THE NEW KING JAMES VERSION CONCORDANCE

THE NEW KING JAMES VERSION CONCORDANCE

THOMAS NELSON PUBLISHERS
Nashville

B. McCALL BARBOUR
28 GEORGE IV BRIDGE
EDINBURGH EH1 1ES, SCOTLAND

Published in Nashville, Tennessee, by Thomas Nelson, Inc.

Library of Congress Cataloging-in-Publication Data

The NKJV concordance.—Complete and unabridged.
Includes indexes.
ISBN 0-8407-4261-4 (HC)
1. Bible—Concordances, English—New King James. I. Thomas Nelson Publishers. II. Title: New King James Version concordance.
BS425.N55 1992
220.5'2033—dc20 92–28532
CIP

Printed in the United States of America
1 2 3 4 5 6 7 8 9 10 — 08 07 06 05 04 03 02 01 00

Table of Contents

Introduction to the NKJV Concordance vii
Main Concordance 1
Appendix 1173

Introduction to the
NKJV CONCORDANCE

A Bible concordance is a word index—a listing in alphabetical order of the words from a translation. It also includes all references to book, chapter, and verse in which these words appear. A brief phrase or context line is usually given for each occurrence of all but the most common words in order to help a user find a specific verse in which the word appears. An exhaustive Bible concordance, such as this one, indexes *every* word in a translation. The term *exhaustive* applies to the nature of the concordance itself; that is, it indexes *every* word in the Bible text.

The *NKJV Concordance* indexes every word in the NKJV translation of the Bible. There are over 13,300 in the main body of the concordance, with more than 340,000 context lines. To facilitate ease of use, there is a separate index of 100 words which are less commonly used to locate references, such as articles, conjunctions, and prepositions.

NKJV Concordance Entries

ACCOMPLISH (8/8) ACCOMPLISHED, ACCOMPLISHING, ACCOMPLISHMENT

Ex	14:13	which He will ***a*** for you today.
2 Chr	2:14	to make any engraving and to ***a***
Job	35: 6	what do you ***a*** against Him?
Eccl	2: 2	and of mirth, "What does it ***a***?
Isa	55:11	But it shall ***a*** what I please,
Ezek	13:15	Thus will I ***a*** My wrath on the
Dan	9: 2	that He would ***a*** seventy years
Lk	9:31	which He was about to ***a*** at

Headings

This is a sample entry from the main index. It begins with a heading, which includes the indexed word, frequency count, and a list of related words. The first number of the frequency count refers to the number of times the word *occurs* in the NKJV. The second number refers to the actual number of *verses* in which the indexed word appears: *Accomplish* thus appears eight times in eight verses.

Each indexed word appears exactly as it is spelled in the NKJV. If the word appears in other forms, if there are other words sharing common elements, or if near synonyms have been supplied, these words are listed following the frequency count. All of these related words are indexed separately, allowing for greater study of the subject. For example, *Accomplished, Accomplishing,* and *Accomplishment* are each listed separately.

References with Context Lines

The second part of the entry displays the biblical *references* for the indexed word. References are listed in biblical order Each includes the book, chapter, and verse for easy location of the indexed word. (A chart showing the abbreviations for the books of the Bible appears at the end of the Introduction.)

Each reference comes before a *context line,* which provides a portion of the verse in which the word appears. Within a context line, the indexed word is shown abbreviated with its first letter set in bold italic type. For example, the line from Isaiah 55:11, "But it shall accomplish what I please," is listed under *Accomplish* as "But it shall ***a*** what I please."

For proper names of God, the context lines throughout the main concordance faithfully retain the capitalization used in the NKJV. Under the entries GOD and LORD, the abbreviated initial character reflect the capitalization of the NKJV. For example, "LORD" from the NKJV is abbreviated in the context line as "***L***," and "lord," as "***l***."

Every effort has been made to create context lines that are clear and concise within the space limitations of one line. Since these are basically intended to enable the reader to find specific verses in the Bible, the precise contextual meaning of the verse might be easily misunderstood when read in this shortened reference. For example under the entry GOD the line from Psalm 14:1 states, "his heart, 'There is no God.' Only by reading the entire verse is it discovered that this is what a fool has said. To avoid such misunderstandings, the reader should consult at least the entire verse in the NKJV.

Special Features of the NKJV Concordance

Appendix—Index of Articles, Conjunctions, Prepositions, etc.

AM (900/835) See APPENDIX

Words that are not commonly used to locate references but that appear repeatedly throughout the entire Bible—such as articles, conjunctions, prepositions, and pronouns—are grouped together in the Appendix. These words are listed in the main concordance with their frequency of occurrence, followed by "See APPENDIX." In this Appendix, book, chapter, and verse references in which these words appear are given in biblical order, but without context lines. These words appear so often that providing the many thousands of context lines would double the size of this concordance, but with little benefit to the reader.

These 100 words are listed in the main concordance with a "See" notation, referring the reader to the Appendix.

A
Above
Against
Ago
Am
Among
An
And
Any
Are
Around
As
At
Be
Because
Been
But
By
Down
For
From
Had
Has
Have
He
Her
Hers
Herself
Him
Himself
His
However
I
If
In
Into
Is
It
Its
Itself
Like
May
Me
My
Myself
No
Not
Now
O
Of
Oh
On
Or
Our
Ours
Ourselves
Out
Over
Shall
She
So
Than
That
The
Their
Theirs
Themselves
Then
There
Therefore
Thereupon
These
They
This
Those
Through
Thus
To
Too
Unto
Up
Upon
Us
Very
Was
We
Were
When
Which
Who
Whom
Whose
Will
With
Yet
You
Your
Yours
Yourself
Yourselves

Key Phrases

ANGEL OF THE LORD (68/64)

Gen	16: 7	Now the *A* found her by a spring
	16: 9	The *A* said to her, "Return to
	16:10	Then the *A* said to her, "I will
	16:11	And the *A* said to her:

Phrases of special theological importance, such as "Day of Atonement," "kingdom of God," and "day of the LORD," are listed throughout the main concordance with context lines for each appearance. A total of thirty-two significant phrases appear:

Angel of the Lord
As I Live
Body of Christ
Book of Life
Chief Cornerstone
Children of God
Church of God
Day of Atonement
Day of Christ
Day of the Lord
Eyes of the Lord
Face to Face
Fear of the Lord
Gospel of Christ
Hear, O Israel
I Am
In My Name
It Is Written

Kingdom of God
Law of Moses
Love One Another
Love the Lord Your God
Love Your Neighbor
Mercy Seat
Only Son
Remission of Sins
Signs and Wonders
Son of David
Son of God
Son of Man
Assuredly I Say to You
With All Your Heart

Special Words

The words *had, has,* and *have* do appear in the main concordance, but they do not include all of their occurrences. The main concordance listing includes only the references where these words are used as verbs in their own right, denoting ownership. For example, *had,* which has 420 references listed in the main concordance, has an actual total occurrence of 2,582. The remainder of occurrences of *had* when used as an auxiliary verb, are listed in the Appendix.

Likewise, *will,* used in the sense of volition, i.e., "the will of God," has 105 references in the main concordance, out of a total of 6,401 occurrences. *On,* with 4 listings out of 4,232 occurrences, and *So,* with 1 listing out of 3,469 occurrences, are shown in the main concordance only when they appear as proper names.

KJV Words Cross-Referenced to NKJV Equivalents

BRASEN (KJV) See BRONZE, COPPER
DESCRY (KJV) See SPY (OUT)

Over one thousand important KJV words familiar to longtime readers of this translation have been included with their NKJV equivalents. If a word is common to both KJV and NKJV, it will not be listed as a KJV word, since it has references and context lines in the NKJV.

Occasionally a word used in the KJV has a two-word equivalent in the NKJV. For example, *descry* in the KJV is consistently rendered as *spy out* in the NKJV. However, since *spy out* is not a key phrase included in the concordance, the reader is encouraged to look up the word not in parentheses—*spy*—and then search among the context lines for the two-word phrase "**s** out."

Fan-Tab™ Thumb-Index Reference System

This exclusive reference system provides easy access to each letter of the alphabet. The easy-to-use tabs are readily visible on the right hand side of each page, enabling the user to quickly fan pages through the book to the desired letter of the alphabet.

Words from NKJV Textual Features

ASCENTS (15/15)
Ps 120: A Song of *A*.
121: A Song of *A*.
122: A Song of *A*.

Words from editorial *titles or superscriptions of the Psalms* are part of the Hebrew text and are indexed in the concordance. Since these superscriptions occur before the first verse of Psalms in the English Bible, references to them lack a verse number, as shown above.

However, words from *subject headings* throughout the books of the Bible as well as identification of speakers in the Song of Solomon have been inserted by the translators and editors of the NKJV. These words are not indexed in the concordance; nor are the names of Hebrew letters marking divisions in Psalm 119 (*Aleph, Beth,* etc.).

Abbreviations

The following abbreviations are used for the books of the Bible.

Old Testament

Gen	Genesis	2 Chr	2 Chronicles	Dan	Daniel
Ex	Exodus	Ezra	Ezra	Hos	Hosea
Lev	Leviticus	Neh	Nehemiah	Joel	Joel
Num	Numbers	Esth	Esther	Am	Amos
Deut	Deuteronomy	Job	Job	Ob	Obadiah
Josh	Joshua	Ps	Psalms	Jon	Jonah
Judg	Judges	Prov	Proverbs	Mic	Micah
Ruth	Ruth	Eccl	Ecclesiastes	Nah	Nahum
1 Sam	1 Samuel	Song	Song of Solomon	Hab	Habakkuk
2 Sam	2 Samuel	Isa	Isaiah	Zeph	Zephaniah
1 Ki	1 Kings	Jer	Jeremiah	Hag	Haggai
2 Ki	2 Kings	Lam	Lamentations	Zech	Zechariah
1 Chr	1 Chronicles	Ezek	Ezekiel	Mal	Malachi

New Testament

Mt	Matthew	Eph	Ephesians	Heb	Hebrews
Mk*	Mark	Phil	Philippians	Jas	James
Lk	Luke	Col	Colossians	1 Pe	1 Peter
Jn	John	1 Th	1 Thessalonians	2 Pe	2 Peter
Acts	Acts of the Apostles	2 Th	2 Thessalonians	1 Jn	1 John
Rom	Romans	1 Tim	1 Timothy	2 Jn	2 John
1 Cor	1 Corinthians	2 Tim	2 Timothy	3 Jn	3 John
2 Cor	2 Corinthians	Titus	Titus	Jude	Jude
Gal	Galatians	Phm	Philemon	Rev	Revelation

NKJV CONCORDANCE

A

A (8721/6520) See APPENDIX

AARON (322/306) AARON'S, AARONITES

Ex 4:14 Is not *A* the Levite your
4:27 And the LORD said to *A*,
4:28 So Moses told *A* all the words of
4:29 Then Moses and *A* went and
4:30 And *A* spoke all the words which
5: 1 Afterward Moses and *A* went in
5: 4 *A*, why do you take the people
5:20 they met Moses and *A* who stood
6:13 the LORD spoke to Moses and *A*,
6:20 and she bore him *A* and Moses.
6:23 *A* took to himself Elisheba,
6:26 These are the same *A* and
6:27 are the same Moses and *A*.
7: 1 and *A* your brother shall be
7: 2 And *A* your brother shall speak
7: 6 Then Moses and *A* did so; just
7: 7 was eighty years old and *A*
7: 8 the LORD spoke to Moses and *A*,
7: 9 then you shall say to *A*,
7:10 So Moses and *A* went in to
7:10 And *A* cast down his rod before
7:19 spoke to Moses, "Say to *A*,
7:20 And Moses and *A* did so, just as
8: 5 spoke to Moses, "Say to *A*,
8: 6 So *A* stretched out his hand over
8: 8 Pharaoh called for Moses and *A*,
8:12 Then Moses and *A* went out from
8:16 LORD said to Moses, "Say to *A*,
8:17 For *A* stretched out his hand
8:25 Pharaoh called for Moses and *A*,
9: 8 the LORD said to Moses and *A*,
9:27 sent and called for Moses and *A*,
10: 3 So Moses and *A* came in to
10: 8 So Moses and *A* were brought
10:16 Pharaoh called for Moses and *A*
11:10 So Moses and *A* did all these
12: 1 the LORD spoke to Moses and *A*
12:28 LORD had commanded Moses and *A*,
12:31 he called for Moses and *A* by
12:43 the LORD said to Moses and *A*,
12:50 the LORD commanded Moses and *A*,
15:20 the prophetess, the sister of *A*,
16: 2 complained against Moses and *A*
16: 6 Then Moses and *A* said to all the
16: 9 Then Moses spoke to *A*,
16:10 as *A* spoke to the whole
16:33 And Moses said to *A*,
16:34 so *A* laid it up before the
17:10 with Amalek. And Moses, *A*,
17:12 And *A* and Hur supported his
18:12 And *A* came with all the elders
19:24 you and *A* with you. But do not
24: 1 up to the LORD, you and *A*,
24: 9 Then Moses went up, also *A*,
24:14 Indeed *A* and Hur are with you.
27:21 *A* and his sons shall tend it
28: 1 Now take *A* your brother, and his
28: 1 *A* and Aaron's sons: Nadab,
28: 2 shall make holy garments for *A*
28: 4 shall make holy garments for *A*
28:12 So *A* shall bear their names
28:29 So *A* shall bear the names of the
28:30 So *A* shall bear the judgment of
28:35 And it shall be upon *A* when he
28:38 that *A* may bear the iniquity of
28:41 So you shall put them on *A* your
28:43 They shall be on *A* and on his
29: 4 And *A* and his sons you shall
29: 5 garments, put the tunic on *A*,
29: 9 *A* and his sons, and put the
29: 9 So you shall consecrate *A* and
29:10 and *A* and his sons shall put
29:15 and *A* and his sons shall put
29:19 and *A* and his sons shall put
29:20 the tip of the right ear of *A*
29:21 and sprinkle it on *A* and on
29:24 put all these in the hands of *A*
29:27 of that which is for *A* and of
29:28 the children of Israel for *A*
29:29 And the holy garments of *A*
29:32 Then *A* and his sons shall eat
29:35 Thus you shall do to *A* and his
29:44 I will also consecrate both *A*
30: 7 *A* shall burn on it sweet incense
30: 8 And when *A* lights the lamps at
30:10 And *A* shall make atonement upon
30:19 for *A* and his sons shall wash
30:30 And you shall anoint *A* and his
31:10 the holy garments for *A* the
32: 1 people gathered together to *A*,
32: 2 And *A* said to them, "Break off
32: 3 ears, and brought them to *A*.
32: 5 So when *A* saw it, he built an
32: 5 And *A* made a proclamation and
32:21 And Moses said to *A*,
32:22 So *A* said, "Do not let the
32:25 were unrestrained (for *A* had
32:35 they did with the calf which *A*
34:30 So when *A* and all the children
34:31 and *A* and all the rulers of the
35:19 the holy garments for *A* the
38:21 son of *A* the priest.
39: 1 made the holy garments for *A*,
39:27 linen, for *A* and his sons,
39:41 the holy garments for *A* the
40:12 Then you shall bring *A* and his
40:13 put the holy garments on *A*,
40:31 and Moses, *A*, and his sons
Lev 1: 7 The sons of *A* the priest shall
3:13 and the sons of *A* shall
6: 9 Command *A* and his sons, saying,
6:14 The sons of *A* shall offer it on
6:16 And the remainder of it *A* and
6:18 males among the children of *A*
6:20 This is the offering of *A* and
6:25 Speak to *A* and to his sons,
7:10 belong to all the sons of *A*,
7:33 'He among the sons of *A*,
7:34 and I have given them to *A* the
7:35 the consecrated portion for *A*
8: 2 Take *A* and his sons with him,
8: 6 Then Moses brought *A* and his
8:14 Then *A* and his sons laid their
8:18 And *A* and his sons laid their
8:22 Then *A* and his sons laid their
8:30 altar, and sprinkled it on *A*,
8:30 with him; and he consecrated *A*,
8:31 And Moses said to *A* and his
8:31 *A* and his sons shall eat it.'
8:36 So *A* and his sons did all the
9: 1 eighth day that Moses called *A*
9: 2 And he said to *A*, "Take for
9: 7 Moses said to *A*, "Go to the
9: 8 *A* therefore went to the altar
9: 9 Then the sons of *A* brought the
9:21 breasts and the right thigh *A*
9:22 Then *A* lifted his hand toward
9:23 And Moses and *A* went into the
10: 1 Nadab and Abihu, the sons of *A*,
10: 3 And Moses said to *A*, "This is
10: 3 So *A* held his peace.
10: 4 sons of Uzziel the uncle of *A*,
10: 6 And Moses said to *A*,
10: 8 Then the LORD spoke to *A*,
10:12 And Moses spoke to *A*,
10:16 the sons of *A* who were left,
10:19 And *A* said to Moses, "Look,
11: 1 the LORD spoke to Moses and *A*,
13: 1 the LORD spoke to Moses and *A*,
13: 2 then he shall be brought to *A*
14:33 the LORD spoke to Moses and *A*,
15: 1 the LORD spoke to Moses and *A*,
16: 1 the death of the two sons of *A*,
16: 2 Tell *A* your brother not to come
16: 3 Thus *A* shall come into the Holy
16: 6 *A* shall offer the bull as a sin
16: 8 Then *A* shall cast lots for the
16: 9 And *A* shall bring the goat on
16:11 And *A* shall bring the bull of
16:21 *A* shall lay both his hands on
16:23 Then *A* shall come into the
17: 2 'Speak to *A*, to his sons,
21: 1 to the priests, the sons of *A*,
21:17 'Speak to *A*, saying: 'No man
21:21 'No man of the descendants of *A*
21:24 And Moses told it to *A* and his
22: 2 Speak to *A* and his sons, that
22: 4 man of the descendants of *A*,
22:18 Speak to *A* and his sons, and to
24: 3 *A* shall be in charge of it from
24: 9 And it shall be for *A* and his
Num 1: 3 You and *A* shall number them by
1:17 Then Moses and *A* took these men
1:44 whom Moses and *A* numbered, with
2: 1 the LORD spoke to Moses and *A*,
3: 1 Now these are the records of *A*
3: 2 are the names of the sons of *A*:
3: 3 are the names of the sons of *A*,
3: 4 as priests in the presence of *A*
3: 6 and present them before *A* the
3: 9 you shall give the Levites to *A*
3:10 So you shall appoint *A* and his
3:32 And Eleazar the son of *A* the
3:38 of meeting, were Moses, *A*,
3:39 whom Moses and *A* numbered at
3:48 to *A* and his sons."
3:51 their redemption money to *A*
4: 1 the LORD spoke to Moses and *A*,
4: 5 *A* and his sons shall come, and
4:15 And when *A* and his sons have
4:16 duty of Eleazar the son of *A*
4:17 the LORD spoke to Moses and *A*,
4:19 *A* and his sons shall go in and
4:27 *A* and his sons shall assign all
4:28 of Ithamar the son of *A* the
4:33 of Ithamar the son of *A* the
4:34 And Moses, *A*, and the leaders
4:37 whom Moses and *A* numbered
4:41 whom Moses and *A* numbered
4:45 whom Moses and *A* numbered
4:46 of the Levites, whom Moses, *A*,
6:23 Speak to *A* and his sons, saying,
7: 8 of Ithamar the son of *A* the
8: 2 'Speak to *A*, and say to him,
8: 3 And *A* did so; he arranged the
8:11 and *A* shall offer the Levites
8:13 stand the Levites before *A* and
8:19 the Levites as a gift to *A* and
8:20 Thus Moses and *A* and all the
8:21 then *A* presented them, like a
8:21 and *A* made atonement for them
8:22 tabernacle of meeting before *A*
9: 6 they came before Moses and *A*
10: 8 'The sons of *A*, the priests,
12: 1 Then Miriam and *A* spoke against
12: 4 the LORD said to Moses, *A*,
12: 5 and called *A* and Miriam. And
12:10 Then *A* turned toward Miriam,
12:11 So *A* said to Moses, "Oh, my
13:26 and came back to Moses and *A*
14: 2 complained against Moses and *A*,
14: 5 Then Moses and *A* fell on their

14:26 the LORD spoke to Moses and *A*,
15:33 brought him to Moses and *A*,
16: 3 together against Moses and *A*,
16:11 And what is *A* that you
16:16 and they, as well as *A*.
16:17 fifty censers; both you and *A*,
16:18 of meeting with Moses and *A*.
16:20 the LORD spoke to Moses and *A*,
16:37 the son of *A* the priest, to
16:40 who is not a descendant of *A*,
16:41 murmured against Moses and *A*,
16:42 gathered against Moses and *A*,
16:43 Then Moses and *A* came before the
16:46 So Moses said to *A*,
16:47 Then *A* took it as Moses
16:50 So *A* returned to Moses at the
17: 6 and the rod of *A* was among
17: 8 and behold, the rod of *A*,
18: 1 Then the LORD said to *A*:
18: 8 And the LORD spoke to *A*:
18:20 Then the LORD said to *A*:
18:28 heave offering from it to *A*
19: 1 the LORD spoke to Moses and *A*,
20: 2 together against Moses and *A*.
20: 6 So Moses and *A* went from the
20: 8 you and your brother *A* gather
20:10 And Moses and *A* gathered the
20:12 the LORD spoke to Moses and *A*,
20:23 the LORD spoke to Moses and *A*
20:24 *A* shall be gathered to his
20:25 Take *A* and Eleazar his son, and
20:26 and strip *A* of his garments and
20:26 for *A* shall be gathered to
20:28 Moses stripped *A* of his garments
20:28 and *A* died there on the top of
20:29 all the congregation saw that *A*
20:29 house of Israel mourned for *A*
25: 7 the son of *A* the priest, saw
25:11 the son of *A* the priest, has
26: 1 Moses and Eleazar the son of *A*
26: 9 contended against Moses and *A*
26:59 and to Amram she bore *A* and
26:60 To *A* were born Nadab and Abihu,
26:64 were numbered by Moses and *A*
27:13 as *A* your brother was gathered.
33: 1 under the hand of Moses and *A*.
33:38 Then *A* the priest went up to
33:39 *A* was one hundred and
Deut 9:20 the LORD was very angry with *A*
9:20 so I prayed for *A* also at the
10: 6 where *A* died, and where he was
32:50 just as *A* your brother died on
Josh 21: 4 And the children of *A* the
21:10 were for the children of *A*,
21:13 Thus to the children of *A* the
21:19 the cities of the children of *A*,
24: 5 'Also I sent Moses and *A*,
24:33 And Eleazar the son of *A* died.
Judg 20:28 son of Eleazar, the son of *A*,
1 Sam 12: 6 LORD who raised up Moses and *A*,
12: 8 then the LORD sent Moses and *A*,
1 Chr 6: 3 The children of Amram were *A*,
6: 3 And the sons of *A* were Nadab,
6:49 But *A* and his sons offered
6:50 Now these are the sons of *A*:
6:54 given by lot to the sons of *A*,
6:57 And to the sons of *A* they gave
15: 4 assembled the children of *A*
23:13 *A* and Moses; and Aaron was set
23:13 and *A* was set apart, he and his
23:28 was to help the sons of *A* in
23:32 and the needs of the sons of *A*
24: 1 the divisions of the sons of *A*.
24: 1 The sons of *A* were Nadab,
24:19 ordinance by the hand of *A*
24:31 as their brothers the sons of *A*
2 Chr 13: 9 of the LORD, the sons of *A*,
13:10 to the LORD are the sons of *A*,
26:18 for the priests, the sons of *A*,
29:21 the priests, the sons of *A*,
31:19 Also for the sons of *A* the
35:14 the priests, the sons of *A*,
35:14 for the priests, the sons of *A*.
Ezra 7: 5 the son of *A* the chief priest—
Neh 10:38 the priest, the descendant of *A*,
12:47 them for the children of *A*.
Ps 77:20 By the hand of Moses and *A*.
99: 6 Moses and *A* were among His
105:26 And *A* whom He had chosen.
106:16 And *A* the saint of the LORD,
115:10 O house of *A*,
115:12 He will bless the house of *A*.
118: 3 Let the house of *A* now say,
133: 2 on the beard, The beard of *A*,
135:19 Bless the LORD, O house of *A*!
Mic 6: 4 And I sent before you Moses, *A*,
Lk 1: 5 wife was of the daughters of *A*,
Acts 7:40 'saying to *A*, 'Make us gods
Heb 5: 4 called by God, just as *A* was.
7:11 according to the order of *A*?

AARON'S (28/28) AARON

Ex 6:25 *A* son, took for himself one of
7:12 But *A* rod swallowed up their
28: 1 Aaron and *A* sons: Nadab,
28: 3 that they may make *A* garments,
28:30 and they shall be over *A* heart
28:38 So it shall be on *A* forehead,
28:40 For *A* sons you shall make
29:26 take the breast of the ram of *A*
Lev 1: 5 *A* sons, shall bring the blood
1: 8 *A* sons, shall lay the parts,
1:11 *A* sons, shall sprinkle its
2: 2 He shall bring it to *A* sons, the
2: 3 the grain offering shall be *A*
2:10 the grain offering shall be *A*
3: 2 and *A* sons, the priests, shall
3: 5 and *A* sons shall burn it on the
3: 8 and *A* sons shall sprinkle its
7:31 but the breast shall be *A* and
8:12 some of the anointing oil on *A*
8:13 Then Moses brought *A* sons and
8:23 and put it on the tip of *A*
8:24 Then he brought *A* sons.
8:27 and he put all these in *A* hands
9:12 and *A* sons presented to him the
9:18 And *A* sons presented to him the
Num 17: 3 And you shall write *A* name on
17:10 Bring *A* rod back before the
Heb 9: 4 *A* rod that budded, and the

AARONITES (2/2) AARON

1 Chr 12:27 Jehoiada, the leader of the *A*,
27:17 the son of Kemuel; over the *A*,

ABADDON (1/1)

Rev 9:11 pit, whose name in Hebrew is *A*,

ABAGTHA (1/1)

Esth 1:10 Biztha, Harbona, Bigtha, *A*,

ABANAH (1/1)

2 Ki 5:12 Are not the *A* and the Pharpar,

ABANDON (1/1) ABANDONED

Prov 19: 7 yet they ***a*** him.

ABANDONED (1/1) ABANDON

Lam 2: 7 He has ***a*** His sanctuary; He

ABARIM (7/7)

Num 27:12 "Go up into this Mount *A*,
33:47 camped in the mountains of *A*,
33:48 from the mountains of *A* and
Deut 32:49 "Go up this mountain of the *A*,
Jer 22:20 voice in Bashan; Cry from *A*,

ABASED (1/1) HUMBLED

Phil 4:12 I know how to be ***a***,

ABASHED (1/1)

Mic 3: 7 be ashamed, And the diviners ***a***;

ABATED (KJV) See DEDUCTED, DIMINISHED, RECEDED, SUBSIDED

ABBA (3/3) FATHER

Mk 14:36 '*A*, Father, all things are
Rom 8:15 by whom we cry out, "*A*,
Gal 4: 6 your hearts, crying out, "*A*,

ABDA (2/2)

1 Ki 4: 6 and Adoniram the son of *A*,
Neh 11:17 and *A* the son of Shammua, the

ABDEEL (1/1)

Jer 36:26 and Shelemiah the son of *A*,

ABDI (3/3)

1 Chr 6:44 the son of Kishi, the son of *A*,
2 Chr 29:12 Kish the son of *A* and Azariah
Ezra 10:26 Mattaniah, Zechariah, Jehiel, *A*,

ABDIEL (1/1)

1 Chr 5:15 Ahi the son of *A*,

ABDON (8/8)

Josh 21:30 *A* with its common-land,
Judg 12:13 *A* the son of Hillel the
12:15 Then *A* the son of Hillel the
1 Chr 6:74 *A* with its common-lands,
8:23 *A*, Zichri, Hanan,
8:30 And his firstborn son was *A*,
9:36 His firstborn son was *A*,
2 Chr 34:20 *A* the son of Micah, Shaphan the

ABED-NEGO (15/14)

Dan 1: 7 Meshach; and to Azariah, *A*.
2:49 and *A* over the affairs of the
3:12 Shadrach, Meshach, and *A*;
3:13 bring Shadrach, Meshach, and *A*.
3:14 true, Shadrach, Meshach, and *A*,
3:16 and *A* answered and said to the
3:19 toward Shadrach, Meshach, and *A*.
3:20 bind Shadrach, Meshach, and *A*,
3:22 up Shadrach, Meshach, and *A*.
3:23 men, Shadrach, Meshach, and *A*,
3:26 "Shadrach, Meshach, and *A*,
3:26 and *A* came from the midst of
3:28 God of Shadrach, Meshach, and *A*,
3:29 and *A* shall be cut in pieces,
3:30 and *A* in the province of

ABEL (25/22)

Gen 4: 2 again, this time his brother *A*.
4: 2 Now *A* was a keeper of sheep,
4: 4 *A* also brought of the firstborn
4: 4 And the LORD respected *A* and
4: 8 Now Cain talked with *A* his
4: 8 that Cain rose up against *A* his
4: 9 'Where is *A* your brother?"
4:25 seed for me instead of *A*,
1 Sam 6:18 far as the large stone of *A*
2 Sam 20:14 all the tribes of Israel to *A*
20:15 came and besieged him in *A* of
20:18 surely seek guidance at *A*,
Mt 23:35 from the blood of righteous *A*
Lk 11:51 from the blood of *A* to the blood
Heb 11: 4 By faith *A* offered to God a
12:24 better things than that of *A*.

ABEL ACACIA GROVE (1/1)

Num 33:49 Beth Jesimoth as far as the *A*

ABEL BETH MAACHAH (2/2)

1 Ki 15:20 He attacked Ijon, Dan, *A*,
2 Ki 15:29 Assyria came and took Ijon, *A*,

ABEL KERAMIM (1/1)

Judg 11:33 Minnith—twenty cities—and to *A*,

ABEL MAIM (1/1)

2 Chr 16: 4 They attacked Ijon, Dan, *A*,

ABEL MEHOLAH (3/3)

Judg 7:22 as far as the border of *A*,
1 Ki 4:12 Jezreel, from Beth Shean to *A*,
19:16 Elisha the son of Shaphat of *A*

ABEL MIZRAIM (1/1)

Gen 50:11 Therefore its name was called *A*,

ABEZ (1/1)

Josh 19:20 Rabbith, Kishion, *A*,

ABHOR (21/20) ABHORRED, ABHORRENCE, ABHORRENT, ABHORS

Lev 20:23 and therefore I ***a*** them.
26:11 and My soul shall not ***a*** you.
26:30 and My soul shall ***a*** you.
26:44 nor shall I ***a*** them, to utterly
Deut 7:26 detest it and utterly ***a*** it,
23: 7 You shall not ***a*** an Edomite, for
23: 7 You shall not ***a*** an Egyptian,
1 Sam 27:12 his people Israel utterly ***a***
Job 9:31 And my own clothes will ***a*** me.
19:19 All my close friends ***a*** me, And
30:10 They ***a*** me, they keep far from
42: 6 Therefore I ***a*** myself, And
Ps 36: 4 He does not ***a*** evil.
119:163 I hate and ***a*** lying, But I
Prov 24:24 Nations will ***a*** him.
Jer 14:21 Do not ***a*** us, for Your name's
Am 5:10 And they ***a*** the one who speaks
6: 8 I ***a*** the pride of Jacob, And
Mic 3: 9 Who ***a*** justice And pervert all
Rom 2:22 You who ***a*** idols, do you rob
12: 9 *A* what is evil. Cling to what

ABHORRED (12/12) ABHOR

Lev 26:43 and because their soul ***a*** My
1 Sam 2:17 for men ***a*** the offering of the
2 Sam 16:21 will hear that you are ***a*** by
1 Ki 11:25 and he ***a*** Israel, and reigned
Ps 22:24 For He has not despised nor ***a***
78:59 And greatly ***a*** Israel,
89:38 But You have cast off and ***a***,
106:40 So that He ***a*** His own
107:18 Their soul ***a*** all manner of
Prov 22:14 He who is ***a*** by the LORD will
Ezek 16:25 and made your beauty to be ***a***.
Zech 11: 8 and their soul also ***a*** me.

ABHORRENCE (1/1) ABHOR

Isa 66:24 They shall be an ***a*** to all

ABHORRENT (1/1) ABHOR

Ex 5:21 because you have made us ***a*** in

ABHORS (4/4) ABHOR

Lev 26:15 or if your soul ***a*** My judgments,
Job 33:20 So that his life ***a*** bread, And
Ps 5: 6 The LORD ***a*** the bloodthirsty
Isa 49: 7 To Him whom the nation ***a***,

ABI (1/1)

2 Ki 18: 2 His mother's name was *A* the

ABI-ALBON (1/1)

2 Sam 23:31 *A* the Arbathite, Azmaveth the

ABIASAPH (1/1) EBIASAPH

Ex 6:24 were Assir, Elkanah, and *A*.

ABIATHAR (30/28) ABIATHAR'S

1 Sam 22:20 the son of Ahitub, named *A*,
22:21 And *A* told David that Saul had
22:22 So David said to *A*,
23: 6 when *A* the son of Ahimelech
23: 9 he said to *A* the priest,
30: 7 Then David said to *A* the
30: 7 And *A* brought the ephod to
2 Sam 8:17 and Ahimelech the son of *A*
15:24 and *A* went up until all the
15:27 son, and Jonathan the son of *A*.
15:29 Therefore Zadok and *A* carried
15:35 do you not have Zadok and *A*
15:35 you shall tell to Zadok and *A*
17:15 Hushai said to Zadok and *A* the
19:11 King David sent to Zadok and *A*
20:25 Zadok and *A* were the priests;
1 Ki 1: 7 the son of Zeruiah and with *A*
1:19 *A* the priest, and Joab the
1:25 and *A* the priest; and look!
1:42 the son of *A* the priest.
2:22 and for *A* the priest, and for
2:26 And to *A* the priest the king
2:27 So Solomon removed *A* from being
2:35 the priest in the place of *A*.
4: 4 over the army; Zadok and *A*,
1 Chr 15:11 David called for Zadok and *A*
18:16 and Abimelech the son of *A*
24: 6 priest, Ahimelech the son of *A*,
27:34 the son of Benaiah, then *A*.
Mk 2:26 of God in the days of *A* the

ABIATHAR'S (1/1) ABIATHAR

2 Sam 15:36 *A* son; and by them you shall

ABIB (7/5) NISAN

Ex 13: 4 are going out, in the month *A*.
23:15 appointed in the month of *A*,
34:18 time of the month of *A*;
34:18 for in the month of *A* you came
Deut 16: 1 "Observe the month of *A*,
16: 1 for in the month of *A* the LORD

ABIDA (1/1) ABIDAH

1 Chr 1:33 were Ephah, Epher, Hanoch, *A*,

ABIDAH (1/1) ABIDA

Gen 25: 4 were Ephah, Epher, Hanoch, *A*,

ABIDAN (5/5)

Num 1:11 *A* the son of Gideoni;
2:22 of Benjamin shall be *A* the
7:60 On the ninth day *A* the son of
7:65 This was the offering of *A* the
10:24 the children of Benjamin was *A*

ABIDE (36/32) ABIDES, ABIDING, DWELL, REMAIN

Deut 12:11 God chooses to make His name *a*.
14:23 He chooses to make His name *a*,
16: 6 God chooses to make His name *a*,
16:11 God chooses to make His name *a*.
26: 2 God chooses to make His name *a*.
Job 24:13 do not know its ways Nor *a* in
Ps 15: 1 who may *a* in Your tabernacle?
61: 4 I will *a* in Your tabernacle
61: 7 He shall *a* before God forever.
91: 1 place of the Most High Shall *a*
Prov 15:31 the rebukes of life Will *a*
19:23 And he who has it will *a*
Hos 3: 4 the children of Israel shall *a*
Joel 3:20 But Judah shall *a* forever, And
Mic 5: 4 His God; And they shall *a*,
Lk 24:29 *A* with us, for it is toward
Jn 8:31 If you *a* in My word, you are My
8:35 And a slave does not *a* in the
12:46 believes in Me should not *a* in
14:16 that He may *a* with you forever—
15: 4 *A* in Me, and I in you. As the
15: 4 unless you *a* in Me.
15: 6 If anyone does not *a* in Me, he
15: 7 If you *a* in Me, and My words
15: 7 and My words *a* in you, you will
15: 9 have loved you; *a* in My love.
15:10 you will *a* in My love, just as
15:10 My Father's commandments and *a*
1 Cor 13:13 And now *a* faith, hope, love,
1 Jn 2:24 Therefore let that *a* in you
2:24 you also will *a* in the Son and
2:27 you will *a* in Him.
2:28 *a* in Him, that when He appears,
3:17 how does the love of God *a* in
4:13 By this we know that we *a* in
2 Jn 9 transgresses and does not *a* in

ABIDES (26/24) ABIDE

Ps 55:19 Even He who *a* from of old.
119:90 established the earth, and it *a*.
125: 1 be moved, but *a* forever.
Eccl 1: 4 But the earth *a* forever.
Jn 3:36 but the wrath of God *a* on
6:56 My flesh and drinks My blood *a*
8:35 but a son *a* forever.
15: 4 unless it *a* in the vine,
15: 5 He who *a* in Me, and I in him,
1 Pe 1:23 word of God which lives and *a*
1 Jn 2: 6 He who says he *a* in Him ought
2:10 He who loves his brother *a* in
2:14 and the word of God *a* in you,
2:17 he who does the will of God *a*
2:24 you heard from the beginning *a*
2:27 you have received from Him *a*
3: 6 Whoever *a* in Him does not sin.
3:14 does not love his brother *a*
3:24 he who keeps His commandments *a*
3:24 And by this we know that He *a*
4:12 God *a* in us, and His love has
4:15 God *a* in him, and he in God.
4:16 and he who *a* in love abides in
4:16 and he who abides in love *a* in
2 Jn 2 because of the truth which *a* in
9 He who *a* in the doctrine of

ABIDING (2/2) ABIDE

Jn 5:38 you do not have His word *a*
1 Jn 3:15 no murderer has eternal life *a*

ABIEL (3/3)

1 Sam 9: 1 name was Kish the son of *A*,
14:51 of Abner was the son of *A*.
1 Chr 11:32 *A* the Arbathite,

ABIEZER (6/6) ABIEZRITE, EZER, JEEZER

Josh 17: 2 families: for the children of *A*,
Judg 8: 2 better than the vintage of *A*?
2 Sam 23:27 *A* the Anathothite, Mebunnai the
1 Chr 7:18 Hammoleketh bore Ishhod, *A*,
11:28 *A* the Anathothite,
27:12 for the ninth month was *A* the

ABIEZRITE (1/1) ABIEZER, ABIEZRITES

Judg 6:11 which belonged to Joash the *A*,

ABIEZRITES (3/3) ABIEZRITE

Judg 6:24 it is still in Ophrah of the *A*.
6:34 and the *A* gathered behind him.
8:32 his father, in Ophrah of the *A*.

ABIGAIL (17/17)

1 Sam 25: 3 and the name of his wife *A*.
25:14 one of the young men told *A*,
25:18 Then *A* made haste and took two
25:23 Now when *A* saw David, she
25:32 Then David said to *A*:
25:36 Now *A* went to Nabal, and there
25:39 David sent and proposed to *A*,
25:40 of David had come to *A* at
25:42 So *A* rose in haste and rode on a
27: 3 and *A* the Carmelitess, Nabal's
30: 5 and *A* the widow of Nabal the
2 Sam 2: 2 and *A* the widow of Nabal the
3: 3 by *A* the widow of Nabal the
17:25 who had gone in to *A* the
1 Chr 2:16 sisters were Zeruiah and *A*.
2:17 *A* bore Amasa; and the father of
3: 1 by *A* the Carmelitess;

ABIHAIL (6/6)

Num 3:35 Merari was Zuriel the son of *A*.
1 Chr 2:29 of the wife of Abishur was *A*,
5:14 These were the children of *A*
2 Chr 11:18 and of *A* the daughter of
Esth 2:15 for Esther the daughter of *A*
9:29 Queen Esther, the daughter of *A*,

ABIHU (12/12)

Ex 6:23 wife; and she bore him Nadab, *A*,
24: 1 you and Aaron, Nadab and *A*,
24: 9 up, also Aaron, Nadab, and *A*,
28: 1 and Aaron's sons: Nadab, *A*,
Lev 10: 1 Then Nadab and *A*, the sons of
Num 3: 2 Nadab, the firstborn, and *A*,
3: 4 Nadab and *A* had died before the
26:60 To Aaron were born Nadab and *A*,
26:61 And Nadab and *A* died when they
1 Chr 6: 3 sons of Aaron were Nadab, *A*,
24: 1 sons of Aaron were Nadab, *A*,
24: 2 And Nadab and *A* died before

ABIHUD (1/1)

1 Chr 8: 3 of Bela were Addar, Gera, *A*,

ABIJAH (28/27) ABIJAM

1 Sam 8: 2 and the name of his second, *A*;
1 Ki 14: 1 At that time *A* the son of
1 Chr 2:24 Hezron's wife *A* bore him Ashhur
3:10 *A* was his son, Asa his son,
6:28 firstborn, and *A* the second.
7: 8 Elioenai, Omri, Jerimoth, *A*,
24:10 to Hakkoz, the eighth to *A*,
2 Chr 11:20 of Absalom; and she bore him *A*,
11:22 And Rehoboam appointed *A* the son
12:16 Then *A* his son reigned in his
13: 1 *A* became king over Judah.
13: 2 And there was war between *A* and
13: 3 *A* set the battle in order with
13: 4 Then *A* stood on Mount Zemaraim,
13:15 and all Israel before *A* and
13:17 Then *A* and his people struck
13:19 And *A* pursued Jeroboam and took
13:20 strength again in the days of *A*;
13:21 But *A* grew mighty, married
13:22 Now the rest of the acts of *A*,
14: 1 So *A* rested with his fathers,
29: 1 His mother's name was *A* the
Neh 10: 7 Meshullam, *A*, Mijamin,
12: 4 Iddo, Ginnethoi, *A*,
12:17 of *A*, Zichri; the son of
Mt 1: 7 Rehoboam, Rehoboam begot *A*,
1: 7 and *A* begot Asa.
Lk 1: 5 Zacharias, of the division of *A*.

ABIJAM (5/4) ABIJAH

1 Ki 14:31 Then *A* his son reigned in his
15: 1 *A* became king over Judah.
15: 7 Now the rest of the acts of *A*,
15: 7 And there was war between *A* and
15: 8 So *A* rested with his fathers,

ABILENE (1/1)

Lk 3: 1 and Lysanias tetrarch of *A*,

ABILITY (11/10) ABLE, GIFT, SKILL, SUFFICIENCY, TALENT

Ex 35:34 He has put in his heart the *a*
Lev 27: 8 according to the *a* of him who
1 Chr 26: 6 they were men of great *a*.
Ezra 2:69 According to their *a*,
Neh 5: 8 According to our *a* we have
Dan 1: 4 who had *a* to serve in the
Mt 25:15 to each according to his own *a*;
Acts 11:29 each according to his *a*,
2 Cor 8: 3 that according to their *a*,
8: 3 yes, and beyond their *a*,
1 Pe 4:11 let him do it as with the *a*

ABIMAEL (2/2)

Gen 10:28 Obal, *A*, Sheba,
1 Chr 1:22 Ebal, *A*, Sheba,

ABIMELECH (65/61) ABIMELECH'S, AHIMELECH

Gen 20: 2 And *A* king of Gerar sent and
20: 3 But God came to *A* in a dream by
20: 4 But *A* had not come near her; and
20: 8 So *A* rose early in the morning,
20: 9 And *A* called Abraham and said to
20:10 Then *A* said to Abraham, "What
20:14 Then *A* took sheep, oxen, and
20:15 And *A* said, "See, my land is
20:17 prayed to God; and God healed *A*,
20:18 all the wombs of the house of *A*
21:22 to pass at that time that *A*
21:25 Then Abraham rebuked *A* because
21:26 And *A* said, "I do not know who
21:27 and oxen and gave them to *A*,
21:29 Then *A* asked Abraham, "What is
21:32 So *A* rose with Phichol, the
26: 1 And Isaac went to *A* king of the
26: 8 that *A* king of the Philistines
26: 9 Then *A* called Isaac and said,
26:10 And *A* said, "What is this you
26:11 So *A* charged all his people,
26:16 And *A* said to Isaac, "Go away
26:26 Then *A* came to him from Gerar
Judg 8:31 a son, whose name he called *A*.
9: 1 Then *A* the son of Jerubbaal went
9: 3 heart was inclined to follow *A*,
9: 4 with which *A* hired worthless
9: 6 and they went and made *A* king
9:16 and sincerity in making *A* king,
9:18 sons on one stone, and made *A*,
9:19 this day, then rejoice in *A*,
9:20 let fire come from *A* and devour
9:20 from Beth Millo and devour *A*!
9:21 for fear of *A* his brother.
9:22 After *A* had reigned over Israel
9:23 a spirit of ill will between *A*
9:23 dealt treacherously with *A*,
9:24 and their blood be laid on *A*
9:25 that way; and it was told *A*.
9:27 and ate and drank, and cursed *A*.
9:28 son of Ebed said, "Who is *A*,
9:29 Then I would remove *A*.
9:29 Abimelech." So he said to *A*,
9:31 And he sent messengers to *A*
9:34 So *A* and all the people who
9:35 *A* and the people who were with
9:38 with which you said, 'Who is *A*,
9:39 of Shechem, and fought with *A*.
9:40 And *A* chased him, and he fled
9:41 Then *A* dwelt at Arumah, and
9:42 into the field, and they told *A*.
9:44 Then *A* and the company that was
9:45 So *A* fought against the city all
9:47 And it was told *A* that all the
9:48 Then *A* went up to Mount Zalmon,
9:48 And *A* took an ax in his hand

9:49 his own bough and followed *A*,
9:50 Then *A* went to Thebez, and he
9:52 So *A* came as far as the tower
9:55 the men of Israel saw that *A*
9:56 God repaid the wickedness of *A*,
10: 1 After *A* there arose to save
2 Sam 11:21 Who struck *A* the son of
1 Chr 18:16 Zadok the son of Ahitub and *A*
Ps 34: he pretended madness before *A*,

ABIMELECH'S (2/2) ABIMELECH

Gen 21:25 of a well of water which *A*
Judg 9:53 an upper millstone on *A* head

ABINADAB (12/11)

1 Sam 7: 1 brought it into the house of *A*
16: 8 So Jesse called *A*,
17:13 the firstborn, next to him *A*,
31: 2 Philistines killed Jonathan, *A*,
2 Sam 6: 3 it out of the house of *A*,
6: 3 Uzzah and Ahio, the sons of *A*,
6: 4 it out of the house of *A*,
1 Chr 2:13 *A* the second, Shimea the third,
8:33 begot Jonathan, Malchishua, *A*,
9:39 begot Jonathan, Malchishua, *A*,
10: 2 Philistines killed Jonathan, *A*,
13: 7 a new cart from the house of *A*,

ABINOAM (4/4)

Judg 4: 6 called for Barak the son of *A*
4:12 Sisera that Barak the son of *A*
5: 1 Deborah and Barak the son of *A*
5:12 captives away, O son of *A*!

ABIRAM (11/9)

Num 16: 1 with Dathan and *A* the sons of
16:12 sent to call Dathan and *A* the
16:24 tents of Korah, Dathan, and *A*.
16:25 rose and went to Dathan and *A*,
16:27 tents of Korah, Dathan, and *A*;
16:27 and Dathan and *A* came out and
26: 9 were Nemuel, Dathan, and *A*.
26: 9 These are the Dathan and *A*,
Deut 11: 6 what He did to Dathan and *A*
1 Ki 16:34 He laid its foundation with *A*
Ps 106:17 And covered the faction of *A*.

ABISHAG (5/5)

1 Ki 1: 3 and found *A* the Shunammite, and
1:15 and *A* the Shunammite was
2:17 that he may give me *A* the
2:21 Let *A* the Shunammite be given to
2:22 Now why do you ask *A* the

ABISHAI (25/24)

1 Sam 26: 6 Ahimelech the Hittite and to *A*
26: 6 And *A* said, "I will go down
26: 7 So David and *A* came to the
26: 8 Then *A* said to David, "God has
26: 9 And David said to *A*, "Do not
2 Sam 2:18 Joab and *A* and Asahel. And
2:24 Joab and *A* also pursued Abner.
3:30 So Joab and *A* his brother killed
10:10 he put under the command of *A*
10:14 they also fled before *A*,
16: 9 Then *A* the son of Zeruiah said
16:11 And David said to *A* and all his
18: 2 one third under the hand of *A*
18: 5 the king had commanded Joab, *A*,
18:12 the king commanded you and *A*
19:21 But *A* the son of Zeruiah
20: 6 David said to *A*, "Now Sheba
20:10 Then Joab and *A* his brother
21:17 But *A* the son of Zeruiah came to
23:18 Now *A* the brother of Joab, the
1 Chr 2:16 And the sons of Zeruiah were *A*,
11:20 *A* the brother of Joab was chief
18:12 Moreover *A* the son of Zeruiah
19:11 he put under the command of *A*
19:15 they also fled before *A* his

ABISHALOM (2/2) ABSALOM

1 Ki 15: 2 Maachah the granddaughter of *A*.
15:10 Maachah the granddaughter of *A*.

ABISHUA (5/5)

1 Chr 6: 4 Phinehas, and Phinehas begot *A*;
6: 5 *A* begot Bukki, and Bukki begot
6:50 Phinehas his son, *A* his son,
8: 4 *A*, Naaman, Ahoah,
Ezra 7: 5 the son of *A*, the son of

ABISHUR (2/2)

1 Chr 2:28 of Shammai were Nadab and *A*.
2:29 And the name of the wife of *A*

ABITAL (2/2)

2 Sam 3: 4 fifth, Shephatiah the son of *A*;
1 Chr 3: 3 the fifth, Shephatiah, by *A*;

ABITUB (1/1)

1 Chr 8:11 And by Hushim he begot *A* and

ABIUD (2/1)

Mt 1:13 Zerubbabel begot *A*,
1:13 *A* begot Eliakim, and Eliakim

ABJECTS (KJV) See ATTACKERS

ABLE (167/163) ABILITY, ENABLE, ENABLED, QUALIFIED, STRONG, SUFFICIENT

Gen 13: 6 Now the land was not *a* to
15: 5 count the stars if you are *a*
33:14 are *a* to endure, until I come
Ex 10: 5 so that no one will be *a* to see
18:18 you are not *a* to perform it by
18:21 select from all the people *a*
18:23 then you will be *a* to endure,
18:25 And Moses chose *a* men out of all
40:35 And Moses was not *a* to enter the
Lev 5: 7 If he is not *a* to bring a lamb,
5:11 But if he is not *a* to bring two
12: 8 And if she is not *a* to bring a
14:22 such as he is *a* to afford: one
14:31 such as he is *a* to afford, the
25:26 but he himself becomes *a* to
25:28 But if he is not *a* to have it
25:49 or if he is *a* he may redeem
Num 1: 3 all who are *a* to go to war in
1:20 all who were *a* to go to war:
1:22 all who were *a* to go to war:
1:24 all who were *a* to go to war:
1:26 all who were *a* to go to war:
1:28 all who were *a* to go to war:
1:30 all who were *a* to go to war:
1:32 all who were *a* to go to war:
1:34 all who were *a* to go to war:
1:36 all who were *a* to go to war:
1:38 all who were *a* to go to war:
1:40 all who were *a* to go to war:
1:42 all who were *a* to go to war:
1:45 all who were *a* to go to war
6:21 whatever else his hand is *a* to
11:14 I am not *a* to bear all these
13:30 for we are well *a* to overcome
13:31 We are not *a* to go up against
14:16 Because the LORD was not *a* to
22: 6 Perhaps I shall be *a* to defeat
22:11 perhaps I shall be *a* to
22:37 Am I not *a* to honor you?"
26: 2 all who are *a* to go to war in
Deut 1: 9 I alone am not *a* to bear you.
7:24 no one shall be *a* to stand
9:28 Because the LORD was not *a* to
11:25 No man shall be *a* to stand
14:24 so that you are not *a* to carry
16:17 man shall give as he is *a*,
Josh 1: 5 No man shall be *a* to stand
14:12 and I shall be *a* to drive them
23: 9 no one has been *a* to stand
Judg 8: 3 And what was I *a* to do in
1 Sam 6:20 Who is *a* to stand before this
17: 9 If he is *a* to fight with me and
17:33 You are not *a* to go against this
1 Ki 3: 9 For who is *a* to judge this
9:21 of Israel had not been *a* to
2 Ki 3:21 all who were *a* to bear arms and
18:23 if you are *a* on your part to put
18:29 for he shall not be *a* to
1 Chr 5:18 men *a* to bear shield and sword,
9:13 They were very *a* men for the
12:36 *a* to keep battle formation,
26: 7 Elihu and Semachiah were *a*
26: 8 *a* men with strength for the
26: 9 and brethren, eighteen *a* men.
26:30 one thousand seven hundred *a*
26:32 two thousand seven hundred *a*
29:14 That we should be *a* to offer
2 Chr 2: 6 But who is *a* to build Him a
7: 7 Solomon had made was not *a* to
20: 6 so that no one is *a* to
20:37 so that they were not *a* to go
25: 5 *a* to go to war, who could
25: 9 The LORD is *a* to give you much
32:13 of those lands in any way *a* to
32:14 that your God should be *a* to
32:15 of any nation or kingdom was *a*
Ezra 10:13 and we are not *a* to stand
Neh 4:10 much rubbish that we are not *a*
Job 41:10 Who then is *a* to stand against
Ps 21:11 a plot which they are not *a*
36:12 been cast down and are not *a*
40:12 so that I am not *a* to look up;
Prov 27: 4 But who is *a* to stand before
Eccl 8:17 he will not be *a* to find it.
Isa 36: 8 if you are *a* on your part to put
36:14 for he will not be *a* to deliver
47:11 You will not be *a* to put it
47:12 Perhaps you will be *a* to
Jer 3: 5 evil things, As you were *a*.
10:10 And the nations will not be *a*
11:11 them which they will not be *a*
49:10 And he shall not be *a* to hide
Lam 1:14 of those whom I am not *a* to
Ezek 7:19 and their gold will not be *a*
33:12 nor shall the righteous be *a* to
Dan 2:26 Are you *a* to make known to me
3:17 our God whom we serve is *a* to
4:18 men of my kingdom are not *a*
4:18 interpretation; but you are *a*,
4:37 who walk in pride He is *a* to
6:20 been *a* to deliver you from the
Am 7:10 The land is not *a* to bear all
Zeph 1:18 nor their gold Shall be *a* to
Mt 3: 9 For I say to you that God is *a*
9:28 Do you believe that I am *a* to do
10:28 But rather fear Him who is *a* to
18:25 But as he was not *a* to pay, his
19:12 He who is *a* to accept it, let
20:22 Are you *a* to drink the cup that
20:22 They said to Him, "We are *a*.
22:46 And no one was *a* to answer Him a
26:61 I am *a* to destroy the temple of
Mk 4:33 word to them as they were *a* to
10:38 Are you *a* to drink the cup that
10:39 They said to Him, "We are *a*.
Lk 1:20 you will be mute and not *a* to
3: 8 For I say to you that God is *a*
12:26 If you then are not *a* to do the
13:24 seek to enter and will not be *a*.
14:29 and is not *a* to finish, all who
14:30 began to build and was not *a*
14:31 and consider whether he is *a*
21:15 your adversaries will not be *a*
Jn 8:43 Because you are not *a* to listen
10:29 and no one is *a* to snatch them
21: 6 and now they were not *a* to draw
Acts 6:10 And they were not *a* to resist
15:10 our fathers nor we were *a* to
20:32 which is *a* to build you up and
Rom 4:21 He had promised He was also *a*
8:39 shall be *a* to separate us from
11:23 for God is *a* to graft them in
14: 4 for God is *a* to make him stand.
15:14 *a* also to admonish one another.
16:25 Now to Him who is *a* to
1 Cor 3: 2 for until now you were not *a*
3: 2 even now you are still not *a*;
6: 5 who will be *a* to judge between
10:13 tempted beyond what you are *a*,
10:13 that you may be *a* to bear it.
2 Cor 1: 4 that we may be *a* to comfort
9: 8 And God is *a* to make all grace
Eph 3:18 may be *a* to comprehend with all
3:20 Now to Him who is *a* to do
6:11 that you may be *a* to stand
6:13 that you may be *a* to withstand
6:16 faith with which you will be *a*
Phil 3:21 to the working by which He is *a*
1 Tim 3: 2 hospitable, *a* to teach;
2 Tim 1:12 and am persuaded that He is *a*
2: 2 to faithful men who will be *a*
2:24 *a* to teach, patient,
3: 7 always learning and never *a* to
3:15 which are *a* to make you wise
Titus 1: 9 been taught, that he may be *a*,
Heb 2:18 He is *a* to aid those who are
5: 7 and tears to Him who was *a* to
7:25 Therefore He is also *a* to save
11:19 concluding that God was *a* to
Jas 1:21 which is *a* to save your souls.
3: 2 *a* also to bridle the whole
4:12 who is *a* to save and to
Jude 24 Now to Him who is *a* to keep you
Rev 5: 3 earth or under the earth was *a*
6:17 and who is *a* to stand?"
13: 4 Who is *a* to make war with
15: 8 and no one was *a* to enter the

ABNER (62/52) ABNER'S

1 Sam 14:50 commander of his army was *A*
14:51 and Ner the father of *A* was
17:55 the Philistine, he said to *A*,
17:55 the commander of the army, "*A*,
17:55 And *A* said, "As your soul
17:57 *A* took him and brought him
20:25 and *A* sat by Saul's side, but
26: 5 and *A* the son of Ner, the
26: 7 And *A* and the people lay all
26:14 out to the people and to *A* the
26:14 saying, "Do you not answer, *A*?
26:14 Then *A* answered and said,
26:15 So David said to *A*,
2 Sam 2: 8 But *A* the son of Ner, commander
2:12 Now *A* the son of Ner, and the
2:14 Then *A* said to Joab, "Let the
2:17 and *A* and the men of Israel
2:19 So Asahel pursued *A*,
2:19 or to the left from following *A*.
2:20 Then *A* looked behind him and
2:21 And *A* said to him, "Turn aside
2:22 So *A* said again to Asahel,
2:23 Therefore *A* struck him in the
2:24 and Abishai also pursued *A*.
2:25 gathered together behind *A* and
2:26 Then *A* called to Joab and said,
2:29 Then *A* and his men went on all
2:30 Joab returned from pursuing *A*.
3: 6 that *A* was strengthening his
3: 7 So Ishbosheth said to *A*,
3: 8 Then *A* became very angry at the
3: 9 "May God do so to *A*,
3:11 And he could not answer *A*
3:12 Then *A* sent messengers on his
3:16 So *A* said to him, "Go,
3:17 Now *A* had communicated with the
3:19 And *A* also spoke in the hearing
3:19 Then *A* also went to speak in
3:20 So *A* and twenty men with him
3:20 And David made a feast for *A*
3:21 Then *A* said to David, "I will
3:21 So David sent *A* away, and he

3:22 But ***A*** was not with David in
3:23 ***A*** the son of Ner came to the
3:24 ***A*** came to you; why is it that
3:25 Surely you realize that ***A*** the
3:26 he sent messengers after ***A***,
3:27 Now when ***A*** had returned to
3:28 forever of the blood of ***A*** the
3:30 Abishai his brother killed ***A***,
3:31 with sackcloth, and mourn for ***A***.
3:32 So they buried ***A*** in Hebron; and
3:32 and wept at the grave of ***A***,
3:33 the king sang a lament over ***A***
3:33 Should ***A*** die as a fool dies?
3:37 the king's intent to kill ***A***
4: 1 When Saul's son heard that ***A*** had
4:12 buried it in the tomb of ***A*** in
1 Ki 2: 5 to ***A*** the son of Ner and Amasa
2:32 ***A*** the son of Ner, the commander
1 Chr 26:28 ***A*** the son of Ner, and Joab the
27:21 Benjamin, Jaasiel the son of ***A***;

ABNER'S (1/1) ABNER

2 Sam 2:31 of Benjamin and ***A*** men, three

ABOARD (1/1)

Acts 21: 2 we went ***a*** and set sail.

ABODE (1/1)

Jude 6 domain, but left their own ***a***,

ABODEST (KJV) See SIT

ABOLISH (1/1) ABOLISHED, ANNUL, DESTROY

Isa 2:18 the idols He shall utterly ***a***.

ABOLISHED (4/4) ABOLISH

Isa 51: 6 My righteousness will not be ***a***.
Ezek 6: 6 down, and your works may be ***a***.
Eph 2:15 having ***a*** in His flesh the
2 Tim 1:10 who has ***a*** death and brought

ABOMINABLE (21/21) ABOMINABLY, HORRIBLE, HATEFUL, LOATHSOME, VILE

Lev 7:21 or any ***a*** unclean thing, and who
11:43 shall not make yourselves ***a***
18:30 do not commit any of these ***a***
20:25 shall not make yourselves ***a*** by
1 Chr 21: 6 for the king's word was ***a*** to
2 Chr 15: 8 and removed the ***a*** idols from
Job 15:16 who is ***a*** and filthy, Who
Ps 14: 1 They have done ***a*** works, There
53: 1 and have done ***a*** iniquity;
Isa 14:19 out of your grave Like an ***a***
65: 4 And the broth of ***a*** things is
Jer 16:18 of their detestable and ***a***
44: 4 do not do this ***a*** thing that I
Ezek 4:14 nor has ***a*** flesh ever come into
8:10 ***a*** beasts, and all the idols of
16:36 and with all your ***a*** idols, and
16:52 you committed were more ***a*** than
Nah 3: 6 I will cast ***a*** filth upon you,
Titus 1:16 in works they deny Him, being ***a***,
1 Pe 4: 3 parties, and ***a*** idolatries.
Rev 21: 8 the cowardly, unbelieving, ***a***,

ABOMINABLY (1/1) ABOMINABLE

1 Ki 21:26 And he behaved very ***a*** in

ABOMINATION (78/71) ABOMINABLE, ABOMINABLY, ABOMINATIONS

Gen 43:32 for that is an ***a*** to the
46:34 for every shepherd is an ***a*** to
Ex 8:26 we would be sacrificing the ***a***
8:26 If we sacrifice the ***a*** of the
Lev 7:18 it shall be an ***a*** to him who
11:10 they are an ***a*** to you.
11:11 They shall be an ***a*** to you; you
11:11 regard their carcasses as an ***a***.
11:12 that shall be an ***a*** to you.
11:13 these you shall regard as an ***a***
11:13 not be eaten, they are an ***a***:
11:20 on all fours shall be an ***a***
11:23 have four feet shall be an ***a***
11:41 on the earth shall be an ***a***.
11:42 not eat, for they are an ***a***.
18:22 as with a woman. It is an ***a***.
19: 7 on the third day, it is an ***a***.
20:13 of them have committed an ***a***.
Deut 7:25 for it is an ***a*** to the LORD
7:26 Nor shall you bring an ***a*** into
12:31 for every ***a*** to the LORD which
13:14 and certain that such an ***a***
17: 1 for that is an ***a*** to the LORD
17: 4 and certain that such an ***a***
18:12 who do these things are an ***a***
22: 5 for all who do so are an ***a*** to
23:18 for both of these are an ***a*** to
24: 4 for that is an ***a*** before the
25:16 are an ***a*** to the LORD your
27:15 an ***a*** to the LORD, the work of
1 Sam 13: 4 Israel had also become an ***a*** to
1 Ki 11: 5 and after Milcom the ***a*** of the
11: 7 a high place for Chemosh the ***a***
11: 7 and for Molech the ***a*** of the
2 Ki 23:13 had built for Ashtoreth the ***a***
23:13 for Chemosh the ***a*** of the
23:13 and for Milcom the ***a*** of the
Ps 88: 8 You have made me an ***a*** to them;
Prov 3:32 the perverse person is an ***a***
6:16 seven are an ***a*** to Him:
8: 7 Wickedness is an ***a*** to my
11: 1 Dishonest scales are an ***a*** to
11:20 of a perverse heart are an ***a***
12:22 Lying lips are an ***a*** to the
13:19 But it is an ***a*** to fools to
15: 8 of the wicked is an ***a*** to the
15: 9 way of the wicked is an ***a*** to
15:26 of the wicked are an ***a*** to the
16: 5 proud in heart is an ***a*** to the
16:12 It is an ***a*** for kings to
17:15 Both of them alike are an ***a***
20:10 an ***a*** to the LORD.
20:23 Diverse weights are an ***a*** to
21:27 of the wicked is an ***a***;
24: 9 And the scoffer is an ***a*** to
28: 9 law, Even his prayer is an ***a***.
29:27 An unjust man is an ***a*** to the
29:27 upright in the way is an ***a*** to
Isa 1:13 Incense is an ***a*** to Me.
41:24 He who chooses you is an ***a***.
44:19 I make the rest of it an ***a***?
66:17 swine's flesh and the ***a*** and
Jer 2: 7 land And made My heritage an ***a***.
6:15 when they had committed ***a***?
8:12 when they had committed ***a***?
32:35 mind that they should do this ***a***,
Ezek 16:50 were haughty and committed ***a***
18:12 to the idols, Or committed ***a***;
22:11 One commits ***a*** with his
Dan 11:31 and place there the ***a*** of
12:11 and the ***a*** of desolation is set
Hos 9:10 They became an ***a*** like the
Mic 6:10 short measure that is an ***a***?
Mal 2:11 And an ***a*** has been committed in
Mt 24:15 ***a*** of desolation,' spoken of by
Mk 13:14 ***a*** of desolation,' spoken of by
Lk 16:15 esteemed among men is an ***a*** in
Rev 21:27 or causes an ***a*** or a lie, but

ABOMINATIONS (75/73) ABOMINATION

Lev 18:26 not commit any of these ***a***,
18:27 (for all these ***a*** the men of the
18:29 whoever commits any of these ***a***,
Deut 18: 9 not learn to follow the ***a*** of
18:12 and because of these ***a*** the
20:18 to do according to all their ***a***
29:17 and you saw their ***a*** and their
32:16 With ***a*** they provoked Him to
1 Ki 14:24 did according to all the ***a*** of
2 Ki 16: 3 according to the ***a*** of the
21: 2 according to the ***a*** of the
21:11 king of Judah has done these ***a***
23:24 all the ***a*** that were seen in the
2 Chr 28: 3 according to the ***a*** of the
33: 2 according to the ***a*** of the
34:33 Thus Josiah removed all the ***a***
36: 8 the ***a*** which he did, and what
36:14 according to all the ***a*** of the
Ezra 9: 1 with respect to the ***a*** of the
9:11 with their ***a*** which have filled
9:14 the people committing these ***a***?
Prov 26:25 For there are seven ***a*** in his
Isa 66: 3 their soul delights in their ***a***,
Jer 4: 1 if you will put away your ***a***
7:10 delivered to do all these ***a***'?
7:30 They have set their ***a*** in the
13:27 Your ***a*** on the hills in the
32:34 But they set their ***a*** in the
44:22 doings and because of the ***a***
Ezek 5: 9 do again, because of all your ***a***.
5:11 things and with all your ***a***,
6: 9 they committed in all their ***a***.
6:11 for all the evil ***a*** of the house
7: 3 I will repay you for all your ***a***.
7: 4 And your ***a*** will be in your
7: 8 I will repay you for all your ***a***.
7: 9 And your ***a*** will be in your
7:20 from it The images of their ***a***—
8: 6 the great ***a*** that the house of
8: 6 again, you will see greater ***a***.
8: 9 and see the wicked ***a*** which they
8:13 and you will see greater ***a***
8:15 you will see greater ***a*** than
8:17 house of Judah to commit the ***a***
9: 4 who sigh and cry over all the ***a***
11:18 things and all its ***a*** from
11:21 detestable things and their ***a***,
12:16 they may declare all their ***a***
14: 6 your faces away from all your ***a***.
16: 2 cause Jerusalem to know her ***a***,
16:22 And in all your ***a*** and acts of
16:43 in addition to all your ***a***.
16:47 nor act according to their ***a***;
16:51 but you have multiplied your ***a***
16:51 your sisters by all the ***a***
16:58 for your lewdness and your ***a***,
18:13 If he has done any of these ***a***,
18:24 and does according to all the ***a***
20: 4 Then make known to them the ***a***
20: 7 throw away the ***a*** which are
20: 8 did not all cast away the ***a***
20:30 harlotry according to their ***a***?
22: 2 show her all her ***a***!
23:36 Then declare to them their ***a***.
33:26 on your sword, you commit ***a***,
33:29 because of all their ***a*** which
36:31 for your iniquities and your ***a***.
43: 8 defiled My holy name by the ***a***
44: 6 us have no more of all your ***a***.
44: 7 covenant because of all your ***a***.
44:13 bear their shame and their ***a***
Dan 9:27 And on the wing of ***a*** shall be
Zech 9: 7 And the ***a*** from between his
Rev 17: 4 her hand a golden cup full of ***a***
17: 5 THE ***A*** OF THE EARTH.

ABOUND (21/19) ABOUNDED, ABOUNDING, ABOUNDS, INCREASE, OVERFLOW

Gen 1:20 Let the waters ***a*** with an
8:17 so that they may ***a*** on the
Deut 30: 9 LORD your God will make you ***a***
Prov 28:20 A faithful man will ***a*** with
Mt 24:12 because lawlessness will ***a***,
Rom 5:20 that the offense might ***a***.
6: 1 in sin that grace may ***a***?
15:13 that you may ***a*** in hope by the
2 Cor 1: 5 as the sufferings of Christ ***a***
4:15 may cause thanksgiving to ***a*** to
8: 7 But as you ***a*** in everything—in
8: 7 see that you ***a*** in this grace
9: 8 is able to make all grace ***a***
Eph 1: 8 which He made to ***a*** toward us in
Phil 1: 9 that your love may ***a*** still more
4:12 be abased, and I know how to ***a***.
4:12 both to ***a*** and to suffer need.
4:18 Indeed I have all and ***a***.
1 Th 3:12 Lord make you increase and ***a***
4: 1 Lord Jesus that you should ***a***
2 Pe 1: 8 if these things are yours and ***a***,

ABOUNDED, ABOUNDETH (KJV) See ABOUNDS

ABOUNDED (6/5) ABOUND

Gen 1:21 moves, with which the waters ***a***,
Ps 105:30 Their land ***a*** with frogs, Even
Rom 5:15 Man, Jesus Christ, ***a*** to many.
5:20 might abound. But where sin ***a***,
5:20 grace ***a*** much more,
2 Cor 8: 2 joy and their deep poverty ***a***

ABOUNDING (6/6) ABOUND

Ex 34: 6 and ***a*** in goodness and truth,
Ps 103: 8 Slow to anger, and ***a*** in mercy.
Prov 8:24 there were no fountains ***a***
1 Cor 15:58 always ***a*** in the work of the
2 Cor 9:12 but also is ***a*** through many
Col 2: 7 ***a*** in it with thanksgiving.

ABOUNDS (4/4) ABOUND

Prov 29:22 And a furious man ***a*** in
2 Cor 1: 5 so our consolation also ***a***
Phil 4:17 but I seek the fruit that ***a*** to
2 Th 1: 3 love of every one of you all ***a***

ABOUT (381/364)

Gen 7:18 and the ark moved ***a*** on the
21:16 from him at a distance of ***a*** a
24:33 not eat until I have told ***a*** my
25:32 I am ***a*** to die; so what is
26: 7 the men of the place asked ***a***
26:32 servants came and told him ***a***
29:13 when Laban heard the report ***a***
31:34 And Laban searched all ***a*** the
32:29 Why is it that you ask ***a*** My
35:22 and Israel heard ***a*** it. Now
38:24 ***a*** three months after, that
39:11 But it happened ***a*** this time,
41:25 shown Pharaoh what He is ***a*** to
41:28 shown Pharaoh what He is ***a*** to
42: 9 dreams which he had dreamed ***a***
43: 7 The man asked us pointedly ***a***
43:27 Then he asked them ***a*** their
45:20 Also do not be concerned ***a*** your
50:20 in order to bring it ***a*** as it
Ex 9:18 tomorrow ***a*** this time I will
11: 4 ***A*** midnight I will go out into
12:37 ***a*** six hundred thousand men on
13:15 when Pharaoh was stubborn ***a***
18: 7 And they asked each other ***a***
21:19 if he rises again and walks ***a***
25:22 ***a*** everything which I will give
32:28 And ***a*** three thousand men of the
Lev 6: 2 by lying to his neighbor ***a***
6: 2 or ***a*** a pledge, or about a
6: 2 or ***a*** a robbery, or if he has
6: 5 or all that ***a*** which he has sworn
10:16 Moses made careful inquiry ***a***
19:16 You shall not go ***a*** as a
Num 11: 8 The people went ***a*** and gathered
11:31 ***a*** a day's journey on this side
11:31 journey on this side and ***a*** a
11:31 and ***a*** two cubits above the
14:37 who brought the evil report ***a***
Deut 2: 4 You are ***a*** to pass through the
12:10 from all your enemies round ***a***,
26: 5 ***a*** to perish, and he went down

Josh 3: 4 *a* two thousand cubits by
4:13 *A* forty thousand prepared for
6:15 *a* the dawning of the day, and
7: 3 but let *a* two or three thousand
7: 4 So *a* three thousand men went up
7: 5 And the men of Ai struck down *a*
8: 5 the city; and it will come *a*,
8:12 So he took *a* five thousand men
9: 1 the Jebusite—heard *a* it,
10:13 not hasten to go down for *a* a
11: 6 for tomorrow *a* this time I will
23: 1 from all their enemies round *a*,
Judg 3:29 And at that time they killed *a*
6:13 which our fathers told us *a*,
8:10 *a* fifteen thousand, all who
8:15 *a* whom you ridiculed me,
9:42 And it came *a* on the next day
9:49 *a* a thousand men and women.
16:27 *a* three thousand men and women
20:31 *a* thirty men of Israel.
20:39 had begun to strike and kill *a*
Ruth 1: 4 And they dwelt there *a* ten
2:17 and it was *a* an ephah of
1 Sam 4: 2 who killed *a* four thousand men
4:20 And *a* the time of her death the
9: 5 lest my father cease caring *a*
9: 5 donkeys and become worried *a*
9:13 for *a* this time you will find
9:16 Tomorrow *a* this time I will send
9:20 do not be anxious *a* them, for
9:22 there were *a* thirty persons.
9:26 and it was *a* the dawning of the
10: 2 father has ceased caring *a* the
10: 2 the donkeys and is worrying *a*
10: 2 What shall I do *a* my son?"'
10:16 But *a* the matter of the
13:15 *a* six hundred men.
13:22 So it came *a*, on the day of
14: 2 who were with him were *a* six
14:14 and his armorbearer made was *a*
14:14 was about twenty men within *a*
17:42 when the Philistine looked *a*
19: 3 I will speak with my father *a*
19: 5 and the LORD brought *a* a great
21: 2 not let anyone know anything *a*
21: 5 have been kept from us *a*
22: 2 And there were *a* four hundred
22: 6 and all his servants standing *a*
22: 7 to his servants who stood *a*
22:17 said to the guards who stood *a*
23:13 *a* six hundred, arose and
25:13 And *a* four hundred men went
25:38 after *a* ten days, that the
2 Sam 4: 4 five years old when the news *a*
4: 5 set out and came at *a* the heat
7: 6 but have moved *a* in a tent and
7: 7 Wherever I have moved *a* with all
11: 3 So David sent and inquired *a* the
14: 1 king's heart was concerned *a*
14:20 To bring *a* this change of
18: 3 they will not care *a* us; nor if
18: 3 will they care *a* us. But you
18:29 I did not know what it was *a*.
19:10 why do you say nothing *a*
23:10 The LORD brought *a* a great
23:12 And the LORD brought *a* a great
1 Ki 1:18 you do not know *a* it.
10: 2 she spoke with him *a* all that
10: 6 which I heard in my own land *a*
14: 5 coming to ask you something *a*
18:26 Then they leaped *a* the altar
19: 2 of one of them by tomorrow *a*
20: 6 my servants to you tomorrow *a*
21:27 and went *a* mourning.
22: 6 *a* four hundred men, and said to
2 Ki 2: 1 when the LORD was *a* to take up
4:16 *A* this time next year you shall
7: 1 Tomorrow *a* this time a seah of
7:18 shall be sold tomorrow *a* this
1 Chr 11:14 So the LORD brought *a* a great
15:13 we did not consult Him *a* the
17: 6 Wherever I have moved *a* with all
19: 5 some went and told David *a*
2 Chr 2: 9 for the temple which I am *a* to
9: 1 she spoke with him *a* all that
9: 5 which I heard in my own land *a*
18:34 and *a* the time of sunset he
24:27 and the many oracles *a* him, and
25: 9 But what shall we do *a* the
32:31 they sent to him to inquire *a*
Neh 13:15 And I warned them *a* the day on
Esth 9:29 to confirm this second letter *a*
Job 15:23 He wanders *a* for bread,
20:23 When he is *a* to fill his
21:21 For what does he care *a* his
27:11 I will teach you *a* the hand of
28:22 We have heard a report *a* it with
30:18 It binds me *a* as the collar of
30:28 I go *a* mourning, but not in the
37:12 And they swirl *a*,
38:41 And wander *a* for lack of food?
Ps 26: 6 So I will go *a* Your altar, O
35:14 I paced *a* as though he were
39: 6 Surely every man walks *a* like a
48:12 Walk *a* Zion, And go all around
77:17 Your arrows also flashed *a*.
82: 5 They walk *a* in darkness; All
97: 3 burns up His enemies round *a*.
104:20 beasts of the forest creep *a*.
104:26 There the ships sail *a*;
119:59 I thought *a* my ways, And
130:11 the night shall be light *a* me;

Prov 1: 9 And chains *a* your neck.
16:30 purses his lips and brings *a*
20:19 He who goes *a* as a talebearer
27: 1 Do not boast *a* tomorrow, For
Eccl 1: 6 The wind whirls *a* continually,
12: 5 And the mourners go *a* the
Song 3: 2 And go *a* the city; In the
3: 3 The watchmen who go *a* the city
5: 7 The watchmen who went *a* the
7: 2 is a heap of wheat Set *a*
Isa 14: 9 from beneath is excited *a*
23:16 go *a* the city, You forgotten
27:13 who are *a* to perish in the land
31: 5 Like birds flying *a*,
56: 1 For My salvation is *a* to
Jer 2:36 Why do you gad *a* so much to
5:12 They have lied *a* the LORD,
6:26 in sackcloth And roll *a* in
12: 1 Yet let me talk with You *a*
14:18 both prophet and priest go *a* in
25:34 and cry! Roll *a* in the
30:15 Why do you cry *a* your
31:22 How long will you gad *a*,
48:39 And a dismay to all those *a*
50:43 Babylon has heard the report *a*
Lam 5:18 With foxes walking *a* on it.
Ezek 8:16 were *a* twenty-five men with
11:15 are those *a* whom the
12:22 that you people have *a* the
27:30 They will roll *a* in ashes;
33:30 of your people are talking *a*
36: 8 for they are *a* to come.
38: 7 companies that are gathered *a*
Dan 1:20 of wisdom and understanding *a*
2:29 *a* what would come to pass
4:29 twelve months he was walking *a*
5:31 being *a* sixty-two years old.
7:19 I wished to know the truth *a*
8:27 afterward I arose and went *a*
9:21 reached me *a* the time of the
Joel 1: 3 Tell your children *a* it, Let
Jon 1: 4 so that the ship was *a* to be
4: 9 it right for you to be angry *a*
Mt 1:11 Jeconiah and his brothers *a*
1:20 But while he thought *a* these
4:23 And Jesus went *a* all Galilee,
6:25 do not worry *a* your life, what
6:25 nor *a* your body, what you will
6:28 So why do you worry *a* clothing?
6:34 Therefore do not worry *a*
6:34 for tomorrow will worry *a* its
8:18 Jesus saw great multitudes *a*
9:31 they spread the news *a* Him in
9:35 Then Jesus went *a* all the
10:19 do not worry *a* how or what you
11: 2 John had heard in prison *a* the
14: 1 the tetrarch heard the report *a*
14:21 Now those who had eaten were *a*
15: 7 Well did Isaiah prophesy *a* you,
17:12 the Son of Man is also *a* to
17:22 The Son of Man is *a* to be
20: 3 And he went out *a* the third hour
20: 5 Again he went out *a* the sixth
20: 6 And *a* the eleventh hour he went
20: 9 those came who were hired *a*
20:22 to drink the cup that I am *a*
22: 7 But when the king heard *a* it,
22:16 nor do You care *a* anyone, for
22:42 What do you think *a* the Christ?
27:46 And *a* the ninth hour Jesus cried
Mk 1:30 and they told Him *a* her at
2: 8 Why do you reason *a* these things
3:10 as had afflictions pressed *a*
3:21 when His own people heard *a*
3:34 in a circle at those who sat *a*
4:10 Him with the twelve asked Him *a*
5:13 the swine (there were *a* two
5:16 and *a* the swine.
5:27 When she heard *a* Jesus, she came
6: 6 Then He went *a* the villages in
6:44 who had eaten the loaves were *a*
6:48 Now *a* the fourth watch of the
6:52 For they had not understood *a*
6:55 and began to carry *a* on beds
7:25 had an unclean spirit heard *a*
8: 9 Now those who had eaten were *a*
8:30 that they should tell no one *a*
10:10 also asked Him again *a* the
12:14 and care *a* no one; for You do
14:72 And when he thought *a* it, he
Lk 1:56 And Mary remained with her *a*
2:37 this woman was a widow of *a*
2:49 you not know that I must be *a*
3:15 all reasoned in their hearts *a*
3:23 began His ministry at *a*
4:37 And the report *a* Him went out
5: 1 as the multitude pressed *a* Him
7: 3 So when he heard *a* Jesus, he
7:17 And this report *a* Him went
8:42 for he had an only daughter *a*
9:11 them and spoke to them *a* the
9:14 For there were *a* five thousand
9:28 *a* eight days after these
9:31 of His decease which He was *a*
9:44 for the Son of Man is *a* to be
9:45 they were afraid to ask Him *a*
10: 1 place where He Himself was *a*
10:41 you are worried and troubled *a*
11:53 and to cross-examine Him *a* many
12:11 do not worry *a* how or what you
12:22 do not worry *a* your life, what
12:22 nor *a* the body, what you will

13: 1 season some who told Him *a* the
16: 2 'What is this I hear *a* you?
21: 7 be when these things are *a* to
22:41 He was withdrawn from them *a* a
22:59 Then after *a* an hour had passed,
23: 8 he had heard many things *a* Him,
23:44 Now it was *a* the sixth hour,
24: 4 they were greatly perplexed *a*
24:35 And they told *a* the things that
Jn 1:22 What do you say *a* yourself?"
1:39 Him that day (now it was *a* the
3:25 John's disciples and the Jews *a*
4: 6 It was *a* the sixth hour.
5:46 for he wrote *a* Me.
6:10 in number *a* five thousand.
6:15 perceived that they were *a* to
6:19 So when they had rowed *a* three
6:41 The Jews then complained *a* Him,
6:61 that His disciples complained *a*
7:14 Now *a* the middle of the feast
9:17 What do you say *a* Him because He
10:13 a hireling and does not care *a*
10:41 the things that John spoke *a*
11:13 thought that He was speaking *a*
11:18 *a* two miles away.
12:16 these things were written *a*
13:22 perplexed *a* whom He spoke.
16:19 inquiring among yourselves *a*
16:25 but I will tell you plainly *a*
18:19 high priest then asked Jesus *a*
18:34 you speaking for yourself *a*
19:14 and *a* the sixth hour. And he
19:39 *a* a hundred pounds.
21: 8 but *a* two hundred cubits),
21:21 what *a* this man?"
Acts 1:15 the number of names was *a* a
2:41 and that day *a* three thousand
3: 3 seeing Peter and John *a* to go
4: 4 number of the men came to be *a*
5: 7 Now it was *a* three hours later
5:36 *a* four hundred, joined him.
9:13 I have heard from many *a* this
10: 3 *A* the ninth hour of the day he
10: 9 *a* the sixth hour.
10:19 While Peter thought *a* the
10:38 who went *a* doing good and
12: 1 Now *a* that time Herod the king
12: 6 And when Herod was *a* to bring
12:18 stir among the soldiers *a* what
13:18 Now for a time of *a* forty years
13:20 that He gave them judges for *a*
15: 2 and elders, *a* this question.
16:27 drew his sword and was *a* to
18:14 And when Paul was *a* to open his
19: 7 Now the men were *a* twelve in
19:23 And *a* that time there arose a
19:23 arose a great commotion *a* the
19:34 with one voice cried out for *a*
20: 3 against him as he was *a* to
21:21 but they have been informed *a*
21:37 Then as Paul was *a* to be led
22: 6 and came near Damascus at *a*
22:29 immediately those who were *a*
23:20 going to inquire more fully *a*
23:27 seized by the Jews and was *a*
24:25 Now as he reasoned *a*
25: 7 down from Jerusalem stood *a*
25:15 *a* whom the chief priests and the
25:19 some questions against him *a*
25:19 about their own religion and *a*
25:24 you see this man *a* whom the
27:27 *a* midnight the sailors sensed
27:33 And as day was *a* to dawn, Paul
28:15 when the brethren heard *a* us,
Rom 4: 2 he has something to boast *a*,
4:15 because the law brings *a* wrath;
4:19 already dead (since he was *a* a
10: 5 For Moses writes *a* the
15:19 from Jerusalem and round *a* to
1 Cor 7:21 Do not be concerned *a* it; but
7:33 But he who is married cares *a*
7:34 The unmarried woman cares *a* the
7:34 But she who is married cares *a*
9: 9 Is it oxen God is concerned *a*?
16:17 I am glad *a* the coming of
2 Cor 4:10 always carrying *a* in the body
7:14 I have boasted to him *a* you,
8:23 If anyone inquires *a* Titus,
8:23 our brethren are inquired *a*,
9: 2 *a* which I boast of you to the
10: 8 I should boast somewhat more *a*
Gal 2:14 were not straightforward *a* the
4:20 for I have doubts *a* you.
Eph 4:14 to and fro and carried *a* with
Col 4: 7 will tell you all the news *a*
4:10 Mark the cousin of Barnabas (*a*
1 Tim 5:13 wandering *a* from house to
2 Tim 2:14 the Lord not to strive *a* words
Titus 3: 9 and strivings *a* the law; for
Heb 8: 5 instructed when he was *a* to
11:37 They wandered *a* in sheepskins
13: 9 Do not be carried *a* with various
1 Pe 5: 8 adversary the devil walks *a*
1 Jn 5:16 not say that he should pray *a*
Jude 9 when he disputed *a* the body of
12 carried *a* by the winds; late
14 prophesied *a* these men also,
Rev 1:13 down to the feet and girded *a*
2:10 of those things which you are *a*
2:10 the devil is *a* to throw some
8: 1 was silence in heaven for *a*
8:13 of the three angels who are *a*

10: 4 I was *a* to write; but I heard a
10: 7 when he is *a* to sound, the
10:11 You must prophesy again *a* many
16:21 each hailstone *a* the weight

ABOVE (234/221) See APPENDIX

ABRAHAM (232/217) ABRAHAM'S, ABRAM

Gen 17: 5 Abram, but your name shall be *A*;
17: 9 God said to *A*: "As for you,
17:15 God said to *A*, "As for Sarai
17:17 Then *A* fell on his face and
17:18 And *A* said to God, "Oh, that
17:22 him, and God went up from *A*.
17:23 So *A* took Ishmael his son, all
17:24 *A* was ninety-nine years old
17:26 That very same day *A* was
18: 6 So *A* hurried into the tent to
18: 7 And *A* ran to the herd, took a
18:11 Now *A* and Sarah were old, well
18:13 And the LORD said to *A*,
18:16 and *A* went with them to send
18:17 Shall I hide from *A* what I am
18:18 since *A* shall surely become a
18:19 that the LORD may bring to *A*
18:22 but *A* still stood before the
18:23 And *A* came near and said,
18:27 Then *A* answered and said,
18:33 He had finished speaking with *A*;
18:33 and *A* returned to his place.
19:27 And *A* went early in the morning
19:29 plain, that God remembered *A*,
20: 1 And *A* journeyed from there to
20: 2 Now *A* said of Sarah his wife,
20: 9 And Abimelech called *A* and said
20:10 Then Abimelech said to *A*,
20:11 And *A* said, "Because I thought,
20:14 servants, and gave them to *A*;
20:17 So *A* prayed to God; and God
21: 2 For Sarah conceived and bore *A*
21: 3 And *A* called the name of his son
21: 4 Then *A* circumcised his son Isaac
21: 5 Now *A* was one hundred years old
21: 7 Who would have said to *A* that
21: 8 And *A* made a great feast on the
21: 9 whom she had borne to *A*,
21:10 Therefore she said to *A*,
21:12 God said to *A*, "Do not let
21:14 So *A* rose early in the morning,
21:22 of his army, spoke to *A*,
21:24 And *A* said, "I will swear."
21:25 Then *A* rebuked Abimelech
21:27 So *A* took sheep and oxen and
21:28 And *A* set seven ewe lambs of the
21:29 Then Abimelech asked *A*,
21:33 Then *A* planted a tamarisk tree
21:34 And *A* stayed in the land of the
22: 1 these things that God tested *A*,
22: 1 *A*!" And he said, "Here I am."
22: 3 So *A* rose early in the morning
22: 4 Then on the third day *A* lifted
22: 5 And *A* said to his young men,
22: 6 So *A* took the wood of the burnt
22: 7 But Isaac spoke to *A* his father
22: 8 And *A* said, "My son, God will
22: 9 And *A* built an altar there and
22:10 And *A* stretched out his hand and
22:11 him from heaven and said, "*A*,
22:11 *A*!" So he said, "Here I am."
22:13 Then *A* lifted his eyes and
22:13 So *A* went and took the ram, and
22:14 And *A* called the name of the
22:15 Angel of the LORD called to *A*
22:19 So *A* returned to his young men,
22:19 and *A* dwelt at Beersheba.
22:20 these things that it was told *A*,
23: 2 and *A* came to mourn for Sarah
23: 3 Then *A* stood up from before his
23: 5 And the sons of Heth answered *A*,
23: 7 Then *A* stood up and bowed
23:10 Ephron the Hittite answered *A*
23:12 Then *A* bowed himself down before
23:14 And Ephron answered *A*,
23:16 And *A* listened to Ephron; and
23:16 and *A* weighed out the silver
23:18 to *A* as a possession in the
23:19 *A* buried Sarah his wife in the
23:20 is in it were deeded to *A* by
24: 1 Now *A* was old, well advanced in
24: 1 and the LORD had blessed *A* in
24: 2 So *A* said to the oldest servant
24: 6 But *A* said to him, "Beware that
24: 9 his hand under the thigh of *A*
24:12 "O LORD God of my master *A*,
24:12 show kindness to my master *A*.
24:27 the LORD God of my master *A*,
24:42 'O LORD God of my master *A*,
24:48 the LORD God of my master *A*,
25: 1 *A* again took a wife, and her
25: 5 And *A* gave all that he had to
25: 6 But *A* gave gifts to the sons of
25: 6 sons of the concubines which *A*
25: 8 Then *A* breathed his last and
25:10 the field which *A* purchased from
25:10 There *A* was buried, and Sarah
25:11 to pass, after the death of *A*,
25:12 Sarah's maidservant, bore to *A*.
25:19 *A* begot Isaac.
26: 1 that was in the days of *A*.
26: 3 the oath which I swore to *A*
26: 5 because *A* obeyed My voice and
26:15 had dug in the days of *A* his
26:18 they had dug in the days of *A*
26:18 them up after the death of *A*.
26:24 am the God of your father *A*;
28: 4 And give you the blessing of *A*,
28: 4 stranger, Which God gave to *A*.
28:13 I am the LORD God of *A* your
31:42 the God of *A* and the Fear of
31:53 "The God of *A*,
32: 9 O God of my father *A* and God of
35:12 The land which I gave *A* and
35:27 where *A* and Isaac had dwelt.
48:15 before whom my fathers *A* and
48:16 And the name of my fathers *A*
49:30 which *A* bought with the field
49:31 There they buried *A* and Sarah
50:13 which *A* bought with the field
50:24 the land of which He swore to *A*,
Ex 2:24 remembered His covenant with *A*,
3: 6 God of your father—the God of *A*,
3:15 of your fathers, the God of *A*,
3:16 of your fathers, the God of *A*,
4: 5 of their fathers, the God of *A*,
6: 3 "I appeared to *A*,
6: 8 land which I swore to give to *A*,
32:13 'Remember *A*, Isaac, and
33: 1 the land of which I swore to *A*,
Lev 26:42 Isaac and My covenant with *A* I
Num 32:11 the land of which I swore to *A*,
Deut 1: 8 swore to your fathers—to *A*,
6:10 He swore to your fathers, to *A*,
9: 5 swore to your fathers, to *A*,
9:27 'Remember Your servants, *A*,
29:13 has sworn to your fathers, to *A*,
30:20 swore to your fathers, to *A*,
34: 4 land of which I swore to give *A*,
Josh 24: 2 the father of *A* and the father
24: 3 Then I took your father *A* from
1 Ki 18:36 near and said, "LORD God of *A*,
2 Ki 13:23 because of His covenant with *A*,
1 Chr 1:27 and Abram, who is *A*.
1:28 The sons of *A* were Isaac and
1:34 And *A* begot Isaac. The sons of
16:16 covenant which He made with *A*,
29:18 "O LORD God of *A*,
2 Chr 20: 7 gave it to the descendants of *A*
30: 6 return to the LORD God of *A*,
Neh 9: 7 And gave him the name *A*;
Ps 47: 9 The people of the God of *A*.
105: 6 O seed of *A* His servant, You
105: 9 covenant which He made with *A*,
105:42 And *A* His servant.
Isa 29:22 says the LORD, who redeemed *A*,
41: 8 The descendants of *A* My
51: 2 Look to *A* your father, And to
63:16 Though *A* was ignorant of us,
Jer 33:26 over the descendants of *A*,
Ezek 33:24 *A* was only one, and he inherited
Mic 7:20 truth to Jacob And mercy to *A*,
Mt 1: 1 the Son of David, the Son of *A*:
1: 2 *A* begot Isaac, Isaac begot
1:17 So all the generations from *A* to
3: 9 We have *A* as our father.' For I
3: 9 able to raise up children to *A*
8:11 and west, and sit down with *A*,
22:32 'I am the God of *A*,
Mk 12:26 'I am the God of *A*,
Lk 1:55 To *A* and to his seed
1:73 which He swore to our father *A*:
3: 8 We have *A* as our father.' For I
3: 8 able to raise up children to *A*
3:34 son of Isaac, the son of *A*,
13:16 woman, being a daughter of *A*,
13:28 when you see *A* and Isaac and
16:23 he lifted up his eyes and saw *A*
16:24 he cried and said, 'Father *A*,
16:25 But *A* said, 'Son, remember that
16:29 *A* said to him, 'They have Moses
16:30 "And he said, 'No, father *A*;
19: 9 because he also is a son of *A*;
20:37 the Lord 'the God of *A*,
Jn 8:39 *A* is our father." Jesus said to
8:39 you would do the works of *A*.
8:40 *A* did not do this.
8:52 know that You have a demon! *A*
8:53 You greater than our father *A*,
8:56 Your father *A* rejoiced to see My
8:57 years old, and have You seen *A*?
8:58 before *A* was, I AM."
Acts 3:13 'The God of *A*, Isaac, and
3:25 with our fathers, saying to *A*,
7: 2 glory appeared to our father *A*
7: 5 But even when *A* had no child,
7: 8 and so *A* begot Isaac and
7:16 and laid in the tomb that *A*
7:17 near which God had sworn to *A*,
7:32 your fathers—the God of *A*,
13:26 sons of the family of *A*,
Rom 4: 1 What then shall we say that *A*
4: 2 For if *A* was justified by works,
4: 3 *A* believed God, and it was
4: 9 that faith was accounted to *A*
4:12 of the faith which our father *A*
4:13 of the world was not to *A* or
4:16 those who are of the faith of *A*,
9: 7 because they are the seed of *A*;
11: 1 an Israelite, of the seed of *A*,
2 Cor 11:22 am I. Are they the seed of *A*?
Gal 3: 6 just as *A* "believed God, and
3: 7 who are of faith are sons of *A*.
3: 8 preached the gospel to *A*
3: 9 are blessed with believing *A*.
3:14 that the blessing of *A* might
3:16 Now to *A* and his Seed were the
3:18 but God gave it to *A* by
4:22 For it is written that *A* had two
Heb 2:16 does give aid to the seed of *A*.
6:13 when God made a promise to *A*,
7: 1 who met *A* returning from the
7: 2 to whom also *A* gave a tenth part
7: 4 to whom even the patriarch *A*
7: 5 have come from the loins of *A*;
7: 6 them received tithes from *A*
7: 9 tithes, paid tithes through *A*,
11: 8 By faith *A* obeyed when he was
11:17 By faith *A*, when he was tested,
Jas 2:21 Was not *A* our father justified
2:23 *A* believed God, and it was
1 Pe 3: 6 as Sarah obeyed *A*,

ABRAHAM'S (19/19) ABRAHAM

Gen 17:23 male among the men of *A* house,
20:18 because of Sarah, *A* wife.
21:11 was very displeasing in *A* sight
22:23 bore to Nahor, *A* brother.
24:15 *A* brother, came out with her
24:34 I am *A* servant.
24:52 when *A* servant heard their
24:59 and *A* servant and his men.
25: 7 the sum of the years of *A* life
25:12 *A* son, whom Hagar the Egyptian,
25:19 *A* son. Abraham begot Isaac.
26:24 for My servant *A* sake."
28: 9 *A* son, the sister of Nebajoth,
1 Chr 1:32 *A* concubine, were Zimran,
Lk 16:22 by the angels to *A* bosom.
Jn 8:33 We are *A* descendants, and have
8:37 that you are *A* descendants,
8:39 If you were *A* children, you
Gal 3:29 then you are *A* seed, and heirs

ABRAM (54/46) ABRAHAM, ABRAM'S

Gen 11:26 seventy years, and begot *A*,
11:27 of Terah: Terah begot *A*,
11:29 Then *A* and Nahor took wives: the
11:31 And Terah took his son *A* and
12: 1 Now the LORD had said to *A*:
12: 4 So *A* departed as the LORD had
12: 4 And *A* was seventy-five years
12: 5 Then *A* took Sarai his wife and
12: 6 *A* passed through the land to the
12: 7 Then the LORD appeared to *A* and
12: 9 So *A* journeyed, going on still
12:10 and *A* went down to Egypt to
12:14 when *A* came into Egypt, that
12:16 He treated *A* well for her sake.
12:18 And Pharaoh called *A* and said,
13: 1 Then *A* went up from Egypt, he
13: 2 *A* was very rich in livestock,
13: 4 And there *A* called on the name
13: 5 Lot also, who went with *A*,
13: 8 So *A* said to Lot, "Please let
13:12 *A* dwelt in the land of Canaan,
13:14 And the LORD said to *A*,
13:18 Then *A* moved his tent, and went
14:13 who had escaped came and told *A*
14:13 and they were allies with *A*.
14:14 Now when *A* heard that his
14:19 Blessed be *A* of God Most High,
14:21 the king of Sodom said to *A*,
14:22 But *A* said to the king of Sodom,
14:23 I have made *A* rich'—
15: 1 word of the LORD came to *A* in
15: 1 saying, "Do not be afraid, *A*.
15: 2 But *A* said, "Lord GOD, what
15: 3 Then *A* said, "Look, You have
15:11 *A* drove them away.
15:12 down, a deep sleep fell upon *A*;
15:13 Then He said to *A*:
15:18 LORD made a covenant with *A*,
16: 2 So Sarai said to *A*,
16: 2 And *A* heeded the voice of
16: 3 and gave her to her husband *A*
16: 3 after *A* had dwelt ten years in
16: 5 Then Sarai said to *A*,
16: 6 So *A* said to Sarai, "Indeed
16:15 So Hagar bore *A* a son; and
16:15 and *A* named his son, whom Hagar
16:16 *A* was eighty-six years old when
16:16 when Hagar bore Ishmael to *A*.
17: 1 When *A* was ninety-nine years
17: 1 the LORD appeared to *A* and
17: 3 Then *A* fell on his face, and God
17: 5 shall your name be called *A*,
1 Chr 1:27 and *A*, who is Abraham.
Neh 9: 7 the LORD God, Who chose *A*,

ABRAM'S (7/7) ABRAHAM'S, ABRAM

Gen 11:29 the name of *A* wife was Sarai,
11:31 his son *A* wife, and they went
12:17 because of Sarai, *A* wife.
13: 7 between the herdsmen of *A*
14:12 *A* brother's son who dwelt in
16: 1 *A* wife, had borne him no
16: 3 *A* wife, took Hagar her maid,

ABROAD (15/15)

Gen 11: 4 lest we be scattered *a* over the

11: 8 So the LORD scattered them ***a***
11: 9 the LORD scattered them ***a***
28:14 you shall spread ***a*** to the west
Ex 5:12 So the people were scattered ***a***
Ps 112: 9 He has dispersed ***a***,
Prov 5:16 your fountains be dispersed ***a***,
Isa 24: 1 its surface And scatters ***a***
44:24 Who spreads ***a*** the earth by
Ezek 34:21 horns, and scattered them ***a***,
Zech 2: 6 for I have spread you ***a*** like the
Mt 12:30 not gather with Me scatters ***a***.
Jn 11:52 of God who were scattered ***a***.
2 Cor 9: 9 "He has dispersed ***a***,
Jas 1: 1 tribes which are scattered ***a***:

ABRONAH (2/2)

Num 33:34 from Jotbathah and camped at *A*.
33:35 They departed from *A* and camped

ABSALOM (102/85) ABISHALOM, ABSALOM'S

2 Sam 3: 3 *A* the son of Maacah, the
13: 1 After this *A* the son of David
13:20 And *A* her brother said to her,
13:22 And *A* spoke to his brother Amnon
13:22 For *A* hated Amnon, because he
13:23 that *A* had sheepshearers in
13:23 so *A* invited all the king's
13:24 Then *A* came to the king and
13:25 But the king said to *A*,
13:26 Then *A* said, "If not, please
13:27 But *A* urged him; so he let Amnon
13:28 Now *A* had commanded his
13:29 So the servants of *A* did to
13:29 of Absalom did to Amnon as *A*
13:30 *A* has killed all the king's
13:32 For by the command of *A* this
13:34 Then *A* fled. And the young man
13:37 But *A* fled and went to Talmai
13:38 So *A* fled and went to Geshur,
13:39 King David longed to go to *A*.
14: 1 heart was concerned about *A*.
14:21 bring back the young man *A*.
14:23 and brought *A* to Jerusalem.
14:24 So *A* returned to his own
14:25 who was praised as much as *A*
14:27 To *A* were born three sons, and
14:28 And *A* dwelt two full years in
14:29 Therefore *A* sent for Joab, to
14:32 And *A* answered Joab, "Look, I
14:33 And when he had called for *A*,
14:33 king. Then the king kissed *A*.
15: 1 After this it happened that *A*
15: 2 Now *A* would rise early and stand
15: 2 that *A* would call to him and
15: 3 Then *A* would say to him, "Look,
15: 4 Moreover *A* would say, "Oh, that
15: 6 In this manner *A* acted toward
15: 6 So *A* stole the hearts of the
15: 7 pass after forty years that *A*
15:10 Then *A* sent spies throughout
15:10 *A* reigns in Hebron!'"
15:11 And with *A* went two hundred men
15:12 Then *A* sent for Ahithophel the
15:12 for the people with *A*
15:13 of the men of Israel are with *A*.
15:14 or we shall not escape from *A*.
15:31 among the conspirators with *A*.
15:34 to the city, and say to *A*,
15:37 And *A* came into Jerusalem.
16: 8 the kingdom into the hand of *A*.
16:15 Meanwhile *A* and all the people,
16:16 David's friend, came to *A*,
16:16 Absalom, that Hushai said to *A*,
16:17 So *A* said to Hushai, "Is this
16:18 And Hushai said to *A*,
16:20 Then *A* said to Ahithophel,
16:21 And Ahithophel said to *A*,
16:22 So they pitched a tent for *A* on
16:22 and *A* went in to his father's
16:23 both with David and with *A*.
17: 1 Moreover Ahithophel said to *A*,
17: 4 And the saying pleased *A* and all
17: 5 Then *A* said, "Now call Hushai
17: 6 And when Hushai came to *A*,
17: 6 *A* spoke to him, saying,
17: 7 So Hushai said to *A*:
17: 9 among the people who follow *A*.
17:14 So *A* and all the men of Israel
17:14 LORD might bring disaster on *A*.
17:15 and so Ahithophel advised *A*
17:18 a lad saw them, and told *A*.
17:24 And *A* crossed over the Jordan,
17:25 And *A* made Amasa captain of the
17:26 So Israel and *A* encamped in the
18: 5 my sake with the young man *A*.
18: 5 captains orders concerning *A*.
18: 9 Then *A* met the servants of
18: 9 *A* rode on a mule. The mule went
18:10 I just saw *A* hanging in a
18:12 anyone touch the young man *A*!
18:15 bore Joab's armor surrounded *A*,
18:17 And they took *A* and cast him
18:18 Now *A* in his lifetime had taken
18:29 Is the young man *A* safe?"
18:32 'Is the young man *A* safe?"
18:33 he said thus: "O my son *A*—
18:33 son Absalom—my son, my son *A*—
18:33 I had died in your place! O *A*
19: 1 is weeping and mourning for *A*.
19: 4 O my son *A*! O Absalom, my son,
19: 4 voice, "O my son Absalom! O *A*,
19: 6 for today I perceive that if *A*
19: 9 fled from the land because of *A*.
19:10 'But *A*, whom we anointed
20: 6 will do us more harm than *A*.
1 Ki 1: 6 mother had borne him after *A*.
2: 7 came to me when I fled from *A*
2:28 though he had not defected to *A*.
1 Chr 3: 2 *A* the son of Maacah, the
2 Chr 11:20 Maacah the granddaughter of *A*;
11:21 Maachah the granddaughter of *A*
Ps 3: of David when he fled from *A*

ABSALOM'S (7/7) ABSALOM

2 Sam 13: 4 my brother *A* sister."
13:20 desolate in her brother *A* house
14:30 And *A* servants set the field
14:31 Joab arose and came to *A* house,
17:20 And when *A* servants came to the
18:14 and thrust them through *A* heart,
18:18 day it is called *A* Monument.

ABSENCE (2/2) ABSENT

Lk 22: 6 to betray Him to them in the ***a***
Phil 2:12 only, but now much more in my ***a***,

ABSENT (11/11) ABSENCE

Gen 31:49 you and me when we are ***a*** one
1 Cor 5: 3 as ***a*** in body but present in
2 Cor 5: 6 at home in the body we are ***a***
5: 8 well pleased rather to be ***a***
5: 9 our aim, whether present or ***a***,
10: 1 but being ***a*** am bold toward you.
10:11 word by letters when we are ***a***,
13: 2 and now being ***a*** I write to
13:10 I write these things being ***a***,
Phil 1:27 I come and see you or am ***a***,
Col 2: 5 For though I am ***a*** in the flesh,

ABSTAIN (8/8) ABSTINENCE

Deut 23:22 But if you ***a*** from vowing, it
Josh 6:18 by all means ***a*** from the
Acts 15:20 that we write to them to ***a***
15:29 that you ***a*** from things offered
1 Th 4: 3 that you should ***a*** from sexual
5:22 *A* from every form of evil.
1 Tim 4: 3 and commanding to ***a*** from
1 Pe 2:11 ***a*** from fleshly lusts which war

ABSTINENCE (1/1) ABSTAIN, SELF-CONTROL

Acts 27:21 But after long ***a*** from food, then

ABUNDANCE (79/77) ABUNDANT

Gen 1:20 the waters abound with an ***a*** of
Deut 28:47 for the ***a*** of everything,
33:19 they shall partake of the ***a***
1 Sam 1:16 for out of the ***a*** of my
2 Sam 12:30 spoil of the city in great ***a***.
1 Ki 1:19 fattened cattle and sheep in ***a***,
1:25 fattened cattle and sheep in ***a***,
10:10 There never again came such ***a***
18:41 for there is the sound of ***a***
1 Chr 20: 2 spoil of the city in great ***a***.
22: 3 And David prepared iron in ***a*** for
22: 3 and bronze in ***a*** beyond measure,
22: 4 and cedar trees in ***a***;
22:15 are workmen with you in ***a***:
29: 2 stones, and marble slabs in ***a***.
29:16 all this ***a*** that we have
29:21 and sacrifices in ***a*** for all
2 Chr 2: 9 to prepare timber for me in ***a***,
4:18 articles made in such great ***a***
9: 1 that bore spices, gold in ***a***,
9: 9 of gold, spices in great ***a***,
11:23 he gave them provisions in ***a***.
14:15 off sheep and camels in ***a***,
17: 5 he had riches and honor in ***a***.
18: 1 had riches and honor in ***a***;
18: 2 killed sheep and oxen in ***a*** for
20:25 they found among them an ***a*** of
24:11 by day, and gathered money in ***a***.
29:35 the burnt offerings were in ***a***,
31: 5 of Israel brought in ***a*** the
31:10 what is left is this great ***a***.
32: 5 made weapons and shields in ***a***.
32:29 of flocks and herds in ***a***;
Neh 5:18 and once every ten days an ***a*** of
9:25 groves, And fruit trees in ***a***.
Esth 1: 7 the other, with royal wine in ***a***,
Job 22:11 And an ***a*** of water covers you.
36:31 peoples; He gives food in ***a***.
38:34 That an ***a*** of water may cover
Ps 18:14 the foe, Lightnings in ***a***,
37:11 delight themselves in the ***a*** of
52: 7 But trusted in the ***a*** of his
65:11 And Your paths drip with ***a***.
72: 7 And ***a*** of peace, Until the
72:16 There will be an ***a*** of grain in
73: 7 Their eyes bulge with ***a***;
78:15 And gave them drink in ***a*** like
Eccl 5:10 silver; Nor he who loves ***a***,
5:12 But the ***a*** of the rich will not
Isa 7:22 from the ***a*** of milk they give,
15: 7 Therefore the ***a*** they have
47: 9 For the great ***a*** of your
55: 2 your soul delight itself in ***a***.
60: 5 Because the ***a*** of the sea shall
66:11 and be delighted With the ***a***
Jer 31:14 the soul of the priests with ***a***,
33: 6 them and reveal to them the ***a***
40:12 wine and summer fruit in ***a***.
Ezek 16:49 and ***a*** of idleness; neither did
26:10 Because of the ***a*** of his horses,
27:16 your merchant because of the ***a***
27:18 your merchant because of the ***a***
28:16 By the ***a*** of your trading You
31: 5 became long because of the ***a***
Zech 14:14 silver, and apparel in great ***a***.
Mt 12:34 For out of the ***a*** of the heart
13:12 be given, and he will have ***a***;
25:29 be given, and he will have ***a***;
Mk 12:44 they all put in out of their ***a***,
Lk 6:45 For out of the ***a*** of the heart
12:15 life does not consist in the ***a***
21: 4 for all these out of their ***a***
Rom 5:17 much more those who receive ***a***
2 Cor 8: 2 trial of affliction the ***a*** of
8:14 that now at this time your ***a***
8:14 that their ***a*** also may supply
9: 8 may have an ***a*** for every good
12: 7 exalted above measure by the ***a***
Rev 18: 3 have become rich through the ***a***

ABUNDANT (23/23) ABUNDANCE, ABUNDANTLY, PLENTIFUL

Num 14:18 LORD is longsuffering and ***a***
1 Ki 10:27 and he made cedar trees as ***a*** as
1 Chr 22: 5 So David made ***a*** preparations
22:14 beyond measure, for it is so ***a***.
2 Chr 1:15 and he made cedars as ***a*** as the
9:27 and he made cedar trees as ***a*** as
Neh 9:17 *A* in kindness, And did not
9:27 And according to Your ***a***
Job 37:23 In judgment and ***a*** justice;
Ps 86: 5 And ***a*** in mercy to all those
86:15 Longsuffering and ***a*** in mercy
130: 7 And with Him is ***a*** redemption.
Isa 56:12 be as today, And much more ***a***.
Jer 51:13 *A* in treasures, Your end has
Ezek 17: 5 He placed it by ***a*** waters
31: 7 its roots reached to ***a*** waters.
Dan 4:12 were lovely, Its fruit ***a***,
4:21 were lovely and its fruit ***a***,
Jon 4: 2 slow to anger and ***a*** in
2 Cor 11:23 am more: in labors more ***a***,
Phil 1:26 rejoicing for me may be more ***a***
1 Tim 1:14 of our Lord was exceedingly ***a***,
1 Pe 1: 3 who according to His ***a*** mercy

ABUNDANTLY (23/23) ABUNDANT

Gen 9: 7 Bring forth ***a*** in the earth
41:47 the ground brought forth ***a***.
Ex 1: 7 were fruitful and increased ***a***,
8: 3 river shall bring forth frogs ***a***,
Num 20:11 his rod; and water came out ***a***,
1 Chr 12:40 and oil and oxen and sheep ***a***,
2 Chr 31: 5 and they brought in ***a*** the tithe
Job 8: 7 latter end would increase ***a***.
36:28 clouds drop down And pour ***a***
Ps 36: 8 They are ***a*** satisfied with the
65:10 You water its ridges ***a***,
132:15 I will ***a*** bless her provision;
Isa 35: 2 It shall blossom ***a*** and rejoice,
55: 7 For He will ***a*** pardon.
Jn 10:10 that they may have it more ***a***.
1 Cor 15:10 but I labored more ***a*** than they
2 Cor 1:12 and more ***a*** toward you.
2: 4 the love which I have so ***a*** for
12:15 though the more ***a*** I love you,
Eph 3:20 who is able to do exceedingly ***a***
Titus 3: 6 whom He poured out on us ***a***
Heb 6:17 determining to show more ***a*** to
2 Pe 1:11 will be supplied to you ***a*** into

ABUSE (5/5) ABUSED, DAMAGE, HARM, OPPRESS

1 Sam 31: 4 and thrust me through and ***a*** me.
1 Chr 10: 4 uncircumcised men come and ***a***
Jer 38:19 and they ***a*** me."
Acts 14: 5 to ***a*** and stone them,
1 Cor 9:18 that I may not ***a*** my authority

ABUSED (2/2) ABUSE

Num 22:29 Because you have ***a*** me. I wish
Judg 19:25 And they knew her and ***a*** her all

ABYSS (2/2)

Lk 8:31 them to go out into the ***a***.
Rom 10: 7 will descend into the ***a***?

ACACIA (30/30) ACACIAS

Ex 25: 5 badger skins, and ***a*** wood;
25:10 shall make an ark of ***a*** wood;
25:13 you shall make poles of ***a*** wood,
25:23 also make a table of ***a*** wood;
25:28 shall make the poles of ***a*** wood,
26:15 shall make the boards of ***a*** wood,
26:26 you shall make bars of ***a*** wood:
26:32 upon the four pillars of ***a*** wood
26:37 screen five pillars of ***a*** wood,
27: 1 shall make an altar of ***a*** wood,
27: 6 poles of ***a*** wood, and overlay

30: 1 you shall make it of ***a*** wood.
30: 5 shall make the poles of ***a*** wood,
35: 7 badger skins, and ***a*** wood;
35:24 with whom was found ***a*** wood
36:20 he made boards of ***a*** wood,
36:31 And he made bars of ***a*** wood:
36:36 for it four pillars of ***a*** wood,
37: 1 Bezalel made the ark of ***a*** wood;
37: 4 He made poles of ***a*** wood, and
37:10 He made the table of ***a*** wood;
37:15 And he made the poles of ***a*** wood
37:25 the incense altar of ***a*** wood.
37:28 And he made the poles of ***a*** wood,
38: 1 of burnt offering of ***a*** wood;
38: 6 And he made the poles of ***a*** wood,
Num 25: 1 Now Israel remained in ***A*** Grove,
Deut 10: 3 So I made an ark of ***a*** wood,
Josh 2: 1 of Nun sent out two men from ***A***
3: 1 and they set out from ***A*** Grove
Isa 41:19 the cedar and the ***a*** tree
Mic 6: 5 From ***A*** Grove to Gilgal, That

ACACIAS (1/1) ACACIA

Joel 3:18 And water the Valley of ***A***.

ACCAD (1/1)

Gen 10:10 his kingdom was Babel, Erech, ***A***,

ACCEPT (35/33) ACCEPTABLE, ACCEPTABLY, ACCEPTANCE, ACCEPTED, ACCEPTING, ACCEPTS

Gen 32:20 perhaps he will ***a*** me."
Ex 8: 9 ***A*** the honor of saying when I
22:11 and the owner of it shall ***a***
Lev 26:41 and they ***a*** their guilt—
26:43 they will ***a*** their guilt,
Num 7: 5 ***A*** these from them, that they
Deut 20:11 it shall be that if they ***a***
33:11 And ***a*** the work of his hands;
1 Sam 26:19 let Him ***a*** an offering. But if
2 Sam 24:23 May the LORD your God ***a*** you."
Esth 4: 4 but he would not ***a*** them.
Job 2:10 Shall we indeed ***a*** good from
2:10 and shall we not ***a*** adversity?"
42: 8 For I will ***a*** him, lest I deal
Ps 20: 3 And ***a*** your burnt sacrifice.
119:108 ***A***, I pray, the freewill
Prov 6:35 He will ***a*** no recompense, Nor
Jer 14:10 the LORD does not ***a*** them;
14:12 I will not ***a*** them. But I will
Ezek 20:40 there I will ***a*** them, and there
20:41 I will ***a*** you as a sweet aroma
43:27 and I will ***a*** you,' says the
Hos 8:13 But the LORD does not ***a***
Am 5:22 I will not ***a*** them, Nor will
Mal 1: 8 Would he ***a*** you favorably?"
1: 9 Will He ***a*** you favorably?"
1:10 Nor will I ***a*** an offering from
1:13 bring an offering! Should I ***a***
Mt 19:11 All cannot ***a*** this saying, but
19:12 He who is able to ***a*** it, let
19:12 let him ***a*** it."
Mk 4:20 ***a*** it, and bear fruit: some
Acts 24: 3 we ***a*** it always and in all
24:15 which they themselves also ***a***,
1 Cor 6: 7 Why do you not rather ***a*** wrong?

ACCEPTABLE (24/24) ACCEPT, ACCEPTABLY

Lev 22:20 for it shall not be ***a*** on your
Ps 19:14 meditation of my heart Be ***a***
69:13 in the ***a*** time; O God, in the
Prov 10:32 of the righteous know what is ***a***,
21: 3 and justice Is more ***a*** to the
Eccl 12:10 The Preacher sought to find ***a***
Isa 49: 8 In an ***a*** time I have heard You,
58: 5 And an ***a*** day to the LORD?
61: 2 To proclaim the ***a*** year of the
Jer 6:20 burnt offerings are not ***a***,
42: 2 let our petition be ***a*** to you,
Dan 4:27 let my advice be ***a*** to you;
Lk 4:19 To proclaim the ***a*** year of
Rom 12: 1 ***a*** to God, which is your
12: 2 prove what is that good and ***a***
14:18 Christ in these things is ***a***
15:16 of the Gentiles might be ***a***,
15:31 service for Jerusalem may be ***a***
2 Cor 6: 2 In an ***a*** time I have heard
Eph 5:10 finding out what is ***a*** to the
Phil 4:18 an ***a*** sacrifice, well pleasing
1 Tim 2: 3 For this is good and ***a*** in the
5: 4 for this is good and ***a*** before
1 Pe 2: 5 up spiritual sacrifices ***a*** to

ACCEPTABLY (1/1) ACCEPTABLE

Heb 12:28 by which we may serve God ***a***

ACCEPTANCE (4/4) ACCEPT, ACCEPTABLE, ACCEPTING

Isa 60: 7 They shall ascend with ***a*** on My
Rom 11:15 what will their ***a*** be but life
1 Tim 1:15 saying and worthy of all ***a***,
4: 9 saying and worthy of all ***a***.

ACCEPTED (26/26) ACCEPT

Gen 4: 7 you do well, will you not be ***a***?
Ex 28:38 that they may be ***a*** before the
Lev 1: 4 and it will be ***a*** on his behalf
7:18 third day, it shall not be ***a***,
10:19 would it have been ***a*** in the
19: 7 abomination. It shall not be ***a***.
22:21 it must be perfect to be ***a***;
22:23 but for a vow it shall not be ***a***.
22:25 They shall not be ***a*** on your
22:27 and thereafter it shall be ***a***
23:11 to be ***a*** on your behalf; on the
Judg 13:23 He would not have ***a*** a burnt
1 Sam 18: 5 and he was ***a*** in the sight of
Esth 9:23 So the Jews ***a*** the custom which
Job 42: 9 for the LORD had ***a*** Job.
Eccl 9: 7 For God has already ***a*** your
Isa 56: 7 their sacrifices Will be ***a***
Jer 37:20 let my petition be ***a*** before
Lk 4:24 no prophet is ***a*** in his own
Acts 10:35 and works righteousness is ***a***
2 Cor 6: 2 now is the ***a*** time; behold, now
8:12 it is ***a*** according to what one
8:17 For he not only ***a*** the
11: 4 gospel which you have not ***a***—
Eph 1: 6 by which He has made us ***a*** in
Heb 10:34 and joyfully ***a*** the plundering

ACCEPTING (1/1) ACCEPT

Heb 11:35 not ***a*** deliverance, that they

ACCEPTS (1/1) ACCEPT

Prov 17:23 A wicked man ***a*** a bribe behind

ACCESS (4/4)

Esth 1:14 who had ***a*** to the king's
Rom 5: 2 through whom also we have ***a*** by
Eph 2:18 For through Him we both have ***a***
3:12 in whom we have boldness and ***a***

ACCHO (KJV) See ACCO

ACCIDENTALLY (4/4)

Num 35:11 who kills any person ***a*** may
35:15 anyone who kills a person ***a***
Josh 20: 3 the slayer who kills a person ***a***
20: 9 that whoever killed a person ***a***

ACCO (1/1)

Judg 1:31 drive out the inhabitants of ***A***

ACCOMPANIED (12/12) ACCOMPANY

1 Sam 25:15 miss anything as long as we ***a***
1 Chr 15:16 brethren to be the singers ***a***
2 Chr 30:21 ***a*** by loud instruments.
Jer 17:25 ***a*** by the men of Judah and the
22: 4 ***a*** by servants and people, kings
Acts 1:21 of these men who have ***a*** us all
10:23 and some brethren from Joppa ***a***
11:12 Moreover these six brethren ***a***
20: 4 And Sopater of Berea ***a*** him to
20:38 And they ***a*** him to the ship.
21: 5 and they all ***a*** us, with wives
1 Pe 3: 2 observe your chaste conduct ***a***

ACCOMPANY (1/1) ACCOMPANIED, ACCOMPANYING

Heb 6: 9 things that ***a*** salvation, though

ACCOMPANYING (2/2) ACCOMPANY

2 Sam 6: 4 ***a*** the ark of God; and Ahio went
Mk 16:20 the word through the ***a*** signs.

ACCOMPLISH (8/8) ACCOMPLISHED, ACCOMPLISHING, ACCOMPLISHMENT

Ex 14:13 which He will ***a*** for you today.
2 Chr 2:14 to make any engraving and to ***a***
Job 35: 6 what do you ***a*** against Him?
Eccl 2: 2 and of mirth, "What does it ***a***?
Isa 55:11 But it shall ***a*** what I please,
Ezek 13:15 Thus will I ***a*** My wrath on the
Dan 9: 2 that He would ***a*** seventy years
Lk 9:31 which He was about to ***a*** at

ACCOMPLISHED (16/16) ACCOMPLISH

1 Sam 11:13 for today the LORD has ***a***
14:45 who has ***a*** this great
2 Chr 7:11 and Solomon successfully ***a*** all
Job 15:32 It will be ***a*** before his time,
Prov 13:19 A desire ***a*** is sweet to the
Isa 26:18 We have not ***a*** any deliverance
Lam 4:22 of your iniquity is ***a***,
Dan 11:36 till the wrath has been ***a***;
Lk 12:50 distressed I am till it is ***a***!
18:31 the Son of Man will be ***a***.
22:37 is written must still be ***a*** in
Jn 19:28 that all things were now ***a***,
Acts 19:21 When these things were ***a***,
Rom 15:18 things which Christ has not ***a***
2 Cor 12:12 the signs of an apostle were ***a***
Eph 3:11 the eternal purpose which He ***a***

ACCOMPLISHING (1/1) ACCOMPLISH

Jn 12:19 You see that you are ***a*** nothing.

ACCOMPLISHMENT (1/1) ACCOMPLISH

2 Cor 10:16 in another man's sphere of ***a***.

ACCORD (22/22) ACCORDANCE, ACCORDING, ACCORDINGLY, ACCORDS

Lev 25: 5 What grows of its own ***a*** of your
25:11 reap what grows of its own ***a***,
Josh 9: 2 Joshua and Israel with one ***a***.
1 Ki 22:13 of the prophets with one ***a***
2 Chr 18:12 of the prophets with one ***a***
Zeph 3: 9 LORD, To serve Him with one ***a***.
Lk 14:18 But they all with one ***a*** began
Acts 1:14 These all continued with one ***a***
2: 1 they were all with one ***a*** in one
2:46 So continuing daily with one ***a***
4:24 their voice to God with one ***a***
5:12 And they were all with one ***a*** in
7:57 ears, and ran at him with one ***a***;
8: 6 And the multitudes with one ***a***
12:10 opened to them of its own ***a***;
12:20 but they came to him with one ***a***,
15:25 us, being assembled with one ***a***,
18:12 the Jews with one ***a*** rose up
19:29 into the theater with one ***a***,
2 Cor 6:15 And what ***a*** has Christ with
8:17 he went to you of his own ***a***.
Phil 2: 2 the same love, being of one ***a***,

ACCORDANCE (3/3) ACCORD

Judg 8:35 of Jerubbaal (Gideon) in ***a***
Esth 1: 8 In ***a*** with the law, the drinking
Rom 2: 5 But in ***a*** with your hardness and

ACCORDING (898/802)

Gen 1:11 tree that yields fruit ***a*** to
1:12 the herb that yields seed ***a*** to
1:12 whose seed is in itself ***a*** to
1:21 ***a*** to their kind, and every
1:21 and every winged bird ***a*** to its
1:24 forth the living creature ***a*** to
1:24 each ***a*** to its kind"; and it
1:25 made the beast of the earth ***a***
1:25 cattle ***a*** to its kind, and
1:25 that creeps on the earth ***a*** to
1:26 ***a*** to Our likeness; let them
6:22 ***a*** to all that God commanded
7: 5 And Noah did ***a*** to all that the
8:19 ***a*** to their families, went out
10: 5 everyone ***a*** to his language,
10: 5 ***a*** to their families, into their
10:20 ***a*** to their families, according
10:20 ***a*** to their languages, in their
10:31 ***a*** to their families, according
10:31 ***a*** to their languages, in their
10:31 ***a*** to their nations.
10:32 ***a*** to their generations, in
18:10 will certainly return to you ***a***
18:14 ***a*** to the time of life, and
18:21 they have done altogether ***a*** to
21:23 but that ***a*** to the kindness that
25:13 ***a*** to their generations: The
25:16 twelve princes ***a*** to their
27: 8 obey my voice ***a*** to what I
30:34 that it were ***a*** to your word!"
34:12 and I will give ***a*** to what you
36:30 ***a*** to their chiefs in the land
36:40 ***a*** to their families and their
36:43 ***a*** to their dwelling places in
40:13 Pharaoh's cup in his hand ***a*** to
41:11 Each of us dreamed ***a*** to the
41:12 to each man he interpreted ***a*** to
41:40 all my people shall be ruled ***a***
43: 7 And we told him ***a*** to these
43:33 the firstborn ***a*** to his
43:33 birthright and the youngest ***a***
44: 2 So he did ***a*** to the word that
44:10 Now also let it be ***a*** to your
45:21 ***a*** to the command of Pharaoh,
47:12 ***a*** to the number in their
49:28 he blessed each one ***a*** to his
Ex 6:16 names of the sons of Levi ***a*** to
6:17 were Libni and Shimi ***a*** to
6:19 are the families of Levi ***a*** to
6:25 houses of the Levites ***a*** to
6:26 from the land of Egypt ***a*** to
8:10 Let it be ***a*** to your word,
8:13 So the LORD did ***a*** to the word
8:31 And the LORD did ***a*** to the word
12: 3 ***a*** to the house of his father,
12: 4 next to his house take it ***a***
12: 4 ***a*** to each man's need you shall
12:21 take lambs for yourselves ***a*** to
12:35 children of Israel had done ***a*** to
12:51 out of the land of Egypt ***a*** to
16:16 Let every man gather it ***a*** to
16:16 ***a*** to the number of persons;
16:18 Every man had gathered ***a*** to
16:21 every man ***a*** to his need.
17: 1 ***a*** to the commandment of the
21: 9 he shall deal with her ***a*** to the

21:31 *a* to this judgment it shall be
22:17 he shall pay money *a* to the
23:24 nor do *a* to their works; but
24: 4 and twelve pillars *a* to the
24: 8 the LORD has made with you *a*
25: 9 *A* to all that I show you, that
25:35 *a* to the six branches that
25:40 to it that you make them *a* to
26:30 raise up the tabernacle *a* to
28:15 Artistically woven *a* to the
28:21 twelve *a* to their names, like
28:21 they shall be *a* to the twelve
29:35 *a* to all that I have commanded
30:13 half a shekel *a* to the shekel
30:24 *a* to the shekel of the
30:25 an ointment compounded *a* to the
30:32 *a* to its composition. It is
30:35 a compound *a* to the art of the
30:37 *a* to its composition. It shall
31:11 *A* to all that I have commanded
32:28 So the sons of Levi did *a* to the
34:27 for *a* to the tenor of these
36: 1 shall do *a* to all that the
37:21 *a* to the six branches extending
37:29 *a* to the work of the perfumer.
38:21 which was counted *a* to the
38:24 *a* to the shekel of the
38:25 *a* to the shekel of the
38:26 *a* to the shekel of the
39:14 There were twelve stones *a* to
39:14 *a* to their names, engraved
39:14 each one with its own name *a* to
39:32 the children of Israel did *a*
39:42 *A* to all that the LORD had
40:16 *a* to all that the LORD had
Lev 4:35 *a* to the offerings made by fire
5:10 second as a burnt offering *a*
5:12 and burn it on the altar *a* to
5:15 in shekels of silver *a* to the
9:16 offering and offered it *a* to
10: 7 And they did *a* to the word of
18: 3 *A* to the doings of the land of
18: 3 and *a* to the doings of the land
25:15 *A* to the number of years after
25:15 and *a* to the number of years of
25:16 *A* to the multitude of years you
25:16 and *a* to the fewer number of
25:16 for he sells to you *a* to the
25:50 of his release shall be *a* to
25:50 it shall be *a* to the time of
25:51 *a* to them he shall repay the
25:52 and *a* to his years he shall
26:21 more plagues, *a* to your sins.
27: 2 *a* to your valuation,
27: 3 *a* to the shekel of the
27: 8 *a* to the ability of him who
27:16 then your valuation shall be *a*
27:17 *a* to your valuation it shall
27:18 reckon to him the money due *a*
27:25 all your valuations shall be *a*
27:27 then he shall redeem it *a* to
27:27 then it shall be sold *a* to your
Num 1: 2 *a* to the number of names, every
1:18 *a* to the number of names, from
1:20 *a* to the number of names, every
1:22 *a* to the number of names, every
1:24 *a* to the number of names, from
1:26 *a* to the number of names, from
1:28 *a* to the number of names, from
1:30 *a* to the number of names, from
1:32 *a* to the number of names, from
1:34 *a* to the number of names, from
1:36 *a* to the number of names, from
1:38 *a* to the number of names, from
1:40 *a* to the number of names, from
1:42 *a* to the number of names, from
1:52 *a* to their armies;
1:54 *a* to all that the LORD
2: 3 forces with Judah shall camp *a*
2: 9 All who were numbered *a* to their
2:10 of the forces with Reuben *a* to
2:16 All who were numbered *a* to their
2:18 of the forces with Ephraim *a*
2:24 All who were numbered *a* to their
2:25 shall be on the north side *a*
2:32 All who were numbered *a* to
2:34 the children of Israel did *a*
2:34 *a* to their fathers' houses.
3:16 So Moses numbered them *a* to the
3:22 *a* to the number of all the
3:26 *a* to all the work relating to
3:28 *A* to the number of all the
3:34 *a* to the number of all the
3:43 *a* to the number of names from a
3:50 *a* to the shekel of the
3:51 *a* to the word of the LORD, as
4:37 Moses and Aaron numbered *a* to
4:41 Moses and Aaron numbered *a* to
4:45 Moses and Aaron numbered *a* to
4:49 *A* to the commandment of the
4:49 each *a* to his service and
4:49 according to his service and *a*
6:21 *a* to the vow which he takes, so
6:21 so he must do *a* to the law of
7: 5 to every man *a* to his
7: 7 *a* to their service;
7: 8 *a* to their service, under the
7:13 *a* to the shekel of the
7:19 *a* to the shekel of the
7:25 *a* to the shekel of the
7:31 *a* to the shekel of the
7:37 *a* to the shekel of the
7:43 *a* to the shekel of the
7:49 *a* to the shekel of the
7:55 *a* to the shekel of the
7:61 *a* to the shekel of the
7:67 *a* to the shekel of the
7:73 *a* to the shekel of the
7:79 *a* to the shekel of the
7:85 *a* to the shekel of the
7:86 *a* to the shekel of the
8: 4 *A* to the pattern which the
8:20 *a* to all that the LORD
9: 3 *A* to all its rites and
9: 5 *a* to all that the LORD
9:12 *A* to all the ordinances of the
9:14 he must do so *a* to the rite of
9:14 the rite of the Passover and *a*
9:20 *a* to the command of the LORD
9:20 and *a* to the command of the
10:13 out for the first time *a* to
10:14 of Judah set out first *a* to
10:18 of the camp of Reuben set out *a*
10:22 children of Ephraim set out *a*
10:25 of all the camps) set out *a* to
10:28 *a* to their armies, when they
13: 3 from the Wilderness of Paran *a*
14:19 *a* to the greatness of Your
14:20 have pardoned, *a* to your word;
14:29 *a* to your entire number, from
14:34 *A* to the number of the days in
15:12 *A* to the number that you
15:12 so you shall do with everyone *a*
15:24 *a* to the ordinance, and one kid
17: 2 all their leaders *a* to their
17: 6 for each leader *a* to their
18:16 *a* to your valuation, for five
18:16 *a* to the shekel of the
24: 2 and saw Israel encamped *a* to
26:12 The sons of Simeon *a* to their
26:15 The sons of Gad *a* to their
26:18 families of the sons of Gad *a*
26:20 And the sons of Judah *a* to their
26:22 are the families of Judah *a*
26:23 The sons of Issachar *a* to their
26:25 the families of Issachar *a* to
26:26 The sons of Zebulun *a* to their
26:27 families of the Zebulunites *a*
26:28 The sons of Joseph *a* to their
26:35 are the sons of Ephraim *a* to
26:37 of the sons of Ephraim *a* to
26:37 are the sons of Joseph *a* to
26:38 The sons of Benjamin *a* to their
26:41 ARE the sons of Benjamin *a* to
26:42 These are the sons of Dan *a* to
26:42 are the families of Dan *a* to
26:43 *a* to those who were numbered of
26:44 The sons of Asher *a* to their
26:47 of the sons of Asher *a* to
26:48 The sons of Naphtali *a* to their
26:50 the families of Naphtali *a* to
26:53 *a* to the number of names.
26:54 be given its inheritance *a* to
26:55 they shall inherit *a* to the
26:56 *A* to the lot their inheritance
26:57 were numbered of the Levites *a*
29: 6 *a* to their ordinance, as a
29:18 *a* to the ordinance;
29:21 *a* to the ordinance;
29:24 *a* to the ordinance;
29:27 *a* to the ordinance;
29:30 *a* to the ordinance;
29:33 *a* to the ordinance;
29:37 *a* to the ordinance;
30: 2 he shall do *a* to all that
33: 2 these are their journeys *a* to
33:54 You shall inherit *a* to the
34:14 of the children of Reuben *a* to
34:14 tribe of the children of Gad *a*
35:24 and the avenger of blood *a* to
36: 5 the children of Israel *a* to
Deut 1: 3 to the children of Israel *a* to
1:30 *a* to all He did for you in
1:46 *a* to the days that you spent
3:11 *a* to the standard cubit.
4: 5 that you should act *a* to them
4:34 *a* to all that the LORD your
10: 4 And He wrote on the tablets *a* to
12:15 *a* to the blessing of the LORD
16:17 *a* to the blessing of the LORD
16:18 *a* to your tribes, and they
17:10 You shall do *a* to the sentence
17:10 you shall be careful to do *a*
17:11 *A* to the sentence of the law in
17:11 *a* to the judgment which they
18:16 *a* to all you desired of the
20:18 lest they teach you to do *a* to
24: 8 you carefully observe and do *a*
25: 2 *a* to his guilt, with a certain
26:13 *a* to all Your commandments
26:14 and have done *a* to all that You
29:21 *a* to all the curses of the
30: 2 *a* to all that I command you
31: 5 that you may do to them *a* to
32: 8 boundaries of the peoples *A*
34: 5 *a* to the word of the LORD.
Josh 1: 7 that you may observe to do *a* to
1: 8 that you may observe to do *a* to
2:21 *A* to your words, so be it."
4: 5 *a* to the number of the tribes
4: 8 *a* to the number of the tribes
4:10 *a* to all that Moses had
7:14 you shall be brought *a* to your
7:14 the LORD takes shall come *a*
8: 8 *A* to the commandment of the
8:27 *a* to the word of the LORD
8:34 *a* to all that is written in the
10:32 *a* to all that he had done to
10:35 *a* to all that he had done to
10:37 *a* to all that he had done to
11:23 *a* to all that the LORD had
11:23 as an inheritance to Israel *a*
12: 7 of Israel as a possession *a*
13:15 of Reuben an inheritance *a*
13:23 of the children of Reuben *a* to
13:24 to the children of Gad *a* to
13:28 of the children of Gad *a* to
13:29 of the children of Manasseh *a*
13:31 of the children of Machir *a* to
15: 1 of the children of Judah *a* to
15:12 children of Judah all around *a*
15:13 *a* to the commandment of the
15:20 of the children of Judah *a* to
16: 5 *a* to their families, was thus:
16: 8 of the children of Ephraim *a*
17: 2 of the children of Manasseh *a*
17: 2 of Manasseh the son of Joseph *a*
17: 4 *a* to the commandment of the
18: 4 survey it *a* to their
18:10 to the children of Israel *a* to
18:11 children of Benjamin came up *a*
18:20 *a* to its boundaries all around,
18:20 *a* to their families.
18:21 *a* to their families, were
18:28 of the children of Benjamin *a*
19: 1 of the children of Simeon *a* to
19: 8 of the children of Simeon *a* to
19:10 for the children of Zebulun *a*
19:16 of the children of Zebulun *a*
19:17 for the children of Issachar *a*
19:23 of the children of Issachar *a*
19:24 of the children of Asher *a* to
19:31 of the children of Asher *a* to
19:32 for the children of Naphtali *a*
19:39 of the children of Naphtali *a*
19:40 tribe of the children of Dan *a*
19:48 tribe of the children of Dan *a*
19:49 the land as an inheritance *a*
19:50 *A* to the word of the LORD they
21: 7 The children of Merari *a* to
21:33 cities of the Gershonites *a* to
21:40 for the children of Merari *a*
21:44 *a* to all that He had sworn to
22: 9 which they had obtained *a* to
24: 5 *a* to what I did among them.
Judg 11:10 if we do not do *a* to your
11:36 do to me *a* to what has gone out
Ruth 3: 6 the threshing floor and did *a*
1 Sam 2:35 priest who shall do *a* to what
6: 4 *a* to the number of the lords
6:18 *a* to the number of all the
8: 8 *A* to all the works which they
13: 8 *a* to the time set by Samuel.
14: 7 *a* to your heart."
17:23 and he spoke *a* to the same
23:20 come down *a* to all the desire
25: 9 they spoke to Nabal *a* to all
25:30 LORD has done for my lord *a*
2 Sam 3:39 shall repay the evildoer *a* to
7:17 *A* to all these words and
7:17 to all these words and *a* to
7:21 and *a* to Your own heart, You
7:22 *a* to all that we have heard
9:11 *A* to all that my lord the king
14:20 *a* to the wisdom of the angel of
14:26 head at two hundred shekels *a*
22:21 The LORD rewarded me *a* to my
22:21 *A* to the cleanness of my hands
22:25 the LORD has recompensed me *a*
22:25 *A* to my cleanness in His eyes.
24:19 *a* to the word of Gad, went up
1 Ki 2: 6 Therefore do *a* to your wisdom,
3:12 I have done *a* to your words;
4:28 each man *a* to his charge.
5: 6 you wages for your servants *a*
5:10 cedar and cypress logs *a* to
6:38 in all its details and *a* to
8:32 the righteous by giving him *a*
8:39 and give to everyone *a* to all
8:43 and do *a* to all for which the
8:56 *a* to all that He promised.
9: 4 to do *a* to all that I have
10:13 what Solomon had given her *a*
12:14 and he spoke to them *a* to the
12:24 *a* to the word of the LORD.
13: 5 *a* to the sign which the man of
13:26 *a* to the word of the LORD
14:18 *a* to the word of the LORD
14:24 They did *a* to all the
15:29 *a* to the word of the LORD
16:12 *a* to the word of the LORD,
16:34 *a* to the word of the LORD,
17: 5 So he went and did *a* to the word
17:15 So she went away and did *a* to
17:16 *a* to the word of the LORD
18:31 *a* to the number of the tribes
21:26 *a* to all that the Amorites had
22:38 *a* to the word of the LORD
22:53 *a* to all that his father had
2 Ki 1:17 So Ahaziah died *a* to the word
2:22 *a* to the word of Elisha which
4:44 *a* to the word of the LORD.
5:14 *a* to the saying of the man of
6:18 He struck them with blindness *a*
7:16 *a* to the word of the LORD.
8: 2 So the woman arose and did *a* to

9:26 *a* to the word of the LORD."
10:17 *a* to the word of the LORD
11: 9 captains of the hundreds did *a*
11:14 king standing by a pillar *a* to
14: 6 *a* to what is written in the
14:25 *a* to the word of the LORD God
15: 3 *a* to all that his father
15:34 he did *a* to all that his father
16: 3 *a* to the abominations of the
16:10 *a* to all its workmanship.
16:11 the priest built an altar *a* to
16:16 *a* to all that King Ahaz
17:13 *a* to all the law which I
17:33 *a* to the rituals of the nations
18: 3 *a* to all that his father David
21: 2 *a* to the abominations of the
21: 8 if they are careful to do *a* to
21: 8 and *a* to all the law that My
22:13 to do *a* to all that is written
23:16 and defiled it *a* to the word of
23:19 and he did to them *a* to all the
23:25 *a* to all the Law of Moses; nor
23:32 *a* to all that his fathers had
23:35 taxed the land to give money *a*
23:35 from every one *a* to his
23:37 *a* to all that his fathers had
24: 2 *a* to the word of the LORD
24: 3 *a* to all that he had done,
24: 9 *a* to all that his father had
24:19 *a* to all that Jehoiakim had
1 Chr 5: 1 the genealogy is not listed *a*
6:19 the families of the Levites *a*
6:32 they served in their office *a*
6:49 *a* to all that Moses the servant
7: 4 *a* to their fathers' houses,
7: 9 were recorded by genealogy *a*
9: 9 *a* to their generations—nine
11: 3 *a* to the word of the LORD by
11:10 *a* to the word of the LORD
12:23 *a* to the word of the LORD:
15:15 as Moses had commanded *a* to the
15:20 with strings *a* to Alamoth;
16:40 and to do *a* to all that is
17:15 *A* to all these words and
17:15 to all these words and *a* to
17:17 and have regarded me *a* to the
17:19 and *a* to Your own heart, You
17:20 *a* to all that we have heard
23:31 by number *a* to the ordinance
24: 3 divided them *a* to the schedule
24:19 into the house of the LORD *a*
24:30 the sons of the Levites *a* to
25: 2 who prophesied *a* to the order
26:13 *a* to their father's house.
26:31 was head of the Hebronites *a*
27: 1 *a* to their number, the heads of
28:15 *a* to the use of each lampstand.
2 Chr 3: 3 was sixty cubits (by cubits *a*
3: 8 Its length was *a* to the width
4: 7 made ten lampstands of gold *a*
6:23 the righteous by giving him *a*
6:30 and give to everyone *a* to all
6:33 and do *a* to all for which the
7:17 and do *a* to all that I have
8:13 *a* to the daily rate, offering
8:13 offering *a* to the commandment
8:14 *a* to the order of David his
10:14 and he spoke to them *a* to the
17: 4 in His commandments and not *a*
17:14 *a* to their fathers' houses.
23: 8 Levites and all Judah did *a* to
24: 6 *a* to the commandment of
25: 5 *a* to their fathers' houses,
26: 4 *a* to all that his father
26:11 *a* to the number on their roll
27: 2 *a* to all that his father Uzziah
28: 3 *a* to the abominations of the
29: 2 *a* to all that his father David
29:15 and went *a* to the commandment
29:25 *a* to the commandment of David,
30: 6 and spoke *a* to the command of
30:16 They stood in their place *a* to
30:16 *a* to the Law of Moses the man
30:19 though he is not cleansed *a*
31: 2 the priests and the Levites *a*
31: 2 each man *a* to his service, the
31:17 written in the genealogy *a* to
31:17 from twenty years old and up *a*
32:25 But Hezekiah did not repay *a* to
33: 2 *a* to the abominations of the
33: 8 *a* to the whole law and the
34:21 to do *a* to all that is written
34:32 inhabitants of Jerusalem did *a*
35: 4 Prepare yourselves *a* to your
35: 4 *a* to your divisions, following
35: 5 stand in the holy place *a*
35: 5 and *a* to the division of the
35: 6 that they may do *a* to the word
35:10 *a* to the king's command.
35:13 OFFERINGS with fire *a* to the
35:15 *a* to the command of David,
35:16 *a* to the command of King
35:26 *a* to what was written in the
36:14 *a* to all the abominations of
Ezra 2:69 *A* to their ability, they gave to
3: 7 *a* to the permission which they
3:10 *a* to the ordinance of David
6: 9 *a* to the request of the priests
6:13 companions diligently did *a* to
6:14 *a* to the commandment of the God
6:14 and *a* to the command of Cyrus,
6:17 *a* to the number of the tribes
7: 6 *a* to the hand of the LORD his
7: 9 *a* to the good hand of his God
7:18 do it *a* to the will of your
7:25 *a* to your God-given wisdom, set
10: 3 *a* to the advice of my master
10: 3 and let it be done *a* to the
10: 5 an oath that they would do *a*
10: 8 *a* to the instructions of the
Neh 2: 8 the king granted them to me *a*
4:13 and I set the people *a* to their
5: 8 *A* to our ability we have
5:12 from them that they would do *a*
5:13 Then the people did *a* to this
5:19 *a* to all that I have done for
6: 6 *a* to these rumors, you are
6:14 *a* to these their works, and the
8:18 *a* to the prescribed manner.
9:27 And *a* to Your abundant mercies
9:28 times You delivered them *a* to
10:34 *a* to our fathers' houses, at
12:24 *a* to the command of David the
12:45 *a* to the command of David and
13:22 and spare me *a* to the greatness
13:24 but spoke *a* to the language of
Esth 1: 7 *a* to the generosity of the
1: 8 that they should do *a* to each
1:15 *a* to law, because she did not
1:21 and the king did *a* to the word
2:12 *a* to the regulations for the
2:18 the provinces and gave gifts *a*
3:12 and a decree was written *a* to
3:12 to every province *a* to its
4:17 went his way and did *a* to all
8: 9 *a* to all that Mordecai
9:13 Shushan to do again tomorrow *a*
9:27 *a* to the written instructions
9:27 written instructions and *a* to
Job 1: 5 and offer burnt offerings *a*
34:11 For He repays man *a* to his
34:11 makes man to find a reward *a*
34:33 Should He repay it *a* to your
42: 8 lest I deal with you *a* to
Ps 7: 8 *a* to my righteousness, And
7: 8 And *a* to my integrity within
7:17 I will praise the LORD *a* to
18:20 The LORD rewarded me *a* to my
18:20 *A* to the cleanness of my hands
18:24 the LORD has recompensed me *a*
18:24 *A* to the cleanness of my hands
20: 4 May He grant you *a* to your
25: 7 *A* to Your mercy remember me,
28: 4 Give them *a* to their deeds,
28: 4 And *a* to the wickedness of
28: 4 Give them *a* to the work of
35:24 *a* to Your righteousness; And
48:10 *A* to Your name, O God, So is
51: 1 *A* to Your lovingkindness;
51: 1 *A* to the multitude of Your
62:12 For You render to each one *a*
69:16 Turn to me *a* to the multitude
78:72 So he shepherded them *a* to the
79:11 *A* to the greatness of Your
90:15 Make us glad *a* to the days in
103:10 He has not dealt with us *a* to
103:10 Nor punished us *a* to our
106:45 And relented *a* to the
109:26 save me *a* to Your mercy,
110: 4 You are a priest forever *A* to
119: 9 By taking heed *a* to Your word.
119:25 Revive me *a* to Your word.
119:28 Strengthen me *a* to Your word.
119:41 Your salvation *a* to Your word.
119:58 Be merciful to me *a* to Your
119:65 *a* to Your word.
119:76 *A* to Your word to Your
119:85 Which is not *a* to Your law.
119:88 Revive me *a* to Your
119:91 They continue this day *a* to
119:107 *a* to Your word.
119:116 Uphold me *a* to Your word, that
119:124 Deal with Your servant *a* to
119:149 Hear my voice *a* to Your
119:149 revive me *a* to Your justice.
119:154 Revive me *a* to Your word.
119:156 Revive me *a* to Your judgments.
119:159 *a* to Your lovingkindness.
119:169 Give me understanding *a* to
119:170 Deliver me *a* to Your word.
150: 2 Praise Him *a* to His excellent
Prov 12: 8 A man will be commended *a* to
24:12 He not render to each man *a*
24:29 I will render to the man *a* to
26: 4 Do not answer a fool *a* to his
26: 5 Answer a fool *a* to his folly,
Eccl 8:14 just men to whom it happens *a*
8:14 men to whom it happens *a* to
Isa 8:20 If they do not speak *a* to this
9: 3 They rejoice before You *A* to
21:16 *a* to the year of a hired man,
23:15 *a* to the days of one king.
27: 7 Or has He been slain *a* to the
44:13 *A* to the beauty of a man, that
59:18 *A* to their deeds, accordingly
63: 7 *A* to all that the LORD has
63: 7 He has bestowed on them *a* to
63: 7 *A* to the multitude of His
65: 2 *A* to their own thoughts;
Jer 2:28 For *a* to the number of your
3:15 I will give you shepherds *a* to
9:13 nor walked *a* to it,
9:14 but they have walked *a* to the
11: 4 and do *a* to all that I command
11:13 For *a* to the number of your
11:13 and *a* to the number of the
13: 2 So I got a sash *a* to the word of
17:10 Even to give every man *a* to
17:10 *A* to the fruit of his doings.
18:12 is hopeless! So we will walk *a*
21: 2 the LORD will deal with us *a*
21:14 But I will punish you *a* to the
23:17 And to everyone who walks *a*
25:14 and I will repay them *a* to
25:14 according to their deeds and *a*
26:20 city and against this land *a*
27:12 to Zedekiah king of Judah *a* to
30:18 And the palace shall remain *a*
31:32 not *a* to the covenant that I
32: 8 me in the court of the prison *a*
32:11 both that which was sealed *a*
32:19 to give everyone *a* to his ways
32:19 according to his ways and *a* to
35:10 and have obeyed and done *a* to
35:18 all his precepts and done *a* to
36: 8 Baruch the son of Neriah did *a*
38:27 And he told them *a* to all these
42: 4 pray to the LORD your God *a*
42: 5 if we do not do *a* to everything
42:20 and *a* to all that the LORD
50:21 And do *a* to all that I have
50:29 Repay her *a* to her work;
50:29 *A* to all she has done, do to
52: 2 *a* to all that Jehoiakim had
Lam 3:32 He will show compassion *A* to
3:64 *A* to the work of their hands.
Ezek 4: 4 *A* to the number of the days
4: 5 *a* to the number of the days,
5: 7 nor even done *a* to the
7: 3 I will judge you *a* to your
7: 8 I will judge you *a* to your
7: 9 I will repay you *a* to your
7:27 I will do to them *a* to their
7:27 And *a* to what they deserve I
11:12 but have done *a* to the customs
14: 4 *a* to the multitude of his
16:47 walk in their ways nor act *a*
18:24 and does *a* to all the
18:30 every one *a* to his ways," says
20:30 and committing harlotry *a* to
20:44 not *a* to your wicked ways nor
20:44 to your wicked ways nor *a* to
23:24 And they shall judge you *a* to
24:14 *A* to your ways And according
24:14 According to your ways And *a*
24:24 *a* to all that he has done you
25:14 that they may do in Edom *a* to
25:14 according to My anger and *a* to
33:20 I will judge every one of you *a*
35:11 I will do *a* to your anger and
35:11 according to your anger and *a*
36:19 I judged them *a* to their ways
39:24 *A* to their uncleanness and
39:24 to their uncleanness and *a* to
40:24 its gateposts and archways *a*
40:28 the southern gateway *a* to
40:29 and its archways were *a* to
40:32 he measured the gateway *a* to
40:33 and its archways were *a* to
40:35 gateway and measured it *a* to
42:11 exits and entrances were *a* to
44:24 and judge it *a* to My
45: 8 *a* to their tribes."
45:11 their measure shall be *a* to the
45:25 *a* to the sin offering, the
47:21 this land among yourselves *a*
Dan 4: 8 *a* to the name of my god; in him
4:35 He does *a* to His will in the
6: 8 *a* to the law of the Medes and
6:12 *a* to the law of the Medes and
8: 4 but he did *a* to his will and
9:16 *a* to all Your righteousness, I
11: 3 and do *a* to his will.
11: 4 not among his posterity nor *a*
11:16 comes against him shall do *a*
11:36 Then the king shall do *a* to his
Hos 7:12 I will chastise them *A* to
10: 1 *A* to the multitude of his
10: 1 *A* to the bounty of his land
12: 2 And will punish Jacob *a* to his
12: 2 *A* to his deeds He will
13: 2 *a* to their skill; All of it
Jon 3: 3 *a* to the word of the LORD.
Hag 2: 5 *A* to the word that I
Zech 1: 6 *A* to our ways and according to
1: 6 According to our ways and *a* to
5: 3 *a* to this side of the
5: 3 *a* to that side of it."
Mt 2:16 *a* to the time which he had
9:29 *A* to your faith let it be to
16:27 and then He will reward each *a*
23: 3 but do not do *a* to their works;
25:15 to each *a* to his own ability;
Mk 7: 5 do Your disciples not walk *a*
Lk 1: 9 *a* to the custom of the
1:38 of the Lord! Let it be to me *a*
2:22 the days of her purification *a*
2:24 and to offer a sacrifice *a* to
2:27 to do for Him *a* to the custom
2:29 *A* to Your word;
2:39 had performed all things *a* to
2:42 they went up to Jerusalem *a* to
12:47 not prepare himself or do *a*
23:56 they rested on the Sabbath *a*
Jn 2: 6 *a* to the manner of purification
7:24 Do not judge *a* to appearance,

8:15 You judge *a* to the flesh; I
18:31 You take Him and judge Him *a* to
19: 7 and *a* to our law He ought to
Acts 2:30 *a* to the flesh, He would raise
7:44 instructing Moses to make it *a*
11:29 each *a* to his ability,
13:23 *a* to the promise, God raised
15: 1 Unless you are circumcised *a* to
21:21 their children nor to walk *a*
22: 3 taught *a* to the strictness of
22:12 a devout man *a* to the law,
23: 3 For you sit to judge me *a* to
24: 6 and wanted to judge him *a* to
24:14 that *a* to the Way which they
26: 5 that *a* to the strictest sect of
Rom 1: 3 born of the seed of David *a* to
1: 4 the Son of God with power *a* to
2: 2 that the judgment of God is *a*
2: 6 render to each one *a*
2:16 *a* to my gospel.
4: 1 Abraham our father has found *a*
4:16 of faith that it might be *a*
4:18 *a* to what was spoken, "So
5:14 those who had not sinned *a* to
7:22 I delight in the law of God *a*
8: 1 who do not walk *a* to the flesh,
8: 1 but *a* to the Spirit.
8: 4 in us who do not walk *a* to the
8: 4 according to the flesh but *a*
8: 5 For those who live *a* to the
8: 5 but those who live *a* to the
8:12 to live *a* to the flesh.
8:13 For if you live *a* to the flesh
8:27 intercession for the saints *a*
8:28 to those who are the called *a*
9: 3 my countrymen *a* to the flesh,
9: 5 *a* to the flesh, Christ came,
9:11 that the purpose of God *a* to
10: 2 but not *a* to knowledge.
11: 5 time there is a remnant *a* to
12: 6 Having then gifts differing *a* to
15: 5 *a* to Christ Jesus,
16:25 who is able to establish you *a*
16:25 *a* to the revelation of the
16:26 *a* to the commandment of the
1 Cor 1:26 that not many wise *a* to the
3: 8 will receive his own reward *a*
3:10 *A* to the grace of God which was
7:40 *a* to my judgment—and I think I
15: 3 Christ died for our sins *a* to
15: 4 He rose again the third day *a*
2 Cor 1:17 do I plan *a* to the flesh, that
4:13 *a* to what is written, "I
5:10 *a* to what he has done, whether
5:16 we regard no one *a* to the
5:16 though we have known Christ *a*
8: 3 For I bear witness that *a* to
8:12 it is accepted *a* to what one
8:12 and not *a* to what he does not
10: 2 think of us as if we walked *a*
10: 3 we do not war *a* to the flesh.
10: 7 Do you look at things *a* to the
11:15 whose end will be *a* to their
11:17 I speak not *a* to the Lord, but
11:18 Seeing that many boast *a* to the
13:10 *a* to the authority which the
Gal 1: 4 *a* to the will of our God and
1:11 was preached by me is not *a* to
3:29 and heirs *a* to the promise.
4:23 of the bondwoman was born *a* to
4:29 as he who was born *a* to the
4:29 him who was born *a* to the
6:16 And as many as walk *a* to this
Eph 1: 5 *a* to the good pleasure of His
1: 7 *a* to the riches of His grace
1: 9 *a* to His good pleasure which He
1:11 being predestined *a* to the
1:11 of Him who works all things *a*
1:19 *a* to the working of His mighty
2: 2 in which you once walked *a* to
2: 2 *a* to the prince of the power of
3: 7 of which I became a minister *a*
3:11 *a* to the eternal purpose which
3:16 *a* to the riches of His glory,
3:20 *a* to the power that works in
4: 7 one of us grace was given *a* to
4:16 *a* to the effective working by
4:22 old man which grows corrupt *a*
4:24 new man which was created *a* to
6: 5 to those who are your masters *a*
Phil 1:20 *a* to my earnest expectation and
3:21 *a* to the working by which He is
4:19 shall supply all your need *a*
Col 1:11 *a* to His glorious power, for
1:25 of which I became a minister *a*
1:29 striving *a* to His working which
2: 8 *a* to the tradition of men,
2: 8 *a* to the basic principles of
2: 8 and not *a* to Christ.
2:22 *a* to the commandments and
3:10 who is renewed in knowledge *a*
3:22 in all things your masters *a*
2 Th 1:12 *a* to the grace of our God and
2: 9 of the lawless one is *a* to
3: 6 who walks disorderly and not *a*
1 Tim 1:11 *a* to the glorious gospel of the
1:18 *a* to the prophecies previously
2 Tim 1: 1 *a* to the promise of life which
1: 8 sufferings for the gospel *a* to
1: 9 not *a* to our works, but
1: 9 but *a* to His own purpose and
2: 5 crowned unless he competes *a*
2: 8 was raised from the dead *a* to
4: 3 but *a* to their own desires,
4:14 May the Lord repay him *a* to his
Titus 1: 1 *a* to the faith of God's elect
1: 3 which was committed to me *a* to
3: 5 but *a* to His mercy He saved us,
3: 7 grace we should become heirs *a*
Heb 2: 4 *a* to His own will?
4:11 lest anyone fall *a* to the same
5: 6 are a priest forever *A*
5:10 *a* to the order of
6:20 become High Priest forever *a*
7: 5 tithes from the people *a* to
7:11 another priest should rise *a*
7:11 and not be called *a* to the
7:16 not *a* to the law of a fleshly
7:16 but *a* to the power of an
7:17 are a priest forever *A*
7:21 are a priest forever *A*
8: 4 priests who offer the gifts *a*
8: 5 you make all things *a* to
8: 9 not *a* to the covenant that
9:19 precept to all the people *a* to
9:22 And *a* to the law almost all
10: 8 are offered *a* to the law),
11: 7 of the righteousness which is *a*
Jas 2: 8 fulfill the royal law *a* to
1 Pe 1: 2 elect *a* to the foreknowledge of
1: 3 who *a* to His abundant mercy has
1:17 without partiality judges *a* to
4: 6 that they might be judged *a* to
4: 6 but live *a* to God in the
4:19 let those who suffer *a* to the
2 Pe 2:10 especially those who walk *a* to
2:22 But it has happened to them *a* to
3: 3 walking *a* to their own lusts,
3:13 *a* to His promise, look for new
3:15 *a* to the wisdom given to him,
1 Jn 5:14 that if we ask anything *a* to
2 Jn 6 that we walk *a* to His
Jude 16 walking *a* to their own lusts;
18 the last time who would walk *a*
Rev 2:23 will give to each one of you *a*
18: 6 and repay her double *a* to her
20:12 And the dead were judged *a* to
20:13 each one *a* to his works.
21:17 *a* to the measure of a man,
22:12 to give to every one *a* to his

ACCORDINGLY (3/3)

Ex 21:22 he shall surely be punished *a*
Ezra 5: 4 *a*, we told them the names of
Isa 59:18 *a* He will repay, Fury to His

ACCORDS (2/2)

1 Tim 6: 3 and to the doctrine which *a*
Titus 1: 1 of the truth which *a* with

ACCOUNT (28/28) ACCOUNTED, ACCOUNTING, ACCOUNTS

Gen 20:11 and they will kill me on *a* of
26: 9 Lest I die on *a* of her.'"
Deut 3:26 was angry with me on your *a*,
Josh 22:23 LORD Himself require an *a*.
2 Ki 12:15 they did not require an *a* from
16:18 on *a* of the king of Assyria.
1 Chr 27:24 the number recorded in the *a*
Esth 10: 2 and the *a* of the greatness of
Ps 10:13 "You will not require an *a*.
106:32 it went ill with Moses on *a* of
Eccl 3:15 And God requires an *a* of what
Isa 2:22 For of what *a* is he?
Dan 6: 2 that the satraps might give *a*
7:28 "This is the end of the *a*.
Joel 3: 2 judgment with them there On *a*
Mt 12:36 they will give *a* of it in the
Lk 1: 3 to write to you an orderly *a*,
16: 2 Give an *a* of your stewardship,
Jn 12:11 because on *a* of him many of the
Acts 1: 1 The former *a* I made, O
19:40 reason which we may give to *a*
Rom 8: 3 on *a* of sin: He condemned sin
14:12 So then each of us shall give *a*
Phil 4:17 fruit that abounds to your *a*.
Phm 1:18 owes anything, put that on my *a*.
Heb 4:13 of Him to whom we must give *a*.
13:17 souls, as those who must give *a*.
1 Pe 4: 5 They will give an *a* to Him who

ACCOUNTED (14/14) ACCOUNT

Gen 15: 6 and He *a* it to him for
Num 18:30 then the rest shall be *a* to
1 Ki 10:21 for this was *a* as nothing in
2 Chr 9:20 for this was *a* as nothing in
Ps 44:22 We are *a* as sheep for the
106:31 And that was *a* to him for
Rom 4: 3 and it was *a* to him for
4: 5 his faith is *a* for
4: 9 For we say that faith was *a* to
4:10 How then was it *a*?
4:22 it was *a* to him for
8:36 We are *a* as sheep for
Gal 3: 6 and it was *a* to him for
Jas 2:23 and it was *a* to him for

ACCOUNTING (2/2) ACCOUNT

2 Ki 22: 7 However there need be no *a* made
Job 33:13 For He does not give an *a* of

ACCOUNTS (3/3) ACCOUNT

Mt 18:23 king who wanted to settle *a*
18:24 when he had begun to settle *a*,
25:19 servants came and settled *a*

ACCUMULATED (2/2)

2 Ki 20:17 and what your fathers have *a*
Isa 39: 6 and what your fathers have *a*

ACCURATE (1/1) ACCURATELY

Acts 24:22 having more *a* knowledge of the

ACCURATELY (2/2) ACCURATE

Acts 18:25 he spoke and taught *a* the
18:26 to him the way of God more *a*.

ACCURSED (24/20)

Deut 7:26 for it is an *a* thing.
13:17 So none of the *a* things shall
21:23 for he who is hanged is *a* of
Josh 6:18 by all means abstain from the *a*
6:18 lest you become *a* when you take
6:18 when you take of the *a* things,
7: 1 a trespass regarding the *a*
7: 1 took of the *a* things; so the
7:11 have even taken some of the *a*
7:12 unless you destroy the *a* from
7:13 There is an *a* thing in your
7:13 until you take away the *a*
7:15 he who is taken with the *a*
22:20 commit a trespass in the *a*
2 Ki 9:34 see to this *a* woman, and bury
1 Chr 2: 7 who transgressed in the *a*
Isa 65:20 hundred years old shall be *a*.
Jn 7:49 that does not know the law is *a*.
Rom 9: 3 wish that I myself were *a* from
1 Cor 12: 3 the Spirit of God calls Jesus *a*,
16:22 Lord Jesus Christ, let him be *a*.
Gal 1: 8 preached to you, let him be *a*.
1: 9 you have received, let him be *a*.
2 Pe 2:14 and are *a* children.

ACCUSATION (12/12) ACCUSE, ACCUSER, ACCUSERS

Ezra 4: 6 they wrote an *a* against the
Mt 27:37 they put up over His head the *a*
Mk 15:26 And the inscription of His *a* was
Lk 6: 7 that they might find an *a*
16: 1 and an *a* was brought to him
19: 8 anything from anyone by false *a*,
Jn 18:29 What *a* do you bring against this
Acts 24: 2 upon, Tertullus began his *a*,
25:18 they brought no *a* against him
1 Tim 5:19 Do not receive an *a* against an
2 Pe 2:11 do not bring a reviling *a*
Jude 9 bring against him a reviling *a*,

ACCUSE (13/13) ACCUSATION, ACCUSED, ACCUSER, ACCUSES, ACCUSING

Mt 12:10 that they might *a* Him.
Mk 3: 2 so that they might *a* Him.
Lk 3:14 Do not intimidate anyone or *a*
11:54 that they might *a* Him.
23: 2 And they began to *a* Him, saying,
23:14 those things of which you *a*
Jn 5:45 Do not think that I shall *a* you
8: 6 have something of which to *a*
Acts 24: 8 all these things of which we *a*
24:13 the things of which they now *a*
25: 5 you go down with me and *a*
25:11 things of which these men *a* me,
28:19 I had anything of which to *a*

ACCUSED (13/13) ACCUSE

Dan 3: 8 Chaldeans came forward and *a*
6:24 brought those men who had *a*
Mt 27:12 And while He was being *a* by the
Mk 15: 3 And the chief priests *a* Him of
Lk 23:10 scribes stood and vehemently *a*
Acts 22:30 know for certain why he was *a*
23:28 to know the reason they *a* him,
23:29 I found out that he was *a*
25:16 man to destruction before the *a*
26: 2 all the things of which I am *a*
26: 7 I am *a* by the Jews.
Titus 1: 6 having faithful children not *a*
Rev 12:10 who *a* them before our God day

ACCUSER (2/2) ACCUSE, ACCUSERS

Ps 109: 6 And let an *a* stand at his
Rev 12:10 for the *a* of our brethren, who

ACCUSERS (9/9) ACCUSE

Ps 109: 4 for my love they are my *a*,
109:20 be the LORD's reward to my *a*,
109:29 Let my *a* be clothed with shame,
Jn 8:10 where are those *a* of yours?
Acts 23:30 and also commanded his *a* to
23:35 I will hear you when your *a* also
24: 8 commanding his *a* to come to you.

25:16 before the accused meets the **a**
25:18 When the **a** stood up, they

ACCUSES (1/1) ACCUSE
Jn 5:45 there is one who **a** you—Moses,

ACCUSING (1/1) ACCUSE
Rom 2:15 themselves their thoughts **a**

ACCUSTOMED (6/6)
1 Sam 30:31 himself and his men were **a** to
Jer 13:23 may you also do good who are **a**
Mt 27:15 at the feast the governor was **a**
Mk 10: 1 to Him again, and as He was **a**,
15: 6 Now at the feast he was **a** to
Lk 22:39 Mount of Olives, as He was **a**,

ACELDAMA (KJV) See AKEL (DAMA)

ACHAIA (11/11)
Acts 18:12 When Gallio was proconsul of **A**,
18:27 when he desired to cross to **A**,
19:21 passed through Macedonia and **A**,
Rom 15:26 those from Macedonia and **A** to
16: 5 who is the firstfruits of **A** to
1 Cor 16:15 that it is the firstfruits of **A**,
2 Cor 1: 1 all the saints who are in all **A**:
9: 2 that **A** was ready a year ago;
11:10 boasting in the regions of **A**.
1 Th 1: 7 to all in Macedonia and **A** who
1: 8 not only in Macedonia and **A**,

ACHAICUS (1/1)
1 Cor 16:17 of Stephanas, Fortunatus, and **A**,

ACHAN (6/6) ACHAR
Josh 7: 1 for **A** the son of Carmi, the son
7:18 and **A** the son of Carmi, the son
7:19 Now Joshua said to **A**,
7:20 And **A** answered Joshua and said,
7:24 took **A** the son of Zerah, the
22:20 Did not **A** the son of Zerah

ACHAR (1/1) ACHAN
1 Chr 2: 7 The son of Carmi was **A**,

ACHAZ (KJV) See AHAZ

ACHBOR (7/7)
Gen 36:38 Baal-Hanan the son of **A** reigned
36:39 when Baal-Hanan the son of **A**
2 Ki 22:12 **A** the son of Michaiah, Shaphan
22:14 Hilkiah the priest, Ahikam, **A**,
1 Chr 1:49 Baal-Hanan the son of **A** reigned
Jer 26:22 to Egypt: Elnathan the son of **A**,
36:12 Shemaiah, Elnathan the son of **A**,

ACHIM (2/1)
Mt 1:14 Azor begot Zadok, Zadok begot **A**,
1:14 and **A** begot Eliud.

ACHISH (21/20)
1 Sam 21:10 and went to **A** the king of Gath.
21:11 And the servants of **A** said to
21:12 and was very much afraid of **A**
21:14 Then **A** said to his servants,
27: 2 men who were with him to **A**
27: 3 So David dwelt with **A** at Gath,
27: 5 Then David said to **A**,
27: 6 So **A** gave him Ziklag that day.
27: 9 and returned and came to **A**.
27:10 Then **A** would say, "Where have
27:12 So **A** believed David, saying,
28: 1 And **A** said to David, "You
28: 2 And David said to **A**,
28: 2 And **A** said to David,
29: 2 in review at the rear with **A**.
29: 3 And **A** said to the princes of
29: 6 Then **A** called David and said to
29: 8 So David said to **A**,
29: 9 Then **A** answered and said to
1 Ki 2:39 slaves of Shimei ran away to **A**
2:40 and went to **A** at Gath to seek

ACHMETHA (1/1)
Ezra 6: 2 And at **A**, in the palace

ACHOR (5/5)
Josh 7:24 brought them to the Valley of **A**.
7:26 been called the Valley of **A** to
15: 7 Debir from the Valley of **A**,
Isa 65:10 And the Valley of **A** a place
Hos 2:15 And the Valley of **A** as a door

ACHSA (KJV) See ACHSAH

ACHSAH (5/5)
Josh 15:16 to him I will give **A** my
15:17 and he gave him **A** his daughter
Judg 1:12 him I will give my daughter **A**
1:13 so he gave him his daughter **A**
1 Chr 2:49 the daughter of Caleb was **A**.

ACHSHAPH (3/3)
Josh 11: 1 of Shimron, to the king of **A**,
12:20 Meron, one; the king of **A**,
19:25 Helkath, Hali, Beten, **A**,

ACHZIB (4/4) CHEZIB
Josh 15:44 Keilah, **A**, and Mareshah:
19:29 at the sea by the region of **A**.
Judg 1:31 of Sidon, or of Ahlab, **A**,
Mic 1:14 The houses of **A** shall be a

ACKNOWLEDGE (15/15) ACKNOWLEDGED, ACKNOWLEDGES, ACKNOWLEDGMENT
Deut 21:17 But he shall **a** the son of the
33: 9 Nor did he **a** his brothers, Or
Ps 51: 3 For I **a** my transgressions, And
Prov 3: 6 In all your ways **a** Him, And He
Isa 33:13 who are near, **a** My might."
61: 9 All who see them shall **a** them,
63:16 And Israel does not **a** us.
Jer 3:13 Only **a** your iniquity, That you
14:20 We **a**, O LORD, our wickedness
24: 5 so will I **a** those who are
Dan 11:39 a foreign god, which he shall **a**,
Hos 5:15 again to My place Till they **a**
8: 4 but I did not **a** them.
1 Cor 14:37 let him **a** that the things which
16:18 Therefore **a** such men.

ACKNOWLEDGED (4/4) ACKNOWLEDGE
Gen 38:26 So Judah **a** them and said, "She
Ex 2:25 and God **a** them.
Ps 32: 5 I **a** my sin to You, And my
Acts 15: 8 **a** them by giving them the Holy

ACKNOWLEDGES (3/3) ACKNOWLEDGE
1 Ki 2:44 "You know, as your heart **a**,
Ps 142: 4 For there is no one who **a**
1 Jn 2:23 he who **a** the Son has the Father

ACKNOWLEDGMENT (2/2) ACKNOWLEDGE
Titus 1: 1 faith of God's elect and the **a**
Phm 1: 6 may become effective by the **a**

ACQUAINT (1/1) ACQUAINTANCE, ACQUAINTED
Job 22:21 Now **a** yourself with Him, and be

ACQUAINTANCE (1/1) ACQUAINT, ACQUAINTANCES
Ps 55:13 equal, My companion and my **a**.

ACQUAINTANCES (9/9) ACQUAINTANCE
2 Ki 10:11 his great men and his close **a**
Job 19:13 And my **a** are completely
42:11 all those who had been his **a**
Ps 31:11 And am repulsive to my **a**;
88: 8 You have put away my **a** far from
88:18 And my **a** into darkness.
Jer 20:10 we will report it!" All my **a**
Lk 2:44 among their relatives and **a**.
23:49 But all His **a**, and the women

ACQUAINTED (2/2) ACQUAINT
Ps 139: 3 And are **a** with all my ways.
Isa 53: 3 A Man of sorrows and **a** with

ACQUIRE (1/1) ACQUIRED, ACQUIRES
Gen 34:10 and **a** possessions for

ACQUIRED (15/15) ACQUIRE
Gen 4: 1 I have **a** a man from the LORD."
12: 5 and the people whom they had **a**
31: 1 what was our father's he has **a**
31:18 his **a** livestock which he had
46: 6 which they had **a** in the land of
Ruth 4:10 I have **a** as my wife, to
1 Ki 9:28 and **a** four hundred and twenty
2 Chr 1:17 They also **a** and imported from
8:18 and **a** four hundred and fifty
Ps 78:54 which His right hand had **a**.
Eccl 2: 7 I **a** male and female servants,
2: 8 I **a** male and female singers,
Jer 13: 4 "Take the sash that you **a**,
48:36 the riches they have **a** have
Ezek 38:12 who have **a** livestock and goods,

ACQUIRES (1/1) ACQUIRE
Prov 18:15 The heart of the prudent **a**

ACQUIT (3/3) ACQUITTED
Job 10:14 And will not **a** me of my
Joel 3:21 For I will **a** them of the guilt
Nah 1: 3 And will not at all **a** the

ACQUITTED (4/4) ACQUIT
Ex 21:19 he who struck him shall be **a**.
21:28 owner of the ox shall be **a**.
Isa 43:26 your case, that you may be **a**.
Joel 3:21 of bloodshed, whom I had not **a**;

ACRE (1/1) ACRES
1 Sam 14:14 men within about half an **a** of

ACRES (1/1) ACRE
Isa 5:10 For ten **a** of vineyard shall

ACROSS (33/32)
Gen 1:20 let birds fly above the earth **a**
21:16 Then she went and sat down **a**
Ex 26:35 and the lampstand **a** from the
40:24 **a** from the table, on the south
Num 22: 1 on the side of the Jordan **a**
26: 3 **a** from Jericho, saying:
26:63 **a** from Jericho.
31:12 **a** from Jericho.
33:48 **a** from Jericho.
33:50 **a** from Jericho, saying,
34:15 **a** from Jericho eastward,
35: 1 of Moab by the Jordan **a** from
36:13 **a** from Jericho.
Deut 32:49 **a** from Jericho; view the land
34: 1 which is **a** from Jericho.
2 Sam 19:15 to escort the king **a** the
19:18 Then a ferryboat went **a** to carry
19:31 down from Rogelim and went **a**
19:31 to escort him **a** the Jordan.
19:33 Come **a** with me, and I will
19:36 servant will go a little way **a**
19:41 and all David's men with him **a**
1 Ki 6: 3 was twenty cubits long **a** the
6:21 He stretched gold chains **a** the
1 Chr 6:78 **a** from Jericho, on the east
2 Chr 3: 4 was twenty cubits long **a** the
Neh 12: 9 stood **a** from them in their
12:24 with their brothers **a** from
Esth 5: 1 **a** from the king's house, while
7: 8 Haman had fallen **a** the couch
Job 1:19 a great wind came from **a** the
Jer 25:22 of the coastlands which are **a**
Dan 8: 5 **a** the surface of the whole

ACT (24/23) ACTED, ACTING, ACTIONS, ACTIVE, ACTIVITIES, ACTIVITY, ACTS, ACTUALLY
Deut 4: 5 that you should **a** according to
4:16 lest you **a** corruptly and make
4:25 and **a** corruptly and make a
11: 7 eyes have seen every great **a**
17:13 and no longer **a** presumptuously.
Judg 19:23 do not **a** so wickedly! Seeing
2 Sam 14: 2 but **a** like a woman who has been
1 Ki 8:32 "then hear in heaven, and **a**,
8:39 place, and forgive, and **a**,
2 Chr 6:23 "then hear from heaven, and **a**,
19: 9 Thus you shall **a** in the fear of
Neh 6:13 that I should be afraid and **a**
Ps 119:126 It is time for You to **a**,
Isa 28:16 Whoever believes will not **a**
28:21 work, And bring to pass His **a**,
28:21 to pass His act, His unusual **a**.
59: 6 And the **a** of violence is in
Ezek 8:18 Therefore I also will **a** in fury.
16:47 not walk in their ways nor **a**
Dan 9:19 listen and **a**! Do not delay for
11:23 is made with him he shall **a**
11:39 Thus he shall **a** against the
Jn 8: 4 in adultery, in the very **a**.
Rom 5:18 through one Man's righteous **a**

ACTED (18/18) ACT
Gen 42: 7 but he **a** as a stranger to them
Deut 9:12 you brought out of Egypt have **a**
Judg 9:16 if you have **a** in truth and
9:19 if then you have **a** in truth and
2 Sam 15: 6 In this manner Absalom **a** toward
2 Ki 10:19 But Jehu **a** deceptively, with
21:11 these abominations (he has **a**
2 Chr 20:35 who **a** very wickedly.
27: 2 But still the people **a**
Neh 1: 7 We have **a** very corruptly against
9:10 For You knew that they **a**
9:16 But they and our fathers **a**
9:29 Yet they **a** proudly, And did
Job 36: 9 That they have **a** defiantly.
Ps 78:57 But turned back and **a**
Ezek 20: 9 But I **a** for My name's sake, that
20:14 But I **a** for My name's sake, that
20:22 I withdrew My hand and **a** for

ACTING (3/3) ACT
Gen 19: 9 and he keeps **a** as a judge; now
Num 16:13 that you should keep **a** like a
Acts 17: 7 and these are all **a** contrary to

ACTIONS (1/1)
1 Sam 2: 3 And by Him ***a*** are weighed.

ACTIVE (3/3) ACTIVITY
Lev 13:51 the plague is an ***a*** leprosy.
13:52 for it is an ***a*** leprosy; the
14:44 it is an ***a*** leprosy in the

ACTIVITIES (1/1) ACTIVITY
1 Cor 12: 6 And there are diversities of ***a***,

ACTIVITY (1/1) ACTIVE, ACTIVITIES
Eccl 5: 3 a dream comes through much ***a***,

ACTS (74/72) ACT
Ex 21:14 But if a man ***a*** with
Deut 11: 3 His signs and His ***a*** which He did
17:12 the man who ***a*** presumptuously
Judg 5:11 shall recount the righteous ***a***
5:11 The righteous ***a*** for His
1 Sam 12: 7 concerning all the righteous ***a***
1 Ki 11:41 the rest of the ***a*** of Solomon,
11:41 written in the book of the ***a***
14:19 the rest of the ***a*** of Jeroboam,
14:29 the rest of the ***a*** of Rehoboam,
15: 7 Now the rest of the ***a*** of Abijam,
15:23 The rest of all the ***a*** of Asa,
15:31 Now the rest of the ***a*** of Nadab,
16: 5 the rest of the ***a*** of Baasha,
16:14 Now the rest of the ***a*** of Elah,
16:20 Now the rest of the ***a*** of Zimri,
16:27 Now the rest of the ***a*** of Omri
22:39 Now the rest of the ***a*** of Ahab,
22:45 rest of the ***a*** of Jehoshaphat,
2 Ki 1:18 Now the rest of the ***a*** of Ahaziah
8:23 Now the rest of the ***a*** of Joram,
10:34 Now the rest of the ***a*** of Jehu,
12:19 Now the rest of the ***a*** of Joash,
13: 8 the rest of the ***a*** of Jehoahaz,
13:12 Now the rest of the ***a*** of Joash,
14:15 the rest of the ***a*** of Jehoash
14:18 the rest of the ***a*** of Amaziah,
14:28 the rest of the ***a*** of Jeroboam,
15: 6 the rest of the ***a*** of Azariah,
15:11 rest of the ***a*** of Zechariah,
15:15 the rest of the ***a*** of Shallum,
15:21 the rest of the ***a*** of Menahem,
15:26 the rest of the ***a*** of Pekahiah,
15:31 Now the rest of the ***a*** of Pekah,
15:36 the rest of the ***a*** of Jotham,
16:19 Now the rest of the ***a*** of Ahaz
20:20 rest of the ***a*** of Hezekiah—all
21:17 rest of the ***a*** of Manasseh—all
21:25 Now the rest of the ***a*** of Amon
23:28 the rest of the ***a*** of Josiah,
24: 5 rest of the ***a*** of Jehoiakim,
1 Chr 29:29 Now the ***a*** of King David, first
2 Chr 9:29 the rest of the ***a*** of Solomon,
12:15 The ***a*** of Rehoboam, first and
13:22 Now the rest of the ***a*** of Abijah,
16:11 Note that the ***a*** of Asa, first
17: 4 and not according to the ***a*** of
20:34 rest of the ***a*** of Jehoshaphat,
25:26 the rest of the ***a*** of Amaziah,
26:22 the rest of the ***a*** of Uzziah,
27: 7 the rest of the ***a*** of Jotham,
28:26 Now the rest of his ***a*** and all
32:32 the rest of the ***a*** of Hezekiah,
33:18 the rest of the ***a*** of Manasseh,
35:26 Now the rest of the ***a*** of Josiah
36: 8 the rest of the ***a*** of Jehoiakim,
Esth 10: 2 Now all the ***a*** of his power and
Job 15:25 And ***a*** defiantly against the
Ps 103: 7 His ***a*** to the children of
106: 2 Who can utter the mighty ***a*** of
145: 4 shall declare Your mighty ***a***.
145: 6 of the might of Your awesome ***a***,
145:12 to the sons of men His mighty ***a***,
150: 2 Praise Him for His mighty ***a***;
Prov 13:16 Every prudent man ***a*** with
14:17 A quick-tempered man ***a***
21:24 He ***a*** with arrogant pride.
Isa 64: 4 Who ***a*** for the one who waits
Ezek 16:20 Were your ***a*** of harlotry a
16:22 in all your abominations and ***a***
16:25 and multiplied your ***a*** of
16:26 and increased your ***a*** of
16:29 you multiplied your ***a***
Rev 19: 8 fine linen is the righteous ***a***

ACTUALLY (5/5)
Gen 50:15 and may ***a*** repay us for all the
2 Ki 4:14 And Gehazi answered, "*A*,
1 Cor 5: 1 It is ***a*** reported that there
Phil 1:12 which happened to me have ***a***
2 Pe 2:18 the ones who have ***a*** escaped

ADADAH (1/1)
Josh 15:22 Kinah, Dimonah, *A*,

ADAH (8/8)
Gen 4:19 wives: the name of one was *A*,
4:20 And *A* bore Jabal. He was the
4:23 *A* and Zillah, hear my voice;
36: 2 *A* the daughter of Elon the
36: 4 Now *A* bore Eliphaz to Esau, and
36:10 Eliphaz the son of *A* the wife
36:12 These were the sons of *A*,
36:16 They were the sons of *A*.

ADAIAH (9/9)
2 Ki 22: 1 was Jedidah the daughter of *A*
1 Chr 6:41 the son of Zerah, the son of *A*,
8:21 *A*, Beraiah, and Shimrath were
9:12 *A* the son of Jeroham, the son of
2 Chr 23: 1 of Obed, Maaseiah the son of *A*,
Ezra 10:29 of Bani: Meshullam, Malluch, *A*,
10:39 Shelemiah, Nathan, *A*,
Neh 11: 5 son of Hazaiah, the son of *A*,
11:12 and *A* the son of Jeroham, the

ADALIA (1/1)
Esth 9: 8 Poratha, *A*, Aridatha,

ADAM (30/26)
Gen 2:19 and brought them to *A* to see
2:19 And whatever *A* called each
2:20 So *A* gave names to all cattle,
2:20 But for *A* there was not found a
2:21 a deep sleep to fall on *A*,
2:23 And *A* said: "This is now
3: 8 and *A* and his wife hid
3: 9 the LORD God called to *A* and
3:17 Then to *A* He said, "Because you
3:20 And *A* called his wife's name
3:21 Also for *A* and his wife the
4: 1 Now *A* knew Eve his wife, and she
4:25 And *A* knew his wife again, and
5: 1 the book of the genealogy of *A*.
5: 3 And *A* lived one hundred and
5: 4 the days of *A* were eight
5: 5 So all the days that *A* lived
Deut 32: 8 He separated the sons of *A*,
Josh 3:16 in a heap very far away at *A*,
1 Chr 1: 1 *A*, Seth, Enosh,
Job 31:33 covered my transgressions as *A*,
Lk 3:38 son of Seth, the son of *A*,
Rom 5:14 death reigned from *A* to Moses,
5:14 of the transgression of *A*,
1 Cor 15:22 For as in *A* all die, even so in
15:45 The first man *A* became a
15:45 The last *A* became a
1 Tim 2:13 For *A* was formed first, then
2:14 And *A* was not deceived, but the
Jude 14 Now Enoch, the seventh from *A*,

ADAMAH (1/1)
Josh 19:36 *A*, Ramah, Hazor,

ADAMANT (1/1)
Ezek 3: 9 Like ***a*** stone, harder than flint,

ADAMI (1/1)
Josh 19:33 *A* Nekeb, and Jabneel, as far as

ADAR (10/10) ADDAR
Josh 15: 3 along to Hezron, went up to *A*,
Ezra 6:15 the third day of the month of *A*,
Esth 3: 7 which is the month of *A*.
3:13 which is the month of *A*,
8:12 month, which is the month of *A*.
9: 1 month, that is, the month of *A*,
9:15 day of the month of *A* and
9:17 day of the month of *A*.
9:19 day of the month of *A* with
9:21 days of the month of *A*,

ADBEEL (2/2)
Gen 25:13 Nebajoth; then Kedar, *A*,
1 Chr 1:29 was Nebajoth; then Kedar, *A*,

ADD (34/34) ADDED, ADDING, ADDITION, ADDS
Gen 30:24 The LORD shall ***a*** to me another
Lev 5:16 and shall ***a*** one-fifth to it and
6: 5 ***a*** one-fifth more to it, and
22:14 and ***a*** one-fifth to it.
27:13 then he must ***a*** one-fifth to
27:15 then he must ***a*** one-fifth of the
27:19 then he must ***a*** one-fifth of the
27:27 and shall ***a*** one-fifth to it; or
27:31 he shall ***a*** one-fifth to it.
Num 35: 6 And to these you shall ***a***
Deut 4: 2 You shall not ***a*** to the word
12:32 you shall not ***a*** to it nor take
19: 9 then you shall ***a*** three more
2 Sam 24: 3 Now may the LORD your God ***a*** to
1 Ki 12:11 I will ***a*** to your yoke; my
12:14 but I will ***a*** to your yoke; my
2 Ki 20: 6 And I will ***a*** to your days
1 Chr 22:14 and you may ***a*** to them.
2 Chr 10:11 I will ***a*** to your yoke; my
10:14 but I will ***a*** to it; my father
28:13 You intend to ***a*** to our sins and
Ps 69:27 *A* iniquity to their iniquity,
Prov 3: 2 life And peace they will ***a*** to
30: 6 Do not ***a*** to His words, Lest He
Isa 5: 8 They ***a*** field to field, Till
29: 1 the city where David dwelt! *A*
30: 1 That they may ***a*** sin to sin;
38: 5 surely I will ***a*** to your days
Jer 7:21 *A* your burnt offerings to your
Mt 6:27 of you by worrying can ***a***
Lk 12:25 which of you by worrying can ***a***
Phil 1:16 supposing to ***a*** affliction to my
2 Pe 1: 5 ***a*** to your faith virtue, to
Rev 22:18 God will ***a*** to him the plagues

ADDAN (1/1)
Ezra 2:59 Melah, Tel Harsha, Cherub, *A*,

ADDAR (4/4) ADAR
1 Chr 8: 3 The sons of Bela were *A*,

ADDED (19/19) ADD
Num 36: 3 and it will be ***a*** to the
36: 4 their inheritance will be ***a*** to
Deut 5:22 and He ***a*** no more. And He wrote
1 Sam 12:19 for we have ***a*** to all our sins
Neh 13:18 Yet you bring ***a*** wrath on Israel
Prov 9:11 And years of life will be ***a*** to
Eccl 3:14 Nothing can be ***a*** to it, And
Jer 36:32 there were ***a*** to them many
45: 3 is me now! For the LORD has ***a***
Dan 4:36 and excellent majesty was ***a*** to
Mt 6:33 all these things shall be ***a*** to
Lk 3:20 also ***a*** this, above all, that he
12:31 all these things shall be ***a*** to
Acts 2:41 three thousand souls were ***a***
2:47 And the Lord ***a*** to the church
5:14 believers were increasingly ***a***
11:24 And a great many people were ***a***
Gal 2: 6 who seemed to be something ***a***
3:19 ***a*** because of transgressions,

ADDERS' (KJV) See ASPS

ADDI (1/1)
Lk 3:28 son of Melchi, the son of *A*,

ADDING (2/2) ADD
Ezra 10:10 ***a*** to the guilt of Israel.
Eccl 7:27 *A* one thing to the other to

ADDITION (3/3) ADD
Gen 28: 9 to be his wife in ***a*** to the
Num 5: 8 in ***a*** to the ram of the
Ezek 16:43 shall not commit lewdness in ***a***

ADDON (1/1)
Neh 7:61 Melah, Tel Harsha, Cherub, *A*,

ADDS (6/6) ADD
Job 34:37 For he ***a*** rebellion to his sin;
Prov 10:22 And He ***a*** no sorrow with it.
16:23 And ***a*** learning to his lips.
Gal 3:15 no one annuls or ***a*** to it.
Heb 10:17 then He ***a***, "Their sins
Rev 22:18 If anyone ***a*** to these things,

ADER (KJV) See EDER

ADHERE (1/1) ADHERES
Dan 2:43 but they will not ***a*** to one

ADHERES (1/1) ADHERE
Job 31: 7 Or if any spot ***a*** to my hands,

ADIEL (3/3)
1 Chr 4:36 Jaakobah, Jeshohaiah, Asaiah, *A*,
9:12 Malchijah; Maasai the son of *A*,
27:25 And Azmaveth the son of *A* was

ADIN (4/4)
Ezra 2:15 the people of *A*,
8: 6 of the sons of *A*,
Neh 7:20 the sons of *A*,
10:16 Adonijah, Bigvai, *A*,

ADINA (1/1)
1 Chr 11:42 *A* the son of Shiza the Reubenite

ADINO (1/1)
2 Sam 23: 8 He was called *A* the Eznite,

ADITHAIM (1/1)
Josh 15:36 Sharaim, *A*, Gederah,

ADJACENT (3/3)
Ezek 45: 6 ***a*** to the district of the holy
48:18 It shall be ***a*** to the district
48:21 ***a*** to the tribal portions; it

ADJOIN (1/1) ADJOINED, ADJOINING
Gen 49:13 And his border shall ***a*** Sidon.

ADJOINED (1/1) ADJOIN
Josh 19:34 it ***a*** Zebulun on the south side

ADJOINING (2/2) ADJOIN
Josh 17:10 Manasseh's territory was ***a***
Acts 2:10 Egypt and the parts of Libya ***a***

ADJOURNED (1/1)
Acts 24:22 he ***a*** the proceedings and said,

ADJURE (KJV) See EXORCISE, IMPLORE, MAKE

ADLAI (1/1)
1 Chr 27:29 and Shaphat the son of *A* was

ADMAH (5/5)
Gen 10:19 go toward Sodom, Gomorrah, *A*,
14: 2 of Gomorrah, Shinab king of *A*,
14: 8 king of Gomorrah, the king of *A*,
Deut 29:23 of Sodom and Gomorrah, *A*,
Hos 11: 8 How can I make you like *A*?

ADMATHA (1/1)
Esth 1:14 him being Carshena, Shethar, *A*,

ADMINISTER (2/2) ADMINISTERED, ADMINISTERS, ADMINISTRATION, ADMINISTRATOR
1 Ki 3:28 wisdom of God was in him to ***a***
Ps 9: 8 And He shall ***a*** judgment for

ADMINISTERED (5/5) ADMINISTER
Deut 33:21 He ***a*** the justice of the LORD,
2 Sam 8:15 and David ***a*** judgment and
1 Chr 18:14 and ***a*** judgment and justice to
2 Cor 8:19 which is ***a*** by us to the glory
8:20 in this lavish gift which is ***a***

ADMINISTERS (1/1) ADMINISTER
Deut 10:18 He ***a*** justice for the fatherless

ADMINISTRATION (1/1) ADMINISTER, ADMINISTRATIONS
2 Cor 9:12 For the ***a*** of this service not

ADMINISTRATIONS (1/1) ADMINISTRATOR
1 Cor 12:28 gifts of healings, helps, ***a***,

ADMINISTRATOR (1/1) ADMINISTER, ADMINISTRATION, ADMINISTRATIONS, ADMINISTRATORS
Dan 2:48 and chief ***a*** over all the wise

ADMINISTRATORS (4/4) ADMINISTRATOR
Dan 3: 2 together the satraps, the ***a***,
3: 3 So the satraps, the ***a***,
3:27 And the satraps, ***a***,
6: 7 the ***a*** and satraps, the

ADMIRED (1/1)
2 Th 1:10 in His saints and to be ***a***

ADMONISH (5/5) ADMONISHED, ADMONISHING, ADMONITION
Ps 81: 8 and I will ***a*** you! O Israel, if
Rom 15:14 able also to ***a*** one another.
1 Th 5:12 are over you in the Lord and ***a***
2 Th 3:15 but ***a*** him as a brother.
Titus 2: 4 that they ***a*** the young women to

ADMONISHED (4/4) ADMONISH
Eccl 4:13 and foolish king who will be ***a***
12:12 be ***a*** by these. Of making many
Jer 42:19 Know certainly that I have ***a***
Zech 3: 6 Then the Angel of the LORD ***a***

ADMONISHING (1/1) ADMONISH
Col 3:16 teaching and ***a*** one another in

ADMONITION (3/3) ADMONISH
1 Cor 10:11 and they were written for our ***a***,
Eph 6: 4 them up in the training and ***a***
Titus 3:10 after the first and second ***a***,

ADNA (2/2) ADNAH
Ezra 10:30 of the sons of Pahath-Moab: *A*,
Neh 12:15 of Harim, *A*; of Meraioth,

ADNAH (2/2) ADNA
1 Chr 12:20 who defected to him were *A*,
2 Chr 17:14 *A* the captain, and with him

ADO (KJV) See COMMOTION

ADONI-BEZEK (3/3) BEZEK
Judg 1: 5 And they found *A* in Bezek, and
1: 6 Then *A* fled, and they pursued
1: 7 And *A* said, "Seventy kings with

ADONI-ZEDEK (2/2)
Josh 10: 1 Now it came to pass when *A* king
10: 3 Therefore *A* king of Jerusalem

ADONIJAH (26/26)
2 Sam 3: 4 *A* the son of Haggith; the
1 Ki 1: 5 Then *A* the son of Haggith
1: 7 and they followed and helped *A*.
1: 8 to David were not with *A*.
1: 9 And *A* sacrificed sheep and oxen
1:11 Have you not heard that *A* the
1:13 Why then has *A* become king?'
1:18 *A* has become king; and
1:24 *A* shall reign after me, and he
1:25 Long live King *A*!'
1:41 Now *A* and all the guests who
1:42 And *A* said to him, "Come in,
1:43 Jonathan answered and said to *A*,
1:49 all the guests who were with *A*
1:50 Now *A* was afraid of Solomon; so
1:51 Indeed *A* is afraid of King
2:13 Now *A* the son of Haggith came
2:19 Solomon, to speak to him for *A*.
2:21 the Shunammite be given to *A*
2:22 Abishag the Shunammite for *A*?
2:23 if *A* has not spoken this word
2:24 *A* shall be put to death
2:28 for Joab had defected to *A*,
1 Chr 3: 2 *A* the son of Haggith;
2 Chr 17: 8 Shemiramoth, Jehonathan, *A*,
Neh 10:16 *A*, Bigvai, Adin,

ADONIKAM (3/3)
Ezra 2:13 the people of *A*,
8:13 of the last sons of *A*,
Neh 7:18 the sons of *A*,

ADONIRAM (2/2) ADORAM
1 Ki 4: 6 and *A* the son of Abda, over the
5:14 *A* was in charge of the labor

ADOPTION (5/5)
Rom 8:15 you received the Spirit of ***a***
8:23 eagerly waiting for the ***a***,
9: 4 to whom pertain the ***a***,
Gal 4: 5 that we might receive the ***a*** as
Eph 1: 5 having predestined us to ***a*** as

ADORAIM (1/1)
2 Chr 11: 9 *A*, Lachish, Azekah,

ADORAM (2/2) ADONIRAM
2 Sam 20:24 *A* was in charge of revenue;
1 Ki 12:18 Then King Rehoboam sent *A*,

ADORN (5/5) ADORNED, ADORNMENT, ADORNS
Job 40:10 Then ***a*** yourself with majesty
Jer 4:30 Though you ***a*** yourself with
Mt 23:29 the tombs of the prophets and ***a***
1 Tim 2: 9 that the women ***a*** themselves in
Titus 2:10 that they may ***a*** the doctrine of

ADORNED (13/13) ADORN
2 Ki 9:30 she put paint on her eyes and ***a***
Job 26:13 By His Spirit He ***a*** the heavens;
Jer 31: 4 You shall again be ***a*** with
Ezek 16:11 I ***a*** you with ornaments, put
16:13 Thus you were ***a*** with gold and
16:16 some of your garments and ***a***
23:40 and ***a*** yourself with ornaments.
Lk 21: 5 how it was ***a*** with beautiful
1 Pe 3: 5 women who trusted in God also ***a***
Rev 17: 4 and ***a*** with gold and precious
18:16 and ***a*** with gold and precious
21: 2 prepared as a bride ***a*** for her
21:19 of the wall of the city were ***a***

ADORNMENT (1/1) ADORN
1 Pe 3: 3 Do not let your ***a*** be merely

ADORNS (2/2) ADORN
Ps 93: 5 Holiness ***a*** Your house, O
Isa 61:10 And as a bride ***a*** herself with

ADRAMMELECH (3/3)
2 Ki 17:31 their children in fire to *A*
19:37 that his sons *A* and Sharezer
Isa 37:38 that his sons *A* and Sharezer

ADRAMYTTIUM (1/1)
Acts 27: 2 So, entering a ship of *A*,

ADRIATIC (1/1)
Acts 27:27 driven up and down in the *A*

ADRIEL (2/2)
1 Sam 18:19 that she was given to *A* the
2 Sam 21: 8 whom she brought up for *A* the

ADRIFT (1/1)
Ps 88: 5 ***A*** among the dead, Like the

ADULLAM (8/8) ADULLAMITE
Josh 12:15 of Libnah, one; the king of *A*,
15:35 Jarmuth, *A*, Socoh,
1 Sam 22: 1 and escaped to the cave of *A*.
2 Sam 23:13 came to David at the cave of *A*.
1 Chr 11:15 to David, into the cave of *A*;
2 Chr 11: 7 Beth Zur, Sochoh, *A*,
Neh 11:30 Zanoah, *A*, and their villages;
Mic 1:15 glory of Israel shall come to *A*.

ADULLAMITE (3/3) ADULLAM
Gen 38: 1 and visited a certain *A* whose
38:12 he and his friend Hirah the *A*.
38:20 by the hand of his friend the *A*,

ADULTERER (3/3) ADULTERERS, ADULTERY
Lev 20:10 the ***a*** and the adulteress, shall
Job 24:15 The eye of the ***a*** waits for the
Isa 57: 3 You offspring of the ***a*** and the

ADULTERERS (9/9) ADULTERER
Ps 50:18 have been a partaker with ***a***.
Jer 9: 2 from them! For they are all ***a***,
23:10 For the land is full of ***a***;
Hos 7: 4 "They are all ***a***.
Mal 3: 5 Against sorcerers, Against ***a***,
Lk 18:11 men—extortioners, unjust, ***a***,
1 Cor 6: 9 nor idolaters, nor ***a***,
Heb 13: 4 but fornicators and ***a*** God will
Jas 4: 4 ***A*** and adulteresses! Do you not

ADULTERESS (4/3) ADULTERESSES, ADULTERY
Lev 20:10 wife, the adulterer and the ***a***,
Prov 6:26 And an ***a*** will prey upon his
Rom 7: 3 man, she will be called an ***a***;
7: 3 that law, so that she is no ***a***,

ADULTERESSES (3/2) ADULTERESS
Ezek 23:45 them after the manner of ***a***,
23:45 shed blood, because they are ***a***,
Jas 4: 4 Adulterers and ***a***! Do you not

ADULTERIES (5/5) ADULTERY
Jer 13:27 I have seen your ***a*** And your
Ezek 23:43 her who had grown old in ***a***,
Hos 2: 2 And her ***a*** from between her
Mt 15:19 evil thoughts, murders, ***a***,
Mk 7:21 men, proceed evil thoughts, ***a***,

ADULTEROUS (6/6) ADULTERY
Prov 30:20 This is the way of an ***a***
Ezek 6: 9 I was crushed by their ***a*** heart
16:32 You are an ***a*** wife, who takes
Mt 12:39 An evil and ***a*** generation seeks
16: 4 A wicked and ***a*** generation seeks
Mk 8:38 of Me and My words in this ***a***

ADULTERY (40/33) ADULTERER, ADULTERERS, ADULTERESS, ADULTERESSES, ADULTERIES, ADULTEROUS
Ex 20:14 "You shall not commit ***a***.
Lev 20:10 The man who commits ***a*** with
20:10 he who commits ***a*** with his
Deut 5:18 'You shall not commit ***a***.
Prov 6:32 Whoever commits ***a*** with a woman
Jer 3: 8 Israel had committed ***a***,
3: 9 the land and committed ***a*** with
5: 7 Then they committed ***a*** And
7: 9 you steal, murder, commit ***a***,
23:14 They commit ***a*** and walk in
29:23 have committed ***a*** with their
Ezek 23:37 "For they have committed ***a***,
23:37 They have committed ***a*** with
Hos 3: 1 by a lover and is committing ***a***,
4: 2 and stealing and committing ***a***,
4:13 And your brides commit ***a***.
4:14 your brides when they commit ***a***;
Mt 5:27 'You shall not commit ***a***.
5:28 for her has already committed ***a***
5:32 causes her to commit ***a***;
5:32 woman who is divorced commits ***a***.
19: 9 and marries another, commits ***a***;
19: 9 her who is divorced commits ***a***.
19:18 'You shall not commit ***a***,
Mk 10:11 and marries another commits ***a***

10:12 marries another, she commits *a*.
10:19 'Do not commit *a*,
Lk 16:18 and marries another commits *a*;
16:18 from her husband commits *a*.
18:20 'Do not commit *a*,
Jn 8: 3 to Him a woman caught in *a*.
8: 4 this woman was caught in *a*,
Rom 2:22 You who say, "Do not commit *a*,
2:22 adultery," do you commit *a*?
13: 9 "You shall not commit *a*,
Gal 5:19 flesh are evident, which are: *a*,
Jas 2:11 who said, "Do not commit *a*,
2:11 Now if you do not commit *a*,
2 Pe 2:14 having eyes full of *a* and that
Rev 2:22 and those who commit *a* with her

ADUMMIM (2/2)

Josh 15: 7 is before the Ascent of *A*,
18:17 which is before the Ascent of *A*,

ADVANCE (7/7) ADVANCED, ADVANTAGE

Num 10: 5 "When you sound the *a*,
10: 6 When you sound the *a* the second
10: 7 shall blow, but not sound the *a*.
Josh 6: 7 and let him who is armed *a*
2 Sam 5:24 then you shall *a* quickly.
Prov 30:27 Yet they all *a* in ranks;
Dan 11:39 and *a* its glory; and he shall

ADVANCED (17/16) ADVANCE

Josh 6: 8 rams' horns before the LORD *a*
13: 1 *a* in years. And the LORD said
13: 1 *a* in years, and there remains
23: 1 Joshua was old, *a* in age.
23: 2 'I am old, *a* in age.
Judg 11:29 and from Mizpah of Gilead he *a*
11:32 So Jephthah *a* toward the people
1 Sam 17:12 *a* in years, in the days of
1 Ki 1: 1 *a* in years; and they put covers
Esth 3: 1 and *a* him and set his seat
5:11 and how he had *a* him above the
10: 2 to which the king *a* him, are
Gal 1:14 And I *a* in Judaism beyond many

ADVANTAGE (11/11)

Job 35: 3 'What *a* will it be to You?
Eccl 3:19 man has no *a* over animals, for
Jn 16: 7 It is to your *a* that I go away;
Rom 3: 1 What *a* then has the Jew, or what
1 Cor 15:32 what *a* is it to me? If the
2 Cor 2:11 lest Satan should take *a* of us;
8:10 It is to your *a* not only to be
12:17 Did I take *a* of you by any of
12:18 Did Titus take *a* of you? Did we
1 Th 4: 6 that no one should take *a* of and
Jude 16 flattering people to gain *a*.

ADVERSARIES (35/35) ADVERSARY

Ex 23:22 and an adversary to your *a*.
Deut 32:27 Lest their *a* should
32:43 And render vengeance to His *a*;
Josh 5:13 "Are You for us or for our *a*?
1 Sam 2:10 The *a* of the LORD shall be
2 Sam 19:22 that you should be *a* to me
Ezra 4: 1 Now when the *a* of Judah and
Neh 4:11 And our *a* said, "They will
Job 22:20 Surely our *a* are cut down, And
Ps 27:12 deliver me to the will of my *a*;
38:20 evil for good, They are my *a*,
69:19 My *a* are all before You.
71:13 and consumed Who are *a* of my
81:14 turn My hand against their *a*.
89:42 exalted the right hand of his *a*;
Isa 1:24 I will rid Myself of My *a*,
9:11 the LORD shall set up The *a*
11:13 And the *a* of Judah shall be
59:18 He will repay, Fury to His *a*,
63:18 Our *a* have trodden down Your
64: 2 make Your name known to Your *a*,
Jer 30:16 be devoured; And all your *a*,
46:10 He may avenge Himself on His *a*.
50: 7 And their *a* said, 'We have not
Lam 1: 5 Her *a* have become the master,
1: 7 The *a* saw her And mocked at
1:17 those around him become his *a*;
2:17 has exalted the horn of your *a*.
Mic 5: 9 shall be lifted against your *a*,
Nah 1: 2 will take vengeance on His *a*,
Lk 13:17 all His *a* were put to shame;
21:15 and wisdom which all your *a*
1 Cor 16: 9 to me, and there are many *a*.
Phil 1:28 in any way terrified by your *a*,
Heb 10:27 which will devour the *a*.

ADVERSARY (21/20) ADVERSARIES

Ex 23:22 enemy to your enemies and an *a*
Num 22:22 His stand in the way as an *a*
1 Sam 29: 4 in the battle he become our *a*.
1 Ki 5: 4 there is neither *a* nor evil
11:14 Now the LORD raised up an *a*
11:23 And God raised up another *a*
11:25 He was an *a* of Israel all the
Esth 7: 6 The *a* and enemy is this wicked
Job 16: 9 My *a* sharpens His gaze on me.
Ps 74:10 how long will the *a* reproach?
Isa 50: 8 stand together. Who is My *a*?

Lam 1:10 The *a* has spread his hand Over
2: 4 With His right hand, like an *a*,
4:12 not have believed That the *a*
Am 3:11 An *a* shall be all around the
Mt 5:25 Agree with your *a* quickly, while
5:25 lest your *a* deliver you to the
Lk 12:58 When you go with your *a* to the
18: 3 'Get justice for me from my *a*.
1 Tim 5:14 give no opportunity to the *a* to
1 Pe 5: 8 because your *a* the devil walks

ADVERSITIES (3/3) ADVERSITY

1 Sam 10:19 saved you from all your *a* and
Ps 31: 7 You have known my soul in *a*,
Jer 36: 3 of Judah will hear all the *a*

ADVERSITY (20/20) ADVERSITIES

Deut 29:21 all the tribes of Israel for *a*,
2 Sam 4: 9 has redeemed my life from all *a*,
12:11 I will raise up *a* against you
2 Chr 15: 6 God troubled them with every *a*.
Job 2:10 God, and shall we not accept *a*?
2:11 friends heard of all this *a*
42:11 and comforted him for all the *a*
Ps 10: 6 moved; I shall never be in *a*.
35:15 But in my *a* they rejoiced And
94:13 him rest from the days of *a*,
Prov 17:17 And a brother is born for *a*.
24:10 If you faint in the day of *a*,
Eccl 7:14 But in the day of *a* consider:
Isa 30:20 Lord gives you The bread of *a*
Jer 15:11 with you In the time of *a* and
21:10 My face against this city for *a*
39:16 My words upon this city for *a*
44:27 I will watch over them for *a*
44:29 surely stand against you for *a*.
45: 5 I will bring *a* on all flesh,"

ADVERTISE (KJV) See ADVISE, INFORM

ADVICE (29/26) ADVISE

Gen 41:37 So the *a* was good in the eyes
Judg 20: 7 give your *a* and counsel here
1 Sam 25:33 And blessed is your *a* and
2 Sam 16:23 Now the *a* of Ahithophel, which
16:23 So was all the *a* of Ahithophel
17: 7 The *a* that Ahithophel has given
17:14 The *a* of Hushai the Archite is
17:14 Archite is better than the *a*
17:14 purposed to defeat the good *a*
17:23 when Ahithophel saw that his *a*
1 Ki 1:12 please, let me now give you *a*,
12: 8 But he rejected the *a* which the
12: 9 What *a* do you give? How should
12:13 and rejected the *a* which the
12:14 to them according to the *a* of
12:28 Therefore the king asked *a*,
2 Chr 10: 8 But he rejected the *a* which the
10: 9 What *a* do you give? How should
10:13 King Rehoboam rejected the *a* of
10:14 to them according to the *a* of
22: 5 He also followed their *a*,
25:16 this and have not heeded my *a*.
25:17 Amaziah king of Judah asked *a*
Ezra 10: 3 according to the *a* of my master
Job 26: 3 how have you declared sound *a*
Isa 30: 2 Egypt, And have not asked My *a*,
Jer 38:15 to death? And if I give you *a*,
Dan 4:27 let my *a* be acceptable to you;
2 Cor 8:10 And in this I give *a*:

ADVISE (5/5) ADVICE, ADVISED, ADVISORS, WELL-ADVISED

Num 24:14 I will *a* you what this people
2 Sam 17:11 Therefore I *a* that all Israel be
19:43 were we not the first to *a*
1 Ki 12: 6 How do you *a* me to answer these
2 Chr 10: 6 How do you *a* me to answer these

ADVISED (9/8) ADVISE

2 Sam 17:15 Thus and so Ahithophel *a* Absalom
17:15 and thus and so I have *a*.
17:21 For thus has Ahithophel *a*
2 Ki 5: 6 of Israel, which said, Now be *a*,
2 Chr 22: 3 for his mother *a* him to do
Esth 2:15 the custodian of the women, *a*.
Jn 18:14 Now it was Caiaphas who *a* the
Acts 27: 9 already over, Paul *a* them,
27:12 the majority *a* to set sail from

ADVISORS (1/1) ADVISE

Dan 6: 7 satraps, the counselors and *a*,

ADVOCATE (1/1)

1 Jn 2: 1 we have an *A* with the Father,

AENEAS (2/2)

Acts 9:33 he found a certain man named *A*,
9:34 And Peter said to him, "*A*,

AENON (1/1)

Jn 3:23 John also was baptizing in *A*

AFAR (54/54)

Gen 22: 4 his eyes and saw the place *a*
37:18 Now when they saw him *a* off,
Ex 2: 4 And his sister stood *a* off, to
20:18 they trembled and stood *a* off.
20:21 So the people stood *a* off, but
24: 1 of Israel, and worship from *a*.
Deut 28:49 a nation against you from *a*,
1 Sam 26:13 stood on the top of a hill *a*
2 Ki 4:25 when the man of God saw her *a*
Ezra 3:13 and the sound was heard *a* off.
Neh 12:43 joy of Jerusalem was heard *a*
Job 2:12 they raised their eyes from *a*,
36: 3 will fetch my knowledge from *a*;
36:25 it; Man looks on it from *a*.
39:25 He smells the battle from *a*,
39:29 prey; Its eyes observe from *a*.
Ps 10: 1 Why do You stand *a* off, O
38:11 And my relatives stand *a* off.
138: 6 But the proud He knows from *a*.
139: 2 You understand my thought *a*
Prov 31:14 She brings her food from *a*.
Isa 5:26 a banner to the nations from *a*,
10: 3 which will come from *a*?
22: 3 They have fled from *a*.
30:27 name of the LORD comes from *a*,
33:13 you who are *a* off, what I
43: 6 Bring My sons from *a*,
49: 1 you peoples from *a*! The LORD
49:12 Surely these shall come from *a*;
59:14 And righteousness stands *a*
60: 4 Your sons shall come from *a*,
60: 9 To bring your sons from *a*,
66:19 to the coastlands *a* off who
Jer 5:15 a nation against you from *a*,
23:23 And not a God *a* off?
30:10 behold, I will save you from *a*,
31:10 declare it in the isles *a* off,
46:27 behold, I will save you from *a*,
51:50 Remember the LORD *a* off,
Ezek 23:40 you sent for men to come from *a*,
Mic 4: 3 And rebuke strong nations *a*
Hab 1: 8 Their cavalry comes from *a*;
Zech 6:15 Even those from *a* shall come and
Mt 27:55 were there looking on from *a*,
Mk 5: 6 When he saw Jesus from *a*,
8: 3 some of them have come from *a*.
11:13 And seeing from *a* a fig tree
15:40 also women looking on from *a*,
Lk 16:23 up his eyes and saw Abraham *a*
17:12 lepers, who stood *a* off.
18:13 standing *a* off, would not so
Acts 2:39 and to all who are *a* off, as
Eph 2:17 peace to you who were *a* off
Heb 11:13 but having seen them *a* off were

AFFAIRS (9/9)

2 Sam 14:20 bring about this change of *a*
1 Chr 26:32 pertaining to God and the *a* of
Ps 112: 5 He will guide his *a* with
Dan 2:49 and Abed-Nego over the *a* of the
3:12 whom you have set over the *a*
Eph 6:21 that you also may know my *a*
6:22 that you may know our *a*,
Phil 1:27 am absent, I may hear of your *a*,
2 Tim 2: 4 entangles himself with the *a*

AFFECTED (1/1) AFFECTS

Dan 3:27 nor were their garments *a*,

AFFECTION (4/4) AFFECTIONATE, AFFECTIONS

1 Chr 29: 3 because I have set my *a* on the
1 Cor 7: 3 render to his wife the *a* due
Phil 1: 8 I long for you all with the *a*
2: 1 if any *a* and mercy,

AFFECTIONATE (1/1) AFFECTION, AFFECTIONATELY

Rom 12:10 Be kindly *a* to one another with

AFFECTIONATELY (1/1) AFFECTIONATE

1 Th 2: 8 *a* longing for you, we were well

AFFECTIONS (2/2) AFFECTION

2 Cor 6:12 are restricted by your own *a*.
7:15 And his *a* are greater for you as

AFFECTS (1/1) AFFECTED, AFFECTIONATELY

Job 35: 8 Your wickedness *a* a man such as

AFFINITY (KJV) See TREATY

AFFIRM (4/4) AFFIRMED

Rom 3: 8 reported and as some *a* that we
1 Cor 15:31 I *a*, by the boasting in you
1 Tim 1: 7 say nor the things which they *a*.
Titus 3: 8 these things I want you to *a*

AFFIRMED (2/2) AFFIRM

Lk 22:59 passed, another confidently *a*,

Acts 25:19 whom Paul **a** to be alive.

AFFLICT (31/30) AFFLICTED, AFFLICTING, AFFLICTION, AFFLICTIONS

Gen 15:13 and they will **a** them four
31:50 If you **a** my daughters, or if you
Ex 1:11 set taskmasters over them to **a**
22:22 You shall not **a** any widow or
22:23 If you **a** them in any way, and
Lev 16:29 you shall **a** your souls, and do
16:31 and you shall **a** your souls.
23:27 you shall **a** your souls, and
23:32 and you shall **a** your souls; on
Num 24:24 And they shall **a** Asshur and
24:24 they shall afflict Asshur and **a**
29: 7 You shall **a** your souls; you
30:13 vow and every binding oath to **a**
Deut 7:15 and will **a** you with none of the
Judg 16: 5 that we may bind him to **a** him;
16: 6 what you may be bound to **a** you.
1 Ki 8:35 from their sin because You **a**
11:39 And I will **a** the descendants of
2 Chr 6:26 from their sin because You **a**
Ps 55:19 and **a** them, Even He who abides
89:22 Nor the son of wickedness **a**
94: 5 And **a** Your heritage.
143:12 And destroy all those who **a** my
Isa 51:23 it into the hand of those who **a**
58: 5 A day for a man to **a** his soul?
64:12 and **a** us very severely?
Jer 31:28 down, to destroy, and to **a**,
Lam 3:33 For He does not **a** willingly,
Am 6:14 And they will **a** you from the
Nah 1:12 I will **a** you no more;
Zeph 3:19 I will deal with all who **a**

AFFLICTED (49/48) AFFLICT

Ex 1:12 But the more they **a** them, the
Lev 23:29 For any person who is not **a** in
Num 11:11 'Why have You **a** Your servant?
20:15 and the Egyptians **a** us and our
Deut 26: 6 **a** us, and laid hard bondage on
Ruth 1:21 and the Almighty has **a** me?"
1 Ki 2:26 and because you were **a** every
2:26 every time my father was **a**.
2 Ki 17:20 **a** them, and delivered them into
Job 6:14 "To him who is **a**,
30:11 has loosed my bowstring and **a**
34:28 For He hears the cry of the **a**.
Ps 22:24 the affliction of the **a**;
25:16 me, For I am desolate and **a**.
44: 2 You **a** the peoples, and cast
82: 3 Do justice to the **a** and needy.
88: 7 And You have **a** me with all
88:15 I have been **a** and ready to
90:15 the days in which You have **a**
102: A Prayer of the **a** when he is
107:17 of their iniquities, were **a**.
116:10 I spoke, "I am greatly **a**.
119:67 Before I was **a** I went astray,
119:71 good for me that I have been **a**,
119:75 in faithfulness You have **a** me.
119:107 I am **a** very much; Revive me, O
129: 1 Many a time they have **a** me from
129: 2 Many a time they have **a** me from
140:12 maintain The cause of the **a**,
Prov 15:15 All the days of the **a** are
22:22 Nor oppress the **a** at the gate;
31: 5 the justice of all the **a**.
Isa 49:13 And will have mercy on His **a**.
51:21 please hear this, you **a**,
53: 4 Smitten by God, and **a**.
53: 7 He was oppressed and He was **a**,
54:11 O you **a** one, Tossed with
58: 3 Why have we **a** our souls, and
58:10 the hungry And satisfy the **a**
60:14 Also the sons of those who **a**
63: 9 all their affliction He was **a**,
Lam 1: 4 sigh, Her virgins are **a**,
1: 5 For the LORD has **a** her
Mic 4: 6 And those whom I have **a**;
Nah 1:12 Though I have **a** you, I will
Mt 4:24 Him all sick people who were **a**
2 Cor 1: 6 if we are **a**, it is for your
1 Tim 5:10 feet, if she has relieved the **a**,
Heb 11:37 goatskins, being destitute, **a**,

AFFLICTING (1/1)

Am 5:12 **A** the just and taking bribes;

AFFLICTION (68/66) AFFLICT, AFFLICTIONS

Gen 16:11 the LORD has heard your **a**.
29:32 LORD has surely looked on my **a**.
31:42 God has seen my **a** and the labor
41:52 be fruitful in the land of my **a**.
Ex 3:17 will bring you up out of the **a**
4:31 that He had looked on their **a**,
Deut 16: 3 the bread of **a** (for you came
26: 7 our voice and looked on our **a**
1 Sam 1:11 You will indeed look on the **a**
2 Sam 16:12 the LORD will look on my **a**,
1 Ki 22:27 and feed him with bread of **a**
22:27 of affliction and water of **a**,
2 Ki 14:26 For the LORD saw that the **a** of
2 Chr 18:26 and feed him with bread of **a**
18:26 of affliction and water of **a**
20: 9 and cry out to You in our **a**,
21:14 your people with a serious **a**—
33:12 Now when he was in **a**,
Neh 9: 9 You saw the **a** of our fathers in
Job 5: 6 For **a** does not come from the
30:16 The days of **a** take hold of me.
30:27 Days of **a** confront me.
36: 8 Held in the cords of **a**,
36:15 delivers the poor in their **a**,
36:21 have chosen this rather than **a**.
Ps 22:24 despised nor abhorred the **a** of
25:18 Look on my **a** and my pain, And
44:24 And forget our **a** and our
66:11 You laid **a** on our backs.
88: 9 eye wastes away because of **a**.
106:44 He regarded their **a**,
107:10 Bound in **a** and irons—
107:39 Through oppression, **a** and
107:41 the poor on high, far from **a**,
119:50 This is my comfort in my **a**,
119:92 then have perished in my **a**.
119:153 Consider my **a** and deliver me,
Eccl 6: 2 vanity, and it is an evil **a**.
Isa 30:20 of adversity and the water of **a**,
48:10 tested you in the furnace of **a**.
63: 9 In all their **a** He was
Jer 4:15 from Dan And proclaims **a** from
15:11 adversity and in the time of **a**.
16:19 My refuge in the day of **a**,
30:12 Your **a** is incurable, Your
30:15 Why do you cry about your **a**?
48:16 And his **a** comes quickly.
Lam 1: 3 Under **a** and hard servitude;
1: 7 In the days of her **a** and
1: 9 "O LORD, behold my **a**,
3: 1 I am the man who has seen **a**
3:19 Remember my **a** and roaming,
Hos 5:15 In their **a** they will earnestly
Am 6: 6 But are not grieved for the **a**
Ob 13 not have gazed on their **a** In
Jon 2: 2 to the LORD because of my **a**,
Nah 1: 9 **A** will not rise up a second
Hab 3: 7 I saw the tents of Cushan in **a**;
Zech 10:11 pass through the sea with **a**,
Mk 5:29 that she was healed of the **a**.
5:34 peace, and be healed of your **a**.
2 Cor 2: 4 For out of much **a** and anguish of
4:17 For our light **a**,
8: 2 that in a great trial of **a** the
Phil 1:16 supposing to add **a** to my
1 Th 1: 6 received the word in much **a**,
3: 7 in all our **a** and distress we
Heb 11:25 choosing rather to suffer **a** with

AFFLICTIONS (8/8) AFFLICT

Ps 34:19 Many are the **a** of the
132: 1 remember David And all his **a**;
Mk 3:10 so that as many as had **a**
Lk 7:21 He cured many of infirmities, **a**,
Col 1:24 flesh what is lacking in the **a**
1 Th 3: 3 one should be shaken by these **a**;
2 Tim 3:11 persecutions, **a**, which happened
4: 5 in all things, endure **a**,

AFFORD (5/5)

Lev 14:21 if he is poor and cannot **a** it,
14:22 such as he is able to **a**:
14:30 young pigeons, such as he can **a**—
14:31 "such as he is able to **a**,
14:32 who cannot **a** the usual

AFFRIGHT (KJV) See FRIGHTEN

AFLAME (1/1)

Prov 29: 8 Scoffers set a city **a**,

AFOREHAND (KJV) See BEFOREHAND

AFRAID (216/212)

Gen 3:10 and I was **a** because I was
15: 1 a vision, saying, "Do not be **a**,
18:15 did not laugh," for she was **a**.
19:30 for he was **a** to dwell in Zoar.
20: 8 and the men were very much **a**.
26: 7 for he was **a** to say, "She is
28:17 And he was **a** and said, "How
31:31 to Laban, "Because I was **a**,
32: 7 So Jacob was greatly **a** and
42:28 failed them and they were **a**,
42:35 bundles of money, they were **a**.
43:18 Now the men were **a** because they
43:23 be with you, do not be **a**.
50:19 said to them, "Do not be **a**,
50:21 "Now therefore, do not be **a**;
Ex 3: 6 for he was **a** to look upon God.
14:10 after them. So they were very **a**,
14:13 to the people, "Do not be **a**.
15:14 people will hear and be **a**;
34:30 and they were **a** to come near
Lev 26: 6 down, and none will make you **a**;
Num 12: 8 Why then were you not **a** To
22: 3 And Moab was exceedingly **a** of
Deut 1:17 you shall not be **a** in any man's
1:29 'Do not be terrified, or **a** of
2: 4 and they will be **a** of you.
5: 5 for you were **a** because of the
7:18 you shall not be **a** of them, but
7:19 the peoples of whom you are **a**.
9:19 For I was **a** of the anger and hot
18:22 you shall not be **a** of him.
20: 1 do not be **a** of them; for the
20: 3 your heart faint, do not be **a**,
28:10 and they shall be **a** of you.
28:60 of Egypt, of which you were **a**,
31: 6 do not fear nor be **a** of them;
Josh 1: 9 of good courage; do not be **a**,
8: 1 said to Joshua: "Do not be **a**,
9:24 therefore we were very much **a**
10:25 said to them, "Do not be **a**,
11: 6 Do not be **a** because of them, for
Judg 7: 3 'Whoever is fearful and **a**,
7:10 But if you are **a** to go down, go
8:20 draw his sword; for he was **a**,
1 Sam 3:15 And Samuel was **a** to tell Eli
4: 7 So the Philistines were **a**,
7: 7 they were **a** of the Philistines.
17:11 were dismayed and greatly **a**.
17:24 from him and were dreadfully **a**.
18:12 Now Saul was **a** of David,
18:15 he was **a** of him.
18:29 and Saul was still more **a** of
21: 1 And Ahimelech was **a** when he met
21:12 and was very much **a** of Achish
23: 3 we are **a** here in Judah.
28: 5 of the Philistines, he was **a**,
28:13 king said to her, "Do not be **a**.
28:20 and was dreadfully **a** because of
31: 4 would not, for he was greatly **a**.
2 Sam 1:14 How was it you were not **a** to put
6: 9 David was **a** of the LORD that
10:19 So the Syrians were **a** to help
12:18 the servants of David were **a**
13:28 then kill him. Do not be **a**.
14:15 the people have made me **a**.
17: 2 weary and weak, and make him **a**.
22: 5 floods of ungodliness made me **a**.
1 Ki 1:49 who were with Adonijah were **a**,
1:50 Now Adonijah was **a** of Solomon;
1:51 Indeed Adonijah is **a** of King
2 Ki 1:15 do not be **a** of him." So he
10: 4 But they were exceedingly **a**,
19: 6 Do not be **a** of the words which
25:24 Do not be **a** of the servants of
25:26 for they were **a** of the
1 Chr 10: 4 would not, for he was greatly **a**.
13:12 David was **a** of God that day,
21:30 for he was **a** of the sword of
2 Chr 20:15 Do not be **a** nor dismayed because
32: 7 do not be **a** nor dismayed before
Neh 2: 2 So I became dreadfully **a**,
4:14 'Do not be **a** of them.
6: 9 all were trying to make us **a**,
6:13 that I should be **a** and act that
6:14 who would have made me **a**.
Job 5:21 And you shall not be **a** of
5:22 And you shall not be **a** of the
6:21 You see terror and are **a**.
9:28 I am **a** of all my sufferings; I
11:19 and no one would make you **a**;
13:11 not His excellence make you **a**,
13:21 not the dread of You make me **a**.
15:24 Trouble and anguish make him **a**;
19:29 Be **a** of the sword for
23:15 I am **a** of Him.
32: 6 very old; Therefore I was **a**,
41:25 himself up, the mighty are **a**;
Ps 3: 6 I will not be **a** of ten
18: 4 floods of ungodliness made me **a**.
27: 1 my life; Of whom shall I be **a**?
49:16 Do not be **a** when one becomes
56: 3 Whenever I am **a**,
56:11 put my trust; I will not be **a**.
65: 8 in the farthest parts are **a** of
77:16 waters saw You, they were **a**;
91: 5 You shall not be **a** of the
112: 7 He will not be **a** of evil
112: 8 established; He will not be **a**,
119:120 And I am **a** of Your judgments.
Prov 3:24 you lie down, you will not be **a**;
3:25 Do not be **a** of sudden terror,
31:21 She is not **a** of snow for her
Eccl 12: 5 Also they are **a** of height, And
Isa 8:12 Nor be **a** of their threats, nor
10:24 do not be **a** of the Assyrian.
10:29 up lodging at Geba. Ramah is **a**,
12: 2 I will trust and not be **a**;
13: 8 And they will be **a**.
17: 2 and no one will make them **a**.
19:16 and will be **a** and fear because
19:17 makes mention of it will be **a**
20: 5 Then they shall be **a** and ashamed
31: 4 He will not be **a** of their
31: 9 And his princes shall be **a** of
33:14 The sinners in Zion are **a**;
37: 6 Do not be **a** of the words which
40: 9 Lift it up, be not **a**;
41: 5 The ends of the earth were **a**;
44: 8 Do not fear, nor be **a**;
51: 7 Nor be **a** of their insults.
51:12 are you that you should be **a**
57:11 "And of whom have you been **a**,
Jer 1: 8 Do not be **a** of their faces,
2:12 at this, And be horribly **a**;
10: 5 Do not be **a** of them, For they
26:21 he was **a** and fled, and went to
30:10 And no one shall make him **a**.
36:24 Yet they were not **a**,
38:19 I am **a** of the Jews who have
39:17 of the men of whom you are **a**.

40: 9 Do not be ***a*** to serve the
41:18 for they were ***a*** of them,
42:11 Do not be ***a*** of the king of
42:11 of Babylon, of whom you are ***a***;
42:11 do not be ***a*** of him,' says the
42:16 the famine of which you were ***a***
46:27 ease; No one shall make him ***a***.
Ezek 2: 6 do not be ***a*** of them nor be
2: 6 not be afraid of them nor be ***a***
2: 6 do not be ***a*** of their words or
3: 9 do not be ***a*** of them, nor be
27:35 Their kings will be greatly ***a***,
30: 9 make the careless Ethiopians ***a***,
32:10 kings shall be horribly ***a*** of
34:28 and no one shall make them ***a***.
39:26 land and no one made them ***a***.
Dan 4: 5 I saw a dream which made me ***a***,
8:17 and when he came I was ***a*** and
Joel 2:22 Do not be ***a***, you beasts of
Am 3: 6 city, will not the people be ***a***?
Jon 1: 5 Then the mariners were ***a***;
1:10 the men were exceedingly ***a***,
Mic 4: 4 And no one shall make them ***a***;
7:17 They shall be ***a*** of the LORD
Nah 2:11 cub, And no one made them ***a***?
Hab 2:17 of beasts which made them ***a***,
3: 2 heard your speech and was ***a***;
Zeph 3:13 And no one shall make them ***a***.
Mt 1:20 do not be ***a*** to take to you Mary
2:22 he was ***a*** to go there. And being
14:27 cheer! It is I; do not be ***a***.
14:30 wind was boisterous, he was ***a***;
17: 6 their faces and were greatly ***a***.
17: 7 said, "Arise, and do not be ***a***.
25:25 'And I was ***a***, and went and hid
28: 5 to the women, "Do not be ***a***,
28:10 said to them, "Do not be ***a***.
Mk 5:15 his right mind. And they were ***a***.
5:36 of the synagogue, "Do not be ***a***;
6:50 It is I; do not be ***a***."
9: 6 to say, for they were greatly ***a***.
9:32 and were ***a*** to ask Him.
10:32 as they followed they were ***a***.
16: 8 to anyone, for they were ***a***.
Lk 1:13 said to him, "Do not be ***a***,
1:30 said to her, "Do not be ***a***,
2: 9 them, and they were greatly ***a***.
2:10 said to them, "Do not be ***a***,
5:10 said to Simon, "Do not be ***a***.
8:25 your faith?" And they were ***a***,
8:35 his right mind. And they were ***a***.
8:50 him, saying, "Do not be ***a***;
9:45 and they were ***a*** to ask Him
12: 4 do not be ***a*** of those who kill
24: 5 as they were ***a*** and bowed their
Jn 6:19 near the boat; and they were ***a***.
6:20 to them, "It is I; do not be ***a***.
14:27 troubled, neither let it be ***a***.
19: 8 that saying, he was the more ***a***,
Acts 9:26 but they were all ***a*** of him, and
10: 4 when he observed him, he was ***a***,
16:38 and they were ***a*** when they heard
18: 9 by a vision, "Do not be ***a***,
22: 9 indeed saw the light and were ***a***,
22:29 and the commander was also ***a***
24:25 Felix was ***a*** and answered, "Go
27:24 "saying, 'Do not be ***a***,
Rom 13: 4 But if you do evil, be ***a***;
Gal 4:11 I am ***a*** for you, lest I have
Heb 11:23 and they were not ***a*** of the
12:21 I am exceedingly ***a*** and
1 Pe 3: 6 if you do good and are not ***a***
3:14 And do not be ***a*** of their
2 Pe 2:10 They are not ***a*** to speak evil of
Rev 1:17 me, saying to me, "Do not be ***a***;
11:13 and the rest were ***a*** and gave

AFRESH (1/1)

Job 7: 5 is cracked and breaks out ***a***.

AFTER (688/664) AFTERNOON, AFTERWARD, AFTERWARDS

Gen 4:17 called the name of the city ***a***
5: 3 ***a*** his image, and named him
5: 4 ***A*** he begot Seth, the days of
5: 7 ***A*** he begot Enosh, Seth lived
5:10 ***A*** he begot Cainan, Enosh lived
5:13 ***A*** he begot Mahalalel, Cainan
5:16 ***A*** he begot Jared, Mahalalel
5:19 ***A*** he begot Enoch, Jared lived
5:22 ***A*** he begot Methuselah, Enoch
5:26 ***A*** he begot Lamech, Methuselah
5:30 ***A*** he begot Noah, Lamech lived
6:20 Of the birds ***a*** their kind, of
6:20 of animals ***a*** their kind, and of
6:20 creeping thing of the earth ***a***
7: 4 For ***a*** seven more days I will
7:10 And it came to pass ***a*** seven days
7:14 they and every beast ***a*** its kind,
7:14 all cattle ***a*** their kind, every
7:14 that creeps on the earth ***a*** its
7:14 and every bird ***a*** its kind,
9: 9 you and with your descendants ***a***
9:28 And Noah lived ***a*** the flood
10: 1 And sons were born to them ***a***
10:32 were divided on the earth ***a***
11:10 and begot Arphaxad two years ***a***
11:11 ***A*** he begot Arphaxad, Shem lived
11:13 ***A*** he begot Salah, Arphaxad lived
11:15 ***A*** he begot Eber, Salah lived
11:17 ***A*** he begot Peleg, Eber lived
11:19 ***A*** he begot Reu, Peleg lived two
11:21 ***A*** he begot Serug, Reu lived two
11:23 ***A*** he begot Nahor, Serug lived
11:25 ***A*** he begot Terah, Nahor lived
13:14 ***a*** Lot had separated from him:
14:17 ***a*** his return from the defeat of
15: 1 ***A*** these things the word of the
16: 3 ***a*** Abram had dwelt ten years in
17: 7 and you and your descendants ***a***
17: 7 to you and your descendants ***a***
17: 8 to you and your descendants ***a***
17: 9 you and your descendants ***a*** you
17:10 and you and your descendants ***a***
17:19 and with his descendants ***a***
18: 5 ***A*** that you may pass by,
18:12 ***A*** I have grown old, shall I have
18:19 children and his household ***a***
22: 1 Now it came to pass ***a*** these
22:20 Now it came to pass ***a*** these
23:19 And ***a*** this, Abraham buried Sarah
24:55 ***a*** that she may go."
24:67 So Isaac was comforted ***a*** his
25:11 ***a*** the death of Abraham, that
26:18 had stopped them up ***a*** the
35:12 and to your descendants ***a*** you I
37:17 So Joseph went ***a*** his
38:24 to pass, about three months ***a***,
39: 7 And it came to pass ***a*** these
39:19 Your servant did to me ***a*** this
40: 1 It came to pass ***a*** these things
41: 3 seven other cows came up ***a*** them
41: 6 sprang up ***a*** them.
41:19 seven other cows came up ***a***
41:23 sprang up ***a*** them.
41:27 and ugly cows which came up ***a***
41:30 but ***a*** them seven years of famine
45:15 and ***a*** that his brothers talked
48: 1 Now it came to pass ***a*** these
48: 4 land to your descendants ***a*** you
48: 6 offspring whom you beget ***a***
50:14 And ***a*** he had buried his father,
Ex 3:20 and ***a*** that he will let you go.
5:19 that they were in trouble ***a***
7:25 And seven days passed ***a*** the
10:14 nor shall there be such ***a*** them.
11: 8 the people who follow you!' ***A***
14:10 the Egyptians marched ***a*** them.
14:23 Egyptians pursued and went ***a***
14:28 that came into the sea ***a*** them.
15:20 and all the women went out ***a***
16: 1 day of the second month ***a*** they
18: 2 ***a*** he had sent her back,
19: 1 In the third month ***a*** the
23: 2 a dispute so as to turn aside ***a***
28:43 to him and his descendants ***a***
29:29 of Aaron shall be his sons' ***a***
Lev 11:14 and the falcon ***a*** its kind;
11:15 every raven ***a*** its kind,
11:16 and the hawk ***a*** its kind;
11:19 the heron ***a*** its kind, the
11:22 the locust ***a*** its kind, the
11:22 the destroying locust ***a*** its
11:22 the cricket ***a*** its kind, and the
11:22 and the grasshopper ***a*** its kind.
11:29 and the large lizard ***a*** its
13: 7 ***a*** he has been seen by the
13:35 at all spread over the skin ***a***
13:55 shall examine the plague ***a*** it
13:56 indeed the plague has faded ***a***
14: 8 ***A*** that he shall come into the
14:43 ***a*** he has taken away the stones,
14:43 ***a*** he has scraped the house, and
14:43 and ***a*** it is plastered,
14:48 has not spread in the house ***a***
15:28 and ***a*** that she shall be clean.
16: 1 Now the LORD spoke to Moses ***a***
17: 7 ***a*** whom they have played the
19:31 do not seek ***a*** them, to be
23:11 on the day ***a*** the Sabbath the
23:15 for yourselves from the day ***a***
23:16 Count fifty days to the day ***a***
25:15 to the number of years ***a*** the
25:29 it within a whole year ***a*** it is
25:46 for your children ***a*** you,
25:48 ***a*** he is sold he may be redeemed
26:18 And ***a*** all this, if you do not
26:27 And ***a*** all this, if you do not
26:33 nations and draw out a sword ***a***
27:18 if he dedicates his field ***a***
Num 1: 1 in the second year ***a*** they had
6:19 the hands of the Nazirite ***a*** he
6:20 ***A*** that the Nazirite may drink
7:88 offering for the altar ***a*** it
8:15 ***A*** that the Levites shall go in
8:22 ***A*** that the Levites went in to do
9: 1 month of the second year ***a***
9:17 ***a*** that the children of Israel
13:25 from spying out the land ***a***
25: 8 and he went ***a*** the man of Israel
25:13 be to him and his descendants ***a***
26: 1 ***a*** the plague, that the LORD
30:15 if he does make them void ***a*** he
32:42 called it Nobah, ***a*** his own
33: 3 on the day ***a*** the Passover the
33:38 there in the fortieth year ***a***
35:28 But ***a*** the death of the high
Deut 1: 4 ***a*** he had killed Sihon king of
1: 8 to them and their descendants ***a***
3:14 and called Bashan ***a*** his own
4:37 He chose their descendants ***a***
4:40 you and with your children ***a***
4:45 to the children of Israel ***a***
4:46 children of Israel defeated ***a***
6:14 You shall not go ***a*** other gods,
9: 4 ***a*** the LORD your God has cast
10:15 He chose their descendants ***a***
11:28 to go ***a*** other gods which you
12:25 with you and your children ***a***
12:28 with you and your children ***a***
12:30 ***a*** they are destroyed from
12:30 and that you do not inquire ***a***
13: 2 Let us go ***a*** other gods'—which
13: 4 You shall walk ***a*** the LORD your
14:13 and the kite ***a*** their kinds;
14:14 every raven ***a*** its kind;
14:15 and the hawk ***a*** their kinds;
14:18 the heron ***a*** its kind, and the
21:13 ***a*** that you may go in to her and
24: 4 take her back to be his wife ***a***
28:14 to go ***a*** other gods to serve
29:22 of your children who rise up ***a***
31:27 then how much more ***a*** my death?
31:29 For I know that ***a*** my death you
Josh 1: 1 ***A*** the death of Moses the
3: 2 ***a*** three days, that the officers
3: 3 out from your place and go ***a***
5: 4 ***a*** they had come out of Egypt.
5:11 of the land on the day ***a*** the
5:12 the manna ceased on the day ***a***
6: 9 and the rear guard came ***a*** the
6:13 But the rear guard came ***a*** the
7:25 they burned them with fire ***a***
8: 6 For they will come out ***a*** us till
8:17 or Bethel who did not go out ***a***
9:16 ***a*** they had made a covenant with
10:14 before it or ***a*** it, that the
19:47 ***a*** the name of Dan their father.
22:27 and us and our generations ***a***
23: 1 a long time ***a*** the LORD had
24:20 ***a*** He has done you good."
24:29 Now it came to pass ***a*** these
Judg 1: 1 Now ***a*** the death of Joshua it
2:10 another generation arose ***a*** them
3:22 Even the hilt went in ***a*** the
3:28 So they went down ***a*** him,
3:31 ***A*** him was Shamgar the son of
5:14 ***A*** you, Benjamin, with your
9:22 ***A*** Abimelech had reigned over
10: 1 ***A*** Abimelech there arose to save
10: 3 ***A*** him arose Jair, a Gileadite
11: 4 It came to pass ***a*** a time that
12: 8 ***A*** him, Ibzan of Bethlehem
12:11 ***A*** him, Elon the Zebulunite
12:13 ***A*** him, Abdon the son of Hillel
14: 8 ***A*** some time, when he returned to
15: 1 ***A*** a while, in the time of wheat
15: 7 and ***a*** that I will cease."
16:22 his head began to grow again ***a***
18:29 ***a*** the name of Dan their father,
19: 3 her husband arose and went ***a***
Ruth 1:15 return ***a*** your sister-in-law."
1:16 to turn back from following ***a***
2: 2 and glean heads of grain ***a*** him
2: 3 and gleaned in the field ***a*** the
2: 7 let me glean and gather ***a*** the
2: 9 and go ***a*** them. Have I not
2:18 to her what she had kept back ***a***
3: 7 And ***a*** Boaz had eaten and drunk,
3:10 in that you did not go ***a*** young
4: 4 and I am next ***a*** you.'
1 Sam 1: 9 So Hannah arose ***a*** they had
5: 9 ***a*** they had carried it away,
6:12 of the Philistines went ***a*** them
7: 2 the house of Israel lamented ***a***
8: 3 they turned aside ***a*** dishonest
10: 5 ***A*** that you shall come to the
12:21 for then you would go ***a***
13:14 has sought for Himself a man ***a***
14:12 Come up ***a*** me, for the LORD has
14:13 knees with his armorbearer ***a***
14:13 And as he came ***a*** him, his
14:22 they also followed hard ***a*** them
14:36 Let us go down ***a*** the Philistines
14:37 Shall I go down ***a*** the
15:31 So Samuel turned back ***a*** Saul,
17:35 I went out ***a*** it and struck it,
20:37 Jonathan cried out ***a*** the lad
20:38 And Jonathan cried out ***a*** the
22:20 escaped and fled ***a*** David.
24:14 ***A*** whom has the king of Israel
24:21 not cut off my descendants ***a***
25:19 I am coming ***a*** you." But she
25:38 ***a*** about ten days, that the
26: 3 and he saw that Saul came ***a*** him
31: 2 the Philistines followed hard ***a***
2 Sam 1: 1 Now it came to pass ***a*** the death
1: 6 and horsemen followed hard ***a***
1:10 sure that he could not live ***a***
2: 1 It happened ***a*** this that David
3:26 he sent messengers ***a*** Abner, who
5:13 ***a*** he had come from Hebron. Also
7:12 I will set up your seed ***a*** you,
8: 1 ***A*** this it came to pass that
10: 1 It happened ***a*** this that the king
12:28 the city and it be called ***a*** my
13: 1 ***A*** this Absalom the son of David
13: 4 becoming thinner day ***a*** day?
13:23 ***a*** two full years, that Absalom
15: 1 ***A*** this it happened that Absalom
15: 7 Now it came to pass ***a*** forty
15:16 out with all his household ***a***
15:17 went out with all the people ***a***
17:21 ***a*** they had departed, that they

18:18 He called the pillar ***a*** his
18:22 please let me also run ***a*** the
20: 7 went out ***a*** him. And they went
20:13 all the people went on ***a*** Joab
20:14 together and also went ***a***
21: 1 year ***a*** year; and David inquired
21:12 ***a*** the Philistines had struck
21:14 And ***a*** that God heeded the
23: 4 By clear shining ***a*** rain.'
23: 9 And ***a*** him was Eleazar the son
23:10 and the people returned ***a*** him
23:11 And ***a*** him was Shammah the son
24:10 David's heart condemned him ***a***
1 Ki 1: 6 His mother had borne him ***a***
1:13 your son Solomon shall reign ***a***
1:14 I also will come in ***a*** you and
1:17 Solomon your son shall reign ***a***
1:20 throne of my lord the king ***a***
1:24 Adonijah shall reign ***a*** me, and
1:27 throne of my lord the king ***a***
1:30 your son shall be king ***a*** me,
1:35 Then you shall come up ***a*** him,
1:40 And all the people went up ***a***
3:12 nor shall any like you arise ***a***
3:18 the third day ***a*** I had given
6: 1 hundred and eightieth year ***a***
9:21 who were left in the land ***a***
11: 2 will turn away your hearts ***a***
11: 4 his wives turned his heart ***a***
11: 5 For Solomon went ***a*** Ashtoreth the
11: 5 and ***a*** Milcom the abomination of
11:10 that he should not go ***a*** other
11:15 ***a*** he had killed every male in
13:14 and went ***a*** the man of God, and
13:23 ***a*** he had eaten bread and after
13:23 after he had eaten bread and ***a***
13:31 ***a*** he had buried him, that he
13:33 ***A*** this event Jeroboam did not
15: 4 by setting up his son ***a*** him and
16:24 ***a*** the name of Shemer, owner of
17: 7 And it happened ***a*** a while that
17:17 Now it happened ***a*** these things
18: 1 And it came to pass ***a*** many days
19:11 and ***a*** the wind an earthquake,
19:12 and ***a*** the earthquake a fire,
19:12 and ***a*** the fire a still small
19:20 And he left the oxen and ran ***a***
20:15 and ***a*** them he mustered all the
21: 1 And it came to pass ***a*** these
2 Ki 1: 1 rebelled against Israel ***a*** the
5:20 I will run ***a*** him and take
5:21 When Naaman saw him running ***a***
6:23 and ***a*** they ate and drank, he
6:24 And it happened ***a*** this that
7:15 And they went ***a*** them to the
14:17 lived fifteen years ***a*** the death
14:19 but they sent ***a*** him to Lachish
14:22 ***a*** the king rested with his
17:15 and went ***a*** the nations who
18: 5 so that ***a*** him was none like him
23:25 nor ***a*** him did any arise like
1 Chr 2:24 ***A*** Hezron died in Caleb
5:25 and played the harlot ***a*** the
6:31 ***a*** the ark came to rest.
8: 8 ***a*** he had sent away Hushim and
10: 2 the Philistines followed hard ***a***
11:12 ***A*** him was Eleazar the son of
14:14 You shall not go up ***a*** them;
17:11 that I will set up your seed ***a***
18: 1 ***A*** this it came to pass that
19: 1 It happened ***a*** this that Nahash
23: 4 thousand were to look ***a*** the
27: 7 and Zebadiah his son ***a*** him; in
27:34 ***A*** Ahithophel was Jehoiada the
28: 8 for your children ***a*** you
2 Chr 1:12 nor shall any ***a*** you have the
2:17 ***a*** the census in which David his
8: 8 who were left in the land ***a***
10: 5 Come back to me ***a*** three days."
11:16 And ***a*** the Levites left, those
11:20 ***A*** her he took Maacah the
18: 2 ***A*** some years he went down to
20: 1 It happened ***a*** this that the
20:35 ***A*** this Jehoshaphat king of
21:18 ***A*** all this the LORD struck him
21:19 ***a*** the end of two years, that
22: 4 for they were his counselors ***a***
24: 4 Now it happened ***a*** this that
24:17 Now ***a*** the death of Jehoiada the
25:14 ***a*** Amaziah came from the
25:25 lived fifteen years ***a*** the death
25:27 ***A*** the time that Amaziah turned
25:27 but they sent ***a*** him to Lachish
26: 2 ***a*** the king rested with his
26:17 So Azariah the priest went in ***a***
32: 1 ***A*** these deeds of faithfulness,
32: 9 ***A*** this Sennacherib king of
33:14 ***A*** this he built a wall outside
35:20 ***A*** all this, when Josiah had
Ezra 7: 1 Now ***a*** these things, in the reign
9:10 what shall we say ***a*** this?
9:13 And ***a*** all that has come upon us
Neh 3:16 ***A*** him Nehemiah the son of Azbuk,
3:17 ***A*** him the Levites, under Rehum
3:18 ***A*** him their brethren, under
3:20 ***A*** him Baruch the son of Zabbai
3:21 ***A*** him Meremoth the son of
3:22 And ***a*** him the priests, the men
3:23 ***A*** him Benjamin and Hasshub made
3:23 ***A*** them Azariah the son of
3:24 ***A*** him Binnui the son of Henadad
3:25 ***A*** him Pedaiah the son of Parosh
3:27 ***A*** them the Tekoites repaired
3:29 ***A*** them Zadok the son of Immer
3:29 ***A*** him Shemaiah the son of
3:30 ***A*** him Hananiah the son of
3:30 ***A*** him Meshullam the son of
3:31 ***A*** him Malchijah, one of the
5: 7 ***A*** serious thought, I rebuked the
9:28 But ***a*** they had rest, They again
11: 8 and ***a*** him Gabbai and Sallai,
12:32 ***A*** them went Hoshaiah and half of
13: 6 Then ***a*** certain days I obtained
13:19 they must not be opened till ***a***
Esth 2: 1 ***A*** these things, when the wrath
2:12 to go in to King Ahasuerus ***a***
3: 1 ***A*** these things King Ahasuerus
9:26 ***a*** the name Pur. Therefore,
Job 3: 1 ***A*** this Job opened his mouth and
19:26 And ***a*** my skin is destroyed,
21: 3 And ***a*** I have spoken, keep
21:21 he care about his household ***a***
29:22 ***A*** my words they did not speak
31: 7 Or my heart walked ***a*** my eyes,
37: 4 ***A*** it a voice roars
39: 8 And he searches ***a*** every green
42: 7 ***a*** the LORD had spoken these
42:16 ***A*** this Job lived one hundred and
Ps 16: 4 be multiplied who hasten ***a***
35: 4 to dishonor Who seek ***a*** my
49:11 They call their lands ***a*** their
49:17 His glory shall not descend ***a***
51: ***a*** he had gone in to Bathsheba.
54: 3 And oppressors have sought ***a***
68:25 on instruments followed ***a***;
104:21 The young lions roar ***a*** their
119:150 They draw near who follow ***a***
Prov 6:25 Do not lust ***a*** her beauty in
7:22 Immediately he went ***a*** her, as
20: 7 His children are blessed ***a***
28:22 man with an evil eye hastens ***a***
Eccl 1:11 come By those who will come ***a***.
2:18 it to the man who will come ***a***
3:22 him to see what will happen ***a***
6:12 tell a man what will happen ***a***
7:14 out nothing that will come ***a***
9: 3 and ***a*** that they go to the
10:14 can tell him what will be ***a***
11: 1 For you will find it ***a*** many
12: 2 the clouds do not return ***a*** the
Song 1: 4 OF JERUSALEM We will run ***a***
Isa 1:23 And follows ***a*** rewards.
24:22 ***A*** many days they will be
43:10 Nor shall there be ***a*** Me.
48: 2 For they call themselves ***a*** the
49:20 ***A*** you have lost the others,
51: 1 you who follow ***a*** righteousness,
66:17 To go to the gardens ***A*** an
Jer 2: 2 When you went ***a*** Me in the
2: 8 And walked ***a*** things that do
2:23 I have not gone ***a*** the Baals'?
2:25 and ***a*** them I will go.'
3: 7 ***a*** she had done all these
5: 8 Every one neighed ***a*** his
7: 6 or walk ***a*** other gods to your
7: 9 and walk ***a*** other gods whom you
8: 2 which they have served and ***a***
9:14 of their own hearts and ***a*** the
9:16 And I will send a sword ***a*** them
9:22 Like cuttings ***a*** the harvester,
11:10 and they have gone ***a*** other gods
12: 6 they have called a multitude ***a***
12:15 ***a*** I have plucked them out, that
13: 6 Now it came to pass ***a*** many days
13:10 and walk ***a*** other gods to serve
16:11 they have walked ***a*** other gods
24: 1 ***a*** Nebuchadnezzar king of
25: 6 Do not go ***a*** other gods to serve
25:26 king of Sheshach shall drink ***a***
28:12 ***a*** Hananiah the prophet had
29: 2 (This happened ***a*** Jeconiah the
29:10 ***A*** seventy years are completed
31:19 ***a*** my turning, I repented; And
31:19 And ***a*** I was instructed, I
31:26 ***A*** this I awoke and looked
31:33 make with the house of Israel ***a***
32:18 the bosom of their children ***a***
32:39 of them and their children ***a***
34: 8 ***a*** King Zedekiah had made a
35:15 and do not go ***a*** other gods to
36:27 Now ***a*** the king had burned the
39:12 Take him and look ***a*** him, and do
40: 1 to Jeremiah from the LORD ***a***
40: 4 and I will look ***a*** you. But if
41: 4 on the second day ***a*** he had
41:16 Ishmael the son of Nethaniah ***a***
42: 7 And it happened ***a*** ten days that
42:16 afraid shall follow close ***a***
49:37 And I will send the sword ***a*** them
51:46 And ***a*** that, in another year
Ezek 5: 2 I will draw out a sword ***a*** them.
5:12 and I will draw out a sword ***a***
6: 9 eyes which play the harlot ***a***
9: 5 Go ***a*** him through the city and
12:14 and I will draw out the sword ***a***
16:23 ***a*** all your wickedness—'Woe, woe
20:16 for their heart went ***a*** their
23:30 you have gone as a harlot ***a***
23:39 For ***a*** they had slain their
23:45 men will judge them ***a*** the
23:45 and ***a*** the manner of women who
38: 8 ***A*** many days you will be visited.
39:26 ***a*** they have borne their shame,
40: 1 in the fourteenth year ***a*** the
40:24 ***A*** that he brought me toward the
44:10 who strayed away from Me ***a***
44:26 ***A*** he is cleansed, they shall
46:12 and ***a*** he goes out the gate
46:17 ***a*** which it shall return to the
48:31 of the city shall be named ***a***
Dan 2:29 what would come to pass ***a*** this;
2:39 But ***a*** you shall arise another
2:45 king what will come to pass ***a***
4:26 ***a*** you come to know that Heaven
7: 6 ***A*** this I looked, and there was
7: 7 ***A*** this I saw in the night
7:24 And another shall rise ***a*** them;
8: 1 ***a*** the one that appeared to me
9:26 And ***a*** the sixty-two weeks
11:18 ***A*** this he shall turn his face to
11:23 And ***a*** the league is made with
Hos 2: 5 I will go ***a*** my lovers, Who give
2:13 And went ***a*** her lovers; But Me
6: 2 ***A*** two days He will revive us
7: 4 ceases stirring the fire ***a***
11:10 'They shall walk ***a*** the LORD.
Joel 2: 2 will there ever be any such ***a***
Am 2: 7 They pant ***a*** the dust of the
4:10 I sent among you a plague ***a*** the
7: 1 it was the late crop ***a*** the
Ob 6 treasures shall be sought ***a***!
Zech 2: 8 He sent Me ***a*** glory, to the
6: 6 the white are going ***a*** them, and
7:14 Thus the land became desolate ***a***
Mt 1:12 And ***a*** they were brought to
1:18 ***A*** His mother Mary was betrothed
2: 1 Now ***a*** Jesus was born in
3:11 but He who is coming ***a*** me is
6:32 For ***a*** all these things the
10:38 take his cross and follow ***a*** Me
12:39 adulterous generation seeks ***a***
15:23 for she cries out ***a*** us."
16: 4 adulterous generation seeks ***a***
16:24 If anyone desires to come ***a*** Me,
17: 1 Now ***a*** six days Jesus took Peter,
18:32 ***a*** he had called him, said to
22:25 The first died ***a*** he had
24:29 Immediately ***a*** the tribulation
25:19 ***A*** a long time the lord of those
26: 2 You know that ***a*** two days is the
26:32 But ***a*** I have been raised, I will
27:53 and coming out of the graves ***a***
27:63 ***A*** three days I will rise.'
28: 1 Now ***a*** the Sabbath, as the first
Mk 1: 7 There comes One ***a*** me who is
1:14 Now ***a*** John was put in prison,
1:20 and went ***a*** Him.
2: 1 again He entered Capernaum ***a***
4:28 ***a*** that the full grain in the
8:31 and ***a*** three days rise again.
8:34 Whoever desires to come ***a*** Me,
9: 2 Now ***a*** six days Jesus took
9:31 And ***a*** He is killed, He will
12:34 But ***a*** that no one dared
13:24 ***a*** that tribulation, the sun
14: 1 ***A*** two days it was the Passover
14:28 But ***a*** I have been raised, I will
15:15 ***a*** he had scourged Him, to be
16:12 ***A*** that, He appeared in another
16:14 those who had seen Him ***a*** He
16:19 ***a*** the Lord had spoken to them,
Lk 1:24 Now ***a*** those days his wife
2:46 Now so it was that ***a*** three days
5:27 ***A*** these things He went out and
6: 1 on the second Sabbath ***a*** the
7:11 Now it happened, the day ***a***,
9:23 If anyone desires to come ***a*** Me,
9:28 about eight days ***a*** these
10: 1 ***A*** these things the Lord
12: 4 and ***a*** that have no more that
12: 5 ***a*** He has killed, has power to
12:30 the nations of the world seek ***a***,
13: 9 ***a*** that you can cut it down.'"
14:27 not bear his cross and come ***a***
14:29 ***a*** he has laid the foundation,
15: 4 and go ***a*** the one which is lost
15:13 "And not many days ***a***,
17:23 Look there!' Do not go ***a*** them
19:14 and sent a delegation ***a*** him,
20:40 But ***a*** that they dared not
21: 8 Therefore do not go ***a*** them.
22:20 He also took the cup ***a*** supper,
22:58 And ***a*** a little while another saw
22:59 Then ***a*** about an hour had passed,
23:26 cross that he might bear it ***a***
23:55 Him from Galilee followed ***a***,
Jn 1:15 He who comes ***a*** me is preferred
1:27 coming ***a*** me, is preferred
1:30 ***A*** me comes a Man who is
2:12 ***A*** this He went down to
3:22 ***A*** these things Jesus and His
4:43 Now ***a*** the two days He departed
5: 1 ***A*** this there was a feast of the
5: 4 ***a*** the stirring of the water,
6: 1 ***A*** these things Jesus went over
6:23 place where they ate bread ***a***
7: 1 ***A*** these things Jesus walked in
11: 7 Then ***a*** this He said to the
11:11 and ***a*** that He said to them,
12:19 the world has gone ***a*** Him!"
13: 5 ***A*** that, He poured water into a
13: 7 but you will know ***a*** this."
13:27 Now ***a*** the piece of bread, Satan
19:28 ***A*** this, Jesus, knowing that all
19:38 ***A*** this, Joseph of Arimathea,
20:26 And ***a*** eight days His disciples

21: 1 ***A*** these things Jesus showed
21:14 Himself to His disciples ***a*** He
Acts 1: 2 ***a*** He through the Holy Spirit
1: 3 also presented Himself alive ***a***
5: 4 And ***a*** it was sold, was it not
5:37 ***A*** this man, Judas of Galilee
5:37 and drew away many people ***a***
7: 5 and to his descendants ***a*** him.
7: 7 and ***a*** that they shall come
7:36 ***a*** he had shown wonders and
9:23 Now ***a*** many days were past, the
10:37 and began from Galilee ***a*** the
10:41 us who ate and drank with Him ***a***
11:19 those who were scattered ***a*** the
12: 4 bring him before the people ***a***
13:15 And ***a*** the reading of the Law and
13:20 ***A*** that He gave them judges for
13:22 a man ***a*** My own heart, who
13:24 ***a*** John had first preached,
13:25 there comes One ***a*** me, the
13:36 ***a*** he had served his own
14:24 And ***a*** they had passed through
15:13 And ***a*** they had become silent,
15:16 ***A*** this I will return And
15:33 And ***a*** they had stayed there for
15:36 Then ***a*** some days Paul said to
16: 7 ***A*** they had come to Mysia, they
16:10 Now ***a*** he had seen the vision,
18: 1 ***A*** these things Paul departed
18:23 ***A*** he had spent some time there,
19: 4 on Him who would come ***a*** him,
19:21 ***A*** I have been there, I must also
20: 1 ***A*** the uproar had ceased, Paul
20: 6 we sailed away from Philippi ***a***
20:29 that ***a*** my departure savage
20:30 to draw away the disciples ***a***
21:15 And ***a*** those days we packed and
21:36 of the people followed ***a***,
22:29 commander was also afraid ***a*** he
24: 1 Now ***a*** five days Ananias the high
24:10 ***a*** the governor had nodded to
24:17 Now ***a*** many years I came to bring
24:24 And ***a*** some days, when Felix came
24:27 But ***a*** two years Porcius Festus
25: 1 ***a*** three days he went up from
25:13 And ***a*** some days King Agrippa
25:26 so that ***a*** the examination has
27:14 But not long ***a***, a tempestuous
27:21 But ***a*** long abstinence from food,
28: 6 But ***a*** they had looked for a
28:11 ***A*** three months we sailed in an
28:13 And ***a*** one day the south wind
28:17 And it came to pass ***a*** three
28:25 they departed ***a*** Paul had said
Rom 3:11 is none who seeks ***a*** God.
1 Cor 1:22 and Greeks seek ***a*** wisdom;
10: 6 that we should not lust ***a*** evil
10:18 Observe Israel ***a*** the flesh: Are
11:25 manner He also took the cup ***a***
12:28 ***a*** that miracles, then gifts of
15: 6 ***A*** that He was seen by over five
15: 7 ***A*** that He was seen by James,
Gal 1:18 Then ***a*** three years I went up to
2: 1 Then ***a*** fourteen years I went up
3:25 But ***a*** faith has come, we are no
4: 9 But now ***a*** you have known God, or
Eph 1:13 ***a*** you heard the word of truth,
1:15 ***a*** I heard of your faith in the
1 Th 2: 2 But even ***a*** we had suffered
1 Tim 5:15 have already turned aside ***a***
Titus 3:10 Reject a divisive man ***a*** the
Heb 4: 7 ***a*** such a long time, as it has
6:15 ***a*** he had patiently endured, he
7:28 which came ***a*** the law, appoints
8:10 the house of Israel ***a***
9:17 For a testament is in force ***a***
9:27 but ***a*** this the judgment,
10:12 ***a*** He had offered one sacrifice
10:15 for ***a*** He had said before,
10:16 I will make with them ***a***
10:26 For if we sin willfully ***a*** we
10:32 ***a*** you were illuminated, you
10:36 so that ***a*** you have done the
11:30 walls of Jericho fell down ***a***
1 Pe 5:10 ***a*** you have suffered a while,
2 Pe 1:15 a reminder of these things ***a***
2:20 ***a*** they have escaped the
Jude 7 to sexual immorality and gone ***a***
Rev 1:19 things which will take place ***a***
4: 1 ***A*** these things I looked, and
4: 1 things which must take place ***a***
7: 1 ***A*** these things I saw four angels
7: 9 ***A*** these things I looked, and
9:12 two more woes are coming ***a***
11:11 Now ***a*** the three-and-a-half days
12:15 out of his mouth like a flood ***a***
15: 5 ***A*** these things I looked, and
18: 1 ***A*** these things I saw another
19: 1 ***A*** these things I heard a loud
20: 3 But ***a*** these things he must be

AFTERNOON (1/1)

Judg 19: 8 So they delayed until ***a***;

AFTERWARD (86/86)

Gen 6: 4 earth in those days, and also ***a***,
10:18 ***A*** the families of the
15:14 ***a*** they shall come out with
25:26 ***A*** his brother came out, and his
30:21 ***A*** she bore a daughter, and
32:20 and ***a*** I will see his face;
33: 7 ***A*** Joseph and Rachel came near,
38:30 ***A*** his brother came out who had
Ex 5: 1 ***A*** Moses and Aaron went in and
11: 1 ***A*** he will let you go from here.
34:32 ***A*** all the children of Israel
Lev 14:19 ***A*** he shall kill the burnt
14:36 and ***a*** the priest shall go in to
16:26 and ***a*** he may come into the
16:28 and ***a*** he may come into the
22: 7 and ***a*** he may eat the holy
Num 5:26 and ***a*** make the woman drink the
12:14 and ***a*** she may be received
12:16 And ***a*** the people moved from
19: 7 and ***a*** he shall come into the
31: 2 ***A*** you shall be gathered to your
31:24 and ***a*** you may come into the
32:22 then ***a*** you may return and be
Deut 13: 9 and ***a*** the hand of all the
17: 7 and ***a*** the hands of all the
24:21 you shall not glean it ***a***;
Josh 2:16 ***A*** you may go your way."
8:34 And ***a*** he read all the words of
10:26 And ***a*** Joshua struck them and
24: 5 ***A*** I brought you out.
Judg 1: 9 And ***a*** the children of Judah went
7:11 and ***a*** your hands shall be
16: 4 ***A*** it happened that he loved a
19: 5 and ***a*** go your way."
1 Sam 9:13 ***a*** those who are invited will
24: 5 Now it happened ***a*** that David's
24: 8 David also arose ***a***,
2 Sam 3:28 ***A***, when David heard it,
21:18 Now it happened ***a*** that there
1 Ki 17:13 and ***a*** make some for yourself
1 Chr 2:21 Now ***a*** Hezron went in to the
20: 4 Now it happened ***a*** that war
2 Chr 35:14 Then ***a*** they prepared portions
Neh 6:10 ***A*** I came to the house of
Esth 6:12 ***A*** Mordecai went back to the
Job 18: 2 and ***a*** we will speak.
Ps 73:24 And ***a*** receive me to glory.
Prov 20:17 But ***a*** his mouth will be filled
20:25 And ***a*** to reconsider his vows.
24:27 And ***a*** build your house.
28:23 a man will find more favor ***a***
Eccl 4:16 Yet those who come ***a*** will not
Isa 1:26 ***A*** you shall be called the city
9: 1 And ***a*** more heavily oppressed
Jer 16:16 and ***a*** I will send for many
21: 7 'And ***a***,' says the LORD,
34:11 But ***a*** they changed their minds
46:26 ***A*** it shall be inhabited as in
49: 6 But ***a*** I will bring back The
Ezek 43: 1 ***A*** he brought me to the gate, the
Dan 8:27 ***a*** I arose and went about the
Hos 3: 5 ***A*** the children of Israel shall
Joel 2:28 And it shall come to pass ***a***
Mt 4: 2 ***a*** He was hungry.
21:29 but ***a*** he regretted it and
21:32 you did not ***a*** relent and
25:11 ***A*** the other virgins came also,
Mk 4:17 so endure only for a time. ***A***,
9:39 a miracle in My name can soon ***a***
Lk 4: 2 days He ate nothing, and ***a***,
8: 1 Now it came to pass, ***a***,
17: 8 and ***a*** you will eat and drink'?
18: 4 but ***a*** he said within himself,
Jn 5:14 ***A*** Jesus found him in the temple,
13:36 now, but you shall follow Me ***a***.
Acts 13:21 And ***a*** they asked for a king; so
1 Cor 15:23 ***a*** those who are Christ's at
15:46 and ***a*** the spiritual.
Gal 1:21 ***A*** I went into the regions of
3:23 for the faith which would ***a*** be
Heb 3: 5 things which would be spoken ***a***,
4: 8 then He would not ***a*** have spoken
12:11 ***a*** it yields the peaceable fruit
12:17 For you know that ***a***,
2 Pe 2: 6 them an example to those who ***a***
Jude 5 ***a*** destroyed those who did not

AFTERWARDS (1/1)

Ezra 3: 5 ***A*** they offered the regular

AGABUS (2/2)

Acts 11:28 Then one of them, named ***A***,
21:10 a certain prophet named ***A*** came

AGAG (8/6) AGAGITE

Num 24: 7 king shall be higher than ***A***,
1 Sam 15: 8 He also took ***A*** king of the
15: 9 Saul and the people spared ***A***
15:20 and brought back ***A*** king of
15:32 Bring ***A*** king of the Amalekites
15:32 So ***A*** came to him cautiously.
15:32 And ***A*** said, "Surely the
15:33 And Samuel hacked ***A*** in pieces

AGAGITE (5/5) AGAG

Esth 3: 1 the son of Hammedatha the ***A***,
3:10 the son of Hammedatha the ***A***,
8: 3 the evil of Haman the ***A***,
8: 5 the son of Hammedatha the ***A***,
9:24 the son of Hammedatha the ***A***,

AGAIN (428/412)

Gen 4: 2 Then she bore ***a***,
4:25 And Adam knew his wife ***a***,
8:10 and ***a*** he sent the dove out from
8:12 which did not return ***a*** to him
8:21 I will never ***a*** curse the ground
8:21 nor will I ***a*** destroy every
9:11 Never ***a*** shall all flesh be cut
9:11 never ***a*** shall there be a flood
9:15 the waters shall never ***a*** become
18:29 And he spoke to Him yet ***a*** and
25: 1 Abraham ***a*** took a wife, and her
26:18 And Isaac dug ***a*** the wells of
29:33 Then she conceived ***a*** and bore a
29:34 She conceived ***a*** and bore a son,
29:35 And she conceived ***a*** and bore a
30: 7 maid Bilhah conceived ***a*** and
30:19 Then Leah conceived ***a*** and bore
30:31 I will ***a*** feed and keep your
35: 9 Then God appeared to Jacob ***a***,
38: 4 She conceived ***a*** and bore a son,
38: 5 And she conceived yet ***a*** and bore
38:26 And he never knew her ***a***.
40:21 butler to his butlership ***a***,
42:24 Then he returned to them ***a***,
46: 4 also surely bring you up ***a***;
Ex 4: 7 "Put your hand in your bosom ***a***.
4: 7 he put his hand in his bosom ***a***,
10: 8 Moses and Aaron were brought ***a***
10:29 I will never see your face ***a***.
11: 6 before, nor shall be like it ***a***.
14:13 you shall see ***a*** no more
21:19 if he rises ***a*** and walks about
23: 4 surely bring it back to him ***a***.
34:35 put the veil on his face ***a***,
Lev 13: 6 the priest shall examine him ***a***
13: 7 shall be seen by the priest ***a***.
13:16 flesh changes and turns white ***a***,
13:57 But if it appears ***a*** in the
14:39 And the priest shall come ***a*** on
20: 2 '***A***, you shall say to the
25:48 he is sold he may be redeemed ***a***.
Num 11: 4 children of Israel also wept ***a***
11:25 although they never did so ***a***.
12:14 she may be received ***a***.
12:15 till Miriam was brought in ***a***.
15:17 ***A*** the LORD spoke to Moses,
15:37 ***A*** the LORD spoke to Moses,
22:15 Then Balak ***a*** sent princes, more
22:25 the wall; so he struck her ***a***.
32:15 He will once ***a*** leave them in
Deut 13:11 and not ***a*** do such wickedness as
13:16 it shall not be built ***a***.
17:16 shall not return that way ***a***.
18:16 Let me not hear ***a*** the voice of
19:20 and hereafter they shall not ***a***
22: 4 surely help him lift them up ***a***.
24:13 case return the pledge to him ***a***
24:20 shall not go over the boughs ***a***;
28:68 you, 'You shall never see it ***a***.
30: 3 and gather you ***a*** from all the
30: 8 And you will ***a*** obey the voice of
30: 9 For the LORD will ***a*** rejoice
33:11 hate him, that they rise not ***a***.
Josh 5: 2 the sons of Israel ***a*** the
Judg 3:12 And the children of Israel ***a***
4: 1 the children of Israel ***a*** did
8:33 that the children of Israel ***a***
9:37 So Gaal spoke ***a*** and said, "See,
10: 6 Then the children of Israel ***a***
11: 8 That is why we have turned ***a*** to
11:14 So Jephthah ***a*** sent messengers to
13: 1 ***A*** the children of Israel did
13: 8 God whom You sent come to us ***a***
13: 9 of God came to the woman ***a*** as
16:22 of his head began to grow ***a***
19: 7 urged him; so he lodged there ***a***.
20:22 encouraged themselves and ***a***
20:23 Shall I ***a*** draw near for battle
20:28 Shall I yet ***a*** go out to battle
Ruth 1:14 up their voices and wept ***a***;
1:21 the LORD has brought me home ***a***
1 Sam 3: 5 "I did not call; lie down ***a***.
3: 6 Then the LORD called yet ***a***,
3: 6 not call, my son; lie down ***a***.
3: 8 And the LORD called Samuel ***a***
3:21 Then the LORD appeared ***a*** in
5: 3 Dagon and set it in its place ***a***.
9: 8 And the servant answered Saul ***a***
19: 8 And there was war ***a***;
19:21 Then Saul sent messengers ***a*** the
20: 3 Then David took an oath ***a***,
20:17 Now Jonathan ***a*** caused David to
23: 4 inquired of the LORD once ***a***.
2 Sam 1: 9 "He said to me ***a***, 'Please stand
2:22 So Abner said ***a*** to Asahel,
3:34 all the people wept over him ***a***.
5:22 the Philistines went up once ***a***
6: 1 ***A*** David gathered all the choice
12:23 I fast? Can I bring him back ***a***?
14:13 bring his banished one home ***a***.
14:14 which cannot be gathered up ***a***.
14:29 And when he sent ***a*** the second
18:22 the son of Zadok said ***a*** to
19:37 let your servant turn back ***a***,
20:10 and he did not strike him ***a***.
21:15 the Philistines were at war ***a***
21:18 afterward that there was ***a*** a
21:19 ***A*** there was war at Gob with the
21:20 Yet ***a*** there was war at Gath,
22:38 Neither did I turn back ***a*** till
24: 1 ***A*** the anger of the LORD was
1 Ki 10:10 There never ***a*** came such
10:12 There never ***a*** came such almug

13:33 but ***a*** he made priests from
18:37 their hearts back to You ***a***.
18:43 And seven times he said, "Go ***a***.
19: 6 ate and drank, and lay down ***a***.
19:20 And he said to him, "Go back ***a***,
2 Ki 1:13 ***A***, he sent a third captain
4:35 and ***a*** went up and stretched
4:43 one hundred men?" He said ***a***,
19: 9 So he ***a*** sent messengers to
19:30 of the house of Judah Shall ***a***
1 Chr 14:13 Then the Philistines once ***a***
14:14 Therefore David inquired ***a*** of
20: 5 ***A*** there was war with the
20: 6 Yet ***a*** there was war at Gath,
2 Chr 13:20 did not recover strength ***a*** in
19: 4 and he went out ***a*** among the
28:17 For ***a*** the Edomites had come,
33: 8 and I will not ***a*** remove the foot
Ezra 9:14 should we ***a*** break Your
Neh 9:28 They ***a*** did evil before You.
13:21 the wall? If you do so ***a***,
Esth 2:14 would not go in to the king ***a***
5:12 and tomorrow I am ***a*** invited by
7: 2 the king ***a*** said to Esther,
8: 3 Now Esther spoke ***a*** to the king,
9:13 who are in Shushan to do ***a***
9:15 in Shushan gathered together ***a***
Job 2: 1 ***A*** there was a day when the sons
7: 7 a breath! My eye will never ***a***
10: 9 will You turn me into dust ***a***?
10:16 And ***a*** You show Yourself
14: 7 cut down, that it will sprout ***a***,
14:14 a man dies, shall he live ***a***?
17:10 "But please, come back ***a***,
20:15 riches And vomits them up ***a***;
29:22 my words they did not speak ***a***,
41: 8 Never do it ***a***!
Ps 18:37 Neither did I turn back ***a*** till
60: 1 Oh, restore us ***a***!
71:20 troubles, Shall revive me ***a***,
71:20 And bring me up ***a*** from the
78:39 passes away and does not come ***a***.
78:41 ***a*** and again they tempted God,
78:41 again and ***a*** they tempted God,
85: 6 Will You not revive us ***a***,
107:26 They go down ***a*** to the depths;
126: 6 Shall doubtless come ***a*** with
140:10 pits, that they rise not up ***a***.
Prov 19:19 him, you will have to do it ***a***.
19:24 much as bring it to his mouth ***a***.
24:16 fall seven times And rise ***a***,
Eccl 1: 6 And comes ***a*** on its circuit.
1: 7 come, There they return ***a***.
4: 4 ***A***, I saw that for all toil
4:11 ***A***, if two lie down together,
8:14 to the work of the wicked; ***a***,
Song 5: 3 robe; How can I put it on ***a***?
Isa 1: 5 Why should you be stricken ***a***?
7:10 Moreover the LORD spoke ***a*** to
8: 5 The LORD also spoke to me ***a***,
10:20 Will never ***a*** depend on him who
11:11 the LORD shall set His hand ***a***
24:20 it will fall, and not rise ***a***.
29:14 I will ***a*** do a marvelous work
37:31 of the house of Judah Shall ***a***
49:20 Will say ***a*** in your ears, 'The
Jer 3: 1 man's, May he return to her ***a***?
18: 4 so he made it ***a*** into another
19:11 which cannot be made whole ***a***;
24: 4 ***A*** the word of the LORD came to
31: 4 ***A*** I will build you, and you
31: 4 virgin of Israel! You shall ***a***
31:23 They shall ***a*** use this speech in
31:39 The surveyor's line shall ***a***
32:15 vineyards shall be possessed ***a***
33:10 ***A*** there shall be heard in this
33:12 there shall ***a*** be a dwelling
33:13 the flocks shall ***a*** pass under
38:22 And they have turned away ***a***.
Lam 3: 3 against me Time and time ***a***
Ezek 3:20 '***A***, when a righteous man
4: 6 lie ***a*** on your right side; then
5: 4 Then take some of them ***a*** and
5: 9 like of which I will never do ***a***,
8: 6 from My sanctuary? Now turn ***a***,
8:13 And He said to me, "Turn ***a***,
8:15 this, O son of man? Turn ***a***,
11:14 ***A*** the word of the LORD came to
12:26 ***A*** the word of the LORD came to
14:12 The word of the LORD came ***a*** to
16: 1 ***A*** the word of the LORD came to
16: 8 When I passed by you ***a*** and
18: 1 word of the LORD came to me ***a***,
18:27 '***A***, when a wicked man
21: 8 ***A*** the word of the LORD came to
21:18 word of the LORD came to me ***a***,
23: 1 The word of the LORD came ***a*** to
24: 1 ***A***, in the ninth year,
26:21 for, you will never be found ***a***,
27: 1 The word of the LORD came ***a*** to
28: 1 word of the LORD came to me ***a***,
29:15 it shall never ***a*** exalt itself
30: 1 word of the LORD came to me ***a***,
31:14 trees by the waters may ever ***a***
33: 1 ***A*** the word of the LORD came to
33:14 '***A***, when I say to the wicked,
36:30 so that you need never ***a*** bear
37: 4 ***A*** He said to me, "Prophesy to
37:15 ***A*** the word of the LORD came to
37:22 be divided into two kingdoms ***a***.
38:12 the waste places that are ***a***
47: 4 ***A*** he measured one thousand and
47: 4 ***A*** he measured one thousand and
47: 5 ***A*** he measured one thousand, and
Dan 2: 7 They answered ***a*** and said, "Let
9:25 The street shall be built ***a***,
10:18 Then ***a***, the one having the
Hos 1: 6 And she conceived ***a*** and bore a
3: 1 the LORD said to me, "Go ***a***,
5:15 I will return ***a*** to My place
11: 9 I will not ***a*** destroy Ephraim.
12: 9 I will ***a*** make you dwell in
Joel 3:17 shall ever pass through her ***a***.
Am 7:13 But never ***a*** prophesy at Bethel,
8:14 shall fall and never rise ***a***.
Jon 2: 4 Yet I will look ***a*** toward Your
Mic 7:19 He will ***a*** have compassion on
Hag 2:20 And ***a*** the word of the LORD
Zech 1:17 ***A*** proclaim, saying, 'Thus says
1:17 My cities shall ***a*** spread out
1:17 The LORD will ***a*** comfort Zion,
1:17 And will ***a*** choose Jerusalem.'
2:12 and will ***a*** choose Jerusalem.
8: 1 ***A*** the word of the LORD of hosts
8: 4 Old men and old women shall ***a***
8:15 So ***a*** in these days I am
12: 6 Jerusalem shall be inhabited ***a***
Mal 3:18 Then you shall ***a*** discern
Mt 4: 7 said to him, "It is written ***a***,
4: 8 ***A***, the devil took Him up on
5:33 ***A*** you have heard that it was
13:44 ***A***, the kingdom of heaven is
13:45 ***A***, the kingdom of heaven is
13:47 ***A***, the kingdom of heaven is
18:19 ***A*** I say to you that if two of
19:24 And ***a*** I say to you, it is easier
20: 5 ***A*** he went out about the sixth
20:19 the third day He will rise ***a***.
21:19 no fruit grow on you ever ***a***.
21:36 ***A*** he sent other servants, more
22: 1 answered and spoke to them ***a***
22: 4 '***A***, he sent out other servants,
26:42 ***A***, a second time, He went
26:43 He came and found them asleep ***a***,
26:44 So He left them, went away ***a***,
26:72 But ***a*** he denied with an oath,
27:50 And Jesus cried out ***a*** with a
Mk 2: 1 And ***a*** He entered Capernaum after
2:13 Then He went out ***a*** by the sea;
3: 1 And He entered the synagogue ***a***,
3:20 the multitude came together ***a***,
4: 1 And ***a*** He began to teach by the
5:21 when Jesus had crossed over ***a***
7:31 ***A***, departing from the region
8:13 and getting into the boat ***a***,
8:25 He put His hands on his eyes ***a***
8:31 and after three days rise ***a***.
10: 1 multitudes gathered to Him ***a***,
10: 1 accustomed, He taught them ***a***.
10:10 His disciples also asked Him ***a***
10:24 But Jesus answered ***a*** and said
10:32 He took the twelve aside ***a*** and
10:34 the third day He will rise ***a***.
11:14 one eat fruit from you ever ***a***.
11:27 Then they came ***a*** to Jerusalem.
12: 4 ***A*** he sent them another servant,
12: 5 And ***a*** he sent another, and him
14:39 ***A*** He went away and prayed, and
14:40 He found them asleep ***a***,
14:61 ***A*** the high priest asked Him,
14:69 And the servant girl saw him ***a***,
14:70 But he denied it ***a***.
14:70 who stood by said to Peter ***a***,
15: 4 Then Pilate asked Him ***a***,
15:12 answered and said to them ***a***,
15:13 So they cried out ***a***,
Lk 9: 8 of the old prophets had risen ***a***.
9:19 of the old prophets has risen ***a***.
10:35 more you spend, when I come ***a***,
13:20 And ***a*** He said, "To what shall
15:24 my son was dead and is alive ***a***;
15:32 brother was dead and is alive ***a***,
18:33 the third day He will rise ***a***.
20:11 ***A*** he sent another servant; and
20:12 And ***a*** he sent a third; and they
23:20 ***a*** called out to them.
24: 7 and the third day rise ***a***.
Jn 1:35 ***A***, the next day, John
3: 3 to you, unless one is born ***a***,
3: 7 to you, 'You must be born ***a***.'
4: 3 He left Judea and departed ***a*** to
4:13 of this water will thirst ***a***,
4:46 So Jesus came ***a*** to Cana of
4:54 This ***a*** is the second sign Jesus
6:15 He departed ***a*** to the mountain
8: 2 early in the morning He came ***a***
8: 8 And ***a*** He stooped down and wrote
8:12 Then Jesus spoke to them ***a***,
8:21 Then Jesus said to them ***a***,
9:15 the Pharisees also asked him ***a***
9:17 They said to the blind man ***a***,
9:24 So they ***a*** called the man who was
9:26 Then they said to him ***a***,
9:27 Why do you want to hear it ***a***?
10: 7 Then Jesus said to them ***a***,
10:17 My life that I may take it ***a***.
10:18 and I have power to take it ***a***.
10:19 there was a division ***a*** among
10:31 the Jews took up stones ***a*** to
10:39 Therefore they sought ***a*** to seize
10:40 And He went away ***a*** beyond the
11: 7 "Let us go to Judea ***a***."
11: 8 You, and are You going there ***a***?
11:23 her, "Your brother will rise ***a***."
11:24 I know that he will rise ***a*** in
11:38 ***a*** groaning in Himself, came to
12:28 it and will glorify it ***a***."
12:39 believe, because Isaiah said ***a***:
13:12 His garments, and sat down ***a***,
14: 3 I will come ***a*** and receive you
16:16 and ***a*** a little while, and you
16:17 and ***a*** a little while, and you
16:19 and ***a*** a little while, and you
16:22 but I will see you ***a*** and your
16:28 and have come into the world. ***A***,
18: 7 Then He asked them ***a***,
18:27 Peter then denied ***a***;
18:33 Pilate entered the Praetorium ***a***,
18:38 he went out ***a*** to the Jews, and
18:40 Then they all cried ***a***,
19: 4 Pilate then went out ***a***,
19: 9 and went ***a*** into the Praetorium,
19:37 And ***a*** another Scripture says,
20: 9 that He must rise ***a*** from the
20:10 Then the disciples went away ***a***
20:21 So Jesus said to them ***a***,
20:26 eight days His disciples were ***a***
21: 1 things Jesus showed Himself ***a***
21:16 He said to him ***a*** a second time,
Acts 10:15 And a voice spoke to him ***a*** the
10:16 was taken up into heaven ***a***.
11: 9 But the voice answered me ***a*** from
11:10 and all were drawn up ***a*** into
17: 3 had to suffer and rise ***a*** from
17:32 We will hear you ***a*** on this
18:21 but I will return ***a*** to you, God
27:28 they took soundings ***a*** and found
Rom 8:15 the spirit of bondage ***a*** to
11:23 God is able to graft them in ***a***.
14: 9 died and rose and lived ***a***,
15:10 And ***a*** he says: "Rejoice, O
15:11 And ***a***: "Praise the LORD,
15:12 And ***a***, Isaiah says: "There
1 Cor 3:20 and ***a***, "The LORD knows the
7: 5 and come together ***a*** so that
8:13 I will never ***a*** eat meat, lest I
12:21 nor ***a*** the head to the feet, "I
15: 4 and that He rose ***a*** the third
2 Cor 1:16 to come ***a*** from Macedonia to
2: 1 that I would not come ***a*** to you
3: 1 Do we begin ***a*** to commend
5:12 we do not commend ourselves ***a***
5:15 who died for them and rose ***a***.
10: 7 let him ***a*** consider this in
11:16 I say ***a***, let no one think
12:19 ***A***, do you think that we
12:21 lest, when I come ***a***,
13: 2 that if I come ***a*** I will not
Gal 1: 9 said before, so now I say ***a***,
1:17 and returned ***a*** to Damascus.
2: 1 fourteen years I went up ***a*** to
2:18 For if I build ***a*** those things
4: 9 how is it that you turn ***a*** to
4: 9 to which you desire ***a*** to be in
4:19 for whom I labor in birth ***a***
5: 1 and do not be entangled ***a*** with
5: 3 And I testify ***a*** to every man who
Phil 1:26 Christ by my coming to you ***a***.
2:28 that when you see him ***a*** you may
4: 4 ***A*** I will say, rejoice!
4:10 care for me has flourished ***a***;
4:16 you sent aid once and ***a*** for
1 Th 2:18 to you—even I, Paul, time and ***a***—
4:14 that Jesus died and rose ***a***,
Heb 1: 5 have begotten You"? And ***a***:
1: 6 But when He ***a*** brings the
2:13 And ***a***: "I will put My
2:13 My trust in Him." And ***a***:
4: 5 and ***a*** in this place: "They
4: 7 ***a*** He designates a certain day,
5:12 need someone to teach you ***a***
6: 1 not laying ***a*** the foundation of
6: 6 to renew them ***a*** to repentance,
6: 6 since they crucify ***a*** for
10:30 repay," says the Lord. And ***a***,
11:35 their dead raised to life ***a***.
Jas 5:18 And he prayed ***a***,
1 Pe 1: 3 mercy has begotten us ***a*** to a
1:23 having been born ***a***,
2 Pe 2:20 they are ***a*** entangled in them
1 Jn 2: 8 ***A***, a new commandment I write
Rev 10: 8 from heaven spoke to me ***a*** and
10:11 You must prophesy ***a*** about many
19: 3 ***A*** they said, "Alleluia!
20: 5 rest of the dead did not live ***a***

AGAINST (1615/1341) See APPENDIX

AGAR (KJV) See HAGAR

AGATE (2/2)

Ex 28:19 third row, a jacinth, an ***a***,
39:12 the third row, a jacinth, an ***a***,

AGATES (KJV) See RUBIES

AGE (63/60) AGED, AGES

Gen 15:15 shall be buried at a good old ***a***.
18:11 were old, well advanced in ***a***;
18:11 and Sarah had passed the ***a*** of
21: 2 bore Abraham a son in his old ***a***,
21: 7 borne him a son in his old ***a***.
24: 1 was old, well advanced in ***a***;

25: 8 last and died in a good old *a*,
37: 3 he was the son of his old *a*.
44:20 man, and a child of his old *a*,
48:10 eyes of Israel were dim with *a*,
Num 8:25 and at the *a* of fifty years they
Josh 23: 1 Joshua was old, advanced in *a*.
23: 2 them: "I am old, advanced in *a*.
Judg 8:32 of Joash died at a good old *a*,
Ruth 4:15 and a nourisher of your old *a*;
1 Sam 2:33 die in the flower of their *a*.
1 Ki 14: 4 were glazed by reason of his *a*.
15:23 But in the time of his old *a* he
1 Chr 23: 3 were numbered from the *a* of
23:24 from the *a* of twenty years and
29:28 So he died in a good old *a*,
Job 5:26 come to the grave at a full *a*,
8: 8 please, of the former *a*,
32: 7 *A* should speak, And multitude
Ps 39: 5 And my *a* is as nothing before
71: 9 me off in the time of old *a*;
92:14 shall still bear fruit in old *a*;
Isa 46: 4 Even to your old *a*,
Dan 1:10 the young men who are your *a*?
Zech 8: 4 in his hand Because of great *a*.
Mt 12:32 either in this *a* or in the age
12:32 in this age or in the *a* to
13:39 the harvest is the end of the *a*,
13:40 it will be at the end of this *a*.
13:49 it will be at the end of the *a*.
24: 3 coming, and of the end of the *a*?
28:20 even to the end of the *a*.
Mk 5:42 for she was twelve years of *a*.
10:30 and in the *a* to come, eternal
Lk 1:36 conceived a son in her old *a*;
2:36 of Asher. She was of a great *a*,
3:23 at about thirty years of *a*,
8:42 about twelve years of *a*,
18:30 and in the *a* to come eternal
20:34 The sons of this *a* marry and are
20:35 counted worthy to attain that *a*,
Jn 9:21 eyes we do not know. He is of *a*;
9:23 his parents said, "He is of *a*;
1 Cor 1:20 is the disputer of this *a*?
2: 6 yet not the wisdom of this *a*,
2: 6 nor of the rulers of this *a*,
2: 8 none of the rulers of this *a*
3:18 you seems to be wise in this *a*,
2 Cor 4: 4 whose minds the god of this *a*
Gal 1: 4 us from this present evil *a*,
Eph 1:21 not only in this *a* but also in
6:12 of the darkness of this *a*,
1 Tim 6:17 who are rich in this present *a*
Titus 2:12 and godly in the present *a*,
Heb 5:14 to those who are of full *a*,
6: 5 of God and the powers of the *a*
11:11 a child when she was past the *a*,
11:24 Moses, when he became of *a*,

AGED (9/9) AGE

2 Sam 19:32 Now Barzillai was a very *a* man,
2 Chr 36:17 on the *a* or the weak; He gave
Job 12:12 Wisdom is with *a* men, And
15:10 the gray-haired and the *a* are
29: 8 And the *a* arose and stood;
32: 9 Nor do the *a* always
Jer 6:11 The *a* with him who is full
Lam 3: 4 He has *a* my flesh and my skin,
Phm 1: 9 such a one as Paul, the *a*,

AGEE (1/1)

2 Sam 23:11 him was Shammah the son of *A*

AGENTS (2/2)

1 Ki 10:29 and thus, through their *a*,
2 Chr 1:17 fifty; thus, through their *a*,

AGES (7/7) AGE

1 Cor 2: 7 God ordained before the *a* for
10:11 upon whom the ends of the *a*
Eph 2: 7 that in the *a* to come He might
3: 5 which in other *a* was not made
3: 9 from the beginning of the *a*
Col 1:26 which has been hidden from *a*
Heb 9:26 now, once at the end of the *a*,

AGITATED (1/1)

Ezek 16:43 but *a* Me with all these

AGO (18/18) See APPENDIX

AGONE (KJV) See AGO

AGONY (2/2)

Isa 23: 5 They also will be in *a* at the
Lk 22:44 And being in *a*,

AGREE (9/9) AGREEABLE, AGREED, AGREEMENT, AGREEMENTS

Mt 5:25 *A* with your adversary quickly,
18:19 to you that if two of you *a* on
20:13 Did you not *a* with me for a
Mk 14:56 but their testimonies did not *a*.
14:59 even then did their testimony *a*.
Acts 15:15 the words of the prophets *a*,
28:25 So when they did not *a* among
Rom 7:16 I *a* with the law that it is
1 Jn 5: 8 and these three *a* as one.

AGREEABLE (1/1) AGREE

Zech 11:12 If it is *a* to you, give me my

AGREED (11/11) AGREE

2 Ki 12: 8 And the priests *a* that they
2 Chr 30: 2 assembly in Jerusalem had *a* to
30:23 Then the whole assembly *a* to
Dan 2: 9 decree for you! For you have *a*
Am 3: 3 together, unless they are *a*?
Mt 20: 2 Now when he had *a* with the
Lk 22: 5 and *a* to give him money.
Jn 9:22 for the Jews had *a* already that
Acts 5: 9 How is it that you have *a*
5:40 And they *a* with him, and when
23:20 The Jews have *a* to ask that you

AGREEMENT (12/11) AGREE, AGREEMENTS

Num 30: 2 oath to bind himself by some *a*,
30: 3 and binds herself by some *a*
30: 4 father hears her vow and the *a*
30: 4 and every *a* with which she has
30:10 or bound herself by an *a* with
30:11 and every *a* by which she bound
30:12 her vows or concerning the *a*
1 Chr 12:19 Philistines sent him away by *a*,
Isa 28:15 And with Sheol we are in *a*.
28:18 And your *a* with Sheol will not
Dan 11: 6 king of the North to make an *a*;
2 Cor 6:16 And what *a* has the temple of God

AGREEMENTS (3/3) AGREEMENT

Num 30: 5 none of her vows nor her *a* by
30: 7 and her *a* by which she bound
30:14 all her vows or all the *a* that

AGRIPPA (12/12)

Acts 25:13 And after some days King *A* and
25:22 Then *A* said to Festus, "I also
25:23 when *A* and Bernice had come
25:24 King *A* and all the men who are
25:26 especially before you, King *A*,
26: 1 Then *A* said to Paul, "You are
26: 2 "I think myself happy, King *A*,
26: 7 For this hope's sake, King *A*,
26:19 "Therefore, King *A*,
26:27 'King *A*, do you believe
26:28 Then *A* said to Paul, "You
26:32 Then *A* said to Festus, "This

AGROUND (4/4)

Acts 27:17 fearing lest they should run *a*
27:26 we must run *a* on a certain
27:29 fearing lest we should run *a* on
27:41 seas met, they ran the ship *a*;

AGUE (KJV) See FEVER

AGUR (1/1)

Prov 30: 1 The words of *A* the son of Jakeh,

AH (13/13)

Ps 35:25 not say in their hearts, "*A*,
Isa 1:24 the Mighty One of Israel, "*A*,
44:16 *A*! I am warm, I have seen the
Jer 1: 6 Then said I: "*A*, Lord GOD!
4:10 Then I said, "*A*, Lord GOD!
14:13 Then I said, "*A*, Lord GOD!
32:17 '*A*, Lord GOD! Behold,
Ezek 4:14 So I said, "*A*, Lord GOD!
9: 8 and cried out, and said, "*A*,
11:13 a loud voice, and said, "*A*,
20:49 Then I said, "*A*, Lord GOD!
21:15 *A*! It is made bright; It
Jon 4: 2 to the LORD, and said, "*A*,

AHA (11/8)

Job 39:25 *A*!' He smells the battle from
Ps 35:21 against me, And said, "*A*,
35:21 *a*! Our eyes have seen it."
40:15 Who say to me, "*A*, aha!"
40:15 Who say to me, "Aha, *a*!"
70: 3 their shame, Who say, "*A*, aha!"
70: 3 their shame, Who say, "Aha, *a*!"
Ezek 25: 3 *A*!' against My sanctuary when it
26: 2 *A*! She is broken who was the
36: 2 *A*! The ancient heights have
Mk 15:29 *A*! You who destroy the temple

AHAB (91/80) AHAB'S

1 Ki 16:28 Then *A* his son reigned in his
16:29 *A* the son of Omri became king
16:29 and *A* the son of Omri reigned
16:30 Now *A* the son of Omri did evil
16:33 And *A* made a wooden image.
16:33 *A* did more to provoke the LORD
17: 1 of Gilead, said to *A*,
18: 1 "Go, present yourself to *A*,
18: 2 went to present himself to *A*;
18: 3 And *A* had called Obadiah, who
18: 5 And *A* had said to Obadiah, "Go
18: 6 *A* went one way by himself, and
18: 9 your servant into the hand of *A*,
18:12 know; so when I go and tell *A*,
18:16 So Obadiah went to meet *A*,
18:16 and *A* went to meet Elijah.
18:17 when *A* saw Elijah, that Ahab
18:17 that *A* said to him, "Is that
18:20 So *A* sent for all the children
18:41 Then Elijah said to *A*,
18:42 So *A* went up to eat and drink.
18:44 So he said, "Go up, say to *A*,
18:45 So *A* rode away and went to
18:46 up his loins and ran ahead of *A*
19: 1 And *A* told Jezebel all that
20: 2 messengers into the city to *A*
20:13 a prophet approached *A* king of
20:14 So *A* said, "By whom?" And he
20:34 Then *A* said, "I will send
21: 1 next to the palace of *A* king of
21: 2 So *A* spoke to Naboth, saying,
21: 3 But Naboth said to *A*,
21: 4 So *A* went into his house sullen
21:15 dead, that Jezebel said to *A*,
21:16 when *A* heard that Naboth was
21:16 that *A* got up and went down to
21:18 go down to meet *A* king of
21:20 So *A* said to Elijah, "Have you
21:21 and will cut off from *A* every
21:24 shall eat whoever belongs to *A*
21:25 But there was no one like *A* who
21:27 when *A* heard those words, that
21:29 See how *A* has humbled himself
22:20 Who will persuade *A* to go up,
22:39 Now the rest of the acts of *A*,
22:40 So *A* rested with his fathers.
22:41 Judah in the fourth year of *A*
22:49 Then Ahaziah the son of *A* said
22:51 Ahaziah the son of *A* became
2 Ki 1: 1 Israel after the death of *A*.
3: 1 Now Jehoram the son of *A* became
3: 5 when *A* died, that the king of
8:16 year of Joram the son of *A*,
8:18 just as the house of *A* had
8:18 for the daughter of *A* was his
8:25 year of Joram the son of *A*,
8:27 in the way of the house of *A*,
8:27 the LORD, like the house of *A*,
8:27 son-in-law of the house of *A*.
8:28 he went with Joram the son of *A*
8:29 down to see Joram the son of *A*
9: 7 strike down the house of *A*
9: 8 For the whole house of *A* shall
9: 8 and I will cut off from *A* all
9: 9 So I will make the house of *A*
9:25 I were riding together behind *A*
9:29 year of Joram the son of *A*,
10: 1 Now *A* had seventy sons in
10:10 spoke concerning the house of *A*;
10:11 who remained of the house of *A*
10:17 he killed all who remained to *A*
10:18 *A* served Baal a little, Jehu
10:30 have done to the house of *A*
21: 3 as *A* king of Israel had done;
21:13 the plummet of the house of *A*;
2 Chr 18: 1 he allied himself with *A*.
18: 2 years he went down to visit *A*
18: 2 and *A* killed sheep and oxen in
18: 3 So *A* king of Israel said to
18:19 Who will persuade *A* king of
21: 6 just as the house of *A* had
21: 6 for he had the daughter of *A* as
21:13 the harlotry of the house of *A*,
22: 3 in the ways of the house of *A*,
22: 4 the LORD, like the house of *A*;
22: 5 went with Jehoram the son of *A*
22: 6 to see Jehoram the son of *A* in
22: 7 to cut off the house of *A*.
22: 8 judgment on the house of *A*,
Jer 29:21 concerning *A* the son of
29:22 make you like Zedekiah and *A*,

AHAB'S (3/3) AHAB

1 Ki 21: 8 And she wrote letters in *A* name,
2 Ki 10: 1 and to those who reared *A*
Mic 6:16 All the works of *A* house are

AHARAH (1/1) AHER, AHIRAM, EHI

1 Chr 8: 1 Ashbel the second, *A* the third,

AHARHEL (1/1)

1 Chr 4: 8 and the families of *A* the son

AHASAI (KJV) See AHZAI

AHASBAI (1/1)

2 Sam 23:34 Eliphelet the son of *A*,

AHASUERUS (31/30)

Ezra 4: 6 In the reign of *A*,
Esth 1: 1 came to pass in the days of *A*
1: 1 of Ahasuerus (this was the *A*
1: 2 in those days when King *A* sat on
1: 9 which belonged to King *A*.
1:10 in the presence of King *A*,
1:15 not obey the command of King *A*
1:16 in all the provinces of King *A*.

1:17 King *A* commanded Queen Vashti
1:19 come no more before King *A*;
2: 1 when the wrath of King *A*
2:12 turn came to go in to King *A*
2:16 So Esther was taken to King *A*,
2:21 sought to lay hands on King *A*.
3: 1 After these things King *A*
3: 6 the whole kingdom of *A*—
3: 7 in the twelfth year of King *A*,
3: 8 Then Haman said to King *A*,
3:12 In the name of King *A* it was
6: 2 sought to lay hands on King *A*.
7: 5 So King *A* answered and said to
8: 1 On that day King *A* gave Queen
8: 7 Then King *A* said to Queen
8:10 he wrote in the name of King *A*,
8:12 in all the provinces of King *A*,
9: 2 all the provinces of King *A* to
9:20 in all the provinces of King *A*,
9:30 provinces of the kingdom of *A*,
10: 1 And King *A* imposed tribute on
10: 3 the Jew was second to King *A*,
Dan 9: 1 year of Darius the son of *A*,

AHAVA (3/3) IVAH

Ezra 8:15 by the river that flows to *A*,
8:21 a fast there at the river of *A*,
8:31 we departed from the river of *A*

AHAZ (45/41)

2 Ki 15:38 Then *A* his son reigned in
16: 1 *A* the son of Jotham, king of
16: 2 *A* was twenty years old when he
16: 5 and they besieged *A* but could
16: 7 So *A* sent messengers to
16: 8 And *A* took the silver and gold
16:10 Now King *A* went to Damascus to
16:10 and King *A* sent to Urijah the
16:11 according to all that King *A*
16:11 priest made it before King *A*
16:15 Then King *A* commanded Urijah the
16:16 according to all that King *A*
16:17 And King *A* cut off the panels
16:19 Now the rest of the acts of *A*
16:20 So *A* rested with his fathers,
17: 1 In the twelfth year of *A* king of
18: 1 that Hezekiah the son of *A*,
20:11 gone down on the sundial of *A*.
23:12 roof, the upper chamber of *A*,
1 Chr 3:13 *A* his son, Hezekiah his son,
8:35 Pithon, Melech, Tarea, and *A*.
8:36 And *A* begot Jehoaddah; Jehoaddah
9:41 Pithon, Melech, Tahrea, and *A*.
9:42 And *A* begot Jarah; Jarah begot
2 Chr 27: 9 Then *A* his son reigned in his
28: 1 *A* was twenty years old when he
28:16 At the same time King *A* sent to
28:19 brought Judah low because of *A*
28:21 For *A* took part of the
28:22 the time of his distress King *A*
28:22 This is that King *A*.
28:24 So *A* gathered the articles of
28:27 So *A* rested with his fathers,
29:19 all the articles which King *A*
Isa 1: 1 the days of Uzziah, Jotham, *A*,
7: 1 came to pass in the days of *A*
7: 3 Isaiah, "Go out now to meet *A*,
7:10 the LORD spoke again to *A*,
7:12 But *A* said, "I will not ask,
14:28 came in the year that King *A*
38: 8 the sun on the sundial of *A*,
Hos 1: 1 the days of Uzziah, Jotham, *A*,
Mic 1: 1 in the days of Jotham, *A*,
Mt 1: 9 begot Jotham, Jotham begot *A*,
1: 9 and *A* begot Hezekiah.

AHAZIAH (36/30) AHAZIAH'S, AZARIAH, JEHOAHAZ

1 Ki 22:40 Then *A* his son reigned in his
22:49 Then *A* the son of Ahab said to
22:51 *A* the son of Ahab became king
2 Ki 1: 2 Now *A* fell through the lattice
1:17 So *A* died according to the
1:18 Now the rest of the acts of *A*
8:24 Then *A* his son reigned in his
8:25 *A* the son of Jehoram, king of
8:26 *A* was twenty-two years old when
8:29 And *A* the son of Jehoram, king
9:16 and *A* king of Judah had come
9:21 Then Joram king of Israel and *A*
9:23 around and fled, and said to *A*,
9:23 to Ahaziah, "Treachery, *A*!"
9:27 But when *A* king of Judah saw
9:29 *A* had become king over Judah.
10:13 Jehu met with the brothers of *A*
10:13 "We are the brothers of *A*;
11: 1 When Athaliah the mother of *A*
11: 2 of King Joram, sister of *A*,
11: 2 took Joash the son of *A*,
12:18 Jehoshaphat and Jehoram and *A*,
13: 1 year of Joash the son of *A*,
14:13 son of Jehoash, the son of *A*,
1 Chr 3:11 *A* his son, Joash his son,
2 Chr 20:35 of Judah allied himself with *A*
20:37 you have allied yourself with *A*,
22: 1 of Jerusalem made *A* his
22: 1 So *A* the son of Jehoram, king
22: 2 *A* was forty-two years old when
22: 8 Ahaziah's brothers who served *A*,
22: 9 Then he searched for *A*;
22: 9 So the house of *A* had no one
22:10 when Athaliah the mother of *A*
22:11 king, took Joash the son of *A*,
22:11 (for she was the sister of *A*),

AHAZIAH'S (2/2) AHAZIAH

2 Chr 22: 7 God's occasion for *A* downfall;
22: 8 Judah and the sons of *A* brothers

AHBAN (1/1)

1 Chr 2:29 and she bore him *A* and Molid.

AHEAD (18/18)

Gen 33:14 Please let my lord go on *a*
Ex 10:10 for evil is *a* of you.
1 Sam 9:12 just *a* of you. Hurry now; for
9:27 Tell the servant to go on *a* of
1 Ki 18:46 girded up his loins and ran *a*
2 Ki 4:31 Now Gehazi went on *a* of them,
5:23 and they carried them on *a* of
6:32 And the king sent a man *a* of
Prov 4:25 Let your eyes look straight *a*,
Am 4: 3 Each one straight *a* of her,
Hab 1: 8 Their chargers charge *a*;
Lk 19: 4 So he ran *a* and climbed up into
19:28 He had said this, He went on *a*,
Acts 20: 5 These men, going *a*,
20:13 Then we went *a* to the ship and
1 Cor 11:21 one takes his own supper *a* of
2 Cor 9: 5 the brethren to go to you *a* of
Phil 3:13 to those things which are *a*,

AHER (1/1) AHARAH

1 Chr 7:12 and Hushim was the son of *A*.

AHI (2/2)

1 Chr 5:15 *A* the son of Abdiel, the son of
7:34 The sons of Shemer were *A*,

AHIAM (2/2)

2 Sam 23:33 *A* the son of Sharar the
1 Chr 11:35 *A* the son of Sacar the Hararite,

AHIAN (1/1)

1 Chr 7:19 And the sons of Shemida were *A*,

AHIEZER (6/6)

Num 1:12 *A* the son of Ammishaddai;
2:25 children of Dan shall be *A*
7:66 On the tenth day *A* the son of
7:71 This was the offering of *A* the
10:25 over their army was *A* the son
1 Chr 12: 3 The chief was *A*,

AHIHUD (2/2)

Num 34:27 *A* the son of Shelomi;
1 Chr 8: 7 to move. He begot Uzza and *A*.

AHIJAH (24/23) AHIMELECH

1 Sam 14: 3 *A* the son of Ahitub, Ichabod's
14:18 And Saul said to *A*,
1 Ki 4: 3 Elihoreph and *A*,
11:29 that the prophet *A* the
11:30 Then *A* took hold of the new
12:15 the LORD had spoken by *A* the
14: 2 *A* the prophet is there, who
14: 4 and came to the house of *A*.
14: 4 But *A* could not see, for his
14: 5 Now the LORD had said to *A*,
14: 6 when *A* heard the sound of her
14:18 He spoke through His servant *A*
15:27 Then Baasha the son of *A*,
15:29 He had spoken by His servant *A*
15:33 Baasha the son of *A* became king
21:22 house of Baasha the son of *A*,
2 Ki 9: 9 house of Baasha the son of *A*.
1 Chr 2:25 and Bunah, Oren, Ozem, and *A*.
8: 7 Naaman, *A*, and Gera who forced
11:36 *A* the Pelonite,
26:20 *A* was over the treasuries of
2 Chr 9:29 in the prophecy of *A* the
10:15 He had spoken by the hand of *A*
Neh 10:26 *A*, Hanan, Anan,

AHIKAM (20/20)

2 Ki 22:12 *A* the son of Shaphan, Achbor
22:14 So Hilkiah the priest, *A*,
25:22 he made Gedaliah the son of *A*,
2 Chr 34:20 *A* the son of Shaphan, Abdon the
Jer 26:24 Nevertheless the hand of *A* the
39:14 him to Gedaliah the son of *A*,
40: 5 back to Gedaliah the son of *A*,
40: 6 went to Gedaliah the son of *A*,
40: 7 had made Gedaliah the son of *A*
40: 9 And Gedaliah the son of *A*,
40:11 over them Gedaliah the son of *A*,
40:14 But Gedaliah the son of *A* did
40:16 But Gedaliah the son of *A* said
41: 1 men to Gedaliah the son of *A*,
41: 2 struck Gedaliah the son of *A*,
41: 6 Come to Gedaliah the son of *A*!"
41:10 to Gedaliah the son of *A*.
41:16 murdered Gedaliah the son of *A*—
41:18 murdered Gedaliah the son of *A*,
43: 6 left with Gedaliah the son of *A*,

AHILUD (5/5)

2 Sam 8:16 Jehoshaphat the son of *A* was
20:24 Jehoshaphat the son of *A* was
1 Ki 4: 3 Jehoshaphat the son of *A*,
4:12 Baana the son of *A*,
1 Chr 18:15 Jehoshaphat the son of *A* was

AHIMAAZ (15/15)

1 Sam 14:50 was Ahinoam the daughter of *A*.
2 Sam 15:27 *A* your son, and Jonathan the
15:36 with them their two sons, *A*,
17:17 Now Jonathan and *A* stayed at En
17:20 'Where are *A* and Jonathan?"
18:19 Then *A* the son of Zadok said,
18:22 And *A* the son of Zadok said
18:23 Then *A* ran by way of the
18:27 first is like the running of *A*
18:28 And *A* called out and said to the
18:29 *A* answered, "When Joab sent
1 Ki 4:15 *A*, in Naphtali; he also took
1 Chr 6: 8 begot Zadok, and Zadok begot *A*;
6: 9 *A* begot Azariah, and Azariah
6:53 and *A* his son.

AHIMAN (4/4)

Num 13:22 the South and came to Hebron; *A*,
Josh 15:14 of Anak from there: Sheshai, *A*,
Judg 1:10 And they killed Sheshai, *A*,
1 Chr 9:17 were Shallum, Akkub, Talmon, *A*,

AHIMELECH (16/15) ABIMELECH, AHIJAH, AHIMELECH'S

1 Sam 21: 1 to *A* the priest. And Ahimelech
21: 1 And *A* was afraid when he met
21: 2 So David said to *A* the priest,
21: 8 And David said to *A*,
22: 9 to *A* the son of Ahitub.
22:11 So the king sent to call *A* the
22:14 So *A* answered the king and said,
22:16 said, "You shall surely die, *A*,
22:20 Now one of the sons of *A* the
23: 6 when Abiathar the son of *A* fled
26: 6 and said to *A* the Hittite and
2 Sam 8:17 Zadok the son of Ahitub and *A*
1 Chr 24: 3 and *A* of the sons of Ithamar,
24: 6 *A* the son of Abiathar, and the
24:31 of King David, Zadok, *A*,
Ps 52: has gone to the house of *A*.

AHIMELECH'S (1/1) AHIMELECH

1 Sam 30: 7 *A* son, "Please bring the ephod

AHIMOTH (1/1) MAHATH

1 Chr 6:25 of Elkanah were Amasai and *A*.

AHINADAB (1/1)

1 Ki 4:14 *A* the son of Iddo, in Mahanaim;

AHINOAM (7/7)

1 Sam 14:50 The name of Saul's wife was *A*
25:43 David also took *A* of Jezreel,
27: 3 *A* the Jezreelitess, and Abigail
30: 5 *A* the Jezreelitess, and Abigail
2 Sam 2: 2 *A* the Jezreelitess, and Abigail
3: 2 His firstborn was Amnon by *A*
1 Chr 3: 1 by *A* the Jezreelitess; the

AHIO (6/6)

2 Sam 6: 3 on the hill; and Uzzah and *A*,
6: 4 and *A* went before the ark.
1 Chr 8:14 *A*, Shashak, Jeremoth,
8:31 Gedor, *A*, Zecher,
9:37 Gedor, *A*, Zechariah,
13: 7 and Uzza and *A* drove the cart.

AHIRA (5/5)

Num 1:15 *A* the son of Enan."
2:29 of Naphtali shall be *A* the
7:78 On the twelfth day *A* the son of
7:83 This was the offering of *A* the
10:27 the children of Naphtali was *A*

AHIRAM (1/1) AHARAH, AHIRAMITES

Num 26:38 family of the Ashbelites; of *A*,

AHIRAMITES (1/1) AHIRAM

Num 26:38 of Ahiram, the family of the *A*;

AHISAMACH (3/3)

Ex 31: 6 with him Aholiab the son of *A*,
35:34 him and Aholiab the son of *A*,
38:23 him was Aholiab the son of *A*,

AHISHAHAR (1/1)

1 Chr 7:10 Zethan, Tharshish, and *A*.

AHISHAR (1/1)
1 Ki 4: 6 *A*, over the household;

AHITHOPHEL (20/17)
2 Sam 15:12 Then Absalom sent for *A* the
15:31 *A* is among the conspirators
15:31 turn the counsel of *A* into
15:34 you may defeat the counsel of *A*
16:15 and *A* was with him.
16:20 Then Absalom said to *A*,
16:21 And *A* said to Absalom, "Go in
16:23 Now the advice of *A*,
16:23 So was all the advice of *A*
17: 1 Moreover *A* said to Absalom,
17: 6 *A* has spoken in this manner.
17: 7 The advice that *A* has given is
17:14 is better than the advice of *A*.
17:14 to defeat the good advice of *A*,
17:15 Thus and so *A* advised Absalom
17:21 For thus has *A* advised against
17:23 Now when *A* saw that his advice
23:34 Eliam the son of *A* the
1 Chr 27:33 *A* was the king's counselor, and
27:34 After *A* was Jehoiada the son of

AHITUB (15/15)
1 Sam 14: 3 Ahijah the son of *A*,
22: 9 Nob, to Ahimelech the son of *A*.
22:11 the priest, the son of *A*,
22:12 son of *A*!" And he answered,
22:20 sons of Ahimelech the son of *A*,
2 Sam 8:17 Zadok the son of *A* and Ahimelech
1 Chr 6: 7 Amariah, and Amariah begot *A*;
6: 8 *A* begot Zadok, and Zadok begot
6:11 Amariah, and Amariah begot *A*;
6:12 *A* begot Zadok, and Zadok begot
6:52 Amariah his son, *A* his son,
9:11 son of Meraioth, the son of *A*,
18:16 Zadok the son of *A* and Abimelech
Ezra 7: 2 the son of Zadok, the son of *A*,
Neh 11:11 son of Meraioth, the son of *A*,

AHLAB (1/1)
Judg 1:31 inhabitants of Sidon, or of *A*,

AHLAI (2/2)
1 Chr 2:31 and Sheshan's child was *A*.
11:41 the Hittite, Zabad the son of *A*,

AHOAH (1/1) AHOHITE
1 Chr 8: 4 Abishua, Naaman, *A*,

AHOHITE (5/5) AHOAH
2 Sam 23: 9 Eleazar the son of Dodo, the *A*,
23:28 Zalmon the *A*, Maharai the
1 Chr 11:12 Eleazar the son of Dodo, the *A*,
11:29 the Hushathite, Ilai the *A*,
27: 4 second month was Dodai an *A*,

AHOLAH (KJV) See OHOLAH

AHOLIAB (5/5)
Ex 31: 6 have appointed with him *A* the
35:34 in him and *A* the son of
36: 1 "And Bezalel and *A*,
36: 2 Moses called Bezalel and *A*,
38:23 And with him was *A* the son of

AHOLIBAH (KJV) See AHOLIBAH

AHOLIBAMAH (8/7)
Gen 36: 2 *A* the daughter of Anah, the
36: 5 And *A* bore Jeush, Jaalam, and
36:14 These were the sons of *A*,
36:18 And these were the sons of *A*,
36:18 chiefs who descended from *A*,
36:25 Dishon and *A* the daughter of
36:41 Chief *A*, Chief Elah, Chief
1 Chr 1:52 Chief *A*, Chief Elah, Chief

AHUMAI (1/1)
1 Chr 4: 2 and Jahath begot *A* and Lahad.

AHUZZAM (1/1)
1 Chr 4: 6 Naarah bore him *A*,

AHUZZATH (1/1)
Gen 26:26 came to him from Gerar with *A*,

AHZAI (1/1)
Neh 11:13 the son of Azarel, the son of *A*,

AI (39/32) AIATH, AIJA
Gen 12: 8 with Bethel on the west and *A*
13: 3 beginning, between Bethel and *A*,
Josh 7: 2 sent men from Jericho to *A*,
7: 2 the men went up and spied out *A*.
7: 3 thousand men go up and attack *A*.
7: 3 for the people of *A* are
7: 4 they fled before the men of *A*.
7: 5 And the men of *A* struck down
8: 1 with you, and arise, go up to *A*.
8: 1 into your hand the king of *A*,
8: 2 And you shall do to *A* and its
8: 3 of war, to go up against *A*;
8: 9 and stayed between Bethel and *A*,
8: 9 and Ai, on the west side of *A*;
8:10 Israel, before the people to *A*.
8:11 camped on the north side of *A*.
8:11 valley lay between them and *A*.
8:12 in ambush between Bethel and *A*,
8:14 when the king of *A* saw it,
8:16 all the people who were in *A*
8:17 There was not a man left in *A* or
8:18 that is in your hand toward *A*,
8:20 And when the men of *A* looked
8:21 and struck down the men of *A*.
8:23 But the king of *A* they took
8:24 all the inhabitants of *A* in
8:24 the Israelites returned to *A*
8:25 thousand—all the people of *A*.
8:26 all the inhabitants of *A*.
8:28 So Joshua burned *A* and made it a
8:29 And the king of *A* he hanged on a
9: 3 had done to Jericho and *A*,
10: 1 heard how Joshua had taken *A*
10: 1 so he had done to *A* and its
10: 2 because it was greater than *A*,
12: 9 of Jericho, one; the king of *A*,
Ezra 2:28 the men of Bethel and *A*,
Neh 7:32 the men of Bethel and *A*,
Jer 49: 3 for *A* is plundered! Cry, you

AIAH (4/4) AIJA, AJAH
2 Sam 3: 7 was Rizpah, the daughter of *A*.
21: 8 of Rizpah the daughter of *A*,
21:10 Now Rizpah the daughter of *A*
21:11 what Rizpah the daughter of *A*,

AIATH (1/1) AI
Isa 10:28 He has come to *A*,

AID (6/5) AIDE, AIDED, AIDES
2 Sam 21:17 son of Zeruiah came to his *a*,
2 Ki 23:29 king of Egypt went to the *a* of
Phil 4:16 in Thessalonica you sent *a*
Heb 2:16 For indeed He does not give *a* to
2:16 but He does give *a* to the seed
2:18 He is able to *a* those who are

AIDE (1/1)
Acts 12:20 Blastus the king's personal *a*

AIDED (2/2) AID
Judg 9:24 who *a* him in the killing of his
Dan 11:34 they shall be *a* with a little

AIDES (1/1) AID
2 Ki 5:15 man of God, he and all his *a*,

AIJA (1/1) AI, AIAH
Neh 11:31 from Geba dwelt in Michmash, *A*,

AIJALON (10/10)
Josh 10:12 And Moon, in the Valley of *A*.
19:42 Shaalabbin, *A*, Jethlah,
21:24 *A* with its common-land, and
Judg 1:35 to dwell in Mount Heres, in *A*,
12:12 died and was buried at *A* in
1 Sam 14:31 that day from Michmash to *A*.
1 Chr 6:69 *A* with its common-lands, and
8:13 houses of the inhabitants of *A*,
2 Chr 11:10 Zorah, *A*, and Hebron,
28:18 and had taken Beth Shemesh, *A*,

AILS (5/5)
Gen 21:17 What *a* you, Hagar? Fear not, for
Judg 18:23 What *a* you, that you have
18:24 What *a* you?'"
Ps 114: 5 What *a* you, O sea, that you
Isa 22: 1 What *a* you now, that you have

AIM (2/2) AIMLESS
Rom 15:20 And so I have made it my *a* to
2 Cor 5: 9 Therefore we make it our *a*,

AIMLESS (1/1) AIM
1 Pe 1:18 from your *a* conduct received

AIN (5/5)
Num 34:11 to Riblah on the east side of *A*;
Josh 15:32 Lebaoth, Shilhim, *A*,
19: 7 *A*, Rimmon, Ether, and Ashan:
21:16 *A* with its common-land, Juttah
1 Chr 4:32 their villages were Etam, *A*,

AIR (43/43)
Gen 1:26 sea, over the birds of the *a*,
1:28 sea, over the birds of the *a*,
1:30 earth, to every bird of the *a*,
2:19 field and every bird of the *a*,
2:20 cattle, to the birds of the *a*,
6: 7 thing and birds of the *a*,
7: 3 seven each of birds of the *a*,
7:23 thing and bird of the *a*.
9: 2 earth, on every bird of the *a*,
Deut 4:17 winged bird that flies in the *a*,
28:26 for all the birds of the *a* and
1 Sam 17:44 flesh to the birds of the *a*
17:46 to the birds of the *a* and the
2 Sam 21:10 not allow the birds of the *a*
1 Ki 14:11 and the birds of the *a* shall
16: 4 and the birds of the *a* shall
21:24 and the birds of the *a* shall
Job 12: 7 you; And the birds of the *a*,
28:21 from the birds of the *a*.
41:16 is so near another That no *a*
Ps 8: 8 The birds of the *a*,
Prov 30:19 The way of an eagle in the *a*,
Eccl 10:20 For a bird of the *a* may carry
Hos 2:18 field, With the birds of the *a*,
4: 3 field And the birds of the *a*;
7:12 them down like birds of the *a*;
Mt 6:26 "Look at the birds of the *a*,
8:20 have holes and birds of the *a*
13:32 so that the birds of the *a* come
Mk 4: 4 and the birds of the *a* came and
4:32 so that the birds of the *a* may
Lk 8: 5 and the birds of the *a* devoured
9:58 have holes and birds of the *a*
13:19 and the birds of the *a* nested
Acts 10:12 things, and birds of the *a*.
11: 6 things, and birds of the *a*.
22:23 and threw dust into the *a*,
1 Cor 9:26 not as one who beats the *a*.
14: 9 you will be speaking into the *a*.
Eph 2: 2 prince of the power of the *a*,
1 Th 4:17 to meet the Lord in the *a*.
Rev 9: 2 So the sun and the *a* were
16:17 poured out his bowl into the *a*,

AJAH (2/2) AIAH
Gen 36:24 both *A* and Anah. This was the
1 Chr 1:40 The sons of Zibeon were *A* and

AJALON (KJV) See AIJALON

AKAN (1/1) JAAKAN, JACHAN
Gen 36:27 of Ezer: Bilhan, Zaavan, and *A*.

AKEL (1/1)
Acts 1:19 *A* Dama, that is, Field of

AKKUB (8/8)
1 Chr 3:24 Hodaviah, Eliashib, Pelaiah, *A*,
9:17 gatekeepers were Shallum, *A*,
Ezra 2:42 sons of Talmon, the sons of *A*,
2:45 sons of Hagabah, the sons of *A*,
Neh 7:45 sons of Talmon, the sons of *A*,
8: 7 Bani, Sherebiah, Jamin, *A*,
11:19 Moreover the gatekeepers, *A*,
12:25 and *A* were gatekeepers keeping

AKRABBIM (3/3)
Num 34: 4 side of the Ascent of *A*,
Josh 15: 3 side of the Ascent of *A*,
Judg 1:36 was from the Ascent of *A*,

ALABASTER (4/4)
Esth 1: 6 on a mosaic pavement of *a*,
Mt 26: 7 a woman came to Him having an *a*
Mk 14: 3 a woman came having an *a* flask
Lk 7:37 brought an *a* flask of fragrant

ALAMETH (KJV) See ALEMETH

ALAMMELECH (1/1)
Josh 19:26 *A*, Amad, and Mishal;

ALAMOTH (2/2)
1 Chr 15:20 with strings according to *A*;
Ps 46: the sons of Korah. A Song for *A*.

ALARM (6/6) ALARMED
Num 10: 9 then you shall sound an *a* with
2 Chr 13:12 trumpets to sound the *a*
Jer 4:19 The *a* of war.
49: 2 I will cause to be heard an *a*
Joel 2: 1 And sound an *a* in My holy
Zeph 1:16 A day of trumpet and *a* Against

ALARMED (2/2) ALARM
Mk 16: 5 the right side; and they were *a*.
16: 6 he said to them, "Do not be *a*.

ALAS (25/18)
Num 24:23 *A*! Who shall live when God does
Josh 7: 7 And Joshua said, "*A*,
Judg 6:22 the LORD. So Gideon said, "*A*,
11:35 tore his clothes, and said, "*A*,
1 Ki 13:30 mourned over him, saying, "*A*,
2 Ki 3:10 *A*! For the LORD has called
6: 5 and he cried out and said, "*A*,

6:15 his servant said to him, "*A*,
Isa 1: 4 *A*, sinful nation, A people
Jer 22:18 lament for him, Saying, '*A*,
22:18 'Alas, my brother!' or '*A*,
22:18 lament for him, Saying, '*A*,
22:18 Saying, 'Alas, master!' or '*A*,
30: 7 *A*! For that day is great, So
34: 5 lament for you, saying, "*A*,
Ezek 6:11 stamp your feet, and say, '*A*,
Joel 1:15 *A* for the day! For the day of
Am 5:16 *A*! Alas!' They shall call the
5:16 Alas! *A*!' They shall call the
Rev 18:10 fear of her torment, saying, '*A*,
18:10 her torment, saying, 'Alas, *a*,
18:16 'and saying, '*A*, alas,
18:16 "and saying, 'Alas, *a*,
18:19 and wailing, and saying, '*A*,
18:19 wailing, and saying, 'Alas, *a*,

ALEMETH (4/4)

1 Chr 6:60 *A* with its common-lands, and
7: 8 Abijah, Anathoth, and *A*.
8:36 Jehoaddah; Jehoaddah begot *A*,
9:42 Ahaz begot Jarah; Jarah begot *A*,

ALEXANDER (6/5) ALEXANDRIA, ALEXANDRIAN, ALEXANDRIANS

Mk 15:21 the father of *A* and Rufus, as
Acts 4: 6 priest, Caiaphas, John, and *A*,
19:33 And they drew *A* out of the
19:33 And *A* motioned with his hand,
1 Tim 1:20 of whom are Hymenaeus and *A*,
2 Tim 4:14 *A* the coppersmith did me much

ALEXANDRIA (1/1) ALEXANDRIAN

Acts 18:24 Jew named Apollos, born at *A*,

ALEXANDRIAN (2/2) ALEXANDRIA, ALEXANDRIANS

Acts 27: 6 There the centurion found an *A*
28:11 three months we sailed in an *A*

ALEXANDRIANS (1/1) ALEXANDRIAN

Acts 6: 9 of the Freedmen (Cyrenians, *A*,

ALGUM (3/3) ALMUG

2 Chr 2: 8 send me cedar and cypress and *a*
9:10 brought *a* wood and precious
9:11 king made walkways of the *a*

ALIAH (1/1) ALVAH, ALVAN

1 Chr 1:51 Edom were Chief Timnah, Chief *A*,

ALIAN (1/1) ALVAN

1 Chr 1:40 The sons of Shobal were *A*,

ALIEN (12/12) ALIENATE, ALIENATED, ALIENS

Deut 14:21 you may give it to the *a* who
23: 7 because you were an *a* in his
28:43 The *a* who is among you shall
2 Sam 1:13 "I am the son of an *a*,
Job 15:19 And no *a* passed among them:
19:15 I am an *a* in their sight.
Ps 69: 8 And an *a* to my mother's
Jer 2:21 the degenerate plant of an *a*
3:13 scattered your charms To *a*
19: 4 forsaken Me and made this an *a*
Zech 7:10 The *a* or the poor. Let none
Mal 3: 5 those who turn away an *a*—

ALIENATE (1/1) ALIENATED

Ezek 48:14 they may not *a* this best part

ALIENATED (7/6) ALIENATE

Ezek 23:17 and *a* herself from them.
23:18 Then I *a* Myself from her, As
23:18 As I had *a* Myself from her
23:22 From whom you have *a* yourself,
23:28 hand of those from whom you *a*
Eph 4:18 being *a* from the life of God,
Col 1:21 who once were *a* and enemies in

ALIENS (17/17) ALIEN

Deut 24:14 your brethren or one of the *a*
1 Chr 22: 2 commanded to gather the *a* who
29:15 For we are *a* and pilgrims
2 Chr 2:17 Solomon numbered all the *a* who
Prov 5:10 Lest *a* be filled with your
Isa 25: 5 You will reduce the noise of *a*,
Jer 2:25 No! For I have loved *a*,
5:19 so you shall serve *a* in a land
Lam 5: 2 has been turned over to *a*,
Ezek 28:10 uncircumcised By the hand of *a*;
30:12 is in it, By the hand of *a*.
31:12 'And *a*, the most terrible of
Hos 7: 9 *A* have devoured his strength,
8: 7 *A* would swallow it up.
Joel 3:17 And no *a* shall ever pass
Eph 2:12 being *a* from the commonwealth

Heb 11:34 to flight the armies of the *a*.

ALIGHT (1/1) ALIGHTED, ALIGHTING

Prov 26: 2 curse without cause shall not *a*.

ALIGHTED (1/1) ALIGHT

Judg 4:15 and Sisera *a* from his chariot

ALIGHTING (1/1) ALIGHT

Mt 3:16 descending like a dove and *a*

ALIKE (14/14)

Deut 12:15 of the gazelle and the deer *a*.
12:22 the unclean and the clean *a* may
15:22 and the clean person *a* may
1 Sam 30:24 supplies; they shall share *a*.
Job 21:26 They lie down *a* in the dust,
Ps 139:12 and the light are both *a* to
Prov 17:15 Both of them *a* are an
20:10 measures, They are both *a*,
27:15 And a contentious woman are *a*;
Eccl 9: 2 All things come *a* to all: One
11: 6 Or whether both *a* will be
Isa 46: 5 compare Me, that we should be *a*?
Ezek 10:10 appearance, all four looked *a*—
Rom 14: 5 another esteems every day *a*.

ALIVE (91/89)

Gen 6:19 to keep them *a* with you; they
6:20 come to you to keep them *a*.
7: 3 to keep the species *a* on the
7:23 with him in the ark remained *a*.
43: 7 'Is your father still *a*?
43:27 whom you spoke? Is he still *a*?
43:28 in good health; he is still *a*.
45:26 saying, "Joseph is still *a*,
45:28 Joseph my son is still *a*.
46:30 face, because you are still *a*.
50:20 this day, to save many people *a*.
Ex 1:17 but saved the male children *a*.
1:18 and saved the male children *a*?
1:22 every daughter you shall save *a*.
4:18 see whether they are still *a*.
21:21 if he remains *a* a day or two,
22: 4 the theft is certainly found *a*
Lev 16:10 scapegoat shall be presented *a*
18:18 nakedness while the other is *a*.
Num 14:38 the son of Jephunneh remained *a*,
16:30 and they go down *a* into the
16:33 all those with them went down *a*
31:15 "Have you kept all the women *a*?
31:18 But keep *a* for yourselves all
Deut 4: 4 to the LORD your God are *a*
5: 3 today, all of us who are *a*.
6:24 that He might preserve us *a*,
20:16 nothing that breathes remain *a*,
31:27 while I am yet *a* with you, you
32:39 Me; I kill and I make *a*;
Josh 8:23 But the king of Ai they took *a*,
14:10 behold, the LORD has kept me *a*,
Judg 21:14 women whom they had saved *a* of
1 Sam 2: 6 "The LORD kills and makes *a*;
15: 8 Agag king of the Amalekites *a*,
27: 9 he left neither man nor woman *a*,
27:11 save neither man nor woman *a*,
2 Sam 8: 2 full line those to be kept *a*.
12:18 "Indeed, while the child was *a*,
12:21 for the child while he was *a*,
12:22 said, "While the child was *a*,
18:14 while he was still *a* in the
1 Ki 18: 5 to keep the horses and mules *a*,
20:18 come out for peace, take them *a*;
20:18 come out for war, take them *a*.
20:32 And he said, "Is he still *a*?
21:15 for money; for Naboth is not *a*,
2 Ki 5: 7 "Am I God, to kill and make *a*,
7: 4 the Syrians. If they keep us *a*,
7:12 the city, we shall catch them *a*,
10:14 Take them *a*!" So they took them
10:14 So they took them *a*,
2 Chr 25:12 took captive ten thousand *a*,
Ps 22:29 he who cannot keep himself *a*.
30: 3 the grave; You have kept me *a*,
33:19 And to keep them *a* in famine.
41: 2 preserve him and keep him *a*,
55:15 Let them go down *a* into hell,
124: 3 they would have swallowed us *a*,
Prov 1:12 Let us swallow them *a* like
Eccl 4: 2 than the living who are still *a*.
Isa 7:21 day That a man will keep *a* a
Jer 49:11 I will preserve them *a*;
Ezek 7:13 sold, Though he may still be *a*;
13:18 people, and keep yourselves *a*?
13:19 and keeping people *a* who should
18:27 right, he preserves himself *a*.
Dan 5:19 whomever he wished, he kept *a*;
Mt 27:63 remember, while He was still *a*,
Mk 16:11 when they heard that He was *a*
Lk 15:24 this my son was dead and is *a*
15:32 your brother was dead and is *a*
24:23 of angels who said He was *a*.
Acts 1: 3 He also presented Himself *a*
9:41 and widows, he presented her *a*.
20:12 they brought the young man in *a*,
25:19 whom Paul affirmed to be *a*.
Rom 6:11 but *a* to God in Christ Jesus
6:13 yourselves to God as being *a*
7: 9 I was *a* once without the law,

1 Cor 15:22 in Christ all shall be made *a*.
15:36 what you sow is not made *a*
Eph 2: 1 And you He made *a*,
2: 5 made us *a* together with Christ
Col 2:13 He has made *a* together with
1 Th 4:15 that we who are *a* and remain
4:17 Then we who are *a* and remain
1 Pe 3:18 death in the flesh but made *a*
Rev 1:18 I am *a* forevermore. Amen. And I
3: 1 you have a name that you are *a*,
19:20 These two were cast *a* into the

ALL (5677/4719)

Gen 1:26 over *a* the earth and over every
1:29 which is on the face of *a* the
2: 1 and *a* the host of them, were
2: 2 on the seventh day from *a* His
2: 3 because in it He rested from *a*
2:20 So Adam gave names to *a* cattle,
3:14 You are cursed more than *a*
3:14 And you shall eat dust *A* the
3:17 toil you shall eat of it *A*
3:20 she was the mother of *a* living.
4:21 He was the father of *a* those
5: 5 So *a* the days that Adam lived
5: 8 So *a* the days of Seth were nine
5:11 So *a* the days of Enosh were nine
5:14 So *a* the days of Cainan were
5:17 So *a* the days of Mahalalel were
5:20 So *a* the days of Jared were nine
5:23 So *a* the days of Enoch were
5:27 So *a* the days of Methuselah were
5:31 So *a* the days of Lamech were
6: 2 took wives for themselves of *a*
6:12 for *a* flesh had corrupted their
6:13 The end of *a* flesh has come
6:17 to destroy from under heaven *a*
6:19 of every living thing of *a*
6:21 shall take for yourself of *a*
6:22 according to *a* that God
7: 1 you and *a* your household,
7: 3 species alive on the face of *a*
7: 4 from the face of the earth *a*
7: 5 And Noah did according to *a* that
7:11 on that day *a* the fountains of
7:14 *a* cattle after their kind,
7:15 of *a* flesh in which is the
7:16 male and female of *a* flesh,
7:19 and *a* the high hills under the
7:21 And *a* flesh died that moved on
7:22 *A* in whose nostrils was the
7:22 *a* that was on the dry land,
7:23 So He destroyed *a* living things
8: 1 and *a* the animals that were
8:17 you every living thing of *a*
9: 2 on *a* that move on the earth,
9: 2 and on *a* the fish of the sea.
9: 3 I have given you *a* things, even
9:10 of *a* that go out of the ark,
9:11 Never again shall *a* flesh be
9:15 and every living creature of *a*
9:15 become a flood to destroy *a*
9:16 and every living creature of *a*
9:17 established between Me and *a*
9:29 So *a* the days of Noah were nine
10:21 the father of *a* the children of
10:29 *A* these were the sons of
11: 6 the people are one and they *a*
11: 8 from there over the face of *a*
11: 9 confused the language of *a* the
11: 9 them abroad over the face of *a*
12: 3 And in you *a* the families of
12: 5 and *a* their possessions that
12:20 with his wife and *a* that he
13: 1 he and his wife and *a* that he
13:10 Lot lifted his eyes and saw *a*
13:11 Then Lot chose for himself *a* the
13:15 for *a* the land which you see I
14: 3 *A* these joined together in the
14: 7 and attacked *a* the country of
14:11 Then they took *a* the goods of
14:11 and *a* their provisions, and
14:16 So he brought back *a* the goods,
14:20 And he gave him a tithe of *a*.
15:10 Then he brought *a* these to Him
16:12 dwell in the presence of *a* his
17: 8 *a* the land of Canaan, as an
17:23 *a* who were born in his house
17:23 were born in his house and *a*
17:27 and *a* the men of his house, born
18:18 and *a* the nations of the earth
18:25 Shall not the Judge of *a* the
18:26 then I will spare *a* the place
18:28 would You destroy *a* of the city
19: 4 *a* the people from every
19:25 *a* the plain, all the
19:25 *a* the inhabitants of the
19:28 and toward *a* the land of the
19:31 in to us as is the custom of *a*
20: 7 you and *a* who are yours."
20: 8 called *a* his servants, and told
20: 8 and told *a* these things in
20:16 this vindicates you before *a*
20:18 for the LORD had closed up *a*
21: 6 and *a* who hear will laugh with
21:22 God is with you in *a* that you
22:18 In your seed *a* the nations of
23:10 *a* who entered at the gate of
23:17 and *a* the trees that were in
23:17 which were within *a* the
23:18 before *a* who went in at the

24: 1 LORD had blessed Abraham in **a**
24: 2 who ruled over **a** that he had,
24:10 for **a** his master's goods were
24:20 and drew for **a** his camels.
24:36 and to him he has given **a** that
24:54 him ate and drank and stayed **a**
24:66 And the servant told Isaac **a** the
25: 4 **A** these were the children of
25: 5 And Abraham gave **a** that he had
25:18 He died in the presence of **a**
25:22 If **a** is well, why am I like
25:25 He was like a hairy garment **a**
26: 3 and your descendants I give **a**
26: 4 will give to your descendants **a**
26: 4 and in your seed **a** the nations
26:11 So Abimelech charged **a** his
26:15 Philistines had stopped up **a**
27:33 I ate **a** of it before you
27:37 and **a** his brethren I have given
28:11 place and stayed there **a** night,
28:14 and in you and in your seed **a**
28:22 and of **a** that You give me I
29: 3 Now **a** the flocks would be
29: 8 We cannot until **a** the flocks are
29:13 So he told Laban **a** these
29:22 And Laban gathered together **a**
30:32 Let me pass through **a** your flock
30:32 removing from there **a** the
30:32 and **a** the brown ones among the
30:35 **a** the female goats that were
30:35 and **a** the brown ones among the
30:40 face toward the streaked and **a**
31: 1 Jacob has taken away **a** that was
31: 1 our father's he has acquired **a**
31: 6 And you know that with **a** my
31: 8 then **a** the flocks bore
31: 8 then **a** the flocks bore
31:12 **a** the rams which leap on the
31:12 for I have seen **a** that Laban is
31:16 For **a** these riches which God has
31:18 And he carried away **a** his
31:18 away all his livestock and **a**
31:21 So he fled with **a** that he had.
31:34 And Laban searched **a** about the
31:37 Although you have searched **a** my
31:43 **a** that you see is mine. But
31:54 And they ate bread and stayed **a**
32:10 am not worthy of the least of **a**
32:10 of all the mercies and of **a**
32:19 and **a** who followed the droves,
33: 8 What do you mean by **a** this
33:13 **a** the flock will die.
34:19 He was more honorable than **a**
34:24 And **a** who went out of the gate
34:24 **a** who went out of the gate of
34:25 upon the city and killed **a** the
34:29 and **a** their wealth. All their
34:29 **A** their little ones and their
34:29 and they plundered even **a** that
35: 2 said to his household and to **a**
35: 4 So they gave Jacob **a** the foreign
35: 5 upon the cities that were **a**
35: 6 he and **a** the people who were
36: 6 and **a** the persons of his
36: 6 his cattle and **a** his animals,
36: 6 and **a** his goods which he had
37: 3 loved Joseph more than **a** his
37: 4 father loved him more than **a**
37: 7 and indeed your sheaves stood **a**
37:35 And **a** his sons and all his
37:35 And all his sons and **a** his
39: 3 him and that the LORD made **a**
39: 4 and **a** that he had he put under
39: 5 him overseer of his house and **a**
39: 5 blessing of the LORD was on **a**
39: 6 Thus he left **a** that he had in
39: 8 and he has committed **a** that he
39:22 committed to Joseph's hand **a**
40:17 the uppermost basket were **a**
40:20 that he made a feast for **a** his
41: 8 and he sent and called for **a**
41: 8 the magicians of Egypt and **a**
41:19 as I have never seen in **a** the
41:29 plenty will come throughout **a**
41:30 and **a** the plenty will be
41:35 And let them gather **a** the food
41:37 of Pharaoh and in the eyes of **a**
41:39 as God has shown you **a** this,
41:40 and **a** my people shall be ruled
41:41 I have set you over **a** the land
41:43 So he set him over **a** the
41:44 may lift his hand or foot in **a**
41:45 So Joseph went out over **a** the
41:46 and went throughout **a** the land
41:48 So he gathered up **a** the food of
41:51 For God has made me forget **a** my
41:51 me forget all my toil and **a** my
41:54 The famine was in **a** lands, but
41:54 but in **a** the land of Egypt
41:55 So when **a** the land of Egypt was
41:55 Then Pharaoh said to **a** the
41:56 The famine was over **a** the face
41:56 and Joseph opened **a** the
41:57 So **a** countries came to Joseph in
41:57 the famine was severe in **a**
42: 6 and it was he who sold to **a** the
42:11 We are **a** one man's sons; we
42:17 So he put them **a** together in
42:29 land of Canaan and told him **a**
42:36 **A** these things are against
45: 1 not restrain himself before **a**
45: 8 and lord of **a** his house, and a
45: 8 and a ruler throughout **a** the
45: 9 God has made me lord of **a** Egypt;
45:10 and **a** that you have.
45:11 and **a** that you have, come to
45:13 you shall tell my father of **a**
45:13 and of **a** that you have seen;
45:15 Moreover he kissed **a** his
45:20 for the best of **a** the land of
45:22 He gave to **a** of them, to each
45:26 and he is governor over **a** the
45:27 But when they told him **a** the
46: 1 Israel took his journey with **a**
46: 6 Jacob and **a** his descendants
46: 7 and **a** his descendants he
46:15 **A** the persons, his sons and his
46:22 to Jacob: fourteen persons in **a**.
46:25 to Jacob: seven persons in **a**.
46:26 **A** the persons who went with
46:26 were sixty-six persons in **a**.
46:27 **A** the persons of the house of
46:32 and **a** that they have.'
47: 1 flocks and their herds and **a**
47:12 and **a** his father's household
47:13 Now there was no bread in **a**
47:14 And Joseph gathered up **a** the
47:15 **a** the Egyptians came to Joseph
47:17 with bread in exchange for **a**
47:20 Then Joseph bought **a** the land
48:15 The God who has fed me **a** my
48:16 who has redeemed me from **a**
49:28 **A** these are the twelve tribes
50: 7 and with him went up **a** the
50: 7 and **a** the elders of the land of
50: 8 as well as **a** the house of
50:14 he and his brothers and **a** who
50:15 and may actually repay us for **a**
Ex 1: 5 **A** those who were descendants of
1: 6 **a** his brothers, and all that
1: 6 and **a** that generation.
1:14 and in **a** manner of service in
1:14 **A** their service in which they
1:22 So Pharaoh commanded **a** his
3:15 and this is My memorial to **a**
3:20 My hand and strike Egypt with **a**
4:19 for **a** the men who sought your
4:21 see that you do **a** those wonders
4:28 So Moses told Aaron **a** the words
4:28 and **a** the signs which He had
4:29 went and gathered together **a**
4:30 And Aaron spoke **a** the words
5:12 scattered abroad throughout **a**
5:23 You delivered Your people at **a**.
6:29 to Pharaoh king of Egypt **a**
7: 2 You shall speak **a** that I command
7:19 and over **a** their pools of
7:19 shall be blood throughout **a**
7:20 And **a** the waters that were in
7:21 So there was blood throughout **a**
7:24 So **a** the Egyptians dug all
7:24 So all the Egyptians dug **a**
8: 2 I will smite **a** your territory
8: 4 and on **a** your servants." ' "
8:16 it may become lice throughout **a**
8:17 **A** the dust of the land became
8:17 land became lice throughout **a**
8:24 and into **a** the land of Egypt.
9: 4 So nothing shall die of **a** that
9: 6 and **a** the livestock of Egypt
9: 9 it will become fine dust in **a**
9: 9 on man and beast throughout **a**
9:11 were on the magicians and on **a**
9:14 at this time I will send **a**
9:14 there is none like Me in **a**
9:16 My name may be declared in **a**
9:19 gather your livestock and **a**
9:22 that there may be hail in **a** the
9:24 there was none like it in **a**
9:25 **a** that was in the field, both
10: 6 the houses of **a** your servants,
10: 6 and the houses of **a** the
10:12 **a** that the hail has left."
10:13 an east wind on the land **a**
10:13 on the land all that day and **a**
10:14 And the locusts went up over **a**
10:14 land of Egypt and rested on **a**
10:15 every herb of the land and **a**
10:15 of the field throughout **a** the
10:19 remained not one locust in **a**
10:22 there was thick darkness in **a**
10:23 But **a** the children of Israel
11: 5 and **a** the firstborn in the land
11: 5 and **a** the firstborn of the
11: 6 be a great cry throughout **a**
11: 8 And **a** these your servants shall
11: 8 and **a** the people who follow
11:10 So Moses and Aaron did **a** these
12: 3 Speak to **a** the congregation of
12: 9 nor boiled at **a** with water, but
12:12 and will strike **a** the firstborn
12:12 and against **a** the gods of Egypt
12:20 in **a** your dwellings you shall
12:21 Then Moses called for **a** the
12:29 that the LORD struck **a** the
12:29 and **a** the firstborn of
12:30 **a** his servants, and all the
12:30 and **a** the Egyptians; and there
12:33 We shall **a** be dead."
12:41 it came to pass that **a** the
12:42 a solemn observance for **a** the
12:47 **A** the congregation of Israel
12:48 let **a** his males be circumcised,
12:50 Thus **a** the children of Israel
13: 2 Consecrate to Me **a** the
13: 7 leaven be seen among you in **a**
13:12 shall set apart to the LORD **a**
13:13 And **a** the firstborn of man
13:15 that the LORD killed **a** the
13:15 I sacrifice to the LORD **a**
13:15 but **a** the firstborn of my sons
14: 4 honor over Pharaoh and over **a**
14: 7 and **a** the chariots of Egypt
14: 9 **a** the horses and chariots of
14:17 honor over Pharaoh and over **a**
14:20 did not come near the other **a**
14:21 back by a strong east wind **a**
14:23 **a** Pharaoh's horses, his
14:28 and **a** the army of Pharaoh that
15:15 **A** the inhabitants of Canaan
15:20 and **a** the women went out after
15:26 to His commandments and keep **a**
16: 1 and **a** the congregation of the
16: 6 Then Moses and Aaron said to **a**
16: 9 Say to **a** the congregation of the
16:13 in the morning the dew lay **a**
16:22 And **a** the rulers of the
16:23 and lay up for yourselves **a**
17: 1 Then **a** the congregation of the
18: 1 heard of **a** that God had done
18: 8 Moses told his father-in-law **a**
18: 8 **a** the hardship that had come
18: 9 Then Jethro rejoiced for **a** the
18:11 the LORD is greater than **a**
18:12 And Aaron came with **a** the
18:14 when Moses' father-in-law saw **a**
18:14 and **a** the people stand before
18:21 you shall select from **a** the
18:22 let them judge the people at **a**
18:23 and **a** this people will also go
18:24 of his father-in-law and did **a**
18:25 Moses chose able men out of **a**
18:26 So they judged the people at **a**
19: 5 special treasure to Me above **a**
19: 5 for **a** the earth is Mine.
19: 7 and laid before them **a** these
19: 8 Then **a** the people answered
19: 8 **A** that the LORD has spoken we
19:11 Mount Sinai in the sight of **a**
19:12 set bounds for the people **a**
19:16 so that **a** the people who were
20: 1 And God spoke **a** these words,
20: 9 days you shall labor and do **a**
20:11 and **a** that is in them, and
20:18 Now **a** the people witnessed the
22:23 and they cry at **a** to Me, I
23:13 And in **a** that I have said to
23:17 Three times in the year **a** your
23:22 indeed obey His voice and do **a**
23:27 I will cause confusion among **a**
23:27 and will make **a** your enemies
24: 3 came and told the people **a** the
24: 3 the words of the LORD and **a**
24: 3 And **a** the people answered with
24: 3 **A** the words which the LORD has
24: 4 And Moses wrote **a** the words of
24: 7 **A** that the LORD has said we
24: 8 made with you according to **a**
25: 9 According to **a** that I show you,
25: 9 and the pattern of **a** its
25:11 make on it a molding of gold **a**
25:24 and make a molding of gold **a**
25:25 it a frame of a handbreadth **a**
25:25 a gold molding for the frame **a**
25:36 **a** of it shall be one hammered
25:39 with **a** these utensils.
26: 8 and the eleven curtains shall **a**
26:17 Thus you shall make for **a** the
27: 3 you shall make **a** its utensils
27:17 **A** the pillars around the court
27:19 **A** the utensils of the tabernacle
27:19 of the tabernacle for **a** its
27:19 **a** its pegs, and all the pegs of
27:19 and **a** the pegs of the court,
28: 3 So you shall speak to **a** who
28:31 make the robe of the ephod **a**
28:32 it shall have a woven binding **a**
28:33 **a** around its hem, and bells of
28:33 bells of gold between them **a**
28:34 upon the hem of the robe **a**
28:38 children of Israel hallow in **a**
29:12 and pour **a** the blood beside the
29:13 And you shall take **a** the fat
29:16 its blood and sprinkle it **a**
29:20 and sprinkle the blood **a** around
29:24 and you shall put **a** these in the
29:35 according to **a** that I have
30: 3 its sides **a** around, and its
30: 3 make for it a molding of gold **a**
30:27 the table and **a** its utensils,
30:28 altar of burnt offering with **a**
31: 3 and in **a** manner of
31: 5 and to work in **a** manner of
31: 6 put wisdom in the hearts of **a**
31: 6 that they may make **a** that I
31: 7 and **a** the furniture of the
31: 8 the pure gold lampstand with **a**
31: 9 altar of burnt offering with **a**
31:11 According to **a** that I have
32: 3 So **a** the people broke off the
32:13 and **a** this land that I have
32:26 And **a** the sons of Levi
33: 8 that **a** the people rose, and
33:10 **A** the people saw the pillar of
33:10 and **a** the people rose and
33:16 from **a** the people who are upon

33:19 I will make *a* My goodness pass
34: 3 let no man be seen throughout *a*
34:10 Before *a* your people I will do
34:10 as have not been done in *a* the
34:10 and *a* the people among whom you
34:19 *A* that open the womb are Mine,
34:20 *A* the firstborn of your sons
34:23 Three times in the year *a* your
34:30 So when Aaron and *a* the children
34:31 and Aaron and *a* the rulers of
34:32 Afterward *a* the children of
34:32 he gave them as commandments *a*
35: 1 Then Moses gathered *a* the
35: 4 And Moses spoke to *a* the
35:10 *A* who are gifted artisans
35:10 you shall come and make *a* that
35:13 *a* its utensils, and the
35:16 *a* its utensils, and the laver
35:20 And *a* the congregation of the
35:21 for *a* its service, and for the
35:22 *a* jewelry of gold, that is,
35:25 *A* the women WHO were gifted
35:26 And *a* the women whose heart
35:29 *a* the men and women whose
35:29 to bring material for *a* kinds
35:31 in knowledge and *a* manner of
35:33 and to work in *a* manner of
35:35 filled them with skill to do *a*
36: 1 to know how to do *a* manner of
36: 1 shall do according to *a* that
36: 3 And they received from Moses *a*
36: 4 Then *a* the craftsmen who were
36: 4 the craftsmen who were doing *a*
36: 7 they had was sufficient for *a*
36: 8 Then *a* the gifted artisans
36: 9 the curtains were *a* the same
36:22 Thus he made for *a* the boards
37: 2 and made a molding of gold *a*
37:11 and made a molding of gold *a*
37:12 made a frame of a handbreadth *a*
37:12 of gold for the frame *a* around
37:22 *a* of it was one hammered piece
37:24 with *a* its utensils.
37:26 its sides *a* around, and its
37:26 made for it a molding of gold *a*
38: 3 He made *a* the utensils for the
38: 3 *a* its utensils he made of
38:16 *A* the hangings of the court all
38:16 All the hangings of the court *a*
38:17 and *a* the pillars of the court
38:20 *A* the pegs of the tabernacle,
38:20 and of the court *a* around,
38:22 made *a* that the LORD had
38:24 *A* the gold that was used in all
38:24 the gold that was used in *a*
38:30 and *a* the utensils for the
38:31 the sockets for the court *a*
38:31 *a* the pegs for the tabernacle,
38:31 and *a* the pegs for the court
38:31 all the pegs for the court *a*
39:22 ephod of woven work, *a* of blue.
39:23 with a woven binding *a* around
39:25 on the hem of the robe *a*
39:26 *a* around the hem of the robe to
39:32 Thus *a* the work of the
39:32 of Israel did according to *a*
39:33 the tent and *a* its furnishings:
39:36 *a* its utensils, and the
39:37 *a* its utensils, and the oil for
39:39 and *a* its utensils; the laver
39:40 *a* the utensils for the service
39:42 According to *a* that the LORD
39:42 so the children of Israel did *a*
39:43 Then Moses looked over *a* the
40: 8 You shall set up the court *a*
40: 9 and anoint the tabernacle and *a*
40: 9 and you shall hallow it and *a*
40:10 of the burnt offering and *a*
40:16 according to *a* that the LORD
40:33 And he raised up the court *a*
40:36 of Israel would go onward in *a*
40:38 in the sight of *a* the house of
40:38 throughout *a* their journeys.
Lev 1: 5 blood and sprinkle the blood *a*
1: 9 And the priest shall burn *a* on
1:11 shall sprinkle its blood *a*
1:13 the priest shall bring it *a*
2: 2 of fine flour and oil with *a*
2:13 With *a* your offerings you shall
2:16 with *a* the frankincense, as an
3: 2 shall sprinkle the blood *a*
3: 3 that covers the entrails and *a*
3: 8 sons shall sprinkle its blood *a*
3: 9 that covers the entrails and *a*
3:13 shall sprinkle its blood *a*
3:14 that covers the entrails and *a*
3:16 *a* the fat is the LORD's.
3:17 your generations in *a* your
4: 8 He shall take from it *a* the fat
4: 8 that covers the entrails and *a*
4:11 But the bull's hide and *a* its
4:19 He shall take *a* the fat from it
4:26 And he shall burn *a* its fat on
4:30 and pour *a* the remaining
4:31 He shall remove *a* its fat, as
4:34 and pour *a* the remaining
4:35 He shall remove *a* its fat, as
6: 5 or *a* that about which he has
6: 9 on the hearth upon the altar *a*
6:15 and *a* the frankincense which
6:18 *A* the males among the children
6:29 *A* the males among the priests
7: 2 its blood he shall sprinkle *a*
7: 3 And he shall offer from it *a* its
7: 9 that is baked in the oven and *a*
7:10 shall belong to *a* the sons of
7:18 peace offering is eaten at *a*
7:19 *a* who are clean may eat of it.
8: 3 and gather *a* the congregation
8:10 anointed the tabernacle and *a*
8:11 anointed the altar and *a* its
8:15 on the horns of the altar *a*
8:16 Then he took *a* the fat that was
8:19 Then he sprinkled the blood *a*
8:24 And Moses sprinkled the blood *a*
8:25 *a* the fat that was on the
8:27 and he put *a* these in Aaron's
8:36 So Aaron and his sons did *a* the
9: 5 And *a* the congregation drew
9:12 which he sprinkled *a* around on
9:18 which he sprinkled *a* around on
9:23 of the LORD appeared to *a* the
9:24 When *a* the people saw it, they
10: 3 And before *a* the people I
10: 6 and wrath come upon *a* the
10:11 teach the children of Israel *a*
11: 2 which you may eat among *a* the
11: 9 These you may eat of *a* that
11:10 But *a* in the seas or in the
11:10 *a* that move in the water or any
11:20 *A* flying insects that creep on
11:20 insects that creep on *a* fours
11:21 insect that creeps on *a* fours:
11:23 But *a* other flying insects
11:27 among *a* kinds of animals that
11:27 kinds of animals that go on *a*
11:31 are unclean to you among *a*
11:42 whatever goes on *a* fours, or
11:42 whatever has many feet among *a*
13: 7 But if the scab should at *a*
13:12 And if leprosy breaks out *a*
13:12 and the leprosy covers *a* the
13:13 if the leprosy has covered *a*
13:13 It has *a* turned white. He is
13:22 and if it should at *a* spread
13:27 If it has at *a* spread over the
13:35 But if the scale should at *a*
13:46 *A* the days he has the sore he
14: 8 shave off *a* his hair, and wash
14: 9 seventh day he shall shave *a*
14: 9 *a* his hair he shall shave off.
14:36 that *a* that is in the house
14:41 *a* around, and the dust that
14:45 and *a* the plaster of the house,
14:46 he who goes into the house at *a*
15:16 then he shall wash *a* his body
15:24 if any man lies with her at *a*,
15:25 *a* the days of her unclean
15:26 Every bed on which she lies *a*
16:16 for *a* their sins; and so he
16:17 and for *a* the assembly of
16:18 it on the horns of the altar *a*
16:21 over it *a* the iniquities
16:21 and *a* their transgressions,
16:21 concerning *a* their sins,
16:22 goat shall bear on itself *a*
16:29 your souls, and do no work at *a*,
16:30 that you may be clean from *a*
16:33 for the priests and for *a* the
16:34 for *a* their sins, once a
17: 2 and to *a* the children of
17:14 for it is the life of *a* flesh.
17:14 for the life of *a* flesh is its
18:24 for by *a* these the nations are
18:27 (for *a* these abominations the
19: 2 Speak to *a* the congregation of
19: 7 And if it is eaten at *a* on the
19:13 shall not remain with you *a*
19:20 and who has not at *a* been
19:23 and have planted *a* kinds of
19:24 But in the fourth year *a* its
19:37 'Therefore you shall observe *a*
19:37 observe all My statutes and *a*
20: 5 and *a* who prostitute themselves
20:22 You shall therefore keep *a* My
20:22 keep all My statutes and *a* My
20:23 for they commit *a* these things,
21:24 and to *a* the children of
22: 3 Whoever of *a* your descendants
22:18 and to *a* the children of
23: 3 the Sabbath of the LORD in *a*
23:14 your generations in *a* your
23:21 be a statute forever in *a*
23:31 your generations in *a* your
23:38 besides *a* your vows, and
23:38 and besides *a* your freewill
23:42 *A* who are native Israelites
24:14 then let *a* who heard him lay
24:14 and let *a* the congregation
24:16 *A* the congregation shall
25: 7 *a* its produce shall be for food.
25: 9 trumpet to sound throughout *a*
25:10 proclaim liberty throughout *a*
25:10 throughout all the land to *a*
25:24 And in *a* the land of your
26:14 and do not observe *a* these
26:15 so that you do not perform *a* My
26:18 And after *a* this, if you do not
26:27 And after *a* this, if you do not
26:44 Yet for *a* that, when they are in
27: 9 *a* that anyone gives to the
27:10 and if he at *a* exchanges animal
27:13 But if he wants at *a* to redeem
27:25 And *a* your valuations shall be
27:28 may devote to the LORD of *a*
27:30 And *a* the tithe of the land,
27:31 If a man wants at *a* to redeem
27:33 it; and if he exchanges it at *a*,
Num 1: 2 Take a census of *a* the
1: 3 *a* who are able to go to war
1:18 and they assembled *a* the
1:20 *a* who were able to go to
1:22 *a* who were able to go to
1:24 *a* who were able to go to
1:26 *a* who were able to go to
1:28 *a* who were able to go to
1:30 *a* who were able to go to
1:32 *a* who were able to go to
1:34 *a* who were able to go to
1:36 *a* who were able to go to
1:38 *a* who were able to go to
1:40 *a* who were able to go to
1:42 *a* who were able to go to
1:45 So *a* who were numbered of the
1:45 *a* who were able to go to
1:46 *a* who were numbered were six
1:50 over *a* its furnishings, and
1:50 and over *a* things that belong
1:50 carry the tabernacle and *a* its
1:54 according to *a* that the LORD
2: 9 *A* who were numbered according to
2:16 *A* who were numbered according to
2:24 *A* who were numbered according to
2:31 *A* who were numbered of the
2:32 *A* who were numbered according
2:34 of Israel did according to *a*
3: 8 Also they shall attend to *a* the
3:13 because *a* the firstborn are
3:13 On the day that I struck *a* the
3:13 I sanctified to Myself *a* the
3:22 according to the number of *a*
3:26 according to *a* the work
3:28 According to the number of *a* the
3:31 and *a* the work relating to
3:34 according to the number of *a*
3:36 *a* the work relating to them,
3:37 and the pillars of the court *a*
3:39 *A* who were numbered of the
3:39 *a* the males from a month old
3:40 Number *a* the firstborn males of
3:41 instead of *a* the firstborn among
3:41 of the Levites instead of *a*
3:42 So Moses numbered *a* the
3:43 And *a* the firstborn males,
3:45 Take the Levites instead of *a*
4: 3 *a* who enter the service to do
4: 9 and *a* its oil vessels, with
4:10 Then they shall put it with *a*
4:12 Then they shall take *a* the
4:14 They shall put on it *a* its
4:14 and *a* the utensils of the
4:15 covering the sanctuary and *a*
4:16 the oversight of *a* the
4:16 of *a* that is in it, with the
4:23 *a* who enter to perform the
4:26 *a* the furnishings for their
4:26 for their service and *a* that
4:27 and his sons shall assign *a*
4:27 *a* their tasks and all their
4:27 all their tasks and *a* their
4:27 And you shall appoint to them *a*
4:31 is what they must carry as *a*
4:32 with *a* their furnishings and
4:32 all their furnishings and *a*
4:33 as *a* their service for the
4:37 *a* who might serve in the
4:41 of *a* who might serve in the
4:46 *A* who were numbered of the
5: 9 Every offering of *a* the holy
5:30 and the priest shall execute *a*
6: 4 *A* the days of his separation he
6: 5 *A* the days of the vow of his
6: 6 *A* the days that he separates
6: 8 *A* the days of his separation he
7: 1 it and consecrated it and *a*
7: 1 and the altar and *a* its
7:85 *A* the silver of the vessels
7:86 *a* the gold of the pans weighed
7:87 *A* the oxen for the burnt
7:88 And *a* the oxen for the sacrifice
8: 7 and let them shave *a* their
8:16 them for Myself instead of *a*
8:16 the firstborn of *a* the children
8:17 For *a* the firstborn among the
8:17 on the day that I struck *a* the
8:18 taken the Levites instead of *a*
8:20 Thus Moses and Aaron and *a* the
8:20 according to *a* that the LORD
9: 3 According to *a* its rites and
9: 5 according to *a* that the LORD
9:12 According to *a* the ordinances
10: 3 *a* the congregation shall gather
10:25 of Dan (the rear guard of *a*
11: 6 there is nothing at *a* except
11:11 You have laid the burden of *a*
11:12 Did I conceive *a* these people?
11:13 am I to get meat to give to *a*
11:13 For they weep *a* over me,
11:14 I am not able to bear *a* these
11:22 Or shall *a* the fish of the sea
11:29 that *a* the LORD's people were
11:31 *a* around the camp, and about
11:32 And the people stayed up *a* that
11:32 *a* night, and all the next day,
11:32 and *a* the next day, and
11:32 them out for themselves *a*

12: 3 more than *a* men who were on
12: 7 He is faithful in *a* My house.
13: 3 *a* of them men who were heads
13:26 back to Moses and Aaron and *a*
13:26 back word to them and to *a* the
13:32 and *a* the people whom we saw in
14: 1 So *a* the congregation lifted up
14: 2 And *a* the children of Israel
14: 5 fell on their faces before *a*
14: 7 and they spoke to *a* the
14:10 And *a* the congregation said to
14:10 tabernacle of meeting before *a*
14:11 with *a* the signs which I have
14:21 *a* the earth shall be filled
14:22 because *a* these men who have
14:29 *a* of you who were numbered,
14:35 I will surely do so to *a* this
14:36 who returned and made *a* the
14:39 Moses told these words to *a*
15:13 *A* who are native-born shall do
15:22 and do not observe *a* these
15:23 *a* that the LORD has commanded
15:26 because *a* the people did it
15:33 and to *a* the congregation.
15:35 *a* the congregation shall stone
15:36 *a* the congregation brought him
15:39 may look upon it and remember *a*
15:40 that you may remember and do *a*
16: 3 for *a* the congregation is
16: 5 and he spoke to Korah and *a* his
16: 6 Korah and *a* your company;
16:10 you and *a* your brethren, the
16:11 Therefore you and *a* your company
16:16 you and *a* your company be
16:19 And Korah gathered *a* the
16:19 of the LORD appeared to *a* the
16:22 the God of the spirits of *a*
16:22 and You be angry with *a* the
16:26 lest you be consumed in *a* their
16:28 the LORD has sent me to do *a*
16:29 these men die naturally like *a*
16:29 by the common fate of *a* men,
16:30 and swallows them up with *a*
16:31 as he finished speaking *a* these
16:32 with their households and *a* the
16:32 with *a* their goods.
16:33 So they and *a* those with them
16:34 Then *a* Israel who were around
16:41 On the next day *a* the
17: 2 *a* their leaders according to
17: 9 Then Moses brought out *a* the
17: 9 from before the LORD to *a* the
17:12 die, we perish, we *a* perish!
17:13 Shall we *a* utterly die?"
18: 3 attend to your needs and *a* the
18: 4 for *a* the work of the
18: 8 *a* the holy gifts of the
18:11 with *a* the wave offerings of
18:12 *A* the best of the oil, all the
18:12 *a* the best of the new wine and
18:15 that first opens the womb of *a*
18:19 *A* the heave offerings of the
18:21 given the children of Levi *a*
18:28 offering to the LORD from *a*
18:29 Of *a* your gifts you shall offer
18:29 from *a* the best of them, the
19:14 *A* who come into the tent and
19:14 who come into the tent and *a*
19:18 on *a* the vessels, on the
20:14 You know *a* the hardship that has
20:27 to Mount Hor in the sight of *a*
20:29 Now when *a* the congregation saw
20:29 *a* the house of Israel mourned
21:17 O well! *A* of you sing to it—
21:23 So Sihon gathered *a* his people
21:25 So Israel took *a* these cities,
21:25 and Israel dwelt in *a* the
21:25 in Heshbon and in *a* its
21:26 and had taken *a* his land from
21:33 he and *a* his people, to battle
21:34 with *a* his people and his land;
21:35 and *a* his people, until there
22: 2 Balak the son of Zippor saw *a*
22:38 have I any power at *a* to say
23: 6 he and *a* the princes of Moab.
23:13 them, and shall not see them *a*;
23:25 "Neither curse them at *a*,
23:25 nor bless them at *a*!"
23:26 *A* that the LORD speaks, that I
24:17 And destroy *a* the sons of
25: 4 Take *a* the leaders of the people
25: 6 of Moses and in the sight of *a*
26: 2 Take a census of *a* the
26: 2 *a* who are able to go to war in
26:43 *A* the families of the
27: 2 and before the leaders and *a*
27:16 the God of the spirits of *a*
27:19 the priest and before *a* the
27:20 that *a* the congregation of the
27:21 he and *a* the children of Israel
27:21 *a* the congregation."
27:22 the priest and before *a* the
30: 2 he shall do according to *a* that
30: 4 then *a* her vows shall stand,
30:11 then *a* her vows shall stand,
30:14 then he confirms *a* her vows or
30:14 he confirms all her vows or *a*
31: 4 thousand from each tribe of *a*
31: 7 and they killed *a* the males.
31: 9 and took as spoil *a* their
31: 9 *a* their flocks, and all their
31: 9 and *a* their goods.
31:10 They also burned with fire *a* the
31:10 and *a* their forts.
31:11 And they took *a* the spoil and
31:11 they took all the spoil and *a*
31:13 and *a* the leaders of the
31:15 Have you kept *a* the women alive?
31:18 keep alive for yourselves *a*
31:23 But *a* that cannot endure fire
31:27 and *a* the congregation.
31:30 from *a* the livestock, and give
31:35 thousand persons in *a*,
31:51 *a* the fashioned ornaments.
31:52 And *a* the gold of the offering
32:13 until *a* the generation that had
32:15 and you will destroy *a* these
32:21 and *a* your armed men cross over
32:26 and *a* our livestock will be
33: 3 boldness in the sight of *a* the
33: 4 the Egyptians were burying *a*
33:52 then you shall drive out *a* the
33:52 destroy *a* their engraved
33:52 destroy *a* their molded images,
33:52 and demolish *a* their high
35: 3 and for *a* their animals.
35: 4 outward a thousand cubits *a*
35: 7 So *a* the cities you will give to
35:29 your generations in *a* your
Deut 1: 1 words which Moses spoke to *a*
1: 3 of Israel according to *a* that
1: 7 to *a* the neighboring places in
1:18 I commanded you at that time *a*
1:19 and went through *a* that great
1:30 according to *a* He did for you
1:31 in *a* the way that you went
1:32 for *a* that, you did not believe
2: 7 your God has blessed you in *a*
2:14 until *a* the generation of the
2:16 when *a* the men of war had
2:32 Then Sihon and *a* his people came
2:33 and *a* his people.
2:34 We took *a* his cities at that
2:36 the LORD our God delivered *a*
3: 1 he and *a* his people, to battle
3: 2 for I have delivered him and *a*
3: 3 with *a* his people, and we
3: 4 And we took *a* his cities at that
3: 4 *a* the region of Argob, the
3: 5 *A* these cities were fortified
3: 7 But *a* the livestock and the
3:10 *a* the cities of the plain, all
3:10 *a* Gilead, and all Bashan, as
3:10 and *a* Bashan, as far as Salcah
3:13 and *a* Bashan, the kingdom of
3:13 (*A* the region of Argob, with
3:13 with *a* Bashan, was called the
3:14 the son of Manasseh took *a* the
3:18 *A* you men of valor shall cross
3:21 Your eyes have seen *a* that the
3:21 so will the LORD do to *a* the
4: 3 has destroyed from among you *a*
4: 6 of the peoples who will hear *a*
4: 8 judgments as are in *a* this law
4: 9 they depart from your heart *a*
4:10 they may learn to fear Me *a*
4:19 *a* the host of heaven, you feel
4:19 LORD your God has given to *a*
4:29 Him if you seek Him with *a*
4:29 with all your heart and with *a*
4:30 and *a* these things come upon
4:34 according to *a* that the LORD
4:40 your God is giving you for *a*
4:49 and *a* the plain on the east side
5: 1 And Moses called *a* Israel, and
5: 3 *a* of us who are alive.
5:13 days you shall labor and do *a*
5:22 words the LORD spoke to *a*
5:23 *a* the heads of your tribes and
5:26 For who is there of *a* flesh
5:27 You go near and hear *a* that the
5:27 and tell us *a* that the LORD
5:28 They are right in *a* that they
5:29 fear Me and always keep *a* My
5:31 and I will speak to you *a* the
5:33 You shall walk in *a* the ways
6: 2 to keep *a* His statutes and His
6: 2 *a* the days of your life, and
6: 5 love the LORD your God with *a*
6: 5 with *a* your soul, and with all
6: 5 and with *a* your strength.
6:11 houses full of *a* good things,
6:14 gods of the peoples who are *a*
6:19 to cast out *a* your enemies from
6:22 and *a* his household.
6:24 LORD commanded us to observe *a*
6:25 if we are careful to observe *a*
7: 6 a special treasure above *a* the
7: 7 for you were the least of *a*
7:14 You shall be blessed above *a*
7:15 LORD will take away from you *a*
7:15 but will lay them on *a* those
7:16 And you shall destroy *a* the
7:18 God did to Pharaoh and to *a*
7:19 the LORD your God do to *a* the
8: 2 the LORD your God led you *a*
8:13 and *a* that you have is
9:10 and on them were *a* the words
9:18 because of *a* your sin which you
10:12 to walk in *a* His ways and to
10:12 the LORD your God with *a* your
10:12 with all your heart and with *a*
10:14 also the earth with *a* that is
10:15 you above *a* peoples, as it is
11: 3 and to *a* his land;
11: 6 and *a* the substance that was
11: 6 in the midst of *a* Israel—
11:13 your God and serve Him with *a*
11:13 with all your heart and with *a*
11:22 For if you carefully keep *a*
11:22 to walk in *a* His ways, and to
11:23 the LORD will drive out *a*
11:25 you and the fear of you upon *a*
11:32 shall be careful to observe *a*
12: 1 *a* the days that you live on the
12: 2 You shall utterly destroy *a* the
12: 5 out of *a* your tribes, to put
12: 7 and you shall rejoice in *a* to
12: 8 You shall not at *a* do as we are
12:10 and He gives you rest from *a*
12:11 There you shall bring *a* that I
12:11 and *a* your choice offerings
12:14 and there you shall do *a* that I
12:15 and eat meat within *a* your
12:18 before the LORD your God in *a*
12:28 Observe and obey *a* these words
13: 3 love the LORD your God with *a*
13: 3 with all your heart and with *a*
13: 7 gods of the people which are *a*
13: 9 and afterward the hand of *a* the
13:11 So *a* Israel shall hear and fear,
13:15 *a* that is in it and its
13:16 And you shall gather *a* its
13:16 burn with fire the city and *a*
13:18 to keep *a* His commandments
14: 2 a special treasure above *a* the
14: 9 These you may eat of *a* that
14: 9 you may eat *a* that have fins
14:11 *A* clean birds you may eat.
14:20 You may eat *a* clean birds.
14:22 You shall truly tithe *a* the
14:29 your God may bless you in *a*
15: 5 to observe with care *a* these
15:10 your God will bless you in *a*
15:10 you in all your works and in *a*
15:18 your God will bless you in *a*
15:19 *A* the firstborn males that come
16: 3 out of the land of Egypt *a* the
16: 4 shall be seen among you in *a*
16:15 your God will bless you in *a*
16:15 in all your produce and in *a*
16:16 Three times a year *a* your males
16:18 judges and officers in *a* your
17: 7 and afterward the hands of *a*
17:10 be careful to do according to *a*
17:13 And *a* the people shall hear and
17:14 will set a king over me like *a*
17:19 and he shall read it *a* the days
17:19 God and be careful to observe *a*
18: 1 *a* the tribe of Levi—shall have
18: 5 God has chosen him out of *a*
18: 6 from where he dwells among *a*
18: 6 and comes with *a* the desire of
18: 7 name of the LORD his God as *a*
18:12 For *a* who do these things are
18:16 according to *a* you desired of
18:18 and He shall speak to them *a*
19: 9 and if you keep *a* these
20:11 then *a* the people who are
20:14 and *a* that is in the city, all
20:14 *a* its spoil, you shall plunder
20:15 Thus you shall do to *a* the
20:18 teach you to do according to *a*
21: 6 And *a* the elders of that city
21:17 him a double portion of *a* that
21:21 Then *a* the men of his city shall
21:21 and *a* Israel shall hear and
22: 5 for *a* who do so are an
22:19 he cannot divorce her *a* his
22:29 be permitted to divorce her *a*
23: 6 peace nor their prosperity *a*
23:20 your God may bless you in *a* to
24: 8 observe and do according to *a*
24:19 your God may bless you in *a*
25:16 For *a* who do such things, all
25:16 *a* who behave unrighteously,
25:18 *a* the stragglers at your rear,
25:19 you rest from your enemies *a*
26: 2 take some of the first of *a*
26:12 have finished laying aside *a*
26:13 according to *a* Your
26:14 and have done according to *a*
26:16 careful to observe them with *a*
26:16 with all your heart and with *a*
26:18 that you should keep *a* His
26:19 He will set you high above *a*
27: 1 Keep *a* the commandments which I
27: 3 You shall write on them *a* the
27: 8 very plainly on the stones *a*
27: 9 spoke to *a* Israel, saying,
27:14 with a loud voice and say to *a*
27:15 And *a* the people shall answer
27:16 And *a* the people shall say,
27:17 And *a* the people shall say,
27:18 And *a* the people shall say,
27:19 And *a* the people shall say,
27:20 And *a* the people shall say,
27:21 And *a* the people shall say,
27:22 And *a* the people shall say,
27:23 And *a* the people shall say,
27:24 And *a* the people shall say,
27:25 And *a* the people shall say,
27:26 the one who does not confirm *a*
27:26 And *a* the people shall say,
28: 1 to observe carefully *a* His
28: 1 God will set you high above *a*

28: 2 And ***a*** these blessings shall come
28: 8 in your storehouses and in ***a***
28:10 Then ***a*** peoples of the earth
28:12 and to bless ***a*** the work of your
28:15 to observe carefully ***a*** His
28:15 that ***a*** these curses will come
28:20 and rebuke in ***a*** that you set
28:25 shall become troublesome to ***a***
28:26 carcasses shall be food for ***a***
28:32 fail with longing for them ***a***
28:37 and a byword among ***a*** nations
28:40 have olive trees throughout ***a***
28:42 Locusts shall consume ***a*** your
28:45 Moreover ***a*** these curses shall
28:52 They shall besiege you at ***a*** your
28:52 come down throughout ***a*** your
28:52 and they shall besiege you at ***a***
28:52 at all your gates throughout ***a***
28:55 enemy shall distress you at ***a***
28:57 enemy shall distress you at ***a***
28:58 you do not carefully observe ***a***
28:60 He will bring back on you ***a***
28:64 LORD will scatter you among ***a***
29: 2 Now Moses called ***a*** Israel and
29: 2 You have seen ***a*** that the LORD
29: 2 to Pharaoh and to ***a*** his
29: 2 to all his servants and to ***a***
29: 9 that you may prosper in ***a*** that
29:10 ***A*** of you stand today before the
29:10 ***a*** the men of Israel,
29:21 would separate him from ***a*** the
29:21 according to ***a*** the curses of
29:24 ***A*** nations would say, 'Why has
29:29 that we may do ***a*** the words of
30: 1 when ***a*** these things come upon
30: 1 you call them to mind among ***a***
30: 2 according to ***a*** that I command
30: 2 with ***a*** your heart and with all
30: 2 with all your heart and with ***a***
30: 3 and gather you again from ***a*** the
30: 6 love the LORD your God with ***a***
30: 6 with all your heart and with ***a***
30: 7 the LORD your God will put ***a***
30: 8 the voice of the LORD and do ***a***
30: 9 God will make you abound in ***a***
30:10 to the LORD your God with ***a***
30:10 with all your heart and with ***a***
31: 1 went and spoke these words to ***a***
31: 7 said to him in the sight of ***a***
31: 9 and to ***a*** the elders of Israel.
31:11 when ***a*** Israel comes to appear
31:11 shall read this law before ***a***
31:12 God and carefully observe ***a***
31:18 face in that day because of ***a***
31:28 Gather to me ***a*** the elders of
31:30 spoke in the hearing of ***a*** the
32: 4 For ***a*** His ways are justice,
32:27 is not the LORD who has done ***a***
32:44 the son of Nun and spoke ***a*** the
32:45 Moses finished speaking ***a*** these
32:45 speaking all these words to ***a***
32:46 Set your hearts on ***a*** the words
32:46 ***a*** the words of this law.
33: 3 ***A*** His saints are in Your
33: 5 ***A*** the tribes of Israel
33:12 Who shelters him ***a*** the day
34: 1 And the LORD showed him ***a*** the
34: 2 ***a*** Naphtali and the land of
34: 2 ***a*** the land of Judah as far as
34:11 in ***a*** the signs and wonders which
34:11 before ***a*** his servants, and in
34:11 and in ***a*** his land,
34:12 and by ***a*** that mighty power and
34:12 by all that mighty power and ***a***
34:12 performed in the sight of ***a***

Josh 1: 2 you and ***a*** this people, to the
1: 4 ***a*** the land of the Hittites, and
1: 5 able to stand before you ***a***
1: 7 observe to do according to ***a***
1: 8 observe to do according to ***a***
1:14 ***a*** your mighty men of valor, and
1:16 ***A*** that you command us we will
1:17 Just as we heeded Moses in ***a***
1:18 in ***a*** that you command him,
2: 3 they have come to search out ***a***
2: 9 and that ***a*** the inhabitants of
2:13 and ***a*** that they have, and
2:18 and ***a*** your father's household
2:22 The pursuers sought them ***a***
2:23 and told him ***a*** that had
2:24 the LORD has delivered ***a*** the
2:24 for indeed ***a*** the inhabitants of
3: 1 he and ***a*** the children of
3: 7 to exalt you in the sight of ***a***
3:11 the covenant of the Lord of ***a***
3:13 the Lord of ***a*** the earth, shall
3:15 (for the Jordan overflows ***a***
3:17 and ***a*** Israel crossed over on
3:17 until ***a*** the people had crossed
4: 1 when ***a*** the people had
4:10 according to ***a*** that Moses had
4:11 when ***a*** the people had
4:14 Joshua in the sight of ***a***
4:14 ***a*** the days of his life.
4:18 to their place and overflowed ***a***
4:24 that ***a*** the peoples of the earth
5: 1 when ***a*** the kings of the
5: 1 and ***a*** the kings of the
5: 4 ***A*** the people who came out of
5: 4 ***a*** the men of war, had died in
5: 5 For ***a*** the people who came out
5: 5 but ***a*** the people born in the
5: 6 till ***a*** the people who were
5: 8 had finished circumcising ***a***
6: 3 ***a*** you men of war; you shall go
6: 3 you shall go ***a*** around the city
6: 5 that ***a*** the people shall shout
6:17 it and ***a*** who are in it.
6:17 she and ***a*** who are with her in
6:18 by ***a*** means abstain from the
6:19 But ***a*** the silver and gold, and
6:21 And they utterly destroyed ***a***
6:22 bring out the woman and ***a*** that
6:23 and ***a*** that she had. So they
6:23 So they brought out ***a*** her
6:24 But they burned the city and ***a***
6:25 and ***a*** that she had. So she
6:27 his fame spread throughout ***a***
7: 3 Do not let ***a*** the people go up,
7: 3 Do not weary ***a*** the people
7: 7 people over the Jordan at ***a***—
7: 9 For the Canaanites and ***a*** the
7:15 he and ***a*** that he has, because
7:23 them to Joshua and to ***a*** the
7:24 and ***a*** Israel with him, took
7:24 and ***a*** that he had, and they
7:25 So ***a*** Israel stoned him with
8: 1 take ***a*** the people of war with
8: 3 and ***a*** the people of war, to go
8: 4 but ***a*** of you be ready.
8: 5 Then I and ***a*** the people who are
8:11 And ***a*** the people of war who
8:13 ***a*** the army that was on the
8:14 he and ***a*** his people, at an
8:15 And Joshua and ***a*** Israel made as
8:16 So ***a*** the people who were in Ai
8:21 Now when Joshua and ***a*** Israel saw
8:24 had made an end of slaying ***a***
8:24 and when they ***a*** had fallen by
8:24 that ***a*** the Israelites returned
8:25 So it was that ***a*** who fell that
8:25 ***a*** the people of Ai.
8:26 he had utterly destroyed ***a*** the
8:33 Then ***a*** Israel, with their elders
8:34 And afterward he read ***a*** the
8:34 according to ***a*** that is written
8:35 There was not a word of ***a*** that
8:35 Joshua did not read before ***a***
9: 1 And it came to pass when ***a*** the
9: 1 and in the lowland and in ***a***
9: 5 and ***a*** the bread of their
9: 9 and ***a*** that He did in Egypt,
9:10 and ***a*** that He did to the two
9:11 Therefore our elders and ***a*** the
9:18 And ***a*** the congregation
9:19 Then ***a*** the rulers said to all
9:19 Then all the rulers said to ***a***
9:21 and water carriers for ***a*** the
9:24 His servant Moses to give you ***a***
9:24 and to destroy ***a*** the
10: 2 and ***a*** its men were mighty.
10: 5 they and ***a*** their armies, and
10: 6 for ***a*** the kings of the Amorites
10: 7 he and ***a*** the people of war with
10: 7 and ***a*** the mighty men of valor.
10: 9 having marched ***a*** night from
10:15 and ***a*** Israel with him, to the
10:21 And ***a*** the people returned to the
10:24 that Joshua called for ***a*** the
10:25 for thus the LORD will do to ***a***
10:28 —***a*** the people who were in it.
10:29 and ***a*** Israel with him, to
10:30 he struck it and ***a*** the people
10:31 and ***a*** Israel with him, to
10:32 and struck it and ***a*** the people
10:32 according to ***a*** that he had done
10:34 and ***a*** Israel with him; and they
10:35 ***a*** the people who were in it he
10:35 according to ***a*** that he had done
10:36 and ***a*** Israel with him, to
10:37 ***a*** its cities, and all the
10:37 and ***a*** the people who were in
10:37 according to ***a*** that he had done
10:37 but utterly destroyed it and ***a***
10:38 and ***a*** Israel with him, to
10:39 he took it and its king and ***a***
10:39 sword and utterly destroyed ***a***
10:40 So Joshua conquered ***a*** the land:
10:40 and ***a*** their kings; he left none
10:40 but utterly destroyed ***a*** that
10:41 and ***a*** the country of Goshen,
10:42 ***A*** these kings and their land
10:43 and ***a*** Israel with him, to the
11: 4 they and ***a*** their armies with
11: 5 And when ***a*** these kings had met
11: 6 this time I will deliver ***a*** of
11: 7 So Joshua and ***a*** the people of
11:10 was formerly the head of ***a***
11:11 And they struck ***a*** the people who
11:12 So ***a*** the cities of those kings,
11:12 and ***a*** their kings, Joshua took
11:14 And ***a*** the spoil of these cities
11:15 He left nothing undone of ***a***
11:16 Thus Joshua took ***a*** this land:
11:16 ***a*** the South, all the land of
11:16 ***a*** the land of Goshen, the
11:17 He captured ***a*** their kings, and
11:18 made war a long time with ***a***
11:19 ***A*** the others they took in
11:21 from ***a*** the mountains of Judah,
11:21 and from ***a*** the mountains of
11:23 according to ***a*** that the LORD
12: 1 and ***a*** the eastern Jordan plain:
12: 5 over ***a*** Bashan, as far as the
12:24 ***a*** the kings, thirty-one.
13: 2 ***a*** the territory of the
13: 2 of the Philistines and ***a*** that
13: 4 ***a*** the land of the Canaanites,
13: 5 and ***a*** Lebanon, toward the
13: 6 ***a*** the inhabitants of the
13: 6 and ***a*** the Sidonians—them I
13: 9 and ***a*** the plain of Medeba as
13:10 ***a*** the cities of Sihon king of
13:11 ***a*** Mount Hermon, and all Bashan
13:11 and ***a*** Bashan as far as Salcah;
13:12 ***a*** the kingdom of Og in Bashan,
13:16 and ***a*** the plain by Medeba;
13:17 Heshbon and ***a*** its cities that
13:21 ***a*** the cities of the plain and
13:21 the cities of the plain and ***a***
13:25 and ***a*** the cities of Gilead, and
13:30 ***a*** Bashan, all the kingdom of Og
13:30 ***a*** the kingdom of Og king of
13:30 and ***a*** the towns of Jair which
15:12 of the children of Judah ***a***
15:32 ***a*** the cities are twenty-nine,
15:46 ***a*** that lay near Ashdod, with
16: 9 ***a*** the cities with their
17:16 and ***a*** the Canaanites who dwell
18:20 according to its boundaries ***a***
19: 8 and ***a*** the villages that were
19: 8 all the villages that were ***a***
20: 9 the cities appointed for ***a*** the
21:19 ***A*** the cities of the children of
21:26 ***A*** the ten cities with their
21:33 ***A*** the cities of the Gershonites
21:39 common-land: four cities in ***a***.
21:40 So ***a*** the cities for the children
21:41 ***A*** the cities of the Levites
21:42 thus were ***a*** these cities.
21:43 So the LORD gave to Israel ***a***
21:44 The LORD gave them rest ***a***
21:44 according to ***a*** that He had
21:44 And not a man of ***a*** their
21:44 the LORD delivered ***a*** their
21:45 ***A*** came to pass.
22: 2 You have kept ***a*** that Moses the
22: 2 and have obeyed my voice in ***a***
22: 5 to walk in ***a*** His ways, to keep
22: 5 and to serve Him with ***a*** your
22: 5 with all your heart and with ***a***
22:20 and wrath fell on ***a*** the
23: 1 had given rest to Israel from ***a***
23: 2 And Joshua called for ***a*** Israel,
23: 3 You have seen ***a*** that the LORD
23: 3 LORD your God has done to ***a***
23: 4 with ***a*** the nations that I have
23: 6 courageous to keep and to do ***a***
23:14 day I am going the way of ***a***
23:14 And you know in ***a*** your hearts
23:14 in all your hearts and in ***a***
23:14 not one thing has failed of ***a***
23:14 ***A*** have come to pass for you;
23:15 that as ***a*** the good things have
23:15 the LORD will bring upon you ***a***
24: 1 Then Joshua gathered ***a*** the
24: 2 And Joshua said to ***a*** the people,
24: 3 led him throughout ***a*** the land
24:17 and preserved us in ***a*** the way
24:17 way that we went and among ***a***
24:18 drove out from before us ***a*** the
24:27 And Joshua said to ***a*** the people,
24:27 for it has heard ***a*** the words of
24:31 Israel served the LORD ***a*** the
24:31 and ***a*** the days of the elders
24:31 who had known ***a*** the works of

Judg 1:25 but they let the man and ***a*** his
2: 4 LORD spoke these words to ***a***
2: 7 the people served the LORD ***a***
2: 7 and ***a*** the days of the elders
2: 7 who had seen ***a*** the great works
2:10 When ***a*** that generation had been
2:12 gods of the people who were ***a***
2:14 the hands of their enemies ***a***
2:18 of the hand of their enemies ***a***
3: 1 ***a*** who had not known any of the
3: 3 ***a*** the Canaanites, the
3:19 Keep silence!" And ***a*** who
3:29 ***a*** stout men of valor; not a man
4:13 So Sisera gathered together ***a***
4:13 and ***a*** the people who were with
4:15 the LORD routed Sisera and ***a***
4:15 and all his chariots and ***a***
4:16 and ***a*** the army of Sisera fell
5:31 Thus let ***a*** Your enemies perish,
6: 9 and out of the hand of ***a*** who
6:13 why then has ***a*** this happened to
6:13 And where are ***a*** His miracles
6:31 But Joash said to ***a*** who stood
6:33 Then ***a*** the Midianites and
6:35 he sent messengers throughout ***a***
6:37 and it is dry on ***a*** the
6:39 but on ***a*** the ground let there
6:40 but there was dew on ***a*** the
7: 1 Gideon) and ***a*** the people who
7: 6 but ***a*** the rest of the people
7: 7 Let ***a*** the other people go,
7: 8 And he sent away ***a*** the rest
7:12 ***a*** the people of the East, were
7:18 I and ***a*** who are with me, then
7:21 every man stood in his place ***a***
7:23 and ***a*** Manasseh, and pursued the
7:24 sent messengers throughout ***a***
7:24 Then ***a*** the men of Ephraim
8:10 ***a*** who were left of all the army
8:10 all who were left of ***a*** the army

8:27 And *a* Israel played the harlot
8:34 them from the hands of *a* their
9: 1 and spoke with them and with *a*
9: 2 speak in the hearing of *a* the
9: 2 that *a* seventy of the sons of
9: 3 his mother's brothers spoke *a*
9: 3 him in the hearing of *a* the
9: 6 And *a* the men of Shechem
9: 6 *a* of Beth Millo, and they went
9:14 Then *a* the trees said to the
9:25 and they robbed *a* who passed by
9:34 So Abimelech and *a* the people
9:44 two companies rushed upon *a*
9:45 fought against the city *a* that
9:46 Now when *a* the men of the tower
9:47 it was told Abimelech that *a*
9:48 he and *a* the people who were
9:49 so that *a* the people of the
9:51 and *a* the men and women—all the
9:51 *a* the people of the city—fled
9:57 And *a* the evil of the men of
10: 8 *a* the children of Israel who
10:18 He shall be head over *a* the
11: 8 and be our head over *a* the
11:11 and Jephthah spoke *a* his words
11:20 So Sihon gathered *a* his people
11:21 of Israel delivered Sihon and *a*
11:21 Israel gained possession of *a*
11:22 They took possession of *a* the
11:26 and in *a* the cities along the
12: 4 Jephthah gathered together *a*
13:13 Of *a* that I said to the woman
13:14 *A* that I commanded her let her
13:23 nor would He have shown us *a*
14: 3 or among *a* my people, that you
16: 2 and lay in wait for him *a*
16: 2 They were quiet *a* night,
16: 3 pulled them up, bar and *a*,
16:17 that he told her *a* his heart,
16:18 saw that he had told her *a* his
16:18 for he has told me *a* his
16:27 *A* the lords of the Philistines
16:30 And he pushed with *a* his
16:30 temple fell on the lords and *a*
16:31 And his brothers and *a* his
18:31 *a* the time that the house of
19: 6 Please be content to stay *a*
19:20 let *a* your needs be my
19:25 they knew her and abused her *a*
19:29 and sent her throughout *a* the
19:30 And so it was that *a* who saw it
20: 1 So *a* the children of Israel came
20: 2 And the leaders of *a* the people,
20: 2 *a* the tribes of Israel,
20: 6 and sent her throughout *a* the
20: 7 Look! *A* of you are children of
20: 8 So *a* the people arose as one
20:10 of every hundred throughout *a*
20:10 they may repay *a* the vileness
20:11 So *a* the men of Israel were
20:12 of Israel sent men through *a*
20:16 Among *a* this people were seven
20:17 *a* of these were men of war.
20:25 *a* these drew the sword.
20:26 Then *a* the children of Israel,
20:26 *a* the people, went up and came
20:29 Israel set men in ambush *a*
20:33 So *a* the men of Israel rose from
20:34 ten thousand select men from *a*
20:35 *a* these drew the sword.
20:44 *a* these were men of valor.
20:46 So *a* who fell of Benjamin that
20:46 *a* these WERE men of valor.
20:48 *a* who were found. They also set
20:48 They also set fire to *a* the
21: 5 Who is there among *a* the
Ruth 1:19 that *a* the city was excited
2:11 *a* that you have done for your
2:21 men until they have finished *a*
3: 5 *A* that you say to me I will
3: 6 floor and did according to *a*
3:11 I will do for you *a* that you
3:11 for *a* the people of my town
3:16 Then she told her *a* that the
4: 9 Boaz said to the elders and *a*
4: 9 this day that I have bought *a*
4: 9 and *a* that was Chilion's and
4:11 And *a* the people who were at
1 Sam 1: 4 to Peninnah his wife and to *a*
1:11 I will give him to the LORD *a*
1:21 Now the man Elkanah and *a* his
2:14 would take for himself *a* that
2:14 So they did in Shiloh to *a* the
2:22 everything his sons did to *a*
2:23 of your evil dealings from *a*
2:28 Did I not choose him out of *a*
2:28 to the house of your father *a*
2:29 fat with the best of *a* the
2:32 despite *a* the good which God
2:33 And *a* the descendants of your
3:12 I will perform against Eli *a*
3:17 you hide anything from me of *a*
3:20 And *a* Israel from Dan to
4: 1 the word of Samuel came to *a*
4: 5 *a* Israel shouted so loudly that
4: 8 who struck the Egyptians with *a*
4:13 *a* the city cried out.
5: 8 and gathered to themselves *a*
5:11 sent and gathered together *a*
5:11 destruction throughout *a* the
6: 3 but by *a* means return it to
6: 4 For the same plague was on *a*
6:18 according to the number of *a*
7: 2 And *a* the house of Israel
7: 3 Then Samuel spoke to *a* the house
7: 3 you return to the LORD with *a*
7: 5 Gather *a* Israel to Mizpah, and I
7:13 was against the Philistines *a*
7:15 And Samuel judged Israel *a* the
7:16 and judged Israel in *a* those
8: 4 Then *a* the elders of Israel
8: 5 us a king to judge us like *a*
8: 7 the voice of the people in *a*
8: 8 According to *a* the works which
8:10 So Samuel told *a* the words of
8:20 that we also may be like *a* the
8:21 And Samuel heard *a* the words of
9: 6 *a* that he says surely comes to
9: 7 the bread in our vessels is *a*
9:19 let you go and will tell you *a*
9:20 And on whom is *a* the desire of
9:20 Is it not on you and on *a*
9:21 and my family the least of *a*
10: 9 and *a* those signs came to pass
10:11 when *a* who knew him formerly
10:18 and from the hand of *a*
10:19 who Himself saved you from *a*
10:20 And when Samuel had caused *a* the
10:24 And Samuel said to *a* the people,
10:24 is no one like him among *a*
10:24 So *a* the people shouted and
10:25 And Samuel sent *a* the people
11: 1 and *a* the men of Jabesh said to
11: 2 that I may put out *a* your right
11: 2 and bring reproach on *a*
11: 3 we may send messengers to *a*
11: 4 And *a* the people lifted up
11: 7 and sent them throughout *a* the
11:15 So *a* the people went to Gilgal,
11:15 and there Saul and *a* the men of
12: 1 Now Samuel said to *a* Israel:
12: 1 I have heeded your voice in *a*
12: 7 before the LORD concerning *a*
12:18 and *a* the people greatly feared
12:19 And *a* the people said to
12:19 for we have added to *a* our sins
12:20 You have done *a* this
12:20 but serve the LORD with *a* your
12:24 and serve Him in truth with *a*
13: 3 blew the trumpet throughout *a*
13: 4 Now *a* Israel heard it said that
13: 7 and *a* the people followed him
13:19 to be found throughout *a* the
13:20 But *a* the Israelites would go
14: 7 Do *a* that is in your heart. Go
14:15 and among *a* the people.
14:20 Then Saul and *a* the people who
14:22 Likewise *a* the men of Israel who
14:25 Now *a* the people of the land
14:38 *a* you chiefs of the people, and
14:39 But not a man among *a* the
14:40 Then he said to *a* Israel, "You
14:47 and fought against *a* his
14:52 war with the Philistines *a* the
15: 3 and utterly destroy *a* that they
15: 6 For you showed kindness to *a*
15: 7 from Havilah *a* the way to Shur,
15: 8 and utterly destroyed *a* the
15: 9 and *a* that was good, and were
15:11 and he cried out to the LORD *a*
16:11 'Are *a* the young men here?"
17:11 When Saul and *a* Israel heard
17:19 Now Saul and they and *a* the men
17:24 And *a* the men of Israel, when
17:46 that *a* the earth may know that
17:47 Then *a* this assembly shall know
18: 5 was accepted in the sight of *a*
18: 6 the women had come out of *a*
18:14 And David behaved wisely in *a*
18:16 But *a* Israel and Judah loved
18:22 and *a* his servants love you.
18:30 behaved more wisely than *a* the
19: 1 to Jonathan his son and to *a*
19: 5 about a great deliverance for *a*
19: 7 and Jonathan told him *a* these
19:18 and told him *a* that Saul had
19:24 and lay down naked *a* that day
19:24 down naked all that day and *a*
20: 6 "If your father misses me at *a*,
20: 6 a yearly sacrifice there for *a*
22: 1 And when his brothers and *a* his
22: 4 and they dwelt with him *a* the
22: 6 and *a* his servants standing
22: 7 and make you *a* captains of
22: 8 *A* of you have conspired against
22:11 and *a* his father's house, the
22:11 And they *a* came to the king.
22:14 And who among *a* your servants
22:15 your servant knew nothing of *a*
22:16 you and *a* your father's
22:22 I have caused the death of *a*
23: 8 Then Saul called *a* the people
23:20 come down according to *a* the
23:23 and take knowledge of *a* the
23:23 search for him throughout *a*
24: 2 thousand chosen men from *a*
25: 6 and peace to *a* that you have!
25: 7 anything missing from them *a*
25: 9 spoke to Nabal according to *a*
25:12 and they came and told him *a*
25:16 *a* the time we were with them
25:17 our master and against *a* his
25:21 in vain I have protected *a*
25:21 so that nothing was missed of *a*
25:22 if I leave one male of *a* who
25:30 for my lord according to *a* the
26: 5 with the people encamped *a*
26: 7 And Abner and the people lay *a*
26:12 For they were *a* asleep,
26:24 and let Him deliver me out of *a*
27:11 And thus was his behavior *a* the
28: 3 and *a* Israel had lamented for
28: 4 So Saul gathered *a* Israel
28:20 for he had eaten no food *a* day
28:20 had eaten no food all day or *a*
29: 1 gathered together *a* their
30: 6 because the soul of *a* the
30: 8 and without fail recover *a*.
30:16 spread out over *a* the land,
30:16 because of *a* the great spoil
30:18 So David recovered *a* that the
30:19 from them; David recovered *a*.
30:20 Then David took *a* the flocks and
30:22 Then *a* the wicked and worthless
30:31 and to *a* the places where David
31: 6 and *a* his men died together
31:12 *a* the valiant men arose and
31:12 men arose and traveled *a* night,
2 Sam 1:11 and so did *a* the men who
2: 9 and over *a* Israel.
2:27 surely then by morning *a* the
2:28 and *a* the people stood still
2:29 Abner and his men went on *a*
2:29 and went through *a* Bithron; and
2:30 And when he had gathered *a* the
2:32 And Joab and his men went *a*
3:12 shall be with you to bring *a*
3:18 Philistines and the hand of *a*
3:19 hearing of David in Hebron *a*
3:21 and gather *a* Israel to my lord
3:21 and that you may reign over *a*
3:23 When Joab and *a* the troops that
3:25 and to know *a* that you are
3:29 on the head of Joab and on *a*
3:31 David said to Joab and to *a*
3:32 and *a* the people wept.
3:34 Then *a* the people wept over him
3:35 And when *a* the people came to
3:36 Now *a* the people took note of
3:36 the king did pleased *a* the
3:37 For *a* the people and all Israel
3:37 For all the people and *a* Israel
4: 1 and *a* Israel was troubled.
4: 6 *a* the way into the house, as
4: 7 and were *a* night escaping
4: 9 who has redeemed my life from *a*
5: 1 Then *a* the tribes of Israel came
5: 3 Therefore *a* the elders of Israel
5: 5 thirty-three years over *a*
5: 9 And David built *a* around from
5:17 *a* the Philistines went up to
6: 1 Again David gathered *a* the
6: 2 And David arose and went with *a*
6: 5 Then David and *a* the house of
6: 5 music before the LORD on *a*
6:11 LORD blessed Obed-Edom and *a*
6:12 the house of Obed-Edom and *a*
6:14 danced before the LORD with *a*
6:15 So David and *a* the house of
6:19 Then he distributed among *a* the
6:19 So *a* the people departed,
6:21 me instead of your father and *a*
7: 1 had given him rest from *a* his
7: 1 him rest from all his enemies *a*
7: 3 do *a* that is in your heart,
7: 7 I have moved about with *a* the
7: 9 and have cut off *a* your enemies
7:11 have caused you to rest from *a*
7:17 According to *a* these words and
7:17 these words and according to *a*
7:21 You have done *a* these great
7:22 according to *a* that we have
8: 4 Also David hamstrung *a* the
8: 9 that David had defeated *a* the
8:11 that he had dedicated from *a*
8:14 throughout *a* Edom he put
8:14 and *a* the Edomites became
8:15 So David reigned over *a* Israel;
8:15 judgment and justice to *a* his
9: 7 and will restore to you *a* the
9: 9 given to your master's son *a*
9: 9 that belonged to Saul and to *a*
9:11 According to *a* that my lord the
9:12 And *a* who dwelt in the house of
10: 7 he sent Joab and *a* the army of
10:17 he gathered *a* Israel, crossed
10:19 And when *a* the kings who were
11: 1 and *a* Israel; and they
11: 9 of the king's house with *a* the
11:18 Joab sent and told David *a* the
11:22 and came and told David *a* that
12:12 I will do this thing before *a*
12:16 fasted and went in and lay *a*
12:29 So David gathered *a* the people
12:31 So he did to *a* the cities of
12:31 Then David and *a* the people
13: 9 And they *a* went out from him.
13:21 But when King David heard of *a*
13:23 so Absalom invited *a* the king's
13:25 let us not *a* go now, lest we be
13:27 so he let Amnon and *a* the
13:29 Then *a* the king's sons arose,
13:30 Absalom has killed *a* the king's
13:31 and *a* his servants stood by
13:32 suppose they have killed *a* the
13:33 to think that *a* the king's sons

13:36 Also the king and ***a*** his
14:19 the hand of Joab with you in ***a***
14:19 and he put ***a*** these words in the
14:21 ***A*** right, I have granted this
14:25 Now in ***a*** Israel there was no
15: 6 manner Absalom acted toward ***a***
15:10 sent spies throughout ***a*** the
15:14 So David said to ***a*** his servants
15:16 Then the king went out with ***a***
15:17 And the king went out with ***a*** the
15:18 Then ***a*** his servants passed
15:18 and ***a*** the Cherethites, all the
15:18 ***a*** the Pelethites, and all the
15:18 and ***a*** the Gittites, six hundred
15:22 Then Ittai the Gittite and ***a***
15:22 Gittite and all his men and ***a***
15:23 And ***a*** the country wept with a
15:23 and ***a*** the people crossed over.
15:23 and ***a*** the people crossed over
15:24 and ***a*** the Levites with him,
15:24 and Abiathar went up until ***a***
15:30 And ***a*** the people who were with
16: 4 ***a*** that belongs to Mephibosheth
16: 6 threw stones at David and at ***a***
16: 6 And ***a*** the people and all the
16: 6 And all the people and ***a*** the
16: 8 LORD has brought upon you ***a***
16:11 And David said to Abishai and ***a***
16:14 Now the king and ***a*** the people
16:15 Meanwhile Absalom and ***a*** the
16:18 the LORD and this people and ***a***
16:21 and ***a*** Israel will hear that you
16:21 Then the hands of ***a*** who are
16:22 concubines in the sight of ***a***
16:23 So was ***a*** the advice of
17: 2 And ***a*** the people who are with
17: 3 Then I will bring back ***a*** the
17: 3 When ***a*** return except the man
17: 3 ***a*** the people will be at
17: 4 saying pleased Absalom and ***a***
17:10 For ***a*** Israel knows that your
17:11 Therefore I advise that ***a*** Israel
17:12 And of him and ***a*** the men who
17:13 then ***a*** Israel shall bring ropes
17:14 So Absalom and ***a*** the men of
17:16 lest the king and ***a*** the people
17:22 So David and ***a*** the people who
17:24 he and ***a*** the men of Israel with
18: 4 and ***a*** the people went out by
18: 5 And ***a*** the people heard when
18: 5 heard when the king gave ***a*** the
18:17 Then ***a*** Israel fled, everyone to
18:28 ***A*** is well!" Then he bowed down
18:31 has avenged you this day of ***a***
18:32 and ***a*** who rise against you to
19: 2 was turned into mourning for ***a***
19: 5 Today you have disgraced ***a*** your
19: 6 if Absalom had lived and ***a*** of
19: 7 will be worse for you than ***a***
19: 8 And they told ***a*** the people,
19: 8 So ***a*** the people came before
19: 9 Now ***a*** the people were in a
19: 9 were in a dispute throughout ***a***
19:11 since the words of ***a*** Israel
19:14 So he swayed the hearts of ***a*** the
19:14 you and ***a*** your servants!"
19:20 the first to come today of ***a***
19:28 For ***a*** my father's house were but
19:30 "Rather, let him take it ***a***,
19:39 Then ***a*** the people went over the
19:40 And ***a*** the people of Judah
19:41 Just then ***a*** the men of Israel
19:41 and ***a*** David's men with him
19:42 So ***a*** the men of Judah answered
20: 7 and ***a*** the mighty men, went out
20:12 And when the man saw that ***a*** the
20:13 ***a*** the people went on after Joab
20:14 And he went through ***a*** the
20:14 to Abel and Beth Maachah and ***a***
20:15 And ***a*** the people who were with
20:22 woman in her wisdom went to ***a***
20:23 And Joab was over ***a*** the army
21: 9 ***a*** seven together, and were put
21:14 So they performed ***a*** that the
22: 1 him from the hand of ***a*** his
22:23 For ***a*** His judgments were
22:31 He is a shield to ***a*** who trust
23: 5 Ordered in ***a*** things and
23: 5 For this is ***a*** my salvation
23: 5 is all my salvation and ***a*** my
23: 6 sons of rebellion shall ***a***
23:39 the Hittite: thirty-seven in ***a***.
24: 2 Now go throughout ***a*** the tribes
24: 7 the stronghold of Tyre and to ***a***
24: 8 So when they had gone through ***a***
24:23 ***A*** these, O king, Araunah has
1 Ki 1: 3 young woman throughout ***a*** the
1: 9 he also invited ***a*** his brothers,
1: 9 and ***a*** the men of Judah, the
1:19 and has invited ***a*** the sons of
1:20 the eyes of ***a*** Israel are on
1:25 and has invited ***a*** the king's
1:39 and ***a*** the people said, "Long
1:40 And ***a*** the people went up after
1:41 Now Adonijah and ***a*** the guests
1:49 So ***a*** the guests who were with
2: 2 I go the way of ***a*** the earth; be
2: 3 that you may prosper in ***a*** that
2: 4 walk before Me in truth with ***a***
2: 4 with all their heart and with ***a***
2:15 and ***a*** Israel had set their
2:44 ***a*** the wickedness that you did

3: 1 and the wall ***a*** around
3:13 like you among the kings ***a***
3:15 and made a feast for ***a*** his
3:28 And ***a*** Israel heard of the
4: 1 So King Solomon was king over ***a***
4: 7 had twelve governors over ***a***
4:10 to him belonged Sochoh and ***a***
4:11 in ***a*** the regions of Dor; he
4:12 and ***a*** Beth Shean, which is
4:21 So Solomon reigned over ***a***
4:21 tribute and served Solomon ***a***
4:24 For he had dominion over ***a*** the
4:24 namely over ***a*** the kings on this
4:24 he had peace on every side ***a***
4:25 ***a*** the days of Solomon.
4:27 for King Solomon and for ***a*** who
4:30 excelled the wisdom of ***a*** the
4:30 all the men of the East and ***a***
4:31 For he was wiser than ***a*** men—than
4:31 and his fame was in ***a*** the
4:34 And men of ***a*** nations, from all
4:34 from ***a*** the kings of the earth
5: 8 and I will do ***a*** you desire
5:10 cypress logs according to ***a***
5:13 up a labor force out of ***a***
6: 5 the temple he built chambers ***a***
6: 5 ***a*** around the sanctuary and the
6: 5 Thus he made side chambers ***a***
6:12 keep ***a*** My commandments, and
6:18 ***A*** was cedar; there was no
6:22 until he had finished ***a*** the
6:29 Then he carved ***a*** the walls of
6:29 all the walls of the temple ***a***
6:38 the house was finished in ***a*** its
6:38 its details and according to ***a***
7: 1 so he finished ***a*** his house.
7: 5 And ***a*** the doorways and doorposts
7: 9 ***A*** these were of costly stones
7:14 and skill in working with ***a***
7:14 came to King Solomon and did ***a***
7:18 above the network ***a*** around to
7:20 rows on each of the capitals ***a***
7:24 buds encircling it ***a*** around,
7:24 ***a*** the way around the Sea.
7:25 and ***a*** their back parts pointed
7:33 and their hubs were ***a*** of cast
7:36 with wreaths ***a*** around.
7:37 ***A*** of them were of the same
7:40 So Huram finished doing ***a*** the
7:45 ***A*** these articles which Huram
7:47 And Solomon did not weigh ***a*** the
7:48 Thus Solomon had ***a*** the
7:51 So ***a*** the work that King Solomon
8: 1 the elders of Israel and ***a*** the
8: 2 Therefore ***a*** the men of Israel
8: 3 So ***a*** the elders of Israel came,
8: 4 and ***a*** the holy furnishings that
8: 5 and ***a*** the congregation of
8:14 while ***a*** the assembly of Israel
8:22 the LORD in the presence of ***a***
8:23 who walk before You with ***a***
8:38 or by ***a*** Your people Israel,
8:39 to everyone according to ***a*** his
8:39 You alone know the hearts of ***a***
8:40 that they may fear You ***a*** the
8:43 and do according to ***a*** for which
8:43 that ***a*** peoples of the earth may
8:48 when they return to You with ***a***
8:48 with all their heart and with ***a***
8:50 and ***a*** their transgressions
8:53 You separated them from among ***a***
8:54 Solomon had finished praying ***a***
8:55 Then he stood and blessed ***a*** the
8:56 according to ***a*** that He
8:56 has not failed one word of ***a***
8:58 to walk in ***a*** His ways, and to
8:60 that ***a*** the peoples of the earth
8:62 Then the king and ***a*** Israel with
8:63 So the king and ***a*** the children
8:65 and ***a*** Israel with him, a great
8:66 joyful and glad of heart for ***a***
9: 1 and ***a*** Solomon's desire which he
9: 4 to do according to ***a*** that I
9: 6 But if you or your sons at ***a***
9: 7 a proverb and a byword among ***a***
9: 9 the LORD has brought ***a*** this
9:19 ***a*** the storage cities that
9:19 and in ***a*** the land of his
9:20 ***A*** the people who were left of
10: 2 she spoke with him about ***a*** that
10: 3 So Solomon answered ***a*** her
10: 4 the queen of Sheba had seen ***a***
10:13 gave the queen of Sheba ***a*** she
10:15 from ***a*** the kings of Arabia, and
10:21 ***A*** King Solomon's drinking
10:21 and ***a*** the vessels of the House
10:23 So King Solomon surpassed ***a*** the
10:24 Now ***a*** the earth sought the
10:29 they exported them to ***a*** the
11: 8 And he did likewise for ***a*** his
11:16 Joab remained there with ***a***
11:25 He was an adversary of Israel ***a***
11:28 made him the officer over ***a*** the
11:32 which I have chosen out of ***a***
11:34 I have made him ruler ***a*** the
11:37 and you shall reign over ***a*** your
11:38 if you heed ***a*** that I command
11:41 ***a*** that he did, and his wisdom,
11:42 reigned in Jerusalem over ***a***
12: 1 for ***a*** Israel had gone to
12:12 So Jeroboam and ***a*** the people
12:16 Now when ***a*** Israel saw that the

12:18 but ***a*** Israel stoned him with
12:20 Now it came to pass when ***a***
12:20 and made him king over ***a***
12:21 he assembled ***a*** the house of
12:23 to ***a*** the house of Judah and
13:11 his sons came and told him ***a***
13:32 and against ***a*** the shrines on
14: 8 and who followed Me with ***a*** his
14: 9 you have done more evil than ***a***
14:10 away refuse until it is ***a*** gone.
14:13 And ***a*** Israel shall mourn for him
14:18 and ***a*** Israel mourned for him,
14:21 the LORD had chosen out of ***a***
14:22 more than ***a*** that their fathers
14:24 They did according to ***a*** the
14:26 He also took away ***a*** the gold
14:29 and ***a*** that he did, are they
14:30 Rehoboam and Jeroboam ***a*** their
15: 3 And he walked in ***a*** the sins of
15: 5 that He commanded him ***a*** the
15: 6 Rehoboam and Jeroboam ***a*** the
15: 7 and ***a*** that he did, are they
15:12 and removed ***a*** the idols that
15:14 heart was loyal to the LORD ***a***
15:16 Asa and Baasha king of Israel ***a***
15:18 Then Asa took ***a*** the silver and
15:20 and ***a*** Chinneroth, with all the
15:20 with ***a*** the land of Naphtali.
15:22 a proclamation throughout ***a***
15:23 The rest of ***a*** the acts of Asa,
15:23 ***a*** his might, all that he did,
15:23 ***a*** that he did, and the cities
15:27 while Nadab and ***a*** Israel laid
15:29 that he killed ***a*** the house of
15:31 and ***a*** that he did, are they
15:32 Asa and Baasha king of Israel ***a***
15:33 of Ahijah became king over ***a***
16: 7 because of ***a*** the evil that he
16:11 that he killed ***a*** the household
16:12 Thus Zimri destroyed ***a*** the
16:13 for ***a*** the sins of Baasha and the
16:14 and ***a*** that he did, are they
16:16 So ***a*** Israel made Omri, the
16:17 Then Omri and ***a*** Israel with him
16:25 and did worse than ***a*** who were
16:26 For he walked in ***a*** the ways of
16:30 more than ***a*** who were before
16:33 God of Israel to anger than ***a***
18: 5 Go into the land to ***a*** the
18: 5 the springs of water and to ***a***
18:19 send and gather ***a*** Israel to me
18:20 So Ahab sent for ***a*** the children
18:21 And Elijah came to ***a*** the people,
18:24 So ***a*** the people answered and
18:30 Then Elijah said to ***a*** the
18:30 So ***a*** the people came near to
18:35 So the water ran ***a*** around the
18:36 and that I have done ***a*** these
18:39 Now when ***a*** the people saw it,
19: 1 And Ahab told Jezebel ***a*** that
19: 1 also how he had executed ***a*** the
19:18 ***a*** whose knees have not bowed to
20: 1 the king of Syria gathered ***a***
20: 4 I and ***a*** that I have are
20: 7 So the king of Israel called ***a***
20: 8 And ***a*** the elders and all the
20: 8 And all the elders and ***a*** the
20: 9 ***A*** that you sent for to your
20:13 Have you seen ***a*** this great
20:15 and after them he mustered ***a***
20:15 ***a*** the children of Israel—seven
20:28 therefore I will deliver ***a***
21:26 according to ***a*** that the
22:10 and ***a*** the prophets prophesied
22:12 And ***a*** the prophets prophesied
22:17 I saw ***a*** Israel scattered on the
22:19 and ***a*** the host of heaven
22:22 lying spirit in the mouth of ***a***
22:23 lying spirit in the mouth of ***a***
22:28 "Take heed, ***a*** you people!"
22:39 and ***a*** that he did, the ivory
22:39 house which he built and ***a*** the
22:43 And he walked in ***a*** the ways of
22:53 according to ***a*** that his father
2 Ki 3: 6 at that time and mustered ***a***
3:21 And when ***a*** the Moabites heard
3:21 ***a*** who were able to bear arms
3:25 and they stopped up ***a*** the
3:25 of water and cut down ***a*** the
4: 3 from ***a*** your neighbors—empty
4: 4 then pour it into ***a*** those
4:13 been concerned for us with ***a***
5:12 better than ***a*** the waters of
5:15 he and ***a*** his aides, and came
5:15 that there is no God in ***a***
5:21 and said, "Is ***a*** well?"
5:22 ***A*** is well. My master has sent
6:17 horses and chariots of fire ***a***
6:24 king of Syria gathered ***a*** his
7:13 may either become like ***a***
7:13 they may become like ***a*** the
7:15 and indeed ***a*** the road was full
8: 4 ***a*** the great things Elisha has
8: 6 Restore ***a*** that was hers, and
8: 6 and ***a*** the proceeds of the field
8:21 and ***a*** his chariots with him.
8:23 and ***a*** that he did, are they
9: 7 and the blood of ***a*** the servants
9: 8 and I will cut off from Ahab ***a***
9:11 Is ***a*** well? Why did this madman
9:14 he and ***a*** Israel, against Hazael
10: 5 we will do ***a*** you tell us; but

10: 9 and said to *a* the people, "You
10: 9 but who killed *a* these?
10:11 So Jehu killed *a* who remained of
10:11 and *a* his great men and his
10:17 he killed *a* who remained to
10:18 Then Jehu gathered *a* the people
10:19 call to me *a* the prophets of
10:19 *a* his servants, and all his
10:19 and *a* his priests. Let no one
10:21 Then Jehu sent throughout *a*
10:21 and *a* the worshipers of Baal
10:22 Bring out vestments for *a* the
10:30 done to the house of Ahab *a*
10:31 the LORD God of Israel with *a*
10:32 and Hazael conquered them in *a*
10:33 *a* the land of Gilead—Gad,
10:34 *a* that he did, and all his
10:34 and *a* his might, are they not
11: 1 she arose and destroyed *a* the
11: 8 shall surround the king on *a*
11: 9 the hundreds did according to *a*
11:11 *a* around the king, from the
11:14 *A* the people of the land were
11:18 And *a* the people of the land
11:19 and *a* the people of the land;
11:20 So *a* the people of the land
12: 2 in the sight of the LORD *a*
12: 4 *A* the money of the dedicated
12: 4 and *a* the money that a man
12: 9 who kept the door put there *a*
12:12 and for *a* that was paid out to
12:18 Jehoash king of Judah took *a*
12:18 and *a* the gold found in the
12:19 and *a* that he did, are they
13: 3 son of Hazael, *a* their days.
13: 8 *a* that he did, and his might,
13:11 He did not depart from *a* the
13:12 *a* that he did, and his might
13:22 of Syria oppressed Israel *a*
14:14 And he took *a* the gold and
14:14 *a* the articles that were found
14:21 And *a* the people of Judah took
14:24 he did not depart from *a* the
14:28 and *a* that he did—his might,
15: 3 according to *a* that his father
15: 6 and *a* that he did, are they
15:16 *a* who were there, and its
15:16 *A* the women there who were with
15:18 he did not depart *a* his days
15:20 from *a* the very wealthy, from
15:21 and *a* that he did, are they
15:26 and *a* that he did, indeed they
15:29 *a* the land of Naphtali; and he
15:31 and *a* that he did, indeed they
15:34 he did according to *a* that his
15:36 and *a* that he did, are they
16:10 according to *a* its workmanship.
16:11 built an altar according to *a*
16:15 with the burnt offering of *a*
16:15 and sprinkle on it *a* the blood
16:15 of the burnt offering and *a*
16:16 according to *a* that King Ahaz
17: 5 of Assyria went throughout *a*
17: 9 for themselves high places in *a*
17:11 There they burned incense on *a*
17:13 by *a* of His prophets, every
17:13 according to *a* the law which I
17:15 after the nations who were *a*
17:16 So they left *a* the commandments
17:16 a wooden image and worshiped *a*
17:20 And the LORD rejected *a* the
17:22 children of Israel walked in *a*
17:23 as He had said by *a* His
17:39 deliver you from the hand of *a*
18: 3 according to *a* that his father
18: 5 him was none like him among *a*
18:12 His covenant and *a* that Moses
18:13 of Assyria came up against *a*
18:15 So Hezekiah gave him *a* the
18:21 is Pharaoh king of Egypt to *a*
18:33 of the gods of the nations at *a*
18:35 Who among *a* the gods of the
19: 4 the LORD your God will hear *a*
19:11 kings of Assyria have done to *a*
19:15 of *a* the kingdoms of the earth.
19:19 that *a* the kingdoms of the
19:24 of my feet I have dried up *A*
19:35 there were the corpses—*a* dead.
20:13 and showed them *a* the house of
20:13 and *a* his armory—all that was
20:13 *a* that was found among his
20:13 nothing in his house or in *a*
20:15 They have seen *a* that is in my
20:17 the days are coming when *a* that
20:20 *a* his might, and how he made a
21: 3 and he worshiped *a* the host of
21: 5 And he built altars for *a* the
21: 7 which I have chosen out of *a*
21: 8 careful to do according to *a*
21: 8 and according to *a* the law that
21:11 has acted more wickedly than *a*
21:14 become victims of plunder to *a*
21:17 *a* that he did, and the sin that
21:21 So he walked in *a* the ways that
21:24 people of the land executed *a*
22: 2 and walked in *a* the ways of his
22:13 for the people and for *a* Judah,
22:13 to do according to *a* that is
22:16 *a* the words of the book which
22:17 provoke Me to anger with *a* the
22:20 and your eyes shall not see *a*
23: 1 the king sent them to gather *a*
23: 2 the house of the LORD with *a*
23: 2 and with him *a* the inhabitants
23: 2 priests and the prophets and *a*
23: 2 And he read in their hearing *a*
23: 3 with *a* his heart and all his
23: 3 with all his heart and *a* his
23: 3 And *a* the people took a stand
23: 4 of the temple of the LORD *a*
23: 4 and for *a* the host of heaven;
23: 5 of Judah and in the places *a*
23: 5 and to *a* the host of heaven.
23: 8 And he brought *a* the priests
23:19 Now Josiah also took away *a* the
23:19 he did to them according to *a*
23:20 He executed *a* the priests of the
23:21 Then the king commanded *a* the
23:22 nor in *a* the days of the kings
23:24 *a* the abominations that were
23:25 who turned to the LORD with *a*
23:25 with *a* his soul, and with all
23:25 and with *a* his might, according
23:25 according to *a* the Law of
23:26 because of *a* the provocations
23:28 and *a* that he did, are they
23:32 according to *a* that his fathers
23:37 according to *a* that his fathers
24: 3 according to *a* that he had
24: 5 and *a* that he did, are they
24: 7 the king of Babylon had taken *a*
24: 9 according to *a* that his father
24:13 he carried out from there *a*
24:13 and he cut in pieces *a* the
24:14 he carried into captivity *a*
24:14 *a* the captains and all the
24:14 all the captains and *a* the
24:14 and *a* the craftsmen and smiths.
24:16 *A* the valiant men, seven
24:16 *a* who were strong and fit
24:19 according to *a* that Jehoiakim
25: 1 king of Babylon and *a* his army
25: 1 built a siege wall against it *a*
25: 4 and *a* the men of war fled at
25: 4 were still encamped *a* around
25: 5 *A* his army was scattered from
25: 9 *a* the houses of Jerusalem, that
25: 9 *a* the houses of the great, he
25:10 And *a* the army of the Chaldeans
25:10 down the walls of Jerusalem *a*
25:14 and *a* the bronze utensils with
25:16 the bronze of *a* these articles
25:17 the network and pomegranates *a*
25:17 all around the capital were *a*
25:23 Now when *a* the captains of the
25:26 And *a* the people, small and
25:29 regularly before the king *a*
25:30 *a* the days of his life.

1 Chr 1:23 *A* these were the sons of
1:33 *A* these were the children of
2: 4 *A* the sons of Judah were five.
2: 6 and Dara—five of them in *a*.
2:23) *A* these belonged to the sons
3: 8 and Eliphelet–nine in *a*.
3: 9 These were *a* the sons of
3:20 and Jushab-Hesed—five in *a*.
3:22 Neariah, and Shaphat—six in *a*.
3:23 and Azrikam—three in *a*.
3:24 Delaiah, and Anani—seven in *a*.
4:33 and *a* the villages that were
5:13 Zia, and Eber—seven in *a*.
5:16 and in *a* the common-lands of
5:17 *A* these were registered by
5:20 and *a* who were with them, for
6:49 for *a* the work of the Most Holy
6:49 according to *a* that Moses the
6:60 *A* their cities among their
7: 1 Jashub, and Shimron—four in *a*.
7: 3 *A* five of them were chief men.
7: 5 Now their brethren among *a* the
7: 5 eighty-seven thousand in *a*.
7: 6 and Jediael—three in *a*.
7: 7 Jerimoth, and Iri—five in *a*.
7: 8 *A* these are the sons of
7:11 *A* these sons of Jediael were
7:40 *A* these were the children of
8:38 *A* these were the sons of Azel.
8:40 one hundred and fifty in *a*.
8:40 These were *a* sons of Benjamin.
9: 1 So *a* Israel was recorded by
9: 9 *A* these men were heads of a
9:22 *A* those chosen as gatekeepers
9:27 And they lodged *a* around the
9:29 the furnishings and over *a* the
10: 6 and *a* his house died together.
10: 7 And when *a* the men of Israel who
10:11 And when *a* Jabesh Gilead heard
10:11 when all Jabesh Gilead heard *a*
10:12 *a* the valiant men arose and took
11: 1 Then *a* Israel came together to
11: 3 Therefore *a* the elders of Israel
11: 4 And David and *a* Israel went to
11:10 with *a* Israel, to make him
12:15 when it had overflowed *a* its
12:15 and they put to flight *a* those
12:21 for they were *a* mighty men of
12:32 and *a* their brethren were at
12:33 expert in war with *a* weapons of
12:38 *A* these men of war, who could
12:38 to make David king over *a*
12:38 and *a* the rest of Israel were
13: 2 And David said to *a* the assembly
13: 2 everywhere who are left in *a*
13: 4 Then *a* the assembly said that
13: 4 was right in the eyes of *a* the
13: 5 So David gathered *a* Israel
13: 6 And David and *a* Israel went up
13: 8 Then David and *a* Israel played
13: 8 played music before God with *a*
13:14 the house of Obed-Edom and *a*
14: 8 had been anointed king over *a*
14: 8 *a* the Philistines went up to
14:17 fame of David went out into *a*
14:17 brought the fear of him upon *a*
15: 3 And David gathered *a* Israel
15:27 as were *a* the Levites who bore
15:28 Thus *a* Israel brought up the ark
16: 9 Talk of *a* His wondrous works!
16:14 His judgments are in *a* the
16:23 *a* the earth; Proclaim the good
16:24 His wonders among *a* peoples.
16:25 is also to be feared above *a*
16:26 For *a* the gods of the peoples
16:30 *a* the earth. The world also is
16:32 and *a* its fullness; Let the
16:32 and *a* that is in it.
16:36 And *a* the people said,
16:40 and to do according to *a* that
16:43 Then *a* the people departed,
17: 2 Do *a* that is in your heart, for
17: 6 I have moved about with *a*
17: 8 and have cut off *a* your enemies
17:10 Also I will subdue *a* your
17:15 According to *a* these words and
17:15 these words and according to *a*
17:19 You have done *a* this greatness,
17:19 in making known *a* these great
17:20 according to *a* that we have
18: 4 And David also hamstrung *a* the
18: 9 that David had defeated *a* the
18:10 Hadoram brought with him *a*
18:11 gold that he had brought from *a*
18:13 and *a* the Edomites became
18:14 So David reigned over *a* Israel,
18:14 judgment and justice to *a* his
19: 8 he sent Joab and *a* the army of
19:17 he gathered *a* Israel, crossed
20: 3 So David did to *a* the cities of
20: 3 Then David and *a* the people
21: 3 are they not *a* my lord's
21: 4 departed and went throughout *a*
21: 5 *A* Israel had one million one
21:12 LORD destroying throughout *a*
21:23 grain offering; I give it *a*.
22: 5 and glorious throughout *a*
22: 9 and I will give him rest from *a*
22: 9 him rest from all his enemies *a*
22:15 and *a* types of skillful men for
22:17 David also commanded *a* the
23: 2 And he gathered together *a* the
23: 8 Zetham and Joel—three in *a*.
23: 9 Haziel, and Haran—three in *a*.
23:12 Hebron, and Uzziel—four in *a*.
23:23 Eder, and Jeremoth—three in *a*.
23:28 in the purifying of *a* holy
23:29 with what is mixed and with *a*
25: 5 *A* these were the sons of Heman
25: 6 *A* these were under the
25: 7 *a* who were skillful, was two
26: 8 *A* these were of the sons of
26:11 *a* the sons and brethren of
26:26 and his brethren were over *a*
26:28 And *a* that Samuel the seer, Saul
26:30 west side of the Jordan for *a*
27: 1 out month by month throughout *a*
27: 3 and the chief of *a* the captains
27:31 *A* these were the officials
28: 1 David assembled at Jerusalem *a*
28: 1 and the stewards over *a* the
28: 1 and *a* the mighty men of valor.
28: 4 God of Israel chose me above *a*
28: 4 with me to make me king over *a*
28: 5 And of *a* my sons (for the LORD
28: 8 in the sight of *a* Israel, the
28: 8 be careful to seek out *a* the
28: 9 for the LORD searches *a* hearts
28: 9 all hearts and understands *a*
28:12 and the plans for *a* that he had
28:12 of *a* the chambers all around,
28:12 of all the chambers *a* around,
28:13 for *a* the work of the service
28:13 and for *a* the articles of
28:14 for *a* articles used in every
28:14 also silver for *a* articles of
28:14 for *a* articles used in every
28:19 *A* this," said David, "the
28:19 *a* the works of these plans."
28:20 until you have finished *a* the
28:21 priests and the Levites for *a*
28:21 will be with you for *a*
28:21 also the leaders and *a* the
29: 1 King David said to *a* the
29: 2 my God I have prepared with *a*
29: 2 *a* kinds of precious stones, and
29: 3 over and above *a* that I have
29: 5 and for *a* kinds of work to be
29:10 blessed the LORD before *a* the
29:11 For *a* that is in heaven and
29:11 You are exalted as head over *a*.
29:12 from You, And You reign over *a*.
29:12 And to give strength to *a*.
29:14 For *a* things come from You,
29:15 As were *a* our fathers; Our
29:16 *a* this abundance that we have
29:16 and is *a* Your own.
29:17 I have willingly offered *a*

29:19 to do ***a*** these things, and to
29:20 Then David said to ***a*** the
29:20 So ***a*** the assembly blessed the
29:21 sacrifices in abundance for ***a***
29:23 and ***a*** Israel obeyed him.
29:24 ***A*** the leaders and the mighty
29:24 and also ***a*** the sons of King
29:25 exceedingly in the sight of ***a***
29:26 the son of Jesse reigned over ***a***
29:30 with ***a*** his reign and his might,
29:30 and to ***a*** the kingdoms of the
2 Chr 1: 2 And Solomon spoke to ***a*** Israel,
1: 2 and to every leader in ***a***
1: 3 and ***a*** the assembly with him,
1:17 they exported them to ***a*** the
2: 5 for our God is greater than ***a***
2:17 Then Solomon numbered ***a*** the
4: 3 of oxen encircling it ***a*** around,
4: 3 ***a*** the way around the Sea. The
4: 4 and ***a*** their back parts pointed
4:16 and ***a*** their articles Huram his
4:18 And Solomon had ***a*** these articles
4:19 Thus Solomon had ***a*** the
5: 1 So ***a*** the work that Solomon had
5: 1 the silver and the gold and ***a***
5: 2 the elders of Israel and ***a*** the
5: 3 Therefore ***a*** the men of Israel
5: 4 So ***a*** the elders of Israel came,
5: 5 and ***a*** the holy furnishings that
5: 6 and ***a*** the congregation of
5:11 of the Most Holy Place (for ***a***
5:12 ***a*** those of Asaph and Heman and
6: 3 while ***a*** the assembly of Israel
6:12 the LORD in the presence of ***a***
6:13 down on his knees before ***a*** the
6:14 who walk before You with ***a***
6:29 or by ***a*** Your people Israel,
6:30 to everyone according to ***a*** his
6:33 and do according to ***a*** for which
6:33 that ***a*** peoples of the earth may
6:38 when they return to You with ***a***
6:38 with all their heart and with ***a***
7: 3 When ***a*** the children of Israel
7: 4 Then the king and ***a*** the people
7: 5 So the king and ***a*** the people
7: 6 while ***a*** Israel stood.
7: 8 and ***a*** Israel with him, a very
7:11 successfully accomplished ***a***
7:17 and do according to ***a*** that I
7:20 a proverb and a byword among ***a***
7:22 therefore He has brought ***a*** this
8: 4 and ***a*** the storage cities which
8: 6 also Baalath and ***a*** the storage
8: 6 and ***a*** the chariot cities and
8: 6 and ***a*** that Solomon desired to
8: 6 and in ***a*** the land of his
8: 7 ***A*** the people who were left of
8:16 Now ***a*** the work of Solomon was
9: 1 she spoke with him about ***a*** that
9: 2 So Solomon answered ***a*** her
9:12 gave to the queen of Sheba ***a***
9:14 And ***a*** the kings of Arabia and
9:20 ***A*** King Solomon's drinking
9:20 and ***a*** the vessels of the House
9:22 So King Solomon surpassed ***a*** the
9:23 And ***a*** the kings of the earth
9:26 So he reigned over ***a*** the kings
9:28 Solomon from Egypt and from ***a***
9:30 reigned in Jerusalem over ***a***
10: 1 for ***a*** Israel had gone to
10: 3 And Jeroboam and ***a*** Israel came
10:12 So Jeroboam and ***a*** the people
10:16 Now when ***a*** Israel saw that the
10:16 So ***a*** Israel departed to their
11: 3 and to ***a*** Israel in Judah and
11:13 And from ***a*** their territories
11:13 and the Levites who were in ***a***
11:16 those from ***a*** the tribes of
11:21 of Absalom more than ***a*** his
11:23 some of his sons throughout ***a***
12: 1 and ***a*** Israel along with him.
12:13 the LORD had chosen out of ***a***
12:15 Rehoboam and Jeroboam ***a*** their
13: 4 Jeroboam and ***a*** Israel:
13:15 that God struck Jeroboam and ***a***
14: 5 and the incense altars from ***a***
14: 8 ***a*** these were mighty men of
14:14 Then they defeated ***a*** the cities
14:14 and they plundered ***a*** the
15: 2 and ***a*** Judah and Benjamin.
15: 5 but great turmoil was on ***a*** the
15: 8 the abominable idols from ***a***
15: 9 Then he gathered ***a*** Judah and
15:12 God of their fathers with ***a***
15:12 with all their heart and with ***a***
15:15 And ***a*** Judah rejoiced at the
15:15 for they had sworn with ***a*** their
15:15 heart and sought Him with ***a***
15:15 and the LORD gave them rest ***a***
15:17 the heart of Asa was loyal ***a***
16: 4 and ***a*** the storage cities of
16: 6 Then King Asa took ***a*** Judah, and
17: 2 And he placed troops in ***a*** the
17: 5 and ***a*** Judah gave presents to
17: 9 they went throughout ***a*** the
17:10 the fear of the LORD fell on ***a***
17:19 fortified cities throughout ***a***
18: 9 and ***a*** the prophets prophesied
18:11 And ***a*** the prophets prophesied
18:16 I saw ***a*** Israel scattered on the
18:18 and ***a*** the host of heaven
18:21 lying spirit in the mouth of ***a***
18:27 "Take heed, ***a*** you people!"
19: 5 in the land throughout ***a*** the
19:11 chief priest is over you in ***a***
19:11 for ***a*** the king's matters; also
20: 3 proclaimed a fast throughout ***a***
20: 4 and from ***a*** the cities of Judah
20: 6 and do You not rule over ***a*** the
20:13 Now ***a*** Judah, with their little
20:15 ***a*** you of Judah and you
20:18 and ***a*** Judah and the inhabitants
20:29 And the fear of God was on ***a*** the
20:30 for his God gave him rest ***a***
21: 2 ***a*** these were the sons of
21: 4 himself and killed ***a*** his
21: 9 and ***a*** his chariots with him.
21:14 and ***a*** your possessions;
21:17 and carried away ***a*** the
21:18 After ***a*** this the LORD struck
22: 1 into the camp had killed ***a*** the
22: 9 who sought the LORD with ***a*** his
22:10 she arose and destroyed ***a*** the
23: 2 and gathered the Levites from ***a***
23: 3 Then ***a*** the assembly made a
23: 5 ***A*** the people shall be in the
23: 6 but ***a*** the people shall keep the
23: 7 shall surround the king on ***a***
23: 8 So the Levites and ***a*** Judah did
23: 8 all Judah did according to ***a***
23:10 Then he set ***a*** the people, every
23:10 ***a*** around the king.
23:13 ***A*** the people of the land were
23:17 And ***a*** the people went to the
23:20 and ***a*** the people of the land,
23:21 So ***a*** the people of the land
24: 2 in the sight of the LORD ***a***
24: 5 and gather from ***a*** Israel money
24: 7 and had also presented ***a*** the
24:10 Then ***a*** the leaders and all the
24:10 Then all the leaders and ***a*** the
24:10 them into the chest until ***a***
24:14 of the LORD continually ***a*** the
24:23 and destroyed ***a*** the leaders of
24:23 and sent ***a*** their spoil to the
25: 5 throughout ***a*** Judah and
25:12 so that they ***a*** were dashed in
25:24 And he took ***a*** the gold and
25:24 ***a*** the articles that were found
26: 1 Now ***a*** the people of Judah took
26: 4 according to ***a*** that his father
26:20 Azariah the chief priest and ***a***
27: 2 according to ***a*** that his father
27: 7 and ***a*** his wars and his ways,
28: 6 ***a*** valiant men, because they had
28:14 spoil before the leaders and ***a***
28:15 from the spoil they clothed ***a***
28:15 and they let ***a*** the feeble ones
28:23 were the ruin of him and of ***a***
28:26 the rest of his acts and ***a*** his
29: 2 according to ***a*** that his father
29:16 and brought out ***a*** the debris
29:18 We have cleansed ***a*** the house of
29:18 of burnt offerings with ***a*** its
29:18 table of the showbread with ***a***
29:19 Moreover ***a*** the articles which
29:24 to make an atonement for ***a***
29:24 sin offering be made for ***a***
29:28 So ***a*** the assembly worshiped, the
29:28 ***a*** this continued until the
29:29 the king and ***a*** who were present
29:32 ***a*** these were for a burnt
29:34 so that they could not skin ***a***
29:36 Then Hezekiah and ***a*** the people
30: 1 And Hezekiah sent to ***a*** Israel
30: 2 the king and his leaders and ***a***
30: 4 matter pleased the king and ***a***
30: 5 a proclamation throughout ***a***
30: 6 the runners went throughout ***a***
30:14 and they took away ***a*** the
30:22 gave encouragement to ***a*** the
30:25 ***a*** the assembly that came from
31: 1 Now when ***a*** this was finished,
31: 1 ***a*** Israel who were present went
31: 1 from ***a*** Judah, Benjamin, Ephraim,
31: 1 had utterly destroyed them ***a***.
31: 1 Then ***a*** the children of Israel
31: 5 and of ***a*** the produce of the
31:18 and to ***a*** who were written in the
31:19 to distribute portions to ***a***
31:19 among the priests and to ***a*** who
31:20 Thus Hezekiah did throughout ***a***
31:21 he did it with ***a*** his heart.
32: 4 together who stopped ***a*** the
32: 5 built up ***a*** the wall that was
32: 7 nor before ***a*** the multitude that
32: 9 to Jerusalem (but he and ***a*** the
32: 9 and to ***a*** Judah who were in
32:13 I and my fathers have done to ***a***
32:14 Who was there among ***a*** the gods
32:22 and from the hand of ***a*** others,
32:23 was exalted in the sight of ***a***
32:27 and for ***a*** kinds of desirable
32:28 and stalls for ***a*** kinds of
32:30 Hezekiah prospered in ***a*** his
32:31 that He might know ***a*** that was
32:33 and ***a*** Judah and the inhabitants
33: 3 and he worshiped ***a*** the host of
33: 5 And he built altars for ***a*** the
33: 7 which I have chosen out of ***a***
33: 8 if they are careful to do ***a***
33:14 he put military captains in ***a***
33:15 and ***a*** the altars that he had
33:19 and ***a*** his sin and trespass, and
33:22 for Amon sacrificed to ***a*** the
33:25 people of the land executed ***a***
34: 6 as far as Naphtali and ***a***
34: 7 and cut down ***a*** the incense
34: 7 the incense altars throughout ***a***
34: 9 from ***a*** the remnant of Israel,
34: 9 from ***a*** Judah and Benjamin, and
34:12 ***a*** of whom were skillful with
34:13 and were overseers of ***a*** who
34:16 ***A*** that was committed to your
34:21 to do according to ***a*** that is
34:24 ***a*** the curses that are written
34:25 provoke Me to anger with ***a*** the
34:28 and your eyes shall not see ***a***
34:29 the king sent and gathered ***a***
34:30 with ***a*** the men of Judah and the
34:30 and ***a*** the people, great and
34:30 And he read in their hearing ***a***
34:31 and His statutes with ***a*** his
34:31 with all his heart and ***a*** his
34:32 And he made ***a*** who were present
34:33 Thus Josiah removed ***a*** the
34:33 all the abominations from ***a***
34:33 and made ***a*** who were present in
34:33 ***A*** his days they did not depart
35: 3 to the Levites who taught ***a***
35: 7 ***a*** for Passover offerings for
35: 7 for Passover offerings for ***a***
35:13 divided them quickly among ***a***
35:16 So ***a*** the service of the LORD
35:18 ***a*** Judah and Israel who were
35:20 After ***a*** this, when Josiah had
35:24 And ***a*** Judah and Jerusalem
35:25 And to this day ***a*** the singing
36:14 Moreover ***a*** the leaders of the
36:14 according to ***a*** the
36:17 He gave them ***a*** into his hand.
36:18 And ***a*** the articles from the
36:18 ***a*** these he took to Babylon.
36:19 burned ***a*** its palaces with fire,
36:19 and destroyed ***a*** its precious
36:22 a proclamation throughout ***a***
36:23 ***A*** the kingdoms of the earth the
36:23 Who is among you of ***a*** His
Ezra 1: 1 a proclamation throughout ***a***
1: 2 ***A*** the kingdoms of the earth the
1: 3 Who is among you of ***a*** His
1: 5 with ***a*** whose spirits God had
1: 6 And ***a*** those who were around
1: 6 besides ***a*** that was willingly
1:11 ***A*** the articles of gold and
1:11 ***A*** these Sheshbazzar took with
2:42 hundred and thirty-nine in ***a***.
2:58 ***A*** the Nethinim and the children
2:70 and ***a*** Israel in their cities.
3: 5 those for New Moons and for ***a***
3: 8 and ***a*** those who had come out of
3:11 Then ***a*** the people shouted with
4: 5 to frustrate their purpose ***a***
4:20 who have ruled over ***a*** the
5: 7 —To Darius the king: ***A*** peace.
6:17 and as a sin offering for ***a***
6:20 ***a*** of them were ritually
6:20 the Passover lambs for ***a*** the
6:21 captivity ate together with ***a***
7: 6 The king granted him ***a*** his
7:13 I issue a decree that ***a*** those of
7:16 and whereas ***a*** the silver and
7:16 and gold that you may find in ***a***
7:21 issue a decree to ***a*** the
7:25 and judges who may judge ***a*** the
7:25 ***a*** such as know the laws of your
7:28 and before ***a*** the king's mighty
8:20 ***A*** of them were designated by
8:21 us and our little ones and ***a***
8:22 hand of our God is upon ***a***
8:22 and His wrath are against ***a***
8:25 and ***a*** Israel who were
8:34 ***A*** the weight was written down
8:35 twelve bulls for ***a*** Israel,
8:35 ***A*** this was a burnt offering
9:13 And after ***a*** that has come upon
10: 3 with our God to put away ***a***
10: 5 and ***a*** Israel swear an oath that
10: 7 Judah and Jerusalem to ***a*** the
10: 8 ***a*** his property would be
10: 9 So ***a*** the men of Judah and
10: 9 and ***a*** the people sat in the
10:12 Then ***a*** the assembly answered and
10:14 and let ***a*** those in our cities
10:17 they finished questioning ***a***
10:44 ***A*** these had taken pagan wives,
Neh 4: 8 and ***a*** of them conspired together
4:15 that ***a*** of us returned to the
4:16 and the leaders were behind ***a***
5:13 And ***a*** the assembly said,
5:16 ***A*** my servants were gathered
5:18 ten days an abundance of ***a***
5:19 according to ***a*** that I have
6: 9 For they ***a*** were trying to
6:12 that God had not sent him at ***a***,
6:16 when ***a*** our enemies heard of
6:16 and ***a*** the nations around us saw
7:60 ***A*** the Nethinim, and the sons of
7:73 and ***a*** Israel dwelt in their
8: 1 Now ***a*** the people gathered
8: 2 of men and women and ***a*** who
8: 3 and the ears of ***a*** the people
8: 5 the book in the sight of ***a*** the
8: 5 for he was standing above ***a***
8: 5 ***a*** the people stood up.
8: 6 Then ***a*** the people answered,

8: 9 who taught the people said to *a*
8: 9 For *a* the people wept, when
8:11 So the Levites quieted *a* the
8:12 And *a* the people went their way
8:13 of the fathers' houses of *a*
8:15 announce and proclaim in *a*
9: 2 separated themselves from *a*
9: 5 Which is exalted above *a*
9: 6 with *a* their host, The earth
9: 6 The seas and *a* that is in
9: 6 them, And You preserve them *a*.
9:10 Against *a* his servants, And
9:10 And against *a* the people of
9:25 And possessed houses full of *a*
9:32 Do not let *a* the trouble seem
9:32 Our fathers and on *a* Your
9:33 However You are just in *a* that
9:38 And because of *a* this, We make
10:28 and *a* those who had separated
10:29 and to observe and do *a* the
10:33 and *a* the work of the house of
10:35 and the firstfruits of *a* fruit
10:35 firstfruits of all fruit of *a*
10:37 the fruit from *a* kinds of
10:37 should receive the tithes in *a*
11: 2 And the people blessed *a* the men
11: 6 *A* the sons of Perez who dwelt at
11:18 *A* the Levites in the holy city
11:20 were in *a* the cities of Judah,
11:24 was the king's deputy in *a*
12:27 sought out the Levites in *a*
12:29 had built themselves villages *a*
12:47 and in the days of Nehemiah *a*
13: 3 that they separated *a* the mixed
13: 6 But during *a* this I was not in
13: 8 therefore I threw *a* the
13:12 Then *a* Judah brought the tithe
13:15 and *a* kinds of burdens, which
13:16 who brought in fish and *a* kinds
13:18 and did not our God bring *a*
13:20 the merchants and sellers of *a*
13:26 and God made him king over *a*
13:27 we then hear of your doing *a*
Esth 1: 3 his reign he made a feast for *a*
1: 4 hundred and eighty days in *a*.
1: 5 feast lasting seven days for *a*
1: 8 for so the king had ordered *a*
1:13 the king's manner toward *a* who
1:16 but also *a* the princes, and all
1:16 and *a* the people who are in
1:16 all the people who are in *a*
1:17 will become known to *a* women,
1:18 Persia and Media will say to *a*
1:20 is proclaimed throughout *a* his
1:20 *a* wives will honor their
1:22 Then he sent letters to *a* the
2: 3 the king appoint officers in *a*
2: 3 that they may gather *a* the
2:15 favor in the sight of *a* who
2:17 king loved Esther more than *a*
2:17 favor in his sight more than *a*
2:18 for *a* his officials and
3: 1 him and set his seat above *a*
3: 2 And *a* the king's servants who
3: 6 Haman sought to destroy *a* the
3: 8 among the people in *a* the
3: 8 laws are different from *a*
3:12 was written according to *a*
3:12 to the officials of *a* people,
3:13 were sent by couriers into *a*
3:13 and to annihilate *a* the Jews,
3:14 being published for *a* people,
4: 1 When Mordecai learned *a* that had
4: 7 And Mordecai told him *a* that had
4:11 *A* the king's servants and the
4:11 put *a* to death, except the one
4:13 king's palace any more than *a*
4:16 gather *a* the Jews who are
4:17 his way and did according to *a*
5:13 Yet *a* this avails me nothing, so
5:14 Then his wife Zeresh and *a* his
6:10 Leave nothing undone of *a* that
6:13 told his wife Zeresh and *a* his
8: 5 the Jews who are in *a* the
8: 9 according to *a* that Mordecai
8: 9 twenty-seven provinces in *a*,
8:11 and annihilate *a* the forces of
8:12 on one day in *a* the provinces of
8:13 province and published for *a*
9: 2 in their cities throughout *a*
9: 2 fear of them fell upon *a*
9: 3 And *a* the officials of the
9: 3 and *a* those doing the king's
9: 4 his fame spread throughout *a*
9: 5 Thus the Jews defeated *a* their
9:20 things and sent letters to *a*
9:20 who were in *a* the provinces of
9:24 the enemy of *a* the Jews, had
9:26 because of *a* the words of this
9:27 and their descendants and *a*
9:30 And Mordecai sent letters to *a*
10: 2 Now *a* the acts of his power and
10: 3 people and speaking peace to *a*
Job 1: 3 this man was the greatest of *a*
1: 5 to the number of them *a*.
1:10 and around *a* that he has on
1:11 out Your hand and touch *a* that
1:12 *a* that he has is in your
1:22 In *a* this Job did not sin nor
2: 4 *a* that a man has he will give
2:10 In *a* this Job did not sin
2:11 Job's three friends heard of *a*
4:14 Which made *a* my bones shake.
8:13 So are the paths of *a* who
9:22 It is *a* one thing; Therefore
9:28 I am afraid of *a* my sufferings;
12: 9 Who among *a* these does not know
12:10 And the breath of *a* mankind?
13: 1 my eye has seen *a* this, My
13: 4 You are *a* worthless
13:27 And watch closely *a* my paths.
14:14 *A* the days of my hard service
15:20 wicked man writhes with pain *a*
16: 2 comforters are you *a*!
16: 7 You have made desolate *a* my
17: 7 And *a* my members are like
17:10 *a* of you, For I shall not find
19:12 They encamp *a* around my tent.
19:19 *A* my close friends abhor me,
22:10 Therefore snares are *a* around
24: 4 *A* the poor of the land are
24:24 are taken out of the way like *a*
27:12 Surely *a* of you have seen it;
28:21 is hidden from the eyes of *a*
29:19 And the dew lies *a* night on my
30:23 to the house appointed for *a*
31: 4 And count *a* my steps?
31:12 And would root out *a* my
33: 1 And listen to *a* my words.
33:11 He watches *a* my paths.'
33:29 God works *a* these things,
34:15 *A* flesh would perish together,
34:19 For they are *a* the work of
34:21 And He sees *a* his steps.
36:19 Or *a* the mighty forces, Keep
37: 7 That *a* men may know His work.
38: 7 And *a* the sons of God shouted
38:18 if you know *a* this.
40:20 And *a* the beasts of the field
41:14 With his terrible teeth *a*
41:34 He is king over *a* the
42:11 Then *a* his brothers, all his
42:11 *a* his sisters, and all those
42:11 and *a* those who had been his
42:11 him and comforted him for *a*
42:15 In *a* the land were found no
Ps 2:12 Blessed are *a* those who put
3: 6 set themselves against me *a*
3: 7 my God! For You have struck *a*
5: 5 You hate *a* workers of
5:11 But let *a* those rejoice who put
6: 6 *A* night I make my bed swim; I
6: 7 It grows old because of *a* my
6: 8 *a* you workers of iniquity; For
6:10 Let *a* my enemies be ashamed and
7: 1 Save me from *a* those who
8: 1 excellent is Your name in *a*
8: 6 You have put *a* things under
8: 7 *A* sheep and oxen
8: 9 excellent is Your name in *a*
9: 1 I will tell of *a* Your
9:14 That I may tell of *a* Your
9:17 And *a* the nations that forget
10: 5 As for *a* his enemies, he
12: 3 May the LORD cut off *a*
14: 3 They have *a* turned aside, They
14: 4 Have *a* the workers of iniquity
16: 3 in whom is *a* my delight."
18: him from the hand of *a* his
18:22 For *a* His judgments were
18:30 He is a shield to *a* who trust
19: 4 line has gone out through *a*
20: 3 May He remember *a* your
20: 4 And fulfill *a* your purpose.
20: 5 May the LORD fulfill *a* your
21: 8 Your hand will find *a* Your
22: 7 *A* those who see Me ridicule Me
22:14 And *a* My bones are out of
22:17 I can count *a* My bones.
22:23 praise Him! *A* you descendants
22:23 *a* you offspring of Israel!
22:27 *A* the ends of the world Shall
22:27 And *a* the families of the
22:29 *A* the prosperous of the earth
22:29 *A* those who go down to the
23: 6 and mercy shall follow me *A*
24: 1 and *a* its fullness, The world
25: 5 On You I wait *a* the day.
25:10 *A* the paths of the LORD are
25:18 And forgive *a* my sins.
25:22 Out of *a* their troubles!
26: 7 And tell of *a* Your wondrous
27: 4 in the house of the LORD *A*
27: 6 be lifted up above my enemies *a*
31:11 I am a reproach among *a* my
31:23 *a* you His saints! For the
31:24 *A* you who hope in the LORD.
32: 3 old Through my groaning *a* the
32:11 *a* you upright in heart!
33: 4 And *a* His work is done in
33: 6 And *a* the host of them by the
33: 8 Let *a* the earth fear the LORD;
33: 8 Let *a* the inhabitants of the
33:11 The plans of His heart to *a*
33:13 He sees *a* the sons of men.
33:14 of His dwelling He looks On *a*
33:15 He considers *a* their works.
34: 1 I will bless the LORD at *a*
34: 4 And delivered me from *a* my
34: 6 And saved him out of *a* his
34: 7 angel of the LORD encamps *a*
34:17 And delivers them out of *a*
34:19 delivers him out of them *a*.
34:20 He guards *a* his bones; Not one
35:10 *A* my bones shall say, "LORD,
35:28 And of Your praise *a* the day
38: 6 I go mourning *a* the day long.
38: 9 *a* my desire is before You;
38:12 And plan deception *a* the day
39: 8 Deliver me from *a* my
39:12 as *a* my fathers were.
40:16 Let *a* those who seek You
41: 7 *A* who hate me whisper together
42: 7 *A* Your waves and billows have
42:10 While they say to me *a* day
44: 8 In God we boast *a* day long,
44:13 scorn and a derision to those *a*
44:17 *A* this has come upon us
44:22 for Your sake we are killed *a*
45: 8 *A* Your garments are scented
45:13 The royal daughter is *a*
45:16 You shall make princes in *a*
45:17 Your name to be remembered in *a*
47: 1 *a* you peoples! Shout to God
47: 2 He is a great King over *a*
47: 7 For God is the King of *a* the
48:12 And go *a* around her.
49: 1 *a* peoples; Give ear, all
49: 1 *a* inhabitants of the world,
49:11 Their dwelling places to *a*
50: 3 it shall be very tempestuous *a*
50:11 I know *a* the birds of the
50:12 and *a* its fullness.
51: 9 And blot out *a* my iniquities.
52: 4 You love *a* devouring words,
54: 7 He has delivered me out of *a*
56: 1 Fighting *a* day he oppresses
56: 2 My enemies would hound me *a*
56: 5 *A* day they twist my words
56: 5 *A* their thoughts are against
57: 2 To God who performs *a* things
57: 5 Let Your glory be above *a*
57:11 Let Your glory be above *a*
59: 5 Awake to punish *a* the nations;
59: 6 And go *a* around the city.
59: 8 You shall have *a* the nations
59:14 And go *a* around the city.
62: 3 *a* of you, Like a leaning wall
62: 8 Trust in Him at *a* times, you
64: 8 *A* who see them shall flee
64: 9 *A* men shall fear, And shall
64:10 And *a* the upright in heart
65: 2 To You *a* flesh will come.
65: 5 who are the confidence of *a*
66: 1 shout to God, *a* the earth!
66: 4 *A* the earth shall worship You
66:16 *a* you who fear God, And I will
67: 2 Your salvation among *a*
67: 3 Let *a* the peoples praise You.
67: 5 Let *a* the peoples praise You.
67: 7 And *a* the ends of the earth
69:19 My adversaries are *a* before
70: 4 Let *a* those who seek You
71: 8 And with Your glory *a* the
71:15 And Your salvation *a* the day,
71:24 talk of Your righteousness *a*
72: 5 Throughout *a* generations.
72:11 *a* kings shall fall down before
72:11 *A* nations shall serve Him.
72:17 *A* nations shall call Him
73:14 For *a* day long I have been
73:27 You have destroyed *a* those who
73:28 That I may declare *a* Your
74: 6 *a* at once, With axes and
74: 8 They have burned up *a* the
74:17 You have set *a* the borders of
75: 3 The earth and *a* its inhabitants
75: 8 Surely its dregs shall *a* the
75:10 *A* the horns of the wicked I will
76: 9 To deliver *a* the oppressed of
76:11 Let *a* who are around Him bring
77:12 I will also meditate on *a* Your
78:14 And *a* the night with a light
78:28 *A* around their dwellings.
78:38 And did not stir up *a* His
78:51 And destroyed *a* the firstborn
79: 3 they have shed like water *a*
79:13 show forth Your praise to *a*
80:12 So that *a* who pass by the way
82: 5 *A* the foundations of the earth
82: 6 And *a* of you are children of
82: 8 For You shall inherit *a*
83:11 *a* their princes like Zebah and
83:18 Are the Most High over *a* the
85: 2 You have covered *a* their sin.
85: 3 You have taken away *a* Your
85: 5 You prolong Your anger to *a*
86: 3 For I cry to You *a* day long.
86: 5 And abundant in mercy to *a*
86: 9 *A* nations whom You have made
86:12 with *a* my heart, And I will
87: 2 the gates of Zion More than *a*
87: 7 *A* my springs are in you."
88: 7 You have afflicted me with *a*
88:17 They came around me *a* day long
89: 1 known Your faithfulness to *a*
89: 4 And build up your throne to *a*
89: 7 to be held in reverence by *a*
89:11 The world and *a* its fullness,
89:16 In Your name they rejoice *a* day
89:40 You have broken down *a* his
89:41 *A* who pass by the way plunder
89:42 You have made *a* his enemies
89:47 futility have You created *a*
89:50 my bosom the reproach of *a*
90: 1 been our dwelling place in *a*

90: 9 For a our days have passed away
90:14 we may rejoice and be glad a
91:11 To keep you in a your ways.
92: 7 And when a the workers of
92: 9 A the workers of iniquity
94: 4 A the workers of iniquity
94:15 And a the upright in heart
95: 3 And the great King above a
96: 1 Sing to the LORD, a the earth.
96: 3 His wonders among a peoples.
96: 4 He is to be feared above a
96: 5 For a the gods of the peoples
96: 9 before Him, a the earth.
96:11 sea roar, and a its fullness;
96:12 and a that is in it. Then all
96:12 Then a the trees of the woods
97: 6 And a the peoples see His
97: 7 Let a be put to shame who serve
97: 7 Worship Him, a you gods.
97: 9 are most high above a the
97: 9 You are exalted far above a
98: 3 A the ends of the earth have
98: 4 a the earth; Break forth in
98: 7 and a its fullness, The world
99: 2 And He is high above a the
100: 1 to the LORD, a you lands!
100: 5 And His truth endures to a
101: 8 Early I will destroy a the
101: 8 That I may cut off a the
102: 8 My enemies reproach me a day
102:12 remembrance of Your name to a
102:15 And a the kings of the earth
102:24 Your years are throughout a
102:26 they will a grow old like a
103: 1 And a that is within me,
103: 2 And forget not a His benefits:
103: 3 Who forgives a your iniquities,
103: 3 Who heals a your diseases,
103: 6 And justice for a who are
103:19 And His kingdom rules over a.
103:21 a you His hosts, You
103:22 a His works, In all places of
103:22 In a places of His dominion.
104:20 In which a the beasts of the
104:24 In wisdom You have made them a.
104:27 These a wait for You, That You
105: 2 Talk of a His wondrous works!
105: 7 His judgments are in a the
105:16 He destroyed a the provision
105:21 ruler of a his possessions,
105:31 lice in a their territory.
105:35 And ate up a the vegetation in
105:36 He also destroyed a the
105:36 The first of a their strength.
106: 2 Who can declare a His praise?
106: 3 he who does righteousness at a
106:31 to him for righteousness To a
106:46 made them to be pitied By a
106:48 to everlasting! And let a the
107:18 Their soul abhorred a manner of
107:42 And a iniquity stops its
108: 5 And Your glory above a the
109:11 Let the creditor seize a that
111: 2 Studied by a who have pleasure
111: 7 A His precepts are sure.
111:10 A good understanding have a
113: 4 The LORD is high above a
116:11 A men are liars."
116:12 I render to the LORD For a
116:14 Now in the presence of a His
116:18 Now in the presence of a His
117: 1 a you Gentiles! Laud Him, all
117: 1 Laud Him, a you peoples!
118:10 A nations surrounded me, But
119: 6 When I look into a Your
119:13 my lips I have declared A the
119:14 As much as in a riches.
119:20 For Your judgments at a times.
119:63 I am a companion of a who fear
119:86 A Your commandments are
119:90 faithfulness endures to a
119:91 For a are Your servants.
119:96 have seen the consummation of a
119:97 law! It is my meditation a
119:99 have more understanding than a
119:118 You reject a those who stray
119:119 You put away a the wicked of
119:128 Therefore a Your precepts
119:128 Your precepts concerning a
119:151 And a Your commandments are
119:168 For a my ways are before You.
119:172 For a Your commandments are
121: 7 shall preserve you from a evil;
128: 3 children like olive plants A
128: 5 see the good of Jerusalem A
129: 5 Let a those who hate Zion Be
130: 8 He shall redeem Israel From a
132: 1 remember David And a his
134: 1 A you servants of the LORD,
135: 5 And our Lord is above a gods.
135: 6 In the seas and in a deep
135: 9 Upon Pharaoh and a his
135:11 And a the kingdoms of Canaan—
135:13 throughout a generations.
136:25 Who gives food to a flesh, For
138: 2 magnified Your word above a
138: 4 A the kings of the earth shall
139: 3 And are acquainted with a my
139:16 And in Your book they a were
143: 5 I meditate on a Your works; I
143:12 And destroy a those who
144:13 Supplying a kinds of produce;
145: 9 The LORD is good to a,
145: 9 His tender mercies are over a
145:10 A Your works shall praise You,
145:13 dominion endures throughout a
145:14 The LORD upholds a who fall,
145:14 And raises up a who are
145:15 The eyes of a look expectantly
145:17 The LORD is righteous in a
145:17 Gracious in a His works.
145:18 The LORD is near to a who
145:18 To a who call upon Him in
145:20 The LORD preserves a who love
145:20 But a the wicked He will
145:21 And a flesh shall bless His
146: 6 and a that is in them; Who
146:10 to a generations. Praise the
147: 4 He calls them a by name.
148: 2 Praise Him, a His angels;
148: 2 Praise Him, a His hosts!
148: 3 a you stars of light!
148: 7 You great sea creatures and a
148: 9 Mountains and a hills;
148: 9 Fruitful trees and a cedars;
148:10 Beasts and a cattle; Creeping
148:11 Kings of the earth and a
148:11 Princes and a judges of the
148:14 The praise of a His saints—Of
149: 9 This honor have a His saints.
Prov 1:13 We shall find a kinds of
1:14 Let us a have one purse"—
1:25 Because you disdained a my
3: 5 Trust in the LORD with a your
3: 6 In a your ways acknowledge Him,
3: 9 And with the firstfruits of a
3:15 And a the things you may
3:17 And a her paths are peace.
3:18 And happy are a who retain
4: 7 And in a your getting, get
4:22 And health to a their flesh.
4:23 Keep your heart with a
4:26 And let a your ways be
5:19 her breasts satisfy you at a
5:21 And He ponders a his paths.
6:31 He may have to give up a the
7:26 And a who were slain by her
8: 8 A the words of my mouth are
8: 9 They are a plain to him who
8:11 And a the things one may
8:16 A the judges of the earth.
8:36 A those who hate me love
10:12 But love covers a sins.
14:23 In a labor there is profit,
15:15 A the days of the afflicted
16: 2 A the ways of a man are pure
16: 4 The LORD has made a for
16:11 A the weights in the bag are
17:17 A friend loves at a times, And
18: 1 He rages against a wise
19: 7 A the brothers of the poor hate
20: 8 throne of judgment Scatters a
20:27 Searching a the inner depths
21:26 He covets greedily a day long,
22: 2 LORD is the maker of them a.
22:18 Let them a be fixed upon your
23:17 for the fear of the LORD a
24: 4 the rooms are filled With a
24:31 a overgrown with thorns; Its
27:24 Nor does a crown endure to a
28: 5 who seek the LORD understand a.
29:11 A fool vents a his feelings,
29:12 A his servants become wicked.
30: 4 Who has established a the ends
30:27 Yet they a advance in ranks;
31: 5 And pervert the justice of a
31: 8 In the cause of a who are
31:12 does him good and not evil A
31:21 For a her household is
31:29 well, But you excel them a.
Eccl 1: 2 of vanities, a is vanity."
1: 3 What profit has a man from a
1: 7 A the rivers run into the sea,
1: 8 A things are full of labor
1:13 out by wisdom concerning a
1:14 I have seen a the works that are
1:14 a is vanity and grasping for
1:16 have gained more wisdom than a
2: 3 of men to do under heaven a
2: 5 and I planted a kinds of fruit
2: 7 of herds and flocks than a who
2: 8 and musical instruments of a
2: 9 great and excelled more than a
2:10 For my heart rejoiced in a my
2:10 And this was my reward from a
2:11 Then I looked on a the works
2:11 And indeed a was vanity and
2:14 same event happens to them a.
2:16 Since a that now is will be
2:17 for a is vanity and grasping
2:18 Then I hated a my labor in
2:19 Yet he will rule over a my
2:20 my heart and despaired of a
2:22 For what has man for a his
2:23 For a his days are sorrowful,
3:13 drink and enjoy the good of a
3:19 they a have one breath; man has
3:19 for a is vanity.
3:20 A go to one place: all are from
3:20 a are from the dust, and all
3:20 and a return to dust.
4: 1 I returned and considered a
4: 4 I saw that for a toil and every
4: 8 Yet there is no end to a his
4:15 I saw a the living who walk
4:16 There was no end of a the
5: 9 the profit of the land is for a;
5:17 A his days he also eats in
5:18 and to enjoy the good of a his
5:18 which he toils under the sun a
6: 2 lacks nothing for himself of a
6: 6 Do not a go to one place?
6: 7 A the labor of man is for his
6:12 a the days of his vain life
7: 2 For that is the end of a men;
7:18 fears God will escape them a.
7:23 A this I have proved by
7:28 But a woman among a these I
8: 9 A this I have seen, and applied
8:15 with him in his labor a the
8:17 then I saw a the work of God,
9: 1 For I considered a this in my
9: 1 so that I could declare it a:
9: 2 A things come alike to all:
9: 2 All things come alike to a:
9: 3 This is an evil in a that is
9: 3 that one thing happens to a.
9: 4 But for him who is joined to a
9: 9 with the wife whom you love a
9: 9 a your days of vanity; for that
9:11 and chance happen to them a.
11: 8 years And rejoices in them a,
11: 8 A that is coming is vanity.
11: 9 But know that for a these God
12: 4 And a the daughters of music
12: 8 A is vanity."
12:13 For this is man's a.
Song 1:13 That lies a night between my
3: 6 With a the merchant's fragrant
3: 8 They a hold swords, Being
4: 4 A shields of mighty men.
4: 7 You are a fair, my love, And
4:10 scent of your perfumes Than a
4:14 With a trees of frankincense,
4:14 With a the chief spices—
7:13 A manner, new and old, Which
8: 7 a man would give for love A
Isa 1:25 And take away a your alloy.
2: 2 And a nations shall flow to
2:13 Upon a the cedars of Lebanon
2:13 And upon a the oaks of Bashan;
2:14 Upon a the high mountains, And
2:14 And upon a the hills that
2:16 Upon a the ships of Tarshish,
2:16 And upon a the beautiful
4: 5 For over a the glory there
5:25 For a this His anger is not
5:28 And a their bows bent; Their
7:19 and a of them will rest In the
7:19 And on a thorns and in all
7:19 And on all thorns and in a
7:24 Because a the land will become
8: 7 The king of Assyria and a his
8: 7 He will go up over a his
8: 7 all his channels And go over a
8: 9 a you from far countries.
8:12 Concerning a that this people
9: 9 A the people will know
9:12 For a this His anger is not
9:17 For a this His anger is not
9:21 For a this His anger is not
10: 4 For a this His anger is not
10:12 when the LORD has performed a
10:14 I have gathered a the earth;
10:23 end In the midst of a the
11: 9 not hurt nor destroy in a My
12: 5 This is known in a the earth.
13: 7 Therefore a hands will be limp,
14: 9 A the chief ones of the earth;
14: 9 up from their thrones A the
14:10 They a shall speak and say to
14:18 A the kings of the nations, All
14:18 A of them, sleep in glory,
14:26 that is stretched out over a
14:29 a you of Philistia, Because
14:31 O city! A you of Philistia
15: 2 On a their heads will be
15: 8 For the cry has gone a around
16:14 of Moab will be despised with a
18: 3 A inhabitants of the world and
18: 6 And a the beasts of the earth
19: 8 A those will lament who cast
19:10 A who make wages will be
19:14 have caused Egypt to err in a
21: 2 O Media! A its sighing I have
21: 9 is fallen! And a the carved
21:16 a the glory of Kedar will fail;
22: 1 that you have a gone up to the
22: 3 A your rulers have fled
22: 3 A who are found in you are
22:24 They will hang on him a the
22:24 a vessels of small quantity,
22:24 from the cups to a the
23: 9 to dishonor the pride of a
23: 9 To bring into contempt a the
23:17 and commit fornication with a
24: 7 A the merry-hearted sigh.
24:11 A joy is darkened, The mirth
25: 6 LORD of hosts will make for a
25: 7 of the covering cast over a
25: 7 the veil that is spread over a
25: 8 will wipe away tears from a
25: 8 He will take away from a the
26:12 For You have also done a our
26:14 And made a their memory to
26:15 You have expanded a the

27: 9 And this is ***a*** the fruit of
27: 9 When he makes ***a*** the stones of
28: 8 For ***a*** tables are full of vomit
28:24 the plowman keep plowing ***a*** day
29: 3 I will encamp against you ***a***
29: 7 The multitude of ***a*** the nations
29: 7 Even ***a*** who fight against her
29: 8 So the multitude of ***a*** the
29:20 And ***a*** who watch for iniquity
30: 5 They were ***a*** ashamed of a people
30:18 Blessed are ***a*** those who wait
31: 3 They ***a*** will perish together.
32:13 on ***a*** the happy homes in the
32:20 are you who sow beside ***a***
34: 1 and ***a*** that is in it, The world
34: 1 The world and ***a*** things that
34: 2 of the LORD is against ***a***
34: 2 And His fury against ***a*** their
34: 4 ***A*** the host of heaven shall be
34: 4 ***A*** their host shall fall down
34:12 and ***a*** its princes shall be
36: 1 of Assyria came up against ***a***
36: 6 is Pharaoh king of Egypt to ***a***
36:20 Who among ***a*** the gods of these
37:11 kings of Assyria have done to ***a***
37:16 of ***a*** the kingdoms of the earth.
37:17 and hear ***a*** the words of
37:18 of Assyria have laid waste ***a***
37:20 that ***a*** the kingdoms of the
37:25 of my feet I have dried up ***A***
37:36 there were the corpses—***a*** dead.
38:13 So He breaks ***a*** my bones; From
38:15 I shall walk carefully ***a*** my
38:16 And in ***a*** these things is the
38:17 For You have cast ***a*** my sins
38:20 with stringed instruments ***A***
39: 2 and ***a*** his armory—all that was
39: 2 ***a*** that was found among his
39: 2 nothing in his house or in ***a***
39: 4 They have seen ***a*** that is in my
39: 6 the days are coming when ***a*** that
40: 2 the LORD's hand Double for ***a***
40: 5 And ***a*** flesh shall see it
40: 6 ***A*** flesh is grass, And all its
40: 6 And ***a*** its loveliness is like
40:17 ***A*** nations before Him are as
40:26 He calls them ***a*** by name, By
41:11 ***a*** those who were incensed
41:29 Indeed they are ***a*** worthless;
42:10 and ***a*** that is in it, You
42:15 And dry up ***a*** their vegetation;
42:22 ***A*** of them are snared in holes,
42:25 It has set him on fire ***a***
43: 9 Let ***a*** the nations be gathered
43:14 And bring them ***a*** down as
44: 9 ***a*** of them are useless, And
44:11 Surely ***a*** his companions would
44:11 Let them ***a*** be gathered
44:24 who makes ***a*** things, Who
44:24 stretches out the heavens ***a***
44:28 And he shall perform ***a*** My
45: 7 do ***a*** these things.'
45:12 And ***a*** their host I have
45:13 And I will direct ***a*** his ways;
45:16 ***a*** of them; They shall go in
45:22 ***A*** you ends of the earth!
45:24 And ***a*** shall be ashamed Who
45:25 In the LORD ***a*** the descendants
46: 3 And ***a*** the remnant of the house
46:10 And I will do ***a*** My pleasure,'
48: 6 See ***a*** this. And will you not
48:14 ***A*** of you, assemble yourselves,
49: 9 their pastures shall be on ***a***
49:18 ***A*** these gather together and
49:18 clothe yourselves with them ***a***
49:26 ***A*** flesh shall know That I,
50: 2 Is My hand shortened at ***a*** that
50: 9 Indeed they will ***a*** grow old
50:11 ***a*** you who kindle a fire, Who
51: 3 He will comfort ***a*** her waste
51:18 no one to guide her Among ***a***
51:18 takes her by the hand Among ***a***
51:20 They lie at the head of ***a*** the
52:10 His holy arm In the eyes of ***a***
52:10 And ***a*** the ends of the earth
53: 6 ***A*** we like sheep have gone
53: 6 on Him the iniquity of us ***a***.
54:12 And ***a*** your walls of precious
54:13 ***A*** your children shall be
55:12 And ***a*** the trees of the field
56: 7 called a house of prayer for ***a***
56: 9 ***A*** you beasts of the field,
56: 9 ***A*** you beasts in the forest.
56:10 They are ***a*** ignorant; They
56:10 They are ***a*** dumb dogs, They
56:11 They ***a*** look to their own way,
57:13 But the wind will carry them ***a***
58: 3 And exploit ***a*** your laborers.
59:11 We ***a*** growl like bears, And
60: 4 Lift up your eyes ***a*** around, and
60: 4 They ***a*** gather together, they
60: 6 ***A*** those from Sheba shall come;
60: 7 ***A*** the flocks of Kedar shall be
60:14 And ***a*** those who despised you
60:21 Also your people shall ***a*** be
61: 2 To comfort ***a*** who mourn,
61: 9 ***A*** who see them shall
61:11 to spring forth before ***a*** the
62: 2 And ***a*** kings your glory.
63: 3 And I have stained ***a*** My robes.
63: 7 According to ***a*** that the LORD
63: 9 In ***a*** their affliction He was
63: 9 bore them and carried them ***A***
64: 6 But we are ***a*** like an unclean
64: 6 And ***a*** our righteousnesses are
64: 6 We ***a*** fade as a leaf, And our
64: 8 And ***a*** we are the work of Your
64: 9 we ***a*** are Your people!
64:11 And ***a*** our pleasant things are
65: 2 have stretched out My hands ***a***
65: 5 ***A*** fire that burns ***a*** the day.
65: 8 That I may not destroy them ***a***.
65:12 And you shall ***a*** bow down to
65:25 not hurt nor destroy in ***a*** My
66: 2 For ***a*** those things My hand has
66: 2 And ***a*** those things exist,"
66:10 ***a*** you who love her; Rejoice
66:10 ***a*** you who mourn for her;
66:16 sword The LORD will judge ***a***
66:18 shall be that I will gather ***a***
66:20 Then they shall bring ***a*** your
66:20 offering to the LORD out of ***a***
66:23 ***A*** flesh shall come to worship
66:24 shall be an abhorrence to ***a***

Jer 1: 7 For you shall go to ***a*** to whom
1:14 shall break forth On ***a*** the
1:15 I am calling ***A*** the families of
1:15 Against ***a*** its walls all
1:15 Against all its walls ***a***
1:15 And against ***a*** the cities of
1:16 Against them concerning ***a***
1:17 And speak to them ***a*** that I
2: 3 ***A*** that devour him will offend;
2: 4 O house of Jacob and ***a*** the
2:24 ***A*** those who seek her will not
2:29 You ***a*** have transgressed
2:34 But plainly on ***a*** these things.
3: 7 after she had done ***a*** these
3: 8 Then I saw that for ***a*** the causes
3:10 And yet for ***a*** this her
3:17 and ***a*** the nations shall be
4:17 a field they are against her ***a***
4:24 And ***a*** the hills moved back and
4:25 And ***a*** the birds of the heavens
4:26 And ***a*** its cities were broken
5:16 They are ***a*** mighty men.
5:19 does the LORD our God do ***a***
6: 3 their tents against her ***a***
6:15 No! They were not at ***a***
6:28 They are ***a*** stubborn rebels,
6:28 They are ***a*** corrupters;
7: 2 ***a*** you of Judah who enter in
7:10 We are delivered to do ***a*** these
7:13 because you have done ***a*** these
7:15 as I have cast out ***a*** your
7:23 And walk in ***a*** the ways that I
7:25 I have even sent to you ***a*** My
7:27 Therefore you shall speak ***a***
8: 2 the sun and the moon and ***a*** the
8: 3 be chosen rather than life by ***a***
8: 3 who remain in ***a*** the places
8:12 No! They were not at ***a***
8:16 and devoured the land and ***a***
9: 2 go from them! For they are ***a***
9:25 that I will punish ***a*** who are
9:26 and ***a*** who are in the farthest
9:26 For ***a*** these nations are
9:26 and ***a*** the house of Israel are
10: 7 For among ***a*** the wise men of
10: 7 And in ***a*** their kingdoms,
10: 9 They are ***a*** the work of
10:16 For He is the Maker of ***a***
10:20 And ***a*** my cords are broken; My
10:21 And ***a*** their flocks shall be
11: 4 and do according to ***a*** that I
11: 6 Proclaim ***a*** these words in the
11: 8 I will bring upon them ***a*** the
11:12 they will not save them at ***a***
12: 9 The vultures ***a*** around are
12: 9 assemble ***a*** the beasts of the
12:12 plunderers have come On ***a*** the
12:14 Against ***a*** My evil neighbors who
13:13 I will fill ***a*** the inhabitants
13:13 and ***a*** the inhabitants of
13:19 ***a*** of it; It shall be wholly
14:22 Since You have made ***a*** these.
15: 4 to ***a*** kingdoms of the earth,
15:13 Because of ***a*** your sins,
16:10 when you show this people ***a***
16:10 'Why has the LORD pronounced ***a***
16:15 land of the north and from ***a***
16:17 For My eyes are on ***a*** their
17: 3 ***a*** your treasures, And your
17: 3 high places of sin within ***a***
17: 9 heart is deceitful above ***a***
17:13 ***A*** who forsake You shall be
17:19 and in ***a*** the gates of
17:20 and ***a*** Judah, and all the
17:20 and ***a*** the inhabitants of
18:23 You know ***a*** their counsel Which
19: 8 and hiss because of ***a*** its
19:13 because of ***a*** the houses on
19:13 they have burned incense to ***a***
19:14 the Lord's house and said to ***a***
19:15 bring on this city and on ***a***
19:15 city and on all her towns ***a***
20: 4 a terror to yourself and to ***a***
20: 4 I will give ***a*** Judah into the
20: 5 Moreover I will deliver ***a*** the
20: 5 ***a*** its produce, and all its
20: 5 and ***a*** its precious things; all
20: 5 ***a*** the treasures of the kings of
20: 6 and ***a*** who dwell in your house,
20: 6 you and ***a*** your friends, to whom
20:10 and we will report it!" ***A*** my
21: 2 deal with us according to ***a***
21:14 And it shall devour ***a*** things
22:20 For ***a*** your lovers are
22:22 The wind shall eat up ***a*** your
22:22 ashamed and humiliated For ***a***
23: 3 remnant of My flock out of ***a***
23: 8 the north country and from ***a***
23: 9 ***A*** my bones shake. I am like a
23:14 ***A*** of them are like Sodom to
23:15 has gone out into ***a*** the land.
23:32 not profit this people at ***a***,
24: 9 deliver them to trouble into ***a***
24: 9 in ***a*** places where I shall drive
25: 1 came to Jeremiah concerning ***a***
25: 2 the prophet spoke to ***a*** the
25: 2 the people of Judah and to ***a***
25: 4 the LORD has sent to you ***a***
25: 9 I will send and take ***a*** the
25: 9 and against these nations ***a***
25:13 'So I will bring on that land ***a***
25:13 ***a*** that is written in this book,
25:13 has prophesied concerning ***a***
25:15 and cause ***a*** the nations, to
25:17 and made ***a*** the nations drink,
25:19 and ***a*** his people;
25:20 ***a*** the mixed multitude, all the
25:20 ***a*** the kings of the land of Uz,
25:20 ***a*** the kings of the land of the
25:22 ***a*** the kings of Tyre, all the
25:22 ***a*** the kings of Sidon, and the
25:23 and ***a*** who are in the farthest
25:24 ***a*** the kings of Arabia and all
25:24 all the kings of Arabia and ***a***
25:25 ***a*** the kings of Zimri, all the
25:25 ***a*** the kings of Elam, and all
25:25 and ***a*** the kings of the Medes;
25:26 ***a*** the kings of the north, far
25:26 and ***a*** the kingdoms of the world
25:29 I will call for a sword on ***a***
25:30 prophesy against them ***a*** these
25:30 Against ***a*** the inhabitants of
25:31 He will plead His case with ***a***
26: 2 and speak to ***a*** the cities of
26: 2 ***a*** the words that I command you
26: 6 make this city a curse to ***a***
26: 7 priests and the prophets and ***a***
26: 8 had made an end of speaking ***a***
26: 8 commanded him to speak to ***a***
26: 8 priests and the prophets and ***a***
26: 9 And ***a*** the people were
26:11 spoke to the princes and ***a*** the
26:12 Then Jeremiah spoke to ***a*** the
26:12 spoke to all the princes and ***a***
26:12 and against this city with ***a***
26:15 has sent me to you to speak ***a***
26:16 So the princes and ***a*** the people
26:17 the land rose up and spoke to ***a***
26:18 and spoke to ***a*** the people of
26:19 Hezekiah king of Judah and ***a***
26:20 this land according to ***a*** the
26:21 with ***a*** his mighty men and all
26:21 with all his mighty men and ***a***
27: 6 And now I have given ***a*** these
27: 7 So ***a*** nations shall serve him and
27:12 king of Judah according to ***a***
27:16 I spoke to the priests and to ***a***
27:20 and ***a*** the nobles of Judah and
28: 1 of the priests and of ***a*** the
28: 3 bring back to this place ***a*** the
28: 4 with ***a*** the captives of Judah
28: 5 and in the presence of ***a*** the
28: 6 of the LORD's house and ***a*** who
28: 7 and in the hearing of ***a*** the
28:11 spoke in the presence of ***a*** the
28:11 of Babylon from the neck of ***a***
28:14 a yoke of iron on the neck of ***a***
29: 1 and ***a*** the people whom
29: 4 to ***a*** who were carried away
29:13 when you search for Me with ***a***
29:14 I will gather you from ***a*** the
29:14 all the nations and from ***a*** the
29:16 concerning ***a*** the people who
29:18 them to trouble among ***a*** the
29:18 and a reproach among ***a*** the
29:20 ***a*** you of the captivity, whom I
29:22 a curse shall be taken up by ***a***
29:25 sent letters in your name to ***a***
29:25 and to ***a*** the priests, saying,
29:31 Send to ***a*** those in captivity,
30: 2 'Write in a book for yourself ***a***
30: 6 And ***a*** faces turned pale?
30:11 Though I make a full end of ***a***
30:14 ***A*** your lovers have forgotten
30:16 Therefore ***a*** those who devour you
30:16 And ***a*** your adversaries, every
30:16 And ***a*** who prey upon you I will
30:20 And I will punish ***a*** who
31: 1 I will be the God of ***a*** the
31:12 they shall sorrow no more at ***a***.
31:24 and in ***a*** its cities together,
31:34 for they ***a*** shall know Me, from
31:37 I will also cast off ***a*** the
31:37 all the seed of Israel For ***a***
31:40 and ***a*** the fields as far as the
32:12 before ***a*** the Jews who sat in
32:19 for your eyes are open to ***a***
32:23 They have done nothing of ***a***
32:23 therefore You have caused ***a***
32:27 the God of ***a*** flesh. Is there
32:32 because of ***a*** the evil of the
32:37 I will gather them out of ***a***

32:41 with ***a*** My heart and with all My
32:41 with all My heart and with ***a*** My
32:42 Just as I have brought ***a*** this
32:42 so I will bring on them ***a*** the
33: 5 ***a*** for whose wickedness I have
33: 8 I will cleanse them from ***a*** their
33: 8 and I will pardon ***a*** their
33: 9 and an honor before ***a*** nations
33: 9 who shall hear ***a*** the good that
33: 9 shall fear and tremble for ***a***
33: 9 for all the goodness and ***a*** the
33:12 and in ***a*** its cities, there
34: 1 king of Babylon and ***a*** his army,
34: 1 ***a*** the kingdoms of the earth
34: 1 and ***a*** the people, fought
34: 1 fought against Jerusalem and ***a***
34: 6 Jeremiah the prophet spoke ***a***
34: 7 fought against Jerusalem and ***a***
34: 8 had made a covenant with ***a*** the
34:10 Now when ***a*** the princes and all
34:10 Now when all the princes and ***a***
34:17 deliver you to trouble among ***a***
34:19 and ***a*** the people of the land
35: 3 his brothers and ***a*** his sons,
35: 7 but ***a*** your days you shall dwell
35: 8 in ***a*** that he charged us, to
35: 8 to drink no wine ***a*** our days,
35:10 obeyed and done according to ***a***
35:15 I have also sent to you ***a*** My
35:17 I will bring on Judah and on ***a***
35:17 the inhabitants of Jerusalem ***a***
35:18 and kept ***a*** his precepts and
35:18 and done according to ***a*** that
36: 2 of a book and write on it ***a***
36: 2 and against ***a*** the nations, from
36: 3 the house of Judah will hear ***a***
36: 4 ***a*** the words of the LORD which
36: 6 read them in the hearing of ***a***
36: 8 of Neriah did according to ***a***
36: 9 a fast before the LORD to ***a***
36: 9 and to ***a*** the people who came
36:10 in the hearing of ***a*** the people.
36:11 heard ***a*** the words of the LORD
36:12 and there ***a*** the princes were
36:12 and ***a*** the princes.
36:13 Michaiah declared to them ***a***
36:14 Therefore ***a*** the princes sent
36:16 when they had heard ***a*** the
36:16 will surely tell the king of ***a***
36:17 how did you write ***a*** these
36:18 proclaimed with his mouth ***a***
36:20 and told ***a*** the words in the
36:21 king and in the hearing of ***a***
36:23 until ***a*** the scroll was consumed
36:24 any of his servants who heard ***a***
36:28 and write on it ***a*** the former
36:31 and on the men of Judah ***a*** the
36:32 the instruction of Jeremiah ***a***
37:21 until ***a*** the bread in the city
38: 1 that Jeremiah had spoken to ***a***
38: 4 and the hands of ***a*** the people,
38: 9 these men have done evil in ***a***
38:22 ***a*** the women who are left in the
38:23 So they shall surrender ***a*** your
38:27 Then ***a*** the princes came to
38:27 And he told them according to ***a***
39: 1 king of Babylon and ***a*** his army
39: 3 Then ***a*** the princes of the king
39: 4 the king of Judah and ***a*** the
39: 6 king of Babylon also killed ***a***
39:13 and ***a*** the king of Babylon's
40: 1 him bound in chains among ***a***
40: 4 ***a*** the land is before you;
40: 7 And when ***a*** the captains of the
40:11 when ***a*** the Jews who were in
40:11 and who were in ***a*** the
40:12 then ***a*** the Jews returned out of
40:12 all the Jews returned out of ***a***
40:13 the son of Kareah and ***a*** the
40:15 so that ***a*** the Jews who are
41: 3 Ishmael also struck down ***a*** the
41: 9 into which Ishmael had cast ***a***
41:10 Ishmael carried away captive ***a***
41:10 the king's daughters and ***a*** the
41:11 the son of Kareah and ***a*** the
41:11 that were with him heard of ***a***
41:12 they took ***a*** the men and went to
41:13 when ***a*** the people who were
41:13 and ***a*** the captains of the
41:14 Then ***a*** the people whom Ishmael
41:16 and ***a*** the captains of the
41:16 took from Mizpah ***a*** the rest of
42: 1 Now ***a*** the captains of the
42: 1 and ***a*** the people, from the
42: 2 for ***a*** this remnant (since we
42: 8 ***a*** the captains of the forces
42: 8 and ***a*** the people from the least
42:17 So shall it be with ***a*** the men
42:20 and according to ***a*** that the
43: 1 had stopped speaking to ***a*** the
43: 1 speaking to all the people ***a***
43: 1 him to them, ***a*** these words,
43: 2 and ***a*** the proud men spoke,
43: 4 ***a*** the captains of the forces,
43: 4 and ***a*** the people would not obey
43: 5 the son of Kareah and ***a*** the
43: 5 captains of the forces took ***a***
43: 5 from ***a*** nations where they had
44: 1 came to Jeremiah concerning ***a***
44: 2 You have seen ***a*** the calamity
44: 2 brought on Jerusalem and on ***a***
44: 4 However I have sent to you ***a*** My
44: 8 a curse and a reproach among ***a***
44:11 and for cutting off ***a*** Judah.
44:12 and they shall ***a*** be consumed
44:15 Then ***a*** the men who knew that
44:15 with ***a*** the women who stood by,
44:15 and ***a*** the people who dwelt in
44:20 Then Jeremiah spoke to ***a*** the
44:20 and ***a*** the people who had given
44:24 Moreover Jeremiah said to ***a*** the
44:24 to all the people and to ***a*** the
44:24 ***a*** Judah who are in the land of
44:26 ***a*** Judah who dwell in the land
44:26 mouth of any man of Judah in ***a***
44:27 And ***a*** the men of Judah who are
44:28 and ***a*** the remnant of Judah, who
45: 5 I will bring adversity on ***a***
45: 5 life to you as a prize in ***a***
46: 5 For fear was ***a*** around,"
46:14 For the sword devours ***a*** around
46:28 I will make a complete end of ***a***
47: 2 shall overflow the land and ***a***
47: 2 And ***a*** the inhabitants of the
47: 4 the day that comes to plunder ***a***
48:17 ***a*** you who are around him; And
48:17 And ***a*** you who know his name,
48:24 On ***a*** the cities of the land of
48:31 And I will cry out for ***a*** Moab;
48:37 On ***a*** the hands shall be
48:38 A general lamentation On ***a*** the
48:39 a derision And a dismay to ***a***
49: 5 From ***a*** those who are around you;
49:13 And ***a*** its cities shall be
49:17 astonished And will hiss at ***a***
49:26 And ***a*** the men of war shall be
49:29 ***A*** their vessels and their
49:32 I will scatter to ***a*** winds
49:32 bring their calamity from ***a***
49:36 And scatter them toward ***a***
50: 7 ***A*** who found them have devoured
50:10 ***A*** who plunder her shall be
50:13 be horrified And hiss at ***a***
50:14 in array against Babylon ***a***
50:14 ***A*** you who bend the bow; Shoot
50:15 Shout against her ***a*** around;
50:21 And do according to ***a*** that I
50:27 Slay ***a*** her bulls, Let them go
50:29 ***A*** you who bend the bow, encamp
50:29 encamp against it ***a*** around;
50:29 According to ***a*** she has done,
50:30 And ***a*** her men of war shall be
50:32 And it will devour ***a*** around
50:33 ***A*** who took them captive have
50:37 And against ***a*** the mixed
51: 2 They shall be against her ***a***
51: 3 Utterly destroy ***a*** her army.
51: 7 That made ***a*** the earth drunk.
51:19 For He is the Maker of ***a***
51:24 I will repay Babylon And ***a***
51:24 inhabitants of Chaldea For ***a***
51:25 Who destroys ***a*** the earth,"
51:28 Its governors and ***a*** its
51:28 ***A*** the land of his dominion.
51:31 that his city is taken on ***a***
51:47 And ***a*** her slain shall fall in
51:48 the heavens and the earth and ***a***
51:49 So at Babylon the slain of ***a***
51:52 And throughout ***a*** her land the
51:60 So Jeremiah wrote in a book ***a***
51:60 ***a*** these words that are written
51:61 and read ***a*** these words,
52: 2 according to ***a*** that Jehoiakim
52: 4 king of Babylon and ***a*** his army
52: 4 built a siege wall against it ***a***
52: 7 and ***a*** the men of war fled and
52: 7 were near the city ***a*** around.
52: 8 ***A*** his army was scattered from
52:10 And he killed ***a*** the princes of
52:13 ***a*** the houses of Jerusalem, that
52:13 ***a*** the houses of the great, he
52:14 And ***a*** the army of the Chaldeans
52:14 of the guard broke down ***a*** the
52:14 all the walls of Jerusalem ***a***
52:17 and carried ***a*** their bronze to
52:18 and ***a*** the bronze utensils with
52:20 the bronze of ***a*** these articles
52:22 a network and pomegranates ***a***
52:22 ***a*** of bronze. The second pillar,
52:23 ***a*** the pomegranates, all around
52:23 ***a*** around on the network, were
52:30 ***A*** the persons were four
52:33 regularly before the king ***a***
52:34 ***a*** the days of his life.
Lam 1: 2 Among ***a*** her lovers She has
1: 2 ***A*** her friends have dealt
1: 3 ***A*** her persecutors overtake her
1: 4 ***A*** her gates are desolate; Her
1: 6 from the daughter of Zion ***A***
1: 7 Jerusalem remembers ***a*** her
1: 8 ***A*** who honored her despise her
1:10 has spread his hand Over ***a***
1:11 ***A*** her people sigh, They seek
1:12 ***a*** you who pass by? Behold and
1:13 made me desolate And faint ***a***
1:15 Lord has trampled underfoot ***a***
1:18 ***a*** peoples, And behold my
1:21 ***A*** my enemies have heard of my
1:22 Let ***a*** their wickedness come
1:22 as You have done to me For ***a***
2: 2 up and has not pitied ***A*** the
2: 3 a flaming fire Devouring ***a***
2: 4 He has slain ***a*** who were
2: 5 He has swallowed up ***a*** her
2:15 ***A*** who pass by clap their hands
2:16 ***A*** your enemies have opened
3:14 have become the ridicule of ***a***
3:14 Their taunting song ***a*** the day.
3:34 To crush under one's feet ***A***
3:46 ***A*** our enemies Have opened
3:51 to my soul Because of ***a*** the
3:60 You have seen ***a*** their
3:60 ***A*** their schemes against me.
3:61 ***A*** their schemes against me,
3:62 their whispering against me ***a***
4:12 And ***a*** inhabitants of the
Ezek 1: 4 and brightness was ***a*** around it
1:16 and ***a*** four had the same
1:18 ***a*** around the four of them.
1:27 with the appearance of fire ***a***
1:27 of fire with brightness ***a***
1:28 appearance of the brightness ***a***
3: 7 for ***a*** the house of Israel are
3:10 receive into your heart ***a*** My
4: 2 battering rams against it ***a***
5: 4 a fire will go out into ***a*** the
5: 5 the nations and the countries ***a***
5: 6 than the countries that are ***a***
5: 7 than the nations that are ***a***
5: 7 of the nations that are ***a***
5: 9 because of ***a*** your abominations.
5:10 and ***a*** of you who remain I will
5:10 who remain I will scatter to ***a***
5:11 defiled My sanctuary with ***a***
5:11 detestable things and with ***a***
5:12 shall fall by the sword ***a***
5:12 scatter another third to ***a*** the
5:14 among the nations that are ***a***
5:14 in the sight of ***a*** who pass by.
5:15 to the nations that are ***a***
6: 5 and I will scatter your bones ***a***
6: 6 In ***a*** your dwelling places the
6: 9 evils which they committed in ***a***
6:11 for ***a*** the evil abominations of
6:13 slain are among their idols ***a***
6:13 on ***a*** the mountaintops, under
6:13 they offered sweet incense to ***a***
6:14 in ***a*** their dwelling places.
7: 3 And I will repay you for ***a***
7: 8 And I will repay you for ***a***
7:14 For My wrath is on ***a*** their
7:16 ***A*** of them mourning, Each for
7:18 Baldness on ***a*** their heads.
8:10 and ***a*** the idols of the house of
8:10 portrayed ***a*** around on the
9: 4 the men who sigh and cry over ***a***
9: 8 Lord GOD! Will You destroy ***a***
10:10 ***a*** four looked alike—as it were,
10:12 were full of eyes ***a*** around.
11:12 of the Gentiles which are ***a***
11:15 and ***a*** the house of Israel in
11:18 and they will take away ***a*** its
11:18 all its detestable things and ***a***
11:25 to those in captivity of ***a*** the
12:10 the prince in Jerusalem and ***a***
12:14 will scatter to every wind ***a***
12:14 and ***a*** his troops; and I will
12:16 that they may declare ***a*** their
12:19 her land may be emptied of ***a***
12:19 because of the violence of ***a***
14: 3 let Myself be inquired of at ***a***
14: 5 because they are ***a*** estranged
14: 6 and turn your faces away from ***a***
14:11 nor be profaned anymore with ***a***
14:22 ***a*** that I have brought upon it.
16:22 And in ***a*** your abominations and
16:23 after ***a*** your wickedness—'Woe,
16:30 seeing you do ***a*** these things,
16:33 Men make payment to ***a*** harlots,
16:33 but you made your payments to ***a***
16:33 them to come to you from ***a***
16:36 and with ***a*** your abominable
16:37 I will gather ***a*** your lovers
16:37 ***a*** those you loved, and all
16:37 and ***a*** those you hated; I will
16:37 I will gather them from ***a***
16:37 that they may see ***a*** your
16:43 but agitated Me with ***a*** these
16:43 lewdness in addition to ***a*** your
16:47 more corrupt than they in ***a***
16:51 justified your sisters by ***a***
16:54 own shame and be disgraced by ***a***
16:57 of the daughters of Syria and ***a***
16:63 provide you an atonement for ***a***
17: 9 ***A*** of its spring leaves will
17:18 gave his hand and still did ***a***
17:21 ***A*** his fugitives with all his
17:21 All his fugitives with ***a*** his
17:24 And ***a*** the trees of the field
18: 4 ***a*** souls are Mine; The soul of
18:14 he begets a son Who sees ***a*** the
18:19 and has kept ***a*** My statutes and
18:21 if a wicked man turns from ***a***
18:21 keeps ***a*** My statutes, and does
18:23 Do I have any pleasure at ***a*** that
18:24 and does according to ***a*** the
18:24 ***A*** the righteousness which he
18:28 and turns away from ***a*** the
18:30 and turn from ***a*** your
18:31 Cast away from you ***a*** the
20: 6 the glory of ***a*** lands.
20: 8 They did not ***a*** cast away the
20:15 the glory of ***a*** lands,
20:26 in that they caused ***a*** their
20:28 and they saw ***a*** the high hills
20:28 saw all the high hills and ***a***

A

20:31 you defile yourselves with a
20:40 there a the house of Israel, all
20:40 a of them in the land, shall
20:40 together with a your holy
20:43 shall remember your ways and a
20:43 in your own sight because of a
20:47 and a faces from the south to
20:48 A flesh shall see that I, the
21: 4 go out of its sheath against a
21: 5 that a flesh may know that I,
21: 7 a hands will be feeble, every
21: 7 and a knees will be weak as
21:10 As it does a wood.
21:12 Against a the princes of
21:15 point of the sword against a
21:24 so that in a your doings your
22: 2 show her a her abominations!
22: 4 and a mockery to a countries.
22:18 they are a bronze, tin, iron,
22:19 Because you have a become dross,
23: 6 A of them desirable young men,
23: 7 A of them choice men of
23: 7 And with a for whom she
23: 7 With a their idols, she
23:12 A of them desirable young men.
23:15 A of them looking like
23:23 A the Chaldeans, Pekod, Shoa,
23:23 A the Assyrians with them,
23:23 A of them desirable young men,
23:23 A of them riding on horses.
23:24 and helmet a around. 'I will
23:29 take away a you have worked
23:48 that a women may be taught not
24:24 according to a that he has done
25: 6 and rejoiced in heart with a
25: 8 The house of Judah is like a
26:11 of his horses he will trample a
26:16 Then a the princes of the sea
26:17 their terror to be on a her
27: 5 They made a your planks of fir
27: 9 A the ships of the sea And
27:11 army were on your walls a
27:11 their shields on your walls a
27:21 Arabia and a the princes of
27:22 a kinds of precious stones, and
27:27 A your men of war who are in
27:29 A who handle the oar, The
27:29 A the pilots of the sea Will
27:35 A the inhabitants of the isles
28:18 the earth In the sight of a
28:19 A who knew you among the
28:24 house of Israel from among a
28:26 when I execute judgments on a
29: 2 and against a Egypt.
29: 4 And a the fish in your rivers
29: 5 You and a the fish of your
29: 6 Then a the inhabitants of Egypt
29: 7 You broke and tore a their
29: 7 You broke and made a their
30: 5 a the mingled people, Chub, and
30: 8 set a fire in Egypt And a her
30:12 and a that is in it, By the
31: 4 And sent out rivulets to a the
31: 5 its height was exalted above a
31: 6 A the birds of the heavens made
31: 6 Under its branches a the
31: 6 And in its shadow a great
31: 9 So that a the trees of Eden
31:12 on the mountains and in a the
31:12 its boughs lie broken by a the
31:12 and a the peoples of the earth
31:13 On its ruin will remain a the
31:13 And a the beasts of the field
31:14 For they have a been delivered
31:15 and a the trees of the field
31:16 and a the trees of Eden, the
31:16 a that drink water, were
31:18 This is Pharaoh and a his
32: 4 And cause to settle on you a
32: 8 A the bright lights of the
32:12 a of them the most terrible of
32:12 And a its multitude shall be
32:13 Also I will destroy a its
32:15 the country is destitute of a
32:15 When I strike a who dwell in
32:16 And for a her multitude,'
32:20 Drawing her and a her
32:22 and a her company, With their
32:22 With their graves a around
32:22 A of them slain, fallen by the
32:23 And her company is a around
32:23 A of them slain, fallen by the
32:24 There is Elam and a her
32:24 A around her grave, All of
32:24 A of them slain, fallen by the
32:25 With a her multitude, With
32:25 With her graves a around it,
32:25 A of them uncircumcised, slain
32:26 are Meshech and Tubal and a
32:26 With a their graves around it,
32:26 A of them uncircumcised, slain
32:29 Her kings and a her princes,
32:30 A of them, and all the
32:30 and a the Sidonians, Who have
32:31 them And be comforted over a
32:31 Pharaoh and a his army, Slain
32:32 Pharaoh and a his multitude,"
33:29 land most desolate because of a
34: 5 and they became food for a the
34: 6 My sheep wandered through a the
34:12 sheep and deliver them from a
34:13 in the valleys and in a the
34:21 butted a the weak ones with
34:26 will make them and the places a
35: 8 and in your valleys and in a
35:12 I have heard a your blasphemies
35:15 as well as a of Edom—all of it!
35:15 a of it! Then they shall know
36: 4 to the rest of the nations a
36: 5 of the nations and against a
36:10 a the house of Israel, all of
36:10 a of it; and the cities shall
36:24 gather you out of a countries,
36:25 I will cleanse you from a your
36:25 all your filthiness and from a
36:29 I will deliver you from a your
36:33 day that I cleanse you from a
36:34 desolate in the sight of a who
36:36 the nations which are left a
37: 2 He caused me to pass by them a
37:16 and for a the house of Israel,
37:22 king shall be king over them a;
37:23 but I will deliver them from a
37:24 and they shall a have one
38: 4 with a your army, horses, and
38: 4 a splendidly clothed, a great
38: 4 a of them handling swords.
38: 5 a of them with shield and
38: 6 Gomer and a its troops; the
38: 6 from the far north and a its
38: 7 you and a your companies that
38: 8 and now a of them dwell safely.
38: 9 you and a your troops and many
38:11 a of them dwelling without
38:13 and a their young lions will
38:15 a of them riding on horses, a
38:20 a creeping things that creep on
38:20 and a men who are on the face
38:21 sword against Gog throughout a
39: 4 you and a your troops and the
39:11 there they will bury Gog and a
39:13 Indeed a the people of the land
39:17 Gather together from a sides
39:18 A of them fatlings of Bashan.
39:20 With mighty men And with a
39:21 a the nations shall see My
39:23 and they a fell by the sword.
39:26 and a their unfaithfulness in
40: 5 Now there was a wall a around
40:10 the three were a the same
40:14 and the court a around the
40:16 on the inside of the gateway a
40:16 There were windows a around
40:17 chambers and a pavement made a
40:25 in it and in its archways a
40:29 in it and in its archways a
40:30 There were archways a around,
40:33 in it and in its archways a
40:36 It had windows a around; its
40:43 fastened a around; and the
41: 5 width of each side chamber a
41: 6 were for the side chambers a
41: 7 side chambers became wider a
41: 8 I also saw an elevation a around
41:10 was a width of twenty cubits a
41:11 the terrace was five cubits a
41:12 was five cubits thick a
41:16 And the galleries a around
41:17 and on every wall a around,
41:19 made throughout the temple a
42:11 and a their exits and entrances
42:15 and measured it a around.
42:16 rods by the measuring rod a
42:17 rods by the measuring rod a
42:20 it had a wall a around, five
43:11 And if they are ashamed of a
43:11 its entire design and a its
43:11 a its forms and all its laws.
43:11 all its forms and a its laws.
43:11 may keep its whole design and a
43:13 with a rim a around its edge of
43:17 one cubit a around; and its
44: 5 a that I say to you concerning
44: 5 that I say to you concerning a
44: 5 of the house of the LORD and a
44: 5 who may enter the house and a
44: 6 let us have no more of a your
44: 7 broke My covenant because of a
44:14 for a its work, and for all
44:14 and for a that has to be done
44:24 My laws and My statutes in a
44:30 The best of a firstfruits of any
44:30 sacrifice of any kind from a
45: 1 holy throughout its territory a
45:16 A the people of the land shall
45:17 and at a the appointed seasons
45:22 prepare for himself and for a
46:22 a four corners were the same
46:23 a row of building stones a
46:23 a around the four of them; and
46:23 made under the rows of stones a
47:12 will grow a kinds of trees
48:19 from a the tribes of Israel,
48:35 A the way around shall be
Dan 1: 4 gifted in a wisdom, possessing
1:15 and fatter in flesh than a the
1:17 them knowledge and skill in a
1:17 Daniel had understanding in a
1:19 and among them a none was found
1:20 And in a matters of wisdom and
1:20 them ten times better than a
1:20 astrologers who were in a his
2:12 and gave a command to destroy a
2:38 has made you ruler over them a—
2:39 which shall rule over a the
2:40 break in pieces and crush a
2:44 break in pieces and consume a
2:48 and chief administrator over a
3: 2 and a the officials of the
3: 3 and a the officials of the
3: 5 in symphony with a kinds of
3: 7 when a the people heard the
3: 7 in symphony with a kinds of
3: 7 a the people, nations, and
3:10 in symphony with a kinds of
3:15 in symphony with a kinds of
4: 1 To a peoples, nations, and
4: 1 and languages that dwell in a
4: 6 I issued a decree to bring in a
4:11 could be seen to the ends of a
4:12 And in it was food for a.
4:12 And a flesh was fed from it.
4:18 since a the wise men of my
4:20 and which could be seen by a
4:21 in which was food for a,
4:28 A this came upon King
4:35 A the inhabitants of the earth
4:37 a of whose works are truth,
5: 8 Now a the king's wise men came,
5:19 a peoples, nations, and
5:22 although you knew a this.
5:23 breath in His hand and owns a
6: 7 A the governors of the kingdom,
6:24 and broke a their bones in
6:25 To a peoples, nations, and
6:25 and languages that dwell in a
7: 7 It was different from a the
7:14 That a peoples, nations, and
7:16 and asked him the truth of a
7:19 which was different from a the
7:23 shall be different from a
7:27 And a dominions shall serve
8:12 He did a this and prospered.
9: 6 to our fathers and a the people
9: 7 inhabitants of Jerusalem and a
9: 7 near and those far off in a
9:11 a Israel has transgressed Your
9:13 a this disaster has come upon
9:14 our God is righteous in a the
9:16 according to a Your
9:16 people are a reproach to a
10: 3 nor did I anoint myself at a,
11: 2 be far richer than them a;
11: 2 he shall stir up a against the
11:37 exalt himself above them a.
11:43 and over a the precious things
12: 7 a these things shall be
Hos 2:11 I will also cause a her mirth
2:11 A her appointed feasts.
4: 2 They break a restraint, With
5: 2 Though I rebuke them a.
7: 2 hearts That I remember a
7: 4 They are a adulterers.
7: 6 Their baker sleeps a night;
7: 7 They are a hot, like an oven,
7: 7 A their kings have fallen.
7:10 Nor seek Him for a this.
9: 4 A who eat it shall be defiled.
9: 8 is a fowler's snare in a his
9:15 A their wickedness is in
9:15 A their princes are
10:14 And a your fortresses shall be
11: 7 None at a exalt Him.
12: 8 In a my labors They shall
13: 2 A of it is the work of
13:10 That he may save you in a your
14: 2 Take away a iniquity; Receive
Joel 1: 2 a you inhabitants of the land!
1: 5 a you drinkers of wine,
1:12 A the trees of the field are
1:13 lie a night in sackcloth, You
1:14 Gather the elders And a the
1:19 And a flame has burned a the
2: 1 in My holy mountain! Let a
2: 6 A faces are drained of color.
2:12 Turn to Me with a your heart,
2:28 I will pour out My Spirit on a
3: 2 I will also gather a nations,
3: 4 and a the coasts of Philistia?
3: 9 Let a the men of war draw
3:11 a you nations, And gather
3:11 And gather together a around.
3:12 there I will sit to judge a
3:18 And a the brooks of Judah
Am 1:11 And cast off a pity; His
2: 3 And slay a its princes with
3: 2 You only have I known of a the
3: 2 I will punish you for a your
3: 5 if it has caught nothing at a?
3:11 An adversary shall be a around
4: 6 you cleanness of teeth in a
4: 6 And lack of bread in a your
5:16 shall be wailing in a
5:16 And they shall say in a the
5:17 In a vineyards there shall
6: 8 deliver up the city And a
7:10 The land is not able to bear a
8: 8 A of it shall swell like the
8:10 And a your songs into
9: 1 them on the heads of them a.
9: 5 And a who dwell there mourn;
9: 5 A of it shall swell like the
9: 9 the house of Israel among a
9:10 A the sinners of My people
9:12 And a the Gentiles who are
9:13 And a the hills shall flow

Ob	7	***A*** the men in your confederacy
	15	the day of the LORD upon ***a***
	16	So shall ***a*** the nations drink
Jon	2: 3	***A*** Your billows and Your waves
Mic	1: 2	***a*** you peoples! Listen, O
	1: 2	and ***a*** that is in it! Let the
	1: 5	***A*** this is for the transgression
	1: 7	***A*** her carved images shall be
	1: 7	And ***a*** her pay as a harlot
	1: 7	***A*** her idols I will lay
	1:10	it not in Gath, Weep not at ***a***;
	2:12	I will surely assemble ***a*** of
	3: 7	Indeed they shall ***a*** cover
	3: 9	abhor justice And pervert ***a***
	4: 5	For ***a*** people walk each in the
	5: 9	And ***a*** your enemies shall be
	5:11	of your land And throw down ***a***
	6:16	***A*** the works of Ahab's house
	7: 2	They ***a*** lie in wait for blood;
	7:16	shall see and be ashamed of ***a***
	7:19	You will cast ***a*** our sins Into
Nah	1: 3	And will not at ***a*** acquit the
	1: 4	And dries up ***a*** the rivers.
	1: 5	the world and ***a*** who dwell in
	2:10	And ***a*** their faces are drained
	3: 1	to the bloody city! It is ***a***
	3: 7	It shall come to pass that ***a***
	3:10	And ***a*** her great men were bound
	3:12	***A*** your strongholds are fig
	3:19	***A*** who hear news of you Will
Hab	1: 9	They ***a*** come for violence; Their
	1:15	They take up ***a*** of them with a
	2: 5	He gathers to himself ***a***
	2: 5	And heaps up for himself ***a***
	2: 6	Will not ***a*** these take up a
	2: 8	***A*** the remnant of the people
	2: 8	And of ***a*** who dwell in it.
	2:17	And of ***a*** who dwell in it.
	2:19	in it there is no breath at ***a***.
	2:20	Let ***a*** the earth keep silence
Zeph	1: 4	And against ***a*** the inhabitants
	1: 8	And ***a*** such as are clothed with
	1: 9	the same day I will punish ***A***
	1:11	inhabitants of Maktesh! For ***a***
	1:11	***A*** those who handle money are
	1:18	will make speedy riddance Of ***a***
	2: 3	***a*** you meek of the earth, Who
	2:11	He will reduce to nothing ***a***
	2:11	Indeed ***a*** the shores of the
	3: 7	they rose early and corrupted ***a***
	3: 8	***A*** my fierce anger; All the
	3: 8	***A*** the earth shall be devoured
	3: 9	That they ***a*** may call on the
	3:14	Be glad and rejoice with ***a***
	3:19	that time I will deal with ***a***
	3:20	you fame and praise Among ***a***
Hag	1:11	and on ***a*** the labor of your
	1:12	with ***a*** the remnant of the
	1:14	and the spirit of ***a*** the remnant
	2: 4	***a*** you people of the land,' says
	2: 7	and I will shake ***a*** nations, and
	2: 7	shall come to the Desire of ***A***
	2:17	and mildew and hail in ***a*** the
Zech	1:11	***a*** the earth is resting
	2: 5	will be a wall of fire ***a*** around
	2:13	***a*** flesh, before the LORD, for
	6: 5	station before the Lord of ***a***
	7: 5	Say to ***a*** the people of the land,
	7:14	them with a whirlwind among ***a***
	8:10	For I set ***a*** men, everyone,
	8:12	of this people To possess ***a***
	8:17	For ***a*** these are things that
	9: 1	(For the eyes of men And ***a***
	10:11	***A*** the depths of the River
	11:10	which I had made with ***a*** the
	12: 2	a cup of drunkenness to ***a*** the
	12: 3	a very heavy stone for ***a***
	12: 3	***a*** who would heave it away will
	12: 3	though ***a*** nations of the earth
	12: 6	they shall devour ***a*** the
	12: 9	that I will seek to destroy ***a***
	12:14	***a*** the families that remain,
	13: 8	it shall come to pass in ***a*** the
	14: 2	For I will gather ***a*** the nations
	14: 5	And ***a*** the saints with You.
	14: 9	the LORD shall be King over ***a***
	14:10	***A*** the land shall be turned into
	14:12	which the LORD will strike ***a***
	14:14	And the wealth of ***a*** the
	14:15	And on ***a*** the cattle that will
	14:16	everyone who is left of ***a*** the
	14:19	Egypt and the punishment of ***a***
Mal	2: 9	and base Before ***a*** the people,
	2:10	Have we not ***a*** one Father?
	3:10	Bring ***a*** the tithes into the
	3:12	And ***a*** nations will call you
	4: 1	And ***a*** the proud, yes, all who
	4: 1	***a*** who do wickedly will be
	4: 4	I commanded him in Horeb for ***a***
Mt	1:17	So ***a*** the generations from
	1:22	So ***a*** this was done that it might
	2: 3	and ***a*** Jerusalem with him.
	2: 4	And when he had gathered ***a*** the
	2:16	sent forth and put to death ***a***
	2:16	who were in Bethlehem and in ***a***
	3: 5	***a*** Judea, and all the region
	3: 5	and ***a*** the region around the
	3:15	is fitting for us to fulfill ***a***
	4: 8	and showed Him ***a*** the kingdoms
	4: 9	***A*** these things I will give You
	4:23	And Jesus went about ***a*** Galilee,
	4:23	and healing ***a*** kinds of sickness
	4:23	all kinds of sickness and ***a***
	4:24	Then His fame went throughout ***a***
	4:24	and they brought to Him ***a*** sick
	5:11	and say ***a*** kinds of evil against
	5:15	and it gives light to ***a*** who
	5:18	means pass from the law till ***a***
	5:34	I say to you, do not swear at ***a***:
	6:29	to you that even Solomon in ***a***
	6:32	For after ***a*** these things the
	6:32	Father knows that you need ***a***
	6:33	and ***a*** these things shall be
	8:16	and healed ***a*** who were sick,
	9:26	report of this went out into ***a***
	9:31	spread the news about Him in ***a***
	9:35	Then Jesus went about ***a*** the
	10: 1	and to heal ***a*** kinds of sickness
	10: 1	all kinds of sickness and ***a***
	10:22	And you will be hated by ***a*** for
	10:30	very hairs of your head are ***a***
	11:13	For ***a*** the prophets and the law
	11:27	***A*** things have been delivered to
	11:28	***a*** you who labor and are heavy
	12:15	Him, and He healed them ***a***.
	12:23	And ***a*** the multitudes were amazed
	13:32	indeed is the least of ***a***
	13:33	measures of meal till it was ***a***
	13:34	***A*** these things Jesus spoke to
	13:41	gather out of His kingdom ***a***
	13:44	joy over it he goes and sells ***a***
	13:46	went and sold ***a*** that he had and
	13:51	Have you understood ***a*** these
	13:56	are they not ***a*** with us?
	13:56	Where then did this Man get ***a***
	14:20	So they ***a*** ate and were filled,
	14:35	they sent out into ***a*** that
	14:35	brought to Him ***a*** who were sick,
	15:37	So they ***a*** ate and were filled,
	17:11	coming first and will restore ***a***
	18:25	his wife and children and ***a***
	18:26	with me, and I will pay you ***a***.
	18:29	with me, and I will pay you ***a***.
	18:31	came and told their master ***a***
	18:32	I forgave you ***a*** that
	18:34	until he should pay ***a*** that was
	19:11	***A*** cannot accept this saying, but
	19:20	***A*** these things I have kept from
	19:26	but with God ***a*** things are
	19:27	we have left ***a*** and followed
	20: 6	you been standing here idle ***a***
	20:31	but they cried out ***a*** the more,
	21: 4	***A*** this was done that it might be
	21:10	***a*** the city was moved, saying,
	21:12	temple of God and drove out ***a***
	21:26	for ***a*** count John as a
	21:37	Then last of ***a*** he sent his son
	22: 4	and ***a*** things are ready. Come
	22:10	and gathered together ***a*** whom
	22:27	Last of ***a*** the woman died also.
	22:28	For they ***a*** had her."
	22:37	the LORD your God with ***a***
	22:37	with ***a*** your soul, and
	22:37	and with ***a*** your mind.'
	22:40	these two commandments hang ***a***
	23: 5	But ***a*** their works they do to be
	23: 8	and you are ***a*** brethren.
	23:20	swears by it and by ***a*** things on
	23:27	full of dead men's bones and ***a***
	23:35	that on you may come ***a*** the
	23:36	***a*** these things will come upon
	24: 2	Do you not see ***a*** these things?
	24: 6	for ***a*** these things must come
	24: 8	***A*** these are the beginning of
	24: 9	and you will be hated by ***a***
	24:14	kingdom will be preached in ***a***
	24:14	all the world as a witness to ***a***
	24:30	and then ***a*** the tribes of the
	24:33	when you see ***a*** these things,
	24:34	by no means pass away till ***a***
	24:39	the flood came and took them ***a***
	24:47	he will make him ruler over ***a***
	25: 5	they ***a*** slumbered and slept.
	25: 7	Then ***a*** those virgins arose and
	25:31	and ***a*** the holy angels with Him,
	25:32	***A*** the nations will be gathered
	26: 1	when Jesus had finished ***a*** these
	26:27	'Drink from it, ***a*** of you.
	26:31	***A*** of you will be made to stumble
	26:33	Even if ***a*** are made to stumble
	26:35	not deny You!" And so said ***a***
	26:52	for ***a*** who take the sword will
	26:56	But ***a*** this was done that the
	26:56	Then ***a*** the disciples forsook
	26:59	and ***a*** the council sought false
	26:70	But he denied it before them ***a***,
	27: 1	***a*** the chief priests and elders
	27:22	They ***a*** said to him, "Let
	27:23	But they cried out ***a*** the
	27:24	that he could not prevail at ***a***,
	27:25	And ***a*** the people answered and
	27:45	hour there was darkness over ***a***
	28:11	to the chief priests ***a*** the
	28:18	***A*** authority has been given to Me
	28:19	and make disciples of ***a*** the
	28:20	teaching them to observe ***a***
Mk	1: 5	Then ***a*** the land of Judea, and
	1: 5	went out to him and were ***a***
	1:27	Then they were ***a*** amazed, so that
	1:28	His fame spread throughout ***a***
	1:32	they brought to Him ***a*** who were
	1:39	their synagogues throughout ***a***
	2:12	out in the presence of them ***a***,
	2:12	so that ***a*** were amazed and
	2:13	and ***a*** the multitude came to
	3:28	***a*** sins will be forgiven the
	4:11	***a*** things come in parables,
	4:13	How then will you understand ***a***
	4:31	is smaller than ***a*** the seeds on
	4:32	up and becomes greater than ***a***
	4:34	He explained ***a*** things to His
	5:12	So ***a*** the demons begged Him,
	5:20	to proclaim in Decapolis ***a***
	5:20	and ***a*** marveled.
	5:26	She had spent ***a*** that she had
	5:40	But when He had put them ***a***
	6:30	to Jesus and told Him ***a*** things,
	6:33	and ran there on foot from ***a***
	6:39	commanded them to make them ***a***
	6:41	fish He divided among them ***a***.
	6:42	So they ***a*** ate and were filled.
	6:50	for they ***a*** saw Him and were
	7: 3	For the Pharisees and ***a*** the Jews
	7: 9	***A*** too well you reject the
	7:14	When He had called ***a*** the
	7:19	thus purifying ***a*** foods?"
	7:23	***A*** these evil things come from
	7:37	'He has done ***a*** things well.
	9:12	is coming first and restores ***a***
	9:15	***a*** the people were greatly
	9:23	***a*** things are possible to him
	9:35	he shall be last of ***a*** and
	9:35	be last of all and servant of ***a***.
	10:20	***a*** these things I have kept from
	10:27	for with God ***a*** things are
	10:28	we have left ***a*** and followed
	10:44	to be first shall be slave of ***a***.
	10:48	but he cried out ***a*** the more,
	11:11	when He had looked around at ***a***
	11:17	a house of prayer for ***a***
	11:18	because ***a*** the people were
	11:32	for ***a*** counted John to have been
	12:22	Last of ***a*** the woman died also.
	12:23	For ***a*** seven had her as wife."
	12:28	is the first commandment of ***a***?
	12:29	The first of ***a*** the commandments
	12:30	the LORD your God with ***a***
	12:30	with ***a*** your soul, with
	12:30	with ***a*** your mind, and
	12:30	and with ***a*** your strength.'
	12:33	And to love Him with ***a*** the
	12:33	with ***a*** the understanding, with
	12:33	with ***a*** the soul, and with all
	12:33	and with ***a*** the strength, and to
	12:33	is more than ***a*** the whole burnt
	12:43	widow has put in more than ***a***
	12:44	for they ***a*** put in out of their
	12:44	she out of her poverty put in ***a***
	13: 4	what will be the sign when ***a***
	13:10	must first be preached to ***a***
	13:13	And you will be hated by ***a*** for
	13:23	I have told you ***a*** things
	13:30	by no means pass away till ***a***
	13:37	what I say to you, I say to ***a***:
	14:23	and they ***a*** drank from it.
	14:27	***A*** of you will be made to stumble
	14:29	Even if ***a*** are made to stumble,
	14:31	will not deny You!" And they ***a***
	14:36	***a*** things are possible for You.
	14:50	Then they ***a*** forsook Him and
	14:53	and with him were assembled ***a***
	14:55	Now the chief priests and ***a*** the
	14:64	And they ***a*** condemned Him to
	15:14	But they cried out ***a*** the
	16:15	Go into ***a*** the world and preach
Lk	1: 3	had perfect understanding of ***a***
	1: 6	walking in ***a*** the commandments
	1:48	henceforth ***a*** generations will
	1:63	So they ***a*** marveled.
	1:65	Then fear came on ***a*** who dwelt
	1:65	and ***a*** these sayings were
	1:65	were discussed throughout ***a***
	1:66	And ***a*** those who heard them kept
	1:71	And from the hand of ***a*** who
	1:75	and righteousness before Him ***a***
	2: 1	out from Caesar Augustus that ***a***
	2: 3	So ***a*** went to be registered,
	2:10	of great joy which will be to ***a***
	2:18	And ***a*** those who heard it
	2:19	But Mary kept ***a*** these things and
	2:20	and praising God for ***a*** the
	2:31	prepared before the face of ***a***
	2:38	and spoke of Him to ***a*** those who
	2:39	So when they had performed ***a***
	2:47	And ***a*** who heard Him were
	2:51	but His mother kept ***a*** these
	3: 3	And he went into ***a*** the region
	3: 6	And ***a*** flesh shall see the
	3:15	and ***a*** reasoned in their hearts
	3:16	John answered, saying to ***a***,
	3:19	and for ***a*** the evils which Herod
	3:20	also added this, above ***a***,
	3:21	When ***a*** the people were
	4: 5	showed Him ***a*** the kingdoms of
	4: 6	***A*** this authority I will give
	4: 7	***a*** will be Yours."
	4:14	news of Him went out through ***a***
	4:15	being glorified by ***a***.
	4:20	And the eyes of ***a*** who were in
	4:22	So ***a*** bore witness to Him, and
	4:25	was a great famine throughout ***a***
	4:28	So ***a*** those in the synagogue,
	4:36	Then they were ***a*** amazed and
	4:40	***a*** those who had any that were
	5: 5	we have toiled ***a*** night and
	5: 9	For he and ***a*** who were with him

5:11 they forsook *a* and followed
5:15 went around concerning Him *a*
5:26 And they were *a* amazed, and they
5:28 So he left *a*, rose up, and
6:10 He had looked around at them *a*,
6:12 and continued *a* night in prayer
6:17 multitude of people from *a*
6:19 out from Him and healed them *a*.
6:26 Woe to you when *a* men speak
7: 1 Now when He concluded *a* His
7:16 Then fear came upon *a*,
7:17 about Him went throughout *a*
7:17 throughout all Judea and *a* the
7:18 reported to him concerning *a*
7:29 And when *a* the people heard
7:35 But wisdom is justified by *a* her
8:40 for they were *a* waiting for
8:43 who had spent *a* her livelihood
8:45 When *a* denied it, Peter and
8:47 to Him in the presence of *a*
8:52 Now *a* wept and mourned for her;
8:54 But He put them *a* outside, took
9: 1 them power and authority over *a*
9: 7 Herod the tetrarch heard of *a*
9:10 told Him *a* that they had done.
9:13 we go and buy food for *a* these
9:15 and made them *a* sit down.
9:17 So they *a* ate and were filled,
9:23 Then He said to them *a*,
9:43 And they were *a* amazed at the
9:43 while everyone marveled at *a*
9:48 For he who is least among you *a*
10:19 and over *a* the power of the
10:22 *A* things have been delivered to
10:27 the LORD your God with *a*
10:27 with *a* your soul, with
10:27 with *a* your strength, and
10:27 and with *a* your mind,' and
11:22 he takes from him *a* his armor
11:41 then indeed *a* things are clean
11:42 you tithe mint and rue and *a*
11:50 that the blood of *a* the prophets
12: 1 to His disciples first of *a*,
12: 7 very hairs of your head are *a*
12:18 and there I will store *a* my
12:27 even Solomon in *a* his glory was
12:30 For *a* these things the nations
12:31 and *a* these things shall be
12:41 or to *a* people?"
12:44 he will make him ruler over *a*
12:51 on earth? I tell you, not at *a*,
13: 2 were worse sinners than *a*
13: 3 unless you repent you will *a*
13: 4 they were worse sinners than *a*
13: 5 unless you repent you will *a*
13:17 *a* His adversaries were put to
13:17 and *a* the multitude rejoiced
13:17 the multitude rejoiced for *a*
13:21 measures of meal till it was *a*
13:27 *a* you workers of iniquity.'
13:28 and Isaac and Jacob and *a* the
14:17 for *a* things are now ready.'
14:18 But they *a* with one accord
14:29 *a* who see it begin to mock
14:33 of you does not forsake *a* that
15: 1 Then *a* the tax collectors and
15:13 the younger son gathered *a*
15:14 "But when he had spent *a*,
15:31 and *a* that I have is yours.
16:14 also heard *a* these things, and
16:26 And besides *a* this, between us
17:10 when you have done *a* those
17:27 flood came and destroyed them *a*.
17:29 heaven and destroyed them *a*.
18:12 I give tithes of *a* that I
18:21 *A* these things I have kept from
18:22 Sell *a* that you have and
18:28 we have left *a* and followed
18:31 and *a* things that are written
18:39 but he cried out *a* the more,
18:43 And *a* the people, when they saw
19: 7 they *a* complained, saying, "He
19:37 God with a loud voice for *a*
19:48 for *a* the people were very
20: 6 *a* the people will stone us,
20:32 Last of *a* the woman died also.
20:33 For *a* seven had her as wife."
20:38 for *a* live to Him."
20:45 in the hearing of *a* the people,
21: 3 widow has put in more than *a*;
21: 4 for *a* these out of their
21: 4 she out of her poverty put in *a*
21:12 But before *a* these things, they
21:15 you a mouth and wisdom which *a*
21:17 And you will be hated by *a* for
21:22 that *a* things which are written
21:24 and be led away captive into *a*
21:29 and *a* the trees.
21:32 by no means pass away till *a*
21:35 it will come as a snare on *a*
21:36 be counted worthy to escape *a*
21:38 Then early in the morning *a* the
22:70 Then they *a* said, "Are You then
23: 5 teaching throughout *a* Judea,
23:18 And they *a* cried out at once,
23:44 and there was darkness over *a*
23:49 But *a* His acquaintances, and the
24: 9 from the tomb and told *a* these
24: 9 things to the eleven and to *a*
24:14 And they talked together of *a*
24:19 deed and word before God and *a*
24:21 besides *a* this, today is the
24:25 slow of heart to believe in *a*
24:27 And beginning at Moses and *a* the
24:27 He expounded to them in *a* the
24:44 that *a* things must be fulfilled
24:47 be preached in His name to *a*

Jn 1: 3 *A* things were made through Him,
1: 7 that *a* through him might
1:16 And of His fullness we have *a*
2:15 He drove them *a* out of the
2:24 because He knew *a* men,
3:26 and *a* are coming to Him!"
3:31 who comes from above is above *a*;
3:31 comes from heaven is above *a*.
3:35 and has given *a* things into His
4:25 He will tell us *a* things."
4:29 see a Man who told me *a* things
4:39 He told me *a* that I ever did."
4:45 having seen *a* the things He did
5:18 Therefore the Jews sought *a* the
5:20 and shows Him *a* things that He
5:22 but has committed *a* judgment to
5:23 that *a* should honor the Son just
5:28 the hour is coming in which *a*
6:37 *A* that the Father gives Me will
6:39 that of *a* He has given Me I
6:45 And they shall *a* be taught
7:21 and you *a* marvel.
8: 2 and *a* the people came to Him;
10: 8 *A* who ever came before Me are
10:29 them to Me, is greater than *a*;
10:41 but *a* the things that John
11:49 them, "You know nothing at *a*,
12:32 will draw *a* peoples to
13: 3 that the Father had given *a*
13:10 but not *a* of you."
13:11 You are not *a* clean."
13:18 I do not speak concerning *a* of
13:35 By this *a* will know that you are
14:26 He will teach you *a* things, and
14:26 and bring to your remembrance *a*
15:15 for *a* things that I heard from
15:21 But *a* these things they will do
16:13 He will guide you into *a* truth;
16:15 *A* things that the Father has are
16:30 we are sure that You know *a*
17: 2 have given Him authority over *a*
17: 7 Now they have known that *a*
17:10 And *a* Mine are Yours, and Yours
17:21 that they *a* may be one, as You,
18: 4 knowing *a* things that would
18:38 "I find no fault in Him at *a*.
18:40 Then they *a* cried again, saying,
19:11 You could have no power at *a*
19:28 knowing that *a* things were now
21:17 You know *a* things; You know

Acts 1: 1 of *a* that Jesus began both to
1: 8 and in *a* Judea and Samaria, and
1:14 These *a* continued with one
1:18 burst open in the middle and *a*
1:19 And it became known to *a* those
1:21 men who have accompanied us *a*
1:24 Lord, who know the hearts of *a*,
2: 1 they were *a* with one accord in
2: 4 And they were *a* filled with the
2: 7 Then they were *a* amazed and
2: 7 are not *a* these who speak
2:12 So they were *a* amazed and
2:14 Men of Judea and *a* who dwell in
2:17 out of My Spirit on *a*
2:32 of which we are *a* witnesses.
2:36 Therefore let *a* the house of
2:39 and to *a* who are afar off, as
2:44 Now *a* who believed were
2:44 and had *a* things in common,
2:45 goods, and divided them among *a*,
2:47 God and having favor with *a*
3: 9 And *a* the people saw him walking
3:11 *a* the people ran together to
3:16 in the presence of you *a*.
3:18 God foretold by the mouth of *a*
3:21 the times of restoration of *a*
3:21 has spoken by the mouth of *a*
3:22 Him you shall hear in *a*
3:24 and *a* the prophets, from Samuel
3:25 And in your seed *a* the
4:10 "let it be known to you *a*,
4:10 and to *a* the people of Israel,
4:16 through them is evident to *a*
4:18 them not to speak at *a* nor
4:21 since they *a* glorified God for
4:23 own companions and reported *a*
4:24 and *a* that is in them,
4:29 to Your servants that with *a*
4:31 and they were *a* filled with the
4:32 but they had *a* things in
4:33 And great grace was upon them *a*.
4:34 for *a* who were possessors of
5: 5 So great fear came upon *a* those
5:11 So great fear came upon *a* the
5:11 upon all the church and upon *a*
5:12 And they were *a* with one accord
5:16 and they were *a* healed.
5:17 and *a* those who were with him
5:20 and speak to the people *a* the
5:21 with *a* the elders of the
5:34 of the law held in respect by *a*
5:36 and *a* who obeyed him were
5:37 and *a* who obeyed him were
6:15 And *a* who sat in the council,
7:10 and delivered him out of *a* his
7:10 him governor over Egypt and *a*
7:11 and great trouble came over *a*
7:14 called his father Jacob and *a*
7:22 And Moses was learned in *a* the
7:50 Has My hand not made *a*
8: 1 and they were *a* scattered
8:10 to whom they *a* gave heed, from
8:27 who had charge of *a* her
8:37 If you believe with *a* your
8:40 he preached in *a* the cities
9:14 the chief priests to bind *a*
9:21 Then *a* who heard were amazed,
9:22 But Saul increased *a* the more in
9:26 but they were *a* afraid of him,
9:31 Then the churches throughout *a*
9:32 as Peter went through *a* parts
9:35 So *a* who dwelt at Lydda and
9:39 And *a* the widows stood by him
9:40 But Peter put them *a* out, and
9:42 it became known throughout *a*
10: 2 and one who feared God with *a*
10: 8 So when he had explained *a*
10:12 In it were *a* kinds of
10:22 has a good reputation among *a*
10:33 we are *a* present before God, to
10:33 to hear *a* the things commanded
10:36 Jesus Christ—He is Lord of *a*—
10:37 was proclaimed throughout *a*
10:38 about doing good and healing *a*
10:39 And we are witnesses of *a* things
10:41 not to *a* the people, but to
10:43 To Him *a* the prophets witness
10:44 the Holy Spirit fell upon *a*
11:10 and *a* were drawn up again into
11:14 you words by which you and *a*
11:23 and encouraged them *a* that with
11:28 be a great famine throughout *a*
12:11 the hand of Herod and from *a*
13:10 O full of *a* deceit and all
13:10 O full of all deceit and *a*
13:10 you enemy of *a* righteousness,
13:22 who will do *a* My will.'
13:24 the baptism of repentance to *a*
13:29 Now when they had fulfilled *a*
13:39 believes is justified from *a*
13:49 was being spread throughout *a*
14:15 and *a* things that are in them,
14:16 in bygone generations allowed *a*
14:27 they reported *a* that God had
15: 3 and they caused great joy to *a*
15: 4 and they reported *a* things that
15:12 Then *a* the multitude kept silent
15:17 Even *a* the Gentiles who
15:17 the LORD who does *a*
15:18 to God from eternity are *a* His
16: 3 for they *a* knew that his father
16:26 and immediately *a* the doors
16:28 for we are *a* here."
16:32 of the Lord to him and to *a*
16:33 And immediately he and *a* his
16:34 having believed in God with *a*
17: 5 set *a* the city in an uproar and
17: 7 and these are *a* acting contrary
17:11 they received the word with *a*
17:15 Timothy to come to him with *a*
17:21 For *a* the Athenians and the
17:22 I perceive that in *a* things you
17:25 since He gives to *a* life,
17:25 life, breath, and *a* things.
17:26 nation of men to dwell on *a*
17:30 but now commands *a* men
17:31 given assurance of this to *a*
18: 2 Claudius had commanded *a* the
18: 8 believed on the Lord with *a* his
18:17 Then *a* the Greeks took
18:21 I must by *a* means keep this
18:23 strengthening *a* the disciples.
19: 7 the men were about twelve in *a*.
19:10 so that *a* who dwelt in Asia
19:17 This became known both to *a* Jews
19:17 and fear fell on them *a*,
19:19 burned them in the sight of *a*.
19:26 but throughout almost *a* Asia,
19:27 whom *a* Asia and the world
19:34 *a* with one voice cried out for
20:19 serving the Lord with *a*
20:25 indeed, now I know that you *a*,
20:26 am innocent of the blood of *a*
20:28 heed to yourselves and to *a*
20:32 give you an inheritance among *a*
20:36 down and prayed with them *a*.
20:37 Then they *a* wept freely, and
20:38 sorrowing most of *a* for the
21: 5 and they *a* accompanied us, with
21:18 and *a* the elders were present.
21:20 and they are *a* zealous for the
21:21 about you that you teach *a* the
21:24 and that *a* may know that those
21:28 This is the man who teaches *a*
21:30 And *a* the city was disturbed;
21:31 of the garrison that *a*
22: 2 they kept *a* the more silent.
22: 3 was zealous toward God as you *a*
22: 5 and *a* the council of the
22:10 and there you will be told *a*
22:12 having a good testimony with *a*
22:15 you will be His witness to *a*
22:30 the chief priests and *a* their
23: 1 I have lived in *a* good
24: 3 we accept it always and in *a*
24: 3 with *a* thankfulness.
24: 5 a creator of dissension among *a*
24: 8 yourself you may ascertain *a*
24:14 believing *a* things which are

25: 8 I offended in anything at *a*.
25:24 King Agrippa and *a* the men who
26: 2 myself before you concerning *a*
26: 3 because you are expert in *a*
26: 4 *a* the Jews know.
26:14 And when we *a* had fallen to the
26:20 and throughout *a* the region of
26:29 but also *a* who hear me today,
27:20 *a* hope that we would be saved
27:24 indeed God has granted you *a*
27:33 Paul implored them *a* to take
27:35 God in the presence of them *a*;
27:36 Then they were *a* encouraged, and
27:37 And in *a* we were two hundred and
27:44 And so it was that they *a*
28: 2 kindled a fire and made us *a*
28:30 and received *a* who came to him,
28:31 the Lord Jesus Christ with *a*
Rom 1: 5 obedience to the faith among *a*
1: 7 To *a* who are in Rome, beloved of
1: 8 through Jesus Christ for you *a*,
1:18 revealed from heaven against *a*
1:29 being filled with *a*
3: 9 we better than they? Not at *a*.
3: 9 Jews and Greeks that they are *a*
3:12 They have *a* turned aside;
3:19 and *a* the world may become
3:22 to *a* and on all who believe.
3:22 to all and on *a* who believe.
3:23 for *a* have sinned and fall short
4:11 he might be the father of *a*
4:16 the promise might be sure to *a*
4:16 who is the father of us *a*
5:12 and thus death spread to *a* men,
5:12 because *a* sinned—
5:18 offense judgment came to *a*
5:18 act the free gift came to *a*
6:10 died, He died to sin once for *a*;
7: 8 produced in me *a* manner of
8:28 And we know that *a* things work
8:32 but delivered Him up for us *a*,
8:32 with Him also freely give us *a*
8:36 sake we are killed *a* day
8:37 Yet in *a* these things we are
9: 5 Christ came, who is over *a*,
9: 6 For they are not *a* Israel who
9: 7 nor are they *a* children
9:17 may be declared in *a* the
10:12 for the same Lord over *a* is
10:12 Lord over all is rich to *a* who
10:16 But they have not *a* obeyed the
10:18 sound has gone out to *a*
10:21 *A* day long I have stretched
11:26 And so *a* Israel will be saved,
11:32 For God has committed them *a* to
11:32 that He might have mercy on *a*.
11:36 through Him and to Him are *a*
12: 4 but *a* the members do not have
12:17 good things in the sight of *a*
12:18 live peaceably with *a* men.
13: 7 Render therefore to *a* their due:
13: 9 are *a* summed up in this
14: 2 For one believes he may eat *a*
14:10 For we shall *a* stand before the
14:20 *A* things indeed are pure, but
15:11 *a* you Gentiles! Laud Him,
15:11 Laud Him, *a* you peoples!"
15:13 the God of hope fill you with *a*
15:14 filled with *a* knowledge, able
15:33 the God of peace be with you *a*.
16: 4 but also *a* the churches of the
16:15 and *a* the saints who are with
16:19 obedience has become known to *a*.
16:24 Jesus Christ be with you *a*.
16:26 has been made known to *a*
1 Cor 1: 2 with *a* who in every place call
1: 5 in everything by Him in *a*
1: 5 by Him in all utterance and *a*
1:10 that you *a* speak the same
2:10 For the Spirit searches *a*
2:15 he who is spiritual judges *a*
3:21 For *a* things are yours:
3:22 or things to come—*a* are yours.
4:13 the offscouring of *a* things
6:12 *A* things are lawful for me, but
6:12 but *a* things are not helpful.
6:12 *A* things are lawful for me, but
7: 7 For I wish that *a* men were even
7:17 And so I ordain in *a* the
8: 1 We know that we *a* have
8: 6 of whom are *a* things, and we
8: 6 through whom are *a* things, and
9:12 but endure *a* things lest we
9:19 For though I am free from *a*
9:19 have made myself a servant to *a*,
9:22 I have become *a* things to all
9:22 I have become all things to *a*
9:22 that I might by *a* means save
9:24 that those who run in a race *a*
9:25 the prize is temperate in *a*
10: 1 want you to be unaware that *a*
10: 1 *a* passed through the sea,
10: 2 *a* were baptized into Moses in
10: 3 *a* ate the same spiritual food,
10: 4 and *a* drank the same spiritual
10:11 Now *a* these things happened to
10:17 for we *a* partake of that one
10:23 *A* things are lawful for me, but
10:23 but not *a* things are helpful;
10:23 *a* things are lawful for me, but
10:23 but not *a* things edify.
10:26 and *a* its fullness."
10:28 and *a* its fullness."
10:31 do *a* to the glory of God.
10:33 just as I also please *a* men in
10:33 as I also please all men in *a*
11: 2 that you remember me in *a*
11:12 but *a* things are from God.
11:18 For first of *a*, when you come
12: 6 it is the same God who works *a*
12: 6 the same God who works all in *a*.
12: 7 each one for the profit of *a*:
12:11 one and the same Spirit works *a*
12:12 but *a* the members of that one
12:13 For by one Spirit we were *a*
12:13 and have *a* been made to drink
12:19 And if they were *a* one member,
12:26 *a* the members suffer with it;
12:26 *a* the members rejoice with it.
12:29 Are *a* apostles? Are all
12:29 Are *a* prophets? Are all
12:29 Are *a* teachers? Are all
12:29 Are *a* workers of miracles?
12:30 Do *a* have gifts of healings?
12:30 Do *a* speak with tongues? Do all
12:30 Do *a* interpret?
13: 2 and understand *a* mysteries and
13: 2 understand all mysteries and *a*
13: 2 and though I have *a* faith, so
13: 3 And though I bestow *a* my goods
13: 7 bears *a* things, believes all
13: 7 believes *a* things, hopes all
13: 7 hopes *a* things, endures all
13: 7 endures *a* things.
14: 5 I wish you *a* spoke with tongues,
14:18 with tongues more than you *a*;
14:21 for *a* that, they will not
14:23 and *a* speak with tongues, and
14:24 But if *a* prophesy, and an
14:24 comes in, he is convinced by *a*,
14:24 by all, he is convicted by *a*.
14:26 Let *a* things be done for
14:31 For you can *a* prophesy one by
14:31 that *a* may learn and all may be
14:31 that all may learn and *a* may be
14:33 as in *a* the churches of the
14:40 Let *a* things be done decently
15: 3 I delivered to you first of *a*
15: 7 then by *a* the apostles.
15: 8 Then last of *a* He was seen by me
15:10 more abundantly than they *a*,
15:19 we are of *a* men the most
15:22 For as in Adam *a* die, even so in
15:22 even so in Christ *a* shall be
15:24 when He puts an end to *a* rule
15:24 puts an end to all rule and *a*
15:25 He must reign till He has put *a*
15:27 He has put *a* things under
15:27 *a* things are put under Him,"
15:27 is evident that He who put *a*
15:28 Now when *a* things are made
15:28 be subject to Him who put *a*
15:28 that God may be *a* in all.
15:28 Him, that God may be all in *a*.
15:29 if the dead do not rise at *a*?
15:39 *A* flesh is not the same flesh,
15:51 We shall not *a* sleep, but we
15:51 but we shall *a* be changed—
16:14 Let *a* that you do be done with
16:20 *A* the brethren greet you.
16:24 My love be with you *a* in Christ
2 Cor 1: 1 with *a* the saints who are in
1: 1 all the saints who are in *a*
1: 3 Father of mercies and God of *a*
1: 4 who comforts us in *a* our
1:20 For *a* the promises of God in Him
2: 3 having confidence in you *a* that
2: 3 my joy is the joy of you *a*.
2: 5 but *a* of you to some extent—not
2: 9 whether you are obedient in *a*
3: 2 known and read by *a* men;
3:18 But we *a*, with unveiled face,
4:15 For *a* things are for your
5:10 For we must *a* appear before the
5:14 thus: that if One died for *a*,
5:14 One died for all, then *a* died;
5:15 and He died for *a*,
5:17 *a* things have become new.
5:18 Now *a* things are of God, who
6: 4 But in *a* things we commend
6:10 and yet possessing *a* things.
7: 1 let us cleanse ourselves from *a*
7: 4 I am exceedingly joyful in *a*
7:11 what vindication! In *a* things
7:13 has been refreshed by you *a*.
7:14 But as we spoke *a* things to you
7:15 the obedience of you *a*,
8: 7 in *a* diligence, and in your
8:18 is in the gospel throughout *a*
9: 8 And God is able to make *a* grace
9: 8 always having *a* sufficiency in
9: 8 having all sufficiency in *a*
9:11 enriched in everything for *a*
9:13 sharing with them and *a* men,
10: 6 and being ready to punish *a*
11: 5 I consider that I am not at *a*
11: 6 manifested among you in *a*
11:28 my deep concern for *a* the
12:12 accomplished among you with *a*
12:19 But we do *a* things, beloved,
13: 2 and to *a* the rest, that if I
13:13 *A* the saints greet you.
13:14 the Holy Spirit be with you *a*.
Gal 1: 2 and *a* the brethren who are with
2:14 I said to Peter before them *a*,
3: 8 In you *a* the nations shall
3:10 does not continue in *a*
3:22 the Scripture has confined *a*
3:26 For you are *a* sons of God
3:28 for you are *a* one in Christ
4: 1 does not differ at *a* from a
4: 1 slave, though he is master of *a*,
4:12 You have not injured me at *a*.
4:26 which is the mother of us *a*.
5:14 For *a* the law is fulfilled in
6: 6 is taught the word share in *a*
6:10 let us do good to *a*,
Eph 1: 8 made to abound toward us in *a*
1:10 might gather together in one *a*
1:11 the purpose of Him who works *a*
1:15 Lord Jesus and your love for *a*
1:21 far above *a* principality and
1:22 And He put *a* things under His
1:22 gave Him to be head over *a*
1:23 fullness of Him who fills *a* in
1:23 of Him who fills all in *a*.
2: 3 among whom also we *a* once
3: 8 who am less than the least of *a*
3: 9 and to make *a* see what is the
3: 9 hidden in God who created *a*
3:18 be able to comprehend with *a*
3:19 that you may be filled with *a*
3:20 exceedingly abundantly above *a*
3:21 the church by Christ Jesus to *a*
4: 2 with *a* lowliness and gentleness,
4: 6 one God and Father of *a*,
4: 6 Father of all, who is above *a*,
4: 6 is above all, and through *a*,
4: 6 and through all, and in you *a*.
4:10 One who ascended far above *a*
4:10 that He might fill *a* things.)
4:13 till we *a* come to the unity of
4:15 may grow up in *a* things into
4:19 to work *a* uncleanness with
4:31 Let *a* bitterness, wrath, anger,
4:31 away from you, with *a* malice.
5: 3 But fornication and *a*
5: 9 fruit of the Spirit is in *a*
5:13 But *a* things that are exposed
5:20 giving thanks always for *a*
6:13 the evil day, and having done *a*,
6:16 above *a*, taking the shield
6:16 you will be able to quench *a*
6:18 praying always with *a* prayer and
6:18 watchful to this end with *a*
6:18 and supplication for *a* the
6:21 will make *a* things known to
6:24 Grace be with *a* those who love
Phil 1: 1 To *a* the saints in Christ
1: 4 mine making request for you *a*
1: 7 for me to think this of you *a*,
1: 7 you *a* are partakers with me of
1: 8 how greatly I long for you *a*
1: 9 and more in knowledge and *a*
1:13 and to *a* the rest, that my
1:20 but with *a* boldness, as always,
1:25 remain and continue with you *a*
2:14 Do *a* things without complaining
2:17 am glad and rejoice with you *a*.
2:21 For *a* seek their own, not the
2:26 since he was longing for you *a*,
2:29 therefore in the Lord with *a*
3: 8 Yet indeed I also count *a* things
3: 8 I have suffered the loss of *a*
3:21 He is able even to subdue *a*
4: 5 your gentleness be known to *a*
4: 7 surpasses *a* understanding,
4:12 Everywhere and in *a* things I
4:13 I can do *a* things through Christ
4:18 Indeed I have *a* and abound. I am
4:19 And my God shall supply *a* your
4:22 *A* the saints greet you, but
4:23 Lord Jesus Christ be with you *a*.
Col 1: 4 Jesus and of your love for *a*
1: 6 as it has also in *a* the
1: 9 the knowledge of His will in *a*
1:11 strengthened with *a* might,
1:11 *a* patience and longsuffering
1:15 the firstborn over *a* creation.
1:16 For by Him *a* things were created
1:16 *A* things were created through
1:17 And He is before *a* things, and
1:17 and in Him *a* things consist.
1:18 that in *a* things He may have
1:19 the Father that in Him *a*
1:20 and by Him to reconcile *a* things
1:28 man and teaching every man in *a*
2: 2 and attaining to *a* riches of
2: 3 in whom are hidden *a* the
2: 9 For in Him dwells *a* the fullness
2:10 who is the head of *a*
2:13 having forgiven you *a*
2:19 from whom *a* the body, nourished
2:22 which *a* concern things which
3: 8 you yourselves are to put off *a*
3:11 but Christ is *a* and in all.
3:11 but Christ is all and in *a*.
3:14 But above *a* these things put on
3:16 Christ dwell in you richly in *a*
3:17 do *a* in the name of the Lord
3:20 obey your parents in *a* things,
3:22 obey in *a* things your masters
4: 7 will tell you *a* the news about
4: 9 They will make known to you *a*
4:12 perfect and complete in *a* the
1 Th 1: 2 thanks to God always for you *a*,

1: 7 that you became examples to *a*
2:15 God and are contrary to *a* men,
3: 7 in *a* our affliction and
3: 9 for *a* the joy with which we
3:12 in love to one another and to *a*,
3:13 of our Lord Jesus Christ with *a*
4: 6 the Lord is the avenger of *a*
4:10 and indeed you do so toward *a*
4:10 all the brethren who are in *a*
5: 5 You are *a* sons of light and sons
5:14 the weak, be patient with *a*.
5:15 both for yourselves and for *a*.
5:21 Test *a* things; hold fast what is
5:26 Greet *a* the brethren with a holy
5:27 that this epistle be read to *a*
2 Th 1: 3 the love of every one of you *a*
1: 4 your patience and faith in *a*
1:10 and to be admired among *a*
1:11 and fulfill *a* the good pleasure
2: 4 and exalts himself above *a*
2: 9 with *a* power, signs, and lying
2:10 and with *a* unrighteous deception
2:12 that they *a* may be condemned who
3: 2 for not *a* have faith.
3:11 manner, not working at *a*,
3:16 The Lord be with you *a*.
3:18 Jesus Christ be with you *a*.
1 Tim 1:15 faithful saying and worthy of *a*
1:16 first Jesus Christ might show *a*
2: 1 Therefore I exhort first of *a*
2: 1 giving of thanks be made for *a*
2: 2 for kings and *a* who are in
2: 2 a quiet and peaceable life in *a*
2: 4 who desires *a* men to be saved
2: 6 who gave Himself a ransom for *a*,
2:11 a woman learn in silence with *a*
3: 4 children in submission with *a*
3:11 faithful in *a* things.
4: 8 godliness is profitable for *a*
4: 9 faithful saying and worthy of *a*
4:10 who is the Savior of *a* men,
4:15 progress may be evident to *a*.
5: 2 women as sisters, with *a* purity.
5:20 rebuke in the presence of *a*,
6: 1 their own masters worthy of *a*
6:10 love of money is a root of *a*
6:13 of God who gives life to *a*
6:17 who gives us richly *a* things to
2 Tim 1:15 that *a* those in Asia have
2: 7 give you understanding in *a*
2:10 Therefore I endure *a* things for
2:24 not quarrel but be gentle to *a*,
3: 9 folly will be manifest to *a*,
3:11 And out of them *a* the Lord
3:12 and *a* who desire to live godly
3:16 *A* Scripture is given by
4: 2 with *a* longsuffering and
4: 5 But you be watchful in *a* things,
4: 8 not to me only but also to *a*
4:16 but *a* forsook me. May it not be
4:17 and that *a* the Gentiles might
4:21 and *a* the brethren.
Titus 1:15 To the pure *a* things are pure,
2: 7 in *a* things showing yourself to
2: 9 to be well pleasing in *a*
2:10 but showing *a* good fidelity,
2:10 of God our Savior in *a* things.
2:11 salvation has appeared to *a*
2:15 and rebuke with *a* authority.
3: 2 showing *a* humility to all men.
3: 2 showing all humility to *a* men.
3:15 *A* who are with me greet you
3:15 the faith. Grace be with you *a*.
Phm 1: 5 the Lord Jesus and toward *a*
Heb 1: 2 whom He has appointed heir of *a*
1: 3 and upholding *a* things by the
1: 6 Let *a* the angels of God
1:11 And they will *a* grow old
1:14 Are they not *a* ministering
2: 8 You have put *a* things in
2: 8 For in that He put *a* in
2: 8 But now we do not yet see *a*
2:10 for whom are *a* things and by
2:10 all things and by whom are *a*
2:11 are being sanctified are *a* of
2:15 through fear of death were *a*
2:17 in *a* things He had to be made
3: 2 Moses also was faithful in *a*
3: 4 but He who built *a* things is
3: 5 indeed was faithful in *a* His
3:16 was it not *a* who came out of
4: 4 on the seventh day from *a*
4:13 but *a* things are naked and
4:15 but was in *a* points tempted as
5: 9 of eternal salvation to *a* who
6:16 is for them an end of *a*
7: 2 Abraham gave a tenth part of *a*,
7: 7 Now beyond *a* contradiction the
7:27 for this He did once for *a* when
8: 5 See that you make *a* things
8:11 for *a* shall know Me,
9: 3 is called the Holiest of *A*,
9: 4 of the covenant overlaid on *a*
9: 8 the way into the Holiest of *A*
9:12 the Most Holy Place once for *a*,
9:17 since it has no power at *a*
9:19 had spoken every precept to *a*
9:19 both the book itself and *a* the
9:21 both the tabernacle and *a* the
9:22 according to the law almost *a*
10:10 of Jesus Christ once for *a*.
11:13 These *a* died in faith, not
11:39 And *a* these, having obtained a
12: 8 of which *a* have become
12:14 Pursue peace with *a* people, and
12:23 heaven, to God the Judge of *a*,
13: 4 Marriage is honorable among *a*,
13:18 in *a* things desiring to live
13:24 Greet *a* those who rule over you,
13:24 and *a* the saints. Those from
13:25 Grace be with you *a*.
Jas 1: 2 count it *a* joy when you fall
1: 5 who gives to *a* liberally and
1: 8 unstable in *a* his ways.
1:21 Therefore lay aside *a*
2:10 one point, he is guilty of *a*.
3: 2 For we *a* stumble in many things.
4:16 *A* such boasting is evil.
5:12 But above *a*, my brethren,
1 Pe 1:15 you also be holy in *a* your
1:24 *A* flesh is as grass, And
1:24 And *a* the glory of man
2: 1 laying aside *a* malice, all
2: 1 *a* deceit, hypocrisy, envy, and
2: 1 and *a* evil speaking,
2:17 Honor *a* people. Love the
2:18 to your masters with *a* fear,
3: 8 *a* of you be of one mind,
4: 7 But the end of *a* things is at
4: 8 And above *a* things have fervent
4:11 that in *a* things God may be
5: 5 *a* of you be submissive to one
5: 7 casting *a* your care upon Him,
5:10 But may the God of *a* grace, who
5:14 Peace to you *a* who are in
2 Pe 1: 3 divine power has given to us *a*
1: 5 giving *a* diligence, add to your
3: 4 *a* things continue as they
3: 9 any should perish but that *a*
3:11 since *a* these things will be
3:16 as also in *a* his epistles,
1 Jn 1: 5 and in Him is no darkness at *a*.
1: 7 His Son cleanses us from *a* sin.
1: 9 sins and to cleanse us from *a*
2:16 For *a* that is in the world—the
2:20 and you know *a* things.
2:27 teaches you concerning *a*
3:20 and knows *a* things.
5:17 *A* unrighteousness is sin, and
2 Jn 1 but also *a* those who have known
3 Jn 2 pray that you may prosper in *a*
12 has a good testimony from *a*,
Jude 3 the faith which was once for *a*
15 "to execute judgment on *a*,
15 to convict *a* who are ungodly
15 who are ungodly among them of *a*
15 and of *a* the harsh things which
Rev 1: 2 to *a* things that he saw.
1: 7 And *a* the tribes of the earth
2:23 and *a* the churches shall know
4:11 For You created *a* things, And
5: 6 Spirits of God sent out into *a*
5:13 and *a* that are in them, I heard
7: 4 and forty-four thousand of *a*
7: 9 of *a* nations, tribes, peoples,
7:11 *A* the angels stood around the
8: 3 it with the prayers of *a* the
8: 7 and *a* green grass was burned
11: 6 and to strike the earth with *a*
12: 5 a male Child who was to rule *a*
13: 3 And *a* the world marveled and
13: 8 *A* who dwell on the earth will
13:12 And he exercises *a* the authority
13:16 He causes *a*, both small
14: 8 because she has made *a* nations
15: 4 For *a* nations shall come and
18: 3 For *a* the nations have drunk of
18:14 and *a* the things which are rich
18:14 shall find them no more at *a*.
18:17 *a* who travel by ship, sailors,
18:19 in which *a* who had ships on the
18:23 for by your sorcery *a* the
18:24 and of *a* who were slain on the
19: 5 *a* you His servants and those
19:17 saying to *a* the birds that fly
19:18 and the flesh of *a* people,
19:21 And *a* the birds were filled
21: 5 I make *a* things new." And He
21: 7 who overcomes shall inherit *a*
21: 8 and *a* liars shall have their
21:19 the city were adorned with *a*
21:25 gates shall not be shut at *a*
22:21 Jesus Christ be with you *a*.

ALLAYS (1/1)

Prov 15:18 he who is slow to anger *a*

ALLEGING (KJV) See DEMONSTRATING

ALLELUIA (4/4)

Rev 19: 1 *A*! Salvation and glory and honor
19: 3 *A*! Her smoke rises up forever
19: 4 throne, saying, "Amen! *A*!"
19: 6 *A*! For the Lord God Omnipotent

ALLIED (6/6) ALLIES

2 Chr 18: 1 and by marriage he *a* himself
20:35 Jehoshaphat king of Judah *a*
20:36 And he *a* himself with him to
20:37 Because you have *a* yourself with
Neh 13: 4 was *a* with Tobiah.
Ezek 30: 5 the men of the lands who are *a*,

ALLIES (3/3) ALLIED

Gen 14:13 and they were *a* with Abram.
Job 9:13 The *a* of the proud lie
Jer 2:37 has rejected your trusted *a*,

ALLON (2/2) ELON

1 Chr 4:37 the son of Shiphi, the son of *A*,

ALLON BACHUTH (1/1)

Gen 35: 8 So the name of it was called *A*.

ALLOTMENT (5/5) ALLOTMENTS, ALLOTTED

1 Chr 16:18 the land of Canaan As the *a*
Job 31: 2 For what is the *a* of God from
Ps 105:11 the land of Canaan As the *a*
Ezek 16:27 against you, diminished your *a*,
Acts 13:19 their land to them by *a*.

ALLOTMENTS (1/1) ALLOTMENT

2 Chr 31:15 to distribute *a* to their

ALLOTTED (7/6) ALLOTMENT

Gen 47:22 for the priests had rations *a*
Judg 1: 3 Come up with me to my *a*
1: 3 likewise go with you to your *a*
Job 7: 3 So I have been *a* months of
Ps 78:55 *A* them an inheritance by
125: 3 shall not rest On the land *a*
Prov 30: 8 Feed me with the food *a* to me;

ALLOW (28/28) ALLOWANCE, ALLOWED

Gen 31: 7 but God did not *a* him to hurt
31:28 And you did not *a* me to kiss my
Ex 12:23 pass over the door and not *a*
Lev 2:13 you shall not *a* the salt of the
22:16 or *a* them to bear the guilt of
Num 21:23 But Sihon would not *a* Israel to
Josh 10:19 Do not *a* them to enter their
Judg 1:34 for they would not *a* them to
3:28 and did not *a* anyone to cross
1 Sam 24: 7 and did not *a* them to rise
2 Sam 21:10 And she did not *a* the birds of
Job 9:18 He will not *a* me to catch my
Ps 16:10 Nor will You *a* Your Holy One
66: 9 And does not *a* our feet to be
89:33 Nor *a* My faithfulness to fail.
121: 3 He will not *a* your foot to be
Prov 10: 3 The LORD will not *a* the
Mt 23:13 nor do you *a* those who are
Mk 1:34 and He did not *a* the demons to
11:16 And He would not *a* anyone to
Lk 4:41 did not *a* them to speak, for
Acts 2:27 Nor will You *a* Your Holy
13:35 You will not *a* Your Holy
19:30 the disciples would not *a* him.
28: 4 yet justice does not *a* to
1 Cor 10:13 who will not *a* you to be
Rev 2:20 because you *a* that woman
11: 9 and not *a* their dead bodies to

ALLOWANCE (1/1) ALLOW

Esth 2: 9 to her, besides her *a*.

ALLOWED (6/6) ALLOW

Deut 8: 3 *a* you to hunger, and fed you
Job 31:30 (Indeed I have not *a* my mouth
Mt 3:15 Then he *a* Him.
24:43 he would have watched and not *a*
Lk 12:39 he would have watched and not *a*
Acts 14:16 who in bygone generations *a* all

ALLOY (1/1)

Isa 1:25 And take away all your *a*.

ALLURE (3/3)

Prov 6:25 Nor let her *a* you with her
Hos 2:14 I will *a* her, Will bring her
2 Pe 2:18 they *a* through the lusts of the

ALMIGHTY (57/57)

Gen 17: 1 I am *A* God; walk before Me and
28: 3 May God *A* bless you, And make
35:11 God said to him: "I am God *A*.
43:14 And may God *A* give you mercy
48: 3 God *A* appeared to me at Luz in
49:25 And by the *A* who will bless
Ex 6: 3 Isaac, and to Jacob, as God *A*,
Num 24: 4 Who sees the vision of the *A*,
24:16 Who sees the vision of the *A*,
Ruth 1:20 for the *A* has dealt very
1:21 and the *A* has afflicted me?"
Job 5:17 despise the chastening of the *A*.
6: 4 For the arrows of the *A* are
6:14 he forsakes the fear of the *A*.
8: 3 Or does the *A* pervert justice?
8: 5 make your supplication to the *A*,
11: 7 find out the limits of the *A*?
13: 3 But I would speak to the *A*,

15:25 acts defiantly against the *A*,
21:15 Who is the *A*, that we should
21:20 him drink of the wrath of the *A*.
22: 3 Is it any pleasure to the *A*
22:17 from us! What can the *A* do to
22:23 If you return to the *A*,
22:25 the *A* will be your gold And
22:26 will have your delight in the *A*,
23:16 And the *A* terrifies me;
24: 1 times are not hidden from the *A*,
27: 2 away my justice, And the *A*,
27:10 he delight himself in the *A*?
27:11 What is with the *A* I will not
27:13 oppressors, received from the *A*:
29: 5 When the *A* was yet with me,
31: 2 And the inheritance of the *A*
31:35 that the *A* would answer me,
32: 8 And the breath of the *A* gives
33: 4 And the breath of the *A* gives
34:10 And from the *A* to commit
34:12 Nor will the *A* pervert
35:13 Nor will the *A* regard it.
37:23 As for the *A*, we cannot find
40: 2 the one who contends with the *A*
Ps 68:14 When the *A* scattered kings in
91: 1 abide under the shadow of the *A*.
Isa 13: 6 come as destruction from the *A*.
Ezek 1:24 waters, like the voice of the *A*,
10: 5 like the voice of *A* God when He
Joel 1:15 come as destruction from the *A*.
2 Cor 6:18 daughters, Says the LORD *A*.
Rev 1: 8 was and who is to come, the *A*.
4: 8 holy, holy, Lord God *A*,
11:17 give You thanks, O Lord God *A*,
15: 3 Lord God *A*! Just and true
16: 7 saying, "Even so, Lord God *A*,
16:14 of that great day of God *A*.
19:15 the fierceness and wrath of *A*
21:22 for the Lord God *A* and the Lamb

ALMODAD (2/2)

Gen 10:26 Joktan begot *A*,
1 Chr 1:20 Joktan begot *A*,

ALMON (3/3)

Josh 21:18 and *A* with its common-land:

ALMON DIBLATHAIM (2/2)

Num 33:46 from Dibon Gad and camped at *A*.
33:47 They moved from *A* and camped in

ALMOND (9/7) ALMONDS

Gen 30:37 of green poplar and of the ***a***
Ex 25:33 bowls shall be made like ***a***
25:33 and three bowls made like ***a***
25:34 bowls shall be made like ***a***
37:19 were three bowls made like ***a***
37:19 and three bowls made like ***a***
37:20 were four bowls made like ***a***
Eccl 12: 5 When the ***a*** tree blossoms, The
Jer 1:11 I see a branch of an ***a*** tree."

ALMONDS (2/2) ALMOND

Gen 43:11 and myrrh, pistachio nuts and ***a***.
Num 17: 8 blossoms and yielded ripe ***a***.

ALMOST (10/10)

Ex 17: 4 They are ***a*** ready to stone me!"
Ps 73: 2 my feet had ***a*** stumbled; My
119:87 They ***a*** made an end of me on
Acts 13:44 On the next Sabbath ***a*** the whole
19:26 but throughout ***a*** all Asia, this
21:27 Now when the seven days were ***a***
26:28 You ***a*** persuade me to become a
26:29 might become both ***a*** and
Phil 2:27 For indeed he was sick ***a*** unto
Heb 9:22 And according to the law ***a*** all

ALMS (9/9)

Lk 11:41 But rather give ***a*** of such things
12:33 "Sell what you have and give ***a***;
Acts 3: 2 to ask ***a*** from those who entered
3: 3 go into the temple, asked for ***a***.
3:10 it was he who sat begging ***a*** at
10: 2 who gave ***a*** generously to the
10: 4 Your prayers and your ***a*** have
10:31 and your ***a*** are remembered in
24:17 many years I came to bring ***a***

ALMSDEEDS (KJV) See (CHARITABLE) DEEDS

ALMUG (3/2) ALGUM

1 Ki 10:11 brought great quantities of ***a***
10:12 the king made steps of the ***a***
10:12 There never again came such ***a***

ALOES (5/5)

Num 24: 6 Like ***a*** planted by the LORD,
Ps 45: 8 are scented with myrrh and ***a***
Prov 7:17 perfumed my bed With myrrh, ***a***,
Song 4:14 of frankincense, Myrrh and ***a***,
Jn 19:39 a mixture of myrrh and ***a***,

ALONE (125/123)

Gen 2:18 not good that man should be ***a***;
32:24 Then Jacob was left ***a***;
42:38 is dead, and he is left ***a***.
44:20 and he ***a*** is left of his
Ex 14:12 Let us ***a*** that we may serve the
18:14 Why do you ***a*** sit, and all the
24: 2 And Moses ***a*** shall come near the
32:10 "Now therefore, let Me ***a***,
Lev 13:46 unclean, and he shall dwell ***a***;
Num 11:14 able to bear all these people ***a***,
11:17 you may not bear it yourself ***a***.
23: 9 There! A people dwelling ***a***,
Deut 1: 9 I ***a*** am not able to bear you.
1:12 How can I ***a*** bear your problems
8: 3 man shall not live by bread ***a***;
9:14 'Let Me ***a***, that I may destroy
29:14 and this oath, not with you ***a***,
32:12 So the LORD ***a*** led him, And
33:28 The fountain of Jacob ***a***,
Josh 22:20 And that man did not perish ***a***
Judg 11:37 let me ***a*** for two months, that I
1 Sam 21: 1 said to him, "Why are you ***a***,
2 Sam 16:11 may this Benjamite? Let him ***a***,
18:24 and there was a man, running ***a***.
18:25 the king said, "If he is ***a***,
18:26 running ***a***!" And the king said,
1 Ki 8:39 heart You know (for You ***a*** know
11:29 and the two were ***a*** in the
18:22 I ***a*** am left a prophet of the
19:10 I ***a*** am left; and they seek to
19:14 I ***a*** am left; and they seek to
2 Ki 4:27 man of God said, "Let her ***a***;
17:18 left but the tribe of Judah ***a***.
19:15 cherubim, You are God, You ***a***,
19:19 You are the LORD God, You ***a***.
23:18 And he said, "Let him ***a***;
23:18 So they let his bones ***a***,
1 Chr 29: 1 whom ***a*** God has chosen, is
2 Chr 6:30 heart You know (for You ***a*** know
Ezra 4: 3 but we ***a*** will build to the
6: 7 the work of this house of God ***a***;
Neh 9: 6 You ***a*** are the LORD; You have
Esth 3: 6 to lay hands on Mordecai ***a***,
Job 1:15 and I ***a*** have escaped to tell
1:16 and I ***a*** have escaped to tell
1:17 and I ***a*** have escaped to tell
1:19 and I ***a*** have escaped to tell
7:16 not live forever. Let me ***a***,
7:19 And let me ***a*** till I swallow my
9: 8 He ***a*** spreads out the heavens,
10:20 my days few? Cease! Leave me ***a***,
15:19 To whom ***a*** the land was given,
34:29 is against a nation or a man ***a***?
Ps 4: 8 in peace, and sleep; For You ***a***,
62: 5 soul, wait silently for God ***a***,
83:18 whose name ***a*** is the LORD,
86:10 You ***a*** are God.
102: 7 And am like a sparrow ***a*** on the
136: 4 To Him who ***a*** does great
148:13 For His name ***a*** is exalted;
Prov 9:12 you scoff, you will bear it ***a***.
Eccl 4: 8 There is one ***a***,
4:10 But woe to him who is ***a*** when
4:11 But how can one be warm ***a***?
Isa 2:11 And the LORD ***a*** shall be
2:17 The LORD ***a*** will be exalted in
5: 8 place Where they may dwell ***a***
14:31 And no one will be ***a*** in his
37:16 cherubim, You are God, You ***a***,
37:20 that You are the LORD, You ***a***.
44:24 stretches out the heavens all ***a***,
49:21 these up? There I was, left ***a***;
51: 2 bore you; For I called him ***a***,
63: 3 have trodden the winepress ***a***,
Jer 15:17 I sat ***a*** because of Your hand,
49:31 gates nor bars, Dwelling ***a***.
Lam 3:28 Let him sit ***a*** and keep silent,
Ezek 9: 8 killing them, I was left ***a***;
Dan 10: 7 ***a*** saw the vision, for the men
10: 8 Therefore I was left ***a*** when I
10:13 for I had been left ***a*** there
Hos 4:17 is joined to idols, Let him ***a***.
8: 9 Like a wild donkey ***a*** by
Mt 4: 4 shall not live by bread ***a***,
14:23 He was ***a*** there.
15:14 "Let them ***a***.
18:15 his fault between you and him ***a***.
27:49 The rest said, "Let Him ***a***;
Mk 1:24 Let us ***a***! What have we to do
2: 7 Who can forgive sins but God ***a***?
4:10 But when He was ***a***,
4:34 to them. And when they were ***a***,
6:47 and He was ***a*** on the land.
14: 6 But Jesus said, "Let her ***a***.
15:36 to drink, saying, "Let Him ***a***;
Lk 4: 4 shall not live by bread ***a***,
4:34 Let us ***a***! What have we to do
5:21 Who can forgive sins but God ***a***?
9:18 as He was ***a*** praying, that His
9:36 had ceased, Jesus was found ***a***.
10:40 sister has left me to serve ***a***?
13: 8 let it ***a*** this year also, until
Jn 6:15 to the mountain by Himself ***a***.
6:22 His disciples had gone away ***a***—
8: 9 the last. And Jesus was left ***a***,
8:16 is true; for I am not ***a***,
8:29 The Father has not left Me ***a***,
11:48 If we let Him ***a*** like this,
12: 7 But Jesus said, "Let her ***a***;
12:24 ground and dies, it remains ***a***;
16:32 to his own, and will leave Me ***a***.
16:32 Me alone. And yet I am not ***a***,
17:20 "I do not pray for these ***a***,
Acts 5:38 from these men and let them ***a***;
Rom 4:23 was not written for his sake ***a***
11: 3 and I ***a*** am left, and
16:27 ***a*** wise, be glory through Jesus
Gal 6: 4 have rejoicing in himself ***a***,
1 Th 3: 1 it good to be left in Athens ***a***,
1 Tim 1:17 to God who ***a*** is wise, be honor
5: 5 is really a widow, and left ***a***,
6:16 who ***a*** has immortality, dwelling
Heb 9: 7 part the high priest went ***a***
Jude 25 Who ***a*** is wise, Be glory and
Rev 15: 4 For You ***a*** are holy. For all

ALONG (76/73)

Gen 42:38 calamity should befall him ***a***
45:24 you do not become troubled ***a***
Ex 2: 5 And her maidens walked ***a*** the
27:11 Likewise ***a*** the length of the
27:12 And ***a*** the width of the court on
38:18 and the height ***a*** its width was
Num 13:29 dwell by the sea and ***a*** the
20:17 we will go ***a*** the King's
34: 3 be from the Wilderness of Zin ***a***
34:12 the border shall go down ***a*** the
Deut 2:37 anywhere ***a*** the River Jabbok, or
22: 4 donkey or his ox fall down ***a***
22: 6 happens to be before you ***a*** the
Josh 2:22 The pursuers sought them all ***a***
10:10 chased them ***a*** the road that
15: 3 passed ***a*** to Zin, ascended on
15: 3 passed ***a*** to Hezron, went up to
15:10 passed ***a*** to the side of Mount
15:11 passed ***a*** to Mount Baalah, and
16: 2 passed ***a*** to the border of the
17: 7 and the border went ***a*** south to
18:18 Then it passed ***a*** toward the
18:19 And the border passed ***a*** to the
19:11 and extended ***a*** the brook that
19:12 eastward toward the sunrise ***a***
19:13 And from there it passed ***a*** on
19:26 ***a*** the Brook Shihor Libnath.
Judg 5: 6 And the travelers walked ***a*** the
5:10 And who walk ***a*** the road.
9:25 all who passed by them ***a*** that
11:18 And they went ***a*** through the
11:26 and in all the cities ***a*** the
14: 9 of it in his hands and went ***a***,
1 Sam 6:12 and went ***a*** the highway, lowing
17:52 of the Philistines fell ***a*** the
2 Sam 3:16 Then her husband went ***a*** with her
8:11 ***a*** with the silver and gold that
15:11 and they went ***a*** innocently and
16:13 And as David and his men went ***a***
16:13 Shimei went ***a*** the hillside
2 Ki 15:25 ***a*** with Argob and Arieh; and
1 Chr 18:11 ***a*** with the silver and gold that
2 Chr 12: 1 and all Israel ***a*** with him.
23:10 ***a*** by the altar and by the
Ezra 7:16 ***a*** with the freewill offering of
8:31 of the enemy and from ambush ***a***
Esth 5:12 by her, ***a*** with the king.
Job 30:14 the ruinous storm they roll ***a***.
40:15 which I made ***a*** with you; He
Prov 7: 8 Passing ***a*** the street near her
27:22 in a mortar with a pestle ***a***
Eccl 10: 3 Even when a fool walks ***a*** the
Isa 10:29 They have gone ***a*** the ridge,
49: 9 They shall feed ***a*** the roads,
Jer 41: 6 meet them, weeping as he went ***a***;
50:33 *A* with the children of Judah;
Ezek 47: 7 ***a*** the bank of the river, were
47:12 *A* the bank of the river, on this
47:18 ***a*** the Jordan, and along the
47:18 and ***a*** the eastern side of the
47:19 ***a*** the brook to the Great Sea.
48: 1 From the northern border ***a*** the
48:15 ***a*** the edge of the twenty-five
48:28 ***a*** the brook to the Great Sea.
Am 3:15 will destroy the winter house ***a***
4:10 *A* with your captive horses; I
Zeph 1: 3 And the stumbling blocks ***a***
Mk 4:36 they took Him ***a*** in the boat as
Lk 10: 4 and greet no one ***a*** the road.
12:58 make every effort ***a*** the way to
Acts 8:26 and go toward the south ***a*** the
25: 3 while they lay in ambush ***a*** the
26:13 ***a*** the road I saw a light from
27: 2 meaning to sail ***a*** the coasts of
1 Cor 5: 4 ***a*** with my spirit, with the
9: 5 Do we have no right to take ***a*** a

ALONGSIDE (3/3)

1 Chr 8:32 They also dwelt ***a*** their
9:38 They also dwelt ***a*** their
Ezek 48:18 ***a*** the district of the holy

ALOOF (1/1)

Ps 38:11 ones and my friends stand ***a***

ALOTH (1/1) BEALOTH

1 Ki 4:16 son of Hushai, in Asher and *A*;

ALOUD (23/23)

Gen 45: 2 And he wept ***a***,
1 Ki 18:27 mocked them and said, "Cry ***a***,

18:28 So they cried *a*,
1 Chr 16:42 to sound *a* with trumpets and
Ezra 3:12 Yet many shouted *a* for joy,
Job 19: 7 I am not heard. If I cry *a*,
Ps 51:14 And my tongue shall sing *a* of
55:17 at noon I will pray, and cry *a*,
59:16 I will sing *a* of Your mercy in
81: 1 Sing *a* to God our strength;
132:16 And her saints shall shout *a*
149: 5 Let them sing *a* on their beds.
Prov 1:20 Wisdom calls *a* outside; She
Isa 24:14 of the LORD They shall cry *a*
42:13 He shall cry out, yes, shout *a*;
54: 1 forth into singing, and cry *a*,
58: 1 'Cry *a*, spare not;
Dan 3: 4 Then a herald cried *a*:
4:14 He cried *a* and said thus:
5: 7 The king cried *a* to bring in the
Hos 5: 8 The trumpet in Ramah! Cry *a*
Mic 4: 9 Now why do you cry *a*?
Mk 15: 8 Then the multitude, crying *a*,

ALPHA (4/4)

Rev 1: 8 I am the *A* and the Omega, the
1:11 I am the *A* and the Omega, the
21: 6 It is done! I am the *A* and the
22:13 I am the *A* and the Omega, the

ALPHAEUS (5/5) CLEOPAS

Mt 10: 3 collector; James the son of *A*,
Mk 2:14 He saw Levi the son of *A*
3:18 Thomas, James the son of *A*,
Lk 6:15 and Thomas; James the son of *A*,
Acts 1:13 James the son of *A* and Simon

ALREADY (53/50)

Ex 1: 5 (for Joseph was in Egypt *a*).
Num 16:47 and *a* the plague had begun
1 Sam 25:18 five sheep *a* dressed, five
2 Sam 3:24 and he has *a* gone?
2 Chr 28:13 for we *a* have offended the
Neh 9:25 Cisterns *a* dug, vineyards,
Eccl 1:10 It has *a* been in ancient times
2:12 Only what he has *a* done.
3:15 That which is has *a* been, And
3:15 And what is to be has *a* been;
4: 2 I praised the dead who were *a*
6:10 one is, he has been named *a*,
9: 7 For God has *a* accepted your
Mal 2: 2 Yes, I have cursed them *a*,
Mt 5:28 a woman to lust for her has *a*
14:15 and the hour is *a* late. Send
17:12 to you that Elijah has come *a*,
24:32 When its branch has *a* become
Mk 4:37 so that it was *a* filling.
6:35 and *a* the hour is late.
11:11 as the hour was *a* late, He went
13:28 When its branch has *a* become
15:44 Pilate marveled that He was *a*
Lk 7: 6 And when He was *a* not far from
12:49 and how I wish it were *a*
21:30 When they are *a* budding, you see
Jn 3:18 does not believe is condemned *a*,
4:35 for they are *a* white for
5: 6 and knew that he *a* had been in
6:17 And it was *a* dark, and Jesus
9:22 for the Jews had agreed *a* that
9:27 answered them, "I told you *a*,
11:17 He found that he had *a* been in
13: 2 the devil having *a* put it into
15: 3 You are *a* clean because of the
19:33 to Jesus and saw that He was *a*
Acts 4: 3 for it was *a* evening.
27: 9 because the Fast was *a* over,
Rom 4:19 *a* dead (since he was about a
1 Cor 4: 8 You are *a* full! You are already
4: 8 You are already full! You are *a*
5: 3 have *a* judged (as though I were
6: 7 it is *a* an utter failure for
Eph 3: 3 (as I have briefly written *a*,
Phil 3:12 Not that I have *a* attained, or
3:12 or am *a* perfected; but I press
3:16 to the degree that we have *a*
2 Th 2: 7 mystery of lawlessness is *a* at
1 Tim 5:15 For some have *a* turned aside
2 Tim 2:18 that the resurrection is *a*
4: 6 For I am *a* being poured out as
1 Jn 2: 8 and the true light is *a*
4: 3 and is now *a* in the world.

ALSO (1756/1700)

Gen 1:16 night. He made the stars *a*.
1:30 '*A*, to every beast
2: 9 The tree of life was *a* in the
3: 6 She *a* gave to her husband with
3:21 *A* for Adam and his wife the
3:22 he put out his hand and take *a*
4: 4 Abel *a* brought of the firstborn
4:22 she *a* bore Tubal-Cain, an
4:26 to him *a* a son was born; and he
6: 4 and *a* afterward, when the sons
6:11 The earth *a* was corrupt before
7: 3 *a* seven each of birds of the
8: 2 the windows of heaven were *a*
8: 8 He *a* sent out from himself a
10:21 And children were born *a* to
12:15 The princes of Pharaoh *a* saw her
13: 5 Lot *a*, who went with Abram,
13:16 then your descendants *a* could
14: 7 and *a* the Amorites who dwelt in
14:12 They *a* took Lot, Abram's
14:16 and *a* brought back his brother
15:14 And *a* the nation whom they serve
16:13 Have I *a* here seen Him who sees
17: 8 *A* I give to you and your
17:16 And I will bless her and *a* give
18:12 pleasure, my lord being old *a*?
18:23 Would You *a* destroy the
18:24 would You *a* destroy the place
19:21 you concerning this thing *a*,
19:34 make him drink wine tonight *a*,
19:35 father drink wine that night *a*.
19:38 she *a* bore a son and called his
20: 4 You slay a righteous nation *a*?
20: 6 For I *a* withheld you from
21: 7 She *a* said, "Who would have
21:13 Yet I will *a* make a nation of
22:20 Indeed Milcah *a* has borne
22:24 *a* bore Tebah, Gaham, Thahash,
24:14 and I will *a* give your camels a
24:19 draw water for your camels *a*,
24:44 I will draw for your camels *a*,
24:46 will give your camels a drink *a*.
24:46 she gave the camels a drink *a*.
24:53 He *a* gave precious things to
26:19 *A* Isaac's servants dug in the
26:21 they quarreled over that one *a*.
27:31 He *a* had made savory food, and
27:34 to his father, "Bless me—me *a*,
27:38 my father? Bless me—me *a*,
27:45 Why should I be bereaved *a* of
28: 8 *A* Esau saw that the daughters of
28:14 *A* your descendants shall be as
29:27 and we will give you this one *a*
29:28 his daughter Rachel as wife *a*.
29:30 Then Jacob *a* went in to Rachel,
29:30 and he *a* loved Rachel more than
29:33 therefore given me this son *a*.
30: 3 that I *a* may have children by
30: 6 and He has *a* heard my voice and
30:15 take away my son's mandrakes *a*?
30:30 when shall I *a* provide for my
31:15 and *a* completely consumed our
31:49 *a* Mizpah, because he said, "May
32: 6 and he *a* is coming to meet you,
32:18 he *a* is behind us.' "
32:20 and *a* say, 'Behold, your servant
33: 7 And Leah *a* came near with her
35:11 *A* God said to him: "I am God
35:17 fear; you will have this son *a*.
37: 3 *A* he made him a tunic of many
37: 7 my sheaf arose and *a* stood
38:10 therefore He killed him *a*.
38:11 Lest he *a* die like his
38:22 *A*, the men of the place said
40:15 and *a* I have done nothing here
40:16 I *a* was in my dream, and there
41:22 *A* I saw in my dream, and
41:44 Pharaoh *a* said to Joseph, "I
43: 8 both we and you and *a* our
43:13 "Take your brother *a*,
44: 2 *A* put my cup, the silver cup, in
44: 9 and we *a* will be my lord's
44:10 Now *a* let it be according to
44:16 both we and he *a* with whom the
44:29 But if you take this one *a* from
45:20 *A* do not be concerned about your
46: 4 and I will *a* surely bring you
46:34 both we and *a* our fathers,'
47: 3 both we and *a* our fathers."
47:18 my lord *a* has our herds of
48:11 God has *a* shown me your
48:19 He *a* shall become a people, and
48:19 and he *a* shall be great; but
50:18 Then his brothers *a* went and
50:23 were *a* brought up on Joseph's
Ex 1:10 that they *a* join our enemies
2:19 and he *a* drew enough water for
3: 9 and I have *a* seen the
4:14 he is *a* coming out to meet you.
5:14 *A* the officers of the children
6: 4 I have *a* established My covenant
6: 5 And I have *a* heard the groaning
7:11 But Pharaoh *a* called the wise
7:11 they *a* did in like manner with
8:21 and *a* the ground on which they
8:32 his heart at this time *a*;
10:24 Let your little ones *a* go with
10:25 You must *a* give us sacrifices
10:26 Our livestock *a* shall go with
12:32 *A* take your flocks and your
12:32 and be gone; and bless me *a*.
12:38 multitude went up with them *a*,
14: 7 *A*, he took six hundred
15: 4 His chosen captains *a* are
16: 8 *A* Moses said, "This shall be
17: 5 *A* take in your hand your rod
18:23 and all this people will *a* go
19:22 *A* let the priests who come near
21: 6 He shall *a* bring him to the
21:29 shall be stoned and its owner *a*
21:35 and the dead ox they shall *a*
23: 9 *A* you shall not oppress a
24: 9 *a* Aaron, Nadab, and Abihu, and
25:23 You shall *a* make a table of
25:31 You shall *a* make a lampstand of
26: 7 You shall *a* make curtains of
26:14 You shall *a* make a covering of
26:23 And you shall *a* make two boards
27: 3 *A* you shall make its pans to
27: 9 You shall *a* make the court of
28:13 You shall *a* make settings of
28:36 You shall *a* make a plate of
29:10 You shall *a* have the bull
29:15 You shall *a* take one ram, and
29:19 You shall *a* take the other ram,
29:22 *A* you shall take the fat of the
29:44 I will *a* consecrate both Aaron
30:18 You shall *a* make a laver of
30:18 with its base *a* of bronze, for
30:23 *A* take for yourself quality
31:13 Speak *a* to the children of
33:12 and you have *a* found grace in
33:17 I will *a* do this thing that you
35:14 *a* the lampstand for the light,
36:18 He *a* made fifty bronze clasps to
36:28 He *a* made two boards for the two
36:37 He *a* made a screen for the
37: 6 He *a* made the mercy seat of pure
37:12 *A* he made a frame of a
37:17 He *a* made the lampstand of pure
37:26 He *a* made for it a molding of
37:29 He *a* made the holy anointing
39:16 They *a* made two settings of gold
40: 5 You shall *a* set the altar of
Lev 5: 2 he *a* shall be unclean and
7: 9 *A* every grain offering that is
7:16 next day the remainder of it *a*
7:32 *A* the right thigh you shall give
8: 9 *A* on the turban, on its front,
8:10 *A* Moses took the anointing oil,
8:23 *A* he took some of its blood
9: 4 *a* a bull and a ram as peace
9:18 He *a* killed the bull and the
11:29 These *a* shall be unclean to
11:40 He *a* who carries its carcass
13:47 *A*, if a garment has a
15:18 '*A*, when a woman lies with a
15:20 *a* everything that she sits on
17: 8 *A* you shall say to them:
18:19 *A* you shall not approach a
18:28 lest the land vomit you out *a*
21: 3 *a* his virgin sister who is near
23:27 *A* the tenth day of this seventh
23:39 *A* on the fifteenth day of the
26:16 I *a* will do this to you: I will
26:22 I will *a* send wild beasts among
26:24 then I *a* will walk contrary to
26:28 then I *a* will walk contrary to
26:39 *a* in their fathers' iniquities,
26:40 and that they *a* have walked
26:41 and that I *a* have walked
26:43 The land *a* shall be left empty
Num 3: 8 *A* they shall attend to all the
4:13 *A* they shall take away the ashes
4:22 *A* take a census of the sons of
6:17 the priest shall *a* offer its
10:10 *A* in the day of your gladness,
11: 4 so the children of Israel *a*
11:10 Moses *a* was displeased.
12: 2 Has He not spoken through us *a*?
13:23 They *a* brought some of the
16:10 you seeking the priesthood *a*?
16:34 the earth swallow us up *a*!"
18: 2 *A* bring with you your brethren
18: 3 lest they die—they and you *a*.
18: 8 I Myself have *a* given you
18:11 This *a* is yours: the heave
18:28 Thus you shall *a* offer a heave
22:19 you *a* stay here tonight, that I
22:33 surely I would *a* have killed
24:12 Did I not *a* speak to your
24:18 shall be a possession; Seir *a*,
24:25 Balak *a* went his way.
27:13 you *a* shall be gathered to your
28:15 *A* one kid of the goats as a sin
28:22 *a* one goat as a sin offering,
28:26 *A* on the day of the
28:30 *a* one kid of the goats, to make
29: 5 *a* one kid of the goats as a sin
29:11 *a* one kid of the goats as a sin
29:16 *a* one kid of the goats as a sin
29:19 *a* one kid of the goats as a sin
29:22 *a* one goat as a sin offering,
29:25 *a* one kid of the goats as a sin
29:28 *a* one goat as a sin offering,
29:31 *a* one goat as a sin offering,
29:34 *a* one goat as a sin offering,
29:38 *a* one goat as a sin offering,
30: 9 *A* any vow of a widow or a
31: 8 Balaam the son of Beor they *a*
31:10 They *a* burned with fire all the
32:41 *A* Jair the son of Manasseh went
33: 4 *A* on their gods the LORD had
35: 2 and you shall *a* give the
Deut 1:25 They *a* took some of the fruit
1:37 The LORD was *a* angry with me
2: 6 and you shall *a* buy water from
2:11 They were *a* regarded as giants,
2:20 (That was *a* regarded as a land
3: 3 So the LORD our God *a* delivered
3:15 *A* I gave Gilead to Machir.
3:17 "the plain *a*, with the Jordan
3:20 and they *a* possess the land
7:13 He will *a* bless the fruit of
9: 8 *A* in Horeb you provoked the
9:19 listened to me at that time *a*.
9:20 so I prayed for Aaron *a* at the
9:22 *A* at Taberah and Massah and
10:10 the LORD *a* heard me at that
10:14 *a* the earth with all that is
12:30 I *a* will do likewise.'

14: 8 ***A*** the swine is unclean for you,
14:19 ***A*** every creeping thing that
15:17 ***A*** to your female servant you
17:18 ***A*** it shall be, when he sits on
20: 6 ***A*** what man is there who has
23:12 ***A*** you shall have a place outside
26:13 and ***a*** have given them to the
26:18 ***A*** today the LORD has proclaimed
28:61 ***A*** every sickness and every
29:11 ***a*** the stranger who is in your
30: 7 ***A*** the LORD your God will put
31: 2 ***A*** the LORD has said to me,
32:24 I will ***a*** send against them the
33:28 His heavens shall ***a*** drop dew.
Josh 1:15 and they ***a*** have taken
2:12 that you ***a*** will show kindness
7:11 and they have ***a*** transgressed My
7:11 and they have ***a*** put it among
10:28 He ***a*** did to the king of
10:30 And the LORD ***a*** delivered it and
10:39 as he had done ***a*** to Libnah and
13: 3 the Ekronites; ***a*** the Avites;
13:22 The children of Israel ***a*** killed
13:24 Moses ***a*** had given an
13:29 Moses ***a*** had given an
15:19 give me ***a*** springs of water."
17: 1 There was ***a*** a lot for the tribe
19:30 ***A*** Ummah, Aphek, and Rehob were
20: 1 The LORD ***a*** spoke to Joshua,
21:27 ***A*** to the children of Gershon,
24: 5 ***A*** I sent Moses and Aaron, and I
24:11 ***a*** the Amorites, the Perizzites,
24:12 ***a*** the two kings of the
24:18 We ***a*** will serve the LORD, for
Judg 1:15 give me ***a*** springs of water."
1:18 ***A*** Judah took Gaza with its
1:22 And the house of Joseph ***a*** went
2: 3 Therefore I ***a*** said, 'I will not
2:21 I ***a*** will no longer drive out
3:31 and he ***a*** delivered Israel.
5: 4 The clouds ***a*** poured water;
5:18 the point of death, Naphtali ***a***,
6: 3 ***a*** Amalekites and the people of
6:10 ***A*** I said to you, "I am the
6:35 who ***a*** gathered behind him.
6:35 He ***a*** sent messengers to Asher,
7:18 then you ***a*** blow the trumpets on
8: 9 So he ***a*** spoke to the men of
8:22 your son, and your grandson ***a***;
8:31 who was in Shechem ***a*** bore him
9:19 and let him ***a*** rejoice in you.
10: 4 they ***a*** had thirty towns, which
10: 9 Jordan to fight against Judah ***a***,
10:12 ***A*** the Sidonians and Amalekites
14: 9 and they ***a*** ate. But he did not
19:10 his concubine was ***a*** with him.
19:16 who ***a*** was from the mountains
20:48 They ***a*** set fire to all the
Ruth 1: 5 Then both Mahlon and Chilion ***a***
1:12 a husband tonight and should ***a***
1:17 LORD do so to me, and more ***a***,
2:16 ***A*** let grain from the bundles
2:21 He ***a*** said to me, 'You shall stay
3:15 ***A*** he said, "Bring the shawl
4: 5 you must ***a*** buy it from Ruth
4:17 ***A*** the neighbor women gave him a
1 Sam 1: 3 ***A*** the two sons of Eli, Hophni
1: 6 And her rival ***a*** provoked her
1:28 Therefore I ***a*** have lent him to
2:15 ***A***, before they burned the fat,
3:17 God do so to you, and more ***a***,
4:11 ***A*** the ark of God was captured;
4:17 ***A*** your two sons, Hophni and
7:14 ***A*** there was peace between
8: 8 gods—so they are doing to you ***a***.
8:20 that we ***a*** may be like all the
10:11 Is Saul ***a*** among the
10:12 Is Saul ***a*** among the prophets?"
10:26 And Saul ***a*** went home to Gibeah;
13: 4 and that Israel had ***a*** become
14:15 The garrison and the raiders ***a***
14:21 they ***a*** joined the Israelites
14:22 they ***a*** followed hard after them
14:44 "God do so and more ***a***;
15: 1 Samuel ***a*** said to Saul, "The
15: 8 He ***a*** took Agag king of the
15:23 He ***a*** has rejected you from
15:29 And ***a*** the Strength of Israel
17:38 he ***a*** clothed him with a coat of
18: 5 sight of all the people and ***a***
19:11 Saul ***a*** sent messengers to
19:20 and they ***a*** prophesied.
19:21 time, and they prophesied ***a***.
19:22 Then he ***a*** went to Ramah, and
19:23 Spirit of God was upon him ***a***,
19:24 And he ***a*** stripped off his
19:24 Is Saul ***a*** among the prophets?"
22:17 because their hand ***a*** is with
22:19 ***A*** Nob, the city of the priests,
24: 8 David ***a*** arose afterward, went
25:13 and David ***a*** girded on his
25:22 "May God do so, and more ***a***,
25:43 David ***a*** took Ahinoam of Jezreel,
26:25 both do great things and ***a***
28:19 Moreover the LORD will ***a***
28:19 The LORD will ***a*** deliver the
28:22 heed ***a*** the voice of your
30:21 whom they ***a*** had made to stay at
31: 5 he ***a*** fell on his sword, and
2 Sam 1: 4 and Jonathan his son are dead ***a***.
2: 2 up there, and his two wives ***a***,
2: 6 I ***a*** will repay you this
2: 7 and ***a*** the house of Judah has
2:24 Joab and Abishai ***a*** pursued
3: 9 God do so to Abner, and more ***a***,
3:12 is the land?" saying ***a***,
3:19 And Abner ***a*** spoke in the hearing
3:19 Then Abner ***a*** went to speak in
3:35 "God do so to me, and more ***a***,
4: 2 (For Beeroth ***a*** was part of
5: 2 '***A***, in time past, when Saul
5:13 ***A*** more sons and daughters were
5:18 The Philistines ***a*** went and
7:11 ***A*** the LORD tells you that He
7:19 and You have ***a*** spoken of Your
8: 3 David ***a*** defeated Hadadezer the
8: 4 ***A*** David hamstrung all the
8: 8 ***A*** from Betah and from Berothai,
8:11 King David ***a*** dedicated these to
8:14 He ***a*** put garrisons in Edom;
10:14 they ***a*** fled before Abishai, and
11:12 to Uriah, "Wait here today ***a***,
11:17 and Uriah the Hittite died ***a***.
11:21 Uriah the Hittite is dead ***a***.
11:24 Uriah the Hittite is dead ***a***.
12: 8 I ***a*** would have given you much
12:13 The LORD ***a*** has put away your
12:14 the child ***a*** who is born to
12:30 ***A*** he brought out the spoil of
13:36 ***A*** the king and all his servants
14: 7 and we will destroy the heir ***a***.
15:19 Why are you ***a*** going with us?
15:19 For you are a foreigner and ***a***
15:21 even there ***a*** your servant will
15:23 The king himself ***a*** crossed over
15:24 There was Zadok ***a***,
15:27 The king ***a*** said to Zadok the
15:34 so I will now ***a*** be your
16: 7 ***A*** Shimei said thus when he
17: 5 "Now call Hushai the Archite ***a***,
18: 2 I ***a*** will surely go out with you
18:22 please let me ***a*** run after the
18:26 He ***a*** brings news."
19:13 God do so to me, and more ***a***,
19:40 and ***a*** half the people of
19:43 therefore we ***a*** have more right
20:14 were gathered together and ***a***
21:20 and he ***a*** was born to the giant.
22:10 He bowed the heavens ***a***,
22:20 He ***a*** brought me out into a
22:24 I was ***a*** blameless before Him,
22:36 You have ***a*** given me the shield
22:41 You have ***a*** given me the necks
22:44 You have ***a*** delivered me from the
22:49 You ***a*** lift me up above those
23:20 He ***a*** had gone down and killed a
1 Ki 1: 6 He was ***a*** very good-looking.
1: 9 he ***a*** invited all his brothers,
1:14 I ***a*** will come in after you and
1:22 Nathan the prophet ***a*** came in.
1:33 The king ***a*** said to them, "Take
1:46 ***A*** Solomon sits on the throne of
1:48 ***A*** the king said thus, 'Blessed
2: 5 Moreover you know ***a*** what Joab
2:22 Ask for him the kingdom ***a***—
2:23 God do so to me, and more ***a***,
3:13 And I have ***a*** given you what you
3:18 that this woman ***a*** gave birth.
4:13 to him ***a*** belonged the region
4:15 he ***a*** took Basemath the daughter
4:28 They ***a*** brought barley and straw
4:33 ***A*** he spoke of trees, from the
4:33 he spoke ***a*** of animals, of
6:22 ***a*** he overlaid with gold the
6:28 ***A*** he overlaid the cherubim with
6:33 the door of the sanctuary he ***a***
7: 2 He ***a*** built the House of the
7: 6 He ***a*** made the Hall of Pillars:
7: 8 Solomon ***a*** made a house like
7: 9 and ***a*** on the outside to the
7:20 capitals on the two pillars ***a***
7:27 He ***a*** made ten carts of bronze;
7:31 and ***a*** on the opening were
8: 5 ***A*** King Solomon, and all the
9:26 King Solomon ***a*** built a fleet of
10:11 ***A***, the ships of Hiram,
10:12 ***a*** harps and stringed
10:17 He ***a*** made three hundred shields
10:28 ***A*** Solomon had horses imported
11:26 ***a*** rebelled against the king.
12:25 ***A*** he went out from there and
13: 5 The altar ***a*** was split apart, and
13:11 they ***a*** told their father the
13:24 The lion ***a*** stood by the corpse.
14: 3 ***A*** take with you ten loaves,
14:23 For they ***a*** built for themselves
14:24 And there were ***a*** perverted
14:26 He ***a*** took away all the gold
15:13 ***A*** he removed Maachah his
15:15 He ***a*** brought into the house of
16: 7 And ***a*** the word of the LORD came
16:16 Zimri has conspired and ***a*** has
17:20 have You ***a*** brought tragedy on
18:35 and he ***a*** filled the trench with
19: 1 ***a*** how he had executed all the
19: 2 the gods do to me, and more ***a***,
19:16 ***A*** you shall anoint Jehu the son
20:10 gods do so to me, and more ***a***,
21:19 Have you murdered and ***a*** taken
21:23 concerning Jezebel the LORD ***a***
22: 5 ***A*** Jehoshaphat said to the king
22:22 and ***a*** prevail. Go out and do
22:44 ***A*** Jehoshaphat made peace with
2 Ki 2:13 He ***a*** took up the mantle of
2:14 And when he ***a*** had struck the
3:18 He will ***a*** deliver the Moabites
3:19 ***A*** you shall attack every
5: 1 He was ***a*** a mighty man of valor,
6:31 "God do so to me and more ***a***,
7: 4 And if we sit here, we die ***a***.
7: 8 and carried some from there ***a***,
9:27 Shoot him ***a*** in the chariot."
10: 2 and horses, a fortified city ***a***,
10: 5 of the city, the elders ***a***,
11:17 and ***a*** between the king and the
13: 6 and the wooden image ***a*** remained
16:14 He ***a*** brought the bronze altar
16:18 ***A*** he removed the Sabbath
17: 9 ***A*** the children of Israel
17:19 ***A*** Judah did not keep the
17:41 ***a*** their children and their
19:29 ***A*** in the third year sow and
21: 4 He ***a*** built altars in the house
21: 6 ***A*** he made his son pass through
21:11 and has ***a*** made Judah sin with
22:19 I ***a*** have heard you," says the
23: 8 ***a*** he broke down the high places
23:19 Now Josiah ***a*** took away all the
23:27 I will ***a*** remove Judah from My
24: 4 and ***a*** because of the innocent
24:14 ***A*** he carried into captivity all
24:19 He ***a*** did evil in the sight of
25:14 They ***a*** took away the pots, the
25:19 He ***a*** took out of the city an
1 Chr 1:51 Hadad died ***a***.
2: 9 ***A*** the sons of Hezron who were
2:49 She ***a*** bore Shaaph the father of
3: 6 ***A*** there were Ibhar, Elishama,
4:22 ***a*** Jokim, the men of Chozeba, and
5:21 ***a*** one hundred thousand of their
6:57 ***a*** Libnah with its common-lands,
6:67 ***a*** Gezer with its common-lands,
8:32 They ***a*** dwelt alongside their
9:38 They ***a*** dwelt alongside their
10: 5 he ***a*** fell on his sword and
10:13 and ***a*** because he consulted a
11: 2 '***A***, in time past, even when
11:22 He ***a*** had gone down and killed a
11:26 ***A*** the mighty warriors were
15:27 David ***a*** wore a linen ephod.
16:25 He is ***a*** to be feared above
16:30 The world ***a*** is firmly
17:10 ***A*** I will subdue all your
17:17 and You have ***a*** spoken of Your
18: 4 And David ***a*** hamstrung all the
18: 8 ***A*** from Tibhath and from Chun,
18:11 King David ***a*** dedicated these to
18:13 He ***a*** put garrisons in Edom, and
19: 7 ***A*** the people of Ammon gathered
19:15 they ***a*** fled before Abishai his
20: 2 ***A*** he brought out the spoil of
20: 6 and he ***a*** was born to the giant.
21:23 I ***a*** give you the oxen for
22:14 prepared timber and stone ***a***,
22:17 David ***a*** commanded all the
23: 6 ***A*** David separated them into
23:26 and ***a*** to the Levites, "They
24:30 ***A*** the sons of Mushi were Mahli,
24:31 These ***a*** cast lots just as their
26: 6 ***A*** to Shemaiah his son were sons
26:10 ***A*** Hosah, of the children of
27: 4 and of his division Mikloth ***a***
27:32 ***A*** Jehonathan, David's uncle,
28:13 ***a*** for the division of the
28:14 ***a*** silver for all articles of
28:17 ***a*** pure gold for the forks, the
28:21 ***a*** the leaders and all the
29: 9 and King David ***a*** rejoiced
29:17 'I know ***a***, my God,
29:24 and ***a*** all the sons of King
2 Chr 1:15 ***A*** the king made silver and gold
1:17 They ***a*** acquired and imported
2: 8 ***A*** send me cedar and cypress and
2:12 Hiram ***a*** said: Blessed be the
3: 7 He ***a*** overlaid the house—the
3:12 and the other wing ***a*** was five
3:15 ***A*** he made in front of the
4: 6 He ***a*** made ten lavers, and put
4: 8 He ***a*** made ten tables, and placed
4:14 he ***a*** made carts and the lavers
4:16 ***a*** the pots, the shovels, the
5: 6 ***A*** King Solomon, and all the
7: 6 the Levites ***a*** with instruments
8: 4 He ***a*** built Tadmor in the
8: 6 ***a*** Baalath and all the storage
9:10 ***A***, the servants of Hiram
9:11 ***a*** harps and stringed
9:16 He ***a*** made three hundred
11:12 ***A*** in every city he put shields
11:23 He ***a*** sought many wives for
12: 5 and therefore I ***a*** have left you
12: 9 He ***a*** carried away the gold
12:12 and things ***a*** went well in
13: 3 Jeroboam ***a*** drew up in battle
13:11 they ***a*** set the showbread in
14: 5 He ***a*** removed the high places and
14:15 They ***a*** attacked the livestock
15:16 ***A*** he removed Maachah, the
15:18 He ***a*** brought into the house of
17: 7 ***A*** in the third year of his
17:11 ***A*** some of the Philistines
18:21 You shall persuade him and ***a***
19:11 ***a*** the Levites will be
21: 4 and ***a*** others of the princes of
21:13 and ***a*** have killed your
21:17 and ***a*** his sons and his wives,

22: 3 He ***a*** walked in the ways of the
22: 5 He ***a*** followed their advice, and
23:13 ***a*** the singers with musical
23:18 ***A*** Jehoiada appointed the
24: 7 and had ***a*** presented all the
24:12 and ***a*** those who worked in iron
24:20 He ***a*** has forsaken you.'"
25: 6 He ***a*** hired one hundred thousand
25:12 ***A*** the children of Judah took
26: 8 ***A*** the Ammonites brought tribute
26:10 ***A*** he built towers in the desert.
26:10 he ***a*** had farmers and
26:20 Indeed he ***a*** hurried to get out,
27: 5 He ***a*** fought with the king of the
27: 5 in the second and third years ***a***.
28: 5 Then he was ***a*** delivered into
28: 8 and they ***a*** took away much spoil
28:10 but are you not ***a*** guilty
28:18 The Philistines ***a*** had invaded
28:20 ***A*** Tiglath-Pileser king of
29: 7 They have ***a*** shut up the doors of
29:22 They ***a*** killed the lambs and
29:27 the song of the LORD ***a*** began,
29:35 ***A*** the burnt offerings were in
30: 1 and ***a*** wrote letters to Ephraim
30:12 ***A*** the hand of God was on Judah
30:25 ***a*** the priests and Levites, all
31: 3 The king ***a*** appointed a portion
31: 6 ***a*** the tithe of holy things
31:19 ***A*** for the sons of Aaron the
32: 5 ***a*** he repaired the Millo in the
32:17 He ***a*** wrote letters to revile the
32:30 This same Hezekiah ***a*** stopped the
33: 4 He ***a*** built altars in the house
33: 6 ***A*** he caused his sons to pass
33:16 He ***a*** repaired the altar of the
33:19 ***A*** his prayer and how God
34: 5 He ***a*** burned the bones of the
34:27 I ***a*** have heard you," says the
35: 9 ***A*** Conaniah, his brothers
35:13 ***A*** they roasted the Passover
35:15 ***A*** the gatekeepers were at each
35:25 Jeremiah ***a*** lamented for Josiah.
36: 7 Nebuchadnezzar ***a*** carried off
36:13 And he ***a*** rebelled against King
36:22 and ***a*** put it in writing,
Ezra 1: 1 and ***a*** put it in writing,
1: 7 King Cyrus ***a*** brought out the
3: 4 They ***a*** kept the Feast of
3: 7 They ***a*** gave money to the masons
4: 7 In the days of Artaxerxes ***a***,
4:20 There have ***a*** been mighty kings
5:10 We ***a*** asked them their names to
5:14 '***A***, the gold and silver
6: 5 ***A*** let the gold and silver
6:11 ***A*** I issue a decree that whoever
7:19 ***A*** the articles that are given to
7:24 ***A*** we inform you that it shall
8:14 ***a*** of the sons of Bigvai, Uthai
8:16 ***a*** for Joiarib and Elnathan, men
8:20 ***a*** of the Nethinim, whom David
8:28 LORD; the articles are holy ***a***;
10: 4 We ***a*** are with you. Be of good
10:20 ***A*** of the sons of Immer: Hanani
10:23 ***A*** of the Levites: Jozabad,
10:24 ***A*** of the singers: Eliashib; and
Neh 1: 3 The wall of Jerusalem is ***a***
2: 6 king said to me (the queen ***a***
2:18 and ***a*** of the king's words that
3: 3 ***A*** the sons of Hassenaah built
3: 8 ***A*** next to him Hananiah, one of
4:22 At the same time I ***a*** said to the
5: 3 There were ***a*** some who said,
5: 4 There were ***a*** those who said,
5:10 'I ***a***, with my brethren
5:11 ***a*** a hundredth of the money and
5:16 I ***a*** continued the work on this
5:18 ***A*** fowl were prepared for me,
6: 7 And you have ***a*** appointed
6:17 ***A*** in those days the nobles of
6:19 ***A*** they reported his good deeds
8: 7 ***A*** Jeshua, Bani, Sherebiah,
8:18 ***A*** day by day, from the first day
9:13 You came down ***a*** on Mount Sinai,
9:20 You ***a*** gave Your good Spirit to
9:23 You ***a*** multiplied their children
9:37 ***A*** they have dominion over our
10:32 ***A*** we made ordinances for
11: 4 ***A*** in Jerusalem dwelt some of
11:15 ***A*** of the Levites
11:22 ***A*** the overseer of the Levites
11:31 ***A*** the children of Benjamin from
12: 9 ***A*** Bakbukiah and Unni, their
12:22 a record was ***a*** kept of the
12:42 ***a*** Maaseiah, Shemaiah, Eleazar,
12:43 ***A*** that day they offered great
12:43 the women and the children ***a***
12:47 They ***a*** consecrated holy
13:10 I ***a*** realized that the portions
13:16 Men of Tyre dwelt there ***a***,
13:22 O my God, concerning this ***a***,
13:23 In those days I ***a*** saw Jews who
13:30 I ***a*** assigned duties to the
Esth 1: 9 Queen Vashti ***a*** made a feast for
1:16 but ***a*** all the princes, and all
2: 8 that Esther ***a*** was taken to the
4: 8 He ***a*** gave him a copy of the
7: 8 Will he ***a*** assault the queen
9: 7 ***A*** Parshandatha, Dalphon,
Job 1: 3 ***A***, his possessions were seven
1: 6 and Satan ***a*** came among them.
1:16 another ***a*** came and said, "The
1:17 another ***a*** came and said, "The
1:18 another ***a*** came and said, "Your
2: 1 and Satan came ***a*** among them to
5:25 You shall ***a*** know that your
7: 1 Are not his days ***a*** like the
11:11 men; He sees wickedness ***a***.
11:19 You would ***a*** lie down, and no
13: 2 I ***a*** know; I am not inferior
13:16 He ***a*** shall be my salvation,
16: 4 I ***a*** could speak as you do, If
16:12 He ***a*** has taken me by my neck,
17: 7 My eye has ***a*** grown dim because
19:11 He has ***a*** kindled His wrath
22:28 You will ***a*** declare a thing,
31:28 This ***a*** would be an iniquity
32: 3 ***A*** against his three friends his
32:10 I ***a*** will declare my opinion.'
32:17 I ***a*** will answer my part, I too
33: 6 I ***a*** have been formed out of
33:19 Man is ***a*** chastened with pain on
36: 1 Elihu ***a*** proceeded and said:
36:10 He ***a*** opens their ear to
36:33 declares it, The cattle ***a***,
37: 1 At this ***a*** my heart trembles,
37:11 ***A*** with moisture He saturates
40:14 Then I will ***a*** confess to you
42:13 He ***a*** had seven sons and three
Ps 1: 3 Whose leaf ***a*** shall not wither;
5:11 Let those ***a*** who love Your name
6: 3 My soul ***a*** is greatly troubled;
7:13 He ***a*** prepares for Himself
9: 9 The LORD ***a*** will be a refuge
16: 7 My heart ***a*** instructs me in the
16: 9 My flesh ***a*** will rest in hope.
18: 7 The foundations of the hills ***a***
18: 9 He bowed the heavens ***a***,
18:19 He ***a*** brought me out into a
18:23 I was ***a*** blameless before Him,
18:35 You have ***a*** given me the shield
18:40 You have ***a*** given me the necks
18:48 You ***a*** lift me up above those
19:10 Sweeter ***a*** than honey and the
19:13 Keep back Your servant ***a*** from
26: 1 I have ***a*** trusted in the LORD;
27: 7 with my voice! Have mercy ***a***
28: 9 inheritance; Shepherd them ***a***,
29: 6 He makes them ***a*** skip like a
35: 3 ***A*** draw out the spear, And stop
35:21 They ***a*** opened their mouth wide
37: 4 Delight yourself ***a*** in the
37: 5 Trust ***a*** in Him, And He shall
38:10 it ***a*** has gone from me.
38:12 Those ***a*** who seek my life lay
38:20 Those ***a*** who render evil for
40: 2 He ***a*** brought me up out of a
45:10 ear; Forget your own people ***a***,
52: 6 The righteous ***a*** shall see and
55:10 Iniquity and trouble are ***a*** in
60: 7 Ephraim ***a*** is the helmet for
62:12 ***A*** to You, O Lord, belongs
65: 8 They ***a*** who dwell in the
65:13 The valleys ***a*** are covered with
65:13 shout for joy, they ***a*** sing.
68: 1 Let those ***a*** who hate Him flee
68: 8 The heavens ***a*** dropped rain at
69:11 I ***a*** made sackcloth my garment;
69:21 They ***a*** gave me gall for my
69:31 This ***a*** shall please the LORD
69:36 ***A***, the descendants of His
71:18 Now ***a*** when I am old and
71:19 ***A*** Your righteousness, O God,
71:22 ***A*** with the lute I will praise
71:24 My tongue ***a*** shall talk of Your
72: 8 He shall have dominion ***a*** from
72:12 when he cries, The poor ***a***,
72:15 Prayer ***a*** will be made for Him
74:16 the night ***a*** is Yours; You
75:10 horns of the wicked I will ***a***
76: 2 In Salem ***a*** is His tabernacle,
77:12 I will ***a*** meditate on all Your
77:16 The depths ***a*** trembled.
77:17 Your arrows ***a*** flashed about.
78:14 In the daytime ***a*** He led them
78:16 He ***a*** brought streams out of the
78:20 Can He give bread ***a***?
78:21 And anger ***a*** came up against
78:27 He ***a*** rained meat on them like
78:46 He ***a*** gave their crops to the
78:48 He ***a*** gave up their cattle to
78:55 He ***a*** drove out the nations
78:62 He ***a*** gave His people over to
78:70 He ***a*** chose David His servant,
81:16 He would have fed them ***a*** with
83: 8 Assyria ***a*** has joined with them;
84: 6 The rain ***a*** covers it with
89: 5 Your faithfulness ***a*** in the
89: 8 Your faithfulness ***a*** surrounds
89:11 the earth ***a*** is Yours; The
89:21 ***A*** My arm shall strengthen him.
89:25 ***A*** I will set his hand over the
89:27 ***A*** I will make him My
89:29 His seed ***a*** I will make to
89:43 You have ***a*** turned back the edge
92:11 My eye ***a*** has seen my desire
95: 4 heights of the hills are His ***a***.
96:10 The world ***a*** is firmly
99: 4 The King's strength ***a*** loves
105:23 Israel ***a*** came into Egypt, And
105:33 He struck their vines ***a***,
105:36 He ***a*** destroyed all the
105:37 He ***a*** brought them out with
106: 9 He rebuked the Red Sea ***a***,
106:28 They joined themselves ***a*** to
106:32 They angered Him ***a*** at the
106:42 Their enemies ***a*** oppressed them,
106:46 He ***a*** made them to be pitied By
107:32 Let them exalt Him ***a*** in the
107:38 He ***a*** blesses them, and they
108: 8 Ephraim ***a*** is the helmet for
109: 3 They have ***a*** surrounded me with
109:10 Let them seek their bread ***a***
109:25 I ***a*** have become a reproach to
119: 3 They ***a*** do no iniquity; They
119:23 Princes ***a*** sit and speak
119:24 Your testimonies ***a*** are my
119:41 Let Your mercies come ***a*** to me,
119:46 speak of Your testimonies ***a***
119:48 My hands ***a*** I will lift up to
132:12 Their sons ***a*** shall sit upon
132:16 I will ***a*** clothe her priests
139:17 How precious ***a*** are Your
145:19 He ***a*** will hear their cry and
148: 6 He ***a*** established them forever
Prov 1:26 I ***a*** will laugh at your
4: 4 He ***a*** taught me, and said to me:
9: 2 She has ***a*** furnished her table.
11:25 And he who waters will ***a*** be
17:26 ***A***, to punish the righteous
18: 3 wicked comes, contempt comes ***a***;
19: 2 ***A*** it is not good for a soul
21:13 to the cry of the poor Will ***a***
23:23 ***A*** wisdom and instruction and
23:28 She ***a*** lies in wait as for a
24:23 These things ***a*** belong to the
25: 1 These ***a*** are proverbs of Solomon
26: 4 Lest you ***a*** be like him.
30:31 A greyhound, A male goat ***a***,
31:15 She ***a*** rises while it is yet
31:28 her blessed; Her husband ***a***,
Eccl 1: 5 The sun ***a*** rises, and the sun
1:17 I perceived that this ***a*** is
2: 1 this ***a*** was vanity.
2: 8 I ***a*** gathered for myself silver
2: 9 ***A*** my wisdom remained with me.
2:15 It ***a*** happens to me, And why
2:15 This ***a*** is vanity."
2:19 This ***a*** is vanity.
2:21 This ***a*** is vanity and a great
2:23 This ***a*** is vanity.
2:24 enjoy good in his labor. This ***a***,
2:26 This ***a*** is vanity and grasping
3:11 ***A*** He has put eternity in their
3:13 and ***a*** that every man should eat
3:19 happens to the sons of men ***a***
4: 4 This ***a*** is vanity and grasping
4: 8 This ***a*** is vanity and a
4:16 Surely this ***a*** is vanity and
5: 7 and many words there is ***a***
5:10 This ***a*** is vanity.
5:16 And this ***a*** is a severe
5:17 All his days he ***a*** eats in
6: 9 This ***a*** is vanity and grasping
7: 6 This ***a*** is vanity.
7:18 And ***a*** not remove your hand
7:21 ***A*** do not take to heart
7:22 For many times, ***a***,
8:10 This ***a*** is vanity.
8:14 I said that this ***a*** is vanity.
9: 6 ***A*** their love, their hatred, and
9:12 For man ***a*** does not know his
9:13 This wisdom I have ***a*** seen under
10:14 A fool ***a*** multiplies words.
11: 2 and ***a*** to eight, For you do not
12: 5 ***A*** they are afraid of height,
Song 1:16 pleasant! ***A*** our bed is green.
Isa 2: 7 Their land is ***a*** full of silver
2: 7 Their land is ***a*** full of
2: 8 Their land is ***a*** full of idols;
5: 2 And ***a*** made a winepress in it;
5: 6 I will ***a*** command the clouds
6: 8 ***A*** I heard the voice of the
7:13 but will you weary my God ***a***?
7:20 And will ***a*** remove the beard.
8: 5 The LORD ***a*** spoke to me again,
10:11 Shall I not do ***a*** to Jerusalem
10:13 ***A*** I have removed the
11: 6 The wolf ***a*** shall dwell with the
11:13 ***A*** the envy of Ephraim shall
12: 2 He ***a*** has become my salvation.'
13: 3 I have ***a*** called My mighty ones
13:16 Their children ***a*** will be dashed
13:18 ***A*** their bows will dash the
14:10 Have you ***a*** become as weak as we?
14:13 I will ***a*** sit on the mount of
14:23 I will ***a*** make it a possession
17: 3 The fortress ***a*** will cease from
19: 8 The fishermen ***a*** will mourn;
19:13 They have ***a*** deluded Egypt,
21:12 and ***a*** the night. If you will
22: 9 You ***a*** saw the damage to the
22:11 You ***a*** made a reservoir between
23: 5 They ***a*** will be in agony at the
23:12 There ***a*** you will have no
24: 5 The earth is ***a*** defiled under
26:12 For You have ***a*** done all our
26:21 The earth will ***a*** disclose her
28: 7 But they ***a*** have erred through
28:17 ***A*** I will make justice the
28:29 This ***a*** comes from the LORD of
29:19 The humble ***a*** shall increase
29:24 These ***a*** who erred in spirit
30: 5 But a shame and ***a*** a
30:22 You will ***a*** defile the covering
31: 2 Yet He ***a*** is wise and will

31: 5 He will *a* deliver it; Passing
32: 4 *A* the heart of the rash will
32: 7 *A* the schemes of the schemer
33: 2 Our salvation *a* in the time of
34: 3 *A* their slain shall be thrown
34:11 *A* the owl and the raven shall
34:14 beasts of the desert shall *a*
34:14 *A* the night creature shall
34:15 There *a* shall the hawks be
37:30 *A* in the third year sow and
40:24 When He will *a* blow on them,
44:19 I have *a* baked bread on its
45:16 They shall be ashamed And *a*
46:11 I will *a* bring it to pass. I
46:11 I will *a* do it.
48:12 I am *a* the Last.
48:19 Your descendants *a* would have
48:21 He *a* split the rock, and the
49: 6 I will *a* give You as a light
49: 7 Princes *a* shall worship,
56: 6 *A* the sons of the foreigner
57: 8 *A* behind the doors and their
57:18 I will *a* lead him, And
60:14 *A* the sons of those who
60:17 I will *a* make your officers
60:21 *A* your people shall all be
62: 3 You shall *a* be a crown of glory
66:21 And I will *a* take some of them
Jer 1: 3 It came *a* in the days of
2: 8 The rulers *a* transgressed
2:16 *A* the people of Noph and
2:33 Therefore you have *a* taught
2:34 *A* on your skirts is found The
2:36 *A* you shall be ashamed of
3: 6 The LORD said *a* to me in the
3: 8 went and played the harlot *a*.
4:12 Now I will *a* speak judgment
6:14 They have *a* healed the hurt of
6:17 *A*, I set watchmen over
7:27 You shall *a* call to them, but
9:16 I will scatter them *a* among the
13:23 Then may you *a* do good who
14: 5 the deer *a* gave birth in the
16: 1 The word of the LORD *a* came to
16: 8 *A* you shall not go into the
19: 5 (they have *a* built the high
20: 1 the priest who was *a* chief
23:14 *A* I have seen a horrible thing
23:14 They *a* strengthen the hands of
25:14 kings shall be served by them *a*;
25:26 *A* the king of Sheshach shall
26:20 Now there was *a* a man who
27: 6 beasts of the field I have *a*
27:12 I *a* spoke to Zedekiah king of
27:16 *A* I spoke to the priests and to
28:14 him the beasts of the field *a*.
29:24 You shall *a* speak to Shemaiah
30:19 I will *a* glorify them, and
30:20 Their children *a* shall be as
31:36 the seed of Israel shall *a*
31:37 I will *a* cast off all the seed
33:21 then My covenant may *a* be broken
33:24 He has *a* cast them off"?
35:15 I have *a* sent to you all My
36: 6 And you shall *a* read them in
38:25 and *a* what the king said to
39: 6 the king of Babylon *a* killed
41: 3 Ishmael *a* struck down all the
43:13 He shall *a* break the sacred
44:19 The women *a* said, "And when
46:21 *A* her mercenaries are in her
46:21 For they *a* are turned back,
48: 2 You *a* shall be cut down, O
48: 7 You *a* shall be taken. And
48: 8 The valley *a* shall perish,
48:26 And he shall *a* be in derision.
48:34 For the waters of Nimrim *a*
49:17 Edom *a* shall be an astonishment;
50:24 You have been found and *a*
51:22 With you *a* I will break in
51:23 With you *a* I will break in
52: 2 He *a* did evil in the sight of
52:11 He *a* put out the eyes of
52:18 They *a* took away the pots, the
52:25 He *a* took out of the city an
Lam 3:16 He has *a* broken my teeth with
4:21 land of Uz! The cup shall *a*
Ezek 1: 5 *A* from within it came the
1:27 *A* from the appearance of His
3:13 I *a* heard the noise of the
3:21 *a* you will have delivered your
4: 1 'You *a*, son of man, take
4: 2 it; set camps against it *a*,
4: 4 Lie *a* on your left side, and
4: 9 *A* take for yourself wheat,
4:11 You shall *a* drink water by
5: 3 You shall *a* take a small number
5:11 therefore I will *a* diminish
7:18 They will *a* be girded with
8:18 Therefore I *a* will act in fury.
9:10 "And as for Me *a*,
10:16 the same wheels *a* did not turn
12:13 I will *a* spread My net over him,
13:21 I will *a* tear off your veils and
16:17 You have *a* taken your beautiful
16:19 *A* My food which I gave you—the
16:24 that you *a* built for yourself a
16:26 You *a* committed harlotry with
16:28 You *a* played the harlot with the
16:39 I will *a* give you into their
16:39 They shall *a* strip you of your
16:40 They shall *a* bring up an
16:43 surely I will *a* recompense your
16:52 sisters, bear your own shame *a*,
16:52 than you. Yes, be disgraced *a*,
16:53 then I will *a* bring back
17:13 He *a* took away the mighty of
17:22 I will take *a* one of the
19: 4 The nations *a* heard of him; He
20:12 Moreover I *a* gave them My
20:15 So I *a* raised My hand in an oath
20:23 *A* I raised My hand in an oath to
20:25 Therefore I *a* gave them up to
20:28 There they *a* sent up their
21: 9 a sword is sharpened And *a*
21:17 I *a* will beat My fists together,
23:26 They shall *a* strip you of your
23:36 The LORD *a* said to me: "Son
24: 3 And *a* pour water into it.
24: 5 *A* pile fuel bones under it,
24:15 *A* the word of the LORD came to
25:13 I will *a* stretch out My hand
26: 4 I will *a* scrape her dust from
26: 6 *A* her daughter villages which
30:10 I will *a* make a multitude of
30:13 I will *a* destroy the idols, And
30:18 Tehaphnehes the day shall *a* be
31:17 They *a* went down to hell with
32: 6 I will *a* water the land with the
32: 9 I will *a* trouble the hearts of
32:13 *A* I will destroy all its
32:17 It came to pass *a* in the
36:33 I will *a* enable you to dwell
36:37 I will *a* let the house of Israel
37: 9 *A* He said to me, "Prophesy to
37:24 they shall *a* walk in My
37:27 My tabernacle *a* shall be with
37:28 The nations *a* will know that I,
39:16 name of the city will *a*
39:28 but *a* brought them back to
40: 8 He *a* measured the vestibule of
40:10 *a* the gateposts were of the
40:20 On the outer court was *a* a
40:22 and *a* its palm trees, had the
40:27 There was *a* a gateway on the
40:29 *A* its gate chambers, its
40:33 *A* its gate chambers, its
40:36 *a* its gate chambers, its
40:42 There were *a* four tables of
41: 3 *A* he went inside and measured
41: 8 I *a* saw an elevation all around
41: 9 and so *a* the remaining terrace
41:14 *a* the width of the eastern face
41:26 *a* on the side chambers of the
42:10 *A* there were chambers in the
42:11 was a walk in front of them *a*,
43:21 Then you shall *a* take the bull
43:25 they shall *a* prepare a young
44: 4 *A* He brought me by way of the
44:30 *a* you shall give to the priest
Dan 2:49 *A* Daniel petitioned the king,
6:18 *A* his sleep went from him.
6:22 innocent before Him; and *a*,
7: 6 The beast *a* had four heads, and
8:24 and *a* the holy people.
11: 1 *A* in the first year of Darius
11: 5 *A* the king of the South shall
11: 8 And he shall *a* carry their gods
11: 9 *A* the king of the North
11:14 the king of the South. *A*,
11:17 He shall *a* set his face to enter
11:22 and *a* the prince of the
11:41 He shall *a* enter the Glorious
11:43 *a* the Libyans and Ethiopians
Hos 2:11 I will *a* cause all her mirth to
4: 5 The prophet *a* shall stumble
4: 6 I *a* will reject you from being
4: 6 I *a* will forget your children.
5: 5 Judah *a* stumbles with them.
6:11 *A*, O Judah, a harvest is
7:11 Ephraim *a* is like a silly dove,
8:14 Judah *a* has multiplied
10: 6 The idol *a* shall be carried
10: 8 *A* the high places of Aven, the
12: 1 *A* they make a covenant with
12: 2 The LORD *a* brings a charge
12:10 I have *a* spoken by the
Joel 1:12 tree, The palm tree *a*,
1:20 The beasts of the field *a* cry
2:29 And *a* on My menservants and on
3: 2 I will *a* gather all nations,
3: 2 They have *a* divided up My
3: 6 *A* the people of Judah and the
3:16 The LORD *a* will roar from
Am 1: 5 I will *a* break the gate bar of
2:10 *A* it was I who brought you
3:14 I will *a* visit destruction on
4: 6 *A* I gave you cleanness of teeth
4: 7 I *a* withheld rain from you,
5:26 You *a* carried Sikkuth your king
7: 6 This *a* shall not be," said the
9:14 They shall *a* make gardens and
Mic 2: 2 *A* houses, and seize them.
3: 3 Who *a* eat the flesh of My
4:11 Now *a* many nations have
5:13 Your carved images I will *a* cut
6:13 Therefore I will *a* make you
Nah 3:10 Her young children *a* were
3:11 You *a* will be drunk; You will
3:11 You *a* will seek refuge from
Hab 1: 8 Their horses *a* are swifter than
2:16 shame instead of glory. You *a*—
Zeph 1: 5 But who *a* swear by Milcom;
2:12 "You Ethiopians *a*,
Zech 3: 7 Then you shall *a* judge My
4: 9 His hands shall *a* finish it.
5: 6 He *a* said, "This is their
8: 6 Will it *a* be marvelous in My
8:21 of hosts. I myself will go *a*.
9: 2 *A* against Hamath, which
9: 5 Gaza *a* shall be very
9:11 "As for you *a*,
10:10 I will *a* bring them back from
11: 8 and their soul *a* abhorred me.
13: 2 I will *a* cause the prophets and
14:14 Judah *a* will fight at
14:15 Such *a* shall be the plague On
Mal 1:13 You *a* say, 'Oh, what a
2: 9 Therefore I *a* have made you
Mt 2: 8 I may come and worship Him *a*.
5:39 cheek, turn the other to him *a*.
5:40 let him have your cloak *a*.
6:14 your heavenly Father will *a*
6:21 is, there your heart will be *a*.
7:12 do *a* to them, for this is the
8: 9 For I *a* am a man under
10: 4 who *a* betrayed Him.
10:32 him I will *a* confess before My
10:33 him I will *a* deny before My
12:45 So shall it *a* be with this
13:26 then the tares *a* appeared.
13:29 you gather up the tares you *a*
15: 3 Why do you *a* transgress the
15:16 Are you *a* still without
16:18 And I *a* say to you that you are
17:12 Likewise the Son of Man is *a*
18:33 Should you not *a* have had
18:35 So My heavenly Father *a* will do
19: 3 The Pharisees *a* came to Him,
19:28 you who have followed Me will *a*
20: 4 You *a* go into the vineyard, and
20: 7 You *a* go into the vineyard, and
21:21 but *a* if you say to this
21:24 I *a* will ask you one thing,
22:26 "Likewise the second *a*,
22:27 "Last of all the woman died *a*.
23:26 outside of them may be clean *a*.
23:28 Even so you *a* outwardly appear
24:27 so *a* will the coming of the Son
24:33 'So you *a*, when you see
24:37 so *a* will the coming of the Son
24:39 so *a* will the coming of the Son
24:44 Therefore you *a* be ready, for
25:11 the other virgins came *a*,
25:17 received two gained two more *a*.
25:22 He *a* who had received two
25:41 Then He will *a* say to those on
25:44 Then they *a* will answer Him,
26:13 this woman has done will *a* be
26:69 You *a* were with Jesus of
26:71 This fellow *a* was with Jesus of
26:73 Surely you *a* are one of them,
27:41 Likewise the chief priests *a*,
27:57 who himself had *a* become a
Mk 1:19 who *a* were in the boat mending
1:38 that I may preach there *a*,
2:15 tax collectors and sinners *a*
2:26 and *a* gave some to those who
2:28 Therefore the Son of Man is *a*
3:19 who *a* betrayed Him. And they
4:21 *A* He said to them, "Is a lamp
4:36 And other little boats were *a*
5:10 *A* he begged Him earnestly that
6:10 *A* He said to them, "In whatever
6:23 He *a* swore to her, "Whatever
7:18 thus without understanding *a*?
8: 7 They *a* had a few small fish; and
8: 7 He said to set them *a* before
8:20 '*A*, when I broke the seven
8:34 Himself, with His disciples *a*,
8:38 of him the Son of Man *a* will be
9:13 I say to you that Elijah has *a*
10:10 In the house His disciples *a*
11:25 your Father in heaven may *a*
11:29 I *a* will ask you one question;
12: 6 he *a* sent him to them last,
12:22 Last of all the woman died *a*.
13:29 'So you *a*, when you see
14: 9 this woman has done will *a* be
14:67 You *a* were with Jesus of
15:27 With Him they *a* crucified two
15:31 Likewise the chief priests *a*,
15:40 There were *a* women looking on
15:41 who *a* followed Him and
Lk 1: 3 it seemed good to me *a*,
1:15 He will *a* be filled with the
1:17 He will *a* go before Him in the
1:35 overshadow you; therefore, *a*,
1:36 Elizabeth your relative has *a*
2: 4 Joseph *a* went up from Galilee,
2:35 pierce through your own soul *a*)
3:12 Then tax collectors *a* came to be
3:20 *a* added this, above all, that he
3:21 it came to pass that Jesus *a*
4:23 do *a* here in Your country.'"
4:41 And demons *a* came out of many,
4:43 of God to the other cities *a*,
5:10 and so *a* were James and John,
5:36 and *a* the piece that was taken
6: 4 and *a* gave some to those with
6: 5 The Son of Man is *a* Lord of the
6: 6 happened on another Sabbath, *a*,
6:13 them He chose twelve whom He *a*
6:14 whom He *a* named Peter, and
6:16 and Judas Iscariot who *a* became
6:29 one cheek, offer the other *a*.

6:31 you ***a*** do to them likewise.
6:36 just as your Father ***a*** is
7: 8 For I ***a*** am a man placed under
8:36 They ***a*** who had seen it told
9:61 And another ***a*** said, "Lord, I
10: 1 Lord appointed seventy others ***a***,
10:39 who ***a*** sat at Jesus' feet and
11: 1 as John ***a*** taught his
11: 4 For we ***a*** forgive everyone who
11:18 If Satan ***a*** is divided against
11:30 so ***a*** the Son of Man will be to
11:34 your whole body ***a*** is full of
11:34 your body ***a*** is full of
11:40 the outside make the inside ***a***?
11:45 these things You reproach us ***a***.
11:46 And He said, "Woe to you ***a***,
11:49 Therefore the wisdom of God ***a***
12: 8 ***A*** I say to you, whoever
12: 8 him the Son of Man ***a*** will
12:34 is, there your heart will be ***a***.
12:40 Therefore you ***a*** be ready, for
12:54 Then He ***a*** said to the
13: 6 He ***a*** spoke this parable: "A
13: 8 'Sir, let it alone this year ***a***,
14:12 Then He ***a*** said to him who
14:12 lest they ***a*** invite you back,
14:26 yes, and his own life ***a***,
16: 1 He ***a*** said to His disciples:
16:10 what is least is faithful ***a***
16:10 in what is least is unjust ***a***
16:14 ***a*** heard all these things, and
16:22 The rich man ***a*** died and was
16:28 lest they ***a*** come to this place
17:24 so ***a*** the Son of Man will be in
17:26 so it will be ***a*** in the days of
17:28 Likewise as it was ***a*** in the days
18: 9 ***A*** He spoke this parable to some
18:15 Then they ***a*** brought infants to
19: 9 because he ***a*** is a son of
19:19 You ***a*** be over five cities.'
20: 3 I ***a*** will ask you one thing, and
20:11 servant; and they beat him ***a***,
20:12 and they wounded him ***a*** and cast
20:31 and in like manner the seven ***a***;
20:32 "Last of all the woman died ***a***.
21: 2 and He saw ***a*** a certain poor
21:31 'So you ***a***, when you see
22:20 Likewise He ***a*** took the cup
22:24 Now there was ***a*** a dispute among
22:39 and His disciples ***a*** followed
22:56 This man was ***a*** with Him."
22:58 You ***a*** are of them." But Peter
22:59 Surely this fellow ***a*** was with
22:68 And if I ***a*** ask you, you will by
23: 7 who was ***a*** in Jerusalem at that
23:27 and women who ***a*** mourned and
23:32 There were ***a*** two others,
23:36 The soldiers ***a*** mocked Him,
23:38 And an inscription ***a*** was written
23:51 who himself was ***a*** waiting for
24:23 came saying that they had ***a***
Jn 1:45 and ***a*** the prophets, wrote—Jesus
3:23 Now John ***a*** was baptizing in
4:45 for they ***a*** had gone to the
5:18 but ***a*** said that God was His
5:19 the Son ***a*** does in like manner.
5:27 authority to execute judgment ***a***,
6:24 they ***a*** got into boats and came
6:67 Do you ***a*** want to go away?"
6:69 ***A*** we have come to believe and
7: 3 that Your disciples ***a*** may see
7:10 then He ***a*** went up to the feast,
7:47 Are you ***a*** deceived?
7:52 'Are you ***a*** from Galilee?
8:17 It is ***a*** written in your law that
8:19 would have known My Father ***a***.
9:15 Then the Pharisees ***a*** asked him
9:27 Do you ***a*** want to become His
9:40 said to Him, "Are we blind ***a***?
10:16 them ***a*** I must bring, and they
11:16 Let us ***a*** go, that we may die
11:37 ***a*** have kept this man from
11:52 but ***a*** that He would gather
12: 9 but that they might ***a*** see
12:10 to put Lazarus to death ***a***,
12:18 For this reason the people ***a*** met
12:26 am, there My servant will be ***a***.
13: 9 but ***a*** my hands and my head!"
13:14 you ***a*** ought to wash one
13:32 God will ***a*** glorify Him in
13:34 that you ***a*** love one another.
14: 1 believe ***a*** in Me.
14: 3 where I am, there you may be ***a***.
14: 7 would have known My Father ***a***;
14:12 works that I do he will do ***a***;
14:19 Because I live, you will live ***a***.
15: 9 I ***a*** have loved you; abide in My
15:20 they will ***a*** persecute you. If
15:20 My word, they will keep yours ***a***.
15:23 who hates Me hates My Father ***a***.
15:24 but now they have seen and ***a***
15:27 And you ***a*** will bear witness,
17: 1 that Your Son ***a*** may glorify
17:18 I ***a*** have sent them into the
17:19 that they ***a*** may be sanctified
17:20 but ***a*** for those who will
17:21 that they ***a*** may be one in Us,
17:24 I desire that they ***a*** whom You
18: 2 ***a*** knew the place; for Jesus
18: 5 ***a*** stood with them.
18:17 You are not ***a*** one of this Man's
18:25 You are not ***a*** one of His
19:23 and ***a*** the tunic. Now the tunic
19:39 ***a*** came, bringing a mixture of
20: 8 to the tomb first, went in ***a***;
20:21 I ***a*** send you."
21: 3 him, "We are going with you ***a***.
21:20 who ***a*** had leaned on His breast
21:25 And there are ***a*** many other
Acts 1: 3 to whom He ***a*** presented Himself
1:11 who ***a*** said, "Men of Galilee,
2:22 as you yourselves ***a*** know—
2:26 Moreover my flesh ***a*** will
3:17 as did ***a*** your rulers.
3:24 have ***a*** foretold these days.
4:36 who was ***a*** named Barnabas by the
5: 2 his wife ***a*** being aware of it,
5:16 ***A*** a multitude gathered from the
5:32 and so ***a*** is the Holy Spirit
5:37 He ***a*** perished, and all who
6:13 They ***a*** set up false witnesses
7:43 You ***a*** took up the
7:45 ***a*** brought with Joshua into the
8:13 Then Simon himself ***a*** believed;
8:19 saying, "Give me this power ***a***,
9:32 that he ***a*** came down to the
10:26 I myself am ***a*** a man."
10:45 poured out on the Gentiles ***a***.
11: 1 heard that the Gentiles had ***a***
11:18 Then God has ***a*** granted to the
11:28 which ***a*** happened in the days of
11:30 This they ***a*** did, and sent it to
12: 3 further to seize Peter ***a***.
12:25 and they ***a*** took with them John
13: 5 They ***a*** had John as their
13: 9 who ***a*** is called Paul, filled
13:22 to whom ***a*** He gave testimony and
13:33 As it is ***a*** written in the
13:35 Therefore He ***a*** says in another
14:15 We ***a*** are men with the same
15:22 Judas who was ***a*** named Barsabas,
15:27 who will ***a*** report the same
15:32 themselves being prophets ***a***,
15:35 Paul and Barnabas ***a*** remained in
15:35 of the Lord, with many others ***a***.
17:12 and ***a*** not a few of the Greeks,
17:13 they came there ***a*** and stirred
17:28 as ***a*** some of your own poets
17:28 For we are ***a*** His offspring.'
19:14 ***A*** there were seven sons of
19:19 ***A***, many of those who had
19:21 I must ***a*** see Rome."
19:27 but ***a*** the temple of the great
20: 4 ***a*** Aristarchus and Secundus of
20:21 and ***a*** to Greeks, repentance
20:30 ***A*** from among yourselves men will
21:13 but ***a*** to die at Jerusalem for
21:16 ***A*** some of the disciples from
21:24 but that you yourself ***a*** walk
21:28 and furthermore he ***a*** brought
22: 5 as ***a*** the high priest bears me
22: 5 from whom I ***a*** received letters
22:20 I ***a*** was standing by consenting
22:29 and the commander was ***a*** afraid
23:11 so you must ***a*** bear witness at
23:30 and ***a*** commanded his accusers to
23:33 they ***a*** presented Paul to him.
23:35 hear you when your accusers ***a***
24: 9 And the Jews ***a*** assented,
24:15 which they themselves ***a*** accept,
24:26 Meanwhile he ***a*** hoped that money
25:22 I ***a*** would like to hear the man
26:10 This I ***a*** did in Jerusalem, and
26:26 before whom I ***a*** speak freely,
26:29 but ***a*** all who hear me today,
27:10 cargo and ship, but ***a*** our lives."
27:12 to set sail from there ***a***,
27:36 and ***a*** took food themselves.
28: 9 the island who had diseases ***a***
28:10 They ***a*** honored us in many ways;
Rom 1: 6 among whom you ***a*** are the called
1:13 have some fruit among you ***a***,
1:15 gospel to you who are in Rome ***a***.
1:16 for the Jew first and ***a*** for the
1:24 Therefore God ***a*** gave them up to
1:27 Likewise ***a*** the men, leaving the
1:32 not only do the same but ***a***
2: 9 of the Jew first and ***a*** of the
2:10 to the Jew first and ***a*** to the
2:12 have sinned without law will ***a***
2:15 their conscience ***a*** bearing
3: 7 why am I ***a*** still judged as a
3:29 Is He not ***a*** the God of the
3:29 Yes, of the Gentiles ***a***,
4: 6 just as David ***a*** describes the
4: 9 or upon the uncircumcised ***a***?
4:11 might be imputed to them ***a***,
4:12 but who ***a*** walk in the steps of
4:16 but ***a*** to those who are of the
4:21 what He had promised He was ***a***
4:24 but ***a*** for us. It shall be
5: 2 through whom ***a*** we have access by
5: 3 but we ***a*** glory in tribulations,
5:11 but we ***a*** rejoice in God through
5:19 so ***a*** by one Man's obedience
6: 4 even so we ***a*** should walk in
6: 5 certainly we ***a*** shall be in
6: 8 we believe that we shall ***a*** live
6:11 Likewise you ***a***,
7: 4 you ***a*** have become dead to the
8:11 Christ from the dead will ***a***
8:17 that we may ***a*** be glorified
8:21 because the creation itself ***a***
8:23 but we ***a*** who have the
8:26 Likewise the Spirit ***a*** helps in
8:29 He ***a*** predestined to be
8:30 these He ***a*** called; whom He
8:30 these He ***a*** justified; and whom
8:30 these He ***a*** glorified.
8:32 how shall He not with Him ***a***
8:34 and furthermore is ***a*** risen, who
8:34 who ***a*** makes intercession for
9: 1 my conscience ***a*** bearing me
9:10 but when Rebecca ***a*** had
9:24 but ***a*** of the Gentiles?
9:25 As He says ***a*** in Hosea: "I
9:27 Isaiah ***a*** cries out concerning
11: 1 Certainly not! For I ***a*** am an
11:16 the lump is ***a*** holy; and if
11:22 Otherwise you ***a*** will be cut
11:23 And they ***a***, if they do not
11:31 even so these ***a*** have now been
11:31 the mercy shown you they ***a*** may
13: 5 not only because of wrath but ***a***
13: 6 For because of this you ***a*** pay
15: 7 just as Christ ***a*** received us,
15:14 that you ***a*** are full of
15:14 able ***a*** to admonish one another.
15:22 For this reason I ***a*** have been
15:27 their duty is ***a*** to minister to
16: 2 helper of many and of myself ***a***.
16: 4 but ***a*** all the churches of the
16: 7 who ***a*** were in Christ before me.
1 Cor 1: 8 who will ***a*** confirm you to the
1:16 I ***a*** baptized the household of
2:13 These things we ***a*** speak, not in
4: 8 that we ***a*** might reign with you!
5:12 I to do with judging those ***a***
6:14 raised up the Lord and will ***a***
7: 3 and likewise ***a*** the wife to her
7:40 and I think I ***a*** have the Spirit
9: 5 as do ***a*** the other apostles,
9: 8 does not the law say the same ***a***?
10: 6 after evil things as they ***a***
10: 9 as some of them ***a*** tempted, and
10:10 as some of them ***a*** complained,
10:13 but with the temptation will ***a***
10:33 just as I ***a*** please all men in
11: 1 just as I ***a*** imitate Christ.
11: 6 let her ***a*** be shorn. But if it
11:12 even so man ***a*** comes through
11:19 For there must ***a*** be factions
11:23 from the Lord that which I ***a***
11:25 In the same manner He ***a*** took
12:12 so ***a*** is Christ.
13:12 then I shall know just as I ***a***
14:15 and I will ***a*** pray with the
14:15 and I will ***a*** sing with the
14:19 that I may teach others ***a***,
14:34 as the law ***a*** says.
15: 1 which ***a*** you received and in
15: 2 by which ***a*** you are saved, if you
15: 3 you first of all that which I ***a***
15: 8 last of all He was seen by me ***a***,
15:14 is empty and your faith is ***a***
15:18 Then ***a*** those who have fallen
15:21 by Man ***a*** came the resurrection
15:28 then the Son Himself will ***a*** be
15:40 There are ***a*** celestial bodies
15:42 So ***a*** is the resurrection of the
15:48 so ***a*** are those who are made
15:48 so ***a*** are those who are
15:49 we shall ***a*** bear the image of
16: 1 of Galatia, so you must do ***a***:
16: 4 if it is fitting that I go ***a***,
16:10 work of the Lord, as I ***a*** do.
16:16 that you ***a*** submit to such, and
2 Cor 1: 5 so our consolation ***a*** abounds
1: 6 the same sufferings which we ***a***
1: 7 so ***a*** you will partake of the
1:11 you ***a*** helping together in prayer
1:14 (as ***a*** you have understood us in
1:14 that we are your boast as you ***a***
1:22 who ***a*** has sealed us and given us
2: 9 For to this end I ***a*** wrote, that
2:10 I ***a*** forgive. For if indeed I
3: 6 who ***a*** made us sufficient as
4:10 that the life of Jesus ***a*** may be
4:11 that the life of Jesus ***a*** may be
4:13 we ***a*** believe and therefore
4:14 up the Lord Jesus will ***a*** raise
5: 5 who ***a*** has given us the Spirit
5:11 and I ***a*** trust are well known in
6: 1 workers together with Him ***a***
6:13 you ***a*** be open.
7: 7 but ***a*** by the consolation with
8: 6 so he would ***a*** complete this
8: 7 that you abound in this grace ***a***.
8:11 but now you ***a*** must complete the
8:11 so there ***a*** may be a
8:14 that their abundance ***a*** may
8:19 but who was ***a*** chosen by the
8:21 but ***a*** in the sight of men.
9: 6 He who sows sparingly will ***a***
9: 6 he who sows bountifully will ***a***
9:12 but ***a*** is abounding through many
10:11 such we will ***a*** be in deed
11:12 I will ***a*** continue to do, that I
11:15 great thing if his ministers ***a***
11:16 that I ***a*** may boast a little.
11:18 I ***a*** will boast.
11:21 speak foolishly—I am bold ***a***.
13: 4 For we ***a*** are weak in Him, but
13: 9 And this ***a*** we pray, that you
Gal 2: 1 and ***a*** took Titus with me.
2: 8 to the circumcised ***a*** worked

2:10 the very thing which I *a* was
2:13 And the rest of the Jews *a*
2:17 we ourselves *a* are found
5:21 just as I *a* told you in time
5:25 let us *a* walk in the Spirit.
6: 1 yourself lest you *a* be tempted.
6: 7 that he will *a* reap.
Eph 1:11 In Him *a* we have obtained an
1:13 In Him you *a* trusted, after you
1:13 of your salvation; in whom *a*,
1:15 Therefore I *a*, after I heard
1:21 not only in this age but *a* in
2: 3 among whom *a* we all once
2:22 in whom you *a* are being built
4: 9 does it mean but that He *a*
4:10 He who descended is *a* the One
5: 2 as Christ *a* has loved us and
5:23 as *a* Christ is head of the
5:25 just as Christ *a* loved the
6: 9 knowing that your own Master *a*
6:21 But that you *a* may know my
Phil 1:15 and some *a* from good will:
1:20 so now *a* Christ will be
1:29 but *a* to suffer for His sake,
2: 4 but *a* for the interests of
2: 5 mind be in you which was *a* in
2: 9 Therefore God *a* has highly
2:18 For the same reason you *a* be
2:19 that I *a* may be encouraged when
2:24 the Lord that I myself shall *a*
2:27 and not only on him but on me *a*,
3: 4 though I *a* might have confidence
3: 8 Yet indeed I *a* count all things
3:12 for which Christ Jesus has *a*
3:20 from which we *a* eagerly wait
4: 3 And I urge you *a*,
4: 3 in the gospel, with Clement *a*,
4:15 Now you Philippians know *a* that
Col 1: 6 as it has *a* in all the world,
1: 6 as it is *a* among you since
1: 7 as you *a* learned from Epaphras,
1: 8 who *a* declared to us your love
1: 9 For this reason we *a*,
1:29 To this end I *a* labor, striving
2:11 In Him you were *a* circumcised
2:12 in which you *a* were raised with
3: 4 then you *a* will appear with Him
3:13 so you *a* must do.
3:15 to which *a* you were called in
4: 1 knowing that you *a* have a
4: 3 meanwhile praying *a* for us, that
4: 3 for which I am *a* in chains,
4:16 see that it is read *a* in the
1 Th 1: 5 but *a* in power, and in the Holy
1: 8 but *a* in every place.
2: 8 but *a* our own lives, because
2:10 You are witnesses, and God *a*,
2:13 For this reason we *a* thank God
2:13 which *a* effectively works in
2:14 For you *a* suffered the same
3: 6 as we *a* to see you—
4: 6 as we *a* forewarned you and
4: 8 who has *a* given us His Holy
4:11 that you *a* aspire to lead a
5:11 just as you *a* are doing.
5:24 who *a* will do it.
2 Th 1: 5 for which you *a* suffer;
1:11 Therefore we *a* pray always for
1 Tim 2: 9 *a*, that the women adorn
3:10 But let these *a* first be tested;
5:13 and not only idle but *a* gossips
5:20 that the rest *a* may fear.
6:12 to which you were *a* called and
2 Tim 1: 5 and I am persuaded is in you *a*.
1:12 For this reason I *a* suffer these
2: 2 will be able to teach others *a*.
2: 5 And *a* if anyone competes in
2:10 that they *a* may obtain the
2:11 We shall *a* live with Him.
2:12 We shall *a* reign with Him.
2:12 He *a* will deny us.
2:20 but *a* of wood and clay, some
2:22 Flee *a* youthful lusts; but
3: 8 so do these *a* resist the truth:
3: 9 as theirs *a* was.
4: 8 and not to me only but *a* to all
4:15 You *a* must beware of him, for he
Titus 3: 3 For we ourselves were *a* once
3:14 And let our people *a* learn to
Phm 1: 9 and now *a* a prisoner of Jesus
1:22 *a* prepare a guest room for me,
Heb 1: 2 through whom *a* He made the
2: 4 God *a* bearing witness both with
3: 2 as Moses *a* was faithful in
4:10 entered His rest has himself *a*
5: 2 since he himself is *a* subject
5: 3 so *a* for himself, to offer
5: 5 So *a* Christ did not glorify
5: 6 As He *a* says in another
7: 2 to whom *a* Abraham gave a tenth
7: 2 and then *a* king of Salem,
7:12 of necessity there is *a* a
7:23 *A* there were many priests,
7:25 Therefore He is *a* able to save
8: 3 is necessary that this One *a*
8: 6 inasmuch as He is *a* Mediator of
9:16 there must *a* of necessity be
10:15 But the Holy Spirit *a* witnesses
11:11 By faith Sarah herself *a*
11:19 from which he *a* received him in
11:32 *a* of David and Samuel and the
12: 1 Therefore we *a*, since we are
12:26 the earth, but *a* heaven."
13: 3 yourselves are in the body *a*.
13:12 Therefore Jesus *a*,
Jas 1:11 So the rich man *a* will fade
2: 2 and there should *a* come in a
2:11 *a* said, "Do not murder."
2:17 Thus *a* faith by itself, if it
2:25 was not Rahab the harlot *a*
2:26 faith without works is dead *a*.
3: 2 able *a* to bridle the whole
3: 4 Look *a* at ships: although they
5: 8 You *a* be patient. Establish your
1 Pe 1:15 you *a* be holy in all your
2: 5 you *a*, as living stones,
2: 6 Therefore it is *a* contained in
2: 8 to which they *a* were appointed.
2:18 but *a* to the harsh.
2:21 because Christ *a* suffered for
3: 5 holy women who trusted in God *a*
3:18 For Christ *a* suffered once for
3:19 by whom *a* He went and preached
3:21 There is *a* an antitype which now
4: 1 arm yourselves *a* with the same
4: 6 the gospel was preached *a* to
4:13 you may *a* be glad with
5: 1 and *a* a partaker of the glory
2 Pe 1: 5 But *a* for this very reason,
2: 1 But there were *a* false prophets
2:19 by him *a* he is brought into
3:15 as *a* our beloved brother Paul,
3:16 as *a* in all his epistles,
3:16 as they do *a* the rest of the
3:17 beware lest you *a* fall from
1 Jn 1: 3 that you *a* may have fellowship
2: 2 and not for ours only but *a* for
2: 6 abides in Him ought himself *a*
2:23 the Son has the Father *a*.
2:24 you *a* will abide in the Son and
3: 4 Whoever commits sin *a* commits
3:16 And we *a* ought to lay down our
4:11 we *a* ought to love one another.
4:21 God must love his brother *a*.
5: 1 who loves Him who begot *a*
2 Jn 1 but *a* all those who have known
3 Jn 12 And we *a* bear witness, and you
Jude 8 Likewise *a* these dreamers defile
14 prophesied about these men *a*,
Rev 2: 6 which I *a* hate.
2:15 Thus you *a* have those who hold
2:27 as I *a* have received from My
3:10 I *a* will keep you from the hour
3:21 as I *a* overcame and sat down
11: 8 where *a* our Lord was crucified.
14:10 he himself shall *a* drink of the
14:17 he *a* having a sharp sickle.
17:10 'There are *a* seven kings.
17:11 is himself *a* the eighth, and is
21: 1 *A* there was no more sea.
21:12 *A* she had a great and high wall

ALTAR (378/322) ALTARS

Gen 8:20 Then Noah built an *a* to the
8:20 burnt offerings on the *a*.
12: 7 And there he built an *a* to
12: 8 there he built an *a* to the
13: 4 to the place of the *a* which he
13:18 and built an *a* there to the
22: 9 And Abraham built an *a* there
22: 9 his son and laid him on the *a*,
26:25 So he built an *a* there and
33:20 Then he erected an *a* there and
35: 1 and make an *a* there to God, who
35: 3 and I will make an *a* there to
35: 7 And he built an *a* there and
Ex 17:15 And Moses built an *a* and called
20:24 An *a* of earth you shall make for
20:25 And if you make Me an *a* of
20:26 you go up by steps to My *a*,
21:14 you shall take him from My *a*,
24: 4 and built an *a* at the foot of
24: 6 the blood he sprinkled on the *a*.
27: 1 You shall make an *a* of acacia
27: 1 the *a* shall be square—and its
27: 5 put it under the rim of the *a*
27: 5 network may be midway up the *a*.
27: 6 you shall make poles for the *a*,
27: 7 be on the two sides of the *a*
28:43 or when they come near the *a* to
29:12 put it on the horns of the *a*
29:12 blood beside the base of the *a*.
29:13 them, and burn them on the *a*.
29:16 it all around on the *a*.
29:18 burn the whole ram on the *a*.
29:20 the blood all around on the *a*.
29:21 of the blood that is on the *a*,
29:25 hands and burn them on the *a*
29:36 You shall cleanse the *a* when
29:37 shall make atonement for the *a*
29:37 And the *a* shall be most holy.
29:37 Whatever touches the *a* must be
29:38 what you shall offer on the *a*:
29:44 tabernacle of meeting and the *a*.
30: 1 You shall make an *a* to burn
30:18 tabernacle of meeting and the *a*.
30:20 or when they come near the *a* to
30:27 and the *a* of incense;
30:28 the *a* of burnt offering with all
31: 8 the *a* of incense,
31: 9 the *a* of burnt offering with all
32: 5 he built an *a* before it.
35:15 'the incense *a*,
35:16 the *a* of burnt offering with its
37:25 He made the incense *a* of acacia
38: 1 He made the *a* of burnt offering
38: 3 made all the utensils for the *a*:
38: 4 of bronze network for the *a*,
38: 7 the rings on the sides of the *a*,
38: 7 He made the *a* hollow with
38:30 of meeting, the bronze *a*,
38:30 and all the utensils for the *a*,
39:38 the gold *a*, the anointing oil,
39:39 the bronze *a*, its grate
40: 5 You shall also set the *a* of gold
40: 6 Then you shall set the *a* of the
40: 7 tabernacle of meeting and the *a*,
40:10 You shall anoint the *a* of the
40:10 utensils, and consecrate the *a*.
40:10 The *a* shall be most holy.
40:26 He put the gold *a* in the
40:29 And he put the *a* of burnt
40:30 tabernacle of meeting and the *a*,
40:32 and when they came near the *a*,
40:33 around the tabernacle and the *a*,
Lev 1: 5 the blood all around on the *a*
1: 7 priest shall put fire on the *a*,
1: 8 that is on the fire upon the *a*;
1: 9 priest shall burn all on the *a*
1:11 it on the north side of the *a*
1:11 its blood all around on the *a*.
1:12 that is on the fire upon the *a*;
1:13 it all and burn it on the *a*;
1:15 priest shall bring it to the *a*,
1:15 its head, and burn it on the *a*;
1:15 out at the side of the *a*.
1:16 and cast it beside the *a* on
1:17 priest shall burn it on the *a*,
2: 2 it as a memorial on the *a*,
2: 8 he shall bring it to the *a*.
2: 9 portion, and burn it on the *a*.
2:12 shall not be burned on the *a*
3: 2 the blood all around on the *a*.
3: 5 sons shall burn it on the *a*
3: 8 its blood all around on the *a*.
3:11 shall burn them on the *a* as
3:13 its blood all around on the *a*.
3:16 shall burn them on the *a* as
4: 7 blood on the horns of the *a* of
4: 7 the bull at the base of the *a*
4:10 shall burn them on the *a* of
4:18 the blood on the horns of the *a*
4:18 blood at the base of the *a* of
4:19 from it and burn it on the *a*.
4:25 put it on the horns of the *a*
4:25 its blood at the base of the *a*
4:26 shall burn all its fat on the *a*,
4:30 put it on the horns of the *a*
4:30 blood at the base of the *a*.
4:31 priest shall burn it on the *a*
4:34 put it on the horns of the *a*
4:34 blood at the base of the *a*.
4:35 priest shall burn it on the *a*,
5: 9 offering on the side of the *a*,
5: 9 out at the base of the *a*.
5:12 and burn it on the *a* according
6: 9 be on the hearth upon the *a*
6: 9 and the fire of the *a* shall be
6:10 the fire has consumed on the *a*,
6:10 he shall put them beside the *a*.
6:12 And the fire on the *a* shall be
6:13 always be burning on the *a*;
6:14 Aaron shall offer it on the *a*
6:15 and shall burn it on the *a*
7: 2 sprinkle all around on the *a*.
7: 5 shall burn them on the *a* as
7:31 shall burn the fat on the *a*,
8:11 sprinkled some of it on the *a*
8:11 anointed the *a* and all its
8:15 put some on the horns of the *a*
8:15 his finger, and purified the *a*.
8:15 the blood at the base of the *a*,
8:16 and Moses burned them on the *a*.
8:19 the blood all around on the *a*.
8:21 burned the whole ram on the *a*.
8:24 the blood all around on the *a*.
8:28 hands and burned them on the *a*,
8:30 the blood which was on the *a*,
9: 7 said to Aaron, "Go to the *a*,
9: 8 Aaron therefore went to the *a*
9: 9 put it on the horns of the *a*
9: 9 the blood at the base of the *a*.
9:10 sin offering he burned on the *a*,
9:12 sprinkled all around on the *a*.
9:13 and he burned them on the *a*.
9:14 the burnt offering on the *a*.
9:17 of it, and burned it on the *a*,
9:18 sprinkled all around on the *a*,
9:20 Then he burned the fat on the *a*;
9:24 offering and the fat on the *a*.
10:12 it without leaven beside the *a*;
14:20 and the grain offering on the *a*.
16:12 coals of fire from the *a*
16:18 And he shall go out to the *a*
16:18 put it on the horns of the *a*
16:20 of meeting, and the *a*,
16:25 offering he shall burn on the *a*.
16:33 of meeting and for the *a*,
17: 6 sprinkle the blood on the *a* of
17:11 given it to you upon the *a* to
21:23 near the veil or approach the *a*,
22:22 by fire of them on the *a* to
Num 3:26 around the tabernacle and the *a*,
4:11 Over the golden *a* they shall
4:13 take away the ashes from the *a*,

4:14 and all the utensils of the *a*—
4:26 around the tabernacle and *a*,
5:25 LORD, and bring it to the *a*;
5:26 portion, burn it on the *a*,
7: 1 and the *a* and all its utensils;
7:10 dedication offering for the *a*
7:10 their offering before the *a*.
7:11 for the dedication of the *a*.
7:84 dedication offering for the *a*
7:88 dedication offering for the *a*
16:38 plates as a covering for the *a*.
16:39 out as a covering on the *a*,
16:46 and put fire in it from the *a*,
18: 3 of the sanctuary and the *a*,
18: 5 and the duties of the *a*,
18: 7 for everything at the *a* and
18:17 sprinkle their blood on the *a*,
23: 2 a bull and a ram on each *a*.
23: 4 and I have offered on each *a*
23:14 a bull and a ram on each *a*.
23:30 a bull and a ram on every *a*.
Deut 12:27 on the *a* of the LORD your God;
12:27 shall be poured out on the *a*
16:21 near the *a* which you build for
26: 4 and set it down before the *a*
27: 5 there you shall build an *a*
27: 5 an *a* of stones; you shall not
27: 6 build with whole stones the *a*
33:10 whole burnt sacrifice on Your *a*.
Josh 8:30 Now Joshua built an *a* to the
8:31 an *a* of whole stones over which
9:27 the congregation and for the *a*
22:10 tribe of Manasseh built an *a*
22:10 Jordan—a great, impressive *a*.
22:11 of Manasseh have built an *a* on
22:16 have built for yourselves an *a*,
22:19 by building yourselves an *a*
22:19 an altar besides the *a* of the
22:23 we have built ourselves an *a*
22:26 prepare to build ourselves an *a*,
22:28 Here is the replica of the *a* of
22:29 to build an *a* for burnt
22:29 besides the *a* of the LORD our
22:34 children of Gad called the *a*,
Judg 6:24 So Gideon built an *a* there to
6:25 and tear down the *a* of Baal
6:26 and build an *a* to the LORD your
6:28 there was the *a* of Baal, torn
6:28 bull was being offered on the *a*
6:30 because he has torn down the *a*
6:31 because his *a* has been torn
6:32 because he has torn down his *a*.
13:20 up toward heaven from the *a*—
13:20 ascended in the flame of the *a*!
21: 4 rose early and built an *a*
1 Sam 2:28 My priest, to offer upon My *a*,
2:33 I do not cut off from My *a*
7:17 and there he built an *a* to the
14:35 Then Saul built an *a* to the
14:35 This was the first *a* that he
2 Sam 24:18 erect an *a* to the LORD on the
24:21 to build an *a* to the LORD,
24:25 And David built there an *a* to
1 Ki 1:50 took hold of the horns of the *a*.
1:51 hold of the horns of the *a*,
1:53 to bring him down from the *a*.
2:28 took hold of the horns of the *a*.
2:29 LORD; there he is, by the *a*.
3: 4 burnt offerings on that *a*.
6:20 and overlaid the *a* of cedar.
6:22 with gold the entire *a* that
7:48 the *a* of gold, and the table of
8:22 Solomon stood before the *a* of
8:31 takes an oath before Your *a* in
8:54 he arose from before the *a* of
8:64 because the bronze *a* that was
9:25 and peace offerings on the *a*
9:25 incense with them on the *a*
12:32 and offered sacrifices on the *a*.
12:33 So he made offerings on the *a*
12:33 and offered sacrifices on the *a*
13: 1 and Jeroboam stood by the *a* to
13: 2 he cried out against the *a* by
13: 2 of the LORD, and said, "O *a*,
13: 2 *a*! Thus says the LORD:
13: 3 Surely the *a* shall split apart,
13: 4 who cried out against the *a* in
13: 4 out his hand from the *a*,
13: 5 The *a* also was split apart, and
13: 5 the ashes poured out from the *a*,
13:32 of the LORD against the *a* in
16:32 Then he set up an *a* for Baal in
18:26 Then they leaped about the *a*
18:30 And he repaired the *a* of the
18:32 with the stones he built an *a*
18:32 he made a trench around the *a*
18:35 the water ran all around the *a*;
2 Ki 11:11 by the *a* and the house.
12: 9 lid, and set it beside the *a*,
16:10 and saw an *a* that was at
16:10 the priest the design of the *a*
16:11 Urijah the priest built an *a*
16:12 Damascus, the king saw the *a*;
16:12 and the king approached the *a*
16:13 of his peace offerings on the *a*.
16:14 He also brought the bronze *a*
16:14 from between the new *a* and the
16:14 on the north side of the new *a*.
16:15 On the great new *a* burn the
16:15 And the bronze *a* shall be for
18:22 shall worship before this *a* in
23: 9 did not come up to the *a* of
23:15 Moreover the *a* that was at
23:15 both that *a* and the high place
23:16 tombs and burned them on the *a*,
23:17 you have done against the *a* of
1 Chr 6:49 offered sacrifices on the *a* of
6:49 of burnt offering and on the *a*
16:40 to the LORD on the *a* of burnt
21:18 David should go and erect an *a*
21:22 that I may build an *a* on it to
21:26 And David built there an *a* to
21:26 from heaven by fire on the *a*
21:29 of the LORD and the *a* of the
22: 1 and this is the *a* of burnt
28:18 gold by weight for the *a* of
2 Chr 1: 5 Now the bronze *a* that Bezalel
1: 6 went up there to the bronze *a*
4: 1 Moreover he made a bronze *a*:
4:19 the *a* of gold and the tables on
5:12 stood at the east end of the *a*,
6:12 Solomon stood before the *a* of
6:22 takes an oath before Your *a* in
7: 7 because the bronze *a* which
7: 9 the dedication of the *a* seven
8:12 to the LORD on the *a* of the
15: 8 and he restored the *a* of the
23:10 along by the *a* and by the
26:16 LORD to burn incense on the *a*
26:19 the LORD, beside the incense *a*.
29:18 the *a* of burnt offerings with
29:19 before the *a* of the LORD."
29:21 to offer them on the *a* of the
29:22 and sprinkled it on the *a*.
29:22 sprinkled the blood on the *a*.
29:22 sprinkled the blood on the *a*.
29:24 presented their blood on the *a*
29:27 the burnt offering on the *a*.
32:12 shall worship before one *a*
33:16 He also repaired the *a* of the
35:16 offer burnt offerings on the *a*
Ezra 3: 2 arose and built the *a* of the
3: 3 they set the *a* on its bases;
7:17 and offer them on the *a* of the
Neh 10:34 to burn on the *a* of the LORD
Ps 26: 6 So I will go about Your *a*,
43: 4 Then I will go to the *a* of God,
51:19 shall offer bulls on Your *a*.
118:27 cords to the horns of the *a*.
Isa 6: 6 taken with the tongs from the *a*.
19:19 that day there will be an *a* to
27: 9 makes all the stones of the *a*
36: 7 shall worship before this *a*'?
56: 7 Will be accepted on My *a*;
60: 7 ascend with acceptance on My *a*,
Lam 2: 7 The Lord has spurned His *a*,
Ezek 8: 5 north of the *a* gate, was this
8:16 between the porch and the *a*,
9: 2 and stood beside the bronze *a*.
40:46 who have charge of the *a*;
40:47 The *a* was in front of the
41:22 The *a* was of wood, three cubits
43:13 are the measurements of the *a*
43:13 This is the height of the *a*:
43:15 The *a* hearth is four cubits
43:16 The *a* hearth is twelve cubits
43:18 are the ordinances for the *a*
43:20 it on the four horns of the *a*,
43:22 and they shall cleanse the *a*,
43:26 shall make atonement for the *a*
43:27 your peace offerings on the *a*;
45:19 corners of the ledge of the *a*,
47: 1 of the temple, south of the *a*.
Joel 1:13 you who minister before the *a*;
2:17 between the porch and the *a*;
Am 2: 8 They lie down by every *a* on
3:14 And the horns of the *a* shall
9: 1 saw the Lord standing by the *a*,
Zech 9:15 Like the corners of the *a*.
14:20 be like the bowls before the *a*.
Mal 1: 7 offer defiled food on My *a*.
1:10 would not kindle fire on My *a*
2:13 You cover the *a* of the LORD
Mt 5:23 if you bring your gift to the *a*,
5:24 your gift there before the *a*,
23:18 "And, 'Whoever swears by the *a*,
23:19 the gift or the *a* that
23:20 he who swears by the *a*,
23:35 between the temple and the *a*.
Lk 1:11 on the right side of the *a* of
11:51 who perished between the *a* and
Acts 17:23 I even found an *a* with this
1 Cor 9:13 and those who serve at the *a*
9:13 of the offerings of the *a*?
10:18 sacrifices partakers of the *a*?
Heb 7:13 no man has officiated at the *a*.
13:10 We have an *a* from which those
Jas 2:21 offered Isaac his son on the *a*?
Rev 6: 9 I saw under the *a* the souls of
8: 3 censer, came and stood at the *a*.
8: 3 the saints upon the golden *a*
8: 5 filled it with fire from the *a*,
9:13 the four horns of the golden *a*
11: 1 the temple of God, the *a*,
14:18 angel came out from the *a*,
16: 7 And I heard another from the *a*

ALTARS (63/52) ALTAR

Ex 34:13 "But you shall destroy their *a*,
Lev 26:30 places, cut down your incense *a*,
Num 3:31 the table, the lampstand, the *a*,
23: 1 Build seven *a* for me here, and
23: 4 "I have prepared the seven *a*,
23:14 of Pisgah, and built seven *a*,
23:29 "Build for me here seven *a*,
Deut 7: 5 them: you shall destroy their *a*,
12: 3 "And you shall destroy their *a*,
Judg 2: 2 you shall tear down their *a*.
1 Ki 19:10 Your covenant, torn down Your *a*,
19:14 Your covenant, torn down Your *a*,
2 Ki 11:18 broke in pieces its *a* and
11:18 the priest of Baal before the *a*.
18:22 whose high places and whose *a*
21: 3 he raised up *a* for Baal, and
21: 4 He also built *a* in the house of
21: 5 And he built *a* for all the host
23:12 The *a* that were on the roof,
23:12 and the *a* which Manasseh had
23:20 who were there, on the *a*,
2 Chr 14: 3 for he removed the *a* of the
14: 5 high places and the incense *a*
23:17 They broke in pieces its *a* and
23:17 the priest of Baal before the *a*.
28:24 and made for himself *a* in every
30:14 They arose and took away the *a*
30:14 took away all the incense *a*
31: 1 down the high places and the *a*—
32:12 away His high places and His *a*,
33: 3 he raised up *a* for the Baals,
33: 4 He also built *a* in the house of
33: 5 And he built *a* for all the host
33:15 and all the *a* that he had built
34: 4 They broke down the *a* of the
34: 4 and the incense *a* which were
34: 5 bones of the priests on their *a*,
34: 7 When he had broken down the *a*
34: 7 and cut down all the incense *a*
Ps 84: 3 may lay her young—Even Your *a*,
Isa 17: 8 He will not look to the *a*,
17: 8 wooden images nor the incense *a*.
27: 9 Wooden images and incense *a*
36: 7 whose high places and whose *a*
65: 3 And burn incense on *a* of
Jer 11:13 of Jerusalem you have set up *a*
11:13 *a* to burn incense to Baal.
17: 1 And on the horns of your *a*,
17: 2 children remember Their *a* and
Ezek 6: 4 Then your *a* shall be desolate,
6: 4 your incense *a* shall be broken,
6: 5 your bones all around your *a*.
6: 6 so that your *a* may be laid
6: 6 your incense *a* may be cut down,
6:13 their idols all around their *a*,
Hos 8:11 Ephraim has made many *a* for
8:11 They have become for him *a* for
10: 1 fruit He has increased the *a*;
10: 2 He will break down their *a*;
10: 8 thistle shall grow on their *a*;
12:11 Indeed their *a* shall be
Am 3:14 visit destruction on the *a* of
Rom 11: 3 and torn down Your *a*,

ALTER (4/4) ALTERED, ALTERNATING, ALTERS

Ezra 6:12 people who put their hand to *a*
Ps 89:34 Nor *a* the word that has gone
Dan 6: 8 and Persians, which does not *a*.
6:12 and Persians, which does not *a*.

ALTERED (2/2) ALTER

Esth 1:19 Medes, so that it will not be *a*,
Lk 9:29 appearance of His face was *a*,

ALTERNATING (1/1)

Neh 12:24 group *a* with group, according

ALTERS (1/1) ALTER

Ezra 6:11 I issue a decree that whoever *a*

ALTHOUGH (37/36)

Gen 8:21 *a* the imagination of man's
31:37 *A* you have searched all my
31:50 *a* no man is with us—see, God
Ex 13:17 *a* that was near; for God said,
Num 5:14 *a* she has not defiled herself—
11:25 *a* they never did so again.
Josh 17:18 *A* it is wooded, you shall cut
22:17 *a* there was a plague in the
Judg 19:19 *a* we have both straw and fodder
1 Sam 1: 5 *a* the LORD had closed her
2 Sam 23: 5 *A* my house is not so with God,
1 Chr 5: 2 *a* the birthright was Joseph's—
2 Chr 27: 2 his father Uzziah had done (*a*
Ezra 3: 6 *a* the foundation of the temple
Esth 7: 4 *a* the enemy could never
Job 2: 3 *a* you incited Me against him,
10: 7 *A* You know that I am not
16:17 *A* no violence is in my hands,
35:14 *A* you say you do not see Him,
Eccl 4:14 *A* he was born poor in his
Isa 35: 8 *a* a fool, Shall not go astray.
Jer 35:14 But *a* I have spoken to you,
Ezek 11:16 *A* I have cast them far off among
11:16 and *a* I have scattered them
23:11 Now *a* her sister Oholibah saw
35:10 *a* the LORD was there,
Dan 5:22 *a* you knew all this.
12: 8 *A* I heard, I did not understand.
Mt 14: 5 And *a* he wanted to put him to
Jn 12:37 But *a* He had done so many signs

21:11 and *a* there were so many, the
Rom 1:21 *a* they knew God, they did not
2:14 *a* not having the law, are a law
2 Cor 7:12 *a* I wrote to you, I did not
1 Tim 1:13 *a* I was formerly a blasphemer, a
Heb 4: 3 *a* the works were finished from
Jas 3: 4 *a* they are so large and are

ALTOGETHER (19/19)

Gen 18:21 see whether they have done *a*
Ex 11: 1 surely drive you out of here *a*.
Deut 16:20 You shall follow what is *a* just,
Neh 7:66 *A* the whole assembly was
Ps 19: 9 are true and righteous *a*.
50:21 You thought that I was *a* like
62: 9 They are *a* lighter than
74: 8 "Let us destroy them *a*.
88:17 like water; They engulfed me *a*.
139: 4 behold, O LORD, You know it *a*.
Song 5:16 he is *a* lovely. This is my
Isa 10: 8 Are not my princes *a* kings?
Jer 5: 5 But these have *a* broken the
10: 8 But they are *a* dull-hearted and
30:11 And will not let you go *a*
49:12 are you the one who will *a* go
Acts 1:15 the midst of the disciples (*a*
26:29 might become both almost and *a*
1 Cor 9:10 Or does He say it *a* for our

ALUSH (2/2)

Num 33:13 from Dophkah and camped at *A*.
33:14 They moved from *A* and camped at

ALVAH (1/1) ALIAH

Gen 36:40 names: Chief Timnah, Chief *A*,

ALVAN (1/1) ALIAH, ALIAN

Gen 36:23 were the sons of Shobal: *A*,

ALWAYS (94/89)

Ex 25:30 on the table before Me *a*.
28:38 and it shall *a* be on his
Lev 6:13 A fire shall *a* be burning on the
Num 9:16 So it was *a*: the cloud covered
Deut 5:29 that they would fear Me and *a*
6:24 LORD our God, for our good *a*,
11: 1 and His commandments *a*.
11:12 of the LORD your God are *a*
14:23 to fear the LORD your God *a*.
19: 9 LORD your God and to walk *a*
1 Sam 7:17 But he *a* returned to Ramah, for
2 Sam 9:10 shall eat bread at my table *a*.
1 Ki 5: 1 for Hiram had *a* loved David.
11:36 that My servant David may *a*
2 Chr 18: 7 but *a* evil. He is Micaiah the
Job 27:10 Will he *a* call on God?
32: 9 Great men are not *a* wise, Nor
32: 9 Nor do the aged *a* understand
Ps 9:18 For the needy shall not *a* be
10: 5 His ways are *a* prospering;
16: 8 I have set the LORD *a* before
51: 3 And my sin is *a* before me.
73:12 Who are *a* at ease; They
103: 9 He will not *a* strive with us,
Prov 5:19 And *a* be enraptured with her
8:30 Rejoicing *a* before Him,
28:14 Happy is the man who is *a*
Eccl 9: 8 Let your garments *a* be white,
Isa 57:16 Nor will I *a* be angry; For
Jer 20:17 And her womb *a* enlarged with
Mt 18:10 that in heaven their angels *a*
26:11 you have the poor with you *a*,
26:11 but Me you do not have *a*.
28:20 you; and lo, I am with you *a*,
Mk 5: 5 And *a*, night and day, he was
14: 7 you have the poor with you *a*,
14: 7 good; but Me you do not have *a*.
15: 8 him to do just as he had *a*
Lk 15:31 you are *a* with me, and all that
18: 1 that men *a* ought to pray and
21:36 and pray *a* that you may be
Jn 6:34 "Lord, give us this bread *a*.
7: 6 but your time is *a* ready.
8:29 for I *a* do those things that
11:42 And I know that You *a* hear Me,
12: 8 the poor you have with you *a*,
12: 8 but Me you do not have *a*.
18:20 I *a* taught in synagogues and in
18:20 where the Jews *a* meet, and in
Acts 2:25 I foresaw the LORD *a*
7:51 in heart and ears! You *a*
10: 2 the people, and prayed to God *a*.
20:18 in what manner I *a* lived among
24: 3 we accept it *a* and in all
24:16 I myself *a* strive to have a
Rom 1: 9 I make mention of you *a* in my
11:10 and bow down their back *a*.
1 Cor 1: 4 I thank my God *a* concerning you
15:58 *a* abounding in the work of the
2 Cor 2:14 Now thanks be to God who *a*
4:10 *a* carrying about in the body the
4:11 For we who live are *a* delivered
5: 6 So we are *a* confident, knowing
6:10 yet *a* rejoicing; as poor, yet
9: 8 *a* having all sufficiency in all
Gal 4:18 to be zealous in a good thing *a*,
Eph 5:20 giving thanks *a* for all things
6:18 praying *a* with all prayer and
Phil 1: 4 *a* in every prayer of mine making
1:20 but with all boldness, as *a*,
2:12 as you have *a* obeyed, not as in
4: 4 Rejoice in the Lord *a*.
Col 1: 3 praying *a* for you,
4: 6 Let your speech *a* be with
4:12 *a* laboring fervently for you in
1 Th 1: 2 We give thanks to God *a* for you
2:16 so as *a* to fill up the
3: 6 and that you *a* have good
4:17 And thus we shall *a* be with the
5:15 but *a* pursue what is good both
5:16 Rejoice *a*,
2 Th 1: 3 We are bound to thank God *a* for
1:11 Therefore we also pray *a* for you
2:13 bound to give thanks to God *a*
3:16 peace Himself give you peace *a*
2 Tim 3: 7 *a* learning and never able to
Titus 1:12 Cretans are *a* liars, evil
Phm 1: 4 making mention of you *a* in my
Heb 3:10 They *a* go astray in their
7:25 since He *a* lives to make
9: 6 the priests *a* went into the
1 Pe 3:15 and *a* be ready to give a
2 Pe 1:12 be negligent to remind you *a*
1:15 be careful to ensure that you *a*

AM (909/835) See APPENDIX

AMAD (1/1)

Josh 19:26 Alammelech, *A*, and Mishal;

AMAL (1/1)

1 Chr 7:35 Zophah, Imna, Shelesh, and *A*.

AMALEK (25/24) AMALEKITE

Gen 36:12 and she bore *A* to Eliphaz.
36:16 Chief Gatam, and Chief *A*.
Ex 17: 8 Now *A* came and fought with
17: 9 men and go out, fight with *A*.
17:10 said to him, and fought with *A*.
17:11 let down his hand, *A* prevailed.
17:13 So Joshua defeated *A* and his
17:14 blot out the remembrance of *A*
17:16 LORD will have war with *A*
Num 24:20 Then he looked on *A*,
24:20 *A* was first among the nations,
24:24 afflict Eber, And so shall *A*,
Deut 25:17 Remember what *A* did to you on
25:19 blot out the remembrance of *A*
Judg 3:13 the people of Ammon and *A*,
5:14 those whose roots were in *A*.
1 Sam 15: 2 I will punish *A* for what he did
15: 3 'Now go and attack *A*,
15: 5 And Saul came to a city of *A*,
15:20 and brought back Agag king of *A*;
28:18 execute His fierce wrath upon *A*,
2 Sam 8:12 from the Philistines, from *A*,
1 Chr 1:36 and Kenaz; and by Timna, *A*.
18:11 the Philistines, and from *A*.
Ps 83: 7 Gebal, Ammon, and *A*;

AMALEKITE (3/3) AMALEK, AMALEKITES

1 Sam 30:13 man from Egypt, servant of an *A*;
2 Sam 1: 8 So I answered him, 'I am an *A*.
1:13 am the son of an alien, an *A*.

AMALEKITES (24/23) AMALEKITE

Gen 14: 7 all the country of the *A*,
Num 13:29 The *A* dwell in the land of the
14:25 Now the *A* and the Canaanites
14:43 For the *A* and the Canaanites
14:45 Then the *A* and the Canaanites
Judg 6: 3 also *A* and the people of the
6:33 Then all the Midianites and *A*,
7:12 Now the Midianites and *A*,
10:12 Also the Sidonians and *A* and
12:15 in the mountains of the *A*.
1 Sam 14:48 an army and attacked the *A*,
15: 6 get down from among the *A*,
15: 6 departed from among the *A*.
15: 7 And Saul attacked the *A*,
15: 8 He also took Agag king of the *A*
15:15 have brought them from the *A*;
15:18 destroy the sinners, the *A*,
15:20 I have utterly destroyed the *A*.
15:32 Bring Agag king of the *A* here to
27: 8 the Girzites, and the *A*.
30: 1 that the *A* had invaded the
30:18 David recovered all that the *A*
2 Sam 1: 1 from the slaughter of the *A*,
1 Chr 4:43 defeated the rest of the *A* who

AMAM (1/1)

Josh 15:26 *A*, Shema, Moladah,

AMANA (1/1)

Song 4: 8 Look from the top of *A*,

AMARIAH (16/14)

1 Chr 6: 7 Meraioth begot *A*,
6: 7 and *A* begot Ahitub;
6:11 Azariah begot *A*,
6:11 and *A* begot Ahitub;
6:52 *A* his son, Ahitub his son,
23:19 *A* the second, Jahaziel the
24:23 *A* the second, Jahaziel the
2 Chr 19:11 *A* the chief priest is over you
31:15 Miniamin, Jeshua, Shemaiah, *A*,
Ezra 7: 3 the son of *A*,
10:42 Shallum, *A*, and Joseph;
Neh 10: 3 Pashhur, *A*, Malchijah,
11: 4 son of Zechariah, the son of *A*,
12: 2 *A*, Malluch, Hattush,
12:13 of Ezra, Meshullam; of *A*,
Zeph 1: 1 son of Gedaliah, the son of *A*,

AMASA (17/13)

2 Sam 17:25 And Absalom made *A* captain of
17:25 This *A* was the son of a man
19:13 'And say to *A*, 'Are you not my
20: 4 And the king said to *A*,
20: 5 So *A* went to assemble the men
20: 8 *A* came before them. Now Joab
20: 9 Then Joab said to *A*,
20: 9 And Joab took *A* by the beard
20:10 But *A* did not notice the sword
20:11 one of Joab's men stood near *A*,
20:12 But *A* wallowed in his blood in
20:12 he moved *A* from the highway to
1 Ki 2: 5 to Abner the son of Ner and *A*
2:32 and *A* the son of Jether, the
1 Chr 2:17 Abigail bore *A*;
2:17 and the father of *A* was Jether
2 Chr 28:12 and *A* the son of Hadlai, stood

AMASAI (5/5)

1 Chr 6:25 The sons of Elkanah were *A* and
6:35 the son of Mahath, the son of *A*,
12:18 Then the Spirit came upon *A*,
15:24 Joshaphat, Nethanel, *A*,
2 Chr 29:12 Mahath the son of *A* and Joel

AMASHAI (1/1)

Neh 11:13 and *A* the son of Azarel, the

AMASIAH (1/1)

2 Chr 17:16 and next to him was *A* the son

AMAZED (17/17) AMAZEMENT

Isa 13: 8 They will be *a* at one another;
Mt 12:23 And all the multitudes were *a*
Mk 1:27 Then they were all *a*,
2:12 so that all were *a* and
6:51 And they were greatly *a* in
9:15 all the people were greatly *a*,
10:32 before them; and they were *a*.
16: 8 for they trembled and were *a*.
Lk 2:48 when they saw Him, they were *a*;
4:36 Then they were all *a* and spoke
5:26 And they were all *a*,
9:43 And they were all *a* at the
Acts 2: 7 Then they were all *a* and
2:12 So they were all *a* and
3:11 is called Solomon's, greatly *a*.
8:13 with Philip, and was *a*,
9:21 Then all who heard were *a*,

AMAZEMENT (3/3) AMAZED

Mk 5:42 they were overcome with great *a*.
Acts 3:10 were filled with wonder and *a*
Rev 17: 6 her, I marveled with great *a*.

AMAZIAH (40/39)

2 Ki 12:21 Then *A* his son reigned in his
13:12 with which he fought against *A*
14: 1 *A* the son of Joash, king of
14: 8 Then *A* sent messengers to
14: 9 king of Israel sent to *A* king
14:11 But *A* would not heed.
14:11 so he and *A* king of Judah faced
14:13 king of Israel captured *A* king
14:15 and how he fought with *A* king
14:17 *A* the son of Joash, king of
14:18 Now the rest of the acts of *A*,
14:21 king instead of his father *A*.
14:23 In the fifteenth year of *A* the
15: 1 of Israel, Azariah the son of *A*,
15: 3 to all that his father *A* had
1 Chr 3:12 *A* his son, Azariah his son,
4:34 and Joshah the son of *A*;
6:45 son of Hashabiah, the son of *A*,
2 Chr 24:27 Then *A* his son reigned in his
25: 1 *A* was twenty-five years old
25: 5 Moreover *A* gathered Judah
25: 9 Then *A* said to the man of God,
25:10 So *A* discharged the troops that
25:11 Then *A* strengthened himself,
25:13 soldiers of the army which *A*
25:14 after *A* came from the slaughter
25:15 the LORD was aroused against *A*,
25:17 Now *A* king of Judah asked
25:18 Joash king of Israel sent to *A*
25:20 But *A* would not heed, for it
25:21 and he and *A* king of Judah
25:23 the king of Israel captured *A*
25:25 *A* the son of Joash, king of
25:26 Now the rest of the acts of *A*,
25:27 After the time that *A* turned
26: 1 king instead of his father *A*.

26: 4 to all that his father *A* had
Am 7:10 Then *A* the priest of Bethel
7:12 Then *A* said to Amos: "Go, you
7:14 Amos answered, and said to *A*:

AMBASSADOR (3/3) AMBASSADORS

Prov 13:17 But a faithful *a* brings
Jer 49:14 And an *a* has been sent to the
Eph 6:20 for which I am an *a* in chains;

AMBASSADORS (7/7) AMBASSADOR

Josh 9: 4 and went and pretended to be *a*.
2 Chr 32:31 regarding the *a* of the princes
Isa 18: 2 Which sends *a* by sea, Even in
30: 4 And his *a* came to Hanes.
33: 7 The *a* of peace shall weep
Ezek 17:15 against him by sending his *a*
2 Cor 5:20 we are *a* for Christ, as though

AMBASSAGE (KJV) See DELEGATION

AMBER (3/3)

Ezek 1: 4 its midst like the color of *a*,
1:27 the color of *a* with the
8: 2 brightness, like the color of *a*.

AMBITION (2/2) AMBITIONS

Phil 1:16 preach Christ from selfish *a*,
2: 3 be done through selfish *a* or

AMBITIONS (2/2) AMBITION

2 Cor 12:20 outbursts of wrath, selfish *a*,
Gal 5:20 outbursts of wrath, selfish *a*,

AMBUSH (21/19) AMBUSHED, AMBUSHES

Josh 8: 2 Lay an *a* for the city behind
8: 4 you shall lie in *a* against the
8: 7 you shall rise from the *a*
8: 9 out; and they went to lie in *a*,
8:12 thousand men and set them in *a*
8:14 not know that there was an *a*
8:19 So those in *a* arose quickly
8:21 and all Israel saw that the *a*
Judg 9:25 the men of Shechem set men in *a*
20:29 Then Israel set men in *a* all
20:33 Then Israel's men in *a* burst
20:36 they relied on the men in *a*
20:37 And the men in *a* quickly rushed
20:37 the men in *a* spread out and
20:38 men of Israel and the men in *a*
2 Chr 13:13 But Jeroboam caused an *a* to go
13:13 and the *a* was behind them.
Ezra 8:31 hand of the enemy and from *a*
Lam 3:10 in wait, Like a lion in *a*.
Acts 23:16 sister's son heard of their *a*,
25: 3 while they lay in *a* along the

AMBUSHED (1/1) AMBUSH

1 Sam 15: 2 how he *a* him on the way when he

AMBUSHES (2/2) AMBUSH

2 Chr 20:22 the LORD set *a* against the
Jer 51:12 up the watchmen, Prepare the *a*.

AMEN (77/72)

Num 5:22 Then the woman shall say, "*A*,
Deut 27:15 answer and say, '*A*!'
27:16 people shall say, '*A*!'
27:17 people shall say, '*A*!'
27:18 people shall say, '*A*!'
27:19 people shall say, '*A*!'
27:20 people shall say, '*A*!'
27:21 people shall say, '*A*!'
27:22 people shall say, '*A*!'
27:23 people shall say, '*A*!'
27:24 people shall say, '*A*!'
27:25 people shall say, '*A*!'
27:26 people shall say, '*A*!'
1 Ki 1:36 *A*! May the LORD God of my lord
1 Chr 16:36 *A*!" and praised the LORD.
Neh 5:13 '*A*!" and praised the LORD.
8: 6 people answered, "*A*, Amen!"
8: 6 *A*!" while lifting up their
Ps 41:13 everlasting to everlasting! *A*
41:13 to everlasting! Amen and *A*.
72:19 with His glory. *A* and Amen.
72:19 with His glory. Amen and *A*.
89:52 be the LORD forevermore! *A*
89:52 LORD forevermore! Amen and *A*.
106:48 *A*!" Praise the LORD!
Jer 28: 6 *A*! The LORD do so; the LORD
Mt 6:13 power and the glory forever. *A*.
28:20 to the end of the age." *A*.
Mk 16:20 the accompanying signs. *A*.
Lk 24:53 praising and blessing God. *A*.
Jn 21:25 books that would be written. *A*.
Rom 1:25 who is blessed forever. *A*.
9: 5 the eternally blessed God. *A*.
11:36 to whom be glory forever. *A*.
15:33 of peace be with you all. *A*.
16:20 Jesus Christ be with you. *A*.
16:24 Christ be with you all. *A*.
16:27 through Jesus Christ forever. *A*.
1 Cor 14:16 *A*" at your giving of thanks,
16:24 with you all in Christ Jesus. *A*.
2 Cor 1:20 in Him are Yes, and in Him *A*,
13:14 Holy Spirit be with you all. *A*.
Gal 1: 5 be glory forever and ever. *A*.
6:18 Christ be with your spirit. *A*.
Eph 3:21 forever and ever. *A*.
6:24 Jesus Christ in sincerity. *A*.
Phil 4:20 be glory forever and ever. *A*.
4:23 Jesus Christ be with you all. *A*.
Col 4:18 Grace be with you. *A*.
1 Th 5:28 Jesus Christ be with you. *A*.
2 Th 3:18 Christ be with you all. *A*.
1 Tim 1:17 and glory forever and ever. *A*.
6:16 honor and everlasting power. *A*.
6:21 Grace be with you. *A*.
2 Tim 4:18 glory forever and ever. *A*!
4:22 Grace be with you. *A*.
Titus 3:15 Grace be with you all. *A*.
Phm 1:25 Christ be with your spirit. *A*.
Heb 13:21 be glory forever and ever. *A*.
13:25 Grace be with you all. *A*.
1 Pe 4:11 dominion forever and ever. *A*.
5:11 dominion forever and ever. *A*.
5:14 all who are in Christ Jesus. *A*.
2 Pe 3:18 glory both now and forever. *A*.
1 Jn 5:21 keep yourselves from idols. *A*.
2 Jn 13 your elect sister greet you. *A*.
Jude 25 Both now and forever. *A*.
Rev 1: 6 dominion forever and ever. *A*.
1: 7 because of Him. Even so, *A*.
1:18 I am alive forevermore. *A*.
3:14 'These things says the *A*,
5:14 *A*!" And the twenty-four elders
7:12 *A*! Blessing and glory and
7:12 to our God forever and ever. *A*.
19: 4 saying, "*A*! Alleluia!"
22:20 I am coming quickly." *A*.
22:21 Christ be with you all. *A*.

AMEND (4/4)

Jer 7: 3 *A* your ways and your doings, and
7: 5 For if you thoroughly *a* your
26:13 *a* your ways and your doings,
35:15 *a* your doings, and do not go

AMERCE (KJV) See FINE

AMETHYST (3/3)

Ex 28:19 a jacinth, an agate, and an *a*;
39:12 a jacinth, an agate, and an *a*;
Rev 21:20 jacinth, and the twelfth *a*.

AMI (1/1)

Ezra 2:57 of Zebaim, and the sons of *A*.

AMIABLE (KJV) See LOVELY

AMID (2/2)

Ezek 19:11 And was seen in her height *a*
Am 1:14 *A* shouting in the day of

AMINADAB (KJV) See AMMINIDAB

AMISS (3/3)

Job 5:24 dwelling and find nothing *a*.
Dan 3:29 which speaks anything *a*
Jas 4: 3 not receive, because you ask *a*,

AMITTAI (2/2)

2 Ki 14:25 His servant Jonah the son of *A*,
Jon 1: 1 came to Jonah the son of *A*,

AMMAH (1/1)

2 Sam 2:24 when they came to the hill of *A*,

AMMI (KJV) See (MY) PEOPLE

AMMIEL (6/6) ELIAM

Num 13:12 *A* the son of Gemalli;
2 Sam 9: 4 house of Machir the son of *A*,
9: 5 house of Machir the son of *A*,
17:27 Machir the son of *A* from Lo
1 Chr 3: 5 by Bathshua the daughter of *A*.
26: 5 *A* the sixth, Issachar the

AMMIHUD (10/10)

Num 1:10 Ephraim, Elishama the son of *A*;
2:18 be Elishama the son of *A*.
7:48 day Elishama the son of *A*,
7:53 of Elishama the son of *A*.
10:22 army was Elishama the son of *A*.
34:20 of Simeon, Shemuel the son of *A*;
34:28 Naphtali, Pedahel the son of *A*.
2 Sam 13:37 and went to Talmai the son of *A*,
1 Chr 7:26 *A* his son, Elishama his son,
9: 4 Uthai the son of *A*,

AMMINADAB (16/14)

Ex 6:23 himself Elisheba, daughter of *A*,
Num 1: 7 Judah, Nahshon the son of *A*;
2: 3 and Nahshon the son of *A* shall
7:12 day was Nahshon the son of *A*,
7:17 of Nahshon the son of *A*.
10:14 army was Nahshon the son of *A*.
Ruth 4:19 begot Ram, and Ram begot *A*;
4:20 *A* begot Nahshon, and Nahshon
1 Chr 2:10 Ram begot *A*,
2:10 and *A* begot Nahshon, leader of
6:22 The sons of Kohath were *A* his
15:10 *A* the chief, and one hundred
15:11 Joel, Shemaiah, Eliel, and *A*.
Mt 1: 4 Ram begot *A*,
1: 4 *A* begot Nahshon, and Nahshon
Lk 3:33 the son of *A*,

AMMINADIB (KJV) See (MY NOBLE) PEOPLE

AMMISHADDAI (5/5)

Num 1:12 Dan, Ahiezer the son of *A*;
2:25 shall be Ahiezer the son of *A*.
7:66 tenth day Ahiezer the son of *A*,
7:71 of Ahiezer the son of *A*.
10:25 army was Ahiezer the son of *A*.

AMMIZABAD (1/1)

1 Chr 27: 6 in his division was *A* his son.

AMMON (89/83) AMMONITE, AMMONITES, AMMONITESS

Gen 19:38 the father of the people of *A*
Num 21:24 as far as the people of *A*;
21:24 the border of the people of *A*
Deut 2:19 you come near the people of *A*,
2:19 of the land of the people of *A*
2:37 the land of the people of *A*—
3:11 in Rabbah of the people of *A*?
3:16 the border of the people of *A*;
Josh 13:10 the border of the children of *A*;
Judg 3:13 to himself the people of *A* and
10: 6 the gods of the people of *A*,
10: 7 the hands of the people of *A*.
10: 9 Moreover the people of *A* crossed
10:11 and from the people of *A* and
10:17 Then the people of *A* gathered
10:18 fight against the people of *A*?
11: 4 a time that the people of *A*
11: 5 when the people of *A* made war
11: 6 fight against the people of *A*.
11: 8 fight against the people of *A*,
11: 9 fight against the people of *A*,
11:12 to the king of the people of *A*,
11:13 And the king of the people of *A*
11:14 to the king of the people of *A*,
11:15 nor the land of the people of *A*;
11:27 of Israel and the people of *A*.
11:28 the king of the people of *A* did
11:29 toward the people of *A*.
11:30 indeed deliver the people of *A*
11:31 in peace from the people of *A*,
11:32 toward the people of *A* to
11:33 Thus the people of *A* were
11:36 your enemies, the people of *A*.
12: 1 fight against the people of *A*,
12: 2 struggle with the people of *A*;
12: 3 over against the people of *A*;
1 Sam 14:47 Moab, against the people of *A*,
2 Sam 8:12 from Moab, from the people of *A*,
10: 1 the king of the people of *A*
10: 2 the land of the people of *A*.
10: 3 the princes of the people of *A*
10: 6 When the people of *A* saw that
10: 6 the people of *A* sent and hired
10: 8 Then the people of *A* came out
10:10 array against the people of *A*.
10:11 but if the people of *A* are too
10:14 When the people of *A* saw that
10:14 returned from the people of *A*
10:19 afraid to help the people of *A*
11: 1 they destroyed the people of *A*
12: 9 the sword of the people of *A*.
12:26 Rabbah of the people of *A*,
12:31 the cities of the people of *A*.
17:27 from Rabbah of the people of *A*,
1 Ki 11: 7 abomination of the people of *A*.
11:33 the god of the people of *A*,
2 Ki 23:13 abomination of the people of *A*.
24: 2 and bands of the people of *A*;
1 Chr 18:11 from Moab, from the people of *A*,
19: 1 the king of the people of *A*
19: 2 in the land of the people of *A*
19: 3 the princes of the people of *A*
19: 6 When the people of *A* saw that
19: 6 Hanun and the people of *A* sent
19: 7 Also the people of *A* gathered
19: 9 Then the people of *A* came out
19:11 array against the people of *A*.
19:12 but if the people of *A* are too
19:15 When the people of *A* saw that
19:19 willing to help the people of *A*
20: 1 the country of the people of *A*,
20: 3 the cities of the people of *A*.
2 Chr 20: 1 of Moab with the people of *A*,
20:10 now, here are the people of *A*,
20:22 against the people of *A*,
20:23 For the people of *A* and Moab
27: 5 And the people of *A* gave him in
27: 5 The people of *A* paid this to
Neh 13:23 had married women of Ashdod, *A*,
Ps 83: 7 Gebal, *A*, and Amalek;

Isa 11:14 And the people of *A* shall obey
Jer 9:26 Judah, Edom, the people of *A*,
25:21 Edom, Moab, and the people of *A*;
49: 6 captives of the people of *A*,
Ezek 25: 5 a stable for camels and *A* a
Dan 11:41 and the prominent people of *A*.
Am 1:13 of the people of *A*,
Zeph 2: 8 the insults of the people of *A*,
2: 9 And the people of *A* like

AMMONITE (9/9) AMMON, AMMONITES

Deut 23: 3 An *A* or Moabite shall not enter
1 Sam 11: 1 Then Nahash the *A* came up and
11: 2 And Nahash the *A* answered them,
2 Sam 23:37 Zelek the *A*,
1 Chr 11:39 Zelek the *A*,
Neh 2:10 the Horonite and Tobiah the *A*
2:19 Tobiah the *A* official, and
4: 3 Now Tobiah the *A* was beside
13: 1 it was found written that no *A*

AMMONITES (25/24) AMMONITE

Deut 2:20 But the *A* call them Zamzummim,
Josh 12: 2 which is the border of the *A*,
13:25 and half the land of the *A* as
1 Sam 11:11 and killed *A* until the heat of
12:12 saw that Nahash king of the *A*
1 Ki 11: 1 women of the Moabites, *A*,
11: 5 Milcom the abomination of the *A*.
2 Chr 20: 1 others with them besides the *A*,
26: 8 Also the *A* brought tribute to
27: 5 fought with the king of the *A*
Ezra 9: 1 the Jebusites, the *A*,
Neh 4: 7 Tobiah, the Arabs, the *A*,
Jer 27: 3 king of Moab, the king of the *A*,
40:11 who were in Moab, among the *A*,
40:14 that Baalis the king of the *A*
41:10 departed to go over to the *A*.
41:15 eight men and went to the *A*.
49: 1 Against the *A*.
49: 2 of war In Rabbah of the *A*;
Ezek 21:20 sword to go to Rabbah of the *A*,
21:28 the Lord GOD concerning the *A*
25: 2 set your face against the *A*,
25: 3 "Say to the *A*,
25:10 possession, together with the *A*,
25:10 that the *A* may not be

AMMONITESS (4/4) AMMON

1 Ki 14:21 mother's name was Naamah, an *A*.
14:31 mother's name was Naamah, an *A*.
2 Chr 12:13 mother's name was Naamah, an *A*.
24:26 Zabad the son of Shimeath the *A*,

AMNON (25/20) AMNON'S

2 Sam 3: 2 His firstborn was *A* by Ahinoam
13: 1 and *A* the son of David loved
13: 2 *A* was so distressed over his
13: 2 And it was improper for *A* to do
13: 3 But *A* had a friend whose name
13: 4 *A* said to him, "I love
13: 6 Then *A* lay down and pretended to
13: 6 *A* said to the king, "Please
13: 9 Then *A* said, "Have everyone go
13:10 Then *A* said to Tamar, "Bring
13:10 and brought them to *A* her
13:15 Then *A* hated her exceedingly,
13:15 And *A* said to her, "Arise, be
13:20 Has *A* your brother been with
13:22 Absalom spoke to his brother *A*
13:22 nor bad. For Absalom hated *A*,
13:26 please let my brother *A* go with
13:27 so he let *A* and all the king's
13:28 Strike *A*!' then kill him. Do not
13:29 servants of Absalom did to *A*
13:32 for only *A* is dead. For by the
13:33 For only *A* is dead."
13:39 had been comforted concerning *A*,
1 Chr 3: 1 in Hebron: The firstborn was *A*,
4:20 And the sons of Shimon were *A*,

AMNON'S (3/3) AMNON

2 Sam 13: 7 Now go to your brother *A* house,
13: 8 So Tamar went to her brother *A*
13:28 when *A* heart is merry with

AMOK (2/2)

Neh 12: 7 Sallu, *A*, Hilkiah,
12:20 of Sallai, Kallai; of *A*,

AMON (21/20)

1 Ki 22:26 and return him to *A* the
2 Ki 21:18 Then his son *A* reigned in his
21:19 *A* was twenty-two years old
21:23 Then the servants of *A*
21:24 had conspired against King *A*.
21:25 Now the rest of the acts of *A*
1 Chr 3:14 *A* his son, and Josiah his son.
2 Chr 18:25 and return him to *A* the
33:20 Then his son *A* reigned in his
33:21 *A* was twenty-two years old
33:22 for *A* sacrificed to all the
33:23 but *A* trespassed more and more.
33:25 had conspired against King *A*.
Neh 7:59 of Zebaim, and the sons of *A*.
Jer 1: 2 the days of Josiah the son of *A*,
25: 3 year of Josiah the son of *A*,
46:25 I will bring punishment on *A* of
Nah 3: 8 Are you better than No *A*
Zeph 1: 1 the days of Josiah the son of *A*,
Mt 1:10 Manasseh, Manasseh begot *A*,
1:10 and *A* begot Josiah.

AMONG (983/902) See APPENDIX

AMORITE (14/14) AMORITES

Gen 10:16 the Jebusite, the *A*,
14:13 terebinth trees of Mamre the *A*,
48:22 I took from the hand of the *A*
Ex 33: 2 out the Canaanite and the *A*
34:11 out from before you the *A* and
Deut 2:24 into your hand Sihon the *A*,
20:17 the Hittite and the *A* and the
Josh 9: 1 Lebanon—the Hittite, the *A*,
11: 3 the east and in the west, the *A*,
1 Chr 1:14 the Jebusite, the *A*,
Ezek 16: 3 your father was an *A* and your
16:45 a Hittite and your father an *A*.
Am 2: 9 it was I who destroyed the *A*
2:10 To possess the land of the *A*.

AMORITES (73/72) AMORITE

Gen 14: 7 and also the *A* who dwelt in
15:16 for the iniquity of the *A* is
15:21 'the *A*, the Canaanites,
Ex 3: 8 and the Hittites and the *A* and
3:17 and the Hittites and the *A* and
13: 5 and the Hittites and the *A* and
23:23 you and bring you in to the *A*
Num 13:29 and the *A* dwell in the
21:13 from the border of the *A*;
21:13 of Moab, between Moab and the *A*.
21:21 to Sihon king of the *A*,
21:25 in all the cities of the *A*,
21:26 the city of Sihon king of the *A*,
21:29 To Sihon king of the *A*.
21:31 dwelt in the land of the *A*.
21:32 villages and drove out the *A*
21:34 you did to Sihon king of the *A*,
22: 2 that Israel had done to the *A*.
32:33 kingdom of Sihon king of the *A*
32:39 and dispossessed the *A* who
Deut 1: 4 had killed Sihon king of the *A*,
1: 7 go to the mountains of the *A*,
1:19 way to the mountains of the *A*,
1:20 come to the mountains of the *A*,
1:27 us into the hand of the *A*,
1:44 And the *A* who dwelt in that
3: 2 you did to Sihon king of the *A*,
3: 8 hand of the two kings of the *A*
3: 9 and the *A* call it Senir),
4:46 the land of Sihon king of the *A*,
4:47 of Bashan, two kings of the *A*,
7: 1 and the Girgashites and the *A*
31: 4 the kings of the *A* and their
Josh 2:10 did to the two kings of the *A*
3:10 and the Girgashites and the *A*
5: 1 when all the kings of the *A* who
7: 7 us into the hand of the *A*,
9:10 did to the two kings of the *A*
10: 5 the five kings of the *A*,
10: 6 for all the kings of the *A* who
10:12 the LORD delivered up the *A*
12: 2 king was Sihon king of the *A*,
12: 8 the South—the Hittites, the *A*,
13: 4 Aphek, to the border of the *A*;
13:10 cities of Sihon king of the *A*,
13:21 kingdom of Sihon king of the *A*,
24: 8 you into the land of the *A*,
24:11 fought against you—also the *A*,
24:12 also the two kings of the *A*,
24:15 the River, or the gods of the *A*,
24:18 including the *A* who dwelt in
Judg 1:34 And the *A* forced the children
1:35 and the *A* were determined to
1:36 Now the boundary of the *A* was
3: 5 Canaanites, the Hittites, the *A*,
6:10 do not fear the gods of the *A*,
10: 8 the Jordan in the land of the *A*,
10:11 the Egyptians and from the *A*
11:19 to Sihon king of the *A*,
11:21 of all the land of the *A*,
11:22 of all the territory of the *A*,
11:23 Israel has dispossessed the *A*
1 Sam 7:14 peace between Israel and the *A*.
2 Sam 21: 2 but of the remnant of the *A*;
1 Ki 4:19 country of Sihon king of the *A*,
9:20 people who were left of the *A*,
21:26 according to all that the *A*
2 Ki 21:11 more wickedly than all the *A*
2 Chr 8: 7 were left of the Hittites, *A*,
Ezra 9: 1 the Egyptians, and the *A*.
Neh 9: 8 The Hittites, the *A*,
Ps 135:11 Sihon king of the *A*,
136:19 Sihon king of the *A*,

AMOS (8/8)

Am 1: 1 The words of *A*,
7: 8 And the LORD said to me, "*A*,
7:10 *A* has conspired against you in
7:11 For thus *A* has said: 'Jeroboam
7:12 Then Amaziah said to *A*:
7:14 Then *A* answered, and said to
8: 2 And He said, "*A*,
Lk 3:25 of Mattathiah, the son of *A*,

AMOUNT (3/3) AMOUNTS

Gen 30:30 it has increased to a great *a*;
2 Sam 8: 8 King David took a large *a* of
1 Chr 18: 8 David brought a large *a* of

AMOUNTS (1/1) AMOUNT

Ex 30:34 there shall be equal *a* of each.

AMOZ (13/13)

2 Ki 19: 2 the prophet, the son of *A*.
19:20 Then Isaiah the son of *A* sent
20: 1 the prophet, the son of *A*,
2 Chr 26:22 the prophet Isaiah the son of *A*
32:20 prophet Isaiah, the son of *A*,
32:32 the prophet, the son of *A*,
Isa 1: 1 vision of Isaiah the son of *A*,
2: 1 word that Isaiah the son of *A*
13: 1 which Isaiah the son of *A* saw.
20: 2 spoke by Isaiah the son of *A*,
37: 2 the prophet, the son of *A*.
37:21 Then Isaiah the son of *A* sent
38: 1 the prophet, the son of *A*,

AMPHIPOLIS (1/1)

Acts 17: 1 when they had passed through *A*

AMPLIAS (1/1)

Rom 16: 8 Greet *A*, my beloved in the Lord.

AMRAM (13/12) AMRAM'S, AMRAMITES, HEMDAN

Ex 6:18 And the sons of Kohath were *A*,
6:20 Now *A* took for himself
6:20 And the years of the life of *A*
Num 3:19 of Kohath by their families: *A*,
26:58 Korathites. And Kohath begot *A*.
26:59 and to *A* she bore Aaron and
1 Chr 6: 2 The sons of Kohath were *A*,
6: 3 The children of *A* were Aaron,
6:18 The sons of Kohath were *A*,
23:12 The sons of Kohath: *A*,
23:13 The sons of *A*:
24:20 sons of Levi: of the sons of *A*,
Ezra 10:34 of the sons of Bani: Maadai, *A*,

AMRAM'S (1/1) AMRAM

Num 26:59 The name of *A* wife was Jochebed

AMRAMITES (2/2) AMRAM

Num 3:27 came the family of the *A*,
1 Chr 26:23 Of the *A*, the Izharites,

AMRAPHEL (2/2)

Gen 14: 1 came to pass in the days of *A*
14: 9 *A* king of Shinar, and Arioch

AMZI (2/2)

1 Chr 6:46 the son of *A*,
Neh 11:12 son of Pelaliah, the son of *A*,

AN (1123/1054) See APPENDIX

ANAB (2/2)

Josh 11:21 from Hebron, from Debir, from *A*,
15:50 *A*, Eshtemoh, Anim,

ANAH (12/10)

Gen 36: 2 Aholibamah the daughter of *A*,
36:14 Esau's wife, the daughter of *A*,
36:18 Esau's wife, the daughter of *A*.
36:20 land: Lotan, Shobal, Zibeon, *A*,
36:24 sons of Zibeon: both Ajah and *A*.
36:24 This was the *A* who found the
36:25 These were the children of *A*:
36:25 Aholibamah the daughter of *A*.
36:29 Shobal, Chief Zibeon, Chief *A*,
1 Chr 1:38 were Lotan, Shobal, Zibeon, *A*,
1:40 sons of Zibeon were Ajah and *A*.
1:41 The son of *A* was Dishon.

ANAHARATH (1/1)

Josh 19:19 Haphraim, Shion, *A*,

ANAIAH (2/2)

Neh 8: 4 stood Mattithiah, Shema, *A*,
10:22 Pelatiah, Hanan, *A*,

ANAK (9/8) ANAKIM

Num 13:22 Talmai, the descendants of *A*,
13:28 we saw the descendants of *A*
13:33 giants (the descendants of *A*
Deut 9: 2 before the descendants of *A*?
Josh 15:13 (Arba was the father of *A*).
15:14 drove out the three sons of *A*
15:14 and Talmai, the children of *A*.
21:11 (Arba was the father of *A*),
Judg 1:20 from there the three sons of *A*.

ANAKIM (9/9) ANAK

Deut 1:28 we have seen the sons of the *A*
2:10 and numerous and tall as the *A*.
2:11 regarded as giants, like the *A*,
2:21 and numerous and tall as the *A*.
9: 2 tall, the descendants of the *A*,
Josh 11:21 Joshua came and cut off the *A*
11:22 None of the *A* were left in the
14:12 you heard in that day how the *A*
14:15 the greatest man among the *A*).

ANAKIMS (KJV) See ANAKIM

ANAMIM (2/2)

Gen 10:13 Mizraim begot Ludim, *A*,
1 Chr 1:11 Mizraim begot Ludim, *A*,

ANAMMELECH (1/1)

2 Ki 17:31 in fire to Adrammelech and *A*,

ANAN (1/1)

Neh 10:26 Ahijah, Hanan, *A*,

ANANI (1/1)

1 Chr 3:24 Akkub, Johanan, Delaiah, and *A*—

ANANIAH (2/2) ANANIAS

Neh 3:23 son of Maaseiah, the son of *A*,
11:32 in Anathoth, Nob, *A*;

ANANIAS (11/10) ANANIAH

Acts 5: 1 But a certain man named *A*,
5: 3 But Peter said, "*A*,
5: 5 Then *A*, hearing these words,
9:10 disciple at Damascus named *A*;
9:10 the Lord said in a vision, "*A*.
9:12 he has seen a man named *A*
9:13 Then *A* answered, "Lord, I have
9:17 And *A* went his way and entered
22:12 a certain *A*, a devout man
23: 2 And the high priest *A* commanded
24: 1 Now after five days *A* the high

ANATH (2/2)

Judg 3:31 him was Shamgar the son of *A*,
5: 6 the days of Shamgar, son of *A*,

ANATHEMA (KJV) See ACCURSED

ANATHOTH (16/16) ANATHOTHITE

Josh 21:18 *A* with its common-land, and
1 Ki 2:26 priest the king said, "Go to *A*,
1 Chr 6:60 and *A* with its common-lands.
7: 8 Omri, Jerimoth, Abijah, *A*,
Ezra 2:23 the men of *A*,
Neh 7:27 the men of *A*,
10:19 Hariph, *A*, Nebai,
11:32 in *A*, Nob, Ananiah;
Isa 10:30 as far as Laish—O poor *A*!
Jer 1: 1 of the priests who were in *A*
11:21 LORD concerning the men of *A*
11:23 catastrophe on the men of *A*,
29:27 you not reproved Jeremiah of *A*
32: 7 "Buy my field which is in *A*,
32: 8 buy my field that is in *A*,
32: 9 son of my uncle who was in *A*,

ANATHOTHITE (4/4) ANATHOTH

2 Sam 23:27 Abiezer the *A*,
1 Chr 11:28 the Tekoite, Abiezer the *A*,
12: 3 Berachah, and Jehu the *A*;
27:12 ninth month was Abiezer the *A*,

ANCESTORS (2/2) ANCESTRY

Gen 49:26 excelled the blessings of my ***a***,
Lev 26:45 the covenant of their ***a***,

ANCESTRY (1/1) ANCESTORS

Num 1:18 and they recited their ***a*** by

ANCHOR (1/1) ANCHORED, ANCHORS

Heb 6:19 This hope we have as an ***a*** of

ANCHORED (1/1) ANCHOR

Mk 6:53 to the land of Gennesaret and ***a***

ANCHORS (3/3) ANCHOR

Acts 27:29 they dropped four ***a*** from the
27:30 pretense of putting out ***a*** from
27:40 And they let go the ***a*** and left

ANCIENT (23/23) ANCIENTS

Deut 33:15 With the best things of the ***a***
Judg 5:21 That ***a*** torrent, the torrent of
2 Ki 19:25 From ***a*** times that I formed it?
1 Chr 4:22 Now the records are ***a***.
Ps 77: 5 The years of ***a*** times.
Prov 22:28 Do not remove the ***a*** landmark
23:10 Do not remove the ***a*** landmark,
Eccl 1:10 It has already been in ***a*** times
Isa 19:11 The son of ***a*** kings?"
23: 7 Whose antiquity is from ***a***
37:26 From ***a*** times that I formed it?
44: 7 Since I appointed the ***a***
45:21 Who has declared this from ***a***
46:10 And from ***a*** times things that
51: 9 the LORD! Awake as in the ***a***
Jer 5:15 It is an ***a*** nation, A nation
18:15 From the ***a*** paths, To walk in
Ezek 35: 5 Because you have had an ***a***
36: 2 Aha! The ***a*** heights have become
Dan 7: 9 And the *A* of Days was seated;
7:13 of heaven! He came to the *A*
7:22 until the *A* of Days came, and a
2 Pe 2: 5 and did not spare the ***a*** world,

ANCIENTS (2/2) ANCIENT

1 Sam 24:13 As the proverb of the ***a*** says,
Ps 119:100 I understand more than the ***a***,

ANCLE (KJV) See ANKLE

AND (38260/21831) See APPENDIX

ANDREW (13/12)

Mt 4:18 and *A* his brother, casting a
10: 2 and *A* his brother; James the
Mk 1:16 He saw Simon and *A* his brother
1:29 the house of Simon and *A*,
3:18 *A*, Philip, Bartholomew,
13: 3 and *A* asked Him privately,
Lk 6:14 and *A* his brother; James and
Jn 1:40 speak, and followed Him, was *A*,
1:44 the city of *A* and Peter.
6: 8 One of His disciples, *A*,
12:22 Philip came and told *A*,
12:22 and in turn *A* and Philip told
Acts 1:13 Peter, James, John, and *A*;

ANDRONICUS (1/1)

Rom 16: 7 Greet *A* and Junia, my countrymen

ANEM (1/1)

1 Chr 6:73 and *A* with its common-lands.

ANER (3/3)

Gen 14:13 of Eshcol and brother of *A*;
14:24 of the men who went with me: *A*,
1 Chr 6:70 *A* with its common-lands and

ANETHOTHITE, ANETOTHITE (KJV) See ANATHOTHITE

ANGEL (199/190) ANGEL'S, ANGELS, ANGELS'

Gen 16: 7 Now the *A* of the LORD found
16: 9 The *A* of the LORD said to her,
16:10 Then the *A* of the LORD said to
16:11 And the *A* of the LORD said to
21:17 Then the ***a*** of God called to
22:11 But the *A* of the LORD called to
22:15 Then the *A* of the LORD called
24: 7 He will send His ***a*** before you,
24:40 will send His ***a*** with you and
31:11 Then the *A* of God spoke to me in
48:16 The *A* who has redeemed me from
Ex 3: 2 And the *A* of the LORD appeared
14:19 And the *A* of God, who went
23:20 I send an *A* before you to keep
23:23 For My *A* will go before you and
32:34 My *A* shall go before you.
33: 2 And I will send My *A* before
Num 20:16 heard our voice and sent the *A*
22:22 and the *A* of the LORD took His
22:23 Now the donkey saw the *A* of the
22:24 Then the *A* of the LORD stood in
22:25 And when the donkey saw the *A* of
22:26 Then the *A* of the LORD went
22:27 And when the donkey saw the *A* of
22:31 and he saw the *A* of the LORD
22:32 And the *A* of the LORD said to
22:34 And Balaam said to the *A* of the
22:35 Then the *A* of the LORD said to
Judg 2: 1 Then the *A* of the LORD came up
2: 4 when the *A* of the LORD spoke
5:23 said the ***a*** of the LORD,
6:11 Now the *A* of the LORD came and
6:12 And the *A* of the LORD appeared
6:20 The *A* of God said to him, "Take
6:21 Then the *A* of the LORD put out
6:21 And the *A* of the LORD departed
6:22 perceived that He was the *A*
6:22 GOD! For I have seen the *A* of
13: 3 And the *A* of the LORD appeared
13: 6 like the countenance of the *A*
13: 9 and the *A* of God came to the
13:13 So the *A* of the LORD said to
13:15 Then Manoah said to the *A* of
13:16 And the *A* of the LORD said to
13:16 did not know He was the *A* of
13:17 Then Manoah said to the *A* of the
13:18 And the *A* of the LORD said to
13:20 the *A* of the LORD ascended in
13:21 When the *A* of the LORD appeared
13:21 Manoah knew that He was the *A*
1 Sam 29: 9 as good in my sight as an ***a*** of
2 Sam 14:17 for as the ***a*** of God, so is my
14:20 to the wisdom of the ***a*** of God,
19:27 my lord the king is like the ***a***
24:16 And when the ***a*** stretched out His
24:16 and said to the ***a*** who was
24:16 And the ***a*** of the LORD was by
24:17 to the LORD when he saw the ***a***
1 Ki 13:18 and an ***a*** spoke to me by the
19: 5 suddenly an ***a*** touched him, and
19: 7 And the ***a*** of the LORD came back
2 Ki 1: 3 But the ***a*** of the LORD said to
1:15 And the ***a*** of the LORD said to
19:35 on a certain night that the ***a***
1 Chr 21:12 with the ***a*** of the LORD
21:15 And God sent an ***a*** to Jerusalem
21:15 and said to the ***a*** who was
21:15 And the ***a*** of the LORD stood
21:16 lifted his eyes and saw the ***a***
21:18 the ***a*** of the LORD commanded
21:20 Now Ornan turned and saw the ***a***;
21:27 So the LORD commanded the ***a***,
21:30 afraid of the sword of the ***a***
2 Chr 32:21 Then the LORD sent an ***a*** who cut
Ps 34: 7 The ***a*** of the LORD encamps all
35: 5 And let the ***a*** of the LORD
35: 6 And let the ***a*** of the LORD
Isa 37:36 Then the ***a*** of the LORD went
63: 9 And the *A* of His Presence
Dan 3:28 who sent His *A* and delivered
6:22 My God sent His ***a*** and shut the
Hos 12: 4 he struggled with the *A* and
Zech 1: 9 So the ***a*** who talked with me
1:11 So they answered the *A* of the
1:12 Then the *A* of the LORD
1:13 And the LORD answered the ***a*** who
1:14 So the ***a*** who spoke with me said
1:19 And I said to the ***a*** who talked
2: 3 And there was the ***a*** who talked
2: 3 and another ***a*** was coming out to
3: 1 priest standing before the *A*
3: 3 and was standing before the *A*.
3: 5 And the *A* of the LORD stood
3: 6 Then the *A* of the LORD
4: 1 Now the ***a*** who talked with me
4: 4 I answered and spoke to the ***a***
4: 5 Then the ***a*** who talked with me
5: 5 Then the ***a*** who talked with me
5:10 So I said to the ***a*** who talked
6: 4 I answered and said to the ***a***
6: 5 And the ***a*** answered and said to
12: 8 like the *A* of the LORD before
Mt 1:20 an ***a*** of the Lord appeared to
1:24 did as the ***a*** of the Lord
2:13 an ***a*** of the Lord appeared to
2:19 an ***a*** of the Lord appeared in a
28: 2 for an ***a*** of the Lord descended
28: 5 But the ***a*** answered and said to
Lk 1:11 Then an ***a*** of the Lord appeared
1:13 But the ***a*** said to him, "Do not
1:18 And Zacharias said to the ***a***,
1:19 And the ***a*** answered and said to
1:26 Now in the sixth month the ***a***
1:28 the ***a*** said to her, "Rejoice,
1:30 Then the ***a*** said to her, "Do not
1:34 Then Mary said to the ***a***,
1:35 And the ***a*** answered and said to
1:38 And the ***a*** departed from her.
2: 9 an ***a*** of the Lord stood before
2:10 Then the ***a*** said to them, "Do
2:13 suddenly there was with the ***a***
2:21 the name given by the ***a*** before
22:43 Then an ***a*** appeared to Him from
Jn 5: 4 For an ***a*** went down at a certain
12:29 An ***a*** has spoken to Him."
Acts 5:19 But at night an ***a*** of the Lord
6:15 his face as the face of an ***a***.
7:30 an *A* of the Lord appeared to
7:35 deliverer by the hand of the *A*
7:38 in the wilderness with the *A*
8:26 Now an ***a*** of the Lord spoke to
10: 3 he saw clearly in a vision an ***a***
10: 7 And when the ***a*** who spoke to him
10:22 instructed by a holy ***a*** to
11:13 he told us how he had seen an ***a***
12: 7 an ***a*** of the Lord stood by him,
12: 8 Then the ***a*** said to him, "Gird
12: 9 that what was done by the ***a***
12:10 and immediately the ***a*** departed
12:11 that the Lord has sent His ***a***,
12:15 So they said, "It is his ***a***."
12:23 Then immediately an ***a*** of the
23: 8 and no ***a*** or spirit; but the
23: 9 but if a spirit or an ***a*** has
27:23 stood by me this night an ***a*** of
2 Cor 11:14 transforms himself into an ***a***
Gal 1: 8 or an ***a*** from heaven, preach any
4:14 but you received me as an ***a*** of
Rev 1: 1 and signified it by His ***a*** to
2: 1 To the ***a*** of the church of
2: 8 And to the ***a*** of the church in
2:12 And to the ***a*** of the church in
2:18 And to the ***a*** of the church in
3: 1 And to the ***a*** of the church in
3: 7 And to the ***a*** of the church in
3:14 And to the ***a*** of the church of
5: 2 Then I saw a strong ***a***
7: 2 Then I saw another ***a*** ascending
8: 3 Then another ***a***, having a golden
8: 5 Then the ***a*** took the censer,
8: 7 The first ***a*** sounded: And hail

8: 8 Then the second ***a*** sounded: And
8:10 Then the third ***a*** sounded: And a
8:12 Then the fourth ***a*** sounded: And
8:13 and I heard an ***a*** flying through
9: 1 Then the fifth ***a*** sounded: And I
9:11 had as king over them the ***a*** of
9:13 Then the sixth ***a*** sounded: And I
9:14 saying to the sixth ***a*** who had
10: 1 I saw still another mighty ***a***
10: 5 The ***a*** whom I saw standing on the
10: 7 the sounding of the seventh ***a***,
10: 8 is open in the hand of the ***a***
10: 9 So I went to the ***a*** and said to
11: 1 And the ***a*** stood, saying, "Rise
11:15 Then the seventh ***a*** sounded: And
14: 6 Then I saw another ***a*** flying in
14: 8 And another ***a*** followed, saying,
14: 9 Then a third ***a*** followed them,
14:15 And another ***a*** came out of the
14:17 Then another ***a*** came out of the
14:18 And another ***a*** came out from the
14:19 So the ***a*** thrust his sickle into
16: 3 Then the second ***a*** poured out
16: 4 Then the third ***a*** poured out his
16: 5 And I heard the ***a*** of the waters
16: 8 Then the fourth ***a*** poured out
16:10 Then the fifth ***a*** poured out his
16:12 Then the sixth ***a*** poured out his
16:17 Then the seventh ***a*** poured out
17: 7 But the ***a*** said to me, "Why did
18: 1 these things I saw another ***a***
18:21 Then a mighty ***a*** took up a stone
19:17 Then I saw an ***a*** standing in the
20: 1 Then I saw an ***a*** coming down from
21:17 of a man, that is, of an ***a***.
22: 6 of the holy prophets sent His ***a***
22: 8 before the feet of the ***a*** who
22:16 have sent My ***a*** to testify to

ANGEL OF THE LORD (68/64)

Gen 16: 7 Now the ***A*** found her by a spring
16: 9 The ***A*** said to her, "Return to
16:10 Then the ***A*** said to her, "I will
16:11 And the ***A*** said to her:
22:11 But the ***A*** called to him from
22:15 Then the ***A*** called to Abraham a
Ex 3: 2 And the ***A*** appeared to him in a
Num 22:22 and the ***A*** took His stand in the
22:23 Now the donkey saw the ***A***
22:24 Then the ***A*** stood in a narrow
22:25 And when the donkey saw the ***A***,
22:26 Then the ***A*** went further, and
22:27 And when the donkey saw the ***A***,
22:31 and he saw the ***A*** standing in
22:32 And the ***A*** said to him, "Why
22:34 And Balaam said to the ***A***,
22:35 Then the ***A*** said to Balaam, "Go
Judg 2: 1 Then the ***A*** came up from Gilgal
2: 4 when the ***A*** spoke these words to
5:23 'Curse Meroz,' said the ***a***,
6:11 Now the ***A*** came and sat under
6:12 And the ***A*** appeared to him, and
6:21 Then the ***A*** put out the end of
6:21 And the ***A*** departed out of his
6:22 perceived that He was the ***A***.
6:22 GOD! For I have seen the ***A***
13: 3 And the ***A*** appeared to the woman
13:13 So the ***A*** said to Manoah, "Of
13:15 Then Manoah said to the ***A***,
13:16 And the ***A*** said to Manoah,
13:16 did not know He was the ***A***.
13:17 Then Manoah said to the ***A***,
13:18 And the ***A*** said to him, "Why do
13:20 the ***A*** ascended in the flame of
13:21 When the ***A*** appeared no more to
13:21 Manoah knew that He was the ***A***.
2 Sam 24:16 And the ***a*** was by the
1 Ki 19: 7 And the ***a*** came back the second
2 Ki 1: 3 But the ***a*** said to Elijah the
1:15 And the ***a*** said to Elijah, "Go
19:35 on a certain night that the ***a***
1 Chr 21:12 with the ***a*** destroying
21:15 And the ***a*** stood by the
21:16 lifted his eyes and saw the ***a***
21:18 the ***a*** commanded Gad to say to
21:30 afraid of the sword of the ***a***.
Ps 34: 7 The ***a*** encamps all around those
35: 5 And let the ***a*** chase them.
35: 6 And let the ***a*** pursue them.
Isa 37:36 Then the ***a*** went out, and killed
Zech 1:11 So they answered the ***A***,
1:12 Then the ***A*** answered and said,
3: 1 priest standing before the ***A***,
3: 5 And the ***A*** stood by.
3: 6 Then the ***A*** admonished Joshua,
12: 8 like the ***A*** before them.
Mt 1:20 an ***a*** appeared to him in a
1:24 did as the ***a*** commanded him and
2:13 an ***a*** appeared to Joseph in a
2:19 an ***a*** appeared in a dream to
28: 2 for an ***a*** descended from heaven,
Lk 1:11 Then an ***a*** appeared to him,
2: 9 an ***a*** stood before them, and the
Acts 5:19 But at night an ***a*** opened the
7:30 an ***A*** appeared to him in a flame
8:26 Now an ***a*** spoke to Philip,
12: 7 an ***a*** stood by him, and a light
12:23 Then immediately an ***a*** struck

ANGEL'S (2/2) ANGEL

Rev 8: 4 ascended before God from the ***a***
10:10 the little book out of the ***a***

ANGELS (92/90) ANGEL, ANGELS'

Gen 19: 1 Now the two ***a*** came to Sodom in
19:15 the ***a*** urged Lot to hurry,
28:12 and there the ***a*** of God were
32: 1 and the ***a*** of God met him.
Job 4:18 If He charges His ***a*** with
Ps 8: 5 him a little lower than the ***a***,
78:49 By sending ***a*** of destruction
91:11 For He shall give His ***a*** charge
103:20 Bless the LORD, you His ***a***,
104: 4 Who makes His ***a*** spirits, His
148: 2 Praise Him, all His ***a***;
Mt 4: 6 He shall give His ***a*** charge
4:11 ***a*** came and ministered to Him.
13:39 age, and the reapers are the ***a***.
13:41 Son of Man will send out His ***a***,
13:49 The ***a*** will come forth, separate
16:27 glory of His Father with His ***a***,
18:10 to you that in heaven their ***a***
22:30 but are like ***a*** of God in
24:31 And He will send His ***a*** with a
24:36 not even the ***a*** of heaven, but
25:31 and all the holy ***a*** with Him,
25:41 for the devil and his ***a***:
26:53 more than twelve legions of ***a***?
Mk 1:13 and the ***a*** ministered to Him.
8:38 of His Father with the holy ***a***.
12:25 but are like ***a*** in heaven.
13:27 "And then He will send His ***a***,
13:32 not even the ***a*** in heaven, nor
Lk 2:15 when the ***a*** had gone away from
4:10 He shall give His ***a*** charge
9:26 Father's, and of the holy ***a***.
12: 8 also will confess before the ***a***
12: 9 will be denied before the ***a*** of
15:10 is joy in the presence of the ***a***
16:22 and was carried by the ***a*** to
20:36 for they are equal to the ***a*** and
24:23 had also seen a vision of ***a***
Jn 1:51 and the ***a*** of God ascending and
20:12 And she saw two ***a*** in white
Acts 7:53 the law by the direction of ***a***
Rom 8:38 nor ***a*** nor principalities nor
1 Cor 4: 9 both to ***a*** and to men.
6: 3 not know that we shall judge ***a***?
11:10 on her head, because of the ***a***.
13: 1 the tongues of men and of ***a***,
Gal 3:19 it was appointed through ***a***
Col 2:18 humility and worship of ***a***,
2 Th 1: 7 from heaven with His mighty ***a***,
1 Tim 3:16 in the Spirit, Seen by ***a***,
5:21 Jesus Christ and the elect ***a***
Heb 1: 4 so much better than the ***a***,
1: 5 For to which of the ***a*** did He
1: 6 Let all the ***a*** of God
1: 7 And of the ***a*** He says: "Who
1: 7 Who makes His ***a*** spirits
1:13 But to which of the ***a*** has He
2: 2 if the word spoken through ***a***
2: 5 we speak, in subjection to ***a***.
2: 7 a little lower than the ***a***;
2: 9 made a little lower than the ***a***,
2:16 He does not give aid to ***a***,
12:22 to an innumerable company of ***a***,
13: 2 have unwittingly entertained ***a***.
1 Pe 1:12 things which ***a*** desire to look
3:22 ***a*** and authorities and powers
2 Pe 2: 4 if God did not spare the ***a*** who
2:11 whereas ***a***, who are greater
Jude 6 And the ***a*** who did not keep their
Rev 1:20 The seven stars are the ***a*** of
3: 5 My Father and before His ***a***.
5:11 and I heard the voice of many ***a***
7: 1 After these things I saw four ***a***
7: 2 a loud voice to the four ***a*** to
7:11 All the ***a*** stood around the
8: 2 And I saw the seven ***a*** who stand
8: 6 So the seven ***a*** who had the seven
8:13 of the trumpet of the three ***a***
9:14 Release the four ***a*** who are bound
9:15 So the four ***a***, who had been
12: 7 Michael and his ***a*** fought with
12: 7 and the dragon and his ***a***
12: 9 and his ***a*** were cast out with
14:10 in the presence of the holy ***a***
15: 1 seven ***a*** having the seven last
15: 6 of the temple came the seven ***a***
15: 7 creatures gave to the seven ***a***
15: 8 seven plagues of the seven ***a***
16: 1 temple saying to the seven ***a***,
17: 1 Then one of the seven ***a*** who had
21: 9 Then one of the seven ***a*** who had
21:12 and twelve ***a*** at the gates, and

ANGELS' (1/1) ANGELS

Ps 78:25 Men ate ***a*** food; He sent them

ANGER (233/228) ANGERED, ANGRY

Gen 27:45 until your brother's ***a*** turns
30: 2 And Jacob's ***a*** was aroused
39:19 that his ***a*** was aroused.
44:18 and do not let your ***a*** burn
49: 6 For in their ***a*** they slew a
49: 7 Cursed be their ***a***,
Ex 4:14 So the ***a*** of the LORD was
11: 8 out from Pharaoh in great ***a***.
32:19 So Moses' ***a*** became hot, and he
32:22 Do not let the ***a*** of my lord
Num 11: 1 and His ***a*** was aroused. So the
11:10 and the ***a*** of the LORD was
12: 9 So the ***a*** of the LORD was
22:22 Then God's ***a*** was aroused
22:27 so Balaam's ***a*** was aroused, and
24:10 Then Balak's ***a*** was aroused
25: 3 and the ***a*** of the LORD was
25: 4 that the fierce ***a*** of the LORD
32:10 So the LORD's ***a*** was aroused on
32:13 So the LORD's ***a*** was aroused
32:14 still more the fierce ***a*** of the
Deut 4:25 your God to provoke Him to ***a***,
6:15 lest the ***a*** of the LORD your
7: 4 so the ***a*** of the LORD will be
9:18 the LORD, to provoke Him to ***a***.
9:19 For I was afraid of the ***a*** and
11:17 lest the LORD's ***a*** be aroused
13:17 from the fierceness of His ***a***
19: 6 while his ***a*** is hot, pursue the
29:20 for then the ***a*** of the LORD and
29:23 the LORD overthrew in His ***a***
29:24 does the heat of this great ***a***
29:27 Then the ***a*** of the LORD was
29:28 them from their land in ***a***,
31:17 Then My ***a*** shall be aroused
31:29 to provoke Him to ***a*** through the
32:16 they provoked Him to ***a***.
32:21 They have moved Me to ***a*** by
32:21 I will move them to ***a*** by a
32:22 For a fire is kindled by my ***a***,
Josh 7: 1 so the ***a*** of the LORD burned
7:26 from the fierceness of His ***a***.
23:16 then the ***a*** of the LORD will
Judg 2:12 they provoked the LORD to ***a***.
2:14 And the ***a*** of the LORD was hot
2:20 Then the ***a*** of the LORD was hot
3: 8 Therefore the ***a*** of the LORD was
8: 3 Then their ***a*** toward him
9:30 his ***a*** was aroused.
10: 7 So the ***a*** of the LORD was hot
14:19 So his ***a*** was aroused, and he
1 Sam 11: 6 and his ***a*** was greatly aroused.
17:28 and Eliab's ***a*** was aroused
20:30 Then Saul's ***a*** was aroused
20:34 from the table in fierce ***a***,
2 Sam 6: 7 Then the ***a*** of the LORD was
12: 5 So David's ***a*** was greatly aroused
24: 1 Again the ***a*** of the LORD was
1 Ki 14: 9 images to provoke Me to ***a***,
14:15 provoking the LORD to ***a***.
15:30 the LORD God of Israel to ***a***.
16: 2 to provoke Me to ***a*** with their
16: 7 the LORD in provoking Him to ***a***
16:13 the LORD God of Israel to ***a***
16:26 the LORD God of Israel to ***a***
16:33 the LORD God of Israel to ***a***
21:22 you have provoked Me to ***a***,
22:53 the LORD God of Israel to ***a***,
2 Ki 13: 3 Then the ***a*** of the LORD was
17:11 to provoke the LORD to ***a***,
17:17 the LORD, to provoke Him to ***a***.
21: 6 the LORD, to provoke Him to ***a***.
21:15 and have provoked Me to ***a*** since
22:17 that they might provoke Me to ***a***
23:19 made to provoke the LORD to ***a***;
23:26 with which His ***a*** was aroused
24:20 For because of the ***a*** of the
1 Chr 13:10 Then the ***a*** of the LORD was
2 Chr 25:10 Therefore their ***a*** was greatly
25:10 they returned home in great ***a***.
25:15 Therefore the ***a*** of the LORD was
28:25 and provoked to ***a*** the LORD God
33: 6 the LORD, to provoke Him to ***a***.
34:25 that they might provoke Me to ***a***
Neh 4: 5 they have provoked You to ***a***
9:17 and merciful, Slow to ***a***,
Esth 1:12 and his ***a*** burned within him.
Job 4: 9 And by the breath of His ***a***
9: 5 He overturns them in His ***a***;
9:13 God will not withdraw His ***a***,
18: 4 You who tear yourself in ***a***,
21:17 God distributes in His ***a***?
35:15 He has not punished in His ***a***,
Ps 6: 1 do not rebuke me in Your ***a***,
7: 6 Arise, O LORD, in Your ***a***;
21: 9 oven in the time of Your ***a***;
27: 9 not turn Your servant away in ***a***;
30: 5 For His ***a*** is but for a
37: 8 Cease from ***a***, and forsake
38: 3 in my flesh Because of Your ***a***,
56: 7 In ***a*** cast down the peoples, O
69:24 And let Your wrathful ***a*** take
74: 1 Why does Your ***a*** smoke against
77: 9 Has He in ***a*** shut up His tender
78:21 And ***a*** also came up against
78:38 many a time He turned His ***a***
78:49 on them the fierceness of His ***a***,
78:50 He made a path for His ***a***;
78:58 For they provoked Him to ***a*** with
85: 3 from the fierceness of Your ***a***.
85: 4 And cause Your ***a*** toward us to
85: 5 Will You prolong Your ***a*** to all
90: 7 we have been consumed by Your ***a***,
90:11 Who knows the power of Your ***a***?
103: 8 and gracious, Slow to ***a***,
103: 9 Nor will He keep His A
106:29 Thus they provoked Him to ***a***
145: 8 Slow to ***a*** and great in mercy.

Prov 15: 1 But a harsh word stirs up ***a***.
15:18 But he who is slow to ***a***
16:32 He who is slow to ***a*** is
19:11 of a man makes him slow to ***a***,
20: 2 Whoever provokes him to ***a***
21:14 A gift in secret pacifies ***a***,
22: 8 And the rod of his ***a*** will
27: 4 Wrath is cruel and ***a*** a
Eccl 5:17 much sorrow and sickness and ***a***.
7: 9 For ***a*** rests in the bosom of
Isa 1: 4 They have provoked to ***a*** The
5:25 Therefore the ***a*** of the LORD is
5:25 For all this His ***a*** is not
7: 4 for the fierce ***a*** of Rezin and
9:12 For all this His ***a*** is not
9:17 For all this His ***a*** is not
9:21 For all this His ***a*** is not
10: 4 For all this His ***a*** is not
10: 5 the rod of My ***a*** And the staff
10:25 as will My ***a*** in their
12: 1 Your ***a*** is turned away, and You
13: 3 called My mighty ones for My ***a***—
13: 9 with both wrath and fierce ***a***,
13:13 And in the day of His fierce ***a***.
14: 6 He who ruled the nations in ***a***,
30:27 from afar, Burning with His ***a***,
30:30 the indignation of His ***a*** And
42:25 on him the fury of His ***a*** And
48: 9 name's sake I will defer My ***a***,
63: 3 I have trodden them in My ***a***,
63: 6 down the peoples in My ***a***,
65: 3 A people who provoke Me to ***a***
66:15 To render His ***a*** with fury,
Jer 2:35 Surely His ***a*** shall turn from
3:12 I will not cause My ***a*** to fall on
4: 8 For the fierce ***a*** of the LORD
4:26 of the LORD, By His fierce ***a***.
7:18 that they may provoke Me to ***a***.
7:19 "Do they provoke Me to ***a***?
7:20 My ***a*** and My fury will be poured
8:19 have they provoked Me to ***a***
10:24 with justice; Not in Your ***a***,
11:17 themselves to provoke Me to ***a***
12:13 Because of the fierce ***a*** of
15:14 For a fire is kindled in My ***a***,
17: 4 you have kindled a fire in My ***a***
18:23 them In the time of Your ***a***.
21: 5 even in ***a*** and fury and great
23:20 The ***a*** of the LORD will not
25: 6 and do not provoke Me to ***a*** with
25: 7 you might provoke Me to ***a***
25:37 down Because of the fierce ***a***
25:38 And because of His fierce ***a***.
30:24 The fierce ***a*** of the LORD will
32:29 other gods, to provoke Me to ***a***;
32:30 have provoked Me only to ***a***
32:31 to Me a provocation of My ***a***
32:32 have done to provoke Me to ***a***—
32:37 I have driven them in My ***a***,
33: 5 of men whom I will slay in My ***a***
36: 7 For great is the ***a*** and the
42:18 As My ***a*** and My fury have been
44: 3 committed to provoke Me to ***a***,
44: 6 So My fury and My ***a*** were poured
49:37 upon them, My fierce ***a***,
51:45 himself from the fierce ***a*** of
52: 3 For because of the ***a*** of the
Lam 1:12 In the day of His fierce ***a***.
2: 1 of Zion With a cloud in His ***a***!
2: 1 footstool In the day of His ***a***.
2: 3 He has cut off in fierce ***a***
2:21 them in the day of Your ***a***,
2:22 In the day of the LORD's ***a***
3:43 have covered Yourself with ***a***
3:66 In Your ***a***, Pursue and destroy
4:11 He has poured out His fierce ***a***.
Ezek 5:13 Thus shall My ***a*** be spent, and I
5:15 judgments among you in ***a*** and
7: 3 And I will send My ***a*** against
7: 8 And spend My ***a*** upon you; I
8:17 returned to provoke Me to ***a***.
13:13 be a flooding rain in My ***a***,
16:26 of harlotry to provoke Me to ***a***.
20: 8 fury on them and fulfill My ***a***
20:21 fury on them and fulfill My ***a***
22:20 so I will gather you in My ***a***
25:14 do in Edom according to My ***a***
35:11 I will do according to your ***a***
43: 8 I have consumed them in My ***a***.
Dan 9:16 let Your ***a*** and Your fury be
11:20 but not in ***a*** or in battle.
Hos 8: 5 O Samaria! My ***a*** is aroused
11: 9 execute the fierceness of My ***a***;
12:14 Ephraim provoked Him to ***a*** most
13:11 I gave you a king in My ***a***,
14: 4 For My ***a*** has turned away from
Joel 2:13 and merciful, Slow to ***a***,
Am 1:11 His ***a*** tore perpetually, And
Jon 3: 9 and turn away from His fierce ***a***,
4: 2 slow to ***a*** and abundant in
Mic 5:15 I will execute vengeance in ***a***
7:18 He does not retain His ***a***
Nah 1: 3 The LORD is slow to ***a*** and
1: 6 endure the fierceness of His ***a***?
Hab 3: 8 Was Your ***a*** against the
3:12 You trampled the nations in ***a***.
Zeph 2: 2 Before the LORD's fierce ***a***
2: 2 the day of the LORD's ***a*** comes
2: 3 In the day of the LORD's ***a***.
3: 8 indignation, All my fierce ***a***;
Zech 10: 3 My ***a*** is kindled against the
Mk 3: 5 looked around at them with ***a***,
Rom 10:19 I will move you to ***a*** by
Eph 4:31 Let all bitterness, wrath, ***a***,
Col 3: 8 are to put off all these: ***a***,

ANGERED (1/1) ANGER

Ps 106:32 They ***a*** Him also at the waters

ANGRY (92/89) ANGER

Gen 4: 5 offering. And Cain was very ***a***,
4: 6 said to Cain, "Why are you ***a***?
18:30 said, "Let not the Lord be ***a***,
18:32 said, "Let not the Lord be ***a***,
31:36 Then Jacob was ***a*** and rebuked
34: 7 the men were grieved and very ***a***,
40: 2 And Pharaoh was ***a*** with his two
41:10 When Pharaoh was ***a*** with his
45: 5 not therefore be grieved or ***a***
Ex 16:20 And Moses was ***a*** with them.
Lev 10:16 And he was ***a*** with Eleazar and
Num 16:15 Then Moses was very ***a***,
16:22 and You be ***a*** with all the
31:14 But Moses was ***a*** with the
Deut 1:34 sound of your words, and was ***a***,
1:37 The LORD was also ***a*** with me for
3:26 But the LORD was ***a*** with me on
4:21 Furthermore the LORD was ***a*** with
9: 8 so that the LORD was ***a*** enough
9:19 with which the LORD was ***a***
9:20 And the LORD was very ***a*** with
Josh 22:18 that tomorrow He will be ***a*** with
Judg 6:39 Do not be ***a*** with me, but let me
18:25 lest ***a*** men fall upon you, and
1 Sam 18: 8 Then Saul was very ***a***,
20: 7 be safe. But if he is very ***a***,
29: 4 of the Philistines were ***a*** with
2 Sam 3: 8 Then Abner became very ***a*** at the
6: 8 And David became ***a*** because of
13:21 all these things, he was very ***a***.
19:42 Why then are you ***a*** over this
22: 8 were shaken, Because He was ***a***.
1 Ki 8:46 and You become ***a*** with them and
11: 9 So the LORD became ***a*** with
2 Ki 13:19 And the man of God was ***a*** with
17:18 Therefore the LORD was very ***a***
1 Chr 13:11 And David became ***a*** because of
2 Chr 6:36 and You become ***a*** with them and
16:10 Then Asa was ***a*** with the seer,
26:19 And while he was ***a*** with the
28: 9 God of your fathers was ***a*** with
Ezra 9:14 Would You not be ***a*** with us
Neh 4: 7 closed, that they became very ***a***,
5: 6 And I became very ***a*** when I
Ps 2:12 Kiss the Son, lest He be ***a***,
4: 4 Be ***a***, and do not sin.
7:11 And God is ***a*** with the
18: 7 were shaken, Because He was ***a***.
76: 7 presence When once You are ***a***?
79: 5 Will You be ***a*** forever?
80: 4 How long will You be ***a***
85: 5 Will You be ***a*** with us forever?
Prov 21:19 Than with a contentious and ***a***
22:24 Make no friendship with an ***a***
25:23 And a backbiting tongue an ***a***
29:22 An ***a*** man stirs up strife, And
Eccl 5: 6 Why should God be ***a*** at your
7: 9 hasten in your spirit to be ***a***,
Song 1: 6 My mother's sons were ***a*** with
Isa 12: 1 Though You were ***a*** with me,
28:21 He will be ***a*** as in the Valley
47: 6 I was ***a*** with My people; I have
54: 9 I sworn That I would not be ***a***
57:16 Nor will I always be ***a***;
57:17 of his covetousness I was ***a***
57:17 struck him; I hid and was ***a***,
64: 5 in Your ways. You are indeed ***a***,
Jer 3: 5 Will He remain ***a*** forever?
3:12 I will not remain ***a*** forever.
37:15 Therefore the princes were ***a***
Lam 5:22 And are very ***a*** with us!
Ezek 16:42 and be ***a*** no more.
Dan 2:12 For this reason the king was ***a***
Jon 4: 1 exceedingly, and he became ***a***.
4: 4 "Is it right for you to be ***a***?
4: 9 Is it right for you to be ***a***
4: 9 "It is right for me to be ***a***,
Zech 1: 2 The LORD has been very ***a*** with
1:12 against which You were ***a*** these
1:15 I am exceedingly ***a*** with the
1:15 at ease; For I was a little ***a***,
Mt 2:16 the wise men, was exceedingly ***a***;
5:22 I say to you that whoever is ***a***
18:34 "And his master was ***a***,
Lk 14:21 master of the house, being ***a***,
15:28 But he was ***a*** and would not go
Jn 7:23 are you ***a*** with Me because I
Acts 12:20 Now Herod had been very ***a*** with
Eph 4:26 'Be ***a***, and do not sin":
Heb 3:10 Therefore I was ***a*** with
3:17 Now with whom was He ***a*** forty
Rev 11:18 The nations were ***a***,

ANGUISH (25/25)

Gen 42:21 for we saw the ***a*** of his soul
Ex 6: 9 because of ***a*** of spirit and
Deut 2:25 and shall tremble and be in ***a***
28:65 failing eyes, and ***a*** of soul.
1 Sam 1:10 to the LORD and wept in ***a***.
2 Sam 1: 9 for ***a*** has come upon me, but my
Job 6:10 have comfort; Though in ***a***,
7:11 I will speak in the ***a*** of my
15:24 Trouble and ***a*** make him afraid;
Ps 38:18 I will be in ***a*** over my sin.
77:10 And I said, "This is my ***a***;
119:143 Trouble and ***a*** have overtaken
Prov 1:27 When distress and ***a*** come upon
Isa 8:22 and darkness, gloom of ***a***;
30: 6 a land of trouble and ***a***,
Jer 4:31 The ***a*** as of her who brings
6:24 ***A*** has taken hold of us, Pain
15: 8 I will cause ***a*** and terror to
49:24 ***A*** and sorrows have taken her
50:43 ***A*** has taken hold of him,
Ezek 30: 4 And great ***a*** shall be in
30: 9 And great ***a*** shall come upon
Jn 16:21 she no longer remembers the ***a***,
Rom 2: 9 tribulation and ***a***,
2 Cor 2: 4 out of much affliction and ***a***

ANIAM (1/1)

1 Chr 7:19 Ahian, Shechem, Likhi, and ***A***.

ANIM (1/1)

Josh 15:50 Anab, Eshtemoh, ***A***,

ANIMAL (45/37) ANIMALS

Gen 7: 2 you seven each of every clean ***a***,
8:19 Every ***a***, every creeping thing,
8:20 and took of every clean ***a*** and
34:23 and every ***a*** of theirs be ours?
43:16 and slaughter an ***a*** and make
Ex 9:19 down on every man and every ***a***
13:12 firstborn that comes from an ***a***
21:34 but the dead ***a*** shall be his.
21:36 and the dead ***a*** shall be his
22: 5 be grazed, and lets loose his ***a***,
22:10 or any ***a*** to keep, and it dies,
22:19 Whoever lies with an ***a*** shall
Lev 7:21 uncleanness, an unclean ***a***,
7:24 And the fat of an ***a*** that dies
7:25 whoever eats the fat of the ***a***
11:26 The carcass of any ***a*** which
11:39 And if any ***a*** which you may eat
11:47 and between the ***a*** that may be
11:47 that may be eaten and the ***a***
17:13 who hunts and catches any ***a*** or
18:23 'Nor shall you mate with any ***a***,
18:23 any woman stand before an ***a*** to
20:15 'If a man mates with an ***a***,
20:15 death, and you shall kill the ***a***.
20:16 If a woman approaches any ***a*** and
20:16 shall kill the woman and the ***a***.
24:18 Whoever kills an ***a*** shall make it
24:18 make it good, ***a*** for animal.
24:18 make it good, animal for ***a***.
24:21 And whoever kills an ***a*** shall
27: 9 If it is an ***a*** that men may
27:10 and if he at all exchanges ***a***
27:10 at all exchanges animal for ***a***,
27:11 If it is an unclean ***a*** which
27:11 then he shall present the ***a***
27:27 'And if it is an unclean ***a***,
Deut 4:17 the likeness of any ***a*** that is
14: 6 And you may eat every ***a*** with
27:21 one who lies with any kind of ***a***.
Neh 2:12 nor was there any ***a*** with me,
2:14 there was no room for the ***a***
Prov 12:10 man regards the life of his ***a***,
Eccl 3:21 upward, and the spirit of the ***a***,
Dan 8: 4 so that no ***a*** could withstand
Lk 10:34 and he set him on his own ***a***,

ANIMALS (39/35) ANIMAL

Gen 6:20 of ***a*** after their kind, and of
7: 2 two each of ***a*** that are
7: 8 Of clean ***a***, of animals that are
7: 8 of ***a*** that are unclean, of
8: 1 and all the ***a*** that were with
36: 6 his cattle and all his ***a***,
45:17 Load your ***a*** and depart; go to
Ex 11: 5 and all the firstborn of the ***a***.
Lev 11: 2 These are the ***a*** which you may
11: 2 you may eat among all the ***a***
11: 3 ***a***, whatever divides the hoof,
11:27 among all kinds of ***a*** that go on
11:46 This is the law of the ***a*** and
20:25 distinguish between clean ***a***
27:26 'But the firstborn of the ***a***,
Num 18:15 and the firstborn of unclean ***a***
20: 4 that we and our ***a*** should die
20: 8 to the congregation and their ***a***.
20:11 the congregation and their ***a***
35: 3 herds, and for all their ***a***.
Deut 14: 4 These are the ***a*** which you may
14: 6 chews the cud, among the ***a***.
1 Ki 4:33 of the wall; he spoke also of ***a***,
2 Ki 3: 9 nor for the ***a*** that followed
3:17 and your ***a*** may drink.'
2 Chr 35:11 the Levites skinned the ***a***.
Ps 66:15 You burnt sacrifices of fat ***a***,
Eccl 3:18 they themselves are like ***a***.
3:19 sons of men also happens to ***a***;
3:19 man has no advantage over ***a***,
Ezek 32:13 Also I will destroy all its ***a***
32:13 Nor shall the hooves of ***a***
Joel 1:18 How the ***a*** groan! The herds of
Acts 7:42 you offer Me slaughtered ***a***
10:12 all kinds of four-footed ***a*** of

11: 6 I saw four-footed ***a*** of the
Rom 1:23 and birds and four-footed ***a*** and
1 Cor 15:39 of men, another flesh of ***a***,
Heb 13:11 For the bodies of those ***a***,

ANISE (1/1)

Mt 23:23 For you pay tithe of mint and ***a***

ANKLE (1/1) ANKLES, ANKLETS

Acts 3: 7 and immediately his feet and ***a***

ANKLES (1/1) ANKLE

Ezek 47: 3 the water came up to my ***a***.

ANKLETS (1/1) ANKLE

Isa 3:18 the finery: The jingling ***a***,

ANNA (1/1)

Lk 2:36 Now there was one, ***A***,

ANNALS (2/2)

2 Chr 13:22 sayings are written in the ***a***
24:27 they are written in the ***a*** of

ANNAS (4/4)

Lk 3: 2 while ***A*** and Caiaphas were high
Jn 18:13 And they led Him away to ***A***
18:24 Then ***A*** sent Him bound to
Acts 4: 6 as well as ***A*** the high priest,

ANNIHILATE (5/5) ANNIHILATED

Esth 3:13 and to ***a*** all the Jews, both
8: 5 which he wrote to ***a*** the Jews
8:11 and ***a*** all the forces of any
9:24 plotted against the Jews to ***a***
Dan 11:44 great fury to destroy and ***a***

ANNIHILATED (1/1) ANNIHILATE

Esth 7: 4 to be killed, and to be ***a***.

ANNOUNCE (5/5) ANNOUNCED

Deut 30:18 I ***a*** to you today that you shall
1 Sam 9:27 that I may ***a*** to you the word of
Neh 8:15 and that they should ***a*** and
Am 4: 5 Proclaim and ***a*** the freewill
Acts 21:26 entered the temple to ***a*** the

ANNOUNCED (4/4) ANNOUNCE

Judg 21:13 and ***a*** peace to them.
Lam 1:21 Bring on the day You have ***a***,
Acts 12:14 but ran in and ***a*** that Peter
Rom 15:21 "To whom He was not ***a***,

ANNOYED (1/1)

Acts 16:18 many days. But Paul, greatly ***a***,

ANNUL (3/3) ANNULLED, ANNULLING, ANNULS

Job 40: 8 Would you indeed ***a*** My judgment?
Isa 14:27 And who will ***a*** it? His hand
Gal 3:17 cannot ***a*** the covenant that was

ANNULLED (1/1) ANNUL

Isa 28:18 covenant with death will be ***a***,

ANNULLING (1/1) ANNUL

Heb 7:18 on the one hand there is an ***a***

ANNULS (1/1) ANNUL

Gal 3:15 no one ***a*** or adds to it.

ANOINT (35/34) ANOINTED, ANOINTING

Ex 28:41 You shall ***a*** them, consecrate
29: 7 it on his head, and ***a*** him.
29:36 and you shall ***a*** it to sanctify
30:26 With it you shall ***a*** the
30:30 And you shall ***a*** Aaron and his
40: 9 and ***a*** the tabernacle and all
40:10 You shall ***a*** the altar of the
40:11 And you shall ***a*** the laver and
40:13 and ***a*** him and consecrate him,
40:15 You shall ***a*** them, as you
Deut 28:40 but you shall not ***a*** yourself
Judg 9: 8 trees once went forth to ***a***
9:15 If in truth you ***a*** me as king
Ruth 3: 3 Therefore wash yourself and ***a***
1 Sam 9:16 and you shall ***a*** him commander
15: 1 The LORD sent me to ***a*** you king
15:17 And did not the LORD ***a*** you
16: 3 you shall ***a*** for Me the one I
16:12 ***a*** him; for this is the one!"
2 Sam 14: 2 do not ***a*** yourself with oil, but
1 Ki 1:34 and Nathan the prophet ***a*** him
19:15 ***a*** Hazael as king over Syria.
19:16 Also you shall ***a*** Jehu the son of
19:16 of Abel Meholah you shall ***a***
Ps 23: 5 You ***a*** my head with oil; My
Isa 21: 5 you princes, ***A*** the shield!
Dan 9:24 And to ***a*** the Most Holy.
10: 3 nor did I ***a*** myself at all, till
Am 6: 6 And ***a*** yourselves with the best
Mic 6:15 but not ***a*** yourselves with oil;
Mt 6:17 ***a*** your head and wash your face,
Mk 14: 8 She has come beforehand to ***a*** My
16: 1 that they might come and ***a*** Him.
Lk 7:46 You did not ***a*** My head with oil,
Rev 3:18 and ***a*** your eyes with eye salve,

ANOINTED (101/99) ANOINT

Gen 31:13 where you ***a*** the pillar and
Ex 29: 2 and unleavened wafers ***a*** with
29:29 to be ***a*** in them and to be
40:15 as you ***a*** their father, that
Lev 2: 4 or unleavened wafers ***a*** with
4: 3 if the ***a*** priest sins, bringing
4: 5 Then the ***a*** priest shall take
4:16 The ***a*** priest shall bring some of
6:20 on the day when he is ***a***:
6:22 who is ***a*** in his place, shall
7:12 unleavened wafers ***a*** with oil,
7:36 on the day that He ***a*** them, by
8:10 and ***a*** the tabernacle and all
8:11 ***a*** the altar and all its
8:12 oil on Aaron's head and ***a*** him,
8:26 a cake of bread ***a*** with oil,
16:32 who is ***a*** and consecrated to
Num 3: 3 the ***a*** priests, whom he
6:15 unleavened wafers ***a*** with oil,
7: 1 that he ***a*** it and consecrated it
7: 1 so he ***a*** them and consecrated
7:10 for the altar when it was ***a***;
7:84 of Israel, when it was ***a***:
7:88 for the altar after it was ***a***.
35:25 of the high priest who was ***a***
1 Sam 2:10 And exalt the horn of His ***a***.
2:35 and he shall walk before My ***a***
10: 1 it not because the LORD has ***a***
12: 3 the LORD and before His ***a***:
12: 5 and His ***a*** is witness this day,
16: 6 Surely the LORD's ***a*** is before
16:13 took the horn of oil and ***a*** him
24: 6 to my master, the LORD's ***a***,
24: 6 seeing he is the ***a*** of the
24:10 lord, for he is the LORD's ***a***.
26: 9 his hand against the LORD's ***a***,
26:11 my hand against the LORD's ***a***.
26:16 your master, the LORD's ***a***.
26:23 my hand against the LORD's ***a***.
2 Sam 1:14 hand to destroy the LORD's ***a***?
1:16 'I have killed the LORD's ***a***.
1:21 shield of Saul, not ***a*** with oil.
2: 4 and there they ***a*** David king
2: 7 also the house of Judah has ***a***
3:39 though ***a*** king; and these men,
5: 3 And they ***a*** David king over
5:17 heard that they had ***a*** David
12: 7 I ***a*** you king over Israel, and I
12:20 washed and ***a*** himself, and
19:10 whom we ***a*** over us, has died in
19:21 because he cursed the LORD's ***a***?
22:51 king, And shows mercy to His ***a***,
23: 1 The ***a*** of the God of Jacob,
1 Ki 1:39 oil from the tabernacle and ***a***
1:45 and Nathan the prophet have ***a***
5: 1 he heard that they had ***a*** him
2 Ki 9: 3 I have ***a*** you king over Israel."
9: 6 I have ***a*** you king over the
9:12 I have ***a*** you king over Israel."
11:12 they made him king and ***a*** him,
23:30 ***a*** him, and made him king in his
1 Chr 11: 3 Then they ***a*** David king over
14: 8 heard that David had been ***a***
16:22 Do not touch My ***a*** ones, And do
29:22 and ***a*** him before the LORD to
2 Chr 6:42 turn away the face of Your ***A***;
22: 7 whom the LORD had ***a*** to cut off
23:11 Then Jehoiada and his sons ***a***
28:15 and ***a*** them; and they let all
Ps 2: 2 the LORD and against His ***A***,
18:50 king, And shows mercy to His ***a***,
20: 6 know that the LORD saves His ***a***;
28: 8 is the saving refuge of His ***a***.
45: 7 has ***a*** You With the oil of
84: 9 look upon the face of Your ***a***.
89:20 With My holy oil I have ***a*** him,
89:38 have been furious with Your ***a***.
89:51 the footsteps of Your ***a***.
92:10 I have been ***a*** with fresh oil.
105:15 Do not touch My ***a*** ones, And do
132:10 turn away the face of Your ***A***.
132:17 I will prepare a lamp for My ***A***.
Isa 45: 1 "Thus says the LORD to His ***a***,
61: 1 Because the LORD has ***a*** Me To
Lam 4:20 the ***a*** of the LORD, Was caught
Ezek 16: 9 and I ***a*** you with oil.
28:14 You were the ***a*** cherub who
Hab 3:13 For salvation with Your ***A***.
Zech 4:14 These are the two ***a*** ones, who
Mk 6:13 and ***a*** with oil many who were
Lk 4:18 Because He has ***a*** Me To
7:38 and she kissed His feet and ***a***
7:46 but this woman has ***a*** My feet
Jn 9: 6 and He ***a*** the eyes of the blind
9:11 called Jesus made clay and ***a***
11: 2 It was that Mary who ***a*** the Lord
12: 3 ***a*** the feet of Jesus, and wiped
Acts 4:27 holy Servant Jesus, whom You ***a***,
10:38 how God ***a*** Jesus of Nazareth with
2 Cor 1:21 us with you in Christ and has ***a***
Heb 1: 9 has ***a*** You With the oil

ANOINTING (27/25) ANOINT

Ex 25: 6 and spices for the ***a*** oil and
29: 7 And you shall take the ***a*** oil,
29:21 and some of the ***a*** oil, and
30:25 shall make from these a holy ***a***
30:25 It shall be a holy ***a*** oil.
30:31 This shall be a holy ***a*** oil to Me
31:11 and the ***a*** oil and sweet incense
35: 8 and spices for the ***a*** oil and
35:15 the ***a*** oil, the sweet incense,
35:28 for the ***a*** oil, and for the
37:29 He also made the holy ***a*** oil and
39:38 the ***a*** oil, and the sweet
40: 9 And you shall take the ***a*** oil,
40:15 for their ***a*** shall surely be an
Lev 8: 2 the ***a*** oil, a bull as the sin
8:10 Also Moses took the ***a*** oil, and
8:12 And he poured some of the ***a*** oil
8:30 Then Moses took some of the ***a***
10: 7 for the ***a*** oil of the LORD is
21:10 on whose head the ***a*** oil was
21:12 for the consecration of the ***a***
Num 4:16 the ***a*** oil, the oversight of all
Isa 10:27 be destroyed because of the ***a***
Jas 5:14 ***a*** him with oil in the name of
1 Jn 2:20 But you have an ***a*** from the Holy
2:27 But the ***a*** which you have
2:27 but as the same ***a*** teaches you

ANON (KJV) See IMMEDIATELY, (AT) ONCE

ANOTHER (442/401)

Gen 4:25 For God has appointed ***a*** seed for
8:10 And he waited yet ***a*** seven days,
8:12 So he waited yet ***a*** seven days
11: 3 Then they said to one ***a***,
26:21 Then they dug ***a*** well, and they
26:22 he moved from there and dug ***a***
26:31 and swore an oath with one ***a***;
29:19 that I should give her to ***a***
29:27 you will serve with me still ***a***
29:30 he served with Laban still ***a***
30:24 The LORD shall add to me ***a***
31:49 when we are absent one from ***a***.
37: 9 Then he dreamed still ***a*** dream
37: 9 I have dreamed ***a*** dream.
37:19 Then they said to one ***a***,
42: 1 "Why do you look at one ***a***?
42:21 Then they said to one ***a***,
42:28 were afraid, saying to one ***a***,
43: 6 man whether you had still ***a***
43: 7 Have you ***a*** brother?' And we
43:33 looked in astonishment at one ***a***.
Ex 10:23 They did not see one ***a***;
16:15 saw it, they said to one ***a***,
18:16 and I judge between one and ***a***;
21:10 If he takes ***a*** wife, he shall
22: 5 and it feeds in ***a*** man's field,
22: 9 any kind of lost thing which ***a***
25:20 and they shall face one ***a***;
26: 3 shall be coupled to one ***a***,
26: 3 shall be coupled to one ***a***.
26: 5 loops may be clasped to one ***a***.
26:17 each board for binding one to ***a***.
36:10 coupled five curtains to one ***a***,
36:10 curtains he coupled to one ***a***.
36:12 loops held one curtain to ***a***.
36:13 coupled the curtains to one ***a***
36:22 two tenons for binding one to ***a***.
37: 9 their wings. They faced one ***a***;
Lev 13: 5 the priest shall isolate him ***a***
13:33 the one who has the scale ***a***
13:54 and he shall isolate it ***a*** seven
19:11 deal falsely, nor lie to one ***a***.
19:19 let your livestock breed with ***a***
20:10 who commits adultery with ***a***
25:14 you shall not oppress one ***a***.
25:17 you shall not oppress one ***a***,
25:46 you shall not rule over one ***a***
26:37 They shall stumble over one ***a***,
27:20 if he has sold the field to ***a***
Num 8: 8 and you shall take ***a*** young bull
14: 4 So they said to one ***a***,
23:13 Please come with me to ***a*** place
23:27 I will take you to ***a*** place;
36: 9 hands from one tribe to ***a***,
Deut 4:34 a nation from the midst of ***a***
17: 8 between one judgment or ***a***,
17: 8 or between one punishment or ***a***,
20: 5 he die in the battle and ***a*** man
20: 6 he die in the battle and ***a*** man
20: 7 he die in the battle and ***a*** man
24: 2 and goes and becomes ***a*** man's
28:30 but ***a*** man shall lie with her;
28:32 shall be given to ***a*** people,
29:28 and cast them into ***a*** land, as
Judg 2:10 ***a*** generation arose after them
6:29 So they said to one ***a***,
9:37 and ***a*** company is coming from
10:18 of Gilead, said to one ***a***,
11: 2 for you are the son of ***a***
Ruth 2: 8 Do not go to glean in ***a*** field,
3:14 before one could recognize ***a***.
1 Sam 2:25 "If one man sins against ***a***,
10: 3 ***a*** carrying three loaves of
10: 3 and ***a*** carrying a skin of wine.
10: 6 with them and be turned into ***a***

10: 9 that God gave him **a** heart; and
10:11 that the people said to one **a**,
13:18 **a** company turned to the road to
13:18 and **a** company turned to the
17:30 he turned from him toward **a**
20:41 times. And they kissed one **a**;
21:11 they not sing of him to one **a**
29: 5 of whom they sang to one **a** in
2 Sam 3:11 And he could not answer Abner **a**
11:25 sword devours one as well as **a**.
14:12 let your maidservant speak **a**
18:20 for you shall take the news **a**
18:26 Then the watchman saw **a** man
18:26 There is **a** man, running
23:18 was chief of **a** three.
1 Ki 7: 8 the house where he dwelt had **a**
11:23 And God raised up **a** adversary
13:10 So he went **a** way and did not
14: 5 that she will pretend to be **a**
14: 6 Why do you pretend to be **a**
18: 6 and Obadiah went **a** way by
20:37 And he found **a** man, and said,
21: 6 I will give you **a** vineyard for
22:20 and **a** spoke in that manner.
2 Ki 1:11 Then he sent to him **a** captain of
3:23 swords and have killed one **a**;
4: 6 Bring me **a** vessel." And he said
4: 6 There is not **a** vessel." So
7: 3 gate; and they said to one **a**,
7: 6 army; so they said to one **a**,
7: 8 they came back and entered **a**
7: 9 Then they said to one **a**,
14: 8 let us face one **a** in
14:11 king of Judah faced one **a** at
21:16 Jerusalem from one end to **a**,
1 Chr 2:26 Jerahmeel had **a** wife, whose name
11:20 of Joab was chief of **a** three.
16:20 they went from one nation to **a**,
16:20 And from one kingdom to **a**
17: 5 and from one tabernacle to **a**.
24: 5 divided by lot, one group as **a**,
2 Chr 18:19 and **a** spoke in that manner.
20:23 they helped to destroy one **a**.
25:17 let us face one **a** in
25:21 king of Judah faced one **a** at
30:23 agreed to keep the feast **a**
30:23 and they kept it **a** seven days
32: 5 and built **a** wall outside; also
Ezra 9:11 filled it from one end to **a**
Neh 3:11 son of Pahath-Moab repaired **a**
3:19 repaired **a** section in front of
3:21 repaired **a** section, from the
3:24 the son of Henadad repaired **a**
3:27 them the Tekoites repaired **a**
3:30 repaired **a** section. After him
4:19 we are separated far from one **a**
7: 3 one at his watch station and **a**
9: 3 and for **a** fourth they
Esth 1:19 give her royal position to **a**
4:14 will arise for the Jews from **a**
9:19 for sending presents to one **a**.
9:22 of sending presents to one **a**
Job 1:16 **a** also came and said, "The
1:17 **a** also came and said, "The
1:18 **a** also came and said, "Your
19:27 my eyes shall behold, and not **a**.
21:25 *A* man dies in the bitterness of
31: 8 and **a** eat; Yes, let my harvest
31:10 Then let my wife grind for **a**,
33:14 may speak in one way, or in **a**,
41:16 One is so near **a** That no air
41:17 They are joined one to **a**,
Ps 16: 4 multiplied who hasten after **a**
75: 7 puts down one, And exalts **a**.
105:13 they went from one nation to **a**,
105:13 From one kingdom to **a** people,
109: 8 And let **a** take his office.
145: 4 shall praise Your works to **a**,
Prov 23:35 that I may seek **a** drink?"
25: 9 do not disclose the secret to **a**;
27: 2 Let **a** man praise you, and not
Eccl 1: 4 and **a** generation comes; But
4:12 one may be overpowered by **a**,
8: 9 in which one man rules over **a**
Song 5: 9 is your beloved More than **a**
5: 9 is your beloved More than **a**
Isa 3: 5 Every one by **a** and every one
6: 3 And one cried to **a** and said:
13: 8 They will be amazed at one **a**;
28:11 with stammering lips and **a**
42: 8 My glory I will not give to **a**,
44: 5 *A* will call himself by the
44: 5 *A* will write with his hand,
48:11 I will not give My glory to **a**.
65:15 And call His servants by **a**
65:22 They shall not build and **a**
65:22 They shall not plant and **a**
66:23 That from one New Moon to **a**,
66:23 And from one Sabbath to **a**,
Jer 3: 1 goes from him And becomes **a**
13:14 I will dash them one against **a**,
18: 4 so he made it again into **a**
22:26 into **a** country where you were
25:26 north, far and near, one with **a**;
36:16 looked in fear from one to **a**,
36:28 Take yet **a** scroll, and write on
36:32 Then Jeremiah took **a** scroll and
46:16 fall; Yes, one fell upon **a**.
51:31 One runner will run to meet **a**,
51:31 And one messenger to meet **a**,
51:46 in **a** year A rumor will
Ezek 1: 9 Their wings touched one **a**.
1:11 of each one touched one **a**,
1:23 out straight, one toward **a**.
3:13 creatures that touched one **a**,
4: 8 cannot turn from one side to **a**
4:17 and be dismayed with one **a**,
5:12 and I will scatter **a** third to
10: 9 one wheel by one cherub and **a**
12: 3 your place into captivity to **a**
15: 7 but **a** fire shall devour them.
17: 7 But there was **a** great eagle
19: 5 She took **a** of her cubs and
22:11 **a** lewdly defiles his
22:11 and **a** in you violates his
24:23 iniquities and mourn with one **a**.
33:30 houses; and they speak to one **a**,
37:16 Then take **a** stick and write on
37:17 Then join them one to **a** for
40:49 one on this side and **a** on that
41:11 one door toward the north and **a**
46:21 of the court there was **a**
47:14 inherit it equally with one **a**;
Dan 2:39 But after you shall arise **a**
2:39 inferior to yours; then **a**,
2:43 they will not adhere to one **a**,
5:17 and give your rewards to **a**;
7: 5 And suddenly **a** beast, a second,
7: 6 this I looked, and there was **a**,
7: 8 and there was **a** horn, a little
7:24 And **a** shall rise after them;
8:13 and **a** holy one said to that
Hos 4: 4 let no man contend, or rebuke **a**;
Joel 1: 3 And their children **a**
2: 8 They do not push one **a**;
Am 4: 7 I withheld rain from **a** city.
4: 8 or three cities wandered to **a**
Jon 1: 7 And they said to one **a**,
Nah 2: 4 They jostle one **a** in the broad
Zech 2: 3 and **a** angel was coming out to
8:21 of one city shall go to **a**,
Mal 2:10 deal treacherously with one **a**
3:16 feared the LORD spoke to one **a**,
Mt 2:12 for their own country **a** way.
8: 9 'Go,' and he goes; and to **a**,
8:21 Then **a** of His disciples said to
10:23 you in this city, flee to **a**.
11: 3 Coming One, or do we look for **a**?
13:24 *A* parable He put forth to them,
13:31 *A* parable He put forth to them,
13:33 *A* parable He spoke to them
19: 9 immorality, and marries **a**,
21:33 Hear **a** parable: There was a
21:35 one, killed one, and stoned **a**.
22: 5 **a** to his business.
24: 2 stone shall be left here upon **a**,
24:10 be offended, will betray one **a**,
24:10 another, and will hate one **a**.
25:15 to **a** two, and to another one,
25:15 and to **a** one, to each according
25:16 and made **a** five talents.
25:32 will separate them one from **a**,
26:71 **a** girl saw him and said to
27:38 one on the right and **a** on the
Mk 4:41 exceedingly, and said to one **a**,
9:50 and have peace with one **a**.
10:11 his wife and marries **a** commits
10:12 her husband and marries **a**,
12: 4 Again he sent them **a** servant,
12: 5 "And again he sent **a**,
13: 2 one stone shall be left upon **a**,
14:19 And **a** said, "Is it I?"
14:58 three days I will build **a** made
16:12 He appeared in **a** form to two of
Lk 2:15 the shepherds said to one **a**,
6: 6 Now it happened on **a** Sabbath,
6:11 and discussed with one **a** what
7: 8 'Go,' and he goes; and to **a**,
7:19 Coming One, or do we look for **a**?
7:20 Coming One, or do we look for **a**?
7:32 and calling to one **a**,
8:25 and marveled, saying to one **a**,
9:56 And they went to **a** village.
9:59 Then He said to **a**,
9:61 And **a** also said, "Lord, I will
12: 1 so that they trampled one **a**,
14:19 And **a** said, 'I have bought five
14:20 Still **a** said, 'I have married a
14:31 going to make war against **a**
16: 7 "Then he said to **a**,
16:12 not been faithful in what is **a**
16:18 his wife and marries **a** commits
19:11 He spoke **a** parable, because He
19:20 Then **a** came, saying, 'Master,
19:44 leave in you one stone upon **a**,
20:11 Again he sent **a** servant; and
21: 6 one stone shall be left upon **a**
22:58 And after a little while **a** saw
22:59 **a** confidently affirmed, saying,
24:17 this that you have with one **a**
24:32 And they said to one **a**,
Jn 4:33 the disciples said to one **a**,
4:37 One sows and **a** reaps.'
5: 7 **a** steps down before me."
5:32 There is **a** who bears witness of
5:43 if **a** comes in his own name, him
5:44 who receive honor from one **a**,
13:22 the disciples looked at one **a**,
13:34 to you, that you love one **a**;
13:34 you, that you also love one **a**.
13:35 if you have love for one **a**.
14:16 and He will give you **a** Helper,
15:12 that you love one **a** as I have
15:17 you, that you love one **a**.
18:15 and so did **a** disciple.
19:37 And again **a** Scripture says,
21:18 and **a** will gird you and carry
Acts 1:20 Let **a** take his office.'
2: 7 and marveled, saying to one **a**,
2:12 and perplexed, saying to one **a**,
7:18 till **a** king arose who did not
7:26 why do you wrong one **a**?
10:28 company with or go to one of **a**
12:17 And he departed and went to **a**
13:35 Therefore He also says in **a**
15:39 that they parted from one **a**.
17: 7 saying there is **a** king—Jesus."
19:32 cried one thing and some **a**,
19:38 bring charges against one **a**.
21: 6 we had taken our leave of one **a**,
21:34 cried one thing and some **a**.
28: 4 his hand, they said to one **a**,
Rom 1:27 burned in their lust for one **a**,
2: 1 for in whatever you judge **a** you
2:21 You, therefore, who teach **a**,
7: 3 she marries **a** man, she will be
7: 3 though she has married **a** man.
7: 4 that you may be married to **a**—
7:23 But I see **a** law in my members,
9:21 one vessel for honor and **a** for
12: 5 individually members of one **a**.
12:10 kindly affectionate to one **a**
12:10 giving preference to one **a**;
12:16 of the same mind toward one **a**.
13: 8 anything except to love one **a**,
13: 8 for he who loves **a** has
14: 5 person esteems one day above **a**;
14: 5 **a** esteems every day alike.
14:13 let us not judge one **a** anymore,
14:19 things by which one may edify **a**.
15: 5 to be like-minded toward one **a**,
15: 7 Therefore receive one **a**,
15:14 able also to admonish one **a**.
15:20 lest I should build on **a** man's
16:16 Greet one **a** with a holy kiss.
1 Cor 3: 4 says, "I am of Paul," and **a**,
3:10 and **a** builds on it. But let
4: 7 who makes you differ from **a**?
6: 1 you, having a matter against **a**,
6: 7 you go to law against one **a**.
7: 5 Do not deprive one **a** except with
7: 7 one in this manner and **a** in
10:29 why is my liberty judged by **a**
11:21 and one is hungry and **a** is
11:33 together to eat, wait for one **a**.
12: 8 to **a** the word of knowledge
12: 9 to **a** faith by the same Spirit,
12: 9 to **a** gifts of healings by the
12:10 to **a** the working of miracles, to
12:10 to **a** prophecy, to another
12:10 to **a** discerning of spirits, to
12:10 to **a** different kinds of
12:10 to **a** the interpretation of
12:25 have the same care for one **a**.
14:30 if anything is revealed to **a**
15:39 **a** flesh of animals, another of
15:39 **a** of fish, and another of
15:39 and **a** of birds.
15:40 glory of the terrestrial is **a**.
15:41 **a** glory of the moon, and
15:41 and **a** glory of the stars; for
15:41 for one star differs from **a**
16:20 Greet one **a** with a holy kiss.
2 Cor 10:16 and not to boast in **a** man's
11: 4 For if he who comes preaches **a**
13:12 Greet one **a** with a holy kiss.
Gal 1: 7 which is not **a**;
5:13 but through love serve one **a**.
5:15 if you bite and devour one **a**,
5:15 lest you be consumed by one **a**!
5:17 and these are contrary to one **a**,
5:26 conceited, provoking one **a**,
5:26 one another, envying one **a**.
6: 4 in himself alone, and not in **a**.
Eph 4: 2 bearing with one **a** in love,
4:25 for we are members of one **a**.
4:32 And be kind to one **a**,
4:32 tenderhearted, forgiving one **a**,
5:19 speaking to one **a** in psalms and
5:21 submitting to one **a** in the fear
Col 3: 9 Do not lie to one **a**,
3:13 bearing with one **a**,
3:13 another, and forgiving one **a**,
3:13 has a complaint against **a**;
3:16 teaching and admonishing one **a**
1 Th 3:12 and abound in love to one **a**
4: 9 are taught by God to love one **a**;
4:18 Therefore comfort one **a** with
5:11 each other and edify one **a**,
Titus 3: 3 envy, hateful and hating one **a**.
Heb 3:13 but exhort one **a** daily, while it
4: 8 not afterward have spoken of **a**
5: 6 As He also says in **a** place:
7:11 need was there that **a** priest
7:13 things are spoken belongs to **a**
7:15 there arises **a** priest
9:25 every year with blood of **a**—
10:24 And let us consider one **a** in
10:25 of some, but exhorting one **a**,
Jas 2:25 and sent them out **a** way?
4:11 Do not speak evil of one **a**,
4:12 Who are you to judge **a**?
5: 9 Do not grumble against one **a**,
5:16 your trespasses to one **a**,
5:16 one another, and pray for one **a**,
1 Pe 1:22 love one **a** fervently with a

3: 8 having compassion for one **a**;
4: 8 have fervent love for one **a**,
4: 9 Be hospitable to one **a** without
4:10 a gift, minister it to one **a**,
5: 5 of you be submissive to one **a**,
5:14 Greet one **a** with a kiss of love.
1 Jn 1: 7 we have fellowship with one **a**,
3:11 that we should love one **a**,
3:23 Son Jesus Christ and love one **a**,
4: 7 Beloved, let us love one **a**,
4:11 us, we also ought to love one **a**.
4:12 at any time. If we love one **a**,
2 Jn 5 beginning: that we love one **a**.
Rev 6: 4 **A** horse, fiery red, went out.
6: 4 that people should kill one **a**;
7: 2 Then I saw **a** angel ascending
8: 3 Then **a** angel, having a golden
10: 1 I saw still **a** mighty angel
11:10 merry, and send gifts to one **a**,
12: 3 And **a** sign appeared in heaven:
13:11 Then I saw **a** beast coming up
14: 6 Then I saw **a** angel flying in
14: 8 And **a** angel followed, saying,
14:15 And **a** angel came out of the
14:17 Then **a** angel came out of the
14:18 And **a** angel came out from the
15: 1 Then I saw **a** sign in heaven,
16: 7 And I heard **a** from the altar
18: 1 After these things I saw **a** angel
18: 4 And I heard **a** voice from heaven
20:12 And **a** book was opened, which is

ANOTHER'S (6/6)

Gen 11: 7 they may not understand one **a**
Ex 21:35 "If one man's ox hurts **a**,
Ezek 33:26 and you defile one **a** wives.
Jn 13:14 you also ought to wash one **a**
Rom 14: 4 Who are you to judge **a** servant?
Gal 6: 2 Bear one **a** burdens, and so

ANSWER (148/145)

Gen 30:33 So my righteousness will **a** for
41:16 God will give Pharaoh an **a** of
45: 3 But his brothers could not **a**
Deut 21: 7 Then they shall **a** and say, 'Our
25: 9 and **a** and say, 'So shall it be
26: 5 And you shall **a** and say before
27:15 And all the people shall **a**
Josh 4: 7 Then you shall **a** them that the
Judg 19:28 be going." But there was no **a**.
1 Sam 2:16 he would then **a** him, "No,
4:20 a son." But she did not **a**,
14:37 But He did not **a** him that
26:14 of Ner, saying, "Do you not **a**,
28: 6 the LORD did not **a** him, either
28:15 from me and does not **a** me
2 Sam 3:11 And he could not **a** Abner another
22:42 but He did not **a** them.
24:13 Now consider and see what **a** I
1 Ki 9: 9 "Then they will **a**,
12: 6 How do you advise me to **a** these
12: 7 and **a** them, and speak good
12: 9 How should we **a** this people who
2 Ki 4:29 do not **a** him; but lay my staff
18:36 Do not **a** him."
1 Chr 21:12 Now consider what **a** I should
2 Chr 7:22 "Then they will **a**,
10: 6 How do you advise me to **a** these
10: 9 How should we **a** this people who
Ezra 4:17 The king sent an **a**:
5: 5 Then a written **a** was returned
5:11 And thus they returned us an **a**,
Esth 4:13 And Mordecai told them to **a**
Job 5: 1 Is there anyone who will **a**
9: 3 He could not **a** Him one time
9:14 How then can I **a** Him, And
9:15 I could not **a** Him; I would beg
9:32 That I may **a** Him, And that
13:22 Then call, and I will **a**;
14:15 and I will **a** You; You shall
15: 2 Should a wise man **a** with empty
16: 3 what provokes you that you **a**?
19:16 my servant, but he gives no **a**;
20: 2 my anxious thoughts make me **a**,
20: 3 my understanding causes me to **a**.
23: 5 the words which He would **a** me,
30:20 but You do not **a** me; I stand
31:14 how shall I **a** Him?
31:35 that the Almighty would **a** me,
32: 3 because they had found no **a**,
32: 5 saw that there was no **a** in
32:14 So I will not **a** him with your
32:15 They are dismayed and **a** no
32:17 I also will **a** my part, I too
32:20 I must open my lips and **a**.
33: 5 If you can **a** me, Set your
33:12 I will **a** you, For God is
33:32 **a** me; Speak, for I desire to
35: 4 I will **a** you, And your
35:12 they cry out, but He does not **a**,
38: 3 and you shall **a** Me.
40: 2 let him **a** it."
40: 4 What shall I **a** You? I lay my
40: 5 I have spoken, but I will not **a**;
40: 7 and you shall **a** Me:
42: 4 and you shall **a** Me.'
Ps 18:41 but He did not **a** them.
20: 1 May the LORD **a** you in the day
20: 6 He will **a** him from His holy
20: 9 LORD! May the King **a** us when
27: 7 mercy also upon me, and **a** me.
65: 5 in righteousness You will **a** us,
86: 7 For You will **a** me.
91:15 and I will **a** him; I will be
102: 2 **a** me speedily.
119:42 So shall I have an **a** for him
143: 1 In Your faithfulness **a** me,
143: 7 **A** me speedily, O LORD
Prov 1:28 call on me, but I will not **a**;
15: 1 A soft **a** turns away wrath, But
15:23 A man has joy by the **a** of his
15:28 the righteous studies how to **a**,
16: 1 But the **a** of the tongue is
22:21 That you may **a** words of truth
24:26 He who gives a right **a** kisses
26: 4 Do not **a** a fool according to
26: 5 **A** a fool according to his
26:16 eyes Than seven men who can **a**
27:11 That I may **a** him who
Song 5: 6 called him, but he gave me no **a**.
Isa 14:32 What will they **a** the
30:19 He will **a** you.
36:21 Do not **a** him."
41:28 could **a** a word.
46: 7 yet it cannot **a** Nor save him
50: 2 I called, was there none to **a**?
58: 9 call, and the LORD will **a**;
65:12 when I called, you did not **a**;
65:24 before they call, I will **a**;
Jer 5:19 then you shall **a** them, 'Just
7:13 I called you, but you did not **a**,
7:27 but they will not **a** you.
22: 9 "Then they will **a**,
33: 3 and I will **a** you, and show you
44:20 who had given him that **a**—
Ezek 14: 4 I the LORD will **a** him who
14: 7 I the LORD will **a** him by
21: 7 you sighing?' that you shall **a**,
Dan 3:16 we have no need to **a** you in
Hos 2:21 in that day That I will **a**,
2:21 I will **a** the heavens, And they
2:21 And they shall **a** the earth.
2:22 The earth shall **a** With grain,
2:22 They shall **a** Jezreel.
Joel 2:19 The LORD will **a** and say to His
Mic 3: 7 For there is no **a** from
Hab 2: 1 And what I will **a** when I am
2:11 beam from the timbers will **a**
Zech 13: 6 your arms?' Then he will **a**,
13: 9 And I will **a** them. I will
Mt 22:46 And no one was able to **a** Him a
25:37 Then the righteous will **a** Him,
25:40 And the King will **a** and say to
25:44 Then they also will **a** Him,
25:45 Then He will **a** them, saying,
26:62 Do You **a** nothing? What is it
Mk 11:29 then **a** Me, and I will tell you
11:30 heaven or from men? **A** Me."
14:40 and they did not know what to **a**
14:60 Do You **a** nothing? What is it
15: 4 Do You **a** nothing? See how many
Lk 11: 7 and he will **a** from within and
12:11 about how or what you should **a**,
13:25 and He will **a** and say to you,
14: 6 And they could not **a** Him
20: 3 ask you one thing, and **a** Me:
20:26 And they marveled at His **a** and
21:14 beforehand on what you will **a**;
22:68 you will by no means **a** Me or
Jn 1:22 that we may give an **a** to those
18:22 Do You **a** the high priest like
19: 9 But Jesus gave him no **a**.
Acts 12:13 a girl named Rhoda came to **a**.
24:10 I do the more cheerfully **a** for
25:16 and has opportunity to **a** for
26: 2 because today I shall **a** for
2 Cor 5:12 that you may have an **a** for
Col 4: 6 you may know how you ought to **a**
1 Pe 3:21 but the **a** of a good conscience

ANSWERED (522/518) ANSWER, ANSWERING, ANSWERS

Gen 18:27 Then Abraham **a** and said,
23: 5 And the sons of Heth **a** Abraham,
23:10 and Ephron the Hittite **a**
23:14 And Ephron **a** Abraham, saying to
24:50 Then Laban and Bethuel **a** and
27: 1 And he **a** him, "Here I am."
27:37 Then Isaac **a** and said to Esau,
27:39 Then Isaac his father **a** and
31:14 Then Rachel and Leah **a** and said
31:31 Then Jacob **a** and said to Laban,
31:36 and Jacob **a** and said to Laban:
31:43 And Laban **a** and said to Jacob,
34:13 But the sons of Jacob **a** Shechem
35: 3 who **a** me in the day of my
40:18 So Joseph **a** and said, "This is
41:16 So Joseph **a** Pharaoh, saying,
42:22 And Reuben **a** them, saying, "Did
43:28 And they **a**, "Your servant
Ex 4: 1 Then Moses **a** and said, "But
15:21 And Miriam **a** them: "Sing to
19: 8 Then all the people **a** together
19:19 and God **a** him by voice.
24: 3 And all the people **a** with one
Num 11:28 **a** and said, "Moses my lord,
22:18 Then Balaam **a** and said to the
23:12 So he **a** and said, "Must I not
23:26 So Balaam **a** and said to Balak,
32:31 and the children of Reuben **a**,
Deut 1:14 And you **a** me and said, 'The
1:41 Then you **a** and said to me, 'We
Josh 1:16 So they **a** Joshua, saying, "All
2:14 So the men **a** her, "Our lives
7:20 And Achan **a** Joshua and said,
9:24 So they **a** Joshua and said,
15:19 She **a**, "Give me a
17:15 So Joshua **a** them, "If you are
22:21 half the tribe of Manasseh **a**
24:16 So the people **a** and said: "Far
Judg 5:29 Her wisest ladies **a** her, Yes,
5:29 Yes, she **a** herself,
7:14 Then his companion **a** and said,
8: 8 And the men of Penuel **a** him as
8: 8 him as the men of Succoth had **a**.
8:18 killed at Tabor?" So they **a**,
8:25 So they **a**, "We will gladly give
11:13 king of the people of Ammon **a**
15: 6 has done this?" And they **a**,
15:10 come up against us?" So they **a**,
18:14 spy out the country of Laish **a**
20: 4 **a** and said, "My concubine and
Ruth 2: 4 be with you!" And they **a** him,
2: 6 was in charge of the reapers **a**
2:11 And Boaz **a** and said to her, "It
3: 9 "Who are you?" So she **a**,
1 Sam 1:15 And Hannah **a** and said, "No, my
1:17 Then Eli **a** and said, "Go in
3: 4 LORD called Samuel. And he **a**,
3: 6 I am, for you called me." He **a**,
3:10 Samuel!" And Samuel **a**,
3:16 "Samuel, my son!" And he **a**,
4:17 So the messenger **a** and said,
5: 8 the God of Israel?" And they **a**,
6: 4 shall return to Him?" They **a**,
7: 9 and the LORD **a** him.
9: 8 And the servant **a** Saul again and
9:12 And they **a** them and said, "Yes,
9:19 And Samuel **a** Saul and said, "I
9:21 And Saul **a** and said, "Am I not
10:12 Then a man from there **a** and
10:22 here yet?" And the LORD **a**,
11: 2 And Nahash the Ammonite **a** them,
12: 5 in my hand." And they **a**,
14:39 a man among all the people **a**
14:44 And Saul **a**, "God do so and
16:18 Then one of the servants **a** and
17:27 And the people **a** him in this
17:30 and these people **a** him as the
17:58 you, young man?" So David **a**,
19:17 And Michal **a** Saul, "He said
20:28 So Jonathan **a** Saul, "David
20:32 And Jonathan **a** Saul his father,
21: 4 And the priest **a** David and said,
21: 5 Then David **a** the priest, and
22: 9 Then **a** Doeg the Edomite, who
22:12 now, son of Ahitub!" And he **a**,
22:14 So Ahimelech **a** the king and
23: 4 And the LORD **a** him and said,
25:10 Then Nabal **a** David's servants,
26: 6 Then David **a**, and said to
26:14 Then Abner **a** and said, "Who
26:22 And David **a** and said, "Here is
28:15 by bringing me up?" And Saul **a**,
29: 9 Then Achish **a** and said to David,
30: 8 And He **a** him, "Pursue, for
30:22 of those who went with David **a**
2 Sam 1: 4 Please tell me." And he **a**,
1: 7 me and called to me. And I **a**,
1: 8 So I **a** him, 'I am an
1:13 are you from?" And he **a**,
2:20 said, "Are you Asahel?" He **a**,
4: 9 But David **a** Rechab and Baanah
9: 6 "Mephibosheth?" And he **a**,
13:12 And she **a** him, "No, my brother,
13:32 **a** and said, "Let not my lord
14: 5 troubles you?" And she **a**,
14:18 Then the king **a** and said to the
14:19 And the woman **a** and said,
14:32 And Absalom **a** Joab, "Look, I
15:21 And Ittai **a** the king and said,
18: 3 But the people **a**,
18:29 man Absalom safe?" Ahimaaz **a**,
18:32 So the Cushite **a**,
19:21 Abishai the son of Zeruiah **a**
19:26 And he **a**, "My lord, O king,
19:38 And the king **a**, "Chimham shall
19:42 So all the men of Judah **a** the
19:43 And the men of Israel **a** the men
20:17 said, "Are you Joab?" He **a**,
20:17 of your maidservant." And he **a**,
20:20 And Joab **a** and said, "Far be
21: 1 of the LORD. And the LORD **a**,
21: 5 Then they **a** the king, "As for
1 Ki 1:28 Then King David **a** and said,
1:36 Benaiah the son of Jehoiada **a**
1:43 Then Jonathan **a** and said to
2:22 And King Solomon **a** and said to
2:30 and thus he **a** me."
3:27 So the king **a** and said, "Give
10: 3 So Solomon **a** all her questions;
11:22 to your own country?" So he **a**,
12:13 Then the king **a** the people
12:16 the people **a** the king, saying:
13: 6 Then the king **a** and said to the
18: 8 And he **a** him, "It is I. Go,
18:18 And he **a**, "I have not troubled
18:21 But the people **a** him not a
18:24 So all the people **a** and said,
18:26 there was no voice; no one **a**.
18:29 there was no voice; no one **a**,
20: 4 And the king of Israel **a** and
20:11 So the king of Israel **a** and

	20:14	the battle in order?" And he ***a***,
	21: 6	vineyard for it.' And he ***a***,
	21:20	me, O my enemy?" And he ***a***,
	22:15	And he ***a*** him, "Go and
2 Ki	1: 8	So they ***a*** him, "A hairy man
	1:10	So Elijah ***a*** and said to the
	1:11	And he ***a*** and said to him: "Man
	1:12	So Elijah ***a*** and said to them,
	2: 5	from over you today?" So he ***a***,
	3: 8	way shall we go up?" And he ***a***,
	3:11	of the king of Israel ***a*** and
	4:13	of the army?'" She ***a***,
	4:14	be done for her?" And Gehazi ***a***,
	4:26	with the child?'" And she ***a***,
	6: 2	where we may dwell." So he ***a***,
	6: 3	with your servants." And he ***a***,
	6:16	So he ***a***, "Do not fear,
	6:22	But he ***a***, "You shall not kill
	6:28	is troubling you?" And she ***a***,
	7: 2	on whose hand the king leaned ***a***
	7:13	And one of his servants ***a*** and
	7:19	Then that officer had ***a*** the man
	8:12	is my lord weeping?" He ***a***,
	8:13	gross thing?" And Elisha ***a***,
	8:14	Elisha say to you?" And he ***a***,
	9:19	'Is it peace?'" And Jehu ***a***,
	9:22	it peace, Jehu?" So he ***a***,
	10:13	"Who are you?" So they ***a***,
	10:15	your heart?" And Jehonadab ***a***,
	18:36	people held their peace and ***a***
	20:10	And Hezekiah ***a***, "It is an easy
	20:15	in your house?" So Hezekiah ***a***,
1 Chr	12:17	and ***a*** and said to them, "If
	21: 3	And Joab ***a***, "May the LORD
	21:26	and He ***a*** him from heaven by
	21:28	David saw that the LORD had ***a***
2 Chr	2:11	Then Hiram king of Tyre ***a*** in
	9: 2	So Solomon ***a*** all her questions;
	10:13	Then the king ***a*** them roughly.
	10:16	the people ***a*** the king, saying:
	18: 3	And he ***a*** him, "I am as you
	25: 9	And the man of God ***a***,
	29:31	Then Hezekiah ***a*** and said, "Now
	31:10	***a*** him and said, "Since the
	34:15	Then Hilkiah ***a*** and said to
	34:23	Then she ***a*** them, "Thus says the
Ezra	8:23	and He ***a*** our prayer.
	10:12	Then all the assembly ***a*** and said
Neh	2:20	So I ***a*** them, and said to them,
	6: 4	and I ***a*** them in the same
	8: 6	God. Then all the people ***a***,
Esth	1:16	And Memucan ***a*** before the king
	5: 4	So Esther ***a***, "If it pleases the
	5: 7	Then Esther ***a*** and said, "My
	6: 7	And Haman ***a*** the king, "For the
	7: 3	Then Queen Esther ***a*** and said,
	7: 5	So King Ahasuerus ***a*** and said to
Job	1: 7	So Satan ***a*** the LORD and
	1: 9	So Satan ***a*** the LORD and said,
	2: 2	So Satan ***a*** the LORD and
	2: 4	So Satan ***a*** the LORD and said,
	4: 1	Then Eliphaz the Temanite ***a*** and
	6: 1	Then Job ***a*** and said:
	8: 1	Then Bildad the Shuhite ***a*** and
	9: 1	Then Job ***a*** and said:
	9:16	If I called and He ***a*** me, I
	11: 1	Then Zophar the Naamathite ***a*** and
	11: 2	not the multitude of words be ***a***?
	12: 1	Then Job ***a*** and said:
	12: 4	and He ***a*** him, The just and
	15: 1	Then Eliphaz the Temanite ***a*** and
	16: 1	Then Job ***a*** and said:
	18: 1	Then Bildad the Shuhite ***a*** and
	19: 1	Then Job ***a*** and said:
	20: 1	Then Zophar the Naamathite ***a*** and
	21: 1	Then Job ***a*** and said:
	22: 1	Then Eliphaz the Temanite ***a*** and
	23: 1	Then Job ***a*** and said:
	25: 1	Then Bildad the Shuhite ***a*** and
	26: 1	But Job ***a*** and said:
	32: 6	***a*** and said: "I am young in
	32:12	Or ***a*** his words—
	32:16	they stood still and ***a*** no
	34: 1	Elihu further ***a*** and said:
	35: 1	Moreover Elihu ***a*** and said:
	38: 1	Then the LORD ***a*** Job out of the
	40: 1	Moreover the LORD ***a*** Job, and
	40: 3	Then Job ***a*** the LORD and said:
	40: 6	Then the LORD ***a*** Job out of the
	42: 1	Then Job ***a*** the LORD and said:
Ps	22:21	of the wild oxen! You have ***a***
	81: 7	I ***a*** you in the secret place of
	99: 6	upon the LORD, and He ***a*** them.
	99: 8	You ***a*** them, O LORD our God;
	118: 5	The LORD ***a*** me and set me
	118:21	For You have ***a*** me, And have
	119:26	and You ***a*** me; Teach me Your
	138: 3	You ***a*** me, And made me bold
Isa	6:11	"Lord, how long?" And He ***a***:
	21: 9	pair of horsemen!" Then he ***a***
	36:21	they held their peace and ***a***
	39: 4	in your house?" So Hezekiah ***a***,
	66: 4	when I called, no one ***a***,
Jer	11: 5	'" And I ***a*** and said, "So
	23:35	brother, 'What has the LORD ***a***?
	23:37	What has the LORD ***a*** you?' and,
	35:17	to them but they have not ***a***.
	36:18	So Baruch ***a*** them, "He
	44:15	***a*** Jeremiah, saying:
Ezek	24:20	Then I ***a*** them, "The word of the
	37: 3	can these bones live?" So I ***a***,
Dan	2: 5	The king ***a*** and said to the
	2: 7	They ***a*** again and said, "Let the
	2: 8	The king ***a*** and said, "I know
	2:10	The Chaldeans ***a*** the king, and
	2:14	counsel and wisdom Daniel ***a***
	2:15	he ***a*** and said to Arioch the
	2:20	Daniel ***a*** and said: "Blessed
	2:26	The king ***a*** and said to Daniel,
	2:27	Daniel ***a*** in the presence of the
	2:47	The king ***a*** Daniel, and said,
	3:16	and Abed-Nego ***a*** and said to the
	3:24	They ***a*** and said to the king,
	3:25	'Look!" he ***a***, "I see four men
	4:19	Belteshazzar ***a*** and said, "My
	5:17	Then Daniel ***a***,
	6:12	The king ***a*** and said, "The
	6:13	So they ***a*** and said before the
Am	7:14	Then Amos ***a***,
Jon	2: 2	And He ***a*** me. "Out of the
Mic	6: 5	what Balaam the son of Beor ***a***
Hab	2: 2	Then the LORD ***a*** me and said:
Hag	2:12	Then the priests ***a*** and
	2:13	So the priests ***a*** and said,
	2:14	Then Haggai ***a*** and said, "'So
Zech	1:10	stood among the myrtle trees ***a***
	1:11	So they ***a*** the Angel of the
	1:12	Then the Angel of the LORD ***a***
	1:13	And the LORD ***a*** the angel who
	1:19	So he ***a*** me, "These are the
	3: 4	Then He ***a*** and spoke to those who
	4: 4	So I ***a*** and spoke to the angel
	4: 5	the angel who talked with me ***a***
	4: 6	So he ***a*** and said to me: "This
	4:11	Then I ***a*** and said to him,
	4:12	And I further ***a*** and said to him,
	4:13	Then he ***a*** me and said, "Do you
	5: 2	me, "What do you see?" So I ***a***,
	6: 4	Then I ***a*** and said to the angel
	6: 5	And the angel ***a*** and said to me,
Mt	3:15	But Jesus ***a*** and said to him,
	4: 4	But He ***a*** and said, "It is
	8: 8	The centurion ***a*** and said,
	11: 4	Jesus ***a*** and said to them, "Go
	11:25	At that time Jesus ***a*** and said,
	12:38	of the scribes and Pharisees ***a***,
	12:39	But He ***a*** and said to them, "An
	12:48	But He ***a*** and said to the one who
	13:11	He ***a*** and said to them, "Because
	13:37	He ***a*** and said to them: "He who
	14:28	And Peter ***a*** Him and said,
	15: 3	He ***a*** and said to them, "Why do
	15:13	But He ***a*** and said, "Every plant
	15:15	Then Peter ***a*** and said to Him,
	15:23	But He ***a*** her not a word. And His
	15:24	But He ***a*** and said, "I was not
	15:26	But He ***a*** and said, "It is not
	15:28	Then Jesus ***a*** and said to her,
	16: 2	He ***a*** and said to them, "When it
	16:16	Simon Peter ***a*** and said, "You
	16:17	Jesus ***a*** and said to him,
	17: 4	Then Peter ***a*** and said to Jesus,
	17:11	Jesus ***a*** and said to them,
	17:17	Then Jesus ***a*** and said, "O
	19: 4	And He ***a*** and said to them,
	19:27	Then Peter ***a*** and said to Him,
	20:13	But he ***a*** one of them and said,
	20:22	But Jesus ***a*** and said, "You do
	21:21	So Jesus ***a*** and said to them,
	21:24	But Jesus ***a*** and said to them,
	21:27	So they ***a*** Jesus and said, "We
	21:29	He ***a*** and said, 'I will not,' but
	21:30	And he ***a*** and said, 'I go,
	22: 1	And Jesus ***a*** and spoke to them
	22:29	Jesus ***a*** and said to them, "You
	24: 4	And Jesus ***a*** and said to them:
	25: 9	"But the wise ***a***,
	25:12	But he ***a*** and said, 'Assuredly, I
	25:26	But his lord ***a*** and said to him,
	26:23	He ***a*** and said, "He who dipped
	26:25	***a*** and said, "Rabbi, is it I?"
	26:33	Peter ***a*** and said to Him, "Even
	26:63	And the high priest ***a*** and said
	26:66	They ***a*** and said, "He is
	27:12	He ***a*** nothing.
	27:14	But He ***a*** him not one word, so
	27:21	The governor ***a*** and said to them,
	27:25	And all the people ***a*** and said,
	28: 5	But the angel ***a*** and said to the
Mk	3:33	But He ***a*** them, saying, "Who is
	5: 9	is your name?" And he ***a***,
	6:37	But He ***a*** and said to them, "You
	7: 6	He ***a*** and said to them, "Well
	7:28	And she ***a*** and said to Him,
	8: 4	Then His disciples ***a*** Him, "How
	8:28	So they ***a***, "John the Baptist;
	8:29	Peter ***a*** and said to Him,
	9: 5	Then Peter ***a*** and said to Jesus,
	9:12	Then He ***a*** and told them,
	9:17	Then one of the crowd ***a*** and
	9:19	He ***a*** him and said, "O faithless
	9:38	Now John ***a*** Him, saying,
	10: 3	And He ***a*** and said to them,
	10: 5	And Jesus ***a*** and said to them,
	10:20	And he ***a*** and said to Him,
	10:24	But Jesus ***a*** again and said to
	10:29	So Jesus ***a*** and said,
	10:51	So Jesus ***a*** and said to him,
	11:22	So Jesus ***a*** and said to them,
	11:29	But Jesus ***a*** and said to them,
	11:33	So they ***a*** and said to Jesus,
	11:33	And Jesus ***a*** and said to them,
	12:17	And Jesus ***a*** and said to them,
	12:24	Jesus ***a*** and said to them, "Are
	12:28	perceiving that He had ***a*** them
	12:29	Jesus ***a*** him, "The first of all
	12:34	Now when Jesus saw that he ***a***
	12:35	Then Jesus ***a*** and said, while He
	13: 2	And Jesus ***a*** and said to him,
	14:20	He ***a*** and said to them, "It is
	14:48	Then Jesus ***a*** and said to them,
	14:61	But He kept silent and ***a***
	15: 2	He ***a*** and said to him, "It
	15: 3	but He ***a*** nothing.
	15: 5	But Jesus still ***a*** nothing, so
	15: 9	But Pilate ***a*** them, saying, "Do
	15:12	Pilate ***a*** and said to them again,
Lk	1:19	And the angel ***a*** and said to him,
	1:35	And the angel ***a*** and said to her,
	1:60	His mother ***a*** and said, "No; he
	3:11	He ***a*** and said to them, "He who
	3:16	John ***a***, saying to all,
	4: 4	But Jesus ***a*** him, saying, "It is
	4: 8	And Jesus ***a*** and said to him,
	4:12	And Jesus ***a*** and said to him,
	5: 5	But Simon ***a*** and said to Him,
	5:22	He ***a*** and said to them, "Why
	5:31	Jesus ***a*** and said to them,
	7:22	Jesus ***a*** and said to them, "Go
	7:40	And Jesus ***a*** and said to him,
	7:43	Simon ***a*** and said, "I suppose
	8:21	But He ***a*** and said to them, "My
	8:50	He ***a*** him, saying, "Do not be
	9:19	So they ***a*** and said, "John the
	9:20	Peter ***a*** and said, "The
	9:41	Then Jesus ***a*** and said, "O
	9:49	Now John ***a*** and said, "Master,
	10:27	So he ***a*** and said, "'You
	10:28	You have ***a*** rightly; do this and
	10:30	Then Jesus ***a*** and said: "A
	10:41	And Jesus ***a*** and said to her,
	11:45	Then one of the lawyers ***a*** and
	13: 2	And Jesus ***a*** and said to them,
	13: 8	But he ***a*** and said to him, 'Sir,
	13:14	the ruler of the synagogue ***a***
	13:15	The Lord then ***a*** him and said,
	14: 5	Then He ***a*** them, saying, "Which
	15:29	So he ***a*** and said to his father,
	17:17	So Jesus ***a*** and said, "Were
	17:20	He ***a*** them and said, "The
	17:37	And they ***a*** and said to Him,
	19:40	But He ***a*** and said to them, "I
	20: 3	But He ***a*** and said to them, "I
	20: 7	So they ***a*** that they did not know
	20:24	They ***a*** and said, "Caesar's."
	20:34	And Jesus ***a*** and said to them,
	20:39	Then some of the scribes ***a*** and
	22:51	But Jesus ***a*** and said, "Permit
	23: 3	He ***a*** him and said, "It is
	23: 9	but He ***a*** him nothing.
	24:18	one whose name was Cleopas ***a***
Jn	1:21	you the Prophet?" And he ***a***,
	1:26	John ***a*** them, saying, "I baptize
	1:48	Jesus ***a*** and said to him,
	1:49	Nathanael ***a*** and said to Him,
	1:50	Jesus ***a*** and said to him,
	2:18	So the Jews ***a*** and said to Him,
	2:19	Jesus ***a*** and said to them,
	3: 3	Jesus ***a*** and said to him, "Most
	3: 5	Jesus ***a***, "Most assuredly,
	3: 9	Nicodemus ***a*** and said to Him,
	3:10	Jesus ***a*** and said to him, "Are
	3:27	John ***a*** and said, "A man can
	4:10	Jesus ***a*** and said to her, "If
	4:13	Jesus ***a*** and said to her,
	4:17	The woman ***a*** and said, "I have
	5: 7	The sick man ***a*** Him, "Sir, I
	5:11	He ***a*** them, "He who made me well
	5:17	But Jesus ***a*** them, "My Father
	5:19	Then Jesus ***a*** and said to them,
	6: 7	Philip ***a*** Him, "Two hundred
	6:26	Jesus ***a*** them and said, "Most
	6:29	Jesus ***a*** and said to them, "This
	6:43	Jesus therefore ***a*** and said to
	6:68	But Simon Peter ***a*** Him, "Lord,
	6:70	Jesus ***a*** them, "Did I not choose
	7:16	Jesus ***a*** them and said, "My
	7:20	The people ***a*** and said, "You
	7:21	Jesus ***a*** and said to them, "I
	7:46	The officers ***a***, "No man ever
	7:47	Then the Pharisees ***a*** them, "Are
	7:52	They ***a*** and said to him, "Are
	8:14	Jesus ***a*** and said to them, "Even
	8:19	is Your Father?" Jesus ***a***,
	8:33	They ***a*** Him, "We are Abraham's
	8:34	Jesus ***a*** them, "Most assuredly,
	8:39	They ***a*** and said to Him,
	8:48	Then the Jews ***a*** and said to
	8:49	Jesus ***a***, "I do not have
	8:54	Jesus ***a***, "If I honor Myself,
	9: 3	Jesus ***a***, "Neither this man
	9:11	He ***a*** and said, "A Man called
	9:20	His parents ***a*** them and said,
	9:25	He ***a*** and said, "Whether He is a
	9:27	He ***a*** them, "I told you already,
	9:30	The man ***a*** and said to them,
	9:34	They ***a*** and said to him, "You
	9:36	He ***a*** and said, "Who is He,
	10:25	Jesus ***a*** them, "I told you, and
	10:32	Jesus ***a*** them, "Many good works
	10:33	The Jews ***a*** Him, saying, "For a
	10:34	Jesus ***a*** them, "Is it not
	11: 9	Jesus ***a***, "Are there not twelve
	12:23	But Jesus ***a*** them, saying, "The
	12:30	Jesus ***a*** and said, "This voice
	12:34	The people ***a*** Him, "We have

13: 7 Jesus ***a*** and said to him, "What
13: 8 never wash my feet!" Jesus ***a***
13:26 Jesus ***a***, "It is he to whom
13:36 Jesus ***a*** him, "Where I am
13:38 Jesus ***a*** him, "Will you lay down
14:23 Jesus ***a*** and said to him, "If
16:31 Jesus ***a*** them, "Do you now
18: 5 They ***a*** Him, "Jesus of
18: 8 Jesus ***a***, "I have told you
18:20 Jesus ***a*** him, "I spoke openly to
18:23 Jesus ***a*** him, "If I have spoken
18:30 They ***a*** and said to him, "If He
18:34 Jesus ***a*** him, "Are you speaking
18:35 Pilate ***a***, "Am I a Jew?
18:36 Jesus ***a***, "My kingdom is not
18:37 You a king then?" Jesus ***a***,
19: 7 The Jews ***a*** him, "We have a law,
19:11 Jesus ***a***, "You could have no
19:15 King?" The chief priests ***a***,
19:22 Pilate ***a***, "What I have
20:28 And Thomas ***a*** and said to Him,
21: 5 They ***a*** Him, "No."
Acts 4:19 But Peter and John ***a*** and said to
5: 8 And Peter ***a*** her, "Tell me
5:29 and the other apostles ***a*** and
8:24 Then Simon ***a*** and said, "Pray to
8:34 So the eunuch ***a*** Philip and said,
8:37 And he ***a*** and said, "I
9:13 Then Ananias ***a***, "Lord, I have
10:46 and magnify God. Then Peter ***a***,
11: 9 But the voice ***a*** me again from
15:13 they had become silent, James ***a***,
19:15 And the evil spirit ***a*** and said,
21:13 Then Paul ***a***, "What do you
22: 8 'So I ***a***, 'Who are You,
22:28 The commander ***a***, "With a large
24:10 had nodded to him to speak, ***a***:
24:25 to come, Felix was afraid and ***a***,
25: 4 But Festus ***a*** that Paul should be
25: 8 while he ***a*** for himself,
25: 9 ***a*** Paul and said, "Are you
25:12 conferred with the council, ***a***,
25:16 'To them I ***a***, 'It is not the
26: 1 stretched out his hand and ***a***
Rev 7:13 Then one of the elders ***a***,

ANSWERING (6/6)

Job 32: 1 So these three men ceased ***a*** Job,
Mk 13: 5 ***a*** them, began to say: "Take
Lk 6: 3 But Jesus ***a*** them said, "Have
14: 3 And Jesus, ***a***, spoke to the
23:40 But the other, ***a***, rebuked him,
Titus 2: 9 in all things, not ***a*** back,

ANSWERS (9/9)

1 Sam 20:10 or what if your father ***a*** you
1 Ki 18:24 and the God who ***a*** by fire, He
Job 21:34 falsehood remains in your ***a***?
34:36 Because his ***a*** are like
Prov 18:13 He who ***a*** a matter before he
18:23 But the rich ***a*** roughly.
Eccl 10:19 But money ***a*** everything.
Jer 42: 4 that whatever the LORD ***a*** you,
Lk 2:47 at His understanding and ***a***.

ANT (1/1) ANTS

Prov 6: 6 Go to the ***a***,

ANTELOPE (2/2)

Deut 14: 5 goat, the mountain goat, the ***a***,
Isa 51:20 Like an ***a*** in a net; They are

ANTICHRIST (4/4) ANTICHRISTS

1 Jn 2:18 as you have heard that the ***A***
2:22 He is ***a*** who denies the Father
4: 3 this is the spirit of the ***A***,
2 Jn 7 This is a deceiver and an ***a***.

ANTICHRISTS (1/1) ANTICHRIST

1 Jn 2:18 even now many ***a*** have come, by

ANTICIPATED (1/1)

Mt 17:25 Jesus ***a*** him, saying, "What do

ANTIOCH (19/18)

Acts 6: 5 and Nicolas, a proselyte from ***A***,
11:19 far as Phoenicia, Cyprus, and ***A***,
11:20 who, when they had come to ***A***,
11:22 out Barnabas to go as far as ***A***.
11:26 found him, he brought him to ***A***.
11:26 first called Christians in ***A***.
11:27 came from Jerusalem to ***A***.
13: 1 Now in the church that was at ***A***
13:14 they came to ***A*** in Pisidia, and
14:19 Then Jews from ***A*** and Iconium
14:21 to Lystra, Iconium, and ***A***,
14:26 From there they sailed to ***A***,
15:22 men of their own company to ***A***
15:23 who are of the Gentiles in ***A***,
15:30 were sent off, they came to ***A***;
15:35 and Barnabas also remained in ***A***,
18:22 the church, he went down to ***A***.
Gal 2:11 Now when Peter had come to ***A***,
2 Tim 3:11 which happened to me at ***A***,

ANTIPAS (1/1)

Rev 2:13 even in the days in which ***A***

ANTIPATRIS (1/1)

Acts 23:31 and brought him by night to ***A***.

ANTIQUITY (2/2)

Isa 23: 7 Whose ***a*** is from ancient days,
Ezek 26:20 in places desolate from ***a***,

ANTITYPE (1/1)

1 Pe 3:21 There is also an ***a*** which now

ANTOTHIJAH (1/1)

1 Chr 8:24 Hananiah, Elam, ***A***,

ANTOTHITE (KJV) See ANATHOTHITE

ANTS (1/1)

Prov 30:25 The ***a*** are a people not strong,

ANUB (1/1)

1 Chr 4: 8 and Koz begot ***A***,

ANVIL (1/1)

Isa 41: 7 inspired him who strikes the ***a***,

ANXIETIES (2/2) ANXIETY

Ps 94:19 In the multitude of my ***a*** within
139:23 heart; Try me, and know my ***a***;

ANXIETY (4/4) ANXIETIES, ANXIOUS, ANXIOUSLY

Prov 12:25 ***A*** in the heart of man causes
Ezek 4:16 eat bread by weight and with ***a***,
12:18 your water with trembling and ***a***.
12:19 shall eat their bread with ***a***,

ANXIOUS (7/7) ANXIETY, ANXIOUSLY

1 Sam 9:20 do not be ***a*** about them, for
Job 20: 2 Therefore my ***a*** thoughts make me
Jer 17: 8 And will not be ***a*** in the year
Dan 2: 3 and my spirit is ***a*** to know the
Lk 12:26 why are you ***a*** for the rest?
12:29 nor have an ***a*** mind.
Phil 4: 6 Be ***a*** for nothing, but in

ANXIOUSLY (1/1) ANXIOUS

Lk 2:48 father and I have sought You ***a***.

ANY (493/453) See APPENDIX

ANYMORE (70/63)

Gen 8:12 did not return again to him ***a***.
35:10 shall not be called Jacob ***a***,
Ex 8:29 Pharaoh not deal deceitfully ***a***
Lev 27:20 man, it shall not be redeemed ***a***;
Deut 5:25 voice of the LORD our God ***a***,
18:16 let me see this great fire ***a***,
Josh 7:12 Neither will I be with you ***a***,
1 Sam 7:13 and they did not come ***a*** into
18: 2 go home to his father's house ***a***.
27: 1 to seek me ***a*** in any part of
28:15 me and does not answer me ***a***,
2 Sam 2:28 and did not pursue Israel ***a***,
2:28 anymore, nor did they fight ***a***.
7:10 of wickedness oppress them ***a***,
10:19 to help the people of Ammon ***a***.
14:10 and he shall not touch you ***a***.
14:11 avenger of blood to destroy ***a***,
19:28 have I still to cry out ***a*** to
19:29 Why do you speak ***a*** of your
2 Ki 21: 8 the feet of Israel wander ***a***
24: 7 did not come out of his land ***a***,
1 Chr 17: 9 of wickedness oppress them ***a***,
19:19 to help the people of Ammon ***a***.
Job 7:10 Nor shall his place know him ***a***.
20: 9 will his place behold him ***a***.
Isa 2: 4 Neither shall they learn war ***a***.
30:20 not be moved into a corner ***a***,
54: 4 reproach of your widowhood ***a***.
Jer 3:16 it, nor shall it be made ***a***.
10:20 is no one to pitch my tent ***a***,
20: 9 Nor speak ***a*** in His name."
22:11 "He shall not return here ***a***,
22:30 And ruling ***a*** in Judah.'"
31:40 be plucked up or thrown down ***a***
34:10 should keep them in bondage ***a***,
51:44 shall not stream to him ***a***.
Ezek 14:11 nor be profaned ***a*** with all
16:63 and never open your mouth ***a***
21: 5 sheath; it shall not return ***a***.
23:27 to them, Nor remember Egypt ***a***.
24:13 cleansed of your filthiness ***a***,
29:15 not rule over the nations ***a***.
34:29 the shame of the Gentiles ***a***.
36:14 more, nor bereave your nation ***a***,
36:15 the taunts of the nations ***a***,
36:15 the reproach of the peoples ***a***,
36:15 cause your nation to stumble ***a***,
37:23 shall not defile themselves ***a***
39: 7 them profane My holy name ***a***.
39:29 not hide My face from them ***a***;
Hos 14: 3 Nor will we say ***a*** to the work
14: 8 What have I to do ***a*** with idols?'
Am 7: 8 I will not pass by them ***a***.
8: 2 I will not pass by them ***a***.
Mal 2:13 does not regard the offering ***a***,
Mt 22:46 did anyone dare question Him ***a***.
Mk 9: 8 around, they saw no one ***a***,
Lk 20:36 "nor can they die ***a***,
20:40 they dared not question Him ***a***.
Rom 14:13 let us not judge one another ***a***,
Heb 12:19 should not be spoken to them ***a***.
Rev 7:16 They shall neither hunger ***a*** nor
7:16 hunger anymore nor thirst ***a***;
18:11 no one buys their merchandise ***a***:
18:21 down, and shall not be found ***a***.
18:22 shall not be heard in you ***a***.
18:22 craft shall be found in you ***a***,
18:22 shall not be heard in you ***a***.
18:23 a lamp shall not shine in you ***a***,
18:23 shall not be heard in you ***a***.

ANYONE (192/186)

Gen 4:14 and it will happen that ***a*** who
4:15 lest ***a*** finding him should kill
19:12 Have you ***a*** else here?
Ex 10:23 nor did ***a*** rise from his place
Lev 2: 1 When ***a*** offers a grain offering
4:27 If ***a*** of the common people sins
18: 6 None of you shall approach ***a***
25:49 or ***a*** who is near of kin to him
27: 9 all that ***a*** gives to the LORD
Num 6: 9 And if ***a*** dies very suddenly
9:10 If ***a*** of you or your posterity is
19:11 who touches the dead body of ***a***
19:13 Whoever touches the body of ***a***
21: 9 was, if a serpent had bitten ***a***,
35:15 that ***a*** who kills a person
Deut 18:10 not be found among you ***a*** who
19:11 But if ***a*** hates his neighbor,
21: 1 If ***a*** is found slain, lying in
22: 8 on your household if ***a*** falls
Josh 2:11 remain any more courage in ***a***
23: 7 nor cause ***a*** to swear by
Judg 3:28 and did not allow ***a*** to cross
18: 7 and they had no ties with ***a***
18:28 and they had no ties with ***a***.
21: 5 made a great oath concerning ***a***
1 Sam 21: 2 Do not let ***a*** know anything about
30: 2 to great; they did not kill ***a***,
2 Sam 7: 7 have I ever spoken a word to ***a***
9: 1 Is there still ***a*** who is left of
15: 2 whenever ***a*** who had a lawsuit
15: 5 whenever ***a*** came near to bow
18:12 Beware lest ***a*** touch the young
1 Ki 3:12 so that there has not been ***a***
3:13 so that there shall not be ***a***
8:31 When ***a*** sins against his
8:38 supplication is made by ***a***,
15:29 He did not leave to Jeroboam ***a***
2 Ki 2:16 he said, "You shall not send ***a***.
4:29 be on your way. If you meet ***a***,
4:29 and if ***a*** greets you, do not
10: 5 but we will not make ***a*** king.
2 Chr 6:22 If ***a*** sins against his neighbor,
6:29 supplication is made by ***a***,
Job 5: 1 Is there ***a*** who will answer
21:22 Can ***a*** teach God knowledge,
31:19 If I have seen ***a*** perish for
32:21 I pray, show partiality to ***a***;
34:31 For has ***a*** said to God, 'I
36:29 can ***a*** understand the spreading
Jer 5: 1 If there is ***a*** who executes
15:12 Can ***a*** break iron, The northern
23:24 Can ***a*** hide himself in secret
29:32 he shall not have ***a*** to dwell
Ezek 9: 6 but do not come near ***a*** on whom
14: 7 For ***a*** of the house of Israel, or
18: 7 If he has not oppressed ***a***,
18:16 Has not oppressed ***a***,
39:15 and when ***a*** sees a man's bone,
Dan 1:20 I have more wisdom than ***a***
Zech 13: 3 shall come to pass that if ***a***
Mt 5:40 If ***a*** wants to sue you and take
11:27 Nor does ***a*** know the Father
12:19 Nor will ***a*** hear His
12:32 ***A*** who speaks a word against the
13:19 When ***a*** hears the word of the
16:24 If ***a*** desires to come after Me,
21: 3 And if ***a*** says anything to you,
22:16 truth; nor do You care about ***a***,
22:46 nor from that day on did ***a*** dare
23: 9 Do not call ***a*** on earth your
24:23 Then if ***a*** says to you, 'Look,
Mk 1:44 "See that you say nothing to ***a***;
4:23 If ***a*** has ears to hear, let him
5: 4 neither could ***a*** tame him.
7:16 If ***a*** has ears to hear, let him
8:26 nor tell ***a*** in the town."
9:30 and He did not want ***a*** to know
9:35 If ***a*** desires to be first, he
11: 3 And if ***a*** says to you, 'Why are
11:16 And He would not allow ***a*** to
11:25 if you have anything against ***a***,
13:21 Then if ***a*** says to you, 'Look,
16: 8 And they said nothing to ***a***,
Lk 3:14 Do not intimidate ***a*** or accuse
9:23 If ***a*** desires to come after Me,
12:10 And ***a*** who speaks a word against

14: 8 When you are invited by ***a*** to a
14:26 If ***a*** comes to Me and does not
19: 8 if I have taken anything from ***a***
19:31 And if ***a*** asks you, 'Why are you
Jn 2:25 and had no need that ***a*** should
4:33 Has ***a*** brought Him anything to
6:46 Not that ***a*** has seen the Father,
6:51 If ***a*** eats of this bread, he
7:17 If ***a*** wants to do His will, he
7:37 If ***a*** thirsts, let him come to Me
8:33 have never been in bondage to ***a***.
8:51 if ***a*** keeps My word he shall
8:52 If ***a*** keeps My word he shall
9:22 had agreed already that if ***a***
9:31 but if ***a*** is a worshiper of God
9:32 it has been unheard of that ***a***
10: 9 If ***a*** enters by Me, he will be
10:28 neither shall ***a*** snatch them out
11: 9 If ***a*** walks in the day, he does
11:57 that if ***a*** knew where He was, he
12:26 If ***a*** serves Me, let him follow
12:26 If ***a*** serves Me, him My Father
12:47 And if ***a*** hears My words and does
14:23 If ***a*** loves Me, he will keep My
15: 6 If ***a*** does not abide in Me, he is
16:30 and have no need that ***a*** should
18:31 is not lawful for us to put ***a***
Acts 2:45 among all, as ***a*** had need.
4:32 neither did ***a*** say that any of
4:34 Nor was there ***a*** among them who
4:35 they distributed to each as ***a***
8:19 that ***a*** on whom I lay hands may
10:47 Can ***a*** forbid water, that these
19:38 craftsmen have a case against ***a***,
24:12 in the temple disputing with ***a***
Rom 8: 9 Now if ***a*** does not have the
1 Cor 1:15 lest ***a*** should say that I had
3:11 For no other foundation can ***a***
3:12 Now if ***a*** builds on this
3:17 If ***a*** defiles the temple of God,
3:18 If ***a*** among you seems to be wise
5:11 you not to keep company with ***a***
7:18 Was ***a*** called while circumcised?
7:18 Was ***a*** called while
8: 2 And if ***a*** thinks that he knows
8: 3 But if ***a*** loves God, this one is
8:10 For if ***a*** sees you who have
9:15 for me to die than that ***a***
10:28 But if ***a*** says to you, "This was
11:16 But if ***a*** seems to be
11:34 But if ***a*** is hungry, let him eat
14:27 If ***a*** speaks in a tongue, let
14:37 If ***a*** thinks himself to be a
14:38 But if ***a*** is ignorant, let him be
16:22 If ***a*** does not love the Lord
2 Cor 2: 5 But if ***a*** has caused grief, he
5:17 if ***a*** is in Christ, he is a
8:20 that ***a*** should blame us in this
8:23 If ***a*** inquires about Titus, he
10: 7 If ***a*** is convinced in himself
11:21 for that! But in whatever ***a*** is
12: 6 lest ***a*** should think of me above
Gal 1: 9 if ***a*** preaches any other gospel
6: 3 For if ***a*** thinks himself to be
Eph 2: 9 lest ***a*** should boast.
6: 8 knowing that whatever good ***a***
Phil 3: 4 If ***a*** else thinks he may have
Col 2: 4 Now this I say lest ***a*** should
2: 8 Beware lest ***a*** cheat you through
3:13 if ***a*** has a complaint against
1 Th 5:15 one renders evil for evil to ***a***,
2 Th 3:10 If ***a*** will not work, neither
3:14 And if ***a*** does not obey our word
1 Tim 5: 8 But if ***a*** does not provide for
5:22 Do not lay hands on ***a*** hastily,
6: 3 If ***a*** teaches otherwise and does
2 Tim 2: 5 And also if ***a*** competes in
2:21 Therefore if ***a*** cleanses himself
Heb 4:11 lest ***a*** fall according to the
10:28 ***A*** who has rejected Moses' law
10:38 But if ***a*** draws back, My
12:15 looking carefully lest ***a*** fall
Jas 1:13 nor does He Himself tempt ***a***.
1:23 For if ***a*** is a hearer of the word
1:26 If ***a*** among you thinks he is
3: 2 If ***a*** does not stumble in word,
5:13 Is ***a*** among you suffering?
5:13 Is ***a*** cheerful? Let him sing
5:14 Is ***a*** among you sick? Let him
5:19 if ***a*** among you wanders from the
1 Pe 4:11 If ***a*** speaks, let him speak as
4:11 If ***a*** ministers, let him do
4:16 Yet if ***a*** suffers as a
1 Jn 2: 1 And if ***a*** sins, we have an
2:15 If ***a*** loves the world, the love
2:27 and you do not need that ***a***
5:16 If ***a*** sees his brother sinning a
2 Jn 10 If ***a*** comes to you and does not
Rev 3:20 If ***a*** hears My voice and opens
11: 5 And if ***a*** wants to harm them,
11: 5 And if ***a*** wants to harm them, he
13: 9 If ***a*** has an ear, let him hear.
14: 9 If ***a*** worships the beast and his
20:15 And ***a*** not found written in the
22:18 If ***a*** adds to these things, God
22:19 and if ***a*** takes away from the

ANYONE'S (4/4)

Lev 7: 8 And the priest who offers ***a***
1 Cor 3:14 If ***a*** work which he has built on
3:15 If ***a*** work is burned, he will
2 Th 3: 8 nor did we eat ***a*** bread free of

ANYTHING (139/135)

Gen 14:23 and that I will not take ***a*** that
18:14 'Is ***a*** too hard for the LORD?
19:22 For I cannot do ***a*** until you
22:12 or do ***a*** to him; for now I know
30:31 said, "You shall not give me ***a***.
39: 9 nor has he kept back ***a*** from me
39:23 the prison did not look into ***a***
Ex 20: 4 or any likeness of ***a*** that is
20:17 nor ***a*** that is your
20:23 You shall not make ***a*** to be
22:14 And if a man borrows ***a*** from
Lev 4: 2 of the LORD in ***a*** which
4:13 of the LORD in ***a*** which
4:22 of the LORD his God in ***a***
4:27 of the LORD in ***a*** which
11:32 ***A*** on which any of them falls,
13:48 whether in leather or in ***a*** made
13:49 or in ***a*** made of leather, it is
13:51 in the leather or in ***a*** made of
13:52 or ***a*** of leather, for it is an
13:53 or in ***a*** made of leather,
13:57 or in ***a*** made of leather, it is
13:59 or in ***a*** made of leather, to
15: 6 He who sits on ***a*** on which he who
15:10 Whoever touches ***a*** that was under
15:22 And whoever touches ***a*** that she
15:23 If ***a*** is on her bed or on
15:23 is on her bed or on ***a*** on
19:26 You shall not eat ***a*** with the
22: 4 And whoever touches ***a*** made
25:14 And if you sell ***a*** to your
Num 15:30 But the person who does ***a***
22:38 I any power at all to say ***a***?
35:22 or throws ***a*** at him without
Deut 3:24 or on earth who can do ***a*** like
4:18 the likeness of ***a*** that creeps on
4:23 a carved image in the form of ***a***
4:25 a carved image in the form of ***a***,
4:32 or ***a*** like it has been heard.
5: 8 any likeness of ***a*** that is in
5:21 or ***a*** that is your neighbor's.'
14:21 You shall not eat ***a*** that dies
15: 2 Every creditor who has lent ***a***
22: 5 A woman shall not wear ***a*** that
23:19 on money or food or ***a*** that
24:10 "When you lend your brother ***a***,
Judg 13: 4 and not to eat ***a*** unclean.
13: 7 nor eat ***a*** unclean, for the
13:14 She may not eat ***a*** that comes
13:14 nor eat ***a*** unclean. All that I
18: 7 might put them to shame for ***a***.
18:10 where there is no lack of ***a***
19:19 there is no lack of ***a***.
Ruth 1:17 If ***a*** but death parts you and
4: 7 and exchanging, to confirm ***a***:
1 Sam 3:17 if you hide ***a*** from me of all
12: 4 nor have you taken ***a*** from any
12: 5 that you have not found ***a*** in my
20:26 Saul did not say ***a*** that day,
20:39 But the lad did not know ***a***.
21: 2 Do not let anyone know ***a*** about
22:15 me! Let not the king impute ***a***
25: 7 nor was there ***a*** missing from
25:15 nor did we miss ***a*** as long as we
30:19 spoil or ***a*** which they had taken
2 Sam 3:35 if I taste bread or ***a*** else till
13: 2 was improper for Amnon to do ***a***
14:10 Whoever says ***a*** to you, bring
14:18 Please do not hide from me ***a***
14:19 hand or to the left from ***a***
15:11 innocently and did not know ***a***.
1 Ki 15: 5 and had not turned aside from ***a***
Neh 4:11 will neither know nor see ***a***,
Job 15:18 Not hiding ***a*** received from
20:20 He will not save ***a*** he desires.
33:32 If you have ***a*** to say, answer
Eccl 1:10 Is there ***a*** of which it may be
5: 2 And let not your heart utter ***a***
6: 5 not seen the sun or known ***a***,
9: 1 neither love nor hatred by ***a***
9: 6 will they have a share In ***a***
Jer 32:27 Is there ***a*** too hard for Me?
42:21 or ***a*** which He has sent you by
Ezek 14: 9 prophet is induced to speak ***a***
17:17 army and great company do ***a*** in
44:18 not clothe themselves with ***a***
44:31 "The priests shall not eat ***a***,
Dan 3:29 or language which speaks ***a***
Joel 1: 2 of the land! Has ***a*** like
Jon 3: 7 beast, herd nor flock, taste ***a***;
Mt 18:19 you agree on earth concerning ***a***
21: 3 And if anyone says ***a*** to you, you
24:17 housetop not go down to take ***a***
Mk 2:12 We never saw ***a*** like this!"
4:22 nor has ***a*** been kept secret but
7:12 you no longer let him do ***a*** for
8:23 him, He asked him if he saw ***a***.
9:22 But if You can do ***a***,
11:25 if you have ***a*** against anyone,
13:15 nor enter to take ***a*** out of his
16:18 and if they drink ***a*** deadly, it
Lk 8:17 nor ***a*** hidden that will not be
15:16 ate, and no one gave him ***a***.
19: 8 and if I have taken ***a*** from
19:48 and were unable to do ***a***;
22:35 and sandals, did you lack ***a***?
Jn 1:46 Can ***a*** good come out of
4:33 Has anyone brought Him ***a*** to
7: 4 For no one does ***a*** in secret
14:14 If you ask ***a*** in My name, I will
Acts 10:14 Lord! For I have never eaten ***a***
17:25 hands, as though He needed ***a***,
24:19 you to object if they had ***a***
25: 8 Caesar have I offended in ***a*** at
25:11 or have committed ***a*** deserving
28:19 not that I had ***a*** of which to
Rom 13: 8 Owe no one ***a*** except to love one
14:14 but to him who considers ***a*** to
14:21 meat nor drink wine nor do ***a***
1 Cor 2: 2 For I determined not to know ***a***
3: 7 then neither he who plants is ***a***,
8: 2 anyone thinks that he knows ***a***,
10:19 saying then? That an idol is ***a***,
10:19 what is offered to idols is ***a***?
14:30 But if ***a*** is revealed to another
2 Cor 2:10 Now whom you forgive ***a***,
2:10 For if indeed I have forgiven ***a***,
3: 5 of ourselves to think of ***a*** as
6: 3 We give no offense in ***a***,
7:14 For if in ***a*** I have boasted to
Gal 5: 6 nor uncircumcision avails ***a***,
6:15 nor uncircumcision avails ***a***,
Phil 3:15 and if in ***a*** you think
4: 8 any virtue and if there is ***a***
1 Th 1: 8 so that we do not need to say ***a***.
Phm 1:18 if he has wronged you or owes ***a***,
Jas 1: 7 suppose that he will receive ***a***
1 Jn 5:14 that if we ask ***a*** according to
Rev 21:27 shall by no means enter it ***a***

ANYWAY (1/1)

1 Ki 11:22 "Nothing, but do let me go ***a***.

ANYWHERE (5/5)

Gen 19:17 not look behind you nor stay ***a***
Deut 2:37 ***a*** along the River Jabbok, or to
1 Ki 2:36 and do not go out from there ***a***.
2:42 the day you go out and travel ***a***,
2 Ki 5:25 "Your servant did not go ***a***.

APACE (KJV) See RAPIDLY, SPEEDILY

APART (40/39)

Ex 8:22 And in that day I will set ***a*** the
13:12 that you shall set ***a*** to the
Lev 15:19 she shall be set ***a*** seven days;
Num 16:31 that the ground split ***a*** under
Deut 4:41 Then Moses set ***a*** three cities
Judg 7: 5 you shall set ***a*** by himself;
14: 6 and he tore the lion ***a*** as one
14: 6 apart as one would have torn ***a***
1 Sam 9:23 which I said to you, 'Set it ***a***.
9:24 It was set ***a*** for you. Eat; for
1 Ki 5: 9 and will have them broken ***a***
13: 3 Surely the altar shall split ***a***,
13: 5 The altar also was split ***a***,
1 Chr 23:13 and Moses; and Aaron was set ***a***,
Ezra 10:16 were set ***a*** by the fathers'
Ps 4: 3 know that the LORD has set ***a***
16: 2 My goodness is nothing ***a*** from
Prov 18:18 cease, And keeps the mighty ***a***.
Isa 23:18 gain and her pay will be set ***a***
51: 9 not the arm that cut Rahab ***a***,
Jer 50:23 the whole earth has been cut ***a***
Ezek 22:10 violate women who are set ***a***
39:14 They will set ***a*** men regularly
45: 1 you shall set ***a*** a district for
48: 8 district which you shall set ***a***,
48: 9 district that you shall set ***a***
48:12 district of land that is set ***a***
48:20 You shall set ***a*** the holy
48:22 ***a*** from the possession of the
Hos 4:14 For the men themselves go ***a***
Nah 1:13 you, And burst your bonds ***a***.
Mt 10:29 of them falls to the ground ***a***
Mk 5: 4 the chains had been pulled ***a***
9: 2 them up on a high mountain ***a***
Rom 3:21 now the righteousness of God ***a***
3:28 a man is justified by faith ***a***
4: 6 God imputes righteousness ***a***
7: 8 For ***a*** from the law sin was
Heb 9:28 ***a*** from sin, for salvation.
11:40 should not be made perfect ***a***

APELLES (1/1)

Rom 16:10 Greet ***A***, approved in Christ.

APES (2/2)

1 Ki 10:22 bringing gold, silver, ivory, ***a***,
2 Chr 9:21 bringing gold, silver, ivory, ***a***,

APHARSACHITES, APHARSITES (KJV) See APHARSATHCHITES, PERSIANS

APHARSATHCHITES (1/1)

Ezra 4: 9 of the Dinaites, the ***A***,

APHEK (8/8) APHIK

Josh 12:18 the king of ***A***,
13: 4 to the Sidonians as far as ***A***,
19:30 Also Ummah, ***A***,

1 Sam 4: 1 the Philistines encamped in ***A***.
29: 1 together all their armies at ***A***,
1 Ki 20:26 the Syrians and went up to ***A***
20:30 But the rest fled to ***A***,
2 Ki 13:17 must strike the Syrians at ***A***

APHEKAH (1/1)

Josh 15:53 Janum, Beth Tappuah, ***A***,

APHIAH (1/1)

1 Sam 9: 1 son of Bechorath, the son of ***A***,

APHIK (1/1) APHEK

Judg 1:31 or of Ahlab, Achzib, Helbah, ***A***,

APHSES (KJV) See HAPPIZZEZ

APIECE (5/5)

Num 7:86 incense weighed ten shekels ***a***,
17: 6 their leaders gave him a rod ***a***,
Ezek 41:24 The doors had two panels ***a***,
Lk 9: 3 and do not have two tunics ***a***.
Jn 2: 6 twenty or thirty gallons ***a***.

APOLLONIA (1/1)

Acts 17: 1 passed through Amphipolis and ***A***,

APOLLOS (10/10)

Acts 18:24 Now a certain Jew named ***A***,
19: 1 while ***A*** was at Corinth, that
1 Cor 1:12 am of Paul," or "I am of ***A***,
3: 4 and another, "I am of ***A***,
3: 5 then is Paul, and who is ***A***,
3: 6 ***A*** watered, but God gave the
3:22 whether Paul or ***A*** or Cephas, or
4: 6 transferred to myself and ***A***
16:12 Now concerning our brother ***A***,
Titus 3:13 Send Zenas the lawyer and ***A*** on

APOLLYON (1/1)

Rev 9:11 but in Greek he has the name ***A***.

APOSTLE (19/19) APOSTLES, APOSTLES', APOSTLESHIP

Rom 1: 1 Christ, called to be an ***a***,
11:13 inasmuch as I am an ***a*** to the
1 Cor 1: 1 called TO be an ***a*** of Jesus
9: 1 Am I not an ***a***?
9: 2 If I am not an ***a*** to others, yet
15: 9 am not worthy to be called an ***a***,
2 Cor 1: 1 an ***a*** of Jesus Christ by the
12:12 Truly the signs of an ***a*** were
Gal 1: 1 an ***a*** (not from men nor through
Eph 1: 1 an ***a*** of Jesus Christ by the
Col 1: 1 an ***a*** of Jesus Christ by the
1 Tim 1: 1 an ***a*** of Jesus Christ, by the
2: 7 appointed a preacher and an ***a***—
2 Tim 1: 1 an ***a*** of Jesus Christ by the
1:11 was appointed a preacher, an ***a***,
Titus 1: 1 a bondservant of God and an ***a***
Heb 3: 1 consider the ***A*** and High Priest
1 Pe 1: 1 an ***a*** of Jesus Christ, To the
2 Pe 1: 1 a bondservant and ***a*** of Jesus

APOSTLES (55/54) APOSTLE, APOSTLES'

Mt 10: 2 Now the names of the twelve ***a***
Mk 6:30 Then the ***a*** gathered to Jesus
Lk 6:13 twelve whom He also named ***a***:
9:10 And the ***a***, when they had
11:49 will send them prophets and ***a***,
17: 5 And the ***a*** said to the Lord,
22:14 and the twelve ***a*** with Him.
24:10 who told these things to the ***a***.
Acts 1: 2 had given commandments to the ***a***
1:26 was numbered with the eleven ***a***.
2:37 to Peter and the rest of the ***a***,
2:43 signs were done through the ***a***.
4:33 And with great power the ***a*** gave
4:36 also named Barnabas by the ***a***
5:12 And through the hands of the ***a***
5:18 and laid their hands on the ***a***
5:29 But Peter and the other ***a***
5:34 and commanded them to put the ***a***
5:40 when they had called for the ***a***
6: 6 whom they set before the ***a***;
8: 1 Judea and Samaria, except the ***a***.
8:14 Now when the ***a*** who were at
9:27 him and brought him to the ***a***.
11: 1 Now the ***a*** and brethren who were
14: 4 the Jews, and part with the ***a***.
14:14 But when the ***a*** Barnabas and Paul
15: 2 to the ***a*** and elders, about this
15: 4 by the church and the ***a*** and
15: 6 Now the ***a*** and elders came
15:22 Then it pleased the ***a*** and
15:23 this letter by them: The ***a***,
15:33 from the brethren to the ***a***.
16: 4 which were determined by the ***a***
Rom 16: 7 who are of note among the ***a***,
1 Cor 4: 9 God has displayed us, the ***a***,
9: 5 wife, as do also the other ***a***,
12:28 these in the church: first ***a***,
12:29 Are all ***a***?
15: 7 by James, then by all the ***a***.
15: 9 For I am the least of the ***a***,
2 Cor 11: 5 inferior to the most eminent ***a***.
11:13 For such are false ***a***,
11:13 transforming themselves into ***a***
12:11 was I behind the most eminent ***a***,
Gal 1:17 to those who were ***a*** before
1:19 But I saw none of the other ***a***
Eph 2:20 on the foundation of the ***a*** and
3: 5 by the Spirit to His holy ***a***
4:11 He Himself gave some to be ***a***,
1 Th 2: 6 we might have made demands as ***a***
2 Pe 3: 2 the ***a*** of the Lord and Savior,
Jude 17 were spoken before by the ***a*** of
Rev 2: 2 those who say they are ***a*** and
18:20 and you holy ***a*** and prophets,
21:14 were the names of the twelve ***a***

APOSTLES' (5/5) APOSTLES

Acts 2:42 steadfastly in the ***a*** doctrine
4:35 and laid them at the ***a*** feet;
4:37 money and laid it at the ***a*** feet.
5: 2 part and laid it at the ***a*** feet.
8:18 the laying on of the ***a*** hands

APOSTLESHIP (4/4) APOSTLE

Acts 1:25 part in this ministry and ***a***
Rom 1: 5 we have received grace and ***a***
1 Cor 9: 2 For you are the seal of my ***a*** in
Gal 2: 8 effectively in Peter for the ***a***

APOTHECARIES (KJV) See PERFUMERS

APOTHECARY (KJV) See PERFUMER

APPAIM (2/2)

1 Chr 2:30 sons of Nadab were Seled and ***A***;
2:31 The son of ***A*** was Ishi, the son

APPAREL (23/22) APPARELED

Judg 14:19 of their men, took their ***a***,
1 Sam 27: 9 donkeys, the camels, and the ***a***,
2 Sam 1:24 put ornaments of gold on your ***a***.
13:18 virgin daughters wore such ***a***.
14: 2 mourner, and put on mourning ***a***;
1 Ki 10: 5 of his waiters and their ***a***,
2 Chr 9: 4 of his waiters and their ***a***,
9: 4 his cupbearers and their ***a***,
Ezra 3:10 the priests stood in their ***a***
Esth 8:15 of the king in royal ***a*** of blue
Isa 3:22 the festal ***a***, and the mantles;
4: 1 our own food and wear our own ***a***;
63: 1 One who is glorious in His ***a***,
63: 2 Why is Your ***a*** red, And Your
Ezek 27:24 in chests of multicolored ***a***,
Zeph 1: 8 as are clothed with foreign ***a***.
Zech 14:14 and ***a*** in great abundance.
Acts 1:10 men stood by them in white ***a***,
12:21 day Herod, arrayed in royal ***a***,
20:33 no one's silver or gold or ***a***.
1 Tim 2: 9 adorn themselves in modest ***a***,
Jas 2: 2 man with gold rings, in fine ***a***,
1 Pe 3: 3 gold, or putting on fine ***a***—

APPARELED (1/1) APPAREL

Lk 7:25 those who are gorgeously ***a*** and

APPARENTLY (KJV) See PLAINLY

APPEAL (6/6) APPEALED, APPEALING

2 Ki 8: 3 and she went to make an ***a*** to
Acts 25:11 I ***a*** to Caesar."
28:19 I was compelled to ***a*** to Caesar,
Phm 1: 9 for love's sake I rather ***a*** to
1:10 I ***a*** to you for my son Onesimus,
Heb 13:22 And I ***a*** to you, brethren, bear

APPEALED (4/4) APPEAL

Acts 25:12 You have ***a*** to Caesar? To Caesar
25:21 But when Paul ***a*** to be reserved
25:25 and that he himself had ***a*** to
26:32 been set free if he had not ***a***

APPEALING (2/2) APPEAL

2 Ki 8: 5 ***a*** to the king for her house and
Isa 4: 2 shall be excellent and ***a***

APPEAR (40/39) APPEARANCE, APPEARED, APPEARING, APPEARS

Gen 1: 9 and let the dry land ***a***"; and
Ex 23:15 none shall ***a*** before Me empty);
23:17 the year all your males shall ***a***
34:20 And none shall ***a*** before Me
34:23 the year all your men shall ***a***
34:24 your land when you go up to ***a***
Lev 9: 4 for today the LORD will ***a*** to
9: 6 the glory of the LORD will ***a***
13: 4 and does not ***a*** to be deeper
13:31 and indeed it does not ***a*** deeper
13:32 and the scale does not ***a*** deeper
13:34 and does not ***a*** deeper than the
14:37 which ***a*** to be deep in the wall,
16: 2 for I will ***a*** in the cloud above
Deut 16:16 a year all your males shall ***a***
16:16 and they shall not ***a*** before the
31:11 when all Israel comes to ***a***
1 Sam 1:22 that he may ***a*** before the LORD
Ps 42: 2 When shall I come and ***a*** before
90:16 Let Your work ***a*** to Your
102:16 He shall ***a*** in His glory.
Song 2:12 The flowers ***a*** on the earth;
Isa 1:12 When you come to ***a*** before Me,
Jer 13:26 face, That your shame may ***a***.
Ezek 21:24 in all your doings your sins ***a***—
Mt 6:16 their faces that they may ***a*** to
6:18 so that you do not ***a*** to men to
23:27 tombs which indeed ***a*** beautiful
23:28 Even so you also outwardly ***a***
24:30 sign of the Son of Man will ***a***
Lk 19:11 the kingdom of God would ***a***
Acts 22:30 and all their council to ***a***,
Rom 7:13 that it might ***a*** sin, was
2 Cor 5:10 For we must all ***a*** before the
7:12 in the sight of God might ***a*** to
13: 7 not that we should ***a*** approved,
Col 3: 4 then you also will ***a*** with Him
Heb 9:24 now to ***a*** in the presence of God
9:28 eagerly wait for Him He will ***a***
1 Pe 4:18 ungodly and the sinner ***a***?

APPEARANCE (54/39) APPEAR

Gen 29:17 was beautiful of form and ***a***.
39: 6 was handsome in form and ***a***.
Lev 13:43 as the ***a*** of leprosy on the skin
Num 9:15 the tabernacle like the ***a*** of
9:16 and the ***a*** of fire by night.
1 Sam 16: 7 Do not look at his ***a*** or at the
16: 7 for man looks at the outward ***a***,
25: 3 understanding and beautiful ***a***;
2 Sam 14:27 She was a woman of beautiful ***a***.
Job 4:16 But I could not discern its ***a***.
Lam 4: 7 Like sapphire in their ***a***.
4: 8 Now their ***a*** is blacker than
Ezek 1: 5 And this was their ***a***:
1:13 their ***a*** was like burning coals
1:13 like the ***a*** of torches going
1:14 in ***a*** like a flash of lightning.
1:16 The ***a*** of the wheels and their
1:16 The ***a*** of their workings was,
1:26 in ***a*** like a sapphire stone; on
1:26 was a likeness with the ***a*** of
1:27 Also from the ***a*** of His waist and
1:27 the color of amber with the ***a***
1:27 and from the ***a*** of His waist and
1:27 the ***a*** of fire with brightness
1:28 Like the ***a*** of a rainbow in a
1:28 so was the ***a*** of the brightness
1:28 This was the ***a*** of the likeness
8: 2 like the ***a*** of fire—from the
8: 2 from the ***a*** of His waist and
8: 2 like the ***a*** of brightness, like
10: 1 having the ***a*** of the likeness of
10:10 As for their ***a***,
10:22 their ***a*** and their persons.
40: 3 there was a man whose ***a*** was
40: 3 appearance was like the ***a*** of
41:21 their ***a*** was similar.
42:11 and their ***a*** was like the
43: 3 It was like the ***a*** of the
Dan 1:13 Then let our ***a*** be examined
1:13 and the ***a*** of the young men who
7:20 whose ***a*** was greater than his
8:15 before me one having the ***a*** of
10: 6 his face like the ***a*** of
Joel 2: 4 Their ***a*** is like the appearance
2: 4 appearance is like the ***a*** of
Lk 9:29 the ***a*** of His face was altered,
Jn 7:24 "Do not judge according to ***a***,
2 Cor 5:12 for those who boast in ***a*** and
10: 7 according to the outward ***a***?
Phil 2: 8 And being found in ***a*** as a man,
Col 2:23 These things indeed have an ***a*** of
Jas 1:11 and its beautiful ***a*** perishes.
Rev 4: 3 jasper and a sardius stone in ***a***;
4: 3 in ***a*** like an emerald.

APPEARED (76/73) APPEAR

Gen 12: 7 Then the LORD ***a*** to Abram and
12: 7 who had ***a*** to him.
15:17 there ***a*** a smoking oven and a
17: 1 the LORD ***a*** to Abram and said
18: 1 Then the LORD ***a*** to him by the
26: 2 Then the LORD ***a*** to him and
26:24 And the LORD ***a*** to him the same
35: 1 who ***a*** to you when you fled from
35: 7 because there God ***a*** to him when
35: 9 Then God ***a*** to Jacob again, when
48: 3 God Almighty ***a*** to me at Luz in
Ex 3: 2 And the Angel of the LORD ***a*** to
3:16 ***a*** to me, saying, "I have
4: 1 The LORD has not ***a*** to you.'"
4: 5 has ***a*** to you."
6: 3 I ***a*** to Abraham, to Isaac, and to
14:27 the sea; and when the morning ***a***,
16:10 the glory of the LORD ***a*** in the
Lev 9:23 Then the glory of the LORD ***a***
Num 14:10 Now the glory of the LORD ***a*** in
16:19 Then the glory of the LORD ***a***
16:42 and the glory of the LORD ***a***.
20: 6 And the glory of the LORD ***a*** to
Deut 31:15 Now the LORD ***a*** at the

Judg 6:12 And the Angel of the LORD *a* to
13: 3 And the Angel of the LORD *a* to
13:10 the other day has just now *a*
13:21 When the Angel of the LORD *a* no
1 Sam 3:21 Then the LORD *a* again in
1 Ki 3: 5 At Gibeon the LORD *a* to Solomon
9: 2 that the LORD *a* to Solomon the
9: 2 as He had *a* to him at Gibeon.
11: 9 who had *a* to him twice,
2 Ki 2:11 suddenly a chariot of fire *a*
2 Chr 1: 7 On that night God *a* to Solomon,
3: 1 where the LORD had *a* to his
7:12 Then the LORD *a* to Solomon by
Neh 4:21 from daybreak until the stars *a*.
Jer 31: 3 The LORD has *a* of old to me,
Ezek 10: 1 there *a* something like a
10: 8 The cherubim *a* to have the form
10: 9 the wheels *a* to have the
Dan 1:15 of ten days their features *a*
5: 5 the fingers of a man's hand *a*
8: 1 of King Belshazzar a vision *a*
8: 1 after the one that *a* to me the
Mt 1:20 an angel of the Lord *a* to him
2: 7 from them what time the star *a*.
2:13 an angel of the Lord *a* to
2:19 an angel of the Lord *a* in a
13:26 a crop, then the tares also *a*.
17: 3 Moses and Elijah *a* to them,
27:53 went into the holy city and *a*
Mk 9: 4 And Elijah *a* to them with Moses,
16: 9 He *a* first to Mary Magdalene,
16:12 He *a* in another form to two of
16:14 Later He *a* to the eleven as
Lk 1:11 Then an angel of the Lord *a* to
9: 8 and by some that Elijah had *a*,
9:31 who *a* in glory and spoke of His
22:43 Then an angel *a* to Him from
24:34 and has *a* to Simon!"
Acts 2: 3 Then there *a* to them divided
7: 2 The God of glory *a* to our
7:26 And the next day he *a* to two of
7:30 an Angel of the Lord *a* to him
7:35 by the hand of the Angel who *a*
9:17 who *a* to you on the road as you
16: 9 And a vision *a* to Paul in the
26:16 for I have *a* to you for this
27:20 when neither sun nor stars *a*
Titus 2:11 that brings salvation has *a* to
3: 4 of God our Savior toward man *a*,
Heb 9:26 He has *a* to put away sin by the
Rev 12: 1 Now a great sign *a* in heaven: a
12: 3 And another sign *a* in heaven:

APPEARING (5/5) APPEAR

1 Tim 6:14 until our Lord Jesus Christ's *a*,
2 Tim 1:10 has now been revealed by the *a*
4: 1 living and the dead at His *a*
4: 8 to all who have loved His *a*.
Titus 2:13 blessed hope and glorious *a* of

APPEARS (15/15) APPEAR

Lev 13: 3 and the sore *a* to be deeper
13: 5 and indeed if the sore *a* to be
13:14 But when raw flesh *a* on him, he
13:20 it indeed *a* deeper than the
13:25 and it *a* deeper than the skin,
13:30 and indeed if it *a* deeper than
13:37 But if the scale *a* to be at a
13:57 But if it *a* again in the
Ps 84: 7 Each one *a* before God in
Jer 6: 1 For disaster *a* out of the
Mal 3: 2 And who can stand when He *a*?
Col 3: 4 When Christ who is our life *a*,
Jas 4:14 It is even a vapor that *a* for a
1 Pe 5: 4 and when the Chief Shepherd *a*,
1 Jn 2:28 abide in Him, that when He *a*,

APPEASE (3/3) APPEASED

Gen 32:20 I will *a* him with the present
Prov 16:14 But a wise man will *a* it.
Mt 28:14 we will *a* him and make you

APPEASED (1/1) APPEASE

Prov 6:35 Nor will he be *a* though you

APPERTAIN (KJV) See BELONGS

APPETITE (2/2)

Job 38:39 Or satisfy the *a* of the young
Prov 23: 2 If you are a man given to *a*.

APPHIA (1/1)

Phm 1: 2 to the beloved *A*,

APPII (1/1)

Acts 28:15 came to meet us as far as *A*

APPLE (7/7) APPLES

Deut 32:10 He kept him as the *a* of His
Ps 17: 8 Keep me as the *a* of Your eye;
Prov 7: 2 And my law as the *a* of your
Song 2: 3 Like an *a* tree among the trees
8: 5 I awakened you under the *a*
Joel 1:12 And the *a* tree—All the trees
Zech 2: 8 who touches you touches the *a*

APPLES (3/3) APPLE

Prov 25:11 word fitly spoken is like *a*
Song 2: 5 of raisins, Refresh me with *a*,
7: 8 fragrance of your breath like *a*,

APPLIED (4/4) APPLY

1 Ki 6:35 and overlaid them with gold *a*
Eccl 7:25 I *a* my heart to know, To
8: 9 and *a* my heart to every work
8:16 When I *a* my heart to know

APPLY (4/4) APPLIED

Prov 2: 2 And *a* your heart to
22:17 And *a* your heart to my
23:12 *A* your heart to instruction,
Isa 38:21 and *a* it as a poultice on the

APPOINT (40/39) APPOINTED, APPOINTMENT, APPOINTS

Gen 41:34 and let him *a* officers over the
Ex 21:13 then I will *a* for you a place
30:16 and shall *a* it for the service
Lev 26:16 I will even *a* terror over you,
Num 1:50 but you shall *a* the Levites over
3:10 So you shall *a* Aaron and his
4:19 and his sons shall go in and *a*
4:27 And you shall *a* to them all
35: 6 to the Levites you shall *a*
35:11 then you shall *a* cities to be
35:14 You shall *a* three cities on this
35:14 and three cities you shall *a* in
Deut 16:18 You shall *a* judges and officers
Josh 20: 2 *A* for yourselves cities of
1 Sam 8:11 He will take your sons and *a*
8:12 He will *a* captains over his
2 Sam 6:21 to *a* me ruler over the people
7:10 Moreover I will *a* a place for My
1 Chr 15:16 the leaders of the Levites to *a*
17: 9 Moreover I will *a* a place for My
Neh 7: 3 and *a* guards from among the
Esth 2: 3 and let the king *a* officers in
Job 9:19 who will *a* my day in court?
14:13 That You would *a* me a set
Isa 26: 1 God will *a* salvation for
Jer 15: 3 And I will *a* over them four
49:19 is a chosen man that I may *a*
50:44 is a chosen man that I may *a*
51:27 *A* a general against her;
Ezek 21:19 *a* for yourself two ways for the
21:20 *A* a road for the sword to go to
45: 6 You shall *a* as the property of
Hos 1:11 And *a* for themselves one head;
Zeph 3:19 I will *a* them for praise and
Mt 24:51 and will cut him in two and *a*
Lk 12:46 and will cut him in two and *a*
Acts 6: 3 whom we may *a* over this
1 Cor 6: 4 do you *a* those who are least
1 Th 5: 9 For God did not *a* us to wrath,
Titus 1: 5 and *a* elders in every city as I

APPOINTED (152/150) APPOINT

Gen 4:25 For God has *a* another seed for
18:14 At the *a* time I will return to
24:14 her be the one You have *a*
24:44 the woman whom the LORD has *a*
Ex 9: 5 Then the LORD *a* a set time,
23:15 at the time *a* in the month of
31: 6 have *a* with him Aholiab the son
34:18 in the *a* time of the month of
Lev 23: 4 you shall proclaim at their *a*
Num 3:36 And the *a* duty of the children
4:16 The *a* duty of Eleazar the son of
9: 2 keep the Passover at its *a*
9: 3 you shall keep it at its *a*
9: 7 offering of the LORD at its *a*
9:13 offering of the LORD at its *a*
10:10 in your *a* feasts, and at the
15: 3 freewill offering or in your *a*
28: 2 to offer to Me at their *a* time.
29:39 present to the LORD at your *a*
Deut 18:14 the LORD your God has not *a*
31:10 at the *a* time in the year of
Josh 4: 4 the twelve men whom he had *a*
8:14 at an *a* place before the plain.
20: 7 So they *a* Kedesh in Galilee, in
20: 9 These were the cities *a* for all
Judg 20:38 Now the *a* signal between the men
1 Sam 13:11 did not come within the days *a*,
20:35 into the field at the time *a*
25:30 and has *a* you ruler over
29: 4 to the place which you have *a*
2 Sam 20: 5 the set time which David had *a*
23:23 And David *a* him over his guard.
24:15 from the morning till the *a*
1 Ki 1:35 For I have *a* him to be ruler
20:42 of your hand a man whom I *a*
2 Ki 4:17 and bore a son when the *a* time
7:17 Now the king had *a* the officer
8: 6 So the king *a* a certain officer
10:24 Now Jehu had *a* for himself
11:18 And the priest *a* officers over
17:32 and from every class they *a* for
1 Chr 6:31 these are the men whom David *a*
6:48 were *a* to every kind of
9:22 and Samuel the seer had *a* them
9:29 Some of them were *a* over the
11:25 And David *a* him over his guard.
15:17 So the Levites *a* Heman the son
16: 4 And he *a* some of the Levites to
22: 2 and he *a* masons to cut hewn
2 Chr 8:13 and the three *a* yearly
8:14 he *a* the divisions of the
11:15 Then he *a* for himself priests
11:22 And Rehoboam *a* Abijah the son of
19: 8 Jehoshaphat *a* some of the
20:21 he *a* those who should sing to
23:18 Also Jehoiada *a* the oversight of
31: 2 And Hezekiah *a* the divisions of
31: 3 The king also *a* a portion of
33: 8 from the land which I have *a*
34:22 and those the king had *a*
Ezra 3: 5 for New Moons and for all the *a*
3: 8 began work and *a* the Levites
8:20 David and the leaders had *a*
10:14 taken pagan wives come at *a*
Neh 5:14 from the time that I was *a* to
6: 7 And you have also *a* prophets to
7: 1 and the Levites had been *a*,
9:17 in their rebellion They *a* a
10:34 at the *a* times year by year, to
12:31 and *a* two large thanksgiving
12:44 at the same time some were *a*
13:13 And I *a* as treasurers over the
13:31 and the firstfruits at *a* times.
Esth 4: 5 king's eunuchs whom he had *a*
8: 2 and Esther *a* Mordecai over the
9:31 days of Purim at their *a* time,
Job 1: 4 each on his *a* day, and would
7: 3 wearisome nights have been *a*
14: 5 You have *a* his limits, so that
20:29 The heritage *a* to him by
23:14 For He performs what is *a* for
30:23 And to the house *a* for all
34:13 Or who *a* Him over the whole
Ps 78: 5 And *a* a law in Israel, Which
79:11 Preserve those who are *a* to
102:20 To release those *a* to death,
104:19 He *a* the moon for seasons; The
Prov 7:20 And will come home on the *a*
31: 8 the cause of all who are *a*
Eccl 7:14 Surely God has *a* the one as
Isa 1:14 Your New Moons and your *a*
14:31 no one will be alone in his *a*
28:25 The barley in the *a* place,
33:20 the city of our *a* feasts; Your
44: 7 Since I *a* the ancient people.
Jer 5:24 He reserves for us the *a* weeks
8: 7 in the heavens Knows her *a*
33:25 and if I have not *a* the
43:11 deliver to death those *a*
43:11 and to captivity those *a* for
43:11 and to the sword those *a* for
46:17 He has passed by the *a* time!'
47: 7 There He has *a* it."
Lam 2: 6 The LORD has caused The *a*
Ezek 43:21 and burn it in the *a* place of
44:24 and My statutes in all My *a*
45:17 and at all the *a* seasons of the
46: 9 come before the LORD on the *a*
46:11 At the festivals and the *a* feast
Dan 1: 5 And the king *a* for them a daily
1:10 who has *a* your food and drink.
2:24 whom the king had *a* to destroy
8:19 for at the *a* time the end
10: 1 but the *a* time was long; and
11:27 end will still be at the *a*
11:29 At the *a* time he shall return
11:35 it is still for the *a* time.
Hos 2:11 All her *a* feasts.
6:11 a harvest is *a* for you, When I
9: 5 What will you do in the *a* day,
12: 9 As in the days of the *a* feast.
Mic 6: 9 Hear the Rod! Who has *a* it?
Nah 1:15 keep your *a* feasts, Perform
Hab 1:12 You have *a* them for judgment;
2: 3 the vision is yet for an *a*
Zeph 3:18 those who sorrow over the *a*
Mt 28:16 the mountain which Jesus had *a*
Mk 3:14 Then He *a* twelve, that they
Lk 3:13 no more than what is *a*
10: 1 After these things the Lord *a*
Jn 15:16 but I chose you and *a* you that
Acts 7:44 in the wilderness, as He *a*,
13:48 And as many as had been *a* to
14:23 So when they had *a* elders in
17:31 because He has *a* a day on which
22:10 be told all things which are *a*
28:23 So when they had *a* him a day,
Rom 13: 1 authorities that exist are *a*
1 Cor 12:28 And God has *a* these in the
2 Cor 10:13 of the sphere which God *a* us—
Gal 3:19 and it was *a* through angels
4: 2 and stewards until the time *a*
Phil 1:17 knowing that I am *a* for the
1 Th 3: 3 yourselves know that we are *a*
1 Tim 2: 7 for which I was *a* a preacher and
2 Tim 1:11 to which I was *a* a preacher, an
Heb 1: 2 whom He has *a* heir of all
3: 2 who was faithful to Him who *a*
5: 1 taken from among men is *a* for
8: 3 For every high priest is *a* to
9:27 And as it is *a* for men to die
1 Pe 2: 8 word, to which they also were *a*.

APPOINTMENT (1/1) APPOINT

Job 2:11 For they had made an *a* together

APPOINTS (3/2) APPOINT
Dan 5:21 and *a* over it whomever He
Heb 7:28 For the law *a* as high priests
7:28 *a* the Son who has been

APPORTION (2/2) APPORTIONED
Job 28:25 And *a* the waters by measure.
41: 6 Will they *a* him among the

APPORTIONED (3/3) APPORTION
1 Ki 11:18 *a* food for him, and gave him
2 Ki 12:11 the money, which had been *a*,
Esth 2:12 the days of their preparation *a*:

APPREHEND (KJV) See ARREST

APPREHENDED (1/1)
Phil 3:13 I do not count myself to have *a*;

APPROACH (21/20) APPROACHED, APPROACHES, APPROACHING
Lev 18: 6 None of you shall *a* anyone who
18:14 You shall not *a* his wife; she
18:19 Also you shall not *a* a woman to
21:17 may *a* to offer the bread of his
21:18 who has a defect shall not *a*:
21:23 not go near the veil or *a* the
Num 4:19 live and not die when they *a*
Deut 20: 2 that the priest shall *a* and
31:14 the days *a* when you must die;
Josh 8: 5 people who are with me will *a*
2 Sam 11:20 Why did you *a* so near to the
Job 31:37 Like a prince I would *a* Him.
41:13 Who can *a* him with a double
Ps 65: 4 And cause to *a* You, That he
Jer 30:21 And he shall *a* Me; For who
30:21 who pledged his heart to *a* Me?
Ezek 42:13 where the priests who *a* the
42:14 then they may *a* that which is
43:19 who *a* Me to minister to Me,'
Lk 8:19 and could not *a* Him because of
Heb 10: 1 make those who *a* perfect.

APPROACHED (6/6) APPROACH
Judg 20:24 So the children of Israel *a* the
1 Ki 20:13 Suddenly a prophet *a* Ahab king
2 Ki 16:12 and the king *a* the altar and
Ezek 18: 6 Nor *a* a woman during her
Dan 6:15 Then these men *a* the king, and
Lk 10:40 and she *a* Him and said, "Lord,

APPROACHES (2/2) APPROACH
Lev 20:16 If a woman *a* any animal and
Lk 12:33 where no thief *a* nor moth

APPROACHING (2/2) APPROACH
Isa 58: 2 They take delight in *a* God.
Heb 10:25 the more as you see the Day *a*.

APPROVE (7/7) APPROVED, APPROVES
Ps 49:13 And of their posterity who *a*
Lam 3:36 his cause—The Lord does not *a*.
Lk 11:48 you bear witness that you *a* the
Rom 1:32 only do the same but also *a* of
2:18 and *a* the things that are
1 Cor 16: 3 whomever you *a* by your letters
Phil 1:10 that you may *a* the things that

APPROVED (9/9) APPROVE
Job 29:11 then it *a* me;
Rom 14:18 is acceptable to God and *a* by
16:10 *a* in Christ. Greet those who
1 Cor 11:19 that those who are *a* may be
2 Cor 10:18 he who commends himself is *a*,
13: 7 not that we should appear *a*,
1 Th 2: 4 But as we have been *a* by God to
2 Tim 2:15 diligent to present yourself *a*
Jas 1:12 for when he has been *a*,

APPROVES (1/1) APPROVE
Rom 14:22 condemn himself in what he *a*.

APRONS (1/1)
Acts 19:12 so that even handkerchiefs or *a*

AQUEDUCT (3/3)
2 Ki 18:17 they went and stood by the *a*
Isa 7: 3 at the end of the *a* from the
36: 2 And he stood by the *a* from the

AQUILA (6/6)
Acts 18: 2 he found a certain Jew named *A*,
18:18 and Priscilla and *A* were with
18:26 When *A* and Priscilla heard him,
Rom 16: 3 Greet Priscilla and *A*,
1 Cor 16:19 *A* and Priscilla greet you
2 Tim 4:19 Greet Prisca and *A*,

AR (6/6)
Num 21:15 reaches to the dwelling of *A*,
21:28 It consumed *A* of Moab, The
Deut 2: 9 because I have given *A* to the
2:18 day you are to cross over at *A*,
2:29 and the Moabites who dwell in *A*
Isa 15: 1 Because in the night *A* of Moab

ARA (1/1)
1 Chr 7:38 were Jephunneh, Pispah, and *A*.

ARAB (3/3)
Josh 15:52 *A*, Dumah, Eshean,
Neh 2:19 and Geshem the *A* heard of it,
6: 1 Sanballat, Tobiah, Geshem the *A*,

ARABAH (8/7)
Deut 3:17 east side of the Sea of the *A*
4:49 as far as the Sea of the *A*,
Josh 3:16 went down into the Sea of the *A*,
12: 3 as far as the Sea of the *A*
18:18 toward the north side of *A*,
18:18 of Arabah, and went down to *A*.
2 Ki 14:25 of Hamath to the Sea of the *A*,
Am 6:14 Hamath To the Valley of the *A*.

ARABIA (8/7) ARAB, ARABIAN, ARABIANS, ARABS
1 Ki 10:15 from all the kings of *A*,
2 Chr 9:14 And all the kings of *A* and
Isa 21:13 The burden against *A*.
21:13 In the forest in *A* you will
Jer 25:24 all the kings of *A* and all the
Ezek 27:21 *A* and all the princes of Kedar
Gal 1:17 before me; but I went to *A*,
4:25 this Hagar is Mount Sinai in *A*,

ARABIAN (2/2) ARABIA, ARABIANS
Isa 13:20 Nor will the *A* pitch tents
Jer 3: 2 have sat for them Like an *A*

ARABIANS (4/4) ARABIAN
2 Chr 17:11 and the *A* brought him flocks,
21:16 of the Philistines and the *A*
22: 1 the raiders who came with the *A*
26: 7 against the *A* who lived in Gur

ARABS (2/2) ARAB, ARABIA
Neh 4: 7 when Sanballat, Tobiah, the *A*,
Acts 2:11 "Cretans and *A*—

ARAD (5/5)
Num 21: 1 The king of *A*,
33:40 Now the king of *A*,
Josh 12:14 of Hormah, one; the king of *A*,
Judg 1:16 lies in the South near *A*;
1 Chr 8:15 Zebadiah, *A*, Eder,

ARAH (4/4)
1 Chr 7:39 The sons of Ulla were *A*,
Ezra 2: 5 the people of *A*,
Neh 6:18 of Shechaniah the son of *A*,
7:10 the sons of *A*, six hundred

ARAM (6/6) ARAMAIC, MESOPOTAMIA, SYRIA
Gen 10:22 Asshur, Arphaxad, Lud, and *A*.
10:23 The sons of *A* were Uz, Hul,
22:21 brother, Kemuel the father of *A*,
Num 23: 7 of Moab has brought me from *A*,
1 Chr 1:17 Elam, Asshur, Arphaxad, Lud, *A*,
7:34 Ahi, Rohgah, Jehubbah, and *A*.

ARAMAIC (5/4) ARAM
2 Ki 18:26 speak to your servants in *A*,
Ezra 4: 7 the letter was written in *A*
4: 7 and translated into the *A*
Isa 36:11 speak to your servants in the *A*
Dan 2: 4 spoke to the king in *A*,

ARAMITESS (KJV) See (SYRIAN) CONCUBINE

ARAN (2/2)
Gen 36:28 the sons of Dishan: Uz and *A*.
1 Chr 1:42 sons of Dishan were Uz and *A*.

ARARAT (4/4)
Gen 8: 4 month, on the mountains of *A*.
2 Ki 19:37 they escaped into the land of *A*.
Isa 37:38 they escaped into the land of *A*.
Jer 51:27 together against her: *A*,

ARAUNAH (9/7) ORNAN
2 Sam 24:16 was by the threshing floor of *A*
24:18 on the threshing floor of *A*
24:20 Now *A* looked, and saw the king
24:20 So *A* went out and bowed before
24:21 Then *A* said, "Why has my lord
24:22 Now *A* said to David, "Let my
24:23 *A* has given to the king."
24:23 And *A* said to the king, "May
24:24 Then the king said to *A*,

ARBA (3/3)
Josh 14:15 formerly was Kirjath Arba (*A*
15:13 which is Hebron (*A* was the
21:11 they gave them Kirjath Arba (*A*

ARBAH (KJV) See ARBA

ARBATHITE (2/2)
2 Sam 23:31 Abi-Albon the *A*,
1 Chr 11:32 brooks of Gaash, Abiel the *A*,

ARBITE (1/1) ARAB
2 Sam 23:35 the Carmelite, Paarai the *A*,

ARBITRATE (1/1) ARBITRATOR
Isa 47: 3 And I will not *a* with a man."

ARBITRATOR (1/1) ARBITRATE
Lk 12:14 who made Me a judge or an *a*

ARCHANGEL (2/2)
1 Th 4:16 a shout, with the voice of an *a*,
Jude 9 Yet Michael the *a*,

ARCHELAUS (1/1)
Mt 2:22 But when he heard that *A* was

ARCHER (2/2) ARCHERS
Gen 21:20 the wilderness, and became an *a*.
Jer 51: 3 Against her let the *a* bend his

ARCHERS (13/11) ARCHER
Gen 49:23 The *a* have bitterly grieved
Judg 5:11 Far from the noise of the *a*,
1 Sam 31: 3 The *a* hit him, and he was
31: 3 was severely wounded by the *a*.
2 Sam 11:24 The *a* shot from the wall at your
1 Chr 8:40 Ulam were mighty men of valor—*a*.
10: 3 The *a* hit him, and he was
10: 3 and he was wounded by the *a*.
2 Chr 35:23 And the *a* shot King Josiah; and
Job 16:13 His *a* surround me. He pierces
Isa 21:17 remainder of the number of *a*,
22: 3 They are captured by the *a*.
Jer 50:29 Call together the *a* against

ARCHES (KJV) See ARCHWAYS

ARCHI (KJV) See ACHITES

ARCHIPPUS (2/2)
Col 4:17 And say to *A*, "Take heed
Phm 1: 2 *A* our fellow soldier, and to

ARCHITE (5/5) ARCHITES
2 Sam 15:32 there was Hushai the *A* coming to
16:16 so it was, when Hushai the *A*,
17: 5 Now call Hushai the *A* also, and
17:14 The advice of Hushai the *A* is
1 Chr 27:33 and Hushai the *A* was the

ARCHITES (1/1) ARCHITE
Josh 16: 2 along to the border of the *A*

ARCHIVES (1/1)
Ezra 6: 1 and a search was made in the *a*,

ARCHWAY (2/2) ARCHWAYS
Ezek 40:22 and its *a* was in front of it.
40:26 and its *a* was in front of

ARCHWAYS (13/11) ARCHWAY
Ezek 40:16 and in their intervening *a* on
40:21 side, its gateposts and its *a*,
40:22 Its windows and those of its *a*,
40:24 he measured its gateposts and *a*
40:25 windows in it and in its *a* all
40:29 and its *a* were according to
40:29 windows in it and in its *a* all
40:30 There were *a* all around,
40:31 Its *a* faced the outer court,
40:33 and its *a* were according to
40:33 windows in it and in its *a* all
40:34 Its *a* faced the outer court, and
40:36 its gateposts, and its *a*.

ARCTURUS (KJV) See BEAR

ARD (3/2) ARDITES
Gen 46:21 Rosh, Muppim, Huppim, and *A*.
Num 26:40 And the sons of Bela were *A* and
26:40 were Ard and Naaman: of *A*,

ARDITES (1/1) ARD
Num 26:40 of Ard, the family of the *A*;

ARDON (1/1)
1 Chr 2:18 her sons: Jesher, Shobab, and *A*.

ARE (3507/2977) See APPENDIX

AREA (13/10) AREAS
1 Sam 27:10 Against the southern ***a*** of
27:10 or against the southern ***a*** of
27:10 or against the southern ***a*** of
30:14 an invasion of the southern ***a***
30:14 and of the southern ***a*** of
1 Chr 5:10 tents throughout the entire ***a***
11: 8 the Millo to the surrounding ***a***.
2 Chr 3: 9 and he overlaid the upper ***a***
Ezek 43:12 The whole ***a*** surrounding the
45: 5 An ***a*** twenty-five thousand
45: 6 the property of the city an ***a***
48:13 the Levites shall have an ***a***
48:22 the ***a*** between the border of

AREAS (3/3) AREA
Josh 13:32 These are the ***a*** which Moses
14: 1 These are the ***a*** which the
Ezek 42:20 to separate the holy ***a*** from the

ARELI (2/2) ARELITES
Gen 46:16 Shuni, Ezbon, Eri, Arodi, and *A*.
Num 26:17 family of the Arodites; of *A*,

ARELITES (1/1) ARELI
Num 26:17 of Areli, the family of the *A*.

AREOPAGITE (1/1) AREOPAGUS
Acts 17:34 among them Dionysius the *A*,

AREOPAGUS (2/2) AREOPAGITE
Acts 17:19 him and brought him to the *A*,
17:22 stood in the midst of the *A*

ARETAS (1/1)
2 Cor 11:32 under *A* the king, was guarding

ARGOB (5/5)
Deut 3: 4 cities, all the region of *A*,
3:13 (All the region of *A*,
3:14 took all the region of *A*,
1 Ki 4:13 belonged the region of *A* in
2 Ki 15:25 along with *A* and Arieh; and

ARGUING (1/1) ARGUMENTS
Job 6:25 But what does your ***a*** prove?

ARGUMENTS (3/3) ARGUING
Job 23: 4 Him, And fill my mouth with ***a***.
2 Cor 10: 5 casting down ***a*** and every high
1 Tim 6: 4 is obsessed with disputes and ***a***

ARIDAI (1/1)
Esth 9: 9 Parmashta, Arisai, *A*,

ARIDATHA (1/1)
Esth 9: 8 Poratha, Adalia, *A*,

ARIEH (1/1)
2 Ki 15:25 house, along with Argob and *A*;

ARIEL (6/4) JERUSALEM
Ezra 8:16 Then I sent for Eliezer, *A*,
Isa 29: 1 "Woe to *A*,
29: 1 "Woe to Ariel, to *A*,
29: 2 Yet I will distress *A*;
29: 2 And it shall be to Me as *A*.
29: 7 the nations who fight against *A*,

ARIGHT (4/4)
Ps 50:23 him who orders his conduct ***a***
78: 8 that did not set its heart ***a***,
Prov 11: 5 blameless will direct his way ***a***,
Jer 8: 6 But they do not speak ***a***.

ARIMATHEA (4/4)
Mt 27:57 there came a rich man from *A*,
Mk 15:43 Joseph of *A*, a prominent
Lk 23:51 and deed. He was from *A*,
Jn 19:38 After this, Joseph of *A*,

ARIOCH (7/6)
Gen 14: 1 *A* king of Ellasar, Chedorlaomer
14: 9 and *A* king of Ellasar—four
Dan 2:14 and wisdom Daniel answered *A*,
2:15 he answered and said to *A* the
2:15 Then *A* made the decision
2:24 Therefore Daniel went to *A*,
2:25 Then *A* quickly brought Daniel

ARISAI (1/1)
Esth 9: 9 Parmashta, *A*, Aridai,

ARISE (142/141) ARISEN, ARISES, AROSE, RISE, RISEN
Gen 13:17 '*A*, walk in the land through
19:15 urged Lot to hurry, saying, "*A*,
21:18 '*A*, lift up the lad and hold
27:19 just as you told me; please ***a***,
27:31 Let my father ***a*** and eat of his
27:43 my son, obey my voice: ***a***,
28: 2 '*A*, go to Padan Aram,
31:13 you made a vow to Me. Now ***a***,
35: 1 Then God said to Jacob, "*A*,
35: 3 Then let us ***a*** and go up to
41:30 seven years of famine will ***a***,
43: 8 and we will ***a*** and go, that we
43:13 "Take your brother also, and ***a***,
Deut 9:12 "Then the LORD said to me, '*A*,
10:11 "Then the LORD said to me, '*A*,
17: 8 then you shall ***a*** and go up to
Josh 1: 2 is dead. Now therefore, ***a***,
8: 1 people of war with you, and ***a***,
Judg 5:12 Awake, awake, sing a song! *A*,
7: 9 that the LORD said to him, "*A*,
7:15 camp of Israel, and said, "*A*,
18: 9 So they said, "*A*,
1 Sam 9: 3 of the servants with you, and ***a***,
16:12 And the LORD said, "*A*,
23: 4 answered him and said, "*A*,
2 Sam 2:14 Let the young men now ***a*** and
2:14 And Joab said, "Let them ***a***.
3:21 I will ***a*** and go, and gather all
13:15 And Amnon said to her, "*A*,
15:14 with him at Jerusalem, "*A*,
17: 1 and I will ***a*** and pursue David
17:21 *A* and cross over the water
19: 7 "Now therefore, ***a***,
1 Ki 3:12 nor shall any like you ***a*** after
14: 2 said to his wife, "Please ***a***,
14:12 *A* therefore, go to your own
17: 9 '*A*, go to Zarephath,
19: 5 *A* and eat."
19: 7 *A* and eat, because the journey
21: 7 authority over Israel! *A*,
21:15 that Jezebel said to Ahab, "*A*,
21:18 '*A*, go down to meet Ahab
2 Ki 1: 3 to Elijah the Tishbite, "*A*,
8: 1 *A* and go, you and your
23:25 nor after him did any ***a*** like
1 Chr 22:16 *A* and begin working, and the
22:19 Therefore ***a*** and build the
2 Chr 6:41 "Now therefore, *A*,
Ezra 10: 4 '*A*, for this matter is
Neh 2:20 we His servants will ***a*** and
Esth 4:14 relief and deliverance will ***a***
Job 7: 4 down, I say, 'When shall I ***a***,
19:18 young children despise me; I ***a***,
Ps 3: 7 *A*, O LORD; Save me,
7: 6 *A*, O LORD, in Your anger;
9:19 *A*, O LORD, Do not let man
10:12 *A*, O LORD! O God, lift up
12: 5 of the needy, Now I will ***a***,
17:13 *A*, O LORD, Confront him,
44:23 *A*! Do not cast us off
44:26 *A* for our help, And redeem us
68: 1 Let God ***a***, Let His enemies
74:22 *A*, O God, plead Your
78: 6 That they may ***a*** and declare
82: 8 *A*, O God, judge
88:10 Shall the dead ***a*** and praise
102:13 You will ***a*** and have mercy on
109:28 but You bless; When they ***a***,
132: 8 *A*, O LORD, to Your resting
Prov 28:12 glory; But when the wicked ***a***,
28:28 When the wicked ***a***,
Isa 21: 5 the tower, Eat and drink. *A*,
23:12 virgin daughter of Sidon. *A*,
26:19 with my dead body they shall ***a***.
31: 2 But will ***a*** against the house
49: 7 "Kings shall see and ***a***,
52: 2 yourself from the dust, ***a***;
60: 2 But the LORD will ***a*** over you,
Jer 1:17 prepare yourself and ***a***,
2:27 *A* and save us.'
2:28 for yourselves? Let them ***a***,
6: 4 "Prepare war against her; *A*,
6: 5 *A*, and let us go by night,
13: 4 is around your waist, and ***a***,
13: 6 that the LORD said to me, "*A*,
18: 2 *A* and go down to the potter's
31: 6 will cry on Mount Ephraim, '*A*,
46:16 *A*! Let us go back to our own
49:28 Thus says the LORD: "*A*,
49:31 '*A*, go up to the wealthy
Lam 2:19 '*A*, cry out in the night,
Ezek 3:22 there, and He said to me, "*A*,
38:10 to pass that thoughts will ***a***
Dan 2:39 But after you shall ***a*** another
7: 5 And they said thus to it: '*A*,
7:17 are four kings which ***a*** out of
7:24 are ten kings Who shall ***a***
8:22 four kingdoms shall ***a*** out of
8:23 their fullness, A king shall ***a***,
11: 2 three more kings will ***a*** in
11: 3 "Then a mighty king shall ***a***,
11: 7 of her roots one shall ***a*** in
11:20 There shall ***a*** in his place one
11:21 And in his place shall ***a*** a vile
12:13 and will ***a*** to your inheritance
Hos 10:14 Therefore tumult shall ***a*** among
Ob 1 the nations, saying, "*A*,
Jon 1: 2 '*A*, go to Nineveh,
1: 6 "What do you mean, sleeper? *A*,
3: 2 '*A*, go to Nineveh,
Mic 2:10 *A* and depart, For this is not
4:13 *A* and thresh, O daughter of
6: 1 now what the LORD says: "*A*,
7: 8 enemy; When I fall, I will ***a***;
Hab 2:19 *A*! It shall teach!' Behold, it
Mal 4: 2 Sun of Righteousness shall ***a***
Mt 2:13 Joseph in a dream, saying, "*A*,
2:20 saying, "*A*, take the young
9: 5 or to say, '*A* and walk'?
9: 6 He said to the paralytic, "*A*,
17: 7 and touched them and said, "*A*,
Mk 2: 9 forgiven you,' or to say, '*A*,
2:11 "I say to you, ***a***,
5:41 "Little girl, I say to you, ***a***.
Lk 5:24 paralyzed, "I say to you, ***a***,
6: 8 *A* and stand here." And he arose
7:14 "Young man, I say to you, ***a***.
8:54 saying, "Little girl, ***a***.
15:18 I will ***a*** and go to my father,
17:19 And He said to him, "*A*,
24:38 And why do doubts ***a*** in your
Jn 14:31 gave Me commandment, so I do. *A*,
Acts 8:26 *A* and go toward the south along
9: 6 *A* and go into the city, and you
9:11 *A* and go to the street called
9:34 *A* and make your bed." Then he
9:40 the body he said, "Tabitha, ***a***.
10:20 *A* therefore, go down and go with
12: 7 *A* quickly!" And his chains fell
22:10 *A* and go into Damascus, and
22:16 *A* and be baptized, and wash
Eph 5:14 *A* from the dead, And Christ

ARISEN (3/3) ARISE
Deut 34:10 But since then there has not ***a***
Dan 11: 4 "And when he has ***a***,
Jn 7:52 for no prophet has ***a*** out of

ARISES (11/11) ARISE
Deut 13: 1 If there ***a*** among you a prophet
17: 8 If a matter ***a*** which is too hard
Job 30:12 my right hand the rabble ***a***;
Ps 112: 4 Unto the upright there ***a*** light
Isa 2:19 When He ***a*** to shake the earth
2:21 When He ***a*** to shake the earth
47:11 shall not know from where it ***a***.
Hab 1: 3 is strife, and contention ***a***.
Mt 13:21 tribulation or persecution ***a***
Mk 4:17 tribulation or persecution ***a***
Heb 7:15 there ***a*** another priest

ARISTARCHUS (5/5)
Acts 19:29 having seized Gaius and *A*,
20: 4 also *A* and Secundus of the
27: 2 along the coasts of Asia. *A*,
Col 4:10 *A* my fellow prisoner greets you,
Phm 1:24 as do Mark, *A*, Demas, Luke,

ARISTOBULUS (1/1)
Rom 16:10 who are of the household of *A*.

ARK (229/199)
Gen 6:14 Make yourself an ***a*** of
6:14 gopherwood; make rooms in the ***a***,
6:15 The length of the ***a*** shall be
6:16 shall make a window for the ***a***,
6:16 and set the door of the ***a*** in
6:18 and you shall go into the ***a***—
6:19 two of every sort into the ***a***,
7: 1 said to Noah, "Come into the ***a***,
7: 7 went into the ***a*** because of the
7: 9 by two they went into the ***a*** to
7:13 sons with them, entered the ***a***—
7:15 And they went into the ***a*** to
7:17 increased and lifted up the ***a***,
7:18 and the ***a*** moved about on the
7:23 who were with him in the ***a***
8: 1 that were with him in the ***a***.
8: 4 Then the ***a*** rested in the seventh
8: 6 Noah opened the window of the ***a***
8: 9 and she returned into the ***a*** to
8: 9 and drew her into the ***a*** to
8:10 he sent the dove out from the ***a***.
8:13 removed the covering of the ***a***
8:16 "Go out of the ***a***,
8:19 families, went out of the ***a***.
9:10 of all that go out of the ***a***,
9:18 of Noah who went out of the ***a***
Ex 2: 3 she took an ***a*** of bulrushes for
2: 5 and when she saw the ***a*** among
25:10 And they shall make an ***a*** of
25:14 the rings on the sides of the ***a***,
25:14 that the ***a*** may be carried by
25:15 shall be in the rings of the ***a***;
25:16 And you shall put into the ***a*** the
25:21 the mercy seat on top of the ***a***,
25:21 and in the ***a*** you shall put the
25:22 cherubim which are on the ***a***
26:33 Then you shall bring the ***a*** of
26:34 put the mercy seat upon the ***a***
30: 6 the veil that is before the ***a***

30:26 of meeting and the **a** of the
31: 7 the **a** of the Testimony and the
35:12 the **a** and its poles, with the
37: 1 Then Bezalel made the **a** of
37: 5 the rings at the sides of the **a**,
37: 5 sides of the ark, to bear the **a**.
39:35 the **a** of the Testimony with its
40: 3 You shall put in it the **a** of the
40: 3 and partition off the **a** with
40: 5 for the incense before the **a**
40:20 and put it into the **a**,
40:20 through the rings of the **a**,
40:20 the mercy seat on top of the **a**.
40:21 And he brought the **a** into the
40:21 and partitioned off the **a** of
Lev 16: 2 mercy seat which is on the **a**,
Num 3:31 Their duty included the **a**,
4: 5 covering veil and cover the **a**
7:89 mercy seat that was on the **a**
10:33 and the **a** of the covenant of
10:35 whenever the **a** set out, that
14:44 neither the **a** of the covenant
Deut 10: 1 and make yourself an **a** of wood.
10: 2 and you shall put them in the **a**.
10: 3 So I made an **a** of acacia wood,
10: 5 and put the tablets in the **a**
10: 8 tribe of Levi to bear the **a** of
31: 9 who bore the **a** of the covenant
31:25 who bore the **a** of the covenant
31:26 and put it beside the **a** of the
Josh 3: 3 When you see the **a** of the
3: 6 Take up the **a** of the covenant
3: 6 So they took up the **a** of the
3: 8 the priests who bear the **a** of
3:11 the **a** of the covenant of the
3:13 of the priests who bear the **a**
3:14 with the priests bearing the **a**
3:15 and as those who bore the **a** came
3:15 of the priests who bore the **a**
3:17 the priests who bore the **a** of
4: 5 Cross over before the **a** of the
4: 7 were cut off before the **a** of
4: 9 of the priests who bore the **a**
4:10 So the priests who bore the **a**
4:11 that the **a** of the LORD and the
4:16 the priests who bear the **a** of
4:18 the priests who bore the **a** of
6: 4 of rams' horns before the **a**.
6: 6 Take up the **a** of the covenant,
6: 6 of rams' horns before the **a** of
6: 7 is armed advance before the **a**
6: 8 and the **a** of the covenant of
6: 9 the rear guard came after the **a**,
6:11 So he had the **a** of the LORD
6:12 and the priests took up the **a**
6:13 of rams' horns before the **a** of
6:13 rear guard came after the **a** of
7: 6 earth on his face before the **a**
8:33 stood on either side of the **a**
8:33 who bore the **a** of the covenant
Judg 20:27 inquired of the LORD (the **a**
1 Sam 3: 3 of the LORD where the **a** of
4: 3 Let us bring the **a** of the
4: 4 might bring from there the **a**
4: 4 were there with the **a** of the
4: 5 And when the **a** of the covenant
4: 6 they understood that the **a** of
4:11 Also the **a** of God was captured;
4:13 his heart trembled for the **a**
4:17 and the **a** of God has been
4:18 when he made mention of the **a**
4:19 she heard the news that the **a**
4:21 from Israel!" because the **a**
4:22 for the **a** of God has been
5: 1 the Philistines took the **a** of
5: 2 the Philistines took the **a** of
5: 3 face to the earth before the **a**
5: 4 to the ground before the **a** of
5: 7 The **a** of the God of Israel must
5: 8 What shall we do with the **a** of
5: 8 Let the **a** of the God of Israel
5: 8 So they carried the **a** of the
5:10 Therefore they sent the **a** of
5:10 as the **a** of God came to Ekron,
5:10 They have brought the **a** of the
5:11 Send away the **a** of the God of
6: 1 Now the **a** of the LORD was in
6: 2 What shall we do with the **a** of
6: 3 If you send away the **a** of the
6: 8 Then take the **a** of the LORD and
6:11 And they set the **a** of the LORD
6:13 lifted their eyes and saw the **a**,
6:15 The Levites took down the **a** of
6:18 Abel on which they set the **a**
6:19 they had looked into the **a** of
6:21 have brought back the **a** of the
7: 1 Jearim came and took the **a** of
7: 1 Eleazar his son to keep the **a**
7: 2 So it was that the **a** remained
14:18 Bring the **a** of God here" (for
14:18 here" (for at that time the **a**
2 Sam 6: 2 to bring up from there the **a**
6: 3 So they set the **a** of God on a
6: 4 accompanying the **a** of God; and
6: 4 God; and Ahio went before the **a**.
6: 6 put out his hand to the **a** of
6: 7 and he died there by the **a** of
6: 9 How can the **a** of the LORD come
6:10 So David would not move the **a** of
6:11 The **a** of the LORD remained in
6:12 because of the **a** of God."
6:12 went and brought up the **a** of
6:13 when those bearing the **a** of the
6:15 of Israel brought up the **a** of
6:16 Now as the **a** of the LORD came
6:17 So they brought the **a** of the
7: 2 but the **a** of God dwells inside
11:11 The **a** and Israel and Judah are
15:24 bearing the **a** of the covenant
15:24 And they set down the **a** of God,
15:25 Carry the **a** of God back into the
15:29 and Abiathar carried the **a** of
1 Ki 2:26 because you carried the **a** of
3:15 and stood before the **a** of the
6:19 to set the **a** of the covenant of
8: 1 that they might bring up the **a**
8: 3 and the priests took up the **a**.
8: 4 Then they brought up the **a** of
8: 5 were with him before the **a**,
8: 6 the priests brought in the **a**
8: 7 wings over the place of the **a**,
8: 7 the cherubim overshadowed the **a**
8: 9 Nothing was in the **a** except the
8:21 I have made a place for the **a**,
1 Chr 6:31 after the **a** came to rest.
13: 3 and let us bring the **a** of our
13: 5 to bring the **a** of God from
13: 6 to bring up from there the **a** of
13: 7 So they carried the **a** of God on
13: 9 put out his hand to hold the **a**,
13:10 he put his hand to the **a**;
13:12 How can I bring the **a** of God to
13:13 So David would not move the **a**
13:14 The **a** of God remained with the
15: 1 he prepared a place for the **a**
15: 2 No one may carry the **a** of God
15: 2 has chosen them to carry the **a**
15: 3 to bring up the **a** of the LORD
15:12 that you may bring up the **a** of
15:14 themselves to bring up the **a**
15:15 of the Levites bore the **a** of
15:23 were doorkeepers for the **a**;
15:24 blow the trumpets before the **a**
15:24 Jehiah, doorkeepers for the **a**.
15:25 went to bring up the **a** of the
15:26 the Levites who bore the **a** of
15:27 all the Levites who bore the **a**,
15:28 all Israel brought up the **a** of
15:29 as the **a** of the covenant of
16: 1 So they brought the **a** of God,
16: 4 to minister before the **a** of
16: 6 the trumpets before the **a** of
16:37 brothers there before the **a** of
16:37 LORD to minister before the **a**
17: 1 but the **a** of the covenant of
22:19 to bring the **a** of the covenant
28: 2 a house of rest for the **a** of
28:18 wings and overshadowed the **a**
2 Chr 1: 4 But David had brought up the **a**
5: 2 that they might bring the **a** of
5: 4 and the Levites took up the **a**.
5: 5 Then they brought up the **a**,
5: 6 assembled with him before the **a**,
5: 7 the priests brought in the **a**
5: 8 wings over the place of the **a**,
5: 8 the cherubim overshadowed the **a**
5: 9 the ends of the poles of the **a**
5:10 Nothing was in the **a** except the
6:11 "And there I have put the **a**,
6:41 You and the **a** of Your
8:11 the places to which the **a** of
35: 3 Put the holy **a** in the house
Ps 132: 8 You and the **a** of Your
Jer 3:16 The **a** of the covenant of the
Mt 24:38 the day that Noah entered the **a**,
Lk 17:27 the day that Noah entered the **a**,
Heb 9: 4 the golden censer and the **a** of
11: 7 prepared an **a** for the saving of
1 Pe 3:20 while the **a** was being
Rev 11:19 and the **a** of His covenant was

ARKITE (2/2)

Gen 10:17 the Hivite, the *A*,
1 Chr 1:15 the Hivite, the *A*,

ARM (67/62) ARMED, ARMLETS, ARMPITS, ARMRESTS, ARMS

Ex 6: 6 you with an outstretched **a** and
15:16 By the greatness of Your **a**
Num 11:23 Has the LORD's **a** been
31: 3 *A* some of yourselves for war,
32:20 if you **a** yourselves before the
Deut 4:34 hand and an outstretched **a**,
5:15 hand and by an outstretched **a**;
7:19 hand and the outstretched **a**,
9:29 and by Your outstretched **a**.
11: 2 hand and His outstretched **a**—
26: 8 hand and with an outstretched **a**,
33:20 And tears the **a** and the crown
1 Sam 2:31 that I will cut off your **a** and
2:31 cut off your arm and the **a** of
2 Sam 1:10 the bracelet that was on his **a**,
1 Ki 8:42 hand and Your outstretched **a**),
2 Ki 17:36 power and an outstretched **a**,
2 Chr 6:32 hand and Your outstretched **a**,
32: 8 With him is an **a** of flesh; but
Job 26: 2 How have you saved the **a**
31:22 Then let my **a** fall from my
31:22 Let my **a** be torn from the
35: 9 out for help because of the **a**
38:15 And the upraised **a** is broken.
40: 9 Have you an **a** like God? Or can
Ps 10:15 Break the **a** of the wicked and
44: 3 Nor did their own **a** save them;
44: 3 it was Your right hand, Your **a**,
77:15 You have with Your **a** redeemed
89:10 Your enemies with Your mighty **a**.
89:13 You have a mighty **a**;
89:21 Also My **a** shall strengthen
98: 1 His right hand and His holy **a**
136:12 and with an outstretched **a**,
Song 8: 6 heart, As a seal upon your **a**;
Isa 9:20 eat the flesh of his own **a**.
17: 5 And reaps the heads with his **a**;
30:30 And show the descent of His **a**,
33: 2 Be their **a** every morning, Our
40:10 And His **a** shall rule for Him;
40:11 gather the lambs with His **a**,
48:14 And His **a** shall be against
51: 5 And on My **a** they will trust.
51: 9 O **a** of the LORD! Awake as in
51: 9 Are You not the **a** that cut
52:10 LORD has made bare His holy **a**
53: 1 And to whom has the **a** of the
59:16 Therefore His own **a** brought
62: 8 by His right hand And by the **a**
63: 5 Therefore My own **a** brought
63:12 of Moses, With His glorious **a**,
Jer 21: 5 hand and with a strong **a**,
27: 5 power and by My outstretched **a**,
32:17 great power and outstretched **a**.
32:21 hand and an outstretched **a**,
48:25 And his **a** is broken," says
Ezek 4: 7 your **a** shall be uncovered,
20:33 hand, with an outstretched **a**,
20:34 hand, with an outstretched **a**,
30:21 I have broken the **a** of Pharaoh
31:17 who were its strong **a** dwelt
Zech 11:17 sword shall be against his **a**
11:17 His **a** shall completely wither,
Lk 1:51 has shown strength with His **a**;
Jn 12:38 And to whom has the **a**
Acts 13:17 and with an uplifted **a** He
1 Pe 4: 1 **a** yourselves also with the same

ARMAGEDDON (1/1)

Rev 16:16 the place called in Hebrew, *A*.

ARMED (33/33) ARM

Gen 14:14 he **a** his three hundred and
Num 31: 5 twelve thousand **a** for war.
32:17 "but we ourselves will be **a**,
32:21 and all your **a** men cross over
32:27 every man **a** for war, before the
32:29 every man **a** for battle before
32:30 if they do not cross over **a**
32:32 We will cross over **a** before the
Deut 3:18 men of valor shall cross over **a**
Josh 1:14 pass before your brethren **a**,
4:12 of Manasseh crossed over **a**
6: 7 and let him who is **a** advance
6: 9 The **a** men went before the
6:13 And the **a** men went before them.
Judg 7:11 to the outpost of the **a** men
18:11 **a** with weapons of war.
18:16 The six hundred men **a** with their
18:17 six hundred men who were **a**
1 Sam 17: 5 and he was **a** with a coat of
2 Sam 22:40 For You have **a** me with strength
23: 7 who touches them Must be **a**
1 Chr 12: 2 **a** with bows, using both the
12:24 six thousand eight hundred **a**
12:37 hundred and twenty thousand **a**
20: 1 that Joab led out the **a** forces
2 Chr 17:17 him two hundred thousand men **a**
28:14 So the **a** men left the captives
Ps 18:39 For You have **a** me with strength
78: 9 being **a** and carrying bows,
Prov 6:11 And your need like an **a** man.
24:34 And your need like an **a** man.
Isa 15: 4 Therefore the **a** soldiers of
Lk 11:21 "When a strong man, fully **a**,

ARMENIA (KJV) See ARARAT

ARMIES (52/52) ARMY

Ex 6:26 of Egypt according to their **a**.
7: 4 My hand on Egypt and bring My **a**
12:17 day I will have brought your **a**
12:41 came to pass that all the **a**
12:51 of Egypt according to their **a**.
Num 1: 3 shall number them by their **a**.
1:52 standard, according to their **a**;
2: 3 shall camp according to their **a**;
2: 9 numbered according to their **a**
2:10 Reuben according to their **a**,
2:16 numbered according to their **a**
2:18 Ephraim according to their **a**,
2:24 numbered according to their **a**
2:25 north side according to their **a**,
2:32 numbered according to their **a**
10:14 out first according to their **a**;
10:18 set out according to their **a**;
10:22 set out according to their **a**;
10:25 set out according to their **a**;
10:28 of Israel, according to their **a**,
33: 1 of the land of Egypt by their **a**
Deut 20: 9 shall make captains of the **a**
Josh 10: 5 went up, they and all their **a**,
11: 4 they and all their **a** with them,
Judg 8:10 and their **a** with them, about

1 Sam 17: 1 Philistines gathered their **a**
17: 8 he stood and cried out to the **a**
17:10 I defy the **a** of Israel this day;
17:23 coming up from the **a** of the
17:26 that he should defy the **a** of
17:36 seeing he has defied the **a** of
17:45 the God of the **a** of Israel,
23: 3 we go to Keilah against the **a**
28: 1 Philistines gathered their **a**
29: 1 gathered together all their **a**
1 Ki 2: 5 to the two commanders of the **a**
15:20 and sent the captains of his **a**
2 Ki 25:23 when all the captains of the **a**,
25:26 and the captains of the **a**,
2 Chr 16: 4 and sent the captains of his **a**
Job 25: 3 Is there any number to His **a**?
Ps 44: 9 You do not go out with our **a**.
60:10 who did not go out with our **a**?
68:12 Kings of **a** flee, they flee, And
108:11 who did not go out with our **a**?
Isa 34: 2 His fury against all their **a**;
Jer 40: 7 when all the captains of the **a**
Mt 22: 7 And he sent out his **a**,
Lk 21:20 see Jerusalem surrounded by **a**,
Heb 11:34 turned to flight the **a** of the
Rev 19:14 And the **a** in heaven, clothed in
19:19 kings of the earth, and their **a**,

ARMLETS (1/1) ARM

Num 31:50 **a** and bracelets and signet

ARMONI (1/1)

2 Sam 21: 8 So the king took **A** and

ARMOR (30/30) ARMORBEARER, ARMORY

1 Sam 14: 1 to the young man who bore his **a**,
14: 6 to the young man who bore his **a**,
17: 6 And he had bronze **a** on his
17:38 Saul clothed David with his **a**,
17:39 fastened his sword to his **a**
17:54 but he put his **a** in his tent.
18: 4 gave it to David, with his **a**,
31: 9 his head and stripped off his **a**,
31:10 Then they put his **a** in the
2 Sam 2:21 of the young men and take his **a**
18:15 ten young men who bore Joab's **a**
20: 8 Joab was dressed in battle **a**;
1 Ki 10:25 of silver and gold, garments, **a**,
20:11 not the one who puts on his **a**
22:34 between the joints of his **a**.
1 Chr 10: 9 him and took his head and his **a**,
10:10 Then they put his **a** in the
2 Chr 9:24 of silver and gold, garments, **a**,
18:33 between the joints of his **a**.
26:14 spears, helmets, body **a**,
Neh 4:16 shields, the bows, and wore **a**;
Isa 22: 8 looked in that day to the **a** of
45: 1 before him And loose the **a** of
Jer 46: 4 Put on the **a**!
51: 3 up against her in his **a**.
Lk 11:22 he takes from him all his **a** in
Rom 13:12 and let us put on the **a** of
2 Cor 6: 7 by the **a** of righteousness on
Eph 6:11 Put on the whole **a** of God, that
6:13 Therefore take up the whole **a** of

ARMORBEARER (18/14) ARMOR

Judg 9:54 quickly to the young man, his **a**,
1 Sam 14: 7 So his **a** said to him, "Do all
14:12 called to Jonathan and his **a**,
14:12 Jonathan said to his **a**,
14:13 his hands and knees with his **a**
14:13 his **a** killed them.
14:14 which Jonathan and his **a** made
14:17 Jonathan and his **a** were not
16:21 greatly, and he became his **a**.
31: 4 Then Saul said to his **a**,
31: 4 But his **a** would not, for he
31: 5 And when his **a** saw that Saul was
31: 6 So Saul, his three sons, his **a**,
2 Sam 23:37 Naharai the Beerothite (**a** of
1 Chr 10: 4 Then Saul said to his **a**,
10: 4 But his **a** would not, for he
10: 5 And when his **a** saw that Saul was
11:39 Naharai the Berothite (the **a** of

ARMORY (5/5) ARMOR

2 Ki 20:13 ointment, and all his **a**—
Neh 3:19 in front of the Ascent to the **A**
Song 4: 4 tower of David, Built for an **a**,
Isa 39: 2 ointment, and all his **a**—
Jer 50:25 The LORD has opened His **a**,

ARMPITS (1/1) ARM

Jer 38:12 clothes and rags under your **a**,

ARMRESTS (4/2) ARM

1 Ki 10:19 there were **a** on either side
10:19 two lions stood beside the **a**.
2 Chr 9:18 there were **a** on either side of
9:18 two lions stood beside the **a**.

ARMS (33/31) ARM

Gen 49:24 And the **a** of his hands were
Deut 33:27 are the everlasting **a**;
Judg 15:14 the ropes that were on his **a**
16:12 But he broke them off his **a**
2 Sam 22:35 So that my **a** can bend a bow of
1 Ki 17:19 So he took him out of her **a**
2 Ki 3:21 all who were able to bear **a** and
9:24 and shot Jehoram between his **a**;
Ezra 4:23 and by force of **a** made them
Job 39:21 He gallops into the clash of **a**.
Ps 18:32 It is God who **a** me with
18:34 So that my **a** can bend a bow of
37:17 For the **a** of the wicked shall
129: 7 he who binds sheaves, his **a**.
Prov 5:20 And be embraced in the **a** of a
31:17 And strengthens her **a**.
Isa 44:12 it with the strength of his **a**.
49:22 bring your sons in their **a**,
51: 5 And My **a** will judge the
Ezek 13:20 I will tear them from your **a**,
30:22 of Egypt, and will break his **a**,
30:24 I will strengthen the **a** of the
30:24 but I will break Pharaoh's **a**,
30:25 Thus I will strengthen the **a** of
30:25 but the **a** of Pharaoh shall fall
Dan 2:32 its chest and **a** of silver, its
10: 6 his **a** and feet like burnished
Hos 7:15 and strengthened their **a**,
11: 3 walk, Taking them by their **a**;
Zech 13: 6 are these wounds between your **a**?
Mk 9:36 when He had taken him in His **a**,
10:16 And He took them up in His **a**,
Lk 2:28 he took Him up in his **a** and

ARMY (206/191) ARMIES

Gen 21:22 Phichol, the commander of his **a**,
21:32 Phichol, the commander of his **a**,
26:26 Phichol the commander of his **a**.
Ex 14: 4 over Pharaoh and over all his **a**,
14: 9 Pharaoh, his horsemen and his **a**,
14:17 over Pharaoh and over all his **a**,
14:24 LORD looked down upon the **a**
14:24 and He troubled the **a** of the
14:28 and all the **a** of Pharaoh that
15: 4 Pharaoh's chariots and his **a** He
Num 2: 4 And his **a** was numbered at
2: 6 And his **a** was numbered at
2: 8 And his **a** was numbered at
2:11 And his **a** was numbered at
2:13 And his **a** was numbered at
2:15 And his **a** was numbered at
2:19 And his **a** was numbered at forty
2:21 And his **a** was numbered at
2:23 And his **a** was numbered at
2:26 And his **a** was numbered at
2:28 And his **a** was numbered at
2:30 And his **a** was numbered at
10:14 over their **a** was Nahshon the
10:15 Over the **a** of the tribe of the
10:16 And over the **a** of the tribe of
10:18 over their **a** was Elizur the
10:19 Over the **a** of the tribe of the
10:20 And over the **a** of the tribe of
10:22 over their **a** was Elishama the
10:23 Over the **a** of the tribe of the
10:24 And over the **a** of the tribe of
10:25 over their **a** was Ahiezer the
10:26 Over the **a** of the tribe of the
10:27 And over the **a** of the tribe of
31:14 with the officers of the **a**,
31:48 were over thousands of the **a**,
Deut 11: 4 what He did to the **a** of Egypt,
23: 9 When the **a** goes out against
Josh 5:14 but as Commander of the **a** of
5:15 the Commander of the LORD's **a**
8:13 all the **a** that was on the
Judg 4: 2 The commander of his **a** was
4: 7 the commander of Jabin's **a**,
4:15 his chariots and all his **a**
4:16 pursued the chariots and the **a**
4:16 and all the **a** of Sisera fell by
7:21 and the whole **a** ran and cried
7:22 and the **a** fled to Beth Acacia,
8: 6 we should give bread to your **a**?
8:10 all who were left of all the **a**
8:11 and he attacked the **a** while the
8:12 and routed the whole **a**.
9:29 Increase your **a** and come out!"
1 Sam 4: 2 four thousand men of the **a** in
12: 9 commander of the **a** of Hazor,
14:48 And he gathered an **a** and
14:50 name of the commander of his **a**
17:20 he came to the camp as the **a**
17:21 battle array, **a** against army.
17:21 in battle array, army against **a**.
17:22 the supply keeper, ran to the **a**,
17:48 hastened and ran toward the **a**
17:55 Abner, the commander of the **a**,
26: 5 of Ner, the commander of his **a**.
28: 5 When Saul saw the **a** of the
28:19 LORD will also deliver the **a**
29: 6 coming in with me in the **a** is
2 Sam 2: 8 of Ner, commander of Saul's **a**,
8: 9 David had defeated all the **a**
8:16 son of Zeruiah was over the **a**;
10: 7 he sent Joab and all the **a** of
10:16 the commander of Hadadezer's **a**
10:18 the commander of their **a**,
17:25 made Amasa captain of the **a**
19:13 you are not commander of the **a**
20:23 And Joab was over all the **a** of
24: 2 to Joab the commander of the **a**
24: 4 against the captains of the **a**.
24: 4 Joab and the captains of the **a**
1 Ki 1:19 and Joab the commander of the **a**;
1:25 and the commanders of the **a**,
2:32 the commander of the **a** of
2:32 the commander of the **a** of
2:35 in his place over the **a**,
4: 4 the son of Jehoiada, over the **a**;
11:15 and Joab the commander of the **a**
11:21 Joab the commander of the **a**
16:16 Omri, the commander of the **a**,
20:19 went out of the city with the **a**
20:25 and you shall muster an **a** like
20:25 muster an army like the **a** that
22:36 a shout went throughout the **a**,
2 Ki 3: 9 there was no water for the **a**,
4:13 or to the commander of the **a**?
5: 1 commander of the **a** of the king
6:14 and chariots and a great **a**
6:15 and went out, there was an **a**,
6:24 of Syria gathered all his **a**,
7: 4 let us surrender to the **a** of
7: 6 For the LORD had caused the **a**
7: 6 horses—the noise of a great **a**;
7:14 the direction of the Syrian **a**,
9: 5 were the captains of the **a**
11:15 hundreds, the officers of the **a**,
13: 7 For He left of the **a** of Jehoahaz
18:17 with a great **a** against
25: 1 king of Babylon and all his **a**
25: 5 But the **a** of the Chaldeans
25: 5 All his **a** was scattered from
25:10 And all the **a** of the Chaldeans
25:19 recruiting officer of the **a**,
1 Chr 7:40 by genealogies among the **a** fit
11:15 and the **a** of the Philistines
12:14 sons of Gad, captains of the **a**;
12:21 and they were captains in the **a**.
12:22 him, until it was a great **a**,
12:22 like the **a** of God.
14:16 and they drove back the **a** of
18: 9 David had defeated all the **a**
18:15 son of Zeruiah was over the **a**;
19: 8 he sent Joab and all the **a** of
19:16 the commander of Hadadezer's **a**
19:18 Shophach the commander of the **a**.
25: 1 David and the captains of the **a**
26:26 and the captains of the **a**,
27: 3 of all the captains of the **a**
27: 5 The third captain of the **a** for
27:34 And the general of the king's **a**
2 Chr 13: 3 the battle in order with an **a**
14: 8 And Asa had an **a** of three
14: 9 out against them with an **a** of
14:13 before the LORD and His **a**.
16: 7 therefore the **a** of the king of
16: 8 and the Lubim not a huge **a**
20:21 as they went out before the **a**
23:14 who were set over the **a**,
24:23 spring of the year that the **a**
24:24 For the **a** of the Syrians came
24:24 LORD delivered a very great **a**
25: 7 do not let the **a** of Israel go
25:13 as for the soldiers of the **a**
26:11 Moreover Uzziah had an **a** of
26:13 their authority was an **a** of
26:14 for them, for the entire **a**,
28: 9 and he went out before the **a**
33:11 them the captains of the **a** of
Neh 2: 9 had sent captains of the **a** and
4: 2 before his brethren and the **a**
Job 29:25 So I dwelt as a king in the **a**,
Ps 27: 3 Though an **a** may encamp against
33:16 saved by the multitude of an **a**;
136:15 overthrew Pharaoh and his **a** in
Song 6: 4 Awesome as an **a** with
6:10 Awesome as an **a** with
Isa 13: 4 LORD of hosts musters The **a**
36: 2 the Rabshakeh with a great **a**
43:17 The **a** and the power (They
Jer 32: 2 then the king of Babylon's **a**
34: 1 king of Babylon and all his **a**,
34: 7 when the king of Babylon's **a**
34:21 hand of the king of Babylon's **a**
35:11 to Jerusalem for fear of the **a**
35:11 and for fear of the **a** of the
37: 5 Then Pharaoh's **a** came up from
37: 7 Pharaoh's **a** which has come up
37:10 you had defeated the whole **a**
37:11 when the **a** of the Chaldeans
37:11 for fear of Pharaoh's **a**,
38: 3 hand of the king of Babylon's **a**,
39: 1 king of Babylon and all his **a**
39: 5 But the Chaldean **a** pursued them
46: 2 Concerning the **a** of Pharaoh
46:22 For they shall march with an **a**
51: 3 men; Utterly destroy all her **a**.
52: 4 king of Babylon and all his **a**
52: 8 But the **a** of the Chaldeans
52: 8 All his **a** was scattered from
52:14 And all the **a** of the Chaldeans
52:25 the principal scribe of the **a**
Ezek 1:24 a tumult like the noise of an **a**;
17:17 Pharaoh with his mighty **a** and
26: 7 and an **a** with many people.
27:10 and Libya Were in your **a** as
27:11 Men of Arvad with your **a** were
29:18 king of Babylon caused his **a**
29:18 yet neither he nor his **a**
29:19 will be the wages for his **a**.
32:31 Pharaoh and all his **a**,
37:10 feet, an exceedingly great **a**.

38: 4 lead you out, with all your *a*,
38:13 Have you gathered your *a* to
38:15 a great company and a mighty *a*.
Dan 3:20 of valor who were in his *a* to
4:35 according to His will in the *a*
8:12 an *a* was given over to the
11: 7 place, who shall come with an *a*,
11:13 of some years with a great *a*
11:25 of the South with a great *a*.
11:25 with a very great and mighty *a*;
11:26 his *a* shall be swept away, and
Joel 2:11 LORD gives voice before His *a*,
2:20 far from you the northern *a*,
2:25 My great *a* which I sent among
Zech 9: 8 My house Because of the *a*,
Rev 9:16 Now the number of the *a* of the
19:19 on the horse and against His *a*.

ARNAN (1/1)

1 Chr 3:21 sons of Rephaiah, the sons of *A*,

ARNON (25/23)

Num 21:13 on the other side of the *A*,
21:13 for the *A* is the border of
21:14 in Suphah, The brooks of the *A*,
21:24 of his land from the *A* to the
21:26 from his hand as far as the *A*.
21:28 lords of the heights of the *A*.
22:36 is on the border at the *A*,
Deut 2:24 and cross over the River *A*.
2:36 is on the bank of the River *A*,
3: 8 from the River *A* to Mount
3:12 Aroer, which is by the River *A*,
3:16 Gilead as far as the River *A*,
4:48 is on the bank of the River *A*,
Josh 12: 1 from the River *A* to Mount
12: 2 is on the bank of the River *A*,
13: 9 is on the bank of the River *A*,
13:16 is on the bank of the River *A*,
Judg 11:13 from the *A* as far as the
11:18 on the other side of the *A*.
11:18 for the *A* was the border of
11:22 from the *A* to the Jabbok and
11:26 cities along the banks of the *A*,
2 Ki 10:33 Aroer, which is by the River *A*,
Isa 16: 2 of Moab at the fords of the *A*.
Jer 48:20 Wail and cry! Tell it in *A*,

AROD (1/1) ARODI

Num 26:17 *A*, the family of the Arodites;

ARODI (1/1) AROD, ARODITES

Gen 46:16 Haggi, Shuni, Ezbon, Eri, *A*,

ARODITES (1/1) ARODI

Num 26:17 of Arod, the family of the *A*;

AROER (16/16) AROERITE

Num 32:34 built Dibon and Ataroth and *A*,
Deut 2:36 'From *A*, which is on the bank
3:12 possessed at that time, from *A*,
4:48 from *A*, which is on the bank
Josh 12: 2 ruled half of Gilead, from *A*,
13: 9 from *A* which is on the bank of
13:16 Their territory was from *A*,
13:25 of the Ammonites as far as *A*,
Judg 11:26 in *A* and its villages, and in
11:33 And he defeated them from *A* as
1 Sam 30:28 those who were in *A*,
2 Sam 24: 5 over the Jordan and camped in *A*,
2 Ki 10:33 Reuben, and Manasseh—from *A*,
1 Chr 5: 8 the son of Joel, who dwelt in *A*,
Isa 17: 2 The cities of *A* are forsaken;
Jer 48:19 O inhabitant of *A*,

AROERITE (1/1) AROER

1 Chr 11:44 Jeiel the sons of Hotham the *A*,

AROMA (46/45) AROMAS

Gen 8:21 the LORD smelled a soothing *a*.
Ex 29:18 to the LORD; it is a sweet *a*,
29:25 as a sweet *a* before the LORD.
29:41 in the morning, for a sweet *a*,
Lev 1: 9 a sweet *a* to the LORD.
1:13 a sweet *a* to the LORD.
1:17 a sweet *a* to the LORD.
2: 2 a sweet *a* to the LORD.
2: 9 a sweet *a* to the LORD.
2:12 on the altar for a sweet *a*.
3: 5 a sweet *a* to the LORD.
3:16 made by fire for a sweet *a*;
4:31 it on the altar for a sweet *a*
6:15 it on the altar for a sweet *a*,
6:21 you shall offer for a sweet *a*
8:21 a burnt sacrifice for a sweet *a*,
8:28 offerings for a sweet *a*.
17: 6 and burn the fat for a sweet *a*
23:13 to the LORD, for a sweet *a*;
23:18 made by fire for a sweet *a* to
Num 15: 3 to make a sweet *a* to the LORD,
15: 7 of a HIN of wine as a sweet *a*
15:10 a sweet *a* to the LORD.
15:13 a sweet *a* to the LORD.
15:14 a sweet *a* to the LORD, just as
15:24 as a sweet *a* to the LORD, with
18:17 made by fire for a sweet *a* to
28: 2 made by fire as a sweet *a* to
28: 6 at Mount Sinai for a sweet *a*,
28: 8 a sweet *a* to the LORD.
28:13 as a burnt offering of sweet *a*,
28:24 as a sweet *a* to the LORD; it
28:27 a burnt offering as a sweet *a*
29: 2 a burnt offering as a sweet *a*
29: 6 their ordinance, as a sweet *a*,
29: 8 to the LORD as a sweet *a*:
29:13 made by fire as a sweet *a* to
29:36 made by fire as a sweet *a* to
Ezra 6:10 offer sacrifices of sweet *a* to
Ps 66:15 With the sweet *a* of rams; I
Ezek 20:28 also sent up their sweet *a* and
20:41 will accept you as a sweet *a*
2 Cor 2:16 To the one we are the *a* of
2:16 and to the other the *a* of life
Eph 5: 2 to God for a sweet-smelling *a*.
Phil 4:18 from you, a sweet-smelling *a*,

AROMAS (1/1) AROMA

Lev 26:31 the fragrance of your sweet *a*.

AROSE (196/192) ARISE

Gen 19:33 when she lay down or when she *a*.
19:35 And the younger *a* and lay with
19:35 when she lay down or when she *a*.
22: 3 and *a* and went to the place of
24:10 And he *a* and went to
24:54 Then they *a* in the morning, and
24:61 Then Rebekah and her maids *a*,
25:34 then he ate and drank, *a*,
26:31 Then they *a* early in the morning
31:21 He *a* and crossed the river, and
31:55 early in the morning Laban *a*,
32:22 And he *a* that night and took
37: 7 my sheaf *a* and also stood
37:35 sons and all his daughters *a*
38:19 So she *a* and went away, and laid
43:15 and *a* and went down to Egypt;
46: 5 Then Jacob *a* from Beersheba; and
Ex 1: 8 Now there *a* a new king over
24:13 So Moses *a* with his assistant
Josh 8: 3 So Joshua *a*, and all the
8:19 So those in ambush *a* quickly
18: 8 Then the men *a* to go away; and
24: 9 *a* to make war against Israel,
Judg 2:10 another generation *a* after them
3:20 So he *a* from his seat.
4: 9 Then Deborah *a* and went with
5: 7 in Israel, Until I, Deborah, *a*,
5: 7 *A* a mother in Israel.
6:28 And when the men of the city *a*
8:21 So Gideon *a* and killed Zebah
10: 1 After Abimelech there *a* to save
10: 3 After him *a* Jair, a Gileadite;
13:11 So Manoah *a* and followed his
16: 3 then he *a* at midnight, took
19: 3 Then her husband *a* and went
19: 5 on the fourth day that they *a*
19: 8 Then he *a* early in the morning
19:27 When her master *a* in the
20: 8 So all the people *a* as one man,
20:18 Then the children of Israel *a*
Ruth 1: 6 Then she *a* with her
3:14 and she *a* before one could
1 Sam 1: 9 So Hannah *a* after they had
3: 6 So Samuel *a* and went
3: 8 Then he *a* and went to Eli, and
5: 3 And when the people of Ashdod *a*
5: 4 And when they *a* early the next
9:26 They *a* early; and it was about
9:26 you on your way." And Saul *a*,
13:15 Then Samuel *a* and went up from
16:13 So Samuel *a* and went to Ramah.
17:35 and when it *a* against me, I
17:48 when the Philistine *a* and came
17:52 the men of Israel and Judah *a*
18:27 therefore David *a* and went, he
20:25 by the wall. And Jonathan *a*,
20:34 So Jonathan *a* from the table in
20:41 David *a* from a place toward
20:42 So he *a* and departed, and
21:10 Then David *a* and fled that day
23:13 *a* and departed from Keilah and
23:16 *a* and went to David in the
23:24 So they *a* and went to Ziph
24: 4 And David *a* and secretly
24: 8 David also *a* afterward, went
25: 1 And David *a* and went down to
25:41 Then she *a*, bowed her face
26: 2 Then Saul *a* and went down to the
26: 5 So David *a* and came to the
27: 2 Then David *a* and went over with
28:23 Then he *a* from the ground and
31:12 all the valiant men *a* and
2 Sam 2:15 So they *a* and went over by
6: 2 And David *a* and went with all
11: 2 one evening that David *a* from
12:17 So the elders of his house *a*
12:20 So David *a* from the ground,
12:21 you *a* and ate food."
13:29 Then all the king's sons *a*,
13:31 So the king *a* and tore his
14:23 So Joab *a* and went to Geshur,
14:31 Then Joab *a* and came to
15: 9 So he *a* and went to Hebron.
17:22 the people who were with him *a*
17:23 and *a* and went home to his
19: 8 Then the king *a* and sat in the
23:10 He *a* and attacked the
24:11 Now when David *a* in the morning,
1 Ki 1:49 Adonijah were afraid, and *a*,
1:50 was afraid of Solomon; so he *a*,
2:40 Shimei *a*, saddled his donkey,
3:20 So she *a* in the middle of the
8:54 that he *a* from before the altar
11:18 Then they *a* from Midian and came
11:40 But Jeroboam *a* and fled to
14: 4 she *a* and went to Shiloh, and
14:17 Then Jeroboam's wife *a* and
17:10 So he *a* and went to Zarephath.
19: 3 he *a* and ran for his life, and
19: 8 So he *a*, and ate and drank;
19:21 Then he *a* and followed Elijah,
2 Ki 1:15 So he *a* and went down with
4:30 So he *a* and followed her.
6:15 the servant of the man of God *a*
7: 7 Therefore they *a* and fled at
7:12 So the king *a* in the night and
8: 2 So the woman *a* and did according
9: 6 Then he *a* and went into the
10:12 And he *a* and departed and went
11: 1 she *a* and destroyed all the
12:20 And his servants *a* and formed a
19:35 and when people *a* early in the
25:26 *a* and went to Egypt; for they
1 Chr 10:12 all the valiant men *a* and took
2 Chr 22:10 she *a* and destroyed all the
29:12 Then these Levites *a*:
30:14 They *a* and took away the altars
30:27 *a* and blessed the people, and
36:16 until the wrath of the LORD *a*
Ezra 1: 5 *a* to go up and build the house
3: 2 *a* and built the altar of the
3: 9 *a* as one to oversee those
9: 5 At the evening sacrifice I *a*
10: 5 Then Ezra *a*, and made
Neh 2:12 Then I *a* in the night, I and a
4:14 and *a* and said to the nobles,
Esth 7: 7 Then the king *a* in his wrath
8: 4 So Esther *a* and stood before
Job 1:20 Then Job *a*, tore his robe,
29: 8 And the aged *a* and stood;
Ps 76: 9 When God *a* to judgment, To
Eccl 1: 5 hastens to the place where it *a*.
Song 5: 5 I *a* to open for my beloved,
Isa 37:36 and when people *a* early in the
Jer 41: 2 *a* and struck Gedaliah the son
Ezek 3:23 So I *a* and went out into the
Dan 6:19 Then the king *a* very early in
8:27 afterward I *a* and went about
Jon 1: 3 But Jonah *a* to flee to Tarshish
3: 3 So Jonah *a* and went to Nineveh,
3: 6 and he *a* from his throne and
4: 8 And it happened, when the sun *a*,
Mt 2:14 When he *a*, he took the young
2:21 Then he *a*, took the young Child
8:15 And she *a* and served them.
8:24 And suddenly a great tempest *a*
8:26 Then He *a* and rebuked the
9: 7 And he *a* and departed to his
9: 9 So he *a* and followed Him.
9:19 So Jesus *a* and followed him, and
9:25 her by the hand, and the girl *a*.
25: 7 Then all those virgins *a* and
26:62 And the high priest *a* and said
Mk 2:12 Immediately he *a*, took up
2:14 So he *a* and followed Him.
4:37 And a great windstorm *a*,
4:39 Then He *a* and rebuked the wind,
5:42 Immediately the girl *a* and
7:24 From there He *a* and went to the
9:27 and lifted him up, and he *a*.
10: 1 Then He *a* from there and came to
Lk 1:39 Now Mary *a* in those days and
4:38 Now He *a* from the synagogue and
4:39 And immediately she *a* and
6: 8 And he *a* and stood.
6:48 the rock. And when the flood *a*,
8:24 we are perishing!" Then He *a*
8:55 and she *a* immediately. And He
9:46 Then a dispute *a* among them as
15:14 there *a* a severe famine in that
15:20 And he *a* and came to his father.
23: 1 the whole multitude of them *a*
24:12 But Peter *a* and ran to the tomb;
Jn 3:25 Then there *a* a dispute between
6:18 Then the sea *a* because a great
11:29 she *a* quickly and came to Him.
Acts 5: 6 And the young men *a* and wrapped
6: 1 there *a* a complaint against the
6: 9 Then there *a* some from what is
7:18 till another king *a* who did not
8: 1 that time a great persecution *a*
8:27 So he *a* and went. And behold, a
9: 8 Then Saul *a* from the ground, and
9:18 and he *a* and was baptized.
9:34 Then he *a* immediately.
9:39 Then Peter *a* and went with them.
10:41 and drank with Him after He *a*
11:19 after the persecution that *a*
19:23 And about that time there *a* a
23: 7 a dissension *a* between the
23: 9 Then there *a* a loud outcry.
23: 9 of the Pharisees' party *a* and
23:10 Now when there *a* a great
27:14 a tempestuous head wind *a*,

Heb 7:14 it is evident that our Lord **a**
Rev 9: 2 and smoke **a** out of the pit like

AROUND (379/354) See APPENDIX

AROUSE (1/1) AROUSED

Job 3: 8 Those who are ready to **a**

AROUSED (42/41) AROUSE

Gen 30: 2 And Jacob's anger was **a** against
39:19 manner," that his anger was **a**.
Num 11: 1 heard it, and His anger was **a**.
11:10 of the LORD was greatly **a**;
11:33 the wrath of the LORD was **a**
12: 9 the anger of the LORD was **a**
22:22 Then God's anger was **a** because
22:27 Balaam; so Balaam's anger was **a**,
24:10 Then Balak's anger was **a**
25: 3 the anger of the LORD was **a**
32:10 So the LORD's anger was **a** on
32:13 So the LORD's anger was **a**
Deut 6:15 of the LORD your God be **a**
7: 4 anger of the LORD will be **a**
11:17 lest the LORD's anger be **a**
29:27 the anger of the LORD was **a**
31:17 Then My anger shall be **a** against
Judg 9:30 son of Ebed, his anger was **a**.
14:19 the riddle. So his anger was **a**,
1 Sam 11: 6 and his anger was greatly **a**.
17:28 and Eliab's anger was **a** against
20:30 Then Saul's anger was **a** against
2 Sam 6: 7 the anger of the LORD was **a**
12: 5 So David's anger was greatly **a**
24: 1 the anger of the LORD was **a**
2 Ki 13: 3 the anger of the LORD was **a**
22:13 wrath of the LORD that is **a**
22:17 Therefore My wrath shall be **a**
23:26 with which His anger was **a**
1 Chr 13:10 the anger of the LORD was **a**
2 Chr 25:10 their anger was greatly **a**
25:15 the anger of the LORD was **a**
Job 32: 2 was **a** against Job; his wrath
32: 2 his wrath was **a** because he
32: 3 three friends his wrath was **a**,
32: 5 three men, his wrath was **a**.
42: 7 My wrath is **a** against you and
Isa 5:25 the anger of the LORD is **a**
Hos 8: 5 O Samaria! My anger is **a**
Zech 2:13 for He is **a** from His holy
Mt 1:24 being **a** from sleep, did as the
Rom 7: 5 sinful passions which were **a**

ARPAD (6/6)

2 Ki 18:34 are the gods of Hamath and **A**?
19:13 king of Hamath, the king of **A**,
Isa 10: 9 Is not Hamath like **A**?
36:19 are the gods of Hamath and **A**?
37:13 king of Hamath, the king of **A**,
Jer 49:23 Hamath and **A** are shamed, For

ARPHAD (KJV) See ARPAD

ARPHAXAD (10/10)

Gen 10:22 of Shem were Elam, Asshur, **A**,
10:24 **A** begot Salah, and Salah begot
11:10 and begot **A** two years after the
11:11 After he begot **A**, Shem lived
11:12 **A** lived thirty-five years, and
11:13 **A** lived four hundred and three
1 Chr 1:17 of Shem were Elam, Asshur, **A**,
1:18 **A** begot Shelah, and Shelah begot
1:24 Shem, **A**, Shelah,
Lk 3:36 son of Cainan, the son of **A**,

ARRAIGN (2/2)

Jer 49:19 Who will **a** Me? And who is
50:44 Who will **a** Me? And who is

ARRANGE (3/3) ARRANGED, ARRANGEMENT, ARRANGING

Ex 25:37 and they shall **a** its lamps so
40: 4 shall bring in the table and **a**
Num 8: 2 When you **a** the lamps, the seven

ARRANGED (2/2) ARRANGE

Num 8: 3 he **a** the lamps to face toward
Mt 22: 2 is like a certain king who **a** a

ARRANGEMENT (2/2) ARRANGE

Judg 6:26 of this rock in the proper **a**,
Ezek 43:11 design of the temple and its **a**,

ARRANGING (1/1) ARRANGE

1 Pe 3: 3 **a** the hair, wearing gold, or

ARRAY (27/26) ARRAYED

Judg 20:20 put themselves in battle **a** to
20:22 they had put themselves in **a**
20:30 and put themselves in battle **a**
20:33 and put themselves in battle **a**
1 Sam 4: 2 put themselves in battle **a**
17: 2 and drew up in battle **a** against
17:21 had drawn up in battle **a**,
2 Sam 10: 8 and put themselves in battle **a**
10: 9 best and put them in battle **a**
10:10 he might set them in battle **a**
10:17 set themselves in battle **a**
1 Chr 19: 9 and put themselves in battle **a**
19:10 best and put them in battle **a**
19:11 set themselves in battle **a**
19:17 and set up in battle **a** against
19:17 David had set up in battle **a**
2 Chr 14:10 set the troops in battle **a** in
Esth 6: 9 that he may **a** the man whom the
Job 40:10 and **a** yourself with glory and
Isa 22: 7 shall set themselves in **a** at
Jer 6:23 As men of war set in **a** against
43:12 And he shall **a** himself with the
50: 9 And they shall **a** themselves
50:14 Put yourselves in **a** against
50:42 shall ride on horses, Set in **a**,
Ezek 23:24 They shall **a** against you
Joel 2: 5 a strong people set in battle **a**.

ARRAYED (9/9) ARRAY

Esth 6:11 **a** Mordecai and led him on
Job 6: 4 The terrors of God are **a**
Mt 6:29 in all his glory was not **a**
Lk 12:27 in all his glory was not **a**
23:11 **a** Him in a gorgeous robe, and
Acts 12:21 **a** in royal apparel, sat on his
Rev 7:13 Who are these **a** in white robes,
17: 4 The woman was **a** in purple and
19: 8 to her it was granted to be **a**

ARREST (5/5) ARRESTED

Judg 15:10 We have come up to **a** Samson, to
15:12 We have come down to **a** you, that
1 Ki 13: 4 *A* him!" Then his hand, which he
Mk 13:11 But when they **a** you and deliver
2 Cor 11:32 garrison, desiring to **a** me;

ARRESTED (5/5) ARREST

2 Sam 4:10 I **a** him and had him executed in
Lk 22:54 Having **a** Him, they led Him and
Jn 18:12 and the officers of the Jews **a**
Acts 1:16 became a guide to those who **a**
12: 4 So when he had **a** him, he put

ARRIVAL (1/1) ARRIVALS, ARRIVE, ARRIVED

Num 10:21 would be prepared for their **a**.

ARRIVALS (1/1) ARRIVAL

Deut 32:17 new **a** That your fathers did

ARRIVE (6/6) ARRIVAL, ARRIVED

Gen 19:22 cannot do anything until you **a**
24:41 clear from this oath when you **a**
Ex 10:26 must serve the LORD until we **a**
1 Ki 19:15 of Damascus; and when you **a**,
2 Ki 9: 2 Now when you **a** at that place,
Jer 51:61 When you **a** in Babylon and see

ARRIVED (14/14) ARRIVE

Judg 3:27 And it happened, when he **a**,
12: 5 before the Ephraimites **a**.
2 Ki 9: 5 And when he **a**, there were
2 Chr 22: 7 downfall; for when he **a**,
Esth 4: 3 the king's command and decree **a**,
Mk 6:33 They **a** before them and came
Lk 10:32 when he **a** at the place, came
24:22 who **a** at the tomb early,
Acts 13: 5 And when they **a** in Salamis, they
17:10 by night to Berea. When they **a**,
18:27 to receive him; and when he **a**,
20:15 The following day we **a** at
27: 7 and **a** with difficulty off
2 Tim 1:17 but when he **a** in Rome, he sought

ARROGANCE (6/6) ARROGANT

1 Sam 2: 3 Let no **a** come from your mouth,
Prov 8:13 Pride and **a** and the evil way
Isa 9: 9 Who say in pride and **a** of
13:11 I will halt the **a** of the
Jer 48:29 Of his loftiness and **a** and
Jas 4:16 But now you boast in your **a**.

ARROGANT (7/7) ARROGANCE

Prov 21:24 He acts with **a** pride.
Isa 10:12 will punish the fruit of the **a**
Ezek 24:21 your **a** boast, the desire of
30:18 And her **a** strength shall cease
33:28 her **a** strength shall cease, and
Zeph 2: 8 And made **a** threats against
2:10 they have reproached and made **a**

ARROW (20/18) ARROWS

Ex 19:13 be stoned or shot with an **a**;
1 Sam 20:36 he shot an **a** beyond him.
20:37 come to the place where the **a**
20:37 Is not the **a** beyond you?"
2 Ki 9:24 and the **a** came out at his
13:17 The **a** of the LORD's deliverance
13:17 LORD's deliverance and the **a**
19:32 Nor shoot an **a** there, Nor
Job 41:28 The **a** cannot make him flee;
Ps 11: 2 They make ready their **a** on the
64: 7 shall shoot at them with an **a**;
91: 5 Nor of the **a** that flies by
Prov 7:23 Till an **a** struck his liver.
25:18 a club, a sword, and a sharp **a**.
Isa 34:15 There the **a** snake shall make
37:33 Nor shoot an **a** there, Nor
Jer 9: 8 Their tongue is an **a** shot out;
Lam 3:12 set me up as a target for the **a**.
Zech 9:14 And His **a** will go forth like
Heb 12:20 stoned or shot with an **a**.

ARROWS (43/41) ARROW

Num 24: 8 And pierce them with his **a**.
Deut 32:23 I will spend My **a** on them.
32:42 I will make My **a** drunk with
1 Sam 20:20 Then I will shoot three **a** to the
20:21 a lad, saying, 'Go, find the **a**.
20:21 the **a** are on this side of you;
20:22 the **a** are beyond you'—go your
20:36 find the **a** which I shoot."
20:38 lad gathered up the **a** and came
2 Sam 22:15 He sent out **a** and scattered
2 Ki 13:15 to him, "Take a bow and some **a**.
13:15 took himself a bow and some **a**.
13:18 Take the **a**"; so he took them.
1 Chr 12: 2 stones and shooting **a** with
2 Chr 26:15 to shoot **a** and large stones.
Job 6: 4 For the **a** of the Almighty are
Ps 7:13 He makes His **a** into fiery
18:14 He sent out His **a** and scattered
21:12 You will make ready Your **a**
38: 2 For Your **a** pierce me deeply,
45: 5 Your **a** are sharp in the heart
57: 4 Whose teeth are spears and **a**,
58: 7 Let his **a** be as if cut in
64: 3 their bows to shoot their **a**—
76: 3 There He broke the **a** of the
77:17 Your **a** also flashed about.
120: 4 Sharp **a** of the warrior, With
127: 4 Like **a** in the hand of a
144: 6 Shoot out Your **a** and destroy
Prov 26:18 madman who throws firebrands, **a**,
Isa 5:28 Whose **a** are sharp, And all
7:24 With **a** and bows men will come
Jer 50: 9 Their **a** shall be like those
50:14 bow; Shoot at her, spare no **a**,
51:11 Make the **a** bright! Gather the
Lam 3:13 He has caused the **a** of His
Ezek 5:16 against them the terrible **a** of
21:21 use divination: he shakes the **a**,
39: 3 and cause the **a** to fall out of
39: 9 and bucklers, the bows and **a**,
Hab 3: 9 Oaths were sworn over Your **a**.
3:11 At the light of Your **a** they
3:14 thrust through with his own **a**

ART (3/3) ARTISTIC

Ex 30:25 compounded according to the **a**
30:35 a compound according to the **a**
Acts 17:29 something shaped by **a** and man's

ARTAXERXES (14/13)

Ezra 4: 7 In the days of **A** also, Bishlam,
4: 7 of their companions wrote to **A**
4: 8 against Jerusalem to King **A** in
4:11 that they sent him) To King **A**
6:14 and **A** king of Persia.
7: 1 in the reign of **A** king of
7: 7 in the seventh year of King **A**.
7:11 copy of the letter that King **A**
7:12 **A**, king of kings,
7:21 **A** the king, issue a decree to
8: 1 Babylon, in the reign of King **A**:
Neh 2: 1 in the twentieth year of King **A**,
5:14 thirty-second year of King **A**,
13: 6 in the thirty-second year of **A**

ARTAXERXES' (1/1)

Ezra 4:23 when the copy of King **A** letter

ARTEMAS (1/1)

Titus 3:12 When I send **A** to you, or

ARTICLES (65/53)

Ex 3:22 **a** of silver, articles of gold,
3:22 **a** of gold, and clothing; and
11: 2 **a** of silver and articles of
11: 2 articles of silver and **a** of
12:35 had asked from the Egyptians **a**
12:35 **a** of gold, and clothing.
22: 7 to his neighbor money or **a** to
Num 18: 3 they shall not come near the **a**
31: 6 with the holy **a** and the signal
1 Sam 6: 8 and put the **a** of gold which you
6:15 in which were the **a** of gold,
2 Sam 8:10 and Joram brought with him **a**
8:10 **a** of gold, and articles of
8:10 of gold, and **a** of bronze.
1 Ki 7:45 All these **a** which Huram made
7:47 Solomon did not weigh all the **a**,
10:25 **a** of silver and gold, garments,
2 Ki 12:13 any **a** of gold or articles of
12:13 any articles of gold or **a** of
14:14 all the **a** that were found in
23: 4 temple of the LORD all the **a**

24:13 and he cut in pieces all the ***a***
25:16 the bronze of all these ***a*** was
1 Chr 18: 8 and the ***a*** of bronze.
18:10 with him all kinds of ***a*** of
22:19 of the LORD and the holy ***a*** of
23:26 or any of the ***a*** for its
28:13 and for all the ***a*** of service in
28:14 for all ***a*** used in every kind of
28:14 also silver for all ***a*** of
28:14 for all ***a*** used in every kind of
2 Chr 4:16 and all their ***a*** Huram his master
4:18 And Solomon had all these ***a*** made
9:24 ***a*** of silver and gold, garments,
24:14 they made from it ***a*** for the
24:14 ***a*** for serving and offering,
25:24 all the ***a*** that were found in
28:24 So Ahaz gathered the ***a*** of the
28:24 cut in pieces the ***a*** of the
29:18 burnt offerings with all its ***a***,
29:18 of the showbread with all its ***a***.
29:19 Moreover all the ***a*** which King
36: 7 also carried off some of the ***a***
36:10 with the costly ***a*** from the
36:18 And all the ***a*** from the house of
Ezra 1: 6 them encouraged them with ***a*** of
1: 7 Cyrus also brought out the ***a***
1:10 and one thousand other ***a***.
1:11 All the ***a*** of gold and silver
5:14 the gold and silver ***a*** of the
5:15 he said to him, 'Take these ***a***;
6: 5 Also let the gold and silver ***a***
7:19 Also the ***a*** that are given to you
8:25 the silver, the gold, and the ***a***,
8:26 silver ***a*** weighing one hundred
8:28 the ***a*** are holy also; and the
8:30 silver and the gold and the ***a***
8:33 silver and the gold and the ***a***
Neh 10:39 to the storerooms where the ***a***
13: 5 the frankincense, the ***a***,
13: 9 I brought back into them the ***a***
Jer 52:20 the bronze of all these ***a*** was
Dan 1: 2 with some of the ***a*** of the house
1: 2 and he brought the ***a*** into the
11: 8 princes and their precious ***a***

ARTIFICER, ARTIFICERS (KJV)
See ARTISAN, CRAFTSMAN

ARTILLERY (KJV) See WEAPONS

ARTISAN (3/3) ARTISANS

Ex 36: 1 and every gifted ***a*** in whom the
36: 2 and every gifted ***a*** in whose
Isa 3: 3 counselor and the skillful ***a***,

ARTISANS (5/5) ARTISAN

Ex 28: 3 speak to all who are gifted ***a***,
31: 6 hearts of all who are gifted ***a***,
35:10 All who are gifted ***a*** among
35:25 the women who were gifted ***a***
36: 8 Then all the gifted ***a*** among

ARTISTIC (9/9) ART, ARTISTICALLY

Ex 26: 1 with ***a*** designs of cherubim you
26:31 It shall be woven with an ***a***
31: 4 to design ***a*** works, to work in
35:32 to design ***a*** works, to work in
35:33 and to work in all manner of ***a***
35:35 work and those who design ***a***
36: 8 with ***a*** designs of cherubim
36:35 it was worked with an ***a*** design
39: 3 fine linen, into ***a*** designs.

ARTISTICALLY (4/4) ARTISTIC

Ex 28: 6 woven linen, ***a*** worked.
28:15 ***A*** woven according to the
39: 8 ***a*** woven like the workmanship of
39:27 ***a*** woven of fine linen, for

ARUBBOTH (1/1)

1 Ki 4:10 Ben-Hesed, in ***A***;

ARUMAH (1/1) RUMAH

Judg 9:41 Then Abimelech dwelt at ***A***,

ARVAD (2/2) ARVADITE

Ezek 27: 8 Inhabitants of Sidon and ***A*** were
27:11 Men of ***A*** with your army were

ARVADITE (2/2) ARVAD

Gen 10:18 the ***A***, the Zemarite, and the
1 Chr 1:16 the ***A***, the Zemarite, and the

ARZA (1/1)

1 Ki 16: 9 himself drunk in the house of ***A***,

AS (3767/3029) See APPENDIX

AS I LIVE (27/27)

Num 14:21 'but truly, ***a***, all the earth
14:28 "Say to them, '***A***,
Deut 32:40 And say, "***A*** forever,
Job 27: 6 not reproach me as long ***a***.
Ps 104:33 sing to the LORD as long ***a***;
116: 2 will call upon Him as long ***a***.
Isa 49:18 together and come to you. ***A***,
Jer 22:24 ***A***," says the LORD,
46:18 ***A***," says the King,
Ezek 5:11 'Therefore, ***a***,' says the Lord
14:16 these three men were in it, ***a***,
14:18 these three men were in it, ***a***,
14:20 Daniel, and Job were in it, ***a***,
16:48 ***A***," says the Lord GOD,
17:16 ***A***,' says the Lord GOD,
17:19 thus says the Lord GOD: "***A***,
18: 3 ***A***," says the Lord GOD,
20: 3 you come to inquire of Me? ***A***,
20:31 by you, O house of Israel? ***A***,
20:33 ***A***," says the Lord GOD,
33:11 "Say to them: '***A***,
33:27 'Thus says the Lord GOD: "***A***,
34: 8 ***A***," says the Lord GOD,
35: 6 'therefore, ***a***," says the Lord
35:11 'therefore, ***a***," says the Lord
Zeph 2: 9 Therefore, ***a***," Says the LORD
Rom 14:11 For it is written: "***A***,

ASA (59/53) ASA'S

1 Ki 15: 8 Then ***A*** his son reigned in his
15: 9 ***A*** became king over Judah.
15:11 ***A*** did what was right in the
15:13 And ***A*** cut down her obscene
15:16 Now there was war between ***A*** and
15:17 let none go out or come in to ***A***
15:18 Then ***A*** took all the silver and
15:18 And King ***A*** sent them to
15:20 So Ben-Hadad heeded King ***A***,
15:22 Then King ***A*** made a proclamation
15:22 and with them King ***A*** built Geba
15:23 The rest of all the acts of ***A***,
15:24 So ***A*** rested with his fathers,
15:25 Israel in the second year of ***A***
15:28 him in the third year of ***A***
15:32 And there was war between ***A*** and
15:33 In the third year of ***A*** king of
16: 8 In the twenty-sixth year of ***A***
16:10 in the twenty-seventh year of ***A***
16:15 the twenty-seventh year of ***A***
16:23 In the thirty-first year of ***A***
16:29 In the thirty-eighth year of ***A***
22:41 Jehoshaphat the son of ***A*** had
22:43 in all the ways of his father ***A***.
22:46 in the days of his father ***A***,
1 Chr 3:10 ***A*** his son, Jehoshaphat his son,
9:16 and Berechiah the son of ***A***,
2 Chr 14: 1 Then ***A*** his son reigned in his
14: 2 ***A*** did what was good and right
14: 8 And ***A*** had an army of three
14:10 So ***A*** went out against him, and
14:11 And ***A*** cried out to the LORD his
14:12 struck the Ethiopians before ***A***
14:13 And ***A*** and the people who were
15: 2 And he went out to meet ***A***,
15: 2 and said to him: "Hear me, ***A***,
15: 8 And when ***A*** heard these words
15:10 year of the reign of ***A***.
15:16 the mother of ***A*** the king, from
15:16 and ***A*** cut down her obscene
15:17 Nevertheless the heart of ***A*** was
15:19 year of the reign of ***A***.
16: 1 year of the reign of ***A***,
16: 1 let none go out or come in to ***A***
16: 2 Then ***A*** brought silver and gold
16: 4 So Ben-Hadad heeded King ***A***,
16: 6 Then King ***A*** took all Judah, and
16: 7 time Hanani the seer came to ***A***
16:10 Then ***A*** was angry with the seer,
16:10 And ***A*** oppressed some of the
16:11 Note that the acts of ***A***,
16:12 ***A*** became diseased in his feet,
16:13 So ***A*** rested with his fathers;
17: 2 the cities of Ephraim which ***A***
20:32 in the way of his father ***A***,
21:12 or in the ways of ***A*** king of
Jer 41: 9 was the same one ***A*** the king
Mt 1: 7 Abijah, and Abijah begot ***A***.
1: 8 ***A*** begot Jehoshaphat, Jehoshaphat

ASA'S (1/1) ASA

1 Ki 15:14 Nevertheless ***A*** heart was loyal

ASAHEL (18/17)

2 Sam 2:18 there: Joab and Abishai and ***A***.
2:18 And ***A*** was as fleet of foot as
2:19 So ***A*** pursued Abner, and in going
2:20 him and said, "Are you ***A***?
2:21 But ***A*** would not turn aside
2:22 So Abner said again to ***A***,
2:23 as came to the place where ***A***
2:30 servants nineteen men and ***A***.
2:32 Then they took up ***A*** and buried
3:27 he died for the blood of ***A*** his
3:30 he had killed their brother ***A***
23:24 ***A*** the brother of Joab was one
1 Chr 2:16 were Abishai, Joab, and ***A***—
11:26 the mighty warriors were ***A***
27: 7 for the fourth month was ***A***
2 Chr 17: 8 Nethaniah, Zebadiah, ***A***,
31:13 Jehiel, Azaziah, Nahath, ***A***,
Ezra 10:15 Only Jonathan the son of ***A*** and

ASAHIAH (KJV) See ASAIAH

ASAIAH (8/8)

2 Ki 22:12 and ***A*** a servant of the king,
22:14 and ***A*** went to Huldah the
1 Chr 4:36 Jaakobah, Jeshohaiah, ***A***,
6:30 his son, and ***A*** his son.
9: 5 ***A*** the firstborn and his sons.
15: 6 ***A*** the chief, and two hundred
15:11 for the Levites: for Uriel, ***A***,
2 Chr 34:20 and ***A*** a servant of the king,

ASAPH (46/41)

2 Ki 18:18 scribe, and Joah the son of ***A***,
18:37 scribe, and Joah the son of ***A***,
1 Chr 6:39 And his brother ***A***,
6:39 was ***A*** the son of Berachiah,
9:15 the son of Zichri, the son of ***A***;
15:17 ***A*** the son of Berechiah; and of
15:19 the singers, Heman, ***A***,
16: 5 ***A*** the chief, and next to him
16: 5 but ***A*** made music with cymbals;
16: 7 psalm into the hand of ***A*** and
16:37 So he left ***A*** and his brothers
25: 1 service some of the sons of ***A***,
25: 2 Of the sons of ***A***:
25: 2 the sons of ***A*** were under the
25: 2 were under the direction of ***A***,
25: 6 service of the house of God. ***A***,
25: 9 Now the first lot for ***A*** came
26: 1 son of Kore, of the sons of ***A***.
2 Chr 5:12 all those of ***A*** and Heman and
20:14 a Levite of the sons of ***A***,
29:13 and Jeiel; of the sons of ***A***,
29:30 the words of David and of ***A***
35:15 And the singers, the sons of ***A***,
35:15 to the command of David, ***A***,
Ezra 2:41 The singers: the sons of ***A***,
3:10 and the Levites, the sons of ***A***,
Neh 2: 8 and a letter to ***A*** the keeper of
7:44 The singers: the sons of ***A***,
11:17 the son of Zabdi, the son of ***A***,
11:22 son of Micha, of the sons of ***A***,
12:35 the son of Zaccur, the son of ***A***,
12:46 For in the days of David and ***A***
Ps 50: A Psalm of ***A***.
73: A Psalm of ***A***.
74: A Contemplation of ***A***.
75: Not Destroy." A Psalm of ***A***.
76: instruments. A Psalm of ***A***.
77: To Jeduthun. A Psalm of ***A***.
78: A Contemplation of ***A***.
79: A Psalm of ***A***.
80: Lilies." A Testimony of ***A***.
81: of Gath. A Psalm of ***A***.
82: A Psalm of ***A***.
83: A Song. A Psalm of ***A***.
Isa 36: 3 scribe, and Joah the son of ***A***,
36:22 scribe, and Joah the son of ***A***,

ASAREL (1/1)

1 Chr 4:16 Ziph, Ziphah, Tiria, and ***A***.

ASCEND (19/19) ASCENDED, ASCENDING, ASCENDS, ASCENT, DESCEND

Deut 30:12 Who will ***a*** into heaven for us
32:50 die on the mountain which you ***a***,
Ps 24: 3 Who may ***a*** into the hill of the
135: 7 He causes the vapors to ***a*** from
139: 8 If I ***a*** into heaven, You are
Isa 5:24 And their blossom will ***a*** like
14:13 I will ***a*** into heaven, I will
14:14 I will ***a*** above the heights of
34:10 Its smoke shall ***a*** forever.
60: 7 They shall ***a*** with acceptance
Jer 10:13 And He causes the vapors to ***a***
48: 5 in the Ascent of Luhith they ***a***
51:16 He causes the vapors to ***a*** from
Ezek 38: 9 'You will ***a***, coming like a
Ob : 4 Though you ***a*** as high as the
Jn 6:62 you should see the Son of Man ***a***
Acts 2:34 For David did not ***a*** into the
Rom 10: 6 Who will ***a*** into heaven?'"
Rev 17: 8 and will ***a*** out of the

ASCENDED (17/17) ASCEND

Ex 19:18 Its smoke ***a*** like the smoke of a
Josh 8:20 the smoke of the city ***a*** to
8:21 that the smoke of the city ***a***,
10: 7 So Joshua ***a*** from Gilgal, he and
15: 3 ***a*** on the south side of Kadesh
Judg 13:20 the Angel of the LORD ***a*** in the
Ps 68:18 You have ***a*** on high, You have
Prov 30: 4 Who has ***a*** into heaven, or
Ezek 40:22 it was ***a*** by seven steps, and
41: 7 in the wall of the temple ***a***
Jn 3:13 No one has ***a*** to heaven but He
20:17 for I have not yet ***a*** to My
Eph 4: 8 When He ***a*** on high, He led
4: 9 He ***a***"—what does it mean but
4:10 is also the One who ***a*** far
Rev 8: 4 ***a*** before God from the angel's
11:12 And they ***a*** to heaven in a

ASCENDING (6/6) ASCEND

Gen 28:12 there the angels of God were *a*
1 Sam 28:13 I saw a spirit *a* out of the
1 Chr 26:16 the Shallecheth Gate on the *a*
Jn 1:51 and the angels of God *a* and
20:17 I am *a* to My Father and your
Rev 7: 2 Then I saw another angel *a* from

ASCENDS (2/2) ASCEND

Rev 11: 7 the beast that *a* out of the
14:11 the smoke of their torment *a*

ASCENT (14/14) ASCEND

Num 34: 4 the southern side of the *A* of
Josh 11:17 from Mount Halak and the *a* to
12: 7 as far as Mount Halak and the *a*
15: 3 to the southern side of the *A*
15: 7 which is before the *A* of
18:17 which is before the *A* of
Judg 1:36 of the Amorites was from the *A*
8:13 from the *A* of Heres.
2 Sam 15:30 So David went up by the *A* of
2 Ki 9:27 And they shot him at the *A*
2 Chr 20:16 will surely come up by the *A*
Neh 3:19 section in front of the *A* to
Isa 15: 5 For by the *A* of Luhith They
Jer 48: 5 For in the *A* of Luhith they

ASCENTS (15/15)

Ps 120: A Song of *A*.
121: A Song of *A*.
122: A Song of *A*.
123: A Song of *A*.
124: A Song of *A*.
125: A Song of *A*.
126: A Song of *A*.
127: A Song of *A*.
128: A Song of *A*.
129: A Song of *A*.
130: A Song of *A*.
131: A Song of *A*.
132: A Song of *A*.
133: A Song of *A*.
134: A Song of *A*.

ASCERTAIN (3/3)

Acts 21:34 So when he could not *a* the
24: 8 him yourself you may *a* all
24:11 because you may *a* that it is no

ASCRIBE (3/3) ASCRIBED, ASCRIBING

Deut 32: 3 *A* greatness to our God.
Job 36: 3 I will *a* righteousness to my
Ps 68:34 *A* strength to God; His

ASCRIBED (2/1) ASCRIBE

1 Sam 18: 8 They have *a* to David ten
18: 8 and to me they have *a* only

ASCRIBING (1/1)

Hab 1:11 *A* this power to his god."

ASENATH (3/3)

Gen 41:45 And he gave him as a wife *A*,
41:50 years of famine came, whom *A*,
46:20 Manasseh and Ephraim, whom *A*,

ASH (5/5) ASHES

1 Sam 2: 8 lifts the beggar from the *a*
Ps 113: 7 lifts the needy out of the *a*
Lam 4: 5 up in scarlet Embrace *a* heaps.
Dan 2: 5 your houses shall be made an *a*
3:29 houses shall be made an *a* heap;

ASHAMED (117/105)

Gen 2:25 and his wife, and were not *a*.
2 Sam 10: 5 because the men were greatly *a*.
19: 3 as people who are *a* steal away
2 Ki 2:17 they urged him till he was *a*,
8:11 in a stare until he was *a*;
1 Chr 19: 5 because the men were greatly *a*.
2 Chr 30:15 priests and the Levites were *a*,
Ezra 8:22 For I was *a* to request of the
9: 6 I am too *a* and humiliated to
Job 19: 3 You are not *a* that you have
Ps 6:10 Let all my enemies be *a* and
6:10 Let them turn back and be *a*
22: 5 trusted in You, and were not *a*.
25: 2 trust in You; Let me not be *a*;
25: 3 no one who waits on You be *a*;
25: 3 Let those be *a* who deal
25:20 deliver me; Let me not be *a*,
31: 1 my trust; Let me never be *a*;
31:17 Do not let me be *a*,
31:17 upon You; Let the wicked be *a*;
34: 5 And their faces were not *a*.
35:26 Let them be *a* and brought to
37:19 They shall not be *a* in the evil
40:14 Let them be *a* and brought to
69: 6 be *a* because of me; Let not
70: 2 Let them be *a* and confounded
74:21 not let the oppressed return *a*!
86:17 hate me may see it and be *a*,
109:28 When they arise, let them be *a*,
119: 6 Then I would not be *a*,
119:46 kings, And will not be *a*.
119:78 Let the proud be *a*,
119:80 statutes, That I may not be *a*.
119:116 And do not let me be *a* of my
127: 5 of them; They shall not be *a*,
Isa 1:29 For they shall be *a* of the
19: 9 who weave fine fabric will be *a*;
20: 5 they shall be afraid and *a* of
23: 4 Be *a*, O Sidon;
24:23 be disgraced And the sun *a*;
26:11 But they will see and be *a*
29:22 "Jacob shall not now be *a*,
30: 5 They were all *a* of a people
41:11 against you Shall be *a* and
42:17 back, They shall be greatly *a*,
44: 9 nor know, that they may be *a*.
44:11 all his companions would be *a*;
44:11 They shall be *a* together.
45:16 They shall be *a* And also
45:17 You shall not be *a* or
45:24 And all shall be *a* Who are
49:23 For they shall not be *a* who
50: 7 I know that I will not be *a*.
54: 4 not fear, for you will not be *a*;
65:13 rejoice, But you shall be *a*;
66: 5 your joy.' But they shall be *a*.
Jer 2:26 As the thief is *a* when he is
2:26 So is the house of Israel *a*;
2:36 Also you shall be *a* of Egypt
2:36 ashamed of Egypt as you were *a*
3: 3 forehead; You refuse to be *a*.
6:15 Were they *a* when they had
6:15 No! They were not at all *a*;
8: 9 The wise men are *a*,
8:12 Were they *a* when they had
8:12 No! They were not at all *a*,
9:19 plundered! We are greatly *a*,
12:13 But be *a* of your harvest
14: 3 They were *a* and confounded
14: 4 the land, The plowmen were *a*;
15: 9 She has been *a* and confounded.
17:13 All who forsake You shall be *a*.
17:18 Let them be *a* who persecute me,
20:11 They will be greatly *a*,
22:22 Surely then you will be *a* and
31:19 myself on the thigh; I was *a*,
46:24 daughter of Egypt shall be *a*;
48:13 Moab shall be *a* of Chemosh, As
48:13 As the house of Israel was *a*
50:12 Your mother shall be deeply *a*;
50:12 She who bore you shall be *a*.
51:47 Her whole land shall be *a*,
51:51 We are *a* because we have heard
Ezek 16:27 who were *a* of your lewd
16:61 remember your ways and be *a*,
16:63 you may remember and be *a*,
36:32 Be *a* and confounded for your
43:10 that they may be *a* of their
43:11 And if they are *a* of all that
Hos 4:19 And they shall be *a* because of
10: 6 And Israel shall be *a* of his
Joel 1:11 Be *a*, you farmers,
Mic 3: 7 So the seers shall be *a*,
7:16 nations shall see and be *a* of
Zech 13: 4 that every prophet will be *a*
Mk 8:38 For whoever is *a* of Me and My
8:38 the Son of Man also will be *a*
Lk 9:26 For whoever is *a* of Me and My
9:26 of him the Son of Man will be *a*
16: 3 I am *a* to beg.
Rom 1:16 For I am not *a* of the gospel of
6:21 things of which you are now *a*?
2 Cor 7:14 to him about you, I am not *a*.
9: 4 to mention you!) should be *a*
10: 8 destruction, I shall not be *a*—
Phil 1:20 that in nothing I shall be *a*,
2 Th 3:14 with him, that he may be *a*.
2 Tim 1: 8 Therefore do not be *a* of the
1:12 things; nevertheless I am not *a*,
1:16 and was not *a* of my chain;
2:15 who does not need to be *a*,
Titus 2: 8 one who is an opponent may be *a*,
Heb 2:11 for which reason He is not *a* to
11:16 Therefore God is not *a* to be
1 Pe 3:16 good conduct in Christ may be *a*.
4:16 a Christian, let him not be *a*,
1 Jn 2:28 have confidence and not be *a*

ASHAN (4/4)

Josh 15:42 Libnah, Ether, *A*,
19: 7 Ain, Rimmon, Ether, and *A*:
1 Chr 4:32 Ain, Rimmon, Tochen, and *A*—
6:59 *A* with its common-lands, and

ASHARELAH (1/1)

1 Chr 25: 2 Joseph, Nethaniah, and *A*;

ASHBEA (1/1)

1 Chr 4:21 linen workers of the house of *A*;

ASHBEL (3/3) ASHBELITES

Gen 46:21 Benjamin were Belah, Becher, *A*,
Num 26:38 family of the Belaites; of *A*,
1 Chr 8: 1 *A* the second, Aharah the third,

ASHBELITES (1/1) ASHBEL

Num 26:38 of Ashbel, the family of the *A*;

ASHCHENAZ (KJV) See ASHKENAZ

ASHDOD (21/18) ASHDODITES

Josh 11:22 only in Gaza, in Gath, and in *A*.
15:46 the sea, all that lay near *A*,
15:47 *A* with its towns and villages,
1 Sam 5: 1 brought it from Ebenezer to *A*.
5: 3 And when the people of *A* arose
5: 5 on the threshold of Dagon in *A*
5: 6 was heavy on the people of *A*,
5: 6 both *A* and its territory.
5: 7 And when the men of *A* saw how
6:17 to the LORD: one for *A*,
2 Chr 26: 6 of Jabneh, and the wall of *A*;
26: 6 and he built cities around *A*
Neh 13:23 who had married women of *A*,
13:24 spoke the language of *A*,
Isa 20: 1 the year that Tartan came to *A*,
20: 1 and he fought against *A* and
Jer 25:20 Ekron, and the remnant of *A*);
Am 1: 8 cut off the inhabitant from *A*,
3: 9 in the palaces at *A*,
Zeph 2: 4 They shall drive out *A* at
Zech 9: 6 mixed race shall settle in *A*,

ASHDODITES (2/2) ASHDOD

Josh 13: 3 Philistines—the Gazites, the *A*,
Neh 4: 7 and the *A* heard that the walls

ASHDOTHITES (KJV) See ASHDODITES

ASHDOTHPISGAH (KJV) See PISGAH

ASHER (45/43) ASHERAH, ASHERAHS, ASHERITES

Gen 30:13 So she called his name *A*.
35:26 maidservant, were Gad and *A*.
46:17 The sons of *A* were Jimnah,
49:20 Bread from *A* shall be rich,
Ex 1: 4 Dan, Naphtali, Gad, and *A*.
Num 1:13 'from *A*, Pagiel the son of
1:40 From the children of *A*,
1:41 were numbered of the tribe of *A*
2:27 him shall be the tribe of *A*,
2:27 the leader of the children of *A*
7:72 leader of the children of *A*,
10:26 the tribe of the children of *A*
13:13 from the tribe of *A*,
26:44 The sons of *A* according to
26:46 the name of the daughter of *A*
26:47 the families of the sons of *A*
34:27 the tribe of the children of *A*,
Deut 27:13 Ebal to curse: Reuben, Gad, *A*,
33:24 And of *A* he said: "Asher is
33:24 *A* is most blessed of sons; Let
Josh 17: 7 of Manasseh was from *A* to
17:10 territory was adjoining *A* on
17:11 And in Issachar and in *A*,
19:24 the tribe of the children of *A*
19:31 the tribe of the children of *A*
19:34 on the south side and *A* on the
21: 6 Issachar, from the tribe of *A*,
21:30 and from the tribe of *A*,
Judg 1:31 Nor did *A* drive out the
5:17 *A* continued at the seashore,
6:35 He also sent messengers to *A*,
7:23 together from Naphtali, *A*,
1 Ki 4:16 in *A* and Aloth;
1 Chr 2: 2 Benjamin, Naphtali, Gad, and *A*.
6:62 Issachar, from the tribe of *A*,
6:74 And from the tribe of *A*:
7:30 The sons of *A* were Imnah,
7:40 these were the children of *A*,
12:36 of *A*, those who could go out
2 Chr 30:11 Nevertheless some from *A*,
Ezek 48: 2 the west, one section for *A*;
48: 3 "by the border of *A*,
48:34 gate for Gad, one gate for *A*,
Lk 2:36 of Phanuel, of the tribe of *A*.
Rev 7: 6 of the tribe of *A* twelve

ASHERAH (5/5) ASHERAHS

1 Ki 15:13 had made an obscene image of *A*.
18:19 the four hundred prophets of *A*,
2 Ki 21: 7 He even set a carved image of *A*
23: 4 that were made for Baal, for *A*,
2 Chr 15:16 had made an obscene image of *A*;

ASHERAHS (1/1) ASHERAH

Judg 3: 7 God, and served the Baals and *A*.

ASHERITES (1/1) ASHER

Judg 1:32 So the *A* dwelt among the

ASHES (43/41) ASH

Gen 18:27 I who am but dust and *a* have
Ex 9: 8 for yourselves handfuls of *a*
9:10 Then they took *a* from the
27: 3 make its pans to receive its *a*,

Lev 1:16 east side, into the place for *a*.
4:12 where the *a* are poured out, and
4:12 where the *a* are poured out it
6:10 and take up the *a* of the burnt
6:11 and carry the *a* outside the
Num 4:13 they shall take away the *a*
19: 9 clean shall gather up the *a* of
19:10 And the one who gathers the *a* of
19:17 they shall take some of the *a*
2 Sam 13:19 Then Tamar put *a* on her head,
1 Ki 13: 3 and the *a* on it shall be poured
13: 5 and the *a* poured out from the
2 Ki 23: 4 and carried their *a* to Bethel.
23: 6 Kidron and ground it to *a*,
23: 6 and threw its *a* on the graves
Esth 4: 1 and put on sackcloth and *a*,
4: 3 and many lay in sackcloth and *a*.
Job 2: 8 he sat in the midst of the *a*.
13:12 platitudes are proverbs of *a*,
30:19 I have become like dust and *a*.
42: 6 And repent in dust and *a*.
Ps 102: 9 For I have eaten *a* like bread,
147:16 He scatters the frost like *a*;
Isa 44:20 He feeds on *a*;
58: 5 to spread out sackcloth and *a*?
61: 3 To give them beauty for *a*,
Jer 6:26 sackcloth And roll about in *a*!
25:34 Roll about in the *a*,
31:40 of the dead bodies and of the *a*,
Lam 3:16 gravel, And covered me with *a*.
Ezek 27:30 They will roll about in *a*;
28:18 And I turned you to *a* upon the
Dan 9: 3 with fasting, sackcloth, and *a*.
Jon 3: 6 with sackcloth and sat in *a*.
Mal 4: 3 For they shall be *a* under the
Mt 11:21 long ago in sackcloth and *a*.
Lk 10:13 ago, sitting in sackcloth and *a*.
Heb 9:13 of bulls and goats and the *a*
2 Pe 2: 6 of Sodom and Gomorrah into *a*,

ASHHUR (2/2)

1 Chr 2:24 wife Abijah bore him *A* the
4: 5 And *A* the father of Tekoa had

ASHIMA (1/1)

2 Ki 17:30 the men of Hamath made *A*,

ASHKELON (12/11) ASHKELONITES

Judg 1:18 *A* with its territory, and Ekron
14:19 and he went down to *A* and
1 Sam 6:17 Ashdod, one for Gaza, one for *A*,
2 Sam 1:20 it not in the streets of *A*—
Jer 25:20 of the Philistines (namely, *A*,
47: 5 *A* is cut off With the
47: 7 given it a charge Against *A*
Am 1: 8 who holds the scepter from *A*;
Zeph 2: 4 And *A* desolate; They shall
2: 7 In the houses of *A* they shall
Zech 9: 5 *A* shall see it and fear
9: 5 And *A* shall not be inhabited.

ASHKELONITES (1/1) ASHKELON

Josh 13: 3 Gazites, the Ashdodites, the *A*,

ASHKENAZ (3/3)

Gen 10: 3 The sons of Gomer were *A*,
1 Chr 1: 6 The sons of Gomer were *A*,
Jer 51:27 her: Ararat, Minni, and *A*.

ASHNAH (2/2)

Josh 15:33 the lowland: Eshtaol, Zorah, *A*,
15:43 Jiphtah, *A*, Nezib,

ASHPENAZ (1/1)

Dan 1: 3 Then the king instructed *A*,

ASHRIEL (KJV) See ASRIEL

ASHTAROTH (6/6) ASHTEROTH, ASHTORETH

Deut 1: 4 who dwelt at *A* in Edrei.
Josh 9:10 Og king of Bashan, who was at *A*.
12: 4 who dwelt at *A* and at Edrei,
13:12 who reigned in *A* and Edrei, who
13:31 and *A* and Edrei, cities of the
1 Chr 6:71 with its common-lands and *A*

ASHTERATHITE (1/1)

1 Chr 11:44 Uzzia the *A*,

ASHTEROTH (1/1) ASHTAROTH

Gen 14: 5 and attacked the Rephaim in *A*

ASHTORETH (3/3) ASHTAROTH

1 Ki 11: 5 For Solomon went after *A* the
11:33 and worshiped *A* the goddess of
2 Ki 23:13 king of Israel had built for *A*

ASHTORETHS (6/6) ASHTORETH

Judg 2:13 LORD and served Baal and the *A*.
10: 6 and served the Baals and the *A*,
1 Sam 7: 3 away the foreign gods and the *A*
7: 4 put away the Baals and the *A*,
12:10 and served the Baals and *A*;
31:10 armor in the temple of the *A*,

ASHUR (KJV) See ASHHUR

ASHURITES (2/2)

2 Sam 2: 9 king over Gilead, over the *A*,
Ezek 27: 6 The company of *A* have inlaid

ASHVATH (1/1)

1 Chr 7:33 were Pasach, Bimhal, and *A*.

ASIA (21/20)

Acts 2: 9 and Cappadocia, Pontus and *A*,
6: 9 and those from Cilicia and *A*),
16: 6 Spirit to preach the word in *A*.
19:10 so that all who dwelt in *A*
19:22 but he himself stayed in *A* for
19:26 but throughout almost all *A*,
19:27 whom all *A* and the world
19:31 Then some of the officials of *A*,
20: 4 of Berea accompanied him to *A*—
20: 4 and Tychicus and Trophimus of *A*.
20:16 not have to spend time in *A*;
20:18 the first day that I came to *A*,
21:27 almost ended, the Jews from *A*,
24:18 midst of which some Jews from *A*
27: 2 to sail along the coasts of *A*.
1 Cor 16:19 The churches of *A* greet you.
2 Cor 1: 8 trouble which came to us in *A*:
2 Tim 1:15 that all those in *A* have turned
1 Pe 1: 1 Pontus, Galatia, Cappadocia, *A*,
Rev 1: 4 seven churches which are in *A*:
1:11 seven churches which are in *A*:

ASIDE (101/94)

Gen 38:19 and laid *a* her veil and put on
Ex 3: 3 I will now turn *a* and see this
3: 4 the LORD saw that he turned *a*
23: 2 in a dispute so as to turn *a*
32: 8 They have turned *a* quickly out
Num 20:17 we will not turn *a* to the right
21:22 We will not turn *a* into fields
22:23 and the donkey turned *a* out of
22:33 donkey saw Me and turned *a*
22:33 If she had not turned *a* from
Deut 5:32 you shall not turn *a* to the
9:12 they have quickly turned *a* from
9:16 a molded calf! You had turned *a*
11:16 and you turn *a* and serve other
11:28 but turn *a* from the way which I
17:11 you shall not turn *a* to the
17:20 that he may not turn *a* from the
26:12 you have finished laying *a* all
28:14 So you shall not turn *a* from any
31:29 and turn *a* from the way which I
Josh 23: 6 lest you turn *a* from it to the
Judg 4:18 and said to him, "Turn *a*,
4:18 turn *a* to me; do not fear."
4:18 And when he had turned *a* with
14: 8 he turned *a* to see the carcass
18: 3 They turned *a* and said to him,
18:15 So they turned *a* there, and came
19:11 and let us turn *a* into this
19:12 We will not turn *a* here into a
19:15 They turned *a* there to go in to
Ruth 4: 1 came by. So Boaz said, "Come *a*,
4: 1 So he came *a* and sat down.
1 Sam 6:12 and did not turn *a* to the right
8: 3 they turned *a* after dishonest
12:20 yet do not turn *a* from
12:21 "And do not turn *a*;
2 Sam 2:21 Turn *a* to your right hand or to
2:21 But Asahel would not turn *a*
2:22 'Turn *a* from following me.
2:23 However, he refused to turn *a*.
3:27 Joab took him *a* in the gate to
6:10 but David took it *a* into the
18:30 Turn *a* and stand here." So he
18:30 So he turned *a* and stood
1 Ki 15: 5 and had not turned *a* from
22:32 Therefore they turned *a* to
22:43 He did not turn *a* from them,
2 Ki 4: 4 and set *a* the full ones."
22: 2 he did not turn *a* to the right
1 Chr 13:13 but took it *a* into the house of
2 Chr 20:32 and did not turn *a* from it,
29:19 Ahaz in his reign had cast *a*
34: 2 he did not turn *a* to the
Job 6:18 The paths of their way turn *a*,
23:11 kept His way and not turned *a*.
Ps 14: 3 They have all turned *a*,
40: 4 nor such as turn *a* to lies.
53: 3 Every one of them has turned *a*;
78:57 They were turned *a* like a
119:51 Yet I do not turn *a* from Your
125: 5 As for such as turn *a* to their
Prov 7:25 Do not let your heart turn *a* to
Song 6: 1 has your beloved turned *a*,
Isa 29:21 And turn *a* the just by empty
30:11 Turn *a* from the path, Cause
44:20 deceived heart has turned him *a*;
Jer 14: 8 like a traveler who turns *a*
15: 5 Or who will turn *a* to ask how
Lam 3:11 He has turned *a* my ways and
3:35 To turn *a* the justice due a
Ezek 1:17 they did not turn *a* when they
10:11 they did not turn *a* when they
10:11 They did not turn *a* when they
26:16 lay *a* their robes, and take off
Jon 3: 6 from his throne and laid *a* his
Zech 10: 6 as though I had not cast them *a*;
Mt 2:22 he turned *a* into the region of
16:22 Then Peter took Him *a* and began
20:17 took the twelve disciples *a* on
Mk 6:31 Come *a* by yourselves to a
7: 8 For laying *a* the commandment of
7:33 And He took him *a* from the
8:32 And Peter took Him *a* and began
10:32 Then He took the twelve *a* again
10:50 And throwing *a* his garment, he
Lk 9:10 Then He took them and went *a*
18:31 Then He took the twelve *a* and
Jn 13: 4 rose from supper and laid *a* His
Acts 4:15 had commanded them to go *a* out
18:26 they took him *a* and explained
23:19 went *a* and asked privately,
26:31 and when they had gone *a*,
Rom 3:12 They have all turned *a*;
1 Cor 16: 2 each one of you lay something *a*,
Gal 2:21 I do not set *a* the grace of God;
1 Tim 1: 6 have turned *a* to idle talk,
5:15 For some have already turned *a*
2 Tim 4: 4 and be turned *a* to fables.
Heb 12: 1 let us lay *a* every weight, and
Jas 1:21 Therefore lay *a* all filthiness
1 Pe 2: 1 laying *a* all malice, all

ASIEL (1/1)

1 Chr 4:35 son of Seraiah, the son of *A*;

ASK (119/113) ASKED, ASKING, ASKS

Gen 24:57 call the young woman and *a* her
32:29 Why is it that you *a* about My
34:12 *A* me ever so much dowry and
Ex 3:22 But every woman shall *a* of her
11: 2 and let every man *a* from his
Deut 4:32 For *a* now concerning the days
4:32 and *a* from one end of heaven
13:14 and *a* diligently. And if it
32: 7 *A* your father, and he will
Josh 4: 6 among you when your children *a*
4:21 When your children *a* their
9:14 but they did not *a* counsel of
15:18 that she persuaded him to *a* her
Judg 1:14 that she urged him to *a* her
13: 6 but I did not *a* Him where He
13:18 Why do you *a* My name, seeing it
1 Sam 25: 8 *A* your young men, and they will
25:40 to *a* you to become his wife."
28:16 Why then do you *a* me, seeing the
2 Sam 14:18 hide from me anything that I *a*
1 Ki 2:16 Now I *a* one petition of you; do
2:20 *A* it, my mother, for I will not
2:22 Now why do you *a* Abishag the
2:22 *A* for him the kingdom also—for
3: 5 *A*! What shall I give you?"
14: 5 coming to *a* you something about
2 Ki 2: 9 *A*! What may I do for you, before
4:28 Did I *a* a son of my lord? Did I
2 Chr 1: 7 *A*! What shall I give you?"
20: 4 So Judah gathered together to *a*
Neh 2: 5 I *a* that you send me to Judah,
Job 12: 7 But now *a* the beasts, and they
Ps 2: 8 *A* of Me, and I will give You
35:11 They *a* me things that I do
Isa 7:11 *A* a sign for yourself from the
7:11 *a* it either in the depth or in
7:12 But Ahaz said, "I will not *a*,
45:11 *A* Me of things to come
58: 2 They *a* of Me the ordinances of
65: 1 by those who did not *a* for
Jer 6:16 And *a* for the old paths, where
15: 5 Or who will turn aside to *a*
18:13 *A* now among the Gentiles, Who
23:33 or the prophet or the priest *a*
30: 6 *A* now, and see, Whether a man
38:14 'I will *a* you something.
48:19 *A* him who flees And her who
50: 5 They shall *a* the way to Zion,
Lam 4: 4 The young children *a* for
Hos 4:12 My people *a* counsel from their
Hag 2:11 *a* the priests concerning the
Zech 7: 3 and to *a* the priests who were
10: 1 *A* the LORD for rain In the
Mt 6: 8 you have need of before you *a*
7: 7 *A*, and it will be given to
7:11 give good things to those who *a*
14: 7 give her whatever she might *a*.
18:19 concerning anything that they *a*,
20:22 "You do not know what you *a*.
21:22 And whatever things you *a* in
21:24 I also will *a* you one thing,
27:20 multitudes that they should *a*
Mk 6:22 *A* me whatever you want, and I
6:23 Whatever you *a* me, I will give
6:24 to her mother, "What shall I *a*?
9:32 and were afraid to *a* Him.
10:35 You to do for us whatever we *a*.
10:38 "You do not know what you *a*.
11:24 whatever things you *a* when you
11:29 I also will *a* you one question;
15: 8 began to *a* him to do just as
Lk 6: 9 I will *a* you one thing: Is it
6:30 takes away your goods do not *a*
9:45 and they were afraid to *a* Him
11: 9 "So I say to you, *a*,

11:13 the Holy Spirit to those who *a*
12:48 of him they will *a* the more.
14:12 do not *a* your friends, your
14:18 I *a* you to have me excused.'
14:19 I *a* you to have me excused.'
20: 3 I also will *a* you one thing, and
22:68 And if I also *a* you, you will
Jn 1:19 and Levites from Jerusalem to *a*
4: 9 *a* a drink from me, a Samaritan
9:21 *a* him. He will speak for
9:23 'He is of age; *a* him."
11:22 now I know that whatever You *a*
13:24 therefore motioned to him to *a*
14:13 And whatever you *a* in My name,
14:14 If you *a* anything in My name, I
15: 7 you will *a* what you desire, and
15:16 that whatever you *a* the Father
16:19 knew that they desired to *a*
16:23 And in that day you will *a* Me
16:23 whatever you *a* the Father in My
16:24 asked nothing in My name. *A*,
16:26 In that day you will *a* in My
18:21 Why do you *a* Me? Ask those who
18:21 *A* those who have heard Me what
21:12 none of the disciples dared *a*
Acts 3: 2 to *a* alms from those who
8:34 I *a* you, of whom does the
10:29 as soon as I was sent for. I *a*,
23:20 The Jews have agreed to *a* that
Rom 10:20 to those who did not *a*
1 Cor 14:35 let them *a* their own husbands
Eph 3:13 Therefore I *a* that you do not
3:20 abundantly above all that we *a*
Col 1: 9 and to *a* that you may be filled
2 Th 2: 1 together to Him, we *a* you,
Jas 1: 5 let him *a* of God, who gives to
1: 6 But let him *a* in faith, with no
4: 2 not have because you do not *a*.
4: 3 You *a* and do not receive,
4: 3 because you *a* amiss, that you
1 Jn 3:22 And whatever we *a* we receive
5:14 that if we *a* anything according
5:15 that He hears us, whatever we *a*,
5:16 not lead to death, he will *a*,

ASKED (153/147)

Gen 21:29 Then Abimelech *a* Abraham, "What
24:47 Then I *a* her, and said, 'Whose
26: 7 And the men of the place *a* about
32:29 Then Jacob *a*, saying, "Tell me
37:15 And the man *a* him, saying,
38:21 Then he *a* the men of that place,
40: 7 So he *a* Pharaoh's officers who
43: 7 The man *a* us pointedly about
43:27 Then he *a* them about their
44:19 My lord *a* his servants, saying,
Ex 5:14 them, were beaten and were *a*,
12:35 and they had *a* from the
18: 7 And they *a* each other about
Josh 19:50 gave him the city which he *a*
Judg 1: 1 that the children of Israel *a*
5:25 He *a* for water, she gave milk;
6:29 when they had inquired and *a*,
20:23 and *a* counsel of the LORD,
1 Sam 1:17 your petition which you have *a*
1:20 Because I have *a* for him from
1:27 me my petition which I *a* of
8:10 the LORD to the people who *a*
14:37 So Saul *a* counsel of God,
19:22 well that is at Sechu. So he *a*,
20: 6 David earnestly *a* permission of
20:28 David earnestly *a* permission of
2 Sam 11: 7 David *a* how Joab was doing, and
1 Ki 3:10 that Solomon had *a* this thing.
3:11 Because you have *a* this thing,
3:11 and have not *a* long life for
3:11 nor have *a* riches for yourself,
3:11 nor have *a* the life of your
3:11 but have *a* for yourself
3:13 given you what you have not *a*:
10:13 all she desired, whatever she *a*,
12:28 Therefore the king *a* advice,
2 Ki 2:10 You have *a* a hard thing.
8: 6 And when the king *a* the woman,
2 Chr 1:11 and you have not *a* riches or
1:11 nor have you *a* long life—but
1:11 but have *a* wisdom and knowledge
9:12 all she desired, whatever she *a*,
25:17 Now Amaziah king of Judah *a*
Ezra 5: 9 Then we *a* those elders, and
5:10 We also *a* them their names to
Neh 1: 2 and I *a* them concerning the
Esth 6: 6 and the king *a* him, "What
Job 21:29 Have you not *a* those who travel
42: 3 You *a*, 'Who is this who hides
Ps 21: 4 He *a* life from You, and You
105:40 The people *a*, and He brought
137: 3 who carried us away captive *a*
Isa 30: 2 And have not *a* My advice, To
41:28 when I *a* of them, could answer
Jer 36:17 And they *a* Baruch, saying,
37:17 The king *a* him secretly in his
38:27 princes came to Jeremiah and *a*
Dan 2:10 or ruler has ever *a* such
2:16 So Daniel went in and *a* the king
2:23 now made known to me what we *a*
7:16 and *a* him the truth of all
Zech 5: 6 So I *a*, "What is it?"
Mt 12:10 And they *a* Him, saying, "Is it
16: 1 and testing Him *a* that He would
16:13 He *a* His disciples, saying,
17:10 And His disciples *a* Him, saying,
22:23 came to Him and *a* Him,
22:35 *a* Him a question, testing
22:41 together, Jesus *a* them,
27:11 And the governor *a* Him, saying,
27:58 This man went to Pilate and *a*
Mk 4:10 around Him with the twelve *a*
5: 9 Then He *a* him, "What is your
6:25 in with haste to the king and *a*,
7: 5 the Pharisees and scribes *a*
7:17 His disciples *a* Him concerning
8: 5 He *a* them, "How many loaves do
8:23 He *a* him if he saw anything.
8:27 and on the road He *a* His
9:11 And they *a* Him, saying, "Why do
9:16 And He *a* the scribes, "What are
9:21 So He *a* his father, "How long
9:28 His disciples *a* Him privately,
9:33 when He was in the house He *a*
10: 2 The Pharisees came and *a* Him,
10:10 the house His disciples also *a*
10:17 and *a* Him, "Good Teacher, what
12:18 and they *a* Him, saying:
12:28 *a* Him, "Which is the first
13: 3 and Andrew *a* Him privately,
14:60 stood up in the midst and *a*
14:61 Again the high priest *a* Him,
15: 2 Then Pilate *a* Him, "Are You the
15: 4 Then Pilate *a* Him again, saying,
15:43 went in to Pilate and *a* for the
15:44 he *a* him if He had been dead
Lk 1:63 And he *a* for a writing tablet,
3:10 So the people *a* him, saying,
3:14 Likewise the soldiers *a* him,
5: 3 and *a* him to put out a little
7:36 Then one of the Pharisees *a* Him
8: 9 Then His disciples *a* Him,
8:30 Jesus *a* him, saying, "What is
8:37 region of the Gadarenes *a* Him
9:18 and He *a* them, saying, "Who do
11:37 a certain Pharisee *a* Him to
15:26 one of the servants and *a* what
17:20 Now when He was *a* by the
18:18 Now a certain ruler *a* Him,
18:36 he *a* what it meant.
18:40 he had come near, He *a* him,
20:21 Then they *a* Him, saying,
20:27 came to Him and *a* Him,
21: 7 So they *a* Him, saying,
22:31 Satan has *a* for you, that he
22:64 struck Him on the face and *a*
23: 3 Then Pilate *a* Him, saying,
23: 6 he *a* if the Man were a
23:52 This man went to Pilate and *a*
Jn 1:21 And they *a* him, "What then?
1:25 And they *a* him, saying, "Why
4:10 you would have *a* Him, and He
5:12 Then they *a* him, "Who is the
9: 2 And His disciples *a* Him, saying,
9:15 Then the Pharisees also *a* him
9:19 And they *a* them, saying, "Is
12:21 and *a* him, saying, "Sir, we
16:24 Until now you have *a* nothing in
18: 7 Then He *a* them again, "Whom are
18:19 The high priest then *a* Jesus
19:31 the Jews *a* Pilate that their
19:38 *a* Pilate that he might take
Acts 1: 6 they *a* Him, saying, "Lord,
3: 3 into the temple, *a* for alms.
3:14 and *a* for a murderer to be
4: 7 set them in the midst, they *a*,
5:27 And the high priest *a* them,
7:46 found favor before God and *a*
8:31 And he *a* Philip to come up
9: 2 and *a* letters from him to the
10:18 And they called and *a* whether
10:48 Then they *a* him to stay a few
12:20 they *a* for peace, because their
13:21 And afterward they *a* for a king;
13:28 they *a* Pilate that He should be
16:39 and *a* them to depart from the
18:20 When they *a* him to stay a
21:33 and he *a* who he was and what he
23:18 called me to him and *a* me to
23:19 went aside and *a* privately,
23:34 he *a* what province he was from.
25:20 I *a* whether he was willing to
1 Jn 5:15 the petitions that we have *a*

ASKELON (KJV) See ASHKELON

ASKING (12/12)

1 Sam 12:17 in *a* a king for yourselves."
12:19 to all our sins the evil of *a*
Job 31:30 allowed my mouth to sin By *a*
Ps 78:18 God in their heart By *a* for
Mt 20:20 kneeling down and *a* something
Mk 7:26 and she kept *a* Him to cast the
Lk 2:46 both listening to them and *a*
Jn 8: 7 So when they continued *a* Him, He
Acts 25: 3 *a* a favor against him, that he
25:15 *a* for a judgment against him.
1 Cor 10:25 *a* no questions for conscience'
10:27 *a* no question for conscience'

ASKS (18/17)

Gen 32:17 my brother meets you and *a* you,
Ex 13:14 when your son *a* you in time to
Deut 6:20 When your son *a* you in time to
Eccl 4: 8 But he never *a*,
Mic 7: 3 The prince *a* for gifts, The
Mt 5:42 Give to him who *a* you, and from
7: 8 For everyone who *a* receives, and
7: 9 if his son *a* for bread, will
7:10 Or if he *a* for a fish, will he
Lk 6:30 Give to everyone who *a* of you.
11:10 For everyone who *a* receives, and
11:11 If a son *a* for bread from any
11:11 Or if he *a* for a fish, will
11:12 Or if he *a* for an egg, will he
14:32 he sends a delegation and *a*
19:31 And if anyone *a* you, 'Why are
Jn 16: 5 and none of you *a* Me, 'Where
1 Pe 3:15 a defense to everyone who *a*

ASLEEP (19/19) SLEEP

Judg 4:21 for he was fast *a* and weary. So
1 Sam 26:12 or awoke. For they were all *a*,
Job 3:13 quiet, I would have been *a*;
Jon 1: 5 had lain down, and was fast *a*.
Mt 8:24 with the waves. But He was *a*.
26:40 the disciples and found them *a*,
26:43 And He came and found them *a*
27:52 of the saints who had fallen *a*
Mk 4:38 *a* on a pillow. And they awoke
14:40 He found them *a* again, for
Lk 8:23 But as they sailed He fell *a*.
Acts 7:60 he had said this, he fell *a*.
13:36 by the will of God, fell *a*,
1 Cor 15: 6 present, but some have fallen *a*.
15:18 also those who have fallen *a*
15:20 of those who have fallen *a*.
1 Th 4:13 those who have fallen *a*,
4:15 means precede those who are *a*.
2 Pe 3: 4 For since the fathers fell *a*,

ASNAH (1/1)

Ezra 2:50 the sons of *A*,

ASNAPPER (KJV) See OSNAPPER

ASP (KJV) See COBRA'S

ASPATHA (1/1)

Esth 9: 7 Also Parshandatha, Dalphon, *A*,

ASPHALT (3/3)

Gen 11: 3 and they had *a* for mortar.
14:10 of Siddim was full of *a*
Ex 2: 3 daubed it with *a* and pitch, put

ASPIRE (1/1)

1 Th 4:11 that you also *a* to lead a quiet

ASPS (2/2)

Ps 140: 3 The poison of *a* is under
Rom 3:13 The poison of *a* is under

ASRIEL (3/3) ASRIELITES

Num 26:31 of *A*, the family of
Josh 17: 2 of Helek, the children of *A*,
1 Chr 7:14 of Gilead, the father of *A*.

ASRIELITES (1/1) ASRIEL

Num 26:31 of Asriel, the family of the *A*;

ASS, ASS'S, ASSES (KJV) See DONKEY

ASSAIL (1/1)

Lk 11:53 and the Pharisees began to *a*

ASSASSINS (1/1)

Acts 21:38 and led the four thousand *a*

ASSAULT (3/3)

Deut 21: 5 every controversy and every *a*
Esth 7: 8 Will he also *a* the queen while I
8:11 or province that would *a* them,

ASSAULTED (KJV) See ATTACKED

ASSAY (KJV) See ATTEMPTS

ASSAYER (1/1)

Jer 6:27 I have set you as an *a* and a

ASSEMBLE (19/19) ASSEMBLED, ASSEMBLES, ASSEMBLIES, ASSEMBLING, ASSEMBLY

2 Sam 20: 4 *A* the men of Judah for me within
20: 5 So Amasa went to *a* the men of
Isa 11:12 And will *a* the outcasts of
45:20 *A* yourselves and come; Draw
48:14 *a* yourselves, and hear!
54:15 Indeed they shall surely *a*,
Jer 4: 5 *A* yourselves, And let us go
8:14 *A* yourselves, And let us
12: 9 *a* all the beasts of the field,

21: 4 and I will *a* them in the midst
Ezek 11:17 *a* you from the countries where
39:17 *A* yourselves and come; Gather
Dan 11:10 and *a* a multitude of great
Hos 7:14 They *a* together for grain and
Joel 2:16 *A* the elders, Gather the
3:11 *A* and come, all you nations,
Am 3: 9 *A* on the mountains of Samaria;
Mic 2:12 I will surely *a* all of you, O
4: 6 I will *a* the lame, I will

ASSEMBLED (33/33) ASSEMBLE

Ex 38: 8 of the serving women who *a* at
Num 1:18 and they *a* all the congregation
Josh 18: 1 of the children of Israel *a*
Judg 10:17 And the children of Israel *a*
1 Sam 2:22 they lay with the women who *a*
14:20 the people who were with him *a*,
1 Ki 8: 1 Now Solomon *a* the elders of
8: 2 all the men of Israel *a* with
8: 5 of Israel who were *a* with him,
12:21 he *a* all the house of Judah
1 Chr 15: 4 Then David *a* the children of
28: 1 Now David *a* at Jerusalem all the
2 Chr 5: 2 Now Solomon *a* the elders of
5: 3 all the men of Israel *a* with
5: 6 of Israel who were *a* with him
11: 1 he *a* from the house of Judah
20:26 And on the fourth day they *a* in
Ezra 9: 4 words of the God of Israel *a*
Neh 9: 1 the children of Israel were *a*
Esth 9:18 the Jews who were at Shushan *a*
Ps 48: 4 For behold, the kings *a*,
Isa 43: 9 And let the people be *a*.
Jer 5: 7 they committed adultery And *a*
Dan 6:11 Then these men *a* and found
Mt 26: 3 and the elders of the people *a*
26:57 scribes and the elders were *a*.
28:12 When they had *a* with the elders
Mk 14:53 and with him were *a* all the
Jn 20:19 shut where the disciples were *a*,
Acts 1: 4 And being *a* together with
4:31 the place where they were *a*
11:26 that for a whole year they *a*
15:25 being *a* with one accord, to

ASSEMBLES (1/1) ASSEMBLE

Isa 54:15 Whoever *a* against you shall

ASSEMBLIES (3/3) ASSEMBLY

Isa 1:13 Sabbaths, and the calling of *a*—
4: 5 of Mount Zion, and above her *a*,
Am 5:21 I do not savor your sacred *a*.

ASSEMBLING (1/1) ASSEMBLE

Heb 10:25 not forsaking the *a* of ourselves

ASSEMBLY (132/125) ASSEMBLE, ASSEMBLIES

Gen 28: 3 That you may be an *a* of
49: 6 my honor be united to their *a*;
Ex 12: 6 Then the whole *a* of the
16: 3 to kill this whole *a* with
Lev 4:13 hidden from the eyes of the *a*,
4:14 then the *a* shall offer a young
4:21 It is a sin offering for the *a*.
16:17 and for all the *a* of Israel.
16:33 and for all the people of the *a*.
23:36 to the LORD. It is a sacred *a*,
Num 10: 7 And when the *a* is to be gathered
14: 5 on their faces before all the *a*
15:15 shall be for you of the *a*
16: 3 exalt yourselves above the *a*
16:33 they perished from among the *a*.
16:47 and ran into the midst of the *a*;
19:20 be cut off from among the *a*,
20: 4 Why have you brought up the *a* of
20: 6 from the presence of the *a* to
20:10 Moses and Aaron gathered the *a*
20:12 you shall not bring this *a*
29:35 day you shall have a sacred *a*.
Deut 5:22 the LORD spoke to all your *a*,
9:10 of the fire in the day of the *a*.
10: 4 of the fire in the day of the *a*;
16: 8 there shall be a sacred *a* to
18:16 in Horeb in the day of the *a*,
23: 1 shall not enter the *a* of the
23: 2 birth shall not enter the *a* of
23: 2 descendants shall enter the *a*
23: 3 Moabite shall not enter the *a*
23: 3 descendants shall enter the *a*
23: 8 born to them may enter the *a*
31:30 in the hearing of all the *a* of
Josh 8:35 did not read before all the *a*
Judg 20: 2 presented themselves in the *a*
21: 5 who did not come up with the *a*
21: 8 from Jabesh Gilead to the *a*.
1 Sam 17:47 Then all this *a* shall know that
1 Ki 8:14 around and blessed the whole *a*
8:14 while all the *a* of Israel was
8:22 in the presence of all the *a*
8:55 he stood and blessed all the *a*
8:65 a great *a* from the entrance of
12: 3 Then Jeroboam and the whole *a*
2 Ki 10:20 Proclaim a solemn *a* for Baal."
1 Chr 13: 2 And David said to all the *a* of
13: 4 Then all the *a* said that they
28: 8 the *a* of the LORD, and in the
29: 1 King David said to all the *a*:
29:10 the LORD before all the *a*;
29:20 Then David said to all the *a*,
29:20 So all the *a* blessed the
2 Chr 1: 3 and all the *a* with him, went to
1: 5 Solomon and the *a* sought Him
6: 3 around and blessed the whole *a*
6: 3 while all the *a* of Israel was
6:12 in the presence of all the *a*
6:13 on his knees before all the *a*
7: 8 a very great *a* from the
7: 9 eighth day they held a sacred *a*,
20: 5 Jehoshaphat stood in the *a* of
20:14 of Asaph, in the midst of the *a*.
23: 3 Then all the *a* made a covenant
24: 6 of the LORD and of the *a* of
28:14 the leaders and all the *a*.
29:23 before the king and the *a*,
29:28 So all the *a* worshiped, the
29:31 So the *a* brought in sacrifices
29:32 the burnt offerings which the *a*
30: 2 and his leaders and all the *a*
30: 4 pleased the king and all the *a*.
30:13 many people, a very great *a*
30:17 For there were many in the *a*
30:23 Then the whole *a* agreed to keep
30:24 king of Judah gave to the *a* a
30:24 and the leaders gave to the *a*
30:25 The whole *a* of Judah rejoiced,
30:25 all the *a* that came from
Ezra 2:64 The whole *a* together was
10: 1 a very large *a* of men, women,
10: 8 would be separated from the *a*
10:12 Then all the *a* answered and said
10:14 let the leaders of our entire *a*
Neh 5: 7 So I called a great *a* against
5:13 And all the *a* said, "Amen!"
7:66 Altogether the whole *a* was
8: 2 brought the Law before the *a*
8:17 So the whole *a* of those who had
8:18 day there was a sacred *a*,
13: 1 should ever come into the *a* of
Job 30:28 I stand up in the *a* and cry
Ps 22:22 In the midst of the *a* I will
22:25 be of You in the great *a*;
26: 5 I have hated the *a* of
35:18 give You thanks in the great *a*;
40: 9 righteousness In the great *a*;
40:10 Your truth From the great *a*.
89: 5 faithfulness also in the *a* of
89: 7 greatly to be feared in the *a*
107:32 them exalt Him also in the *a*
111: 1 In the *a* of the upright and
149: 1 And His praise in the *a* of
Prov 5:14 In the midst of the *a* and
21:16 Will rest in the *a* of the
26:26 will be revealed before the *a*.
Jer 6:11 And on the *a* of young men
9: 2 An *a* of treacherous men.
15:17 I did not sit in the *a* of the
26:17 rose up and spoke to all the *a*
50: 9 come up against Babylon An *a*
Lam 1:10 commanded Not to enter Your *a*.
1:15 He has called an *a* against me
2: 6 has destroyed His place of *a*;
Ezek 13: 9 they shall not be in the *a* of
16:40 They shall also bring up an *a*
23:46 Bring up an *a* against them, give
23:47 The *a* shall stone them with
Joel 1:14 a fast, Call a sacred *a*;
2:15 a fast, Call a sacred *a*;
Mic 2: 5 boundaries by lot In the *a* of
Zeph 3: 8 to gather the nations To My *a*
3:18 who sorrow over the appointed *a*,
Acts 19:32 for the *a* was confused, and
19:39 be determined in the lawful *a*.
19:41 things, he dismissed the *a*.
21:22 The *a* must certainly meet, for
23: 7 and the *a* was divided.
25:24 man about whom the whole *a* of
Heb 2:12 In the midst of the *a* I
12:23 to the general *a* and church of
Jas 2: 2 there should come into your *a*

ASSENT (KJV) See ACCORD

ASSENTED (1/1)

Acts 24: 9 And the Jews also *a*,

ASSESSED (1/1) ASSESSMENT

2 Ki 18:14 And the king of Assyria *a*

ASSESSMENT (2/2) ASSESSED

2 Ki 12: 4 each man's *a* money—and all the
23:35 every one according to his *a*,

ASSHUR (4/4) ASSHURIM

Gen 10:22 The sons of Shem were Elam, *A*,
Num 24:22 How long until *A* carries you
24:24 And they shall afflict *A* and
1 Chr 1:17 The sons of Shem were Elam, *A*,

ASSHURIM (1/1) ASSHUR

Gen 25: 3 And the sons of Dedan were *A*,

ASSIGN (2/2) ASSIGNED, ASSIGNMENT

Num 4:27 Aaron and his sons shall *a* all
4:32 and you shall *a* to each man

A

ASSIGNED (9/9) ASSIGN

Josh 20: 8 they *a* Bezer in the wilderness
2 Sam 11:16 that he *a* Uriah to a place
1 Chr 9:24 The gatekeepers were *a* to the
23:11 therefore they were *a* as one
2 Chr 23:18 whom David had *a* in the house
Ezra 6:18 They *a* the priests to their
Neh 13:30 I also *a* duties to the priests
Job 36:23 Who has *a* Him His way, Or who
Prov 8:29 When He *a* to the sea its limit,

ASSIGNMENT (1/1) ASSIGN

1 Chr 9:23 house of the tabernacle, by *a*.

ASSIR (5/5)

Ex 6:24 And the sons of Korah were *A*,
1 Chr 3:17 the sons of Jeconiah were *A*,
6:22 Korah his son, *A* his son,
6:23 Ebiasaph his son, *A* his son,
6:37 the son of Tahath, the son of *A*,

ASSIST (2/2) ASSISTANT, ASSISTANTS

2 Chr 28:20 and did not *a* him.
Rom 16: 2 and *a* her in whatever business

ASSISTANT (4/4) ASSIST, ASSISTANTS

Ex 24:13 So Moses arose with his *a*
Num 11:28 Joshua the son of Nun, Moses' *a*,
Josh 1: 1 Joshua the son of Nun, Moses' *a*,
Acts 13: 5 They also had John as their *a*.

ASSISTANTS (1/1) ASSISTANT

2 Chr 31:15 his faithful *a* in the cities

ASSOCIATE (3/3) ASSOCIATED, ASSOCIATES

Prov 20:19 Therefore do not *a* with one
24:21 Do not *a* with those given to
Rom 12:16 but *a* with the humble. Do not

ASSOCIATED (1/1) ASSOCIATE

Num 18: 1 you shall bear the iniquity *a*

ASSOCIATES (3/3) ASSOCIATE

2 Ki 9: 2 him rise up from among his *a*,
25:19 five men of the king's close *a*
Jer 52:25 men of the king's close *a* who

ASSOS (2/2)

Acts 20:13 to the ship and sailed to *A*,
20:14 And when he met us at *A*,

ASSUME (1/1)

2 Chr 22: 9 of Ahaziah had no one to *a*

ASSUR (KJV) See ASSYRIA

ASSURANCE (7/7) ASSURE, ASSURED, ASSUREDLY

Deut 28:66 and have no *a* of life.
Isa 32:17 quietness and *a* forever.
Acts 17:31 He has given *a* of this to all
Col 2: 2 to all riches of the full *a* of
1 Th 1: 5 the Holy Spirit and in much *a*,
Heb 6:11 same diligence to the full *a*
10:22 with a true heart in full *a* of

ASSURE (1/1) ASSURANCE, ASSURED, ASSUREDLY

1 Jn 3:19 and shall *a* our hearts before

ASSURED (4/4) ASSURE

Jer 14:13 but I will give you *a* peace in
Dan 4:26 your kingdom shall be *a* to you,
2 Tim 3:14 you have learned and been *a* of,
Heb 11:13 seen them afar off were *a* of

ASSUREDLY (83/83) ASSURE

1 Sam 28: 1 You *a* know that you will go out
1 Ki 1:13 *A* your son Solomon shall reign
1:17 *A* Solomon your son shall reign
1:30 *A* Solomon your son shall be king
Jer 32:41 and I will *a* plant them in this
49:12 not to drink of the cup have *a*
Mt 5:18 'For *a*, I say to you, till
5:26 '*A*, I say to you, you will by
6: 2 they may have glory from men. *A*,
6: 5 that they may be seen by men. *A*,
6:16 appear to men to be fasting. *A*,
8:10 said to those who followed, "*A*,
10:15 '*A*, I say to you, it will be
10:23 city, flee to another. For *a*,
10:42 in the name of a disciple, *a*,
11:11 '*A*, I say to you, among those

13:17 **a**, I say to you that many
16:28 '*A*, I say to you, there are
17:20 of your unbelief; for **a**,
18: 3 and said, "*A*, I say to you,
18:13 "And if he should find it, **a**,
18:18 '*A*, I say to you, whatever you
19:23 said to His disciples, "*A*,
19:28 *A* I say to you, that in the
21:21 answered and said to them, "*A*,
21:31 Jesus said to them, "*A*,
23:36 '*A*, I say to you, all these
24: 2 you not see all these things? *A*,
24:34 '*A*, I say to you, this
24:47 '*A*, I say to you that he will
25:12 "But he answered and said, '*A*,
25:40 will answer and say to them, '*A*,
25:45 He will answer them, saying, '*A*,
26:13 '*A*, I say to you, wherever
26:21 they were eating, He said, "*A*,
26:34 Jesus said to him, "*A*,
Mk 3:28 *A*, I say to you, all sins
6:11 as a testimony against them. *A*,
8:12 this generation seek a sign? *A*,
9: 1 And He said to them, "*A*,
9:41 because you belong to Christ, **a**,
10:15 '*A*, I say to you, whoever does
10:29 So Jesus answered and said, "*A*,
11:23 'For **a**, I say to you, whoever
12:43 Himself and said to them, "*A*,
13:30 '*A*, I say to you, this
14: 9 '*A*, I say to you, wherever
14:18 sat and ate, Jesus said, "*A*,
14:25 '*A*, I say to you, I will no
14:30 Jesus said to him, "*A*,
Lk 4:24 Then He said, "*A*,
12:37 he comes, will find watching. *A*,
13:35 is left to you desolate; and **a**,
18:17 '*A*, I say to you, whoever
18:29 So He said to them, "*A*,
21:32 '*A*, I say to you, this
23:43 And Jesus said to him, "*A*,
Jn 1:51 And He said to him, "Most **a**,
3: 3 and said to him, "Most **a**,
3: 5 Jesus answered, "Most **a**,
3:11 'Most **a**, I say to you, We
5:19 and said to them, "Most **a**,
5:24 Most **a**, I say to you, he who
5:25 'Most **a**, I say to you, the hour
6:26 them and said, "Most **a**,
6:32 Jesus said to them, "Most **a**,
6:47 'Most **a**, I say to you, he who
6:53 Jesus said to them, "Most **a**,
8:34 Jesus answered them, "Most **a**,
8:51 'Most **a**, I say to you, if
8:58 Jesus said to them, "Most **a**,
10: 1 'Most **a**, I say to you, he who
10: 7 said to them again, "Most **a**,
12:24 'Most **a**, I say to you, unless
13:16 'Most **a**, I say to you, a
13:20 'Most **a**, I say to you, he who
13:21 testified and said, "Most **a**,
13:38 your life for My sake? Most **a**,
14:12 Most **a**, I say to you, he who
16:20 'Most **a**, I say to you that you
16:23 you will ask Me nothing. Most **a**,
21:18 'Most **a**, I say to you, when you
Acts 2:36 all the house of Israel know **a**

ASSWAGE (KJV) See RELIEVE

ASSYRIA (130/120) ASSYRIAN, ASSYRIANS

Gen 2:14 which goes toward the east of *A*.
10:11 From that land he went to *A* and
25:18 of Egypt as you go toward *A*.
2 Ki 15:19 Pul king of *A* came against the
15:20 to give to the king of *A*.
15:20 So the king of *A* turned back,
15:29 Tiglath-Pileser king of *A* came
15:29 he carried them captive to *A*.
16: 7 to Tiglath-Pileser king of *A*,
16: 8 as a present to the king of *A*.
16: 9 So the king of *A* heeded him; for
16: 9 for the king of *A* went up
16:10 meet Tiglath-Pileser king of *A*,
16:18 on account of the king of *A*.
17: 3 Shalmaneser king of *A* came up
17: 4 And the king of *A* uncovered a
17: 4 no tribute to the king of *A*,
17: 4 Therefore the king of *A* shut
17: 5 Now the king of *A* went
17: 6 the king of *A* took Samaria and
17: 6 and carried Israel away to *A*,
17:23 away from their own land to *A*,
17:24 Then the king of *A* brought
17:26 So they spoke to the king of *A*,
17:27 Then the king of *A* commanded,
18: 7 rebelled against the king of *A*
18: 9 that Shalmaneser king of *A*
18:11 Then the king of *A* carried
18:11 Israel away captive to *A*,
18:13 Sennacherib king of *A* came up
18:14 of Judah sent to the king of *A*
18:14 And the king of *A* assessed
18:16 and gave it to the king of *A*.
18:17 Then the king of *A* sent the
18:19 the great king, the king of *A*:
18:23 to my master the king of *A*,
18:28 the king of *A*!
18:30 into the hand of the king of *A*.
18:31 for thus says the king of *A*:
18:33 from the hand of the king of *A*?
19: 4 whom his master the king of *A*
19: 6 the servants of the king of *A*
19: 8 and found the king of *A*
19:10 into the hand of the king of *A*.
19:11 have heard what the kings of *A*
19:17 the kings of *A* have laid waste
19:20 against Sennacherib king of *A*,
19:32 LORD concerning the king of *A*:
19:36 So Sennacherib king of *A*
20: 6 from the hand of the king of *A*;
23:29 to the aid of the king of *A*,
1 Chr 5: 6 whom Tiglath-Pileser king of *A*
5:26 up the spirit of Pul king of *A*,
5:26 is, Tiglath-Pileser king of *A*.
2 Chr 28:16 Ahaz sent to the kings of *A* to
28:20 Also Tiglath-Pileser king of *A*
28:21 he gave it to the king of *A*;
30: 6 from the hand of the kings of *A*.
32: 1 Sennacherib king of *A* came and
32: 4 Why should the kings of *A* come
32: 7 dismayed before the king of *A*,
32: 9 this Sennacherib king of *A*
32:10 says Sennacherib king of *A*:
32:11 from the hand of the king of *A*'
32:21 in the camp of the king of *A*.
32:22 of Sennacherib the king of *A*,
33:11 of the army of the king of *A*,
Ezra 4: 2 days of Esarhaddon king of *A*,
6:22 the heart of the king of *A*
Neh 9:32 from the days of the kings of *A*
Ps 83: 8 *A* also has joined with them
Isa 7:17 LORD will bring the king of *A*
7:18 bee that is in the land of *A*.
7:20 the River, with the king of *A*,
8: 4 taken away before the king of *A*.
8: 7 The king of *A* and all his
10: 5 Woe to *A*, the rod of My
10:12 arrogant heart of the king of *A*,
11:11 From *A* and Egypt, From
11:16 people Who will be left from *A*,
19:23 be a highway from Egypt to *A*,
19:23 Egypt and the Egyptian into *A*,
19:24 one of three with Egypt and *A*—
19:25 and *A* the work of My hands, and
20: 1 when Sargon the king of *A* sent
20: 4 so shall the king of *A* lead away
20: 6 be delivered from the king of *A*;
23:13 *A* founded it for wild beasts
27:13 to perish in the land of *A*,
30:31 the voice of the LORD *A* will
31: 8 Then *A* shall fall by a sword not
36: 1 that Sennacherib king of *A*
36: 2 Then the king of *A* sent the
36: 4 the great king, the king of *A*:
36: 8 to my master the king of *A*,
36:13 the king of *A*!
36:15 into the hand of the king of *A*.
36:16 for thus says the king of *A*:
36:18 from the hand of the king of *A*?
37: 4 whom his master the king of *A*
37: 6 the servants of the king of *A*
37: 8 and found the king of *A* warring
37:10 into the hand of the king of *A*.
37:11 have heard what the kings of *A*
37:18 the kings of *A* have laid waste
37:21 against Sennacherib king of *A*,
37:33 LORD concerning the king of *A*:
37:37 So Sennacherib king of *A*
38: 6 from the hand of the king of *A*,
Jer 2:18 Or why take the road to *A*,
2:36 Egypt as you were ashamed of *A*.
50:17 First the king of *A* devoured
50:18 I have punished the king of *A*.
Ezek 23: 7 All of them choice men of *A*;
27:23 Eden, the merchants of Sheba, *A*,
31: 3 Indeed *A* was a cedar in
32:22 *A* is there, and all her
Hos 5:13 Then Ephraim went to *A* And
7:11 call to Egypt, They go to *A*.
8: 9 For they have gone up to *A*,
9: 3 shall eat unclean things in *A*.
10: 6 also shall be carried to *A*
11:11 Like a dove from the land of *A*.
14: 3 *A* shall not save us, We will
Mic 5: 6 with the sword the land of *A*,
7:12 they shall come to you From *A*
Nah 3:18 shepherds slumber, O king of *A*;
Zeph 2:13 against the north, Destroy *A*,
Zech 10:10 Egypt, And gather them from *A*.
10:11 Then the pride of *A* shall be

ASSYRIAN (7/7) ASSYRIA, ASSYRIANS

Isa 10:24 Zion, do not be afraid of the *A*.
14:25 That I will break the *A* in My
19:23 and the *A* will come into Egypt
52: 4 Then the *A* oppressed them
Hos 11: 5 But the *A* shall be his king,
Mic 5: 5 When the *A* comes into our
5: 6 He shall deliver us from the *A*,

ASSYRIANS (10/10) ASSYRIAN

2 Ki 19:35 and killed in the camp of the *A*
Isa 19:23 Egyptians will serve with the *A*.
37:36 and killed in the camp of the *A*
Lam 5: 6 to the Egyptians And the *A*,
Ezek 16:28 played the harlot with the *A*,
23: 5 her lovers, the neighboring *A*,
23: 9 lovers, Into the hand of the *A*,
23:12 lusted for the neighboring *A*,
23:23 All the *A* with them, All of
Hos 12: 1 they make a covenant with the *A*,

ASTAROTH (KJV) See ASHTAROTH

ASTONISHED (46/46) ASTONISHING, ASTONISHMENT

Lev 26:32 who dwell in it shall be **a** at
1 Ki 9: 8 who passes by it will be **a** and
2 Chr 7:21 who passes by it will be **a** and
Ezra 9: 3 head and beard, and sat down **a**.
9: 4 and I sat **a** until the evening
Job 17: 8 Upright men are **a** at this,
18:20 Those in the west are **a** at his
21: 5 Look at me and be **a**;
26:11 And are **a** at His rebuke.
Isa 52:14 Just as many were **a** at you, So
Jer 2:12 Be **a**, O heavens, at this,
4: 9 The priests shall be **a**,
14: 9 Why should You be like a man **a**,
18:16 who passes by it will be **a**
19: 8 who passes by it will be **a** and
49:17 who goes by it will be **a** And
Ezek 3:15 and remained there **a** among them
26:16 and be **a** at you.
27:35 of the isles will be **a** at you;
28:19 you among the peoples are **a** at
32:10 I will make many peoples **a** at
Dan 3:24 Then King Nebuchadnezzar was **a**;
4:19 was **a** for a time, and his
5: 9 changed, and his lords were **a**.
8:27 I was **a** by the vision, but no
Mt 7:28 that the people were **a** at His
13:54 so that they were **a** and said,
19:25 heard it, they were greatly **a**,
22:33 they were **a** at His teaching.
Mk 1:22 And they were **a** at His teaching,
6: 2 And many hearing Him were **a**,
7:37 And they were **a** beyond measure,
10:24 And the disciples were **a** at His
10:26 And they were greatly **a**,
11:18 because all the people were **a**
Lk 2:47 And all who heard Him were **a** at
4:32 And they were **a** at His teaching,
5: 9 all who were with him were **a**
8:56 And her parents were **a**,
24:22 at the tomb early, **a** us.
Acts 8: 9 sorcery in the city and **a** the
8:11 heeded him because he had **a**
9: 6 So he, trembling and **a**,
10:45 who believed were **a**,
12:16 door and saw him, they were **a**.
13:12 being **a** at the teaching of the

ASTONISHING (1/1) ASTONISHED

Jer 5:30 An **a** and horrible thing Has

ASTONISHMENT (13/13) ASTONISHED

Gen 43:33 and the men looked in **a** at one
Deut 28:37 "And you shall become an **a**,
Jer 8:21 *A* has taken hold of me.
25: 9 them, and make them an **a**,
25:11 shall be a desolation and an **a**,
25:18 to make them a desolation, an **a**,
29:18 the earth—to be a curse, an **a**,
42:18 And you shall be an oath, an **a**,
44:12 and they shall be an oath, an **a**,
44:22 your land is a desolation, an **a**,
49:17 "Edom also shall be an **a**;
51:37 An **a** and a hissing, Without
Ezek 5:15 and an **a** to the nations that

ASTOUNDED (1/1)

Hab 1: 5 Be utterly **a**! For I will

ASTRAY (32/30)

Ex 23: 4 ox or his donkey going **a**,
Num 5:12 If any man's wife goes **a** and
5:19 and if you have not gone **a** to
5:20 But if you have gone **a** while
5:29 goes **a** and defiles herself,
Deut 22: 1 ox or his sheep going **a**,
2 Chr 21:11 harlotry, and led Judah **a**.
Ps 58: 3 They go **a** as soon as they are
95:10 It is a people who go **a** in
119:67 I was afflicted I went **a**,
119:176 I have gone **a** like a lost
Prov 5:23 of his folly he shall go **a**.
10:17 who refuses correction goes **a**.
12:26 way of the wicked leads them **a**.
14:22 Do they not go **a** who devise
20: 1 And whoever is led **a** by it is
28:10 causes the upright to go **a** in
Isa 35: 8 a fool, Shall not go **a**.
53: 6 All we like sheep have gone **a**;
Jer 50: 6 shepherds have led them **a**;
Ezek 44:10 far from Me, when Israel went **a**,
44:15 the children of Israel went **a**
48:11 who did not go **a** when the
48:11 the children of Israel went **a**,
48:11 astray, as the Levites went **a**.
Am 2: 4 Their lies lead them **a**,
Mt 18:12 sheep, and one of them goes **a**,
18:13 ninety-nine that did not go **a**.
Heb 3:10 They always go **a** in their

5: 2 who are ignorant and going ***a***,
1 Pe 2:25 For you were like sheep going ***a***,
2 Pe 2:15 the right way and gone ***a***,

ASTROLOGER (1/1) ASTROLOGERS

Dan 2:10 such things of any magician, ***a***,

ASTROLOGERS (8/8) ASTROLOGER

Isa 47:13 your counsels; Let now the ***a***,
Dan 1:20 than all the magicians and ***a***
2: 2 to call the magicians, the ***a***,
2:27 demanded, the wise men, the ***a***,
4: 7 Then the magicians, the ***a***,
5: 7 cried aloud to bring in the ***a***,
5:11 him chief of the magicians, ***a***,
5:15 "Now the wise men, the ***a***,

ASUPPIM (KJV) See STOREHOUSE

ASYNCRITUS (1/1)

Rom 16:14 Greet ***A***, Phlegon, Hermas,

AT (1815/1673) See APPENDIX

ATAD (2/2)

Gen 50:10 to the threshing floor of ***A***,
50:11 at the threshing floor of ***A***,

ATARAH (1/1)

1 Chr 2:26 another wife, whose name was ***A***;

ATAROTH (4/4) ATROTH, JOAB

Num 32: 3 '***A***, Dibon, Jazer, Nimrah,
32:34 of Gad built Dibon and ***A*** and
Josh 16: 2 the border of the Archites at ***A***,
16: 7 it went down from Janohah to ***A***

ATAROTH-ADAR (KJV) See ATAROTH ADDAR

ATAROTH ADDAR (2/2)

Josh 16: 5 on the east side was ***A*** as far
18:13 and the border descended to ***A***,

ATE (115/113) EAT

Gen 3: 6 she took of its fruit and ***a***.
3: 6 her husband with her, and he ***a***.
3:12 gave me of the tree, and I ***a***.
3:13 serpent deceived me, and I ***a***.
18: 8 them under the tree as they ***a***.
19: 3 unleavened bread, and they ***a***.
24:54 the men who were with him ***a***
25:28 Isaac loved Esau because he ***a***
25:34 then he ***a*** and drank, arose, and
26:30 and they ***a*** and drank.
27:25 it near to him, and he ***a***;
27:33 I ***a*** all of it before you
31:46 and they ***a*** there on the heap.
31:54 And they ***a*** bread and stayed all
39: 6 except for the bread which he ***a***.
40:17 and the birds ***a*** them out of the
41: 4 And the ugly and gaunt cows ***a*** up
41:20 And the gaunt and ugly cows ***a*** up
43:32 and the Egyptians who ***a*** with
47:22 and they ***a*** their rations which
Ex 10:15 and they ***a*** every herb of the
16: 3 the pots of meat and when we ***a***
16:35 And the children of Israel ***a***
16:35 they ***a*** manna until they came to
24:11 and they ***a*** and drank.
34:28 he neither ***a*** bread nor drank
Num 11: 5 remember the fish which we ***a***
25: 2 and the people ***a*** and bowed down
Deut 9: 9 I neither ***a*** bread nor drank
9:18 I neither ***a*** bread nor drank
32:38 Who ***a*** the fat of their
Josh 5:11 And they ***a*** of the produce of the
5:12 but they ***a*** the food of the land
Judg 9:27 and ***a*** and drank, and cursed
14: 9 some to them, and they also ***a***.
19: 4 So they ***a*** and drank and lodged
19: 6 and the two of them ***a*** and drank
19: 8 afternoon; and both of them ***a***.
19:21 and ***a*** and drank.
Ruth 2:14 and she ***a*** and was satisfied,
1 Sam 1:18 So the woman went her way and ***a***,
9:24 So Saul ***a*** with Samuel that
14:32 and the people ***a*** them with the
20:34 and ***a*** no food the second day of
28:25 and his servants, and they ***a***.
30:11 they gave him bread and he ***a***,
2 Sam 9:13 for he ***a*** continually at the
11:13 he ***a*** and drank before him; and
12: 3 It ***a*** of his own food and drank
12:20 set food before him, and he ***a***.
12:21 you arose and ***a*** food."
1 Ki 13:19 and ***a*** bread in his house, and
13:22 ***a*** bread, and drank water in the
17:15 she and he and her household ***a***
19: 6 So he ***a*** and drank, and lay down
19: 8 and ***a*** and drank; and he went in
19:21 it to the people, and they ***a***.
2 Ki 4:44 and they ***a*** and had some left
6:23 and after they ***a*** and drank, he
6:29 and ***a*** him. And I said to her on
7: 8 they went into one tent and ***a***
9:34 he ***a*** and drank. Then he said,
23: 9 but they ***a*** unleavened bread
25:29 and he ***a*** bread regularly before
1 Chr 29:22 So they ***a*** and drank before the
2 Chr 30:18 yet they ***a*** the Passover
30:22 and they ***a*** throughout the feast
Ezra 6:21 returned from the captivity ***a***
10: 6 he ***a*** no bread and drank no
Neh 5:14 neither I nor my brothers ***a*** the
9:25 So they ***a*** and were filled and
Job 42:11 came to him and ***a*** food with him
Ps 41: 9 Who ***a*** my bread, Has lifted up
78:25 Men ***a*** angels' food; He sent
78:29 So they ***a*** and were well filled,
105:35 And ***a*** up all the vegetation in
106:28 And ***a*** sacrifices made to the
Jer 15:16 and I ***a*** them, And Your word
41: 1 And there they ***a*** bread together
52:33 and he ***a*** bread regularly before
Lam 4: 5 Those who ***a*** delicacies Are
Ezek 3: 3 that I give you." So I ***a***,
16:13 You ***a*** pastry of fine flour,
Dan 1:15 than all the young men who ***a***
4:33 he was driven from men and ***a***
10: 3 I ***a*** no pleasant food, no meat or
Mt 12: 4 entered the house of God and ***a***
14:20 So they all ***a*** and were filled,
15:37 So they all ***a*** and were filled,
15:38 Now those who ***a*** were four
Mk 1: 6 and he ***a*** locusts and wild
2:26 and ***a*** the showbread, which is
6:42 So they all ***a*** and were filled.
8: 8 So they ***a*** and were filled, and
14:18 Now as they sat and ***a***,
Lk 4: 2 And in those days He ***a*** nothing,
6: 1 the heads of grain and ***a*** them,
6: 4 took and ***a*** the showbread, and
9:17 So they all ***a*** and were filled,
13:26 We ***a*** and drank in Your presence,
15:16 with the pods that the swine ***a***,
17:27 'They ***a***, they drank, they
17:28 also in the days of Lot: They ***a***,
24:43 And He took it and ***a*** in their
Jn 6:23 near the place where they ***a***
6:26 but because you ***a*** of the loaves
6:31 Our fathers ***a*** the manna in the
6:49 Your fathers ***a*** the manna in the
6:58 not as your fathers ***a*** the manna,
Acts 2:46 they ***a*** their food with gladness
9: 9 and neither ***a*** nor drank.
10:41 even to us who ***a*** and drank
11: 3 in to uncircumcised men and ***a***
1 Cor 10: 3 all ***a*** the same spiritual food,
Rev 10:10 out of the angel's hand and ***a***

ATER (5/5)

Ezra 2:16 the people of ***A*** of Hezekiah,
2:42 sons of Shallum, the sons of ***A***,
Neh 7:21 the sons of ***A*** of Hezekiah,
7:45 sons of Shallum, the sons of ***A***,
10:17 ***A***, Hezekiah, Azzur,

ATHACH (1/1)

1 Sam 30:30 those who were in ***A***,

ATHAIAH (1/1)

Neh 11: 4 ***A*** the son of Uzziah, the son of

ATHALIAH (17/17)

2 Ki 8:26 His mother's name was ***A*** the
11: 1 When ***A*** the mother of Ahaziah saw
11: 2 nurse in the bedroom, from ***A***,
11: 3 while ***A*** reigned over the land.
11:13 Now when ***A*** heard the noise of
11:14 So ***A*** tore her clothes and cried
11:20 for they had slain ***A*** with the
1 Chr 8:26 Shamsherai, Shehariah, ***A***,
2 Chr 22: 2 His mother's name was ***A*** the
22:10 Now when ***A*** the mother of
22:11 hid him from ***A*** so that she did
22:12 while ***A*** reigned over the land.
23:12 Now when ***A*** heard the noise of
23:13 So ***A*** tore her clothes and said,
23:21 for they had slain ***A*** with the
24: 7 For the sons of ***A***,
Ezra 8: 7 of Elam, Jeshaiah the son of ***A***,

ATHARIM (1/1)

Num 21: 1 was coming on the road to ***A***,

ATHENIANS (1/1) ATHENS

Acts 17:21 For all the ***A*** and the foreigners

ATHENS (5/5) ATHENIANS

Acts 17:15 conducted Paul brought him to ***A***;
17:16 while Paul waited for them at ***A***,
17:22 Areopagus and said, "Men of ***A***,
18: 1 things Paul departed from ***A***
1 Th 3: 1 it good to be left in ***A*** alone,

ATHLAI (1/1)

Ezra 10:28 Hananiah, Zabbai, and ***A***;

ATHLETICS (1/1)

2 Tim 2: 5 also if anyone competes in ***a***,

ATONED (1/1) ATONEMENT, ATONING

1 Sam 3:14 of Eli's house shall not be ***a***

ATONEMENT (99/86) ATONED

Ex 29:33 those things with which the ***a***
29:36 day as a sin offering for ***a***.
29:36 the altar when you make ***a*** for
29:37 Seven days you shall make ***a*** for
30:10 And Aaron shall make ***a*** upon its
30:10 blood of the sin offering of ***a***;
30:10 once a year he shall make ***a***
30:15 to make ***a*** for yourselves.
30:16 And you shall take the ***a*** money
30:16 to make ***a*** for yourselves."
32:30 perhaps I can make ***a*** for your
Lev 1: 4 on his behalf to make ***a*** for
4:20 So the priest shall make ***a*** for
4:26 So the priest shall make ***a*** for
4:31 So the priest shall make ***a*** for
4:35 So the priest shall make ***a*** for
5: 6 So the priest shall make ***a*** for
5:10 So the priest shall make ***a*** on
5:13 The priest shall make ***a*** for him,
5:16 So the priest shall make ***a*** for
5:18 So the priest shall make ***a*** for
6: 7 So the priest shall make ***a*** for
6:30 to make ***a*** in the holy place,
7: 7 the priest who makes ***a*** with it
8:15 to make ***a*** for it.
8:34 to make ***a*** for you.
9: 7 and make ***a*** for yourself and for
9: 7 and make ***a*** for them, as the
10:17 to make ***a*** for them before the
12: 7 and make ***a*** for her. And she
12: 8 So the priest shall make ***a*** for
14:18 So the priest shall make ***a*** for
14:19 and make ***a*** for him who is to be
14:20 So the priest shall make ***a*** for
14:21 to make ***a*** for him, one-tenth
14:29 to make ***a*** for him before the
14:31 So the priest shall make ***a*** for
14:53 and make ***a*** for the house, and
15:15 So the priest shall make ***a*** for
15:30 and the priest shall make ***a*** for
16: 6 and make ***a*** for himself and for
16:10 to make ***a*** upon it, and to let
16:11 and make ***a*** for himself and for
16:16 So he shall make ***a*** for the Holy
16:17 when he goes in to make ***a*** in
16:17 that he may make ***a*** for himself,
16:18 and make ***a*** for it, and shall
16:24 and make ***a*** for himself and for
16:27 blood was brought in to make ***a***
16:30 day the priest shall make ***a***
16:32 father's place, shall make ***a***,
16:33 then he shall make ***a*** for the
16:33 and he shall make ***a*** for the
16:33 and he shall make ***a*** for the
16:34 to make ***a*** for the children of
17:11 to you upon the altar to make ***a***
17:11 it is the blood that makes ***a***
19:22 The priest shall make ***a*** for him
23:27 month shall be the Day of ***A***.
23:28 day, for it is the Day of ***A***,
23:28 to make ***a*** for you before the
25: 9 on the Day of ***A*** you shall make
Num 5: 8 in addition to the ram of the ***a***
5: 8 of the atonement with which ***a***
6:11 and make ***a*** for him, because he
8:12 to make ***a*** for the Levites.
8:19 and to make ***a*** for the children
8:21 and Aaron made ***a*** for them to
15:25 So the priest shall make ***a*** for
15:28 So the priest shall make ***a*** for
15:28 to make ***a*** for him; and it shall
16:46 to the congregation and make ***a***
16:47 put in the incense and made ***a***
25:13 and made ***a*** for the children of
28:22 to make ***a*** for you.
28:30 to make ***a*** for you.
29: 5 to make ***a*** for you;
29:11 besides the sin offering for ***a***,
31:50 to make ***a*** for ourselves before
35:33 and no ***a*** can be made for the
Deut 21: 8 'Provide ***a***, O LORD, for Your
21: 8 And ***a*** shall be provided on
32:43 He will provide ***a*** for His land
2 Sam 21: 3 And with what shall I make ***a***,
1 Chr 6:49 and to make ***a*** for Israel,
2 Chr 29:24 as a sin offering to make an ***a***
30:18 May the good LORD provide ***a*** for
Neh 10:33 for the sin offerings to make ***a***
Ps 65: 3 You will provide ***a*** for them.
79: 9 and provide ***a*** for our sins,
Prov 16: 6 In mercy and truth ***A*** is
Isa 22:14 iniquity there will be no ***a***
Jer 18:23 Provide no ***a*** for their
Ezek 16:63 when I provide you an ***a*** for all
43:20 you shall cleanse it and make ***a***
43:26 Seven days they shall make ***a*** for
45:15 to make ***a*** for them," says the
45:17 the peace offerings to make ***a***
45:20 Thus you shall make ***a*** for the

A

ATONING (1/1) ATONED

Lev 16:20 when he has made an end of *a*

ATROTH (1/1) ATAROTH

Num 32:35 *A* and Shophan and Jazer and

ATROTH BETH JOAB (1/1)

1 Chr 2:54 Bethlehem, the Netophathites, *A*,

ATTACHED (12/12)

Gen 29:34 time my husband will become *a*
Ex 29:13 the fatty lobe *a* to the liver,
29:22 the fatty lobe *a* to the liver,
Lev 3: 4 and the fatty lobe *a* to the
3:10 and the fatty lobe *a* to the
3:15 and the fatty lobe *a* to the
4: 9 and the fatty lobe *a* to the
7: 4 and the fatty lobe *a* to the
8:16 the fatty lobe *a* to the
8:25 the fatty lobe *a* to the
9:19 and the fatty lobe *a* to the
1 Ki 6:10 they were *a* to the temple with

ATTACK (20/19) ATTACKED, ATTACKERS, ATTACKING, ATTACKS

Gen 32:11 lest he come and *a* me and the
Num 25:17 the Midianites, and *a* them;
Josh 7: 3 three thousand men go up and *a*
9:18 children of Israel did not *a*
10: 4 that we may *a* Gibeon, for it
10:19 and *a* their rear guard. Do not
1 Sam 15: 3 Now go and *a* Amalek, and utterly
23: 2 Shall I go and *a* these
23: 2 Go and *a* the Philistines, and
2 Sam 11:25 Strengthen your *a* against the
1 Ki 20:12 And they got ready to *a* the
2 Ki 3:19 Also you shall *a* every fortified
7: 6 the kings of the Egyptians to *a*
2 Chr 18:31 they surrounded him to *a*;
Neh 4: 8 together to come and *a*
Ps 62: 3 How long will you *a* a man?
Jer 18:18 Come and let us *a* him with the
Dan 11:40 the king of the South shall *a*
Zech 11: 6 They shall *a* the land, and I
Acts 18:10 and no one will *a* you to hurt

ATTACKED (39/38) ATTACK

Gen 14: 5 that were with him came and *a*
14: 7 and *a* all the country of the
14:15 and he and his servants *a* them
36:35 who *a* Midian in the field of
Num 14:45 that mountain came down and *a*
Deut 3: 3 and we *a* him until he had no
25:18 he met you on the way and *a*
Josh 11: 7 and they *a* them.
11: 8 they *a* them until they left
Judg 1:17 and they *a* the Canaanites who
8:11 and he *a* the army while the
9:43 and he rose against them and *a*
15: 8 So he *a* them hip and thigh with
1 Sam 13: 3 And Jonathan *a* the garrison of
13: 4 heard it said that Saul had *a*
14:48 And he gathered an army and *a*
15: 7 And Saul *a* the Amalekites, from
27: 9 Whenever David *a* the land, he
30: 1 *a* Ziklag and burned it with
30:17 Then David *a* them from twilight
2 Sam 8: 1 it came to pass that David *a*
23:10 He arose and *a* the Philistines
1 Ki 15:20 He *a* Ijon, Dan, Abel Beth
20:21 king of Israel went out and *a*
2 Ki 3:24 Israel rose up and *a* the
3:25 the slingers surrounded and *a*
8:21 Then he rose by night and *a* the
15:16 Menahem *a* Tiphsah, all who
15:16 therefore he *a* it. All the
1 Chr 1:46 who *a* Midian in the field of
4:41 and they *a* their tents and the
18: 1 it came to pass that David *a*
2 Chr 14:15 They also *a* the livestock
16: 4 They *a* Ijon, Dan, Abel Maim,
21: 9 And he rose by night and *a* the
28:17 *a* Judah, and carried away
Jer 47: 1 before Pharaoh *a* Gaza.
Dan 8: 7 *a* the ram, and broke his two
Acts 17: 5 all the city in an uproar and *a*

ATTACKERS (1/1) ATTACK

Ps 35:15 *A* gathered against me, And I

ATTACKING (2/2) ATTACK

Deut 25:11 from the hand of the one *a* him,
2 Chr 11: 4 and turned back from *a*

ATTACKS (5/5) ATTACK

Gen 32: 8 comes to the one company and *a*
Deut 27:24 Cursed is the one who *a* his
Josh 15:16 He who *a* Kirjath Sepher and
Judg 1:12 Whoever *a* Kirjath Sepher and
1 Chr 11: 6 Whoever *a* the Jebusites first

ATTAI (4/4)

1 Chr 2:35 as wife, and she bore him *A*.
2:36 *A* begot Nathan, and Nathan begot
12:11 *A* the sixth, Eliel the seventh,
2 Chr 11:20 and she bore him Abijah, *A*,

ATTAIN (10/10) ATTAINED, ATTAINING

2 Sam 23:19 he did not *a* to the first
23:23 but he did not *a* to the first
1 Chr 11:21 However he did not *a* to the
11:25 but he did not *a* to the first
Ps 139: 6 It is high, I cannot *a* it.
Prov 1: 5 a man of understanding will *a*
Hos 8: 5 How long until they *a* to
Lk 20:35 who are counted worthy to *a*
Acts 26: 7 God night and day, hope to *a*.
Phil 3:11 I may *a* to the resurrection

ATTAINED (6/6) ATTAIN

Gen 47: 9 and they have not *a* to the days
Eccl 1:16 I have *a* greatness, and have
Rom 9:30 have *a* to righteousness, even
9:31 has not *a* to the law of
Phil 3:12 Not that I have already *a*,
3:16 degree that we have already *a*,

ATTAINING (1/1) ATTAIN

Col 2: 2 and *a* to all riches of the

ATTALIA (1/1)

Acts 14:25 in Perga, they went down to *A*.

ATTEMPT (2/2) ATTEMPTED, ATTEMPTING, ATTEMPTS

Acts 14: 5 And when a violent *a* was made by
Gal 5: 4 you who *a* to be justified by

ATTEMPTED (1/1) ATTEMPT

Acts 9:29 but they *a* to kill him.

ATTEMPTING (1/1) ATTEMPT

Heb 11:29 *a* to do so, were drowned.

ATTEMPTS (2/2) ATTEMPT

Job 4: 2 If one *a* a word with you, will
Eccl 8:17 though a wise man *a* to know

ATTEND (20/20) ATTENDANT, ATTENDED, ATTENDING

Num 1:50 they shall *a* to it and camp
3: 7 And they shall *a* to his needs
3: 8 Also they shall *a* to all the
3:10 and they shall *a* to their
8:26 to *a* to needs, but they
18: 3 They shall *a* to your needs and
18: 4 shall be joined with you and *a*
18: 5 And you shall *a* to the duties of
18: 7 and your sons with you shall *a*
1 Sam 24: 3 and Saul went in to *a* to his
1 Chr 23:32 and that they should *a* to the
2 Chr 13:10 and the Levites *a* to their
Esth 4: 5 whom he had appointed to *a* her,
Ps 17: 1 *A* to my cry; Give ear to my
55: 2 *A* to me, and hear me
61: 1 *A* to my prayer.
86: 6 And *a* to the voice of my
142: 6 *A* to my cry, For I am brought
Prov 27:23 And *a* to your herds;
Jer 23: 2 I will *a* to you for the evil of

ATTENDANT (1/1) ATTEND

Lk 4:20 and gave it back to the *a* and

ATTENDED (9/9) ATTEND

Judg 3:19 Keep silence!" And all who *a*
1 Sam 25:42 *a* by five of her maidens; and
2 Sam 13:17 he called his servant who *a*
2 Chr 7: 6 And the priests *a* to their
Esth 2: 2 Then the king's servants who *a*
6: 3 And the king's servants who *a*
Ps 66:19 He has *a* to the voice of my
Isa 10:28 At Michmash he has *a* to his
Jer 23: 2 and not *a* to them. Behold, I

ATTENDING (2/2) ATTEND

Judg 3:24 He is probably *a* to his needs in
Rom 13: 6 for they are God's ministers *a*

ATTENTION (12/12) ATTENTIVE, ATTENTIVELY

1 Ki 18:29 no one answered, no one paid *a*.
2 Ki 21: 9 But they paid no *a*, and Manasseh
Job 32:12 I paid close *a* to you; And
Prov 4: 1 And give *a* to know
4:20 give *a* to my words; Incline
5: 1 pay *a* to my wisdom; Lend your
7:24 Pay *a* to the words of my
29:12 If a ruler pays *a* to lies, All
Acts 3: 5 So he gave them his *a*,
26:26 of these things escapes his *a*,
1 Tim 4:13 give *a* to reading,
Jas 2: 3 and you pay *a* to the one wearing

ATTENTIVE (8/8) ATTENTION, ATTENTIVELY

2 Ki 20:13 And Hezekiah was *a* to them, and
2 Chr 6:40 open and let Your ears be *a*
7:15 will be open and My ears *a* to
Neh 1: 6 please let Your ear be *a* and
1:11 please let Your ear be *a* to the
8: 3 of all the people were *a* to
Ps 130: 2 my voice! Let Your ears be *a*
Lk 19:48 for all the people were very *a*

ATTENTIVELY (1/1) ATTENTIVE

Job 37: 2 Hear *a* the thunder of His

ATTESTED (1/1)

Acts 2:22 a Man *a* by God to you by

ATTIRE (3/3) ATTIRED

Judg 5:10 donkeys, Who sit in judges' *a*,
Prov 7:10 With the *a* of a harlot, and a
Jer 2:32 ornaments, Or a bride her *a*?

ATTIRED (1/1) ATTIRE

Lev 16: 4 the linen turban he shall be *a*.

ATTRACTED (1/1)

Gen 34: 3 His soul was strongly *a* to Dinah

ATTRIBUTES (1/1)

Rom 1:20 of the world His invisible *a*

AUDITORIUM (1/1)

Acts 25:23 and had entered the *a* with the

AUGMENT (KJV) See INCREASE

AUGUSTAN (1/1) AUGUSTUS

Acts 27: 1 a centurion of the *A* Regiment.

AUGUSTUS (3/3) AUGUSTAN, CAESAR

Lk 2: 1 a decree went out from Caesar *A*
Acts 25:21 reserved for the decision of *A*,
25:25 he himself had appealed to *A*,

AUL (KJV) See AWL

AUNT (1/1)

Lev 18:14 his wife; she is your *a*.

AUSTERE (2/2)

Lk 19:21 because you are an *a* man.
19:22 You knew that I was an *a* man,

AUTHOR (3/3) AUTHORITIES, AUTHORITY

1 Cor 14:33 For God is not the *a* of
Heb 5: 9 He became the *a* of eternal
12: 2 the *a* and finisher of our

AUTHORITIES (6/5) AUTHORITY

Lk 12:11 and magistrates and *a*,
Acts 16:19 into the marketplace to the *a*.
Rom 13: 1 be subject to the governing *a*.
13: 1 and the *a* that exist are
Titus 3: 1 to be subject to rulers and *a*,
1 Pe 3:22 angels and *a* and powers having

AUTHORITY (90/85) AUTHORITIES

Gen 39: 4 that he had he put under his *a*.
39:23 that was under Joseph's *a*,
41:35 and store up grain under the *a*
Num 4:28 duties shall be under the *a*
4:33 under the *a* of Ithamar the son
5:19 while under your husband's *a*,
5:20 while under your husband's *a*,
5:29 while under her husband's *a*,
7: 8 under the *a* of Ithamar the son
27:20 you shall give some of your *a*
Judg 9:29 this people were under my *a*!
1 Ki 21: 7 You now exercise *a* over Israel!
2 Ki 8:20 Edom revolted against Judah's *a*,
8:22 in revolt against Judah's *a* to
1 Chr 25: 6 and Heman were under the *a* of
2 Chr 21: 8 revolted against Judah's *a*,
21:10 in revolt against Judah's *a* to
26:13 And under their *a* was an army
Neh 13: 4 having *a* over the storerooms of
Esth 9:29 wrote with full *a* to confirm
Prov 29: 2 When the righteous are in *a*,
Dan 11: 6 not retain the power of her *a*,
11: 6 and neither he nor his *a* shall
Mt 7:29 He taught them as one having *a*,
8: 9 "For I also am a man under *a*,
20:25 those who are great exercise *a*
21:23 'By what *a* are You doing these
21:23 And who gave You this *a*?"
21:24 will tell you by what *a* I do
21:27 will I tell you by what *a* I do
28:18 All *a* has been given to Me in

Mk 1:22 He taught them as one having *a*,
1:27 For with *a* He commands even the
10:42 and their great ones exercise *a*
11:28 By what *a* are You doing these
11:28 And who gave You this *a* to do
11:29 and I will tell you by what *a*
11:33 will I tell you by what *a* I do
13:34 who left his house and gave *a*
Lk 4: 6 All this *a* I will give You, and
4:32 for His word was with *a*.
4:36 a word this is! For with *a*
7: 8 I also am a man placed under *a*,
9: 1 and gave them power and *a* over
10:19 I give you the *a* to trample on
19:17 have *a* over ten cities.'
20: 2 by what *a* are You doing these
20: 2 who is he who gave You this *a*?
20: 8 will I tell you by what *a* I do
20:20 Him to the power and the *a* of
22:25 and those who exercise *a* over
Jn 5:27 and has given Him *a* to execute
7:17 whether I speak on My own *a*.
11:51 he did not say on his own *a*;
12:49 I have not spoken on My own *a*;
14:10 you I do not speak on My own *a*;
16:13 He will not speak on His own *a*,
17: 2 as You have given Him *a* over all
Acts 1: 7 the Father has put in His own *a*.
8:27 a eunuch of great *a* under
9:14 And here he has *a* from the chief
25: 5 let those who have *a* among you
26:10 having received *a* from the
26:12 I journeyed to Damascus with *a*
Rom 13: 1 For there is no *a* except from
13: 2 whoever resists the *a* resists
13: 3 want to be unafraid of the *a*?
1 Cor 7: 4 The wife does not have *a* over
7: 4 the husband does not have *a*
9:18 that I may not abuse my *a* in
11:10 ought to have a symbol of *a*
15:24 an end to all rule and all *a*
2 Cor 10: 8 boast somewhat more about our *a*,
10:14 ourselves (as though our *a*
13:10 according to the *a* which the
2 Th 3: 9 not because we do not have *a*,
1 Tim 2: 2 for kings and all who are in *a*,
2:12 a woman to teach or to have *a*
Titus 2:15 exhort, and rebuke with all *a*.
2 Pe 2:10 of uncleanness and despise *a*.
Jude : 8 defile the flesh, reject *a*,
Rev 9: 5 And they were not given *a* to
13: 2 power, his throne, and great *a*.
13: 4 the dragon who gave *a* to the
13: 5 and he was given *a* to continue
13: 7 And *a* was given him over every
13:12 And he exercises all the *a* of
17:12 but they receive *a* for one hour
17:13 will give their power and *a* to
18: 1 from heaven, having great *a*,

AUTUMN (1/1)

Jude :12 late *a* trees without fruit,

AVA (1/1) IVAH

2 Ki 17:24 people from Babylon, Cuthah, *A*,

AVAIL (1/1) AVAILS

Job 41:26 sword reaches him, it cannot *a*;

AVAILS (4/4) AVAIL

Esth 5:13 Yet all this *a* me nothing, so
Gal 5: 6 nor uncircumcision *a* anything,
6:15 nor uncircumcision *a* anything,
Jas 5:16 prayer of a righteous man *a*

AVEN (3/3)

Ezek 30:17 The young men of *A* and Pi
Hos 10: 8 Also the high places of *A*,
Am 1: 5 inhabitant from the Valley of *A*,

AVENGE (14/14) AVENGED, AVENGER, AVENGES, AVENGING

Deut 32:43 For He will *a* the blood of His
1 Sam 24:12 and let the LORD *a* me on you.
2 Ki 9: 7 that I may *a* the blood of My
Esth 8:13 would be ready on that day to *a*
Jer 5: 9 And shall I not *a* Myself on such
5:29 Shall I not *a* Myself on such a
9: 9 Shall I not *a* Myself on such a
46:10 That He may *a* Himself on His
Hos 1: 4 in a little while I will *a*
Lk 18: 5 widow troubles me I will *a* her,
18: 7 And shall God not *a* His own
18: 8 I tell you that He will *a* them
Rom 12:19 do not *a* yourselves,
Rev 6:10 until You judge and *a* our blood

AVENGED (10/10) AVENGE

Gen 4:24 If Cain shall be *a* sevenfold,
Judg 11:36 because the LORD has *a* you of
1 Sam 25:31 or that my lord has *a* himself.
2 Sam 4: 8 and the LORD has *a* my lord the
18:19 how the LORD has *a* him of his
18:31 the king! For the LORD has *a*
Ezek 5:13 rest upon them, and I will be *a*;
Acts 7:24 he defended and *a* him who was

Rev 18:20 for God has *a* you on her!"
19: 2 and He has *a* on her the blood

AVENGER (17/16) AVENGE

Num 35:12 of refuge for you from the *a*,
35:19 The *a* of blood himself shall put
35:21 The *a* of blood shall put the
35:24 the manslayer and the *a* of
35:25 from the hand of the *a* of
35:27 and the *a* of blood finds him
35:27 and the *a* of blood kills the
Deut 19: 6 lest the *a* of blood, while his
19:12 him over to the hand of the *a*
Josh 20: 3 be your refuge from the *a* of
20: 5 Then if the *a* of blood pursues
20: 9 not die by the hand of the *a*
2 Sam 14:11 and do not permit the *a* of
Ps 8: 2 may silence the enemy and the *a*.
44:16 Because of the enemy and the *a*.
Rom 13: 4 an *a* to execute wrath on him
1 Th 4: 6 because the Lord is the *a* of

AVENGES (5/4) AVENGE

2 Sam 22:48 It is God who *a* me, And
Ps 9:12 When He *a* blood, He remembers
18:47 It is God who *a* me, And
Nah 1: 2 is jealous, and the LORD *a*;
1: 2 The LORD *a* and is furious.

AVENGING (4/4) AVENGE

1 Sam 25:26 coming to bloodshed and from *a*
25:33 coming to bloodshed and from *a*
Ps 79:10 nations in our sight The *a* of
Ezek 25:12 and has greatly offended by *a*

AVERSE (KJV) See RETURNED

AVIM (2/2) AVITES

Deut 2:23 And the *A*, who dwelt in villages
Josh 18:23 *A*, Parah, Ophrah,

AVIMS (KJV) See AVIM

AVITES (2/2) AVIM

Josh 13: 3 and the Ekronites; also the *A*;
2 Ki 17:31 and the *A* made Nibhaz and

AVITH (2/2)

Gen 36:35 And the name of his city was *A*.
1 Chr 1:46 The name of his city was *A*.

AVOID (5/5) AVOIDING

Job 36:18 ransom would not help you *a*
Prov 4:15 *A* it, do not travel on it
Rom 16:17 which you learned, and *a* them.
2 Tim 2:23 But *a* foolish and ignorant
Titus 3: 9 But *a* foolish disputes,

AVOIDING (2/2) AVOID

2 Cor 8:20 *a* this: that anyone should blame
1 Tim 6:20 *a* the profane and idle

AWAIT (1/1) AWAITING

Acts 20:23 that chains and tribulations *a*

AWAITING (1/1) AWAIT

Ps 65: 1 Praise is *a* You, O God, in

AWAKE (42/34) AWAKEN, AWAKENED, AWAKENS, AWAKES, AWAKING, AWOKE

Judg 5:12 '*A*, awake, Deborah!
5:12 'Awake, *a*, Deborah!
5:12 "Awake, awake, Deborah! *A*,
5:12 awake, Deborah! Awake, *a*,
Job 8: 6 Surely now He would *a* for you,
14:12 They will not *a* Nor be roused
Ps 17:15 I shall be satisfied when I *a*
35:23 and *a* to my vindication, To my
44:23 *A*! Why do You sleep, O Lord
57: 8 *A*, my glory! Awake, lute and
57: 8 Awake, my glory! *A*,
59: 4 *A* to help me, and behold!
59: 5 *A* to punish all the nations;
73:20 awakes, So, Lord, when You *a*,
102: 7 I lie *a*, And am like a sparrow
108: 2 *A*, lute and harp! I will
119:148 My eyes are *a* through the
127: 1 The watchman stays *a* in vain.
139:18 number than the sand; When I *a*,
Prov 6:22 will keep you; And when you *a*,
23:35 not feel it. When shall I *a*,
Song 4:16 *A*, O north wind, And come,
5: 2 I sleep, but my heart is *a*;
Isa 26:19 *A* and sing, you who dwell in
51: 9 *A*, awake, put on strength,
51: 9 Awake, *a*, put on strength,
51: 9 O arm of the LORD! *A* as in
51:17 *A*, awake! Stand up, O
51:17 *a*! Stand up, O Jerusalem, You
52: 1 *A*, awake! Put on your
52: 1 *a*! Put on your strength, O

Jer 51:39 a perpetual sleep And not *a*,
51:57 a perpetual sleep And not *a*,
Dan 12: 2 the dust of the earth shall *a*,
Joel 1: 5 *A*, you drunkards, and weep;
Hab 2:19 *A*!' To silent stone, 'Arise! It
Zech 13: 7 *A*, O sword, against My
Mal 2:12 being *a* and aware, Yet who
Lk 9:32 and when they were fully *a*,
Rom 13:11 now it is high time to *a* out
1 Cor 15:34 *A* to righteousness, and do not
Eph 5:14 Therefore He says: "*A*,

AWAKEN (6/6) AWAKE, AWAKENED, AWAKENS

Ps 57: 8 lute and harp! I will *a* the
108: 2 lute and harp! I will *a* the
Song 2: 7 Do not stir up nor *a* love
3: 5 Do not stir up nor *a* love
8: 4 Do not stir up nor *a* love
Hab 2: 7 Will they not *a* who oppress

AWAKENED (3/3) AWAKEN

1 Ki 18:27 he is sleeping and must be *a*.
2 Ki 4:31 saying, "The child has not *a*.
Song 8: 5 I *a* you under the apple tree.

AWAKENS (2/1) AWAKEN

Isa 50: 4 He *a* Me morning by morning,
50: 4 He *a* My ear To hear as the

AWAKES (3/2) AWAKE

Ps 73:20 As a dream when one *a*,
Isa 29: 8 And look—he eats; But he *a*,
29: 8 And look—he drinks; But he *a*,

AWAKING (1/1) AWAKE

Acts 16:27 *a* from sleep and seeing the

AWARE (12/12)

Song 6:12 Before I was even *a*,
Jer 50:24 O Babylon, And you were not *a*;
Ob : 7 No one is *a* of it.
Mal 2:12 does this, being awake and *a*,
Mt 16: 8 being *a* of it, said to them,
24:50 at an hour that he is not *a* of,
26:10 But when Jesus was *a* of it, He
Mk 8:17 being *a* of it, said to them,
Lk 11:44 who walk over them are not *a*
12:46 and at an hour when he is not *a*,
Acts 5: 2 his wife also being *a* of it,
14: 6 they became *a* of it and fled to

AWAY (888/832)

Gen 9:23 Their faces were turned *a*,
12:20 him; and they sent him *a*,
15:11 carcasses, Abram drove them *a*.
18:22 Then the men turned *a* from
21:14 boy to Hagar, and sent her *a*.
24:54 Send me *a* to my master."
24:56 send me *a* so that I may go to
24:59 So they sent *a* Rebekah their
25: 6 *a* from Isaac his son, to the
26:16 Go *a* from us, for you are much
26:27 you hate me and have sent me *a*
26:29 but good and have sent you *a*
26:31 another; and Isaac sent them *a*,
27:35 with deceit and has taken *a*
27:36 He took *a* my birthright, and
27:36 he has taken *a* my blessing!"
27:44 your brother's fury turns *a*,
27:45 your brother's anger turns *a*
28: 5 So Isaac sent Jacob *a*,
28: 6 blessed Jacob and sent him *a*
30:15 matter that you have taken *a*
30:15 Would you take *a* my son's
30:23 God has taken *a* my reproach."
30:25 said to Laban, "Send me *a*,
31: 1 Jacob has taken *a* all that was
31: 9 So God has taken *a* the livestock
31:18 And he carried *a* all his
31:20 And Jacob stole *a*,
31:26 that you have stolen *a* unknown
31:26 and carried *a* my daughters like
31:27 Why did you flee *a* secretly, and
31:27 and steal *a* from me, and not
31:27 for I might have sent you *a*
31:42 now you would have sent me *a*
35: 2 Put *a* the foreign gods that are
36: 6 and went to a country *a* from
38:19 So she arose and went *a*,
40:15 For indeed I was stolen *a* from
42:24 And he turned himself *a* from
44: 3 dawned, the men were sent *a*,
45:24 So he sent his brothers *a*,
Ex 2: 9 Take this child *a* and nurse him
2:17 shepherds came and drove them *a*;
8: 8 the LORD that He may take *a*
8:28 you shall not go very far *a*.
10:17 that He may take *a* from me this
10:19 which took the locusts *a* and
10:28 Get *a* from me! Take heed to
12:28 the children of Israel went *a*
13:22 He did not take *a* the pillar of
14:11 have you taken us *a* to die in
15:15 of Canaan will melt *a*.
19:24 *A*! Get down and then come up,

22:10 it dies, is hurt, or driven **a**,
23:25 And I will take sickness **a** from
33:23 Then I will take **a** My hand, and
Lev 13:55 the fire; it continues eating **a**,
14:40 shall command that they take **a**
14:43 after he has taken **a** the
16:21 and shall send it **a** into the
26:39 you who are left shall waste **a**
26:39 with them, they shall waste **a**.
26:44 enemies, I will not cast them **a**,
Num 4:13 Also they shall take **a** the ashes
9:10 or is far **a** on a journey, he
14:43 because you have turned **a** from
16:24 Get **a** from the tents of Korah,
16:27 So they got **a** from around the
16:37 the fire some distance **a**.
16:45 Get **a** from among this
17:10 you may put their complaints **a**
20:21 so Israel turned **a** from him.
21: 7 to the LORD that He take **a**
24:22 long until Asshur carries you **a**
25: 4 anger of the LORD may turn **a**
32: 8 fathers did when I sent them **a**
32:15 For if you turn **a** from following
36: 4 inheritance will be taken **a**
Deut 2: 8 **a** from the road of the plain,
2: 8 **a** from Elath and Ezion Geber,
7: 4 they will turn your sons **a**
7:15 And the LORD will take **a** from
12:32 shall not add to it nor take **a**
13: 5 spoken in order to turn you **a**
13: 5 So you shall put **a** the evil
13:10 he sought to entice you **a** from
15:13 And when you send him **a** free
15:13 you shall not let him go **a**
15:16 I will not go **a** from you,'
15:18 hard to you when you send him **a**
17: 7 So you shall put **a** the evil
17:12 So you shall put **a** the evil
17:17 himself, lest his heart turn **a**;
19:13 but you shall put **a** the guilt
19:19 so you shall put **a** the evil
21: 9 So you shall put **a** the guilt
21:21 so you shall put **a** the evil
22:21 So you shall put **a** the evil
22:22 so you shall put **a** the evil
22:24 so you shall put **a** the evil
23:14 and turn **a** from you.
24: 7 and you shall put **a** the evil
28:26 no one shall frighten them **a**.
28:31 shall be violently taken **a**
29:18 whose heart turns **a** today from
30:17 But if your heart turns **a** so
30:17 do not hear, and are drawn **a**,
Josh 2:21 be it." And she sent them **a**,
3:16 and rose in a heap very far **a**
5: 9 This day I have rolled **a** the
7:13 your enemies until you take **a**
8: 3 men of valor and sent them **a**
8:16 Joshua and were drawn **a** from
18: 8 Then the men arose to go **a**;
22: 6 blessed them and sent them **a**,
22: 7 when Joshua sent them **a** to
22:16 to turn **a** this day from
22:18 but that you must turn **a** this
24:14 and put **a** the gods which your
24:23 put **a** the foreign gods which
Judg 3:18 he sent **a** the people who had
4:15 from his chariot and fled **a**
4:17 Sisera had fled **a** on foot to
5:12 Barak, and lead your captives **a**,
5:21 torrent of Kishon swept them **a**,
7: 8 And he sent **a** all the rest
9:21 And Jotham ran **a** and fled; and
10:16 So they put **a** the foreign gods
11:13 Because Israel took **a** my land
11:15 Israel did not take **a** the land
11:38 And he sent her **a** for two
12: 9 And he gave **a** thirty daughters
18:24 You have taken **a** my gods which I
18:24 the priest, and you have gone **a**.
19: 2 and went **a** from him to her
20:31 and were drawn **a** from the
20:32 Let us flee and draw them **a** from
1 Sam 1:14 Put your wine **a** from you!"
5: 8 the God of Israel be carried **a**
5: 8 the ark of the God of Israel **a**.
5: 9 after they had carried it **a**,
5:11 Send **a** the ark of the God of
6: 3 If you send **a** the ark of the God
6: 7 their calves home, **a** from them.
6: 8 by its side. Then send it **a**,
7: 3 then put **a** the foreign gods
7: 4 So the children of Israel put **a**
10:25 Samuel sent all the people **a**,
12:25 wickedly, you shall be swept **a**,
13: 2 rest of the people he sent **a**,
14:16 was the multitude, melting **a**;
15:27 as Samuel turned around to go **a**,
17:26 this Philistine and takes **a**
19:10 but he slipped **a** from Saul's
19:17 like this, and sent my enemy **a**,
20:13 report it to you and send you **a**,
20:22 for the LORD has sent you **a**.
20:29 please let me get **a** and see my
21: 6 on the day when it was taken **a**.
23: 5 and took **a** their livestock.
23:26 So David made haste to get **a**
24:19 will he let him get **a** safely?
25:10 servants nowadays who break **a**
26:12 by Saul's head, and they got **a**;
27: 9 but took **a** the sheep, the oxen,

28:25 Then they rose and went **a** that
30: 2 but carried them **a** and went
30:18 the Amalekites had carried **a**,
30:22 that they may lead them **a** and
2 Sam 1:21 shield of the mighty is cast **a**
3:21 So David sent Abner **a**,
3:22 Hebron, for he had sent him **a**,
3:23 to the king, and he sent him **a**,
3:24 why is it that you sent him **a**,
5:21 and his men carried them **a**.
10: 4 their buttocks, and sent them **a**.
12:13 The LORD also has put **a** your
13:16 This evil of sending me **a** is
13:17 **a** from me, and bolt the door
13:19 her hand on her head and went **a**
14:14 Yet God does not take **a** a life;
17:18 But both of them went **a** quickly
18: 3 not go out! For if we flee **a**,
19: 3 people who are ashamed steal **a**
19:41 stolen you **a** and brought the
22:46 The foreigners fade **a**,
23: 6 all be as thorns thrust **a**,
24:10 take **a** the iniquity of Your
1 Ki 2:31 that you may take **a** from me and
2:39 two slaves of Shimei ran **a** to
5: 9 then you can take them **a**.
8:48 of their enemies who led them **a**
8:66 eighth day he sent the people **a**;
11: 2 Surely they will turn **a** your
11: 3 and his wives turned **a** his
11:11 will surely tear the kingdom **a**
11:13 However I will not tear **a** the
14: 8 and tore the kingdom **a** from the
14:10 I will take **a** the remnant of
14:10 as one takes **a** refuse until it
14:26 And he took **a** the treasures of
14:26 he took **a** everything. He also
14:26 He also took **a** all the gold
15:22 And they took **a** the stones and
16: 3 surely I will take **a** the
17: 3 Get **a** from here and turn
17:15 So she went **a** and did according
18:45 So Ahab rode **a** and went to
20:34 I will send you **a** with this
20:34 treaty with him and sent him **a**.
20:41 hastened to take the bandage **a**
21: 4 and turned **a** his face, and
21:21 I will take **a** your posterity,
22:43 high places were not taken **a**,
2 Ki 2: 3 know that the LORD will take **a**
2: 5 know that the LORD will take **a**
2: 9 before I am taken **a** from you?"
3: 2 for he put **a** the sacred pillar
4:27 Gehazi came near to push her **a**.
5:11 and went **a** and said, "Indeed,
5:12 So he turned and went **a** in a
5:24 and stored them **a** in the
6:23 he sent them **a** and they went to
6:32 has sent someone to take **a** my
7:15 which the Syrians had thrown **a**
10:29 However Jehu did not turn **a**
11: 2 and stole him **a** from among the
12: 3 high places were not taken **a**;
12:18 Then he went **a** from Jerusalem.
14: 4 high places were not taken **a**,
17: 6 Samaria and carried Israel **a**
17:11 whom the LORD had carried **a**
17:23 So Israel was carried **a** from
17:28 whom they had carried **a** from
17:33 among whom they were carried **a**.
18:11 of Assyria carried Israel **a**
18:14 turn **a** from me; whatever you
18:22 altars Hezekiah has taken **a**,
18:32 until I come and take you **a** to a
19:36 of Assyria departed and went **a**,
20:18 And they shall take **a** some of
23:19 Now Josiah also took **a** all the
23:24 Moreover Josiah put **a** those who
25:11 captain of the guard carried **a**
25:14 They also took **a** the pots, the
25:15 the captain of the guard took **a**.
25:21 Thus Judah was carried **a**
1 Chr 5:21 Then they took **a** their
7:21 they came down to take **a** their
8: 8 after he had sent **a** Hushim and
9: 1 But Judah was carried **a** captive
12:19 of the Philistines sent him **a**
12:40 from as far **a** as Issachar and
17:13 and I will not take My mercy **a**
19: 4 their buttocks, and sent them **a**.
21: 8 take **a** the iniquity of Your
2 Chr 6:42 do not turn **a** the face of Your
7:10 month he sent the people **a** to
7:19 But if you turn **a** and forsake
12: 9 and took **a** the treasures of the
12: 9 He also carried **a** the gold
14:13 And they carried **a** very much
16: 6 and they carried **a** the stones
20:25 and his people came to take **a**
20:25 more than they could carry **a**;
20:33 high places were not taken **a**,
21:17 carried **a** all the possessions
22:11 and stole him **a** from among the
25:27 the time that Amaziah turned **a**
28: 5 and carried **a** a great multitude
28: 8 children of Israel carried **a**
28: 8 and they also took **a** much spoil
28:17 and carried **a** captives.
29: 6 have turned their faces **a** from
29:10 His fierce wrath may turn **a**
30: 8 of His wrath may turn **a** from
30:14 They arose and took **a** the altars

30:14 and they took **a** all the incense
32:12 not the same Hezekiah taken **a**
33:15 He took **a** the foreign gods and
35:23 to his servants, "Take me **a**,
36:20 from the sword he carried **a** to
Ezra 2: 1 of those who had been carried **a**,
2: 1 king of Babylon had carried **a**
5:12 and carried the people **a** to
8:35 of those who had been carried **a**
9: 4 of those who had been carried **a**
10: 3 covenant with our God to put **a**
10:14 wrath of our God is turned **a**
10:19 promise that they would put **a**
Neh 7: 6 of those who had been carried **a**,
7: 6 king of Babylon had carried **a**,
Esth 2: 6 Kish had been carried **a** from
2: 6 king of Babylon had carried **a**.
4: 4 and take his sackcloth **a** from
Job 1:15 raided them and took them **a**—
1:17 the camels and took them **a**,
1:21 gave, and the LORD has taken **a**;
4:21 not their own excellence go **a**?
6:15 of the brooks that pass **a**,
7: 9 cloud disappears and vanishes **a**,
7:19 Will You not look **a** from me,
7:21 And take **a** my iniquity?
8: 4 He has cast them **a** for their
8:20 God will not cast **a** the
9:12 If He takes **a**, who can hinder
9:25 than a runner; They flee **a**,
9:34 Let Him take His rod **a** from me,
11:14 hand, and you put it far **a**,
11:16 as waters that have passed **a**,
12:17 He leads counselors **a**
12:19 He leads princes **a** plundered,
12:20 And takes **a** the discernment of
12:24 He takes **a** the understanding of
14: 2 forth like a flower and fades **a**;
14: 6 Look **a** from him that he may
14:10 But man dies and is laid **a**;
14:18 mountain falls and crumbles **a**,
14:19 As water wears **a** stones, And
14:19 And as torrents wash **a** the
14:20 his countenance and send him **a**.
15:12 does your heart carry you **a**,
15:30 of His mouth he will go **a**.
20: 8 He will fly **a** like a dream, and
20: 8 he will be chased **a** like a
20:28 And his goods will flow **a**
21:18 chaff that a storm carries **a**.
22: 9 You have sent widows **a** empty,
22:16 foundations were swept **a** by a
24: 3 They drive **a** the donkey of the
24:10 And they take **a** the sheaves
24:22 But God draws the mighty **a** with
27: 2 who has taken **a** my justice,
27: 5 Till I die I will not put **a** my
27: 8 If God takes **a** his life?
27:20 A tempest steals him **a** in the
27:21 The east wind carries him **a**,
28: 4 He breaks open a shaft **a** from
28: 4 by feet They hang far **a** from
30:12 They push **a** my feet, And they
32:22 my Maker would soon take me **a**.
33:21 His flesh wastes **a** from sight,
34: 5 But God has taken **a** my
34:20 people are shaken and pass **a**;
34:20 The mighty are taken **a** without
36:18 beware lest He take you **a** with
Ps 1: 4 chaff which the wind drives **a**.
2: 3 bonds in pieces And cast **a**
6: 7 My eye wastes **a** because of
17: 4 I have kept **a** from the paths
18:22 And I did not put **a** His
18:45 The foreigners fade **a**,
27: 9 Do not turn Your servant **a** in
28: 3 Do not take me **a** with the
31: 9 My eye wastes **a** with grief,
31:10 iniquity, And my bones waste **a**.
31:13 They scheme to take **a** my life.
34: Abimelech, who drove him **a**,
36:11 hand of the wicked drive me **a**.
37:20 Into smoke they shall vanish **a**.
37:36 Yet he passed **a**,
39:11 You make his beauty melt **a**
39:13 Before I go **a** and am no
48: 5 were troubled, they hastened **a**.
49:17 dies he shall carry nothing **a**;
51:11 Do not cast me **a** from Your
52: 5 forever; He shall take you **a**,
55: 6 like a dove! I would fly **a**
58: 7 Let them flow **a** as waters
58: 8 be like a snail which melts **a**
58: 9 He shall take them **a** as with a
64: 8 All who see them shall flee **a**.
66:20 Who has not turned **a** my
68: 2 As smoke is driven **a**,
68: 2 driven away, So drive them **a**;
78:38 a time He turned His anger **a**,
78:39 A breath that passes **a** and
85: 3 You have taken **a** all Your
88: 8 You have put **a** my acquaintances
88: 9 My eye wastes **a** because of
90: 5 You carry them **a** like a flood;
90: 9 all our days have passed **a** in
90:10 is soon cut off, and we fly **a**.
101: 3 the work of those who fall **a**;
102:10 have lifted me up and cast me **a**.
102:11 And I wither **a** like grass.
102:24 Do not take me **a** in the midst
104: 7 of Your thunder they hastened **a**.
104:29 You take **a** their breath, they

106:23 To turn ***a*** His wrath, lest He
106:46 all those who carried them ***a***
112:10 will gnash his teeth and melt ***a***;
119:37 Turn ***a*** my eyes from looking at
119:39 Turn ***a*** my reproach which I
119:119 You put ***a*** all the wicked of the
125: 5 The LORD shall lead them ***a***
132:10 Do not turn ***a*** the face of Your
137: 3 there those who carried us ***a***
148: 6 a decree which shall not pass ***a***.
Prov 1:19 It takes ***a*** the life of its
1:32 For the turning ***a*** of the simple
4: 5 nor turn ***a*** from the words of my
4:15 Turn ***a*** from it and pass on.
4:16 And their sleep is taken ***a***
4:24 Put ***a*** from you a deceitful
6:33 reproach will not be wiped ***a***.
10: 3 But He casts ***a*** the desire of
13:14 To turn one ***a*** from the snares
14:27 To turn one ***a*** from the snares
15: 1 A soft answer turns ***a*** wrath,
15:24 That he may turn ***a*** from hell
19:26 his father and chases ***a*** his
20:30 Blows that hurt cleanse ***a*** evil,
22:27 Why should he take ***a*** your bed
23: 5 They fly ***a*** like an eagle
24:18 And He turn ***a*** His wrath from
25: 4 Take ***a*** the dross from silver,
25: 5 Take ***a*** the wicked from before
25:20 Like one who takes ***a*** a garment
27:10 nearby than a brother far ***a***.
28: 9 One who turns ***a*** his ear from
29: 8 But wise men turn ***a*** wrath.
30:30 beasts And does not turn ***a***
Eccl 1: 4 One generation passes ***a***,
3: 5 A time to cast ***a*** stones, And a
3: 6 to keep, And a time to throw ***a***;
5:15 labor Which he may carry ***a*** in
11:10 And put ***a*** evil from your
Song 1: 4 Draw me ***a***! We will run
2:10 love, my fair one, And come ***a***.
2:13 And come ***a***!
2:17 breaks And the shadows flee ***a***,
4: 6 breaks And the shadows flee ***a***,
5: 6 But my beloved had turned ***a***
5: 7 of the walls Took my veil ***a***
6: 5 Turn your eyes ***a*** from me, For
Isa 1: 4 They have turned ***a*** backward.
1:16 Put ***a*** the evil of your doings
1:25 And thoroughly purge ***a*** your
1:25 And take ***a*** all your alloy.
2:20 In that day a man will cast ***a***
3: 1 Takes ***a*** from Jerusalem and
3:18 that day the Lord will take ***a***
4: 1 To take ***a*** our reproach."
4: 4 When the Lord has washed ***a*** the
5: 5 I will take ***a*** its hedge, and
5:23 And take ***a*** justice from the
5:25 this His anger is not turned ***a***,
5:29 They will carry it ***a*** safely,
6: 7 lips; Your iniquity is taken ***a***,
6:12 LORD has removed men far ***a***,
8: 4 of Samaria will be taken ***a***
9:12 this His anger is not turned ***a***,
9:17 this His anger is not turned ***a***,
9:21 this His anger is not turned ***a***,
10: 4 this His anger is not turned ***a***,
10:18 be as when a sick man wastes ***a***.
10:27 his burden will be taken ***a***
12: 1 me, Your anger is turned ***a***,
15: 6 the green grass has withered ***a***;
15: 7 They will carry ***a*** to the Brook
16:10 Gladness is taken ***a***,
17:13 them and they will flee far ***a***,
18: 5 with pruning hooks And take ***a***
19: 7 Will wither, be driven ***a***,
20: 4 the king of Assyria lead ***a*** the
22: 4 Look ***a*** from me, I will weep
22:17 the LORD will throw you ***a***
24: 4 The earth mourns and fades ***a***,
24: 4 world languishes and fades ***a***;
25: 8 And the Lord GOD will wipe ***a***
25: 8 of His people He will take ***a***
27: 8 In measure, by sending it ***a***,
27: 9 is all the fruit of taking ***a***
28:17 The hail will sweep ***a*** the
29: 5 ones Like chaff that passes ***a***;
30:22 You will throw them ***a*** as an
30:22 will say to them, "Get ***a***!"
31: 7 day every man shall throw ***a***
35:10 sorrow and sighing shall flee ***a***.
36: 7 altars Hezekiah has taken ***a***,
36:17 until I come and take you ***a*** to a
37:37 of Assyria departed and went ***a***,
39: 7 And they shall take ***a*** some of
40:24 the whirlwind will take them ***a***
41: 9 you and have not cast you ***a***:
41:16 the wind shall carry them ***a***,
49:17 who laid you waste Shall go ***a***
49:19 swallowed you up will be far ***a***.
49:25 of the mighty shall be taken ***a***,
50: 1 divorce, Whom I have put ***a***?
50: 1 your mother has been put ***a***.
50: 5 rebellious, Nor did I turn ***a***.
51: 6 For the heavens will vanish ***a***
51:11 and sighing shall flee ***a***.
52: 5 That My people are taken ***a*** for
57: 1 Merciful men are taken ***a***,
57: 1 That the righteous is taken ***a***
57:13 the wind will carry them all ***a***,
58: 9 If you take ***a*** the yoke from your
58:13 If you turn ***a*** your foot from
64: 6 like the wind, Have taken us ***a***.
Jer 1: 3 until the carrying ***a*** of
1:13 and it is facing ***a*** from the
2:24 of mating, who can turn her ***a***?
3: 8 I had put her ***a*** and given her a
3:19 And not turn ***a*** from Me.'
4: 1 And if you will put ***a*** your
4: 4 And take ***a*** the foreskins of
5:10 Take ***a*** her branches, For they
5:25 have turned these things ***a***,
6: 4 Woe to us, for the day goes ***a***,
7:29 off your hair and cast it ***a***,
7:33 no one will frighten them ***a***.
8: 4 Will one turn ***a*** and not
8:13 I have given them shall pass ***a***
13:19 Judah shall be carried ***a***
13:19 It shall be wholly carried ***a***
13:24 like stubble That passes ***a*** by
15:15 patience, do not take me ***a***.
16: 5 for I have taken ***a*** My peace
17:16 I have not hurried ***a*** from
18:20 To turn ***a*** Your wrath from
21: 2 that the king may go ***a*** from
22:10 bitterly for him who goes ***a***,
23: 2 My flock, driven them ***a***,
24: 1 king of Babylon had carried ***a***
24: 5 those who are carried ***a***
27:20 when he carried ***a*** captive
28: 3 king of Babylon took ***a*** from
28: 6 and all who were carried ***a***
29: 1 the elders who were carried ***a***
29: 1 Nebuchadnezzar had carried ***a***
29: 4 to all who were carried ***a***
29: 4 I have caused to be carried ***a***
29: 7 have caused you to be carried ***a***
29:14 I cause you to be carried ***a***
32:40 that I will not turn ***a*** from
33:26 then I will cast ***a*** the
38:22 And they have turned ***a***
39: 9 captain of the guard carried ***a***
40: 1 among all who were carried ***a***
40: 1 who were carried ***a*** captive to
40: 7 land who had not been carried ***a***
41:10 Then Ishmael carried ***a*** captive
41:10 son of Nethaniah carried them ***a***
41:14 whom Ishmael had carried ***a***
43: 3 put us to death or carry us ***a***
43:12 burn them and carry them ***a***
46: 6 "Do not let the swift flee ***a***,
46:15 are your valiant men swept ***a***?
46:15 Because the LORD drove them ***a***.
46:21 They have fled ***a*** together.
48: 9 That she may flee and get ***a***;
49:19 I will suddenly make him run ***a***
49:29 their flocks they shall take ***a***.
49:30 get far ***a***! Dwell in the depths,
50: 6 They have turned them ***a*** on
50:17 The lions have driven him ***a***.
50:44 I will make them suddenly run ***a***
51:50 Get ***a***! Do not stand still!
52:15 captain of the guard carried ***a***
52:18 They also took ***a*** the pots, the
52:19 the captain of the guard took ***a***.
52:27 Thus Judah was carried ***a***
52:28 whom Nebuchadnezzar carried ***a***
52:29 of Nebuchadnezzar he carried ***a***
52:30 captain of the guard carried ***a***
Lam 1: 8 Yes, she sighs and turns ***a***.
4: 9 of hunger; For these pine ***a***,
4:15 cried out to them, "Go ***a***,
4:15 "Go away, unclean! Go ***a***,
4:15 away, unclean! Go away, go ***a***,
Ezek 3:14 lifted me up and took me ***a***,
4:17 and waste ***a*** because of their
8: 6 to make Me go far ***a*** from My
11:15 Get far ***a*** from the LORD; this
11:18 and they will take ***a*** all its
12:11 they shall be carried ***a*** into
14: 6 turn ***a*** from your idols, and
14: 6 and turn your faces ***a*** from all
16:50 therefore I took them ***a*** as I
17:13 He also took ***a*** the mighty of
18:24 when a righteous man turns ***a***
18:26 When a righteous man turns ***a***
18:27 when a wicked man turns ***a*** from
18:28 he considers and turns ***a*** from
18:31 Cast ***a*** from you all the
20: 7 throw ***a*** the abominations which
20: 8 They did not all cast ***a*** the
23:10 Took ***a*** her sons and daughters,
23:26 you of your clothes And take ***a***
23:29 take ***a*** all you have worked for,
24:16 I take ***a*** from you the desire of
24:23 but you shall pine ***a*** in your
29:19 he shall take ***a*** her wealth,
30: 4 And they take ***a*** her wealth,
33: 4 the sword comes and takes him ***a***,
33: 6 he is taken ***a*** in his iniquity;
33:10 and we pine ***a*** in them, how can
34: 4 brought back what was driven ***a***,
34:16 bring back what was driven ***a***,
38:13 to carry ***a*** silver and gold, to
38:13 to take ***a*** livestock and goods,
42: 5 because the galleries took ***a***
43: 9 carcasses of their kings far ***a***
44:10 who strayed ***a*** from Me after
Dan 1:16 Thus the steward took ***a*** their
2:35 the wind carried them ***a*** so that
7:12 they had their dominion taken ***a***,
7:14 Which shall not pass ***a***,
7:26 And they shall take ***a*** his
8:11 daily sacrifices were taken ***a***,
9:16 and Your fury be turned ***a*** from
11:12 When he has taken ***a*** the
11:22 a flood they shall be swept ***a***
11:26 him; his army shall be swept ***a***,
11:31 then they shall take ***a*** the
12:11 the daily sacrifice is taken ***a***,
Hos 1: 6 But I will utterly take them ***a***.
2: 2 I her Husband! Let her put ***a***
2: 9 I will return and take ***a*** My
4: 3 who dwells there will waste ***a***
4: 3 fish of the sea will be taken ***a***.
5:14 I, will tear them and go ***a***;
5:14 go away; I will take them ***a***,
6: 4 like the early dew it goes ***a***.
9:11 their glory shall fly ***a*** like a
9:17 My God will cast them ***a***,
13: 3 the early dew that passes ***a***,
13:11 And took him ***a*** in My wrath.
14: 2 Take ***a*** all iniquity; Receive
14: 4 For My anger has turned ***a*** from
Joel 1: 7 it bare and thrown it ***a***;
1:12 Surely joy has withered ***a*** from
2:20 And will drive him ***a*** into a
Am 1: 3 I will not turn ***a*** its
1: 6 I will not turn ***a*** its
1: 9 I will not turn ***a*** its
1:11 I will not turn ***a*** its
1:13 I will not turn ***a*** its
2: 1 I will not turn ***a*** its
2: 4 I will not turn ***a*** its
2: 6 I will not turn ***a*** its
4: 2 you When He will take you ***a***
5:23 Take ***a*** from Me the noise of
7:11 Israel shall surely be led ***a***
7:17 Israel shall surely be led ***a***
9: 1 flees from them shall not get ***a***,
Jon 3: 9 and turn ***a*** from His fierce
Mic 1:11 Its place to stand is taken ***a***
2: 9 children You have taken ***a*** My
6:14 You may carry some ***a***,
Nah 2: 7 She shall be led ***a*** captive,
2: 8 pool of water, Now they flee ***a***.
3:10 Yet she was carried ***a***,
3:16 locust plunders and flies ***a***.
3:17 When the sun rises they flee ***a***,
Zeph 3:11 For then I will take ***a*** from
3:15 The LORD has taken ***a*** your
Hag 1: 9 brought it home, I blew it ***a***.
Zech 3: 4 Take ***a*** the filthy garments from
9: 7 I will take ***a*** the blood from
12: 3 all who would heave it ***a*** will
Mal 2: 3 And one will take you ***a*** with
2: 6 And turned many ***a*** from
3: 5 And against those who turn ***a***
3: 7 your fathers You have gone ***a***
Mt 1:11 the time they were carried ***a***
1:19 was minded to put her ***a***
4:10 ***A*** with you, Satan! For it is
5:18 till heaven and earth pass ***a***,
5:40 wants to sue you and take ***a***
5:42 borrow from you do not turn ***a***.
8:31 permit us to go ***a*** into the herd
8:33 and they went ***a*** into the city
9:15 the bridegroom will be taken ***a***
9:16 for the patch pulls ***a*** from the
13: 6 had no root they withered ***a***.
13:12 what he has will be taken ***a***
13:19 one comes and snatches ***a*** what
13:36 Jesus sent the multitude ***a*** and
13:48 vessels, but threw the bad ***a***.
14:12 his disciples came and took ***a***
14:15 Send the multitudes ***a***,
14:16 "They do not need to go ***a***.
14:22 while He sent the multitudes ***a***.
14:23 He had sent the multitudes ***a***,
15:23 urged Him, saying, "Send her ***a***,
15:32 I do not want to send them ***a***
15:39 And He sent ***a*** the multitude, got
19: 7 of divorce, and to put her ***a***?
19:22 he went ***a*** sorrowful, for he had
21:19 the fig tree withered ***a***.
21:20 How did the fig tree wither ***a*** so
22:13 him hand and foot, take him ***a***,
24:34 will by no means pass ***a*** till
24:35 "Heaven and earth will pass ***a***,
24:35 words will by no means pass ***a***.
24:39 flood came and took them all ***a***,
25:29 what he has will be taken ***a***.
25:46 And these will go ***a*** into
26:42 He went ***a*** and prayed, saying,
26:42 if this cup cannot pass ***a*** from
26:44 went ***a*** again, and prayed the
26:57 laid hold of Jesus led Him ***a***
27: 2 they led Him ***a*** and delivered
27:31 and led Him ***a*** to be crucified.
27:64 come by night and steal Him ***a***,
28:13 came at night and stole Him ***a***
28:16 the eleven disciples went ***a***
Mk 1:43 warned him and sent him ***a*** at
2:20 the bridegroom will be taken ***a***
2:21 or else the new piece pulls ***a***
4: 6 it had no root it withered ***a***.
4:15 comes immediately and takes ***a***
4:25 what he has will be taken ***a***.
6:29 they came and took ***a*** his corpse
6:36 'Send them ***a***, that they may go
6:45 while He sent the multitude ***a***.
6:46 And when He had sent them ***a***,
7:17 When He had entered a house ***a***
8: 3 And if I send them ***a*** hungry to
8: 9 And He sent them ***a***,
8:26 Then He sent him ***a*** to his house,

10:22 and went ***a*** sorrowful, for he
11:21 which You cursed has withered ***a***.
12: 3 and beat him and sent him ***a***
12: 4 and sent him ***a*** shamefully
12:12 So they left Him and went ***a***.
13:30 will by no means pass ***a*** till
13:31 "Heaven and earth will pass ***a***,
13:31 words will by no means pass ***a***.
14:36 Take this cup ***a*** from Me;
14:39 Again He went ***a*** and prayed, and
14:44 seize Him and lead Him ***a***
14:53 And they led Jesus ***a*** to the
15: 1 they bound Jesus, led Him ***a***,
15:16 Then the soldiers led Him ***a***
16: 3 Who will roll ***a*** the stone from
16: 4 the stone had been rolled ***a***—
Lk 1:25 to take ***a*** my reproach among
1:53 And the rich He has sent ***a***
2:15 when the angels had gone ***a*** from
5:35 the bridegroom will be taken ***a***
6:29 And from him who takes ***a*** your
6:30 And from him who takes ***a*** your
8: 6 it withered ***a*** because it lacked
8:12 the devil comes and takes ***a***
8:13 in time of temptation fall ***a***.
8:38 with Him. But Jesus sent him ***a***,
9:12 When the day began to wear ***a***,
9:12 to Him, "Send the multitude ***a***,
10:42 which will not be taken ***a*** from
11:52 For you have taken ***a*** the
13:15 and lead it ***a*** to water it?
16: 3 is taking the stewardship ***a***
16:17 for heaven and earth to pass ***a***
17:31 not come down to take them ***a***.
19:20 which I have kept put ***a*** in a
19:26 what he has will be taken ***a***
20:10 beat him and sent him ***a***
20:11 and sent him ***a*** empty-handed.
21:24 and be led ***a*** captive into all
21:32 will by no means pass ***a*** till
21:33 "Heaven and earth will pass ***a***,
21:33 words will by no means pass ***a***.
22:42 take this cup ***a*** from Me;
23:18 ***A*** with this Man, and release to
23:26 Now as they led Him ***a***,
24: 2 they found the stone rolled ***a***
Jn 1:29 The Lamb of God who takes ***a***
2:16 Take these things ***a***! Do not make
4: 8 For His disciples had gone ***a***
6:22 but His disciples had gone ***a***
6:67 "Do you also want to go ***a***?
8:21 to them again, "I am going ***a***,
10:40 And He went ***a*** again beyond the
11:18 Jerusalem, about two miles ***a***.
11:39 Take ***a*** the stone." Martha, the
11:41 Then they took ***a*** the stone from
11:46 But some of them went ***a*** to the
11:48 the Romans will come and take ***a***
12:11 of him many of the Jews went ***a***
14:28 I am going ***a*** and coming back to
15: 2 does not bear fruit He takes ***a***;
16: 5 But now I go ***a*** to Him who sent
16: 7 to your advantage that I go ***a***;
16: 7 I go away; for if I do not go ***a***,
18:13 And they led Him ***a*** to Annas
19:15 ***A*** with Him, away with Him!
19:15 ***a*** with Him! Crucify Him!"
19:16 they took Jesus and led Him ***a***.
19:31 and that they might be taken ***a***.
19:38 Pilate that he might take ***a***
20: 1 the stone had been taken ***a***
20: 2 They have taken ***a*** the Lord out
20:10 Then the disciples went ***a*** again
20:13 Because they have taken ***a*** my
20:15 if You have carried Him ***a***,
20:15 laid Him, and I will take Him ***a***.
Acts 3:26 in turning ***a*** every one of you
5:37 and drew ***a*** many people after
5:38 keep ***a*** from these men and let
7:21 Pharaoh's daughter took him ***a***
7:27 his neighbor wrong pushed him ***a***,
7:43 And I will carry you ***a***
8:33 His justice was taken ***a***,
8:39 of the Lord caught Philip ***a***,
10:23 On the next day Peter went ***a***
13: 3 on them, they sent them ***a***.
13: 8 to turn the proconsul ***a*** from
17:10 sent Paul and Silas ***a*** by night
17:14 the brethren sent Paul ***a***,
19:26 Paul has persuaded and turned ***a***
20: 6 But we sailed ***a*** from Philippi
20:30 to draw ***a*** the disciples after
21:36 crying out, "***A*** with him!"
22:16 and wash ***a*** your sins, calling
22:22 ***A*** with such a fellow from the
24:25 Go ***a*** for now; when I have a
27:32 Then the soldiers cut ***a*** the
27:42 lest any of them should swim ***a***
Rom 6: 6 the body of sin might be done ***a***
11: 1 has God cast ***a*** His people?
11: 2 God has not cast ***a*** His people
11:15 For if their being cast ***a*** is
11:26 And He will turn ***a***
11:27 When I take ***a*** their
1 Cor 5: 2 done this deed might be taken ***a***
5:13 put ***a*** from yourselves the
7:31 form of this world is passing ***a***.
12: 2 carried ***a*** to these dumb idols,
13: 8 is knowledge, it will vanish ***a***.
13:10 which is in part will be done ***a***.
13:11 I put ***a*** childish things.
2 Cor 3: 7 which glory was passing ***a***,
3:11 For if what is passing ***a*** was
3:13 the end of what was passing ***a***.
3:14 because the veil is taken ***a*** in
3:16 the Lord, the veil is taken ***a***.
5:17 old things have passed ***a***;
Gal 1: 6 marvel that you are turning ***a***
2:13 even Barnabas was carried ***a***
Eph 4:25 putting ***a*** lying, "Let each
4:31 and evil speaking be put ***a*** from
Col 1:23 and are not moved ***a*** from the
1 Th 2:17 having been taken ***a*** from you
2 Th 2: 3 not come unless the falling ***a***
2 Tim 1:15 all those in Asia have turned ***a***
3: 5 And from such people turn ***a***!
3: 6 led ***a*** by various lusts,
4: 4 they will turn their ears ***a***
Heb 2: 1 we have heard, lest we drift ***a***.
6: 6 if they fall ***a***, to renew them
8:13 old is ready to vanish ***a***.
9:26 He has appeared to put ***a*** sin by
10: 4 of bulls and goats could take ***a***
10: 9 He takes ***a*** the first that He
10:11 which can never take ***a*** sins.
10:35 Therefore do not cast ***a*** your
11: 5 By faith Enoch was taken ***a*** so
12:25 we not escape if we turn ***a***
Jas 1:10 of the field he will pass ***a***.
1:11 the rich man also will fade ***a***
1:14 is tempted when he is drawn ***a***
1:24 for he observes himself, goes ***a***,
4:14 little time and then vanishes ***a***.
1 Pe 1: 4 and that does not fade ***a***,
1:24 And its flower falls ***a***,
3:11 Let him turn ***a*** from evil
5: 4 of glory that does not fade ***a***.
2 Pe 3:10 which the heavens will pass ***a***
3:17 being led ***a*** with the error of
1 Jn 2: 8 the darkness is passing ***a***,
2:17 And the world is passing ***a***,
3: 5 He was manifested to take ***a***
Rev 7:17 And God will wipe ***a*** every tear
12:15 cause her to be carried ***a*** by
16:20 Then every island fled ***a***,
17: 3 So he carried me ***a*** in the Spirit
20:11 the earth and the heaven fled ***a***.
21: 1 the first earth had passed ***a***.
21: 4 And God will wipe ***a*** every tear
21: 4 the former things have passed ***a***.
21:10 And he carried me ***a*** in the
22:19 and if anyone takes ***a*** from the
22:19 God shall take ***a*** his part from

AWE (2/2) AWESOME

Ps 33: 8 of the world stand in ***a*** of Him.
119:161 But my heart stands in ***a*** of

AWESOME (38/38) AWE

Gen 28:17 How ***a*** is this place! This is
Ex 34:10 For it is an ***a*** thing that I
Deut 7:21 the great and ***a*** God, is among
10:17 the great God, mighty and ***a***,
10:21 done for you these great and ***a***
28:58 may fear this glorious and ***a***
Judg 13: 6 of the Angel of God, very ***a***;
2 Sam 7:23 to do for Yourself great and ***a***
1 Chr 17:21 Yourself a name by great and ***a***
Neh 1: 5 O great and ***a*** God, You who
4:14 Remember the Lord, great and ***a***,
9:32 and ***a*** God, Who keeps covenant
Job 10:16 And again You show Yourself ***a***
37:22 With God is ***a*** majesty.
Ps 45: 4 right hand shall teach You ***a***
47: 2 For the LORD Most High is ***a***;
65: 5 By ***a*** deeds in righteousness
66: 3 How ***a*** are Your works! Through
66: 5 He is ***a*** in His doing
68:35 You are more ***a*** than Your holy
76:12 He is ***a*** to the kings of the
99: 3 them praise Your great and ***a***
106:22 ***A*** things by the Red Sea.
111: 9 Holy and ***a*** is His name.
145: 6 speak of the might of Your ***a***
Song 6: 4 ***A*** as an army with banners!
6:10 ***A*** as an army with banners?
Isa 28:21 His ***a*** work, And bring to pass
64: 3 When You did ***a*** things for
Jer 20:11 ***a*** One. Therefore my
Lam 1: 9 Therefore her collapse was ***a***;
Ezek 1:18 they were so high they were ***a***;
1:22 was like the color of an ***a***
Dan 2:31 before you; and its form was ***a***.
9: 4 great and ***a*** God, who keeps His
Joel 2:31 the coming of the great and ***a***
Zeph 2:11 The LORD will be ***a*** to them,
Acts 2:20 of the great and ***a*** day

AWHILE (1/1)

1 Sam 9:27 went on. "But you stand here ***a***,

AWL (2/2)

Ex 21: 6 shall pierce his ear with an ***a***;
Deut 15:17 then you shall take an ***a*** and

AWOKE (15/15) AWAKE

Gen 9:24 So Noah ***a*** from his wine, and
28:16 Then Jacob ***a*** from his sleep and
41: 4 and fat cows. So Pharaoh ***a***.
41: 7 and full heads. So Pharaoh ***a***,
41:21 as at the beginning. So I ***a***.
Judg 16:14 Samson!" But he ***a*** from his
16:20 Samson!" So he ***a*** from his
1 Sam 26:12 no man saw it or knew it or ***a***.
1 Ki 3:15 Then Solomon ***a***; and indeed
Ps 3: 5 I lay down and slept; I ***a***,
78:65 Then the Lord ***a*** as from sleep,
Jer 31:26 After this I ***a*** and looked
Mt 8:25 disciples came to Him and ***a***
Mk 4:38 And they ***a*** Him and said to Him,
Lk 8:24 And they came to Him and ***a*** Him,

AWRY (1/1)

Prov 15:22 Without counsel, plans go ***a***,

AX (10/10) AXES

Deut 19: 5 swings a stroke with the ***a*** to
20:19 its trees by wielding an ***a***
Judg 9:48 And Abimelech took an ***a*** in his
1 Sam 13:20 plowshare, his mattock, his ***a***,
2 Ki 6: 5 the iron ***a*** head fell into the
Eccl 10:10 If the ***a*** is dull, And one does
Isa 10:15 Shall the ***a*** boast itself
Jer 10: 3 of the workman, with the ***a***.
Mt 3:10 And even now the ***a*** is laid to
Lk 3: 9 And even now the ***a*** is laid to

AXES (8/8) AX

1 Sam 13:21 mattocks, the forks, and the ***a***,
2 Sam 12:31 saws and iron picks and iron ***a***,
1 Chr 20: 3 with iron picks, and with ***a***.
2 Chr 34: 6 Naphtali and all around, with ***a***.
Ps 74: 5 seem like men who lift up ***A***
74: 6 With ***a*** and hammers.
Jer 46:22 And come against her with ***a***,
Ezek 26: 9 and with his ***a*** he will break

AXLE (1/1) AXLES

1 Ki 7:33 their ***a*** pins, their rims, their

AXLES (2/2) AXLE

1 Ki 7:30 had four bronze wheels and ***a***
7:32 and the ***a*** of the wheels were

AXLETREES (KJV) See AXLES

AYYAH (1/1)

1 Chr 7:28 as far as ***A*** and its towns;

AZAL (1/1)

Zech 14: 5 valley shall reach to ***A***.

AZALIAH (2/2)

2 Ki 22: 3 the scribe, the son of ***A***,
2 Chr 34: 8 he sent Shaphan the son of ***A***,

AZANIAH (1/1)

Neh 10: 9 Levites: Jeshua the son of ***A***,

AZARAEL, AZAREEL (KJV) See AZAREL

AZAREL (6/6)

1 Chr 12: 6 Elkanah, Jisshiah, ***A***,
25:18 the eleventh for ***A***,
27:22 ***A*** the son of Jeroham.
Ezra 10:41 ***A***, Shelemiah, Shemariah,
Neh 11:13 and Amashai the son of ***A***,
12:36 and his brethren, Shemaiah, ***A***,

AZARIAH (48/45) AHAZIAH, EZRA

1 Ki 4: 2 ***A*** the son of Zadok, the priest;
4: 5 ***A*** the son of Nathan, over the
2 Ki 14:21 all the people of Judah took ***A***,
15: 1 ***A*** the son of Amaziah, king of
15: 6 Now the rest of the acts of ***A***,
15: 7 So ***A*** rested with his fathers,
15: 8 In the thirty-eighth year of ***A***
15:17 In the thirty-ninth year of ***A***
15:23 In the fiftieth year of ***A*** king
15:27 In the fifty-second year of ***A***
1 Chr 2: 8 The son of Ethan was ***A***.
2:38 begot Jehu, and Jehu begot ***A***;
2:39 ***A*** begot Helez, and Helez begot
3:12 ***A*** his son, Jotham his son,
6: 9 Ahimaaz begot ***A***,
6: 9 and ***A*** begot Johanan;
6:10 Johanan begot ***A*** (it was he who
6:11 ***A*** begot Amariah, and Amariah
6:13 Hilkiah, and Hilkiah begot ***A***;
6:14 ***A*** begot Seraiah, and Seraiah
6:36 the son of Joel, the son of ***A***,
9:11 ***A*** the son of Hilkiah, the son of
2 Chr 15: 1 the Spirit of God came upon ***A***
21: 2 the sons of Jehoshaphat: ***A***,
22: 6 And ***A*** the son of Jehoram, king
23: 1 ***A*** the son of Jeroham, Ishmael
23: 1 ***A*** the son of Obed, Maaseiah the
26:17 So ***A*** the priest went in after
26:20 And ***A*** the chief priest and all
28:12 ***A*** the son of Johanan, Berechiah
29:12 of Amasai and Joel the son of ***A***,

29:12 Kish the son of Abdi and *A* the
31:10 And *A* the chief priest, from the
31:13 of Hezekiah the king and *A* the
Ezra 7: 1 son of Seraiah, the son of *A*,
7: 3 son of Amariah, the son of *A*,
Neh 3:23 After them *A* the son of
3:24 from the house of *A* to the
7: 7 were Jeshua, Nehemiah, *A*,
8: 7 Hodijah, Maaseiah, Kelita, *A*,
10: 2 Seraiah, *A*, Jeremiah,
12:33 and *A*, Ezra, Meshullam,
Jer 43: 2 that *A* the son of Hoshaiah,
Dan 1: 6 Hananiah, Mishael, and *A*.
1: 7 to Mishael, Meshach; and to *A*,
1:11 Hananiah, Mishael, and *A*,
1:19 Hananiah, Mishael, and *A*;
2:17 to Hananiah, Mishael, and *A*,

AZARYAHU (1/1)

2 Chr 21: 2 Azariah, Jehiel, Zechariah, *A*,

AZAZ (1/1)

1 Chr 5: 8 and Bela the son of *A*,

AZAZIAH (3/3)

1 Chr 15:21 Obed-Edom, Jeiel, and *A*,
27:20 of Ephraim, Hoshea the son of *A*;
2 Chr 31:13 Jehiel, *A*, Nahath, Asahel,

AZBUK (1/1)

Neh 3:16 After him Nehemiah the son of *A*,

AZEKAH (7/7)

Josh 10:10 struck them down as far as *A*
10:11 from heaven on them as far as *A*,
15:35 Jarmuth, Adullam, Socoh, *A*,
1 Sam 17: 1 encamped between Sochoh and *A*,
2 Chr 11: 9 Adoraim, Lachish, *A*,
Neh 11:30 in *A* and its villages.
Jer 34: 7 left, against Lachish and *A*;

AZEL (6/4)

1 Chr 8:37 and *A* his son.
8:38 *A* had six sons whose names were
8:38 All these were the sons of *A*.
9:43 and *A* his son.
9:44 And *A* had six sons whose names
9:44 these were the sons of *A*.

AZEM (KJV) See EZEM

AZGAD (4/4)

Ezra 2:12 the people of *A*, one thousand
8:12 of the sons of *A*, Johanan
Neh 7:17 the sons of *A*, two thousand
10:15 Bunni, *A*, Bebai,

AZIEL (1/1)

1 Chr 15:20 Zechariah, *A*, Shemiramoth,

AZIZA (1/1)

Ezra 10:27 Jeremoth, Zabad, and *A*;

AZMAVETH (8/8)

2 Sam 23:31 *A* the Barhumite,
1 Chr 8:36 Jehoaddah begot Alemeth, *A*,
9:42 Jarah; Jarah begot Alemeth, *A*,
11:33 *A* the Baharumite, Eliahba the
12: 3 Jeziel and Pelet the sons of *A*;
27:25 And *A* the son of Adiel was
Ezra 2:24 the people of *A*,
Neh 12:29 from the fields of Geba and *A*;

AZMON (3/3) HESHMON

Num 34: 4 Hazar Addar, and continue to *A*;
34: 5 the border shall turn from *A* to
Josh 15: 4 there it passed toward *A* and

AZNOTH TABOR (1/1)

Josh 19:34 border extended westward to *A*,

AZOR (2/2)

Mt 1:13 Eliakim, and Eliakim begot *A*.
1:14 *A* begot Zadok, Zadok begot

AZOTUS (1/1)

Acts 8:40 But Philip was found at *A*.

AZRIEL (3/3)

1 Chr 5:24 houses: Epher, Ishi, Eliel, *A*,
27:19 Naphtali, Jerimoth the son of *A*;
Jer 36:26 son, Seraiah the son of *A*,

AZRIKAM (6/6)

1 Chr 3:23 were Elioenai, Hezekiah, and *A*—
8:38 sons whose names were these: *A*,
9:14 son of Hasshub, the son of *A*,
9:44 sons whose names were these: *A*,
2 Chr 28: 7 *A* the officer over the house,
Neh 11:15 son of Hasshub, the son of *A*,

AZUBAH (4/4)

1 Ki 22:42 His mother's name was *A* the
1 Chr 2:18 son of Hezron had children by *A*,
2:19 When *A* died, Caleb took Ephrath
2 Chr 20:31 His mother's name was *A* the

AZUR (1/1) AZZUR

Jer 28: 1 that Hananiah the son of *A* the

AZZAH (KJV) See GAZA

AZZAN (1/1)

Num 34:26 Issachar, Paltiel the son of *A*;

AZZUR (2/2) AZUR

Neh 10:17 Ater, Hezekiah, *A*,
Ezek 11: 1 I saw Jaazaniah the son of *A*,

B

BAAL (67/55) BAAL'S, BAALS, BEL

Num 22:41 him up to the high places of *B*,
25: 3 So Israel was joined to *B* of
25: 5 his men who were joined to *B*
Deut 4: 3 you all the men who followed *B*
Judg 2:13 forsook the LORD and served *B*
6:25 and tear down the altar of *B*
6:28 there was the altar of *B*,
6:30 he has torn down the altar of *B*,
6:31 him, "Would you plead for *B*?
6:32 Let *B* plead against him, because
1 Ki 16:31 and he went and served *B* and
16:32 Then he set up an altar for *B* in
16:32 for Baal in the temple of *B*,
18:19 hundred and fifty prophets of *B*,
18:21 is God, follow Him; but if *B*,
18:25 said to the prophets of *B*,
18:26 and called on the name of *B*
18:26 even till noon, saying, "O *B*,
18:40 Seize the prophets of *B*! Do not
19:18 whose knees have not bowed to *B*,
22:53 for he served *B* and worshiped
2 Ki 3: 2 away the sacred pillar of *B*
10:18 Ahab served *B* a little, Jehu
10:19 to me all the prophets of *B*,
10:19 I have a great sacrifice for *B*.
10:19 destroying the worshipers of *B*.
10:20 a solemn assembly for *B*.
10:21 and all the worshipers of *B*
10:21 they came into the temple of *B*,
10:21 and the temple of *B* was full
10:22 for all the worshipers of *B*.
10:23 went into the temple of *B*,
10:23 and said to the worshipers of *B*,
10:23 but only the worshipers of *B*.
10:25 inner room of the temple of *B*.
10:26 pillars out of the temple of *B*
10:27 down the sacred pillar of *B*,
10:27 and tore down the temple of *B*
10:28 Thus Jehu destroyed *B* from
11:18 land went to the temple of *B*,
11:18 killed Mattan the priest of *B*
17:16 host of heaven, and served *B*.
21: 3 he raised up altars for *B*,
23: 4 articles that were made for *B*,
23: 5 those who burned incense to *B*,
1 Chr 4:33 around these cities as far as *B*.
5: 5 Reaiah his son, *B* his son,
8:30 was Abdon, then Zur, Kish, *B*,
9:36 was Abdon, then Zur, Kish, *B*,
2 Chr 23:17 people went to the temple of *B*,
23:17 killed Mattan the priest of *B*
Ps 106:28 joined themselves also to *B* of
Jer 2: 8 The prophets prophesied by *B*,
7: 9 falsely, burn incense to *B*,
11:13 altars to burn incense to *B*.
11:17 anger in offering incense to *B*.
12:16 taught My people to swear by *B*,
19: 5 also built the high places of *B*,
19: 5 fire for burnt offerings to *B*,
23:13 They prophesied by *B* And
23:27 fathers forgot My name for *B*.
32:29 they have offered incense to *B*
32:35 they built the high places of *B*
Hos 2: 8 they prepared for *B*.
13: 1 But when he offended through *B*
Zeph 1: 4 will cut off every trace of *B*
Rom 11: 4 not bowed the knee to *B*.

BAAL GAD (3/3)

Josh 11:17 even as far as *B* in the Valley
12: 7 from *B* in the Valley of Lebanon
13: 5 from *B* below Mount Hermon as

BAAL HAMON (1/1)

Song 8:11 Solomon had a vineyard at *B*;

BAAL HAZOR (1/1)

2 Sam 13:23 Absalom had sheepshearers in *B*,

BAAL HERMON (2/2)

Judg 3: 3 from Mount *B* to the entrance of
1 Chr 5:23 increased from Bashan to *B*,

BAAL MEON (3/3)

Num 32:38 Nebo and *B* (their names being
1 Chr 5: 8 in Aroer, as far as Nebo and *B*.
Ezek 25: 9 the country, Beth Jeshimoth, *B*,

BAAL PEOR (2/2)

Deut 4: 3 seen what the LORD did at *B*
Hos 9:10 But they went to *B* Peor, And

BAAL PERAZIM (4/2)

2 Sam 5:20 So David went to *B*,
5:20 called the name of that place *B*.
1 Chr 14:11 So they went up to *B*,
14:11 called the name of that place *B*.

BAAL SHALISHA (1/1)

2 Ki 4:42 Then a man came from *B*,

BAAL TAMAR (1/1)

Judg 20:33 themselves in battle array at *B*.

BAAL ZEPHON (3/3)

Ex 14: 2 Migdol and the sea, opposite *B*;
14: 9 beside Pi Hahiroth, before *B*.
Num 33: 7 Hahiroth, which is east of *B*;

BAAL-BERITH (2/2) BERITH

Judg 8:33 and made *B* their god.
9: 4 of silver from the temple of *B*,

BAAL-HANAN (5/5) HANAN

Gen 36:38 *B* the son of Achbor reigned in
36:39 And when *B* the son of Achbor
1 Chr 1:49 *B* the son of Achbor reigned in
1:50 And when *B* died, Hadad reigned
27:28 *B* the Gederite was over the

BAAL-ZEBUB (4/4) BEELZEBUB

2 Ki 1: 2 to them, "Go, inquire of *B*,
1: 3 you are going to inquire of *B*,
1: 6 you are sending to inquire of *B*,
1:16 sent messengers to inquire of *B*,

BAAL'S (1/1) BAAL

1 Ki 18:22 but *B* prophets are four

BAALAH (5/5) BILHAH

Josh 15: 9 And the border went around to *B*
15:10 border turned westward from *B*
15:11 passed along to Mount *B*,
15:29 *B*, Ijim, Ezem,
1 Chr 13: 6 and all Israel went up to *B*,

BAALATH (3/3)

Josh 19:44 Eltekeh, Gibbethon, *B*,
1 Ki 9:18 *B*, and Tadmor in the wilderness,
2 Chr 8: 6 also *B* and all the storage

BAALATH BEER (1/1)

Josh 19: 8 around these cities as far as *B*,

BAALE JUDAH (1/1)

2 Sam 6: 2 who were with him from *B* to

BAALI (KJV) See (MY) MASTER

BAALIM (KJV) See BAALS

BAALIS (1/1)

Jer 40:14 Do you certainly know that *B* the

BAALS (18/18) BAAL

Judg 2:11 of the LORD, and served the *B*;
3: 7 and served the *B* and Asherahs.
8:33 played the harlot with the *B*,
10: 6 and served the *B* and the
10:10 our God and served the *B*!"
1 Sam 7: 4 of Israel put away the *B* and
12:10 the LORD and served the *B* and
1 Ki 18:18 LORD and have followed the *B*.
2 Chr 17: 3 David; he did not seek the *B*,
24: 7 the house of the LORD to the *B*.
28: 2 made molded images for the *B*.
33: 3 he raised up altars for the *B*,
34: 4 broke down the altars of the *B*
Jer 2:23 I have not gone after the *B*'?
9:14 own hearts and after the *B*,
Hos 2:13 her For the days of the *B* to
2:17 her mouth the names of the *B*,
11: 2 them; They sacrificed to the *B*,

BAANA (2/2) BAANAH

1 Ki 4:12 **B** the son of Ahilud, in
Neh 3: 4 Next to them Zadok the son of **B**

BAANAH (10/10) BAANA

2 Sam 4: 2 The name of one was **B** and the
4: 5 the Beerothite, Rechab and **B**,
4: 6 Then Rechab and **B** his brother
4: 9 David answered Rechab and **B**
23:29 Heleb the son of **B** (the
1 Ki 4:16 **B** the son of Hushai, in Asher
1 Chr 11:30 Heled the son of **B** the
Ezra 2: 2 Mispar, Bigvai, Rehum, and **B**.
Neh 7: 7 Mispereth, Bigvai, Nehum, and **B**.
10:27 Malluch, Harim, and **B**.

BAARA (1/1)

1 Chr 8: 8 he had sent away Hushim and **B**

BAASEIAH (1/1)

1 Chr 6:40 son of Michael, the son of **B**,

BAASHA (28/26)

1 Ki 15:16 was war between Asa and **B** king
15:17 And **B** king of Israel came up
15:19 and break your treaty with **B**
15:21 when **B** heard it, that he
15:22 which **B** had used for building;
15:27 Then **B** the son of Ahijah, of the
15:27 And **B** killed him at Gibbethon,
15:28 **B** killed him in the third year
15:32 was war between Asa and **B** king
15:33 **B** the son of Ahijah became king
16: 1 the son of Hanani, against **B**,
16: 3 take away the posterity of **B**
16: 4 shall eat whoever belongs to **B**
16: 5 Now the rest of the acts of **B**,
16: 6 So **B** rested with his fathers and
16: 7 the son of Hanani against **B**
16: 8 Elah the son of **B** became king
16:11 killed all the household of **B**;
16:12 all the household of **B**,
16:12 which He spoke against **B** by
16:13 for all the sins of **B** and the
21:22 and like the house of **B** the son
2 Ki 9: 9 and like the house of **B** the son
2 Chr 16: 1 **B** king of Israel came up
16: 3 break your treaty with **B** king
16: 5 when **B** heard it, that he
16: 6 which **B** had used for building;
Jer 41: 9 the king had made for fear of **B**

BABBLE (1/1) BABBLER, BABBLERS, BABBLINGS

2 Ki 9:11 "You know the man and his **b**.

BABBLER (2/2)

Eccl 10:11 The **b** is no different.
Acts 17:18 What does this **b** want to say?"

BABBLERS (1/1) BABBLER

Isa 44:25 frustrates the signs of the **b**,

BABBLINGS (2/2) BABBLE

1 Tim 6:20 the profane and idle **b** and
2 Tim 2:16 But shun profane and idle **b**,

BABE (5/5) BABES, BABIES, BABY

Lk 1:41 that the **b** leaped in her womb;
1:44 the **b** leaped in my womb for
2:12 You will find a **B** wrapped in
2:16 and the **B** lying in a manger.
Heb 5:13 of righteousness, for he is a **b**.

BABEL (2/2) BABYLON

Gen 10:10 beginning of his kingdom was **B**,
11: 9 Therefore its name is called **B**,

BABES (11/11) BABE

Ps 8: 2 Out of the mouth of **b** and
17:14 their possession for their **b**.
Isa 3: 4 And **b** shall rule over them.
Joel 2:16 the children and nursing **b**;
Mt 11:25 and have revealed them to **b**.
21:16 Out of the mouth of **b** and
Lk 10:21 prudent and revealed them to **b**.
Rom 2:20 of the foolish, a teacher of **b**,
1 Cor 3: 1 to carnal, as to **b** in Christ.
14:20 however, in malice be **b**,
1 Pe 2: 2 as newborn **b**, desire the pure

BABIES (4/4) BABY

Mt 24:19 and to those who are nursing **b**
Mk 13:17 and to those who are nursing **b**
Lk 21:23 and to those who are nursing **b**
Acts 7:19 making them expose their **b**,

BABY (1/1) BABE

Ex 2: 6 the **b** wept. So she had

BABYLON (287/253) BABEL, BABYLONIAN, BABYLON'S, CHALDEA, SHESHACH

2 Ki 17:24 Assyria brought people from **B**,
17:30 The men of **B** made Succoth
20:12 the son of Baladan, king of **B**,
20:14 came from a far country, from **B**.
20:17 this day, shall be carried to **B**;
20:18 in the palace of the king of **B**.
24: 1 days Nebuchadnezzar king of **B**
24: 7 for the king of **B** had taken all
24:10 of Nebuchadnezzar king of **B**
24:11 And Nebuchadnezzar king of **B**
24:12 went out to the king of **B**;
24:12 of Babylon; and the king of **B**,
24:15 carried Jehoiachin captive to **B**.
24:15 captivity from Jerusalem to **B**.
24:16 these the king of **B** brought
24:16 of Babylon brought captive to **B**.
24:17 Then the king of **B** made
24:20 rebelled against the king of **B**.
25: 1 that Nebuchadnezzar king of **B**
25: 6 him up to the king of **B** at
25: 7 fetters, and took him to **B**.
25: 8 King Nebuchadnezzar king of **B**),
25: 8 a servant of the king of **B**,
25:11 had deserted to the king of **B**,
25:13 and carried their bronze to **B**.
25:20 brought them to the king of **B**
25:21 Then the king of **B** struck them
25:22 whom Nebuchadnezzar king of **B**
25:23 heard that the king of **B** had
25:24 land and serve the king of **B**,
25:27 that Evil-Merodach king of **B**,
25:28 kings who were with him in **B**.
1 Chr 9: 1 was carried away captive to **B**
2 Chr 32:31 ambassadors of the princes of **B**,
33:11 and carried him off to **B**.
36: 6 Nebuchadnezzar king of **B** came up
36: 6 fetters to carry him off to **B**.
36: 7 the house of the LORD to **B**,
36: 7 and put them in his temple at **B**.
36:10 summoned him and took him to **B**,
36:18 all these he took to **B**.
36:20 the sword he carried away to **B**,
Ezra 1:11 who were brought from **B** to
2: 1 Nebuchadnezzar the king of **B**
2: 1 Babylon had carried away to **B**,
4: 9 of Persia and Erech and **B** and
5:12 of Nebuchadnezzar king of **B**,
5:12 carried the people away to **B**.
5:13 first year of Cyrus king of **B**,
5:14 carried into the temple of **B**—
5:14 Cyrus took from the temple of **B**,
5:17 house, which is there in **B**,
6: 1 the treasures were stored in **B**.
6: 5 in Jerusalem and brought to **B**,
7: 6 this Ezra came up from **B**;
7: 9 he began his journey from **B**,
7:16 find in all the province of **B**,
8: 1 who went up with me from **B**,
Neh 7: 6 Nebuchadnezzar the king of **B**
13: 6 year of Artaxerxes king of **B** I
Esth 2: 6 Nebuchadnezzar the king of **B**
Ps 87: 4 make mention of Rahab and **B** to
137: 1 By the rivers of **B**,
137: 8 O daughter of **B**, who are to be
Isa 13: 1 The burden against **B** which
13:19 And **B**, the glory of kingdoms,
14: 4 proverb against the king of **B**,
14:22 And cut off from **B** the name and
21: 9 **B** is fallen, is fallen! And all
39: 1 the son of Baladan, king of **B**,
39: 3 me from a far country, from **B**.
39: 6 this day, shall be carried to **B**;
39: 7 in the palace of the king of **B**.
43:14 your sake I will send to **B**,
47: 1 dust, O virgin daughter of **B**;
48:14 He shall do His pleasure on **B**,
48:20 Go forth from **B**! Flee from
Jer 20: 4 into the hand of the king of **B**,
20: 4 shall carry them captive to **B**
20: 5 seize them, and carry them to **B**.
20: 6 captivity. You shall go to **B**,
21: 2 for Nebuchadnezzar king of **B**
21: 4 you fight against the king of **B**
21: 7 of Nebuchadnezzar king of **B**,
21:10 into the hand of the king of **B**,
22:25 of Nebuchadnezzar king of **B**
24: 1 after Nebuchadnezzar king of **B**
24: 1 and had brought them to **B**.
25: 1 of Nebuchadnezzar king of **B**),
25: 9 Nebuchadnezzar the king of **B**,
25:11 shall serve the king of **B**
25:12 I will punish the king of **B**
27: 6 of Nebuchadnezzar the king of **B**,
27: 8 Nebuchadnezzar the king of **B**,
27: 8 under the yoke of the king of **B**,
27: 9 shall not serve the king of **B**.
27:11 the yoke of the king of **B** and
27:12 under the yoke of the king of **B**,
27:13 will not serve the king of **B**?
27:14 shall not serve the king of **B**,
27:16 shortly be brought back from **B**'
27:17 to them; serve the king of **B**,
27:18 at Jerusalem, do not go to **B**.
27:20 Nebuchadnezzar king of **B**
27:20 of Judah, from Jerusalem to **B**,
27:22 'They shall be carried to **B**,
28: 2 the yoke of the king of **B**.
28: 3 that Nebuchadnezzar king of **B**
28: 3 this place and carried to **B**.
28: 4 captives of Judah who went to **B**,
28: 4 break the yoke of the king of **B**.
28: 6 from **B** to this place.
28:11 of Nebuchadnezzar king of **B**
28:14 serve Nebuchadnezzar king of **B**;
29: 1 captive from Jerusalem to **B**.
29: 3 king of Judah sent to **B**,
29: 3 to Nebuchadnezzar king of **B**,
29: 4 away from Jerusalem to **B**:
29:10 years are completed at **B**,
29:15 raised up prophets for us in **B**'
29:20 I have sent from Jerusalem to **B**.
29:21 of Nebuchadnezzar king of **B**,
29:22 of Judah who are in **B**,
29:22 whom the king of **B** roasted in
29:28 For he has sent to us in **B**,
32: 3 into the hand of the king of **B**,
32: 4 into the hand of the king of **B**,
32: 5 he shall lead Zedekiah to **B**,
32:28 of Nebuchadnezzar king of **B**,
32:36 into the hand of the king of **B**
34: 1 when Nebuchadnezzar king of **B**
34: 2 into the hand of the king of **B**,
34: 3 see the eyes of the king of **B**,
34: 3 to face, and you shall go to **B**.
35:11 when Nebuchadnezzar king of **B**
36:29 in it that the king of **B** will
37: 1 whom Nebuchadnezzar king of **B**
37:17 into the hand of the king of **B**!
37:19 The king of **B** will not come
38:23 by the hand of the king of **B**.
39: 1 Nebuchadnezzar king of **B** and
39: 3 the princes of the king of **B**
39: 3 of the princes of the king of **B**.
39: 5 up to Nebuchadnezzar king of **B**,
39: 6 Then the king of **B** killed the
39: 6 the king of **B** also killed all
39: 7 fetters to carry him off to **B**.
39: 9 carried away captive to **B** the
39:11 Now Nebuchadnezzar king of **B**
40: 1 were carried away captive to **B**.
40: 4 to you to come with me to **B**,
40: 4 for you to come with me to **B**,
40: 5 whom the king of **B** has made
40: 7 heard that the king of **B** had
40: 7 been carried away captive to **B**,
40: 9 land and serve the king of **B**,
40:11 heard that the king of **B** had
41: 2 killed him whom the king of **B**
41:18 whom the king of **B** had made
42:11 not be afraid of the king of **B**,
43: 3 or carry us away captive to **B**.
43:10 Nebuchadnezzar the king of **B**,
44:30 of Nebuchadnezzar king of **B**,
46: 2 which Nebuchadnezzar king of **B**
46:13 how Nebuchadnezzar king of **B**
46:26 of Nebuchadnezzar king of **B**
49:28 which Nebuchadnezzar king of **B**
49:30 For Nebuchadnezzar king of **B** has
50: 1 that the LORD spoke against **B**
50: 2 **B** is taken, Bel is shamed.
50: 8 "Move from the midst of **B**,
50: 9 and cause to come up against **B**
50:13 Everyone who goes by **B** shall
50:14 yourselves in array against **B**
50:16 Cut off the sower from **B**,
50:17 this Nebuchadnezzar king of **B**
50:18 I will punish the king of **B** and
50:23 cut apart and broken! How **B**
50:24 have indeed been trapped, O **B**,
50:28 and escape from the land of **B**
50:29 together the archers against **B**.
50:34 disquiet the inhabitants of **B**.
50:35 "Against the inhabitants of **B**,
50:42 Against you, O daughter of **B**.
50:43 The king of **B** has heard the
50:45 that He has taken against **B**,
50:46 the noise of the taking of **B**
51: 1 I will raise up against **B**,
51: 2 And I will send winnowers to **B**,
51: 6 Flee from the midst of **B**,
51: 7 **B** was a golden cup in the
51: 8 **B** has suddenly fallen and been
51: 9 We would have healed **B**,
51:11 For His plan is against **B** to
51:12 the standard on the walls of **B**;
51:12 against the inhabitants of **B**.
51:24 And I will repay **B** And all the
51:29 shall be performed against **B**,
51:29 To make the land of **B** a
51:30 The mighty men of **B** have ceased
51:31 To show the king of **B** that his
51:33 The daughter of **B** is like a
51:34 Nebuchadnezzar the king of **B**
51:35 to me and my flesh be upon **B**,
51:37 **B** shall become a heap, A
51:41 How **B** has become desolate among
51:42 The sea has come up over **B**;
51:44 I will punish Bel in **B**,
51:44 the wall of **B** shall fall.
51:47 on the carved images of **B**;
51:48 Shall sing joyously over **B**;
51:49 As **B** has caused the slain of
51:49 So at **B** the slain of all the
51:53 Though **B** were to mount up to
51:54 sound of a cry comes from **B**,
51:55 the LORD is plundering **B** And
51:56 comes against her, against **B**,
51:58 The broad walls of **B** shall be
51:59 the king of Judah to **B** in the

51:60 the evil that would come upon **B**,
51:60 that are written against **B**.
51:61 When you arrive in **B** and see it,
51:64 Thus **B** shall sink and not rise
52: 3 rebelled against the king of **B**.
52: 4 that Nebuchadnezzar king of **B**
52: 9 him up to the king of **B** at
52:10 Then the king of **B** killed the
52:11 and the king of **B** bound him in
52:11 bronze fetters, took him to **B**,
52:12 King Nebuchadnezzar king of **B**),
52:12 who served the king of **B**,
52:15 had deserted to the king of **B**,
52:17 carried all their bronze to **B**.
52:26 brought them to the king of **B**
52:27 Then the king of **B** struck them
52:31 that Evil-Merodach king of **B**,
52:32 kings who were with him in **B**.
52:34 given him by the king of **B**,
Ezek 12:13 My snare. I will bring him to **B**,
17:12 Indeed the king of **B** went to
17:12 and led them with him to **B**.
17:16 with him in the midst of **B** he
17:20 I will bring him to **B** and try
19: 9 brought him to the king of **B**;
21:19 for the sword of the king of **B**
21:21 For the king of **B** stands at the
24: 2 the king of **B** started his siege
26: 7 north Nebuchadnezzar king of **B**,
29:18 Nebuchadnezzar king of **B** caused
29:19 to Nebuchadnezzar king of **B**;
30:10 of Nebuchadnezzar king of **B**.
30:24 the arms of the king of **B** and
30:25 the arms of the king of **B**,
30:25 into the hand of the king of **B**
32:11 The sword of the king of **B** shall
Dan 1: 1 Nebuchadnezzar king of **B** came
2:12 destroy all the wise men of **B**.
2:14 out to kill the wise men of **B**;
2:18 the rest of the wise men of **B**.
2:24 to destroy the wise men of **B**.
2:24 not destroy the wise men of **B**;
2:48 over the whole province of **B**,
2:48 over all the wise men of **B**.
2:49 affairs of the province of **B**;
3: 1 of Dura, in the province of **B**.
3:12 affairs of the province of **B**:
3:30 Abed-Nego in the province of **B**.
4: 6 bring in all the wise men of **B**
4:29 about the royal palace of **B**.
4:30 saying, "Is not this great **B**,
5: 7 saying to the wise men of **B**,
7: 1 year of Belshazzar king of **B**,
Mic 4:10 And to **B** you shall go.
Zech 2: 7 dwell with the daughter of **B**.
6:10 Jedaiah, who have come from **B**—
Mt 1:11 they were carried away to **B**.
1:12 after they were brought to **B**,
1:17 David until the captivity in **B**
1:17 and from the captivity in **B**
Acts 7:43 carry you away beyond **B**.
1 Pe 5:13 She who is in **B**, elect together
Rev 14: 8 **B** is fallen, is fallen, that
16:19 And great **B** was remembered
17: 5 **B** THE GREAT, THE MOTHER OF
18: 2 **B** the great is fallen, is
18:10 'Alas, alas, that great city **B**,
18:21 with violence the great city **B**

BABYLON'S (8/8) BABYLON

Jer 32: 2 For then the king of **B** army
34: 7 when the king of **B** army fought
34:21 into the hand of the king of **B**
38: 3 into the hand of the king of **B**
38:17 surrender to the king of **B**
38:18 not surrender to the king of **B**
38:22 surrendered to the king of **B**
39:13 and all the king of **B** chief

BABYLONIAN (1/1) BABYLON, BABYLONIANS

Josh 7:21 among the spoils a beautiful **B**

BABYLONIANS (3/3) BABYLONIAN

Ezek 23:15 In the manner of the **B** of
23:17 Then the **B** came to her, into the
23:23 The **B**, All the Chaldeans,

BABYLONISH (KJV) See BABYLONIAN

BACA (1/1)

Ps 84: 6 pass through the Valley of **B**,

BACHRITES (1/1) BECHER

Num 26:35 of Becher, the family of the **B**;

BACK (408/396) BACKBITE, BACKBONE, BACKSLIDING, BACKWARD

Gen 14: 7 Then they turned **b** and came to
14:16 So he brought **b** all the goods,
14:16 and also brought **b** his brother
19: 9 Stand **b**!" Then they said,
19:26 But his wife looked **b** behind
22: 5 and we will come **b** to you."
24: 5 Must I take your son **b** to the
24: 6 that you do not take my son **b**
24: 8 only do not take my son **b**
24:20 ran **b** to the well to draw
28:15 and will bring you **b** to this
28:21 so that I come **b** to my father's
29: 3 and put the stone **b** in its
37:14 and bring **b** word to me." So he
37:22 and bring him **b** to his father.
38:29 as he drew **b** his hand, that his
39: 9 nor has he kept **b** anything from
42:37 sons if I do not bring him **b**
42:37 and I will bring him **b** to
43: 2 father said to them, "Go **b**,
43: 9 If I do not bring him **b** to you
43:12 and take **b** in your hand the
43:13 and arise, go **b** to the man.
43:21 so we have brought it **b** in our
44: 8 we brought **b** to you from the
44:25 Go **b** and buy us a little food.'
44:32 If I do not bring him **b** to you,
48:21 be with you and bring you **b** to
50: 5 my father, and I will come **b**.
Ex 3: 1 And he led the flock to the **b**
4:21 When you go **b** to Egypt, see that
5: 4 Get **b** to your labor."
10:24 flocks and your herds be kept **b**.
14:21 LORD caused the sea to go **b**
14:26 that the waters may come **b** upon
15:19 and the LORD brought **b** the
18: 2 wife, after he had sent her **b**,
19: 8 So Moses brought **b** the words
23: 4 you shall surely bring it **b** to
24:14 here for us until we come **b** to
26:12 shall hang over the **b** of the
26:23 make two boards for the two **b**
29:25 You shall receive them **b** from
33:23 My hand, and you shall see My **b**;
36:28 made two boards for the two **b**
Lev 14:43 Now if the plague comes **b** and
26:26 and they shall bring **b** your
Num 13:26 Now they departed and came **b** to
13:26 they brought **b** word to them and
14:45 and drove them **b** as far as
17:10 Bring Aaron's rod **b** before the
22: 8 and I will bring **b** word to you,
22:13 Go **b** to your land, for the LORD
22:23 the donkey to turn her **b** onto
22:34 displeases You, I will turn **b**.
23:16 Go **b** to Balak, and thus you
24:11 the LORD has kept you **b** from
25:11 has turned **b** My wrath from the
33: 7 moved from Etham and turned **b**
Deut 1:22 and bring **b** word to us of the
1:25 and they brought **b** word to us,
1:44 and drove you **b** from Seir to
22: 1 shall certainly bring them **b**
23:15 You shall not give **b** to his
24: 4 her must not take her **b** to be
24:19 you shall not go **b** to get it;
28:60 Moreover He will bring **b** on you
28:68 And the LORD will take you **b** to
30: 3 your God will bring you **b** from
Josh 7: 8 I say when Israel turns its **b**
8:20 to the wilderness turned **b** on
8:21 they turned **b** and struck down
8:26 For Joshua did not draw **b** his
11:10 Joshua turned **b** at that time
14: 7 and I brought **b** word to him as
18: 4 inheritance, and come **b** to me.
18: 8 and come **b** to me, that I may
22:32 and brought **b** word to them.
23:12 else, if indeed you do go **b**,
Judg 3:19 But he himself turned **b** from the
6:18 "I will wait until you come **b**.
8: 9 When I come **b** in peace, I will
11: 9 If you take me **b** home to fight
11:35 and I cannot go **b** on it."
14:19 and he went **b** up to his
18: 8 Then the spies came **b** to their
18:26 he turned and went **b** to his
19: 3 kindly to her and bring her **b**,
20: 8 nor will any turn **b** to his
20:41 when the men of Israel turned **b**,
20:48 And the men of Israel turned **b**
21:14 So Benjamin came **b** at that time,
Ruth 1:11 But Naomi said, "Turn **b**,
1:12 'Turn **b**, my daughters, go—for
1:15 your sister-in-law has gone **b**
1:16 Or to turn **b** from following
2: 6 young Moabite woman who came **b**
2:14 was satisfied, and kept some **b**.
2:18 gave to her what she had kept **b**
4: 3 who has come **b** from the country
4: 4 Buy it **b** in the presence of the
1 Sam 5:11 and let it go **b** to its own
6:21 Philistines have brought **b**
7:11 and drove them **b** as far as
9:24 "Here it is, what was kept **b**.
10: 9 when he had turned his **b** to go
14:31 Now they had driven **b** the
15:11 for he has turned **b** from
15:20 and brought **b** Agag king of
15:31 So Samuel turned **b** after Saul,
17:18 and bring **b** news of them."
19:15 Saul sent the messengers **b** to
20:38 up the arrows and came **b** to
23:23 and come **b** to me with
25:12 on their heels and went **b**;
25:26 since the LORD has held you **b**
25:34 who has kept me **b** from hurting
29: 4 that he may go **b** to the place
30:12 his strength came **b** to him; for
2 Sam 1:22 bow of Jonathan did not turn **b**,
2:23 the spear came out of his **b**;
3:26 who brought him **b** from the well
5:25 and he drove **b** the Philistines
11:23 then we drove them **b** as far as
12:23 Can I bring him **b** again?
14:21 bring **b** the young man
15: 8 the LORD indeed brings me **b**
15:20 and take your brethren **b**.
15:25 Carry the ark of God **b** into the
15:25 He will bring me **b** and show me
15:29 carried the ark of God **b** to
17: 3 Then I will bring **b** all the
18:16 For Joab held **b** the people.
19: 3 And the people stole **b** into the
19:10 say nothing about bringing **b**
19:11 the last to bring the king **b**
19:12 are you the last to bring **b**
19:30 as my lord the king has come **b**
19:37 let your servant turn **b**
19:43 the first to advise bringing **b**
22:38 Neither did I turn **b** again
24:13 what answer I should take **b** to
1 Ki 2:30 And Benaiah brought **b** word to
2:41 to Gath and had come **b**.
7:25 and all their **b** parts pointed
8:33 and when they turn **b** to You and
8:34 and bring them **b** to the land
10:19 the throne was round at the **b**;
12: 5 then come **b** to me." And the
12:12 Come **b** to me the third day."
12:20 heard that Jeroboam had come **b**,
12:24 word of the LORD, and turned **b**,
12:27 of this people will turn **b** to
12:27 and they will kill me and go **b**
13: 4 so that he could not pull it **b**
13:18 Bring him **b** with you to your
13:19 So he went **b** with him, and ate
13:20 prophet who had brought him **b**;
13:22 'but you came **b**, ate bread,
13:23 prophet whom he had brought **b**.
13:26 prophet who had brought him **b**
13:29 on the donkey, and brought it **b**.
14: 9 and have cast Me behind your **b**—
14:28 then brought them **b** into the
17:21 let this child's soul come **b** to
17:22 the soul of the child came **b**
18:37 You have turned their hearts **b**
19: 7 the angel of the LORD came **b**
19:20 Go **b** again, for what have I done
19:21 So Elisha turned **b** from him,
20: 5 Then the messengers came **b** and
20: 9 departed and brought **b** word to
22:33 that they turned **b** from
2 Ki 1: 5 to them, "Why have you come **b**?
2:13 and went **b** and stood by the
2:18 And when they came **b** to him, for
4:22 to the man of God and come **b**.
4:31 Therefore he went **b** to meet
4:35 He returned and walked **b** and
5: 2 and had brought **b** captive a
5:26 you when the man turned **b**
7: 8 then they came **b** and entered
8:29 Then King Joram went **b** to
9:18 to them, but is not coming **b**.
9:20 up to them and is not coming **b**;
9:36 Therefore they came **b** and told
15:20 So the king of Assyria turned **b**,
16:11 it before King Ahaz came **b**
16:12 And when the king came **b** from
19:21 shaken her head behind your **b**!
19:28 And I will turn you **b** By the
22:20 So they brought **b** word
1 Chr 13: 3 us bring the ark of our God **b**
14:16 and they drove **b** the army of
21:12 what answer I should take **b** to
2 Chr 4: 4 and all their **b** parts pointed
6:25 and bring them **b** to the land
10: 5 Come **b** to me after three days."
10:12 Come **b** to me the third day."
11: 4 and turned **b** from attacking
12:11 then they would take them **b**
18:32 that they turned **b** from
19: 4 and brought them **b** to the LORD
20:27 to go **b** to Jerusalem with joy,
24:19 to bring them **b** to the LORD;
25:10 to go **b** home. Therefore their
30: 9 so that they may come **b** to this
33:13 and brought him **b** to Jerusalem
34: 9 and which they had brought **b**
34:28 So they brought **b** word
Ezra 2: 1 of the province who came **b**
6: 5 be restored and taken **b** to the
Neh 2:15 then I turned **b** and entered by
7: 6 of the province who came **b**
9:29 That You might bring them **b** to
13: 9 and I brought **b** into them the
13:10 who did the work had gone **b** to
Esth 6:12 Afterward Mordecai went **b** to
Job 1: 7 and from walking **b** and forth on
2: 2 and from walking **b** and forth on
17:10 come **b** again, all of you, For
33:18 He keeps **b** his soul from the
33:30 To bring **b** his soul from the
34:27 Because they turned **b** from Him,
39:22 Nor does he turn **b** from the
Ps 6:10 Let them turn **b** and be
7:12 If he does not turn **b**,
9: 3 When my enemies turn **b**,
14: 7 When the LORD brings **b** the
18:37 Neither did I turn **b** again
19:13 Keep **b** Your servant also from
21:12 You will make them turn their **b**;

35: 4 Let those be turned **b** and
44:10 You make us turn **b** from the
44:18 Our heart has not turned **b**,
53: 6 out of Zion! When God brings **b**
56: 9 Then my enemies will turn **b**;
68:22 I will bring **b** from Bashan, I
68:22 I will bring them **b** from the
70: 2 Let them be turned **b** and
70: 3 Let them be turned **b** because of
78: 9 Turned **b** in the day of battle.
78:57 But turned **b** and acted
78:66 And He beat **b** His enemies; He
80:18 Then we will not turn **b** from
85: 1 You have brought **b** the
85: 8 But let them not turn **b** to
89:43 You have also turned **b** the edge
114: 3 it and fled; Jordan turned **b**.
114: 5 O Jordan, that you turned **b**?
126: 1 When the LORD brought **b** the
126: 4 Bring **b** our captivity, O LORD,
129: 3 The plowers plowed on my **b**;
129: 5 Be put to shame and turned **b**.
Prov 3:28 neighbor, "Go, and come **b**,
10:13 But a rod is for the **b** of him
17:23 accepts a bribe behind the **b**
19:17 And He will pay **b** what he has
21:14 And a bribe behind the **b**,
24:11 And hold **b** those stumbling to
26: 3 And a rod for the fool's **b**.
26:15 It wearies him to bring it **b**
26:27 a stone will have it roll **b** on
29:11 But a wise man holds them **b**.
Isa 14:27 out, And who will turn it **b**?
21:12 Return! Come **b**!"
28: 6 strength to those who turn **b**
31: 2 And will not call **b** His words,
37:22 shaken her head behind your **b**!
37:29 And I will turn you **b** By the
38:17 cast all my sins behind Your **b**.
42:17 They shall be turned **b**,
43: 6 Do not keep them **b**!' Bring My
49: 5 To bring Jacob **b** to Him, So
50: 6 I gave My **b** to those who struck
52: 8 to eye When the LORD brings **b**
59:14 Justice is turned **b**,
Jer 2:27 For they have turned their **b**
4: 8 of the LORD Has not turned **b**
4:24 And all the hills moved **b** and
4:28 Nor will I turn **b** from it.
6: 9 put your hand **b** into the
8: 5 Why has this people slidden **b**,
11:10 They have turned **b** to the
12:15 on them and bring them **b**,
15:19 Then I will bring you **b**,
16:15 For I will bring them **b** into
18:17 I will show them the **b** and not
20: 9 I was weary of holding it **b**,
21: 4 I will turn **b** the weapons of
23: 3 and bring them **b** to their
23:14 So that no one turns **b** from
23:20 of the LORD will not turn **b**
24: 6 and I will bring them **b** to this
27:16 will now shortly be brought **b**
28: 3 two full years I will bring **b**
28: 4 And I will bring **b** to this place
28: 6 to bring **b** the vessels of the
29:14 and I will bring you **b** from
30: 3 that I will bring **b** from
30:18 I will bring **b** the captivity of
31:16 And they shall come **b** from the
31:17 your children shall come **b** to
31:21 way in which you went. Turn **b**,
31:21 Turn **b** to these your cities.
31:23 when I bring **b** their captivity:
32:33 they have turned to Me the **b**,
32:37 I will bring them **b** to this
34:16 and every one of you brought **b**
34:16 and brought them **b** into
34:21 army which has gone **b** from you.
37: 8 the Chaldeans shall come **b**
40: 5 Jeremiah had not yet gone **b**,
40: 5 Go **b** to Gedaliah the son of
41:14 Mizpah turned around and came **b**,
41:16 whom he had brought **b** from
42: 4 I will keep nothing **b** from
46: 5 them dismayed and turned **b**?
46: 5 fled, And did not look **b**,
46:16 Arise! Let us go **b** to our own
46:21 For they also are turned **b**,
47: 3 The fathers will not look **b**
48:10 And cursed is he who keeps **b**
48:39 How Moab has turned her **b**
48:47 Yet I will bring **b** the captives
49: 6 But afterward I will bring **b**
49: 8 Flee, turn **b**, dwell in the
49:39 I will bring **b** the captives of
50:19 But I will bring **b** Israel to
Lam 1:13 for my feet And turned me **b**;
2: 3 He has drawn **b** His right hand
2:14 To bring **b** your captives, But
3:40 And turn **b** to the LORD;
5:21 Turn us **b** to You, O LORD, and
Ezek 1:13 appearance of torches going **b**
1:14 And the living creatures ran **b**
7:13 And it shall not turn **b**;
9:11 reported **b** and said, "I have
10:12 their whole body, with their **b**,
16:53 When I bring **b** their captives,
16:53 then I will also bring **b**
23:35 Me and cast Me behind your **b**,
24:14 will do it; I will not hold **b**,
27:19 traversing **b** and forth.
28:14 You walked **b** and forth in the
29:14 I will bring **b** the captives of
31:15 the great waters were held **b**.
33:15 gives **b** what he has stolen, and
34: 4 nor brought **b** what was driven
34:16 seek what was lost and bring **b**
38: 8 the land of those brought **b**
39:25 Now I will bring **b** the captives
39:27 When I have brought them **b** from
39:28 but also brought them **b** to
44: 1 Then He brought me **b** to the
47: 1 Then he brought me **b** to the door
Dan 7: 6 which had on its **b** four wings
11:18 he shall turn **b** on him.
Hos 2: 9 And will take **b** My wool and My
Joel 2:20 the eastern sea And his **b**
3: 1 When I bring **b** the captives of
Am 9:14 I will bring **b** the captives of
Nah 2: 8 they cry; But no one turns **b**.
Zeph 1: 6 Those who have turned **b** from
3:20 that time I will bring you **b**,
Zech 4: 1 who talked with me came **b** and
8: 8 I will bring them **b**,
10: 6 of Joseph. I will bring them **b**,
10:10 I will also bring them **b** from
Mt 2: 8 bring **b** word to me, that I may
7: 2 it will be measured **b** to you.
24:18 who is in the field not go **b**
25:27 coming I would have received **b**
27: 3 was remorseful and brought **b**
28: 2 and came and rolled **b** the stone
Mk 13:16 who is in the field not go **b**
Lk 4:20 and gave it **b** to the attendant
6:30 your goods do not ask them **b**.
6:34 from whom you hope to receive **b**,
6:34 to sinners to receive as much **b**.
6:38 it will be measured **b** to you."
9:42 and gave him **b** to his father.
9:62 hand to the plow, and looking **b**,
14:12 lest they also invite you **b**,
17:31 the field, let him not turn **b**.
23:11 and sent Him **b** to Pilate.
23:15 for I sent you **b** to him; and
Jn 6:66 many of His disciples went **b**
9: 7 and washed, and came **b** seeing.
13:25 leaning **b** on Jesus' breast, he
14:28 I am going away and coming **b** to
18: 6 they drew **b** and fell to the
Acts 5: 2 And he kept **b** part of the
5: 3 to the Holy Spirit and keep **b**
7:16 And they were carried **b** to
7:39 in their hearts they turned **b**
15:33 they were sent **b** with greetings
15:36 Let us now go **b** and visit our
20:20 how I kept **b** nothing that was
Rom 11:10 and bow down their **b**
Titus 2: 9 in all things, not answering **b**,
Phm 1:12 I am sending him **b**.
Heb 10:38 But if anyone draws **b**,
10:39 we are not of those who draw **b**
Jas 5: 4 which you kept **b** by fraud, cry
5:19 truth, and someone turns him **b**,
Rev 4: 6 full of eyes in front and in **b**.
5: 1 written inside and on the **b**,

BACKBITE (1/1) BACK, BACKBITERS, BACKBITING, BACKBITINGS

Ps 15: 3 He who does not **b** with his

BACKBITERS (1/1) BACKBITE

Rom 1:30 **b**, haters of God, violent,

BACKBITING (1/1) BACKBITE, BACKBITINGS

Prov 25:23 And a **b** tongue an angry

BACKBITINGS (1/1) BACKBITING

2 Cor 12:20 of wrath, selfish ambitions, **b**,

BACKBONE (1/1) BACK

Lev 3: 9 he shall remove close to the **b**.

BACKS (10/10) BACK

Ex 23:27 all your enemies turn their **b**
Josh 7:12 but turned their **b** before
Judg 20:42 they turned their **b** before
2 Chr 29: 6 and turned their **b** on Him.
Neh 9:26 Cast Your law behind their **b**
Ps 66:11 You laid affliction on our **b**.
Prov 19:29 And beatings for the **b** of
Isa 30: 6 carry their riches on the **b** of
Ezek 8:16 twenty-five men with their **b**
29: 7 You broke and made all their **b**

BACKSLIDER (1/1) BACKSLIDING

Prov 14:14 The **b** in heart will be filled

BACKSLIDING (12/12) BACK, BACKSLIDER, BACKSLIDINGS

Isa 57:17 And he went on **b** in the way of
Jer 3: 6 Have you seen what **b** Israel has
3: 8 for all the causes for which **b**
3:11 **B** Israel has shown herself more
3:12 **b** Israel,' says the LORD; 'I
3:14 O **b** children," says the LORD;
3:22 you **b** children, And I will
8: 5 Jerusalem, in a perpetual **b**?
31:22 O you **b** daughter? For the
49: 4 O **b** daughter? Who trusted in
Hos 11: 7 My people are bent on **b** from
14: 4 "I will heal their **b**,

BACKSLIDINGS (4/4) BACKSLIDING

Jer 2:19 And your **b** will rebuke you.
3:22 And I will heal your **b**.
5: 6 Their **b** have increased.
14: 7 For our **b** are many, We have

BACKWARD (14/14) BACK

Gen 9:23 and went **b** and covered the
49:17 So that its rider shall fall **b**.
1 Sam 4:18 that Eli fell off the seat **b** by
2 Ki 20: 9 go forward ten degrees or go **b**
20:10 but let the shadow go **b** ten
20:11 the shadow ten degrees **b**,
Job 23: 8 but He is not there, And **b**,
Ps 40:14 Let them be driven **b** and
Isa 1: 4 They have turned away **b**.
28:13 That they might go and fall **b**,
38: 8 sundial of Ahaz, ten degrees **b**.
44:25 mad; Who turns wise men **b**,
Jer 7:24 and went **b** and not forward.
15: 6 the LORD, "You have gone **b**.

BAD (44/35)

Gen 24:50 we cannot speak to you either **b**
31:24 to Jacob neither good nor **b**.
31:29 to Jacob neither good nor **b**.
37: 2 and Joseph brought a **b** report
Ex 33: 4 when the people heard this **b**
Lev 27:10 good for **b** or bad for good; and
27:10 good for bad or **b** for good; and
27:12 for it, whether it is good or **b**;
27:14 for it, whether it is good or **b**;
27:33 inquire whether it is good or **b**,
Num 13:19 they dwell in is good or **b**;
13:32 gave the children of Israel a **b**
14:36 against him by bringing a **b**
24:13 to do good or **b** of my own will.
Deut 22:14 and brings a **b** name on her, and
22:19 because he has brought a **b** name
2 Sam 13:22 Amnon neither good nor **b**.
19:35 discern between the good and **b**?
1 Ki 14: 6 have been sent to you with **b**
2 Ki 2:19 lord sees; but the water is **b**,
Prov 25:19 time of trouble Is like a **b**
Jer 24: 2 the other basket had very **b**
24: 2 not be eaten, they were so **b**.
24: 3 good figs, very good; and the **b**,
24: 3 very good; and the bad, very **b**,
24: 3 cannot be eaten, they are so **b**.
24: 8 And as the **b** figs which cannot
24: 8 cannot be eaten, they are so **b**'—
29:17 cannot be eaten, they are so **b**.
49:23 For they have heard **b** news.
Am 8: 6 Even sell the **b** wheat?"
Mt 6:23 "But if your eye is **b**,
7:17 but a **b** tree bears bad fruit.
7:17 but a bad tree bears **b** fruit.
7:18 A good tree cannot bear **b** fruit,
7:18 nor can a **b** tree bear good
12:33 or else make the tree **b** and its
12:33 the tree bad and its fruit **b**;
13:48 but threw the **b** away.
22:10 both **b** and good. And the
Lk 6:43 a good tree does not bear **b**
6:43 nor does a **b** tree bear good
11:34 But when your eye is **b**,
2 Cor 5:10 he has done, whether good or **b**.

BADGER (14/14) BADGERS

Ex 25: 5 **b** skins, and acacia wood;
26:14 and a covering of **b** skins above
35: 7 **b** skins, and acacia wood;
35:23 and **b** skins, brought them.
36:19 and a covering of **b** skins above
39:34 the covering of **b** skins, and
Num 4: 6 shall put on it a covering of **b**
4: 8 the same with a covering of **b**
4:10 its utensils in a covering of **b**
4:11 cover it with a covering of **b**
4:12 cover them with a covering of **b**
4:14 spread on it a covering of **b**
4:25 the covering of **b** skins that
Ezek 16:10 and gave you sandals of **b** skin;

BADGERS (2/2) BADGER

Ps 104:18 are a refuge for the rock **b**.
Prov 30:26 The rock **b** are a feeble folk,

BAG (15/15) BAGS

Deut 25:13 You shall not have in your **b**
1 Sam 17:40 and put them in a shepherd's **b**,
17:49 David put his hand in his **b**
Job 14:17 is sealed up in a **b**,
Prov 7:20 He has taken a **b** of money with
16:11 All the weights in the **b** are
Isa 46: 6 They lavish gold out of the **b**,
Mic 6:11 And with the **b** of deceitful
Hag 1: 6 Earns wages to put into a **b**
Mt 10:10 nor **b** for your journey, nor two
Mk 6: 8 the journey except a staff—no **b**,

Lk 9: 3 neither staffs nor ***b*** nor bread
10: 4 "Carry neither money ***b***,
22:35 I sent you without money ***b***,
22:36 "But now, he who has a money ***b***,

BAGS (3/3) BAG

2 Ki 5:23 two talents of silver in two ***b***,
12:10 priest came up and put it in ***b***,
Lk 12:33 provide yourselves money ***b***

BAHARUMITE (1/1)

1 Chr 11:33 Azmaveth the ***B***,

BAHURIM (5/5)

2 Sam 3:16 went along with her to ***B***,
16: 5 Now when King David came to ***B***,
17:18 and came to a man's house in ***B***,
19:16 a Benjamite, who was from ***B***,
1 Ki 2: 8 son of Gera, a Benjamite from ***B***,

BAJITH (KJV) See TEMPLE

BAKBAKKAR (1/1)

1 Chr 9:15 ***B***, Heresh, Galal,

BAKBUK (2/2)

Ezra 2:51 the sons of ***B***, the sons of
Neh 7:53 the sons of ***B***, the sons of

BAKBUKIAH (3/3)

Neh 11:17 the thanksgiving with prayer; ***B***,
12: 9 Also ***B*** and Unni, their brethren,
12:25 Mattaniah, ***B***, Obadiah,

BAKE (7/6) BAKED, BAKER, BAKERS, BAKERS', BAKES

Gen 11: 3 let us make bricks and ***b*** them
Ex 16:23 ***B*** what you will bake today,
16:23 Bake what you will ***b*** today,
Lev 24: 5 you shall take fine flour and ***b***
26:26 ten women shall ***b*** your bread in
Ezek 4:12 and ***b*** it using fuel of human
46:20 and where they shall ***b*** the

BAKED (16/16) BAKE

Gen 19: 3 and ***b*** unleavened bread, and
40:17 basket were all kinds of ***b***
Ex 12:39 And they ***b*** unleavened cakes of
Lev 2: 4 an offering a grain offering ***b***
2: 5 is a grain offering ***b*** in a
2: 7 IS a grain offering ***b*** in a
6:17 'It shall not be ***b*** with leaven.
6:21 The ***b*** pieces of the grain
7: 9 every grain offering that is ***b***
23:17 they shall be ***b*** with leaven.
1 Sam 28:24 and ***b*** unleavened bread from it.
2 Sam 13: 8 his sight, and ***b*** the cakes.
1 Ki 19: 6 by his head was a cake ***b*** on
1 Chr 9:31 over the things that were ***b*** in
23:29 cakes and what is ***b*** in the
Isa 44:19 I have also ***b*** bread on its

BAKEMEATS (KJV) See (BAKED) GOODS

BAKER (9/9) BAKE, BAKERS

Gen 40: 1 that the butler and the ***b*** of
40: 2 chief butler and the chief ***b***.
40: 5 Then the butler and the ***b*** of
40:16 When the chief ***b*** saw that the
40:20 chief butler and of the chief ***b***
40:22 But he hanged the chief ***b***,
41:10 guard, both me and the chief ***b***,
Hos 7: 4 Like an oven heated by a ***b***—
7: 6 Their ***b*** sleeps all night; In

BAKERS (1/1) BAKER, BAKERS'

1 Sam 8:13 to be perfumers, cooks, and ***b***.

BAKERS' (1/1) BAKERS

Jer 37:21 of bread from the ***b*** street,

BAKES (1/1) BAKE

Isa 44:15 he kindles it and ***b*** bread;

BALAAM (59/56) BALAAM'S

Num 22: 5 Then he sent messengers to ***B*** the
22: 7 and they came to ***B*** and spoke to
22: 8 princes of Moab stayed with ***B***.
22: 9 Then God came to ***B*** and said,
22:10 So ***B*** said to God, "Balak the
22:12 And God said to ***B***, "You shall
22:13 So ***B*** rose in the morning and
22:14 ***B*** refuses to come with us."
22:16 And they came to ***B*** and said to
22:18 Then ***B*** answered and said to the
22:20 And God came to ***B*** at night and
22:21 So ***B*** rose in the morning,
22:23 So ***B*** struck the donkey to turn
22:27 the LORD, she lay down under ***B***;
22:28 the donkey, and she said to ***B***,
22:29 And ***B*** said to the donkey,
22:30 So the donkey said to ***B***,
22:34 And ***B*** said to the Angel of the
22:35 Angel of the LORD said to ***B***,
22:35 So ***B*** went with the princes of
22:36 Now when Balak heard that ***B*** was
22:37 Then Balak said to ***B***,
22:38 And ***B*** said to Balak, "Look, I
22:39 So ***B*** went with Balak, and they
22:40 and he sent some to ***B*** and to
22:41 that Balak took ***B*** and brought
23: 1 Then ***B*** said to Balak, "Build
23: 2 And Balak did just as ***B*** had
23: 2 and Balak and ***B*** offered a bull
23: 3 Then ***B*** said to Balak, "Stand by
23: 4 And God met ***B***, and he said
23:11 Then Balak said to ***B***,
23:16 Then the LORD met ***B***,
23:25 Then Balak said to ***B***,
23:26 So ***B*** answered and said to Balak,
23:27 Then Balak said to ***B***,
23:28 So Balak took ***B*** to the top of
23:29 Then ***B*** said to Balak, "Build
23:30 And Balak did as ***B*** had said, and
24: 1 Now when ***B*** saw that it pleased
24: 2 And ***B*** raised his eyes, and saw
24: 3 The utterance of ***B*** the son of
24:10 anger was aroused against ***B***,
24:10 together; and Balak said to ***B***,
24:12 So ***B*** said to Balak, "Did I not
24:15 The utterance of ***B*** the son of
24:25 So ***B*** rose and departed and
31: 8 ***B*** the son of Beor they also
31:16 through the counsel of ***B***,
Deut 23: 4 they hired against you ***B*** the
23: 5 your God would not listen to ***B***,
Josh 13:22 also killed with the sword ***B***
24: 9 and sent and called ***B*** the son
24:10 'But I would not listen to ***B***;
Neh 13: 2 but hired ***B*** against them to
Mic 6: 5 And what ***B*** the son of Beor
2 Pe 2:15 following the way of ***B*** the son
Jude 11 run greedily in the error of ***B***
Rev 2:14 who hold the doctrine of ***B***,

BALAAM'S (4/4)

Num 22:25 against the wall and crushed ***B***
22:27 so ***B*** anger was aroused, and he
22:31 Then the LORD opened ***B*** eyes,
23: 5 Then the LORD put a word in ***B***

BALADAN (2/2) BERODACH-BALADAN, MERODACH-BALADAN

2 Ki 20:12 Berodach-Baladan the son of ***B***,
Isa 39: 1 Merodach-Baladan the son of ***B***,

BALAH (1/1)

Josh 19: 3 Hazar Shual, ***B***, Ezem,

BALAK (43/41) BALAK'S

Num 22: 2 Now ***B*** the son of Zippor saw all
22: 4 And ***B*** the son of Zippor was
22: 7 and spoke to him the words of ***B***.
22:10 ***B*** the son of Zippor, king of
22:13 and said to the princes of ***B***,
22:14 of Moab rose and went to ***B***,
22:15 Then ***B*** again sent princes, more
22:16 Thus says ***B*** the son of Zippor:
22:18 and said to the servants of ***B***,
22:18 Though ***B*** were to give me his
22:35 went with the princes of ***B***.
22:36 Now when ***B*** heard that Balaam
22:37 Then ***B*** said to Balaam, "Did I
22:38 And Balaam said to ***B***,
22:39 So Balaam went with ***B***,
22:40 Then ***B*** offered oxen and sheep,
22:41 that ***B*** took Balaam and brought
23: 1 Then Balaam said to ***B***,
23: 2 And ***B*** did just as Balaam had
23: 2 and ***B*** and Balaam offered a bull
23: 3 Then Balaam said to ***B***,
23: 5 mouth, and said, "Return to ***B***,
23: 7 ***B*** the king of Moab has brought
23:11 Then ***B*** said to Balaam, "What
23:13 Then ***B*** said to him, "Please
23:15 And he said to ***B***, "Stand here
23:16 mouth, and said, "Go back to ***B***,
23:17 And ***B*** said to him, "What has
23:18 oracle and said: "Rise up, ***B***,
23:25 Then ***B*** said to Balaam,
23:26 Balaam answered and said to ***B***,
23:27 Then ***B*** said to Balaam, "Please
23:28 So ***B*** took Balaam to the top of
23:29 Then Balaam said to ***B***,
23:30 And ***B*** did as Balaam had said,
24:10 and ***B*** said to Balaam, "I
24:12 So Balaam said to ***B***,
24:13 If ***B*** were to give me his house
24:25 ***B*** also went his way.
Josh 24: 9 Then ***B*** the son of Zippor, king
Judg 11:25 are you any better than ***B*** the
Mic 6: 5 remember now What ***B*** king of
Rev 2:14 who taught ***B*** to put a stumbling

BALAK'S (1/1) BALAK

Num 24:10 Then ***B*** anger was aroused

BALANCE (1/1) BALANCED, BALANCES

Isa 40:12 in scales And the hills in a ***b***?

BALANCED (1/1)

Job 37:16 you know how the clouds are ***b***,

BALANCES (1/1) BALANCE

Dan 5:27 You have been weighed in the ***b***,

BALD (14/10) BALDHEAD, BALDNESS

Lev 13:40 fallen from his head, he is ***b***,
13:41 he is ***b*** on the forehead, but
13:42 And if there is on the ***b*** head or
13:42 there is on the bald head or ***b***
13:42 leprosy breaking out on his ***b***
13:42 out on his bald head or his ***b***
13:43 sore is reddish-white on his ***b***
13:43 on his bald head or on his ***b***
21: 5 They shall not make any ***b***
Jer 16: 6 nor make themselves ***b*** for them.
48:37 "For every head shall be ***b***,
Ezek 27:31 shave themselves completely ***b***
29:18 Tyre; every head was made ***b***,
Mic 1:16 Make yourself ***b*** and cut off

BALDHEAD (2/1) BALD

2 Ki 2:23 'Go up, you ***b***!
2:23 Go up, you ***b***!"

BALDNESS (7/7) BALD

Isa 3:24 Instead of well-set hair, ***b***;
15: 2 On all their heads will be ***b***,
22:12 For ***b*** and for girding with
Jer 47: 5 ***B*** has come upon Gaza, Ashkelon
Ezek 7:18 ***B*** on all their heads.
Am 8:10 And ***b*** on every head; I will
Mic 1:16 Enlarge your ***b*** like an eagle,

BALL (1/1)

Isa 22:18 and toss you like a ***b*** Into a

BALM (6/6)

Gen 37:25 their camels, bearing spices, ***b***,
43:11 a little ***b*** and a little honey,
Jer 8:22 Is there no ***b*** in Gilead, Is
46:11 "Go up to Gilead and take ***b***,
51: 8 Wail for her! Take ***b*** for her
Ezek 27:17 millet, honey, oil, and ***b***.

BAMAH (1/1) BAMOTH

Ezek 20:29 So its name is called ***B*** to

BAMOTH (2/2) BAMAH

Num 21:19 to Nahaliel, from Nahaliel to ***B***,
21:20 and from ***B***, in the valley that

BAMOTH BAAL (1/1)

Josh 13:17 are in the plain: Dibon, ***B***,

BAN (1/1)

Lev 27:29 'No person under the ***b***,

BAND (16/16) BANDAGE, BANDAGED, BANDED, BANDS

Gen 49:15 And became a ***b*** of slaves.
Ex 28: 8 And the intricately woven ***b*** of
28:27 above the intricately woven ***b***
28:28 above the intricately woven ***b***
29: 5 with the intricately woven ***b***
39: 5 And the intricately woven ***b*** of
39:20 above the intricately woven ***b***
39:21 above the intricately woven ***b***
Lev 8: 7 with the intricately woven ***b***
1 Ki 11:24 him and became captain over a ***b***
2 Ki 13:21 that suddenly they spied a ***b***
Job 38: 9 thick darkness its swaddling ***b***;
Dan 4:15 Bound with a ***b*** of iron and
4:23 bound with a ***b*** of iron and
Hos 7: 1 A ***b*** of robbers takes spoil
Rev 1:13 about the chest with a golden ***b***.

BANDAGE (2/2) BANDAGED

1 Ki 20:38 and disguised himself with a ***b***
20:41 And he hastened to take the ***b***

BANDAGED (2/2) BANDAGE

Ezek 30:21 it has not been ***b*** for healing,
Lk 10:34 So he went to him and ***b*** his

BANDED (2/2) BAND

Judg 11: 3 and worthless men ***b*** together
Acts 23:12 some of the Jews ***b*** together and

BANDS (23/19) BAND

Ex 27:10 of the pillars and their ***b***
27:11 of the pillars and their ***b*** of
27:17 around the court shall have ***b***

38:10 of the pillars and their **b**
38:11 of the pillars and their **b**
38:12 of the pillars and their **b**
38:17 of the pillars and their **b**
38:17 the pillars of the court had **b**
38:19 of their capitals and their **b**
38:28 and made **b** for them.
Lev 26:13 I have broken the **b** of your
2 Ki 6:23 So the **b** of Syrian raiders
13:20 And the raiding **b** from Moab
24: 2 sent against him raiding **b** of
24: 2 **b** of Syrians, bands of
24: 2 **b** of Moabites, and bands of the
24: 2 and **b** of the people of Ammon;
1 Chr 12:21 helped David against the **b** of
Job 1:17 "The Chaldeans formed three **b**,
Ezek 34:27 when I have broken the **b** of
Hos 6: 9 As **b** of robbers lie in wait for
11: 4 With **b** of love, And I was to
Rev 15: 6 chests girded with golden **b**.

BANI (15/14)

2 Sam 23:36 ***B*** the Gadite,
1 Chr 6:46 the son of Amzi, the son of ***B***,
9: 4 the son of Imri, the son of ***B***,
Ezra 2:10 the people of ***B***,
10:29 of the sons of ***B***: Meshullam,
10:34 of the sons of ***B***: Maadai,
10:38 ***B***, Binnui, Shimei,
Neh 3:17 under Rehum the son of ***B***,
8: 7 Also Jeshua, ***B***,
9: 4 Then Jeshua, ***B***,
9: 4 Shebaniah, Bunni, Sherebiah, ***B***,
9: 5 the Levites, Jeshua, Kadmiel, ***B***,
10:13 Hodijah, ***B***, and Beninu.
10:14 Pahath-Moab, Elam, Zattu, ***B***,
11:22 was Uzzi the son of ***B***,

BANISHED (5/5) BANISHMENT

2 Sam 14:13 the king does not bring his **b**
14:14 so that His **b** ones are not
1 Ki 15:12 And he **b** the perverted persons
22:46 he **b** from the land.
Prov 14:32 The wicked is **b** in his

BANISHMENT (1/1) BANISHED

Ezra 7:26 whether it be death, or **b**,

BANK (15/15) BANKERS, BANKS

Gen 41: 3 by the other cows on the **b** of
41:17 in my dream I stood on the **b** of
Ex 2: 3 in the reeds by the river's **b**.
7:15 shall stand by the river's **b**
Deut 2:36 which is on the **b** of the River
4:48 which is on the **b** of the River
Josh 12: 2 which is on the **b** of the River
13: 9 from Aroer which is on the **b** of
13:16 which is on the **b** of the River
13:23 children of Reuben was the **b**
2 Ki 2:13 went back and stood by the **b**
Ezek 47: 6 me and returned me to the **b** of
47: 7 along the **b** of the river, were
47:12 Along the **b** of the river, on
Lk 19:23 you not put my money in the **b**,

BANKERS (1/1) BANK

Mt 25:27 deposited my money with the **b**,

BANKS (8/8) BANK

Num 13:29 by the sea and along the **b** of
Josh 3:15 the Jordan overflows all its **b**
4:18 place and overflowed all its **b**
Judg 11:26 in all the cities along the **b**
1 Chr 12:15 it had overflowed all its **b**;
Song 5:13 ***B*** of scented herbs. His lips
Isa 8: 7 channels And go over all his **b**.
Dan 8:16 a man's voice between the **b**

BANNER (12/12) BANNERS

Ps 60: 4 You have given a **b** to those who
Song 2: 4 And his **b** over me was love.
Isa 5:26 He will lift up a **b** to the
11:10 Who shall stand as a **b** to the
11:12 He will set up a **b** for the
13: 2 Lift up a **b** on the high
18: 3 When he lifts up a **b** on the
30:17 top of a mountain And as a **b**
31: 9 shall be afraid of the **b**,
62:10 Lift up a **b** for the peoples!
Jer 51:27 Set up a **b** in the land, Blow
Zech 9:16 Lifted like a **b** over His land—

BANNERS (4/4) BANNER

Ps 20: 5 our God we will set up our **b**!
74: 4 They set up their **b** for
Song 6: 4 Awesome as an army with **b**!
6:10 Awesome as an army with **b**?

BANQUET (12/12) BANQUETING, BANQUETS

Esth 5: 4 and Haman come today to the **b**
5: 5 king and Haman went to the **b**
5: 6 At the **b** of wine the king said
5: 8 king and Haman come to the **b**
5:12 come in with the king to the **b**
5:14 merrily with the king to the **b**.
6:14 to bring Haman to the **b** which
7: 2 at the **b** of wine, the king
7: 7 arose in his wrath from the **b**
7: 8 garden to the place of the **b**
Job 41: 6 your companions make a **b** of
Dan 5:10 came to the **b** hall. The queen

BANQUETING (1/1) BANQUET

Song 2: 4 He brought me to the **b** house,

BANQUETS (1/1) BANQUET

Am 6: 7 And those who recline at **b**

BAPTISM (22/22) BAPTISMS, BAPTIST, BAPTIST'S, BAPTIZE, BAPTIZED, BAPTIZES, BAPTIZING

Mt 3: 7 and Sadducees coming to his **b**,
20:22 and be baptized with the **b** that
20:23 and be baptized with the **b** that
21:25 The **b** of John—where was it from?
Mk 1: 4 wilderness and preaching a **b**
10:38 and be baptized with the **b** that
10:39 and with the **b** I am baptized
11:30 The **b** of John—was it from heaven
Lk 3: 3 preaching a **b** of repentance for
7:29 been baptized with the **b** of
12:50 But I have a **b** to be baptized
20: 4 The **b** of John—was it from heaven
Acts 1:22 beginning from the **b** of John to
10:37 began from Galilee after the **b**
13:24 the **b** of repentance to all the
18:25 though he knew only the **b** of
19: 3 So they said, "Into John's **b**.
19: 4 John indeed baptized with a **b** of
Rom 6: 4 were buried with Him through **b**
Eph 4: 5 one Lord, one faith, one **b**;
Col 2:12 buried with Him in **b**,
1 Pe 3:21 **b** (not the removal of the filth

BAPTISMS (1/1) BAPTISM

Heb 6: 2 of the doctrine of **b**,

BAPTIST (14/14) BAPTIST'S, BAPTIZE, JOHN

Mt 3: 1 In those days John the ***B*** came
11:11 one greater than John the ***B***;
11:12 from the days of John the ***B***
14: 2 servants, "This is John the ***B***;
16:14 said, "Some say John the ***B***,
17:13 He spoke to them of John the ***B***.
Mk 6:14 John the ***B*** is risen from the
6:24 The head of John the ***B***!"
6:25 at once the head of John the ***B***
8:28 So they answered, "John the ***B***;
Lk 7:20 John the ***B*** has sent us to You,
7:28 greater prophet than John the ***B***;
7:33 For John the ***B*** came neither
9:19 answered and said, "John the ***B***,

BAPTIST'S (1/1) BAPTIST

Mt 14: 8 Give me John the ***B*** head here on

BAPTIZE (10/8) BAPTISM, BAPTIST, BAPTIZED, BAPTIZES, BAPTIZING

Mt 3:11 I indeed **b** you with water unto
3:11 He will **b** you with the Holy
Mk 1: 8 but He will **b** you with the Holy
Lk 3:16 I indeed **b** you with water; but
3:16 He will **b** you with the Holy
Jn 1:25 Why then do you **b** if you are not
1:26 I **b** with water, but there stands
1:33 but He who sent me to **b** with
4: 2 (though Jesus Himself did not **b**,
1 Cor 1:17 For Christ did not send me to **b**,

BAPTIZED (59/49) BAPTIZE

Mt 3: 6 and were **b** by him in the Jordan,
3:13 to John at the Jordan to be **b**
3:14 I need to be **b** by You, and are
3:16 When He had been **b**,
20:22 and be **b** with the baptism that
20:22 with the baptism that I am **b**
20:23 and be **b** with the baptism that
20:23 with the baptism that I am **b**
Mk 1: 5 went out to him and were all **b**
1: 8 I indeed **b** you with water, but
1: 9 and was **b** by John in the
10:38 and be **b** with the baptism that
10:38 with the baptism that I am **b**
10:39 and with the baptism I am **b**
10:39 am baptized with you will be **b**;
16:16 He who believes and is **b** will be
Lk 3: 7 that came out to be **b** by him,
3:12 collectors also came to be **b**,
3:21 When all the people were **b**,
3:21 to pass that Jesus also was **b**;
7:29 having been **b** with the baptism
7:30 not having been **b** by him.
12:50 But I have a baptism to be **b**
Jn 3:22 He remained with them and **b**.
3:23 And they came and were **b**.
4: 1 had heard that Jesus made and **b**
Acts 1: 5 for John truly **b** with water, but
1: 5 but you shall be **b** with the
2:38 and let every one of you be **b**
2:41 gladly received his word were **b**;
8:12 both men and women were **b**.
8:13 and when he was **b** he continued
8:16 They had only been **b** in the
8:36 What hinders me from being **b**?
8:38 into the water, and he **b** him.
9:18 at once; and he arose and was **b**.
10:47 that these should not be **b** who
10:48 And he commanded them to be **b** in
11:16 John indeed **b** with water, but
11:16 but you shall be **b** with the
16:15 she and her household were **b**,
16:33 he and all his family were **b**.
18: 8 hearing, believed and were **b**.
19: 3 "Into what then were you **b**?
19: 4 John indeed **b** with a baptism of
19: 5 they were **b** in the name of the
22:16 are you waiting? Arise and be **b**,
Rom 6: 3 that as many of us as were **b**
6: 3 into Christ Jesus were **b** into
1 Cor 1:13 Or were you **b** in the name of
1:14 I thank God that I **b** none of you
1:15 anyone should say that I had **b**
1:16 I also **b** the household of
1:16 I do not know whether I **b** any
10: 2 all were **b** into Moses in the
12:13 For by one Spirit we were all **b**
15:29 what will they do who are **b** for
15:29 Why then are they **b** for the
Gal 3:27 For as many of you as were **b**

BAPTIZES (1/1) BAPTIZE

Jn 1:33 this is He who **b** with the Holy

BAPTIZING (7/7) BAPTIZE

Mt 28:19 **b** them in the name of the
Mk 1: 4 John came **b** in the wilderness
Jn 1:28 the Jordan, where John was **b**.
1:31 therefore I came **b** with
3:23 Now John also was **b** in Aenon
3:26 have testified—behold, He is **b**,
10:40 to the place where John was **b**

BAR (5/5) BARS

Ex 26:28 The middle **b** shall pass through
36:33 And he made the middle **b** to pass
Judg 16: 3 **b** and all, put them on his
Neh 7: 3 let them shut and **b** the doors;
Am 1: 5 I will also break the gate **b**

BAR-JESUS (1/1)

Acts 13: 6 a Jew whose name was ***B***,

BAR-JONAH (1/1) SIMON

Mt 16:17 him, "Blessed are you, Simon ***B***,

BARABBAS (11/10)

Mt 27:16 a notorious prisoner called ***B***.
27:17 want me to release to you? ***B***,
27:20 that they should ask for ***B*** and
27:21 They said, "***B***!"
27:26 Then he released ***B*** to them; and
Mk 15: 7 And there was one named ***B***,
15:11 he should rather release ***B*** to
15:15 released ***B*** to them; and he
Lk 23:18 and release to us ***B***"—
Jn 18:40 but ***B***!" Now Barabbas was a
18:40 but Barabbas!" Now ***B*** was a

BARACHEL (2/2)

Job 32: 2 the son of ***B*** the Buzite, of the
32: 6 the son of ***B*** the Buzite,

BARACHIAS (KJV) See BERECHIAH

BARAK (14/13)

Judg 4: 6 Then she sent and called for ***B***
4: 8 And ***B*** said to her, "If you will
4: 9 Deborah arose and went with ***B***
4:10 And ***B*** called Zebulun and
4:12 they reported to Sisera that ***B***
4:14 Then Deborah said to ***B***,
4:14 So ***B*** went down from Mount
4:15 the edge of the sword before ***B***;
4:16 But ***B*** pursued the chariots and
4:22 as ***B*** pursued Sisera, Jael came
5: 1 Then Deborah and ***B*** the son of
5:12 awake, sing a song! Arise, ***B***,
5:15 so was ***B*** Sent into the valley
Heb 11:32 me to tell of Gideon and ***B*** and

BARBARIAN (1/1) BARBARIANS

Col 3:11 nor uncircumcised, **b**,

BARBARIANS (1/1) BARBARIAN

Rom 1:14 debtor both to Greeks and to **b**,

BARBAROUS [PEOPLE] (KJV) See NATIVES

BARBER'S (1/1)

Ezek 5: 1 take it as a **b** razor, and pass

BARE (15/15) BAREFOOT

Lev 13:45 shall be torn and his head **b**;
Ps 29: 9 And strips the forests **b**;
Isa 32:11 yourselves, make yourselves **b**,
52:10 The LORD has made **B** His holy
Jer 13:22 uncovered, Your heels made **b**.
26:18 of the temple Like the **b**
49:10 But I have made Esau **b**;
Ezek 16: 7 grew, but you were naked and **b**.
16:22 when you were naked and **b**,
16:39 and leave you naked and **b**.
23:29 for, and leave you naked and **b**.
Joel 1: 7 He has stripped it **b** and
Mic 3:12 of the temple Like the **b**
Hab 3:13 By laying **b** from foundation to
Zeph 2:14 For He will lay **b** the cedar

BAREFOOT (4/4) BARE

2 Sam 15:30 had his head covered and went **b**.
Isa 20: 2 he did so, walking naked and **b**.
20: 3 Isaiah has walked naked and **b**
20: 4 young and old, naked and **b**,

BARHUMITE (1/1)

2 Sam 23:31 the Arbathite, Azmaveth the **B**,

BARIAH (1/1)

1 Chr 3:22 Shemaiah were Hattush, Igal, **B**,

BARK (1/1)

Isa 56:10 all dumb dogs, They cannot **b**;

BARKOS (2/2)

Ezra 2:53 the sons of **B**, the sons of
Neh 7:55 the sons of **B**, the sons of

BARLEY (36/35)

Ex 9:31 Now the flax and the **b** were
9:31 for the **b** was in the head and
Lev 27:16 A homer of **b** seed shall be
Num 5:15 one-tenth of an EPHAH of **b**
Deut 8: 8 "a land of wheat and **b**,
Judg 7:13 a loaf of **b** bread tumbled into
Ruth 1:22 at the beginning of **b** harvest.
2:17 and it was about an ephah of **b**.
2:23 to glean until the end of **b**
3: 2 he is winnowing **b** tonight at
3:15 he measured six ephahs of **b**,
3:17 These six ephahs of **b** he gave
2 Sam 14:30 and he has **b** there; go and set
17:28 **b** and flour, parched grain and
21: 9 in the beginning of **b** harvest.
1 Ki 4:28 They also brought **b** and straw to
2 Ki 4:42 twenty loaves of **b** bread, and
7: 1 and two seahs of **b** for a
7:16 and two seahs of **b** for a
7:18 Two seahs of **b** for a shekel, and
1 Chr 11:13 was a piece of ground full of **b**.
2 Chr 2:10 twenty thousand kors of **b**,
2:15 Now therefore, the wheat, the **b**,
27: 5 of wheat, and ten thousand of **b**.
Job 31:40 wheat, And weeds instead of **b**.
Isa 28:25 The **b** in the appointed place,
Jer 41: 8 we have treasures of wheat, **b**,
Ezek 4: 9 take for yourself wheat, **b**,
4:12 And you shall eat it as **b**
13:19 My people for handfuls of **b**
45:13 of an ephah from a homer of **b**.
Hos 3: 2 one and one-half homers of **b**.
Joel 1:11 For the wheat and the **b**;
Jn 6: 9 is a lad here who has five **b**
6:13 the fragments of the five **b**
Rev 6: 6 and three quarts of **b** for a

BARN (5/5) BARNS

Hag 2:19 'Is the seed still in the **b**?
Mt 3:12 and gather His wheat into the **b**;
13:30 but gather the wheat into my **b**.
Lk 3:17 and gather the wheat into His **b**;
12:24 have neither storehouse nor **b**;

BARNABAS (29/28) JOSES

Acts 4:36 who was also named **B** by the
9:27 But **B** took him and brought him
11:22 and they sent out **B** to go as
11:25 Then **B** departed for Tarsus to
11:30 to the elders by the hands of **B**
12:25 And **B** and Saul returned from
13: 1 prophets and teachers: **B**,
13: 2 Now separate to Me **B** and Saul
13: 7 This man called for **B** and Saul
13:43 proselytes followed Paul and **B**,
13:46 Then Paul and **B** grew bold and
13:50 persecution against Paul and **B**,
14:12 And **B** they called Zeus, and
14:14 But when the apostles **B** and Paul
14:20 next day he departed with **B** to
15: 2 when Paul and **B** had no small
15: 2 determined that Paul and **B** and
15:12 kept silent and listened to **B**
15:22 to Antioch with Paul and **B**,
15:25 men to you with our beloved **B**
15:35 Paul and **B** also remained in
15:36 after some days Paul said to **B**,
15:37 Now **B** was determined to take
15:39 And so **B** took Mark and sailed
1 Cor 9: 6 Or is it only **B** and I who
Gal 2: 1 up again to Jerusalem with **B**,
2: 9 they gave me and **B** the right
2:13 so that even **B** was carried away
Col 4:10 with Mark the cousin of **B**

BARNS (5/5) BARN

Ps 144:13 That our **b** may be full,
Prov 3:10 So your **b** will be filled with
Joel 1:17 **B** are broken down, For the
Mt 6:26 sow nor reap nor gather into **b**;
Lk 12:18 I will pull down my **b** and build

BARRACKS (6/6)

Acts 21:34 him to be taken into the **b**.
21:37 was about to be led into the **b**,
22:24 him to be brought into the **b**,
23:10 them, and bring him into the **b**.
23:16 he went and entered the **b** and
23:32 with him, and returned to the **b**.

BARREL, BARRELS (KJV) See BIN

BARREN (24/24) BARRENNESS

Gen 11:30 But Sarai was **b**; she had no
25:21 his wife, because she was **b**;
29:31 her womb; but Rachel was **b**.
Ex 23:26 suffer miscarriage or be **b** in
Deut 7:14 shall not be a male or female **b**
Judg 13: 2 and his wife was **b** and had no
13: 3 you are **b** and have borne no
1 Sam 2: 5 Even the **b** has borne seven,
2 Ki 2:19 water is bad, and the ground **b**.
Job 3: 7 may that night be **b**! May no
15:34 of hypocrites will be **b**,
24:21 For he preys on the **b** who do
39: 6 And the **b** land his dwelling?
Ps 113: 9 He grants the **b** woman a home,
Prov 30:16 The **b** womb, The earth that
Song 4: 2 And none is **b** among them.
6: 6 And none is **b** among them.
Isa 54: 1 'Sing, O **b**, You who have
Joel 2:20 will drive him away into a **b**
Lk 1: 7 child, because Elizabeth was **b**,
1:36 month for her who was called **b**.
23:29 will say, 'Blessed are the **b**,
Gal 4:27 is written: "Rejoice, O **b**,
2 Pe 1: 8 you will be neither **b** nor

BARRENNESS (2/2) BARREN

2 Ki 2:21 shall be no more death or **b**.
Ps 107:34 A fruitful land into **b**,

BARS (36/32) BAR

Ex 26:26 And you shall make **b** of acacia
26:27 five **b** for the boards on the
26:27 and five **b** for the boards of
26:29 of gold as holders for the **b**,
26:29 and overlay the **b** with gold.
35:11 its clasps, its boards, its **b**,
36:31 And he made **b** of acacia wood:
36:32 five **b** for the boards on the
36:32 and five **b** for the boards of
36:34 gold to be holders for the **b**,
36:34 and overlaid the **b** with gold.
39:33 its clasps, its boards, its **b**,
40:18 set up its boards, put in its **b**,
Num 3:36 boards of the tabernacle, its **b**,
4:31 boards of the tabernacle, its **b**,
Deut 3: 5 with high walls, gates, and **b**,
1 Sam 23: 7 a town that has gates and **b**.
2 Chr 8: 5 with walls, gates, and **b**,
14: 7 them, and towers, gates, and **b**,
Neh 3: 3 its doors with its bolts and **b**.
3: 6 its doors, with its bolts and **b**.
3:13 its doors with its bolts and **b**,
3:14 its doors with its bolts and **b**.
3:15 its doors with its bolts and **b**,
Job 38:10 And set **b** and doors;
40:18 His ribs like **b** of iron.
Ps 107:16 And cut the **b** of iron in two.
147:13 For He has strengthened the **b**
Prov 18:19 contentions are like the **b** of
Isa 45: 2 gates of bronze And cut the **b**
Jer 49:31 has neither gates nor **b**,
51:30 The **b** of her gate are broken.
Lam 2: 9 has destroyed and broken her **b**.
Ezek 38:11 and having neither **b** nor
Jon 2: 6 The earth with its **b** closed
Nah 3:13 Fire shall devour the **b** of

BARSABAS (2/2) JOSEPH, JUDAS, JUSTUS

Acts 1:23 proposed two: Joseph called **B**,
15:22 Judas who was also named **B**,

BARTERED (1/1)

Ezek 27:13 They **b** human lives and vessels

BARTHOLOMEW (4/4) NATHANAEL

Mt 10: 3 Philip and **B**; Thomas and
Mk 3:18 Andrew, Philip, **B**,
Lk 6:14 James and John; Philip and **B**;
Acts 1:13 **B** and Matthew; James the son

BARTIMAEUS (1/1) TIMAEUS

Mk 10:46 and a great multitude, blind **B**,

BARUCH (26/24)

Neh 3:20 After him **B** the son of Zabbai
10: 6 Daniel, Ginnethon, **B**,
11: 5 and Maaseiah the son of **B**,
Jer 32:12 I gave the purchase deed to **B**
32:13 Then I charged **B** before them,
32:16 the purchase deed to **B** the son
36: 4 Then Jeremiah called **B** the son
36: 4 and **B** wrote on a scroll of a
36: 5 And Jeremiah commanded **B**,
36: 8 And **B** the son of Neriah did
36:10 Then **B** read from the book the
36:13 words that he had heard when **B**
36:14 the son of Cushi, to **B**,
36:14 So **B** the son of Neriah took
36:15 So **B** read it in their
36:16 one to another, and said to **B**,
36:17 And they asked **B**,
36:18 So **B** answered them, "He
36:19 Then the princes said to **B**,
36:26 to seize **B** the scribe and
36:27 scroll with the words which **B**
36:32 scroll and gave it to **B** the
43: 3 But **B** the son of Neriah has set
43: 6 and Jeremiah the prophet and **B**
45: 1 the prophet spoke to **B** the son
45: 2 the God of Israel, to you, O **B**:

BARZILLAI (12/10)

2 Sam 17:27 and **B** the Gileadite from
19:31 And **B** the Gileadite came down
19:32 Now **B** was a very aged man,
19:33 And the king said to **B**,
19:34 But **B** said to the king, "How
19:39 the king kissed **B** and blessed
21: 8 up for Adriel the son of **B** the
1 Ki 2: 7 show kindness to the sons of **B**
Ezra 2:61 sons of Koz, and the sons of **B**,
2:61 a wife of the daughters of **B**
Neh 7:63 the sons of Koz, the sons of **B**,
7:63 a wife of the daughters of **B**

BASE (26/26) BASES, BASIC

Ex 19:12 to the mountain or touch its **b**.
29:12 all the blood beside the **b** of
30:18 with its **b** also of bronze, for
30:28 and the laver and its **b**.
31: 9 and the laver and its **b**—
35:16 and the laver and its **b**;
38: 8 the laver of bronze and its **b**
39:39 utensils; the laver with its **b**;
40:11 anoint the laver and its **b**,
Lev 4: 7 blood of the bull at the **b** of
4:18 the remaining blood at the **b**
4:25 and pour its blood at the **b** of
4:30 the remaining blood at the **b**
4:34 the remaining blood at the **b**
5: 9 shall be drained out at the **b**
8:11 and the laver and its **b**,
8:15 he poured the blood at the **b**
9: 9 and poured the blood at the **b**
2 Sam 6:20 as one of the **b** fellows
Isa 3: 5 And the **b** toward the
Ezek 43:13 the **b** one cubit high and one
43:14 from the **b** on the ground to the
43:17 half a cubit around it; its **b**,
Zech 5:11 will be set there on its **b**.
Mal 2: 9 made you contemptible and **b**
1 Cor 1:28 and the **b** things of the world

BASEMATH (7/7)

Gen 26:34 and **B** the daughter of Elon the
36: 3 and **B**, Ishmael's daughter,
36: 4 and **B** bore Reuel.
36:10 and Reuel the son of **B** the wife
36:13 These were the sons of **B**,
36:17 These were the sons of **B**,
1 Ki 4:15 he also took **B** the daughter of

BASES (4/4) BASE

Ex 38:27 of the sanctuary and the **b** of
38:31 the **b** for the court gate, all
Ezra 3: 3 they set the altar on its **b**;
Song 5:15 pillars of marble Set on **b** of

BASEST (KJV) See LOWEST, LOWLIEST

BASHAN (60/53)

Num 21:33 and went up by the way to **B**.
21:33 So Og king of **B** went out
32:33 and the kingdom of Og king of **B**,
Deut 1: 4 in Heshbon, and Og king of **B**,
3: 1 and went up the road to **B**;
3: 1 and Og king of **B** came out
3: 3 into our hands Og king of **B**,
3: 4 Argob, the kingdom of Og in **B**.
3:10 plain, all Gilead, and all **B**,
3:10 of the kingdom of Og in **B**.
3:11 For only Og king of **B** remained
3:13 "The rest of Gilead, and all **B**,
3:13 the region of Argob, with all **B**,
3:14 and called **B** after his own
4:43 and Golan in **B** for the
4:47 and the land of Og king of **B**,
29: 7 of Heshbon and Og king of **B**
32:14 And rams of the breed of **B**,
33:22 whelp; He shall leap from **B**.
Josh 9:10 of Heshbon, and Og king of **B**,
12: 4 other king was Og king of **B**
12: 5 Hermon, over Salcah, over all **B**,
13:11 and all **B** as far as Salcah;
13:12 all the kingdom of Og in **B**,
13:30 was from Mahanaim, all **B**,
13:30 all the kingdom of Og king of **B**,
13:30 towns of Jair which are in **B**,
13:31 of the kingdom of Og in **B**,
17: 1 he was given Gilead and **B**.
17: 5 the land of Gilead and **B**,
20: 8 tribe of Gad, and Golan in **B**,
21: 6 the half-tribe of Manasseh in **B**.
21:27 they gave Golan in **B** with its
22: 7 had given a possession in **B**,
1 Ki 4:13 the region of Argob in **B**—
4:19 Amorites, and of Og king of **B**.
2 Ki 10:33 Arnon, including Gilead and **B**.
1 Chr 5:11 next to them in the land of **B**
5:12 then Jaanai and Shaphat in **B**,
5:16 in **B** and in its villages, and
5:23 numbers increased from **B** to
6:62 from the tribe of Manasseh in **B**.
6:71 were given Golan in **B** with
Neh 9:22 And the land of Og king of **B**.
Ps 22:12 Strong bulls of **B** have
68:15 of God is the mountain of **B**;
68:15 peaks is the mountain of **B**.
68:22 "I will bring back from **B**,
135:11 of the Amorites, Og king of **B**,
136:20 And Og king of **B**,
Isa 2:13 up, And upon all the oaks of **B**;
33: 9 And **B** and Carmel shake off
Jer 22:20 And lift up your voice in **B**;
50:19 he shall feed on Carmel and **B**;
Ezek 27: 6 Of oaks from **B** they made your
39:18 All of them fatlings of **B**.
Am 4: 1 Hear this word, you cows of **B**,
Mic 7:14 Let them feed in **B** and
Nah 1: 4 **B** and Carmel wither, And the
Zech 11: 2 are ruined. Wail, O oaks of **B**,

BASHAN-HAVOTH-JAIR (KJV) See BASHAN

BASHEMATH (KJV) See BASEMATH

BASIC (2/2)

Col 2: 8 according to the **b** principles
2:20 you died with Christ from the **b**

BASIN (3/2) BASINS

Ex 12:22 in the blood that is in the **b**,
12:22 the blood that is in the **b**.
Jn 13: 5 He poured water into a **b** and

BASINS (15/14) BASIN

Ex 24: 6 half the blood and put it in **b**,
27: 3 and its shovels and its **b** and
38: 3 the pans, the shovels, the **b**,
Num 4:14 the forks, the shovels, the **b**,
2 Sam 17:28 brought beds and **b**,
1 Ki 7:50 the **b**, the trimmers, the bowls,
2 Ki 12:13 for the house of the LORD **b**
25:15 The firepans and the **b**,
1 Chr 28:17 pure gold for the forks, the **b**,
Ezra 1:10 thirty gold **b**, four hundred and
1:10 four hundred and ten silver **b**
8:27 twenty gold **b** worth a thousand
Neh 7:70 thousand gold drachmas, fifty **b**,
Jer 52:19 The **b**, the firepans, the bowls,
Zech 9:15 be filled with blood like **b**,

BASKET (32/29) BASKETS

Gen 40:17 In the uppermost **b** were all
40:17 birds ate them out of the **b** on
Ex 29: 3 You shall put them in one **b** and
29: 3 basket and bring them in the **b**,
29:23 and one wafer from the **b** of the
29:32 and the bread that is in the **b**,
Lev 8: 2 and a **b** of unleavened bread;
8:26 and from the **b** of unleavened
8:31 the bread that is in the **b** of
Num 6:15 a **b** of unleavened bread, cakes
6:17 with the **b** of unleavened bread;
6:19 one unleavened cake from the **b**,
Deut 26: 2 and put it in a **b** and go to
26: 4 the priest shall take the **b**
28: 5 Blessed shall be your **b** and
28:17 Cursed shall be your **b** and
Judg 6:19 The meat he put in a **b**,
Jer 24: 2 One **b** had very good figs, like
24: 2 and the other **b** had very bad
Am 8: 1 a **b** of summer fruit.
8: 2 A **b** of summer fruit." Then the
Zech 5: 6 It is a **b** that is going
5: 7 a woman sitting inside the **b**";
5: 8 he thrust her down into the **b**,
5: 9 and they lifted up the **b**
5:10 "Where are they carrying the **b**?
5:11 the **b** will be set there on
Mt 5:15 a lamp and put it under a **b**,
Mk 4:21 brought to be put under a **b** or
Lk 11:33 in a secret place or under a **b**,
Acts 9:25 through the wall in a large **b**.
2 Cor 11:33 but I was let down in a **b**

BASKETS (15/15) BASKET

Gen 40:16 and there were three white **b**
40:18 The three **b** are three days.
2 Ki 10: 7 put their heads in **b** and sent
Ps 81: 6 hands were freed from the **b**.
Jer 24: 1 and there were two **b** of figs
Mt 14:20 and they took up twelve **b** full
15:37 and they took up seven large **b**
16: 9 five thousand and how many **b**
16:10 thousand and how many large **b**
Mk 6:43 And they took up twelve **b** full
8: 8 and they took up seven large **b**
8:19 how many **b** full of fragments
8:20 how many large **b** full of
Lk 9:17 and twelve **b** of the leftover
Jn 6:13 and filled twelve **b** with the

BASMATH (KJV) See BASEMATH

BASON, BASONS (KJV) See BASIN, BASINS

BASTARD, BASTARDS (KJV) See DESCENDANTS, ILLEGITIMATE

BAT (2/2) BATS

Lev 11:19 its kind, the hoopoe, and the **b**.
Deut 14:18 kind, and the hoopoe and the **b**.

BATH (7/5) BATHE, BATHED, BATHING, BATHS

Isa 5:10 of vineyard shall yield one **b**,
Ezek 45:10 honest ephah, and an honest **b**.
45:11 The ephah and the **b** shall be of
45:11 so that the **b** contains
45:14 the **b** of oil, is one-tenth of
45:14 is one-tenth of a **b** from a

BATH RABBIM (1/1)

Song 7: 4 in Heshbon By the gate of **B**.

BATHE (19/19) BATHED, BATHING

Ex 2: 5 of Pharaoh came down to **b** at
Lev 15: 5 shall wash his clothes and **b**
15: 6 shall wash his clothes and **b**
15: 7 shall wash his clothes and **b**
15: 8 he shall wash his clothes and **b**
15:10 shall wash his clothes and **b**
15:11 he shall wash his clothes and **b**
15:13 and **b** his body in running
15:18 they shall **b** in water, and be
15:21 shall wash his clothes and **b**
15:22 on shall wash his clothes and **b**
15:27 he shall wash his clothes and **b**
16:26 shall wash his clothes and **b**
16:28 shall wash his clothes and **b**
17:15 both wash his clothes and **b** in
17:16 if he does not wash them or **b**
Num 19: 7 he shall **b** in water, and
19: 8 **b** in water, and shall be
19:19 and **b** in water; and at evening

BATHED (4/4) BATHE

1 Ki 22:38 his blood while the harlots **b**,
Job 29: 6 When my steps were **b** with
Isa 34: 5 For My sword shall be **b** in
Jn 13:10 He who is **b** needs only to wash

BATHING (1/1) BATHE

2 Sam 11: 2 from the roof he saw a woman **b**,

BATHS (10/7) BATH

1 Ki 7:26 It contained two thousand **b**.
7:38 each laver contained forty **b**,
2 Chr 2:10 twenty thousand **b** of wine, and
2:10 and twenty thousand **b** of oil.
4: 5 It contained three thousand **b**.
Ezra 7:22 one hundred **b** of wine, one
7:22 one hundred **b** of oil, and salt
Ezek 45:14 A kor is a homer or ten **b**,
45:14 for ten **b** are a homer.
Hag 2:16 wine vat to draw out fifty **b**

BATHSHEBA (11/11) BATHSHUA

2 Sam 11: 3 someone said, "Is this not **B**,
12:24 Then David comforted **B** his
1 Ki 1:11 So Nathan spoke to **B** the mother
1:15 So **B** went into the chamber to
1:16 And **B** bowed and did homage to
1:28 Call **B** to me." So she came into
1:31 Then **B** bowed with her face to
2:13 the son of Haggith came to **B**
2:18 So **B** said, "Very well, I will
2:19 **B** therefore went to King
Ps 51: him, after he had gone in to **B**.

BATHSHUA (1/1) BATHSHEBA

1 Chr 3: 5 four by **B** the daughter of

BATS (1/1)

Isa 2:20 to worship, To the moles and **b**,

BATTEN (2/1)

Judg 16:14 wove it tightly with the **b** of
16:14 and pulled out the **b** and the

BATTER (1/1) BATTERED, BATTERING

Num 24:17 And **b** the brow of Moab, And

BATTERED (1/1) BATTER

2 Sam 20:15 people who were with Joab **b**

BATTERING (4/3) BATTER

Ezek 4: 2 and place **b** rams against it all
21:22 to set up **b** rams, to call for a
21:22 to set **b** rams against the
26: 9 He will direct his **b** rams

BATTLE (184/171) BATTLE-AX, BATTLEFIELD, BATTLEMENT, BATTLES

Gen 14: 8 out and joined together in **b**
Num 21:33 all his people, to **b** at Edrei.
31:14 who had come from the **b**.
31:21 of war who had gone to the **b**,
31:27 in the war, who went out to **b**,
31:28 men of war who went out to **b**:
32:27 for war, before the LORD to **b**,
32:29 every man armed for **b** before
Deut 2: 9 nor contend with them in **b**,
2:24 it, and engage him in **b**.
3: 1 all his people, to **b** at Edrei.
20: 1 When you go out to **b** against
20: 2 when you are on the verge of **b**,
20: 3 you are on the verge of **b** with
20: 5 lest he die in the **b** and
20: 6 lest he die in the **b** and
20: 7 lest he die in the **b** and
29: 7 Bashan came out against us to **b**,
Josh 4:13 over before the LORD for **b**,
8:14 went out against Israel to **b**,
11:19 All the others they took in **b**.
11:20 should come against Israel in **b**,
22:33 more of going against them in **b**,
Judg 8:13 son of Joash returned from **b**,
20:14 to go to **b** against the children
20:18 of us shall go up first to **b**
20:20 the men of Israel went out to **b**
20:20 of Israel put themselves in **b**
20:22 and again formed the **b** line at
20:23 Shall I again draw near for **b**
20:28 Shall I yet again go out to **b**
20:30 and put themselves in **b** array
20:33 place and put themselves in **b**
20:34 and the **b** was fierce. But the
20:39 men of Israel would turn in **b**.
20:39 before us, as in the first **b**.
20:42 but the **b** overtook them, and
1 Sam 4: 1 Now Israel went out to **b**
4: 2 put themselves in **b** array
4: 2 And when they joined **b**,
4:12 man of Benjamin ran from the **b**
4:16 "I am he who came from the **b**.
4:16 And I fled today from the **b**
7:10 the Philistines drew near to **b**
11: 7 out with Saul and Samuel to **b**,
13:22 it came about, on the day of **b**,
14:20 and they went to the **b**;
14:22 hard after them in the **b**.
14:23 and the **b** shifted to Beth Aven.
17: 1 their armies together to **b**,
17: 2 and drew up in **b** array against
17: 8 you come out to line up for **b**?
17:13 gone to follow Saul to the **b**.
17:13 three sons who went to the **b**
17:20 fight and shouting for the **b**.
17:21 Philistines had drawn up in **b**
17:28 you have come down to see the **b**.
17:47 for the **b** is the LORD's, and
26:10 or he shall go out to **b** and
28: 1 you will go out with me to **b**,
29: 4 let him go down with us to **b**,
29: 4 lest in the **b** he become our
29: 9 not go up with us to the **b**.
30:24 part is who goes down to the **b**,
31: 3 The **b** became fierce against
2 Sam 1: 4 people have fled from the **b**,
1:25 fallen in the midst of the **b**!

2:17 So there was a very fierce ***b***
3:30 Asahel at Gibeon in the ***b***.
10: 8 out and put themselves in ***b***
10: 9 When Joab saw that the ***b*** line
10: 9 best and put them in ***b*** array
10:10 that he might set them in ***b***
10:13 with him drew near for the ***b***
10:17 the Syrians set themselves in ***b***
11: 1 time when kings go out to ***b***,
11:15 the forefront of the hottest ***b***,
17:11 and that you go to ***b*** in person.
18: 6 went out into the field of ***b***
18: 6 And the ***b*** was in the woods of
18: 8 For the ***b*** there was scattered
19: 3 steal away when they flee in ***b***.
19:10 anointed over us, has died in ***b***.
20: 8 Now Joab was dressed in ***b***
21:17 go out no more with us to ***b***,
21:18 that there was again a ***b*** with
22:40 me with strength for the ***b***;
23: 9 who were gathered there for ***b***,
1 Ki 8:44 When Your people go out to ***b***
20:14 Who will set the ***b*** in order?"
20:29 that on the seventh day the ***b***
20:39 out into the midst of the ***b***;
22:30 disguise myself and go into ***b***;
22:30 himself and went into ***b***.
22:34 around and take me out of the ***b***,
22:35 The ***b*** increased that day; and
2 Ki 3:26 the king of Moab saw that the ***b***
14: 8 let us face one another in ***b***.
1 Chr 5:20 they cried out to God in the ***b***.
7:11 fit to go out for war and ***b***.
7:40 among the army fit for ***b***;
10: 3 The ***b*** became fierce against
11:13 Philistines were gathered for ***b***,
12: 8 men of valor, men trained for ***b***,
12:19 going with the Philistines to ***b***
12:33 thousand who went out to ***b***,
12:35 of the Danites who could keep ***b***
12:36 able to keep ***b*** formation, forty
12:37 and twenty thousand armed for ***b***
14:15 then you shall go out to ***b***,
19: 7 their cities, and came to ***b***.
19: 9 out and put themselves in ***b***
19:10 When Joab saw that the ***b*** line
19:10 best and put them in ***b*** array
19:11 and they set themselves in ***b***
19:14 with him drew near for the ***b***
19:17 and set up in ***b*** array against
19:17 So when David had set up in ***b***
20: 1 at the time kings go out to ***b***,
2 Chr 6:34 When Your people go out to ***b***
13: 3 Abijah set the ***b*** in order with
13: 3 Jeroboam also drew up in ***b***
13:14 to their surprise the ***b*** line
14:10 and they set the troops in ***b***
18:29 disguise myself and go into ***b***;
18:29 himself, and they went into ***b***.
18:33 around and take me out of the ***b***,
18:34 The ***b*** increased that day, and
20: 1 came to ***b*** against Jehoshaphat.
20:15 for the ***b*** is not yours, but
20:17 not need to fight in this ***b***.
25: 8 be gone! Be strong in ***b***! Even
25:13 they would not go with him to ***b***,
25:17 let us face one another in ***b***.
Job 15:24 him, like a king ready for ***b***.
38:23 For the day of ***b*** and war?
39:25 Aha!' He smells the ***b*** from
41: 8 hand on him; Remember the ***b***—
Ps 18:39 me with strength for the ***b***;
24: 8 mighty, The LORD mighty in ***b***.
55:18 my soul in peace from the ***b***
76: 3 bow, The shield and sword of ***b***.
78: 9 Turned back in the day of ***b***.
89:43 have not sustained him in the ***b***.
140: 7 covered my head in the day of ***b***.
144: 1 for war, And my fingers for ***b***—
Prov 21:31 is prepared for the day of ***b***,
Eccl 9:11 Nor the ***b*** to the strong, Nor
Isa 9: 5 sandal from the noisy ***b***,
13: 4 hosts musters The army for ***b***.
16: 9 For ***b*** cries have fallen Over
22: 2 with the sword, Nor dead in ***b***.
27: 4 and thorns Against Me in ***b***?
28: 6 to those who turn back the ***b***
42:25 anger And the strength of ***b***;
Jer 8: 6 As the horse rushes into the ***b***.
18:21 be slain By the sword in ***b***.
46: 3 And draw near to ***b***!
49:14 And rise up to ***b***!
50:22 A sound of ***b*** is in the land,
50:42 in array, like a man for the ***b***,
Ezek 7:14 ready, But no one goes to ***b***;
13: 5 house of Israel to stand in ***b***
Dan 11:20 but not in anger or in ***b***.
11:25 South shall be stirred up to ***b***
Hos 1: 7 them by bow, Nor by sword or ***b***,
2:18 Bow and sword of ***b*** I will
10: 9 The ***b*** in Gibeah against the
10:14 Beth Arbel in the day of ***b***—
Joel 2: 5 Like a strong people set in ***b***
Am 1:14 Amid shouting in the day of ***b***,
Ob 1 us rise up against her for ***b***'
Zech 9:10 The ***b*** bow shall be cut off.
10: 3 as His royal horse in the ***b***.
10: 4 From him the ***b*** bow, From him
10: 5 mire of the streets in the ***b***.
14: 2 gather all the nations to ***b***
14: 3 As He fights in the day of ***b***.
1 Cor 14: 8 who will prepare himself for ***b***?
Heb 11:34 strong, became valiant in ***b***,
Rev 9: 7 was like horses prepared for ***b***.
9: 9 with many horses running into ***b***.
16:14 to gather them to the ***b*** of that
20: 8 to gather them together to ***b***,

BATTLE-AX (2/2)

Jer 51:20 You are My ***b*** and weapons of
Ezek 9: 2 each with his ***b*** in his hand.

BATTLEFIELD (1/1) BATTLE

Judg 5:18 also, on the heights of the ***b***.

BATTLEMENT (1/1) BATTLE

Song 8: 9 We will build upon her A ***b*** of

BATTLES (6/6) BATTLE

1 Sam 8:20 out before us and fight our ***b***.
18:17 for me, and fight the LORD's ***b***.
25:28 because my lord fights the ***b*** of
1 Chr 26:27 Some of the spoils won in ***b*** they
2 Chr 32: 8 to help us and to fight our ***b***.
Isa 30:32 And in ***b*** of brandishing He

BAVAI (1/1)

Neh 3:18 under ***B*** the son of Henadad,

BAY (4/4)

Josh 15: 2 from the ***b*** that faces
15: 5 quarter began at the ***b*** of the
18:19 border ended at the north ***b*** at
Acts 27:39 but they observed a ***b*** with a

BAZLITH (1/1) BAZLUTH

Neh 7:54 the sons of ***B***, the sons of

BAZLUTH (1/1) BAZLITH

Ezra 2:52 the sons of ***B***, the sons of

BDELLIUM (2/2)

Gen 2:12 ***B*** and the onyx stone are
Num 11: 7 its color like the color of ***b***.

BE (5747/4673) See APPENDIX

BE ESHTERAH (1/1)

Josh 21:27 and ***B*** with its common-land: two

BEACH (1/1)

Acts 27:39 they observed a bay with a ***b***,

BEACON (KJV) See POLE

BEALIAH (1/1)

1 Chr 12: 5 Eluzai, Jerimoth, ***B***,

BEALOTH (1/1) ALOTH

Josh 15:24 Ziph, Telem, ***B***,

BEAM (8/8) BEAMS

Num 4:10 and put it on a carrying ***b***.
4:12 and put them on a carrying ***b***.
1 Sam 17: 7 spear was like a weaver's ***b***,
2 Sam 21:19 spear was like a weaver's ***b***.
2 Ki 6: 2 and let every man take a ***b*** from
1 Chr 11:23 was a spear like a weaver's ***b***;
20: 5 spear was like a weaver's ***b***.
Hab 2:11 And the ***b*** from the timbers

BEAMS (15/15)

1 Ki 6: 6 so that the support ***b*** would
6: 9 he paneled the temple with ***b***
6:10 to the temple with cedar ***b***.
6:36 hewn stone and a row of cedar ***b***.
7: 2 and cedar ***b*** on the pillars.
7: 3 paneled with cedar above the ***b***
7:12 stones and a row of cedar ***b***.
2 Chr 3: 7 the ***b*** and doorposts, its walls
34:11 buy hewn stone and timber for ***b***,
Neh 2: 8 must give me timber to make ***b***
3: 3 they laid its ***b*** and hung its
3: 6 they laid its ***b*** and hung its
Job 40:18 His bones are like ***b*** of
Ps 104: 3 He lays the ***b*** of His upper
Song 1:17 The ***b*** of our houses are cedar,

BEANS (2/2)

2 Sam 17:28 and flour, parched grain and ***b***,
Ezek 4: 9 for yourself wheat, barley, ***b***,

BEAR (225/215) BEARERS, BEARING, BEARS, BORE, BORNE

Gen 4:13 is greater than I can ***b***!
16:11 And you shall ***b*** a son.
17:17 years old, ***b*** a child?"
17:19 Sarah your wife shall ***b*** you a
17:21 whom Sarah shall ***b*** to you at
18:13 Shall I surely ***b*** a child,
30: 3 and she will ***b*** a child on my
43: 9 then let me ***b*** the blame
44:32 then I shall ***b*** the blame before
49:15 He bowed his shoulder to ***b*** a
Ex 18:22 for they will ***b*** the burden
20:16 You shall not ***b*** false witness
25:27 as holders for the poles to ***b***
27: 7 two sides of the altar to ***b*** it.
28:12 So Aaron shall ***b*** their names
28:29 So Aaron shall ***b*** the names of
28:30 So Aaron shall ***b*** the judgment
28:38 that Aaron may ***b*** the iniquity
30: 4 for the poles with which to ***b***
37: 5 sides of the ark, to ***b*** the ark.
37:14 as holders for the poles to ***b***
37:15 the poles of acacia wood to ***b***
37:27 for the poles with which to ***b***
38: 7 with which to ***b*** it. He made the
Lev 5:17 yet he is guilty and shall ***b***
7:18 person who eats of it shall ***b***
10:17 God has given it to you to ***b***
16:22 The goat shall ***b*** on itself all
17:16 then he shall ***b*** his guilt."
19: 8 everyone who eats it shall ***b***
19:17 and not ***b*** sin because of him.
19:18 nor ***b*** any grudge against the
20:17 He shall ***b*** his guilt.
20:19 They shall ***b*** their guilt.
20:20 They shall ***b*** their sin; they
22: 9 lest they ***b*** sin for it and die
22:16 or allow them to ***b*** the guilt of
24:15 'Whoever curses his God shall ***b***
Num 5:31 but that woman shall ***b*** her
9:13 that man shall ***b*** his sin.
11:14 I am not able to ***b*** all these
11:17 and they shall ***b*** the burden of
11:17 that you may not ***b*** it yourself
14:27 How long shall I ***b*** with this
14:33 and ***b*** the brunt of your
14:34 for each day you shall ***b*** your
18: 1 house with you shall ***b*** the
18: 1 and your sons with you shall ***b***
18:22 lest they ***b*** sin and die.
18:23 and they shall ***b*** their
18:32 And you shall ***b*** no sin because
30:15 then he shall ***b*** her guilt."
Deut 1: 9 I alone am not able to ***b*** you.
1:12 How can I alone ***b*** your problems
5:20 You shall not ***b*** false witness
10: 8 the tribe of Levi to ***b*** the ark
29:23 it is not sown, nor does it ***b***,
Josh 3: 8 command the priests who ***b*** the
3:13 the feet of the priests who ***b***
4:16 Command the priests who ***b*** the
6: 4 And seven priests shall ***b*** seven
6: 6 and let seven priests ***b*** seven
Judg 5:14 And from Zebulun those who ***b***
13: 3 but you shall conceive and ***b*** a
13: 5 you shall conceive and ***b*** a son.
13: 7 you shall conceive and ***b*** a son.
Ruth 1:12 tonight and should also ***b*** sons,
1 Sam 17:34 and when a lion or a ***b*** came and
17:36 has killed both lion and ***b***;
17:37 lion and from the paw of the ***b***,
2 Sam 17: 8 like a ***b*** robbed of her cubs in
1 Ki 21:10 before him to ***b*** witness against
2 Ki 3:21 all who were able to ***b*** arms and
19:30 And ***b*** fruit upward.
1 Chr 5:18 men able to ***b*** shield and sword,
2 Chr 2: 2 seventy thousand men to ***b***
Job 9: 9 He made the ***B***, Orion, and the
21: 3 ***B*** with me that I may speak,
24:21 on the barren who do not ***b***,
36: 2 ***B*** with me a little, and I will
38:32 Or can you guide the Great ***B***
39: 1 when the wild mountain goats ***b***
39: 2 you know the time when they ***b***
Ps 28: 9 And ***b*** them up forever.
55:12 Then I could ***b*** it. Nor is
89:50 How I ***b*** in my bosom the
91:12 In their hands they shall ***b***
92:14 They shall still ***b*** fruit in old
Prov 9:12 you will ***b*** it alone."
17:12 Let a man meet a ***b*** robbed of
18:14 But who can ***b*** a broken spirit?
28:15 a roaring lion and a charging ***b***
30:21 for four it cannot ***b*** up:
Isa 7:14 virgin shall conceive and ***b*** a
11: 7 The cow and the ***b*** shall graze;
37:31 And ***b*** fruit upward.
46: 4 I have made, and I will ***b***;
46: 7 They ***b*** it on the shoulder, they
52:11 You who ***b*** the vessels of the
53:11 For He shall ***b*** their
Jer 10:19 And I must ***b*** it."
12: 2 they ***b*** fruit. You are near in
17:21 and ***b*** no burden on the Sabbath
29: 6 so that they may ***b*** sons and
44:22 the LORD could no longer ***b***
Lam 3:10 He has been to me a ***b*** lying
3:27 It is good for a man to ***b***
5: 7 But we ***b*** their iniquities.
Ezek 4: 4 you shall ***b*** their iniquity.
4: 5 so you shall ***b*** the iniquity of
4: 6 then you shall ***b*** the iniquity
12: 6 In their sight you shall ***b*** them
12:12 who is among them shall ***b***
14:10 And they shall ***b*** their iniquity;
16:52 ***b*** your own shame also, because
16:52 and ***b*** your own shame, because
16:54 that you may ***b*** your own shame

17: 8 **b** fruit, And become a
17:23 and **b** fruit, and be a majestic
18:19 Why should the son not **b** the
18:20 The son shall not **b** the guilt
18:20 nor the father **b** the guilt of
23:35 Therefore you shall **b** the
32:24 Now they **b** their shame with
32:25 Yet they **b** their shame With
32:30 And **b** their shame with those
34:29 nor **b** the shame of the Gentiles
36: 7 that are around you shall **b**
36:11 and they shall increase and **b**
36:15 nor **b** the reproach of the
36:30 so that you need never again **b**
44:10 they shall **b** their iniquity.
44:12 that they shall **b** their
44:13 but they shall **b** their shame
47:12 They will **b** fruit every month,
47:22 who dwell among you and who **b**
Dan 7: 5 beast, a second, like a **b**.
Hos 9:16 They shall **b** no fruit.
9:16 were they to **b** children, I
13: 8 I will meet them like a **b**
Am 5:19 And a **b** met him! Or as
7:10 The land is not able to **b** all
Mic 6:16 Therefore you shall **b** the
7: 9 I will **b** the indignation of the
Zech 6:13 He shall **b** the glory, And
Mal 3:11 Nor shall the vine fail to **b**
Mt 1:23 and **b** a Son, and they
3: 8 Therefore **b** fruits worthy of
3:10 every tree which does not **b**
4: 6 their hands they shall **b**
7:18 A good tree cannot **b** bad fruit,
7:18 nor can a bad tree **b** good
7:19 Every tree that does not **b** good
17:17 How long shall I **b** with you?
19:18 You shall not **b** false
23: 4 bind heavy burdens, hard to **b**,
27:32 Him they compelled to **b** His
Mk 4:20 and **b** fruit: some thirtyfold,
9:19 How long shall I **b** with you?
10:19 Do not **b** false witness,' 'Do
15:21 and passing by, to **b** His cross.
Lk 1:13 and your wife Elizabeth will **b**
3: 8 Therefore **b** fruits worthy of
3: 9 every tree which does not **b**
4:11 their hands they shall **b**
6:43 For a good tree does not **b** bad
6:43 nor does a bad tree **b** good
8:15 keep it and **b** fruit with
9:41 long shall I be with you and **b**
11:46 load men with burdens hard to **b**,
11:48 you **b** witness that you approve
14:27 And whoever does not **b** his cross
18:20 Do not **b** false witness,'
23:26 laid the cross that he might **b**
Jn 1: 7 to **b** witness of the Light, that
1: 8 but was sent to **b** witness of
3:28 You yourselves **b** me witness,
5:31 If I **b** witness of Myself, My
5:36 **b** witness of Me, that the Father
8:13 You **b** witness of Yourself; Your
8:14 Even if I **b** witness of Myself,
10:25 they **b** witness of Me.
15: 2 branch in Me that does not **b**
15: 2 that it may **b** more fruit.
15: 4 As the branch cannot **b** fruit of
15: 8 that you **b** much fruit; so you
15:16 you that you should go and **b**
15:27 And you also will **b** witness,
16:12 but you cannot **b** them now.
18:23 **b** witness of the evil; but if
18:37 that I should **b** witness to the
Acts 9:15 is a chosen vessel of Mine to **b**
15:10 fathers nor we were able to **b**?
18:14 would be reason why I should **b**
23:11 so you must also **b** witness at
Rom 7: 4 that we should **b** fruit to God.
7: 5 at work in our members to **b**
10: 2 For I **b** them witness that they
13: 4 for he does not **b** the sword in
13: 9 You shall not **b** false
15: 1 then who are strong ought to **b**
1 Cor 10:13 that you may be able to **b** it.
15:49 we shall also **b** the image of
16: 3 your letters I will send to **b**
2 Cor 8: 3 For I **b** witness that according
11: 1 that you would **b** with me in a
11: 1 and indeed you do **b** with me.
Gal 4:15 For I **b** you witness that, if
4:27 You who do not **b**! Break
5:10 but he who troubles you shall **b**
6: 2 **B** one another's burdens, and so
6: 5 For each one shall **b** his own
6:17 for I **b** in my body the marks of
Col 4:13 For I **b** him witness that he has
1 Tim 5:14 **b** children, manage the house,
Heb 9:28 so Christ was offered once to **b**
13:22 **b** with the word of exhortation,
Jas 3:12 **b** olives, or a grapevine bear
3:12 or a grapevine **b** figs? Thus no
1 Jn 1: 2 and **b** witness, and declare to
5: 7 For there are three that **b**
5: 8 And there are three that **b**
3 Jn 12 And we also **b** witness, and you
Rev 2: 2 and that you cannot **b** those who
13: 2 were like the feet of a **b**,

BEARD (15/14) BEARDS

Lev 13:29 has a sore on the head or the **b**,
13:30 scaly leprosy of the head or **b**.
14: 9 the hair off his head and his **b**
19:27 disfigure the edges of your **b**.
1 Sam 17:35 me, I caught it by its **b**,
21:13 his saliva fall down on his **b**.
2 Sam 20: 9 And Joab took Amasa by the **b**
Ezra 9: 3 of the hair of my head and **b**,
Ps 133: 2 head, Running down on the **b**,
133: 2 The **b** of Aaron, Running down
Isa 7:20 And will also remove the **b**.
15: 2 And every **b** cut off.
50: 6 to those who plucked out the **b**;
Jer 48:37 and every **b** clipped; On all
Ezek 5: 1 it over your head and your **b**;

BEARDS (5/5) BEARD

Lev 21: 5 shave the edges of their **b** nor
2 Sam 10: 4 shaved off half of their **b**,
10: 5 Wait at Jericho until your **b**
1 Chr 19: 5 Wait at Jericho until your **b**
Jer 41: 5 eighty men with their **b** shaved

BEARERS (2/2) BEAR

2 Chr 2:18 seventy thousand of them **b** of
34:13 were over the burden **b** and

BEARING (25/25) BEAR

Gen 16: 2 LORD has restrained me from **b**
29:35 name Judah. Then she stopped **b**.
30: 9 Leah saw that she had stopped **b**,
37:25 **b** spices, balm, and myrrh, on
Num 4:47 of service and the work of **b**
Deut 29:18 may not be among you a root **b**
Josh 3: 3 **b** it, then you shall set out
3:14 with the priests **b** the ark of
6: 8 that the seven priests **b** the
6:13 Then seven priests **b** seven
2 Sam 6:13 when those **b** the ark of the
15:24 **b** the ark of the covenant of
21:16 who was **b** a new sword, thought
1 Chr 12:24 of the sons of Judah **b** shield
Ps 126: 6 **B** seed for sowing, Shall
Isa 1:14 I am weary of **b** them.
Mt 21:43 you and given to a nation **b**
Jn 19:17 **b** His cross, went out to a
Acts 14: 3 who was **b** witness to the word
Rom 2:15 their conscience also **b**
9: 1 my conscience also **b** me witness
Eph 4: 2 **b** with one another in love,
Col 3:13 **b** with one another, and
Heb 2: 4 God also **b** witness both with
13:13 the camp, **b** His reproach.

BEARS (27/25) BEAR

Lev 5: 1 does not tell it, he **b** guilt.
12: 5 But if she **b** a female child,
Deut 25: 6 the firstborn son which she **b**
28:57 and her children whom she **b**;
2 Ki 2:24 And two female **b** came out of
Job 16: 8 rises up against me And **b**
Prov 25:18 A man who **b** false witness
Song 4: 2 Every one of which **b** twins,
6: 6 Every one **b** twins, And none
Isa 59:11 We all growl like **b**,
Joel 2:22 And the tree **b** its fruit; The
Mt 7:17 every good tree **b** good fruit,
7:17 but a bad tree **b** bad fruit.
13:23 who indeed **b** fruit and
Lk 13: 9 And if it **b** fruit, well. But if
18: 7 though He **b** long with them?
Jn 5:32 There is another who **b** witness
8:18 I am One who **b** witness of
8:18 and the Father who sent Me **b**
15: 2 and every branch that **b** fruit
15: 5 **b** much fruit; for without Me
Acts 22: 5 as also the high priest **b** me
Rom 8:16 The Spirit Himself **b** witness
1 Cor 13: 7 **b** all things, believes all
Heb 6: 7 and **b** herbs useful for those by
6: 8 but if it **b** thorns and briars,
1 Jn 5: 6 And it is the Spirit who **b**

BEAST (127/117) BEASTS

Gen 1:24 and creeping thing and **b** of
1:25 And God made the **b** of the earth
1:30 to every **b** of the earth, to
2:19 the LORD God formed every **b**
2:20 and to every **b** of the field.
3: 1 was more cunning than any **b** of
3:14 And more than every **b** of the
6: 7 of the earth, both man and **b**,
7:14 they and every **b** after its kind,
9: 2 of you shall be on every **b** of
9: 5 from the hand of every **b** I will
9:10 and every **b** of the earth with
9:10 every **b** of the earth.
37:20 Some wild **b** has devoured him.'
37:33 A wild **b** has devoured him.
Ex 8:17 and it became lice on man and **b**.
8:18 So there were lice on man and **b**.
9: 9 break out in sores on man and **b**
9:10 break out in sores on man and **b**.
9:22 the land of Egypt—on man, on **b**,
9:25 in the field, both man and **b**;
11: 7 its tongue, against man or **b**,
12:12 land of Egypt, both man and **b**;
13: 2 of Israel, both of man and **b**;
13:15 of man and the firstborn of **b**.
19:13 an arrow; whether man or **b**,
22:13 it is torn to pieces by a **b**,
23:29 land become desolate and the **b**
Lev 5: 2 is the carcass of an unclean **b**,
7:26 whether of bird or **b**.
20:25 yourselves abominable by **b** or
27:28 that he has, both man and **b**,
Num 3:13 in Israel, both man and **b**.
8:17 are Mine, both man and **b**;
18:15 to the LORD, whether man or **b**,
31:11 and all the booty—of man and **b**.
31:26 that was taken–of man and **b**—
31:47 fifty, drawn from man and **b**,
2 Ki 14: 9 and a wild **b** that was in
2 Chr 25:18 and a wild **b** that was in
Job 39:15 Or that a wild **b** may break
Ps 36: 6 LORD, You preserve man and **b**.
50:10 For every **b** of the forest is
73:22 I was like a **b** before You.
74:19 Your turtledove to the wild **b**!
80:13 And the wild **b** of the field
104:11 They give drink to every **b** of
135: 8 of Egypt, Both of man and **b**.
147: 9 He gives to the **b** its food,
Isa 35: 9 Nor shall any ravenous **b** go
43:20 The **b** of the field will honor
46: 1 A burden to the weary **b**.
63:14 As a **b** goes down into the
Jer 7:20 on this place—on man and on **b**,
21: 6 of this city, both man and **b**;
27: 5 the man and the **b** that are on
31:27 seed of man and the seed of **b**.
32:43 is desolate, without man or **b**;
33:10 without man and without **b**"—in
33:10 inhabitant and without **b**,
33:12 without man and without **b**,
36:29 and cause man and **b** to cease
50: 3 shall depart, Both man and **b**.
51:62 remain in it, neither man nor **b**,
Ezek 14:13 and cut off man and **b** from it.
14:17 and I cut off man and **b** from
14:19 and cut off from it man and **b**,
14:21 to cut off man and **b** from it?
25:13 cut off man and **b** from it, and
29: 8 and cut off from you man and **b**.
29:11 pass through it nor foot of **b**
34: 8 flock became food for every **b**
36:11 multiply upon you man and **b**;
39:17 sort of bird and to every **b** of
44:31 not eat anything, bird or **b**,
Dan 4:16 him be given the heart of a **b**,
7: 5 "And suddenly another **b**,
7: 6 The **b** also had four heads, and
7: 7 visions, and behold, a fourth **b**,
7:11 I watched till the **b** was slain,
7:19 the truth about the fourth **b**,
7:23 The fourth **b** shall be A fourth
Hos 13: 8 The wild **b** shall tear them.
Jon 3: 7 saying, Let neither man nor **b**,
3: 8 But let man and **b** be covered
Zeph 1: 3 "I will consume man and **b**;
2:14 Every **b** of the nation.
Zech 8:10 for man nor any hire for **b**;
Heb 12:20 And if so much as a **b**
Jas 3: 7 For every kind of **b** and bird, of
Rev 11: 7 the **b** that ascends out of the
13: 1 And I saw a **b** rising up out of
13: 2 Now the **b** which I saw was like a
13: 3 marveled and followed the **b**.
13: 4 who gave authority to the **b**;
13: 4 beast; and they worshiped the **b**,
13: 4 saying, "Who is like the **b**?
13:11 Then I saw another **b** coming up
13:12 the authority of the first **b**
13:12 in it to worship the first **b**,
13:14 to do in the sight of the **b**,
13:14 to make an image to the **b** who
13:15 breath to the image of the **b**,
13:15 that the image of the **b** should
13:15 not worship the image of the **b**
13:17 the mark or the name of the **b**,
13:18 calculate the number of the **b**,
14: 9 If anyone worships the **b** and his
14:11 who worship the **b** and his
15: 2 who have the victory over the **b**,
16: 2 men who had the mark of the **b**
16:10 his bowl on the throne of the **b**,
16:13 out of the mouth of the **b**,
17: 3 a woman sitting on a scarlet **b**
17: 7 of the woman and of the **b** that
17: 8 The **b** that you saw was, and is
17: 8 when they see the **b** that was,
17:11 And the **b** that was, and is not,
17:12 one hour as kings with the **b**.
17:13 power and authority to the **b**.
17:16 horns which you saw on the **b**,
17:17 to give their kingdom to the **b**,
19:19 And I saw the **b**,
19:20 Then the **b** was captured, and
19:20 who received the mark of the **b**
20: 4 who had not worshiped the **b** or
20:10 fire and brimstone where the **b**

BEASTS (100/97) BEAST

Gen 7:21 birds and cattle and **b** and
31:39 That which was torn by **b** I did
Ex 22:31 shall not eat meat torn by **b**
23:11 the **b** of the field may eat. In
Lev 7:24 fat of what is torn by wild **b**,
17:15 or what was torn by **b**,
22: 8 naturally or is torn by **b**

25: 7 for your livestock and the **b**
26: 6 I will rid the land of evil **b**,
26:22 I will also send wild **b** among
Deut 7:22 lest the **b** of the field become
28:26 the birds of the air and the **b**
32:24 against them the teeth of **b**,
Judg 20:48 every city, men and **b**,
1 Sam 17:44 the birds of the air and the **b**
17:46 of the air and the wild **b** of
2 Sam 21:10 rest on them by day nor the **b**
Job 5:22 shall not be afraid of the **b**
5:23 And the **b** of the field shall
12: 7 "But now ask the **b**,
18: 3 Why are we counted as **b**,
35:11 teaches us more than the **b** of
37: 8 The **b** go into dens, And remain
40:20 And all the **b** of the field
Ps 8: 7 Even the **b** of the field,
49:12 He is like the **b** that perish.
49:20 Is like the **b** that perish.
50:11 And the wild **b** of the field
68:30 Rebuke the **b** of the reeds, The
79: 2 flesh of Your saints to the **b**
104:20 In which all the **b** of the
148:10 **B** and all cattle;
Prov 30:30 which is mighty among **b** And
Isa 13:21 But wild **b** of the desert will
18: 6 birds of prey And for the **b**
18: 6 And all the **b** of the earth
23:13 Assyria founded it for wild **b**
30: 6 The burden against the **b** of the
34:14 The wild **b** of the desert shall
40:16 Nor its **b** sufficient for a
46: 1 Their idols were on the **b** and
56: 9 All you **b** of the field, come
56: 9 All you **b** in the forest.
Jer 7:33 of the heaven and for the **b** of
9:10 birds of the heavens and the **b**
12: 4 The **b** and birds are consumed,
12: 9 assemble all the **b** of the
15: 3 birds of the heavens and the **b**
16: 4 birds of heaven and for the **b**
19: 7 of the heaven and for the **b** of
27: 6 and the **b** of the field I have
28:14 I have given him the **b** of the
34:20 birds of the heaven and the **b**
50:39 Therefore the wild desert **b**
Ezek 4:14 died of itself or was torn by **b**,
5:17 against you famine and wild **b**,
8:10 of creeping thing, abominable **b**,
14:15 If I cause wild **b** to pass
14:15 pass through because of the **b**,
14:21 sword and famine and wild **b**
29: 5 given you as food To the **b** of
31: 6 Under its branches all the **b**
31:13 And all the **b** of the field
32: 4 with you I will fill the **b** of
33:27 field I will give to the **b** to
34: 5 they became food for all the **b**
34:25 and cause wild **b** to cease from
34:28 nor shall **b** of the land devour
38:20 the **b** of the field, all
39: 4 of every sort and to the **b** of
44:31 or was torn by wild **b**.
Dan 2:38 or the **b** of the field and the
4:12 The **b** of the field found shade
4:14 Let the **b** get out from under
4:15 And let him graze with the **b**
4:21 under which the **b** of the field
4:23 and let him graze with the **b** of
4:25 dwelling shall be with the **b**
4:32 dwelling shall be with the **b**
5:21 his heart was made like the **b**,
7: 3 And four great **b** came up from
7: 7 was different from all the **b**
7:12 "As for the rest of the **b**,
7:17 'Those great **b**, which are four,
Hos 2:12 And the **b** of the field shall
2:18 a covenant for them With the **b**
4: 3 will waste away With the **b** of
Joel 1:20 The **b** of the field also cry out
2:22 you **b** of the field; For the
Mic 5: 8 Like a lion among the **b** of the
Hab 2:17 And the plunder of **b** which
Zeph 2:15 A place for **b** to lie down!
Mk 1:13 Satan, and was with the wild **b**;
Acts 10:12 animals of the earth, wild **b**,
11: 6 animals of the earth, wild **b**,
1 Cor 15:32 I have fought with **b** at
Titus 1:12 are always liars, evil **b**,
2 Pe 2:12 like natural brute **b** made to be
Jude 10 know naturally, like brute **b**,
Rev 6: 8 and by the **b** of the earth.

BEAT (40/40) BEATEN, BEATING, BEATINGS, BEATS

Ex 30:36 And you shall **b** some of it very
39: 3 And they **b** the gold into thin
Num 11: 8 ground it on millstones or **b**
Deut 24:20 When you **b** your olive trees, you
25: 3 he should exceed this and **b**
Judg 19:22 surrounded the house and **b** on
Ruth 2:17 and **b** out what she had gleaned,
2 Sam 22:43 Then I **b** them as fine as the
Ps 18:42 Then I **b** them as fine as the
78:66 And He **b** back His enemies;
89:23 I will **b** down his foes before
Prov 23:13 For if you **b** him with a rod,
23:14 You shall **b** him with a rod,
Isa 2: 4 They shall **b** their swords into
41:15 thresh the mountains and **b**
Ezek 21:17 I also will **b** My fists together,
22:13 I **b** My fists at the dishonest
Joel 3:10 **B** your plowshares into swords
Jon 4: 8 and the sun **b** on Jonah's head,
Mic 4: 3 They shall **b** their swords into
4:13 You shall **b** in pieces many
Mt 7:25 and the winds blew and **b** on
7:27 and the winds blew and **b** on
21:35 **b** one, killed one, and stoned
24:49 and begins to **b** his fellow
26:67 they spat in His face and **b**
Mk 4:37 and the waves **b** into the boat,
12: 3 And they took him and **b** him and
14:65 and to **b** Him, and to say to
Lk 6:48 the stream **b** vehemently against
6:49 against which the stream **b**
12:45 and begins to **b** the male and
18:13 but **b** his breast, saying, 'God,
20:10 But the vinedressers **b** him and
20:11 and they **b** him also, treated
22:63 who held Jesus mocked Him and **b**
23:48 **b** their breasts and returned.
Acts 18:17 and **b** him before the judgment
22:19 synagogue I imprisoned and **b**
27:20 and no small tempest **b** on us,

BEATEN (27/26) BEAT

Ex 5:14 were **b** and were asked, "Why
5:16 And indeed your servants are **b**,
37: 7 He made two cherubim of **b** gold;
Lev 2:14 grain **b** from full heads.
2:16 part of its **b** grain and part
16:12 hands full of sweet incense **b**
Deut 25: 2 the wicked man deserves to be **b**,
25: 2 cause him to lie down and be **b**
Josh 8:15 Israel made as if they were **b**
2 Sam 2:17 and the men of Israel were **b**
2 Chr 34: 7 had **b** the carved images into
Prov 23:35 They have **b** me, but I did not
Isa 27: 9 Like chalkstones that are **b**
28:27 But the black cummin is **b** out
30:31 of the LORD Assyria will be **b**
Jer 10: 9 Silver is **b** into plates; It is
46: 5 Their mighty ones are **b** down;
Mic 1: 7 her carved images shall be **b**
Mk 13: 9 and you will be **b** in the
Lk 12:47 shall be **b** with many stripes.
12:48 shall be **b** with few.
Acts 5:40 called for the apostles and **b**
16:22 and commanded them to be **b**
16:37 They have **b** us openly,
1 Cor 4:11 we are poorly clothed, and **b**,
2 Cor 11:25 Three times I was **b** with rods;
1 Pe 2:20 when you are **b** for your faults,

BEATING (4/4) BEAT

Ex 2:11 And he saw an Egyptian **b** a
Nah 2: 7 of doves, **B** their breasts.
Mk 12: 5 **b** some and killing some.
Acts 21:32 they stopped **b** Paul.

BEATINGS (1/1) BEAT

Prov 19:29 And **b** for the backs of fools.

BEATS (2/2) BEAT

Ex 21:20 And if a man **b** his male or
1 Cor 9:26 not as one who **b** the air.

BEAUTIES (1/1) BEAUTIFY

Ps 110: 3 In the **b** of holiness, from the

BEAUTIFUL (53/53) BEAUTY

Gen 6: 2 of men, that they were **b**;
12:11 know that you are a woman of **b**
12:14 the woman, that she was very **b**.
24:16 the young woman was very **b** to
26: 7 because she is **b** to behold."
29:17 but Rachel was **b** of form and
49:21 He uses **b** words.
Ex 2: 2 when she saw that he was a **b**
Lev 23:40 on the first day the fruit of **b**
Deut 6:10 to give you large and **b** cities
8:12 and have built **b** houses and
21:11 you see among the captives a **b**
Josh 7:21 I saw among the spoils a **b**
1 Sam 25: 3 of good understanding and **b**
2 Sam 11: 2 and the woman was very **b** to
14:27 She was a woman of **b**
Esth 1:11 for she was **b** to behold.
2: 2 Let **b** young virgins be sought
2: 3 that they may gather all the **b**
2: 7 young woman was lovely and **b**.
Job 42:15 land were found no women so **b**
Ps 33: 1 praise from the upright is **b**.
48: 2 **B** in elevation, The joy of the
147: 1 is pleasant, and praise is **b**.
Eccl 3:11 He has made everything **b** in its
Song 6: 4 you are as **b** as Tirzah,
7: 1 How **b** are your feet in sandals,
Isa 2:16 And upon all the **b** sloops.
4: 2 Branch of the LORD shall be **b**
5: 9 Great and **b** ones, without
52: 1 Put on your **b** garments, O
52: 7 How **b** upon the mountains Are
64:11 Our holy and **b** temple, Where
Jer 3:19 A **b** heritage of the hosts of
13:20 given to you, Your **b** sheep?
48:17 staff is broken, The **b** rod!'
Ezek 16: 7 matured, and became very **b**.
16:12 and a **b** crown on your head.
16:13 and oil. You were exceedingly **b**,
16:17 You have also taken your **b**
16:39 take your **b** jewelry, and leave
23:26 clothes And take away your **b**
23:42 on their wrists and **b** crowns
31: 7 Thus it was **b** in greatness and
31: 9 I made it **b** with a multitude of
Mt 13:45 is like a merchant seeking **b**
23:27 tombs which indeed appear **b**
Lk 21: 5 how it was adorned with **b**
Acts 3: 2 of the temple which is called **B**,
3:10 who sat begging alms at the **B**
Rom 10:15 How **b** are the feet of
Heb 11:23 because they saw he was a **b**
Jas 1:11 and its **b** appearance perishes.

BEAUTIFY (4/4) BEAUTIES, BEAUTIFYING, BEAUTY

Ezra 7:27 to **b** the house of the LORD
Ps 149: 4 He will **b** the humble with
Isa 60:13 To **b** the place of My
Jer 2:33 Why do you **b** your way to seek

BEAUTIFYING (1/1) BEAUTIFY

Esth 2:12 and preparations for **b** women.

BEAUTY (49/49) BEAUTIES, BEAUTIFUL, BEAUTIFY, BEAUTIFYING

Ex 28: 2 brother, for glory and for **b**.
28:40 hats for them, for glory and **b**.
2 Sam 1:19 The **b** of Israel is slain on your
1 Chr 16:29 worship the LORD in the **b** of
2 Chr 3: 6 with precious stones for **b**,
20:21 and who should praise the **b** of
Esth 1:11 in order to show her **b** to the
2: 3 And let **b** preparations be given
2: 9 he readily gave **b** preparations
Job 40:10 array yourself with glory and **b**.
Ps 27: 4 To behold the **b** of the LORD,
29: 2 Worship the LORD in the **b** of
39:11 You make his **b** melt away like
45:11 King will greatly desire your **b**;
49:14 And their **b** shall be consumed
50: 2 of Zion, the perfection of **b**,
90:17 And let the **b** of the LORD our
96: 6 Strength and **b** are in His
96: 9 worship the LORD in the **b** of
Prov 6:25 Do not lust after her **b** in your
31:30 Charm is deceitful and **b** is
Isa 3:24 And branding instead of **b**.
13:19 The **b** of the Chaldeans' pride,
28: 1 Whose glorious **b** is a fading
28: 4 And the glorious **b** is a fading
28: 5 of glory and a diadem of **b** To
33:17 eyes will see the King in His **b**;
44:13 According to the **b** of a man,
53: 2 There is no **b** that we should
61: 3 To give them **b** for ashes, The
Lam 2: 1 heaven to the earth The **b** of
2:15 is called 'The perfection of **b**,
Ezek 7:20 As for the **b** of his ornaments,
16:14 the nations because of your **b**,
16:15 you trusted in your own **b**,
16:25 and made your **b** to be abhorred.
27: 3 have said, 'I am perfect in **b**.
27: 4 builders have perfected your **b**.
27:11 They made your **b** perfect.
28: 7 their swords against the **b** of
28:12 of wisdom and perfect in **b**.
28:17 was lifted up because of your **b**;
31: 8 garden of God was like it in **b**.
32:19 'Whom do you surpass in **b**?
Hos 14: 6 His **b** shall be like an olive
Zech 9:17 goodness And how great its **b**!
11: 7 two staffs: the one I called **B**,
11:10 And I took my staff, **B**,
1 Pe 3: 4 with the incorruptible **b** of a

BEBAI (6/5)

Ezra 2:11 the people of **B**,
8:11 of the sons of **B**,
8:11 Bebai, Zechariah the son of **B**,
10:28 of the sons of **B**:
Neh 7:16 the sons of **B**, six hundred
10:15 Bunni, Azgad, **B**,

BECAME (269/263)

Gen 2: 7 and man **b** a living being.
2:10 parted and **b** four riverheads.
9:21 and **b** uncovered in his tent.
16: 4 her mistress **b** despised in her
16: 5 I **b** despised in her eyes. The
19:11 so that they **b** weary trying to
19:26 and she **b** a pillar of salt.
20:12 and she **b** my wife.
21:20 and **b** an archer.
24:67 and he took Rebekah and she **b**
26:13 prospering until he **b** very
30:43 Thus the man **b** exceedingly
41:56 And the famine **b** severe in the
44:32 For your servant **b** surety for
47:20 So the land **b** Pharaoh's.
49:15 And **b** a band of slaves.
Ex 2:10 and he **b** her son. So she called

4: 3 and it **b** a serpent; and Moses
4: 4 and it **b** a rod in his hand),
7:10 and it **b** a serpent.
7:12 and they **b** serpents.
8:17 and it **b** lice on man and beast.
8:17 All the dust of the land **b** lice
9: 7 But the heart of Pharaoh **b**
9:24 the land of Egypt since it **b** a
16:21 And when the sun **b** hot, it
17:12 But Moses' hands **b** heavy; so
19:19 the trumpet sounded long and **b**
32:19 So Moses' anger **b** hot, and he
Num 9: 7 We **b** defiled by a human corpse.
12:10 suddenly Miriam **b** leprous, as
21: 4 and the soul of the people **b**
22:30 ever since I **b** yours, to this
26:10 and they **b** a sign.
Deut 26: 5 and there he **b** a nation, great,
Josh 7: 5 of the people melted and **b**
14:14 Hebron therefore **b** the
Judg 1:35 the house of Joseph **b** greater,
8:27 It **b** a snare to Gideon and to
11:39 And it **b** a custom in Israel
15:14 ropes that were on his arms **b**
15:18 Then he **b** very thirsty; so he
16:21 and he **b** a grinder in the
17: 5 his sons, who **b** his priest.
17:11 and the young man **b** like one of
17:12 and the young man **b** his priest,
Ruth 4:13 So Boaz took Ruth and she **b** his
4:16 and **b** a nurse to him.
1 Sam 10:12 Therefore it **b** a proverb:
16:21 and he **b** his armorbearer.
18:29 So Saul **b** David's enemy
18:30 so that his name **b** highly
22: 2 So he **b** captain over them.
25:37 and he **b** like a stone.
25:42 of David, and **b** his wife.
31: 3 The battle **b** fierce against
2 Sam 2:25 together behind Abner and **b** a
3: 8 Then Abner **b** very angry at the
4: 4 that he fell and **b** lame.
5:10 So David went on and **b** great,
6: 8 And David **b** angry because of the
8: 2 So the Moabites **b** David's
8: 6 and the Syrians **b** David's
8:14 and all the Edomites **b** David's
11:27 and she **b** his wife and bore him
12:15 bore to David, and it **b** ill.
13: 2 over his sister Tamar that he **b**
16:14 the people who were with him **b**
23:19 Therefore he **b** their captain.
1 Ki 11: 9 So the LORD **b** angry with
11:24 So he gathered men to him and **b**
12:30 Now this thing **b** a sin, for the
13: 6 to him, and **b** as before.
13:33 and he **b** one of the priests of
14: 1 Abijah the son of Jeroboam **b**
14:21 forty-one years old when he **b**
15: 1 Abijam **b** king over Judah.
15: 9 Asa **b** king over Judah.
15:25 Nadab the son of Jeroboam **b**
15:29 when he **b** king, that he killed
15:33 Baasha the son of Ahijah **b** king
16: 8 Elah the son of Baasha **b** king
16:23 Omri **b** king over Israel, and
16:29 Ahab the son of Omri **b** king
17:17 the woman who owned the house **b**
18:45 in the meantime that the sky **b**
19:21 and **b** his servant.
22:42 years old when he **b** king,
22:51 Ahaziah the son of Ahab **b** king
2 Ki 1:17 Jehoram **b** king in his place, in
3: 1 Now Jehoram the son of Ahab **b**
4:34 and the flesh of the child **b**
5:11 But Naaman **b** furious, and went
8:17 thirty-two years old when he **b**
8:26 twenty-two years old when he **b**
11:21 was seven years old when he **b**
12: 1 Jehoash **b** king, and he reigned
13: 1 Jehoahaz the son of Jehu **b** king
13:10 Jehoash the son of Jehoahaz **b**
14: 1 king of Judah, **b** king.
14: 2 years old when he **b** king,
14:23 **b** king in Samaria, and
15: 1 king of Judah, **b** king.
15: 2 was sixteen years old when he **b**
15:13 Shallum the son of Jabesh **b**
15:17 Menahem the son of Gadi **b** king
15:23 Pekahiah the son of Menahem **b**
15:27 Pekah the son of Remaliah **b**
15:33 years old when he **b** king,
16: 2 was twenty years old when he **b**
17: 1 Hoshea the son of Elah **b** king
17: 3 and Hoshea **b** his vassal, and
17:15 **b** idolaters, and went after
18: 2 years old when he **b** king,
21: 1 was twelve years old when he **b**
21:19 twenty-two years old when he **b**
22: 1 was eight years old when he **b**
23:31 years old when he **b** king,
23:36 years old when he **b** king,
24: 1 and Jehoiakim **b** his vassal for
24: 8 eighteen years old when he **b**
24:18 twenty-one years old when he **b**
1 Chr 10: 3 The battle **b** fierce against
11: 6 went up first, and **b** chief.
11: 9 Then David went on and **b** great,
11:21 Therefore he **b** their captain.
13:11 And David **b** angry because of the
18: 2 and the Moabites **b** David's
18: 6 and the Syrians **b** David's
18:13 and all the Edomites **b** David's
19:19 made peace with David and **b**
2 Chr 12:13 forty-one years old when he **b**
13: 1 Abijah **b** king over Judah.
16:12 Asa **b** diseased in his feet, and
17:12 So Jehoshaphat **b** increasingly
20:31 years old when he **b** king,
21: 5 thirty-two years old when he **b**
21:20 thirty-two years old when he **b**
22: 2 forty-two years old when he **b**
24: 1 was seven years old when he **b**
25: 1 years old when he **b** king,
26: 3 sixteen years old when he **b**
26: 8 for he **b** exceedingly strong.
26:15 marvelously helped till he **b**
26:19 Then Uzziah **b** furious; and he
27: 1 years old when he **b** king,
27: 6 So Jotham **b** mighty, because he
27: 8 years old when he **b** king,
28: 1 was twenty years old when he **b**
28:22 of his distress King Ahaz **b**
29: 1 Hezekiah **b** king when he was
33: 1 was twelve years old when he **b**
33:21 twenty-two years old when he **b**
34: 1 was eight years old when he **b**
36: 2 years old when he **b** king,
36: 5 years old when he **b** king,
36: 9 was eight years old when he **b**
36:11 twenty-one years old when he **b**
36:20 where they **b** servants to him
Neh 2: 2 So I **b** dreadfully afraid,
4: 7 that they **b** very angry,
5: 6 And I **b** very angry when I heard
Esth 2:21 **b** furious and sought to lay
2:22 So the matter **b** known to
8:17 of the people of the land **b**
9: 4 for this man Mordecai **b**
Ps 69:10 That **b** my reproach.
69:11 I **b** a byword to them.
83:10 Who **b** as refuse on the
106:36 Which **b** a snare to them.
114: 2 Judah **b** His sanctuary, And
Eccl 2: 9 So I **b** great and excelled more
Song 8:10 Then I **b** in his eyes As one
Isa 63: 8 So He **b** their Savior.
Jer 51:30 They **b** like women; They have
52: 1 twenty-one years old when he **b**
Lam 4:10 They **b** food for them In the
Ezek 7:19 Because it **b** their stumbling
16: 7 and **b** very beautiful. Your
16: 8 and you **b** Mine," says the Lord
16:47 you **b** more corrupt than they in
17: 6 And it grew and **b** a spreading
17: 6 So it **b** a vine, Brought forth
19: 3 And he **b** a young lion; He
19: 6 And **b** a young lion; He
23:10 She **b** a byword among women,
23:11 she **b** more corrupt in her lust
27: 8 They **b** your pilots.
28:16 of your trading You **b** filled
31: 5 And its branches **b** long
34: 5 and they **b** food for all the
34: 8 surely because My flock **b** a
34: 8 and My flock **b** food for every
36: 3 so that you **b** the possession of
36: 4 which **b** plunder and mockery to
41: 7 the side chambers **b** wider all
Dan 2:35 and **b** like chaff from the
2:35 stone that struck the image **b**
4:11 The tree grew and **b** strong;
4:20 which grew and **b** strong, whose
8: 4 did according to his will and **b**
8: 8 but when he **b** strong, the large
10:15 my face toward the ground and **b**
Hos 9:10 They **b** an abomination like the
Jon 4: 1 and he **b** angry.
Zech 7:14 Thus the land **b** desolate after
Mt 17: 2 and His clothes **b** as white as
28: 4 and **b** like dead men.
Mk 9: 3 His clothes **b** shining,
9:26 And he **b** as one dead, so that
Lk 1:80 So the child grew and **b** strong
2:40 And the Child grew and **b** strong
6:16 and Judas Iscariot who also **b**
9:29 and His robe **b** white and
11:30 For as Jonah **b** a sign to the
13:19 and it grew and **b** a large tree,
18:23 he **b** very sorrowful, for he was
18:24 And when Jesus saw that he **b**
22:44 Then His sweat **b** like great
23:12 very day Pilate and Herod **b**
Jn 1:14 And the Word **b** flesh and dwelt
Acts 1:16 who **b** a guide to those who
1:19 And it **b** known to all those
7:13 and Joseph's family **b** known to
7:29 Moses fled and **b** a dweller in
9:24 But their plot **b** known to Saul.
9:37 in those days that she **b** sick
9:42 And it **b** known throughout all
10:10 Then he **b** very hungry and wanted
11:18 they heard these things they **b**
14: 6 they **b** aware of it and fled to
15:39 Then the contention **b** so sharp
19:17 This **b** known both to all Jews
Rom 1:21 but **b** futile in their thoughts,
1:22 to be wise, they **b** fools,
4:18 so that he **b** the father of many
6:18 you **b** slaves of righteousness.
11:17 and with them **b** a partaker of
1 Cor 1:30 who **b** for us wisdom from
9:20 and to the Jews I **b** as a Jew,
9:22 to the weak I **b** as weak, that I
10: 6 Now these things **b** our examples,
13:11 but when I **b** a man, I put away
15:45 The first man Adam **b** a
15:45 The last Adam **b** a
2 Cor 8: 9 yet for your sakes He **b** poor,
Gal 4:12 for I **b** like you. You have not
Eph 3: 7 of which I **b** a minister
Phil 2: 8 He humbled Himself and **b**
Col 1:23 which I, Paul, **b** a minister.
1:25 of which I **b** a minister
1 Th 1: 6 And you **b** followers of us and of
1: 7 so that you **b** examples to all in
2:14 **b** imitators of the churches of
Heb 5: 9 He **b** the author of eternal
10:33 and partly while you **b**
11: 7 he condemned the world and **b**
11:24 when he **b** of age, refused to be
11:34 **b** valiant in battle, turned to
Rev 6:12 and the sun **b** black as
6:12 and the moon **b** like blood.
8: 8 and a third of the sea **b** blood.
8:11 A third of the waters **b**
10:10 my stomach **b** bitter.
16: 3 and it **b** blood as of a dead
16: 4 and they **b** blood.
16:10 and his kingdom **b** full of
18:15 who **b** rich by her, will stand
18:19 all who had ships on the sea **b**

BECAUSE (1476/1373) See APPENDIX

BECHER (5/4) BACHRITES

Gen 46:21 sons of Benjamin were Belah, **B**,
Num 26:35 of the Shuthalhites; of **B**,
1 Chr 7: 6 sons of Benjamin were Bela, **B**,
7: 8 The sons of **B** were Zemirah,
7: 8 All these are the sons of **B**.

BECHORATH (1/1)

1 Sam 9: 1 the son of Zeror, the son of **B**,

BECKONED (1/1)

Lk 1:22 for he **b** to them and remained

BECOME (295/285) BECAME, BECOMES, BECOMING

Gen 2:24 and they shall **b** one flesh.
3:22 the man has **b** like one of Us,
9:15 the waters shall never again **b**
18:18 since Abraham shall surely **b** a
24:35 and he has **b** great; and He has
24:60 may you **b** The mother of
27:40 when you **b** restless, That you
29:34 this time my husband will **b**
32:10 and now I have **b** two companies.
34:15 If you will **b** as we are, if
34:16 and we will **b** one people.
37:20 We shall see what will **b** of
45:24 See that you do not **b** troubled
47:26 which did not **b** Pharaoh's.
48:19 He also shall **b** a people, and
48:19 and his descendants shall **b** a
49:13 He shall **b** a haven for
Ex 4: 9 you take from the river will **b**
7: 9 and let it **b** a serpent.'"
7:19 that they may **b** blood.
8:16 so that it may **b** lice
9: 9 And it will **b** fine dust in all
15: 2 And He has **b** my salvation; He
15: 6 has **b** glorious in power; Your
22:24 and My wrath will **b** hot, and I
23:29 lest the land **b** desolate and
23:29 and the beast of the field **b**
32: 1 we do not know what has **b** of
32:22 not let the anger of my lord **b**
32:23 we do not know what has **b** of
Lev 11:24 By these you shall **b** unclean;
19:29 and the land **b** full of
22: 5 any person by whom he would **b**
25:45 and they shall **b** your property.
27:29 who may **b** doomed to destruction
Num 5:24 curse shall enter her to **b**
5:27 a curse will enter her and **b**
5:27 and the woman will **b** a curse
14: 3 our wives and children should **b**
16:40 that he might not **b** like Korah
Deut 7:22 lest the beasts of the field **b**
15: 9 and it **b** sin among you.
27: 9 This day you have **b** the people
28:25 and you shall **b** troublesome to
28:37 And you shall **b** an astonishment,
31:29 that after my death you will **b**
Josh 6:18 lest you **b** accursed when you
7:12 because they have **b** doomed to
9:13 and our sandals have **b** old
16:10 to this day and have **b** forced
24:32 and which had **b** an inheritance
Judg 16: 7 then I shall **b** weak, and be
16:11 then I shall **b** weak, and be
16:17 and I shall **b** weak, and be like
18: 4 and I have **b** his priest."
1 Sam 2: 5 she who has many children has **b**
4: 9 that you do not **b** servants of
9: 5 caring about the donkeys and **b**
13: 4 and that Israel had also **b** an
16:23 Then Saul would **b** refreshed and
18:22 **b** the king's son-in-law.'"
18:26 it pleased David well to **b** the

18:27 that he might **b** the king's
25:40 to ask you to **b** his wife."
28:16 has departed from you and has **b**
29: 4 lest in the battle he **b** our
2 Sam 7:24 have **b** their God.
14:14 For we will surely die and **b**
15:33 then you will **b** a burden to me.
1 Ki 1:11 the son of Haggith has **b** king,
1:13 Why then has Adonijah **b** king?'
1:18 look! Adonijah has **b** king; and
2:15 and has **b** my brother's; for it
8:46 and You **b** angry with them and
14: 3 he will tell you what will **b** of
22:41 the son of Asa had **b** king over
2 Ki 7:13 they may either **b** like all
7:13 they may **b** like all the
8:13 has shown me that you will **b**
9:29 Ahaziah had **b** king over Judah.
13:14 Elisha had **b** sick with the
21:14 and they shall **b** victims of
22:19 that they would **b** a desolation
25: 3 fourth month the famine had **b**
1 Chr 17:22 You, LORD, have **b** their God.
2 Chr 6:36 and You **b** angry with them and
21:15 and you will **b** very sick with
Esth 1:17 the queen's behavior will **b**
Job 4: 2 will you **b** weary? But who can
15:28 Which are destined to **b** ruins.
17: 6 And I have **b** one in whose face
21: 7 Why do the wicked live and **b**
21: 7 **b** mighty in power?
30:19 And I have **b** like dust and
30:21 But You have **b** cruel to me;
41:28 Slingstones **b** like stubble to
Ps 14: 3 They have together **b** corrupt;
28: 1 I **b** like those who go down to
53: 3 They have together **b** corrupt;
69: 8 I have **b** a stranger to my
69:22 Let their table **b** a snare
71: 7 I have **b** as a wonder to many,
79: 4 We have **b** a reproach to our
109: 7 And let his prayer **b** sin.
109:25 I also have **b** a reproach to
118:14 And He has **b** my salvation.
118:21 And have **b** my salvation.
118:22 the builders rejected Has **b**
119:56 This has **b** mine, Because I
119:83 For I have **b** like a wineskin in
119:173 Let Your hand **b** my help, For I
Prov 6: 1 if you **b** surety for your
10: 9 he who perverts his ways will **b**
19:25 and the simple will **b** wary;
25:17 Lest he **b** weary of you and
29:12 All his servants **b** wicked.
Isa 1: 9 We would have **b** like Sodom,
1:21 How the faithful city has **b** a
1:22 Your silver has **b** dross, Your
7:24 Because all the land will **b**
7:25 But it will **b** a range for oxen
12: 2 He also has **b** my salvation.'
14:10 Have you also **b** as weak as we?
14:10 Have you **b** like us?
19:13 The princes of Zoan have **b**
22:23 And he will **b** a glorious
29:11 The whole vision has **b** to you
31: 8 And his young men shall **b**
32:14 The forts and towers will **b**
34: 9 Its land shall **b** burning
35: 7 The parched ground shall **b** a
59: 6 Their webs will not **b** garments,
60: 5 Then you shall see and **b**
60:22 A little one shall **b** a
63:19 We have **b** like those of old,
Jer 2: 5 And have **b** idolaters?
5:13 And the prophets **b** wind, For
5:27 Therefore they have **b** great
7:11 **b** a den of thieves in your
10:21 For the shepherds have **b**
13:11 that they may **b** My people, for
18:21 Let their wives **b** widows And
22: 5 that this house shall **b** a
25:33 they shall **b** refuse on the
26:18 Jerusalem shall **b** heaps of
30:16 Those who plunder you shall **b**
49:13 that Bozrah shall **b** a
50:10 And Chaldea shall **b** plunder;
50:23 and broken! How Babylon has **b**
50:37 And they will **b** like women.
51:37 Babylon shall **b** a heap, A
51:41 is seized! How Babylon has **b**
52: 6 the famine had **b** so severe in
Lam 1: 1 among the provinces Has **b** a
1: 2 They have **b** her enemies.
1: 5 Her adversaries have **b** the
1: 6 Her princes have **b** like deer
1: 8 Therefore she has **b** vile.
1:17 That those around him **b** his
1:17 Jerusalem has **b** an unclean
1:21 That they may **b** like me.
3:14 I have **b** the ridicule of all my
4: 1 How the gold has **b** dim! How
4: 8 It has **b** as dry as wood.
4:21 over to you And you shall **b**
5: 3 We have **b** orphans and waifs,
Ezek 12:20 and the land shall **b** desolate;
17: 8 And **b** a majestic vine." '
19:14 and has **b** a lamentation.
22: 4 You have **b** guilty by the blood
22:18 the house of Israel has **b** dross
22:18 they have **b** dross from silver.
22:19 Because you have all **b** dross,
23:30 because you have **b** defiled by
24:11 That it may **b** hot and its
26: 5 it shall **b** plunder for the
27:36 You will **b** a horror, and be
28:19 You have **b** a horror, And
29: 9 And the land of Egypt shall **b**
36: 2 The ancient heights have **b** our
36:35 land that was desolate has **b**
37:17 and they will **b** one in your
46:17 it shall **b** theirs.
Dan 4:22 who have grown and **b** strong;
11: 5 the king of the South shall **b**
11:23 for he shall come up and **b**
Hos 8:11 They have **b** for him altars for
12: 8 Surely I have **b** rich, I have
13:15 Then his spring shall **b** dry,
Jon 1:12 then the sea will **b** calm for
4: 5 till he might see what would **b**
Mic 3:12 Jerusalem shall **b** heaps of
Hab 2: 7 And you will **b** their booty.
Zeph 1:13 Therefore their goods shall **b**
2:15 How has she **b** a desolation,
Hag 2:12 will it **b** holy?" '" Then the
Zech 2: 9 and they shall **b** spoil for
2:11 and they shall **b** My people.
4: 7 Zerubbabel you shall **b** a
12: 7 of Jerusalem shall not **b**
Mt 4: 3 command that these stones **b**
18: 3 unless you are converted and **b**
19: 5 and the two shall **b** one
20:26 but whoever desires to **b** great
21:42 builders rejected Has **b**
24:32 When its branch has already **b**
27:57 who himself had also **b** a
Mk 1:17 and I will make you **b** fishers
6:14 for His name had **b** well known.
10: 8 and the two shall **b** one
10:43 but whoever desires to **b** great
12:10 builders rejected Has **b**
13:28 When its branch has already **b**
Lk 4: 3 command this stone to **b**
20:17 builders rejected Has **b**
20:33 whose wife does she **b**?
Jn 1:12 to them He gave the right to **b**
4:14 that I shall give him will **b**
9:27 Do you also want to **b** His
12:36 that you may **b** sons of light."
Acts 1:22 one of these must **b** a witness
4:11 which has **b** the chief
7:40 do not know what has **b**
7:52 of whom you now have **b** the
12:18 the soldiers about what had **b**
15:13 And after they had **b** silent,
26:28 You almost persuade me to **b** a
26:29 might **b** both almost and
Rom 2:25 your circumcision has **b**
3:12 They have together **b**
3:19 and all the world may **b** guilty
6:22 and having **b** slaves of God, you
7: 4 you also have **b** dead to the law
7:13 Has then what is good **b** death
7:13 through the commandment might **b**
9:29 We would have **b** like
11: 9 Let their table **b** a snare
11:34 Or who has **b** His
15: 8 I say that Jesus Christ has **b**
16:19 For your obedience has **b** known
1 Cor 3:13 each one's work will **b** clear;
3:18 let him **b** a fool that he may
3:18 him become a fool that he may **b**
6:16 shall **b** one flesh."
7:18 Let him not **b** uncircumcised.
7:23 do not **b** slaves of men.
8: 9 this liberty of yours **b** a
9:22 I have **b** all things to all
9:27 I myself should **b** disqualified.
10: 7 And do not **b** idolaters as were
13: 1 I have **b** sounding brass or a
15:20 and has **b** the firstfruits of
2 Cor 5:17 all things have **b** new.
5:21 that we might **b** the
8: 9 you through His poverty might **b**
12:11 I have **b** a fool in boasting;
13:11 **B** complete. Be of good comfort,
Gal 3:13 having **b** a curse for us (for it
4:12 I urge you to **b** like me, for I
4:16 Have I therefore **b** your enemy
5: 2 say to you that if you **b**
5: 4 You have **b** estranged from
5:26 Let us not **b** conceited,
Eph 5:31 and the two shall **b** one
Phil 1:13 so that it has **b** evident to the
1:14 having **b** confident by my
2:15 that you may **b** blameless and
Col 3:21 lest they **b** discouraged.
1 Th 2: 8 because you had **b** dear to us.
Titus 3: 7 by His grace we should **b** heirs
Phm 1: 6 the sharing of your faith may **b**
Heb 1: 4 having **b** so much better than the
3:14 For we have **b** partakers of
5: 5 did not glorify Himself to **b**
5:11 since you have **b** dull of
6: 4 and have **b** partakers of the
6:12 that you do not **b** sluggish, but
6:20 having **b** High Priest forever
7:21 (for they have **b** priests without
7:22 by so much more Jesus has **b** a
7:26 and has **b** higher than the
12: 3 lest you **b** weary and
12: 8 of which all have **b** partakers,
12:15 and by this many **b** defiled;
Jas 2: 4 and **b** judges with evil
2:11 you have **b** a transgressor of
3: 1 let not many of you **b** teachers,
1 Pe 2: 7 builders rejected Has **b**
3:13 he who will harm you if you **b**
3 Jn 8 that we may **b** fellow workers
Rev 2: 3 My name's sake and have not **b**
3:17 have **b** wealthy, and have need
11:15 kingdoms of this world have **b**
18: 2 and has **b** a dwelling place of
18: 3 merchants of the earth have **b**

BECOMES (35/32)

Ex 22:14 and it **b** injured or dies, the
29:30 That son who **b** priest in his
Lev 4:14 sin which they have committed **b**
11:34 food upon which water falls **b**
11:34 that may be drunk from it **b**
11:36 touches any such carcass **b**
11:38 it **b** unclean to you.
13: 2 and it **b** on the skin of his
13:24 the raw flesh of the burn **b** a
25:25 If one of your brethren **b** poor,
25:26 but he himself **b** able to redeem
25:35 If one of your brethren **b** poor,
25:39 brethren who dwells by you **b**
25:47 or stranger close to you **b**
25:47 brethren who dwells by him **b**
Num 5: 2 and whoever **b** defiled by a
5:14 comes upon him and he **b**
5:14 comes upon him and he **b**
5:30 and he **b** jealous of his wife;
11:20 out of your nostrils and **b**
Deut 23:10 is any man among you who **b**
24: 2 and goes and **b** another man's
Job 14:11 And a river **b** parched and
20:14 It **b** cobra venom within him.
Ps 49:16 Do not be afraid when one **b**
Prov 10: 4 He who has a slack hand **b** poor,
17:18 And **b** surety for his friend.
Isa 32:15 And the wilderness **b** a
Jer 3: 1 And she goes from him And **b**
Mt 13:22 and he **b** unfruitful.
13:32 greater than the herbs and **b** a
Mk 4:19 and it **b** unfruitful.
4:32 it grows up and **b** greater than
9:18 and **b** rigid. So I spoke to Your
Gal 5: 3 again to every man who **b**

BECOMING (5/5)

2 Sam 13: 4 **b** thinner day after day?
Prov 17: 7 Excellent speech is not **b** to a
Acts 7: 9 **b** envious, sold Joseph into
17: 5 **b** envious, took some of the
Heb 8:13 Now what is **b** obsolete and

BED (89/87) BIDDING

Gen 47:31 himself on the head of the **b**.
48: 2 himself and sat up on the **b**.
49: 4 you went up to your father's **b**;
49:33 he drew his feet up into the **b**
Ex 8: 3 into your bedroom, on your **b**,
21:18 die but is confined to his **b**,
Lev 15: 4 Every **b** is unclean on which he
15: 5 And whoever touches his **b** shall
15:21 Whoever touches her **b** shall wash
15:23 If anything is on her **b** or on
15:24 and every **b** on which he lies
15:26 Every **b** on which she lies all
15:26 shall be to her as the **b** of
Deut 22:30 nor uncover his father's **b**.
27:20 he has uncovered his father's **b**.
1 Sam 19:13 an image and laid it in the **b**,
19:15 "Bring him up to me in the **b**,
19:16 there was the image in the **b**,
28:23 the ground and sat on the **b**.
2 Sam 4: 5 who was lying on his **b** at noon.
4: 7 he was lying on his **b** in his
4:11 in his own house on his **b**?
11: 2 that David arose from his **b**
11:13 he went out to lie on his **b**
13: 5 Lie down on your **b** and pretend
1 Ki 1:47 the king bowed himself on the **b**.
17:19 and laid him on his own **b**.
21: 4 And he lay down on his **b**,
2 Ki 1: 4 shall not come down from the **b**
1: 6 shall not come down from the **b**
1:16 shall not come down from the **b**
4:10 and let us put a **b** for him
4:21 went up and laid him on the **b**
4:32 the child, lying dead on his **b**.
1 Chr 5: 1 he defiled his father's **b**,
2 Chr 16:14 and they laid him in the **b**
24:25 priest, and killed him on his **b**.
Job 7:13 My **b** will comfort me, My couch
17:13 If I make my **b** in the
33:19 chastened with pain on his **b**,
39: 9 Will he **b** by your manger?
Ps 4: 4 within your heart on your **b**,
6: 6 All night I make my **b** swim; I
36: 4 He devises wickedness on his **b**;
41: 3 will strengthen him on his **b**
63: 6 When I remember You on my **b**,
132: 3 go up to the comfort of my **b**;
139: 8 If I make my **b** in hell,
Prov 7:16 I have spread my **b** with
7:17 I have perfumed my **b** With
22:27 Why should he take away your **b**
26:14 does the lazy man on his **b**.
Song 1:16 pleasant! Also our **b** is
3: 1 By night on my **b** I sought the

5:13 His cheeks are like a **b** of
Isa 28:20 For the **b** is too short to
57: 7 mountain You have set your **b**;
57: 8 You have enlarged your **b** And
57: 8 them; You have loved their **b**,
Ezek 23:17 into the **b** of love, And they
32:25 They have set her **b** in the
Dan 2:28 of your head upon your **b**,
2:29 to your mind while on your **b**,
4: 5 and the thoughts on my **b** and
4:10 of my head while on my **b**:
4:13 of my head while on my **b**,
7: 1 of his head while on his **b**.
Am 3:12 In the corner of a **b** and on the
Mt 9: 2 to Him a paralytic lying on a **b**.
9: 6 "Arise, take up your **b**,
Mk 2: 4 they let down the **b** on which
2: 9 take up your **b** and walk'?
2:11 to you, arise, take up your **b**,
2:12 he arose, took up the **b**,
4:21 put under a basket or under a **b**?
7:30 and her daughter lying on the **b**.
Lk 5:18 men brought on a **b** a man who
5:19 and let him down with his **b**
5:24 to you, arise, take up your **b**,
8:16 a vessel or puts it under a **b**,
11: 7 my children are with me in **b**;
17:34 there will be two men in one **b**:
Jn 5: 8 take up your **b** and walk."
5: 9 was made well, took up his **b**,
5:10 lawful for you to carry your **b**.
5:11 Take up your **b** and walk.'"
5:12 Take up your **b** and walk'?"
Acts 9:34 Arise and make your **b**."
Heb 13: 4 and the **b** undefiled; but

BEDAD (2/2)
Gen 36:35 Husham died, Hadad the son of **B**,
1 Chr 1:46 Husham died, Hadad the son of **B**,

BEDAN (2/2)
1 Sam 12:11 the LORD sent Jerubbaal, **B**,
1 Chr 7:17 The son of Ulam was **B**.

BEDCHAMBER (KJV) See BEDROOM

BEDEIAH (1/1)
Ezra 10:35 Benaiah, **B**, Cheluh,

BEDRIDDEN (1/1) BED
Acts 9:33 who had been **b** eight years and

BEDROOM (8/7) BED
Ex 8: 3 into your house, into your **b**,
2 Sam 4: 7 was lying on his bed in his **b**;
13:10 "Bring the food into the **b**,
13:10 to Amnon her brother in the **b**.
2 Ki 6:12 words that you speak in your **b**.
11: 2 hid him and his nurse in the **b**,
2 Chr 22:11 put him and his nurse in a **b**.
Eccl 10:20 curse the rich, even in your **b**;

BEDS (10/10) BED
2 Sam 17:28 brought **b** and basins, earthen
Job 33:15 While slumbering on their **b**,
Ps 149: 5 Let them sing aloud on their **b**.
Song 6: 2 To the **b** of spices, To feed
Isa 57: 2 They shall rest in their **b**,
Hos 7:14 When they wailed upon their **b**.
Am 6: 4 Who lie on **b** of ivory, Stretch
Mic 2: 1 And work out evil on their **b**!
Mk 6:55 and began to carry about on **b**
Acts 5:15 the streets and laid them on **b**

BEDSTEAD (2/1) BED
Deut 3:11 Indeed his **b** was an iron
3:11 his bedstead was an iron **b**.

BEE (1/1) BEES
Isa 7:18 And for the **b** that is in the

BEELIADA (1/1)
1 Chr 14: 7 Elishama, **B**, and Eliphelet.

BEELZEBUB (7/7) BAAL-ZEBUB
Mt 10:25 the master of the house **B**,
12:24 not cast out demons except by **B**,
12:27 "And if I cast out demons by **B**,
Mk 3:22 from Jerusalem said, "He has **B**,
Lk 11:15 "He casts out demons by **B**,
11:18 you say I cast out demons by **B**.
11:19 "And if I cast out demons by **B**,

BEEN (583/548) See APPENDIX

BEER (2/2)
Num 21:16 From there they went to **B**,
Judg 9:21 and he went to **B** and dwelt

BEER ELIM (1/1)
Isa 15: 8 to Eglaim And its wailing to **B**.

BEER LAHAI ROI (3/3)
Gen 16:14 Therefore the well was called **B**;
24:62 Isaac came from the way of **B**,
25:11 son Isaac. And Isaac dwelt at **B**.

BEERA (1/1)
1 Chr 7:37 Shilshah, Jithran, and **B**.

BEERAH (1/1)
1 Chr 5: 6 and **B** his son, whom

BEERI (2/2)
Gen 26:34 wives Judith the daughter of **B**
Hos 1: 1 that came to Hosea the son of **B**,

BEEROTH (5/5) BEEROTHITE
Josh 9:17 were Gibeon, Chephirah, **B**,
18:25 Gibeon, Ramah, **B**,
2 Sam 4: 2 (For **B** also was part of
Ezra 2:25 Kirjath Arim, Chephirah, and **B**,
Neh 7:29 Jearim, Chephirah, and **B**,

BEEROTHITE (4/4) BEEROTH, BEEROTHITES, BEROTHITE
2 Sam 4: 2 the sons of Rimmon the **B**,
4: 5 Then the sons of Rimmon the **B**,
4: 9 the sons of Rimmon the **B**,
23:37 Naharai the **B** (armorbearer of

BEEROTHITES (1/1) BEEROTHITE
2 Sam 4: 3 because the **B** fled to Gittaim

BEERSHEBA (34/33)
Gen 21:14 wandered in the Wilderness of **B**.
21:31 he called that place **B**,
21:32 Thus they made a covenant at **B**.
21:33 planted a tamarisk tree in **B**,
22:19 rose and went together to **B**;
22:19 and Abraham dwelt at **B**.
26:23 he went up from there to **B**.
26:33 the name of the city is **B** to
28:10 Now Jacob went out from **B** and
46: 1 all that he had, and came to **B**,
46: 5 Then Jacob arose from **B**;
Josh 15:28 Hazar Shual, **B**, Bizjothjah,
19: 2 They had in their inheritance **B**
Judg 20: 1 Israel came out, from Dan to **B**,
1 Sam 3:20 And all Israel from Dan to **B**
8: 2 Abijah; they were judges in **B**.
2 Sam 3:10 and over Judah, from Dan to **B**.
17:11 gathered to you, from Dan to **B**,
24: 2 tribes of Israel, from Dan to **B**,
24: 7 to South Judah as far as **B**.
24:15 From Dan to **B** seventy thousand
1 Ki 4:25 fig tree, from Dan as far as **B**,
19: 3 ran for his life, and went to **B**,
2 Ki 12: 1 mother's name was Zibiah of **B**.
23: 8 burned incense, from Geba to **B**;
1 Chr 4:28 They dwelt at **B**,
21: 2 number Israel from **B** to Dan,
2 Chr 19: 4 again among the people from **B**
24: 1 mother's name was Zibiah of **B**.
30: 5 from **B** to Dan, that they should
Neh 11:27 and **B** and its villages;
11:30 They dwelt from **B** to the Valley
Am 5: 5 Gilgal, Nor pass over to **B**;
8:14 'As the way of **B** lives!'

BEES (3/3) BEE
Deut 1:44 you and chased you as **b** do,
Judg 14: 8 a swarm of **b** and honey were in
Ps 118:12 They surrounded me like **b**;

BEESH-TERAH (KJV) See BE ESHTERAH

BEETLE (KJV) See CRICKET

BEEVES (KJV) See CATTLE

BEFALL (6/6) BEFALLEN, BEFALLS
Gen 42: 4 Lest some calamity **b** him."
42:38 If any calamity should **b** him
49: 1 I may tell you what shall **b**
Deut 31:17 many evils and troubles shall **b**
31:29 and evil will **b** you in the
Ps 91:10 No evil shall **b** you, Nor shall

BEFALLEN (5/5) BEFALL
Lev 10:19 and such things have **b** me! If
Num 20:14 all the hardship that has **b** us,
Josh 2:23 and told him all that had **b**
2 Sam 19: 7 than all the evil that had **b**
Neh 9:33 are just in all that has **b** us;

BEFALLS (2/2) BEFALL
Gen 44:29 and calamity **b** him, you shall
Eccl 3:19 one thing **b** them: as one dies,

BEFITTING (1/1)
Acts 26:20 and do works **b** repentance.

BEFORE (1677/1546)
Gen 2: 5 **b** any plant of the field was in
2: 5 field was in the earth and **b**
6:11 The earth also was corrupt **b**
6:13 end of all flesh has come **b** Me,
7: 1 that you are righteous **b** Me
10: 9 He was a mighty hunter **b** the
10: 9 Nimrod the mighty hunter **b** the
11:28 And Haran died **b** his father
13: 9 Is not the whole land **b** you?
13:10 well watered everywhere (**b** the
17: 1 walk **b** Me and be blameless.
17:18 that Ishmael might live **b**
18: 8 and set it **b** them; and he
18:22 but Abraham still stood **b** the
19: 4 Now **b** they lay down, the men of
19:13 against them has grown great **b**
19:27 the place where he had stood **b**
20:15 my land is **b** you; dwell where
20:16 indeed this vindicates you **b**
20:16 all who are with you and **b**
23: 3 Then Abraham stood up from **b** his
23:12 Abraham bowed himself down **b**
23:17 which was **b** Mamre, the field
23:18 **b** all who went in at the gate
23:19 **b** Mamre (that is, Hebron) in
24: 7 He will send His angel **b** you,
24:15 **b** he had finished speaking,
24:33 Food was set **b** him to eat, but
24:40 **b** whom I walk, will send His
24:45 But **b** I had finished speaking
24:51 Here is Rebekah **b** you; take
25: 9 which is **b** Mamre, in the field
27: 4 that my soul may bless you **b** I
27: 7 in the presence of the LORD **b**
27:10 and that he may bless you **b** his
27:33 I ate all of it **b** you came,
29:26 to give the younger **b** the
30:30 For what you had **b** I came was
30:33 the subject of my wages comes **b**
30:38 he set **b** the flocks in the
30:39 So the flocks conceived **b** the
30:41 that Jacob placed the rods **b**
31: 2 not favorable toward him as **b**.
31: 5 not favorable toward me as **b**;
31:35 my lord that I cannot rise **b**
31:37 Set it here **b** my brethren and
32: 3 Then Jacob sent messengers **b**
32:16 Pass over **b** me, and put some
32:20 with the present that goes **b**
32:21 So the present went on over **b**
33: 3 Then he crossed over **b** them and
33:12 and I will go **b** you."
33:14 let my lord go on ahead **b** his
33:14 which the livestock that go **b**
33:18 and he pitched his tent **b** the
34:10 and the land shall be **b** you.
36:31 reigned in the land of Edom **b**
37:10 to bow down to the earth **b** you?
37:18 even **b** he came near them, they
40: 9 in my dream a vine was **b** me,
41:43 and they cried out **b** him, "Bow
41:46 years old when he stood **b**
41:50 to Joseph were born two sons **b**
42: 6 brothers came and bowed down **b**
42:24 from them and bound him **b**
43: 9 him back to you and set him **b**
43:14 God Almighty give you mercy **b**
43:15 and they stood **b** Joseph.
43:26 and bowed down **b** him to the
43:33 And they sat **b** him, the
43:34 he took servings to them from **b**
44:14 and they fell **b** him on the
44:32 then I shall bear the blame **b**
45: 1 could not restrain himself **b**
45: 5 for God sent me **b** you to
45: 7 And God sent me **b** you to
45:28 I will go and see him **b** I
46:28 Then he sent Judah **b** him to
46:28 to point out **b** him the way to
47: 6 The land of Egypt is **b** you.
47: 7 his father Jacob and set him **b**
47:10 and went out from **b** Pharaoh.
47:19 Why should we die **b** your eyes,
48: 5 to you in the land of Egypt **b**
48:15 **b** whom my fathers Abraham and
48:20 ' And thus he set Ephraim **b**
49: 8 children shall bow down **b** you.
49:30 which is **b** Mamre in the land
50:13 **b** Mamre, which Abraham bought
50:16 **B** your father died he commanded,
50:18 also went and fell down **b** his
Ex 1:19 are lively and give birth **b**
4:10 neither **b** nor since You have
4:21 that you do all those wonders **b**
5: 7 people straw to make brick as **b**.
5: 8 of bricks which they made **b**.
5:14 both yesterday and today, as **b**?
6:12 And Moses spoke **b** the LORD,
6:30 But Moses said **b** the LORD,
7: 9 Take your rod and cast it **b**
7:10 And Aaron cast down his rod **b**
7:10 his rod before Pharaoh and **b**
8:20 in the morning and stand **b**
8:26 abomination of the Egyptians **b**
9:10 from the furnace and stood **b**
9:11 the magicians could not stand **b**

9:13 in the morning and stand **b**
10: 1 may show these signs of Mine **b**
10: 3 refuse to humble yourself **b** Me?
11: 6 such as was not like it **b**,
11:10 Aaron did all these wonders **b**
12:34 the people took their dough **b**
13:21 And the LORD went **b** them by day
13:22 of fire by night from **b** the
14: 2 that they turn and camp **b** Pi
14: 2 you shall camp **b** it by the sea.
14: 9 Pi Hahiroth, **b** Baal Zephon.
14:19 who went **b** the camp of Israel,
14:19 the pillar of cloud went from **b**
16: 9 Come near **b** the LORD, for He
16:33 and lay it up **b** the LORD, to
16:34 so Aaron laid it up **b** the
17: 5 Go on **b** the people, and take
17: 6 I will stand **b** you there on the
18:12 with Moses' father-in-law **b**
18:13 and the people stood **b** Moses
18:14 and all the people stand **b** you
18:19 Stand **b** God for the people, so
19: 2 So Israel camped there **b** the
19: 7 and laid **b** them all these words
20: 3 shall have no other gods **b** Me.
20:20 and that His fear may be **b** you,
21: 1 which you shall set **b** them:
22: 9 of both parties shall come **b**
22:26 you shall return it to him **b**
23:15 none shall appear **b** Me empty);
23:17 all your males shall appear **b**
23:20 I send an Angel **b** you to keep
23:23 For My Angel will go **b** you and
23:27 I will send My fear **b** you, I
23:28 And I will send hornets **b** you,
23:28 and the Hittite from **b** you.
23:29 will not drive them out from **b**
23:30 I will drive them out from **b**
23:31 and you shall drive them out **b**
25:30 the showbread on the table **b**
27:21 outside the veil which is **b**
27:21 it from evening until morning **b**
28:12 Aaron shall bear their names **b**
28:29 as a memorial **b** the LORD
28:30 heart when he goes in **b** the
28:30 of Israel over his heart **b** the
28:35 he goes into the holy place **b**
28:38 that they may be accepted **b** the
29:10 also have the bull brought **b**
29:11 you shall kill the bull **b**
29:23 the unleavened bread that is **b**
29:24 them as a wave offering **b** the
29:25 as a sweet aroma **b** the LORD.
29:26 wave it as a wave offering **b**
29:42 of the tabernacle of meeting **b**
30: 6 And you shall put it **b** the veil
30: 6 it before the veil that is **b**
30: 6 **b** the mercy seat that is over
30: 8 a perpetual incense **b** the LORD
30:16 for the children of Israel **b**
30:36 and put some of it **b** the
32: 1 make us gods that shall go **b**
32: 5 he built an altar **b** it.
32:23 Make us gods that shall go **b** us;
32:34 My Angel shall go **b** you.
33: 2 And I will send My Angel **b** you,
33:19 make all My goodness pass **b**
33:19 the name of the LORD **b** you.
34: 3 flocks nor herds feed **b** that
34: 6 And the LORD passed **b** him and
34:10 **B** all your people I will do
34:11 I am driving out from **b** you the
34:20 And none shall appear **b** Me
34:23 all your men shall appear **b**
34:24 I will cast out the nations **b**
34:24 when you go up to appear **b** the
34:34 But whenever Moses went in **b** the
40: 5 of gold for the incense **b** the
40: 6 altar of the burnt offering **b**
40:23 the bread in order upon it **b**
40:25 and he lit the lamps **b** the
40:29 the altar of burnt offering **b**
Lev 1: 3 of the tabernacle of meeting **b**
1: 5 He shall kill the bull **b** the
1:11 the north side of the altar **b**
3: 1 offer it without blemish **b** the
3: 7 then he shall offer it **b** the
3: 8 and kill it **b** the tabernacle of
3:12 then he shall offer it **b** the
3:13 hand on its head and kill it **b**
4: 4 of the tabernacle of meeting **b**
4: 4 and kill the bull **b** the LORD.
4: 6 of the blood seven times **b** the
4: 7 of the altar of sweet incense **b**
4:14 and bring it **b** the tabernacle
4:15 on the head of the bull **b** the
4:15 the bull shall be killed **b** the
4:17 and sprinkle it seven times **b**
4:18 horns of the altar which is **b**
4:24 they kill the burnt offering **b**
6: 7 shall make atonement for him **b**
6:14 shall offer it on the altar **b**
6:25 sin offering shall be killed **b**
7:30 be waved as a wave offering **b**
8:26 of unleavened bread that was **b**
8:27 them as a wave offering **b** the
8:29 waved it as a wave offering **b**
9: 2 and offer them **b** the LORD.
9: 4 to sacrifice **b** the LORD, and a
9: 5 brought what Moses commanded **b**
9: 5 drew near and stood **b** the
9:21 waved as a wave offering **b**
9:24 and fire came out from **b** the
10: 1 and offered profane fire **b** the
10: 2 and they died **b** the LORD.
10: 3 And **b** all the people I must
10: 4 carry your brethren from **b** the
10:15 to offer as a wave offering **b**
10:17 to make atonement for them **b**
10:19 and their burnt offering **b** the
12: 7 Then he shall offer it **b** the
14:11 **b** the LORD, at the door of
14:12 them as a wave offering **b** the
14:16 with his finger seven times **b**
14:18 shall make atonement for him **b**
14:23 of meeting, **b** the LORD.
14:24 them as a wave offering **b** the
14:27 in his left hand seven times **b**
14:29 to make atonement for him **b** the
14:31 for him who is to be cleansed **b**
14:36 **b** the priest goes into it to
15:14 and come **b** the LORD, to the
15:15 shall make atonement for him **b**
15:30 shall make atonement for her **b**
16: 1 they offered profane fire **b**
16: 2 **b** the mercy seat which is on
16: 7 two goats and present them **b**
16:10 shall be presented alive **b** the
16:12 coals of fire from the altar **b**
16:13 put the incense on the fire **b**
16:14 and **b** the mercy seat he shall
16:15 it on the mercy seat and **b** the
16:18 go out to the altar that is **b**
16:30 be clean from all your sins **b**
17: 4 an offering to the LORD **b** the
18:23 Nor shall any woman stand **b** an
18:24 which I am casting out **b** you.
18:27 who were **b** you, and thus the
18:28 out the nations that were **b**
18:30 customs which were committed **b**
19:14 nor put a stumbling block **b** the
19:22 ram of the trespass offering **b**
19:32 You shall rise **b** the gray
20:23 which I am casting out **b** you;
23:11 He shall wave the sheaf **b** the
23:20 as a wave offering **b** the
23:28 to make atonement for you **b** the
23:40 and you shall rejoice **b** the
24: 3 it from evening until morning **b**
24: 4 on the pure gold lampstand **b**
24: 6 on the pure gold table **b** the
24: 8 he shall set it in order **b** the
26: 7 they shall fall by the sword **b**
26: 8 shall fall by the sword **b** you.
26:37 as it were **b** a sword, when no
26:37 have no power to stand **b** your
27: 8 he shall present himself **b** the
27:11 he shall present the animal **b**
Num 3: 4 Nadab and Abihu had died **b** the
3: 4 they offered profane fire **b**
3: 6 and present them **b** Aaron the
3: 7 of the whole congregation **b**
3:38 those who were to camp **b** the
3:38 **b** the tabernacle of meeting,
5:16 and set her **b** the LORD.
5:18 priest shall stand the woman **b**
5:25 shall wave the offering **b** the
5:30 he shall stand the woman **b** the
6:16 the priest shall bring them **b**
6:20 wave them as a wave offering **b**
7: 3 they brought their offering **b**
7: 3 and they presented them **b** the
7:10 offered their offering **b** the
8: 9 you shall bring the Levites **b**
8:10 you shall bring the Levites **b**
8:11 shall offer the Levites **b** the
8:13 you shall stand the Levites **b**
8:21 like a wave offering **b** the
8:22 in the tabernacle of meeting **b**
9: 6 and they came **b** Moses and Aaron
10: 3 the congregation shall gather **b**
10: 9 and you will be remembered **b**
10:10 shall be a memorial for you **b**
10:33 covenant of the LORD went **b**
10:35 let those who hate You flee **b**
11: 6 at all except this manna **b**
11:20 and have wept **b** Him, saying,
11:33 **b** it was chewed, the wrath of
13:22 Hebron was built seven years **b**
13:30 Caleb quieted the people **b**
14: 5 and Aaron fell on their faces **b**
14:10 in the tabernacle of meeting **b**
14:14 and You go **b** them in a pillar
14:37 died by the plague **b** the LORD.
14:43 and the Canaanites are there **b**
15:15 so shall the stranger be **b** the
15:25 and their sin offering **b** the
15:28 when he sins unintentionally **b**
16: 2 and they rose up **b** Moses with
16: 7 them and put incense in them **b**
16: 9 and to stand **b** the congregation
16:16 all your company be present **b**
16:17 each of you bring his censer **b**
16:38 Because they presented them **b**
16:40 come near to offer incense **b**
16:43 Then Moses and Aaron came **b** the
17: 4 in the tabernacle of meeting **b**
17: 7 And Moses placed the rods **b** the
17: 9 out all the rods from **b** the
17:10 Bring Aaron's rod back **b** the
18: 2 and your sons are with you **b**
18:19 a covenant of salt forever **b**
19: 3 and it shall be slaughtered **b**
20: 3 died when our brethren died **b**
20: 8 Speak to the rock **b** their eyes,
20: 9 So Moses took the rod from **b** the
20:10 the assembly together **b** the
22:32 your way is perverse **b** Me.
25: 4 and hang the offenders **b** the
26:61 they offered profane fire **b**
27: 2 And they stood **b** Moses, before
27: 2 **b** Eleazar the priest, and
27: 2 and **b** the leaders and all the
27: 5 So Moses brought their case **b**
27:14 to hallow Me at the waters **b**
27:17 who may go out **b** them and go in
27:17 go out before them and go in **b**
27:19 set him **b** Eleazar the priest and
27:19 Eleazar the priest and **b** all
27:21 He shall stand **b** Eleazar the
27:21 who shall inquire **b** the LORD
27:22 He took Joshua and set him **b**
27:22 Eleazar the priest and **b** all
31:50 make atonement for ourselves **b**
31:54 for the children of Israel **b**
32: 4 which the LORD defeated **b** the
32:17 ready to go **b** the children of
32:20 if you arm yourselves **b** the
32:21 men cross over the Jordan **b**
32:21 driven out His enemies from **b**
32:22 and the land is subdued **b** the
32:22 may return and be blameless **b**
32:22 before the LORD and **b** Israel;
32:22 shall be your possession **b** the
32:27 **b** the LORD to battle, just as
32:29 every man armed for battle **b**
32:29 and the land is subdued **b** you,
32:32 We will cross over armed **b** the
33: 8 They departed from **b** Hahiroth
33:47 mountains of Abarim, **b** Nebo.
33:52 inhabitants of the land from **b**
33:55 inhabitants of the land from **b**
35:12 may not die until he stands **b**
35:32 return to dwell in the land **b**
36: 1 came near and spoke **b** Moses and
36: 1 and spoke before Moses and **b**
Deut 1: 8 I have set the land **b** you; go
1:21 your God has set the land **b**
1:22 Let us send men **b** us, and let
1:30 who goes **b** you, He will fight
1:30 all He did for you in Egypt **b**
1:33 who went in the way **b** you to
1:38 who stands **b** you, he shall go
1:42 lest you be defeated **b** your
1:45 Then you returned and wept **b** the
2:12 them and destroyed them from **b**
2:21 But the LORD destroyed them **b**
2:22 He destroyed the Horites from **b**
3:18 valor shall cross over armed **b**
3:28 for he shall go over **b** this
4: 8 in all this law which I set **b**
4:10 the day you stood **b** the LORD
4:32 which were **b** you, since the day
4:34 your God did for you in Egypt **b**
4:38 driving out from **b** you nations
4:44 is the law which Moses set **b**
5: 7 shall have no other gods **b** Me.
6:19 out all your enemies from **b**
6:22 showed signs and wonders **b** our
6:25 all these commandments **b** the
7: 1 and has cast out many nations **b**
7:22 will drive out those nations **b**
8:20 which the LORD destroys **b** you,
9: 2 Who can stand **b** the descendants
9: 3 God is He who goes over **b** you
9: 3 them and bring them down **b** you;
9: 4 your God has cast them out **b**
9: 4 is driving them out from **b** you.
9: 5 God drives them out from **b** you,
9:17 my two hands and broke them **b**
9:18 And I fell down **b** the LORD, as
9:25 Thus I prostrated myself **b** the
10: 8 to stand **b** the LORD to
10:11 begin your journey **b** the
11:23 out all these nations from **b**
11:26 I set **b** you today a blessing
11:32 and judgments which I set **b**
12: 7 And there you shall eat **b** the
12:12 And you shall rejoice **b** the
12:18 But you must eat them **b** the
12:18 and you shall rejoice **b** the
12:29 LORD your God cuts off from **b**
12:30 they are destroyed from **b** you,
14:23 And you shall eat **b** the LORD
14:26 you shall eat there **b** the LORD
15:20 your household shall eat it **b**
16:11 You shall rejoice **b** the LORD
16:16 all your males shall appear **b**
16:16 and they shall not appear **b** the
17:12 who stands to minister there **b**
17:18 from the one **b** the priests,
18: 7 who stand there **b** the LORD.
18:12 God drives them out from **b** you.
18:13 You shall be blameless **b** the
19:17 the controversy shall stand **b**
19:17 **b** the priests and the judges
22: 6 a bird's nest happens to be **b**
22:17 they shall spread the cloth **b**
24: 4 for that is an abomination **b**
24:13 be righteousness to you **b** the
26: 4 of your hand and set it down **b**
26: 5 you shall answer and say **b**
26:10 Then you shall set it **b** the
26:10 and worship **b** the LORD your
26:13 then you shall say **b** the LORD
27: 7 and rejoice **b** the LORD your

B

28: 7 against you to be defeated **b**
28: 7 against you one way and flee **b**
28:25 will cause you to be defeated **b**
28:25 them and flee seven ways **b**
28:31 ox shall be slaughtered **b**
28:31 be violently taken away from **b**
28:66 life shall hang in doubt **b** you;
29: 2 seen all that the LORD did **b**
29:10 All of you stand today **b** the
29:15 who stands here with us today **b**
30: 1 the curse which I have set **b**
30:15 I have set **b** you today life and
30:19 that I have set **b** you life and
31: 3 God Himself crosses over **b** you;
31: 3 destroy these nations from **b**
31: 3 Joshua himself crosses over **b**
31: 8 He is the one who goes **b** you.
31:11 all Israel comes to appear **b**
31:11 you shall read this law **b** all
31:21 even **b** I have brought them to
32:52 Yet you shall see the land **b**
33: 1 the children of Israel **b** his
33:10 They shall put incense **b** You,
33:27 thrust out the enemy from **b**
34:11 **b** Pharaoh, before all his
34:11 **b** all his servants, and in all
Josh 1: 5 man shall be able to stand **b**
1:14 But you shall pass **b** your
2: 8 Now **b** they lay down, she came
3: 1 and lodged there **b** they crossed
3: 4 you have not passed this way **b**.
3: 6 the covenant and cross over **b**
3: 6 ark of the covenant and went **b**
3:10 without fail drive out from **b**
3:11 the earth is crossing over **b**
3:14 the ark of the covenant **b** the
4: 5 Cross over **b** the ark of the
4: 7 of the Jordan were cut off **b**
4:12 Manasseh crossed over armed **b**
4:13 for war crossed over **b** the
4:18 overflowed all its banks as **b**.
4:23 up the waters of the Jordan **b**
4:23 which He dried up **b** us until we
5: 1 the waters of the Jordan from **b**
6: 4 trumpets of rams' horns **b** the
6: 5 go up every man straight **b** him.
6: 6 trumpets of rams' horns **b** the
6: 7 let him who is armed advance **b**
6: 8 trumpets of rams' horns **b** the
6: 9 The armed men went **b** the priests
6:13 trumpets of rams' horns **b** the
6:13 And the armed men went **b** them.
6:20 every man straight **b** him, and
6:26 Cursed be the man **b** the LORD
7: 4 but they fled **b** the men of Ai.
7: 5 for they chased them from **b**
7: 6 to the earth on his face **b** the
7: 8 when Israel turns its back **b**
7:12 of Israel could not stand **b**
7:12 but turned their backs **b**
7:13 you cannot stand **b** your enemies
7:23 and laid them out **b** the LORD.
8: 5 that we shall flee **b** them.
8: 6 They are fleeing **b** us as at
8: 6 Therefore we will flee **b** them.
8:10 **b** the people to Ai.
8:11 and they came **b** the city and
8:14 at an appointed place **b** the
8:15 made as if they were beaten **b**
8:33 on either side of the ark **b**
8:33 of the LORD had commanded **b**,
8:35 which Joshua did not read **b**
9:24 inhabitants of the land from **b**
10: 5 and camped **b** Gibeon and made
10: 8 not a man of them shall stand **b**
10:10 So the LORD routed them **b**
10:11 as they fled **b** Israel and were
10:12 delivered up the Amorites **b**
10:14 **b** it or after it, that the
11: 6 deliver all of them slain **b**
13: 6 them I will drive out from **b** the
13:25 which is **b** Rabbah,
15: 7 which is **b** the Ascent of
15: 8 of the mountain that lies **b**
17: 4 And they came near **b** Eleazar the
17: 4 **b** Joshua the son of Nun, and
17: 4 and **b** the rulers, saying, "The
18: 1 And the land was subdued **b**
18: 6 I may cast lots for you here **b**
18: 8 I may cast lots for you here **b**
18:10 cast lots for them in Shiloh **b**
18:14 from the hill that lies **b** Beth
18:16 of the mountain that lies **b**
18:17 which is **b** the Ascent of
19:51 inheritance by lot in Shiloh **b**
20: 6 in that city until he stands **b**
20: 9 of blood until he stood **b** the
22:27 the service of the LORD **b** Him
22:29 the LORD our God which is **b**
23: 5 God will expel them from **b** you
23: 9 the LORD has driven out from **b**
23:13 drive out these nations from **b**
24: 1 and they presented themselves **b**
24: 8 and I destroyed them from **b**
24:12 I sent the hornet **b** you which
24:12 you which drove them out from **b**
24:18 the LORD drove out from **b**
Judg 2: 3 I will not drive them out **b** you;
2:14 they could no longer stand **b**
2:21 also will no longer drive out **b**
4:14 Has not the LORD gone out **b**
4:15 with the edge of the sword **b**
5: 5 The mountains gushed **b** the
5: 5 **b** the LORD God of Israel.
6: 9 and drove them out **b** you and
6:18 out my offering and set it **b**
8:28 Thus Midian was subdued **b** the
11:11 Jephthah spoke all his words **b**
11:23 the Amorites from **b** His people
11:24 our God takes possession of **b**
11:33 people of Ammon were subdued **b**
12: 5 the fords of the Jordan **b** the
14:18 to him on the seventh day **b**
16:20 and said, "I will go out as **b**,
20: 1 gathered together as one man **b**
20:23 of Israel went up and wept **b**
20:26 They sat there **b** the LORD and
20:26 and peace offerings **b** the
20:28 stood **b** it in those days),
20:32 They are defeated **b** us, as at
20:35 The LORD defeated Benjamin **b**
20:39 Surely they are defeated **b** us,
20:42 they turned their backs **b**
21: 2 and remained there **b** God till
Ruth 2:11 people whom you did not know **b**.
3:14 and she arose **b** one could
1 Sam 1:12 as she continued praying **b** the
1:15 but have poured out my soul **b**
1:19 in the morning and worshiped **b**
1:22 that he may appear **b** the LORD
2:11 ministered to the LORD **b** Eli
2:15 **b** they burned the fat, the
2:17 the young men was very great **b**
2:18 But Samuel ministered **b** the
2:21 the child Samuel grew **b** the
2:28 and to wear an ephod **b** Me?
2:30 of your father would walk **b** Me
2:35 and he shall walk **b** My anointed
3: 1 ministered to the LORD **b** Eli.
3: 3 and **b** the lamp of God went out
4: 3 the LORD defeated us today **b**
4: 7 a thing has never happened **b**.
4:17 Israel has fled **b** the
5: 3 on its face to the earth **b** the
5: 4 on its face to the ground **b**
6:20 Who is able to stand **b** this holy
7: 6 and poured it out **b** the LORD.
7:10 them that they were overcome **b**
8:11 and some will run **b** his
8:20 king may judge us and go out **b**
9:13 you will surely find him **b** he
9:15 Samuel in his ear the day **b**
9:19 Go up **b** me to the high place,
9:24 its upper part and set it **b**
10: 5 and a harp **b** them; and they
10: 8 You shall go down **b** me to
10:19 present yourselves **b** the LORD
10:25 it in a book and laid it up **b**
11:15 and there they made Saul king **b**
11:15 of peace offerings **b** the LORD,
12: 2 walking **b** you; and I am old and
12: 2 I have walked **b** you from my
12: 3 Witness against me **b** the LORD
12: 3 me before the LORD and **b** His
12: 7 that I may reason with you **b**
12:16 which the LORD will do **b** your
14:13 and they fell **b** Jonathan.
14:21 were with the Philistines **b**
14:24 **b** I have taken vengeance on my
15:30 **b** the elders of my people and
15:30 the elders of my people and **b**
15:33 Samuel hacked Agag in pieces **b**
16: 6 the LORD's anointed is **b** Him.
16: 8 and made him pass **b** Samuel.
16:10 made seven of his sons pass **b**
16:16 who are **b** you, to seek out a
16:21 David came to Saul and stood **b**
16:22 Please let David stand **b** me, for
17: 7 and a shield-bearer went **b** him.
17:41 man who bore the shield went **b**
17:57 took him and brought him **b**
18:13 and he went out and came in **b**
18:16 he went out and came in **b** them.
19:24 his clothes and prophesied **b**
20: 1 and what is my sin **b** your
21: 6 which had been taken from **b**
21: 7 detained **b** the LORD. And his
21:10 arose and fled that day from **b**
21:13 So he changed his behavior **b**
22: 4 So he brought them **b** the king of
23:18 two of them made a covenant **b**
23:24 they arose and went to Ziph **b**
25:19 Go on **b** me; see, I am coming
25:23 fell on her face **b** David, and
26:19 may they be cursed **b** the
26:20 my blood fall to the earth **b**
28:22 let me set a piece of bread **b**
28:25 So she brought it **b** Saul and
30:20 and herds they had driven **b**
31: 1 the men of Israel fled from **b**
2 Sam 2:14 men now arise and compete **b** us.
2:17 the men of Israel were beaten **b**
2:24 which is **b** Giah by the road to
3:28 kingdom and I are guiltless **b**
3:34 As a man falls **b** wicked men,
5: 3 covenant with them at Hebron **b**
5:20 broken through my enemies **b** me,
5:24 then the LORD will go out **b**
6: 4 and Ahio went **b** the ark.
6: 5 of Israel played music **b** the
6:14 Then David danced **b** the LORD
6:16 David leaping and whirling **b**
6:17 and peace offerings **b** the
6:21 It was **b** the LORD, who chose
6:21 Therefore I will play music **b**
7: 9 cut off all your enemies from **b**
7:15 whom I removed from **b** you.
7:16 shall be established forever **b**
7:18 King David went in and sat **b**
7:23 **b** Your people whom You redeemed
7:26 servant David be established **b**
7:29 that it may continue forever **b**
10: 9 battle line was against him **b**
10:13 and they fled **b** him.
10:14 they also fled **b** Abishai, and
10:16 of Hadadezer's army went **b**
10:18 Then the Syrians fled **b** Israel;
11:13 he ate and drank **b** him; and he
12:11 and I will take your wives **b**
12:12 but I will do this thing **b** all
12:12 before all Israel, **b** the sun.'
12:20 they set food **b** him, and he
13: 9 the pan and placed them out **b**
14:33 on his face to the ground **b**
15: 1 and fifty men to run **b** him.
15:18 Then all his servants passed **b**
15:18 passed **b** the king.
16: 4 I humbly bow **b** you, that I may
18: 7 Israel were overthrown there **b**
18:28 with his face to the earth **b**
19: 8 So all the people came **b** the
19:13 not commander of the army **b** me
19:17 and they went over the Jordan **b**
19:18 the son of Gera fell down **b**
19:28 house were but dead men **b** my
20: 8 Amasa came **b** them. Now Joab was
21: 6 and we will hang them **b** the
21: 9 they hanged them on the hill **b**
22:13 From the brightness **b** Him
22:23 For all His judgments were **b**
22:24 I was also blameless **b** Him,
24:13 shall you flee three months **b**
24:20 So Araunah went out and bowed **b**
1 Ki 1: 2 and let her stand **b** the king,
1: 5 and fifty men to run **b** him.
1:23 And when he came in **b** the
1:23 he bowed down **b** the king with
1:25 They are eating and drinking **b**
1:28 the king's presence and stood **b**
1:32 So they came **b** the king.
1:53 And he came and fell down **b**
2: 4 to walk **b** Me in truth with all
2:26 the ark of the Lord GOD **b** my
2:45 of David shall be established **b**
3: 6 because he walked **b** You in
3:12 has not been anyone like you **b**
3:15 came to Jerusalem and stood **b**
3:16 and stood **b** him.
3:22 Thus they spoke **b** the king.
3:24 So they brought a sword **b** the
8: 5 were with him **b** the ark,
8:22 Then Solomon stood **b** the altar
8:23 with Your servants who walk **b**
8:25 not fail to have a man sit **b**
8:25 that they walk **b** Me as you have
8:25 before Me as you have walked **b**
8:28 Your servant is praying **b** You
8:31 and comes and takes an oath **b**
8:33 people Israel are defeated **b**
8:50 and grant them compassion **b**
8:54 that he arose from **b** the altar
8:59 I have made supplication **b** the
8:62 with him offered sacrifices **b**
8:64 the bronze altar that was **b**
8:65 **b** the LORD our God, seven days
9: 3 that you have made **b** Me;
9: 4 Now if you walk **b** Me as your
9: 6 My statutes which I have set **b**
9:25 on the altar that was **b**
10: 8 who stand continually **b** you
11:36 David may always have a lamp **b**
12: 6 the elders who stood **b** his
12: 8 who stood **b** him.
12:30 the people went to worship **b**
13: 6 to him, and became as **b**.
14: 9 more evil than all who were **b**
14:24 which the LORD had cast out **b**
15: 3 which he had done **b** him; his
16:25 did worse than all who were **b**
16:30 more than all who were **b** him.
16:33 the kings of Israel who were **b**
17: 1 **b** whom I stand, there shall not
18:15 **b** whom I stand, I will surely
18:44 and go down **b** the rain stops
19:11 and stand on the mountain **b** the
19:11 and broke the rocks in pieces **b**
19:19 with twelve yoke of oxen **b**
20:27 children of Israel encamped **b**
21:10 **b** him to bear witness against
21:13 came in and sat **b** him; and the
21:26 whom the LORD had cast out **b**
21:29 how Ahab has humbled himself **b**
21:29 he has humbled himself **b** Me,
22:10 all the prophets prophesied **b**
22:21 came forward and stood **b** the
2 Ki 1:13 came and fell on his knees **b**
2: 9 **b** I am taken away from you?"
2:15 and bowed to the ground **b** him.
3:14 **b** whom I stand, surely were it
3:24 so that they fled **b** them; and
4:12 she stood **b** him.
4:38 of the prophets were sitting **b**
4:43 Shall I set this **b** one hundred
4:44 So he set it **b** them; and they
5:15 and came and stood **b** him; and
5:16 **b** whom I stand, I will receive

5:25 Now he went in and stood **b** his
6:22 Set food and water **b** them, that
6:32 but **b** the messenger came to
8: 9 and he came and stood **b** him,
11:18 Mattan the priest of Baal **b**
13: 5 dwelt in their tents as **b**.
16: 3 the LORD had cast out from **b**
16:11 So Urijah the priest made it **b**
16:14 the bronze altar which was **b**
17: 2 the kings of Israel who were **b**
17: 8 the LORD had cast out from **b**
17:11 the LORD had carried away **b**
18: 5 nor who were **b** him.
18:22 You shall worship **b** this altar
19:14 and spread it **b** the LORD.
19:15 Then Hezekiah prayed **b** the
19:26 And grain blighted **b** it is
19:32 Nor come **b** it with shield,
20: 3 how I have walked **b** You in
20: 4 **b** Isaiah had gone out into the
21: 2 whom the LORD had cast out **b**
21: 9 whom the LORD had destroyed **b**
21:11 all the Amorites who were **b**
22:10 And Shaphan read it **b** the
22:19 and you humbled yourself **b** the
22:19 tore your clothes and wept **b**
23: 3 a pillar and made a covenant **b**
23:23 this Passover was held **b** the
23:25 Now **b** him there was no king like
25: 7 killed the sons of Zedekiah **b**
25:24 And Gedaliah took an oath **b** them
25:29 and he ate bread regularly **b**
1 Chr 1:43 reigned in the land of Edom **b**
5:25 whom God had destroyed **b** them.
6:32 were ministering with music **b**
10: 1 the men of Israel fled from **b**
11: 3 covenant with them at Hebron **b**
13: 8 and all Israel played music **b**
13:10 and he died there **b** God.
14:15 for God has gone out **b** you to
15: 2 ark of God and to minister **b**
15:24 were to blow the trumpets **b** the
16: 1 and peace offerings **b** God.
16: 4 of the Levites to minister **b**
16: 6 regularly blew the trumpets **b**
16:27 Honor and majesty are **b** Him;
16:29 and come **b** Him. Oh, worship
16:30 Tremble **b** Him, all the earth.
16:33 of the woods shall rejoice **b**
16:37 Asaph and his brothers there **b**
16:37 of the LORD to minister **b** the
16:39 **b** the tabernacle of the LORD
17: 8 cut off all your enemies from **b**
17:13 I took it from him who was **b**
17:16 King David went in and sat **b**
17:21 by driving out nations from **b**
17:24 servant David be established **b**
17:25 it in his heart to pray **b**
17:27 that it may continue **b** You
19: 7 who came and encamped **b** Medeba.
19: 9 themselves in battle array **b**
19:10 battle line was against him **b**
19:14 and they fled **b** him.
19:15 they also fled **b** Abishai his
19:16 of Hadadezer's army went **b**
19:18 Then the Syrians fled **b** Israel;
21:21 and bowed **b** David with his
21:30 But David could not go **b** it to
22: 5 made abundant preparations **b**
22:18 and the land is subdued **b** the
22:18 subdued before the LORD and **b**
23:13 to burn incense **b** the LORD, to
23:31 regularly **b** the LORD;
24: 2 And Nadab and Abihu died **b** their
24: 6 wrote them down **b** the king, the
29:10 David blessed the LORD **b** all
29:15 we are aliens and pilgrims **b**
29:20 and prostrated themselves **b**
29:22 So they ate and drank **b** the
29:22 and anointed him **b** the LORD
29:25 as had not been on any king **b**
2 Chr 1: 5 he put **b** the tabernacle of the
1: 6 up there to the bronze altar **b**
1:10 that I may go out and come in **b**
1:12 the kings have had who were **b**
1:13 from **b** the tabernacle of
2: 4 to burn **b** Him sweet incense,
2: 6 except to burn sacrifice **b** Him?
3:17 Then he set up the pillars **b** the
5: 6 who were assembled with him **b**
6:12 Then Solomon stood **b** the altar
6:13 knelt down on his knees **b** all
6:14 with Your servants who walk **b**
6:16 not fail to have a man sit **b**
6:16 in My law as you have walked **b**
6:19 Your servant is praying **b** You:
6:22 and comes and takes an oath **b**
6:24 people Israel are defeated **b**
6:24 pray and make supplication **b**
7: 4 the people offered sacrifices **b**
7:17 if you walk **b** Me as your father
7:19 which I have set **b** you,
8:12 the LORD which he had built **b**
8:14 duties (to praise and serve **b**
9: 7 who stand continually **b** you and
9:11 none such as these seen **b** in
10: 6 the elders who stood **b** his
10: 8 who stood **b** him.
13:15 Jeroboam and all Israel **b**
13:16 the children of Israel fled **b**
14: 7 while the land is yet **b** us,
14:12 LORD struck the Ethiopians **b**
14:13 for they were broken **b** the
15: 8 altar of the LORD that was **b**
15:14 Then they took an oath **b** the
18: 9 all the prophets prophesied **b**
18:20 came forward and stood **b** the
19:11 Levites will be officials **b**
20: 5 **b** the new court,
20: 7 the inhabitants of this land **b**
20: 9 we will stand **b** this temple and
20:13 stood **b** the LORD.
20:16 them at the end of the brook **b**
20:18 of Jerusalem bowed **b** the LORD,
20:21 as they went out **b** the army and
23:17 Mattan the priest of Baal **b**
24:14 the rest of the money **b** the
25: 8 God shall make you fall **b** the
25:14 and bowed down **b** them and
26:19 **b** the priests in the house of
27: 6 because he prepared his ways **b**
28: 3 whom the LORD had cast out **b**
28: 9 and he went out **b** the army that
28:10 are you not also guilty **b** the
28:14 the captives and the spoil **b**
29:11 has chosen you to stand **b** Him,
29:19 **b** the altar of the LORD."
29:23 goats for the sin offering **b**
31:20 was good and right and true **b**
32: 7 do not be afraid nor dismayed **b**
32: 7 nor **b** all the multitude that
32:12 You shall worship **b** one altar
33: 2 whom the LORD had cast out **b**
33: 9 whom the LORD had destroyed **b**
33:12 and humbled himself greatly **b**
33:19 **b** he was humbled, indeed they
33:23 And he did not humble himself **b**
34:18 And Shaphan read it **b** the
34:24 the book which they have read **b**
34:27 and you humbled yourself **b** God
34:27 and you humbled yourself **b** Me,
34:27 tore your clothes and wept **b**
34:31 his place and made a covenant **b**
36:12 and did not humble himself **b**
Ezra 3:12 of this temple was laid **b**
4:18 to us has been clearly read **b**
4:23 Artaxerxes' letter was read **b**
7:19 deliver in full **b** the God of
7:28 and has extended mercy to me **b**
7:28 and **b** all the king's mighty
8:21 we might humble ourselves **b**
8:29 them until you weigh them **b**
9:15 Here we are **b** You, in our
9:15 though no one can stand **b** You
10: 1 and bowing down **b** the house of
10: 6 Then Ezra rose up from **b** the
Neh 1: 4 I was fasting and praying **b** the
1: 6 of Your servant which I pray **b**
2: 1 when wine was **b** him, that I
2: 1 been sad in his presence **b**.
4: 2 And he spoke **b** his brethren and
4: 5 sin be blotted out from **b** You;
4: 5 have provoked You to anger **b**
5:15 former governors who were **b**
6: 5 sent his servant to me as **b**,
6:19 they reported his good deeds **b**
8: 2 the priest brought the Law **b**
8: 3 **b** the men and women and those
9: 8 found his heart faithful **b** You,
9:11 And You divided the sea **b** them,
9:24 You subdued **b** them the
9:28 They again did evil **b** You.
9:32 all the trouble seem small **b**
9:35 and rich land which You set **b**
12:36 Ezra the scribe went **b** them.
13: 4 Now **b** this, Eliashib the
13:19 as it began to be dark **b** the
Esth 1: 3 of the provinces being **b** him—
1:11 to bring Queen Vashti **b** the
1:16 And Memucan answered **b** the king
1:17 Vashti to be brought in **b** him,
1:19 Vashti shall come no more **b**
3: 7 **b** Haman to determine the day
4: 8 to him and plead **b** him for her
5: 9 he did not stand or tremble **b**
6: 1 and they were read **b** the king.
6: 9 and proclaim **b** him: 'Thus shall
6:11 and proclaimed **b** him, "Thus
6:13 **b** whom you have begun to fall,
6:13 him but will surely fall **b** him.
7: 6 So Haman was terrified **b** the
7: 7 but Haman stood **b** Queen Esther,
8: 1 And Mordecai came **b** the king,
8: 4 So Esther arose and stood **b** the
9:25 but when Esther came **b** the
Job 1: 6 came to present themselves **b**
2: 1 came to present themselves **b**
2: 1 them to present himself **b** the
3:24 For my sighing comes **b** I eat,
4:15 Then a spirit passed **b** my face;
4:16 A form was **b** my eyes; There
4:19 Who are crushed **b** a moth?
8:12 It withers **b** any other plant.
9: 2 how can a man be righteous **b**
10:21 ***B*** I go to the place from
13:15 I will defend my own ways **b**
13:16 a hypocrite could not come **b**
15: 4 And restrain prayer **b** God.
15: 7 Or were you made **b** the hills?
15:32 It will be accomplished **b** his
18:14 And they parade him **b** the king
21: 8 And their offspring **b** their
21:18 They are like straw **b** the wind,
21:33 As countless have gone **b**
22:16 Who were cut down **b** their time,
23: 4 I would present my case **b** Him,
25: 4 then can man be righteous **b**
26: 6 Sheol is naked **b** Him, And
30:11 have cast off restraint **b** me.
33: 5 Set your words in order **b**
33: 6 I am as your spokesman **b** God;
34:23 That he should go **b** God in
35:14 Yet justice is **b** Him, and
41:22 And sorrow dances **b** him.
42:10 Job twice as much as he had **b**.
42:11 had been his acquaintances **b**,
Ps 5: 8 Make Your way straight **b** my
16: 8 I have set the LORD always **b**
18: 6 And my cry came **b** Him, even
18:12 From the brightness **b** Him, His
18:22 For all His judgments were **b**
18:23 I was also blameless **b** Him,
18:42 them as fine as the dust **b** the
22:25 I will pay My vows **b** those who
22:27 of the nations Shall worship **b**
22:29 down to the dust Shall bow **b**
23: 5 You prepare a table **b** me in the
26: 3 For Your lovingkindness is **b**
31:22 I am cut off from **b** Your eyes";
34: when he pretended madness **b**
35: 5 Let them be like chaff **b** the
36: 1 There is no fear of God **b**
38: 9 all my desire is **b** You; And
38:17 my sorrow is continually **b** me.
39: 1 While the wicked are **b** me."
39: 5 And my age is as nothing **b**
39:13 ***B*** I go away and am no more."
41:12 And set me **b** Your face
42: 2 shall I come and appear **b** God?
44:15 My dishonor is continually **b**
50: 3 A fire shall devour **b** Him,
50: 8 Which are continually **b** Me.
50:21 And set them in order **b** your
51: 3 And my sin is always **b** me.
54: 3 They have not set God **b** them.
56:13 That I may walk **b** God In the
57: 6 They have dug a pit **b** me;
58: 9 ***B*** your pots can feel the
61: 7 He shall abide **b** God forever.
62: 8 Pour out your heart **b** Him;
68: 1 those also who hate Him flee **b**
68: 2 As wax melts **b** the fire, So
68: 3 Let them rejoice **b** God; Yes,
68: 4 And rejoice **b** Him.
68: 7 when You went out **b** Your
68:25 The singers went **b**,
69:19 My adversaries are all **b** You.
69:22 their table become a snare **b**
72: 6 down like rain upon the grass **b**
72: 9 in the wilderness will bow **b**
72:11 all kings shall fall down **b**
73:22 I was like a beast **b** You.
78:55 also drove out the nations **b**
79:11 of the prisoner come **b** You;
80: 2 ***B*** Ephraim, Benjamin, and
83:13 Like the chaff **b** the wind!
84: 7 Each one appears **b** God in
85:13 Righteousness will go **b** Him,
86: 9 made Shall come and worship **b**
86:14 And have not set You **b** them.
88: 1 have cried out day and night **b**
88: 2 Let my prayer come **b** You;
88:13 the morning my prayer comes **b**
89:14 Mercy and truth go **b** Your
89:23 I will beat down his foes **b** his
89:36 And his throne as the sun **b**
90: 2 ***B*** the mountains were brought
90: 8 You have set our iniquities **b**
95: 2 Let us come **b** His presence with
95: 6 Let us kneel **b** the LORD our
96: 6 Honor and majesty are **b** Him;
96: 9 beauty of holiness! Tremble **b**
96:12 of the woods will rejoice **b**
97: 3 A fire goes **b** Him, And burns
98: 6 Shout joyfully **b** the LORD,
98: 8 the hills be joyful together **b**
100: 2 Come **b** His presence with
101: 3 I will set nothing wicked **b** my
102: and pours out his complaint **b**
102:28 will be established **b** You.
105:17 sent a man **b** them—Joseph—who
106:23 Moses His chosen one stood **b**
109:14 of his fathers be remembered **b**
109:15 Let them be continually **b** the
116: 9 I will walk **b** the LORD In the
119:30 Your judgments I have laid **b**
119:46 of Your testimonies also **b**
119:67 ***B*** I was afflicted I went
119:147 I rise **b** the dawning of the
119:168 For all my ways are **b** You.
119:169 Let my cry come **b** You, O
119:170 Let my supplication come **b** You;
129: 6 Which withers **b** it grows up,
138: 1 ***B*** the gods I will sing praises
139: 5 have hedged me behind and **b**,
141: 2 Let my prayer be set **b** You as
142: 2 I pour out my complaint **b** Him;
142: 2 I declare **b** Him my trouble.
147:17 Who can stand **b** His cold?
Prov 4:25 And your eyelids look right **b**
5:21 For the ways of man are **b** the
8:22 ***B*** His works of old.
8:23 **b** there was ever an earth.
8:25 ***B*** the mountains were settled,
8:25 ***B*** the hills, I was brought
8:30 Rejoicing always **b** Him,

14:19 The evil will bow **b** the good,
15:11 Hell and Destruction are **b** the
15:33 And **b** honor is humility.
16:18 Pride goes **b** destruction, And
16:18 And a haughty spirit **b** a fall.
17:14 Therefore stop contention **b** a
18:12 ***B*** destruction the heart of a
18:12 And **b** honor is humility.
18:13 He who answers a matter **b** he
18:16 And brings him **b** great men.
22:29 He will stand **b** kings; He
22:29 He will not stand **b** unknown
23: 1 Consider carefully what is **b**
25: 5 Take away the wicked from **b** the
25:26 A righteous man who falters **b**
26:26 wickedness will be revealed **b**
27: 4 But who is able to stand **b**
30: 7 of You (Deprive me not **b** I
Eccl 1:10 been in ancient times **b** us.
1:16 wisdom than all who were **b** me
2: 7 all who were in Jerusalem **b** me.
2: 9 more than all who were **b** me in
2:26 give to him who is good **b**
3:14 that men should fear **b** Him.
5: 2 heart utter anything hastily **b**
5: 6 nor say **b** the messenger of
6: 8 Who knows how to walk **b** the
7:17 Why should you die **b** your
8:12 fear God, who fear **b** Him.
8:13 because he does not fear **b** God.
9: 1 by anything they see **b** them.
12: 1 ***B*** the difficult days come,
12: 6 Remember your Creator **b** the
Song 6:12 ***B*** I was even aware, My soul
8:12 My own vineyard is **b** me. You,
Isa 1:12 When you come to appear **b** Me,
1:16 the evil of your doings from **b**
1:23 the cause of the widow come **b**
7:16 For **b** the Child shall know to
8: 4 for **b** the child shall have
8: 4 of Samaria will be taken away **b**
9: 3 They rejoice **b** You According
9:12 The Syrians **b** and the
13:16 also will be dashed to pieces **b**
17:13 the chaff of the mountains **b**
17:13 Like a rolling thing **b** the
17:14 trouble! And **b** the morning,
18: 5 For **b** the harvest, when the bud
23:18 will be for those who dwell **b**
24:23 Jerusalem And **b** His elders,
28: 4 Like the first fruit **b** the
30: 8 write it **b** them on a tablet,
30:11 Israel To cease from **b** us."
36: 7 You shall worship **b** this
37:14 and spread it **b** the LORD.
37:27 And grain blighted **b** it is
37:33 Nor come **b** it with shield,
38: 3 how I have walked **b** You in
40:10 And His work **b** Him.
40:17 All nations **b** Him are as
41: 1 Keep silence **b** Me, O coastlands,
41: 2 Who gave the nations **b** him,
42: 9 ***B*** they spring forth I tell you
42:16 I will make darkness light **b**
43:10 ***B*** Me there was no God formed,
43:13 Indeed **b** the day was, I am
44:17 He falls down **b** it and
44:19 Shall I fall down **b** a block of
45: 1 To subdue nations **b** him And
45: 1 To open **b** him the double
45: 2 I will go **b** you And make the
47:14 Nor a fire to sit **b**!
48: 5 ***B*** it came to pass I proclaimed
48: 7 And **b** this day you have not
48:19 cut off Nor destroyed from **b**
49:16 Your walls are continually **b**
52:12 For the LORD will go **b** you,
53: 2 For He shall grow up **b** Him as a
53: 7 And as a sheep **b** its shearers
55:12 break forth into singing **b** you,
57:16 For the spirit would fail **b**
58: 8 your righteousness shall go **b**
59:12 are multiplied **b** You,
61:11 and praise to spring forth **b**
62:11 And His work **b** Him.'"
63:12 Dividing the water **b** them To
65: 6 it is written **b** Me: I will
65:12 But did evil **b** My eyes, And
65:24 shall come to pass That **b**
66: 4 But they did evil **b** My eyes,
66: 7 ***B*** she was in labor, she gave
66: 7 ***B*** her pain came, She
66:22 I will make shall remain **b** Me,
66:23 flesh shall come to worship **b**
Jer 1: 5 ***B*** I formed you in the womb I
1: 5 ***B*** you were born I sanctified
1:17 Do not be dismayed **b** their
1:17 Lest I dismay you **b** them.
2:21 How then have you turned **b** Me
2:22 your iniquity is marked **b** Me,
6: 7 ***B*** Me continually are grief
6:21 I will lay stumbling blocks **b**
7:10 and then come and stand **b** Me in
8: 2 They shall spread them **b** the sun
9:13 forsaken My law which I set **b**
13:16 glory to the LORD your God ***B***
13:16 And **b** your feet stumble On
15: 1 if Moses and Samuel stood **b** Me,
15: 9 I will deliver to the sword ***B***
15:19 You shall stand **b** Me; If you
16: 9 **b** your eyes and in your days,
17:16 It was right there **b** You.
18:17 them as with an east wind **b**
18:20 Remember that I stood **b** You
18:23 But let them be overthrown **b**
19: 7 them to fall by the sword **b**
20:12 For I have pleaded my cause **b**
21: 8 I set **b** you the way of life and
24: 1 were two baskets of figs set **b**
26: 4 in My law which I have set **b**
28: 8 The prophets who have been **b** me
28: 8 who have been before me and **b**
29:21 and he shall slay them **b** your
30:20 children also shall be as **b**,
30:20 shall be established **b** Me;
31:36 ordinances depart From **b** Me,
31:36 cease From being a nation **b**
32:12 **b** all the Jews who sat in the
32:13 Then I charged Baruch **b** them,
32:30 of Judah have done only evil **b**
32:31 so I will remove it from **b** My
33: 9 and an honor **b** all nations of
33:18 man to offer burnt offerings **b**
33:24 should no more be a nation **b**
34: 5 the former kings who were **b**
34:15 and you made a covenant **b** Me in
34:18 the covenant which they made **b**
35: 5 Then I set **b** the sons of the
35:19 not lack a man to stand **b** Me
36: 7 present their supplication **b**
36: 9 that they proclaimed a fast **b**
36:22 fire burning on the hearth **b**
37:20 let my petition be accepted **b**
38:10 prophet out of the dungeon **b**
38:26 I presented my request **b** the
39: 6 killed the sons of Zedekiah **b**
39:16 be performed in that day **b**
40: 4 all the land is **b** you;
40: 9 took an oath **b** them and their
42: 9 me to present your petition **b**
44:10 or in My statutes that I set **b**
47: 1 **b** Pharaoh attacked Gaza.
49:37 cause Elam to be dismayed **b**
49:37 before their enemies And **b**
50: 8 And be like the rams **b** the
52:10 killed the sons of Zedekiah **b**
52:33 and he ate bread regularly **b**
Lam 1: 5 have gone into captivity **b** the
1: 6 That flee without strength ***B***
1:22 all their wickedness come **b**
2: 3 back His right hand From **b**
2:19 out your heart like water **b**
3:35 the justice due a man ***B*** the
Ezek 2:10 Then He spread it **b** me; and
3:20 and I lay a stumbling block **b**
4: 1 a clay tablet and lay it **b** you,
6: 4 cast down your slain men **b**
6: 5 of the children of Israel **b**
8: 1 the elders of Judah sitting **b**
8:11 And there stood **b** them seventy
9: 6 with the elders who were **b**
14: 1 of Israel came to me and sat **b**
14: 3 and put **b** them that which
14: 4 and puts **b** him what causes him
14: 7 idols in his heart and puts **b**
16:18 you set My oil and My incense **b**
16:19 you set it **b** them as sweet
16:50 and committed abomination **b** Me;
16:57 **b** your wickedness was uncovered.
20: 1 of the LORD, and sat **b** me.
20: 7 the abominations which are **b**
20: 8 the abominations which were **b**
20: 9 it should not be profaned **b**
20:14 it should not be profaned **b**
20:41 and I will be hallowed in you **b**
21: 6 and sigh with bitterness **b**
22:30 and stand in the gap **b** Me on
23:41 with a table prepared **b** it, on
28: 9 Will you still say **b** him who
28:17 I laid you **b** kings, That they
30:24 and he will groan **b** him with
32:10 you when I brandish My sword **b**
33:22 had been upon me the evening **b**
33:31 they sit **b** you as My people,
36:23 when I am hallowed in you **b**
37:20 write will be in your hand **b**
38:16 O Gog, **b** their eyes."
41:22 This is the table that is **b**
43:24 When you offer them **b** the LORD,
44: 3 he may sit in it to eat bread **b**
44:11 and they shall stand **b** them to
44:12 they ministered to them **b**
44:15 and they shall stand **b** Me to
46: 3 the entrance to this gateway **b**
46: 9 the people of the land come **b**
Dan 1: 5 that time they might serve **b**
1:10 you would endanger my head **b**
1:13 our appearance be examined **b**
1:18 the eunuchs brought them in **b**
1:19 therefore they served **b** the
2: 2 So they came and stood **b** the
2: 9 lying and corrupt words **b** me
2:24 take me **b** the king, and I will
2:25 quickly brought Daniel **b** the
2:31 stood **b** you; and its form was
2:36 the interpretation of it **b** the
2:46 prostrate **b** Daniel, and
3: 3 and they stood **b** the image that
3:13 So they brought these men **b** the
4: 6 all the wise men of Babylon **b**
4: 8 But at last Daniel came **b** me
4: 8 and I told the dream **b** him,
5:13 Then Daniel was brought in **b**
5:15 have been brought in **b** me, that
5:17 and said **b** the king, "Let your
5:19 trembled and feared **b** him.
5:23 the vessels of His house **b** you,
6: 6 and satraps thronged **b** the
6:10 and prayed and gave thanks **b**
6:11 and making supplication **b** his
6:12 And they went **b** the king, and
6:13 So they answered and said **b** the
6:18 and no musicians were brought **b**
6:22 because I was found innocent **b**
6:22 I have done no wrong **b** you."
6:24 all their bones in pieces **b**
6:26 men must tremble and fear **b**
7: 7 all the beasts that were **b** it,
7: 8 **b** whom three of the first horns
7:10 issued And came forth from **b**
7:10 times ten thousand stood **b** Him.
7:13 And they brought Him near **b**
7:20 **b** which three fell, namely,
8:15 that suddenly there stood **b** me
9:10 which He set **b** us by His
9:13 we have not made our prayer **b**
9:18 not present our supplications **b**
9:20 presenting my supplication **b**
10:12 and to humble yourself **b** your
10:16 saying to him who stood **b** me,
11:22 shall be swept away from **b** him
Hos 7: 2 They are **b** My face.
Joel 1:13 you who minister **b** the altar;
1:16 Is not the food cut off **b** our
2: 3 A fire devours **b** them, And
2: 3 is like the Garden of Eden **b**
2: 6 ***B*** them the people writhe in
2:10 The earth quakes **b** them, The
2:11 The LORD gives voice **b** His
2:31 ***B*** the coming of the great and
Am 1: 1 two years **b** the earthquake.
2: 9 I who destroyed the Amorite **b**
9: 4 they go into captivity **b** their
Jon 1: 2 their wickedness has come up **b**
Mic 1: 4 valleys will split Like wax **b**
2:13 who breaks open will come up **b**
2:13 Their king will pass **b** them,
6: 1 plead your case **b** the
6: 4 And I sent **b** you Moses, Aaron,
6: 6 With what shall I come **b** the
6: 6 And bow myself **b** the High
6: 6 Shall I come **b** Him with burnt
Nah 1: 5 The mountains quake **b** Him, The
1: 6 Who can stand **b** His
2: 1 He who scatters has come up **b**
Hab 1: 3 plundering and violence are **b**
2:20 all the earth keep silence **b**
3: 5 ***B*** Him went pestilence, And
Zeph 2: 2 ***B*** the decree is issued, Or
2: 2 ***B*** the LORD's fierce anger
2: 2 ***B*** the day of the LORD's anger
3:20 When I return your captives **b**
Hag 2:14 and so is this nation **b** Me,'
2:15 from **b** stone was laid upon
Zech 2:13 **b** the LORD, for He is aroused
3: 1 the high priest standing **b** the
3: 3 and was standing **b** the Angel.
3: 4 and spoke to those who stood **b**
3: 8 and your companions who sit **b**
3: 9 the stone That I have laid **b**
4: 7 ***B*** Zerubbabel you shall
6: 5 go out from their station **b**
7: 2 to pray **b** the LORD,
8:10 For **b** these days There were
8:21 us continue to go and pray **b**
8:22 And to pray **b** the LORD.'
12: 8 like the Angel of the LORD **b**
14:20 shall be like the bowls **b** the
Mal 2: 5 feared Me And was reverent **b**
2: 9 you contemptible and base ***B***
3: 1 And he will prepare the way **b**
3:14 we have walked as mourners ***B***
3:16 of remembrance was written **b**
4: 5 send you Elijah the prophet ***B***
Mt 1:18 **b** they came together, she was
2: 9 had seen in the East went **b**
5:12 the prophets who were **b** you.
5:16 Let your light so shine **b** men,
5:24 leave your gift there **b** the
6: 1 not do your charitable deeds **b**
6: 2 do not sound a trumpet **b** you as
6: 8 the things you have need of **b**
7: 6 nor cast your pearls **b** swine,
8:29 You come here to torment us **b**
10:18 You will be brought **b** governors
10:23 through the cities of Israel **b**
10:32 whoever confesses Me **b** men,
10:32 him I will also confess **b** My
10:33 But whoever denies Me **b** men, him
10:33 him I will also deny **b** My
11:10 I send My messenger **b**
11:10 will prepare Your way **b**
14: 6 daughter of Herodias danced **b**
14:22 get into the boat and go **b** Him
17: 2 and He was transfigured **b** them.
18:26 servant therefore fell down **b**
21: 9 Then the multitudes who went **b**
21:31 enter the kingdom of God **b** you.
24:38 For as in the days **b** the flood,
25:32 the nations will be gathered **b**
26:32 I will go **b** you to Galilee."
26:34 **b** the rooster crows, you will
26:70 But he denied it **b** them all,
26:75 ***B*** the rooster crows, you will
27:11 Now Jesus stood **b** the governor.
27:24 water and washed his hands **b**

27:29 And they bowed the knee ***b*** Him
28: 7 and indeed He is going ***b*** you
Mk 1: 2 I send My messenger ***b***
1: 2 will prepare Your way ***b***
1:35 having risen a long while ***b***
3:11 fell down ***b*** Him and cried out,
5:33 came and fell down ***b*** Him and
6:33 They arrived ***b*** them and came
6:41 to His disciples to set ***b*** them;
6:45 get into the boat and go ***b*** Him
8: 6 them to His disciples to set ***b***
8: 6 and they set them ***b*** the
8: 7 He said to set them also ***b***
9: 2 and He was transfigured ***b*** them.
10:17 knelt ***b*** Him, and asked Him,
10:32 and Jesus was going ***b*** them; and
11: 9 Then those who went ***b*** and those
13: 9 You will be brought ***b*** rulers
14:28 I will go ***b*** you to Galilee."
14:30 ***b*** the rooster crows twice, you
14:72 ***B*** the rooster crows twice, you
15:42 the day ***b*** the Sabbath,
16: 7 that He is going ***b*** you into
Lk 1: 6 And they were both righteous ***b***
1: 8 he was serving as priest ***b*** God
1:17 He will also go ***b*** Him in the
1:75 holiness and righteousness ***b***
1:76 For you will go ***b*** the face of
2: 9 an angel of the Lord stood ***b***
2:21 the name given by the angel ***b***
2:26 that he would not see death ***b***
2:31 Which You have prepared ***b*** the
4: 7 if You will worship ***b*** me, all
5:18 sought to bring in and lay ***b***
5:19 the tiling into the midst ***b***
5:25 Immediately he rose up ***b*** them,
7:27 I send My messenger ***b***
7:27 will prepare Your way ***b***
8:28 fell down ***b*** Him, and with a
8:47 and falling down ***b*** Him, she
9:16 to the disciples to set ***b*** the
9:52 and sent messengers ***b*** His face.
10: 1 and sent them two by two ***b*** His
10: 8 eat such things as are set ***b***
11: 6 and I have nothing to set ***b***
11:38 that He had not first washed ***b***
12: 6 not one of them is forgotten ***b***
12: 8 whoever confesses Me ***b*** men, him
12: 8 Son of Man also will confess ***b***
12: 9 But he who denies Me ***b*** men will
12: 9 Me before men will be denied ***b***
14: 2 there was a certain man ***b*** Him
15:18 sinned against heaven and ***b***
16:15 those who justify yourselves ***b***
18:39 Then those who went ***b*** warned him
19:27 and slay them ***b*** me.'"
21:12 But ***b*** all these things, they
21:12 You will be brought ***b*** kings and
21:36 and to stand ***b*** the Son of
22:15 eat this Passover with you ***b*** I
22:34 shall not crow this day ***b*** you
22:47 went ***b*** them and drew near to
22:61 ***B*** the rooster crows, you will
23:53 where no one had ever lain ***b***.
24:19 mighty in deed and word ***b*** God
Jn 1:15 comes after me is preferred ***b***
1:15 for He was ***b*** me.'"
1:27 is preferred ***b*** me, whose sandal
1:30 comes a Man who is preferred ***b***
1:30 for He was ***b*** me.'
1:48 ***B*** Philip called you, when you
3:28 I have been sent ***b*** Him.'
4:49 come down ***b*** my child dies!"
5: 7 another steps down ***b*** me."
6:62 of Man ascend where He was ***b***?
7:51 Does our law judge a man ***b*** it
8:58 ***b*** Abraham was, I AM."
10: 4 he goes ***b*** them; and the sheep
10: 8 All who ever came ***b*** Me are
11:55 the country up to Jerusalem ***b***
12: 1 six days ***b*** the Passover, Jesus
12:37 He had done so many signs ***b***
13: 1 Now ***b*** the feast of the Passover,
13:19 Now I tell you ***b*** it comes, that
14:29 And now I have told you ***b*** it
15:18 you know that it hated Me ***b*** it
17: 5 glory which I had with You ***b***
17:24 for You loved Me ***b*** the
Acts 1:16 which the Holy Spirit spoke ***b***
2:20 ***B*** the coming of the
2:25 the LORD always ***b*** my
3:20 who was preached to you ***b***,
4:10 by Him this man stands here ***b***
4:28 and Your purpose determined ***b***
5:23 the guards standing outside ***b***
5:27 they set them ***b*** the council.
6: 6 whom they set ***b*** the apostles;
7: 2 ***b*** he dwelt in Haran,
7:40 Make us gods to go ***b*** us;
7:45 whom God drove out ***b*** the face
7:46 who found favor ***b*** God and asked
8:32 And as a lamb ***b*** its
9:15 of Mine to bear My name ***b***
10: 4 have come up for a memorial ***b***
10:17 and stood ***b*** the gate.
10:30 a man stood ***b*** me in bright
10:33 we are all present ***b*** God, to
10:41 but to witnesses chosen ***b*** by
11:11 three men stood ***b*** the house
12: 4 intending to bring him ***b*** the
12: 6 and the guards ***b*** the door were
12:14 announced that Peter stood ***b***
13:24 ***b*** His coming, the baptism of
16:29 and fell down trembling ***b*** Paul
16:34 he set food ***b*** them; and he
18:17 and beat him ***b*** the judgment
19: 9 but spoke evil of the Way ***b*** the
22: 1 hear my defense ***b*** you now."
22:30 Paul down and set him ***b*** them.
23: 1 lived in all good conscience ***b***
23:15 but we are ready to kill him ***b***
23:28 I brought him ***b*** their council.
23:30 his accusers to state ***b*** you
24:19 ought to have been here ***b***
24:20 in me while I stood ***b*** the
25: 9 and there be judged ***b*** me
25:14 Festus laid Paul's case ***b*** the
25:16 any man to destruction ***b*** the
25:26 I have brought him out ***b*** you,
25:26 and especially ***b*** you, King
26: 2 I shall answer for myself ***b***
26:26 ***b*** whom I also speak freely,
27:24 you must be brought ***b*** Caesar;
Rom 1: 2 which He promised ***b*** through His
3:18 is no fear of God ***b***
3:19 the world may become guilty ***b***
4: 2 to boast about, but not ***b*** God.
9:29 And as Isaiah said ***b***:
14:10 For we shall all stand ***b*** the
14:22 Have it to yourself ***b*** God.
15: 4 whatever things were written ***b***
16: 7 who also were in Christ ***b*** me.
1 Cor 2: 7 wisdom which God ordained ***b***
4: 5 Therefore judge nothing ***b*** the
6: 1 go to law ***b*** the unrighteous,
6: 1 and not ***b*** the saints?
6: 6 and that ***b*** unbelievers!
10:27 eat whatever is set ***b*** you,
2 Cor 1:15 I intended to come to you ***b***,
5:10 For we must all appear ***b*** the
7: 3 for I have said ***b*** that you are
8:24 and ***b*** the churches the proof of
12:19 We speak ***b*** God in Christ.
12:21 for many who have sinned ***b*** and
13: 2 I have told you ***b***,
13: 2 to those who have sinned ***b***,
Gal 1: 9 As we have said ***b***,
1:17 to those who were apostles ***b***
1:20 ***b*** God, I do not lie.)
2:12 for ***b*** certain men came from
2:14 I said to Peter ***b*** them all,
3: 1 ***b*** whose eyes Jesus Christ was
3:17 covenant that was confirmed ***b***
3:23 But ***b*** faith came, we were kept
Eph 1: 4 just as He chose us in Him ***b*** the
1: 4 be holy and without blame ***b***
Col 1: 5 of which you heard ***b*** in the
1:17 And He is ***b*** all things, and in
1 Th 2: 2 even after we had suffered ***b***
3: 4 we told you ***b*** when we were with
3: 9 we rejoice for your sake ***b*** our
3:13 hearts blameless in holiness ***b***
1 Tim 5: 4 this is good and acceptable ***b***
5:21 I charge you ***b*** God and the Lord
6:13 and ***b*** Christ Jesus who
6:13 the good confession ***b*** Pontius
2 Tim 1: 9 given to us in Christ Jesus ***b***
2:14 charging them ***b*** the Lord not
4: 1 I charge you therefore ***b*** God
4:21 Do your utmost to come ***b*** winter.
Titus 1: 2 promised ***b*** time began,
Heb 6:18 to lay hold of the hope set ***b***
10:15 to us; for after He had said ***b***,
11: 5 for ***b*** he was taken he had this
12: 1 the race that is set ***b*** us,
12: 2 who for the joy that was set ***b***
Jas 1:27 Pure and undefiled religion ***b***
1 Pe 1:20 He indeed was foreordained ***b*** the
2:20 this is commendable ***b*** God.
2 Pe 2:11 accusation against them ***b*** the
3: 2 the words which were spoken ***b***
1 Jn 2:28 and not be ashamed ***b*** Him at
3:19 and shall assure our hearts ***b***
3 Jn 6 borne witness of your love ***b***
Jude 17 the words which were spoken ***b***
24 to present you faultless ***B***
Rev 1: 4 the seven Spirits who are ***b***
2:14 to put a stumbling block ***b*** the
3: 2 not found your works perfect ***b***
3: 5 but I will confess his name ***b***
3: 5 his name before My Father and ***b***
3: 8 I have set ***b*** you an open door,
3: 9 make them come and worship ***b***
4: 5 lamps of fire were burning ***b***
4: 6 ***B*** the throne there was a sea
4:10 twenty-four elders fall down ***b***
4:10 and cast their crowns ***b*** the
5: 8 twenty-four elders fell down ***b***
7: 9 standing ***b*** the throne and
7: 9 before the throne and ***b*** the
7:11 and fell on their faces ***b*** the
7:15 Therefore they are ***b*** the throne
8: 2 the seven angels who stand ***b***
8: 3 the golden altar which was ***b***
8: 4 ascended ***b*** God from the angel's
9:13 of the golden altar which is ***b***
11: 4 the two lampstands standing ***b***
11:16 twenty-four elders who sat ***b***
12: 4 And the dragon stood ***b*** the
12:10 who accused them ***b*** our God day
14: 3 sang as it were a new song ***b***
14: 3 ***b*** the four living creatures,
14: 5 for they are without fault ***b***
15: 4 shall come and worship ***b*** You,
16:19 great Babylon was remembered ***b***
20:12 standing ***b*** God, and books were
22: 8 I fell down to worship ***b*** the

BEFOREHAND (13/13)

Josh 20: 5 but did not hate him ***b***.
Mt 24:25 "See, I have told you ***b***.
Mk 13:11 deliver you up, do not worry ***b***,
13:23 I have told you all things ***b***.
14: 8 She has come ***b*** to anoint My
Lk 21:14 your hearts not to meditate ***b***
Rom 9:23 which He had prepared ***b*** for
2 Cor 9: 5 prepare your generous gift ***b***,
Gal 3: 8 the gospel to Abraham ***b***,
5:21 the like; of which I tell you ***b***,
Eph 2:10 which God prepared ***b*** that we
1 Pe 1:11 indicating when He testified ***b***
2 Pe 3:17 beloved, since you know this ***b***,

BEG (16/16) BEGGAR, BEGGARLY, BEGGED, BEGGING

Gen 50:17 I ***b*** you, please forgive the
Josh 2:12 I ***b*** you, swear to me by the
7:19 I ***b*** you, give glory to the
Judg 19:23 my brethren! I ***b*** you, do not
Job 9:15 I would ***b*** mercy of my Judge.
19:16 I ***b*** him with my mouth.
Ps 109:10 continually be vagabonds, and ***b***;
Prov 20: 4 He will ***b*** during harvest and
Lk 8:28 I ***b*** You, do not torment me!"
16: 3 I cannot dig; I am ashamed to ***b***.
16:27 I ***b*** you therefore, father, that
Acts 24: 4 I ***b*** you to hear, by your
26: 3 Therefore I ***b*** you to hear me
Rom 15:30 Now I ***b*** you, brethren, through
2 Cor 10: 2 But I ***b*** you that when I am
1 Pe 2:11 I ***b*** you as sojourners and

BEGAN (131/129) BEGIN

Gen 4:26 Then men ***b*** to call on the name
6: 1 when men ***b*** to multiply on the
9:20 And Noah ***b*** to be a farmer,
10: 8 he ***b*** to be a mighty one on the
26:13 The man ***b*** to prosper, and
41:54 the seven years of famine ***b*** to
44:12 He ***b*** with the oldest and left
Num 10:28 when they ***b*** their journey.
25: 1 and the people ***b*** to commit
Deut 1: 5 Moses ***b*** to explain this law,
Josh 15: 2 And their southern border ***b*** at
15: 5 on the northern quarter ***b*** at
18:12 border on the north side ***b*** at
18:15 The south side ***b*** at the end of
19:33 And their border ***b*** at Heleph,
Judg 13:25 And the Spirit of the LORD ***b*** to
16:19 Then she ***b*** to torment him, and
16:22 the hair of his head ***b*** to grow
19:25 and when the day ***b*** to break,
20:31 They ***b*** to strike down and kill
20:40 But when the cloud ***b*** to rise
1 Sam 17:41 and ***b*** drawing near to David,
2 Sam 2:10 was forty years old when he ***b***
5: 4 thirty years old when he ***b*** to
1 Ki 6: 1 that he ***b*** to build the house of
16:11 when he ***b*** to reign, as soon as
2 Ki 8:16 the son of Jehoshaphat ***b*** to
8:25 king of Judah, ***b*** to reign.
10:32 In those days the LORD ***b*** to
15:32 king of Judah, ***b*** to reign.
15:37 In those days the LORD ***b*** to
16: 1 king of Judah, ***b*** to reign.
18: 1 king of Judah, ***b*** to reign.
25:27 in the year that he ***b*** to reign,
1 Chr 1:10 he ***b*** to be a mighty one on the
27:24 Joab the son of Zeruiah ***b*** a
2 Chr 3: 1 Now Solomon ***b*** to build the house
3: 2 And he ***b*** to build on the second
20:22 Now when they ***b*** to sing and to
29:17 Now they ***b*** to sanctify on the
29:27 And when the burnt offering ***b***,
29:27 the song of the LORD also ***b***,
31: 7 In the third month they ***b***
31:10 Since the people ***b*** to bring
31:21 And in every work that he ***b*** in
34: 3 he ***b*** to seek the God of his
34: 3 and in the twelfth year he ***b*** to
Ezra 3: 6 of the seventh month they ***b*** to
3: 8 ***b*** work and appointed the
5: 2 son of Jozadak rose up and ***b***
7: 9 day of the first month he ***b***
Neh 11:17 the leader who ***b*** the
13:19 as it ***b*** to be dark before the
Job 38:12 the morning since your days ***b***,
Ezek 9: 6 So they ***b*** with the elders who
Dan 2:13 and they ***b*** killing the wise
Hos 1: 2 When the LORD ***b*** to speak by
Jon 3: 4 And Jonah ***b*** to enter the city on
Mt 4:17 From that time Jesus ***b*** to preach
11: 7 Jesus ***b*** to say to the
11:20 Then He ***b*** to rebuke the cities
12: 1 and ***b*** to pluck heads of grain
16:21 From that time Jesus ***b*** to show
16:22 Peter took Him aside and ***b*** to
26:22 and each of them ***b*** to say to
26:37 and He ***b*** to be sorrowful and
26:74 Then he ***b*** to curse and swear,
28: 1 as the first day of the week ***b***
Mk 1:45 he went out and ***b*** to proclaim
2:23 as they went His disciples ***b***

4: 1 And again He **b** to teach by the
5:17 Then they **b** to plead with Him to
5:20 And he departed and **b** to
6: 2 He **b** to teach in the synagogue.
6: 7 and **b** to send them out two by
6:34 So He **b** to teach them many
6:55 and **b** to carry about on beds
8:11 the Pharisees came out and **b**
8:31 And He **b** to teach them that the
8:32 And Peter took Him aside and **b**
10:28 Then Peter **b** to say to Him,
10:32 the twelve aside again and **b**
10:41 they **b** to be greatly displeased
10:47 he **b** to cry out and say,
11:15 went into the temple and **b** to
12: 1 Then He **b** to speak to them in
13: 5 **b** to say: "Take heed that no
14:19 And they **b** to be sorrowful, and
14:33 and He **b** to be troubled and
14:65 Then some **b** to spit on Him, and
14:69 and **b** to say to those who stood
14:71 Then he **b** to curse and swear,
15: 8 **b** to ask him to do just as
15:18 and **b** to salute Him, "Hail,
Lk 1:70 have been since the world **b**,
3:23 Now Jesus Himself **b** His
4:21 And He **b** to say to them, "Today
5: 7 so that they **b** to sink.
5:21 scribes and the Pharisees **b** to
7:15 So he who was dead sat up and **b**
7:24 He **b** to speak to the multitudes
7:38 and she **b** to wash His feet with
7:49 sat at the table with Him **b** to
9:12 When the day **b** to wear away, the
11:29 He **b** to say, "This is an evil
11:53 scribes and the Pharisees **b** to
12: 1 He **b** to say to His disciples
14:18 they all with one accord **b** to
14:30 This man **b** to build and was not
15:14 and he **b** to be in want.
15:24 And they **b** to be merry.
19:37 multitude of the disciples **b**
19:45 He went into the temple and **b**
20: 9 Then He **b** to tell the people
22:23 Then they **b** to question among
23: 2 And they **b** to accuse Him,
Jn 9:32 Since the world **b** it has been
13: 5 water into a basin and **b** to
Acts 1: 1 of all that Jesus **b** both to do
2: 4 with the Holy Spirit and **b** to
3:21 holy prophets since the world **b**.
10:37 and **b** from Galilee after the
11:15 And as I **b** to speak, the Holy
18:26 So he **b** to speak boldly in the
24: 2 Tertullus **b** his accusation,
27:35 when he had broken it he **b** to
Rom 16:25 kept secret since the world **b**
2 Cor 8:10 not only to be doing what you **b**
2 Tim 1: 9 in Christ Jesus before time **b**,
Titus 1: 2 lie, promised before time **b**,
Heb 2: 3 which at the first **b** to be

BEGAT, BEGET, BEGGETTEST, BEGETTETH (KJV) See BEGETS, BEGETTING, BEGOT

BEGET (9/9) BEGETS, BEGETTING, BEGOT, BEGOTTEN

Gen 17:20 He shall **b** twelve princes, and
48: 6 Your offspring whom you **b** after
Lev 25:45 which they **b** in your land; and
Num 11:12 Did I **b** them, that You should
Deut 4:25 When you **b** children and
28:41 You shall **b** sons and daughters,
2 Ki 20:18 from you, whom you will **b**;
Isa 39: 7 from you, whom you will **b**;
Jer 29: 6 Take wives and **b** sons and

BEGETS (6/6) BEGET

Prov 17:21 He who **b** a scoffer does so to
23:24 And he who **b** a wise child
Eccl 5:14 When he **b** a son, there is
6: 3 If a man **b** a hundred children
Ezek 18:10 If he **b** a son who is a robber
18:14 he **b** a son Who sees all the

BEGETTING (1/1) BEGET

Isa 45:10 to his father, 'What are you **b**?

BEGGAR (3/3) BEG

1 Sam 2: 8 from the dust And lifts the **b**
Lk 16:20 But there was a certain **b** named
16:22 So it was that the **b** died, and

BEGGARLY (1/1)

Gal 4: 9 turn again to the weak and **b**

BEGGED (21/21) BEG

Mt 8:31 So the demons **b** Him, saying,
8:34 they **b** Him to depart from
14:36 and **b** Him that they might only
18:29 fell down at his feet and **b**
18:32 all that debt because you **b** me.
Mk 5:10 Also he **b** Him earnestly that He
5:12 So all the demons **b** Him, saying,
5:18 who had been demon-possessed **b**
5:23 and **b** Him earnestly, saying,
6:56 and **b** Him that they might just
7:32 and they **b** Him to put His hand
8:22 and **b** Him to touch him.
Lk 7: 4 they **b** Him earnestly, saying
8:31 And they **b** Him that He would not
8:32 So they **b** Him that He would
8:38 whom the demons had departed **b**
8:41 fell down at Jesus' feet and **b**
Jn 9: 8 "Is not this he who sat and **b**?
Acts 13:42 the Gentiles **b** that these words
16:15 she **b** us, saying, "If you
Heb 12:19 so that those who heard it **b**

BEGGING (4/4) BEG

Ps 37:25 Nor his descendants **b** bread.
Mk 10:46 of Timaeus, sat by the road **b**.
Lk 18:35 blind man sat by the road **b**.
Acts 3:10 knew that it was he who sat **b**

BEGIN (27/25) BEGAN, BEGINNING, BEGINNINGS, BEGINS, BEGUN

Gen 11: 6 and this is what they **b** to do;
Num 10: 5 on the east side shall then **b**
10: 6 lie on the south side shall **b**
10: 6 sound the call for them to **b**
Deut 2:24 ***B*** to possess it, and engage
2:25 This day I will **b** to put the
2:31 ***B*** to possess it, that you may
10:11 **b** your journey before the
16: 9 **b** to count the seven weeks from
16: 9 weeks from the time you **b**
Josh 3: 7 This day I will **b** to exalt you
Judg 10:18 Who is the man who will **b** the
13: 5 and he shall **b** to deliver
1 Sam 22:15 Did I then **b** to inquire of God
1 Chr 22:16 Arise and **b** working, and the
Eccl 10:13 The words of his mouth **b** with
Jer 25:29 I **b** to bring calamity on the
Ezek 9: 6 and **b** at My sanctuary."
Lk 3: 8 and do not **b** to say to
13:25 and you **b** to stand outside and
13:26 then you will **b** to say, 'We ate
14: 9 and then you **b** with shame to
14:29 all who see it **b** to mock him,
21:28 Now when these things **b** to
23:30 Then they will **b** 'to say to
2 Cor 3: 1 Do we **b** again to commend
1 Pe 4:17 has come for judgment to **b**

BEGINNING (105/103) BEGINNINGS

Gen 1: 1 In the **b** God created the
10:10 And the **b** of his kingdom was
13: 3 his tent had been at the **b**,
41:21 were just as ugly as at the **b**.
49: 3 My might and the **b** of my
Ex 12: 2 This month shall be your **b** of
Lev 6:20 **b** on the day when he is
Num 10:10 and at the **b** of your months,
Deut 11:12 from the **b** of the year to the
21:17 for he is the **b** of his
Judg 7:19 outpost of the camp at the **b**
Ruth 1:22 came to Bethlehem at the **b** of
3:10 at the end than at the **b**,
1 Sam 3:12 his house, from **b** to end.
2 Sam 21: 9 in the **b** of barley harvest.
21:10 from the **b** of harvest until the
2 Ki 17:25 at the **b** of their dwelling
Ezra 4: 6 in the **b** of his reign, they
Neh 4: 7 restored and the gaps were **b**
Job 8: 7 Though your **b** was small, Yet
42:12 days of Job more than his **b**;
Ps 111:10 fear of the LORD is the **b** of
Prov 1: 7 fear of the LORD is the **b** of
8:22 LORD possessed me at the **b** of
8:23 from everlasting, From the **b**,
9:10 fear of the LORD is the **b** of
17:14 The **b** of strife is like
20:21 gained hastily at the **b** Will
Eccl 3:11 the work that God does from **b**
7: 8 a thing is better than its **b**;
Isa 1:26 your counselors as at the **b**.
18: 2 a people terrible from their **b**
18: 7 a people terrible from their **b**
40:21 it not been told you from the **b**?
41: 4 the generations from the **b**?
41:26 Who has declared from the **b**,
46:10 Declaring the end from the **b**,
48: 3 the former things from the **b**;
48: 5 Even from the **b** I have declared
48: 7 created now and not from the **b**;
48:16 not spoken in secret from the **b**;
64: 4 For since the **b** of the world
Jer 17:12 high throne from the **b** Is
26: 1 In the **b** of the reign of
27: 1 In the **b** of the reign of
28: 1 at the **b** of the reign of
49:34 in the **b** of the reign of
Lam 2:19 At the **b** of the watches; Pour
Ezek 40: 1 at the **b** of the year, on the
Dan 9:21 had seen in the vision at the **b**,
9:23 At the **b** of your supplications
Am 7: 1 formed locust swarms at the **b**
Mic 1:13 swift steeds (She was the **b**
Mt 14:30 and **b** to sink he cried out,
19: 4 He who made them at the **b** '
19: 8 but from the **b** it was not so.
20: 8 **b** with the last to the first.'
24: 8 All these are the **b** of sorrows.
24:21 as has not been since the **b** of
Mk 1: 1 The **b** of the gospel of Jesus
10: 6 But from the **b** of the creation,
13:19 as has not been since the **b** of
Lk 1: 2 just as those who from the **b**
23: 5 **b** from Galilee to this place."
24:27 And **b** at Moses and all the
24:47 all nations, **b** at Jerusalem.
Jn 1: 1 In the **b** was the Word, and the
1: 2 He was in the **b** with God.
2:10 Every man at the **b** sets out the
2:11 This **b** of signs Jesus did in
6:64 For Jesus knew from the **b** who
8: 9 **b** with the oldest even to the
8:25 been saying to you from the **b**.
8:44 He was a murderer from the **b**,
15:27 have been with Me from the **b**.
16: 4 I did not say to you at the **b**,
Acts 1:22 **b** from the baptism of John to
8:35 and **b** at this Scripture,
11: 4 it to them in order from the **b**,
11:15 upon them, as upon us at the **b**.
26: 4 which was spent from the **b**
Eph 3: 9 which from the **b** of the ages
Phil 4:15 know also that in the **b** of the
Col 1:18 body, the church, who is the **b**,
2 Th 2:13 because God from the **b** chose
Heb 1:10 in the **b** laid the
3:14 of Christ if we hold the **b** of
7: 3 having neither **b** of days nor
2 Pe 2:20 is worse for them than the **b**.
3: 4 as they were from the **b** of
1 Jn 1: 1 That which was from the **b**,
2: 7 which you have had from the **b**.
2: 7 word which you heard from the **b**.
2:13 known Him who is from the **b**.
2:14 known Him who is from the **b**.
2:24 you which you heard from the **b**.
2:24 If what you heard from the **b**
3: 8 the devil has sinned from the **b**.
3:11 that you heard from the **b**,
2 Jn 5 which we have had from the **b**:
6 as you have heard from the **b**,
Rev 1: 8 the ***B*** and the End," says the
3:14 the ***B*** of the creation of God:
21: 6 the ***B*** and the End. I will give
22:13 the ***B*** and the End, the First

BEGINNINGS (3/3) BEGINNING

Num 28:11 At the **b** of your months you
Ezek 36:11 better for you than at your **b**.
Mk 13: 8 These are the **b** of sorrows.

BEGINS (3/3)

Mt 24:49 and **b** to beat his fellow
Lk 12:45 and **b** to beat the male and
1 Pe 4:17 and if it **b** with us first,

BEGOT (211/133) BEGET

Gen 4:18 and Irad **b** Mehujael, and
4:18 and Mehujael **b** Methushael, and
4:18 and Methushael **b** Lamech.
5: 3 and **b** a son in his own
5: 4 After he **b** Seth, the days of
5: 6 and five years, and **b** Enosh.
5: 7 After he **b** Enosh, Seth lived
5: 9 ninety years, and **b** Cainan.
5:10 After he **b** Cainan, Enosh lived
5:12 and **b** Mahalalel.
5:13 After he **b** Mahalalel, Cainan
5:15 sixty-five years, and **b** Jared.
5:16 After he **b** Jared, Mahalalel
5:18 sixty-two years, and **b** Enoch.
5:19 After he **b** Enoch, Jared lived
5:21 and **b** Methuselah.
5:22 After he **b** Methuselah, Enoch
5:25 years, and **b** Lamech.
5:26 After he **b** Lamech, Methuselah
5:30 After he **b** Noah, Lamech lived
5:32 and Noah **b** Shem, Ham, and
6:10 And Noah **b** three sons: Shem,
10: 8 Cush **b** Nimrod; he began to be a
10:13 Mizraim **b** Ludim, Anamim,
10:15 Canaan **b** Sidon his firstborn,
10:24 Arphaxad **b** Salah, and Salah
10:24 and Salah **b** Eber.
10:26 Joktan **b** Almodad, Sheleph,
11:10 and **b** Arphaxad two years after
11:11 After he **b** Arphaxad, Shem lived
11:11 and **b** sons and daughters.
11:12 thirty-five years, and **b** Salah.
11:13 After he **b** Salah, Arphaxad lived
11:13 and **b** sons and daughters.
11:14 thirty years, and **b** Eber.
11:15 After he **b** Eber, Salah lived
11:15 and **b** sons and daughters.
11:16 thirty-four years, and **b** Peleg.
11:17 After he **b** Peleg, Eber lived
11:17 and **b** sons and daughters.
11:18 thirty years, and **b** Reu.
11:19 After he **b** Reu, Peleg lived two
11:19 and **b** sons and daughters.
11:20 years, and **b** Serug.
11:21 After he **b** Serug, Reu lived two
11:21 and **b** sons and daughters.
11:22 thirty years, and **b** Nahor.
11:23 After he **b** Nahor, Serug lived
11:23 and **b** sons and daughters.

11:24 years, and ***b*** Terah.
11:25 After he ***b*** Terah, Nahor lived
11:25 and ***b*** sons and daughters.
11:26 and ***b*** Abram, Nahor, and Haran.
11:27 Terah ***b*** Abram, Nahor, and
11:27 and Haran. Haran ***b*** Lot.
22:23 And Bethuel ***b*** Rebekah.
25: 3 Jokshan ***b*** Sheba and Dedan.
25:19 Abraham ***b*** Isaac.
Num 26:29 and Machir ***b*** Gilead; of Gilead,
26:58 And Kohath ***b*** Amram.
Deut 32:18 Of the Rock who ***b*** you, you are
Judg 11: 1 and Gilead ***b*** Jephthah.
Ruth 4:18 Perez ***b*** Hezron;
4:19 Hezron ***b*** Ram, and Ram begot
4:19 and Ram ***b*** Amminadab;
4:20 Amminadab ***b*** Nahshon, and
4:20 and Nahshon ***b*** Salmon;
4:21 Salmon ***b*** Boaz, and Boaz begot
4:21 and Boaz ***b*** Obed;
4:22 Obed ***b*** Jesse, and Jesse begot
4:22 and Jesse ***b*** David.
1 Chr 1:10 Cush ***b*** Nimrod; he began to be a
1:11 Mizraim ***b*** Ludim, Anamim,
1:13 Canaan ***b*** Sidon, his firstborn,
1:18 Arphaxad ***b*** Shelah, and Shelah
1:18 and Shelah ***b*** Eber.
1:20 Joktan ***b*** Almodad, Sheleph,
1:34 And Abraham ***b*** Isaac. The sons
2:10 Ram ***b*** Amminadab, and
2:10 and Amminadab ***b*** Nahshon, leader
2:11 Nahshon ***b*** Salma, and Salma begot
2:11 and Salma ***b*** Boaz;
2:12 Boaz ***b*** Obed, and Obed begot
2:12 and Obed ***b*** Jesse;
2:13 Jesse ***b*** Eliab his firstborn,
2:20 And Hur ***b*** Uri, and Uri begot
2:20 and Uri ***b*** Bezalel.
2:22 Segub ***b*** Jair, who had
2:36 Attai ***b*** Nathan, and Nathan begot
2:36 and Nathan ***b*** Zabad;
2:37 Zabad ***b*** Ephlal, and Ephlal begot
2:37 and Ephlal ***b*** Obed;
2:38 Obed ***b*** Jehu, and Jehu begot
2:38 and Jehu ***b*** Azariah;
2:39 Azariah ***b*** Helez, and Helez begot
2:39 and Helez ***b*** Eleasah;
2:40 Eleasah ***b*** Sismai, and Sismai
2:40 and Sismai ***b*** Shallum;
2:41 Shallum ***b*** Jekamiah, and Jekamiah
2:41 and Jekamiah ***b*** Elishama.
2:44 Shema ***b*** Raham the father of
2:44 and Rekem ***b*** Shammai.
2:46 and Haran ***b*** Gazez.
4: 2 And Reaiah the son of Shobal ***b***
4: 2 and Jahath ***b*** Ahumai and Lahad.
4: 8 and Koz ***b*** Anub, Zobebah, and the
4:11 the brother of Shuhah ***b*** Mehir,
4:12 And Eshton ***b*** Beth-Rapha, Paseah,
4:14 and Meonothai who ***b*** Ophrah.
4:14 Seraiah ***b*** Joab the father of Ge
6: 4 Eleazar ***b*** Phinehas, and
6: 4 and Phinehas ***b*** Abishua;
6: 5 Abishua ***b*** Bukki, and Bukki begot
6: 5 and Bukki ***b*** Uzzi;
6: 6 Uzzi ***b*** Zerahiah, and Zerahiah
6: 6 and Zerahiah ***b*** Meraioth;
6: 7 Meraioth ***b*** Amariah, and Amariah
6: 7 and Amariah ***b*** Ahitub;
6: 8 Ahitub ***b*** Zadok, and Zadok begot
6: 8 and Zadok ***b*** Ahimaaz;
6: 9 Ahimaaz ***b*** Azariah, and Azariah
6: 9 and Azariah ***b*** Johanan;
6:10 Johanan ***b*** Azariah (it was he who
6:11 Azariah ***b*** Amariah, and Amariah
6:11 and Amariah ***b*** Ahitub;
6:12 Ahitub ***b*** Zadok, and Zadok begot
6:12 and Zadok ***b*** Shallum;
6:13 Shallum ***b*** Hilkiah, and Hilkiah
6:13 and Hilkiah ***b*** Azariah;
6:14 Azariah ***b*** Seraiah, and Seraiah
6:14 and Seraiah ***b*** Jehozadak.
7:15 but Zelophehad ***b*** only
7:32 And Heber ***b*** Japhlet, Shomer,
8: 1 Now Benjamin ***b*** Bela his
8: 7 He ***b*** Uzza and Ahihud.
8: 9 By Hodesh his wife he ***b*** Jobab,
8:11 And by Hushim he ***b*** Abitub and
8:32 who ***b*** Shimeah. They also dwelt
8:33 Ner ***b*** Kish, Kish begot Saul, and
8:33 Kish ***b*** Saul, and Saul begot
8:33 and Saul ***b*** Jonathan,
8:34 and Merib-Baal ***b*** Micah.
8:36 And Ahaz ***b*** Jehoaddah; Jehoaddah
8:36 Jehoaddah ***b*** Alemeth, Azmaveth,
8:36 and Zimri ***b*** Moza.
8:37 Moza ***b*** Binea, Raphah his son,
9:38 And Mikloth ***b*** Shimeam. They also
9:39 Ner ***b*** Kish, Kish begot Saul, and
9:39 Kish ***b*** Saul, and Saul begot
9:39 and Saul ***b*** Jonathan,
9:40 and Merib-Baal ***b*** Micah.
9:42 And Ahaz ***b*** Jarah; Jarah begot
9:42 Jarah ***b*** Alemeth, Azmaveth, and
9:42 and Zimri ***b*** Moza;
9:43 Moza ***b*** Binea, Rephaiah his son,
14: 3 and David ***b*** more sons and
2 Chr 11:21 and ***b*** twenty-eight sons and
13:21 and ***b*** twenty-two sons and
Neh 12:10 Jeshua ***b*** Joiakim, Joiakim begot
12:10 Joiakim ***b*** Eliashib, Eliashib
12:10 Eliashib ***b*** Joiada,
12:11 Joiada ***b*** Jonathan, and Jonathan
12:11 and Jonathan ***b*** Jaddua.
Prov 23:22 Listen to your father who ***b***
Jer 16: 3 them and their fathers who ***b***
Dan 11: 6 and with him who ***b*** her, and
Zech 13: 3 his father and mother who ***b***
13: 3 And his father and mother who ***b***
Mt 1: 2 Abraham ***b*** Isaac, Isaac begot
1: 2 Isaac ***b*** Jacob, and Jacob begot
1: 2 and Jacob ***b*** Judah and his
1: 3 Judah ***b*** Perez and Zerah by
1: 3 Perez ***b*** Hezron, and Hezron
1: 3 and Hezron ***b*** Ram.
1: 4 Ram ***b*** Amminadab, Amminadab
1: 4 Amminadab ***b*** Nahshon, and
1: 4 and Nahshon ***b*** Salmon.
1: 5 Salmon ***b*** Boaz by Rahab, Boaz
1: 5 by Rahab, Boaz ***b*** Obed by Ruth,
1: 5 by Ruth, Obed ***b*** Jesse,
1: 6 and Jesse ***b*** David the king.
1: 6 David the king ***b*** Solomon by
1: 7 Solomon ***b*** Rehoboam, Rehoboam
1: 7 Rehoboam ***b*** Abijah, and Abijah
1: 7 and Abijah ***b*** Asa.
1: 8 Asa ***b*** Jehoshaphat, Jehoshaphat
1: 8 Jehoshaphat ***b*** Joram, and Joram
1: 8 and Joram ***b*** Uzziah.
1: 9 Uzziah ***b*** Jotham, Jotham begot
1: 9 Jotham ***b*** Ahaz, and Ahaz begot
1: 9 and Ahaz ***b*** Hezekiah.
1:10 Hezekiah ***b*** Manasseh, Manasseh
1:10 Manasseh ***b*** Amon, and Amon begot
1:10 and Amon ***b*** Josiah.
1:11 Josiah ***b*** Jeconiah and his
1:12 Jeconiah ***b*** Shealtiel, and
1:12 and Shealtiel ***b*** Zerubbabel.
1:13 Zerubbabel ***b*** Abiud, Abiud begot
1:13 Abiud ***b*** Eliakim, and Eliakim
1:13 and Eliakim ***b*** Azor.
1:14 Azor ***b*** Zadok, Zadok begot Achim,
1:14 Zadok ***b*** Achim, and Achim begot
1:14 and Achim ***b*** Eliud.
1:15 Eliud ***b*** Eleazar, Eleazar begot
1:15 Eleazar ***b*** Matthan, and Matthan
1:15 and Matthan ***b*** Jacob.
1:16 And Jacob ***b*** Joseph the husband
Acts 7: 8 and so Abraham ***b*** Isaac and
7: 8 and Isaac ***b*** Jacob, and Jacob
7: 8 and Jacob ***b*** the twelve
1 Jn 5: 1 everyone who loves Him who ***b***

BEGOTTEN (18/18) BEGET

Lev 18:11 ***b*** by your father—she is your
Job 38:28 Or who has ***b*** the drops of dew?
Ps 2: 7 Today I have ***b*** You.
Isa 49:21 Who has ***b*** these for me, Since I
Hos 5: 7 For they have ***b*** pagan
Jn 1:14 the glory as of the only ***b*** of
1:18 The only ***b*** Son, who is in the
3:16 world that He gave His only ***b***
3:18 in the name of the only ***b*** Son
Acts 13:33 Today I have ***b*** You.'
1 Cor 4:15 for in Christ Jesus I have ***b***
Phm 1:10 whom I have ***b*** while in my
Heb 1: 5 Today I have ***b*** You"?
5: 5 Today I have ***b*** You."
11:17 promises offered up his only ***b***
1 Pe 1: 3 to His abundant mercy has ***b*** us
1 Jn 4: 9 that God has sent His only ***b***
5: 1 begot also loves him who is ***b***

BEGUILE, BEGUILED, BEGUILING (KJV) See CHEAT, DECEIVE, ENTICING, SEDUCED

BEGUN (13/13) BEGIN

Num 16:46 the LORD. The plague has ***b***.
16:47 and already the plague had ***b***
Deut 2:31 I have ***b*** to give Sihon and his
3:24 You have ***b*** to show Your servant
Judg 20:39 Now Benjamin had ***b*** to strike
1 Sam 3: 2 and when his eyes had ***b*** to grow
Esth 6:13 before whom you have ***b*** to fall,
9:23 the custom which they had ***b***,
Mt 18:24 And when he had ***b*** to settle
2 Cor 8: 6 urged Titus, that as he had ***b***,
Gal 3: 3 Having ***b*** in the Spirit, are you
Phil 1: 6 that He who has ***b*** a good work
1 Tim 5:11 for when they have ***b*** to grow

BEHALF (24/24)

Ex 27:21 to their generations on ***b*** of
Lev 1: 4 it will be accepted on his ***b***
5:10 shall make atonement on his ***b***
22:20 not be acceptable on your ***b***.
22:25 shall not be accepted on your ***b***.
23:11 LORD, to be accepted on your ***b***;
Deut 21: 8 shall be provided on their ***b***
2 Sam 3:12 Abner sent messengers on his ***b***
2 Ki 4:13 you want me to speak on your ***b***
2 Chr 16: 9 to show Himself strong on ***b*** of
Esth 7: 9 who spoke good on the king's ***b***,
Job 36: 2 yet words to speak on God's ***b***.
Isa 8:19 they seek the dead on ***b*** of
Ezek 22:30 in the gap before Me on ***b*** of
Rom 16:19 Therefore I am glad on your ***b***;
1 Cor 4: 6 of you may be puffed up on ***b***
2 Cor 1:11 given by many persons on our ***b***
5:12 opportunity to boast on our ***b***,
5:20 we implore you on Christ's ***b***,
7: 4 great is my boasting on your ***b***.
8:24 and of our boasting on your ***b***.
Phil 1:29 to you it has been granted on ***b***
Col 1: 7 minister of Christ on your ***b***,
Phm 1:13 that on your ***b*** he might

B

BEHAVE (6/6) BEHAVED, BEHAVES, BEHAVING, BEHAVIOR

Deut 25:16 all who ***b*** unrighteously, are
2 Chr 19:11 ***B*** courageously, and the LORD
Job 27:12 Why then do you ***b*** with
Ps 101: 2 I will ***b*** wisely in a perfect
Ezek 24:19 signify to us, that you ***b*** so?"
1 Cor 13: 5 does not ***b*** rudely, does not seek

BEHAVED (10/10) BEHAVE

Ex 18:11 the very thing in which they ***b***
Num 5:27 she has defiled herself and ***b***
Judg 2:19 that they reverted and ***b*** more
1 Sam 18: 5 and ***b*** wisely. And Saul set him
18:14 And David ***b*** wisely in all his
18:15 when Saul saw that he ***b*** very
18:30 that David ***b*** more wisely than
1 Ki 21:26 And he ***b*** very abominably in
Hos 2: 5 She who conceived them has ***b***
1 Th 2:10 and justly and blamelessly we ***b***

BEHAVES (1/1) BEHAVE

Num 5:12 man's wife goes astray and ***b***

BEHAVING (2/2) BEHAVE

1 Cor 3: 3 are you not carnal and ***b*** like
7:36 But if any man thinks he is ***b***

BEHAVIOR (11/11) BEHAVE

Deut 31:21 know the inclination of their ***b***
1 Sam 8: 9 and show them the ***b*** of the king
8:11 This will be the ***b*** of the king
10:25 explained to the people the ***b***
21:13 So he changed his ***b*** before them,
27:11 And thus was his ***b*** all the
Esth 1:17 For the queen's ***b*** will become
1:18 that they have heard of the ***b***
Ezek 16:27 who were ashamed of your lewd ***b***.
1 Tim 3: 2 sober-minded, of good ***b***,
Titus 2: 3 that they be reverent in ***b***,

BEHEADED (6/6)

2 Sam 4: 7 ***b*** him and took his head, and
Mt 14:10 So he sent and had John ***b*** in
Mk 6:16 said, "This is John, whom I ***b***;
6:27 And he went and ***b*** him in
Lk 9: 9 Herod said, "John I have ***b***,
Rev 20: 4 souls of those who had been ***b***

BEHELD (5/5) BEHOLD

Jer 4:23 I ***b*** the earth, and indeed it
4:24 I ***b*** the mountains, and indeed
4:25 ***b***, and indeed there was no
4:26 ***b***, and indeed the fruitful
Jn 1:14 and we ***b*** His glory, the glory

BEHEMOTH (1/1)

Job 40:15 "Look now at the ***b***,

BEHIND (96/93)

Gen 18:10 in the tent door which was ***b***
19: 6 shut the door ***b*** him,
19:17 for your life! Do not look ***b***
19:26 But his wife looked back ***b*** him,
22:13 and there ***b*** him was a ram
32:18 he also is ***b*** us.'"
32:20 your servant Jacob is ***b*** us.'
33: 2 front, Leah and her children ***b***,
Ex 10:26 us; not a hoof shall be left ***b***.
11: 5 of the female servant who is ***b***
14:19 moved and went ***b*** them; and the
14:19 from before them and stood ***b***
26:33 ***b*** the veil. The veil shall be a
Num 3:23 the Gershonites were to camp ***b***
18: 7 everything at the altar and ***b***
Deut 28:54 his children whom he leaves ***b***,
Josh 8: 2 Lay an ambush for the city ***b***
8: 4 ***b*** the city. Do not go very far
8:14 was an ambush against him ***b***
8:20 And when the men of Ai looked ***b***
Judg 3:23 the doors of the upper room ***b***
6:34 and the Abiezrites gathered ***b***
6:35 who also gathered ***b*** him.
20:40 the Benjamites looked ***b*** them,
1 Sam 11: 5 coming ***b*** the herd from the
21: 9 wrapped in a cloth ***b*** the ephod.
24: 8 And when Saul looked ***b*** him,
30: 9 those stayed who were left ***b***.
30:10 for two hundred stayed ***b***,
30:13 and my master left me ***b***,
2 Sam 1: 7 Now when he looked ***b*** him, he saw
2:20 Then Abner looked ***b*** him and
2:25 of Benjamin gathered together ***b***
3:16 weeping ***b*** her. So Abner said to
5:23 circle around ***b*** them, and come

10: 9 was against him before and **b**,
13:17 and bolt the door **b** her."
13:18 her out and bolted the door **b**
13:34 the road on the hillside **b** him.
1 Ki 14: 9 and have cast Me **b** your back—
2 Ki 4: 4 you shall shut the door **b** you
4: 5 from him and shut the door **b**
4:33 shut the door **b** the two of
6:32 sound of his master's feet **b**
9:25 and I were riding together **b**
11: 6 and one-third at the gate **b** the
19:21 Has shaken her head **b** your
1 Chr 19:10 was against him before and **b**,
2 Chr 13:13 an ambush to go around **b** them;
13:13 and the ambush was **b** them.
Neh 4:13 Therefore I positioned men **b**
4:16 and the leaders were **b** all the
9:26 Cast Your law **b** their backs
12:38 and I was **b** them with half of
Job 39:10 Or will he plow the valleys **b**
41:32 He leaves a shining wake **b** him;
Ps 50:17 And cast My words **b** you?
63: 8 My soul follows close **b** You;
139: 5 You have hedged me **b** and
Prov 17:23 wicked man accepts a bribe **b**
21:14 And a bribe **b** the back, strong
Song 2: 9 he stands **b** our wall; He is
4: 1 You have dove's eyes **b** your
4: 3 Your temples **b** your veil Are
6: 7 Are your temples **b** your veil.
Isa 9:12 before and the Philistines **b**;
26:20 And shut your doors **b** you;
30:21 Your ears shall hear a word **b**
37:22 Has shaken her head **b** your
38:17 You have cast all my sins **b**
45:14 They shall walk **b** you, They
57: 8 Also **b** the doors and their
Ezek 3:12 and I heard **b** me a great
23:35 have forgotten Me and cast Me **b**
24:21 and daughters whom you left **b**
41:15 the length of the building **b**
Hos 5: 8 Look **b** you, O Benjamin!'
Joel 2: 3 And **b** them a flame burns;
2: 3 And **b** them a desolate
2:14 And leave a blessing **b** Him—A
Jon 2: 6 earth with its bars closed **b**
Zech 1: 8 and **b** him were horses: red,
Mt 9:20 for twelve years came from **b**
16:23 Get **b** Me, Satan! You are an
Mk 5:27 she came **b** Him in the crowd
8:33 Get **b** Me, Satan! For you are not
12:19 dies, and leaves his wife **b**,
Lk 2:43 the Boy Jesus lingered **b** in
4: 8 Get **b** Me, Satan! For it is
7:38 and stood at His feet **b** Him
8:44 came from **b** and touched the
2 Cor 12:11 for in nothing was I **b** the most
Phil 3:13 those things which are **b** and
Heb 6:19 which enters the Presence **b**
9: 3 and **b** the second veil, the part
Rev 1:10 and I heard **b** me a loud voice,

BEHOLD (593/581) BEHELD, BEHOLDING, BEHOLDS

Gen 3:22 Then the LORD God said, "**B**,
6:13 violence through them; and **b**,
6:17 'And **b**, I Myself am bringing
8:11 to him in the evening, and **b**,
9: 9 'And as for Me, **b**, I
15: 4 And **b**, the word of the LORD
15:12 sleep fell upon Abram; and **b**,
15:17 down and it was dark, that **b**,
16:11 of the LORD said to her: "**B**,
17: 4 'As for Me, **b**, My covenant
17:20 Ishmael, I have heard you. **B**,
18: 2 his eyes and looked, and **b**,
18:10 to the time of life, and **b**,
19:28 of the plain; and he saw, and **b**,
20:16 Then to Sarah he said, "**B**,
24:13 '**B**, here I stand by the well
24:15 had finished speaking, that **b**,
24:16 woman was very beautiful to **b**,
24:43 '**b**, I stand by the well of
26: 7 because she is beautiful to **b**.
27: 2 **B** now, I am old. I do not know
27:39 answered and said to him: "**B**,
28:12 Then he dreamed, and **b**,
28:13 And **b**, the LORD stood above it
28:15 '**B**, I am with you and will keep
29: 2 saw a well in the field; and **b**,
29:25 to pass in the morning, that **b**,
31:10 eyes and saw in a dream, and **b**,
32:18 sent to my lord Esau; and **b**,
32:20 'and also say, '**B**, your servant
37: 7 sheaves in the field. Then **b**,
38:27 time for giving birth, that **b**,
40: 9 to Joseph, and said to him, "**B**,
41: 1 that Pharaoh had a dream; and **b**,
41: 3 Then **b**, seven other cows came up
41: 6 Then **b**, seven thin heads,
41:17 Pharaoh said to Joseph: "**B**,
41:19 'Then **b**, seven other cows came
41:23 'Then **b**, seven heads, withered,
42:22 would not listen? Therefore **b**,
45:12 'And **b**, your eyes and the eyes
48: 4 'and said to me, '**B**, I will
48:21 Then Israel said to Joseph, "**B**,
50: 5 made me swear, saying, "**B**,
50:18 his face, and they said, "**B**,
Ex 2: 6 it, she saw the child, and **b**,
2:13 he went out the second day, **b**,
3: 2 of a bush. So he looked, and **b**,
3: 9 'Now therefore, **b**, the cry of
4: 6 and when he took it out, **b**,
4: 7 drew it out of his bosom, and **b**,
6:30 said before the LORD, "**B**,
7:17 know that I am the LORD. **B**,
8: 2 you refuse to let them go, **b**,
8:21 will not let My people go, **b**,
9: 3 '**b**, the hand of the LORD will
9:18 '**B**, tomorrow about this time I
10: 4 refuse to let My people go, **b**,
14:10 Israel lifted their eyes, and **b**,
16: 4 the LORD said to Moses, "**B**,
16:10 toward the wilderness, and **b**,
17: 6 '**B**, I will stand before you
19: 9 the LORD said to Moses, "**B**,
23:20 **B**, I send an Angel before you
32:34 which I have spoken to you. **B**,
34:10 And He said: "**B**, I make a
34:11 what I command you this day. **B**,
34:30 children of Israel saw Moses, **b**,
Num 3:12 'Now **b**, I Myself have taken the
17: 8 tabernacle of witness, and **b**,
18: 6 '**B**, I Myself have taken your
18:21 **B**, I have given the children
22:32 donkey these three times? **B**,
23: 9 And from the hills I **b** him;
23:20 **B**, I have received a command
24:17 I **b** Him, but not near; A Star
25:12 'Therefore say, '**B**, I give to
Deut 3:27 **b** it with your eyes, for you
9:16 "And I looked, and **b**,
11:26 **B**, I set before you today a
26:10 'and now, **b**, I have brought
31:14 the LORD said to Moses, "**B**,
31:16 the LORD said to Moses: "**B**,
Josh 2: 2 king of Jericho, saying, "**B**,
3:11 '**B**, the ark of the covenant of
5:13 his eyes and looked, and **b**,
8: 4 he commanded them, saying: "**B**,
8:20 behind them, they saw, and **b**,
14:10 'And now, **b**, the LORD has kept
22:11 Israel heard someone say, "**B**,
23:14 **B**, this day I am going the
24:27 said to all the people, "**B**,
Judg 13: 5 'For **b**, you shall conceive and
13: 7 "And He said to me, '**B**,
14: 8 the carcass of the lion. And **b**,
Ruth 2: 4 Now **b**, Boaz came from
4: 1 gate and sat down there; and **b**,
1 Sam 2:31 '**B**, the days are coming that I
3:11 the LORD said to Samuel: "**B**,
15:22 the voice of the LORD? **B**,
24: 4 which the LORD said to you, '**B**,
2 Sam 1: 2 on the third day, **b**, it happened
11: 2 woman was very beautiful to **b**.
12:11 "Thus says the LORD: '**B**,
19: 1 And Joab was told, "**B**,
1 Ki 3:12 '**b**, I have done according to
5: 5 And **b**, I propose to build a
8:27 indeed dwell on the earth? **B**,
11:31 LORD, the God of Israel: '**B**,
13: 1 And **b**, a man of God went from
13: 2 Thus says the LORD: '**B**,
14:10 therefore **b**! I will bring
19: 9 the night in that place; and **b**,
19:11 before the LORD." And **b**,
20:13 all this great multitude? **B**,
21:21 '**B**, I will bring calamity on
2 Ki 6:17 young man, and he saw. And **b**,
20:17 '**B**, the days are coming when
21:12 the LORD God of Israel: '**B**,
22:16 "Thus says the LORD: '**B**,
1 Chr 22: 9 '**B**, a son shall be born to
2 Chr 2: 4 **B**, I am building a temple
6:18 dwell with men on the earth? **B**,
21:14 **b**, the LORD will strike your
23: 3 And he said to them, "**B**,
34:24 "Thus says the LORD: '**B**,
Esth 1:11 for she was beautiful to **b**.
Job 1:12 the LORD said to Satan, "**B**,
2: 6 the LORD said to Satan, "**B**,
5:17 **B**, happy is the man whom
5:27 **B**, this we have searched out;
8:19 **B**, this is the joy of His
8:20 **B**, God will not cast away the
13: 1 '**B**, my eye has seen all this,
19:27 myself, And my eyes shall **b**,
20: 9 Nor will his place **b** him
23: 9 I cannot **b** Him; When He turns
28:28 And to man He said, '**B**,
33:29 '**B**, God works all these
35: 5 And **b** the clouds—They are
36: 5 '**B**, God is mighty, but
36:22 **B**, God is exalted by His
36:26 '**B**, God is great, and we do
40: 4 '**B**, I am vile; What shall I
Ps 7:14 **B**, the wicked brings forth
11: 4 is in heaven; His eyes **b**,
27: 4 To **b** the beauty of the LORD,
33:18 **B**, the eye of the LORD is on
37:36 Yet he passed away, and **b**,
40: 7 Then I said, "**B**, I come;
46: 8 **b** the works of the LORD, Who
48: 4 For **b**, the kings assembled,
51: 5 **B**, I was brought forth in
51: 6 **B**, You desire truth in the
54: 4 **B**, God is my helper;
59: 4 Awake to help me, and **b**!
73:12 **B**, these are the ungodly,
73:15 said, "I will speak thus," **B**,
78:20 **B**, He struck the rock,
83: 2 For **b**, Your enemies make a
84: 9 **b** our shield, And look upon
87: 4 to those who know Me; **B**,
92: 9 For **b**, Your enemies, O LORD,
92: 9 Your enemies, O LORD, For **b**,
113: 6 Who humbles Himself to **b** The
119:40 **B**, I long for Your precepts;
121: 4 **B**, He who keeps Israel
123: 2 **B**, as the eyes of servants
127: 3 **B**, children are a heritage
128: 4 **B**, thus shall the man be
132: 6 **B**, we heard of it in Ephrathah;
133: 1 **B**, how good and how pleasant
134: 1 **B**, bless the LORD, All you
139: 4 a word on my tongue, But **b**,
139: 8 in hell, **b**, You are there.
Eccl 11: 7 is pleasant for the eyes to **b**
Song 1:15 **B**, you are fair, my love!
1:15 you are fair, my love! **B**,
1:16 **B**, you are handsome, my
2: 8 The voice of my beloved! **B**,
2: 9 a gazelle or a young stag. **B**,
3: 7 **B**, it is Solomon's couch,
4: 1 **B**, you are fair, my love!
4: 1 you are fair, my love! **B**,
Isa 3: 1 For **b**, the Lord, the LORD of
5: 7 He looked for justice, but **b**,
5: 7 For righteousness, but **b**,
5:30 if one looks to the land, **B**,
6: 7 with it, and said: "**B**,
7:14 Himself will give you a sign: **B**,
8: 7 Now therefore, **b**, the Lord
10:33 **B**, the Lord, The LORD of
12: 2 **B**, God is my salvation, I
13: 9 **B**, the day of the LORD comes,
13:17 **B**, I will stir up the Medes
17: 1 burden against Damascus. "**B**,
17:14 Then **b**, at eventide, trouble!
19: 1 The burden against Egypt. **B**d,
23:13 **B**, the land of the Chaldeans,
24: 1 **B**, the LORD makes the earth
25: 9 will be said in that day: "**B**,
26:10 And will not **b** the majesty of
26:21 For **b**, the LORD comes out of
28: 2 **B**, the Lord has a mighty
28:16 Lord GOD: "**B**, I lay in Zion
29:14 Therefore, **b**, I will again do
30:27 **B**, the name of the LORD
32: 1 **B**, a king will reign in
35: 4 **B**, your God will come with
38: 8 '**B**, I will bring the shadow on
39: 6 '**B**, the days are coming when
40: 9 of Judah, "**B** your God!"
40:10 **B**, the Lord GOD shall come
40:10 **B**, His reward is with Him,
40:15 **B**, the nations are as a drop
41:11 '**B**, all those who were
41:15 '**B**, I will make you into a
42: 1 **B**! My Servant whom I uphold, My
42: 9 **B**, the former things have come
43:19 **B**, I will do a new thing,
47:14 **B**, they shall be as stubble,
48:10 **B**, I have refined you, but not
49:22 '**B**, I will lift My hand
52: 6 who speaks: '**B**, it is I.'
52:13 **B**, My Servant shall deal
54:11 **B**, I will lay your stones
54:16 '**B**, I have created the
59: 1 **B**, the LORD's hand is not
60: 2 For **b**, the darkness shall
62:11 **B**, His reward is with Him,
65: 6 '**B**, it is written before Me:
65:13 '**B**, My servants shall eat,
65:13 **B**, My servants shall drink,
65:13 **B**, My servants shall rejoice,
65:14 **B**, My servants shall sing
65:17 For **b**, I create new
65:18 For **b**, I create Jerusalem
66:12 '**B**, I will extend peace to
66:15 For **b**, the LORD will come with
Jer 1: 6 **B**, I cannot speak, for
1: 9 '**B**, I have put My words in
1:15 For **b**, I am calling
1:18 For **b**, I have made you this
2:35 **B**, I will plead My case
3: 5 **B**, you have spoken and done
4:13 '**B**, he shall come up like
5:14 **B**, I will make My words in
5:15 **B**, I will bring a nation
6:10 **B**, the word of the LORD is
6:19 **B**, I will certainly bring
6:21 '**B**, I will lay stumbling blocks
6:22 '**B**, a people comes from the
7: 8 **B**, you trust in lying words
7:11 **B**, I, even I, have seen
7:20 '**B**, My anger and My fury will
7:32 Therefore **b**, the days are
8: 9 **B**, they have rejected the
8:17 'For **b**, I will send serpents
9: 7 '**B**, I will refine them and
9:15 '**B**, I will feed them,
9:25 **B**, the days are coming,"
10:18 '**B**, I will throw out at
10:22 **B**, the noise of the report
11:11 '**B**, I will surely bring
11:22 '**B**, I will punish them.
12:14 —**b**, I will pluck them out
13:13 '**B**, I will fill all the
14:13 **B**, the prophets say to them,
14:18 **b**, those slain with the sword!
14:18 **b**, those sick from famine!
16: 9 '**B**, I will cause to cease

16:12 for **b**, each one follows the
16:14 Therefore **b**, the days are
16:16 **B**, I will send for many
16:21 Therefore **b**, I will
18:11 '**B**, I am fashioning a disaster
19: 3 '**B**, I will bring such a
19: 6 'therefore **b**, the days are
19:15 '**B**, I will bring on this city
20: 4 '**B**, I will make you a terror
21: 4 '**B**, I will turn back the
21: 8 '**B**, I set before you the way
21:13 **B**, I am against you,
23: 2 **B**, I will attend to you for
23: 5 **B**, the days are coming,"
23: 7 Therefore, **b**, the days are
23:15 '**B**, I will feed them with
23:19 **B**, a whirlwind of the LORD
23:30 Therefore **b**, I am against
23:31 '**B**, I am against the
23:32 '**B**, I am against those who
23:39 'therefore **b**, I, even I,
25: 9 '**b**, I will send and take all
25:29 'For **b**, I begin to bring
25:32 '**B**, disaster shall go forth
27:16 '**B**, the vessels of the LORD's
28:16 '**B**, I will cast you from the
29:17 **B**, I will send on them the
29:21 **B**, I will deliver them into
29:32 **B**, I will punish Shemaiah
30: 3 'For **b**, the days are coming,'
30:10 For **b**, I will save you from
30:18 '**B**, I will bring back the
30:23 **B**, the whirlwind of the LORD
31: 8 **B**, I will bring them from
31:27 **B**, the days are coming,
31:31 **B**, the days are coming,
31:38 **B**, the days are coming,
32: 3 '**B**, I will give this city
32: 7 '**B**, Hanamel the son of
32:17 **B**, You have made the
32:27 '**B**, I am the LORD, the God
32:28 '**B**, I will give this city
32:37 '**B**, I will gather them out
33: 6 '**B**, I will bring it health
33:14 **B**, the days are coming,'
34: 2 '**B**, I will give this city into
34:17 **B**, I proclaim liberty to you,'
34:22 '**B**, I will command,' says the
35:17 '**B**, I will bring on Judah
37: 7 '**B**, Pharaoh's army which has
38:22 'Now **b**, all the women who
39:16 '**B**, I will bring My words
43:10 '**B**, I will send and bring
44: 2 and **b**, this day they are a
44:11 '**B**, I will set My face against
44:26 '**B**, I have sworn by My great
44:27 '**B**, I will watch over them
44:30 '**B**, I will give Pharaoh
45: 4 '**B**, what I have built
45: 5 for **b**, I will bring adversity
46:25 '**B**, I will bring punishment
46:27 For **b**, I will save you from
47: 2 '**B**, waters rise out of the
48:12 'Therefore **b**, the days are
48:40 '**B**, one shall fly like an
49: 2 Therefore **b**, the days are
49: 5 **B**, I will bring fear upon
49:12 '**B**, those whose judgment was
49:19 '**B**, he shall come up like a
49:22 **B**, He shall come up and fly
49:35 '**B**, I will break the bow of
50: 9 For **b**, I will raise and cause
50:12 **B**, the least of the nations
50:18 '**B**, I will punish the king
50:31 '**B**, I am against you,
50:41 **B**, a people shall come
50:44 '**B**, he shall come up like a
51: 1 '**B**, I will raise up against
51:25 '**B**, I am against you,
51:36 '**B**, I will plead your case
51:47 Therefore **b**, the days are
51:52 Therefore **b**, the days are
Lam 1: 9 'O LORD, **b** my affliction,
1:12 **B** and see If there is any
1:18 And **b** my sorrow; My virgins
5: 1 Look, and **b** our reproach!
Ezek 1: 4 Then I looked, and **b**,
1:15 **b**, a wheel was on the earth
2: 9 and **b**, a scroll of a book was
3: 8 '**B**, I have made your face
3:23 and **b**, the glory of the LORD
7: 5 **B**, it has come!
7: 6 **B**, it has come!
7:10 **B**, the day! Behold,
7:10 Behold, the day! **B**, it
8: 4 And **b**, the glory of the God
13:20 '**B**, I am against your magic
14:22 'Yet **b**, there shall be left
16:27 '**B**, therefore, I stretched out
17: 7 And **b**, this vine bent its
17:10 **B**, it is planted, Will it
18: 4 '**B**, all souls are Mine;
18:18 **B**, he shall die for his
20:47 '**B**, I will kindle a fire
21: 3 LORD: "**B**, I am against you,
21: 7 **B**, it is coming and shall
22:13 **B**, therefore, I beat My
22:19 therefore **b**, I will gather you
23:22 '**B**, I will stir up your
24:16 'Son of man, **b**, I take away
24:21 '**B**, I will profane My sanctuary,
25: 9 **b**, I will clear the territory
26: 3 '**B**, I am against you, O Tyre,
26: 7 '**B**, I will bring against Tyre
28: 3 (**B**, you are wiser than
28: 7 **B**, therefore, I will bring
28:22 '**B**, I am against you,
29: 3 '**B**, I am against you,
34:10 '**B**, I am against the
34:17 '**B**, I shall judge between
34:20 '**B**, I Myself will judge
35: 3 '**B**, O Mount Seir, I am
36: 6 '**B**, I have spoken in My
37: 2 and **b**, there were very many
37:12 '**B**, O My people, I will open
38: 3 '**B**, I am against you, O Gog,
39: 1 '**B**, I am against you, O Gog,
40: 3 and **b**, there was a man whose
43: 2 And **b**, the glory of the God
43: 5 and **b**, the glory of the LORD
43:12 **B**, this is the law of the
44: 4 so I looked, and **b**, the glory
Dan 2:31 were watching; and **b**, a great
4:10 looking, and **b**, A tree in the
7: 2 **b**, the four winds of heaven
7: 7 **b**, a fourth beast, dreadful
7:13 And **b**, One like the Son of
10: 5 and **b**, a certain man clothed
10:13 and **b**, Michael, one of the
11: 2 **B**, three more kings will arise
Hos 2: 6 Therefore, **b**, I will hedge
2:14 Therefore, **b**, I will allure
Joel 2:19 '**B**, I will send you grain
3: 1 'For **b**, in those days and at
3: 7 '**B**, I will raise them
Am 2:13 **B**, I am weighed down by
4: 2 '**B**, the days shall come upon
4:13 **b**, He who forms mountains,
6:11 **b**, the LORD gives a command:
6:14 'But, **b**, I will raise up a
7: 1 GOD showed me: **B**, He formed
7: 4 GOD showed me: **B**, the Lord GOD
7: 7 He showed me: **B**, the Lord
7: 8 '**B**, I am setting a plumb
8: 1 GOD showed me: **B**, a basket
8:11 **B**, the days are coming,"
9: 8 '**B**, the eyes of the Lord GOD
9:13 **B**, the days are coming,"
Ob 2 '**B**, I will make you small
Mic 1: 3 For **b**, the LORD is coming
2: 3 '**B**, against this family
Nah 1:15 **B**, on the mountains The feet
2:13 **B**, I am against you," says
3: 5 **B**, I am against you,"
Hab 1:13 are of purer eyes than to **b**
2: 4 **B** the proud, His soul is not
2:13 **B**, is it not of the LORD
2:19 **B**, it is overlaid with gold
Zeph 3:19 **B**, at that time I will deal
Zech 1: 8 I saw by night, and **b**, a man
1:11 fro throughout the earth, and **b**,
2: 1 my eyes and looked, and **b**,
2:10 For **b**, I am coming and I will
3: 8 For **b**, I am bringing forth
3: 9 For **b**, the stone That I
3: 9 **B**, I will engrave its
6: 1 my eyes and looked, and **b**,
6:12 '**B**, the Man whose name is
8: 7 '**B**, I will save My people
9: 4 **B**, the LORD will cast her out;
9: 9 O daughter of Jerusalem! **B**,
12: 2 '**B**, I will make Jerusalem
14: 1 **B**, the day of the LORD is
Mal 2: 3 '**B**, I will rebuke your
3: 1 '**B**, I send My messenger,
3: 1 **B**, He is coming," Says
4: 1 'For **b**, the day is coming,
4: 5 **B**, I will send you Elijah
Mt 1:20 thought about these things, **b**,
1:23 '**B**, the virgin shall be
2: 1 the days of Herod the king, **b**,
2: 9 the king, they departed; and **b**,
2:13 Now when they had departed, **b**,
2:19 But when Herod was dead, **b**,
3:16 from the water; and **b**,
4:11 Then the devil left Him, and **b**,
8: 2 And **b**, a leper came and
8:34 And **b**, the whole city came
9: 2 Then **b**, they brought to Him
9:10 the table in the house, that **b**,
9:18 spoke these things to them, **b**,
9:32 As they went out, **b**,
10:16 **B**, I send you out as
11:10 of whom it is written: '**B**,
12:10 And **b**, there was a man who
12:18 **B**! My Servant whom I have
12:46 talking to the multitudes, **b**,
13: 3 them in parables, saying: "**B**,
15:22 And **b**, a woman of Canaan
17: 3 And **b**, Moses and Elijah
17: 5 While he was still speaking, **b**,
19:16 Now **b**, one came and said
20:18 '**B**, we are going up to
20:30 And **b**, two blind men
21: 5 the daughter of Zion, '**B**,
25: 6 midnight a cry was heard: '**B**,
26:45 still sleeping and resting? **B**,
26:47 while He was still speaking, **b**,
27:51 Then, **b**, the veil of the
28: 2 And **b**, there was a great
28: 7 there you will see Him. **B**,
28: 9 went to tell His disciples, **b**,
28:11 Now while they were going, **b**,
Mk 1: 2 written in the Prophets: "**B**,
4: 3 'Listen! **B**, a sower went
5:22 And **b**, one of the rulers
10:33 '**B**, we are going up
14:41 is enough! The hour has come; **b**,
Lk 1:20 'But **b**, you will be mute
1:31 'And **b**, you will conceive
1:38 **B** the maidservant of the Lord!
1:48 of His maidservant; For **b**,
2: 9 And **b**, an angel of the Lord
2:10 them, "Do not be afraid, for **b**,
2:25 And **b**, there was a man
2:34 said to Mary His mother, "**B**,
5:12 was in a certain city, that **b**,
5:18 Then **b**, men brought on a
7:12 near the gate of the city, **b**,
7:27 of whom it is written: '**B**,
7:37 And **b**, a woman in the city
8:41 And **b**, there came a man
9:30 And **b**, two men talked with
9:39 'And **b**, a spirit seizes him,
10: 3 "Go your way; **b**,
10:19 '**B**, I give you the authority
10:25 And **b**, a certain lawyer
13:11 And **b**, there was a woman
13:32 them, "Go, tell that fox, '**B**,
14: 2 And **b**, there was a certain
18:31 aside and said to them, "**B**,
19: 2 Now **b**, there was a man
22:10 And He said to them, "**B**,
22:21 'But **b**, the hand of My
22:47 while He was still speaking, **b**,
23:50 Now **b**, there was a man
24: 4 perplexed about this, that **b**,
24:13 Now **b**, two of them were
24:39 **B** My hands and My feet, that it
24:49 '**B**, I send the Promise
Jn 1:29 **B**! The Lamb of God who takes
1:36 **B** the Lamb of God!"
1:47 Him, and said of him, "**B**,
3:26 to whom you have testified—**b**,
4:35 and then comes the harvest'? **B**,
11: 3 sent to Him, saying, "Lord, **b**,
12:15 not, daughter of Zion; **B**,
17:24 that they may **b** My glory which
19: 4 again, and said to them, "**B**,
19: 5 said to them, "**B** the Man!"
19:14 to the Jews, "**B** your King!"
19:26 'Woman, **b** your son!"
19:27 **B** your mother!" And from that
Acts 1:10 toward heaven as He went up, **b**,
8:27 So he arose and went. And **b**,
9:11 called Saul of Tarsus, for **b**,
10:17 which he had seen meant, **b**,
10:19 the Spirit said to him, "**B**,
10:30 I prayed in my house, and **b**,
12: 7 Now **b**, an angel of the Lord
13:25 think I am? I am not He. But **b**,
13:41 '**B**, you despisers,
13:46 unworthy of everlasting life, **b**,
16: 1 came to Derbe and Lystra. And **b**,
Rom 9:33 As it is written: "**B**,
1 Cor 15:51 **B**, I tell you a mystery:
2 Cor 5:17 old things have passed away; **b**,
6: 2 I have helped you." **B**,
6: 2 now is the accepted time; **b**,
6: 9 and **b** we live; as chastened,
Heb 8: 8 fault with them, He says: "**B**,
10: 7 Then I said, '**B**,
10: 9 then He said, "**B**,
Jas 5: 9 lest you be condemned. **B**,
1 Pe 2: 6 in the Scripture, "**B**,
1 Jn 3: 1 **B** what manner of love the Father
Jude 14 these men also, saying, "**B**,
Rev 1: 7 **B**, He is coming with clouds,
1:18 who lives, and was dead, and **b**,
3:11 '**B**, I am coming quickly!
3:20 '**B**, I stand at the door
4: 1 these things I looked, and **b**,
4: 2 I was in the Spirit; and **b**,
5: 5 said to me, "Do not weep. **B**,
5: 6 And I looked, and **b**,
6: 2 And I looked, and **b**,
6: 5 and see." So I looked, and **b**,
6: 8 So I looked, and **b**,
6:12 He opened the sixth seal, and **b**,
7: 9 these things I looked, and **b**,
9:12 One woe is past. **B**,
11:14 The second woe is past. **B**,
12: 3 sign appeared in heaven: **b**,
14: 1 Then I looked, and **b**,
14:14 Then I looked, and **b**,
15: 5 these things I looked, and **b**,
16:15 '**B**, I am coming as a thief.
19:11 Now I saw heaven opened, and **b**,
21: 3 voice from heaven saying, "**B**,
21: 5 who sat on the throne said, "**B**,
22: 7 '**B**, I am coming quickly!
22:12 And **b**, I am coming

BEHOLDING (1/1) BEHOLD

2 Cor 3:18 **b** as in a mirror the glory of

BEHOLDS (2/2) BEHOLD

Job 41:34 He **b** every high thing; He is
Ps 11: 7 His countenance **b** the upright.

BEHOVED (KJV) See LUK 24:46 (WAS NECESSARY); HEB 2:17 (HAD TO BE)

BEING (243/235) BE

Gen 2: 7 life; and man became a living **b**.
18:12 my lord **b** old also?"
19:16 the LORD **b** merciful to him,
24:27 **b** on the way, the LORD led me
35:29 **b** old and full of days. And
37: 2 **b** seventeen years old, was
50:26 **b** one hundred and ten years
Ex 22:14 the owner of it not **b** with it,
Lev 21: 4 **b** a chief man among his
24: 8 **b** taken from the children of
Num 4:20 while the holy things are **b**
11: 6 but now our whole **b** is dried
32:38 and Baal Meon (their names **b**
Deut 32:31 Even our enemies themselves **b**
Josh 2: 5 it happened as the gate was **b**
9:23 of you shall be freed from **b**
24:29 **b** one hundred and ten years
Judg 6:28 and the second bull was **b**
1 Sam 15:23 also has rejected you from **b**
15:26 LORD has rejected you from **b**
26:13 a great distance **b** between
2 Sam 13:14 and **b** stronger than she, he
1 Ki 2:27 removed Abiathar from **b** priest
6: 7 when it was **b** built, was built
6: 7 in the temple while it was **b**
15:13 his grandmother from **b** queen
16: 7 in **b** like the house of
2 Ki 11: 2 the king's sons who were **b**
2 Chr 15:16 from **b** queen mother, because
22:11 the king's sons who were **b**
Ezra 5: 8 which is **b** built with heavy
5: 8 and timber is **b** laid in the
7:14 And whereas you are **b** sent by
10:19 and **b** guilty, they presented
Neh 4: 7 the walls of Jerusalem were **b**
6: 8 such things as you say are **b**
Esth 1: 3 the princes of the provinces **b**
1: 7 each vessel **b** different from
1:14 those closest to him **b**
3:14 **b** published for all people,
Job 4: 7 who ever perished **b** innocent?
21:23 **B** wholly at ease and secure;
37:12 **b** turned by His guidance, That
Ps 65: 6 **B** clothed with power;
69: 4 **B** my enemies wrongfully;
78: 9 **b** armed and carrying bows,
78:38 **b** full of compassion, forgave
83: 4 let us cut them off from **b** a
104:33 to my God while I have my **b**.
139:16 **b** yet unformed. And in Your
146: 2 to my God while I have my **b**.
Prov 3:26 And will keep your foot from **b**
11:15 But one who hates **b** surety is
23:16 my inmost **b** will rejoice When
Song 3: 8 **B** expert in war. Every man
Isa 3:26 And she **b** desolate shall sit
16:11 And my inner **b** for Kir Heres.
17: 1 Damascus will cease from **b** a
65:20 But the sinner **b** one hundred
Jer 2:25 Withhold your foot from **b**
17:16 I have not hurried away from **b**
31:36 shall also cease From **b** a
Ezek 20:27 by **b** unfaithful to Me.
40: 5 each **b** a cubit and a
Dan 4:27 break off your sins by **b**
5:31 **b** about sixty-two years old.
9:21 **b** caused to fly swiftly,
Hos 4: 6 I also will reject you from **b**
Mal 1: 9 While this is **b** done by your
2:12 **b** awake and aware, Yet who
Mt 1:19 **b** a just man, and not wanting
1:24 **b** aroused from sleep, did as
2:12 **b** divinely warned in a dream
2:22 And **b** warned by God in a dream,
7:11 **b** evil, know how to give good
12:34 **b** evil, speak good things?
16: 8 **b** aware of it, said to them,
26:45 and the Son of Man is **b**
27:12 And while He was **b** accused by
Mk 3: 5 **b** grieved by the hardness of
8: 1 the multitude **b** very great and
8:17 **b** aware of it, said to them,
9:31 The Son of Man is **b** betrayed
14: 3 And **b** in Bethany at the house
14:41 the Son of Man is **b** betrayed
Lk 1:74 **B** delivered from the hand of
3: 1 Pontius Pilate **b** governor of
3: 1 Herod **b** tetrarch of Galilee,
3:19 **b** rebuked by him concerning
3:23 **b** (as was supposed) the son of
4: 1 **b** filled with the Holy Spirit,
4: 2 **b** tempted for forty days by the
4:15 **b** glorified by all.
7:12 a dead man was **b** carried out,
11:13 **b** evil, know how to give good
13:16 **b** a daughter of Abraham, whom
14:21 **b** angry, said to his servant,
16:23 And **b** in torments in Hades, he
20:36 **b** sons of the resurrection.
22:44 And **b** in agony, He prayed more
Jn 4: 6 **b** wearied from His journey,
4: 9 **b** a Jew, ask a drink from me, a
5:13 a multitude **b** in that place.
6:71 **b** one of the twelve.
7:50 **b** one of them) said to them,
8: 9 **b** convicted by their
10:33 **b** a Man, make Yourself God."
11:49 **b** high priest that year, said
11:51 but **b** high priest that year he
13: 2 And supper **b** ended, the devil
14:25 I have spoken to you while **b**
16:21 for joy that a human **b** has been
19:38 **b** a disciple of Jesus, but
20:19 **b** the first day of the week,
20:26 the doors **b** shut, and stood in
Acts 1: 3 **b** seen by them during forty
1: 4 And **b** assembled together with
2:23 **b** delivered by the determined
2:30 **b** a prophet, and knowing that
2:33 Therefore **b** exalted to the right
2:47 church daily those who were **b**
4: 2 **b** greatly disturbed that they
4:23 And **b** let go, they went to
5: 2 his wife also **b** aware of it,
7:55 **b** full of the Holy Spirit,
8:36 What hinders me from **b**
13: 4 **b** sent out by the Holy Spirit,
13:12 **b** astonished at the teaching of
13:49 And the word of the Lord was **b**
15: 3 **b** sent on their way by the
15:21 **b** read in the synagogues every
15:25 **b** assembled with one accord, to
15:32 themselves **b** prophets also,
15:40 **b** commended by the brethren to
16:20 **b** Jews, exceedingly trouble our
16:21 **b** Romans, to receive or
17:28 we live and move and have our **b**,
18:25 and **b** fervent in spirit, he
19:40 For we are in danger of **b** called
19:40 there **b** no reason which we may
22:11 **b** led by the hand of those who
23: 6 of the dead I am **b** judged!"
24: 2 and prosperity is **b** brought to
24:16 This **b** so, I myself always
24:21 of the dead I am **b** judged by
26:11 and **b** exceedingly enraged
27:41 but the stern was **b** broken up
Rom 1:20 **b** understood by the things that
1:29 **b** filled with all
2:18 **b** instructed out of the law,
3:21 **b** witnessed by the Law and the
3:24 **b** justified freely by His grace
4:19 And not **b** weak in faith, he did
4:21 and **b** fully convinced that what
6:13 present yourselves to God as **b**
9:11 (for the children not yet **b**
10: 3 For they **b** ignorant of God's
11:15 For if their **b** cast away is the
11:17 **b** a wild olive tree, were
12: 5 **b** many, are one body in
1 Cor 1:18 but to us who are **b** saved it is
4:12 **B** reviled, we bless; being
4:12 **b** persecuted, we endure;
4:13 **b** defamed, we entreat. We have
8: 7 **b** weak, is defiled.
9:21 as without law (not **b** without
12:12 **b** many, are one body, so also
15:45 Adam became a living **b**.
2 Cor 2:15 of Christ among those who are **b**
3: 5 to think of anything as **b**
3:18 are **b** transformed into the same
4:16 yet the inward man is **b**
5: 4 **b** burdened, not because we want
8:17 but **b** more diligent, he went to
10: 1 but **b** absent am bold toward
10: 6 and **b** ready to punish all
11: 9 everything I kept myself from **b**
12:16 **b** crafty, I caught you by
13: 2 and now **b** absent I write to
13:10 I write these things **b** absent,
13:10 lest **b** present I should use
Gal 1:14 **b** more exceedingly zealous for
2: 3 **b** a Greek, was compelled to be
2:14 **b** a Jew, live in the manner of
3: 3 are you now **b** made perfect by
Eph 1:11 **b** predestined according to the
1:18 eyes of your understanding **b**
2:12 **b** aliens from the commonwealth
2:20 Jesus Christ Himself **b** the
2:21 **b** joined together, grows into a
2:22 in whom you also are **b** built
3:17 **b** rooted and grounded in love,
4:18 **b** alienated from the life of
4:19 **b** past feeling, have given
6:18 **b** watchful to this end with all
Phil 1: 6 **b** confident of this very thing,
1:11 **b** filled with the fruits of
1:25 And **b** confident of this, I know
2: 2 fulfill my joy by **b** like-minded,
2: 2 **b** of one accord, of one mind.
2: 6 **b** in the form of God, did not
2: 8 And **b** found in appearance as a
2:17 and if I am **b** poured out as a
3:10 **b** conformed to His death,
Col 1:10 **b** fruitful in every good work
2: 2 **b** knit together in love, and
2:13 **b** dead in your trespasses and
4: 2 **b** vigilant in it with
1 Tim 2:14 but the woman **b** deceived, fell
3: 6 lest **b** puffed up with pride he
3:10 **b** found blameless.
2 Tim 1: 4 **b** mindful of your tears, that I
3:13 deceiving and **b** deceived.
4: 6 For I am already **b** poured out
Titus 1:16 **b** abominable, disobedient, and
3:11 sinning, **b** self-condemned.
Phm 1: 9 **b** such a one as Paul, the aged,
Heb 1: 3 who **b** the brightness of His
2:11 sanctifies and those who are **b**
2:18 **b** tempted, He is able to aid
4: 2 not **b** mixed with faith in those
6: 8 it is rejected and near to **b**
7: 2 first **b** translated "king of
7:12 For the priesthood **b** changed, of
10:14 forever those who are **b**
11: 4 and through it he **b** dead still
11: 7 **b** divinely warned of things not
11:37 **b** destitute, afflicted,
12:27 of those things that are **b**
1 Pe 1: 7 **b** much more precious than gold
2: 5 are **b** built up a spiritual
2: 8 **b** disobedient to the word, to
3: 5 **b** submissive to their own
3: 7 and as **b** heirs together of the
3:18 **b** put to death in the flesh but
3:20 while the ark was **b** prepared,
5: 3 nor as **b** lords over those
5: 3 but **b** examples to the flock;
2 Pe 3: 6 **b** flooded with water.
3:12 **b** on fire, and the elements
3:17 **b** led away with the error of
Rev 12: 2 Then **b** with child, she cried out
14: 4 **b** firstfruits to God and to

BEKAH (1/1)

Ex 38:26 a **b** for each man (that is,

BEL (3/3) BAAL

Isa 46: 1 **B** bows down, Nebo stoops
Jer 50: 2 **B** is shamed. Merodach is
51:44 I will punish **B** in Babylon,

BELA (13/13) BELAH, BELAITES

Gen 14: 2 and the king of **B** (that is,
14: 8 and the king of **B** (that is,
36:32 **B** the son of Beor reigned in
36:33 And when **B** died, Jobab the son
Num 26:38 to their families were: of **B**,
26:40 And the sons of **B** were Ard and
1 Chr 1:43 **B** the son of Beor, and the name
1:44 And when **B** died, Jobab the son
5: 8 and **B** the son of Azaz, the son
7: 6 The sons of Benjamin were **B**,
7: 7 The sons of **B** were Ezbon, Uzzi,
8: 1 Now Benjamin begot **B** his
8: 3 The sons of **B** were Addar, Gera,

BELAH (1/1) BELA

Gen 46:21 The sons of Benjamin were **B**,

BELAITES (1/1) BELA

Num 26:38 of Bela, the family of the **B**;

BELCH (1/1)

Ps 59: 7 they **b** with their mouth;

BELIAL (1/1)

2 Cor 6:15 what accord has Christ with **B**?

BELIEF (1/1) BELIEVE, UNBELIEF

2 Th 2:13 by the Spirit and **b** in the

BELIEVE (178/163) BELIEF, BELIEVED, BELIEVER, BELIEVERS, BELIEVES, BELIEVING

Gen 45:26 because he did not **b** them.
Ex 4: 1 But suppose they will not **b** me
4: 5 that they may **b** that the LORD
4: 8 if they do not **b** you, nor heed
4: 8 that they may **b** the message of
4: 9 if they do not **b** even these two
19: 9 and **b** you forever." So Moses
Num 14:11 And how long will they not **b**
20:12 Because you did not **b** Me, to
Deut 1:32 you did not **b** the LORD your
9:23 and you did not **b** Him nor obey
1 Ki 10: 7 However I did not **b** the words
2 Ki 17:14 who did not **b** in the LORD
2 Chr 9: 6 However I did not **b** their words
20:20 **B** in the LORD your God, and
20:20 **b** His prophets, and you shall
32:15 and do not **b** him; for no god of
Job 9:16 I would not **b** that He was
15:22 He does not **b** that he will
29:24 they did not **b** it, And the
Ps 78:22 Because they did not **b** in God,
78:32 AND did not **b** in His wondrous
106:24 They did not **b** His word,
119:66 For I **b** Your commandments.
Prov 26:25 do not **b** him, For there are
Isa 7: 9 If you will not **b**,
43:10 That you may know and **b** Me,
Jer 12: 6 Do not **b** them, Even though
40:14 the son of Ahikam did not **b**
Hab 1: 5 days Which you would not **b**,
Mt 9:28 Do you **b** that I am able to do
18: 6 one of these little ones who **b**
21:25 Why then did you not **b** him?'
21:32 and you did not **b** him; but tax
21:32 did not afterward relent and **b**
24:23 There!' do not **b** it.
24:26 in the inner rooms!' do not **b**
27:42 and we will **b** Him.
Mk 1:15 Repent, and **b** in the gospel."
5:36 "Do not be afraid; only **b**.
9:23 said to him, "If you can **b**,

9:24 said with tears, "Lord, I ***b***;
9:42 one of these little ones who ***b***
11:24 ***b*** that you receive them, and
11:31 Why then did you not ***b*** him?'
13:21 He is there!' do not ***b*** it.
15:32 cross, that we may see and ***b***.
16:11 seen by her, they did not ***b***.
16:13 but they did not ***b*** them
16:14 because they did not ***b*** those
16:16 but he who does not ***b*** will be
16:17 signs will follow those who ***b***:
Lk 1:20 because you did not ***b*** my words
8:12 lest they should ***b*** and be
8:13 who ***b*** for a while and in time
8:50 "Do not be afraid; only ***b***,
20: 5 Why then did you not ***b*** him?'
22:67 you, you will by no means ***b***.
24:11 and they did not ***b*** them.
24:25 and slow of heart to ***b*** in all
24:41 But while they still did not ***b***
Jn 1: 7 that all through him might ***b***.
1:12 to those who ***b*** in His name:
1:50 under the fig tree,' do you ***b***?
3:12 earthly things and you do not ***b***,
3:12 how will you ***b*** if I tell you
3:18 but he who does not ***b*** is
3:36 and he who does not ***b*** the Son
4:21 ***b*** Me, the hour is coming when
4:42 said to the woman, "Now we ***b***,
4:48 wonders, you will by no means ***b***.
5:38 whom He sent, Him you do not ***b***.
5:44 'How can you ***b***, who receive
5:46 you would ***b*** Me; for he wrote
5:47 But if you do not ***b*** his
5:47 how will you ***b*** My words?"
6:29 that you ***b*** in Him whom He
6:30 that we may see it and ***b*** You?
6:36 have seen Me and yet do not ***b***.
6:64 are some of you who do not ***b***.
6:64 who they were who did not ***b***,
6:69 Also we have come to ***b*** and know
7: 5 even His brothers did not ***b*** in
8:24 for if you do not ***b*** that I am
8:45 the truth, you do not ***b*** Me.
8:46 why do you not ***b*** Me?
9:18 But the Jews did not ***b***
9:35 Do you ***b*** in the Son of God?"
9:36 that I may ***b*** in Him?"
9:38 I ***b***!" And he worshiped Him.
10:25 "I told you, and you do not ***b***.
10:26 "But you do not ***b***,
10:37 of My Father, do not ***b*** Me;
10:38 though you do not ***b*** Me, believe
10:38 ***b*** the works, that you may know
10:38 that you may know and ***b*** that
11:15 I was not there, that you may ***b***.
11:26 never die. Do you ***b*** this?"
11:27 I ***b*** that You are the Christ,
11:40 say to you that if you would ***b***
11:42 that they may ***b*** that You sent
11:48 everyone will ***b*** in Him, and the
12:36 ***b*** in the light, that you may
12:37 they did not ***b*** in Him,
12:39 Therefore they could not ***b***,
12:47 hears My words and does not ***b***,
13:19 you may ***b*** that I am He.
14: 1 you ***b*** in God, believe also in
14: 1 believe in God, ***b*** also in Me.
14:10 Do you not ***b*** that I am in the
14:11 ***B*** Me that I am in the Father
14:11 or else ***b*** Me for the sake of
14:29 it does come to pass, you may ***b***.
16: 9 because they do not ***b*** in Me;
16:30 By this we ***b*** that You came
16:31 answered them, "Do you now ***b***?
17:20 but also for those who will ***b***
17:21 that the world may ***b*** that You
19:35 the truth, so that you may ***b***.
20:25 into His side, I will not ***b***.
20:31 are written that you may ***b***
Acts 8:37 If you ***b*** with all your heart,
8:37 I ***b*** that Jesus Christ is the Son
9:26 and did not ***b*** that he was a
13:41 you will by no means ***b***,
15: 7 the word of the gospel and ***b***.
15:11 But we ***b*** that through the grace
16:31 ***B*** on the Lord Jesus Christ, and
19: 4 the people that they should ***b***
19: 9 were hardened and did not ***b***,
21:25 concerning the Gentiles who ***b***,
22:19 and beat those who ***b*** on You.
26:27 do you ***b*** the prophets? I know
26:27 I know that you do ***b***."
27:25 for I ***b*** God that it will be
Rom 3: 3 For what if some did not ***b***?
3:22 Christ, to all and on all who ***b***.
4:11 the father of all those who ***b***,
4:24 It shall be imputed to us who ***b***
6: 8 we ***b*** that we shall also live
10: 9 mouth the Lord Jesus and ***b*** in
10:14 And how shall they ***b*** in Him of
15:31 those in Judea who do not ***b***,
1 Cor 1:21 preached to save those who ***b***.
7:12 has a wife who does not ***b***,
7:13 has a husband who does not ***b***,
10:27 If any of those who do not ***b***
11:18 among you, and in part I ***b*** it.
14:22 not to those who ***b*** but to
14:22 unbelievers but for those who ***b***.
2 Cor 4: 4 age has blinded, who do not ***b***,
4:13 we also ***b*** and therefore
Gal 3:22 might be given to those who ***b***.
Eph 1:19 of His power toward us who ***b***,
Phil 1:29 not only to ***b*** in Him, but also
1 Th 1: 7 in Macedonia and Achaia who ***b***.
2:10 ourselves among you who ***b***;
2:13 effectively works in you who ***b***.
4:14 For if we ***b*** that Jesus died and
2 Th 1:10 admired among all those who ***b***,
2:11 that they should ***b*** the lie,
2:12 may be condemned who did not ***b***
1 Tim 1:16 to those who are going to ***b*** on
4: 3 thanksgiving by those who ***b***
4:10 men, especially of those who ***b***.
Heb 10:39 but of those who ***b*** to the
11: 6 for he who comes to God must ***b***
11:31 perish with those who did not ***b***,
Jas 2:19 You ***b*** that there is one God.
2:19 You do well. Even the demons ***b***—
1 Pe 1:21 who through Him ***b*** in God, who
2: 7 Therefore, to you who ***b***,
1 Jn 3:23 that we should ***b*** on the name of
4: 1 do not ***b*** every spirit, but test
5:10 he who does not ***b*** God has made
5:13 I have written to you who ***b*** in
5:13 that you may continue to ***b***
Jude 5 destroyed those who did not ***b***.

BELIEVED (82/80) BELIEVE

Gen 15: 6 And he ***b*** in the LORD, and He
Ex 4:31 So the people ***b***;
14:31 and ***b*** the LORD and His servant
1 Sam 27:12 So Achish ***b*** David, saying, "He
Ps 27:13 unless I had ***b*** That I would
106:12 Then they ***b*** His words; They
116:10 I ***b***, therefore I spoke,
Isa 53: 1 Who has ***b*** our report? And to
Lam 4:12 Would not have ***b*** That the
Dan 6:23 because he ***b*** in his God.
Jon 3: 5 So the people of Nineveh ***b*** God,
Mt 8:13 your way; and as you have ***b***,
21:32 tax collectors and harlots ***b***
Lk 1:45 "Blessed is she who ***b***,
Jn 2:11 and His disciples ***b*** in Him.
2:22 and they ***b*** the Scripture and
2:23 many ***b*** in His name when they
3:18 because he has not ***b*** in the
4:39 the Samaritans of that city ***b***
4:41 And many more ***b*** because of His
4:50 So the man ***b*** the word that
4:53 son lives." And he himself ***b***,
5:46 For if you ***b*** Moses, you would
7:31 And many of the people ***b*** in Him,
7:48 the rulers or the Pharisees ***b***
8:30 these words, many ***b*** in Him.
8:31 Jesus said to those Jews who ***b***
10:42 And many ***b*** in Him there.
11:45 things Jesus did, ***b*** in Him.
12:11 of the Jews went away and ***b*** in
12:38 who has ***b*** our report?
12:42 even among the rulers many ***b***
16:27 and have ***b*** that I came forth
17: 8 and they have ***b*** that You sent
20: 8 went in also; and he saw and ***b***.
20:29 you have seen Me, you have ***b***.
20:29 have not seen and yet have ***b***.
Acts 2:44 Now all who ***b*** were together, and
4: 4 of those who heard the word ***b***;
4:32 the multitude of those who ***b***
8:12 But when they ***b*** Philip as he
8:13 Then Simon himself also ***b***;
9:42 and many ***b*** on the Lord.
10:45 of the circumcision who ***b*** were
11:17 gift as He gave us when we ***b***
11:21 and a great number ***b*** and turned
13:12 Then the proconsul ***b***,
13:48 appointed to eternal life ***b***.
14: 1 of the Jews and of the Greeks ***b***.
14:23 to the Lord in whom they had ***b***.
15: 5 the sect of the Pharisees who ***b***
16: 1 of a certain Jewish woman who ***b***,
16:34 having ***b*** in God with all his
17:12 Therefore many of them ***b***,
17:34 some men joined him and ***b***,
18: 8 ***b*** on the Lord with all his
18: 8 ***b*** and were baptized.
18:27 greatly helped those who had ***b***
19: 2 the Holy Spirit when you ***b***?
19:18 And many who had ***b*** came
21:20 of Jews there are who have ***b***,
Rom 4: 3 Abraham ***b*** God, and it was
4:17 the presence of Him whom he ***b***—
4:18 contrary to hope, in hope ***b***,
10:14 on Him in whom they have not ***b***?
10:16 who has ***b*** our report?"
13:11 nearer than when we first ***b***.
1 Cor 3: 5 ministers through whom you ***b***,
15: 2 unless you ***b*** in vain.
15:11 they, so we preach and so you ***b***.
2 Cor 4:13 I ***b*** and therefore I
Gal 2:16 even we have ***b*** in Christ Jesus,
3: 6 ***b*** God, and it was accounted
Eph 1:13 in whom also, having ***b***,
2 Th 1:10 our testimony among you was ***b***.
1 Tim 3:16 ***B*** on in the world, Received
2 Tim 1:12 for I know whom I have ***b*** and am
Titus 3: 8 that those who have ***b*** in God
Heb 4: 3 For we who have ***b*** do enter that
Jas 2:23 Abraham ***b*** God, and it was
1 Jn 4:16 And we have known and ***b*** the love
5:10 because he has not ***b*** the

BELIEVER (1/1) BELIEVE, BELIEVERS, UNBELIEVER

2 Cor 6:15 Or what part has a ***b*** with an

BELIEVERS (3/3) BELIEVER

Acts 5:14 And ***b*** were increasingly added to
1 Tim 4:12 but be an example to the ***b*** in
6: 2 those who are benefited are ***b***

BELIEVES (34/33) BELIEVE

Prov 14:15 The simple ***b*** every word, But
Isa 28:16 Whoever ***b*** will not act
Mk 9:23 are possible to him who ***b***.
11:23 but ***b*** that those things he says
16:16 He who ***b*** and is baptized will be
Jn 3:15 that whoever ***b*** in Him should not
3:16 that whoever ***b*** in Him should
3:18 He who ***b*** in Him is not
3:36 He who ***b*** in the Son has
5:24 he who hears My word and ***b*** in
6:35 and he who ***b*** in Me shall never
6:40 who sees the Son and ***b*** in Him
6:47 he who ***b*** in Me has everlasting
7:38 He who ***b*** in Me, as the Scripture
11:25 He who ***b*** in Me, though he may
11:26 And whoever lives and ***b*** in Me
12:44 He who ***b*** in Me, believes not in
12:44 ***b*** not in Me but in Him who sent
12:46 that whoever ***b*** in Me should not
14:12 he who ***b*** in Me, the works that
Acts 10:43 whoever ***b*** in Him will receive
13:39 and by Him everyone who ***b*** is
Rom 1:16 to salvation for everyone who ***b***,
4: 5 to him who does not work but ***b***
9:33 And whoever ***b*** on Him
10: 4 righteousness to everyone who ***b***.
10:10 For with the heart one ***b*** unto
10:11 Whoever ***b*** on Him will not
14: 2 For one ***b*** he may eat all things,
1 Cor 13: 7 ***b*** all things, hopes all things,
1 Pe 2: 6 And he who ***b*** on Him
1 Jn 5: 1 Whoever ***b*** that Jesus is the
5: 5 but he who ***b*** that Jesus is the
5:10 He who ***b*** in the Son of God has

BELIEVING (11/11) BELIEVE

Mt 21:22 things you ask in prayer, ***b***,
Jn 7:39 whom those ***b*** in Him would
20:27 Do not be unbelieving, but ***b***.
20:31 and that ***b*** you may have life in
Acts 24:14 ***b*** all things which are written
Rom 15:13 you with all joy and peace in ***b***,
1 Cor 9: 5 have no right to take along a ***b***
Gal 3: 9 of faith are blessed with ***b***
1 Tim 5:16 If any ***b*** man or woman has
6: 2 And those who have ***b*** masters,
1 Pe 1: 8 now you do not see Him, yet ***b***,

BELL (4/2) BELLS

Ex 28:34 a golden ***b*** and a pomegranate, a
28:34 a golden ***b*** and a pomegranate,
39:26 a ***b*** and a pomegranate, a bell
39:26 a ***b*** and a pomegranate, all

BELLOW (1/1) BELLOWS

Jer 50:11 And you ***b*** like bulls,

BELLOWS (1/1) BELLOW

Jer 6:29 The ***b*** blow fiercely, The lead

BELLS (4/3) BELL

Ex 28:33 and ***b*** of gold between them all
39:25 And they made ***b*** of pure gold,
39:25 and put the ***b*** between the
Zech 14:20 shall be engraved on the ***b*** of

BELLY (18/18)

Gen 3:14 On your ***b*** you shall go, And
Lev 11:42 'Whatever crawls on its ***b***,
Num 5:21 makes your thigh rot and your ***b***
5:22 and make your ***b*** swell and
5:27 and her ***b*** will swell, her thigh
Judg 3:21 thigh, and thrust it into his ***b***.
3:22 draw the dagger out of his ***b***;
Job 20:15 God casts them out of his ***b***.
32:19 Indeed my ***b*** is like wine that
Ps 17:14 And whose ***b*** You fill with Your
Ezek 3: 3 me, "Son of man, feed your ***b***,
Dan 2:32 its ***b*** and thighs of bronze,
Jon 1:17 And Jonah was in the ***b*** of the
2: 1 LORD his God from the fish's ***b***.
2: 2 Out of the ***b*** of Sheol I cried,
Mt 12:40 days and three nights in the ***b***
Rom 16:18 Jesus Christ, but their own ***b***,
Phil 3:19 whose god is their ***b***,

BELONG (33/31) BELONGED, BELONGING, BELONGINGS, BELONGS

Gen 32:17 you, saying, 'To whom do you ***b***,

38:25 "By the man to whom these **b**,
40: 8 Do not interpretations **b** to God?
Lev 7:10 shall **b** to all the sons of
7:14 It shall **b** to the priest who
25:30 in the walled city shall **b**
27:19 and it shall **b** to him.
Num 1:50 and over all things that **b** to
35: 5 This shall **b** to them as
Deut 10:14 and the highest heavens **b** to
29:29 The secret things **b** to the
29:29 which are revealed **b** to us
1 Sam 25:22 I leave one male of all who **b**
30:13 to him, "To whom do you **b**,
Job 25: 2 Dominion and fear **b** to Him; He
Ps 47: 9 the shields of the earth **b** to
68:20 And to GOD the Lord **b**
Prov 14:22 But mercy and truth **b** to
16: 1 preparations of the heart **b**
24:23 These things also **b** to the
Ezek 45: 5 and ten thousand wide shall **b**
45: 6 it shall **b** to the whole house
46:16 it shall **b** to his sons; it is
46:17 But his inheritance shall **b** to
48:10 holy district shall **b**:
48:21 The rest shall **b** to the
48:21 it shall **b** to the prince.
48:22 the border of Benjamin shall **b**
Dan 9: 9 To the Lord our God **b** mercy and
Mk 9:41 because you **b** to Christ,
Acts 27:23 an angel of the God to whom I **b**
1 Pe 4:11 to whom **b** the glory and the
Rev 19: 1 glory and honor and power **b**

BELONGED (25/24) BELONG

Josh 17: 8 on the border of Manasseh **b**
Judg 6:11 which **b** to Joash the
18:27 and the priest who had **b** to
Ruth 4: 3 the piece of land which **b** to
1 Sam 21: 7 chief of the herdsmen who **b**
27: 6 Therefore Ziklag has **b** to the
2 Sam 8: 7 the shields of gold that had **b**
9: 9 to your master's son all that **b**
1 Ki 1: 8 and the mighty men who **b** to
4:10 to him **b** Sochoh and all the
4:13 to him **b** the towns of Jair the
4:13 to him also **b** the region of
15:27 which **b** to the Philistines,
16:15 which **b** to the Philistines.
2 Ki 11:10 and shields which had **b** to
12:16 It **b** to the priests.
14:28 what had **b** to Judah—are
24: 7 of Babylon had taken all that **b**
1 Chr 2:23 All these **b** to the sons of
13: 6 which **b** to Judah, to bring up
2 Chr 23: 9 small shields which had **b** to
26:23 in the field of burial which **b**
34:33 from all the country that **b**
Esth 1: 9 in the royal palace which **b**
Lk 23: 7 as soon as he knew that He **b**

BELONGING (6/6) BELONG, BELONGINGS

Num 31:43 now the half **b** to the
Josh 24:33 They buried him in a hill **b**
Ruth 2: 3 to the part of the field **b** to
1 Sam 6:18 cities of the Philistines **b**
Ezek 45: 4 **b** to the priests, the ministers
Lk 9:10 into a deserted place **b** to the

BELONGINGS (5/5) BELONGING

Ezek 12: 3 prepare your **b** for captivity,
12: 4 day you shall bring out your **b**
12: 5 and carry your **b** out through
12: 7 I brought out my **b** by day, as
12:12 among them shall bear his **b**

BELONGS (34/33) BELONG

Ex 9: 4 shall die of all that **b** to
Lev 6: 5 and give it to whomever it **b**,
7:20 of the peace offering that **b**
7:21 of the peace offering that **b**
Num 16:30 them up with all that **b** to
Josh 13: 4 and Mearah that **b** to the
Judg 18:28 It was in the valley that **b** to
19:14 Gibeah, which **b** to Benjamin.
20: 4 which **b** to Benjamin, to spend
1 Sam 17: 1 which **b** to Judah; they
25:21 was missed of all that **b** to
30:14 in the territory which **b** to
2 Sam 3: 8 Am I a dog's head that **b** to
6:12 of Obed-Edom and all that **b**
16: 4 all that **b** to Mephibosheth is
1 Ki 14:11 The dogs shall eat whoever **b** to
16: 4 The dogs shall eat whoever **b** to
17: 9 which **b** to Sidon, and dwell
19: 3 which **b** to Judah, and left his
21:24 The dogs shall eat whoever **b** to
2 Ki 14:11 Shemesh, which **b** to Judah.
2 Chr 25:21 which **b** to Judah.
Ps 3: 8 Salvation **b** to the LORD.
62:11 That power **b** to God.
62:12 **b** mercy; For You render to
89:18 For our shield **b** to the LORD,
94: 1 LORD God, to whom vengeance **b**—
94: 1 God, to whom vengeance **b**,
Ezek 48:22 are in the midst of what **b**
Dan 9: 7 righteousness **b** to You, but to
9: 8 to us **b** shame of face, to our
Heb 5:14 But solid food **b** to those who
7:13 whom these things are spoken **b**
Rev 7:10 Salvation **b** to our God who sits

BELOVED (122/110) BELOVED'S, WELL-BELOVED

Deut 33:12 The **b** of the LORD shall dwell
2 Sam 1:23 Saul and Jonathan were **b** and
Neh 13:26 who was **b** of his God; and God
Ps 60: 5 That Your **b** may be delivered,
108: 6 That Your **b** may be delivered,
127: 2 For so He gives His **b** sleep.
Song 1:13 A bundle of myrrh is my **b** to
1:14 My **b** is to me a cluster of
1:16 my **b**! Yes, pleasant! Also our
2: 1 lily of the valleys.
2: 3 So is my **b** among the sons.
2: 8 The voice of my **b**! Behold, he
2: 9 My **b** is like a gazelle or a
2:10 My **b** spoke, and said to me:
2:16 My **b** is mine, and I am his.
2:17 shadows flee away, Turn, my **b**,
4:16 Let my **b** come to his garden
5: 1 O **b** ones!
5: 2 It is the voice of my **b**!
5: 4 My **b** put his hand By the latch
5: 5 I arose to open for my **b**,
5: 6 I opened for my **b**,
5: 6 But my **b** had turned away and
5: 8 of Jerusalem, If you find my **b**,
5: 9 What is your **b** More than
5: 9 beloved More than another **b**,
5: 9 What is your **b** More than
5: 9 beloved More than another **b**,
5:10 My **b** is white and ruddy,
5:16 This is my **b**,
6: 1 Where has your **b** gone, O
6: 1 Where has your **b** turned aside,
6: 2 My **b** has gone to his garden,
6: 3 And my **b** is mine. He feeds
7: 9 goes down smoothly for my **b**,
7:11 Come, my **b**, Let us go
7:13 I have laid up for you, my **b**.
8: 5 wilderness, Leaning upon her **b**?
8:12 fruit two hundred.
8:14 Make haste, my **b**,
Isa 5: 1 my Well-beloved A song of my **B**
Jer 11:15 What has My **b** to do in My house,
12: 7 I have given the dearly **b** of
Dan 9:23 you, for you are greatly **b**;
10:11 me, "O Daniel, man greatly **b**,
10:19 And he said, "O man greatly **b**,
Mt 3:17 This is My **b** Son, in whom I am
12:18 My **B** in whom My soul is
17: 5 This is My **b** Son, in whom I am
Mk 1:11 You are My **b** Son, in whom I am
9: 7 This is My **b** Son. Hear Him!"
12: 6 still having one son, his **b**,
Lk 3:22 You are My **b** Son; in You I am
9:35 This is My **b** Son. Hear Him!"
20:13 I will send my **b** son. Probably
Acts 15:25 chosen men to you with our **b**
Rom 1: 7 **b** of God, called to be
9:25 not My people, And her **b**,
9:25 beloved, who was not **b**.
11:28 the election they are **b** for
12:19 **B**, do not avenge yourselves,
16: 5 Greet my **b** Epaenetus, who is
16: 8 Amplias, my **b** in the Lord.
16: 9 in Christ, and Stachys, my **b**.
16:12 Greet the **b** Persis, who labored
1 Cor 4:14 but as my **b** children I warn
4:17 who is my **b** and faithful son in
10:14 Therefore, my **b**, flee from
15:58 my **b** brethren, be steadfast,
2 Cor 7: 1 having these promises, **b**,
12:19 But we do all things, **b**,
Eph 1: 6 has made us accepted in the **B**.
6:21 a **b** brother and faithful
Phil 2:12 Therefore, my **b**, as you have
4: 1 my **b** and longed-for brethren,
4: 1 so stand fast in the Lord, **b**.
Col 3:12 the elect of God, holy and **b**,
4: 7 a **b** brother, faithful minister,
4: 9 a faithful and **b** brother, who
4:14 Luke the **b** physician and Demas
1 Th 1: 4 **b** brethren, your election by
2 Th 2:13 brethren **b** by the Lord, because
1 Tim 6: 2 benefited are believers and **b**.
2 Tim 1: 2 a **b** son: Grace, mercy, and
Phm 1: 1 To Philemon our **b** friend and
1: 2 to the **b** Apphia, Archippus our
1:16 a **b** brother, especially to me
Heb 6: 9 But, **b**, we are confident
Jas 1:16 be deceived, my **b** brethren.
1:19 my **b** brethren, let every man be
2: 5 my **b** brethren: Has God not
1 Pe 2:11 **B**, I beg you as sojourners
4:12 **B**, do not think it strange
2 Pe 1:17 This is My **b** Son, in whom I am
3: 1 **B**, I now write to you this
3: 8 But, **b**, do not forget this
3:14 Therefore, **b**, looking forward
3:15 as also our **b** brother Paul,
3:17 You therefore, **b**, since you
1 Jn 3: 2 **B**, now we are children of
3:21 **B**, if our heart does not
4: 1 **B**, do not believe every
4: 7 **B**, let us love one another,
4:11 **B**, if God so loved us, we also
3 Jn 1 To the **b** Gaius, whom I love in
2 **B**, I pray that you may prosper
5 **B**, you do faithfully whatever
11 **B**, do not imitate what is evil,
Jude 3 **B**, while I was very diligent
17 But you, **b**, remember the words
20 But you, **b**, building
Rev 20: 9 camp of the saints and the **b**

BELOVED'S (2/2) BELOVED

Song 6: 3 I am my **b**, And my beloved
7:10 I am my **b**, And his desire

BELOW (16/16)

Gen 35: 8 and she was buried **b** Bethel
Deut 3:17 **b** the slopes of Pisgah.
4:49 **b** the slopes of Pisgah.
Josh 11: 3 and the Hivite **b** Hermon in the
11:17 Gad in the Valley of Lebanon **b**
12: 3 and southward **b** the slopes of
13: 5 from Baal Gad **b** Mount Hermon as
Judg 7: 8 Now the camp of Midian was **b**
1 Sam 7:11 and drove them back as far as **b**
1 Ki 4:12 which is beside Zaretan **b**
7:24 **B** its brim were ornamental buds
7:29 **B** the lions and oxen were
8:23 in heaven above or on earth **b**
Job 18:16 His roots are dried out **b**,
Prov 15:24 he may turn away from hell **b**.
Mk 14:66 Now as Peter was **b** in the

BELSHAZZAR (8/8)

Dan 5: 1 **B** the king made a great feast
5: 2 **B** gave the command to bring the
5: 9 Then King **B** was greatly
5:22 "But you his son, **B**,
5:29 Then **B** gave the command, and
5:30 That very night **B**,
7: 1 In the first year of **B** king of
8: 1 year of the reign of King **B** a

BELT (17/15) BELTS

Ex 12:11 with a **b** on your waist, your
1 Sam 18: 4 his sword and his bow and his **b**.
2 Sam 18:11 ten shekels of silver and a **b**.
20: 8 on it was a **b** with a sword
1 Ki 2: 5 put the blood of war on his **b**
2 Ki 1: 8 hairy man wearing a leather **b**
Job 12:18 And binds their waist with a **b**.
38:31 Or loose the **b** of Orion?
Ps 109:19 And for a **b** with which he
Isa 5:27 Nor will the **b** on their loins
11: 5 Righteousness shall be the **b** of
11: 5 And faithfulness the **b** of His
22:21 And strengthen him with your **b**;
Mt 3: 4 with a leather **b** around his
Mk 1: 6 hair and with a leather **b**
Acts 21:11 come to us, he took Paul's **b**,
21:11 bind the man who owns this **b**,

BELTESHAZZAR (10/8) DANIEL

Dan 1: 7 he gave Daniel the name **B**;
2:26 to Daniel, whose name was **B**,
4: 8 came before me (his name is **B**,
4: 9 '**B**, chief of the magicians,
4:18 have seen. Now you, **B**,
4:19 Then Daniel, whose name was **B**,
4:19 the king spoke, and said, "**B**,
4:19 **B** answered and said, "My
5:12 Daniel, whom the king named **B**,
10: 1 Daniel, whose name was called **B**.

BELTS (3/3) BELT

Ezek 23:15 Girded with **b** around their
Mt 10: 9 nor copper in your money **b**,
Mk 6: 8 no copper in their money **b**—

BEMOAN (5/5) BEMOANING

Jer 15: 5 Or who will **b** you? Or who
16: 5 nor go to lament or **b** them; for
22:10 nor **b** him; Weep bitterly for
48:17 **B** him, all you who are around
Nah 3: 7 is laid waste! Who will **b** her?

BEMOANED (KJV) See CONSOLED

BEMOANING (1/1) BEMOAN

Jer 31:18 have surely heard Ephraim **b**

BEN (1/1)

1 Chr 15:18 the second rank: Zechariah, **B**,

BEN-ABINADAB (1/1)

1 Ki 4:11 **B**, in all the regions of Dor;

BEN-AMMI (1/1)

Gen 19:38 a son and called his name **B**;

BEN-DEKER (1/1)
1 Ki 4: 9 ***B***, in Makaz, Shaalbim,

BEN-GEBER (1/1)
1 Ki 4:13 ***B***, in Ramoth Gilead;

BEN-HADAD (27/26) HADAD
1 Ki 15:18 And King Asa sent them to ***B*** the
15:20 So ***B*** heeded King Asa, and sent
20: 1 Now ***B*** the king of Syria gathered
20: 2 and said to him, "Thus says ***B***:
20: 5 back and said, "Thus speaks ***B***,
20: 9 he said to the messengers of ***B***,
20:10 Then ***B*** sent to him and said,
20:12 And it happened when ***B*** heard
20:16 Meanwhile ***B*** and the thirty-two
20:17 And ***B*** sent out a patrol, and
20:20 and ***B*** the king of Syria escaped
20:26 that ***B*** mustered the Syrians and
20:30 And ***B*** fled and went into the
20:32 Your servant ***B*** says, 'Please let
20:33 and said, "Your brother ***B***.
20:33 Then ***B*** came out to him; and
20:34 So ***B*** said to him, "The cities
2 Ki 6:24 it happened after this that ***B***
8: 7 and ***B*** king of Syria was sick;
8: 9 Your son ***B*** king of Syria has
13: 3 and into the hand of ***B*** the son
13:24 Then ***B*** his son reigned in his
13:25 recaptured from the hand of ***B***,
2 Chr 16: 2 and sent to ***B*** king of Syria,
16: 4 So ***B*** heeded King Asa, and sent
Jer 49:27 shall consume the palaces of ***B***.
Am 1: 4 shall devour the palaces of ***B***.

BEN-HAIL (1/1)
2 Chr 17: 7 reign he sent his leaders, ***B***,

BEN-HANAN (1/1)
1 Chr 4:20 Shimon were Amnon, Rinnah, ***B***,

BEN-HESED (1/1)
1 Ki 4:10 ***B***, in Arubboth; to him

BEN-HUR (1/1)
1 Ki 4: 8 These are their names: ***B***,

BEN-JAHAZIEL (1/1)
Ezra 8: 5 of the sons of Shechaniah, ***B***,

BEN-JOSIPHIAH (1/1)
Ezra 8:10 of the sons of Shelomith, ***B***,

BEN-ONI (1/1)
Gen 35:18 that she called his name ***B***;

BEN-ZOHETH (1/1) ZOHETH
1 Chr 4:20 sons of Ishi were Zoheth and ***B***.

BENAIAH (42/41)
2 Sam 8:18 ***B*** the son of Jehoiada was over
20:23 ***B*** the son of Jehoiada was over
23:20 ***B*** was the son of Jehoiada, the
23:22 These things ***B*** the son of
23:30 ***B*** a Pirathonite, Hiddai from the
1 Ki 1: 8 ***B*** the son of Jehoiada, Nathan
1:10 invite Nathan the prophet, ***B***,
1:26 nor ***B*** the son of Jehoiada, nor
1:32 and ***B*** the son of Jehoiada."
1:36 ***B*** the son of Jehoiada answered
1:38 ***B*** the son of Jehoiada, the
1:44 ***B*** the son of Jehoiada, the
2:25 Solomon sent by the hand of ***B***
2:29 Then Solomon sent ***B*** the son
2:30 So ***B*** went to the tabernacle of
2:30 And ***B*** brought back word to
2:34 So ***B*** the son of Jehoiada went up
2:35 The king put ***B*** the son of
2:46 So the king commanded ***B*** the son
4: 4 ***B*** the son of Jehoiada, over the
1 Chr 4:36 Asaiah, Adiel, Jesimiel, and ***B***;
11:22 ***B*** was the son of Jehoiada, the
11:24 These things ***B*** the son of
11:31 ***B*** the Pirathonite,
15:18 Jehiel, Unni, Eliab, ***B***,
15:20 Unni, Eliab, Maaseiah, and ***B***,
15:24 Nethanel, Amasai, Zechariah, ***B***,
16: 5 Jehiel, Mattithiah, Eliab, ***B***,
16: 6 ***B*** and Jahaziel the priests
18:17 ***B*** the son of Jehoiada was over
27: 5 army for the third month was ***B***,
27: 6 This was the ***B*** who was mighty
27:14 for the eleventh month was ***B***
27:34 was Jehoiada the son of ***B***,
2 Chr 20:14 son of Zechariah, the son of ***B***,
31:13 and ***B*** were overseers under the
Ezra 10:25 Eleazar, Malchijah, and ***B***;
10:30 of Pahath-Moab: Adna, Chelal, ***B***,
10:35 ***B***, Bedeiah, Cheluh,
10:43 Zebina, Jaddai, Joel, and ***B***.
Ezek 11: 1 and Pelatiah the son of ***B***,
11:13 that Pelatiah the son of ***B***

BEND (8/8) BENDS, BENT
2 Sam 22:35 So that my arms can ***b*** a bow of
Ps 11: 2 For look! The wicked ***b*** their
18:34 So that my arms can ***b*** a bow of
64: 3 And ***b*** their bows to shoot
Jer 46: 9 the Lydians who handle and ***b***
50:14 All you who ***b*** the bow; Shoot
50:29 All you who ***b*** the bow, encamp
51: 3 Against her let the archer ***b***

BENDS (2/2) BEND
Ps 7:12 He ***b*** His bow and makes it
58: 7 When he ***b*** his bow, Let his

BENE BERAK (1/1)
Josh 19:45 Jehud, ***B***, Gath Rimmon,

BENE JAAKAN (3/3)
Num 33:31 from Moseroth and camped at ***B***.
33:32 They moved from ***B*** and camped at
Deut 10: 6 journeyed from the wells of ***B***

BENEATH (16/16)
Gen 49:25 of the deep that lies ***b***,
Ex 20: 4 or that is in the earth ***b***,
27: 5 it under the rim of the altar ***b***,
Deut 4:18 fish that is in the water ***b***
4:39 heaven above and on the earth ***b***;
5: 8 or that is in the earth ***b***,
28:13 be above only, and not be ***b***,
33:13 the dew, And the deep lying ***b***,
Josh 2:11 in heaven above and on earth ***b***.
Job 9:13 of the proud lie prostrate ***b***
Isa 14: 9 Hell from ***b*** is excited about
51: 6 And look on the earth ***b***.
Jer 31:37 of the earth searched out ***b***,
Am 2: 9 fruit above And his roots ***b***.
Jn 8:23 said to them, "You are from ***b***;
Acts 2:19 And signs in the earth ***b***:

BENEFACTORS (1/1)
Lk 22:25 over them are called '***b***.

BENEFIT (5/4) BENEFACTORS, BENEFITED, BENEFITS
Ps 106: 5 That I may see the ***b*** of Your
Isa 30: 5 of a people who could not ***b***
30: 5 benefit them, Or be help or ***b***,
Jer 18:10 with which I said I would ***b*** it.
2 Cor 1:15 that you might have a second ***b***—

BENEFITED (1/1)
1 Tim 6: 2 them because those who are ***b***

BENEFITS (3/3) BENEFIT
Ps 68:19 Who daily loads us with ***b***,
103: 2 soul, And forget not all His ***b***:
116:12 to the LORD For all His ***b***

BENINU (1/1)
Neh 10:13 Hodijah, Bani, and ***B***.

BENJAMIN (162/158) BENJAMIN'S, BENJAMITE, BENJAMITES
Gen 35:18 but his father called him ***B***.
35:24 of Rachel were Joseph and ***B***;
42: 4 did not send Joseph's brother ***B***
42:36 more, and you want to take ***B***.
43:14 your other brother and ***B***.
43:15 the men took that present and ***B***,
43:16 When Joseph saw ***B*** with them, he
43:29 his eyes and saw his brother ***B***,
45:12 and the eyes of my brother ***B***
45:14 and ***B*** wept on his neck.
45:22 but to ***B*** he gave three hundred
46:19 wife, were Joseph and ***B***.
46:21 The sons of ***B*** were Belah,
49:27 ***B*** is a ravenous wolf; In the
Ex 1: 3 Issachar, Zebulun, and ***B***;
Num 1:11 'from ***B***, Abidan the son of
1:36 From the children of ***B***,
1:37 were numbered of the tribe of ***B***
2:22 "Then comes the tribe of ***B***,
2:22 the leader of the children of ***B***
7:60 leader of the children of ***B***,
10:24 the tribe of the children of ***B***
13: 9 from the tribe of ***B***,
26:38 The sons of ***B*** according to
26:41 These are the sons of ***B***
34:21 "from the tribe of ***B***,
Deut 27:12 Judah, Issachar, Joseph, and ***B***;
33:12 Of ***B*** he said: "The beloved
Josh 18:11 the tribe of the children of ***B***
18:20 of the children of ***B***,
18:21 the tribe of the children of ***B***,
18:28 of the children of ***B*** according
21: 4 Simeon, and from the tribe of ***B***.
21:17 and from the tribe of ***B***,
Judg 1:21 But the children of ***B*** did not
1:21 dwell with the children of ***B***
5:14 were in Amalek. After you, ***B***,
10: 9 against Judah also, against ***B***,
19:14 near Gibeah, which belongs to ***B***.
20: 3 (Now the children of ***B*** heard
20: 4 into Gibeah, which belongs to ***B***,
20:10 when they come to Gibeah in ***B***,
20:12 men through all the tribe of ***B***,
20:13 But the children of ***B*** would
20:14 the children of ***B*** gathered
20:15 at that time the children of ***B***
20:17 Now besides ***B***, the men of
20:18 against the children of ***B***?
20:20 went out to battle against ***B***,
20:21 Then the children of ***B*** came out
20:23 the children of my brother ***B***?
20:24 approached the children of ***B***
20:25 And ***B*** went out against them from
20:28 the children of my brother ***B***,
20:30 up against the children of ***B***
20:31 So the children of ***B*** went out
20:32 And the children of ***B*** said,
20:35 The LORD defeated ***B*** before
20:36 So the children of ***B*** saw that
20:39 Now ***B*** had begun to strike and
20:41 the men of ***B*** panicked, for they
20:44 And eighteen thousand men of ***B***
20:46 So all who fell of ***B*** that day
20:48 back against the children of ***B***,
21: 1 us shall give his daughter to ***B***
21: 6 of Israel grieved for ***B*** their
21:13 word to the children of ***B*** who
21:14 So ***B*** came back at that time, and
21:15 And the people grieved for ***B***,
21:16 since the women of ***B*** have been
21:17 for the survivors of ***B***,
21:18 the one who gives a wife to ***B***.
21:20 instructed the children of ***B***,
21:21 then go to the land of ***B***.
21:23 And the children of ***B*** did so;
1 Sam 4:12 Then a man of ***B*** ran from the
9: 1 There was a man of ***B*** whose name
9:16 you a man from the land of ***B***,
9:21 the families of the tribe of ***B***?
10: 2 tomb in the territory of ***B*** at
10:20 the tribe of ***B*** was chosen.
10:21 he had caused the tribe of ***B***
13: 2 with Jonathan in Gibeah of ***B***.
13:15 up from Gilgal to Gibeah of ***B***.
13:16 them remained in Gibeah of ***B***.
14:16 of Saul in Gibeah of ***B*** looked,
2 Sam 2: 9 Jezreel, over Ephraim, over ***B***,
2:15 over by number, twelve from ***B***,
2:25 Now the children of ***B*** gathered
2:31 of ***B*** and Abner's men, three
3:19 also spoke in the hearing of ***B***.
3:19 Israel and the whole house of ***B***.
4: 2 of the children of ***B***.
4: 2 Beeroth also was part of ***B***,
19:17 were a thousand men of ***B*** with
21:14 his son in the country of ***B*** in
23:29 Gibeah of the children of ***B***,
1 Ki 4:18 Shimei the son of Elah, in ***B***;
12:21 of Judah with the tribe of ***B***,
12:23 to all the house of Judah and ***B***,
15:22 them King Asa built Geba of ***B***,
1 Chr 2: 2 Dan, Joseph, ***B***, Naphtali,
6:60 And from the tribe of ***B***:
6:65 the tribe of the children of ***B***
7: 6 The sons of ***B*** were Bela,
7:10 sons of Bilhan were Jeush, ***B***,
8: 1 Now ***B*** begot Bela his firstborn,
8:40 These were all sons of ***B***.
9: 3 and some of the children of ***B***,
9: 7 Of the sons of ***B***: Sallu the
11:31 of Gibeah, of the sons of ***B***,
12: 2 with the bow. They were of ***B***,
12:16 Then some of the sons of ***B*** and
12:29 of the sons of ***B***, relatives of
21: 6 But he did not count Levi and ***B***
27:21 the son of Zechariah; over ***B***,
2 Chr 11: 1 from the house of Judah and ***B***
11: 3 to all Israel in Judah and ***B***,
11:10 which are in Judah and ***B***,
11:12 having Judah and ***B*** on his side.
11:23 the territories of Judah and ***B***,
14: 8 and from ***B*** two hundred and
15: 2 me, Asa, and all Judah and ***B***.
15: 8 all the land of Judah and ***B***
15: 9 he gathered all Judah and ***B***,
17:17 Of ***B***: Eliada a mighty man
25: 5 throughout all Judah and ***B***;
31: 1 the altars—from all Judah, ***B***,
34: 9 of Israel, from all Judah and ***B***,
34:32 were present in Jerusalem and ***B***
Ezra 1: 5 fathers' houses of Judah and ***B***,
4: 1 the adversaries of Judah and ***B***
10: 9 So all the men of Judah and ***B***
10:32 ***B***, Malluch, and Shemariah;
Neh 3:23 After him ***B*** and Hasshub made
11: 4 Judah and of the children of ***B***.
11: 7 And these are the sons of ***B***:
11:31 Also the children of ***B*** from
11:36 divisions of Levites were in ***B***.
12:34 Judah, ***B***, Shemaiah, Jeremiah,
Ps 68:27 There is little ***B***,
80: 2 Before Ephraim, ***B***,
Jer 1: 1 in Anathoth in the land of ***B***,
6: 1 "O you children of ***B***,
17:26 from the land of ***B*** and from the
20: 2 were in the high gate of ***B***,
32: 8 which is in the country of ***B***;
32:44 witnesses, in the land of ***B***,
33:13 of the South, in the land of ***B***,

37:12 to go into the land of **B** to
37:13 when he was in the Gate of **B**,
38: 7 was sitting at the Gate of **B**,
Ezek 48:22 of Judah and the border of **B**
48:23 **B** shall have one section;
48:24 "by the border of **B**,
48:32 gate for Joseph, one gate for **B**,
Hos 5: 8 Look behind you, O **B**!'
Ob 19 **B** shall possess Gilead.
Acts 13:21 Kish, a man of the tribe of **B**,
Rom 11: 1 of Abraham, of the tribe of **B**.
Phil 3: 5 of Israel, of the tribe of **B**,
Rev 7: 8 of the tribe of **B** twelve

BENJAMIN'S (4/4)

Gen 43:34 but **B** serving was five times as
44:12 the cup was found in **B** sack
45:14 he fell on his brother **B** neck
Zech 14:10 in her place from **B** Gate

BENJAMITE (9/9)

Judg 3:15 Ehud the son of Gera, the **B**,
1 Sam 9: 1 the son of Aphiah, a **B**,
9:21 and said, "Am I not a **B**,
2 Sam 16:11 How much more now may this **B**?
19:16 And Shimei the son of Gera, a **B**,
20: 1 Sheba the son of Bichri, a **B**.
1 Ki 2: 8 a **B** from Bahurim, who cursed me
Esth 2: 5 of Shimei, the son of Kish, a **B**.
Ps 7: the words of Cush, a **B**.

BENJAMITES (9/9)

Judg 19:16 the men of the place were **B**.
20:34 But the **B** did not know that
20:35 thousand one hundred **B**;
20:36 had given ground to the **B**,
20:40 the **B** looked behind them, and
20:43 They surrounded the **B**,
1 Sam 9: 4 through the land of the **B**,
22: 7 you **B**! Will the son of Jesse
1 Chr 27:12 the Anathothite, of the **B**;

BENO (2/2)

1 Chr 24:26 the son of Jaaziah, **B**.
24:27 of Merari by Jaaziah were **B**,

BENT (11/11) BEND

Ps 37:14 drawn the sword And have ***b***
Isa 5:28 sharp, And all their bows ***b***;
21:15 From the ***b*** bow, and from the
Jer 9: 3 like their bow they have ***b***
Lam 2: 4 He has ***b*** His bow; With His
3:12 He has ***b*** His bow And set me up
Ezek 17: 7 this vine ***b*** its roots toward
Dan 11:27 kings' hearts shall be ***b*** on
Hos 11: 7 My people are ***b*** on backsliding
Zech 9:13 For I have ***b*** Judah, My bow,
Lk 13:11 and was ***b*** over and could in no

BEON (1/1)

Num 32: 3 Elealeh, Shebam, Nebo, and **B**,

BEOR (11/11)

Gen 36:32 Bela the son of **B** reigned in
Num 22: 5 to Balaam the son of **B** at
24: 3 of Balaam the son of **B**,
24:15 of Balaam the son of **B**,
31: 8 Balaam the son of **B** they also
Deut 23: 4 you Balaam the son of **B** from
Josh 13:22 the sword Balaam the son of **B**,
24: 9 and called Balaam the son of **B**
1 Chr 1:43 of Israel: Bela the son of **B**,
Mic 6: 5 And what Balaam the son of **B**
2 Pe 2:15 the way of Balaam the son of **B**,

BEQUEATHS (1/1)

Deut 21:16 on the day he ***b*** his possessions

BERA (1/1)

Gen 14: 2 that they made war with **B** king

BERACHAH (3/2)

1 Chr 12: 3 Pelet the sons of Azmaveth; **B**,
2 Chr 20:26 assembled in the Valley of **B**,
20:26 was called The Valley of **B**

BERACHIAH (1/1)

1 Chr 6:39 hand, was Asaph the son of **B**,

BERAIAH (1/1)

1 Chr 8:21 Adaiah, **B**, and Shimrath

BEREA (3/3)

Acts 17:10 and Silas away by night to **B**.
17:13 God was preached by Paul at **B**,
20: 4 And Sopater of **B** accompanied him

BEREAVE (6/6) BEREAVED, BEREAVES

Jer 15: 7 I will ***b*** them of children;
Ezek 5:17 and they will ***b*** you.
36:12 no more shall you ***b*** them of
36:13 You devour men and ***b*** your nation
36:14 nor ***b*** your nation anymore,"
Hos 9:12 Yet I will ***b*** them to the last

BEREAVED (5/4) BEREAVE

Gen 27:45 Why should I be ***b*** also of you
42:36 You have ***b*** me: Joseph is no
43:14 brother and Benjamin. If I am ***b***,
43:14 I am bereaved, I am ***b***!"
Jer 18:21 wives become widows And ***b*** of

BEREAVES (1/1) BEREAVE

Lam 1:20 Outside the sword ***b***,

BERECHIAH (11/11)

1 Chr 3:20 and Hashubah, Ohel, **B**,
9:16 and **B** the son of Asa, the son
15:17 brethren, Asaph the son of **B**;
15:23 **B** and Elkanah were doorkeepers
2 Chr 28:12 **B** the son of Meshillemoth,
Neh 3: 4 to them Meshullam the son of **B**,
3:30 him Meshullam the son of **B**
6:18 of Meshullam the son of **B**.
Zech 1: 1 came to Zechariah the son of **B**,
1: 7 came to Zechariah the son of **B**,
Mt 23:35 blood of Zechariah, son of **B**,

BERED (2/2)

Gen 16:14 it is between Kadesh and **B**.
1 Chr 7:20 **B** his son, Tahath his son,

BERI (1/1) BERIAH, BERITES

1 Chr 7:36 were Suah, Harnepher, Shual, **B**,

BERIAH (11/10) BERI

Gen 46:17 were Jimnah, Ishuah, Isui, **B**,
46:17 And the sons of **B** were Heber
Num 26:44 family of the Jesuites; of **B**,
26:45 Of the sons of **B**:
1 Chr 7:23 a son; and he called his name **B**,
7:30 were Imnah, Ishvah, Ishvi, **B**,
7:31 The sons of **B** were Heber and
8:13 and **B** and Shema, who were heads
8:16 and Joha were the sons of **B**.
23:10 Jahath, Zina, Jeush, and **B**.
23:11 But Jeush and **B** did not have

BERIITES (1/1)

Num 26:44 of Beriah, the family of the **B**.

BERITES (1/1) BERI

2 Sam 20:14 and Beth Maachah and all the **B**.

BERITH (1/1) BAAL-BERITH

Judg 9:46 of the temple of the god **B**.

BERNICE (3/3)

Acts 25:13 some days King Agrippa and **B**
25:23 when Agrippa and **B** had come
26:30 as well as the governor and **B**

BERODACH-BALADAN (1/1) BALADAN, MERODACH-BALADAN

2 Ki 20:12 At that time **B** the son of

BEROTHAH (1/1) BEROTHAI

Ezek 47:16 'Hamath, **B**, Sibraim

BEROTHAI (1/1) BEROTHAH

2 Sam 8: 8 Also from Betah and from **B**,

BEROTHITE (1/1) BEEROTHITE

1 Chr 11:39 Naharai the **B** (the armorbearer

BERRIES (KJV) See OLIVES

BERYL (8/8)

Ex 28:20 "and the fourth row, a ***b***,
39:13 the fourth row, a ***b***,
Song 5:14 are rods of gold Set with ***b***.
Ezek 1:16 was like the color of ***b***,
10: 9 to have the color of a ***b***
28:13 sardius, topaz, and diamond, **B**,
Dan 10: 6 His body was like ***b***,
Rev 21:20 chrysolite, the eighth ***b***,

BESAI (2/2)

Ezra 2:49 sons of Paseah, the sons of **B**,
Neh 7:52 the sons of **B**, the sons of

BESEECH (3/3)

Ps 80:14 we ***b*** You, O God of hosts; Look
Rom 12: 1 I ***b*** you therefore, brethren, by
Eph 4: 1 ***b*** you to walk worthy of the

BESEECHING, BESOUGHT (KJV)

See ENTREATED, IMPLORED, IMPLORING, PLEADED, PLEADING

BESIDE (65/64)

Gen 48: 7 Rachel died ***b*** me in the land of
48:12 So Joseph brought them from ***b***
Ex 14: 9 them camping by the sea ***b*** Pi
29:12 and pour all the blood ***b*** the
Lev 1:16 its feathers and cast it ***b*** the
6:10 and he shall put them ***b*** the
10:12 and eat it without leaven ***b*** the
Num 2: 2 ***b*** the emblems of his father's
6: 9 if anyone dies very suddenly ***b***
24: 6 Like cedars ***b*** the waters.
Deut 11:30 ***b*** the terebinth trees of Moreh?
31:26 and put it ***b*** the ark of the
Josh 3:16 the city that is ***b*** Zaretan.
7: 2 which is ***b*** Beth Aven, on the
12: 9 which is ***b*** Bethel, one;
Judg 4:11 Zaanaim, which is ***b*** Kedesh.
6:25 the wooden image that is ***b*** it;
6:28 the wooden image that was ***b***
6:30 the wooden image that was ***b***
7: 1 him rose early and encamped ***b***
9: 6 went and made Abimelech king ***b***
Ruth 2:14 So she sat ***b*** the reapers, and
1 Sam 4: 1 and encamped ***b*** Ebenezer; and
19: 3 And I will go out and stand ***b*** my
2 Sam 15: 2 would rise early and stand ***b***
18: 4 So the king stood ***b*** the gate,
1 Ki 4:12 which is ***b*** Zaretan below
7:30 supports of cast bronze ***b***
10:19 and two lions stood ***b*** the
13:31 lay my bones ***b*** his bones.
2 Ki 12: 9 and set it ***b*** the altar, on the
2 Chr 9:18 and two lions stood ***b*** the
26:19 ***b*** the incense altar.
Neh 2: 6 to me (the queen also sitting ***b***
4: 3 Now Tobiah the Ammonite was ***b***
4:18 who sounded the trumpet was ***b***
8: 4 and ***b*** him, at his right hand,
Job 1:14 and the donkeys feeding ***b*** them,
18: 6 And his lamp ***b*** him is put out.
41:25 of his crashings they are ***b***
Ps 23: 2 He leads me ***b*** the still
Prov 8: 2 **B** the way, where the paths
8:30 Then I was ***b*** Him as a master
Song 1: 8 And feed your little goats **B**
Isa 32:20 Blessed are you who sow ***b*** all
Jer 36:21 of all the princes who stood ***b***
Ezek 1:15 a wheel was on the earth ***b***
1:19 the wheels went ***b*** them; and
3:13 and the noise of the wheels ***b***
9: 2 They went in and stood ***b*** the
10: 6 that he went in and stood ***b***
10:16 the wheels went ***b*** them; and
10:16 also did not turn from ***b*** them.
10:19 the wheels were ***b*** them; and
11:22 with the wheels ***b*** them, and the
32:13 all its animals From ***b*** its
32:29 their might Are laid ***b*** those
33:30 people are talking about you ***b***
43: 6 while a man stood ***b*** me.
Dan 8: 3 standing ***b*** the river, was a ram
8: 6 which I had seen standing ***b*** the
Zech 4:14 who stand ***b*** the Lord of the
Acts 12:15 You are ***b*** yourself!" Yet she
26:24 you are ***b*** yourself!
2 Cor 5:13 For if we are ***b*** ourselves, it

BESIDES (91/86)

Gen 26: 1 ***b*** the first famine that was in
31:50 or if you take other wives ***b***
46:26 ***b*** Jacob's sons' wives, were
Ex 12:37 men on foot, ***b*** children.
Lev 7:13 **B** the cakes, as his offering he
9:17 ***b*** the burnt sacrifice of the
23:38 ***b*** the Sabbaths of the LORD,
23:38 ***b*** your gifts, besides all your
23:38 ***b*** all your vows, and besides
23:38 and ***b*** all your freewill
Num 6:21 and ***b*** that, whatever else his
16:49 ***b*** those who died in the Korah
28:10 ***b*** the regular burnt offering
28:15 ***b*** the regular burnt offering
28:23 You shall offer these ***b*** the
28:24 it shall be offered ***b*** the
28:31 ***b*** the regular burnt offering
29: 6 ***b*** the burnt offering with its
29:11 ***b*** the sin offering for
29:16 ***b*** the regular burnt offering,
29:19 ***b*** the regular burnt offering
29:22 ***b*** the regular burnt offering,
29:25 ***b*** the regular burnt offering,
29:28 ***b*** the regular burnt offering,
29:31 ***b*** the regular burnt offering,
29:34 ***b*** the regular burnt offering,
29:38 ***b*** the regular burnt offering,
29:39 at your appointed feasts (***b***
Deut 3: 5 ***b*** a great many rural towns.
4:35 there is none other ***b*** Him.
18: 8 ***b*** what comes from the sale of
19: 9 more cities for yourself ***b***

29: 1 **b** the covenant which He made
32:39 And there is no God **b** Me; I
Josh 17: 5 **b** the land of Gilead and
22:19 building yourselves an altar **b**
22:29 **b** the altar of the LORD our
Judg 8:26 **b** the crescent ornaments,
8:26 and **b** the chains that were
11:34 **B** her he had neither son nor
20:15 **b** the inhabitants of Gibeah,
20:17 Now **b** Benjamin, the men of
1 Sam 2: 2 For there is none **b** You,
2 Sam 7:22 nor is there any God **b** You,
1 Ki 4:23 **b** deer, gazelles, roebucks, and
5:16 **b** three thousand three hundred
10:13 **b** what Solomon had given her
10:15 **b** that from the traveling
11:25 all the days of Solomon (**b** the
2 Ki 21:16 **b** his sin by which he made
1 Chr 3: 9 **b** the sons of the concubines,
17:20 nor is there any God **b** You,
2 Chr 9:14 **b** what the traveling merchants
17:19 **b** those the king put in the
20: 1 and others with them **b** the
31:16 **B** those males from three years
Ezra 1: 4 **b** the freewill offerings for
1: 6 **b** all that was willingly
2:65 **b** their male and female
Neh 5:15 **b** forty shekels of silver.
5:17 **b** those who came to us from the
7:67 **b** their male and female
Esth 2: 9 **b** her allowance. Then seven
5:12 Moreover Haman said, "**B**,
Ps 73:25 upon earth that I desire **b**
Isa 26:13 masters **b** You Have had
43:11 And **b** Me there is no savior.
44: 6 **B** Me there is no God.
44: 8 Is there a God **b** Me?
45: 5 There is no God **b** Me.
45: 6 That there is none **b** Me.
45:21 And there is no other God **b**
45:21 There is none **b** Me.
47: 8 and there is no one else **b**
47:10 and there is no one else **b**
56: 8 I will gather to him Others **b**
64: 4 has the eye seen any God **b** You,
Jer 36:32 had burned in the fire. And **b**,
Dan 11: 4 even for others **b** these.
Hos 13: 4 For there is no Savior **b** Me.
Zeph 2:15 and there is none **b** me."
Mt 14:21 **b** women and children.
15:38 **b** women and children.
25:20 have gained five more talents **b**
25:22 have gained two more talents **b**
Lk 16:26 And **b** all this, between us and
24:21 **b** all this, today is the third
1 Cor 1:16 the household of Stephanas. **B**,
2 Cor 11:28 **b** the other things, what comes
1 Tim 5:13 And **b** they learn to be idle,
Phm 1:19 you owe me even your own self **b**.

BESIEGE (9/8) BESIEGED, BESIEGES, BESIEGING

Deut 20:12 then you shall **b** it.
20:19 When you **b** a city for a long
28:52 They shall **b** you at all your
28:52 and they shall **b** you at all
1 Sam 23: 8 to go down to Keilah to **b** David
2 Chr 6:28 when their enemies **b** them in
Isa 21: 2 Go up, O Elam! **B**,
Jer 21: 4 and the Chaldeans who **b** you
21: 9 defects to the Chaldeans who **b**

BESIEGED (22/22) BESIEGE

2 Sam 11: 1 the people of Ammon and **b**
11:16 while Joab **b** the city, that he
20:15 Then they came and **b** him in Abel
1 Ki 16:17 Gibbethon, and they **b** Tirzah.
20: 1 And he went up and **b** Samaria,
2 Ki 6:24 and went up and **b** Samaria.
6:25 and indeed they **b** it until a
16: 5 and they **b** Ahaz but could not
17: 5 and went up to Samaria and **b** it
18: 9 came up against Samaria and **b**
24:10 Jerusalem, and the city was **b**.
25: 2 So the city was **b** until the
1 Chr 20: 1 and came and **b** Rabbah.
Eccl 9:14 **b** it, and built great snares
Isa 1: 8 of cucumbers, As a **b** city.
Jer 32: 2 the king of Babylon's army **b**
39: 1 Jerusalem, and **b** it.
52: 5 So the city was **b** until the
Lam 3: 5 He has **b** me And surrounded me
Ezek 4: 3 against it, and it shall be **b**,
6:12 and he who remains and is **b**
Dan 1: 1 came to Jerusalem and **b** it.

BESIEGES (1/1) BESIEGE

1 Ki 8:37 when their enemy **b** them in the

BESIEGING (2/2) BESIEGE

2 Ki 24:11 as his servants were **b** it.
Jer 37: 5 when the Chaldeans who were **b**

BESODEIAH (1/1)

Neh 3: 6 and Meshullam the son of **B**

BESOM (KJV) See BROOM

BESOR (3/3)

1 Sam 30: 9 him, and came to the Brook **B**,
30:10 could not cross the Brook **B**.
30:21 had made to stay at the Brook **B**.

BEST (49/44)

Gen 43:11 Take some of the **b** fruits of
45:18 I will give you the **b** of the
45:20 for the **b** of all the land of
47: 6 and brothers dwell in the **b** of
47:11 in the **b** of the land, in the
Ex 22: 5 make restitution from the **b** of
22: 5 of his own field and the **b** of
Num 18:12 All the **b** of the oil, all the
18:12 all the **b** of the new wine and
18:29 from all the **b** of them, the
18:30 When you have lifted up the **b** of
18:32 when you have lifted up the **b**
36: 6 them marry whom they think **b**,
Deut 23:16 where it seems **b** to him; you
33:15 With the **b** things of the
Judg 10:15 Do to us whatever seems **b** to
14:20 who had been his **b** man.
Ruth 3: 3 put on your **b** garment and go
1 Sam 1:23 Do what seems **b** to you; wait
2:29 make yourselves fat with the **b**
8:14 And he will take the **b** of your
15: 9 people spared Agag and the **b**
15:15 for the people spared the **b** of
15:21 the **b** of the things which
2 Sam 10: 9 he chose some of Israel's **b** and
18: 4 Whatever seems **b** to you I will
2 Ki 10: 3 choose the **b** qualified of your
1 Chr 19:10 he chose some of Israel's **b** and
Esth 2: 9 and her maidservants to the **b**
Ps 39: 5 Certainly every man at his **b**
Prov 16:28 a whisperer separates the **b** of
Song 7: 9 roof of your mouth like the **b**
Ezek 31:16 the choice and **b** of Lebanon,
44:30 The **b** of all firstfruits of any
48:14 they may not alienate this **b**
Am 6: 6 anoint yourselves with the **b**
Mic 7: 4 The **b** of them is like a brier;
Mt 23: 6 They love the **b** places at
23: 6 the **b** seats in the synagogues,
Mk 12:39 the **b** seats in the synagogues,
12:39 and the **b** places at feasts,
Lk 11:43 Pharisees! For you love the **b**
14: 7 He noted how they chose the **b**
14: 8 do not sit down in the **b** place,
15:22 Bring out the **b** robe and put it
20:46 the **b** seats in the synagogues,
20:46 and the **b** places at feasts,
1 Cor 12:31 But earnestly desire the **b**
Heb 12:10 chastened us as seemed **b** to

BESTOW (5/5) BESTOWED

Ex 32:29 that He may **b** on you a blessing
Deut 21:16 that he must not **b** firstborn
Lk 22:29 And I **b** upon you a kingdom, just
1 Cor 12:23 on these we **b** greater honor;
13: 3 And though I **b** all my goods to

BESTOWED (8/7) BESTOW

1 Chr 29:25 and **b** on him such royal
Esth 6: 3 honor or dignity has been **b** on
Isa 63: 7 to all that the LORD has **b** on
63: 7 Which He has **b** on them
Ezek 16:14 My splendor which I had **b** on
Lk 22:29 just as My Father **b** one upon
2 Cor 8: 1 to you the grace of God **b** on
1 Jn 3: 1 of love the Father has **b** on us,

BETAH (1/1)

2 Sam 8: 8 Also from **B** and from Berothai,

BETEN (1/1)

Josh 19:25 included Helkath, Hali, **B**,

BETH ACACIA (1/1)

Judg 7:22 and the army fled to **B**,

BETH ANATH (3/2)

Josh 19:38 Iron, Migdal El, Horem, **B**,
Judg 1:33 Shemesh or the inhabitants of **B**;
1:33 of Beth Shemesh and **B** were put

BETH ANOTH (1/1)

Josh 15:59 Maarath, **B**, and Eltekon:

BETH APHRAH (1/1)

Mic 1:10 In **B** Roll yourself in the

BETH ARABAH (3/3)

Josh 15: 6 Hoglah and passed north of **B**;
15:61 In the wilderness: **B**,
18:22 **B**, Zemaraim, Bethel,

BETH ARBEL (1/1)

Hos 10:14 As Shalman plundered **B** in the

BETH AVEN (7/7)

Josh 7: 2 to Ai, which is beside **B**,
18:12 it ended at the Wilderness of **B**.
1 Sam 13: 5 in Michmash, to the east of **B**.
14:23 and the battle shifted to **B**.
Hos 4:15 up to Gilgal, Nor go up to **B**,
5: 8 in Ramah! Cry aloud at **B**,
10: 5 fear Because of the calf of **B**.

B

BETH AZMAVETH (1/1)

Neh 7:28 the men of **B**, forty-two;

BETH BAAL MEON (1/1)

Josh 13:17 plain: Dibon, Bamoth Baal, **B**,

BETH BARAH (2/1)

Judg 7:24 the watering places as far as **B**
7:24 the watering places as far as **B**

BETH BIRI (1/1)

1 Chr 4:31 Beth Marcaboth, Hazar Susim, **B**,

BETH CAR (1/1)

1 Sam 7:11 them back as far as below **B**.

BETH DAGON (2/2)

Josh 15:41 **B**, Naamah, and Makkedah:
19:27 turned toward the sunrise to **B**;

BETH DIBLATHAIM (1/1)

Jer 48:22 On Dibon and Nebo and **B**,

BETH EDEN (1/1)

Am 1: 5 who holds the scepter from **B**.

BETH EKED (2/2)

2 Ki 10:12 at **B** of the Shepherds,
10:14 killed them at the well of **B**,

BETH EMEK (1/1)

Josh 19:27 then northward beyond **B** and

BETH EZEL (1/1)

Mic 1:11 **B** mourns; Its place to stand

BETH GADER (1/1)

1 Chr 2:51 and Hareph the father of **B**.

BETH GAMUL (1/1)

Jer 48:23 On Kirjathaim and **B** and Beth

BETH HACCEREM (2/2)

Neh 3:14 leader of the district of **B**,
Jer 6: 1 And set up a signal-fire in **B**;

BETH HAGGAN (1/1)

2 Ki 9:27 this, he fled by the road to **B**.

BETH HARAM (1/1)

Josh 13:27 and in the valley **B**,

BETH HARAN (1/1)

Num 32:36 Beth Nimrah and **B**,

BETH HOGLAH (3/3)

Josh 15: 6 The border went up to **B** and
18:19 along to the north side of **B**;
18:21 their families, were Jericho, **B**,

BETH HORON (14/13)

Josh 10:10 along the road that goes to **B**,
10:11 and were on the descent of **B**,
16: 3 far as the boundary of Lower **B**
16: 5 Ataroth Addar as far as Upper **B**.
18:13 on the south side of Lower **B**.
18:14 the hill that lies before **B**
21:22 and **B** with its common-land:
1 Sam 13:18 turned to the road to **B**,
1 Ki 9:17 Solomon built Gezer, Lower **B**,
1 Chr 6:68 **B** with its common-lands,
7:24 who built Lower and Upper **B** and
2 Chr 8: 5 He built Upper **B** and Lower Beth
8: 5 Upper Beth Horon and Lower **B**,
25:13 of Judah from Samaria to **B**,

BETH JESHIMOTH (3/3)

Josh 12: 3 (the Salt Sea), the road to **B**,
13:20 the slopes of Pisgah, and **B**—
Ezek 25: 9 the glory of the country, **B**,

BETH JESIMOTH (1/1)

Num 33:49 from **B** as far as the Abel

BETH JOAB (1/1)

1 Chr 2:54 Netophathites, Atroth *B*, half of

BETH LEBAOTH (1/1)

Josh 19: 6 *B*, and Sharuhen: thirteen

BETH MAACHAH (4/4)

2 Sam 20:14 tribes of Israel to Abel and *B*
20:15 and besieged him in Abel of *B*;
1 Ki 15:20 He attacked Ijon, Dan, Abel *B*,
2 Ki 15:29 came and took Ijon, Abel *B*,

BETH MARCABOTH (2/2)

Josh 19: 5 Ziklag, *B*, Hazar Susah,
1 Chr 4:31 *B*, Hazar Susim, Beth Biri,

BETH MEON (1/1)

Jer 48:23 Kirjathaim and Beth Gamul and *B*,

BETH MILLO (3/2)

Judg 9: 6 gathered together, all of *B*,
9:20 devour the men of Shechem and *B*;
9:20 the men of Shechem and from *B*

BETH NIMRAH (2/2)

Num 32:36 *B* and Beth Haran, fortified
Josh 13:27 and in the valley Beth Haram, *B*,

BETH PAZZEZ (1/1)

Josh 19:21 En Gannim, En Haddah, and *B*.

BETH PELET (2/2)

Josh 15:27 Hazar Gaddah, Heshmon, *B*,
Neh 11:26 in Jeshua, Moladah, *B*,

BETH PEOR (4/4)

Deut 3:29 stayed in the valley opposite *B*.
4:46 in the valley opposite *B*,
34: 6 in the land of Moab, opposite *B*;
Josh 13:20 *B*,

BETH REHOB (3/3)

Judg 18:28 in the valley that belongs to *B*.
2 Sam 10: 6 and hired the Syrians of *B* and
10: 8 And the Syrians of Zoba, *B*,

BETH SHAN (3/3)

1 Sam 31:10 his body to the wall of *B*.
31:12 of his sons from the wall of *B*;
2 Sam 21:12 them from the street of *B*,

BETH SHEAN (6/5)

Josh 17:11 Manasseh had *B* and its towns
17:16 those who are of *B* and its towns
Judg 1:27 inhabitants of *B* and its villages
1 Ki 4:12 *B*, which is beside Zaretan below
4:12 from *B* to Abel Meholah, as far
1 Chr 7:29 Manasseh were *B* and its towns

BETH SHEMESH (23/21)

Josh 15:10 is Chesalon), went down to *B*,
19:22 to Tabor, Shahazimah, and *B*;
19:38 El, Horem, Beth Anath, and *B*:
21:16 and *B* with its common-land:
Judg 1:33 drive out the inhabitants of *B*
1:33 the inhabitants of *B* and Beth
1 Sam 6: 9 road to its own territory, to *B*,
6:12 straight for the road to *B*,
6:12 after them to the border of *B*.
6:13 Now the people of *B* were
6:14 into the field of Joshua of *B*,
6:15 Then the men of *B* offered burnt
6:18 day in the field of Joshua of *B*.
6:19 Then He struck the men of *B*,
6:20 And the men of *B* said, "Who is
1 Ki 4: 9 in Makaz, Shaalbim, *B*,
2 Ki 14:11 of Judah faced one another at *B*,
14:13 the son of Ahaziah, at *B*;
1 Chr 6:59 and *B* with its common-lands.
2 Chr 25:21 of Judah faced one another at *B*,
25:23 the son of Jehoahaz, at *B*;
28:18 South of Judah, and had taken *B*,
Jer 43:13 break the sacred pillars of *B*

BETH TAPPUAH (1/1)

Josh 15:53 Janum, *B*, Aphekah,

BETH ZUR (4/4)

Josh 15:58 Halhul, *B*, Gedor,
1 Chr 2:45 and Maon was the father of *B*.
2 Chr 11: 7 *B*, Sochoh, Adullam,
Neh 3:16 district of *B*, made repairs

BETH-HACCEREM (KJV) See BETH HACCEREM

BETH-HOGLA (KJV) See BETH HOGLAH

BETH-LEHEM-JUDAH (KJV) See BETHLEHEM (IN JUDAH)

BETH-MEON (KJV) See BETH MEON

BETH-PALET (KJV) See BETH PELET

BETH-RAPHA (1/1) RAPHA

1 Chr 4:12 And Eshton begot *B*,

BETH-SHEAN (KJV) See BETH SHEAN

BETH-SHEMITE (KJV) See BETH SHEMESH

BETHABARA (1/1)

Jn 1:28 These things were done in *B*

BETHANY (11/11)

Mt 21:17 and went out of the city to *B*,
26: 6 And when Jesus was in *B* at the
Mk 11: 1 Jerusalem, to Bethphage and *B*,
11:11 He went out to *B* with the
11:12 when they had come out from *B*,
14: 3 And being in *B* at the house of
Lk 19:29 He came near to Bethphage and *B*,
24:50 He led them out as far as *B*,
Jn 11: 1 man was sick, Lazarus of *B*,
11:18 Now *B* was near Jerusalem, about
12: 1 the Passover, Jesus came to *B*,

BETHARAM (KJV) See BETH HARAM

BETHBIREI (KJV) See BETH BIRI

BETHEL (69/62)

Gen 12: 8 there to the mountain east of *B*,
12: 8 he pitched his tent with *B* on
13: 3 from the South as far as *B*,
13: 3 beginning, between *B* and Ai,
28:19 called the name of that place *B*;
31:13 'I am the God of *B*,
35: 1 go up to *B* and dwell there; and
35: 3 let us arise and go up to *B*;
35: 6 Jacob came to Luz (that is, *B*),
35: 7 there and called the place El *B*,
35: 8 and she was buried below *B*
35:15 where God spoke with him, *B*.
35:16 Then they journeyed from *B*.
Josh 7: 2 Aven, on the east side of *B*,
8: 9 and stayed between *B* and Ai, on
8:12 set them in ambush between *B*
8:17 was not a man left in Ai or *B*
12: 9 king of Ai, which is beside *B*,
12:16 of Makkedah, one; the king of *B*,
16: 1 through the mountains to *B*,
16: 2 then went out from *B* to Luz,
18:13 the side of Luz (which is *B*)
18:22 Beth Arabah, Zemaraim, *B*,
Judg 1:22 Joseph also went up against *B*,
1:23 of Joseph sent men to spy out *B*.
4: 5 of Deborah between Ramah and *B*
20:31 (one of which goes up to *B* and
21:19 in Shiloh, which is north of *B*,
21:19 highway that goes up from *B* to
1 Sam 7:16 year to year on a circuit to *B*,
10: 3 three men going up to God at *B*
13: 2 and in the mountains of *B*,
30:27 to those who were in *B*,
1 Ki 12:29 And he set up one in *B*,
12:32 on the altar. So he did at *B*,
12:32 And at *B* he installed the
12:33 altar which he had made at *B*
13: 1 of God went from Judah to *B* by
13: 4 out against the altar in *B*,
13:10 return by the way he came to *B*.
13:11 Now an old prophet dwelt in *B*,
13:11 of God had done that day in *B*;
13:32 LORD against the altar in *B*,
16:34 In his days Hiel of *B* built
2 Ki 2: 2 the LORD has sent me on to *B*.
2: 2 So they went down to *B*.
2: 3 of the prophets who were at *B*
2:23 he went up from there to *B*;
10:29 golden calves that were at *B*
17:28 Samaria came and dwelt in *B*,
23: 4 and carried their ashes to *B*.
23:15 the altar that was at *B*,
23:17 done against the altar of *B*.
23:19 all the deeds he had done in *B*.
1 Chr 7:28 and dwelling places were *B*
2 Chr 13:19 *B* with its villages, Jeshanah
Ezra 2:28 the men of *B* and Ai, two hundred
Neh 7:32 the men of *B* and Ai, one hundred
11:31 dwelt in Michmash, Aija, and *B*,
Jer 48:13 of Israel was ashamed of *B*,
Hos 10:15 it shall be done to you, O *B*,
12: 4 from Him. He found Him in *B*,
Am 3:14 destruction on the altars of *B*;
4: 4 Come to *B* and transgress, At
5: 5 But do not seek *B*,
5: 5 And *B* shall come to nothing.
5: 6 With no one to quench it in *B*—
7:10 Then Amaziah the priest of *B*
7:13 But never again prophesy at *B*,

BETHELITE (KJV) See (HIEL OF) BETHEL

BETHER (1/1)

Song 2:17 stag Upon the mountains of *B*.

BETHESDA (1/1)

Jn 5: 2 which is called in Hebrew, *B*,

BETHLEHEM (49/47) BETHLEHEMITE

Gen 35:19 way to Ephrath (that is, *B*).
48: 7 the way to Ephrath (that is, *B*).
Josh 19:15 Shimron, Idalah, and *B*:
Judg 12: 8 Ibzan of *B* judged Israel.
12:10 Ibzan died and was buried at *B*.
17: 7 there was a young man from *B*
17: 8 departed from the city of *B* in
17: 9 I am a Levite from *B* in Judah,
19: 1 for himself a concubine from *B*
19: 2 him to her father's house at *B*
19:18 We are passing from *B* in Judah
19:18 I went to *B* in Judah; now I am
Ruth 1: 1 And a certain man of *B*,
1: 2 and Chilion—Ephrathites of *B*,
1:19 them went until they came to *B*.
1:19 when they had come to *B*,
1:22 Now they came to *B* at the
2: 4 Now behold, Boaz came from *B*,
4:11 in Ephrathah and be famous in *B*.
1 Sam 16: 4 the LORD said, and went to *B*.
17:12 the son of that Ephrathite of *B*
17:15 to feed his father's sheep at *B*.
20: 6 me that he might run over to *B*,
20:28 permission of me to go to *B*.
2 Sam 2:32 father's tomb, which was in *B*.
23:14 the Philistines was then in *B*.
23:15 of the water from the well of *B*,
23:16 drew water from the well of *B*
23:24 Elhanan the son of Dodo of *B*,
1 Chr 2:51 Salma the father of *B*,
2:54 The sons of Salma were *B*,
4: 4 of Ephrathah the father of *B*.
11:16 the Philistines was then in *B*.
11:17 of water from the well of *B*,
11:18 drew water from the well of *B*
11:26 Elhanan the son of Dodo of *B*,
2 Chr 11: 6 And he built *B*, Etam, Tekoa,
Ezra 2:21 the people of *B*,
Neh 7:26 the men of *B* and Netophah, one
Jer 41:17 of Chimham, which is near *B*,
Mic 5: 2 *B* Ephrathah, Though you are
Mt 2: 1 Now after Jesus was born in *B* of
2: 5 In *B* of Judea, for thus it is
2: 6 'But you, *B*, in the land
2: 8 And he sent them to *B* and said,
2:16 the male children who were in *B*
Lk 2: 4 of David, which is called *B*,
2:15 Let us now go to *B* and see this
Jn 7:42 of David and from the town of *B*,

BETHLEHEMITE (4/4) BETHLEHEM, LAHMI

1 Sam 16: 1 I am sending you to Jesse the *B*.
16:18 have seen a son of Jesse the *B*,
17:58 son of your servant Jesse the *B*.
2 Sam 21:19 the son of Jaare-Oregim the *B*

BETHPHAGE (3/3)

Mt 21: 1 near Jerusalem, and came to *B*,
Mk 11: 1 to *B* and Bethany, at the Mount
Lk 19:29 when He came near to *B* and

BETHPHELET (KJV) See BETH PELET

BETHSAIDA (7/7)

Mt 11:21 *B*! For if the mighty works
Mk 6:45 Him to the other side, to *B*,
8:22 Then He came to *B*;
Lk 9:10 belonging to the city called *B*.
10:13 *B*! For if the mighty works
Jn 1:44 Now Philip was from *B*,
12:21 who was from *B* of Galilee, and

BETHUEL (10/10) BETHUL

Gen 22:22 Hazo, Pildash, Jidlaph, and *B*.
22:23 And *B* begot Rebekah. These eight
24:15 Rebekah, who was born to *B*,
24:24 him, "I am the daughter of *B*,
24:47 she said, 'The daughter of *B*,
24:50 Then Laban and *B* answered and
25:20 the daughter of *B* the Syrian of
28: 2 to the house of *B* your mother's
28: 5 to Laban the son of *B* the
1 Chr 4:30 *B*, Hormah, Ziklag,

BETHUL (1/1) BETHUEL

Josh 19: 4 Eltolad, *B*, Hormah,

BETIMES (KJV) See EARLY, EARNESTLY, PROMPTLY

BETONIM (1/1)

Josh 13:26 Heshbon to Ramath Mizpah and ***B***,

BETRAY (18/18) BETRAYED, BETRAYER, BETRAYERS, BETRAYING, BETRAYS

1 Chr 12:17 but if to ***b*** me to my enemies,
Isa 16: 3 Do not ***b*** him who escapes.
Mt 24:10 will ***b*** one another, and will
26:16 he sought opportunity to ***b*** Him.
26:21 one of you will ***b*** Me."
26:23 with Me in the dish will ***b*** Me.
Mk 13:12 Now brother will ***b*** brother to
14:10 went to the chief priests to ***b***
14:11 how he might conveniently ***b***
14:18 of you who eats with Me will ***b***
Lk 22: 4 how he might ***b*** Him to them.
22: 6 and sought opportunity to ***b***
Jn 6:64 and who would ***b*** Him.
6:71 for it was he who would ***b*** Him,
12: 4 who would ***b*** Him, said,
13: 2 Simon's son, to ***b*** Him,
13:11 For He knew who would ***b*** Him;
13:21 one of you will ***b*** Me."

BETRAYED (16/16) BETRAY

Mt 10: 4 Iscariot, who also ***b*** Him.
17:22 Son of Man is about to be ***b***
20:18 and the Son of Man will be ***b*** to
26:24 by whom the Son of Man is ***b***!
26:45 and the Son of Man is being ***b***
Mk 3:19 who also ***b*** Him. And they went
9:31 The Son of Man is being ***b*** into
10:33 and the Son of Man will be ***b*** to
14:21 by whom the Son of Man is ***b***!
14:41 the Son of Man is being ***b*** into
Lk 9:44 the Son of Man is about to be ***b***
21:16 You will be ***b*** even by parents
22:22 to that man by whom He is ***b***!"
Jn 18: 2 who ***b*** Him, also knew the place;
18: 5 who ***b*** Him, also stood with
1 Cor 11:23 same night in which He was ***b***

BETRAYER (6/6) BETRAY, BETRAYERS

Mt 26:46 My ***b*** is at hand."
26:48 Now His ***b*** had given them a sign,
27: 3 Then Judas, His ***b***,
Mk 14:42 My ***b*** is at hand."
14:44 Now His ***b*** had given them a
Lk 22:21 the hand of My ***b*** is with Me on

BETRAYERS (1/1) BETRAYER

Acts 7:52 whom you now have become the ***b***

BETRAYING (3/3) BETRAY

Mt 26:25 who was ***b*** Him, answered and
27: 4 I have sinned by ***b*** innocent
Lk 22:48 are you ***b*** the Son of Man with a

BETRAYS (2/2) BETRAY

Mt 26:73 for your speech ***b*** you."
Jn 21:20 who is the one who ***b*** You?"

BETROTH (4/3) BETROTHAL, BETROTHED

Deut 28:30 You shall ***b*** a wife, but another
Hos 2:19 I will ***b*** you to Me forever;
2:19 I will ***b*** you to Me In
2:20 I will ***b*** you to Me in

BETROTHAL (1/1) BETROTH

Jer 2: 2 your youth, The love of your ***b***,

BETROTHED (14/14) BETROTH

Ex 21: 8 who has ***b*** her to himself, then
21: 9 And if he has ***b*** her to his son,
22:16 entices a virgin who is not ***b***,
Lev 19:20 with a woman who is ***b*** to a
Deut 20: 7 what man is there who is ***b***
22:23 woman who is a virgin is ***b***
22:25 But if a man finds a ***b*** young
22:27 and the ***b*** young woman cried
22:28 who is a virgin, who is not ***b***,
2 Sam 3:14 whom I ***b*** to myself for a
Mt 1:18 After His mother Mary was ***b*** to
Lk 1:27 to a virgin ***b*** to a man whose
2: 5 his ***b*** wife, who was with child.
2 Cor 11: 2 For I have ***b*** you to one

BETTER (122/119)

Gen 29:19 It is ***b*** that I give her to you
Ex 10:10 The LORD had ***b*** be with you when
14:12 For it would have been ***b***
Num 14: 3 Would it not be ***b*** for us to
Judg 8: 2 of the grapes of Ephraim ***b***
9: 2 Which is ***b*** for you, that all
11:25 are you any ***b*** than Balak the
15: 2 Is not her younger sister ***b***
18:19 Is it ***b*** for you to be a
Ruth 4:15 who is ***b*** to you than seven
1 Sam 1: 8 Am I not ***b*** to you than ten
14:30 How much ***b*** if the people had
15:22 to obey is ***b*** than sacrifice,
15:28 who is ***b*** than you.
27: 1 There is nothing ***b*** for me
2 Sam 14:32 It would be ***b*** for me to be
17:14 the Archite is ***b*** than the advice
1 Ki 1:47 God make the name of Solomon ***b***
2:32 two men more righteous and ***b***
19: 4 for I am no ***b*** than my
21: 2 it I will give you a vineyard ***b***
2 Ki 5:12 ***b*** than all the waters of
2 Chr 21:13 who were ***b*** than yourself,
Esth 1:19 position to another who is ***b***
Ps 37:16 Is ***b*** than the riches of many
63: 3 Your lovingkindness is ***b*** than
69:31 also shall please the LORD ***b***
84:10 For a day in Your courts is ***b***
118: 8 It is ***b*** to trust in the LORD
118: 9 It is ***b*** to trust in the LORD
119:72 The law of Your mouth is ***b*** to
Prov 3:14 For her proceeds are ***b*** than
8:11 For wisdom is ***b*** than rubies,
8:19 My fruit is ***b*** than gold, yes,
12: 9 ***B*** is the one who is slighted
15:16 ***B*** is a little with the fear of
15:17 ***B*** is a dinner of herbs where
16: 8 ***B*** is a little with
16:16 How much ***b*** to get wisdom than
16:19 ***B*** to be of a humble spirit
16:32 who is slow to anger is ***b***
17: 1 ***B*** is a dry morsel with
19: 1 ***B*** is the poor who walks in his
19:22 And a poor man is ***b*** than a
21: 9 ***B*** to dwell in a corner of a
21:19 ***B*** to dwell in the wilderness,
25: 7 For it is ***b*** that he say to
25:24 It is ***b*** to dwell in a corner
27: 5 Open rebuke is ***b*** Than love
27:10 ***B*** is a neighbor nearby than a
28: 6 ***B*** is the poor who walks in his
Eccl 2:24 Nothing is ***b*** for a man than
3:12 I know that nothing is ***b*** for
3:22 I perceived that nothing is ***b***
4: 3 ***b*** than both is he who has
4: 6 ***B*** a handful with quietness
4: 9 Two are ***b*** than one, Because
4:13 ***B*** a poor and wise youth Than
5: 5 ***B*** not to vow than to vow and
6: 3 that a stillborn child is ***b***
6: 9 ***B*** is the sight of the eyes
6:11 vanity, How is man the ***b***?
7: 1 A good name is ***b*** than precious
7: 2 ***B*** to go to the house of
7: 3 Sorrow is ***b*** than laughter,
7: 3 countenance the heart is made ***b***.
7: 5 It is ***b*** to hear the rebuke of
7: 8 The end of a thing is ***b*** than
7: 8 The patient in spirit is ***b***
7:10 Why were the former days ***b*** than
8:15 because a man has nothing ***b***
9: 4 for a living dog is ***b*** than a
9:16 Wisdom is ***b*** than strength.
9:18 Wisdom is ***b*** than weapons of
Song 1: 2 For your love is ***b*** than wine.
4:10 my spouse! How much ***b*** than
Isa 56: 5 My walls a place and a name ***B***
Lam 4: 9 slain by the sword are ***b*** off
Ezek 15: 2 how is the wood of the vine ***b***
36:11 and do ***b*** for you than at your
Dan 1:15 days their features appeared ***b***
1:20 he found them ten times ***b*** than
Hos 2: 7 For then it was ***b*** for me
Am 6: 2 Are you ***b*** than these
Jon 4: 3 for it is ***b*** for me to die
4: 8 It is ***b*** for me to die than to
Nah 3: 8 Are you ***b*** than No Amon That
Mt 18: 6 it would be ***b*** for him if a
18: 8 It is ***b*** for you to enter into
18: 9 It is ***b*** for you to enter into
19:10 it is ***b*** not to marry."
Mk 5:26 all that she had and was no ***b***,
9:42 it would be ***b*** for him if a
9:43 It is ***b*** for you to enter into
9:45 It is ***b*** for you to enter life
9:47 It is ***b*** for you to enter the
Lk 5:39 new; for he says, 'The old is ***b***.
17: 2 It would be ***b*** for him if a
Jn 4:52 of them the hour when he got ***b***.
Rom 3: 9 Are we ***b*** than they? Not at
1 Cor 7: 9 For it is ***b*** to marry than to
7:38 give her in marriage does ***b***.
8: 8 neither if we eat are we the ***b***,
9:15 for it would be ***b*** for me to
11:17 you come together not for the ***b***
Phil 1:23 with Christ, which is far ***b***.
2: 3 mind let each esteem others ***b***
Heb 1: 4 having become so much ***b*** than the
6: 9 we are confident of ***b*** things
7: 7 the lesser is blessed by the ***b***.
7:19 bringing in of a ***b*** hope
7:22 a surety of a ***b*** covenant.
8: 6 as He is also Mediator of a ***b***
8: 6 was established on ***b*** promises.
9:23 themselves with ***b*** sacrifices
10:34 ***b*** and enduring possession
11:16 But now they desire a ***b***,
11:35 might obtain a ***b*** resurrection.
11:40 God having provided something ***b***
12:24 of sprinkling that speaks ***b***
1 Pe 3:17 For it is ***b***, if it is the will
2 Pe 2:21 it would have been ***b*** for them

BETWEEN (230/209)

Gen 3:15 And I will put enmity ***B*** you
3:15 And ***b*** your seed and her Seed;
9:12 of the covenant which I make ***b***
9:13 for the sign of the covenant ***b***
9:15 My covenant which is ***b*** Me and
9:16 the everlasting covenant ***b*** God
9:17 which I have established ***b*** Me
10:12 and Resen ***b*** Nineveh and Calah
13: 3 beginning, ***b*** Bethel and Ai,
13: 7 And there was strife ***b*** the
13: 8 let there be no strife ***b*** you
13: 8 and ***b*** my herdsmen and your
15:17 a burning torch that passed ***b***
16: 5 The LORD judge ***b*** you and me."
16:14 it is ***b*** Kadesh and Bered.
17: 2 And I will make My covenant ***b*** Me
17: 7 I will establish My covenant ***b***
17:10 ***b*** Me and you and your
17:11 be a sign of the covenant ***b*** Me
20: 1 and dwelt ***b*** Kadesh and Shur,
23:15 What is that ***b*** you and me?
26:28 Let there now be an oath ***b*** us,
26:28 ***b*** you and us; and let us make a
30:36 he put three days' journey ***b***
31:37 that they may judge ***b*** us both!
31:44 and let it be a witness ***b*** you
31:48 This heap is a witness ***b*** you
31:49 May the LORD watch ***b*** you and me
31:50 God is witness ***b*** you and me!"
31:51 which I have placed ***b*** you and
31:53 God of their father judge ***b*** us.
32:16 and put some distance ***b***
49:10 Nor a lawgiver from ***b*** his
49:14 Lying down ***b*** two burdens;
Ex 8:23 I will make a difference ***b*** My
9: 4 LORD will make a difference ***b***
11: 7 LORD does make a difference ***b***
13: 9 your hand and as a memorial ***b***
13:16 on your hand and as frontlets ***b***
14: 2 ***b*** Migdol and the sea, opposite
14:20 So it came ***b*** the camp of the
16: 1 which is ***b*** Elim and Sinai, on
18:16 and I judge ***b*** one and another;
22:11 an oath of the LORD shall be ***b***
25:22 from ***b*** the two cherubim which
26:33 shall be a divider for you ***b***
28:33 and bells of gold ***b*** them all
30:18 You shall put it ***b*** the
31:13 for it is a sign ***b*** Me and you
31:17 It is a sign ***b*** Me and the
39:25 and put the bells ***b*** the
39:25 hem of the robe all around ***b***
40: 7 And you shall set the laver ***b***
40:30 He set the laver ***b*** the
Lev 10:10 that you may distinguish ***b*** holy
10:10 and ***b*** unclean and clean,
11:47 to distinguish ***b*** the unclean and
11:47 and ***b*** the animal that may be
20:25 shall therefore distinguish ***b***
20:25 ***b*** unclean birds and clean, and
26:46 and laws which the LORD made ***b***
Num 7:89 from ***b*** the two cherubim; thus
11:33 But while the meat was still ***b***
13:23 they carried it ***b*** two of them
16:48 And he stood ***b*** the dead and the
21:13 ***b*** Moab and the Amorites.
22:24 LORD stood in a narrow path ***b***
26:56 inheritance shall be divided ***b***
30:16 ***b*** a man and his wife, and
30:16 and ***b*** a father and his daughter
31:27 ***b*** those who took part in the
35:24 the congregation shall judge ***b***
Deut 1: 1 ***b*** Paran, Tophel, Laban,
1:16 Hear the cases ***b*** your
1:16 and judge righteously ***b*** a man
5: 5 I stood ***b*** the LORD and you at
6: 8 they shall be as frontlets ***b***
11:18 they shall be as frontlets ***b***
17: 8 ***b*** degrees of guilt for
17: 8 ***b*** one judgment or another, or
17: 8 or ***b*** one punishment or another,
25: 1 If there is a dispute ***b*** men, and
28:57 which comes out from ***b*** her
33:12 And he shall dwell ***b*** His
Josh 3: 4 Yet there shall be a space ***b*** you
8: 9 and stayed ***b*** Bethel and Ai, on
8:11 Now a valley lay ***b*** them and
8:12 men and set them in ambush ***b***
18:11 of their lot came out ***b*** the
22:25 has made the Jordan a border ***b***
22:27 that it may be a witness ***b***
22:28 but it is a witness ***b*** you and
22:34 For it is a witness ***b*** us that
24: 7 and He put darkness ***b*** you and
Judg 4: 5 the palm tree of Deborah ***b***
4:17 for there was peace ***b*** Jabin
9:23 God sent a spirit of ill will ***b***
11:10 The LORD will be a witness ***b***
11:27 render judgment this day ***b*** the
13:25 move upon him at Mahaneh Dan ***b***
15: 4 and put a torch ***b*** each pair of
16:25 And they stationed him ***b*** the
16:31 him up and buried him ***b*** Zorah
20:38 Now the appointed signal ***b*** the
1 Sam 4: 4 who dwells ***b*** the cherubim.
7:12 took a stone and set it up ***b***
7:14 Also there was peace ***b*** Israel
14: 4 ***B*** the passes, by which Jonathan
14:42 Cast lots ***b*** my son Jonathan and
17: 1 they encamped ***b*** Sochoh and

17: 3 with a valley **b** them.
17: 6 his legs and a bronze javelin **b**
20: 3 there is but a step **b** me and
20:23 indeed the LORD be **b** you and
20:42 May the LORD be **b** you and me,
20:42 and **b** your descendants and my
24:12 Let the LORD judge **b** you and
24:15 and judge **b** you and me, and see
26:13 a great distance being **b** them.
2 Sam 3: 1 Now there was a long war **b** the
3: 6 while there was war **b** the house
6: 2 who dwells **b** the cherubim.
18: 9 so he was left hanging **b** heaven
18:24 Now David was sitting **b** the two
19:35 Can I discern **b** the good and
21: 7 of the LORD's oath that was **b**
21: 7 **b** David and Jonathan the son of
1 Ki 3: 9 that I may discern **b** good and
5:12 and there was peace **b** Hiram and
7:28 and the panels were **b** frames;
7:29 on the panels that were **b** the
7:46 **b** Succoth and Zaretan.
14:30 And there was war **b** Rehoboam and
15: 6 And there was war **b** Rehoboam and
15: 7 And there was war **b** Abijam and
15:16 Now there was war **b** Asa and
15:19 Let there be a treaty **b** you
15:19 as there was **b** my father and
15:32 And there was war **b** Asa and
18: 6 So they divided the land **b** them
18:21 How long will you falter **b** two
18:42 and put his face **b** his knees,
22: 1 years passed without war **b**
22:34 and struck the king of Israel **b**
2 Ki 9:24 strength and shot Jehoram **b**
11:17 Jehoiada made a covenant **b** the
11:17 and also **b** the king and the
16:14 from **b** the new altar and the
19:15 the One who dwells **b** the
25: 4 at night by way of the gate **b**
1 Chr 13: 6 who dwells **b** the cherubim,
21:16 angel of the LORD standing **b**
2 Chr 4:17 **b** Succoth and Zeredah.
12:15 And there were wars **b**
13: 2 And there was war **b** Abijah and
16: 3 Let there be a treaty **b** you
16: 3 as there was **b** my father and
18:33 and struck the king of Israel **b**
23:16 Jehoiada made a covenant **b**
Neh 3:32 And **b** the upper room at the
Job 9:33 Nor is there any mediator **b** us,
41:16 That no air can come **b** them;
Ps 80: 1 You who dwell **b** the cherubim,
99: 1 peoples tremble! He dwells **b**
Song 1:13 That lies all night **b** my
Isa 2: 4 He shall judge **b** the nations,
5: 3 **b** Me and My vineyard.
22:11 You also made a reservoir **b** the
37:16 the One who dwells **b** the
Jer 7: 5 thoroughly execute judgment **b**
34:18 the calf in two and passed **b**
34:19 of the land who passed **b** the
39: 4 by the gate **b** the two walls.
42: 5 a true and faithful witness **b**
52: 7 at night by way of the gate **b**
Ezek 4: 3 and set it as an iron wall **b**
8: 3 and the Spirit lifted me up **b**
8:16 **b** the porch and the altar,
18: 8 And executed true judgment **b**
20:12 to be a sign **b** them and Me,
20:20 and they will be a sign **b** Me
22:26 they have not distinguished **b**
22:26 made known the difference **b**
34:17 I shall judge **b** sheep and
34:17 **b** rams and goats.
34:20 I Myself will judge **b** the fat
34:22 and I will judge **b** sheep and
40: 7 **b** the gate chambers was a
41:10 And **b** it and the wall
41:18 a palm tree **b** cherub and
43: 8 with a wall **b** them and Me, they
44:23 My people the difference **b**
44:23 and cause them to discern **b** the
47:16 Sibraim (which is **b** the border
47:18 mark out the border from **b**
47:18 and **b** Gilead and the land of
48:22 the area **b** the border of
Dan 7: 5 had three ribs in its mouth **b**
8: 5 the goat had a notable horn **b**
8:16 And I heard a man's voice **b** the
8:21 The large horn that is **b** its
11:45 the tents of his palace **b** the
Hos 2: 2 And her adulteries from **b** her
Joel 2: 8 Though they lunge **b** the
2:17 Weep **b** the porch and the
Jon 4:11 persons who cannot discern **b**
Mic 4: 3 He shall judge **b** many peoples,
Zech 5: 9 and they lifted up the basket **b**
6: 1 chariots were coming from **b**
6:13 the counsel of peace shall be **b**
9: 7 And the abominations from **b**
11:14 I might break the brotherhood **b**
13: 6 What are these wounds **b** your
Mal 2:14 the LORD has been witness **B**
3:18 you shall again discern **B** the
3:18 **B** one who serves God And one
Mt 18:15 go and tell him his fault **b** you
23:35 whom you murdered **b** the temple
Lk 11:51 of Zechariah who perished **b**
16:26 **b** us and you there is a great
Jn 3:25 Then there arose a dispute **b**
Acts 12: 6 bound with two chains **b** two
15: 9 and made no distinction **b** us and
23: 7 a dissension arose **b** the
Rom 2:15 and **b** themselves their
10:12 For there is no distinction **b**
1 Cor 6: 5 who will be able to judge **b** his
7:34 There is a difference **b** a wife
Phil 1:23 For I am hard pressed **b** the two,
1 Tim 2: 5 is one God and one Mediator **b**

BEULAH (1/1)

Isa 62: 4 Hephzibah, and your land ***B***;

BEVELED (5/5)

1 Ki 6: 4 for the house windows with **b**
7: 4 There were windows with **b**
Ezek 40:16 There were **b** window frames in
41:16 their doorposts and the **b** window
41:26 There were **b** window frames

BEVERAGE (1/1)

Song 7: 2 goblet; It lacks no blended **b**.

BEWAIL (3/3) BEWAILED, BEWAILING

Lev 10: 6 **b** the burning which the LORD
Judg 11:37 wander on the mountains and **b**
Isa 16: 9 Therefore I will **b** the vine of

BEWAILED (1/1) BEWAIL

Judg 11:38 and **b** her virginity on the

BEWAILING (1/1) BEWAIL

Jer 4:31 voice of the daughter of Zion **b**

BEWARE (30/28)

Gen 24: 6 **B** that you do not take my son
Ex 10:10 you and your little ones go! **B**,
23:21 **B** of Him and obey His voice; do
Deut 6:12 then **b**, lest you forget
8:11 **B** that you do not forget the
15: 9 **B** lest there be a wicked thought
2 Sam 18:12 **B** lest anyone touch the young
2 Ki 6: 9 **B** that you do not pass this
Job 36:18 **b** lest He take you away with
Isa 36:18 **B** lest Hezekiah persuade you,
Mt 7:15 **B** of false prophets, who come
10:17 But **b** of men, for they will
16: 6 Take heed and **b** of the leaven of
16:11 but to **b** of the leaven of the
16:12 He did not tell them to **b** of
Mk 8:15 **b** of the leaven of the
12:38 **B** of the scribes, who desire to
Lk 12: 1 **B** of the leaven of the
12:15 Take heed and **b** of covetousness,
20:46 **B** of the scribes, who desire to
Acts 13:40 **B** therefore, lest what has been
1 Cor 8: 9 But **b** lest somehow this liberty
Gal 5:15 **b** lest you be consumed by one
Phil 3: 2 **B** of dogs, beware of evil
3: 2 **b** of evil workers, beware of
3: 2 **b** of the mutilation!
Col 2: 8 **B** lest anyone cheat you through
2 Tim 4:15 You also must **b** of him, for he
Heb 3:12 **B**, brethren, lest there be
2 Pe 3:17 **b** lest you also fall from your

BEWILDERED (1/1)

Ex 14: 3 They are **b** by the land; the

BEWITCHED (1/1)

Gal 3: 1 O foolish Galatians! Who has **b**

BEWRAY (KJV) See BETRAY

BEYOND (83/80)

Gen 31:52 that I will not pass **b** this
31:52 and you will not pass **b** this
35:21 and pitched his tent **b** the
50:10 which is **b** the Jordan, and
50:11 which is **b** the Jordan.
Lev 15:25 or if it runs **b** her usual
Num 22:18 I could not go **b** the word of
24:13 I could not go **b** the word of
32:19 other side of the Jordan and **b**,
Deut 2: 8 And when we passed **b** our
3:20 your God is giving them **b** the
3:25 over and see the good land **b**
30:13 Nor is it **b** the sea, that you
Josh 9:10 of the Amorites who were **b**
13: 8 **b** the Jordan eastward, as Moses
18: 7 received their inheritance **b**
19:27 then northward **b** Beth Emek and
19:47 of the children of Dan went **b**
Judg 3:26 and passed **b** the stone images
5:17 Gilead stayed **b** the Jordan,
1 Sam 20:22 the arrows are **b** you'—go your
20:36 he shot an arrow **b** him.
20:37 Is not the arrow **b** you?"
2 Sam 10:16 out the Syrians who were **b**
1 Ki 14:15 and will scatter them **b** the
2 Ki 25:16 of all these articles was **b**
1 Chr 19:16 brought the Syrians who were **b**
22: 3 and bronze in abundance **b**
22:14 and bronze and iron **b** measure,
2 Chr 20: 2 is coming against you from **b**
Ezra 4:10 of Samaria and the remainder **b**
4:11 the men of the region **b** the
4:16 you will have no dominion **b**
4:17 and to the remainder **b** the
4:20 ruled over all the region **b**
5: 3 the governor of the region **b**
5: 6 The governor of the region **b**
5: 6 who were in the region **b**
6: 6 governor of the region **b** the
6: 6 the Persians who are **b** the
6: 8 from taxes on the region **b**
6:13 governor of the region **b** the
7:21 who are in the region **b**
7:25 who are in the region **b**
8:36 governors in the region **b**
Neh 2: 7 governors of the region **b**
2: 9 governors in the region **b**
3: 7 the governor of the region **b**
3:28 **B** the Horse Gate the priests
12:37 **b** the house of David, as far as
Isa 5:14 itself And opened its mouth **b**
7:20 With those from **b** the River,
9: 1 **b** the Jordan, In Galilee of
18: 1 Which is **b** the rivers of
33:19 **b** perception, Of a stammering
Jer 2:10 For pass **b** the coasts of Cyprus
5:22 that it cannot pass **b** it?
22:19 Dragged and cast out **b** the
52:20 of all these articles was **b**
Ezek 41: 4 **b** the sanctuary; and he said to
Am 5:27 will send you into captivity **b**
Zeph 3:10 From **b** the rivers of Ethiopia
Mal 1: 5 The LORD is magnified **b** the
Mt 4:15 **b** the Jordan, Galilee of
4:25 Judea, and **b** the Jordan.
19: 1 came to the region of Judea **b**
Mk 3: 8 and Jerusalem and Idumea and **b**
6:51 greatly amazed in themselves **b**
7:37 And they were astonished **b**
Jn 1:28 were done in Bethabara **b** the
3:26 He who was with you **b** the
10:40 And He went away again **b** the
Acts 7:43 I will carry you away **b**
1 Cor 4: 6 may learn in us not to think **b**
10:13 not allow you to be tempted **b**
2 Cor 1: 8 that we were burdened **b**
8: 3 and **b** their ability, they
10:13 will not boast **b** measure, but
10:15 not boasting of things **b**
10:16 the gospel in the regions **b**
Gal 1:13 persecuted the church of God **b**
1:14 And I advanced in Judaism **b** many
Heb 7: 7 Now **b** all contradiction the

BEZAI (3/3)

Ezra 2:17 the people of ***B***,
Neh 7:23 the sons of ***B***, three
10:18 Hodijah, Hashum, ***B***,

BEZALEL (9/9)

Ex 31: 2 I have called by name ***B*** the son
35:30 the LORD has called by name ***B***
36: 1 And ***B*** and Aholiab, and every
36: 2 Then Moses called ***B*** and
37: 1 Then ***B*** made the ark of acacia
38:22 ***B*** the son of Uri, the son of
1 Chr 2:20 Hur begot Uri, and Uri begot ***B***.
2 Chr 1: 5 Now the bronze altar that ***B*** the
Ezra 10:30 Benaiah, Maaseiah, Mattaniah, ***B***,

BEZEK (3/3) ADONI-BEZEK

Judg 1: 4 killed ten thousand men at ***B***.
1: 5 And they found Adoni-Bezek in ***B***,
1 Sam 11: 8 When he numbered them in ***B***,

BEZER (5/5)

Deut 4:43 ***B*** in the wilderness on the
Josh 20: 8 they assigned ***B*** in the
21:36 ***B*** with its common-land, Jahaz
1 Chr 6:78 ***B*** in the wilderness with its
7:37 ***B***, Hod, Shamma, Shilshah,

BICHRI (8/8)

2 Sam 20: 1 name was Sheba the son of ***B***,
20: 2 followed Sheba the son of ***B***.
20: 6 Now Sheba the son of ***B*** will do
20: 7 to pursue Sheba the son of ***B***.
20:10 pursued Sheba the son of ***B***.
20:13 to pursue Sheba the son of ***B***.
20:21 Sheba the son of ***B*** by name, has
20:22 the head of Sheba the son of ***B***,

BID (1/1)

Lk 9:61 but let me first go and **b** them

BIDDEN, BIDDETH (KJV) See GREETS, INVITED

BIDDING (1/1) BID

1 Sam 22:14 son-in-law, who goes at your **b**,

BIDKAR (1/1)

2 Ki 9:25 Then Jehu said to ***B*** his

BIG (9/9)
Ex 29:20 their right hand and on the ***b***
Lev 8:23 and on the ***b*** toe of his right
8:24 and on the ***b*** toes of their
14:14 and on the ***b*** toe of his right
14:17 and on the ***b*** toe of his right
14:25 and on the ***b*** toe of his right
14:28 and on the ***b*** toe of his right
Judg 1: 6 and cut off his thumbs and ***b***
1: 7 kings with their thumbs and ***b***

BIGTHA (1/1)
Esth 1:10 Mehuman, Biztha, Harbona, ***B***,

BIGTHAN (1/1) BIGTHANA
Esth 2:21 ***B*** and Teresh, doorkeepers,

BIGTHANA (1/1) BIGTHAN
Esth 6: 2 that Mordecai had told of ***B***

BIGVAI (6/6)
Ezra 2: 2 Mordecai, Bilshan, Mispar, ***B***,
2:14 the people of ***B***,
8:14 also of the sons of ***B***,
Neh 7: 7 Mordecai, Bilshan, Mispereth, ***B***,
7:19 the sons of ***B***, two thousand
10:16 Adonijah, ***B***, Adin,

BILDAD (5/5)
Job 2:11 ***B*** the Shuhite, and Zophar the
8: 1 Then ***B*** the Shuhite answered and
18: 1 Then ***B*** the Shuhite answered and
25: 1 Then ***B*** the Shuhite answered and
42: 9 So Eliphaz the Temanite and ***B***

BILE (1/1)
Lam 2:11 My ***b*** is poured on the ground

BILEAM (1/1) IBLEAM
1 Chr 6:70 with its common-lands and ***B***

BILGAH (3/3)
1 Chr 24:14 the fifteenth to ***B***,
Neh 12: 5 Mijamin, Maadiah, ***B***,
12:18 of ***B***, Shammua; of Shemaiah,

BILGAI (1/1)
Neh 10: 8 Maaziah, ***B***, and Shemaiah.

BILHAH (11/11) BAALAH
Gen 29:29 And Laban gave his maid ***B*** to his
30: 3 she said, "Here is my maid ***B***;
30: 4 Then she gave him ***B*** her maid as
30: 5 And ***B*** conceived and bore Jacob a
30: 7 And Rachel's maid ***B*** conceived
35:22 Reuben went and lay with ***B*** his
35:25 the sons of ***B***, Rachel's
37: 2 the lad was with the sons of ***B***
46:25 These were the sons of ***B***,
1 Chr 4:29 ***B***, Ezem, Tolad,
7:13 and Shallum, the sons of ***B***.

BILHAN (4/3)
Gen 36:27 These were the sons of Ezer: ***B***,
1 Chr 1:42 The sons of Ezer were ***B***,
7:10 The son of Jediael was ***B***,
7:10 and the sons of ***B*** were Jeush,

BILL (2/2)
Lk 16: 6 So he said to him, 'Take your ***b***,
16: 7 he said to him, 'Take your ***b***,

BILLOWS (2/2)
Ps 42: 7 All Your waves and ***b*** have gone
Jon 2: 3 All Your ***b*** and Your waves

BILSHAN (2/2)
Ezra 2: 2 Seraiah, Reelaiah, Mordecai, ***B***,
Neh 7: 7 Raamiah, Nahamani, Mordecai, ***B***,

BIMHAL (1/1)
1 Chr 7:33 sons of Japhlet were Pasach, ***B***,

BIN (3/3)
1 Ki 17:12 only a handful of flour in a ***b***,
17:14 The ***b*** of flour shall not be used
17:16 The ***b*** of flour was not used up,

BIND (37/37) BINDING, BINDS, BOUND
Ex 28:28 They shall ***b*** the breastplate by
Num 30: 2 or swears an oath to ***b*** himself
30:14 or all the agreements that ***b***
Deut 6: 8 You shall ***b*** them as a sign on
11:18 and ***b*** them as a sign on your
Josh 2:18 you ***b*** this line of scarlet cord
Judg 16: 5 that we may ***b*** him to afflict
16: 7 If they ***b*** me with seven fresh
16:11 If they ***b*** me securely with new
Job 31:36 And ***b*** it on me like a crown;
38:31 Can you ***b*** the cluster of the
39:10 Can you ***b*** the wild ox in the
40:13 ***B*** their faces in hidden
Ps 105:22 To ***b*** his princes at his
118:27 ***B*** the sacrifice with cords to
149: 8 To ***b*** their kings with chains,
Prov 3: 3 ***B*** them around your neck,
6:21 ***B*** them continually upon your
7: 3 ***B*** them on your fingers
Isa 8:16 ***B*** up the testimony, Seal the
49:18 And ***b*** them on you as a bride
Ezek 3:25 will put ropes on you and ***b***
5: 3 a small number of them and ***b***
24:17 ***b*** your turban on your head, and
30:21 nor a splint put on to ***b*** it, to
34:16 ***b*** up the broken and strengthen
Dan 3:20 who were in his army to ***b***
Hos 6: 1 but He will ***b*** us up.
10:10 against them When I ***b*** them
Mt 13:30 together the tares and ***b*** them
16:19 and whatever you ***b*** on earth
18:18 whatever you ***b*** on earth will be
22:13 ***B*** him hand and foot, take him
23: 4 For they ***b*** heavy burdens, hard
Mk 5: 3 and no one could ***b*** him, not
Acts 9:14 from the chief priests to ***b***
21:11 shall the Jews at Jerusalem ***b***

BINDING (10/10) BIND
Gen 37: 7 ***b*** sheaves in the field.
49:11 ***B*** his donkey to the vine, And
Ex 26:17 shall be in each board for ***b***
28:32 it shall have a woven ***b*** all
36:22 board had two tenons for ***b*** one
39:23 with a woven ***b*** all around the
Num 30:12 or concerning the agreement ***b***
30:13 Every vow and every ***b*** oath to
Ps 56:12 Vows made to You are ***b*** upon
Acts 22: 4 ***b*** and delivering into prisons

BINDS (12/12) BIND
Num 30: 3 and ***b*** herself by some
Job 5:18 but He ***b*** up; He wounds, but
12:18 And ***b*** their waist with a belt.
26: 8 He ***b*** up the water in His thick
30:18 It ***b*** me about as the collar of
36:13 do not cry for help when He ***b***
Ps 129: 7 Nor he who ***b*** sheaves, his
147: 3 heals the brokenhearted And ***b***
Prov 26: 8 Like one who ***b*** a stone in a
Isa 30:26 In the day that the LORD ***b*** up
Mt 12:29 unless he first ***b*** the strong
Mk 3:27 unless he first ***b*** the strong

BINEA (2/2)
1 Chr 8:37 Moza begot ***B***, Raphah his son,
9:43 Moza begot ***B***, Rephaiah his son,

BINNUI (7/7)
Ezra 8:33 Jeshua and Noadiah the son of ***B***,
10:30 Maaseiah, Mattaniah, Bezalel, ***B***,
10:38 Bani, ***B***, Shimei,
Neh 3:24 After him ***B*** the son of Henadad
7:15 the sons of ***B***, six hundred
10: 9 ***B*** of the sons of Henadad, and
12: 8 the Levites were Jeshua, ***B***,

BIRD (44/38) BIRD'S, BIRDS, BIRDS'
Gen 1:21 and every winged ***b*** according to
1:30 to every ***b*** of the air, and to
2:19 beast of the field and every ***b***
7:14 and every ***b*** after its kind,
7:14 every ***b*** of every sort.
7:23 creeping thing and ***b*** of the
8:19 every creeping thing, every ***b***,
8:20 animal and of every clean ***b***,
9: 2 on every ***b*** of the air, on all
Lev 7:26 whether of ***b*** or beast.
14: 6 "As for the living ***b***,
14: 6 and dip them and the living ***b***
14: 6 bird in the blood of the ***b***
14: 7 and shall let the living ***b***
14:51 the scarlet, and the living ***b***,
14:51 in the blood of the slain ***b***
14:52 house with the blood of the ***b***
14:52 running water and the living ***b***,
14:53 he shall let the living ***b***
17:13 and catches any animal or ***b***
20:25 abominable by beast or by ***b***,
Deut 4:17 or the likeness of any winged ***b***
Job 28: 7 That path no ***b*** knows, Nor has
41: 5 you play with him as with a ***b***,
Ps 11: 1 Flee as a ***b*** to your mountain"?
124: 7 Our soul has escaped as a ***b***
Prov 1:17 spread In the sight of any ***b***;
6: 5 And like a ***b*** from the hand of
7:23 As a ***b*** hastens to the snare,
27: 8 Like a ***b*** that wanders from its
Eccl 10:20 For a ***b*** of the air may carry
10:20 And a ***b*** in flight may tell the
12: 4 rises up at the sound of a ***b***,
Isa 16: 2 it shall be as a wandering ***b***
46:11 Calling a ***b*** of prey from the
Lam 3:52 cause Hunted me down like a ***b***.
Ezek 39:17 Speak to every sort of ***b*** and to
44:31 ***b*** or beast, that died naturally
Dan 7: 6 on its back four wings of a ***b***.
Hos 9:11 glory shall fly away like a ***b***—
11:11 shall come trembling like a ***b***
Am 3: 5 Will a ***b*** fall into a snare on
Jas 3: 7 For every kind of beast and ***b***,
Rev 18: 2 for every unclean and hated ***b***!

BIRD'S (1/1) BIRD
Deut 22: 6 If a ***b*** nest happens to be

BIRDS (87/85) BIRD, BIRDS'
Gen 1:20 and let ***b*** fly above the earth
1:22 and let ***b*** multiply on the
1:26 over the ***b*** of the air, and over
1:28 over the ***b*** of the air, and over
2:20 to the ***b*** of the air, and to
6: 7 creeping thing and ***b*** of the
6:20 Of the ***b*** after their kind, of
7: 3 also seven each of ***b*** of the air,
7: 8 animals that are unclean, of ***b***,
7:21 ***b*** and cattle and beasts and
8:17 ***b*** and cattle and every creeping
9:10 that is with you: the ***b***,
15:10 but he did not cut the ***b*** in
40:17 and the ***b*** ate them out of the
40:19 and the ***b*** will eat your flesh
Lev 1:14 offering to the LORD is of ***b***,
11:13 as an abomination among the ***b***;
11:46 law of the animals and the ***b***
14: 4 two living and clean ***b***,
14: 5 command that one of the ***b*** be
14:49 to cleanse the house, two ***b***,
14:50 he shall kill one of the ***b*** in
20:25 between unclean ***b*** and clean,
Deut 14:11 All clean ***b*** you may eat.
14:20 "You may eat all clean ***b***.
28:26 shall be food for all the ***b*** of
1 Sam 17:44 I will give your flesh to the ***b***
17:46 of the Philistines to the ***b*** of
2 Sam 21:10 And she did not allow the ***b*** of
1 Ki 4:33 he spoke also of animals, of ***b***,
14:11 and the ***b*** of the air shall eat
16: 4 and the ***b*** of the air shall eat
21:24 and the ***b*** of the air shall eat
Job 12: 7 And the ***b*** of the air, and they
28:21 And concealed from the ***b*** of
35:11 And makes us wiser than the ***b***
Ps 8: 8 The ***b*** of the air, And the fish
50:11 I know all the ***b*** of the
79: 2 have given as food for the ***b***
104:12 By them the ***b*** of the heavens
104:17 Where the ***b*** make their nests;
Eccl 9:12 Like ***b*** caught in a snare, So
Isa 18: 6 together for the mountain ***b*** of
18: 6 The ***b*** of prey will summer on
31: 5 Like ***b*** flying about, So will
Jer 4:25 And all the ***b*** of the heavens
5:27 As a cage is full of ***b***,
7:33 people will be food for the ***b***
9:10 Both the ***b*** of the heavens and
12: 4 The beasts and ***b*** are consumed,
15: 3 the ***b*** of the heavens and the
16: 4 shall be meat for the ***b*** of
19: 7 I will give as meat for the ***b***
34:20 shall be for meat for the ***b*** of
Ezek 13:20 you hunt souls there like ***b***.
13:20 go, the souls you hunt like ***b***.
17:23 Under it will dwell ***b*** of every
29: 5 of the field And to the ***b*** of
31: 6 All the ***b*** of the heavens made
31:13 its ruin will remain all the ***b***
32: 4 to settle on you all the ***b*** of
38:20 the ***b*** of the heavens, the
39: 4 I will give you to ***b*** of prey of
Dan 2:38 beasts of the field and the ***b***
4:12 The ***b*** of the heavens dwelt in
4:14 And the ***b*** from its branches.
4:21 and in whose branches the ***b*** of
Hos 2:18 With the ***b*** of the air, And
4: 3 beasts of the field And the ***b***
7:12 I will bring them down like ***b***
Zeph 1: 3 I will consume the ***b*** of the
Mt 6:26 Look at the ***b*** of the air, for
8:20 Foxes have holes and ***b*** of the
13: 4 and the ***b*** came and devoured
13:32 so that the ***b*** of the air come
Mk 4: 4 and the ***b*** of the air came and
4:32 so that the ***b*** of the air may
Lk 8: 5 and the ***b*** of the air devoured
9:58 Foxes have holes and ***b*** of the
12:24 more value are you than the ***b***?
13:19 and the ***b*** of the air nested in
Acts 10:12 and ***b*** of the air.
11: 6 things, and ***b*** of the air.
Rom 1:23 and ***b*** and four-footed animals
1 Cor 15:39 of fish, and another of ***b***.
Rev 19:17 saying to all the ***b*** that fly in
19:21 And all the ***b*** were filled with

BIRDS' (1/1) BIRDS
Dan 4:33 feathers and his nails like ***b***

BIRSHA (1/1)
Gen 14: 2 ***B*** king of Gomorrah, Shinab king

BIRTH (48/46) BIRTHDAY, BIRTHRIGHT, BIRTHSTOOLS, BORN, CHILDBIRTH

Gen 25:24 fulfilled for her to give **b**,
38:27 pass, at the time for giving **b**,
38:28 it was, when she was giving **b**,
Ex 1:19 for they are lively and give **b**
21:22 that she gives **b** prematurely,
28:10 stone, in order of their **b**.
Deut 23: 2 One of illegitimate **b** shall not
Ruth 2:11 mother and the land of your **b**,
1 Sam 4:19 she bowed herself and gave **b**,
1 Ki 3:17 and I gave **b** while she was in
3:18 third day after I had given **b**,
3:18 that this woman also gave **b**.
2 Ki 19: 3 for the children have come to **b**,
Job 3: 1 and cursed the day of his **b**.
3:11 "Why did I not die at **b**?
38:29 frost of heaven, who gives it **b**?
39: 1 you mark when the deer gives **b**?
Ps 22:10 I was cast upon You from **b**.
29: 9 the LORD makes the deer give **b**,
48: 6 as of a woman in **b** pangs,
71: 6 You I have been upheld from **b**;
Eccl 7: 1 death than the day of one's **b**;
Isa 37: 3 for the children have come to **b**,
46: 3 have been upheld by Me from **b**,
66: 7 she was in labor, she gave **b**;
66: 8 the earth be made to give **b** in
66: 8 She gave **b** to her children.
66: 9 Shall I bring to the time of **b**,
Jer 2:27 You gave **b** to me.' For they
14: 5 the deer also gave **b** in the
48:41 Like the heart of a woman in **b**
49:22 Like the heart of a woman in **b**
Ezek 16: 3 Your **b** and your nativity are
Hos 9:11 fly away like a bird—No **b**,
Mic 4:10 Like a woman in **b** pangs.
5: 3 she who is in labor has given **b**;
Mt 1:18 Now the **b** of Jesus Christ was
Mk 7:26 a Greek, a Syro-Phoenician by **b**,
Lk 1:14 and many will rejoice at his **b**.
Jn 9: 1 saw a man who was blind from **b**.
16:21 but as soon as she has given **b**
Rom 8:22 groans and labors with **b** pangs
Gal 4:19 for whom I labor in **b** again
4:24 from Mount Sinai which gives **b**
Jas 1:15 it gives **b** to sin; and sin,
Rev 12: 2 in labor and in pain to give **b**.
12: 4 woman who was ready to give **b**,
12:13 the woman who gave **b** to the

BIRTHDAY (3/3) BIRTH

Gen 40:20 day, which was Pharaoh's **b**,
Mt 14: 6 But when Herod's **b** was
Mk 6:21 day came when Herod on his **b**

BIRTHRIGHT (10/9) BIRTH

Gen 25:31 Sell me your **b** as of this day."
25:32 so what is this **b** to me?"
25:33 and sold his **b** to Jacob.
25:34 Thus Esau despised his **b**.
27:36 two times. He took away my **b**,
43:33 firstborn according to his **b**
1 Chr 5: 1 his **b** was given to the sons of
5: 1 not listed according to the **b**;
5: 2 although the **b** was Joseph's—
Heb 12:16 one morsel of food sold his **b**.

BIRTHSTOOLS (1/1) BIRTH

Ex 1:16 women, and see them on the **b**,

BIRZAITH (1/1)

1 Chr 7:31 who was the father of **B**.

BISHLAM (1/1)

Ezra 4: 7 the days of Artaxerxes also, **B**,

BISHOP (3/3) BISHOPS

1 Tim 3: 1 man desires the position of a **b**,
3: 2 A **b** then must be blameless, the
Titus 1: 7 For a **b** must be blameless, as a

BISHOPRICK (KJV) See OFFICE

BISHOPS (1/1) BISHOP

Phil 1: 1 with the **b** and deacons:

BIT (3/3) BITE, BITS

Num 21: 6 and they **b** the people; and many
Ps 32: 9 must be harnessed with **b** and
Am 5:19 And a serpent **b** him!

BITE (4/4) BIT, BITES, BITTEN

Eccl 10:11 A serpent may **b** when it is
Jer 8:17 And they shall **b** you," says
Am 9: 3 and it shall **b** them;
Gal 5:15 But if you **b** and devour one

BITES (2/2) BITE

Gen 49:17 That **b** the horse's heels So
Prov 23:32 At the last it **b** like a

BITHIAH (1/1)

1 Chr 4:18 And these were the sons of **B**

BITHRON (1/1)

2 Sam 2:29 Jordan, and went through all **B**;

BITHYNIA (2/2)

Acts 16: 7 Mysia, they tried to go into **B**,
1 Pe 1: 1 Cappadocia, Asia, and **B**,

BITS (2/2) BIT

Am 6:11 break the great house into **b**,
Jas 3: 3 we put **b** in horses' mouths that

BITTEN (3/3) BITE

Num 21: 8 shall be that everyone who is **b**,
21: 9 if a serpent had **b** anyone, when
Eccl 10: 8 through a wall will be **b** by a

BITTER (43/41) BITTERLY, BITTERNESS

Gen 27:34 an exceedingly great and **b** cry,
Ex 1:14 And they made their lives **b** with
12: 8 bread and with **b** herbs they
15:23 of Marah, for they were **b**.
Num 5:18 have in his hand the **b** water
5:19 be free from this **b** water that
5:23 scrape them off into the **b**
5:24 the woman drink the **b** water
5:24 shall enter her to become **b**.
5:27 will enter her and become **b**,
9:11 unleavened bread and **b** herbs.
Deut 32:24 by pestilence and **b** destruction;
32:32 of gall, Their clusters are **b**.
2 Sam 2:26 you not know that it will be **b**
2 Ki 14:26 of Israel was very **b**;
Esth 4: 1 He cried out with a loud and **b**
Job 3:20 And life to the **b** of soul,
13:26 For You write **b** things against
23: 2 "Even today my complaint is **b**;
27: 2 who has made my soul **b**,
Ps 64: 3 their arrows—**b** words,
Prov 5: 4 But in the end she is **b** as
27: 7 a hungry soul every **b** thing
31: 6 And wine to those who are **b** of
Eccl 7:26 And I find more **b** than death
Isa 5:20 Who put **b** for sweet, and sweet
5:20 for sweet, and sweet for **b**!
24: 9 Strong drink is **b** to those who
Jer 2:19 it is an evil and **b** thing
4:18 wickedness, Because it is **b**,
6:26 most **b** lamentation; For the
31:15 Lamentation and **b** weeping,
Ezek 27:31 bitterness of heart and **b**
Am 8:10 And its end like a **b** day.
Mic 2: 4 And lament with a **b**
Hab 1: 6 A **b** and hasty nation Which
Zeph 1:14 of the day of the LORD is **b**;
Col 3:19 love your wives and do not be **b**
Jas 3:11 send forth fresh water and **b**
3:14 But if you have **b** envy and
Rev 8:11 water, because it was made **b**.
10: 9 and it will make your stomach **b**,
10:10 eaten it, my stomach became **b**.

BITTERLY (20/20) BITTER

Gen 49:23 The archers have **b** grieved him,
Judg 5:23 'Curse its inhabitants **b**,
21: 2 up their voices and wept **b**,
Ruth 1:20 the Almighty has dealt very **b**
2 Sam 13:19 her head and went away crying **b**.
13:36 all his servants wept very **b**.
2 Ki 20: 3 And Hezekiah wept **b**.
Ezra 10: 1 for the people wept very **b**.
Neh 13: 8 And it grieved me **b**;
Isa 15: 3 Everyone will wail, weeping **b**.
22: 4 away from me, I will weep **b**;
33: 7 of peace shall weep **b**.
38: 3 And Hezekiah wept **b**.
Jer 13:17 My eyes will weep **b** And run
22:10 Weep **b** for him who goes away,
Lam 1: 2 She weeps **b** in the night, Her
Ezek 27:30 They will cry **b** and cast dust
Hos 12:14 provoked Him to anger most **b**;
Mt 26:75 So he went out and wept **b**.
Lk 22:62 So Peter went out and wept **b**.

BITTERN (1/1)

Zeph 2:14 Both the pelican and the **b**

BITTERNESS (21/21) BITTER

Deut 29:18 be among you a root bearing **b**
1 Sam 1:10 And she was in **b** of soul, and
15:32 Surely the **b** of death is past."
Job 7:11 I will complain in the **b** of my
9:18 my breath, But fills me with **b**.
10: 1 I will speak in the **b** of my
21:25 Another man dies in the **b** of
Prov 14:10 The heart knows its own **b**,
17:25 And **b** to her who bore him.
Isa 38:15 all my years In the **b** of my
38:17 own peace That I had great **b**;
Lam 1: 4 afflicted, And she is in **b**.
3: 5 me And surrounded me with **b**
3:15 He has filled me with **b**,
Ezek 3:14 took me away, and I went in **b**,
21: 6 and sigh with **b** before their
27:31 And weep for you With **b** of
Acts 8:23 see that you are poisoned by **b**
Rom 3:14 is full of cursing and **b**.
Eph 4:31 Let all **b**, wrath, anger,
Heb 12:15 lest any root of **b** springing up

BIZJOTHJAH (1/1)

Josh 15:28 Hazar Shual, Beersheba, **B**,

BIZTHA (1/1)

Esth 1:10 wine, he commanded Mehuman, **B**,

BLACK (16/15) BLACKER, BLACKNESS, BLACKSMITH

Lev 13:31 and there is no **b** hair in it,
13:37 and there is **b** hair grown up in
1 Ki 18:45 meantime that the sky became **b**
Esth 1: 6 and white and **b** marble.
Job 30:30 My skin grows **b** and falls from
Prov 7: 9 In the **b** and dark night.
Song 5:11 And **b** as a raven.
Isa 28:25 Does he not sow the **b** cummin
28:27 For the **b** cummin is not
28:27 But the **b** cummin is beaten out
Jer 4:28 And the heavens above be **b**,
Zech 6: 2 with the second chariot **b**
6: 6 The one with the **b** horses is
Mt 5:36 cannot make one hair white or **b**.
Rev 6: 5 a **b** horse, and he who sat on it
6:12 and the sun became **b** as

BLACKER (1/1) BLACK

Lam 4: 8 Now their appearance is **b** than

BLACKNESS (6/6) BLACK

Job 3: 5 May the **b** of the day terrify
Isa 50: 3 I clothe the heavens with **b**,
59: 9 brightness, but we walk in **b**!
Heb 12:18 and to **b** and darkness and
2 Pe 2:17 for whom is reserved the **b** of
Jude 13 for whom is reserved the **b** of

BLACKSMITH (3/3)

1 Sam 13:19 Now there was no **b** to be found
Isa 44:12 The **b** with the tongs works one
54:16 I have created the **b** Who blows

BLADE (4/3)

Judg 3:22 the hilt went in after the **b**,
3:22 and the fat closed over the **b**,
Ezek 21:16 Thrust right! Set your **b**!
Mk 4:28 crops by itself: first the **b**,

BLAINS (KJV) See SORES

BLAME (4/4) BLAMED, BLAMELESS, BLAMELESSLY

Gen 43: 9 then let me bear the **b** forever.
44:32 then I shall bear the **b** before
2 Cor 8:20 that anyone should **b** us in this
Eph 1: 4 we should be holy and without **b**

BLAMED (2/2) BLAME

2 Cor 6: 3 that our ministry may not be **b**.
Gal 2:11 face, because he was to be **b**;

BLAMELESS (47/45) BLAME, BLAMELESSLY

Gen 17: 1 God; walk before Me and be **b**.
44:10 be my slave, and you shall be **b**.
Num 32:22 you may return and be **b** before
Deut 18:13 You shall be **b** before the LORD
Josh 2:17 We will be **b** of this oath of
Judg 15: 3 This time I shall be **b** regarding
2 Sam 22:24 I was also **b** before Him, And I
22:26 With a **b** man You will show
22:26 man You will show Yourself **b**;
Job 1: 1 and that man was **b** and upright,
1: 8 a **b** and upright man, one who
2: 3 a **b** and upright man, one who
8:20 God will not cast away the **b**,
9:20 condemn me; Though I were **b**,
9:21 'I am **b**, yet I do not know
9:22 He destroys the **b** and the
12: 4 The just and **b** who is
22: 3 Him that you make your ways **b**?
Ps 18:23 I was also **b** before Him, And I
18:25 With a **b** man You will show
18:25 man You will show Yourself **b**;
19:13 over me. Then I shall be **b**,
37:37 Mark the **b** man, and observe
51: 4 And **b** when You judge.
64: 4 may shoot in secret at the **b**;
119:80 Let my heart be **b** regarding
Prov 2:21 And the **b** will remain in it;
11: 5 The righteousness of the **b** will
11:20 But the **b** in their ways are
13: 6 guards him whose way is **b**,
28:10 But the **b** will inherit good.
29:10 The bloodthirsty hate the **b**,
Mt 12: 5 profane the Sabbath, and are **b**?

Lk 1: 6 and ordinances of the Lord **b**.
1 Cor 1: 8 that you may be **b** in the
Phil 2:15 that you may become **b** and
3: 6 which is in the law, **b**.
Col 1:22 to present you holy, and **b**,
1 Th 3:13 He may establish your hearts **b**
5:23 and body be preserved **b** at the
1 Tim 3: 2 A bishop then must be **b**,
3:10 as deacons, being found **b**.
5: 7 command, that they may be **b**.
6:14 **b** until our Lord Jesus Christ's
Titus 1: 6 if a man is **b**, the husband of
1: 7 For a bishop must be **b**,
2 Pe 3:14 in peace, without spot and **b**;

BLAMELESSLY (2/2) BLAMELESS

Prov 28:18 Whoever walks **b** will be saved,
1 Th 2:10 how devoutly and justly and **b**

BLANKET (1/1)

Judg 4:18 tent, she covered him with a **b**.

BLASPHEME (6/6) BLASPHEMED, BLASPHEMES, BLASPHEMING, BLASPHEMOUSLY

2 Sam 12:14 the enemies of the LORD to **b**,
Ps 74:10 Will the enemy **b** Your name
Acts 26:11 and compelled them to **b**;
1 Tim 1:20 that they may learn not to **b**.
Jas 2: 7 Do they not **b** that noble name by
Rev 13: 6 to **b** His name, His tabernacle,

BLASPHEMED (23/23) BLASPHEME

Lev 24:11 And the Israelite woman's son **b**
1 Ki 21:10 You have **b** God and the king."
21:13 Naboth has **b** God and the king!"
2 Ki 19: 6 of the king of Assyria have **b**
19:22 have you reproached and **b**?
Ps 74:18 that a foolish people has **b**
Isa 37: 6 of the king of Assyria have **b**
37:23 have you reproached and **b**?
52: 5 And My name is **b** continually
65: 7 on the mountains And **b** Me on
Ezek 20:27 this too your fathers have **b**
Mt 27:39 And those who passed by **b** Him,
Mk 15:29 And those who passed by **b** Him,
Lk 23:39 the criminals who were hanged **b**
Acts 18: 6 But when they opposed him and **b**,
Rom 2:24 the name of God is **b** among
1 Tim 6: 1 and His doctrine may not be **b**.
Titus 2: 5 the word of God may not be **b**.
1 Pe 4:14 upon you. On their part He is **b**,
2 Pe 2: 2 whom the way of truth will be **b**.
Rev 16: 9 and they **b** the name of God who
16:11 They **b** the God of heaven because
16:21 Men **b** God because of the plague

BLASPHEMER (1/1) BLASPHEME, BLASPHEMERS, BLASPHEMIES, BLASPHEMOUS, BLASPHEMY

1 Tim 1:13 although I was formerly a **b**,

BLASPHEMERS (2/2) BLASPHEMER

Acts 19:37 robbers of temples nor **b** of
2 Tim 3: 2 of money, boasters, proud, **b**,

BLASPHEMES (5/4) BLASPHEME

Lev 24:16 And whoever **b** the name of the
24:16 When he **b** the name of the
Mt 9: 3 themselves, "This Man **b**!"
Mk 3:29 but he who **b** against the Holy
Lk 12:10 but to him who **b** against the

BLASPHEMIES (7/7) BLASPHEMY

Ezek 35:12 I have heard all your **b** which
Dan 11:36 shall speak **b** against the God
Mt 15:19 thefts, false witness, **b**.
Mk 2: 7 Why does this Man speak **b** like
3:28 and whatever **b** they may utter;
Lk 5:21 "Who is this who speaks **b**?
Rev 13: 5 speaking great things and **b**,

BLASPHEMING (2/2) BLASPHEME

Jn 10:36 sent into the world, 'You are **b**,
Acts 13:45 envy; and contradicting and **b**,

BLASPHEMOUS (3/3) BLASPHEME, BLASPHEMOUSLY

Acts 6:11 We have heard him speak **b** words
6:13 man does not cease to speak **b**
Rev 13: 1 and on his heads a **b** name.

BLASPHEMOUSLY (1/1) BLASPHEMOUS

Lk 22:65 And many other things they **b**

BLASPHEMY (13/11) BLASPHEME, BLASPHEMIES

2 Ki 19: 3 of trouble, and rebuke, and **b**;
Isa 37: 3 day of trouble and rebuke and **b**;
Mt 12:31 every sin and **b** will be
12:31 but the **b** against the Spirit
26:65 He has spoken **b**! What further
26:65 now you have heard His **b**!
Mk 7:22 lewdness, an evil eye, **b**,
14:64 You have heard the **b**! What do
Jn 10:33 we do not stone You, but for **b**,
Col 3: 8 these: anger, wrath, malice, **b**,
Rev 2: 9 and I know the **b** of those who
13: 6 Then he opened his mouth in **b**
17: 3 which was full of names of **b**,

BLAST (8/8) BLASTED, BLASTS

Ex 15: 8 And with the **b** of Your nostrils
19:19 And when the **b** of the trumpet
Josh 6: 5 when they make a long **b** with
2 Sam 22:16 At the **b** of the breath of His
Job 4: 9 By the **b** of God they perish,
39:25 At the **b** of the trumpet he
Ps 18:15 At the **b** of the breath of Your
Isa 25: 4 For the **b** of the terrible ones

BLASTED (1/1) BLAST

Am 4: 9 I **b** you with blight and mildew.

BLASTS (1/1) BLAST

Rev 8:13 because of the remaining **b** of

BLASTUS (1/1)

Acts 12:20 and having made **B** the king's

BLAZE (1/1) BLAZED, BLAZING

Num 16:37 up the censers out of the **b**,

BLAZED (1/1) BLAZE

Lam 2: 3 He has **b** against Jacob like a

BLAZING (1/1) BLAZE

Ezek 20:47 the **b** flame shall not be

BLEAT (1/1) BLEATING

Isa 34:14 And the wild goat shall **b** to

BLEATING (1/1) BLEAT

1 Sam 15:14 What then is this **b** of the

BLEMISH (56/50) BLEMISHED, BLEMISHES

Ex 12: 5 'Your lamb shall be without **b**,
29: 1 bull and two rams without **b**,
Lev 1: 3 let him offer a male without **b**;
1:10 he shall bring a male without **b**.
3: 1 he shall offer it without **b**
3: 6 he shall offer it without **b**.
4: 3 sinned a young bull without **b**
4:23 of the goats, a male without **b**.
4:28 the goats, a female without **b**,
4:32 shall bring a female without **b**.
5:15 offering a ram without **b** from
5:18 to the priest a ram without **b**
6: 6 a ram without **b** from the flock,
9: 2 as a burnt offering, without **b**,
9: 3 of the first year, without **b**,
14:10 take two male lambs without **b**,
14:10 of the first year without **b**,
22:19 own free will a male without **b**
23:12 of the first year, without **b**,
23:18 of the first year, without **b**,
Num 6:14 in its first year without **b** as
6:14 in its first year without **b** as
6:14 one ram without **b** as a peace
19: 2 you a red heifer without **b**,
28: 3 in their first year without **b**,
28: 9 in their first year, without **b**,
28:11 in their first year, without **b**;
28:19 Be sure they are without **b**.
28:31 'Be sure they are without **b**.
29: 2 in their first year, without **b**.
29: 8 Be sure they are without **b**.
29:13 They shall be without **b**.
29:17 in their first year without **b**,
29:20 in their first year without **b**,
29:23 in their first year, without **b**,
29:26 in their first year without **b**,
29:29 in their first year without **b**,
29:32 in their first year without **b**,
29:36 in their first year without **b**,
Deut 17: 1 a bull or sheep which has any **b**
32: 5 children, Because of their **b**:
2 Sam 14:25 of his head there was no **b** in
Ezek 43:22 a kid of the goats without **b**
43:23 offer a young bull without **b**,
43:23 a ram from the flock without **b**.
43:25 from the flock, both without **b**.
45:18 take a young bull without **b**
45:23 bulls and seven rams without **b**,
46: 4 shall be six lambs without **b**,
46: 4 blemish, and a ram without **b**;
46: 6 be a young bull without **b**,
46: 6 a ram; they shall be without **b**.
46:13 of the first year without **b**;
Dan 1: 4 men in whom there was no **b**,
Eph 5:27 should be holy and without **b**.
1 Pe 1:19 as of a lamb without **b** and

BLEMISHED (1/1) BLEMISH

Mal 1:14 to the Lord what is **b**—

BLEMISHES (1/1) BLEMISH

2 Pe 2:13 They are spots and **b**,

BLENDED (2/2)

Lev 7:12 or cakes of **b** flour mixed with
Song 7: 2 It lacks no **b** beverage.

BLESS (133/123) BLESSED, BLESSEDNESS, BLESSES, BLESSING, BLESSINGS

Gen 12: 2 I will **b** you And make your
12: 3 I will **b** those who bless you,
12: 3 I will bless those who **b** you,
17:16 And I will **b** her and also give
17:16 then I will **b** her, and she
22:17 blessing I will **b** you, and
26: 3 and I will be with you and **b**
26:24 I will **b** you and multiply your
27: 4 that my soul may **b** you before I
27: 7 that I may eat it and **b** you in
27:10 and that he may **b** you before
27:19 that your soul may **b** me."
27:25 so that my soul may **b** you."
27:29 And blessed be those who **b**
27:31 that your soul may **b** me."
27:34 **B** me—me also, O my father!"
27:38 **B** me—me also, O my father!"
28: 3 May God Almighty **b** you, And
32:26 not let You go unless You **b**
48: 9 and I will **b** them."
48:16 **B** the lads; Let my name be
48:20 saying, "By you Israel will **b**,
49:25 by the Almighty who will **b** you
Ex 12:32 be gone; and **b** me also."
20:24 come to you, and I will **b** you.
23:25 and He will **b** your bread and
Num 6:23 This is the way you shall **b** the
6:24 The LORD **b** you and keep you;
6:27 and I will **b** them."
22: 6 for I know that he whom you **b**
23:20 have received a command to **b**;
23:25 nor **b** them at all!"
24: 1 that it pleased the LORD to **b**
Deut 1:11 and **b** you as He has promised
7:13 And He will love you and **b** you
7:13 He will also **b** the fruit of
8:10 then you shall **b** the LORD your
10: 8 to minister to Him and to **b** in
14:29 that the LORD your God may **b**
15: 4 for the LORD will greatly **b**
15: 6 For the LORD your God will **b**
15:10 the LORD your God will **b** you
15:18 Then the LORD your God will **b**
16:15 the LORD your God will **b** you
21: 5 to minister to Him and to **b** in
23:20 that the LORD your God may **b**
24:13 sleep in his own garment and **b**
24:19 that the LORD your God may **b**
26:15 and **b** Your people Israel and
27:12 stand on Mount Gerizim to **b**
28: 8 and He will **b** you in the land
28:12 and to **b** all the work of your
30:16 and the LORD your God will **b**
33:11 **B** his substance, LORD, And
Josh 8:33 that they should **b** the people
24:10 therefore he continued to **b**
Judg 5: 2 themselves, **B** the LORD!
5: 9 the people. **B** the LORD!
Ruth 2: 4 The LORD **b** you!"
1 Sam 2:20 And Eli would **b** Elkanah and his
9:13 because he must **b** the
2 Sam 6:20 Then David returned to **b** his
7:29 let it please You to **b** the
8:10 to greet him and **b** him, because
21: 3 that you may **b** the inheritance
1 Ki 1:47 king's servants have gone to **b**
1 Chr 4:10 that You would **b** me indeed, and
16:43 and David returned to **b** his
17:27 You have been pleased to **b**
18:10 to greet him and **b** him, because
29:20 'Now **b** the LORD your God."
Neh 9: 5 Stand up and **b** the LORD your
Ps 5:12 will **b** the righteous; With
16: 7 I will **b** the LORD who has
26:12 In the congregations I will **b**
28: 9 And **b** Your inheritance;
29:11 The LORD will **b** His people
34: 1 I will **b** the LORD at all
62: 4 They **b** with their mouth, But
63: 4 Thus I will **b** You while I live;
65:10 You **b** its growth.
66: 8 **b** our God, you peoples!
67: 1 God be merciful to us and **b** us,
67: 6 our own God, shall **b** us.
67: 7 God shall **b** us, And all the
68:26 **B** God in the congregations,
96: 2 **b** His name; Proclaim the good
100: 4 and **b** His name.
103: 1 **B** the LORD, O my soul
103: 1 **b** His holy name!
103: 2 **B** the LORD, O my soul, And
103:20 **B** the LORD, you His angels,

103:21 **B** the LORD, all you His
103:22 **B** the LORD, all His works, In
103:22 **B** the LORD, O my soul!
104: 1 **B** the LORD, O my soul!
104:35 **B** the LORD, O my soul!
109:28 Let them curse, but You **b**;
115:12 He will **b** us; He will bless
115:12 He will **b** the house of Israel;
115:12 He will **b** the house of Aaron.
115:13 He will **b** those who fear the
115:18 But we will **b** the LORD From
128: 5 The LORD **b** you out of Zion,
129: 8 We **b** you in the name of the
132:15 I will abundantly **b** her
134: 1 **b** the LORD, All you servants
134: 2 And **b** the LORD.
134: 3 who made heaven and earth **B**
135:19 **B** the LORD, O house of Israel!
135:19 O house of Israel! **B** the
135:20 **B** the LORD, O house of Levi!
135:20 fear the LORD, **b** the LORD!
145: 1 And I will **b** Your name forever
145: 2 Every day I will **b** You, And I
145:10 And Your saints shall **b** You.
145:21 And all flesh shall **b** His holy
Prov 30:11 And does not **b** its mother.
Isa 19:25 whom the LORD of hosts shall **b**,
65:16 himself in the earth Shall **b**
Jer 4: 2 The nations shall **b** themselves
31:23 The LORD **b** you, O home of
Hag 2:19 But from this day I will **b**
Mt 5:44 **b** those who curse you, do good
Lk 6:28 **b** those who curse you, and pray
Acts 3:26 sent Him to **b** you, in turning
Rom 12:14 **B** those who persecute you; bless
12:14 **b** and do not curse.
1 Cor 4:12 own hands. Being reviled, we **b**;
10:16 The cup of blessing which we **b**,
14:16 if you **b** with the spirit, how
Heb 6:14 Surely blessing I will **b**
Jas 3: 9 With it we **b** our God and Father,

BLESSED (303/287) BLESS

Gen 1:22 And God **b** them, saying, "Be
1:28 Then God **b** them, and God said to
2: 3 Then God **b** the seventh day and
5: 2 and **b** them and called them
9: 1 So God **b** Noah and his sons, and
9:26 **B** be the LORD, The God of
12: 3 of the earth shall be **b**.
14:19 And he **b** him and said:
14:19 **B** be Abram of God Most High,
14:20 And **b** be God Most High, Who
17:20 I have **b** him, and will make him
18:18 of the earth shall be **b** in him?
22:18 nations of the earth shall be **b**,
24: 1 and the LORD had **b** Abraham in
24:27 **B** be the LORD God of my master
24:31 O **b** of the LORD! Why do you
24:35 The LORD has **b** my master
24:48 and **b** the LORD God of my
24:60 And they **b** Rebekah and said to
25:11 that God **b** his son Isaac.
26: 4 nations of the earth shall be **b**;
26:12 and the LORD **b** him.
26:29 You are now the **b** of the
27:23 Esau's hands; so he **b** him.
27:27 and **b** him and said: "Surely,
27:27 a field Which the LORD has **b**.
27:29 And **b** be those who bless
27:33 and I have **b** him—and indeed he
27:33 him—and indeed he shall be **b**.
27:41 with which his father **b** him,
28: 1 Then Isaac called Jacob and **b**
28: 6 Esau saw that Isaac had **b** Jacob
28: 6 and that as he **b** him he gave
28:14 of the earth shall be **b**.
30:13 the daughters will call me **b**.
30:27 that the LORD has **b** me for
30:30 the LORD has **b** you since my
31:55 his sons and daughters and **b**
32:29 And He **b** him there.
35: 9 Padan Aram, and **b** him.
39: 5 that the LORD **b** the Egyptian's
47: 7 and Jacob **b** Pharaoh.
47:10 So Jacob **b** Pharaoh, and went out
48: 3 in the land of Canaan and **b** me,
48:15 And he **b** Joseph, and said:
48:20 So he **b** them that day, saying,
49:28 And he **b** them; he blessed each
49:28 he **b** each one according to his
Ex 18:10 **B** be the LORD, who has
20:11 Therefore the LORD **b** the
39:43 And Moses **b** them.
Lev 9:22 **b** them, and came down from
9:23 and came out and **b** the people.
Num 22: 6 that he whom you bless is **b**,
22:12 the people, for they are **b**.
23:11 you have **b** them bountifully!"
23:20 a command to bless; He has **b**,
24: 9 **B** is he who blesses you, And
24:10 you have bountifully **b** them
Deut 2: 7 For the LORD your God has **b** you
7:14 You shall be **b** above all
12: 7 which the LORD your God has **b**
14:24 when the LORD your God has **b**
15:14 From what the LORD has **b** you
28: 3 **B** shall you be in the city,
28: 3 and **b** shall you be in the
28: 4 **B** shall be the fruit of your
28: 5 **B** shall be your basket and
28: 6 **B** shall you be when you come
28: 6 and **b** shall you be when you
33: 1 which Moses the man of God **b**
33:13 **B** of the LORD is his land,
33:20 **B** is he who enlarges Gad; He
33:24 Asher is most **b** of sons; Let
Josh 14:13 And Joshua **b** him, and gave
17:14 inasmuch as the LORD has **b** us
22: 6 So Joshua **b** them and sent them
22: 7 to their tents, he **b** them,
22:33 and the children of Israel **b**
Judg 5:24 Most **b** among women is Jael, The
5:24 **B** is she among women in tents.
13:24 and the LORD **b** him.
17: 2 May you be **b** by the LORD, my
Ruth 2:19 **B** be the one who took notice of
2:20 **B** be he of the LORD, who has
3:10 **B** are you of the LORD, my
4:14 **B** be the LORD, who has not
1 Sam 15:13 **B** are you of the LORD! I have
23:21 **B** are you of the LORD, for you
25:32 **B** is the LORD God of Israel,
25:33 And **b** is your advice and
25:33 blessed is your advice and **b**
25:39 **B** be the LORD, who has pleaded
26:25 said to David, "May you be **b**,
2 Sam 2: 5 You are **b** of the LORD, for you
6:11 And the LORD **b** Obed-Edom and
6:12 The LORD has **b** the house of
6:18 he **b** the people in the name of
7:29 the house of Your servant be **b**
13:25 would not go; and he **b** him.
18:28 **B** be the LORD your God, who
19:39 the king kissed Barzillai and **b**
22:47 The LORD lives! **B** be my Rock!
1 Ki 1:48 **B** be the LORD God of Israel,
2:45 "But King Solomon shall be **b**,
5: 7 **B** be the LORD this day, for
8:14 the king turned around and **b**
8:15 **B** be the LORD God of Israel,
8:55 Then he stood and **b** all the
8:56 **B** be the LORD, who has given
8:66 and they **b** the king, and went
10: 9 **B** be the LORD your God, who
1 Chr 13:14 And the LORD **b** the house of
16: 2 he **b** the people in the name of
16:36 **B** be the LORD God of Israel
17:27 for You have **b** it, O LORD, and
17:27 and it shall be **b** forever."
26: 5 the eighth; for God **b** him.
29:10 Therefore David **b** the LORD
29:10 **B** are You, LORD God of Israel,
29:20 So all the assembly **b** the
2 Chr 2:12 **B** be the LORD God of Israel,
6: 3 the king turned around and **b**
6: 4 **B** be the LORD God of Israel,
9: 8 **B** be the LORD your God, who
20:26 for there they **b** the LORD;
30:27 arose and **b** the people, and
31: 8 they **b** the LORD and His people
31:10 for the LORD has **b** His people;
Ezra 7:27 **B** be the LORD God of our
Neh 8: 6 And Ezra **b** the LORD, the great
9: 5 **B** be Your glorious name, Which
11: 2 And the people **b** all the men who
Job 1:10 You have **b** the work of his
1:21 **B** be the name of the LORD."
29:11 then it **b** me, And when the eye
31:20 If his heart has not **b** me, And
42:12 Now the LORD **b** the latter days
Ps 1: 1 **B** is the man Who walks not in
2:12 **B** are all those who put their
18:46 The LORD lives! **B** be my
21: 6 For You have made him most **b**
28: 6 **B** be the LORD, Because He
31:21 **B** be the LORD, For He has
32: 1 **B** is he whose transgression
32: 2 **B** is the man to whom the LORD
33:12 **B** is the nation whose God is
34: 8 **B** is the man who trusts in
37:22 For those **b** by Him shall
37:26 And his descendants are **b**.
40: 4 **B** is that man who makes the
41: 1 **B** is he who considers the poor
41: 2 And he will be **b** on the
41:13 **B** be the LORD God of Israel
45: 2 Therefore God has **b** You
65: 4 **B** is the man You choose,
66:20 **B** be God, Who has not turned
68:19 **B** be the Lord, Who daily
68:35 to His people. **B** be God!
72:17 And men shall be **b** in Him;
72:17 All nations shall call Him **b**.
72:18 **B** be the LORD God, the God of
72:19 And **b** be His glorious name
84: 4 **B** are those who dwell in Your
84: 5 **B** is the man whose strength
84:12 **B** is the man who trusts in
89:15 **B** are the people who know the
89:52 **B** be the LORD forevermore!
94:12 **B** is the man whom You
106: 3 **B** are those who keep justice,
106:48 **B** be the LORD God of Israel
112: 1 Praise the LORD! **B** is the
112: 2 of the upright will be **b**.
113: 2 **B** be the name of the LORD
115:15 May you be **b** by the LORD,
118:26 **B** is he who comes in the name
118:26 name of the LORD! We have **b**
119: 1 **B** are the undefiled in the
119: 2 **B** are those who keep His
119:12 **B** are You, O LORD! Teach me
124: 6 **B** be the LORD, Who has not
128: 1 **B** is every one who fears the
128: 4 thus shall the man be **b** Who
135:21 **B** be the LORD out of Zion,
144: 1 **B** be the LORD my Rock, Who
147:13 He has **b** your children within
Prov 5:18 Let your fountain be **b**,
8:32 For **b** are those who keep my
8:34 **B** is the man who listens to me,
10: 7 memory of the righteous is **b**,
20: 7 His children are **b** after him.
20:21 at the beginning Will not be **b**
22: 9 has a generous eye will be **b**,
31:28 children rise up and call her **b**;
Eccl 10:17 **B** are you, O land, when your
Song 6: 9 saw her And called her **b**,
Isa 19:25 **B** is Egypt My people, and
30:18 **B** are all those who wait for
32:20 **B** are you who sow beside all
51: 2 And **b** him and increased him."
56: 2 **B** is the man who does this,
61: 9 posterity whom the LORD has **b**.
65:23 be the descendants of the **B**
Jer 17: 7 **B** is the man who trusts in the
20:14 Let the day not be **b** in
Ezek 3:12 **B** is the glory of the LORD
Dan 2:19 So Daniel **b** the God of heaven.
2:20 **B** be the name of God forever and
3:28 **B** be the God of Shadrach,
4:34 and I **b** the Most High and
12:12 **B** is he who waits, and comes to
Zech 11: 5 **B** be the LORD, for I am rich';
Mal 3:12 all nations will call you **b**,
3:15 So now we call the proud **b**,
Mt 5: 3 **B** are the poor in spirit, For
5: 4 **B** are those who mourn, For
5: 5 **B** are the meek, For they
5: 6 **B** are those who hunger and
5: 7 **B** are the merciful, For they
5: 8 **B** are the pure in heart, For
5: 9 **B** are the peacemakers, For
5:10 **B** are those who are persecuted
5:11 **B** are you when they revile and
11: 6 And **b** is he who is not offended
13:16 But **b** are your eyes for they
14:19 He **b** and broke and gave the
16:17 **B** are you, Simon Bar-Jonah, for
21: 9 **B** is He who comes in the
23:39 **B** is He who comes in the
24:46 **B** is that servant whom his
25:34 you **b** of My Father, inherit the
26:26 **b** and broke it, and gave it
Mk 6:41 **b** and broke the loaves, and
8: 7 and having **b** them, He said to
10:16 hands on them, and **b** them.
11: 9 **B** is He who comes in the
11:10 **B** is the kingdom of our father
14:22 **b** and broke it, and gave it
14:61 the Christ, the Son of the **B**?
Lk 1:28 **b** are you among women!"
1:42 **B** are you among women, and
1:42 and **b** is the fruit of your
1:45 **B** is she who believed, for
1:48 all generations will call me **b**.
1:68 **B** is the Lord God of Israel,
2:28 took Him up in his arms and **b**
2:34 Then Simeon **b** them, and said to
6:20 **B** are you poor, For yours is
6:21 **B** are you who hunger now,
6:21 **B** are you who weep now, For
6:22 **B** are you when men hate you,
7:23 And **b** is he who is not offended
9:16 He **b** and broke them, and gave
10:23 **B** are the eyes which see the
11:27 **B** is the womb that bore You,
11:28 **b** are those who hear the word
12:37 **B** are those servants whom the
12:38 **b** are those servants.
12:43 **B** is that servant whom his
13:35 **B** is He who comes in the
14:14 "And you will be **b**,
14:15 **B** is he who shall eat bread in
19:38 **B** is the King who comes in
23:29 **B** are the barren, wombs that
24:30 **b** and broke it, and gave it to
24:50 He lifted up His hands and **b**
24:51 while He **b** them, that He was
Jn 12:13 **B** is He who comes in the
13:17 **b** are you if you do them.
20:29 **B** are those who have not seen
Acts 3:25 of the earth shall be **b**.
20:35 It is more **b** to give than to
Rom 1:25 who is **b** forever. Amen.
4: 7 **B** are those whose lawless
4: 8 **B** is the man to whom the
9: 5 the eternally **b** God. Amen.
2 Cor 1: 3 **B** be the God and Father of our
11:31 who is **b** forever, knows that I
Gal 3: 8 the nations shall be **b**.
3: 9 those who are of faith are **b**
Eph 1: 3 **B** be the God and Father of our
1: 3 who has **b** us with every
1 Tim 1:11 to the glorious gospel of the **b**
6:15 He who is the **b** and only
Titus 2:13 looking for the **b** hope and
Heb 7: 1 slaughter of the kings and **b**
7: 6 tithes from Abraham and **b** him
7: 7 contradiction the lesser is **b**
11:20 By faith Isaac **b** Jacob and Esau
11:21 **b** each of the sons of Joseph,
Jas 1:12 **B** is the man who endures
1:25 this one will be **b** in what he

5:11 Indeed we count them **b** who
1 Pe 1: 3 **B** be the God and Father of our
3:14 sake, you are **b**.
4:14 **b** are you, for the Spirit of
Rev 1: 3 **B** is he who reads and those who
14:13 **B** are the dead who die in the
16:15 **B** is he who watches, and keeps
19: 9 **B** are those who are called to
20: 6 **B** and holy is he who has part
22: 7 I am coming quickly! **B** is he
22:14 **B** are those who do His

BLESSEDNESS (2/2) BLESS

Rom 4: 6 as David also describes the **b**
4: 9 Does this **b** then come upon

BLESSES (10/10) BLESS

Num 24: 9 Blessed is he who **b** you, And
Deut 16:10 give as the LORD your God **b**
29:19 that he **b** himself in his heart,
Ps 10: 3 He **b** the greedy and renounces
49:18 Though while he lives he **b**
107:38 He also **b** them, and they
Prov 3:33 But He **b** the home of the just.
27:14 He who **b** his friend with a loud
Isa 65:16 So that he who **b** himself in the
66: 3 as if he **b** an idol. Just as

BLESSING (67/64) BLESS, BLESSINGS

Gen 12: 2 great; And you shall be a **b**.
22:17 **b** I will bless you, and
27:12 a curse on myself and not a **b**.
27:30 as soon as Isaac had finished **b**
27:35 and has taken away your **b**.
27:36 he has taken away my **b**!"
27:36 Have you not reserved a **b** for
27:38 father, "Have you only one **b**,
27:41 hated Jacob because of the **b**
28: 4 And give you the **b** of Abraham,
33:11 take my **b** that is brought to
39: 5 and the **b** of the LORD was on
49:28 each one according to his own **b**.
Ex 32:29 that He may bestow on you a **b**
Lev 25:21 Then I will command My **b** on you
Deut 11:26 I set before you today a **b** and
11:27 'the **b**, if you obey the
11:29 that you shall put the **b** on
12:15 according to the **b** of the LORD
16:17 according to the **b** of the LORD
23: 5 God turned the curse into a **b**
28: 8 The LORD will command the **b** on
30: 1 the **b** and the curse which I
30:19 **b** and cursing; therefore choose
33: 1 Now this is the **b** with which
33:16 Let the **b** come 'on the head
33:23 And full of the **b** of the
Josh 15:19 She answered, "Give me a **b**;
Judg 1:15 she said to him, "Give me a **b**;
2 Sam 7:29 and with Your **b** let the house
1 Chr 23:13 and to give the **b** in His name
Neh 9: 5 Which is exalted above all **b**
13: 2 God turned the curse into a **b**.
Job 29:13 The **b** of a perishing man came
Ps 3: 8 Your **b** is upon Your people.
24: 5 He shall receive **b** from the
109:17 As he did not delight in **b**,
129: 8 The **b** of the LORD be upon you;
133: 3 there the LORD commanded the **b**—
Prov 10:22 The **b** of the LORD makes one
11:11 By the **b** of the upright the
11:26 But **b** will be on the head of
24:25 And a good **b** will come upon
Isa 19:24 a **b** in the midst of the land,
44: 3 And My **b** on your offspring;
65: 8 For a **b** is in it,' So will I
Ezek 34:26 places all around My hill a **b**;
34:26 there shall be showers of **b**.
44:30 to cause a **b** to rest on your
Joel 2:14 And leave a **b** behind Him—A
Zech 8:13 save you, and you shall be a **b**.
Mal 3:10 And pour out for you such **b**
Lk 24:53 in the temple praising and **b**
Rom 15:29 come in the fullness of the **b**
1 Cor 10:16 The cup of **b** which we bless, is
Gal 3:14 that the **b** of Abraham might come
4:15 What then was the **b** you
Eph 1: 3 us with every spiritual **b** in
Heb 6: 7 receives **b** from God;
6:14 Surely **b** I will bless you,
12:17 when he wanted to inherit the **b**,
Jas 3:10 Out of the same mouth proceed **b**
1 Pe 3: 9 reviling, but on the contrary **b**,
3: 9 this, that you may inherit a **b**.
Rev 5:12 and honor and glory and **b**!"
5:13 **B** and honor and glory and power
7:12 Amen! **B** and glory and wisdom,

BLESSINGS (11/8) BLESSING

Gen 49:25 who will bless you With **b** of
49:25 **B** of the deep that lies
49:25 **B** of the breasts and of the
49:26 The **b** of your father Have
49:26 father Have excelled the **b** of
Deut 28: 2 And all these **b** shall come upon
Josh 8:34 the **b** and the cursings,
Ps 21: 3 For You meet him with the **b** of
Prov 10: 6 **B** are on the head of the
28:20 faithful man will abound with **b**,

Mal 2: 2 you, And I will curse your **b**.

BLEW (25/25) BLOW

Ex 10:19 took the locusts away and **b**
15:10 You **b** with Your wind, The sea
Josh 6: 8 the LORD advanced and **b** the
6: 9 went before the priests who **b**
6:13 went on continually and **b** with
6:16 when the priests **b** the
6:20 shouted when the priests **b**
Judg 3:27 that he **b** the trumpet in the
6:34 then he **b** the trumpet, and the
7:19 and they **b** the trumpets and
7:20 Then the three companies **b** the
7:22 When the three hundred **b** the
1 Sam 13: 3 Then Saul **b** the trumpet
2 Sam 2:28 So Joab **b** a trumpet; and all the
18:16 So Joab **b** the trumpet, and the
20: 1 And he **b** a trumpet, and said:
20:22 Then he **b** a trumpet, and they
1 Ki 1:39 And they **b** the horn, and all
2 Ki 9:13 and they **b** trumpets, saying,
1 Chr 16: 6 the priests regularly **b** the
Hag 1: 9 I **b** it away. Why?" says the
Mt 7:25 and the winds **b** and beat on
7:27 and the winds **b** and beat on
Acts 27:13 When the south wind **b** softly,
28:13 after one day the south wind **b**;

BLIGHT (4/4) BLIGHTED

1 Ki 8:37 pestilence or **b** or mildew,
2 Chr 6:28 pestilence or **b** or mildew,
Am 4: 9 I blasted you with **b** and mildew.
Hag 2:17 I struck you with **b** and mildew

BLIGHTED (5/5) BLIGHT

Gen 41: 6 **b** by the east wind, sprang up
41:23 and **b** by the east wind, sprang
41:27 and the seven empty heads **b** by
2 Ki 19:26 on the housetops And grain **b**
Isa 37:27 on the housetops And grain **b**

BLIND (82/73) BLINDED, BLINDFOLD, BLINDFOLDED, BLINDNESS, BLINDS

Ex 4:11 the deaf, the seeing, or the **b**?
Lev 19:14 a stumbling block before the **b**,
21:18 a man **b** or lame, who has a
22:22 Those that are **b** or broken or
Deut 15:21 if it is lame or **b** or has
27:18 is the one who makes the **b** to
28:29 as a **b** man gropes in darkness;
1 Sam 12: 3 any bribe with which to **b** my
2 Sam 5: 6 but the **b** and the lame will
5: 8 Jebusites (the lame and the **b**,
5: 8 The **b** and the lame shall not
Job 29:15 I was eyes to the **b**,
Ps 146: 8 opens the eyes of the **b**;
Isa 29: 9 **B** yourselves and be blind!
29: 9 Blind yourselves and be **b**!
29:18 And the eyes of the **b** shall
35: 5 Then the eyes of the **b** shall be
42: 7 To open **b** eyes, To bring out
42:16 I will bring the **b** by a way
42:18 you deaf; And look, you **b**,
42:19 Who is **b** but My servant, Or
42:19 Who is **b** as he who is
42:19 And **b** as the LORD's servant?
43: 8 Bring out the **b** people who
56:10 His watchmen are **b**,
59:10 grope for the wall like the **b**,
Jer 31: 8 Among them the **b** and the
Lam 4:14 They wandered **b** in the streets;
Zeph 1:17 And they shall walk like **b**
Mal 1: 8 And when you offer the **b** as a
Mt 9:27 two **b** men followed Him, crying
9:28 the **b** men came to Him.
11: 5 The **b** see and the lame walk;
12:22 **b** and mute; and He healed him,
12:22 so that the **b** and mute man both
15:14 They are **b** leaders of the
15:14 They are blind leaders of the **b**.
15:14 And if the **b** leads the blind,
15:14 And if the blind leads the **b**,
15:30 having with them the lame, **b**,
15:31 and the **b** seeing; and they
20:30 two **b** men sitting by the road,
21:14 Then the **b** and the lame came
23:16 **b** guides, who say, 'Whoever
23:17 Fools and **b**! For which is
23:19 Fools and **b**! For which is
23:24 **B** guides, who strain out a gnat
23:26 **B** Pharisee, first cleanse the
Mk 8:22 and they brought a **b** man to
8:23 So He took the **b** man by the hand
10:46 **b** Bartimaeus, the son of
10:49 Then they called the **b** man,
10:51 The **b** man said to Him,
Lk 4:18 of sight to the **b**,
6:39 'Can the **b** lead the blind?
6:39 "Can the blind lead the **b**?
7:21 and to many **b** He gave sight.
7:22 that the **b** see, the lame
14:13 the maimed, the lame, the **b**.
14:21 maimed and the lame and the **b**.
18:35 that a certain **b** man sat by the
Jn 5: 3 multitude of sick people, **b**,
9: 1 He saw a man who was **b** from
9: 2 his parents, that he was born **b**?
9: 6 He anointed the eyes of the **b**
9: 8 had seen that he was **b** said,
9:13 brought him who formerly was **b**
9:17 They said to the **b** man again,
9:18 that he had been **b** and received
9:19 son, who you say was born **b**?
9:20 our son, and that he was born **b**;
9:24 again called the man who was **b**,
9:25 I know: that though I was **b**,
9:32 the eyes of one who was born **b**.
9:39 those who see may be made **b**.
9:40 Are we **b** also?"
9:41 said to them, "If you were **b**,
10:21 a demon open the eyes of the **b**?
11:37 who opened the eyes of the **b**,
Acts 13:11 upon you, and you shall be **b**,
Rom 2:19 yourself are a guide to the **b**,
Rev 3:17 wretched, miserable, poor, **b**,

BLINDED (6/6) BLIND

Zech 11:17 right eye shall be totally **b**.
Jn 12:40 He has **b** their eyes and
Rom 11: 7 it, and the rest were **b**.
2 Cor 3:14 But their minds were **b**.
4: 4 minds the god of this age has **b**,
1 Jn 2:11 because the darkness has **b** his

BLINDFOLD (1/1) BLIND, BLINDFOLDED

Mk 14:65 and to **b** Him, and to beat Him,

BLINDFOLDED (1/1) BLINDFOLD

Lk 22:64 And having **b** Him, they struck

BLINDNESS (8/7) BLIND

Gen 19:11 the doorway of the house with **b**,
Deut 28:28 strike you with madness and **b**
2 Ki 6:18 this people, I pray, with **b**.
6:18 And He struck them with **b**
Zech 12: 4 horse of the peoples with **b**.
Rom 11:25 that **b** in part has happened to
Eph 4:18 because of the **b** of their
2 Pe 1: 9 is shortsighted, even to **b**,

BLINDS (2/2) BLIND

Ex 23: 8 for a bribe **b** the discerning
Deut 16:19 for a bribe **b** the eyes of the

BLOCK (10/10) BLOCKED, BLOCKS

Lev 19:14 nor put a stumbling **b** before
Isa 44:19 Shall I fall down before a **b**
57:14 Take the stumbling **b** out of
Ezek 3:20 and I lay a stumbling **b** before
7:19 it became their stumbling **b** of
Rom 11: 9 A stumbling **b** and a
14:13 not to put a stumbling **b** or a
1 Cor 1:23 to the Jews a stumbling **b** and
8: 9 of yours become a stumbling **b**
Rev 2:14 Balak to put a stumbling **b**

BLOCKED (2/2) BLOCK

Jer 51:32 The passages are **b**,
Lam 3: 9 He has **b** my ways with hewn

BLOCKS (2/2) BLOCK

Jer 6:21 I will lay stumbling **b** before
Zeph 1: 3 And the stumbling **b** along with

BLOOD (424/357) BLOODLINE, BLOODSHED, BLOODTHIRSTY, BLOODY, LIFEBLOOD

Gen 4:10 The voice of your brother's **b**
4:11 to receive your brother's **b**
9: 4 with its life, that is, its **b**.
9: 6 "Whoever sheds man's **b**,
9: 6 By man his **b** shall be shed;
37:22 said to them, "Shed no **b**,
37:26 our brother and conceal his **b**?
37:31 and dipped the tunic in the **b**.
42:22 his **b** is now required of us."
49:11 And his clothes in the **b** of
Ex 4: 9 from the river will become **b**
4:25 you are a husband of **b**
4:26 a husband of **b**!"—because
7:17 and they shall be turned to **b**.
7:19 water, that they may become **b**.
7:19 And there shall be **b** throughout
7:20 in the river were turned to **b**.
7:21 So there was **b** throughout all
12: 7 they shall take some of the **b**
12:13 Now the **b** shall be a sign for
12:13 you are. And when I see the **b**,
12:22 dip it in the **b** that is in
12:22 the two doorposts with the **b**
12:23 and when He sees the **b** on the
23:18 You shall not offer the **b** of My
24: 6 And Moses took half the **b** and
24: 6 and half the **b** he sprinkled on
24: 8 And Moses took the **b**,
24: 8 This is the **b** of the covenant
29:12 You shall take some of the **b** of
29:12 and pour all the **b** beside the
29:16 and you shall take its **b** and

29:20 and take some of its ***b*** and put
29:20 and sprinkle the ***b*** all around
29:21 you shall take some of the ***b***
30:10 horns once a year with the ***b***
34:25 You shall not offer the ***b*** of My
Lev 1: 5 shall bring the ***b*** and sprinkle
1: 5 the blood and sprinkle the ***b***
1:11 shall sprinkle its ***b*** all around
1:15 its ***b*** shall be drained out at
3: 2 shall sprinkle the ***b*** all around
3: 8 sons shall sprinkle its ***b*** all
3:13 of Aaron shall sprinkle its ***b***
3:17 you shall eat neither fat nor ***b***.
4: 5 take some of the bull's ***b*** and
4: 6 shall dip his finger in the ***b***
4: 6 and sprinkle some of the ***b***
4: 7 priest shall put some of the ***b***
4: 7 he shall pour the remaining ***b***
4:16 bring some of the bull's ***b*** to
4:17 shall dip his finger in the ***b***
4:18 he shall put some of the ***b*** on
4:18 he shall pour the remaining ***b***
4:25 shall take some of the ***b*** of
4:25 and pour its ***b*** at the base of
4:30 shall take some of its ***b*** with
4:30 and pour all the remaining ***b***
4:34 shall take some of the ***b*** of
4:34 and pour all the remaining ***b***
5: 9 shall sprinkle some of the ***b***
5: 9 and the rest of the ***b*** shall be
6:27 And when its ***b*** is sprinkled on
6:30 from which any of the ***b*** is
7: 2 And its ***b*** he shall sprinkle all
7:14 the priest who sprinkles the ***b***
7:26 you shall not eat any ***b*** in any
7:27 'Whoever eats any ***b***,
7:33 who offers the ***b*** of the peace
8:15 killed it. Then he took the ***b***,
8:15 And he poured the ***b*** at the base
8:19 Then he sprinkled the ***b*** all
8:23 Also he took some of its ***b*** and
8:24 And Moses put some of the ***b*** on
8:24 And Moses sprinkled the ***b*** all
8:30 oil and some of the ***b*** which
9: 9 sons of Aaron brought the ***b*** to
9: 9 he dipped his finger in the ***b***,
9: 9 and poured the ***b*** at the base of
9:12 sons presented to him the ***b***,
9:18 sons presented to him the ***b***,
10:18 See! Its ***b*** was not brought
12: 4 shall then continue in the ***b***
12: 5 she shall continue in the ***b*** of
12: 7 be clean from the flow of her ***b***.
14: 6 and the living bird in the ***b***
14:14 shall take some of the ***b*** of
14:17 on the ***b*** of the trespass
14:25 shall take some of the ***b*** of
14:28 on the place of the ***b*** of the
14:51 and dip them in the ***b*** of the
14:52 cleanse the house with the ***b***
15:19 discharge from her body is ***b***,
15:25 a woman has a discharge of ***b***
16: 3 with the ***b*** of a young bull
16:14 He shall take some of the ***b*** of
16:14 he shall sprinkle some of the ***b***
16:15 bring its ***b*** inside the veil, do
16:15 do with that ***b*** as he did with
16:15 blood as he did with the ***b*** of
16:18 and shall take some of the ***b*** of
16:18 of the bull and some of the ***b***
16:19 he shall sprinkle some of the ***b***
16:27 whose ***b*** was brought in to make
17: 4 to that man. He has shed ***b***;
17: 6 priest shall sprinkle the ***b*** on
17:10 dwell among you, who eats any ***b***,
17:10 against that person who eats ***b***,
17:11 life of the flesh is in the ***b***,
17:11 for it is the ***b*** that makes
17:12 'No one among you shall eat ***b***,
17:12 who dwells among you eat ***b***.
17:13 he shall pour out its ***b*** and
17:14 Its ***b*** sustains its life.
17:14 You shall not eat the ***b*** of any
17:14 the life of all flesh is its ***b***.
19:26 not eat anything with the ***b***,
20: 9 His ***b*** shall be upon him.
20:11 Their ***b*** shall be upon them.
20:12 Their ***b*** shall be upon them.
20:13 Their ***b*** shall be upon them.
20:16 Their ***b*** is upon them.
20:18 has uncovered the flow of her ***b***.
20:27 Their ***b*** shall be upon them.'
Num 18:17 You shall sprinkle their ***b*** on
19: 4 shall take some of its ***b*** with
19: 4 and sprinkle some of its ***b***
19: 5 its hide, its flesh, its ***b***,
23:24 And drinks the ***b*** of the
35:19 The avenger of ***b*** himself shall
35:21 The avenger of ***b*** shall put the
35:24 manslayer and the avenger of ***b***
35:25 the hand of the avenger of ***b***,
35:27 and the avenger of ***b*** finds him
35:27 and the avenger of ***b*** kills the
35:27 he shall not be guilty of ***b***,
35:33 for ***b*** defiles the land, and no
35:33 for the ***b*** that is shed on it,
35:33 except by the ***b*** of him who shed
Deut 12:16 "Only you shall not eat the ***b***;
12:23 sure that you do not eat the ***b***,
12:23 for the ***b*** is the life; you may
12:27 offerings, the meat and the ***b***,
12:27 and the ***b*** of your sacrifices
15:23 "Only you shall not eat its ***b***;
19: 6 "lest the avenger of ***b***,
19:10 lest innocent ***b*** be shed in the
19:12 to the hand of the avenger of ***b***,
19:13 away the guilt of innocent ***b***
21: 7 'Our hands have not shed this ***b***,
21: 8 and do not lay innocent ***b*** to
21: 8 on their behalf for the ***b***.
21: 9 away the guilt of innocent ***b***
32:14 the ***b*** of the grapes.
32:42 make My arrows drunk with ***b***,
32:42 With the ***b*** of the slain and
32:43 For He will avenge the ***b*** of
Josh 2:19 his ***b*** shall be on his own
2:19 his ***b*** shall be on our head if
20: 3 refuge from the avenger of ***b***.
20: 5 Then if the avenger of ***b*** pursues
20: 9 by the hand of the avenger of ***b***
Judg 9:24 might be settled and their ***b***
1 Sam 14:32 the people ate them with the ***b***.
14:33 the LORD by eating with the ***b***!
14:34 the LORD by eating with the ***b***.
19: 5 will you sin against innocent ***b***,
25:31 either that you have shed ***b***
26:20 do not let my ***b*** fall to the
2 Sam 1:16 Your ***b*** is on your own head, for
1:22 From the ***b*** of the slain, From
3:27 so that he died for the ***b*** of
3:28 the LORD forever of the ***b*** of
4:11 shall I not now require his ***b***
14:11 do not permit the avenger of ***b***
16: 8 has brought upon you all the ***b***
20:12 But Amasa wallowed in his ***b*** in
23:17 do this! Is this not the ***b***
1 Ki 2: 5 And he shed the ***b*** of war in
2: 5 and put the ***b*** of war on his
2: 9 hair down to the grave with ***b***.
2:31 of my father the innocent ***b***
2:32 the LORD will return his ***b***
2:33 Their ***b*** shall therefore return
2:37 your ***b*** shall be on your own
18:28 until the ***b*** gushed out on them.
21:19 place where dogs licked the ***b***
21:19 Naboth, dogs shall lick your ***b***,
22:35 The ***b*** ran out from the wound
22:38 and the dogs licked up his ***b***
2 Ki 3:22 on the other side as red as ***b***.
3:23 And they said, "This is ***b***;
9: 7 that I may avenge the ***b*** of My
9: 7 and the ***b*** of all the servants
9:26 Surely I saw yesterday the ***b*** of
9:26 the blood of Naboth and the ***b***
9:33 and some of her ***b*** spattered on
16:13 offering and sprinkled the ***b***
16:15 and sprinkle on it all the ***b*** of
16:15 burnt offering and all the ***b***
21:16 shed very much innocent ***b***,
24: 4 also because of the innocent ***b***
24: 4 Jerusalem with innocent ***b***,
1 Chr 11:19 do this! Shall I drink the ***b***
22: 8 You have shed much ***b*** and have
22: 8 because you have shed much ***b*** on
28: 3 a man of war and have shed ***b***.
2 Chr 24:25 against him because of the ***b***
29:22 and the priests received the ***b***
29:22 the rams and sprinkled the ***b***
29:22 the lambs and sprinkled the ***b***
29:24 and they presented their ***b*** on
30:16 the priests sprinkled the ***b***
35:11 the priests sprinkled the ***b***
Job 16:18 "O earth, do not cover my ***b***,
39:30 Its young ones suck up ***b***;
Ps 9:12 When He avenges ***b***,
16: 4 Their drink offerings of ***b*** I
30: 9 profit is there in my ***b***,
50:13 Or drink the ***b*** of goats?
58:10 shall wash his feet in the ***b***
68:23 your foot may crush them in ***b***,
72:14 And precious shall be their ***b***
78:44 Turned their rivers into ***b***,
79: 3 Their ***b*** they have shed like
79:10 sight The avenging of the ***b***
94:21 And condemn innocent ***b***.
105:29 He turned their waters into ***b***,
106:38 And shed innocent ***b***,
106:38 The ***b*** of their sons and
106:38 the land was polluted with ***b***.
Prov 1:11 Let us lie in wait to shed ***b***;
1:16 And they make haste to shed ***b***.
1:18 lie in wait for their own ***b***,
6:17 Hands that shed innocent ***b***,
12: 6 are, "Lie in wait for ***b***,
30:33 wringing the nose produces ***b***,
Isa 1:11 I do not delight in the ***b*** of
1:15 Your hands are full of ***b***.
4: 4 and purged the ***b*** of Jerusalem
9: 5 And garments rolled in ***b***,
15: 9 of Dimon will be full of ***b***;
26:21 earth will also disclose her ***b***,
34: 3 shall be melted with their ***b***.
34: 6 of the LORD is filled with ***b***,
34: 6 With the ***b*** of lambs and goats,
34: 7 land shall be soaked with ***b***,
49:26 be drunk with their own ***b*** as
59: 3 your hands are defiled with ***b***,
59: 7 make haste to shed innocent ***b***;
63: 3 Their ***b*** is sprinkled upon My
66: 3 as if he offers swine's ***b***;
Jer 2:34 on your skirts is found The ***b***
7: 6 and do not shed innocent ***b*** in
18:21 And pour out their ***b*** By the
19: 4 filled this place with the ***b***
22: 3 nor shed innocent ***b*** in this
22:17 For shedding innocent ***b***,
26:15 will surely bring innocent ***b***
46:10 and made drunk with their ***b***;
48:10 who keeps back his sword from ***b***.
51:35 And my ***b*** be upon the inhabitants
Lam 4:13 Who shed in her midst The ***b***
4:14 have defiled themselves with ***b***,
Ezek 3:18 but his ***b*** I will require at
3:20 but his ***b*** I will require at
5:17 Pestilence and ***b*** shall pass
7:23 land is filled with crimes of ***b***,
14:19 and pour out My fury on it in ***b***,
16: 6 you struggling in your own ***b***,
16: 6 blood, I said to you in your ***b***,
16: 6 Yes, I said to you in your ***b***,
16: 9 I thoroughly washed off your ***b***,
16:22 and bare, struggling in your ***b***.
16:36 and because of the ***b*** of your
16:38 who break wedlock or shed ***b***
16:38 I will bring ***b*** upon you in fury
18:10 is a robber Or a shedder of ***b***,
18:13 His ***b*** shall be upon him.
21:32 Your ***b*** shall be in the midst
22: 3 The city sheds ***b*** in her own
22: 4 have become guilty by the ***b***
22: 6 has used his power to shed ***b***
22:12 you they take bribes to shed ***b***;
22:27 tearing the prey, to shed ***b***,
23:37 and ***b*** is on their hands.
23:45 the manner of women who shed ***b***,
23:45 and ***b*** is on their hands.
24: 7 For her ***b*** is in her midst; She
24: 8 I have set her ***b*** on top of a
28:23 And ***b*** in her streets; The
32: 6 land with the flow of your ***b***,
33: 4 his ***b*** shall be on his own
33: 5 his ***b*** shall be upon himself.
33: 6 but his ***b*** I will require at the
33: 8 but his ***b*** I will require at
33:25 GOD: "You eat meat with ***b***,
33:25 toward your idols, and shed ***b***.
35: 5 and have shed the ***b*** of the
35: 6 "I will prepare you for ***b***,
35: 6 and ***b*** shall pursue you; since
35: 6 you; since you have not hated ***b***,
35: 6 therefore ***b*** shall pursue you.
36:18 out My fury on them for the ***b***
39:17 you may eat flesh and drink ***b***.
39:18 Drink the ***b*** of the princes of
39:19 And drink ***b*** till you are
43:18 and for sprinkling ***b*** on it.
43:20 You shall take some of its ***b*** and
44: 7 My food, the fat and the ***b***,
44:15 offer to Me the fat and the ***b***,
45:19 shall take some of the ***b*** of
Hos 6: 8 evildoers, And defiled with ***b***.
Joel 2:30 ***B*** and fire and pillars of
2:31 darkness, And the moon into ***b***,
3:19 For they have shed innocent ***b***
Jon 1:14 not charge us with innocent ***b***;
Mic 7: 2 They all lie in wait for ***b***;
Hab 2: 8 Because of men's ***b*** And the
2:17 Because of men's ***b*** And the
Zeph 1:17 Their ***b*** shall be poured out
Zech 9: 7 I will take away the ***b*** from his
9:11 Because of the ***b*** of your
9:15 They shall be filled with ***b***
Mt 9:20 a woman who had a flow of ***b*** for
16:17 for flesh and ***b*** has not
23:30 partakers with them in the ***b***
23:35 may come all the righteous ***b***
23:35 from the ***b*** of righteous Abel to
23:35 of righteous Abel to the ***b*** of
26:28 For this is My ***b*** of the new
27: 4 sinned by betraying innocent ***b***.
27: 6 because they are the price of ***b***.
27: 8 has been called the Field of ***B***
27:24 I am innocent of the ***b*** of this
27:25 His ***b*** be on us and on our
Mk 5:25 a certain woman had a flow of ***b***
5:29 the fountain of her ***b*** was
14:24 This is My ***b*** of the new
Lk 8:43 having a flow of ***b*** for twelve
8:44 And immediately her flow of ***b***
11:50 that the ***b*** of all the prophets
11:51 from the ***b*** of Abel to the blood
11:51 the blood of Abel to the ***b*** of
13: 1 Him about the Galileans whose ***b***
22:20 is the new covenant in My ***b***,
22:44 became like great drops of ***b***
Jn 1:13 who were born, not of ***b***,
6:53 the Son of Man and drink His ***b***,
6:54 eats My flesh and drinks My ***b***
6:55 and My ***b*** is drink indeed.
6:56 eats My flesh and drinks My ***b***
19:34 and immediately ***b*** and water
Acts 1:19 Akel Dama, that is, Field of ***B***.
2:19 ***B*** and fire and vapor of
2:20 And the moon into ***b***,
5:28 intend to bring this Man's ***b***
15:20 things strangled, and from ***b***.
15:29 things offered to idols, from ***b***,
17:26 And He has made from one ***b*** every
18: 6 Your ***b*** be upon your own heads;
20:26 that I am innocent of the ***b***
20:28 He purchased with His own ***b***.
21:25 offered to idols, from ***b***,
22:20 And when the ***b*** of Your martyr
Rom 3:15 feet are swift to shed ***b***;
3:25 as a propitiation by His ***b***,
5: 9 now been justified by His ***b***,

1 Cor 10:16 it not the communion of the **b**
11:25 cup is the new covenant in My **b**.
11:27 be guilty of the body and **b** of
15:50 that flesh and **b** cannot inherit
Gal 1:16 confer with flesh and **b**,
Eph 1: 7 have redemption through His **b**,
2:13 been brought near by the **b** of
6:12 not wrestle against flesh and **b**,
Col 1:14 have redemption through His **b**,
1:20 made peace through the **b** of
Heb 2:14 have partaken of flesh and **b**,
9: 7 once a year, not without **b**,
9:12 Not with the **b** of goats and
9:12 but with His own **b** He entered
9:13 For if the **b** of bulls and goats
9:14 how much more shall the **b** of
9:18 was dedicated without **b**.
9:19 he took the **b** of calves and
9:20 This is the **b** of the
9:21 likewise he sprinkled with **b**
9:22 all things are purified with **b**,
9:22 and without shedding of **b** there
9:25 Holy Place every year with **b**
10: 4 is not possible that the **b** of
10:19 to enter the Holiest by the **b**
10:29 counted the **b** of the covenant
11:28 and the sprinkling of **b**,
12:24 and to the **b** of sprinkling that
13:11 whose **b** is brought into the
13:12 the people with His own **b**,
13:20 through the **b** of the
1 Pe 1: 2 and sprinkling of the **b** of
1:19 but with the precious **b** of
1 Jn 1: 7 and the **b** of Jesus Christ His
5: 6 is He who came by water and **b**—
5: 6 by water, but by water and **b**.
5: 8 Spirit, the water, and the **b**;
Rev 1: 5 us from our sins in His own **b**,
5: 9 redeemed us to God by Your **b**
6:10 You judge and avenge our **b** on
6:12 and the moon became like **b**.
7:14 and made them white in the **b**
8: 7 fire followed, mingled with **b**,
8: 8 and a third of the sea became **b**.
11: 6 over waters to turn them to **b**,
12:11 they overcame him by the **b**
14:20 and **b** came out of the
16: 3 and it became **b** as of a dead
16: 4 of water, and they became **b**.
16: 6 For they have shed the **b** of
16: 6 And You have given them **b** to
17: 6 drunk with the **b** of the saints
17: 6 of the saints and with the **b**
18:24 And in her was found the **b** of
19: 2 He has avenged on her the **b** of
19:13 clothed with a robe dipped in **b**,

BLOODLINE (1/1) BLOOD

Ezek 19:10 was like a vine in your **b**,

BLOODSHED (24/23) BLOOD

Ex 22: 2 shall be no guilt for his **b**.
22: 3 shall be guilt for his **b**.
Lev 17: 4 the guilt of **b** shall be imputed
Deut 17: 8 between degrees of guilt for **b**,
19:10 and thus guilt of **b** be upon
22: 8 you may not bring guilt of **b**
1 Sam 25:26 held you back from coming to **b**
25:33 me this day from coming to **b**
2 Chr 19:10 whether of **b** or offenses
Ps 51:14 Deliver me from the guilt of **b**,
Prov 28:17 A man burdened with **b** will flee
Isa 33:15 his ears from hearing of **b**,
Ezek 9: 9 and the land is full of **b**,
22: 9 are men who slander to cause **b**;
22:13 and at the **b** which has been in
38:22 judgment with pestilence and **b**;
Hos 1: 4 while I will avenge the **b** of
4: 2 With **b** upon bloodshed.
4: 2 With bloodshed upon **b**.
12:14 will leave the guilt of his **b**
Joel 3:21 acquit them of the guilt of **b**,
Mic 3:10 Who build up Zion with **b** And
Hab 2:12 to him who builds a town with **b**,
Heb 12: 4 You have not yet resisted to **b**,

BLOODTHIRSTY (9/9) BLOOD

2 Sam 16: 7 Come out! Come out! You **b** man,
16: 8 because you are a **b** man!"
21: 1 is because of Saul and his **b**
Ps 5: 6 The LORD abhors the **b** and
26: 9 Nor my life with **b** men,
55:23 **B** and deceitful men shall not
59: 2 And save me from **b** men.
139:19 from me, therefore, you **b** men.
Prov 29:10 The **b** hate the blameless, But

BLOODY (4/4) BLOOD

Ezek 22: 2 will you judge the **b** city?
24: 6 Woe to the **b** city, To the pot
24: 9 Woe to the **b** city! I too will
Nah 3: 1 Woe to the **b** city! It is all

BLOOM (1/1) BLOOMED, BLOOMS, BLOSSOM

Song 7:12 And the pomegranates are in **b**.

BLOOMED (1/1) BLOOM

Song 6:11 And the pomegranates had **b**.

BLOOMS (1/1) BLOOM

Song 1:14 is to me a cluster of henna **b**

BLOSSOM (9/9) BLOSSOMED, BLOSSOMS

Num 17: 5 of the man whom I choose will **b**;
1 Ki 7:26 brim of a cup, like a lily **b**.
2 Chr 4: 5 brim of a cup, like a lily **b**.
Job 15:33 And cast off his **b** like an
Isa 5:24 And their **b** will ascend like
27: 6 Israel shall **b** and bud, And
35: 1 the desert shall rejoice and **b**
35: 2 It shall **b** abundantly and
Hab 3:17 Though the fig tree may not **b**,

BLOSSOMED (1/1) BLOSSOM

Ezek 7:10 has gone out; The rod has **b**,

BLOSSOMS (10/8) BLOSSOM, BLOSSOMS

Gen 40:10 its **b** shot forth, and its
Ex 25:33 shall be made like almond **b**
25:33 bowls made like almond **b** on
25:34 shall be made like almond **b**,
37:19 bowls made like almond **b** on
37:19 bowls made like almond **b** on
37:20 four bowls made like almond **b**,
Num 17: 8 had produced **b** and yielded ripe
Eccl 12: 5 way; When the almond tree **b**,
Song 7:12 Whether the grape **b** are open,

BLOT (11/11) BLOTS, BLOTTED

Ex 17:14 that I will utterly **b** out the
32:32 **b** me out of Your book which You
32:33 I will **b** him out of My book.
Deut 9:14 that I may destroy them and **b**
25:19 that you will **b** out the
29:20 and the LORD would **b** out his
2 Ki 14:27 did not say that He would **b**
Ps 51: 1 **B** out my transgressions.
51: 9 And **b** out all my iniquities.
Jer 18:23 Nor **b** out their sin from Your
Rev 3: 5 and I will not **b** out his name

BLOTS (1/1) BLOT

Isa 43:25 am He who **b** out your

BLOTTED (8/8) BLOT

Deut 25: 6 that his name may not be **b** out
Neh 4: 5 and do not let their sin be **b**
Ps 9: 5 You have **b** out their name
69:28 Let them be **b** out of the book
109:13 following let their name be **b**
109:14 not the sin of his mother be **b**
Isa 44:22 I have **b** out, like a thick
Acts 3:19 that your sins may be **b** out, so

BLOW (35/34) BLEW, BLOWING, BLOWN, BLOWS

Num 10: 3 When they **b** both of them, all
10: 4 But if they **b** only one, then
10: 7 gathered together, you shall **b**,
10: 8 shall **b** the trumpets; and these
10:10 you shall **b** the trumpets over
Josh 6: 4 and the priests shall **b** the
Judg 7:18 When I **b** the trumpet, I and all
7:18 then you also **b** the trumpets on
16:28 that I may with one **b** take
1 Sam 19: 8 and struck them with a mighty **b**,
23: 5 struck them with a mighty **b**,
1 Ki 1:34 and **b** the horn, and say, 'Long
1 Chr 15:24 were to **b** the trumpets before
Job 36:18 He take you away with one **b**;
Ps 39:10 I am consumed by the **b** of Your
78:26 He caused an east wind to **b** in
81: 3 **B** the trumpet at the time of
147:18 them; He causes His wind to **b**,
Song 4:16 O south! **B** upon my garden,
Isa 40:24 When He will also **b** on them,
Jer 4: 5 **B** the trumpet in the land; Cry,
6: 1 the midst of Jerusalem! **B** the
6:29 The bellows **b** fiercely, The
14:17 stroke, with a very severe **b**.
51:27 **B** the trumpet among the
Ezek 21:31 I will **b** against you with the
22:20 to **b** fire on it, to melt it;
22:21 I will gather you and **b** on you
33: 6 the sword coming and does not **b**
Hos 5: 8 **B** the ram's horn in Gibeah,
Joel 2: 1 **B** the trumpet in Zion, And
2:15 **B** the trumpet in Zion,
Zech 9:14 The Lord GOD will **b** the
Lk 12:55 when you see the south wind **b**,
Rev 7: 1 that the wind should not **b** on

BLOWING (8/8) BLOW

Lev 23:24 a memorial of **b** of trumpets, a
Num 29: 1 For you it is a day of **b** the
Josh 6: 9 the priests continued **b** the
6:13 the priests continued **b** the
Judg 7:20 in their right hands for **b**—
2 Ki 11:14 the land were rejoicing and **b**
2 Chr 23:13 the land were rejoicing and **b**
Jn 6:18 because a great wind was **b**.

BLOWN (4/4) BLOW

Isa 27:13 The great trumpet will be **b**;
Ezek 7:14 They have **b** the trumpet and made
Hos 13: 3 Like chaff **b** off from a
Am 3: 6 If a trumpet is **b** in a city,

BLOWS (13/12) BLOW

Deut 25: 2 with a certain number of **b**.
25: 3 Forty **b** he may give him and no
25: 3 this and beat him with many **b**
2 Sam 7:14 the rod of men and with the **b**
Prov 17:10 a wise man Than a hundred **b**
18: 6 And his mouth calls for **b**.
20:30 **B** that hurt cleanse away evil,
Isa 18: 3 And when he **b** a trumpet, you
40: 7 the breath of the LORD **b** upon
54:16 created the blacksmith Who **b**
Jer 4:11 of the desolate heights **b** in
Ezek 33: 3 if he **b** the trumpet and warns
Jn 3: 8 The wind **b** where it wishes, and

BLUE (48/48)

Ex 25: 4 '**b**, purple, and scarlet
26: 1 of fine woven linen and **b**,
26: 4 shall make loops of **b** yarn
26:31 shall make a veil woven of **b**,
26:36 of the tabernacle, woven of **b**,
27:16 cubits long, woven of **b**,
28: 5 "They shall take the gold, **b**,
28: 6 shall make the ephod of gold, **b**,
28: 8 workmanship, made of gold, **b**,
28:15 you shall make it: of gold, **b**,
28:28 using a **b** cord, so that it is
28:31 the robe of the ephod all of **b**.
28:33 shall make pomegranates of **b**,
28:37 you shall put it on a **b** cord,
35: 6 '**b**, purple, and scarlet thread,
35:23 man, with whom was found **b**,
35:25 what they had spun, of **b** ,
35:35 and the tapestry maker, in **b**,
36: 8 woven of fine linen, and of **b**,
36:11 He made loops of **b** yarn on the
36:35 And he made a veil of **b**,
36:37 for the tabernacle door, of **b**,
38:18 of the court was woven of **b**,
38:23 and designer, a weaver of **b**,
39: 1 Of the **b**, purple, and scarlet
39: 2 He made the ephod of gold, **b**,
39: 3 to work it in with the **b**,
39: 5 workmanship, woven of gold, **b**,
39: 8 of the ephod, of gold, **b**,
39:21 the rings of the ephod with a **b**
39:22 ephod of woven work, all of **b**.
39:24 of the robe pomegranates of **b**,
39:29 sash of fine woven linen with **b**,
39:31 And they tied to it a **b** cord, to
Num 4: 6 that a cloth entirely of **b**;
4: 7 they shall spread a **b** cloth,
4: 9 And they shall take a **b** cloth
4:11 altar they shall spread a **b**
4:12 put them in a **b** cloth, cover
15:38 and to put a **b** thread in the
2 Chr 2: 7 in purple and crimson and **b**,
2:14 stone and wood, purple and **b**,
3:14 And he made the veil of **b**,
Esth 1: 6 There were white and **b** linen
8:15 the king in royal apparel of **b**
Jer 10: 9 **B** and purple are their
Ezek 27: 7 **B** and purple from the coasts
Rev 9:17 of fiery red, hyacinth **b**,

BLUNT (1/1)

2 Sam 2:23 him in the stomach with the **b**

BLUSH (2/2)

Jer 6:15 Nor did they know how to **b**.
8:12 Nor did they know how to **b**.

BOANERGES (1/1)

Mk 3:17 to whom He gave the name **B**,

BOAR (1/1)

Ps 80:13 The **b** out of the woods uproots

BOARD (11/9) BOARDED, BOARDS

Ex 26:16 shall be the length of a **b**,
26:16 shall be the width of each **b**.
26:17 tenons shall be in each **b**
26:25 sockets under each **b**.
36:21 The length of each **b** was ten
36:21 and the width of each **b** a cubit
36:22 Each **b** had two tenons for
Acts 20:13 intending to take Paul on **b**;
20:14 we took him on **b** and came to
27: 6 to Italy, and he put us on **b**.
27:17 When they had taken it on **b**,

BOARDED (1/1) BOARD

Acts 21: 6 we **b** the ship, and they

BOARDS (45/38) BOARD

Ex 26:15 you shall make the ***b*** of acacia
26:17 you shall make for all the ***b***
26:18 And you shall make the ***b*** for the
26:18 twenty ***b*** for the south side.
26:19 of silver under the twenty ***b***:
26:19 two sockets under each of the ***b***
26:20 there shall be twenty ***b***
26:21 two sockets under each of the ***b***.
26:22 westward, you shall make six ***b***.
26:23 And you shall also make two ***b***
26:25 So there shall be eight ***b*** with
26:26 five for the ***b*** on one side of
26:27 five bars for the ***b*** on the other
26:27 and five bars for the ***b*** of the
26:28 pass through the midst of the ***b***
26:29 You shall overlay the ***b*** with
27: 8 shall make it hollow with ***b***;
35:11 its covering, its clasps, its ***b***,
36:20 For the tabernacle he made ***b*** of
36:22 Thus he made for all the ***b*** of
36:23 And he made ***b*** for the
36:23 twenty ***b*** for the south side.
36:24 made to go under the twenty ***b***:
36:24 two sockets under each of the ***b***
36:25 north side, he made twenty ***b***
36:26 two sockets under each of the ***b***.
36:27 of the tabernacle he made six ***b***.
36:28 He also made two ***b*** for the two
36:30 So there were eight ***b*** and their
36:30 sockets under each of the ***b***.
36:31 five for the ***b*** on one side of
36:32 five bars for the ***b*** on the other
36:32 and five bars for the ***b*** of the
36:33 bar to pass through the ***b*** from
36:34 He overlaid the ***b*** with gold,
38: 7 He made the altar hollow with ***b***.
39:33 furnishings: its clasps, its ***b***,
40:18 its sockets, set up its ***b***,
Num 3:36 of Merari included the ***b*** of
4:31 the ***b*** of the tabernacle, its
1 Ki 6: 9 the temple with beams and ***b*** of
6:15 of the temple with cedar ***b***;
6:16 floor to ceiling, with cedar ***b***;
Song 8: 9 We will enclose her With ***b*** of
Acts 27:44 some on ***b*** and some on parts of

BOAST (46/41) BOASTED, BOASTERS, BOASTFUL, BOASTFULLY, BOASTING, BOASTS

1 Ki 20:11 one who puts on his armor ***b***
2 Chr 25:19 your heart is lifted up to ***b***.
Ps 34: 2 My soul shall make its ***b*** in the
44: 8 In God we ***b*** all day long, And
49: 6 trust in their wealth And ***b***
52: 1 Why do you ***b*** in evil, O mighty
90:10 Yet their ***b*** is only labor and
94: 4 All the workers of iniquity ***b***
97: 7 Who ***b*** of idols. Worship Him,
Prov 27: 1 Do not ***b*** about tomorrow, For
Isa 10:15 Shall the ax ***b*** itself against
61: 6 And in their glory you shall ***b***.
Jer 49: 4 Why do you ***b*** in the valleys,
Ezek 24:21 My sanctuary, your arrogant ***b***,
Rom 2:17 and make your ***b*** in God,
2:23 You who make your ***b*** in the law,
4: 2 he has something to ***b*** about,
11:18 do not ***b*** against the branches.
11:18 the branches. But if you do ***b***,
1 Cor 3:21 Therefore let no one ***b*** in men.
4: 7 why do you ***b*** as if you had not
9:16 I have nothing to ***b*** of, for
2 Cor 1:14 that we are your ***b*** as you also
5:12 but give you opportunity to ***b***
5:12 an answer for those who ***b*** in
9: 2 about which I ***b*** of you to the
10: 8 For even if I should ***b*** somewhat
10:13 will not ***b*** beyond measure, but
10:16 and not to ***b*** in another man's
11:12 in the things of which they ***b***.
11:16 that I also may ***b*** a little.
11:18 Seeing that many ***b*** according to
11:18 to the flesh, I also will ***b***.
11:30 If I must ***b***, I will boast in
11:30 I will ***b*** in the things which
12: 1 not profitable for me to ***b***.
12: 5 Of such a one I will ***b***;
12: 5 yet of myself I will not ***b***,
12: 6 For though I might desire to ***b***,
12: 9 most gladly I will rather ***b*** in
Gal 6:13 circumcised that they may ***b*** in
6:14 But God forbid that I should ***b***
Eph 2: 9 of works, lest anyone should ***b***.
2 Th 1: 4 so that we ourselves ***b*** of you
Jas 3:14 do not ***b*** and lie against the
4:16 But now you ***b*** in your arrogance.

BOASTED (2/2) BOAST

Ezek 35:13 with your mouth you have ***b***
2 Cor 7:14 For if in anything I have ***b*** to

BOASTERS (2/2) BOAST

Rom 1:30 of God, violent, proud, ***b***,
2 Tim 3: 2 themselves, lovers of money, ***b***,

BOASTFUL (3/3) BOAST, BOASTFULLY

Ps 5: 5 The ***b*** shall not stand in Your
73: 3 For I was envious of the ***b***,
75: 4 'I said to the ***b***,

BOASTFULLY (1/1) BOASTFUL

Ps 75: 4 to the boastful, 'Do not deal ***b***,

BOASTING (14/14) BOAST

Rom 3:27 Where is ***b*** then? It is
1 Cor 9:15 that anyone should make my ***b***
15:31 by the ***b*** in you which I have in
2 Cor 1:12 For our ***b*** is this: the
7: 4 great is my ***b*** on your behalf.
7:14 even so our ***b*** to Titus was
8:24 of your love and of our ***b*** on
9: 3 lest our ***b*** of you should be in
9: 4 be ashamed of this confident ***b***.
10:15 not ***b*** of things beyond measure,
11:10 one shall stop me from this ***b***
11:17 in this confidence of ***b***.
12:11 I have become a fool in ***b***;
Jas 4:16 All such ***b*** is evil.

BOASTS (4/4) BOAST

Ps 10: 3 For the wicked ***b*** of his heart's
Prov 20:14 he has gone his way, then he ***b***.
25:14 Whoever falsely ***b*** of giving
Jas 3: 5 is a little member and ***b*** great

BOAT (43/41) BOATS

Mt 4:21 in the ***b*** with Zebedee their
4:22 and immediately they left the ***b***
8:23 Now when He got into a ***b***,
8:24 so that the ***b*** was covered with
9: 1 So He got into a ***b***,
13: 2 so that He got into a ***b*** and
14:13 He departed from there by ***b*** to
14:22 His disciples get into the ***b***
14:24 But the ***b*** was now in the middle
14:29 had come down out of the ***b***,
14:32 And when they got into the ***b***,
14:33 Then those who were in the ***b***
15:39 the multitude, got into the ***b***,
Mk 1:19 who also were in the ***b*** mending
1:20 their father Zebedee in the ***b***
3: 9 His disciples that a small ***b***
4: 1 so that He got into a ***b*** and sat
4:36 they took Him along in the ***b*** as
4:37 and the waves beat into the ***b***,
5: 2 when He had come out of the ***b***,
5:18 And when He got into the ***b***,
5:21 had crossed over again by ***b*** to
6:32 to a deserted place in the ***b***
6:45 His disciples get into the ***b***
6:47 the ***b*** was in the middle of the
6:51 Then He went up into the ***b*** to
6:54 And when they came out of the ***b***,
8:10 immediately got into the ***b*** with
8:13 and getting into the ***b*** again,
8:14 one loaf with them in the ***b***.
Lk 5: 3 the multitudes from the ***b***.
5: 7 their partners in the other ***b***
8:22 that He got into a ***b*** with His
8:37 And He got into the ***b*** and
Jn 6:17 got into the ***b***, and went over
6:19 the sea and drawing near the ***b***;
6:21 received Him into the ***b***,
6:21 and immediately the ***b*** was at
6:22 saw that there was no other ***b***
6:22 Jesus had not entered the ***b***
21: 3 and immediately got into the ***b***,
21: 6 net on the right side of the ***b***,
21: 8 disciples came in the little ***b***

BOATS (7/7) BOAT

Mk 4:36 And other little ***b*** were also
Lk 5: 2 and saw two ***b*** standing by the
5: 3 Then He got into one of the ***b***,
5: 7 they came and filled both the ***b***,
5:11 when they had brought their ***b***
Jn 6:23 other ***b*** came from Tiberias,
6:24 they also got into ***b*** and came

BOAZ (28/24)

Ruth 2: 1 of Elimelech. His name was ***B***.
2: 3 of the field belonging to ***B***,
2: 4 ***B*** came from Bethlehem, and said
2: 5 Then ***B*** said to his servant who
2: 8 Then ***B*** said to Ruth, "You will
2:11 And ***B*** answered and said to her,
2:14 Now ***B*** said to her at mealtime,
2:15 ***B*** commanded his young men,
2:19 with whom I worked today is ***B***.
2:23 close by the young women of ***B***,
3: 2 'Now ***B***, whose young women
3: 7 And after ***B*** had eaten and drunk,
4: 1 Now ***B*** went up to the gate and
4: 1 the close relative of whom ***B***
4: 1 So ***B*** said, "Come aside,
4: 5 Then ***B*** said, "On the day you
4: 8 the close relative said to ***B***,
4: 9 And ***B*** said to the elders and all
4:13 So ***B*** took Ruth and she became
4:21 Salmon begot ***B***, and Boaz begot
4:21 and ***B*** begot Obed;
1 Ki 7:21 the left and called its name ***B***.
1 Chr 2:11 begot Salma, and Salma begot ***B***;
2:12 ***B*** begot Obed, and Obed begot
2 Chr 3:17 name of the one on the left ***B***.
Mt 1: 5 Salmon begot ***B*** by Rahab, Boaz
1: 5 ***B*** begot Obed by Ruth, Obed
Lk 3:32 son of Obed, the son of ***B***,

BOCHERU (2/2)

1 Chr 8:38 names were these: Azrikam, ***B***,
9:44 names were these: Azrikam, ***B***,

BOCHIM (2/2)

Judg 2: 1 LORD came up from Gilgal to ***B***,
2: 5 called the name of that place ***B***;

BODIES (38/35) BODY

Gen 47:18 the sight of my lord but our ***b***
1 Sam 31:12 the body of Saul and the ***b*** of
1 Chr 10:12 the body of Saul and the ***b*** of
2 Chr 20:24 and there were their dead ***b***,
20:25 of valuables on the dead ***b***,
Neh 9:37 they have dominion over our ***b***
Ps 79: 2 The dead ***b*** of Your servants
110: 6 fill the places with dead ***b***,
Jer 31:40 the whole valley of the dead ***b***
33: 5 their places with the dead ***b***
34:20 Their dead ***b*** shall be for meat
41: 9 had cast all the dead ***b*** of the
Ezek 1:11 and two covered their ***b***.
39:14 the land and bury those ***b***
44:18 and linen trousers on their ***b***;
Dan 3:27 they saw these men on whose ***b***
3:28 word, and yielded their ***b***,
Am 6:10 with one who will burn the ***b***,
6:10 picks up the ***b*** to take them out
8: 3 Many dead ***b*** everywhere, They
Nah 3: 3 of slain, A great number of ***b***,
Mt 27:52 and many ***b*** of the saints who
Jn 19:31 that the ***b*** should not remain on
Rom 1:24 to dishonor their ***b*** among
8:11 also give life to your mortal ***b***
12: 1 that you present your ***b*** a
1 Cor 6:15 Do you not know that your ***b*** are
10: 5 for their ***b*** were scattered in
15:40 There are also celestial ***b*** and
15:40 bodies and terrestrial ***b***;
2 Cor 7: 5 our ***b*** had no rest, but we were
Eph 5:28 their own wives as their own ***b***;
Heb 10:22 an evil conscience and our ***b***
13:11 For the ***b*** of those animals,
Rev 11: 8 And their dead ***b*** will lie in
11: 9 nations will see their dead ***b***
11: 9 and not allow their dead ***b*** to
18:13 and ***b*** and souls of men.

BODILY (4/4) BODY

Lk 3:22 the Holy Spirit descended in ***b***
2 Cor 10:10 but his ***b*** presence is weak,
Col 2: 9 the fullness of the Godhead ***b***;
1 Tim 4: 8 For ***b*** exercise profits a little,

BODY (224/196) BODIES, BODILY, BODYGUARDS

Gen 15: 4 who will come from your own ***b***
25:23 shall be separated from your ***b***;
35:11 kings shall come from your ***b***.
46:26 to Egypt, who came from his ***b***,
Lev 6:10 trousers he shall put on his ***b***,
13: 2 a man has on the skin of his ***b***
13: 2 it becomes on the skin of his ***b***
13: 3 the sore on the skin of the ***b***;
13: 3 deeper than the skin of his ***b***,
13: 4 is white on the skin of his ***b***,
13:11 leprosy on the skin of his ***b***.
13:13 leprosy has covered all his ***b***,
13:18 If the ***b*** develops a boil in the
13:24 Or if the ***b*** receives a burn on
13:38 spots on the skin of the ***b***,
13:39 spots on the skin of the ***b***
13:43 of leprosy on the skin of the ***b***,
14: 9 his clothes and wash his ***b*** in
15: 2 man has a discharge from his ***b***,
15: 3 whether his ***b*** runs with his
15: 3 or his ***b*** is stopped up by his
15: 7 And he who touches the ***b*** of him
15:13 and bathe his ***b*** in running
15:16 then he shall wash all his ***b*** in
15:19 and the discharge from her ***b***
16: 4 and the linen trousers on his ***b***;
16: 4 Therefore he shall wash his ***b***
16:24 And he shall wash his ***b*** with
16:26 his clothes and bathe his ***b*** in
16:28 his clothes and bathe his ***b*** in
17:16 not wash them or bathe his ***b***,
21:11 shall he go near any dead ***b***,
22: 6 unless he washes his ***b*** with
Num 6: 6 he shall not go near a dead ***b***.
8: 7 and let them shave all their ***b***,
19:11 He who touches the dead ***b*** of
19:13 Whoever touches the ***b*** of anyone
25: 8 and the woman through her ***b***.
Deut 21:23 his ***b*** shall not remain overnight
28: 4 shall be the fruit of your ***b***,
28:11 goods, in the fruit of your ***b***,
28:18 shall be the fruit of your ***b***
28:53 eat the fruit of your own ***b***,
30: 9 hand, in the fruit of your ***b***,
1 Sam 31:10 and they fastened his ***b*** to the
31:12 and took the ***b*** of Saul and the

2 Sam 7:12 you, who will come from your **b**,
16:11 my son who came from my own **b**
1 Ki 8:19 son who will come from your **b**,
21:27 and put sackcloth on his **b**,
2 Ki 6:30 he had sackcloth on his **b**.
23:30 Then his servants moved his **b** in
1 Chr 10:12 men arose and took the **b** of
2 Chr 6: 9 son who will come from your **b**,
26:14 **b** armor, bows, and slings to
Job 4:15 The hair on my **b** stood up.
7:15 And death rather than my **b**.
19:17 to the children of my own **b**.
20:25 drawn, and comes out of the **b**;
Ps 31: 9 Yes, my soul and my **b**!
44:25 Our **b** clings to the ground.
109:18 So let it enter his **b** like
132:11 your throne the fruit of your **b**.
Prov 5:11 When your flesh and your **b** are
14:30 sound heart is life to the **b**,
18: 8 they go down into the inmost **b**.
26:22 they go down into the inmost **b**.
Song 5:14 His **b** is carved ivory Inlaid
Isa 10:18 field, Both soul and **b**;
20: 2 the sackcloth from your **b**,
26:19 Together with my dead **b** they
48:19 And the offspring of your **b**
51:23 And you have laid your **b** like
Jer 26:23 the sword and cast his dead **b**
36:30 and his dead **b** shall be cast
Lam 4: 7 They were more ruddy in **b** than
Ezek 1:23 covered the other side of the **b**.
10:12 And their whole **b**, with their
Dan 4:33 his **b** was wet with the dew of
5:21 and his **b** was wet with the dew
7:11 and its **b** destroyed and given
7:15 in my spirit within my **b**,
10: 6 His **b** was like beryl, his face
Mic 6: 7 The fruit of my **b** for the sin
Hab 3:16 my **b** trembled; My lips
Hag 2:13 unclean because of a dead **b**
Mt 5:29 than for your whole **b** to be
5:30 than for your whole **b** to be
6:22 The lamp of the **b** is the eye.
6:22 your whole **b** will be full of
6:23 your whole **b** will be full of
6:25 will drink; nor about your **b**,
6:25 life more than food and the **b**
10:28 not fear those who kill the **b**
10:28 to destroy both soul and **b** in
14:12 came and took away the **b** and
26:12 this fragrant oil on My **b**,
26:26 said, "Take, eat; this is My **b**.
27:58 to Pilate and asked for the **b**
27:58 Then Pilate commanded the **b** to
27:59 When Joseph had taken the **b**,
Mk 5:29 and she felt in her **b** that she
14: 8 come beforehand to anoint My **b**
14:22 said, "Take, eat; this is My **b**.
14:51 thrown around his naked **b**.
15:43 to Pilate and asked for the **b**
15:45 he granted the **b** to Joseph.
Lk 11:34 The lamp of the **b** is the eye.
11:34 your whole **b** also is full of
11:34 your **b** also is full of
11:36 If then your whole **b** is full of
11:36 the whole **b** will be full of
12: 4 afraid of those who kill the **b**,
12:22 you will eat; nor about the **b**,
12:23 and the **b** is more than
17:37 Wherever the **b** is, there the
22:19 This is My **b** which is given for
23:52 to Pilate and asked for the **b**
23:55 the tomb and how His **b** was
24: 3 went in and did not find the **b**
24:23 "When they did not find His **b**,
Jn 2:21 speaking of the temple of His **b**.
19:38 that he might take away the **b**
19:38 So he came and took the **b** of
19:40 Then they took the **b** of Jesus,
20:12 where the **b** of Jesus had lain.
Acts 2:30 him that of the fruit of his **b**,
9:40 And turning to the **b** he said,
19:12 aprons were brought from his **b**
Rom 4:19 he did not consider his own **b**,
6: 6 that the **b** of sin might be done
6:12 let sin reign in your mortal **b**,
7: 4 dead to the law through the **b**
7:24 will deliver me from this **b** of
8:10 the **b** is dead because of sin,
8:13 put to death the deeds of the **b**,
8:23 the redemption of our **b**.
12: 4 we have many members in one **b**,
12: 5 are one **b** in Christ, and
1 Cor 5: 3 as absent in **b** but present in
6:13 Now the **b** is not for sexual
6:13 Lord, and the Lord for the **b**.
6:16 is joined to a harlot is one **b**
6:18 a man does is outside the **b**,
6:18 sins against his own **b**.
6:19 Or do you not know that your **b**
6:20 glorify God in your **b** and in
7: 4 have authority over her own **b**,
7: 4 have authority over his own **b**,
7:34 that she may be holy both in **b**
9:27 But I discipline my **b** and bring
10:16 it not the communion of the **b**
10:17 many, are one bread and one **b**;
11:24 this is My **b** which is broken
11:27 manner will be guilty of the **b**
11:29 not discerning the Lord's **b**.
12:12 For as the **b** is one and has
12:12 all the members of that one **b**,
12:12 one body, being many, are one **b**,
12:13 we were all baptized into one **b**—
12:14 For in fact the **b** is not one
12:15 not a hand, I am not of the **b**,
12:15 is it therefore not of the **b**?
12:16 not an eye, I am not of the **b**,
12:16 is it therefore not of the **b**?
12:17 If the whole **b** were an eye,
12:18 in the **b** just as He pleased.
12:19 where would the **b** be?
12:20 are many members, yet one **b**.
12:22 those members of the **b** which
12:23 And those members of the **b**
12:24 no need. But God composed the **b**,
12:25 should be no schism in the **b**,
12:27 Now you are the **b** of Christ, and
13: 3 and though I give my **b** to be
15:35 And with what **b** do they come?"
15:37 you do not sow that **b** that
15:38 But God gives it a **b** as He
15:38 and to each seed its own **b**.
15:42 The **b** is sown in corruption,
15:44 It is sown a natural **b**,
15:44 it is raised a spiritual **b**.
15:44 body. There is a natural **b**,
15:44 and there is a spiritual **b**.
2 Cor 4:10 always carrying about in the **b**
4:10 also may be manifested in our **b**.
5: 6 while we are at home in the **b**
5: 8 rather to be absent from the **b**
5:10 the things done in the **b**,
12: 2 whether in the **b** I do not know,
12: 2 or whether out of the **b** I do
12: 3 whether in the **b** or out of the
12: 3 in the body or out of the **b** I
Gal 6:17 for I bear in my **b** the marks of
Eph 1:23 which is His **b**, the fullness
2:16 them both to God in one **b**
3: 6 be fellow heirs, of the same **b**,
4: 4 There is one **b** and one Spirit,
4:12 for the edifying of the **b** of
4:16 from whom the whole **b**,
4:16 causes growth of the **b** for the
5:23 and He is the Savior of the **b**.
5:30 For we are members of His **b**,
Phil 1:20 will be magnified in my **b**,
3:21 who will transform our lowly **b**
3:21 be conformed to His glorious **b**,
Col 1:18 And He is the head of the **b**,
1:22 in the **b** of His flesh through
1:24 Christ, for the sake of His **b**,
2:11 by putting off the **b** of the
2:19 the Head, from whom all the **b**,
2:23 humility, and neglect of the **b**,
3:15 also you were called in one **b**;
1 Th 5:23 and **b** be preserved blameless at
Heb 10: 5 But a **b** You have
10:10 through the offering of the **b**
13: 3 you yourselves are in the **b**
Jas 2:16 which are needed for the **b**,
2:26 For as the **b** without the spirit
3: 2 able also to bridle the whole **b**.
3: 3 us, and we turn their whole **b**.
3: 6 that it defiles the whole **b**,
1 Pe 2:24 bore our sins in His own **b** on
Jude 9 when he disputed about the **b** of

BODY OF CHRIST (4/4)

Rom 7: 4 dead to the law through the **b**,
1 Cor 10:16 it not the communion of the **b**?
12:27 Now you are the **b**,
Eph 4:12 for the edifying of the **b**,

BODYGUARDS (2/2) BODY

2 Ki 11: 4 of the **b** and the escorts—and
11:19 the captains of hundreds, the **b**,

BOHAN (2/2)

Josh 15: 6 went up to the stone of ***B*** the
18:17 and descended to the stone of ***B***

BOIL (19/18) BOILED, BOILING, BOILS

Ex 16:23 and **b** what you will boil; and
16:23 and boil what you will **b**;
23:19 You shall not **b** a young goat in
29:31 ram of the consecration and **b**
34:26 You shall not **b** a young goat in
Lev 8:31 ***B*** the flesh at the door of the
13:18 If the body develops a **b** in the
13:19 and in the place of the **b** there
13:20 which has broken out of the **b**.
13:23 it is the scar of the **b**;
Deut 14:21 You shall not **b** a young goat in
2 Ki 4:38 and **b** stew for the sons of the
20: 7 they took and laid it on the **b**,
Job 41:31 He makes the deep **b** like a pot;
Isa 38:21 it as a poultice on the **b**,
64: 2 As fire causes water to **b**—
Ezek 24: 5 Make it **b** well, And let the
46:20 where the priests shall **b** the
46:24 of the temple shall **b** the

BOILED (8/7) BOIL

Ex 12: 9 nor **b** at all with water, but
Lev 6:28 vessel in which it is **b** shall
6:28 And if it is **b** in a bronze pot,
Num 6:19 the priest shall take the **b**
1 Sam 2:15 for he will not take **b** meat
1 Ki 19:21 oxen and slaughtered them and **b**
2 Ki 6:29 'So we **b** my son, and ate him.
2 Chr 35:13 other holy offerings they **b**

BOILING (3/3) BOIL

1 Sam 2:13 his hand while the meat was **b**.
Job 41:20 As from a **b** pot and burning
Jer 1:13 I see a **b** pot, and it is facing

BOILS (7/6) BOIL

Ex 9: 9 and it will cause **b** that break
9:10 And they caused **b** that break
9:11 before Moses because of the **b**,
9:11 for the **b** were on the magicians
Deut 28:27 will strike you with the **b** of
28:35 and on the legs with severe **b**
Job 2: 7 and struck Job with painful **b**

BOISTEROUS (1/1)

Mt 14:30 he saw that the wind was **b**,

BOLD (12/10) BOLDLY, BOLDNESS

Ps 138: 3 And made me **b** with strength
Prov 28: 1 But the righteous are **b** as a
Acts 13:46 Then Paul and Barnabas grew **b**
Rom 10:20 But Isaiah is very **b** and says:
2 Cor 10: 1 but being absent am **b** toward
10: 2 I am present I may not be **b**
10: 2 by which I intend to be **b**
11:21 But in whatever anyone is **b**—
11:21 foolishly—I am **b** also.
Phil 1:14 are much more **b** to speak the
1 Th 2: 2 we were **b** in our God to speak
Phm 1: 8 though I might be very **b** in

BOLDLY (12/12) BOLD

Gen 34:25 each took his sword and came **b**
Jn 7:26 "But look! He speaks **b**,
Acts 9:27 and how he had preached **b** at
9:29 And he spoke **b** in the name of
14: 3 speaking **b** in the Lord, who was
18:26 So he began to speak **b** in the
19: 8 into the synagogue and spoke **b**
Rom 15:15 I have written more **b** to you on
Eph 6:19 that I may open my mouth **b** to
6:20 that in it I may speak **b**,
Heb 4:16 Let us therefore come **b** to the
13: 6 So we may **b** say: "The LORD

BOLDNESS (12/12) BOLD

Ex 14: 8 of Israel went out with **b**.
Num 33: 3 of Israel went out with **b** in
Acts 4:13 Now when they saw the **b** of
4:29 Your servants that with all **b**
4:31 spoke the word of God with **b**.
2 Cor 3:12 we use great **b** of speech—
7: 4 Great is my **b** of speech toward
Eph 3:12 in whom we have **b** and access
Phil 1:20 be ashamed, but with all **b**,
1 Tim 3:13 a good standing and great **b** in
Heb 10:19 having **b** to enter the Holiest
1 Jn 4:17 that we may have **b** in the day

BOLSTER (KJV) See HEAD

BOLT (1/1) BOLTED, BOLTS

2 Sam 13:17 and **b** the door behind her."

BOLTED (1/1) BOLT

2 Sam 13:18 his servant put her out and **b**

BOLTS (6/6) BOLT

2 Sam 22:15 scattered them; Lightning **b**,
Neh 3: 3 and hung its doors with its **b**
3: 6 with its **b** and bars.
3:13 hung its doors with its **b** and
3:14 and hung its doors with its **b**
3:15 hung its doors with its **b** and

BOND (9/9) BONDAGE, BONDS, BONDSERVANT, BONDSERVANTS, BONDWOMAN

Deut 32:36 remaining, **b** or free.
1 Ki 14:10 **b** and free; I will take away
21:21 both **b** and free.
2 Ki 9: 8 both **b** and free.
14:26 and whether **b** or free, there
Ezek 20:37 I will bring you into the **b** of
Lk 13:16 be loosed from this **b** on the
Eph 4: 3 unity of the Spirit in the **b**
Col 3:14 which is the **b** of perfection.

BONDAGE (42/41) BOND

Ex 1:14 their lives bitter with hard **b**—
2:23 Israel groaned because of the **b**,
2:23 came up to God because of the **b**.
6: 5 whom the Egyptians keep in **b**,
6: 6 I will rescue you from their **b**,
6: 9 anguish of spirit and cruel **b**.
13: 3 of Egypt, out of the house of **b**;
13:14 of Egypt, out of the house of **b**.

20: 2 of Egypt, out of the house of **b**.
Deut 5: 6 of Egypt, out of the house of **b**.
6:12 of Egypt, from the house of **b**.
7: 8 you from the house of **b**,
8:14 of Egypt, from the house of **b**;
13: 5 you from the house of **b**,
13:10 of Egypt, from the house of **b**.
26: 6 and laid hard **b** on us.
Josh 24:17 of Egypt, from the house of **b**,
Judg 6: 8 you out of the house of **b**;
Ezra 9: 8 a measure of revival in our **b**.
9: 9 God did not forsake us in our **b**;
Neh 5:18 because the **b** was heavy on this
9:17 a leader To return to their **b**.
Isa 14: 3 from your fear and the hard **b**
Jer 34: 9 keep a Jewish brother in **b**.
34:10 no one should keep them in **b**
34:13 of Egypt, out of the house of **b**,
Mic 6: 4 you from the house of **b**;
Jn 8:33 and have never been in **b** to
Acts 7: 6 they would bring them into **b**
7: 7 whom they will be in **b**
Rom 8:15 did not receive the spirit of **b**
8:21 will be delivered from the **b**
1 Cor 7:15 or a sister is not under **b** in
2 Cor 11:20 it if one brings you into **b**,
Gal 2: 4 they might bring us into **b**),
4: 3 were in **b** under the elements of
4: 9 you desire again to be in **b**?
4:24 Sinai which gives birth to **b**,
4:25 and is in **b** with her children—
5: 1 again with a yoke of **b**.
Heb 2:15 all their lifetime subject to **b**.
2 Pe 2:19 him also he is brought into **b**.

BONDMAID, BONDMAIDS (KJV)
See BONDWOMAN, CONCUBINE, SLAVES

BONDMAN, BONDMEN (KJV)
See SERVANT, SLAVE, SLAVES

BONDS (17/17) BOND

Judg 15:14 and his **b** broke loose from his
Job 12:18 He loosens the **b** of kings, And
39: 5 Who loosed the **b** of the
Ps 2: 3 Let us break Their **b** in pieces
116:16 You have loosed my **b**.
Isa 28:22 Lest your **b** be made strong;
52: 2 Loose yourself from the **b** of
58: 6 To loose the **b** of wickedness,
Jer 2:20 your yoke and burst your **b**;
5: 5 the yoke And burst the **b**.
27: 2 Make for yourselves **b** and yokes,
30: 8 neck, And will burst your **b**;
Nah 1:13 And burst your **b** apart."
Zech 11: 7 and the other I called **B**;
11:14 I cut in two my other staff, **B**,
Lk 8:29 and he broke the **b** and was
Acts 22:30 he released him from his **b**,

BONDSERVANT (8/8) BOND

Rom 1: 1 a **b** of Jesus Christ, called to
Gal 1:10 I would not be a **b** of Christ.
Phil 2: 7 taking the form of a **b**,
Col 4:12 a **b** of Christ, greets you,
Titus 1: 1 a **b** of God and an apostle of
Jas 1: 1 a **b** of God and of the Lord
2 Pe 1: 1 a **b** and apostle of Jesus
Jude 1 a **b** of Jesus Christ, and

BONDSERVANTS (9/9) BOND

2 Cor 4: 5 and ourselves your **b** for Jesus'
Eph 6: 5 **B**, be obedient to those
6: 6 but as **b** of Christ, doing the
Phil 1: 1 **b** of Jesus Christ, To all the
Col 3:22 **B**, obey in all things
4: 1 give your **b** what is just and
1 Tim 6: 1 Let as many **b** as are under the
Titus 2: 9 Exhort **b** to be obedient to
1 Pe 2:16 for vice, but as **b** of God.

BONDWOMAN (9/7) BOND

Gen 21:10 Cast out this **b** and her son; for
21:10 for the son of this **b** shall not
21:12 of the lad or because of your **b**.
21:13 a nation of the son of the **b**,
Gal 4:22 had two sons: the one by a **b**,
4:23 But he who was of the **b** was
4:30 Cast out the **b** and her
4:30 for the son of the **b**
4:31 we are not children of the **b**

BONDWOMEN (KJV) See SLAVES

BONE (16/15) BONES

Gen 2:23 This is now **b** of my bones And
29:14 Surely you are my **b** and my
Num 19:16 or a **b** of a man, or a grave,
19:18 or on the one who touched a **b**,
Judg 9: 2 that I am your own flesh and **b**.
2 Sam 5: 1 Indeed we are your **b** and your
19:12 you are my **b** and my flesh.
19:13 Are you not my **b** and my flesh?
1 Chr 11: 1 Indeed we are your **b** and your
Job 2: 5 and touch his **b** and his flesh,
19:20 My **b** clings to my skin and to
Prov 25:15 And a gentle tongue breaks a **b**.
Ezek 37: 7 came together, **b** to bone.
37: 7 bones came together, bone to **b**.
39:15 when anyone sees a man's **b**,
Zeph 3: 3 wolves That leave not a **b**

BONES (94/81) BONE

Gen 2:23 This is now bone of my **b** And
50:25 and you shall carry up my **b**
Ex 12:46 shall you break one of its **b**.
13:19 And Moses took the **b** of Joseph
13:19 and you shall carry up my **b**
Num 9:12 morning, nor break one of its **b**.
24: 8 He shall break their **b** And
Josh 24:32 The **b** of Joseph, which the
1 Sam 31:13 Then they took their **b** and
2 Sam 21:12 Then David went and took the **b**
21:12 and the **b** of Jonathan his son,
21:13 So he brought up the **b** of Saul
21:13 up the bones of Saul and the **b**
21:13 and they gathered the **b** of
21:14 They buried the **b** of Saul and
1 Ki 13: 2 and men's **b** shall be burned on
13:31 lay my **b** beside his bones.
13:31 lay my bones beside his **b**.
2 Ki 13:21 was let down and touched the **b**
23:14 filled their places with the **b**
23:16 And he sent and took the **b** out
23:18 alone; let no one move his **b**.
23:18 So they let his **b** alone, with
23:18 with the **b** of the prophet who
23:20 and burned men's **b** on them; and
1 Chr 10:12 and buried their **b** under the
2 Chr 34: 5 He also burned the **b** of the
Job 4:14 Which made all my **b** shake.
10:11 And knit me together with **b**
20:11 His **b** are full of his youthful
21:24 And the marrow of his **b** is
30:17 My **b** are pierced in me at
30:30 My **b** burn with fever.
33:19 strong pain in many of his **b**,
33:21 And his **b** stick out which
40:18 His **b** are like beams of
Ps 6: 2 for my **b** are troubled.
22:14 And all My **b** are out of joint;
22:17 I can count all My **b**.
31:10 And my **b** waste away.
32: 3 my **b** grew old Through my
34:20 He guards all his **b**;
35:10 All my **b** shall say, "LORD,
38: 3 Nor any health in my **b**
42:10 As with a breaking of my **b**,
51: 8 That the **b** You have broken
53: 5 For God has scattered the **b** of
102: 3 And my **b** are burned like a
102: 5 the sound of my groaning My **b**
109:18 water, And like oil into his **b**.
141: 7 Our **b** are scattered at the
Prov 3: 8 flesh, And strength to your **b**.
12: 4 is like rottenness in his **b**.
14:30 envy is rottenness to the **b**.
15:30 And a good report makes the **b**
16:24 to the soul and health to the **b**.
17:22 a broken spirit dries the **b**.
Eccl 11: 5 Or how the **b** grow in the
Isa 38:13 a lion, So He breaks all my **b**;
58:11 drought, And strengthen your **b**;
66:14 And your **b** shall flourish like
Jer 8: 1 they shall bring out the **b** of
8: 1 and the **b** of its princes, and
8: 1 and the **b** of the priests, and
8: 1 and the **b** of the prophets, and
8: 1 and the **b** of the inhabitants of
20: 9 a burning fire Shut up in my **b**;
23: 9 All my **b** shake. I am like a
50:17 of Babylon has broken his **b**.
Lam 1:13 He has sent fire into my **b**,
3: 4 and my skin, And broken my **b**.
4: 8 Their skin clings to their **b**,
Ezek 6: 5 and I will scatter your **b** all
24: 5 Also pile fuel **b** under it,
32:27 iniquities will be on their **b**,
37: 1 valley; and it was full of **b**.
37: 3 can these **b** live?" So I
37: 4 to me, "Prophesy to these **b**,
37: 4 and say to them, 'O dry **b**,
37: 5 says the Lord GOD to these **b**:
37: 7 and the **b** came together, bone
37:11 these **b** are the whole house of
37:11 Our **b** are dry, our hope is lost,
Dan 6:24 and broke all their **b** in pieces
Am 2: 1 Because he burned the **b** of the
Mic 3: 2 And the flesh from their **b**;
3: 3 skin from them, Break their **b**,
Hab 3:16 voice; Rottenness entered my **b**;
Mt 23:27 are full of dead men's **b** and
Lk 24:39 does not have flesh and **b** as
Jn 19:36 Not one of His **b** shall be
Acts 3: 7 his feet and ankle **b** received
Eph 5:30 body, of His flesh and of His **b**.
Heb 11:22 instructions concerning his **b**.

BONNETS (KJV)
See HATS, HEADDRESSES, TURBANS

BOOK (178/165) BOOKS

Gen 5: 1 This is the **b** of the genealogy
Ex 17:14 this for a memorial in the **b**
24: 7 Then he took the **B** of the
32:32 blot me out of Your **b** which You
32:33 Me, I will blot him out of My **b**.
Num 5:23 shall write these curses in a **b**,
21:14 Therefore it is said in the **B** of
Deut 17:18 a copy of this law in a **b**,
28:58 law that are written in this **b**,
28:61 is not written in this **B** of
29:20 curse that is written in this **b**
29:21 that are written in this **B** of
29:27 curse that is written in this **b**.
30:10 which are written in this **B** of
31:24 the words of this law in a **b**,
31:26 Take this **B** of the Law, and put
Josh 1: 8 This **B** of the Law shall not
8:31 as it is written in the **B** of
8:34 to all that is written in the **B**
10:13 Is this not written in the **B**
18: 9 and wrote the survey in a **b** in
23: 6 do all that is written in the **B**
24:26 wrote these words in the **B** of
1 Sam 10:25 and wrote it in a **b** and laid
2 Sam 1:18 it is written in the **B** of
1 Ki 11:41 are they not written in the **b**
14:19 they are written in the **b** of
14:29 are they not written in the **b**
15: 7 are they not written in the **b**
15:23 are they not written in the **b**
15:31 are they not written in the **b**
16: 5 are they not written in the **b**
16:14 are they not written in the **b**
16:20 are they not written in the **b**
16:27 are they not written in the **b**
22:39 are they not written in the **b**
22:45 are they not written in the **b**
2 Ki 1:18 are they not written in the **b**
8:23 are they not written in the **b**
10:34 are they not written in the **b**
12:19 are they not written in the **b**
13: 8 are they not written in the **b**
13:12 are they not written in the **b**
14: 6 to what is written in the **B** of
14:15 they not written in the **b**
14:18 are they not written in the **b**
14:28 they not written in the **b**
15: 6 are they not written in the **b**
15:11 they are written in the **b** of
15:15 they are written in the **b** of
15:21 are they not written in the **b**
15:26 they are written in the **b** of
15:31 they are written in the **b** of
15:36 are they not written in the **b**
16:19 are they not written in the **b**
20:20 they not written in the **b**
21:17 they not written in the **b**
21:25 are they not written in the **b**
22: 8 I have found the **B** of the Law in
22: 8 And Hilkiah gave the **b** to
22:10 the priest has given me a **b**.
22:11 king heard the words of the **B**
22:13 concerning the words of this **b**
22:13 not obeyed the words of this **b**,
22:16 all the words of the **b** which the
23: 2 hearing all the words of the **B**
23: 3 that were written in this **b**.
23:21 as it is written in this **B** of
23:24 law which were written in the **b**
23:28 are they not written in the **b**
24: 5 are they not written in the **b**
1 Chr 9: 1 they were inscribed in the **b**
29:29 they are written in the **b** of
29:29 in the **b** of Nathan the prophet,
29:29 and in the **b** of Gad the seer,
2 Chr 9:29 are they not written in the **b**
12:15 are they not written in the **b**
16:11 are indeed written in the **b** of
17: 9 and had the **B** of the Law of
20:34 they are written in the **b** of
20:34 which is mentioned in the **b** of
24:27 written in the annals of the **b**
25: 4 written in the Law in the **B** of
25:26 are they not written in the **b**
27: 7 they are written in the **b** of
28:26 they are written in the **b** of
32:32 and in the **b** of the kings of
33:18 they are written in the **b** of
34:14 Hilkiah the priest found the **B**
34:15 I have found the **B** of the Law in
34:15 And Hilkiah gave the **b** to
34:16 So Shaphan carried the **b** to the
34:18 the priest has given me a **b**.
34:21 concerning the words of the **b**
34:21 all that is written in this **b**.
34:24 that are written in the **b**
34:30 hearing all the words of the **B**
34:31 that were written in this **b**.
35:12 as it is written in the **B** of
35:27 they are written in the **b** of
36: 8 they are written in the **b** of
Ezra 4:15 search may be made in the **b** of
4:15 And you will find in the **b** of
6:18 as it is written in the **B** of
Neh 8: 1 Ezra the scribe to bring the **B**
8: 3 were attentive to the **B** of
8: 5 And Ezra opened the **b** in the
8: 8 they read distinctly from the **b**,
8:18 he read from the **B** of the Law
9: 3 place and read from the **B** of
12:23 were written in the **b** of the
13: 1 that day they read from the **B**
Esth 2:23 and it was written in the **b** of
6: 1 was commanded to bring the **b**
9:32 and it was written in the **b**.

10: 2 are they not written in the ***b***
Job 19:23 they were inscribed in a ***b***!
31:35 my Prosecutor had written a ***b***!
Ps 40: 7 In the scroll of the ***b*** it is
56: 8 Are they not in Your ***b***?
69:28 them be blotted out of the ***b***
139:16 And in Your ***b*** they all were
Isa 29:11 to you like the words of a ***b***
29:12 Then the ***b*** is delivered to one
29:18 shall hear the words of the ***b***,
34:16 Search from the ***b*** of the LORD,
Jer 25:13 all that is written in this ***b***,
30: 2 Write in a ***b*** for yourself all
36: 2 Take a scroll of a ***b*** and write
36: 4 Baruch wrote on a scroll of a ***b***,
36: 8 reading from the ***b*** the words of
36:10 Then Baruch read from the ***b*** the
36:11 words of the LORD from the ***b***,
36:13 heard when Baruch read the ***b***
36:18 I wrote them with ink in the ***b***.
36:32 all the words of the ***b*** which
45: 1 had written these words in a ***b***
51:60 So Jeremiah wrote in a ***b*** all the
51:63 have finished reading this ***b***,
Ezek 2: 9 a scroll of a ***b*** was in it.
Dan 12: 1 who is found written in the ***b***.
12: 4 and seal the ***b*** until the time
Nah 1: 1 The ***b*** of the vision of Nahum
Mal 3:16 So a ***b*** of remembrance was
Mt 1: 1 The ***b*** of the genealogy of Jesus
Mk 12:26 have you not read in the ***b*** of
Lk 3: 4 as it is written in the ***b*** of the
4:17 And He was handed the ***b*** of the
4:17 And when He had opened the ***b***,
4:20 Then He closed the ***b***,
20:42 David himself said in the ***B*** of
Jn 20:30 which are not written in this ***b***;
Acts 1:20 For it is written in the ***b*** of
7:42 as it is written in the ***b*** of
Gal 3:10 are written in the ***b*** of
Phil 4: 3 whose names are in the ***B*** of
Heb 9:19 and sprinkled both the ***b*** itself
10: 7 In the volume of the ***b***
Rev 1:11 write in a ***b*** and send it to
3: 5 blot out his name from the ***B***
10: 2 He had a little ***b*** open in his
10: 8 take the little ***b*** which is open
10: 9 to him, "Give me the little ***b***.
10:10 Then I took the little ***b*** out of
13: 8 have not been written in the ***B***
17: 8 names are not written in the ***B***
20:12 And another ***b*** was opened, which
20:12 which is the ***B*** of Life.
20:15 not found written in the ***B*** of
21:27 are written in the Lamb's ***B*** of
22: 7 words of the prophecy of this ***b***.
22: 9 who keep the words of this ***b***.
22:10 words of the prophecy of this ***b***,
22:18 words of the prophecy of this ***b***:
22:18 that are written in this ***b***;
22:19 away from the words of the ***b***
22:19 take away his part from the ***B***
22:19 which are written in this ***b***.

BOOK OF LIFE (8/8)

Phil 4: 3 whose names are in the ***B***.
Rev 3: 5 blot out his name from the ***B***;
13: 8 have not been written in the ***B***
17: 8 names are not written in the ***B***
20:12 was opened, which is the ***B***.
20:15 not found written in the ***B*** was
21:27 who are written in the Lamb's ***B***.
22:19 take away his part from the ***B***,

BOOKS (8/7) BOOK

Eccl 12:12 Of making many ***b*** there is no
Dan 7:10 And the ***b*** were opened.
9: 2 understood by the ***b*** the number
Jn 21:25 itself could not contain the ***b***
Acts 19:19 magic brought their ***b*** together
2 Tim 4:13 Troas when you come—and the ***b***,
Rev 20:12 and ***b*** were opened. And another
20:12 which were written in the ***b***.

BOOTH (2/2) BOOTHS

Job 27:18 Like a ***b*** which a watchman
Isa 1: 8 of Zion is left as a ***b*** in a

BOOTHS (10/8) BOOTH

Gen 33:17 and made ***b*** for his livestock.
Lev 23:42 You shall dwell in ***b*** for seven
23:42 Israelites shall dwell in ***b***,
23:43 children of Israel dwell in ***b***
2 Ki 23: 7 he tore down the ritual ***b*** of
Neh 8:14 of Israel should dwell in ***b***
8:15 of leafy trees, to make ***b***,
8:16 them and made themselves ***b***,
8:17 from the captivity made ***b*** and
8:17 made booths and sat under the ***b***;

BOOTY (12/12)

Num 31:11 all the spoil and all the ***b***—
31:12 brought the captives, the ***b***,
31:32 The ***b*** remaining from the
Deut 3: 7 of the cities we took as ***b*** for
Josh 8: 2 its cattle you shall take as ***b***
8:27 of that city Israel took as ***b***
11:14 children of Israel took as ***b***
Jer 49:32 Their camels shall be for ***b***,
Ezek 38:12 "to take plunder and to take ***b***,
38:13 gathered your army to take ***b***,
Hab 2: 7 And you will become their ***b***.
Zeph 1:13 their goods shall become ***b***,

BOOZ (KJV) See BOAZ

BORDER (148/112) BORDERING, BORDERS

Gen 10:19 And the ***b*** of the Canaanites was
49:13 And his ***b*** shall adjoin Sidon.
Ex 16:35 manna until they came to the ***b***
Num 20:16 a city on the edge of your ***b***.
20:23 Aaron in Mount Hor by the ***b*** of
21:13 that extends from the ***b*** of the
21:13 for the Arnon is the ***b*** of
21:15 And lies on the ***b*** of Moab."
21:24 for the ***b*** of the people of
22:36 which is on the ***b*** at the
33:44 at the ***b*** of Moab.
34: 3 Your southern ***b*** shall be from
34: 3 Wilderness of Zin along the ***b***
34: 3 then your southern ***b*** shall
34: 4 your ***b*** shall turn from the
34: 5 the ***b*** shall turn from Azmon to
34: 6 'As for the western ***b***,
34: 6 have the Great Sea for a ***b***;
34: 6 this shall be your western ***b***.
34: 7 this shall be your northern ***b***:
34: 7 Sea you shall mark out your ***b***
34: 8 you shall mark out your ***b*** to
34: 8 then the direction of the ***b***
34: 9 the ***b*** shall proceed to Ziphron,
34: 9 This shall be your northern ***b***.
34:10 shall mark out your eastern ***b***
34:11 the ***b*** shall go down from Shepham
34:11 the ***b*** shall go down and reach
34:12 the ***b*** shall go down along the
Deut 3:14 as far as the ***b*** of the
3:16 middle of the river as the ***b***,
3:16 the ***b*** of the people of Ammon;
3:17 also, with the Jordan as the ***b***,
12:20 LORD your God enlarges your ***b***
Josh 4:19 camped in Gilgal on the east ***b***
12: 2 which is the ***b*** of the
12: 5 as far as the ***b*** of the
12: 5 over half of Gilead to the ***b***
13: 3 as far as the ***b*** of Ekron
13: 4 to the ***b*** of the Amorites;
13:10 as far as the ***b*** of the children
13:11 and the ***b*** of the Geshurites and
13:23 And the ***b*** of the children of
13:26 and from Mahanaim to the ***b*** of
13:27 with the Jordan as its ***b***,
15: 1 The ***b*** of Edom at the Wilderness
15: 2 And their southern ***b*** began at
15: 4 and the ***b*** ended at the sea.
15: 4 This shall be your southern ***b***.
15: 5 The east ***b*** was the Salt Sea as
15: 5 And the ***b*** on the northern
15: 6 The ***b*** went up to Beth Hoglah and
15: 6 and the ***b*** went up to the stone
15: 7 Then the ***b*** went up toward Debir
15: 7 The ***b*** continued toward the
15: 8 And the ***b*** went up by the Valley
15: 8 The ***b*** went up to the top of the
15: 9 Then the ***b*** went around from the
15: 9 And the ***b*** went around to Baalah
15:10 Then the ***b*** turned westward from
15:11 And the ***b*** went out to the side
15:11 Then the ***b*** went around to
15:11 and the ***b*** ended at the sea.
15:12 The west ***b*** was the coastline of
15:21 toward the ***b*** of Edom in the
16: 2 passed along to the ***b*** of the
16: 5 The ***b*** of the children of
16: 5 The ***b*** of their inheritance on
16: 6 And the ***b*** went out toward the
16: 6 then the ***b*** went around eastward
16: 8 The ***b*** went out from Tappuah
17: 7 and the ***b*** went along south to
17: 8 but Tappuah on the ***b*** of
17: 9 And the ***b*** descended to the Brook
17: 9 The ***b*** of Manasseh was on the
17:10 and the sea was its ***b***.
18:12 Their ***b*** on the north side began
18:12 and the ***b*** went up to the side
18:13 The ***b*** went over from there
18:13 and the ***b*** descended to Ataroth
18:14 Then the ***b*** extended around the
18:15 and the ***b*** extended on the west
18:16 Then the ***b*** came down to the end
18:19 And the ***b*** passed along to the
18:19 then the ***b*** ended at the north
18:20 The Jordan was its ***b*** on the east
19:10 and the ***b*** of their inheritance
19:11 Their ***b*** went toward the west and
19:12 toward the sunrise along the ***b***
19:14 Then the ***b*** went around it on the
19:22 And the ***b*** reached to Tabor,
19:22 their ***b*** ended at the Jordan:
19:29 And the ***b*** turned to Ramah and to
19:29 then the ***b*** turned to Hosah, and
19:33 And their ***b*** began at Heleph,
19:34 From Heleph the ***b*** extended
19:47 And the ***b*** of the children of Dan
22:25 LORD has made the Jordan a ***b***
24:30 they buried him within the ***b***
Judg 2: 9 they buried him within the ***b***
7:22 as far as the ***b*** of Abel
11:18 But they did not enter the ***b*** of
11:18 for the Arnon was the ***b*** of
1 Sam 6:12 went after them to the ***b*** of
13:18 turned to the road of the ***b***
1 Ki 4:21 as far as the ***b*** of Egypt.
2 Ki 3:21 and they stood at the ***b***.
2 Chr 9:26 as far as the ***b*** of Egypt.
Ps 78:54 He brought them to His holy ***b***,
Isa 19:19 a pillar to the LORD at its ***b***.
Jer 31:17 shall come back to their own ***b***.
50:26 against her from the farthest ***b***;
Ezek 11:10 I will judge you at the ***b*** of
11:11 I will judge you at the ***b*** of
29:10 as far as the ***b*** of Ethiopia.
45: 7 from the west ***b*** to the east
45: 7 the west border to the east ***b***.
47:15 This shall be the ***b*** of the
47:16 (which is between the ***b*** of
47:16 border of Damascus and the ***b***
47:16 Hatticon (which is on the ***b***
47:17 the ***b*** of Damascus; and as for
47:17 it is the ***b*** of Hamath.
47:18 side you shall mark out the ***b***
48: 1 From the northern ***b*** along the
48: 1 the ***b*** of Damascus northward, in
48: 2 by the ***b*** of Dan, from the east
48: 3 by the ***b*** of Asher, from the east
48: 4 by the ***b*** of Naphtali, from the
48: 5 by the ***b*** of Manasseh, from the
48: 6 by the ***b*** of Ephraim, from the
48: 7 by the ***b*** of Reuben, from the
48: 8 by the ***b*** of Judah, from the
48:12 a thing most holy by the ***b*** of
48:13 Opposite the ***b*** of the priests,
48:21 as far as the eastern ***b***,
48:21 as far as the western ***b***,
48:22 the area between the ***b*** of
48:22 the border of Judah and the ***b***
48:24 by the ***b*** of Benjamin, from the
48:25 by the ***b*** of Simeon, from the
48:26 by the ***b*** of Issachar, from the
48:27 by the ***b*** of Zebulun, from the
48:28 by the ***b*** of Gad, on the south
48:28 the ***b*** shall be from Tamar to
Ob 7 Shall force you to the ***b***;
Mal 1: 5 is magnified beyond the ***b*** of
Lk 8:44 from behind and touched the ***b***

BORDERING (1/1) BORDER

Ezek 45: 7 and ***b*** on the holy district and

BORDERS (22/22) BORDER

Gen 23:17 within all the surrounding ***b***,
47:21 from one end of the ***b*** of Egypt
Ex 34:24 before you and enlarge your ***b***;
Num 32:33 with its cities within the ***b***,
Josh 19:13 to Rimmon, which ***b*** on Neah.
19:49 according to their ***b***,
2 Ki 19:23 enter the extremity of its ***b***,
1 Chr 5:16 of Sharon within their ***b***.
7:29 and by the ***b*** of the children of
Ps 74:17 You have set all the ***b*** of the
147:14 He makes peace in your ***b***,
Isa 15: 8 cry has gone all around the ***b***
26:15 You have expanded all the ***b*** of
60:18 nor destruction within your ***b***;
Jer 17: 3 places of sin within all your ***b***.
Ezek 27: 4 Your ***b*** are in the midst of the
47:13 These are the ***b*** by which you
Joel 3: 6 remove them far from their ***b***.
Mic 5: 6 when he treads within our ***b***.
Zeph 2: 8 threats against their ***b***.
Zech 9: 2 which ***b*** on it, And against
Mt 23: 5 broad and enlarge the ***b*** of

BORE (148/143) BEAR

Gen 4: 1 and she conceived and ***b*** Cain,
4: 2 Then she ***b*** again, this time his
4:17 and she conceived and ***b*** Enoch.
4:20 And Adah ***b*** Jabal. He was the
4:22 she also ***b*** Tubal-Cain, an
4:25 and she ***b*** a son and named him
6: 4 the daughters of men and they ***b***
16:15 So Hagar ***b*** Abram a son; and
16:15 named his son, whom Hagar ***b***,
16:16 years old when Hagar ***b*** Ishmael
19:37 The firstborn ***b*** a son and called
19:38 she also ***b*** a son and called his
20:17 Then they ***b*** children;
21: 2 For Sarah conceived and ***b***
21: 3 whom Sarah ***b*** to him—Isaac.
22:23 These eight Milcah ***b*** to Nahor,
22:24 also ***b*** Tebah, Gaham, Thahash,
24:24 whom she ***b*** to Nahor."
24:36 And Sarah my master's wife ***b*** a
24:47 whom Milcah ***b*** to him.' So I put
25: 2 And she ***b*** him Zimran, Jokshan,
25:12 maidservant, ***b*** to Abraham.
25:26 was sixty years old when she ***b***
29:32 So Leah conceived and ***b*** a son,
29:33 Then she conceived again and ***b***
29:34 She conceived again and ***b*** a son,
29:35 And she conceived again and ***b*** a
30: 1 Now when Rachel saw that she ***b***
30: 5 And Bilhah conceived and ***b*** Jacob
30: 7 Bilhah conceived again and ***b***
30:10 And Leah's maid Zilpah ***b*** Jacob a
30:12 And Leah's maid Zilpah ***b*** Jacob a

B

30:17 and she conceived and **b** Jacob a
30:19 Then Leah conceived again and **b**
30:21 Afterward she **b** a daughter, and
30:23 And she conceived and **b** a son,
31: 8 then all the flocks **b**
31: 8 then all the flocks **b**
31:39 I **b** the loss of it.
36: 4 Now Adah **b** Eliphaz to Esau, and
36: 4 and Basemath **b** Reuel.
36: 5 And Aholibamah **b** Jeush, Jaalam,
36:12 and she **b** Amalek to Eliphaz.
36:14 And she **b** to Esau: Jeush,
38: 3 So she conceived and **b** a son,
38: 4 She conceived again and **b** a son,
38: 5 she conceived yet again and **b**
38: 5 He was at Chezib when she **b**
41:50 priest of On, **b** to him.
44:27 You know that my wife **b** me two
46:15 whom she **b** to Jacob in Padan
46:18 and these she **b** to Jacob:
46:20 priest of On, **b** to him.
46:25 and she **b** these to Jacob: seven
Ex 2: 2 So the woman conceived and **b** a
2:22 And she **b** him a son, and he
6:20 and she **b** him Aaron and Moses.
6:23 and she **b** him Nadab, Abihu,
6:25 and she **b** him Phinehas.
19: 4 and how I **b** you on eagles'
Num 26:59 and to Amram she **b** Aaron and
Deut 31: 9 who **b** the ark of the covenant
31:25 who **b** the ark of the covenant
Josh 3:15 and as those who **b** the ark came
3:15 the feet of the priests who **b**
3:17 Then the priests who **b** the ark
4: 9 the feet of the priests who **b**
4:10 So the priests who **b** the ark
4:18 when the priests who **b** the ark
8:33 who **b** the ark of the covenant
Judg 8:31 who was in Shechem also **b** him
11: 2 Gilead's wife **b** sons; and when
13:24 So the woman **b** a son and called
Ruth 4:12 whom Tamar **b** to Judah, because
4:13 conception, and she **b** a son.
1 Sam 1:20 that Hannah conceived and **b** a
2:21 so that she conceived and **b**
14: 1 said to the young man who **b**
14: 6 said to the young man who **b**
17:41 and the man who **b** the shield
2 Sam 11:27 and she became his wife and **b**
12:15 the child that Uriah's wife **b**
12:24 So she **b** a son, and he called
18:15 And ten young men who **b** Joab's
21: 8 whom she **b** to Saul; and the
1 Ki 10: 2 with camels that **b** spices, very
11:20 Then the sister of Tahpenes **b**
2 Ki 4:17 and **b** a son when the appointed
1 Chr 2: 4 **b** him Perez and Zerah. All the
2:17 Abigail **b** Amasa; and the father
2:19 as his wife, who **b** him Hur.
2:21 and she **b** him Segub.
2:24 Hezron's wife Abijah **b** him
2:29 and she **b** him Ahban and Molid.
2:35 and she **b** him Attai.
2:46 **b** Haran, Moza, and Gazez; and
2:48 **b** Sheber and Tirhanah.
2:49 She also **b** Shaaph the father of
4: 6 Naarah **b** him Ahuzzam, Hepher,
4: 9 Because I **b** him in pain."
4:17 And Mered's wife **b** Miriam,
4:18 (His wife Jehudijah **b** Jered the
7:14 his Syrian concubine **b** him
7:16 (Maachah the wife of Machir **b** a
7:18 His sister Hammoleketh **b** Ishhod,
7:23 she conceived and **b** a son; and
15:15 the children of the Levites **b**
15:26 God helped the Levites who **b**
15:27 as were all the Levites who **b**
2 Chr 9: 1 camels that **b** spices, gold in
11:19 And she **b** him children: Jeush,
11:20 and she **b** him Abijah, Attai,
Neh 5:15 even their servants **b** rule over
Prov 17:25 And bitterness to her who **b**
23:25 And let her who **b** you rejoice.
Song 6: 9 The favorite of the one who **b**
8: 5 There she who **b** you brought
Isa 8: 3 and she conceived and **b** a son.
22: 6 Elam **b** the quiver With
51: 2 And to Sarah who **b** you; For
53:12 And He **b** the sin of many, And
63: 9 And He **b** them and carried them
Jer 16: 3 concerning their mothers who **b**
20:14 be blessed in which my mother **b**
22:26 and your mother who **b** you, into
31:19 Because I **b** the reproach of my
50:12 She who **b** you shall be
Ezek 12: 7 and I **b** them on my shoulder
16:20 whom you **b** to Me, and these you
23: 4 And they **b** sons and daughters.
23:37 their sons whom they **b** to Me,
Hos 1: 3 and she conceived and **b** him a
1: 6 And she conceived again and **b**
1: 8 she conceived and **b** a son.
Mt 8:17 our infirmities And **b**
Mk 14:56 For many **b** false witness against
14:57 Then some rose up and **b** false
Lk 4:22 So all **b** witness to Him, and
11:27 Blessed is the womb that **b** You,
23:29 the barren, wombs that never **b**,
Jn 1:15 John **b** witness of Him and cried
1:32 And John **b** witness, saying, "I
12:17 from the dead, **b** witness.
Heb 11:11 and she **b** a child when she was
1 Pe 2:24 who Himself **b** our sins in His
Rev 1: 2 who **b** witness to the word of
12: 5 She **b** a male Child who was to
22: 2 which **b** twelve fruits, each

BORED (1/1)

2 Ki 12: 9 **b** a hole in its lid, and set it

BORN (144/138) BEAR, BIRTH, BORNE

Gen 4:18 To Enoch was **b** Irad; and Irad
4:26 Seth, to him also a son was **b**;
6: 1 and daughters were **b** to them,
10: 1 And sons were **b** to them after
10:21 And children were **b** also to
10:25 To Eber were **b** two sons: the
14:14 trained servants who were **b**
15: 3 indeed one **b** in my house is my
17:12 he who is **b** in your house or
17:13 He who is **b** in your house and he
17:17 Shall a child be **b** to a man
17:23 all who were **b** in his house and
17:27 **b** in the house or bought with
21: 3 the name of his son who was **b**
21: 5 old when his son Isaac was **b**
24:15 who was **b** to Bethuel, son of
35:26 the sons of Jacob who were **b**
36: 5 the sons of Esau who were **b** to
41:50 And to Joseph were **b** two sons
46:20 in the land of Egypt were **b**
46:22 who were **b** to Jacob: fourteen
46:27 the sons of Joseph who were **b**
48: 5 who were **b** to you in the land
Ex 1:22 Every son who is **b** you shall
Lev 18: 9 whether **b** at home or
19:34 you shall be to you as one **b**
22:11 and one who is **b** in his house
22:27 bull or a sheep or a goat is **b**,
24:16 as well as him who is **b** in the
Num 26:59 who was **b** to Levi in Egypt; and
26:60 To Aaron were **b** Nadab and Abihu,
Deut 23: 8 of the third generation **b** to
Josh 5: 5 but all the people **b** in the
8:33 as well as he who was **b** among
Judg 13: 8 do for the child who will be **b**.
18:29 who was **b** to Israel.
Ruth 4:17 'There is a son **b** to Naomi."
2 Sam 3: 2 Sons were **b** to David in Hebron:
3: 5 These were **b** to David in
5:13 more sons and daughters were **b**
5:14 the names of those who were **b**
12:14 the child also who is **b** to
14:27 To Absalom were **b** three sons,
21:20 and he also was **b** to the giant.
21:22 These four were **b** to the giant
1 Ki 13: 2 shall be **b** to the house of
1 Chr 1:19 To Eber were **b** two sons: the
1:32 Now the sons **b** to Keturah,
2: 3 These three were **b** to him by
2: 9 the sons of Hezron who were **b**
3: 1 the sons of David who were **b**
3: 4 These six were **b** to him in
3: 5 And these were **b** to him in
7:21 The men of Gath who were **b** in
20: 6 and he also was **b** to the giant.
20: 8 These were **b** to the giant in
22: 9 a son shall be **b** to you, who
26: 6 to Shemaiah his son were sons **b**
Ezra 10: 3 and those who have been **b** to
Job 1: 2 and three daughters were **b** to
3: 3 the day perish on which I was **b**,
5: 7 Yet man is **b** to trouble, As
8: 9 For we were **b** yesterday, and
11:12 a wild donkey's colt is **b** a
14: 1 Man who is **b** of woman Is of
15: 7 you the first man who was **b**?
15:14 And he who is **b** of a woman,
25: 4 how can he be pure who is **b**
38:21 because you were **b** then, Or
Ps 22:31 to a people who will be **b**,
58: 3 go astray as soon as they are **b**,
78: 6 The children who would be **b**,
87: 4 This one was **b** there.'"
87: 5 one and that one were **b**
87: 6 This one was **b** there." Selah
Prov 17:17 And a brother is **b** for
Eccl 2: 7 And had servants **b** in my house.
3: 2 A time to be **b**, And a time
4:14 Although he was **b** poor in his
Isa 9: 6 For unto us a Child is **b**,
66: 8 Or shall a nation be **b** at
Jer 1: 5 Before you were **b** I sanctified
16: 3 sons and daughters who are **b**
20:14 be the day in which I was **b**!
20:15 A male child has been **b** to
22:26 country where you were not **b**;
Ezek 16: 4 on the day you were **b** your
16: 5 loathed on the day you were **b**.
Hos 2: 3 her, as in the day she was **b**,
13:13 stay long where children are **b**.
Mt 1:16 of whom was **b** Jesus who is
2: 1 Now after Jesus was **b** in
2: 2 Where is He who has been **b** King
2: 4 where the Christ was to be **b**.
11:11 among those **b** of women there
19:12 there are eunuchs who were **b**
26:24 that man if he had not been **b**.
Mk 14:21 that man if he had never been **b**.
Lk 1:35 that Holy One who is to be **b**
2:11 For there is **b** to you this day
7:28 among those **b** of women there is
Jn 1:13 who were **b**, not of blood,
3: 3 unless one is **b** again, he
3: 4 How can a man be **b** when he is
3: 4 into his mother's womb and be **b**?
3: 5 unless one is **b** of water and
3: 6 That which is **b** of the flesh is
3: 6 and that which is **b** of the
3: 7 You must be **b** again.'
3: 8 So is everyone who is **b** of the
8:41 We were not **b** of fornication; we
9: 2 that he was **b** blind?"
9:19 who you say was **b** blind?
9:20 and that he was **b** blind;
9:32 the eyes of one who was **b**
9:34 You were completely **b** in sins,
16:21 that a human being has been **b**
18:37 a king. For this cause I was **b**,
Acts 2: 8 own language in which we were **b**?
7:20 "At this time Moses was **b**,
18: 2 **b** in Pontus, who had recently
18:24 **b** at Alexandria, an eloquent
22: 3 **b** in Tarsus of Cilicia, but
22:28 But I was **b** a citizen."
Rom 1: 3 who was **b** of the seed of David
9:11 the children not yet being **b**,
1 Cor 15: 8 as by one **b** out of due time.
Gal 4: 4 **b** of a woman, born under the
4: 4 **b** under the law,
4:23 was of the bondwoman was **b**
4:29 as he who was **b** according to
4:29 persecuted him who was **b**
Heb 11:12 were **b** as many as the stars
11:23 By faith Moses, when he was **b**,
1 Pe 1:23 having been **b** again, not of
1 Jn 2:29 practices righteousness is **b**
3: 9 Whoever has been **b** of God does
3: 9 because he has been **b** of God.
4: 7 and everyone who loves is **b** of
5: 1 that Jesus is the Christ is **b**
5: 4 For whatever is **b** of God
5:18 We know that whoever is **b** of
5:18 but he who has been **b** of God
Rev 12: 4 her Child as soon as it was **b**.

BORNE (32/32) BEAR

Gen 16: 1 had **b** him no children. And she
21: 7 For I have **b** him a son in his
21: 9 whom she had **b** to Abraham,
22:20 Indeed Milcah also has **b**
29:34 because I have **b** him three
30:20 because I have **b** him six
30:25 when Rachel had **b** Joseph, that
31:43 their children whom they have **b**?
34: 1 whom she had **b** to Jacob, went
Ex 21: 4 and she has **b** him sons or
Lev 12: 2 and **b** a male child, then she
12: 7 is the law for her who has **b**
Deut 21:15 and they have **b** him children,
Judg 13: 3 you are barren and have **b** no
Ruth 4:15 than seven sons, has **b** him."
1 Sam 2: 5 Even the barren has **b** seven,
4:20 for you have **b** a son." But she
1 Ki 1: 6 His mother had **b** him after
3:21 he was not my son whom I had **b**.
Job 34:31 I have **b** chastening; I will
Ps 69: 7 Because for Your sake I have **b**
Isa 53: 4 Surely He has **b** our griefs
54: 1 You who have not **b**!
Jer 15: 9 She languishes who has **b** seven;
15:10 That you have **b** me, A man of
Lam 2:22 Those whom I have **b** and
Ezek 36: 6 because you have **b** the shame of
39:26 after they have **b** their shame,
Mt 20:12 them equal to us who have **b**
Jn 5:33 and he has **b** witness to the
1 Cor 15:49 And as we have **b** the image of
3 Jn 6 who have **b** witness of your love

BORROW (4/4) BORROWED, BORROWER, BORROWS

Deut 15: 6 nations, but you shall not **b**;
28:12 nations, but you shall not **b**.
2 Ki 4: 3 **b** vessels from everywhere, from
Mt 5:42 and from him who wants to **b**

BORROWED (2/2) BORROW

2 Ki 6: 5 "Alas, master! For it was **b**.
Neh 5: 4 We have **b** money for the king's

BORROWER (2/2) BORROW

Prov 22: 7 And the **b** is servant to the
Isa 24: 2 with the lender, so with the **b**;

BORROWS (2/2) BORROW

Ex 22:14 And if a man **b** anything from
Ps 37:21 The wicked **b** and does not

BOSCATH (KJV) See BOZKATH

BOSOM (35/31)

Ex 4: 6 "Now put your hand in your **b**.
4: 6 And he put his hand in his **b**,
4: 7 Put your hand in your **b** again."
4: 7 So he put his hand in his **b**
4: 7 again, and drew it out of his **b**,
Num 11:12 to me, 'Carry them in your **b**,

Deut 13: 6 daughter, the wife of your ***b***,
28:54 toward the wife of his ***b***,
28:56 refuse to the husband of her ***b***,
Ruth 4:16 the child and laid him on her ***b***,
2 Sam 12: 3 his own cup and lay in his ***b***;
1 Ki 1: 2 and let her lie in your ***b***,
3:20 slept, and laid him in her ***b***,
3:20 and laid her dead child in my ***b***.
Job 31:33 By hiding my iniquity in my ***b***,
Ps 74:11 Take it out of Your ***b*** and
79:12 sevenfold into their ***b*** Their
89:50 How I bear in my ***b*** the
Prov 6:27 Can a man take fire to his ***b***,
Eccl 7: 9 For anger rests in the ***b*** of
Isa 40:11 arm, And carry them in His ***b***,
65: 6 repay—Even repay into their ***b***—
65: 7 their former work into their ***b***.
66:11 With the consolation of her ***b***,
Jer 32:18 of the fathers into the ***b*** of
Lam 2:12 poured out In their mothers' ***b***.
Ezek 23: 3 Their virgin ***b*** was there
23: 8 with her, Pressed her virgin ***b***,
23:21 the Egyptians pressed your ***b***
Mic 7: 5 From her who lies in your ***b***.
Lk 6:38 over will be put into your ***b***.
16:22 by the angels to Abraham's ***b***.
16:23 afar off, and Lazarus in his ***b***.
Jn 1:18 who is in the ***b*** of the Father,
13:23 there was leaning on Jesus' ***b***

BOSOR (KJV) See BEOR

BOTH (308/306)

Gen 2:25 And they were ***b*** naked, the man
3: 7 Then the eyes of ***b*** of them were
3:18 ***B*** thorns and thistles it shall
6: 7 ***b*** man and beast, creeping thing
7:23 ***b*** man and cattle, creeping
9:23 laid it on ***b*** their shoulders,
19: 4 ***b*** old and young, all the people
19:11 ***b*** small and great, so that they
19:36 Thus ***b*** the daughters of Lot
24:25 We have ***b*** straw and feed enough,
27:45 I be bereaved also of you ***b*** in
31:37 they may judge between us ***b***!
36:24 ***b*** Ajah and Anah. This was the
40: 5 ***b*** of them, each man's dream in
41:10 ***b*** me and the chief baker,
43: 8 ***b*** we and you and also our
44:16 ***b*** we and he also with whom the
46:34 ***b*** we and also our fathers,'
47: 3 ***b*** we and also our fathers."
47:19 ***b*** we and our land? Buy us and
48:13 And Joseph took them ***b***,
50: 9 And there went up with him ***b***
Ex 5:14 your task in making brick ***b***
7:19 ***b*** in buckets of wood and
9:25 ***b*** man and beast; and the hail
12:12 ***b*** man and beast; and against
12:31 ***b*** you and the children of
13: 2 ***b*** of man and beast; it is
13:15 ***b*** the firstborn of man and the
18:18 ***B*** you and these people who are
22: 9 the cause of ***b*** parties shall
22:11 LORD shall be between them ***b***,
26:24 Thus it shall be for ***b*** of them.
29:44 I will also consecrate ***b*** Aaron
30: 4 under the molding on ***b*** its
32:15 The tablets were written on ***b***
35:22 ***b*** men and women, as many as had
36:29 Thus he made ***b*** of them for the
37:27 by its two corners on ***b*** sides,
Lev 6:28 it shall be ***b*** scoured and
7: 7 there is one law for them ***b***:
9: 3 ***b*** of the first year, without
16:21 Aaron shall lay ***b*** his hands on
17:15 he shall ***b*** wash his clothes and
20:11 ***b*** of them shall surely be put
20:12 ***b*** of them shall surely be put
20:13 ***b*** of them have committed an
20:14 ***b*** he and they, that there may
20:18 ***B*** of them shall be cut off from
21:22 ***b*** the most holy and the holy;
22:28 do not kill ***b*** her and her young
27:10 then ***b*** it and the one exchanged
27:28 ***b*** man and beast, or the field
27:33 then ***b*** it and the one exchanged
Num 3:13 ***b*** man and beast. They shall be
5: 3 You shall put out ***b*** male and
7:13 ***b*** of them full of fine flour
7:19 ***b*** of them full of fine flour
7:25 ***b*** of them full of fine flour
7:31 ***b*** of them full of fine flour
7:37 ***b*** of them full of fine flour
7:43 ***b*** of them full of fine flour
7:49 ***b*** of them full of fine flour
7:55 ***b*** of them full of fine flour
7:61 ***b*** of them full of fine flour
7:67 ***b*** of them full of fine flour
7:73 ***b*** of them full of fine flour
7:79 ***b*** of them full of fine flour
8:17 ***b*** man and beast; on the day
9:14 ***b*** for the stranger and the
10: 3 When they blow ***b*** of them, all
11:30 ***b*** he and the elders of Israel.
12: 5 And they ***b*** went forward.
16:17 ***b*** you and Aaron, each with his
25: 8 into the tent and thrust ***b*** of
Deut 19:17 then ***b*** men in the controversy
21:15 ***b*** the loved and the unloved,
22:22 then ***b*** of them shall die—the
22:24 then you shall bring them ***b*** out
23:18 for ***b*** of these are an
30:19 that ***b*** you and your descendants
Josh 6:21 ***b*** man and woman, young and old,
7:11 and have ***b*** stolen and deceived;
8:25 ***b*** men and women, were twelve
14:11 ***b*** for going out and for coming
17:16 ***b*** those who are of Beth
Judg 6: 5 ***b*** they and their camels were
8:22 ***b*** you and your son, and your
9:13 Which cheers ***b*** God and men,
10:10 because we have ***b*** forsaken our
15: 5 and burned up ***b*** the shocks and
19: 8 and ***b*** of them ate.
19:19 although we have ***b*** straw and
Ruth 1: 5 Then ***b*** Mahlon and Chilion also
1 Sam 2:26 and in favor ***b*** with the LORD
2:34 they shall die, ***b*** of them.
3:11 something in Israel at which ***b***
5: 4 The head of Dagon and ***b*** the
5: 6 ***b*** Ashdod and its territory.
5: 9 ***b*** small and great, and tumors
6:18 ***b*** fortified cities and country
9:26 and ***b*** of them went outside, he
12:14 then ***b*** you and the king who
12:25 ***b*** you and your king."
14:11 So ***b*** of them showed themselves
15: 3 But kill ***b*** man and woman,
17:36 Your servant has killed ***b*** lion
20:11 So ***b*** of them went out into
20:42 since we have ***b*** sworn in the
22:19 ***b*** men and women, children and
25:16 They were a wall to us ***b*** by
25:43 and so ***b*** of them were his
26:25 my son David! You shall ***b*** do
2 Sam 6:19 ***b*** the women and the men, to
8:18 son of Jehoiada was over ***b***
9:13 And he was lame in ***b*** his feet.
15:25 bring me back and show me ***b***
16:23 all the advice of Ahithophel ***b***
17:18 But ***b*** of them went away quickly
1 Ki 3:13 ***b*** riches and honor, so that
6:25 ***b*** cherubim were of the same
6:29 ***b*** the inner and outer
6:30 ***b*** the inner and outer
7:50 ***b*** for the doors of the inner
8:24 You have ***b*** spoken with Your
21:21 in Israel, ***b*** bond and free.
2 Ki 9: 8 in Israel, ***b*** bond and free.
21:12 ***b*** his ears will tingle.
23: 2 ***b*** small and great. And he read
23:15 ***b*** that altar and the high place
1 Chr 12: 2 using ***b*** the right hand and the
16: 3 ***b*** man and woman, to everyone a
23:29 ***b*** with the showbread and the
29:12 ***B*** riches and honor come from
2 Chr 6:15 You have ***b*** spoken with Your
13:14 the battle line was at ***b***
24:16 ***b*** toward God and His house.
26:10 ***b*** in the lowlands and in the
Ezra 3: 3 ***b*** the morning and evening
Neh 1: 6 ***B*** my father's house and I have
12:27 ***b*** with thanksgivings and
12:45 ***B*** the singers and the
Esth 1:20 ***b*** great and small."
2:23 and ***b*** were hanged on a gallows;
3:13 ***b*** young and old, little
8:11 ***b*** little children and women,
Job 9:33 Who may lay his hand on us ***b***.
15:10 ***B*** the gray-haired and the aged
Ps 4: 8 I will ***b*** lie down in peace, and
49: 2 ***B*** low and high, Rich and poor
64: 6 ***B*** the inward thought and the
76: 6 ***B*** the chariot and horse were
87: 7 ***B*** the singers and the players
104:25 Living things ***b*** small and
115:13 ***B*** small and great.
135: 8 ***B*** of man and beast.
139:12 darkness and the light are ***b***
148:12 ***B*** young men and maidens
Prov 17:15 ***B*** of them alike are an
20:10 They are ***b*** alike, an
20:12 eye, The LORD has made them ***b***.
27: 3 wrath is heavier than ***b*** of
29:13 gives light to the eyes of ***b***.
Eccl 4: 3 better than ***b*** is he who has
4: 6 with quietness Than ***b*** hands
8: 5 a wise man's heart discerns ***b***
11: 6 Or whether ***b*** alike will be
Isa 1:31 ***B*** will burn together, And no
7:16 you dread will be forsaken by ***b***
8:14 and a rock of offense To ***b***
10:18 ***B*** soul and body; And they
13: 9 with ***b*** wrath and fierce anger,
18: 5 He will ***b*** cut off the sprigs
31: 3 ***B*** he who helps will fall, And
38:15 He has ***b*** spoken to me, And He
Jer 5:24 ***b*** the former and the latter, in
9:10 ***B*** the birds of the heavens and
14:18 ***b*** prophet and priest go about
16: 6 ***B*** the great and the small shall
21: 6 ***b*** man and beast; they shall die
23:11 For ***b*** prophet and priest are
26: 5 ***b*** rising up early and sending
32:11 ***b*** that which was sealed
32:14 ***b*** this purchase deed which is
46:12 They ***b*** have fallen
50: 3 ***B*** man and beast.
51:12 For the LORD has ***b*** devised
Ezek 14:22 ***b*** sons and daughters; surely
15: 4 the fire devours ***b*** ends of it,
21: 3 out of its sheath and cut off ***b***
21: 4 Because I will cut off ***b***
21:19 ***b*** of them shall go from the
23:13 ***B*** took the same way.
23:29 ***b*** your lewdness and your
30:22 ***b*** the strong one and the one
39: 9 ***b*** the shields and bucklers, the
43:25 ***b*** without blemish.
Dan 8:13 the giving of ***b*** the sanctuary
11:27 ***B*** these kings' hearts shall be
Mic 5: 8 ***B*** treads down and tears in
7: 3 may successfully do evil with ***b***
Zeph 2:14 ***B*** the pelican and the bittern
Zech 6:13 peace shall be between them ***b***.
14: 8 In ***b*** summer and winter it
Mt 9:17 and ***b*** are preserved."
10:28 Him who is able to destroy ***b***
12:22 that the blind and mute man ***b***
13:30 Let ***b*** grow together until the
15:14 ***b*** will fall into a ditch."
22:10 ***b*** bad and good. And the wedding
Mk 6:30 ***b*** what they had done and what
7:37 He makes ***b*** the deaf to hear and
9:22 And often he has thrown him ***b***
Lk 1: 6 And they were ***b*** righteous before
1: 7 and they were ***b*** well advanced
2:46 ***b*** listening to them and asking
5: 7 And they came and filled ***b*** the
5:38 and ***b*** are preserved.
6:39 Will they not ***b*** fall into the
7:42 repay, he freely forgave them ***b***.
22:33 ***b*** to prison and to death."
22:66 ***b*** chief priests and scribes,
Jn 2: 2 Now ***b*** Jesus and His disciples
4:36 that ***b*** he who sows and he who
7:28 You ***b*** know Me, and you know
9:37 You have ***b*** seen Him and it is He
11:48 will come and take away ***b*** our
11:57 Now ***b*** the chief priests and the
12:28 I have ***b*** glorified it and will
15:24 have seen and also hated ***b*** Me
20: 4 So they ***b*** ran together, and the
Acts 1: 1 of all that Jesus began ***b*** to do
2:10 ***b*** Jews and proselytes,
2:29 that he is ***b*** dead and buried,
2:36 ***b*** Lord and Christ."
4:27 ***b*** Herod and Pontius Pilate,
5:14 multitudes of ***b*** men and women,
8:12 ***b*** men and women were baptized.
8:38 And ***b*** Philip and the eunuch
10:39 of all things which He did ***b***
14: 1 spoke that a great multitude ***b***
14: 5 a violent attempt was made by ***b***
17:14 but ***b*** Silas and Timothy
18: 4 and persuaded ***b*** Jews and
19:10 ***b*** Jews and Greeks.
19:17 This became known ***b*** to all Jews
21:12 ***b*** we and those from that place
22: 4 and delivering into prisons ***b***
23: 8 but the Pharisees confess ***b***.
24:15 ***b*** of the just and the unjust.
25:24 ***b*** at Jerusalem and here, crying
26:16 you a minister and a witness ***b***
26:22 witnessing ***b*** to small and
26:29 might become ***b*** almost and
28:23 them concerning Jesus from ***b***
Rom 1:12 with you by the mutual faith ***b***
1:14 I am a debtor ***b*** to Greeks and to
1:14 ***b*** to wise and to unwise.
3: 9 we have previously charged ***b***
11:33 the depth of the riches ***b*** of
14: 9 that He might be Lord of ***b*** the
1 Cor 1: 2 ***b*** theirs and ours:
1:24 ***b*** Jews and Greeks, Christ the
4: 5 who will ***b*** bring to light the
4: 9 ***b*** to angels and to men.
4:11 To the present hour we ***b*** hunger
6:13 but God will destroy ***b*** it and
6:14 And God ***b*** raised up the Lord and
7:34 that she may be holy ***b*** in body
Eph 1:10 ***b*** which are in heaven and which
2:14 who has made ***b*** one, and has
2:16 that He might reconcile them ***b***
2:18 For through Him we ***b*** have access
Phil 1: 7 inasmuch as ***b*** in my chains and
2:13 it is God who works in you ***b***
4:12 in all things I have learned ***b***
4:12 ***b*** to abound and to suffer need.
Col 2: 2 ***b*** of the Father and of Christ,
1 Th 2:15 who killed ***b*** the Lord Jesus and
5:15 always pursue what is good ***b***
2 Th 3: 4 ***b*** that you do and will do the
1 Tim 4:10 For to this end we ***b*** labor and
4:16 in doing this you will save ***b***
Titus 1: 9 ***b*** to exhort and convict those
1:10 ***b*** idle talkers and deceivers,
Phm 1:16 ***b*** in the flesh and in the Lord.
Heb 2: 4 God also bearing witness ***b*** with
2:11 For ***b*** He who sanctifies and
5: 1 that he may offer ***b*** gifts and
5:14 senses exercised to discern ***b***
6:19 ***b*** sure and steadfast, and which
8: 3 priest is appointed to offer ***b***
9: 9 for the present time in which ***b***
9:19 and sprinkled ***b*** the book itself
9:21 he sprinkled with blood ***b*** the
10:33 you were made a spectacle ***b*** by
Jas 3:12 Thus no spring yields ***b*** salt
2 Pe 3: 1 you this second epistle (in ***b***
3:10 ***b*** the earth and the works that
3:18 To Him be the glory ***b*** now and
2 Jn 9 in the doctrine of Christ has ***b***

Jude 25 **b** now and forever. Amen.
Rev 1: 9 **b** your brother and companion in
6:11 until **b** the number of their
13:15 the image of the beast should **b**
13:16 **b** small and great, rich and
19: 5 **b** small and great!"
19:18 **b** small and great."

BOTTLE (4/3) BOTTLES

Ps 56: 8 Put my tears into Your **b**;
Jer 13:12 Every **b** shall be filled with
13:12 not certainly know that every **b**
Hab 2:15 Pressing him to your **b**,

BOTTLES (2/2) BOTTLE

Job 38:37 Or who can pour out the **b** of
Jer 48:12 his vessels And break the **b**.

BOTTOM (8/8) BOTTOMLESS

Ex 15: 5 They sank to the **b** like a
26:24 be coupled together at the **b**
36:29 And they were coupled at the **b**
38: 4 its rim, midway from the **b**.
Dan 6:24 before they ever came to the **b**
Am 9: 3 hide from My sight at the **b** of
Mt 27:51 was torn in two from top to **b**;
Mk 15:38 was torn in two from top to **b**.

BOTTOMLESS (7/7) BOTTOM

Rev 9: 1 him was given the key to the **b**
9: 2 And he opened the **b** pit, and
9:11 over them the angel of the **b**
11: 7 that ascends out of the **b** pit
17: 8 and will ascend out of the **b**
20: 1 having the key to the **b** pit and
20: 3 and he cast him into the **b** pit,

BOUGH (7/6) BOUGHS

Gen 49:22 "Joseph is a fruitful **b**,
49:22 A fruitful **b** by a well; His
Judg 9:48 ax in his hand and cut down a **b**
9:49 likewise cut down his own **b**
Isa 10:33 Will lop off the **b** with
17: 6 at the top of the uppermost **b**,
17: 9 cities will be as a forsaken **b**

BOUGHS (14/14) BOUGH

Lev 23:40 the **b** of leafy trees, and
Deut 24:20 you shall not go over the **b**
2 Sam 18: 9 mule went under the thick **b** of
Ps 80:10 the mighty cedars with its **b**.
80:11 She sent out her **b** to the Sea,
Isa 27:11 When its **b** are withered, they
Ezek 17:23 it; and it will bring forth **b**,
31: 3 its top was among the thick **b**.
31: 5 Its **b** were multiplied, And
31: 6 made their nests in its **b**;
31: 8 fir trees were not like its **b**,
31:10 set its top among the thick **b**,
31:12 its **b** lie broken by all the
31:14 their tops among the thick **b**,

BOUGHT (44/44) BUY

Gen 17:12 who is born in your house or **b**
17:13 in your house and he who is **b**
17:23 in his house and all who were **b**
17:27 born in the house or **b** with
33:19 And he **b** the parcel of land,
39: 1 **b** him from the Ishmaelites who
47:14 for the grain which they **b**;
47:20 Then Joseph **b** all the land of
47:23 Indeed I have **b** you and your
49:30 which Abraham **b** with the field
50:13 which Abraham **b** with the field
Ex 12:44 every man's servant who is **b**
Lev 25:28 in the hand of him who **b** it
25:30 permanently to him who **b** it,
25:50 he shall reckon with him who **b**
25:51 the money with which he was **b**.
27:22 LORD a field which he has **b**,
27:24 to him from whom it was **b**,
Deut 32: 6 who **b** you? Has He not made you
Josh 24:32 of ground which Jacob had **b**
Ruth 4: 9 this day that I have **b** all
2 Sam 12: 3 little ewe lamb which he had **b**
24:24 So David **b** the threshing
1 Ki 10:28 the king's merchants **b** them in
16:24 And he **b** the hill of Samaria
2 Chr 1:16 the king's merchants **b** them in
Isa 43:24 You have **b** Me no sweet cane
Jer 32: 9 So I **b** the field from Hanamel,
32:43 And fields will be **b** in this
Hos 3: 2 So I **b** her for myself for
Mt 13:46 and sold all that he had and **b**
21:12 and drove out all those who **b**
27: 7 they consulted together and **b**
Mk 11:15 began to drive out those who **b**
15:46 Then he **b** fine linen, took Him
16: 1 and Salome **b** spices, that they
Lk 14:18 I have **b** a piece of ground, and
14:19 I have **b** five yoke of oxen, and
17:28 They ate, they drank, they **b**,
19:45 began to drive out those who **b**
Acts 7:16 in the tomb that Abraham **b** for
1 Cor 6:20 For you were **b** at a price;
7:23 You were **b** at a price; do not
2 Pe 2: 1 even denying the Lord who **b**

BOUND (91/89) BIND

Gen 22: 9 and he **b** Isaac his son and laid
38:28 took a scarlet thread and **b**
42:24 he took Simeon from them and **b**
44:30 since his life is **b** up in the
49:26 Up to the utmost **b** of the
Ex 12:34 having their kneading bowls **b**
39:21 And they **b** the breastplate by
Num 30: 4 agreement by which she has **b**
30: 4 agreement with which she has **b**
30: 5 agreements by which she has **b**
30: 6 while **b** by her vows or by a
30: 6 from her lips by which she **b**
30: 7 her agreements by which she **b**
30: 8 by which she **b** herself, and the
30: 9 by which she has **b** herself,
30:10 or **b** herself by an agreement
30:11 every agreement by which she **b**
Josh 2:21 And she **b** the scarlet cord in
Judg 15:13 And they **b** him with two new
16: 6 and with what you may be **b** to
16: 8 and she **b** him with them.
16:10 tell me what you may be **b** with.
16:12 Delilah took new ropes and **b**
16:13 Tell me what you may be **b**
16:21 They **b** him with bronze fetters,
1 Sam 25:29 the life of my lord shall be **b**
2 Sam 3:34 Your hands were not **b** Nor your
2 Ki 5:23 and **b** two talents of silver in
17: 4 and **b** him in prison.
25: 7 **b** him with bronze fetters, and
2 Chr 33:11 **b** him with bronze fetters, and
36: 6 and **b** him in bronze fetters to
Job 36: 8 And if they are **b** in fetters,
Ps 68: 6 He brings out those who are **b**
107:10 **B** in affliction and irons—
119:61 cords of the wicked have **b** me,
Prov 22:15 Foolishness is **b** up in the
30: 4 Who has **b** the waters in a
Isa 1: 6 have not been closed or **b** up,
22: 3 All who are found in you are **b**
61: 1 prison to those who are **b**;
Jer 5:22 have placed the sand as the **b**
30:13 That you may be **b** up; You
39: 7 and **b** him with bronze fetters
40: 1 when he had taken him **b** in
52:11 and the king of Babylon **b** him
Lam 1:14 yoke of my transgressions was **b**;
Ezek 34: 4 nor **b** up the broken, nor
Dan 3:21 Then these men were **b** in their
3:23 fell down **b** into the midst of
3:24 Did we not cast three men **b** into
4:15 **B** with a band of iron and
4:23 **b** with a band of iron and
Hos 13:12 iniquity of Ephraim is **b**
Nah 3:10 And all her great men were **b**
Mt 14: 3 had laid hold of John and **b**
16:19 you bind on earth will be **b** in
18:18 you bind on earth will be **b** in
27: 2 And when they had **b** Him, they
Mk 5: 4 because he had often been **b** with
6:17 and **b** him in prison for the
15: 1 and they **b** Jesus, led Him
Lk 8:29 **b** with chains and shackles; and
13:16 of Abraham, whom Satan has **b**—
Jn 11:44 And he who had died came out **b**
18:12 the Jews arrested Jesus and **b**
18:24 Then Annas sent Him **b** to
19:40 and **b** it in strips of linen
Acts 8:23 poisoned by bitterness and **b**
9: 2 he might bring them **b** to
9:21 so that he might bring them **b**
10:11 an object like a great sheet **b**
12: 6 **b** with two chains between two
20:22 now I go **b** in the spirit to
21:11 **b** his own hands and feet, and
21:13 For I am ready not only to be **b**,
21:33 and commanded him to be **b** with
22:25 And as they **b** him with thongs,
22:29 and because he had **b** him.
23:12 the Jews banded together and **b**
23:14 We have **b** ourselves under a
23:21 men who have **b** themselves by an
24:27 the Jews a favor, left Paul **b**.
28:20 for the hope of Israel I am **b**
Rom 7: 2 woman who has a husband is **b**
1 Cor 7:27 Are you **b** to a wife? Do not seek
7:39 A wife is **b** by law as long as
2 Th 1: 3 We are **b** to thank God always
2:13 But we are **b** to give thanks to
Rev 9:14 the four angels who are **b** at
20: 2 and **b** him for a thousand years;

BOUNDARIES (7/7) BOUNDARY

Num 34: 2 land of Canaan to its **b**.
34:12 land with its surrounding **b**.
Deut 32: 8 He set the **b** of the peoples
Josh 18:20 according to its **b** all around,
Isa 10:13 Also I have removed the **b** of
Mic 2: 5 have no one to determine **b** by
Acts 17:26 preappointed times and the **b**

BOUNDARY (14/13) BOUNDARIES, BOUNDLESS, BOUNDS

Num 22:36 the **b** of the territory.
33:37 on the **b** of the land of Edom.
Deut 2:18 over at Ar, the **b** of Moab.
Josh 15: 1 was the extreme southern **b**.
15:12 This is the **b** of the children
16: 3 went down westward to the **b** of
16: 3 as far as the **b** of Lower Beth
18:19 This was the southern **b**.
Judg 1:36 Now the **b** of the Amorites was
Job 26:10 At the **b** of light and
Ps 104: 9 You have set a **b** that they may
Prov 15:25 But He will establish the **b** of
Ezek 47:17 Thus the **b** shall be from the Sea
47:20 from the southern **b** until one

BOUNDLESS (1/1) BOUNDS

Nah 3: 9 her strength, And it was **b**;

BOUNDS (3/3) BOUNDLESS

Ex 19:12 You shall set **b** for the people
19:23 Set **b** around the mountain and
23:31 And I will set your **b** from the

BOUNTIFUL (2/2) BOUNTIFULLY, BOUNTY

Isa 32: 5 Nor the miser said to be **b**;
Jer 2: 7 I brought you into a **b** country,

BOUNTIFULLY (8/7) BOUNTIFUL

Num 23:11 you have blessed them **b**!"
24:10 you have **b** blessed them these
Ps 13: 6 Because He has dealt **b** with
116: 7 For the LORD has dealt **b** with
119:17 Deal **b** with Your servant,
142: 7 For You shall deal **b** with
2 Cor 9: 6 and he who sows **b** will also
9: 6 bountifully will also reap **b**.

BOUNTY (2/2) BOUNTIFUL

Neh 9:36 To eat its fruit and its **b**,
Hos 10: 1 According to the **b** of his land

BOW (98/94) BOWED, BOWING, BOWMEN, BOWS, BOWSHOT, BOWSTRING

Gen 27: 3 weapons, your quiver and your **b**,
27:29 And nations **b** down to you.
27:29 And let your mother's sons **b**
37:10 your brothers indeed come to **b**
41:43 **B** the knee!" So he set him over
48:22 Amorite with my sword and my **b**.
49: 8 father's children shall **b** down
49:24 But his **b** remained in strength,
Ex 11: 8 shall come down to me and **b**
20: 5 you shall not **b** down to them nor
23:24 You shall not **b** down to their
Lev 26: 1 to **b** down to it; for I am the
Deut 5: 9 you shall not **b** down to them nor
Josh 23: 7 you shall not serve them nor **b**
24:12 with your sword or with your **b**.
Judg 2:19 to serve them and **b** down to
1 Sam 2:36 in your house will come and **b**
18: 4 even to his sword and his **b** and
2 Sam 1:18 of Judah the Song of the **B**;
1:22 The **b** of Jonathan did not turn
15: 5 whenever anyone came near to **b**
16: 4 I humbly **b** before you, that I
22:35 So that my arms can bend a **b**
1 Ki 22:34 Now a certain man drew a **b** at
2 Ki 5:18 and I **b** down in the temple of
5:18 when I **b** down in the temple of
6:22 with your sword and your **b**?
9:24 Now Jehu drew his **b** with full
13:15 'Take a **b** and some arrows."
13:15 So he took himself a **b** and
13:16 "Put your hand on the **b**.
17:35 nor **b** down to them nor serve
1 Chr 5:18 and sword, to shoot with the **b**,
12: 2 and shooting arrows with the **b**.
2 Chr 17:17 thousand men armed with **b** and
18:33 Now a certain man drew a **b** at
Esth 3: 2 But Mordecai would not **b** or pay
3: 5 saw that Mordecai did not **b** or
Job 20:24 A bronze **b** will pierce him
29:20 And my **b** is renewed in my
31:10 And let others **b** down over
39: 3 They **b** down, They bring forth
Ps 7:12 He bends His **b** and makes it
11: 2 The wicked bend their **b**,
18:34 So that my arms can bend a **b**
22:29 go down to the dust Shall **b**
31: 2 **B** down Your ear to me, Deliver
37:14 sword And have bent their **b**,
44: 6 For I will not trust in my **b**,
46: 9 He breaks the **b** and cuts the
58: 7 When he bends his **b**,
72: 9 dwell in the wilderness will **b**
76: 3 He broke the arrows of the **b**,
78:57 turned aside like a deceitful **b**.
86: 1 **B** down Your ear, O LORD, hear
95: 6 let us worship and **b** down; Let
144: 5 **B** down Your heavens, O LORD,
Prov 14:19 The evil will **b** before the
Eccl 12: 3 And the strong men **b** down;
Isa 2: 9 People **b** down, And each man
10: 4 Without Me they shall **b** down
21:15 drawn sword, From the bent **b**,
41: 2 As driven stubble to his **b**?
45:14 And they shall **b** down to you.

45:23 That to Me every knee shall ***b***,
46: 2 they ***b*** down together; They
49:23 They shall ***b*** down to you with
58: 5 Is it to ***b*** down his head
65:12 And you shall all ***b*** down to
66:19 and Pul and Lud, who draw the ***b***,
Jer 6:23 They will lay hold on ***b*** and
9: 3 And like their ***b*** they have bent
46: 9 who handle and bend the ***b***.
49:35 I will break the ***b*** of Elam,
50:14 around, All you who bend the ***b***;
50:29 All you who bend the ***b***,
50:42 They shall hold the ***b*** and the
51: 3 her let the archer bend his ***b***,
Lam 2: 4 an enemy, He has bent His ***b***;
2:10 The virgins of Jerusalem ***B***
3:12 He has bent His ***b*** And set me
Ezek 39: 3 Then I will knock the ***b*** out of
Hos 1: 5 day That I will break the ***b***
1: 7 And will not save them by ***b***,
2:18 ***B*** and sword of battle I will
7:16 They are like a treacherous ***b***.
Am 2:15 not stand who handles the ***b***,
Mic 6: 6 And ***b*** myself before the High
Hab 3: 9 Your ***b*** was made quite ready;
Zech 9:10 The battle ***b*** shall be cut off.
9:13 For I have bent Judah, My ***b***,
9:13 Fitted the ***b*** with Ephraim,
10: 4 peg, From him the battle ***b***,
Rom 11:10 and ***b*** down their back
14:11 Every knee shall ***b*** to
Eph 3:14 For this reason I ***b*** my knees to
Phil 2:10 of Jesus every knee should ***b***,
Rev 6: 2 He who sat on it had a ***b***;

BOWED (75/73) BOW

Gen 18: 2 and ***b*** himself to the ground,
19: 1 and he ***b*** himself with his face
23: 7 Then Abraham stood up and ***b***
23:12 Then Abraham ***b*** himself down
24:26 Then the man ***b*** down his head and
24:48 And I ***b*** my head and worshiped
33: 3 crossed over before them and ***b***
33: 6 their children, and ***b*** down.
33: 7 and they ***b*** down.
33: 7 came near, and they ***b*** down.
37: 7 sheaves stood all around and ***b***
37: 9 and the eleven stars ***b*** down to
42: 6 Joseph's brothers came and ***b***
43:26 and ***b*** down before him to the
43:28 And they ***b*** their heads down
47:31 So Israel ***b*** himself on the head
48:12 and he ***b*** down with his face to
49:15 He ***b*** his shoulder to bear a
Ex 4:31 then they ***b*** their heads and
12:27 So the people ***b*** their heads
18: 7 ***b*** down, and kissed him.
34: 8 So Moses made haste and ***b*** his
Num 22:31 and he ***b*** his head and fell flat
25: 2 and the people ate and ***b*** down
Josh 23:16 and ***b*** down to them, then the
Judg 2:12 and they ***b*** down to them; and
2:17 and ***b*** down to them. They turned
Ruth 2:10 ***b*** down to the ground, and said
1 Sam 4:19 she ***b*** herself and gave birth,
20:41 and ***b*** down three times.
24: 8 to the earth, and ***b*** down.
25:23 and ***b*** down to the ground.
25:41 ***b*** her face to the earth, and
28:14 his face to the ground and ***b***
2 Sam 9: 8 Then he ***b*** himself, and said,
14:22 to the ground on his face and ***b***
14:33 he came to the king and ***b***
18:21 So the Cushite ***b*** himself to
18:28 All is well!" Then he ***b*** down
22:10 He ***b*** the heavens also, and came
24:20 So Araunah went out and ***b***
1 Ki 1:16 And Bathsheba ***b*** and did homage
1:23 he ***b*** down before the king with
1:31 Then Bathsheba ***b*** with her face
1:47 Then the king ***b*** himself on the
2:19 king rose up to meet her and ***b***
18:42 then he ***b*** down on the ground,
19:18 all whose knees have not ***b*** to
2 Ki 2:15 and ***b*** to the ground before him.
4:37 and ***b*** to the ground; then she
1 Chr 21:21 and ***b*** before David with his
29:20 and ***b*** their heads and
2 Chr 7: 3 they ***b*** their faces to the
20:18 And Jehoshaphat ***b*** his head with
20:18 the inhabitants of Jerusalem ***b***
24:17 the leaders of Judah came and ***b***
25:14 and ***b*** down before them and
29:29 all who were present with him ***b***
29:30 and they ***b*** their heads and
Neh 8: 6 And they ***b*** their heads and
Esth 3: 2 were within the king's gate ***b***
Ps 18: 9 He ***b*** the heavens also, and came
20: 8 They have ***b*** down and fallen;
35:14 I ***b*** down heavily, as one who
38: 6 I am ***b*** down greatly; I go
44:25 For our soul is ***b*** down to the
57: 6 My soul is ***b*** down; They have
145:14 And raises up all who are ***b***
146: 8 LORD raises those who are ***b***
Isa 2:11 haughtiness of men shall be ***b***
2:17 loftiness of man shall be ***b***
Hab 3: 6 The perpetual hills ***b***.
Mt 27:29 And they ***b*** the knee before Him
Lk 24: 5 as they were afraid and ***b***
Rom 11: 4 men who have not ***b*** the

BOWING (5/5) BOW

Gen 24:52 ***b*** himself to the earth.
Ezra 10: 1 and ***b*** down before the house of
Isa 60:14 afflicted you Shall come ***b*** to
Mk 15:19 and ***b*** the knee, they worshiped
Jn 19:30 It is finished!" And ***b*** His

BOWL (31/30) BOWL-SHAPED, BOWLFUL, BOWLS

Num 7:13 and one silver ***b*** of seventy
7:19 and one silver ***b*** of seventy
7:25 and one silver ***b*** of seventy
7:31 and one silver ***b*** of seventy
7:37 and one silver ***b*** of seventy
7:43 and one silver ***b*** of seventy
7:49 and one silver ***b*** of seventy
7:55 and one silver ***b*** of seventy
7:61 and one silver ***b*** of seventy
7:67 and one silver ***b*** of seventy
7:73 and one silver ***b*** of seventy
7:79 and one silver ***b*** of seventy
7:85 and thirty shekels and each ***b***
Deut 28: 5 your basket and your kneading ***b***.
28:17 your basket and your kneading ***b***.
Judg 5:25 brought out cream in a lordly ***b***.
2 Ki 2:20 And he said, "Bring me a new ***b***,
1 Chr 28:17 gold by weight for every ***b***;
28:17 silver by weight for every ***b***;
Prov 19:24 man buries his hand in the ***b***,
26:15 man buries his hand in the ***b***;
Eccl 12: 6 Or the golden ***b*** is broken, Or
Zech 4: 2 of solid gold with a ***b*** on top
4: 3 one at the right of the ***b*** and
Rev 16: 2 went and poured out his ***b*** upon
16: 3 second angel poured out his ***b***
16: 4 third angel poured out his ***b***
16: 8 fourth angel poured out his ***b***
16:10 fifth angel poured out his ***b***
16:12 sixth angel poured out his ***b***
16:17 seventh angel poured out his ***b***

BOWL-SHAPED (6/4) BOWL

1 Ki 7:41 the two ***b*** capitals that were
7:41 two networks covering the two ***b***
7:42 to cover the two ***b*** capitals
2 Chr 4:12 the two pillars and the ***b***
4:12 two networks covering the two ***b***
4:13 to cover the two ***b*** capitals

BOWLFUL (1/1)

Judg 6:38 of the fleece, a ***b*** of water.

BOWLS (32/29) BOWL

Ex 8: 3 ovens, and into your kneading ***b***.
12:34 having their kneading ***b*** bound
25:29 and its ***b*** for pouring.
25:31 Its shaft, its branches, its ***b***,
25:33 Three ***b*** shall be made like
25:33 and three ***b*** made like almond
25:34 the lampstand itself four ***b***
37:16 its dishes, its cups, its ***b***,
37:17 Its shaft, its branches, its ***b***,
37:19 There were three ***b*** made like
37:19 and three ***b*** made like almond
37:20 lampstand itself were four ***b***
Num 4: 7 it the dishes, the pans, the ***b***,
7:84 platters, twelve silver ***b***,
1 Ki 7:40 and the shovels and the ***b***.
7:45 pots, the shovels, and the ***b***.
7:50 the basins, the trimmers, the ***b***,
1 Chr 28:17 of pure gold, and the golden ***b***—
28:17 bowl; and for the silver ***b***,
2 Chr 4: 8 And he made one hundred ***b*** of
4:11 pots and the shovels and the ***b***.
4:22 the trimmers, the ***b***,
Jer 35: 5 the house of the Rechabites ***b***
52:18 shovels, the trimmers, the ***b***,
52:19 The basins, the firepans, the ***b***,
Am 6: 6 Who drink wine from ***b***,
Zech 14:20 house shall be like the ***b***
Rev 5: 8 and golden ***b*** full of incense,
15: 7 the seven angels seven golden ***b***
16: 1 Go and pour out the ***b*** of the
17: 1 angels who had the seven ***b***
21: 9 angels who had the seven ***b***

BOWMEN (1/1) BOW

Jer 4:29 the noise of the horsemen and ***b***.

BOWS (17/17) BOW, BOWMEN, BOWSHOT, BOWSTRING, BOWSTRINGS

Gen 49: 9 He ***b*** down, he lies down as a
Num 24: 9 He ***b*** down, he lies down as a
1 Sam 2: 4 The ***b*** of the mighty men are
1 Chr 12: 2 armed with ***b***, using both the
2 Chr 14: 8 who carried shields and drew ***b***;
26:14 spears, helmets, body armor, ***b***,
Neh 4:13 their spears, and their ***b***.
4:16 the spears, the shields, the ***b***,
Ps 37:15 And their ***b*** shall be broken.
64: 3 And bend their ***b*** to shoot
78: 9 being armed and carrying ***b***,
Isa 5:28 And all their ***b*** bent; Their
7:24 With arrows and ***b*** men will come
13:18 Also their ***b*** will dash the
46: 1 Bel ***b*** down, Nebo stoops; Their
Jer 51:56 Every one of their ***b*** is
Ezek 39: 9 the ***b*** and arrows, the javelins

BOWSHOT (1/1) BOW

Gen 21:16 him at a distance of about a ***b***;

BOWSTRING (1/1) BOW, BOWSTRINGS

Job 30:11 Because He has loosed my ***b*** and

BOWSTRINGS (3/3) BOWSTRING

Judg 16: 7 they bind me with seven fresh ***b***,
16: 8 brought up to her seven fresh ***b***,
16: 9 Samson!" But he broke the ***b*** as

BOX (4/4) BOXES

Isa 41:19 tree and the pine And the ***b***
60:13 and the ***b*** tree together, To
Jn 12: 6 a thief, and had the money ***b***;
13:29 because Judas had the money ***b***,

BOXES (1/1) BOX

Isa 3:20 the headbands; The perfume ***b***,

BOY (8/8) BOY'S, BOYS

Gen 21:14 he gave it and the ***b*** to Hagar,
21:15 and she placed the ***b*** under one
21:16 me not see the death of the ***b***.
42:22 'Do not sin against the ***b***';
1 Sam 3: 1 Then the ***b*** Samuel ministered to
3: 8 that the LORD had called the ***b***.
Joel 3: 3 Have given a ***b*** as payment
Lk 2:43 the ***B*** Jesus lingered behind in

BOY'S (1/1) BOY

Judg 13:12 What will be the ***b*** rule of

BOYS (3/3) BOY

Gen 25:27 So the ***b*** grew. And Esau was a
Lam 5:13 ***B*** staggered under loads of
Zech 8: 5 of the city Shall be full of ***b***

BOZEZ (1/1)

1 Sam 14: 4 And the name of one was ***B***,

BOZKATH (2/2)

Josh 15:39 Lachish, ***B***, Eglon,
2 Ki 22: 1 the daughter of Adaiah of ***B***.

BOZRAH (8/8)

Gen 36:33 Jobab the son of Zerah of ***B***
1 Chr 1:44 Jobab the son of Zerah of ***B***
Isa 34: 6 the LORD has a sacrifice in ***B***,
63: 1 With dyed garments from ***B***,
Jer 48:24 On Kerioth and ***B***,
49:13 that ***B*** shall become a
49:22 And spread His wings over ***B***;
Am 1:12 shall devour the palaces of ***B***.

BRACED (1/1) BRACELET, BRACELETS

Judg 16:29 and he ***b*** himself against them,

BRACELET (1/1) BRACELETS

2 Sam 1:10 that was on his head and the ***b***

BRACELETS (7/7) BRACELET

Gen 24:22 and two ***b*** for her wrists
24:30 and the ***b*** on his sister's
24:47 ring on her nose and the ***b*** on
Num 31:50 armlets and ***b*** and signet rings
Isa 3:19 The pendants, the ***b***,
Ezek 16:11 put ***b*** on your wrists, and a
23:42 who put ***b*** on their wrists and

BRAIDED (9/8)

Ex 28:14 two chains of pure gold like ***b***
28:14 and fasten the ***b*** chains to the
28:22 like ***b*** cords of pure gold.
28:24 you shall put the two ***b*** chains
28:25 other two ends of the two ***b***
39:15 like ***b*** cords of pure gold.
39:17 And they put the two ***b*** chains of
39:18 The two ends of the two ***b*** chains
1 Tim 2: 9 not with ***b*** hair or gold or

BRAMBLE (4/3) BRAMBLES

Judg 9:14 all the trees said to the ***b***,
9:15 And the ***b*** said to the trees,
9:15 let fire come out of the ***b*** And
Lk 6:44 do they gather grapes from a ***b***

BRAMBLES (1/1) BRAMBLE

Isa 34:13 Nettles and ***b*** in its

BRANCH (34/30) BRANCHES

Ex 25:33 like almond blossoms on one ***b***,
25:33 almond blossoms on the other ***b***,
37:19 like almond blossoms on one ***b***,

37:19 almond blossoms on the other **b**,
Num 13:23 and there cut down a **b** with one
Job 15:32 And his **b** will not be green.
18:16 And his **b** withers above.
29:19 the dew lies all night on my **b**.
Ps 80:15 And the **b** that You made
Isa 4: 2 In that day the **B** of the LORD
9:14 Palm **b** and bulrush in one day.
11: 1 And a **B** shall grow out of his
14:19 grave Like an abominable **b**,
17: 9 bough And an uppermost **b**,
19:15 Palm **b** or bulrush, may do.
60:21 The **b** of My planting, The
Jer 1:11 I see a **b** of an almond tree."
23: 5 I will raise to David a **B**
33:15 cause to grow up to David A **B**
Ezek 8:17 Indeed they put the **b** to their
15: 2 the vine **b** which is among the
17: 3 from the cedar the highest **b**.
19:14 So that she has no strong **b**—
Dan 11: 7 But from a **b** of her roots one
Zech 3: 8 bringing forth My Servant the **B**.
6:12 the Man whose name is the **B**!
6:12 From His place He shall **b** out,
Mal 4: 1 leave them neither root nor **b**.
Mt 24:32 When its **b** has already become
Mk 13:28 When its **b** has already become
Jn 15: 2 Every **b** in Me that does not bear
15: 2 and every **b** that bears fruit
15: 4 As the **b** cannot bear fruit of
15: 6 he is cast out as a **b** and is

BRANCHES (84/67) BRANCH

Gen 40:10 "and in the vine were three **b**;
40:12 The three **b** are three days.
49:22 His **b** run over the wall.
Ex 25:31 hammered work. Its shaft, its **b**,
25:32 And six **b** shall come out of its
25:32 three **b** of the lampstand out of
25:32 and three **b** of the lampstand
25:33 and so for the six **b** that come
25:35 a knob under the first two **b**
25:35 a knob under the second two **b**
25:35 a knob under the third two **b**
25:35 according to the six **b** that
25:36 Their knobs and their **b** shall
37:17 the lampstand. Its shaft, its **b**,
37:18 And six **b** came out of its sides:
37:18 three **b** of the lampstand out of
37:18 and three **b** of the lampstand
37:19 and so for the six **b** coming out
37:21 a knob under the first two **b**
37:21 a knob under the second two **b**
37:21 a knob under the third two **b**
37:21 to the six **b** extending
37:22 Their knobs and their **b** were of
Lev 23:40 **b** of palm trees, the boughs of
Neh 8:15 the mountain, and bring olive **b**,
8:15 **b** of oil trees, myrtle
8:15 branches of oil trees, myrtle **b**,
8:15 trees, myrtle branches, palm **b**,
8:15 and **b** of leafy trees, to make
Job 8:16 And his **b** spread out in his
14: 9 it will bud And bring forth **b**
15:30 The flame will dry out his **b**,
Ps 80:11 And her **b** to the River.
104:12 home; They sing among the **b**.
Song 7: 8 I will take hold of its **b**.
Isa 16: 8 Her **b** are stretched out, They
17: 6 or five in its most fruitful **b**,
18: 5 take away and cut down the **b**.
27:10 lie down And consume its **b**.
Jer 5:10 complete end. Take away her **b**,
6: 9 put your hand back into the **b**.
11:16 And its **b** are broken.
Ezek 17: 6 Its **b** turned toward him, But
17: 6 became a vine, Brought forth **b**,
17: 7 And stretched its **b** toward
17: 8 many waters, To bring forth **b**,
17:22 also one of the highest **b** of
17:23 in the shadow of its **b** they
19:10 Fruitful and full of **b**
19:11 She had strong **b** for scepters
19:11 in stature above the thick **b**,
19:12 Her strong **b** were broken and
19:14 come out from a rod of her **b**
31: 3 With fine **b** that shaded the
31: 5 And its **b** became long because
31: 6 Under its **b** all the beasts of
31: 7 and in the length of its **b**,
31: 8 trees were not like its **b**;
31: 9 beautiful with a multitude of **b**,
31:12 its **b** have fallen on the
31:13 of the field will come to its **b**—
36: 8 you shall shoot forth your **b**
Dan 4:12 of the heavens dwelt in its **b**,
4:14 down the tree and cut off its **b**,
4:14 it, And the birds from its **b**.
4:21 and in whose **b** the birds of the
Hos 14: 6 His **b** shall spread; His beauty
Joel 1: 7 Its **b** are made white.
Nah 2: 2 out And ruined their vine **b**.
Zech 4:12 What are these two olive **b**
Mt 13:32 the air come and nest in its **b**.
21: 8 others cut down **b** from the
Mk 4:32 herbs, and shoots out large **b**,
11: 8 and others cut down leafy **b**
Lk 13:19 of the air nested in its **b**.
Jn 12:13 took **b** of palm trees and went
15: 5 "I am the vine, you are the **b**.
Rom 11:16 root is holy, so are the **b**.
11:17 And if some of the **b** were broken
11:18 do not boast against the **b**.
11:19 **B** were broken off that I might
11:21 God did not spare the natural **b**,
11:24 will these, who are natural **b**,
Rev 7: 9 with palm **b** in their hands,

BRAND (1/1) BRANDING, BRANDISH, BRANDISHED, BRANDISHING

Zech 3: 2 rebuke you! Is this not a **b**

BRANDING (1/1) BRAND

Isa 3:24 And **b** instead of beauty.

BRANDISH (1/1) BRANDISHED, BRANDISHING

Ezek 32:10 afraid of you when I **b** My

BRANDISHED (1/1) BRANDISH

Nah 2: 3 And the spears are **b**.

BRANDISHING (1/1) BRANDISH

Isa 30:32 And in battles of **b** He will

BRASEN (KJV) See BRONZE, COPPER

BRASS (4/4)

1 Cor 13: 1 I have become sounding **b** or a
Rev 1:15 His feet were like fine **b**,
2:18 fire, and His feet like fine **b**:
9:20 and idols of gold, silver, **b**,

BRAVE (1/1)

1 Cor 16:13 stand fast in the faith, be **b**,

BRAVERY (KJV) See FINERY

BRAWLER (1/1)

Prov 20: 1 a mocker, Strong drink is a **b**,

BRAY (1/1) BRAYED

Job 6: 5 Does the wild donkey **b** when it

BRAYED (1/1) BRAY

Job 30: 7 Among the bushes they **b**,

BRAZEN (1/1)

Ezek 16:30 the deeds of a **b** harlot.

BREACH (4/4) BREACHED, BREACHES

Gen 38:29 This **b** be upon you!"
Ps 106:23 one stood before Him in the **b**,
Isa 30:13 shall be to you Like a **b**
58:12 be called the Repairer of the **B**,

BREACHED (1/1) BREACH

Ezek 26:10 enter a city that has been **b**.

BREACHES (1/1) BREACH

Ps 60: 2 have broken it; Heal its **b**,

BREAD (346/315)

Gen 3:19 of your face you shall eat **b**
14:18 king of Salem brought out **b**
18: 5 I will bring a morsel of **b**,
19: 3 a feast, and baked unleavened **b**,
21:14 and took **b** and a skin of water;
25:34 And Jacob gave Esau **b** and stew
27:17 gave the savory food and the **b**,
28:20 and give me **b** to eat and
31:54 called his brethren to eat **b**.
31:54 And they ate **b** and stayed all
39: 6 what he had except for the **b**
41:54 the land of Egypt there was **b**.
41:55 people cried to Pharaoh for **b**.
43:25 heard that they would eat **b**
43:31 and said, "Serve the **b**.
45:23 donkeys loaded with grain, **b**,
47:12 his father's household with **b**,
47:13 Now there was no **b** in all the
47:15 to Joseph and said, "Give us **b**,
47:16 and I will give you **b** for your
47:17 and Joseph gave them **b** in
47:17 Thus he fed them with **b** in
47:19 Buy us and our land for **b**,
49:20 **B** from Asher shall be rich,
Ex 2:20 Call him, that he may eat **b**.
12: 8 with unleavened **b** and with
12:15 days you shall eat unleavened **b**.
12:15 For whoever eats leavened **b**
12:17 the Feast of Unleavened **B**,
12:18 you shall eat unleavened **b**,
12:20 you shall eat unleavened **b**.
13: 3 No leavened **b** shall be eaten.
13: 6 days you shall eat unleavened **b**,
13: 7 Unleavened **b** shall be eaten
13: 7 And no leavened **b** shall be seen
16: 3 of meat and when we ate **b** to
16: 4 I will rain **b** from heaven for
16: 8 and in the morning **b** to the
16:12 you shall be filled with **b**.
16:15 This is the **b** which the LORD
16:22 they gathered twice as much **b**,
16:29 He gives you on the sixth day **b**
16:32 that they may see the **b** with
18:12 the elders of Israel to eat **b**
23:15 keep the Feast of Unleavened **B**
23:15 (you shall eat unleavened **b**
23:18 of My sacrifice with leavened **b**;
23:25 and He will bless your **b** and
29: 2 "and unleavened **b**,
29:23 'one loaf of **b**, one cake made
29:23 the basket of the unleavened **b**
29:32 and the **b** that is in the
29:34 offerings, or of the **b**,
34:18 The Feast of Unleavened **B** you
34:18 days you shall eat unleavened **b**,
34:28 he neither ate **b** nor drank
40:23 and he set the **b** in order upon
Lev 6:16 with unleavened **b** it shall be
7:13 he shall offer leavened **b** with
8: 2 and a basket of unleavened **b**;
8:26 from the basket of unleavened **b**
8:26 a cake of **b** anointed with
8:31 and eat it there with the **b**
8:32 of the flesh and of the **b** you
21: 6 and the **b** of their God;
21: 8 for he offers the **b** of your
21:17 may approach to offer the **b** of
21:21 not come near to offer the **b**
21:22 He may eat the **b** of his God,
22:25 offer any of these as the **b** of
23: 6 is the Feast of Unleavened **B**
23: 6 days you must eat unleavened **b**.
23:14 You shall eat neither **b** nor
23:18 'And you shall offer with the **b**
23:20 shall wave them with the **b** of
24: 7 that it may be on the **b** for a
26: 5 you shall eat your **b** to the
26:26 I have cut off your supply of **b**,
26:26 ten women shall bake your **b** in
26:26 they shall bring back your **b**
Num 6:15 'a basket of unleavened **b**,
6:17 with the basket of unleavened **b**;
9:11 shall eat it with unleavened **b**
14: 9 the land, for they are our **b**;
15:19 when you eat of the **b** of the
21: 5 soul loathes this worthless **b**.
28:17 unleavened **b** shall be eaten for
Deut 8: 3 that man shall not live by **b**
8: 9 land in which you will eat **b**
9: 9 I neither ate **b** nor drank
9:18 I neither ate **b** nor drank
16: 3 You shall eat no leavened **b** with
16: 3 days you shall eat unleavened **b**
16: 3 the **b** of affliction (for you
16: 8 days you shall eat unleavened **b**,
16:16 at the Feast of Unleavened **B**,
23: 4 they did not meet you with **b**
29: 6 "You have not eaten **b**,
Josh 5:11 unleavened **b** and parched grain,
9: 5 and all the **b** of their
9:12 This **b** of ours we took hot for
Judg 6:19 and unleavened **b** from an ephah
6:20 the meat and the unleavened **b**
6:21 the meat and the unleavened **b**;
6:21 the meat and the unleavened **b**.
7:13 a loaf of barley **b** tumbled into
8: 5 Please give loaves of **b** to the
8: 6 that we should give **b** to your
8:15 that we should give **b** to your
19: 5 your heart with a morsel of **b**,
19:19 and **b** and wine for myself, for
Ruth 1: 6 His people by giving them **b**.
2:14 "Come here, and eat of the **b**,
2:14 and dip your piece of **b** in the
1 Sam 2: 5 have hired themselves out for **b**,
2:36 of silver and a morsel of **b**,
2:36 that I may eat a piece of **b**.
9: 7 For the **b** in our vessels is all
10: 3 carrying three loaves of **b**,
10: 4 and give you two loaves of **b**,
16:20 took a donkey loaded with **b**,
21: 3 Give me five loaves of **b** in
21: 4 There is no common **b** on hand;
21: 4 on hand; but there is holy **b**,
21: 5 and the **b** is in effect
21: 6 So the priest gave him holy **b**;
21: 6 for there was no **b** there but
21: 6 in order to put hot **b** in its
22:13 in that you have given him **b**
25:11 Shall I then take my **b** and my
25:18 took two hundred loaves of **b**,
28:22 and let me set a piece of **b**
28:24 and baked unleavened **b** from it.
30:11 and they gave him **b** and he ate,
30:12 for he had eaten no **b** nor drunk
2 Sam 3:29 by the sword, or who lacks **b**.
3:35 if I taste **b** or anything else
6:19 men, to everyone a loaf of **b**,
9: 7 and you shall eat **b** at my table
9:10 your master's son shall eat **b**
16: 1 them two hundred loaves of **b**,
16: 2 the **b** and summer fruit for the
1 Ki 13: 8 nor would I eat **b** nor drink
13: 9 saying, 'You shall not eat **b**,
13:15 "Come home with me and eat **b**.
13:16 neither can I eat **b** nor drink
13:17 You shall not eat **b** nor drink
13:18 that he may eat **b** and drink
13:19 and ate **b** in his house, and

13:22 'but you came back, ate **b**,
13:22 Eat no **b** and drink no water,"
13:23 after he had eaten **b** and after
17: 6 The ravens brought him **b** and
17: 6 and **b** and meat in the evening;
17:11 Please bring me a morsel of **b** in
17:12 your God lives, I do not have **b**,
18: 4 and had fed them with **b** and
18:13 and fed them with **b** and water?
22:27 and feed him with **b** of
2 Ki 4:42 and brought the man of God **b** of
4:42 twenty loaves of barley **b**,
18:32 a land of **b** and vineyards, a
23: 9 but they ate unleavened **b** among
25:29 and he ate **b** regularly before
1 Chr 16: 3 woman, to everyone a loaf of **b**,
2 Chr 8:13 Feast of Unleavened **B**,
18:26 and feed him with **b** of
30:13 keep the Feast of Unleavened **B**
30:21 kept the Feast of Unleavened **B**
35:17 and the Feast of Unleavened **B**
Ezra 6:22 kept the Feast of Unleavened **B**
10: 6 he ate no **b** and drank no water,
Neh 5:15 and took from them **b** and wine,
9:15 You gave them **b** from heaven for
13: 2 the children of Israel with **b**
Job 15:23 He wanders about for **b**,
22: 7 And you have withheld **b** from
27:14 shall not be satisfied with **b**.
28: 5 for the earth, from it comes **b**,
33:20 So that his life abhors **b**,
Ps 14: 4 eat up my people as they eat **b**,
37:25 Nor his descendants begging **b**.
41: 9 whom I trusted, Who ate my **b**,
53: 4 eat up my people as they eat **b**,
78:20 Can He give **b** also? Can He
78:24 And given them of the **b** of
80: 5 You have fed them with the **b** of
102: 4 So that I forget to eat my **b**.
102: 9 For I have eaten ashes like **b**,
104:15 And **b** which strengthens man's
105:16 all the provision of **b**.
105:40 And satisfied them with the **b**
109:10 Let them seek their **b** also
127: 2 To eat the **b** of sorrows; For
132:15 I will satisfy her poor with **b**.
Prov 4:17 For they eat the **b** of
6:26 is reduced to a crust of **b**;
9: 5 eat of my **b** And drink of the
9:17 And **b** eaten in secret is
12: 9 who honors himself but lacks **b**.
12:11 land will be satisfied with **b**,
20:13 you will be satisfied with **b**.
20:17 **B** gained by deceit is sweet to
22: 9 For he gives of his **b** to the
23: 6 Do not eat the **b** of a miser,
25:21 give him **b** to eat; And if he
28:19 his land will have plenty of **b**,
28:21 Because for a piece of **b** a man
31:27 And does not eat the **b** of
Eccl 9: 7 eat your **b** with joy, And drink
9:11 Nor **b** to the wise, Nor riches
11: 1 Cast your **b** upon the waters,
Isa 3: 1 The whole supply of **b** and the
21:14 With their **b** they met him who
28:28 **B** flour must be ground
30:20 the Lord gives you The **b** of
30:23 And **b** of the increase of the
33:16 **B** will be given him, His
36:17 a land of **b** and vineyards.
44:15 he kindles it and bakes **b**;
44:19 I have also baked **b** on its
51:14 And that his **b** should not
55: 2 spend money for what is not **b**,
55:10 give seed to the sower And **b**
58: 7 Is it not to share your **b**
Jer 5:17 eat up your harvest and your **b**,
16: 7 Nor shall men break **b** in
37:21 give him daily a piece of **b**
37:21 until all the **b** in the city was
38: 9 For there is no more **b** in the
41: 1 And there they ate **b** together
42:14 trumpet, nor be hungry for **b**,
52:33 and he ate **b** regularly before
Lam 1:11 her people sigh, They seek **b**;
4: 4 The young children ask for **b**,
5: 6 to be satisfied with **b**.
5: 9 We get our **b** at the risk of
Ezek 4: 9 make **b** of them for yourself.
4:13 of Israel eat their defiled **b**
4:15 and you shall prepare your **b**
4:16 I will cut off the supply of **b**
4:16 they shall eat **b** by weight and
4:17 that they may lack **b** and water,
5:16 and cut off your supply of **b**.
12:18 eat your **b** with quaking, and
12:19 They shall eat their **b** with
13:19 of barley and for pieces of **b**,
14:13 I will cut off its supply of **b**,
18: 7 But has given his **b** to the
18:16 But has given his **b** to the
24:17 and do not eat man's **b** of
24:22 your lips nor eat man's **b** of
44: 3 he may sit in it to eat **b**
45:21 unleavened **b** shall be eaten.
Hos 2: 5 Who give me my **b** and my water,
9: 4 It shall be like **b** of
9: 4 For their **b** shall be for
Am 4: 6 And lack of **b** in all your
7:12 the land of Judah. There eat **b**,
8:11 on the land, Not a famine of **b**,
Ob 7 Those who eat your **b** shall
Hag 2:12 and with the edge he touches **b**
Mt 4: 3 that these stones become **b**.
4: 4 Man shall not live by **b**
6:11 Give us this day our daily **b**.
7: 9 you who, if his son asks for **b**,
15: 2 their hands when they eat **b**.
15:26 good to take the children's **b**
15:33 Where could we get enough **b** in
16: 5 they had forgotten to take **b**.
16: 7 is because we have taken no **b**.
16: 8 because you have brought no **b**?
16:11 not speak to you concerning **b**?
16:12 to beware of the leaven of **b**,
26:17 the Feast of the Unleavened **B**
26:26 they were eating, Jesus took **b**,
Mk 3:20 they could not so much as eat **b**.
6: 8 except a staff—no bag, no **b**,
6:36 villages and buy themselves **b**;
6:37 two hundred denarii worth of **b**
7: 2 saw some of His disciples eat **b**
7: 5 eat **b** with unwashed hands?"
7:27 good to take the children's **b**
8: 4 one satisfy these people with **b**
8:14 had forgotten to take **b**,
8:16 "It is because we have no **b**.
8:17 reason because you have no **b**?
14: 1 and the Feast of Unleavened **B**.
14:12 the first day of Unleavened **B**,
14:22 they were eating, Jesus took **b**,
Lk 4: 3 command this stone to become **b**.
4: 4 Man shall not live by **b**
7:33 Baptist came neither eating **b**
9: 3 neither staffs nor bag nor **b**
11: 3 Give us day by day our daily **b**.
11:11 If a son asks for **b** from any
14: 1 of the Pharisees to eat **b** on
14:15 is he who shall eat **b**
15:17 father's hired servants have **b**
22: 1 Now the Feast of Unleavened **B**
22: 7 came the Day of Unleavened **B**,
22:19 And He took **b**, gave thanks and
24:30 table with them, that He took **b**,
24:35 to them in the breaking of **b**.
Jn 6: 5 Philip, "Where shall we buy **b**,
6: 7 hundred denarii worth of **b**
6:23 near the place where they ate **b**
6:31 He gave them **b** from heaven
6:32 Moses did not give you the **b**
6:32 My Father gives you the true **b**
6:33 For the **b** of God is He who comes
6:34 'Lord, give us this **b** always."
6:35 I am the **b** of life. He who comes
6:41 I am the **b** which came down from
6:48 I am the **b** of life.
6:50 This is the **b** which comes down
6:51 I am the living **b** which came
6:51 If anyone eats of this **b**,
6:51 and the **b** that I shall give is
6:58 This is the **b** which came down
6:58 He who eats this **b** will live
13:18 He who eats **b** with Me has
13:26 whom I shall give a piece of **b**
13:26 And having dipped the **b**,
13:27 Now after the piece of **b**, Satan
13:30 Having received the piece of **b**,
21: 9 and fish laid on it, and **b**.
21:13 Jesus then came and took the **b**
Acts 2:42 in the breaking of **b**,
2:46 and breaking **b** from house to
12: 3 the Days of Unleavened **B**.
20: 6 after the Days of Unleavened **B**,
20: 7 came together to break **b**,
20:11 had broken **b** and eaten, and
27:35 he took **b** and gave thanks to
1 Cor 5: 8 but with the unleavened **b** of
10:16 The **b** which we break, is it not
10:17 are one **b** and one body; for we
10:17 we all partake of that one **b**.
11:23 in which He was betrayed took **b**;
11:26 For as often as you eat this **b**
11:27 Therefore whoever eats this **b**
11:28 and so let him eat of the **b** and
2 Cor 9:10 and **b** for food, supply and
2 Th 3: 8 nor did we eat anyone's **b** free
3:12 quietness and eat their own **b**.

BREADTH (7/6)

Judg 20:16 sling a stone at a hair's **b**
Job 38:18 Have you comprehended the **b** of
Isa 8: 8 of his wings Will fill the **b**
Hab 1: 6 Which marches through the **b**
Rev 20: 9 They went up on the **b** of the
21:16 its length is as great as its **b**.
21:16 furlongs. Its length, **b**,

BREAK (138/131) BREACH, BREAKER, BREAKERS, BREAKING, BREAKS, BREAKTHROUGH, BROKE, BROKEN, BROKENHEARTED

Gen 19: 9 and came near to **b** down the
27:40 That you shall **b** his yoke from
38:29 'How did you **b** through?
Ex 9: 9 and it will cause boils that **b**
9:10 And they caused boils that **b**
12:46 nor shall you **b** one of its
13:13 then you shall **b** its neck.
19:21 lest they **b** through to gaze at
19:22 lest the LORD **b** out against
19:24 the priests and the people **b**
19:24 lest He **b** out against them."
23:24 them and completely **b** down
32: 2 **B** off the golden earrings which
32:24 let them **b** it off.' So they
34:13 **b** their sacred pillars, and
34:20 then you shall **b** his neck.
Lev 2: 6 You shall **b** it in pieces and
11:33 any of them falls you shall **b**;
14:45 And he shall **b** down the house,
26:15 but **b** My covenant,
26:19 I will **b** the pride of your
26:44 to utterly destroy them and **b**
Num 2: 9 these shall **b** camp first.
2:16 they shall be the second to **b**
2:24 they shall be the third to **b**
2:31 they shall **b** camp last, with
9:12 nor **b** one of its bones.
24: 8 He shall **b** their bones And
30: 2 he shall not **b** his word; he
Deut 7: 5 **b** down their sacred pillars,
12: 3 **b** their sacred pillars, and
21: 4 and they shall **b** the heifer's
31:16 and they will forsake Me and **b**
31:20 and they will provoke Me and **b**
Judg 2: 1 I will never **b** My covenant with
19:25 and when the day began to **b**,
1 Sam 25:10 many servants nowadays who **b**
1 Ki 15:19 Come and **b** your treaty with
2 Ki 3:26 to **b** through to the king of
2 Chr 16: 3 **b** your treaty with Baasha king
Ezra 9:14 should we again **b** Your
Neh 4: 3 he will **b** down their stone
Job 19: 2 And **b** me in pieces with words?
24:16 In the dark they **b** into houses
30:13 They **b** up my path, They
39:15 Or that a wild beast may **b**
Ps 2: 3 Let us **b** Their bonds in pieces
2: 9 You shall **b** them with a rod of
10:15 **B** the arm of the wicked and the
46: 5 just at the **b** of dawn.
48: 7 As when You **b** the ships of
58: 6 **B** their teeth in their mouth, O
58: 6 O God! **B** out the fangs of the
72: 4 And will **b** in pieces the
74: 6 And now they **b** down its carved
89:31 If they **b** My statutes And do
89:34 My covenant I will not **b**,
94: 5 They **b** in pieces Your people, O
98: 4 **B** forth in song, rejoice, and
Eccl 3: 3 A time to **b** down, And a time
Isa 5: 5 And **b** down its wall, and it
14: 7 They **b** forth into singing.
14:25 That I will **b** the Assyrian in
28:28 **B** it with his cartwheel, Or
30:14 And He shall **b** it like the
42: 3 A bruised reed He will not **b**,
44:23 **B** forth into singing, you
45: 2 I will **b** in pieces the gates
49:13 O earth! And **b** out in singing,
52: 9 **B** forth into joy, sing
54: 1 You who have not borne! **B**
55:12 and the hills Shall **b** forth
58: 6 And that you **b** every yoke?
58: 8 Then your light shall **b** forth
Jer 1:14 of the north calamity shall **b**
4: 3 **B** up your fallow ground, And do
14:21 do not **b** Your covenant with us.
15:12 Can anyone **b** iron, The
16: 7 Nor shall men **b** bread in
19:10 Then you shall **b** the flask in
19:11 Even so I will **b** this people and
28: 4 for I will **b** the yoke of the
28:11 Even so I will **b** the yoke of
30: 8 That I will **b** his yoke from
31:28 to **b** down, to throw down, to
33:20 If you can **b** My covenant with
43:13 He shall also **b** the sacred
45: 4 what I have built I will **b**
48:12 And empty his vessels And **b**
49:35 I will **b** the bow of Elam, The
51:20 For with you I will **b** the
51:21 With you I will **b** in pieces the
51:21 With you I will **b** in pieces
51:22 With you also I will **b** in
51:22 With you I will **b** in pieces
51:22 With you I will **b** in pieces
51:23 With you also I will **b** in
51:23 With you I will **b** in pieces
51:23 And with you I will **b** in
Ezek 13:13 will cause a stormy wind to **b**
13:14 So I will **b** down the wall you
16:38 I will judge you as women who **b**
16:39 throw down your shrines and **b**
17:15 Can he **b** a covenant and still
23:34 You shall **b** its shards, And
26: 4 the walls of Tyre and **b** down
26: 9 and with his axes he will **b**
26:12 they will **b** down your walls and
30:18 When I **b** the yokes of Egypt
30:22 and will **b** his arms, both the
30:24 but I will **b** Pharaoh's arms,
Dan 2:40 that kingdom will **b** in pieces
2:44 it shall **b** in pieces and
4:27 **b** off your sins by being
7:23 Trample it and **b** it in pieces.
Hos 1: 5 in that day That I will **b** the
4: 2 They **b** all restraint, With
10: 2 He will **b** down their altars;
10:11 Jacob shall **b** his clods."
10:12 **B** up your fallow ground, For
Joel 2: 7 And they do not **b** ranks.
Am 1: 5 I will also **b** the gate bar of

5: 6 Lest He **b** out like fire in
6:11 He will **b** the great house into
9: 1 And **b** them on the heads of
Mic 2:13 They will **b** out, Pass through
3: 3 **B** their bones, And chop them
Nah 1:13 For now I will **b** off his yoke
Zech 11:10 that I might **b** the covenant
11:14 that I might **b** the brotherhood
Mt 6:19 destroy and where thieves **b** in
6:20 and where thieves do not **b** in
9:17 or else the wineskins **b**,
12:20 reed He will not **b**,
Jn 19:33 they did not **b** His legs.
Acts 20: 7 disciples came together to **b**
1 Cor 10:16 of Christ? The bread which we **b**,
Gal 4:27 You who do not bear! **B**

BREAKER (1/1) BREAK, BREAKERS

Rom 2:25 but if you are a **b** of the law,

BREAKERS (1/1) BREAKER

Job 30:14 They come as broad **b**;

BREAKFAST (2/2)

Jn 21:12 said to them, "Come and eat **b**.
21:15 So when they had eaten **b**,

BREAKING (20/20) BREAK

Gen 32:24 wrestled with him until the **b**
Ex 22: 2 If the thief is found **b** in, and
Lev 13:42 it is leprosy **b** out on his
Ps 42:10 As with a **b** of my bones, My
144:14 That there be no **b** in or
Isa 22: 5 **B** down the walls And of crying
28:24 he keep turning his soil and **b**
30:13 Whose **b** comes suddenly, in an
30:14 He shall break it like the **b**
Jer 2:23 You are a swift dromedary **b**
Ezek 16:59 who despised the oath by **b** the
17:18 he despised the oath by **b** the
21: 6 with a **b** heart, and sigh with
Dan 7: 7 **b** in pieces, and trampling the
Lk 5: 6 of fish, and their net was **b**.
24:35 He was known to them in the **b**
Acts 2:42 in the **b** of bread, and in
2:46 **b** bread from house to house,
21:13 do you mean by weeping and **b**
Rom 2:23 do you dishonor God through **b**

BREAKS (31/31) BREAK

Gen 32:26 "Let Me go, for the day **b**.
Ex 22: 6 If fire **b** out and catches in
Lev 13:12 And if leprosy **b** out all over
14:43 if the plague comes back and **b**
Judg 16: 9 as a strand of yarn **b** when it
Neh 6: 1 and that there were no **b** left
Job 7: 5 My skin is cracked and **b** out
12:14 If He **b** a thing down, it
16:14 He **b** me with wound upon wound;
19:10 He **b** me down on every side,
26:12 And by His understanding He **b**
28: 4 He **b** open a shaft away from
34:24 He **b** in pieces mighty men
Ps 29: 5 The voice of the LORD **b** the
46: 9 He **b** the bow and cuts the
119:20 My soul **b** with longing For
141: 7 As when one plows and **b** up the
Prov 15: 4 But perverseness in it **b** the
25:15 And a gentle tongue **b** a bone.
Eccl 10: 8 And whoever **b** through a wall
Song 2:17 Until the day **b** And the
4: 6 Until the day **b** And the
Isa 38:13 So He **b** all my bones; From
59: 5 which is crushed a viper **b** out.
66: 3 as if he **b** a dog's neck; He
Jer 19:11 as one **b** a potter's vessel,
23:29 And like a hammer that **b** the
Lam 4: 4 But no one **b** it for them.
Dan 2:40 inasmuch as iron **b** in pieces
Mic 2:13 The one who **b** open will come up
Mt 5:19 Whoever therefore **b** one of the

BREAKTHROUGH (2/2)

2 Sam 5:20 like a **b** of water."
1 Chr 14:11 my enemies by my hand like a **b**

BREAST (16/15) BREASTPLATE, BREASTPLATES, BREASTS

Ex 29:26 Then you shall take the **b** of the
29:27 you shall consecrate the **b** of
Lev 7:30 The fat with the **b** he shall
7:30 that the **b** may be waved as a
7:31 but the **b** shall be Aaron's and
7:34 For the **b** of the wave offering
8:29 And Moses took the **b** and waved
10:14 The **b** of the wave offering and
10:15 of the heave offering and the **b**
Num 6:20 together with the **b** of the wave
18:18 just as the wave **b** and the
Job 24: 9 the fatherless from the **b**,
Isa 60:16 And milk the **b** of kings; You
Lk 18:13 eyes to heaven, but beat his **b**,
Jn 13:25 Then, leaning back on Jesus' **b**,
21:20 who also had leaned on His **b** at

BREASTPLATE (28/24) BREAST, BREASTPLATES

Ex 25: 7 set in the ephod and in the **b**.
28: 4 which they shall make: a **b**,
28:15 You shall make the **b** of
28:22 shall make chains for the **b** at
28:23 two rings of gold for the **b**,
28:23 rings on the two ends of the **b**.
28:24 which are on the ends of the **b**;
28:26 them on the two ends of the **b**,
28:28 They shall bind the **b** by means
28:28 and so that the **b** does not come
28:29 of the sons of Israel on the **b**
28:30 And you shall put in the **b** of
29: 5 the ephod, the ephod, and the **b**,
35: 9 set in the ephod and in the **b**.
35:27 set in the ephod and in the **b**,
39: 8 And he made the **b**, artistically
39: 9 They made the **b** square by
39:15 And they made chains for the **b**
39:16 rings on the two ends of the **b**.
39:17 two rings on the ends of the **b**.
39:19 them on the two ends of the **b**,
39:21 And they bound the **b** by means of
39:21 and that the **b** would not come
Lev 8: 8 Then he put the **b** on him, and he
8: 8 Urim and the Thummim in the **b**.
Isa 59:17 He put on righteousness as a **b**,
Eph 6:14 having put on the **b** of
1 Th 5: 8 putting on the **b** of faith and

BREASTPLATES (3/2) BREASTPLATE

Rev 9: 9 And they had **b** like breastplates
9: 9 they had breastplates like **b**
9:17 those who sat on them had **b** of

BREASTS (27/27) BREAST

Gen 49:25 Blessings of the **b** and of the
Lev 9:20 and they put the fat on the **b**.
9:21 but the **b** and the right thigh
Job 3:12 knees receive me? Or why the **b**,
Ps 22: 9 trust while on My mother's **b**.
Prov 5:19 Let her **b** satisfy you at all
Song 1:13 lies all night between my **b**.
4: 5 Your two **b** are like two fawns,
7: 3 Your two **b** are like two fawns,
7: 7 And your **b** like its clusters.
7: 8 Let now your **b** be like
8: 1 Who nursed at my mother's **b**!
8: 8 sister, And she has no **b**.
8:10 And my **b** like towers; Then I
Isa 28: 9 Those just drawn from the **b**?
32:12 shall mourn upon their **b** For
Lam 4: 3 the jackals present their **b**
Ezek 16: 7 Your **b** were formed, your hair
23: 3 Their **b** were there embraced,
23:21 Because of your youthful **b**.
23:34 shards, And tear at your own **b**;
Hos 2: 2 adulteries from between her **b**;
9:14 a miscarrying womb And dry **b**!
Nah 2: 7 of doves, Beating their **b**.
Lk 11:27 and the **b** which nursed You!"
23:29 and **b** which never nursed!'
23:48 beat their **b** and returned.

BREATH (54/51) BREATHE

Gen 2: 7 into his nostrils the **b** of
6:17 all flesh in which is the **b**
7:15 of all flesh in which is the **b**
7:22 in whose nostrils was the **b**
2 Sam 22:16 At the blast of the **b** of His
1 Ki 17:17 so serious that there was no **b**
Job 4: 9 And by the **b** of His anger they
7: 7 remember that my life is a **b**!
7:16 For my days are but a **b**.
9:18 will not allow me to catch my **b**,
12:10 And the **b** of all mankind?
15:30 And by the **b** of His mouth he
19:17 My **b** is offensive to my wife,
27: 3 As long as my **b** is in me, And
27: 3 the **b** of God in my nostrils,
32: 8 And the **b** of the Almighty
33: 4 And the **b** of the Almighty
34:14 to Himself His Spirit and His **b**,
37:10 By the **b** of God ice is given,
41:21 His **b** kindles coals, And a
Ps 18:15 At the blast of the **b** of Your
33: 6 all the host of them by the **b**
78:39 A **b** that passes away and does
104:29 You take away their **b**,
135:17 Nor is there any **b** in their
144: 4 Man is like a **b**;
150: 6 Let everything that has **b**
Eccl 3:19 Surely, they all have one **b**;
Song 7: 8 The fragrance of your **b** like
Isa 2:22 Whose **b** is in his nostrils;
11: 4 And with the **b** of His lips He
30:28 His **b** is like an overflowing
30:33 The **b** of the LORD, like a
33:11 bring forth stubble; Your **b**,
40: 7 Because the **b** of the LORD
42: 5 Who gives **b** to the people on
57:13 A **b** will take them. But he
Jer 10:14 And there is no **b** in them.
51:17 And there is no **b** in them.
Lam 4:20 The **b** of our nostrils, the
Ezek 37: 5 Surely I will cause **b** to enter
37: 6 cover you with skin and put **b**
37: 8 but there was no **b** in them.
37: 9 said to me, "Prophesy to the **b**,
37: 9 son of man, and say to the **b**,
37: 9 "Come from the four winds, O **b**,
37:10 and **b** came into them, and they
Dan 5:23 and the God who holds your **b**
10:17 nor is any **b** left in me."
Hab 2:19 Yet in it there is no **b** at
Acts 17:25 since He gives to all life, **b**,
2 Th 2: 8 Lord will consume with the **b**
Rev 11:11 three-and-a-half days the **b** of
13:15 He was granted power to give **b**

BREATHE (2/2) BREATH, BREATHED, BREATHES, BREATHING

Ps 27:12 And such as **b** out violence.
Ezek 37: 9 and **b** on these slain, that they

BREATHED (15/15) BREATHE

Gen 2: 7 and **b** into his nostrils the
25: 8 Then Abraham **b** his last and died
25:17 and he **b** his last and died, and
35:29 So Isaac **b** his last and died,
49:33 his feet up into the bed and **b**
Josh 10:40 utterly destroyed all that **b**,
1 Ki 15:29 leave to Jeroboam anyone that **b**,
Jer 15: 9 She has **b** her last; Her sun
Lam 1:19 My priests and my elders **B**
Mk 15:37 and **b** His last.
15:39 He cried out like this and **b**
Lk 23:46 He **b** His last.
Jn 20:22 He **b** on them, and said to
Acts 5: 5 fell down and **b** his last.
5:10 she fell down at his feet and **b**

BREATHES (2/2) BREATHE

Deut 20:16 you shall let nothing that **b**
Job 14:10 Indeed he **b** his last And

BREATHING (3/3) BREATHE

Josh 11:11 There was none left **b**.
11:14 them, and they left none **b**.
Acts 9: 1 still **b** threats and murder

BRED (2/2) BREED

Ex 16:20 and it **b** worms and stank.
Esth 8:10 riding on royal horses **b** from

BREECHES (KJV) See TROUSERS

BREED (2/2) BRED, BREEDS

Lev 19:19 shall not let your livestock **b**
Deut 32:14 And rams of the **b** of Bashan,

BREEDS (1/1) BREED

Job 21:10 Their bull **b** without failure;

BRETHREN (398/389) BROTHER

Gen 9:25 servants He shall be to his **b**.
13: 8 your herdsmen; for we are **b**.
16:12 in the presence of all his **b**.
19: 7 and said, "Please, my **b**,
24:27 to the house of my master's **b**.
25:18 in the presence of all his **b**.
27:29 to you. Be master over your **b**,
27:37 and all his **b** I have given to
29: 4 And Jacob said to them, "My **b**,
31:23 Then he took his **b** with him and
31:25 and Laban with his **b** pitched in
31:32 live. In the presence of our **b**,
31:37 Set it here before my **b** and
31:37 before my brethren and your **b**,
31:46 Then Jacob said to his **b**,
31:54 and called his **b** to eat bread.
50:24 And Joseph said to his **b**,
Ex 2:11 that he went out to his **b** and
2:11 beating a Hebrew, one of his **b**.
4:18 let me go and return to my **b**
Lev 10: 4 carry your **b** from before the
10: 6 all the people. But let your **b**,
21:10 is the high priest among his **b**,
25:25 If one of your **b** becomes poor,
25:35 If one of your **b** becomes poor,
25:39 And if one of your **b** who
25:46 But regarding your **b**,
25:47 and one of your **b** who
Num 8:26 may minister with their **b**
16:10 Himself, you and all your **b**,
18: 2 Also bring with you your **b** of
18: 6 I Myself have taken your **b** the
20: 3 only we had died when our **b**
25: 6 came and presented to his **b** a
32: 6 Shall your **b** go to war while you
Deut 1:16 the cases between your **b**,
1:28 Our **b** have discouraged our
2: 4 through the territory of your **b**,
2: 8 when we passed beyond our **b**,
3:18 cross over armed before your **b**,
3:20 LORD has given rest to your **b**
10: 9 nor inheritance with his **b**;
15: 7 among you a poor man of your **b**,
17:15 one from among your **b** you
17:20 may not be lifted above his **b**,
18: 2 no inheritance among their **b**;
18: 7 the LORD his God as all his **b**

18:15 me from your midst, from your ***b***.
18:18 like you from among their ***b***,
20: 8 lest the heart of his ***b*** faint
24: 7 found kidnapping any of his ***b***
24:14 whether one of your ***b*** or one
Josh 1:14 you shall pass before your ***b***
1:15 the LORD has given your ***b***
14: 8 Nevertheless my ***b*** who went up
22: 3 You have not left your ***b*** these
22: 4 God has given rest to your ***b***,
22: 7 a possession among their ***b***
22: 8 of your enemies with your ***b***.
Judg 14: 3 among the daughters of your ***b***,
18: 8 spies came back to their ***b*** at
18: 8 and their ***b*** said to them,
18:14 answered and said to their ***b***,
19:23 my ***b***! I beg you, do not act so
20:13 listen to the voice of their ***b***,
Ruth 4:10 not be cut off from among his ***b***
1 Sam 30:23 But David said, "My ***b***,
2 Sam 2:26 to return from pursuing their ***b***?
2:27 have given up pursuing their ***b***.
15:20 and take your ***b*** back. Mercy and
19:12 'You are my ***b***, you are my bone
19:41 to the king, "Why have our ***b***,
1 Ki 12:24 go up nor fight against your ***b***
2 Ki 23: 9 unleavened bread among their ***b***.
1 Chr 5: 7 And his ***b*** by their families,
5:13 and their ***b*** of their father's
6:44 Their ***b***, the sons of Merari,
6:48 And their ***b***, the Levites, were
7: 5 Now their ***b*** among all the
7:22 and his ***b*** came to comfort him.
8:32 in Jerusalem, with their ***b***.
9: 6 of Zerah: Jeuel, and their ***b***—
9: 9 and their ***b***, according to their
9:13 and their ***b***, heads of their
9:17 Talmon, Ahiman, and their ***b***.
9:19 the son of Korah, and his ***b***,
9:25 And their ***b*** in their villages
9:32 And some of their ***b*** of the sons
9:38 in Jerusalem, with their ***b***.
12: 2 were of Benjamin, Saul's ***b***.
12:32 and all their ***b*** were at their
12:39 for their ***b*** had prepared for
13: 2 let us send out to our ***b***
15: 5 one hundred and twenty of his ***b***;
15: 6 two hundred and twenty of his ***b***;
15: 7 one hundred and thirty of his ***b***;
15: 8 chief, and two hundred of his ***b***;
15: 9 the chief, and eighty of his ***b***;
15:10 one hundred and twelve of his ***b***.
15:12 yourselves, you and your ***b***,
15:16 the Levites to appoint their ***b***
15:17 the son of Joel; and of his ***b***,
15:17 of Berechiah; and of their ***b***,
15:18 and with them their ***b*** of the
16: 7 the hand of Asaph and his ***b***,
16:38 with his sixty-eight ***b***,
16:39 and Zadok the priest and his ***b***
23:22 but only daughters; and their ***b***,
23:32 of the sons of Aaron their ***b***
24:31 did just as their younger ***b***.
25: 7 with their ***b*** who were
25: 9 him with his ***b*** and sons,
25:10 for Zaccur, his sons and his ***b***,
25:11 for Jizri, his sons and his ***b***,
25:12 Nethaniah, his sons and his ***b***,
25:13 for Bukkiah, his sons and his ***b***,
25:14 Jesharelah, his sons and his ***b***,
25:15 Jeshaiah, his sons and his ***b***,
25:16 Mattaniah, his sons and his ***b***,
25:17 for Shimei, his sons and his ***b***,
25:18 for Azarel, his sons and his ***b***,
25:19 Hashabiah, his sons and his ***b***,
25:20 for Shubael, his sons and his ***b***,
25:21 Mattithiah, his sons and his ***b***,
25:22 Jeremoth, his sons and his ***b***,
25:23 Hananiah, his sons and his ***b***,
25:24 his sons and his ***b***, twelve;
25:25 for Hanani, his sons and his ***b***,
25:26 Mallothi, his sons and his ***b***,
25:27 Eliathah, his sons and his ***b***,
25:28 for Hothir, his sons and his ***b***,
25:29 Giddalti, his sons and his ***b***,
25:30 Mahazioth, his sons and his ***b***,
25:31 his sons and his ***b***, twelve.
26: 8 they and their sons and their ***b***,
26: 9 And Meshelemiah had sons and ***b***,
26:11 all the sons and ***b*** of Hosah
26:12 duties just like their ***b***,
26:25 And his ***b*** by Eliezer were
26:26 This Shelomith and his ***b*** were
26:28 the hand of Shelomith and his ***b***.
26:30 Hebronites, Hashabiah and his ***b***,
26:32 And his ***b*** were two thousand
28: 2 my ***b*** and my people: I had it
2 Chr 5:12 with their sons and their ***b***,
11: 4 go up or fight against your ***b***!
19:10 case comes to you from your ***b***
19:10 wrath come upon you and your ***b***.
28: 8 away captive of their ***b*** two
28:11 have taken captive from your ***b***,
28:15 So they brought them to their ***b***
29:15 And they gathered their ***b***,
29:34 therefore their ***b*** the Levites
30: 7 be like your fathers and your ***b***,
30: 9 your ***b*** and your children will
31:15 allotments to their ***b*** by
35: 5 the fathers' houses of your ***b***
35: 6 and prepare them for your ***b***,
35:15 because their ***b*** the Levites
Ezra 3: 2 the son of Jozadak and his ***b***
3: 2 the son of Shealtiel and his ***b***,
3: 8 and the rest of their ***b*** the
3: 9 with their sons and their ***b***
6:20 for their ***b*** the priests, and
7:18 seems good to you and your ***b***
8:17 should say to Iddo and his ***b***
8:24 and ten of their ***b*** with them—
Neh 1: 2 that Hanani one of my ***b*** came
3: 1 high priest rose up with his ***b***
3:18 After him their ***b***, under Bavai
4: 2 And he spoke before his ***b*** and
4:14 awesome, and fight for your ***b***,
4:23 So neither I, my ***b***, my servants,
5: 1 wives against their Jewish ***b***.
5: 5 flesh is as the flesh of our ***b***,
5: 8 we have redeemed our Jewish ***b***
5: 8 will you even sell your ***b***?
5:10 with my ***b*** and my servants, am
10:10 Their ***b***: Shebaniah, Hodijah,
10:29 these joined with their ***b***,
11:12 Their ***b*** who did the work of the
11:13 and his ***b***, heads of the fathers'
11:14 their ***b***, mighty men of valor,
11:17 the second among his ***b***;
11:19 and their ***b*** who kept the gates,
12: 7 of the priests and their ***b*** in
12: 8 psalms, he and his ***b***.
12: 9 Bakbukiah and Unni, their ***b***,
12:36 and his ***b***, Shemaiah, Azarel,
13:13 was to distribute to their ***b***.
Esth 10: 3 by the multitude of his ***b***,
Ps 22:22 will declare Your name to My ***b***;
122: 8 For the sake of my ***b*** and
133: 1 how pleasant it is For ***b*** to
Prov 6:19 one who sows discord among ***b***.
Isa 66: 5 Your ***b*** who hated you, Who cast
66:20 they shall bring all your ***b***
Jer 7:15 as I have cast out all your ***b***—
29:16 and concerning your ***b*** who have
41: 8 did not kill them among their ***b***.
49:10 His ***b*** and his neighbors, And
Ezek 11:15 "Son of man, your ***b***,
Hos 2: 1 Say to your ***b***, 'My people,'
13:15 he is fruitful among his ***b***,
Mic 5: 3 Then the remnant of His ***b***
Mt 5:47 And if you greet your ***b*** only,
23: 8 the Christ, and you are all ***b***.
25:40 one of the least of these My ***b***,
28:10 Go and tell My ***b*** to go to
Lk 22:32 to Me, strengthen your ***b***.
Jn 20:17 but go to My ***b*** and say to them,
21:23 saying went out among the ***b***
Acts 1:16 'Men and ***b***, this Scripture
2:29 'Men and ***b***, let me speak
2:37 of the apostles, "Men and ***b***,
3:17 'Yet now, ***b***, I know that you
3:22 like me from your ***b***.
6: 3 'Therefore, ***b***, seek out from
7: 2 ***B*** and fathers, listen: The God
7:23 into his heart to visit his ***b***,
7:25 For he supposed that his ***b*** would
7:26 them, saying, 'Men, you are ***b***;
7:37 like me from your ***b***.
9:30 When the ***b*** found out, they
10:23 and some ***b*** from Joppa
11: 1 Now the apostles and ***b*** who were
11:12 these six ***b*** accompanied
11:29 to send relief to the ***b***
12:17 things to James and to the ***b***.
13:15 to them, saying, "Men and ***b***,
13:26 'Men and ***b***, sons of the family
13:38 let it be known to you, ***b***,
14: 2 their minds against the ***b***.
15: 1 from Judea and taught the ***b***,
15: 3 caused great joy to all the ***b***.
15: 7 and said to them: "Men and ***b***,
15:13 answered, saying, "Men and ***b***,
15:22 Silas, leading men among the ***b***.
15:23 apostles, the elders, and the ***b***,
15:23 To the ***b*** who are of the
15:32 and strengthened the ***b*** with
15:33 back with greetings from the ***b***
15:36 us now go back and visit our ***b***
15:40 being commended by the ***b*** to the
16: 2 He was well spoken of by the ***b***
16:40 and when they had seen the ***b***,
17: 6 they dragged Jason and some ***b***
17:10 Then the ***b*** immediately sent
17:14 Then immediately the ***b*** sent Paul
18:18 Then he took leave of the ***b*** and
18:27 the ***b*** wrote, exhorting the
20:32 'So now, ***b***, I commend you
21: 7 to Ptolemais, greeted the ***b***,
21:17 the ***b*** received us gladly.
22: 1 ***B*** and fathers, hear my defense
22: 5 also received letters to the ***b***,
23: 1 the council, said, "Men and ***b***,
23: 5 Paul said, "I did not know, ***b***,
23: 6 in the council, "Men and ***b***,
28:14 where we found ***b***,
28:15 when the ***b*** heard about us, they
28:17 he said to them: "Men and ***b***,
28:21 nor have any of the ***b*** who came
Rom 1:13 not want you to be unaware, ***b***,
7: 1 ***b*** (for I speak to those who
7: 4 Therefore, my ***b***, you also have
8:12 ***b***, we are debtors—not
8:29 be the firstborn among many ***b***.
9: 3 accursed from Christ for my ***b***,
10: 1 ***B***, my heart's desire and prayer
11:25 For I do not desire, ***b***,
12: 1 I beseech you therefore, ***b***,
15:14 confident concerning you, my ***b***,
15:15 Nevertheless, ***b***, I have written
15:30 Now I beg you, ***b***, through the
16:14 and the ***b*** who are with them.
16:17 Now I urge you, ***b***, note those
1 Cor 1:10 Now I plead with you, ***b***,
1:11 to me concerning you, my ***b***,
1:26 For you see your calling, ***b***,
2: 1 And I, ***b***, when I came to you,
3: 1 And I, ***b***, could not speak to you
4: 6 Now these things, ***b***, I have
6: 5 be able to judge between his ***b***?
6: 8 do these things to your ***b***!
7:24 ***B***, let each one remain with God
7:29 But this I say, ***b***, the time is
8:12 when you thus sin against the ***b***,
10: 1 ***b***, I do not want you to be
11: 2 Now I praise you, ***b***,
11:33 Therefore, my ***b***, when you come
12: 1 concerning spiritual gifts, ***b***,
14: 6 But now, ***b***, if I come to you
14:20 ***B***, do not be children in
14:26 How is it then, ***b***?
14:39 Therefore, ***b***, desire earnestly
15: 1 Moreover, ***b***, I declare to you
15: 6 seen by over five hundred ***b*** at
15:50 Now this I say, ***b***, that flesh
15:58 Therefore, my beloved ***b***,
16:11 I am waiting for him with the ***b***.
16:12 him to come to you with the ***b***,
16:15 I urge you, ***b***—you know the
16:20 All the ***b*** greet you. Greet one
2 Cor 1: 8 not want you to be ignorant, ***b***,
8: 1 Moreover, ***b***, we make known to
8:23 Or if our ***b*** are inquired
9: 3 Yet I have sent the ***b***,
9: 5 it necessary to exhort the ***b***
11: 9 for what I lacked the ***b*** who
11:26 sea, in perils among false ***b***;
13:11 Finally, ***b***, farewell.
Gal 1: 2 and all the ***b*** who are with me,
1:11 But I make known to you, ***b***,
2: 4 occurred because of false ***b***
3:15 ***B***, I speak in the manner of
4:12 ***B***, I urge you to become like me,
4:28 Now we, ***b***, as Isaac was, are
4:31 So then, ***b***, we are not children
5:11 And I, ***b***, if I still preach
5:13 For you, ***b***, have been called to
6: 1 ***B***, if a man is overtaken in any
6:18 ***B***, the grace of our Lord Jesus
Eph 6:10 Finally, my ***b***, be strong in
6:23 Peace to the ***b***, and love with
Phil 1:12 But I want you to know, ***b***,
1:14 and most of the ***b*** in the Lord,
3: 1 Finally, my ***b***, rejoice in the
3:13 ***B***, I do not count myself to have
3:17 ***B***, join in following my example
4: 1 my beloved and longed-for ***b***,
4: 8 Finally, ***b***, whatever things are
4:21 The ***b*** who are with me greet
Col 1: 2 To the saints and faithful ***b*** in
4:15 Greet the ***b*** who are in Laodicea,
1 Th 1: 4 knowing, beloved ***b***, your
2: 1 For you yourselves know, ***b***,
2: 9 For you remember, ***b***, our labor
2:14 For you, ***b***, became imitators of
2:17 But we, ***b***, having been taken
3: 7 therefore, ***b***, in all our
4: 1 Finally then, ***b***, we urge and
4:10 you do so toward all the ***b*** who
4:10 But we urge you, ***b***,
4:13 not want you to be ignorant, ***b***,
5: 1 the times and the seasons, ***b***,
5: 4 But you, ***b***, are not in darkness,
5:12 And we urge you, ***b***,
5:14 Now we exhort you, ***b***, warn those
5:25 ***B***, pray for us.
5:26 Greet all the ***b*** with a holy
5:27 be read to all the holy ***b***.
2 Th 1: 3 to thank God always for you, ***b***,
2: 1 Now, ***b***, concerning the coming
2:13 ***b*** beloved by the Lord, because
2:15 Therefore, ***b***, stand fast and
3: 1 Finally, ***b***, pray for us, that
3: 6 But we command you, ***b***,
3:13 But as for you, ***b***,
1 Tim 4: 6 If you instruct the ***b*** in these
6: 2 them because they are ***b***,
2 Tim 4:21 Linus, Claudia, and all the ***b***.
Heb 2:11 is not ashamed to call them ***b***,
2:12 declare Your name to My ***b***;
2:17 He had to be made like His ***b***,
3: 1 Therefore, holy ***b***, partakers of
3:12 Beware, ***b***, lest there be in any
7: 5 the law, that is, from their ***b***,
10:19 Therefore, ***b***, having boldness
13:22 And I appeal to you, ***b***,
Jas 1: 2 My ***b***, count it all joy when you
1:16 not be deceived, my beloved ***b***.
1:19 So then, my beloved ***b***,
2: 1 My ***b***, do not hold the faith of
2: 5 Listen, my beloved ***b***:
2:14 What does it profit, my ***b***,
3: 1 My ***b***, let not many of you become
3:10 blessing and cursing. My ***b***,
3:12 Can a fig tree, my ***b***, bear
4:11 speak evil of one another, ***b***.
5: 7 Therefore be patient, ***b***,
5: 9 grumble against one another, ***b***,
5:10 My ***b***, take the prophets, who

5:12 But above all, my **b**, do not
5:19 **B**, if anyone among you wanders
1 Pe 1:22 Spirit in sincere love of the **b**,
2 Pe 1:10 Therefore, **b**, be even more
1 Jn 2: 7 **B**, I write no new commandment to
3:13 Do not marvel, my **b**,
3:14 to life, because we love the **b**.
3:16 lay down our lives for the **b**.
3 Jn 3 For I rejoiced greatly when **b**
5 whatever you do for the **b** and
10 himself does not receive the **b**,
Rev 6:11 fellow servants and their **b**,
12:10 come, for the accuser of our **b**,
19:10 and of your **b** who have the
22: 9 and of your **b** the prophets, and

BRIARS (1/1)

Heb 6: 8 but if it bears thorns and **b**,

BRIBE (15/13) BRIBERY, BRIBES

Ex 23: 8 "And you shall take no **b**,
23: 8 for a **b** blinds the discerning
Deut 10:17 no partiality nor takes a **b**.
16:19 show partiality, nor take a **b**,
16:19 for a **b** blinds the eyes of the
27:25 is the one who takes a **b** to
1 Sam 12: 3 hand have I received any **b**
Job 6:22 Offer a **b** for me from your
Ps 15: 5 Nor does he take a **b** against
Prov 17:23 A wicked man accepts a **b**
21:14 And a **b** behind the back,
Eccl 7: 7 And a **b** debases the heart.
Isa 5:23 Who justify the wicked for a **b**,
Mic 3:11 Her heads judge for a **b**,
7: 3 gifts, The judge seeks a **b**,

BRIBERY (1/1) BRIBE

Job 15:34 will consume the tents of **b**.

BRIBES (9/9) BRIBE

1 Sam 8: 3 after dishonest gain, took **b**,
2 Chr 19: 7 no partiality, nor taking of **b**.
Ps 26:10 whose right hand is full of **b**.
Prov 15:27 But he who hates **b** will live.
29: 4 But he who receives **b**
Isa 1:23 of thieves; Everyone loves **b**,
33:15 with his hands, refusing **b**,
Ezek 22:12 In you they take **b** to shed
Am 5:12 the just and taking **b**;

BRICK (9/9) BRICKS

Gen 11: 3 They had **b** for stone, and
Ex 1:14 hard bondage—in mortar, in **b**,
5: 7 the people straw to make **b** as
5:14 your task in making **b** both
5:16 Make **b**!' And indeed your
2 Sam 12:31 made them cross over to the **b**
Isa 65: 3 burn incense on altars of **b**;
Jer 43: 9 in the clay in the **b** courtyard
Nah 3:14 the mortar! Make strong the **b**

BRICKKILN (KJV) See BRICK (COURTYARDS), BRICK (KILN), BRICK (WORKS)

BRICKS (5/5) BRICK

Gen 11: 3 let us make **b** and bake them
Ex 5: 8 lay on them the quota of **b**
5:18 shall deliver the quota of **b**.
5:19 You shall not reduce any **b** from
Isa 9:10 The **b** have fallen down, But we

BRIDE (14/14) BRIDE-PRICE, BRIDEGROOM, BRIDEGROOM'S, BRIDES

Isa 49:18 And bind them on you as a **b**
61:10 And as a **b** adorns herself
62: 5 bridegroom rejoices over the **b**,
Jer 2:32 Or a **b** her attire? Yet My
7:34 and the voice of the **b**.
16: 9 and the voice of the **b**.
25:10 and the voice of the **b**,
33:11 and the voice of the **b**,
Joel 2:16 And the **b** from her dressing
Jn 3:29 He who has the **b** is the
Rev 18:23 the voice of bridegroom and **b**
21: 2 prepared as a **b** adorned for her
21: 9 "Come, I will show you the **b**,
22:17 And the Spirit and the **b** say,

BRIDE-PRICE (2/2) BRIDE

Ex 22:16 he shall surely pay the **b** for
22:17 pay money according to the **b**

BRIDECHAMBER (KJV) See BRIDEGROOM

BRIDEGROOM (26/20) BRIDE, BRIDEGROOM'S

Ps 19: 5 Which is like a **b** coming out
Isa 61:10 As a **b** decks himself with
62: 5 And as the **b** rejoices over
Jer 7:34 the voice of the **b** and the
16: 9 the voice of the **b** and the
25:10 the voice of the **b** and the
33:11 the voice of the **b** and the
Joel 2:16 Let the **b** go out from his
Mt 9:15 Can the friends of the **b** mourn
9:15 mourn as long as the **b** is with
9:15 the days will come when the **b**
25: 1 and went out to meet the **b**.
25: 5 But while the **b** was delayed,
25: 6 the **b** is coming; go out to meet
25:10 the **b** came, and those who were
Mk 2:19 Can the friends of the **b** fast
2:19 bridegroom fast while the **b** is
2:19 As long as they have the **b** with
2:20 the days will come when the **b**
Lk 5:34 you make the friends of the **b**
5:34 bridegroom fast while the **b** is
5:35 the days will come when the **b**
Jn 2: 9 of the feast called the **b**.
3:29 "He who has the bride is the **b**;
3:29 but the friend of the **b**,
Rev 18:23 and the voice of **b** and bride

BRIDEGROOM'S (1/1) BRIDEGROOM

Jn 3:29 greatly because of the **b** voice.

BRIDES (2/2) BRIDE

Hos 4:13 And your **b** commit adultery.
4:14 Nor your **b** when they commit

BRIDLE (8/8) BRIDLES

2 Ki 19:28 My hook in your nose And My **b**
Job 41:13 approach him with a double **b**?
Ps 32: 9 be harnessed with bit and **b**,
Prov 26: 3 A **b** for the donkey, And a rod
Isa 30:28 And there shall be a **b** in
37:29 My hook in your nose And My **b**
Jas 1:26 and does not **b** his tongue but
3: 2 able also to **b** the whole body.

BRIDLES (1/1) BRIDLE

Rev 14:20 winepress, up to the horses' **b**,

BRIEFLY (2/2)

Eph 3: 3 to me the mystery (as I have **b**
1 Pe 5:12 him, I have written to you **b**,

BRIER (3/3) BRIERS

Isa 55:13 And instead of the **b** shall
Ezek 28:24 no longer be a pricking **b** or a
Mic 7: 4 The best of them is like a **b**;

BRIERS (11/11) BRIER

Judg 8: 7 of the wilderness and with **b**!
8:16 thorns of the wilderness and **b**,
Isa 5: 6 But there shall come up **b** and
7:23 It will be for **b** and thorns.
7:24 all the land will become **b** and
7:25 not go there for fear of **b** and
9:18 It shall devour the **b** and
10:17 devour His thorns and his **b**
27: 4 Who would set **b** and thorns
32:13 will come up thorns and **b**,
Ezek 2: 6 though **b** and thorns are with

BRIGANDINE (KJV) See ARMOR

BRIGHT (26/25) BRIGHTENED, BRIGHTER, BRIGHTNESS

Lev 13: 2 or a **b** spot, and it becomes on
13: 4 But if the **b** spot is white on
13:19 a white swelling or a **b** spot,
13:23 But if the **b** spot stays in one
13:24 flesh of the burn becomes a **b**
13:25 if the hair of the **b** spot has
13:26 are no white hairs in the **b**
13:28 But if the **b** spot stays in one
13:38 If a man or a woman has **b** spots
13:38 specifically white **b** spots,
13:39 and indeed if the **b** spots on
14:56 swelling and a scab and a **b** spot
1 Sam 16:12 with **b** eyes, and good-looking.
Job 37:11 He scatters His **b** clouds.
37:21 at the light when it is **b**
Jer 51:11 Make the arrows **b**! Gather the
Ezek 1:13 The fire was **b**,
21:15 Ah! It is made **b**;
32: 8 All the **b** lights of the heavens
Nah 3: 3 Horsemen charge with **b** sword
Mt 17: 5 a **b** cloud overshadowed them;
Lk 11:36 as when the **b** shining of a lamp
Acts 10:30 stood before me in **b** clothing,
Rev 15: 6 clothed in pure **b** linen, and
19: 8 in fine linen, clean and **b**,
22:16 the **B** and Morning Star."

BRIGHTENED (2/2) BRIGHT

1 Sam 14:27 mouth; and his countenance **b**.
14:29 how my countenance has **b**

BRIGHTER (4/4) BRIGHT

Job 11:17 And your life would be **b** than
Prov 4:18 That shines ever **b** unto the
Lam 4: 7 Her Nazirites were **b** than snow
Acts 26:13 **b** than the sun, shining around

BRIGHTNESS (19/19) BRIGHT

2 Sam 22:13 From the **b** before Him Coals of
Job 31:26 Or the moon moving in **b**,
Ps 18:12 From the **b** before Him, His
Isa 59: 9 but there is darkness! For **b**,
60: 3 And kings to the **b** of your
60:19 Nor for **b** shall the moon give
62: 1 righteousness goes forth as **b**,
Ezek 1: 4 and **b** was all around it and
1:27 the appearance of fire with **b**
1:28 so was the appearance of the **b**
8: 2 like the appearance of **b**,
10: 4 the court was full of the **b** of
Dan 12: 3 wise shall shine Like the **b**
Joel 2:10 And the stars diminish their **b**.
3:15 the stars will diminish their **b**.
Am 5:20 very dark, with no **b** in it?
Hab 3: 4 His **b** was like the light; He
2 Th 2: 8 mouth and destroy with the **b**
Heb 1: 3 who being the **b** of His glory

BRIM (8/6)

1 Ki 7:23 ten cubits from one **b** to the
7:24 Below its **b** were ornamental
7:26 and its **b** was shaped like the
7:26 its brim was shaped like the **b**
2 Chr 4: 2 ten cubits from one **b** to the
4: 5 and its **b** was shaped like the
4: 5 its brim was shaped like the **b**
Jn 2: 7 they filled them up to the **b**.

BRIMSTONE (14/14)

Gen 19:24 Then the LORD rained **b** and fire
Deut 29:23 'The whole land is **b**,
Job 18:15 **B** is scattered on his
Ps 11: 6 Fire and **b** and a burning wind
Isa 30:33 the LORD, like a stream of **b**,
34: 9 pitch, And its dust into **b**;
Ezek 38:22 great hailstones, fire, and **b**.
Lk 17:29 of Sodom it rained fire and **b**
Rev 9:17 mouths came fire, smoke, and **b**.
9:18 fire and the smoke and the **b**
14:10 be tormented with fire and **b**
19:20 the lake of fire burning with **b**.
20:10 into the lake of fire and **b**
21: 8 which burns with fire and **b**,

BRING (710/677) BRINGING, BRINGS, BROUGHT

Gen 1:11 Let the earth **b** forth grass, the
1:24 Let the earth **b** forth the living
3:16 In pain you shall **b** forth
3:18 thorns and thistles it shall **b**
6:19 thing of all flesh you shall **b**
8:17 **B** out with you every living
9: 7 **B** forth abundantly in the
9:14 when I **b** a cloud over the
15: 9 **B** Me a three-year-old heifer, a
18: 5 And I will **b** a morsel of bread,
18:19 that the LORD may **b** to Abraham
19: 5 **B** them out to us that we may
19: 8 let me **b** them out to you, and
27: 4 and **b** it to me that I may eat,
27: 5 the field to hunt game and to **b**
27: 7 **B** me game and make savory food
27: 9 Go now to the flock and **b** me
27:12 and I shall **b** a curse on myself
27:25 **B** it near to me, and I will eat
27:45 then I will send and **b** you from
28:15 and will **b** you back to this
31:39 torn by beasts I did not **b**
37:14 and **b** back word to me." So he
37:22 and **b** him back to his father.
38:24 **B** her out and let her be
41:32 and God will shortly **b** it to
42:16 and let him **b** your brother; and
42:20 And **b** your youngest brother to
42:34 And **b** your youngest brother to
42:37 my two sons if I do not **b**
42:37 and I will **b** him back to you."
42:38 then you would **b** down my gray
43: 7 **B** your brother down'?"
43: 9 If I do not **b** him back to you
44:21 **B** him down to me, that I may set
44:29 you shall **b** down my gray hair
44:31 So your servants will **b** down
44:32 If I do not **b** him back to you,
45:13 and you shall hurry and **b** my
45:18 **B** your father and your
45:19 **b** your father and come.
46: 4 and I will also surely **b** you up
48: 9 Please **b** them to me, and I will
48:21 but God will be with you and **b**
50:20 in order to **b** it about as it
50:24 and **b** you out of this land to
Ex 3: 8 and to **b** them up from that land
3:10 you to Pharaoh that you may **b**
3:11 that I should **b** the children
3:17 and I have said I will **b** you up
6: 6 I will **b** you out from under the
6: 8 And I will **b** you into the land
6:13 to **b** the children of Israel out
6:26 **B** out the children of Israel
6:27 to **b** out the children of Israel
7: 4 may lay My hand on Egypt and **b**

7: 5 out My hand on Egypt and **b** out
8: 3 So the river shall **b** forth frogs
8:18 with their enchantments to **b**
10: 4 tomorrow I will **b** locusts into
11: 1 I will **b** yet one more plague on
14:11 to **b** us up out of Egypt?
15:17 You will **b** them in and plant
16: 5 they shall prepare what they **b**
18:19 so that you may **b** the
18:22 great matter they shall **b** to
21: 6 then his master shall **b** him to
21: 6 He shall also **b** him to the
22:13 then he shall **b** it as evidence,
23: 4 you shall surely **b** it back to
23:19 of your land you shall **b** into
23:20 to keep you in the way and to **b**
23:23 Angel will go before you and **b**
25: 2 that they **b** Me an offering.
26:33 Then you shall **b** the ark of the
27:20 children of Israel that they **b**
29: 3 put them in one basket and **b**
29: 4 Aaron and his sons you shall **b**
29: 8 Then you shall **b** his sons and
32: 2 daughters, and **b** them to me."
33:12 **B** up this people.' But You have
33:15 do not **b** us up from here.
34:26 of your land you shall **b** to
35: 5 let him **b** it as an offering to
35:29 whose hearts were willing to **b**
36: 5 The people **b** much more than
40: 4 'You shall **b** in the table and
40: 4 you shall **b** in the lampstand
40:12 Then you shall **b** Aaron and his
40:14 And you shall **b** his sons and
Lev 1: 2 you shall **b** your offering of
1: 5 shall **b** the blood and sprinkle
1:10 he shall **b** a male without
1:13 Then the priest shall **b** it all
1:14 then he shall **b** his offering of
1:15 The priest shall **b** it to the
2: 2 He shall **b** it to Aaron's sons,
2: 4 And if you **b** as an offering a
2: 8 You shall **b** the grain offering
2: 8 he shall **b** it to the altar.
2:11 'No grain offering which you **b**
4: 4 He shall **b** the bull to the door
4: 5 some of the bull's blood and **b**
4:14 and **b** it before the tabernacle
4:16 The anointed priest shall **b** some
4:23 he shall **b** as his offering a
4:28 then he shall **b** as his offering
4:32 he shall **b** a female without
5: 6 and he shall **b** his trespass
5: 7 If he is not able to **b** a lamb,
5: 7 then he shall **b** to the LORD,
5: 8 And he shall **b** them to the
5:11 But if he is not able to **b** two
5:11 then he who sinned shall **b** for
5:12 'Then he shall **b** it to the
5:15 then he shall **b** to the LORD as
5:18 And he shall **b** to the priest a
6: 6 And he shall **b** his trespass
6:21 you shall **b** it in. The baked
7:29 offering to the LORD shall **b**
7:30 His own hands shall **b** the
7:30 fat with the breast he shall **b**,
10:15 the wave offering they shall **b**
12: 6 she shall **b** to the priest a
12: 8 And if she is not able to **b** a
12: 8 then she may **b** two turtledoves
14:23 He shall **b** them to the priest on
15:29 and **b** them to the priest, to
16: 9 And Aaron shall **b** the goat on
16:11 And Aaron shall **b** the bull of
16:12 and **b** it inside the veil.
16:15 **b** its blood inside the veil, do
16:20 he shall **b** the live goat.
17: 4 and does not **b** it to the door of
17: 5 the children of Israel may **b**
17: 5 that they may **b** them to the
17: 9 and does not **b** it to the door of
19:21 And he shall **b** his trespass
23:10 then you shall **b** a sheaf of the
23:17 You shall **b** from your dwellings
24: 2 children of Israel that they **b**
25:21 and it will **b** forth produce
26:21 I will **b** on you seven times
26:25 And I will **b** a sword against you
26:26 and they shall **b** back your
26:31 lay your cities waste and **b**
26:32 I will **b** the land to desolation,
27: 9 is an animal that men may **b**
Num 3: 6 **B** the tribe of Levi near, and
5: 9 which they **b** to the priest,
5:15 then the man shall **b** his wife to
5:15 He shall **b** the offering
5:16 And the priest shall **b** her
5:25 and **b** it to the altar;
6:10 on the eighth day he shall **b**
6:12 and **b** a male lamb in its first
6:16 Then the priest shall **b** them
8: 9 And you shall **b** the Levites
8:10 So you shall **b** the Levites
9:13 because he did not **b** the
11:16 **b** them to the tabernacle of
13:20 And **b** some of the fruit of the
14: 8 then He will **b** us into this
14:16 the LORD was not able to **b**
14:24 I will **b** into the land where he
14:31 I will **b** in, and they shall
15: 4 offering to the LORD shall **b**
15:10 and you shall **b** as the drink
15:18 into the land to which I **b** you,
15:25 they shall **b** their offering, an
15:27 then he shall **b** a female goat
16: 9 to **b** you near to Himself, to do
16:17 and each of you **b** his censer
17:10 **B** Aaron's rod back before the
18: 2 Also **b** with you your brethren of
18:13 which they **b** to the LORD,
18:15 which they **b** to the LORD,
19: 2 that they **b** you a red heifer
20: 5 to **b** us to this evil place?
20: 8 thus you shall **b** water for them
20:10 you rebels! Must we **b** water for
20:12 therefore you shall not **b** this
20:25 and **b** them up to Mount Hor;
22: 8 and I will **b** back word to you,
27:17 who may lead them out and **b**
28:26 when you **b** a new grain offering
Deut 1:17 **b** to me, and I will hear it.'
1:22 and **b** back word to us of the
4:38 to **b** you in, to give you their
6:23 that He might **b** us in, to give
7:26 Nor shall you **b** an abomination
9: 3 He will destroy them and **b** them
9:28 the LORD was not able to **b**
12:11 There you shall **b** all that I
14:28 every third year you shall **b**
17: 5 then you shall **b** out to your
19:12 of his city shall send and **b**
21: 4 elders of that city shall **b**
21:12 then you shall **b** her home to
21:19 shall take hold of him and **b**
22: 1 you shall certainly **b** them back
22: 2 then you shall **b** it to your own
22: 8 that you may not **b** guilt of
22:15 young woman shall take and **b**
22:21 then they shall **b** out the young
22:24 then you shall **b** them both out
23:18 You shall not **b** the wages of a
24: 4 and you shall not **b** sin on the
24: 5 and **b** happiness to his wife
24:11 man to whom you lend shall **b**
26: 2 which you shall **b** from your
28:36 The LORD will **b** you and the
28:49 The LORD will **b** a nation
28:59 then the LORD will **b** upon you
28:60 Moreover He will **b** back on you
28:61 will the LORD **b** upon you until
28:63 over you to destroy you and **b**
29:27 to **b** on it every curse that is
30: 3 the LORD your God will **b**
30: 4 and from there He will **b** you.
30: 5 the LORD your God will **b**
30:12 into heaven for us and **b** it to
30:13 go over the sea for us and **b**
31:23 for you shall **b** the children of
33: 7 And **b** him to his people; Let
Josh 2: 3 **B** out the men who have come to
2:18 and unless you **b** your father,
6:22 and from there **b** out the woman
10:22 and **b** out those five kings to
18: 6 the land in seven parts and **b**
23:15 so the LORD will **b** upon you
Judg 6:13 Did not the LORD **b** us up from
6:18 until I come to You and **b** out
6:30 **B** out your son, that he may die,
7: 4 **b** them down to the water, and I
19: 3 to speak kindly to her and **b**
19:22 **B** out the man who came to your
19:24 let me **b** them out now.
Ruth 3:15 **B** the shawl that is on you and
1 Sam 2:19 and **b** it to him year by year
4: 3 us **b** the ark of the covenant
4: 4 that they might **b** from there
9: 7 what shall we **b** the man?
9: 7 and there is no present to **b**
9:23 **B** the portion which I gave you,
11: 2 and **b** reproach on all Israel."
11:12 **B** the men, that we may put
13: 9 **B** a burnt offering and peace
14:18 **B** the ark of God here" (for at
14:34 **B** me here every man's ox and
15:32 **B** Agag king of the Amalekites
16:11 Send and **b** him. For we will not
16:17 play well, and **b** him to me."
17:18 and **b** back news of them."
19:15 **B** him up to me in the bed, that
20: 8 for why should you **b** me to your
20:31 send and **b** him to me, for he
23: 9 **B** the ephod here."
27:11 to **b** news to Gath, saying,
28: 8 and **b** up for me the one I shall
28:11 'Whom shall I **b** up for you?"
28:11 **B** up Samuel for me."
30: 7 Please **b** the ephod here to me."
2 Sam 3:12 hand shall be with you to **b**
3:13 see my face unless you first **b**
6: 2 with him from Baale Judah to **b**
9:10 you shall **b** in the harvest,
12:23 Can I **b** him back again? I shall
13:10 **B** the food into the bedroom,
14:10 **b** him to me, and he shall not
14:13 in that the king does not **b**
14:20 To **b** about this change of
14:21 **b** back the young man Absalom."
15:14 he overtake us suddenly and **b**
15:25 He will **b** me back and show me
17: 3 Then I will **b** back all the
17:13 then all Israel shall **b** ropes
17:14 intent that the LORD might **b**
19:11 Why are you the last to **b** the
19:12 Why then are you the last to **b**
22:28 that You may **b** them down.
1 Ki 1:42 and **b** good news."
1:53 So King Solomon sent them to **b**
2: 9 but **b** his gray hair down to the
3:24 **B** me a sword." So they brought
5: 9 My servants shall **b** them down
8: 1 that they might **b** up the ark of
8:34 and **b** them back to the land
13:18 **B** him back with you to your
14:10 therefore behold! I will **b**
17:10 Please **b** me a little water in a
17:11 Please **b** me a morsel of bread in
17:13 and **b** it to me; and afterward
17:18 Have you come to me to **b** my sin
20:33 **b** him." Then Ben-Hadad came
21:21 I will **b** calamity on you.
21:29 I will not **b** the calamity in
21:29 In the days of his son I will **b**
22: 9 **B** Micaiah the son of Imlah
2 Ki 2:20 **B** me a new bowl, and put salt in
3:15 'But now **b** me a musician."
4: 6 **B** me another vessel." And he
4:41 Then **b** some flour." And he put
6:19 and I will **b** you to the man
10:22 **B** out vestments for all the
12: 4 man purposes in his heart to **b**
19: 3 but there is no strength to **b**
22:16 I will **b** calamity on this place
22:20 the calamity which I will **b** on
23: 4 to **b** out of the temple of the
1 Chr 12:17 God of our fathers look and **b**
13: 3 and let us **b** the ark of our God
13: 5 to **b** the ark of God from
13: 6 to **b** up from there the ark of
13:12 How can I **b** the ark of God to
15: 3 to **b** up the ark of the LORD to
15:12 that you may **b** up the ark of
15:14 sanctified themselves to **b** up
15:25 over thousands went to **b** up
16:29 **B** an offering, and come before
21: 2 and **b** the number of them to me
22:19 to **b** the ark of the covenant of
2 Chr 2:16 we will **b** it to you in rafts by
5: 2 that they might **b** the ark of
6:25 and **b** them back to the land
12:11 the guard would go and **b** them
18: 8 **B** Micaiah the son of Imla
24: 6 not required the Levites to **b**
24: 9 Judah and Jerusalem to **b** to
24:19 to **b** them back to the LORD;
28:13 You shall not **b** the captives
28:27 but they did not **b** him into the
29:31 and **b** sacrifices and thank
31:10 Since the people began to **b**
34:24 I will **b** calamity on this place
34:28 the calamity which I will **b** on
Ezra 3: 7 people of Sidon and Tyre to **b**
8:17 that they should **b** us servants
8:30 to **b** them to Jerusalem to the
Neh 1: 9 and **b** them to the place which I
8: 1 they told Ezra the scribe to **b**
8:15 and **b** olive branches, branches
9:29 That You might **b** them back to
10:35 And we made ordinances to **b**
10:36 to **b** the firstborn of our sons
10:37 to **b** the firstfruits of our
10:37 and to **b** the tithes of our land
10:38 and the Levites shall **b** up a
10:39 the children of Levi shall **b**
11: 1 of the people cast lots to **b**
12:27 to **b** them to Jerusalem to
13:18 and did not our God **b** all this
13:18 Yet you **b** added wrath on Israel
Esth 1:11 to **b** Queen Vashti before the
3: 9 to **b** it into the king's
5: 5 **B** Haman quickly, that he may do
6: 1 So one was commanded to **b** the
6:14 and hastened to **b** Haman to the
Job 6:22 **B** something to me'? Or, 'Offer
14: 3 And **b** me to judgment with
14: 4 Who can **b** a clean thing out of
14: 9 of water it will bud And **b**
15:35 They conceive trouble and **b**
30:23 For I know that You will **b** me
33:30 To **b** back his soul from the
38:32 Can you **b** out Mazzaroth in its
39: 3 They **b** forth their young,
39:12 Will you trust him to **b** home
40:12 and **b** him low; Tread down the
40:19 Only He who made him can **b**
Ps 18:27 But will **b** down haughty looks.
25:17 **B** me out of my distresses!
37: 5 And He shall **b** it to pass.
37: 6 He shall **b** forth your
38: To **b** to remembrance.
43: 3 Let them **b** me to Your holy
55: 3 For they **b** down trouble upon
55:23 shall **b** them down to the pit of
59:11 And **b** them down, O Lord our
60: 9 Who will **b** me to the strong
68:22 I will **b** back from Bashan, I
68:22 I will **b** them back from the
68:29 Kings will **b** presents to You.
70: To **b** to remembrance.
71:20 And **b** me up again from the
72: 3 The mountains will **b** peace to
72: 4 He will **b** justice to the poor
72:10 and of the isles Will **b**
76:11 Let all who are around Him **b**
96: 8 **B** an offering, and come into
104:14 That he may **b** forth food from
108:10 Who will **b** me into the strong

B

126: 4 ***B*** back our captivity, O LORD,
142: 7 ***B*** my soul out of prison, That
143:11 Your righteousness' sake ***b*** my
144:13 That our sheep may ***b*** forth
Prov 4: 8 She will ***b*** you honor, when you
19:24 And will not so much as ***b*** it
24:22 knows the ruin those two can ***b***?
26:15 It wearies him to ***b*** it back to
27: 1 do not know what a day may ***b***
29:23 A man's pride will ***b*** him low,
Eccl 3:22 For who can ***b*** him to see what
11: 9 that for all these God will ***b***
12:14 For God will ***b*** every work into
Song 8: 2 I would lead you and ***b*** you
8:11 Everyone was to ***b*** for its
Isa 1:13 ***B*** no more futile sacrifices
5: 2 So He expected it to ***b*** forth
5: 4 when I expected it to ***b*** forth
5: 4 Did it ***b*** forth wild grapes?
7:17 The LORD will ***b*** the king of
14: 2 people will take them and ***b***
15: 9 Because I will ***b*** more upon
21:14 ***B*** water to him who is thirsty;
23: 4 nor ***b*** forth children; Neither
23: 4 Nor ***b*** up virgins."
23: 9 To ***b*** to dishonor the pride of
23: 9 To ***b*** into contempt all the
25:11 And He will ***b*** down their pride
25:12 fort of your walls He will ***b***
25:12 And ***b*** to the ground, down to
28: 2 Who will ***b*** them down to the
28:21 And ***b*** to pass His act, His
31: 2 He also is wise and will ***b***
33:11 You shall ***b*** forth stubble;
37: 3 but there is no strength to ***b***
38: 8 I will ***b*** the shadow on the
40: 9 You who ***b*** good tidings, Get
40: 9 You who ***b*** good tidings, Lift
41:21 ***B*** forth your strong reasons,"
41:22 Let them ***b*** forth and show us
42: 1 He will ***b*** forth justice to the
42: 3 He will ***b*** forth justice for
42: 7 To ***b*** out prisoners from the
42:16 I will ***b*** the blind by a way
43: 5 I will ***b*** your descendants from
43: 6 Do not keep them back!' ***B*** My
43: 8 ***B*** out the blind people who
43: 9 Let them ***b*** out their witnesses,
43:14 And ***b*** them all down as
45: 8 let them ***b*** forth salvation,
45:21 Tell and ***b*** forth your case;
46:11 I will also ***b*** it to pass.
46:13 I ***b*** My righteousness near, it
49: 5 To ***b*** Jacob back to Him, So
49:22 They shall ***b*** your sons in
55:10 And make it ***b*** forth and bud,
56: 7 Even them I will ***b*** to My holy
56:12 I will ***b*** wine, And we will fill
58: 7 And that you ***b*** to your house
59: 4 They conceive evil and ***b*** forth
60: 6 They shall ***b*** gold and incense,
60: 9 To ***b*** your sons from afar,
60:11 That men may ***b*** to you the
60:17 Instead of bronze I will ***b***
60:17 Instead of iron I will ***b***
65: 9 I will ***b*** forth descendants from
65:23 Nor ***b*** forth children for
66: 4 And ***b*** their fears on them;
66: 9 Shall I ***b*** to the time of birth,
66:20 Then they shall ***b*** all your
66:20 as the children of Israel ***b*** an
Jer 2: 9 Therefore I will yet ***b*** charges
2: 9 children's children I will ***b***
3:14 and I will ***b*** you to Zion.
4: 6 Do not delay! For I will ***b***
5:15 I will ***b*** a nation against you
6:19 I will certainly ***b*** calamity on
8: 1 they shall ***b*** out the bones of
10:24 lest You ***b*** me to nothing.
11: 8 therefore I will ***b*** upon them
11:11 I will surely ***b*** calamity on
11:23 for I will ***b*** catastrophe on the
12: 9 ***B*** them to devour!
12:15 have compassion on them and ***b***
15: 8 I will ***b*** against them,
15:19 Then I will ***b*** you back; You
16:15 For I will ***b*** them back into
17:18 ***B*** on them the day of doom,
17:21 nor ***b*** it in by the gates of
17:24 to ***b*** no burden through the gates
18: 8 disaster that I thought to ***b***
18:22 When You ***b*** a troop suddenly
19: 3 I will ***b*** such a catastrophe on
19:15 I will ***b*** on this city and on
23: 3 and ***b*** them back to their folds;
23:12 For I will ***b*** disaster on them,
23:40 And I will ***b*** an everlasting
24: 6 and I will ***b*** them back to this
25: 9 and will ***b*** them against this
25:13 So I will ***b*** on that land all My
25:29 I begin to ***b*** calamity on the
26: 3 calamity which I purpose to ***b***
26:15 you will surely ***b*** innocent
27:11 But the nations that ***b*** their
27:12 ***B*** your necks under the yoke of
27:22 Then I will ***b*** them up and
28: 3 'Within two full years I will ***b***
28: 4 And I will ***b*** back to this place
28: 6 to ***b*** back the vessels of the
29:14 and I will ***b*** you back from your
29:14 and I will ***b*** you to the place
30: 3 that I will ***b*** back from
30:18 I will ***b*** back the captivity of
31: 8 I will ***b*** them from the north
31:23 when I ***b*** back their captivity:
32:37 I will ***b*** them back to this
32:42 so I will ***b*** on them all the
33: 6 I will ***b*** it health and healing;
33:11 and of those who will ***b*** the
35: 2 and ***b*** them into the house of
35:17 I will ***b*** on Judah and on all
36: 3 which I purpose to ***b*** upon them,
36:21 So the king sent Jehudi to ***b*** the
36:31 and I will ***b*** on them, on the
39:16 I will ***b*** My words upon this
41: 5 to ***b*** them to the house of the
42:17 from the disaster that I will ***b***
43:10 I will send and ***b*** Nebuchadnezzar
45: 5 I will ***b*** adversity on all
46:25 I will ***b*** punishment on Amon of
48:44 upon it I will ***b*** The year of
48:47 Yet I will ***b*** back the captives
49: 5 I will ***b*** fear upon you," Says
49: 6 But afterward I will ***b*** back
49: 8 of Dedan! For I will ***b*** the
49:16 I will ***b*** you down from
49:32 And I will ***b*** their calamity
49:36 Against Elam I will ***b*** the four
49:37 I will ***b*** disaster upon them,
49:39 I will ***b*** back the captives of
50:19 But I will ***b*** back Israel to his
51:40 I will ***b*** them down Like lambs
51:44 And I will ***b*** out of his mouth
51:47 days are coming That I will ***b***
51:52 That I will ***b*** judgment on her
51:64 the catastrophe that I will ***b***
Lam 1:21 ***B*** on the day You have
2:14 To ***b*** back your captives, But
3:51 My eyes ***b*** suffering to my soul
Ezek 5:17 and I will ***b*** the sword against
6: 3 will ***b*** a sword against you, and
6:10 not said in vain that I would ***b***
7:24 Therefore I will ***b*** the worst of
11: 7 but I shall ***b*** you out of the
11: 8 and I will ***b*** a sword upon
11: 9 And I will ***b*** you out of its
12: 4 By day you shall ***b*** out your
12:13 I will ***b*** him to Babylon, to
13:14 and ***b*** it down to the ground, so
14:17 Or if I ***b*** a sword on that
16:38 I will ***b*** blood upon you in fury
16:40 They shall also ***b*** up an assembly
16:53 When I ***b*** back their captives,
16:53 then I will also ***b*** back
17: 8 To ***b*** forth branches, bear
17:20 I will ***b*** him to Babylon and try
17:23 and it will ***b*** forth boughs, and
20: 6 to ***b*** them out of the land of
20: 9 to ***b*** them out of the land of
20:15 that I would not ***b*** them into
20:34 I will ***b*** you out from the
20:35 And I will ***b*** you into the
20:37 and I will ***b*** you into the bond
20:38 I will ***b*** them out of the
20:41 you as a sweet aroma when I ***b***
20:42 when I ***b*** you into the land of
21:23 but he will ***b*** their iniquity to
21:29 To ***b*** you on the necks of the
23:22 And I will ***b*** them against you
23:46 ***B*** up an assembly against them,
24: 6 ***B*** it out piece by piece,
26: 7 I will ***b*** against Tyre from the
26:19 when I ***b*** the deep upon you, and
26:20 then I will ***b*** you down with
28: 7 I will ***b*** strangers against you,
29: 4 I will ***b*** you up out of the
29: 8 Surely I will ***b*** a sword upon you
29:14 I will ***b*** back the captives of
32: 8 And ***b*** darkness upon your
32: 9 when I ***b*** your destruction among
33: 2 When I ***b*** the sword upon a land,
34:13 And I will ***b*** them out from the
34:13 and will ***b*** them to their own
34:16 will seek what was lost and ***b***
36:24 and ***b*** you into your own land.
36:29 and ***b*** no famine upon you.
37: 6 will put sinews on you and ***b***
37:12 and ***b*** you into the land of
37:21 them from every side and ***b***
38:16 the latter days that I will ***b***
38:17 in those days that I would ***b***
38:22 And I will ***b*** him to judgment
39: 2 and ***b*** you against the mountains
39:25 Now I will ***b*** back the captives
46:20 so that they do not ***b*** them out
Dan 1: 3 to ***b*** some of the children of
3:13 gave the command to ***b*** Shadrach,
4: 6 I issued a decree to ***b*** in all
5: 2 gave the command to ***b*** the gold
5: 7 The king cried aloud to ***b*** in the
9:24 To ***b*** in everlasting
9:27 middle of the week He shall ***b***
11:18 But a ruler shall ***b*** the
Hos 1: 4 And ***b*** an end to the kingdom of
2: 2 ***B*** charges against your mother,
2: 2 ***b*** charges; For she is not My
2:14 Will ***b*** her into the
7:12 I will ***b*** them down like birds
9:12 they ***b*** up their children,
9:13 So Ephraim will ***b*** out his
Joel 3: 1 When I ***b*** back the captives of
3: 2 And ***b*** them down to the Valley
Am 4: 1 ***B*** wine, let us drink!"
4: 4 ***B*** your sacrifices every
8:10 I will ***b*** sackcloth on every
9: 2 From there I will ***b*** them down;
9: 7 Did I not ***b*** up Israel from the
9:14 I will ***b*** back the captives of
Ob 3 Who will ***b*** me down to the
4 From there I will ***b*** you
Jon 3:10 that He had said He would ***b***
Mic 1:15 I will yet ***b*** an heir to you,
4:10 and labor to ***b*** forth, O
7: 9 He will ***b*** me forth to the
Zeph 1:17 I will ***b*** distress upon men, And
3:10 Shall ***b*** My offering.
3:20 At that time I will ***b*** you back,
Hag 1: 6 and ***b*** in little; You eat, but
1: 8 Go up to the mountains and ***b***
Zech 4: 7 a plain! And he shall ***b*** forth
8: 8 I will ***b*** them back, And they
10: 6 I will ***b*** them back, Because I
10:10 I will also ***b*** them back from
10:10 I will ***b*** them into the land of
13: 9 I will ***b*** the one-third through
Mal 1:13 And you ***b*** the stolen, the lame,
1:13 Thus you ***b*** an offering!
3:10 ***B*** all the tithes into the
Mt 1:21 And she will ***b*** forth a Son, and
2: 8 ***b*** back word to me, that I may
2:13 and stay there until I ***b*** you
5:23 Therefore if you ***b*** your gift to
10:34 not think that I came to ***b***
10:34 I did not come to ***b*** peace but a
14:18 ***B*** them here to Me."
17:17 ***B*** him here to Me."
21: 2 Loose them and ***b*** them to Me.
28: 8 and ran to ***b*** His disciples
Mk 9:19 ***B*** him to Me."
11: 2 Loose it and ***b*** it.
12:15 ***B*** Me a denarius that I may see
Lk 1:19 was sent to speak to you and ***b***
1:31 conceive in your womb and ***b***
2:10 I ***b*** you good tidings of great
2:32 A light to ***b*** revelation to the
5:18 whom they sought to ***b*** in and
5:19 not find how they might ***b*** him
8:14 and ***b*** no fruit to maturity.
9:41 ***B*** your son here."
12:11 Now when they ***b*** you to the
14:21 and ***b*** in here the poor and
15:22 ***B*** out the best robe and put it
15:23 And ***b*** the fatted calf here and
19:27 But ***b*** here those enemies of
19:30 Loose it and ***b*** it here.
Jn 10:16 this fold; them also I must ***b***,
14:26 and ***b*** to your remembrance all
18:29 What accusation do you ***b*** against
21:10 ***B*** some of the fish which you
Acts 5:28 and intend to ***b*** this Man's
7: 6 and that they would ***b*** them into
9: 2 he might ***b*** them bound to
9:21 so that he might ***b*** them bound
12: 4 intending to ***b*** him before the
12: 6 And when Herod was about to ***b***
17: 5 and sought to ***b*** them out to the
19:38 Let them ***b*** charges against one
22: 5 and went to Damascus to ***b*** in
23:10 and ***b*** him into the barracks.
23:18 me to him and asked me to ***b***
23:20 have agreed to ask that you ***b***
23:24 and ***b*** him safely to Felix the
24:17 after many years I came to ***b***
Rom 7:10 which was to ***b*** life, I found
7:10 I found to ***b*** death.
8:33 Who shall ***b*** a charge against
10: 6 to ***b*** Christ down from above)
10: 7 to ***b*** Christ up from the dead).
10:15 Who ***b*** glad tidings of
13: 2 and those who resist will ***b***
1 Cor 1:19 And ***b*** to nothing the
1:28 to ***b*** to nothing the things that
4: 5 who will both ***b*** to light the
9:27 But I discipline my body and ***b***
Gal 2: 4 that they might ***b*** us into
3:24 the law was our tutor to ***b***
Eph 6: 4 but ***b*** them up in the training
1 Th 4:14 even so God will ***b*** with Him
2 Tim 4:11 Get Mark and ***b*** him with you,
4:13 ***B*** the cloak that I left with
1 Pe 3:18 that He might ***b*** us to God,
2 Pe 2: 1 who will secretly ***b*** in
2: 1 and ***b*** on themselves swift
2:11 do not ***b*** a reviling accusation
2 Jn 10 comes to you and does not ***b***
Jude 9 dared not ***b*** against him a
Rev 21:24 and the kings of the earth ***b***
21:26 And they shall ***b*** the glory and

BRINGING (44/42)

Gen 6:17 I Myself am ***b*** floodwaters on
Ex 12:42 observance to the LORD for ***b***
36: 3 So they continued ***b*** to him
36: 6 people were restrained from ***b***,
Lev 4: 3 ***b*** guilt on the people, then let
18: 3 where I am ***b*** you, you shall not
20:22 that the land where I am ***b*** you
Num 5:15 for ***b*** iniquity to remembrance.
14:36 complain against him by ***b*** a
Deut 8: 7 For the LORD your God is ***b*** you
1 Sam 28:15 have you disturbed me by ***b***
2 Sam 19:10 why do you say nothing about ***b***
19:43 we not the first to advise ***b***
1 Ki 8:32 ***b*** his way on his head, and
10:22 the merchant ships came ***b*** gold,

2 Ki 21:12 I am **b** such calamity upon
22: 9 **b** the king word, saying, "Your
1 Chr 12:40 were **b** food on donkeys and
2 Chr 6:23 **b** retribution on the wicked by
6:23 retribution on the wicked by **b**
9:21 **b** gold, silver, ivory, apes,
34:16 **b** the king word, saying, "All
Neh 10:34 for **b** the wood offering into
13:15 and **b** in sheaves, and loading
13:31 and to **b** the wood offering and
Ps 126: 6 **B** his sheaves with him.
Jer 17:26 **b** burnt offerings and
17:26 **b** sacrifices of praise to the
Ezek 39: 2 **b** you up from the far north,
Dan 9:12 by **b** upon us a great disaster;
Zech 3: 8 I am **b** forth My Servant the
Mk 2: 3 **b** a paralytic who was carried
Lk 8: 1 preaching and **b** the glad
24: 1 came to the tomb **b** the spices
Jn 19: 4 I am **b** Him out to you, that you
19:39 **b** a mixture of myrrh and aloes,
Acts 5:16 **b** sick people and those who
17:20 For you are **b** some strange
Rom 7:23 and **b** me into captivity to the
2 Cor 10: 5 **b** every thought into captivity
Col 1: 6 and is **b** forth fruit, as it
Heb 2:10 in **b** many sons to glory, to
7:19 there is the **b** in of a
2 Pe 2: 5 **b** in the flood on the world of

BRINGS (81/74)

Ex 6: 7 I am the LORD your God who **b**
13: 5 when the LORD **b** you into the
13:11 when the LORD **b** you into the
Lev 1: 2 When any one of you **b** an
4:32 If he **b** a lamb as his sin
11:45 For I am the LORD who **b** you up
Num 5:18 hand the bitter water that **b** a
5:19 from this bitter water that **b**
5:24 drink the bitter water that **b**
5:24 and the water that **b** the curse
5:27 that the water that **b** a curse
15:30 that one **b** reproach on the
23:22 God **b** them out of Egypt; He
24: 8 God **b** him out of Egypt; He has
Deut 6:10 when the LORD your God **b** you
7: 1 When the LORD your God **b** you
22:14 and **b** a bad name on her, and
1 Sam 2: 6 He **b** down to the grave and
2: 6 brings down to the grave and **b**
2: 7 He **b** low and lifts up.
2 Sam 15: 8 If the LORD indeed **b** me back to
18:26 He also **b** news."
Job 12:22 And **b** the shadow of death to
19:29 For wrath **b** the punishment of
28:11 What is hidden he **b** forth to
Ps 1: 3 That **b** forth its fruit in its
7:14 the wicked **b** forth iniquity;
7:14 he conceives trouble and **b**
14: 7 out of Zion! When the LORD **b**
33:10 The LORD **b** the counsel of the
37: 7 Because of the man who **b**
53: 6 come out of Zion! When God **b**
68: 6 He **b** out those who are bound
107:28 And He **b** them out of their
135: 7 He **b** the wind out of His
Prov 10:31 The mouth of the righteous **b**
13:17 But a faithful ambassador **b**
16:30 He purses his lips and **b**
18:16 And **b** him before great men.
19:26 a son who causes shame and **b**
20:26 And **b** the threshing wheel over
21:22 And **b** down the trusted
21:27 How much more when he **b** it
25:23 The north wind **b** forth rain,
29:15 a child left to himself **b**
29:25 The fear of man **b** a snare, But
31:14 She **b** her food from afar.
Eccl 10:10 But wisdom **b** success.
Isa 8: 7 the Lord **b** up over them The
26: 5 For He **b** down those who dwell
26: 5 He **b** it down to the dust.
40:23 He **b** the princes to nothing;
40:26 Who **b** out their host by
41:27 give to Jerusalem one who **b**
43:17 Who **b** forth the chariot and
52: 7 Are the feet of him who **b**
52: 7 Who **b** glad tidings of good
52: 8 eye to eye When the LORD **b**
54:16 Who **b** forth an instrument for
61:11 For as the earth **b** forth its
Jer 4:31 The anguish as of her who **b**
10:13 He **b** the wind out of His
51:16 He **b** the wind out of His
Hos 4: 1 For the LORD **b** a charge
10: 1 He **b** forth fruit for himself.
12: 2 The LORD also **b** a charge
Nah 1:15 The feet of him who **b** good
Zeph 3: 5 Every morning He **b** His justice
Hag 1:11 on whatever the ground **b** forth,
Mal 2:12 Yet who **b** an offering to the
Mt 12:35 good treasure of his heart **b**
12:35 man out of the evil treasure **b**
13:52 is like a householder who **b**
Lk 6:45 good treasure of his heart **b**
6:45 evil treasure of his heart **b**
Jn 10: 4 And when he **b** out his own sheep,
Rom 4:15 because the law **b** about wrath;
2 Cor 11:20 For you put up with it if one **b**
Titus 2:11 For the grace of God that **b**
Heb 1: 6 But when He again **b** the
Jas 1:15 is full-grown, **b** forth death.

BRISTLING (1/1)

Jer 51:27 horses to come up like the **b**

BROAD (16/16) BROADER

2 Sam 22:20 also brought me out into a **b**
1 Chr 4:40 pasture, and the land was **b**,
Neh 3: 8 Jerusalem as far as the **B** Wall.
12:38 of the Ovens as far as the **B**
Job 30:14 They come as **b** breakers; Under
36:16 Into a **b** place where there
37:10 And the **b** waters are frozen.
Ps 18:19 also brought me out into a **b**
118: 5 me and set me in a **b** place.
119:96 commandment is exceedingly **b**.
Isa 33:21 will be for us A place of **b**
Jer 51:58 The **b** walls of Babylon shall be
Am 8: 9 I will darken the earth in **b**
Nah 2: 4 jostle one another in the **b**
Mt 7:13 for wide is the gate and **b** is
23: 5 They make their phylacteries **b**

BROADER (1/1) BROAD

Job 11: 9 longer than the earth And **b**

BROIDED (KJV) See BRAIDED

BROILED (1/1)

Lk 24:42 gave Him a piece of a **b** fish

BROKE (79/76) BREAK

Ex 9:25 every herb of the field and **b**
32: 3 So all the people **b** off the
32:19 tablets out of his hands and **b**
34: 1 the first tablets which you **b**.
Num 2:34 their standards and so they **b**
Deut 9:17 them out of my two hands and **b**
10: 2 the first tablets, which you **b**;
Judg 7:19 they blew the trumpets and **b**
7:20 blew the trumpets and **b** the
15:14 and his bonds **b** loose from his
16: 9 Samson!" But he **b** the
16:12 But he **b** them off his arms like
1 Sam 5: 9 and tumors **b** out on them.
2 Sam 23:16 So the three mighty men **b**
1 Ki 19:11 tore into the mountains and **b**
2 Ki 10:27 Then they **b** down the sacred
11:18 They thoroughly **b** in pieces its
14:13 and **b** down the wall of
18: 4 removed the high places and **b**
18: 4 down the wooden image and **b** in
23: 8 also he **b** down the high places
23:12 the king **b** down and pulverized
23:14 And he **b** in pieces the sacred
23:15 altar and the high place he **b**
25:10 the captain of the guard **b**
25:13 the Chaldeans **b** in pieces, and
1 Chr 11:18 So the three **b** through the camp
15:13 the LORD our God **b** out against
20: 4 happened afterward that war **b**
2 Chr 14: 3 and **b** down the sacred pillars
23:17 They **b** in pieces its altars and
25:23 and **b** down the wall of
26: 6 and **b** down the wall of Gath,
26:19 leprosy **b** out on his forehead,
31: 1 to the cities of Judah and **b**
34: 4 They **b** down the altars of the
34: 4 and the molded images he **b** in
36:19 **b** down the wall of Jerusalem,
Job 29:17 I **b** the fangs of the wicked,
Ps 74:13 You **b** the heads of the sea
74:14 You **b** the heads of Leviathan in
74:15 You **b** open the fountain and the
76: 3 There He **b** the arrows of the
106:29 And the plague **b** out among
107:14 And **b** their chains in pieces.
Isa 22:10 And the houses you **b** down To
Jer 28:10 prophet Jeremiah's neck and **b**
31:32 Egypt, My covenant which they **b**,
39: 8 and **b** down the walls of
52:14 with the captain of the guard **b**
52:17 the Chaldeans **b** in pieces, and
Ezek 17:16 and whose covenant he **b**—
17:19 and My covenant which he **b**,
27:26 But the east wind **b** you in the
29: 7 You **b** and tore all their
29: 7 You **b** and made all their backs
44: 7 then they **b** My covenant because
Dan 2:34 and clay, and **b** them in pieces.
2:45 and that it **b** in pieces the
6:24 and **b** all their bones in pieces
7:19 **b** in pieces, and trampled the
8: 7 and **b** his two horns. There was
Mt 14:19 He blessed and **b** and gave the
15:36 **b** them and gave them to His
26:26 blessed and **b** it, and gave it
Mk 6:41 blessed and **b** the loaves, and
8: 6 **b** them and gave them to His
8:19 When I **b** the five loaves for the
8:20 when I **b** the seven for the four
14: 3 Then she **b** the flask and poured
14:22 blessed and **b** it, and gave it
Lk 8:29 and he **b** the bonds and was
9:16 He blessed and **b** them, and
22:19 gave thanks and **b** it, and gave
24:30 blessed and **b** it, and gave it
Jn 5:18 because He not only **b** the
19:32 Then the soldiers came and **b** the
1 Cor 11:24 He **b** it and said, "Take, eat;
Rev 12: 7 And war **b** out in heaven:

BROKEN (166/160) BREAK, BROKENHEARTED

Gen 7:11 of the great deep were **b** up,
17:14 he has **b** My covenant."
Lev 6:28 which it is boiled shall be **b**.
11:35 it shall be **b** down; for they
13:20 is a leprous sore which has **b**
13:25 it is leprosy **b** out in the
15:12 discharge touches shall be **b**,
21:19 a man who has a **b** foot or broken
21:19 man who has a broken foot or **b**
22:22 Those that are blind or **b** or
26:13 I have **b** the bands of your yoke
Num 15:31 and has **b** His commandment, that
Deut 21: 6 the heifer whose neck was **b** in
1 Sam 2: 4 bows of the mighty men are **b**,
2:10 of the LORD shall be **b** in
4:18 and his neck was **b** and he died,
5: 4 the palms of its hands were **b**
2 Sam 5:20 The LORD has **b** through my
1 Ki 5: 9 and will have them **b** apart
18:30 of the LORD that was **b** down.
2 Ki 11: 6 the house, lest it be **b** down.
18:21 in the staff of this **b** reed,
25: 4 Then the city wall was **b**
1 Chr 14:11 God has **b** through my enemies by
2 Chr 14:13 for they were **b** before the
24: 7 had **b** into the house of God,
32: 5 up all the wall that was **b**,
33: 3 Hezekiah his father had **b** down;
34: 7 When he had **b** down the altars
Neh 1: 3 wall of Jerusalem is also **b**
2:13 of Jerusalem which were **b** down
Job 4:10 teeth of the young lions are **b**.
4:20 They are **b** in pieces from
17: 1 "My spirit is **b**,
17:11 My purposes are **b** off, Even
24:20 And wickedness should be **b**
26: 8 Yet the clouds are not **b** under
38:15 And the upraised arm is **b**.
Ps 3: 7 You have **b** the teeth of the
31:12 I am like a **b** vessel.
34:18 is near to those who have a **b**
34:20 bones; Not one of them is **b**.
37:15 And their bows shall be **b**.
37:17 arms of the wicked shall be **b**,
38: 8 I am feeble and severely **b**;
44:19 But You have severely **b** us in
51: 8 That the bones You have **b** may
51:17 The sacrifices of God are a **b**
51:17 **b** and a contrite heart—These,
55:20 He has **b** his covenant.
60: 1 You have **b** us down; You have
60: 2 You have **b** it; Heal its
69:20 Reproach has **b** my heart, And I
80:12 Why have You **b** down her hedges,
89:10 You have **b** Rahab in pieces, as
89:40 You have **b** down all his hedges;
107:16 For He has **b** the gates of
109:16 That he might even slay the **b**
124: 7 of the fowlers; The snare is **b**,
Prov 3:20 knowledge the depths were **b** up,
6:15 Suddenly he shall be **b** without
15:13 of the heart the spirit is **b**.
17:22 But a **b** spirit dries the bones.
18:14 But who can bear a **b** spirit?
24:31 Its stone wall was **b** down.
25:28 own spirit Is like a city **b**
Eccl 4:12 threefold cord is not quickly **b**.
12: 6 Or the golden bowl is **b**,
12: 6 Or the wheel **b** at the well.
Isa 5:27 the strap of their sandals be **b**;
7: 8 years Ephraim will be **b**,
8: 9 and be **b** in pieces! Give ear,
8: 9 but be **b** in pieces; Gird
8: 9 but be **b** in pieces.
8:15 They shall fall and be **b**,
9: 4 For You have **b** the yoke of his
14: 5 The LORD has **b** the staff of
14:29 the rod that struck you is **b**;
16: 8 lords of the nations have **b**
19:10 And its foundations will be **b**.
21: 9 images of her gods He has **b**
24: 5 **B** the everlasting covenant.
24:10 The city of confusion is **b**
24:19 The earth is violently **b**,
27:11 they will be **b** off; The women
28:13 and be **b** And snared and
30:14 Which is **b** in pieces; He
33: 8 He has **b** the covenant, He has
33:20 Nor will any of its cords be **b**.
36: 6 in the staff of this **b** reed,
Jer 2:13 **b** cisterns that can hold no
2:16 of Noph and Tahpanhes Have **b**
2:20 For of old I have **b** your yoke
4:26 And all its cities were **b** down
5: 5 But these have altogether **b**
10:20 And all my cords are **b**;
11:10 and the house of Judah have **b**
11:16 on it, And its branches are **b**.
14:17 of my people Has been **b** with
22:28 **b** idol—A vessel in which is
23: 9 My heart within me is **b**
28: 2 I have **b** the yoke of the king of
28:12 Hananiah the prophet had **b** the
28:13 You have **b** the yokes of wood,

33:21 'then My covenant may also be **b**
48:17 'How the strong staff is **b**,
48:20 for he is **b** down. Wail and
48:25 is cut off, And his arm is **b**,
48:38 For I have **b** Moab like a
48:39 How she is **b** down! How Moab has
50: 2 Merodach is **b** in pieces; Her
50: 2 Her images are **b** in pieces.'
50:17 king of Babylon has **b** his
50:23 earth has been cut apart and **b**!
51:30 The bars of her gate are **b**.
51:56 Every one of their bows is **b**;
51:58 of Babylon shall be utterly **b**,
52: 7 Then the city wall was **b**
Lam 2: 9 He has destroyed and **b** her
3: 4 And **b** my bones.
3:16 He has also **b** my teeth with
Ezek 6: 4 your incense altars shall be **b**,
6: 6 your idols may be **b** and made to
19:12 Her strong branches were **b** and
26: 2 Aha! She is **b** who was the
27:34 But you are **b** by the seas in
30: 4 And her foundations are **b**
30:21 I have **b** the arm of Pharaoh
30:22 one and the one that was **b**;
31:12 its boughs lie **b** by all the
32:28 you shall be **b** in the midst of
34: 4 were sick, nor bound up the **b**,
34:16 bind up the **b** and strengthen
34:27 when I have **b** the bands of
Dan 8: 8 strong, the large horn was **b**,
8:22 As for the **b** horn and the four
8:25 But he shall be **b** without
11: 4 his kingdom shall be **b** up and
11:22 away from before him and be **b**,
Hos 5:11 Ephraim is oppressed and **b** in
8: 6 the calf of Samaria shall be **b**
Joel 1:17 Barns are **b** down, For the
Am 4: 3 You will go out through **b**
Jon 1: 4 the ship was about to be **b** up.
Zech 11:11 So it was **b** on that day.
11:16 nor heal those that are **b**,
Mt 21:44 falls on this stone will be **b**;
24:43 not allowed his house to be **b**
Mk 2: 4 So when they had **b** through,
5: 4 and the shackles **b** in pieces;
Lk 12:39 not allowed his house to be **b**
20:18 falls on that stone will be **b**;
Jn 7:23 law of Moses should not be **b**,
10:35 (and the Scripture cannot be **b**)
19:31 that their legs might be **b**,
19:36 of His bones shall be **b**.
21:11 were so many, the net was not **b**.
Acts 13:43 when the congregation had **b** up,
20:11 had **b** bread and eaten, and
27:35 and when he had **b** it he began
27:41 but the stern was being **b** up by
Rom 11:17 if some of the branches were **b**
11:19 Branches were **b** off that I might
11:20 of unbelief they were **b** off,
1 Cor 11:24 this is My body which is **b** for
Eph 2:14 and has **b** down the middle wall

BROKENHEARTED (3/3) BROKEN, HEART

Ps 147: 3 He heals the **b** And binds up
Isa 61: 1 He has sent Me to heal the **b**,
Lk 4:18 sent Me to heal the **b**,

BRONZE (161/138)

Gen 4:22 of every craftsman in **b** and
Ex 25: 3 from them: gold, silver, and **b**;
26:11 shall make fifty **b** clasps,
26:37 shall cast five sockets of **b**
27: 2 And you shall overlay it with **b**.
27: 3 make all its utensils of **b**.
27: 4 a grate for it, a network of **b**;
27: 4 you shall make four **b** rings
27: 6 wood, and overlay them with **b**.
27:10 twenty sockets shall be **b**.
27:11 and their twenty sockets of **b**,
27:17 silver and their sockets of **b**.
27:18 linen, and its sockets of **b**.
27:19 of the court, shall be of **b**.
30:18 shall also make a laver of **b**,
30:18 bronze, with its base also of **b**,
31: 4 work in gold, in silver, in **b**,
35: 5 the LORD: gold, silver, and **b**;
35:16 of burnt offering with its **b**
35:24 an offering of silver or **b**
35:32 work in gold and silver and **b**,
36:18 He also made fifty **b** clasps to
36:38 but their five sockets were **b**.
38: 2 And he overlaid it with **b**.
38: 3 all its utensils he made of **b**.
38: 4 And he made a grate of **b** network
38: 5 four corners of the **b** grating,
38: 6 wood, and overlaid them with **b**.
38: 8 He made the laver of **b** and its
38: 8 of bronze and its base of **b**,
38: 8 from the **b** mirrors of the
38:10 with twenty **b** sockets.
38:11 and their twenty **b** sockets.
38:17 sockets for the pillars were **b**,
38:19 with their four sockets of **b**;
38:20 the court all around, were **b**.
38:29 The offering of **b** was seventy
38:30 the **b** altar, the bronze grating
38:30 the **b** grating for it, and all
39:39 the **b** altar, its grate of
39:39 bronze altar, its grate of **b**,
Lev 6:28 And if it is boiled in a **b** pot,
26:19 like iron and your earth like **b**.
Num 16:39 the priest took the **b** censers,
21: 9 So Moses made a **b** serpent, and
21: 9 he looked at the **b** serpent,
31:22 the gold, the silver, the **b**,
Deut 28:23 are over your head shall be **b**,
33:25 sandals shall be iron and **b**;
Josh 6:19 and vessels of **b** and iron, are
6:24 and the vessels of **b** and iron,
22: 8 with silver, with gold, with **b**,
Judg 16:21 They bound him with **b** fetters,
1 Sam 17: 5 He had a **b** helmet on his head,
17: 5 was five thousand shekels of **b**.
17: 6 And he had **b** armor on his legs
17: 6 on his legs and a **b** javelin
17:38 and he put a **b** helmet on his
2 Sam 8: 8 David took a large amount of **b**.
8:10 of gold, and articles of **b**.
21:16 the weight of whose **b** spear
22:35 my arms can bend a bow of **b**.
1 Ki 4:13 with walls and **b** gate-bars;
7:14 a **b** worker; he was filled with
7:14 in working with all kinds of **b**
7:15 And he cast two pillars of **b**,
7:16 he made two capitals of cast **b**,
7:23 And he made the Sea of cast **b**,
7:27 He also made ten carts of **b**;
7:30 Every cart had four **b** wheels and
7:30 bronze wheels and axles of **b**,
7:30 laver were supports of cast **b**
7:33 their hubs were all of cast **b**.
7:38 Then he made ten lavers of **b**;
7:45 the LORD were of burnished **b**.
7:47 the weight of the **b** was not
8:64 because the **b** altar that was
14:27 Then King Rehoboam made **b**
2 Ki 16:14 He also brought the **b** altar
16:15 And the **b** altar shall be for me
16:17 down the Sea from the **b** oxen
18: 4 broke in pieces the **b** serpent
25: 7 bound him with **b** fetters, and
25:13 The **b** pillars that were in the
25:13 and the carts and the **b** Sea
25:13 and carried their **b** to Babylon.
25:14 and all the **b** utensils with
25:16 the **b** of all these articles was
25:17 and the capital on it was of **b**.
25:17 the capital were all of **b**.
1 Chr 15:19 were to sound the cymbals of **b**;
18: 8 brought a large amount of **b**,
18: 8 with which Solomon made the **b**
18: 8 pillars, and the articles of **b**.
18:10 articles of gold, silver, and **b**.
22: 3 and **b** in abundance beyond
22:14 and **b** and iron beyond measure,
22:16 Of gold and silver and **b** and
29: 2 **b** for things of bronze, iron
29: 2 bronze for things of **b**,
29: 7 eighteen thousand talents of **b**,
2 Chr 1: 5 Now the **b** altar that Bezalel the
1: 6 went up there to the **b** altar
2: 7 in **b** and iron, in purple and
2:14 **b** and iron, stone and wood,
4: 1 Moreover he made a **b** altar:
4: 2 he made the Sea of cast **b**,
4: 9 he overlaid these doors with **b**.
4:16 craftsman made of burnished **b**
4:18 that the weight of the **b** was
6:13 (for Solomon had made a **b**
7: 7 because the **b** altar which
12:10 Rehoboam made **b** shields
24:12 those who worked in iron and **b**
33:11 bound him with **b** fetters, and
36: 6 and bound him in **b** fetters to
Ezra 8:27 two vessels of fine polished **b**,
Job 6:12 of stones? Or is my flesh **b**?
20:24 A **b** bow will pierce him
40:18 bones are like beams of **b**,
41:27 And **b** as rotten wood.
Ps 18:34 my arms can bend a bow of **b**.
107:16 He has broken the gates of **b**,
Isa 45: 2 break in pieces the gates of **b**
48: 4 an iron sinew, And your brow **b**,
60:17 Instead of **b** I will bring gold,
60:17 silver, Instead of wood, **b**,
Jer 1:18 And **b** walls against the whole
6:28 They are **b** and iron, They
15:12 The northern iron and the **b**?
15:20 people a fortified **b** wall;
39: 7 and bound him with **b** fetters to
52:11 king of Babylon bound him in **b**
52:17 The **b** pillars that were in the
52:17 and the carts and the **b** Sea
52:17 and carried all their **b** to
52:18 and all the **b** utensils with
52:20 the twelve **b** bulls which were
52:20 the **b** of all these articles was
52:22 A capital of **b** was on it; and
52:22 around the capital, all of **b**.
Ezek 1: 7 like the color of burnished **b**.
9: 2 and stood beside the **b** altar.
22:18 dross to Me; they are all **b**,
22:20 'As men gather silver, **b**,
24:11 it may become hot and its **b**
27:13 human lives and vessels of **b**
40: 3 was like the appearance of **b**.
Dan 2:32 its belly and thighs of **b**,
2:35 the iron, the clay, the **b**,
2:39 another, a third kingdom of **b**,
2:45 broke in pieces the iron, the **b**,
4:15 with a band of iron and **b**,
4:23 with a band of iron and **b** in
5: 4 **b** and iron, wood and stone.
5:23 **b** and iron, wood and stone,
7:19 of iron and its nails of **b**,
10: 6 arms and feet like burnished **b**
Mic 4:13 And I will make your hooves **b**;
Zech 6: 1 mountains were mountains of **b**.
Rev 18:12 object of most precious wood, **b**,

BROOD (8/8) BROODS

Num 32:14 a **b** of sinful men, to increase
Isa 1: 4 A **b** of evildoers, Children
14:20 The **b** of evildoers shall never
Mt 3: 7 **B** of vipers! Who warned you to
12:34 **B** of vipers! How can you, being
23:33 **b** of vipers! How can you escape
Lk 3: 7 **B** of vipers! Who warned you to
13:34 as a hen gathers her **b** under

BROODS (1/1) BROOD

Jer 17:11 As a partridge that **b** but does

BROOK (50/47) BROOKS

Gen 32:23 took them, sent them over the **b**,
Lev 23:40 trees, and willows of the **b**;
Num 34: 5 shall turn from Azmon to the **B**
Deut 9:21 and I threw its dust into the **b**
Josh 11: 8 to the **B** Misrephoth, and to the
13: 6 from Lebanon as far as the **B**
15: 4 Azmon and went out to the **B** of
15:47 as far as the **B** of Egypt and the
16: 8 from Tappuah westward to the **B**
17: 9 the border descended to the **B**
17: 9 Brook Kanah, southward to the **b**.
17: 9 was on the north side of the **b**;
19:11 and extended along the **b** that
19:26 along the **B** Shihor Libnath.
1 Sam 17:40 five smooth stones from the **b**,
30: 9 and came to the **B** Besor, where
30:10 that they could not cross the **B**
30:21 also had made to stay at the **B**
2 Sam 15:23 also crossed over the **B** Kidron,
17:20 have gone over the water **b**.
1 Ki 2:37 day you go out and cross the **B**
8:65 entrance of Hamath to the **B** of
15:13 image and burned it by the **B**
17: 3 and hide by the **B** Cherith,
17: 4 you shall drink from the **b**,
17: 5 for he went and stayed by the **B**
17: 6 and he drank from the **b**.
17: 7 after a while that the **b** dried
18:40 brought them down to the **B**
2 Ki 23: 6 to the **B** Kidron outside
23: 6 burned it at the **B** Kidron and
23:12 and threw their dust into the **B**
24: 7 to the king of Egypt from the **B**
2 Chr 7: 8 entrance of Hamath to the **B** of
15:16 and burned it by the **B** Kidron.
20:16 find them at the end of the **b**
29:16 out and carried it to the **B**
30:14 and cast them into the **B**
32: 4 all the springs and the **b** that
Job 6:15 have dealt deceitfully like a **b**,
40:22 The willows by the **b** surround
Ps 83: 9 As with Jabin at the **B**
110: 7 He shall drink of the **b** by the
Prov 18: 4 of wisdom is a flowing **b**.
Isa 15: 7 They will carry away to the **B**
27:12 channel of the River to the **B**
Jer 31:40 all the fields as far as the **B**
Ezek 47:19 along the **b** to the Great Sea.
48:28 along the **b** to the Great Sea.
Jn 18: 1 with His disciples over the **B**

BROOKS (14/14) BROOK

Num 21:14 The **b** of the Arnon,
21:15 And the slope of the **b** That
Deut 8: 7 a land of **b** of water, of
2 Sam 23:30 Hiddai from the **b** of Gaash,
1 Ki 18: 5 of water and to all the **b**;
2 Ki 19:24 I have dried up All the **b** of
1 Chr 11:32 Hurai of the **b** of Gaash, Abiel
Job 6:15 Like the streams of the **b** that
22:24 Ophir among the stones of the **b**.
Ps 42: 1 the deer pants for the water **b**,
Isa 19: 6 The **b** of defense will be
37:25 I have dried up All the **b** of
Joel 1:20 For the water **b** are dried up,
3:18 And all the **b** of Judah shall

BROOM (5/5)

1 Ki 19: 4 and came and sat down under a **b**
19: 5 as he lay and slept under a **b**
Job 30: 4 And **b** tree roots for their
Ps 120: 4 With coals of the **b** tree!
Isa 14:23 I will sweep it with the **b** of

BROTH (3/3)

Judg 6:19 and he put the **b** in a pot; and
6:20 this rock, and pour out the **b**.
Isa 65: 4 And the **b** of abominable things

BROTHER (357/322) BRETHREN, BROTHERHOOD, BROTHERLY, BROTHER'S, BROTHERS

Gen 4: 2 this time his **b** Abel. Now Abel
4: 8 Now Cain talked with Abel his **b**;
4: 8 rose up against Abel his **b** and
4: 9 Cain, "Where is Abel your **b**?
9: 5 From the hand of every man's **b**
10:21 the **b** of Japheth the elder.
14:13 **b** of Eshcol and brother of
14:13 brother of Eshcol and **b** of
14:14 Now when Abram heard that his **b**
14:16 and also brought back his **b** Lot
20: 5 she herself said, 'He is my **b**.
20:13 we go, say of me, "He is my **b**.
20:16 I have given your **b** a thousand
22:20 has borne children to your **b**
22:21 "Huz his firstborn, Buz his **b**,
22:23 bore to Nahor, Abraham's **b**.
24:15 the wife of Nahor, Abraham's **b**,
24:29 Now Rebekah had a **b** whose name
24:48 the daughter of my master's **b**
24:53 gave precious things to her **b**
24:55 But her **b** and her mother said,
25:26 Afterward his **b** came out, and
27: 6 father speak to Esau your **b**,
27:11 Esau my **b** is a hairy man, and
27:23 his hands were hairy like his **b**
27:30 that Esau his **b** came in from
27:35 Your **b** came with deceit and has
27:40 And you shall serve your **b**;
27:41 then I will kill my **b** Jacob."
27:42 Surely your **b** Esau comforts
27:43 flee to my **b** Laban in Haran.
28: 2 of Laban your mother's **b**.
28: 5 the **b** of Rebekah, the mother of
29:10 of Laban his mother's **b**,
29:10 sheep of Laban his mother's **b**,
29:10 flock of Laban his mother's **b**.
32: 3 before him to Esau his **b** in
32: 6 We came to your **b** Esau, and he
32:11 I pray, from the hand of my **b**,
32:13 as a present for Esau his **b**:
32:17 When Esau my **b** meets you and
33: 3 until he came near to his **b**.
33: 9 said, "I have enough, my **b**;
35: 1 from the face of Esau your **b**.
35: 7 he fled from the face of his **b**.
36: 6 away from the presence of his **b**
37:26 is there if we kill our **b**
37:27 for he is our **b** and our
38: 8 and raise up an heir to your **b**.
38: 9 he should give an heir to his **b**.
38:29 that his **b** came out
38:30 Afterward his **b** came out who had
42: 4 Jacob did not send Joseph's **b**
42:15 place unless your youngest **b**
42:16 you, and let him bring your **b**;
42:20 And bring your youngest **b** to me;
42:21 truly guilty concerning our **b**,
42:34 And bring your youngest **b** to me;
42:34 I will grant your **b** to you, and
42:38 for his **b** is dead, and he is
43: 3 not see my face unless your **b**
43: 4 If you send our **b** with us, we
43: 5 not see my face unless your **b**
43: 6 you had still another **b**?
43: 7 Have you another **b**?'
43: 7 Bring your **b** down'?"
43:13 Take your **b** also, and arise, go
43:14 he may release your other **b**
43:29 lifted his eyes and saw his **b**
43:29 Is this your younger **b** of whom
43:30 Now his heart yearned for his **b**;
44:19 'Have you a father or a **b**?
44:20 his **b** is dead, and he alone is
44:23 Unless your youngest **b** comes
44:26 if our youngest **b** is with us,
44:26 face unless our youngest **b** is
45: 4 he said: "I am Joseph your **b**,
45:12 your eyes and the eyes of my **b**
45:14 Then he fell on his **b** Benjamin's
48:19 but truly his younger **b** shall
Ex 4:14 not Aaron the Levite your **b**?
7: 1 and Aaron your **b** shall be your
7: 2 And Aaron your **b** shall speak to
28: 1 "Now take Aaron your **b**,
28: 2 holy garments for Aaron your **b**,
28: 4 holy garments for Aaron your **b**
28:41 shall put them on Aaron your **b**
32:27 and let every man kill his **b**,
32:29 has opposed his son and his **b**.
Lev 16: 2 Tell Aaron your **b** not to come at
18:14 nakedness of your father's **b**.
19:17 You shall not hate your **b** in
21: 2 son, his daughter, and his **b**;
25:25 then he may redeem what his **b**
25:36 that your **b** may live with you.
Num 6: 7 for his **b** or his sister, when
20: 8 you and your **b** Aaron gather the
20:14 Thus says your **b** Israel: 'You
27:13 as Aaron your **b** was gathered.
36: 2 give the inheritance of our **b**
Deut 1:16 between a man and his **b** or the
13: 6 If your **b**, the son of your
15: 2 it of his neighbor or his **b**,
15: 3 claim to what is owed by your **b**,
15: 7 shut your hand from your poor **b**,
15: 9 eye be evil against your poor **b**
15:11 open your hand wide to your **b**,
15:12 If your **b**, a Hebrew man,
17:15 over you, who is not your **b**.
19:18 testified falsely against his **b**,
19:19 thought to have done to his **b**;
22: 1 bring them back to your **b**.
22: 2 And if your **b** is not near you,
22: 2 remain with you until your **b**
23: 7 an Edomite, for he is your **b**.
23:19 not charge interest to your **b**—
23:20 but to your **b** you shall not
24:10 When you lend your **b** anything,
25: 3 and your **b** be humiliated in
25: 5 her husband's **b** shall go in to
25: 5 the duty of a husband's **b** to
25: 6 to the name of his dead **b**,
25: 7 My husband's **b** refuses to raise
25: 7 to raise up a name to his **b** in
25: 7 the duty of my husband's **b**.
28:54 will be hostile toward his **b**,
32:50 just as Aaron your **b** died on
Josh 15:17 the **b** of Caleb, took it; and he
Judg 1: 3 So Judah said to Simeon his **b**,
1:13 son of Kenaz, Caleb's younger **b**,
1:17 And Judah went with his **b**
3: 9 son of Kenaz, Caleb's younger **b**.
9: 3 for they said, "He is our **b**.
9:18 Shechem, because he is your **b**—
9:21 for fear of Abimelech his **b**.
9:24 be laid on Abimelech their **b**,
20:23 against the children of my **b**
20:28 against the children of my **b**
21: 6 grieved for Benjamin their **b**,
Ruth 4: 3 land which belonged to our **b**
1 Sam 14: 3 the son of Ahitub, Ichabod's **b**,
17:28 Now Eliab his oldest **b** heard
20:29 and my **b** has commanded me to
26: 6 **b** of Joab, saying, "Who will
2 Sam 1:26 my **b** Jonathan; You have been
2:22 How then could I face your **b**
3:27 for the blood of Asahel his **b**.
3:30 So Joab and Abishai his **b** killed
3:30 because he had killed their **b**
4: 6 Then Rechab and Baanah his **b**
4: 9 Rechab and Baanah his **b**,
10:10 the command of Abishai his **b**,
13: 3 the son of Shimeah, David's **b**.
13: 4 my **b** Absalom's sister."
13: 7 Now go to your **b** Amnon's house,
13: 8 So Tamar went to her **b** Amnon's
13:10 brought them to Amnon her **b**
13:12 she answered him, "No, my **b**,
13:20 And Absalom her **b** said to her,
13:20 Has Amnon your **b** been with you?
13:20 peace, my sister. He is your **b**;
13:20 remained desolate in her **b**
13:22 And Absalom spoke to his **b** Amnon
13:26 please let my **b** Amnon go with
13:32 the son of Shimeah, David's **b**,
14: 7 'Deliver him who struck his **b**,
14: 7 him for the life of his **b** whom
18: 2 the son of Zeruiah, Joab's **b**,
20: 9 "Are you in health, my **b**?
20:10 Then Joab and Abishai his **b**
21:19 the Bethlehemite killed the **b**
21:21 the son of Shimea, David's **b**,
23:18 Now Abishai the **b** of Joab, the
23:24 Asahel the **b** of Joab was one
1 Ki 1:10 mighty men, or Solomon his **b**.
2: 7 when I fled from Absalom your **b**.
2:21 be given to Adonijah your **b** as
2:22 also—for he is my older **b**—
9:13 which you have given me, my **b**?
13:30 saying, "Alas, my **b**!"
20:32 he still alive? He is my **b**.
20:33 Your **b** Ben-Hadad." So he said,
1 Chr 2:32 the **b** of Shammai, were Jether
2:42 descendants of Caleb the **b** of
4:11 Chelub the **b** of Shuhah begot
6:39 And his **b** Asaph, who stood at
7:16 The name of his **b** was Sheresh,
7:35 And the sons of his **b** Helem
8:39 And the sons of Eshek his **b**
11:20 Abishai the **b** of Joab was chief
11:26 warriors were Asahel the **b** of
11:38 Joel the **b** of Nathan, Mibhar the
11:45 son of Shimri, and Joha his **b**,
19:11 the command of Abishai his **b**,
19:15 also fled before Abishai his **b**,
20: 5 son of Jair killed Lahmi the **b**
20: 7 the son of Shimea, David's **b**,
24:25 The **b** of Michah, Isshiah; of the
26:22 Jehieli, Zetham and Joel his **b**,
27: 7 fourth month was Asahel the **b**
2 Chr 31:12 and Shimei his **b** was the next.
31:13 of Cononiah and Shimei his **b**,
36: 4 of Egypt made Jehoahaz's **b**
36: 4 And Necho took Jehoahaz his **b**
36:10 made Zedekiah, Jehoiakim's **b**,
Neh 5: 7 is exacting usury from his **b**.
7: 2 the charge of Jerusalem to my **b**
Job 22: 6 have taken pledges from your **b**
30:29 I am a **b** of jackals, And a
Ps 35:14 he were my friend or **b**;
49: 7 can by any means redeem his **b**,
50:20 sit and speak against your **b**;
Prov 17:17 And a **b** is born for adversity.
18: 9 is slothful in his work Is a **b**
18:19 A **b** offended is harder to
18:24 who sticks closer than a **b**.
27:10 is a neighbor nearby than a **b**
Eccl 4: 8 He has neither son nor **b**.
Song 8: 1 Oh, that you were like my **b**,
Isa 3: 6 a man takes hold of his **b** In
9:19 fire; No man shall spare his **b**.
19: 2 will fight against his **b**,
41: 6 neighbor, And said to his **b**,
Jer 9: 4 And do not trust any **b**;
9: 4 For every **b** will utterly
22:18 my **b**!' or 'Alas, my sister!'
23:35 and every one to his **b**,
31:34 neighbor, and every man his **b**,
34: 9 no one should keep a Jewish **b**
34:14 every man set free his Hebrew **b**,
34:17 every one to his **b** and every
Ezek 18:18 Robbed his **b** by violence, And
33:30 everyone saying to his **b**,
38:21 sword will be against his **b**.
44:25 for **b** or unmarried sister may
Hos 12: 3 He took his **b** by the heel in
Am 1:11 Because he pursued his **b** with
Ob 10 For violence against your **b**
12 gazed on the day of your **b** In
Mic 7: 2 Every man hunts his **b** with a
Hag 2:22 one by the sword of his **b**.
Zech 7: 9 compassion Everyone to his **b**.
7:10 in his heart Against his **b**
Mal 1: 2 Was not Esau Jacob's **b**?"
Mt 4:18 called Peter, and Andrew his **b**,
4:21 son of Zebedee, and John his **b**,
5:22 whoever is angry with his **b**
5:22 And whoever says to his **b**,
5:23 and there remember that your **b**
5:24 First be reconciled to your **b**,
7: 4 "Or how can you say to your **b**,
10: 2 called Peter, and Andrew his **b**;
10: 2 son of Zebedee, and John his **b**;
10:21 Now **b** will deliver up brother to
10:21 Now brother will deliver up **b** to
12:50 of My Father in heaven is My **b**
14: 3 his **b** Philip's wife.
17: 1 Peter, James, and John his **b**,
18:15 Moreover if your **b** sins against
18:15 you, you have gained your **b**.
18:21 how often shall my **b** sin
18:35 does not forgive his **b** his
22:24 his **b** shall marry his wife and
22:24 raise up offspring for his **b**.
22:25 left his wife to his **b**.
Mk 1:16 He saw Simon and Andrew his **b**
1:19 son of Zebedee, and John his **b**,
3:17 son of Zebedee and John the **b**
3:35 does the will of God is My **b**
5:37 and John the **b** of James.
6: 3 and **b** of James, Joses, Judas,
6:17 his **b** Philip's wife; for he had
12:19 wrote to us that if a man's **b**
12:19 his **b** should take his wife and
12:19 raise up offspring for his **b**.
13:12 Now **b** will betray brother to
13:12 Now brother will betray **b** to
Lk 3: 1 his **b** Philip tetrarch of Iturea
3:19 his **b** Philip's wife, and for
6:14 named Peter, and Andrew his **b**;
6:42 "Or how can you say to your **b**,
6:42 can you say to your brother, '**B**,
12:13 'Teacher, tell my **b** to divide
15:27 Your **b** has come, and because he
15:32 for your **b** was dead and is
17: 3 If your **b** sins against you,
20:28 wrote to us that if a man's **b**
20:28 his **b** should take his wife and
20:28 raise up offspring for his **b**.
Jn 1:40 was Andrew, Simon Peter's **b**.
1:41 He first found his own **b** Simon,
6: 8 Andrew, Simon Peter's **b**,
11: 2 whose **b** Lazarus was sick.
11:19 comfort them concerning their **b**.
11:21 my **b** would not have died.
11:23 Your **b** will rise again."
11:32 my **b** would not have died."
Acts 9:17 **B** Saul, the Lord Jesus, who
12: 2 Then he killed James the **b** of
21:20 they said to him, "You see, **b**,
22:13 '**B** Saul, receive your sight.'
Rom 14:10 But why do you judge your **b**?
14:10 do you show contempt for your **b**?
14:15 Yet if your **b** is grieved because
14:21 do anything by which your **b**
16:23 greets you, and Quartus, a **b**.
1 Cor 1: 1 of God, and Sosthenes our **b**,
5:11 company with anyone named a **b**,
6: 6 But **b** goes to law against
6: 6 brother goes to law against **b**,
7:12 If any **b** has a wife who does
7:15 a **b** or a sister is not under
8:11 your knowledge shall the weak **b**
8:13 if food makes my **b** stumble, I
8:13 lest I make my **b** stumble.
16:12 Now concerning our **b** Apollos, I
2 Cor 1: 1 will of God, and Timothy our **b**,
2:13 I did not find Titus my **b**;
8:18 And we have sent with him the **b**
8:22 we have sent with them our **b**
12:18 and sent our **b** with him.
Gal 1:19 except James, the Lord's **b**.
Eph 6:21 a beloved **b** and faithful
Phil 2:25 send to you Epaphroditus, my **b**,
Col 1: 1 will of God, and Timothy our **b**,
4: 7 Tychicus, a beloved **b**,
4: 9 a faithful and beloved **b**,
1 Th 3: 2 our **b** and minister of God, and
4: 6 advantage of and defraud his **b**
2 Th 3: 6 that you withdraw from every **b**
3:15 enemy, but admonish him as a **b**.

Phm 1: 1 Jesus, and Timothy our ***b***,
1: 7 have been refreshed by you, ***b***.
1:16 more than a slave—a beloved ***b***,
1:20 Yes, ***b***, let me have joy from you
Heb 8:11 neighbor, and none his ***b***,
13:23 Know that our ***b*** Timothy has
Jas 1: 9 Let the lowly ***b*** glory in his
2:15 If a ***b*** or sister is naked and
4:11 He who speaks evil of a ***b*** and
4:11 of a brother and judges his ***b***,
1 Pe 5:12 our faithful ***b*** as I consider
2 Pe 3:15 as also our beloved ***b*** Paul,
1 Jn 2: 9 in the light, and hates his ***b***,
2:10 He who loves his ***b*** abides in the
2:11 But he who hates his ***b*** is in
3:10 is he who does not love his ***b***.
3:12 wicked one and murdered his ***b***.
3:14 He who does not love his ***b***
3:15 Whoever hates his ***b*** is a
3:17 and sees his ***b*** in need, and
4:20 "I love God," and hates his ***b***,
4:20 for he who does not love his ***b***
4:21 who loves God must love his ***b***
5:16 If anyone sees his ***b*** sinning a
Jude 1 and ***b*** of James, To those who
Rev 1: 9 both your ***b*** and companion in

BROTHER'S (34/30) BROTHER

Gen 4: 9 Am I my ***b*** keeper?"
4:10 The voice of your ***b*** blood cries
4:11 to receive your ***b*** blood
4:21 His ***b*** name was Jubal. He was
10:25 and his ***b*** name was Joktan.
12: 5 his wife and Lot his ***b*** son,
14:12 Abram's ***b*** son who dwelt in
27:44 until your ***b*** fury turns away,
27:45 until your ***b*** anger turns away
38: 8 Go in to your ***b*** wife and marry
38: 9 when he went in to his ***b*** wife,
Lev 18:16 the nakedness of your ***b*** wife;
18:16 it is your ***b*** nakedness.
20:21 If a man takes his ***b*** wife, it
20:21 has uncovered his ***b*** nakedness.
Deut 22: 1 You shall not see your ***b*** ox or
22: 3 with any lost thing of your ***b***,
22: 4 You shall not see your ***b*** donkey
25: 7 does not want to take his ***b*** wife,
25: 7 then let his ***b*** wife go up to
25: 9 then his ***b*** wife shall come to
25: 9 will not build up his ***b*** house.
1 Ki 2:15 over, and has become my ***b***;
1 Chr 1:19 and his ***b*** name was Joktan.
Job 1:13 wine in their oldest ***b*** house;
1:18 wine in their oldest ***b*** house,
Prov 27:10 Nor go to your ***b*** house in the
Mt 7: 3 look at the speck in your ***b*** eye,
7: 5 to remove the speck from your ***b***
Mk 6:18 for you to have your ***b*** wife.
Lk 6:41 at the speck in your ***b*** eye,
6:42 the speck that is in your ***b***
Rom 14:13 cause to fall in our ***b*** way.
1 Jn 3:12 evil and his ***b*** righteousness.

BROTHERHOOD (4/4) BROTHER

Am 1: 9 not remember the covenant of ***b***.
Zech 11:14 that I might break the ***b***
1 Pe 2:17 Honor all people. Love the ***b***.
5: 9 are experienced by your ***b*** in

BROTHERLY (5/4) BROTHER

Rom 12:10 to one another with ***b*** love,
1 Th 4: 9 But concerning ***b*** love you have
Heb 13: 1 Let ***b*** love continue.
2 Pe 1: 7 to godliness ***b*** kindness, and to
1: 7 and to ***b*** kindness love.

BROTHERS (173/164) BROTHER

Gen 9:22 and told his two ***b*** outside.
34:11 said to her father and her ***b***,
34:25 Simeon and Levi, Dinah's ***b***,
37: 2 feeding the flock with his ***b***.
37: 4 But when his ***b*** saw that their
37: 4 loved him more than all his ***b***,
37: 5 dream, and he told it to his ***b***;
37: 8 And his ***b*** said to him, "Shall
37: 9 dream and told it to his ***b***,
37:10 it to his father and his ***b***;
37:10 your mother and I and your ***b***
37:11 And his ***b*** envied him, but his
37:12 Then his ***b*** went to feed their
37:13 Are not your ***b*** feeding the
37:14 see if it is well with your ***b***
37:16 So he said, "I am seeking my ***b***.
37:17 ' So Joseph went after his ***b***
37:23 when Joseph had come to his ***b***,
37:26 So Judah said to his ***b***,
37:27 And his ***b*** listened.
37:28 so the ***b*** pulled Joseph up and
37:30 And he returned to his ***b*** and
38: 1 that Judah departed from his ***b***,
38:11 "Lest he also die like his ***b***.
42: 3 So Joseph's ten ***b*** went down to
42: 4 brother Benjamin with his ***b***,
42: 6 And Joseph's ***b*** came and bowed
42: 7 Joseph saw his ***b*** and recognized
42: 8 So Joseph recognized his ***b***,
42:13 "Your servants are twelve ***b***,
42:19 let one of your ***b*** be confined
42:28 So he said to his ***b***, "My money
42:32 'We are twelve ***b***, sons of our
42:33 Leave one of your ***b*** here with
44:14 So Judah and his ***b*** came to
44:33 let the lad go up with his ***b***.
45: 1 made himself known to his ***b***.
45: 3 Then Joseph said to his ***b***,
45: 3 But his ***b*** could not answer
45: 4 And Joseph said to his ***b***,
45:15 Moreover he kissed all his ***b*** and
45:15 and after that his ***b*** talked
45:16 Joseph's ***b*** have come." So it
45:17 said to Joseph, "Say to your ***b***,
45:24 So he sent his ***b*** away, and they
46:31 Then Joseph said to his ***b*** and to
46:31 My ***b*** and those of my father's
47: 1 and said, "My father and my ***b***,
47: 2 took five men from among his ***b***
47: 3 Then Pharaoh said to his ***b***,
47: 5 Your father and your ***b*** have come
47: 6 Have your father and ***b*** dwell in
47:11 situated his father and his ***b***,
47:12 provided his father, his ***b***,
48: 6 called by the name of their ***b***
48:22 to you one portion above your ***b***,
49: 5 "Simeon and Levi are ***b***;
49: 8 you are he whom your ***b*** shall
49:26 him who was separate from his ***b***.
50: 8 all the house of Joseph, his ***b***,
50:14 he and his ***b*** and all who went
50:15 When Joseph's ***b*** saw that their
50:17 forgive the trespass of your ***b***
50:18 Then his ***b*** also went and fell
Ex 1: 6 And Joseph died, all his ***b***,
Lev 25:48 One of his ***b*** may redeem him;
Num 27: 4 possession among our father's ***b***.
27: 7 among their father's ***b***,
27: 9 give his inheritance to his ***b***.
27:10 'If he has no ***b***, then you shall
27:10 inheritance to his father's ***b***.
27:11 'And if his father has no ***b***,
36:11 to the sons of their father's ***b***.
Deut 25: 5 If ***b*** dwell together, and one of
33: 9 Nor did he acknowledge his ***b***,
33:16 who was separate from his ***b***.
33:24 Let him be favored by his ***b***,
Josh 2:13 my father, my mother, my ***b***,
2:18 father, your mother, your ***b***,
6:23 her father, her mother, her ***b***,
17: 4 us an inheritance among our ***b***.
17: 4 among their father's ***b***.
Judg 8:19 Then he said, "They were my ***b***,
9: 1 to Shechem, to his mother's ***b***,
9: 3 And his mother's ***b*** spoke all
9: 5 at Ophrah and killed his ***b***,
9:24 him in the killing of his ***b***.
9:26 the son of Ebed came with his ***b***
9:31 Gaal the son of Ebed and his ***b***
9:41 Zebul drove out Gaal and his ***b***,
9:56 father by killing his seventy ***b***.
11: 3 Then Jephthah fled from his ***b***
16:31 And his ***b*** and all his father's
21:22 when their fathers or their ***b***
1 Sam 16:13 him in the midst of his ***b***;
17:17 Take now for your ***b*** an ephah of
17:17 and run to your ***b*** at the camp.
17:18 and see how your ***b*** fare, and
17:22 and came and greeted his ***b***.
20:29 let me get away and see my ***b***.
22: 1 And when his ***b*** and all his
2 Sam 3: 8 of Saul your father, to his ***b***,
1 Ki 1: 9 he also invited all his ***b***,
2 Ki 10:13 Jehu met with the ***b*** of Ahaziah
10:13 We are the ***b*** of Ahaziah; we
1 Chr 4: 9 was more honorable than his ***b***,
4:27 but his ***b*** did not have many
5: 2 yet Judah prevailed over his ***b***,
16:37 So he left Asaph and his ***b***
24:31 also cast lots just as their ***b***
26: 7 whose ***b*** Elihu and Semachiah
27:18 Judah, Elihu, one of David's ***b***;
2 Chr 11:22 to be leader among his ***b***;
21: 2 He had ***b***, the sons of
21: 4 himself and killed all his ***b***
21:13 and also have killed your ***b***,
22: 8 and the sons of Ahaziah's ***b***
35: 9 his ***b*** Shemaiah and Nethanel,
Ezra 3: 9 Jeshua with his sons and ***b***,
8:18 Sherebiah, with his sons and ***b***,
8:19 his ***b*** and their sons, twenty
10:18 the son of Jozadak, and his ***b***:
Neh 5:14 neither I nor my ***b*** ate the
12:24 with their ***b*** across from them,
Job 6:15 My ***b*** have dealt deceitfully
19:13 He has removed my ***b*** far from
42:11 Then all his ***b***, all his sisters,
42:15 an inheritance among their ***b***.
Ps 69: 8 have become a stranger to my ***b***,
Prov 17: 2 an inheritance among the ***b***.
19: 7 All the ***b*** of the poor hate him;
Jer 12: 6 For even your ***b***, the house of
35: 3 his ***b*** and all his sons, and the
Mt 1: 2 and Jacob begot Judah and his ***b***.
1:11 begot Jeconiah and his ***b*** about
4:18 the Sea of Galilee, saw two ***b***,
4:21 from there, He saw two other ***b***,
12:46 His mother and ***b*** stood outside,
12:47 Your mother and Your ***b*** are
12:48 is My mother and who are My ***b***?
12:49 Here are My mother and My ***b***!
13:55 And His ***b*** James, Joses, Simon,
19:29 who has left houses or ***b*** or
20:24 displeased with the two ***b***.
22:25 there were with us seven ***b***.
Mk 3:31 Then His ***b*** and His mother came,
3:32 Your mother and Your ***b*** are
3:33 "Who is My mother, or My ***b***?
3:34 Here are My mother and My ***b***!
10:29 no one who has left house or ***b***
10:30 houses and ***b*** and sisters and
12:20 "Now there were seven ***b***.
Lk 8:19 Then His mother and ***b*** came to
8:20 Your mother and Your ***b*** are
8:21 My mother and My ***b*** are these who
14:12 do not ask your friends, your ***b***,
14:26 ***b*** and sisters, yes, and his own
16:28 'for I have five ***b***, that he may
18:29 has left house or parents or ***b***
20:29 "Now there were seven ***b***.
21:16 betrayed even by parents and ***b***,
Jn 2:12 He, His mother, His ***b***,
7: 3 His ***b*** therefore said to Him,
7: 5 For even His ***b*** did not believe
7:10 But when His ***b*** had gone up,
Acts 1:14 mother of Jesus, and with His ***b***.
7:13 Joseph was made known to his ***b***,
28:11 whose figurehead was the Twin ***B***,
1 Cor 9: 5 the ***b*** of the Lord, and Cephas?
1 Tim 5: 1 as a father, younger men as ***b***,
1 Pe 3: 8 for one another; love as ***b***,

BROUGHT (843/802)

Gen 1:12 And the earth ***b*** forth grass, the
2:19 and ***b*** them to Adam to see what
2:22 and He ***b*** her to the man.
4: 3 it came to pass that Cain ***b*** an
4: 4 Abel also ***b*** of the firstborn of
14:16 So he ***b*** back all the goods, and
14:16 and also ***b*** back his brother Lot
14:18 Melchizedek king of Salem ***b***
15: 5 Then He ***b*** him outside and said,
15: 7 who ***b*** you out of Ur of the
15:10 Then he ***b*** all these to Him and
18: 4 let a little water be ***b***,
19:16 and they ***b*** him out and set him
19:17 when they had ***b*** them outside,
20: 9 that you have ***b*** on me and on my
24:53 Then the servant ***b*** out jewelry
24:67 Then Isaac ***b*** her into his mother
26:10 and you would have ***b*** guilt on
27:14 And he went and got them and ***b***
27:20 Because the LORD your God ***b*** it
27:25 So he ***b*** it near to him, and
27:25 and he ***b*** him wine, and he
27:31 and ***b*** it to his father, and
27:33 the one who hunted game and ***b***
29:13 and ***b*** him to his house. So he
29:23 he took Leah his daughter and ***b***
30:14 and ***b*** them to his mother Leah.
30:39 and the flocks ***b*** forth
33:11 take my blessing that is ***b*** to
37: 2 and Joseph ***b*** a bad report of
37:32 and they ***b*** it to their father
38:25 When she was ***b*** out, she sent to
39:14 he has ***b*** in to us a Hebrew to
39:17 The Hebrew servant whom you ***b*** to
40:10 and its clusters ***b*** forth ripe
41:14 and they ***b*** him quickly out of
41:47 plentiful years the ground ***b***
43: 2 up the grain which they had ***b***
43:17 and the man ***b*** the men into
43:18 were afraid because they were ***b***
43:18 that we are ***b*** in, so that he
43:21 so we have ***b*** it back in our
43:22 And we have ***b*** down other money
43:23 Then he ***b*** Simeon out to them.
43:24 So the man ***b*** the men into
43:26 they ***b*** him the present which
44: 8 we ***b*** back to you from the land
46: 7 and all his descendants he ***b***
46:32 and they have ***b*** their flocks,
47: 7 Then Joseph ***b*** in his father
47:14 and Joseph ***b*** the money into
47:17 So they ***b*** their livestock to
48:10 Then Joseph ***b*** them near him,
48:12 So Joseph ***b*** them from beside his
48:13 and ***b*** them near him.
50:23 were also ***b*** up on Joseph's
Ex 2:10 and she ***b*** him to Pharaoh's
3:12 When you have ***b*** the people out
5:22 why have You ***b*** trouble on this
8: 7 and ***b*** up frogs on the land of
8:12 the frogs which He had ***b***
9:19 in the field and is not ***b*** home;
10: 8 So Moses and Aaron were ***b*** again
10:13 and the LORD ***b*** an east wind on
10:13 the east wind ***b*** the locusts.
12:17 on this same day I will have ***b***
12:39 of the dough which they had ***b***
12:51 that the LORD ***b*** the children
13: 3 by strength of hand the LORD ***b***
13: 9 a strong hand the LORD has ***b***
13:14 strength of hand the LORD ***b***
13:16 by strength of hand the LORD ***b***
15:19 and the LORD ***b*** back the waters
15:22 So Moses ***b*** Israel from the Red
15:26 diseases on you which I have ***b***
16: 3 to the full! For you have ***b*** us
16: 6 know that the LORD has ***b*** you
16:32 when I ***b*** you out of the land of
17: 3 Why is it you have ***b*** us up out
18: 1 that the LORD had ***b*** Israel out
18:26 the hard cases they ***b*** to Moses,

19: 4 you on eagles' wings and ***b*** you
19: 8 So Moses ***b*** back the words of
19:17 And Moses ***b*** the people out of
20: 2 who ***b*** you out of the land of
22: 8 master of the house shall be ***b***
29:10 shall also have the bull ***b***
29:46 who ***b*** them up out of the land
32: 1 the man who ***b*** us up out of the
32: 3 and ***b*** them to Aaron.
32: 4 that ***b*** you out of the land of
32: 6 and ***b*** peace offerings; and the
32: 7 For your people whom you ***b*** out
32: 8 that ***b*** you out of the land of
32:11 Your people whom You have ***b***
32:12 He ***b*** them out to harm them, to
32:21 do to you that you have ***b*** so
32:23 the man who ***b*** us out of the
33: 1 and the people whom you have ***b***
35:21 and they ***b*** the LORD's offering
35:22 and ***b*** earrings and nose rings,
35:23 and badger skins, ***b*** them.
35:24 offering of silver or bronze ***b***
35:24 any work of the service, ***b*** it.
35:25 and ***b*** what they had spun, of
35:27 The rulers ***b*** onyx stones, and
35:29 The children of Israel ***b*** a
36: 3 the children of Israel had ***b***
39:33 And they ***b*** the tabernacle to
40:21 And he ***b*** the ark into the
Lev 6:30 which any of the blood is ***b***
8: 6 Then Moses ***b*** Aaron and his sons
8:13 Then Moses ***b*** Aaron's sons and
8:14 And he ***b*** the bull for the sin
8:18 Then he ***b*** the ram as the burnt
8:22 And he ***b*** the second ram, the
8:24 Then he ***b*** Aaron's sons.
9: 5 So they ***b*** what Moses commanded
9: 9 Then the sons of Aaron ***b*** the
9:15 Then he ***b*** the people's
9:16 And he ***b*** the burnt offering and
9:17 Then he ***b*** the grain offering,
10:18 See! Its blood was not ***b*** inside
13: 2 then he shall be ***b*** to Aaron the
13: 9 then he shall be ***b*** to the
14: 2 He shall be ***b*** to the priest.
16:27 whose blood was ***b*** in to make
19:36 who ***b*** you out of the land of
22:33 who ***b*** you out of the land of
23:14 the same day that you have ***b***
23:15 from the day that you ***b*** the
23:43 dwell in booths when I ***b*** them
24:11 and so they ***b*** him to Moses.
25:38 who ***b*** you out of the land of
25:42 whom I ***b*** out of the land of
25:55 they are My servants whom I ***b***
26:13 who ***b*** you out of the land of
26:41 contrary to them and have ***b***
26:45 whom I ***b*** out of the land of
Num 6:13 he shall be ***b*** to the door of
7: 3 And they ***b*** their offering before
11:31 and it ***b*** quail from the sea and
12:15 not journey till Miriam was ***b***
13:23 They also ***b*** some of the
13:26 they ***b*** back word to them and to
14: 3 Why has the LORD ***b*** us to this
14:13 for by Your might You ***b*** these
14:37 those very men who ***b*** the evil
15:33 found him gathering sticks ***b***
15:36 all the congregation ***b*** him
15:41 who ***b*** you out of the land of
16:10 and that He has ***b*** you near to
16:13 a small thing that you have ***b***
16:14 Moreover you have not ***b*** us into
17: 9 Then Moses ***b*** out all the rods
20: 4 Why have you ***b*** up the assembly
20:16 voice and sent the Angel and ***b***
21: 5 Why have you ***b*** us up out of
22:41 that Balak took Balaam and ***b***
23: 7 Balak the king of Moab has ***b*** me
23:14 So he ***b*** him to the field of
27: 5 So Moses ***b*** their case before the
31:12 Then they ***b*** the captives, the
31:50 Therefore we have ***b*** an offering
31:54 and ***b*** it into the tabernacle of
32:17 of Israel until we have ***b*** them
Deut 1:25 the land in their hands and ***b***
1:25 and they ***b*** back word to us,
1:27 He has ***b*** us out of the land of
4:20 the LORD has taken you and ***b***
4:37 and He ***b*** you out of Egypt with
5: 6 am the LORD your God who ***b***
5:15 and the LORD your God ***b*** you
6:12 you forget the LORD who ***b*** you
6:21 and the LORD ***b*** us out of Egypt
6:23 Then He ***b*** us out from there,
7: 8 the LORD has ***b*** you out with a
7:19 by which the LORD your God ***b***
8:14 the LORD your God who ***b*** you
8:15 who ***b*** water for you out of the
9: 4 righteousness the LORD has ***b***
9:12 for your people whom you ***b*** out
9:26 whom You have ***b*** out of Egypt
9:28 'lest the land from which You ***b***
9:28 He has ***b*** them out to kill them
9:29 whom You ***b*** out by Your mighty
11:29 when the LORD your God has ***b***
13: 5 who ***b*** you out of the land of
13:10 who ***b*** you out of the land of
16: 1 of Abib the LORD your God ***b***
20: 1 who ***b*** you up from the land of
22:19 because he has ***b*** a bad name on
26: 8 So the LORD ***b*** us out of Egypt
26: 9 He has ***b*** us to this place and
26:10 I have ***b*** the firstfruits of the
29:25 He made with them when He ***b***
31:20 When I have ***b*** them to the land
31:21 even before I have ***b*** them to
Josh 2: 6 (But she had ***b*** them up to the
6:23 had been spies went in and ***b***
6:23 So they ***b*** out all her relatives
7: 7 why have You ***b*** this people over
7:14 therefore you shall be ***b***
7:16 rose early in the morning and ***b***
7:17 He ***b*** the clan of Judah, and he
7:17 and he ***b*** the family of the
7:18 Then he ***b*** his household man by
7:23 ***b*** them to Joshua and to all the
7:24 and they ***b*** them to the Valley
8:23 alive, and ***b*** him to Joshua.
10:23 and ***b*** out those five kings to
10:24 when they ***b*** out those kings to
14: 7 and I ***b*** back word to him as it
22:32 and ***b*** back word to them.
24: 5 Afterward I ***b*** you out.
24: 6 Then I ***b*** your fathers out of
24: 7 ***b*** the sea upon them, and
24: 8 And I ***b*** you into the land of the
24:17 the LORD our God is He who ***b***
24:32 the children of Israel had ***b***
Judg 1: 7 Then they ***b*** him to Jerusalem,
2: 1 I led you up from Egypt and ***b***
2:12 who had ***b*** them out of the land
3:17 So he ***b*** the tribute to Eglon
5:25 She ***b*** out cream in a lordly
6: 8 I ***b*** you up from Egypt and
6: 8 you up from Egypt and ***b*** you
6:19 and he ***b*** them out to Him under
7: 5 So he ***b*** the people down to the
7:25 They pursued Midian and ***b*** the
11:35 my daughter! You have ***b*** me very
12: 9 and ***b*** in thirty daughters from
14:11 that they ***b*** thirty companions
15:13 him with two new ropes and ***b***
16: 8 the lords of the Philistines ***b***
16:18 came up to her and ***b*** the money
16:21 and ***b*** him down to Gaza.
16:31 and ***b*** him up and buried him
18: 3 Who ***b*** you here? What are you
19: 3 So she ***b*** him into her father's
19:21 So he ***b*** him into his house, and
19:25 man took his concubine and ***b***
21:12 and they ***b*** them to the camp at
Ruth 1:21 and the LORD has ***b*** me home
2:18 So she ***b*** out and gave to her
1 Sam 1:24 and ***b*** him to the house of the
1:25 and ***b*** the child to Eli.
2:14 all that the fleshhook ***b*** up.
5: 1 took the ark of God and ***b*** it
5: 2 they ***b*** it into the temple of
5:10 They have ***b*** the ark of the God
6:21 The Philistines have ***b*** back the
7: 1 and ***b*** it into the house of
8: 8 done since the day that I ***b***
9:22 took Saul and his servant and ***b***
10:18 I ***b*** up Israel out of Egypt, and
10:23 So they ran and ***b*** him from
10:27 and ***b*** him no presents. But he
12: 6 and who ***b*** your fathers up from
12: 8 who ***b*** your fathers out of Egypt
14:34 So every one of the people ***b*** his
15:15 They have ***b*** them from the
15:20 and ***b*** back Agag king of Amalek;
16:12 So he sent and ***b*** him in. Now he
17:54 head of the Philistine and ***b***
17:57 Abner took him and ***b*** him before
18:27 And David ***b*** their foreskins,
19: 5 and the LORD ***b*** about a great
19: 7 So Jonathan ***b*** David to Saul,
20: 8 for you have ***b*** your servant
21: 8 For I have ***b*** neither my sword
21:14 Why have you ***b*** him to me?
21:15 that you have ***b*** this fellow to
22: 4 So he ***b*** them before the king of
25:27 which your maidservant has ***b***
25:35 from her hand what she had ***b***
28:25 So she ***b*** it before Saul and his
30: 7 And Abiathar ***b*** the ephod to
30:11 and ***b*** him to David; and they
30:16 And when he had ***b*** him down,
2 Sam 1:10 and have ***b*** them here to my
2: 3 And David ***b*** up the men who were
2: 8 the son of Saul and ***b*** him over
3:22 and Joab came from a raid and ***b***
3:26 who ***b*** him back from the well of
4: 8 And they ***b*** the head of
4:10 thinking to have ***b*** good news,
5: 2 one who led Israel out and ***b***
6: 3 and ***b*** it out of the house of
6: 4 And they ***b*** it out of the house
6:12 So David went and ***b*** up the
6:15 and all the house of Israel ***b***
6:17 So they ***b*** the ark of the LORD,
7: 6 a house since the time that I ***b***
7:18 that You have ***b*** me this far?
8: 2 and ***b*** tribute.
8: 6 and ***b*** tribute. The LORD
8: 7 and ***b*** them to Jerusalem.
8:10 and Joram ***b*** with him articles
9: 5 Then King David sent and ***b*** him
10:16 Then Hadadezer sent and ***b*** out
11:27 David sent and ***b*** her to his
12:30 Also he ***b*** out the spoil of the
12:31 And he ***b*** out the people who
13:10 and ***b*** them to Amnon her
13:11 Now when she had ***b*** them to him
14: 2 And Joab sent to Tekoa and ***b***
14:23 and ***b*** Absalom to Jerusalem.
16: 8 The LORD has ***b*** upon you all the
17:28 ***b*** beds and basins, earthen
19:41 stolen you away and ***b*** the king,
21: 8 whom she ***b*** up for Adriel the
21:13 So he ***b*** up the bones of Saul and
22:20 He also ***b*** me out into a broad
23:10 The LORD ***b*** about a great
23:12 And the LORD ***b*** about a great
23:16 and took it and ***b*** it to David.
1 Ki 1: 3 and ***b*** her to the king.
2:30 And Benaiah ***b*** back word to
2:40 And Shimei went and ***b*** his
3: 1 then he ***b*** her to the City of
3:24 So they ***b*** a sword before the
4:21 They ***b*** tribute and served
4:28 They also ***b*** barley and straw to
7:13 Now King Solomon sent and ***b***
7:51 and Solomon ***b*** in the things
8: 4 Then they ***b*** up the ark of the
8: 4 The priests and the Levites ***b***
8: 6 Then the priests ***b*** in the ark of
8:16 Since the day that I ***b*** My people
8:21 when He ***b*** them out of the land
8:51 whom You ***b*** out of Egypt, out of
8:53 when You ***b*** our fathers out of
9: 9 who ***b*** their fathers out of the
9: 9 therefore the LORD has ***b*** all
9:28 and ***b*** it to King Solomon.
10:11 which ***b*** gold from Ophir,
10:11 ***b*** great quantities of almug
10:25 Each man ***b*** his present: articles
12:28 which ***b*** you up from the land of
13:20 came to the prophet who had ***b***
13:23 the prophet whom he had ***b*** back.
13:26 Now when the prophet who had ***b***
13:29 and ***b*** it back. So the old
14:28 then ***b*** them back into the
15:15 He also ***b*** into the house of the
17: 6 The ravens ***b*** him bread and meat
17:20 have You also ***b*** tragedy on the
17:23 And Elijah took the child and ***b***
18:40 and Elijah ***b*** them down to the
20: 9 the messengers departed and ***b***
20:39 a man came over and ***b*** a man to
22:37 and was ***b*** to Samaria. And they
2 Ki 2:20 So they ***b*** it to him.
4: 5 who ***b*** the vessels to her; and
4:20 When he had taken him and ***b*** him
4:42 and ***b*** the man of God bread of
5: 2 and had ***b*** back captive a young
5: 6 Then he ***b*** the letter to the king
5:20 from his hands what he ***b***;
10: 8 They have ***b*** the heads of the
10:22 So he ***b*** out vestments for
10:24 any of the men whom I have ***b***
10:26 And they ***b*** the sacred pillars
11: 4 year Jehoiada sent and ***b*** the
11: 4 and ***b*** them into the house of the
11:12 And he ***b*** out the king's son, put
11:19 and they ***b*** the king down from
12: 4 the dedicated gifts that are ***b***
12: 9 door put there all the money ***b***
12:13 from the money ***b*** into the house
12:16 the sin offerings was not ***b***
14:20 Then they ***b*** him on horses, and
16:14 He also ***b*** the bronze altar which
17: 4 and ***b*** no tribute to the king of
17: 7 who had ***b*** them up out of the
17:24 Then the king of Assyria ***b***
17:27 one of the priests whom you ***b***
17:36 who ***b*** you up from the land of
19:25 Now I have ***b*** it to pass, That
20:11 and He ***b*** the shadow ten degrees
20:20 made a pool and a tunnel and ***b***
22: 4 the money which has been ***b***
22:20 So they ***b*** back word to
23: 6 And he ***b*** out the wooden image
23: 8 And he ***b*** all the priests from
23:30 ***b*** him to Jerusalem, and buried
24:16 these the king of Babylon ***b***
25: 6 So they took the king and ***b*** him
25:20 took these and ***b*** them to the
1 Chr 9:28 for they ***b*** them in and took
10:12 and they ***b*** them to Jabesh, and
11: 2 one who led Israel out and ***b***
11:14 So the LORD ***b*** about a great
11:18 and took it and ***b*** it to
11:19 the risk of their lives they ***b***
14:17 and the LORD ***b*** the fear of him
15:28 Thus all Israel ***b*** up the ark of
16: 1 So they ***b*** the ark of God, and
17: 5 a house since the time that I ***b***
17:16 that You have ***b*** me this far?
18: 2 and ***b*** tribute.
18: 6 and ***b*** tribute. So the LORD
18: 7 and ***b*** them to Jerusalem.
18: 8 David ***b*** a large amount of
18:10 and Hadoram ***b*** with him all
18:11 silver and gold that he had ***b***
19:16 they sent messengers and ***b*** the
20: 2 Also he ***b*** out the spoil of the
20: 3 And he ***b*** out the people who
22: 4 and those from Tyre ***b*** much
2 Chr 1: 4 But David had ***b*** up the ark of
5: 1 and Solomon ***b*** in the things
5: 5 Then they ***b*** up the ark, the
5: 5 The priests and the Levites ***b***
5: 7 Then the priests ***b*** in the ark of
6: 5 Since the day that I ***b*** My people

B

7:22 who **b** them out of the land of
7:22 therefore He has **b** all this
8:11 Now Solomon **b** the daughter of
8:18 and **b** it to King Solomon.
9:10 who **b** gold from Ophir, brought
9:10 **b** algum wood and precious
9:12 much more than she had **b** to
9:14 merchants and traders **b**.
9:14 and governors of the country **b**
9:24 Each man **b** his present: articles
9:28 And they **b** horses to Solomon
15:11 sheep from the spoil they had **b**.
15:18 He also **b** into the house of God
16: 2 Then Asa **b** silver and gold from
17:11 Also some of the Philistines **b**
17:11 and the Arabians **b** him flocks,
19: 4 and **b** them back to the LORD
22: 9 and **b** him to Jehu. When they
23:11 And they **b** out the king's son,
23:14 And Jehoiada the priest **b** out
23:20 and **b** the king down from the
24:10 **b** their contributions, and put
24:11 when the chest was **b** to the
24:14 they **b** the rest of the money
25:12 **b** them to the top of the rock,
25:14 that he **b** the gods of the
25:23 and he **b** him to Jerusalem, and
25:28 Then they **b** him on horses and
26: 8 Also the Ammonites **b** tribute to
28: 5 and **b** them to Damascus.
28: 8 and **b** the spoil to Samaria.
28:15 they **b** them to their brethren
28:19 For the LORD **b** Judah low
29: 4 Then he **b** in the priests and the
29:16 and **b** out all the debris that
29:21 And they **b** seven bulls, seven
29:23 Then they **b** out the male goats
29:31 So the assembly **b** in sacrifices
29:31 as were of a willing heart **b**
29:32 offerings which the assembly **b**
30:15 and **b** the burnt offerings to
31: 5 the children of Israel **b** in
31: 5 and they **b** in abundantly the
31: 6 **b** the tithe of oxen and sheep;
31:12 Then they faithfully **b** in the
32:23 And many **b** gifts to the LORD at
32:30 and **b** the water by tunnel to
33:11 Therefore the LORD **b** upon them
33:13 and **b** him back to Jerusalem
34: 9 delivered the money that was **b**
34: 9 and which they had **b** back to
34:14 Now when they **b** out the money
34:14 out the money that was **b** into
34:28 So they **b** back word to
35:24 and they **b** him to Jerusalem.
36:17 Therefore He **b** against them the
Ezra 1: 7 King Cyrus also **b** out the
1: 8 and Cyrus king of Persia **b** them
1:11 with the captives who were **b**
4: 2 king of Assyria, who **b** us here."
6: 5 which is in Jerusalem and **b**
8:18 they **b** us a man of
Neh 4:15 and that God had **b** their plot
5: 5 of our daughters have been **b**
8: 2 So Ezra the priest **b** the Law
8:16 Then the people went out and **b**
9: 7 And **b** him out of Ur of the
9:15 And **b** them water out of the
9:18 This is your god That **b** you up
9:23 And **b** them into the land
10:31 if the peoples of the land **b**
12:31 So I **b** the leaders of Judah up
13: 9 and I **b** back into them the
13:12 Then all Judah **b** the tithe of
13:15 which they **b** into Jerusalem on
13:16 who **b** in fish and all kinds of
13:19 that no burdens would be **b** in
Esth 1:12 command **b** by his eunuchs;
1:15 command of King Ahasuerus **b**
1:17 commanded Queen Vashti to be **b**
2: 7 And Mordecai had **b** up Hadassah,
2:20 of Mordecai as when she was **b**
6: 8 let a royal robe be **b** which the
9:11 in Shushan the citadel was **b**
Job 4:12 Now a word was secretly **b** to
10:18 Why then have You **b** me out of
14:21 They are **b** low, and he does
21:30 They shall be **b** out on the day
21:32 Yet he shall be **b** to the grave,
24:24 They are **b** low; They are
36:16 Indeed He would have **b** you out
42:11 adversity that the LORD had **b**
Ps 18:19 He also **b** me out into a broad
22:15 You have **b** Me to the dust of
30: 3 You **b** my soul up from the
35: 4 those be put to shame and **b** to
35: 4 those be turned back and **b** to
35:26 Let them be ashamed and **b** to
40: 2 He also **b** me up out of a
40:14 Let them be ashamed and **b** to
40:14 them be driven backward and **b**
45:14 She shall be **b** to the King in
45:14 follow her, shall be **b** to You.
45:15 and rejoicing they shall be **b**;
51: 5 I was **b** forth in iniquity, And
66:11 You **b** us into the net; You
66:12 But You **b** us out to rich
71:24 For they are **b** to shame Who
73:19 how they are **b** to desolation,
78:16 He also **b** streams out of the
78:26 And by His power He **b** in the
78:54 And He **b** them to His holy
78:71 the ewes that had young He **b**
79: 8 For we have been **b** very low.
80: 8 You have **b** a vine out of Egypt;
81:10 Who **b** you out of the land of
85: 1 You have **b** back the captivity
89:40 You have **b** his strongholds to
90: 2 Before the mountains were **b**
94:23 He has **b** on them their own
105:37 He also **b** them out with silver
105:40 and He **b** quail, And satisfied
105:43 He **b** out His people with joy,
106:42 And they were **b** into subjection
106:43 And were **b** low for their
107:12 Therefore He **b** down their heart
107:14 He **b** them out of darkness and
107:39 they are diminished and **b** low
116: 6 I was **b** low, and He saved me.
126: 1 When the LORD **b** back the
136:11 And **b** out Israel from among
142: 6 For I am **b** very low; Deliver
Prov 8:24 there were no depths I was **b**
8:25 the hills, I was **b** forth;
Eccl 12: 4 the daughters of music are **b**
Song 1: 4 SHULAMITE The king has **b** me
2: 4 He **b** me to the banqueting
3: 4 Until I had **b** him to the house
8: 5 There your mother **b** you forth;
8: 5 There she who bore you **b** you
Isa 1: 2 I have nourished and **b** up
2:12 And it shall be **b** low—
2:17 haughtiness of men shall be **b**
3: 9 to their soul! For they have **b**
5: 2 But it **b** forth wild grapes.
5:15 People shall be **b** down, Each
14:11 Your pomp is **b** down to Sheol,
14:15 Yet you shall be **b** down to
18: 7 that time a present will be **b**
23:13 And **b** it to ruin.
26:18 **b** forth wind; We have not
29: 4 You shall be **b** down, You shall
29:20 For the terrible one is **b** to
32:19 And the city is **b** low in
37:26 Now I have **b** it to pass, That
40: 4 And every mountain and hill **b**
43:23 You have not **b** Me the sheep for
45:10 What have you **b** forth?' "
48:15 I have **b** him, and his way will
49:21 And who has **b** these up?
51:18 Among all the sons she has **b**
51:18 Among all the sons she has **b**
59:16 Therefore His own arm **b**
62: 9 Those who have **b** it together
63: 5 Therefore My own arm **b**
63: 6 And **b** down their strength to
63:11 Where is He who **b** them up out
Jer 2: 6 Who **b** us up out of the land of
2: 7 I **b** you into a bountiful
2:17 Have you not **b** this on
7:22 them in the day that I **b** them
10: 9 It is **b** from Tarshish, And
11: 4 your fathers in the day I **b**
11: 7 your fathers in the day I **b**
11:19 I was like a docile lamb **b** to
16:14 The LORD lives who **b** up the
16:15 The LORD lives who **b** up the
20: 3 on the next day that Pashhur **b**
20:15 Let the man be cursed Who **b**
23: 7 As the LORD lives who **b** up the
23: 8 As the LORD lives who **b** up and
24: 1 and had **b** them to Babylon.
26:23 And they **b** Urijah from Egypt and
26:23 Urijah from Egypt and **b** him to
27:16 house will now shortly be **b**
32:21 You have **b** Your people Israel
32:42 Just as I have **b** all this great
34:11 and **b** them into subjection as
34:13 fathers in the day that I **b**
34:16 and every one of you **b** back his
34:16 **b** them back into subjection,
35: 4 and I **b** them into the house of
37:14 So Irijah seized Jeremiah and **b**
38:14 and had Jeremiah the prophet **b**
39: 5 they **b** him up to Nebuchadnezzar
40: 3 Now the LORD has **b** it, and has
41:16 whom he had **b** back from Gibeon.
42:10 the disaster that I have **b**
44: 2 all the calamity that I have **b**
50:25 And has **b** out the weapons of
52: 9 So they took the king and **b** him
52:26 of the guard took these and **b**
52:31 Jehoiachin king of Judah and **b**
Lam 1:12 Which has been **b** on me, Which
2: 2 He has **b** them down to the
2:22 Those whom I have borne and **b**
4: 5 Those who were **b** up in scarlet
Ezek 8: 3 and **b** me in visions of God to
8: 7 So He **b** me to the door of the
8:14 So He **b** me to the door of the
8:16 So He **b** me into the inner court
11: 1 the Spirit lifted me up and **b**
11:24 the Spirit took me up and **b** me
12: 7 I **b** out my belongings by day,
12: 7 I **b** them out at twilight, and
14:22 in it a remnant who will be **b**
14:22 the disaster that I have **b**
14:22 all that I have **b** upon it.
17: 6 *B* forth branches, And put
17:14 that the kingdom might be **b** low
17:24 have **b** down the high tree and
19: 3 She **b** up one of her cubs, And
19: 4 And they **b** him with chains to
19: 9 And **b** him to the king of
19: 9 They **b** him in nets, That his
20:10 out of the land of Egypt and **b**
20:14 in whose sight I had **b** them
20:22 in whose sight I had **b** them
20:28 When I **b** them into the land
21: 7 it is coming and shall be **b** to
23: 8 her harlotry **b** from Egypt,
23:27 harlotry *B* from the land of
23:42 and Sabeans were **b** from the
27:15 They **b** you ivory tusks and
27:26 Your oarsmen **b** you into many
28:18 Therefore I **b** fire from your
30:11 Shall be **b** to destroy the
31: 6 all the beasts of the field **b**
31:18 Yet you shall be **b** down with
34: 4 nor **b** back what was driven
37: 1 of the LORD came upon me and **b**
37:13 and **b** you up from your graves.
38: 8 come into the land of those **b**
38: 8 they were **b** out of the nations,
39:27 When I have **b** them back from the
39:28 but also **b** them back to their
40: 4 for you were **b** here so that I
40:17 Then he **b** me into the outer
40:24 After that he **b** me toward the
40:28 Then he **b** me to the inner court
40:32 And he **b** me into the inner
40:35 Then he **b** me to the north
40:48 Then he **b** me to the vestibule of
41: 1 Then he **b** me into the sanctuary
42: 1 Then he **b** me out into the outer
42: 1 and he **b** me into the chamber
42:15 he **b** me out through the gateway
43: 1 Afterward he **b** me to the gate,
43: 5 The Spirit lifted me up and **b** me
44: 1 Then He **b** me back to the outer
44: 4 Also He **b** me by way of the
44: 7 When you **b** in foreigners,
46:19 Now he **b** me through the
46:21 Then he **b** me out into the outer
47: 1 Then he **b** me back to the door of
47: 2 He **b** me out by way of the north
47: 3 and he **b** me through the waters;
47: 4 he measured one thousand and **b**
47: 4 he measured one thousand and **b**
47: 6 Then he **b** me and returned me
Dan 1: 2 and he **b** the articles into the
1: 9 Now God had **b** Daniel into the
1:18 had said that they should be **b**
1:18 the chief of the eunuchs **b** them
2:25 Then Arioch quickly **b** Daniel
3:13 So they **b** these men before the
5: 3 Then they **b** the gold vessels
5:13 Then Daniel was **b** in before the
5:13 whom my father the king **b** from
5:15 have been **b** in before me, that
5:23 They have **b** the vessels of His
6:16 and they **b** Daniel and cast him
6:17 Then a stone was **b** and laid on
6:18 and no musicians were **b** before
6:24 and they **b** those men who had
7:13 And they **b** Him near before
9:14 and **b** it upon us; for the LORD
9:15 who **b** Your people out of the
11: 6 with those who **b** her, and with
Hos 12:13 By a prophet the LORD **b** Israel
Am 2:10 Also it was I who **b** you up
3: 1 the whole family which I **b** up
Jon 2: 6 Yet You have **b** up my life from
Mic 6: 4 For I **b** you up from the land of
Nah 2: 7 She shall be **b** up; And her
Hag 1: 9 and when you **b** it home, I blew
Zech 10:11 the pride of Assyria shall be **b**
Mt 1:12 And after they were **b** to
1:25 did not know her till she had **b**
4:24 and they **b** to Him all sick
8:16 they **b** to Him many who were
9: 2 they **b** to Him a paralytic lying
9:32 they **b** to Him a man, mute and
10:18 You will be **b** before governors
11:23 will be **b** down to Hades; for if
12:22 Then one was **b** to Him who was
12:25 divided against itself is **b** to
14:11 And his head was **b** on a platter
14:11 and she **b** it to her mother.
14:35 **b** to Him all who were sick,
16: 8 yourselves because you have **b**
17:16 So I **b** him to Your disciples,
18:24 one was **b** to him who owed him
19:13 Then little children were **b** to
21: 7 They **b** the donkey and the colt,
22:19 So they **b** Him a denarius.
25:20 five talents came and **b** five
27: 3 was remorseful and **b** back the
Mk 1:32 they **b** to Him all who were sick
4:21 Is a lamp **b** to be put under a
6:27 and commanded his head to be **b**.
6:28 **b** his head on a platter, and
7:32 Then they **b** to Him one who was
8:22 and they **b** a blind man to Him,
9:17 I **b** You my son, who has a mute
9:20 Then they **b** him to Him. And when
10:13 Then they **b** little children to
10:13 disciples rebuked those who **b**
11: 7 Then they **b** the colt to Jesus
12:16 So they **b** it. And He said to
13: 9 You will be **b** before rulers and
15:22 And they **b** Him to the place
Lk 1:57 and she **b** forth a son.
2: 7 And she **b** forth her firstborn
2:22 they **b** Him to Jerusalem to
2:27 And when the parents **b** in the

3: 5 every mountain and hill **b**
4: 9 Then he **b** Him to Jerusalem, set
4:16 where He had been **b** up. And as
4:40 sick with various diseases **b**
5:11 So when they had **b** their boats
5:18 men **b** on a bed a man who was
7:37 **b** an alabaster flask of
10:15 will be **b** down to Hades.
10:34 **b** him to an inn, and took care
11:17 divided against itself is **b** to
16: 1 and an accusation was **b** to him
18:15 Then they also **b** infants to Him
18:40 and commanded him to be **b** to
19:35 Then they **b** him to Jesus.
21:12 You will be **b** before kings and
22:54 they led Him and **b** Him into
23:14 You have **b** this Man to me, as
Jn 1:42 And he **b** him to Jesus. Now when
4:33 Has anyone **b** Him anything to
7:45 Why have you not **b** Him?"
8: 3 the scribes and Pharisees **b** to
9:13 They **b** him who formerly was
18:16 kept the door, and **b** Peter in.
19:13 he **b** Jesus out and sat down in
Acts 4:34 and **b** the proceeds of the
4:37 and **b** the money and laid it at
5: 2 and **b** a certain part and laid
5:15 so that they **b** the sick out into
5:19 opened the prison doors and **b**
5:21 to the prison to have them **b**.
5:26 went with the officers and **b**
5:27 And when they had **b** them, they
6:12 and **b** him to the council.
7:20 and he was **b** up in his father's
7:21 daughter took him away and **b**
7:36 He **b** them out, after he had
7:40 as for this Moses who **b**
7:45 also **b** with Joshua into the
9: 8 they led him by the hand and **b**
9:27 But Barnabas took him and **b** him
9:30 they **b** him down to Caesarea and
9:39 they **b** him to the upper room.
11:26 he **b** him to Antioch. So it was
12:17 to them how the Lord had **b** him
13: 1 Manaen who had been **b** up with
13:17 and with an uplifted arm He **b**
14:13 **b** oxen and garlands to the
16:16 who **b** her masters much profit
16:20 And they **b** them to the
16:30 And he **b** them out and said,
16:34 Now when he had **b** them into his
16:39 and pleaded with them and **b**
17:15 So those who conducted Paul **b**
17:19 And they took him and **b** him to
18:12 rose up against Paul and **b** him
19:12 handkerchiefs or aprons were **b**
19:19 those who had practiced magic **b**
19:24 **b** no small profit to the
19:37 For you have **b** these men here
20:12 And they **b** the young man in
21:16 Caesarea went with us and **b**
21:28 and furthermore he also **b**
21:29 they supposed that Paul had **b**
22: 3 but **b** up in this city at the
22:24 commander ordered him to be **b**
22:30 and **b** Paul down and set him
23:15 to the commander that he be **b**
23:18 So he took him and **b** him to the
23:28 I **b** him before their council.
23:31 took Paul and **b** him by night
24: 2 and prosperity is being **b** to
25: 6 seat, he commanded Paul to be **b**.
25:17 and commanded the man to be **b**
25:18 they **b** no accusation against
25:23 at Festus' command Paul was **b**
25:26 Therefore I have **b** him out
27:24 you must be **b** before Caesar;
1 Cor 6:12 but I will not be **b** under the
15:54 then shall be **b** to pass the
Gal 2: 4 of false brethren secretly **b**
Eph 2:13 once were far off have been **b**
1 Th 3: 6 and **b** us good news of your
1 Tim 5:10 if she has **b** up children, if
6: 7 For we **b** nothing into this
2 Tim 1:10 who has abolished death and **b**
Heb 13:11 whose blood is **b** into the
13:20 may the God of peace who **b** up
Jas 1:18 Of His own will He **b** us forth by
1 Pe 1:13 upon the grace that is to be **b**
2 Pe 2:19 him also he is **b** into bondage.

BROW (4/4)

Num 24:17 And batter the **b** of Moab, And
Isa 48: 4 iron sinew, And your **b** bronze,
Jer 48:45 And shall devour the **b** of
Lk 4:29 and they led Him to the **b** of

BROWN (4/4)

Gen 30:32 and all the **b** ones among the
30:33 and **b** among the lambs, will be
30:35 and all the **b** ones among the
30:40 the streaked and all the **b** in

BRUISE (4/3) BRUISED, BRUISES, BRUISING

Gen 3:15 He shall **b** your head, And you
3:15 And you shall **b** His heel."
Isa 30:26 that the LORD binds up the **b**
53:10 it pleased the LORD to **b** Him;

BRUISED (4/4) BRUISE

Lev 22:24 offer to the LORD what is **b**
Isa 42: 3 A **b** reed He will not break,
53: 5 He was **b** for our iniquities;
Mt 12:20 A **b** reed He will not

BRUISES (2/2) BRUISE

Job 5:18 For He **b**, but He binds up;
Isa 1: 6 But wounds and **b** and

BRUISING (1/1) BRUISE

Lk 9:39 with great difficulty, **b** him.

BRUIT (KJV) See NEWS, REPORT

BRUNT (1/1)

Num 14:33 and bear the **b** of your

BRUSHWOOD (1/1)

Isa 64: 2 As fire burns **b**,

BRUTAL (2/2) BRUTALLY, BRUTE

Ezek 21:31 you into the hands of **b** men
2 Tim 3: 3 without self-control, **b**,

BRUTALLY (1/1) BRUTAL

Deut 21:14 you shall not treat her **b**,

BRUTE (2/2) BRUTAL, BRUTALLY

2 Pe 2:12 like natural **b** beasts made to
Jude 10 like **b** beasts, in these things

BUCKET (1/1) BUCKETS

Isa 40:15 nations are as a drop in a **b**,

BUCKETS (2/2) BUCKET

Ex 7:19 both in **b** of wood and
Num 24: 7 He shall pour water from his **b**,

BUCKLER (4/4) BUCKLERS

Ps 35: 2 Take hold of shield and **b**,
91: 4 shall be your shield and **b**.
Jer 46: 3 Order the **b** and shield, And
Ezek 23:24 shall array against you **B**,

BUCKLERS (3/3) BUCKLER

Song 4: 4 On which hang a thousand **b**,
Ezek 38: 4 a great company with **b** and
39: 9 weapons, both the shields and **b**,

BUD (7/7) BUDDED, BUDDING, BUDS

Ex 9:31 the head and the flax was in **b**.
Job 14: 9 at the scent of water it will **b**
Isa 18: 5 when the **b** is perfect And the
27: 6 Israel shall blossom and **b**,
55:10 And make it bring forth and **b**,
61:11 as the earth brings forth its **b**,
Hos 8: 7 The stalk has no **b**;

BUDDED (5/5) BUD

Gen 40:10 it was as though it **b**,
Song 6:11 To see whether the vine had **b**
7:12 Let us see if the vine has **b**,
Ezek 7:10 rod has blossomed, Pride has **b**.
Heb 9: 4 the manna, Aaron's rod that **b**,

BUDDING (1/1) BUD

Lk 21:30 "When they are already **b**,

BUDS (4/3) BUD

Num 17: 8 had sprouted and put forth **b**,
1 Ki 6:18 carved with ornamental **b** and
7:24 its brim were ornamental **b**
7:24 The ornamental **b** were cast in

BUFFET (1/1)

2 Cor 12: 7 a messenger of Satan to **b** me,

BUILD (161/153) BUILDER, BUILDERS, BUILDING, BUILDINGS, BUILDS, BUILT

Gen 11: 4 let us **b** ourselves a city, and
Ex 20:25 you shall not **b** it of hewn
Num 23: 1 **B** seven altars for me here, and
23:29 **B** for me here seven altars, and
32:16 We will **b** sheepfolds here for
32:24 **B** cities for your little ones
Deut 6:10 cities which you did not **b**,
16:21 near the altar which you **b** for
20:20 to **b** siegeworks against the
22: 8 When you **b** a new house, then
25: 9 done to the man who will not **b**
27: 5 And there you shall **b** an altar
27: 6 You shall **b** with whole stones
28:30 you shall **b** a house, but you
Josh 22:26 Let us now prepare to **b**
22:29 to **b** an altar for burnt
24:13 and cities which you did not **b**,
Judg 6:26 and **b** an altar to the LORD your
1 Sam 2:35 I will **b** him a sure house, and
2 Sam 7: 5 Would you **b** a house for Me to
7:13 He shall **b** a house for My name,
7:27 'I will **b** you a house.'
24:21 to **b** an altar to the LORD,
1 Ki 2:36 **B** yourself a house in Jerusalem
5: 3 my father David could not **b** a
5: 5 I propose to **b** a house for the
5: 5 he shall **b** the house for My
5:18 timber and stones to **b** the
6: 1 that he began to **b** the house of
7: 1 took thirteen years to **b** his
8:16 of Israel in which to **b** a
8:17 heart of my father David to **b**
8:18 it was in your heart to **b** a
8:19 Nevertheless you shall not **b** the
8:19 he shall **b** the temple for My
9:15 to **b** the house of the LORD,
9:19 whatever Solomon desired to **b**
11:38 then I will be with you and **b**
2 Ki 19:32 Nor **b** a siege mound against
1 Chr 14: 1 carpenters, to **b** him a house.
17: 4 You shall not **b** Me a house to
17:10 tell you that the LORD will **b**
17:12 He shall **b** Me a house, and I
17:25 to Your servant that You will **b**
21:22 that I may **b** an altar on it to
22: 2 masons to cut hewn stones to **b**
22: 6 and charged him to **b** a house
22: 7 it was in my mind to **b** a house
22: 8 you shall not **b** a house for My
22:10 He shall **b** a house for My name,
22:11 and **b** the house of the LORD
22:19 Therefore arise and **b** the
28: 2 I had it in my heart to **b** a
28: 2 and had made preparations to **b**
28: 3 You shall not **b** a house for My
28: 6 your son Solomon who shall **b**
28:10 the LORD has chosen you to **b**
29:16 that we have prepared to **b** You
29:19 and to **b** the temple for which I
2 Chr 2: 1 Then Solomon determined to **b** a
2: 3 and sent him cedars to **b**
2: 5 And the temple which I **b** will
2: 6 But who is able to **b** Him a
2: 6 that I should **b** Him a temple,
2: 9 temple which I am about to **b**
2:12 who will **b** a temple for the
3: 1 Now Solomon began to **b** the house
3: 2 And he began to **b** on the second
6: 5 of Israel in which to **b** a
6: 7 heart of my father David to **b**
6: 8 it was in your heart to **b** a
6: 9 Nevertheless you shall not **b** the
6: 9 he shall **b** the temple for My
8: 6 all that Solomon desired to **b**
14: 7 Let us **b** these cities and make
36:23 And He has commanded me to **b**
Ezra 1: 2 And He has commanded me to **b**
1: 3 and **b** the house of the LORD
1: 5 arose to go up and **b** the house
4: 2 Let us **b** with you, for we seek
4: 3 may do nothing with us to **b** a
4: 3 but we alone will **b** to the
5: 2 Jozadak rose up and began to **b**
5: 3 Who has commanded you to **b** this
5: 9 Who commanded you to **b** this
5:13 King Cyrus issued a decree to **b**
5:17 was issued by King Cyrus to **b**
6: 7 and the elders of the Jews **b**
Neh 2:17 Come and let us **b** the wall of
2:18 said, "Let us rise up and **b**.
2:20 His servants will arise and **b**,
4: 3 and he said, "Whatever they **b**,
4:10 that we are not able to **b** the
Job 19:12 troops come together And **b** up
20:19 a house which he did not **b**.
Ps 28: 5 shall destroy them And not **b**
51:18 **B** the walls of Jerusalem.
69:35 For God will save Zion And **b**
89: 4 And **b** up your throne to all
102:16 For the LORD shall **b** up Zion;
127: 1 They labor in vain who **b** it;
Prov 24:27 And afterward **b** your house.
Eccl 3: 3 And a time to **b** up;
Song 8: 9 We will **b** upon her A
Isa 37:33 Nor **b** a siege mound against
45:13 He shall **b** My city And let My
58:12 Those from among you Shall **b**
60:10 sons of foreigners shall **b** up
62:10 **B** up, Build up the highway!
62:10 **B** up the highway! Take out
65:21 They shall **b** houses and inhabit
65:22 They shall not **b** and another
66: 1 is the house that you will **b**
Jer 1:10 To **b** and to plant."
6: 6 And **b** a mound against
18: 9 kingdom, to **b** and to plant it,
22:14 I will **b** myself a wide house
24: 6 I will **b** them and not pull
29: 5 **B** houses and dwell in them;
29:28 **b** houses and dwell in them,
31: 4 Again I will **b** you, and you
31:28 so I will watch over them to **b**
35: 7 You shall not **b** a house, sow
35: 9 nor to **b** ourselves houses to
42:10 then I will **b** you and not pull
Ezek 4: 2 **b** a siege wall against it, and
11: 3 The time is not near to **b**

13: 5 not gone up into the gaps to **b**
17:17 heap up a siege mound and **b** a
21:22 mound, and to **b** a wall.
26: 8 **b** a wall against you, and raise
28:26 **b** houses, and plant vineyards;
Dan 9:25 the command To restore and **b**
11:15 of the North shall come and **b**
Am 9:14 They shall **b** the waste cities
Mic 3:10 Who **b** up Zion with bloodshed
Zeph 1:13 They shall **b** houses, but not
Hag 1: 8 mountains and bring wood and **b**
Zech 5:11 To **b** a house for it in the land
6:12 And He shall **b** the temple of
6:13 He shall **b** the temple of the
6:15 from afar shall come and **b** the
Mal 1: 4 But we will return and **b** the
1: 4 LORD of hosts: "They may **b**,
Mt 16:18 and on this rock I will **b** My
23:29 hypocrites! Because you **b** the
26:61 the temple of God and to **b** it
27:40 who destroy the temple and **b**
Mk 14:58 and within three days I will **b**
15:29 who destroy the temple and **b**
Lk 11:47 Woe to you! For you **b** the tombs
11:48 and you **b** their tombs.
12:18 I will pull down my barns and **b**
14:28 intending to **b** a tower, does
14:30 This man began to **b** and was not
19:43 you when your enemies will **b**
Jn 2:20 has taken forty-six years to **b**
Acts 7:49 What house will you **b**
20:32 which is able to **b** you up and
Rom 15:20 lest I should **b** on another
Gal 2:18 For if I **b** again those things

BUILDER (2/2) BUILD, BUILDERS

1 Cor 3:10 as a wise master **b** I have laid
Heb 11:10 whose **b** and maker is God.

BUILDERS (15/14) BUILDER

1 Ki 5:18 Solomon's **b**, Hiram's builders,
5:18 Solomon's builders, Hiram's **b**,
2 Ki 12:11 it out to the carpenters and **b**
22: 6 to carpenters and **b** and
2 Chr 34:11 it to the craftsmen and **b** to
Ezra 3:10 When the **b** laid the foundation
Neh 4: 5 You to anger before the **b**.
4:18 Every one of the **b** had his sword
Ps 118:22 The stone which the **b** rejected
Ezek 27: 4 Your **b** have perfected your
Mt 21:42 The stone which the **b**
Mk 12:10 The stone which the **b**
Lk 20:17 The stone which the **b**
Acts 4:11 was rejected by you **b**,
1 Pe 2: 7 The stone which the **b**

BUILDING (31/30) BUILD, BUILDINGS

Gen 11: 8 and they ceased **b** the city.
Josh 22:19 by **b** yourselves an altar
1 Ki 3: 1 David until he had finished **b**
6:12 this temple which you are **b**,
6:38 So he was seven years in **b** it.
9: 1 when Solomon had finished **b** the
15:21 that he stopped **b** Ramah, and
15:22 which Baasha had used for **b**;
2 Chr 2: 4 I am **b** a temple for the name of
3: 3 which Solomon laid for **b** the
16: 5 that he stopped **b** Ramah and
16: 6 which Baasha had used for **b**;
Ezra 4: 1 of the captivity were **b** the
4: 4 They troubled them in **b**,
4:12 and are **b** the rebellious and
5: 4 who were constructing this **b**.
6: 8 for the **b** of this house of God:
Eccl 10:18 Because of laziness the **b**
Ezek 41:12 The **b** that faced the separating
41:12 the wall of the **b** was five
41:13 courtyard with the **b** and its
41:15 He measured the length of the **b**
42: 1 and which was opposite the **b**
42: 5 and middle stories of the **b**.
42:10 courtyard and opposite the **b**.
46:23 There was a row of **b** stones
Lk 6:48 He is like a man **b** a house, who
1 Cor 3: 9 God's field, you are God's **b**.
2 Cor 5: 1 we have a **b** from God, a house
Eph 2:21 in whom the whole **b**,
Jude 20 **b** yourselves up on your most

BUILDINGS (3/3) BUILDING

Mt 24: 1 came up to show Him the **b** of
Mk 13: 1 manner of stones and what **b**
13: 2 him, "Do you see these great **b**?

BUILDS (12/11) BUILD

Josh 6:26 the LORD who rises up and **b**
Job 27:18 He **b** his house like a moth,
Ps 127: 1 Unless the LORD **b** the house,
147: 2 The LORD **b** up Jerusalem; He
Prov 14: 1 The wise woman **b** her house,
Jer 22:13 Woe to him who **b** his house by
Ezek 13:10 and one **b** a wall, and they
Am 9: 6 He who **b** His layers in the sky,
Hab 2:12 Woe to him who **b** a town with
1 Cor 3:10 and another **b** on it. But let
3:10 each one take heed how he **b** on
3:12 Now if anyone **b** on this

BUILT (214/197) BUILD

Gen 4:17 And he **b** a city, and called the
8:20 Then Noah **b** an altar to the
10:11 land he went to Assyria and **b**
11: 5 which the sons of men had **b**.
12: 7 And there he **b** an altar to
12: 8 there he **b** an altar to the
13:18 and **b** an altar there to the
22: 9 And Abraham **b** an altar there
26:25 So he **b** an altar there and
33:17 **b** himself a house, and made
35: 7 And he **b** an altar there and
Ex 1:11 And they **b** for Pharaoh supply
17:15 And Moses **b** an altar and called
24: 4 and **b** an altar at the foot of
32: 5 he **b** an altar before it.
Num 13:22 (Now Hebron was **b** seven years
21:27 to Heshbon, let it be **b**;
23:14 and **b** seven altars, and offered
32:34 And the children of Gad **b** Dibon
32:37 And the children of Reuben **b**
32:38 to the cities which they **b**.
Deut 8:12 and have **b** beautiful houses and
13:16 it shall not be **b** again.
20: 5 What man is there who has **b** a
Josh 8:30 Now Joshua **b** an altar to the
19:50 and he **b** the city and dwelt in
22:10 half the tribe of Manasseh **b**
22:11 the tribe of Manasseh have **b**
22:16 in that you have **b** for
22:23 If we have **b** ourselves an altar
Judg 1:26 **b** a city, and called its name
6:24 So Gideon **b** an altar there to
6:28 the altar which had been **b**.
21: 4 the people rose early and **b** an
Ruth 4:11 the two who **b** the house of
1 Sam 7:17 and there he **b** an altar to the
14:35 Then Saul **b** an altar to the
14:35 was the first altar that he **b**
2 Sam 5: 9 And David **b** all around from the
5:11 And they **b** David a house.
7: 7 Why have you not **b** Me a house of
24:25 And David **b** there an altar to
1 Ki 3: 2 because there was no house **b**
6: 2 the house which King Solomon **b**
6: 5 the wall of the temple he **b**
6: 7 the temple, when it was being **b**,
6: 7 was **b** with stone finished at
6: 7 the temple while it was being **b**.
6: 9 So he **b** the temple and finished
6:10 And he **b** side chambers against
6:14 So Solomon **b** the temple and
6:15 And he **b** the inside walls of the
6:16 Then he **b** the twenty-cubit room
6:16 he **b** it inside as the inner
6:36 And he **b** the inner court with
7: 2 He also **b** the House of the
8:13 I have surely **b** You an exalted
8:20 and I have **b** a temple for the
8:27 this temple which I have **b**!
8:43 this temple which I have **b** is
8:44 and the temple which I have **b**
8:48 and the temple which I have **b**
9: 3 this house which you have **b** to
9:10 when Solomon had **b** the two
9:17 And Solomon **b** Gezer, Lower Beth
9:24 her house which Solomon had **b**
9:24 Then he **b** the Millo.
9:25 on the altar which he had **b**
9:26 King Solomon also **b** a fleet of
10: 4 the house that he had **b**,
11: 7 Then Solomon **b** a high place for
11:27 Solomon had **b** the Millo and
11:38 as I **b** for David, and will give
12:25 Then Jeroboam **b** Shechem in the
12:25 he went out from there and **b**
14:23 For they also **b** for themselves
15:17 and **b** Ramah, that he might let
15:22 and with them King Asa **b** Geba
15:23 did, and the cities which he **b**,
16:24 then he **b** on the hill, and
16:24 the name of the city which he **b**,
16:32 which he had **b** in Samaria.
16:34 In his days Hiel of Bethel **b**
18:32 Then with the stones he **b** an
22:39 the ivory house which he **b** and
22:39 and all the cities that he **b**,
2 Ki 14:22 He **b** Elath and restored it to
15:35 He **b** the Upper Gate of the
16:11 Then Urijah the priest **b** an
16:18 pavilion which they had **b** in
17: 9 and they **b** for themselves high
21: 4 He also **b** altars in the house of
21: 5 And he **b** altars for all the host
23:13 Solomon king of Israel had **b**
25: 1 and they **b** a siege wall against
1 Chr 6:10 in the temple that Solomon **b**
6:32 until Solomon had **b** the house
7:24 who **b** Lower and Upper Beth
8:12 who **b** Ono and Lod with its
11: 8 And he **b** the city around it,
15: 1 David **b** houses for himself in
17: 6 Why have you not **b** Me a house of
21:26 And David **b** there an altar to
22: 5 and the house to be **b** for the
22:19 into the house that is to be **b**
2 Chr 6: 2 I have surely **b** You an exalted
6:10 and I have **b** the temple for the
6:18 this temple which I have **b**!
6:33 this temple which I have **b** is
6:34 and the temple which I have **b**
6:38 the temple which I have **b** for
8: 1 in which Solomon had **b** the
8: 2 Solomon **b** them; and he settled
8: 4 He also **b** Tadmor in the
8: 4 the storage cities which he **b**
8: 5 He **b** Upper Beth Horon and Lower
8:11 of David to the house he had **b**
8:12 of the LORD which he had **b**
9: 3 the house that he had **b**,
11: 5 and **b** cities for defense in
11: 6 And he **b** Bethlehem, Etam, Tekoa,
14: 6 And he **b** fortified cities in
14: 7 So they **b** and prospered.
16: 1 came up against Judah and **b**
16: 6 and with them he **b** Geba and
17:12 and he **b** fortresses and storage
20: 8 and have **b** You a sanctuary in
26: 2 He **b** Elath and restored it to
26: 6 and he **b** cities around Ashdod
26: 9 And Uzziah **b** towers in Jerusalem
26:10 Also he **b** towers in the desert.
27: 3 He **b** the Upper Gate of the house
27: 3 and he **b** extensively on the
27: 4 Moreover he **b** cities in the
27: 4 and in the forests he **b**
32: 5 **b** up all the wall that was
32: 5 and **b** another wall outside;
33: 4 He also **b** altars in the house of
33: 5 And he **b** altars for all the host
33:14 After this he **b** a wall outside
33:15 all the altars that he had **b**
33:19 and the sites where he **b** high
35: 3 son of David, king of Israel, **b**.
Ezra 3: 2 arose and **b** the altar of the
4:13 if this city is **b** and the walls
4:21 that this city may not be **b**
5: 8 which is being **b** with heavy
5:11 the temple that was **b** many
5:11 which a great king of Israel **b**
6:14 So the elders of the Jews **b**,
6:14 And they **b** and finished it,
Neh 3: 1 his brethren the priests and **b**
3: 1 They **b** as far as the Tower of
3: 2 Eliashib the men of Jericho **b**.
3: 2 them Zaccur the son of Imri **b**.
3: 3 Also the sons of Hassenaah **b**
3:13 They **b** it, hung its doors with
3:14 he **b** it and hung its doors with
3:15 he **b** it, covered it, hung its
4: 6 So we **b** the wall, and the
4:17 Those who **b** on the wall, and
4:18 girded at his side as he **b**.
7: 1 when the wall was **b** and I had
12:29 had **b** themselves villages
Job 3:14 Who **b** ruins for themselves,
22:23 you will be **b** up; You will
Ps 78:69 And He **b** His sanctuary like the
89: 2 Mercy shall be **b** up forever;
122: 3 Jerusalem is **b** As a city that
Prov 9: 1 Wisdom has **b** her house, She
24: 3 Through wisdom a house is **b**,
Eccl 2: 4 I **b** myself houses, and planted
9:14 and **b** great snares around it.
Song 4: 4 **B** for an armory, On which
Isa 5: 2 He **b** a tower in its midst,
44:26 of Judah, 'You shall be **b**,
44:28 to Jerusalem, "You shall be **b**,
Jer 7:31 And they have **b** the high places
19: 5 (they have also **b** the high
30:18 The city shall be **b** upon its
31:38 that the city shall be **b** for
32:31 fury from the day that they **b**
32:35 And they **b** the high places of
45: 4 what I have **b** I will break
52: 4 and they **b** a siege wall
Ezek 16:24 that you also **b** for yourself a
16:25 You **b** your high places at the
16:31 and **b** your high place in every
Dan 4:30 that I have **b** for a royal
9:25 The street shall be **b** again,
Hos 8:14 And has **b** temples; Judah also
Am 5:11 Though you have **b** houses of
Mic 7:11 day when your walls are to be **b**,
Hag 1: 2 the LORD's house should be **b**.
Zech 1:16 My house shall be **b** in it,"
8: 9 That the temple might be **b**.
9: 3 For Tyre **b** herself a tower,
Mt 7:24 liken him to a wise man who **b**
7:26 be like a foolish man who **b**
21:33 dug a winepress in it and **b** a
Mk 12: 1 place for the wine vat and **b**
Lk 4:29 hill on which their city was **b**,
6:49 nothing is like a man who **b** a
7: 5 and has **b** us a synagogue."
17:28 they sold, they planted, they **b**;
Acts 7:47 But Solomon **b** Him a house.
1 Cor 3:14 If anyone's work which he has **b**
Eph 2:20 having been **b** on the foundation
2:22 in whom you also are being **b**
Col 2: 7 rooted and **b** up in Him and
Heb 3: 3 inasmuch as He who **b** the house
3: 4 For every house is **b** by someone,
3: 4 but He who **b** all things is
1 Pe 2: 5 are being **b** up a spiritual

BUKKI (5/4)

Num 34:22 **B** the son of Jogli;
1 Chr 6: 5 Abishua begot **B**,
6: 5 and **B** begot Uzzi;
6:51 **B** his son, Uzzi his son,
Ezra 7: 4 the son of Uzzi, the son of **B**,

BUKKIAH (2/2)

1 Chr 25: 4 Of Heman, the sons of Heman: ***B***,
25:13 the sixth for ***B***, his sons and

BUL (1/1)

1 Ki 6:38 year, in the month of ***B***,

BULGE (2/2)

Ps 73: 7 Their eyes ***b*** with abundance;
Isa 30:13 A ***b*** in a high wall, Whose

BULL (104/94) BULL'S, BULLS

Ex 29: 1 Take one young ***b*** and two rams
29: 3 with the ***b*** and the two rams.
29:10 You shall also have the ***b***
29:10 hands on the head of the ***b***.
29:11 Then you shall kill the ***b*** before
29:12 some of the blood of the ***b***
29:14 "But the flesh of the ***b***,
29:36 And you shall offer a ***b*** every
Lev 1: 5 He shall kill the ***b*** before the
4: 3 which he has sinned a young ***b***
4: 4 He shall bring the ***b*** to the door
4: 4 and kill the ***b*** before the
4: 7 the remaining blood of the ***b***
4: 8 from it all the fat of the ***b***
4:10 as it was taken from the ***b*** of
4:12 the whole ***b*** he shall carry
4:14 assembly shall offer a young ***b***
4:15 hands on the head of the ***b***
4:15 Then the ***b*** shall be killed
4:20 And he shall do with the ***b*** as he
4:20 the bull as he did with the ***b***
4:21 Then he shall carry the ***b***
4:21 it as he burned the first ***b***.
8: 2 a ***b*** as the sin offering, two
8:14 And he brought the ***b*** for the
8:14 hands on the head of the ***b*** for
8:17 But the ***b***, its hide, its flesh,
9: 2 Take for yourself a young ***b*** as a
9: 4 also a ***b*** and a ram as peace
9:18 He also killed the ***b*** and the
9:19 and the fat from the ***b*** and the
16: 3 with the blood of a young ***b***
16: 6 Aaron shall offer the ***b*** as a
16:11 And Aaron shall bring the ***b*** of
16:11 and shall kill the ***b*** as the sin
16:14 some of the blood of the ***b*** and
16:15 he did with the blood of the ***b***,
16:18 some of the blood of the ***b*** and
16:27 The ***b*** for the sin offering and
22:23 Either a ***b*** or a lamb that has
22:27 When a ***b*** or a sheep or a goat is
23:18 without blemish, one young ***b***,
Num 7:15 one young ***b***, one ram, and one
7:21 one young ***b***, one ram, and one
7:27 one young ***b***, one ram, and one
7:33 one young ***b***, one ram, and one
7:39 one young ***b***, one ram, and one
7:45 one young ***b***, one ram, and one
7:51 one young ***b***, one ram, and one
7:57 one young ***b***, one ram, and one
7:63 one young ***b***, one ram, and one
7:69 one young ***b***, one ram, and one
7:75 one young ***b***, one ram, and one
7:81 one young ***b***, one ram, and one
8: 8 Then let them take a young ***b***
8: 8 you shall take another young ***b***
15: 8 'And when you prepare a young ***b***
15: 9 be offered with the young ***b*** a
15:11 shall be done for each young ***b***,
15:24 shall offer one young ***b*** as a
23: 2 Balak and Balaam offered a ***b***
23: 4 offered on each altar a ***b*** and
23:14 and offered a ***b*** and a ram on
23:30 and offered a ***b*** and a ram on
28:12 mixed with oil, for each ***b***;
28:14 be half a hin of wine for a ***b***,
28:20 ephah you shall offer for a ***b***,
28:28 of an ephah for each ***b***,
29: 2 aroma to the LORD: one young ***b***,
29: 3 of an ephah for the ***b***,
29: 8 as a sweet aroma: one young ***b***,
29: 9 of an ephah for the ***b***,
29:36 sweet aroma to the LORD: one ***b***,
29:37 their drink offerings for the ***b***,
Deut 17: 1 to the LORD your God a ***b*** or
18: 3 whether it is ***b*** or sheep:
33:17 glory is like a firstborn ***b***,
Judg 6:25 "Take your father's young ***b***,
6:25 the second ***b*** of seven years
6:26 and take the second ***b*** and offer
6:28 and the second ***b*** was being
1 Sam 1:25 Then they slaughtered a ***b***,
1 Ki 18:23 and let them choose one ***b*** for
18:23 and I will prepare the other ***b***,
18:25 Choose one ***b*** for yourselves and
18:26 So they took the ***b*** which was
18:33 cut the ***b*** in pieces, and laid
2 Chr 13: 9 himself with a young ***b*** and
Job 21:10 Their ***b*** breeds without failure;
Ps 50: 9 I will not take a ***b*** from your
69:31 LORD better than an ox or ***b***,
Isa 66: 3 He who kills a ***b*** is as if he
Jer 31:18 chastised, Like an untrained ***b***;
Ezek 43:19 You shall give a young ***b*** for a
43:21 'Then you shall also take the ***b***
43:22 as they cleansed it with the ***b***.
43:23 you shall offer a young ***b***
43:25 shall also prepare a young ***b***
45:18 you shall take a young ***b***
45:22 all the people of the land a ***b***
45:24 of one ephah for each ***b*** and
46: 6 Moon it shall be a young ***b***
46: 7 offering of an ephah for a ***b***,
46:11 shall be an ephah for a ***b***,

BULLOCK (KJV) See BULL, OX

BULL'S (4/4) BULL

Lev 4: 4 lay his hand on the ***b*** head, and
4: 5 shall take some of the ***b*** blood
4:11 But the ***b*** hide and all its
4:16 shall bring some of the ***b***

BULLS (59/56) BULL

Gen 32:15 colts, forty cows and ten ***b***,
Num 7:87 offering were twelve young ***b***,
7:88 offerings were twenty-four ***b***,
8:12 on the heads of the young ***b***,
23: 1 and prepare for me here seven ***b***
23:29 and prepare for me here seven ***b***
28:11 to the LORD: two young ***b***,
28:19 to the LORD: two young ***b***,
28:27 aroma to the LORD: two young ***b***,
29:13 to the LORD: thirteen young ***b***,
29:14 for each of the thirteen ***b***,
29:17 day present twelve young ***b***,
29:18 their drink offerings for the ***b***,
29:20 the third day present eleven ***b***,
29:21 their drink offerings for the ***b***,
29:23 the fourth day present ten ***b***,
29:24 their drink offerings for the ***b***,
29:26 the fifth day present nine ***b***,
29:27 their drink offerings for the ***b***,
29:29 the sixth day present eight ***b***,
29:30 their drink offerings for the ***b***,
29:32 seventh day present seven ***b***,
29:33 their drink offerings for the ***b***,
1 Sam 1:24 him up with her, with three ***b***,
1 Ki 8:63 twenty-two thousand ***b*** and one
18:23 let them give us two ***b***;
1 Chr 15:26 that they offered seven ***b*** and
29:21 on the next day: a thousand ***b***,
2 Chr 7: 5 of twenty-two thousand ***b*** and
15:11 at that time seven hundred ***b***
29:21 And they brought seven ***b***,
29:22 So they killed the ***b***,
29:32 assembly brought was seventy ***b***,
29:33 things were six hundred ***b*** and
30:24 to the assembly a thousand ***b***
30:24 to the assembly a thousand ***b***
Ezra 6: 9 And whatever they need—young ***b***,
6:17 house of God, one hundred ***b***,
7:17 to buy with this money ***b***,
8:35 twelve ***b*** for all Israel,
Job 42: 8 take for yourselves seven ***b*** and
Ps 22:12 Many ***b*** have surrounded Me;
22:12 Strong ***b*** of Bashan have
50:13 Will I eat the flesh of ***b***,
51:19 Then they shall offer ***b*** on
66:15 I will offer ***b*** with goats.
68:30 The herd of ***b*** with the calves
Isa 1:11 not delight in the blood of ***b***,
34: 7 And the young ***b*** with the
34: 7 young bulls with the mighty ***b***;
Jer 46:21 are in her midst like fat ***b***,
50:11 grain, And you bellow like ***b***,
50:27 Slay all her ***b***, Let them go
52:20 the twelve bronze ***b*** which were
Ezek 39:18 rams and lambs, Of goats and ***b***,
45:23 seven ***b*** and seven rams without
Hos 12:11 Though they sacrifice ***b*** in
Heb 9:13 For if the blood of ***b*** and goats
10: 4 possible that the blood of ***b***

BULRUSH (3/3) BULRUSHES

Isa 9:14 Palm branch and ***b*** in one day.
19:15 head or tail, Palm branch or ***b***,
58: 5 to bow down his head like a ***b***,

BULRUSHES (1/1) BULRUSH

Ex 2: 3 she took an ark of ***b*** for him,

BULWARKS (2/2)

Ps 48:13 Mark well her ***b***;
Isa 26: 1 salvation for walls and ***b***.

BUNAH (1/1)

1 Chr 2:25 were Ram, the firstborn, and ***B***,

BUNCH (1/1)

Ex 12:22 And you shall take a ***b*** of

BUNDLE (4/4) BUNDLES

Gen 42:35 that surprisingly each man's ***b***
1 Sam 25:29 my lord shall be bound in the ***b***
Song 1:13 A ***b*** of myrrh is my beloved to
Acts 28: 3 But when Paul had gathered a ***b***

BUNDLES (3/3) BUNDLE

Gen 42:35 and their father saw the ***b*** of
Ruth 2:16 Also let grain from the ***b*** fall
Mt 13:30 the tares and bind them in ***b***

BUNNI (3/3)

Neh 9: 4 Bani, Kadmiel, Shebaniah, ***B***,
10:15 ***B***, Azgad, Bebai,
11:15 son of Hashabiah, the son of ***B***;

BURDEN (56/56) BURDENED, BURDENS, BURDENSOME

Gen 49:15 his shoulder to bear a ***b***,
Ex 18:22 for they will bear the ***b*** with
23: 5 who hates you lying under its ***b***,
Num 11:11 that You have laid the ***b*** of all
11:14 because the ***b*** is too heavy for
11:17 and they shall bear the ***b*** of
2 Sam 13:25 lest we be a ***b*** to you."
15:33 then you will become a ***b*** to me.
19:35 your servant be a further ***b*** to
2 Ki 9:25 that the LORD laid this ***b*** upon
2 Chr 6:29 when each one knows his own ***b***
34:13 were over the ***b*** bearers and
35: 3 It shall no longer be a ***b*** on
Job 7:20 So that I am a ***b*** to myself?
Ps 38: 4 Like a heavy ***b*** they are too
55:22 Cast your ***b*** on the LORD, And
81: 6 removed his shoulder from the ***b***;
Eccl 12: 5 The grasshopper is a ***b***,
Isa 9: 4 have broken the yoke of his ***b***
10:27 pass in that day That his ***b***
13: 1 The ***b*** against Babylon which
14:25 And his ***b*** removed from their
14:28 This is the ***b*** which came in the
15: 1 The ***b*** against Moab. Because in
17: 1 The ***b*** against Damascus.
19: 1 The ***b*** against Egypt.
21: 1 The ***b*** against the Wilderness of
21:11 The ***b*** against Dumah. He calls
21:13 The ***b*** against Arabia. In the
22: 1 The ***b*** against the Valley of
22:25 and the ***b*** that was on it will
23: 1 The ***b*** against Tyre. Wail, you
30: 6 The ***b*** against the beasts of the
30:27 And His ***b*** is heavy; His
46: 1 A ***b*** to the weary beast.
46: 2 They could not deliver the ***b***,
Jer 17:21 and bear no ***b*** on the Sabbath
17:22 nor carry a ***b*** out of your houses
17:24 to bring no ***b*** through the gates
17:27 such as not carrying a ***b*** when
Ezek 12:10 This ***b*** concerns the prince in
Hos 8:10 Because of the ***b*** of the king
Nah 1: 1 The ***b*** against Nineveh. The book
Hab 1: 1 The ***b*** which the prophet
Zeph 3:18 To whom its reproach is a ***b***.
Zech 9: 1 The ***b*** of the word of the LORD
12: 1 The ***b*** of the word of the LORD
Mal 1: 1 The ***b*** of the word of the LORD
Mt 11:30 For My yoke is easy and My ***b*** is
20:12 to us who have borne the ***b*** and
Acts 15:28 to lay upon you no greater ***b***
2 Cor 11: 9 I was a ***b*** to no one, for what I
12:16 I did not ***b*** you.
1 Th 2: 9 that we might not be a ***b*** to any
2 Th 3: 8 that we might not be a ***b*** to any
Rev 2:24 I will put on you no other ***b***.

BURDENED (6/6) BURDEN

Prov 28:17 A man ***b*** with bloodshed will
Isa 43:24 But you have ***b*** Me with your
2 Cor 1: 8 that we were ***b*** beyond measure,
5: 4 in this tent groan, being ***b***,
8:13 should be eased and you ***b***;
1 Tim 5:16 and do not let the church be ***b***,

BURDENS (19/18) BURDEN

Gen 49:14 Lying down between two ***b***;
Ex 1:11 to afflict them with their ***b***.
2:11 brethren and looked at their ***b***.
6: 6 bring you out from under the ***b***
6: 7 you out from under the ***b*** of
Num 4:47 and the work of bearing ***b*** in
Deut 1:12 bear your problems and your ***b***
1 Ki 5:15 seventy thousand who carried ***b***,
2 Chr 2: 2 seventy thousand men to bear ***b***,
2:18 thousand of them bearers of ***b***,
Neh 4:17 wall, and those who carried ***b***,
5:15 who were before me laid ***b*** on
13:15 figs, and all kinds of ***b***,
13:19 so that no ***b*** would be brought
Isa 58: 6 To undo the heavy ***b***,
Mt 23: 4 "For they bind heavy ***b***,
Lk 11:46 For you load men with ***b*** hard
11:46 yourselves do not touch the ***b***
Gal 6: 2 Bear one another's ***b***,

BURDENSOME (9/9) BURDEN

1 Ki 12: 4 lighten the ***b*** service of your
2 Chr 10: 4 lighten the ***b*** service of your
Eccl 1:13 this ***b*** task God has given to
2:23 are sorrowful, and his work ***b***;
Isa 15: 4 His life will be ***b*** to him.
2 Cor 11: 9 I kept myself from being ***b*** to
12:13 except that I myself was not ***b***
12:14 And I will not be ***b*** to you; for
1 Jn 5: 3 And His commandments are not ***b***.

BURIAL (17/16) BURY

Gen 23: 4 Give me property for a ***b*** place
23: 6 dead in the choicest of our ***b***
23: 6 us will withhold from you his ***b***
23: 9 as property for a ***b*** place among
23:20 of Heth as property for a ***b***
47:30 of Egypt and bury me in their ***b***
49:30 as a possession for a ***b*** place.
50:13 the Hittite as property for a ***b***
2 Chr 26:23 his fathers in the field of ***b***
Eccl 6: 3 goodness, or indeed he has no ***b***,
Isa 14:20 not be joined with them in ***b***,
Jer 22:19 He shall be buried with the ***b***
Ezek 39:11 day that I will give Gog a ***b***
Mt 26:12 My body, she did it for My ***b***.
Mk 14: 8 to anoint My body for ***b***.
Jn 12: 7 kept this for the day of My ***b***.
Acts 8: 2 men carried Stephen to his ***b***,

BURIED (104/101) BURY

Gen 15:15 you shall be ***b*** at a good old
23:19 Abraham ***b*** Sarah his wife in the
25: 9 his sons Isaac and Ishmael ***b***
25:10 of Heth. There Abraham was ***b***,
35: 8 and she was ***b*** below Bethel
35:19 So Rachel died and was ***b*** on the
35:29 And his sons Esau and Jacob ***b***
48: 7 and I ***b*** her there on the way to
49:31 There they ***b*** Abraham and Sarah
49:31 there they ***b*** Isaac and Rebekah
49:31 and there I ***b*** Leah.
50:13 and ***b*** him in the cave of the
50:14 And after he had ***b*** his father,
Num 11:34 because there they ***b*** the people
20: 1 and Miriam died there and was ***b***
Deut 10: 6 Aaron died, and where he was ***b***;
34: 6 And He ***b*** him in a valley in the
Josh 24:30 And they ***b*** him within the border
24:32 they ***b*** at Shechem, in the plot
24:33 They ***b*** him in a hill belonging
Judg 2: 9 And they ***b*** him within the border
8:32 and was ***b*** in the tomb of Joash
10: 2 and he died and was ***b*** in
10: 5 And Jair died and was ***b*** in
12: 7 the Gileadite died and was ***b***
12:10 Then Ibzan died and was ***b*** at
12:12 the Zebulunite died and was ***b***
12:15 the Pirathonite died and was ***b***
16:31 and brought him up and ***b*** him
Ruth 1:17 die, And there will I be ***b***.
1 Sam 25: 1 and ***b*** him at his home in Ramah.
28: 3 had lamented for him and ***b*** him
31:13 they took their bones and ***b***
2 Sam 2: 4 Gilead were the ones who ***b***
2: 5 to Saul, and have ***b*** him.
2:32 Then they took up Asahel and ***b***
3:32 So they ***b*** Abner in Hebron; and
4:12 the head of Ishbosheth and ***b***
17:23 and he was ***b*** in his father's
21:14 They ***b*** the bones of Saul and
1 Ki 2:10 and was ***b*** in the City of David.
2:34 and he was ***b*** in his own house
11:43 and was ***b*** in the City of David
13:31 after he had ***b*** him, that he
13:31 tomb where the man of God is ***b***;
14:18 And they ***b*** him; and all Israel
14:31 and was ***b*** with his fathers in
15: 8 and they ***b*** him in the City of
15:24 and was ***b*** with his fathers in
16: 6 with his fathers and was ***b*** in
16:28 with his fathers and was ***b*** in
22:37 And they ***b*** the king in Samaria.
22:50 and was ***b*** with his fathers in
2 Ki 8:24 and was ***b*** with his fathers in
9:28 and ***b*** him in his tomb with his
10:35 and they ***b*** him in Samaria.
12:21 and they ***b*** him with his fathers
13: 9 and they ***b*** him in Samaria.
13:13 And Joash was ***b*** in Samaria with
13:20 and they ***b*** him. And the
14:16 and was ***b*** in Samaria with the
14:20 and he was ***b*** at Jerusalem with
15: 7 and they ***b*** him with his fathers
15:38 and was ***b*** with his fathers in
16:20 and was ***b*** with his fathers in
21:18 and was ***b*** in the garden of his
21:26 And he was ***b*** in his tomb in the
23:30 and ***b*** him in his own tomb.
1 Chr 10:12 and ***b*** their bones under the
2 Chr 9:31 and was ***b*** in the City of David
12:16 and was ***b*** in the City of David.
14: 1 and they ***b*** him in the City of
16:14 They ***b*** him in his own tomb,
21: 1 and was ***b*** with his fathers in
21:20 However they ***b*** him in the City
22: 9 they ***b*** him, "because," they
24:16 And they ***b*** him in the City of
24:25 And they ***b*** him in the City of
25:28 brought him on horses and ***b***
26:23 and they ***b*** him with his fathers
27: 9 and they ***b*** him in the City of
28:27 and they ***b*** him in the city, in
32:33 and they ***b*** him in the upper
33:20 and they ***b*** him in his own
35:24 and was ***b*** in one of the tombs
Job 27:15 who survive him shall be ***b*** in
Eccl 8:10 Then I saw the wicked ***b***,
Jer 8: 2 shall not be gathered nor ***b***;
16: 4 be lamented nor shall they be ***b***,
16: 6 this land. They shall not be ***b***;
20: 6 and be ***b*** there, you and all
22:19 He shall be ***b*** with the burial
25:33 be lamented, or gathered, or ***b***;
Ezek 39:15 till the buriers have ***b*** it in
Mt 14:12 and took away the body and ***b***
Lk 16:22 rich man also died and was ***b***.
Acts 2:29 that he is both dead and ***b***,
5: 6 carried him out, and ***b*** him.
5: 9 the feet of those who have ***b***
5:10 ***b*** her by her husband.
13:36 was ***b*** with his fathers, and saw
Rom 6: 4 Therefore we were ***b*** with Him
1 Cor 15: 4 and that He was ***b***, and that He
Col 2:12 ***b*** with Him in baptism, in which

BURIERS (1/1) BURY

Ezek 39:15 till the ***b*** have buried it in

BURIES (2/2) BURY

Prov 19:24 A lazy man ***b*** his hand in the
26:15 The lazy man ***b*** his hand in the

BURN (144/137) BURNED, BURNING, BURNINGS, BURNS, BURNT

Gen 44:18 and do not let your anger ***b***
Ex 3: 3 sight, why the bush does not ***b***.
12:10 of it until morning you shall ***b***
21:25 ***b*** for burn, wound for wound,
21:25 'burn for ***b***, wound for wound,
27:20 to cause the lamp to ***b***
29:13 and ***b*** them on the altar.
29:14 you shall ***b*** with fire outside
29:18 And you shall ***b*** the whole ram on
29:25 back from their hands and ***b***
29:34 then you shall ***b*** the remainder
30: 1 You shall make an altar to ***b***
30: 7 Aaron shall ***b*** on it sweet
30: 7 he shall ***b*** incense on it.
30: 8 he shall ***b*** incense on it, a
30:20 to ***b*** an offering made by fire
32:10 that My wrath may ***b*** hot against
32:11 why does Your wrath ***b*** hot
Lev 1: 9 And the priest shall ***b*** all on
1:13 shall bring it all and ***b*** it
1:15 and ***b*** it on the altar; its
1:17 and the priest shall ***b*** it on
2: 2 And the priest shall ***b*** it as
2: 9 and ***b*** it on the altar. It is
2:11 for you shall ***b*** no leaven nor
2:16 Then the priest shall ***b*** the
3: 5 and Aaron's sons shall ***b*** it on
3:11 and the priest shall ***b*** them on
3:16 and the priest shall ***b*** them on
4:10 and the priest shall ***b*** them on
4:12 and ***b*** it on wood with fire;
4:19 take all the fat from it and ***b***
4:21 and ***b*** it as he burned the first
4:26 And he shall ***b*** all its fat on
4:31 and the priest shall ***b*** it on
4:35 Then the priest shall ***b*** it on
5:12 and ***b*** it on the altar
6:12 And the priest shall ***b*** wood on
6:12 and he shall ***b*** on it the fat of
6:15 and shall ***b*** it on the altar
7: 5 and the priest shall ***b*** them on
7:31 And the priest shall ***b*** the fat
8:32 and of the bread you shall ***b***
13:24 Or if the body receives a ***b*** on
13:24 and the raw flesh of the ***b***
13:25 is leprosy broken out in the ***b***.
13:28 it is a swelling from the ***b***.
13:28 for it is the scar from the ***b***.
13:52 He shall therefore ***b*** that
13:55 and you shall ***b*** it in the fire;
13:57 you shall ***b*** with fire that in
16:25 of the sin offering he shall ***b***
16:27 And they shall ***b*** in the fire
17: 6 and ***b*** the fat for a sweet aroma
24: 2 to make the lamps ***b***
Num 5:26 ***b*** it on the altar, and
18:17 and ***b*** their fat as an offering
Deut 7: 5 and ***b*** their carved images with
7:25 You shall ***b*** the carved images of
12: 3 and ***b*** their wooden images with
12:31 for they ***b*** even their sons and
13:16 and completely ***b*** with fire the
29:20 LORD and His jealousy would ***b***
32:22 And shall ***b*** to the lowest
Josh 11: 6 hamstring their horses and ***b***
23:16 the anger of the LORD will ***b***
Judg 9:52 the door of the tower to ***b*** it
12: 1 We will ***b*** your house down on
14:15 or else we will ***b*** you and your
1 Sam 2:16 They should really ***b*** the fat
2:28 to ***b*** incense, and to wear an
1 Ki 13: 1 stood by the altar to ***b***
13: 2 of the high places who ***b***
2 Ki 16:15 On the great new altar ***b*** the
23: 5 of Judah had ordained to ***b***
1 Chr 23:13 to ***b*** incense before the LORD,
2 Chr 2: 4 to ***b*** before Him sweet incense,
2: 6 except to ***b*** sacrifice before
4:20 to ***b*** in the prescribed manner
13:11 And they ***b*** to the LORD every
13:11 of gold with its lamps to ***b***
26:16 the temple of the LORD to ***b***
26:18 to ***b*** incense to the LORD, but
26:18 who are consecrated to ***b***
26:19 had a censer in his hand to ***b***
28:25 Judah he made high places to ***b***
29:11 should minister to Him and ***b***
32:12 worship before one altar and ***b***
Neh 10:34 to ***b*** on the altar of the LORD
Job 30:30 My bones ***b*** with fever.
Ps 79: 5 Will Your jealousy ***b*** like
89:46 Will Your wrath ***b*** like fire?
Isa 1:31 Both will ***b*** together, And no
10:17 It will ***b*** and devour His
27: 4 I would ***b*** them together.
40:16 Lebanon is not sufficient to ***b***,
44:15 it shall be for a man to ***b***,
47:14 The fire shall ***b*** them; They
65: 3 And ***b*** incense on altars of
Jer 4: 4 And ***b*** so that no one can
7: 9 ***b*** incense to Baal, and walk
7:20 And it will ***b*** and not be
7:31 to ***b*** their sons and their
9:12 does the land perish and ***b*** up
11:13 altars to ***b*** incense to Baal.
15:14 Which shall ***b*** upon you."
17: 4 fire in My anger which shall ***b***
19: 5 to ***b*** their sons with fire for
21:10 and he shall ***b*** it with fire."
21:12 fury go forth like fire And ***b***
32:29 set fire to this city and ***b*** it,
34: 2 and he shall ***b*** it with fire.
34: 5 so they shall ***b*** incense for you
34:22 against it and take it and ***b***
36:25 implored the king not to ***b*** the
37: 8 and take it and ***b*** it with
37:10 and ***b*** the city with fire.'"
38:18 they shall ***b*** it with fire, and
43:12 and he shall ***b*** them and carry
43:13 of the Egyptians he shall ***b***
44: 3 in that they went to ***b*** incense
44: 5 to ***b*** no incense to other gods.
44:17 to ***b*** incense to the queen of
44:25 to ***b*** incense to the queen of
Ezek 5: 2 You shall ***b*** with fire one-third
5: 4 and ***b*** them in the fire.
16:41 They shall ***b*** your houses with
23:47 and ***b*** their houses with fire.
24:11 become hot and its bronze may ***b***,
39: 9 go out and set on fire and ***b***
43:21 and ***b*** it in the appointed place
Hos 4:13 And ***b*** incense on the hills,
Am 6:10 with one who will ***b*** the
Nah 2:13 I will ***b*** your chariots in smoke,
Hab 1:16 And ***b*** incense to their dragnet;
Mal 4: 1 the day which is coming shall ***b***
Mt 3:12 but He will ***b*** up the chaff with
13:30 and bind them in bundles to ***b***
Lk 1: 9 his lot fell to ***b*** incense when
3:17 but the chaff He will ***b*** with
24:32 Did not our heart ***b*** within us
1 Cor 7: 9 it is better to marry than to ***b***
2 Cor 11:29 I do not ***b*** with indignation?
Rev 17:16 eat her flesh and ***b*** her with

BURNED (167/159) BURN

Gen 38:24 her out and let her be ***b***!
Ex 32:20 ***b*** it in the fire, and ground
40:27 and he ***b*** sweet incense on it, as
Lev 2:12 but they shall not be ***b*** on the
4:12 are poured out it shall be ***b***.
4:21 and burn it as he ***b*** the first
6:22 the LORD. It shall be wholly ***b***.
6:23 the priest shall be wholly ***b***.
6:30 It shall be ***b*** in the fire.
7:17 on the third day must be ***b***
7:19 It shall be ***b*** with fire. And as
8:16 and Moses ***b*** them on the altar.
8:17 he ***b*** with fire outside the
8:20 and Moses ***b*** the head, the
8:21 And Moses ***b*** the whole ram on
8:28 them from their hands and ***b***
9:10 liver of the sin offering he ***b***
9:11 The flesh and the hide he ***b*** with
9:13 and he ***b*** them on the altar.
9:14 and ***b*** them with the burnt
9:17 and ***b*** it on the altar, besides
9:20 Then he ***b*** the fat on the altar;
10:16 ***b*** up. And he was angry with
13:52 the garment shall be ***b*** in the
19: 6 it shall be ***b*** in the fire.
20:14 They shall be ***b*** with fire, both
21: 9 She shall be ***b*** with fire.
Num 11: 1 So the fire of the LORD ***b***
11: 3 the fire of the LORD had ***b***
16:39 which those who were ***b*** up had
19: 5 Then the heifer shall be ***b*** in
19: 5 blood, and its offal shall be ***b***.
24:22 Nevertheless Kain shall be ***b***.
31:10 They also ***b*** with fire all the
Deut 4:11 and the mountain ***b*** with fire to
9:15 and the mountain ***b*** with fire;
9:21 and ***b*** it with fire and crushed
Josh 6:24 But they ***b*** the city and all that
7: 1 so the anger of the LORD ***b***
7:15 the accursed thing shall be ***b***
7:25 and they ***b*** them with fire after
8:28 So Joshua ***b*** Ai and made it a
11: 9 he hamstrung their horses and ***b***
11:11 Then he ***b*** Hazor with fire.
11:13 Israel ***b*** none of them, except
11:13 Hazor only, which Joshua ***b***.
Judg 15: 5 and ***b*** up both the shocks and
15: 6 the Philistines came up and ***b***
15:14 arms became like flax that is ***b***
18:27 the edge of the sword and ***b***

1 Sam 2:15 before they **b** the fat, the
30: 1 attacked Ziklag and **b** it with
30: 3 **b** with fire; and their wives,
30:14 and we **b** Ziklag with fire."
31:12 and they came to Jabesh and **b**
2 Sam 23: 7 And they shall be utterly **b**
1 Ki 3: 3 except that he sacrificed and **b**
9:16 gone up and taken Gezer and **b**
9:25 and he **b** incense with them on
11: 8 who **b** incense and sacrificed to
12:33 sacrifices on the altar and **b**
13: 2 and men's bones shall be **b** on
15:13 down her obscene image and **b**
16:18 of the king's house and **b** the
22:43 people offered sacrifices and **b**
2 Ki 1:14 come down from heaven and **b** up
10:26 out of the temple of Baal and **b**
12: 3 people still sacrificed and **b**
14: 4 people still sacrificed and **b**
15: 4 people still sacrificed and **b**
15:35 people still sacrificed and **b**
16: 4 And he sacrificed and **b** incense
16:13 So he **b** his burnt offering and
17:11 There they **b** incense on all the
17:31 and the Sepharvites **b** their
18: 4 days the children of Israel **b**
22:17 they have forsaken Me and **b**
23: 4 and he **b** them outside Jerusalem
23: 5 and those who **b** incense to
23: 6 **b** it at the Brook Kidron and
23: 8 places where the priests had **b**
23:11 and he **b** the chariots of the
23:15 and he **b** the high place and
23:15 and **b** the wooden image.
23:16 bones out of the tombs and **b**
23:20 and **b** men's bones on them; and
25: 9 He **b** the house of the LORD and
25: 9 of the great, he **b** with fire.
1 Chr 14:12 and they were **b** with fire.
2 Chr 15:16 then crushed and **b** it by the
25:14 bowed down before them and **b**
28: 3 He **b** incense in the Valley of
28: 3 and **b** his children in the fire,
28: 4 And he sacrificed and **b** incense
29: 7 and have not **b** incense or
34: 5 He also **b** the bones of the
34:25 they have forsaken Me and **b**
36:19 Then they **b** the house of God,
36:19 **b** all its palaces with fire,
Neh 1: 3 and its gates are **b** with
2: 3 and its gates are **b** with
2:13 down and its gates which were **b**
2:17 and its gates are **b** with fire.
4: 2 of rubbish—stones that are **b**?
Esth 1:12 and his anger **b** within him.
Job 1:16 of God fell from heaven and **b**
Ps 39: 3 While I was musing, the fire **b**.
74: 8 They have **b** up all the
80:16 It is **b** with fire, it is
102: 3 And my bones are **b** like a
106:18 The flame **b** up the wicked.
Prov 6:27 And his clothes not be **b**?
Isa 1: 7 Your cities are **b** with fire;
5: 5 its hedge, and it shall be **b**;
9:19 LORD of hosts The land is **b**
24: 6 inhabitants of the earth are **b**,
33:12 thorns cut up they shall be **b**
42:25 And it **b** him, Yet he did not
43: 2 the fire, you shall not be **b**,
44:19 I have **b** half of it in the fire,
64:11 Is **b** up with fire; And all
65: 7 Who have **b** incense on the
Jer 1:16 **B** incense to other gods, And
2:15 land waste; His cities are **b**,
9:10 Because they are **b** up, So
18:15 They have **b** incense to
19: 4 because they have **b** incense in
19:13 on whose roofs they have **b**
36:27 Now after the king had **b** the
36:28 the king of Judah has **b**.
36:29 You have **b** this scroll, saying,
36:32 Jehoiakim king of Judah had **b**
38:17 this city shall not be **b** with
38:23 shall cause this city to be **b**
39: 8 And the Chaldeans **b** the king's
44:15 who knew that their wives had **b**
44:19 And when we **b** incense to the
44:21 The incense that you **b** in the
44:23 Because you have **b** incense and
49: 2 And her villages shall be **b**
51:30 They have **b** her dwelling
51:32 The reeds they have **b** with
51:58 And her high gates shall be **b**
52:13 He **b** the house of the LORD and
52:13 of the great, he **b** with fire.
Ezek 15: 4 ends of it, and its middle is **b**.
15: 5 has devoured it, and it is **b**?
24:10 And let the cuts be **b** up.
Hos 2:13 of the Baals to which she **b**
11: 2 And **b** incense to carved
Joel 1:19 And a flame has **b** all the
Am 2: 1 Because he **b** the bones of the
Mic 1: 7 her pay as a harlot shall be **b**
Mt 13:40 as the tares are gathered and **b**
22: 7 murderers, and **b** up their city.
Jn 15: 6 into the fire, and they are **b**.
Acts 19:19 their books together and **b**
Rom 1:27 **b** in their lust for one
1 Cor 3:15 If anyone's work is **b**,
13: 3 though I give my body to be **b**,
Heb 6: 8 cursed, whose end is to be **b**.
12:18 that may be touched and that **b**
13:11 sin, are **b** outside the camp.
2 Pe 3:10 works that are in it will be **b**
Rev 8: 7 a third of the trees were **b** up,
8: 7 and all green grass was **b** up.
18: 8 And she will be utterly **b** with

BURNING (58/55) BURN, BURNINGS

Gen 15:17 a smoking oven and a **b** torch
Ex 3: 2 the bush was **b** with fire, but
Lev 6: 9 of the altar shall be kept **b**
6:12 on the altar shall be kept **b**
6:13 A fire shall always be **b** on the
10: 6 bewail the **b** which the LORD
16:12 shall take a censer full of **b**
Num 19: 6 into the midst of the fire **b**
Deut 5:23 while the mountain was **b** with
28:22 with severe **b** fever, with the
29:23 land is brimstone, salt, and **b**;
2 Chr 16:14 They made a very great **b** for
21:19 And his people made no **b** for
21:19 like the **b** for his fathers.
Job 41:19 Out of his mouth go **b** lights;
41:20 As from a boiling pot and **b**
Ps 11: 6 Fire and brimstone and a **b**
58: 9 your pots can feel the **b**
58: 9 As in His living and **b** wrath.
140:10 Let **b** coals fall upon them;
Prov 16:27 it is on his lips like a **b**
26:21 As charcoal is to **b** coals,
Isa 4: 4 judgment and by the spirit of **b**,
9: 5 Will be used for **b** and fuel
10:16 his glory He will kindle a **b**
10:16 kindle a burning Like the **b**
30:27 **B** with His anger, And His
34: 9 Its land shall become **b** pitch.
Jer 20: 9 word was in my heart like a **b**
36:22 with a fire **b** on the hearth
44: 8 **b** incense to other gods in the
44:18 But since we stopped **b** incense
Lam 2: 6 In His **b** indignation He has
Ezek 1:13 their appearance was like **b**
36: 5 Surely I have spoken in My **b**
Dan 3: 6 into the midst of a **b** fiery
3:11 be cast into the midst of a **b**
3:15 into the midst of a **b** fiery
3:17 able to deliver us from the **b**
3:20 and cast them into the **b**
3:21 cast into the midst of the **b**
3:23 bound into the midst of the **b**
3:26 went near the mouth of the **b**
7: 9 Its wheels a **b** fire;
7:11 destroyed and given to the **b**
Am 4:11 a firebrand plucked from the **b**;
Mal 4: 1 **B** like an oven, And all the
Mk 12:26 in the **b** bush passage, how
Lk 12:35 be girded and your lamps **b**;
20:37 even Moses showed in the **b**
Jn 5:35 He was the **b** and shining lamp,
Jas 1:11 has the sun risen with a **b**
Rev 4: 5 Seven lamps of fire were **b**
8: 8 like a great mountain **b** with
8:10 **b** like a torch, and it fell on
18: 9 they see the smoke of her **b**,
18:18 they saw the smoke of her **b**,
19:20 alive into the lake of fire **b**

BURNINGS (2/2) BURNING

Isa 33:12 people shall be like the **b** of
33:14 shall dwell with everlasting **b**?

BURNISHED (4/4)

1 Ki 7:45 of the LORD were of **b** bronze.
2 Chr 4:16 craftsman made of **b** bronze
Ezek 1: 7 sparkled like the color of **b**
Dan 10: 6 his arms and feet like **b** bronze

BURNS (15/15) BURN

Lev 16:28 Then he who **b** them shall wash
Num 19: 8 And the one who **b** it shall wash
Ps 46: 9 He **b** the chariot in the fire.
83:14 As the fire **b** the woods, And
97: 3 And **b** up His enemies round
Isa 9:18 For wickedness **b** as the fire;
44:16 He **b** half of it in the fire;
62: 1 her salvation as a lamp that **b**.
64: 2 As fire **b** brushwood, As fire
65: 5 A fire that **b** all the day.
66: 3 He who **b** incense, as if he
Jer 48:35 in the high places And **b**
Hos 7: 6 In the morning it **b** like a
Joel 2: 3 And behind them a flame **b**;
Rev 21: 8 their part in the lake which **b**

BURNT (294/267) BURNT

Gen 8:20 and offered **b** offerings on the
22: 2 and offer him there as a **b**
22: 3 and he split the wood for the **b**
22: 6 Abraham took the wood of the **b**
22: 7 but where is the lamb for a **b**
22: 8 for Himself the lamb for a **b**
22:13 and offered it up for a **b**
Ex 10:25 also give us sacrifices and **b**
18:12 took a **b** offering and other
20:24 shall sacrifice on it your **b**
24: 5 who offered **b** offerings and
29:18 It is a **b** offering to the
29:25 burn them on the altar as a **b**
29:42 shall be a continual **b**
30: 9 or a **b** offering, or a grain
30:28 the altar of **b** offering with all
31: 9 the altar of **b** offering with all
32: 6 offered **b** offerings, and
35:16 the altar of **b** offering with its
38: 1 He made the altar of **b** offering
40: 6 shall set the altar of the **b**
40:10 shall anoint the altar of the **b**
40:29 And he put the altar of **b**
40:29 and offered upon it the **b**
Lev 1: 3 If his offering is a **b**
1: 4 his hand on the head of the **b**
1: 6 And he shall skin the **b** offering
1: 9 burn all on the altar as a **b**
1:10 as a **b** sacrifice, he shall bring
1:13 it is a **b** sacrifice, an
1:14 And if the **b** sacrifice of his
1:17 It is a **b** sacrifice, an
3: 5 burn it on the altar upon the **b**
4: 7 the base of the altar of the **b**
4:10 burn them on the altar of the **b**
4:18 at the base of the altar of **b**
4:24 the place where they kill the **b**
4:25 on the horns of the altar of **b**
4:25 at the base of the altar of **b**
4:29 offering at the place of the **b**
4:30 on the horns of the altar of **b**
4:33 the place where they kill the **b**
4:34 on the horns of the altar of **b**
5: 7 offering and the other as a **b**
5:10 shall offer the second as a **b**
6: 9 This is the law of the **b**
6: 9 The **b** offering shall be on
6:10 and take up the ashes of the **b**
6:12 and lay the **b** offering in order
6:25 In the place where the **b**
7: 2 the place where they kill the **b**
7: 8 priest who offers anyone's **b**
7: 8 for himself the skin of the **b**
7:37 This is the law of the **b**
8:18 he brought the ram as the **b**
8:21 It was a **b** sacrifice for a
8:28 on the **b** offering. They were
9: 2 a sin offering and a ram as a **b**
9: 3 as a **b** offering,
9: 7 your sin offering and your **b**
9:12 And he killed the **b** offering;
9:13 Then they presented the **b**
9:14 and burned them with the **b**
9:16 And he brought the **b** offering
9:17 besides the **b** sacrifice of the
9:22 the **b** offering, and peace
9:24 the LORD and consumed the **b**
10:19 their sin offering and their **b**
12: 6 a lamb of the first year as a **b**
12: 8 one as a **b** offering and the
14:13 the sin offering and the **b**
14:19 Afterward he shall kill the **b**
14:20 the priest shall offer the **b**
14:22 sin offering and the other a **b**
14:31 offering and the other as a **b**
15:15 offering and the other as a **b**
15:30 offering and the other as a **b**
16: 3 and of a ram as a **b** offering.
16: 5 and one ram as a **b** offering.
16:24 come out and offer his **b**
16:24 his burnt offering and the **b**
17: 8 who offers a **b** offering or
22:18 they offer to the LORD as a **b**
23:12 as a **b** offering to the LORD.
23:18 They shall be as a **b** offering
23:37 a **b** offering and a grain
Num 6:11 offering and the other as a **b**
6:14 year without blemish as a **b**
6:16 his sin offering and his **b**
7:15 first year, as a **b** offering;
7:21 first year, as a **b** offering;
7:27 first year, as a **b** offering;
7:33 first year, as a **b** offering;
7:39 first year, as a **b** offering;
7:45 first year, as a **b** offering;
7:51 first year, as a **b** offering;
7:57 first year, as a **b** offering;
7:63 first year, as a **b** offering;
7:69 first year, as a **b** offering;
7:75 first year, as a **b** offering;
7:81 first year, as a **b** offering;
7:87 All the oxen for the **b** offering
8:12 offering and the other as a **b**
10:10 blow the trumpets over your **b**
15: 3 a **b** offering or a sacrifice, to
15: 5 you shall prepare with the **b**
15: 8 you prepare a young bull as a **b**
15:24 offer one young bull as a **b**
19:17 of the ashes of the heifer **b**
23: 3 Stand by your **b** offering, and I
23: 6 standing by his **b** offering, he
23:15 Stand here by your **b** offering
23:17 standing by his **b** offering, and
28: 3 as a regular **b** offering.
28: 6 It is a regular **b** offering
28:10 this is the **b** offering for
28:10 besides the regular **b** offering
28:11 months you shall present a **b**
28:13 as a **b** offering of sweet aroma,
28:14 this is the **b** offering for
28:15 besides the regular **b** offering
28:19 an offering made by fire as a **b**
28:23 shall offer these besides the **b**
28:23 which is for a regular **b**
28:24 offered besides the regular **b**
28:27 You shall present a **b** offering

28:31 besides the regular ***b*** offering
29: 2 You shall offer a ***b*** offering as
29: 6 besides the ***b*** offering with its
29: 6 the regular ***b*** offering with its
29: 8 You shall present a ***b*** offering
29:11 the regular ***b*** offering with its
29:13 You shall present a ***b*** offering,
29:16 besides the regular ***b*** offering,
29:19 besides the regular ***b*** offering
29:22 besides the regular ***b*** offering,
29:25 besides the regular ***b*** offering,
29:28 besides the regular ***b*** offering,
29:31 besides the regular ***b*** offering,
29:34 besides the regular ***b*** offering,
29:36 You shall present a ***b*** offering,
29:38 besides the regular ***b*** offering,
29:39 freewill offerings) as your ***b***
Deut 12: 6 There you shall take your ***b***
12:11 your ***b*** offerings, your
12:13 that you do not offer your ***b***
12:14 there you shall offer your ***b***
12:27 And you shall offer your ***b***
27: 6 and offer ***b*** offerings on it to
33:10 And a whole ***b*** sacrifice on
Josh 8:31 And they offered on it ***b***
22:23 if to offer on it ***b*** offerings
22:26 not for ***b*** offering nor for
22:27 the LORD before Him with our ***b***
22:28 though not for ***b*** offerings nor
22:29 to build an altar for ***b***
Judg 6:26 the second bull and offer a ***b***
11:31 and I will offer it up as a ***b***
13:16 But if you offer a ***b*** offering,
13:23 He would not have accepted a ***b***
20:26 and they offered ***b*** offerings
21: 4 and offered ***b*** offerings and
1 Sam 6:14 and offered the cows as a ***b***
6:15 men of Beth Shemesh offered ***b***
7: 9 and offered it as a whole ***b***
7:10 as Samuel was offering up the ***b***
10: 8 come down to you to offer ***b***
13: 9 Bring a ***b*** offering and peace
13: 9 he offered the ***b*** offering.
13:10 had finished presenting the ***b***
13:12 and offered a ***b*** offering."
15:22 LORD as great delight in ***b***
2 Sam 6:17 Then David offered ***b*** offerings
6:18 David had finished offering ***b***
24:22 are oxen for ***b*** sacrifice,
24:24 nor will I offer ***b*** offerings to
24:25 and offered ***b*** offerings and
1 Ki 3: 4 Solomon offered a thousand ***b***
3:15 offered up ***b*** offerings, offered
8:64 there he offered ***b*** offerings,
8:64 was too small to receive the ***b***
9:25 times a year Solomon offered ***b***
18:33 and pour it on the ***b*** sacrifice
18:38 LORD fell and consumed the ***b***
2 Ki 3:27 and offered him as a ***b***
5:17 will no longer offer either ***b***
10:24 in to offer sacrifices and ***b***
10:25 made an end of offering the ***b***
16:13 So he burned his ***b*** offering and
16:15 new altar burn the morning ***b***
16:15 the king's ***b*** sacrifice, and his
16:15 with the ***b*** offering of all the
16:15 on it all the blood of the ***b***
1 Chr 6:49 sacrifices on the altar of ***b***
16: 1 Then they offered ***b*** offerings
16: 2 had finished offering the ***b***
16:40 to offer ***b*** offerings to the
16:40 to the LORD on the altar of ***b***
21:23 also give you the oxen for ***b***
21:24 nor offer ***b*** offerings with
21:26 and offered ***b*** offerings and
21:26 by fire on the altar of ***b***
21:29 LORD and the altar of the ***b***
22: 1 and this is the altar of ***b***
23:31 at every presentation of a ***b***
29:21 to the LORD and offered ***b***
2 Chr 1: 6 and offered a thousand ***b***
2: 4 for the ***b*** offerings morning and
4: 6 as they offered for the ***b***
7: 1 from heaven and consumed the ***b***
7: 7 there he offered ***b*** offerings
7: 7 was not able to receive the ***b***
8:12 Then Solomon offered ***b***
13:11 morning and every evening ***b***
23:18 to offer the ***b*** offerings of the
24:14 And they offered ***b*** offerings in
29: 7 not burned incense or offered ***b***
29:18 the altar of ***b*** offerings with
29:24 the king commanded that the ***b***
29:27 commanded them to offer the ***b***
29:27 And when the ***b*** offering began,
29:28 this continued until the ***b***
29:31 of a willing heart brought ***b***
29:32 And the number of the ***b***
29:32 all these were for a ***b***
29:34 they could not skin all the ***b***
29:35 Also the ***b*** offerings were in
29:35 drink offerings for every ***b***
30:15 and brought the ***b*** offerings to
31: 2 the priests and Levites for ***b***
31: 3 of his possessions for the ***b***
31: 3 for the morning and evening ***b***
31: 3 ***b*** offerings for the Sabbaths
35:12 they removed the ***b*** offerings
35:14 were busy in offering ***b***
35:16 the Passover and to offer ***b***
Ezra 3: 2 to offer ***b*** offerings on it, as
3: 3 and they offered ***b*** offerings on
3: 3 both the morning and evening ***b***
3: 4 and offered the daily ***b***
3: 5 they offered the regular ***b***
3: 6 month they began to offer ***b***
6: 9 and lambs for the ***b*** offerings
8:35 offered ***b*** offerings to the God
8:35 All this was a ***b*** offering to
Neh 10:33 for the regular ***b*** offering of
Job 1: 5 in the morning and offer ***b***
42: 8 and offer up for yourselves a ***b***
Ps 20: 3 And accept your ***b*** sacrifice.
40: 6 ***B*** offering and sin offering
50: 8 for your sacrifices Or your ***b***
51:16 You do not delight in ***b***
51:19 With ***b*** offering and whole
51:19 burnt offering and whole ***b***
66:13 will go into Your house with ***b***
66:15 I will offer You ***b*** sacrifices
Isa 1:11 I have had enough of ***b*** offerings
40:16 its beasts sufficient for a ***b***
43:23 brought Me the sheep for your ***b***
56: 7 Their ***b*** offerings and their
61: 8 I hate robbery for ***b*** offering;
Jer 6:20 Your ***b*** offerings are not
7:21 Add your ***b*** offerings to your
7:22 concerning ***b*** offerings or
14:12 and when they offer ***b*** offering
17:26 bringing ***b*** offerings and
19: 5 their sons with fire for ***b***
33:18 lack a man to offer ***b*** offerings
51:25 And make you a ***b*** mountain.
Ezek 40:38 where they washed the ***b***
40:39 to slay the ***b*** offering,
40:42 tables of hewn stone for the ***b***
40:42 which they slaughtered the ***b***
43:18 for sacrificing ***b*** offerings on
43:24 they will offer them up as a ***b***
43:27 the priests shall offer your ***b***
44:11 they shall slay the ***b*** offering
45:15 ***b*** offerings, and peace
45:17 the prince's part to give ***b***
45:17 the ***b*** offering, and the peace
45:23 the feast he shall prepare a ***b***
45:25 the ***b*** offering, the grain
46: 2 The priests shall prepare his ***b***
46: 4 The ***b*** offering that the prince
46:12 the prince makes a voluntary ***b***
46:12 and he shall prepare his ***b***
46:13 You shall daily make a ***b***
46:15 as a regular ***b*** offering every
Hos 6: 6 knowledge of God more than ***b***
Am 5:22 Though you offer Me ***b*** offerings
Mic 6: 6 Shall I come before Him with ***b***
Mk 12:33 is more than all the whole ***b***
Heb 10: 6 In ***b*** offerings and
10: 8 ***b*** offerings, and offerings

BURST (10/10) BURSTING, BURSTS

Judg 20:33 Then Israel's men in ambush ***b***
Job 32:19 It is ready to ***b*** like new
38: 8 When it ***b*** forth and issued
Isa 35: 6 For waters shall ***b*** forth in
Jer 2:20 I have broken your yoke and ***b***
5: 5 broken the yoke And ***b*** the
30: 8 And will ***b*** your bonds;
Nah 1:13 And ***b*** your bonds apart."
Lk 5:37 or else the new wine will ***b*** the
Acts 1:18 he ***b*** open in the middle and all

BURSTING (1/1) BURST

Ezek 32: 2 ***B*** forth in your rivers,

BURSTS (1/1) BURST

Mk 2:22 or else the new wine ***b*** the

BURY (39/36) BURIAL, BURIED, BURIERS, BURIES, BURYING

Gen 23: 4 that I may ***b*** my dead out of my
23: 6 ***b*** your dead in the choicest of
23: 6 that you may ***b*** your dead."
23: 8 If it is your wish that I ***b*** my
23:11 it to you. ***B*** your dead!"
23:13 take it from me and I will ***b***
23:15 So ***b*** your dead."
47:29 Please do not ***b*** me in Egypt,
47:30 carry me out of Egypt and ***b*** me
49:29 ***b*** me with my fathers in the
50: 5 there you shall ***b*** me."
50: 5 please let me go up and ***b*** my
50: 6 Go up and ***b*** your father, as he
50: 7 So Joseph went up to ***b*** his
50:14 all who went up with him to ***b***
Deut 21:23 but you shall surely ***b*** him that
1 Ki 2:31 and strike him down and ***b*** him,
11:15 of the army had gone up to ***b***
13:29 city to mourn, and to ***b*** him.
13:31 then ***b*** me in the tomb where the
14:13 shall mourn for him and ***b*** him,
2 Ki 9:10 and there shall be none to ***b***
9:34 and ***b*** her, for she was a king's
9:35 So they went to ***b*** her, but they
2 Chr 24:25 but they did not ***b*** him in the
Ps 79: 3 And there was no one to ***b***
Jer 7:32 for they will ***b*** in Tophet until
14:16 they will have no one to ***b***
19:11 and they shall ***b*** them in
19:11 till there is no place to ***b***.
Ezek 39:11 because there they will ***b*** Gog
39:14 to pass through the land and ***b***
Hos 9: 6 Memphis shall ***b*** them.
Mt 8:21 let me first go and ***b*** my
8:22 and let the dead ***b*** their own
27: 7 field, to ***b*** strangers in.
Lk 9:59 let me first go and ***b*** my
9:60 Let the dead ***b*** their own dead,
Jn 19:40 the custom of the Jews is to ***b***.

BURYING (4/4) BURY

Num 33: 4 For the Egyptians were ***b*** all
2 Ki 13:21 as they were ***b*** a man, that
Ezek 39:12 the house of Israel will be ***b***
39:13 people of the land will be ***b***,

BUSH (11/9) BUSHES

Ex 3: 2 of fire from the midst of a ***b***.
3: 2 the ***b*** was burning with fire,
3: 2 but the ***b*** was not consumed.
3: 3 why the ***b*** does not burn."
3: 4 to him from the midst of the ***b***
Deut 33:16 favor of Him who dwelt in the ***b***.
Mk 12:26 in the burning ***b*** passage, how
Lk 6:44 gather grapes from a bramble ***b***.
20:37 Moses showed in the burning ***b***
Acts 7:30 him in a flame of fire in a ***b***,
7:35 who appeared to him in the ***b***.

BUSHES (2/2) BUSH

Job 30: 4 Who pluck mallow by the ***b***,
30: 7 Among the ***b*** they brayed, Under

BUSHY (KJV) See WAVY

BUSINESS (20/19)

Deut 24: 5 to war or be charged with any ***b***;
Josh 2:14 if none of you tell this ***b*** of
2:20 And if you tell this ***b*** of ours,
1 Sam 21: 2 king has ordered me on some ***b***,
21: 2 know anything about the ***b*** on
21: 8 because the king's ***b*** required
25: 2 was a man in Maon whose ***b***
1 Chr 26:30 of the Jordan for all the ***b*** of
Neh 11:16 had the oversight of the ***b***
Job 20:18 From the proceeds of ***b*** He
Ps 107:23 Who do ***b*** on great waters,
Eccl 8:16 to know wisdom and to see the ***b***
Dan 8:27 and went about the king's ***b***.
Mt 22: 5 his own farm, another to his ***b***.
Lk 2:49 I must be about My Father's ***b***?
19:13 Do ***b*** till I come.'
Jn 2:14 and the moneychangers doing ***b***.
Acts 6: 3 whom we may appoint over this ***b***;
Rom 16: 2 and assist her in whatever ***b***
1 Th 4:11 quiet life, to mind your own ***b***,

BUSTLING (1/1)

Isa 32:14 The ***b*** city will be deserted.

BUSY (5/5) BUSYBODIES, BUSYBODY

1 Ki 18:27 he is meditating, or he is ***b***,
20:40 While your servant was ***b*** here
2 Chr 35:14 were ***b*** in offering burnt
Ps 39: 6 Surely they ***b*** themselves in
Eccl 5:20 because God keeps him ***b*** with

BUSYBODIES (2/2) BUSYBODY

2 Th 3:11 not working at all, but are ***b***.
1 Tim 5:13 idle but also gossips and ***b***,

BUSYBODY (1/1) BUSYBODIES

1 Pe 4:15 or as a ***b*** in other people's

BUT (4309/4075) See APPENDIX

BUTLER (9/9) BUTLERSHIP

Gen 40: 1 after these things that the ***b***
40: 2 the chief ***b*** and the chief
40: 5 Then the ***b*** and the baker of the
40: 9 Then the chief ***b*** told his dream
40:13 manner, when you were his ***b***.
40:20 up the head of the chief ***b*** and
40:21 Then he restored the chief ***b*** to
40:23 Yet the chief ***b*** did not remember
41: 9 Then the chief ***b*** spoke to

BUTLERSHIP (1/1) BUTLER

Gen 40:21 the chief butler to his ***b***

BUTTED (1/1)

Ezek 34:21 ***b*** all the weak ones with your

BUTTER (3/3)

Gen 18: 8 So he took ***b*** and milk and the
Ps 55:21 his mouth were smoother than ***b***,
Prov 30:33 the churning of milk produces ***b***,

BUTTOCKS (3/3)

2 Sam 10: 4 in the middle, at their ***b***,
1 Chr 19: 4 in the middle, at their ***b***,

Isa 20: 4 with their ***b*** uncovered, to the

BUTTRESS (5/5)

2 Chr 26: 9 and at the corner ***b*** of the
Neh 3:19 Ascent to the Armory at the ***b***.
3:20 from the ***b*** to the door of the
3:24 the house of Azariah to the ***b***,
3:25 made repairs opposite the ***b***,

BUY (58/53) BOUGHT, BUYER, BUYING, BUYS

Gen 41:57 came to Joseph in Egypt to ***b***
42: 2 go down to that place and ***b*** for
42: 3 ten brothers went down to ***b***
42: 5 the sons of Israel went to ***b***
42: 7 From the land of Canaan to ***b***
42:10 your servants have come to ***b***
43: 2 ***b*** us a little food."
43: 4 we will go down and ***b*** you food.
43:20 came down the first time to ***b***
43:22 other money in our hands to ***b***
44:25 Go back and ***b*** us a little
47:19 ***B*** us and our land for bread,
47:22 of the priests he did not ***b***;
Ex 21: 2 If you ***b*** a Hebrew servant, he
Lev 25:14 anything to your neighbor or ***b***
25:15 after the Jubilee you shall ***b***
25:44 from them you may ***b*** male and
25:45 Moreover you may ***b*** the children
Deut 2: 6 You shall ***b*** food from them with
2: 6 and you shall also ***b*** water from
28:68 but no one will ***b*** you."
Ruth 4: 4 ***B*** it back in the presence of
4: 5 On the day you ***b*** the field from
4: 5 you must also ***b*** it from Ruth
4: 8 ***B*** it for yourself." So he took
2 Sam 24:21 To ***b*** the threshing floor from
24:24 but I will surely ***b*** it from
2 Ki 22: 6 and to ***b*** timber and hewn stone
1 Chr 21:24 but I will surely ***b*** it for the
2 Chr 34:11 the craftsmen and builders to ***b***
Ezra 7:17 be careful to ***b*** with this money
Neh 5: 3 that we might ***b*** grain because
5:16 and we did not ***b*** any land.
10:31 we would not ***b*** it from them on
Prov 23:23 ***B*** the truth, and do not sell
Isa 55: 1 ***b*** and eat. Yes, come, buy wine
55: 1 ***b*** wine and milk Without money
Jer 32: 7 ***B*** my field which is in
32: 7 of redemption is yours to ***b***
32: 8 Please ***b*** my field that is in
32: 8 ***b*** it for yourself.' Then I
32:25 ***B*** the field for money, and take
32:44 Men will ***b*** fields for money,
Am 8: 6 That we may ***b*** the poor for
Mt 14:15 may go into the villages and ***b***
25: 9 and ***b*** for yourselves.'
25:10 "And while they went to ***b***,
Mk 6:36 country and villages and ***b***
6:37 Shall we go and ***b*** two hundred
Lk 9:13 unless we go and ***b*** food for all
22:36 let him sell his garment and ***b***
Jn 4: 8 gone away into the city to ***b***
6: 5 Where shall we ***b*** bread, that
13:29 ***B*** those things we need for the
1 Cor 7:30 those who ***b*** as though they did
Jas 4:13 ***b*** and sell, and make a
Rev 3:18 I counsel you to ***b*** from Me gold
13:17 and that no one may ***b*** or sell

BUYER (3/3) BUY

Prov 20:14 good for nothing," cries the ***b***;
Isa 24: 2 her mistress; As with the ***b***,
Ezek 7:12 Let not the ***b*** rejoice, Nor the

BUYING (1/1) BUY

2 Ki 12:12 and for ***b*** timber and hewn

BUYS (4/4) BUY

Lev 22:11 But if the priest ***b*** a person
Prov 31:16 She considers a field and ***b*** it;
Mt 13:44 and sells all that he has and ***b***
Rev 18:11 for no one ***b*** their merchandise

BUZ (3/3)

Gen 22:21 ***B*** his brother, Kemuel the
1 Chr 5:14 the son of Jahdo, the son of ***B***;
Jer 25:23 Dedan, Tema, ***B***, and all who

BUZI (1/1) BUZITE

Ezek 1: 3 the priest, the son of ***B***,

BUZITE (2/2) BUZI

Job 32: 2 the son of Barachel the ***B***,
32: 6 the son of Barachel the ***B***,

BUZZARD (2/2)

Lev 11:13 the eagle, the vulture, the ***b***,
Deut 14:12 the eagle, the vulture, the ***b***,

BUZZING (1/1)

Isa 18: 1 to the land shadowed with ***b***

BY (2852/2453) See APPENDIX

BYGONE (1/1)

Acts 14:16 who in ***b*** generations allowed all

BYPASSED (1/1) BYPASSING

Judg 11:18 through the wilderness and ***b***

BYPASSING (2/2) BYPASSED

Josh 19:12 toward Daberath, ***b*** Japhia.
19:27 ***b*** Cabul which was on the

BYWAYS (1/1)

Judg 5: 6 travelers walked along the ***b***.

BYWORD (10/10)

Deut 28:37 and a ***b*** among all nations where
1 Ki 9: 7 will be a proverb and a ***b***
2 Chr 7:20 will make it a proverb and a ***b***
Job 17: 6 But He has made me a ***b*** of the
30: 9 song; Yes, I am their ***b***.
Ps 44:14 You make us a ***b*** among the
69:11 I became a ***b*** to them.
Jer 24: 9 to be a reproach and a ***b***,
Ezek 16:56 your sister Sodom was not a ***b***
23:10 She became a ***b*** among women,

C

CABBON (1/1)

Josh 15:40 ***C***, Lahmas, Kithlish,

CABINS (KJV) See CELLS

CABLES (1/1)

Acts 27:17 they used ***c*** to undergird the

CABUL (2/2)

Josh 19:27 bypassing ***C*** which was on the
1 Ki 9:13 he called them the land of ***C***,

CAESAR (21/20) AUGUSTUS, CAESAR'S, CLAUDIUS, TIBERIUS

Mt 22:17 Is it lawful to pay taxes to ***C***,
22:21 Render therefore to ***C*** the things
Mk 12:14 Is it lawful to pay taxes to ***C***,
12:17 Render to ***C*** the things that are
Lk 2: 1 that a decree went out from ***C***
3: 1 year of the reign of Tiberius ***C***,
20:22 for us to pay taxes to ***C*** or
20:25 Render therefore to ***C*** the things
23: 2 forbidding to pay taxes to ***C***,
Jn 19:12 himself a king speaks against ***C***.
19:15 We have no king but ***C***!"
Acts 11:28 in the days of Claudius ***C***.
17: 7 contrary to the decrees of ***C***,
25: 8 nor against ***C*** have I offended
25:11 me to them. I appeal to ***C***.
25:12 "You have appealed to ***C***?
25:12 To ***C*** you shall go!"
25:21 kept till I could send him to ***C***.
26:32 if he had not appealed to ***C***.
27:24 you must be brought before ***C***;
28:19 I was compelled to appeal to ***C***,

CAESAR'S (9/8) CAESAR

Mt 22:21 They said to Him, "***C***.
22:21 to Caesar the things that are ***C***,
Mk 12:16 They said to Him, "***C***."
12:17 to Caesar the things that are ***C***,
Lk 20:24 They answered and said, "***C***.
20:25 to Caesar the things that are ***C***,
Jn 19:12 you are not ***C*** friend.
Acts 25:10 I stand at ***C*** judgment seat,
Phil 4:22 especially those who are of ***C***

CAESAREA (17/17)

Acts 8:40 the cities till he came to ***C***.
9:30 they brought him down to ***C*** and
10: 1 There was a certain man in ***C***
10:24 following day they entered ***C***.
11:11 having been sent to me from ***C***.
12:19 he went down from Judea to ***C***,
18:22 And when he had landed at ***C***,
21: 8 departed and came to ***C***,
21:16 some of the disciples from ***C***
23:23 hundred spearmen to go to ***C*** at
23:33 When they came to ***C*** and had
25: 1 three days he went up from ***C***
25: 4 that Paul should be kept at ***C***,
25: 6 ten days, he went down to ***C***.
25:13 Agrippa and Bernice came to ***C***

CAESAREA PHILIPPI (2/2)

Mt 16:13 Jesus came into the region of ***C***,
Mk 8:27 went out to the towns of ***C***;

CAGE (4/4)

Jer 5:27 As a ***c*** is full of birds, So
Ezek 19: 9 They put him in a ***c*** with
Hos 13: 8 I will tear open their rib ***c***,
Rev 18: 2 and a ***c*** for every unclean and

CAIAPHAS (9/9)

Mt 26: 3 high priest, who was called ***C***,
26:57 of Jesus led Him away to ***C***
Lk 3: 2 while Annas and ***C*** were high
Jn 11:49 And one of them, ***C***,
18:13 he was the father-in-law of ***C***
18:14 Now it was ***C*** who advised the
18:24 Then Annas sent Him bound to ***C***
18:28 Then they led Jesus from ***C*** to
Acts 4: 6 as Annas the high priest, ***C***,

CAIN (19/16)

Gen 4: 1 and she conceived and bore ***C***,
4: 2 but ***C*** was a tiller of the
4: 3 of time it came to pass that ***C***
4: 5 but He did not respect ***C*** and his
4: 5 And ***C*** was very angry, and his
4: 6 So the LORD said to ***C***,
4: 8 Now ***C*** talked with Abel his
4: 8 that ***C*** rose up against Abel his
4: 9 Then the LORD said to ***C***,
4:13 And ***C*** said to the LORD, "My
4:15 "Therefore, whoever kills ***C***,
4:15 And the LORD set a mark on ***C***,
4:16 Then ***C*** went out from the
4:17 And ***C*** knew his wife, and she
4:24 If ***C*** shall be avenged
4:25 of Abel, whom ***C*** killed."
Heb 11: 4 more excellent sacrifice than ***C***,
1 Jn 3:12 not as ***C*** who was of the wicked
Jude 11 they have gone in the way of ***C***,

CAINAN (8/8)

Gen 5: 9 lived ninety years, and begot ***C***.
5:10 After he begot ***C***, Enosh lived
5:12 ***C*** lived seventy years, and
5:13 ***C*** lived eight hundred and forty
5:14 So all the days of ***C*** were nine
1 Chr 1: 2 ***C***, Mahalalel, Jared,
Lk 3:36 the son of ***C***, the son of
3:37 of Mahalalel, the son of ***C***,

CAKE (13/12) CAKED, CAKES

Ex 29:23 one ***c*** made with oil, and one
Lev 7:14 from it he shall offer one ***c***
8:26 LORD he took one unleavened ***c***,
8:26 a ***c*** of bread anointed with
24: 5 an ephah shall be in each ***c***.
Num 6:19 one unleavened ***c*** from the
15:20 You shall offer up a ***c*** of the
1 Sam 30:12 they gave him a piece of a ***c***
2 Sam 6:19 and a ***c*** of raisins. So all the
1 Ki 17:13 but make me a small ***c*** from it
19: 6 and there by his head was a ***c***
1 Chr 16: 3 of meat, and a ***c*** of raisins.
Hos 7: 8 Ephraim is a ***c*** unturned.

CAKED (1/1) CAKE

Job 7: 5 My flesh is ***c*** with worms and

CAKES (24/21) CAKE

Gen 18: 6 fine meal; knead it and make ***c***.
Ex 12:39 And they baked unleavened ***c*** of
29: 2 unleavened ***c*** mixed with oil,
Lev 2: 4 it shall be unleavened ***c*** of
7:12 unleavened ***c*** mixed with oil,
7:12 or ***c*** of blended flour mixed
7:13 'Besides the ***c***, as his offering
24: 5 fine flour and bake twelve ***c***
Num 6:15 ***c*** of fine flour mixed with oil,
11: 8 and made ***c*** of it; and its taste
1 Sam 25:18 and two hundred ***c*** of figs, and
2 Sam 13: 6 come and make a couple of ***c***
13: 8 made ***c*** in his sight, and baked
13: 8 in his sight, and baked the ***c***.
13:10 And Tamar took the ***c*** which
1 Ki 14: 3 with you ten loaves, some ***c***,
1 Chr 12:40 provisions of flour and ***c*** of
12:40 flour and cakes of figs and ***c***
23:29 with the unleavened ***c*** and what
Song 2: 5 Sustain me with ***c*** of raisins,
Jer 7:18 to make ***c*** for the queen of
44:19 did we make ***c*** for her, to
Ezek 4:12 you shall eat it as barley ***c***;
Hos 3: 1 gods and love the raisin ***c***

CALAH (2/2)

Gen 10:11 built Nineveh, Rehoboth Ir, ***C***,
10:12 and Resen between Nineveh and ***C***

CALAMITIES (1/1) CALAMITY

Ps 57: 1 Until these ***c*** have passed by.

CALAMITY (49/46) CALAMITIES

Gen 42: 4 Lest some *c* befall him."
42:38 If any *c* should befall him
44:29 and *c* befalls him, you shall
Deut 32:35 For the day of their *c* is at
Judg 2:15 LORD was against them for *c*,
2 Sam 22:19 me in the day of my *c*,
1 Ki 9: 9 LORD has brought all this *c*
21:21 I will bring *c* on you. I will
21:29 I will not bring the *c* in his
21:29 of his son I will bring the *c*
2 Ki 6:33 Surely this *c* is from the
21:12 I am bringing such *c* upon
22:16 I will bring *c* on this place
22:20 eyes shall not see all the *c*
2 Chr 7:22 He has brought all this *c* on
34:24 I will bring *c* on this place
34:28 eyes shall not see all the *c*
Job 6: 2 And my *c* laid with it on the
30:13 up my path, They promote my *c*;
Ps 18:18 me in the day of my *c*,
Prov 1:26 I also will laugh at your *c*;
6:15 Therefore his *c* shall come
17: 5 He who is glad at *c* will not
24:16 But the wicked shall fall by *c*.
24:22 For their *c* will rise suddenly,
27:10 house in the day of your *c*;
28:14 his heart will fall into *c*.
Isa 45: 7 I make peace and create *c*;
Jer 1:14 Out of the north *c* shall break
6:19 I will certainly bring *c* on
11:11 I will surely bring *c* on them
18:17 the face In the day of their *c*.
25:29 I begin to bring *c* on the city
26: 3 I may relent concerning the *c*
32:23 You have caused all this *c* to
32:42 I have brought all this great *c*
44: 2 You have seen all the *c* that I
44:23 therefore this *c* has happened
46:21 For the day of their *c* had
48:16 The *c* of Moab is near at hand,
49: 8 Dedan! For I will bring the *c*
49:32 And I will bring their *c* from
Ezek 6:10 vain that I would bring this *c*
35: 5 sword at the time of their *c*,
Am 3: 6 If there is *c* in a city, will
9:10 The *c* shall not overtake nor
Ob 13 people In the day of their *c*.
13 In the day of their *c*,
13 In the day of their *c*.

CALAMUS (1/1)

Song 4:14 *C* and cinnamon, With all

CALCOL (1/1) CHALCOL

1 Chr 2: 6 were Zimri, Ethan, Heman, *C*,

CALCULATE (1/1) CALCULATED

Rev 13:18 Let him who has understanding *c*

CALCULATED (1/1) CALCULATE

Isa 40:12 heaven with a span And *c* the

CALDRON (5/5) CALDRONS

1 Sam 2:14 into the pan, or kettle, or *c*,
Ezek 11: 3 houses; this city is the *c*,
11: 7 meat, and this city is the *c*;
11:11 city shall not be your *c*,
Mic 3: 3 the pot, Like flesh in the *c*.

CALDRONS (1/1) CALDRON

2 Chr 35:13 they boiled in pots, in *c*,

CALEB (33/33) CALEB'S, CHELUB, CHELUBAI

Num 13: 6 *C* the son of Jephunneh;
13:30 Then *C* quieted the people
14: 6 Joshua the son of Nun and *C*
14:24 'But My servant *C*,
14:30 Except for *C* the son of
14:38 But Joshua the son of Nun and *C*
26:65 except *C* the son of Jephunneh
32:12 except *C* the son of Jephunneh,
34:19 *C* the son of Jephunneh;
Deut 1:36 except *C* the son of Jephunneh;
Josh 14: 6 And *C* the son of Jephunneh the
14:13 and gave Hebron to *C* the son of
14:14 became the inheritance of *C*
15:13 Now to *C* the son of Jephunneh
15:14 *C* drove out the three sons of
15:16 And *C* said, "He who attacks
15:17 son of Kenaz, the brother of *C*,
15:18 and *C* said to her, "What do
21:12 and its villages they gave to *C*
Judg 1:12 Then *C* said, "Whoever attacks
1:14 and *C* said to her, "What do
1:15 And *C* gave her the upper
1:20 And they gave Hebron to *C*,
1 Sam 25: 3 he was of the house of *C*.
30:14 and of the southern area of *C*;
1 Chr 2:18 *C* the son of Hezron had
2:19 *C* took Ephrath as his wife, who
2:42 The descendants of *C* the
2:49 And the daughter of *C* was
2:50 were the descendants of *C*:
4:15 The sons of *C* the son of
6:56 and its villages they gave to *C*

CALEB EPHRATHAH (1/1)

1 Chr 2:24 After Hezron died in *C*,

CALEB'S (4/4) CALEB

Judg 1:13 *C* younger brother, took it; so
3: 9 *C* younger brother.
1 Chr 2:46 *C* concubine, bore Haran, Moza,
2:48 *C* concubine, bore Sheber and

CALF (31/31) CALVES

Gen 18: 7 herd, took a tender and good *c*,
18: 8 took butter and milk and the *c*
Ex 32: 4 tool, and made a molded *c*.
32: 8 have made themselves a molded *c*,
32:19 that he saw the *c* and the
32:20 Then he took the *c* which they
32:24 and this *c* came out."
32:35 of what they did with the *c*
Lev 9: 3 and a *c* and a lamb, both of
9: 8 to the altar and killed the *c*
Deut 9:16 made for yourselves a molded *c*!
9:21 the *c* which you had made, and
1 Sam 28:24 Now the woman had a fatted *c* in
2 Chr 11:15 and the *c* idols which he had
Neh 9:18 when they made a molded *c*
Ps 29: 6 makes them also skip like a *c*,
106:19 They made a *c* in Horeb, And
Prov 15:17 Than a fatted *c* with hatred.
Isa 11: 6 The *c* and the young lion and
27:10 There the *c* will feed, and
Jer 34:18 when they cut the *c* in two and
34:19 between the parts of the *c*—
Hos 4:16 is stubborn Like a stubborn *c*;
8: 5 Your *c* is rejected, O Samaria!
8: 6 But the *c* of Samaria shall be
10: 5 Samaria fear Because of the *c*
Lk 15:23 And bring the fatted *c* here and
15:27 father has killed the fatted *c*.
15:30 you killed the fatted *c* for
Acts 7:41 And they made a *c* in those days,
Rev 4: 7 second living creature like a *c*,

CALL (187/182) CALLED, CALLING, CALLS, SO-CALLED

Gen 2:19 to Adam to see what he would *c*
4:26 Then men began to *c* on the
16:11 You shall *c* his name Ishmael,
17:15 you shall not *c* her name Sarai,
17:19 and you shall *c* his name Isaac;
24:57 We will *c* the young woman and
30:13 for the daughters will *c* me
Ex 2: 7 Shall I go and *c* a nurse for you
2:20 *C* him, that he may eat bread."
Num 10: 6 they shall sound the *c* for them
16:12 And Moses sent to *c* Dathan and
22: 5 to *c* him, saying: "Look, a
22:20 If the men come to *c* you, rise
Deut 2:11 but the Moabites *c* them Emim.
2:20 But the Ammonites *c* them
3: 9 (the Sidonians *c* Hermon Sirion,
3: 9 and the Amorites *c* it Senir),
4: 7 for whatever reason we may *c*
4:26 I *c* heaven and earth to witness
25: 8 the elders of his city shall *c*
30: 1 and you *c* them to mind among
30:19 I *c* heaven and earth as
31:14 *c* Joshua, and present
31:28 words in their hearing and *c*
33:19 They shall *c* the peoples to
Judg 12: 1 and did not *c* us to go with
16:25 *C* for Samson, that he may
18:12 (Therefore they *c* that place
Ruth 1:20 Do not *c* me Naomi; call me Mara,
1:20 *c* me Mara, for the Almighty has
1:21 Why do you *c* me Naomi, since
1 Sam 3: 5 And he said, "I did not *c*;
3: 6 He answered, "I did not *c*,
3: 8 for you did *c* me." Then Eli
12:17 I will *c* to the LORD, and He
14:17 Now *c* the roll and see who has
22:11 So the king sent to *c* Ahimelech
2 Sam 15: 2 that Absalom would *c* to him and
17: 5 Now *c* Hushai the Archite also,
22: 4 I will *c* upon the LORD, who
1 Ki 1:28 *C* Bathsheba to me." So she came
1:32 *C* to me Zadok the priest, Nathan
8:52 listen to them whenever they *c*
18:24 Then you *c* on the name of your
18:24 and I will *c* on the name of the
18:25 and *c* on the name of your god,
22:13 the messenger who had gone to *c*
2 Ki 4:12 '*C* this Shunammite woman."
4:15 *C* her." When he had called her,
4:36 *C* this Shunammite woman." So he
5:11 and stand and *c* on the name of
10:19 *c* to me all the prophets of
1 Chr 16: 8 give thanks to the LORD! *C*
2 Chr 18:12 the messenger who had gone to *c*
Job 5: 1 *C* out now; Is there anyone who
13:22 Then *c*, and I will answer;
14:15 You shall *c*, and I will
19:16 I *c* my servant, but he gives no
27:10 Will he always *c* on God?
Ps 4: 1 Hear me when I *c*, O God of my
4: 3 The LORD will hear when I *c*
14: 4 And do not *c* on the LORD?
18: 3 I will *c* upon the LORD, who
20: 9 the King answer us when we *c*.
49:11 They *c* their lands after
50: 4 He shall *c* to the heavens from
50:15 *C* upon Me in the day of trouble
53: 4 And do not *c* upon God?
55:16 I will *c* upon God, And the
72:17 All nations shall *c* Him
77: 6 I *c* to remembrance my song in
79: 6 on the kingdoms that do not *c*
80:18 and we will *c* upon Your name.
86: 5 in mercy to all those who *c*
86: 7 the day of my trouble I will *c*
91:15 He shall *c* upon Me, and I will
102: 2 ear to me; In the day that I *c*,
105: 1 give thanks to the LORD! *C*
116: 2 Therefore I will *c* upon Him
116:13 And *c* upon the name of the
116:17 And will *c* upon the name of
145:18 LORD is near to all who *c*
145:18 To all who *c* upon Him in
Prov 1:28 Then they will *c* on me, but I
7: 4 And *c* understanding your
8: 4 "To you, O men, I *c*,
9:15 To *c* to those who pass by, Who
31:28 Her children rise up and *c* her
Isa 5:20 Woe to those who *c* evil good,
7:14 and shall *c* His name Immanuel.
8: 3 LORD said to me, "*C* his name
8:12 all that this people *c* a
12: 4 *c* upon His name; Declare His
22:20 That I will *c* My servant
31: 2 And will not *c* back His words,
34:12 They shall *c* its nobles to the
41:25 rising of the sun he shall *c*
44: 5 Another will *c* himself by the
45: 3 Who *c* you by your name, Am
48: 2 For they *c* themselves after the
48:13 When I *c* to them, They stand
55: 5 Surely you shall *c* a nation you
55: 6 *C* upon Him while He is near.
58: 5 Would you *c* this a fast, And
58: 9 Then you shall *c*, and the LORD
58:13 And *c* the Sabbath a delight,
60:14 And they shall *c* you The City
60:18 But you shall *c* your walls
61: 6 They shall *c* you the servants
62:12 And they shall *c* them The Holy
65:15 And *c* His servants by another
65:24 to pass That before they *c*,
Jer 3:19 You shall *c* Me, "My Father,"
6:30 People will *c* them rejected
7:27 You shall also *c* to them, but
9:17 Consider and *c* for the mourning
10:25 on the families who do not *c*
25:29 for I will *c* for a sword on all
29:12 Then you will *c* upon Me and go
33: 3 *C* to Me, and I will answer you,
50:29 *C* together the archers against
51:27 *C* the kingdoms together
Ezek 21:22 to *c* for a slaughter, to lift
36:29 I will *c* for the grain and
38:21 I will *c* for a sword against Gog
39:11 Therefore they will *c* it the
Dan 2: 2 the king gave the command to *c*
Hos 1: 4 *C* his name Jezreel, For in a
1: 6 *C* her name Lo-Ruhamah, For I
1: 9 *C* his name Lo-Ammi, For you
2:16 you will *c* Me 'My Husband,'
2:16 no longer *c* Me 'My Master,'
7:11 They *c* to Egypt, They go to
11: 7 Though they *c* to the Most
Joel 1:14 *C* a sacred assembly; Gather
2:15 *C* a sacred assembly;
Am 5:16 Alas! Alas!' They shall *c* the
Jon 1: 6 *c* on your God; perhaps your God
Zeph 3: 9 That they all may *c* on the
Zech 13: 9 They will *c* on My name, And I
Mal 3:12 And all nations will *c* you
3:15 So now we *c* the proud blessed,
Mt 1:21 and you shall *c* His name
1:23 and they shall *c* His name
9:13 For I did not come to *c* the
10:25 how much more will they *c*
19:17 Why do you *c* Me good? No one is
20: 8 *C* the laborers and give them
22: 3 sent out his servants to *c*
22:43 does David in the Spirit *c* Him
23: 9 Do not *c* anyone on earth your
Mk 2:17 I did not come to *c* the
10:18 Why do you *c* Me good? No one is
15:12 me to do with Him whom you *c*
Lk 1:13 and you shall *c* his name John.
1:31 and shall *c* His name JESUS.
1:48 all generations will *c* me
5:32 I have not come to *c* the
6:46 But why do you *c* Me 'Lord,
18:19 Why do you *c* Me good? No one is
Jn 4:16 *c* your husband, and come
13:13 You *c* me Teacher and Lord, and
15:15 No longer do I *c* you servants,
Acts 2:39 many as the Lord our God will *c*.
9:14 priests to bind all who *c* on
10:15 God has cleansed you must not *c*
10:28 shown me that I should not *c*
10:32 Send therefore to Joppa and *c*
11: 9 God has cleansed you must not *c*
11:13 and *c* for Simon whose surname
19:13 took it upon themselves to *c*
24:14 to the Way which they *c* a sect,
24:25 a convenient time I will *c* for

Rom 9:25 I will **c** them My people,
10:12 over all is rich to all who **c**
10:14 How then shall they **c** on Him in
1 Cor 1: 2 with all who in every place **c**
2 Cor 1:23 Moreover I **c** God as witness
Phil 3:14 for the prize of the upward **c**
1 Th 4: 7 For God did not **c** us to
2 Tim 1: 5 when I **c** to remembrance the
2:22 peace with those who **c** on the
Heb 2:11 reason He is not ashamed to **c**
Jas 5:14 Let him **c** for the elders of the
1 Pe 1:17 And if you **c** on the Father, who
2 Pe 1:10 more diligent to make your **c**
3 Jn 10 I will **c** to mind his deeds

CALLED (619/593) CALL

Gen 1: 5 God **c** the light Day, and the
1: 5 and the darkness He **c** Night.
1: 8 And God **c** the firmament Heaven.
1:10 And God **c** the dry land Earth,
1:10 together of the waters He **c**
2:19 And whatever Adam **c** each living
2:23 She shall be **c** Woman, Because
3: 9 Then the LORD God **c** to Adam
3:20 And Adam **c** his wife's name Eve,
4:17 and **c** the name of the city
5: 2 and blessed them and **c** them
5:29 And he **c** his name Noah, saying,
11: 9 Therefore its name is **c** Babel,
12: 8 an altar to the LORD and **c** on
12:18 And Pharaoh **c** Abram and said,
13: 4 And there Abram **c** on the name
16:13 Then she **c** the name of the LORD
16:14 Therefore the well was **c** Beer
17: 5 longer shall your name be **c**
19: 5 And they **c** to Lot and said to
19:22 the name of the city was **c**
19:37 The firstborn bore a son and **c**
19:38 she also bore a son and **c** his
20: 8 **c** all his servants, and told
20: 9 And Abimelech **c** Abraham and said
21: 3 And Abraham **c** the name of his
21:12 in Isaac your seed shall be **c**.
21:17 Then the angel of God **c** to
21:31 Therefore he **c** that place
21:33 and there **c** on the name of the
22:11 But the Angel of the LORD **c** to
22:14 And Abraham **c** the name of the
22:15 Then the Angel of the LORD **c**
24:58 Then they **c** Rebekah and said to
25:25 so they **c** his name Esau.
25:26 so his name was **c** Jacob.
25:30 Therefore his name was **c** Edom.
26: 9 Then Abimelech **c** Isaac and said,
26:18 He **c** them by the names which
26:18 names which his father had **c**
26:20 So he **c** the name of the well
26:21 So he **c** its name Sitnah.
26:22 So he **c** its name Rehoboth,
26:25 he built an altar there and **c**
26:33 So he **c** it Shebah. Therefore the
27: 1 that he **c** Esau his older son
27:42 So she sent and **c** Jacob her
28: 1 Then Isaac **c** Jacob and blessed
28:19 And he **c** the name of that place
29:32 and she **c** his name Reuben; for
29:33 And she **c** his name Simeon.
29:34 Therefore his name was **c**
29:35 Therefore she **c** his name
30: 6 Therefore she **c** his name Dan.
30: 8 So she **c** his name Naphtali.
30:11 A troop comes!" So she **c** his
30:13 So she **c** his name Asher.
30:18 So she **c** his name Issachar.
30:20 So she **c** his name Zebulun.
30:21 and **c** her name Dinah.
30:24 So she **c** his name Joseph, and
31: 4 So Jacob sent and **c** Rachel and
31:47 Laban **c** it Jegar Sahadutha, but
31:47 but Jacob **c** it Galeed.
31:48 its name was **c** Galeed,
31:54 and **c** his brethren to eat
32: 2 And he **c** the name of that
32:28 name shall no longer be **c**
32:30 And Jacob **c** the name of the
33:17 the name of the place is **c**
33:20 he erected an altar there and **c**
35: 7 he built an altar there and **c**
35: 8 So the name of it was **c** Allon
35:10 your name shall not be **c** Jacob
35:10 So He **c** his name Israel.
35:15 And Jacob **c** the name of the
35:18 that she **c** his name Ben-Oni;
35:18 but his father **c** him Benjamin.
38: 3 and he **c** his name Er.
38: 4 and she **c** his name Onan.
38: 5 and **c** his name Shelah. He was
38:29 Therefore his name was **c** Perez.
38:30 And his name was **c** Zerah.
39:14 that she **c** to the men of her
41: 8 and he sent and **c** for all the
41:14 Then Pharaoh sent and **c** Joseph,
41:45 And Pharaoh **c** Joseph's name
41:51 Joseph **c** the name of the
41:52 And the name of the second he **c**
47:29 he **c** his son Joseph and said to
48: 6 they will be **c** by the name of
49: 1 And Jacob **c** his sons and said,
50:11 Therefore its name was **c** Abel
Ex 1:18 So the king of Egypt **c** for the
2: 8 So the maiden went and **c** the
2:10 So she **c** his name Moses,
2:22 and he **c** his name Gershom; for
3: 4 God **c** to him from the midst of
7:11 But Pharaoh also **c** the wise men
8: 8 Then Pharaoh **c** for Moses and
8:25 Then Pharaoh **c** for Moses and
9:27 And Pharaoh sent and **c** for
10:16 Then Pharaoh **c** for Moses and
10:24 Then Pharaoh **c** to Moses and
12:21 Then Moses **c** for all the elders
12:31 Then he **c** for Moses and Aaron
15:23 Therefore the name of it was **c**
16:31 And the house of Israel **c** its
17: 7 So he **c** the name of the place
17:15 And Moses built an altar and **c**
19: 3 and the LORD **c** to him from the
19: 7 So Moses came and **c** for the
19:20 And the LORD **c** Moses to the
24:16 And on the seventh day He **c** to
31: 2 I have **c** by name Bezalel the
33: 7 and **c** it the tabernacle of
34:31 Then Moses **c** to them, and Aaron
35:30 the LORD has **c** by name Bezalel
36: 2 Then Moses **c** Bezalel and
Lev 1: 1 Now the LORD **c** to Moses, and
9: 1 on the eighth day that Moses **c**
10: 4 And Moses **c** Mishael and
Num 11: 3 So he **c** the name of the place
11:34 So he **c** the name of that place
12: 5 and **c** Aaron and Miriam.
13:16 And Moses **c** Hoshea the son of
13:24 The place was **c** the Valley of
21: 3 So the name of that place was **c**
24:10 I **c** you to curse my enemies, and
32:41 and **c** them Havoth Jair.
32:42 and he **c** it Nobah, after his
Deut 3:13 was **c** the land of the giants.
3:14 and **c** Bashan after his own
5: 1 And Moses **c** all Israel, and said
15: 2 because it is **c** the LORD's
25:10 And his name shall be **c** in
28:10 earth shall see that you are **c**
29: 2 Now Moses **c** all Israel and said
31: 7 Then Moses **c** Joshua and said to
Josh 4: 4 Then Joshua **c** the twelve men
5: 9 the name of the place is **c**
6: 6 Then Joshua the son of Nun **c**
7:26 name of that place has been **c**
8:16 people who were in Ai were **c**
9:22 Then Joshua **c** for them, and he
10:24 that Joshua **c** for all the men
19:47 They **c** Leshem, Dan, after the
22: 1 Then Joshua **c** the Reubenites,
22:34 and the children of Gad **c** the
23: 2 And Joshua **c** for all Israel, for
24: 1 of Israel to Shechem and **c** for
24: 9 and sent and **c** Balaam the son
Judg 1:17 So the name of the city was **c**
1:26 and **c** its name Luz, which is
2: 5 Then they **c** the name of that
4: 6 Then she sent and **c** for Barak
4:10 And Barak **c** Zebulun and Naphtali
6:24 and **c** it The-Lord-Is-PEACE.
6:32 Therefore on that day he **c** him
8:31 whose name he **c** Abimelech.
9:54 Then he **c** quickly to the young
10: 4 had thirty towns, which are **c** '
12: 2 and when I **c** you, you did not
13:24 So the woman bore a son and **c**
15:17 and **c** that place Ramath Lehi.
15:19 Therefore he **c** its name En
16:18 she sent and **c** for the lords of
16:19 and **c** for a man and had him
16:25 So they **c** for Samson from the
16:28 Then Samson **c** to the LORD,
18:23 And they **c** out to the children
18:29 And they **c** the name of the city
Ruth 4:17 And they **c** his name Obed.
1 Sam 1:20 and **c** his name Samuel, saying,
3: 4 that the LORD **c** Samuel. And he
3: 5 for you **c** me." And he said,
3: 6 Then the LORD **c** yet again,
3: 6 for you **c** me." He answered,
3: 8 And the LORD **c** Samuel again the
3: 8 perceived that the LORD had **c**
3:10 the LORD came and stood and **c**
3:16 Then Eli **c** Samuel and said,
6: 2 And the Philistines **c** for the
7:12 and **c** its name Ebenezer,
9: 9 for he who is now **c** a
9: 9 a prophet was formerly **c** a
9:26 of the day that Samuel **c** to
10:17 Then Samuel **c** the people
12:18 So Samuel **c** to the LORD, and
13: 4 And the people were **c** together
14:12 Then the men of the garrison **c**
14:17 And when they had **c** the roll,
16: 8 So Jesse **c** Abinadab, and made
19: 7 Then Jonathan **c** David, and
23: 8 Then Saul **c** all the people
23:28 so they **c** that place the Rock
24: 8 and **c** out to Saul, saying, "My
26:14 And David **c** out to the people
28:15 Therefore I have **c** you, that
29: 6 Then Achish **c** David and said to
2 Sam 1: 7 he saw me and **c** to me. And I
1:15 Then David **c** one of the young
2:16 Therefore that place was **c** the
2:26 Then Abner **c** to Joab and said,
5: 9 and **c** it the City of David. And
5:20 Therefore he **c** the name of
6: 2 whose name is **c** by the Name,
6: 8 and he **c** the name of the place
9: 2 So when they had **c** him to
9: 9 And the king **c** to Ziba, Saul's
11:13 Now when David **c** him, he ate and
12:24 and he **c** his name Solomon. Now
12:25 So he **c** his name Jedidiah,
12:28 I take the city and it be **c**
13:17 Then he **c** his servant who
14:33 And when he had **c** for Absalom,
18:18 He **c** the pillar after his own
18:18 And to this day it is **c**
18:26 and the watchman **c** to the
18:28 And Ahimaaz **c** out and said to
21: 2 So the king **c** the Gibeonites and
22: 7 In my distress I **c** upon the
23: 8 He was **c** Adino the Eznite,
1 Ki 2:36 Then the king sent and **c** for
2:42 Then the king sent and **c** for
7:21 the pillar on the right and **c**
7:21 up the pillar on the left and **c**
8:43 temple which I have built is **c**
9:13 he **c** them the land of Cabul,
12: 3 that they sent and **c** him.
12:20 they sent for him and **c** him to
16:24 and **c** the name of the city
17:10 And he **c** to her and said,
17:11 he **c** to her and said, "Please
18: 3 And Ahab had **c** Obadiah, who was
18:26 and **c** on the name of Baal from
20: 7 So the king of Israel **c** all the
22: 9 Then the king of Israel **c** an
2 Ki 3:10 Alas! For the LORD has **c** these
3:13 for the LORD has **c** these three
4:12 When he had **c** her, she stood
4:15 When he had **c** her, she stood
4:22 Then she **c** to her husband, and
4:36 And he **c** Gehazi and said, "Call
4:36 So he **c** her. And when she came
6:11 and he **c** his servants and said
7:10 So they went and **c** to the
7:11 And the gatekeepers **c** out, and
8: 1 the LORD has **c** for a famine,
9: 1 And Elisha the prophet **c** one of
12: 7 So King Jehoash **c** Jehoiada the
14: 7 and **c** its name Joktheel to this
18: 4 and **c** it Nehushtan.
18:18 And when they had **c** to the king,
18:28 the Rabshakeh stood and **c** out
1 Chr 4: 9 and his mother **c** his name
4:10 And Jabez **c** on the God of Israel
6:65 these cities which are **c** by
7:16 and she **c** his name Peresh.
7:23 and he **c** his name Beriah,
11: 7 therefore they **c** it the City of
13:11 therefore that place is **c** Perez
14:11 Therefore they **c** the name of
15:11 And David **c** for Zadok and
21:26 and **c** on the LORD; and He
22: 6 Then he **c** for his son Solomon,
2 Chr 3:17 he **c** the name of the one on the
6:33 temple which I have built is **c**
7:14 if My people who are **c** by My
10: 3 Then they sent for him and **c**
18: 8 Then the king of Israel **c** one
20:26 the name of that place was **c**
24: 6 So the king **c** Jehoiada the chief
32:18 Then they **c** out with a loud
Ezra 2:61 and was **c** by their name.
Neh 5: 7 So I **c** a great assembly
5:12 Then I **c** the priests, and
7:63 and was **c** by their name.
Esth 2:14 the king delighted in her and **c**
3:12 the king's scribes were **c** on
4: 5 Then Esther **c** Hathach, one of
4:11 to the king, who has not been **c**,
4:11 Yet I myself have not been **c** to
5:10 and he sent and **c** for his
8: 9 So the king's scribes were **c** at
9:26 So they **c** these days Purim,
Job 9:16 If I **c** and He answered me, I
12: 4 Who **c** on God, and He answered
42:14 And he **c** the name of the first
Ps 17: 6 I have **c** upon You, for You will
18: 6 In my distress I **c** upon the
31:17 for I have **c** upon You; Let the
50: 1 Has spoken and **c** the earth
81: 7 You **c** in trouble, and I
88: 9 I have **c** daily upon You; I
99: 6 Samuel was among those who **c**
99: 6 They **c** upon the LORD, and He
105:16 Moreover He **c** for a famine in
116: 4 Then I **c** upon the name of the
118: 5 I **c** on the LORD in distress;
Prov 1:24 Because I have **c** and you
16:21 The wise in heart will be **c**
24: 8 plots to do evil Will be **c** a
Song 5: 6 I **c** him, but he gave me no
6: 9 The daughters saw her And **c**
Isa 1:26 Afterward you shall be **c** the
4: 1 Only let us be **c** by your name,
4: 3 remains in Jerusalem will be **c**
9: 6 And His name will be **c**
13: 3 I have also **c** My mighty ones
19:18 one will be **c** the City of
22:12 day the Lord GOD of hosts **C**
30: 7 Therefore I have **c** her
32: 5 person will no longer be **c**
35: 8 And it shall be **c** the Highway
36:13 the Rabshakeh stood and **c** out
41: 2 Who in righteousness **c** him to
41: 9 **c** from its farthest regions,
42: 6 have **c** You in righteousness,

43: 1 I have **c** you by your name;
43: 7 Everyone who is **c** by My name,
43:22 But you have not **c** upon Me,
45: 4 I have even **c** you by your
47: 1 For you shall no more be **c**
47: 5 For you shall no longer be **c**
48: 1 Who are **c** by the name of
48: 8 And were **c** a transgressor from
48:12 Me, O Jacob, And Israel, My **c**:
48:15 I have **c** him, I have brought
49: 1 from afar! The LORD has **c** Me
50: 2 there no man? Why, when I **c**,
51: 2 For I **c** him alone, And
54: 5 He is **c** the God of the whole
54: 6 For the LORD has **c** you Like a
56: 7 For My house shall be **c** a
58:12 you shall be **c** the Repairer
61: 3 That they may be **c** trees of
62: 2 You shall be **c** by a new name,
62: 4 But you shall be **c** Hephzibah,
62:12 And you shall be **c** Sought Out,
63:19 Those who were never **c** by Your
65: 1 To a nation that was not **c**
65:12 slaughter; Because, when I **c**,
66: 4 on them; Because, when I **c**,
Jer 3:17 that time Jerusalem shall be **c**
7:10 Me in this house which is **c** by
7:11 which is **c** by My name, become a
7:13 and I **c** you, but you did not
7:14 do to the house which is **c** by
7:30 in the house which is **c** by My
7:32 when it will no more be **c**
11:16 The LORD **c** your name, Green
12: 6 they have **c** a multitude after
14: 9 And we are **c** by Your name; Do
15:16 For I am **c** by Your name,
19: 6 this place shall no more be **c**
20: 3 The LORD has not **c** your name
23: 6 His name by which He will be **c**:
25:29 on the city which is **c** by My
30:17 Because they **c** you an outcast
32:34 in the house which is **c** by My
33:16 name by which she will be **c**:
34:15 Me in the house which is **c** by
35:17 and I have **c** to them but they
36: 4 Then Jeremiah **c** Baruch the son
42: 8 Then he **c** Johanan the son of
Lam 1:15 He has **c** an assembly against
1:19 I **c** for my lovers, But they
2:15 Is this the city that is **c**
3:55 I **c** on Your name, O LORD,
3:57 You drew near on the day I **c** on
Ezek 9: 1 Then He **c** out in my hearing with
9: 3 And He **c** to the man clothed
10:13 they were **c** in my hearing,
20:29 So its name is **c** Bamah to this
23:21 Thus you **c** to remembrance the
Dan 5:12 now let Daniel be **c**,
8:16 the banks of the Ulai, who **c**,
9:18 and the city which is **c** by Your
9:19 city and Your people are **c** by
10: 1 whose name was **c** Belteshazzar.
Hos 11: 1 And out of Egypt I **c** My son.
11: 2 As they **c** them, So they went
Am 7: 4 the Lord GOD **c** for conflict by
9:12 all the Gentiles who are **c** by
Hag 1:11 For I **c** for a drought on the
Zech 6: 8 And He **c** to me, and spoke to me,
7:13 so they **c** out and I would not
8: 3 Jerusalem shall be **c** the City
11: 7 the one I **c** Beauty, and the
11: 7 and the other I **c** Bonds; and I
Mal 1: 4 They shall be **c** the Territory
Mt 1:16 of whom was born Jesus who is **c**
1:25 And he **c** His name ***JESUS***.
2: 7 when he had secretly **c** the wise
2:15 Out of Egypt I **c** My Son."
2:23 he came and dwelt in a city **c**
2:23 He shall be **c** a Nazarene."
4:18 Simon **c** Peter, and Andrew his
4:21 their nets. He **c** them,
5: 9 For they shall be **c** sons of
5:19 shall be **c** least in the kingdom
5:19 he shall be **c** great in the
10: 1 And when He had **c** His twelve
10: 2 who is **c** Peter, and Andrew his
10:25 If they have **c** the master of
13:55 Is not His mother **c** Mary?
15:10 When He had **c** the multitude to
15:32 Now Jesus **c** His disciples to
18: 2 Then Jesus **c** a little child to
18:32 after he had **c** him, said to
20:16 the first last. For many are **c**,
20:25 But Jesus **c** them to Himself and
20:32 So Jesus stood still and **c** them,
21:13 My house shall be **c** a
22:14 'For many are **c**, but few are
23: 7 and to be **c** by men, 'Rabbi,
23: 8 "But you, do not be **c** '
23:10 And do not be **c** teachers; for
25:14 who **c** his own servants and
26: 3 priest, who was **c** Caiaphas,
26:14 **c** Judas Iscariot, went to the
26:36 came with them to a place **c**
27: 8 that field has been **c** the
27:16 they had a notorious prisoner **c**
27:17 or Jesus who is **c** Christ?"
27:22 shall I do with Jesus who is **c**
27:33 when they had come to a place **c**
Mk 1:20 And immediately He **c** them, and
3:13 went up on the mountain and **c**
3:23 So He **c** them to Himself and
6: 7 He **c** the twelve to Himself,
7:14 When He had **c** all the multitude
8: 1 Jesus **c** His disciples to Him
8:34 When He had **c** the people to
9:35 **c** the twelve, and said to them,
10:42 But Jesus **c** them to Himself and
10:49 still and commanded him to be **c**.
10:49 Then they **c** the blind man,
11:17 My house shall be **c** a
12:43 He **c** His disciples to Himself
14:72 Then Peter **c** to mind the word
15:16 led Him away into the hall **c**
15:16 and they **c** together the whole
Lk 1:32 and will be **c** the Son of the
1:35 One who is to be born will be **c**
1:36 sixth month for her who was **c**
1:59 and they would have **c** him by
1:60 'No; he shall be **c** John."
1:61 among your relatives who is **c**
1:62 father—what he would have him **c**.
1:76 will be **c** the prophet of the
2: 4 which is **c** Bethlehem, because
2:21 His name was **c** JESUS, the name
2:23 the womb shall be **c** holy
6:13 He **c** His disciples to Himself;
6:15 and Simon **c** the Zealot;
7:11 that He went into a city **c**
8: 2 Mary **c** Magdalene, out of whom
8:54 took her by the hand and **c**,
9: 1 Then He **c** His twelve disciples
9:10 place belonging to the city **c**
10:39 And she had a sister **c** Mary, who
13:12 He **c** her to Him and said to
15:19 I am no longer worthy to be **c**
15:21 and am no longer worthy to be **c**
15:26 So he **c** one of the servants and
16: 2 So he **c** him and said to him,
16: 5 So he **c** every one of his
18:16 But Jesus **c** them to Him and
19:13 So he **c** ten of his servants,
19:15 to be **c** to him, that he might
19:29 at the mountain **c** Olivet, that
19:39 And some of the Pharisees **c** to
20:37 when he **c** the Lord 'the God
21:37 and stayed on the mountain **c**
22: 1 which is **c** Passover.
22:25 authority over them are **c** '
22:47 and he who was **c** Judas, one of
23:13 when he had **c** together the
23:20 Jesus, again **c** out to them.
23:33 they had come to the place **c**
24:13 that same day to a village **c**
Jn 1:42 You shall be **c** Cephas" (which
1:48 Before Philip **c** you, when you
2: 9 the master of the feast **c** the
4: 5 to a city of Samaria which is **c**
4:25 Messiah is coming" (who is **c**
5: 2 which is **c** in Hebrew, Bethesda,
9:11 A Man **c** Jesus made clay and
9:18 until they **c** the parents of him
9:24 So they again **c** the man who was
10:35 If He **c** them gods, to whom the
11:16 who is **c** the Twin, said to his
11:28 she went her way and secretly **c**
11:54 to a city **c** Ephraim, and there
12:17 who were with Him when He **c**
15:15 but I have **c** you friends, for
18:33 **c** Jesus, and said to Him, "Are
19:13 seat in a place that is **c** The
19:17 went out to a place **c** the
19:17 which is **c** in Hebrew, Golgotha,
20:24 **c** the Twin, one of the twelve,
21: 2 Thomas **c** the Twin, Nathanael of
Acts 1:12 to Jerusalem from the mount **c**
1:19 so that field is **c** in their own
1:23 Joseph **c** Barsabas, who was
3: 2 gate of the temple which is **c**
3:11 to them in the porch which is **c**
4:18 And they **c** them and commanded
5:21 and those with him came and **c**
5:40 and when they had **c** for the
6: 9 arose some from what is **c** the
7:14 Then Joseph sent and **c** his
8: 9 But there was a certain man **c**
9:11 Arise and go to the street **c**
9:11 the house of Judas for one **c**
9:21 he who destroyed those who **c**
9:41 and when he had **c** the saints
10: 1 was a certain man in Caesarea **c**
10: 1 a centurion of what was **c** the
10: 7 Cornelius **c** two of his
10:18 And they **c** and asked whether
10:24 and had **c** together his
11:26 And the disciples were first **c**
13: 1 Simeon who was **c** Niger, Lucius
13: 2 for the work to which I have **c**
13: 7 This man **c** for Barnabas and
13: 9 who also is **c** Paul, filled
14:12 And Barnabas they **c** Zeus, and
15:17 the Gentiles who are **c**
15:37 to take with them John **c** Mark.
16:10 concluding that the Lord had **c**
16:28 But Paul **c** with a loud voice,
16:29 Then he **c** for a light, ran in,
19:25 He **c** them together with the
19:40 we are in danger of being **c** in
20: 1 Paul **c** the disciples
20:17 he sent to Ephesus and **c** for
23:17 Then Paul **c** one of the
23:18 Paul the prisoner **c** me to him
23:23 And he **c** for two centurions,
24: 2 And when he was **c** upon,
27: 8 we came to a place **c** Fair
27:14 head wind arose, **c** Euroclydon.
27:16 the shelter of an island **c**
28: 1 found out that the island was **c**
28:17 after three days that Paul **c**
28:20 this reason therefore I have **c**
Rom 1: 1 **c** to be an apostle, separated
1: 6 among whom you also are the **c** of
1: 7 **c** to be saints: Grace to you
2:17 Indeed you are **c** a Jew, and
7: 3 she will be **c** an adulteress;
8:28 who are the **c** according to His
8:30 He predestined, these He also **c**;
8:30 these He also called; whom He **c**,
9: 7 your seed shall be **c**.
9:24 even us whom He **c**,
9:26 There they shall be **c**
1 Cor 1: 1 **c** to be an apostle of Jesus
1: 2 **c** to be saints, with all who
1: 9 by whom you were **c** into the
1:24 but to those who are **c**,
1:26 mighty, not many noble, are **c**.
7:15 But God has **c** us to peace.
7:17 as the Lord has **c** each one, so
7:18 Was anyone **c** while circumcised?
7:18 anyone **c** while uncircumcised?
7:20 same calling in which he was **c**.
7:21 Were you **c** while a slave?
7:22 For he who is **c** in the Lord
7:22 Likewise he who is **c** while
7:24 that state in which he was **c**.
15: 9 who am not worthy to be **c** an
Gal 1: 6 away so soon from Him who **c**
1:15 me from my mother's womb and **c**
5:13 have been **c** to liberty; only do
Eph 2:11 who are **c** Uncircumcision by what
2:11 Uncircumcision by what is **c**
4: 1 calling with which you were **c**,
4: 4 just as you were **c** in one hope
Col 3:15 to which also you were **c** in one
4:11 and Jesus who is **c** Justus.
2 Th 2: 4 himself above all that is **c**
2:14 to which He **c** you by our gospel,
1 Tim 6:12 to which you were also **c** and
6:20 of what is falsely **c** knowledge—
2 Tim 1: 9 who has saved us and **c** us with
Heb 3:13 while it is **c** "Today," lest
5: 4 but he who is **c** by God, just as
5:10 **c** by God as High Priest
7:11 and not be **c** according to the
9: 2 which is **c** the sanctuary;
9: 3 of the tabernacle which is **c**
9:15 that those who are **c** may
11: 8 Abraham obeyed when he was **c**
11:15 And truly if they had **c** to mind
11:16 God is not ashamed to be **c**
11:18 your seed shall be **c**,
11:24 refused to be **c** the son of
Jas 2: 7 noble name by which you are **c**?
2:23 And he was **c** the friend of
1 Pe 1:15 but as He who **c** you is holy,
2: 9 the praises of Him who **c** you
2:21 For to this you were **c**,
3: 9 knowing that you were **c** to
5:10 who **c** us to His eternal glory
2 Pe 1: 3 the knowledge of Him who **c** us
1 Jn 3: 1 that we should be **c** children of
Jude 1 of James, To those who are **c**,
Rev 1: 9 was on the island that is **c**
11: 8 city which spiritually is **c**
12: 9 **c** the Devil and Satan, who
16:16 them together to the place **c**
17:14 those who are with Him are **c**,
19: 9 Blessed are those who are **c** to
19:11 And He who sat on him was **c**
19:13 and His name is **c** The Word of

CALLING (29/29) CALL

Num 10: 2 you shall use them for **c** the
22:37 **c** for you? Why did you not come
Judg 8: 1 you done this to us by not **c**
1 Sam 26:14 are you, **c** out to the king?"
Isa 1:13 and the **c** of assemblies—I
41: 4 ***C*** the generations from the
46:11 ***C*** a bird of prey from the east,
Jer 1:15 I am **c** All the families of the
Ezek 23:19 multiplied her harlotry In **c**
Mt 11:16 in the marketplaces and **c** to
27:47 This Man is **c** for Elijah!"
Mk 3:31 they sent to Him, **c** Him.
10:49 Rise, He is **c** you."
15:35 'Look, He is **c** for Elijah!"
Lk 7:19 **c** two of his disciples to him,
7:32 in the marketplace and **c** to
Jn 11:28 The Teacher has come and is **c**
Acts 7:59 stoned Stephen as he was **c** on
22:16 **c** on the name of the Lord.'
Rom 11:29 For the gifts and the **c** of God
1 Cor 1:26 For you see your **c**, brethren,
7:20 each one remain in the same **c**
Eph 1:18 know what is the hope of His **c**,
4: 1 you to walk worthy of the **c**
4: 4 called in one hope of your **c**;
2 Th 1:11 count you worthy of this **c**,
2 Tim 1: 9 us and called us with a holy **c**,
Heb 3: 1 partakers of the heavenly **c**,
1 Pe 3: 6 **c** him lord, whose daughters you

CALLS (33/32) CALL

Gen 46:33 when Pharaoh **c** you and says,

Deut 18:11 or one who c up the dead.
1 Sam 3: 9 if He c you, that you must say,
1 Ki 8:43 all for which the foreigner c
2 Chr 6:33 all for which the foreigner c
Ps 42: 7 Deep c unto deep at the noise
147: 4 He c them all by name.
Prov 1:20 Wisdom c aloud outside; She
18: 6 And his mouth c for blows.
Isa 21:11 He c to me out of Seir,
40:26 He c them all by name, By the
59: 4 No one c for justice, Nor does
64: 7 And there is no one who c on
Hos 7: 7 None among them c upon Me.
Joel 2:32 come to pass That whoever c
2:32 the remnant whom the LORD c.
Am 5: 8 He c for the waters of the sea
9: 6 Who c for the waters of the
Mt 22:45 If David then c Him 'Lord,' how
Mk 12:37 Therefore David himself c Him
Lk 15: 6 he c together his friends and
15: 9 c her friends and neighbors
20:44 Therefore David c Him 'Lord';
Jn 10: 3 and he c his own sheep by name
Acts 2:21 to pass That whoever c
Rom 4:17 gives life to the dead and c
9:11 not of works but of Him who c),
10:13 whoever c on the name of
1 Cor 12: 3 by the Spirit of God c Jesus
Gal 5: 8 does not come from Him who c
1 Th 2:12 would walk worthy of God who c
5:24 He who c you is faithful, who
Rev 2:20 who c herself a prophetess, to

CALM (6/6) CALMED, CALMS

Prov 17:27 man of understanding is of a c
Jon 1:11 do to you that the sea may be c
1:12 then the sea will become c for
Mt 8:26 sea, and there was a great c.
Mk 4:39 ceased and there was a great c.
Lk 8:24 they ceased, and there was a c.

CALMED (1/1) CALM

Ps 131: 2 Surely I have c and quieted my

CALMS (1/1) CALM

Ps 107:29 He c the storm, So that its

CALNEH (2/2) CANNEH

Gen 10:10 was Babel, Erech, Accad, and C,
Am 6: 2 Go over to C and see; And from

CALNO (1/1)

Isa 10: 9 Is not C like Carchemish?

CALVARY (1/1) GOLGOTHA

Lk 23:33 had come to the place called C,

CALVES (16/16) CALF, CALVES'

1 Sam 6: 7 and take their c home, away
6:10 and shut up their c at home.
14:32 and took sheep, oxen, and c,
1 Ki 12:28 made two c of gold, and said to
12:32 sacrificing to the c that he
2 Ki 10:29 from the golden c that were at
17:16 a molded image and two c,
2 Chr 13: 8 and with you are the gold c
Job 21:10 cow c without miscarriage.
Ps 68:30 The herd of bulls with the c
Hos 13: 2 men who sacrifice kiss the c!
Am 6: 4 lambs from the flock And c
Mic 6: 6 With c a year old?
Mal 4: 2 And grow fat like stall-fed c.
Heb 9:12 with the blood of goats and c,
9:19 he took the blood of c and

CALVES' (1/1) CALVES

Ezek 1: 7 feet were like the soles of c

CAME (1710/1614)

Gen 4: 3 in the process of time it c to
4: 8 and it c to pass, when they
6: 1 Now it c to pass, when men began
6: 4 when the sons of God c in to
7:10 And it c to pass after seven
8: 6 So it c to pass, at the end of
8:11 Then the dove c to him in the
8:13 And it c to pass in the six
10:14 and Casluhim (from whom c the
11: 2 And it c to pass, as they
11: 5 But the LORD c down to see the
11:31 and they c to Haran and dwelt
12: 5 So they c to the land of
12:11 And it c to pass, when he was
12:14 when Abram c into Egypt, that
14: 1 And it c to pass in the days of
14: 5 the kings that were with him c
14: 7 Then they turned back and c to
14:13 Then one who had escaped c and
15: 1 things the word of the LORD c
15: 4 the word of the LORD c to
15:11 And when the vultures c down on
15:17 And it c to pass, when the sun
18:23 And Abraham c near and said,
19: 1 Now the two angels c to Sodom in
19: 5 Where are the men who c to you
19: 9 This one c in to stay here, and
19: 9 and c near to break down the
19:17 So it c to pass, when they had
19:29 And it c to pass, when God
20: 3 But God c to Abimelech in a
20:13 And it c to pass, when God
21:22 And it c to pass at that time
22: 1 Now it c to pass after these
22: 9 Then they c to the place of
22:20 Now it c to pass after these
23: 2 and Abraham c to mourn for
24: 5 to the land from which you c?
24:15 c out with her pitcher on her
24:16 filled her pitcher, and c up.
24:30 So it c to pass, when he saw the
24:32 Then the man c to the house.
24:42 And this day I c to the well
24:52 And it c to pass, when
24:62 Now Isaac c from the way of Beer
25:11 And it c to pass, after the
25:25 And the first c out red.
25:26 Afterward his brother c out, and
25:29 and Esau c in from the field,
26: 8 Now it c to pass, when he had
26:26 Then Abimelech c to him from
26:32 It c to pass the same day that
26:32 day that Isaac's servants c
27: 1 Now it c to pass, when Isaac was
27:27 And he c near and kissed him;
27:30 that Esau his brother c in from
27:33 I ate all of it before you c,
27:35 Your brother c with deceit and
28:11 So he c to a certain place and
29: 1 went on his journey and c to
29: 9 Rachel c with her father's
29:10 And it c to pass, when Jacob saw
29:13 Then it c to pass, when Laban
29:23 Now it c to pass in the evening,
29:25 So it c to pass in the morning,
30:16 When Jacob c out of the field in
30:25 And it c to pass, when Rachel
30:30 For what you had before I c
30:38 troughs where the flocks c to
30:38 should conceive when they c to
30:41 And it c to pass, whenever the
32: 6 We c to your brother Esau, and
32:13 and took what c to his hand as
33: 3 until he c near to his brother.
33: 6 Then the maidservants c near,
33: 7 And Leah also c near with her
33: 7 Afterward Joseph and Rachel c
33:18 Then Jacob c safely to the city
33:18 when he c from Padan Aram; and
34: 5 held his peace until they c.
34: 7 And the sons of Jacob c in from
34:20 Hamor and Shechem his son c to
34:25 Now it c to pass on the third
34:25 each took his sword and c
34:27 The sons of Jacob c upon the
35: 6 So Jacob c to Luz (that is,
35: 9 when he c from Padan Aram, and
35:17 Now it c to pass, when she was
35:27 Then Jacob c to his father
37:18 even before he c near them,
37:23 So it c to pass, when Joseph
38: 1 It c to pass at that time that
38: 9 and it c to pass, when he went
38:24 And it c to pass, about three
38:27 Now it c to pass, at the time
38:28 This one c out first."
38:29 that his brother c out
38:30 Afterward his brother c out who
39: 7 And it c to pass after these
39:14 He c in to me to lie with me,
39:16 with her until his master c
39:17 whom you brought to us c in to
40: 1 It c to pass after these things
40: 6 And Joseph c in to them in the
40:20 Now it c to pass on the third
41: 1 Then it c to pass, at the end of
41: 2 Suddenly there c up out of the
41: 3 seven other cows c up after
41: 5 seven heads of grain c up on
41: 8 Now it c to pass in the morning
41:13 And it c to pass, just as he
41:14 and c to Pharaoh.
41:18 Suddenly seven cows c up out of
41:19 seven other cows c up after
41:22 and suddenly seven heads c up
41:27 thin and ugly cows which c up
41:50 before the years of famine c,
41:57 So all countries c to Joseph in
42: 6 And Joseph's brothers c and
43: 2 And it c to pass, when they had
43:20 we indeed c down the first time
43:21 when we c to the encampment,
43:26 And when Joseph c home, they
43:31 Then he washed his face and c
44:14 So Judah and his brothers c to
44:18 Then Judah c near to him and
45: 4 So they c near. Then he said:
45:25 and c to the land of Canaan to
46: 1 and c to Beersheba, and offered
46:26 who c from his body, besides
46:28 And they c to the land of
47:15 all the Egyptians c to Joseph
47:18 they c to him the next year and
48: 1 Now it c to pass after these
48: 5 in the land of Egypt before I c
48: 7 when I c from Padan, Rachel
50:10 Then they c to the threshing
Ex 1: 1 of the children of Israel who c
1: 1 each man and his household c
2: 5 the daughter of Pharaoh c down
2:11 Now it c to pass in those days,
2:16 And they c and drew water, and
2:17 Then the shepherds c and drove
2:18 When they c to Reuel their
2:23 and their cry c up to God
3: 1 and c to Horeb, the mountain of
4:24 And it c to pass on the way, at
5:15 children of Israel c and cried
5:20 as they c out from Pharaoh,
5:23 For since I c to Pharaoh to
6:28 And it c to pass, on the day
8: 6 and the frogs c up and covered
8:24 Thick swarms of flies c into
10: 3 So Moses and Aaron c in to
12:29 And it c to pass at midnight
12:41 And it c to pass at the end of
12:41 it c to pass that all the armies
12:51 And it c to pass, on that very
13: 8 the LORD did for me when I c
13:15 And it c to pass, when Pharaoh
13:17 Then it c to pass, when Pharaoh
14:20 So it c between the camp of the
14:24 Now it c to pass, in the morning
14:28 all the army of Pharaoh that c
15:23 Now when they c to Marah, they
15:27 Then they c to Elim, where
16: 1 of the children of Israel c to
16:10 Now it c to pass, as Aaron spoke
16:13 So it was that quails c up at
16:22 rulers of the congregation c
16:35 until they c to an inhabited
16:35 they ate manna until they c to
17: 8 Now Amalek c and fought with
18: 5 c with his sons and his wife to
18:12 And Aaron c with all the elders
19: 1 they c to the Wilderness of
19: 7 So Moses c and called for the
19:16 Then it c to pass on the third
19:20 Then the LORD c down upon Mount
22:15 it c for its hire.
23:15 for in it you c out of Egypt;
24: 3 So Moses c and told the people
32:19 as soon as he c near the camp,
32:24 and this calf c out."
32:30 Now it c to pass on the next
33: 7 And it c to pass that everyone
33: 9 And it c to pass, when Moses
34:18 for in the month of Abib you c
34:29 when Moses c down from Mount
34:29 were in Moses' hand when he c
34:32 all the children of Israel c
34:34 take the veil off until he c
35:21 Then everyone c whose heart was
35:22 They c, both men and women,
36: 4 all the work of the sanctuary c,
37:18 And six branches c out of its
40:17 And it c to pass in the first
40:32 and when they c near the altar,
Lev 9: 1 It c to pass on the eighth day
9:22 and c down from offering the
9:23 and c out and blessed the
9:24 and fire c out from before the
Num 3:21 From Gershon c the family of
3:27 From Kohath c the family of
3:33 From Merari c the family of
3:38 but the outsider who c near was
4:47 everyone who c to do the work
7: 1 Now it c to pass, when Moses had
9: 6 and they c before Moses and
10:11 Now it c to pass on the
11:25 Then the LORD c down in the
12: 4 of meeting!" So the three c
12: 5 Then the LORD c down in the
13:22 up through the South and c to
13:23 Then they c to the Valley of
13:26 Now they departed and c back to
13:33 (the descendants of Anak c
14:45 who dwelt in that mountain c
16:27 and Dathan and Abiram c out and
16:31 Now it c to pass, as he
16:35 And a fire c out from the LORD
16:43 Then Moses and Aaron c before
17: 8 Now it c to pass on the next
20: 1 c into the Wilderness of Zin in
20:11 and water c out abundantly, and
20:20 So Edom c out against them
20:22 journeyed from Kadesh and c to
20:28 Then Moses and Eleazar c down
21: 7 Therefore the people c to
21:23 and he c to Jahaz and fought
22: 7 and they c to Balaam and spoke
22: 9 Then God c to Balaam and said,
22:16 And they c to Balaam and said to
22:20 And God c to Balaam at night and
22:39 and they c to Kirjath Huzoth.
23:17 So he c to him, and there he
24: 2 and the Spirit of God c upon
25: 6 one of the children of Israel c
26: 1 And it c to pass, after the
26: 4 the children of Israel who c
27: 1 Then c the daughters of
31:48 of hundreds, c near to Moses;
32: 2 and the children of Reuben c
32:11 Surely none of the men who c up
32:16 Then they c near to him and
33: 9 They moved from Marah and c to
36: 1 c near and spoke before Moses
Deut 1: 3 Now it c to pass in the fortieth
1:19 Then we c to Kadesh Barnea.

1:22 And everyone of you *c* near to me
1:24 and *c* to the Valley of Eshcol,
1:31 way that you went until you *c*
1:44 who dwelt in that mountain *c*
2:23 who *c* from Caphtor, destroyed
2:32 Sihon and all his people *c* out
3: 1 and Og king of Bashan *c* out
4:11 Then you *c* near and stood at the
4:45 of Israel after they *c* out of
4:46 of Israel defeated after they *c*
5:23 that you *c* near to me, all the
9: 7 the land of Egypt until you *c*
9:11 And it *c* to pass, at the end of
9:15 So I turned and *c* down from the
10: 5 Then I turned and *c* down from
11: 5 in the wilderness until you *c*
16: 3 bread of affliction (for you *c*
16: 3 the day in which you *c* out of
16: 6 at the time you *c* out of Egypt.
22:14 and when I *c* to her I found she
23: 4 water on the road when you *c*
24: 9 to Miriam on the way when you *c*
29: 7 And when you *c* to this place,
29: 7 and Og king of Bashan *c* out
29:16 the land of Egypt and that we *c*
32:44 So Moses *c* with Joshua the son
33: 2 The LORD *c* from Sinai, And
33: 2 And He *c* with ten thousands of
33: 2 From His right hand *C* a
33:21 He *c* with the heads of the
Josh 1: 1 it *c* to pass that the LORD
2: 1 and *c* to the house of a harlot
2: 4 the men *c* to me, but I did not
2: 8 she *c* up to them on the roof,
2:10 the Red Sea for you when you *c*
2:23 and they *c* to Joshua the son of
3: 1 out from Acacia Grove and *c* to
3:15 as those who bore the ark *c* to
3:16 that the waters which *c* down
4: 1 And it *c* to pass, when all the
4:11 Then it *c* to pass, when all the
4:18 And it *c* to pass, when the
4:19 Now the people *c* up from the
5: 4 All the people who *c* out of
5: 5 For all the people who *c* out had
5: 5 on the way as they *c* out of
5: 6 who *c* out of Egypt, were
5:13 And it *c* to pass, when Joshua
6: 1 none went out, and none *c* in.
6: 9 and the rear guard *c* after the
6:11 Then they *c* into the camp and
6:13 But the rear guard *c* after the
6:15 But it *c* to pass on the seventh
8:11 and they *c* before the city and
8:22 Then the others *c* out of the
8:24 And it *c* to pass when Israel
9: 1 And it *c* to pass when all the
9:17 of Israel journeyed and *c* to
10: 1 Now it *c* to pass when
10: 9 Joshua therefore *c* upon them
10:33 Then Horam king of Gezer *c* up to
11: 1 And it *c* to pass, when Jabin
11: 5 they *c* and camped together at
11: 7 the people of war with him *c*
11:21 And at that time Joshua *c* and
14: 6 Then the children of Judah *c* to
15:18 when she *c* to him, that she
16: 7 and *c* out at the Jordan.
17: 4 And they *c* near before Eleazar
18: 9 and they *c* to Joshua at the
18:11 of the children of Benjamin *c*
18:11 the territory of their lot *c*
18:16 Then the border *c* down to the
19: 1 The second lot *c* out for Simeon,
19:10 The third lot *c* out for the
19:17 The fourth lot *c* out to
19:24 The fifth lot *c* out for the
19:32 The sixth lot *c* out to the
19:40 The seventh lot *c* out for the
21: 1 houses of the Levites *c* near
21: 4 Now the lot *c* out for the
21:45 All *c* to pass.
22:10 And when they *c* to the region
22:15 Then they *c* to the children of
23: 1 Now it *c* to pass, a long time
24: 6 and you *c* to the sea; and the
24:11 you went over the Jordan and *c*
24:29 Now it *c* to pass after these
Judg 1: 1 after the death of Joshua it *c*
1:14 when she *c* to him, that she
1:28 And it *c* to pass, when Israel
2: 1 Then the Angel of the LORD *c* up
2:19 And it *c* to pass, when the judge
3:10 The Spirit of the LORD *c* upon
3:20 And Ehud *c* to him (now he was
3:22 and his entrails *c* out.
3:24 Eglon's servants *c* to look, and
4: 5 And the children of Israel *c* up
4:22 Jael *c* out to meet him, and
5:13 Then the survivors *c* down, the
5:13 The LORD *c* down for me
5:14 From Machir rulers *c* down,
5:19 The kings *c* and fought, Then
6: 7 And it *c* to pass, when the
6:11 Now the Angel of the LORD *c*
6:25 Now it *c* to pass the same night
6:34 But the Spirit of the LORD *c*
6:35 and they *c* up to meet them.
7:13 it *c* to a tent and struck it so
7:19 men who were with him *c* to
8: 4 When Gideon *c* to the Jordan, he
8:15 Then he *c* to the men of Succoth
9:26 Now Gaal the son of Ebed *c* with
9:42 And it *c* about on the next day
9:52 So Abimelech *c* as far as the
9:57 and on them *c* the curse of
11: 4 It *c* to pass after a time that
11:13 took away my land when they *c*
11:16 for when Israel *c* up from Egypt,
11:16 as far as the Red Sea and *c* to
11:18 *c* to the east side of the land
11:29 the Spirit of the LORD *c* upon
11:34 When Jephthah *c* to his house at
11:35 And it *c* to pass, when he saw
13: 6 So the woman *c* and told her
13: 6 A Man of God *c* to me, and His
13: 9 and the Angel of God *c* to the
13:10 the Man who *c* to me the other
13:11 When he *c* to the Man, he said
14: 5 and *c* to the vineyards of
14: 5 a young lion *c* roaring against
14: 6 And the Spirit of the LORD *c*
14: 9 When he *c* to his father and
14:14 Out of the eater *c* something to
14:14 And out of the strong *c*
14:15 But it *c* to pass on the seventh
14:19 the Spirit of the LORD *c* upon
15: 6 So the Philistines *c* up and
15:14 When he *c* to Lehi, the
15:14 the Philistines *c* shouting
15:14 Then the Spirit of the LORD *c*
15:19 and water *c* out, and he drank;
16: 5 the lords of the Philistines *c*
16:16 And it *c* to pass, when she
16:18 the lords of the Philistines *c*
16:31 all his father's household *c*
17: 8 Then he *c* to the mountains of
18: 8 Then the spies *c* back to their
18:13 and *c* to the house of Micah.
18:15 and *c* to the house of the young
19: 1 And it *c* to pass in those days,
19: 5 Then it *c* to pass on the fourth
19:10 and *c* to opposite Jebus (that
19:16 Just then an old man *c* in from
19:22 Bring out the man who *c* to your
19:26 Then the woman *c* as the day was
19:30 that the children of Israel *c*
20: 1 So all the children of Israel *c*
20:21 the children of Benjamin *c* out
20:26 went up and *c* to the house of
20:34 select men from all Israel *c*
20:42 and whoever *c* out of the
20:48 fire to all the cities they *c*
21: 2 Then the people *c* to the house
21:14 So Benjamin *c* back at that time,
Ruth 1: 1 Now it *c* to pass, in the days
1:19 two of them went until they *c*
1:22 Now they *c* to Bethlehem at the
2: 4 Boaz *c* from Bethlehem, and said
2: 6 the young Moabite woman who *c*
2: 7 So she *c* and has continued
3: 7 and she *c* softly, uncovered his
3:14 it be known that the woman *c*
3:16 So when she *c* to her
4: 1 of whom Boaz had spoken *c* by.
4: 1 So he *c* aside and sat down.
1 Sam 1: 4 And whenever the time *c* for
1:19 and returned and *c* to their
1:20 So it *c* to pass in the process
2:14 to all the Israelites who *c*
2:19 to him year by year when she *c*
2:27 Then a man of God *c* to Eli and
3: 2 And it *c* to pass at that time,
3:10 Now the LORD *c* and stood and
4: 1 And the word of Samuel *c* to all
4: 5 of the covenant of the LORD *c*
4:12 and *c* to Shiloh with his
4:13 Now when he *c*, there was Eli,
4:13 And when the man *c* into the
4:14 And the man *c* quickly and
4:16 I am he who *c* from the battle.
4:19 for her labor pains *c* upon her.
5:10 as the ark of God *c* to Ekron,
6:14 Then the cart *c* into the field
7: 1 the men of Kirjath Jearim *c*
8: 1 Now it *c* to pass when Samuel was
8: 4 Israel gathered together and *c*
9:12 for today he *c* to this city,
9:15 his ear the day before Saul *c*,
10: 9 and all those signs *c* to pass
10:10 When they *c* there to the hill,
10:10 then the Spirit of God *c* upon
11: 1 Then Nahash the Ammonite *c* up
11: 4 So the messengers *c* to Gibeah
11: 6 Then the Spirit of God *c* upon
11: 7 and they *c* out with one
11: 9 said to the messengers who *c*,
11: 9 Then the messengers *c* and
11:11 and they *c* into the midst of
12:12 Nahash king of the Ammonites *c*
13: 5 And they *c* up and encamped in
13:10 burnt offering, that Samuel *c*;
13:17 Then raiders *c* out of the camp
13:22 So it *c* about, on the day of
14:13 And as he *c* after him,
14:25 all the people of the land *c*
15: 2 him on the way when he *c* up
15: 5 And Saul *c* to a city of Amalek,
15: 6 children of Israel when they *c*
15:10 Now the word of the LORD *c* to
15:32 So Agag *c* to him cautiously.
16: 6 So it was, when they *c*,
16:13 and the Spirit of the LORD *c*
16:21 So David *c* to Saul and stood
17:20 And he *c* to the camp as the
17:22 and *c* and greeted his brothers.
17:34 and when a lion or a bear *c* and
17:41 So the Philistine *c*,
17:48 the Philistine arose and *c* and
18:10 distressing spirit from God *c*
18:13 and he went out and *c* in before
18:16 because he went out and *c* in
19: 9 spirit from the LORD *c* upon
19:20 the Spirit of God *c* upon the
19:22 and *c* to the great well that
19:23 on and prophesied until he *c*
20:38 gathered up the arrows and *c*
21: 1 Now David *c* to Nob, to Ahimelech
21: 5 us about three days since I *c*
22:11 And they all *c* to the king.
23:19 Then the Ziphites *c* up to Saul
23:27 But a messenger *c* to Saul,
24: 3 So he *c* to the sheepfolds by the
25: 9 So when David's young men *c*,
25:12 and they *c* and told him all
25:38 Then it *c* about, after about
26: 1 Now the Ziphites *c* to Saul at
26: 3 and he saw that Saul *c* after
26: 5 So David arose and *c* to the
26: 7 So David and Abishai *c* to the
26:15 For one of the people *c* in to
27: 9 and returned and *c* to Achish.
28: 4 and *c* and encamped at Shunem.
28: 8 and they *c* to the woman by
28:21 And the woman *c* to Saul and saw
30: 1 when David and his men *c* to
30: 3 So David and his men *c* to the
30: 9 and *c* to the Brook Besor, where
30:12 his strength *c* back to him;
30:21 Now David *c* to the two hundred
30:21 And when David *c* near the
30:23 into our hand the troop that *c*
30:26 Now when David *c* to Ziklag, he
31: 7 and the Philistines *c* and dwelt
31: 8 when the Philistines *c* to strip
31:12 and they *c* to Jabesh and burned
2 Sam 1: 1 Now it *c* to pass after the
1: 2 it happened that a man *c* from
1: 2 when he *c* to David, that he
2: 4 Then the men of Judah *c*,
2:23 so that the spear *c* out of his
2:23 So it was that as many as *c* to
2:24 sun was going down when they *c*
2:29 and they *c* to Mahanaim.
2:32 and they *c* to Hebron at
3:20 and twenty men with him *c* to
3:22 servants of David and Joab *c*
3:23 Abner the son of Ner *c* to the
3:24 Then Joab *c* to the king and
3:24 Abner *c* to you; why is it
3:25 that Abner the son of Ner *c* to
3:35 And when all the people *c* to
4: 4 news about Saul and Jonathan *c*
4: 5 set out and *c* at about the heat
4: 6 And they *c* there, all the way
4: 7 For when they *c* into the house,
5: 1 all the tribes of Israel *c* to
5: 3 all the elders of Israel *c* to
6: 6 And when they *c* to Nachon's
6:16 Now as the ark of the LORD *c*
6:20 Michal the daughter of Saul *c*
7: 1 Now it *c* to pass when the king
7: 4 that the word of the LORD *c*
8: 1 After this it *c* to pass that
8: 5 When the Syrians of Damascus *c*
10: 2 And David's servants *c* into the
10: 8 Then the people of Ammon *c* out
10:16 and they *c* to Helam.
10:17 and *c* to Helam. And the Syrians
11: 4 and she *c* to him, and he lay
11:17 Then the men of the city *c* out
11:22 and *c* and told David all that
11:23 men prevailed against us and *c*
12: 1 And he *c* to him, and said to
12: 4 And a traveler *c* to the rich
12:18 Then on the seventh day it *c* to
13: 6 and when the king *c* to see him,
13:23 And it *c* to pass, after two
13:24 Then Absalom *c* to the king and
13:30 And it *c* to pass, while they
13:30 that news *c* to David, saying,
13:36 that the king's sons indeed *c*,
14:31 Then Joab arose and *c* to
14:33 he *c* to the king and bowed
15: 2 anyone who had a lawsuit *c* to
15: 5 whenever anyone *c* near to bow
15: 6 acted toward all Israel who *c*
15: 7 Now it *c* to pass after forty
15:13 Now a messenger *c* to David,
15:20 you *c* only yesterday. Should I
15:37 And Absalom *c* into Jerusalem.
16: 5 Now when King David *c* to
16: 5 He *c* out, cursing continuously
16: 5 cursing continuously as he *c*.
16:11 See how my son who *c* from my own
16:15 *c* to Jerusalem; and Ahithophel
16:16 *c* to Absalom, that Hushai said
17: 6 And when Hushai *c* to Absalom,
17:18 of them went away quickly and *c*
17:20 And when Absalom's servants *c* to
17:21 Now it *c* to pass, after they had
17:21 that they *c* up out of the well
18:25 And he *c* rapidly and drew
18:31 Just then the Cushite *c*;
19: 5 Then Joab *c* into the house to
19: 8 So all the people *c* before

19:15 Then the king returned and ***c*** to
19:15 And Judah ***c*** to Gilgal, to go to
19:16 hastened and ***c*** down with the
19:24 Mephibosheth the son of Saul ***c***
19:31 And Barzillai the Gileadite ***c***
19:41 then all the men of Israel ***c***
20: 3 Now David ***c*** to his house at
20: 8 Amasa ***c*** before them. Now Joab
20:12 when he saw that everyone who ***c***
20:15 Then they ***c*** and besieged him in
21:17 Abishai the son of Zeruiah ***c***
22:10 and ***c*** down With darkness under
23:13 down at harvest time and ***c*** to
24: 6 Then they ***c*** to Gilead and to the
24: 6 they ***c*** to Dan Jaan and around
24: 7 and they ***c*** to the stronghold of
24: 8 they ***c*** to Jerusalem at the end
24:11 the word of the LORD ***c*** to the
24:13 So Gad ***c*** to David and told him;
24:18 And Gad ***c*** that day to David and
1 Ki 1:22 Nathan the prophet also ***c*** in.
1:23 And when he ***c*** in before the
1:28 So she ***c*** into the king's
1:32 So they ***c*** before the king.
1:42 there ***c*** Jonathan, the son of
1:53 And he ***c*** and fell down before
2: 7 for so they ***c*** to me when I fled
2: 8 But he ***c*** down to meet me at the
2:13 Adonijah the son of Haggith ***c***
2:28 Then news ***c*** to Joab, for Joab
3:15 And he ***c*** to Jerusalem and stood
3:16 two women who were harlots ***c***
4:27 King Solomon and for all who ***c***
4:34 ***c*** to hear the wisdom of
6: 1 And it ***c*** to pass in the four
6:11 Then the word of the LORD ***c*** to
7:14 So he ***c*** to King Solomon and did
8: 3 So all the elders of Israel ***c***,
8: 9 when they ***c*** out of the land of
8:10 And it ***c*** to pass, when the
8:10 when the priests ***c*** out of the
9: 1 And it ***c*** to pass, when Solomon
9:24 But Pharaoh's daughter ***c*** up
10: 1 she ***c*** to test him with hard
10: 2 She ***c*** to Jerusalem with a very
10: 2 and when she ***c*** to Solomon, she
10: 7 not believe the words until I ***c***
10:10 There never again ***c*** such
10:12 There never again ***c*** such almug
10:14 The weight of gold that ***c*** to
10:22 years the merchant ships ***c***
11:18 they arose from Midian and ***c***
11:18 men with them from Paran and ***c***
12: 3 the whole assembly of Israel ***c***
12:12 Jeroboam and all the people ***c***
12:20 Now it ***c*** to pass when all Israel
12:21 And when Rehoboam ***c*** to
12:22 But the word of God ***c*** to
13: 4 So it ***c*** to pass when King
13: 9 return by the same way you ***c***.
13:10 did not return by the way he ***c***
13:11 and his sons ***c*** and told him all
13:12 way the man of God went who ***c***
13:14 Are you the man of God who ***c***
13:17 return by going the way you ***c***.
13:20 that the word of the LORD ***c*** to
13:21 out to the man of God who ***c***
13:22 but you ***c*** back, ate bread, and
13:29 So the old prophet ***c*** to the
14: 4 and ***c*** to the house of Ahijah.
14: 6 sound of her footsteps as she ***c***
14:17 and ***c*** to Tirzah. When she came
14:17 When she ***c*** to the threshold of
14:25 that Shishak king of Egypt ***c***
15:17 And Baasha king of Israel ***c*** up
16: 1 Then the word of the LORD ***c*** to
16: 7 also the word of the LORD ***c***
16:11 Then it ***c*** to pass, when he began
16:31 And it ***c*** to pass, as though it
17: 2 Then the word of the LORD ***c*** upon
17: 8 Then the word of the LORD ***c*** to
17:10 And when he ***c*** to the gate of
17:22 and the soul of the child ***c***
18: 1 And it ***c*** to pass after many
18: 1 that the word of the LORD ***c***
18:21 And Elijah ***c*** to all the people,
18:30 So all the people ***c*** near to
18:36 And it ***c*** to pass, at the time
18:36 that Elijah the prophet ***c*** near
18:44 Then it ***c*** to pass the seventh
18:46 Then the hand of the LORD ***c***
19: 4 and ***c*** and sat down under a
19: 7 And the angel of the LORD ***c***
19: 9 the word of the LORD ***c*** to
19:13 Suddenly a voice ***c*** to him, and
20: 5 Then the messengers ***c*** back and
20:22 And the prophet ***c*** to the king of
20:28 Then a man of God ***c*** and spoke
20:32 and ***c*** to the king of Israel and
20:33 Then Ben-Hadad ***c*** out to him;
20:39 a man ***c*** over and brought a man
20:43 and ***c*** to Samaria.
21: 1 And it ***c*** to pass after these
21: 5 But Jezebel his wife ***c*** to him,
21:13 ***c*** in and sat before him; and
21:15 And it ***c*** to pass, when Jezebel
21:17 Then the word of the LORD ***c*** to
21:28 And the word of the LORD ***c*** to
22: 2 Then it ***c*** to pass, in the third
22:15 Then he ***c*** to the king; and the
22:21 Then a spirit ***c*** forward and
2 Ki 1: 6 A man ***c*** up to meet us, and said
1: 7 kind of man was it who ***c*** up
1:10 And fire ***c*** down from heaven
1:12 And the fire of God ***c*** down
1:13 and ***c*** and fell on his knees
2: 1 And it ***c*** to pass, when the LORD
2: 3 prophets who were at Bethel ***c***
2: 4 not leave you!" So they ***c*** to
2: 5 who were at Jericho ***c*** to
2:15 And they ***c*** to meet him, and
2:18 And when they ***c*** back to him, for
2:23 some youths ***c*** from the city and
2:24 And two female bears ***c*** out of
3:15 that the hand of the LORD ***c***
3:20 that suddenly water ***c*** by way of
3:24 So when they ***c*** to the camp of
4: 6 Now it ***c*** to pass, when the
4: 7 Then she ***c*** and told the man of
4:11 it happened one day that he ***c***
4:27 Now when she ***c*** to the man of God
4:27 but Gehazi ***c*** near to push her
4:32 When Elisha ***c*** into the house,
4:36 And when she ***c*** in to him, he
4:39 and ***c*** and sliced them into the
4:42 Then a man ***c*** from Baal
5:13 And his servants ***c*** near and
5:15 and ***c*** and stood before him;
5:24 When he ***c*** to the citadel, he
6: 4 And when they ***c*** to the Jordan,
6:14 and they ***c*** by night and
6:18 So when the Syrians ***c*** down to
6:23 the bands of Syrian raiders ***c***
6:32 but before the messenger ***c*** to
7: 8 And when these lepers ***c*** to the
7: 8 then they ***c*** back and entered
7:17 who spoke when the king ***c*** down
8: 3 It ***c*** to pass, at the end of
8: 9 and he ***c*** and stood before him,
8:14 and ***c*** to his master, who said
9:11 Then Jehu ***c*** out to the servants
9:17 saw the company of Jehu as he ***c***,
9:19 out a second horseman who ***c*** to
9:24 and the arrow ***c*** out at his
9:36 Therefore they ***c*** back and told
10: 7 when the letter ***c*** to them, that
10: 8 Then a messenger ***c*** and told him,
10:17 And when he ***c*** to Samaria, he
10:21 all the worshipers of Baal ***c***,
10:21 So they ***c*** into the temple of
11: 9 and ***c*** to Jehoiada the priest.
11:13 she ***c*** to the people in the
12:10 scribe and the high priest ***c***
13:14 Then Joash the king of Israel ***c***
15:14 ***c*** to Samaria, and struck
15:19 Pul king of Assyria ***c*** against
15:29 king of Assyria ***c*** and took
16: 5 ***c*** up to Jerusalem to make war;
16:11 made it before King Ahaz ***c***
16:12 And when the king ***c*** back from
17: 3 Shalmaneser king of Assyria ***c*** up
17:28 had carried away from Samaria ***c***
18: 1 Now it ***c*** to pass in the third
18: 9 Now it ***c*** to pass in the fourth
18: 9 Shalmaneser king of Assyria ***c***
18:13 Sennacherib king of Assyria ***c***
18:17 And they went up and ***c*** to
18:18 the recorder, ***c*** out to them.
18:37 ***c*** to Hezekiah with their
19: 5 servants of King Hezekiah ***c*** to
19:28 back By the way which you ***c***.
19:33 By the way that he ***c***,
19:35 And it ***c*** to pass on a certain
19:37 Now it ***c*** to pass, as he was
20: 4 that the word of the LORD ***c*** to
20:14 They ***c*** from a far country, from
21:15 since the day their fathers ***c***
22: 3 Now it ***c*** to pass, in the
23:17 tomb of the man of God who ***c***
23:18 the bones of the prophet who ***c***
24: 1 king of Babylon ***c*** up,
24: 3 of the LORD this ***c*** upon
24:10 king of Babylon ***c*** up against
24:11 king of Babylon ***c*** against the
25: 1 Now it ***c*** to pass in the ninth
25: 1 of Babylon and all his army ***c***
25: 8 ***c*** to Jerusalem.
25:23 they ***c*** to Gedaliah at
25:25 ***c*** with ten men and struck and
25:27 Now it ***c*** to pass in the
1 Chr 1:12 Casluhim (from whom ***c*** the
2:53 From these ***c*** the Zorathites and
2:55 These were the Kenites who ***c***
4:41 These recorded by name ***c*** in the
5: 2 and from him ***c*** a ruler,
6:31 after the ark ***c*** to rest.
7:21 killed them because they ***c***
7:22 and his brethren ***c*** to comfort
10: 7 then the Philistines ***c*** and
10: 8 when the Philistines ***c*** to strip
11: 1 Then all Israel ***c*** together to
11: 3 all the elders of Israel ***c*** to
12: 1 Now these were the men who ***c*** to
12:16 sons of Benjamin and Judah ***c***
12:18 Then the Spirit ***c*** upon Amasai,
12:22 For at that time they ***c*** to
12:23 and ***c*** to David at Hebron to
12:38 ***c*** to Hebron with a loyal heart,
13: 9 And when they ***c*** to Chidon's
15:29 of the covenant of the LORD ***c***
17: 1 Now it ***c*** to pass, when David was
17: 3 night that the word of God ***c***
18: 1 After this it ***c*** to pass that
18: 5 the Syrians of Damascus ***c*** to
19: 2 And David's servants ***c*** to Hanun
19: 7 who ***c*** and encamped before
19: 7 their cities, and ***c*** to battle.
19: 9 Then the people of Ammon ***c*** out
19:17 crossed over the Jordan and ***c***
20: 1 and ***c*** and besieged Rabbah.
21: 4 throughout all Israel and ***c*** to
21:11 So Gad ***c*** to David and said to
21:21 Then David ***c*** to Ornan, and Ornan
22: 8 but the word of the LORD ***c*** to
25: 9 Now the first lot for Asaph ***c***
26:14 and his lot ***c*** out for the North
26:16 Shuppim and Hosah the lot ***c***
27: 1 These divisions ***c*** in and went
27:24 for wrath ***c*** upon Israel because
2 Chr 1:13 So Solomon ***c*** to Jerusalem from
5: 4 So all the elders of Israel ***c***,
5:11 And it ***c*** to pass when the
5:11 to pass when the priests ***c*** out
5:13 indeed it ***c*** to pass, when the
7: 1 fire ***c*** down from heaven and
7: 3 of Israel saw how the fire ***c***
7:11 accomplished all that ***c*** into
8: 1 It ***c*** to pass at the end of
9: 1 she ***c*** to Jerusalem to test
9: 1 and when she ***c*** to Solomon, she
9: 6 believe their words until I ***c***
9:13 The weight of gold that ***c*** to
9:21 years the merchant ships ***c***,
10: 3 And Jeroboam and all Israel ***c***
10:12 Jeroboam and all the people ***c***
11: 1 Now when Rehoboam ***c*** to
11: 2 But the word of the LORD ***c*** to
11:14 and their possessions and ***c*** to
11:16 ***c*** to Jerusalem to sacrifice to
12: 1 Now it ***c*** to pass, when Rehoboam
12: 2 that Shishak king of Egypt ***c***
12: 3 and people without number who ***c***
12: 4 cities of Judah and ***c*** to
12: 5 Then Shemaiah the prophet ***c*** to
12: 7 the word of the LORD ***c*** to
12: 9 So Shishak king of Egypt ***c*** up
14: 9 Then Zerah the Ethiopian ***c*** out
14: 9 and he ***c*** to Mareshah.
14:14 for the fear of the LORD ***c***
15: 1 Now the Spirit of God ***c*** upon
15: 5 nor to the one who ***c*** in, but
15: 9 for they ***c*** over to him in great
16: 1 Baasha king of Israel ***c*** up
16: 7 at that time Hanani the seer ***c***
18:14 Then he ***c*** to the king; and the
18:20 Then a spirit ***c*** forward and
20: 1 ***c*** to battle against
20: 2 Then some ***c*** and told
20: 4 all the cities of Judah they ***c***
20:10 let Israel invade when they ***c***
20:14 the Spirit of the LORD ***c*** upon
20:24 So when Judah ***c*** to a place
20:25 Jehoshaphat and his people ***c***
20:28 So they ***c*** to Jerusalem, with
21:12 And a letter ***c*** to him from
21:17 And they ***c*** up into Judah and
21:19 that his intestines ***c*** out
22: 1 for the raiders who ***c*** with the
23: 2 and they ***c*** to Jerusalem.
23:12 she ***c*** to the people in the
24:11 and the high priest's officer ***c***
24:17 the leaders of Judah ***c*** and
24:18 and wrath ***c*** upon Judah and
24:20 Then the Spirit of God ***c*** upon
24:23 year that the army of Syria ***c***
24:23 and they ***c*** to Judah and
24:24 For the army of the Syrians ***c***
25: 7 But a man of God ***c*** to him,
25:14 after Amaziah ***c*** from the
25:20 for it ***c*** from God, that He
28: 9 out before the army that ***c*** to
28:12 stood up against those who ***c***
28:20 king of Assyria ***c*** to him and
29:17 eighth day of the month they ***c***
30:11 humbled themselves and ***c*** to
30:25 all the assembly that ***c*** from
30:25 the sojourners who ***c*** from the
30:27 and their prayer ***c*** up to His
31: 8 Hezekiah and the leaders ***c*** and
32: 1 Sennacherib king of Assyria ***c***
34: 9 When they ***c*** to Hilkiah the high
35:20 Necho king of Egypt ***c*** up to
35:22 So he ***c*** to fight in the Valley
36: 6 king of Babylon ***c*** up against
Ezra 2: 1 people of the province who ***c***
2: 2 Those who ***c*** with Zerubbabel
2:59 these were the ones who ***c*** up
2:68 when they ***c*** to the house of the
4: 2 they ***c*** to Zerubbabel and the
4:12 to the king that the Jews who ***c***
5: 3 and their companions ***c*** to them
5:16 Then the same Sheshbazzar ***c*** and
7: 6 this Ezra ***c*** up from Babylon; and
7: 7 and the Nethinim ***c*** up to
7: 8 And Ezra ***c*** to Jerusalem in the
7: 9 day of the fifth month he ***c***
8:32 So we ***c*** to Jerusalem, and stayed
9: 1 the leaders ***c*** to me, saying,
10: 6 and when he ***c*** there, he ate no
Neh 1: 1 It ***c*** to pass in the month of
1: 2 Hanani one of my brethren ***c***
2: 1 And it ***c*** to pass in the month of
2:11 So I ***c*** to Jerusalem and was
4:12 the Jews who dwelt near them ***c***,
5:17 besides those who ***c*** to us from
6:10 Afterward I ***c*** to the house of

	6:17	and the letters of Tobiah c
	7: 6	people of the province who c
	7: 7	Those who c with Zerubbabel
	7:61	these were the ones who c up
	7:73	When the seventh month c,
	9:13	You c down also on Mount Sinai,
	12: 1	priests and the Levites who c
	13: 7	and I c to Jerusalem and
	13:21	From that time on they c no
Esth	1: 1	Now it c to pass in the days of
	2:12	Each young woman's turn c to go
	2:15	Now when the turn c for Esther
	4: 4	Esther's maids and eunuchs c
	6: 6	So Haman c in, and the king
	6:14	with him, the king's eunuchs c,
	8: 1	And Mordecai c before the king,
	8:17	the king's command and decree c,
	9: 1	the time c for the king's
	9:25	but when Esther c before the
Job	1: 6	a day when the sons of God c
	1: 6	and Satan also c among them.
	1:14	and a messenger c to Job and
	1:16	another also c and said, "The
	1:17	another also c and said, "The
	1:18	another also c and said, "Your
	1:19	and suddenly a great wind c from
	1:21	Naked I c from my mother's womb,
	2: 1	a day when the sons of God c
	2: 1	and Satan c also among them to
	2:11	each one c from his own
	3:11	did I not perish when I c
	4:14	Fear c upon me, and trembling,
	26: 4	And whose spirit c from you?
	29:13	blessing of a perishing man c
	30:26	evil c to me; And when I
	30:26	then c darkness.
	42:11	c to him and ate food with him
Ps	18: 6	And my cry c before Him,
	18: 9	and c down With darkness under
	27: 2	When the wicked c against me
	78:21	And anger also c up against
	78:31	The wrath of God c against
	88:17	They c around me all day long
	105:19	the time that his word c to
	105:23	Israel also c into Egypt, And
	105:31	and there c swarms of flies,
	105:34	He spoke, and locusts c,
Prov	7:15	So I c out to meet you,
Eccl	5:15	As he c from his mother's womb,
	5:15	shall he return, To go as he c;
	5:16	evil—Just exactly as he c,
	9:14	and a great king c against it,
Isa	7: 1	Now it c to pass in the days of
	11:16	Israel In the day that he c
	14:28	This is the burden which c in
	20: 1	In the year that Tartan c to
	30: 4	And his ambassadors c to
	30: 6	From which c the lioness and
	36: 1	Now it c to pass in the
	36: 1	Sennacherib king of Assyria c
	36: 3	the recorder, c out to him.
	36:22	c to Hezekiah with their
	37: 5	servants of King Hezekiah c to
	37:29	back By the way which you c.
	37:34	By the way that he c,
	37:38	Now it c to pass, as he was
	38: 4	And the word of the LORD c to
	39: 3	They c to me from a far country,
	41: 5	They drew near and c.
	48: 3	and they c to pass.
	48: 5	Before it c to pass I
	50: 2	when I c, was there no man?
	64: 3	You c down, The mountains
	66: 7	gave birth; Before her pain c,
Jer	1: 2	to whom the word of the LORD c
	1: 3	It c also in the days of
	1: 4	Then the word of the LORD c to
	1:11	the word of the LORD c to me,
	1:13	And the word of the LORD c to
	2: 1	the word of the LORD c to me,
	3: 9	So it c to pass, through her
	7: 1	The word that c to Jeremiah from
	7:25	the day that your fathers c
	8:15	for peace, but no good c;
	11: 1	The word that c to Jeremiah from
	13: 3	And the word of the LORD c to
	13: 6	Now it c to pass after many days
	13: 8	Then the word of the LORD c to
	14: 1	The word of the LORD that c to
	16: 1	The word of the LORD also c to
	17:16	You know what c out of my
	18: 1	The word which c to Jeremiah
	18: 5	Then the word of the LORD c to
	19:14	Then Jeremiah c from Tophet,
	21: 1	The word which c to Jeremiah
	24: 4	Again the word of the LORD c
	25: 1	The word that c to Jeremiah
	26: 1	this word c from the LORD,
	26:10	they c up from the king's house
	27: 1	this word c to Jeremiah from
	28:12	Now the word of the LORD c to
	29:30	Then the word of the LORD c to
	30: 1	The word that c to Jeremiah from
	32: 1	The word that c to Jeremiah from
	32: 6	The word of the LORD c to me,
	32: 8	Then Hanamel my uncle's son c to
	32:23	And they c in and took
	32:26	Then the word of the LORD c to
	33: 1	the word of the LORD c to
	33:19	And the word of the LORD c to
	33:23	the word of the LORD c to
	34: 1	The word which c to Jeremiah
	34: 8	This is the word that c to
	34:12	the word of the LORD c to
	35: 1	The word which c to Jeremiah
	35:11	But it c to pass, when
	35:11	king of Babylon c up into the
	35:12	Then c the word of the LORD to
	36: 1	Now it c to pass in the fourth
	36: 1	that this word c to Jeremiah
	36: 9	Now it c to pass in the fifth
	36: 9	and to all the people who c
	36:14	the scroll in his hand and c
	36:27	the word of the LORD c to
	37: 5	Then Pharaoh's army c up from
	37: 6	Then the word of the LORD c to
	38:27	Then all the princes c to
	39: 1	of Babylon and all his army c
	39: 3	of the king of Babylon c in
	40: 1	The word that c to Jeremiah from
	40: 8	then they c to Gedaliah at
	40:12	and c to the land of Judah, to
	40:13	that were in the fields c to
	41: 1	Now it c to pass in the seventh
	41: 1	c with ten men to Gedaliah the
	41: 5	that certain men c from Shechem,
	41: 7	when they c into the midst of
	41:14	from Mizpah turned around and c
	42: 1	least to the greatest, c near
	42: 7	that the word of the LORD c
	43: 8	Then the word of the LORD c to
	44: 1	The word that c to Jeremiah
	46: 1	The word of the LORD which c to
	47: 1	The word of the LORD that c to
	49: 9	If grape-gatherers c to you,
	49:34	The word of the LORD that c to
	52: 4	Now it c to pass in the ninth
	52: 4	of Babylon and all his army c
	52:12	of Babylon, c to Jerusalem.
	52:31	Now it c to pass in the
Ezek	1: 1	Now it c to pass in the
	1: 3	the word of the LORD c
	1: 5	Also from within it c the
	1:25	A voice c from above the
	3:15	Then I c to the captives at Tel
	3:16	Now it c to pass at the end of
	3:16	that the word of the LORD c
	6: 1	Now the word of the LORD c to
	7: 1	the word of the LORD c to me,
	8: 1	And it c to pass in the sixth
	9: 2	And suddenly six men c from the
	11:14	Again the word of the LORD c
	12: 1	Now the word of the LORD c to
	12: 8	the word of the LORD c to me,
	12:17	the word of the LORD c to me,
	12:21	And the word of the LORD c to
	12:26	Again the word of the LORD c
	13: 1	And the word of the LORD c to
	14: 1	some of the elders of Israel c
	14: 2	And the word of the LORD c to
	14:12	The word of the LORD c again
	15: 1	Then the word of the LORD c to
	16: 1	Again the word of the LORD c to
	17: 1	And the word of the LORD c to
	17: 3	C to Lebanon And took from
	17:11	the word of the LORD c to me,
	18: 1	The word of the LORD c to me
	20: 1	It c to pass in the seventh
	20: 1	of the elders of Israel c to
	20: 2	Then the word of the LORD c to
	20:45	the word of the LORD c to me,
	21: 1	And the word of the LORD c to
	21: 8	Again the word of the LORD c
	21:18	The word of the LORD c to me
	22: 1	the word of the LORD c to me,
	22:17	The word of the LORD c to me,
	22:23	And the word of the LORD c to
	23: 1	The word of the LORD c again to
	23:17	Then the Babylonians c to her,
	23:39	on the same day they c into My
	23:40	was sent; and there they c.
	24: 1	the word of the LORD c to me,
	24:15	Also the word of the LORD c to
	24:20	The word of the LORD c to me,
	25: 1	The word of the LORD c to me,
	26: 1	And it c to pass in the eleventh
	26: 1	that the word of the LORD c
	27: 1	The word of the LORD c again to
	28: 1	The word of the LORD c to me
	28:11	the word of the LORD c to me,
	28:20	Then the word of the LORD c to
	29: 1	the word of the LORD c to me,
	29:17	And it c to pass in the
	29:17	that the word of the LORD c to
	30: 1	The word of the LORD c to me
	30:20	And it c to pass in the
	30:20	that the word of the LORD c
	31: 1	Now it c to pass in the eleventh
	31: 1	that the word of the LORD c
	32: 1	And it c to pass in the twelfth
	32: 1	that the word of the LORD c
	32:17	It c to pass also in the
	32:17	that the word of the LORD c to
	33: 1	Again the word of the LORD c to
	33:21	And it c to pass in the twelfth
	33:21	had escaped from Jerusalem c
	33:22	me the evening before the man c
	33:22	so when he c to me in the
	33:23	Then the word of the LORD c to
	34: 1	And the word of the LORD c to
	35: 1	the word of the LORD c to me,
	35: 5	when their iniquity c to an
	36:16	the word of the LORD c to me,
	36:20	When they c to the nations,
	37: 1	The hand of the LORD c upon me
	37: 7	and the bones c together, bone
	37: 8	the sinews and the flesh c upon
	37:10	and breath c into them, and
	37:15	Again the word of the LORD c
	38: 1	Now the word of the LORD c to
	42:19	He c around to the west side
	43: 2	glory of the God of Israel c
	43: 3	vision which I saw when I c to
	43: 4	And the glory of the LORD c
	46: 9	of the gate through which he c,
	47: 3	the water c up to my
	47: 4	the water c up to my knees.
	47: 4	the water c up to my waist.
Dan	1: 1	king of Babylon c to Jerusalem
	2: 2	So they c and stood before the
	2:29	thoughts c to your mind
	3: 8	that time certain Chaldeans c
	3:26	and Abed-Nego c from the midst
	4: 7	and the soothsayers c in, and I
	4: 8	But at last Daniel c before me
	4:28	All this c upon King
	5: 8	Now all the king's wise men c,
	5:10	c to the banquet hall.
	6:20	And when he c to the den, he
	6:24	in pieces before they ever c
	7: 3	And four great beasts c up from
	7:10	A fiery stream issued And c
	7:13	the clouds of heaven! He c to
	7:16	I c near to one of those who
	7:20	and the other horn which c up,
	7:22	"until the Ancient of Days c,
	7:22	and the time c for the saints
	8: 3	and the higher one c up last.
	8: 5	suddenly a male goat c from the
	8: 6	Then he c to the ram that had
	8: 8	of it four notable ones c up
	8: 9	And out of one of them c a
	8:17	So he c near where I stood, and
	8:17	and when he c I was afraid and
	10: 3	no meat or wine c into my
	10:13	c to help me, for I had been
Hos	1: 1	The word of the LORD that c to
	2:15	As in the day when she c up
Joel	1: 1	The word of the LORD that c to
Jon	1: 1	Now the word of the LORD c to
	1: 6	So the captain c to him, and
	3: 1	Now the word of the LORD c to
	3: 6	Then word c to the king of
	4:10	which c up in a night and
Mic	1: 1	The word of the LORD that c to
	1:12	But disaster c down from the
	7:15	As in the days when you c out of
Hab	3: 3	God c from Teman, The Holy
	3:14	They c out like a whirlwind to
Zeph	1: 1	The word of the LORD which c
Hag	1: 1	the word of the LORD c by
	1: 3	Then the word of the LORD c by
	1: 9	but indeed it c to little;
	1:14	and they c and worked on the
	2: 1	the word of the LORD c by
	2: 5	covenanted with you when you c
	2:10	the word of the LORD c by
	2:16	when one c to a heap of twenty
	2:16	when one c to the wine vat to
	2:20	again the word of the LORD c
Zech	1: 1	the word of the LORD c to
	1: 7	the word of the LORD c to
	4: 1	the angel who talked with me c
	4: 8	the word of the LORD c to me,
	5: 5	the angel who talked with me c
	6: 9	Then the word of the LORD c to
	7: 1	year of King Darius it c to
	7: 1	that the word of the LORD c
	7: 4	word of the LORD of hosts c
	7: 8	Then the word of the LORD c to
	7:12	Thus great wrath c from the
	8: 1	word of the LORD of hosts c,
	8:10	for whoever went out or c in;
	8:18	word of the LORD of hosts c
	14:16	left of all the nations which c
Mt	1:18	before they c together, she was
	2: 1	wise men from the East c to
	2: 9	till it c and stood over where
	2:21	and c into the land of Israel.
	2:23	And he c and dwelt in a city
	3: 1	those days John the Baptist c
	3:13	Then Jesus c from Galilee to
	3:16	Jesus c up immediately from the
	3:17	And suddenly a voice c from
	4: 3	Now when the tempter c to Him,
	4:11	angels c and ministered to Him.
	4:13	He c and dwelt in Capernaum,
	5: 1	He was seated His disciples c
	5:17	Do not think that I c to
	7:25	rain descended, the floods c,
	7:27	rain descended, the floods c,
	8: 2	a leper c and worshiped Him,
	8: 5	a centurion c to Him, pleading
	8:19	Then a certain scribe c and said
	8:25	Then His disciples c to Him and
	8:34	the whole city c out to meet
	9: 1	and c to His own city.
	9:10	tax collectors and sinners c
	9:14	Then the disciples of John c to
	9:18	a ruler c and worshiped Him,
	9:20	of blood for twelve years c
	9:23	When Jesus c into the ruler's
	9:28	the blind men c to Him.
	10:34	Do not think that I c to bring
	11: 1	Now it c to pass, when Jesus
	11:18	For John c neither eating nor

11:19 The Son of Man ***c*** eating and
12:42 for she ***c*** from the ends of the
12:44 to my house from which I ***c***.
13: 4 and the birds ***c*** and devoured
13:10 And the disciples ***c*** and said to
13:25 his enemy ***c*** and sowed tares
13:27 the servants of the owner ***c***
13:36 And His disciples ***c*** to Him,
13:53 Now it ***c*** to pass, when Jesus
14:12 Then his disciples ***c*** and took
14:15 His disciples ***c*** to Him, saying,
14:23 to pray. Now when evening ***c***,
14:33 those who were in the boat ***c***
14:34 they ***c*** to the land of
15: 1 who were from Jerusalem ***c*** to
15:12 Then His disciples ***c*** and said to
15:22 a woman of Canaan ***c*** from that
15:23 And His disciples ***c*** and urged
15:25 Then she ***c*** and worshiped Him,
15:30 Then great multitudes ***c*** to Him,
15:39 and ***c*** to the region of Magdala.
16: 1 the Pharisees and Sadducees ***c***,
16:13 When Jesus ***c*** into the region of
17: 5 and suddenly a voice ***c*** out of
17: 7 But Jesus ***c*** and touched them and
17: 9 Now as they ***c*** down from the
17:14 a man ***c*** to Him, kneeling down
17:18 and it ***c*** out of him; and the
17:19 Then the disciples ***c*** to Jesus
17:24 who received the temple tax ***c***
18: 1 At that time the disciples ***c*** to
18:21 Then Peter ***c*** to Him and said,
18:31 and ***c*** and told their master all
19: 1 Now it ***c*** to pass, when Jesus had
19: 1 He departed from Galilee and ***c***
19: 3 The Pharisees also ***c*** to Him,
19:16 one ***c*** and said to Him, "Good
20: 9 And when those ***c*** who were
20:10 "But when the first ***c***,
20:20 the mother of Zebedee's sons ***c***
21: 1 and ***c*** to Bethphage, at the
21:14 the blind and the lame ***c*** to
21:19 He ***c*** to it and found nothing on
21:23 Now when He ***c*** into the temple,
21:28 and he ***c*** to the first and said,
21:30 Then he ***c*** to the second and said
21:32 For John ***c*** to you in the way of
22:11 But when the king ***c*** in to see
22:23 ***c*** to Him and asked Him,
24: 1 and His disciples ***c*** up to show
24: 3 the disciples ***c*** to Him
24:39 did not know until the flood ***c***
25:10 went to buy, the bridegroom ***c***,
25:11 Afterward the other virgins ***c***
25:19 the lord of those servants ***c***
25:20 who had received five talents ***c***
25:22 who had received two talents ***c***
25:24 had received the one talent ***c***
25:36 I was in prison and you ***c*** to
26: 1 Now it ***c*** to pass, when Jesus had
26: 7 a woman ***c*** to Him having an
26:17 Bread the disciples ***c*** to Jesus,
26:36 Then Jesus ***c*** with them to a
26:40 Then He ***c*** to the disciples and
26:43 And He ***c*** and found them asleep
26:45 Then He ***c*** to His disciples and
26:47 ***c*** from the chief priests and
26:50 Then they ***c*** and laid hands on
26:60 though many false witnesses ***c***
26:60 at last two false witnesses ***c***
26:69 And a servant girl ***c*** to him,
26:73 later those who stood by ***c*** up
27: 1 When morning ***c***,
27:32 Now as they ***c*** out, they found a
27:57 there ***c*** a rich man from
28: 1 Magdalene and the other Mary ***c***
28: 2 and ***c*** and rolled back the stone
28: 9 Rejoice!" So they ***c*** and held
28:11 some of the guard ***c*** into the
28:13 His disciples ***c*** at night and
28:18 And Jesus ***c*** and spoke to them,
Mk 1: 4 John ***c*** baptizing in the
1: 9 It ***c*** to pass in those days
1: 9 in those days that Jesus ***c***
1:11 Then a voice ***c*** from heaven,
1:14 Jesus ***c*** to Galilee, preaching
1:26 he ***c*** out of him.
1:31 So He ***c*** and took her by the hand
1:40 Now a leper ***c*** to Him, imploring
1:45 and they ***c*** to Him from every
2: 3 Then they ***c*** to Him, bringing a
2:13 and all the multitude ***c*** to Him,
2:18 Then they ***c*** and said to Him,
3: 8 things He was doing, ***c*** to Him.
3:13 And they ***c*** to Him.
3:20 Then the multitude ***c*** together
3:22 And the scribes who ***c*** down from
3:31 His brothers and His mother ***c***,
4: 4 and the birds of the air ***c*** and
5: 1 Then they ***c*** to the other side of
5:15 Then they ***c*** to Jesus, and saw
5:22 the rulers of the synagogue ***c***,
5:27 she ***c*** behind Him in the crowd
5:33 ***c*** and fell down before Him and
5:35 some ***c*** from the ruler of the
5:38 Then He ***c*** to the house of the
5:39 When He ***c*** in, He said to them,
6: 1 He went out from there and ***c***
6:21 Then an opportune day ***c*** when
6:22 Herodias' daughter herself ***c***
6:25 Immediately she ***c*** in with haste
6:29 they ***c*** and took away his corpse
6:33 They arrived before them and ***c***
6:34 when He ***c*** out, saw a great
6:35 His disciples ***c*** to Him and
6:47 Now when evening ***c***,
6:48 fourth watch of the night He ***c***
6:53 they ***c*** to the land of
6:54 And when they ***c*** out of the boat,
7: 1 and some of the scribes ***c***
7:25 and she ***c*** and fell at His feet.
7:31 He ***c*** through the midst of the
8:10 and ***c*** to the region of
8:11 Then the Pharisees ***c*** out and
8:22 Then He ***c*** to Bethsaida; and
9: 7 And a cloud ***c*** and overshadowed
9: 7 and a voice ***c*** out of the cloud,
9: 9 Now as they ***c*** down from the
9:14 And when He ***c*** to the disciples,
9:25 Jesus saw that the people ***c***
9:26 and ***c*** out of him. And he became
9:33 Then He ***c*** to Capernaum.
10: 1 Then He arose from there and ***c***
10: 2 The Pharisees ***c*** and asked Him,
10:17 one ***c*** running, knelt before
10:35 ***c*** to Him, saying, "Teacher, we
10:46 Now they ***c*** to Jericho. As He
10:50 he rose and ***c*** to Jesus.
11:13 When He ***c*** to it, He found
11:15 So they ***c*** to Jerusalem.
11:27 Then they ***c*** again to Jerusalem.
11:27 and the elders ***c*** to Him.
12:18 ***c*** to Him; and they asked Him,
12:28 Then one of the scribes ***c***,
12:42 Then one poor widow ***c*** and threw
14: 3 a woman ***c*** having an alabaster
14:16 and ***c*** into the city, and found
14:17 In the evening He ***c*** with the
14:32 Then they ***c*** to a place which
14:37 Then He ***c*** and found them
14:41 Then He ***c*** the third time and
14:43 ***c*** from the chief priests and
14:66 girls of the high priest ***c***.
15:41 and many other women who ***c*** up
16: 2 they ***c*** to the tomb when the sun
Lk 1:22 But when he ***c*** out, he could not
1:57 Now Elizabeth's full time ***c*** for
1:59 that they ***c*** to circumcise the
1:65 Then fear ***c*** on all who dwelt
2: 1 And it ***c*** to pass in those days
2:16 And they ***c*** with haste and found
2:27 So he ***c*** by the Spirit into the
2:51 He went down with them and ***c***
3: 2 the word of God ***c*** to John the
3: 7 said to the multitudes that ***c***
3:12 Then tax collectors also ***c*** to be
3:21 it ***c*** to pass that Jesus also
3:22 and a voice ***c*** from heaven which
4:16 So He ***c*** to Nazareth, where He
4:35 it ***c*** out of him and did not
4:41 And demons also ***c*** out of many,
4:42 And the crowd sought Him and ***c***
5: 7 And they ***c*** and filled both the
5:15 and great multitudes ***c*** together
6:12 Now it ***c*** to pass in those days
6:17 And He ***c*** down with them and
6:17 who ***c*** to hear Him and be healed
7: 4 And when they ***c*** to Jesus, they
7:12 And when He ***c*** near the gate of
7:14 Then He ***c*** and touched the open
7:16 Then fear ***c*** upon all, and they
7:33 For John the Baptist ***c*** neither
7:45 My feet since the time I ***c*** in.
8: 1 Now it ***c*** to pass, afterward,
8:19 His mother and brothers ***c*** to
8:23 And a windstorm ***c*** down on the
8:24 And they ***c*** to Him and awoke Him,
8:35 and ***c*** to Jesus, and found the
8:41 there ***c*** a man named Jairus, and
8:44 ***c*** from behind and touched the
8:47 she ***c*** trembling; and falling
8:49 someone ***c*** from the ruler of the
8:51 When He ***c*** into the house, He
9:12 the twelve ***c*** and said to Him,
9:28 Now it ***c*** to pass, about eight
9:34 a cloud ***c*** and overshadowed
9:35 And a voice ***c*** out of the cloud,
9:51 Now it ***c*** to pass, when the time
10:31 by chance a certain priest ***c***
10:32 ***c*** and looked, and passed by on
10:33 ***c*** where he was. And when he saw
11: 1 Now it ***c*** to pass, as He was
11:24 to my house from which I ***c***.
11:31 for she ***c*** from the ends of the
12:49 I ***c*** to send fire on the earth,
12:51 Do you suppose that I ***c*** to give
13: 6 and he ***c*** seeking fruit on it
13:31 that very day some Pharisees ***c***,
14:21 So that servant ***c*** and reported
15:17 But when he ***c*** to himself, he
15:20 And he arose and ***c*** to his
15:25 And as he ***c*** and drew near to
15:28 Therefore his father ***c*** out and
15:30 as soon as this son of yours ***c***,
16:21 Moreover the dogs ***c*** and licked
17:27 and the flood ***c*** and destroyed
18: 3 and she ***c*** to him, saying, 'Get
19: 5 And when Jesus ***c*** to the place,
19: 6 So he made haste and ***c*** down,
19:16 Then ***c*** the first, saying,
19:18 'And the second ***c***, saying,
19:20 'Then another ***c***, saying,
19:29 And it ***c*** to pass, when He came
19:29 when He ***c*** near to Bethphage and
20:27 ***c*** to Him and asked Him,
21:38 in the morning all the people ***c***
22: 7 Then ***c*** the Day of Unleavened
22:40 When He ***c*** to the place, He said
22:66 ***c*** together and led Him into
23:48 And the whole crowd who ***c***
24: 1 ***c*** to the tomb bringing the
24:23 they ***c*** saying that they had
24:30 Now it ***c*** to pass, as He sat at
24:51 Now it ***c*** to pass, while He
Jn 1: 7 This man ***c*** for a witness, to
1:11 He ***c*** to His own, and His own did
1:17 but grace and truth ***c*** through
1:31 therefore I ***c*** baptizing with
1:39 They ***c*** and saw where He was
2: 9 and did not know where it ***c***
3: 2 This man ***c*** to Jesus by night and
3:13 to heaven but He who ***c*** down
3:22 Jesus and His disciples ***c*** into
3:23 And they ***c*** and were baptized.
3:26 And they ***c*** to John and said to
4: 5 So He ***c*** to a city of Samaria
4: 7 A woman of Samaria ***c*** to draw
4:27 at this point His disciples ***c***,
4:30 went out of the city and ***c*** to
4:45 So when He ***c*** to Galilee, the
4:46 So Jesus ***c*** again to Cana of
6:16 Now when evening ***c***,
6:23 other boats ***c*** from Tiberias,
6:24 they also got into boats and ***c***
6:41 I am the bread which ***c*** down from
6:51 I am the living bread which ***c***
6:58 This is the bread which ***c*** down
7:45 Then the officers ***c*** to the
7:50 Nicodemus (he who ***c*** to Jesus by
8: 2 Now early in the morning He ***c***
8: 2 and all the people ***c*** to Him;
8:14 for I know where I ***c*** from and
8:42 for I proceeded forth and ***c***
9: 7 and washed, and ***c*** back seeing.
10: 8 All who ever ***c*** before Me are
10:35 to whom the word of God ***c*** (and
10:41 Then many ***c*** to Him and said,
11:17 So when Jesus ***c***,
11:29 she arose quickly and ***c*** to Him.
11:32 when Mary ***c*** where Jesus was,
11:33 and the Jews who ***c*** with her
11:38 ***c*** to the tomb. It was a cave,
11:44 And he who had died ***c*** out bound
12: 1 Jesus ***c*** to Bethany, where
12: 9 that He was there; and they ***c***,
12:20 Greeks among those who ***c*** up to
12:21 Then they ***c*** to Philip, who was
12:22 Philip ***c*** and told Andrew, and in
12:27 But for this purpose I ***c*** to
12:28 Then a voice ***c*** from heaven,
13: 6 Then He ***c*** to Simon Peter.
16:27 and have believed that I ***c***
16:28 I ***c*** forth from the Father and
16:30 By this we believe that You ***c***
17: 8 and have known surely that I ***c***
18: 3 ***c*** there with lanterns, torches,
19: 5 Then Jesus ***c*** out, wearing the
19:32 Then the soldiers ***c*** and broke
19:33 But when they ***c*** to Jesus and saw
19:34 immediately blood and water ***c***
19:38 So he ***c*** and took the body of
19:39 who at first ***c*** to Jesus by
19:39 came to Jesus by night, also ***c***,
20: 2 Then she ran and ***c*** to Simon
20: 4 disciple outran Peter and ***c*** to
20: 6 Then Simon Peter ***c***,
20: 8 who ***c*** to the tomb first, went
20:18 Mary Magdalene ***c*** and told the
20:19 Jesus ***c*** and stood in the midst,
20:24 was not with them when Jesus ***c***.
20:26 and Thomas with them. Jesus ***c***,
21: 8 But the other disciples ***c*** in the
21:13 Jesus then ***c*** and took the bread
Acts 2: 2 And suddenly there ***c*** a sound
2: 6 the multitude ***c*** together,
2:43 Then fear ***c*** upon every soul,
4: 1 and the Sadducees ***c*** upon them,
4: 4 and the number of the men ***c*** to
4: 5 And it ***c*** to pass, on the next
5: 5 So great fear ***c*** upon all those
5: 7 hours later when his wife ***c*** in,
5:10 And the young men ***c*** in and
5:11 So great fear ***c*** upon all the
5:21 priest and those with him ***c***
5:22 But when the officers ***c*** and did
5:25 So one ***c*** and told them, saying,
5:36 him were scattered and ***c*** to
6:12 and they ***c*** upon him, seized
7: 4 Then he ***c*** out of the land of the
7:11 a famine and great trouble ***c***
7:23 it ***c*** into his heart to visit
7:31 the voice of the Lord ***c*** to him,
8: 7 ***c*** out of many who were
8:36 they ***c*** to some water. And the
8:39 Now when they ***c*** up out of the
8:40 in all the cities till he ***c*** to
9: 3 As he journeyed he ***c*** near
9:17 to you on the road as you ***c***,
9:32 Now it ***c*** to pass, as Peter went
9:32 that he also ***c*** down to the
10:13 And a voice ***c*** to him, "Rise,
10:29 Therefore I ***c*** without objection
10:45 as many as ***c*** with Peter,
11: 2 And when Peter ***c*** up to
11: 5 and it ***c*** to me.
11:22 Then news of these things ***c*** to

11:23 When he **c** and had seen the grace
11:27 And in these days prophets **c**
12:10 they **c** to the iron gate that
12:12 he **c** to the house of Mary, the
12:13 a girl named Rhoda **c** to answer.
12:20 but they **c** to him with one
13:13 they **c** to Perga in Pamphylia;
13:14 they **c** to Antioch in Pisidia,
13:31 for many days by those who **c**
13:44 Sabbath almost the whole city **c**
13:51 and **c** to Iconium.
14:19 Jews from Antioch and Iconium **c**
14:24 they **c** to Pamphylia.
15: 1 And certain men **c** down from
15: 6 Now the apostles and elders **c**
15:30 they **c** to Antioch; and when
16: 1 Then he **c** to Derbe and Lystra.
16: 8 they **c** down to Troas.
16:11 and the next day **c** to
16:18 And he **c** out that very hour.
16:39 Then they **c** and pleaded with
17: 1 they **c** to Thessalonica, where
17:13 they **c** there also and stirred
18: 2 and he **c** to them.
18:19 And he **c** to Ephesus, and left
18:24 the Scriptures, **c** to Ephesus.
19: 1 **c** to Ephesus. And finding some
19: 6 the Holy Spirit **c** upon them,
19:18 And many who had believed **c**
20: 2 with many words, he **c** to Greece
20: 7 when the disciples **c** together
20:14 we took him on board and **c** to
20:15 and the next day **c** opposite
20:15 The next day we **c** to Miletus.
20:18 from the first day that I **c** to
21: 1 Now it **c** to pass, that when we
21: 1 running a straight course we **c**
21: 7 we **c** to Ptolemais, greeted the
21: 8 companions departed and **c** to
21:10 certain prophet named Agabus **c**
21:31 news **c** to the commander of the
21:33 Then the commander **c** near and
22: 6 as I journeyed and **c** near
22:11 I **c** into Damascus.
22:13 **c** to me; and he stood and said
22:27 Then the commander **c** and said to
23:14 They **c** to the chief priests and
23:33 When they **c** to Caesarea and had
24: 1 days Ananias the high priest **c**
24: 7 But the commander Lysias **c** by
24:17 Now after many years I **c** to
24:24 when Felix **c** with his wife
25:13 King Agrippa and Bernice **c** to
27: 5 we **c** to Myra, a city of
27: 8 we **c** to a place called Fair
28: 3 a viper **c** out because of the
28: 9 island who had diseases also **c**
28:13 and the next day we **c** to
28:15 they **c** to meet us as far as
28:16 Now when we **c** to Rome, the
28:17 And it **c** to pass after three
28:21 have any of the brethren who **c**
28:23 many **c** to him at his lodging,
28:30 and received all who **c** to him,
Rom 5:16 is not like that which **c**
5:16 For the judgment which **c** from
5:16 but the free gift which **c**
5:18 one man's offense judgment **c**
5:18 act the free gift **c** to all
7: 9 law, but when the commandment **c**,
9: 5 to the flesh, Christ **c**,
1 Cor 2: 1 when I **c** to you, did not come
11:12 For as woman **c** from man, even
15:21 For since by man **c** death, by
15:21 by Man also **c** the resurrection
2 Cor 1: 8 of our trouble which **c** to us in
1:23 that to spare you I **c** no more
2: 3 thing to you, lest, when I **c**,
2:12 when I **c** to Troas to preach
7: 5 when we **c** to Macedonia, our
10:14 for it was to you that we **c**
11: 9 I lacked the brethren who **c**
Gal 1:12 but it **c** through the
2: 4 secretly brought in (who **c** in
2:12 for before certain men **c** from
2:12 the Gentiles; but when they **c**,
3:23 But before faith **c**,
Eph 2:17 And He **c** and preached peace to
Phil 2:30 for the work of Christ he **c**
1 Tim 1:15 that Christ Jesus **c** into the
Heb 3:16 was it not all who **c** out of
7:28 which **c** after the law,
9:11 But Christ **c** as High Priest of
10: 5 when He **c** into the world, He
2 Pe 1:17 and glory when such a voice **c**
1:18 And we heard this voice which **c**
1:21 for prophecy never **c** by the will
1 Jn 5: 6 This is He who **c** by water and
3 Jn 3 greatly when brethren **c** and
Rev 2: 8 who was dead, and **c** to life:
5: 7 Then He **c** and took the scroll
8: 3 **c** and stood at the altar.
9: 3 Then out of the smoke locusts **c**
9:17 and out of their mouths **c** fire,
9:18 and the brimstone which **c** out
14:15 And another angel **c** out of the
14:17 Then another angel **c** out of the
14:18 And another angel **c** out from the
14:20 and blood **c** out of the
15: 6 And out of the temple **c** the
16: 2 and a foul and loathsome sore **c**
16:17 and a loud voice **c** out of the
17: 1 who had the seven bowls **c** and
18:17 in one hour such great riches **c**
19: 5 Then a voice **c** from the throne,
20: 9 And fire **c** down from God out of
21: 9 with the seven last plagues **c**

CAMEL (9/9) CAMEL-LOADS, CAMEL'S, CAMELS, CAMELS'

Gen 24:64 Isaac she dismounted from her **c**;
Lev 11: 4 that have cloven hooves: the **c**,
Deut 14: 7 not eat, such as these: the **c**,
1 Sam 15: 3 ox and sheep, **c** and donkey.'
Zech 14:15 On the **c** and the donkey, And
Mt 19:24 it is easier for a **c** to go
23:24 out a gnat and swallow a **c**!
Mk 10:25 It is easier for a **c** to go
Lk 18:25 For it is easier for a **c** to go

CAMEL-LOADS (1/1) CAMEL

2 Ki 8: 9 good thing of Damascus, forty **c**;

CAMEL'S (3/3) CAMEL

Gen 31:34 put them in the **c** saddle, and
Mt 3: 4 John himself was clothed in **c**
Mk 1: 6 Now John was clothed with **c** hair

CAMELS (45/43) CAMEL, CAMELS'

Gen 12:16 servants, female donkeys, and **c**.
24:10 took ten of his master's **c** and
24:11 And he made his **c** kneel down
24:14 and I will also give your **c** a
24:19 I will draw water for your **c**
24:20 water, and drew for all his **c**.
24:22 when the **c** had finished
24:30 And there he stood by the **c** at
24:31 house, and a place for the **c**.
24:32 And he unloaded the **c**,
24:32 straw and feed for the **c**,
24:35 and **c** and donkeys.
24:44 and I will draw for your **c**
24:46 and I will give your **c** a drink
24:46 and she gave the **c** a drink
24:61 and they rode on the **c** and
24:63 the **c** were coming.
30:43 and **c** and donkeys.
31:17 set his sons and his wives on **c**.
32: 7 and the flocks and herds and **c**,
32:15 thirty milk **c** with their colts,
37:25 coming from Gilead with their **c**,
Ex 9: 3 on the donkeys, on the **c**,
Judg 6: 5 both they and their **c** were
7:12 and their **c** were without
1 Sam 27: 9 the oxen, the donkeys, the **c**,
30:17 young men who rode on **c** and
1 Ki 10: 2 with **c** that bore spices, very
1 Chr 5:21 thousand of their **c**,
12:40 bringing food on donkeys and **c**,
27:30 the Ishmaelite was over the **c**,
2 Chr 9: 1 **c** that bore spices, gold in
14:15 and carried off sheep and **c** in
Ezra 2:67 their **c** four hundred and
Neh 7:69 their **c** four hundred and
Job 1: 3 sheep, three thousand **c**,
1:17 raided the **c** and took them
42:12 thousand sheep, six thousand **c**,
Isa 21: 7 of donkeys, and a chariot of **c**,
30: 6 treasures on the humps of **c**,
60: 6 The multitude of **c** shall cover
66:20 in litters, on mules and on **c**,
Jer 49:29 All their vessels and their **c**;
49:32 Their **c** shall be for booty,
Ezek 25: 5 make Rabbah a stable for **c** and

CAMELS' (2/2) CAMELS

Judg 8:21 that were on their **c** necks.
8:26 that were around their **c**

CAMPHIRE (KJV) See HENNA

CAMON (1/1)

Judg 10: 5 Jair died and was buried in **C**.

CAMP (181/164) CAMPED, CAMPING, CAMPS, ENCAMP

Gen 32: 2 he said, "This is God's **c**.
32:21 lodged that night in the **c**.
Ex 14: 2 that they turn and **c** before Pi
14: 2 you shall **c** before it by the
14:19 who went before the **c** of
14:20 So it came between the **c** of the
14:20 of the Egyptians and the **c** of
16:13 up at evening and covered the **c**,
16:13 the dew lay all around the **c**.
19:16 the people who were in the **c**
19:17 the people out of the **c** to
29:14 burn with fire outside the **c**.
32:17 is a noise of war in the **c**.
32:19 as soon as he came near the **c**,
32:26 stood in the entrance of the **c**,
32:27 to entrance throughout the **c**,
33: 7 and pitched it outside the **c**,
33: 7 the camp, far from the **c**,
33: 7 which was outside the **c**.
33:11 And he would return to the **c**,
36: 6 be proclaimed throughout the **c**,
Lev 4:12 he shall carry outside the **c**
4:21 carry the bull outside the **c**,
6:11 carry the ashes outside the **c**
8:17 burned with fire outside the **c**,
9:11 burned with fire outside the **c**.
10: 4 the sanctuary out of the **c**.
10: 5 by their tunics out of the **c**,
13:46 shall be outside the **c**.
14: 3 priest shall go out of the **c**,
14: 8 that he shall come into the **c**,
16:26 he may come into the **c**.
16:27 shall be carried outside the **c**.
16:28 he may come into the **c**.
17: 3 an ox or lamb or goat in the **c**,
17: 3 or who kills it outside the **c**,
24:10 fought each other in the **c**.
24:14 Take outside the **c** him who has
24:23 and they took outside the **c** him
Num 1:50 they shall attend to it and **c**
1:52 tents, everyone by his own **c**,
1:53 but the Levites shall **c** around
2: 2 the children of Israel shall **c**
2: 2 they shall **c** some distance from
2: 3 the forces with Judah shall **c**
2: 5 Those who **c** next to him shall
2: 9 these shall break **c** first.
2:12 Those who **c** next to him shall
2:16 shall be the second to break **c**.
2:17 shall move out with the **c** of
2:17 middle of the camps; as they **c**,
2:24 shall be the third to break **c**.
2:27 Those who **c** next to him shall
2:31 they shall break **c** last, with
2:34 standards and so they broke **c**,
3:23 of the Gershonites were to **c**
3:29 children of Kohath were to **c**
3:35 These were to **c** on the north
3:38 Moreover those who were to **c**
4: 5 When the **c** prepares to journey,
4:15 when the **c** is set to go, then
5: 2 that they put out of the **c**
5: 3 shall put them outside the **c**,
5: 4 so, and put them outside the **c**;
9:18 of the LORD they would **c**;
10:14 The standard of the **c** of the
10:18 And the standard of the **c** of
10:22 And the standard of the **c** of
10:25 Then the standard of the **c** of
10:31 as you know how we are to **c** in
10:34 when they went out from the **c**.
11: 1 some in the outskirts of the **c**.
11: 9 And when the dew fell on the **c**
11:26 two men had remained in the **c**:
11:26 yet they prophesied in the **c**.
11:27 Medad are prophesying in the **c**.
11:30 And Moses returned to the **c**,
11:31 them fluttering near the **c**,
11:31 other side, all around the **c**,
11:32 for themselves all around the **c**.
12:14 Let her be shut out of the **c**
12:15 So Miriam was shut out of the **c**
14:44 nor Moses departed from the **c**.
15:35 him with stones outside the **c**.
15:36 brought him outside the **c** and
19: 3 he may take it outside the **c**,
19: 7 he shall come into the **c**;
19: 9 and store them outside the **c**
31:12 to the **c** in the plains of Moab
31:13 went to meet them outside the **c**.
31:19 remain outside the **c** seven
31:24 you may come into the **c**.
Deut 2:14 from the midst of the **c**,
2:15 them from the midst of the **c**
23:10 then he shall go outside the **c**;
23:10 he shall not come inside the **c**.
23:11 sets, he may come into the **c**.
23:12 have a place outside the **c**,
23:14 walks in the midst of your **c**,
23:14 therefore your **c** shall be holy,
29:11 the stranger who is in your **c**,
Josh 1:11 Pass through the **c** and command
3: 2 the officers went through the **c**;
3:14 people set out from their **c** to
5: 8 in their places in the **c** till
6:11 Then they came into the **c** and
6:11 the camp and lodged in the **c**.
6:14 city once and returned to the **c**.
6:18 and make the **c** of Israel a
6:23 and left them outside the **c** of
9: 6 to the **c** at Gilgal, and said to
10: 6 Gibeon sent to Joshua at the **c**
10:15 to the **c** at Gilgal.
10:21 the people returned to the **c**,
10:43 to the **c** at Gilgal.
18: 9 they came to Joshua at the **c**
Judg 7: 1 so that the **c** of the Midianites
7: 8 Now the **c** of Midian was below
7: 9 "Arise, go down against the **c**,
7:10 go down to the **c** with Purah
7:11 to go down against the **c**.
7:11 armed men who were in the **c**.
7:13 bread tumbled into the **c** of
7:14 Midian and the whole **c**.
7:15 He returned to the **c** of Israel,
7:15 the LORD has delivered the **c**
7:17 I come to the edge of the **c**
7:18 on every side of the whole **c**,
7:19 came to the outpost of the **c**
7:21 in his place all around the **c**;
7:22 throughout the whole **c**;
8:11 attacked the army while the **c**
21: 8 no one had come to the **c** from

21:12 and they brought them to the *c*
1 Sam 4: 3 the people had come into the *c*,
4: 5 of the LORD came into the *c*,
4: 6 of this great shout in the *c*
4: 6 the LORD had come into the *c*.
4: 7 'God has come into the *c*!"
11:11 came into the midst of the *c*
13:17 Then raiders came out of the *c*
14:15 there was trembling in the *c*,
14:19 the noise which was in the *c*
14:21 went up with them into the *c*
17: 4 a champion went out from the *c*
17:17 run to your brothers at the *c*.
17:20 And he came to the *c* as the
17:46 give the carcasses of the *c* of
26: 5 Now Saul lay within the *c*,
26: 6 down with me to Saul in the *c*?
26: 7 Saul lay sleeping within the *c*,
2 Sam 1: 2 that a man came from Saul's *c*
1: 3 I have escaped from the *c* of
5:24 out before you to strike the *c*
17: 8 and will not *c* with the people.
23:16 mighty men broke through the *c*
1 Ki 16:16 over Israel that day in the *c*.
2 Ki 3:24 So when they came to the *c* of
6: 8 My *c* will be in such and such
7: 5 at twilight to go to the *c* of
7: 5 the outskirts of the Syrian *c*,
7: 7 and left the *c* intact—their
7: 8 came to the outskirts of the *c*,
7:10 "We went to the Syrian *c*,
7:12 they have gone out of the *c* to
19:35 and killed in the *c* of the
1 Chr 9:19 of the entrance to the *c* of
11:18 the three broke through the *c*
14:15 out before you to strike the *c*
2 Chr 22: 1 with the Arabians into the *c*
31: 2 to praise in the gates of the *c*
32:21 and captain in the *c* of the
Ps 78:28 fall in the midst of their *c*,
106:16 they envied Moses in the *c*,
Isa 37:36 and killed in the *c* of the
Joel 2:11 For His *c* is very great; For
Nah 3:17 Which *c* in the hedges on a
Zech 9: 8 I will *c* around My house
Heb 13:11 sin, are burned outside the *c*.
13:13 go forth to Him, outside the *c*,
Rev 20: 9 the earth and surrounded the *c*

CAMPED (62/61) CAMP

Ex 13:20 journey from Succoth and *c* in
15:27 so they *c* there by the waters.
17: 1 and *c* in Rephidim; but there
19: 2 and *c* in the wilderness.
19: 2 So Israel *c* there before the
Num 2:34 so they *c* by their standards
11:35 and *c* at Hazeroth.
12:16 moved from Hazeroth and *c* in
21:10 of Israel moved on and *c* in
21:11 journeyed from Oboth and *c* at
21:12 From there they moved and *c* in
21:13 From there they moved and *c* on
22: 1 and *c* in the plains of Moab on
33: 5 moved from Rameses and *c* at
33: 6 departed from Succoth and *c* at
33: 7 and they *c* near Migdol.
33: 8 and *c* at Marah.
33: 9 so they *c* there.
33:10 They moved from Elim and *c* by
33:11 moved from the Red Sea and *c*
33:12 the Wilderness of Sin and *c* at
33:13 departed from Dophkah and *c* at
33:14 They moved from Alush and *c* at
33:15 departed from Rephidim and *c*
33:16 the Wilderness of Sinai and *c*
33:17 from Kibroth Hattaavah and *c*
33:18 departed from Hazeroth and *c*
33:19 departed from Rithmah and *c* at
33:20 from Rimmon Perez and *c* at
33:21 They moved from Libnah and *c* at
33:22 journeyed from Rissah and *c* at
33:23 went from Kehelathah and *c* at
33:24 moved from Mount Shepher and *c*
33:25 They moved from Haradah and *c* at
33:26 moved from Makheloth and *c* at
33:27 departed from Tahath and *c* at
33:28 They moved from Terah and *c* at
33:29 They went from Mithkah and *c* at
33:30 departed from Hashmonah and *c*
33:31 departed from Moseroth and *c*
33:32 moved from Bene Jaakan and *c*
33:33 went from Hor Hagidgad and *c*
33:34 moved from Jotbathah and *c* at
33:35 departed from Abronah and *c* at
33:36 moved from Ezion Geber and *c*
33:37 They moved from Kadesh and *c* at
33:41 departed from Mount Hor and *c*
33:42 departed from Zalmonah and *c*
33:43 They departed from Punon and *c*
33:44 They departed from Oboth and *c*
33:45 They departed from Ijim and *c* at
33:46 moved from Dibon Gad and *c* at
33:47 from Almon Diblathaim and *c* in
33:48 the mountains of Abarim and *c*
33:49 They *c* by the Jordan, from Beth
Josh 4:19 and they *c* in Gilgal on the
5:10 Now the children of Israel *c* in
8:11 came before the city and *c* on
10: 5 and *c* before Gibeon and made
11: 5 they came and *c* together at the
2 Sam 24: 5 crossed over the Jordan and *c*

Ezra 8:15 and we *c* there three days.

CAMPING (1/1) CAMP

Ex 14: 9 and overtook them *c* by the sea

CAMPS (12/12) CAMP

Num 2:17 Levites in the middle of the *c*;
5: 3 they may not defile their *c* in
10: 2 directing the movement of the *c*.
10: 5 the *c* that lie on the east side
10: 6 then the *c* that lie on the
10:25 (the rear guard of all the *c*)
13:19 they inhabit are like *c* or
1 Chr 9:18 been gatekeepers for the *c* of
Song 6:13 it were, the dance of the two *c*?
Ezek 4: 2 set *c* against it also, and
Am 4:10 I made the stench of your *c*
Zech 14:15 cattle that will be in those *c*.

CAN (344/309)

Gen 4:13 is greater than I *c* bear!
31:43 But what *c* I do this day to
39: 9 How then *c* I do this great
41:15 and there is no one who *c*
41:15 it said of you that you *c*
41:38 *C* we find such a one as this,
44: 1 as much as they *c* carry, and
44:15 not know that such a man as I *c*
Ex 4:14 I know that he *c* speak well.
5:11 yourselves straw where you *c*
32:30 perhaps I *c* make atonement for
Lev 14:30 such as he *c* afford—
Num 10:31 and you *c* be our eyes.
23:10 Who *c* count the dust of Jacob,
31:23 everything that *c* endure fire,
35:33 and no atonement *c* be made for
Deut 1:12 How *c* I alone bear your problems
1:28 Where *c* we go up? Our brethren
3:24 in heaven or on earth who *c* do
7:17 how *c* I dispossess them?'—
8: 9 and out of whose hills you *c*
9: 2 Who *c* stand before the
20:19 if you *c* eat of them, do not
31: 2 I *c* no longer go out and come
32:39 Nor is there any who *c*
Josh 9: 7 so how *c* we make a covenant
Judg 6:15 how *c* I save Israel? Indeed my
14:12 If you *c* correctly solve and
16:15 How *c* you say, 'I love you,'
16:26 so that I *c* lean on them."
18:24 How *c* you say to me, 'What ails
1 Sam 9: 6 perhaps he *c* show us the way
10:27 'How *c* this man save us?"
16: 2 How *c* I go? If Saul hears it,
16:17 Provide me now a man who *c* play
18: 8 Now what more *c* he have but
21: 3 or whatever *c* be found."
26: 9 for who *c* stretch out his hand
28: 2 you know what your servant *c*
30:15 *C* you take me down to this
2 Sam 6: 9 How *c* the ark of the LORD come
7:20 Now what more *c* David say to
12:18 How *c* we tell him that the
12:22 Who *c* tell whether the LORD
12:23 *C* I bring him back again?
14:19 no one *c* turn to the right hand
19:35 *C* I discern between the good
19:35 *C* your servant taste what I eat
19:35 *C* I hear any longer the voice
22:30 For by You I *c* run against a
22:30 By my God I *c* leap over a
22:35 So that my arms *c* bend a bow
1 Ki 5: 9 then you *c* take them away.
13:16 neither *c* I eat bread nor drink
2 Ki 4:10 he *c* turn in there."
4:13 What *c* I do for you? Do you
6:27 where *c* I find help for you?
8: 1 and stay wherever you *c*;
10: 4 how then *c* we stand?"
1 Chr 13:12 How *c* I bring the ark of God to
17:18 What more *c* David say to You
2 Chr 1:10 for who *c* judge this great
Ezra 9:15 though no one *c* stand before
Esth 8: 6 For how *c* I endure to see the
8: 6 Or how *c* I endure to see the
8: 8 the king's signet ring no one *c*
Job 3:22 And are glad when they *c* find
4: 2 But who *c* withhold himself
4:17 *C* a mortal be more righteous
4:17 *C* a man be more pure than his
6: 6 *C* flavorless food be eaten
8:11 *C* the papyrus grow up without a
8:11 *C* the reeds flourish without
9: 2 But how *c* a man be righteous
9:12 who *c* hinder Him? Who can say
9:12 Who *c* say to Him, 'What are
9:14 How then *c* I answer Him, And
10: 7 And there is no one who *c*
11: 7 *C* you search out the deep things
11: 7 *C* you find out the limits of
11: 8 what *c* you do? Deeper than
11: 8 what *c* you know?
11:10 Then who *c* hinder Him?
12:14 there *c* be no release.
13: 9 Or *c* you mock Him as one mocks
14: 4 Who *c* bring a clean thing out
15: 3 by speeches with which he *c* do
17:15 As for my hope, who *c* see it?
21:22 *C* anyone teach God knowledge,

21:34 How then *c* you comfort me with
22: 2 *C* a man be profitable to God,
22:13 *C* He judge through the deep
22:17 What *c* the Almighty do to
23:13 and who *c* make Him change?
25: 4 How then *c* man be righteous
25: 4 Or how *c* he be pure who is
26:14 the thunder of His power who *c*
28:12 But where *c* wisdom be found?
28:15 Nor *c* silver be weighed for
28:17 Neither gold nor crystal *c*
28:17 Nor *c* it be exchanged for
28:19 Nor *c* it be valued in pure
33: 5 If you *c* answer me, Set your
34:29 who then *c* make trouble?
34:29 who then *c* see Him, Whether
36:26 Nor *c* the number of His years
36:29 *c* anyone understand the
37:19 For we *c* prepare nothing
38:31 *C* you bind the cluster of the
38:32 *C* you bring out Mazzaroth in
38:32 Or *c* you guide the Great Bear
38:33 *C* you set their dominion over
38:34 *C* you lift up your voice to the
38:35 *C* you send out lightnings, that
38:37 Who *c* number the clouds by
38:37 Or who *c* pour out the bottles
38:39 *C* you hunt the prey for the
39: 1 Or *c* you mark when the deer
39: 2 *C* you number the months that
39:10 *C* you bind the wild ox in the
39:20 *C* you frighten him like a
40: 9 Or *c* you thunder with a voice
40:14 you That your own right hand *c*
40:19 Only He who made him *c* bring
41: 1 *C* you draw out Leviathan with a
41: 2 *C* you put a reed through his
41: 7 *C* you fill his skin with
41:13 Who *c* remove his outer coat?
41:13 Who *c* approach him with a
41:14 Who *c* open the doors of his
41:16 so near another That no air *c*
42: 2 I know that You *c* do everything,
42: 2 that no purpose of Yours *c*
Ps 11: 1 How *c* you say to my soul,
11: 3 What *c* the righteous do?
18:29 For by You I *c* run against a
18:29 By my God I *c* leap over a
18:34 So that my arms *c* bend a bow
19:12 Who *c* understand his errors?
22:17 I *c* count all My bones.
40: 5 They are more than *c* be
49: 7 None of them *c* by any means
56: 4 What *c* flesh do to me?
56:11 What *c* man do to me?
58: 9 Before your pots *c* feel the
78:19 *C* God prepare a table in the
78:20 *C* He give bread also? Can He
78:20 *C* He provide meat for His
89: 6 For who in the heavens *c* be
89: 6 among the sons of the mighty *c*
89:48 What man *c* live and not see
89:48 *C* he deliver his life from the
106: 2 Who *c* utter the mighty acts of
106: 2 Who *c* declare all His praise?
118: 6 What *c* man do to me?
119: 9 How *c* a young man cleanse his
139: 7 Where *c* I go from Your Spirit?
139: 7 Or where *c* I flee from Your
147:17 Who *c* stand before His cold?
Prov 6:27 *C* a man take fire to his bosom,
6:28 *C* one walk on hot coals, And
18:14 But who *c* bear a broken
20: 3 Since any fool *c* start a
20: 6 But who *c* find a faithful man?
20: 9 Who *c* say, "I have made my
20:24 How then *c* a man understand
24:22 who knows the ruin those two *c*
26:16 Than seven men who *c* answer
31:10 Who *c* find a virtuous wife?
Eccl 2:12 For what *c* the man do who
2:25 For who *c* eat, or who can have
2:25 or who *c* have enjoyment, more
3:11 except that no one *c* find out
3:14 Nothing *c* be added to it,
3:22 For who *c* bring him to see what
4:11 But how *c* one be warm alone?
4:12 two *c* withstand him. And a
6:12 Who *c* tell a man what will
7:13 For who *c* make straight what
7:14 So that man *c* find out nothing
7:24 Who *c* find it out?
8: 7 So who *c* tell him when it will
10:14 Who *c* tell him what will be
Song 5: 3 How *c* I put it on again?
5: 3 How *c* I defile them?
8: 7 Nor *c* the floods drown it.
Isa 43: 9 Who among them *c* declare this,
43:13 And there is no one who *c*
44: 7 And who *c* proclaim as I do?
49:15 *C* a woman forget her nursing
Jer 2:13 broken cisterns that *c* hold no
2:23 How *c* you say, 'I am not
2:24 who *c* turn her away? All those
2:28 If they *c* save you in the time
2:32 *C* a virgin forget her
3:19 How *c* I put you among the
4: 4 And burn so that no one *c*
5: 1 If you *c* find a man,
5:15 Nor *c* you understand what they
8: 8 How *c* you say, 'We are wise,
9:10 So that no one *c* pass through;

9:10 Nor *c* men hear the voice of
9:12 so that no one *c* pass through?
10: 5 Nor *c* they do any good."
12: 5 Then how *c* you contend with
13:23 *C* the Ethiopian change his skin
14:22 the idols of the nations that *c*
14:22 Or *c* the heavens give showers?
15:12 *C* anyone break iron, The
17: 9 Who *c* know it?
18: 6 *c* I not do with you as this
20:10 'Perhaps he *c* be induced;
21:12 fire And burn so that no one *c*
23:24 *C* anyone hide himself in secret
31:37 If heaven above *c* be measured,
33:20 If you *c* break My covenant with
38: 5 For the king *c* do nothing
42: 2 a few of many, as you *c* see),
47: 7 How *c* it be quiet, Seeing the
48:14 How *c* you say, 'We are mighty
Lam 2:13 Who *c* heal you?
Ezek 15: 3 Or *c* men make a peg from it to
17:15 *C* he break a covenant and still
22:14 *C* your heart endure, or can your
22:14 or *c* your hands remain strong,
28: 3 There is no secret that *c* be
33:10 how *c* we then live?" '
33:32 who has a pleasant voice and *c*
37: 3 *c* these bones live?"
Dan 2: 9 and I shall know that you *c*
2:10 is not a man on earth who *c*
2:11 and there is no other who *c*
3:29 there is no other God who *c*
4:35 No one *c* restrain His hand Or
5:16 that you *c* give interpretations
5:16 Now if you *c* read the writing
10:17 For how *c* this servant of my
Hos 11: 8 How *c* I give you up, Ephraim?
11: 8 How *c* I hand you over,
11: 8 How *c* I make you like Admah?
11: 8 How *c* I set you like Zeboiim?
Joel 2:11 Who *c* endure it?
Am 3: 3 *C* two walk together, unless
3: 8 Who *c* but prophesy?
Jon 3: 9 Who *c* tell if God will turn and
Mic 3:11 No harm *c* come upon us."
5: 8 And none *c* deliver.
Nah 1: 6 Who *c* stand before His
1: 6 And who *c* endure the
Mal 3: 2 But who *c* endure the day of His
3: 2 And who *c* stand when He
Mt 6:24 No one *c* serve two masters; for
6:27 Which of you by worrying *c* add
7: 4 Or how *c* you say to your
7:18 nor *c* a bad tree bear good
8: 2 You *c* make me clean."
8:27 Who *c* this be, that even the
9:15 *C* the friends of the bridegroom
12:29 Or how *c* one enter a strong
12:34 Brood of vipers! How *c* you,
19:25 Who then *c* be saved?"
23:33 brood of vipers! How *c* you
Mk 1:40 You *c* make me clean."
2: 7 Who *c* forgive sins but God
2:19 *C* the friends of the bridegroom
3:23 How *c* Satan cast out Satan?
3:27 No one *c* enter a strong man's
4:41 Who *c* this be, that even the
7:15 a man from outside which *c*
8: 4 How *c* one satisfy these people
9: 3 such as no launderer on earth *c*
9:22 But if You *c* do anything, have
9:23 If you *c* believe, all things
9:29 This kind *c* come out by nothing
9:39 works a miracle in My name *c*
10:26 Who then *c* be saved?"
Lk 1:34 How *c* this be, since I do not
5:12 You *c* make me clean."
5:21 Who *c* forgive sins but God
5:34 *C* you make the friends of the
6:39 '*C* the blind lead the blind?
6:42 Or how *c* you say to your
8:25 Who *c* this be? For He commands
12: 4 that have no more that they *c*
12:25 which of you by worrying *c*
12:56 Hypocrites! You *c* discern the
13: 9 after that you *c* cut it down.'
16: 2 for you *c* no longer be
16:13 No servant *c* serve two masters;
16:26 nor *c* those from there pass to
17: 6 you *c* say to this mulberry
18:26 Who then *c* be saved?"
20:36 nor *c* they die anymore, for they
20:41 How *c* they say that the Christ
Jn 1:46 *C* anything good come out of
3: 2 for no one *c* do these signs
3: 4 How *c* a man be born when he is
3: 4 *C* he enter a second time into
3: 9 How *c* these things be?"
3:27 A man *c* receive nothing unless
5:19 Son *c* do nothing of Himself,
5:30 'I *c* of Myself do nothing.
5:44 How *c* you believe, who receive
6:44 No one *c* come to Me unless the
6:52 How *c* this Man give us His
6:60 who *c* understand it?"
6:65 have said to you that no one *c*
8:33 How *c* you say, 'You will be
9: 4 night is coming when no one *c*
9:16 How *c* a man who is a sinner do
10:21 *C* a demon open the eyes of the
12:34 and how *c* You say, 'The Son of
13:37 why *c* I not follow You now?
14: 5 and how *c* we know the way?"
14: 9 so how *c* you say, 'Show us the
15: 4 neither *c* you, unless you abide
15: 5 without Me you *c* do nothing.
Acts 8:31 How *c* I, unless someone guides
10:47 *C* anyone forbid water, that
21:37 *C* you speak Greek?
24:13 Nor *c* they prove the things of
25:11 no one *c* deliver me to them.
Rom 8: 7 nor indeed *c* be.
8:31 who *c* be against us?
1 Cor 2:14 nor *c* he know them, because
3:11 For no other foundation *c* anyone
7:21 but if you *c* be made free,
12: 3 and no one *c* say that Jesus is
14:31 For you *c* all prophesy one by
2 Cor 13: 8 For we *c* do nothing against the
Phil 4:13 I *c* do all things through Christ
1 Th 3: 9 For what thanks *c* we render to
1 Tim 6: 7 and it is certain we *c* carry
6:16 whom no man has seen or *c* see,
Heb 5: 2 He *c* have compassion on those
10: 1 *c* never with these same
10:11 which *c* never take away sins.
13: 6 What *c* man do to me?"
Jas 2:14 *C* faith save him?
3: 8 But no man *c* tame the tongue.
3:12 *C* a fig tree, my brethren, bear
1 Jn 4:20 how *c* he love God whom he has
Rev 3: 8 and no one *c* shut it; for you
9:20 which *c* neither see nor hear

CANA (4/4) CANAAN, CANANITE

Jn 2: 1 day there was a wedding in *C*
2:11 of signs Jesus did in *C* of
4:46 So Jesus came again to *C* of
21: 2 Nathanael of *C* in Galilee, the

CANAAN (93/90) CANAANITE, CANAANITES, CANAANITESS, CANANITE

Gen 9:18 And Ham was the father of *C*.
9:22 And Ham, the father of *C*,
9:25 Then he said: "Cursed be *C*;
9:26 And may *C* be his servant.
9:27 And may *C* be his servant."
10: 6 were Cush, Mizraim, Put, and *C*.
10:15 *C* begot Sidon his firstborn,
11:31 to go to the land of *C*;
12: 5 departed to go to the land of *C*.
12: 5 So they came to the land of *C*.
13:12 Abram dwelt in the land of *C*,
16: 3 ten years in the land of *C*.
17: 8 a stranger, all the land of *C*,
23: 2 is, Hebron) in the land of *C*,
23:19 is, Hebron) in the land of *C*.
28: 1 a wife from the daughters of *C*.
28: 6 a wife from the daughters of *C*,
28: 8 saw that the daughters of *C*
31:18 father Isaac in the land of *C*.
33:18 which is in the land of *C*,
35: 6 which is in the land of *C*,
36: 2 wives from the daughters of *C*:
36: 5 born to him in the land of *C*.
36: 6 he had gained in the land of *C*,
37: 1 a stranger, in the land of *C*.
42: 5 the famine was in the land of *C*.
42: 7 From the land of *C* to buy
42:13 of one man in the land of *C*;
42:29 their father in the land of *C*
42:32 this day in the land of *C*.
44: 8 back to you from the land of *C*
45:17 and depart; go to the land of *C*.
45:25 and came to the land of *C* to
46: 6 had acquired in the land of *C*,
46:12 and Onan died in the land of *C*)
46:31 who were in the land of *C*,
47: 1 have come from the land of *C*;
47: 4 is severe in the land of *C*.
47:13 land of Egypt and the land of *C*
47:14 of Egypt and in the land of *C*,
47:15 of Egypt and in the land of *C*,
48: 3 to me at Luz in the land of *C*
48: 7 beside me in the land of *C* on
49:30 before Mamre in the land of *C*,
50: 5 dug for myself in the land of *C*,
50:13 carried him to the land of *C*,
Ex 6: 4 to give them the land of *C*,
15:15 All the inhabitants of *C* will
16:35 to the border of the land of *C*.
Lev 14:34 have come into the land of *C*,
18: 3 to the doings of the land of *C*,
25:38 to give you the land of *C* and
Num 13: 2 men to spy out the land of *C*,
13:17 them to spy out the land of *C*,
26:19 and Onan died in the land of *C*.
32:30 among you in the land of *C*.
32:32 the LORD into the land of *C*,
33:40 in the South in the land of *C*,
33:51 the Jordan into the land of *C*,
34: 2 you come into the land of *C*,
34: 2 the land of *C* to its boundaries.
34:29 of Israel in the land of *C*.
35:10 the Jordan into the land of *C*,
35:14 shall appoint in the land of *C*,
Deut 32:49 Jericho; view the land of *C*,
Josh 5:12 ate the food of the land of *C*
14: 1 inherited in the land of *C*,
21: 2 them at Shiloh in the land of *C*,
22: 9 which is in the land of *C*,
22:10 which is in the land of *C*,
22:11 the frontier of the land of *C*,
22:32 land of Gilead to the land of *C*,
24: 3 throughout all the land of *C*,
Judg 3: 1 not known any of the wars in *C*
4: 2 the hand of Jabin king of *C*,
4:23 God subdued Jabin king of *C* in
4:24 against Jabin king of *C*,
4:24 had destroyed Jabin king of *C*.
5:19 Then the kings of *C* fought In
21:12 which is in the land of *C*.
1 Chr 1: 8 were Cush, Mizraim, Put, and *C*.
1:13 *C* begot Sidon, his firstborn,
16:18 you I will give the land of *C*
Ps 105:11 you I will give the land of *C*
106:38 sacrificed to the idols of *C*;
135:11 And all the kingdoms of *C*—
Isa 19:18 will speak the language of *C*
23:11 given a commandment against *C*
Ezek 16: 3 are from the land of *C*;
Zeph 2: 5 the LORD is against you, O *C*,
Mt 15:22 a woman of *C* came from that
Acts 7:11 all the land of Egypt and *C*,
13:19 seven nations in the land of *C*,

CANAANITE (14/14) CANAAN, CANAANITES

Gen 38: 2 there a daughter of a certain *C*
46:10 the son of a *C* woman.
Ex 6:15 and Shaul the son of a *C* woman.
23:28 drive out the Hivite, the *C*,
33: 2 and I will drive out the *C* and
34:11 you the Amorite and the *C* and
Num 21: 1 The king of Arad, the *C*,
33:40 Now the king of Arad, the *C*,
Deut 20:17 and the Amorite and the *C* and
Josh 9: 1 Hittite, the Amorite, the *C*,
13: 3 (which is counted as *C*);
Hos 12: 7 A cunning *C*! Deceitful scales
Zech 14:21 there shall no longer be a *C*
Mt 10: 4 Simon the *C*, and Judas

CANAANITES (57/55) CANAANITE

Gen 10:18 the families of the *C* were
10:19 And the border of the *C* was from
12: 6 And the *C* were then in the
13: 7 The *C* and the Perizzites then
15:21 "the Amorites, the *C*,
24: 3 son from the daughters of the *C*,
24:37 son from the daughters of the *C*,
34:30 among the *C* and the Perizzites;
50:11 inhabitants of the land, the *C*,
Ex 3: 8 to the place of the *C* and the
3:17 of Egypt to the land of the *C*
13: 5 you into the land of the *C* and
13:11 you into the land of the *C*,
23:23 and the Perizzites and the *C*
Num 13:29 and the *C* dwell by the sea and
14:25 Now the Amalekites and the *C*
14:43 For the Amalekites and the *C*
14:45 Then the Amalekites and the *C*
21: 3 Israel and delivered up the *C*,
Deut 1: 7 to the land of the *C* and to
7: 1 and the Amorites and the *C* and
11:30 in the land of the *C* who dwell
Josh 3:10 out from before you the *C* and
5: 1 and all the kings of the *C* who
7: 9 For the *C* and all the
11: 3 to the *C* in the east and in the
12: 8 Hittites, the Amorites, the *C*,
13: 4 south, all the land of the *C*,
16:10 they did not drive out the *C*
16:10 but the *C* dwell among the
17:12 but the *C* were determined to
17:13 that they put the *C* to forced
17:16 and all the *C* who dwell in the
17:18 for you shall drive out the *C*,
24:11 Amorites, the Perizzites, the *C*,
Judg 1: 1 to go up for us against the *C*
1: 3 that we may fight against the *C*;
1: 4 and the LORD delivered the *C*
1: 5 and they defeated the *C* and the
1: 9 down to fight against the *C*
1:10 Then Judah went against the *C*
1:17 and they attacked the *C* who
1:27 for the *C* were determined to
1:28 that they put the *C* under
1:29 did Ephraim drive out the *C*
1:29 so the *C* dwelt in Gezer among
1:30 so the *C* dwelt among them, and
1:32 the Asherites dwelt among the *C*,
1:33 but they dwelt among the *C*,
3: 3 of the Philistines, all the *C*,
3: 5 of Israel dwelt among the *C*,
2 Sam 24: 7 cities of the Hivites and the *C*.
1 Ki 9:16 had killed the *C* who dwelt in
Ezra 9: 1 to the abominations of the *C*,
Neh 9: 8 him To give the land of the *C*,
9:24 inhabitants of the land, The *C*,
Ob 20 possess the land of the *C*

CANAANITESS (1/1) CANAAN

1 Chr 2: 3 by the daughter of Shua, the *C*.

CANANITE (1/1)

Mk 3:18 Thaddaeus, Simon the *C*;

CANCER (1/1)
2 Tim 2:17 message will spread like **c**.

CANDACE (1/1)
Acts 8:27 of great authority under **C** the

CANDLE (KJV) See LAMP

CANE (4/4)
Ex 30:23 shekels of sweet-smelling **c**,
Isa 43:24 You have bought Me no sweet **c**
Jer 6:20 And sweet **c** from a far
Ezek 27:19 and **c** were among your

CANKER (KJV) See CANCER

CANKERWORM (KJV) See LOCUST

CANNEH (1/1) CALNEH
Ezek 27:23 'Haran, **C**, Eden,

CANNOT (206/194)
Gen 19:19 but I **c** escape to the
19:22 For I **c** do anything until you
24:50 we **c** speak to you either bad or
29: 8 We **c** until all the flocks are
31:35 not displease my lord that I **c**
32:12 which **c** be numbered for
34:14 We **c** do this thing, to give our
38:22 and said, "I **c** find her.
44:22 The lad **c** leave his father, for
44:26 We **c** go down; if our youngest
Ex 19:23 The people **c** come up to Mount
33:20 You **c** see My face; for no man
Lev 14:21 But if he is poor and **c** afford
14:32 who **c** afford the usual
Num 23:20 and I **c** reverse it.
31:23 But all that **c** endure fire you
Deut 22:19 he **c** divorce her all his days.
28:27 from which you **c** be healed.
28:35 legs with severe boils which **c**
Josh 7:13 you **c** stand before your enemies
24:19 You **c** serve the LORD, for He
Judg 11:35 and I **c** go back on it."
14:13 But if you **c** explain it to me,
21:18 we **c** give them wives from our
Ruth 4: 6 I **c** redeem it for myself, lest
4: 6 for I **c** redeem it."
1 Sam 12:21 go after empty things which **c**
17:39 I **c** walk with these, for I have
25:17 such a scoundrel that one **c**
2 Sam 5: 6 David **c** come in here."
14:14 which **c** be gathered up again.
18:14 I **c** linger with you." And he
23: 6 Because they **c** be taken with
1 Ki 8:27 and the heaven of heavens **c**
13:16 I **c** return with you nor go in
18:12 and he **c** find you, he will kill
20: 9 but this thing I **c** do.'
2 Chr 2: 6 and the heaven of heavens **c**
6:18 and the heaven of heavens **c**
24:20 so that you **c** prosper?
Neh 6: 3 so that I **c** come down.
Job 5:12 So that their hands **c** carry
6:30 **C** my taste discern the
10:15 I **c** lift up my head. I am
12:14 it **c** be rebuilt; If He
14: 5 limits, so that he **c** pass.
19: 8 so that I **c** pass; And He has
22:11 Or darkness so that you **c**
22:14 cover Him, so that He **c** see,
23: 8 but I **c** perceive Him;
23: 9 I **c** behold Him; When He turns
23: 9 I **c** see Him.
28:15 It **c** be purchased for gold,
28:16 It **c** be valued in the gold of
28:19 The topaz of Ethiopia **c** equal
30:27 My heart is in turmoil and **c**
31:23 of His magnificence I **c** endure.
37: 5 does great things which we **c**
37:21 Even now men **c** look at the
37:23 the Almighty, we **c** find Him;
41:17 They stick together and **c** be
41:23 They are firm on him and **c** be
41:26 it **c** avail; Nor does spear,
41:28 The arrow **c** make him flee;
Ps 22:29 Even he who **c** keep himself
40: 5 Your thoughts toward us **C** be
77: 4 I am so troubled that I **c**
88: 8 and I **c** get out;
93: 1 so that it **c** be moved.
125: 1 Which **c** be moved, but abides
139: 6 It is high, I **c** attain it.
Prov 3:15 all the things you may desire **c**
8:11 the things one may desire **c** be
12: 3 the root of the righteous **c** be
30:21 for four it **c** bear up:
Eccl 1: 8 Man **c** express it. The eye is
1:15 What is crooked **c** be made
1:15 And what is lacking **c** be
6:10 And he **c** contend with Him who
7:28 my soul still seeks but I **c**
8:17 that a man **c** find out the work
Song 8: 7 Many waters **c** quench love, Nor
Isa 1:13 I **c** endure iniquity and the
3: 7 I **c** cure your ills, For in my
28:20 covering so narrow that one **c**
29:11 And he says, "I **c**, for it
33:19 stammering tongue that you **c**
38:18 For Sheol **c** thank You, Death
38:18 Death **c** praise You; Those who
38:18 who go down to the pit **c** hope
44:18 so that they **c** see, And their
44:18 so that they **c** understand.
44:20 And he **c** deliver his soul,
45:20 And pray to a god that **c**
46: 7 yet it **c** answer Nor save him
50: 2 hand shortened at all that it **c**
56:10 all dumb dogs, They **c** bark;
56:11 And they are shepherds Who **c**
57:20 When it **c** rest, Whose waters
59: 1 shortened, That it **c** save;
59: 1 ear heavy, That it **c** hear.
59:14 And equity **c** enter.
Jer 1: 6 I **c** speak, for I am a
4:19 I **c** hold my peace, Because
5:22 that it **c** pass beyond it?
5:22 Yet they **c** prevail; Though
5:22 yet they **c** pass over it.
6:10 And they **c** give heed.
7: 8 you trust in lying words that **c**
8:17 Vipers which **c** be charmed,
10: 5 And they **c** speak; They must
10: 5 Because they **c** go by
10: 5 For they **c** do evil, Nor can
14: 9 Like a mighty one who **c** save?
19:11 which **c** be made whole again;
24: 3 which **c** be eaten, they are so
24: 8 And as the bad figs which **c** be
29:17 them like rotten figs that **c**
33:22 As the host of heaven **c** be
36: 5 I **c** go into the house of the
46:23 Though it **c** be searched,
49:23 It **c** be quiet.
Lam 3: 7 has hedged me in so that I **c**
Ezek 3: 6 whose words you **c** understand.
3:25 so that you **c** go out among
4: 8 will restrain you so that you **c**
12: 6 so that you **c** see the ground,
12:12 so that he **c** see the ground
Dan 2:27 and the soothsayers **c** declare
6: 8 so that it **c** be changed,
Hos 1:10 Which **c** be measured or
2: 6 So that she **c** find her paths.
5:13 Yet he **c** cure you, Nor heal
Jon 4:11 twenty thousand persons who **c**
Mic 2: 3 From which you **c** remove your
Hab 1:13 And **c** look on wickedness.
2: 5 and **c** be satisfied, He gathers
Mt 5:14 A city that is set on a hill **c**
5:36 because you **c** make one hair
6:24 You **c** serve God and mammon.
7:18 A good tree **c** bear bad fruit,
10:28 those who kill the body but **c**
16: 3 but you **c** discern the signs of
19:11 All **c** accept this saying, but
26:42 if this cup **c** pass away from Me
26:53 Or do you think that I **c** now
27:42 Himself He **c** save. If He is the
Mk 2:19 the bridegroom with them they **c**
3:24 that kingdom **c** stand.
3:25 that house **c** stand.
3:26 he **c** stand, but has an end.
7:18 enters a man from outside **c**
15:31 Himself He **c** save.
Lk 11: 7 I **c** rise and give to you'?
13:33 for it **c** be that a prophet
14:14 because they **c** repay you; for
14:20 and therefore I **c** come.'
14:26 he **c** be My disciple.
14:27 his cross and come after Me **c**
14:33 not forsake all that he has **c**
16: 3 I **c** dig; I am ashamed to beg.
16:13 You **c** serve God and mammon."
16:26 want to pass from here to you **c**,
Jn 3: 3 he **c** see the kingdom of God."
3: 5 he **c** enter the kingdom of God.
3: 8 but **c** tell where it comes from
7: 7 The world **c** hate you, but it
7:34 and where I am you **c** come."
7:36 and where I am you **c** come'?"
8:21 Where I go you **c** come."
8:22 Where I go you **c** come'?"
10:35 God came (and the Scripture **c**
13:33 you **c** come,' so now I say to
13:36 Where I am going you **c** follow Me
14:17 whom the world **c** receive,
15: 4 As the branch **c** bear fruit of
16:12 but you **c** bear them now.
Acts 4:16 and we **c** deny it.
4:20 For we **c** but speak the things
5:39 you **c** overthrow it—lest you
15: 1 you **c** be saved."
19:36 since these things **c** be denied,
27:31 the ship, you **c** be saved."
Rom 8: 8 those who are in the flesh **c**
8:26 for us with groanings which **c**
1 Cor 7: 9 but if they **c** exercise
10:21 You **c** drink the cup of the Lord
10:21 you **c** partake of the Lord's
12:21 And the eye **c** say to the hand,
15:50 that flesh and blood **c** inherit
Gal 3:17 **c** annul the covenant that was
Phil 1:22 yet what I shall choose I **c**
1 Tim 5:25 and those that are otherwise **c**
2 Tim 2:13 He **c** deny Himself.
Titus 1: 2 who **c** lie, promised before time
2: 8 sound speech that **c** be
Heb 4:15 do not have a High Priest who **c**
9: 5 Of these things we **c** now speak
9: 9 sacrifices are offered which **c**
12:27 that the things which **c** be
12:28 receiving a kingdom which **c** be
Jas 1:13 for God **c** be tempted by evil,
4: 2 You murder and covet and **c**
2 Pe 2:14 full of adultery and that **c**
1 Jn 3: 9 and he **c** sin, because he has
Rev 2: 2 and that you **c** bear those who

CANOPIES (2/2) CANOPY
2 Sam 22:12 He made darkness **c** around Him,
Ezek 41:26 of the temple and on the **c**.

CANOPY (4/4) CANOPIES
1 Ki 7: 6 and a **c** was in front of them.
Job 36:29 clouds, The thunder from His **c**?
Ps 18:11 His **c** around Him was dark
Ezek 41:25 A wooden **c** was on the front of

CAPABLE (1/1)
1 Chr 26:31 there were found among them **c**

CAPER (1/1)
Isa 13:21 And wild goats will **c** there.

CAPERNAUM (16/16)
Mt 4:13 He came and dwelt in **C**,
8: 5 Now when Jesus had entered **C**,
11:23 'And you, **C**, who are exalted
17:24 When they had come to **C**,
Mk 1:21 Then they went into **C**,
2: 1 And again He entered **C** after
9:33 Then He came to **C**.
Lk 4:23 we have heard done in **C**,
4:31 Then He went down to **C**,
7: 1 of the people, He entered **C**.
10:15 'And you, **C**, who are exalted
Jn 2:12 After this He went down to **C**,
4:46 whose son was sick at **C**.
6:17 and went over the sea toward **C**.
6:24 got into boats and came to **C**,
6:59 the synagogue as He taught in **C**.

CAPHTOR (3/3) CAPHTORIM
Deut 2:23 Caphtorim, who came from **C**,
Jer 47: 4 remnant of the country of **C**.
Am 9: 7 Egypt, The Philistines from **C**,

CAPHTORIM (3/3) CAPHTOR
Gen 10:14 came the Philistines and **C**).
Deut 2:23 villages as far as Gaza—the **C**,
1 Chr 1:12 came the Philistines and the **C**)

CAPITAL (12/6) CAPITALS
1 Ki 7:16 The height of one **c** was five
7:16 and the height of the other **c**
7:17 seven chains for one **c** and
7:17 and seven for the other **c**.
7:18 and thus he did for the other **c**.
2 Ki 25:17 and the **c** on it was of bronze.
25:17 The height of the **c** was three
25:17 pomegranates all around the **c**
2 Chr 3:15 and the **c** that was on the top
Jer 52:22 A **c** of bronze was on it; and
52:22 and the height of one **c** was
52:22 pomegranates all around the **c**,

CAPITALS (17/14) CAPITAL
Ex 36:38 And he overlaid their **c** and
38:17 and the overlay of their **c** was
38:19 and the overlay of their **c** and
38:28 the pillars, overlaid their **c**,
1 Ki 7:16 Then he made two **c** of cast
7:17 for the **c** which were on top of
7:18 all around to cover the **c** that
7:19 The **c** which were on top of the
7:20 The **c** on the two pillars also
7:20 in rows on each of the **c** all
7:41 the two bowl-shaped **c** that
7:41 covering the two bowl-shaped **c**
7:42 to cover the two bowl-shaped **c**
2 Chr 4:12 pillars and the bowl-shaped **c**
4:12 covering the two bowl-shaped **c**
4:13 to cover the two bowl-shaped **c**
Zeph 2:14 bittern Shall lodge on the **c**

CAPPADOCIA (2/2)
Acts 2: 9 in Mesopotamia, Judea and **C**,
1 Pe 1: 1 in Pontus, Galatia, **C**,

CAPSTONE (1/1)
Zech 4: 7 And he shall bring forth the **c**

CAPTAIN (72/71) CAPTAINS
Gen 37:36 an officer of Pharaoh and **c** of
39: 1 **c** of the guard, an Egyptian,
40: 3 custody in the house of the **c**
40: 4 And the **c** of the guard charged
41:10 custody in the house of the **c**
41:12 a servant of the **c** of the

1 Sam 17:18 these ten cheeses to the c of
18:13 and made him his c over a
22: 2 So he became c over them.
2 Sam 5: 8 he shall be chief and c.
17:25 And Absalom made Amasa c of the
23:19 Therefore he became their c.
1 Ki 11:24 men to him and became c over a
2 Ki 1: 9 Then the king sent to him a c
1:10 answered and said to the c of
1:11 Then he sent to him another c of
1:13 he sent a third c of fifty with
1:13 And the third c of fifty went
9:25 Then Jehu said to Bidkar his c,
18:24 How then will you repel one c of
25: 8 Nebuzaradan the c of the guard,
25:10 who were with the c of the
25:11 Then Nebuzaradan the c of the
25:12 But the c of the guard left
25:15 the c of the guard took away.
25:18 And the c of the guard took
25:20 c of the guard, took these and
1 Chr 11: 6 first shall be chief and c.
11:21 Therefore he became their c.
27: 5 The third c of the army for the
27: 7 The fourth c for the fourth
27: 8 The fifth c for the fifth month
27: 9 The sixth c for the sixth month
27:10 The seventh c for the seventh
27:11 The eighth c for the eighth
27:12 The ninth c for the ninth month
27:13 The tenth c for the tenth month
27:14 The eleventh c for the eleventh
27:15 The twelfth c for the twelfth
2 Chr 17:14 of thousands: Adnah the c,
17:15 to him was Jehohanan the c,
32:21 and c in the camp of the king
Prov 6: 7 Which, having no c,
Isa 3: 3 The c of fifty and the
36: 9 How then will you repel one c of
Jer 37:13 a c of the guard was there
39: 9 Then Nebuzaradan the c of the
39:10 But Nebuzaradan the c of the
39:11 Jeremiah to Nebuzaradan the c
39:13 So Nebuzaradan the c of the
40: 1 LORD after Nebuzaradan the c
40: 2 And the c of the guard took
40: 5 So the c of the guard gave
41:10 whom Nebuzaradan the c of the
43: 6 person whom Nebuzaradan the c
52:12 the c of the guard, who served
52:14 Chaldeans who were with the c
52:15 Then Nebuzaradan the c of the
52:16 But Nebuzaradan the c of the
52:19 the c of the guard took away.
52:24 The c of the guard took Seraiah
52:26 And Nebuzaradan the c of the
52:30 Nebuzaradan the c of the guard
Dan 2:14 the c of the king's guard, who
2:15 and said to Arioch the king's c,
Jon 1: 6 So the c came to him, and said
Jn 18:12 of troops and the c and the
Acts 4: 1 the c of the temple, and the
5:24 the c of the temple, and the
5:26 Then the c went with the
28:16 the prisoners to the c of the
Heb 2:10 to make the c of their

CAPTAINS (100/87) CAPTAIN

Ex 14: 7 the chariots of Egypt with c
15: 4 His chosen c also are drowned
Num 31:14 with the c over thousands and
31:14 captains over thousands and c
31:48 the c of thousands and captains
31:48 captains of thousands and c of
31:52 from the c of thousands and
31:52 captains of thousands and c of
31:54 received the gold from the c
Deut 20: 9 that they shall make c of the
Josh 10:24 and said to the c of the men of
1 Sam 8:12 He will appoint c over his
8:12 over his thousands and c over
22: 7 and make you all c of
22: 7 captains of thousands and c of
2 Sam 4: 2 son had two men who were c
18: 1 and set c of thousands and
18: 1 captains of thousands and c of
18: 5 when the king gave all the c
23: 8 Tachmonite, chief among the c.
24: 4 against Joab and against the c
24: 4 Therefore Joab and the c of the
1 Ki 9:22 servants: his officers, his c,
14:27 them to the hands of the c of
15:20 and sent the c of his armies
20:24 and put c in their places;
22:31 had commanded the thirty-two c
22:32 when the c of the chariots saw
22:33 when the c of the chariots saw
2 Ki 1:14 and burned up the first two c
8:21 had surrounded him and the c
9: 5 there were the c of the army
10:25 said to the guard and to the c,
11: 4 sent and brought the c of
11: 9 So the c of the hundreds did
11:10 And the priest gave the c of
11:15 the priest commanded the c of
11:19 Then he took the c of hundreds,
24:14 all the c and all the mighty
25:23 Now when all the c of the
25:26 and the c of the armies, arose
1 Chr 4:42 having as their c Pelatiah,
11:11 of a Hachmonite, chief of the c;
12:14 c of the army; the least was
12:18 upon Amasai, chief of the c,
12:18 and made them c of the troop.
12:20 c of the thousands who were
12:21 and they were c in the army.
12:28 his father's house twenty-two c;
12:34 of Naphtali one thousand c,
13: 1 David consulted with the c of
15:25 and the c over thousands went
25: 1 Moreover David and the c of the
26:26 the c over thousands and
26:26 and the c of the army, had
27: 1 the c of thousands and hundreds
27: 3 and the chief of all the c of
28: 1 of the tribes and the c of the
28: 1 the c over thousands and
28: 1 captains over thousands and c
29: 6 the c of thousands and of
2 Chr 1: 2 to the c of thousands and of
8: 9 c of his officers, captains of
8: 9 c of his chariots, and his
11:11 and put c in them, and stores
12:10 them to the hands of the c of
16: 4 and sent the c of his armies
17:14 the c of thousands: Adnah the
18:30 of Syria had commanded the c
18:31 when the c of the chariots saw
18:32 when the c of the chariots saw
21: 9 had surrounded him and the c
23: 1 made a covenant with the c
23: 9 the priest gave to the c of
23:14 the priest brought out the c
23:20 Then he took the c of hundreds,
25: 5 together and set over them c
25: 5 captains of thousands and c of
26:11 Hananiah, one of the king's c.
32: 6 Then he set military c over the
33:11 LORD brought upon them the c
33:14 Then he put military c in all
Neh 2: 9 Now the king had sent c of the
Job 39:25 The thunder of c and shouting.
Jer 40: 7 And when all the c of the
40:13 son of Kareah and all the c of
41:11 son of Kareah and all the c of
41:13 and all the c of the forces who
41:16 and all the c of the forces
42: 1 Now all the c of the forces,
42: 8 all the c of the forces which
43: 4 all the c of the forces, and
43: 5 son of Kareah and all the c of
Ezek 23: 6 C and rulers, All of them
23:12 C and rulers, Clothed most
23:15 All of them looking like c,
23:23 C and men of renown, All of
Lk 22: 4 with the chief priests and c,
22:52 c of the temple, and the elders
Rev 19:18 flesh of kings, the flesh of c,

CAPTIVE (88/82) CAPTIVES, CAPTIVITY, CAPTURED

Gen 14:14 that his brother was taken c,
34:29 and their wives they took c;
Ex 12:29 to the firstborn of the c who
Num 24:22 until Asshur carries you away c?
31: 9 took the women of Midian c,
Deut 21:10 your hand, and you take them c,
1 Sam 30: 2 and had taken c the women and
30: 3 daughters had been taken c.
30: 5 the Carmelite, had been taken c.
1 Ki 8:46 and they take them c to the
8:47 land where they were carried c,
8:47 land of those who took them c,
8:48 enemies who led them away c,
8:50 before those who took them c,
2 Ki 5: 2 and had brought back c a young
6:22 those whom you have taken c
15:29 and he carried them c to
16: 9 carried its people c to Kir,
18:11 Assyria carried Israel away c
24:15 And he carried Jehoiachin c to
24:16 the king of Babylon brought c
25:11 of the guard carried away c
25:21 Thus Judah was carried away c
1 Chr 9: 1 But Judah was carried away c to
2 Chr 6:36 and they take them c to a land
6:37 land where they were carried c,
6:38 where they have been carried c,
25:12 the children of Judah took c
28: 8 of Israel carried away c of
28:11 whom you have taken c from your
30: 9 by those who lead them c,
Ezra 4:10 and noble Osnapper took c and
8:35 who had been carried away c,
9: 4 who had been carried away c,
Ps 68:18 high, You have led captivity c;
106:46 those who carried them away c.
137: 3 those who carried us away c
Song 7: 5 A king is held c by your
Isa 14: 2 they will take them c whose
49:21 children and am desolate, A c,
51:14 The c exile hastens, that he
52: 2 O c daughter of Zion!
Jer 1: 3 carrying away of Jerusalem c
13:17 LORD's flock has been taken c.
13:19 Judah shall be carried away c,
13:19 shall be wholly carried away c.
20: 4 and he shall carry them c to
22:12 place where they have led him c,
24: 1 of Babylon had carried away c
24: 5 those who are carried away c
27:20 when he carried away c Jeconiah
28: 6 and all who were carried away c,
29: 1 elders who were carried away c—
29: 1 had carried away c from
29: 4 to all who were carried away c,
29: 7 caused you to be carried away c,
29:14 cause you to be carried away c.
39: 9 of the guard carried away c to
40: 1 all who were carried away c
40: 1 who were carried away c to
40: 7 had not been carried away c to
41:10 Then Ishmael carried away c all
41:10 Nethaniah carried them away c
41:14 whom Ishmael had carried away c
43: 3 us to death or carry us away c
43:12 burn them and carry them away c.
48:46 your sons have been taken c,
48:46 captive, And your daughters c.
50:33 All who took them c have held
52:15 of the guard carried away c
52:27 Thus Judah was carried away c
52:28 Nebuchadnezzar carried away c:
52:29 he carried away c from
52:30 of the guard carried away c of
Ezek 6: 9 where they are carried c,
39:28 and left none of them c any
Dan 11: 8 shall also carry their gods c
Am 1: 5 people of Syria shall go c to
1: 6 Because they took c the whole
4:10 Along with your c horses; I
6: 7 Therefore they shall now go c
7:11 shall surely be led away c
7:17 shall surely be led away c
Ob 11 day that strangers carried c
Nah 2: 7 She shall be led away c,
Lk 21:24 and be led away c into all
Eph 4: 8 high, He led captivity c,
2 Tim 2:26 having been taken c by him to

CAPTIVES (54/49)

Gen 31:26 away my daughters like c
Num 31:12 Then they brought the c,
31:19 purify yourselves and your c on
Deut 21:11 and you see among the c a
32:42 blood of the slain and the c,
Judg 5:12 and lead your c away, O son of
2 Ki 24:14 men of valor, ten thousand c,
2 Chr 28: 5 a great multitude of them as c,
28:11 me, therefore, and return the c,
28:13 You shall not bring the c here,
28:14 So the armed men left the c and
28:15 by name rose up and took the c,
28:17 Judah, and carried away c.
Ezra 1:11 Sheshbazzar took with the c
Esth 2: 6 away from Jerusalem with the c
Isa 14: 2 will take them captive whose c
20: 4 and the Ethiopians as c,
49:24 Or the c of the righteous be
49:25 Even the c of the mighty shall
61: 1 To proclaim liberty to the c,
Jer 28: 4 with all the c of Judah who
32:44 for I will cause their c to
33: 7 And I will cause the c of Judah
33: 7 captives of Judah and the c of
33:11 For I will cause the c of the
33:26 For I will cause their c to
48:47 Yet I will bring back the c of
49: 6 I will bring back The c of
49:39 I will bring back the c of
Lam 2:14 iniquity, To bring back your c,
Ezek 1: 1 as I was among the c by the
3:11 "And go, get to the c,
3:15 Then I came to the c at Tel
16:53 "When I bring back their c,
16:53 the c of Sodom and her
16:53 and the c of Samaria and her
16:53 will also bring back the c
29:14 I will bring back the c of Egypt
39:25 Now I will bring back the c of
Dan 2:25 I have found a man of the c of
5:13 that Daniel who is one of the c
6:13 who is one of the c from Judah,
Hos 6:11 When I return the c of My
Joel 3: 1 When I bring back the c of
Am 6: 7 captive as the first of the c,
9:14 I will bring back the c of My
Ob 20 And the c of this host of the
20 The c of Jerusalem who are in
Hab 1: 9 They gather c like sand.
Zeph 2: 7 for them, And return their c.
3:20 When I return your c before
Zech 6:10 "Receive the gift from the c—
Lk 4:18 proclaim liberty to the c
2 Tim 3: 6 into households and make c of

CAPTIVITY (106/98) CAPTIVE

Num 21:29 And his daughters into c,
Deut 21:13 put off the clothes of her c,
28:41 yours; for they shall go into c.
30: 3 God will bring you back from c,
Judg 18:30 of Dan until the day of the c
2 Ki 24:14 Also he carried into c all
24:15 of the land he carried into c
25:27 thirty-seventh year of the c
1 Chr 5: 6 king of Assyria carried into c.
5:22 in their place until the c.
5:26 half-tribe of Manasseh into c.
6:15 Jehozadak went into c when the
6:15 Judah and Jerusalem into c by
2 Chr 6:37 to You in the land of their c,
6:38 soul in the land of their c,

29: 9 and our wives are in *c*.
Ezra 2: 1 who came back from the *c*,
3: 8 who had come out of the *c* to
4: 1 that the descendants of the *c*
6:16 of the descendants of the *c*,
6:19 And the descendants of the *c*
6:20 all the descendants of the *c*,
6:21 who had returned from the *c*
8:35 who had come from the *c*,
9: 7 the lands, to the sword, to *c*,
10: 6 the guilt of those from the *c*.
10: 7 to all the descendants of the *c*,
10: 8 assembly of those from the *c*.
10:16 Then the descendants of the *c*
Neh 1: 2 escaped, who had survived the *c*,
1: 3 who are left from the *c* in the
4: 4 them as plunder to a land of *c*!
7: 6 who came back from the *c*,
8:17 who had returned from the *c*
Ps 14: 7 the LORD brings back the *c* of
53: 6 When God brings back the *c* of
68:18 You have led *c* captive; You
78:61 delivered His strength into *c*,
85: 1 You have brought back the *c* of
126: 1 the LORD brought back the *c*
126: 4 Bring back our *c*,
Isa 5:13 my people have gone into *c*,
46: 2 have themselves gone into *c*.
Jer 15: 2 And such as are for the *c*,
15: 2 for the captivity, to the *c*.
20: 6 in your house, shall go into *c*.
22:22 your lovers shall go into *c*;
29:14 will bring you back from your *c*;
29:16 not gone out with you into *c*—
29:20 of the LORD, all you of the *c*,
29:22 shall be taken up by all the *c*
29:28 This *c* is long; build houses
29:31 Send to all those in *c*,
30: 3 that I will bring back from *c* My
30:10 seed from the land of their *c*.
30:16 one of them, shall go into *c*;
30:18 I will bring back the *c* of
31:23 when I bring back their *c*:
43:11 and to *c* those appointed for
43:11 those appointed for *c*,
46:19 Prepare yourself to go into *c*!
46:27 from the land of their *c*;
48: 7 Chemosh shall go forth into *c*,
48:11 vessel, Nor has he gone into *c*.
49: 3 For Milcom shall go into *c*
52:31 thirty-seventh year of the *c*
Lam 1: 3 Judah has gone into *c*,
1: 5 Her children have gone into *c*
1:18 my young men Have gone into *c*.
4:22 will no longer send you into *c*.
Ezek 1: 2 year of King Jehoiachin's *c*,
11:24 God into Chaldea, to those in *c*.
11:25 So I spoke to those in *c* of all
12: 3 prepare your belongings for *c*,
12: 3 and go into *c* by day in their
12: 3 go from your place into *c* to
12: 4 sight, as though going into *c*;
12: 4 sight, like those who go into *c*.
12: 7 by day, as though going into *c*,
12:11 shall be carried away into *c*.
16:53 back the captives of your *c*
25: 3 of Judah when they went into *c*,
30:17 these cities shall go into *c*.
30:18 her daughters shall go into *c*.
33:21 in the twelfth year of our *c*,
39:23 the house of Israel went into *c*
39:28 who sent them into *c* among the
40: 1 the twenty-fifth year of our *c*,
Dan 11:33 by *c* and plundering.
Am 1: 6 they took captive the whole *c*
1: 9 they delivered up the whole *c*
1:15 Their king shall go into *c*,
5: 5 Gilgal shall surely go into *c*,
5:27 I will send you into *c* beyond
9: 4 Though they go into *c* before
Ob 12 brother In the day of his *c*;
Mic 1:16 they shall go from you into *c*.
Nah 3:10 carried away, She went into *c*;
Zech 14: 2 of the city shall go into *c*,
Mt 1:17 from David until the *c* in
1:17 and from the *c* in Babylon until
Rom 7:23 and bringing me into *c* to the
2 Cor 10: 5 bringing every thought into *c*
Eph 4: 8 He led *c* captive, And
Rev 13:10 He who leads into *c* shall go
13:10 into captivity shall go into *c*;

CAPTURED (19/19) CAPTIVE

Josh 11:17 He *c* all their kings, and
Judg 7:25 And they *c* two princes of the
1 Sam 4:11 Also the ark of God was *c*;
4:17 and the ark of God has been *c*.
4:19 news that the ark of God was *c*,
4:21 the ark of God had been *c* and
4:22 for the ark of God has been *c*.
2 Ki 14:13 Then Jehoash king of Israel *c*
16: 6 that time Rezin king of Syria *c*
2 Chr 25:23 Then Joash the king of Israel *c*
Esth 2: 6 the captives who had been *c*
Ps 56: of David when the Philistines *c*
Isa 13:15 And everyone who is *c* will
22: 3 They are *c* by the archers.
Jer 39: 5 And when they had *c* him, they
50: 9 From there she shall be *c*.
Ezek 33:21 The city has been *c*!"
40: 1 year after the city was *c*,
Rev 19:20 Then the beast was *c*,

CARAVANS (1/1)

Job 6:19 The *c* of Tema look, The

CARBUNCLE, CARBUNCLES (KJV) See CRYSTAL, EMERALD

CARCAS (1/1)

Esth 1:10 Bigtha, Abagtha, Zethar, and *C*,

CARCASE, CARCASES (KJV) See CARCASS, CORPSE

CARCASS (20/16) CARCASSES

Lev 5: 2 whether it is the *c* of an
5: 2 or the *c* of unclean livestock,
5: 2 or the *c* of unclean creeping
11:24 whoever touches the *c* of any of
11:25 whoever carries part of the *c* of
11:26 The *c* of any animal which
11:27 Whoever touches any such *c*
11:28 Whoever carries any such *c*
11:35 which a part of any such *c*
11:36 but whatever touches any such *c*
11:37 And if a part of any such *c*
11:38 and if a part of any such *c*
11:39 he who touches its *c* shall be
11:40 He who eats of its *c* shall wash
11:40 He also who carries its *c* shall
Judg 14: 8 he turned aside to see the *c* of
14: 8 bees and honey were in the *c*
14: 9 taken the honey out of the *c*
Ezek 32: 5 fill the valleys with your *c*.
Mt 24:28 For wherever the *c* is, there the

CARCASSES (15/15) CARCASS

Gen 15:11 the vultures came down on the *c*,
Lev 11: 8 and their *c* you shall not
11:11 but you shall regard their *c* as
26:30 and cast your *c* on the lifeless
Num 14:29 The *c* of you who have complained
14:32 your *c* shall fall in this
14:33 until your *c* are consumed in
Deut 14: 8 flesh or touch their dead *c*.
28:26 Your *c* shall be food for all the
1 Sam 17:46 And this day I will give the *c*
Isa 5:25 Their *c* were as refuse in the
Jer 9:22 Even the *c* of men shall fall as
16:18 My inheritance with the *c* of
Ezek 43: 7 by their harlotry or with the *c*
43: 9 put their harlotry and the *c*

CARCHEMISH (3/3)

2 Chr 35:20 came up to fight against *C* by
Isa 10: 9 Is not Calno like *C*?
Jer 46: 2 was by the River Euphrates in *C*,

CARE (32/30) CARED, CAREFREE, CAREFUL, CARELESS, CARES, CARING

Deut 15: 5 to observe with *c* all these
2 Sam 18: 3 they will not *c* about us; nor
18: 3 will they *c* about us. But you
1 Ki 1: 2 and let her *c* for him; and let
2 Ki 4:13 for us with all this *c*.
1 Chr 22:13 if you take *c* to fulfill the
2 Chr 19: 7 take *c* and do it, for there
Esth 2: 8 into the *c* of Hegai the
Job 10:12 And Your *c* has preserved my
21:21 For what does he *c* about his
Ps 27:10 Then the LORD will take *c* of
Isa 21: 7 listened earnestly with great *c*.
Zech 11:16 in the land who will not *c*
Mt 22:16 nor do You *c* about anyone, for
Mk 4:38 do You not *c* that we are
12:14 and *c* about no one; for You do
Lk 10:34 and took *c* of him.
10:35 Take *c* of him; and whatever more
10:40 do You not *c* that my sister has
Jn 10:13 he is a hireling and does not *c*
Acts 22:26 Take *c* what you do, for this man
27: 3 go to his friends and receive *c*.
1 Cor 7:32 But I want you to be without *c*.
12:25 members should have the same *c*
2 Cor 7:12 but that our *c* for you in the
8:16 God who puts the same earnest *c*
Phil 2:20 who will sincerely *c* for your
4:10 that now at last your *c* for me
4:10 again; though you surely did *c*,
1 Tim 3: 5 how will he take *c* of the
Heb 2: 6 of man that You take *c*
1 Pe 5: 7 casting all your *c* upon Him, for

CAREAH (1/1) KAREAH

2 Ki 25:23 Nethaniah, Johanan the son of *C*,

CARED (3/3) CARE

2 Sam 19:24 And he had not *c* for his feet,
1 Ki 1: 4 and she *c* for the king, and
Jn 12: 6 not that he *c* for the poor, but

CAREFREE (1/1) CARE

Ezek 23:42 The sound of a *c* multitude was

CAREFUL (34/34) CARE, CAREFULLY

Gen 31:24 Be *c* that you speak to Jacob
31:29 Be *c* that you speak to Jacob
Lev 10:16 Then Moses made *c* inquiry about
Num 28: 2 you shall be *c* to offer to Me
Deut 4: 6 Therefore be *c* to observe them;
4:15 Take *c* heed to yourselves, for
5: 1 you may learn them and be *c* to
5:32 Therefore you shall be *c* to do
6: 3 and be *c* to observe it, that
6:25 if we are *c* to observe all
8: 1 you today you must be *c* to
11:32 And you shall be *c* to observe
12: 1 judgments which you shall be *c*
12:32 be *c* to observe it; you shall
16:12 and you shall be *c* to observe
17:10 And you shall be *c* to do
17:19 the LORD his God and be *c* to
19:18 And the judges shall make *c*
24: 8 so you shall be *c* to do.
26:16 therefore you shall be *c* to
28:13 and are *c* to observe them.
32:46 command your children to be *c*
Josh 22: 5 But take *c* heed to do the
23:11 Therefore take *c* heed to
Judg 13: 4 please be *c* not to drink wine
13:13 said to the woman let her be *c*.
2 Ki 17:37 you shall be *c* to observe
21: 8 only if they are *c* to do
1 Chr 28: 8 be *c* to seek out all the
2 Chr 33: 8 only if they are *c* to do all
Ezra 7:17 be *c* to buy with this money
Ezek 20:21 and were not *c* to observe My
Titus 3: 8 believed in God should be *c* to
2 Pe 1:15 Moreover I will be *c* to ensure

CAREFULLY (26/26) CAREFUL

Deut 2: 4 Therefore watch yourselves *c*.
11:22 For if you *c* keep all these
15: 5 only if you *c* obey the voice of
24: 8 that you *c* observe and do
28: 1 to observe *c* all His
28:15 to observe *c* all His
28:58 If you do not *c* observe all the
31:12 fear the LORD your God and *c*
Neh 3:20 him Baruch the son of Zabbai *c*
Job 13:17 Listen *c* to my speech, And to
21: 2 Listen *c* to my speech, And let
Ps 37:10 you will look *c* for his place,
Prov 12:26 should choose his friends *c*,
23: 1 Consider *c* what is before
27: 5 rebuke is better Than love *c*
Isa 38:15 I shall walk *c* all my years
55: 2 Listen *c* to Me, and eat what
Jer 12:16 if they will learn *c* the ways
17:24 it shall be, if you heed Me *c*,
Hag 2:15 *c* consider from this day
Mt 2: 8 Go and search *c* for the young
Lk 15: 8 and search *c* until she finds
1 Tim 4: 6 good doctrine which you have *c*
2 Tim 3:10 But you have *c* followed my
Heb 12:15 looking *c* lest anyone fall short
1 Pe 1:10 have inquired and searched *c*,

CARELESS (2/2) CARE

Prov 19:16 But he who is *c* of his ways
Ezek 30: 9 from Me in ships To make the *c*

CARES (11/10) CARE

Deut 11:12 for which the LORD your God *c*;
Ps 142: 4 No one *c* for my soul.
Mt 13:22 and the *c* of this world and the
Mk 4:19 and the *c* of this world, the
Lk 8:14 go out and are choked with *c*,
21:34 and *c* of this life, and that
1 Cor 7:32 He who is unmarried *c* for the
7:33 But he who is married *c* about
7:34 The unmarried woman *c* about the
7:34 But she who is married *c* about
1 Pe 5: 7 for He *c* for you.

CARGO (3/3)

Jon 1: 5 and threw the *c* that was in
Acts 21: 3 the ship was to unload her *c*.
27:10 not only of the *c* and ship, but

CARING (2/2) CARE

1 Sam 9: 5 lest my father cease *c* about
10: 2 now your father has ceased *c*

CARMEL (24/23) CARMELITE, CARMELITESS

Josh 12:22 one; the king of Jokneam in *C*,
15:55 Maon, *C*, Ziph, Juttah,
19:26 it reached to Mount *C* westward,
1 Sam 15:12 saying, "Saul went to *C*,
25: 2 Maon whose business was in *C*,
25: 2 he was shearing his sheep in *C*.
25: 5 to the young men, "Go up to *C*,
25: 7 all the while they were in *C*.
25:40 David had come to Abigail at *C*,
1 Ki 18:19 all Israel to me on Mount *C*,

18:20 prophets together on Mount ***C***.
18:42 Elijah went up to the top of ***C***;
2 Ki 2:25 he went from there to Mount ***C***,
4:25 to the man of God at Mount ***C***.
2 Chr 26:10 in the mountains and in ***C***,
Song 7: 5 head crowns you like Mount ***C***,
Isa 33: 9 And Bashan and ***C*** shake off
35: 2 The excellence of ***C*** and
Jer 46:18 among the mountains And as ***C***
50:19 And he shall feed on ***C*** and
Am 1: 2 And the top of ***C*** withers."
9: 3 hide themselves on top of ***C***,
Mic 7:14 a woodland, In the midst of ***C***;
Nah 1: 4 Bashan and ***C*** wither, And the

CARMELITE (5/5) CARMEL

1 Sam 30: 5 the widow of Nabal the ***C***,
2 Sam 2: 2 the widow of Nabal the ***C***.
3: 3 the widow of Nabal the ***C***;
23:35 Hezrai the ***C***,
1 Chr 11:37 Hezro the ***C***,

CARMELITESS (2/2) CARMEL

1 Sam 27: 3 Jezreelitess, and Abigail the ***C***,
1 Chr 3: 1 Daniel, by Abigail the ***C***;

CARMI (8/8) CARMITES

Gen 46: 9 Hanoch, Pallu, Hezron, and ***C***.
Ex 6:14 Hanoch, Pallu, Hezron, and ***C***.
Num 26: 6 family of the Hezronites; of ***C***,
Josh 7: 1 things, for Achan the son of ***C***,
7:18 by man, and Achan the son of ***C***,
1 Chr 2: 7 The son of ***C*** was Achar, the
4: 1 of Judah were Perez, Hezron, ***C***,
5: 3 Hanoch, Pallu, Hezron, and ***C***.

CARMITES (1/1) CARMI

Num 26: 6 of Carmi, the family of the ***C***.

CARNAL (7/6) CARNALLY

Rom 7:14 law is spiritual, but I am ***c***,
8: 7 Because the ***c*** mind is enmity
1 Cor 3: 1 spiritual people but as to ***c***,
3: 3 for you are still ***c***.
3: 3 are you not ***c*** and behaving like
3: 4 am of Apollos," are you not ***c***?
2 Cor 10: 4 of our warfare are not ***c*** but

CARNALLY (6/6) CARNAL

Gen 19: 5 to us that we may know them ***c***.
Lev 18:20 Moreover you shall not lie ***c***
19:20 Whoever lies ***c*** with a woman who
Num 5:13 'and a man lies with her ***c***,
Judg 19:22 that we may know him ***c***!"
Rom 8: 6 For to be ***c*** minded is death,

CAROUSE (1/1) CAROUSING

2 Pe 2:13 who count it pleasure to ***c*** in

CAROUSING (2/2) CAROUSE

Lk 21:34 hearts be weighed down with ***c***,
2 Pe 2:13 ***c*** in their own deceptions while

CARPENTER (1/1) CARPENTER'S, CARPENTERS

Mk 6: 3 "Is this not the ***c***,

CARPENTER'S (1/1) CARPENTER

Mt 13:55 Is this not the ***c*** son? Is not

CARPENTERS (6/6) CARPENTER'S

2 Sam 5:11 and ***c*** and masons. And they
2 Ki 12:11 and they paid it out to the ***c***
22: 6 to ***c*** and builders and masons—and
1 Chr 14: 1 cedar trees, with masons and ***c***,
2 Chr 24:12 and they hired masons and ***c*** to
Ezra 3: 7 money to the masons and the ***c***,

CARPUS (1/1)

2 Tim 4:13 the cloak that I left with ***C***

CARRIAGES (1/1)

Isa 46: 1 Your ***c*** were heavily loaded,

CARRIED (153/141) CARRY

Gen 31:18 And he ***c*** away all his livestock
31:26 and ***c*** away my daughters like
46: 5 and the sons of Israel ***c*** their
50:13 For his sons ***c*** him to the land
Ex 25:14 that the ark may be ***c*** by them.
25:28 that the table may be ***c*** with
Lev 10: 5 So they went near and ***c*** them by
16:27 shall be ***c*** outside the camp.
Num 7: 9 which they ***c*** on their
13:23 they ***c*** it between two of them
Deut 1:31 saw how the LORD your God ***c***
Josh 4: 8 and ***c*** them over with them to
Judg 3:18 sent away the people who had ***c***
11:39 and he ***c*** out his vow with her
16: 3 and ***c*** them to the top of the
1 Sam 5: 8 ark of the God of Israel be ***c***
5: 8 So they ***c*** the ark of the God
5: 9 after they had ***c*** it away, that
30: 2 but ***c*** them away and went their
30:18 all that the Amalekites had ***c***
2 Sam 5:21 and David and his men ***c*** them
15:29 Therefore Zadok and Abiathar ***c***
1 Ki 2:26 because you ***c*** the ark of the
5:15 had seventy thousand who ***c***
8:47 in the land where they were ***c***
14:28 the guards ***c*** them, then brought
17:19 took him out of her arms and ***c***
2 Ki 5:23 and they ***c*** them on ahead of
7: 8 and ***c*** from it silver and gold
7: 8 and ***c*** some from there also,
9:28 And his servants ***c*** him in the
15:29 and he ***c*** them captive to
16: 9 ***c*** its people captive to Kir,
17: 6 of Assyria took Samaria and ***c***
17:11 nations whom the LORD had ***c***
17:23 So Israel was ***c*** away from their
17:28 of the priests whom they had ***c***
17:33 from among whom they were ***c***
18:11 Then the king of Assyria ***c***
20:17 shall be ***c*** to Babylon; nothing
23: 4 and ***c*** their ashes to Bethel.
24:13 And he ***c*** out from there all the
24:14 Also he ***c*** into captivity all
24:15 And he ***c*** Jehoiachin captive to
24:15 and the mighty of the land he ***c***
25:11 the captain of the guard ***c***
25:13 and ***c*** their bronze to Babylon.
25:21 Thus Judah was ***c*** away captive
1 Chr 5: 6 king of Assyria ***c*** into
5:26 He ***c*** the Reubenites, the
6:15 captivity when the LORD ***c***
9: 1 But Judah was ***c*** away captive to
13: 7 So they ***c*** the ark of God on a
2 Chr 6:37 in the land where they were ***c***
6:38 where they have been ***c*** captive,
12: 9 He also ***c*** away the gold shields
14: 8 thousand from Judah who ***c***
14: 8 and eighty thousand men who ***c***
14:13 And they ***c*** away very much
14:15 and ***c*** off sheep and camels in
16: 6 and they ***c*** away the stones and
21:17 and ***c*** away all the possessions
28: 5 and ***c*** away a great multitude of
28: 8 And the children of Israel ***c***
28:17 and ***c*** away captives.
29:16 the Levites took it out and ***c***
33:11 and ***c*** him off to Babylon.
34:16 So Shaphan ***c*** the book to the
36: 4 Jehoahaz his brother and ***c*** him
36: 7 Nebuchadnezzar also ***c*** off some
36:20 who escaped from the sword he ***c***
Ezra 2: 1 of those who had been ***c*** away,
2: 1 the king of Babylon had ***c*** away
5:12 destroyed this temple and ***c***
5:14 that was in Jerusalem and ***c***
8:35 of those who had been ***c*** away
9: 4 of those who had been ***c*** away
Neh 4:17 and those who ***c*** burdens, loaded
7: 6 of those who had been ***c*** away,
7: 6 the king of Babylon had ***c*** away,
Esth 2: 6 Kish had been ***c*** away from
2: 6 the king of Babylon had ***c*** away.
Job 10:19 I would have been ***c*** from the
Ps 46: 2 And though the mountains be ***c***
106:46 be pitied By all those who ***c***
137: 3 For there those who ***c*** us away
Isa 23: 7 Whose feet ***c*** her far off to
39: 6 shall be ***c*** to Babylon; nothing
46: 3 Who have been ***c*** from the womb:
49:22 And your daughters shall be ***c***
53: 4 He has borne our griefs And ***c***
63: 9 And He bore them and ***c*** them
66:12 On her sides shall you be ***c***,
Jer 10: 5 cannot speak; They must be ***c***,
13:19 Judah shall be ***c*** away captive,
13:19 It shall be wholly ***c*** away
24: 1 king of Babylon had ***c*** away
24: 5 I acknowledge those who are ***c***
27:20 when he ***c*** away captive Jeconiah
27:22 They shall be ***c*** to Babylon, and
28: 3 away from this place and ***c*** to
28: 6 house and all who were ***c*** away
29: 1 of the elders who were ***c*** away
29: 1 whom Nebuchadnezzar had ***c*** away
29: 4 to all who were ***c*** away captive,
29: 4 whom I have caused to be ***c*** away
29: 7 I have caused you to be ***c*** away
29:14 from which I cause you to be ***c***
39: 9 the captain of the guard ***c***
40: 1 in chains among all who were ***c***
40: 1 who were ***c*** away captive to
40: 7 of the land who had not been ***c***
41:10 Then Ishmael ***c*** away captive all
41:10 Ishmael the son of Nethaniah ***c***
41:14 the people whom Ishmael had ***c***
52:15 the captain of the guard ***c***
52:17 and ***c*** all their bronze to
52:27 Thus Judah was ***c*** away captive
52:28 people whom Nebuchadnezzar ***c***
52:29 year of Nebuchadnezzar he ***c***
52:30 the captain of the guard ***c***
Ezek 6: 9 the nations where they are ***c***
12:11 they shall be ***c*** away into
17: 4 its topmost young twig And ***c***
Dan 1: 2 which he ***c*** into the land of
2:35 the wind ***c*** them away so that no
Hos 10: 6 The idol also shall be ***c*** to
12: 1 And oil is ***c*** to Egypt.
Joel 3: 5 And have ***c*** into your temples
Am 5:26 You also ***c*** Sikkuth your king
Ob 11 In the day that strangers ***c***
Nah 3:10 Yet she was ***c*** away, She went
Mt 1:11 about the time they were ***c***
Mk 2: 3 bringing a paralytic who was ***c***
Lk 7:12 a dead man was being ***c*** out, the
7:14 and those who ***c*** him stood
16:22 and was ***c*** by the angels to
24:51 He was parted from them and ***c***
Jn 20:15 if You have ***c*** Him away, tell me
Acts 3: 2 from his mother's womb was ***c***,
5: 6 ***c*** him out, and buried him.
7:16 And they were ***c*** back to Shechem
8: 2 And devout men ***c*** Stephen to
21:35 he had to be ***c*** by the soldiers
1 Cor 12: 2 ***c*** away to these dumb idols,
Gal 2:13 so that even Barnabas was ***c***
Eph 4:14 tossed to and fro and ***c*** about
Heb 13: 9 Do not be ***c*** about with various
2 Pe 2:17 clouds ***c*** by a tempest, for whom
Jude 12 ***c*** about by the winds; late
Rev 12:15 that he might cause her to be ***c***
17: 3 So he ***c*** me away in the Spirit
21:10 And he ***c*** me away in the Spirit

CARRIERS (4/4) CARRY

Josh 9:21 be woodcutters and water ***c*** for
9:23 woodcutters and water ***c*** for the
9:27 them woodcutters and water ***c***
Ezek 27:25 The ships of Tarshish were ***c*** of

CARRIES (11/11) CARRY

Lev 11:25 whoever ***c*** part of the carcass of
11:28 Whoever ***c*** any such carcass
11:40 He also who ***c*** its carcass shall
15:10 He who ***c*** any of those things
Num 11:12 as a guardian ***c*** a nursing
24:22 How long until Asshur ***c*** you
Deut 1:31 as a man ***c*** his son, in all the
Job 21:18 And like chaff that a storm ***c***
27:21 The east wind ***c*** him away, and
Hag 2:12 If one ***c*** holy meat in the fold
Rev 17: 7 woman and of the beast that ***c***

CARRION (2/2)

Lev 11:18 and the ***c*** vulture;
Deut 14:17 the ***c*** vulture, the fisher owl,

CARRY (80/77) CARRIAGES, CARRIED, CARRIERS, CARRIES, CARRYING

Gen 37:25 on their way to ***c*** them down to
42:19 go and ***c*** grain for the famine
43:11 the land in your vessels and ***c***
44: 1 food, as much as they can ***c***,
45:27 which Joseph had sent to ***c*** him,
46: 5 which Pharaoh had sent to ***c***
47:30 you shall ***c*** me out of Egypt and
50:25 and you shall ***c*** up my bones
Ex 12:46 you shall not ***c*** any of the
13:19 and you shall ***c*** up my bones
Lev 4:12 the whole bull he shall ***c***
4:21 Then he shall ***c*** the bull outside
6:11 and ***c*** the ashes outside the
10: 4 ***c*** your brethren from before the
14:45 and he shall ***c*** them outside
Num 1:50 they shall ***c*** the tabernacle and
4:15 sons of Kohath shall come to ***c***
4:15 the sons of Kohath are to ***c***.
4:25 They shall ***c*** the curtains of the
4:31 And this is what they must ***c*** as
4:32 by name the items he must ***c***.
11:12 ***C*** them in your bosom, as a
Deut 14:24 so that you are not able to ***c***
28:38 You shall ***c*** much seed out to the
Josh 4: 3 You shall ***c*** them over with you
1 Sam 17:18 And ***c*** these ten cheeses to the
20:40 ***c*** them to the city."
2 Sam 15:25 ***C*** the ark of God back into the
19:18 a ferryboat went across to ***c***
1 Ki 18:12 the Spirit of the LORD will ***c***
2 Ki 4:19 ***C*** him to his mother."
1 Chr 15: 2 No one may ***c*** the ark of God but
15: 2 the LORD has chosen them to ***c***
23:26 They shall no longer ***c*** the
2 Chr 2:16 and you will ***c*** it up to
20:25 more than they could ***c*** away;
29: 5 and ***c*** out the rubbish from the
36: 6 him in bronze fetters to ***c***
Ezra 5:15 ***c*** them to the temple site that
7:15 and whereas you are to ***c*** the
Job 5:12 So that their hands cannot ***c***
15:12 Why does your heart ***c*** you away,
31:36 Surely I would ***c*** it on my
Ps 49:17 For when he dies he shall ***c***
90: 5 You ***c*** them away like a flood;
Eccl 5:15 from his labor Which he may ***c***
10:20 For a bird of the air may ***c***
Isa 5:29 They will ***c*** it away safely,
15: 7 They will ***c*** away to the Brook
30: 6 They will ***c*** their riches on
40:11 And ***c*** them in His bosom,
41:16 the wind shall ***c*** them away,
45:20 Who ***c*** the wood of their carved
46: 4 even to gray hairs I will ***c***
46: 4 and I will bear; Even I will ***c***,

46: 7 they c it And set it in its
57:13 But the wind will c them all
Jer 17:22 nor c a burden out of your
20: 4 and he shall c them captive to
20: 5 and c them to Babylon.
39: 7 him with bronze fetters to c
43: 3 they may put us to death or c
43:12 and he shall burn them and c
Ezek 12: 5 and c your belongings out
12: 6 them on your shoulders and c
12:12 shall dig through the wall to c
29:19 c off her spoil, and remove her
38:13 to c away silver and gold, to
Dan 11: 8 And he shall also c their gods
11:32 and c out great exploits.
Mic 6:14 You may c some away, but
Mt 3:11 sandals I am not worthy to c.
Mk 6:55 and began to c about on beds
11:16 He would not allow anyone to c
Lk 10: 4 C neither money bag, knapsack,
Jn 5:10 it is not lawful for you to c
21:18 and another will gird you and c
Acts 5: 9 and they will c you out."
7:43 And I will c you away
1 Tim 6: 7 and it is certain we can c

CARRYING (17/15) CARRY

Num 4:10 and put it on a c beam.
4:12 and put them on a c beam.
4:24 Gershonites, in serving and c:
10:17 c the tabernacle.
10:21 c the holy things.
Deut 32:11 C them on its wings,
1 Sam 10: 3 one c three young goats,
10: 3 another c three loaves of
10: 3 and another c a skin of wine.
Ps 78: 9 being armed and c bows,
Jer 1: 3 until the c away of Jerusalem
17:27 such as not c a burden when
Zech 5:10 Where are they c the basket?"
Mk 14:13 and a man will meet you c a
Lk 22:10 a man will meet you c a pitcher
Acts 5:10 and c her out, buried her by
2 Cor 4:10 always c about in the body the

CARSHENA (1/1)

Esth 1:14 those closest to him being C,

CART (21/15) CARTS, CARTWHEEL

Num 7: 3 a c for every two of the
1 Sam 6: 7 "Now therefore, make a new c,
6: 7 and hitch the cows to the c;
6: 8 the LORD and set it on the c;
6:10 cows and hitched them to the c,
6:11 the ark of the LORD on the c,
6:14 Then the c came into the field
6:14 So they split the wood of the c
2 Sam 6: 3 set the ark of God on a new c,
6: 3 of Abinadab, drove the new c.
1 Ki 7:27 was the length of each c,
7:30 Every c had four bronze wheels
7:32 wheels were joined to the c.
7:34 at the four corners of each c;
7:34 supports were part of the c
7:35 On the top of the c,
7:35 round. And on the top of the c,
1 Chr 13: 7 the ark of God on a new c from
13: 7 and Uzza and Ahio drove the c.
Isa 5:18 And sin as if with a c rope;
Am 2:13 As a c full of sheaves is

CARTS (23/21) CART

Gen 45:19 Take c out of the land of Egypt
45:21 did so; and Joseph gave them c,
45:27 and when he saw the c which
46: 5 in the c which Pharaoh had sent
Num 7: 3 six covered c and twelve oxen,
7: 6 So Moses took the c and the
7: 7 Two c and four oxen he gave to
7: 8 and four c and eight oxen he
1 Ki 7:27 He also made ten c of bronze;
7:28 this was the design of the c:
7:37 Thus he made the ten c.
7:38 On each of the ten c was a
7:39 And he put five c on the right
7:43 the ten c, and ten lavers on
7:43 carts, and ten lavers on the c;
2 Ki 16:17 cut off the panels of the c,
25:13 and the c and the bronze Sea
25:16 two pillars, one Sea, and the c,
2 Chr 4:14 he also made c and the lavers on
4:14 carts and the lavers on the c;
Jer 27:19 the Sea, concerning the c,
52:17 and the c and the bronze Sea
52:20 were under it, and the c,

CARTWHEEL (2/2) CART

Isa 28:27 Nor is a c rolled over the
28:28 forever, Break it with his c,

CARVE (1/1) CARVED, CARVES, CARVING

Hab 2:18 that its maker should c it,

CARVED (59/56) CARVE

Ex 20: 4 shall not make for yourself a c
Lev 26: 1 neither a c image nor a sacred
Deut 4:16 and make for yourselves a c
4:23 and make for yourselves a c
4:25 and act corruptly and make a c
5: 8 shall not make for yourself a c
7: 5 and burn their c images with
7:25 You shall burn the c images of
12: 3 you shall cut down the c images
27:15 is the one who makes a c or
Judg 17: 3 to make a c image and a molded
17: 4 and he made it into a c image
18:14 a c image, and a molded image?
18:17 they took the c image, the
18:18 Micah's house and took the c
18:20 and the c image, and took his
18:30 Dan set up for themselves the c
18:31 set up for themselves Micah's c
1 Ki 6:18 c with ornamental buds and open
6:29 Then he c all the walls of the
6:29 with c figures of cherubim,
6:32 and he c on them figures of
6:35 Then he c cherubim, palm trees,
6:35 gold applied evenly on the c
2 Ki 17:41 yet served their c images; also
21: 7 He even set a c image of Asherah
2 Chr 3: 5 and he c palm trees and
3: 7 and he c cherubim on the walls.
33: 7 He even set a c image, the idol
33:19 and set up wooden images and c
33:22 Amon sacrificed to all the c
34: 3 the c images, and the molded
34: 4 the c images, and the molded
34: 7 had beaten the c images into
Ps 74: 6 And now they break down its c
78:58 Him to jealousy with their c
97: 7 all be put to shame who serve c
Song 5:14 His body is c ivory Inlaid
Isa 10:10 Whose c images excelled those
21: 9 And all the c images of her
40:20 workman To prepare a c image
42: 8 Nor My praise to c images.
42:17 Who trust in c images, Who
44:15 He makes it a c image, and
44:17 into a god, His c image.
45:20 Who carry the wood of their c
48: 5 And my c image and my molded
Jer 8:19 Me to anger With their c
50:38 For it is the land of c
51:17 is put to shame by the c image;
51:47 I will bring judgment on the c
51:52 I will bring judgment on her c
Ezek 41:20 cherubim and palm trees were c.
41:25 and palm trees were c on the
41:25 temple just as they were c on
Hos 11: 2 And burned incense to c
Mic 1: 7 All her c images shall be
5:13 Your c images I will also cut
Nah 1:14 your gods I will cut off the c

CARVES (1/1) CARVE

Isa 22:16 Who c a tomb for himself in a

CARVING (3/3) CARVE

Ex 31: 5 in c wood, and to work in all
35:33 in c wood, and to work in all
2 Chr 3:10 two cherubim, fashioned by c,

CASE (34/33) CASES

Gen 30: 6 said, "God has judged my c;
43:18 so that he may make a c against
Ex 18:26 but they judged every small c
Num 27: 5 So Moses brought their c before
Deut 1:17 The c that is too hard for you,
19: 4 And this is the c of the
24:13 You shall in any c return the
Josh 20: 4 and declares his c in the
1 Sam 24:15 and me, and see and plead my c,
2 Sam 15: 3 your c is good and right; but
2 Chr 19:10 Whatever c comes to you from
Job 13:18 See now, I have prepared my c,
23: 4 I would present my c before
29:16 And I searched out the c that
Prov 25: 9 Debate your c with your
Isa 41:21 "Present your c,
43:26 together; State your c,
45:21 Tell and bring forth your c;
Jer 2:35 I will plead My c against you,
25:31 He will plead His c with all
50:34 will thoroughly plead their c,
51:36 I will plead your c and take
Lam 3:58 You have pleaded the c for my
3:59 how I am wronged; Judge my c.
Ezek 20:35 and there I will plead My c
20:36 Just as I pleaded My c with your
20:36 so I will plead My c with
Dan 3:17 "If that is the c,
Mic 6: 1 plead your c before the
7: 9 Until He pleads my c And
Mt 19:10 If such is the c of the man with
Acts 19:38 his fellow craftsmen have a c
24:22 will make a decision on your c.
25:14 Festus laid Paul's c before the

CASEMENT (KJV) See LATTICE

CASES (3/3) CASE

Ex 18:26 the hard c they brought to
Deut 1:16 Hear the c between your
1 Cor 7:15 is not under bondage in such c.

CASIPHIA (2/1)

Ezra 8:17 the chief man at the place C,
8:17 the Nethinim at the place C—

CASLUHIM (2/2)

Gen 10:14 and C (from whom came the
1 Chr 1:12 C (from whom came the

CASSIA (3/3)

Ex 30:24 "five hundred shekels of c,
Ps 45: 8 with myrrh and aloes and c,
Ezek 27:19 back and forth. Wrought iron, c,

CAST (323/307) CASTING, CASTS

Gen 21:10 C out this bondwoman and her
37:20 let us now kill him and c him
37:22 but c him into this pit which
37:24 Then they took him and c him
39: 7 things that his master's wife c
Ex 1:22 son who is born you shall c
4: 3 C it on the ground." So he cast
4: 3 So he c it on the ground, and
4:25 the foreskin of her son and c
7: 9 Take your rod and c it before
7:10 And Aaron c down his rod before
15: 4 chariots and his army He has c
15:25 When he c it into the waters,
25:12 You shall c four rings of gold
26:37 and you shall c five sockets of
32:19 and he c the tablets out of his
32:24 and I c it into the fire, and
34:24 For I will c out the nations
36:36 and he c four sockets of silver
37: 3 And he c for it four rings of
37:13 And he c for it four rings of
38: 5 He c four rings for the four
38:27 talents of silver were c the
Lev 1:16 crop with its feathers and c
14:40 and they shall c them into an
16: 8 Then Aaron shall c lots for the
26:30 and c your carcasses on the
26:44 I will not c them away, nor
Num 19: 6 and c them into the midst of
Deut 6:19 to c out all your enemies from
7: 1 and has c out many nations
9: 4 after the LORD your God has c
29:28 and c them into another land,
Josh 8:29 c it at the entrance of the
10:11 that the LORD c down large
10:27 c them into the cave where they
13:12 for Moses had defeated and c
18: 6 that I may c lots for you here
18: 8 that I may c lots for you here
18:10 Then Joshua c lots for them in
1 Sam 14:42 C lots between my son Jonathan
18:11 And Saul c the spear, for he
20:33 Then Saul c a spear at him to
2 Sam 1:21 the shield of the mighty is c
11:21 Was it not a woman who c a
18:17 And they took Absalom and c him
20:15 and they c up a siege mound
1 Ki 7:15 And he c two pillars of bronze,
7:16 Then he made two capitals of c
7:23 And he made the Sea of c
7:24 The ornamental buds were c in
7:24 cast in two rows when it was c.
7:30 the laver were supports of c
7:33 and their hubs were all of c
7:46 of Jordan the king had them c
9: 7 for My name I will c out of My
14: 9 and have c Me behind your back—
14:24 nations which the LORD had c
21:26 whom the LORD had c out before
2 Ki 2:16 LORD has taken him up and c
2:21 and c in the salt there, and
13:23 not yet destroy them or c them
16: 3 nations whom the LORD had c
17: 8 nations whom the LORD had c
17:20 until He had c them from His
19:18 and have c their gods into the
21: 2 nations whom the LORD had c
23:27 and will c off this city
24:20 that He finally c them out from
1 Chr 24:31 These also c lots just as their
25: 8 And they c lots for their duty,
26:13 And they c lots for each gate,
26:14 Then they c lots for his son
28: 9 He will c you off forever.
2 Chr 4: 2 Then he made the Sea of c
4: 3 The oxen were c in two rows,
4: 3 cast in two rows, when it was c.
4:17 of Jordan the king had them c
7:20 for My name I will c out of My
13: 9 Have you not c out the priests
25:12 and c them down from the top of
26:14 and slings to c stones.
28: 3 nations whom the LORD had c
29:19 King Ahaz in his reign had c
30:14 all the incense altars and c
33: 2 nations whom the LORD had c
33:15 and he c them out of the city.
Neh 1: 9 though some of you were c out
9:26 C Your law behind their backs
10:34 We c lots among the priests, the
11: 1 the rest of the people c lots
Esth 3: 7 they c Pur (that is, the lot),

9:24 and had **c** Pur (that is, the
Job 8: 4 He has **c** them away for their
8:20 God will not **c** away the
15: 4 you **c** off fear, And restrain
15:33 And **c** off his blossom like an
18: 8 For he is **c** into a net by his
20:23 God will **c** on him the fury of
22:29 When they **c** you down, and you
29:24 my countenance they did not **c**
30:11 They have **c** off restraint
30:19 He has **c** me into the mire, And
37:18 Strong as a **c** metal mirror?
Ps 2: 3 Their bonds in pieces And **c**
5:10 **C** them out in the multitude of
17:13 **c** him down; Deliver my life
18:42 I **c** them out like dirt in the
22:10 I was **c** upon You from birth.
22:18 And for My clothing they **c**
36:12 They have been **c** down and are
37:14 To **c** down the poor and needy,
37:24 he shall not be utterly **c** down;
42: 5 Why are you **c** down, O my soul?
42: 6 my soul is **c** down within me;
42:11 Why are you **c** down, O my soul?
43: 2 Why do You **c** me off? Why do I
43: 5 Why are you **c** down, O my soul?
44: 2 the peoples, and **c** them out.
44: 9 But You have **c** us off and put
44:23 Arise! Do not **c** us off
50:17 you hate instruction And **c** My
51:11 Do not **c** me away from Your
55:22 **C** your burden on the LORD,
56: 7 In anger **c** down the peoples, O
60: 1 You have **c** us off; You have
60: 8 Over Edom I will **c** My shoe;
60:10 who **c** us off? And You, O God,
62: 4 They only consult to **c** him
71: 9 Do not **c** me off in the time of
73:18 You **c** them down to
74: 1 why have You **c** us off forever?
76: 6 the chariot and horse were **c**
77: 7 Will the Lord **c** off forever?
78:49 He **c** on them the fierceness of
80: 8 You have **c** out the nations,
88:14 why do You **c** off my soul? Why
89:38 But You have **c** off and
89:44 And **c** his throne down to the
94:14 For the LORD will not **c** off
102:10 You have lifted me up and **c** me
108: 9 Over Edom I will **c** My shoe;
108:11 who **c** us off? And You, O
140:10 Let them be **c** into the fire,
Prov 1:14 **C** in your lot among us, Let us
7:26 For she has **c** down many
16:33 The lot is **c** into the lap, But
22:10 **C** out the scoffer, and
29:18 the people **c** off restraint;
Eccl 3: 5 A time to **c** away stones, And a
11: 1 **C** your bread upon the waters,
Isa 2:20 In that day a man will **c** away
14:19 But you are **c** out of your grave
19: 8 All those will lament who **c**
25: 7 The surface of the covering **c**
26:19 And the earth shall **c** out the
34:17 He has **c** the lot for them, And
37:19 and have **c** their gods into the
38:17 For You have **c** all my sins
41: 9 have chosen you and have not **c**
57:20 Whose waters **c** up mire and
58: 7 your house the poor who are **c**
66: 5 Who **c** you out for My name's
Jer 6:15 They shall be **c** down," says
7:15 And I will **c** you out of My
7:15 as I have **c** out all your
7:29 Cut off your hair and **c** it
8:12 They shall be **c** down,"
9:19 Because we have been **c** out of
14:16 whom they prophesy shall be **c**
15: 1 **C** them out of My sight, and
16:13 Therefore I will **c** you out of
22: 7 down your choice cedars And **c**
22:19 Dragged and **c** out beyond the
22:26 So I will **c** you out, and your
22:28 Why are they **c** out, he and his
22:28 And **c** into a land which they
23:39 and will **c** you out of My
26:23 him with the sword and **c** his
28:16 I will **c** you from the face of
31:37 I will also **c** off all the seed
33:24 He has also **c** them off"?
33:26 then I will **c** away the
36:23 with the scribe's knife and **c**
36:30 and his dead body shall be **c**
38: 6 So they took Jeremiah and **c** him
38: 9 whom they have **c** into the
41: 7 Nethaniah killed them and **c**
41: 9 pit into which Ishmael had **c**
50:26 **C** her up as heaps of ruins,
52: 3 till He finally **c** them out from
Lam 2: 1 He **c** down from heaven to the
3:31 For the Lord will not **c** off
Ezek 6: 4 and I will **c** down your slain
11:16 Although I have **c** them far off
18:31 **C** away from you all the
19:12 She was **c** down to the ground,
20: 8 They did not all **c** away the
23:35 you have forgotten Me and **c** Me
27:30 They will cry bitterly and **c**
28:16 Therefore I **c** you as a profane
28:17 I **c** you to the ground, I laid
31:16 when I **c** it down to hell
32: 4 I will **c** you out on the open
32:18 And **c** them down to the depths
Dan 3: 6 down and worship shall be **c**
3:11 down and worship shall be **c**
3:15 you shall be **c** immediately into
3:20 and **c** them into the burning
3:21 and were **c** into the midst of
3:24 Did we not **c** three men bound
6: 7 shall be **c** into the den of
6:12 shall be **c** into the den of
6:16 and they brought Daniel and **c**
6:24 and they **c** them into the den
8: 7 but he **c** him down to the ground
8:10 and it **c** down some of the host
8:11 place of His sanctuary was **c**
8:12 and he **c** truth down to the
11:12 and he will **c** down tens of
Hos 9:17 My God will **c** them away,
Joel 3: 3 They have **c** lots for My people,
Am 1:11 And **c** off all pity; His anger
4: 3 And you will be **c** into
Ob 11 entered his gates And **c** lots
Jon 1: 7 let us **c** lots, that we may know
1: 7 So they **c** lots, and the lot
2: 3 For You **c** me into the deep,
2: 4 I have been **c** out of Your sight;
Mic 2: 9 The women of My people you **c**
7:19 You will **c** all our sins Into
Nah 3: 6 I will **c** abominable filth upon
3:10 They **c** lots for her honorable
Zeph 3:15 He has **c** out your enemy.
Zech 1:21 to **c** out the horns of the
9: 4 the LORD will **c** her out; He
10: 6 shall be as though I had not **c**
Mt 5:29 pluck it out and **c** it from
5:29 for your whole body to be **c**
5:30 cut it off and **c** it from you;
5:30 for your whole body to be **c**
7: 6 nor **c** your pearls before swine,
7:22 **c** out demons in Your name, and
8:12 sons of the kingdom will be **c**
8:16 And He **c** out the spirits with a
8:31 If You **c** us out, permit us to go
9:33 And when the demon was **c** out,
10: 1 to **c** them out, and to heal all
10: 8 raise the dead, **c** out demons.
12:24 This fellow does not **c** out
12:27 And if I **c** out demons by
12:27 by whom do your sons **c** them
12:28 But if I **c** out demons by the
13:42 and will **c** them into the furnace
13:47 is like a dragnet that was **c**
13:50 and **c** them into the furnace of
17:19 Why could we not **c** it out?"
17:27 **c** in a hook, and take the fish
18: 8 cut it off and **c** it from you.
18: 8 to be **c** into the everlasting
18: 9 pluck it out and **c** it from
18: 9 to be **c** into hell fire.
21:21 Be removed and be **c** into the
21:39 So they took him and **c** him out
22:13 and **c** him into outer darkness;
25:30 And **c** the unprofitable servant
27:35 for My clothing they **c**
Mk 1:34 and **c** out many demons; and He
3:15 to heal sicknesses and to **c**
3:23 How can Satan **c** out Satan?
6:13 And they **c** out many demons, and
7:26 and she kept asking Him to **c**
9:18 that they should **c** it out, but
9:28 Why could we not **c** it out?"
9:45 to be **c** into hell, into the
9:47 to be **c** into hell fire—
11:23 Be removed and be **c** into the
12: 8 took him and killed him and **c**
16: 9 out of whom He had **c** seven
16:17 In My name they will **c** out
Lk 6:22 and **c** out your name as evil,
9:40 I implored Your disciples to **c**
11:18 Because you say I **c** out demons
11:19 And if I **c** out demons by
11:19 by whom do your sons **c** them
11:20 But if I **c** out demons with the
12: 5 has power to **c** into hell; yes,
13:32 I **c** out demons and perform
20:12 and they wounded him also and **c**
20:15 So they **c** him out of the
23:34 they divided His garments and **c**
Jn 6:37 to Me I will by no means **c** out.
9:34 And they **c** him out.
9:35 Jesus heard that they had **c** him
12:31 ruler of this world will be **c**
15: 6 he is **c** out as a branch and is
19:24 but **c** lots for it, whose it
19:24 for My clothing they **c**
21: 6 **C** the net on the right side of
21: 6 will find some." So they **c**,
Acts 1:26 And they **c** their lots, and the
7:58 and they **c** him out of the city
26:10 I **c** my vote against them.
Rom 11: 1 has God **c** away His people?
11: 2 God has not **c** away His people
11:15 For if their being **c** away is
13:12 Therefore let us **c** off the
Gal 4:30 **C** out the bondwoman and her
1 Tim 5:12 because they have **c** off their
Heb 10:35 Therefore do not **c** away your
2 Pe 2: 4 but **c** them down to hell and
Rev 2:22 Indeed I will **c** her into a
4:10 and **c** their crowns before the
12: 9 So the great dragon was **c** out,
12: 9 he was **c** to the earth, and his
12: 9 and his angels were **c** out with
12:10 has been **c** down.
12:13 dragon saw that he had been **c**
19:20 These two were **c** alive into the
20: 3 and he **c** him into the bottomless
20:10 was **c** into the lake of fire and
20:14 Then Death and Hades were **c** into
20:15 in the Book of Life was **c** into

CASTAWAY (KJV) See DISQUALIFIED

CASTING (15/15) CAST

Lev 18:24 which I am **c** out before you.
20:23 of the nation which I am **c** out
1 Ki 7:35 its panels were of the same **c**.
Ps 89:39 have profaned his crown by **c**
Prov 18:18 **C** lots causes contentions to
Mt 4:18 **c** a net into the sea; for they
27:35 **c** lots, that it might be
Mk 1:16 Simon and Andrew his brother **c**
1:39 and **c** out demons.
9:38 who does not follow us **c** out
15:24 **c** lots for them to determine
Lk 9:49 we saw someone **c** out demons in
11:14 And He was **c** out a demon, and
2 Cor 10: 5 **c** down arguments and every high
1 Pe 5: 7 **c** all your care upon Him, for He

CASTLE (1/1)

Prov 18:19 are like the bars of a **c**.

CASTLES (KJV) See FORTRESSES, SETTLEMENTS

CASTS (12/12) CAST

Job 18: 7 And his own counsel **c** him
20:15 God **c** them out of his belly.
Ps 147: 6 He **c** the wicked down to the
147:17 He **c** out His hail like morsels;
Prov 10: 3 But He **c** away the desire of
19:15 Laziness **c** one into a deep
Isa 40:19 And the silversmith **c** silver
Mt 9:34 He **c** out demons by the ruler of
12:26 If Satan **c** out Satan, he is
Mk 3:22 the ruler of the demons He **c**
Lk 11:15 He **c** out demons by Beelzebub,
1 Jn 4:18 but perfect love **c** out fear,

CASUAL (1/1)

Jer 3: 9 through her **c** harlotry, that

CATASTROPHE (4/4)

Jer 11:23 for I will bring **c** on the men
19: 3 I will bring such a **c** on this
44:11 set My face against you for **c**
51:64 sink and not rise from the **c**

CATCH (17/17) CATCHES, CAUGHT

Judg 21:21 and every man **c** a wife for
2 Ki 7:12 we shall **c** them alive, and get
Job 9:18 He will not allow me to **c** my
Ps 10: 9 He lies in wait to **c** the poor;
35: 8 his net that he has hidden **c**
Prov 12:12 The wicked covet the **c** of evil
Song 2:15 **C** us the foxes, The little
Jer 5:26 They set a trap; They **c** men.
Ezek 19: 3 He learned to **c** prey, And he
19: 6 He learned to **c** prey; He
Hab 1:15 They **c** them in their net, And
Mk 12:13 to **c** Him in His words.
Lk 5: 4 and let down your nets for a **c**.
5: 9 him were astonished at the **c**
5:10 From now on you will **c** men."
11:54 and seeking to **c** Him in
20:26 But they could not **c** Him in His

CATCHES (6/6) CATCH

Ex 22: 6 If fire breaks out and **c** in
Lev 17:13 who hunts and **c** any animal or
Job 5:13 He **c** the wise in their own
Ps 10: 9 He **c** the poor when he draws
Jn 10:12 and the wolf **c** the sheep and
1 Cor 3:19 He **c** the wise in their own

CATERPILLAR (2/2)

Ps 78:46 also gave their crops to the **c**,
Isa 33: 4 Like the gathering of the **c**;

CATERPILLERS (KJV) See GRASSHOPPERS

CATTLE (59/59)

Gen 1:24 **c** and creeping thing and beast
1:25 **c** according to its kind, and
1:26 of the air, and over the **c**,
2:20 So Adam gave names to all **c**,
3:14 are cursed more than all **c**,
7:14 all **c** after their kind, every
7:21 birds and **c** and beasts and
7:23 of the ground: both man and **c**,
8:17 birds and **c** and every creeping
9:10 is with you: the birds, the **c**,
29: 7 it is not time for the **c** to
36: 6 his **c** and all his animals, and

47:17 the **c** of the herds, and for the
Ex 9: 3 of the LORD will be on your **c**
20:10 your female servant, nor your **c**,
Lev 22:19 male without blemish from the **c**,
22:21 a freewill offering from the **c**
Num 31: 9 and took as spoil all their **c**,
31:28 hundred of the persons, the **c**,
31:30 drawn from the persons, the **c**,
31:33 seventy-two thousand **c**,
31:38 The **c** were thirty-six thousand,
31:44 thirty-six thousand **c**,
35: 3 shall be for their **c**,
Deut 5:14 your donkey, nor any of your **c**,
7:13 the increase of your **c** and the
28: 4 the increase of your **c** and the
28:18 the increase of your **c** and the
28:51 or the increase of your **c** or
32:14 Curds from the **c**,
Josh 8: 2 Only its spoil and its **c** you
1 Ki 1: 9 sheep and oxen and fattened **c**
1:19 sacrificed oxen and fattened **c**
1:25 sacrificed oxen and fattened **c**
2 Ki 3:17 with water, so that you, your **c**,
1 Chr 5: 9 because their **c** had multiplied
7:21 came down to take away their **c**.
2 Chr 35: 7 as well as three thousand **c**;
35: 8 flock, and three hundred **c**.
35: 9 the flock and five hundred **c**.
35:12 And so they did with the **c**.
Neh 9:37 over our bodies and our **c** At
10:36 firstborn of our sons and our **c**,
Job 36:33 The **c** also, concerning the
Ps 50:10 And the **c** on a thousand
78:48 He also gave up their **c** to the
104:14 the grass to grow for the **c**,
107:38 And He does not let their **c**
148:10 Beasts and all **c**;
Isa 1:11 of rams And the fat of fed **c**.
30:23 In that day your **c** will feed
46: 1 were on the beasts and on the **c**.
Jer 9:10 men hear the voice of the **c**.
49:32 And the multitude of their **c**
Joel 1:18 animals groan! The herds of **c**
Zech 13: 5 for a man taught me to keep **c**
14:15 And on all the **c** that will be
Mt 22: 4 my oxen and fatted **c** are
Rev 18:13 **c** and sheep, horses and

CAUGHT (44/44) CATCH

Gen 22:13 there behind him was a ram **c**
39:12 that she **c** him by his garment,
Ex 4: 4 he reached out his hand and **c**
Num 5:13 against her, nor was she **c**—
Josh 8:22 so they were **c** in the midst of
Judg 1: 6 and they pursued him and **c** him
8:14 And he **c** a young man of the men
15: 4 Then Samson went and **c** three
21:23 those who danced, whom they **c**.
1 Sam 17:35 I **c** it by its beard, and
2 Sam 16: 8 So now you are **c** in your own
18: 9 and his head **c** in the
2 Ki 4:27 she **c** him by the feet, but
2 Chr 22: 9 and they **c** him (he was hiding
Ps 9:15 they hid, their own foot is **c**.
10: 2 Let them be **c** in the plots
Prov 3:26 keep your foot from being **c**.
5:22 And he is **c** in the cords of
7:13 So she **c** him and kissed him;
11: 6 But the unfaithful will be **c**
Eccl 9:12 Like birds **c** in a snare, So
Isa 24:18 midst of the pit Shall be **c**
28:13 and be broken And snared and **c**.
Jer 48:44 gets out of the pit shall be **c**
50:24 You have been found and also **c**,
Lam 4:20 Was **c** in their pits, Of whom
Ezek 12:13 and he shall be **c** in My snare.
Am 3: 4 if he has **c** nothing?
3: 5 if it has **c** nothing at all?
Mt 14:31 stretched out His hand and **c**
Lk 5: 5 we have toiled all night and **c**
5: 6 they **c** a great number of fish,
Jn 8: 3 brought to Him a woman **c** in
8: 4 this woman was **c** in adultery,
21: 3 and that night they **c** nothing.
21:10 the fish which you have just **c**.
Acts 8:39 the Spirit of the Lord **c** Philip
27:15 So when the ship was **c**,
2 Cor 12: 2 such a one was **c** up to the third
12: 4 how he was **c** up into Paradise
12:16 I **c** you by cunning!
1 Th 4:17 alive and remain shall be **c**
2 Pe 2:12 brute beasts made to be **c** and
Rev 12: 5 And her Child was **c** up to God

CAUL, CAULS (KJV) See LOBE

CAULK (1/1) CAULKERS

Ezek 27: 9 its wise men Were in you to **c**

CAULKERS (1/1) CAULK

Ezek 27:27 Your **c** and merchandisers, All

CAUSE (219/210) CAUSED, CAUSES, CAUSING

Gen 7: 4 after seven more days I will **c**
Ex 8: 5 and **c** frogs to come up on the
9: 9 and it will **c** boils that break
9:18 about this time I will **c** very
22: 9 the **c** of both parties shall
23:27 I will **c** confusion among all
27:20 to **c** the lamp to burn
Lev 14:41 And he shall **c** the house to be
19:29 to **c** her to be a harlot, lest
25: 9 Then you shall **c** the trumpet of
26:16 shall consume the eyes and **c**
26:36 sound of a shaken leaf shall **c**
Num 16: 5 and will **c** him to come near to
16: 5 one whom He chooses He will **c**
27: 7 and **c** the inheritance of their
27: 8 then you shall **c** his
Deut 1:38 for he shall **c** Israel to
3:28 and he shall **c** them to inherit
17:16 nor **c** the people to return to
25: 2 that the judge will **c** him to
28: 7 The LORD will **c** your enemies
28:25 The LORD will **c** you to be
31: 7 and you shall **c** them to inherit
Josh 23: 7 nor **c** anyone to swear by
Judg 8: 7 So Gideon said, "For this **c**,
1 Sam 17:29 I done now? Is there not a **c**?
19: 5 to kill David without a **c**?
25:31 you have shed blood without **c**,
25:39 who has pleaded the **c** of my
28: 9 to **c** me to die?"
2 Sam 15: 4 everyone who has any suit or **c**
1 Ki 8:45 and maintain their **c**.
8:49 and maintain their **c**,
8:59 that He may maintain the **c** of
8:59 cause of His servant and the **c**
2 Ki 19: 7 and I will **c** him to fall by the
1 Chr 4:10 that I may not **c** pain!" So God
21: 3 Why should he be a **c** of guilt
2 Chr 6:35 and maintain their **c**.
6:39 and maintain their **c**,
Ezra 4:15 for which **c** this city was
Neh 4:11 midst and kill them and **c** the
6:13 so that they might have **c** for
Job 2: 3 him, to destroy him without **c**.
5: 8 And to God I would commit my **c**—
6:24 **C** me to understand wherein I
9:17 multiplies my wounds without **c**.
24:10 They **c** the poor to go naked,
30:22 lift me up to the wind and **c**
31:13 If I have despised the **c** of my
38:26 To **c** it to rain on a land
38:27 And **c** to spring forth the
Ps 7: 4 plundered my enemy without **c**,
9: 4 maintained my right and my **c**;
10:17 You will **c** Your ear to hear,
17: 1 Hear a just **c**, O LORD,
25: 3 deal treacherously without **c**.
32: 6 For this **c** everyone who is
35: 1 Plead my **c**, O LORD,
35: 7 For without **c** they have hidden
35: 7 they have dug without **c** for my
35:19 the eye who hate me without a **c**.
35:23 to my vindication, To my **c**,
35:27 glad, Who favor my righteous **c**;
43: 1 And plead my **c** against an
65: 4 And **c** to approach You, That
67: 1 And **c** His face to shine upon
69: 4 Those who hate me without a **c**
71: 2 and **c** me to escape; Incline
74:22 Arise, O God, plead Your own **c**;
80: 3 **C** Your face to shine, And we
80: 7 **C** Your face to shine, And we
80:19 **C** Your face to shine, And we
85: 4 And **c** Your anger toward us to
109: 3 fought against me without a **c**.
119:154 Plead my **c** and redeem me;
119:161 persecute me without a **c**,
140:12 the LORD will maintain The **c**
143: 8 **C** me to hear Your
143: 8 **C** me to know the way in which
Prov 1:11 for the innocent without **c**;
3:30 not strive with a man without **c**,
8:21 That I may **c** those who love me
18:17 The first one to plead his **c**
22:23 the LORD will plead their **c**,
23:11 He will plead their **c** against
23:29 Who has wounds without **c**?
24:28 against your neighbor without **c**,
26: 2 So a curse without **c** shall not
29: 7 The righteous considers the **c**
31: 8 In the **c** of all who are
31: 9 And plead the **c** of the poor
Eccl 5: 6 Do not let your mouth **c** your
10: 1 And **c** it to give off a foul
Song 8: 2 I would **c** you to drink of
Isa 1:23 Nor does the **c** of the widow
3:12 My people! Those who lead you **c**
9:16 the leaders of this people **c**
10:30 O daughter of Gallim! **C** it to
13:10 And the moon will not **c** its
27: 6 Those who come He shall **c** to
28:12 rest with which You may **c**
30:11 **C** the Holy One of Israel To
30:30 The LORD will **c** His glorious
32: 6 And he will **c** the drink of the
34: 8 year of recompense for the **c**
37: 7 and I will **c** him to fall by the
42: 2 Nor **c** His voice to be heard in
49: 8 To **c** them to inherit the
51:22 Who pleads the **c** of His
52: 4 oppressed them without **c**.
58:14 And I will **c** you to ride on
61:11 So the Lord GOD will **c**
66: 9 and not **c** delivery?" says the
66: 9 Shall I who **c** delivery shut up
Jer 3:12 I will not **c** My anger to fall on
5:28 They do not plead the **c**,
5:28 The **c** of the fatherless; Yet
7: 3 and I will **c** you to dwell in
7: 7 then I will **c** you to dwell in
7:34 Then I will **c** to cease from the
11:20 to You I have revealed my **c**.
14:22 of the nations that can **c** rain?
15: 8 I will **c** anguish and terror to
15:11 Surely I will **c** the enemy to
16: 9 I will **c** to cease from this
16:21 I will this once **c** them to
16:21 I will **c** them to know My hand
17: 4 And I will **c** you to serve your
18: 2 and there I will **c** you to hear
19: 7 and I will **c** them to fall by
19: 9 And I will **c** them to eat the
20:12 For I have pleaded my **c** before
22:16 He judged the **c** of the poor and
23:32 and **c** My people to err by their
25:15 and **c** all the nations, to whom
29: 8 to your dreams which you **c** to
29:10 and **c** you to return to this
29:14 you to the place from which I **c**
30: 3 And I will **c** them to return to
30:13 is no one to plead your **c**,
30:21 Then I will **c** him to draw
31: 9 I will **c** them to walk by the
32:35 to **c** their sons and their
32:35 to **c** Judah to sin.'
32:37 and I will **c** them to dwell
32:44 for I will **c** their captives to
33: 7 And I will **c** the captives of
33:11 For I will **c** the captives of
33:15 and at that time I will **c** to
33:26 For I will **c** their captives to
34:22 and **c** them to return to this
36:29 and **c** man and beast to cease
38:23 And you shall **c** this city to be
42:12 he may have mercy on you and **c**
48:35 I will **c** to cease in Moab The
49: 2 That I will **c** to be heard an
49:37 For I will **c** Elam to be
50: 9 I will raise and **c** to come up
51:27 **C** the horses to come up like
Lam 3:36 Or subvert a man in his **c**—
3:52 My enemies without **c** Hunted me
Ezek 5:13 and I will **c** My fury to rest
7:24 I will **c** the pomp of the
13:13 I will **c** a stormy wind to break
14:15 If I **c** wild beasts to pass
14:23 I have done nothing without **c**
16: 2 **c** Jerusalem to know her
21:17 And I will **c** My fury to rest;
22: 9 you are men who slander to **c**
23:48 Thus I will **c** lewdness to cease
25: 7 and I will **c** you to perish from
26: 3 and will **c** many nations to come
29: 4 And **c** the fish of your rivers
29:14 the captives of Egypt and **c**
29:21 In that day I will **c** the horn
30:13 And **c** the images to cease from
32: 4 And **c** to settle on you all the
32:12 I will **c** your multitude to
34:10 I will **c** them to cease feeding
34:25 and **c** wild beasts to cease from
34:26 and I will **c** showers to come
36:12 I will **c** men to walk on you, My
36:15 nor shall you **c** your nation to
36:27 put My Spirit within you and **c**
37: 5 Surely I will **c** breath to enter
37:12 I will open your graves and **c**
39: 3 and **c** the arrows to fall out of
44:23 and **c** them to discern between
44:30 to **c** a blessing to rest on your
Dan 8:25 his cunning He shall **c** deceit
9:17 and for the Lord's sake **c** Your
11:39 and he shall **c** them to rule
Hos 2:11 I will also **c** all her mirth to
Joel 2:23 And He will **c** the rain to come
3:11 **C** Your mighty ones to go down
Am 6: 3 Who **c** the seat of violence to
Jon 1: 7 that we may know for whose **c**
1: 8 Please tell us! For whose **c** is
Hab 1: 3 And **c** me to see trouble?
Zech 8:12 I will **c** the remnant of this
13: 2 I will also **c** the prophets and
Mt 5:22 with his brother without a **c**
10:21 rise up against parents and **c**
Mk 13:12 rise up against parents and **c**
Jn 15:25 hated Me without a **c**.
18:37 For this **c** I was born, and for
18:37 and for this **c** I have come into
Acts 13:28 And though they found no **c** for
28:18 because there was no **c** for
Rom 14:13 to put a stumbling block or a **c**
16:17 note those who **c** divisions and
2 Cor 4:15 may **c** thanksgiving to abound to
1 Tim 1: 4 which **c** disputes rather than
Heb 12:15 of bitterness springing up **c**
1 Jn 2:10 and there is no **c** for stumbling
Jude 19 who **c** divisions, not having the
Rev 12:15 that he might **c** her to be
13:15 beast should both speak and **c**

CAUSED (79/78) CAUSE

Gen 2: 5 For the LORD God had not **c** it
2:21 And the LORD God **c** a deep sleep
20:13 when God **c** me to wander from my
41:52 For God has **c** me to be fruitful
Ex 9:10 And they **c** boils that break
14:21 and the LORD **c** the sea to go

36: 6 and they **c** it to be proclaimed
Lev 24:20 as he has **c** disfigurement of a
Num 31:16 these women **c** the children of
Deut 34: 4 I have **c** you to see it with
1 Sam 10:20 And when Samuel had **c** all the
10:21 When he had **c** the tribe of
20:17 Now Jonathan again **c** David to
22:22 I have **c** the death of all the
2 Sam 7:11 and have **c** you to rest from all
1 Ki 11:25 the trouble that Hadad **c**);
11:27 And this is what **c** him to rebel
2 Ki 7: 6 For the LORD had **c** the army of
17:17 And they **c** their sons and
2 Chr 13:13 But Jeroboam **c** an ambush to go
21:11 and **c** the inhabitants of
33: 6 Also he **c** his sons to pass
Neh 13:26 Nevertheless pagan women **c** even
Job 29:13 And I **c** the widow's heart to
31:16 Or **c** the eyes of the widow to
31:39 Or **c** its owners to lose their
34:28 So that they **c** the cry of the
38:12 And **c** the dawn to know its
Ps 66:12 You have **c** men to ride over our
76: 8 You **c** judgment to be heard from
78:13 He divided the sea and **c** them
78:16 And **c** waters to run down like
78:26 He **c** an east wind to blow in
80: 9 And **c** it to take deep root,
119:49 Upon which You have **c** me to
Prov 7:21 her enticing speech she **c** him
Isa 19:14 And they have **c** Egypt to err
43:23 I have not **c** you to serve with
48: 3 and I **c** them to hear it.
48:21 He **c** the waters to flow from
Jer 12:14 the inheritance which I have **c**
13:11 so I have **c** the whole house of
18:15 And they have **c** themselves to
23:13 prophesied by Baal And **c** My
23:22 And had **c** My people to hear My
29: 4 whom I have **c** to be carried
29: 7 of the city where I have **c** you
29:31 and he has **c** you to trust in a
32:23 therefore You have **c** all this
48: 4 Her little ones have **c** a cry
48:33 I have **c** wine to fail from the
51:49 As Babylon has **c** the slain
Lam 2: 6 The LORD has **c** The appointed
2: 8 Therefore He has **c** the rampart
2:17 And He has **c** an enemy to
3:13 He has **c** the arrows of His
Ezek 3: 2 and He **c** me to eat that scroll.
20:26 in that they **c** all their
22: 4 You have **c** your days to draw
24:13 Till I have **c** My fury to rest
26:17 Who **c** their terror to be on
29:18 king of Babylon **c** his army to
31:15 I **c** mourning. I covered the
31:15 I **c** Lebanon to mourn for it,
32:23 Who **c** terror in the land of
32:24 Who **c** their terror in the land
32:25 Though their terror was **c** In
32:26 Though they **c** their terror in
32:30 at the terror which they **c** by
32:32 For I have **c** My terror in the
37: 2 Then He **c** me to pass by them all
44:12 them before their idols and **c**
46:21 out into the outer court and **c**
Dan 9:21 being **c** to fly swiftly, reached
Hos 4:12 the spirit of harlotry has **c**
Jon 3: 7 And he **c** it to be proclaimed
Mal 2: 8 You have **c** many to stumble at
Acts 15: 3 and they **c** great joy to all the
2 Cor 2: 5 But if anyone has **c** grief, he

CAUSES (50/50) CAUSE

Ex 22: 5 If a man **c** a field or vineyard
Lev 24:19 If a man **c** disfigurement of his
Num 5:22 and may this water that **c** the
Ezra 6:12 And may the God who **c** His name
Job 20: 3 spirit of my understanding **c**
37:13 He **c** it to come, Whether for
37:15 And **c** the light of His cloud
Ps 37: 8 it only **c** harm.
104:14 He **c** the grass to grow for the
107:40 And **c** them to wander in the
119:165 And nothing **c** them to stumble.
135: 7 He **c** the vapors to ascend from
147:18 He **c** His wind to blow, and
Prov 10: 5 in harvest is a son who **c**
10:10 He who winks with the eye **c**
12: 4 But she who **c** shame is like
12:25 Anxiety in the heart of man **c**
14:35 wrath is against him who **c**
17: 2 will rule over a son who **c**
18:18 Casting lots **c** contentions to
19:26 Is a son who **c** shame
28:10 Whoever **c** the upright to go
Isa 61:11 As the garden **c** the things
63:14 the Spirit of the LORD **c** him
64: 2 As fire **c** water to boil—To
Jer 3: 8 Then I saw that for all the **c**
10:13 And He **c** the vapors to ascend
13:16 the LORD your God Before He **c**
51:16 He **c** the vapors to ascend from
Lam 3:32 Though He **c** grief, Yet He will
Ezek 14: 3 put before them that which **c**
14: 4 and puts before him what **c** him
14: 7 and puts before him what **c** him
26: 3 as the sea **c** its waves to come
44:18 with anything that **c** sweat.
Mt 5:29 If your right eye **c** you to sin,
5:30 And if your right hand **c** you to
5:32 except sexual immorality **c** her
18: 6 But whoever **c** one of these
18: 8 If your hand or foot **c** you to
18: 9 And if your eye **c** you to sin,
Mk 9:42 But whoever **c** one of these
9:43 If your hand **c** you to sin, cut
9:45 And if your foot **c** you to sin,
9:47 And if your eye **c** you to sin,
2 Cor 9:11 which **c** thanksgiving through us
Eph 4:16 **c** growth of the body for the
Rev 13:12 and **c** the earth and those who
13:16 He **c** all, both small and great,
21:27 or **c** an abomination or a lie,

CAUSEWAY (KJV) See HIGHWAY

CAUSING (3/3) CAUSE

Isa 30:28 **C** them to err.
Jer 33:12 a dwelling place of shepherds **c**
Ezek 16:21 offered them up to them by **c**

CAUTIOUSLY (1/1)

1 Sam 15:32 to me." So Agag came to him **c**.

CAVALRY (6/6)

1 Ki 9:19 chariots and cities for his **c**,
9:22 of his chariots, and his **c**.
20:20 escaped on a horse with the **c**.
2 Chr 8: 6 cities and the cities of the **c**,
8: 9 of his chariots, and his **c**.
Hab 1: 8 Their **c** comes from afar; They

CAVE (33/31) CAVE'S, CAVES

Gen 19:30 his two daughters dwelt in a **c**.
23: 9 that he may give me the **c** of
23:11 I give you the field and the **c**
23:17 the field and the **c** which was
23:19 buried Sarah his wife in the **c**
23:20 So the field and the **c** that is
25: 9 Ishmael buried him in the **c** of
49:29 me with my fathers in the **c**
49:30 in the **c** that is in the field
49:32 The field and the **c** that is
50:13 and buried him in the **c** of the
Josh 10:16 and hidden themselves in a **c**
10:17 been found hidden in the **c** at
10:18 against the mouth of the **c**,
10:22 said, "Open the mouth of the **c**,
10:22 five kings to me from the **c**.
10:23 five kings to him from the **c**:
10:27 cast them into the **c** where they
1 Sam 22: 1 there and escaped to the **c** of
24: 3 the road, where there was a **c**;
24: 3 in the recesses of the **c**.
24: 7 And Saul got up from the **c** and
24: 8 afterward, went out of the **c**,
24:10 you today into my hand in the **c**,
2 Sam 23:13 and came to David at the **c** of
1 Ki 18: 4 and hidden them, fifty to a **c**,
18:13 LORD's prophets, fifty to a **c**,
19: 9 And there he went into a **c**,
19:13 stood in the entrance of the **c**.
1 Chr 11:15 into the **c** of Adullam; and the
Ps 57: he fled from Saul into the **c**.
142: A Prayer when he was in the **c**.
Jn 11:38 came to the tomb. It was a **c**,

CAVE'S (2/2) CAVE

Josh 10:27 stones against the **c** mouth,
Jer 48:28 In the sides of the **c** mouth.

CAVES (8/8) CAVE

Judg 6: 2 for themselves the dens, the **c**,
1 Sam 13: 6 then the people hid in **c**,
Job 30: 6 In **c** of the earth and the
Isa 2:19 And into the **c** of the earth,
Ezek 33:27 are in the strongholds and **c**
Nah 2:12 Filled his **c** with prey, And
Heb 11:38 in dens and **c** of the earth.
Rev 6:15 hid themselves in the **c** and in

CEASE (72/72) CEASED, CEASES, CEASING

Gen 8:22 And day and night Shall not **c**.
Ex 9:29 the LORD; the thunder will **c**,
Num 8:25 age of fifty years they must **c**
Deut 15:11 For the poor will never **c** from
32:26 make the memory of them to **c**
Josh 22:25 would make our descendants **c**
Judg 2:19 They did not **c** from their own
9: 9 Should I **c** giving my oil, With
9:11 Should I **c** my sweetness and my
9:13 Should I **c** my new wine, Which
15: 7 on you, and after that I will **c**.
20:28 brother Benjamin, or shall I **c**?
1 Sam 7: 8 Do not **c** to cry out to the LORD
9: 5 lest my father **c** caring about
2 Chr 25:16 **C**! Why should you be killed?"
Ezra 4:21 the command to make these men **c**,
4:23 by force of arms made them **c**.
5: 5 that they could not make them **c**
Neh 4:11 them and cause the work to **c**.
6: 3 Why should the work **c** while I
Job 3:17 There the wicked **c** from
6:17 they **c** to flow; When it is
10:20 **C**! Leave me alone, that I may
14: 7 its tender shoots will not **c**.
Ps 35:15 tore at me and did not **c**;
37: 8 **C** from anger, and forsake wrath
46: 9 He makes wars **c** to the end of
49: 8 And it shall **c** forever—
85: 4 cause Your anger toward us to **c**.
89:44 You have made his glory **c**,
Prov 18:18 lots causes contentions to **c**,
19:27 **C** listening to instruction, my
22:10 strife and reproach will **c**.
23: 4 your own understanding, **c**!
Eccl 12: 3 When the grinders **c** because
Isa 1:16 **C** to do evil,
10:25 and the indignation will **c**,
16:10 I have made their shouting **c**.
17: 1 Damascus will **c** from being a
17: 3 The fortress also will **c** from
21: 2 its sighing I have made to **c**.
30:11 the Holy One of Israel To **c**
33: 1 When you **c** plundering,
Jer 7:34 Then I will cause to **c** from the
14:17 and day, And let them not **c**;
16: 9 I will cause to **c** from this
17: 8 Nor will **c** from yielding
31:36 the seed of Israel shall also **c**
36:29 and cause man and beast to **c**
48:35 I will cause to **c** in Moab The
Lam 3:49 My eyes flow and do not **c**,
Ezek 6: 6 may be broken and made to **c**,
7:24 the pomp of the strong to **c**,
16:41 and I will make you **c** playing
23:27 Thus I will make you **c** your
23:48 I will cause lewdness to **c**
30:10 make a multitude of Egypt to **c**
30:13 And cause the images to **c** from
30:18 her arrogant strength shall **c**
33:28 her arrogant strength shall **c**,
34:10 I will cause them to **c** feeding
34:25 and cause wild beasts to **c** from
Hos 2:11 also cause all her mirth to **c**,
Am 7: 5 Then I said: "O Lord GOD, **c**,
Acts 5:42 they did not **c** teaching and
6:13 This man does not **c** to speak
13:10 will you not **c** perverting the
20:31 for three years I did not **c** to
1 Cor 13: 8 are tongues, they will **c**;
Eph 1:16 do not **c** to give thanks for you,
Col 1: 9 do not **c** to pray for you, and
2 Pe 2:14 of adultery and that cannot **c**

CEASED (35/33) CEASE

Gen 11: 8 and they **c** building the city.
Ex 9:33 then the thunder and the hail **c**,
9:34 the hail, and the thunder had **c**,
Josh 5:12 Then the manna **c** on the day
Judg 5: 7 Village life **c**,
5: 7 it **c** in Israel, Until I,
1 Sam 2: 5 And the hungry have **c** to
10: 2 And now your father has **c**
2 Ki 4: 6 another vessel." So the oil **c**.
2 Chr 16: 5 he stopped building Ramah and **c**
25:16 Then the prophet **c**, and said,
Ezra 4:24 of God which is at Jerusalem **c**,
Job 32: 1 So these three men **c** answering
Ps 36: 3 He has **c** to be wise and to do
77: 8 Has His mercy **c** forever?
Isa 14: 4 "How the oppressor has **c**,
14: 4 The golden city **c**!
Jer 51:30 mighty men of Babylon have **c**
Lam 5:14 The elders have **c** gathering
5:15 The joy of our heart has **c**;
Hos 4:10 Because they have **c** obeying
Jon 1:15 and the sea **c** from its raging.
Mt 14:32 got into the boat, the wind **c**.
Mk 4:39 be still!" And the wind **c** and
6:51 boat to them, and the wind **c**.
Lk 7:45 but this woman has not **c** to
8:24 raging of the water. And they **c**,
9:36 When the voice had **c**,
11: 1 in a certain place, when He **c**,
Acts 20: 1 After the uproar had **c**,
21:14 he would not be persuaded, we **c**,
Gal 5:11 the offense of the cross has **c**.
Heb 4:10 His rest has himself also **c**
10: 2 For then would they not have **c**
1 Pe 4: 1 has suffered in the flesh has **c**

CEASES (8/7) CEASE

Num 9:13 and **c** to keep the Passover,
Ps 12: 1 for the godly man **c**! For the
Prov 26:20 is no talebearer, strife **c**.
Isa 16: 4 is at an end, Devastation **c**,
24: 8 The mirth of the tambourine **c**,
24: 8 ends, The joy of the harp **c**.
33: 8 lie waste, The traveling man **c**.
Hos 7: 4 He **c** stirring the fire after

CEASING (7/7) CEASE

1 Sam 12:23 sin against the LORD in **c** to
Ps 77: 2 out in the night without **c**;
Rom 1: 9 that without **c** I make mention
1 Th 1: 3 remembering without **c** your work
2:13 we also thank God without **c**,
5:17 pray without **c**,

2 Tim 1: 3 as without **c** I remember you in

CEDAR (52/49) CEDARS

Lev 14: 4 **c** wood, scarlet, and hyssop.
14: 6 the **c** wood and the scarlet and
14:49 **c** wood, scarlet, and hyssop.
14:51 and he shall take the **c** wood,
14:52 with the **c** wood, the hyssop,
Num 19: 6 And the priest shall take **c** wood
2 Sam 5:11 and **c** trees, and carpenters and
7: 2 now, I dwell in a house of **c**,
7: 7 you not built Me a house of **c**?
1 Ki 4:33 from the **c** tree of Lebanon even
5: 8 all you desire concerning the **c**
5:10 Then Hiram gave Solomon **c** and
6: 9 with beams and boards of **c**.
6:10 attached to the temple with **c**
6:15 walls of the temple with **c**
6:16 with **c** boards; he built it
6:18 The inside of the temple was **c**,
6:18 and open flowers. All was **c**;
6:20 and overlaid the altar of **c**.
6:36 of hewn stone and a row of **c**
7: 2 with four rows of **c** pillars,
7: 2 and **c** beams on the pillars.
7: 3 And it was paneled with **c**
7: 7 and it was paneled with **c**
7:11 hewn to size, and **c** wood.
7:12 of hewn stones and a row of **c**
9:11 had supplied Solomon with **c**
10:27 and he made **c** trees as abundant
2 Ki 14: 9 was in Lebanon sent to the **c**
1 Chr 14: 1 and **c** trees, with masons and
17: 1 now, I dwell in a house of **c**,
17: 6 you not built Me a house of **c**?
22: 4 and **c** trees in abundance; for
22: 4 those from Tyre brought much **c**
2 Chr 2: 8 Also send me **c** and cypress and
9:27 and he made **c** trees as abundant
25:18 was in Lebanon sent to the **c**
Ezra 3: 7 of Sidon and Tyre to bring **c**
Job 40:17 He moves his tail like a **c**;
Ps 92:12 He shall grow like a **c** in
Song 1:17 The beams of our houses are **c**,
8: 9 enclose her With boards of **c**.
Isa 41:19 plant in the wilderness the **c**
Jer 22:14 Paneling it with **c** And
22:15 you enclose yourself in **c**?
Ezek 17: 3 to Lebanon And took from the **c**
17:22 highest branches of the high **c**
17:23 bear fruit, and be a majestic **c**.
27: 5 They took a **c** from Lebanon to
31: 3 Indeed Assyria was a **c** in
Zeph 2:14 For He will lay bare the **c**
Zech 11: 2 for the **c** has fallen, Because

CEDARS (22/21) CEDAR

Num 24: 6 Like **c** beside the waters.
Judg 9:15 the bramble And devour the **c**
1 Ki 5: 6 command that they cut down **c**
2 Ki 19:23 I will cut down its tall **c**
2 Chr 1:15 and he made **c** as abundant as
2: 3 and sent him **c** to build himself
Ps 29: 5 voice of the LORD breaks the **c**,
29: 5 the LORD splinters the **c** of
80:10 And the mighty **c** with its
104:16 The **c** of Lebanon which He
148: 9 Fruitful trees and all **c**;
Song 5:15 Lebanon, Excellent as the **c**.
Isa 2:13 Upon all the **c** of Lebanon that
9:10 we will replace them with **c**.
14: 8 And the **c** of Lebanon,
37:24 I will cut down its tall **c**
44:14 He cuts down **c** for himself,
Jer 22: 7 shall cut down your choice **c**
22:23 Making your nest in the **c**,
Ezek 31: 8 The **c** in the garden of God
Am 2: 9 was like the height of the **c**,
Zech 11: 1 That fire may devour your **c**.

CEDRON (KJV) See KIDRON

CEILING (3/3)

1 Ki 6:15 floor of the temple to the **c**
6:16 of the temple, from floor to **c**,
7: 7 with cedar from floor to **c**.

CELEBRATE (5/5) CELEBRATED

Lev 23:32 you shall **c** your sabbath."
23:41 You shall **c** it in the seventh
Neh 12:27 to bring them to Jerusalem to **c**
Esth 9:21 among them that they should **c**
9:27 that without fail they should **c**

CELEBRATED (3/3) CELEBRATE

Ezra 6:16 **c** the dedication of this house
Esth 9:19 dwelt in the unwalled towns **c**
Mt 14: 6 But when Herod's birthday was **c**,

CELESTIAL (2/1)

1 Cor 15:40 There are also **c** bodies and
15:40 but the glory of the **c** is one,

CELLARS (KJV) See PRODUCE, STORE

CELLS (1/1)

Jer 37:16 entered the dungeon and the **c**,

CENCHREA (2/2)

Acts 18:18 He had his hair cut off at **C**,
Rom 16: 1 is a servant of the church in **C**,

CENSER (12/10) CENSERS

Lev 10: 1 each took his **c** and put fire in
16:12 Then he shall take a **c** full of
Num 16:17 Let each take his **c** and put
16:17 and each of you bring his **c**
16:17 you and Aaron, each with his **c**.
16:18 So every man took his **c**,
16:46 Take a **c** and put fire in it from
2 Chr 26:19 and he had a **c** in his hand to
Ezek 8:11 Each man had a **c** in his hand,
Heb 9: 4 which had the golden **c** and the
Rev 8: 3 angel, having a golden **c**,
8: 5 Then the angel took the **c**,

CENSERS (7/7) CENSER

Num 16: 6 "Do this: Take **c**,
16:17 LORD, two hundred and fifty **c**;
16:37 to pick up the **c** out of the
16:38 The **c** of these men who sinned
16:39 the priest took the bronze **c**,
1 Ki 7:50 and the **c** of pure gold; and the
2 Chr 4:22 and the **c** of pure gold. As for

CENSUS (13/12)

Ex 30:12 When you take the **c** of the
Num 1: 2 Take a **c** of all the congregation
1:49 nor take a **c** of them among the
4: 2 Take a **c** of the sons of Kohath
4:22 Also take a **c** of the sons of
26: 2 Take a **c** of all the congregation
26: 4 Take a **c** of the people
2 Ki 12: 4 each man's **c** money, each man's
1 Chr 27:24 the son of Zeruiah began a **c**,
27:24 upon Israel because of this **c**;
2 Chr 2:17 after the **c** in which David his
Lk 2: 2 This **c** first took place while
Acts 5:37 rose up in the days of the **c**,

CENTER (6/6)

Judg 9:37 are coming down from the **c** of
Ezek 48: 8 with the sanctuary in the **c**.
48:10 of the LORD shall be in the **c**.
48:15 and the city shall be in the **c**.
48:21 the temple shall be in the **c**.
Jn 19:18 either side, and Jesus in the **c**.

CENTURION (20/20) CENTURION'S, CENTURIONS

Mt 8: 5 a **c** came to Him, pleading with
8: 8 The **c** answered and said, "Lord,
8:13 Then Jesus said to the **c**,
27:54 So when the **c** and those with
Mk 15:39 So when the **c**, who stood
15:44 dead; and summoning the **c**,
15:45 So when he found out from the **c**,
Lk 7: 6 the **c** sent friends to Him,
23:47 So when the **c** saw what had
Acts 10: 1 a **c** of what was called the
10:22 they said, "Cornelius the **c**,
22:25 Paul said to the **c** who stood
22:26 When the **c** heard that, he went
24:23 So he commanded the **c** to keep
27: 1 a **c** of the Augustan Regiment.
27: 6 There the **c** found an Alexandrian
27:11 Nevertheless the **c** was more
27:31 Paul said to the **c** and the
27:43 But the **c**, wanting to save
28:16 the **c** delivered the prisoners

CENTURION'S (1/1) CENTURION

Lk 7: 2 And a certain **c** servant, who was

CENTURIONS (3/3) CENTURION

Acts 21:32 immediately took soldiers and **c**,
23:17 Then Paul called one of the **c** to
23:23 And he called for two **c**,

CEPHAS (6/6) PETER, SIMON

Jn 1:42 You shall be called **C**" (which
1 Cor 1:12 am of Apollos," or "I am of **C**,
3:22 whether Paul or Apollos or **C**,
9: 5 the brothers of the Lord, and **C**?
15: 5 and that He was seen by **C**,
Gal 2: 9 and when James, **C**, and John,

CERAMIC (2/2)

Dan 2:41 the iron mixed with **c** clay.
2:43 As you saw iron mixed with **c**

CEREMONIALLY (1/1) CEREMONY

Num 8: 6 of Israel and cleanse them **c**.

CEREMONIES (2/2) CEREMONY

Num 9: 3 to all its rites and **c** you
Jer 34: 5 as in the **c** of your fathers,

CEREMONY (1/1) CEREMONIALLY, CEREMONIES

Num 9:14 Passover and according to its **c**;

CERTAIN (136/134) CERTAINLY, CERTAINTY, UNCERTAIN

Gen 28:11 So he came to a **c** place and
37:15 Now a **c** man found him, and there
38: 1 and visited a **c** Adullamite
38: 2 a daughter of a **c** Canaanite
Ex 16: 4 go out and gather a **c** quota
Lev 27: 2 consecrates by a vow **c** persons
Num 9: 6 Now there were **c** men who were
Deut 13:14 if it is indeed true and **c**
17: 4 if it is indeed true and **c**
25: 2 with a **c** number of blows.
Josh 23:13 know for **c** that the LORD your
Judg 9:53 But a **c** woman dropped an upper
13: 2 Now there was a **c** man from
19: 1 that there was a **c** Levite
19:22 suddenly **c** men of the city,
Ruth 1: 1 And a **c** man of Bethlehem,
1 Sam 1: 1 Now there was a **c** man of
21: 7 Now a **c** man of the servants of
2 Sam 18:10 Now a **c** man saw it and told
1 Ki 2:37 know for **c** you shall surely
2:42 Know for **c** that on the day you
11:17 he and **c** Edomites of his
20:35 Now a **c** man of the sons of the
22:34 Now a **c** man drew a bow at
2 Ki 4: 1 A **c** woman of the wives of the
8: 6 king appointed a **c** officer
19:35 And it came to pass on a **c**
2 Chr 18:33 Now a **c** man drew a bow at
Ezra 10:16 with **c** heads of the fathers'
Neh 11:23 them that a **c** portion should
13: 6 Then after **c** days I obtained
Esth 2: 5 the citadel there was a **c** Jew
3: 8 There is a **c** people scattered
Jer 26:15 But know for **c** that if you put
26:17 Then **c** of the elders of the land
41: 5 that **c** men came from Shechem,
Ezek 20: 1 that **c** of the elders of Israel
Dan 2: 8 I know for **c** that you would gain
2:45 pass after this. The dream is **c**,
3: 8 at that time **c** Chaldeans
3:12 There are **c** Jews whom you have
3:20 And he commanded **c** mighty men of
8:13 holy one said to that **c** one
10: 5 a **c** man clothed in linen, whose
Mt 8:19 Then a **c** scribe came and said to
18:23 of heaven is like a **c** king
21:33 There was a **c** landowner who
22: 2 kingdom of heaven is like a **c**
26:18 Go into the city to a **c** man, and
Mk 5:25 Now a **c** woman had a flow of
14:51 Now a **c** young man followed Him,
15:21 Then they compelled a **c** man,
Lk 1: 5 a **c** priest named Zacharias, of
5:12 when He was in a **c** city,
5:17 Now it happened on a **c** day, as
7: 2 And a **c** centurion's servant, who
7:41 There was a **c** creditor who had
8: 2 and **c** women who had been healed
8:22 on a **c** day, that He got into a
8:27 there met Him a **c** man from the
10:25 a **c** lawyer stood up and tested
10:30 A **c** man went down from
10:31 Now by chance a **c** priest came
10:33 But a **c** Samaritan, as he
10:38 that He entered a **c** village
10:38 and a **c** woman named Martha
11: 1 as He was praying in a **c** place,
11:27 that a **c** woman from the crowd
11:37 a **c** Pharisee asked Him to dine
12:16 The ground of a **c** rich man
13: 6 A **c** man had a fig tree planted
14: 2 there was a **c** man before Him
14:16 A **c** man gave a great supper and
15:11 A **c** man had two sons.
16: 1 There was a **c** rich man who had a
16:19 There was a **c** rich man who was
16:20 But there was a **c** beggar named
17:12 Then as He entered a **c** village,
18: 2 There was in a **c** city a judge
18:18 Now a **c** ruler asked Him,
18:35 that a **c** blind man sat by the
19:12 A **c** nobleman went into a far
20: 9 A **c** man planted a vineyard,
21: 2 and He saw also a **c** poor widow
22:56 And a **c** servant girl, seeing him
23:19 into prison for a **c** rebellion
23:26 they laid hold of a **c** man,
24: 1 and **c** other women with them,
24:22 and **c** women of our company, who
24:24 And **c** of those who were with
Jn 4:46 And there was a **c** nobleman
5: 4 angel went down at a **c** time
5: 5 Now a **c** man was there who had an
11: 1 Now a **c** man was sick, Lazarus
12:20 Now there were **c** Greeks among
Acts 3: 2 And a **c** man lame from his
5: 1 But a **c** man named Ananias, with
5: 2 and brought a **c** part and laid
8: 9 But there was a **c** man called
9:10 Now there was a **c** disciple at
9:33 There he found a **c** man named
9:36 At Joppa there was a **c** disciple

10: 1 There was a c man in Caesarea
12:11 Now I know for c that the Lord
13: 1 Antioch there were c prophets
13: 6 they found a c sorcerer, a
14: 8 And in Lystra a c man without
15: 1 And c men came down from Judea
15: 2 Paul and Barnabas and c others
16: 1 a c disciple was there, named
16: 1 the son of a c Jewish woman
16:14 Now a c woman named Lydia heard
16:16 that a c slave girl possessed
17:18 Then c Epicurean and Stoic
18: 2 And he found a c Jew named
18: 7 and entered the house of a c man
18:24 Now a c Jew named Apollos, born
19:24 For a c man named Demetrius, a
20: 9 And in a window sat a c young
21:10 a c prophet named Agabus came
21:16 brought with them a c Mnason
22:12 Then a c Ananias, a devout man
22:30 he wanted to know for c why he
24: 1 with the elders and a c orator
25:14 There is a c man left a prisoner
25:19 religion and about a c Jesus
25:26 I have nothing c to write to my
27:26 run aground on a c island.
Rom 15:26 Achaia to make a c contribution
Gal 2:12 for before c men came from
1 Tim 6: 7 and it is c we can carry
Heb 2: 6 But one testified in a c place,
4: 4 For He has spoken in a c place
4: 7 again He designates a c day,
10:27 but a c fearful expectation of
Jude 4 For c men have crept in

CERTAINLY (51/51) CERTAIN

Gen 15:13 Know c that your descendants
18:10 I will c return to you according
26:28 We have c seen that the LORD is
44:15 know that such a man as I can c
Ex 3:12 I will c be with you. And this
22: 4 If the theft is c found alive in
Lev 5:19 he has c trespassed against the
24:16 All the congregation shall c
Num 14:23 they c shall not see the land of
22:17 for I will c honor you greatly,
Deut 21:14 but you c shall not sell her
22: 1 you shall c bring them back to
1 Sam 14:45 C not! As the LORD lives, not
20: 3 Your father c knows that I have
20: 9 For if I knew c that evil was
23:10 Your servant has c heard that
25:28 For the LORD will c make for
1 Ki 1:30 so I c will do this day."
2 Ki 8:10 You shall c recover.' However
Ps 39: 5 C every man at his best state
66:19 But c God has heard me; He
Prov 23: 5 For riches c make themselves
Jer 6:19 I will c bring calamity on this
8: 8 the false pen of the scribe c
13:12 Do we not c know that every
25:28 You shall c drink!
36:29 that the king of Babylon will c
40:14 Do you c know that Baalis the
42:19 Do not go to Egypt!' Know c that
42:22 know c that you shall die by
44:17 But we will c do whatever has
Dan 11:10 and one shall c come and
11:13 and shall c come at the end of
Lk 20:16 heard it they said, "C not!"
23:47 C this was a righteous Man!"
Acts 21:22 The assembly must c meet, for
Rom 3: 4 C not! Indeed, let God be true
3: 6 C not! For then how will God
3:31 C not! On the contrary, we
6: 2 C not! How shall we who died to
6: 5 c we also shall be in the
6:15 law but under grace? C not!
7: 7 C not! On the contrary, I would
7:13 C not! But sin, that it might
9:14 with God? C not!
11: 1 C not! For I also am an
11:11 C not! But through their fall,
1 Cor 5:10 Yet I c did not mean with the
6:15 members of a harlot? C not!
Gal 2:17 a minister of sin? C not!
3:21 C not! For if there had been a

CERTAINTY (3/3) CERTAIN

1 Sam 23:23 and come back to me with c,
Prov 22:21 I may make you know the c of
Lk 1: 4 that you may know the c of those

CERTIFICATE (7/7) CERTIFIED

Deut 24: 1 and he writes her a c of
24: 3 detests her and writes her a c
Isa 50: 1 Where is the c of your mother's
Jer 3: 8 put her away and given her a c
Mt 5:31 let him give her a c of
19: 7 did Moses command to give a c
Mk 10: 4 permitted a man to write a c

CERTIFIED (1/1) CERTIFICATE

Jn 3:33 received His testimony has c

CHAFF (15/15)

Job 21:18 And like c that a storm
Ps 1: 4 But are like the c which the
35: 5 Let them be like c before the
83:13 Like the c before the wind!
Isa 5:24 And the flame consumes the c,
17:13 And be chased like the c of
29: 5 of the terrible ones Like c
33:11 You shall conceive c,
41:15 And make the hills like c.
Jer 23:28 What is the c to the wheat?"
Dan 2:35 and became like c from the
Hos 13: 3 Like c blown off from a
Zeph 2: 2 Or the day passes like c,
Mt 3:12 but He will burn up the c with
Lk 3:17 but the c He will burn with

CHAIN (10/10) CHAINED, CHAINS, CHAINWORK

Gen 41:42 of fine linen and put a gold c
Lam 3: 7 He has made my c heavy.
Ezek 7:23 Make a c, For the land is
16:11 and a c on your neck.
Dan 5: 7 with purple and have a c of
5:16 with purple and have a c of
5:29 with purple and put a c of
Acts 28:20 Israel I am bound with this c.
2 Tim 1:16 me, and was not ashamed of my c;
Rev 20: 1 bottomless pit and a great c

CHAINED (3/3) CHAIN

Mk 15: 7 who was c with his fellow
2 Tim 2: 9 but the word of God is not c.
Heb 13: 3 Remember the prisoners as if c

CHAINS (49/47) CHAIN

Ex 28:14 and you shall make two c of pure
28:14 and fasten the braided c to the
28:22 You shall make c for the
28:24 shall put the two braided c
28:25 two ends of the two braided c
39:15 And they made c for the
39:17 And they put the two braided c
39:18 two ends of the two braided c
Judg 8:26 and besides the c that were
1 Ki 6:21 He stretched gold c across the
7:17 seven c for one capital and
Ps 107:14 And broke their c in pieces.
149: 8 To bind their kings with c,
Prov 1: 9 And c about your neck.
Song 1:10 Your neck with c of gold.
Isa 40:19 the silversmith casts silver c.
45:14 you, They shall come over in c;
Jer 40: 1 he had taken him bound in c
40: 4 I free you this day from the c
Ezek 19: 4 And they brought him with c to
19: 9 They put him in a cage with c,
Nah 3:10 her great men were bound in c.
Mk 5: 3 could bind him, not even with c,
5: 4 been bound with shackles and c.
5: 4 And the c had been pulled apart
Lk 8:29 bound with c and shackles; and
Acts 12: 6 bound with two c between two
12: 7 Arise quickly!" And his c fell
16:26 were opened and everyone's c
20:23 saying that c and tribulations
21:33 him to be bound with two c;
22: 5 went to Damascus to bring in c
23:29 him deserving of death or c.
26:29 as I am, except for these c.
26:31 nothing deserving of death or c.
Eph 6:20 which I am an ambassador in c;
Phil 1: 7 inasmuch as both in my c and in
1:13 that my c are in Christ;
1:14 having become confident by my c,
1:16 to add affliction to my c;
Col 4: 3 for which I am also in c,
4:18 own hand—Paul. Remember my c.
2 Tim 2: 9 even to the point of c;
Phm 1:10 I have begotten while in my c,
1:13 he might minister to me in my c
Heb 10:34 had compassion on me in my c,
11:36 and of c and imprisonment.
2 Pe 2: 4 and delivered them into c of
Jude 6 has reserved in everlasting c

CHAINWORK (4/3) CHAIN

1 Ki 7:17 network, with wreaths of c,
2 Chr 3: 5 and he carved palm trees and c
3:16 He made wreaths of c,
3:16 put them on the wreaths of c.

CHAIR (1/1)

2 Ki 4:10 and a table and a c and a

CHALCEDONY (1/1)

Rev 21:19 second sapphire, the third c,

CHALCOL (1/1) CALCOL

1 Ki 4:31 the Ezrahite, and Heman, C,

CHALDEA (7/7) BABYLON, CHALDEAN, CHALDEANS, CHALDEANS'

Jer 50:10 And C shall become plunder;
51:24 And all the inhabitants of C
51:35 be upon the inhabitants of C!
Ezek 11:24 by the Spirit of God into C,
16:29 as the land of the trader, C;
23:15 manner of the Babylonians of C,
23:16 sent messengers to them in C.

CHALDEAN (3/3) CHALDEA, CHALDEANS

Ezra 5:12 king of Babylon, the C,
Jer 39: 5 But the C army pursued them and
Dan 2:10 any magician, astrologer, or C.

CHALDEANS (79/79) CHALDEA, CHALDEAN, CHALDEANS', CHALDEES

Gen 11:28 his native land, in Ur of the C.
11:31 out with them from Ur of the C
15: 7 brought you out of Ur of the C,
2 Ki 24: 2 against him raiding bands of C,
25: 4 even though the C were still
25: 5 But the army of the C pursued
25:10 And all the army of the C who
25:13 the C broke in pieces, and
25:24 afraid of the servants of the C.
25:25 as well as the C who were with
25:26 for they were afraid of the C.
2 Chr 36:17 against them the king of the C,
Neh 9: 7 brought him out of Ur of the C,
Job 1:17 The C formed three bands, raided
Isa 23:13 Behold, the land of the C,
43:14 all down as fugitives—The C,
47: 1 O daughter of the C! For you
47: 5 darkness, O daughter of the C;
48:14 arm shall be against the C.
48:20 from Babylon! Flee from the C!
Jer 21: 4 the king of Babylon and the C
21: 9 goes out and defects to the C
22:25 Babylon and the hand of the C.
24: 5 good, into the land of the C.
25:12 that nation, the land of the C,
32: 4 escape from the hand of the C,
32: 5 "though you fight with the C,
32:24 given into the hand of the C
32:25 given into the hand of the C.
32:28 city into the hand of the C,
32:29 And the C who fight against this
32:43 given into the hand of the C.
33: 5 'They come to fight with the C,
35:11 for fear of the army of the C
37: 5 and when the C who were
37: 8 And the C shall come back and
37: 9 The C will surely depart from
37:10 the whole army of the C who
37:11 when the army of the C left
37:13 You are defecting to the C!"
37:14 I am not defecting to the C.
38: 2 but he who goes over to the C
38:18 be given into the hand of the C;
38:19 Jews who have defected to the C,
38:23 wives and children to the C.
39: 8 And the C burned the king's
40: 9 not be afraid to serve the C.
40:10 at Mizpah and serve the C who
41: 3 and the C who were found there,
41:18 because of the C;
43: 3 us into the hand of the C,
50: 1 and against the land of the C
50: 8 Go out of the land of the C;
50:25 of hosts In the land of the C.
50:35 "A sword is against the C,
50:45 against the land of the C:
51: 4 shall fall in the land of the C,
51:54 from the land of the C,
52: 7 even though the C were near
52: 8 But the army of the C pursued
52:14 And all the army of the C who
52:17 the C broke in pieces, and
Ezek 1: 3 in the land of the C by the
12:13 Babylon, to the land of the C;
23:14 Images of C portrayed in
23:23 The Babylonians, All the C,
Dan 1: 4 and literature of the C.
2: 2 and the C to tell the king his
2: 4 Then the C spoke to the king in
2: 5 king answered and said to the C,
2:10 The C answered the king, and
3: 8 at that time certain C came
4: 7 the astrologers, the C,
5: 7 bring in the astrologers, the C,
5:11 the magicians, astrologers, C,
5:30 night Belshazzar, king of the C,
9: 1 king over the realm of the C—
Hab 1: 6 indeed I am raising up the C,
Acts 7: 4 came out of the land of the C

CHALDEANS' (1/1) CHALDEANS

Isa 13:19 The beauty of the C pride,

CHALDEES (KJV) See CHALDEANS

CHALK (1/1) CHALKSTONES

Isa 44:13 rule, He marks one out with c;

CHALKSTONES (1/1) CHALK

Isa 27: 9 the stones of the altar Like c

CHAMBER (32/30) CHAMBERS

Gen 43:30 And he went into his c and
Judg 3:20 upstairs in his cool private c)

3:24 to his needs in the cool **c**.
2 Sam 18:33 and went up to the **c** over the
1 Ki 1:15 So Bathsheba went into the **c** to
6: 6 The lowest **c** was five cubits
20:30 into the city, into an inner **c**.
22:25 when you go into an inner **c** to
2 Ki 23:11 by the **c** of Nathan-Melech, the
23:12 the upper **c** of Ahaz, which the
2 Chr 18:24 when you go into an inner **c** to
Ezra 10: 6 and went into the **c** of
Job 37: 9 From the **c** of the south
Ps 19: 5 bridegroom coming out of his **c**,
132: 3 I will not go into the **c** of my
Song 3: 4 And into the **c** of her who
Jer 35: 4 into the **c** of the sons of Hanan
35: 4 which was by the **c** of the
35: 4 above the **c** of Maaseiah the son
36:10 in the **c** of Gemariah the son of
36:12 house, into the scribe's **c**;
36:20 stored the scroll in the **c** of
36:21 it from Elishama the scribe's **c**.
Ezek 40: 7 Each gate **c** was one rod long
40:13 from the roof of one gate **c**
40:38 There was a **c** and its
40:45 This **c** which faces south is for
40:46 The **c** which faces north is for
41: 5 The width of each side **c** all
42: 1 and he brought me into the **c**
42:14 not go out of the holy **c** into
Joel 2:16 bridegroom go out from his **c**,

CHAMBERLAIN (KJV) See (PERSONAL) AIDE, OFFICER

CHAMBERS (58/48) CHAMBER

1 Ki 6: 5 wall of the temple he built **c**
6: 5 Thus he made side **c** all around
6:10 And he built side **c** against the
1 Chr 9:26 And they had charge over the **c**
9:33 Levites, who lodged in the **c**,
23:28 in the courts and in the **c**,
28:11 its treasuries, its upper **c**,
28:11 its upper chambers, its inner **c**,
28:12 of all the **c** all around, of the
Ezra 8:29 in the **c** of the house of the
Job 9: 9 And the **c** of the south;
Ps 104: 3 lays the beams of His upper **c**
104:13 the hills from His upper **c**;
105:30 Even in the **c** of their kings.
Prov 7:27 Descending to the **c** of death.
Song 1: 4 king has brought me into his **c**.
Isa 26:20 Come, my people, enter your **c**,
Jer 22:13 by unrighteousness And his **c**
22:14 a wide house with spacious **c**,
35: 2 of the LORD, into one of the **c**,
Ezek 21:14 That enters their private **c**.
40: 7 between the gate **c** was a
40:10 gateway were three gate **c** on
40:12 a space in front of the gate **c**,
40:12 the gate **c** were six cubits on
40:16 window frames in the gate **c**
40:17 and there were **c** and a
40:17 thirty **c** faced the pavement.
40:21 Its gate **c**, three on this
40:29 Also its gate **c**,
40:33 Also its gate **c**,
40:36 also its gate **c**,
40:44 the inner gate were the **c** for
41: 6 The side **c** were in three
41: 6 thirty **c** in each story; they
41: 6 which were for the side **c** all
41: 7 the side **c** became wider all
41: 8 the foundation of the side **c**,
41: 9 of the outer wall of the side **c**
41: 9 by the place of the side **c** of
41:10 between it and the wall **c**
41:11 The doors of the side **c** opened
41:26 also on the side **c** of the temple
42: 4 In front of the **c**,
42: 5 Now the upper **c** were shorter,
42: 7 outside ran parallel to the **c**,
42: 7 chambers, at the front of the **c**,
42: 8 The length of the **c** toward the
42: 9 At the lower **c** was the entrance
42:10 Also there were **c** in the
42:11 appearance was like the **c**
42:12 to the doors of the **c** that
42:13 The north **c** and the south
42:13 north chambers and the south **c**,
42:13 are the holy **c** where the
44:19 leave them in the holy **c**,
45: 5 they shall have twenty **c** as a
46:19 into the holy **c** of the priests

CHAMELEON (1/1)

Lev 11:30 the sand lizard, and the **c**.

CHAMOIS (KJV) See (MOUNTAIN) SHEEP

CHAMPAIGN (KJV) See PLAIN

CHAMPION (3/3)

1 Sam 17: 4 And a **c** went out from the camp
17:23 with them, there was the **c**,
17:51 Philistines saw that their **c**

CHANAAN (KJV) See CANAAN

CHANCE (4/4)

1 Sam 6: 9 us— it happened to us by **c**.
2 Sam 1: 6 As I happened by **c** to be on
Eccl 9:11 But time and **c** happen to them
Lk 10:31 Now by **c** a certain priest came

CHANCELLOR (KJV) See COMMANDER

CHANGE (23/23) CHANGED, CHANGERS, CHANGERS', CHANGES, UNCHANGEABLE

Gen 35: 2 and **c** your garments.
Ex 13:17 Lest perhaps the people **c** their
Num 36: 7 children of Israel shall not **c**
36: 9 Thus no inheritance shall **c**
Deut 28:24 The LORD will **c** the rain of
2 Sam 14:20 To bring about this **c** of affairs
Job 14:14 will wait, Till my **c** comes.
14:20 You **c** his countenance and send
17:12 They **c** the night into day;
23:13 unique, and who can make Him **c**?
Ps 15: 4 to his own hurt and does not **c**;
55:19 Selah Because they do not **c**,
102:26 Like a cloak You will **c** them,
Prov 24:21 associate with those given to **c**;
Jer 2:36 do you gad about so much to **c**
13:23 Can the Ethiopian **c** his skin or
Dan 5:10 you, nor let your countenance **c**.
7:25 And shall intend to **c** times
Hos 4: 7 I will **c** their glory into
Mal 3: 6 I am the LORD, I do not **c**;
Acts 6:14 will destroy this place and **c**
Gal 4:20 present with you now and to **c**
Heb 7:12 of necessity there is also a **c**

CHANGED (37/36) CHANGE

Gen 31: 7 father has deceived me and **c**
31:41 and you have **c** my wages ten
41:14 **c** his clothing, and came to
Lev 13:55 if the plague has not **c** its
Num 32:38 Meon (their names being **c**)
1 Sam 21:13 So he **c** his behavior before
2 Sam 12:20 and **c** his clothes; and he went
2 Ki 23:34 and **c** his name to Jehoiakim.
24:17 and **c** his name to Zedekiah.
25:29 So Jehoiachin **c** from his prison
2 Chr 36: 4 and **c** his name to Jehoiakim.
Ps 102:26 them, And they will be **c**.
106:20 Thus they **c** their glory Into
Eccl 8: 1 the sternness of his face is **c**.
Isa 24: 5 **C** the ordinance, Broken the
Jer 2:11 Has a nation **c** its gods,
2:11 But My people have **c** their
34:11 But afterward they **c** their minds
48:11 him, And his scent has not **c**.
52:33 So Jehoiachin **c** from his prison
Lam 4: 1 gold has become dim! How **c**
Dan 2: 9 before me till the time has **c**.
3:19 the expression on his face **c**
4:16 Let his heart be **c** from that
5: 6 Then the king's countenance **c**,
5: 9 troubled, his countenance was **c**,
6: 8 writing, so that it cannot be **c**,
6:15 the king establishes may be **c**.
6:17 Daniel might not be **c**.
7:28 me, and my countenance **c**;
Mic 2: 4 utterly destroyed! He has **c**
Acts 28: 6 they **c** their minds and said
Rom 1:23 and **c** the glory of the
1 Cor 15:51 sleep, but we shall all be **c**—
15:52 and we shall be **c**.
Heb 1:12 up, And they will be **c**.
7:12 For the priesthood being **c**,

CHANGERS (2/2)

Mt 21:12 the tables of the money **c** and
Mk 11:15 the tables of the money **c** and

CHANGERS' (1/1) CHANGE

Jn 2:15 and poured out the **c** money and

CHANGES (12/11) CHANGE

Gen 45:22 **c** of garments; but to Benjamin
45:22 pieces of silver and five **c**
Lev 13:16 Or if the raw flesh **c** and turns
Judg 14:12 linen garments and thirty **c** of
14:13 linen garments and thirty **c** of
14:19 and gave the **c** of clothing to
2 Ki 5: 5 and ten **c** of clothing.
5:22 a talent of silver and two **c**
5:23 with two **c** of garments, and
Job 10:17 **C** and war are ever with me.
Dan 2:21 And He **c** the times and the
Hab 1:11 Then his mind **c**,

CHANNEL (2/2) CHANNELS

Job 38:25 Who has divided a **c** for the
Isa 27:12 From the **c** of the River to the

CHANNELS (4/4) CHANNEL

2 Sam 22:16 Then the **c** of the sea were
Job 28:10 He cuts out **c** in the rocks,
Ps 18:15 Then the **c** of the sea were

Isa 8: 7 He will go up over all his **c**

CHANT (1/1)

Mic 3: 5 people stray; Who **c** "Peace"

CHAPEL (KJV) See SANCTUARY

CHAPITER, CHAPITERS (KJV) See CAPITAL, CAPITALS

C

CHARACTER (3/2)

Rom 5: 4 and perseverance, **c**;
5: 4 perseverance, character; and **c**,
Phil 2:22 But you know his proven **c**,

CHARASHIM (KJV) See GE HARASHIM

CHARCHEMISH (KJV) See CARCHEMISH

CHARCOAL (1/1)

Prov 26:21 As **c** is to burning coals, and

CHARGE (98/93) CHARGED, CHARGERS, CHARGES, CHARGING

Gen 26: 5 obeyed My voice and kept My **c**,
28: 6 he blessed him he gave him a **c**,
Ex 22:25 you shall not **c** him interest.
Lev 8:35 and keep the **c** of the LORD, so
24: 3 Aaron shall be in **c** of it from
24: 4 He shall be in **c** of the lamps on
Num 1:53 and the Levites shall keep **c** of
3:28 thousand six hundred keeping **c**
3:32 oversight of those who kept **c**
3:38 keeping **c** of the sanctuary, to
9:19 children of Israel kept the **c**
9:23 they kept the **c** of the LORD,
18: 8 I Myself have also given you **c**
31:30 them to the Levites who keep **c**
31:47 who kept **c** of the tabernacle of
Deut 11: 1 LORD your God, and keep His **c**,
21: 8 lay innocent blood to the **c** of
23:19 You shall not **c** interest to
23:20 To a foreigner you may **c**
23:20 to your brother you shall not **c**
Josh 22: 3 but have kept the **c** of the
Ruth 2: 5 to his servant who was in **c** of
2: 6 So the servant who was in **c** of
1 Sam 13:21 and the **c** for a sharpening was a
14:27 had not heard his father **c** the
2 Sam 3: 8 and you **c** me today with a fault
20:24 Adoram was in **c** of revenue;
1 Ki 2: 3 And keep the **c** of the LORD your
4:28 each man according to his **c**.
5:14 Adoniram was in **c** of the labor
12:18 who was in **c** of the revenue;
18: 3 who was in **c** of his house.
2 Ki 7:17 whose hand he leaned to have **c**
10: 5 And he who was in **c** of the
10: 5 and he who was in **c** of the
10:22 And he said to the one in **c** of
25:19 the city an officer who had **c**
1 Chr 9:19 were in **c** of the work of the
9:23 and their children were in **c**
9:26 And they had **c** over the
9:27 and they were in **c** of opening
9:28 Now some of them were in **c** of
9:32 of the Kohathites were in **c**
15:22 was instructor in **c** of the
22:12 and give you **c** concerning
2 Chr 10:18 who was in **c** of revenue; but
30:17 therefore the Levites had **c** of
31:12 Cononiah the Levite had **c** of
Neh 7: 2 that I gave the **c** of Jerusalem
11:22 the singers in **c** of the service
12:45 and the gatekeepers kept the **c**
12:45 charge of their God and the **c**
Job 1:22 all this Job did not sin nor **c**
24:12 Yet God does not **c** them with
34:13 Who gave Him **c** over the earth?
Ps 91:11 For He shall give His angels **c**
Song 2: 7 I **c** you, O daughters of
3: 5 I **c** you, O daughters of
5: 8 I **c** you, O daughters of
5: 9 That you so **c** us?
8: 4 I **c** you, O daughters of
Isa 10: 6 of My wrath I will give him **c**,
Jer 39:11 king of Babylon gave **c**
47: 7 the LORD has given it a **c**
52:25 the city an officer who had **c**
Ezek 9: 1 Let those who have **c** over the
40:45 is for the priests who have **c**
40:46 is for the priests who have **c**
44: 8 And you have not kept **c** of My
44: 8 you have set others to keep **c**
44:14 I will make them keep **c** of the
44:15 who kept **c** of My sanctuary when
44:16 to Me, and they shall keep My **c**.
48:11 sanctified, who have kept My **c**,
Dan 6: 4 satraps sought to find some **c**
6: 4 but they could find no **c** or
6: 5 We shall not find any **c** against
Hos 4: 1 For the LORD brings a **c**
12: 2 The LORD also brings a **c**
Jon 1:14 and do not **c** us with innocent
Nah 3: 3 Horsemen **c** with bright sword

Hab 1: 8 Their chargers c ahead;
Zech 3: 7 And likewise have c of My
Mt 4: 6 shall give His angels c
Lk 4:10 shall give His angels c
Acts 7:60 do not c them with this sin."
8:27 who had c of all her treasury,
16:24 Having received such a c,
25:16 for himself concerning the c
Rom 8:33 Who shall bring a c against
1 Cor 9:18 the gospel of Christ without c,
2 Cor 11: 7 gospel of God to you free of c?
1 Th 5:27 I c you by the Lord that this
2 Th 3: 8 we eat anyone's bread free of c,
1 Tim 1: 3 in Ephesus that you may c some
1:18 This c I commit to you, son
5:21 I c you before God and the Lord
2 Tim 4: 1 I c you therefore before God

CHARGED (28/28) CHARGE

Gen 26:11 So Abimelech c all his people,
28: 1 and c him, and said to him:
40: 4 And the captain of the guard c
49:29 Then he c them and said to
Deut 22:17 Now he has c her with shameful
24: 5 not go out to war or be c with
Josh 6:26 Then Joshua c them at that
18: 8 and Joshua c those who went to
1 Sam 14:28 Your father strictly c the
2 Sam 11:19 and c the messenger, saying,
1 Ki 2: 1 and he c Solomon his son,
2 Ki 17:15 whom the LORD had c them that
17:35 had made a covenant and c them,
1 Chr 22: 6 and c him to build a house for
22:13 with which the LORD c Moses
Neh 5:11 that you have c them."
13:19 and c that they must not be
Esth 2:10 for Mordecai had c her not to
2:20 just as Mordecai had c her, for
Jer 32:13 Then I c Baruch before them,
35: 8 in all that he c us, to drink
Mk 8:15 Then He c them, saying, "Take
Lk 5:14 And He c him to tell no one,
8:56 but He c them to tell no one
Acts 23:29 but had nothing c against him
Rom 3: 9 For we have previously c both
1 Th 2:11 and c every one of you, as a
2 Tim 4:16 May it not be c against them.

CHARGER (KJV) See PLATTER

CHARGERS (1/1) CHARGE

Hab 1: 8 Their c charge ahead;

CHARGES (9/7) CHARGE

Deut 22:14 and c her with shameful conduct,
Job 4:18 If He c His angels with
Jer 2: 9 Therefore I will yet bring c
2: 9 children I will bring c.
Hos 2: 2 Bring c against your mother,
2: 2 against your mother, bring c;
Acts 19:38 Let them bring c against one
23:30 to state before you the c
25:27 and not to specify the c

CHARGING (2/2) CHARGE

Prov 28:15 Like a roaring lion and a c
2 Tim 2:14 c them before the Lord not to

CHARIOT (62/54) CHARIOTEERS, CHARIOTS

Gen 41:43 he had him ride in the second c
46:29 So Joseph made ready his c and
Ex 14: 6 So he made ready his c and took
14:25 And He took off their c wheels,
Judg 4:15 and Sisera alighted from his c
5:28 Why is his c so long in coming?
2 Sam 8: 4 Also David hamstrung all the c
1 Ki 7:33 like the workmanship of a c
10:26 whom he stationed in the c
10:29 Now a c that was imported from
12:18 King Rehoboam mounted his c in
18:44 say to Ahab, 'Prepare your c,
20:25 horse for horse and c for
20:25 for horse and chariot for c.
20:33 he had him come up into the c.
22:34 he said to the driver of his c,
22:35 king was propped up in his c,
22:35 wound onto the floor of the c.
22:38 Then someone washed the c at a
2 Ki 2:11 that suddenly a c of fire
2:12 the c of Israel and its
5: 9 went with his horses and c,
5:21 he got down from the c to meet
5:26 the man turned back from his c
9:16 So Jehu rode in a c and went to
9:21 And his c was made ready.
9:21 Judah went out, each in his c;
9:24 and he sank down in his c.
9:27 said, "Shoot him also in the c.
9:28 servants carried him in the c
10:15 took him up to him into the c.
10:16 So they had him ride in his c.
23:30 servants moved his body in a c
1 Chr 18: 4 David also hamstrung all the c
28:18 for the construction of the c,
2 Chr 1:14 whom he stationed in the c
1:17 and imported from Egypt a c
8: 6 and all the c cities and the
9:25 whom he stationed in the c
10:18 King Rehoboam mounted his c
18:33 he said to the driver of his c,
18:34 propped himself up in his c
35:24 took him out of that c and put
35:24 and put him in the second c
Ps 46: 9 He burns the c in the fire.
76: 6 Both the c and horse were cast
104: 3 Who makes the clouds His c,
Isa 21: 7 And he saw a c with a pair of
21: 7 A c of donkeys, and a chariot
21: 7 and a c of camels, And he
21: 9 here comes a c of men with a
43:17 Who brings forth the c and
Jer 51:21 I will break in pieces the c
Mic 1:13 Harness the c to the swift
Zech 6: 2 With the first c were red
6: 2 with the second c black horses,
6: 3 with the third c white horses,
6: 3 and with the fourth c dappled
9:10 I will cut off the c from
Acts 8:28 returning. And sitting in his c,
8:29 "Go near and overtake this c.
8:38 So he commanded the c to stand

CHARIOTEERS (2/2) CHARIOT

2 Sam 10:18 David killed seven hundred c
1 Chr 19:18 David killed seven thousand c

CHARIOTS (110/101) CHARIOT

Gen 50: 9 there went up with him both c
Ex 14: 7 he took six hundred choice c,
14: 7 and all the c of Egypt with
14: 9 all the horses and c of
14:17 and over all his army, his c,
14:18 for Myself over Pharaoh, his c,
14:23 all Pharaoh's horses, his c,
14:26 upon the Egyptians, on their c,
14:28 returned and covered the c,
15: 4 Pharaoh's c and his army He has
15:19 of Pharaoh went with his c and
Deut 11: 4 to their horses and their c:
20: 1 and see horses and c and
Josh 11: 4 with very many horses and c.
11: 6 their horses and burn their c
11: 9 horses and burned their c with
17:16 the land of the valley have c
17:18 though they have iron c and
24: 6 pursued your fathers with c
Judg 1:19 because they had c of iron.
4: 3 for Jabin had nine hundred c of
4: 7 with his c and his multitude at
4:13 gathered together all his c,
4:13 nine hundred c of iron, and all
4:15 routed Sisera and all his c
4:16 But Barak pursued the c and the
5:28 tarries the clatter of his c?
1 Sam 8:11 and appoint them for his own c
8:11 and some will run before his c.
8:12 of war and equipment for his c.
13: 5 thirty thousand c and six
2 Sam 1: 6 and indeed the c and horsemen
8: 4 took from him one thousand c,
8: 4 of them for one hundred c.
15: 1 provided himself with c and
1 Ki 1: 5 and he prepared for himself c
4:26 stalls of horses for his c,
9:19 cities for his c and cities for
9:22 captains, commanders of his c,
10:26 And Solomon gathered c and
10:26 had one thousand four hundred c
16: 9 Zimri, commander of half his c,
20: 1 with him, with horses and c.
20:21 and attacked the horses and c,
22:31 thirty-two captains of his c,
22:32 when the captains of the c saw
22:33 when the captains of the c saw
2 Ki 6:14 Therefore he sent horses and c
6:15 the city with horses and c.
6:17 was full of horses and c of
7: 6 Syrians to hear the noise of c
7:14 Therefore they took two c with
8:21 and all his c with him. Then he
8:21 him and the captains of the c;
10: 2 and you have c and horses, a
13: 7 only fifty horsemen, ten c,
13:14 the c of Israel and their
18:24 put your trust in Egypt for c
19:23 By the multitude of my c I have
23:11 and he burned the c of the sun
1 Chr 18: 4 took from him one thousand c,
18: 4 of them for one hundred c.
19: 6 to hire for themselves c and
19: 7 thirty-two thousand c,
2 Chr 1:14 And Solomon gathered c and
1:14 had one thousand four hundred c
8: 9 his officers, captains of his c,
9:25 stalls for horses and c,
12: 3 with twelve hundred c,
14: 9 million men and three hundred c,
16: 8 a huge army with very many c
18:30 the captains of the c who
18:31 when the captains of the c saw
18:32 when the captains of the c saw
21: 9 and all his c with him. And he
21: 9 him and the captains of the c.
Ps 20: 7 Some trust in c,
68:17 The c of God are twenty
Song 1: 9 To my filly among Pharaoh's c.
6:12 soul had made me As the c of
Isa 2: 7 And there is no end to their c.
22: 6 Elam bore the quiver With c of
22: 7 valleys Shall be full of c,
22:18 and there your glorious c
31: 1 Who trust in c because they
36: 9 put your trust in Egypt for c
37:24 By the multitude of my c I have
66:15 come with fire And with His c,
66:20 on horses and in c and in
Jer 4:13 And his c like a whirlwind.
17:25 riding in c and on horses, they
22: 4 riding on horses and in c,
46: 9 O c! And let the mighty men
47: 3 At the rushing of his c,
50:37 their horses, Against their c,
Ezek 23:24 shall come against you With c,
26: 7 of kings, with horses, with c,
26:10 horsemen, the wagons, and the c,
Dan 11:40 him like a whirlwind, with c,
Joel 2: 5 With a noise like c Over
Mic 5:10 your midst And destroy your c.
Nah 2: 3 The c come with flaming
2: 4 The c rage in the streets,
2:13 I will burn your c in smoke, and
3: 2 Of clattering c!
Hab 3: 8 Your c of salvation?
Hag 2:22 I will overthrow the c And
Zech 6: 1 four c were coming from
Rev 9: 9 wings was like the sound of c
18:13 cattle and sheep, horses and c,

CHARITABLE (5/5)

Mt 6: 1 heed that you do not do your c
6: 2 when you do a c deed, do not
6: 3 But when you do a c deed, do not
6: 4 that your c deed may be in
Acts 9:36 was full of good works and c

CHARITY (KJV) See LOVE

CHARM (1/1) CHARMED, CHARMERS, CHARMING, CHARMS

Prov 31:30 C is deceitful and beauty is

CHARMED (2/2) CHARM

Eccl 10:11 may bite when it is not c;
Jer 8:17 you, Vipers which cannot be c,

CHARMERS (2/2) CHARM

Ps 58: 5 will not heed the voice of c,
Isa 19: 3 consult the idols and the c,

CHARMING (1/1) CHARM

Ps 58: 5 C ever so skillfully.

CHARMS (4/4) CHARM

Isa 3:20 The perfume boxes, the c,
Jer 3:13 And have scattered your c To
Ezek 13:18 to the women who sew magic c
13:20 I am against your magic c by

CHARRAN (KJV) See HARAN

CHASE (6/6) CHASED, CHASES, CHASING

Lev 26: 7 You will c your enemies, and
26: 8 Five of you shall c a hundred,
Deut 32:30 How could one c a thousand,
Josh 23:10 One man of you shall c a
Ps 35: 5 let the angel of the LORD c
Hos 2: 7 She will c her lovers, But not

CHASED (9/9) CHASE

Deut 1:44 came out against you and c you
Josh 7: 5 for they c them from before
10:10 c them along the road that goes
11: 8 who defeated them and c them to
Judg 9:40 And Abimelech c him, and he fled
20:43 c them, and easily trampled
Job 18:18 And c out of the world.
20: 8 he will be c away like a vision
Isa 17:13 And be c like the chaff of the

CHASES (1/1) CHASE

Prov 19:26 mistreats his father and c

CHASING (1/1) CHASE

1 Sam 17:53 of Israel returned from c the

CHASTE (3/3) CHASTEN, CHASTENED, CHASTENING, CHASTENS

2 Cor 11: 2 that I may present you as a c
Titus 2: 5 to be discreet, c,
1 Pe 3: 2 when they observe your c conduct

CHASTEN (7/7) CHASTENED, CHASTENING, CHASTENS, CHASTISE

2 Sam 7:14 I will c him with the rod of
Ps 6: 1 Nor c me in Your hot

38: 1 Nor c me in Your hot
Prov 19:18 C your son while there is hope,
Hos 10:10 I will c them. Peoples shall
Heb 12: 7 there whom a father does not c?
Rev 3:19 many as I love, I rebuke and c.

CHASTENED (9/9) CHASTEN

Deut 21:18 when they have c him, will not
Job 33:19 Man is also c with pain on his
Ps 69:10 When I wept and c my soul
73:14 And c every morning.
118:18 The LORD has c me severely,
Jer 2:30 In vain I have c your children;
1 Cor 11:32 we are c by the Lord, that we
2 Cor 6: 9 dying, and behold we live; as c,
Heb 12:10 they indeed for a few days c

CHASTENING (9/9) CHASTEN

Deut 11: 2 and who have not seen the c of
Job 5:17 do not despise the c of the
34:31 said to God, 'I have borne c;
Prov 3:11 do not despise the c of the
Isa 26:16 out a prayer when Your c was
Heb 12: 5 do not despise the c of
12: 7 If you endure c, God deals
12: 8 But if you are without c,
12:11 Now no c seems to be joyful for

CHASTENS (3/2) CHASTEN

Deut 8: 5 in your heart that as a man c
8: 5 so the LORD your God c you.
Heb 12: 6 whom the LORD loves He c,

CHASTISE (8/8) CHASTEN, CHASTISED, CHASTISEMENT

Lev 26:28 will c you seven times for your
1 Ki 12:11 but I will c you with
12:14 but I will c you with
2 Chr 10:11 but I will c you with
10:14 but I will c you with
Hos 7:12 I will c them According to
Lk 23:16 I will therefore c Him and
23:22 I will therefore c Him and let

CHASTISED (6/5) CHASTISE

1 Ki 12:11 my father c you with whips, but
12:14 my father c you with whips, but
2 Chr 10:11 my father c you with whips, but
10:14 my father c you with whips, but
Jer 31:18 You have c me, and I was
31:18 have chastised me, and I was c,

CHASTISEMENT (2/2) CHASTISE

Isa 53: 5 The c for our peace was upon
Jer 30:14 With the c of a cruel one,

CHATTER (1/1) CHATTERED

Prov 14:23 But idle c leads only to

CHATTERED (1/1) CHATTER

Isa 38:14 a crane or a swallow, so I c;

CHEAT (4/4)

Lev 19:13 You shall not c your neighbor,
1 Cor 6: 8 you yourselves do wrong and c,
Col 2: 8 Beware lest anyone c you through
2:18 Let no one c you of your reward,

CHEATED (4/4)

1 Sam 12: 3 have I taken, or whom have I c?
12: 4 You have not c us or oppressed
1 Cor 6: 7 rather let yourselves be c?
2 Cor 7: 2 we have c no one.

CHEBAR (8/8)

Ezek 1: 1 the captives by the River C,
1: 3 of the Chaldeans by the River C;
3:15 Abib, who dwelt by the River C;
3:23 which I saw by the River C;
10:15 creature I saw by the River C.
10:20 God of Israel by the River C,
10:22 which I had seen by the River C,
43: 3 which I saw by the River C;

CHECKER WORK (KJV) See LATTICE

CHEDORLAOMER (5/5)

Gen 14: 1 C king of Elam, and Tidal king
14: 4 Twelve years they served C,
14: 5 In the fourteenth year C and
14: 9 against C king of Elam, Tidal
14:17 his return from the defeat of C

CHEEK (7/7) CHEEKBONE, CHEEKS

1 Ki 22:24 and struck Micaiah on the c,
2 Chr 18:23 and struck Micaiah on the c,
Job 16:10 me reproachfully on the c,
Lam 3:30 Let him give his c to the one
Mic 5: 1 of Israel with a rod on the c.
Mt 5:39 slaps you on your right c,
Lk 6:29 who strikes you on the one c,

CHEEKBONE (1/1) CHEEK

Ps 3: 7 struck all my enemies on the c;

CHEEKS (5/5) CHEEK

Deut 18: 3 the priest the shoulder, the c,
Song 1:10 Your c are lovely with
5:13 His c are like a bed of
Isa 50: 6 And My c to those who plucked
Lam 1: 2 night, Her tears are on her c;

CHEER (9/9) CHEERFUL, CHEERFULLY, CHEERFULNESS, CHEERS

Eccl 11: 9 And let your heart c you in
Mt 9: 2 paralytic, "Son, be of good c;
9:22 saw her He said, "Be of good c,
14:27 Be of good c! It is I; do not be
Mk 6:50 Be of good c! It is I; do not be
10:49 saying to him, "Be of good c.
Lk 8:48 her, "Daughter, be of good c;
Jn 16:33 tribulation; but be of good c,
Acts 23:11 by him and said, "Be of good c,

CHEERFUL (6/6) CHEER, CHEERFULLY, CHEERFULNESS

Ruth 3: 7 and drunk, and his heart was c,
1 Ki 21: 7 food, and let your heart be c;
Prov 15:13 A merry heart makes a c
Zech 8:19 be joy and gladness and c
2 Cor 9: 7 for God loves a c giver.
Jas 5:13 Let him pray. Is anyone c?

CHEERFULLY (1/1) CHEERFUL

Acts 24:10 I do the more c answer for

CHEERFULNESS (1/1) CHEERFUL

Rom 12: 8 he who shows mercy, with c.

CHEERS (1/1) CHEER

Judg 9:13 Which c both God and men,

CHEESE (2/2) CHEESES

2 Sam 17:29 sheep and c of the herd, for
Job 10:10 milk, And curdle me like c,

CHEESES (1/1) CHEESE

1 Sam 17:18 And carry these ten c to the

CHELAL (1/1)

Ezra 10:30 sons of Pahath-Moab: Adna, C,

CHELUB (2/2) CALEB

1 Chr 4:11 C the brother of Shuhah begot
27:26 Ezri the son of C was over those

CHELUBAI (1/1) CALEB

1 Chr 2: 9 him were Jerahmeel, Ram, and C.

CHELUH (1/1)

Ezra 10:35 Benaiah, Bedeiah, C,

CHELLUH (KJV) See CHELUH

CHEMARIMS (KJV) See (IDOLATROUS) PRIESTS

CHEMOSH (8/8)

Num 21:29 O people of C! He has given
Judg 11:24 you not possess whatever C
1 Ki 11: 7 built a high place for C the
11:33 C the god of the Moabites, and
2 Ki 23:13 for C the abomination of the
Jer 48: 7 And C shall go forth into
48:13 Moab shall be ashamed of C,
48:46 O Moab! The people of C

CHENAANAH (5/5)

1 Ki 22:11 Now Zedekiah the son of C had
22:24 Now Zedekiah the son of C went
1 Chr 7:10 were Jeush, Benjamin, Ehud, C,
2 Chr 18:10 Now Zedekiah the son of C had
18:23 Then Zedekiah the son of C went

CHENANI (1/1)

Neh 9: 4 and C stood on the stairs of

CHENANIAH (3/3) CONONIAH

1 Chr 15:22 C, leader of the Levites,
15:27 and C the music master with
26:29 C and his sons performed

CHEPHAR HAAMMONI (1/1)

Josh 18:24 C, Ophni, and Gaba:

CHEPHAR-HAAMMONA (KJV) See CHEPHAR HAAMMONI

CHEPHIRAH (4/4)

Josh 9:17 their cities were Gibeon, C,
18:26 Mizpah, C, Mozah,
Ezra 2:25 the people of Kirjath Arim, C,
Neh 7:29 the men of Kirjath Jearim, C,

CHERAN (2/2)

Gen 36:26 Hemdan, Eshban, Ithran, and C.
1 Chr 1:41 Hamran, Eshban, Ithran, and C.

CHERETHIMS (KJV) See CHERETHITES

CHERETHITES (10/10)

1 Sam 30:14 of the southern area of the C,
2 Sam 8:18 Jehoiada was over both the C
15:18 before him; and all the C,
20: 7 So Joab's men, with the C,
20:23 son of Jehoiada was over the C
1 Ki 1:38 the son of Jehoiada, the C,
1:44 the son of Jehoiada, the C,
1 Chr 18:17 son of Jehoiada was over the C
Ezek 25:16 and I will cut off the C and
Zeph 2: 5 The nation of the C! The word

CHERISHES (2/2)

Eph 5:29 but nourishes and c it, just as
1 Th 2: 7 just as a nursing mother c her

CHERITH (2/2)

1 Ki 17: 3 and hide by the Brook C,
17: 5 went and stayed by the Brook C,

CHERUB (30/21) CHERUBIM

Ex 25:19 Make one c at one end, and the
25:19 and the other c at the other
37: 8 one c at one end on this side,
37: 8 and the other c at the other
2 Sam 22:11 He rode upon a c,
1 Ki 6:24 One wing of the c was five
6:24 and the other wing of the c
6:25 And the other c was ten cubits;
6:26 The height of one c was ten
6:26 cubits, and so was the other c.
6:27 and the wing of the other c
2 Chr 3:11 one wing of the one c was
3:11 the wing of the other c;
3:12 one wing of the other c was
3:12 the wing of the other c.
Ezra 2:59 from Tel Melah, Tel Harsha, C,
Neh 7:61 from Tel Melah, Tel Harsha, C,
Ps 18:10 And He rode upon a c,
Ezek 9: 3 Israel had gone up from the c,
10: 2 among the wheels, under the c,
10: 4 of the LORD went up from the c,
10: 7 And the c stretched out his hand
10: 9 one wheel by one c and another
10: 9 another wheel by each other c;
10:14 first face was the face of a c,
28:14 You were the anointed c who
28:16 I destroyed you, O covering c,
41:18 a palm tree between c and
41:18 palm tree between cherub and c.
41:18 Each c had two faces,

CHERUBIM (66/58) CHERUB

Gen 3:24 and He placed c at the east of
Ex 25:18 And you shall make two c of
25:19 you shall make the c at the two
25:20 And the c shall stretch out
25:20 the faces of the c shall be
25:22 from between the two c which
26: 1 with artistic designs of c you
26:31 with an artistic design of c.
36: 8 with artistic designs of c
36:35 with an artistic design of c.
37: 7 He made two c of beaten gold;
37: 8 He made the c at the two ends
37: 9 The c spread out their wings
37: 9 the faces of the c were toward
Num 7:89 from between the two c;
1 Sam 4: 4 who dwells between the c.
2 Sam 6: 2 who dwells between the c.
1 Ki 6:23 inner sanctuary he made two c
6:25 both c were of the same size
6:27 Then he set the c inside the
6:27 out the wings of the c so that
6:28 Also he overlaid the c with
6:29 with carved figures of c,
6:32 he carved on them figures of c,
6:32 and he spread gold on the c and
6:35 Then he carved c,
7:29 frames were lions, oxen, and c.
7:36 and on its panels he engraved c,
8: 6 under the wings of the c.
8: 7 For the c spread their two
8: 7 and the c overshadowed the ark
2 Ki 19:15 One who dwells between the c,
1 Chr 13: 6 who dwells between the c,
28:18 the gold c that spread their
2 Chr 3: 7 and he carved c on the walls.
3:10 Most Holy Place he made two c,
3:11 The wings of the c were twenty
3:13 The wings of these c spanned
3:14 and wove c into it.

C

5: 7 under the wings of the **c**.
5: 8 For the **c** spread their wings
5: 8 and the **c** overshadowed the ark
Ps 80: 1 You who dwell between the **c**,
99: 1 He dwells between the **c**;
Isa 37:16 One who dwells between the **c**,
Ezek 10: 1 was above the head of the **c**,
10: 2 coals of fire from among the **c**,
10: 3 Now the **c** were standing on the
10: 5 the sound of the wings of the **c**
10: 6 the wheels, from among the **c**,
10: 7 out his hand from among the **c**
10: 7 the fire that was among the **c**,
10: 8 The **c** appeared to have the form
10: 9 there were four wheels by the **c**,
10:15 And the **c** were lifted up.
10:16 When the **c** went, the wheels went
10:16 and when the **c** lifted their
10:17 When the **c** stood still, the
10:18 the temple and stood over the **c**.
10:19 And the **c** lifted their wings and
10:20 Chebar, and I knew they were **c**.
11:22 So the **c** lifted up their wings,
41:18 And it was made with **c** and
41:20 **c** and palm trees were carved.
41:25 **C** and palm trees were carved on
Heb 9: 5 and above it were the **c** of glory

CHESALON (1/1)

Josh 15:10 on the north (which is **C**),

CHESED (1/1)

Gen 22:22 '**C**, Hazo, Pildash, Jidlaph,

CHESIL (1/1)

Josh 15:30 Eltolad, **C**, Hormah,

CHEST (11/10) CHESTNUT, CHESTS

1 Sam 6: 8 as a trespass offering in a **c**
6:11 and the **c** with the gold rats
6:15 the ark of the LORD and the **c**
2 Ki 12: 9 Jehoiada the priest took a **c**,
12:10 there was much money in the **c**,
2 Chr 24: 8 king's command they made a **c**,
24:10 and put them into the **c** until
24:11 when the **c** was brought to the
24:11 officer came and emptied the **c**,
Dan 2:32 its **c** and arms of silver, its
Rev 1:13 the feet and girded about the **c**

CHESTNUT (2/2)

Gen 30:37 poplar and of the almond and **c**
Ezek 31: 8 And the **c** trees were not like

CHESTS (2/2) CHEST

Ezek 27:24 in **c** of multicolored apparel,
Rev 15: 6 and having their **c** girded with

CHESULLOTH (1/1)

Josh 19:18 to Jezreel, and included **C**,

CHEW (7/6) CHEWED, CHEWING, CHEWS

Lev 11: 4 not eat among those that **c** the
11: 7 yet does not **c** the cud, is
11:26 not cloven-hoofed or does not **c**
Deut 14: 7 of those that **c** the cud or have
14: 7 for they **c** the cud but do not
14: 8 yet does not **c** the cud; you
Mic 3: 5 Peace" While they **c** with their

CHEWED (1/1) CHEW

Num 11:33 their teeth, before it was **c**,

CHEWING (3/3) CHEW

Lev 11: 3 having cloven hooves and **c** the
Joel 1: 4 What the **c** locust left, the
2:25 And the **c** locust, My great

CHEWS (4/4) CHEW

Lev 11: 4 because it **c** the cud but does
11: 5 because it **c** the cud but does
11: 6 because it **c** the cud but does
Deut 14: 6 and that **c** the cud, among the

CHEZIB (1/1) ACHZIB, CHOZEBA

Gen 38: 5 He was at **C** when she bore him.

CHICKENS (KJV) See CHICKS

CHICKS (1/1)

Mt 23:37 as a hen gathers her **c** under

CHIDE (KJV) See CONTENDED, REPRIMANDED, STRIVE

CHIDON (KJV) See CHIDON'S

CHIDON'S (1/1) NACHON'S

1 Chr 13: 9 And when they came to **C**

CHIEF (271/238) CHIEFLY, CHIEFS, CHIEFTAINS

Gen 36:15 were **C** Teman, Chief Omar, Chief
36:15 **C** Omar, Chief Zepho, Chief
36:15 **C** Zepho, Chief Kenaz,
36:15 Chief Zepho, **C** Kenaz,
36:16 **C** Korah, Chief Gatam, and Chief
36:16 **C** Gatam, and Chief Amalek.
36:16 and **C** Amalek. These were the
36:17 **C** Nahath, Chief Zerah, Chief
36:17 **C** Zerah, Chief Shammah, and
36:17 **C** Shammah, and Chief Mizzah.
36:17 and **C** Mizzah. These were the
36:18 **C** Jeush, Chief Jaalam, and
36:18 **C** Jaalam, and Chief Korah.
36:18 and **C** Korah. These were the
36:29 **C** Lotan, Chief Shobal, Chief
36:29 **C** Shobal, Chief Zibeon, Chief
36:29 **C** Zibeon, Chief Anah,
36:29 Chief Zibeon, **C** Anah,
36:30 **C** Dishon, Chief Ezer, and Chief
36:30 **C** Ezer, and Chief Dishan. These
36:30 and **C** Dishan. These were the
36:40 **C** Timnah, Chief Alvah, Chief
36:40 **C** Alvah, Chief Jetheth,
36:40 Chief Alvah, **C** Jetheth,
36:41 **C** Aholibamah, Chief Elah, Chief
36:41 **C** Elah, Chief Pinon,
36:41 Chief Elah, **C** Pinon,
36:42 **C** Kenaz, Chief Teman, Chief
36:42 **C** Teman, Chief Mibzar,
36:42 Chief Teman, **C** Mibzar,
36:43 **C** Magdiel, and Chief Iram.
36:43 and **C** Iram. These were the
40: 2 the **c** butler and the chief
40: 2 the chief butler and the **c**
40: 9 Then the **c** butler told his
40:16 When the **c** baker saw that the
40:20 he lifted up the head of the **c**
40:20 the chief butler and of the **c**
40:21 Then he restored the **c** butler to
40:22 But he hanged the **c** baker, as
40:23 Yet the **c** butler did not
41: 9 Then the **c** butler spoke to
41:10 both me and the **c** baker,
47: 6 then make them **c** herdsmen over
Lev 21: 4 being a **c** man among his
Num 3:32 the priest was to be **c** over
31:26 Eleazar the priest and the **c**
32:28 and to the **c** fathers of the
36: 1 Now the **c** fathers of the
36: 1 the **c** fathers of the children
Josh 22:14 one ruler each from the **c** house
1 Sam 21: 7 the **c** of the herdsmen who
28: 2 I will make you one of my **c**
2 Sam 5: 8 he shall be **c** and
8:18 and David's sons were **c**
20:26 and Ira the Jairite was a **c**
23: 8 **c** among the captains. He was
23:13 Then three of the thirty **c** men
23:18 was **c** of another three.
1 Ki 8: 1 the **c** fathers of the children
2 Ki 25:18 of the guard took Seraiah the **c**
25:19 the **c** recruiting officer of the
1 Chr 1:51 And the chiefs of Edom were **C**
1:51 **C** Aliah, Chief Jetheth,
1:51 Chief Aliah, **C** Jetheth,
1:52 **C** Aholibamah, Chief Elah, Chief
1:52 **C** Elah, Chief Pinon,
1:52 Chief Elah, **C** Pinon,
1:53 **C** Kenaz, Chief Teman, Chief
1:53 **C** Teman, Chief Mibzar,
1:53 Chief Teman, **C** Mibzar,
1:54 **C** Magdiel, and Chief Iram. These
1:54 and **C** Iram. These were the
5: 7 was registered: the **c**,
5:12 Joel was the **c**,
5:15 was **c** of their father's house.
7: 3 All five of them were **c** men.
7:40 men of valor, **c** leaders.
8:28 **c** men. These dwelt in
9:17 Shallum was the **c**.
9:26 trusted office were four **c**
11: 6 the Jebusites first shall be **c**
11: 6 went up first, and became **c**.
11:11 **c** of the captains; he had
11:15 Now three of the thirty **c** men
11:20 the brother of Joab was **c** of
11:42 of Shiza the Reubenite (a **c** of
12: 3 The **c** was Ahiezer, then Joash,
12:18 **c** of the captains, and he
15: 5 the sons of Kohath, Uriel the **c**,
15: 6 sons of Merari, Asaiah the **c**,
15: 7 the sons of Gershom, Joel the **c**,
15: 8 of Elizaphan, Shemaiah the **c**,
15: 9 the sons of Hebron, Eliel the **c**,
15:10 sons of Uzziel, Amminadab the **c**,
16: 5 Asaph the **c**, and next to
18:17 and David's sons were **c**
24:31 The **c** fathers did just as
26:12 among the **c** men, having duties
27: 3 and the **c** of all the captains
27: 5 Jehoiada the priest, who was **c**;
2 Chr 5: 2 the **c** fathers of the children
11:22 Abijah the son of Maachah as **c**,
19: 8 and some of the **c** fathers of
19:11 Amariah the **c** priest is over
23: 2 and the **c** fathers of Israel,
24: 6 the king called Jehoiada the **c**
26:12 The total number of **c** officers
26:20 And Azariah the **c** priest and all
31:10 And Azariah the **c** priest, from
35: 9 **c** of the Levites, gave to the
Ezra 5:10 names of the men who were **c**
7: 5 the son of Aaron the **c** priest—
8:17 them a command for Iddo the **c**
Job 29:25 the way for them, and sat as **c**;
Ps 4: To the **C** Musician. With stringed
5: To the **C** Musician. With flutes.
6: To the **C** Musician. With stringed
8: To the **C** Musician. On the
9: To the **C** Musician. To the tune
11: To the **C** Musician. A Psalm of
12: To the **C** Musician. On an
13: To the **C** Musician. A Psalm of
14: To the **C** Musician. A Psalm of
18: To the **C** Musician. A Psalm of
19: To the **C** Musician. A Psalm of
20: To the **C** Musician. A Psalm of
21: To the **C** Musician. A Psalm of
22: To the **C** Musician. Set to "The
31: To the **C** Musician. A Psalm of
36: To the **C** Musician. A Psalm of
39: To the **C** Musician. To Jeduthun.
40: To the **C** Musician. A Psalm of
41: To the **C** Musician. A Psalm of
42: To the **C** Musician.
44: To the **C** Musician.
45: To the **C** Musician. Set to "The
46: To the **C** Musician. A Psalm of
47: To the **C** Musician. A Psalm of
49: To the **C** Musician. A Psalm of
51: To the **C** Musician. A Psalm of
52: To the **C** Musician.
53: To the **C** Musician. Set to
54: To the **C** Musician. With stringed
55: To the **C** Musician. With stringed
56: To the **C** Musician. Set to "The
57: To the **C** Musician. Set to "Do
58: To the **C** Musician. Set to "Do
59: To the **C** Musician. Set to "Do
60: To the **C** Musician. Set to "Lily
61: To the **C** Musician. On a stringed
62: To the **C** Musician. To Jeduthun.
64: To the **C** Musician. A Psalm of
65: To the **C** Musician. A Psalm of
66: To the **C** Musician. A Song.
67: To the **C** Musician. On stringed
68: To the **C** Musician. A Psalm of
69: To the **C** Musician. Set to "The
70: To the **C** Musician. A Psalm of
75: To the **C** Musician. Set to "Do
76: To the **C** Musician. On stringed
77: To the **C** Musician. To Jeduthun.
80: To the **C** Musician. Set to "The
81: To the **C** Musician. On an
84: To the **C** Musician. On an
85: To the **C** Musician. A Psalm of
88: To the **C** Musician. Set to
109: To the **C** Musician. A Psalm of
118:22 rejected Has become the **c**
137: 6 not exalt Jerusalem Above my **c**
139: For the **C** Musician. A Psalm of
140: To the **C** Musician. A Psalm of
Prov 1:21 She cries out in the **c**
Song 4:14 With all the **c** spices—
5:10 **C** among ten thousand.
Isa 14: 9 All the **c** ones of the earth;
Jer 20: 1 the priest who was also **c**
31: 7 And shout among the **c** of the
39:13 and all the king of Babylon's **c**
52:24 of the guard took Seraiah the **c**
Dan 1: 7 To them the **c** of the eunuchs
1: 8 he requested of the **c** of the
1: 9 favor and goodwill of the **c** of
1:10 And the **c** of the eunuchs said to
1:11 said to the steward whom the **c**
1:18 the **c** of the eunuchs brought
2:48 and **c** administrator over all
4: 9 **c** of the magicians, because I
5:11 made him **c** of the magicians,
10:13 one of the **c** princes, came to
Am 6: 1 Notable persons in the **c**
Hab 3:19 To the **C** Musician. With my
Mt 2: 4 when he had gathered all the **c**
16:21 things from the elders and **c**
20:18 Man will be betrayed to the **c**
21:15 But when the **c** priests and
21:23 the **c** priests and the elders of
21:42 rejected Has become the **c**
21:45 Now when the **c** priests and
26: 3 Then the **c** priests, the scribes,
26:14 went to the **c** priests
26:47 came from the **c** priests and
26:59 Now the **c** priests, the elders,
27: 1 all the **c** priests and elders of
27: 3 pieces of silver to the **c**
27: 6 But the **c** priests took the
27:12 He was being accused by the **c**
27:20 But the **c** priests and elders
27:41 Likewise the **c** priests also,
27:62 the **c** priests and Pharisees
28:11 the city and reported to the **c**
Mk 6:21 and the **c** men of Galilee.
8:31 be rejected by the elders and **c**
10:33 Man will be betrayed to the **c**
11:18 And the scribes and **c** priests
11:27 the **c** priests, the scribes, and
12:10 rejected Has become the **c**

14: 1 And the **c** priests and the
14:10 went to the **c** priests to betray
14:43 came from the **c** priests and the
14:53 him were assembled all the **c**
14:55 Now the **c** priests and all the
15: 1 the **c** priests held a
15: 3 And the **c** priests accused Him of
15:10 For he knew that the **c** priests
15:11 But the **c** priests stirred up the
15:31 Likewise the **c** priests also,
Lk 9:22 be rejected by the elders and **c**
19: 2 man named Zacchaeus who was a **c**
19:47 But the **c** priests, the scribes,
20: 1 that the **c** priests and the
20:17 rejected Has become the **c**
20:19 And the **c** priests and the
22: 2 And the **c** priests and the
22: 4 way and conferred with the **c**
22:52 Then Jesus said to the **c**
22:66 both **c** priests and scribes,
23: 4 So Pilate said to the **c** priests
23:10 And the **c** priests and scribes
23:13 he had called together the **c**
23:23 of these men and of the **c**
24:20 and how the **c** priests and our
Jn 7:32 and the Pharisees and the **c**
7:45 the officers came to the **c**
11:47 Then the **c** priests and the
11:57 Now both the **c** priests and the
12:10 But the **c** priests plotted to put
18: 3 and officers from the **c** priests
18:35 Your own nation and the **c**
19: 6 when the **c** priests and officers
19:15 The **c** priests answered, "We
19:21 Therefore the **c** priests of the
Acts 4:11 which has become the **c**
4:23 and reported all that the **c**
5:24 and the **c** priests heard these
9:14 he has authority from the **c**
9:21 might bring them bound to the **c**
13:50 and prominent women and the **c**
14:12 because he was the **c** speaker.
19:14 a Jewish **c** priest, who did so.
22:30 and commanded the **c** priests and
23:14 They came to the **c** priests and
25: 2 Then the high priest and the **c**
25:15 about whom the **c** priests and the
26:10 received authority from the **c**
26:12 and commission from the **c**
Eph 2:20 Christ Himself being the **c**
1 Tim 1:15 to save sinners, of whom I am **c**.
1 Pe 2: 6 I lay in Zion A **c**
2: 7 rejected Has become the **c**
5: 4 and when the **C** Shepherd appears,

CHIEF CORNERSTONE (8/8)

Ps 118:22 rejected Has become the **c**.
Mt 21:42 rejected Has become the **c**.
Mk 12:10 rejected Has become the **c**.
Lk 20:17 Has become the **c**'?
Acts 4:11 which has become the **c**.
Eph 2:20 Christ Himself being the **c**,
1 Pe 2: 6 I lay in Zion A **c**,
2: 7 rejected Has become the **c**,

CHIEFLY (1/1) CHIEF

Rom 3: 2 Much in every way! **C** because to

CHIEFS (21/20) CHIEF

Gen 36:15 These were the **c** of the sons
36:16 These were the **c** of Eliphaz in
36:17 These were the **c** of Reuel in
36:18 These were the **c** who
36:19 Edom, and these were their **c**.
36:21 These were the **c** of the
36:29 These were the **c** of the
36:30 These were the **c** of the
36:30 according to their **c** in the
36:40 these were the names of the **c**
36:43 These were the **c** of Edom,
Ex 15:15 Then the **c** of Edom will be
1 Sam 14:38 all you **c** of the people, and
1 Ki 5:16 three hundred from the **c** of
9:23 Others were **c** of the officials
1 Chr 1:51 And the **c** of Edom were Chief
1:54 These were the **c** of Edom.
12:32 their **c** were two hundred; and
2 Chr 8:10 And others were **c** of the
Neh 12:46 Asaph of old there were **c** of
Job 12:24 the understanding of the **c** of

CHIEFTAINS (1/1) CHIEF

Jer 13:21 you have taught them To be **c**,

CHILD (181/160) CHILD'S, CHILDBEARING, CHILDBIRTH, CHILDHOOD, CHILDISH, CHILDLESS, CHILDREN, CHILDREN'S

Gen 11:30 Sarai was barren; she had no **c**.
16:11 "Behold, you are with **c**,
17:10 Every male **c** among you shall be
17:12 every male **c** in your
17:14 "And the uncircumcised male **c**,
17:17 Shall a **c** be born to a man who
17:17 is ninety years old, bear a **c**?
18:13 'Shall I surely bear a **c**,
19:36 daughters of Lot were with **c**
21: 8 So the **c** grew and was weaned.
30: 3 and she will bear a **c** on my
38:24 furthermore she is with **c** by
38:25 whom these belong, I am with **c**.
44:20 and a **c** of his old age, who
Ex 2: 2 saw that he was a beautiful **c**,
2: 3 put the **c** in it, and laid it
2: 6 had opened it, she saw the **c**,
2: 7 that she may nurse the **c** for
2: 9 Take this **c** away and nurse him
2: 9 So the woman took the **c** and
2:10 And the **c** grew, and she brought
21:22 fight, and hurt a woman with **c**,
22:22 any widow or fatherless **c**.
Lev 12: 2 conceived, and borne a male **c**,
12: 5 'But if she bears a female **c**,
22:13 widow or divorced, and has no **c**,
Num 11:12 a guardian carries a nursing **c**,
Deut 32:25 The nursing **c** with the man of
Judg 11:34 and she was his only **c**.
13: 5 for the **c** shall be a Nazirite
13: 7 for the **c** shall be a Nazirite
13: 8 us what we shall do for the **c**
13:24 and the **c** grew, and the LORD
Ruth 4:16 Then Naomi took the **c** and laid
1 Sam 1:11 give Your maidservant a male **c**,
1:22 Not until the **c** is weaned; then
1:24 And the **c** was young.
1:25 and brought the **c** to Eli.
1:27 For this **c** I prayed, and the
2:11 But the **c** ministered to the
2:18 before the LORD, even as a **c**,
2:21 Meanwhile the **c** Samuel grew
2:26 And the **c** Samuel grew in
4:19 Phinehas' wife, was with **c**,
4:21 Then she named the **c** Ichabod,
15: 3 and woman, infant and nursing **c**,
2 Sam 11: 5 David, and said, "I am with **c**.
12:14 the **c** also who is born to you
12:15 And the LORD struck the **c**
12:16 pleaded with God for the **c**,
12:18 day it came to pass that the **c**
12:18 afraid to tell him that the **c**
12:18 while the **c** was alive, we spoke
12:18 How can we tell him that the **c**
12:19 David perceived that the **c** was
12:19 Is the **c** dead?" And they said,
12:21 You fasted and wept for the **c**
12:21 but when the **c** died, you arose
12:22 While the **c** was alive, I fasted
12:22 that the **c** may live?'
1 Ki 3: 7 David, but I am a little **c**;
3:20 and laid her dead **c** in my
3:25 Divide the living **c** in two, and
3:26 my lord, give her the living **c**,
3:27 the first woman the living **c**,
11:17 Hadad was still a little **c**.
13: 2 says the LORD: 'Behold, a **c**,
14: 3 you what will become of the **c**.
14:12 the **c** shall die.
14:17 the house, the **c** died.
17:21 stretched himself out on the **c**
17:22 and the soul of the **c** came back
17:23 And Elijah took the **c** and
2 Ki 4:18 And the **c** grew. Now it happened
4:26 Is it well with the **c**?
4:29 my staff on the face of the **c**.
4:30 And the mother of the **c** said,
4:31 the staff on the face of the **c**;
4:31 The **c** has not awakened."
4:32 into the house, there was the **c**,
4:34 And he went up and lay on the **c**,
4:34 stretched himself out on the **c**,
4:34 and the flesh of the **c** became
4:35 then the **c** sneezed seven times,
4:35 and the **c** opened his eyes.
5:14 like the flesh of a little **c**,
8:12 and rip open their women with **c**.
15:16 women there who were with **c** he
1 Chr 2:31 and Sheshan's **c** was Ahlai.
Job 3: 3 A male **c** is conceived.'
3:16 I not hidden like a stillborn **c**,
Ps 58: 8 Like a stillborn **c** of a
131: 2 Like a weaned **c** with his
131: 2 Like a weaned **c** is my soul
Prov 20:11 Even a **c** is known by his deeds,
22: 6 Train up a **c** in the way he
22:15 bound up in the heart of a **c**;
23:13 withhold correction from a **c**,
23:24 And he who begets a wise **c**
29:15 But a **c** left to himself
Eccl 6: 3 I say that a stillborn **c** is
10:16 O land, when your king is a **c**,
11: 5 the womb of her who is with **c**,
Isa 3: 5 The **c** will be insolent toward
7:16 For before the **C** shall know to
8: 4 for before the **c** shall have
9: 6 For unto us a **C** is born, Unto
10:19 be so few in number That a **c**
11: 6 And a little **c** shall lead
11: 8 The nursing **c** shall play by the
11: 8 And the weaned **c** shall put his
26:17 As a woman with **c** Is in pain
26:18 We have been with **c**,
49:15 a woman forget her nursing **c**,
54: 1 who have not labored with **c**!
65:20 For the **c** shall die one
66: 7 came, She delivered a male **c**.
Jer 4:31 who brings forth her first **c**,
20:15 A male **c** has been born to you!"
30: 6 a man is ever in labor with **c**?
31: 8 The woman with **c** And the one
31: 8 And the one who labors with **c**,
31:20 dear son? Is he a pleasant **c**?
44: 7 **c** and infant, out of Judah,
Hos 11: 1 "When Israel was a **c**,
13:16 And their women with **c** ripped
Am 1:13 ripped open the women with **c**
Mt 1:18 she was found with **c** of the
1:23 virgin shall be with **c**,
2: 8 carefully for the young **C**,
2: 9 stood over where the young **C**
2:11 they saw the young **C** with Mary
2:13 take the young **C** and His
2:13 Herod will seek the young **C** to
2:14 he took the young **C** and His
2:20 take the young **C** and His
2:21 took the young **C** and His
10:21 to death, and a father his **c**;
17:18 and the **c** was cured from that
18: 2 Then Jesus called a little **c** to
18: 4 himself as this little **c** is
18: 5 Whoever receives one little **c**
Mk 5:39 The **c** is not dead, but
5:40 father and the mother of the **c**,
5:40 and entered where the **c** was
5:41 Then He took the **c** by the hand,
9:24 the father of the **c** cried out
9:36 Then He took a little **c** and set
10:15 kingdom of God as a little **c**
13:12 to death, and a father his **c**;
Lk 1: 7 But they had no **c**,
1:59 they came to circumcise the **c**;
1:66 What kind of **c** will this be?"
1:76 'And you, **c**, will be called
1:80 So the **c** grew and became strong
2: 5 betrothed wife, who was with **c**.
2:17 was told them concerning this **C**.
2:21 for the circumcision of the **C**,
2:27 the parents brought in the **C**
2:34 this **C** is destined for the
2:40 And the **C** grew and became strong
9:38 on my son, for he is my only **c**.
9:42 unclean spirit, healed the **c**,
9:47 took a little **c** and set him by
9:48 receives this little **c**
18:17 kingdom of God as a little **c**
Jn 4:49 come down before my **c** dies!"
16:21 as she has given birth to the **c**,
Acts 7: 5 But even when Abraham had no **c**,
1 Cor 13:11 When I was a **c**, I spoke as a
13:11 I was a child, I spoke as a **c**,
13:11 as a child, I understood as a **c**,
13:11 as a child, I thought as a **c**;
Gal 4: 1 the heir, as long as he is a **c**,
Heb 11:11 and she bore a **c** when she was
11:23 they saw he was a beautiful **c**;
Rev 12: 2 Then being with **c**, she cried
12: 4 to devour her **C** as soon as it
12: 5 She bore a male **C** who was to
12: 5 And her **C** was caught up to God
12:13 who gave birth to the male **C**.

CHILD'S (4/4) CHILD

Ex 2: 8 maiden went and called the **c**
1 Ki 17:21 let this **c** soul come back to
Job 33:25 flesh shall be young like a **c**,
Mt 2:20 those who sought the young **C**

CHILDBEARING (2/2)

Gen 18:11 Sarah had passed the age of **c**.
1 Tim 2:15 she will be saved in **c** if they

CHILDBIRTH (4/4) BIRTH

Gen 35:16 Ephrath, Rachel labored in **c**,
Isa 13: 8 will be in pain as a woman in **c**;
Jer 50:43 him, Pangs as of a woman in **c**.
Hos 13:13 The sorrows of a woman in **c**

CHILDHOOD (5/5) CHILD

1 Sam 12: 2 walked before you from my **c** to
Prov 29:21 who pampers his servant from **c**
Eccl 11:10 For **c** and youth are vanity.
Mk 9:21 to him?" And he said, "From **c**.
2 Tim 3:15 and that from **c** you have known

CHILDISH (1/1) CHILD

1 Cor 13:11 I put away **c** things.

CHILDLESS (7/6) CHILD

Gen 15: 2 will You give me, seeing I go **c**,
Lev 20:20 their sin; they shall die **c**.
20:21 They shall be **c**.
1 Sam 15:33 your sword has made women **c**,
15:33 so shall your mother be **c** among
Jer 22:30 'Write this man down as **c**,
Lk 20:30 took her as wife, and he died **c**.

CHILDREN (1350/1186) CHILD, CHILDREN'S, GRANDCHILDREN

Gen 3:16 pain you shall bring forth **c**;
6: 4 of men and they bore **c** to
10:21 And **c** were born also to Shem,
10:21 the father of all the **c** of
16: 1 wife, had borne him no **c**.
16: 2 restrained me from bearing **c**.

	16: 2	perhaps I shall obtain **c** by
	18:19	that he may command his **c** and
	20:17	servants. Then they bore **c**;
	21: 7	that Sarah would nurse **c**?
	22:20	Milcah also has borne **c**
	25: 4	All these were the **c** of
	25:22	But the **c** struggled together
	30: 1	saw that she bore Jacob no **c**,
	30: 1	and said to Jacob, "Give me **c**,
	30: 3	that I also may have **c** by
	30:26	Give me my wives and my **c** for
	31:43	and these **c** are my children,
	31:43	and these children are my **c**,
	31:43	my daughters or to their **c**
	32:11	me and the mother with the **c**.
	32:32	Therefore to this day the **c** of
	33: 1	So he divided the **c** among Leah,
	33: 2	the maidservants and their **c**
	33: 2	Leah and her **c** behind, and
	33: 5	eyes and saw the women and **c**,
	33: 5	The **c** whom God has graciously
	33: 6	came near, they and their **c**,
	33: 7	Leah also came near with her **c**,
	33:13	My lord knows that the **c** are
	33:14	that go before me, and the **c**,
	33:19	from the **c** of Hamor, Shechem's
	36:25	These were the **c** of Anah:
	36:31	any king reigned over the **c** of
	37: 3	Joseph more than all his **c**,
	44:20	alone is left of his mother's **c**,
	45:10	be near to me, you and your **c**,
	45:10	children, your children's **c**,
	46: 8	these were the names of the **c**
	49: 8	Your father's **c** shall bow down
	50:23	Joseph saw Ephraim's **c** to the
	50:23	The **c** of Machir, the son of
	50:25	Joseph took an oath from the **c**
Ex	1: 1	these are the names of the **c**
	1: 7	But the **c** of Israel were
	1: 9	the people of the **c** of Israel
	1:12	they were in dread of the **c** of
	1:13	So the Egyptians made the **c** of
	1:17	but saved the male **c** alive.
	1:18	and saved the male **c** alive?"
	2: 6	"This is one of the Hebrews' **c**.
	2:23	Then the **c** of Israel groaned
	2:25	And God looked upon the **c** of
	3: 9	the cry of the **c** of Israel has
	3:10	the **c** of Israel, out of
	3:11	and that I should bring the **c**
	3:13	when I come to the **c** of Israel
	3:14	Thus you shall say to the **c** of
	3:15	Thus you shall say to the **c** of
	4:29	all the elders of the **c** of
	4:31	the LORD had visited the **c** of
	5:14	Also the officers of the **c** of
	5:15	Then the officers of the **c** of
	5:19	And the officers of the **c** of
	6: 5	heard the groaning of the **c** of
	6: 6	Therefore say to the **c** of
	6: 9	So Moses spoke thus to the **c** of
	6:11	king of Egypt to let the **c** of
	6:12	The **c** of Israel have not heeded
	6:13	gave them a command for the **c**
	6:13	to bring the **c** of Israel out of
	6:26	Bring out the **c** of Israel from
	6:27	to bring out the **c** of Israel
	7: 2	speak to Pharaoh to send the **c**
	7: 4	the **c** of Israel, out of the
	7: 5	on Egypt and bring out the **c**
	9: 4	of all that belongs to the **c**
	9: 6	but of the livestock of the **c**
	9:26	where the **c** of Israel were,
	9:35	neither would he let the **c** of
	10:20	and he did not let the **c** of
	10:23	But all the **c** of Israel had
	11: 7	But against none of the **c** of
	11:10	and he did not let the **c** of
	12:26	when your **c** say to you, 'What
	12:27	over the houses of the **c** of
	12:28	Then the **c** of Israel went away
	12:31	both you and the **c** of Israel.
	12:35	Now the **c** of Israel had done
	12:37	Then the **c** of Israel journeyed
	12:37	thousand men on foot, besides **c**.
	12:40	Now the sojourn of the **c** of
	12:42	observance for all the **c** of
	12:50	Thus all the **c** of Israel did;
	12:51	that the LORD brought the **c** of
	13: 2	opens the womb among the **c** of
	13:18	And the **c** of Israel went up in
	13:19	for he had placed the **c** of
	14: 2	Speak to the **c** of Israel, that
	14: 3	For Pharaoh will say of the **c** of
	14: 8	and he pursued the **c** of Israel;
	14: 8	and the **c** of Israel went out
	14:10	the **c** of Israel lifted their
	14:10	and the **c** of Israel cried out
	14:15	Tell the **c** of Israel to go
	14:16	And the **c** of Israel shall go on
	14:22	So the **c** of Israel went into the
	14:29	But the **c** of Israel had walked
	15: 1	Then Moses and the **c** of Israel
	15:19	But the **c** of Israel went on dry
	16: 1	all the congregation of the **c**
	16: 2	whole congregation of the **c** of
	16: 3	And the **c** of Israel said to
	16: 6	and Aaron said to all the **c** of
	16: 9	all the congregation of the **c**
	16:10	whole congregation of the **c** of
	16:12	heard the complaints of the **c**
	16:15	So when the **c** of Israel saw it,
	16:17	Then the **c** of Israel did so and
	16:35	And the **c** of Israel ate manna
	17: 1	all the congregation of the **c**
	17: 3	to kill us and our **c** and our
	17: 7	of the contention of the **c** of
	19: 1	In the third month after the **c**
	19: 3	and tell the **c** of Israel:
	19: 6	which you shall speak to the **c**
	20: 5	of the fathers on the **c** to the
	20:22	Thus you shall say to the **c** of
	21: 4	the wife and her **c** shall be her
	21: 5	my master, my wife, and my **c**;
	22:24	and your **c** fatherless.
	24: 5	he sent young men of the **c** of
	24:11	But on the nobles of the **c** of
	24:17	mountain in the eyes of the **c**
	25: 2	Speak to the **c** of Israel, that
	25:22	you in commandment to the **c** of
	27:20	And you shall command the **c** of
	27:21	generations on behalf of the **c**
	28: 1	from among the **c** of Israel,
	28:30	bear the judgment of the **c** of
	28:38	of the holy things which the **c**
	29:28	It shall be from the **c** of Israel
	29:28	be a heave offering from the **c**
	29:43	there I will meet with the **c**
	29:45	I will dwell among the **c** of
	30:12	you take the census of the **c**
	30:16	the atonement money of the **c**
	30:16	it may be a memorial for the **c**
	30:31	And you shall speak to the **c** of
	31:13	Speak also to the **c** of Israel,
	31:16	Therefore the **c** of Israel shall
	31:17	a sign between Me and the **c** of
	32:20	on the water and made the **c** of
	33: 5	Say to the **c** of Israel, 'You
	33: 6	So the **c** of Israel stripped
	34: 7	of the fathers upon the **c** and
	34: 7	children and the children's **c**
	34:30	So when Aaron and all the **c** of
	34:32	Afterward all the **c** of Israel
	34:34	come out and speak to the **c** of
	34:35	And whenever the **c** of Israel saw
	35: 1	all the congregation of the **c**
	35: 4	all the congregation of the **c**
	35:20	all the congregation of the **c**
	35:29	The **c** of Israel brought a
	35:30	And Moses said to the **c** of
	36: 3	all the offering which the **c**
	39:32	And the **c** of Israel did
	39:42	so the **c** of Israel did all the
	40:36	the **c** of Israel would go onward
Lev	1: 2	Speak to the **c** of Israel, and
	4: 2	Speak to the **c** of Israel,
	6:18	All the males among the **c** of
	7:23	Speak to the **c** of Israel,
	7:29	Speak to the **c** of Israel,
	7:34	I have taken from the **c** of
	7:34	and to his sons from the **c** of
	7:36	to be given to them by the **c**
	7:38	day when He commanded the **c** of
	9: 3	And to the **c** of Israel you shall
	10:11	and that you may teach the **c** of
	10:14	of peace offerings of the **c** of
	11: 2	Speak to the **c** of Israel,
	12: 2	Speak to the **c** of Israel,
	15: 2	Speak to the **c** of Israel, and
	15:31	'Thus you shall separate the **c**
	16: 5	from the congregation of the **c**
	16:16	of the uncleanness of the **c** of
	16:19	from the uncleanness of the **c**
	16:21	it all the iniquities of the **c**
	16:34	to make atonement for the **c** of
	17: 2	and to all the **c** of Israel, and
	17: 5	to the end that the **c** of Israel
	17:12	Therefore I said to the **c** of
	17:13	Whatever man of the **c** of Israel,
	17:14	Therefore I said to the **c** of
	18: 2	Speak to the **c** of Israel, and
	19: 2	all the congregation of the **c** of
	19:18	bear any grudge against the **c**
	20: 2	you shall say to the **c** of
	20: 2	Whoever of the **c** of Israel, or
	21:24	and to all the **c** of Israel.
	22: 2	from the holy things of the **c**
	22: 3	the holy things which the **c** of
	22:15	the holy offerings of the **c**
	22:18	and to all the **c** of Israel, and
	22:32	I will be hallowed among the **c**
	23: 2	Speak to the **c** of Israel, and
	23:10	Speak to the **c** of Israel, and
	23:24	Speak to the **c** of Israel,
	23:34	Speak to the **c** of Israel,
	23:43	may know that I made the **c** of
	23:44	So Moses declared to the **c** of
	24: 2	Command the **c** of Israel that
	24: 8	being taken from the **c** of
	24:10	went out among the **c** of Israel;
	24:15	Then you shall speak to the **c** of
	24:23	Then Moses spoke to the **c** of
	24:23	So the **c** of Israel did as the
	25: 2	Speak to the **c** of Israel, and
	25:33	their possession among the **c**
	25:41	he and his **c** with him—and shall
	25:45	Moreover you may buy the **c** of
	25:46	as an inheritance for your **c**
	25:46	the **c** of Israel, you shall not
	25:54	he and his **c** with him.
	25:55	For the **c** of Israel are
	26:22	which shall rob you of your **c**,
	26:46	made between Himself and the **c**
	27: 2	Speak to the **c** of Israel, and
	27:34	commanded Moses for the **c** of
Num	1: 2	all the congregation of the **c**
	1:20	Now the **c** of Reuben, Israel's
	1:22	From the **c** of Simeon, their
	1:24	From the **c** of Gad, their
	1:26	From the **c** of Judah, their
	1:28	From the **c** of Issachar, their
	1:30	From the **c** of Zebulun, their
	1:32	the **c** of Ephraim, their
	1:34	From the **c** of Manasseh, their
	1:36	From the **c** of Benjamin, their
	1:38	From the **c** of Dan, their
	1:40	From the **c** of Asher, their
	1:42	From the **c** of Naphtali, their
	1:45	all who were numbered of the **c**
	1:49	a census of them among the **c**
	1:52	The **c** of Israel shall pitch
	1:53	on the congregation of the **c**
	1:54	Thus the **c** of Israel did;
	2: 2	Everyone of the **c** of Israel
	2: 3	shall be the leader of the **c**
	2: 5	shall be the leader of the **c**
	2: 7	shall be the leader of the **c**
	2:10	and the leader of the **c** of
	2:12	and the leader of the **c** of
	2:14	and the leader of the **c** of Gad
	2:18	and the leader of the **c** of
	2:20	and the leader of the **c** of
	2:22	and the leader of the **c** of
	2:25	and the leader of the **c** of Dan
	2:27	and the leader of the **c** of
	2:29	and the leader of the **c** of
	2:32	who were numbered of the **c** of
	2:33	were not numbered among the **c**
	2:34	Thus the **c** of Israel did
	3: 4	of Sinai; and they had no **c**.
	3: 8	and to the needs of the **c** of
	3: 9	to him from among the **c** of
	3:12	the Levites from among the **c**
	3:12	who opens the womb among the **c**
	3:15	Number the **c** of Levi by their
	3:25	The duties of the **c** of Gershon
	3:29	The families of the **c** of Kohath
	3:36	the appointed duty of the **c** of
	3:38	to meet the needs of the **c** of
	3:40	the firstborn males of the **c**
	3:41	all the firstborn among the **c**
	3:41	among the livestock of the **c**
	3:42	all the firstborn among the **c**
	3:45	all the firstborn among the **c**
	3:46	of the firstborn of the **c** of
	3:50	From the firstborn of the **c** of
	4: 2	of Kohath from among the **c** of
	5: 2	Command the **c** of Israel that
	5: 4	And the **c** of Israel did so, and
	5: 4	so the **c** of Israel did.
	5: 6	Speak to the **c** of Israel: 'When
	5: 9	of all the holy things of the **c**
	5:12	Speak to the **c** of Israel, and
	5:28	be free and may conceive **c**.
	6: 2	Speak to the **c** of Israel, and
	6:23	the way you shall bless the **c**
	6:27	shall put My name on the **c** of
	7:24	leader of the **c** of Zebulun,
	7:30	leader of the **c** of Reuben,
	7:36	leader of the **c** of Simeon,
	7:42	leader of the **c** of Gad,
	7:48	leader of the **c** of Ephraim,
	7:54	leader of the **c** of Manasseh,
	7:60	leader of the **c** of Benjamin,
	7:66	leader of the **c** of Dan,
	7:72	leader of the **c** of Asher,
	7:78	leader of the **c** of Naphtali,
	8: 6	the Levites from among the **c**
	8: 9	whole congregation of the **c** of
	8:10	and the **c** of Israel shall lay
	8:11	a wave offering from the **c** of
	8:14	the Levites from among the **c**
	8:16	given to Me from among the **c**
	8:16	the firstborn of all the **c** of
	8:17	all the firstborn among the **c**
	8:18	of all the firstborn of the **c**
	8:19	and his sons from among the **c**
	8:19	to do the work for the **c** of
	8:19	to make atonement for the **c** of
	8:19	there be no plague among the **c**
	8:19	children of Israel when the **c**
	8:20	all the congregation of the **c** of
	8:20	so the **c** of Israel did to them.
	9: 2	Let the **c** of Israel keep the
	9: 4	So Moses told the **c** of Israel
	9: 5	so the **c** of Israel did.
	9: 7	its appointed time among the **c**
	9:10	Speak to the **c** of Israel,
	9:17	after that the **c** of Israel
	9:17	there the **c** of Israel would
	9:18	the command of the LORD the **c**
	9:19	the **c** of Israel kept the charge
	9:22	the **c** of Israel would remain
	10:12	And the **c** of Israel set out from
	10:14	standard of the camp of the **c**
	10:15	the army of the tribe of the **c**
	10:16	the army of the tribe of the **c**
	10:19	the army of the tribe of the **c**
	10:20	the army of the tribe of the **c**
	10:22	standard of the camp of the **c**
	10:23	the army of the tribe of the **c**
	10:24	the army of the tribe of the **c**
	10:25	standard of the camp of the **c**
	10:26	the army of the tribe of the **c**
	10:27	the army of the tribe of the **c**
	10:28	the order of march of the **c** of

11: 4 so the ***c*** of Israel also wept
13: 2 which I am giving to the ***c*** of
13: 3 men who were heads of the ***c***
13:26 all the congregation of the ***c***
13:32 And they gave the ***c*** of Israel a
14: 2 And all the ***c*** of Israel
14: 3 that our wives and ***c*** should
14: 5 of the congregation of the ***c***
14: 7 all the congregation of the ***c***
14:10 of meeting before all the ***c*** of
14:18 of the fathers on the ***c*** to the
14:27 the complaints which the ***c*** of
14:39 told these words to all the ***c***
15: 2 Speak to the ***c*** of Israel, and
15:18 Speak to the ***c*** of Israel, and
15:25 whole congregation of the ***c*** of
15:26 whole congregation of the ***c*** of
15:29 who is native-born among the ***c***
15:32 Now while the ***c*** of Israel were
15:38 Speak to the ***c*** of Israel: Tell
16: 2 Moses with some of the ***c*** of
16:27 their sons, and their little ***c***.
16:38 they shall be a sign to the ***c***
16:40 to be a memorial to the ***c*** of
16:41 all the congregation of the ***c***
17: 2 Speak to the ***c*** of Israel, and
17: 5 of the complaints of the ***c*** of
17: 6 So Moses spoke to the ***c*** of
17: 9 before the LORD to all the ***c***
17:12 So the ***c*** of Israel spoke to
18: 5 may be no more wrath on the ***c***
18: 6 the Levites from among the ***c***
18: 8 all the holy gifts of the ***c*** of
18:11 the wave offerings of the ***c*** of
18:19 which the ***c*** of Israel offer to
18:20 your inheritance among the ***c***
18:21 I have given the ***c*** of Levi all
18:22 Hereafter the ***c*** of Israel shall
18:23 that among the ***c*** of Israel they
18:24 For the tithes of the ***c*** of
18:24 Among the ***c*** of Israel they shall
18:26 When you take from the ***c*** of
18:28 which you receive from the ***c***
18:32 the holy gifts of the ***c*** of
19: 2 Speak to the ***c*** of Israel, that
19: 9 for the congregation of the ***c***
19:10 be a statute forever to the ***c***
20: 1 Then the ***c*** of Israel, the whole
20:12 hallow Me in the eyes of the ***c***
20:13 because the ***c*** of Israel
20:19 So the ***c*** of Israel said to him,
20:22 Then the ***c*** of Israel, the whole
20:24 which I have given to the ***c*** of
21:10 Now the ***c*** of Israel moved on
22: 1 Then the ***c*** of Israel moved, and
22: 3 with dread because of the ***c*** of
25: 6 one of the ***c*** of Israel came and
25: 6 all the congregation of the ***c***
25: 8 plague was stopped among the ***c***
25:11 back My wrath from the ***c*** of
25:11 so that I did not consume the ***c***
25:13 and made atonement for the ***c*** of
26: 2 all the congregation of the ***c***
26: 4 commanded Moses and the ***c*** of
26: 5 The ***c*** of Reuben were: of
26:11 Nevertheless the ***c*** of Korah did
26:51 who were numbered of the ***c*** of
26:62 not numbered among the other ***c***
26:62 given to them among the ***c*** of
26:63 who numbered the ***c*** of Israel in
26:64 when they numbered the ***c*** of
27: 8 And you shall speak to the ***c*** of
27:11 And it shall be to the ***c*** of
27:12 which I have given to the ***c*** of
27:20 all the congregation of the ***c***
27:21 he and all the ***c*** of Israel with
28: 2 Command the ***c*** of Israel, and say
29:40 So Moses told the ***c*** of Israel
30: 1 of the tribes concerning the ***c***
31: 2 on the Midianites for the ***c*** of
31: 9 And the ***c*** of Israel took the
31:12 to the congregation of the ***c***
31:16 these women caused the ***c*** of
31:30 And from the ***c*** of Israel's half
31:42 And from the ***c*** of Israel's
31:47 and from the ***c*** of Israel's half
31:54 as a memorial for the ***c*** of
32: 1 Now the ***c*** of Reuben and the
32: 1 children of Reuben and the ***c***
32: 2 the ***c*** of Gad and the children of
32: 2 the children of Gad and the ***c*** of
32: 6 And Moses said to the ***c*** of Gad
32: 6 children of Gad and to the ***c***
32: 7 discourage the heart of the ***c***
32: 9 discouraged the heart of the ***c***
32:17 ready to go before the ***c*** of
32:18 homes until every one of the ***c***
32:25 And the ***c*** of Gad and the
32:25 the children of Gad and the ***c***
32:28 fathers of the tribes of the ***c***
32:29 If the ***c*** of Gad and the children
32:29 the children of Gad and the ***c***
32:31 Then the ***c*** of Gad and the
32:31 the children of Gad and the ***c***
32:33 So Moses gave to the ***c*** of Gad,
32:33 to the ***c*** of Reuben, and to half
32:34 And the ***c*** of Gad built Dibon and
32:37 And the ***c*** of Reuben built
32:39 And the ***c*** of Machir the son of
33: 1 are the journeys of the ***c*** of
33: 3 day after the Passover the ***c***
33: 5 Then the ***c*** of Israel moved from
33:38 the fortieth year after the ***c***
33:40 heard of the coming of the ***c*** of
33:51 Speak to the ***c*** of Israel, and
34: 2 Command the ***c*** of Israel, and say
34:13 Then Moses commanded the ***c*** of
34:14 For the tribe of the ***c*** of Reuben
34:14 and the tribe of the ***c*** of Gad
34:20 from the tribe of the ***c*** of
34:22 leader from the tribe of the ***c***
34:23 leader from the tribe of the ***c***
34:24 leader from the tribe of the ***c***
34:25 leader from the tribe of the ***c***
34:26 leader from the tribe of the ***c***
34:27 leader from the tribe of the ***c***
34:28 leader from the tribe of the ***c***
34:29 the inheritance among the ***c*** of
35: 2 Command the ***c*** of Israel that
35: 8 from the possession of the ***c*** of
35:10 Speak to the ***c*** of Israel, and
35:15 shall be for refuge for the ***c***
35:34 I the LORD dwell among the ***c***
36: 1 of the families of the ***c*** of
36: 1 the chief fathers of the ***c*** of
36: 2 an inheritance by lot to the ***c***
36: 3 of the other tribes of the ***c***
36: 4 And when the Jubilee of the ***c*** of
36: 5 Then Moses commanded the ***c*** of
36: 7 So the inheritance of the ***c*** of
36: 7 for every one of the ***c*** of
36: 8 in any tribe of the ***c*** of
36: 8 so that the ***c*** of Israel each
36: 9 but every tribe of the ***c*** of
36:12 into the families of the ***c*** of
36:13 the LORD commanded the ***c*** of
Deut 1: 3 that Moses spoke to the ***c*** of
1:36 and to him and his ***c*** I am
1:39 your little ones and your ***c***,
3: 6 women, and ***c*** of every city.
3:18 brethren, the ***c*** of Israel.
4: 9 And teach them to your ***c*** and
4:10 that they may teach their ***c***.
4:25 When you beget ***c*** and
4:40 well with you and with your ***c***
4:44 which Moses set before the ***c***
4:45 which Moses spoke to the ***c*** of
4:46 whom Moses and the ***c*** of Israel
5: 9 of the fathers upon the ***c*** to
5:29 well with them and with their ***c***
6: 7 teach them diligently to your ***c***,
10: 6 (Now the ***c*** of Israel journeyed
11: 2 I do not speak with your ***c***,
11:19 shall teach them to your ***c***,
11:21 days and the days of your ***c***
12:25 may go well with you and your ***c***
12:28 may go well with you and your ***c***
14: 1 You are the ***c*** of the LORD your
17:20 he and his ***c*** in the midst of
21:15 and they have borne him ***c***,
23: 8 The ***c*** of the third generation
24: 7 any of his brethren of the ***c***
24:16 be put to death for their ***c***,
24:16 nor shall the ***c*** be put to death
28:54 and toward the rest of his ***c***
28:55 any of them the flesh of his ***c***
28:57 from between her feet and her ***c***
29: 1 Moses to make with the ***c*** of
29:22 the coming generation of your ***c***
29:29 belong to us and to our ***c***
30: 2 you today, you and your ***c***,
31:13 "and that their ***c***,
31:19 and teach it to the ***c*** of
31:19 a witness for Me against the ***c***
31:22 and taught it to the ***c*** of
31:23 for you shall bring the ***c*** of
32: 5 They are not His ***c***,
32: 8 to the number of the ***c*** of
32:20 ***C*** in whom is no faith.
32:46 which you shall command your ***c***
32:49 which I give to the ***c*** of Israel
32:51 against Me among the ***c*** of
32:51 Me in the midst of the ***c*** of
32:52 which I am giving to the ***c*** of
33: 1 the man of God blessed the ***c***
33: 9 brothers, Or know his own ***c***;
34: 8 And the ***c*** of Israel wept for
34: 9 so the ***c*** of Israel heeded him,
Josh 1: 2 to them—the ***c*** of Israel.
2: 2 come here tonight from the ***c***
3: 1 he and all the ***c*** of Israel, and
3: 9 So Joshua said to the ***c*** of
4: 4 he had appointed from the ***c*** of
4: 5 number of the tribes of the ***c***
4: 6 be a sign among you when your ***c***
4: 7 be for a memorial to the ***c*** of
4: 8 And the ***c*** of Israel did so,
4: 8 number of the tribes of the ***c***
4:12 over armed before the ***c*** of
4:21 Then he spoke to the ***c*** of
4:21 When your ***c*** ask their fathers in
4:22 then you shall let your ***c*** know,
5: 1 of the Jordan from before the ***c***
5: 1 any longer because of the ***c*** of
5: 6 For the ***c*** of Israel walked forty
5:10 Now the ***c*** of Israel camped in
5:12 and the ***c*** of Israel no longer
6: 1 shut up because of the ***c*** of
7: 1 But the ***c*** of Israel committed a
7: 1 the LORD burned against the ***c***
7:12 Therefore the ***c*** of Israel could
7:23 to Joshua and to all the ***c*** of
8:31 the LORD had commanded the ***c***
8:32 in the presence of the ***c*** of
9:17 Then the ***c*** of Israel journeyed
9:18 But the ***c*** of Israel did not
9:26 them out of the hand of the ***c***
10: 4 with Joshua and with the ***c*** of
10:11 from the hailstones than the ***c***
10:12 up the Amorites before the ***c***
10:20 while Joshua and the ***c*** of
10:21 tongue against any of the ***c*** of
11:14 the ***c*** of Israel took as booty
11:19 that made peace with the ***c*** of
11:22 were left in the land of the ***c***
12: 1 kings of the land whom the ***c***
12: 6 servant of the LORD and the ***c***
12: 7 country which Joshua and the ***c***
13: 6 drive out from before the ***c*** of
13:10 as far as the border of the ***c***
13:13 Nevertheless the ***c*** of Israel did
13:15 given to the tribe of the ***c*** of
13:22 The ***c*** of Israel also killed with
13:23 And the border of the ***c*** of
13:23 was the inheritance of the ***c***
13:24 to the ***c*** of Gad according to
13:28 is the inheritance of the ***c***
13:29 for half the tribe of the ***c*** of
13:31 were for the ***c*** of Machir the
13:31 for half of the ***c*** of Machir
14: 1 are the areas which the ***c***
14: 1 fathers of the tribes of the ***c***
14: 4 For the ***c*** of Joseph were two
14: 5 so the ***c*** of Israel did; and
14: 6 Then the ***c*** of Judah came to
15: 1 the lot of the tribe of the ***c***
15:12 This is the boundary of the ***c***
15:13 he gave a share among the ***c*** of
15:14 and Talmai, the ***c*** of Anak.
15:20 of the tribe of the ***c*** of Judah
15:21 limits of the tribe of the ***c***
15:63 the ***c*** of Judah could not drive
15:63 the Jebusites dwell with the ***c***
16: 1 The lot fell to the ***c*** of Joseph
16: 4 So the ***c*** of Joseph, Manasseh and
16: 5 The border of the ***c*** of Ephraim,
16: 8 of the tribe of the ***c*** of
16: 9 The separate cities for the ***c*** of
16: 9 among the inheritance of the ***c***
17: 2 a lot for the rest of the ***c***
17: 2 for the ***c*** of Abiezer, the
17: 2 the ***c*** of Helek, the children of
17: 2 the ***c*** of Asriel, the children
17: 2 the ***c*** of Shechem, the children
17: 2 the ***c*** of Hepher, and the
17: 2 and the ***c*** of Shemida; these
17: 2 these were the male ***c*** of
17: 8 of Manasseh belonged to the ***c***
17:12 Yet the ***c*** of Manasseh could not
17:13 when the ***c*** of Israel grew
17:14 Then the ***c*** of Joseph spoke to
17:16 But the ***c*** of Joseph said, "The
18: 1 whole congregation of the ***c*** of
18: 2 But there remained among the ***c***
18: 3 Then Joshua said to the ***c*** of
18:10 divided the land to the ***c*** of
18:11 the lot of the tribe of the ***c***
18:11 lot came out between the ***c*** of
18:11 children of Judah and the ***c*** of
18:14 a city of the ***c*** of Judah.
18:20 was the inheritance of the ***c***
18:21 cities of the tribe of the ***c***
18:28 was the inheritance of the ***c***
19: 1 for the tribe of the ***c*** of
19: 1 the inheritance of the ***c*** of
19: 8 of the tribe of the ***c*** of
19: 9 The inheritance of the ***c*** of
19: 9 in the share of the ***c*** of Judah,
19: 9 for the share of the ***c*** of Judah
19: 9 Therefore the ***c*** of Simeon had
19:10 third lot came out for the ***c***
19:16 was the inheritance of the ***c***
19:17 for the ***c*** of Issachar according
19:23 of the tribe of the ***c*** of
19:24 out for the tribe of the ***c*** of
19:31 of the tribe of the ***c*** of Asher
19:32 sixth lot came out to the ***c*** of
19:32 for the ***c*** of Naphtali according
19:39 of the tribe of the ***c*** of
19:40 out for the tribe of the ***c*** of
19:47 And the border of the ***c*** of Dan
19:47 because the ***c*** of Dan went up to
19:48 of the tribe of the ***c*** of Dan
19:49 the ***c*** of Israel gave an
19:51 fathers of the tribes of the ***c***
20: 2 Speak to the ***c*** of Israel,
20: 9 cities appointed for all the ***c***
21: 1 houses of the tribes of the ***c***
21: 3 So the ***c*** of Israel gave to the
21: 4 And the ***c*** of Aaron the priest,
21: 5 The rest of the ***c*** of Kohath had
21: 6 And the ***c*** of Gershon had
21: 7 The ***c*** of Merari according to
21: 8 And the ***c*** of Israel gave these
21: 9 gave from the tribe of the ***c***
21: 9 and from the tribe of the ***c*** of
21:10 which were for the ***c*** of Aaron,
21:10 who were of the ***c*** of Levi;
21:13 Thus to the ***c*** of Aaron the
21:19 All the cities of the ***c*** of
21:20 And the families of the ***c*** of
21:20 the rest of the ***c*** of Kohath,
21:26 rest of the families of the ***c***
21:27 Also to the ***c*** of Gershon, of
21:34 And to the families of the ***c*** of
21:40 So all the cities for the ***c*** of

C

21:41 within the possession of the *c*
22: 9 So the *c* of Reuben, the children
22: 9 the *c* of Gad, and half the
22: 9 and departed from the *c* of
22:10 the *c* of Reuben, the children
22:10 the *c* of Gad, and half the
22:11 Now the *c* of Israel heard
22:11 the *c* of Reuben, the children
22:11 the *c* of Gad, and half the
22:11 on the *c* of Israel's side."
22:12 And when the *c* of Israel heard
22:12 whole congregation of the *c* of
22:13 Then the *c* of Israel sent
22:13 of Eleazar the priest to the *c*
22:13 to the *c* of Gad, and to half
22:15 Then they came to the *c* of
22:15 to the *c* of Gad, and to half
22:21 Then the *c* of Reuben, the
22:21 the *c* of Gad, and half the
22:25 you *c* of Reuben and children
22:25 you children of Reuben and *c*
22:30 heard the words that the *c* of
22:30 the *c* of Gad, and the children
22:30 and the *c* of Manasseh spoke, it
22:31 the priest said to the *c* of
22:31 the *c* of Gad, and the children
22:31 and the *c* of Manasseh, "This
22:31 Now you have delivered the *c* of
22:32 returned from the *c* of Reuben
22:32 children of Reuben and the *c*
22:32 to the *c* of Israel, and brought
22:33 So the thing pleased the *c* of
22:33 and the *c* of Israel blessed
22:33 to destroy the land where the *c*
22:34 The *c* of Reuben and the children
22:34 children of Reuben and the *c*
24: 4 but Jacob and his *c* went down
24:32 which the *c* of Israel had
24:32 become an inheritance of the *c*
Judg 1: 1 it came to pass that the *c* of
1: 8 Now the *c* of Judah fought
1: 9 And afterward the *c* of Judah
1:16 Now the *c* of the Kenite, Moses'
1:16 the City of Palms with the *c*
1:21 But the *c* of Benjamin did not
1:21 the Jebusites dwell with the *c*
1:34 And the Amorites forced the *c*
2: 4 spoke these words to all the *c*
2: 6 the *c* of Israel went each to
2:11 Then the *c* of Israel did evil
3: 2 that the generations of the *c*
3: 5 Thus the *c* of Israel dwelt
3: 7 So the *c* of Israel did evil in
3: 8 and the *c* of Israel served
3: 9 When the *c* of Israel cried out
3: 9 up a deliverer for the *c* of
3:12 And the *c* of Israel again did
3:14 So the *c* of Israel served Eglon
3:15 But when the *c* of Israel cried
3:15 By him the *c* of Israel sent
3:27 and the *c* of Israel went down
4: 1 the *c* of Israel again did evil
4: 3 And the *c* of Israel cried out to
4: 3 he harshly oppressed the *c* of
4: 5 And the *c* of Israel came up to
4:11 of the *c* of Hobab the
4:23 in the presence of the *c* of
4:24 And the hand of the *c* of Israel
6: 1 Then the *c* of Israel did evil in
6: 2 the *c* of Israel made for
6: 6 and the *c* of Israel cried out
6: 7 when the *c* of Israel cried out
6: 8 LORD sent a prophet to the *c*
8:28 was subdued before the *c* of
8:33 that the *c* of Israel again
8:34 Thus the *c* of Israel did not
10: 6 Then the *c* of Israel again did
10: 8 harassed and oppressed the *c*
10: 8 all the *c* of Israel who were on
10:10 And the *c* of Israel cried out
10:11 So the LORD said to the *c* of
10:15 And the *c* of Israel said to the
10:17 And the *c* of Israel assembled
11:27 this day between the *c* of
11:33 were subdued before the *c* of
13: 1 Again the *c* of Israel did evil
13: 2 wife was barren and had no *c*.
13: 3 are barren and have borne no *c*,
18: 2 So the *c* of Dan sent five men of
18:16 who were of the *c* of Dan,
18:22 together and overtook the *c* of
18:23 And they called out to the *c* of
18:25 And the *c* of Dan said to him,
18:26 Then the *c* of Dan went their
18:30 Then the *c* of Dan set up for
19:12 who are not of the *c* of
19:30 or seen from the day that the *c*
20: 1 So all the *c* of Israel came out,
20: 3 (Now the *c* of Benjamin heard
20: 3 of Benjamin heard that the *c*
20: 3 Then the *c* of Israel said,
20: 7 All of you are *c* of
20:13 evil from Israel!" But the *c*
20:13 brethren, the *c* of Israel.
20:14 the *c* of Benjamin gathered
20:14 to go to battle against the *c*
20:15 cities at that time the *c* of
20:18 Then the *c* of Israel arose and
20:18 first to battle against the *c*
20:19 So the *c* of Israel rose in the
20:21 Then the *c* of Benjamin came out
20:23 Then the *c* of Israel went up and
20:23 near for battle against the *c*
20:24 So the *c* of Israel approached
20:24 of Israel approached the *c* of
20:25 thousand more of the *c* of
20:26 Then all the *c* of Israel, that
20:27 So the *c* of Israel inquired of
20:28 go out to battle against the *c*
20:30 And the *c* of Israel went up
20:30 of Israel went up against the *c*
20:31 So the *c* of Benjamin went out
20:32 And the *c* of Benjamin said,
20:32 But the *c* of Israel said,
20:35 And the *c* of Israel destroyed
20:36 So the *c* of Benjamin saw that
20:48 turned back against the *c* of
21: 5 The *c* of Israel said, "Who is
21: 6 And the *c* of Israel grieved for
21:10 including the women and *c*.
21:13 sent word to the *c* of
21:18 for the *c* of Israel have sworn
21:20 they instructed the *c* of
21:23 And the *c* of Benjamin did so;
21:24 So the *c* of Israel departed from
1 Sam 1: 2 other Peninnah. Peninnah had *c*,
1: 2 children, but Hannah had no *c*.
2: 5 And she who has many *c* has
2:28 all the offerings of the *c* of
7: 4 So the *c* of Israel put away the
7: 6 And Samuel judged the *c* of
7: 7 Philistines heard that the *c*
7: 7 And when the *c* of Israel heard
7: 8 So the *c* of Israel said to
9: 2 person than he among the *c* of
10:18 and said to the *c* of Israel,
11: 8 the *c* of Israel were three
14:18 the ark of God was with the *c*
15: 6 showed kindness to all the *c*
17:53 Then the *c* of Israel returned
22:19 *c* and nursing infants, oxen and
26:19 But if it is the *c* of men,
30:22 for every man's wife and *c*,
2 Sam 1:18 he told them to teach the *c*
2:25 Now the *c* of Benjamin gathered
4: 2 of the *c* of Benjamin.
6:23 the daughter of Saul had no *c*
7: 6 the time that I brought the *c*
7: 7 moved about with all the *c* of
12: 3 with him and with his *c*.
21: 2 Gibeonites were not of the *c*
21: 2 the *c* of Israel had sworn
21: 2 them in his zeal for the *c* of
23:29 of Ribai from Gibeah of the *c*
1 Ki 6: 1 and eightieth year after the *c*
6:13 And I will dwell among the *c* of
8: 1 the chief fathers of the *c* of
8: 9 made a covenant with the *c*
8:63 So the king and all the *c* of
9:20 who were not of the *c* of
9:21 whom the *c* of Israel had not
9:22 But of the *c* of Israel Solomon
11: 2 the LORD had said to the *c* of
12:17 Rehoboam reigned over the *c* of
12:24 against your brethren the *c* of
12:33 he ordained a feast for the *c*
14:24 had cast out before the *c* of
18:20 So Ahab sent for all the *c* of
19:10 for the *c* of Israel have
19:14 because the *c* of Israel have
20: 3 your loveliest wives and *c* are
20: 5 your wives and your *c*";
20: 7 sent to me for my wives, my *c*,
20:15 all the *c* of Israel—seven
20:27 And the *c* of Israel were
20:27 Now the *c* of Israel encamped
20:29 and the *c* of Israel killed one
21:26 had cast out before the *c* of
2 Ki 8:12 evil that you will do to the *c*
8:12 and you will dash their *c*,
13: 5 and the *c* of Israel dwelt in
14: 6 But the *c* of the murderers he
14: 6 not be put to death for their *c*,
14: 6 nor shall *c* be put to death for
16: 3 had cast out from before the *c*
17: 7 For so it was that the *c* of
17: 8 had cast out from before the *c*
17: 9 Also the *c* of Israel secretly
17:22 For the *c* of Israel walked in
17:24 of Samaria instead of the *c* of
17:31 the Sepharvites burned their *c*
17:34 the LORD had commanded the *c*
17:41 also their *c* and their
17:41 and their children's *c* have
18: 4 for until those days the *c* of
19: 3 for the *c* have come to birth,
21: 2 had cast out before the *c* of
21: 9 had destroyed before the *c* of
1 Chr 1:33 All these were the *c* of
1:43 a king reigned over the *c* of
2:10 leader of the *c* of Judah;
2:18 Caleb the son of Hezron had *c*
2:30 Appaim; Seled died without *c*.
2:32 Jonathan; Jether died without *c*.
4:27 brothers did not have many *c*,
4:27 multiply as much as the *c* of
5:11 And the *c* of Gad dwelt next to
5:14 These were the *c* of Abihail the
5:23 So the *c* of the half-tribe of
6: 3 The *c* of Amram were Aaron,
6:64 So the *c* of Israel gave these
6:65 by lot from the tribe of the *c*
6:65 from the tribe of the *c* of
6:65 and from the tribe of the *c* of
6:77 of Zebulun the rest of the *c*
7:29 and by the borders of the *c* of
7:29 In these dwelt the *c* of Joseph,
7:33 These were the *c* of Japhlet.
7:40 All these were the *c* of Asher,
8: 8 And Shaharaim had *c* in the
9: 3 Now in Jerusalem the *c* of Judah
9: 3 and some of the *c* of Benjamin,
9: 3 and of the *c* of Ephraim and
9:18 for the camps of the *c* of Levi
9:23 So they and their *c* were in
14: 4 these are the names of his *c*
15: 4 Then David assembled the *c* of
15:15 And the *c* of the Levites bore
16:13 You *c* of Jacob, His chosen
24: 2 their father, and had no *c*;
26:10 of the *c* of Merari, had sons:
27: 1 And the *c* of Israel, according
27: 3 he was of the *c* of Perez, and
27:10 of the *c* of Ephraim; in his
27:14 of the *c* of Ephraim; in his
27:20 over the *c* of Ephraim, Hoshea
28: 8 as an inheritance for your *c*
2 Chr 5: 2 the chief fathers of the *c* of
5:10 made a covenant with the *c*
6:11 LORD which He made with the *c*
7: 3 When all the *c* of Israel saw how
8: 2 and he settled the *c* of Israel
8: 8 whom the *c* of Israel did not
8: 9 But Solomon did not make the *c*
10:17 Rehoboam reigned over the *c* of
10:18 but the *c* of Israel stoned him
11:19 And she bore him *c*:
13:12 O *c* of Israel, do not fight
13:16 And the *c* of Israel fled before
13:18 Thus the *c* of Israel were
13:18 and the *c* of Judah prevailed,
20:13 ones, their wives, and their *c*,
20:19 Then the Levites of the *c* of the
20:19 of the Kohathites and of the *c*
21:14 a serious affliction—your *c*,
25: 4 he did not execute their *c*,
25: 4 not be put to death for their *c*,
25: 4 nor shall the *c* be put to death
25: 7 not with any of the *c* of
25:12 Also the *c* of Judah took captive
28: 3 and burned his *c* in the fire,
28: 3 had cast out before the *c* of
28: 8 And the *c* of Israel carried away
28:10 now you propose to force the *c*
28:12 some of the heads of the *c* of
30: 6 *C* of Israel, return to the LORD
30: 9 your brethren and your *c* will
30:21 So the *c* of Israel who were
31: 1 Then all the *c* of Israel
31: 5 the *c* of Israel brought in
31: 6 And the *c* of Israel and Judah,
33: 2 had cast out before the *c* of
33: 9 had destroyed before the *c* of
34:33 that belonged to the *c* of
35:17 And the *c* of Israel who were
Ezra 2:58 All the Nethinim and the *c* of
3: 1 and the *c* of Israel were in
6:16 Then the *c* of Israel, the
6:21 Then the *c* of Israel who had
7: 7 Some of the *c* of Israel, the
8:35 The *c* of those who had been
9:12 it as an inheritance to your *c*
10: 1 and *c* gathered to him from
10:44 had wives by whom they had *c*.
Neh 1: 6 for the *c* of Israel Your
1: 6 and confess the sins of the *c*
2:10 to seek the well-being of the *c*
5: 5 our *c* as their children; and
5: 5 our children as their *c*;
7:73 the *c* of Israel were in their
8:14 that the *c* of Israel should
8:17 of Nun until that day the *c* of
9: 1 day of this month the *c* of
9:23 You also multiplied their *c* as
10:39 For the *c* of Israel and the
10:39 children of Israel and the *c*
11: 4 Jerusalem dwelt some of the *c*
11: 4 children of Judah and of the *c*
11: 4 The *c* of Judah: Athaiah the
11: 4 of the *c* of Perez;
11:24 of the *c* of Zerah the son of
11:25 some of the *c* of Judah dwelt
11:31 Also the *c* of Benjamin from
12:43 the women and the *c* also
12:47 consecrated them for the *c* of
13: 2 because they had not met the *c*
13:16 them on the Sabbath to the *c*
13:24 And half of their *c* spoke the
Esth 3:13 little *c* and women, in one day,
5:11 riches, the multitude of his *c*,
8:11 both little *c* and women, and
Job 17: 5 Even the eyes of his *c* will
19:17 And I am repulsive to the *c* of
19:18 Even young *c* despise me;
20:10 His *c* will seek the favor of
21:11 And their *c* dance.
21:19 up one's iniquity for his *c*';
24: 5 food for them and for their *c*.
27:14 If his *c* are multiplied, it
29: 5 When my *c* were around me;
41:34 He is king over all the *c* of
42:16 and saw his *c* and grandchildren
Ps 14: 2 down from heaven upon the *c* of
17:14 They are satisfied with *c*,
34:11 Come, you *c*, listen to me;
36: 7 O God! Therefore the *c* of men

53: 2 down from heaven upon the c of
69: 8 And an alien to my mother's c;
72: 4 He will save the c of the
73:15 to the generation of Your c.
78: 4 not hide them from their c,
78: 5 make them known to their c;
78: 6 The c who would be born,
78: 6 and declare them to their c,
78: 9 The c of Ephraim, being armed
82: 6 And all of you are c of the
83: 8 They have helped the c of Lot.
89:47 have You created all the c of
90: 3 'Return, O c of men."
90:16 And Your glory to their c.
102:28 The c of Your servants will
103: 7 His acts to the c of Israel.
103:13 As a father pities his c,
103:17 righteousness to children's c,
105: 6 You c of Jacob, His chosen
107: 8 His wonderful works to the c
107:15 His wonderful works to the c
107:21 His wonderful works to the c
107:31 His wonderful works to the c
109: 9 Let his c be fatherless, And
109:10 Let his c continually be
109:12 any to favor his fatherless c.
113: 9 Like a joyful mother of c.
115:14 more and more, You and your c.
115:16 earth He has given to the c of
127: 3 c are a heritage from the
127: 4 So are the c of one's youth.
128: 3 Your c like olive plants All
128: 6 may you see your children's c.
147:13 He has blessed your c within
148:12 men and maidens; Old men and c.
148:14 Of the c of Israel, A people
149: 2 Let the c of Zion be joyful in
Prov 4: 1 Hear, my c, the instruction
5: 7 Therefore hear me now, my c,
7:24 therefore, listen to me, my c;
8:32 therefore, listen to me, my c,
13:22 inheritance to his children's c,
14:26 And His c will have a place of
17: 6 Children's c are the crown of
17: 6 And the glory of c is their
20: 7 His c are blessed after him.
31:28 Her c rise up and call her
Eccl 6: 3 If a man begets a hundred c
Isa 1: 2 have nourished and brought up c,
1: 4 C who are corrupters!
2: 6 they are pleased with the c of
3: 4 I will give c to be their
3:12 c are their oppressors, And
8:18 Here am I and the c whom the
13:16 Their c also will be dashed to
13:18 Their eye will not spare c.
14:21 Prepare slaughter for his c
17: 3 will be as the glory of the c
17: 9 they left because of the c of
23: 4 do not labor, nor bring forth c;
27:12 O you c of Israel.
29:23 But when he sees his c,
30: 1 "Woe to the rebellious c,
30: 9 a rebellious people, Lying c,
30: 9 C who will not hear the law
31: 6 to Him against whom the c of
37: 3 for the c have come to birth,
38:19 make known Your truth to the c.
47: 8 shall I know the loss of c';
47: 9 in one day: The loss of c,
49:20 The c you will have, After you
49:21 Since I have lost my c and am
49:25 you, And I will save your c.
54: 1 For more are the c of
54: 1 of the desolate Than the c of
54:13 All your c shall be taught by
54:13 shall be the peace of your c.
57: 4 Are you not c of
57: 5 Slaying the c in the valleys,
63: 8 C who will not lie." So He
65:23 Nor bring forth c for trouble;
66: 8 labor, She gave birth to her c.
66:20 as the c of Israel bring an
Jer 2: 9 And against your children's c I
2:30 vain I have chastened your c;
3:14 "Return, O backsliding c,
3:19 How can I put you among the c
3:21 and supplications of the c of
3:22 "Return, you backsliding c,
4:22 known Me. They are silly c,
5: 7 Your c have forsaken Me And
6: 1 O you c of Benjamin, Gather
6:11 I will pour it out on the c
7:18 The c gather wood, the fathers
7:30 For the c of Judah have done
9:21 our palaces, To kill off the c—
10:20 My c have gone from me, And
15: 7 I will bereave them of c;
16:14 lives who brought up the c of
16:15 lives who brought up the c of
17: 2 While their c remember Their
17:19 and stand in the gate of the c
18:21 Therefore deliver up their c to
18:21 widows And bereaved of their c.
23: 7 lives who brought up the c of
30:20 Their c also shall be as
31:15 Rachel weeping for her c,
31:15 to be comforted for her c,
31:17 That your c shall come back
32:18 into the bosom of their c
32:30 because the c of Israel and the
32:30 children of Israel and the c
32:30 For the c of Israel have
32:32 of all the evil of the c of
32:32 children of Israel and the c
32:39 the good of them and their c
38:23 surrender all your wives and c
40: 7 committed to him men, women, c,
41:16 of war and the women and the c
43: 6 men, women, c, the king's
47: 3 will not look back for their c,
49:11 Leave your fatherless c,
50: 4 The c of Israel shall come,
50: 4 They and the c of Judah
50:33 The c of Israel were oppressed,
50:33 Along with the c of Judah;
Lam 1: 5 Her c have gone into captivity
1:16 My c are desolate Because the
2:11 Because the c and the infants
2:19 For the life of your young c,
2:20 The c they have cuddled?
3:33 Nor grieve the c of men.
4: 4 The young c ask for bread,
4:10 women Have cooked their own c;
Ezek 2: 3 I am sending you to the c of
2: 4 are impudent and stubborn c.
3:11 to the c of your people, and
4:13 So shall the c of Israel eat
6: 5 I will lay the corpses of the c
9: 6 maidens and little c and women;
16:21 that you have slain My c and
16:36 because of the blood of your c
16:45 loathing husband and c;
16:45 loathed their husbands and c;
20:18 But I said to their c in the
20:21 the c rebelled against Me;
23:39 after they had slain their c
31:14 Among the c of men who go down
33: 2 speak to the c of your people,
33:12 say to the c of your people:
33:17 Yet the c of your people say,
33:30 the c of your people are
35: 5 shed the blood of the c of
36:12 shall you bereave them of c.
36:13 and bereave your nation of c,
37:16 For Judah and for the c of
37:18 And when the c of your people
37:21 Surely I will take the c of
37:25 dwell there, they, their c,
37:25 and their children's c,
43: 7 dwell in the midst of the c of
44: 9 foreigner who is among the c
44:15 of My sanctuary when the c of
47:22 dwell among you and who bear c
47:22 you as native-born among the c
48:11 did not go astray when the c
Dan 1: 3 to bring some of the c of
2:38 and wherever the c of men dwell,
6:24 the den of lions—them, their c,
Hos 1: 2 a wife of harlotry And c of
1:10 Yet the number of the c of
1:11 Then the c of Judah and the
1:11 children of Judah and the c of
2: 4 will not have mercy on her c,
2: 4 For they are the c of
3: 1 love of the LORD for the c of
3: 4 For the c of Israel shall abide
3: 5 Afterward the c of Israel shall
4: 1 You c of Israel, For the
4: 6 God, I also will forget your c.
5: 7 For they have begotten pagan c.
9:12 Though they bring up their c,
9:13 Ephraim will bring out his c
9:16 Yes, were they to bear c,
10: 9 battle in Gibeah against the c
10:14 dashed in pieces upon her c.
13:13 he should not stay long where c
Joel 1: 3 Tell your c about it, Let
1: 3 Let your c tell their
1: 3 your children tell their c,
1: 3 And their c another
2:16 Gather the c and nursing
2:23 you c of Zion, And rejoice in
3:16 And the strength of the c of
Am 2:11 O you c of Israel?" Says the
3: 1 O c of Israel, against the
3:12 So shall the c of Israel be
4: 5 You c of Israel!" Says the
9: 7 O c of Israel?" says the
Ob 12 you have rejoiced over the c
20 captives of this host of the c
Mic 1:16 Because of your precious c;
2: 9 From their c You have taken
5: 3 Shall return to the c of
Nah 3:10 Her young c also were dashed
Zeph 1: 8 the princes and the king's c,
Zech 10: 7 their c shall see it and be
10: 9 live, together with their c,
Mal 4: 6 hearts of the fathers to the c,
4: 6 And the hearts of the c to
Mt 2:16 and put to death all the male c
2:18 Rachel weeping for her c,
3: 9 that God is able to raise up c
7:11 to give good gifts to your c,
10:21 and c will rise up against
11:16 It is like c sitting in the
11:19 wisdom is justified by her c.
14:21 men, besides women and c.
15:38 men, besides women and c.
18: 3 and become as little c,
18:25 with his wife and c and all
19:13 Then little c were brought to
19:14 Let the little c come to Me, and
19:29 father or mother or wife or c
21:15 and the c crying out in the
22:24 that if a man dies, having no c,
23:37 often I wanted to gather your c
27: 9 whom they of the c of Israel
27:25 blood be on us and on our c.
Mk 7:27 Let the c be filled first, for
9:37 receives one of these little c
10:13 Then they brought little c to
10:14 Let the little c come to Me, and
10:24 again and said to them, "C,
10:29 father or mother or wife or c
10:30 and sisters and mothers and c
12:19 wife behind, and leaves no c,
13:12 and c will rise up against
Lk 1:16 he will turn many of the c
1:17 of the fathers to the c,
3: 8 that God is able to raise up c
7:32 They are like c sitting in the
7:35 is justified by all her c.
11: 7 and my c are with me in bed;
11:13 to give good gifts to your c,
13:34 often I wanted to gather your c
14:26 father and mother, wife and c,
18:16 Let the little c come to Me, and
18:29 or brothers or wife or c,
19:44 and your c within you, to the
20:28 a wife, and he dies without c,
20:29 took a wife, and died without c.
20:31 seven also; and they left no c,
23:28 for yourselves and for your c.
Jn 1:12 He gave the right to become c
8:39 them, "If you were Abraham's c,
11:52 gather together in one the c
13:33 'Little c, I shall be with
21: 5 Then Jesus said to them, "C,
Acts 2:39 promise is to you and to your c,
5:21 with all the elders of the c of
7:23 his brethren, the c of Israel.
7:37 is that Moses who said to the c
9:15 and the c of Israel.
10:36 word which God sent to the c
13:33 fulfilled this for us their c,
21: 5 us, with wives and c,
21:21 not to circumcise their c nor
Rom 8:16 with our spirit that we are c
8:17 and if c, then heirs—heirs
8:21 the glorious liberty of the c
9: 7 nor are they all c because
9: 8 those who are the c of the
9: 8 these are not the c of God;
9: 8 but the c of the promise are
9:11 (for the c not yet being born,
9:27 the number of the c of
1 Cor 4:14 but as my beloved c I warn
7:14 otherwise your c would be
14:20 do not be c in understanding;
2 Cor 3: 7 so that the c of Israel could
3:13 over his face so that the c of
6:13 for the same (I speak as to c),
12:14 For the c ought not to lay up
12:14 but the parents for the c.
Gal 4: 3 Even so we, when we were c,
4:19 My little c, for whom I labor
4:25 and is in bondage with her c—
4:27 desolate has many more c
4:28 are c of promise.
4:31 we are not c of the bondwoman
Eph 2: 3 and were by nature c of wrath,
4:14 that we should no longer be c,
5: 1 be imitators of God as dear c.
5: 8 Walk as c of light
6: 1 C, obey your parents in the
6: 4 do not provoke your c to wrath,
Phil 2:15 c of God without fault in the
Col 3:20 C, obey your parents in all
3:21 Fathers, do not provoke your c,
1 Th 2: 7 mother cherishes her own c.
2:11 as a father does his own c,
1 Tim 3: 4 having his c in submission
3:12 ruling their c and their own
5: 4 But if any widow has c or
5:10 works: if she has brought up c,
5:14 younger widows marry, bear c,
Titus 1: 6 having faithful c not accused
2: 4 their husbands, to love their c,
Heb 2:13 Here am I and the c whom
2:14 Inasmuch then as the c have
11:22 of the departure of the c of
1 Pe 1:14 as obedient c, not conforming
2 Pe 2:14 practices, and are accursed c.
1 Jn 2: 1 My little c, these things I
2:12 I write to you, little c,
2:13 I write to you, little c,
2:18 Little c, it is the last
2:28 And now, little c, abide
3: 1 that we should be called c of
3: 2 now we are c of God; and it has
3: 7 Little c, let no one deceive
3:10 In this the c of God and the
3:10 the children of God and the c
3:18 My little c, let us not love
4: 4 You are of God, little c,
5: 2 we know that we love the c of
5:21 Little c, keep yourselves
2 Jn 1 To the elect lady and her c,
4 I have found some of your c
13 The c of your elect sister greet
3 Jn 4 joy than to hear that my c
Rev 2:14 a stumbling block before the c
2:23 I will kill her c with death,
7: 4 of all the tribes of the c of
21:12 of the twelve tribes of the c

C

CHILDREN OF GOD (10/10)

Jn 1:12 He gave the right to become **c**,
11:52 gather together in one the **c**
Rom 8:16 with our spirit that we are **c**,
8:21 the glorious liberty of the **c**.
9: 8 the flesh, these are not the **c**;
Phil 2:15 **c** without fault in the midst of
1 Jn 3: 1 that we should be called **c**!
3: 2 Beloved, now we are **c**;
3:10 In this the **c** and the children
5: 2 this we know that we love the **c**,

CHILDREN'S (16/16) CHILDREN

Gen 31:16 are really ours and our **c**;
45:10 your **c** children, your flocks
Ex 34: 7 upon the children and the **c**
Josh 14: 9 be your inheritance and your **c**
2 Ki 17:41 also their children and their **c**
Ps 103:17 And His righteousness to **c**
128: 6 may you see your **c** children.
Prov 13:22 leaves an inheritance to his **c**
17: 6 **C** children are the crown of
Jer 2: 9 And against your **c** children I
31:29 And the **c** teeth are set on
Ezek 18: 2 And the **c** teeth are set on
37:25 and their **c** children, forever;
Mt 15:26 It is not good to take the **c**
Mk 7:27 it is not good to take the **c**
7:28 under the table eat from the **c**

CHILEAB (1/1)

2 Sam 3: 3 his second, **C**, by Abigail

CHILION (2/2) CHILION'S

Ruth 1: 2 his two sons were Mahlon and **C**—
1: 5 Then both Mahlon and **C** also

CHILION'S (1/1) CHILION

Ruth 4: 9 and all that was **C** and

CHILMAD (1/1)

Ezek 27:23 and **C** were your merchants.

CHIMHAM (4/4)

2 Sam 19:37 But here is your servant **C**;
19:38 **C** shall cross over with me, and
19:40 and **C** went on with him. And all
Jer 41:17 dwelt in the habitation of **C**,

CHIMNEY (1/1)

Hos 13: 3 floor And like smoke from a **c**.

CHINNERETH (4/4) CHINNEROTH, GENNESARET

Num 34:11 eastern side of the Sea of **C**;
Deut 3:17 from **C** as far as the east side
Josh 13:27 far as the edge of the Sea of **C**,
19:35 Zer, Hammath, Rakkath, **C**,

CHINNEROTH (3/3) CHINNERETH

Josh 11: 2 in the plain south of **C**,
12: 3 Jordan plain from the Sea of **C**
1 Ki 15:20 Abel Beth Maachah, and all **C**,

CHIOS (1/1)

Acts 20:15 the next day came opposite **C**.

CHISEL (1/1)

1 Ki 6: 7 so that no hammer or **c** or any

CHISLEU (KJV) See CHISLEV

CHISLEV (2/2)

Neh 1: 1 came to pass in the month of **C**,
Zech 7: 1 day of the ninth month, **C**,

CHISLON (1/1)

Num 34:21 Benjamin, Elidad the son of **C**;

CHISLOTH TABOR (1/1)

Josh 19:12 sunrise along the border of **C**,

CHISLOTH-TABOR (KJV) See CHISLOTH TABOR

CHITTIM (KJV) See CYPRUS

CHIUN (1/1) REMPHAN

Am 5:26 Sikkuth your king And **C**,

CHLOE'S (1/1)

1 Cor 1:11 by those of **C** household, that

CHOICE (31/30) CHOICEST, CHOOSE

Gen 27: 9 bring me from there two **c** kids
27:15 Then Rebekah took the **c** clothes
49:11 donkey's colt to the **c** vine,
Ex 14: 7 he took six hundred **c** chariots,
Num 11:28 one of his **c** men, answered and
Deut 12:11 and all your **c** offerings which
1 Sam 9: 2 And he had a **c** and handsome son
2 Sam 6: 1 David gathered all the **c** men
2 Ki 3:19 fortified city and every **c** city,
19:23 cedars And its **c** cypress
1 Chr 7:40 **c** men, mighty men of valor,
2 Chr 13: 3 four hundred thousand **c** men.
13: 3 with eight hundred thousand **c**
13:17 so five hundred thousand **c** men
25: 5 to be three hundred thousand **c**
Neh 5:18 daily was one ox and six **c**
Esth 2: 9 Then seven **c** maidservants were
Ps 78:31 And struck down the **c** men of
Prov 8:10 knowledge rather than **c** gold;
8:19 And my revenue than **c** silver.
10:20 of the righteous is **c** silver;
Isa 16: 8 have broken down its **c** plants,
25: 6 people A feast of **c** pieces,
37:24 its tall cedars And its **c**
Jer 22: 7 shall cut down your **c** cedars
Ezek 23: 7 All of them **c** men of Assyria;
24: 4 Fill it with **c** cuts;
24: 5 Take the **c** of the flock.
27:24 were your merchants in **c** items
31:16 the **c** and best of Lebanon, all
Dan 11:15 Even his **c** troops shall have

CHOICEST (5/5) CHOICE

Gen 23: 6 bury your dead in the **c** of our
Deut 32:14 With the **c** wheat; And you
Isa 5: 2 And planted it with the **c**
22: 7 shall come to pass that your **c**
Ezek 27:22 traded for your wares the **c**

CHOIR (1/1) CHOIRS

Neh 12:38 The other thanksgiving **c** went

CHOIRS (2/2) CHOIR

Neh 12:31 two large thanksgiving **c**.
12:40 So the two thanksgiving **c** stood

CHOKE (2/2)

Mt 13:22 the deceitfulness of riches **c**
Mk 4:19 for other things entering in **c**

CHOKED (4/4) CHOKE

Mt 13: 7 and the thorns sprang up and **c**
Mk 4: 7 and the thorns grew up and **c**
Lk 8: 7 thorns sprang up with it and **c**
8:14 go out and are **c** with cares,

CHOLER (KJV) See RAGE

CHOOSE (39/39) CHOICE, CHOOSES, CHOOSING, CHOSE, CHOSEN

Ex 17: 9 **C** us some men and go out, fight
Num 17: 5 the rod of the man whom I **c**
Deut 1:13 **C** wise, understanding, and
7: 7 not set His love on you nor **c**
30:19 therefore **c** life, that both you
Josh 9:27 in the place which He would **c**,
24:15 **c** for yourselves this day whom
1 Sam 2:28 Did I not **c** him out of all the
17: 8 **C** a man for yourselves, and let
2 Sam 16:18 and all the men of Israel **c**,
17: 1 Now let me **c** twelve thousand
24:12 **c** one of them for yourself,
1 Ki 18:23 and let them **c** one bull for
18:25 **C** one bull for yourselves and
2 Ki 10: 3 **c** the best qualified of your
1 Chr 21:10 **c** one of them for yourself,
21:11 the LORD: '**C** for yourself,
2 Chr 6: 5 nor did I **c** any man to be a
Job 9:14 And **c** my words to reason
15: 5 And you **c** the tongue of the
34: 4 Let us **c** justice for ourselves;
34:33 you disavow it? You must **c**,
Ps 47: 4 He will **c** our inheritance for
65: 4 Blessed is the man You **c**,
75: 2 When I **c** the proper time, I
78:67 And did not **c** the tribe of
Prov 1:29 hated knowledge And did not **c**
3:31 And **c** none of his ways;
12:26 The righteous should **c** his
Isa 7:15 know to refuse the evil and **c**
7:16 know to refuse the evil and **c**
14: 1 and will still **c** Israel, and
56: 4 And **c** what pleases Me, And
66: 4 So will I **c** their delusions,
Zech 1:17 And will again **c** Jerusalem."
2:12 and will again **c** Jerusalem.
Jn 6:70 Did I not **c** you, the twelve, and
15:16 You did not **c** Me, but I chose
Phil 1:22 yet what I shall **c** I cannot

CHOOSES (32/32) CHOOSE

Num 16: 5 That one whom He **c** He will
16: 7 that the man whom the LORD **c**
Deut 12: 5 where the LORD your God **c**,
12:11 where the LORD your God **c** to
12:14 in the place which the LORD **c**,
12:18 which the LORD your God **c**,
12:21 where the LORD your God **c** to
12:26 to the place which the LORD **c**.
14:23 in the place where He **c** to make
14:24 where the LORD your God **c** to
14:25 which the LORD your God **c**.
15:20 in the place which the LORD **c**.
16: 2 in the place where the LORD **c**
16: 6 where the LORD your God **c** to
16: 7 which the LORD your God **c**,
16:11 where the LORD your God **c** to
16:15 in the place which the LORD **c**,
16:16 God in the place which He **c**:
17: 8 which the LORD your God **c**.
17:10 in that place which the LORD **c**.
17:15 you whom the LORD your God **c**;
18: 6 to the place which the LORD **c**,
23:16 in the place which he **c** within
26: 2 where the LORD your God **c** to
31:11 God in the place which He **c**,
Job 7:15 So that my soul **c** strangling
Ps 25:12 shall He teach in the way He **c**.
Isa 40:20 for such a contribution **C** a
41:24 He who **c** you is an
Dan 4:25 and gives it to whomever He **c**.
4:32 and gives it to whomever He **c**.
5:21 appoints over it whomever He **c**.

CHOOSING (1/1) CHOOSE

Heb 11:25 **c** rather to suffer affliction

CHOP (4/4) CHOPS

Jer 46:22 Like those who **c** wood.
Dan 4:14 **C** down the tree and cut off its
4:23 **C** down the tree and destroy it,
Mic 3: 3 And **c** them in pieces Like

CHOPS (1/1) CHOP

Isa 10:15 boast itself against him who **c**

CHORASHAN (1/1)

1 Sam 30:30 Hormah, those who were in **C**,

CHORAZIN (2/2)

Mt 11:21 **C**! Woe to you, Bethsaida!
Lk 10:13 **C**! Woe to you, Bethsaida!

CHOSE (35/35) CHOOSE

Gen 6: 2 themselves of all whom they **c**.
13:11 Then Lot **c** for himself all the
Ex 18:25 And Moses **c** able men out of all
Deut 4:37 therefore He **c** their
10:10 and the LORD **c** not to destroy
10:15 and He **c** their descendants
Josh 8: 3 and Joshua **c** thirty thousand
Judg 5: 8 They **c** new gods; Then there
1 Sam 13: 2 Saul **c** for himself three
17:40 and he **c** for himself five
2 Sam 6:21 who **c** me instead of your father
10: 9 he **c** some of Israel's best and
21: 6 of Saul, whom the LORD **c**.
1 Ki 8:16 but I **c** David to be over My
11:34 whom I **c** because he kept My
1 Chr 19:10 he **c** some of Israel's best and
28: 4 the LORD God of Israel **c** me
Neh 9: 7 Who **c** Abram, And brought him
Job 29:25 I **c** the way for them, and sat
Ps 78:68 But **c** the tribe of Judah,
78:70 He also **c** David His servant,
Isa 65:12 And **c** that in which I do not
66: 4 And **c** that in which I do not
Ezek 20: 5 On the day when I **c** Israel and
Mk 13:20 for the elect's sake, whom He **c**,
Lk 6:13 and from them He **c** twelve whom
14: 7 when He noted how they **c** the
Jn 15:16 but I **c** you and appointed you
15:19 but I **c** you out of the world,
Acts 6: 5 And they **c** Stephen, a man full
13:17 God of this people Israel **c**
15: 7 that a good while ago God **c**
15:40 but Paul **c** Silas and departed,
Eph 1: 4 just as He **c** us in Him before
2 Th 2:13 God from the beginning **c** you

CHOSEN (108/105) CHOOSE

Ex 15: 4 His **c** captains also are
Num 1:16 These were **c** from the
Deut 7: 6 the LORD your God has **c** you to
14: 2 and the LORD has **c** you to be a
18: 5 For the LORD your God has **c** him
21: 5 for the LORD your God has **c**
Josh 24:22 yourselves that you have **c** the
Judg 10:14 to the gods which you have **c**;
1 Sam 8:18 of your king whom you have **c**
10:20 the tribe of Benjamin was **c**.
10:21 the family of Matri was **c**.
10:21 And Saul the son of Kish was **c**.
10:24 see him whom the LORD has **c**,
12:13 is the king whom you have **c**
16: 8 Neither has the LORD **c** this
16: 9 Neither has the LORD **c** this
16:10 The LORD has not **c** these."
20:30 Do I not know that you have **c**
24: 2 Saul took three thousand **c** men
26: 2 having three thousand **c** men of
1 Ki 3: 8 of Your people whom You have **c**,
8:16 I have **c** no city from any tribe
8:44 the city which You have **c** and

8:48 the city which You have c and
11:13 of Jerusalem which I have c.
11:32 the city which I have c out of
11:36 the city which I have c for
12:21 hundred and eighty thousand c
14:21 the city which the LORD had c
2 Ki 21: 7 which I have c out of all the
23:27 city Jerusalem which I have c,
1 Chr 9:22 All those c as gatekeepers were
15: 2 for the LORD has c them to
16:13 of Jacob, His c ones!
16:41 and the rest who were c,
28: 4 for He has c Judah to be the
28: 5 given me many sons) He has c
28: 6 for I have c him to be My
28:10 for the LORD has c you to
29: 1 Solomon, whom alone God has c,
2 Chr 6: 5 I have c no city from any tribe
6: 6 Yet I have c Jerusalem, that My
6: 6 and I have c David to be over
6:34 this city which You have c and
6:38 the city which You have c,
7:12 and have c this place for
7:16 For now I have c and sanctified
11: 1 hundred and eighty thousand c
12:13 the city which the LORD had c
29:11 for the LORD has c you to
33: 7 which I have c out of all the
Neh 1: 9 to the place which I have c as
Job 36:21 For you have c this rather
Ps 33:12 The people He has c as His own
89: 3 have made a covenant with My c,
89:19 I have exalted one c from the
105: 6 of Jacob, His c ones!
105:26 And Aaron whom He had c.
105:43 His c ones with gladness.
106: 5 I may see the benefit of Your c
106:23 Had not Moses His c one stood
119:30 I have c the way of truth;
119:173 For I have c Your precepts.
132:13 For the LORD has c Zion;
135: 4 For the LORD has c Jacob for
Prov 16:16 to get understanding is to be c
22: 1 A good name is to be c rather
Isa 1:29 the gardens Which you have c.
41: 8 servant, Jacob whom I have c,
41: 9 I have c you and have not cast
43:10 "And My servant whom I have c,
43:20 give drink to My people, My c.
44: 1 And Israel whom I have c.
44: 2 you, Jeshurun, whom I have c.
49: 7 And He has c You."
58: 5 Is it a fast that I have c,
58: 6 this not the fast that I have c:
65:15 your name as a curse to My c;
66: 3 Just as they have c their own
Jer 8: 3 Then death shall be c rather
33:24 families which the LORD has c,
48:15 Her c young men have gone down
49:19 And who is a c man that I
50:44 And who is a c man that I
Hag 2:23 for I have c you,' says the
Zech 3: 2 The LORD who has c Jerusalem
Mt 12:18 My Servant whom I have c,
20:16 For many are called, but few c.
22:14 many are called, but few are c.
Lk 10:42 and Mary has c that good part,
23:35 the Christ, the c of God."
Jn 13:18 of you. I know whom I have c;
Acts 1: 2 to the apostles whom He had c,
1:24 which of these two You have c
9:15 for he is a c vessel of Mine to
10:41 but to witnesses c before by
15:22 to send c men of their own
15:25 to send c men to you with our
22:14 The God of our fathers has c you
Rom 16:13 c in the Lord, and his mother
1 Cor 1:27 But God has c the foolish things
1:27 and God has c the weak things
1:28 which are despised God has c,
2 Cor 8:19 but who was also c by the
Jas 2: 5 Has God not c the poor of this
1 Pe 2: 4 but c by God and precious,
2: 9 But you are a c generation, a
Rev 17:14 are with Him are called, c,

CHOZEBA (1/1) CHEZIB

1 Chr 4:22 also Jokim, the men of C,

CHRIST (554/521) CHRIST'S, CHRISTIAN, CHRISTIANS, CHRISTS

Mt 1: 1 of the genealogy of Jesus C,
1:16 was born Jesus who is called C.
1:17 in Babylon until the C are
1:18 Now the birth of Jesus C was as
2: 4 he inquired of them where the C
11: 2 in prison about the works of C,
16:16 and said, "You are the C,
16:20 no one that He was Jesus the C.
22:42 "What do you think about the C?
23: 8 for One is your Teacher, the C,
23:10 for One is your Teacher, the C.
24: 5 in My name, saying, 'I am the C,
24:23 here is the C!' or 'There!' do
26:63 God: Tell us if You are the C,
26:68 C! Who is the one who struck
27:17 or Jesus who is called C?
27:22 I do with Jesus who is called C?
Mk 1: 1 of the gospel of Jesus C,
8:29 said to Him, "You are the C.
9:41 name, because you belong to C,
12:35 the scribes say that the C is
13:21 here is the C!' or, 'Look, He
14:61 saying to Him, "Are You the C,
15:32 'Let the C, the King of
Lk 2:11 a Savior, who is C the Lord.
2:26 before he had seen the Lord's C.
3:15 whether he was the C or not,
4:41 out and saying, "You are the C,
4:41 for they knew that He was the C.
9:20 and said, "The C of God."
20:41 How can they say that the C is
22:67 "If You are the C,
23: 2 saying that He Himself is C,
23:35 Him save Himself if He is the C,
23:39 Him, saying, "If You are the C,
24:26 Ought not the C to have suffered
24:46 it was necessary for the C to
Jn 1:17 and truth came through Jesus C.
1:20 but confessed, "I am not the C.
1:25 baptize if you are not the C,
1:41 (which is translated, the C).
3:28 that I said, 'I am not the C,
4:25 is coming" (who is called C).
4:29 I ever did. Could this be the C?
4:42 know that this is indeed the C,
6:69 and know that You are the C,
7:26 indeed that this is truly the C?
7:27 but when the C comes, no one
7:31 When the C comes, will He do
7:41 Others said, "This is the C.
7:41 Will the C come out of Galilee?
7:42 the Scripture said that the C
9:22 confessed that He was C,
10:24 us in doubt? If You are the C,
11:27 I believe that You are the C,
12:34 heard from the law that the C
17: 3 and Jesus C whom You have sent.
20:31 may believe that Jesus is the C,
Acts 2:30 He would raise up the C to sit
2:31 the resurrection of the C,
2:36 you crucified, both Lord and C.
2:38 in the name of Jesus C for the
3: 6 In the name of Jesus C of
3:18 that the C would suffer, He has
3:20 "and that He may send Jesus C,
4:10 that by the name of Jesus C of
4:26 LORD and against His C.
5:42 and preaching Jesus as the C.
8: 5 city of Samaria and preached C
8:12 of God and the name of Jesus C,
8:37 I believe that Jesus C is the
9:20 Immediately he preached the C
9:22 that this Jesus is the C.
9:34 Jesus the C heals you. Arise
10:36 preaching peace through Jesus C—
11:17 we believed on the Lord Jesus C,
15:11 the grace of the Lord Jesus C
15:26 the name of our Lord Jesus C.
16:18 you in the name of Jesus C to
16:31 "Believe on the Lord Jesus C,
17: 3 and demonstrating that the C
17: 3 whom I preach to you is the C.
18: 5 the Jews that Jesus is the C.
18:28 Scriptures that Jesus is the C.
19: 4 him, that is, on C Jesus."
20:21 faith toward our Lord Jesus C.
24:24 him concerning the faith in C.
26:23 that the C would suffer, that He
28:31 which concern the Lord Jesus C
Rom 1: 1 Paul, a bondservant of Jesus C,
1: 3 concerning His Son Jesus C our
1: 6 also are the called of Jesus C;
1: 7 our Father and the Lord Jesus C.
1: 8 I thank my God through Jesus C
1:16 not ashamed of the gospel of C,
2:16 the secrets of men by Jesus C,
3:22 God, through faith in Jesus C,
3:24 the redemption that is in C
5: 1 God through our Lord Jesus C,
5: 6 in due time C died for the
5: 8 still sinners, C died for us.
5:11 in God through our Lord Jesus C,
5:15 grace of the one Man, Jesus C,
5:17 life through the One, Jesus C.
5:21 to eternal life through Jesus C
6: 3 of us as were baptized into C
6: 4 that just as C was raised from
6: 8 Now if we died with C,
6: 9 that C, having been raised
6:11 but alive to God in C Jesus our
6:23 of God is eternal life in C
7: 4 the law through the body of C,
7:25 —through Jesus C our Lord!
8: 1 to those who are in C Jesus,
8: 2 law of the Spirit of life in C
8: 9 does not have the Spirit of C,
8:10 And if C is in you, the body
8:11 He who raised C from the dead
8:17 of God and joint heirs with C,
8:34 It is C who died, and
8:35 separate us from the love of C?
8:39 the love of God which is in C
9: 1 I tell the truth in C,
9: 3 I myself were accursed from C
9: 5 C came, who is over all, the
10: 4 For C is the end of the law for
10: 6 to bring C down from above)
10: 7 to bring C up from the dead).
12: 5 being many, are one body in C,
13:14 But put on the Lord Jesus C,
14: 9 For to this end C died and rose
14:10 before the judgment seat of C.
14:15 your food the one for whom C
14:18 For he who serves C in these
15: 3 For even C did not please
15: 5 according to C Jesus,
15: 6 and Father of our Lord Jesus C.
15: 7 just as C also received us, to
15: 8 Now I say that Jesus C has
15:16 might be a minister of Jesus C
15:17 I have reason to glory in C
15:18 of any of those things which C
15:19 fully preached the gospel of C.
15:20 not where C was named, lest I
15:29 the blessing of the gospel of C.
15:30 through the Lord Jesus C,
16: 3 my fellow workers in C Jesus,
16: 5 the firstfruits of Achaia to C.
16: 7 who also were in C before me.
16: 9 Urbanus, our fellow worker in C,
16:10 Greet Apelles, approved in C.
16:16 The churches of C greet you.
16:18 do not serve our Lord Jesus C,
16:20 The grace of our Lord Jesus C
16:24 The grace of our Lord Jesus C
16:25 and the preaching of Jesus C,
16:27 be glory through Jesus C
1 Cor 1: 1 to be an apostle of Jesus C
1: 2 those who are sanctified in C
1: 2 call on the name of Jesus C
1: 3 our Father and the Lord Jesus C.
1: 4 God which was given to you by C
1: 6 even as the testimony of C was
1: 7 revelation of our Lord Jesus C,
1: 8 in the day of our Lord Jesus C.
1: 9 of His Son, Jesus C our Lord.
1:10 by the name of our Lord Jesus C,
1:12 am of Cephas," or "I am of C.
1:13 Is C divided? Was Paul crucified
1:17 For C did not send me to
1:17 lest the cross of C should be
1:23 but we preach C crucified, to
1:24 C the power of God and the
1:30 But of Him you are in C Jesus,
2: 2 among you except Jesus C and
2:16 But we have the mind of C.
3: 1 as to carnal, as to babes in C.
3:11 which is laid, which is Jesus C.
3:23 Christ's, and C is God's.
4: 1 as servants of C and stewards
4:10 but you are wise in C!
4:15 ten thousand instructors in C,
4:15 for in C Jesus I have begotten
4:17 will remind you of my ways in C,
5: 4 In the name of our Lord Jesus C,
5: 4 the power of our Lord Jesus C,
5: 7 are unleavened. For indeed C,
6:15 your bodies are members of C?
6:15 I then take the members of C
8: 6 and one Lord Jesus C, through
8:11 for whom C died?
8:12 conscience, you sin against C.
9: 1 Have I not seen Jesus C our
9:12 lest we hinder the gospel of C.
9:18 I may present the gospel of C
9:21 God, but under law toward C),
10: 4 them, and that Rock was C.
10: 9 nor let us tempt C,
10:16 the communion of the blood of C?
10:16 the communion of the body of C?
11: 1 me, just as I also imitate C.
11: 3 that the head of every man is C,
11: 3 and the head of C is God.
12:12 are one body, so also is C.
12:27 Now you are the body of C,
15: 3 that C died for our sins
15:12 Now if C is preached that He
15:13 then C is not risen.
15:14 And if C is not risen, then our
15:15 of God that He raised up C,
15:16 then C is not risen.
15:17 And if C is not risen, your
15:18 who have fallen asleep in C
15:19 life only we have hope in C,
15:20 But now C is risen from the
15:22 even so in C all shall be made
15:23 C the firstfruits, afterward
15:31 in you which I have in C Jesus
15:57 through our Lord Jesus C.
16:22 does not love the Lord Jesus C,
16:23 The grace of our Lord Jesus C
16:24 My love be with you all in C
2 Cor 1: 1 an apostle of Jesus C by the
1: 2 our Father and the Lord Jesus C.
1: 3 and Father of our Lord Jesus C,
1: 5 For as the sufferings of C
1: 5 also abounds through C.
1:19 For the Son of God, Jesus C,
1:21 establishes us with you in C
2:10 your sakes in the presence of C,
2:14 always leads us in triumph in C,
2:15 are to God the fragrance of C
2:17 speak in the sight of God in C.
3: 3 you are an epistle of C,
3: 4 we have such trust through C
3:14 the veil is taken away in C.
4: 4 of the gospel of the glory of C,
4: 5 but C Jesus the Lord, and
4: 6 of God in the face of Jesus C.
5:10 before the judgment seat of C,
5:14 For the love of C compels us,
5:16 Even though we have known C
5:17 Therefore, if anyone is in C,

C

5:18 us to Himself through Jesus *C*,
5:19 that God was in *C* reconciling
5:20 then, we are ambassadors for *C*,
6:15 And what accord has *C* with
8: 9 the grace of our Lord Jesus *C*,
8:23 of the churches, the glory of *C*.
9:13 confession to the gospel of *C*,
10: 1 meekness and gentleness of *C*—
10: 5 captivity to the obedience of *C*,
10:14 we came with the gospel of *C*;
11: 2 you as a chaste virgin to *C*.
11: 3 the simplicity that is in *C*.
11:10 As the truth of *C* is in me, no
11:13 themselves into apostles of *C*.
11:23 Are they ministers of *C*?
11:31 and Father of our Lord Jesus *C*,
12: 2 I know a man in *C* who fourteen
12: 9 that the power of *C* may rest
12:19 We speak before God in *C*.
13: 3 since you seek a proof of *C*
13: 5 that Jesus *C* is in you?—unless
13:14 The grace of the Lord Jesus *C*,
Gal 1: 1 but through Jesus *C* and God the
1: 3 the Father and our Lord Jesus *C*,
1: 6 called you in the grace of *C*,
1: 7 want to pervert the gospel of *C*.
1:10 would not be a bondservant of *C*.
1:12 the revelation of Jesus *C*.
1:22 of Judea which were in *C*.
2: 4 our liberty which we have in *C*
2:16 the law but by faith in Jesus *C*,
2:16 even we have believed in *C*
2:16 be justified by faith in *C* and
2:17 we seek to be justified by *C*,
2:17 is *C* therefore a minister of
2:20 "I have been crucified with *C*;
2:20 but *C* lives in me; and the
2:21 then *C* died in vain."
3: 1 before whose eyes Jesus *C* was
3:13 *C* has redeemed us from the curse
3:14 come upon the Gentiles in *C*
3:16 to your Seed," who is *C*.
3:17 confirmed before by God in *C*,
3:22 the promise by faith in Jesus *C*
3:24 our tutor to bring us to *C*,
3:26 sons of God through faith in *C*
3:27 of you as were baptized into *C*
3:27 into Christ have put on *C*.
3:28 for you are all one in *C* Jesus.
4: 7 then an heir of God through *C*.
4:14 even as *C* Jesus.
4:19 I labor in birth again until *C*
5: 1 in the liberty by which *C* has
5: 2 *C* will profit you nothing.
5: 4 have become estranged from *C*,
5: 6 For in *C* Jesus neither
6: 2 and so fulfill the law of *C*.
6:12 persecution for the cross of *C*.
6:14 the cross of our Lord Jesus *C*,
6:15 For in *C* Jesus neither
6:18 the grace of our Lord Jesus *C*
Eph 1: 1 an apostle of Jesus *C* by the
1: 1 and faithful in *C* Jesus:
1: 2 our Father and the Lord Jesus *C*.
1: 3 and Father of our Lord Jesus *C*,
1: 3 in the heavenly places in *C*,
1: 5 to adoption as sons by Jesus *C*
1:10 together in one all things in *C*,
1:12 that we who first trusted in *C*
1:17 the God of our Lord Jesus *C*,
1:20 which He worked in *C* when He
2: 5 made us alive together with *C*
2: 6 in the heavenly places in *C*
2: 7 in His kindness toward us in *C*
2:10 created in *C* Jesus for good
2:12 at that time you were without *C*,
2:13 But now in *C* Jesus you who once
2:13 brought near by the blood of *C*.
2:20 Jesus *C* Himself being the chief
3: 1 the prisoner of *C* Jesus for you
3: 4 knowledge in the mystery of *C*),
3: 6 partakers of His promise in *C*
3: 8 the unsearchable riches of *C*,
3: 9 all things through Jesus *C*;
3:11 which He accomplished in *C*
3:14 the Father of our Lord Jesus *C*,
3:17 that *C* may dwell in your hearts
3:19 to know the love of *C* which
3:21 be glory in the church by *C*
4:12 the edifying of the body of *C*,
4:13 stature of the fullness of *C*;
4:15 into Him who is the head—*C*—
4:20 But you have not so learned *C*,
4:32 just as God in *C* forgave you.
5: 2 as *C* also has loved us and
5: 5 in the kingdom of *C* and God.
5:14 And *C* will give you light."
5:20 in the name of our Lord Jesus *C*,
5:23 as also *C* is head of the
5:24 as the church is subject to *C*,
5:25 just as *C* also loved the church
5:32 but I speak concerning *C* and
6: 5 in sincerity of heart, as to *C*;
6: 6 but as bondservants of *C*,
6:23 the Father and the Lord Jesus *C*.
6:24 who love our Lord Jesus *C* in
Phil 1: 1 bondservants of Jesus *C*,
1: 1 To all the saints in *C* Jesus
1: 2 our Father and the Lord Jesus *C*.
1: 6 it until the day of Jesus *C*;
1: 8 with the affection of Jesus *C*.
1:10 offense till the day of *C*,
1:11 which are by Jesus *C*,
1:13 rest, that my chains are in *C*;
1:15 Some indeed preach *C* even from
1:16 The former preach *C* from selfish
1:18 *C* is preached; and in this I
1:19 supply of the Spirit of Jesus *C*,
1:20 so now also *C* will be magnified
1:21 For to me, to live is *C*,
1:23 desire to depart and be with *C*,
1:26 be more abundant in Jesus *C* by
1:27 be worthy of the gospel of *C*,
1:29 has been granted on behalf of *C*,
2: 1 there is any consolation in *C*,
2: 5 be in you which was also in *C*
2:11 should confess that Jesus *C*
2:16 I may rejoice in the day of *C*
2:21 not the things which are of *C*
2:30 because for the work of *C* he
3: 3 rejoice in *C* Jesus, and have no
3: 7 these I have counted loss for *C*.
3: 8 of the knowledge of *C* Jesus my
3: 8 that I may gain *C*
3: 9 which is through faith in *C*,
3:12 lay hold of that for which *C*
3:14 of the upward call of God in *C*
3:18 the enemies of the cross of *C*:
3:20 the Savior, the Lord Jesus *C*,
4: 7 your hearts and minds through *C*
4:13 I can do all things through *C*
4:19 to His riches in glory by *C*
4:21 Greet every saint in *C* Jesus.
4:23 The grace of our Lord Jesus *C* be
Col 1: 1 an apostle of Jesus *C* by the
1: 2 and faithful brethren in *C*
1: 2 our Father and the Lord Jesus *C*.
1: 3 and Father of our Lord Jesus *C*,
1: 4 we heard of your faith in *C*
1: 7 is a faithful minister of *C* on
1:24 lacking in the afflictions of *C*,
1:27 which is *C* in you, the hope of
1:28 present every man perfect in *C*
2: 2 both of the Father and of *C*,
2: 5 of your faith in *C*.
2: 6 you have therefore received *C*
2: 8 world, and not according to *C*.
2:11 flesh, by the circumcision of *C*,
2:17 come, but the substance is of *C*.
2:20 if you died with *C* from the
3: 1 If then you were raised with *C*,
3: 1 where *C* is, sitting at the
3: 3 and your life is hidden with *C*
3: 4 When *C* who is our life
3:11 but *C* is all and in all.
3:13 even as *C* forgave you, so you
3:16 Let the word of *C* dwell in you
3:24 for you serve the Lord *C*.
4: 3 word, to speak the mystery of *C*,
4:12 one of you, a bondservant of *C*,
1 Th 1: 1 the Father and the Lord Jesus *C*:
1: 1 our Father and the Lord Jesus *C*.
1: 3 of hope in our Lord Jesus *C* in
2: 6 made demands as apostles of *C*.
2:14 of God which are in Judea in *C*
2:19 presence of our Lord Jesus *C*
3: 2 laborer in the gospel of *C*,
3:11 Himself, and our Lord Jesus *C*,
3:13 the coming of our Lord Jesus *C*
4:16 And the dead in *C* will rise
5: 9 through our Lord Jesus *C*,
5:18 this is the will of God in *C*
5:23 the coming of our Lord Jesus *C*.
5:28 The grace of our Lord Jesus *C*
2 Th 1: 1 our Father and the Lord Jesus *C*:
1: 2 our Father and the Lord Jesus *C*.
1: 8 the gospel of our Lord Jesus *C*.
1:12 the name of our Lord Jesus *C*
1:12 of our God and the Lord Jesus *C*.
2: 1 the coming of our Lord Jesus *C*
2: 2 as though the day of *C* had
2:14 the glory of our Lord Jesus *C*.
2:16 Now may our Lord Jesus *C*
3: 5 God and into the patience of *C*.
3: 6 in the name of our Lord Jesus *C*,
3:12 through our Lord Jesus *C* that
3:18 The grace of our Lord Jesus *C*
1 Tim 1: 1 Paul, an apostle of Jesus *C*,
1: 1 our Savior and the Lord Jesus *C*,
1: 2 God our Father and Jesus *C* our
1:12 And I thank *C* Jesus our Lord
1:14 faith and love which are in *C*
1:15 that *C* Jesus came into the
1:16 that in me first Jesus *C* might
2: 5 God and men, the Man *C* Jesus,
2: 7 I am speaking the truth in *C*
3:13 in the faith which is in *C*
4: 6 be a good minister of Jesus *C*,
5:11 begun to grow wanton against *C*,
5:21 God and the Lord Jesus *C* and
6: 3 the words of our Lord Jesus *C*,
6:13 and before *C* Jesus who
2 Tim 1: 1 an apostle of Jesus *C* by the
1: 1 promise of life which is in *C*
1: 2 peace from God the Father and *C*
1: 9 which was given to us in *C*
1:10 appearing of our Savior Jesus *C*,
1:13 faith and love which are in *C*
2: 1 in the grace that is in *C*
2: 3 as a good soldier of Jesus *C*.
2: 8 Remember that Jesus *C*,
2:10 the salvation which is in *C*
2:19 who names the name of *C* depart
3:12 who desire to live godly in *C*
3:15 through faith which is in *C*
4: 1 before God and the Lord Jesus *C*,
4:22 The Lord Jesus *C* be with your
Titus 1: 1 God and an apostle of Jesus *C*,
1: 4 the Father and the Lord Jesus *C*
2:13 great God and Savior Jesus *C*,
3: 6 us abundantly through Jesus *C*
Phm 1: 1 a prisoner of *C* Jesus, and
1: 3 our Father and the Lord Jesus *C*.
1: 6 good thing which is in you in *C*
1: 8 I might be very bold in *C* to
1: 9 now also a prisoner of Jesus *C*—
1:23 my fellow prisoner in *C* Jesus,
1:25 The grace of our Lord Jesus *C*
Heb 3: 1 of our confession, *C* Jesus,
3: 6 but *C* as a Son over His own
3:14 we have become partakers of *C*
5: 5 So also *C* did not glorify
6: 1 the elementary principles of *C*,
9:11 But *C* came as High Priest of
9:14 much more shall the blood of *C*,
9:24 For *C* has not entered the holy
9:28 so *C* was offered once to bear
10:10 of the body of Jesus *C* once
11:26 esteeming the reproach of *C*
13: 8 Jesus *C* is the same yesterday,
13:21 in His sight, through Jesus *C*,
Jas 1: 1 of God and of the Lord Jesus *C*,
2: 1 the faith of our Lord Jesus *C*,
1 Pe 1: 1 Peter, an apostle of Jesus *C*,
1: 2 of the blood of Jesus *C*:
1: 3 and Father of our Lord Jesus *C*,
1: 3 the resurrection of Jesus *C*
1: 7 at the revelation of Jesus *C*,
1:11 the Spirit of *C* who was in them
1:11 beforehand the sufferings of *C*
1:13 at the revelation of Jesus *C*;
1:19 with the precious blood of *C*,
2: 5 to God through Jesus *C*.
2:21 because *C* also suffered for us,
3:16 revile your good conduct in *C*
3:18 For *C* also suffered once for
3:21 the resurrection of Jesus *C*,
4: 1 since *C* suffered for us in the
4:11 be glorified through Jesus *C*,
4:14 reproached for the name of *C*,
5: 1 witness of the sufferings of *C*,
5:10 us to His eternal glory by *C*
5:14 Peace to you all who are in *C*
2 Pe 1: 1 and apostle of Jesus *C*,
1: 1 of our God and Savior Jesus *C*:
1: 8 knowledge of our Lord Jesus *C*.
1:11 of our Lord and Savior Jesus *C*.
1:14 just as our Lord Jesus *C* showed
1:16 and coming of our Lord Jesus *C*,
2:20 of the Lord and Savior Jesus *C*,
3:18 of our Lord and Savior Jesus *C*.
1 Jn 1: 3 Father and with His Son Jesus *C*.
1: 7 and the blood of Jesus *C* His
2: 1 Jesus *C* the righteous.
2:22 who denies that Jesus is the *C*?
3:23 on the name of His Son Jesus *C*
4: 2 that confesses that Jesus *C*
4: 3 does not confess that Jesus *C*
5: 1 believes that Jesus is the *C*
5: 6 came by water and blood—Jesus *C*;
5:20 who is true, in His Son Jesus *C*.
2 Jn 3 and from the Lord Jesus *C*,
7 who do not confess Jesus *C* as
9 not abide in the doctrine of *C*
9 who abides in the doctrine of *C*
Jude 1 Jude, a bondservant of Jesus *C*,
1 and preserved in Jesus *C*:
4 Lord God and our Lord Jesus *C*.
17 apostles of our Lord Jesus *C*:
21 the mercy of our Lord Jesus *C*
Rev 1: 1 The Revelation of Jesus *C*,
1: 2 and to the testimony of Jesus *C*,
1: 5 from Jesus *C*, the faithful
1: 9 kingdom and patience of Jesus *C*,
1: 9 for the testimony of Jesus *C*.
11:15 of our Lord and of His *C*,
12:10 and the power of His *C* have
12:17 have the testimony of Jesus *C*.
20: 4 they lived and reigned with *C*
20: 6 be priests of God and of *C*,
22:21 The grace of our Lord Jesus *C*

CHRIST'S (15/13) CHRIST

1 Cor 3:23 And you are *C*, and Christ
4:10 We are fools for *C* sake, but
7:22 called while free is *C* slave.
15:23 afterward those who are *C* at
2 Cor 2:12 to Troas to preach *C* gospel,
5:20 we implore you on *C* behalf, be
10: 7 in himself that he is *C*,
10: 7 himself, that just as he is *C*,
10: 7 is Christ's, even so we are *C*.
12:10 for *C* sake. For when I am weak,
Gal 3:29 And if you are *C*, then you are
5:24 And those who are *C* have
Eph 4: 7 to the measure of *C* gift.
1 Tim 6:14 our Lord Jesus *C* appearing,
1 Pe 4:13 you partake of *C* sufferings,

CHRISTIAN (2/2) CHRISTIANS

Acts 26:28 persuade me to become a *C*.
1 Pe 4:16 Yet if anyone suffers as a *C*,

CHRISTIANS (1/1) CHRISTIAN

Acts 11:26 disciples were first called *C*

CHRISTS (2/2) CHRIST

Mt 24:24 For false *c* and false prophets
Mk 13:22 For false *c* and false prophets

CHRONICLES (38/38)

1 Ki 14:19 written in the book of the *c*
14:29 written in the book of the *c*
15: 7 written in the book of the *c*
15:23 written in the book of the *c*
15:31 written in the book of the *c*
16: 5 written in the book of the *c*
16:14 written in the book of the *c*
16:20 written in the book of the *c*
16:27 written in the book of the *c*
22:39 written in the book of the *c*
22:45 written in the book of the *c*
2 Ki 1:18 written in the book of the *c*
8:23 written in the book of the *c*
10:34 written in the book of the *c*
12:19 written in the book of the *c*
13: 8 written in the book of the *c*
13:12 written in the book of the *c*
14:15 written in the book of the *c*
14:18 written in the book of the *c*
14:28 written in the book of the *c*
15: 6 written in the book of the *c*
15:11 written in the book of the *c*
15:15 written in the book of the *c*
15:21 written in the book of the *c*
15:26 written in the book of the *c*
15:31 written in the book of the *c*
15:36 written in the book of the *c*
16:19 written in the book of the *c*
20:20 written in the book of the *c*
21:17 written in the book of the *c*
21:25 written in the book of the *c*
23:28 written in the book of the *c*
24: 5 written in the book of the *c*
1 Chr 27:24 in the account of the *c* of
Neh 12:23 written in the book of the *c*.
Esth 2:23 written in the book of the *c*
6: 1 book of the records of the *c*;
10: 2 written in the book of the *c*

CHRYSOLITE (1/1)

Rev 21:20 sixth sardius, the seventh *c*,

CHRYSOPRASE (1/1)

Rev 21:20 the ninth topaz, the tenth *c*,

CHUB (1/1)

Ezek 30: 5 all the mingled people, *C*,

CHUN (1/1)

1 Chr 18: 8 Also from Tibhath and from *C*,

CHURCH (74/73) CHURCHES

Mt 16:18 on this rock I will build My *c*,
18:17 to hear them, tell it to the *c*.
18:17 he refuses even to hear the *c*,
Acts 2:47 And the Lord added to the *c*
5:11 great fear came upon all the *c*
8: 1 arose against the *c* which was
8: 3 Saul, he made havoc of the *c*,
11:22 came to the ears of the *c* in
11:26 year they assembled with the *c*
12: 1 hand to harass some from the *c*.
12: 5 offered to God for him by the *c*.
13: 1 Now in the *c* that was at Antioch
14:23 had appointed elders in every *c*,
14:27 had come and gathered the *c*
15: 3 sent on their way by the *c*,
15: 4 they were received by the *c* and
15:22 and elders, with the whole *c*,
18:22 and gone up and greeted the *c*,
20:17 called for the elders of the *c*.
20:28 to shepherd the *c* of God which
Rom 16: 1 who is a servant of the *c* in
16: 5 Likewise greet the *c* that is in
16:23 and the host of the whole *c*,
1 Cor 1: 2 To the *c* of God which is at
4:17 I teach everywhere in every *c*.
6: 4 are least esteemed by the *c* to
10:32 or to the Greeks or to the *c*
11:18 when you come together as a *c*,
11:22 Or do you despise the *c* of God
12:28 has appointed these in the *c*:
14: 4 he who prophesies edifies the *c*.
14: 5 that the *c* may receive
14:12 for the edification of the *c*
14:19 yet in the *c* I would rather
14:23 Therefore if the whole *c* comes
14:28 let him keep silent in *c*,
14:35 for women to speak in *c*.
15: 9 because I persecuted the *c* of
16:19 with the *c* that is in their
2 Cor 1: 1 To the *c* of God which is at
Gal 1:13 how I persecuted the *c* of God
Eph 1:22 head over all things to the *c*,
3:10 might be made known by the *c*
3:21 to Him be glory in the *c* by
5:23 as also Christ is head of the *c*;
5:24 just as the *c* is subject to
5:25 as Christ also loved the *c* and
5:27 her to Himself a glorious *c*,
5:29 just as the Lord does the *c*.
5:32 concerning Christ and the *c*.
Phil 3: 6 zeal, persecuting the *c*;
4:15 no *c* shared with me concerning
Col 1:18 is the head of the body, the *c*,
1:24 of His body, which is the *c*,
4:15 and Nymphas and the *c* that is
4:16 that it is read also in the *c*
1 Th 1: 1 To the *c* of the Thessalonians
2 Th 1: 1 To the *c* of the Thessalonians
1 Tim 3: 5 how will he take care of the *c*
3:15 which is the *c* of the living
5:16 and do not let the *c* be
Phm 1: 2 and to the *c* in your house:
Heb 12:23 to the general assembly and *c* of
Jas 5:14 call for the elders of the *c*,
3 Jn 6 of your love before the *c*.
9 I wrote to the *c*,
10 to, putting them out of the *c*.
Rev 2: 1 To the angel of the *c* of Ephesus
2: 8 And to the angel of the *c* in
2:12 And to the angel of the *c* in
2:18 And to the angel of the *c* in
3: 1 And to the angel of the *c* in
3: 7 And to the angel of the *c* in
3:14 And to the angel of the *c* of

CHURCH OF GOD (8/8)

Acts 20:28 to shepherd the *c* which He
1 Cor 1: 2 To the *c* which is at Corinth, to
10:32 or to the Greeks or to the *c*,
11:22 Or do you despise the *c* and
15: 9 because I persecuted the *c*.
2 Cor 1: 1 To the *c* which is at Corinth,
Gal 1:13 how I persecuted the *c* beyond
1 Tim 3: 5 how will he take care of the *c*?

CHURCHES (36/35) CHURCH

Acts 9:31 Then the *c* throughout all
15:41 Cilicia, strengthening the *c*.
16: 5 So the *c* were strengthened in
Rom 16: 4 but also all the *c* of the
16:16 The *c* of Christ greet you.
1 Cor 7:17 And so I ordain in all the *c*.
11:16 nor do the *c* of God.
14:33 as in all the *c* of the saints.
14:34 your women keep silent in the *c*,
16: 1 as I have given orders to the *c*
16:19 The *c* of Asia greet you. Aquila
2 Cor 8: 1 grace of God bestowed on the *c*
8:18 the gospel throughout all the *c*,
8:19 who was also chosen by the *c*
8:23 they are messengers of the *c*,
8:24 and before the *c* the proof of
11: 8 I robbed other *c*,
11:28 my deep concern for all the *c*.
12:13 you were inferior to other *c*,
Gal 1: 2 To the *c* of Galatia:
1:22 I was unknown by face to the *c*
1 Th 2:14 became imitators of the *c* of
2 Th 1: 4 boast of you among the *c* of
Rev 1: 4 to the seven *c* which are in
1:11 and send it to the seven *c*
1:20 are the angels of the seven *c*,
1:20 which you saw are the seven *c*.
2: 7 what the Spirit says to the *c*.
2:11 what the Spirit says to the *c*.
2:17 what the Spirit says to the *c*.
2:23 and all the *c* shall know that I
2:29 what the Spirit says to the *c*.
3: 6 what the Spirit says to the *c*.
3:13 what the Spirit says to the *c*.
3:22 what the Spirit says to the *c*.
22:16 to you these things in the *c*.

CHURNING (1/1) CHURNS

Prov 30:33 For as the *c* of milk produces

CHURNS (1/1) CHURNING

Hos 11: 8 My heart *c* within Me;

CHUZA (1/1)

Lk 8: 3 and Joanna the wife of *C*,

CIELED (KJV) See PANELED, PANELING

CILICIA (8/8)

Acts 6: 9 and those from *C* and Asia),
15:23 in Antioch, Syria, and *C*:
15:41 And he went through Syria and *C*,
21:39 "I am a Jew from Tarsus, in *C*,
22: 3 a Jew, born in Tarsus of *C*,
23:34 understood that he was from *C*,
27: 5 over the sea which is off *C*
Gal 1:21 into the regions of Syria and *C*.

CINNAMON (4/4)

Ex 30:23 half as much sweet-smelling *c*
Prov 7:17 bed With myrrh, aloes, and *c*.
Song 4:14 and saffron, Calamus and *c*,
Rev 18:13 and *c* and incense, fragrant oil

CINNEROTH (KJV) See CHINNEROTH

CIRCLE (7/7) CIRCLED, CIRCUIT, CIRCULAR, CIRCULATE, CIRCUMSISE, CIRCUMFERENCE, CIRCUMSPECT

Josh 6:11 he had the ark of the LORD *c*
2 Sam 5:23 *c* around behind them, and come
1 Chr 14:14 *c* around them, and come upon
Job 22:14 And He walks above the *c* of
Prov 8:27 When He drew a *c* on the face
Isa 40:22 is He who sits above the *c* of
Mk 3:34 And He looked around in a *c* at

CIRCLED (1/1) CIRCLE

Acts 28:13 From there we *c* round and

CIRCUIT (4/4)

1 Sam 7:16 went from year to year on a *c*
Ps 19: 6 And its *c* to the other end;
Eccl 1: 6 And comes again on its *c*.
Mk 6: 6 went about the villages in a *c*,

CIRCULAR (1/1) CIRCLE

Job 26:10 He drew a *c* horizon on the face

CIRCULATE (1/1) CIRCULATED

Ex 23: 1 You shall not *c* a false report.

CIRCULATED (1/1) CIRCULATE

2 Chr 31: 5 soon as the commandment was *c*,

CIRCUMCISE (8/8) CIRCLE, CIRCUMCISED, CIRCUMCISING, CIRCUMCISION, UNCIRCUMCISED

Deut 10:16 Therefore *c* the foreskin of your
30: 6 And the LORD your God will *c*
Josh 5: 2 and *c* the sons of Israel again
Jer 4: 4 *C* yourselves to the LORD, And
Lk 1:59 that they came to *c* the child;
Jn 7:22 and you *c* a man on the Sabbath.
Acts 15: 5 It is necessary to *c* them, and
21:21 saying that they ought not to *c*

CIRCUMCISED (48/42) CIRCUMCISE

Gen 17:10 male child among you shall be *c*;
17:11 and you shall be *c* in the flesh
17:12 days old among you shall be *c*,
17:13 with your money must be *c*,
17:14 who is not *c* in the flesh of
17:23 and *c* the flesh of their
17:24 years old when he was *c* in the
17:25 years old when he was *c* in the
17:26 very same day Abraham was *c*,
17:27 were *c* with him.
21: 4 Then Abraham *c* his son Isaac
34:15 are, if every male of you is *c*,
34:17 you will not heed us and be *c*,
34:22 if every male among us is *c* as
34:22 is circumcised as they are *c*.
34:24 his son; every male was *c*,
Ex 12:44 when you have *c* him, then he
12:48 LORD, let all his males be *c*,
Lev 12: 3 of his foreskin shall be *c*.
Josh 5: 3 and *c* the sons of Israel at the
5: 4 is the reason why Joshua *c*
5: 5 people who came out had been *c*,
5: 5 out of Egypt, had not been *c*.
5: 7 Then Joshua *c* their sons whom
5: 7 because they had not been *c* on
Jer 9:25 I will punish all who are *c*
Acts 7: 8 so Abraham begot Isaac and *c*
15: 1 Unless you are *c* according to
15:24 You must be *c* and keep the
16: 3 And he took him and *c* him
Rom 3:30 one God who will justify the *c*
4: 9 then come upon the *c* only,
4:10 it accounted? While he was *c*,
4:10 or uncircumcised? Not while *c*,
1 Cor 7:18 Was anyone called while *c*?
7:18 uncircumcised? Let him not be *c*.
Gal 2: 3 a Greek, was compelled to be *c*.
2: 7 as the gospel for the *c* was
2: 8 for the apostleship to the *c*
2: 9 the Gentiles and they to the *c*.
5: 2 say to you that if you become *c*,
5: 3 to every man who becomes *c*
6:12 these would compel you to be *c*,
6:13 For not even those who are *c*
6:13 but they desire to have you *c*
Phil 3: 5 *c* the eighth day, of the stock
Col 2:11 In Him you were also *c* with the
3:11 *c* nor uncircumcised, barbarian,

CIRCUMCISING (1/1) CIRCUMCISE

Josh 5: 8 when they had finished *c* all

CIRCUMCISION (29/26) CIRCUMCISE

Ex 4:26 of blood!"—because of the **c**.
Lk 2:21 days were completed for the **c**
Jn 7:22 'Moses therefore gave you **c** (not
7:23 If a man receives **c** on the
Acts 7: 8 He gave him the covenant of **c**;
10:45 And those of the **c** who believed
11: 2 those of the **c** contended with
Rom 2:25 For **c** is indeed profitable if
2:25 your **c** has become
2:26 uncircumcision be counted as **c**?
2:27 with your written code and **c**,
2:28 nor is **c** that which is
2:29 and **c** is that of the heart,
3: 1 or what is the profit of **c**?
4:11 And he received the sign of **c**,
4:12 and the father of **c** to those who
4:12 who not only are of the **c**,
15: 8 has become a servant to the **c**
1 Cor 7:19 **C** is nothing and uncircumcision
Gal 2:12 fearing those who were of the **c**.
5: 6 For in Christ Jesus neither **c**
5:11 brethren, if I still preach **c**,
6:15 For in Christ Jesus neither **c**
Eph 2:11 by what is called the **C** made
Phil 3: 3 For we are the **c**,
Col 2:11 also circumcised with the **c**
2:11 by the **c** of Christ,
4:11 kingdom of God who are of the **c**;
Titus 1:10 especially those of the **c**,

CIRCUMFERENCE (4/4)

1 Ki 7:15 of twelve cubits measured the **c**
7:23 of thirty cubits measured its **c**.
2 Chr 4: 2 of thirty cubits measured its **c**.
Jer 52:21 cubits could measure its **c**,

CIRCUMSPECT (1/1) CIRCUMSPECTLY

Ex 23:13 be **c** and make no mention of the

CIRCUMSPECTLY (1/1) CIRCUMSPECT

Eph 5:15 See then that you walk **c**,

CIRCUMSTANCES (1/1)

Col 4: 8 that he may know your **c** and

CIS (KJV) See KISH

CISTERN (5/5) CISTERNS

Lev 11:36 'Nevertheless a spring or a **c**,
2 Ki 18:31 drink the waters of his own **c**;
Prov 5:15 Drink water from your own **c**,
Isa 30:14 Or to take water from the **c**.
36:16 drink the waters of his own **c**;

CISTERNS (4/3) CISTERN

Neh 9:25 **C** already dug, vineyards,
Jer 2:13 waters, And hewn themselves **c**—
2:13 broken **c** that can hold no water.
14: 3 They went to the **c** and found

CITADEL (17/17) CITADELS

1 Ki 16:18 that he went into the **c** of the
2 Ki 5:24 When he came to the **c**,
15:25 in the **c** of the king's house,
Neh 1: 1 year, as I was in Shushan the **c**,
2: 8 beams for the gates of the **c**
7: 2 Hananiah the leader of the **c**,
Esth 1: 2 which was in Shushan the **c**,
1: 5 were present in Shushan the **c**,
2: 3 young virgins to Shushan the **c**,
2: 5 In Shushan the **c** there was a
2: 8 were gathered at Shushan the **c**,
3:15 was proclaimed in Shushan the **c**.
8:14 was issued in Shushan the **c**.
9: 6 And in Shushan the **c** the Jews
9:11 were killed in Shushan the **c**
9:12 hundred men in Shushan the **c**,
Dan 8: 2 that I was in Shushan, the **c**,

CITADELS (1/1) CITADEL

Isa 13:22 hyenas will howl in their **c**,

CITIES (440/388) CITY

Gen 13:12 and Lot dwelt in the **c** of the
19:25 So He overthrew those **c**,
19:25 all the inhabitants of the **c**,
19:29 when God destroyed the **c** of the
19:29 when He overthrew the **c** in
35: 5 terror of God was upon the **c**
41:35 and let them keep food in the **c**.
41:48 and laid up the food in the **c**;
47:21 he moved them into the **c**,
Ex 1:11 they built for Pharaoh supply **c**,
Lev 25:32 Nevertheless the **c** of the
25:32 and the houses in the **c** of
25:33 for the houses in the **c** of the
25:34 of the common-land of their **c**
26:25 together within your **c** I will
26:31 I will lay your **c** waste and
26:33 shall be desolate and your **c**
Num 13:19 whether the **c** they inhabit are
13:28 the **c** are fortified and very
21: 2 I will utterly destroy their **c**.
21: 3 destroyed them and their **c**.
21:25 So Israel took all these **c**,
21:25 and Israel dwelt in all the **c**
31:10 also burned with fire all the **c**
32:16 and **c** for our little ones,
32:17 will dwell in the fortified **c**
32:24 Build **c** for your little ones and
32:26 will be there in the **c** of
32:33 the land with its **c** within the
32:33 the **c** of the surrounding
32:36 and Beth Haran, fortified **c**,
32:38 they gave other names to the **c**
35: 2 that they give the Levites **c**
35: 2 common-land around the **c**.
35: 3 They shall have the **c** to dwell
35: 4 The common-land of the **c** which
35: 5 them as common-land for the **c**.
35: 6 Now among the **c** which you will
35: 6 you shall appoint six **c** of
35: 6 these you shall add forty-two **c**.
35: 7 So all the **c** you will give to
35: 8 And the **c** which you will give
35: 8 Each shall give some of its **c**
35:11 then you shall appoint **c** to be
35:11 shall appoint cities to be **c**
35:12 They shall be **c** of refuge for
35:13 And of the **c** which you give, you
35:13 you shall have six **c** of refuge.
35:14 You shall appoint three **c** on
35:14 and three **c** you shall appoint
35:14 which will be **c** of refuge.
35:15 These six **c** shall be for refuge
Deut 1:22 and of the **c** into which we
1:28 the **c** are great and fortified
2:34 We took all his **c** at that time,
2:35 with the spoil of the **c** which
2:37 or to the **c** of the mountains,
3: 4 And we took all his **c** at that
3: 4 did not take from them: sixty **c**,
3: 5 All these **c** were fortified with
3: 7 and the spoil of the **c** we took
3:10 all the **c** of the plain, all
3:10 **c** of the kingdom of Og in
3:12 mountains of Gilead and its **c**,
3:19 shall stay in your **c** which I
4:41 Then Moses set apart three **c** on
4:42 by fleeing to one of these **c**
6:10 give you large and beautiful **c**
9: 1 **c** great and fortified up to
13:12 hear someone in one of your **c**,
19: 1 them and dwell in their **c** and
19: 2 you shall separate three **c** for
19: 5 shall flee to one of these **c**
19: 7 You shall separate three **c** for
19: 9 you shall add three more **c** for
19:11 and he flees to one of these **c**,
20:15 you shall do to all the **c**
20:15 which are not of the **c** of
20:16 But of the **c** of these peoples
21: 2 slain man to the surrounding **c**.
Josh 9:17 journeyed and came to their **c**
9:17 Now their **c** were Gibeon,
10: 2 city, like one of the royal **c**,
10:19 not allow them to enter their **c**,
10:20 who escaped entered fortified **c**.
10:37 the sword—its king, all its **c**,
10:39 it and its king and all its **c**;
11:12 So all the **c** of those kings, and
11:13 But as for the **c** that stood on
11:14 And all the spoil of these **c** and
11:21 destroyed them with their **c**.
13:10 all the **c** of Sihon king of the
13:17 Heshbon and all its **c** that are
13:21 all the **c** of the plain and all
13:23 the **c** and their villages.
13:25 and all the **c** of Gilead, and
13:28 the **c** and their villages.
13:30 which are in Bashan, sixty **c**;
13:31 **c** of the kingdom of Og in
14: 4 except **c** to dwell in, with
14:12 and that the **c** were great
15: 9 and extended to the **c** of Mount
15:21 The **c** at the limits of the tribe
15:32 all the **c** are twenty-nine,
15:36 fourteen **c** with their villages;
15:41 sixteen **c** with their villages;
15:44 nine **c** with their villages;
15:51 eleven **c** with their villages;
15:54 nine **c** with their villages;
15:57 ten **c** with their villages;
15:59 six **c** with their villages;
15:60 two **c** with their villages.
15:62 six **c** with their villages.
16: 9 The separate **c** for the children
16: 9 all the **c** with their villages.
17: 9 These **c** of Ephraim are among
17: 9 of Ephraim are among the **c** of
17:12 the inhabitants of those **c**,
18: 9 in a book in seven parts by **c**;
18:21 Now the **c** of the tribe of the
18:24 twelve **c** with their villages;
18:28 fourteen **c** with their villages.
19: 6 thirteen **c** and their villages;
19: 7 four **c** and their villages;
19: 8 that were all around these **c**
19:15 twelve **c** with their villages.
19:16 these **c** with their villages.
19:22 sixteen **c** with their villages.
19:23 the **c** and their villages.
19:30 twenty-two **c** with their
19:31 these **c** with their villages.
19:35 And the fortified **c** are Ziddim,
19:38 nineteen **c** with their villages.
19:39 the **c** and their villages.
19:48 these **c** with their villages.
20: 2 Appoint for yourselves **c** of
20: 4 when he flees to one of those **c**,
20: 9 These were the **c** appointed for
21: 2 through Moses to give us **c** to
21: 3 these **c** and their common-lands:
21: 4 had thirteen **c** by lot from the
21: 5 children of Kohath had ten **c**
21: 6 of Gershon had thirteen **c** by
21: 7 to their families had twelve **c**
21: 8 of Israel gave these **c** with
21: 9 the children of Simeon these **c**
21:16 nine **c** from those two tribes;
21:18 with its common-land: four **c**.
21:19 All the **c** of the children of
21:19 were thirteen **c** with their
21:20 even they had the **c** of their
21:22 with its common-land: four **c**;
21:24 with its common-land: four **c**;
21:25 with its common-land: two **c**.
21:26 All the ten **c** with their
21:27 with its common-land: two **c**;
21:29 with its common-land: four **c**;
21:31 with its common-land: four **c**;
21:32 with its common-land: three **c**.
21:33 All the **c** of the Gershonites
21:33 families were thirteen **c** with
21:35 with its common-land: four **c**;
21:37 with its common-land: four **c**;
21:39 common-land: four **c** in all.
21:40 So all the **c** for the children of
21:40 were by their lot twelve **c**.
21:41 All the **c** of the Levites within
21:41 of Israel were forty-eight **c**
21:42 Every one of these **c** had its
21:42 it; thus were all these **c**.
24:13 and **c** which you did not build,
Judg 11:26 and in all the **c** along the
11:33 as far as Minnith—twenty **c**—
12: 7 and was buried in among the **c**
20:14 gathered together from their **c**
20:15 And from their **c** at that time
20:42 and whoever came out of the **c**
20:48 They also set fire to all the **c**
21:23 and they rebuilt the **c** and
1 Sam 6:18 to the number of all the **c** of
6:18 both fortified **c** and country
7:14 Then the **c** which the Philistines
18: 6 had come out of all the **c** of
30:29 those who were in the **c** of
30:29 those who were in the **c** of
31: 7 they forsook the **c** and fled;
2 Sam 2: 1 Shall I go up to any of the **c** of
2: 3 So they dwelt in the **c** of
8: 8 **c** of Hadadezer, King David took
10:12 for our people and for the **c**
12:31 So he did to all the **c** of the
20: 6 he find for himself fortified **c**,
24: 7 of Tyre and to all the **c** of
1 Ki 4:13 sixty large **c** with walls and
8:37 them in the land of their **c**;
9:11 then gave Hiram twenty **c** in
9:12 went from Tyre to see the **c**
9:13 What kind of **c** are these
9:19 all the storage **c** that Solomon
9:19 **c** for his chariots and cities
9:19 cities for his chariots and **c**
10:26 he stationed in the chariot **c**
12:17 of Israel who dwelt in the **c**
13:32 places which are in the **c** of
15:20 of his armies against the **c** of
15:23 and the **c** which he built, are
20:34 The **c** which my father took from
22:39 which he built and all the **c**
2 Ki 3:25 Then they destroyed the **c**,
13:25 the **c** which he had taken out of
13:25 him and recaptured the **c** of
17: 6 and in the **c** of the Medes.
17: 9 high places in all their **c**,
17:24 and placed them in the **c** of
17:24 of Samaria and dwelt in its **c**.
17:26 removed and placed in the **c** of
17:29 every nation in the **c** where
18:11 and in the **c** of the Medes,
18:13 up against all the fortified **c**
19:25 be For crushing fortified **c**
23: 5 on the high places in the **c** of
23: 8 all the priests from the **c** of
23:19 places that were in the **c** of
1 Chr 2:22 who had twenty-three **c** in the
4:31 These were their **c** until the
4:32 Tochen, and Ashan—five **c**—
4:33 that were around these **c** as
6:57 Aaron they gave one of the **c**
6:60 All their **c** among their
6:61 they gave by lot ten **c** from
6:62 they gave thirteen **c** from the
6:63 they gave twelve **c** from the
6:64 of Israel gave these **c** with
6:65 children of Benjamin these **c**
6:66 sons of Kohath were given **c**
6:67 they gave them one of the **c**
9: 2 in their possessions in their **c**
10: 7 they forsook their **c** and fled;
13: 2 Levites who are in their **c**
18: 8 **c** of Hadadezer, David brought a
19: 7 gathered together from their **c**,

19:13 for our people and for the **c**
20: 3 So David did to all the **c** of
27:25 in the field, in the **c**,
2 Chr 1:14 he stationed in the chariot **c**
6:28 them in the land of their **c**;
8: 2 that the **c** which Hiram had given
8: 4 and all the storage **c** which he
8: 5 fortified **c** with walls, gates,
8: 6 Baalath and all the storage **c**
8: 6 and all the chariot **c** and the
8: 6 the chariot cities and the **c**
9:25 he stationed in the chariot **c**
10:17 of Israel who dwelt in the **c**
11: 5 and built **c** for defense in
11:10 Judah and Benjamin, fortified **c**.
12: 4 And he took the fortified **c** of
13:19 pursued Jeroboam and took **c**
14: 5 incense altars from all the **c**
14: 6 And he built fortified **c** in
14: 7 Let us build these **c** and make
14:14 Then they defeated all the **c**
14:14 and they plundered all the **c**,
15: 8 and Benjamin and from the **c**
16: 4 of his armies against the **c** of
16: 4 and all the storage **c** of
17: 2 troops in all the fortified **c**
17: 2 the land of Judah and in the **c**
17: 7 to teach in the **c** of Judah.
17: 9 they went throughout all the **c**
17:12 built fortresses and storage **c**
17:13 He had much property in the **c** of
17:19 the king put in the fortified **c**
19: 5 throughout all the fortified **c**
19:10 brethren who dwell in their **c**,
20: 4 and from all the **c** of Judah
21: 3 with fortified **c** in Judah; but
23: 2 the Levites from all the **c** of
24: 5 Go out to the **c** of Judah, and
25:13 they raided the **c** of Judah from
26: 6 and he built **c** around Ashdod
27: 4 Moreover he built **c** in the
28:18 also had invaded the **c** of the
31: 1 were present went out to the **c**
31: 1 Israel returned to their own **c**,
31: 6 who dwelt in the **c** of Judah,
31:15 faithful assistants in the **c**
31:19 of the common-lands of their **c**,
32: 1 against the fortified **c**,
32:29 Moreover he provided **c** for
33:14 in all the fortified **c** of
34: 6 And so he did in the **c** of
Ezra 2:70 the Nethinim, dwelt in their **c**,
2:70 and all Israel in their **c**.
3: 1 of Israel were in the **c**,
4:10 captive and settled in the **c**
10:14 and let all those in our **c** who
10:14 elders and judges of their **c**,
Neh 7:73 and all Israel dwelt in their **c**.
7:73 of Israel were in their **c**.
8:15 and proclaim in all their **c**
9:25 And they took strong **c** and a
11: 1 were to dwell in other **c**.
11: 3 (But in the **c** of Judah everyone
11: 3 his own possession in their **c**—
11:20 were in all the **c** of Judah,
12:44 them from the fields of the **c**
Esth 9: 2 gathered together in their **c**
Job 15:28 He dwells in desolate **c**,
Ps 9: 6 And you have destroyed **c**;
69:35 save Zion And build the **c** of
Isa 1: 7 Your **c** are burned with fire;
6:11 Until the **c** are laid waste and
14:17 wilderness And destroyed its **c**,
14:21 the face of the world with **c**.
17: 2 The **c** of Aroer are forsaken;
17: 9 In that day his strong **c** will
19:18 In that day five **c** in the land
33: 8 He has despised the **c**,
36: 1 up against all the fortified **c**
37:26 be For crushing fortified **c**
40: 9 Say to the **c** of Judah,
42:11 Let the wilderness and its **c**
44:26 To the **c** of Judah, 'You shall
54: 3 And make the desolate **c**
61: 4 they shall repair the ruined **c**,
64:10 Your holy **c** are a wilderness,
Jer 1:15 And against all the **c** of
2:15 His **c** are burned, without
2:28 to the number of your **c** Are
4: 5 let us go into the fortified **c**.
4: 7 Your **c** will be laid waste,
4:16 their voice against the **c** of
4:26 And all its **c** were broken down
5: 6 leopard will watch over their **c**.
5:17 shall destroy your fortified **c**,
7:17 not see what they do in the **c**
7:34 will cause to cease from the **c**
8:14 let us enter the fortified **c**,
9:11 I will make the **c** of Judah
10:22 To make the **c** of Judah
11: 6 all these words in the **c** of
11:12 Then the **c** of Judah and the
11:13 to the number of your **c** were
13:19 The **c** of the South shall be
17:26 they shall come from the **c**
20:16 And let that man be like the **c**
22: 6 **C** which are not inhabited.
25:18 Jerusalem and the **c** of Judah,
26: 2 and speak to all the **c** of
31:21 Turn back to these your **c**.
31:23 the land of Judah and in its **c**,
31:24 and in all its **c** together,
32:44 in the **c** of Judah, in the
32:44 in the **c** of the mountains, in
32:44 in the **c** of the lowland, and in
32:44 and in the **c** of the South; for
33:10 in the **c** of Judah, in the
33:12 without beast, and in all its **c**,
33:13 In the **c** of the mountains, in
33:13 in the **c** of the lowland, in the
33:13 in the **c** of the South, in the
33:13 and in the **c** of Judah, the
34: 1 against Jerusalem and all its **c**,
34: 7 Jerusalem and all the **c** of
34: 7 for only these fortified **c**
34: 7 cities remained of the **c** of
34:22 and I will make the **c** of Judah
36: 6 all Judah who come from their **c**.
36: 9 the people who came from the **c**
40: 5 has made governor over the **c**
40:10 and dwell in your **c** that you
44: 2 on Jerusalem and on all the **c**
44: 6 out and kindled in the **c** of
44:17 in the **c** of Judah and in the
44:21 that you burned in the **c** of
48: 9 For her **c** shall be desolate,
48:15 and gone up from her **c**;
48:24 On all the **c** of the land of
48:28 Leave the **c** and dwell in the
49: 1 And his people dwell in its **c**?
49:13 And all its **c** shall be
50:32 I will kindle a fire in his **c**,
51:43 Her **c** are a desolation, A dry
Lam 5:11 The maidens in the **c** of Judah.
Ezek 6: 6 all your dwelling places the **c**
12:20 Then the **c** that are inhabited
19: 7 places, And laid waste their **c**;
25: 9 the territory of Moab of **c**,
25: 9 of the **c** on its frontier, the
26:19 like **c** that are not inhabited,
29:12 and among the **c** that are laid
29:12 her **c** shall be desolate forty
30: 7 And her **c** shall be in the
30: 7 shall be in the midst of the **c**
30:17 And these **c** shall go into
35: 4 I shall lay your **c** waste, And
35: 9 your **c** shall be uninhabited;
36: 4 and the **c** that have been
36:10 and the **c** shall be inhabited
36:33 enable you to dwell in the **c**,
36:35 and ruined **c** are now
36:38 so shall the ruined **c** be filled
39: 9 those who dwell in the **c**
Hos 8:14 also has multiplied fortified **c**;
8:14 I will send fire upon his **c**,
11: 6 the sword shall slash in his **c**,
13:10 he may save you in all your **c**?
Am 4: 6 of teeth in all your **c**.
4: 8 So two or three **c** wandered to
9:14 They shall build the waste **c**
Ob 20 Sepharad Shall possess the **c**
Mic 5:11 I will cut off the **c** of your
5:14 Thus I will destroy your **c**.
7:12 Assyria and the fortified **c**,
Zeph 1:16 alarm Against the fortified **c**
3: 6 Their **c** are destroyed;
Zech 1:12 on Jerusalem and on the **c** of
1:17 My **c** shall again spread out
7: 7 when Jerusalem and the **c**
8:20 come, Inhabitants of many **c**;
Mt 9:35 Jesus went about all the **c** and
10:23 not have gone through the **c** of
11: 1 teach and to preach in their **c**.
11:20 Then He began to rebuke the **c**
14:13 followed Him on foot from the **c**.
Mk 6:33 there on foot from all the **c**.
6:56 He entered into villages, **c**,
Lk 4:43 kingdom of God to the other **c**
13:22 And He went through the **c** and
19:17 have authority over ten **c**.
19:19 him, 'You also be over five **c**.
Acts 5:16 from the surrounding **c** to
8:40 he preached in all the **c** till
14: 6 **c** of Lycaonia, and to the
16: 4 And as they went through the **c**,
26:11 them even to foreign **c**.
2 Pe 2: 6 and turning the **c** of Sodom and
Jude 7 and the **c** around them in a
Rev 16:19 and the **c** of the nations fell.

CITIZEN (4/4) CITIZENS, CITIZENSHIP

Lk 15:15 went and joined himself to a **c**
Acts 21:39 a **c** of no mean city; and I
22:28 said, "But I was born a **c**.
28: 7 was an estate of the leading **c**

CITIZENS (2/2) CITIZEN

Lk 19:14 But his **c** hated him, and sent a
Eph 2:19 but fellow **c** with the saints

CITIZENSHIP (2/2)

Acts 22:28 a large sum I obtained this **c**.
Phil 3:20 For our **c** is in heaven, from

CITRON (1/1)

Rev 18:12 every kind of **c** wood, every

CITY (851/765) CITIES, CITY'S

Gen 4:17 bore Enoch. And he built a **c**,
4:17 and called the name of the **c**
10:12 (that is the principal **c**).
11: 4 let us build ourselves a **c**,
11: 5 LORD came down to see the **c**
11: 8 and they ceased building the **c**.
18:24 fifty righteous within the **c**;
18:26 fifty righteous within the **c**,
18:28 would You destroy all of the **c**
19: 4 they lay down, the men of the **c**,
19:12 and whomever you have in the **c**—
19:14 the LORD will destroy this **c**!
19:15 in the punishment of the **c**.
19:16 out and set him outside the **c**.
19:20 this **c** is near enough to flee
19:21 I will not overthrow this **c**
19:22 Therefore the name of the **c**
23:10 entered at the gate of his **c**,
23:18 went in at the gate of his **c**.
24:10 to the **c** of Nahor.
24:11 kneel down outside the **c** by a
24:13 daughters of the men of the **c**
26:33 Therefore the name of the **c** is
28:19 but the name of that **c** had been
33:18 Jacob came safely to the **c** of
33:18 pitched his tent before the **c**.
34:20 son came to the gate of their **c**,
34:20 spoke with the men of their **c**,
34:24 went out of the gate of his **c**
34:24 went out of the gate of his **c**.
34:25 and came boldly upon the **c** and
34:27 the slain, and plundered the **c**,
34:28 what was in the **c** and what
36:32 and the name of his **c** was
36:35 And the name of his **c** was
36:39 and the name of his **c** was Pau.
41:48 he laid up in every **c** the food
44: 4 When they had gone out of the **c**,
44:13 donkey and returned to the **c**.
Ex 9:29 as I have gone out of the **c**,
9:33 So Moses went out of the **c** from
Lev 14:40 an unclean place outside the **c**.
14:41 an unclean place outside the **c**.
14:45 carry them outside the **c** to
14:53 bird loose outside the **c** in
25:29 man sells a house in a walled **c**,
25:30 then the house in the walled **c**
25:33 house that was sold in the **c**
Num 20:16 a **c** on the edge of your border.
21:26 For Heshbon was the **c** of Sihon
21:27 Let the **c** of Sihon be
21:28 A flame from the **c** of Sihon;
22:36 went out to meet him at the **c**
24:19 destroy the remains of the **c**.
35: 4 extend from the wall of the **c**
35: 5 shall measure outside the **c** on
35: 5 The **c** shall be in the middle.
35:25 shall return him to the **c** of
35:26 outside the limits of the **c** of
35:27 outside the limits of his **c** of
35:28 should have remained in his **c**
35:32 for him who has fled to his **c**
Deut 2:34 and little ones of every **c**;
2:36 and from the **c** that is in the
2:36 there was not one **c** too strong
3: 4 there was not a **c** which we did
3: 6 women, and children of every **c**.
13:13 the inhabitants of their **c**,
13:15 the inhabitants of that **c** with
13:16 burn with fire the **c** and all
19:12 then the elders of his **c** shall
20:10 When you go near a **c** to fight
20:12 Now if the **c** will not make
20:14 and all that is in the **c**,
20:19 When you besiege a **c** for a long
20:20 build siegeworks against the **c**
21: 3 be that the elders of the **c**
21: 4 The elders of that **c** shall bring
21: 6 And all the elders of that **c**
21:19 him out to the elders of his **c**,
21:19 his city, to the gate of his **c**.
21:20 say to the elders of his **c**,
21:21 Then all the men of his **c** shall
22:15 to the elders of the **c** at the
22:17 before the elders of the **c**.
22:18 Then the elders of that **c** shall
22:21 and the men of her **c** shall
22:23 and a man finds her in the **c**
22:24 both out to the gate of that **c**,
22:24 she did not cry out in the **c**,
25: 8 Then the elders of his **c** shall
28: 3 shall you be in the **c**,
28:16 shall you be in the **c**,
34: 3 the **c** of palm trees, as far as
Josh 2:15 for her house was on the **c**
3:16 the **c** that is beside Zaretan.
6: 3 "You shall march around the **c**,
6: 3 you shall go all around the **c**
6: 4 you shall march around the **c**
6: 5 then the wall of the **c** will
6: 7 and march around the **c**,
6:11 ark of the LORD circle the **c**,
6:14 day they marched around the **c**
6:15 and marched around the **c** seven
6:15 only they marched around the **c**
6:16 the LORD has given you the **c**!
6:17 Now the **c** shall be doomed by the
6:20 the people went up into the **c**,
6:20 before him, and they took the **c**.
6:21 all that was in the **c**,
6:24 But they burned the **c** and all
6:26 who rises up and builds this **c**
8: 1 king of Ai, his people, his **c**,
8: 2 Lay an ambush for the **c** behind

8: 4 lie in ambush against the **c**,
8: 4 against the city, behind the **c**.
8: 4 Do not go very far from the **c**,
8: 5 with me will approach the **c**;
8: 6 we have drawn them from the **c**,
8: 7 from the ambush and seize the **c**,
8: 8 be, when you have taken the **c**,
8: 8 that you shall set the **c** on
8:11 and they came before the **c** and
8:12 Ai, on the west side of the **c**.
8:13 that was on the north of the **c**,
8:13 rear guard on the west of the **c**,
8:14 that the men of the **c** hurried
8:14 ambush against him behind the **c**.
8:16 and were drawn away from the **c**.
8:17 So they left the **c** open and
8:18 was in his hand toward the **c**.
8:19 and they entered the **c** and took
8:19 and hurried to set the **c** on
8:20 the smoke of the **c** ascended to
8:21 the ambush had taken the **c** and
8:21 and that the smoke of the **c**
8:22 the others came out of the **c**
8:27 and the spoil of that **c** Israel
8:29 entrance of the gate of the **c**,
10: 2 because Gibeon was a great **c**,
11:19 There was not a **c** that made
13:16 and the **c** that is in the midst
15: 8 slope of the Jebusite **c**
15:62 the **C** of Salt, and En Gedi: six
18:14 a **c** of the children of Judah.
18:16 to the side of the Jebusite **c**
19:29 to Ramah and to the fortified **c**
19:50 the LORD they gave him the **c**
19:50 and he built the **c** and dwelt in
20: 4 entrance of the gate of the **c**,
20: 4 hearing of the elders of that **c**,
20: 4 they shall take him into the **c**
20: 6 And he shall dwell in that **c**
20: 6 return and come to his own **c**
20: 6 to the **c** from which he fled.'
21:12 But the fields of the **c** and its
21:13 with its common-land (a **c** of
21:21 the mountains of Ephraim (a **c**
21:27 with its common-land (a **c** of
21:32 with its common-land (a **c** of
21:38 with its common-land (a **c** of
Judg 1: 8 of the sword and set the **c** on
1:16 went up from the **C** of Palms
1:17 So the name of the **c** was called
1:23 (The name of the **c** was
1:24 saw a man coming out of the **c**,
1:24 show us the entrance to the **c**,
1:25 them the entrance to the **c**,
1:25 and they struck the **c** with the
1:26 land of the Hittites, built a **c**,
3:13 and took possession of the **C** of
6:27 household and the men of the **c**
6:28 And when the men of the **c** arose
6:30 Then the men of the **c** said to
8:16 And he took the elders of the **c**,
8:17 and killed the men of the **c**.
8:27 an ephod and set it up in his **c**,
9:30 When Zebul, the ruler of the **c**,
9:31 fortifying the **c** against you.
9:33 rise early and rush upon the **c**;
9:35 stood in the entrance to the **c**
9:43 the people, coming out of the **c**;
9:44 entrance of the gate of the **c**;
9:45 Abimelech fought against the **c**
9:45 he took the **c** and killed the
9:45 and he demolished the **c** and
9:51 was a strong tower in the **c**,
9:51 women—all the people of the **c**—
14:18 So the men of the **c** said to him
16: 2 all night at the gate of the **c**.
16: 3 the doors of the gate of the **c**
17: 8 The man departed from the **c** of
18:27 of the sword and burned the **c**
18:28 So they rebuilt the **c** and dwelt
18:29 they called the name of the **c**
18:29 the name of the **c** formerly was
19:11 let us turn aside into this **c**
19:12 not turn aside here into a **c**
19:15 in the open square of the **c**,
19:17 in the open square of the **c**;
19:22 suddenly certain men of the **c**,
20:11 were gathered against the **c**,
20:31 and were drawn away from the **c**.
20:32 and draw them away from the **c**
20:37 out and struck the whole **c**
20:38 of smoke rise up from the **c**,
20:40 cloud began to rise from the **c**
20:40 and there was the whole **c** going
20:48 edge of the sword—from every **c**,
Ruth 1:19 that all the **c** was excited
2:18 took it up and went into the **c**,
3:15 Then she went into the **c**.
4: 2 ten men of the elders of the **c**,
1 Sam 1: 3 This man went up from his **c**
4:13 when the man came into the **c**
4:13 all the **c** cried out.
5: 9 of the LORD was against the **c**
5: 9 and He struck the men of the **c**,
5:11 throughout all the **c**;
5:12 and the cry of the **c** went up to
8:22 Israel, "Every man go to his **c**.
9: 6 there is in this **c** a man of
9:10 So they went to the **c** where
9:11 they went up the hill to the **c**,
9:12 for today he came to this **c**,
9:13 soon as you come into the **c**,
9:14 So they went up to the **c**.
9:14 As they were coming into the **c**,
9:25 from the high place into the **c**,
9:27 down to the outskirts of the **c**,
10: 5 you have come there to the **c**,
15: 5 And Saul came to a **c** of Amalek,
20: 6 run over to Bethlehem, his **c**,
20:29 family has a sacrifice in the **c**,
20:40 him, "Go, carry them to the **c**.
20:42 and Jonathan went into the **c**.
22:19 the **c** of the priests, he struck
23:10 to Keilah to destroy the **c** for
27: 5 servant dwell in the royal **c**
28: 3 him in Ramah, in his own **c**.
30: 3 David and his men came to the **c**,
2 Sam 5: 7 (that is, the **C** of David).
5: 9 and called it the **C** of David.
6:10 the LORD with him into the **C**
6:12 house of Obed-Edom to the **C** of
6:16 of the LORD came into the **C**
10: 3 servants to you to search the **c**,
10:14 Abishai, and entered the **c**.
11:16 was, while Joab besieged the **c**,
11:17 Then the men of the **c** came out
11:20 you approach so near to the **c**
11:25 your attack against the **c**,
12: 1 "There were two men in one **c**,
12:26 of Ammon, and took the royal **c**.
12:28 and encamp against the **c** and
12:28 lest I take the **c** and it be
12:30 brought out the spoil of the **c**
15: 2 What **c** are you from?" And he
15:12 David's counselor, from his **c**—
15:14 and strike the **c** with the edge
15:24 crossing over from the **c**.
15:25 the ark of God back into the **c**.
15:27 Return to the **c** in peace, and
15:34 "But if you return to the **c**,
15:37 David's friend, went into the **c**.
17:13 if he has withdrawn into a **c**,
17:13 shall bring ropes to that **c**;
17:17 not be seen coming into the **c**;
17:23 home to his house, to his **c**.
18: 3 now more help to us in the **c**.
19: 3 people stole back into the **c**
19:37 that I may die in my own **c**,
20:15 up a siege mound against the **c**,
20:16 wise woman cried out from the **c**,
20:19 You seek to destroy a **c** and a
20:21 and I will depart from the **c**.
20:22 and they withdrew from the **c**,
1 Ki 1:41 Why is the **c** in such a noisy
1:45 so that the **c** is in an uproar.
2:10 and was buried in the **C** of
3: 1 then he brought her to the **C** of
8: 1 of the LORD from the **C** of
8:16 I have chosen no **c** from any
8:44 pray to the LORD toward the **c**
8:48 the **c** which You have chosen and
9:16 Canaanites who dwelt in the **c**,
9:24 daughter came up from the **C** of
11:27 repaired the damages to the **C**
11:32 the **c** which I have chosen out
11:36 the **c** which I have chosen for
11:43 and was buried in the **C** of
13:25 they went and told it in the **c**
13:29 the old prophet came to the **c**
14:11 to Jeroboam and dies in the **c**,
14:12 When your feet enter the **c**,
14:21 the **c** which the LORD had
14:31 with his fathers in the **C** of
15: 8 and they buried him in the **C** of
15:24 with his fathers in the **C** of
16: 4 to Baasha and dies in the **c**,
16:18 when Zimri saw that the **c** was
16:24 and called the name of the **c**
17:10 he came to the gate of the **c**,
20: 2 he sent messengers into the **c**
20:12 they got ready to attack the **c**.
20:19 the provinces went out of the **c**
20:30 rest fled to Aphek, into the **c**;
20:30 fled and went into the **c**,
21: 8 who were dwelling in the **c**
21:11 So the men of his **c**,
21:11 who were inhabitants of his **c**,
21:13 they took him outside the **c**
21:24 to Ahab and dies in the **c**,
22:26 to Amon the governor of the **c**
22:36 saying, "Every man to his **c**,
22:50 with his fathers in the **C** of
2 Ki 2:19 Then the men of the **c** said to
2:19 the situation of this **c** is
2:23 some youths came from the **c** and
3:19 shall attack every fortified **c**
3:19 city and every choice **c**,
6:14 by night and surrounded the **c**.
6:15 surrounding the **c** with horses
6:19 not the way, nor is this the **c**.
7: 4 we say, 'We will enter the **c**,
7: 4 city,' the famine is in the **c**,
7:10 to the gatekeepers of the **c**,
7:12 'When they come out of the **c**,
7:12 them alive, and get into the **c**.
7:13 horses which are left in the **c**.
8:24 with his fathers in the **C** of
9:15 leave or escape from the **c** to
9:28 tomb with his fathers in the **C**
10: 2 a fortified **c** also, and
10: 5 he who was in charge of the **c**,
10: 6 with the great men of the **c**,
11:20 and the **c** was quiet, for they
12:21 him with his fathers in the **C**
14:20 with his fathers in the **C** of
15: 7 him with his fathers in the **C**
15:38 with his fathers in the **C** of
16:20 with his fathers in the **C** of
17: 9 from watchtower to fortified **c**.
18: 8 from watchtower to fortified **c**.
18:30 this **c** shall not be given into
19:13 and the king of the **c** of
19:32 shall not come into this **c**,
19:33 he shall not come into this **c**,
19:34 'For I will defend this **c**,
20: 6 I will deliver you and this **c**
20: 6 and I will defend this **c** for My
20:20 and brought water into the **c**—
23: 8 of Joshua the governor of the **c**,
23: 8 were to the left of the **c**
23:17 So the men of the **c** told him,
23:27 and will cast off this **c**
24:10 and the **c** was besieged.
24:11 of Babylon came against the **c**,
25: 2 So the **c** was besieged until the
25: 3 had become so severe in the **c**
25: 4 Then the **c** wall was broken
25: 4 all around against the **c**.
25:11 people who remained in the **c**
25:19 He also took out of the **c** an
25:19 who were found in the **c**,
25:19 land who were found in the **c**.
1 Chr 1:43 and the name of his **c** was
1:46 The name of his **c** was Avith.
1:50 and the name of his **c** was Pai.
6:56 But the fields of the **c** and its
11: 5 (that is, the **C** of David).
11: 7 therefore they called it the **C**
11: 8 And he built the **c** around it,
11: 8 Joab repaired the rest of the **c**.
13:13 the ark with him into the **C** of
15: 1 houses for himself in the **C** of
15:29 of the LORD came to the **C** of
19: 9 array before the gate of the **c**,
19:15 his brother, and entered the **c**.
20: 2 brought out the spoil of the **c**
2 Chr 5: 2 of the LORD up from the **C** of
6: 5 I have chosen no **c** from any
6:34 they pray to You toward this **c**
6:38 the **c** which You have chosen,
8:11 of Pharaoh up from the **C** of
9:31 and was buried in the **C** of
11:12 Also in every **c** he put shields
11:23 Benjamin, to every fortified **c**;
12:13 the **c** which the LORD had
12:16 and was buried in the **C** of
14: 1 and they buried him in the **C** of
15: 6 and **c** by city, for God troubled
15: 6 by nation, and city by **c**,
16:14 had made for himself in the **C**
18:25 to Amon the governor of the **c**
19: 5 cities of Judah, **c** by city,
19: 5 cities of Judah, city by **c**,
21: 1 with his fathers in the **C** of
21:20 they buried him in the **C** of
23:21 and the **c** was quiet, for they
24:16 And they buried him in the **C** of
24:25 And they buried him in the **C** of
25:28 him with his fathers in the **C**
27: 9 and they buried him in the **C** of
28:15 the **c** of palm trees. Then they
28:25 And in every single **c** of Judah
28:27 and they buried him in the **c**,
29:20 gathered the rulers of the **c**,
30:10 So the runners passed from **c** to
30:10 runners passed from city to **c**
31:19 their cities, in every single **c**,
32: 3 which were outside the **c**;
32: 5 he repaired the Millo in the **C**
32: 6 him in the open square of the **c**
32:18 that they might take the **c**.
32:30 to the west side of the **C** of
33:14 he built a wall outside the **C**
33:15 and he cast them out of the **c**.
34: 8 Maaseiah the governor of the **c**,
Ezra 2: 1 Judah, everyone to his own **c**.
4:12 the rebellious and evil **c**,
4:13 if this **c** is built and the
4:15 records and know that this **c**
4:15 this city is a rebellious **c**,
4:15 incited sedition within the **c**
4:15 for which cause this **c** was
4:16 inform the king that if this **c**
4:19 and it was found that this **c** in
4:21 that this **c** may not be built
Neh 2: 3 my face not be sad, when the **c**,
2: 5 to the **c** of my fathers' tombs,
2: 8 for the **c** wall, and for the
3:15 stairs that go down from the **C**
7: 4 Now the **c** was large and
7: 6 and Judah, everyone to his **c**.
11: 1 dwell in Jerusalem, the holy **c**,
11: 9 Senuah was second over the **c**.
11:18 All the Levites in the holy **c**
12:37 went up the stairs of the **C** of
13:18 disaster on us and on this **c**?
Esth 3:15 but the **c** of Shushan was
4: 1 out into the midst of the **c**.
4: 6 went out to Mordecai in the **c**
6: 9 him on horseback through the **c**
6:11 him on horseback through the **c**
8:11 the Jews who were in every **c**
8:15 and the **c** of Shushan rejoiced
8:17 And in every province and **c**,
9:28 every province, and every **c**,
Job 24:12 The dying groan in the **c**,

29: 7 I went out to the gate by the c,
39: 7 He scorns the tumult of the c;
Ps 31:21 kindness in a strong c!
46: 4 streams shall make glad the c
48: 1 to be praised In the c of our
48: 2 The c of the great King.
48: 8 So we have seen In the c of
48: 8 In the c of our God: God will
55: 9 violence and strife in the c.
59: 6 a dog, And go all around the c.
59:14 a dog, And go all around the c.
60: 9 will bring me to the strong c?
72:16 And those of the c shall
87: 3 O c of God! Selah
101: 8 all the evildoers from the c
107: 4 They found no c to dwell in.
107: 7 That they might go to a c for
107:36 That they may establish a c
108:10 bring me into the strong c?
122: 3 Jerusalem is built As a c that
127: 1 Unless the LORD guards the c,
Prov 1:21 openings of the gates in the c
8: 3 gates, at the entry of the c,
9: 3 the highest places of the c,
9:14 by the highest places of the c,
10:15 man's wealth is his strong c;
11:10 the c rejoices; And when the
11:11 blessing of the upright the c
16:32 spirit than he who takes a c.
18:11 man's wealth is his strong c,
18:19 to win than a strong c,
21:22 A wise man scales the c of the
25:28 his own spirit Is like a c
29: 8 Scoffers set a c aflame, But
Eccl 7:19 More than ten rulers of the c.
8:10 they were forgotten in the c
9:14 There was a little c with few
9:15 by his wisdom delivered the c.
10:15 even know how to go to the c!
Song 3: 2 I said, "And go about the c;
3: 3 watchmen who go about the c
5: 7 watchmen who went about the c
Isa 1: 8 of cucumbers, As a besieged c.
1:21 How the faithful c has become
1:26 you shall be called the c of
1:26 righteousness, the faithful c.
14: 4 The golden c ceased!
14:31 O c! All you of Philistia are
17: 1 will cease from being a c,
19: 2 C against city, kingdom
19: 2 his neighbor, City against c,
19:18 one will be called the C of
22: 2 full of noise, A tumultuous c,
22: 2 A tumultuous city, a joyous c?
22: 9 also saw the damage to the c
23: 7 Is this your joyous c,
23: 8 against Tyre, the crowning c,
23:16 "Take a harp, go about the c,
24:10 The c of confusion is broken
24:12 In the c desolation is left,
25: 2 For You have made a c a ruin,
25: 2 A fortified c a ruin, A
25: 2 palace of foreigners to be a c
25: 3 The c of the terrible nations
26: 1 Judah: "We have a strong c;
26: 5 who dwell on high, The lofty c;
27:10 Yet the fortified c will be
29: 1 the c where David dwelt!
32:13 happy homes in the joyous c;
32:14 The bustling c will be
32:19 And the c is brought low in
33:20 the c of our appointed feasts;
36:15 this c will not be given into
37:13 and the king of the c of
37:33 shall not come into this c,
37:34 he shall not come into this c,
37:35 'For I will defend this c,
38: 6 I will deliver you and this c
38: 6 and I will defend this c.
45:13 He shall build My c And let
48: 2 themselves after the holy c,
52: 1 O Jerusalem, the holy c!
60:14 And they shall call you The C
62:12 A C Not Forsaken.
66: 6 The sound of noise from the c!
Jer 1:18 you this day A fortified c
3:14 one from a c and two from a
4:29 The whole c shall flee from the
4:29 Every c shall be forsaken,
6: 6 This is the c to be punished.
8:16 The c and those who dwell in
14:18 And if I enter the c,
17:24 through the gates of this c on
17:25 shall enter the gates of this c
17:25 and this c shall remain
19: 8 I will make this c desolate and
19:11 break this people and this c,
19:12 and make this c like Tophet.
19:15 I will bring on this c and on
20: 5 all the wealth of this c,
21: 4 them in the midst of this c.
21: 6 the inhabitants of this c,
21: 7 and such as are left in this c
21: 9 He who remains in this c shall
21:10 set My face against this c for
22: 8 nations will pass by this c;
22: 8 LORD done so to this great c?
23:39 and the c that I gave you and
25:29 to bring calamity on the c
26: 6 and will make this c a curse to
26: 9 and this c shall be desolate,
26:11 has prophesied against this c,
26:12 this house and against this c
26:15 blood on yourselves, on this c,
26:20 who prophesied against this c
27:17 and live! Why should this c be
27:19 vessels that remain in this c,
29: 7 And seek the peace of the c
29:16 the people who dwell in this c,
30:18 The c shall be built upon its
31:38 that the c shall be built for
32: 3 I will give this c into the
32:24 They have come to the c to
32:24 and the c has been given into
32:25 yet the c has been given into
32:28 I will give this c into the
32:29 who fight against this c shall
32:29 come and set fire to this c
32:31 For this c has been to Me a
32:36 concerning this c of which you
33: 4 the houses of this c and the
33: 5 have hidden My face from this c.
34: 2 I will give this c into the
34:22 cause them to return to this c.
37: 8 back and fight against this c,
37:10 and burn the c with fire.'"
37:21 until all the bread in the c
38: 2 He who remains in this c shall
38: 3 This c shall surely be given
38: 4 men of war who remain in this c,
38: 9 is no more bread in the c.
38:17 this c shall not be burned with
38:18 then this c shall be given into
38:23 And you shall cause this c to
39: 2 the c was penetrated.
39: 4 fled and went out of the c by
39: 9 people who remained in the c
39:16 bring My words upon this c for
41: 7 came into the midst of the c,
46: 8 I will destroy the c and its
47: 2 The c and those who dwell
48: 8 shall come against every c;
49:25 Why is the c of praise not
49:25 the c of My joy?
51:31 the king of Babylon that his c
52: 5 So the c was besieged until the
52: 6 had become so severe in the c
52: 7 Then the c wall was broken
52: 7 war fled and went out of the c
52: 7 the Chaldeans were near the c
52:15 people who remained in the c,
52:25 He also took out of the c an
52:25 who were found in the c,
52:25 found in the midst of the c.
Lam 1: 1 How lonely sits the c That
1:19 Breathed their last in the c,
2:11 Faint in the streets of the c.
2:12 In the streets of the c,
2:15 Is this the c that is called
3:51 of all the daughters of my c.
Ezek 4: 1 you, and portray on it a c,
4: 3 iron wall between you and the c.
5: 2 one-third in the midst of the c,
7:15 And whoever is in the c,
7:23 And the c is full of violence.
9: 1 who have charge over the c
9: 4 "Go through the midst of the c,
9: 5 Go after him through the c and
9: 7 went out and killed in the c.
9: 9 and the c full of perversity;
10: 2 and scatter them over the c.
11: 2 give wicked counsel in this c,
11: 3 this c is the caldron, and we
11: 6 multiplied your slain in this c,
11: 7 and this c is the caldron;
11:11 This c shall not be your
11:23 up from the midst of the c and
11:23 is on the east side of the c.
17: 4 He set it in a c of merchants.
21:19 the head of the road to the c.
22: 2 will you judge the bloody c?
22: 3 The c sheds blood in her own
24: 6 GOD: "Woe to the bloody c,
24: 9 Woe to the bloody c! I too will
26:10 as men enter a c that has been
26:17 by seafaring men, O renowned c,
26:19 'When I make you a desolate c,
27:32 What c is like Tyre,
33:21 The c has been captured!"
39:16 The name of the c will also
40: 1 the fourteenth year after the c
40: 2 like the structure of a c.
43: 3 when I came to destroy the c.
45: 6 as the property of the c an
48:15 be for general use by the c,
48:15 and the c shall be in the
48:17 The common-land of the c shall
48:18 food for the workers of the c.
48:19 "The workers of the c,
48:20 with the property of the c.
48:22 and the possession of the c
48:30 are the exits of the c.
48:31 (the gates of the c shall be
48:35 and the name of the c from
Dan 9:16 fury be turned away from Your c
9:18 and the c which is called by
9:19 for Your c and Your people are
9:24 your people and for your holy c,
9:26 is to come Shall destroy the c
11:15 mound, and take a fortified c;
Hos 6: 8 Gilead is a c of evildoers,
Joel 2: 9 They run to and fro in the c,
Am 3: 6 If a trumpet is blown in a c,
3: 6 If there is calamity in a c,
4: 7 I made it rain on one c,
4: 7 I withheld rain from another c.
4: 8 cities wandered to another c
5: 3 The c that goes out by a
6: 8 I will deliver up the c And
7:17 wife shall be a harlot in the c;
Jon 1: 2 go to Nineveh, that great c,
3: 2 go to Nineveh, that great c,
3: 3 was an exceedingly great c,
3: 4 And Jonah began to enter the c
4: 5 So Jonah went out of the c and
4: 5 sat on the east side of the c.
4: 5 see what would become of the c.
4:11 not pity Nineveh, that great c,
Mic 4:10 you shall go forth from the c,
6: 9 LORD's voice cries to the c—
Nah 3: 1 Woe to the bloody c! It is
Hab 2: 8 violence of the land and the c,
2:12 Who establishes a c by
2:17 violence of the land and the c,
Zeph 2:15 This is the rejoicing c That
3: 1 To the oppressing c!
Zech 8: 3 shall be called the C of Truth,
8: 5 The streets of the c Shall be
8:21 The inhabitants of one c shall
14: 2 The c shall be taken, The
14: 2 Half of the c shall go into
14: 2 shall not be cut off from the c.
Mt 2:23 And he came and dwelt in a c
4: 5 took Him up into the holy c,
5:14 A c that is set on a hill
5:35 for it is the c of the great
8:33 and they went away into the c
8:34 the whole c came out to meet
9: 1 over, and came to His own c.
10: 5 and do not enter a c of the
10:11 Now whatever c or town you
10:14 you depart from that house or c,
10:15 of judgment than for that c!
10:23 they persecute you in this c,
12:25 and every c or house divided
21:10 all the c was moved, saying,
21:17 them and went out of the c to
21:18 as He returned to the c,
22: 7 and burned up their c.
23:34 and persecute from c to city,
23:34 and persecute from city to c,
26:18 Go into the c to a certain man,
27:53 they went into the holy c and
28:11 of the guard came into the c
Mk 1:33 And the whole c was gathered
1:45 no longer openly enter the c,
5:14 and they told it in the c and
6:11 of judgment than for that c!"
11:19 had come, He went out of the c.
14:13 said to them, "Go into the c,
14:16 went out, and came into the c,
Lk 1:26 Gabriel was sent by God to a c
1:39 to a c of Judah,
2: 3 everyone to his own c.
2: 4 out of the c of Nazareth, into
2: 4 to the c of David, which is
2:11 born to you this day in the c
2:39 to Galilee, to their own c.
4:29 up and thrust Him out of the c;
4:29 of the hill on which their c
4:31 a c of Galilee, and was
5:12 when He was in a certain c,
7:11 that He went into a c called
7:12 He came near the gate of the c,
7:12 And a large crowd from the c
7:37 a woman in the c who was a
8: 1 that He went through every c
8: 4 had come to Him from every c,
8:27 Him a certain man from the c
8:34 fled and told it in the c and
8:39 throughout the whole c what
9: 5 you, when you go out of that c,
9:10 place belonging to the c
10: 1 before His face into every c
10: 8 Whatever c you enter, and they
10:10 But whatever c you enter, and
10:11 The very dust of your c which
10:12 Day for Sodom than for that c.
14:21 the streets and lanes of the c,
18: 2 There was in a certain c a judge
18: 3 there was a widow in that c;
19:41 He saw the c and wept over it,
22:10 when you have entered the c,
23:19 certain rebellion made in the c,
23:51 a c of the Jews, who himself
24:49 but tarry in the c of Jerusalem
Jn 1:44 the c of Andrew and Peter.
4: 5 So He came to a c of Samaria
4: 8 had gone away into the c to
4:28 went her way into the c,
4:30 Then they went out of the c and
4:39 of the Samaritans of that c
11:54 to a c called Ephraim, and
19:20 was crucified was near the c;
Acts 7:58 and they cast him out of the c
8: 5 Then Philip went down to the c
8: 8 there was great joy in that c.
8: 9 practiced sorcery in the c and
9: 6 him, "Arise and go into the c,
10: 9 journey and drew near the c,
11: 5 I was in the c of Joppa praying;
12:10 iron gate that leads to the c,
13:44 next Sabbath almost the whole c
13:50 and the chief men of the c,
14: 4 But the multitude of the c was
14:13 temple was in front of their c,

14:19 and dragged him out of the c,
14:20 he rose up and went into the c.
14:21 preached the gospel to that c
15:21 those who preach him in every c,
15:36 visit our brethren in every c
16:12 which is the foremost c of that
16:12 And we were staying in that c
16:13 day we went out of the c to
16:14 a seller of purple from the c
16:20 Jews, exceedingly trouble our c;
16:39 them to depart from the c.
17: 5 set all the c in an uproar and
17: 6 brethren to the rulers of the c,
17: 8 crowd and the rulers of the c
17:16 him when he saw that the c was
18:10 I have many people in this c.
19:29 So the whole c was filled with
19:35 And when the c clerk had quieted
19:35 who does not know that the c
20:23 Spirit testifies in every c,
21: 5 till we were out of the c.
21:29 the Ephesian with him in the c,
21:30 And all the c was disturbed; and
21:39 Cilicia, a citizen of no mean c;
22: 3 but brought up in this c at the
24:12 in the synagogues or in the c.
25:23 and the prominent men of the c,
27: 5 came to Myra, a c of Lycia.
27: 8 near the c of Lasea.
Rom 16:23 Erastus, the treasurer of the c,
2 Cor 11:26 Gentiles, in perils in the c,
11:32 was guarding the c of the
Titus 1: 5 and appoint elders in every c
Heb 11:10 for he waited for the c which
11:16 for He has prepared a c for
12:22 to Mount Zion and to the c of
13:14 here we have no continuing c,
Jas 4:13 we will go to such and such a c,
Rev 3:12 of My God and the name of the c
11: 2 And they will tread the holy c
11: 8 in the street of the great c
11:13 and a tenth of the c fell.
14: 8 fallen, is fallen, that great c,
14:20 was trampled outside the c,
16:19 Now the great c was divided into
17:18 whom you saw is that great c
18:10 that great c Babylon, that
18:10 that mighty c! For in one hour
18:16 that great c that was clothed
18:18 'What is like this great c?
18:19 'Alas, alas, that great c,
18:21 with violence the great c
20: 9 of the saints and the beloved c.
21: 2 Then I, John, saw the holy c,
21:10 and showed me the great c,
21:14 Now the wall of the c had twelve
21:15 a gold reed to measure the c,
21:16 The c is laid out as a square;
21:16 And he measured the c with the
21:18 and the c was pure gold, like
21:19 of the wall of the c were
21:21 And the street of the c was
21:23 The c had no need of the sun or
22:14 through the gates into the c.
22:19 Book of Life, from the holy c,

CITY'S (4/3) CITY

2 Sam 12:27 and I have taken the c water
Ezek 45: 7 district and the c property;
45: 7 on the holy district and the c
48:21 district and of the c property,

CLAD (1/1)

Isa 59:17 And was c with zeal as a

CLAIM (5/5) CLAIMING, CLAIMS

Deut 15: 3 but you shall give up your c to
Judg 7: 2 lest Israel c glory for itself
Job 3: 5 and the shadow of death c it;
Isa 40:27 And my just c is passed over
Jer 37:12 into the land of Benjamin to c

CLAIMING (2/2) CLAIM

Acts 5:36 c to be somebody. A number of
8: 9 c that he was someone great,

CLAIMS (1/1) CLAIM

Ex 22: 9 of lost thing which another c

CLAMOR (1/1) CLAMOROUS

Eph 4:31 all bitterness, wrath, anger, c,

CLAMOROUS (1/1) CLAMOR

Prov 9:13 A foolish woman is c;

CLAN (2/2) CLANS

Josh 7:17 He brought the c of Judah, and
Judg 6:15 Indeed my c is the weakest in

CLANGING (1/1)

1 Cor 13: 1 become sounding brass or a c

CLANS (2/2) CLAN

1 Sam 10:19 by your tribes and by your c.

23:23 for him throughout all the c

CLAP (6/6) CLAPPED, CLAPS

Job 27:23 Men shall c their hands at
Ps 47: 1 c your hands, all you peoples!
98: 8 Let the rivers c their hands;
Isa 55:12 the trees of the field shall c
Lam 2:15 All who pass by c their hands
Nah 3:19 who hear news of you Will c

CLAPPED (2/2) CLAP

2 Ki 11:12 and they c their hands and
Ezek 25: 6 Because you c your hands,

CLAPS (1/1) CLAP

Job 34:37 He c his hands among us,

CLARITY (1/1) CLEAR

Ex 24:10 like the very heavens in its c.

CLASH (1/1)

Job 39:21 He gallops into the c of arms.

CLASHING (1/1)

Ps 150: 5 Praise Him with c cymbals!

CLASPED (1/1) CLASPS

Ex 26: 5 that the loops may be c to one

CLASPS (10/7) CLASPED

Ex 26: 6 And you shall make fifty c of
26: 6 curtains together with the c,
26:11 you shall make fifty bronze c,
26:11 put the c into the loops, and
26:33 shall hang the veil from the c.
35:11 its tent, its covering, its c,
36:13 And he made fifty c of gold, and
36:13 to one another with the c,
36:18 He also made fifty bronze c to
39:33 and all its furnishings: its c,

CLASS (4/4)

1 Ki 12:31 and made priests from every c
13:33 he made priests from every c
2 Ki 17:32 and from every c they appointed
2 Cor 10:12 For we dare not c ourselves or

CLATTER (1/1) CLATTERING

Judg 5:28 Why tarries the c of his

CLATTERING (1/1) CLATTER

Nah 3: 2 Of c chariots!

CLAUDA (1/1)

Acts 27:16 shelter of an island called C,

CLAUDIA (1/1)

2 Tim 4:21 as well as Pudens, Linus, C,

CLAUDIUS (3/3) CAESAR

Acts 11:28 also happened in the days of C
18: 2 his wife Priscilla (because C
23:26 C Lysias, to the most excellent

CLAVE (KJV) See (STRONGLY) ATTRACTED, CLUNG, JOINED, SPLIT

CLAWS (1/1)

Dan 4:33 and his nails like birds' c.

CLAY (35/32)

1 Ki 7:46 the king had them cast in c
2 Chr 4:17 the king had them cast in c
Job 4:19 those who dwell in houses of c,
10: 9 that You have made me like c.
13:12 defenses are defenses of c.
27:16 And piles up clothing like c—
33: 6 also have been formed out of c.
38:14 It takes on form like c under
Ps 40: 2 pit, Out of the miry c,
Isa 29:16 the potter be esteemed as the c;
41:25 mortar, As the potter treads c.
45: 9 of the earth! Shall the c say
64: 8 are our Father; We are the c,
Jer 18: 4 the vessel that he made of c
18: 6 as the c is in the potter's
43: 9 in the c in the brick courtyard
Lam 4: 2 How they are regarded as c
Ezek 4: 1 take a c tablet and lay it
Dan 2:33 partly of iron and partly of c.
2:34 image on its feet of iron and c,
2:35 "Then the iron, the c,
2:41 partly of potter's c and partly
2:41 the iron mixed with ceramic c.
2:42 partly of iron and partly of c,
2:43 saw iron mixed with ceramic c,
2:43 as iron does not mix with c.
2:45 the iron, the bronze, the c,
Nah 3:14 Go into the c and tread the
Jn 9: 6 spat on the ground and made c
9: 6 of the blind man with the c.
9:11 A Man called Jesus made c and
9:14 a Sabbath when Jesus made the c
9:15 He put c on my eyes, and I
Rom 9:21 potter have power over the c,
2 Tim 2:20 silver, but also of wood and c,

CLEAN (114/99) CLEANNESS, CLEANSE, CLEANSED, CLEANSING, UNCLEAN

Gen 7: 2 with you seven each of every c
7: 8 Of c animals, of animals that
8:20 and took of every c animal and
8:20 clean animal and of every c
Lev 4:12 carry outside the camp to a c
6:11 ashes outside the camp to a c
7:19 And as for the c flesh, all
7:19 all who are c may eat of it.
10:10 and between unclean and c,
10:14 offering you shall eat in a c
11:32 evening; then it shall be c.
11:36 is plenty of water, shall be c,
11:37 is to be sown, it remains c.
11:47 between the unclean and the c,
12: 7 And she shall be c from the
12: 8 for her, and she will be c.
13: 6 priest shall pronounce him c;
13: 6 shall wash his clothes and be c.
13:13 he shall pronounce him c who
13:13 has all turned white. He is c.
13:17 priest shall pronounce him c
13:17 who has the sore. He is c.
13:23 priest shall pronounce him c.
13:28 priest shall pronounce him c,
13:34 priest shall pronounce him c,
13:34 shall wash his clothes and be c.
13:37 the scale has healed. He is c,
13:37 priest shall pronounce him c.
13:39 grows on the skin. He is c.
13:40 he is bald, but he is c.
13:41 on the forehead, but he is c.
13:58 a second time, and shall be c.
13:59 to pronounce it c or to
14: 4 be cleansed two living and c
14: 7 and shall pronounce him c,
14: 8 in water, that he may be c.
14: 9 in water, and he shall be c.
14:11 the priest who makes him c
14:11 the man who is to be made c,
14:20 for him, and he shall be c.
14:48 shall pronounce the house c,
14:53 the house, and it shall be c.
14:57 is unclean and when it is c.
15: 8 discharge spits on him who is c,
15:13 water; then he shall be c.
15:28 and after that she shall be c.
16:30 that you may be c from all
17:15 Then he shall be c.
20:25 distinguish between c animals
20:25 between unclean birds and c,
22: 4 holy offerings until he is c.
22: 7 the sun goes down he shall be c;
Num 5:28 not defiled herself, and is c,
8: 7 and so make themselves c.
9:13 But the man who is c and is not
18:11 Everyone who is c in your house
18:13 Everyone who is c in your house
19: 9 Then a man who is c shall
19: 9 them outside the camp in a c
19:12 seventh day; then he will be c.
19:12 seventh day, he will not be c.
19:18 A c person shall take hyssop and
19:19 The c person shall sprinkle the
19:19 and at evening he shall be c.
31:23 the fire, and it shall be c;
31:24 on the seventh day and be c,
Deut 12:15 the unclean and the c may eat
12:22 the unclean and the c alike may
14:11 All c birds you may eat.
14:20 You may eat all c birds.
15:22 the unclean and the c person
2 Ki 5:10 to you, and you shall be c.
5:12 I not wash in them and be c?
5:13 says to you, 'Wash, and be c'?
5:14 of a little child, and he was c.
2 Chr 30:17 for everyone who was not c,
Ezra 6:20 all of them were ritually c.
Job 11: 4 And I am c in your eyes.'
14: 4 Who can bring a c thing out of
17: 9 And he who has c hands will be
Ps 19: 9 The fear of the LORD is c,
24: 4 He who has c hands and a pure
51: 7 with hyssop, and I shall be c;
51:10 Create in me a c heart, O God,
Prov 14: 4 no oxen are, the trough is c;
20: 9 say, "I have made my heart c,
Eccl 9: 2 the wicked; To the good, the c,
Isa 1:16 yourselves, make yourselves c;
28: 8 and filth; No place is c.
52:11 from the midst of her, Be c,
66:20 Israel bring an offering in a c
Jer 13:27 Will you still not be made c?
Ezek 22:26 between the unclean and the c;
36:25 Then I will sprinkle c water on
36:25 on you, and you shall be c;
44:23 between the unclean and the c.
Zech 3: 5 Let them put a c turban on his
3: 5 So they put a c turban on his

Mt 3:12 and He will thoroughly **c** out
8: 2 are willing, You can make me **c**.
23:26 the outside of them may be **c**
27:59 he wrapped it in a **c** linen
Mk 1:40 are willing, You can make me **c**.
Lk 3:17 and He will thoroughly **c** out
5:12 are willing, You can make me **c**.
11:39 outside of the cup and dish **c**,
11:41 then indeed all things are **c** to
Jn 13:10 his feet, but is completely **c**;
13:10 completely clean; and you are **c**,
13:11 He said, "You are not all **c**.
15: 3 You are already **c** because of the
Acts 18: 6 upon your own heads; I am **c**.
Rev 19: 8 **c** and bright, for the fine
19:14 in fine linen, white and **c**,

CLEANNESS (5/5) CLEAN

2 Sam 22:21 According to the **c** of my hands
22:25 According to my **c** in His eyes.
Ps 18:20 According to the **c** of my hands
18:24 According to the **c** of my hands
Am 4: 6 Also I gave you **c** of teeth in

CLEANSE (38/38) CLEAN, CLEANSED, CLEANSES, CLEANSING

Ex 29:36 You shall **c** the altar when you
Lev 14:49 to **c** the house, two birds,
14:52 And he shall **c** the house with
16:19 **c** it, and consecrate it from
16:30 to **c** you, that you may be
Num 8: 6 the children of Israel and **c**
8: 7 you shall do to them to **c**
8:15 So you shall **c** them and offer
8:21 made atonement for them to **c**
2 Chr 29:15 to **c** the house of the LORD.
29:16 of the house of the LORD to **c**
Neh 13: 9 Then I commanded them to **c** the
13:22 the Levites that they should **c**
Job 9:30 And **c** my hands with soap,
Ps 19:12 **C** me from secret faults.
51: 2 And **c** me from my sin.
119: 9 How can a young man **c** his way?
Prov 20:30 Blows that hurt **c** away evil,
Jer 4:11 My people—Not to fan or to **c**—
33: 8 I will **c** them from all their
Ezek 16: 4 were you washed in water to **c**
36:25 I will **c** you from all your
36:33 On the day that I **c** you from all
37:23 and will **c** them. Then they
39:12 in order to **c** the land.
39:14 in order to **c** it. At the end of
39:16 Thus they shall **c** the land." '
43:20 thus you shall **c** it and make
43:22 and they shall **c** the altar, as
45:18 bull without blemish and **c** the
Mt 10: 8 **c** the lepers, raise the dead,
23:25 hypocrites! For you **c** the
23:26 first **c** the inside of the cup
2 Cor 7: 1 let us **c** ourselves from all
Eph 5:26 that He might sanctify and **c** her
Heb 9:14 **c** your conscience from dead
Jas 4: 8 **C** your hands, you sinners;
1 Jn 1: 9 forgive us our sins and to **c**

CLEANSED (41/38) CLEANSE

Lev 14: 4 to take for him who is to be **c**
14: 7 times on him who is to be **c**
14: 8 He who is to be **c** shall wash his
14:14 right ear of him who is to be **c**,
14:17 right ear of him who is to be **c**,
14:18 the head of him who is to be **c**.
14:19 for him who is to be **c** from
14:25 right ear of him who is to be **c**,
14:28 right ear of him who is to be **c**,
14:29 the head of him who is to be **c**,
14:31 for him who is to be **c** before
15:13 he who has a discharge is **c** of
15:28 But if she is **c** of her
Josh 22:17 from which we are not **c** until
2 Sam 11: 4 for she was **c** from her
2 Chr 29:18 We have **c** all the house of the
30:18 had not **c** themselves, yet they
30:19 though he is not **c** according
34: 5 and **c** Judah and Jerusalem.
Neh 13:30 Thus I **c** them of everything
Ps 73:13 Surely I have **c** my heart in
Ezek 22:24 You are a land that is not **c** or
24:13 Because I have **c** you, and you
24:13 you, and you were not **c**,
24:13 You will not be **c** of your
43:22 as they **c** it with the bull.
44:26 'After he is **c**, they shall
Dan 8:14 then the sanctuary shall be **c**.
Mt 8: 3 saying, "I am willing; be **c**.
8: 3 Immediately his leprosy was **c**.
11: 5 the lepers are **c** and the deaf
Mk 1:41 to him, "I am willing; be **c**.
1:42 leprosy left him, and he was **c**.
Lk 4:27 and none of them was **c** except
5:13 saying, "I am willing; be **c**.
7:22 lame walk, the lepers are **c**,
17:14 that as they went, they were **c**.
17:17 said, "Were there not ten **c**?
Acts 10:15 What God has **c** you must not call
11: 9 What God has **c** you must not call
2 Pe 1: 9 and has forgotten that he was **c**

CLEANSES (2/2) CLEANSE

2 Tim 2:21 Therefore if anyone **c** himself
1 Jn 1: 7 of Jesus Christ His Son **c** us

CLEANSING (10/10) CLEANSE

Lev 13: 7 seen by the priest for his **c**,
13:35 over the skin after his **c**,
14: 2 the leper for the day of his **c**:
14:23 on the eighth day for his **c**,
14:32 who cannot afford the usual **c**.
15:13 himself seven days for his **c**,
Num 6: 9 his head on the day of his **c**;
Ezek 43:23 When you have finished **c** it,
Mk 1:44 and offer for your **c** those
Lk 5:14 and make an offering for your **c**,

CLEAR (16/16) CLARITY, CLEARED, CLEARING, CLEARLY, CLEARS

Gen 24:41 You will be **c** from this oath
44:16 Or how shall we **c** ourselves?
Lev 26:10 and **c** out the old because of
Josh 17:15 to the forest country and **c** a
2 Sam 23: 4 By **c** shining after rain.'
1 Ki 7:36 wherever there was a **c** space on
Song 6:10 **C** as the sun, Awesome as an
Isa 18: 4 from My dwelling place Like **c**
Ezek 25: 9 I will **c** the territory of Moab
32:14 I will make their waters **c**,
34:18 and to have drunk of the **c**
1 Cor 3:13 each one's work will become **c**;
2 Cor 7:11 you proved yourselves to be **c**
Rev 21:11 jasper stone, **c** as crystal.
21:18 was pure gold, like **c** glass.
22: 1 **c** as crystal, proceeding from

CLEARED (2/2) CLEAR

Job 37:21 the wind has passed and **c** them.
Isa 5: 2 He dug it up and **c** out its

CLEARING (2/2)

Ex 34: 7 by no means **c** the guilty,
2 Cor 7:11 what **c** of yourselves, what

CLEARLY (13/13) CLEAR

Josh 9:24 Because your servants were **c**
1 Sam 2:27 Did I not **c** reveal Myself to the
Ezra 4:18 you sent to us has been **c** read
Mt 7: 5 and then you will see **c** to
Mk 8:25 was restored and saw everyone **c**.
Lk 6:42 and then you will see **c** to
Jn 3:21 that his deeds may be **c** seen,
Acts 10: 3 ninth hour of the day he saw **c**
Rom 1:20 His invisible attributes are **c**
2 Cor 3: 3 **c** you are an epistle of
Gal 3: 1 whose eyes Jesus Christ was **c**
1 Tim 5:24 Some men's sins are **c** evident,
5:25 the good works of some are **c**

CLEARS (1/1) CLEAR

Num 14:18 but He by no means **c** the

CLEAVE, CLEAVED, CLEAVETH (KJV) See CLING, DIVIDED, JOIN, JOINED, PERSISTED, SPLIT, STUCK

CLEFT (3/3) CLEFTS

Ex 33:22 that I will put you in the **c** of
Judg 15: 8 he went down and dwelt in the **c**
15:11 of Judah went down to the **c** of

CLEFTS (7/7) CLEFT

Job 30: 6 They had to live in the **c** of
Song 2:14 in the **c** of the rock, In the
Isa 2:21 To go into the **c** of the rocks,
7:19 desolate valleys and in the **c**
57: 5 Under the **c** of the rocks?
Jer 49:16 O you who dwell in the **c** of
Ob 3 You who dwell in the **c** of the

CLEMENCY (KJV) See COURTESY

CLEMENT (1/1)

Phil 4: 3 with **C** also, and the rest of my

CLEOPAS (1/1) ALPHAEUS

Lk 24:18 Then the one whose name was **C**

CLEOPHAS (KJV) See CLOPAS

CLERK (1/1)

Acts 19:35 And when the city **c** had quieted

CLIFF (3/3) CLIFFS

Ps 141: 6 by the sides of the **c**,
Song 2:14 In the secret places of the **c**,
Lk 4:29 might throw Him down over the **c**.

CLIFFS (1/1) CLIFF

Ps 104:18 The **c** are a refuge for the

CLIFT (KJV) See CLEFT

CLIMB (4/4) CLIMBED, CLIMBS

Jer 4:29 shall go into thickets and **c**
Joel 2: 7 They **c** the wall like men of
2: 9 They **c** into the houses, They
Am 9: 2 Though they **c** up to heaven,

CLIMBED (2/2) CLIMB

1 Sam 14:13 And Jonathan **c** up on his hands
Lk 19: 4 So he ran ahead and **c** up into a

CLIMBS (2/2) CLIMB

2 Sam 5: 8 Whoever **c** up by way of the water
Jn 10: 1 but **c** up some other way, the

CLING (15/15) CLINGS, CLUNG

Deut 28:21 LORD will make the plague **c**
28:60 and they shall **c** to you.
30:20 and that you may **c** to Him, for
Josh 23:12 and **c** to the remnant of these
2 Ki 5:27 the leprosy of Naaman shall **c**
Job 38:38 And the clods **c** together?
Ps 101: 3 It shall not **c** to me.
102: 5 of my groaning My bones **c** to
119:31 I **c** to Your testimonies;
137: 6 Let my tongue **c** to the roof of
Isa 14: 1 and they will **c** to the house of
Jer 13:11 the whole house of Judah to **c**
Ezek 3:26 I will make your tongue **c** to the
Jn 20:17 Do not **c** to Me, for I have not
Rom 12: 9 **C** to what is good.

CLINGS (9/9) CLING

Job 19:20 My bone **c** to my skin and to my
Ps 22:15 And My tongue **c** to My jaws;
41: 8 they say, "**c** to him.
44:25 Our body **c** to the ground.
119:25 My soul **c** to the dust;
Jer 13:11 For as the sash **c** to the waist
Lam 4: 4 The tongue of the infant **c** To
4: 8 Their skin **c** to their bones,
Lk 10:11 very dust of your city which **c**

CLIPPED (1/1)

Jer 48:37 be bald, and every beard **c**;

CLOAK (8/8)

Ps 102:26 Like a **c** You will change them,
Isa 59:17 And was clad with zeal as a **c**.
Mt 5:40 let him have your **c** also.
Lk 6:29 from him who takes away your **c**,
1 Th 2: 5 nor a **c** for covetousness—God
2 Tim 4:13 Bring the **c** that I left with
Heb 1:12 Like a **c** You will fold
1 Pe 2:16 yet not using liberty as a **c**

CLODS (5/5)

Job 21:33 The **c** of the valley shall be
38:38 And the **c** cling together?
Isa 28:24 his soil and breaking the **c**?
Hos 10:11 Jacob shall break his **c**."
Joel 1:17 The seed shrivels under the **c**,

CLOPAS (1/1)

Jn 19:25 sister, Mary the wife of **C**,

CLOSE (33/32) CLOSED, CLOSELY, CLOSER, CLOSEST

Gen 12:11 when he was **c** to entering
Ex 25:27 The rings shall be **c** to the
37:14 The rings were **c** to the frame,
Lev 3: 9 tail which he shall remove **c**
25:47 or stranger **c** to you becomes
25:47 to the stranger or sojourner **c**
Ruth 2: 8 but stay **c** by my young women.
2:20 one of our **c** relatives."
2:21 You shall stay **c** by my young men
2:23 So she stayed **c** by the young
3: 9 for you are a **c** relative."
3:12 true that I am a **c** relative;
3:13 he will perform the duty of a **c**
4: 1 the **c** relative of whom Boaz had
4: 3 Then he said to the **c** relative,
4: 6 And the **c** relative said, "I
4: 8 Therefore the **c** relative said to
4:14 this day without a **c** relative;
2 Sam 19:42 Because the king is a **c**
2 Ki 10:11 great men and his **c** acquaintances
25:19 men of the king's **c** associates
Neh 6:10 and let us **c** the doors of the
Job 19:14 And my **c** friends have
19:19 All my **c** friends abhor me, And
32:12 I paid **c** attention to you;
Ps 63: 8 My soul follows **c** behind You;
Jer 38:22 Your **c** friends have set upon you
42:16 you were afraid shall follow **c**
52:25 seven men of the king's **c**
Lk 19:43 surround you and **c** you in on

Acts 10:24 his relatives and c friends.
27:13 they sailed c by Crete.
Phil 2:30 of Christ he came c to death,

CLOSED (17/17) CLOSE

Gen 2:21 and c up the flesh in its
20:18 for the LORD had c up all the
Ex 14: 3 the wilderness has c them in.'
Num 16:33 the earth c over them, and they
Judg 3:22 and the fat c over the blade,
1 Sam 1: 5 although the LORD had c her
1: 6 because the LORD had c her
Neh 4: 7 the gaps were beginning to be c,
Ps 17:10 They have c up their fat
Isa 1: 6 They have not been c or bound
29:10 And has c your eyes, namely,
Dan 12: 9 for the words are c up and
Jon 2: 5 The deep c around me;
2: 6 The earth with its bars c
Mt 13:15 their eyes they have c,
Lk 4:20 Then He c the book, and gave it
Acts 28:27 their eyes they have c,

CLOSELY (5/5) CLOSE

1 Ki 20:33 Now the men were watching c to
Job 13:27 And watch c all my paths.
Mk 3: 2 So they watched Him c,
Lk 6: 7 and Pharisees watched Him c,
14: 1 that they watched Him c.

CLOSER (2/2) CLOSE

Ruth 3:12 there is a relative c than I.
Prov 18:24 is a friend who sticks c than

CLOSEST (2/2) CLOSE

Num 27:11 inheritance to the relative c
Esth 1:14 those c to him being Carshena,

CLOSET (KJV) See ROOM

CLOTH (18/18) CLOTHS

Num 4: 6 and spread over that a c
4: 7 they shall spread a blue c,
4: 8 spread over them a scarlet c,
4: 9 And they shall take a blue c and
4:11 they shall spread a blue c,
4:12 put them in a blue c,
4:13 and spread a purple c over it.
Deut 22:17 And they shall spread the c
1 Sam 21: 9 wrapped in a c behind the
2 Ki 8:15 day that he took a thick c and
Ezek 16:10 clothed you in embroidered c
16:13 linen, silk, and embroidered c.
Mt 9:16 one puts a piece of unshrunk c
27:59 wrapped it in a clean linen c,
Mk 2:21 one sews a piece of unshrunk c
14:51 having a linen c thrown around
14:52 and he left the linen c and fled
Jn 11:44 his face was wrapped with a c.

CLOTHE (21/21) CLOTH, CLOTHED, CLOTHES, CLOTHING, CLOTHS, UNCLOTHED

Ex 40:14 you shall bring his sons and c
Esth 4: 4 Then she sent garments to c
Job 10:11 C me with skin and flesh, And
Ps 132:16 I will also c her priests with
132:18 His enemies I will c with
Prov 23:21 And drowsiness will c a man
Isa 15: 3 In their streets they will c
22:21 I will c him with your robe
49:18 You shall surely c yourselves
50: 3 I c the heavens with blackness,
Jer 4: 8 c yourself with sackcloth,
4:30 Though you c yourself with
Ezek 26:16 they will c themselves with
34: 3 You eat the fat and c yourselves
44:18 they shall not c themselves
Hag 1: 6 You c yourselves, but no one
Zech 3: 4 and I will c you with rich
Mt 6:30 will He not much more c you,
25:38 or naked and c You?
25:43 naked and you did not c Me,
Lk 12:28 how much more will He c you,

CLOTHED (76/73) CLOTHE

Gen 3:21 tunics of skin, and c them.
41:42 and he c him in garments of
Lev 8: 7 c him with the robe, and put
1 Sam 17:38 So Saul c David with his armor,
17:38 he also c him with a coat of
2 Sam 1:24 Who c you in scarlet, with
1 Ki 11:29 and he had c himself with a new
1 Chr 15:27 David was c with a robe of fine
21:16 c in sackcloth, fell on their
2 Chr 5:12 c in white linen, having
6:41 be c with salvation, And let
18: 9 c in their robes, sat each on
28:15 and from the spoil they c all
Esth 4: 2 might enter the king's gate c
Job 8:22 Those who hate you will be c
29:14 and it c me; My justice was
39:19 Have you c his neck with
Ps 30:11 put off my sackcloth and c me
35:26 Let them be c with shame and
65: 6 Being c with power;
65:13 The pastures are c with flocks;
93: 1 He is c with majesty;
93: 1 with majesty; The LORD is c,
104: 1 You are c with honor and
109:18 As he c himself with cursing as
109:29 Let my accusers be c with
132: 9 Let Your priests be c with
Prov 31:21 For all her household is c
Isa 61:10 For He has c me with the
Ezek 7:27 The prince will be c with
9: 2 One man among them was c with
9: 3 And He called to the man c with
9:11 the man c with linen, who had
10: 2 Then He spoke to the man c with
10: 6 when He commanded the man c in
10: 7 into the hands of the man c
16:10 I c you in embroidered cloth and
16:10 I c you with fine linen and
23: 6 Who were c in purple,
23:12 C most gorgeously, Horsemen
38: 4 and horsemen, all splendidly c,
Dan 5: 7 shall be c with purple and
5:16 you shall be c with purple and
5:29 and they c Daniel with purple
10: 5 a certain man c in linen, whose
12: 6 And one said to the man c in
12: 7 Then I heard the man c in linen,
Zeph 1: 8 And all such as are c with
Zech 3: 3 Now Joshua was c with filthy
Mt 3: 4 And John himself was c in
11: 8 A man c in soft garments?
25:36 I was naked and you c Me; I was
Mk 1: 6 Now John was c with camel's hair
5:15 sitting and c and in his right
15:17 And they c Him with purple; and
16: 5 they saw a young man c in a
Lk 7:25 A man c in soft garments?
8:35 c and in his right mind.
16:19 a certain rich man who was c
1 Cor 4:11 and thirst, and we are poorly c,
2 Cor 5: 2 earnestly desiring to be c with
5: 3 if indeed, having been c,
5: 4 to be unclothed, but further c,
1 Pe 5: 5 and be c with humility, for
Rev 1:13 c with a garment down to the
3: 5 He who overcomes shall be c in
3:18 garments, that you may be c,
4: 4 c in white robes; and they had
7: 9 c with white robes, with palm
10: 1 c with a cloud. And a rainbow
11: 3 sixty days, c in sackcloth."
12: 1 a woman c with the sun, with
15: 6 c in pure bright linen, and
18:16 that great city that was c in
19:13 He was c with a robe dipped in
19:14 c in fine linen, white and

CLOTHES (115/112) CLOTHE, CLOTHING

Gen 27:15 Then Rebekah took the choice c
37:29 in the pit; and he tore his c.
37:34 Then Jacob tore his c,
44:13 Then they tore their c,
49:11 And his c in the blood of
Ex 12:34 bowls bound up in their c on
19:10 and let them wash their c.
19:14 people, and they washed their c.
Lev 10: 6 your heads nor tear your c,
11:25 of any of them shall wash his c
11:28 such carcass shall wash his c
11:40 of its carcass shall wash his c
11:40 its carcass shall wash his c
13: 6 and he shall wash his c and be
13:34 He shall wash his c and be
13:45 his c shall be torn and his
14: 8 to be cleansed shall wash his c,
14: 9 He shall wash his c and wash
14:47 in the house shall wash his c,
14:47 in the house shall wash his c.
15: 5 his bed shall wash his c and
15: 6 discharge sat shall wash his c
15: 7 the discharge shall wash his c
15: 8 then he shall wash his c and
15:10 those things shall wash his c
15:11 he shall wash his c and bathe
15:13 for his cleansing, wash his c,
15:21 her bed shall wash his c and
15:22 she sat on shall wash his c
15:27 he shall wash his c and bathe
16:26 the scapegoat shall wash his c
16:28 who burns them shall wash his c
16:32 and put on the linen c,
17:15 he shall both wash his c and
21:10 uncover his head nor tear his c;
Num 8: 7 body, and let them wash their c,
8:21 themselves and washed their c;
14: 6 out the land, tore their c;
19: 7 the priest shall wash his c,
19: 8 who burns it shall wash his c
19:10 of the heifer shall wash his c,
19:19 purify himself, wash his c,
19:21 purification shall wash his c;
31:24 And you shall wash your c on the
Deut 21:13 She shall put off the c of her
29: 5 Your c have not worn out on
Josh 7: 6 Then Joshua tore his c,
Judg 3:16 and fastened it under his c on
11:35 he saw her, that he tore his c,
17:10 of silver per year, a suit of c,
1 Sam 4:12 and came to Shiloh with his c
19:13 head, and covered it with c.
19:24 And he also stripped off his c
28: 8 himself and put on other c,
2 Sam 1: 2 from Saul's camp with his c
1:11 David took hold of his own c
3:31 were with him, "Tear your c,
12:20 himself, and changed his c;
13:31 servants stood by with their c
19:24 his mustache, nor washed his c,
1 Ki 21:27 that he tore his c and put
2 Ki 2:12 And he took hold of his own c
5: 7 that he tore his c and said,
5: 8 king of Israel had torn his c,
5: 8 "Why have you torn your c?
6:30 the woman, that he tore his c;
11:14 So Athaliah tore her c and
18:37 came to Hezekiah with their c
19: 1 heard it, that he tore his c,
22:11 of the Law, that he tore his c.
22:19 and you tore your c and wept
2 Chr 23:13 So Athaliah tore her c and
34:19 of the Law, that he tore his c.
34:27 and you tore your c and wept
Neh 4:23 who followed me took off our c,
9:21 Their c did not wear out And
Esth 4: 1 he tore his c and put on
Job 9:31 And my own c will abhor me.
Prov 6:27 And his c not be burned?
Isa 36:22 came to Hezekiah with their c
37: 1 heard it, that he tore his c,
Jer 38:11 and took from there old c and
38:12 Please put these old c and rags
41: 5 beards shaved and their c torn,
Ezek 16:39 shall also strip you of your c,
23:26 shall also strip you of your c
27:24 in choice items—in purple c,
Am 2: 8 lie down by every altar on c
Zech 3: 5 and they put the c on him.
Mt 6:30 Now if God so c the grass of the
17: 2 and His c became as white as
21: 7 laid their c on them, and set
21: 8 great multitude spread their c
24:18 field not go back to get his c.
26:65 Then the high priest tore his c,
27:31 put His own c on Him, and led
Mk 5:28 "If only I may touch His c,
5:30 and said, "Who touched My c?
9: 3 His c became shining,
11: 7 to Jesus and threw their c on
11: 8 And many spread their c on the
13:16 field not go back to get his c.
14:63 the high priest tore his c and
15:20 put His own c on Him, and led
Lk 8:27 a long time. And he wore no c,
12:28 If then God so c the grass,
19:35 And they threw their own c on
19:36 many spread their c on the
Acts 7:58 witnesses laid down their c at
14:14 they tore their c and ran in
16:22 magistrates tore off their c
22:20 and guarding the c of those who
22:23 out and tore off their c and
Jas 2: 2 come in a poor man in filthy c,
2: 3 to the one wearing the fine c

CLOTHING (49/49) CLOTHES

Gen 24:53 silver, jewelry of gold, and c,
27:27 he smelled the smell of his c,
28:20 and give me bread to eat and c
41:14 and he shaved, changed his c,
Ex 3:22 silver, articles of gold, and c;
12:35 silver, articles of gold, and c.
21:10 not diminish her food, her c,
22: 9 an ox, a donkey, a sheep, or c,
Lev 11:32 it is any item of wood or c
Deut 10:18 stranger, giving him food and c.
22:12 on the four corners of the c
Josh 22: 8 with iron, and with very much c.
Judg 14:12 and thirty changes of c.
14:13 and thirty changes of c.
14:19 and gave the changes of c to
2 Ki 5: 5 of gold, and ten changes of c.
5:26 receive money and to receive c,
7: 8 from it silver and gold and c,
Job 22: 6 stripped the naked of their c.
24: 7 the night naked, without c,
24:10 poor to go naked, without c;
27:16 And piles up c like clay—
31:19 anyone perish for lack of c,
Ps 22:18 And for My c they cast lots.
35:13 My c was sackcloth;
45:13 Her c is woven with gold.
Prov 27:26 lambs will provide your c,
31:22 Her c is fine linen and
31:25 Strength and honor are her c;
Isa 3: 6 father, saying, "You have c;
3: 7 my house is neither food nor c;
23:18 sufficiently, and for fine c.
59:17 the garments of vengeance for c,
Jer 10: 9 Blue and purple are their c;
Ezek 16:13 and your c was of fine linen,
18: 7 And covered the naked with c;
18:16 And covered the naked with c;
Mt 6:25 food and the body more than c?
6:28 "So why do you worry about c?
7:15 who come to you in sheep's c,
11: 8 those who wear soft c are in
27:35 And for My c they cast
28: 3 and his c as white as snow.
Lk 10:30 who stripped him of his c,
12:23 and the body is more than c.
Jn 19:24 And for My c they cast

Acts 10:30 man stood before me in bright *c*,
1 Tim 2: 9 or gold or pearls or costly *c*,
6: 8 And having food and *c*,

CLOTHS (7/7) CLOTH

Ezek 16: 4 salt nor wrapped in swaddling *c*.
Lk 2: 7 and wrapped Him in swaddling *c*,
2:12 a Babe wrapped in swaddling *c*,
24:12 he saw the linen *c* lying by
Jn 20: 5 saw the linen *c* lying there;
20: 6 and he saw the linen *c* lying
20: 7 not lying with the linen *c*,

CLOUD (108/96) CLOUDS, CLOUDY

Gen 9:13 "I set My rainbow in the *c*,
9:14 when I bring a *c* over the
9:14 rainbow shall be seen in the *c*;
9:16 "The rainbow shall be in the *c*,
Ex 13:21 them by day in a pillar of *c*
13:22 not take away the pillar of *c*
14:19 and the pillar of *c* went from
14:20 Thus it was a *c* and darkness
14:24 the pillar of fire and *c*,
16:10 of the LORD appeared in the *c*.
19: 9 I come to you in the thick *c*,
19:16 and a thick *c* on the mountain;
24:15 and a *c* covered the mountain.
24:16 and the *c* covered it six days.
24:16 Moses out of the midst of the *c*.
24:18 went into the midst of the *c*
33: 9 that the pillar of *c* descended
33:10 the people saw the pillar of *c*
34: 5 the LORD descended in the *c*
40:34 Then the *c* covered the
40:35 because the *c* rested above it,
40:36 Whenever the *c* was taken up from
40:37 But if the *c* was not taken up,
40:38 For the *c* of the LORD was
Lev 16: 2 for I will appear in the *c*
16:13 that the *c* of incense may cover
Num 9:15 the *c* covered the tabernacle,
9:16 the *c* covered it by day, and
9:17 Whenever the *c* was taken up from
9:17 and in the place where the *c*
9:18 as long as the *c* stayed above
9:19 Even when the *c* continued long,
9:20 when the *c* was above the
9:21 when the *c* remained only from
9:21 when the *c* was taken up in the
9:21 whenever the *c* was taken up,
9:22 or a year that the *c* remained
10:11 that the *c* was taken up from
10:12 then the *c* settled down in the
10:34 And the *c* of the LORD was
11:25 the LORD came down in the *c*,
12: 5 came down in the pillar of *c*
12:10 And when the *c* departed from
14:14 seen face to face and Your *c*
14:14 go before them in a pillar of *c*
16:42 and suddenly the *c* covered it,
Deut 1:33 the fire by night and in the *c*
4:11 of heaven, with darkness, *c*,
5:22 the midst of the fire, the *c*,
31:15 the tabernacle in a pillar of *c*,
31:15 and the pillar of *c* stood above
Judg 20:38 that they would make a great *c*
20:40 But when the *c* began to rise
1 Ki 8:10 that the *c* filled the house of
8:11 ministering because of the *c*;
8:12 He would dwell in the dark *c*.
18:44 that he said, "There is a *c*,
2 Chr 5:13 the LORD, was filled with a *c*,
5:14 ministering because of the *c*;
6: 1 He would dwell in the dark *c*.
Neh 9:19 The pillar of the *c* did not
Job 3: 5 May a *c* settle on it; May the
7: 9 As the *c* disappears and
26: 9 And spreads His *c* over it.
30:15 prosperity has passed like a *c*.
37:15 And causes the light of His *c*
Ps 78:14 also He led them with the *c*,
105:39 He spread a *c* for a covering,
Prov 16:15 And his favor is like a *c* of
Isa 4: 5 a *c* and smoke by day and the
18: 4 Like a *c* of dew in the heat of
19: 1 the LORD rides on a swift *c*,
25: 5 As heat in the shadow of a *c*,
44:22 blotted out, like a thick *c*,
44:22 transgressions, And like a *c*,
60: 8 are these who fly like a *c*,
Lam 2: 1 the daughter of Zion With a *c*
3:44 have covered Yourself with a *c*,
Ezek 1: 4 a great *c* with raging fire
1:28 appearance of a rainbow in a *c*
8:11 and a thick *c* of incense went
10: 3 and the *c* filled the inner
10: 4 the house was filled with the *c*,
30:18 a *c* shall cover her, And her
32: 7 I will cover the sun with a *c*,
38: 9 covering the land like a *c*,
38:16 My people Israel like a *c*,
Hos 6: 4 is like a morning *c*,
13: 3 shall be like the morning *c*
Mt 17: 5 a bright *c* overshadowed them;
17: 5 a voice came out of the *c*,
Mk 9: 7 And a *c* came and overshadowed
9: 7 and a voice came out of the *c*,
Lk 9:34 a *c* came and overshadowed them;
9:34 fearful as they entered the *c*.
9:35 And a voice came out of the *c*,
12:54 Whenever you see a *c* rising out
21:27 the Son of Man coming in a *c*
Acts 1: 9 and a *c* received Him out of
1 Cor 10: 1 our fathers were under the *c*,
10: 2 baptized into Moses in the *c*
Heb 12: 1 are surrounded by so great a *c*
Rev 10: 1 from heaven, clothed with a *c*.
11:12 they ascended to heaven in a *c*,
14:14 I looked, and behold, a white *c*,
14:14 and on the *c* sat One like the
14:15 voice to Him who sat on the *c*,
14:16 So He who sat on the *c* thrust in

CLOUDS (56/53) CLOUD

Deut 33:26 And in His excellency on the *c*.
Judg 5: 4 The *c* also poured water;
2 Sam 22:12 Dark waters and thick *c* of
23: 4 sun rises, A morning without *c*,
1 Ki 18:45 the sky became black with *c*
Job 20: 6 And his head reaches to the *c*,
22:14 Thick *c* cover Him, so that He
26: 8 up the water in His thick *c*,
26: 8 Yet the *c* are not broken under
35: 5 And behold the *c*—They are
36:28 Which the *c* drop down And
36:29 understand the spreading of *c*,
37:11 He saturates the thick *c*;
37:11 He scatters His bright *c*.
37:16 Do you know how the *c* are
38: 9 When I made the *c* its garment,
38:34 you lift up your voice to the *c*,
38:37 Who can number the *c* by wisdom?
Ps 18:11 was dark waters And thick *c*
18:12 His thick *c* passed with
36: 5 faithfulness reaches to the *c*.
57:10 And Your truth unto the *c*.
68: 4 Extol Him who rides on the *c*,
68:34 And His strength is in the *c*.
77:17 The *c* poured out water;
78:23 Yet He had commanded the *c*
97: 2 *C* and darkness surround Him
104: 3 Who makes the *c* His chariot,
108: 4 Your truth reaches to the *c*.
147: 8 Who covers the heavens with *c*,
148: 8 Fire and hail, snow and *c*;
Prov 3:20 And *c* drop down the dew.
8:28 When He established the *c*
25:14 boasts of giving Is like *c*
Eccl 11: 3 If the *c* are full of rain,
11: 4 And he who regards the *c* will
12: 2 And the *c* do not return after
Isa 5: 6 I will also command the *c*
5:30 the light is darkened by the *c*.
14:14 above the heights of the *c*,
Jer 4:13 he shall come up like *c*,
Ezek 30: 3 near; It will be a day of *c*,
Dan 7:13 Coming with the *c* of heaven!
Joel 2: 2 A day of *c* and thick darkness,
2: 2 Like the morning *c* spread
Nah 1: 3 And the *c* are the dust of His
Zeph 1:15 A day of *c* and thick darkness,
Zech 10: 1 The LORD will make flashing *c*;
Mt 24:30 the Son of Man coming on the *c*
26:64 and coming on the *c* of
Mk 13:26 the Son of Man coming in the *c*
14:62 and coming with the *c* of
1 Th 4:17 up together with them in the *c*
2 Pe 2:17 *c* carried by a tempest, for
Jude 12 They are *c* without water,
Rev 1: 7 Behold, He is coming with *c*,

CLOUDY (3/3) CLOUD

Neh 9:12 You led them by day with a *c*
Ps 99: 7 He spoke to them in the *c*
Ezek 34:12 they were scattered on a *c* and

CLOVEN (10/8) CLOVEN-HOOFED

Lev 11: 3 having *c* hooves and chewing
11: 4 the cud or those that have *c*
11: 4 the cud but does not have *c*
11: 5 the cud but does not have *c*
11: 6 the cud but does not have *c*
11: 7 having *c* hooves, yet does not
Deut 14: 6 you may eat every animal with *c*
14: 7 that chew the cud or have *c*
14: 7 chew the cud but do not have *c*
14: 8 because it has *c* hooves, yet

CLOVEN-HOOFED (1/1) CLOVEN

Lev 11:26 but is not *c* or does not chew

CLUB (1/1) CLUBS

Prov 25:18 his neighbor Is like a *c*,

CLUBS (5/5) CLUB

Mt 26:47 multitude with swords and *c*,
26:55 with swords and *c* to take Me?
Mk 14:43 multitude with swords and *c*,
14:48 with swords and *c* to take Me?
Lk 22:52 a robber, with swords and *c*?

CLUMPS (1/1)

Job 38:38 When the dust hardens in *c*,

CLUNG (2/2) CLING

Ruth 1:14 but Ruth *c* to her.
1 Ki 11: 2 Solomon *c* to these in love.

CLUSTER (6/6) CLUSTERS

Num 13:23 cut down a branch with one *c*
13:24 because of the *c* which the men
Job 38:31 Can you bind the *c* of the
Song 1:14 My beloved is to me a *c* of
Isa 65: 8 the new wine is found in the *c*,
Mic 7: 1 There is no *c* to eat Of

CLUSTERS (8/8) CLUSTER

Gen 40:10 and its *c* brought forth ripe
Deut 32:32 Their *c* are bitter.
1 Sam 25:18 one hundred *c* of raisins, and
30:12 of a cake of figs and two *c* of
2 Sam 16: 1 one hundred *c* of raisins, one
Song 7: 7 And your breasts like its *c*.
7: 8 now your breasts be like *c* of
Rev 14:18 sharp sickle and gather the *c*

CNIDUS (1/1)

Acts 27: 7 arrived with difficulty off *C*,

COAL (2/2) COALS

Isa 6: 6 having in his hand a live *c*
47:14 It shall not be a *c* to be

COALS (23/23) COAL

Lev 16:12 a censer full of burning *c* of
2 Sam 22: 9 *C* were kindled by it.
22:13 the brightness before Him *C*
1 Ki 19: 6 his head was a cake baked on *c*,
Job 41:21 His breath kindles *c*,
Ps 11: 6 Upon the wicked He will rain *c*;
18: 8 *C* were kindled by it.
18:12 passed with hailstones and *c*
18:13 Hailstones and *c* of fire.
120: 4 With *c* of the broom tree!
140:10 Let burning *c* fall upon them;
Prov 6:28 Can one walk on hot *c*,
25:22 For so you will heap *c* of fire
26:21 As charcoal is to burning *c*,
Isa 44:12 the tongs works one in the *c*,
44:19 have also baked bread on its *c*;
54:16 blacksmith Who blows the *c* in
Ezek 1:13 appearance was like burning *c*
10: 2 fill your hands with *c* of fire
24:11 set the pot empty on the *c*,
Jn 18:18 who had made a fire of *c* stood
21: 9 they saw a fire of *c* there, and
Rom 12:20 so doing you will heap *c*

COARSE (2/2)

Zech 13: 4 they will not wear a robe of *c*
Eph 5: 4 nor *c* jesting, which are not

COAST (1/1) COASTLAND, COASTLANDS, COASTLINE, COASTS

Zeph 2: 7 The *c* shall be for the remnant

COASTLAND (3/3) COAST, COASTLANDS

Gen 10: 5 From these the *c* peoples of the
Isa 23: 2 still, you inhabitants of the *c*,
23: 6 you inhabitants of the *c*!

COASTLANDS (19/18) COASTLAND

Isa 24:15 LORD God of Israel in the *c*
41: 1 "Keep silence before Me, O *c*,
41: 5 The *c* saw it and feared,
42: 4 And the *c* shall wait for His
42:10 You *c* and you inhabitants of
42:12 declare His praise in the *c*.
42:15 I will make the rivers *c*,
49: 1 'Listen, O *c*, to Me,
51: 5 The *c* will wait upon Me, And
59:18 The *c* He will fully repay.
60: 9 Surely the *c* shall wait for Me;
66:19 to the *c* afar off who have not
Jer 25:22 and the kings of the *c* which
Ezek 26:15 Will the *c* not shake at the
26:18 Now the *c* tremble on the day of
26:18 the *c* by the sea are troubled
27: 3 of the peoples on many *c*,
39: 6 who live in security in the *c*.
Dan 11:18 he shall turn his face to the *c*,

COASTLINE (2/2) COAST

Josh 15:12 The west border was the *c* of
15:47 and the Great Sea with its *c*.

COASTS (7/7) COAST

Num 24:24 ships shall come from the *c*
Josh 9: 1 in the lowland and in all the *c*
Jer 2:10 For pass beyond the *c* of Cyprus
Ezek 27: 6 planks With ivory from the *c*
27: 7 Blue and purple from the *c* of
Joel 3: 4 and all the *c* of Philistia?
Acts 27: 2 meaning to sail along the *c* of

COAT (7/6) COATS
Ex 28:32 like the opening in a **c** of
39:23 like the opening in a **c** of
1 Sam 17: 5 and he was armed with a **c** of
17: 5 and the weight of the **c** was
17:38 he also clothed him with a **c** of
Job 30:18 me about as the collar of my **c**.
41:13 Who can remove his outer **c**?

COAT OF MANY COLORS (KJV) See TUNIC (OF MANY COLORS)

COATS (1/1) COAT
Dan 3:21 these men were bound in their **c**,

COBRA (3/3) COBRA'S, COBRAS
Job 20:14 It becomes **c** venom within him.
Ps 58: 4 They are like the deaf **c**
91:13 tread upon the lion and the **c**,

COBRA'S (1/1) COBRA
Isa 11: 8 child shall play by the **c** hole,

COBRAS (2/2) COBRA
Deut 32:33 And the cruel venom of **c**.
Job 20:16 He will suck the poison of **c**;

COCK (KJV) See ROOSTER

COCKATRICE (KJV) See VIPER

COCKCROWING (KJV) See CROWING

COCKLE (KJV) See WEEDS

CODE (1/1)
Rom 2:27 even with your written **c** and

COFFER (KJV) See CHEST

COFFIN (3/3)
Gen 50:26 and he was put in a **c** in Egypt.
2 Sam 3:31 And King David followed the **c**.
Lk 7:14 He came and touched the open **c**,

COGITATIONS (KJV) See THOUGHTS

COIN (2/2) COINS
Mt 10:29 sparrows sold for a copper **c**?
Lk 15: 8 coins, if she loses one **c**,

COINS (4/4) COIN
Ps 119:72 to me Than thousands of **c**
Song 8:11 its fruit A thousand silver **c**.
Lk 12: 6 sparrows sold for two copper **c**?
15: 8 what woman, having ten silver **c**,

COL-HOZEH (2/2)
Neh 3:15 Shallun the son of **C**,
11: 5 the son of Baruch, the son of **C**,

COLD (17/16)
Gen 8:22 **C** and heat, Winter and
Job 24: 7 And have no covering in the **c**.
37: 9 And **c** from the scattering
Ps 147:17 Who can stand before His **c**?
Prov 25:13 Like the **c** of snow in time of
25:20 who takes away a garment in **c**
25:25 As **c** water to a weary soul,
Jer 18:14 Will the **c** flowing waters be
Nah 3:17 camp in the hedges on a **c** day;
Mt 10:42 little ones only a cup of **c**
24:12 the love of many will grow **c**.
Jn 18:18 coals stood there, for it was **c**,
Acts 28: 2 falling and because of the **c**.
2 Cor 11:27 in **c** and nakedness—
Rev 3:15 that you are neither **c** nor hot.
3:15 I could wish you were **c** or hot.
3:16 and neither **c** nor hot, I will

COLLAPSE (2/2) COLLAPSED
Jer 13:18 down, For your rule shall **c**,
Lam 1: 9 Therefore her **c** was awesome;

COLLAPSED (1/1) COLLAPSE
Judg 7:13 and overturned, and the tent **c**.

COLLAR (1/1)
Job 30:18 It binds me about as the **c** of

COLLECT (3/3) COLLECTED, COLLECTING, COLLECTION, COLLECTIONS, COLLECTOR, COLLECTORS
Gen 41:34 to **c** one-fifth of the
Lk 3:13 **C** no more than what is appointed
19:21 You **c** what you did not deposit,

COLLECTED (1/1) COLLECT
Lk 19:23 at my coming I might have **c** it

COLLECTING (2/2) COLLECT
Eccl 2:26 the work of gathering and **c**,
Lk 19:22 **c** what I did not deposit and

COLLECTION (4/4) COLLECT, COLLECTIONS
2 Chr 24: 6 Judah and from Jerusalem the **c**,
24: 9 to bring to the LORD the **c**
Isa 57:13 Let your **c** of idols deliver
1 Cor 16: 1 Now concerning the **c** for the

COLLECTIONS (1/1) COLLECTION
1 Cor 16: 2 that there be no **c** when I come.

COLLECTOR (7/7) COLLECT, COLLECTORS
Mt 10: 3 Thomas and Matthew the tax **c**;
18:17 you like a heathen and a tax **c**.
Lk 5:27 He went out and saw a tax **c**
18:10 Pharisee and the other a tax **c**.
18:11 or even as this tax **c**.
18:13 'And the tax **c**, standing afar
19: 2 Zacchaeus who was a chief tax **c**,

COLLECTORS (16/15) COLLECTOR
Mt 5:46 Do not even the tax **c** do the
5:47 Do not even the tax **c** do so?
9:10 many tax **c** and sinners came and
9:11 your Teacher eat with tax **c**
11:19 a friend of tax **c** and sinners!'
21:31 I say to you that tax **c** and
21:32 but tax **c** and harlots believed
Mk 2:15 that many tax **c** and sinners
2:16 saw Him eating with the tax **c**
2:16 He eats and drinks with tax **c**
Lk 3:12 Then tax **c** also came to be
5:29 were a great number of tax **c**
5:30 do You eat and drink with tax **c**
7:29 even the tax **c** justified God,
7:34 a friend of tax **c** and sinners!'
15: 1 Then all the tax **c** and the

COLLEGE (KJV) See (SECOND) QUARTER

COLONY (1/1)
Acts 16:12 of that part of Macedonia, a **c**.

COLOR (13/12) COLORED, COLORFUL, COLORS
Lev 13:55 plague has not changed its **c**,
Num 11: 7 and its **c** like the color of
11: 7 and its color like the **c** of
Ezek 1: 4 out of its midst like the **c** of
1: 7 They sparkled like the **c** of
1:16 their workings was like the **c**
1:22 creatures was like the **c** of
1:27 the **c** of amber with the
8: 2 like the **c** of amber.
10: 9 appeared to have the **c** of a
Dan 10: 6 feet like burnished bronze in **c**,
Joel 2: 6 All faces are drained of **c**.
Nah 2:10 their faces are drained of **c**.

COLORED (1/1) COLOR
Prov 7:16 **C** coverings of Egyptian linen.

COLORFUL (1/1) COLOR
Isa 54:11 I will lay your stones with **c**

COLORS (8/8) COLOR
Gen 37: 3 he made him a tunic of many **c**.
37:23 the tunic of many **c** that was
37:32 they sent the tunic of many **c**,
2 Sam 13:18 Now she had on a robe of many **c**,
13:19 and tore her robe of many **c**
1 Chr 29: 2 glistening stones of various **c**,
Ps 45:14 to the King in robes of many **c**;
Ezek 17: 3 Full of feathers of various **c**,

COLOSSE (1/1)
Col 1: 2 in Christ who are in **C**:

COLT (15/14) COLT
Gen 49:11 And his donkey's **c** to the
Job 11:12 When a wild donkey's **c** is born
Zech 9: 9 and riding on a donkey, A **c**,
Mt 21: 2 and a **c** with her. Loose them
21: 5 sitting on a donkey, A **c**,
21: 7 brought the donkey and the **c**,
Mk 11: 2 entered it you will find a **c**
11: 4 and found the **c** tied by the
11: 5 are you doing, loosing the **c**?
11: 7 Then they brought the **c** to Jesus
Lk 19:30 as you enter you will find a **c**
19:33 But as they were loosing the **c**,
19:33 "Why are you loosing the **c**?
19:35 their own clothes on the **c**,
Jn 12:15 Sitting on a donkey's **c**.

COLTS (1/1) COLT
Gen 32:15 thirty milk camels with their **c**,

COLUMN (2/2) COLUMNS
Judg 20:40 to rise from the city in a **c**
Joel 2: 8 Every one marches in his own **c**.

COLUMNS (1/1)
Jer 36:23 Jehudi had read three or four **c**,

COME (1702/1588) BECOME, COMELINESS, COMES, COMING
Gen 6:13 The end of all flesh has **c**
6:20 two of every kind will **c** to
7: 1 **C** into the ark, you and all your
11: 3 they said to one another, "**C**,
11: 4 And they said, "**C**,
11: 7 '**C**, let Us go down and there
15: 4 but one who will **c** from your
15:14 afterward they shall **c** out with
16: 8 where have you **c** from, and
17: 6 and kings shall **c** from you.
18: 5 inasmuch as you have **c** to your
18:21 outcry against it that has **c**
19: 8 this is the reason they have **c**
19:31 is no man on the earth to **c**
19:32 '**C**, let us make our father
20: 4 But Abimelech had not **c** near
22: 5 and we will **c** back to you."
24:31 **C** in, O blessed of the LORD!
24:43 and it shall **c** to pass that
26:27 Why have you **c** to me, since you
27:21 Please **c** near, that I may feel
27:26 **C** near now and kiss me, my
27:40 And it shall **c** to pass, when
28:21 so that I **c** back to my father's
30:16 You must **c** in to me, for I have
30:33 will answer for me in time to **c**,
31:24 But God had **c** to Laban the
31:44 therefore, **c**, let us make
32:11 lest he **c** and attack me and
33:14 until I **c** to my lord in Seir."
35:11 and kings shall **c** from your
37:10 I and your brothers indeed **c**
37:13 the flock in Shechem? **C**,
37:20 **C** therefore, let us now kill him
37:23 when Joseph had **c** to his
37:27 **C** and let us sell him to the
38:16 Please let me **c** in to you"; for
38:16 that you may **c** in to me?"
41:29 years of great plenty will **c**
41:54 years of famine began to **c**,
42: 7 Where do you **c** from?" And they
42: 9 You are spies! You have **c** to
42:10 but your servants have **c** to buy
42:12 but you have **c** to see the
42:21 therefore this distress has **c**
44:30 when I **c** to your servant my
44:34 I see the evil that would **c**
45: 4 Please **c** near to me." So they
45: 9 **c** down to me, do not tarry.
45:11 **c** to poverty; for there are
45:16 "Joseph's brothers have **c**.
45:18 and your households and **c** to
45:19 wives; bring your father and **c**
46:31 land of Canaan, have **c** to me.
47: 1 have **c** from the land of Canaan;
47: 4 We have **c** to dwell in the land,
47: 5 and your brothers have **c** to
47:24 And it shall **c** to pass in the
50: 5 and I will **c** back.'"
Ex 1:10 '**c**, let us deal shrewdly with
1:19 birth before the midwives **c** to
2:18 How is it that you have **c** so
3: 8 So I have **c** down to deliver them
3: 9 of the children of Israel has **c**
3:10 **C** now, therefore, and I will
3:13 when I **c** to the children of
3:18 your voice; and you shall **c**,
8: 3 which shall go up and **c** into
8: 4 And the frogs shall **c** up on you,
8: 5 and cause frogs to **c** up on the
9:19 for the hail shall **c** down on
10:12 that they may **c** upon the land
11: 8 all these your servants shall **c**
12:23 not allow the destroyer to **c**
12:25 It will **c** to pass when you come
12:25 will come to pass when you **c**
12:48 and then let him **c** near and
13:14 your son asks you in time to **c**,
14:20 so that the one did not **c** near
14:26 that the waters may **c** back upon
16: 9 **C** near before the LORD, for He
17: 6 and water will **c** out of it,
18: 8 all the hardship that had **c**
18:15 Because the people **c** to me to
18:16 they **c** to me, and I judge
19: 2 had **c** to the Wilderness of
19: 9 I **c** to you in the thick cloud,
19:11 the third day the LORD will **c**
19:13 they shall **c** near the
19:15 do not **c** near your wives."
19:22 Also let the priests who **c** near
19:23 The people cannot **c** up to Mount

19:24 Away! Get down and then *c* up,
19:24 the people break through to *c*
20:20 for God has *c* to test you, and
20:24 I record My name I will *c* to
22: 9 cause of both parties shall *c*
23:27 all the people to whom you *c*,
24: 1 *C* up to the LORD, you and
24: 2 And Moses alone shall *c* near the
24: 2 but they shall not *c* near; nor
24:12 *C* up to Me on the mountain and
24:14 Wait here for us until we *c* back
25:32 And six branches shall *c* out of
25:33 so for the six branches that *c*
28:28 that the breastplate does not *c*
28:43 and on his sons when they *c*
28:43 or when they *c* near the altar
30:20 or when they *c* near the altar
32: 1 to Aaron, and said to him, "*C*,
32:26 *c* to me." And all the sons of
33: 5 I could *c* up into your midst in
34: 2 and *c* up in the morning to
34: 3 And no man shall *c* up with you,
34:30 and they were afraid to *c* near
34:34 and he would *c* out and speak to
35:10 artisans among you shall *c* and
36: 2 to *c* and do the work.
39:21 the breastplate would not *c*
Lev 10: 3 By those who *c* near Me I must
10: 4 *C* near, carry your brethren from
10: 6 and wrath *c* upon all the
12: 4 nor *c* into the sanctuary until
13:16 he shall *c* to the priest.
14: 8 After that he shall *c* into the
14:34 When you have *c* into the land of
14:39 And the priest shall *c* again on
14:44 then the priest shall *c* and
15:14 and *c* before the LORD, to the
16: 2 Aaron your brother not to *c* at
16: 3 Thus Aaron shall *c* into the Holy
16:23 Then Aaron shall *c* into the
16:24 *c* out and offer his burnt
16:26 and afterward he may *c* into the
16:28 and afterward he may *c* into the
19:19 of mixed linen and wool *c* upon
19:23 When you *c* into the land, and
21:21 shall *c* near to offer the
21:21 he shall not *c* near to offer
23:10 When you *c* into the land which I
25: 2 When you *c* into the land which I
Num 1: 1 second year after they had *c*
4: 5 Aaron and his sons shall *c*,
4:15 the sons of Kohath shall *c* to
6: 5 his separation no razor shall *c*
8:19 when the children of Israel *c*
9: 1 second year after they had *c*
10:29 *C* with us, and we will treat
11:17 Then I will *c* down and talk with
11:20 Why did we ever *c* up out of
12: 4 *C* out, you three, to the
15: 2 When you have *c* into the land
15:18 When you *c* into the land to
16: 5 and will cause him to *c* near
16: 5 He chooses He will cause to *c*
16:12 We will not *c* up!
16:14 We will not *c* up!"
16:40 should *c* near to offer incense
18: 3 but they shall not *c* near the
18: 4 but an outsider shall not *c*
18:22 children of Israel shall not *c*
19: 2 on which a yoke has never *c*.
19: 7 and afterward he shall *c* into
19:14 All who *c* into the tent and all
20: 5 And why have you made us *c* up
20:18 lest I *c* out against you with
21:27 *C* to Heshbon, let it be built;
22: 5 a people has *c* from Egypt. See,
22: 6 Therefore please *c* at once,
22:11 a people has *c* out of Egypt,
22:11 *C* now, curse them for me;
22:14 Balaam refuses to *c* with us."
22:17 say to me. Therefore please *c*,
22:20 If the men *c* to call you, rise
22:32 I have *c* out to stand against
22:37 Why did you not *c* to me? Am I
22:38 I have *c* to you! Now, have I
23: 3 perhaps the LORD will *c* to
23: 7 the mountains of the east. '*C*,
23: 7 curse Jacob for me, And *c*,
23:13 Please *c* with me to another
23:27 said to Balaam, "Please *c*,
24:14 I am going to my people. *C*,
24:17 A Star shall *c* out of Jacob;
24:24 But ships shall *c* from the
27:21 and at his word they shall *c*
31:14 who had *c* from the battle.
31:24 and afterward you may *c* into
33:38 the children of Israel had *c*
34: 2 When you *c* into the land of
Deut 1:20 You have *c* to the mountains of
1:22 cities into which we shall *c*.
2:14 And the time we took to *c* from
2:19 And when you *c* near the people
4:30 and all these things *c* upon you
6:20 your son asks you in time to *c*,
7:12 Then it shall *c* to pass,
10: 1 and *c* up to Me on the mountain
11:10 of Egypt from which you have *c*,
12: 9 for as yet you have not *c* to the
14:29 may *c* and eat and be satisfied,
15:19 the firstborn males that *c*
17: 9 And you shall *c* to the priests,
17:14 When you *c* to the land which
18: 9 When you *c* into the land which
18:22 the thing does not happen or *c*
21: 5 shall *c* near, for the LORD
23:10 he shall not *c* inside the camp.
23:11 he may *c* into the camp.
23:24 When you *c* into your neighbor's
23:25 When you *c* into your neighbor's
25: 1 and they *c* to court, that the
25: 9 his brother's wife shall *c* to
26: 1 when you *c* into the land which
26: 3 LORD your God that I have *c*
28: 1 Now it shall *c* to pass, if you
28: 2 all these blessings shall *c*
28: 6 shall you be when you *c* in,
28: 7 they shall *c* out against you
28:15 But it shall *c* to pass, if you
28:15 that all these curses will *c*
28:19 shall you be when you *c* in,
28:24 from the heaven it shall *c* down
28:43 and you shall *c* down lower and
28:45 all these curses shall *c* upon
28:52 *c* down throughout all your
30: 1 Now it shall *c* to pass, when all
30: 1 when all these things *c* upon
31: 2 I can no longer go out and *c*
31:17 Have not these evils *c* upon us
31:21 many evils and troubles have *c*
32:35 And the things to *c* hasten
33:16 Let the blessing *c* 'on
Josh 2: 2 men have *c* here tonight from
2: 3 Bring out the men who have *c* to
2: 3 for they have *c* to search out
2:18 when we *c* into the land, you
3: 4 Do not *c* near it, that you may
3: 8 When you have *c* to the edge of
3: 9 *C* here, and hear the words of
3:13 And it shall *c* to pass, as soon
3:13 the waters that *c* down from
4: 6 your children ask in time to *c*,
4:16 the ark of the Testimony to *c*
4:17 *C* up from the Jordan."
4:18 the covenant of the LORD had *c*
4:21 ask their fathers in time to *c*,
5: 4 after they had *c* out of Egypt.
5:14 army of the LORD I have now *c*.
6: 5 It shall *c* to pass, when they
6:19 they shall *c* into the treasury
7:14 which the LORD takes shall *c*
7:14 which the LORD takes shall *c*
7:14 which the LORD takes shall *c*
8: 5 and it will *c* about, when they
8: 5 when they *c* out against us as
8: 6 For they will *c* out after us
9: 6 We have *c* from a far country;
9: 8 and where do you *c* from?"
9: 9 country your servants have *c*,
9:12 on the day we departed to *c* to
10: 4 *C* up to me and help me, that we
10: 6 *c* up to us quickly, save us and
10:24 *C* near, put your feet on the
11:20 that they should *c* against
18: 4 and *c* back to me.
18: 8 and *c* back to me, that I may
20: 6 the slayer may return and *c* to
22:24 In time to *c* your descendants
22:27 to our descendants in time to *c*,
22:28 to our generations in time to *c*,
23:14 All have *c* to pass for you; not
23:15 Therefore it shall *c* to pass,
23:15 as all the good things have *c*
Judg 1: 3 *C* up with me to my allotted
1:34 they would not allow them to *c*
4:22 meet him, and said to him, "*C*,
5:23 Because they did not *c* to the
6: 3 Midianites would *c* up; also
6: 3 the people of the East would *c*
6: 5 For they would *c* up with their
6:18 until I *c* to You and bring out
6:18 I will wait until you *c* back."
7:13 And when Gideon had *c*,
7:17 and when I *c* to the edge of the
7:24 *C* down against the Midianites,
8: 9 When I *c* back in peace, I will
9:10 You *c* and reign over us!'
9:12 You *c* and reign over us!'
9:14 You *c* and reign over us!'
9:15 Then *c* and take shelter in
9:15 let fire *c* out of the bramble
9:20 let fire *c* from Abimelech and
9:20 and let fire *c* from the men of
9:29 Increase your army and *c* out!"
9:31 of Ebed and his brothers have *c*
9:33 the people who are with him *c*
11: 6 *C* and be our commander, that we
11: 7 Why have you *c* to me now when
11:12 that you have *c* to fight
12: 3 Why then have you *c* up to me
13: 5 And no razor shall *c* upon his
13: 8 the Man of God whom You sent *c*
13:12 Now let Your words *c* to pass!
13:17 that when Your words *c* to
15:10 Why have you *c* up against us?"
15:10 We have *c* up to arrest Samson,
15:12 We have *c* down to arrest you,
16: 2 'Samson has *c* here!"
16:17 No razor has ever *c* upon my
16:18 *C* up once more, for he has told
17: 9 'Where do you *c* from?"
18:10 you will *c* to a secure people
18:19 and *c* with us; be a father and
19:11 servant said to his master, "*C*,
19:13 So he said to his servant, "*C*,
19:17 and where do you *c* from?"
19:23 Seeing this man has *c* into my
20:10 that when they *c* to Gibeah in
20:41 they saw that disaster had *c*
21: 3 why has this *c* to pass in
21: 5 tribes of Israel who did not *c*
21: 5 anyone who had not *c* up to the
21: 8 tribes of Israel who did not *c*
21: 8 no one had *c* to the camp from
21:21 when the daughters of Shiloh *c*
21:21 then *c* out from the vineyards,
21:22 fathers or their brothers *c* to
Ruth 1:19 when they had *c* to Bethlehem,
2: 3 And she happened to *c* to the
2:11 and have *c* to a people whom you
2:12 under whose wings you have *c*
2:14 *C* here, and eat of the bread,
4: 1 *C* aside, friend, sit down
4: 3 who has *c* back from the country
1 Sam 1:11 and no razor shall *c* upon his
2: 3 Let no arrogance *c* from your
2:13 the priest's servant would *c*
2:15 the priest's servant would *c*
2:34 be a sign to you that will *c*
2:36 And it shall *c* to pass that
2:36 is left in your house will *c*
4: 3 And when the people had *c* into
4: 6 that the ark of the LORD had *c*
4: 7 God has *c* into the camp!" And
5: 5 priests of Dagon nor any who *c*
6:21 *c* down and take it up with
7:13 and they did not *c* anymore into
9: 5 When they had *c* to the land of
9: 5 servant who was with him, "*C*,
9: 9 of God, he spoke thus: "*C*,
9:10 to his servant, "Well said; *c*,
9:13 As soon as you *c* into the city,
9:16 because their cry has *c* to
9:25 When they had *c* down from the
10: 3 go on forward from there and *c*
10: 5 After that you shall *c* to the
10: 5 when you have *c* there to the
10: 6 the Spirit of the LORD will *c*
10: 7 when these signs *c* to you,
10: 8 and surely I will *c* down to you
10: 8 till I *c* to you and show you
10:11 What is this that has *c* upon
10:20 all the tribes of Israel to *c*
10:21 the tribe of Benjamin to *c*
10:22 'Has the man *c* here yet?"
11: 3 we will *c* out to you."
11:10 Tomorrow we will *c* out to you,
11:14 Samuel said to the people, "*C*,
13: 8 But Samuel did not *c* to Gilgal;
13:11 and that you did not *c* within
13:12 The Philistines will now *c* down
14: 1 man who bore his armor, "*C*,
14: 6 man who bore his armor, "*C*,
14: 9 Wait until we *c* to you,' then we
14:10 *C* up to us,' then we will go up.
14:12 *C* up to us, and we will show you
14:12 *C* up after me, for the LORD has
14:26 And when the people had *c* into
14:38 *C* over here, all you chiefs of
16: 2 I have *c* to sacrifice to the
16: 4 Do you *c* peaceably?"
16: 5 I have *c* to sacrifice to the
16: 5 *c* with me to the sacrifice."
17: 8 Why have you *c* out to line up
17: 8 and let him *c* down to me.
17:25 you seen this man who has *c* up?
17:25 Surely he has *c* up to defy
17:28 'Why did you *c* down here?
17:28 for you have *c* down to see the
17:43 that you *c* to me with sticks?"
17:44 *C* to me, and I will give your
17:45 You *c* to me with a sword, with a
17:45 But I *c* to you in the name of
18: 6 that the women had *c* out of all
19:16 And when the messengers had *c*
20: 9 determined by my father to *c*
20:11 And Jonathan said to David, "*C*,
20:19 go down quickly and *c* to the
20:21 side of you; get them and *c*'—
20:24 And when the New Moon had *c*,
20:27 has the son of Jesse not *c*
20:29 Therefore he has not *c* to the
20:37 When the lad had *c* to the place
21:15 Shall this fellow *c* into my
22: 3 let my father and mother *c*
23:10 heard that Saul seeks to *c* to
23:11 Will Saul *c* down, as Your
23:11 He will *c* down."
23:15 So David saw that Saul had *c* out
23:20 *c* down according to all the
23:20 the desire of your soul to *c*
23:23 and *c* back to me with
23:27 to Saul, saying, "Hasten and *c*,
24:14 whom has the king of Israel *c*
25: 8 for we *c* on a feast day.
25:30 And it shall *c* to pass, when the
25:34 unless you had hastened and *c*
25:40 the servants of David had *c* to
26: 4 that Saul had indeed *c*.
26:10 or his day shall *c* to die, or
26:20 For the king of Israel has *c*
26:22 Let one of the young men *c* over
28:10 no punishment shall *c* upon you
29:10 master's servants who have *c*
31: 4 lest these uncircumcised men *c*
2 Sam 1: 3 'Where have you *c* from?"
1: 9 for anguish has *c* upon me, but

C

3:13 when you *c* to see my face."
3:23 that were with him had *c*,
5: 6 You shall not *c* in here; but the
5: 6 David cannot *c* in here."
5: 8 blind and the lame shall not *c*
5:13 after he had *c* from Hebron.
5:23 and *c* upon them in front of the
6: 9 can the ark of the LORD *c*
7:12 who will *c* from your body, and
7:19 house for a great while to *c*.
9: 6 had *c* to David, he fell on his
10:11 then I will *c* and help you.
11: 7 When Uriah had *c* to him, David
11:10 Did you not *c* from a journey?
12: 4 the wayfaring man who had *c* to
12: 4 it for the man who had *c* to
13: 5 Please let my sister Tamar *c* and
13: 6 Please let Tamar my sister *c* and
13:11 of her and said to her, "*C*,
14:15 I have *c* to speak of this thing
14:29 but he would not *c* to him.
14:29 the second time, he would not *c*.
14:32 *C* here, so that I may send you
14:32 'Why have I *c* from Geshur?
15: 4 has any suit or cause would *c*
15:32 it happened when David had *c*
16: 7 '*C* out! Come out!
16: 7 *C* out! You bloodthirsty man,
17: 2 I will *c* upon him while he is
17:12 So we will *c* upon him in some
17:17 so a female servant would *c* and
17:27 when David had *c* to Mahanaim,
19:11 the words of all Israel have *c*
19:20 the first to *c* today of all the
19:25 when he had *c* to Jerusalem to
19:30 as my lord the king has *c* back
19:33 *C* across with me, and I will
20:16 *C* nearby, that I may speak with
20:17 When he had *c* near to her, the
22:46 And *c* frightened from their
24:13 Shall seven years of famine *c* to
24:21 Why has my lord the king *c* to
1 Ki 1:12 '*C*, please, let me now give
1:14 I also will *c* in after you and
1:35 Then you shall *c* up after him,
1:35 and he shall *c* and sit on my
1:42 *C* in, for you are a prominent
2:13 'Do you *c* peaceably?"
2:30 *C* out!'" And he said, "No,
2:41 Jerusalem to Gath and had *c*
3: 7 do not know how to go out or *c*
6: 1 the children of Israel had *c*
8:19 but your son who will *c* from
8:26 let Your word *c* true, which You
8:41 but has *c* from a far country
8:47 yet when they *c* to themselves
12: 5 then *c* back to me." And the
12:12 *C* back to me the third day."
12:20 heard that Jeroboam had *c* back,
13: 7 *C* home with me and refresh
13:15 *C* home with me and eat bread."
13:22 your corpse shall not *c* to
13:32 will surely *c* to pass."
14: 6 *C* in, wife of Jeroboam. Why do
14:13 one of Jeroboam who shall *c* to
15:17 he might let none go out or *c*
15:19 *C* and break your treaty with
17:18 Have you *c* to me to bring my
17:21 let this child's soul *c* back to
18:12 And it shall *c* to pass, as
18:30 *C* near to me." So all the
18:31 the word of the LORD had *c*,
20:18 If they have *c* out for peace,
20:18 and if they have *c* out for war,
20:22 year the king of Syria will *c*
20:33 any sign of mercy would *c*
20:33 and he had him *c* up into the
22:27 until I *c* in peace."'"
2 Ki 1: 4 You shall not *c* down from the
1: 5 Why have you *c* back?"
1: 6 Therefore you shall not *c* down
1: 9 the king has said, '*C* down!'
1:10 then let fire *c* down from
1:11 *C* down quickly!'"
1:12 let fire *c* down from heaven and
1:14 fire has *c* down from heaven and
1:16 Therefore you shall not *c* down
3:21 heard that the kings had *c* up
4: 4 And when you have *c* in, you
4:17 when the appointed time had *c*,
4:22 may run to the man of God and *c*
5: 8 Please let him *c* to me, and he
5:11 He will surely *c* out to me,
5:22 sons of the prophets have *c* to
6:20 when they had *c* to Samaria,
7: 4 we die also. Now therefore, *c*,
7: 5 and when they had *c* to the
7: 9 some punishment will *c* upon us.
7: 9 come upon us. Now therefore, *c*,
7:12 When they *c* out of the city, we
8: 1 it will *c* upon the land for
8: 7 The man of God has *c* here."
9:11 Why did this madman *c* to you?"
9:16 and Ahaziah king of Judah had *c*
9:30 Now when Jehu had *c* to Jezreel,
10: 6 and *c* to me at Jezreel by this
10:13 we have *c* down to greet the
10:16 *C* with me, and see my zeal for
10:21 not a man left who did not *c*.
10:25 let no one *c* out!" And they
11: 5 One-third of you who *c* on duty
14: 8 king of Israel, saying, "*C*,

16: 7 *C* up and save me from the hand
18:17 When they had *c* up, they went
18:25 Have I now *c* up without the
18:31 with me by a present and *c* out
18:32 until I *c* and take you away to a
19: 3 for the children have *c* to
19: 9 he has *c* out to make war with
19:23 of my chariots I have *c* up to
19:28 Me and your tumult Have *c* up
19:32 He shall not *c* into this city,
19:32 Nor *c* before it with shield,
19:33 And he shall not *c* into this
20:14 and from where did they *c* to
23: 9 of the high places did not *c*
24: 7 And the king of Egypt did not *c*
1 Chr 7:23 because tragedy had *c* upon his
9:25 in their villages had to *c*
10: 4 lest these uncircumcised men *c*
11: 5 You shall not *c* in here!"
12:17 If you have *c* peaceably to me to
12:31 were designated by name to *c*
14:14 and *c* upon them in front of the
16:29 and *c* before Him. Oh, worship
17:17 house for a great while to *c*,
19: 3 Did his servants not *c* to you
19: 9 and the kings who had *c* were
29:12 Both riches and honor *c* from
29:14 For all things *c* from You,
2 Chr 1:10 that I may go out and *c* in
5:10 when they had *c* out of Egypt.
6: 9 but your son who will *c* from
6:17 let Your word *c* true, which You
6:32 when they *c* and pray in this
6:37 yet when they *c* to themselves
8:11 the ark of the LORD has *c* are
10: 5 *C* back to me after three days."
10:12 *C* back to me the third day."
16: 1 he might let none go out or *c*
16: 3 sent you silver and gold; *c*,
19:10 against the LORD and wrath *c*
20:16 They will surely *c* up by the
20:22 who had *c* against Judah; and
21:15 until your intestines *c* out by
23: 6 But let no one *c* into the house
25:10 the troops that had *c* to him
25:17 king of Israel, saying, "*C*,
28:17 For again the Edomites had *c*,
29:31 *c* near, and bring sacrifices
30: 1 that they should *c* to the house
30: 5 that they should *c* to keep the
30: 9 so that they may *c* back to this
32: 2 saw that Sennacherib had *c*,
32: 4 should the kings of Assyria *c*
32:26 wrath of the LORD did not *c*
35:21 I have not *c* against you
Ezra 3: 1 when the seventh month had *c*,
3: 3 Though fear had *c* upon them
3: 8 and all those who had *c* out of
4:12 who came up from you have *c* to
8:35 who had *c* from the captivity,
9:13 And after all that has *c* upon us
10: 8 and that whoever would not *c*
10:14 who have taken pagan wives *c*
Neh 2: 7 me to pass through till I *c* to
2:10 disturbed that a man had *c* to
2:17 *C* and let us build the wall of
4: 8 of them conspired together to *c*
4:11 till we *c* into their midst and
6: 2 Geshem sent to me, saying, "*C*,
6: 3 so that I cannot *c* down.
6: 7 be reported to the king. So *c*,
6:10 at night they will *c* to kill
7: 5 genealogy of those who had *c*
9:32 small before You That has *c*
13: 1 or Moabite should ever *c* into
Esth 1:12 But Queen Vashti refused to *c* at
1:17 before him, but she did not *c*.
1:19 that Vashti shall *c* no more
4:14 who knows whether you have *c*
5: 4 let the king and Haman *c* today
5: 8 then let the king and Haman *c*
5:12 invited no one but me to *c* in
6: 5 Let him *c* in."
8: 6 to see the evil that will *c* to
Job 1: 7 to Satan, "From where do you *c*?
2: 2 to Satan, "From where do you *c*?
2:11 all this adversity that had *c*
2:11 an appointment together to *c*
3: 6 May it not *c* into the number
3: 7 May no joyful shout *c* into
3:21 for death, but it does not *c*,
3:25 thing I greatly feared has *c*
5: 6 For affliction does not *c* from
5:26 You shall *c* to the grave at a
6:20 They *c* there and are confused.
7: 9 down to the grave does not *c*
8:22 place of the wicked will *c* to
13:13 Then let *c* on me what may!
13:16 For a hypocrite could not *c*
14:21 His sons *c* to honor, and he
17:10 *c* back again, all of you, For
19:12 His troops *c* together And
20:22 Every hand of misery will *c*
20:25 Terrors *c* upon him;
21:17 does their destruction *c* upon
22:21 Thereby good will *c* to you.
22:29 Exaltation will *c*!' Then He
23: 3 That I might *c* to His seat!
23:10 I shall *c* forth as gold.
28:20 where then does wisdom *c*?
30:14 They *c* as broad breakers;
33: 3 My words *c* from my upright

34:28 the cry of the poor to *c* to
37:13 He causes it to *c*,
38:11 I said, 'This far you may *c*,
39:24 Nor does he *c* to a halt
41:16 near another That no air can *c*
Ps 5: 7 I will *c* into Your house in the
7: 9 the wickedness of the wicked *c*
7:16 his violent dealing shall *c*
14: 7 salvation of Israel would *c*
17: 2 Let my vindication *c* from Your
18:45 And *c* frightened from their
22:31 They will *c* and declare His
24: 7 And the King of glory shall *c*
24: 9 And the King of glory shall *c*
32: 6 great waters They shall not *c*
32: 9 Else they will not *c* near you.
34:11 *C*, you children, listen to
35: 8 Let destruction *c* upon him
36:11 Let not the foot of pride *c*
40: 7 Then I said, "Behold, I *c*;
42: 2 When shall I *c* and appear
44:17 All this has *c* upon us; But we
45:12 the daughter of Tyre will *c*
46: 8 *C*, behold the works of the
50: 3 Our God shall *c*,
53: 6 the salvation of Israel would *c*
55: 5 and trembling have *c* upon me,
59:10 My God of mercy shall *c* to meet
65: 2 To You all flesh will *c*.
66: 5 *C* and see the works of God
66:16 *C* and hear, all you who fear
68:31 Envoys will *c* out of Egypt;
69: 1 O God! For the waters have *c*
69: 2 I have *c* into deep waters,
69:27 And let them not *c* into Your
71:18 power to everyone who is to *c*.
72: 6 He shall *c* down like rain upon
78: 4 to the generation to *c*
78: 6 That the generation to *c* might
78:39 that passes away and does not *c*
79: 1 the nations have *c* into Your
79: 8 Let Your tender mercies *c* speedily
79:11 the groaning of the prisoner *c*
80: 2 And *c* and save us!
83: 4 They have said, "*C*,
86: 9 whom You have made Shall *c*
88: 2 Let my prayer *c* before You;
91: 7 But it shall not *c* near you.
91:10 Nor shall any plague *c* near
95: 1 *c*, let us sing to the LORD!
95: 2 Let us *c* before His presence
95: 6 Oh *c*, let us worship and bow
96: 8 and *c* into His courts.
100: 2 *C* before His presence with
101: 2 when will You *c* to me? I will
102: 1 And let my cry *c* to You.
102:13 her, Yes, the set time, has *c*.
102:18 written for the generation to *c*,
109:17 so let it *c* to him; As he did
119:41 Let Your mercies *c* also to me,
119:77 Let Your tender mercies *c* to
119:169 Let my cry *c* before You, O
119:170 Let my supplication *c* before
126: 6 Shall doubtless *c* again with
144: 5 and *c* down; Touch the
Prov 1:11 *C* with us, Let us lie in wait
1:27 When distress and anguish *c*
2: 6 From His mouth *c* knowledge
3:28 and *c* back, And tomorrow I
6: 3 For you have *c* into the hand
6:11 So shall your poverty *c* on you
6:15 his calamity shall *c* suddenly;
7:18 *C*, let us take our fill of
7:20 And will *c* home on the
8: 6 the opening of my lips will *c*
9: 5 '*C*, eat of my bread And
10:24 The fear of the wicked will *c*
10:29 But destruction will *c* to
11:27 But trouble will *c* to him who
12:13 But the righteous will *c*
13:18 Poverty and shame will *c* to
20:13 lest you *c* to poverty; Open
21:15 But destruction will *c* to
22:16 will surely *c* to poverty.
23:21 and the glutton will *c* to
24:25 And a good blessing will *c*
24:34 So shall your poverty *c* like a
25: 7 *C* up here," Than that you
28:22 consider that poverty will *c*
31:25 She shall rejoice in time to *c*.
Eccl 1: 7 place from which the rivers *c*,
1:11 of things that are to *c* By
1:11 to come By those who will *c*
2: 1 *C* now, I will test you with
2:16 be forgotten in the days to *c*.
2:18 leave it to the man who will *c*
4:16 Yet those who *c* afterward will
7:14 find out nothing that will *c*
8:10 who had *c* and gone from the
9: 2 All things *c* alike to all:
12: 1 Before the difficult days *c*,
Song 2:10 my fair one, And *c* away.
2:12 The time of singing has *c*,
2:13 my fair one, And *c* away!
4: 2 of shorn sheep Which have *c*
4: 8 *C* with me from Lebanon, my
4:16 Awake, O north wind, And *c*,
4:16 Let my beloved *c* to his garden
5: 1 I have *c* to my garden, my
6: 6 a flock of sheep Which have *c*
7:11 *C*, my beloved, Let us go forth
Isa 1:12 When you *c* to appear before Me,

1:18 *C* now, and let us reason
1:23 does the cause of the widow *c*
2: 2 Now it shall *c* to pass in the
2: 3 Many people shall *c* and say,
2: 3 people shall come and say, "*C*,
2: 5 *c* and let us walk In the light
2:12 the LORD of hosts Shall *c*
4: 3 And it shall *c* to pass that he
5: 6 But there shall *c* up briers
5:19 One of Israel draw near and *c*,
5:26 Surely they shall *c* with
7: 7 Nor shall it *c* to pass.
7:17 days that have not *c* since the
7:18 And it shall *c* to pass in that
7:19 They will *c*, and all of them
7:24 arrows and bows men will *c*
8:10 but it will *c* to nothing;
10: 3 in the desolation which will *c*
10:12 Therefore it shall *c* to pass,
10:20 And it shall *c* to pass in that
10:27 It shall *c* to pass in that day
10:28 He has *c* to Aiath, He has
11: 1 There shall *c* forth a Rod from
11:11 It shall *c* to pass in that day
13: 5 They *c* from a far country,
13: 6 LORD is at hand! It will *c*
13:22 Her time is near to *c*,
14: 3 It shall *c* to pass in the day
14: 8 No woodsman has *c* up against
14:24 so it shall *c* to pass, And as
14:29 of the serpent's roots will *c*
14:31 For smoke will *c* from the
16:12 And it shall *c* to pass, When
16:12 That he will *c* to his
17: 4 In that day it shall *c* to pass
19: 1 And will *c* into Egypt;
19:23 and the Assyrian will *c* into
21:12 Return! *C* back!"
22: 7 It shall *c* to pass that your
23:15 Now it shall *c* to pass in that
24:21 It shall *c* to pass in that day
26:20 *C*, my people, enter your
27: 6 Those who *c* He shall cause to
27:11 The women *c* and set them on
27:12 And it shall *c* to pass in that
27:13 will be blown; They will *c*,
28:15 It will not *c* to us, For we
29: 1 Let feasts *c* around.
29:24 who erred in spirit will *c* to
30: 8 That it may be for time to *c*,
30:29 To *c* into the mountain of the
31: 4 So the LORD of hosts will *c*
32:10 fail, The gathering will not *c*.
32:13 the land of my people will *c*
34: 1 *C* near, you nations, to hear
34: 1 world and all things that *c*
34: 5 Indeed it shall *c* down on
34: 7 The wild oxen shall *c* down with
34:13 And thorns shall *c* up in its
35: 4 your God will *c* with
35: 4 He will *c* and save you."
35:10 And *c* to Zion with singing,
36:10 Have I now *c* up without the
36:16 with me by a present and *c*
36:17 until I *c* and take you away to a
37: 3 for the children have *c* to
37: 9 He has *c* out to make war with
37:24 of my chariots I have *c* up to
37:29 Me and your tumult Have *c* up
37:33 He shall not *c* into this city,
37:33 Nor *c* before it with shield,
37:34 And he shall not *c* into this
39: 3 and from where did they *c* to
40:10 the Lord GOD shall *c* with a
41: 1 their strength! Let them *c*
41: 1 Let us *c* near together for
41:22 Or declare to us things to *c*.
41:23 Show the things that are to *c*
41:25 from the north, And he shall *c*;
41:25 And he shall *c* against princes
42: 9 the former things have *c* to
42:23 and hear for the time to *c*?
44: 7 that are coming and shall *c*,
45:11 Ask Me of things to *c* concerning
45:14 Shall *c* over to you, and they
45:14 They shall *c* over in chains;
45:20 "Assemble yourselves and *c*;
45:24 To Him men shall *c*,
47: 1 '*C* down and sit in the dust,
47: 9 But these two things shall *c*
47: 9 They shall *c* upon you in their
47:11 Therefore evil shall *c* upon
47:11 And desolation shall *c* upon
47:13 and save you From what shall *c*
48: 1 And have *c* forth from the
48:16 *C* near to Me, hear this: I have
49:12 Surely these shall *c* from afar;
49:18 these gather together and *c*
50: 8 Let him *c* near Me.
51:11 And *c* to Zion with singing,
51:19 These two things have *c* to
52: 1 the unclean Shall no longer *c*
54:14 for it shall not *c* near you.
55: 1 *C* to the waters; And you who
55: 1 And you who have no money, *C*,
55: 1 Come, buy and eat. Yes, *c*,
55: 3 and *c* to Me. Hear, and your
55:13 Instead of the thorn shall *c* up
55:13 instead of the brier shall *c*
56: 1 My salvation is about to *c*,
56: 9 *c* to devour, All you beasts in
56:12 '*C*,' one says, "I will bring
57: 3 But *c* here, You sons of the
59:20 The Redeemer will *c* to Zion,
60: 1 For your light has *c*! And the
60: 3 The Gentiles shall *c* to your
60: 4 they *c* to you; Your sons shall
60: 4 Your sons shall *c* from afar,
60: 5 wealth of the Gentiles shall *c*
60: 6 All those from Sheba shall *c*;
60: 9 the ships of Tarshish will *c*
60:13 The glory of Lebanon shall *c* to
60:14 who afflicted you Shall *c*
63: 4 the year of My redeemed has *c*.
64: 1 the heavens! That You would *c*
65: 5 Do not *c* near me, For I am
65:17 shall not be remembered or *c*
65:24 It shall *c* to pass That before
66:15 the LORD will *c* with fire And
66:18 and they shall *c* and see My
66:23 And it shall *c* to pass That
66:23 All flesh shall *c* to worship
Jer 1:15 They shall *c* and each one set
2: 3 Disaster will *c* upon them,"
2:31 We will *c* no more to You'?
3:16 Then it shall *c* to pass, when
3:16 It shall not *c* to mind, nor
3:18 and they shall *c* together out
3:22 Indeed we do *c* to You, For You
4: 4 Lest My fury *c* forth like
4: 7 The lion has *c* up from his
4: 9 And it shall *c* to pass in that
4:12 too strong for these will *c*
4:13 he shall *c* up like clouds, And
4:16 That watchers *c* from a far
5:12 Neither will evil *c* upon us,
6: 3 with their flocks shall *c* to
6:26 the plunderer will suddenly *c*
7:10 and then *c* and stand before Me
7:31 nor did it *c* into My heart.
8:16 For they have *c* and devoured
9:17 That they may *c*; And send for
9:17 wailing women, That they may *c*.
9:21 For death has *c* through our
10:22 the noise of the report has *c*,
12: 9 all around are against her. *C*,
12:12 The plunderers have *c* On all
13:20 your eyes and see Those who *c*
13:22 Why have these things *c* upon
16:19 The Gentiles shall *c* to You
17:15 Let it *c* now!"
17:19 by which the kings of Judah *c*
17:26 And they shall *c* from the cities
18:18 *C* and let us devise plans
18:18 *C* and let us attack him with
19: 5 nor did it *c* into My mind),
20:18 Why did I *c* forth from the womb
21:13 'Who shall *c* down against us?
22:23 will you be when pangs *c* upon
23:17 No evil shall *c* upon you.'"
25: 3 the word of the LORD has *c* to
25:12 Then it will *c* to pass, when
25:31 A noise will *c* to the ends of
26: 2 which *c* to worship in the
27: 3 hand of the messengers who *c*
30: 8 For it shall *c* to pass in that
30:21 And their governor shall *c*
31: 9 They shall *c* with weeping, And
31:12 Therefore they shall *c* and sing
31:16 And they shall *c* back from the
31:17 That your children shall *c*
31:28 And it shall *c* to pass, that as
32: 7 of Shallum your uncle will *c*
32:23 caused all this calamity to *c*
32:24 the siege mounds! They have *c*
32:29 against this city shall *c* and
32:35 nor did it *c* into My mind that
33: 5 They *c* to fight with the
35:11 into the land, that we said, '*C*,
36: 6 the hearing of all Judah who *c*
36:14 hearing of the people, and *c*.
36:29 of Babylon will certainly *c*
37: 7 Pharaoh's army which has *c* up
37: 8 And the Chaldeans shall *c* back
37:19 'The king of Babylon will not *c*
38:25 and they *c* to you and say to
39:15 the word of the LORD had *c* to
40: 3 therefore this thing has *c* upon
40: 4 If it seems good to you to *c*
40: 4 to come with me to Babylon, *c*,
40: 4 if it seems wrong for you to *c*
40:10 and serve the Chaldeans who *c*
41: 6 *C* to Gedaliah the son of
44:21 and did it not *c* into His
46: 9 *C* up, O horses, and rage, O
46: 9 And let the mighty men *c*
46:13 king of Babylon would *c* and
46:18 by the sea, so he shall *c*.
46:21 the day of their calamity had *c*
46:22 shall march with an army And *c*
47: 5 Baldness has *c* upon Gaza,
48: 2 devised evil against her: '*C*,
48: 8 And the plunderer shall *c*
48:18 *C* down from your glory, And
48:18 the plunderer of Moab has *c*
48:21 And judgment has *c* on the plain
48:45 But a fire shall *c* out of
49: 4 Who will *c* against me?'
49:14 *c* against her, And rise up to
49:19 he shall *c* up like a lion from
49:22 He shall *c* up and fly like the
49:39 But it shall *c* to pass in the
50: 4 children of Israel shall *c*,
50: 4 continual weeping they shall *c*,
50: 5 *C* and let us join ourselves to
50: 9 I will raise and cause to *c* up
50:26 *C* against her from the farthest
50:27 to them! For their day has *c*,
50:31 of hosts; "For your day has *c*,
50:41 a people shall *c* from the
50:44 he shall *c* up like a lion from
51:10 *C* and let us declare in Zion
51:13 in treasures, Your end has *c*,
51:27 Cause the horses to *c* up like
51:33 the time of her harvest will *c*.
51:42 The sea has *c* up over Babylon;
51:46 in the land (A rumor will *c*
51:46 another year A rumor will *c*,
51:48 For the plunderers shall *c* to
51:50 And let Jerusalem *c* to your
51:51 For strangers have *c* into the
51:53 from Me plunderers would *c* to
51:60 book all the evil that would *c*
Lam 1:22 Let all their wickedness *c*
3:47 Fear and a snare have *c* upon
4:18 were over, For our end had *c*.
5: 1 what has *c* upon us; Look, and
Ezek 4:14 nor has abominable flesh ever *c*
7: 2 An end! The end has *c* upon the
7: 3 Now the end has *c* upon you,
7: 5 disaster; Behold, it has *c*!
7: 6 An end has *c*, The end has
7: 6 end has come, The end has *c*;
7: 6 Behold, it has *c*!
7: 7 Doom has *c* to you, you who
7: 7 in the land; The time has *c*,
7:10 it has *c*! Doom has gone out;
7:12 The time has *c*,
7:26 Disaster will *c* upon disaster,
9: 6 but do not *c* near anyone on
11: 5 for I know the things that *c*
12:25 the word which I speak will *c*
14:22 surely they will *c* out to you,
16:33 and hired them to *c* to you from
19:14 Fire has *c* out from a rod of
20: 3 'Have you *c* to inquire of Me?
21:24 because you have *c* to
21:25 of Israel, whose day has *c*,
21:29 the slain Whose day has *c*,
22: 3 own midst, that her time may *c*;
22: 4 and have *c* to the end of
23:24 And they shall *c* against you
23:40 you sent for men to *c* from
24:14 It shall *c* to pass, and I will
24:26 day one who escapes will *c* to
26: 3 will cause many nations to *c*
26: 3 the sea causes its waves to *c*
26:16 the princes of the sea will *c*
27:29 the pilots of the sea Will *c*
30: 4 The sword shall *c* upon Egypt,
30: 6 the pride of her power shall *c*
30: 9 And great anguish shall *c* upon
31:13 the beasts of the field will *c*
32:11 of the king of Babylon shall *c*
33:30 Please *c* and hear what the word
33:31 So they *c* to you as people do,
33:33 comes to pass—surely it will *c*—
34:26 and I will cause showers to *c*
36: 8 Israel, for they are about to *c*.
37: 9 *C* from the four winds, O breath,
37:12 your graves and cause you to *c*
38: 8 In the latter years you will *c*
38:10 On that day it shall *c* to pass
38:13 'Have you *c* to take plunder?
38:15 Then you will *c* from your place
38:16 You will *c* up against My people
38:18 And it will *c* to pass at the
39:11 It will *c* to pass in that day
39:17 "Assemble yourselves and *c*;
40:46 who *c* near the LORD to
44:13 And they shall not *c* near Me to
44:13 nor *c* near any of My holy
44:15 they shall *c* near Me to
44:16 and they shall *c* near My table
44:17 no wool shall *c* upon them while
45: 4 who *c* near to minister to the
46: 9 when the people of the land *c*
Dan 2:29 about what would *c* to pass
2:45 known to the king what will *c*
3: 2 to *c* to the dedication of the
3:26 *c* out, and come here."
3:26 and *c* here." Then Shadrach,
4:24 which has *c* upon my lord the
4:26 after you *c* to know that Heaven
9:13 all this disaster has *c* upon
9:22 I have now *c* forth to give you
9:23 and I have *c* to tell you, for
9:26 of the prince who is to *c*
10:12 and I have *c* because of your
10:14 Now I have *c* to make you
10:14 to many days yet to *c*.
10:20 Do you know why I have *c* to you?
10:20 the prince of Greece will *c*.
11: 7 who shall *c* with an army, enter
11: 9 king of the North shall *c*
11:10 and one shall certainly *c* and
11:13 and shall certainly *c* at the
11:15 the king of the North shall *c*
11:21 but he shall *c* in peaceably,
11:23 for he shall *c* up and become
11:30 For ships from Cyprus shall *c*
11:40 the king of the North shall *c*
11:45 yet he shall *c* to his end, and
Hos 1: 5 It shall *c* to pass in that day
1:10 And it shall *c* to pass In the
1:11 And they shall *c* up out of the

2:21 It shall *c* to pass in that day
4:15 Do not *c* up to Gilgal, Nor go
6: 1 *C*, and let us return to the
6: 3 He will *c* to us like the rain,
8: 1 to your mouth! He shall *c*
9: 4 It shall not *c* into the house
9: 7 The days of punishment have *c*;
9: 7 The days of recompense have *c*.
11: 9 And I will not *c* with terror.
11:10 Then His sons shall *c*
11:11 They shall *c* trembling like a
13:13 a woman in childbirth shall *c*
13:15 brethren, An east wind shall *c*;
13:15 The wind of the LORD shall *c*
Joel 1: 6 For a nation has *c* up against
1:13 minister before the altar; *C*,
1:15 It shall *c* as destruction from
2: 2 the mountains. A people *c*,
2:20 His stench will *c* up, And his
2:23 He will cause the rain to *c*
2:28 And it shall *c* to pass
2:32 And it shall *c* to pass That
3: 9 Let them *c* up.
3:11 Assemble and *c*,
3:12 and *c* up to the Valley of
3:13 for the harvest is ripe. *C*,
3:18 And it will *c* to pass in that
Am 4: 2 the days shall *c* upon you When
4: 4 *C* to Bethel and transgress, At
4:10 the stench of your camps *c* up
5: 5 And Bethel shall *c* to nothing.
6: 3 the seat of violence to *c* near;
6: 9 Then it shall *c* to pass, that if
8: 2 The end has *c* upon My people
8: 9 And it shall *c* to pass in that
Ob 5 If thieves had *c* to you, If
5 If grape-gatherers had *c* to
21 Then saviors shall *c* to Mount
Jon 1: 2 for their wickedness has *c* up
1: 7 they said to one another, "*C*,
1: 7 cause this trouble has *c*
1: 8 And where do you *c* from?
4: 6 prepared a plant and made it *c*
Mic 1: 3 He will *c* down And tread on
1: 9 For it has *c* to Judah; It has
1: 9 It has *c* to the gate of My
1:15 The glory of Israel shall *c* to
2:13 one who breaks open will *c* up
3:11 No harm can *c* upon us."
4: 1 Now it shall *c* to pass in the
4: 2 Many nations shall *c* and say,
4: 2 shall come and say, "*C*,
4: 8 of Zion, To you shall it *c*,
4: 8 the former dominion shall *c*,
5: 2 Yet out of you shall *c* forth
6: 6 With what shall I *c* before the
6: 6 Shall I *c* before Him with
7:12 In that day they shall *c* to
Nah 2: 1 He who scatters has *c* up before
2: 3 The chariots *c* with flaming
3: 7 It shall *c* to pass that all
Hab 1: 9 'They all *c* for violence;
2: 3 Because it will surely *c*,
Zeph 1:12 And it shall *c* to pass at that
Hag 1: 2 says, "The time has not *c*,
2: 7 and they shall *c* to the Desire
2:22 and their riders shall *c* down,
Zech 6:10 who have *c* from Babylon—and go
6:15 Even those from afar shall *c* and
6:15 And this shall *c* to pass if
8:13 And it shall *c* to pass That
8:20 'Peoples shall yet *c*,
8:22 and strong nations Shall *c* to
11: 2 For the thick forest has *c*
12: 9 destroy all the nations that *c*
13: 3 It shall *c* to pass that if
13: 8 And it shall *c* to pass in all
14: 5 Thus the LORD my God will *c*,
14: 6 It shall *c* to pass in that day
14:13 It shall *c* to pass in that day
14:16 And it shall *c* to pass that
14:17 families of the earth do not *c*
14:18 the family of Egypt will not *c*
14:18 the nations who do not *c* up to
14:19 all the nations that do not *c*
14:21 who sacrifices shall *c* and
Mal 3: 1 Will suddenly *c* to His temple,
3: 5 And I will *c* near you for
4: 6 Lest I *c* and strike the earth
Mt 2: 2 star in the East and have *c* to
2: 6 For out of you shall *c*
2: 8 that I may *c* and worship Him
2:11 And when they had *c* into the
3: 7 you to flee from the wrath to *c*?
5:17 I did not *c* to destroy but to
5:24 and then *c* and offer your gift.
6:10 Your kingdom *c*.
7:15 who *c* to you in sheep's
8: 1 When He had *c* down from the
8: 7 I will *c* and heal him."
8: 8 am not worthy that You should *c*
8: 9 and he goes; and to another, '*C*,
8:11 I say to you that many will *c*
8:14 Now when Jesus had *c* into
8:16 When evening had *c*,
8:28 When He had *c* to the other
8:29 Have You *c* here to torment us
8:32 So when they had *c* out, they
9:13 For I did not *c* to call the
9:15 But the days will *c* when the
9:18 but *c* and lay Your hand on her
9:28 And when He had *c* into the
10:13 let your peace *c* upon it.
10:34 I did not *c* to bring peace but
10:35 For I have *c* to 'set a man
11:14 it, he is Elijah who is to *c*.
11:28 *C* to Me, all you who labor and
12:28 the kingdom of God has *c* upon
12:32 in this age or in the age to *c*.
13:32 so that the birds of the air *c*
13:49 The angels will *c* forth,
13:54 And when He had *c* to His own
14:28 command me to *c* to You on the
14:29 So He said, "*C*.
14:29 And when Peter had *c* down out
15:18 proceed out of the mouth *c*
16: 5 Now when His disciples had *c* to
16:24 If anyone desires to *c* after Me,
16:27 For the Son of Man will *c* in the
17:10 scribes say that Elijah must *c*
17:12 I say to you that Elijah has *c*
17:14 And when they had *c* to the
17:24 When they had *c* to Capernaum,
17:25 And when he had *c* into the
18: 7 offenses! For offenses must *c*,
18:11 For the Son of Man has *c* to save
19:14 Let the little children *c* to Me,
19:21 have treasure in heaven; and *c*,
20: 8 "So when evening had *c*,
20:28 as the Son of Man did not *c* to
21:10 And when He had *c* into
21:38 'This is the heir. *C*,
22: 3 and they were not willing to *c*.
22: 4 *C* to the wedding." '
22:12 how did you *c* in here without a
23:35 that on you may *c* all the
23:36 all these things will *c* upon
24: 5 For many will *c* in My name,
24: 6 for all these things must *c*
24:14 and then the end will *c*.
24:43 what hour the thief would *c*,
24:50 master of that servant will *c*
25:34 to those on His right hand, '*C*,
25:39 or in prison, and *c* to You?'
26:20 When evening had *c*, He sat
26:50 him, "Friend, why have you *c*?
26:55 Have you *c* out, as against a
27:33 And when they had *c* to a place
27:40 *c* down from the cross."
27:42 let Him now *c* down from the
27:49 let us see if Elijah will *c* to
27:57 Now when evening had *c*,
27:64 lest His disciples *c* by night
28: 6 for He is risen, as He said. *C*,
Mk 1:24 Did You *c* to destroy us? I know
1:25 and *c* out of him!"
1:29 Now as soon as they had *c* out
1:38 for this purpose I have *c*
2: 4 And when they could not *c* near
2:17 I did not *c* to call the
2:20 But the days will *c* when the
4:11 all things *c* in parables,
4:22 secret but that it should *c* to
4:29 because the harvest has *c*.
4:35 same day, when evening had *c*,
5: 2 And when He had *c* out of the
5: 8 *C* out of the man, unclean
5:23 *C* and lay Your hands on her,
6: 2 And when the Sabbath had *c*,
6:31 *C* aside by yourselves to a
7: 1 having *c* from Jerusalem.
7: 4 When they *c* from the
7:15 but the things which *c* out of
7:23 All these evil things *c* from
7:30 And when she had *c* to her house,
8: 3 for some of them have *c* from
8:34 Whoever desires to *c* after Me,
9:11 scribes say that Elijah must *c*
9:13 to you that Elijah has also *c*,
9:25 *c* out of him and enter him no
9:28 And when He had *c* into the
9:29 This kind can *c* out by nothing
10:14 Let the little children *c* to Me,
10:21 have treasure in heaven; and *c*,
10:30 in the age to *c*,
10:45 even the Son of Man did not *c*
11:12 when they had *c* out from
11:19 When evening had *c*,
12: 7 'This is the heir. *C*,
12: 9 He will *c* and destroy the
12:14 When they had *c*,
13: 6 For many will *c* in My name,
14: 8 She has *c* beforehand to anoint
14:41 It is enough! The hour has *c*;
14:45 As soon as He had *c*,
14:48 Have you *c* out, as against a
15:30 and *c* down from the cross!"
15:33 Now when the sixth hour had *c*,
15:36 let us see if Elijah will *c* to
15:42 Now when evening had *c*,
16: 1 that they might *c* and anoint
Lk 1:28 And having *c* in, the angel said
1:35 The Holy Spirit will *c* upon
1:43 the mother of my Lord should *c*
2:15 and see this thing that has *c*
3: 7 you to flee from the wrath to *c*?
4:34 Did You *c* to destroy us?
4:35 and *c* out of him!" And when
4:36 and they *c* out."
5: 7 in the other boat to *c* and
5:17 who had *c* out of every town of
5:32 I have not *c* to call the
5:35 But the days will *c* when the
7: 3 pleading with Him to *c* and heal
7: 7 even think myself worthy to *c*
7: 8 and he goes; and to another, '*C*,
7:20 When the men had *c* to Him, they
7:34 The Son of Man has *c* eating and
8: 2 out of whom had *c* seven demons,
8: 4 and they had *c* to Him from
8:17 that will not be known and *c*
8:29 the unclean spirit to *c* out of
8:41 feet and begged Him to *c* to
9:23 If anyone desires to *c* after Me,
9:37 when they had *c* down from the
9:51 when the time had *c* for Him to
9:54 want us to command fire to *c*
9:56 For the Son of Man did not *c* to
10: 9 The kingdom of God has *c* near to
10:11 that the kingdom of God has *c*
10:35 when I *c* again, I will repay
11: 2 be Your name. Your kingdom *c*.
11: 6 for a friend of mine has *c* to me
11:20 the kingdom of God has *c* upon
11:33 that those who *c* in may see the
12:37 and will *c* and serve them.
12:38 And if he should *c* in the second
12:38 or *c* in the third watch, and
12:39 what hour the thief would *c*,
12:46 master of that servant will *c*
13: 7 for three years I have *c*
13:14 therefore *c* and be healed on
13:29 They will *c* from the east and
14: 9 he who invited you and him *c*
14:17 to those who were invited, '*C*,
14:20 wife, and therefore I cannot *c*.
14:23 and compel them to *c* in, that
14:27 does not bear his cross and *c*
15:27 to him, 'Your brother has *c*,
16:28 lest they also *c* to this place
17: 1 that no offenses should *c*,
17: 1 him through whom they do *c*!
17: 7 will say to him when he has *c*
17: 7 *C* at once and sit down to eat'?
17:20 when the kingdom of God would *c*,
17:20 The kingdom of God does not *c*
17:22 The days will *c* when you will
17:31 let him not *c* down to take them
18:16 Let the little children *c* to Me,
18:22 have treasure in heaven; and *c*,
18:30 and in the age to *c* eternal
18:40 And when he had *c* near, He
19: 5 make haste and *c* down, for
19: 9 Today salvation has *c* to this
19:10 for the Son of Man has *c* to seek
19:13 to them, 'Do business till I *c*.
19:43 For days will *c* upon you when
20:14 saying, 'This is the heir. *C*,
20:16 He will *c* and destroy those
21: 6 the days will *c* in which not
21: 8 For many will *c* in My name,
21: 9 for these things must *c* to pass
21: 9 but the end will not *c*
21:34 and that Day *c* on you
21:35 For it will *c* as a snare on all
21:36 all these things that will *c*
22:14 When the hour had *c*,
22:45 and had *c* to His disciples, He
22:52 and the elders who had *c* to
22:52 Have you *c* out, as against a
23:33 And when they had *c* to the place
23:42 remember me when You *c* into
23:55 And the women who had *c* with Him
Jn 1:39 *C* and see." They came and saw
1:46 'Can anything good *c* out of
1:46 said to him, "*C* and see."
2: 4 with Me? My hour has not yet *c*.
3: 2 know that You are a teacher *c*
3:19 that the light has *c* into the
3:20 hates the light and does not *c*
4:15 nor *c* here to draw."
4:16 your husband, and *c* here."
4:29 '*C*, see a Man who told me
4:40 So when the Samaritans had *c* to
4:47 When he heard that Jesus had *c*
4:47 to Him and implored Him to *c*
4:49 *c* down before my child dies!"
4:54 sign Jesus did when He had *c*
5:14 lest a worse thing *c* upon
5:24 and shall not *c* into judgment,
5:29 and *c* forth—those who have done
5:40 But you are not willing to *c* to
5:43 I have *c* in My Father's name,
6:14 truly the Prophet who is to *c*
6:15 that they were about to *c* and
6:17 and Jesus had not *c* to them.
6:25 when did You *c* here?"
6:37 the Father gives Me will *c* to
6:38 For I have *c* down from heaven,
6:42 I have *c* down from heaven'?"
6:44 No one can *c* to Me unless the
6:65 said to you that no one can *c*
6:69 Also we have *c* to believe and
7: 6 them, "My time has not yet *c*,
7: 8 for My time has not yet fully *c*.
7:28 and I have not *c* of Myself, but
7:30 because His hour had not yet *c*.
7:34 and where I am you cannot *c*.
7:36 and where I am you cannot *c*'?
7:37 let him *c* to Me and drink.
7:41 Will the Christ *c* out of
8:14 but you do not know where I *c*
8:20 Him, for His hour had not yet *c*.
8:21 sin. Where I go you cannot *c*.
8:22 says, 'Where I go you cannot *c*'?
8:42 nor have I *c* of Myself, but He

9:39 For judgment I have **c** into this
10:10 The thief does not **c** except to
10:10 I have **c** that they may have
11:27 who is to **c** into the world."
11:28 The Teacher has **c** and is calling
11:30 Now Jesus had not yet **c** into the
11:34 to Him, "Lord, **c** and see."
11:43 'Lazarus, **c** forth!"
11:45 many of the Jews who had **c** to
11:48 and the Romans will **c** and take
11:56 that He will not **c** to the
12:12 a great multitude that had **c**
12:23 The hour has **c** that the Son of
12:30 This voice did not **c** because of
12:46 I have **c** as a light into the
12:47 for I did not **c** to judge the
13: 1 Jesus knew that His hour had **c**
13: 3 and that He had **c** from God and
13:19 that when it does **c** to pass,
13:33 'Where I am going, you cannot **c**,
14: 3 I will **c** again and receive you
14:18 I will **c** to you.
14:23 and We will **c** to him and make
14:29 that when it does **c** to pass,
15:22 If I had not **c** and spoken to
16: 7 the Helper will not **c** to you;
16: 8 "And when He has **c**,
16:13 He, the Spirit of truth, has **c**,
16:13 He will tell you things to **c**.
16:21 sorrow because her hour has **c**;
16:28 from the Father and have **c**
16:32 hour is coming, yes, has now **c**,
17: 1 said: "Father, the hour has **c**.
17:11 and I **c** to You. Holy Father,
17:13 But now I **c** to You, and these
18: 4 all things that would **c** upon
18:37 and for this cause I have **c**
21: 4 But when the morning had now **c**,
21: 9 as soon as they had **c** to land,
21:12 '**C** and eat breakfast."
21:22 I will that he remain till I **c**,
21:23 I will that he remain till I **c**,
Acts 1: 6 when they had **c** together, they
1: 8 when the Holy Spirit has **c**
1:11 will so **c** in like manner as you
2: 1 Day of Pentecost had fully **c**,
2:17 And it shall **c** to pass in
2:21 And it shall **c** to pass
3:19 that times of refreshing may **c**
5:38 it will **c** to nothing;
7: 3 and **c** to a land that I
7: 7 after that they shall **c**
7:34 their groaning and have **c**
7:34 deliver them. And now **c**,
8:15 when they had **c** down, prayed
8:24 which you have spoken may **c**
8:27 and had **c** to Jerusalem to
8:31 And he asked Philip to **c** up
9:21 and has **c** here for that
9:26 And when Saul had **c** to
9:39 went with them. When he had **c**,
10: 4 prayers and your alms have **c**
10:21 For what reason have you **c**?
10:27 in and found many who had **c**
10:33 and you have done well to **c**.
11:20 when they had **c** to Antioch,
12:11 And when Peter had **c** to himself,
13:40 been spoken in the prophets **c**
14:11 The gods have **c** down to us in
14:27 Now when they had **c** and gathered
15: 4 And when they had **c** to
16: 7 After they had **c** to Mysia, they
16: 9 **C** over to Macedonia and help
16:15 **c** to my house and stay."
16:18 the name of Jesus Christ to **c**
16:37 No indeed! Let them **c**
17: 6 the world upside down have **c**
17:15 for Silas and Timothy to **c** to
18: 2 who had recently **c** from Italy
18: 5 When Silas and Timothy had **c**
19: 4 believe on Him who would **c**
19:32 did not know why they had **c**
20:11 Now when he had **c** up, had broken
20:18 And when they had **c** to him, he
20:29 departure savage wolves will **c**
21: 5 When we had **c** to the end of
21:11 When he had **c** to us, he took
21:17 And when we had **c** to Jerusalem,
21:22 they will hear that you have **c**.
23:35 when your accusers also have **c**.
24: 8 commanding his accusers to **c** to
24:25 and the judgment to **c**,
25: 1 Now when Festus had **c** to the
25: 7 When he had **c**, the Jews who
25: 7 the Jews who had **c** down from
25:17 Therefore when they had **c**
25:23 when Agrippa and Bernice had **c**
26:22 prophets and Moses said would **c**—
27:27 when the fourteenth night had **c**,
27:29 stern, and prayed for day to **c**.
28: 6 a long time and saw no harm **c**
28:17 So when they had **c** together, he
Rom 1:10 a way in the will of God to **c**
1:13 that I often planned to **c** to
3: 8 us do evil that good may **c**'
4: 9 this blessedness then **c** upon
5:14 is a type of Him who was to **c**.
8:38 things present nor things to **c**,
9: 9 At this time I will **c** and
9:26 And it shall **c** to pass in
11:11 salvation has **c** to the
11:25 fullness of the Gentiles has **c**
11:26 The Deliverer will **c** out of
15:23 desire these many years to **c**
15:24 I shall **c** to you. For I hope to
15:29 But I know that when I **c** to you,
15:29 I shall **c** in the fullness of
15:32 that I may **c** to you with joy by
1 Cor 1: 7 so that you **c** short in no gift,
2: 1 did not **c** with excellence of
3:22 things present or things to **c**—
4: 5 Then each one's praise will **c**
4:19 But I will **c** to you shortly, if
4:21 Shall I **c** to you with a rod, or
7: 5 and **c** together again so that
10:11 the ends of the ages have **c**.
11:17 since you **c** together not for
11:18 when you **c** together as a
11:20 Therefore when you **c** together in
11:33 when you **c** together to eat,
11:34 lest you **c** together for
11:34 I will set in order when I **c**.
13:10 that which is perfect has **c**,
14: 6 if I **c** to you speaking with
14:23 and there **c** in those who are
14:26 Whenever you **c** together, each
14:36 Or did the word of God **c**
15:35 And with what body do they **c**?
16: 2 be no collections when I **c**.
16: 3 And when I **c**, whomever you
16: 5 Now I will **c** to you when I pass
16:11 that he may **c** to me; for I am
16:12 I strongly urged him to **c** to
16:12 he was quite unwilling to **c** at
16:12 he will **c** when he has a
16:22 him be accursed. O Lord, **c**!
2 Cor 1:15 confidence I intended to **c** to
1:16 to **c** again from Macedonia to
2: 1 that I would not **c** again to you
6:17 **C** out from among them And
9: 4 lest if some Macedonians **c** with
12: 1 I will **c** to visions and
12:14 the third time I am ready to **c**
12:20 For I fear lest, when I **c**,
12:21 when I **c** again, my God will
13: 2 that if I **c** again I will not
Gal 2:11 Now when Peter had **c** to
3:14 the blessing of Abraham might **c**
3:19 till the Seed should **c** to whom
3:25 But after faith has **c**,
4: 4 the fullness of the time had **c**,
5: 8 This persuasion does not **c** from
Eph 1:21 but also in that which is to **c**.
2: 7 that in the ages to **c** He might
4:13 till we all **c** to the unity of
Phil 1:27 so that whether I **c** and see you
2:24 Lord that I myself shall also **c**
Col 1: 6 which has **c** to you, as it has
2:17 are a shadow of things to **c**,
1 Th 1: 5 For our gospel did not **c** to you
1:10 delivers us from the wrath to **c**.
2: 3 For our exhortation did not **c**
2:16 but wrath has **c** upon them to
2:18 Therefore we wanted to **c** to
3: 6 But now that Timothy has **c** to
2 Th 2: 2 though the day of Christ had **c**.
2: 3 for that Day will not **c**
1 Tim 2: 4 all men to be saved and to **c**
3:14 though I hope to **c** to you
4: 8 is and of that which is to **c**.
4:13 Till I **c**, give attention to
6: 4 from which **c** envy, strife,
6:19 foundation for the time to **c**,
2 Tim 2:26 and that they may **c** to their
3: 1 last days perilous times will **c**:
3: 7 learning and never able to **c**
4: 3 For the time will **c** when they
4: 9 Be diligent to **c** to me quickly;
4:13 with Carpus at Troas when you **c**—
4:21 Do your utmost to **c** before
Titus 3:12 be diligent to **c** to me at
Heb 2: 5 He has not put the world to **c**,
4: 1 lest any of you seem to have **c**
4:16 Let us therefore **c** boldly to the
5:12 and you have **c** to need milk and
6: 5 and the powers of the age to **c**,
7: 5 though they have **c** from the
7:16 who has **c**, not according to
7:25 to the uttermost those who **c**
9:11 Priest of the good things to **c**,
10: 1 shadow of the good things to **c**,
10: 7 I said, 'Behold, I have **c**—
10: 9 I have **c** to do Your
10:37 He who is coming will **c**
11:15 country from which they had **c**
11:20 and Esau concerning things to **c**.
12:18 For you have not **c** to the
12:22 But you have **c** to Mount Zion and
13:14 city, but we seek the one to **c**.
Jas 2: 2 For if there should **c** into your
2: 2 and there should also **c** in a
4: 1 Where do wars and fights **c** from
4: 1 Do they not **c** from your
4:13 **C** now, you who say, "Today or
5: 1 **C** now, you rich, weep and howl
1 Pe 1:10 of the grace that would **c**
4:17 For the time has **c** for
2 Pe 3: 3 that scoffers will **c** in the
3: 9 perish but that all should **c**
3:10 the day of the Lord will **c** as
1 Jn 2:18 now many antichrists have **c**,
4: 2 that Jesus Christ has **c** in the
4: 3 that Jesus Christ has **c** in the
5:20 know that the Son of God has **c**
2 Jn 12 but I hope to **c** to you and
3 Jn 10 Therefore, if I **c**, I will call
Rev 1: 4 is and who was and who is to **c**,
1: 8 is and who was and who is to **c**,
2: 5 or else I will **c** to you quickly
2:16 or else I will **c** to you quickly
2:25 fast what you have till I **c**.
3: 3 I will **c** upon you as a thief,
3: 3 not know what hour I will **c**
3: 9 indeed I will make them **c** and
3:10 the hour of trial which shall **c**
3:20 I will **c** in to him and dine
4: 1 **C** up here, and I will show you
4: 8 Who was and is and is to **c**!"
6: 1 like thunder, "**C** and see."
6: 3 creature saying, "**C** and see."
6: 5 **C** and see." So I looked, and
6: 7 creature saying, "**C** and see."
6:17 great day of His wrath has **c**,
7:13 and where did they **c** from?"
7:14 These are the ones who **c** out of
11:12 **C** up here." And they ascended
11:17 is and who was and who is to **c**,
11:18 angry, and Your wrath has **c**,
12:10 the power of His Christ have **c**,
12:12 the sea! For the devil has **c**
13:13 so that he even makes fire **c**
14: 7 the hour of His judgment has **c**;
14:15 for the time has **c** for You to
15: 4 For all nations shall **c** and
17: 1 with me, saying to me, "**C**,
17:10 and the other has not yet **c**.
18: 4 **C** out of her, my people, lest
18: 8 Therefore her plagues will **c** in
18:10 in one hour your judgment has **c**.
19: 7 the marriage of the Lamb has **c**,
19:17 **C** and gather together for the
21: 9 and talked with me, saying, "**C**,
22:17 **C**!" And let him who hears say,
22:17 **C**!" And let him who thirsts
22:17 And let him who thirsts **c**.
22:20 quickly." Amen. Even so, **c**,

COMELINESS (1/1)

Isa 53: 2 He has no form or **c**;

COMES (272/257)

Gen 24:43 to pass that when the virgin **c**
24:50 The thing **c** from the LORD; we
30:11 A troop **c**!" So she called his
30:33 when the subject of my wages **c**
32: 8 If Esau **c** to the one company and
42:15 unless your youngest brother **c**
44:23 'Unless your youngest brother **c**
49:10 his feet, Until Shiloh **c**;
Ex 8:20 stand before Pharaoh as he **c**
13:12 every firstborn that **c** from an
21: 3 If he **c** in by himself, he shall
21: 3 if he **c** in married, then his
28:35 before the LORD and when he **c**
Lev 4:23 sin which he has committed **c**
4:28 sin which he has committed **c**
13:19 the place of the boil there **c**
14:35 and he who owns the house **c** and
14:43 Now if the plague **c** back and
14:48 But if the priest **c** in and
16:17 until he **c** out, that he may
25:22 until its produce **c** in, you
25:25 if his redeeming relative **c** to
Num 1:51 The outsider who **c** near shall
2: 7 Then **c** the tribe of Zebulun,
2:14 Then **c** the tribe of Gad, and
2:20 Next to him **c** the tribe of
2:22 Then **c** the tribe of Benjamin,
2:29 Then **c** the tribe of Naphtali,
3:10 but the outsider who **c** near
5:14 if the spirit of jealousy **c** upon
5:14 or if the spirit of jealousy **c**
5:30 when the spirit of jealousy **c**
11:20 until it **c** out of your nostrils
12:12 is half consumed when he **c** out
17:13 Whoever even **c** near the
18: 7 but the outsider who **c** near
36: 4 of the children of Israel **c**,
Deut 13: 2 and the sign or the wonder **c** to
18: 6 So if a Levite **c** from any of
18: 6 and **c** with all the desire of
18: 8 besides what **c** from the sale of
23:11 it shall be, when evening **c**,
28:57 her placenta which **c** out from
29:22 and the foreigner who **c** from a
31:11 when all Israel **c** to appear
Judg 4:20 and if any man **c** and inquires
5:31 Him be like the sun When it **c**
11:31 it will be that whatever **c** out
13:14 may not eat anything that **c**
1 Sam 4: 3 that when it **c** among us it may
9: 6 all that he says surely **c** to
9:13 people will not eat until he **c**,
16:11 we will not sit down till he **c**
25: 8 Please give whatever **c** to your
2 Sam 13: 5 And when your father **c** to see
15:28 of the wilderness until word **c**
18:27 and **c** with good news."
1 Ki 8:31 and **c** and takes an oath before
8:42 when he **c** and prays toward this
14: 5 when she **c** in, that she will
2 Ki 4:10 whenever he **c** to us, he can
5: 6 when this letter **c** to you, that
6:32 Look, when the messenger **c**,

10: 2 Now as soon as this letter **c** to
11: 8 and whoever **c** within range, let
11: 8 as he goes out and as he **c** in.
12: 9 on the right side as one **c** into
2 Chr 6:22 and **c** and takes an oath before
6:32 but who **c** from a far country
13: 9 so that whoever **c** to consecrate
19:10 Whatever case **c** to you from your
20: 9 If disaster **c** upon us—sword,
23: 7 and whoever **c** into the house,
23: 7 to be with the king when he **c**
Job 3:24 For my sighing **c** before I eat,
3:26 I have no rest, for trouble **c**.
4: 5 But now it **c** upon you, and you
5:13 the counsel of the cunning **c**
5:21 afraid of destruction when it **c**.
14: 2 He **c** forth like a flower and
14:14 I will wait, Till my change **c**.
15:21 In prosperity the destroyer **c**
20:25 and **c** out of the body; Yes,
20:25 the glittering point **c** out of
27: 9 hear his cry When trouble **c**
28: 5 from it **c** bread, But
37: 2 And the rumbling that **c** from
37: 9 the chamber of the south **c**
37:22 He **c** from the north as golden
38:29 From whose womb **c** the ice?
Ps 30: 5 But joy **c** in the morning.
41: 6 And if he **c** to see me, he
62: 1 From Him **c** my salvation.
75: 6 For exaltation **c** neither from
88:13 And in the morning my prayer **c**
118:26 Blessed is he who **c** in the
121: 1 From whence **c** my help?
121: 2 My help **c** from the LORD, Who
Prov 1:26 I will mock when your terror **c**,
1:27 When your terror **c** like a
1:27 And your destruction **c** like a
3:25 from the wicked when it **c**;
11: 2 When pride **c**, then comes shame;
11: 2 then **c** shame; But with the
11: 8 And it **c** to the wicked
13: 5 wicked man is loathsome and **c**
13:10 By pride **c** nothing but strife,
13:12 sick, But when the desire **c**,
14: 4 But much increase **c** by the
18: 3 When the wicked **c**,
18: 3 contempt **c** also; And with
18: 3 And with dishonor **c** reproach.
18:17 Until his neighbor **c** and
29:26 But justice for man **c** from
Eccl 1: 4 away, and another generation **c**;
1: 6 And **c** again on its circuit.
4:14 For he **c** out of prison to be
5: 3 For a dream **c** through much
6: 4 for it **c** in vanity and departs
Song 2: 8 he **c** Leaping upon the
Isa 13: 9 Behold, the day of the LORD **c**,
21: 1 So it **c** from the desert, from
21: 9 here **c** a chariot of men with a
21:12 watchman said, "The morning **c**,
24:18 And he who **c** up from the midst
26:21 the LORD **c** out of His place
28:29 This also **c** from the LORD of
30:13 Whose breaking **c** suddenly, in
30:27 the name of the LORD **c** from
32:19 Though hail **c** down on the
42: 5 the earth and that which **c**
55:10 For as the rain **c** down, and the
59:19 When the enemy **c** in like a
63: 1 Who is this who **c** from Edom,
Jer 6:20 For what purpose to Me **C**
6:22 a people **c** from the north
17: 6 And shall not see when good **c**,
17: 8 And will not fear when heat **c**;
18:14 Which **c** from the rock of the
27: 7 until the time of his land **c**;
28: 9 when the word of the prophet **c**
43:11 'When he **c**, he shall strike
46:20 heifer, But destruction **c**,
46:20 it **c** from the north.
47: 4 Because of the day that **c** to
48:16 And his affliction **c** quickly.
50: 3 out of the north a nation **c** up
51:54 The sound of a cry **c** from
51:56 Because the plunderer **c** against
Lam 1: 4 to Zion mourn Because no one **c**
3:37 is he who speaks and it **c** to
5: 4 And our wood **c** at a price.
Ezek 7:25 Destruction **c**; They will seek
14: 4 and then **c** to the prophet, I
14: 4 the LORD will answer him who **c**,
14: 7 then **c** to a prophet to inquire
21: 7 'Because of the news; when it **c**,
21:27 Until He **c** whose right it is,
24:24 you shall do; and when this **c**,
33: 4 if the sword **c** and takes him
33: 6 and the sword **c** and takes any
33:30 hear what the word is that **c**
33:33 And when this **c** to pass—surely
38:18 when Gog **c** against the land of
47:20 southern boundary until one **c**
Dan 11:16 But he who **c** against him shall
12:12 and **c** to the one thousand three
Hos 7: 1 A thief **c** in; A band of
10:12 Till He **c** and rains
Am 5: 9 So that fury **c** upon the
6: 1 To whom the house of Israel **c**!
Mic 5: 5 When the Assyrian **c** into our
5: 6 When he **c** into our land And
7: 4 watchman and your punishment **c**;
Nah 1:11 From you **c** forth one Who
Hab 1: 8 Their cavalry **c** from afar;
3:16 When he **c** up to the people,
Zeph 2: 2 the LORD's fierce anger **c**
2: 2 the day of the LORD's anger **c**
Zech 10: 4 From him **c** the cornerstone,
Mt 8: 9 to another, 'Come,' and he **c**;
10:23 Israel before the Son of Man **c**.
12:44 which I came.' And when he **c**,
13:19 then the wicked one **c** and
15:11 but what **c** out of the mouth,
17:27 and take the fish that **c** up
18: 7 that man by whom the offense **c**!
21: 9 Blessed is He who **c** in the
21:40 the owner of the vineyard **c**,
23:39 Blessed is He who **c** in the
24:27 For as the lightning **c** from the
24:46 whom his master, when he **c**,
25:31 When the Son of Man **c** in His
28:14 And if this **c** to the governor's
Mk 1: 7 There **c** One after me who is
4:15 Satan **c** immediately and takes
7:20 What **c** out of a man, that
8:38 also will be ashamed when He **c**
11: 9 Blessed is He who **c** in the
11:10 of our father David That **c** in
Lk 6:47 Whoever **c** to Me, and hears My
7: 8 to another, 'Come,' and he **c**;
8:12 then the devil **c** and takes away
9:26 Man will be ashamed when He **c**
11:22 But when a stronger than he **c**
11:25 "And when he **c**, he finds it
12:36 that when he **c** and knocks they
12:37 whom the master, when he **c**,
12:43 will find so doing when he **c**.
13:35 not see Me until the time **c**
13:35 Blessed is He who **c** in the
14:10 that when he who invited you **c**
14:26 If anyone **c** to Me and does not
14:31 ten thousand to meet him who **c**
15: 6 And when he **c** home, he calls
18: 8 when the Son of Man **c**,
19:38 is the King who **c**
22:18 vine until the kingdom of God **c**.
Jn 1:15 He who **c** after me is preferred
1:30 After me **c** a Man who is
3: 8 but cannot tell where it **c** from
3:21 But he who does the truth **c** to
3:31 He who **c** from above is above
3:31 He who **c** from heaven is above
4:25 is called Christ). "When He **c**,
4:35 still four months and then **c**
5:43 if another **c** in his own name,
5:44 do not seek the honor that **c**
6:33 the bread of God is He who **c**
6:35 He who **c** to Me shall never
6:37 and the one who **c** to Me I will
6:45 and learned from the Father **c**
6:50 This is the bread which **c** down
7:27 is from; but when the Christ **c**,
7:31 and said, "When the Christ **c**,
7:42 said that the Christ **c** from
12:13 Blessed is He who **c** in the
13:19 "Now I tell you before it **c**,
14: 6 No one **c** to the Father except
14:29 now I have told you before it **c**,
15:26 "But when the Helper **c**,
16: 4 told you, that when the time **c**,
Acts 3:16 the faith which **c** through Him
10:32 a tanner, by the sea. When he **c**,
13:25 there **c** One after me, the
23:15 ready to kill him before he **c**
24:22 When Lysias the commander **c**
Rom 10:17 So then faith **c** by hearing, and
1 Cor 4: 5 the time, until the Lord **c**,
11:12 even so man also **c** through
11:26 the Lord's death till He **c**.
14:23 if the whole church **c** together
14:24 or an uninformed person **c** in,
15:24 Then **c** the end, when He
16:10 Now if Timothy **c**,
2 Cor 11: 4 For if he who **c** preaches another
11:28 what **c** upon me daily: my deep
Gal 2:21 for if righteousness **c** through
Eph 5: 6 things the wrath of God **c** upon
Col 4:10 if he **c** to you, welcome him),
1 Th 5: 2 that the day of the Lord so **c**
5: 3 then sudden destruction **c** upon
2 Th 1:10 when He **c**, in that Day,
2: 3 come unless the falling away **c**
Heb 6: 7 in the rain that often **c** upon
11: 6 for he who **c** to God must
13:23 whom I shall see you if he **c**
Jas 1:17 and **c** down from the Father of
2 Jn 10 If anyone **c** to you and does not
Jude 14 the Lord **c** with ten thousands
Rev 3:12 which **c** down out of heaven from
17:10 has not yet come. And when he **c**,

COMFORT (59/55) COMFORTED, COMFORTER, COMFORTING, COMFORTS

Gen 5:29 This one will **c** us concerning
37:35 all his daughters arose to **c**
2 Sam 10: 2 the hand of his servants to **c**
19: 7 go out and speak **c** to your
1 Chr 7:22 and his brethren came to **c** him.
19: 2 So David sent messengers to **c**
19: 2 of the people of Ammon to **c**
Job 2:11 mourn with him, and to **c** him.
6:10 Then I would still have **c**;
7:13 My bed will **c** me, My couch will
10:20 that I may take a little **c**,
16: 5 And the **c** of my lips would
21:34 How then can you **c** me with
Ps 23: 4 rod and Your staff, they **c** me.
71:21 And **c** me on every side.
119:50 This is my **c** in my affliction,
119:76 merciful kindness be for my **c**,
119:82 When will You **c** me?"
132: 3 Or go up to the **c** of my bed;
Isa 12: 1 is turned away, and You **c** me.
22: 4 Do not labor to **c** me Because
40: 1 '**C**, yes, comfort My
40: 1 **c** My people!" Says your God.
40: 2 Speak **c** to Jerusalem, and cry
51: 3 For the LORD will **c** Zion, He
51: 3 He will **c** all her waste
51:19 By whom will I **c** you?
57: 6 Should I receive **c** in these?
61: 2 To **c** all who mourn,
66:13 So I will **c** you; And you
Jer 8:18 I would **c** myself in sorrow;
16: 7 to **c** them for the dead;
31:13 Will **c** them, And make them
Lam 1: 2 her lovers She has none to **c**
2:13 that I may **c** you, O virgin
Ezek 14:23 And they will **c** you, when you
Hos 2:14 And speak **c** to her.
Zech 1:17 The LORD will again **c** Zion,
10: 2 They **c** in vain.
Jn 11:19 to **c** them concerning their
Acts 9:31 fear of the Lord and in the **c**
Rom 15: 4 we through the patience and **c**
15: 5 may the God of patience and **c**
1 Cor 14: 3 and exhortation and **c** to men.
2 Cor 1: 3 of mercies and God of all **c**,
1: 4 that we may be able to **c** those
1: 4 with the **c** with which we
2: 7 ought rather to forgive and **c**
7: 4 your behalf. I am filled with **c**.
7:13 have been comforted in your **c**.
13:11 Become complete. Be of good **c**,
Eph 6:22 and that he may **c** your hearts.
Phil 2: 1 if any **c** of love, if any
Col 4: 8 know your circumstances and **c**
4:11 they have proved to be a **c** to
1 Th 4:18 Therefore **c** one another with
5:11 Therefore **c** each other and edify
5:14 **c** the fainthearted, uphold the
2 Th 2:17 **c** your hearts and establish you

COMFORTED (31/31) COMFORT

Gen 24:67 So Isaac was **c** after his
37:35 but he refused to be **c**,
38:12 wife, died; and Judah was **c**,
50:21 And he **c** them and spoke
Ruth 2:13 for you have **c** me, and have
2 Sam 12:24 Then David **c** Bathsheba his
13:39 For he had been **c** concerning
Job 42:11 and they consoled him and **c** him
Ps 77: 2 My soul refused to be **c**.
86:17 have helped me and **c** me.
119:52 And have **c** myself.
Isa 49:13 For the LORD has **c** His
52: 9 For the LORD has **c** His
54:11 with tempest, and not **c**,
66:13 And you shall be **c** in
Jer 31:15 Refusing to be **c** for her
Ezek 14:22 Then you will be **c** concerning
16:54 by all that you did when you **c**
31:16 were **c** in the depths of the
32:31 will see them And be **c** over
Mt 2:18 Refusing to be **c**,
5: 4 who mourn, For they shall be **c**.
Lk 16:25 but now he is **c** and you are
Acts 20:12 and they were not a little **c**.
2 Cor 1: 4 with which we ourselves are **c**
1: 6 we also suffer. Or if we are **c**,
7: 6 **c** us by the coming of Titus,
7: 7 with which he was **c** in you,
7:13 Therefore we have been **c** in
1 Th 2:11 you know how we exhorted, and **c**,
3: 7 and distress we were **c**

COMFORTER (4/3) COMFORT, COMFORTERS

Eccl 4: 1 oppressed, But they have no **c**—
4: 1 is power, But they have no **c**.
Lam 1: 9 was awesome; She had no **c**.
1:16 with water; Because the **c**,

COMFORTERS (5/5) COMFORTER

2 Sam 10: 3 father because he has sent **c**
1 Chr 19: 3 father because he has sent **c**
Job 16: 2 Miserable **c** are you all!
Ps 69:20 there was none; And for **c**,
Nah 3: 7 Where shall I seek **c** for

COMFORTING (3/3) COMFORT

2 Sam 14:17 my lord the king will now be **c**;
Zech 1:13 with good and **c** words.
Jn 11:31 and **c** her, when they saw that

COMFORTS (10/10) COMFORT

Gen 27:42 Surely your brother Esau **c**
Job 29:25 As one who **c** mourners.
Ps 94:19 Your **c** delight my soul.
Isa 51:12 I, even I, am He who **c** you.

57:18 And restore **c** to him And to
66:13 As one whom his mother **c**,
Lam 1:17 But no one **c** her; The LORD
1:21 But no one **c** me. All my
2 Cor 1: 4 who **c** us in all our tribulation,
7: 6 who **c** the downcast, comforted

COMING (260/254)

Gen 24:13 of the men of the city are **c**
24:45 **c** out with her pitcher on her
24:63 and there, the camels were **c**.
29: 6 his daughter Rachel is **c** with
30:30 has blessed you since my **c**.
32: 6 and he also is **c** to meet you,
33: 1 looked, and there, Esau was **c**,
37:19 this dreamer is **c**!
37:25 **c** from Gilead with their
41:35 of those good years that are **c**,
43:25 present ready for Joseph's **c**
48: 2 your son Joseph is **c** to you";
Ex 4:14 he is also **c** out to meet you.
18: 6 am **c** to you with your wife and
32: 1 saw that Moses delayed **c** down
37:19 and so for the six branches **c**
Num 21: 1 heard that Israel was **c** on the
22:16 let nothing hinder you from **c**
22:36 Balak heard that Balaam was **c**,
33:40 heard of the **c** of the children
Deut 25:17 to you on the way as you were **c**
29:22 so that the **c** generation of your
Josh 14:11 both for going out and for **c**
Judg 1:24 And when the spies saw a man **c**
5:28 is his chariot so long in **c**?
6: 5 **c** in as numerous as locusts;
9:36 people are **c** down from the tops
9:37 people are **c** down from the
9:37 and another company is **c** from
9:43 **c** out of the city; and he rose
11:34 **c** out to meet him with timbrels
19: 9 the day is **c** to an end; lodge
Ruth 4:11 LORD make the woman who is **c**
1 Sam 2:31 the days are **c** that I will cut
9:14 As they were **c** into the city,
9:14 **c** out toward them on his way up
10: 5 will meet a group of prophets **c**
11: 5 **c** behind the herd from the
14:11 the Hebrews are **c** out of the
16: 4 of the town trembled at his **c**,
17:23 **c** up from the armies of the
18: 6 it had happened as they were **c**
25:19 I am **c** after you." But she did
25:20 **c** down toward her, and she met
25:26 LORD has held you back from **c**
25:33 have kept me this day from **c**
28:14 An old man is **c** up, and he is
29: 6 and your going out and your **c**
29: 6 in you since the day of your **c**
2 Sam 3:25 know your going out and your **c**
13:34 many people were **c** from the
13:35 "Look, the king's sons are **c**;
15:32 was Hushai the Archite **c**
16: 5 **c** from there. He came out,
17:17 for they dared not be seen **c**
24:20 saw the king and his servants **c**
1 Ki 14: 5 **c** to ask you something about
20:17 Men are **c** out of Samaria!"
2 Ki 4: 1 And the creditor is **c** to take
6: 9 for the Syrians are **c** down
6:33 **c** down to him; and then the
9:18 but is not **c** back."
9:20 went up to them and is not **c**
10:15 **c** to meet him; and he greeted
19:27 Your going out and your **c** in,
20:17 the days are **c** when all that
1 Chr 16:33 For He is **c** to judge the
24:19 of their service for **c** into
2 Chr 20: 2 A great multitude is **c** against
20:11 rewarding us by **c** to throw us
20:12 this great multitude that is **c**
Ezra 3: 8 of the second year of their **c**
Neh 6:10 for they are **c** to kill you;
Ps 19: 5 Which is like a bridegroom **c**
37:13 For He sees that his day is **c**.
96:13 For He is **c**, for He is coming
96:13 for He is **c** to judge the earth.
98: 9 For He is **c** to judge the earth.
121: 8 your going out and your **c** in
Eccl 11: 8 All that is **c** is vanity.
Song 3: 6 Who is this **c** out of the
8: 5 Who is this **c** up from the
Isa 14: 9 you, To meet you at your **c**;
37:28 Your going out and your **c** in,
39: 6 the days are **c** when all that
44: 7 And the things that are **c** and
62:11 'Surely your salvation is **c**;
Jer 7:32 behold, the days are **c**,
8: 7 Observe the time of their **c**.
9:25 "Behold, the days are **c**,
16:14 behold, the days are **c**,
19: 6 behold, the days are **c**,
23: 5 "Behold, the days are **c**,
23: 7 behold, the days are **c**,
30: 3 'For behold, the days are **c**,
31:27 "Behold, the days are **c**,
31:31 "Behold, the days are **c**,
31:38 "Behold, the days are **c**,
33:14 'Behold, the days are **c**,
37: 4 Now Jeremiah was **c** and going
46: 7 Who is this **c** up like a flood,
48:12 behold, the days are **c**,
49: 2 behold, the days are **c**,
51:47 the days are **c** That I will
51:52 behold, the days are **c**,
Ezek 1: 4 a whirlwind was **c** out of the
21: 7 it is **c** and shall be brought to
30: 9 For indeed it is **c**!"
33: 3 when he sees the sword **c** upon
33: 6 the watchman sees the sword **c**
38: 9 **c** like a storm, covering the
39: 8 "Surely it is **c**,
44:25 not defile themselves by **c**
Dan 4:13 **c** down from heaven.
4:23 **c** down from heaven and saying,
7: 8 **c** up among them, before whom
7:13 ***C*** with the clouds of heaven!
Joel 2: 1 For the day of the LORD is **c**,
2:31 Before the **c** of the great and
Am 8:11 "Behold, the days are **c**,
9:13 "Behold, the days are **c**,
Mic 1: 3 the LORD is **c** out of His
Zech 1:21 'What are these **c** to do?"
1:21 but the craftsmen are **c** to
2: 3 and another angel was **c** out to
2:10 I am **c** and I will dwell in your
5: 9 **c** with the wind in their wings;
6: 1 four chariots were **c** from
9: 9 your King is **c** to you; He is
14: 1 the day of the LORD is **c**,
Mal 3: 1 you delight. Behold, He is **c**,
3: 2 who can endure the day of His **c**?
4: 1 "For behold, the day is **c**,
4: 1 And the day which is **c** shall
4: 5 the prophet Before the **c** of
Mt 3: 7 the Pharisees and Sadducees **c**
3:11 but He who is **c** after me is
3:14 and are You **c** to me?"
8:28 **c** out of the tombs, exceedingly
11: 3 Are You the ***C*** One, or do we look
16:28 till they see the Son of Man **c**
17:11 Elijah is **c** first and will
21: 5 your King is **c** to you,
24: 3 will be the sign of Your **c**,
24:27 so also will the **c** of the Son
24:30 they will see the Son of Man **c**
24:37 so also will the **c** of the Son
24:39 so also will the **c** of the Son
24:42 know what hour your Lord is **c**.
24:44 for the Son of Man is **c** at an
24:48 'My master is delaying his **c**,
25: 6 'Behold, the bridegroom is **c**;
25:13 in which the Son of Man is **c**.
25:27 and at my **c** I would have
26:64 and **c** on the clouds of
27:53 and **c** out of the graves after
Mk 1:10 **c** up from the water, He saw the
6:31 For there were many **c** and
9:12 Elijah is **c** first and restores
13:26 they will see the Son of Man **c**
13:35 the master of the house is **c**—
13:36 **c** suddenly, he find you
14:62 and **c** with the clouds of
15:21 as he was **c** out of the country
15:43 **c** and taking courage, went in
Lk 2:38 And **c** in that instant she gave
3:16 but One mightier than I is **c**,
7:19 Are You the ***C*** One, or do we look
7:20 Are You the ***C*** One, or do we look
9:42 And as he was still **c**,
12:40 for the Son of Man is **c** at an
12:45 'My master is delaying his **c**,
12:54 you say, 'A shower is **c**';
18: 5 lest by her continual **c** she
18:35 as He was **c** near Jericho, that
19:23 that at my **c** I might have
21:26 of those things which are **c** on
21:27 they will see the Son of Man **c**
22:39 ***C*** out, He went to the Mount of
23:26 who was **c** from the country, and
23:29 For indeed the days are **c** in
23:36 **c** and offering Him sour wine,
Jn 1: 9 gives light to every man **c**
1:27 **c** after me, is preferred before
1:29 The next day John saw Jesus **c**
1:47 Jesus saw Nathanael **c** toward
3:26 and all are **c** to Him!"
4:21 the hour is **c** when you will
4:23 "But the hour is **c**,
4:25 'I know that Messiah is **c**"
5: 7 is stirred up; but while I am **c**,
5:25 I say to you, the hour is **c**,
5:28 for the hour is **c** in which all
6: 5 and seeing a great multitude **c**
9: 4 the night is **c** when no one can
10:12 sees the wolf **c** and leaves the
11:20 as she heard that Jesus was **c**,
12:12 they heard that Jesus was **c** to
12:15 Behold, your King is **c**,
14:28 I am going away and **c** back to
14:30 the ruler of this world is **c**,
16: 2 the time is **c** that whoever
16:25 but the time is **c** when I will
16:32 "Indeed the hour is **c**,
Acts 2:20 Before the **c** of the
7:52 those who foretold the **c** of
9:12 has seen a man named Ananias **c**
9:28 **c** in and going out.
9:38 him not to delay in **c** to them.
10: 3 in a vision an angel of God **c**
10:25 As Peter was **c** in, Cornelius met
13:24 first preached, before His **c**,
18:21 must by all means keep this **c**
23:27 ***C*** with the troops I rescued
Rom 15:22 have been much hindered from **c**
1 Cor 2: 6 who are **c** to nothing.
4:18 as though I were not **c** to you.
15:23 who are Christ's at His **c**.
16:17 I am glad about the **c** of
2 Cor 7: 6 comforted us by the **c** of Titus,
7: 7 and not only by his **c**,
13: 1 be the third time I am **c** to
Phil 1:26 in Jesus Christ by my **c** to you
2: 7 and **c** in the likeness of men.
Col 3: 6 things the wrath of God is **c**
1 Th 2: 1 that our **c** to you was not in
2:19 our Lord Jesus Christ at His **c**?
3:13 our God and Father at the **c** of
4:15 alive and remain until the **c**
5:23 be preserved blameless at the **c**
2 Th 2: 1 concerning the **c** of our Lord
2: 8 with the brightness of His **c**.
2: 9 The **c** of the lawless one is
Heb 8: 8 "Behold, the days are **c**,
10:37 And He who is **c** will
Jas 5: 1 for your miseries that are **c**
5: 7 until the **c** of the Lord.
5: 8 for the **c** of the Lord is at
1 Pe 2: 4 ***C*** to Him as to a living
2 Pe 1:16 known to you the power and **c**
3: 4 "Where is the promise of His **c**?
3:12 for and hastening the **c** of the
1 Jn 2:18 heard that the Antichrist is **c**,
2:28 be ashamed before Him at His **c**.
4: 3 which you have heard was **c**,
2 Jn 7 not confess Jesus Christ as **c**
Rev 1: 7 He is **c** with clouds, and every
3:11 I am **c** quickly! Hold fast what
9:12 still two more woes are **c** after
10: 1 still another mighty angel **c**
11:14 the third woe is **c** quickly.
13:11 Then I saw another beast **c** up
16:13 unclean spirits like frogs **c**
16:15 I am **c** as a thief. Blessed is
18: 1 things I saw another angel **c**
20: 1 Then I saw an angel **c** down from
21: 2 **c** down out of heaven from God,
22: 7 I am **c** quickly! Blessed is he
22:12 I am **c** quickly, and My reward
22:20 Surely I am **c** quickly." Amen.

COMMAND (202/195) COMMANDED, COMMANDER, COMMANDING, COMMANDMENT, COMMANDS

Gen 18:19 in order that he may **c** his
27: 8 my voice according to what I **c**
42:25 Then Joseph gave a **c** to fill
45:21 according to the **c** of Pharaoh,
Ex 6:13 and gave them a **c** for the
7: 2 You shall speak all that I **c**
8:27 the LORD our God as He will **c**
27:20 And you shall **c** the children of
34:11 Observe what I **c** you this day.
Lev 6: 9 ***C*** Aaron and his sons, saying,
13:54 then the priest shall **c** that
14: 4 then the priest shall **c** to take
14: 5 And the priest shall **c** that one
14:36 then the priest shall **c** that
14:40 then the priest shall **c** that
24: 2 ***C*** the children of Israel that
25:21 Then I will **c** My blessing on you
Num 5: 2 ***C*** the children of Israel that
9: 8 may hear what the LORD will **c**
9:18 At the **c** of the LORD the
9:18 and at the **c** of the LORD they
9:20 according to the **c** of the LORD
9:20 and according to the **c** of the
9:23 At the **c** of the LORD they
9:23 and at the **c** of the LORD they
9:23 at the **c** of the LORD by the
10:13 first time according to the **c**
13: 3 of Paran according to the **c** of
14:41 why do you transgress the **c** of
23:20 I have received a **c** to bless;
27:14 you rebelled against My **c** to
28: 2 ***C*** the children of Israel, and
31:49 men of war who are under our **c**,
32:28 So Moses gave **c** concerning them
33: 2 of their journeys at the **c** of
33:38 went up to Mount Hor at the **c**
34: 2 ***C*** the children of Israel, and
35: 2 ***C*** the children of Israel that
Deut 1:26 but rebelled against the **c** of
1:43 but rebelled against the **c** of
2: 4 And **c** the people, saying, "You
3:28 But **c** Joshua, and encourage him
4: 2 not add to the word which I **c**
4: 2 of the LORD your God which I **c**
4:40 and His commandments which I **c**
6: 2 and His commandments which I **c**
6: 6 And these words which I **c** you
7:11 and the judgments which I **c** you
8: 1 Every commandment which I **c** you
8:11 and His statutes which I **c** you
10:13 and His statutes which I **c** you
11: 8 every commandment which I **c**
11:13 obey My commandments which I **c**
11:22 these commandments which I **c**
11:27 of the LORD your God which I **c**
11:28 aside from the way which I **c**
12:11 you shall bring all that I **c**
12:14 you shall do all that I **c** you.
12:28 obey all these words which I **c**

12:32 Whatever I **c** you, be careful to
13:18 all His commandments which I **c**
15: 5 these commandments which I **c**
15:11 therefore I **c** you, saying, 'You
15:15 therefore I **c** you this thing
18:18 speak to them all that I **c** Him.
19: 7 Therefore I **c** you, saying, 'You
19: 9 which I **c** you today, to love
24:18 therefore I **c** you to do this
24:22 therefore I **c** you to do this
27: 1 all the commandments which I **c**
27: 4 which I **c** you today, and you
27:10 and His statutes which I **c** you
28: 1 all His commandments which I **c**
28: 8 The LORD will **c** the blessing on
28:13 which I **c** you today, and are
28:14 any of the words which I **c** you
28:15 and His statutes which I **c** you
30: 2 according to all that I **c** you
30: 8 all His commandments which I **c**
30:11 this commandment which I **c** you
30:16 in that I **c** you today to love
32:46 which you shall **c** your children
Josh 1:11 Pass through the camp and **c** the
1:16 All that you **c** us we will do,
1:18 Whoever rebels against your **c**
1:18 in all that you **c** him, shall be
3: 8 You shall **c** the priests who bear
4: 3 and **c** them, saying, 'Take for
4:16 **C** the priests who bear the ark
Judg 4:10 ten thousand men under his **c**,
5:15 into the valley under his **c**;
1 Sam 16:16 Let our master now **c** your
2 Sam 10:10 the people he put under the **c**
13:32 For by the **c** of Absalom this
1 Ki 5: 6 **c** that they cut down cedars for
11:38 if you heed all that I **c** you,
20:12 kings were drinking at the **c**
20:16 him were getting drunk at the **c**
2 Ki 23:35 give money according to the **c**
1 Chr 12:32 their brethren were at their **c**;
19:11 the people he put under the **c**
28:21 will be completely at your **c**.
2 Chr 7:13 or **c** the locusts to devour the
8:15 They did not depart from the **c**
13:11 for we keep the **c** of the LORD
24: 8 Then at the king's **c** they made
24:21 and at the **c** of the king they
30: 6 and spoke according to the **c** of
30:12 of heart to obey the **c** of the
35:10 according to the king's **c**.
35:15 according to the **c** of David,
35:16 according to the **c** of King
Ezra 4:19 And I gave the **c**,
4:21 Now give the **c** to make these men
4:21 may not be built until the **c**
6:14 and according to the **c** of
8:17 And I gave them a **c** for Iddo the
Neh 11:23 For it was the king's **c**
12:24 according to the **c** of David the
12:45 according to the **c** of David
Esth 1:12 refused to come at the king's **c**
1:15 because she did not obey the **c**
2: 8 when the king's **c** and decree
2:20 for Esther obeyed the **c** of
3: 3 do you transgress the king's **c**?
3:15 out, hastened by the king's **c**;
4: 3 province where the king's **c**
4: 5 and she gave him a **c** concerning
4: 8 and that he might **c** her to go
4:10 and gave him a **c** for Mordecai:
8:14 and pressed on by the king's **c**.
8:17 wherever the king's **c** and
9: 1 time came for the king's **c**
Job 39:27 the eagle mount up at your **c**,
Ps 42: 8 The LORD will **c** His
44: 4 **C** victories for Jacob.
147:15 He sends out His **c** to the
Prov 6:20 My son, keep your father's **c**,
8:29 would not transgress His **c**,
Eccl 8: 5 He who keeps his **c** will
Isa 5: 6 I will also **c** the clouds That
45:11 work of My hands, you **c** Me.
Jer 1: 7 And whatever I **c** you, you
1:17 speak to them all that I **c** you.
7:22 or **c** them in the day that I
7:31 in the fire, which I did not **c**,
11: 4 do according to all that I **c**
19: 5 which I did not **c** or speak, nor
23:32 Yet I did not send them or **c**
26: 2 all the words that I **c** you to
27: 4 And **c** them to say to their
32:35 which I did not **c** them, nor did
34:22 I will **c**,' says the LORD,
Dan 2: 2 Then the king gave the **c** to call
2:12 and gave a **c** to destroy all the
3:13 gave the **c** to bring Shadrach,
3:22 because the king's **c** was
4:26 inasmuch as they gave the **c** to
5: 2 Belshazzar gave the **c** to bring
5:29 Then Belshazzar gave the **c**,
6:16 So the king gave the **c**,
6:24 And the king gave the **c**,
9:23 of your supplications the **c**
9:25 from the going forth of the **c**
Am 6:11 behold, the LORD gives a **c**:
9: 3 From there I will **c** the
9: 4 From there I will **c** the sword,
9: 9 "For surely I will **c**,
Nah 1:14 The LORD has given a **c**
Zech 3: 7 And if you will keep My **c**,
Mt 4: 3 **c** that these stones become
8:18 He gave a **c** to depart to the
14:28 **c** me to come to You on the
19: 7 Why then did Moses **c** to give a
27:64 Therefore **c** that the tomb be
Mk 9:25 I **c** you, come out of him and
10: 3 What did Moses **c** you?"
Lk 4: 3 **c** this stone to become bread."
8:31 begged Him that He would not **c**
9:54 do You want us to **c** fire to
Jn 10:18 This **c** I have received from My
11:57 and the Pharisees had given a **c**,
12:49 Father who sent Me gave Me a **c**,
12:50 And I know that His **c** is
15:14 friends if you do whatever I **c**
15:17 These things I **c** you, that you
Acts 5:28 Did we not strictly **c** you not to
15: 5 and to **c** them to keep the law
16:18 I **c** you in the name of Jesus
17:15 and receiving a **c** for Silas and
23: 3 and do you **c** me to be struck
25:23 at Festus' **c** Paul was brought
1 Cor 7:10 Now to the married I **c**,
2 Th 3: 4 do and will do the things we **c**
3: 6 But we **c** you, brethren, in the
3:12 Now those who are such we **c** and
1 Tim 4:11 These things **c** and teach.
5: 7 And these things **c**,
6:17 **C** those who are rich in this
Phm 1: 8 be very bold in Christ to **c**
Heb 11:23 were not afraid of the king's **c**.
Rev 3:10 Because you have kept My **c** to

COMMANDED (450/437) COMMAND

Gen 2:16 And the LORD God **c** the man,
3:11 from the tree of which I **c** you
3:17 from the tree of which I **c** you,
6:22 according to all that God **c**
7: 5 to all that the LORD **c** him.
7: 9 as God had **c** Noah.
7:16 went in as God had **c** him; and
12:20 So Pharaoh **c** his men concerning
21: 4 as God had **c** him.
32: 4 And he **c** them, saying, "Speak
32:17 And he **c** the first one, saying,
32:19 So he **c** the second, the third,
44: 1 And he **c** the steward of his
45:19 'Now you are **c**—do this:
47:11 of Rameses, as Pharaoh had **c**.
50: 2 And Joseph **c** his servants the
50:12 did for him just as he had **c**
50:16 "Before your father died he **c**,
Ex 1:17 not do as the king of Egypt **c**
1:22 So Pharaoh **c** all his people,
4:28 all the signs which He had **c**
5: 6 So the same day Pharaoh **c** the
7: 6 just as the LORD **c** them, so
7:10 did so, just as the LORD **c**.
7:20 did so, just as the LORD **c**.
12:28 just as the LORD had **c** Moses
12:50 as the LORD **c** Moses and Aaron,
16:16 the thing which the LORD has **c**:
16:24 it up till morning, as Moses **c**;
16:32 the thing which the LORD has **c**:
16:34 As the LORD **c** Moses, so Aaron
19: 7 these words which the LORD **c**
23:15 as I **c** you, at the time
29:35 according to all that I have **c**
31: 6 may make all that I have **c** you:
31:11 According to all that I have **c**
32: 8 out of the way which I **c** them.
34: 4 as the LORD had **c** him; and he
34:18 as I **c** you, in the appointed
34:34 Israel whatever he had been **c**.
35: 1 the words which the LORD has **c**
35: 4 is the thing which the LORD **c**,
35:10 make all that the LORD has **c**:
35:29 of Moses, had **c** to be done.
36: 1 to all that the LORD has **c**.
36: 5 of the work which the LORD **c**
38:22 made all that the LORD had **c**
39: 1 as the LORD had **c** Moses.
39: 5 as the LORD had **c** Moses.
39: 7 as the LORD had **c** Moses.
39:21 as the LORD had **c** Moses.
39:26 as the LORD had **c** Moses.
39:29 as the LORD had **c** Moses.
39:31 as the LORD had **c** Moses.
39:32 to all that the LORD had **c**
39:42 to all that the LORD had **c**
39:43 had done it; as the LORD had **c**,
40:16 to all that the LORD had **c**
40:19 as the LORD had **c** Moses.
40:21 as the LORD had **c** Moses.
40:23 as the LORD had **c** Moses.
40:25 as the LORD had **c** Moses.
40:27 as the LORD had **c** Moses.
40:29 as the LORD had **c** Moses.
40:32 as the LORD had **c** Moses.
Lev 7:36 The LORD **c** this to be given to
7:38 which the LORD **c** Moses on Mount
7:38 on the day when He **c** the
8: 4 So Moses did as the LORD **c** him.
8: 5 This is what the LORD **c** to be
8: 9 as the LORD had **c** Moses.
8:13 as the LORD had **c** Moses.
8:17 as the LORD had **c** Moses.
8:21 as the LORD had **c** Moses.
8:29 as the LORD had **c** Moses.
8:31 consecration offerings, as I **c**,
8:34 so the LORD has **c** to do, to
8:35 not die; for so I have been **c**.
8:36 things that the LORD had **c** by
9: 5 So they brought what Moses **c**
9: 6 is the thing which the LORD **c**
9: 7 for them, as the LORD **c**.
9:10 as the LORD had **c** Moses.
9:21 the LORD, as Moses had **c**.
10: 1 which He had not **c** them.
10:13 the LORD; for so I have been **c**.
10:15 forever, as the LORD has **c**.
10:18 it in a holy place, as I **c**.
16:34 And he did as the LORD **c**
17: 2 the thing which the LORD has **c**,
24:23 of Israel did as the LORD **c**
27:34 commandments which the LORD **c**
Num 1:19 As the LORD **c** Moses, so he
1:54 to all that the LORD **c** Moses,
2:33 just as the LORD **c** Moses.
2:34 to all that the LORD **c** Moses;
3:16 word of the LORD, as he was **c**.
3:42 as the LORD **c** him.
3:51 as the LORD **c** Moses.
4:49 as the LORD **c** Moses.
8: 3 as the LORD **c** Moses.
8:20 to all that the LORD **c** Moses
8:22 as the LORD **c** Moses concerning
9: 5 to all that the LORD **c** Moses,
15:23 all that the LORD has **c** you by
15:36 as the LORD **c** Moses, all the
16:47 Then Aaron took it as Moses **c**,
17:11 just as the LORD had **c** him, so
19: 2 the law which the LORD has **c**,
20: 9 from before the LORD as He **c**
20:27 Moses did just as the LORD **c**,
26: 4 just as the LORD **c** Moses and
27:11 just as the LORD **c** Moses.
27:22 So Moses did as the LORD **c** him.
27:23 just as the LORD **c** by the hand
29:40 just as the LORD **c** Moses.
30: 1 the thing which the LORD has **c**:
30:16 the statutes which the LORD **c**
31: 7 just as the LORD **c** Moses, and
31:21 of the law which the LORD **c**
31:31 the priest did as the LORD **c**
31:41 as the LORD **c** Moses.
31:47 as the LORD **c** Moses.
34:13 Then Moses **c** the children of
34:13 which the LORD has **c** to give
34:29 are the ones the LORD **c** to
36: 2 The LORD **c** my lord Moses to
36: 2 and my lord was **c** by the LORD
36: 5 Then Moses **c** the children of
36:10 Just as the LORD **c** Moses, so
36:13 the judgments which the LORD **c**
Deut 1:16 Then I **c** your judges at that
1:18 And I **c** you at that time all the
1:19 as the LORD our God had **c** us.
1:41 just as the LORD our God **c**
3:18 Then I **c** you at that time,
3:21 And I **c** Joshua at that time,
4: 5 just as the LORD my God **c** me,
4:13 to you His covenant which He **c**
4:14 And the LORD **c** me at that time
5:12 as the LORD your God **c** you.
5:15 therefore the LORD your God **c**
5:16 as the LORD your God has **c**
5:32 do as the LORD your God has **c**
5:33 which the LORD your God has **c**
6: 1 which the LORD your God has **c**
6:17 and His statutes which He has **c**
6:20 which the LORD our God has **c**
6:24 And the LORD **c** us to observe
6:25 as He has **c** us.'
9:12 aside from the way which I **c**
9:16 the way which the LORD had **c**
10: 5 just as the LORD **c** me."
12:21 just as I have **c** you, and you
13: 5 in which the LORD your God **c**
17: 3 of heaven, which I have not **c**,
18:20 which I have not **c** him to
20:17 as the LORD your God has **c**
24: 8 just as I **c** them, so you shall
26:13 commandments which You have **c**
26:14 to all that You have **c** me.
27: 1 **c** the people, saying: "Keep
27:11 And Moses **c** the people on the
28:45 and His statutes which He **c**
29: 1 the covenant which the LORD **c**
31: 5 commandment which I have **c** you.
31:10 And Moses **c** them, saying: "At
31:25 that Moses **c** the Levites, who
31:29 from the way which I have **c**
33: 4 Moses **c** a law for us, A
34: 9 and did as the LORD had **c**
Josh 1: 7 law which Moses My servant **c**
1: 9 Have I not **c** you? Be strong and
1:10 Then Joshua **c** the officers of
1:13 the servant of the LORD **c** you,
3: 3 and they **c** the people, saying,
4: 8 Israel did so, just as Joshua **c**,
4:10 finished that the LORD had **c**
4:10 to all that Moses had **c** Joshua;
4:17 Joshua therefore **c** the priests,
6:10 Now Joshua had **c** the people,
7:11 My covenant which I **c** them.
8: 4 And he **c** them, saying: "Behold,
8: 8 See, I have **c** you."
8:27 of the LORD which He had **c**
8:29 Joshua **c** that they should take
8:31 the servant of the LORD had **c**
8:33 the servant of the LORD had **c**
8:35 a word of all that Moses had **c**
9:24 told that the LORD your God **c**

10:27 down of the sun that Joshua **c**,
10:40 the LORD God of Israel had **c**.
11:12 the servant of the LORD had **c**.
11:15 As the LORD had **c** Moses his
11:15 so Moses **c** Joshua, and so
11:15 of all that the LORD had **c**
11:20 as the LORD had **c** Moses.
13: 6 as I have **c** you.
14: 2 as the LORD had **c** by the hand
14: 5 As the LORD had **c** Moses, so the
17: 4 The LORD **c** Moses to give us an
21: 2 The LORD **c** through Moses to
21: 8 as the LORD had **c** by the hand
22: 2 the servant of the LORD **c** you,
22: 2 my voice in all that I **c** you.
22: 5 the servant of the LORD **c** you,
23:16 which He **c** you, and have gone
Judg 2:20 My covenant which I **c** their
3: 4 which He had **c** their fathers by
4: 6 not the LORD God of Israel **c**,
13:14 All that I **c** her let her
21:10 and **c** them, saying, "Go and
Ruth 2: 9 Have I not **c** the young men not
2:15 Boaz **c** his young men, saying,
1 Sam 2:29 and My offering which I have **c**
13:13 which He **c** you. For now the
13:14 and the LORD has **c** him to be
13:14 have not kept what the LORD **c**
17:20 and went as Jesse had **c** him.
18:22 And Saul **c** his servants,
20:29 and my brother has **c** me to be
21: 2 or what I have **c** you.'
2 Sam 4:12 So David **c** his young men, and
5:25 as the LORD **c** him; and he
7: 7 whom I **c** to shepherd My people
7:11 since the time that I **c** judges
9:11 all that my lord the king has **c**
13:28 Now Absalom had **c** his servants,
13:28 Have I not **c** you? Be courageous
13:29 did to Amnon as Absalom had **c**.
14:19 For your servant Joab **c** me, and
18: 5 Now the king had **c** Joab,
18:12 For in our hearing the king **c**
21:14 performed all that the king **c**.
24:19 of Gad, went up as the LORD **c**.
1 Ki 2:46 So the king **c** Benaiah the son of
5:17 And the king **c** them to quarry
8:58 which He **c** our fathers.
9: 4 according to all that I have **c**
11:10 and had **c** him concerning this
11:10 not keep what the LORD had **c**.
11:11 which I have **c** you, I will
13: 9 For so it was **c** me by the word
13:21 which the LORD your God **c** you,
15: 5 aside from anything that He **c**
17: 4 and I have **c** the ravens to feed
17: 9 I have **c** a widow there to
22:31 Now the king of Syria had **c** the
2 Ki 11: 5 Then he **c** them, saying, "This
11: 9 all that Jehoiada the priest **c**.
11:15 And Jehoiada the priest **c** the
14: 6 of Moses, in which the LORD **c**,
16:15 Then King Ahaz **c** Urijah the
16:16 to all that King Ahaz **c**.
17:13 to all the law which I **c** your
17:27 Then the king of Assyria **c**,
17:34 which the LORD had **c** the
18: 6 which the LORD had **c** Moses.
18:12 the servant of the LORD had **c**;
21: 8 according to all that I have **c**
21: 8 the law that My servant Moses **c**
22:12 Then the king **c** Hilkiah the
23: 4 And the king **c** Hilkiah the high
23:21 Then the king **c** all the people,
1 Chr 6:49 Moses the servant of God had **c**.
14:16 So David did as God **c** him, and
15:15 as Moses had **c** according to the
16:15 forever, The word which He **c**,
16:40 the Law of the LORD which He **c**
17: 6 whom I **c** to shepherd My people,
17:10 since the time that I **c** judges
21:17 Was it not I who **c** the people to
21:18 the angel of the LORD **c** Gad to
21:27 So the LORD **c** the angel, and he
22: 2 So David **c** to gather the aliens
22:17 David also **c** all the leaders of
24:19 the LORD God of Israel had **c**
2 Chr 7:17 according to all that I have **c**
8:14 so David the man of God had **c**.
14: 4 He **c** Judah to seek the LORD God
18:30 Now the king of Syria had **c** the
19: 9 And he **c** them, saying, "Thus
23: 8 all that Jehoiada the priest **c**.
25: 4 of Moses, where the LORD **c**,
29:21 Then he **c** the priests, the sons
29:24 for the king **c** that the burnt
29:27 Then Hezekiah **c** them to offer
29:30 Hezekiah and the leaders **c** the
31: 4 Moreover he **c** the people who
31:11 Now Hezekiah **c** them to prepare
32:12 and **c** Judah and Jerusalem,
33: 8 to do all that I have **c** them,
33:16 and **c** Judah to serve the LORD
34:20 Then the king **c** Hilkiah, Ahikam
35:21 for God **c** me to make haste.
36:23 And He has **c** me to build Him a
Ezra 1: 2 And He has **c** me to build Him a
4: 3 Cyrus the king of Persia has **c**
5: 3 Who has **c** you to build this
5: 9 Who **c** you to build this temple
7:23 Whatever is **c** by the God of
9:11 which You **c** by Your servants the
Neh 1: 7 nor the ordinances which You **c**
1: 8 the word that You **c** Your
8: 1 which the LORD had **c** Israel.
8:14 which the LORD had **c** by Moses,
9:14 And **c** them precepts, statutes
13: 5 which were **c** to be given to
13: 9 Then I **c** them to cleanse the
13:19 that I **c** the gates to be shut,
13:22 And I **c** the Levites that they
Esth 1:10 he **c** Mehuman, Biztha, Harbona,
1:17 King Ahasuerus **c** Queen Vashti to
3: 2 for so the king had **c**
3:12 according to all that Haman **c**—
4:17 according to all that Esther **c**
6: 1 So one was **c** to bring the book
8: 9 to all that Mordecai **c**,
9:14 So the king **c** this to be done;
9:25 he **c** by letter that this wicked
Job 38:12 Have you **c** the morning since
42: 9 went and did as the LORD **c**
Ps 7: 6 me to the judgment You have **c**!
33: 9 spoke, and it was done; He **c**,
68:28 Your God has **c** your strength;
78: 5 Which He **c** our fathers, That
78:23 Yet He had **c** the clouds above,
105: 8 forever, The word which He **c**,
106:34 whom the LORD had **c** them,
111: 9 He has **c** His covenant forever:
119: 4 You have **c** us To keep Your
119:138 testimonies, which You have **c**,
133: 3 For there the LORD **c** the
148: 5 For He **c** and they were
Isa 13: 3 I have **c** My sanctified ones;
34:16 For My mouth has **c** it, and His
45:12 And all their host I have **c**.
48: 5 and my molded image Have **c**
Jer 7:23 But this is what I **c** them,
7:23 in all the ways that I have **c**
11: 4 which I **c** your fathers in the
11: 8 which I **c** them to do, but
13: 5 as the LORD **c** me.
13: 6 from there the sash which I **c**
14:14 **c** them, nor spoken to them;
17:22 as I **c** your fathers.
26: 8 all that the LORD had **c** him
29:23 which I have not **c** them.
32:23 done nothing of all that You **c**
35: 6 **c** us, saying, 'You shall drink
35:10 all that Jonadab our father **c**
35:14 which he **c** his sons, not to
35:16 which he **c** them, but this
35:18 according to all that he **c** you,
36: 5 And Jeremiah **c** Baruch, saying,
36: 8 all that Jeremiah the prophet **c**
36:26 And the king **c** Jerahmeel the
37:21 Then Zedekiah the king **c** that
38:10 Then the king **c** Ebed-Melech the
38:27 these words that the king had **c**.
50:21 according to all that I have **c**
51:59 which Jeremiah the prophet **c**
Lam 1:10 Those whom You **c** Not to enter
1:17 The LORD has **c** concerning
2:17 fulfilled His word Which He **c**
3:37 When the Lord has not **c** it?
Ezek 9:11 I have done as You **c** me."
10: 6 when He **c** the man clothed in
12: 7 So I did as I was **c**.
24:18 next morning I did as I was **c**.
37: 7 So I prophesied as I was **c**;
37:10 So I prophesied as He **c** me, and
Dan 2:46 and **c** that they should present
3: 4 cried aloud: "To you it is **c**,
3:19 He spoke and **c** that they heat
3:20 And he **c** certain mighty men of
6:23 and **c** that they should take
Am 2:12 And **c** the prophets saying,
Zech 1: 6 Which I **c** My servants the
Mal 4: 4 Which I **c** him in Horeb for all
Mt 1:24 did as the angel of the Lord **c**
8: 4 and offer the gift that Moses **c**,
10: 5 twelve Jesus sent out and **c**
14: 9 he **c** it to be given to her.
14:19 Then He **c** the multitudes to sit
15: 4 'For God **c**, saying, 'Honor
15:35 So He **c** the multitude to sit
16:20 Then He **c** His disciples that
17: 9 Jesus **c** them, saying, "Tell
18:25 his master **c** that he be sold,
21: 6 went and did as Jesus **c** them.
27:58 Then Pilate **c** the body to be
28:20 all things that I have **c** you;
Mk 1:44 those things which Moses **c**,
5:43 But He **c** them strictly that no
6: 8 He **c** them to take nothing for
6:27 king sent an executioner and **c**
6:39 Then He **c** them to make them all
7:36 Then He **c** them that they should
7:36 but the more He **c** them, the
8: 6 So He **c** the multitude to sit
9: 9 He **c** them that they should tell
10:49 So Jesus stood still and **c** him
11: 6 to them just as Jesus had **c**.
13:34 and **c** the doorkeeper to watch.
Lk 5:14 to them, just as Moses **c**.
8:29 For He had **c** the unclean spirit
8:55 And He **c** that she be given
9:21 And He strictly warned and **c**
14:22 'Master, it is done as you **c**,
17: 9 he did the things that were **c**
17:10 those things which you are **c**,
18:40 So Jesus stood still and **c** him
19:15 he then **c** these servants, to
Jn 8: 5 **c** us that such should be
Acts 1: 4 He **c** them not to depart from
4:15 But when they had **c** them to go
4:18 And they called them and **c** them
5:34 and **c** them to put the apostles
5:40 they **c** that they should not
8:38 So he **c** the chariot to stand
10:33 to hear all the things **c** you by
10:42 And He **c** us to preach to the
10:48 And he **c** them to be baptized in
12:19 he examined the guards and **c**
13:47 'For so the Lord has **c** us:
16:22 tore off their clothes and **c**
18: 2 (because Claudius had **c** all
21:33 and **c** him to be bound with two
21:34 he **c** him to be taken into the
22:30 and **c** the chief priests and all
23: 2 And the high priest Ananias **c**
23:10 **c** the soldiers to go down and
23:22 and **c** him, "Tell no one that
23:30 and also **c** his accusers to
23:31 the soldiers, as they were **c**,
23:35 And he **c** him to be kept in
24:23 So he **c** the centurion to keep
25: 6 he **c** Paul to be brought.
25:17 sat on the judgment seat and **c**
25:21 I **c** him to be kept till I could
27:43 and **c** that those who could swim
1 Cor 9:14 Even so the Lord has **c** that
2 Cor 4: 6 For it is the God who **c** light to
1 Th 4:11 your own hands, as we **c** you,
2 Th 3:10 we **c** you this: If anyone will
Titus 1: 5 elders in every city as I **c**
Heb 9:20 covenant which God has **c**
12:20 could not endure what was **c**:
Rev 9: 4 They were **c** not to harm the

COMMANDER (55/53) COMMAND, COMMANDERS

Gen 21:22 the **c** of his army, spoke to
21:32 the **c** of his army, and they
26:26 and Phichol the **c** of his army.
Josh 5:14 but as **C** of the army of the
5:15 Then the **C** of the LORD's army
Judg 4: 2 The **c** of his army was Sisera,
4: 7 the **c** of Jabin's army, with his
11: 6 Jephthah, "Come and be our **c**,
11:11 the people made him head and **c**
1 Sam 9:16 and you shall anoint him **c** over
10: 1 the LORD has anointed you **c**
12: 9 **c** of the army of Hazor, into
13:14 has commanded him to be **c**
14:50 And the name of the **c** of his
17:55 the **c** of the army, "Abner,
26: 5 the **c** of his army. Now Saul lay
2 Sam 2: 8 **c** of Saul's army, took
10:16 And Shobach the **c** of
10:18 and struck Shobach the **c** of
19:13 if you are not **c** of the army
24: 2 So the king said to Joab the **c**
1 Ki 1:19 and Joab the **c** of the army; but
2:32 the **c** of the army of Israel,
2:32 the **c** of the army of
11:15 and Joab the **c** of the army had
11:21 and that Joab the **c** of the army
16: 9 **c** of half his chariots,
16:16 the **c** of the army, king over
2 Ki 4:13 behalf to the king or to the **c**
5: 1 **c** of the army of the king of
9: 5 "I have a message for you, **C**.
9: 5 And he said, "For you, **C**."
1 Chr 19:16 and Shophach the **c** of
19:18 and killed Shophach the **c** of
Ezra 4: 8 Rehum the **c** and Shimshai the
4: 9 From Rehum the **c**,
4:17 sent an answer: To Rehum the **c**,
Isa 55: 4 A leader and **c** for the people.
Acts 21:31 news came to the **c** of the
21:32 And when they saw the **c** and the
21:33 Then the **c** came near and took
21:37 the barracks, he said to the **c**,
22:24 the **c** ordered him to be brought
22:26 that, he went and told the **c**,
22:27 Then the **c** came and said to him,
22:28 The **c** answered, "With a large
22:29 and the **c** was also afraid after
23:10 arose a great dissension, the **c**,
23:15 suggest to the **c** that he be
23:17 "Take this young man to the **c**,
23:18 him and brought him to the **c**
23:19 Then the **c** took him by the hand,
23:22 So the **c** let the young man
24: 7 But the **c** Lysias came by and
24:22 When Lysias the **c** comes down, I

COMMANDERS (7/7) COMMANDER

1 Ki 1:25 and the **c** of the army, and
2: 5 and what he did to the two **c**
9:22 **c** of his chariots, and his
2 Chr 32: 3 with his leaders and **c** to stop
Nah 3:17 Your **c** are like swarming
Acts 25:23 the auditorium with the **c** and
Rev 6:15 great men, the rich men, the **c**,

COMMANDING (5/5) COMMAND

Gen 49:33 And when Jacob had finished **c**
Mt 11: 1 when Jesus finished **c** His
Acts 16:23 **c** the jailer to keep them
24: 8 **c** his accusers to come to you.

1 Tim 4: 3 and c to abstain from foods

COMMANDMENT (112/108) COMMAND, COMMANDMENTS

Ex 17: 1 according to the c of the
25:22 which I will give you in c to
36: 6 So Moses gave a c,
38:21 was counted according to the c
Num 3:39 and Aaron numbered at the c of
4:37 numbered according to the c of
4:41 numbered according to the c of
4:49 According to the c of the LORD
15:23 from the day the LORD gave c
15:31 the LORD, and has broken His c,
Deut 6: 1 "Now this is the c,
7:11 you shall keep the c,
8: 1 Every c which I command you
9:23 you rebelled against the c of
11: 8 you shall keep every c which I
17:20 may not turn aside from the c
30:11 For this c which I command you
31: 5 do to them according to every c
Josh 8: 8 According to the c of the LORD
15:13 according to the c of the LORD
17: 4 according to the c of the
21: 3 at the c of the LORD, these
22: 3 have kept the charge of the c
22: 5 take careful heed to do the c
1 Sam 12:14 and do not rebel against the c
12:15 but rebel against the c of the
13:13 You have not kept the c of the
15:13 LORD! I have performed the c
15:24 for I have transgressed the c
2 Sam 12: 9 Why have you despised the c of
1 Ki 2:43 the oath of the LORD and the c
13:21 and have not kept the c which
2 Ki 17:34 or the law and c which the
17:37 and the c which He wrote for
18:36 for the king's c was, "Do not
24: 3 Surely at the c of the LORD
1 Chr 14:12 gods there, David gave a c,
2 Chr 8:13 offering according to the c of
14: 4 to observe the law and the c.
19:10 or offenses against law or c,
24: 6 according to the c of Moses
29:15 and went according to the c of
29:25 according to the c of David, of
29:25 for thus was the c of the
31: 5 As soon as the c was
31:13 at the c of Hezekiah the king
31:21 of God, in the law and in the c,
Ezra 6:14 according to the c of the God
10: 3 of those who tremble at the c
Job 23:12 I have not departed from the c
Ps 19: 8 The c of the LORD is pure,
71: 3 You have given the c to save
119:96 But Your c is exceedingly
Prov 6:23 For the c is a lamp, And the
13:13 But he who fears the c will be
19:16 He who keeps the c keeps his
Eccl 8: 2 Keep the king's c for the sake
Isa 23:11 The LORD has given a c
29:13 toward Me is taught by the c
36:21 for the king's c was, "Do not
Jer 35:14 none, and obey their father's c.
35:16 of Rechab have performed the c
35:18 Because you have obeyed the c of
Lam 1:18 For I rebelled against His c.
Mal 2: 1 this c is for you.
2: 4 know that I have sent this c
Mt 15: 3 do you also transgress the c
15: 6 Thus you have made the c of
22:36 which is the great c in the
22:38 is the first and great c.
Mk 7: 8 For laying aside the c of God,
7: 9 too well you reject the c of
12:28 Which is the first c of all?"
12:30 This is the first c.
12:31 There is no other c greater
Lk 15:29 I never transgressed your c at
23:56 the Sabbath according to the c.
Jn 13:34 A new c I give to you, that you
14:31 and as the Father gave Me c,
15:12 'This is My c, that you love
Acts 15:24 whom we gave no such c—
Rom 7: 8 taking opportunity by the c,
7: 9 but when the c came, sin
7:10 And the c, which was to bring
7:11 sin, taking occasion by the c,
7:12 and the c holy and just and
7:13 so that sin through the c might
13: 9 and if there is any other c,
16:26 according to the c of the
1 Cor 7: 6 as a concession, not as a c.
7:25 I have no c from the Lord; yet
2 Cor 8: 8 I speak not by c,
Eph 6: 2 which is the first c with
1 Tim 1: 1 by the c of God our Savior and
1: 5 Now the purpose of the c is love
6:14 that you keep this c without
Titus 1: 3 to me according to the c of
Heb 7: 5 have a c to receive tithes from
7:16 to the law of a fleshly c,
7:18 is an annulling of the former c
2 Pe 2:21 to turn from the holy c
3: 2 and of the c of us, the
1 Jn 2: 7 I write no new c to you, but an
2: 7 but an old c which you have had
2: 7 The old c is the word which you
2: 8 a new c I write to you, which
3:23 And this is His c:
3:23 one another, as He gave us c.
4:21 And this c we have from Him:
2 Jn 4 as we received c from the
5 not as though I wrote a new c
6 His commandments. This is the c,

COMMANDMENTS (159/156) COMMANDMENT

Gen 26: 5 voice and kept My charge, My c,
Ex 15:26 give ear to His c and keep all
16:28 do you refuse to keep My c and
20: 6 those who love Me and keep My c.
24:12 and the law and c which I have
34:28 of the covenant, the Ten C.
34:32 and he gave them as c all that
Lev 4: 2 against any of the c of the
4:13 against any of the c of the
4:22 against any of the c of the
4:27 against any of the c of the
5:17 forbidden to be done by the c
22:31 you shall keep My c,
26: 3 in My statutes and keep My c,
26:14 and do not observe all these c,
26:15 you do not perform all My c,
27:34 These are the c which the
Num 15:22 and do not observe all these c
15:39 upon it and remember all the c
15:40 may remember and do all My c,
36:13 These are the c and the
Deut 1: 3 the LORD had given him as c
4: 2 that you may keep the c of the
4:13 you to perform, the Ten C;
4:40 keep His statutes and His c
5:10 those who love Me and keep My c.
5:29 Me and always keep all My c,
5:31 I will speak to you all the c,
6: 2 keep all His statutes and His c
6:17 shall diligently keep the c of
6:25 careful to observe all these c
7: 9 who love Him and keep His c;
8: 2 whether you would keep His c or
8: 6 you shall keep the c
8:11 your God by not keeping His c,
10: 4 to the first writing, the Ten C,
10:13 and to keep the c of the LORD
11: 1 and His c always.
11:13 that if you earnestly obey My c
11:22 you carefully keep all these c
11:27 if you obey the c of the LORD
11:28 if you do not obey the c of the
13: 4 and keep His c and obey His
13:18 to keep all His c which I
15: 5 observe with care all these c
19: 9 and if you keep all these c and
26:13 according to all Your c which
26:13 I have not transgressed Your c,
26:17 and keep His statutes, His c,
26:18 that you should keep all His c,
27: 1 Keep all the c which I command
27:10 and observe His c and His
28: 1 to observe carefully all His c
28: 9 if you keep the c of the LORD
28:13 if you heed the c of the LORD
28:15 to observe carefully all His c
28:45 to keep His c and His statutes
30: 8 of the LORD and do all His c
30:10 to keep His c and His statutes
30:16 in His ways, and to keep His c,
Josh 22: 5 in all His ways, to keep His c,
Judg 2:17 in obeying the c of the LORD;
3: 4 whether they would obey the c
1 Sam 15:11 Me, and has not performed My c.
1 Ki 2: 3 to keep His statutes, His c,
3:14 to keep My statutes and My c,
6:12 My judgments, keep all My c,
8:58 and to keep His c and His
8:61 in His statutes and keep His c,
9: 6 and do not keep My c and My
11:34 I chose because he kept My c
11:38 to keep My statutes and My c,
14: 8 who kept My c and who followed
18:18 in that you have forsaken the c
2 Ki 17:13 and keep My c and My statutes,
17:16 So they left all the c of the
17:19 Also Judah did not keep the c
18: 6 following Him, but kept His c,
23: 3 the LORD and to keep His c
1 Chr 28: 7 he is steadfast to observe My c
28: 8 careful to seek out all the c
29:19 a loyal heart to keep Your c
2 Chr 7:19 forsake My statutes and My c
17: 4 and walked in His c and not
24:20 Why do you transgress the c of
34:31 and to keep His c and His
Ezra 7:11 expert in the words of the c of
9:10 For we have forsaken Your c,
9:14 "should we again break Your c,
Neh 1: 5 who love You and observe Your c,
1: 7 You, and have not kept the c,
1: 9 and keep My c and do them,
9:13 true laws, Good statutes and c.
9:16 necks, And did not heed Your c.
9:29 And did not heed Your c,
9:34 Nor heeded Your c and Your
10:29 to observe and do all the c of
Ps 78: 7 works of God, But keep His c;
89:31 statutes And do not keep My c,
103:18 to those who remember His c to
111:10 have all those who do His c.
112: 1 Who delights greatly in His c.
119: 6 When I look into all Your c.
119:10 let me not wander from Your c!
119:19 Do not hide Your c from me.
119:21 cursed, Who stray from Your c.
119:32 will run the course of Your c,
119:35 me walk in the path of Your c,
119:47 I will delight myself in Your c,
119:48 also I will lift up to Your c,
119:60 did not delay To keep Your c.
119:66 For I believe Your c.
119:73 that I may learn Your c.
119:86 All Your c are faithful;
119:98 You, through Your c,
119:115 For I will keep the c of my
119:127 Therefore I love Your c More
119:131 For I longed for Your c.
119:143 Yet Your c are my delights.
119:151 And all Your c are truth.
119:166 salvation, And I do Your c.
119:172 For all Your c are
119:176 For I do not forget Your c.
Eccl 12:13 Fear God and keep His c,
Isa 48:18 that you had heeded My c!
Dan 9: 4 and with those who keep His c,
Am 2: 4 LORD, And have not kept His c.
Mt 5:19 one of the least of these c,
15: 9 as doctrines the c of
19:17 to enter into life, keep the c.
22:40 On these two c hang all the Law
Mk 7: 7 as doctrines the c of
10:19 "You know the c:
12:29 The first of all the c is:
Lk 1: 6 walking in all the c and
18:20 "You know the c:
Jn 14:15 "If you love Me, keep My c.
14:21 He who has My c and keeps them,
15:10 "If you keep My c,
15:10 as I have kept My Father's c
Acts 1: 2 the Holy Spirit had given c to
Rom 13: 9 For the c, "You shall not
1 Cor 7:19 but keeping the c of God is
14:37 which I write to you are the c
Eph 2:15 the law of c contained in
Col 2:22 according to the c and doctrines
1 Th 4: 2 for you know what c we gave you
Titus 1:14 heed to Jewish fables and c of
1 Jn 2: 3 we know Him, if we keep His c.
2: 4 Him," and does not keep His c,
3:22 because we keep His c and do
3:24 Now he who keeps His c abides
5: 2 when we love God and keep His c.
5: 3 love of God, that we keep His c.
5: 3 And His c are not burdensome.
2 Jn 6 that we walk according to His c.
Rev 12:17 who keep the c of God and have
14:12 here are those who keep the c
22:14 Blessed are those who do His c,

COMMANDS (20/20) COMMAND

Ex 18:23 and God so c you, then you
Num 32:25 servants will do as my lord c.
36: 6 This is what the LORD c
Deut 26:16 day the LORD your God c
2 Sam 15:15 do whatever my lord the king c.
Job 9: 7 He c the sun, and it does not
36:10 And c that they turn from
36:32 And c it to strike.
37:12 they may do whatever He c them
Ps 107:25 For He c and raises the stormy
Prov 2: 1 And treasure my c within you,
3: 1 But let your heart keep my c;
4: 4 retain my words; Keep my c,
7: 1 And treasure my c within you.
7: 2 Keep my c and live, And my law
10: 8 wise in heart will receive c,
Mk 1:27 For with authority He c even
Lk 4:36 with authority and power He c
8:25 For He c even the winds and
Acts 17:30 but now c all men everywhere to

COMMEMORATE (1/1)

1 Chr 16: 4 the ark of the LORD, to c,

COMMEND (7/7) COMMENDABLE, COMMENDATION, COMMENDED, COMMENDING, COMMENDS

Acts 20:32 I c you to God and to the word
Rom 16: 1 I c to you Phoebe our sister,
1 Cor 8: 8 But food does not c us to God;
2 Cor 3: 1 Do we begin again to c
5:12 For we do not c ourselves again
6: 4 But in all things we c
10:12 ourselves with those who c

COMMENDABLE (2/2) COMMEND

1 Pe 2:19 For this is c,
2:20 this is c before God.

COMMENDATION (2/1) COMMEND

2 Cor 3: 1 epistles of c to you or
3: 1 to you or letters of c from

COMMENDED (8/8) COMMEND

Gen 12:15 of Pharaoh also saw her and c
Prov 12: 8 A man will be c according to

Eccl 8:15 So I **c** enjoyment, because a man
Lk 16: 8 So the master **c** the unjust
Acts 14:23 they **c** them to the Lord in whom
14:26 where they had been **c** to the
15:40 being **c** by the brethren to the
2 Cor 12:11 For I ought to have been **c** by

COMMENDING (1/1) COMMEND

2 Cor 4: 2 by manifestation of the truth **c**

COMMENDS (2/1) COMMEND

2 Cor 10:18 For not he who **c** himself is
10:18 approved, but whom the Lord **c**.

COMMISSION (1/1)

Acts 26:12 Damascus with authority and **c**

COMMIT (65/60) COMMITS, COMMITTED, COMMITTING

Ex 20:14 You shall not **c** adultery.
Lev 18:26 and shall not **c** any of these
18:29 the persons who **c** them shall
18:30 so that you do not **c** any of
20: 5 themselves with him to **c**
20:23 for they **c** all these things,
Num 5: 6 commits any sin that men **c** in
25: 1 and the people began to **c**
Deut 5:18 You shall not **c** adultery.
19:20 they shall not again **c** such
Josh 22:20 not Achan the son of Zerah **c** a
Judg 19:23 do not **c** this outrage.
2 Ki 17:21 and made them **c** a great sin.
2 Chr 21:11 inhabitants of Jerusalem to **c**
Job 5: 8 And to God I would **c** my cause—
34:10 And from the Almighty to **c**
Ps 31: 5 Into Your hand I **c** my spirit;
37: 5 ***C*** your way to the LORD, Trust
Prov 16: 3 ***C*** your works to the LORD, And
16:12 an abomination for kings to **c**
Isa 22:21 I will **c** your responsibility
23:17 and **c** fornication with all the
Jer 7: 9 **c** adultery, swear falsely, burn
9: 5 They weary themselves to **c**
23:14 They **c** adultery and walk in
37:21 commanded that they should **c**
44: 7 Why do you **c** this great evil
Ezek 8:17 to the house of Judah to **c** the
8:17 the abominations which they **c**
16:43 And you shall not **c** lewdness in
16:51 Samaria did not **c** half of your
22: 9 in your midst they **c** lewdness.
23:43 Will they **c** harlotry with her
33:26 you **c** abominations, and you
Hos 4:10 They shall **c** harlotry, but not
4:13 Therefore your daughters **c**
4:13 And your brides **c** adultery.
4:14 your daughters when they **c**
4:14 Nor your brides when they **c**
4:18 They **c** harlotry continually.
5: 3 you **c** harlotry; Israel is
6: 9 Surely they **c** lewdness.
Mt 5:27 You shall not **c** adultery.'
5:32 immorality causes her to **c**
19:18 You shall not **c** adultery,'
Mk 10:19 Do not **c** adultery,' 'Do not
Lk 16:11 who will **c** to your trust the
18:20 Do not **c** adultery,' 'Do not
23:46 into Your hands I **c** My
Jn 2:24 But Jesus did not **c** Himself to
Rom 2:22 Do not **c** adultery," do you
2:22 do you **c** adultery? You who
13: 9 You shall not **c** adultery,"
1 Cor 10: 8 Nor let us **c** sexual immorality,
2 Cor 11: 7 Did I **c** sin in humbling myself
1 Tim 1:18 This charge I **c** to you, son
2 Tim 2: 2 **c** these to faithful men who
Jas 2: 9 you **c** sin, and are convicted by
2:11 Do not **c** adultery," also
2:11 Now if you do not **c** adultery,
1 Pe 4:19 according to the will of God **c**
1 Jn 5:16 give him life for those who **c**
Rev 2:14 and to **c** sexual immorality.
2:20 and seduce My servants to **c**
2:22 and those who **c** adultery with

COMMITS (30/26) COMMIT

Lev 5:15 If a person **c** a trespass, and
5:17 and **c** any of these things which
6: 2 If a person sins and **c** a
18:29 For whoever **c** any of these
20:10 The man who **c** adultery with
20:10 he who **c** adultery with his
Num 5: 6 When a man or woman **c** any sin
Deut 19:15 iniquity or any sin that he **c**;
2 Sam 7:14 If he **c** iniquity, I will
Ps 10:14 The helpless **c** himself to You;
Prov 6:32 Whoever **c** adultery with a woman
Ezek 3:20 from his righteousness and **c**
8: 6 that the house of Israel **c**
18:24 from his righteousness and **c**
18:26 **c** iniquity, and dies in it, it
22:11 One **c** abomination with his
33:13 in his own righteousness and **c**
33:18 from his righteousness and **c**
Hab 1:11 He **c** offense, Ascribing this
Mt 5:32 a woman who is divorced **c**
19: 9 **c** adultery; and whoever marries
19: 9 marries her who is divorced **c**
Mk 10:11 his wife and marries another **c**
10:12 another, she **c** adultery."
Lk 16:18 his wife and marries another **c**
16:18 is divorced from her husband **c**
Jn 8:34 whoever **c** sin is a slave of
1 Cor 6:18 but he who **c** sexual immorality
1 Jn 3: 4 Whoever **c** sin also commits
3: 4 Whoever commits sin also **c**

COMMITTED (112/106) COMMIT

Gen 39: 8 and he has **c** all that he has to
39:22 And the keeper of the prison **c**
Ex 32:30 You have **c** a great sin. So now I
32:31 these people have **c** a great
Lev 4:14 'when the sin which they have **c**
4:23 or if his sin which he has **c**
4:28 or if his sin which he has **c**
4:28 for his sin which he has **c**.
4:35 for his sin that he has **c**.
5: 6 for his sin which he has **c**,
5: 7 for his trespass which he has **c**,
5:10 for his sin which he has **c**,
5:13 for his sin that he has **c** in
18:30 customs which were **c** before
19:22 for his sin which he has **c**.
19:22 And the sin which he has **c**
20:12 They have **c** perversion.
20:13 both of them have **c** an
Num 5: 7 confess the sin which he has **c**.
15:24 be, if it is unintentionally **c**,
Deut 9:18 of all your sin which you **c** in
13:14 that such an abomination was **c**
17: 4 such an abomination has been **c**
17: 5 that man or woman who has **c**
21:22 If a man has **c** a sin deserving
Josh 7: 1 But the children of Israel **c** a
22:16 is this that you have **c**
22:31 because you have not **c** this
Judg 20: 6 because they **c** lewdness and
1 Ki 8:47 we have **c** wickedness';
14:22 with their sins which they **c**,
14:27 and **c** them to the hands of the
16:19 of the sins which he had **c** in
16:19 and in his sin which he had **c**
16:20 of Zimri, and the treason he **c**,
2 Ki 21:17 he did, and the sin that he **c**—
1 Chr 10:13 unfaithfulness which he had **c**
2 Chr 6:37 and have **c** wickedness';
12:10 and **c** them to the hands of the
34:16 All that was **c** to your servants
Ps 106: 6 We have **c** iniquity, We have
Jer 2:13 For My people have **c** two evils:
3: 8 which backsliding Israel had **c**
3: 9 that she defiled the land and **c**
5: 7 Then they **c** adultery And
5:30 and horrible thing Has been **c**
6:15 they ashamed when they had **c**
8:12 they ashamed when they had **c**
16:10 what is our sin that we have **c**
29:23 have **c** adultery with their
37:18 What offense have I **c** against
39:14 and **c** him to Gedaliah the son
40: 7 and had **c** to him men, women,
41:10 the captain of the guard had **c**
44: 3 wickedness which they have **c**
44: 9 which they **c** in the land of
44:22 of the abominations which you **c**.
Ezek 6: 9 for the evils which they **c** in
16:26 You also **c** harlotry with the
16:50 And they were haughty and **c**
16:52 because the sins which you **c**
17:20 for the treason which he **c**
18:12 Or **c** abomination;
18:21 all his sins which he has **c**,
18:22 transgressions which he has **c**
18:24 and the sin which he has **c**,
18:27 from the wickedness which he **c**,
18:28 the transgressions which he **c**,
18:31 transgressions which you have **c**,
20:43 all the evils that you have **c**.
22:29 **c** robbery, and mistreated the
23: 3 They **c** harlotry in Egypt,
23: 3 They **c** harlotry in their
23: 7 Thus she **c** her harlotry with
23:37 For they have **c** adultery, and
23:37 They have **c** adultery with their
33:13 of the iniquity that he has **c**,
33:16 of his sins which he has **c**
33:29 abominations which they have **c**.
43: 8 the abominations which they **c**;
44:13 abominations which they have **c**.
Dan 9: 5 we have sinned and **c** iniquity,
9: 7 which they have **c** against You.
Hos 1: 2 For the land has **c** great
7: 1 For they have **c** fraud;
Mal 2:11 And an abomination has been **c**
Mt 5:28 to lust for her has already **c**
Mk 15: 7 they had **c** murder in the
Lk 12:48 yet **c** things deserving of
12:48 and to whom much has been **c**,
Jn 5:22 but has **c** all judgment to the
Acts 25:11 or have **c** anything deserving of
25:25 when I found that he had **c**
Rom 3: 2 Chiefly because to them were **c**
3:25 the sins that were previously **c**,
11:32 For God has **c** them all to
2 Cor 5:19 and has **c** to us the word of
Gal 2: 7 the uncircumcised had been **c**
1 Tim 1:11 of the blessed God which was **c**
6:20 O Timothy! Guard what was **c** to
2 Tim 1:12 is able to keep what I have **c**
1:14 That good thing which was **c** to
Titus 1: 3 which was **c** to me according to
Heb 9: 7 and for the people's sins **c**
Jas 5:15 And if he has **c** sins, he will
1 Pe 2:22 Who **c** no sin, Nor was
2:23 but **c** Himself to Him who
Jude 15 deeds which they have **c** in an
Rev 17: 2 whom the kings of the earth **c**
18: 3 the kings of the earth have **c**
18: 9 The kings of the earth who **c**
20: 4 and judgment was **c** to them.

COMMITTING (7/7) COMMIT

Ezra 9:14 in marriage with the people **c**
Ezek 20:30 and **c** harlotry according to
33:15 the statutes of life without **c**
Hos 3: 1 is loved by a lover and is **c**
4: 2 Killing and stealing and **c**
Acts 8: 3 **c** them to prison.
Rom 1:27 men with men **c** what is

COMMON (28/28) COMMON-LAND, COMMONLY

Lev 4:27 If anyone of the **c** people sins
Num 16:29 they are visited by the **c** fate
1 Sam 21: 4 There is no **c** bread on hand;
21: 5 and the bread is in effect **c**,
1 Ki 10:27 The king made silver as **c** in
2 Ki 23: 6 ashes on the graves of the **c**
2 Chr 1:15 king made silver and gold as **c**
9:27 The king made silver as **c** in
Prov 22: 2 and the poor have this in **c**,
29:13 the oppressor have this in **c**:
Eccl 6: 1 and it is **c** among men:
Jer 26:23 body into the graves of the **c**
Ezek 7:27 And the hands of the **c** people
23:42 with men of the **c** sort, who put
42:20 the holy areas from the **c**.
Mk 12:37 And the **c** people heard Him
Acts 2:44 and had all things in **c**,
4:32 but they had all things in **c**.
5:18 and put them in the **c** prison.
10:14 I have never eaten anything **c**
10:15 cleansed you must not call **c**.
10:28 I should not call any man **c** or
11: 8 Lord! For nothing **c** or unclean
11: 9 cleansed you must not call **c**.
1 Cor 10:13 you except such as is **c** to man;
Titus 1: 4 a true son in our **c** faith:
Heb 10:29 he was sanctified a **c** thing,
Jude 3 you concerning our **c** salvation,

COMMON-LAND (59/34) COMMON, COMMON-LANDS

Lev 25:34 But the field of the **c** of their
Num 35: 2 shall also give the Levites **c**
35: 3 and their **c** shall be for their
35: 4 The **c** of the cities which you
35: 5 This shall belong to them as **c**
35: 7 you shall give with their **c**.
Josh 21:11 with the **c** surrounding it.
21:13 they gave Hebron with its **c** (a
21:13 the slayer), Libnah with its **c**,
21:14 Jattir with its **c**,
21:14 Eshtemoa with its **c**,
21:15 Holon with its **c**,
21:15 common-land, Debir with its **c**,
21:16 Ain with its **c**,
21:16 common-land, Juttah with its **c**,
21:16 and Beth Shemesh with its **c**:
21:17 of Benjamin, Gibeon with its **c**,
21:17 common-land, Geba with its **c**,
21:18 Anathoth with its **c**,
21:18 and Almon with its **c**:
21:21 gave them Shechem with its **c**
21:21 the slayer), Gezer with its **c**,
21:22 Kibzaim with its **c**,
21:22 and Beth Horon with its **c**:
21:23 of Dan, Eltekeh with its **c**,
21:23 Gibbethon with its **c**,
21:24 Aijalon with its **c**,
21:24 and Gath Rimmon with its **c**:
21:25 Tanach with its **c** and Gath
21:25 and Gath Rimmon with its **c**:
21:27 Golan in Bashan with its **c** (a
21:27 and Be Eshterah with its **c**:
21:28 of Issachar, Kishion with its **c**,
21:28 Daberath with its **c**,
21:29 Jarmuth with its **c**,
21:29 and En Gannim with its **c**:
21:30 of Asher, Mishal with its **c**,
21:30 common-land, Abdon with its **c**,
21:31 Helkath with its **c**,
21:31 and Rehob with its **c**:
21:32 Kedesh in Galilee with its **c** (a
21:32 slayer), Hammoth Dor with its **c**,
21:32 and Kartan with its **c**:
21:34 of Zebulun, Jokneam with its **c**,
21:34 common-land, Kartah with its **c**,
21:35 Dimnah with its **c**,
21:35 and Nahalal with its **c**:
21:36 of Reuben, Bezer with its **c**,
21:36 common-land, Jahaz with its **c**,
21:37 Kedemoth with its **c**,
21:37 and Mephaath with its **c**:
21:38 Ramoth in Gilead with its **c** (a
21:38 slayer), Mahanaim with its **c**,
21:39 Heshbon with its **c**,

21:39 and Jazer with its **c**:
21:42 one of these cities had its **c**
Ezek 27:28 The **c** will shake at the sound
48:15 the city, for dwellings and **c**;
48:17 'The **c** of the city shall be:

COMMON-LANDS (54/33) COMMON-LAND

Josh 14: 4 with their **c** for their
21: 2 with their **c** for our
21: 3 LORD, these cities and their **c**:
21: 8 gave these cities with their **c**
21:19 thirteen cities with their **c**.
21:26 All the ten cities with their **c**
21:33 thirteen cities with their **c**.
21:41 forty-eight cities with their **c**.
1 Chr 5:16 and in all the **c** of Sharon
6:55 Judah, with its surrounding **c**.
6:57 Hebron; also Libnah with its **c**,
6:57 Jattir, Eshtemoa with its **c**,
6:58 Hilen with its **c**,
6:58 common-lands, Debir with its **c**,
6:59 Ashan with its **c**,
6:59 and Beth Shemesh with its **c**.
6:60 of Benjamin: Geba with its **c**,
6:60 Alemeth with its **c**,
6:60 and Anathoth with its **c**.
6:64 these cities with their **c** to
6:67 of refuge, Shechem with its **c**,
6:67 Ephraim, also Gezer with its **c**,
6:68 Jokmeam with its **c**,
6:68 Beth Horon with its **c**,
6:69 Aijalon with its **c**,
6:69 and Gath Rimmon with its **c**.
6:70 Aner with its **c** and Bileam with
6:70 and Bileam with its **c**,
6:71 Golan in Bashan with its **c** and
6:71 and Ashtaroth with its **c**.
6:72 of Issachar: Kedesh with its **c**,
6:72 Daberath with its **c**,
6:73 Ramoth with its **c**,
6:73 and Anem with its **c**.
6:74 of Asher: Mashal with its **c**,
6:74 common-lands, Abdon with its **c**,
6:75 Hukok with its **c**,
6:75 and Rehob with its **c**.
6:76 Kedesh in Galilee with its **c**,
6:76 common-lands, Hammon with its **c**,
6:76 and Kirjathaim with its **c**.
6:77 were given Rimmon with its **c**
6:77 and Tabor with its **c**.
6:78 in the wilderness with its **c**,
6:78 common-lands, Jahzah with its **c**,
6:79 Kedemoth with its **c**,
6:79 and Mephaath with its **c**.
6:80 Ramoth in Gilead with its **c**,
6:80 Mahanaim with its **c**,
6:81 Heshbon with its **c**,
6:81 and Jazer with its **c**.
13: 2 in their cities and their **c**,
2 Chr 11:14 For the Levites left their **c** and
31:19 were in the fields of the **c**

COMMONLY (1/1) COMMON

Mt 28:15 and this saying is **c** reported

COMMONWEALTH (1/1)

Eph 2:12 being aliens from the **c** of

COMMOTION (3/3) COMMOTIONS

Jer 10:22 And a great **c** out of the north
Mk 5:39 'Why make this **c** and weep?
Acts 19:23 that time there arose a great **c**

COMMOTIONS (1/1) COMMONTION

Lk 21: 9 when you hear of wars and **c**,

COMMUNED (1/1) COMMUNION

Eccl 1:16 I **c** with my heart, saying,

COMMUNICATE (1/1) COMMUNICATED

1 Sam 18:22 **C** with David secretly, and say,

COMMUNICATED (2/2) COMMUNICATE

2 Sam 3:17 Now Abner had **c** with the elders
Gal 2: 2 and **c** to them that gospel which

COMMUNION (4/3) COMMUNED

1 Cor 10:16 is it not the **c** of the blood of
10:16 is it not the **c** of the body of
2 Cor 6:14 And what **c** has light with
13:14 and the **c** of the Holy Spirit

COMMUNITIES (1/1)

Neh 10:37 the tithes in all our farming **c**.

COMPACT (1/1)

Ps 122: 3 is built As a city that is **c**

COMPANIES (12/12) COMPANY

Gen 32: 7 herds and camels, into two **c**.
32:10 and now I have become two **c**.
Judg 7:16 three hundred men into three **c**,
7:20 Then the three **c** blew the
9:34 wait against Shechem in four **c**.
9:43 divided them into three **c**,
9:44 and the other two **c** rushed
1 Sam 11:11 Saul put the people in three **c**;
13:17 of the Philistines in three **c**.
2 Chr 26:11 men who went out to war by **c**,
Isa 21:13 O you traveling **c** of
Ezek 38: 7 you and all your **c** that are

COMPANION (25/25) COMPANIONS

Ex 2:13 "Why are you striking your **c**?
32:27 his brother, every man his **c**,
Judg 7:13 a man telling a dream to his **c**.
7:14 Then his **c** answered and said,
7:22 every man's sword against his **c**
14:20 wife was given to his **c**,
15: 2 therefore I gave her to your **c**.
15: 6 his wife and given her to his **c**.
1 Chr 27:33 the Archite was the king's **c**.
Job 30:29 And a **c** of ostriches.
Ps 55:13 My **c** and my acquaintance.
119:63 I am a **c** of all who fear You,
Prov 2:17 Who forsakes the **c** of her
13:20 But the **c** of fools will be
28: 7 But a **c** of gluttons shames his
28:24 The same is **c** to a
29: 3 But a **c** of harlots wastes his
Eccl 4: 8 There is one alone, without **c**:
4:10 fall, one will lift up his **c**.
Isa 34:14 wild goat shall bleat to its **c**;
Mic 7: 5 not put your confidence in a **c**;
Zech 13: 7 Against the Man who is My **C**,
Mal 2:14 Yet she is your **c** And your
Phil 4: 3 And I urge you also, true **c**,
Rev 1: 9 both your brother and **c** in the

COMPANIONS (32/31) COMPANION

Num 16:40 not become like Korah and his **c**,
Judg 14:11 that they brought thirty **c** to
Ezra 4: 7 and the rest of their **c** wrote
4: 9 scribe, and the rest of their **c**—
4:17 to the rest of their **c** who
4:23 the scribe, and their **c**,
5: 3 and Shethar-Boznai and their **c**
5: 6 and Shethar-Boznai, and his **c**,
6: 6 and your **c** the Persians who
6:13 and their **c** diligently did
Job 35: 4 And your **c** with you.
41: 6 Will your **c** make a banquet of
Ps 45: 7 of gladness more than Your **c**.
45:14 her **c** who follow her, shall be
122: 8 the sake of my brethren and **c**,
Song 1: 7 By the flocks of your **c**?
8:13 The **c** listen for your
Isa 1:23 rebellious, And **c** of thieves;
44:11 Surely all his **c** would be
Ezek 37:16 the children of Israel, his **c**.
37:16 all the house of Israel, his **c**.
37:19 and the tribes of Israel, his **c**;
Dan 2:13 they sought Daniel and his **c**,
2:17 Mishael, and Azariah, his **c**,
2:18 so that Daniel and his **c** might
Zech 3: 8 You and your **c** who sit before
Mt 11:16 and calling to their **c**,
Acts 4:23 they went to their own **c** and
19:29 Macedonians, Paul's travel **c**.
21: 8 next day we who were Paul's **c**
Heb 1: 9 gladness more than Your **c**.
10:33 and partly while you became **c**

COMPANY (51/47) COMPANIES

Gen 32: 8 If Esau comes to the one **c** and
32: 8 then the other **c** which is left
33: 8 do you mean by all this **c**
35:11 a nation and a **c** of nations
37:25 and there was a **c** of
Num 16: 5 he spoke to Korah and all his **c**,
16: 6 censers, Korah and all your **c**;
16:11 Therefore you and all your **c**
16:16 you and all your **c** be present
22: 4 Now this **c** will lick up
26: 9 Moses and Aaron in the **c** of
26:10 with Korah when that **c** died,
27: 3 but he was not in the **c** of
27: 3 in **c** with Korah, but he died in
Judg 9:37 and another **c** is coming from
9:44 Then Abimelech and the **c** that
18:23 that you have gathered such a **c**?
1 Sam 13:17 One **c** turned to the road to
13:18 another **c** turned to the road to
13:18 and another **c** turned to the
2 Ki 9:17 and he saw the **c** of Jehu as he
9:17 I see a **c** of men." And Joram
2 Chr 24:24 Syrians came with a small **c** of
31:18 the whole **c** of them—for in
Job 15:34 For the **c** of hypocrites will
16: 7 have made desolate all my **c**.
34: 8 Who goes in **c** with the workers
Ps 68:11 Great was the **c** of those who
68:27 princes of Judah and their **c**,
106:18 A fire was kindled in their **c**;
107:32 And praise Him in the **c** of the
Ezek 17:17 his mighty army and great **c**
27: 6 The **c** of Ashurites have inlaid
27:27 And the entire **c** which is in
27:34 merchandise and the entire **c**
32: 3 My net over you with a **c** of
32:22 is there, and all her **c**,
32:23 And her **c** is all around her
38: 4 a great **c** with bucklers and
38:15 a great **c** and a mighty army.
Hos 6: 9 So the **c** of priests murder on
Lk 2:44 Him to have been in the **c**,
24:22 and certain women of our **c**,
Acts 10:28 is for a Jewish man to keep **c**
15:22 send chosen men of their own **c**
Rom 15:24 if first I may enjoy your **c**
1 Cor 5: 9 you in my epistle not to keep **c**
5:11 written to you not to keep **c**
15:33 Evil **c** corrupts good habits."
2 Th 3:14 that person and do not keep **c**
Heb 12:22 to an innumerable **c** of angels,

COMPARABLE (2/2) COMPARE

Gen 2:18 I will make him a helper **c** to
2:20 there was not found a helper **c**

COMPARE (6/6) COMPARABLE, COMPARED, COMPARING, COMPARISON

Prov 3:15 things you may desire cannot **c**
Isa 40:18 Or what likeness will you **c** to
46: 5 and make Me equal And **c** Me,
Lam 2:13 What shall I **c** with you, that
Lk 13:18 And to what shall I **c** it?
2 Cor 10:12 dare not class ourselves or **c**

COMPARED (4/4) COMPARE

Ps 89: 6 who in the heavens can be **c** to
Prov 8:11 one may desire cannot be **c**
Song 1: 9 I have **c** you, my love, To my
Rom 8:18 time are not worthy to be **c**

COMPARING (2/2) COMPARE

1 Cor 2:13 **c** spiritual things with
2 Cor 10:12 and **c** themselves among

COMPARISON (3/3) COMPARE

Judg 8: 2 What have I done now in **c** with
8: 3 And what was I able to do in **c**
Hag 2: 3 In **c** with it, is this not in

COMPASS (1/1)

Isa 44:13 He marks it out with the **c**,

COMPASSION (47/44) COMPASSIONATE, COMPASSIONS

Ex 2: 6 So she had **c** on him, and said,
33:19 and I will have **c** on whom I
33:19 on whom I will have **c**.
Deut 13:17 have **c** on you and multiply you,
30: 3 and have **c** on you, and gather
32:36 judge His people And have **c**
1 Sam 23:21 for you have **c** on me.
1 Ki 3:26 for she yearned with **c** for her
8:50 and grant them **c** before those
8:50 that they may have **c** on them
2 Ki 13:23 had **c** on them, and regarded
2 Chr 30: 9 will be treated with **c** by
36:15 because He had **c** on His people
36:17 and had no **c** on young man or
Ps 78:38 But He, being full of **c**,
86:15 O Lord, are a God full of **c**,
90:13 And have **c** on Your servants.
111: 4 is gracious and full of **c**.
112: 4 is gracious, and full of **c**,
135:14 And He will have **c** on His
145: 8 is gracious and full of **c**,
Isa 49:15 And not have **c** on the son of
Jer 12:15 that I will return and have **c**
Lam 3:32 Yet He will show **c** According
Ezek 16: 5 to have **c** on you; but you were
Mic 7:19 He will again have **c** on us,
Zech 7: 9 Show mercy and **c** Everyone to
Mt 9:36 He was moved with **c** for them,
14:14 and He was moved with **c** for
15:32 I have **c** on the multitude,
18:27 that servant was moved with **c**,
18:33 'Should you not also have had **c**
20:34 So Jesus had **c** and touched their
Mk 1:41 Then Jesus, moved with **c**,
5:19 and how He has had **c** on you."
6:34 multitude and was moved with **c**
8: 2 I have **c** on the multitude,
9:22 have **c** on us and help us."
Lk 7:13 He had **c** on her and said to
10:33 And when he saw him, he had **c**.
15:20 his father saw him and had **c**,
Rom 9:15 and I will have **c** on
9:15 on whomever I will have **c**.
Heb 5: 2 He can have **c** on those who are
10:34 for you had **c** on me in my
1 Pe 3: 8 having **c** for one another; love
Jude 22 And on some have **c**,

COMPASSIONATE (2/2) COMPASSION

Lam 4:10 The hands of the **c** women Have

Jas 5:11 that the Lord is very **c** and

COMPASSIONS (1/1) COMPASSION

Lam 3:22 Because His **c** fail not.

COMPEL (4/4) COMPELLED, COMPELS

Lev 25:39 you shall not **c** him to serve as
Lk 14:23 and **c** them to come in, that my
Gal 2:14 why do you **c** Gentiles to live
6:12 these would **c** you to be

COMPELLED (8/8) COMPEL

1 Sam 13:12 the LORD.' Therefore I felt **c**,
Mt 27:32 Him they **c** to bear His cross.
Mk 15:21 Then they **c** a certain man,
Acts 18: 5 Paul was **c** by the Spirit, and
26:11 often in every synagogue and **c**
28:19 I was **c** to appeal to Caesar,
2 Cor 12:11 you have **c** me. For I ought to
Gal 2: 3 was **c** to be circumcised.

COMPELS (3/3) COMPEL

Job 32:18 The spirit within me **c** me.
Mt 5:41 And whoever **c** you to go one
2 Cor 5:14 For the love of Christ **c** us,

COMPENSATE (1/1)

Esth 7: 4 the enemy could never **c** for

COMPETE (1/1) COMPETES

2 Sam 2:14 the young men now arise and **c**

COMPETENT (1/1)

Gen 47: 6 And if you know any **c** men

COMPETES (3/2) COMPETE

1 Cor 9:25 And everyone who **c** for the
2 Tim 2: 5 And also if anyone **c** in
2: 5 he is not crowned unless he **c**

COMPLACENCY (2/2) COMPLACENT

Prov 1:32 And the **c** of fools will
Zeph 1:12 the men Who are settled in **c**,

COMPLACENT (3/3) COMPLACENCY

Isa 32: 9 You **c** daughters, Give ear to
32:10 will be troubled, you **c** women;
32:11 Be troubled, you **c** ones;

COMPLAIN (8/8) COMPLAINED, COMPLAINERS, COMPLAINT

Ex 16: 7 that you **c** against us?"
Num 14:27 this evil congregation who **c**
14:36 and made all the congregation **c**
16:11 And what is Aaron that you **c**
Judg 21:22 their brothers come to us to **c**,
Job 7:11 I will **c** in the bitterness of
Lam 3:39 Why should a living man **c**,
1 Cor 10:10 nor **c**, as some of them also

COMPLAINED (19/19) COMPLAIN

Ex 15:24 And the people **c** against Moses,
16: 2 of the children of Israel **c**
17: 3 and the people **c** against Moses,
Num 11: 1 Now when the people **c**,
14: 2 all the children of Israel **c**
14:29 carcasses of you who have **c**
Deut 1:27 and you **c** in your tents, and
Josh 9:18 And all the congregation **c**
Job 31:13 or female servant When they **c**
Ps 77: 3 God, and was troubled; I **c**,
106:25 But **c** in their tents, And did
Isa 29:24 And those who **c** will learn
Mt 20:11 they **c** against the landowner,
Lk 5:30 scribes and the Pharisees **c**
15: 2 And the Pharisees and scribes **c**,
19: 7 when they saw it, they all **c**,
Jn 6:41 The Jews then **c** about Him,
6:61 in Himself that His disciples **c**
1 Cor 10:10 as some of them also **c**,

COMPLAINERS (1/1) COMPLAIN

Jude 16 These are grumblers, **c**,

COMPLAINING (2/2)

Jn 7:12 And there was much **c** among the
Phil 2:14 Do all things without **c** and

COMPLAINT (13/12) COMPLAIN, COMPLAINTS

1 Sam 1:16 out of the abundance of my **c**
Job 7:13 My couch will ease my **c**,'
9:27 If I say, 'I will forget my **c**,
10: 1 will give free course to my **c**,
21: 4 is my **c** against man? And if
23: 2 'Even today my **c** is bitter;
Ps 55: 2 hear me; I am restless in my **c**,
102: and pours out his **c** before the
142: 2 I pour out my **c** before Him;
Mic 6: 2 O you mountains, the LORD's **c**,
6: 2 For the LORD has a **c** against
Acts 6: 1 there arose a **c** against the
Col 3:13 if anyone has a **c** against

COMPLAINTS (11/10) COMPLAINT

Ex 16: 7 for He hears your **c** against the
16: 8 for the LORD hears your **c**
16: 8 Your **c** are not against us but
16: 9 LORD, for He has heard your **c**.
16:12 I have heard the **c** of the
Num 14:27 I have heard the **c** which the
17: 5 I will rid Myself of the **c** of
17:10 that you may put their **c** away
Deut 1:12 and your burdens and your **c**?
Prov 23:29 has contentions? Who has **c**?
Acts 25: 7 about and laid many serious **c**

COMPLETE (20/19) COMPLETED, COMPLETELY, COMPLETION

Gen 15:16 of the Amorites is not yet **c**.
Neh 4: 2 Will they **c** it in a day?
Job 27:12 Why then do you behave with **c**
Jer 5:10 But do not make a **c** end.
5:18 I will not make a **c** end of you.
30:11 Yet I will not make a **c** end of
46:28 For I will make a **c** end of all
46:28 But I will not make a **c** end of
Ezek 11:13 Lord GOD! Will You make a **c**
2 Cor 8: 6 so he would also **c** this grace
8:11 but now you also must **c** the
13: 9 we pray, that you may be made **c**.
13:11 brethren, farewell. Become **c**.
Phil 1: 6 a good work in you will **c** it
Col 2:10 and you are **c** in Him, who is the
4:12 you may stand perfect and **c** in
2 Tim 3:17 that the man of God may be **c**,
Heb 13:21 make you **c** in every good work to
Jas 1: 4 that you may be perfect and **c**,
Rev 15: 1 in them the wrath of God is **c**.

COMPLETED (19/19) COMPLETE

Lev 23:15 seven Sabbaths shall be **c**.
Deut 31:24 when Moses had **c** writing the
2 Chr 8:16 So the house of the LORD was **c**.
24:13 and the work was **c** by them;
Ezra 4:13 city is built and the walls **c**,
4:16 is rebuilt and its walls are **c**,
5:11 king of Israel built and **c**.
Esth 1: 5 And when these days were **c**,
2:12 King Ahasuerus after she had **c**
Jer 25:12 pass, when seventy years are **c**,
29:10 After seventy years are **c** at
Ezek 4: 6 And when you have **c** them, lie
Lk 1:23 the days of his service were **c**,
2: 6 the days were **c** for her to be
2:21 And when eight days were **c** for
2:22 to the law of Moses were **c**,
Acts 14:26 for the work which they had **c**.
Rev 6:11 be killed as they were, was **c**.
15: 8 of the seven angels were **c**.

COMPLETELY (27/27) COMPLETE

Gen 31:15 and also **c** consumed our money.
Ex 19:18 Now Mount Sinai was **c** in smoke,
23:24 utterly overthrow them and **c**
Lev 1:17 but shall not divide it **c**;
5: 8 but shall not divide it **c**.
Num 15:31 that person shall be **c** cut off;
Deut 13:16 and **c** burn with fire the city
Josh 3:17 all the people had crossed **c**
4: 1 when all the people had **c**
4:11 when all the people had **c**
Judg 1:28 but did not **c** drive them out.
2 Sam 17:10 heart of a lion, will melt **c**.
1 Ki 7:23 it was **c** round. Its height
9:21 had not been able to destroy **c**—
1 Chr 28:21 and all the people will be **c**
2 Chr 4: 2 it was **c** round. Its height
12:12 so as not to destroy him **c**;
Esth 4:14 For if you remain **c** silent at
Job 19:13 And my acquaintances are **c**
Ezek 22:15 and remove your filthiness **c**
27:31 They will shave themselves **c**
Dan 12: 7 of the holy people has been **c**
Zech 11:17 His arm shall **c** wither, And
Jn 7:23 with Me because I made a man **c**
9:34 You were **c** born in sins, and are
13:10 but is **c** clean; and you are
1 Th 5:23 of peace Himself sanctify you **c**;

COMPLETION (1/1) COMPLETE

2 Cor 8:11 so there also may be a **c** out

COMPOSED (1/1) COMPOSITION

1 Cor 12:24 But God **c** the body, having

COMPOSITION (3/3) COMPOSED

Ex 30:32 like it, according to its **c**.
30:37 yourselves, according to its **c**.
Ps 45: 1 I recite my **c** concerning the

COMPOUND (1/1) COMPOUNDED, COMPOUNDS

Ex 30:35 a **c** according to the art of the

COMPOUNDED (1/1) COMPOUND

Ex 30:25 an ointment **c** according to the

COMPOUNDS (1/1) COMPOUND

Ex 30:33 Whoever **c** any like it, or

COMPREHEND (5/5) COMPREHENDED

Job 37: 5 great things which we cannot **c**.
Ps 139: 3 You **c** my path and my lying
Lk 24:45 that they might **c** the
Jn 1: 5 and the darkness did not **c** it.
Eph 3:18 may be able to **c** with all the

C

COMPREHENDED (1/1) COMPREHEND

Job 38:18 Have you **c** the breadth of the

COMPRISED (2/1)

1 Ki 6:34 two panels **c** one folding door,
6:34 and two panels **c** the other

COMPULSION (2/2) COMPULSORY

Phm 1:14 good deed might not be by **c**,
1 Pe 5: 2 not by **c** but willingly, not for

COMPULSORY (1/1) COMPULSION

Esth 1: 8 the law, the drinking was not **c**;

CONANIAH (1/1)

2 Chr 35: 9 Also **C**, his brothers

CONCEAL (8/8) CONCEALED, CONCEALS

Gen 37:26 if we kill our brother and **c**
Deut 13: 8 nor shall you spare him or **c**
Job 14:13 That You would **c** me until Your
27:11 with the Almighty I will not **c**.
33:17 And **c** pride from man,
41:12 I will not **c** his limbs, His
Prov 25: 2 It is the glory of God to **c**
Jer 50: 2 do not **c** it—Say, 'Babylon is

CONCEALED (5/5) CONCEAL

Num 5:13 and it is **c** that she has
Job 6:10 For I have not **c** the words of
28:21 And **c** from the birds of the
Ps 40:10 I have not **c** Your
Prov 27: 5 better Than love carefully **c**.

CONCEALS (2/2) CONCEAL

Prov 11:13 who is of a faithful spirit **c**
12:23 A prudent man **c** knowledge, But

CONCEDE (1/1)

Job 6:29 there be no injustice! Yes, **c**,

CONCEIT (1/1) CONCEITED, CONCEITS

Phil 2: 3 through selfish ambition or **c**,

CONCEITED (1/1) CONCEIT

Gal 5:26 Let us not become **c**,

CONCEITS (1/1) CONCEIT

2 Cor 12:20 backbitings, whisperings, **c**,

CONCEIVE (13/13) CONCEIVED, CONCEIVES, CONCEIVING, CONCEPTION

Gen 30:38 so that they should **c** when they
30:41 that they might **c** among the
Num 5:28 she shall be free and may **c**
11:12 'Did I **c** all these people?
Judg 13: 3 but you shall **c** and bear a son.
13: 5 you shall **c** and bear a son.
13: 7 you shall **c** and bear a son.
Job 15:35 They **c** trouble and bring forth
Isa 7:14 the virgin shall **c** and bear a
33:11 You shall **c** chaff, You shall
59: 4 They **c** evil and bring forth
Lk 1:31 you will **c** in your womb and
Heb 11:11 also received strength to **c**

CONCEIVED (46/45) CONCEIVE

Gen 4: 1 and she **c** and bore Cain, and
4:17 and she **c** and bore Enoch. And
16: 4 he went in to Hagar, and she **c**.
16: 4 And when she saw that she had **c**,
16: 5 and when she saw that she had **c**,
21: 2 For Sarah **c** and bore Abraham a
25:21 plea, and Rebekah his wife **c**.
29:32 So Leah **c** and bore a son, and
29:33 Then she **c** again and bore a son,
29:34 She **c** again and bore a son, and
29:35 And she **c** again and bore a son,
30: 5 And Bilhah **c** and bore Jacob a
30: 7 And Rachel's maid Bilhah **c** again

30:17 and she *c* and bore Jacob a
30:19 Then Leah *c* again and bore Jacob
30:23 And she *c* and bore a son, and
30:39 So the flocks *c* before the rods,
30:41 the stronger livestock *c*,
31:10 at the time when the flocks *c*,
38: 3 So she *c* and bore a son, and he
38: 4 She *c* again and bore a son, and
38: 5 And she *c* yet again and bore a
38:18 and she *c* by him.
Ex 2: 2 So the woman *c* and bore a son.
Lev 12: 2 saying: 'If a woman has *c*,
1 Sam 1:20 process of time that Hannah *c*
2:21 so that she *c* and bore three
2 Sam 11: 5 And the woman *c*;
2 Ki 4:17 But the woman *c*,
1 Chr 7:23 she *c* and bore a son; and he
Job 3: 3 was said, 'A male child is *c*.
Ps 51: 5 And in sin my mother *c* me.
Song 3: 4 into the chamber of her who *c*
Isa 8: 3 And she *c* and bore a son.
Jer 49:30 And has *c* a plan against you.
Hos 1: 3 and she *c* and bore him a son.
1: 6 And she *c* again and bore a
1: 8 she *c* and bore a son.
2: 5 She who *c* them has behaved
Mt 1:20 for that which is *c* in her is
Lk 1:24 those days his wife Elizabeth *c*;
1:36 your relative has also *c* a son
2:21 by the angel before He was *c*
Acts 5: 4 Why have you *c* this thing in
Rom 9:10 but when Rebecca also had *c* by
Jas 1:15 Then, when desire has *c*,

CONCEIVES (1/1) CONCEIVE

Ps 7:14 he *c* trouble and brings forth

CONCEIVING (1/1) CONCEIVE

Isa 59:13 *C* and uttering from the heart

CONCEPTION (3/3) CONCEIVE

Gen 3:16 multiply your sorrow and your *c*;
Ruth 4:13 in to her, the LORD gave her *c*,
Hos 9:11 no pregnancy, and no *c*!

CONCERN (10/9) CONCERNED, CONCERNS

Job 39:16 labor is in vain, without *c*,
Ps 131: 1 Neither do I *c* myself with
Ezek 36:21 But I had *c* for My holy name,
Dan 4:19 may the dream *c* those who hate
4:19 and its interpretation *c* your
Jn 2: 4 what does your *c* have to do
Acts 28:31 and teaching the things which *c*
2 Cor 11:28 my deep *c* for all the churches.
11:30 boast in the things which *c* my
Col 2:22 which all *c* things which perish

CONCERNED (6/6) CONCERN

Gen 45:20 Also do not be *c* about your
2 Sam 14: 1 that the king's heart was *c*
2 Ki 4:13 you have been *c* for us with all
1 Cor 7:21 Do not be *c* about it; but if
9: 9 Is it oxen God is *c* about?
Heb 9:10 *c* only with foods and drinks,

CONCERNING (289/271)

Gen 5:29 This one will comfort us *c* our
12:20 So Pharaoh commanded his men *c*
19:21 I have favored you *c* this thing
24: 9 and swore to him *c* this matter.
27:42 Esau comforts himself *c* you
42:21 We are truly guilty *c* our
Ex 8:12 Moses cried out to the LORD *c*
Lev 4:26 shall make atonement for him *c*
5: 6 shall make atonement for him *c*
6: 3 found what was lost and lies *c*
6:18 forever in your generations *c*
16:21 *c* all their sins, putting them
27:32 And *c* the tithe of the herd or
Num 8:20 the LORD commanded Moses *c*
8:22 as the LORD commanded Moses *c*
9: 8 what the LORD will command *c*
30: 1 to the heads of the tribes *c*
30:12 proceeded from her lips *c* her
30:12 lips concerning her vows or *c*
32:28 So Moses gave command *c* them to
36: 6 is what the LORD commands *c*
Deut 4:10 especially *c* the day you stood
4:32 For ask now *c* the days that are
19:15 shall not rise against a man *c*
Josh 14: 6 said to Moses the man of God *c*
23:14 the LORD your God spoke *c* you.
Judg 9: 3 spoke all these words *c* him in
21: 5 they had made a great oath *c*
Ruth 4: 7 in former times in Israel *c*
1 Sam 3:12 Eli all that I have spoken *c*
12: 7 with you before the LORD *c*
25:30 the good that He has spoken *c*
2 Sam 3: 8 charge me today with a fault *c*
7:25 word which You have spoken *c*
7:25 concerning Your servant and *c*
10: 2 his servants to comfort him *c*
11:18 and told David all the things *c*
13:39 For he had been comforted *c*
14: 8 and I will give orders *c* you."
18: 5 gave all the captains orders *c*
1 Ki 2: 4 His word which He spoke *c* me,
2:27 of the LORD which He spoke *c*
5: 8 I will do all you desire *c* the
6:12 *C* this temple which you are
8:41 *c* a foreigner, who is not of
10: 1 heard of the fame of Solomon *c*
11:10 and had commanded him *c* this
21:23 And *c* Jezebel the LORD also
22: 8 he does not prophesy good *c* me,
22:18 he would not prophesy good *c*
2 Ki 10:10 LORD which the LORD spoke *c*
17:15 *c* whom the LORD had charged
19: 9 And the king heard *c* Tirhakah
19:21 which the LORD has spoken *c*
19:32 thus says the LORD *c* the king
22:13 *c* the words of this book that
22:13 to all that is written *c* us.
22:18 *C* the words which you have
1 Chr 11:10 to the word of the LORD *c*
17:23 word which You have spoken *c*
17:23 concerning Your servant and *c*
19: 2 messengers to comfort him *c*
22:12 and give you charge *c* Israel,
22:13 which the LORD charged Moses *c*
24:21 *C* Rehabiah, of the sons of
26: 1 *C* the divisions of the
2 Chr 6:32 *c* a foreigner, who is not of
8:15 to the priests and Levites *c*
8:15 concerning any matter or *c* the
9:29 the visions of Iddo the seer *c*
12:15 and of Iddo the seer *c*
18: 7 he never prophesies good *c* me,
18:17 he would not prophesy good *c*
24:27 Now *c* his sons, and the many
31: 9 the priests and the Levites *c*
34:21 *c* the words of the book that is
34:26 *C* the words which you have
Ezra 5: 5 a written answer was returned *c*
5:17 the king send us his pleasure *c*
6: 3 King Cyrus issued a decree *c*
7:14 seven counselors to inquire *c*
Neh 1: 2 and I asked them *c* the Jews who
1: 2 the captivity, and *c* Jerusalem.
6: 7 prophets to proclaim *c* you at
11:23 it was the king's command *c*
11:24 king's deputy in all matters *c*
13:14 *c* this, and do not wipe out my
13:22 *c* this also, and spare me
Esth 3: 2 for so the king had commanded *c*
4: 5 and she gave him a command *c*
8: 8 yourselves write a decree *c*
9:26 what they had seen *c* this
9:31 and their descendants *c*
Job 19: 7 If I cry out *c* wrong, I am not
34: 6 Should I lie *c* my right?
36:33 *c* the rising storm.
Ps 7: which he sang to the LORD *c*
17: 4 *C* the works of men, By the
36: 1 An oracle within my heart *c* the
45: 1 I recite my composition *c* the
73: 8 scoff and speak wickedly *c*
106:34 *C* whom the LORD had commanded
119:128 all Your precepts *c* all
119:152 *C* Your testimonies, I have
Eccl 1:13 and search out by wisdom *c* all
3:18 *C* the condition of the sons of
7:10 you do not inquire wisely *c*
Isa 1: 1 which he saw *c* Judah and
2: 1 Isaiah the son of Amoz saw *c*
8: 1 write on it with a man's pen *c*
8:12 *C* all that this people call a
16:13 which the LORD has spoken *c*
29:22 *c* the house of Jacob: "Jacob
37: 9 And the king heard *c* Tirhakah
37:22 which the LORD has spoken *c*
37:33 thus says the LORD *c* the king
45:11 Ask Me of things to come *c* My
45:11 And *c* the work of My hands,
Jer 1:16 My judgments Against them *c*
7:22 *c* burnt offerings or sacrifices
11:21 thus says the LORD *c* the men
14: 1 LORD that came to Jeremiah *c*
14:15 thus says the LORD *c* the
16: 3 For thus says the LORD *c* the
16: 3 and *c* their mothers who bore
18: 7 The instant I speak *c* a nation
18: 7 concerning a nation and *c* a
18: 9 And the instant I speak *c* a
18: 9 concerning a nation and *c* a
18:10 then I will relent *c* the good
21:11 And *c* the house of the king of
22:11 For thus says the LORD *c*
22:18 thus says the LORD *c*
23:15 thus says the LORD of hosts *c*
25: 1 word that came to Jeremiah *c*
25:13 Jeremiah has prophesied *c* all
26: 3 that I may relent *c* the
26:13 then the LORD will relent *c*
26:19 And the Lord relented *c* the
27:19 thus says the LORD of hosts *c*
27:19 *c* the Sea, concerning the
27:19 *c* the carts, and concerning the
27:19 and *c* the remainder of the
27:21 *c* the vessels that remain in
29:16 thus says the LORD *c* the king
29:16 *c* all the people who dwell in
29:16 and *c* your brethren who have
29:21 *c* Ahab the son of Kolaiah, and
29:31 Thus says the LORD *c* Shemaiah
30: 4 words that the LORD spoke *c*
32:36 *c* this city of which you say,
33: 4 *c* the houses of this city and
34: 4 of Judah! Thus says the LORD *c*
36:30 thus says the LORD *c*
39:11 king of Babylon gave charge *c*
40:16 for you speak falsely *c*
42:10 For I relent *c* the disaster
42:19 'The LORD has said *c* you,
44: 1 word that came to Jeremiah *c*
46: 2 *C* the army of Pharaoh Necho,
52:21 Now *c* the pillars: the height
Lam 1:17 The LORD has commanded *c*
Ezek 13:16 of Israel who prophesy *c*
14: 7 a prophet to inquire of him *c*
14:22 Then you will be comforted *c*
18: 2 when you use this proverb *c*
20:28 I brought them into the land *c*
21:28 Thus says the Lord GOD *c* the
21:28 concerning the Ammonites and *c*
23:43 Then I said *c* her who had
36: 6 Therefore prophesy *c* the land of
44: 5 all that I say to you *c* all the
45:14 The ordinance *c* oil, the bath of
Dan 2:18 from the God of heaven *c* this
4:33 hour the word was fulfilled *c*
5:29 and made a proclamation *c* him
6: 4 some charge against Daniel *c*
6: 5 we find it against him *c* the
6:12 and spoke *c* the king's decree:
6:17 that the purpose *c* Daniel might
8:13 *c* the daily sacrifices and
Am 1: 1 which he saw *c* Israel in the
7: 3 So the LORD relented *c* this.
7: 6 So the LORD relented *c* this.
Ob 1 Thus says the Lord GOD *c* Edom
Mic 1: 1 which he saw *c* Samaria and
3: 5 Thus says the LORD *c* the
Nah 1:14 LORD has given a command *c*
Hag 2:11 ask the priests *c* the law,
Mt 11: 7 to say to the multitudes *c*
13:52 every scribe instructed *c* the
16:11 that I did not speak to you *c*
18:19 if two of you agree on earth *c*
22:31 But *c* the resurrection of the
Mk 7:17 His disciples asked Him *c* the
9:12 And how is it written *c* the Son
12:26 But *c* the dead, that they rise,
Lk 2:17 saying which was told them *c*
3:19 being rebuked by him *c*
4:38 and they made request of Him *c*
5:15 the report went around *c* Him
7:18 of John reported to him *c* all
7:24 to speak to the multitudes *c*
18:31 are written by the prophets *c*
22:37 For the things *c* Me have an
23:14 found no fault in this Man *c*
24:19 The things *c* Jesus of Nazareth,
24:27 all the Scriptures the things *c*
24:44 Prophets and the Psalms *c* Me.
Jn 7:12 complaining among the people *c*
7:17 he shall know *c* the doctrine,
7:32 crowd murmuring these things *c*
7:39 But this He spoke *c* the Spirit,
8:26 things to say and to judge *c*
9:18 But the Jews did not believe *c*
11:19 to comfort them *c* their
13:18 'I do not speak *c* all of you.
18:34 or did others tell you this *c*
Acts 1:16 before by the mouth of David *c*
2:25 For David says *c* Him: 'I
2:31 spoke *c* the resurrection of the
8:12 as he preached the things *c*
13:29 all that was written *c* Him,
19: 8 reasoning and persuading *c* the
21:24 of which they were informed *c*
21:25 But *c* the Gentiles who believe,
22:18 not receive your testimony *c*
23: 6 *c* the hope and resurrection of
23:15 to make further inquiries *c*
23:29 found out that he was accused *c*
24:21 *C* the resurrection of the dead I
24:24 sent for Paul and heard him *c*
25: 9 and there be judged before me *c*
25:16 to answer for himself *c* the
25:20 and there be judged *c* these
25:26 certain to write to my lord *c*
26: 2 answer for myself before you *c*
28:21 received letters from Judea *c*
28:22 for *c* this sect, we know that
28:23 persuading them *c* Jesus from
Rom 1: 3 *c* His Son Jesus Christ our Lord,
9:27 Isaiah also cries out *c* Israel:
11:28 *C* the gospel they are enemies
11:28 but *c* the election they are
15:14 Now I myself am confident *c*
16:19 and simple *c* evil.
1 Cor 1: 4 I thank my God always *c* you for
1:11 it has been declared to me *c*
6: 4 If then you have judgments *c*
7: 1 Now *c* the things of which you
7:25 Now *c* virgins: I have no
8: 1 Now *c* things offered to idols:
8: 4 Therefore *c* the eating of things
12: 1 Now *c* spiritual gifts,
16: 1 Now *c* the collection for the
16:12 Now *c* our brother Apollos,
2 Cor 8:23 my partner and fellow worker *c*
9: 1 Now *c* the ministering to the
12: 8 *C* this thing I pleaded with the
Gal 1:20 (Now *c* the things which I write
Eph 4:22 *c* your former conduct, the old
5:32 but I speak *c* Christ and the
Phil 3: 5 *c* the law, a Pharisee;
3: 6 *c* zeal, persecuting the church;

3: 6 **c** the righteousness which is in
4:15 no church shared with me **c**
1 Th 1: 9 For they themselves declare **c** us
3: 2 you and encourage you **c** your
3: 7 distress we were comforted **c**
4: 9 But **c** brotherly love you have
4:13 **c** those who have fallen asleep,
5: 1 But **c** the times and the seasons,
2 Th 2: 1 **c** the coming of our Lord Jesus
3: 4 have confidence in the Lord **c**
1 Tim 1:18 prophecies previously made **c**
1:19 **c** the faith have suffered
6:21 it some have strayed **c** the
2 Tim 2:18 who have strayed **c** the truth,
3: 8 disapproved **c** the faith;
Heb 6: 9 confident of better things **c**
7:14 tribe Moses spoke nothing **c**
11:20 Isaac blessed Jacob and Esau **c**
11:22 and gave instructions **c** his
1 Pe 4:12 do not think it strange **c** the
2 Pe 3: 9 The Lord is not slack **c** His
1 Jn 1: 1 **c** the Word of life—
2:26 things I have written to you **c**
2:27 same anointing teaches you **c**
Jude 3 diligent to write to you **c** our

CONCERNS (4/4) CONCERN

Ex 22: 9 whether it **c** an ox, a
Ps 138: 8 will perfect that which **c** me;
Ezek 7:13 For the vision **c** the whole
12:10 This burden **c** the prince in

CONCESSION (1/1)

1 Cor 7: 6 But I say this as a **c**,

CONCILIATION (1/1)

Eccl 10: 4 For **c** pacifies great offenses.

CONCISION (KJV) See MUTILATION

CONCLUDE (1/1) CONCLUDED, CONCLUDING, CONCLUSION

Rom 3:28 Therefore we **c** that a man is

CONCLUDED (2/2) CONCLUDE

Ruth 3:18 will not rest until he has **c**
Lk 7: 1 Now when He **c** all His sayings in

CONCLUDING (2/2) CONCLUDE

Acts 16:10 **c** that the Lord had called us
Heb 11:19 **c** that God was able to raise

CONCLUSION (2/2) CONCLUDE

Eccl 12:13 Let us hear the **c** of the whole
1 Cor 14:15 What is the **c** then? I will

CONCORD (KJV) See ACCORD

CONCOURSE (KJV) See CONCOURSES, GATHERING

CONCOURSES (1/1)

Prov 1:21 She cries out in the chief **c**,

CONCUBINE (23/22) CONCUBINES

Gen 22:24 His **c**, whose name was Reumah,
35:22 lay with Bilhah his father's **c**;
36:12 Now Timna was the **c** of Eliphaz,
Lev 19:20 is betrothed to a man as a **c**,
Judg 8:31 And his **c** who was in Shechem
19: 1 He took for himself a **c** from
19: 2 But his **c** played the harlot
19: 9 he and his **c** and his servant—his
19:10 his **c** was also with him.
19:24 daughter and the man's **c**;
19:25 So the man took his **c** and
19:27 to go his way, there was his **c**,
19:29 a knife, laid hold of his **c**,
20: 4 My **c** and I went into Gibeah,
20: 5 but instead they ravished my **c**
20: 6 "So I took hold of my **c**,
2 Sam 3: 7 And Saul had a **c**,
3: 7 you gone in to my father's **c**?
21:11 the **c** of Saul, had done.
1 Chr 1:32 born to Keturah, Abraham's **c**,
2:46 Ephah, Caleb's **c**,
2:48 Maachah, Caleb's **c**,
7:14 his Syrian **c** bore him Machir

CONCUBINES (17/16) CONCUBINE

Gen 25: 6 gave gifts to the sons of the **c**
2 Sam 5:13 And David took more **c** and wives
15:16 But the king left ten women, **c**,
16:21 "Go in to your father's **c**,
16:22 went in to his father's **c** in
19: 5 wives and the lives of your **c**,
20: 3 his **c** whom he had left to keep
1 Ki 11: 3 princesses, and three hundred **c**;
1 Chr 3: 9 besides the sons of the **c**,
2 Chr 11:21 than all his wives and his **c**;
11:21 took eighteen wives and sixty **c**,
Esth 2:14 king's eunuch who kept the **c**.
Song 6: 8 are sixty queens And eighty **c**,
6: 9 blessed, The queens and the **c**,
Dan 5: 2 and his **c** might drink from
5: 3 and his **c** drank from them.
5:23 lords, your wives and your **c**,

CONCUPISCENCE (KJV) See EVIL, LUST, PASSION

CONDEMN (25/25) CONDEMNATION, CONDEMNED, CONDEMNING, CONDEMNS, UNCONDEMNED

Ex 22: 9 and whomever the judges **c**
Deut 25: 1 justify the righteous and **c**
Job 9:20 my own mouth would **c** me;
10: 2 Do not **c** me; Show me why You
34:17 Will you **c** Him who is most
40: 8 Would you **c** Me that you may be
Ps 37:33 Nor **c** him when he is judged.
94:21 And **c** innocent blood.
109:31 To save him from those who **c**
Prov 12: 2 of wicked intentions He will **c**.
Isa 50: 9 Who is he who will **c** Me?
54:17 you in judgment You shall **c**.
Mt 12:41 with this generation and **c** it,
12:42 with this generation and **c** it,
20:18 and they will **c** Him to death,
Mk 10:33 and they will **c** Him to death
Lk 6:37 **C** not, and you shall not be
11:31 men of this generation and **c**
11:32 with this generation and **c** it,
Jn 3:17 His Son into the world to **c**
8:11 Neither do I **c** you; go and sin
Rom 2: 1 you judge another you **c**
14:22 Happy is he who does not **c**
2 Cor 7: 3 I do not say this to **c**;
1 Jn 3:21 if our heart does not **c** us, we

CONDEMNATION (16/16) CONDEMN

Mt 23:14 you will receive greater **c**.
23:33 How can you escape the **c** of
Mk 3:29 but is subject to eternal **c**"—
12:40 These will receive greater **c**.
Lk 20:47 These will receive greater **c**.
23:40 seeing you are under the same **c**?
Jn 3:19 "And this is the **c**,
5:29 evil, to the resurrection of **c**.
Rom 3: 8 Their **c** is just.
5:16 one offense resulted in **c**,
5:18 came to all men, resulting in **c**,
8: 1 There is therefore now no **c** to
2 Cor 3: 9 For if the ministry of **c** had
1 Tim 3: 6 pride he fall into the same **c**
5:12 having **c** because they have cast
Jude 4 ago were marked out for this **c**,

CONDEMNED (26/25) CONDEMN

2 Sam 24:10 And David's heart **c** him after
Job 9:29 I am **c**, Why then do I labor
32: 3 and yet had **c** Job.
Ps 34:21 hate the righteous shall be **c**.
34:22 who trust in Him shall be **c**.
Am 2: 8 And drink the wine of the **c**
Mt 12: 7 you would not have **c** the
12:37 and by your words you will be **c**.
27: 3 seeing that He had been **c**,
Mk 14:64 And they all **c** Him to be
16:16 who does not believe will be **c**.
Lk 6:37 not, and you shall not be **c**.
24:20 rulers delivered Him to be **c**
Jn 3:18 who believes in Him is not **c**;
3:18 he who does not believe is **c**
8:10 Has no one **c** you?"
Rom 8: 3 He **c** sin in the flesh,
14:23 But he who doubts is **c** if he
1 Cor 4: 9 as men **c** to death; for we have
11:32 that we may not be **c** with the
2 Th 2:12 that they all may be **c** who did
Titus 2: 8 sound speech that cannot be **c**,
Heb 11: 7 by which he **c** the world and
Jas 5: 6 You have **c**, you have murdered
5: 9 brethren, lest you be **c**.
2 Pe 2: 6 **c** them to destruction, making

CONDEMNING (2/2) CONDEMN

1 Ki 8:32 **c** the wicked, bringing his way
Acts 13:27 have fulfilled them in **c** Him.

CONDEMNS (5/5) CONDEMN

Job 15: 6 Your own mouth **c** you, and not
21:31 Who **c** his way to his face?
Prov 17:15 and he who **c** the just, Both of
Rom 8:34 Who is he who **c**?
1 Jn 3:20 For if our heart **c** us, God is

CONDESCEND (KJV) See ASSOCIATE

CONDITION (6/6) CONDITIONS

Gen 34:15 But on this **c** we will consent
34:22 Only on this **c** will the men
1 Sam 11: 2 On this **c** I will make a
2 Chr 24:13 house of God to its original **c**
Eccl 3:18 Concerning the **c** of the sons of
Jn 5: 6 already had been in that **c**

CONDITIONS (1/1)

Lk 14:32 sends a delegation and asks **c**

CONDUCT (24/23) CONDUCTED

Deut 22:14 charges her with shameful **c**,
22:17 has charged her with shameful **c**,
1 Sam 4: 9 Be strong and **c** yourselves like
4: 9 **C** yourselves like men, and
28: 8 Please **c** a seance for me, and
Ps 37:14 slay those who are of upright **c**.
50:23 And to him who orders his **c**
Gal 1:13 you have heard of my former **c**
Eph 4:22 off, concerning your former **c**,
Phil 1:27 Only let your **c** be worthy of
1 Tim 3:15 you may know how you ought to **c**
4:12 to the believers in word, in **c**,
Heb 13: 5 Let your **c** be without
13: 7 the outcome of their **c**.
Jas 3:13 Let him show by good **c** that
1 Pe 1:15 you also be holy in all your **c**,
1:17 **c** yourselves throughout the
1:18 from your aimless **c** received
2:12 having your **c** honorable among
3: 1 may be won by the **c** of their
3: 2 when they observe your chaste **c**
3:16 those who revile your good **c** in
2 Pe 2: 7 was oppressed by the filthy **c**
3:11 ought you to be in holy **c** and

CONDUCTED (3/3) CONDUCT

Acts 17:15 So those who **c** Paul brought him
2 Cor 1:12 of our conscience that we **c**
Eph 2: 3 among whom also we all once **c**

CONDUIT (KJV) See AQUEDUCT

CONFECTION (KJV) See COMPOUND

CONFECTIONARIES (KJV) See PERFUMERS

CONFEDERACY (2/2)

Ps 83: 5 They form a **c** against You:
Ob 7 All the men in your **c** Shall

CONFER (2/2) CONFERRED

Judg 19:30 until this day. Consider it, **c**,
Gal 1:16 I did not immediately **c** with

CONFERRED (4/4) CONFER

1 Ki 1: 7 Then he **c** with Joab the son of
Lk 22: 4 So he went his way and **c** with
Acts 4:15 they **c** among themselves,
25:12 when he had **c** with the council,

CONFESS (25/25) CONFESSED, CONFESSES, CONFESSING, CONFESSION

Lev 5: 5 that he shall **c** that he has
16:21 **c** over it all the iniquities of
26:40 But if they **c** their iniquity
Num 5: 7 then he shall **c** the sin which he
1 Ki 8:33 they turn back to You and **c**
8:35 pray toward this place and **c**
2 Chr 6:24 and return and **c** Your name, and
6:26 pray toward this place and **c**
Neh 1: 6 and **c** the sins of the children
Job 40:14 Then I will also **c** to you That
Ps 32: 5 I will **c** my transgressions to
Mt 10:32 him I will also **c** before My
Lk 12: 8 him the Son of Man also will **c**
Jn 12:42 of the Pharisees they did not **c**
Acts 23: 8 but the Pharisees **c** both.
24:14 But this I **c** to you, that
Rom 10: 9 that if you **c** with your mouth
14:11 And every tongue shall **c**
15: 9 For this reason I will **c**
Phil 2:11 and that every tongue should **c**
Jas 5:16 **C** your trespasses to one
1 Jn 1: 9 If we **c** our sins, He is faithful
4: 3 every spirit that does not **c**
2 Jn 7 out into the world who do not **c**
Rev 3: 5 but I will **c** his name before My

CONFESSED (7/6) CONFESS

Neh 9: 2 and they stood and **c** their sins
9: 3 and for another fourth they **c**
Jn 1:20 He **c**, and did not deny,
1:20 and did not deny, but **c**,
9:22 already that if anyone **c** that
1 Tim 6:12 you were also called and have **c**
Heb 11:13 embraced them and **c** that they

CONFESSES (5/5) CONFESS

Prov 28:13 But whoever **c** and forsakes
Mt 10:32 Therefore whoever **c** Me before
Lk 12: 8 whoever **c** Me before men, him
1 Jn 4: 2 Every spirit that **c** that Jesus
4:15 Whoever **c** that Jesus is the Son

CONFESSING (5/5) CONFESS

Ezra 10: 1 was praying, and while he was **c**,

Dan 9:20 and **c** my sin and the sin of my
Mt 3: 6 in the Jordan, **c** their sins.
Mk 1: 5 the Jordan River, **c** their sins.
Acts 19:18 many who had believed came **c**

CONFESSION (11/11) CONFESS

Josh 7:19 and make **c** to Him, and tell me
2 Chr 30:22 peace offerings and making **c**
Ezra 10:11 make **c** to the LORD God of your
Dan 9: 4 to the LORD my God, and made **c**,
Rom 10:10 and with the mouth **c** is made
2 Cor 9:13 for the obedience of your **c** to
1 Tim 6:12 and have confessed the good **c**
6:13 Jesus who witnessed the good **c**
Heb 3: 1 and High Priest of our **c**,
4:14 of God, let us hold fast our **c**.
10:23 Let us hold fast the **c** of our

CONFIDENCE (36/35) CONFIDENT

Judg 9:26 the men of Shechem put their **c**
2 Ki 18:19 What **c** is this in which you
Job 4: 6 Is not your reverence your **c**?
8:14 Whose **c** shall be cut off, And
31:24 to fine gold, 'You are my **c**';
Ps 65: 5 You who are the **c** of all
118: 8 in the LORD Than to put **c** in
118: 9 in the LORD Than to put **c** in
Prov 3:26 For the LORD will be your **c**,
14:26 the LORD there is strong **c**,
25:19 ***C*** in an unfaithful man in time
Isa 30:15 In quietness and **c** shall be
36: 4 What **c** is this in which you
Jer 48:13 was ashamed of Bethel, their **c**.
Ezek 29:16 No longer shall it be the **c** of
Mic 7: 5 Do not put your **c** in a
Acts 28:31 Lord Jesus Christ with all **c**,
2 Cor 1:15 And in this **c** I intended to
2: 3 having **c** in you all that my joy
7:16 I rejoice that I have **c** in you
8:22 because of the great **c** which
10: 2 I may not be bold with that **c**
11:17 in this **c** of boasting.
Gal 5:10 I have **c** in you, in the Lord,
Eph 3:12 have boldness and access with **c**
Phil 3: 3 and have no **c** in the flesh,
3: 4 though I also might have **c** in
3: 4 else thinks he may have **c** in
2 Th 3: 4 And we have **c** in the Lord
Phm 1:21 Having **c** in your obedience, I
Heb 3: 6 we are if we hold fast the **c**
3:14 we hold the beginning of our **c**
10:35 do not cast away your **c**,
1 Jn 2:28 we may have **c** and not be
3:21 we have **c** toward God.
5:14 Now this is the **c** that we have

CONFIDENT (13/13) CONFIDENCE, CONFIDENTLY

Job 6:20 because they were **c**;
40:23 he is not disturbed; He is **c**,
Ps 27: 3 In this I will be **c**.
Rom 2:19 and are **c** that you yourself are
15:14 Now I myself am **c** concerning
2 Cor 5: 6 So we are always **c**,
5: 8 We are **c**, yes, well pleased
9: 4 should be ashamed of this **c**
Phil 1: 6 being **c** of this very thing, that
1:14 having become **c** by my chains,
1:25 And being **c** of this, I know that
Heb 6: 9 we are **c** of better things
13:18 for we are **c** that we have a

CONFIDENTLY (1/1) CONFIDENT

Lk 22:59 another **c** affirmed, saying,

CONFINED (10/10)

Gen 39:20 the king's prisoners were **c**.
40: 3 the place where Joseph was **c**.
40: 5 who were **c** in the prison, had
42:19 let one of your brothers be **c**
Ex 21:18 and he does not die but is **c** to
21:29 owner, and he has not kept it **c**,
21:36 and its owner has not kept it **c**,
Josh 17:15 mountains of Ephraim are too **c**
Jer 36: 5 Baruch, saying, "I am **c**,
Gal 3:22 But the Scripture has **c** all

CONFIRM (11/11) CONFIRMATION, CONFIRMED, CONFIRMING, CONFIRMS

Lev 26: 9 multiply you and **c** My covenant
Num 30:13 her husband may **c** it, or her
Deut 27:26 is the one who does not **c**
Ruth 4: 7 to **c** anything: one man took off
1 Ki 1:14 will come in after you and **c**
Esth 9:29 wrote with full authority to **c**
9:31 to **c** these days of Purim at
Dan 9:27 Then he shall **c** a covenant with
11: 1 stood up to **c** and strengthen
Rom 15: 8 to **c** the promises made to the
1 Cor 1: 8 who will also **c** you to the end,

CONFIRMATION (3/3) CONFIRM

Ruth 4: 7 and this was a **c** in Israel.
Phil 1: 7 and in the defense and **c** of
Heb 6:16 and an oath for **c** is for them

CONFIRMED (15/15) CONFIRM

1 Ki 2:24 who has **c** me and set me on the
1 Chr 16:17 And **c** it to Jacob for a
Esth 2:23 made into the matter, it was **c**,
9:32 So the decree of Esther **c** these
Ps 68: 9 Whereby You **c** Your
105:10 And **c** it to Jacob for a
119:106 I have sworn and **c** That I will
Ezek 13: 6 hope that the word may be **c**.
Dan 9:12 And He has **c** His words, which He
1 Cor 1: 6 the testimony of Christ was **c**
Gal 3:15 covenant, yet if it is **c**,
3:17 annul the covenant that was **c**
Heb 2: 3 and was **c** to us by those who
6:17 **c** it by an oath,
2 Pe 1:19 so we have the prophetic word **c**,

CONFIRMING (1/1) CONFIRM

Mk 16:20 Lord working with them and **c**

CONFIRMS (3/2) CONFIRM

Num 30:14 then he **c** all her vows or all
30:14 he **c** them, because he made no
Isa 44:26 Who **c** the word of His servant,

CONFISCATED (1/1) CONFISCATION

Ezra 10: 8 all his property would be **c**,

CONFISCATION (1/1) CONFISCATED

Ezra 7:26 or **c** of goods, or imprisonment.

CONFLICT (4/4) CONFLICTS

Am 7: 4 the Lord GOD called for **c** by
Phil 1:30 having the same **c** which you saw
Col 2: 1 you to know what a great **c** I
1 Th 2: 2 you the gospel of God in much **c**.

CONFLICTS (1/1) CONFLICT

2 Cor 7: 5 Outside were **c**, inside were

CONFORMED (4/4) CONFORMING

Rom 8:29 He also predestined to be **c**
12: 2 And do not be **c** to this world,
Phil 3:10 being **c** to His death,
3:21 lowly body that it may be **c** to

CONFORMING (1/1) CONFORMED

1 Pe 1:14 not **c** yourselves to the former

CONFOUNDED (12/12)

2 Ki 19:26 They were dismayed and **c**;
Ps 40:15 Let them be **c** because of their
69: 6 not those who seek You be **c**
70: 2 Let them be ashamed and **c** Who
71:13 Let them be **c** and consumed
71:24 the day long; For they are **c**,
83:17 Let them be **c** and dismayed
Isa 37:27 They were dismayed and **c**;
Jer 14: 3 They were ashamed and **c** And
15: 9 She has been ashamed and **c**.
Ezek 36:32 Be ashamed and **c** for your own
Acts 9:22 and **c** the Jews who dwelt in

CONFRONT (3/3) CONFRONTED, CONFRONTING

Job 30:27 Days of affliction **c** me.
Ps 17:13 ***C*** him, cast him down;
Am 9:10 shall not overtake nor **c** us.

CONFRONTED (7/7) CONFRONT

2 Sam 22: 6 The snares of death **c** me.
22:19 They **c** me in the day of my
2 Ki 23:29 him at Megiddo when he **c** him.
Ps 18: 5 The snares of death **c** me.
18:18 They **c** me in the day of my
Mt 21:23 and the elders of the people **c**
Lk 20: 1 with the elders, **c** Him

CONFRONTING (1/1) CONFRONT

Dan 8: 7 And I saw him **c** the ram;

CONFUSE (1/1) CONFUSED, CONFUSION

Gen 11: 7 let Us go down and there **c**

CONFUSED (6/6) CONFUSE

Gen 11: 9 because there the LORD **c** the
1 Sam 7:10 and so **c** them that they were
Job 6:20 They come there and are **c**.
Ps 70: 2 Let them be turned back and **c**
Acts 2: 6 came together, and were **c**,
19:32 another, for the assembly was **c**,

CONFUSION (19/19) CONFUSE

Ex 23:27 I will cause **c** among all the
Deut 28:20 will send on you cursing, **c**,
28:28 madness and blindness and **c** of
1 Sam 14:20 and there was very great **c**.
Neh 4: 8 attack Jerusalem and create **c**.
Ps 35: 4 be turned back and brought to **c**
35:26 and brought to mutual **c** Who
40:14 and brought to mutual **c** Who
60: 3 made us drink the wine of **c**.
Isa 24:10 The city of **c** is broken down;
34:11 out over it The line of **c** and
41:29 molded images are wind and **c**.
45:16 They shall go in **c** together,
61: 7 And instead of **c** they shall
Jer 20:11 Their everlasting **c** will
Zech 12: 4 will strike every horse with **c**,
Acts 19:29 whole city was filled with **c**,
1 Cor 14:33 God is not the author of **c**
Jas 3:16 **c** and every evil thing are

CONGEALED (1/1)

Ex 15: 8 The depths **c** in the heart of

CONGREGATION (139/131) CONGREGATIONS

Ex 12: 3 Speak to all the **c** of Israel,
12: 6 the whole assembly of the **c** of
12:19 shall be cut off from the **c** of
12:47 All the **c** of Israel shall keep
16: 1 and all the **c** of the children
16: 2 Then the whole **c** of the children
16: 9 Say to all the **c** of the children
16:10 as Aaron spoke to the whole **c**
16:22 And all the rulers of the **c**
17: 1 Then all the **c** of the children
34:31 and all the rulers of the **c**
35: 1 Then Moses gathered all the **c** of
35: 4 And Moses spoke to all the **c** of
35:20 And all the **c** of the children
38:25 who were numbered of the **c**
Lev 4:13 Now if the whole **c** of Israel
4:15 And the elders of the **c** shall
8: 3 and gather all the **c** together at
8: 4 And the **c** was gathered together
8: 5 And Moses said to the **c**,
9: 5 And all the **c** drew near and
10:17 you to bear the guilt of the **c**,
16: 5 And he shall take from the **c** of
19: 2 Speak to all the **c** of the
24:14 and let all the **c** stone him.
24:16 All the **c** shall certainly stone
Num 1: 2 Take a census of all the **c** of
1:16 These were chosen from the **c**,
1:18 and they assembled all the **c**
1:53 there may be no wrath on the **c**
3: 7 and the needs of the whole **c**
4:34 and the leaders of the **c**
8: 9 gather together the whole **c** of
8:20 Moses and Aaron and all the **c**
10: 2 use them for calling the **c** and
10: 3 all the **c** shall gather before
13:26 Moses and Aaron and all the **c**
13:26 word to them and to all the **c**
14: 1 So all the **c** lifted up their
14: 2 and the whole **c** said to them,
14: 5 all the assembly of the **c** of
14: 7 and they spoke to all the **c** of
14:10 And all the **c** said to stone them
14:27 I bear with this evil **c** who
14:35 do so to all this evil **c** who
14:36 who returned and made all the **c**
15:24 without the knowledge of the **c**,
15:24 that the whole **c** shall offer
15:25 make atonement for the whole **c**
15:26 shall be forgiven the whole **c**
15:33 and Aaron, and to all the **c**.
15:35 all the **c** shall stone him with
15:36 all the **c** brought him outside
16: 2 and fifty leaders of the **c**,
16: 2 representatives of the **c**,
16: 3 for all the **c** is holy, every
16: 9 has separated you from the **c**
16: 9 and to stand before the **c** to
16:19 And Korah gathered all the **c**
16:19 the LORD appeared to all the **c**.
16:21 yourselves from among this **c**,
16:22 and You be angry with all the **c**?
16:24 'Speak to the **c**, saying,
16:26 And he spoke to the **c**,
16:41 On the next day all the **c** of
16:42 when the **c** had gathered against
16:45 "Get away from among this **c**,
16:46 and take it quickly to the **c**
19: 9 they shall be kept for the **c**
20: 1 children of Israel, the whole **c**,
20: 2 there was no water for the **c**;
20: 8 your brother Aaron gather the **c**
20: 8 and give drink to the **c** and
20:11 and the **c** and their animals
20:22 children of Israel, the whole **c**,
20:27 Hor in the sight of all the **c**.
20:29 Now when all the **c** saw that
25: 6 and in the sight of all the **c**
25: 7 he rose from among the **c** and
26: 2 Take a census of all the **c** of
26: 9 representatives of the **c**,
27: 2 the leaders and all the **c**,
27:14 Zin, during the strife of the **c**,
27:16 all flesh, set a man over the **c**,
27:17 that the **c** of the LORD may not
27:19 the priest and before all the **c**,
27:20 that all the **c** of the children
27:21 of Israel with him—all the **c**.
27:22 the priest and before all the **c**.

31:12 and to the c of the children of
31:13 and all the leaders of the c,
31:16 there was a plague among the c
31:26 and the chief fathers of the c;
31:27 out to battle, and all the c.
31:43 now the half belonging to the c
32: 2 and to the leaders of the c,
32: 4 LORD defeated before the c of
35:12 until he stands before the c
35:24 then the c shall judge between
35:25 So the c shall deliver the
35:25 and the c shall return him to
Deut 33: 4 A heritage of the c of Jacob.
Josh 9:15 and the rulers of the c swore
9:18 because the rulers of the c had
9:18 And all the c complained
9:19 the rulers said to all the c,
9:21 water carriers for all the c,
9:27 and water carriers for the c
18: 1 Now the whole c of the children
20: 6 until he stands before the c
20: 9 until he stood before the c.
22:12 the whole c of the children of
22:16 Thus says the whole c of the
22:17 there was a plague in the c of
22:18 will be angry with the whole c
22:20 and wrath fell on all the c of
22:30 priest and the rulers of the c,
Judg 20: 1 and the c gathered together as
21:10 So the c sent out there twelve
21:13 Then the whole c sent word to
21:16 Then the elders of the c said,
1 Ki 8: 5 and all the c of Israel who
12:20 for him and called him to the c,
2 Chr 5: 6 and all the c of Israel who
Ps 1: 5 Nor sinners in the c of the
7: 7 So the c of the peoples shall
22:16 The c of the wicked has
68:10 Your c dwelt in it; You, O
74: 2 Remember Your c,
82: 1 God stands in the c of the
111: 1 of the upright and in the c.
Prov 5:14 the midst of the assembly and c.
Isa 14:13 also sit on the mount of the c
Jer 6:18 you nations, And know, O c,
30:20 And their c shall be
Hos 7:12 According to what their c has
Joel 2:16 the people, Sanctify the c,
Acts 7:38 This is he who was in the c in
13:43 Now when the c had broken up,

CONGREGATIONS (2/2) CONGREGATION

Ps 26:12 In the c I will bless the
68:26 Bless God in the c,

CONIAH (3/3) JECONIAH, JEHOIACHIN

Jer 22:24 though C the son of Jehoiakim,
22:28 Is this man C a despised, broken
37: 1 of Josiah reigned instead of C

CONIES (KJV) See BADGERS

CONJURES (1/1)

Deut 18:11 or one who c spells, or a

CONONIAH (2/2) CHENANIAH

2 Chr 31:12 C the Levite had charge of
31:13 overseers under the hand of C

CONQUER (2/2) CONQUERED, CONQUERING, CONQUERORS

Deut 7: 2 you shall c them and utterly
Rev 6: 2 he went out conquering and to c.

CONQUERED (6/6) CONQUER

Deut 29: 7 us to battle, and we c them.
Josh 10:40 So Joshua c all the land:
10:41 And Joshua c them from Kadesh
12: 6 the children of Israel had c;
12: 7 and the children of Israel c
2 Ki 10:32 and Hazael c them in all the

CONQUERING (1/1) CONQUER

Rev 6: 2 and he went out c and to

CONQUERORS (1/1) CONQUER

Rom 8:37 these things we are more than c

CONSCIENCE (29/28) CONSCIENCE', CONSCIENCES

Jn 8: 9 being convicted by their c,
Acts 23: 1 I have lived in all good c
24:16 always strive to have a c
Rom 2:15 their c also bearing witness,
9: 1 my c also bearing me witness in
13: 5 of wrath but also for c' sake.
1 Cor 8: 7 offered to an idol; and their c,
8:10 will not the c of him who is
8:12 and wound their weak c,
10:25 asking no questions for c'
10:27 asking no questions for c' sake.
10:28 and for c' sake; for "the
10:29 'C," I say, not your own, but
10:29 judged by another man's c?
2 Cor 1:12 the testimony of our c that we
4: 2 ourselves to every man's c in
1 Tim 1: 5 a pure heart, from a good c,
1:19 having faith and a good c,
3: 9 of the faith with a pure c.
4: 2 having their own c seared with
2 Tim 1: 3 God, whom I serve with a pure c,
Titus 1:15 but even their mind and c are
Heb 9: 9 perfect in regard to the c—
9:14 cleanse your c from dead works
10:22 sprinkled from an evil c and
13:18 confident that we have a good c,
1 Pe 2:19 if because of c toward God one
3:16 having a good c,
3:21 but the answer of a good c

CONSCIENCES (1/1) CONSCIENCE

2 Cor 5:11 trust are well known in your c.

CONSCIOUSNESS (2/2)

1 Cor 8: 7 with c of the idol, until now
Heb 10: 2 would have had no more c of

CONSECRATE (35/34) CONSECRATED, CONSECRATES, CONSECRATION

Ex 13: 2 C to Me all the firstborn,
19:10 Go to the people and c them
19:22 who come near the LORD c
19:23 around the mountain and c it.
28: 3 to c him, that he may minister
28:41 c them, and sanctify them, that
29: 9 So you shall c Aaron and his
29:27 of the consecration you shall c
29:33 to c and to sanctify them; but
29:35 Seven days you shall c them.
29:44 So I will c the tabernacle of
29:44 I will also c both Aaron and
30:29 You shall c them, that they may
30:30 and c them, that they may
32:29 C yourselves today to the LORD,
40:10 and c the altar. The altar
40:11 laver and its base, and c it.
40:13 and anoint him and c him, that
Lev 8:11 laver and its base, to c them.
8:12 and anointed him, to c him.
8:33 For seven days he shall c you.
11:44 You shall therefore c
16:19 and c it from the uncleanness
20: 7 C yourselves therefore, and be
21: 8 Therefore you shall c him, for
25:10 And you shall c the fiftieth
Num 6:12 He shall c to the LORD the days
11:18 C yourselves for tomorrow, and
1 Chr 29: 5 Who then is willing to c
2 Chr 13: 9 so that whoever comes to c
35: 6 c yourselves, and prepare them
Ezek 43:26 and purify it, and so c it.
Joel 1:14 C a fast, Call a sacred
2:15 C a fast, Call a sacred
Mic 4:13 I will c their gain to the

CONSECRATED (37/33) CONSECRATE

Ex 29:29 be anointed in them and to be c
Lev 7:35 This is the c portion for
8:10 that was in it, and c them.
8:15 and c it, to make atonement for
8:30 and he c Aaron, his garments,
16:32 who is anointed and c to
21:10 oil was poured and who is c to
Num 3: 3 whom he c to minister as
6: 9 and he defiles his c head, then
6:18 the Nazirite shall shave his c
6:18 shall take the hair from his c
6:19 after he has shaved his c
7: 1 that he anointed it and c it
7: 1 so he anointed them and c them.
18:29 the c part of them.'
Josh 6:19 are c to the LORD; they shall
Judg 17: 5 and he c one of his sons, who
17:12 So Micah c the Levite, and the
1 Sam 7: 1 and c Eleazar his son to keep
16: 5 Then he c Jesse and his sons,
1 Ki 8:64 On the same day the king c the
9: 3 I have c this house which you
9: 7 and this house which I have c
13:33 he c him, and he became one of
2 Chr 7: 7 Furthermore Solomon c the
26:18 who are c to burn incense.
29:31 Now that you have c yourselves
29:33 The c things were six hundred
30: 3 number of priests had not c
31: 6 of holy things which were c to
36:14 of the LORD which He had c in
Ezra 3: 5 feasts of the LORD that were c,
Neh 3: 1 they c it and hung its doors.
3: 1 and c it, then as far as the
12:47 They also c holy things for
12:47 and the Levites c them for the
Heb 10:20 a new and living way which He c

CONSECRATES (2/2) CONSECRATE

Lev 27: 2 When a man c by a vow certain
Num 6: 2 When either a man or woman c an

CONSECRATION (11/11) CONSECRATE, CONSECRATIONS

Ex 29:22 thigh (for it is a ram of c),
29:26 breast of the ram of Aaron's c
29:27 And from the ram of the c you
29:31 you shall take the ram of the c
29:34 if any of the flesh of the c
Lev 8:22 the second ram, the ram of c.
8:28 They were c offerings for a
8:29 was Moses' part of the ram of c,
8:31 that is in the basket of c
8:33 until the days of your c are
21:12 for the c of the anointing oil

CONSECRATIONS (1/1) CONSECRATION

Lev 7:37 the trespass offering, the c,

CONSENT (15/15) CONSENTED, CONSENTING

Gen 34:15 on this condition we will c
34:22 this condition will the men c
34:23 Only let us c to them, and they
41:44 and without your c no man may
Deut 13: 8 you shall not c to him or listen
Judg 11:17 of Moab, but he would not c.
1 Sam 11: 7 and they came out with one c.
1 Ki 20: 8 to him, "Do not listen or c.
2 Ki 6: 3 Please c to go with your
Ps 83: 5 consulted together with one c;
Prov 1:10 sinners entice you, Do not c.
Acts 18:20 time with them, he did not c,
1 Cor 7: 5 one another except with c for
1 Tim 6: 3 otherwise and does not c to
Phm 1:14 But without your c I wanted to

CONSENTED (3/3) CONSENT

Ps 50:18 you c with him, And have been
Dan 1:14 So he c with them in this
Lk 23:51 He had not c to their decision

CONSENTING (2/2) CONSENT

Acts 8: 1 Now Saul was c to his death.
22:20 I also was standing by c to his

CONSIDER (84/83) CONSIDERED, CONSIDERING, CONSIDERS

Ex 33:13 And c that this nation is Your
Lev 13:13 "then the priest shall c;
Deut 4:39 and c it in your heart, that
32: 7 C the years of many
32:29 That they would c their
Judg 18:14 c what you should do."
19:30 C it, confer, and speak up!"
1 Sam 1:16 Do not c your maidservant a
12:24 for c what great things He has
25:17 know and c what you will do,
2 Sam 24:13 Now c and see what answer I
2 Ki 5: 7 his leprosy? Therefore please c,
1 Chr 21:12 Now c what answer I should
28:10 C now, for the LORD has chosen
Job 8: 8 And c the things discovered by
11:11 Will He not then c it?
23:15 When I c this, I am afraid of
34:23 For He need not further c a
34:27 And would not c any of His
37:14 Stand still and c the wondrous
Ps 5: 1 C my meditation.
8: 3 When I c Your heavens, the work
9:13 O LORD! C my trouble from
13: 3 C and hear me, O LORD my God
25:19 C my enemies, for they are many
45:10 C and incline your ear;
48:13 C her palaces; That you may
50:22 Now c this, you who forget God,
64: 9 For they shall wisely c His
119:95 But I will c Your
119:128 concerning all things I c
119:153 C my affliction and deliver
119:159 C how I love Your precepts
Prov 6: 6 you sluggard! C her ways and
23: 1 C carefully what is before
24:12 not He who weighs the hearts c
28:22 And does not c that poverty
Eccl 2:12 Then I turned myself to c
7:13 C the work of God; For who
7:14 But in the day of adversity c:
Isa 1: 3 not know, My people do not c.
5:12 Nor c the operation of His
14:16 And c you, saying: 'Is
41:20 And c and understand together,
41:22 That we may c them, And know
43:18 Nor c the things of old.
52:15 they had not heard they shall c.
Jer 2:10 Send to Kedar and c
9:17 C and call for the mourning
30:24 In the latter days you will c
Lam 1: 9 She did not c her destiny;
1:11 'See, O LORD, and c,
2:20 and c! To whom have You done
Ezek 12: 3 It may be that they will c,
Dan 9:23 therefore c the matter, and
Hos 7: 2 They do not c in their hearts
Jon 1: 6 perhaps your God will c us, so
Hag 1: 5 LORD of hosts: "C your ways!

1: 7 LORD of hosts: "C your ways!
2:15 carefully c from this day
2:18 C now from this day forward,
2:18 LORD's temple was laid—c it:
Mt 6:28 C the lilies of the field, how
7: 3 but do not c the plank in your
Lk 12:24 C the ravens, for they neither
12:27 C the lilies, how they grow:
14:31 does not sit down first and c
Jn 11:50 nor do you c that it is
Acts 15: 6 and elders came together to c
Rom 4:19 he did not c his own body,
8:18 For I c that the sufferings of
11:22 Therefore c the goodness and
1 Cor 4: 1 Let a man so c us, as servants
2 Cor 10: 7 let him again c this in
10:11 Let such a person c this, that
11: 5 For I c that I am not at all
Phil 2: 6 did not c it robbery to be
2 Tim 2: 7 C what I say, and may the Lord
Heb 3: 1 c the Apostle and High Priest
7: 4 Now c how great this man was,
10:24 And let us c one another in
12: 3 For c Him who endured such
1 Pe 5:12 our faithful brother as I c
2 Pe 3:15 and c that the longsuffering of

CONSIDERED (21/21) CONSIDER

Gen 30:33 will be c stolen, if it is
31:15 Are we not c strangers by him?
1 Ki 5: 8 I have c the message which
Neh 13:13 for they were c faithful, and
Job 1: 8 Have you c My servant Job, that
2: 3 Have you c My servant Job, that
Ps 31: 7 For You have c my trouble;
77: 5 I have c the days of old,
Prov 17:28 he is c perceptive.
24:32 I c it well; I looked on it
Eccl 4: 1 Then I returned and c all the
9: 1 For I c all this in my heart, so
Isa 38:13 I have c until morning—Like a
Jer 33:24 Have you not c what these people
Hos 8:12 But they were c a strange
Mk 10:42 You know that those who are c
Lk 1:29 and c what manner of greeting
22:24 as to which of them should be c
Acts 11: 6 I observed it intently and c,
12:12 when he had c this, he came to
Phil 2:25 Yet I c it necessary to send to

CONSIDERING (5/5) CONSIDER

Dan 7: 8 I was c the horns, and there was
8: 5 And as I was c, suddenly a male
Acts 17:23 as I was passing through and c
Gal 6: 1 c yourself lest you also be
Heb 13: 7 c the outcome of their

CONSIDERS (12/12) CONSIDER

Ps 33:15 He c all their works.
41: 1 Blessed is he who c the poor;
Prov 14:15 But the prudent c well his
21:12 The righteous God wisely c the
29: 7 The righteous c the cause of
31:16 She c a field and buys it;
Isa 44:19 And no one c in his heart, Nor
57: 1 While no one c That the
Jer 29:26 man who is demented and c
Ezek 18:14 And c but does not do
18:28 Because he c and turns away from
Rom 14:14 but to him who c anything to be

CONSIST (2/2)

Lk 12:15 for one's life does not c in
Col 1:17 things, and in Him all things c.

CONSOLATION (14/13) CONSOLATIONS, CONSOLE

Job 21: 2 speech, And let this be your c.
Isa 66:11 and be satisfied With the c
Jer 16: 7 men give them the cup of c to
Lk 2:25 waiting for the C of Israel,
6:24 For you have received your c.
2 Cor 1: 5 so our c also abounds through
1: 6 it is for your c and
1: 6 it is for your c and
1: 7 you will partake of the c.
7: 7 but also by the c with which he
Phil 2: 1 Therefore if there is any c in
2 Th 2:16 us and given us everlasting c
Phm 1: 7 For we have great joy and c in
Heb 6:18 to lie, we might have strong c,

CONSOLATIONS (1/1) CONSOLATION

Job 15:11 Are the c of God too small for

CONSOLE (2/2) CONSOLATION, CONSOLED

Isa 61: 3 To c those who mourn in Zion,
Lam 2:13 How shall I c you? To what

CONSOLED (1/1) CONSOLE

Job 42:11 and they c him and comforted

CONSPIRACY (12/11) CONSPIRE

2 Sam 15:12 And the c grew strong, for the
2 Ki 12:20 servants arose and formed a c,
14:19 And they formed a c against him
15:15 and the c which he led, indeed
15:30 Hoshea the son of Elah led a c
17: 4 king of Assyria uncovered a c
2 Chr 25:27 they made a c against him in
Isa 8:12 "Do not say, 'A c,
8:12 all that this people call a c,
Jer 11: 9 A c has been found among the men
Ezek 22:25 The c of her prophets in her
Acts 23:13 forty who had formed this c.

CONSPIRATORS (1/1) CONSPIRE

2 Sam 15:31 Ahithophel is among the c with

CONSPIRE (1/1) CONSPIRACY, CONSPIRATORS, CONSPIRED

Nah 1: 9 What do you c against the

CONSPIRED (19/19) CONSPIRE

Gen 37:18 they c against him to kill him.
1 Sam 22: 8 All of you have c against me,
22:13 Why have you c against me, you
1 Ki 15:27 c against him. And Baasha
16: 9 c against him as he was in
16:16 Zimri has c and also has killed
2 Ki 9:14 c against Joram. (Now Joram had
10: 9 Indeed I c against my master
15:10 Shallum the son of Jabesh c
15:25 c against him and killed him in
21:23 Then the servants of Amon c
21:24 executed all those who had c
2 Chr 24:21 So they c against him, and at
24:25 his own servants c against him
24:26 These are the ones who c
33:24 Then his servants c against him,
33:25 executed all those who had c
Neh 4: 8 and all of them c together to
Am 7:10 Amos has c against you in the

CONSTANT (1/1) CONSTANTLY

Acts 12: 5 but c prayer was offered to God

CONSTANTLY (1/1) CONSTANT

Titus 3: 8 things I want you to affirm c,

CONSTELLATIONS (2/2)

2 Ki 23: 5 the sun, to the moon, to the c,
Isa 13:10 the stars of heaven and their c

CONSTITUENCY (2/2)

2 Ki 12: 5 it themselves, each from his c;
12: 7 take more money from your c,

CONSTRAIN (KJV) See COMPEL

CONSTRAINED (1/1)

Lk 24:29 But they c Him, saying, "Abide

CONSTRUCTING (1/1) CONSTRUCTION

Ezra 5: 4 the names of the men who were c

CONSTRUCTION (5/5) CONSTRUCTING

1 Chr 28:18 and for the c of the chariot,
Ezra 5:16 until now it has been under c,
Neh 4:16 half of my servants worked at c,
4:17 with one hand they worked at c,
Rev 21:18 The c of its wall was of

CONSULT (6/6) CONSULTATION, CONSULTED, CONSULTS

1 Chr 15:13 because we did not c Him about
Ezra 2:63 things till a priest could c
Neh 6: 7 and let us c together.
7:65 things till a priest could c
Ps 62: 4 They only c to cast him down
Isa 19: 3 And they will c the idols and

CONSULTATION (1/1) CONSULT

Mk 15: 1 the chief priests held a c with

CONSULTED (17/17) CONSULT

1 Ki 12: 6 Then King Rehoboam c the elders
12: 8 and c the young men who had
2 Ki 6: 8 and he c with his servants,
21: 6 and c spiritists and mediums.
23:24 Josiah put away those who c
1 Chr 10:13 and also because he c a medium
13: 1 Then David c with the captains
2 Chr 10: 6 Then King Rehoboam c the elders
10: 8 and c the young men who had
20:21 And when he had c with the
32: 3 he c with his leaders and
33: 6 and c mediums and spiritists.
Ps 83: 3 And c together against Your
83: 5 For they have c together with
Dan 6: 7 have c together to establish a
Mt 27: 7 And they c together and bought
28:12 with the elders and c together,

CONSULTS (1/1) CONSULT

Ezek 21:21 he c the images, he looks at

CONSUME (41/39) CONSUMED, CONSUMES, CONSUMING, CONSUMMATION, CONSUMPTION

Ex 32:10 hot against them and I may c
32:12 and to c them from the face of
33: 3 lest I c you on the way, for
33: 5 your midst in one moment and c
Lev 26:16 and fever which shall c the
Num 16:21 that I may c them in a
16:45 that I may c them in a
24: 8 He shall c the nations, his
25:11 so that I did not c the
Deut 5:25 For this great fire will c us;
28:38 for the locust shall c it.
28:42 Locusts shall c all your trees
32:22 It shall c the earth with her
Josh 24:20 turn and do you harm and c you,
1 Sam 2:33 cut off from My altar shall c
2 Ki 1:10 come down from heaven and c
1:12 come down from heaven and c
Neh 9:31 mercy You did not utterly c
Esth 9:24 to c them and destroy them;
Job 15:34 And fire will c the tents of
20:26 An unfanned fire will c him;
24:19 As drought and heat c the snow
Ps 59:13 C them in wrath, consume
59:13 c them, That they may not
Isa 10:18 And it will c the glory of his
27:10 there it will lie down And c
Jer 8:13 I will surely c them," says
14:12 But I will c them by the sword,
49:27 And it shall c the palaces of
Ezek 13:13 great hailstones in fury to c
20:13 in the wilderness, to c them.
35:12 they are given to us to c.
Dan 2:44 it shall break in pieces and c
7:26 To c and destroy it forever.
Hos 11: 6 And c them, Because of their
Zeph 1: 2 I will utterly c everything
1: 3 I will c man and beast; I will
1: 3 I will c the birds of the
Zech 5: 4 the midst of his house And c
Lk 9:54 to come down from heaven and c
2 Th 2: 8 whom the Lord will c with the

CONSUMED (74/73) CONSUME

Gen 19:15 lest you be c in the punishment
31:15 and also completely c our
31:40 I was! In the day the drought c
Ex 3: 2 fire, but the bush was not c.
15: 7 It c them like stubble.
22: 6 grain, or the field is c,
Lev 6:10 offering which the fire has c
9:24 out from before the LORD and c
Num 11: 1 and c some in the outskirts of
12:12 whose flesh is half c when he
14:33 until your carcasses are c in
14:35 this wilderness they shall be c,
16:26 lest you be c in all their
16:35 came out from the LORD and c
21:28 It c Ar of Moab, The lords of
Deut 2:14 of the men of war was c from
2:15 of the camp until they were c.
28:21 cling to you until He has c
Josh 5: 6 who came out of Egypt, were c,
8:24 of the sword until they were c,
Judg 6:21 rose out of the rock and c the
1 Sam 15:18 against them until they are c.
2 Sam 21: 5 As for the man who c us and
1 Ki 18:38 fire of the LORD fell and c
2 Ki 1:10 came down from heaven and c
1:12 God came down from heaven and c
7:13 left from those who are c;
2 Chr 7: 1 came down from heaven and c
Ezra 9:14 angry with us until You had c
Job 1:16 and c them; and I alone have
4: 9 breath of His anger they are c.
Ps 39:10 I am c by the blow of Your
49:14 And their beauty shall be c in
71:13 Let them be confounded and c
73:19 They are utterly c with
78:33 Therefore their days He c in
78:63 The fire c their young men,
90: 7 For we have been c by Your
102: 3 For my days are c like smoke,
104:35 May sinners be c from the
119:139 My zeal has c me, Because my
Prov 5:11 your flesh and your body are c,
Isa 1:28 forsake the LORD shall be c.
16: 4 The oppressors are c out of
29:20 nothing, The scornful one is c,
64: 7 And have c us because of our
66:17 Shall be c together," says
Jer 5: 3 You have c them, But they
6:29 The lead is c by the fire;
9:16 after them until I have c them.
10:25 Devoured him and c him, And
12: 4 The beasts and birds are c,
14:15 those prophets shall be c!
16: 4 They shall be c by the sword
20:18 That my days should be c with

24:10 till they are *c* from the land
27: 8 until I have *c* them by his
36:23 until all the scroll was *c* in
44:12 and they shall all be *c* and
44:12 They shall be *c* by the sword
44:18 everything and have been *c* by
44:27 in the land of Egypt shall be *c*
49:37 after them Until I have *c*
Lam 3:22 LORD's mercies we are not *c*,
Ezek 5:12 and be *c* with famine in your
13:14 and you shall be *c* in the midst
19:12 The fire *c* them.
22:31 I have *c* them with the fire of
24:11 in it, That its scum may be *c*.
34:29 and they shall no longer be *c*
43: 8 therefore I have *c* them in My
Am 7: 4 and it *c* the great deep and
Mal 3: 6 Therefore you are not *c*,
Gal 5:15 beware lest you be *c* by one

CONSUMES (6/6) CONSUME

Job 22:20 And the fire *c* their remnant.'
24:19 So the grave *c* those who
31:12 that would be a fire that *c*
Eccl 4: 5 fool folds his hands And *c*
6: 2 but a foreigner *c* it. This is
Isa 5:24 And the flame *c* the chaff,

CONSUMING (8/8) CONSUME

Ex 24:17 of the LORD was like a *c*
Deut 4:24 the LORD your God is a *c*
9: 3 goes over before you as a *c*
Isa 6:13 And will return and be for *c*,
Ezek 21:28 Polished for slaughter, For *c*,
Joel 1: 4 the *c* locust has eaten.
2:25 The *c* locust, And the chewing
Heb 12:29 For our God is a *c* fire.

CONSUMMATION (2/2) CONSUME

Ps 119:96 I have seen the *c* of all
Dan 9:27 desolate, Even until the *c*,

CONSUMPTION (1/1) CONSUME

Deut 28:22 LORD will strike you with *c*,

CONTAIN (4/4) CONTAINED, CONTAINER, CONTAINING, CONTAINS

1 Ki 8:27 the heaven of heavens cannot *c*
2 Chr 2: 6 the heaven of heavens cannot *c*
6:18 the heaven of heavens cannot *c*
Jn 21:25 the world itself could not *c*

CONTAINED (5/5) CONTAIN

1 Ki 7:26 It *c* two thousand baths.
7:38 each laver *c* forty baths, and
2 Chr 4: 5 It *c* three thousand baths.
Eph 2:15 the law of commandments *c* in
1 Pe 2: 6 Therefore it is also *c* in the

CONTAINER (1/1) CONTAIN

Deut 23:24 shall not put any in your *c*.

CONTAINING (1/1) CONTAIN

Jn 2: 6 *c* twenty or thirty gallons

CONTAINS (3/3) CONTAIN

Job 28: 6 And it *c* gold dust.
Ezek 23:32 in derision; It *c* much.
45:11 so that the bath *c* one-tenth of

CONTEMN (KJV) See RENOUNCE

CONTEMPLATE (1/1)

Ps 119:15 And *c* Your ways.

CONTEMPLATION (13/13)

Ps 32: A Psalm of David. A *C*.
42: A *C* of the sons of Korah.
44: A *C* of the sons of Korah.
45: A *C* of the sons of Korah.
52: A *C* of David when Doeg the
53: A *C* of David.
54: A *C* of David when the Ziphites
55: A *C* of David.
74: A *C* of Asaph.
78: A *C* of Asaph.
88: A *C* of Heman the Ezrahite.
89: A *C* of Ethan the Ezrahite.
142: A *C* of David. A Prayer when he

CONTEMPORARIES (1/1)

Gal 1:14 in Judaism beyond many of my *c*

CONTEMPT (14/14) CONTEMPTIBLE, CONTEMPTUOUSLY

Deut 27:16 his father or his mother with *c*.
Esth 1:18 there will be excessive *c*
Job 12:21 He pours *c* on princes, And
31:34 And dreaded the *c* of families,
Ps 107:40 He pours *c* on princes, And
119:22 Remove from me reproach and *c*,
123: 3 are exceedingly filled with *c*.
123: 4 With the *c* of the proud.
Prov 18: 3 *c* comes also; And with
Isa 23: 9 To bring into *c* all the
Dan 12: 2 to shame and everlasting *c*.
Mk 9:12 things and be treated with *c*?
Lk 23:11 treated Him with *c* and mocked
Rom 14:10 Or why do you show *c* for your

CONTEMPTIBLE (4/4) CONTEMPT

Mal 1: 7 'The table of the LORD is *c*.
1:12 And its fruit, its food, is *c*.
2: 9 I also have made you *c* and
2 Cor 10:10 is weak, and his speech *c*.

CONTEMPTUOUSLY (1/1) CONTEMPT

Ps 31:18 insolent things proudly and *c*

CONTEND (21/20) CONTENDED, CONTENDING, CONTENDS

Ex 17: 2 Why do you *c* with me? Why do you
21:18 If men *c* with each other, and
Deut 2: 9 nor *c* with them in battle, for
Job 9: 3 If one wished to *c* with Him,
10: 2 Show me why You *c* with me.
13: 8 Will you *c* for God?
13:19 Who is he who will *c* with me?
23: 6 Would He *c* with me in His great
33:13 Why do you *c* with Him? For He
Prov 28: 4 But such as keep the law *c*
Eccl 6:10 And he cannot *c* with Him who
Isa 43:26 Let us *c* together; State your
49:25 For I will *c* with him who
50: 8 Who will *c* with Me? Let us
57:16 For I will not *c* forever, Nor
Jer 12: 5 Then how can you *c* with
18:19 to the voice of those who *c*
Hos 4: 4 "Now let no man *c*,
4: 4 people are like those who *c*
Mic 6: 2 And He will *c* with Israel.
Jude 3 write to you exhorting you to *c*

CONTENDED (13/12) CONTEND

Ex 17: 2 Therefore the people *c* with
Num 20: 3 And the people *c* with Moses and
20:13 the children of Israel *c* with
26: 9 who *c* against Moses and Aaron
26: 9 when they *c* against the LORD;
Deut 33: 8 And with whom You *c* at the
Neh 13:11 So I *c* with the rulers, and
13:17 Then I *c* with the nobles of
13:25 So I *c* with them and cursed
Isa 27: 8 You *c* with it. He removes it
41:12 Those who *c* with you. Those
Jer 50:24 Because you have *c* against the
Acts 11: 2 those of the circumcision *c*

CONTENDING (1/1) CONTEND

Jude 9 in *c* with the devil, when he

CONTENDS (3/3) CONTEND

Job 40: 2 Shall the one who *c* with the
Prov 29: 9 If a wise man *c* with a foolish
Isa 49:25 I will contend with him who *c*

CONTENT (10/10) CONTENTMENT

Ex 2:21 Then Moses was *c* to live with
Lev 10:20 Moses heard that, he was *c*.
Josh 7: 7 Oh, that we had been *c*,
Judg 17:11 Then the Levite was *c* to dwell
19: 6 Please be *c* to stay all night,
Lk 3:14 and be *c* with your wages."
Phil 4:11 in whatever state I am, to be *c*:
1 Tim 6: 8 with these we shall be *c*.
Heb 13: 5 be *c* with such things as you
3 Jn 10 And not *c* with that, he himself

CONTENTION (8/8) CONTENTIONS, CONTENTIOUS

Ex 17: 7 because of the *c* of the
Prov 15:18 who is slow to anger allays *c*.
17:14 Therefore stop *c* before a
18: 6 A fool's lips enter into *c*,
22:10 and *c* will leave; Yes, strife
Jer 15:10 A man of strife and a man of *c*
Hab 1: 3 is strife, and *c* arises.
Acts 15:39 Then the *c* became so sharp that

CONTENTIONS (8/8) CONTENTION

Prov 18:18 Casting lots causes *c* to cease,
18:19 And *c* are like the bars of a
19:13 And the *c* of a wife are a
23:29 Who has sorrow? Who has *c*?
1 Cor 1:11 that there are *c* among you.
2 Cor 12:20 do not wish; lest there be *c*,
Gal 5:20 idolatry, sorcery, hatred, *c*,
Titus 3: 9 disputes, genealogies, *c*,

CONTENTIOUS (6/6) CONTENTION

Prov 21: 9 shared with a *c* woman.
21:19 Than with a *c* and angry woman.
25:24 shared with a *c* woman.
26:21 So is a *c* man to kindle
27:15 rainy day And a *c* woman
1 Cor 11:16 But if anyone seems to be *c*,

CONTENTMENT (1/1) CONTENT

1 Tim 6: 6 Now godliness with *c* is great

CONTINGENTS (1/1)

2 Ki 11: 7 The two *c* of you who go off duty

CONTINUAL (10/10) CONTINUALLY, CONTINUE

Ex 29:42 This shall be a *c* burnt
2 Chr 2: 4 for the *c* showbread, for the
Prov 15:15 merry heart has a *c* feast.
19:13 of a wife are a *c* dripping.
27:15 A *c* dripping on a very rainy
Isa 14: 6 in wrath with a *c* stroke,
Jer 48: 5 they ascend with *c* weeping;
50: 4 With *c* weeping they shall
Lk 18: 5 lest by her *c* coming she weary
Rom 9: 2 have great sorrow and *c* grief

CONTINUALLY (75/75) CONTINUAL

Gen 6: 5 of his heart was only evil *c*.
8: 3 And the waters receded *c* from
8: 5 And the waters decreased *c* until
Ex 27:20 to cause the lamp to burn *c*.
28:29 a memorial before the LORD *c*.
28:30 his heart before the LORD *c*.
29:38 of the first year, day by day *c*.
Lev 24: 2 light, to make the lamps burn *c*.
24: 3 morning before the LORD *c*;
24: 4 lampstand before the LORD *c*.
24: 8 it in order before the LORD *c*,
Deut 28:29 only oppressed and plundered *c*,
28:33 be only oppressed and crushed *c*.
Josh 6:13 the ark of the LORD went on *c*
1 Sam 18:29 So Saul became David's enemy *c*.
2 Sam 9: 7 shall eat bread at my table *c*.
9:13 for he ate *c* at the king's
15:12 for the people with Absalom *c*
19:13 of the army before me *c* in
1 Ki 10: 8 who stand *c* before you and
2 Chr 9: 7 who stand *c* before you and hear
24:14 in the house of the LORD *c*
28:19 decline in Judah and had been *c*
Ps 34: 1 His praise shall *c* be in my
35:27 And let them say *c*,
38:17 And my sorrow is *c* before me.
40:11 and Your truth *c* preserve me.
40:16 as love Your salvation say *c*,
42: 3 While they *c* say to me,
44:15 My dishonor is *c* before me,
50: 8 Which are *c* before Me.
52: 1 The goodness of God endures *c*.
58: 7 away as waters which run *c*;
69:23 And make their loins shake *c*.
70: 4 who love Your salvation say *c*,
71: 3 To which I may resort *c*;
71: 6 My praise shall be *c* of You.
71:14 But I will hope *c*,
72:15 also will be made for Him *c*,
73:23 Nevertheless I am *c* with You;
74:23 rise up against You increases *c*.
109:10 Let his children *c* be
109:15 Let them be *c* before the LORD,
109:19 with which he girds himself *c*.
119:44 So shall I keep Your law *c*,
119:109 My life is *c* in my hand, Yet
119:117 I shall observe Your statutes *c*.
126: 6 He who *c* goes forth weeping,
140: 2 They *c* gather together for
Prov 6:14 his heart, He devises evil *c*,
6:21 Bind them *c* upon your heart;
Eccl 1: 6 The wind whirls about *c*,
Isa 21: 8 my Lord! I stand *c* on the
49:16 Your walls are *c* before Me.
51:13 You have feared *c* every day
52: 5 And My name is blasphemed *c*
58:11 The LORD will guide you *c*,
60:11 your gates shall be open *c*;
65: 3 who provoke Me to anger *c* to
Jer 6: 7 Before Me *c* are grief and
23:17 They *c* say to those who despise
33:18 offerings, and to sacrifice *c*.
Dan 6:16 "Your God, whom you serve *c*,
6:20 has your God, whom you serve *c*,
Hos 4:18 They commit harlotry *c*.
12: 6 And wait on your God *c*.
Ob 16 shall all the nations drink *c*;
Nah 3:19 not your wickedness passed *c*?
Lk 24:53 and were *c* in the temple
Acts 6: 4 but we will give ourselves *c* to
10: 7 among those who waited on him *c*.
Rom 13: 6 God's ministers attending *c* to
Heb 7: 3 Son of God, remains a priest *c*.
10: 1 which they offer *c* year by
13:15 Therefore by Him let us *c* offer

CONTINUANCE (1/1) CONTINUE

Rom 2: 7 life to those who by patient *c*

C

CONTINUE (46/45) CONTINUAL, CONTINUANCE, CONTINUED, CONTINUES, CONTINUING, CONTINUOUSLY

Lev	12: 4	She shall then **c** in the blood of
	12: 5	and she shall **c** in the blood of
Num	34: 4	**c** to Zin, and be on the south
	34: 4	and **c** to Azmon;
1 Sam	12:14	king who reigns over you will **c**
	13:14	now your kingdom shall not **c**.
2 Sam	7:29	that it may **c** forever before
1 Ki	8:11	so that the priests could not **c**
2 Ki	17:34	To this day they **c** practicing
1 Chr	17:27	that it may **c** before You
2 Chr	5:14	so that the priests could not **c**
Job	14: 2	like a shadow and does not **c**.
	15:29	be rich, Nor will his wealth **c**,
Ps	36:10	**c** Your lovingkindness to those
	49: 9	That he should **c** to live
	72:17	His name shall **c** as long as
	101: 7	He who tells lies shall not **c**
	102:28	of Your servants will **c**,
	119:91	They **c** this day according to
Isa	5:11	Who **c** until night, till wine
	64: 5	have sinned—In these ways we **c**;
Dan	11: 8	and he shall **c** more years than
Hab	1:17	And **c** to slay nations without
Zech	8:21	Let us **c** to go and pray before
Mal	2: 4	My covenant with Levi may **c**,
Acts	11:23	purpose of heart they should **c**
	13:43	persuaded them to **c** in the
	14:22	exhorting them to **c** in the
Rom	6: 1	Shall we **c** in sin that grace
	11:22	if you **c** in His goodness.
	11:23	if they do not **c** in unbelief,
2 Cor	11:12	I will also **c** to do, that I may
Gal	2: 5	the truth of the gospel might **c**
	3:10	everyone who does not **c**
Phil	1:25	know that I shall remain and **c**
Col	1:23	if indeed you **c** in the faith,
	4: 2	**C** earnestly in prayer, being
1 Tim	2:15	in childbearing if they **c** in
	4:16	**C** in them, for in doing this
2 Tim	3:14	But you must **c** in the things
Heb	8: 9	because they did not **c** in
	13: 1	Let brotherly love **c**.
2 Pe	3: 4	all things **c** as they were
1 Jn	5:13	and that you may **c** to believe
Rev	13: 5	and he was given authority to **c**
	17:10	he must **c** a short time.

CONTINUED (37/37) CONTINUE

Gen	26:13	and **c** prospering until he
Ex	36: 3	So they **c** bringing to him
Num	9:19	Even when the cloud **c** long, many
Josh	6: 9	while the priests **c** blowing
	6:13	while the priests **c** blowing
	15: 7	The border **c** toward the waters
	24:10	therefore he **c** to bless you. So
Judg	5:17	Asher **c** at the seashore, And
Ruth	2: 7	So she came and has **c** from
1 Sam	1:12	as she **c** praying before the
	14:19	the camp of the Philistines **c**
1 Ki	3: 6	You have **c** this great kindness
2 Ki	2:11	as they **c** on and talked, that
	17:29	However every nation **c** to make
	17:41	children's children have **c**
1 Chr	21:20	but Ornan **c** threshing wheat.
2 Chr	29:28	all this **c** until the burnt
Neh	5:16	I also **c** the work on this wall,
Job	27: 1	Moreover Job **c** his discourse,
	29: 1	Job further **c** his discourse, and
Dan	1:21	Thus Daniel **c** until the first
Jon	1:13	for the sea **c** to grow more
Mt	15:32	because they have now **c** with Me
Mk	8: 2	because they have now **c** with Me
Lk	6:12	and **c** all night in prayer to
	22:28	But you are those who have **c**
Jn	8: 7	So when they **c** asking Him, He
Acts	1:14	These all **c** with one accord in
	2:42	And they **c** steadfastly in the
	8:13	and when he was baptized he **c**
	12:16	Now Peter **c** knocking; and when
	18:11	And he **c** there a year and six
	19:10	And this **c** for two years, so
	20: 7	spoke to them and **c** his message
	20: 9	and as Paul **c** speaking, he fell
	27:33	day you have waited and **c**
1 Jn	2:19	they would have **c** with us;

CONTINUES (4/4) CONTINUE

Lev	13:55	it **c** eating away, whether the
1 Tim	5: 5	trusts in God and **c** in
Heb	7:24	because He **c** forever, has an
Jas	1:25	perfect law of liberty and **c**

CONTINUING (5/5) CONTINUE

Jer	30:23	A **c** whirlwind; It will fall
Acts	2:46	So **c** daily with one accord in
Rom	12:12	**c** steadfastly in prayer;
Heb	7:23	were prevented by death from **c**.
	13:14	For here we have no **c** city, but

CONTINUOUSLY (1/1) CONTINUE

2 Sam	16: 5	cursing **c** as he came.

CONTRADICT (2/2) CONTRADICTING, CONTRADICTION, CONTRADICTIONS, CONTRARY

Lk	21:15	will not be able to **c** or
Titus	1: 9	exhort and convict those who **c**.

CONTRADICTING (1/1) CONTRADICT

Acts	13:45	and **c** and blaspheming, they

CONTRADICTION (1/1) CONTRADICT

Heb	7: 7	Now beyond all **c** the lesser is

CONTRADICTIONS (1/1) CONTRADICT

1 Tim	6:20	and idle babblings and **c** of

CONTRARIWISE (KJV) See CONTRARY

CONTRARY (29/29) CONTRADICT

Lev	26:21	if you walk **c** to Me, and are
	26:23	but walk **c** to Me,
	26:24	then I also will walk **c** to you,
	26:27	but walk **c** to Me,
	26:28	then I also will walk **c** to you
	26:40	that they also have walked **c**
	26:41	and that I also have walked **c**
2 Chr	30:18	yet they ate the Passover **c** to
Mt	14:24	the waves, for the wind was **c**.
Lk	22:26	not so among you; on the **c**,
Jn	7:12	others said, "No, on the **c**,
Acts	17: 7	and these are all acting **c** to
	18:13	persuades men to worship God **c**
	23: 3	you command me to be struck **c**
	26: 9	I must do many things **c** to the
	27: 4	because the winds were **c**.
Rom	3:31	On the **c**, we establish the
	4:18	**c** to hope, in hope believed, so
	7: 7	On the **c**, I would not have
	10:21	To a disobedient and **c**
	11:24	and were grafted **c** to nature
	16:17	**c** to the doctrine which you
2 Cor	2: 7	so that, on the **c**,
Gal	2: 7	But on the **c**, when they saw
	5:17	and these are **c** to one another,
Col	2:14	which was **c** to us. And He has
1 Th	2:15	do not please God and are **c** to
1 Tim	1:10	is any other thing that is **c**
1 Pe	3: 9	but on the **c** blessing, knowing

CONTRIBUTE (1/1) CONTRIBUTION

2 Chr	31: 4	who dwelt in Jerusalem to **c**

CONTRIBUTION (2/2) CONTRIBUTE

Isa	40:20	too impoverished for such a **c**
Rom	15:26	and Achaia to make a certain **c**

CONTRIBUTIONS (1/1) CONTRIBUTION

2 Chr	24:10	rejoiced, brought their **c**,

CONTRITE (5/4)

Ps	34:18	such as have a **c** spirit.
	51:17	A broken and a **c** heart—These,
Isa	57:15	With him who has a **c** and
	57:15	the heart of the **c** ones.
	66: 2	is poor and of a **c** spirit,

CONTROL (2/2)

2 Ki	15:19	the kingdom under his **c**.
Acts	5: 4	sold, was it not in your own **c**?

CONTROVERSIES (1/1) CONTROVERSY

2 Chr	19: 8	judgment of the LORD and for **c**,

CONTROVERSY (6/6) CONTROVERSIES

Deut	17: 8	matters of **c** within your gates,
	19:17	then both men in the **c** shall
	21: 5	by their word every **c** and every
Jer	25:31	For the LORD has a **c** with the
Ezek	44:24	In **c** they shall stand as judges,
1 Tim	3:16	And without **c** great is the

CONVENIENT (4/4) CONVENIENTLY

Jer	40: 4	wherever it seems good and **c**
	40: 5	Or go wherever it seems **c** for
Acts	24:25	when I have a **c** time I will
1 Cor	16:12	he will come when he has a **c**

CONVENIENTLY (1/1) CONVENIENT

Mk	14:11	how he might **c** betray Him.

CONVERSATION (2/2) CONVERSED

Jer	38:27	for the **c** had not been heard.
Lk	24:17	What kind of **c** is this that you

CONVERSED (2/2) CONVERSATION

Lk	24:15	while they **c** and reasoned, that
Acts	24:26	sent for him more often and **c**

CONVERSION (1/1) CONVERTED

Acts	15: 3	describing the **c** of the

CONVERTED (3/3) CONVERSION, CONVERTING

Ps	51:13	And sinners shall be **c** to You.
Mt	18: 3	unless you are **c** and become as
Acts	3:19	"Repent therefore and be **c**,

CONVERTING (1/1) CONVERTED

Ps	19: 7	is perfect, **c** the soul;

CONVEX (1/1)

1 Ki	7:20	by the **c** surface which was

CONVEY (KJV) See FLOAT, PASS

CONVEYED (1/1)

Col	1:13	and **c** us into the kingdom of

CONVICT (3/3) CONVICTED, CONVICTS

Jn	16: 8	He will **c** the world of sin, and
Titus	1: 9	both to exhort and **c** those who
Jude	15	to **c** all who are ungodly among

CONVICTED (3/3) CONVICT

Jn	8: 9	being **c** by their conscience,
1 Cor	14:24	he is **c** by all.
Jas	2: 9	and are **c** by the law as

CONVICTS (1/1) CONVICT

Jn	8:46	Which of you **c** Me of sin? And if

CONVINCE (1/1) CONVINCED

2 Tim	4: 2	**C**, rebuke, exhort,

CONVINCED (7/7) CONVINCE

Job	32:12	surely not one of you **c** Job,
Acts	26:26	for I am **c** that none of these
Rom	4:21	and being fully **c** that what He
	14: 5	Let each be fully **c** in his own
	14:14	I know and am **c** by the Lord
1 Cor	14:24	he is **c** by all, he is convicted
2 Cor	10: 7	If anyone is **c** in himself that

CONVOCATION (16/15) CONVOCATIONS

Ex	12:16	day there shall be a holy **c**,
	12:16	day there shall be a holy **c**
Lev	23: 3	of solemn rest, a holy **c**.
	23: 7	day you shall have a holy **c**;
	23: 8	seventh day shall be a holy **c**;
	23:21	same day that it is a holy **c**
	23:24	blowing of trumpets, a holy **c**.
	23:27	It shall be a holy **c** for you;
	23:35	day there shall be a holy **c**.
	23:36	day you shall have a holy **c**,
Num	28:18	day you shall have a holy **c**.
	28:25	day you shall have a holy **c**.
	28:26	Weeks, you shall have a holy **c**.
	29: 1	month, you shall have a holy **c**.
	29: 7	month you shall have a holy **c**.
	29:12	month you shall have a holy **c**.

CONVOCATIONS (3/3) CONVOCATION

Lev	23: 2	shall proclaim to be holy **c**,
	23: 4	holy **c** which you shall proclaim
	23:37	shall proclaim to be holy **c**,

CONVULSED (4/4) CONVULSES

Mk	1:26	when the unclean spirit had **c**
	9:20	immediately the spirit **c** him,
	9:26	**c** him greatly, and came out of
Lk	9:42	the demon threw him down and **c**

CONVULSES (1/1) CONVULSED

Lk	9:39	it **c** him so that he foams at

COOK (4/4) COOKED, COOKING, COOKS

1 Sam	9:23	And Samuel said to the **c**,
	9:24	So the **c** took up the thigh with
Ezek	24:10	**C** the meat well, Mix in the
Zech	14:21	and take them and **c** in them.

COOKED (3/3) COOK

Gen	25:29	Now Jacob **c** a stew; and Esau
Num	11: 8	**c** it in pans, and made cakes
Lam	4:10	the compassionate women Have **c**

COOKING (2/2) COOK

Lev	11:35	whether it is an oven or **c**

Ezek 46:23 and *c* hearths were made under

COOKS (1/1) COOK
1 Sam 8:13 daughters to be perfumers, *c*,

COOL (4/4)
Gen 3: 8 garden in the *c* of the day,
Judg 3:20 in his *c* private chamber).
3:24 to his needs in the *c* chamber.
Lk 16:24 in water and *c* my tongue;

COOS (KJV) See COS

COPIED (1/1) COPY
Prov 25: 1 men of Hezekiah king of Judah *c*:

COPIES (2/2) COPY
Heb 9:23 it was necessary that the *c*
9:24 which are *c* of the true, but

COPPER (7/7) COPPERSMITH
Deut 8: 9 of whose hills you can dig *c*.
Job 28: 2 And *c* is smelted from ore.
Mt 10: 9 neither gold nor silver nor *c*
10:29 sparrows sold for a *c* coin?
Mk 6: 8 no *c* in their money belts—
7: 4 *c* vessels, and couches.
Lk 12: 6 sparrows sold for two *c* coins?

COPPERSMITH (1/1) COPPER
2 Tim 4:14 Alexander the *c* did me much

COPULATION (KJV) See EMISSION (OF SEMEN)

COPY (10/10) COPIED, COPIES
Deut 17:18 he shall write for himself a *c*
Josh 8:32 he wrote on the stones a *c* of
Ezra 4:11 (This is a *c* of the letter that
4:23 Now when the *c* of King
5: 6 This is a *c* of the letter that
7:11 This is a *c* of the letter that
Esth 3:14 A *c* of the document was to be
4: 8 He also gave him a *c* of the
8:13 A *c* of the document was to be
Heb 8: 5 who serve the *c* and shadow of

CORAL (1/1) CORALS
Job 28:18 No mention shall be made of *c*

CORALS (1/1) CORAL
Ezek 27:16 embroidery, fine linen, *c*,

CORBAN (1/1)
Mk 7:11 have received from me is *C*"—'

CORD (11/11) CORDS
Gen 38:18 she said, "Your signet and *c*,
38:25 these are—the signet and *c*,
Ex 28:28 of the ephod, using a blue *c*,
28:37 you shall put it on a blue *c*,
39:21 of the ephod with a blue *c*,
39:31 And they tied to it a blue *c*,
Josh 2:18 bind this line of scarlet *c* in
2:21 And she bound the scarlet *c* in
Eccl 4:12 And a threefold *c* is not
12: 6 Creator before the silver *c*
Ezek 16: 4 day you were born your navel *c*

CORDS (24/24) CORD
Ex 28:14 of pure gold like braided *c*,
28:22 like braided *c* of pure gold.
35:18 pegs of the court, and their *c*;
39:15 like braided *c* of pure gold.
39:40 for the court gate, its *c*,
Num 3:26 and the altar, and their *c*,
3:37 their pegs, and their *c*.
4:26 and altar, and their *c*,
4:32 with their sockets, pegs, and *c*,
Esth 1: 6 curtains fastened with *c* of
Job 36: 8 Held in the *c* of affliction,
Ps 2: 3 pieces And cast away Their *c*
118:27 Bind the sacrifice with *c* to
119:61 The *c* of the wicked have bound
129: 4 He has cut in pieces the *c* of
140: 5 hidden a snare for me, and *c*;
Prov 5:22 And he is caught in the *c* of
Isa 5:18 those who draw iniquity with *c*
33:20 Nor will any of its *c* be
54: 2 Do not spare; Lengthen your *c*,
Jer 10:20 And all my *c* are broken;
Ezek 27:24 apparel, in sturdy woven *c*,
Hos 11: 4 I drew them with gentle *c*,
Jn 2:15 When He had made a whip of *c*,

CORIANDER (2/2)
Ex 16:31 And it was like white *c* seed,
Num 11: 7 Now the manna was like *c* seed,

CORINTH (6/6) CORINTHIANS
Acts 18: 1 from Athens and went to *C*.
19: 1 while Apollos was at *C*,
1 Cor 1: 2 the church of God which is at *C*,
2 Cor 1: 1 the church of God which is at *C*,
1:23 spare you I came no more to *C*.
2 Tim 4:20 Erastus stayed in *C*,

CORINTHIANS (2/2) CORINTH
Acts 18: 8 And many of the *C*,
2 Cor 6:11 O *C*! We have spoken openly to

CORNELIUS (10/10)
Acts 10: 1 man in Caesarea called *C*,
10: 3 saying to him, "*C*!"
10: 7 *C* called two of his household
10:17 men who had been sent from *C*
10:21 who had been sent to him from *C*,
10:22 *C* the centurion, a just man,
10:24 Now *C* was waiting for them, and
10:25 *C* met him and fell down at his
10:30 So *C* said, "Four days ago I was
10:31 'and said, '*C*, your prayer

CORNER (23/21) CORNERS, CORNERSTONE
1 Sam 24: 4 arose and secretly cut off a *c*
24:11 see the *c* of your robe in my
24:11 For in that I cut off the *c* of
2 Ki 14:13 the Gate of Ephraim to the *C*
2 Chr 25:23 the Gate of Ephraim to the *C*
26: 9 towers in Jerusalem at the *C*
26: 9 and at the *c* buttress of the
28:24 for himself altars in every *c*
Neh 3:24 buttress, even as far as the *c*.
3:31 far as the upper room at the *c*.
3:32 between the upper room at the *c*,
Prov 7: 8 along the street near her *c*;
7:12 square, Lurking at every *c*.
21: 9 Better to dwell in a *c* of a
25:24 is better to dwell in a *c* of
Isa 30:20 will not be moved into a *c*
Jer 31:38 the Tower of Hananel to the *C*
31:40 to the *c* of the Horse Gate
51:26 take from you a stone for a *c*
Ezek 46:21 in every *c* of the court there
Am 3:12 In the *c* of a bed and on the
Zech 14:10 of the First Gate and the *C*
Acts 26:26 this thing was not done in a *c*.

CORNERS (39/37) CORNER
Ex 25:12 it, and put them in its four *c*;
25:26 and put the rings on the four *c*
26:23 two boards for the two back *c*
26:24 They shall be for the two *c*.
27: 2 make its horns on its four *c*;
27: 4 four bronze rings at its four *c*.
36:28 two boards for the two back *c*
36:29 made both of them for the two *c*.
37: 3 gold to be set in its four *c*:
37:13 and put the rings on the four *c*
37:27 by its two *c* on both sides, as
38: 2 He made its horns on its four *c*;
38: 5 cast four rings for the four *c*
Lev 19: 9 shall not wholly reap the *c* of
23:22 shall not wholly reap the *c* of
Num 15:38 them to make tassels on the *c*
15:38 thread in the tassels of the *c*.
Deut 22:12 make tassels on the four *c* of
1 Ki 7:34 four supports at the four *c* of
2 Chr 26:15 to be on the towers and the *c*,
Job 1:19 and struck the four *c* of the
Isa 11:12 of Judah From the four *c* of
Jer 9:26 all who are in the farthest *c*,
25:23 all who are in the farthest *c*;
49:32 winds those in the farthest *c*,
Ezek 7: 2 end has come upon the four *c*
41:22 two cubits. Its *c*, its length,
43:16 wide, square at its four *c*;
43:20 on the four *c* of the ledge, and
45:19 on the four *c* of the ledge of
46:21 me to pass by the four *c* of
46:22 In the four *c* of the court were
46:22 all four *c* were the same size.
Zech 9:15 Like the *c* of the altar.
Mt 6: 5 in the synagogues and on the *c*
Acts 10:11 great sheet bound at the four *c*,
11: 5 let down from heaven by four *c*;
Rev 7: 1 angels standing at the four *c*
20: 8 which are in the four *c* of the

CORNERSTONE (11/11) CORNER
Job 38: 6 Or who laid its *c*,
Ps 118:22 Has become the chief *c*.
Isa 28:16 A tried stone, a precious *c*,
Zech 10: 4 From him comes the *c*,
Mt 21:42 Has become the chief *c*.
Mk 12:10 Has become the chief *c*.
Lk 20:17 Has become the chief *c*'?
Acts 4:11 has become the chief *c*.
Eph 2:20 Himself being the chief *c*,
1 Pe 2: 6 I lay in Zion A chief *c*,
2: 7 Has become the chief *c*,

CORNET, CORNETS (KJV) See (RAMS') HORNS, SISTRUMS

CORNFLOOR (KJV) See (THRESHING) FLOOR

CORPSE (20/16) CORPSES
Lev 22: 4 anything made unclean by a *c*,
Num 5: 2 whoever becomes defiled by a *c*.
6:11 he sinned in regard to the *c*;
9: 6 who were defiled by a human *c*,
9: 7 became defiled by a human *c*.
9:10 is unclean because of a *c*,
Josh 8:29 that they should take his *c*
1 Ki 13:22 your *c* shall not come to the
13:24 And his *c* was thrown on the
13:24 The lion also stood by the *c*.
13:25 men passed by and saw the *c*
13:25 and the lion standing by the *c*.
13:28 Then he went and found his *c*
13:28 and the lion standing by the *c*.
13:28 The lion had not eaten the *c*
13:29 And the prophet took up the *c* of
13:30 Then he laid the *c* in his own
2 Ki 9:37 and the *c* of Jezebel shall be as
Isa 14:19 Like a *c* trodden underfoot.
Mk 6:29 they came and took away his *c*

CORPSES (11/10) CORPSE
2 Ki 19:35 the morning, there were the *c*—
Isa 34: 3 stench shall rise from their *c*,
37:36 the morning, there were the *c*—
66:24 go forth and look Upon the *c*
Jer 7:33 The *c* of this people will be
16: 4 and their *c* shall be meat for
19: 7 their *c* I will give as meat for
Ezek 6: 5 And I will lay the *c* of the
Nah 3: 3 number of bodies, Countless *c*—
3: 3 stumble over the *c*—
Heb 3:17 whose *c* fell in the wilderness?

CORRECT (9/9) CORRECTED, CORRECTING, CORRECTION, CORRECTLY, CORRECTS
Job 40: 2 with the Almighty *c* Him?
Ps 39:11 When with rebukes You *c* man for
94:10 the nations, shall He not *c*,
Prov 9: 8 Do not *c* a scoffer, lest he
29:17 *C* your son, and he will give
Jer 2:19 Your own wickedness will *c* you,
10:24 *c* me, but with justice; Not in
30:11 But I will *c* you in justice,
46:28 I will rightly *c* you, For I

CORRECTED (3/3) CORRECT
Prov 29:19 A servant will not be *c* by mere
Hab 2: 1 what I will answer when I am *c*.
Heb 12: 9 had human fathers who *c* us,

CORRECTING (1/1) CORRECT
2 Tim 2:25 in humility *c* those who are in

CORRECTION (18/18) CORRECT
Job 37:13 it to come, Whether for *c*,
Prov 3:11 of the LORD, Nor detest His *c*;
5:12 And my heart despised *c*!
7:22 Or as a fool to the *c* of the
10:17 But he who refuses *c* goes
12: 1 But he who hates *c* is stupid.
13:18 come to him who disdains *c*,
15: 5 But he who receives *c* is
15:10 And he who hates *c* will die.
16:22 But the *c* of fools is folly.
22:15 The rod of *c* will drive it far
23:13 Do not withhold *c* from a child,
Jer 2:30 They received no *c*.
5: 3 they have refused to receive *c*.
7:28 LORD their God nor receive *c*.
Hab 1:12 You have marked them for *c*.
Zeph 3: 2 voice, She has not received *c*;
2 Tim 3:16 doctrine, for reproof, for *c*,

CORRECTLY (1/1) CORRECT
Judg 14:12 If you can *c* solve and explain

CORRECTS (5/5) CORRECT
Job 5:17 happy is the man whom God *c*;
22: 4 of your fear of Him that He *c*
Prov 3:12 For whom the LORD loves He *c*,
9: 7 He who *c* a scoffer gets shame
15:12 does not love one who *c* him,

CORRESPONDING (3/3) CORRESPONDS
Ex 38:18 *c* to the hangings of the court.
Ezek 40:18 *c* to the length of the
42:12 And *c* to the doors of the

CORRESPONDS (1/1) CORRESPONDING
Gal 4:25 and *c* to Jerusalem which now

CORRODED (1/1) CORROSION
Jas 5: 3 Your gold and silver are *c*,

CORROSION (1/1) CORRODED
Jas 5: 3 and their c will be a witness

CORRUPT (20/19) CORRUPTED, CORRUPTERS, CORRUPTIBLE, CORRUPTION, CORRUPTLY, CORRUPTS
Gen 6:11 The earth also was c before
6:12 the earth, and indeed it was c;
Deut 13:13 C men have gone out from among
31:29 death you will become utterly c,
1 Sam 2:12 Now the sons of Eli were c;
Ps 14: 1 is no God." They are c,
14: 3 They have together become c;
53: 1 is no God." They are c,
53: 3 They have together become c;
Ezek 16:47 you became more c than they in
20:44 according to your c doings,
23:11 she became more c in her lust
23:11 and in her harlotry more c than
Dan 2: 9 to speak lying and c words
11:32 the covenant he shall c with
Eph 4:22 the old man which grows c
4:29 Let no c word proceed out of
1 Tim 6: 5 wranglings of men of c minds
2 Tim 3: 8 men of c minds, disapproved
Jude 10 in these things they c

CORRUPTED (12/12) CORRUPT
Gen 6:12 for all flesh had c their way
Ex 8:24 The land was c because of the
32: 7 out of the land of Egypt have c
Deut 32: 5 'They have c themselves;
Ezek 28:17 You c your wisdom for the sake
Hos 9: 9 They are deeply c,
Zeph 3: 7 But they rose early and c all
Mal 2: 8 You have c the covenant of
2 Cor 7: 2 we have c no one, we have
11: 3 so your minds may be c from the
Jas 5: 2 Your riches are c,
Rev 19: 2 great harlot who c the earth

CORRUPTERS (2/2) CORRUPT
Isa 1: 4 evildoers, Children who are c!
Jer 6:28 and iron, They are all c;

CORRUPTIBLE (5/5) CORRUPT
Rom 1:23 an image made like c man—and
1 Cor 15:53 For this c must put on
15:54 So when this c has put on
1 Pe 1:18 not redeemed with c things,
1:23 not of c seed but

CORRUPTION (18/18) CORRUPT
Lev 22:25 because their c is in them,
2 Ki 23:13 on the south of the Mount of C,
Job 17:14 If I say to c, 'You are my
Ps 16:10 allow Your Holy One to see c.
Isa 38:17 my soul from the pit of c,
Acts 2:27 Your Holy One to see c.
2:31 Hades, nor did His flesh see c.
13:34 dead, no more to return to c,
13:35 Your Holy One to see c.
13:36 with his fathers, and saw c;
13:37 He whom God raised up saw no c.
Rom 8:21 from the bondage of c into the
1 Cor 15:42 The body is sown in c,
15:50 nor does c inherit
Gal 6: 8 flesh will of the flesh reap c,
2 Pe 1: 4 having escaped the c that is
2:12 utterly perish in their own c,
2:19 they themselves are slaves of c;

CORRUPTLY (6/6) CORRUPT
Deut 4:16 lest you act c and make for
4:25 and act c and make a carved
9:12 out of Egypt have acted c;
Judg 2:19 reverted and behaved more c
2 Chr 27: 2 But still the people acted c.
Neh 1: 7 We have acted very c against

CORRUPTS (1/1) CORRUPT
1 Cor 15:33 Evil company c good habits."

COS (1/1)
Acts 21: 1 a straight course we came to C,

COSAM (1/1)
Lk 3:28 son of Addi, the son of C,

COST (4/4) COSTLY, COSTS
1 Ki 10:29 that was imported from Egypt c
Ezra 6: 8 Let the c be paid at the king's
Prov 7:23 it would c his life.
Lk 14:28 sit down first and count the c,

COSTLY (10/10) COST
1 Ki 5:17 c stones, and hewn stones, to
7: 9 All these were of c stones
7:10 foundation was of c stones,
7:11 And above were c stones, hewn
2 Chr 36:10 with the c articles from the
Ps 49: 8 redemption of their souls is c,
Mt 26: 7 flask of very c fragrant oil,
Mk 14: 3 alabaster flask of very c oil
Jn 12: 3 took a pound of very c oil
1 Tim 2: 9 gold or pearls or c clothing,

COSTS (2/2) COST
2 Sam 24:24 that which c me nothing."
1 Chr 21:24 that which c me nothing."

COTES (KJV) See FOLDS

COUCH (7/7) COUCHES
Gen 49: 4 defiled it—He went up to my c.
Esth 7: 8 Haman had fallen across the c
Job 7:13 My c will ease my complaint,'
Ps 6: 6 I drench my c with my tears.
Song 3: 7 Behold, it is Solomon's c,
Ezek 23:41 "You sat on a stately c,
Am 3:12 a bed and on the edge of a c!

COUCHES (4/4) COUCH
Esth 1: 6 and the c were of gold and
Am 6: 4 ivory, Stretch out on your c,
Mk 7: 4 pitchers, copper vessels, and c.
Acts 5:15 and laid them on beds and c,

COULD (230/218)
Gen 13: 6 were so great that they c not
13:16 so that if a man c number the
13:16 your descendants also c be
26: 9 so how c you say, 'She is my
27: 1 were so dim that he c not see,
36: 7 c not support them because
37: 4 they hated him and c not speak
41: 8 no one who c interpret them
41:24 no one who c explain it
43: 7 C we possibly have known that
43:32 because the Egyptians c not eat
44: 8 How then c we steal silver or
45: 1 Then Joseph c not restrain
45: 3 But his brothers c not answer
48:10 so that he c not see.
Ex 2: 3 But when she c no longer hide
7:21 and the Egyptians c not drink
7:24 because they c not drink the
8:18 but they c not. So there were
9:11 And the magicians c not stand
12:39 out of Egypt and c not wait,
15:23 they c not drink the waters of
33: 5 I c come up into your midst in
Num 9: 6 so that they c not keep the
22:18 I c not go beyond the word of
24:13 I c not go beyond the word of
35:17 by which one c die, and he does
35:18 by which one c die, and he does
35:23 by which a man c die, throwing
Deut 29:19 as though the drunkard c be
32:30 How c one chase a thousand,
Josh 7:12 the children of Israel c not
15:63 the children of Judah c not
17:12 of Manasseh c not drive
Judg 1:19 but they c not drive out the
2:14 so that they c no longer stand
10:16 And His soul c no longer endure
12: 6 for he c not pronounce it
14:14 Now for three days they c not
17: 8 wherever he c find a place.
20:16 every one c sling a stone at a
Ruth 3:14 before one c recognize
1 Sam 3: 2 grow so dim that he c not see,
4:15 were so dim that he c not see.
10:21 he c not be found.
23:13 and went wherever they c go.
29: 4 For with what c he reconcile
30:10 so weary that they c not cross
30:21 weary that they c not follow
2 Sam 1:10 I was sure that he c not live
2:22 How then c I face your brother
3:11 And he c not answer Abner
13:13 where c I take my shame? And as
17:20 searched and c not find them,
21:16 thought he c kill David.
22:39 So that they c not rise; They
1 Ki 1: 1 but he c not get warm.
5: 3 my father David c not build
8: 5 sheep and oxen that c not be
8: 8 the ends of the poles c be seen
8: 8 but they c not be seen from
8:11 so that the priests c not
10: 3 for the king that he c not
13: 4 so that he c not pull it back
14: 4 But Ahijah c not see, for his
18:10 nation that they c not find
2 Ki 3:26 king of Edom, but they c not.
4:40 And they c not eat it.
5:12 C I not wash in them and be
7: 2 c this thing be?" And he said,
7:19 c such a thing be?" And he had
10: 4 two kings c not stand up to
16: 5 they besieged Ahaz but c not
1 Chr 12: 8 who c handle shield and spear,
12:33 stouthearted men who c keep
12:35 of the Danites who c keep battle
12:36 those who c go out to war, able
12:38 who c keep ranks, came to
21:30 But David c not go before it to
2 Chr 5: 6 sheep and oxen that c not be
5: 9 the poles of the ark c be seen
5: 9 but they c not be seen from
5:14 so that the priests c not
7: 2 And the priests c not enter the
9: 2 for Solomon that he c not
13: 7 and inexperienced and c not
14:13 and they c not recover, for
20:25 more than they c carry away;
25: 5 who c handle spear and shield.
25:15 which c not rescue their own
29:34 so that they c not skin all the
30: 3 For they c not keep it at the
32:14 destroyed that c deliver
Ezra 2:59 but they c not identify their
2:63 till a priest c consult
3:13 so that the people c not discern
5: 5 so that they c not make them
5: 5 them cease till a report c go
Neh 7:61 but they c not identify their
7:65 holy things till a priest c
8: 2 women and all who c hear
8: 3 and those who c understand;
13:24 and c not speak the language of
Esth 6: 1 That night the king c not sleep.
7: 4 although the enemy c never
9: 2 And no one c withstand them,
Job 4:16 But I c not discern its
9: 3 He c not answer Him one time
9:15 I c not answer Him; I would
9:24 who else c it be?
11:15 Then surely you c lift up your
11:15 you c be steadfast, and not
13:16 For a hypocrite c not come
15:14 is man, that he c be pure?
15:14 that he c be righteous?
16: 4 I also c speak as you do, If
16: 4 I c heap up words against you,
23: 7 There the upright c reason with
31:17 So that the fatherless c not
Ps 18:38 So that they c not rise; They
37:36 but he c not be found.
55:12 Then I c bear it. Nor is
55:12 Then I c hide from him.
73: 7 have more than heart c wish.
78:44 that they c not drink.
130: 3 O Lord, who c stand?
Eccl 9: 1 so that I c declare it all:
Song 5: 6 but I c not find him; I called
Isa 5: 4 What more c have been done to
7: 1 but c not prevail against it.
7:23 That wherever there c be a
7:25 And to any hill which c be dug
10:15 As if a rod c wield itself
10:15 Or as if a staff c lift up,
30: 5 a people who c not benefit
33:23 They c not strengthen their
33:23 They c not spread the sail.
41:28 of them, c answer a word.
46: 2 They c not deliver the burden,
Jer 20: 9 holding it back, And I c not.
24: 2 had very bad figs which c not
44:22 So the LORD c no longer bear
52:21 twelve cubits c measure
Lam 4:12 the enemy C enter the gates
4:17 nation that c not save us.
4:18 our steps So that we c not
Ezek 15: 5 no object c be made from it.
20:25 by which they c not live;
31: 8 garden of God c not hide it;
47: 5 a river that I c not cross;
47: 5 a river that c not be crossed.
Dan 2:47 since you c reveal this
4:11 And it c be seen to the ends
4:20 and which c be seen
5: 8 but they c not read the
5:15 but they c not give the
6: 4 but they c find no charge or
8: 4 so that no animal c withstand
8: 4 there any that c deliver
8: 7 was no one that c deliver
Jon 1:13 but they c not, for the sea
Zech 1:21 so that no one c lift up his
7:11 their ears so that they c not
Mt 8:28 so that no one c pass that way.
12:23 C this be the Son of David?"
15:33 Where c we get enough bread in
17:16 but they c not cure him."
17:19 Why c we not cast it out?"
26:40 C you not watch with Me one
26:54 How then c the Scriptures be
27:24 When Pilate saw that he c not
Mk 1:45 so that Jesus c no longer
2: 4 And when they c not come near
3:20 so that they c not so much as
5: 3 and no one c bind him, not even
5: 4 neither c anyone tame him.
6: 5 Now He c do no mighty work
6:19 to kill him, but she c not;
7:24 but He c not be hidden.
9:18 but they c not."
9:28 Why c we not cast it out?"
14: 8 "She has done what she c.
14:37 C you not watch one hour?
Lk 1:22 he c not speak to them;
5:19 And when they c not find how
6:48 and c not shake it, for it was
8:19 and c not approach Him because
8:43 livelihood on physicians and c
9:40 cast it out, but they c not."
13:11 and was bent over and c in no
14: 6 And they c not answer Him
19: 3 but c not because of the crowd,

20:26 But they **c** not catch Him in His
Jn 4:29 **C** this be the Christ?"
9:33 He **c** do nothing."
11:37 **C** not this Man, who opened the
12:39 Therefore they **c** not believe,
19:11 You **c** have no power at all
21:25 world itself **c** not contain
Acts 2:12 Whatever **c** this mean?"
4:14 they **c** say nothing against it.
8:20 gift of God **c** be purchased
11:17 who was I that I **c** withstand
13:39 which you **c** not be justified
14:18 they **c** scarcely restrain the
21:34 So when he **c** not ascertain the
22:11 And since I **c** not see for the
25: 7 which they **c** not prove,
25:21 him to be kept till I **c** send
27:12 if by any means they **c** reach
27:15 and **c** not head into the wind,
27:43 that those who **c** swim
Rom 8: 3 For what the law **c** not do in
9: 3 For I **c** wish that I myself were
1 Cor 3: 1 **c** not speak to you as to
4: 8 and indeed I **c** wish you did
13: 2 so that I **c** remove mountains,
2 Cor 3: 7 children of Israel **c** not look
3:13 children of Israel **c** not look
Gal 3:21 which **c** have given life,
5:12 I **c** wish that those who trouble
1 Th 3: 1 when we **c** no longer endure it,
3: 5 when I **c** no longer endure it, I
Heb 3:19 So we see that they **c** not enter
6:13 because He **c** swear by no one
10: 4 of bulls and goats **c** take
12:20 (For they **c** not endure what was
Rev 3:15 I **c** wish you were cold or hot.
7: 9 which no one **c** number,
14: 3 and no one **c** learn that song

COUNCIL (25/25) COUNCILS

Gen 49: 6 Let not my soul enter their **c**;
Mt 5:22 shall be in danger of the **c**.
26:59 and all the **c** sought false
Mk 14:55 the chief priests and all the **c**
15: 1 and scribes and the whole **c**;
15:43 a prominent **c** member, who was
Lk 22:66 and led Him into their **c**,
23:50 a **c** member, a good and just
Jn 11:47 and the Pharisees gathered a **c**
Acts 4:15 them to go aside out of the **c**,
5:21 with him came and called the **c**
5:27 they set them before the **c**.
5:34 Then one in the **c** stood up, a
5:41 from the presence of the **c**,
6:12 him, and brought him to the **c**.
6:15 And all who sat in the **c**,
22: 5 and all the **c** of the elders,
22:30 chief priests and all their **c**
23: 1 looking earnestly at the **c**,
23: 6 he cried out in the **c**,
23:15 therefore, together with the **c**,
23:20 you bring Paul down to the **c**
23:28 I brought him before their **c**.
24:20 me while I stood before the **c**,
25:12 he had conferred with the **c**,

COUNCILS (2/2) COUNCIL

Mt 10:17 they will deliver you up to **c**
Mk 13: 9 they will deliver you up to **c**,

COUNSEL (90/89) COUNSELED, COUNSELOR, COUNSELS

Ex 18:19 to my voice; I will give you **c**,
Num 31:16 through the **c** of Balaam, to
Deut 32:28 they are a nation void of **c**,
Josh 9:14 but they did not ask **c** of the
Judg 20: 7 give your advice and **c** here and
20:23 and asked **c** of the LORD,
1 Sam 14:37 So Saul asked **c** of God, "Shall
2 Sam 15:31 turn the **c** of Ahithophel into
15:34 then you may defeat the **c** of
16:20 Give **c** as to what we should
Job 5:13 And the **c** of the cunning comes
10: 3 And smile on the **c** of the
12:13 He has **c** and understanding.
15: 8 Have you heard the **c** of God?
18: 7 And his own **c** casts him down.
21:16 The **c** of the wicked is far
22:18 But the **c** of the wicked is far
29: 4 When the friendly **c** of God
29:21 And kept silence for my **c**.
38: 2 Who is this who darkens **c** By
42: 3 Who is this who hides **c** without
Ps 1: 1 man Who walks not in the **c** of
2: 2 And the rulers take **c**
13: 2 How long shall I take **c** in my
14: 6 You shame the **c** of the poor,
16: 7 the LORD who has given me **c**;
31:13 While they take **c** together
33:10 The LORD brings the **c** of the
33:11 The **c** of the LORD stands
55:14 We took sweet **c** together, And
71:10 lie in wait for my life take **c**
73:24 You will guide me with Your **c**,
83: 3 They have taken crafty **c**
106:13 They did not wait for His **c**,
106:43 But they rebelled in their **c**,
107:11 And despised the **c** of the Most
Prov 1: 5 will attain wise **c**,
1:25 Because you disdained all my **c**,
1:30 They would have none of my **c**
3:32 But His secret **c** is with the
8:14 **C** is mine, and sound wisdom
11:14 Where there is no **c**,
12:15 But he who heeds **c** is wise.
15:22 Without **c**, plans go awry,
19:20 Listen to **c** and receive
19:21 Nevertheless the LORD's **c**—
20: 5 **C** in the heart of man is like
20:18 Plans are established by **c**;
20:18 By wise **c** wage war.
21:30 wisdom or understanding Or **c**
24: 6 For by wise **c** you will wage
27: 9 gives delight by hearty **c**.
Isa 5:19 And let the **c** of the Holy One
8:10 Take **c** together, but it will
11: 2 The Spirit of **c** and might,
16: 3 'Take **c**, execute judgment;
19: 3 I will destroy their **c**,
19:11 wise counselors give foolish **c**.
19:17 because of the **c** of the LORD
23: 8 Who has taken this **c** against
28:29 Who is wonderful in **c** and
29:15 who seek deep to hide their **c**
30: 1 says the LORD, "Who take **c**,
40:14 With whom did He take **c**,
44:26 And performs the **c** of His
45:21 let them take **c** together.
46:10 My **c** shall stand, And I will do
46:11 The man who executes My **c**,
Jer 18:18 nor **c** from the wise, nor the
18:23 You know all their **c** Which is
19: 7 And I will make void the **c** of
23:18 For who has stood in the **c** of
23:22 But if they had stood in My **c**,
32:19 You are great in **c** and mighty
49: 7 Has **c** perished from the
49:20 Therefore hear the **c** of the
49:30 king of Babylon has taken **c**
50:45 Therefore hear the **c** of the
Ezek 7:26 And **c** from the elders.
11: 2 iniquity and give wicked **c** in
Dan 2:14 Then with **c** and wisdom Daniel
Hos 4:12 My people ask **c** from their
10: 6 shall be ashamed of his own **c**.
Mic 4:12 Nor do they understand His **c**;
Hab 2:10 You give shameful **c** to your
Zech 6:13 And the **c** of peace shall be
Acts 20:27 to declare to you the whole **c**
Eph 1:11 all things according to the **c**
Heb 6:17 the immutability of His **c**,
Rev 3:18 I **c** you to buy from Me gold

COUNSELED (2/2) COUNSEL

Job 26: 3 How have you **c** one who has
Mic 6: 5 now What Balak king of Moab **c**,

COUNSELOR (12/12) COUNSEL, COUNSELORS

2 Sam 15:12 the Gilonite, David's **c**,
1 Chr 26:14 his son Zechariah, a wise **c**,
27:32 David's uncle, was a **c**,
27:33 Ahithophel was the king's **c**,
2 Chr 25:16 "Have we made you the king's **c**?
Isa 3: 3 The **c** and the skillful
9: 6 will be called Wonderful, **C**,
40:13 Or as His **c** has taught Him?
41:28 them, but there was no **c**,
Mic 4: 9 Has your **c** perished?
Nah 1:11 against the LORD, A wicked **c**.
Rom 11:34 Or who has become His **c**?

COUNSELORS (21/21) COUNSELOR

2 Chr 22: 4 for they were his **c** after the
Ezra 4: 5 and hired **c** against them to
7:14 by the king and his seven **c** to
7:15 gold which the king and his **c**
7:28 to me before the king and his **c**,
8:25 God which the king and his **c**
Job 3:14 With kings and **c** of the earth,
12:17 He leads **c** away plundered, And
Ps 119:24 also are my delight And my **c**.
Prov 11:14 But in the multitude of **c**
12:20 But **c** of peace have joy.
15:22 But in the multitude of **c** they
24: 6 And in a multitude of **c** there
Isa 1:26 And your **c** as at the
19:11 Pharaoh's wise **c** give foolish
Dan 3: 2 the governors, the **c**,
3: 3 the governors, the **c**,
3:24 and spoke, saying to his **c**,
3:27 and the king's **c** gathered
4:36 My **c** and nobles resorted to me,
6: 7 the **c** and advisors, have

COUNSELS (10/10) COUNSEL

Ps 5:10 Let them fall by their own **c**;
81:12 heart, To walk in their own **c**.
Prov 12: 5 But the **c** of the wicked are
22:20 things Of **c** and knowledge,
Isa 25: 1 Your **c** of old are
47:13 in the multitude of your **c**;
Jer 7:24 but followed the **c** and the
Hos 11: 6 them, Because of their own **c**.
Mic 6:16 done; And you walk in their **c**,
1 Cor 4: 5 of darkness and reveal the **c**

COUNT (42/40) COUNTED, COUNTING, COUNTLESS, COUNTS

Gen 15: 5 and **c** the stars if you are able
Ex 12: 4 need you shall make your **c** for
Lev 15:13 then he shall **c** for himself
15:28 then she shall **c** for herself
19:23 then you shall **c** their fruit as
23:15 And you shall **c** for yourselves
23:16 **C** fifty days to the day after
25: 8 And you shall **c** seven sabbaths
25:27 then let him **c** the years since
Num 23:10 Who can **c** the dust of Jacob, Or
31:26 **C** up the plunder that was
31:49 Your servants have taken a **c** of
Deut 16: 9 You shall **c** seven weeks for
16: 9 begin to **c** the seven weeks from
1 Sam 18:27 and they gave them in full **c** to
2 Sam 24: 2 and **c** the people, that I may
24: 4 of the king to **c** the people
2 Ki 22: 4 that he may **c** the money which
1 Chr 9:28 them in and took them out by **c**.
21: 6 But he did not **c** Levi and
Job 19:15 **C** me as a stranger; I am an
31: 4 And **c** all my steps?
Ps 22:17 I can **c** all My bones.
48:12 **C** her towers;
139:18 If I should **c** them, they would
139:22 I **c** them my enemies.
Ezek 44:26 they shall **c** seven days for
Mic 6:11 Shall I **c** pure those with the
Mt 21:26 for all **c** John as a prophet."
Lk 14:28 does not sit down first and **c**
Acts 20:24 nor do I **c** my life dear to
Phil 3: 8 Yet indeed I also **c** all things
3: 8 and **c** them as rubbish, that I
3:13 I do not **c** myself to have
2 Th 1:11 our God would **c** you worthy
3:15 Yet do not **c** him as an enemy,
1 Tim 6: 1 as are under the yoke **c** their
Phm 1:17 If then you **c** me as a partner,
Jas 1: 2 **c** it all joy when you fall into
5:11 Indeed we **c** them blessed who
2 Pe 2:13 as those who **c** it pleasure to
3: 9 as some **c** slackness, but is

COUNTED (35/35) COUNT

Gen 16:10 so that they shall not be **c** for
Ex 38:21 which was **c** according to the
Lev 25:31 no wall around them shall be **c**
Josh 13: 3 of Ekron northward (which is **c**
Judg 21: 9 For when the people were **c**,
1 Ki 1:21 I and my son Solomon will be **c**
3: 8 numerous to be numbered or **c**.
8: 5 and oxen that could not be **c**
2 Ki 12:10 and **c** the money that was found
1 Chr 23:24 fathers' houses as they were **c**
2 Chr 5: 6 and oxen that could not be **c**
Ezra 1: 8 and **c** them out to Sheshbazzar
Job 18: 3 Why are we **c** as beasts, And
Ps 88: 4 I am **c** with those who go down
Prov 17:28 Even a fool is **c** wise when he
27:14 It will be **c** a curse to him.
Isa 32:15 And the fruitful field is **c** as
40:15 And are **c** as the small dust on
40:17 And they are **c** by Him less
Mt 14: 5 because they **c** him as a
26:15 And they **c** out to him thirty
Mk 11:32 for all **c** John to have been a
Lk 20:35 But those who are **c** worthy to
21:36 pray always that you may be **c**
Acts 5:41 rejoicing that they were **c**
19:19 And they **c** up the value of
Rom 2:26 not his uncircumcision be **c** as
4: 4 the wages are not **c** as grace
9: 8 children of the promise are **c**
Phil 3: 7 these I have **c** loss for Christ.
2 Th 1: 5 that you may be **c** worthy of the
1 Tim 1:12 because He **c** me faithful,
5:17 the elders who rule well be **c**
Heb 3: 3 For this One has been **c** worthy
10:29 **c** the blood of the covenant by

COUNTENANCE (39/38) FACE

Gen 4: 5 very angry, and his **c** fell.
4: 6 And why has your **c** fallen?
12:11 you are a woman of beautiful **c**.
31: 2 And Jacob saw the **c** of Laban,
31: 5 them, "I see your father's **c**,
Num 6:26 The LORD lift up His **c** upon
Deut 28:50 "a nation of fierce **c**,
Judg 13: 6 and His **c** was like the
13: 6 countenance was like the **c** of
1 Sam 14:27 and his **c** brightened.
14:29 how my **c** has brightened because
2 Ki 8:11 Then he set his **c** in a stare
Job 14:20 You change his **c** and send him
29:24 And the light of my **c** they did
Ps 4: 6 lift up the light of Your **c**
10: 4 The wicked in his proud **c** does
11: 7 His **c** beholds the upright.
42: 5 Him For the help of His **c**.
42:11 The help of my **c** and my God.
43: 5 The help of my **c** and my God.
44: 3 arm, and the light of Your **c**,
80:16 perish at the rebuke of Your **c**.
89:15 O LORD, in the light of Your **c**.
90: 8 sins in the light of Your **c**.
Prov 15:13 merry heart makes a cheerful **c**,
25:23 a backbiting tongue an angry **c**.

27:17 So a man sharpens the **c** of his
Eccl 7: 3 For by a sad **c** the heart is
Song 5:15 His **c** is like Lebanon,
Isa 3: 9 The look on their **c** witnesses
Ezek 27:35 And their **c** will be troubled.
Dan 5: 6 Then the king's **c** changed, and
5: 9 his **c** was changed, and his
5:10 nor let your **c** change.
7:28 and my **c** changed; but I kept
Mt 6:16 the hypocrites, with a sad **c**.
28: 3 His **c** was like lightning, and
2 Cor 3: 7 because of the glory of his **c**,
Rev 1:16 and His **c** was like the sun

COUNTERACT (1/1)

Esth 8: 3 implored him with tears to **c**

COUNTING (1/1) COUNT

Gen 41:49 of the sea, until he stopped **c**,

COUNTLESS (2/2) COUNT

Job 21:33 As **c** have gone before him.
Nah 3: 3 ***C*** corpses—They stumble over

COUNTRIES (42/40) COUNTRY

Gen 41:57 So all **c** came to Joseph in Egypt
2 Ki 18:35 lands have delivered their **c**
1 Chr 22: 5 and glorious throughout all **c**.
2 Chr 20:29 on all the kingdoms of those **c**
Ezra 3: 3 of the people of those **c**,
Ps 110: 6 execute the heads of many **c**.
Isa 8: 9 Give ear, all you from far **c**.
36:20 lands have delivered their **c**
Jer 23: 3 of My flock out of all **c** where
23: 8 country and from all the **c**
28: 8 old prophesied against many **c**
32:37 I will gather them out of all **c**
40:11 and who were in all the **c**,
Ezek 5: 5 midst of the nations and the **c**
5: 6 My statutes more than the **c**
6: 8 you are scattered through the **c**.
11:16 have scattered them among the **c**,
11:16 sanctuary for them in the **c**
11:17 assemble you from the **c** where
12:15 disperse them throughout the **c**.
20:23 disperse them throughout the **c**,
20:32 like the families in other **c**,
20:34 and gather you out of the **c**
20:41 and gather you out of the **c**
22: 4 nations, and a mockery to all **c**.
22:15 disperse you throughout the **c**,
25: 7 cause you to perish from the **c**;
29:12 desolate in the midst of the **c**
29:12 disperse them throughout the **c**.
30: 7 in the midst of the desolate **c**,
30:23 disperse them throughout the **c**.
30:26 disperse them throughout the **c**.
32: 9 into the **c** which you have not
34:13 and gather them from the **c**,
35:10 two nations and these two **c**
36:19 were dispersed throughout the **c**;
36:24 gather you out of all **c**,
Dan 9: 7 and those far off in all the **c**
11:40 ships; and he shall enter the **c**,
11:41 and many **c** shall be
11:42 out his hand against the **c**,
Zech 10: 9 they shall remember Me in far **c**;

COUNTRY (159/155) COUNTRIES, COUNTRYSIDE

Gen 12: 1 to Abram: "Get out of your **c**,
14: 7 and attacked all the **c** of the
24: 4 but you shall go to my **c** and to
25: 6 to the **c** of the east.
29:26 must not be done so in our **c**,
30:25 go to my own place and to my **c**.
32: 3 land of Seir, the **c** of Edom.
32: 9 Return to your **c** and to your
34: 2 the Hivite, prince of the **c**,
36: 6 and went to a **c** away from the
42:30 and took us for spies of the **c**.
42:33 the man, the lord of the **c**,
47:27 in the **c** of Goshen; and they
Lev 16:29 a native of your own **c** or a
17:15 he is a native of your own **c**
24:22 and for one from your own **c**;
25:31 counted as the fields of the **c**.
Num 20:17 let us pass through your **c**.
21:20 the valley that is in the **c**
32: 4 the **c** which the LORD defeated
32:33 the cities of the surrounding **c**.
Deut 26: 3 God that I have come to the **c**
28: 3 blessed shall you be in the **c**.
28:16 cursed shall you be in the **c**.
Josh 2: 2 of Israel to search out the **c**.
2: 3 come to search out all the **c**.
2:24 all the inhabitants of the **c**
6:22 two men who had spied out the **c**,
6:27 spread throughout all the **c**.
7: 2 "Go up and spy out the **c**.
9: 6 "We have come from a far **c**;
9: 9 From a very far **c** your servants
9:11 all the inhabitants of our **c**
10:40 the mountain **c** and the South
10:41 and all the **c** of Goshen, even
11:16 all this land: the mountain **c**,
12: 7 these are the kings of the **c**
12: 8 in the mountain **c**,
13:21 of Sihon dwelling in the **c**.
15:48 And in the mountain **c**:
17:15 then go up to the forest **c**
17:16 The mountain **c** is not enough for
17:18 but the mountain **c** shall be
19:51 made an end of dividing the **c**.
22: 9 to go to the **c** of Gilead, to
Judg 8:28 And the **c** was quiet for forty
11:21 Amorites, who inhabited that **c**.
12:12 was buried at Aijalon in the **c**
18:14 who had gone to spy out the **c**
Ruth 1: 1 went to dwell in the **c** of Moab,
1: 2 And they went to the **c** of Moab
1: 6 she might return from the **c** of
1: 6 for she had heard in the **c** of
1:22 who returned from the **c** of
2: 6 back with Naomi from the **c** of
4: 3 who has come back from the **c** of
1 Sam 6: 1 ark of the LORD was in the **c**
6:18 both fortified cities and **c**
14:21 camp from the surrounding **c**,
27: 5 a place in some town in the **c**,
27: 7 time that David dwelt in the **c**
27:11 all the time he dwelt in the **c**
2 Sam 15:23 And all the **c** wept with a loud
21:14 and Jonathan his son in the **c**
1 Ki 4:19 in the **c** of Sihon king of the
8:41 but has come from a far **c** for
10:13 turned and went to her own **c**,
10:15 and from the governors of the **c**.
11:21 that I may go to my own **c**.
11:22 you seek to go to your own **c**?
22:36 and every man to his own **c**!"
2 Ki 20:14 said, "They came from a far **c**,
1 Chr 8: 8 had children in the **c** of Moab,
20: 1 armed forces and ravaged the **c**
2 Chr 6:32 but who comes from a far **c** for
9:12 turned and went to her own **c**,
9:14 Arabia and governors of the **c**
30:10 city to city through the **c** of
34:33 the abominations from all the **c**
Prov 25:25 So is good news from a far **c**.
Isa 1: 7 Your **c** is desolate, Your
13: 5 They come from a far **c**,
22:18 you like a ball Into a large **c**;
39: 3 "They came to me from a far **c**,
46:11 My counsel, from a far **c**.
Jer 2: 7 brought you into a bountiful **c**,
4:16 watchers come from a far **c**
6:20 And sweet cane from a far **c**?
6:22 a people comes from the north **c**,
8:19 of my people From a far **c**:
10:22 commotion out of the north **c**,
22:10 no more, Nor see his native **c**.
22:26 into another **c** where you were
23: 8 of Israel from the north **c** and
31: 8 bring them from the north **c**,
32: 8 which is in the **c** of Benjamin;
44: 1 and in the **c** of Pathros,
46:10 a sacrifice In the north **c** by
47: 4 The remnant of the **c** of
48:21 has come on the plain **c**:
50: 9 great nations from the north **c**,
51: 9 let us go everyone to his own **c**;
Ezek 20:38 I will bring them out of the **c**
20:42 into the **c** for which I raised
25: 9 frontier, the glory of the **c**,
32:15 And the **c** is destitute of all
34:13 the inhabited places of the **c**.
36: 5 in order to plunder its open **c**.
Hos 4:16 forage Like a lamb in open **c**.
12:12 Jacob fled to the **c** of Syria;
Jon 1: 8 you come from? What is your **c**?
4: 2 I said when I was still in my **c**?
Zech 6: 6 horses is going to the north **c**,
6: 6 are going toward the south **c**.
6: 8 who go toward the north **c** have
6: 8 to My Spirit in the north **c**.
Mt 2:12 they departed for their own **c**
8:28 to the **c** of the Gergesenes,
9:31 news about Him in all that **c**.
13:54 when He had come to His own **c**,
13:57 honor except in his own **c** and
21:33 and went into a far **c**.
25:14 like a man traveling to a far **c**,
Mk 5: 1 to the **c** of the Gadarenes.
5:10 not send them out of the **c**.
5:14 it in the city and in the **c**.
6: 1 there and came to His own **c**,
6: 4 honor except in his own **c**,
6:36 may go into the surrounding **c**
6:56 villages, cities, or in the **c**,
12: 1 and went into a far **c**.
13:34 is like a man going to a far **c**,
15:21 as he was coming out of the **c**
16:12 they walked and went into the **c**.
Lk 1:39 days and went into the hill **c**
1:65 throughout all the hill **c** of
2: 8 Now there were in the same **c**
4:23 do also here in Your **c**.
4:24 is accepted in his own **c**.
8:26 Then they sailed to the **c** of
8:34 it in the city and in the **c**.
9:12 the surrounding towns and **c**,
15:13 together, journeyed to a far **c**,
15:15 himself to a citizen of that **c**,
19:12 nobleman went into a far **c** to
20: 9 and went into a far **c** for a
21:21 let not those who are in the **c**
23:26 who was coming from the **c**,
Jn 4:44 has no honor in his own **c**.
11:54 but went from there into the **c**
11:55 and many went from the **c** up to
Acts 4:36 a Levite of the **c** of Cyprus,
7: 3 Get out of your **c** and from
9:32 through all parts of the **c**,
12:20 because their **c** was supplied
12:20 with food by the king's **c**.
Heb 11: 9 of promise as in a foreign **c**,
11:15 they had called to mind that **c**
11:16 better, that is, a heavenly **c**.

COUNTRYMAN (1/1)

Rom 16:11 Greet Herodion, my **c**.

COUNTRYMEN (8/8)

Esth 8: 6 to see the destruction of my **c**?
10: 3 and speaking peace to all his **c**.
Ezek 11:15 your relatives, your **c**,
Rom 9: 3 my **c** according to the flesh,
16: 7 my **c** and my fellow prisoners,
16:21 Jason, and Sosipater, my **c**,
2 Cor 11:26 in perils of my own **c**,
1 Th 2:14 the same things from your own **c**,

COUNTRYSIDE (5/5) COUNTRY

Deut 22:25 betrothed young woman in the **c**,
22:27 "For he found her in the **c**,
2 Sam 18: 8 over the face of the whole **c**,
1 Ki 20:27 while the Syrians filled the **c**.
Neh 12:28 gathered together from the **c**

COUNTS (5/5) COUNT

Job 19:11 And He **c** me as one of His
33:10 He **c** me as His enemy;
Ps 147: 4 He **c** the number of the stars;
Isa 33:18 Where is he who **c** the
Jer 33:13 under the hands of him who **c**

COUPLE (9/9) COUPLED

Ex 26: 6 and **c** the curtains together
26: 9 And you shall **c** five curtains by
26:11 and **c** the tent together, that
36:18 made fifty bronze clasps to **c**
39: 4 shoulder straps for it to **c**
Judg 19: 3 having his servant and a **c** of
2 Sam 13: 6 my sister come and make a **c** of
16: 1 who met him with a **c** of saddled
1 Ki 17:12 I am gathering a **c** of sticks

COUPLED (11/7) COUPLE

Ex 26: 3 Five curtains shall be **c** to one
26: 3 five curtains shall be **c** to
26:24 They shall be **c** together at the
26:24 the bottom and they shall be **c**
36:10 And he **c** five curtains to one
36:10 the other five curtains he **c**
36:13 and **c** the curtains to one
36:16 He **c** five curtains by themselves
36:29 And they were **c** at the bottom
36:29 coupled at the bottom and **c**
39: 4 it was **c** together at its two

COURAGE (22/22) COURAGEOUS

Num 13:20 there or not. Be of good **c**.
Deut 31: 6 "Be strong and of good **c**,
31: 7 "Be strong and of good **c**,
31:23 said, "Be strong and of good **c**;
Josh 1: 6 "Be strong and of good **c**,
1: 9 Be strong and of good **c**,
1:18 Only be strong and of good **c**.
2:11 did there remain any more **c** in
10:25 be strong and of good **c**,
2 Sam 10:12 "Be of good **c**,
1 Chr 19:13 "Be of good **c**,
22:13 Israel. Be strong and of good **c**;
28:20 "Be strong and of good **c**,
2 Chr 15: 8 of Oded the prophet, he took **c**,
Ezra 10: 4 are with you. Be of good **c**,
Ps 27:14 on the LORD; Be of good **c**,
31:24 Be of good **c**, And He
Isa 41: 6 Be of good **c**!"
Jer 47: 3 for their children, Lacking **c**,
Dan 11:25 stir up his power and his **c**
Mk 15:43 of God, coming and taking **c**,
Acts 28:15 them, he thanked God and took **c**.

COURAGEOUS (5/5) COURAGE, COURAGEOUSLY

Josh 1: 7 "Only be strong and very **c**,
23: 6 Therefore be very **c** to keep and
2 Sam 13:28 Be **c** and valiant."
2 Chr 32: 7 "Be strong and **c**;
Am 2:16 The most **c** men of might Shall

COURAGEOUSLY (1/1) COURAGEOUS

2 Chr 19:11 Behave **c**, and the LORD will

COURIERS (4/4)

Esth 3:13 And the letters were sent by **c**
3:15 The **c** went out, hastened by the
8:10 and sent letters by **c** on
8:14 The **c** who rode on royal horses

COURSE (12/12) COURSES

2 Chr 21:19 Then it happened in the **c** of
Job 1: 5 of feasting had run their **c**,
10: 1 I will give free **c** to my
Ps 119:32 I will run the **c** of Your
Isa 48: 7 Of **c** I knew them.'
Jer 8: 6 Everyone turned to his own **c**,
23:10 Their **c** of life is evil, And
Acts 13:25 as John was finishing his **c**,
16:11 we ran a straight **c** to
21: 1 running a straight **c** we came to
Eph 2: 2 once walked according to the **c**
Jas 3: 6 and sets on fire the **c** of

COURSES (1/1) COURSE

Judg 5:20 The stars from their **c** fought

COURT (131/108) COURTS, COURTYARD

Ex 27: 9 You shall also make the **c** of
27: 9 shall be hangings for the **c**
27:12 And along the width of the **c** on
27:13 The width of the **c** on the east
27:16 For the gate of the **c** there
27:17 All the pillars around the **c**
27:18 The length of the **c** shall be
27:19 pegs, and all the pegs of the **c**,
35:17 'the hangings of the **c**,
35:17 screen for the gate of the **c**;
35:18 tabernacle, the pegs of the **c**,
38: 9 Then he made the **c** on the south
38: 9 the hangings of the **c** were of
38:15 for the other side of the **c**
38:16 All the hangings of the **c** all
38:17 and all the pillars of the **c**
38:18 screen for the gate of the **c**
38:18 to the hangings of the **c**.
38:20 and of the **c** all around, were
38:31 the sockets for the **c** all
38:31 the bases for the **c** gate, all
38:31 and all the pegs for the **c** all
39:40 the hangings of the **c**,
39:40 the screen for the **c** gate, its
40: 8 You shall set up the **c** all
40: 8 and hang up the screen at the **c**
40:33 And he raised up the **c** all
40:33 and hung up the screen of the **c**
Lev 6:16 in the **c** of the tabernacle of
6:26 in the **c** of the tabernacle of
Num 3:26 screen for the door of the **c**,
3:26 the hangings of the **c** which
3:37 and the pillars of the **c** all
4:26 the door of the gate of the **c**,
4:26 the hangings of the **c** which
4:32 and the pillars around the **c**
Deut 25: 1 between men, and they come to **c**,
2 Sam 17:18 who had a well in his **c**;
1 Ki 6:36 And he built the inner **c** with
7: 8 where he dwelt had another **c**
7: 9 on the outside to the great **c**.
7:12 The great **c** was enclosed with
7:12 So were the inner **c** of the
8:64 the middle of the **c** that was
2 Ki 20: 4 had gone out into the middle **c**,
23:11 the officer who was in the **c**;
2 Chr 4: 9 Furthermore he made the **c** of
4: 9 and the great **c** and doors for
4: 9 great court and doors for the **c**;
6:13 set it in the midst of the **c**;
7: 7 the middle of the **c** that was
20: 5 of the LORD, before the new **c**,
24:21 him with stones in the **c** of
29:16 temple of the LORD to the **c**
Neh 3:25 upper house that was by the **c**
Esth 1: 5 in the **c** of the garden of the
2:11 paced in front of the **c** of the
4:11 who goes into the inner **c** to
5: 1 and stood in the inner **c** of
5: 2 Queen Esther standing in the **c**,
6: 4 king said, "Who is in the **c**?
6: 4 had just entered the outer **c**
6: 5 is there, standing in the **c**.
Job 9:19 who will appoint my day in **c**?
9:32 And that we should go to **c**
11:19 many would **c** your favor.
Prov 25: 8 Do not go hastily to **c**;
Jer 19:14 and he stood in the **c** of the
26: 2 Stand in the **c** of the LORD's
32: 2 prophet was shut up in the **c**
32: 8 son came to me in the **c** of the
32:12 all the Jews who sat in the **c**
33: 1 he was still shut up in the **c**
36:10 in the upper **c** at the entry of
36:20 went to the king, into the **c**;
37:21 commit Jeremiah to the **c** of
37:21 Jeremiah remained in the **c** of
38: 6 which was in the **c** of the
38:13 And Jeremiah remained in the **c**
38:28 Now Jeremiah remained in the **c**
39:14 to take Jeremiah from the **c** of
39:15 while he was shut up in the **c**
Ezek 8: 3 the north gate of the inner **c**,
8: 7 brought me to the door of the **c**;
8:16 He brought me into the inner **c**
10: 3 the cloud filled the inner **c**.
10: 4 and the **c** was full of the
10: 5 was heard even in the outer **c**,
40:14 and the **c** all around the
40:17 he brought me into the outer **c**;
40:17 pavement made all around the **c**;
40:19 to the front of the inner **c**
40:20 On the outer **c** was also a
40:23 A gate of the inner **c** was
40:27 also a gateway on the inner **c**,
40:28 he brought me to the inner **c**
40:31 Its archways faced the outer **c**,
40:32 he brought me into the inner **c**
40:34 Its archways faced the outer **c**,
40:37 Its gateposts faced the outer **c**,
40:44 for the singers in the inner **c**,
40:47 And he measured the **c**,
41:15 temple and the porches of the **c**,
42: 1 brought me out into the outer **c**,
42: 3 Opposite the inner **c** of twenty
42: 3 the pavement of the outer **c**,
42: 7 chambers, toward the outer **c**;
42: 8 the chambers toward the outer **c**
42: 9 goes into them from the outer **c**.
42:10 thickness of the wall of the **c**
42:14 holy chamber into the outer **c**;
43: 5 and brought me into the inner **c**;
44:17 enter the gates of the inner **c**,
44:17 the gates of the inner **c** or
44:19 they go out to the outer **c**,
44:19 to the outer **c** to the people,
44:21 wine when he enters the inner **c**.
44:27 his sin offering in the inner **c**,
45:19 of the gate of the inner **c**.
46: 1 The gateway of the inner **c** that
46:20 them out into the outer **c** to
46:21 me out into the outer **c** and
46:21 by the four corners of the **c**;
46:21 in every corner of the **c** there
46:21 court there was another **c**.
46:22 In the four corners of the **c**
Dan 7:10 The **c** was seated, And the
7:26 But the **c** shall be seated, And
1 Cor 4: 3 judged by you or by a human **c**.
Gal 4:17 They zealously **c** you, but for
Rev 11: 2 But leave out the **c** which is

COURTEOUS (1/1) COURTEOUSLY, COURTESY

1 Pe 3: 8 be tenderhearted, be **c**;

COURTEOUSLY (1/1) COURTEOUS

Acts 28: 7 us and entertained us **c** for

COURTESY (1/1) COURTEOUS

Acts 24: 4 I beg you to hear, by your **c**,

COURTS (26/26) COURT

2 Ki 21: 5 host of heaven in the two **c** of
23:12 Manasseh had made in the two **c**
1 Chr 23:28 in the **c** and in the chambers,
28: 6 shall build My house and My **c**;
28:12 of the **c** of the house of the
2 Chr 23: 5 the people shall be in the **c**
33: 5 host of heaven in the two **c** of
Neh 8:16 or in their courtyards or the **c**
13: 7 a room for him in the **c** of the
Ps 65: 4 That he may dwell in Your **c**.
84: 2 even faints For the **c** of the
84:10 For a day in Your **c** is better
92:13 LORD Shall flourish in the **c**
96: 8 offering, and come into His **c**.
100: 4 And into His **c** with praise.
116:19 In the **c** of the LORD's house,
135: 2 In the **c** of the house of our
Isa 1:12 your hand, To trample My **c**?
62: 9 shall drink it in My holy **c**.
Ezek 9: 7 and fill the **c** with the slain.
42: 6 like the pillars of the **c**;
46:22 of the court were enclosed **c**,
Zech 3: 7 likewise have charge of My **c**;
Lk 7:25 live in luxury are in kings' **c**.
Acts 19:38 the **c** are open and there are
Jas 2: 6 you and drag you into the **c**?

COURTYARD (15/15) COURT, COURTYARDS

Isa 34:13 A **c** for ostriches.
Jer 43: 9 in the clay in the brick **c**
Ezek 41:12 that faced the separating **c** at
41:13 and the separating **c** with the
41:14 including the separating **c**,
41:15 it, facing the separating **c**,
42: 1 was opposite the separating **c**,
42:10 opposite the separating **c** and
42:13 are opposite the separating **c**,
Mt 26:58 distance to the high priest's **c**.
26:69 Now Peter sat outside in the **c**.
Mk 14:54 right into the **c** of the high
14:66 as Peter was below in the **c**,
Lk 22:55 a fire in the midst of the **c**
Jn 18:15 and went with Jesus into the **c**

COURTYARDS (2/2) COURTYARD

Ex 8:13 out of the houses, out of the **c**,
Neh 8:16 or in their **c** or the courts of

COUSIN (1/1)

Col 4:10 with Mark the **c** of Barnabas

COVENANT (313/293) COVENANTED, COVENANTS

Gen 6:18 But I will establish My **c** with
9: 9 I establish My **c** with you and
9:11 Thus I establish My **c** with you:
9:12 This is the sign of the **c** which
9:13 shall be for the sign of the **c**
9:15 and I will remember My **c** which
9:16 to remember the everlasting **c**
9:17 This is the sign of the **c** which
15:18 the same day the LORD made a **c**
17: 2 And I will make My **c** between Me
17: 4 My **c** is with you, and you shall
17: 7 And I will establish My **c**
17: 7 for an everlasting **c**,
17: 9 for you, you shall keep My **c**,
17:10 This is My **c** which you shall
17:11 and it shall be a sign of the **c**
17:13 and My **c** shall be in your flesh
17:13 your flesh for an everlasting **c**.
17:14 his people; he has broken My **c**.
17:19 I will establish My **c** with him
17:19 with him for an everlasting **c**,
17:21 But My **c** I will establish with
21:27 and the two of them made a **c**.
21:32 Thus they made a **c** at Beersheba.
26:28 and let us make a **c** with you,
31:44 come, let us make a **c**,
Ex 2:24 and God remembered His **c** with
6: 4 I have also established My **c**
6: 5 and I have remembered My **c**.
19: 5 obey My voice and keep My **c**,
23:32 You shall make no **c** with them,
24: 7 Then he took the Book of the **C**
24: 8 This is the blood of the **c** which
31:16 generations as a perpetual **c**.
34:10 He said: "Behold, I make a **c**.
34:12 lest you make a **c** with the
34:15 lest you make a **c** with the
34:27 of these words I have made a **c**
34:28 the tablets the words of the **c**,
Lev 2:13 not allow the salt of the **c** of
24: 8 of Israel by an everlasting **c**.
26: 9 multiply you and confirm My **c**
26:15 commandments, but break My **c**,
26:25 execute the vengeance of the **c**;
26:42 then I will remember My **c** with
26:42 and My **c** with Isaac and My
26:42 My covenant with Isaac and My **c**
26:44 destroy them and break My **c**
26:45 sake I will remember the **c** of
Num 10:33 and the ark of the **c** of the
14:44 neither the ark of the **c** of the
18:19 it is a **c** of salt forever
25:12 I give to him My **c** of peace;
25:13 his descendants after him a **c**
Deut 4:13 So He declared to you His **c**
4:23 lest you forget the **c** of the
4:31 nor forget the **c** of your
5: 2 The LORD our God made a **c** with
5: 3 The LORD did not make this **c**
7: 2 You shall make no **c** with them
7: 9 the faithful God who keeps **c**
7:12 God will keep with you the **c**
8:18 that He may establish His **c**
9: 9 the tablets of the **c** which the
9:11 of stone, the tablets of the **c**.
9:15 and the two tablets of the **c**
10: 8 Levi to bear the ark of the **c**
17: 2 God, in transgressing His **c**,
29: 1 These are the words of the **c**
29: 1 besides the **c** which He made
29: 9 keep the words of this **c**,
29:12 that you may enter into **c** with
29:14 I make this **c** and this oath,
29:21 to all the curses of the **c**
29:25 they have forsaken the **c** of
31: 9 who bore the ark of the **c** of
31:16 will forsake Me and break My **c**
31:20 will provoke Me and break My **c**.
31:25 who bore the ark of the **c** of
31:26 put it beside the ark of the **c**
33: 9 Your word And kept Your **c**.
Josh 3: 3 When you see the ark of the **c** of
3: 6 Take up the ark of the **c** and
3: 6 they took up the ark of the **c**
3: 8 who bear the ark of the **c**,
3:11 the ark of the **c** of the Lord of
3:14 bearing the ark of the **c**
3:17 who bore the ark of the **c** of
4: 7 off before the ark of the **c** of
4: 9 who bore the ark of the **c**
4:18 who bore the ark of the **c** of
6: 6 "Take up the ark of the **c**,
6: 8 and the ark of the **c** of the
7:11 have also transgressed My **c**
7:15 he has transgressed the **c** of
8:33 who bore the ark of the **c** of
9: 6 make a **c** with us."
9: 7 so how can we make a **c** with
9:11 make a **c** with us." '
9:15 and made a **c** with them to let
9:16 after they had made a **c** with
23:16 you have transgressed the **c** of
24:25 So Joshua made a **c** with the
Judg 2: 1 I will never break My **c** with
2: 2 And you shall make no **c** with the
2:20 nation has transgressed My **c**
20:27 of the LORD (the ark of the **c**
1 Sam 4: 3 Let us bring the ark of the **c**

4: 4 from there the ark of the **c** of
4: 4 there with the ark of the **c** of
4: 5 And when the ark of the **c** of
11: 1 Make a **c** with us, and we will
11: 2 condition I will make a **c**
18: 3 Jonathan and David made a **c**,
20: 8 brought your servant into a **c**
20:16 So Jonathan made a **c** with the
22: 8 to me that my son has made a **c**
23:18 So the two of them made a **c**
2 Sam 3:12 Make your **c** with me, and indeed
3:13 I will make a **c** with you.
3:21 that they may make a **c** with
5: 3 and King David made a **c** with
15:24 bearing the ark of the **c** of
23: 5 made with me an everlasting **c**,
1 Ki 3:15 stood before the ark of the **c**
6:19 to set the ark of the **c** of the
8: 1 bring up the ark of the **c** of
8: 6 brought in the ark of the **c** of
8: 9 when the LORD made a **c** with
8:21 in which is the **c** of the LORD
8:23 who keep Your **c** and mercy with
11:11 and have not kept My **c** and My
19:10 of Israel have forsaken Your **c**,
19:14 of Israel have forsaken Your **c**,
2 Ki 11: 4 And he made a **c** with them and
11:17 Then Jehoiada made a **c** between
13:23 because of His **c** with Abraham,
17:15 His statutes and His **c** that He
17:35 whom the LORD had made a **c**
17:38 And the **c** that I have made with
18:12 but transgressed His **c** and all
23: 2 the words of the Book of the **C**
23: 3 stood by a pillar and made a **c**
23: 3 to perform the words of this **c**
23: 3 people took a stand for the **c**.
23:21 written in this Book of the **C**.
1 Chr 11: 3 and David made a **c** with them at
15:25 to bring up the ark of the **c**
15:26 who bore the ark of the **c** of
15:28 brought up the ark of the **c** of
15:29 as the ark of the **c** of the
16: 6 before the ark of the **c** of God.
16:15 Remember His **c** forever, The
16:16 The **c** which He made with
16:17 Israel for an everlasting **c**,
16:37 there before the ark of the **c**
17: 1 but the ark of the **c** of the
22:19 to bring the ark of the **c** of
28: 2 of rest for the ark of the **c**
28:18 overshadowed the ark of the **c**
2 Chr 5: 2 might bring the ark of the **c**
5: 7 brought in the ark of the **c** of
5:10 when the LORD made a **c** with
6:11 in which is the **c** of the LORD
6:14 who keep Your **c** and mercy with
13: 5 his sons, by a **c** of salt?
15:12 Then they entered into a **c** to
21: 7 because of the **c** that He had
23: 1 and made a **c** with the
23: 3 Then all the assembly made a **c**
23:16 Then Jehoiada made a **c** between
29:10 it is in my heart to make a **c**
34:30 the words of the Book of the **C**
34:31 stood in his place and made a **c**
34:31 to perform the words of the **c**
34:32 did according to the **c** of God,
Ezra 10: 3 let us make a **c** with our God to
Neh 1: 5 You who keep Your **c** and mercy
9: 8 And made a **c** with him To give
9:32 Who keeps **c** and mercy: Do not
9:38 of all this, We make a sure **c**,
13:29 the priesthood and the **c** of
Job 5:23 For you shall have a **c** with the
31: 1 I have made a **c** with my eyes;
41: 4 Will he make a **c** with you?
Ps 25:10 To such as keep His **c** and His
25:14 And He will show them His **c**.
44:17 we dealt falsely with Your **c**.
50: 5 Those who have made a **c** with
50:16 Or take My **c** in your mouth,
55:20 with him; He has broken his **c**.
74:20 Have respect to the **c**;
78:10 They did not keep the **c** of God;
78:37 were they faithful in His **c**.
89: 3 I have made a **c** with My chosen,
89:28 And My **c** shall stand firm with
89:34 My **c** I will not break, Nor
89:39 You have renounced the **c** of
103:18 To such as keep His **c**,
105: 8 He remembers His **c** forever,
105: 9 The **c** which He made with
105:10 To Israel as an everlasting **c**,
106:45 their sake He remembered His **c**,
111: 5 will ever be mindful of His **c**.
111: 9 He has commanded His **c**
132:12 If your sons will keep My **c**
Prov 2:17 And forgets the **c** of her God.
Isa 24: 5 Broken the everlasting **c**.
28:15 We have made a **c** with death,
28:18 Your **c** with death will be
33: 8 He has broken the **c**,
42: 6 keep You and give You as a **c**
49: 8 You and give You As a **c** to
54:10 Nor shall My **c** of peace be
55: 3 I will make an everlasting **c**
56: 4 pleases Me, And hold fast My **c**,
56: 6 Sabbath, And holds fast My **c**—
57: 8 your bed And made a **c** with
59:21 this is My **c** with them: My
61: 8 make with them an everlasting **c**.
Jer 3:16 The ark of the **c** of the LORD.'
11: 2 "Hear the words of this **c**,
11: 3 not obey the words of this **c**
11: 6 Hear the words of this **c** and do
11: 8 them all the words of this **c**,
11:10 house of Judah have broken My **c**
14:21 do not break Your **c** with us.
22: 9 they have forsaken the **c** of
31:31 when I will make a new **c** with
31:32 not according to the **c** that I
31:32 My **c** which they broke, though I
31:33 But this is the **c** that I will
32:40 I will make an everlasting **c**
33:20 If you can break My **c** with the
33:20 covenant with the day and My **c**
33:21 then My **c** may also be broken
33:25 If My **c** is not with day and
34: 8 King Zedekiah had made a **c**
34:10 who had entered into the **c**,
34:13 I made a **c** with your fathers in
34:15 and you made a **c** before Me in
34:18 men who have transgressed My **c**,
34:18 performed the words of the **c**
50: 5 to the LORD In a perpetual **c**
Ezek 16: 8 to you and entered into a **c**
16:59 the oath by breaking the **c**.
16:60 I will remember My **c** with you
16:60 will establish an everlasting **c**
16:61 but not because of My **c** with
16:62 And I will establish My **c** with
17:13 made a **c** with him, and put him
17:14 but that by keeping his **c** it
17:15 Can he break a **c** and still be
17:16 oath he despised and whose **c**
17:18 the oath by breaking the **c**,
17:19 and My **c** which he broke, I will
20:37 you into the bond of the **c**;
34:25 I will make a **c** of peace with
37:26 Moreover I will make a **c** of
37:26 it shall be an everlasting **c**
44: 7 then they broke My **c** because of
Dan 9: 4 who keeps His **c** and mercy with
9:27 Then he shall confirm a **c** with
11:22 and also the prince of the **c**.
11:28 be moved against the holy **c**;
11:30 in rage against the holy **c**,
11:30 those who forsake the holy **c**.
11:32 who do wickedly against the **c**
Hos 2:18 In that day I will make a **c** for
6: 7 men they transgressed the **c**;
8: 1 they have transgressed My **c**
10: 4 Swearing falsely in making a **c**.
12: 1 Also they make a **c** with the
Am 1: 9 And did not remember the **c** of
Zech 9:11 Because of the blood of your **c**,
11:10 that I might break the **c** which
Mal 2: 4 That My **c** with Levi may
2: 5 My **c** was with him, one of life
2: 8 You have corrupted the **c** of
2:10 another By profaning the **c** of
2:14 companion And your wife by **c**.
3: 1 Even the Messenger of the **c**,
Mt 26:28 this is My blood of the new **c**,
Mk 14:24 "This is My blood of the new **c**,
Lk 1:72 And to remember His holy **c**,
22:20 This cup is the new **c** in My
Acts 3:25 and of the **c** which God made
7: 8 Then He gave him the **c** of
Rom 11:27 For this is My **c** with
1 Cor 11:25 This cup is the new **c** in My
2 Cor 3: 6 as ministers of the new **c**,
Gal 3:15 Though it is only a man's **c**,
3:17 cannot annul the **c** that was
Heb 7:22 become a surety of a better **c**.
8: 6 is also Mediator of a better **c**,
8: 7 For if that first **c** had been
8: 8 when I will make a new **c**
8: 9 not according to the **c** that
8: 9 did not continue in My **c**,
8:10 For this is the **c** that I
8:13 In that He says, "A new **c**,
9: 1 even the first **c** had
9: 4 censer and the ark of the **c**
9: 4 and the tablets of the **c**;
9:15 He is the Mediator of the new **c**,
9:15 under the first **c**,
9:18 not even the first **c** was
9:20 is the blood of the **c**
10:16 This is the **c** that I will
10:29 counted the blood of the **c** by
12:24 Jesus the Mediator of the new **c**,
13:20 the blood of the everlasting **c**,
Rev 11:19 and the ark of His **c** was seen

COVENANTED (2/2) COVENANT

2 Chr 7:18 as I **c** with David your father,
Hag 2: 5 to the word that I **c** with you

COVENANTS (3/3) COVENANT

Rom 9: 4 the adoption, the glory, the **c**,
Gal 4:24 For these are the two **c**:
Eph 2:12 and strangers from the **c** of

COVER (73/72) COVERED, COVERING, COVERINGS, COVERS, UNCOVER

Gen 6:14 and **c** it inside and outside
Ex 10: 5 And they shall **c** the face of the
21:33 a man digs a pit and does not **c**
26:13 on that side, to **c** it.
28:42 linen trousers to **c** their
33:22 and will **c** you with My hand
Lev 13:45 and he shall **c** his mustache,
16:13 the cloud of incense may **c** the
17:13 pour out its blood and **c** it
Num 4: 5 covering veil and **c** the ark
4: 8 and **c** the same with a covering
4: 9 and **c** the lampstand of the
4:11 and **c** it with a covering of
4:12 **c** them with a covering of
19:15 which has no **c** fastened on it,
22: 5 they **c** the face of the earth,
22:11 and they **c** the face of the
Deut 22:12 the clothing with which you **c**
23:13 and turn and **c** your refuse.
1 Sam 19:13 put a **c** of goats' hair for his
19:16 with a **c** of goats' hair for
25:20 that she went down under **c** of
1 Ki 7:18 all around to **c** the capitals
7:42 to **c** the two bowl-shaped
2 Chr 4:13 to **c** the two bowl-shaped
Neh 4: 5 Do not **c** their iniquity, and do
Job 14:17 And You **c** my iniquity.
16:18 do not **c** my blood, And let my
21:26 And worms **c** them.
22:14 Thick clouds **c** Him, so that He
38:34 abundance of water may **c** you?
40:22 The lotus trees **c** him with
Ps 91: 4 He shall **c** you with His
104: 2 Who **c** Yourself with light as
104: 9 That they may not return to **c**
109:29 And let them **c** themselves with
140: 9 Let the evil of their lips **c**
Isa 11: 9 of the LORD As the waters **c**
14:11 And worms **c** you.'
26:21 And will no more **c** her slain.
32: 2 And a **c** from the tempest, As
54: 9 of Noah would no longer **c** the
58: 7 that you **c** him, And not hide
59: 6 Nor will they **c** themselves
60: 2 the darkness shall **c** the earth,
60: 6 camels shall **c** your land,
Jer 46: 8 I will go up and **c** the earth,
Ezek 7:18 Horror will **c** them; Shame
12: 6 you shall **c** your face, so that
12:12 He shall **c** his face, so that he
24: 7 To **c** it with dust.
24:17 do not **c** your lips, and do not
24:22 you shall not **c** your lips nor
26:10 their dust will **c** you;
26:19 and great waters **c** you,
30:18 a cloud shall **c** her, And her
32: 7 I will **c** the heavens, and make
32: 7 I will **c** the sun with a cloud,
37: 6 **c** you with skin and put breath
38:16 to **c** the land. It will be in
Hos 2: 9 Given to **c** her nakedness.
10: 8 to the mountains, "**C** us!"
Ob 10 Shame shall **c** you, And you
Mic 3: 7 Indeed they shall all **c** their
7:10 And shame will **c** her who said
Hab 2:14 As the waters **c** the sea.
2:17 done to Lebanon will **c** you,
Zech 5: 8 and threw the lead **c** over its
Mal 2:13 You **c** the altar of the LORD
Lk 23:30 to the hills, "**C** us!"
1 Cor 11: 7 For a man indeed ought not to **c**
Jas 5:20 save a soul from death and **c** a
1 Pe 4: 8 love will **c** a multitude of

COVERED (99/95) COVER

Gen 7:19 under the whole heaven were **c**.
7:20 and the mountains were **c**.
9:23 and went backward and **c** the
24:65 took a veil and **c** herself.
38:14 **c** herself with a veil and
38:15 because she had **c** her face.
Ex 8: 6 and the frogs came up and **c** the
10:15 For they **c** the face of the whole
14:28 returned and **c** the chariots,
15: 5 The depths have **c** them;
15:10 The sea **c** them; They sank
16:13 came up at evening and **c** the
24:15 and a cloud **c** the mountain.
24:16 and the cloud **c** it six days.
37: 9 and **c** the mercy seat with
40:34 Then the cloud **c** the tabernacle
Lev 2: 7 offering baked in a **c** pan,
7: 9 that is prepared in the **c** pan,
13:13 indeed if the leprosy has **c**
Num 4:20 the holy things are being **c**,
7: 3 six **c** carts and twelve oxen, a
9:15 the cloud **c** the tabernacle, the
9:16 the cloud **c** it by day, and
16:42 and suddenly the cloud **c** it,
Josh 24: 7 and **c** them. And your eyes saw
Judg 4:18 she **c** him with a blanket.
4:19 him a drink, and **c** him.
1 Sam 19:13 and **c** it with clothes.
28:14 and he is **c** with a mantle."
2 Sam 15:30 and he had his head **c** and went
15:30 were with him **c** their heads
19: 4 But the king **c** his face, and the
1 Ki 6:15 and he **c** the floor of the
2 Ki 19: 1 **c** himself with sackcloth, and
19: 2 **c** with sackcloth, to Isaiah the
Neh 3:15 **c** it, hung its doors with its
Esth 6:12 mourning and with his head **c**.
7: 8 they **c** Haman's face.
Job 15:27 Though he has **c** his face with

31:33 If I have **c** my transgressions
Ps 32: 1 is forgiven, Whose sin is **c**.
44:15 the shame of my face has **c** me,
44:19 And **c** us with the shadow of
65:13 The valleys also are **c** with
68:13 wings of a dove **c** with silver,
69: 7 Shame has **c** my face.
71:13 Let them be **c** with reproach
80:10 The hills were **c** with its
85: 2 You have **c** all their sin.
89:45 You have **c** him with shame.
104: 6 You **c** it with the deep as with
106:11 The waters **c** their enemies;
106:17 And **c** the faction of Abiram.
139:13 You **c** me in my mother's womb.
140: 7 You have **c** my head in the day
Prov 24:31 Its surface was **c** with
26:23 Are like earthenware **c** with
26:26 Though his hatred is **c** by
Eccl 6: 4 and its name is **c** with
Song 5: 2 For my head is **c** with dew, My
Isa 6: 2 with two he **c** his face, with
6: 2 with two he **c** his feet, and
27: 9 the iniquity of Jacob will be **c**;
29:10 And He has **c** your heads,
37: 1 **c** himself with sackcloth, and
37: 2 **c** with sackcloth, to Isaiah the
51:16 I have **c** you with the shadow
61:10 He has **c** me with the robe of
Jer 14: 3 confounded And **c** their heads.
14: 4 They **c** their heads.
51:42 She is **c** with the multitude of
51:51 Shame has **c** our faces, For
Lam 2: 1 How the Lord has **c** the daughter
3:16 And **c** me with ashes.
3:43 You have **c** Yourself with
3:44 You have **c** Yourself with a
Ezek 1:11 and two **c** their bodies.
1:23 Each one had two which **c** one
1:23 and each one had two which **c**
16: 8 My wing over you and **c** your
16:10 you with fine linen and **c** you
16:18 garments and **c** them,
18: 7 the hungry And **c** the naked
18:16 the hungry And **c** the naked
24: 8 a rock, That it may not be **c**.
27: 7 of Elishah was what **c** you.
31:15 I **c** the deep because of it.
37: 8 and the skin **c** them over; but
41:16 the windows—the windows were **c**—
Jon 3: 6 **c** himself with sackcloth and
3: 8 But let man and beast be **c** with
Hab 3: 3 Selah His glory **c** the heavens,
Mt 8:24 so that the boat was **c** with the
10:26 For there is nothing **c** that
Lk 12: 2 For there is nothing **c** that will
Rom 4: 7 And whose sins are **c**;
1 Cor 11: 4 prophesying, having his head **c**,
11: 6 For if a woman is not **c**,
11: 6 shorn or shaved, let her be **c**.

COVERING (43/38) COVER, COVERINGS

Gen 8:13 and Noah removed the **c** of the
Ex 22:27 "For that is his only **c**,
25:20 **c** the mercy seat with their
26:14 You shall also make a **c** of ram
26:14 and a **c** of badger skins above
35:11 tabernacle, its tent, its **c**,
35:12 seat, and the veil of the **c**;
36:19 Then he made a **c** for the tent of
36:19 and a **c** of badger skins above
39:34 the **c** of ram skins dyed red, the
39:34 the **c** of badger skins, and the
39:34 skins, and the veil of the **c**;
40:19 the tabernacle and put the **c**
40:21 hung up the veil of the **c**,
Num 3:25 tabernacle, the tent with its **c**,
4: 5 and they shall take down the **c**
4: 6 Then they shall put on it a **c** of
4: 8 and cover the same with a **c** of
4:10 it with all its utensils in a **c**
4:11 and cover it with a **c** of badger
4:12 cover them with a **c** of badger
4:14 they shall spread on it a **c** of
4:15 finished **c** the sanctuary
4:25 of meeting with its **c**,
4:25 the **c** of badger skins that is
16:38 into hammered plates as a **c**
16:39 they were hammered out as a **c**
2 Sam 17:19 the woman took and spread a **c**
1 Ki 7:41 the two networks **c** the two
2 Chr 4:12 the two networks **c** the two
Job 24: 7 And have no **c** in the cold.
26: 6 Him, And Destruction has no **c**.
31:19 Or any poor man without **c**;
Ps 105:39 He spread a cloud for a **c**,
Isa 4: 5 the glory there will be a **c**.
25: 7 mountain The surface of the **c**
28:20 And the **c** so narrow that one
30:22 You will also defile the **c** of
50: 3 And I make sackcloth their **c**.
Ezek 28:13 precious stone was your **c**:
28:16 O **c** cherub, From the midst of
38: 9 **c** the land like a cloud, you
1 Cor 11:15 hair is given to her for a **c**.

COVERINGS (2/2) COVER, COVERING

Gen 3: 7 together and made themselves **c**.
Prov 7:16 Colored **c** of Egyptian linen.

COVERS (29/29) COVER

Ex 29:13 the fat that **c** the entrails,
29:22 the fat that **c** the entrails,
Lev 3: 3 The fat that **c** the entrails and
3: 9 And the fat that **c** the entrails
3:14 The fat that **c** the entrails and
4: 8 The fat that **c** the entrails and
7: 3 the fat that **c** the entrails,
9:19 what **c** the entrails and the
13:12 and the leprosy **c** all the skin
1 Ki 1: 1 and they put **c** on him, but he
Job 9:24 He **c** the faces of its judges.
22:11 an abundance of water **c** you.
26: 9 He **c** the face of His throne,
36:30 And **c** the depths of the sea.
36:32 He **c** His hands with lightning,
Ps 73: 6 Violence **c** them like a
84: 6 The rain also **c** it with pools.
109:19 like the garment which **c** him,
147: 8 Who **c** the heavens with clouds,
Prov 10: 6 But violence **c** the mouth of
10:11 But violence **c** the mouth of
10:12 But love **c** all sins.
12:16 But a prudent man **c** shame.
17: 9 He who **c** a transgression seeks
28:13 He who **c** his sins will not
Jer 3:25 And our reproach **c** us. For we
Ezek 28:14 were the anointed cherub who **c**;
Mal 2:16 For it **c** one's garment with
Lk 8:16 **c** it with a vessel or puts it

COVERT (1/1)

Job 40:21 In a **c** of reeds and marsh.

COVET (10/9) COVETED, COVETOUS, COVETS

Ex 20:17 You shall not **c** your neighbor's
20:17 you shall not **c** your neighbor's
34:24 neither will any man **c** your
Deut 5:21 You shall not **c** your neighbor's
7:25 you shall not **c** the silver or
Prov 12:12 The wicked **c** the catch of evil
Mic 2: 2 They **c** fields and take them by
Rom 7: 7 had said, "You shall not **c**.
13: 9 "You shall not **c**,
Jas 4: 2 You murder and **c** and cannot

COVETED (2/2) COVET

Josh 7:21 I **c** them and took them.
Acts 20:33 I have **c** no one's silver or gold

COVETOUS (6/6) COVET, COVETOUSNESS

1 Cor 5:10 of this world, or with the **c**,
5:11 who is sexually immoral, or **c**,
6:10 nor thieves, nor **c**,
Eph 5: 5 nor **c** man, who is an idolater,
1 Tim 3: 3 gentle, not quarrelsome, not **c**;
2 Pe 2:14 heart trained in **c** practices,

COVETOUSNESS (17/17) COVETOUS

Ex 18:21 God, men of truth, hating **c**;
Ps 119:36 Your testimonies, And not to **c**.
Prov 28:16 But he who hates **c** will
Isa 57:17 For the iniquity of his **c** I
Jer 6:13 them, Everyone is given to **c**;
8:10 Everyone is given to **c**;
22:17 are for nothing but your **c**,
51:13 come, The measure of your **c**.
Mk 7:22 'thefts, **c**, wickedness,
Lk 12:15 "Take heed and beware of **c**,
Rom 1:29 immorality, wickedness, **c**,
7: 7 For I would not have known **c**
Eph 5: 3 and all uncleanness or **c**,
Col 3: 5 passion, evil desire, and **c**,
1 Th 2: 5 as you know, nor a cloak for **c**—
Heb 13: 5 your conduct be without **c**;
2 Pe 2: 3 By **c** they will exploit you with

COVETS (2/2) COVET

Prov 21:26 He **c** greedily all day long,
Hab 2: 9 Woe to him who **c** evil gain for

COW (6/6) COWS

Lev 22:28 Whether it is a **c** or ewe, do
Num 18:17 "But the firstborn of a **c**,
Job 21:10 Their **c** calves without
Isa 7:21 a man will keep alive a young **c**
11: 7 The **c** and the bear shall graze;
Ezek 4:15 I am giving you **c** dung instead

COWARDLY (1/1)

Rev 21: 8 'But the **c**, unbelieving,

COWS (18/14) COW

Gen 32:15 forty **c** and ten bulls, twenty
41: 2 up out of the river seven **c**,
41: 3 seven other **c** came up after
41: 3 and stood by the other **c** on
41: 4 And the ugly and gaunt **c** ate up
41: 4 seven fine looking and fat **c**.
41:18 Suddenly seven **c** came up out of
41:19 seven other **c** came up after
41:20 And the gaunt and ugly **c** ate up
41:20 up the first seven, the fat **c**.
41:26 The seven good **c** are seven
41:27 And the seven thin and ugly **c**
1 Sam 6: 7 take two milk **c** which have
6: 7 and hitch the **c** to the cart;
6:10 they took two milk **c** and
6:12 Then the **c** headed straight for
6:14 of the cart and offered the **c**
Am 4: 1 you **c** of Bashan, who are on

COZ (KJV) See KOZ

COZBI (2/2)

Num 25:15 woman who was killed was ***C***
25:18 of Peor and in the matter of ***C***,

CRACKED (1/1)

Job 7: 5 My skin is **c** and breaks out

CRACKLING (1/1)

Eccl 7: 6 For like the **c** of thorns under

CRACKNELS (KJV) See CAKES

CRAFT (1/1) CRAFTSMAN

Rev 18:22 No craftsman of any **c** shall be

CRAFTILY (2/2) CRAFTY

Josh 9: 4 they worked **c**, and went and
Ps 105:25 To deal **c** with His servants.

CRAFTINESS (6/6) CRAFTY

Job 5:13 catches the wise in their own **c**,
Lk 20:23 But He perceived their **c**,
1 Cor 3:19 the wise in their own **c**'
2 Cor 4: 2 not walking in **c** nor handling
11: 3 serpent deceived Eve by his **c**,
Eph 4:14 in the cunning **c** of deceitful

CRAFTSMAN (10/10) CRAFT, CRAFTSMEN

Gen 4:22 an instructor of every **c** in
Deut 27:15 the work of the hands of the **c**,
1 Chr 28:21 and every willing **c** will be
2 Chr 2:13 Huram my master **c**
4:16 articles Huram his master **c**
Prov 8:30 I was beside Him as a master **c**;
Isa 41: 7 So the **c** encouraged the
44:13 The **c** stretches out his rule,
Jer 10: 9 The work of the **c** And of the
Rev 18:22 No **c** of any craft shall be

CRAFTSMEN (15/15) CRAFTSMAN

Ex 36: 4 Then all the **c** who were doing
2 Ki 24:14 and all the **c** and smiths.
24:16 and **c** and smiths, one thousand,
1 Chr 4:14 of Ge Harashim, for they were **c**.
29: 5 to be done by the hands of **c**.
2 Chr 34:11 They gave it to the **c** and
Neh 11:35 Lod, Ono, and the Valley of ***C***.
Jer 24: 1 the princes of Judah with the **c**
29: 2 of Judah and Jerusalem, the **c**,
52:15 Babylon, and the rest of the **c**.
Hos 13: 2 All of it is the work of **c**.
Zech 1:20 Then the LORD showed me four **c**.
1:21 but the **c** are coming to terrify
Acts 19:24 no small profit to the **c**.
19:38 if Demetrius and his fellow **c**

CRAFTY (7/7) CRAFTILY, CRAFTINESS

1 Sam 23:22 For I am told he is very **c**.
2 Sam 13: 3 Now Jonadab was a very **c** man.
Job 5:12 frustrates the devices of the **c**,
15: 5 you choose the tongue of the **c**.
Ps 83: 3 They have taken **c** counsel
Prov 7:10 a harlot, and a **c** heart.
2 Cor 12:16 Nevertheless, being **c**,

CRAG (1/1) CRAGS

Job 39:28 On the **c** of the rock and the

CRAGS (2/2) CRAG

Prov 30:26 they make their homes in the **c**;
Isa 2:21 And into the **c** of the rugged

CRANE (1/1)

Isa 38:14 Like a **c** or a swallow, so I

CRASHING (1/1) CRASHINGS

Zeph 1:10 And a loud **c** from the hills.

CRASHINGS (1/1) CRASHING

Job 41:25 Because of his **c** they are

CRAVES (1/1) CRAVING

Isa 29: 8 faint, And his soul still **c**:

CRAVING (3/3) CRAVES
Num 11: 4 among them yielded to intense **c**;
11:34 the people who had yielded to **c**.
Ps 78:30 were not deprived of their **c**;

CRAWL (1/1) CRAWLING, CRAWLS
Mic 7:17 They shall **c** from their holes

CRAWLING (3/2) CRAWL
Joel 1: 4 the **c** locust has eaten; And
1: 4 And what the **c** locust left,
2:25 The **c** locust, The consuming

CRAWLS (1/1) CRAWL
Lev 11:42 Whatever **c** on its belly,

CREAM (3/3)
Judg 5:25 She brought out **c** in a lordly
Job 20:17 rivers flowing with honey and **c**.
29: 6 my steps were bathed with **c**,

CREATE (11/9) CREATED, CREATES, CREATION, CREATOR, CREATURE
Neh 4: 8 Jerusalem and **c** confusion.
Ps 51:10 **C** in me a clean heart, O God,
Isa 4: 5 then the LORD will **c** above
45: 7 the light and **c** darkness,
45: 7 I make peace and **c** calamity;
45:18 Who did not **c** it in vain, Who
57:19 I **c** the fruit of the lips:
65:17 I **c** new heavens and a new
65:18 and rejoice forever in what I **c**;
65:18 I **c** Jerusalem as a rejoicing,
Eph 2:15 so as to **c** in Himself one new

CREATED (46/40) CREATE
Gen 1: 1 In the beginning God **c** the
1:21 So God **c** great sea creatures and
1:27 So God **c** man in His own image;
1:27 in the image of God He **c** him;
1:27 male and female He **c** them.
2: 3 all His work which God had **c**
2: 4 and the earth when they were **c**,
5: 1 In the day that God **c** man, He
5: 2 He **c** them male and female, and
5: 2 Mankind in the day they were **c**.
6: 7 will destroy man whom I have **c**
Deut 4:32 since the day that God **c** man on
Ps 89:12 You have **c** them; Tabor and
89:47 For what futility have You **c**
102:18 That a people yet to be **c** may
104:30 forth Your Spirit, they are **c**;
148: 5 He commanded and they were **c**.
Isa 40:26 And see who has **c** these
41:20 the Holy One of Israel has **c**
42: 5 Who **c** the heavens and
43: 1 the LORD, who **c** you, O Jacob,
43: 7 Whom I have **c** for My glory; I
45: 8 I, the LORD, have **c** it.
45:12 And **c** man on it. I—My hands—
45:18 Who **c** the heavens, Who is
48: 7 They are **c** now and not from the
54:16 I have **c** the blacksmith Who
54:16 And I have **c** the spoiler to
Jer 31:22 For the LORD has **c** a new
Ezek 21:30 In the place where you were **c**,
28:13 for you on the day you were **c**.
28:15 ways from the day you were **c**,
Mal 2:10 Has not one God **c** us? Why do
Mk 13:19 of the creation which God **c**
Rom 8:39 nor any other **c** thing, shall be
1 Cor 11: 9 Nor was man **c** for the woman, but
Eph 2:10 **c** in Christ Jesus for good
3: 9 in God who **c** all things
4:24 put on the new man which was **c**
Col 1:16 For by Him all things were **c**
1:16 All things were **c** through Him
3:10 to the image of Him who **c** him,
1 Tim 4: 3 abstain from foods which God **c**
Rev 4:11 For You **c** all things, And by
4:11 Your will they exist and were **c**.
10: 6 who **c** heaven and the things

CREATES (2/2) CREATE
Num 16:30 But if the LORD **c** a new thing,
Am 4:13 And **c** the wind, Who declares

CREATION (13/13) CREATE
Mk 10: 6 from the beginning of the **c**,
13:19 since the beginning of the **c**
Rom 1:20 For since the **c** of the world His
8:19 earnest expectation of the **c**
8:20 For the **c** was subjected to
8:21 because the **c** itself also will
8:22 For we know that the whole **c**
2 Cor 5:17 is in Christ, he is a new **c**;
Gal 6:15 avails anything, but a new **c**.
Col 1:15 God, the firstborn over all **c**.
Heb 9:11 hands, that is, not of this **c**.
2 Pe 3: 4 were from the beginning of **c**.
Rev 3:14 the Beginning of the **c** of God:

CREATOR (7/7) CREATE
Eccl 12: 1 Remember now your **C** in the days
12: 6 Remember your **C** before the
Isa 40:28 The **C** of the ends of the
43:15 The **C** of Israel, your King."
Acts 24: 5 a **c** of dissension among all the
Rom 1:25 the creature rather than the **C**,
1 Pe 4:19 doing good, as to a faithful **C**.

CREATURE (30/26) CREATE, CREATURES
Gen 1:24 earth bring forth the living **c**
2:19 Adam called each living **c**,
9:10 and with every living **c** that is
9:12 and every living **c** that is
9:15 Me and you and every living **c**
9:16 between God and every living **c**
Lev 11:46 the birds and every living **c**
11:46 and of every **c** that creeps on
Isa 34:14 Also the night **c** shall rest
Ezek 1:15 the earth beside each living **c**
10:15 This was the living **c** I saw by
10:17 for the spirit of the living **c**
10:20 This is the living **c** I saw
Mk 16:15 preach the gospel to every **c**.
Acts 28: 4 So when the natives saw the **c**
28: 5 But he shook off the **c** into the
Rom 1:25 and worshiped and served the **c**
Col 1:23 which was preached to every **c**
1 Tim 4: 4 For every **c** of God is good, and
Heb 4:13 And there is no **c** hidden from
Jas 3: 7 of reptile and **c** of the sea, is
Rev 4: 7 The first living **c** was like a
4: 7 the second living **c** like a
4: 7 the third living **c** had a face
4: 7 and the fourth living **c** was
5:13 And every **c** which is in heaven
6: 3 I heard the second living **c**
6: 5 I heard the third living **c** say,
6: 7 voice of the fourth living **c**
16: 3 and every living **c** in the sea

CREATURES (30/28) CREATURE
Gen 1:20 with an abundance of living **c**,
1:21 So God created great sea **c** and
Ps 148: 7 You great sea **c** and all the
Ezek 1: 5 the likeness of four living **c**.
1: 9 The **c** did not turn when they
1:13 the likeness of the living **c**,
1:13 and forth among the living **c**.
1:14 And the living **c** ran back and
1:15 as I looked at the living **c**,
1:19 When the living **c** went, the
1:19 and when the living **c** were
1:20 for the spirit of the living **c**
1:21 for the spirit of the living **c**
1:22 the heads of the living **c** was
3:13 of the wings of the living **c**
Jas 1:18 a kind of firstfruits of His **c**.
Rev 4: 6 were four living **c** full of
4: 8 The four living **c**,
4: 9 Whenever the living **c** give glory
5: 6 throne and of the four living **c**,
5: 8 the four living **c** and the
5:11 around the throne, the living **c**,
5:14 Then the four living **c** said,
6: 1 heard one of the four living **c**
6: 6 the midst of the four living **c**
7:11 elders and the four living **c**,
8: 9 And a third of the living **c** in
14: 3 before the four living **c**,
15: 7 Then one of the four living **c**
19: 4 elders and the four living **c**

CREDIT (4/4) CREDITOR
Lk 6:32 what **c** is that to you? For even
6:33 what **c** is that to you? For even
6:34 what **c** is that to you? For even
1 Pe 2:20 For what **c** is it if, when you

CREDITOR (5/5) CREDIT, CREDITORS
Deut 15: 2 Every **c** who has lent anything
2 Ki 4: 1 And the **c** is coming to take my
Ps 109:11 Let the **c** seize all that he
Isa 24: 2 the borrower; As with the **c**,
Lk 7:41 There was a certain **c** who had

CREDITORS (2/2) CREDITOR
Isa 50: 1 Or which of My **c** is it to
Hab 2: 7 Will not your **c** rise up

CREEP (7/7) CREEPING, CREEPS, CREPT
Lev 11:20 All flying insects that **c** on
11:29 the creeping things that **c** on
11:31 unclean to you among all that **c**.
11:42 all creeping things that **c** on
Ps 104:20 all the beasts of the forest **c**
Ezek 38:20 all creeping things that **c** on
2 Tim 3: 6 of this sort are those who **c**

CREEPING (26/26) CREEP
Gen 1:24 cattle and **c** thing and beast of
1:26 earth and over every **c** thing
6: 7 **c** thing and birds of the air,
6:20 and of every **c** thing of the
7:14 every **c** thing that creeps on
7:21 and beasts and every **c** thing
7:23 **c** thing and bird of the air.
8:17 birds and cattle and every **c**
8:19 every **c** thing, every bird, and
Lev 5: 2 carcass of unclean **c** things,
11:29 to you among the **c** things that
11:41 And every **c** thing that creeps
11:42 many feet among all **c** things
11:43 abominable with any **c** thing
11:44 defile yourselves with any **c**
22: 5 or whoever touches any **c** thing
Deut 14:19 Also every **c** thing that flies is
1 Ki 4:33 of **c** things, and of fish.
Ps 148:10 **C** things and flying fowl;
Ezek 8:10 every sort of **c** thing,
38:20 all **c** things that creep on the
Hos 2:18 And with the **c** things of the
Hab 1:14 Like **c** things that have no
Acts 10:12 **c** things, and birds of the air.
11: 6 **c** things, and birds of the air.
Rom 1:23 animals and **c** things.

CREEPS (15/15) CREEP
Gen 1:25 and everything that **c** on the
1:26 every creeping thing that **c** on
1:30 and to everything that **c** on the
7: 8 and of everything that **c** on the
7:14 every creeping thing that **c** on
7:21 every creeping thing that **c** on
8:17 every creeping thing that **c** on
8:19 and whatever **c** on the earth,
Lev 11:21 of every flying insect that **c**
11:41 every creeping thing that **c** on
11:43 with any creeping thing that **c**;
11:44 with any creeping thing that **c**
11:46 and of every creature that **c** on
20:25 kind of living thing that **c** on
Deut 4:18 likeness of anything that **c** on

CREPT (1/1) CREEP
Jude 4 For certain men have **c** in

CRESCENS (1/1)
2 Tim 4:10 **C** for Galatia, Titus for

CRESCENT (2/2) CRESCENTS
Judg 8:21 and took the **c** ornaments that
8:26 besides the **c** ornaments,

CRESCENTS (1/1) CRESCENT
Isa 3:18 anklets, the scarves, and the **c**;

CREST (1/1)
Esth 6: 8 which has a royal **c** placed on

CRETANS (2/2) CRETE
Acts 2:11 **C** and Arabs—we hear them
Titus 1:12 **C** are always liars, evil

CRETE (5/5) CRETANS
Acts 27: 7 under the shelter of **C** off
27:12 a harbor of **C** opening toward
27:13 to sea, they sailed close by **C**.
27:21 and not have sailed from **C** and
Titus 1: 5 this reason I left you in **C**,

CRETES, CRETIANS (KJV) See CRETANS

CRIB (1/1)
Isa 1: 3 And the donkey its master's **c**;

CRICKET (1/1)
Lev 11:22 the **c** after its kind, and the

CRIED (174/172) CRY
Gen 27:34 he **c** with an exceedingly great
39:14 and I **c** out with a loud voice.
39:15 that I lifted my voice and **c**
39:18 as I lifted my voice and **c** out,
41:43 and they **c** out before him,
41:55 the people **c** to Pharaoh for
45: 1 and he **c** out, "Make everyone
Ex 2:23 and they **c** out; and their cry
5:15 children of Israel came and **c**
8:12 And Moses **c** out to the LORD
14:10 and the children of Israel **c**
15:25 So he **c** out to the LORD, and
17: 4 So Moses **c** out to the LORD,
Num 11: 2 Then the people **c** out to Moses,
12:13 So Moses **c** out to the LORD,
14: 1 lifted up their voices and **c**,
20:16 When we **c** out to the LORD, He
Deut 22:27 the betrothed young woman **c**
26: 7 Then we **c** out to the LORD God
Josh 24: 7 So they **c** out to the LORD; and
Judg 3: 9 When the children of Israel **c**
3:15 when the children of Israel **c**
4: 3 And the children of Israel **c** out
5:28 And **c** out through the lattice,
6: 6 and the children of Israel **c**

6: 7 when the children of Israel **c**
7:20 hands for blowing—and they **c**,
7:21 and the whole army ran and **c**
9: 7 and lifted his voice and **c** out.
10:10 And the children of Israel **c**
10:12 and you **c** out to Me, and I
15:18 so he **c** out to the LORD and
1 Sam 4:13 all the city **c** out.
5:10 that the Ekronites **c** out,
7: 9 Then Samuel **c** out to the LORD
12: 8 and your fathers **c** out to the
12:10 Then they **c** out to the LORD,
15:11 and he **c** out to the LORD all
17: 8 Then he stood and **c** out to the
20:37 Jonathan **c** out after the lad
20:38 And Jonathan **c** out after the
28:12 she **c** out with a loud voice.
2 Sam 18:25 Then the watchman **c** out and told
19: 4 and the king **c** out with a loud
20:16 Then a wise woman **c** out from
22: 7 And **c** out to my God; He heard
1 Ki 13: 2 Then he **c** out against the altar
13: 4 who **c** out against the altar in
13:21 and he **c** out to the man of God
13:32 For the saying which he **c** out by
17:20 Then he **c** out to the LORD and
17:21 and **c** out to the LORD and
18:28 So they **c** aloud, and cut
20:39 he **c** out to the king and said,
22:32 and Jehoshaphat **c** out.
2 Ki 2:12 and he **c** out, "My father, my
4: 1 of the sons of the prophets **c**
4:40 that they **c** out and said, "Man
6: 5 and he **c** out and said, "Alas,
6:26 a woman **c** out to him, saying,
11:14 tore her clothes and **c** out,
20:11 So Isaiah the prophet **c** out to
1 Chr 5:20 for they **c** out to God in the
2 Chr 13:14 and they **c** out to the LORD,
14:11 And Asa **c** out to the LORD his
18:31 but Jehoshaphat **c** out, and the
32:20 prayed and **c** out to heaven.
Neh 9: 4 the stairs of the Levites and **c**
9:27 When they **c** to You, You heard
9:28 Yet when they returned and **c**
Esth 4: 1 He **c** out with a loud and bitter
Job 29:12 I delivered the poor who **c** out,
Ps 3: 4 I **c** to the LORD with my voice,
18: 6 And **c** out to my God; He heard
18:41 They **c** out, but there was
22: 5 They **c** to You, and were
22:24 But when He **c** to Him, He
30: 2 I **c** out to You, And You healed
30: 8 I **c** out to You, O LORD;
31:22 of my supplications When I **c**
34: 6 This poor man **c** out, and the
66:17 I **c** to Him with my mouth, And
77: 1 I **c** out to God with my
88: 1 I have **c** out day and night
88:13 But to You I have **c** out, O
107: 6 Then they **c** out to the LORD in
107:13 Then they **c** out to the LORD in
107:19 Then they **c** out to the LORD in
120: 1 In my distress I **c** to the
130: 1 Out of the depths I have **c** to
138: 3 In the day when I **c** out, You
142: 5 I **c** out to You, O LORD:
Isa 6: 3 And one **c** to another and said:
6: 4 by the voice of him who **c** out,
21: 8 Then he **c**, "A lion, my Lord!
Jer 4:20 upon destruction is **c**,
20: 8 I **c** out; I shouted, "Violence
46:17 They **c** there, 'Pharaoh, king
Lam 2:18 Their heart **c** out to the Lord,
4:15 They **c** out to them, "Go away,
Ezek 9: 8 and I fell on my face and **c**
11:13 Then I fell on my face and **c**
Dan 3: 4 Then a herald **c** aloud: "To you
4:14 He **c** aloud and said thus:
5: 7 The king **c** aloud to bring in the
6:20 he **c** out with a lamenting voice
Jon 1: 5 and every man **c** out to his god,
1:14 Therefore they **c** out to the
2: 2 I **c** out to the LORD because of
2: 2 of the belly of Sheol I **c**,
3: 4 Then he **c** out and said, "Yet
Mt 8:29 And suddenly they **c** out, saying,
14:26 It is a ghost!" And they **c** out
14:30 and beginning to sink he **c** out,
15:22 came from that region and **c**
20:30 **c** out, saying, "Have mercy on
20:31 but they **c** out all the more,
21: 9 and those who followed **c** out,
27:23 But they **c** out all the more,
27:46 about the ninth hour Jesus **c**
27:50 And Jesus **c** out again with a
Mk 1:23 unclean spirit. And he **c** out,
1:26 spirit had convulsed him and **c**
3:11 fell down before Him and **c** out,
5: 7 And he **c** out with a loud voice
6:49 was a ghost, and **c** out;
9:24 the father of the child **c** out
9:26 Then the spirit **c** out,
10:48 but he **c** out all the more,
11: 9 and those who followed **c** out,
15:13 So they **c** out again, "Crucify
15:14 But they **c** out all the more,
15:34 And at the ninth hour Jesus **c**
15:37 And Jesus **c** out with a loud
15:39 saw that He **c** out like this and
Lk 4:33 And he **c** out with a loud voice,
8: 8 He had said these things He **c**,
8:28 he **c** out, fell down before Him,
9:38 a man from the multitude **c** out,
16:24 Then he **c** and said, 'Father
18:38 And he **c** out, saying, "Jesus,
18:39 but he **c** out all the more,
23:18 And they all **c** out at once,
23:46 And when Jesus had **c** out with a
Jn 1:15 John bore witness of Him and **c**
7:28 Then Jesus **c** out, as He taught
7:37 Jesus stood and **c** out, saying,
11:43 He **c** with a loud voice,
12:13 and **c** out: "Hosanna!
12:44 Then Jesus **c** out and said, "He
18:40 Then they all **c** again, saying,
19: 6 they **c** out, saying, "Crucify
19:12 but the Jews **c** out, saying,
19:15 But they **c** out, "Away with
Acts 7:57 Then they **c** out with a loud
7:60 Then he knelt down and **c** out
16:17 and **c** out, saying, "These men
19:28 they were full of wrath and **c**
19:32 Some therefore **c** one thing and
19:34 all with one voice **c** out for
21:34 And some among the multitude **c**
22:23 as they **c** out and tore off
23: 6 he **c** out in the council, "Men
24:21 this one statement which I **c**
Rev 6:10 And they **c** with a loud voice,
7: 2 And he **c** with a loud voice to
10: 3 and **c** with a loud voice, as
10: 3 When he **c** out, seven thunders
12: 2 she **c** out in labor and in pain
14:18 and he **c** with a loud cry to him
18: 2 And he **c** mightily with a loud
18:18 and **c** out when they saw the
18:19 dust on their heads and **c** out,
19:17 and he **c** with a loud voice,

CRIES (18/18) CRY

Gen 4:10 of your brother's blood **c** out
Ex 22:27 will be that when he **c** to Me,
Job 31:38 If my land **c** out against me,
Ps 72:12 deliver the needy when he **c**,
Prov 1:21 She **c** out in the chief
8: 3 She **c** out by the gates, at the
9: 3 She **c** out from the highest
20:14 for nothing," **c** the buyer;
Isa 16: 9 For battle **c** have fallen Over
26:17 with child Is in pain and **c**
46: 7 Though one **c** out to it, yet
Jer 12: 8 It **c** out against Me;
Mic 6: 9 The LORD's voice **c** to the
Mt 15:23 for she **c** out after us."
Lk 9:39 and he suddenly **c** out; it
Rom 9:27 Isaiah also **c** out concerning
Heb 5: 7 with vehement **c** and tears to
Jas 5: 4 and the **c** of the reapers have

CRIME (1/1) CRIMES, CRIMINALS

Judg 9:24 that the **c** done to the seventy

CRIMES (2/2) CRIME

Ezek 7:23 For the land is filled with **c**
Acts 18:14 of wrongdoing or wicked **c**,

CRIMINALS (3/3) CRIME

Lk 23:32 There were also two others, **c**,
23:33 they crucified Him, and the **c**,
23:39 Then one of the **c** who were

CRIMSON (5/5)

2 Chr 2: 7 in purple and **c** and blue, who
2:14 and blue, fine linen and **c**,
3:14 the veil of blue, purple, **c**,
Isa 1:18 Though they are red like **c**,
Jer 4:30 you clothe yourself with **c**,

CRIPPLE (1/1)

Acts 14: 8 a **c** from his mother's womb, who

CRISPUS (2/2)

Acts 18: 8 Then **C**, the ruler of the
1 Cor 1:14 I baptized none of you except **C**

CRITICIZED (1/1)

Mk 14: 5 And they **c** her sharply.

CROOKED (13/13)

Deut 32: 5 A perverse and **c** generation.
Ps 125: 5 turn aside to their **c** ways,
Prov 2:15 Whose ways are **c**,
8: 8 Nothing **c** or perverse is in
Eccl 1:15 What is **c** cannot be made
7:13 straight what He has made **c**?
Isa 40: 4 The **c** places shall be made
42:16 And **c** places straight. These
45: 2 make the **c** places straight;
59: 8 They have made themselves **c**
Lam 3: 9 stone; He has made my paths **c**.
Lk 3: 5 The **c** places shall be
Phil 2:15 fault in the midst of a **c** and

CROP (9/8) CROPPED, CROPS

Lev 1:16 And he shall remove its **c** with
Ezek 17:22 I will **c** off from the topmost
Am 7: 1 at the beginning of the late **c**;
7: 1 indeed it was the late **c**
Mt 13: 8 on good ground and yielded a **c**:
13:26 had sprouted and produced a **c**,
Mk 4: 7 choked it, and it yielded no **c**.
4: 8 on good ground and yielded a **c**
Lk 8: 8 and yielded a **c** a

CROPPED (1/1) CROP

Ezek 17: 4 He **c** off its topmost young twig

CROPS (8/8) CROP

Ex 9:32 struck, for they are late **c**.
Lev 25:15 to the number of years of **c** he
25:16 number of the years of the **c**.
Ps 78:46 He also gave their **c** to the
Mk 4:28 For the earth yields **c** by
Lk 12:17 I have no room to store my **c**?
12:18 and there I will store all my **c**
2 Tim 2: 6 be first to partake of the **c**.

CROSS (85/84) CROSSED, CROSSES, CROSSING, CROSSROADS

Num 32:21 and all your armed men **c** over
32:27 but your servants will **c** over,
32:29 and the children of Reuben **c**
32:30 But if they do not **c** over armed
32:32 We will **c** over armed before the
35:10 When you **c** the Jordan into the
Deut 2:13 Now rise and **c** over the Valley
2:18 This day you are to **c** over at
2:24 and **c** over the River Arnon.
2:29 until I **c** the Jordan to the
3:18 All you men of valor shall **c**
3:25 let me **c** over and see the good
3:27 for you shall not **c** over this
4:14 them in the land which you **c**
4:21 and swore that I would not **c**
4:22 I must not **c** over the Jordan;
4:22 but you shall **c** over and
4:26 from the land which you **c** over
9: 1 You are to **c** over the Jordan
11: 8 possess the land which you **c**
11:11 but the land which you **c** over to
11:31 For you will **c** over the Jordan
12:10 But when you **c** over the Jordan
27: 2 on the day when you **c** over the
30:18 days in the land which you **c**
31: 2 You shall not **c** over this
31:13 live in the land which you **c**
32:47 days in the land which you **c**
34: 4 but you shall not **c** over
Josh 1:11 within three days you will **c**
3: 6 the ark of the covenant and **c**
3:14 set out from their camp to **c**
4: 5 **C** over before the ark of the
22:19 then **c** over to the land of the
Judg 3:28 and did not allow anyone to **c**
12: 1 Why did you **c** over to fight
12: 5 Let me **c** over," the men of
1 Sam 14: 8 let us **c** over to these men,
30:10 so weary that they could not **c**
2 Sam 12:31 and made them **c** over to the
15:22 'Go, and **c** over.'
17:16 but speedily **c** over, lest the
17:21 Arise and **c** over the water
19:37 let him **c** over with my lord the
19:38 Chimham shall **c** over with me,
1 Ki 2:37 on the day you go out and **c** the
Isa 11:15 And make men **c** over dry-shod.
23: 2 Whom those who **c** the sea have
23: 6 **C** over to Tarshish
23:12 Arise, **c** over to Cyprus;
31: 9 He shall **c** over to his
51:10 For the redeemed to **c** over?
Jer 15:14 And I will make you **c** over
Ezek 47: 5 was a river that I could not **c**;
Mt 10:38 he who does not take his **c**
16:24 deny himself, and take up his **c**,
27:32 they compelled to bear His **c**.
27:40 of God, come down from the **c**.
27:42 Him now come down from the **c**,
Mk 4:35 Let us **c** over to the other
8:34 deny himself, and take up his **c**,
10:21 heaven; and come, take up the **c**,
15:21 and passing by, to bear His **c**.
15:30 and come down from the **c**!"
15:32 Israel, descend now from the **c**,
Lk 8:22 Let us **c** over to the other side
9:23 and take up his **c** daily, and
14:27 whoever does not bear his **c**
23:26 and on him they laid the **c** that
Jn 19:17 And He, bearing His **c**,
19:19 a title and put it on the **c**.
19:25 Now there stood by the **c** of
19:31 should not remain on the **c** on
Acts 18:27 And when he desired to **c** to
1 Cor 1:17 lest the **c** of Christ should be
1:18 For the message of the **c** is
Gal 5:11 Then the offense of the **c** has
6:12 suffer persecution for the **c**
6:14 I should boast except in the **c**
Eph 2:16 God in one body through the **c**,
Phil 2: 8 death, even the death of the **c**.
3:18 are the enemies of the **c** of
Col 1:20 through the blood of His **c**.
2:14 way, having nailed it to the **c**.
Heb 12: 2 set before Him endured the **c**,

CROSS-EXAMINE (1/1)

Lk	11:53	and to c Him about many things,

CROSSED (55/50) CROSS

Gen	31:21	He arose and c the river, and
	32:10	for I c over this Jordan with
	32:22	and c over the ford of Jabbok.
	32:31	Just as he c over Penuel the sun
	33: 3	Then he c over before them and
Num	33:51	When you have c the Jordan into
Deut	2:13	So we c over the Valley of the
	2:14	from Kadesh Barnea until we c
	27: 3	when you have c over, that you
	27: 4	when you have c over the
	27:12	when you have c over the
Josh	2:23	and c over; and they came to
	3: 1	and lodged there before they c
	3:16	and the people c over opposite
	3:17	and all Israel c over on dry
	3:17	until all the people had c
	4: 1	all the people had completely c
	4: 7	when it c over the Jordan, the
	4:10	and the people hurried and c
	4:11	all the people had completely c
	4:11	of the LORD and the priests c
	4:12	half the tribe of Manasseh c
	4:13	thousand prepared for war c
	4:22	Israel c over this Jordan on dry
	4:23	before you until you had c
	4:23	up before us until we had c
	5: 1	of Israel until we had c over,
Judg	6:33	and they c over and encamped in
	8: 4	men who were with him c over,
	10: 9	Moreover the people of Ammon c
	12: 1	c over toward Zaphon, and said
	12: 3	took my life in my hands and c
1 Sam	13: 7	And some of the Hebrews c over
2 Sam	2:29	c over the Jordan, and went
	10:17	c over the Jordan, and came to
	15:22	ones who were with him c over.
	15:23	and all the people c over.
	15:23	The king himself also c over
	15:23	and all the people c over
	17:22	who were with him arose and c
	17:24	And Absalom c over the Jordan,
	19:18	before the king when he had c
	19:39	And when the king had c over,
	24: 5	And they c over the Jordan and
2 Ki	2: 8	so that the two of them c over
	2: 9	when they had c over, that
	2:14	and Elisha c over.
1 Chr	12:15	These are the ones who c the
	19:17	c over the Jordan and came upon
Jer	2: 6	Through a land that no one c
Ezek	47: 5	a river that could not be c.
Mt	9: 1	c over, and came to His own
	14:34	When they had c over, they came
Mk	5:21	Now when Jesus had c over again
	6:53	When they had c over, they came

CROSSES (2/1) CROSS

Deut	31: 3	The LORD your God Himself c
	31: 3	Joshua himself c over before

CROSSING (3/3) CROSS

Deut	6: 1	in the land which you are c
Josh	3:11	the Lord of all the earth is c
2 Sam	15:24	all the people had finished c

CROSSROADS (1/1) CROSS

Ob	14	should not have stood at the c

CROUCH (1/1) CROUCHES, CROUCHING

Job	38:40	When they c in their dens,

CROUCHES (1/1) CROUCH

Ps	10:10	So he c, he lies low,

CROUCHING (1/1) CROUCH

Ps	17:11	c down to the earth,

CROW (2/2) CROWED, CROWING, CROWS

Lk	22:34	the rooster shall not c this
Jn	13:38	the rooster shall not c till

CROWD (31/31) CROWDS

Ex	23: 2	You shall not follow a c to do
Mt	9:23	flute players and the noisy c
	9:25	But when the c was put outside,
Mk	2: 4	come near Him because of the c,
	5:27	she came behind Him in the c
	5:30	turned around in the c and
	7:17	entered a house away from the c,
	9:17	Then one of the c answered and
	15:11	chief priests stirred up the c,
	15:15	wanting to gratify the c,
Lk	4:42	And the c sought Him and came
	5:19	bring him in, because of the c,
	6:17	on a level place with a c of
	7: 9	around and said to the c that
	7:11	went with Him, and a large c.
	7:12	And a large c from the city was
	8:19	approach Him because of the c.
	11:27	that a certain woman from the c
	12:13	Then one from the c said to
	13:14	Sabbath; and he said to the c,
	19: 3	but could not because of the c,
	19:39	called to Him from the c,
	23: 4	to the chief priests and the c,
	23:48	And the whole c who came
Jn	7:32	The Pharisees heard the c
	7:40	Therefore many from the c,
	7:49	But this c that does not know
Acts	17: 8	And they troubled the c and the
	19:35	city clerk had quieted the c,
	21:27	stirred up the whole c and laid
	24:12	with anyone nor inciting the c,

CROWDS (3/3) CROWD

Lk	9:18	Who do the c say that I am?"
	11:29	And while the c were thickly
Acts	17:13	there also and stirred up the c.

CROWED (5/5) CROW

Mt	26:74	Immediately a rooster c.
Mk	14:68	on the porch, and a rooster c.
	14:72	A second time the rooster c.
Lk	22:60	still speaking, the rooster c.
Jn	18:27	and immediately a rooster c.

CROWING (1/1) CROW

Mk	13:35	at the c of the rooster, or in

CROWN (60/59) CROWNED, CROWNING, CROWNS

Gen	49:26	And on the c of the head of
Ex	29: 6	and put the holy c on the
	39:30	made the plate of the holy c
Lev	8: 9	the golden plate, the holy c,
Deut	33:16	And on the c of the head of
	33:20	And tears the arm and the c of
2 Sam	1:10	And I took the c that was on
	12:30	Then he took their king's c from
	14:25	his foot to the c of his head
1 Ki	7:31	Its opening inside the c at the
2 Ki	11:12	put the c on him, and gave
1 Chr	20: 2	Then David took their king's c
2 Chr	23:11	put the c on him, gave him
Esth	1:11	the king, wearing her royal c,
	2:17	so he set the royal c upon her
	8:15	with a great c of gold and a
Job	2: 7	foot to the c of his head.
	19: 9	And taken the c from my head.
	31:36	And bind it on me like a c;
Ps	7:16	shall come down on his own c.
	21: 3	You set a c of pure gold upon
	65:11	You c the year with Your
	89:39	You have profaned his c by
	132:18	But upon Himself His c shall
Prov	4: 9	A c of glory she will deliver
	12: 4	An excellent wife is the c of
	14:24	The c of the wise is their
	16:31	silver-haired head is a c of
	17: 6	children are the c of old men,
	27:24	Nor does a c endure to all
Song	3:11	see King Solomon with the c
Isa	3:17	will strike with a scab The c
	28: 1	Woe to the c of pride, to the
	28: 3	The c of pride, the drunkards
	28: 5	of hosts will be For a c of
	62: 3	You shall also be a c of glory
Jer	2:16	broken the c of your head.
	13:18	the c of your glory."
	48:45	The c of the head of the sons
Lam	5:16	The c has fallen from our
Ezek	16:12	and a beautiful c on your head.
	21:26	the turban, and take off the c;
Zech	6:11	and gold, make an elaborate c,
	6:14	Now the elaborate c shall be for
	9:16	be like the jewels of a c,
Mt	27:29	When they had twisted a c of
Mk	15:17	and they twisted a c of thorns,
Jn	19: 2	And the soldiers twisted a c of
	19: 5	wearing the c of thorns and the
1 Cor	9:25	it to obtain a perishable c,
	9:25	but we for an imperishable c.
Phil	4: 1	brethren, my joy and c,
1 Th	2:19	or joy, or c of rejoicing?
2 Tim	4: 8	for me the c of righteousness,
Jas	1:12	he will receive the c of life
1 Pe	5: 4	you will receive the c of glory
Rev	2:10	and I will give you the c of
	3:11	that no one may take your c.
	6: 2	and a c was given to him, and
	14:14	having on His head a golden c,

CROWNED (6/6) CROWN

Ps	8: 5	And You have c him with glory
Prov	14:18	But the prudent are c with
Song	3:11	With which his mother c him
2 Tim	2: 5	he is not c unless he competes
Heb	2: 7	You have c him with
	2: 9	of death c with glory and

CROWNING (1/1) CROWN

Isa	23: 8	the c city, Whose merchants

CROWNS (8/8) CROWN

Ps	103: 4	Who c you with lovingkindness
Song	7: 5	Your head c you like Mount
Ezek	23:42	on their wrists and beautiful c
Rev	4: 4	and they had c of gold on their
	4:10	and cast their c before the
	9: 7	On their heads were c of
	13: 1	horns, and on his horns ten c,
	19:12	and on His head were many c.

CROWS (5/5)

Mt	26:34	night, before the rooster c,
	26:75	to him, "Before the rooster c,
Mk	14:30	before the rooster c twice, you
	14:72	Before the rooster c twice, you
Lk	22:61	to him, "Before the rooster c,

CRUCIFIED (39/39) CRUCIFY

Mt	26: 2	will be delivered up to be c.
	27:22	Let Him be c!"
	27:23	Let Him be c!"
	27:26	he delivered Him to be c.
	27:31	Him, and led Him away to be c.
	27:35	Then they c Him, and divided His
	27:38	Then two robbers were c with
	27:44	Even the robbers who were c with
	28: 5	that you seek Jesus who was c.
Mk	15:15	he had scourged Him, to be c.
	15:24	And when they c Him, they
	15:25	third hour, and they c Him.
	15:27	With Him they also c two
	15:32	Even those who were c with
	16: 6	Jesus of Nazareth, who was c.
Lk	23:23	with loud voices that He be c.
	23:33	there they c Him, and the
	24: 7	hands of sinful men, and be c,
	24:20	condemned to death, and c Him.
Jn	19:16	delivered Him to them to be c.
	19:18	where they c Him, and two others
	19:20	for the place where Jesus was c
	19:23	when they had c Jesus, took His
	19:32	and of the other who was c
	19:41	Now in the place where He was c
Acts	2:23	taken by lawless hands, have c,
	2:36	has made this Jesus, whom you c,
	4:10	Christ of Nazareth, whom you c,
Rom	6: 6	that our old man was c with
1 Cor	1:13	Was Paul c for you? Or were you
	1:23	but we preach Christ c,
	2: 2	except Jesus Christ and Him c.
	2: 8	they would not have c the Lord
2 Cor	13: 4	For though He was c in weakness,
Gal	2:20	I have been c with Christ; it is
	3: 1	portrayed among you as c?
	5:24	who are Christ's have c the
	6:14	by whom the world has been c to
Rev	11: 8	where also our Lord was c.

CRUCIFY (14/10) CRUCIFIED

Mt	20:19	to mock and to scourge and to c.
	23:34	of them you will kill and c,
Mk	15:13	cried out again, "C Him!"
	15:14	all the more, "C Him!"
	15:20	and led Him out to c Him.
Lk	23:21	C Him, crucify Him!"
	23:21	'Crucify Him, c Him!"
Jn	19: 6	C Him, crucify Him!" Pilate
	19: 6	c Him!" Pilate said to them,
	19: 6	You take Him and c Him, for I
	19:10	not know that I have power to c
	19:15	away with Him! C Him!"
	19:15	Shall I c your King?" The chief
Heb	6: 6	since they c again for

CRUEL (19/19) CRUELLY, CRUELTY

Gen	49: 7	their wrath, for it is c!
Ex	6: 9	of spirit and c bondage.
Deut	32:33	And the c venom of cobras.
Job	30:21	But You have become c to me;
Ps	25:19	hate me with c hatred.
	71: 4	of the unrighteous and c man.
Prov	5: 9	And your years to the c one;
	11:17	But he who is c troubles
	12:10	mercies of the wicked are c.
	17:11	Therefore a c messenger will
	27: 4	Wrath is c and anger a
Eccl	9:12	Like fish taken in a c net,
Song	8: 6	Jealousy as c as the grave;
Isa	13: 9	the day of the LORD comes, C,
	19: 4	Into the hand of a c master,
Jer	6:23	They are c and have no mercy;
	30:14	the chastisement of a c one,
	50:42	They are c and shall not show
Lam	4: 3	the daughter of my people is c,

CRUELLY (1/1) CRUEL

Ezek	18:18	Because he c oppressed,

CRUELTY (3/3) CRUEL

Gen	49: 5	Instruments of c are in
Ps	74:20	are full of the haunts of c.
Ezek	34: 4	but with force and c you have

CRUMBLES (1/1)

Job	14:18	as a mountain falls and c

CRUMBS (3/3)

Mt 15:27 even the little dogs eat the **c**
Mk 7:28 table eat from the children's **c**.
Lk 16:21 desiring to be fed with the **c**

CRUSE (KJV) See BOWL, JAR, JUG

CRUSH (10/10) CRUSHED, CRUSHES, CRUSHING

Job 6: 9 would please God to **c** me,
39:15 that a foot may **c** them,
Ps 68:23 That your foot may **c** them in
Isa 28:28 Or **c** it with his horsemen.
Lam 1:15 To **c** my young men;
3:34 To **c** under one's feet All the
Dan 2:40 will break in pieces and **c** all
Am 4: 1 Who **c** the needy, Who say to
Mk 3: 9 lest they should **c** Him.
Rom 16:20 God of peace will **c** Satan

CRUSHED (19/19) CRUSH

Lev 22:24 the LORD what is bruised or **c**,
Num 22:25 **c** Balaam's foot against the
Deut 9:21 burned it with fire and **c** it
28:33 shall be only oppressed and **c**
Judg 9:53 on Abimelech's head and **c** his
2 Ki 23:15 the high place and **c** it
2 Chr 15:16 then **c** and burned it by the
Job 4:19 Who are **c** before a moth?
5: 4 They are **c** in the gate, And
22: 9 of the fatherless was **c**.
34:25 in the night, And they are **c**.
Ps 143: 3 He has **c** my life to the
Prov 26:28 hates those who are **c** by it,
27:22 pestle along with **c** grain,
Isa 59: 5 And from that which is **c** a
Jer 51:34 he has **c** me; He has made me an
Ezek 6: 9 because I was **c** by their
Dan 2:35 and the gold were **c** together,
2 Cor 4: 8 on every side, yet not **c**;

CRUSHES (2/2) CRUSH

Job 9:17 For He **c** me with a tempest,
Dan 2:40 and like iron that **c**,

CRUSHING (4/4) CRUSH

Deut 23: 1 He who is emasculated by **c** or
2 Ki 19:25 For **c** fortified cities
Isa 3:15 What do you mean by **c** My people
37:26 For **c** fortified cities

CRUST (1/1)

Prov 6:26 A man is reduced to a **c**

CRY (172/160) CRIED, CRIES, CRYING

Gen 27:34 exceedingly great and bitter **c**,
Ex 2:23 and their **c** came up to God
3: 7 and have heard their **c** because
3: 9 the **c** of the children of Israel
5: 8 therefore they **c** out, saying,
11: 6 Then there shall be a great **c**
12:30 and there was a great **c** in
14:15 Why do you **c** to Me? Tell the
22:23 and they **c** at all to Me, I
22:23 Me, I will surely hear their **c**;
32:18 Nor the noise of the **c** of
Lev 13:45 shall cover his mustache, and **c**,
Num 16:34 around them fled at their **c**,
Deut 15: 9 and he **c** out to the LORD
22:24 woman because she did not **c**
24:15 lest he **c** out against you to
Judg 10:14 Go and **c** out to the gods which
1 Sam 5:12 and the **c** of the city went up
7: 8 Do not cease to **c** out to the
8:18 And you will **c** out in that day
9:16 because their **c** has come to
2 Sam 19:28 what right have I still to **c**
22: 7 And my **c** entered His ears.
1 Ki 8:28 and listen to the **c** and the
18:27 **C** aloud, for he is a god;
2 Chr 6:19 and listen to the **c** and the
20: 9 and **c** out to You in our
Neh 9: 9 heard their **c** by the Red Sea.
Esth 4: 1 out with a loud and bitter **c**.
Job 16:18 And let my **c** have no resting
19: 7 If I **c** out concerning wrong, I
19: 7 If I **c** aloud, there is no
24:12 the souls of the wounded **c** out;
27: 9 Will God hear his **c** When
30:20 I **c** out to You, but You do not
30:24 If they **c** out when He destroys
30:28 up in the assembly and **c** out
34:28 So that they caused the **c** of
34:28 For He hears the **c** of the
35: 9 of oppressions they **c** out;
35: 9 They **c** out for help because of
35:12 There they **c** out, but He does
36:13 They do not **c** for help when He
38:41 When its young ones **c** to God,
Ps 5: 2 Give heed to the voice of my **c**,
9:12 He does not forget the **c** of
17: 1 cause, O LORD, Attend to my **c**;
18: 6 And my **c** came before Him,
22: 2 I **c** in the daytime, but You do
27: 7 when I **c** with my voice!
28: 1 To You I will **c**,
28: 2 of my supplications When I **c**
34:15 His ears are open to their **c**.
34:17 The righteous **c** out, and the
39:12 O LORD, And give ear to my **c**;
40: 1 inclined to me, And heard my **c**.
55:17 and **c** aloud, And He shall hear
56: 9 When I **c** out to You, Then my
57: 2 I will **c** out to God Most High,
61: 1 HEAR my **c**, O God;
61: 2 the end of the earth I will **c**
84: 2 My heart and my flesh **c** out
86: 3 For I **c** to You all day long.
88: 2 Incline Your ear to my **c**.
89:26 He shall **c** to Me, 'You are my
102: 1 And let my **c** come to You.
106:44 When He heard their **c**;
107:28 Then they **c** out to the LORD in
119:145 I **c** out with my whole heart;
119:146 I **c** out to You; Save me, and I
119:147 And **c** for help; I hope in
119:169 Let my **c** come before You,
141: 1 I **c** out to You; Make haste to
141: 1 Give ear to my voice when I **c**
142: 1 I **c** out to the LORD with my
142: 6 Attend to my **c**, For I am
145:19 He also will hear their **c** and
147: 9 to the young ravens that **c**.
Prov 2: 3 if you **c** out for discernment,
8: 1 Does not wisdom **c** out, And
21:13 shuts his ears to the **c** of the
21:13 cry of the poor Will also **c**
Isa 5: 7 but behold, a **c** for help.
8: 4 to **c** 'My father' and
12: 6 **C** out and shout, O inhabitant
14:31 Wail, O gate! **C**,
15: 4 Heshbon and Elealeh will **c** out,
15: 4 armed soldiers of Moab will **c**
15: 5 My heart will **c** out for Moab;
15: 5 They will raise up a **c** of
15: 8 For the **c** has gone all around
19:20 for they will **c** to the LORD
24:11 There is a **c** for wine in the
24:14 shall **c** aloud from the sea.
30:19 to you at the sound of your **c**;
33: 7 their valiant ones shall **c**
40: 2 and **c** out to her, That her
40: 6 The voice said, "**C** out!"
40: 6 And he said, "What shall I **c**?
42: 2 He will not **c** out, nor raise
42:13 He shall **c** out, yes, shout
42:14 Now I will **c** like a woman in
54: 1 and **c** aloud, You who have not
57:13 When you **c** out, Let your
58: 1 **C** aloud, spare not; Lift up
58: 9 LORD will answer; You shall **c**,
65:14 But you shall **c** for sorrow of
Jer 2: 2 Go and **c** in the hearing of
3: 4 not from this time **c** to Me,
4: 5 **C**, 'Gather together,'
7:16 nor lift up a **c** or prayer for
8:19 The **c** of the daughter of my
11:11 and though they **c** out to Me, I
11:12 of Jerusalem will go and **c** out
11:14 or lift up a **c** or prayer for
11:14 them in the time that they **c**
14: 2 And the **c** of Jerusalem has
14:12 fast, I will not hear their **c**;
18:22 Let a **c** be heard from their
20:16 Let him hear the **c** in the
22:20 to Lebanon, and **c** out,
22:20 **C** from Abarim, For all your
25:34 Wail, shepherds, and **c**!
25:36 A voice of the **c** of the
30:15 Why do you **c** about your
31: 6 day When the watchmen will **c**
46:12 And your **c** has filled the
47: 2 within; Then the men shall **c**,
48: 4 little ones have caused a **c** to
48: 5 the enemies have heard a **c** of
48:20 Wail and **c**! Tell it in Arnon,
48:31 And I will **c** out for all Moab;
48:34 From the **c** of Heshbon to
49: 3 **C**, you daughters of
49:21 At the **c** its noise is heard at
49:29 And they shall **c** out to them,
50:46 And the **c** is heard among the
51:54 The sound of a **c** comes from
Lam 2:19 'Arise, **c** out in the night,
3: 8 Even when I **c** and shout, He
3:56 from my **c** for help."
Ezek 8:18 and though they **c** in My ears
9: 4 of the men who sigh and **c** over
21:12 **C** and wail, son of man; For it
26:15 your fall, when the wounded **c**,
27:28 shake at the sound of the **c** of
27:30 They will **c** bitterly and cast
Hos 5: 8 **C** aloud at Beth Aven,
7:14 They did not **c** out to Me with
8: 2 Israel will **c** to Me, 'My God,
Joel 1:14 And **c** out to the LORD.
1:19 to You I **c** out; For fire has
1:20 beasts of the field also **c** out
Am 3: 4 Will a young lion **c** out of his
Jon 1: 2 and **c** out against it; for their
3: 8 and **c** mightily to God; yes, let
Mic 3: 4 Then they will **c** to the LORD,
4: 9 Now why do you **c** aloud?
Nah 2: 8 'Halt! Halt!' they **c**;
Hab 1: 2 O LORD, how long shall I **c**,
1: 2 Even **c** out to You,
2:11 For the stone will **c** out from
Zeph 1:10 The sound of a mournful **c** from
1:14 There the mighty men shall **c**
Mt 12:19 will not quarrel nor **c**
25: 6 And at midnight a **c** was heard:
Mk 10:47 he began to **c** out and say,
Lk 18: 7 not avenge His own elect who **c**
19:40 the stones would immediately **c**
Rom 8:15 of adoption by whom we **c** out,
Jas 5: 4 **c** out; and the cries of the
Rev 14:18 and he cried with a loud **c** to

CRYING (26/26) CRY

2 Sam 13:19 on her head and went away **c**
Ps 69: 3 I am weary with my **c**;
Isa 22: 5 down the walls And of **c** to
40: 3 The voice of one **c** in the
65:19 in her, Nor the voice of **c**.
Jer 48: 3 A voice of **c** shall be from
Mal 2:13 with tears, With weeping and **c**;
Mt 3: 3 The voice of one **c** in the
9:27 **c** out and saying, "Son of
21:15 and the children **c** out in the
Mk 1: 3 The voice of one **c** in the
5: 5 **c** out and cutting himself with
15: 8 **c** aloud, began to ask him to
Lk 3: 4 The voice of one **c** in the
4:41 **c** out and saying, "You are the
Jn 1:23 The voice of one **c** in the
Acts 8: 7 **c** with a loud voice, came out
14:14 among the multitude, **c** out
17: 6 **c** out, "These who have turned
21:28 **c** out, "Men of Israel, help!
21:36 **c** out, "Away with him!"
25:24 **c** out that he was not fit to
Gal 4: 6 **c** out, "Abba, Father!"
Rev 7:10 and **c** out with a loud voice,
14:15 **c** with a loud voice to Him who
21: 4 more death, nor sorrow, nor **c**.

CRYSTAL (6/6)

Job 28:17 Neither gold nor **c** can equal
Isa 54:12 of rubies, Your gates of **c**,
Ezek 1:22 like the color of an awesome **c**,
Rev 4: 6 was a sea of glass, like **c**.
21:11 like a jasper stone, clear as **c**.
22: 1 of water of life, clear as **c**,

CUB (1/1) CUBS

Nah 2:11 the lioness and lion's **c**,

CUBIT (42/27) CUBITS

Gen 6:16 and you shall finish it to a **c**
Ex 25:10 a **c** and a half its width, and a
25:10 and a **c** and a half its height.
25:17 shall be its length and a **c**
25:23 a **c** its width, and a cubit and
25:23 and a **c** and a half its height.
26:13 And a **c** on one side and a cubit
26:13 a cubit on one side and a **c** on
26:16 and a **c** and a half shall be
30: 2 A **c** shall be its length and a
30: 2 shall be its length and a **c**
36:21 and the width of each board a **c**
37: 1 a **c** and a half its width, and a
37: 1 and a **c** and a half its height.
37: 6 cubits was its length and a **c**
37:10 a **c** its width, and a cubit and
37:10 and a **c** and a half its height.
37:25 Its length was a **c** and its
37:25 was a cubit and its width a **c**—
Deut 3:11 according to the standard **c**.
Judg 3:16 (it was double-edged and a **c**
1 Ki 7:24 it all around, ten to a **c**,
7:31 crown at the top was one **c** in
7:35 cart, at the height of half a **c**,
2 Chr 4: 3 it all around, ten to a **c**,
Ezek 40: 5 each being a **c** and a
40:12 one **c** on this side and one
40:12 on this side and one **c** on
40:42 one **c** and a half long, one
40:42 one **c** and a half wide, and one
40:42 and one **c** high; on these they
42: 4 wide, at a distance of one **c**;
43:13 in cubits (the **c** is one cubit
43:13 in cubits (the cubit is one **c**
43:13 the base one **c** high and one
43:13 base one cubit high and one **c**
43:14 the width of the ledge, one **c**;
43:14 the width of the ledge, one **c**.
43:17 with a rim of half a **c** around
43:17 one **c** all around; and its steps
Mt 6:27 you by worrying can add one **c**
Lk 12:25 you by worrying can add one **c**

CUBITS (234/151) CUBIT

Gen 6:15 ark shall be three hundred **c**,
6:15 cubits, its width fifty **c**,
6:15 cubits, and its height thirty **c**.
7:20 The waters prevailed fifteen **c**
Ex 25:10 two and a half **c** shall be its
25:17 two and a half **c** shall be its
25:23 two **c** shall be its length,
26: 2 shall be twenty-eight **c**,
26: 2 width of each curtain four **c**.
26: 8 curtain shall be thirty **c**,
26: 8 width of each curtain four **c**;
26:16 Ten **c** shall be the length of a
27: 1 five **c** long and five cubits

27: 1 five cubits long and five c
27: 1 its height shall be three c.
27: 9 one hundred c long for one
27:11 be hangings one hundred c
27:12 shall be hangings of fifty c,
27:13 east side shall be fifty c.
27:14 the gate shall be fifteen c,
27:15 be hangings of fifteen c,
27:16 shall be a screen twenty c
27:18 court shall be one hundred c,
27:18 and the height five c,
30: 2 and two c shall be its height.
36: 9 curtain was twenty-eight c,
36: 9 width of each curtain four c;
36:15 of each curtain was thirty c,
36:15 width of each curtain four c;
36:21 length of each board was ten c,
37: 1 two and a half c was its
37: 6 two and a half c was its
37:10 two c was its length, a cubit
37:25 —and two c was its height.
38: 1 five c was its length and five
38: 1 was its length and five c its
38: 1 its height was three c.
38: 9 one hundred c long.
38:11 hangings were one hundred c
38:12 were hangings of fifty c,
38:13 the hangings were fifty c.
38:14 of the gate were fifteen c
38:15 were hangings of fifteen c,
38:18 The length was twenty c,
38:18 along its width was five c,
Num 11:31 and about two c above the
35: 4 the city outward a thousand c
35: 5 on the east side two thousand c,
35: 5 the south side two thousand c,
35: 5 on the west side two thousand c,
35: 5 the north side two thousand c.
Deut 3:11 Nine c is its length and four
3:11 is its length and four c its
Josh 3: 4 about two thousand c by
1 Sam 17: 4 whose height was six c and a
1 Ki 6: 2 LORD, its length was sixty c,
6: 2 twenty, and its height thirty c,
6: 3 of the house was twenty c
6: 3 the vestible extended ten c
6: 6 The lowest chamber was five c
6: 6 the middle was six c wide, and
6: 6 and the third was seven c
6:10 each five c high; they were
6:17 temple sanctuary was forty c
6:20 inner sanctuary was twenty c
6:20 twenty c wide, and twenty
6:20 wide, and twenty c high.
6:23 olive wood, each ten c high.
6:24 wing of the cherub was five c,
6:24 other wing of the cherub five c:
6:24 ten c from the tip of one wing
6:25 And the other cherub was ten c;
6:26 height of one cherub was ten c,
7: 2 its length was one hundred c,
7: 2 cubits, its width fifty c,
7: 2 cubits, and its height thirty c,
7: 6 its length was fifty c,
7: 6 cubits, and its width thirty c;
7:10 some ten c and some eight
7:10 ten cubits and some eight c.
7:15 each one eighteen c high, and a
7:15 and a line of twelve c measured
7:16 of one capital was five c,
7:16 the other capital was five c.
7:19 in the shape of lilies, four c.
7:23 ten c from one brim to the
7:23 round. Its height was five c,
7:23 and a line of thirty c measured
7:27 four c was the length of each
7:27 four c its width, and three
7:27 and three c its height.
7:31 one and a half c in outside
7:32 a wheel was one and a half c.
7:38 and each laver was four c.
2 Ki 14:13 the Corner Gate—four hundred c.
25:17 of one pillar was eighteen c,
25:17 of the capital was three c,
1 Chr 11:23 five c tall. In the Egyptian's
2 Chr 3: 3 The length was sixty c (by
3: 3 (by c according to the former
3: 3 and the width twenty c.
3: 4 the sanctuary was twenty c
3: 8 width of the house, twenty c,
3: 8 cubits, and its width twenty c.
3:11 of the cherubim were twenty c
3:11 the one cherub was five c,
3:11 and the other wing was five c,
3:12 of the other cherub was five c,
3:12 other wing also was five c,
3:13 these cherubim spanned twenty c
3:15 two pillars thirty-five c high,
3:15 top of each of them was five c.
4: 1 twenty c was its length, twenty
4: 1 twenty c its width, and ten
4: 1 and ten c its height.
4: 2 ten c from one brim to the
4: 2 Its height was five c,
4: 2 and a line of thirty c measured
6:13 made a bronze platform five c
6:13 five c wide, and three cubits
6:13 and three c high, and had set
25:23 the Corner Gate—four hundred c.
Ezra 6: 3 its height sixty c and its
6: 3 cubits and its width sixty c,
Neh 3:13 and repaired a thousand c of
Esth 5:14 fifty c high, and in the
7: 9 fifty c high, which Haman made
Jer 52:21 of one pillar was eighteen c,
52:21 a measuring line of twelve c
52:22 of one capital was five c,
Ezek 40: 5 hand was a measuring rod six c
40: 7 was a space of five c;
40: 9 of the gateway, eight c;
40: 9 and the gateposts, two c.
40:11 entrance to the gateway, ten c;
40:11 length of the gate, thirteen c.
40:12 the gate chambers were six c
40:12 cubits on this side and six c
40:13 the width was twenty-five c,
40:14 sixty c high, and the court all
40:15 of the inner gate was fifty c.
40:19 one hundred c toward the east
40:21 its length was fifty c and its
40:21 and its width twenty-five c.
40:23 to gateway, one hundred c.
40:25 its length was fifty c and its
40:25 and its width twenty-five c.
40:27 toward the south, one hundred c.
40:29 it was fifty c long and
40:29 cubits long and twenty-five c
40:30 twenty-five c long and five
40:30 cubits long and five c wide.
40:33 it was fifty c long and
40:33 cubits long and twenty-five c
40:36 its length was fifty c and its
40:36 and its width twenty-five c.
40:47 one hundred c long and one
40:47 cubits long and one hundred c
40:48 five c on this side and five
40:48 cubits on this side and five c
40:48 of the gateway was three c on
40:48 on this side and three c on
40:49 of the vestibule was twenty c,
40:49 cubits, and the width eleven c;
41: 1 six c wide on one side and six
41: 1 wide on one side and six c
41: 2 of the entryway was ten c,
41: 2 of the entrance were five c
41: 2 cubits on this side and five c
41: 2 he measured its length, forty c,
41: 2 cubits, and its width, twenty c.
41: 3 measured the doorposts, two c;
41: 3 six c high; and the width of
41: 3 width of the entrance, seven c.
41: 4 measured the length, twenty c;
41: 4 cubits; and the width, twenty c,
41: 5 the wall of the temple, six c.
41: 5 around the temple was four c
41: 8 that is, six c high.
41: 9 the side chambers was five c,
41:10 was a width of twenty c all
41:11 of the terrace was five c all
41:12 its western end was seventy c
41:12 of the building was five c
41:12 around, and its length ninety c.
41:13 one hundred c long; and the
41:13 its walls was one hundred c
41:14 courtyard, was one hundred c.
41:15 the other side, one hundred c,
41:22 three c high, and its length
41:22 high, and its length two c.
42: 2 which was one hundred c (the
42: 2 cubits (the width was fifty c),
42: 3 the inner court of twenty c,
42: 4 was a walk ten c wide, at a
42: 7 its length was fifty c.
42: 8 the outer court was fifty c,
42: 8 the temple was one hundred c.
42:20 five hundred c long and five
43:13 measurements of the altar in c
43:14 to the lower ledge, two c;
43:14 to the larger ledge, four c;
43:15 The altar hearth is four c
43:16 The altar hearth is twelve c
43:17 fourteen c long and fourteen
45: 1 be twenty-five thousand c,
45: 2 with fifty c around it for an
45: 3 twenty-five thousand c long
45: 5 area twenty-five thousand c
45: 6 city an area five thousand c
46:22 forty c long and thirty wide;
47: 3 he measured one thousand c,
48: 8 twenty-five thousand c in
48: 9 be twenty-five thousand c in
48:10 north twenty-five thousand c
48:13 area twenty-five thousand c
48:15 The five thousand c in width
48:16 four thousand five hundred c,
48:17 north two hundred and fifty c,
48:18 shall be ten thousand c to
48:20 be twenty-five thousand c by
48:20 by twenty-five thousand c,
48:21 to the twenty-five thousand c
48:30 four thousand five hundred c
48:32 four thousand five hundred c,
48:33 four thousand five hundred c,
48:34 four thousand five hundred c,
48:35 shall be eighteen thousand c;
Dan 3: 1 whose height was sixty c and
3: 1 cubits and its width six c.
Zech 5: 2 Its length is twenty c and its
5: 2 cubits and its width ten c.
Jn 21: 8 land, but about two hundred c),
Rev 21:17 one hundred and forty-four c,

CUBS (9/9) CUB

2 Sam 17: 8 like a bear robbed of her c in
Job 4:11 And the c of the lioness are
38:32 guide the Great Bear with its c?
Prov 17:12 man meet a bear robbed of her c,
Ezek 19: 2 young lions she nourished her c.
19: 3 She brought up one of her c,
19: 5 She took another of her c and
Hos 13: 8 a bear deprived of her c;
Nah 2:12 tore in pieces enough for his c,

CUCKOW (KJV) See (SEA) GULL

CUCUMBERS (2/2)

Num 11: 5 we ate freely in Egypt, the c,
Isa 1: 8 As a hut in a garden of c,

CUD (11/9)

Lev 11: 3 hooves and chewing the c—
11: 4 among those that chew the c or
11: 4 because it chews the c but does
11: 5 because it chews the c but does
11: 6 because it chews the c but does
11: 7 hooves, yet does not chew the c,
11:26 or does not chew the c,
Deut 14: 6 parts, and that chews the c,
14: 7 of those that chew the c or
14: 7 for they chew the c but do not
14: 8 yet does not chew the c;

CUDDLED (1/1)

Lam 2:20 The children they have c?

CULTIVATE (1/1) CULTIVATED

Ezek 48:19 tribes of Israel, shall c it.

CULTIVATED (2/2) CULTIVATE

Rom 11:24 contrary to nature into a c
Heb 6: 7 for those by whom it is c,

CUMBERED (KJV) See DISTRACTED

CUMI (1/1)

Mk 5:41 and said to her, "Talitha, c,

CUMMIN (7/3)

Isa 28:25 Does he not sow the black c
28:25 And scatter the c, Plant the
28:27 For the black c is not threshed
28:27 a cartwheel rolled over the c;
28:27 But the black c is beaten out
28:27 And the c with a rod.
Mt 23:23 tithe of mint and anise and c,

CUNNING (6/6) CUNNINGLY

Gen 3: 1 Now the serpent was more c than
Job 5:13 And the counsel of the c comes
Dan 8:25 Through his c He shall cause
Hos 12: 7 A c Canaanite! Deceitful scales
2 Cor 12:16 I caught you by c!
Eph 4:14 in the c craftiness of

CUNNINGLY (1/1) CUNNING

2 Pe 1:16 For we did not follow c devised

CUP (69/60) CUPBEARER, CUPS

Gen 40:11 Then Pharaoh's c was in my
40:11 pressed them into Pharaoh's c,
40:11 and placed the c in Pharaoh's
40:13 and you will put Pharaoh's c in
40:21 and he placed the c in
44: 2 'Also put my c, the silver
44: 2 "Also put my cup, the silver c,
44:12 and the c was found in
44:16 with whom the c was found."
44:17 whose hand the c was found,
2 Sam 12: 3 food and drank from his own c
1 Ki 7:26 was shaped like the brim of a c,
17:10 bring me a little water in a c,
2 Chr 4: 5 was shaped like the brim of a c,
Ps 11: 6 be the portion of their c.
16: 5 of my inheritance and my c;
23: 5 My c runs over.
73:10 And waters of a full c are
75: 8 of the LORD there is a c,
116:13 I will take up the c of
Prov 23:31 red, When it sparkles in the c,
Isa 51:17 the LORD The c of His fury;
51:17 have drunk the dregs of the c
51:22 hand The c of trembling,
51:22 The dregs of the c of My fury;
Jer 16: 7 nor shall men give them the c
25:15 Take this wine c of fury from My
25:17 Then I took the c from the
25:28 if they refuse to take the c
49:12 was not to drink of the c
51: 7 Babylon was a golden c in the
Lam 4:21 The c shall also pass over
Ezek 23:31 therefore I will put her c in
23:32 shall drink of your sister's c,
23:33 The c of horror and
23:33 The c of your sister Samaria.

Hab 2:16 **c** of the LORD's right hand
Zech 12: 2 I will make Jerusalem a **c** of
Mt 10:42 of these little ones only a **c**
20:22 Are you able to drink the **c**
20:23 "You will indeed drink My **c**,
23:25 cleanse the outside of the **c**
23:26 cleanse the inside of the **c**
26:27 Then He took the **c**,
26:39 let this **c** pass from Me;
26:42 if this **c** cannot pass away from
Mk 9:41 For whoever gives you a **c** of
10:38 Are you able to drink the **c**
10:39 You will indeed drink the **c** that
14:23 Then He took the **c**,
14:36 Take this **c** away from Me;
Lk 11:39 make the outside of the **c** and
22:17 Then He took the **c**,
22:20 Likewise He also took the **c**
22:20 This **c** is the new covenant in
22:42 take this **c** away from Me;
Jn 18:11 Shall I not drink the **c** which
1 Cor 10:16 The **c** of blessing which we
10:21 You cannot drink the **c** of the
10:21 and the **c** of demons;
11:25 manner He also took the **c**
11:25 This **c** is the new covenant in My
11:26 eat this bread and drink this **c**,
11:27 this bread or drinks this **c**
11:28 of the bread and drink of the **c**.
Rev 14:10 out full strength into the **c**
16:19 to give her the **c** of the wine
17: 4 having in her hand a golden **c**
18: 6 in the **c** which she has mixed,

CUPBEARER (1/1) CUP, CUPBEARERS

Neh 1:11 For I was the king's **c**.

CUPBEARERS (2/2) CUPBEARER

1 Ki 10: 5 and their apparel, his **c**,
2 Chr 9: 4 his **c** and their apparel, and

CUPS (6/6) CUP

Ex 37:16 on the table: its dishes, its **c**,
Isa 22:24 from the **c** to all the pitchers.
Jer 35: 5 bowls full of wine, and **c**;
52:19 the spoons, and the **c**,
Mk 7: 4 hold, like the washing of **c**,
7: 8 washing of pitchers and **c**,

CURDLE (1/1) CURDS

Job 10:10 And **c** me like cheese,

CURDS (5/4) CURDLE

Deut 32:14 **C** from the cattle, and milk of
2 Sam 17:29 honey and **c**, sheep and cheese
Isa 7:15 **C** and honey He shall eat, that
7:22 they give, That he will eat **c**;
7:22 For **c** and honey everyone will

CURE (4/4) CURED, CURES

Isa 3: 7 I cannot **c** your ills, For in
Hos 5:13 Yet he cannot **c** you, Nor heal
Mt 17:16 but they could not **c** him."
Lk 9: 1 and to **c** diseases.

CURED (5/5) CURE

Isa 30:24 work the ground Will eat **c**
Jer 46:11 medicines; You shall not be **c**.
Mt 17:18 and the child was **c** from that
Lk 7:21 And that very hour He **c** many of
Jn 5:10 therefore said to him who was **c**,

CURES (1/1) CURE

Lk 13:32 I cast out demons and perform **c**

CURRENCY (2/2)

Gen 23:16 **c** of the merchants.
Num 3:47 you shall take them in the **c**

CURRENT (2/2)

1 Ki 10:28 them in Keveh at the **c** price.
2 Chr 1:16 bought them in Keveh at the **c**

CURSE (104/93) CURSED, CURSES, CURSING

Gen 8:21 I will never again **c** the ground
12: 3 And I will **c** him who curses
27:12 and I shall bring a **c** on myself
27:13 Let your **c** be on me, my son;
Ex 22:28 nor **c** a ruler of your people.
Lev 19:14 You shall not **c** the deaf, nor
Num 5:18 bitter water that brings a **c**.
5:19 bitter water that brings a **c**.
5:21 woman under the oath of the **c**,
5:21 the LORD make you a **c** and an
5:22 this water that causes the **c**
5:24 bitter water that brings a **c**,
5:24 and the water that brings the **c**
5:27 that the water that brings a **c**
5:27 and the woman will become a **c**
22: 6 **c** this people for me, for they
22: 6 and he whom you **c** is cursed."
22:11 **c** them for me; perhaps I shall
22:12 you shall not **c** the people, for
22:17 **c** this people for me.'"
23: 7 **c** Jacob for me, And come,
23: 8 How shall I **c** whom God has not
23:11 I took you to **c** my enemies, and
23:13 **c** them for me from there."
23:25 Neither **c** them at all, nor bless
23:27 please God that you may **c** them
24:10 I called you to **c** my enemies,
Deut 11:26 you today a blessing and a **c**:
11:28 'and the **c**, if you do not
11:29 on Mount Gerizim and the **c** on
23: 4 of Mesopotamia, to **c** you.
23: 5 turned the **c** into a blessing
27:13 shall stand on Mount Ebal to **c**:
29:19 he hears the words of this **c**,
29:20 and every **c** that is written in
29:27 to bring on it every **c** that is
30: 1 the blessing and the **c** which I
Josh 6:18 and make the camp of Israel a **c**,
24: 9 the son of Beor to **c** you.
Judg 5:23 '**C** Meroz,' said the angel of the
5:23 **C** its inhabitants bitterly,
9:57 and on them came the **c** of
17: 2 you, and on which you put a **c**,
2 Sam 16: 9 Why should this dead dog **c** my
16:10 sons of Zeruiah? So let him **c**,
16:10 '**C** David.' Who then shall say,
16:11 Let him alone, and let him **c**;
1 Ki 2: 8 cursed me with a malicious **c**
2 Ki 2:24 and pronounced a **c** on them in
22:19 become a desolation and a **c**,
Neh 10:29 and entered into a **c** and an
13: 2 Balaam against them to **c** them.
13: 2 our God turned the **c** into a
Job 1:11 and he will surely **c** You to
2: 5 and he will surely **c** You to
2: 9 **C** God and die!"
3: 8 May those **c** it who curse the
3: 8 May those curse it who **c** the
31:30 to sin By asking for a **c** on
Ps 62: 4 But they **c** inwardly. Selah
109:28 Let them **c**, but You bless;
Prov 3:33 The **c** of the LORD is on the
11:26 The people will **c** him who
24:24 Him the people will **c**;
26: 2 So a **c** without cause shall not
27:14 It will be counted a **c** to him.
30:10 Lest he **c** you, and you be
Eccl 10:20 Do not **c** the king, even in your
10:20 Do not **c** the rich, even in
Isa 8:21 that they will be enraged and **c**
24: 6 Therefore the **c** has devoured
34: 5 And on the people of My **c**,
43:28 I will give Jacob to the **c**,
65:15 shall leave your name as a **c**
Jer 23:10 For because of a **c** the land
24: 9 and a byword, a taunt and a **c**,
25:18 a hissing, and a **c**,
26: 6 and will make this city a **c** to
29:18 kingdoms of the earth—to be a **c**,
29:22 And because of them a **c** shall be
42:18 an oath, an astonishment, a **c**,
44: 8 cut yourselves off and be a **c**
44:12 a **c** and a reproach!
44:22 an astonishment, a **c**,
49:13 a reproach, a waste, and a **c**.
Lam 3:65 Your **c** be upon them!
Dan 9:11 therefore the **c** and the oath
Zech 5: 3 This is the **c** that goes out
5: 4 "I will send out the **c**,
8:13 That just as you were a **c**
Mal 2: 2 I will send a **c** upon you, And I
2: 2 And I will **c** your blessings.
3: 9 You are cursed with a **c**,
4: 6 and strike the earth with a **c**.
Mt 5:44 bless those who **c** you, do good
26:74 Then he began to **c** and swear,
Mk 14:71 Then he began to **c** and swear,
Lk 6:28 bless those who **c** you, and pray
Rom 12:14 bless and do not **c**.
Gal 3:10 of the law are under the **c**;
3:13 has redeemed us from the **c** of
3:13 having become a **c** for us
Jas 3: 9 and with it we **c** men, who have
Rev 22: 3 And there shall be no more **c**,

CURSED (66/63) CURSE

Gen 3:14 You are **c** more than all
3:17 **C** is the ground for your sake;
4:11 So now you are **c** from the
5:29 ground which the LORD has **c**.
9:25 **C** be Canaan; A servant of
27:29 **C** be everyone who curses you,
49: 7 **C** be their anger, for it is
Lev 20: 9 He has **c** his father or his
24:11 the name of the LORD and **c**;
24:14 outside the camp him who has **c**;
24:23 outside the camp him who had **c**,
Num 22: 6 and he whom you curse is **c**.
23: 8 I curse whom God has not **c**?
24: 9 And **c** is he who curses
Deut 27:15 **C** is the one who makes a carved
27:16 **C** is the one who treats his
27:17 **C** is the one who moves his
27:18 **C** is the one who makes the
27:19 **C** is the one who perverts the
27:20 **C** is the one who lies with his
27:21 **C** is the one who lies with any
27:22 **C** is the one who lies with his
27:23 **C** is the one who lies with his
27:24 **C** is the one who attacks his
27:25 **C** is the one who takes a bribe
27:26 **C** is the one who does not
28:16 **C** shall you be in the city,
28:16 and **c** shall you be in the
28:17 **C** shall be your basket and
28:18 **C** shall be the fruit of your
28:19 **C** shall you be when you come
28:19 and **c** shall you be when you
Josh 6:26 **C** be the man before the LORD
9:23 "Now therefore, you are **c**,
Judg 9:27 and **c** Abimelech.
21:18 **C** be the one who gives a wife
1 Sam 14:24 **C** is the man who eats any food
14:28 **C** is the man who eats food this
17:43 And the Philistine **c** David by
26:19 may they be **c** before the
2 Sam 16: 7 Also Shimei said thus when he **c**:
16:13 hillside opposite him and **c** as
19:21 because he **c** the LORD's
1 Ki 2: 8 who **c** me with a malicious curse
Neh 13:25 contended with them and **c** them,
Job 1: 5 my sons have sinned and **c** God
3: 1 Job opened his mouth and **c** the
5: 3 But suddenly I **c** his dwelling
24:18 Their portion should be **c** in
Ps 37:22 But those **c** by Him shall be
119:21 You rebuke the proud—the **c**,
Eccl 7:22 That even you have **c** others.
Jer 11: 3 **C** is the man who does not obey
17: 5 **C** is the man who trusts in man
20:14 **C** be the day in which I was
20:15 Let the man be **c** Who brought
48:10 **C** is he who does the work of
48:10 And **c** is he who keeps back
Mal 1:14 But **c** be the deceiver Who has
2: 2 I have **c** them already, Because
3: 9 You are **c** with a curse, For
Mt 25:41 hand, 'Depart from Me, you **c**,
Mk 11:21 The fig tree which You **c** has
Gal 3:10 **C** is everyone who does not
3:13 **C** is everyone who hangs on
Heb 6: 8 rejected and near to being **c**,

CURSES (18/18) CURSE

Gen 12: 3 And I will curse him who **c**
27:29 Cursed be everyone who **c** you,
Ex 21:17 And he who **c** his father or his
Lev 20: 9 For everyone who **c** his father or
24:15 Whoever **c** his God shall bear his
Num 5:23 the priest shall write these **c**
24: 9 And cursed is he who **c**
Deut 28:15 that all these **c** will come upon
28:45 Moreover all these **c** shall come
29:21 according to all the **c** of the
30: 7 your God will put all these **c**
2 Chr 34:24 all the **c** that are written in
Prov 20:20 Whoever **c** his father or his
28:27 hides his eyes will have many **c**.
30:11 is a generation that **c** its
Jer 15:10 Every one of them **c** me.
Mt 15: 4 He who **c** father or mother,
Mk 7:10 He who **c** father or mother,

CURSING (11/11) CURSE, CURSINGS

Deut 28:20 "The LORD will send on you **c**,
30:19 life and death, blessing and **c**;
2 Sam 16: 5 **c** continuously as he came.
16:12 repay me with good for his **c**
Ps 10: 7 His mouth is full of **c** and
59:12 And for the **c** and lying which
109:17 As he loved **c**, so let it come
109:18 As he clothed himself with **c** as
Eccl 7:21 Lest you hear your servant **c**
Rom 3:14 Whose mouth is full of **c**
Jas 3:10 mouth proceed blessing and **c**.

CURSINGS (2/2) CURSING

Josh 8:34 law, the blessings and the **c**,
Hos 7:16 For the **c** of their tongue.

CURTAIN (25/14) CURTAINS

Ex 26: 2 The length of each **c** shall be
26: 2 and the width of each **c** four
26: 4 yarn on the edge of the **c** on
26: 4 outer edge of the other **c** of
26: 5 you shall make in the one **c**,
26: 5 make on the edge of the **c** that
26: 8 The length of each **c** shall be
26: 8 and the width of each **c** four
26: 9 shall double over the sixth **c**
26:10 loops on the edge of the **c**
26:10 loops on the edge of the **c** of
26:12 the half **c** that remains, shall
36: 9 The length of each **c** was
36: 9 and the width of each **c** four
36:11 yarn on the edge of the **c** on
36:11 outer edge of the other **c** of
36:12 Fifty loops he made on one **c**,
36:12 he made on the edge of the **c**
36:12 the loops held one **c** to
36:15 The length of each **c** was thirty
36:15 and the width of each **c** four
36:17 loops on the edge of the **c**
36:17 he made on the edge of the **c**
Ps 104: 2 out the heavens like a **c**.
Isa 40:22 out the heavens like a **c**,

CURTAINS (32/26) CURTAIN

Ex 26: 1 the tabernacle with ten **c** of
26: 2 And every one of the **c** shall
26: 3 Five **c** shall be coupled to one
26: 3 and the other five **c** shall
26: 6 and couple the **c** together with
26: 7 You shall also make **c** of goats'
26: 7 You shall make eleven **c**.
26: 8 and the eleven **c** shall all have
26: 9 And you shall couple five **c** by
26: 9 by themselves and six **c** by
26:12 remnant that remains of the **c**
26:13 remains of the length of the **c**
36: 8 on the tabernacle made ten **c**
36: 9 the **c** were all the same size.
36:10 And he coupled five **c** to one
36:10 and the other five **c** he
36:13 and coupled the **c** to one
36:14 He made **c** of goats' hair for
36:14 tabernacle; he made eleven **c**.
36:15 the eleven **c** were the same
36:16 He coupled five **c** by themselves
36:16 by themselves and six **c** by
Num 4:25 They shall carry the **c** of the
2 Sam 7: 2 ark of God dwells inside tent **c**.
1 Chr 17: 1 of the LORD is under tent **c**.
Esth 1: 6 were white and blue linen **c**
Song 1: 5 Like the **c** of Solomon.
Isa 54: 2 let them stretch out the **c** of
Jer 4:20 And my **c** in a moment.
10:20 tent anymore, Or set up my **c**.
49:29 take for themselves their **c**,
Hab 3: 7 The **c** of the land of Midian

CURVES (1/1)

Song 7: 1 The **c** of your thighs are

CUSH (10/10) ETHIOPIA

Gen 2:13 goes around the whole land of ***C***.
10: 6 The sons of Ham were ***C***,
10: 7 The sons of ***C*** were Seba,
10: 8 ***C*** begot Nimrod; he began to be a
1 Chr 1: 8 The sons of Ham were ***C***,
1: 9 The sons of ***C*** were Seba,
1:10 ***C*** begot Nimrod; he began to be a
Ps 7: LORD concerning the words of ***C***,
Isa 11:11 and Egypt, From Pathros and ***C***,
45:14 of Egypt and merchandise of ***C***

CUSHAN (1/1)

Hab 3: 7 I saw the tents of ***C*** in

CUSHAN-RISHATHAIM (KJV) See CUSHAN (RISHATHAIM)

CUSHAN-RISHATHAIM (4/2)

Judg 3: 8 He sold them into the hand of ***C***
3: 8 the children of Israel served ***C***
3:10 and the LORD delivered ***C*** king
3:10 and his hand prevailed over ***C***.

CUSHI (2/2)

Jer 36:14 son of Shelemiah, the son of ***C***,
Zeph 1: 1 came to Zephaniah the son of ***C***,

CUSHITE (8/5)

2 Sam 18:21 Then Joab said to the ***C***,
18:21 So the ***C*** bowed himself to
18:22 let me also run after the ***C***.
18:23 of the plain, and outran the ***C***.
18:31 Just then the ***C*** came, and the
18:31 and the ***C*** said, "There is good
18:32 And the king said to the ***C***,
18:32 So the ***C*** answered, "May the

CUSTODIAN (3/3) CUSTODY

Esth 2: 3 king's eunuch, **c** of the women.
2: 8 into the care of Hegai the **c** of
2:15 the **c** of the women, advised.

CUSTODY (9/9) CUSTODIAN

Gen 40: 3 So he put them in **c** in the house
40: 4 so they were in **c** for a while.
40: 7 who were with him in the **c** of
41:10 and put me in **c** in the house of
Lev 24:12 Then they put him in **c**,
Esth 2: 3 under the **c** of Hegai the king's
2: 8 under the **c** of Hegai, that
2:14 to the **c** of Shaashgaz, the
Acts 4: 3 and put them in **c** until the

CUSTOM (27/27) CUSTOMARY, CUSTOMS

Gen 19:31 to come in to us as is the **c**
Ex 21: 9 with her according to the **c** of
Num 15:16 One law and one **c** shall be for
Judg 11:39 And it became a **c** in Israel
Ruth 4: 7 Now this was the **c** in former
1 Sam 2:13 And the priests' **c** with the
1 Ki 18:28 cut themselves, as was their **c**,
2 Ki 11:14 by a pillar according to **c**;
2 Chr 30:16 place according to their **c**,
35:25 They made it a **c** in Israel;
Ezra 4:13 will not pay tax, tribute, or **c**,
4:20 and **c** were paid to them.
7:24 or **c** on any of the priests,
Esth 9:23 So the Jews accepted the **c** which
Ps 119:132 As Your **c** is toward those who
Jer 32:11 according to the law and **c**,
Dan 6:10 as was his **c** since early days.
Lk 1: 9 according to the **c** of the
2:27 do for Him according to the **c**
2:42 to Jerusalem according to the **c**
4:16 And as His **c** was, He went into
Jn 18:39 But you have a **c** that I should
19:40 as the **c** of the Jews is to
Acts 15: 1 circumcised according to the **c**
17: 2 as his **c** was, went in to them,
25:16 It is not the **c** of the Romans to
1 Cor 11:16 contentious, we have no such **c**,

CUSTOMARILY (1/1) CUSTOMARY

Acts 16:13 where prayer was **c** made; and we

CUSTOMARY (19/18) CUSTOM, CUSTOMARILY

Lev 12: 2 in the days of her **c** impurity
12: 5 as in her **c** impurity, and she
15:25 than at the time of her **c**
15:25 be as the days of her **c** impurity.
15:33 is indisposed because of her **c**
18:19 as long as she is in her **c**
23: 7 you shall do no **c** work on it.
23: 8 you shall do no **c** work on
23:21 You shall do no **c** work on it.
23:25 You shall do no **c** work on it;
23:35 You shall do no **c** work on it.
23:36 and you shall do no **c** work on
Num 28:18 You shall do no **c** work.
28:25 You shall do no **c** work.
28:26 You shall do no **c** work.
29: 1 You shall do no **c** work. For you
29:12 You shall do no **c** work, and you
29:35 You shall do no **c** work.
Ezek 36:17 of a woman in her **c** impurity.

CUSTOMS (11/10) CUSTOM

Lev 18:30 any of these abominable **c**
Jer 10: 3 For the **c** of the peoples are
Ezek 11:12 have done according to the **c**
Mt 17:25 the kings of the earth take **c**
Acts 6:14 this place and change the **c**
16:21 and they teach **c** which are not
21:21 nor to walk according to the **c**.
26: 3 you are expert in all **c** and
28:17 against our people or the **c** of
Rom 13: 7 **c** to whom customs, fear to whom
13: 7 are due, customs to whom **c**,

CUT (330/315) CUTS, CUTTING, WOODCUTTERS

Gen 9:11 again shall all flesh be **c** off
15:10 all these to Him and **c** them
15:10 but he did not **c** the birds in
17:14 that person shall be **c** off from
Ex 4:25 took a sharp stone and **c** off
9:15 then you would have been **c** off
12:15 that person shall be **c** off from
12:19 that same person shall be **c** off
23:23 and I will **c** them off.
29:17 Then you shall **c** the ram in
30:33 shall be **c** off from his
30:38 he shall be **c** off from his
31:14 that person shall be **c** off from
34: 1 ***C*** two tablets of stone like the
34: 4 So he **c** two tablets of stone
34:13 and **c** down their wooden images
39: 3 sheets and **c** it into threads,
Lev 1: 6 and **c** it into its pieces.
1:12 And he shall **c** it into its
7:20 that person shall be **c** off from
7:21 that person shall be **c** off from
7:25 who eats it shall be **c** off
7:27 that person shall be **c** off from
8:20 And he **c** the ram into pieces;
17: 4 and that man shall be **c** off
17: 9 that man shall be **c** off from
17:10 and will **c** him off from among
17:14 eats it shall be **c** off.'
18:29 commit them shall be **c** off
19: 8 and that person shall be **c** off
20: 3 and will **c** him off from his
20: 5 and I will **c** him off from his
20: 6 against that person and **c** him
20:17 And they shall be **c** off in the
20:18 Both of them shall be **c** off
22: 3 that person shall be **c** off from
22:24 or crushed, or torn or **c**;
23:29 that same day shall be **c** off
26:26 When I have **c** off your supply of
26:30 **c** down your incense altars, and
Num 4:18 Do not **c** off the tribe of the
9:13 that same person shall be **c** off
13:23 and there **c** down a branch with
13:24 which the men of Israel **c** down
15:30 and he shall be **c** off from
15:31 shall be completely **c** off;
19:13 That person shall be **c** off from
19:20 that person shall be **c** off from
Deut 7: 5 and **c** down their wooden images,
12: 3 you shall **c** down the carved
14: 1 you shall not **c** yourselves nor
19: 1 God has **c** off the nations
19: 5 with his neighbor to **c** timber,
19: 5 a stroke with the ax to **c** down
20:19 do not **c** them down to use in
20:20 you may destroy and **c** down,
25:12 then you shall **c** off her hand;
Josh 3:13 of the Jordan shall be **c** off,
3:16 and were **c** off; and the people
4: 7 waters of the Jordan were **c** off
4: 7 of the Jordan were **c** off.
7: 9 and **c** off our name from the
11:21 that time Joshua came and **c** off
17:18 you shall **c** it down, and its
23: 4 the nations that I have **c** off,
Judg 1: 6 him and caught him and **c** off
1: 7 thumbs and big toes **c** off
6:25 and **c** down the wooden image
6:26 image which you shall **c** down."
6:28 that was beside it was **c** down,
6:30 and because he has **c** down the
9:48 an ax in his hand and **c** down
9:49 the people likewise **c** down
20: 6 **c** her in pieces, and sent her
20:21 and on that day **c** down to the
20:25 and **c** down to the ground
20:45 and they **c** down five thousand
21: 6 One tribe is **c** off from Israel
Ruth 4:10 the dead may not be **c** off
1 Sam 2:31 that I will **c** off your arm
2:33 your men whom I do not **c** off
11: 7 took a yoke of oxen and **c** them
17:51 and **c** off his head with it.
20:15 but you shall not **c** off your
20:15 not when the LORD has **c** off
24: 4 secretly **c** off a corner of
24: 5 because he had **c** Saul's robe.
24:11 **c** off the corner of your robe,
24:21 you will not **c** off my
28: 9 how he has **c** off the mediums
31: 9 And they **c** off his head and
2 Sam 4:12 **c** off their hands and feet, and
7: 9 and have **c** off all your enemies
10: 4 **c** off their garments in the
14:26 And when he **c** the hair of his
14:26 the end of every year he **c** it
14:26 when he **c** it, he weighed the
20:22 And they **c** off the head of
1 Ki 5: 6 command that they **c** down cedars
5: 6 who has skill to **c** timber
7: 9 were of costly stones **c** to
9: 7 then I will **c** off Israel from
11:16 until he had **c** down every male
14:10 and will **c** off from Jeroboam
14:14 over Israel who shall **c** off
15:13 And Asa **c** down her obscene
18:23 **c** it in pieces, and lay it on
18:28 and **c** themselves, as was their
18:33 **c** the bull in pieces, and laid
21:21 and will **c** off from Ahab every
2 Ki 3:19 and shall **c** down every good
3:25 **c** down all the good trees.
6: 4 they **c** down trees.
6: 6 So he **c** off a stick, and threw
9: 8 and I will **c** off from Ahab all
10:32 days the LORD began to **c** off
16:17 And King Ahaz **c** off the panels
18: 4 **c** down the wooden image and
19:23 I will **c** down its tall cedars
23:14 the sacred pillars and **c** down
24:13 and he **c** in pieces all the
1 Chr 17: 8 and have **c** off all your enemies
19: 4 and **c** off their garments in the
22: 2 masons to **c** hewn stones to
2 Chr 2: 8 have skill to **c** timber in
2:10 the woodsmen who **c** timber,
2:16 And we will **c** wood from Lebanon,
14: 3 **c** down the wooden images.
15:16 and Asa **c** down her obscene
22: 7 anointed to **c** off the house
26:21 for he was **c** off from the house
28:24 **c** in pieces the articles of the
31: 1 **c** down the wooden images, and
32:21 sent an angel who **c** down
34: 4 were above them he **c** down;
34: 7 and **c** down all the incense
Job 4: 7 were the upright ever **c** off?
6: 9 loose His hand and **c** me off!
8:12 yet green and not **c** down,
8:14 confidence shall be **c** off,
14: 7 If it is **c** down, that it will
21:21 his months is **c** in half?
22:16 Who were **c** down before their
22:20 our adversaries are **c** down,
23:17 Because I was not **c** off from
36:20 When people are **c** off in their
Ps 12: 3 May the LORD **c** off all
31:22 I am **c** off from before Your
34:16 To **c** off the remembrance of
37: 2 For they shall soon be **c** down
37: 9 For evildoers shall be **c** off;
37:22 cursed by Him shall be **c** off.
37:28 of the wicked shall be **c** off.
37:34 When the wicked are **c** off, you
37:38 of the wicked shall be **c** off.
54: 5 ***C*** them off in Your truth.
58: 7 Let his arrows be as if **c** in
75:10 wicked I will also **c** off,
76:12 He shall **c** off the spirit of
80:16 it is **c** down; They perish at
83: 4 and let us **c** them off from
88: 5 And who are **c** off from Your
88:16 Your terrors have **c** me off.

90: 6 In the evening it is **c** down
90:10 For it is soon **c** off, and we
94:23 And shall **c** them off in their
94:23 The LORD our God shall **c** them
101: 8 That I may **c** off all the
107:16 And **c** the bars of iron in two.
109:13 Let his posterity be **c** off,
109:15 That He may **c** off the memory
129: 4 He has **c** in pieces the cords
143:12 In Your mercy **c** off my enemies,
Prov 2:22 But the wicked will be **c** off
10:31 perverse tongue will be **c** out.
23:18 your hope will not be **c** off.
24:14 your hope will not be **c** off.
Isa 6:13 remains when it is **c** down.
9:10 The sycamores are **c** down,
9:14 Therefore the LORD will **c** off
10: 7 And **c** off not a few nations.
10:34 He will **c** down the thickets of
11:13 of Judah shall be **c** off;
14: 8 'Since you were **c** down,
14:12 How you are **c** down
14:22 And **c** off from Babylon the name
15: 2 And every beard **c** off.
18: 5 He will both **c** off the sprigs
18: 5 And take away and **c** down
22:25 will be removed and be **c** down
22:25 that was on it will be **c** off;
29:20 for iniquity are **c** off—
33:12 Like thorns **c** up they shall
37:24 I will **c** down its tall cedars
38:12 I have **c** off my life like a
45: 2 And **c** the bars of iron.
48: 9 So that I do not **c** you off.
48:19 name would not have been **c** off
51: 9 the arm that **c** Rahab apart,
53: 8 For He was **c** off from the land
55:13 sign that shall not be **c** off.
56: 5 name That shall not be **c** off.
Jer 6: 6 **C** down trees, And build a mound
7:28 perished and has been **c** off
7:29 **C** off your hair and cast it
11:19 and let us **c** him off from the
16: 6 **c** themselves, nor make
22: 7 They shall **c** down your choice
22:14 And **c** out windows for it,
25:37 the peaceful dwellings are **c**
34:18 when they **c** the calf in two and
36:23 that the king **c** it with the
41: 5 having **c** themselves, with
44: 7 to **c** off from you man and
44: 8 that you may **c** yourselves off
46:23 They shall **c** down her forest,"
47: 4 To **c** off from Tyre and Sidon
47: 5 Ashkelon is **c** off With the
47: 5 How long will you **c** yourself?
48: 2 and let us **c** her off as a
48: 2 You also shall be **c** down,
48:25 The horn of Moab is **c** off, And
49:26 the men of war shall be **c** off
50:16 **C** off the sower from Babylon,
50:23 whole earth has been **c** apart
50:30 her men of war shall be **c** off
51: 6 Do not be **c** off in her
51:62 against this place to **c** it off,
Lam 2: 3 He has **c** off in fierce anger
3:54 I said, "I am **c** off!"
Ezek 4:16 surely I will **c** off the supply
5:16 the famine upon you and **c** off
6: 6 incense altars may be **c** down,
14: 8 and I will **c** him off from the
14:13 I will **c** off its supply of
14:13 and **c** off man and beast from
14:17 and I **c** off man and beast from
14:19 and **c** off from it man and
14:21 to **c** off man and beast from it?
16: 4 born your navel cord was not **c**,
17: 9 **C** off its fruit, And leave it
17:17 a wall to **c** off many persons.
21: 3 out of its sheath and **c** off
21: 4 Because I will **c** off both
25: 7 I will **c** you off from the
25:13 **c** off man and beast from it,
25:16 and I will **c** off the
29: 8 a sword upon you and **c** off
30:15 I will **c** off the multitude of
31:12 have **c** it down and left it;
35: 7 and **c** off from it the one who
37:11 and we ourselves are **c** off!'
39:10 from the field nor **c** down any
Dan 2: 5 you shall be **c** in pieces, and
2:34 watched while a stone was **c**
2:45 as you saw that the stone was **c**
3:29 and Abed-Nego shall be **c** in
4:14 Chop down the tree and **c** off its
9:26 Messiah shall be **c** off,
Hos 8: 4 That they might be **c** off.
10: 7 her king is **c** off Like a twig
10:15 king of Israel Shall be **c** off
Joel 1: 5 For it has been **c** off from
1: 9 drink offering Have been **c** off
1:16 Is not the food **c** off before
2: 8 They are not **c** down.
Am 1: 5 And **c** off the inhabitant from
1: 8 I will **c** off the inhabitant
2: 3 And I will **c** off the judge from
3:14 of the altar shall be **c** off
Ob 5 how you will be **c** off!—Would
9 May be **c** off by slaughter.
10 And you shall be **c** off
14 at the crossroads To **c** off
Mic 1:16 Make yourself bald and **c** off
5: 9 your enemies shall be **c** off.
5:10 That I will **c** off your horses
5:11 I will **c** off the cities of your
5:12 I will **c** off sorceries from
5:13 images I will also **c** off,
Nah 1:12 manner they will be **c** down
1:14 I will **c** off the carved image
1:15 He is utterly **c** off.
2:13 I will **c** off your prey from the
3:15 The sword will **c** you off;
Hab 3:17 Though the flock may be **c** off
Zeph 1: 3 I will **c** off man from the face
1: 4 I will **c** off every trace of
1:11 merchant people are **c** down;
1:11 who handle money are **c** off.
3: 6 I have **c** off nations, Their
3: 7 her dwelling would not be **c**
Zech 9: 6 And I will **c** off the pride of
9:10 I will **c** off the chariot from
9:10 The battle bow shall be **c** off.
11:10 and **c** it in two, that I might
11:14 Then I **c** in two my other staff,
11:16 care for those who are **c** off,
12: 3 will surely be **c** in pieces,
13: 2 that I will **c** off the names of
13: 8 it shall be **c** off and die,
14: 2 the people shall not be **c** off
Mal 2:12 May the LORD **c** off from the
Mt 3:10 not bear good fruit is **c** down
5:30 **c** it off and cast it from you;
7:19 not bear good fruit is **c** down
18: 8 **c** it off and cast it from you.
21: 8 others **c** down branches from the
24:51 and will **c** him in two and
26:51 and **c** off his ear.
Mk 9:43 you to sin, **c** it off.
9:45 you to sin, **c** it off.
11: 8 and others **c** down leafy
14:47 and **c** off his ear.
Lk 3: 9 not bear good fruit is **c** down
12:46 and will **c** him in two and
13: 7 **C** it down; why does it use up
13: 9 after that you can **c** it down.'
22:50 of the high priest and **c** off
Jn 18:10 and **c** off his right ear.
18:26 of him whose ear Peter **c** off,
Acts 2:37 they were **c** to the heart, and
7:54 they were **c** to the heart,
18:18 He had his hair **c** off at
27:32 Then the soldiers **c** away the
Rom 9:28 finish the work and **c** it
11:22 you also will be **c** off.
11:24 For if you were **c** out of the
2 Cor 11:12 that I may **c** off the
Gal 5:12 even **c** themselves off!

CUTH (1/1) CUTHAH

2 Ki 17:30 the men of **C** made Nergal, the

CUTHAH (1/1) CUTH

2 Ki 17:24 brought people from Babylon, **C**,

CUTS (12/12) CUT

Deut 12:29 When the LORD your God **c** off
29:11 from the one who **c** your wood to
Job 28:10 He **c** out channels in the rocks,
Ps 46: 9 He breaks the bow and **c** the
Prov 26: 6 by the hand of a fool **C** off
Isa 38:12 He **c** me off from the loom;
44:14 He **c** down cedars for himself,
Jer 10: 3 For one **c** a tree from the
48:37 On all the hands shall be **c**,
Ezek 24: 4 Fill it with choice **c**;
24: 5 And let the **c** simmer in it."
24:10 And let the **c** be burned up.

CUTTING (6/6) CUT, CUTTINGS

Ex 31: 5 in **c** jewels for setting, in
35:33 in **c** jewels for setting, in
2 Ki 6: 5 But as one was **c** down a tree,
Jer 44:11 for catastrophe and for **c** off
Hab 2:10 **C** off many peoples, And sin
Mk 5: 5 crying out and **c** himself with

CUTTINGS (3/3) CUTTING

Lev 19:28 You shall not make any **c** in your
21: 5 of their beards nor make any **c**
Jer 9:22 Like **c** after the harvester,

CYMBAL (1/1) CYMBALS

1 Cor 13: 1 sounding brass or a clanging **c**.

CYMBALS (16/15) CYMBAL

2 Sam 6: 5 on sistrums, and on **c**.
1 Chr 13: 8 on tambourines, on **c**,
15:16 instruments, harps, and **c**,
15:19 were to sound the **c** of bronze;
15:28 horn, with trumpets and with **c**,
16: 5 but Asaph made music with **c**;
16:42 aloud with trumpets and **c** and
25: 1 stringed instruments, and **c**.
25: 6 the house of the LORD, with **c**,
2 Chr 5:12 in white linen, having **c**,
5:13 voice with the trumpets and **c**
29:25 the house of the LORD with **c**,
Ezra 3:10 the sons of Asaph, with **c**,
Neh 12:27 with **c** and stringed
Ps 150: 5 Praise Him with loud **c**;
150: 5 Praise Him with clashing **c**!

CYPRESS (16/16)

1 Ki 5: 8 concerning the cedar and **c**
5:10 Hiram gave Solomon cedar and **c**
6:15 of the temple with planks of **c**.
6:34 And the two doors were of **c**
9:11 Solomon with cedar and **c** and
2 Ki 19:23 tall cedars And its choice **c**
2 Chr 2: 8 Also send me cedar and **c** and
3: 5 larger room he paneled with **c**
Isa 14: 8 Indeed the **c** trees rejoice over
37:24 tall cedars And its choice **c**
41:19 I will set in the desert the **c**
44:14 And takes the **c** and the oak;
55:13 the thorn shall come up the **c**
60:13 The **c**, the pine, and the
Hos 14: 8 I am like a green **c** tree;
Zech 11: 2 Wail, O **c**, for the cedar

CYPRUS (14/14)

Num 24:24 come from the coasts of **C**,
Isa 23: 1 From the land of **C** it is
23:12 Arise, cross over to **C**;
Jer 2:10 pass beyond the coasts of **C**
Ezek 27: 6 ivory from the coasts of **C**.
Dan 11:30 For ships from **C** shall come
Acts 4:36 a Levite of the country of **C**,
11:19 traveled as far as Phoenicia, **C**,
11:20 some of them were men from **C**
13: 4 and from there they sailed to **C**.
15:39 took Mark and sailed to **C**;
21: 3 When we had sighted **C**,
21:16 with them a certain Mnason of **C**,
27: 4 under the shelter of **C**,

CYRENE (4/4) CYRENIAN

Mt 27:32 came out, they found a man of **C**,
Acts 2:10 the parts of Libya adjoining **C**,
11:20 them were men from Cyprus and **C**,
13: 1 was called Niger, Lucius of **C**,

CYRENIAN (2/2) CYRENE, CYRENIANS

Mk 15:21 a certain man, Simon a **C**,
Lk 23:26 of a certain man, Simon a **C**,

CYRENIANS (1/1) CYRENIAN

Acts 6: 9 (**C**, Alexandrians, and those

CYRENIUS (KJV) See QUIRINIUS

CYRUS (23/19)

2 Chr 36:22 Now in the first year of **C** king
36:22 stirred up the spirit of **C**
36:23 Thus says **C** king of Persia: All
Ezra 1: 1 Now in the first year of **C** king
1: 1 stirred up the spirit of **C**
1: 2 Thus says **C** king of Persia: All
1: 7 King **C** also brought out the
1: 8 and **C** king of Persia brought
3: 7 which they had from **C** king of
4: 3 as King **C** the king of Persia
4: 5 purpose all the days of **C** king
5:13 in the first year of **C** king of
5:13 King **C** issued a decree to build
5:14 those King **C** took from the
5:17 a decree was issued by King **C**
6: 3 In the first year of King **C**,
6: 3 King **C** issued a decree
6:14 according to the command of **C**,
Isa 44:28 Who says of **C**, 'He is My
45: 1 LORD to His anointed, To **C**,
Dan 1:21 until the first year of King **C**.
6:28 of Darius and in the reign of **C**
10: 1 In the third year of **C** king of

D

DABAREH (KJV) See DABERATH

DABBASHETH (1/1)

Josh 19:11 west and to Maralah, went to **D**,

DABERATH (3/3)

Josh 19:12 Tabor, and went out toward **D**,
21:28 **D** with its common-land,
1 Chr 6:72 **D** with its common-lands,

DAGGER (3/3)

Judg 3:16 Now Ehud made himself a **d** (it
3:21 took the **d** from his right
3:22 for he did not draw the **d** out

DAGON (13/9) DAGON'S

Judg 16:23 to offer a great sacrifice to **D**
1 Sam 5: 2 it into the temple of **D** and
5: 2 temple of Dagon and set it by **D**.
5: 3 in the morning, there was **D**,

5: 3 So they took ***D*** and set it in
5: 4 the next morning, there was ***D***,
5: 4 The head of ***D*** and both the
5: 5 neither the priests of ***D*** nor
5: 5 tread on the threshold of ***D*** in
5: 7 hand is harsh toward us and ***D***
1 Chr 10:10 his head in the temple of ***D***.

DAGON'S (2/2) DAGON

1 Sam 5: 4 only ***D*** torso was left of it.
5: 5 Dagon nor any who come into ***D***

DAILY (58/57)

Ex 5:13 your ***d*** quota, as when there
5:19 reduce any bricks from your ***d***
16: 5 twice as much as they gather ***d***.
Lev 6:20 an ephah of fine flour as a ***d***
Num 4:16 the ***d*** grain offering, the
28:24 of the offering made by fire ***d***
Judg 16:16 when she pestered him ***d*** with
2 Chr 8:13 according to the ***d*** rate,
31:16 the house of the LORD his ***d***
Ezra 3: 4 and offered the ***d*** burnt
Neh 5:18 Now that which was prepared ***d***
Esth 3: 4 when they spoke to him ***d*** and he
Ps 13: 2 Having sorrow in my heart ***d***?
61: 8 That I may ***d*** perform my vows.
68:19 Who ***d*** loads us with
72:15 And ***d*** He shall be praised.
74:22 foolish man reproaches You ***d***.
88: 9 I have called ***d*** upon You;
Prov 8:30 And I was ***d*** His delight,
8:34 Watching ***d*** at my gates,
Isa 58: 2 Yet they seek Me ***d***,
Jer 7:25 ***d*** rising up early and sending
20: 7 prevailed. I am in derision ***d***;
20: 8 A reproach and a derision ***d***.
37:21 that they should give him ***d*** a
Ezek 30:16 Noph shall be in distress ***d***.
45:23 ***d*** for seven days, and a kid of
45:23 and a kid of the goats ***d*** for a
46:13 You shall ***d*** make a burnt
Dan 1: 5 for them a ***d*** provision
8:11 and by him the ***d*** sacrifices
8:12 to oppose the ***d*** sacrifices;
8:13 concerning the ***d*** sacrifices
11:31 then they shall take away the ***d***
12:11 And from the time that the ***d***
Hos 12: 1 He ***d*** increases lies and
Mt 6:11 Give us this day our ***d*** bread.
26:55 I sat ***d*** with you, teaching in
Mk 14:49 I was ***d*** with you in the temple
Lk 9:23 and take up his cross ***d***,
11: 3 Give us day by day our ***d*** bread.
19:47 And He was teaching ***d*** in the
22:53 When I was with you ***d*** in the
Acts 2:46 So continuing ***d*** with one accord
2:47 the Lord added to the church ***d***
3: 2 whom they laid ***d*** at the gate of
5:42 And ***d*** in the temple, and in
6: 1 widows were neglected in the ***d***
16: 5 and increased in number ***d***.
17:11 and searched the Scriptures ***d***
17:17 and in the marketplace ***d*** with
19: 9 reasoning ***d*** in the school of
1 Cor 15:31 Christ Jesus our Lord, I die ***d***.
2 Cor 11:28 things, what comes upon me ***d***:
Heb 3:13 but exhort one another ***d***,
7:27 who does not need ***d***,
10:11 priest stands ministering ***d***
Jas 2:15 is naked and destitute of ***d***

DAINTIES (1/1)

Gen 49:20 And he shall yield royal ***d***.

DAINTY (KJV) See DELICACIES, RICH, SPLENDID, SUCCULENT

DALAIAH (KJV) See DELAIAH

DALE (KJV) See VALLEY

DALMANUTHA (1/1)

Mk 8:10 and came to the region of ***D***.

DALMATIA (1/1)

2 Tim 4:10 for Galatia, Titus for ***D***.

DALPHON (1/1)

Esth 9: 7 Also Parshandatha, ***D***,

DAMA (1/1)

Acts 1:19 in their own language, Akel ***D***,

DAMAGE (7/7) DAMAGED, DAMAGES

Lev 13:55 whether the ***d*** is outside or
2 Ki 12:12 to repair the ***d*** of the house of
Ezra 4:22 Why should ***d*** increase to the
Isa 22: 9 You also saw the ***d*** to the city
Ezek 21:14 time let the sword do double ***d***.
Dan 11:28 so he shall do ***d*** and return to
11:30 the holy covenant, and do ***d***.

DAMAGED (2/2) DAMAGE

Ps 74: 3 The enemy has ***d*** everything in
Jon 4: 7 and it so ***d*** the plant that it

DAMAGES (8/7) DAMAGE

1 Ki 11:27 the Millo and repaired the ***d***
2 Ki 12: 5 and let them repair the ***d*** of
12: 6 priests had not repaired the ***d***
12: 7 have you not repaired the ***d*** of
12: 7 deliver it for repairing the ***d***
12: 8 nor repair the ***d*** of the temple.
22: 5 to repair the ***d*** of the house—
Am 9:11 fallen down, And repair its ***d***;

DAMARIS (1/1)

Acts 17:34 the Areopagite, a woman named ***D***,

DAMASCENES (1/1) DAMASCUS

2 Cor 11:32 was guarding the city of the ***D***

DAMASCUS (60/55) DAMASCENES

Gen 14:15 as Hobah, which is north of ***D***.
15: 2 of my house is Eliezer of ***D***?
2 Sam 8: 5 When the Syrians of ***D*** came to
8: 6 put garrisons in Syria of ***D***;
1 Ki 11:24 And they went to ***D*** and dwelt
11:24 dwelt there, and reigned in ***D***.
15:18 king of Syria, who dwelt in ***D***,
19:15 your way to the Wilderness of ***D***;
20:34 marketplaces for yourself in ***D***,
2 Ki 5:12 the Pharpar, the rivers of ***D***,
8: 7 Then Elisha went to ***D***,
8: 9 him, of every good thing of ***D***,
14:28 from ***D*** and Hamath, what had
16: 9 of Assyria went up against ***D***
16:10 Now King Ahaz went to ***D*** to meet
16:10 and saw an altar that was at ***D***;
16:11 that King Ahaz had sent from ***D***.
16:11 King Ahaz came back from ***D***.
16:12 when the king came back from ***D***,
1 Chr 18: 5 When the Syrians of ***D*** came to
18: 6 put garrisons in Syria of ***D***;
2 Chr 16: 2 king of Syria, who dwelt in ***D***,
24:23 their spoil to the king of ***D***.
28: 5 and brought them to ***D***.
28:23 he sacrificed to the gods of ***D***
Song 7: 4 Lebanon Which looks toward ***D***.
Isa 7: 8 For the head of Syria is ***D***,
7: 8 And the head of ***D*** is Rezin.
8: 4 the riches of ***D*** and the spoil
10: 9 Arpad? Is not Samaria like ***D***?
17: 1 The burden against ***D***.
17: 1 ***D*** will cease from being a
17: 3 Ephraim, The kingdom from ***D***,
Jer 49:23 Against ***D***. "Hamath and Arpad
49:24 ***D*** has grown feeble
49:27 kindle a fire in the wall of ***D***,
Ezek 27:18 ***D*** was your merchant because of
47:16 is between the border of ***D***
47:17 to Hazar Enan, the border of ***D***;
47:18 from between Hauran and ***D***,
48: 1 the border of ***D*** northward, in
Am 1: 3 three transgressions of ***D***,
1: 5 also break the gate bar of ***D***,
5:27 you into captivity beyond ***D***,
Zech 9: 1 And ***D*** its resting place
Acts 9: 2 from him to the synagogues of ***D***,
9: 3 As he journeyed he came near ***D***,
9: 8 hand and brought him into ***D***.
9:10 was a certain disciple at ***D***
9:19 days with the disciples at ***D***.
9:22 the Jews who dwelt in ***D***,
9:27 he had preached boldly at ***D*** in
22: 5 and went to ***D*** to bring in
22: 6 as I journeyed and came near ***D***
22:10 to me, 'Arise and go into ***D***,
22:11 who were with me, I came into ***D***.
26:12 as I journeyed to ***D*** with
26:20 declared first to those in ***D***
2 Cor 11:32 In ***D*** the governor, under Aretas
Gal 1:17 Arabia, and returned again to ***D***.

DAMNATION (KJV) See CONDEMNATION, DESTRUCTION

DAMS (1/1)

Job 28:11 He ***d*** up the streams from

DAMSEL (KJV) See GIRL, (YOUNG) WOMAN

DAN (74/66) DANITES, LAISH

Gen 14:14 and went in pursuit as far as ***D***.
30: 6 Therefore she called his name ***D***.
35:25 were ***D*** and Naphtali;
46:23 The son of ***D*** was Hushim.
49:16 ***D*** shall judge his people As one
49:17 ***D*** shall be a serpent by the
Ex 1: 4 ***D***, Naphtali, Gad, and Asher.
31: 6 of Ahisamach, of the tribe of ***D***;
35:34 of Ahisamach, of the tribe of ***D***.
38:23 of Ahisamach, of the tribe of ***D***,
Lev 24:11 of Dibri, of the tribe of ***D***.
Num 1:12 'from ***D***, Ahiezer the son of
1:38 From the children of ***D***,
1:39 were numbered of the tribe of ***D***
2:25 standard of the forces with ***D***
2:25 the leader of the children of ***D***
2:31 numbered of the forces with ***D***,
7:66 leader of the children of ***D***,
10:25 the camp of the children of ***D***
13:12 from the tribe of ***D***,
26:42 These are the sons of ***D***
26:42 These are the families of ***D***
34:22 the tribe of the children of ***D***,
Deut 27:13 Reuben, Gad, Asher, Zebulun, ***D***,
33:22 And of ***D*** he said: "Dan is a
33:22 ***D*** is a lion's whelp; He shall
34: 1 the land of Gilead as far as ***D***,
Josh 19:40 the tribe of the children of ***D***
19:47 the border of the children of ***D***
19:47 because the children of ***D*** went
19:47 They called Leshem, ***D***, after
19:47 after the name of ***D*** their
19:48 the tribe of the children of ***D***
21: 5 of Ephraim, from the tribe of ***D***,
21:23 and from the tribe of ***D***,
Judg 1:34 forced the children of ***D*** into
5:17 And why did ***D*** remain on ships?
18: 2 So the children of ***D*** sent five
18:16 who were of the children of ***D***,
18:22 and overtook the children of ***D***.
18:23 called out to the children of ***D***.
18:25 And the children of ***D*** said to
18:26 Then the children of ***D*** went
18:29 called the name of the city ***D***,
18:29 after the name of ***D*** their
18:30 Then the children of ***D*** set up
18:30 were priests to the tribe of ***D***
20: 1 from ***D*** to Beersheba, as well as
1 Sam 3:20 And all Israel from ***D*** to
2 Sam 3:10 from ***D*** to Beersheba."
17:11 from ***D*** to Beersheba, like the
24: 2 from ***D*** to Beersheba, and count
24: 6 they came to ***D*** Jaan and around
24:15 From ***D*** to Beersheba seventy
1 Ki 4:25 from ***D*** as far as Beersheba, all
12:29 and the other he put in ***D***.
12:30 before the one as far as ***D***.
15:20 of Israel. He attacked Ijon, ***D***,
2 Ki 10:29 that were at Bethel and ***D***.
1 Chr 2: 2 ***D***, Joseph, Benjamin, Naphtali,
21: 2 Israel from Beersheba to ***D***,
27:22 over ***D***, Azarel the son of
2 Chr 2:14 a woman of the daughters of ***D***,
16: 4 They attacked Ijon, ***D***,
30: 5 all Israel, from Beersheba to ***D***,
Jer 4:15 For a voice declares from ***D***
8:16 of His horses was heard from ***D***.
Ezek 27:19 ***D*** and Javan paid for your wares,
48: 1 shall be one section for ***D***
48: 2 "by the border of ***D***,
48:32 Benjamin, and one gate for ***D***;
Am 8:14 O ***D***!' And, 'As the way of

DANCE (9/9) DANCED, DANCES, DANCING

Job 21:11 a flock, And their children ***d***.
Ps 149: 3 them praise His name with the ***d***;
150: 4 Him with the timbrel and ***d***;
Eccl 3: 4 time to mourn, And a time to ***d***;
Song 6:13 the ***d*** of the two camps?
Jer 31:13 the virgin rejoice in the ***d***,
Lam 5:15 Our ***d*** has turned into
Mt 11:17 for you, And you did not ***d***;
Lk 7:32 for you, And you did not ***d***;

DANCED (5/5) DANCE

Judg 21:23 their number from those who ***d***,
1 Sam 18: 7 So the women sang as they ***d***,
2 Sam 6:14 Then David ***d*** before the LORD
Mt 14: 6 the daughter of Herodias ***d***
Mk 6:22 daughter herself came in and ***d***,

DANCES (6/6) DANCE

Ex 15:20 her with timbrels and with ***d***.
Judg 21:21 come out to perform their ***d***,
1 Sam 21:11 sing of him to one another in ***d***,
29: 5 they sang to one another in ***d***,
Job 41:22 And sorrow ***d*** before him.
Jer 31: 4 And shall go forth in the ***d*** of

DANCING (6/6) DANCE

Ex 32:19 that he saw the calf and the ***d***.
Judg 11:34 to meet him with timbrels and ***d***;
1 Sam 18: 6 cities of Israel, singing and ***d***,
30:16 land, eating and drinking and ***d***,
Ps 30:11 for me my mourning into ***d***;
Lk 15:25 the house, he heard music and ***d***.

DANDLED (1/1)

Isa 66:12 And be ***d*** on her knees.

DANGER (7/5) DANGEROUS

1 Sam 13: 6 Israel saw that they were in ***d***
Mt 5:21 whoever murders will be in ***d***
5:22 without a cause shall be in ***d***
5:22 Raca!' shall be in ***d*** of the
5:22 You fool!' shall be in ***d*** of hell
Acts 19:27 is this trade of ours in ***d*** of
19:40 For we are in ***d*** of being called

DANGEROUS (1/1) DANGER

Acts 27: 9 and sailing was now **d** because

DANIEL (83/73) BELTESHAZZAR

1 Chr 3: 1 the Jezreelitess; the second, **D**,
Ezra 8: 2 of the sons of Ithamar, **D**;
Neh 10: 6 **D**, Ginnethon, Baruch,
Ezek 14:14 if these three men, Noah, **D**,
14:20 "even though Noah, **D**,
28: 3 you are wiser than **D**!
Dan 1: 6 of the sons of Judah were **D**,
1: 7 he gave **D** the name
1: 8 But **D** purposed in his heart
1: 9 Now God had brought **D** into the
1:10 chief of the eunuchs said to **D**,
1:11 So **D** said to the steward whom
1:11 of the eunuchs had set over **D**,
1:17 and **D** had understanding in all
1:19 them all none was found like **D**,
1:21 Thus **D** continued until the first
2:13 and they sought **D** and his
2:14 Then with counsel and wisdom **D**
2:15 made the decision known to **D**.
2:16 So **D** went in and asked the king
2:17 Then **D** went to his house, and
2:18 so that **D** and his companions
2:19 the secret was revealed to **D**
2:19 So **D** blessed the God of heaven.
2:20 **D** answered and said: "Blessed
2:24 Therefore **D** went to Arioch, whom
2:25 Then Arioch quickly brought **D**
2:26 The king answered and said to **D**,
2:27 **D** answered in the presence of
2:46 on his face, prostrate before **D**,
2:47 The king answered **D**,
2:48 Then the king promoted **D** and
2:49 Also **D** petitioned the king, and
2:49 but **D** sat in the gate of the
4: 8 But at last **D** came before me
4:19 Then **D**, whose name was
5:12 enigmas were found in this **D**,
5:12 now let **D** be called, and he
5:13 Then **D** was brought in before
5:13 The king spoke, and said to **D**,
5:13 Are you that **D** who is one of
5:17 Then **D** answered, and said
5:29 and they clothed **D** with purple
6: 2 of whom **D** was one, that the
6: 3 Then this **D** distinguished
6: 4 to find some charge against **D**
6: 5 find any charge against this **D**
6:10 Now when **D** knew that the
6:11 these men assembled and found **D**
6:13 said before the king, "That **D**,
6:14 and set his heart on **D** to
6:16 and they brought **D** and cast
6:16 the king spoke, saying to **D**,
6:17 that the purpose concerning **D**
6:20 out with a lamenting voice to **D**.
6:20 The king spoke, saying to **D**,
6:20 '**D**, servant of the living
6:21 Then **D** said to the king, "O
6:23 that they should take **D** up out
6:23 So **D** was taken up out of the
6:24 those men who had accused **D**,
6:26 and fear before the God of **D**.
6:27 Who has delivered **D** from the
6:28 So this **D** prospered in the
7: 1 **D** had a dream and visions of
7: 2 **D** spoke, saying, "I saw in my
7:15 I, **D**, was grieved in my
7:28 As for me, **D**, my thoughts
8: 1 vision appeared to me—to me, **D**—
8:15 Then it happened, when I, **D**,
8:27 And I, **D**, fainted and was
9: 2 first year of his reign I, **D**,
9:22 talked with me, and said, "O **D**,
10: 1 a message was revealed to **D**,
10: 2 In those days I, **D**,
10: 7 And I, **D**, alone saw the
10:11 And he said to me, "O **D**,
10:12 he said to me, "Do not fear, **D**,
12: 4 'But you, **D**, shut up the
12: 5 Then I, **D**, looked; and
12: 9 And he said, "Go your way, **D**,
Mt 24:15 spoken of by **D** the prophet,
Mk 13:14 spoken of by **D** the prophet,

DANITES (4/4) DAN

Judg 13: 2 Zorah, of the family of the **D**,
18: 1 those days the tribe of the **D**
18:11 men of the family of the **D**
1 Chr 12:35 of the **D** who could keep battle

DANNAH (1/1)

Josh 15:49 **D**, Kirjath Sannah

DAPPLED (2/2)

Zech 6: 3 fourth chariot **d** horses—strong
6: 6 and the **d** are going toward the

DARA (1/1) DARDA

1 Chr 2: 6 Ethan, Heman, Calcol, and **D**—

DARDA (1/1) DARA

1 Ki 4:31 and Heman, Chalcol, and **D**,

DARE (8/8) DARED

Esth 7: 5 who would **d** presume in his
Job 41:10 that he would **d** stir him up.
Am 6:10 Hold your tongue! For we **d** not
Mt 22:46 did anyone **d** question Him
Rom 5: 7 someone would even **d** to die.
15:18 For I will not **d** to speak of any
1 Cor 6: 1 **D** any of you, having a matter
2 Cor 10:12 For we **d** not class ourselves or

DARED (8/8) DARE

2 Sam 17:17 for they **d** not be seen coming
Job 32: 6 And **d** not declare my opinion
Mk 12:34 no one **d** question Him.
Lk 20:40 But after that they **d** not
Jn 21:12 none of the disciples **d** ask
Acts 5:13 Yet none of the rest **d** join
7:32 And Moses trembled and **d** not
Jude 9 **d** not bring against him a

DARICS (1/1)

1 Chr 29: 7 talents and ten thousand **d** of

DARIUS (25/25)

Ezra 4: 5 even until the reign of **D** king
4:24 second year of the reign of **D**
5: 5 till a report could go to **D**.
5: 6 to **D** the king.
5: 7 To **D** the king: All peace.
6: 1 Then King **D** issued a decree, and
6:12 I **D** issue a decree; let it be
6:13 did according to what King **D**
6:14 to the command of Cyrus, **D**,
6:15 year of the reign of King **D**.
Neh 12:22 During the reign of **D** the
Dan 5:31 And **D** the Mede received the
6: 1 It pleased **D** to set over the
6: 6 and said thus to him: "King **D**,
6: 9 Therefore King **D** signed the
6:25 Then King **D** wrote: To all
6:28 prospered in the reign of **D**
9: 1 In the first year of **D** the son
11: 1 Also in the first year of **D** the
Hag 1: 1 In the second year of King **D**,
1:15 in the second year of King **D**.
2:10 month, in the second year of **D**,
Zech 1: 1 month of the second year of **D**,
1: 7 Shebat, in the second year of **D**,
7: 1 in the fourth year of King **D**

DARK (44/44) DARKEN, DARKER, DARKNESS

Gen 15:17 the sun went down and it was **d**,
Num 12: 8 and not in **d** sayings; And he
Josh 2: 5 was being shut, when it was **d**,
2 Sam 22:12 **D** waters and thick clouds of
1 Ki 8:12 said He would dwell in the **d**
2 Chr 6: 1 said He would dwell in the **d**
Neh 13:19 as it began to be **d** before the
Job 3: 9 the stars of its morning be **d**;
6:16 Which are **d** because of the ice,
10:22 A land as **d** as darkness
11:17 Though you were **d**,
12:25 They grope in the **d** without
18: 6 The light is **d** in his tent,
24:16 In the **d** they break into houses
Ps 18:11 His canopy around Him was **d**
35: 6 Let their way be **d** and
49: 4 I will disclose my **d** saying on
74:20 For the **d** places of the earth
78: 2 I will utter **d** sayings of old,
88:12 Your wonders be known in the **d**?
105:28 sent darkness, and made it **d**;
Prov 7: 9 In the black and **d** night.
Song 1: 5 I am **d**, but lovely,
1: 6 look upon me, because I am **d**,
Isa 29:15 And their works are in the **d**;
45:19 In a **d** place of the earth;
Jer 13:16 your feet stumble On the **d**
Lam 3: 6 He has set me in **d** places Like
Ezek 8:12 the house of Israel do in the **d**,
32: 7 heavens, and make its stars **d**;
32: 8 of the heavens I will make **d**
34:12 scattered on a cloudy and **d**
Joel 2:10 The sun and moon grow **d**,
3:15 The sun and moon will grow **d**,
Am 5: 8 morning And makes the day **d**
5:20 not light? Is it not very **d**,
Mic 3: 6 And the day shall be **d** for
Mt 10:27 "Whatever I tell you in the **d**,
Lk 11:36 full of light, having no part **d**,
12: 3 you have spoken in the **d** will
Jn 6:17 Capernaum. And it was already **d**,
20: 1 early, while it was still **d**,
Acts 13:11 And immediately a **d** mist fell
2 Pe 1:19 as a light that shines in a **d**

DARKEN (1/1) DARK, DARKENED, DARKENS

Am 8: 9 And I will **d** the earth in

DARKENED (15/15) DARKEN

Ex 10:15 earth, so that the land was **d**;
Ps 69:23 Let their eyes be **d**,
Eccl 12: 2 moon and the stars, Are not **d**,
Isa 5:30 And the light is **d** by the
13:10 The sun will be **d** in its going
24:11 in the streets, All joy is **d**,
Ezek 30:18 the day shall also be **d**,
Mt 24:29 of those days the sun will be **d**,
Mk 13:24 tribulation, the sun will be **d**,
Lk 23:45 Then the sun was **d**,
Rom 1:21 and their foolish hearts were **d**.
11:10 Let their eyes be **d**,
Eph 4:18 having their understanding **d**,
Rev 8:12 so that a third of them were **d**.
9: 2 So the sun and the air were **d**

DARKENS (1/1) DARKEN

Job 38: 2 Who is this who **d** counsel By

D

DARKER (1/1) DARK

Gen 49:12 His eyes are **d** than wine, And

DARKNESS (161/141) DARK

Gen 1: 2 and **d** was on the face of the
1: 4 divided the light from the **d**.
1: 5 and the **d** He called Night.
1:18 to divide the light from the **d**.
15:12 horror and great **d** fell upon
Ex 10:21 that there may be **d** over the
10:21 **d** which may even be felt."
10:22 and there was thick **d** in all
14:20 Thus it was a cloud and **d** to
20:21 but Moses drew near the thick **d**
Deut 4:11 to the midst of heaven, with **d**,
4:11 darkness, cloud, and thick **d**.
5:22 the cloud, and the thick **d**,
5:23 voice from the midst of the **d**,
28:29 as a blind man gropes in **d**;
Josh 24: 7 and He put **d** between you and
1 Sam 2: 9 the wicked shall be silent in **d**.
2 Sam 22:10 and came down With **d** under His
22:12 He made **d** canopies around Him,
22:29 The LORD shall enlighten my **d**.
Job 3: 4 May that day be **d**;
3: 5 May **d** and the shadow of death
3: 6 may **d** seize it; May it not
5:14 They meet with **d** in the
10:21 To the land of **d** and the
10:22 A land as dark as **d** itself,
10:22 even the light is like **d**.
12:22 uncovers deep things out of **d**,
15:22 that he will return from **d**,
15:23 He knows that a day of **d** is
15:30 He will not depart from **d**;
17:12 they say, in the face of **d**.
17:13 If I make my bed in the **d**,
18:18 He is driven from light into **d**,
19: 8 And He has set **d** in my paths.
20:26 Total **d** is reserved for his
22:11 Or **d** so that you cannot see;
22:13 He judge through the deep **d**?
23:17 cut off from the presence of **d**,
23:17 And He did not hide deep **d**
26:10 At the boundary of light and **d**.
28: 3 Man puts an end to **d**,
28: 3 every recess For ore in the **d**
29: 3 His light I walked through **d**;
30:26 I waited for light, then came **d**.
34:22 There is no **d** nor shadow of
37:19 nothing because of the **d**.
38: 9 And thick **d** its swaddling
38:19 And **d**, where is its place,
40:13 Bind their faces in hidden **d**.
Ps 18: 9 and came down With **d** under His
18:11 He made **d** His secret place;
18:28 my God will enlighten my **d**.
82: 5 They walk about in **d**;
88: 6 me in the lowest pit, In **d**,
88:18 And my acquaintances into **d**.
91: 6 the pestilence that walks in **d**,
97: 2 Clouds and **d** surround Him;
104:20 You make **d**, and it is night,
105:28 He sent **d**, and made it dark;
107:10 Those who sat in **d** and in the
107:14 He brought them out of **d** and
112: 4 there arises light in the **d**;
139:11 Surely the **d** shall fall on me,"
139:12 the **d** shall not hide from You,
139:12 The **d** and the light are both
143: 3 He has made me dwell in **d**,
Prov 2:13 To walk in the ways of **d**;
4:19 way of the wicked is like **d**;
20:20 lamp will be put out in deep **d**.
Eccl 2:13 excels folly As light excels **d**.
2:14 head, But the fool walks in **d**.
5:17 All his days he also eats in **d**,
6: 4 in vanity and departs in **d**,
6: 4 and its name is covered with **d**.
11: 8 let him remember the days of **d**,
Isa 5:20 Who put **d** for light, and light
5:20 for light, and light for **d**;
5:30 Behold, **d** and sorrow; And the
8:22 earth, and see trouble and **d**,
8:22 they will be driven into **d**.
9: 2 The people who walked in **d**
29:18 out of obscurity and out of **d**.
42: 7 Those who sit in **d** from the
42:16 I will make **d** light before
45: 3 give you the treasures of **d**
45: 7 I form the light and create **d**,
47: 5 in silence, and go into **d**,
49: 9 forth,' To those who are in **d**,
50:10 Who walks in **d** And has no

58:10 your light shall dawn in the **d**,
58:10 And your **d** shall be as the
59: 9 but there is **d**!
60: 2 the **d** shall cover the earth,
60: 2 And deep **d** the people;
Jer 2:31 to Israel, Or a land of **d**?
13:16 your God Before He causes **d**,
13:16 death And makes it dense **d**.
23:12 In the **d** they shall be driven
Lam 3: 2 led me and made me walk In **d**
Ezek 32: 8 And bring **d** upon your land,'
Dan 2:22 He knows what is in the **d**,
Joel 2: 2 A day of **d** and gloominess, A
2: 2 A day of clouds and thick **d**,
2:31 The sun shall be turned into **d**,
Am 4:13 And makes the morning **d**,
5:18 It will be **d**, and not light.
5:20 Is not the day of the LORD **d**,
Mic 3: 6 And you shall have **d** without
7: 8 I will arise; When I sit in **d**,
Nah 1: 8 And **d** will pursue His enemies.
Zeph 1:15 A day of **d** and gloominess, A
1:15 A day of clouds and thick **d**,
Mt 4:16 The people who sat in **d**
6:23 whole body will be full of **d**.
6:23 the light that is in you is **d**,
6:23 how great is that **d**!
8:12 will be cast out into outer **d**.
22:13 and cast him into outer **d**;
25:30 servant into the outer **d**.
27:45 the ninth hour there was **d**
Mk 15:33 there was **d** over the whole land
Lk 1:79 light to those who sit in **d**
11:34 your body also is full of **d**.
11:35 light which is in you is not **d**.
22:53 your hour, and the power of **d**.
23:44 and there was **d** over all the
Jn 1: 5 And the light shines in the **d**,
1: 5 and the **d** did not comprehend
3:19 and men loved **d** rather than
8:12 follows Me shall not walk in **d**,
12:35 lest **d** overtake you; he who
12:35 he who walks in **d** does not know
12:46 in Me should not abide in **d**.
Acts 2:20 shall be turned into **d**,
26:18 order to turn them from **d** to
Rom 2:19 a light to those who are in **d**,
13:12 let us cast off the works of **d**,
1 Cor 4: 5 to light the hidden things of **d**
2 Cor 4: 6 light to shine out of **d**,
6:14 what communion has light with **d**?
Eph 5: 8 For you were once **d**,
5:11 with the unfruitful works of **d**,
6:12 against the rulers of the **d** of
Col 1:13 us from the power of **d** and
1 Th 5: 4 But you, brethren, are not in **d**,
5: 5 are not of the night nor of **d**.
Heb 12:18 and to blackness and **d** and
1 Pe 2: 9 of Him who called you out of **d**
2 Pe 2: 4 them into chains of **d**,
2:17 is reserved the blackness of **d**
1 Jn 1: 5 is light and in Him is no **d** at
1: 6 with Him, and walk in **d**,
2: 8 because the **d** is passing away,
2: 9 is in **d** until now.
2:11 who hates his brother is in **d**
2:11 is in darkness and walks in **d**,
2:11 because the **d** has blinded his
Jude 6 in everlasting chains under **d**
13 is reserved the blackness of **d**
Rev 16:10 his kingdom became full of **d**;

DARKON (2/2)

Ezra 2:56 sons of Jaala, the sons of **D**,
Neh 7:58 sons of Jaala, the sons of **D**,

DARLINGS (1/1)

Hos 9:16 I would kill the **d** of their

DART (1/1) DARTED, DARTS

Job 41:26 Nor does spear, **d**, or

DARTED (1/1) DART

Ex 9:23 and fire **d** to the ground.

DARTS (2/2) DART

Job 41:29 **D** are regarded as straw
Eph 6:16 able to quench all the fiery **d**

DASH (8/8) DASHED, DASHES

Deut 32:26 I will **d** them in pieces, I will
2 Ki 8:12 and you will **d** their children,
Ps 2: 9 You shall **d** them to pieces
91:12 Lest you **d** your foot against a
Isa 13:18 Also their bows will **d** the
Jer 13:14 And I will **d** them one against
Mt 4: 6 Lest you **d** your foot
Lk 4:11 Lest you **d** your foot

DASHED (7/7) DASH

Ex 15: 6 has **d** the enemy in pieces.
2 Chr 25:12 so that they all were **d** in
Isa 13:16 Their children also will be **d**
Hos 10:14 A mother **d** in pieces upon her
13:16 Their infants shall be **d** in
Nah 3:10 young children also were **d** to
Rev 2:27 They shall be **d** to

DASHES (1/1) DASH

Ps 137: 9 Happy the one who takes and **d**

DATHAN (10/8)

Num 16: 1 with **D** and Abiram the sons of
16:12 And Moses sent to call **D** and
16:24 away from the tents of Korah, **D**,
16:25 Then Moses rose and went to **D**
16:27 around the tents of Korah, **D**,
16:27 and **D** and Abiram came out and
26: 9 sons of Eliab were Nemuel, **D**,
26: 9 These are the **D** and Abiram,
Deut 11: 6 and what He did to **D** and Abiram
Ps 106:17 earth opened up and swallowed **D**,

DAUB (KJV) See PLASTER

DAUBED (1/1)

Ex 2: 3 **d** it with asphalt and pitch,

DAUGHTER (302/272)

DAUGHTER-IN-LAW, DAUGHTER'S, DAUGHTERS, GRANDDAUGHTER

Gen 11:29 the **d** of Haran the father of
20:12 She is the **d** of my father, but
20:12 but not the **d** of my mother; and
24:23 Whose **d** are you? Tell me,
24:24 I am the **d** of Bethuel, Milcah's
24:47 Whose **d** are you?' And she said,
24:47 The **d** of Bethuel, Nahor's son,
24:48 the way of truth to take the **d**
25:20 the **d** of Bethuel the Syrian of
26:34 he took as wives Judith the **d**
26:34 and Basemath the **d** of Elon the
28: 9 and took Mahalath the **d** of
29: 6 his **d** Rachel is coming with the
29:10 when Jacob saw Rachel the **d** of
29:18 years for Rachel your younger **d**.
29:23 that he took Leah his **d** and
29:24 gave his maid Zilpah to his **d**
29:28 So he gave him his **d** Rachel as
29:29 gave his maid Bilhah to his **d**
30:21 Afterward she bore a **d**,
34: 1 Now Dinah the **d** of Leah, whom
34: 3 attracted to Dinah the **d** of
34: 5 that he had defiled Dinah his **d**.
34: 7 Israel by lying with Jacob's **d**,
34: 8 my son Shechem longs for your **d**.
34:17 then we will take our **d** and be
34:19 he delighted in Jacob's **d**.
36: 2 Adah the **d** of Elon the Hittite;
36: 2 Aholibamah the **d** of Anah, the
36: 2 the **d** of Zibeon the Hivite;
36: 3 and Basemath, Ishmael's **d**,
36:14 the **d** of Anah, the daughter of
36:14 the **d** of Zibeon. And she bore
36:18 Esau's wife, the **d** of Anah.
36:25 Dishon and Aholibamah the **d** of
36:39 the **d** of Matred, the daughter
36:39 the **d** of Mezahab.
38: 2 And Judah saw there a **d** of a
38:12 in the process of time the **d**
41:45 the **d** of Poti-Pherah priest of
41:50 the **d** of Poti-Pherah priest of
46:15 with his **d** Dinah. All the
46:18 whom Laban gave to Leah his **d**;
46:20 the **d** of Poti-Pherah priest of
46:25 whom Laban gave to Rachel his **d**,
Ex 1:16 kill him; but if it is a **d**,
1:22 and every **d** you shall save
2: 1 went and took as wife a **d** of
2: 5 Then the **d** of Pharaoh came down
2: 7 his sister said to Pharaoh's **d**,
2: 8 And Pharaoh's **d** said to her,
2: 9 Then Pharaoh's **d** said to her,
2:10 she brought him to Pharaoh's **d**,
2:21 and he gave Zipporah his **d** to
6:23 **d** of Amminadab, sister of
20:10 you, nor your son, nor your **d**,
21: 7 And if a man sells his **d** to be
21:31 it has gored a son or gored a **d**,
Lev 12: 6 whether for a son or a **d**,
18: 9 the **d** of your father, or the
18: 9 or the **d** of your mother,
18:10 The nakedness of your son's **d** or
18:10 daughter or your daughter's **d**,
18:11 of your father's wife's **d**,
18:17 nakedness of a woman and her **d**,
18:17 nor shall you take her son's **d**
18:17 daughter or her daughter's **d**,
19:29 'Do not prostitute your **d**,
20:17 his father's **d** or his mother's
20:17 daughter or his mother's **d**,
21: 2 his father, his son, his **d**,
21: 9 The **d** of any priest, if she
22:12 If the priest's **d** is married to
22:13 But if the priest's **d** is a widow
24:11 name was Shelomith the **d** of
Num 25:15 was killed was Cozbi the **d** of
25:18 the **d** of a leader of Midian,
26:46 And the name of the **d** of Asher
26:59 wife was Jochebed the **d** of
27: 8 inheritance to pass to his **d**.
27: 9 'If he has no **d**,
30:16 and between a father and his **d**
36: 8 And every **d** who possesses an
Deut 5:14 you, nor your son, nor your **d**,
7: 3 You shall not give your **d** to
7: 3 nor take their **d** for your son.
12:18 you and your son and your **d**,
13: 6 your mother, your son or your **d**,
16:11 you and your son and your **d**,
16:14 you and your son and your **d**,
18:10 who makes his son or his **d**
22:16 I gave my **d** to this man as wife,
22:17 I found your **d** was not a
27:22 the **d** of his father or the
27:22 of his father or the **d** of his
28:56 bosom, and to her son and her **d**,
Josh 15:16 to him I will give Achsah my **d**
15:17 and he gave him Achsah his **d** as
Judg 1:12 to him I will give my **d** Achsah
1:13 so he gave him his **d** Achsah as
11:34 at Mizpah, there was his **d**,
11:34 her he had neither son nor **d**.
11:35 and said, "Alas, my **d**!
11:40 days each year to lament the **d**
19:24 here is my virgin **d** and the
21: 1 None of us shall give his **d** to
Ruth 2: 2 And she said to her, "Go, my **d**.
2: 8 Ruth, "You will listen, my **d**,
2:22 "It is good, my **d**,
3: 1 said to her, "My **d**,
3:10 of the LORD, my **d**!
3:11 "And now, my **d**,
3:16 she said, "Is that you, my **d**?
3:18 she said, "Sit still, my **d**,
1 Sam 14:50 Saul's wife was Ahinoam the **d**
17:25 riches, will give him his **d**,
18:17 Here is my older **d** Merab; I will
18:19 the time when Merab, Saul's **d**,
18:20 Now Michal, Saul's **d**,
18:27 Saul gave him Michal his **d** as
18:28 and that Michal, Saul's **d**,
25:44 Saul had given Michal his **d**,
2 Sam 3: 3 the **d** of Talmai, king of
3: 7 the **d** of Aiah. So Ishbosheth
3:13 first bring Michal, Saul's **d**,
6:16 City of David, Michal, Saul's **d**,
6:20 And Michal the **d** of Saul came
6:23 Therefore Michal the **d** of Saul
11: 3 the **d** of Eliam, the wife of
12: 3 and it was like a **d** to him.
14:27 and one **d** whose name was
17:25 had gone in to Abigail the **d**
21: 8 the two sons of Rizpah the **d** of
21: 8 the five sons of Michal the **d**
21:10 Now Rizpah the **d** of Aiah took
21:11 was told what Rizpah the **d** of
1 Ki 3: 1 Egypt, and married Pharaoh's **d**;
4:11 he had Taphath the **d** of Solomon
4:15 he also took Basemath the **d** of
7: 8 like this hall for Pharaoh's **d**,
9:16 given it as a dowry to his **d**,
9:24 But Pharaoh's **d** came up from
11: 1 as well as the **d** of Pharaoh:
16:31 he took as wife Jezebel the **d**
22:42 name was Azubah the **d** of
2 Ki 8:18 for the **d** of Ahab was his wife;
9:34 her, for she was a king's **d**.
11: 2 the **d** of King Joram, sister of
14: 9 Give your **d** to my son as wife';
15:33 name was Jerusha the **d** of
18: 2 mother's name was Abi the **d**
19:21 the **d** of Zion, Has despised
19:21 The **d** of Jerusalem Has shaken
21:19 name was Meshullemeth the **d**
22: 1 name was Jedidah the **d** of
23:10 man might make his son or his **d**
23:31 name was Hamutal the **d** of
23:36 name was Zebudah the **d** of
24: 8 name was Nehushta the **d** of
24:18 name was Hamutal the **d** of
1 Chr 1:50 name was Mehetabel the **d** of
1:50 the **d** of Mezahab.
2: 3 were born to him by the **d** of
2:21 Hezron went in to the **d** of
2:35 Sheshan gave his **d** to Jarha his
2:49 And the **d** of Caleb was Achsah.
3: 2 the **d** of Talmai, king of
3: 5 four by Bathshua the **d** of
4:18 were the sons of Bithiah the **d**
7:24 Now his **d** was Sheerah, who
15:29 of David, that Michal, Saul's **d**,
2 Chr 8:11 Now Solomon brought the **d** of
11:18 himself as wife Mahalath the **d**
11:18 and of Abihail the **d** of Eliah
13: 2 name was Michaiah the **d** of
20:31 name was Azubah the **d** of
21: 6 for he had the **d** of Ahab as a
22:11 the **d** of the king, took Joash
22:11 the **d** of King Jehoram, the wife
25:18 Give your **d** to my son as wife';
27: 1 name was Jerushah the **d** of
29: 1 name was Abijah the **d** of
Neh 6:18 Jehohanan had married the **d** of
Esth 2: 7 that is, Esther, his uncle's **d**,
2: 7 Mordecai took her as his own **d**.
2:15 the turn came for Esther the **d**
2:15 who had taken her as his **d**,
9:29 the **d** of Abihail, with Mordecai
Ps 9:14 praise In the gates of the **d**
45:10 Listen, O **d**, Consider and
45:12 And the **d** of Tyre will come
45:13 The royal **d** is all glorious
137: 8 O **d** of Babylon, who are to be
Song 7: 1 O prince's **d**! The curves of

Isa 1: 8 So the **d** of Zion is left as a
10:30 O **d** of Gallim! Cause it to be
10:32 his fist at the mount of the **d**
16: 1 To the mount of the **d** of Zion.
22: 4 of the plundering of the **d** of
23:10 O **d** of Tarshish; There is
23:12 O you oppressed virgin **d** of
37:22 the **d** of Zion, Has despised
37:22 The **d** of Jerusalem Has shaken
47: 1 O virgin **d** of Babylon; Sit on
47: 1 O **d** of the Chaldeans! For you
47: 5 O **d** of the Chaldeans; For you
52: 2 O captive **d** of Zion!
62:11 Say to the **d** of Zion, 'Surely
Jer 4:11 in the wilderness Toward the **d**
4:31 The voice of the **d** of Zion
6: 2 I have likened the **d** of Zion
6:23 against you, O **d** of Zion."
6:26 O **d** of my people, Dress in
8:11 have healed the hurt of the **d**
8:19 The cry of the **d** of my people
8:21 For the hurt of the **d** of my
8:22 For the health of the **d** of my
9: 1 night For the slain of the **d**
9: 7 how shall I deal with the **d** of
14:17 For the virgin **d** of my people
31:22 gad about, O you backsliding **d**?
46:11 the **d** of Egypt; In vain you
46:19 O you **d** dwelling in Egypt,
46:24 The **d** of Egypt shall be
48:18 O **d** inhabiting Dibon, Come down
49: 4 flowing valley, O backsliding **d**?
50:42 Against you, O **d** of Babylon.
51:33 The **d** of Babylon is like a
52: 1 name was Hamutal the **d** of
Lam 1: 6 And from the **d** of Zion All her
1:15 in a winepress The virgin **d**
2: 1 the Lord has covered the **d** of
2: 2 The strongholds of the **d** of
2: 4 On the tent of the **d** of Zion,
2: 5 and lamentation In the **d** of
2: 8 to destroy The wall of the **d**
2:10 The elders of the **d** of Zion
2:11 of the destruction of the **d** of
2:13 O **d** of Jerusalem? What shall
2:13 O virgin **d** of Zion? For your
2:15 shake their heads At the **d** of
2:18 O wall of the **d** of Zion, Let
3:48 For the destruction of the **d**
4: 3 But the **d** of my people is
4: 6 of the iniquity of the **d** of my
4:10 In the destruction of the **d**
4:21 O **d** of Edom, You who dwell in
4:22 O **d** of Zion; He will no
4:22 O **d** of Edom; He will uncover
Ezek 14:20 would deliver neither son nor **d**;
16:44 'Like mother, like **d**!'
16:45 "You are your mother's **d**,
16:49 She and her **d** had pride,
22:11 his sister, his father's **d**.
26: 6 Also her **d** villages which are
26: 8 will slay with the sword your **d**
44:25 father or mother, for son or **d**,
Dan 11: 6 for the **d** of the king of the
11:17 And he shall give him the **d** of
Hos 1: 3 So he went and took Gomer the **d**
1: 6 conceived again and bore a **d**.
Mic 1:13 the beginning of sin to the **d**
4: 8 The stronghold of the **d** of
4: 8 The kingdom of the **d** of
4:10 O **d** of Zion, Like a woman in
4:13 O **d** of Zion; For I will make
5: 1 O **d** of troops; He has laid
7: 6 ***D*** rises against her mother,
Zeph 3:10 The **d** of My dispersed ones,
3:14 O **d** of Zion! Shout, O Israel!
3:14 O **d** of Jerusalem!
Zech 2: 7 you who dwell with the **d** of
2:10 O **d** of Zion! For behold, I am
9: 9 O **d** of Zion! Shout, O daughter
9: 9 O **d** of Jerusalem! Behold, your
Mal 2:11 He has married the **d** of a
Mt 9:18 My **d** has just died, but come and
9:22 He said, "Be of good cheer, **d**;
10:35 a **d** against her mother,
10:37 And he who loves son or **d** more
14: 6 the **d** of Herodias danced before
15:22 Son of David! My **d** is severely
15:28 And her **d** was healed from
21: 5 Tell the **d** of Zion,
Mk 5:23 My little **d** lies at the point of
5:34 And He said to her, "***D***,
5:35 Your **d** is dead. Why trouble the
6:22 And when Herodias' **d** herself
7:25 For a woman whose young **d** had an
7:26 to cast the demon out of her **d**.
7:29 demon has gone out of your **d**.
7:30 and her **d** lying on the bed.
Lk 2:36 the **d** of Phanuel, of the tribe
8:42 for he had an only **d** about
8:48 And He said to her, "***D***,
8:49 Your **d** is dead. Do not trouble
12:53 mother against **d** and daughter
12:53 mother against daughter and **d**
13:16 being a **d** of Abraham, whom
Jn 12:15 **d** of Zion; Behold, your
Acts 7:21 Pharaoh's **d** took him away and
Heb 11:24 called the son of Pharaoh's **d**,

DAUGHTER-IN-LAW (17/16)

DAUGHTER, DAUGHTERS-IN-LAW

Gen 11:31 and his **d** Sarai, his son
38:11 Then Judah said to Tamar his **d**,
38:16 not know that she was his **d**.
38:24 Tamar your **d** has played the
Lev 18:15 uncover the nakedness of your **d**—
20:12 'If a man lies with his **d**,
Ruth 1:22 and Ruth the Moabitess her **d**
2:20 Then Naomi said to her **d**,
2:22 And Naomi said to Ruth her **d**,
4:15 of your old age; for your **d**,
1 Sam 4:19 Now his **d**, Phinehas' wife,
1 Chr 2: 4 And Tamar, his **d**,
Ezek 22:11 another lewdly defiles his **d**;
Mic 7: 6 ***D*** against her mother-in-law;
Mt 10:35 and a **d** against her
Lk 12:53 mother-in-law against her **d** and
12:53 her daughter-in-law and **d**

DAUGHTER'S (3/3) DAUGHTER

Lev 18:10 daughter or your **d** daughter,
18:17 daughter or her **d** daughter,
Deut 22:17 evidences of my **d** virginity.'

DAUGHTERS (253/220) DAUGHTER

Gen 5: 4 years; and he had sons and **d**.
5: 7 seven years, and had sons and **d**.
5:10 years, and had sons and **d**.
5:13 forty years, and had sons and **d**.
5:16 years, and had sons and **d**.
5:19 years, and had sons and **d**.
5:22 years, and had sons and **d**.
5:26 years, and had sons and **d**.
5:30 years, and had sons and **d**.
6: 1 and **d** were born to them,
6: 2 that the sons of God saw the **d**
6: 4 sons of God came in to the **d**
11:11 years, and begot sons and **d**.
11:13 years, and begot sons and **d**.
11:15 years, and begot sons and **d**.
11:17 years, and begot sons and **d**.
11:19 years, and begot sons and **d**.
11:21 years, and begot sons and **d**.
11:23 years, and begot sons and **d**.
11:25 years, and begot sons and **d**.
19: 8 I have two **d** who have not known
19:12 Son-in-law, your sons, your **d**,
19:14 who had married his **d**,
19:15 take your wife and your two **d**
19:16 and the hands of his two **d**,
19:30 and his two **d** were with him;
19:30 And he and his two **d** dwelt in a
19:36 Thus both the **d** of Lot were
24: 3 a wife for my son from the **d**
24:13 and the **d** of the men of the
24:37 a wife for my son from the **d**
27:46 of my life because of the **d** of
27:46 if Jacob takes a wife of the **d**
27:46 like these who are the **d** of
28: 1 not take a wife from the **d** of
28: 2 a wife from there of the **d** of
28: 6 not take a wife from the **d** of
28: 8 Also Esau saw that the **d** of
29:16 Now Laban had two **d**:
30:13 for the **d** will call me
31:26 and carried away my **d** like
31:28 me to kiss my sons and my **d**.
31:31 Perhaps you would take your **d**
31:41 fourteen years for your two **d**,
31:43 These **d** are my daughters, and
31:43 "These daughters are my **d**,
31:43 I do this day to these my **d** or
31:50 "If you afflict my **d**,
31:50 take other wives besides my **d**,
31:55 and kissed his sons and **d** and
34: 1 went out to see the **d** of the
34: 9 give your **d** to us, and take our
34: 9 and take our **d** to yourselves.
34:16 then we will give our **d** to you,
34:16 and we will take your **d** to us;
34:21 Let us take their **d** to us as
34:21 and let us give them our **d**.
36: 2 Esau took his wives from the **d**
36: 6 took his wives, his sons, his **d**,
37:35 And all his sons and all his **d**
46: 7 his **d** and his sons' daughters,
46: 7 his daughters and his sons' **d**,
46:15 the persons, his sons and his **d**,
Ex 2:16 priest of Midian had seven **d**.
2:20 So he said to his **d**,
3:22 on your sons and on your **d**.
6:25 took for himself one of the **d**
10: 9 old; with our sons and our **d**,
21: 4 and she has borne him sons or **d**,
21: 9 according to the custom of **d**.
32: 2 wives, your sons, and your **d**,
34:16 and you take of his **d** for your
34:16 and his **d** play the harlot with
Lev 10:14 and your **d** with you; for they
26:29 shall eat the flesh of your **d**.
Num 18:11 and your sons and **d** with you,
18:19 to you and your sons and **d**
21:29 And his **d** into captivity, To
26:33 of Hepher had no sons, but **d**;
26:33 and the names of the **d** of
27: 1 Then came the **d** of Zelophehad
27: 1 these were the names of his **d**:
27: 7 The **d** of Zelophehad speak what
36: 2 our brother Zelophehad to his **d**.
36: 6 commands concerning the **d** of
36:10 so did the **d** of Zelophehad;
36:11 the **d** of Zelophehad, were
Deut 12:12 you and your sons and your **d**,
12:31 burn even their sons and **d** in
23:17 be no ritual harlot of the **d**
28:32 Your sons and your **d** shall be
28:41 "You shall beget sons and **d**,
28:53 flesh of your sons and your **d**
32:19 of His sons and His **d**.
Josh 7:24 wedge of gold, his sons, his **d**,
17: 3 had no sons, but only **d**.
17: 3 these are the names of his **d**:
17: 6 because the **d** of Manasseh

Judg 3: 6 And they took their **d** to be
3: 6 and gave their **d** to their sons;
11:40 that the **d** of Israel went four
12: 9 And he gave away thirty **d** in
12: 9 and brought in thirty **d** from
14: 1 saw a woman in Timnah of the **d**
14: 2 a woman in Timnah of the **d** of
14: 3 there no woman among the **d** of
21: 7 we will not give them our **d** as
21:18 give them wives from our **d**,
21:21 and just when the **d** of Shiloh
21:21 a wife for himself from the **d**
Ruth 1:11 Naomi said, "Turn back, my **d**;
1:12 "Turn back, my **d**,
1:13 from having husbands? No, my **d**;
1 Sam 1: 4 wife and to all her sons and **d**.
2:21 and bore three sons and two **d**.
8:13 He will take your **d** to be
14:49 And the names of his two **d**
30: 3 and their **d** had been taken
30: 6 man for his sons and his **d**.
30:19 small or great, sons or **d**,
2 Sam 1:20 Lest the **d** of the Philistines
1:20 **d** of the uncircumcised
1:24 O **d** of Israel, weep over Saul,
5:13 Also more sons and **d** were born
13:18 for the king's virgin **d** wore
19: 5 the lives of your sons and **d**,
2 Ki 17:17 they caused their sons and **d**
1 Chr 2:34 Sheshan had no sons, only **d**.
4:27 had sixteen sons and six **d**;
7:15 but Zelophehad begot only **d**.
14: 3 and David begot more sons and **d**.
23:22 and had no sons, but only **d**;
25: 5 Heman fourteen sons and three **d**.
2 Chr 2:14 (the son of a woman of the **d** of
11:21 twenty-eight sons and sixty **d**.
13:21 twenty-two sons and sixteen **d**.
24: 3 for him, and he had sons and **d**.
28: 8 thousand women, sons, and **d**;
29: 9 the sword; and our sons, our **d**,
31:18 their wives, their sons and **d**,
Ezra 2:61 who took a wife of the **d** of
9: 2 have taken some of their **d** as
9:12 do not give your **d** as wives for
9:12 nor take their **d** to your sons;
Neh 3:12 he and his **d** made repairs.
4:14 brethren, your sons, your **d**,
5: 2 and our **d** are many; therefore
5: 5 are forcing our sons and our **d**
5: 5 and some of our **d** have been
7:63 who took a wife of the **d** of
10:28 wives, their sons, and their **d**,
10:30 We would not give our **d** as wives
10:30 nor take their **d** for our sons;
13:25 You shall not give your **d** as
13:25 nor take their **d** for your sons
Job 1: 2 And seven sons and three **d** were
1:13 was a day when his sons and **d**
1:18 Your sons and **d** were eating and
42:13 also had seven sons and three **d**.
42:15 no women so beautiful as the **d**
Ps 45: 9 Kings' **d** are among Your
48:11 Let the **d** of Judah be glad,
97: 8 And the **d** of Judah rejoice
106:37 their sons And their **d** to
106:38 The blood of their sons and **d**,
144:12 That our **d** may be as
Prov 30:15 The leech has two **d**—
31:29 Many **d** have done well, But you
Eccl 12: 4 And all the **d** of music are
Song 1: 4 Draw me away! THE ***D*** OF
1: 4 THE ***D*** OF JERUSALEM We
1: 5 O **d** of Jerusalem, Like the
1:10 THE ***D*** OF JERUSALEM
2: 2 So is my love among the **d**.
2: 3 THE SHULAMITE TO THE ***D***
2: 7 O **d** of Jerusalem, By the
3: 5 O **d** of Jerusalem, By the
3:10 paved with love By the **d** of
3:11 O **d** of Zion, And see King
5: 8 O **d** of Jerusalem, If you find
5: 8 him I am lovesick! THE ***D***
5:16 O **d** of Jerusalem! THE
5:16 of Jerusalem! THE ***D*** OF
6: 9 The **d** saw her And called her
8: 2 (TO THE ***D*** OF JERUSALEM)
8: 4 O **d** of Jerusalem, Do not stir
Isa 3:16 Because the **d** of Zion are
3:17 crown of the head of the **d** of
4: 4 washed away the filth of the **d**
16: 2 So shall be the **d** of Moab at
32: 9 my voice; You complacent **d**,
43: 6 And My **d** from the ends of the
49:22 And your **d** shall be carried on
56: 5 Better than that of sons and **d**;

60: 4 And your **d** shall be nursed at
Jer 3:24 herds, Their sons and their **d**.
5:17 Which your sons and **d** should
7:31 to burn their sons and their **d**
9:20 Teach your **d** wailing, And
11:22 their sons and their **d** shall
14:16 wives, their sons nor their **d**—
16: 2 nor shall you have sons or **d** in
16: 3 concerning the sons and **d** who
19: 9 sons and the flesh of their **d**,
29: 6 Take wives and beget sons and **d**;
29: 6 for your sons and give your **d**
29: 6 that they may bear sons and **d**—
32:35 to cause their sons and their **d**
35: 8 our wives, our sons, or our **d**,
41:10 the king's **d** and all the people
43: 6 women, children, the king's **d**,
48:46 And your **d** captive.
49: 3 you **d** of Rabbah, Gird
Lam 3:51 my soul Because of all the **d**
Ezek 13:17 set your face against the **d** of
14:16 deliver neither sons nor **d**;
14:18 deliver neither sons nor **d**,
14:22 brought out, both sons and **d**;
16:20 you took your sons and your **d**,
16:27 the **d** of the Philistines, who
16:46 who dwells with her **d** to the
16:46 of you, is Sodom and her **d**.
16:48 your sister Sodom nor her **d**
16:48 have done as you and your **d**
16:53 the captives of Sodom and her **d**,
16:53 captives of Samaria and her **d**,
16:55 your sisters, Sodom and her **d**,
16:55 and Samaria and her **d** return to
16:55 then you and your **d** will return
16:57 time of the reproach of the **d**
16:57 and of the **d** of the
16:61 I will give them to you for **d**,
23: 2 The **d** of one mother.
23: 4 Mine, And they bore sons and **d**.
23:10 Took away her sons and **d**,
23:25 shall take your sons and your **d**,
23:47 slay their sons and their **d**,
24:21 and your sons and **d** whom you
24:25 minds, their sons and their **d**:
30:18 And her **d** shall go into
32:16 The **d** of the nations shall
32:18 Her and the **d** of the famous
Hos 4:13 Therefore your **d** commit
4:14 I will not punish your **d** when
Joel 2:28 Your sons and your **d** shall
3: 8 will sell your sons and your **d**
Am 7:17 Your sons and **d** shall fall by
Lk 1: 5 His wife was of the **d** of
23:28 **D** of Jerusalem, do not weep for
Acts 2:17 Your sons and your **d**
21: 9 Now this man had four virgin **d**
2 Cor 6:18 And you shall be My sons and **d**,
1 Pe 3: 6 whose **d** you are if you do good

DAUGHTERS-IN-LAW (3/3)
DAUGHTER-IN-LAW

Ruth 1: 6 Then she arose with her **d** that
1: 7 and her two **d** with her; and
1: 8 And Naomi said to her two **d**,

DAVID (1086/934) DAVID'S

Ruth 4:17 of Jesse, the father of **D**.
4:22 begot Jesse, and Jesse begot **D**.
1 Sam 16:13 of the LORD came upon **D** from
16:19 and said, "Send me your son **D**,
16:20 and sent them by his son **D** to
16:21 So **D** came to Saul and stood
16:22 Please let **D** stand before me,
16:23 that **D** would take a harp and
17:12 Now **D** was the son of that
17:14 **D** was the youngest. And the
17:15 But **D** occasionally went and
17:17 Then Jesse said to his son **D**,
17:20 So **D** rose early in the morning,
17:22 And **D** left his supplies in the
17:23 So **D** heard them.
17:26 Then **D** spoke to the men who
17:28 anger was aroused against **D**,
17:29 And **D** said, "What have I done
17:31 Now when the words which **D**
17:32 Then **D** said to Saul, "Let no
17:33 And Saul said to **D**,
17:34 But **D** said to Saul, "Your
17:37 Moreover **D** said, "The LORD,
17:37 And Saul said to **D**,
17:38 So Saul clothed **D** with his
17:39 **D** fastened his sword to his
17:39 And **D** said to Saul, "I cannot
17:39 So **D** took them off.
17:41 and began drawing near to **D**,
17:42 looked about and saw **D**,
17:43 So the Philistine said to **D**,
17:43 And the Philistine cursed **D**
17:44 And the Philistine said to **D**,
17:45 Then **D** said to the Philistine,
17:48 came and drew near to meet **D**,
17:48 that **D** hastened and ran toward
17:49 Then **D** put his hand in his bag
17:50 So **D** prevailed over the
17:50 was no sword in the hand of **D**.
17:51 Therefore **D** ran and stood over
17:54 And **D** took the head of the
17:55 When Saul saw **D** going out
17:57 as **D** returned from the
17:58 So **D** answered, "I am the
18: 1 was knit to the soul of **D**,
18: 3 Then Jonathan and **D** made a
18: 4 was on him and gave it to **D**,
18: 5 So **D** went out wherever Saul
18: 6 when **D** was returning from the
18: 7 And **D** his ten thousands."
18: 8 They have ascribed to **D** ten
18: 9 So Saul eyed **D** from that day
18:10 So **D** played music with his
18:11 'I will pin **D** to the wall!"
18:11 But **D** escaped his presence
18:12 Now Saul was afraid of **D**,
18:14 And **D** behaved wisely in all his
18:16 all Israel and Judah loved **D**,
18:17 Then Saul said to **D**,
18:18 So **D** said to Saul, "Who am I,
18:19 should have been given to **D**,
18:20 Saul's daughter, loved **D**.
18:21 Therefore Saul said to **D** a
18:22 'Communicate with **D** secretly,
18:23 those words in the hearing of **D**.
18:23 And **D** said, "Does it seem to
18:24 In this manner **D** spoke."
18:25 said, "Thus you shall say to **D**:
18:25 ' But Saul thought to make **D**
18:26 So when his servants told **D**
18:26 it pleased **D** well to become the
18:27 therefore **D** arose and went, he
18:27 And **D** brought their foreskins,
18:28 knew that the LORD was with **D**,
18:29 Saul was still more afraid of **D**.
18:30 that **D** behaved more wisely
19: 1 that they should kill **D**;
19: 1 son, delighted greatly in **D**.
19: 2 So Jonathan told **D**,
19: 4 Thus Jonathan spoke well of **D**
19: 4 against his servant, against **D**,
19: 5 to kill **D** without a cause?"
19: 7 Then Jonathan called **D**,
19: 7 So Jonathan brought **D** to Saul,
19: 8 and **D** went out and fought with
19: 9 And **D** was playing music with
19:10 Then Saul sought to pin **D** to the
19:10 So **D** fled and escaped that
19:12 So Michal let **D** down through a
19:14 Saul sent messengers to take **D**,
19:15 the messengers back to see **D**,
19:18 So **D** fled and escaped, and went
19:19 **D** is at Naioth in Ramah!"
19:20 Saul sent messengers to take **D**.
19:22 said, "Where are Samuel and **D**?
20: 1 Then **D** fled from Naioth in
20: 3 Then **D** took an oath again, and
20: 4 So Jonathan said to **D**,
20: 5 And **D** said to Jonathan, "Indeed
20: 6 **D** earnestly asked permission of
20:10 Then **D** said to Jonathan, "Who
20:11 And Jonathan said to **D**,
20:12 Then Jonathan said to **D**:
20:12 indeed there is good toward **D**,
20:15 every one of the enemies of **D**
20:16 covenant with the house of **D**,
20:17 Now Jonathan again caused **D** to
20:18 Then Jonathan said to **D**,
20:24 Then **D** hid in the field.
20:28 **D** earnestly asked permission of
20:33 by his father to kill **D**.
20:34 month, for he was grieved for **D**,
20:35 at the time appointed with **D**,
20:39 Only Jonathan and **D** knew of the
20:41 **D** arose from a place toward
20:41 wept together, but **D** more so.
20:42 Then Jonathan said to **D**,
21: 1 Now **D** came to Nob, to Ahimelech
21: 1 was afraid when he met **D**,
21: 2 So **D** said to Ahimelech the
21: 4 And the priest answered **D** and
21: 5 Then **D** answered the priest, and
21: 8 And **D** said to Ahimelech, "Is
21: 9 And **D** said, "There is none
21:10 Then **D** arose and fled that day
21:11 Is this not **D** the king of the
21:11 And **D** his ten thousands'?"
21:12 Now **D** took these words to heart,
22: 1 **D** therefore departed from there
22: 3 Then **D** went from there to
22: 4 with him all the time that **D**
22: 5 Now the prophet Gad said to **D**,
22: 5 So **D** departed and went into
22: 6 When Saul heard that **D** and the
22:14 servants is as faithful as **D**,
22:17 their hand also is with **D**,
22:20 escaped and fled after **D**.
22:21 And Abiathar told **D** that Saul
22:22 So **D** said to Abiathar, "I knew
23: 1 Then they told **D**,
23: 2 Therefore **D** inquired of the
23: 2 And the LORD said to **D**,
23: 4 Then **D** inquired of the LORD
23: 5 And **D** and his men went to Keilah
23: 5 So **D** saved the inhabitants of
23: 6 the son of Ahimelech fled to **D**
23: 7 And Saul was told that **D** had
23: 8 go down to Keilah to besiege **D**
23: 9 When **D** knew that Saul plotted
23:10 Then **D** said, "O LORD God of
23:12 Then **D** said, "Will the men of
23:13 So **D** and his men, about six
23:13 Then it was told Saul that **D**
23:14 And **D** stayed in strongholds in
23:15 So **D** saw that Saul had come out
23:15 And **D** was in the Wilderness of
23:16 arose and went to **D** in the
23:18 And **D** stayed in the woods, and
23:19 Is **D** not hiding with us in
23:24 But **D** and his men were in the
23:25 went to seek him, they told **D**.
23:25 he pursued **D** in the Wilderness
23:26 and **D** and his men on the other
23:26 So **D** made haste to get away
23:26 and his men were encircling **D**
23:28 Saul returned from pursuing **D**,
23:29 Then **D** went up from there and
24: 1 Take note! **D** is in the
24: 2 and went to seek **D** and his men
24: 3 (**D** and his men were staying in
24: 4 Then the men of **D** said to him,
24: 4 And **D** arose and secretly
24: 7 So **D** restrained his servants
24: 8 **D** also arose afterward, went
24: 8 **D** stooped with his face to the
24: 9 And **D** said to Saul: "Why do you
24: 9 Indeed **D** seeks your harm'?
24:16 when **D** had finished speaking
24:16 "Is this your voice, my son **D**?
24:17 Then he said to **D**:
24:22 So **D** swore to Saul. And Saul
24:22 but **D** and his men went up to
25: 1 And **D** arose and went down to
25: 4 When **D** heard in the wilderness
25: 5 **D** sent ten young men; and David
25: 5 and **D** said to the young men,
25: 8 your servants and to your son **D**.
25: 9 these words in the name of **D**,
25:10 servants, and said, "Who is **D**,
25:13 Then **D** said to his men, "Every
25:13 and **D** also girded on his sword.
25:13 four hundred men went with **D**,
25:14 **D** sent messengers from the
25:20 and there were **D** and his men,
25:21 Now **D** had said, "Surely in vain
25:22 more also, to the enemies of **D**,
25:23 Now when Abigail saw **D**,
25:23 fell on her face before **D**,
25:32 Then **D** said to Abigail:
25:35 So **D** received from her hand what
25:39 So when **D** heard that Nabal was
25:39 And **D** sent and proposed to
25:40 When the servants of **D** had come
25:40 **D** sent us to you, to ask you to
25:42 followed the messengers of **D**,
25:43 **D** also took Ahinoam of Jezreel,
26: 1 Is **D** not hiding in the hill of
26: 2 to seek **D** in the Wilderness of
26: 3 But **D** stayed in the wilderness,
26: 4 **D** therefore sent out spies, and
26: 5 So **D** arose and came to the
26: 5 And **D** saw the place where Saul
26: 6 Then **D** answered, and said to
26: 7 So **D** and Abishai came to the
26: 8 Then Abishai said to **D**,
26: 9 And **D** said to Abishai, "Do not
26:10 **D** said furthermore, "As the
26:12 So **D** took the spear and the jug
26:13 Now **D** went over to the other
26:14 And **D** called out to the people
26:15 So **D** said to Abner, "Are you
26:17 "Is that your voice, my son **D**?
26:17 And **D** said, "It is my
26:21 have sinned. Return, my son **D**.
26:22 And **D** answered and said, "Here
26:25 Then Saul said to **D**,
26:25 my son **D**! You shall both do
26:25 So **D** went on his way, and
27: 1 And **D** said in his heart, "Now I
27: 2 Then **D** arose and went over with
27: 3 So **D** dwelt with Achish at Gath,
27: 3 and **D** with his two wives,
27: 4 And it was told Saul that **D** had
27: 5 Then **D** said to Achish, "If I
27: 7 Now the time that **D** dwelt in the
27: 8 And **D** and his men went up and
27: 9 Whenever **D** attacked the land, he
27:10 And **D** would say, "Against
27:11 **D** would save neither man nor
27:11 Thus **D** did.'" And thus was
27:12 So Achish believed **D**,
28: 1 Israel. And Achish said to **D**,
28: 2 And **D** said to Achish, "Surely
28: 2 can do." And Achish said to **D**,
28:17 given it to your neighbor, **D**.
29: 2 but **D** and his men passed in
29: 3 Philistines, "Is this not **D**,
29: 5 "Is this not **D**,
29: 5 And **D** his ten thousands'?"
29: 6 Then Achish called **D** and said
29: 8 So **D** said to Achish, "But what
29: 9 Achish answered and said to **D**,
29:11 So **D** and his men rose early to
30: 1 when **D** and his men came to
30: 3 So **D** and his men came to the
30: 4 Then **D** and the people who were
30: 6 Now **D** was greatly distressed,
30: 6 But **D** strengthened himself in
30: 7 Then **D** said to Abiathar the
30: 7 Abiathar brought the ephod to **D**.
30: 8 So **D** inquired of the LORD,
30: 9 So **D** went, he and the six
30:10 But **D** pursued, he and four
30:11 the field, and brought him to **D**;
30:13 Then **D** said to him, "To whom do
30:15 And **D** said to him, "Can you
30:17 Then **D** attacked them from

30:18 So **D** recovered all that the
30:18 and **D** rescued his two wives.
30:19 **D** recovered all.
30:20 Then **D** took all the flocks and
30:21 Now **D** came to the two hundred
30:21 that they could not follow **D**,
30:21 So they went out to meet **D** and
30:21 And when **D** came near the
30:22 men of those who went with **D**
30:23 But **D** said, "My brethren, you
30:26 Now when **D** came to Ziklag, he
30:31 and to all the places where **D**
2 Sam 1: 1 when **D** had returned from the
1: 1 and **D** had stayed two days in
1: 2 So it was, when he came to **D**,
1: 3 And **D** said to him, "Where have
1: 4 Then **D** said to him, "How did
1: 5 So **D** said to the young man who
1:11 Therefore **D** took hold of his
1:13 Then **D** said to the young man who
1:14 So **D** said to him, "How was it
1:15 Then **D** called one of the young
1:16 So **D** said to him, "Your blood
1:17 Then **D** lamented with this
2: 1 It happened after this that **D**
2: 1 **D** said, "Where shall I go
2: 2 So **D** went up there, and his two
2: 3 And **D** brought up the men who
2: 4 and there they anointed **D** king
2: 4 And they told **D**, saying,
2: 5 So **D** sent messengers to the men
2:10 the house of Judah followed **D**.
2:11 And the time that **D** was king in
2:13 Zeruiah, and the servants of **D**,
2:15 twelve from the servants of **D**.
2:17 beaten before the servants of **D**.
2:31 But the servants of **D** had struck
3: 1 of Saul and the house of **D**.
3: 1 But **D** grew stronger and
3: 2 Sons were born to **D** in Hebron:
3: 5 These were born to **D** in Hebron.
3: 6 of Saul and the house of **D**,
3: 8 you into the hand of **D**;
3: 9 if I do not do for **D** as the
3:10 and set up the throne of **D** over
3:12 messengers on his behalf to **D**,
3:13 And **D** said, "Good, I will make
3:14 So **D** sent messengers to
3:17 past you were seeking for **D**
3:18 For the LORD has spoken of **D**,
3:18 'By the hand of My servant **D**,
3:19 to speak in the hearing of **D**
3:20 twenty men with him came to **D**
3:20 And **D** made a feast for Abner
3:21 Then Abner said to **D**,
3:21 So **D** sent Abner away, and he
3:22 that moment the servants of **D**
3:22 But Abner was not with **D** in
3:26 But **D** did not know it.
3:28 when **D** heard it, he said, "My
3:31 Then **D** said to Joab and to all
3:31 And King **D** followed the
3:35 the people came to persuade **D**
3:35 **D** took an oath, saying, "God
4: 8 the head of Ishbosheth to **D** at
4: 9 But **D** answered Rechab and
4:12 So **D** commanded his young men,
5: 1 the tribes of Israel came to **D**
5: 3 and King **D** made a covenant with
5: 3 And they anointed **D** king over
5: 4 **D** was thirty years old when he
5: 6 of the land, who spoke to **D**,
5: 6 **D** cannot come in here."
5: 7 Nevertheless **D** took the
5: 7 Zion (that is, the City of **D**).
5: 8 Now **D** said on that day,
5: 9 Then **D** dwelt in the stronghold,
5: 9 and called it the City of **D**.
5: 9 And **D** built all around from the
5:10 So **D** went on and became great,
5:11 of Tyre sent messengers to **D**,
5:11 And they built **D** a house.
5:12 So **D** knew that the LORD had
5:13 And **D** took more concubines and
5:13 and daughters were born to **D**.
5:17 heard that they had anointed **D**
5:17 went up to search for **D**.
5:17 And **D** heard of it and went
5:19 So **D** inquired of the LORD,
5:19 And the LORD said to **D**,
5:20 So **D** went to Baal Perazim, and
5:20 and **D** defeated them there; and
5:21 and **D** and his men carried them
5:23 Therefore **D** inquired of the
5:25 And **D** did so, as the LORD
6: 1 Again **D** gathered all the choice
6: 2 And **D** arose and went with all
6: 5 Then **D** and all the house of
6: 8 And **D** became angry because of
6: 9 **D** was afraid of the LORD that
6:10 So **D** would not move the ark of
6:10 with him into the City of **D**;
6:10 but **D** took it aside into the
6:12 Now it was told King **D**,
6:12 So **D** went and brought up the
6:12 of Obed-Edom to the City of **D**
6:14 Then **D** danced before the LORD
6:14 and **D** was wearing a linen
6:15 So **D** and all the house of Israel
6:16 LORD came into the City of **D**,
6:16 through a window and saw King **D**
6:17 midst of the tabernacle that **D**
6:17 Then **D** offered burnt offerings
6:18 And when **D** had finished offering
6:20 Then **D** returned to bless his
6:20 of Saul came out to meet **D**,
6:21 So **D** said to Michal, "It was
7: 5 "Go and tell My servant **D**,
7: 8 shall you say to My servant **D**,
7:17 vision, so Nathan spoke to **D**.
7:18 Then King **D** went in and sat
7:20 Now what more can **D** say to You?
7:26 the house of Your servant **D** be
8: 1 this it came to pass that **D**
8: 1 And **D** took Metheg Ammah from
8: 3 **D** also defeated Hadadezer the
8: 4 **D** took from him one thousand
8: 4 Also **D** hamstrung all the
8: 5 **D** killed twenty-two thousand of
8: 6 Then **D** put garrisons in Syria of
8: 6 The LORD preserved **D** wherever
8: 7 And **D** took the shields of gold
8: 8 King **D** took a large amount of
8: 9 Toi king of Hamath heard that **D**
8:10 sent Joram his son to King **D**,
8:11 King **D** also dedicated these to
8:13 And **D** made himself a name when
8:14 And the LORD preserved **D**
8:15 So **D** reigned over all Israel;
8:15 and **D** administered judgment and
9: 1 Now **D** said, "Is there still
9: 2 when they had called him to **D**,
9: 5 Then King **D** sent and brought
9: 6 the son of Saul, had come to **D**,
9: 6 Then **D** said, "Mephibosheth?"
9: 7 So **D** said to him, "Do not fear,
10: 2 Then **D** said, "I will show
10: 2 So **D** sent by the hand of his
10: 3 Do you think that **D** really
10: 3 Has **D** not rather sent his
10: 5 When they told **D**,
10: 6 made themselves repulsive to **D**,
10: 7 Now when **D** heard of it, he
10:17 When it was told **D**,
10:17 in battle array against **D** and
10:18 and **D** killed seven hundred
11: 1 that **D** sent Joab and his
11: 1 But **D** remained at Jerusalem.
11: 2 it happened one evening that **D**
11: 3 So **D** sent and inquired about the
11: 4 Then **D** sent messengers, and took
11: 5 so she sent and told **D**,
11: 6 Then **D** sent to Joab, saying,
11: 6 And Joab sent Uriah to **D**.
11: 7 **D** asked how Joab was doing, and
11: 8 And **D** said to Uriah, "Go down
11:10 So when they told **D**,
11:10 **D** said to Uriah, "Did you
11:11 And Uriah said to **D**,
11:12 Then **D** said to Uriah, "Wait
11:13 Now when **D** called him, he ate
11:14 the morning it happened that **D**
11:17 the people of the servants of **D**
11:18 Then Joab sent and told **D** all
11:22 and came and told **D** all that
11:23 And the messenger said to **D**,
11:25 Then **D** said to the messenger,
11:27 **D** sent and brought her to his
11:27 But the thing that **D** had done
12: 1 Then the LORD sent Nathan to **D**.
12: 7 Then Nathan said to **D**,
12:13 So **D** said to Nathan, "I have
12:13 And Nathan said to **D**,
12:15 that Uriah's wife bore to **D**,
12:16 **D** therefore pleaded with God for
12:16 and **D** fasted and went in and
12:18 And the servants of **D** were
12:19 When **D** saw that his servants
12:19 **D** perceived that the child was
12:19 Therefore **D** said to his
12:20 So **D** arose from the ground,
12:24 Then **D** comforted Bathsheba his
12:27 And Joab sent messengers to **D**,
12:29 So **D** gathered all the people
12:31 Then **D** and all the people
13: 1 this Absalom the son of **D** had
13: 1 and Amnon the son of **D** loved
13: 7 And **D** sent home to Tamar,
13:21 But when King **D** heard of all
13:30 on the way, that news came to **D**,
13:37 And **D** mourned for his son
13:39 And King **D** longed to go to
15:13 Now a messenger came to **D**,
15:14 So **D** said to all his servants
15:22 So **D** said to Ittai, "Go, and
15:30 So **D** went up by the Ascent of
15:31 Then someone told **D**,
15:31 And **D** said, "O LORD, I
15:32 Now it happened when **D** had come
15:33 **D** said to him, "If you go on
16: 1 When **D** was a little past the top
16: 5 Now when King **D** came to
16: 6 And he threw stones at **D** and at
16: 6 at all the servants of King **D**.
16:10 LORD has said to him, 'Curse **D**.
16:11 And **D** said to Abishai and all
16:13 And as **D** and his men went along
16:23 of Ahithophel both with **D** and
17: 1 and I will arise and pursue **D**
17:16 send quickly and tell **D**,
17:17 they would go and tell King **D**.
17:21 well and went and told King **D**,
17:21 told King David, and said to **D**,
17:22 So **D** and all the people who
17:24 Then **D** went to Mahanaim. And
17:27 when **D** had come to Mahanaim,
17:29 for **D** and the people who were
18: 1 And **D** numbered the people who
18: 2 Then **D** sent out one third of the
18: 7 there before the servants of **D**,
18: 9 Absalom met the servants of **D**.
18:24 Now **D** was sitting between the
19:11 So King **D** sent to Zadok and
19:16 the men of Judah to meet King **D**.
19:22 And **D** said, "What have I to do
19:43 we also have more right to **D**
20: 1 'We have no share in **D**,
20: 2 every man of Israel deserted **D**,
20: 3 Now **D** came to his house at
20: 5 than the set time which **D** had
20: 6 And **D** said to Abishai, "Now
20:11 Joab and whoever is for **D**—
20:21 against the king, against **D**.
20:26 was a chief minister under **D**.
21: 1 was a famine in the days of **D**
21: 1 and **D** inquired of the LORD.
21: 3 Therefore **D** said to the
21: 7 between **D** and Jonathan the son
21:11 And **D** was told what Rizpah the
21:12 Then **D** went and took the bones
21:15 **D** and his servants with him
21:15 and **D** grew faint.
21:16 sword, thought he could kill **D**.
21:17 Then the men of **D** swore to him,
21:22 and fell by the hand of **D** and
22: 1 Then **D** spoke to the LORD the
22:51 To **D** and his descendants
23: 1 these are the last words of **D**.
23: 1 Thus says **D** the son of Jesse;
23: 8 names of the mighty men whom **D**
23: 9 of the three mighty men with **D**
23:13 at harvest time and came to **D**
23:14 **D** was then in the stronghold,
23:15 And **D** said with longing, "Oh,
23:16 took it and brought it to **D**.
23:23 And **D** appointed him over his
24: 1 and He moved **D** against them to
24:10 So **D** said to the LORD,
24:11 Now when **D** arose in the morning,
24:12 "Go and tell **D**,
24:13 So Gad came to **D** and told him;
24:14 And **D** said to Gad, "I am in
24:17 Then **D** spoke to the LORD when
24:18 And Gad came that day to **D** and
24:19 So **D**, according to the word
24:21 And **D** said, "To buy the
24:22 Now Araunah said to **D**,
24:24 So **D** bought the threshing
24:25 And **D** built there an altar to
1 Ki 1: 1 Now King **D** was old, advanced in
1: 8 mighty men who belonged to **D**
1:11 and **D** our lord does not know
1:13 Go immediately to King **D** and say
1:28 Then King **D** answered and said,
1:31 Let my lord King **D** live
1:32 And King **D** said, "Call to me
1:37 the throne of my lord King **D**.
1:43 Our lord King **D** has made
1:47 gone to bless our lord King **D**,
2: 1 Now the days of **D** drew near that
2:10 So **D** rested with his fathers,
2:10 and was buried in the City of **D**.
2:11 The period that **D** reigned over
2:12 on the throne of his father **D**;
2:24 and set me on the throne of **D**
2:26 Lord GOD before my father **D**,
2:32 though my father **D** did not know
2:33 But upon **D** and his descendants,
2:44 that you did to my father **D**;
2:45 and the throne of **D** shall be
3: 1 he brought her to the City of **D**
3: 3 in the statutes of his father **D**,
3: 6 great mercy to Your servant **D**
3: 7 king instead of my father **D**,
3:14 as your father **D** walked, then I
5: 1 for Hiram had always loved **D**.
5: 3 You know how my father **D** could
5: 5 the LORD spoke to my father **D**,
5: 7 for He has given **D** a wise son
6:12 which I spoke to your father **D**.
7:51 the things which his father **D**
8: 1 of the LORD from the City of **D**,
8:15 with His mouth to my father **D**,
8:16 but I chose **D** to be over My
8:17 in the heart of my father **D** to
8:18 the LORD said to my father **D**,
8:20 the position of my father **D**,
8:24 You promised Your servant **D** my
8:25 You promised Your servant **D** my
8:26 have spoken to Your servant **D**
8:66 had done for His servant **D**,
9: 4 walk before Me as your father **D**
9: 5 as I promised **D** your father,
9:24 came up from the City of **D** to
11: 4 was the heart of his father **D**.
11: 6 the LORD, as did his father **D**.
11:12 for the sake of your father **D**;
11:13 for the sake of my servant **D**,
11:15 when **D** was in Edom, and Joab
11:21 Hadad heard in Egypt that **D**
11:24 when **D** killed those of Zobah.
11:27 the damages to the City of **D**
11:32 for the sake of My servant **D**,
11:33 judgments, as did his father **D**.
11:34 for the sake of My servant **D**,
11:36 that My servant **D** may always

11:38 as My servant **D** did, then I
11:38 house, as I built for **D**,
11:39 afflict the descendants of **D**
11:43 and was buried in the City of **D**
12:16 "What share have we in **D**?
12:16 your own house, O **D**!"
12:19 against the house of **D** to this
12:20 who followed the house of **D**,
12:26 may return to the house of **D**:
13: 2 shall be born to the house of **D**;
14: 8 away from the house of **D**,
14: 8 have not been as My servant **D**,
14:31 his fathers in the City of **D**.
15: 3 was the heart of his father **D**.
15: 5 because **D** did what was right
15: 8 buried him in the City of **D**.
15:11 the LORD, as did his father **D**.
15:24 his fathers in the City of **D**
22:50 his fathers in the City of **D**
2 Ki 8:19 for the sake of his servant **D**,
8:24 his fathers in the City of **D**.
9:28 his fathers in the City of **D**.
11:10 which had belonged to King **D**,
12:21 his fathers in the City of **D**.
14: 3 yet not like his father **D**;
14:20 his fathers in the City of **D**.
15: 7 his fathers in the City of **D**.
15:38 his fathers in the City of **D**
16: 2 as his father **D** had done.
16:20 his fathers in the City of **D**.
17:21 tore Israel from the house of **D**,
18: 3 to all that his father **D** had
20: 5 the God of **D** your father:
20: 6 for the sake of My servant **D**.
21: 7 which the LORD had said to **D**
22: 2 in all the ways of his father **D**;
1 Chr 2:15 and **D** the seventh.
3: 1 Now these were the sons of **D** who
3: 9 These were all the sons of **D**,
4:31 cities until the reign of **D**.
6:31 Now these are the men whom **D**
7: 2 their number in the days of **D**
9:22 **D** and Samuel the seer had
10:14 turned the kingdom over to **D**
11: 1 all Israel came together to **D**
11: 3 and **D** made a covenant with them
11: 3 Then they anointed **D** king over
11: 4 And **D** and all Israel went to
11: 5 inhabitants of Jebus said to **D**,
11: 5 Nevertheless **D** took the
11: 5 Zion (that is, the City of **D**).
11: 6 Now **D** said, "Whoever attacks
11: 7 Then **D** dwelt in the stronghold;
11: 7 they called it the City of **D**.
11: 9 Then **D** went on and became great,
11:10 heads of the mighty men whom **D**
11:11 of the mighty men whom **D** had:
11:13 He was with **D** at Pasdammim.
11:15 men went down to the rock to **D**,
11:16 **D** was then in the stronghold,
11:17 And **D** said with longing, "Oh,
11:18 took it and brought it to **D**.
11:18 Nevertheless **D** would not drink
11:25 And **D** appointed him over his
12: 1 were the men who came to **D** at
12: 8 Some Gadites joined **D** at the
12:16 of Benjamin and Judah came to **D**
12:17 And **D** went out to meet them, and
12:18 said: "We are yours, O **D**;
12:18 So **D** received them, and made
12:19 from Manasseh defected to **D**
12:21 And they helped **D** against the
12:22 at that time they came to **D**
12:23 and came to **D** at Hebron to
12:31 by name to come and make **D**
12:38 to make **D** king over all Israel;
12:38 were of one mind to make **D**
12:39 And they were there with **D** three
13: 1 Then **D** consulted with the
13: 2 And **D** said to all the assembly
13: 5 So **D** gathered all Israel
13: 6 And **D** and all Israel went up to
13: 8 Then **D** and all Israel played
13:11 And **D** became angry because of
13:12 **D** was afraid of God that day,
13:13 So **D** would not move the ark
13:13 ark with him into the City of **D**,
14: 1 of Tyre sent messengers to **D**,
14: 2 So **D** knew that the LORD had
14: 3 Then **D** took more wives in
14: 3 and **D** begot more sons and
14: 8 the Philistines heard that **D**
14: 8 went up to search for **D**.
14: 8 And **D** heard of it and went
14:10 And **D** inquired of God, saying,
14:11 and **D** defeated them there.
14:11 Then **D** said, "God has broken
14:12 **D** gave a commandment, and they
14:14 Therefore **D** inquired again of
14:16 So **D** did as God commanded him,
14:17 Then the fame of **D** went out into
15: 1 **D** built houses for himself in
15: 1 for himself in the City of **D**;
15: 2 Then **D** said, "No one may carry
15: 3 And **D** gathered all Israel
15: 4 Then **D** assembled the children of
15:11 And **D** called for Zadok and
15:16 Then **D** spoke to the leaders of
15:25 So **D**, the elders of Israel,
15:27 **D** was clothed with a robe of
15:27 **D** also wore a linen ephod.
15:29 the LORD came to the City of **D**,
15:29 through a window and saw King **D**
16: 1 midst of the tabernacle that **D**
16: 2 And when **D** had finished offering
16: 7 On that day **D** first delivered
16:43 and **D** returned to bless his
17: 1 when **D** was dwelling in his
17: 1 that **D** said to Nathan the
17: 2 Then Nathan said to **D**,
17: 4 "Go and tell My servant **D**,
17: 7 shall you say to My servant **D**,
17:15 vision, so Nathan spoke to **D**.
17:16 Then King **D** went in and sat
17:18 What more can **D** say to You for
17:24 the house of Your servant **D** be
18: 1 this it came to pass that **D**
18: 3 And **D** defeated Hadadezer king
18: 4 **D** took from him one thousand
18: 4 And **D** also hamstrung all the
18: 5 **D** killed twenty-two thousand of
18: 6 Then **D** put garrisons in Syria
18: 6 So the LORD preserved **D**
18: 7 And **D** took the shields of gold
18: 8 **D** brought a large amount of
18: 9 Tou king of Hamath heard that **D**
18:10 sent Hadoram his son to King **D**,
18:11 King **D** also dedicated these to
18:13 And the LORD preserved **D**
18:14 So **D** reigned over all Israel,
19: 2 Then **D** said, "I will show
19: 2 So **D** sent messengers to
19: 3 Do you think that **D** really
19: 5 Then some went and told **D** about
19: 6 made themselves repulsive to **D**,
19: 8 Now when **D** heard of it, he
19:17 When it was told **D**,
19:17 So when **D** had set up in battle
19:18 and **D** killed seven thousand
19:19 they made peace with **D** and
20: 1 But **D** stayed at Jerusalem.
20: 2 Then **D** took their king's crown
20: 3 So **D** did to all the cities of
20: 3 Then **D** and all the people
20: 8 and they fell by the hand of **D**
21: 1 and moved **D** to number Israel.
21: 2 So **D** said to Joab and to the
21: 5 the number of the people to **D**.
21: 8 So **D** said to God, "I have
21:10 "Go and tell **D**,
21:11 So Gad came to **D** and said to
21:13 And **D** said to Gad, "I am in
21:16 Then **D** lifted his eyes and saw
21:16 So **D** and the elders, clothed in
21:17 And **D** said to God, "Was it not
21:18 commanded Gad to say to **D** that
21:18 Gad to say to David that **D**
21:19 So **D** went up at the word of Gad,
21:21 Then **D** came to Ornan, and Ornan
21:21 and Ornan looked and saw **D**.
21:21 and bowed before **D** with his
21:22 Then **D** said to Ornan, "Grant me
21:23 And Ornan said to **D**,
21:24 Then King **D** said to Ornan,
21:25 So **D** gave Ornan six hundred
21:26 And **D** built there an altar to
21:28 when **D** saw that the LORD had
21:30 But **D** could not go before it to
22: 1 Then **D** said, "This is the
22: 2 So **D** commanded to gather the
22: 3 And **D** prepared iron in abundance
22: 4 brought much cedar wood to **D**.
22: 5 Now **D** said, "Solomon my son is
22: 5 So **D** made abundant
22: 7 And **D** said to Solomon: "My son,
22:17 **D** also commanded all the
23: 1 So when **D** was old and full of
23: 5 "which I made," said **D**,
23: 6 Also **D** separated them into
23:25 For **D** said, "The LORD God of
23:27 For by the last words of **D** the
24: 3 Then **D** with Zadok of the sons of
24:31 did, in the presence of King **D**,
25: 1 Moreover **D** and the captains of
26:26 dedicated things which King **D**
26:31 year of the reign of **D** they
26:32 whom King **D** made officials over
27:23 But **D** did not take the number
27:24 of the chronicles of King **D**.
28: 1 Now **D** assembled at Jerusalem all
28: 2 Then King **D** rose to his feet and
28:11 Then **D** gave his son Solomon the
28:19 "All this," said **D**,
28:20 And **D** said to his son Solomon,
29: 1 Furthermore King **D** said to all
29: 9 and King **D** also rejoiced
29:10 Therefore **D** blessed the LORD
29:10 and **D** said: "Blessed are
29:20 Then **D** said to all the assembly,
29:22 they made Solomon the son of **D**
29:23 the LORD as king instead of **D**
29:24 and also all the sons of King **D**,
29:26 Thus **D** the son of Jesse reigned
29:29 Now the acts of King **D**,
2 Chr 1: 1 Now Solomon the son of **D** was
1: 4 But **D** had brought up the ark of
1: 4 Jearim to the place **D** had
1: 8 have shown great mercy to **D** my
1: 9 let Your promise to **D** my father
2: 3 As you have dealt with **D** my
2: 7 whom **D** my father provided.
2:12 for He has given King **D** a wise
2:14 the skillful men of my lord **D**
2:17 after the census in which **D** his
3: 1 had appeared to his father **D**,
3: 1 at the place that **D** had
5: 1 the things which his father **D**
5: 2 the LORD up from the City of **D**,
6: 4 with His mouth to my father **D**,
6: 6 and I have chosen **D** to be over
6: 7 in the heart of my father **D** to
6: 8 the LORD said to my father **D**,
6:10 the position of my father **D**,
6:15 You promised Your servant **D** my
6:16 You promised Your servant **D** my
6:17 have spoken to Your servant **D**.
6:42 the mercies of Your servant **D**.
7: 6 which King **D** had made to praise
7: 6 whenever **D** offered praise by
7:10 that the LORD had done for **D**,
7:17 walk before Me as your father **D**
7:18 as I covenanted with **D** your
8:11 Pharaoh up from the City of **D**
8:11 not dwell in the house of **D**
8:14 according to the order of **D** his
8:14 for so **D** the man of God had
9:31 and was buried in the City of **D**
10:16 "What share have we in **D**?
10:16 your own house, O **D**!"
10:19 against the house of **D** to this
11:17 they walked in the way of **D**
11:18 of Jerimoth the son of **D**,
12:16 and was buried in the City of **D**.
13: 5 the dominion over Israel to **D**
13: 6 servant of Solomon the son of **D**,
13: 8 is in the hand of the sons of **D**;
14: 1 buried him in the City of **D**.
16:14 for himself in the City of **D**;
17: 3 the former ways of his father **D**;
21: 1 his fathers in the City of **D**.
21: 7 not destroy the house of **D**,
21: 7 that He had made with **D**,
21:12 the LORD God of your father **D**:
21:20 buried him in the City of **D**,
23: 3 LORD has said of the sons of **D**.
23: 9 which had belonged to King **D**,
23:18 whom **D** had assigned in the
23:18 as it was established by **D**.
24:16 buried him in the City of **D**
24:25 buried him in the City of **D**,
27: 9 buried him in the City of **D**.
28: 1 as his father **D** had done.
29: 2 to all that his father **D** had
29:25 to the commandment of **D**,
29:26 stood with the instruments of **D**,
29:27 and with the instruments of **D**
29:30 the LORD with the words of **D**
30:26 time of Solomon the son of **D**,
32: 5 the Millo in the City of **D**,
32:30 the west side of the City of **D**.
32:33 upper tombs of the sons of **D**;
33: 7 of which God had said to **D** and
33:14 a wall outside the City of **D**
34: 2 in the ways of his father **D**;
34: 3 to seek the God of his father **D**;
35: 3 which Solomon the son of **D**,
35: 4 the written instruction of **D**
35:15 according to the command of **D**,
Ezra 3:10 to the ordinance of **D** king of
8: 2 Daniel; of the sons of **D**,
8:20 whom **D** and the leaders had
Neh 3:15 that go down from the City of **D**.
3:16 in front of the tombs of **D**,
12:24 according to the command of **D**
12:36 the musical instruments of **D**
12:37 up the stairs of the City of **D**,
12:37 the wall, beyond the house of **D**,
12:45 according to the command of **D**
12:46 For in the days of **D** and Asaph
Ps 3: A Psalm of **D** when he fled from
4: A Psalm of **D**.
5: With flutes. A Psalm of **D**.
6: A Psalm of **D**.
7: A Meditation of **D**,
8: of Gath. A Psalm of **D**.
9: of the Son." A Psalm of **D**.
11: Chief Musician. A Psalm of **D**.
12: A Psalm of **D**.
13: Chief Musician. A Psalm of **D**.
14: Chief Musician. A Psalm of **D**.
15: A Psalm of **D**.
16: A Michtam of **D**.
17: A Prayer of **D**.
18: A Psalm of **D** the servant of the
18:50 To **D** and his descendants
19: Chief Musician. A Psalm of **D**.
20: Chief Musician. A Psalm of **D**.
21: Chief Musician. A Psalm of **D**.
22: of the Dawn." A Psalm of **D**.
23: A Psalm of **D**.
24: A Psalm of **D**.
25: A Psalm of **D**.
26: A Psalm of **D**.
27: A Psalm of **D**.
28: A Psalm of **D**.
29: A Psalm of **D**.
30: dedication of the house of **D**.
31: Chief Musician. A Psalm of **D**.
32: A Psalm of **D**.
34: A Psalm of **D** when he pretended
35: A Psalm of **D**.
36: A Psalm of **D** the servant of the
37: A Psalm of **D**.
38: A Psalm of **D**.
39: To Jeduthun. A Psalm of **D**.
40: Chief Musician. A Psalm of **D**.

41: Chief Musician. A Psalm of **D**.
51: A Psalm of **D** when Nathan the
52: A Contemplation of **D** when Doeg
52: **D** has gone to the house of
53: A Contemplation of **D**.
54: A Contemplation of **D** when the
54: Is **D** not hiding with us?"
55: A Contemplation of **D**.
56: A Michtam of **D** when the
57: A Michtam of **D** when he fled
58: Not Destroy." A Michtam of **D**.
59: A Michtam of **D** when Saul sent
60: the Testimony." A Michtam of **D**.
61: A Psalm of **D**.
62: To Jeduthun. A Psalm of **D**.
63: A Psalm of **D** when he was in the
64: Chief Musician. A Psalm of **D**.
65: Chief Musician. A Psalm of **D**.
68: Chief Musician. A Psalm of **D**.
69: to "The Lilies." A Psalm of **D**.
70: Chief Musician. A Psalm of **D**.
72:20 The prayers of **D** the son of
78:70 He also chose **D** His servant,
86: A Prayer of **D**
89: 3 I have sworn to My servant **D**:
89:20 I have found My servant **D**;
89:35 holiness; I will not lie to **D**:
89:49 Which You swore to **D** in Your
101: A Psalm of **D**.
103: A Psalm of **D**.
108: A Song. A Psalm of **D**.
109: Chief Musician. A Psalm of **D**.
110: A Psalm of **D**.
122: A Song of Ascents. Of **D**.
122: 5 The thrones of the house of **D**.
124: A Song of Ascents. Of **D**.
131: A Song of Ascents. Of **D**.
132: 1 remember **D** And all his
132:11 LORD has sworn in truth to **D**;
132:17 I will make the horn of **D** grow;
133: A Song of Ascents. Of **D**.
138: A Psalm of **D**.
139: Chief Musician. A Psalm of **D**.
140: Chief Musician. A Psalm of **D**.
141: A Psalm of **D**.
142: A Contemplation of **D**.
143: A Psalm of **D**.
144: A Psalm of **D**.
144:10 Who delivers **D** His servant
Prov 1: 1 of Solomon the son of **D**,
Eccl 1: 1 of the Preacher, the son of **D**,
Song 4: 4 neck is like the tower of **D**,
Isa 7: 2 it was told to the house of **D**,
7:13 O house of **D**! Is it a small
9: 7 Upon the throne of **D** and over
16: 5 truth, in the tabernacle of **D**,
22: 9 saw the damage to the city of **D**,
22:22 The key of the house of **D** I
29: 1 the city where **D** dwelt!
38: 5 the God of **D** your father:
55: 3 with you—The sure mercies of **D**.
Jer 17:25 sitting on the throne of **D**,
21:12 O house of **D**! Thus says the
22: 2 you who sit on the throne of **D**,
22: 4 who sit on the throne of **D**.
22:30 Sitting on the throne of **D**,
23: 5 That I will raise to **D** a Branch
29:16 who sits on the throne of **D**,
30: 9 And **D** their king, Whom I will
33:15 I will cause to grow up to **D**
33:17 **D** shall never lack a man to sit
33:21 may also be broken with **D** My
33:22 I multiply the descendants of **D**
33:26 the descendants of Jacob and **D**
36:30 one to sit on the throne of **D**,
Ezek 34:23 he shall feed them—My servant **D**.
34:24 and My servant **D** a prince among
37:24 **D** My servant shall be king
37:25 and My servant **D** shall be
Hos 3: 5 seek the LORD their God and **D**
Am 6: 5 musical instruments like **D**;
9:11 raise up The tabernacle of **D**,
Zech 12: 7 the glory of the house of **D**
12: 8 in that day shall be like **D**,
12: 8 and the house of **D** shall be
12:10 I will pour on the house of **D**
12:12 the family of the house of **D** by
13: 1 be opened for the house of **D**
Mt 1: 1 of Jesus Christ, the Son of **D**,
1: 6 and Jesse begot **D** the king.
1: 6 **D** the king begot Solomon by
1:17 generations from Abraham to **D**
1:17 from **D** until the captivity in
1:20 saying, "Joseph, son of **D**,
9:27 out and saying, "Son of **D**,
12: 3 Have you not read what **D** did
12:23 "Could this be the Son of **D**?
15:22 Son of **D**! My daughter is
20:30 on us, O Lord, Son of **D**!"
20:31 on us, O Lord, Son of **D**!"
21: 9 Hosanna to the Son of **D**!
21:15 Hosanna to the Son of **D**!" they
22:42 said to Him, "The Son of **D**.
22:43 How then does **D** in the Spirit
22:45 If **D** then calls Him 'Lord,' how
Mk 2:25 Have you never read what **D** did
10:47 out and say, "Jesus, Son of **D**,
10:48 out all the more, "Son of **D**,
11:10 is the kingdom of our father **D**
12:35 that the Christ is the Son of **D**?
12:36 For **D** himself said by the Holy
12:37 Therefore **D** himself calls Him
Lk 1:27 was Joseph, of the house of **D**.
1:32 Him the throne of His father **D**.
1:69 In the house of His servant **D**,
2: 4 into Judea, to the city of **D**,
2: 4 of the house and lineage of **D**,
2:11 you this day in the city of **D**
3:31 son of Nathan, the son of **D**,
6: 3 what **D** did when he was hungry,
18:38 saying, "Jesus, Son of **D**,
18:39 out all the more, "Son of **D**,
20:41 that the Christ is the Son of **D**?
20:42 Now **D** himself said in the Book
20:44 Therefore **D** calls Him 'Lord';
Jn 7:42 comes from the seed of **D** and
7:42 Bethlehem, where **D** was?"
Acts 1:16 spoke before by the mouth of **D**
2:25 'For **D** says concerning Him:
2:29 to you of the patriarch **D**,
2:34 For **D** did not ascend into the
4:25 by the mouth of Your servant **D**
7:45 our fathers until the days of **D**,
13:22 He raised up for them **D** as
13:22 I have found **D** the son of
13:34 you the sure mercies of **D**.
13:36 'For **D**, after he had served
15:16 the tabernacle of **D**,
Rom 1: 3 who was born of the seed of **D**
4: 6 just as **D** also describes the
11: 9 And **D** says: "Let their
2 Tim 2: 8 Jesus Christ, of the seed of **D**,
Heb 4: 7 a certain day, saying in **D**,
11:32 also of **D** and Samuel and the
Rev 3: 7 who has the key of **D**,
5: 5 tribe of Judah, the Root of **D**,
22:16 the Root and the Offspring of **D**,

DAVID'S (54/53) DAVID

1 Sam 18:29 So Saul became **D** enemy
19:11 sent messengers to **D** house
19:11 **D** wife, told him, saying, "If
20:16 it at the hand of **D** enemies.
20:25 but **D** place was empty.
20:27 that **D** place was empty. And
23: 3 But **D** men said to him, "Look,
24: 5 happened afterward that **D** heart
25: 9 So when **D** young men came, they
25:10 Then Nabal answered **D** servants,
25:12 So **D** young men turned on their
25:44 **D** wife, to Palti the son of
26:17 Then Saul knew **D** voice, and
30: 5 And **D** two wives, Ahinoam the
30:20 This is **D** spoil."
2 Sam 2:30 were missing of **D** servants
3: 5 by **D** wife Eglah. These were
3:26 Joab had gone from **D** presence,
5: 8 who are hated by **D** soul), he
8: 2 Moabites became **D** servants,
8: 6 and the Syrians became **D**
8:14 Edomites became **D** servants.
8:18 and **D** sons were chief
10: 2 And **D** servants came into the
10: 4 Therefore Hanun took **D** servants,
12: 5 So **D** anger was greatly aroused
12:30 And it was set on **D** head.
13: 3 **D** brother. Now Jonadab was a
13:32 **D** brother, answered and said,
15:12 **D** counselor, from his city—from
15:37 **D** friend, went into the city.
16:16 **D** friend, came to Absalom, that
19:41 and all **D** men with him across
21:21 **D** brother, killed him.
24:10 And **D** heart condemned him after
24:11 prophet Gad, **D** seer, saying,
1 Ki 1:38 Solomon ride on King **D** mule,
15: 4 Nevertheless for **D** sake the
2 Ki 19:34 own sake and for My servant **D**
1 Chr 18: 2 Moabites became **D** servants,
18: 6 and the Syrians became **D**
18:13 Edomites became **D** servants.
18:17 and **D** sons were chief
19: 2 And **D** servants came to Hanun in
19: 4 Therefore Hanun took **D** servants,
20: 2 And it was set on **D** head.
20: 7 **D** brother, killed him.
21: 9 Gad, **D** seer, saying,
27:18 one of **D** brothers; over
27:31 officials over King **D** property.
27:32 **D** uncle, was a counselor, a
Ps 132:10 For Your servant **D** sake, Do
Isa 37:35 own sake and for My servant **D**
Jer 13:13 kings who sit on **D** throne,

DAWN (10/10) DAWNED, DAWNING, DAWNS

Job 7: 4 had my fill of tossing till **d**.
38:12 And caused the **d** to know its
Ps 22: Set to "The Deer of the **D**.
46: 5 her, just at the break of **d**.
57: 8 and harp! I will awaken the **d**.
108: 2 and harp! I will awaken the **d**.
Isa 58:10 Then your light shall **d** in the
Hos 10:15 At **d** the king of Israel Shall
Mt 28: 1 day of the week began to **d**,
Acts 27:33 And as day was about to **d**,

DAWNED (6/6) DAWN

Gen 19:15 When the morning **d**,
44: 3 As soon as the morning **d**,
Deut 33: 2 And **d** on them from Seir;
Ezek 7: 6 It has **d** for you; Behold, it
Jon 4: 7 But as morning **d** the next day
Mt 4:16 of death Light has **d**.

DAWNING (6/6) DAWN

Josh 6:15 about the **d** of the day, and
Judg 19:26 the woman came as the day was **d**,
1 Sam 9:26 and it was about the **d** of the
Job 3: 9 And not see the **d** of the day;
Ps 119:147 I rise before the **d** of the
Isa 24:15 glorify the LORD in the **d**

DAWNS (1/1) DAWN

2 Pe 1:19 until the day **d** and the morning

DAY (1563/1390) DAYBREAK, DAYLIGHT, DAY'S, DAYS, DAYSPRING, DAYTIME

Gen 1: 5 God called the light **D**,
1: 5 the morning were the first **d**.
1: 8 the morning were the second **d**.
1:13 the morning were the third **d**.
1:14 of the heavens to divide the **d**
1:16 the greater light to rule the **d**,
1:18 and to rule over the **d** and over
1:19 the morning were the fourth **d**.
1:23 the morning were the fifth **d**.
1:31 the morning were the sixth **d**.
2: 2 And on the seventh **d** God ended
2: 2 and He rested on the seventh **d**
2: 3 Then God blessed the seventh **d**
2: 4 in the **d** that the LORD God
2:17 for in the **d** that you eat of it
3: 5 For God knows that in the **d** you
3: 8 the garden in the cool of the **d**,
4:14 You have driven me out this **d**
5: 1 In the **d** that God created man,
5: 2 called them Mankind in the **d**
7:11 the seventeenth **d** of the month,
7:11 on that **d** all the fountains of
7:13 On the very same **d** Noah and
8: 4 the seventeenth **d** of the month,
8: 5 on the first **d** of the month,
8:13 the first **d** of the month, that
8:14 on the twenty-seventh **d** of the
8:22 And **d** and night Shall not
15:18 On the same **d** the LORD made a
17:23 foreskins that very same **d**,
17:26 That very same **d** Abraham was
18: 1 tent door in the heat of the **d**.
19:34 It happened on the next **d** that
19:37 of the Moabites to this **d**.
19:38 the people of Ammon to this **d**.
21: 8 a great feast on the same **d**
22: 4 Then on the third **d** Abraham
22:14 as it is said to this **d**,
24:12 please give me success this **d**,
24:42 And this **d** I came to the well
25:31 me your birthright as of this **d**.
25:33 "Swear to me as of this **d**.
26:32 It came to pass the same **d** that
26:33 city is Beersheba to this **d**.
27: 2 I do not know the **d** of my
27:45 also of you both in one **d**?
29: 7 "Look, it is still high **d**;
30:35 So he removed that **d** the male
31:22 Laban was told on the third **d**
31:39 whether stolen by **d** or stolen
31:40 There I was! In the **d** the
31:43 But what can I do this **d** to
31:48 between you and me this **d**.
32:24 him until the breaking of **d**.
32:26 for the **d** breaks." But he
32:32 Therefore to this **d** the children
33:13 should drive them hard one **d**,
33:16 So Esau returned that **d** on his
34:25 it came to pass on the third **d**,
35: 3 who answered me in the **d** of my
35:20 of Rachel's grave to this **d**.
39:10 as she spoke to Joseph **d** by
39:10 as she spoke to Joseph day by **d**,
40:20 it came to pass on the third **d**,
41: 9 "I remember my faults this **d**.
42:18 Joseph said to them the third **d**,
42:32 is with our father this **d** in
47:23 you and your land this **d** for
47:26 the land of Egypt to this **d**,
48:15 me all my life long to this **d**,
48:20 So he blessed them that **d**,
50:20 it about as it is this **d**,
Ex 2:13 when he went out the second **d**,
5: 6 So the same **d** Pharaoh commanded
6:28 on the **d** the LORD spoke to
8:22 And in that **d** I will set apart
9: 6 did this thing on the next **d**,
10: 6 since the **d** that they were on
10: 6 were on the earth to this **d**.
10:13 wind on the land all that **d**
10:28 my face no more! For in the **d**
12: 3 On the tenth **d** of this month
12: 6 keep it until the fourteenth **d**
12:14 So this **d** shall be to you a
12:15 On the first **d** you shall remove
12:15 bread from the first **d** until
12:15 first day until the seventh **d**,
12:16 On the first **d** there shall be
12:16 and on the seventh **d** there
12:17 for on this same **d** I will have
12:17 you shall observe this **d**

12:18 on the fourteenth **d** of the
12:18 until the twenty-first **d** of the
12:41 years—on that very same **d**—
12:51 to pass, on that very same **d**,
13: 3 Remember this **d** in which you
13: 4 On this **d** you are going out, in
13: 6 and on the seventh **d** there
13: 8 shall tell your son in that **d**,
13:21 LORD went before them by **d** in
13:21 so as to go by **d** and night.
13:22 away the pillar of cloud by **d**
14:30 the LORD saved Israel that **d**
16: 1 on the fifteenth **d** of the
16: 4 gather a certain quota every **d**,
16: 5 it shall be on the sixth **d**
16:22 And so it was, on the sixth **d**,
16:26 gather it, but on the seventh **d**,
16:27 went out on the seventh **d** to
16:29 He gives you on the sixth **d**
16:29 of his place on the seventh **d**.
16:30 people rested on the seventh **d**.
18:13 And so it was, on the next **d**,
19: 1 land of Egypt, on the same **d**,
19:11 them be ready for the third **d**.
19:11 For on the third **d** the LORD
19:15 "Be ready for the third **d**;
19:16 it came to pass on the third **d**,
20: 8 "Remember the Sabbath **d**,
20:10 but the seventh **d** is the
20:11 them, and rested the seventh **d**.
20:11 the LORD blessed the Sabbath **d**
21:21 if he remains alive a **d** or two,
22:30 on the eighth **d** you shall give
23:12 and on the seventh **d** you shall
24:16 And on the seventh **d** He called
29:36 you shall offer a bull every **d**
29:38 **d** by day continually.
29:38 day by **d** continually.
31:15 does any work on the Sabbath **d**,
31:17 and on the seventh **d** He rested
32: 6 they rose early on the next **d**,
32:28 men of the people fell that **d**.
32:29 bestow on you a blessing this **d**,
32:30 it came to pass on the next **d**
32:34 in the **d** when I visit for
34:11 what I command you this **d**.
34:21 but on the seventh **d** you shall
35: 2 but the seventh **d** shall be a
35: 2 seventh day shall be a holy **d**
35: 3 your dwellings on the Sabbath **d**.
40: 2 On the first **d** of the first
40:17 on the first **d** of the month,
40:37 they did not journey till the **d**
40:38 was above the tabernacle by **d**,
Lev 6: 5 on the **d** of his trespass
6:20 beginning on the **d** when he is
7:15 shall be eaten the same **d** it
7:16 it shall be eaten the same **d**
7:16 but on the next **d** the remainder
7:17 of the sacrifice on the third **d**
7:18 is eaten at all on the third **d**,
7:35 on the **d** when Moses presented
7:36 on the **d** that He anointed them,
7:38 on the **d** when He commanded the
8:34 "As he has done this **d**,
8:35 of the tabernacle of meeting **d**
9: 1 It came to pass on the eighth **d**
10:19 this **d** they have offered their
12: 3 And on the eighth **d** the flesh of
13: 5 examine him on the seventh **d**;
13: 6 him again on the seventh **d**;
13:27 examine him on the seventh **d**.
13:32 And on the seventh **d** the priest
13:34 On the seventh **d** the priest
13:51 the plague on the seventh **d**.
14: 2 the law of the leper for the **d**
14: 9 But on the seventh **d** he shall
14:10 And on the eighth **d** he shall
14:23 to the priest on the eighth **d**
14:39 come again on the seventh **d**
15:14 On the eighth **d** he shall take
15:29 And on the eighth **d** she shall
16:29 on the tenth **d** of the month,
16:30 For on that **d** the priest shall
19: 6 It shall be eaten the same **d** you
19: 6 offer it, and on the next **d**.
19: 6 any remains until the third **d**,
19: 7 is eaten at all on the third **d**,
22:27 and from the eighth **d** and
22:28 her and her young on the same **d**.
22:30 On the same **d** it shall be eaten;
23: 3 but the seventh **d** is a Sabbath
23: 5 On the fourteenth **d** of the
23: 6 And on the fifteenth **d** of the
23: 7 On the first **d** you shall have a
23: 8 The seventh **d** shall be a holy
23:11 on the **d** after the Sabbath the
23:12 'And you shall offer on that **d**,
23:14 fresh grain until the same **d**
23:15 count for yourselves from the **d**
23:15 from the **d** that you brought the
23:16 Count fifty days to the **d** after
23:21 shall proclaim on the same **d**
23:24 on the first **d** of the month,
23:27 Also the tenth **d** of this
23:27 seventh month shall be the ***D***
23:28 shall do no work on that same **d**,
23:28 for it is the ***D*** of Atonement,
23:29 in soul on that same **d** shall
23:30 does any work on that same **d**,
23:32 on the ninth **d** of the month at
23:34 The fifteenth **d** of this seventh
23:35 On the first **d** there shall be
23:36 On the eighth **d** you shall have
23:37 offerings, everything on its **d**—
23:39 Also on the fifteenth **d** of the
23:39 on the first **d** there shall
23:39 and on the eighth **d** a
23:40 for yourselves on the first **d**
25: 9 to sound on the tenth **d** of
25: 9 on the ***D*** of Atonement you shall
27:23 give your valuation on that **d**
Num 1: 1 on the first **d** of the second
1:18 together on the first **d** of
3:13 On the **d** that I struck all the
6: 9 shall shave his head on the **d**
6: 9 on the seventh **d** he shall shave
6:10 Then on the eighth **d** he shall
6:11 sanctify his head that same **d**.
7:11 offering, one leader each **d**,
7:12 his offering on the first **d**
7:18 On the second **d** Nethanel the
7:24 On the third **d** Eliab the son of
7:30 On the fourth **d** Elizur the son
7:36 On the fifth **d** Shelumiel the
7:42 On the sixth **d** Eliasaph the son
7:48 On the seventh **d** Elishama the
7:54 On the eighth **d** Gamaliel the
7:60 On the ninth **d** Abidan the son
7:66 On the tenth **d** Ahiezer the son
7:72 On the eleventh **d** Pagiel the
7:78 On the twelfth **d** Ahira the son
8:17 on the **d** that I struck all the
9: 3 On the fourteenth **d** of this
9: 5 Passover on the fourteenth **d**
9: 6 not keep the Passover on that **d**;
9: 6 before Moses and Aaron that **d**.
9:11 On the fourteenth **d** of the
9:15 Now on the **d** that the
9:16 the cloud covered it by **d**,
9:21 whether by **d** or by night,
10:10 Also in the **d** of your gladness,
10:11 to pass on the twentieth **d** of
10:34 the LORD was above them by **d**
11:19 'You shall eat, not one **d**,
11:32 the people stayed up all that **d**,
11:32 all night, and all the next **d**,
14:14 them in a pillar of cloud by **d**
14:34 for each **d** you shall bear your
15:23 from the **d** the LORD gave
15:32 sticks on the Sabbath **d**.
16:41 On the next **d** all the
17: 8 it came to pass on the next **d**
19:12 with the water on the third **d**
19:12 third day and on the seventh **d**;
19:12 purify himself on the third **d**
19:12 third day and on the seventh **d**,
19:19 the unclean on the third **d** and
19:19 third day and on the seventh **d**;
19:19 and on the seventh **d** he shall
22:30 I became yours, to this **d**?
22:41 So it was the next **d**,
25:18 who was killed in the **d** of the
28: 3 **d** by day, as a regular burnt
28: 3 year without blemish, day by **d**,
28: 9 And on the Sabbath **d** two lambs
28:16 On the fourteenth **d** of the
28:17 And on the fifteenth **d** of this
28:18 On the first **d** you shall have
28:25 And on the seventh **d** you shall
28:26 Also on the **d** of the
29: 1 on the first **d** of the month,
29: 1 For you it is a **d** of blowing
29: 7 On the tenth **d** of this seventh
29:12 On the fifteenth **d** of the
29:17 On the second **d** present twelve
29:20 On the third **d** present eleven
29:23 On the fourth **d** present ten
29:26 On the fifth **d** present nine
29:29 On the sixth **d** present eight
29:32 On the seventh **d** present seven
29:35 On the eighth **d** you shall have
30: 5 father overrules her on the **d**
30: 7 no response to her on the **d**
30: 8 husband overrules her on the **d**
30:12 truly made them void on the **d**
30:14 whatever to her from **d** to day,
30:14 whatever to her from day to **d**,
30:14 no response to her on the **d**
31:19 your captives on the third **d**
31:19 third day and on the seventh **d**.
31:24 your clothes on the seventh **d**
32:10 anger was aroused on that **d**,
33: 3 on the fifteenth **d** of the first
33: 3 on the **d** after the Passover the
33:38 on the first **d** of the fifth
Deut 1: 3 on the first **d** of the month,
1:33 by night and in the cloud by **d**.
2:18 This **d** you are to cross over at
2:22 in their place, even to this **d**.
2:25 This **d** I will begin to put the
2:30 your hand, as it is this **d**.
3:14 name, Havoth Jair, to this **d**.
4: 8 which I set before you this **d**?
4:10 especially concerning the **d**
4:20 inheritance, as you are this **d**.
4:26 to witness against you this **d**,
4:32 since the **d** that God created
4:38 inheritance, as it is this **d**.
4:39 "Therefore know this **d**,
5:12 'Observe the Sabbath **d**,
5:14 but the seventh **d** is the
5:15 you to keep the Sabbath **d**.
5:24 We have seen this **d** that God
6:24 us alive, as it is this **d**.
8:18 your fathers, as it is this **d**.
8:19 I testify against you this **d**
9: 7 From the **d** that you departed
9:10 the midst of the fire in the **d**
9:24 against the LORD from the **d**
10: 4 the midst of the fire in the **d**
10: 8 to bless in His name, to this **d**.
10:15 all peoples, as it is this **d**.
11: 4 has destroyed them to this **d**;
16: 3 that you may remember the **d** in
16: 4 you sacrifice the first **d** at
16: 8 and on the seventh **d** there
18:16 your God in Horeb in the **d** of
21:16 on the **d** he bequeaths his
21:23 shall surely bury him that **d**,
24:15 Each **d** you shall give him his
26:16 This **d** the LORD your God
27: 2 on the **d** when you cross over
27: 9 This **d** you have become the
27:11 the people on the same **d**,
28:14 which I command you this **d**,
28:32 with longing for them all **d**
28:66 you shall fear **d** and night, and
29: 4 ears to hear, to this very **d**.
29:28 another land, as it is this **d**.
31:17 aroused against them in that **d**,
31:17 so that they will say in that **d**,
31:18 surely hide My face in that **d**
31:22 wrote this song the same **d**,
32:35 For the **d** of their calamity
32:48 spoke to Moses that very same **d**,
33:12 Who shelters him all the **d**
34: 6 one knows his grave to this **d**.
Josh 1: 8 but you shall meditate in it **d**
3: 7 This **d** I will begin to exalt you
4: 9 and they are there to this **d**.
4:14 On that **d** the LORD exalted
4:19 the Jordan on the tenth **d** of
5: 9 This **d** I have rolled away the
5: 9 is called Gilgal to this **d**.
5:10 Passover on the fourteenth **d**
5:11 produce of the land on the **d**
5:11 grain, on the very same **d**.
5:12 Then the manna ceased on the **d**
6: 4 But the seventh **d** you shall
6:10 until the **d** I say to you,
6:14 And the second **d** they marched
6:15 came to pass on the seventh **d**
6:15 about the dawning of the **d**,
6:15 On that **d** only they marched
6:25 she dwells in Israel to this **d**,
7:25 LORD will trouble you this **d**.
7:26 stones, still there to this **d**.
7:26 the Valley of Achor to this **d**.
8:25 was that all who fell that **d**,
8:28 forever, a desolation to this **d**.
8:29 stones that remains to this **d**.
9:12 from our houses on the **d** we
9:17 to their cities on the third **d**.
9:27 And that **d** Joshua made them
9:27 He would choose, even to this **d**.
10:12 spoke to the LORD in the **d**
10:13 to go down for about a whole **d**.
10:14 And there has been no **d** like
10:27 remain until this very **d**.
10:28 On that **d** Joshua took Makkedah,
10:32 who took it on the second **d**,
10:35 They took it on that **d** and
10:35 it he utterly destroyed that **d**,
13:13 the Israelites until this **d**.
14: 9 "So Moses swore on that **d**,
14:10 and now, here I am this **d**,
14:11 yet I am as strong this **d**
14:11 as strong this day as on the **d**
14:12 which the LORD spoke in that **d**;
14:12 for you heard in that **d** how the
14:14 the Kenizzite to this **d**,
15:63 of Judah at Jerusalem to this **d**.
16:10 the Ephraimites to this **d** and
22: 3 these many days, up to this **d**,
22:16 to turn away this **d** from
22:16 that you might rebel this **d**
22:17 are not cleansed until this **d**,
22:18 that you must turn away this **d**
22:22 LORD, do not save us this **d**.
22:29 from following the LORD this **d**,
22:31 This **d** we perceive that the
23: 8 God, as you have done to this **d**.
23: 9 to stand against you to this **d**.
23:14 this **d** I am going the way of
24:15 choose for yourselves this **d**
24:25 covenant with the people that **d**,
Judg 1:21 Benjamin in Jerusalem to this **d**.
1:26 which is its name to this **d**.
3:30 So Moab was subdued that **d** under
4:14 For this is the **d** in which
4:23 So on that **d** God subdued Jabin
5: 1 son of Abinoam sang on that **d**,
6:24 To this **d** it is still in
6:27 city too much to do it by **d**,
6:32 Therefore on that **d** he called
9:18 my father's house this **d**,
9:19 and with his house this **d**,
9:42 it came about on the next **d**
9:45 against the city all that **d**;
10: 4 "Havoth Jair" to this **d**,
10:15 to You; only deliver us this **d**,
11:27 render judgment this **d** between
12: 3 have you come up to me this **d**
13: 7 to God from the womb to the **d**
13:10 Man who came to me the other **d**

14:15 came to pass on the seventh **d**
14:17 it happened on the seventh **d**
14:18 said to him on the seventh **d**
15:19 which is in Lehi to this **d**.
18: 1 for until that **d** their
18:12 place Mahaneh Dan to this **d**.
18:30 to the tribe of Dan until the **d**
19: 5 it came to pass on the fourth **d**
19: 8 in the morning on the fifth **d**
19: 9 the **d** is now drawing toward
19: 9 the **d** is coming to an end;
19:11 and the **d** was far spent; and
19:25 and when the **d** began to break,
19:26 Then the woman came as the **d** was
19:30 been done or seen from the **d**
19:30 the land of Egypt until this **d**.
20:21 and on that **d** cut down to the
20:22 in array on the first **d**.
20:24 of Benjamin on the second **d**.
20:25 from Gibeah on the second **d**,
20:26 the LORD and fasted that **d**
20:30 of Benjamin on the third **d**,
20:35 of Israel destroyed that **d**
20:46 all who fell of Benjamin that **d**
Ruth 3:18 has concluded the matter this **d**.
4: 5 On the **d** you buy the field from
4: 9 You are witnesses this **d** that I
4:10 You are witnesses this **d**."
4:14 who has not left you this **d**
1 Sam 2:34 in one **d** they shall die, both
3:12 In that **d** I will perform against
4:12 from the battle line the same **d**,
5: 5 of Dagon in Ashdod to this **d**.
6:15 and made sacrifices the same **d**
6:16 returned to Ekron the same **d**.
6:18 stone remains to this **d** in
7: 6 And they fasted that **d**,
7:10 upon the Philistines that **d**,
8: 8 they have done since the **d**
8: 8 up out of Egypt, even to this **d**—
8:18 you will cry out in that **d**
8:18 will not hear you in that **d**.
9:15 told Samuel in his ear the **d**
9:24 So Saul ate with Samuel that **d**.
9:26 was about the dawning of the **d**
10: 9 those signs came to pass that **d**.
11:11 So it was, on the next **d**,
11:11 until the heat of the **d**.
11:13 shall be put to death this **d**,
12: 2 you from my childhood to this **d**.
12: 5 His anointed is witness this **d**,
12:18 sent thunder and rain that **d**;
13:22 on the **d** of battle, that there
14: 1 Now it happened one **d** that
14:23 the LORD saved Israel that **d**,
14:24 Israel were distressed that **d**,
14:28 the man who eats food this **d**.
14:31 back the Philistines that **d**
14:33 roll a large stone to me this **d**.
14:37 He did not answer him that **d**.
14:45 he has worked with God this **d**.
15:35 no more to see Saul until the **d**
16:13 came upon David from that **d**
17:10 the armies of Israel this **d**;
17:46 This **d** the LORD will deliver
17:46 And this **d** I will give the
18: 2 Saul took him that **d**,
18: 9 So Saul eyed David from that **d**
18:10 And it happened on the next **d**
19:24 and lay down naked all that **d**
20: 5 in the field until the third **d**
20:12 tomorrow, or the third **d**,
20:19 place where you hid on the **d**
20:26 did not say anything that **d**,
20:27 And it happened the next **d**,
20:27 the second **d** of the month,
20:34 and ate no food the second **d** of
21: 5 sanctified in the vessel this **d**.
21: 6 bread in its place on the **d**
21: 7 of Saul was there that **d**,
21:10 David arose and fled that **d**
22: 8 lie in wait, as it is this **d**.
22:13 to lie in wait, as it is this **d**?
22:18 and killed on that **d**
22:22 to Abiathar, "I knew that **d**,
23:14 Saul sought him every **d**,
24: 4 This is the **d** of which the LORD
24:10 this **d** your eyes have seen that
24:18 And you have shown this **d** how
24:19 what you have done to me this **d**.
25: 8 eyes, for we come on a feast **d**.
25:16 wall to us both by night and **d**,
25:32 who sent you this **d** to meet me!
25:33 you have kept me this **d** from
26: 8 enemy into your hand this **d**.
26:10 or his **d** shall come to die, or
26:19 they have driven me out this **d**
26:21 precious in your eyes this **d**.
26:24 life was valued much this **d** in
27: 6 Achish gave him Ziklag that **d**.
27: 6 to the kings of Judah to this **d**.
28:18 done this thing to you this **d**.
28:20 for he had eaten no food all **d**
29: 3 And to this **d** I have found no
29: 6 For to this **d** I have not found
29: 6 found evil in you since the **d**
29: 8 And to this **d** what have you
30: 1 came to Ziklag, on the third **d**,
30:17 until the evening of the next **d**.
30:25 from that **d** forward; he made it
30:25 ordinance for Israel to this **d**.
31: 6 men died together that same **d**.
31: 8 So it happened the next **d**,
2 Sam 1: 2 on the third **d**, behold, it
2:17 was a very fierce battle that **d**,
3:35 eat food while it was still **d**,
3:37 all Israel understood that **d**
3:38 a great man has fallen this **d**
4: 3 sojourners there until this **d**.
4: 5 at about the heat of the **d** to
4: 8 my lord the king this **d** of
5: 8 Now David said on that **d**,
6: 8 the place Perez Uzzah to this **d**.
6: 9 was afraid of the LORD that **d**;
6:23 children to the **d** of her death.
7: 6 up from Egypt, even to this **d**,
11:12 remained in Jerusalem that **d**
12:18 Then on the seventh **d** it came to
13: 4 becoming thinner **d** after day?
13: 4 becoming thinner day after **d**?
13:32 has been determined from the **d**
13:37 mourned for his son every **d**.
16:12 good for his cursing this **d**.
18: 7 took place there that **d**.
18: 8 devoured more people that **d**
18:18 And to this **d** it is called
18:20 shall not take the news this **d**,
18:20 shall take the news another **d**.
18:31 LORD has avenged you this **d**
19: 2 So the victory that **d** was
19: 2 the people heard it said that **d**,
19: 3 stole back into the city that **d**,
19:19 your servant did on the **d** that
19:24 from the **d** the king departed
19:24 the king departed until the **d**
20: 3 So they were shut up to the **d**
21:10 of the air to rest on them by **d**
22: 1 on the **d** when the LORD had
22:19 They confronted me in the **d** of
23:10 about a great victory that **d**;
23:20 the midst of a pit on a snowy **d**.
24:18 And Gad came that **d** to David
1 Ki 1:30 so I certainly will do this **d**.
1:48 one to sit on my throne this **d**,
2: 8 with a malicious curse in the **d**
2:37 on the **d** you go out and cross
2:42 'Know for certain that on the **d**
3: 6 his throne, as it is this **d**.
3:18 the third **d** after I had given
4:22 Solomon's provision for one **d**
5: 7 Blessed be the LORD this **d**,
8: 8 And they are there to this **d**.
8:16 Since the **d** that I brought My
8:24 Your hand, as it is this **d**.
8:29 toward this temple night and **d**,
8:59 be near the LORD our God **d** and
8:59 as each **d** may require,
8:61 His commandments, as at this **d**.
8:64 On the same **d** the king
8:66 On the eighth **d** he sent the
9:13 of Cabul, as they are to this **d**.
9:21 labor, as it is to this **d**.
10:12 the like been seen to this **d**.
12:12 came to Rehoboam the third **d**,
12:12 "Come back to me the third **d**.
12:19 the house of David to this **d**.
12:32 a feast on the fifteenth **d** of
12:33 at Bethel on the fifteenth **d**
13: 3 And he gave a sign the same **d**,
13:11 the man of God had done that **d**
14:14 of Jeroboam; this is the **d**.
16:16 king over Israel that **d** in the
17:14 until the **d** the LORD sends
18:36 let it be known this **d** that You
20:29 So it was that on the seventh **d**
20:29 of the Syrians in one **d**.
22:25 you shall see on that **d** when
22:35 The battle increased that **d**;
2 Ki 2:22 water remains healed to this **d**,
4: 8 Now it happened one **d** that
4:11 And it happened one **d** that he
4:18 Now it happened one **d** that he
6:29 And I said to her on the next **d**,
7: 9 This **d** is a day of good news,
7: 9 This day is a **d** of good news,
8: 6 of the field from the **d** that
8:15 But it happened on the next **d**
8:22 Judah's authority to this **d**.
10:27 made it a refuse dump to this **d**.
14: 7 its name Joktheel to this **d**.
15: 5 he was a leper until the **d** of
16: 6 and dwell there to this **d**.
17:23 Assyria, as it is to this **d**.
17:34 To this **d** they continue
17:41 fathers did, even to this **d**.
19: 3 This **d** is a day of trouble, and
19: 3 This day is a **d** of trouble, and
20: 5 On the third **d** you shall go up
20: 8 house of the LORD the third **d**?
20:17 have accumulated until this **d**,
21:15 Me to anger since the **d** their
21:15 out of Egypt, even to this **d**.
25: 1 on the tenth **d** of the month,
25: 3 By the ninth **d** of the fourth
25: 8 on the seventh **d** of the month
25:27 on the twenty-seventh **d** of the
25:30 the king, a portion for each **d**,
1 Chr 4:41 them, as it is to this **d**.
4:43 They have dwelt there to this **d**.
5:26 the river of Gozan to this **d**.
9:33 were employed in that work **d**
10: 8 So it happened the next **d**,
11:22 the midst of a pit on a snowy **d**.
12:22 time they came to David **d** by
12:22 they came to David day by **d** to
13:11 is called Perez Uzza to this **d**.
13:12 David was afraid of God that **d**,
16: 7 On that **d** David first delivered
16:23 His salvation from **d** to day.
16:23 of His salvation from day to **d**.
17: 5 up Israel, even to this **d**,
26:17 on the north four each **d**,
26:17 day, on the south four each **d**,
28: 7 My judgments, as it is this **d**.
29: 5 to consecrate himself this **d**
29:21 to the LORD on the next **d**:
29:22 with great gladness on that **d**.
2 Chr 3: 2 to build on the second **d** of
5: 9 And they are there to this **d**.
6: 5 Since the **d** that I brought My
6:15 Your hand, as it is this **d**.
6:20 this temple **d** and night,
7: 9 And on the eighth **d** they held a
7:10 On the twenty-third **d** of the
8: 8 labor, as it is to this **d**.
8:14 priests) as the duty of each **d**
8:16 was well-ordered from the **d** of
10:12 came to Rehoboam on the third **d**,
10:12 "Come back to me the third **d**.
10:19 the house of David to this **d**.
18:24 you shall see on that **d**
18:34 The battle increased that **d**,
20:26 And on the fourth **d** they
20:26 Valley of Berachah until this **d**.
21:10 Judah's authority to this **d**.
21:15 of the sickness, **d** by day.
21:15 of the sickness, day by **d**.
24:11 Thus they did **d** by day, and
24:11 Thus they did day by **d**, and
26:21 until the **d** of his death.
28: 6 thousand in Judah in one **d**,
29:17 to sanctify on the first **d** of
29:17 and on the eighth **d** of the
29:17 and on the sixteenth **d** of the
30:15 lambs on the fourteenth **d** of
30:21 priests praised the LORD **d** by
30:21 praised the LORD day by **d**,
35: 1 lambs on the fourteenth **d** of
35:16 LORD was prepared the same **d**,
35:21 not come against you this **d**,
35:25 And to this **d** all the singing
Ezra 3: 4 by ordinance for each **d**.
3: 6 From the first **d** of the seventh
6: 9 let it be given them **d** by day
6: 9 let it be given them day by **d**
6:15 was finished on the third **d** of
6:19 Passover on the fourteenth **d**
7: 9 On the first **d** of the first
7: 9 and on the first **d** of the
8:31 of Ahava on the twelfth **d** of
8:33 Now on the fourth **d** the silver
9: 7 days of our fathers to this **d**
9: 7 humiliation, as it is this **d**.
9:15 as a remnant, as it is this **d**.
10:16 they sat down on the first **d**
10:17 By the first **d** of the first
Neh 1: 6 **d** and night, for the children
1:11 let Your servant prosper this **d**,
4: 2 Will they complete it in a **d**?
4: 9 against them **d** and night.
4:22 night and a working party by **d**.
5:11 now to them, even this **d**,
6:15 on the twenty-fifth **d** of Elul,
8: 2 understanding on the first **d**
8: 9 This **d** is holy to the LORD
8:10 for this **d** is holy to our
8:11 for the **d** is holy; do not be
8:13 Now on the second **d** the heads
8:17 the son of Nun until that **d**
8:18 Also **d** by day, from the first
8:18 Also day by **d**,
8:18 from the first **d** until the last
8:18 the first day until the last **d**,
8:18 and on the eighth **d** there was
9: 1 Now on the twenty-fourth **d** of
9: 3 God for one-fourth of the **d**;
9:10 for Yourself, as it is this **d**.
9:12 Moreover You led them by **d** with
9:19 did not depart from them by **d**,
9:32 kings of Assyria until this **d**.
10:31 grain to sell on the Sabbath **d**,
10:31 on the Sabbath, or on a holy **d**;
11:23 singers, a quota **d** by day.
11:23 the singers, a quota day by **d**.
12:43 Also that **d** they offered great
12:47 a portion for each **d**.
13: 1 On that **d** they read from the
13:15 into Jerusalem on the Sabbath **d**.
13:15 And I warned them about the **d**
13:17 which you profane the Sabbath **d**?
13:19 be brought in on the Sabbath **d**.
13:22 to sanctify the Sabbath **d**.
Esth 1:10 On the seventh **d**,
1:18 This very **d** the noble ladies of
2:11 And every **d** Mordecai paced in
3: 7 Haman to determine the **d** and
3:12 called on the thirteenth **d** of
3:13 children and women, in one **d**,
3:13 on the thirteenth **d** of the
3:14 they should be ready for that **d**.
4:16 for three days, night or **d**.
5: 1 Now it happened on the third **d**
5: 9 So Haman went out that **d** joyful
7: 2 And on the second **d**,
8: 1 On that **d** King Ahasuerus gave
8: 9 Sivan, on the twenty-third **d**;

8:12 on one **d** in all the provinces of
8:12 on the thirteenth **d** of the
8:13 Jews would be ready on that **d**
9: 1 of Adar, on the thirteenth **d**,
9: 1 On the **d** that the enemies of
9:11 On that **d** the number of those
9:15 again on the fourteenth **d** of
9:17 This was on the thirteenth **d**
9:17 And on the fourteenth **d** of the
9:17 they rested and made it a **d** of
9:18 together on the thirteenth **d**,
9:18 and made it a **d** of feasting and
9:19 celebrated the fourteenth **d** of
Job 1: 4 each on his appointed **d**,
1: 6 Now there was a **d** when the sons
1:13 Now there was a **d** when his sons
2: 1 Again there was a **d** when the
3: 1 his mouth and cursed the **d** of
3: 3 May the **d** perish on which I was
3: 4 May that **d** be darkness; May
3: 5 May the blackness of the **d**
3: 8 those curse it who curse the **d**,
3: 9 not see the dawning of the **d**;
9:19 who will appoint my **d** in
14: 6 a hired man he finishes his **d**.
15:23 He knows that a **d** of darkness
17:12 They change the night into **d**;
18:20 west are astonished at his **d**,
20:28 flow away in the **d** of His
21:30 reserved for the **d** of doom;
21:30 brought out on the **d** of wrath.
38:23 For the **d** of battle and war?
Ps 1: 2 law he meditates **d** and night.
7:11 with the wicked every **d**.
18: the words of this song on the **d**
18:18 They confronted me in the **d** of
19: 2 **D** unto day utters speech, And
19: 2 Day unto **d** utters speech, And
20: 1 the LORD answer you in the **d**
25: 5 On You I wait all the **d**.
32: 3 Through my groaning all the **d**
32: 4 For **d** and night Your hand was
35:28 And of Your praise all the **d**
37:13 For He sees that his **d** is
38: 6 I go mourning all the **d** long.
38:12 And plan deception all the **d**
42: 3 have been my food **d** and night,
42:10 While they say to me all **d**
44: 8 In God we boast all **d** long,
44:22 Your sake we are killed all **d**
50:15 Call upon Me in the **d** of
55:10 **D** and night they go around it
56: 1 Fighting all **d** he oppresses
56: 2 enemies would hound me all **d**,
56: 5 All **d** they twist my words; All
59:16 refuge in the **d** of my trouble.
71: 8 with Your glory all the **d**.
71:15 And Your salvation all the **d**,
71:17 And to this **d** I declare Your
71:24 of Your righteousness all the **d**
73:14 For all **d** long I have been
74:16 The **d** is Yours, the night also
77: 2 In the **d** of my trouble I sought
78: 9 Turned back in the **d** of
78:42 The **d** when He redeemed them
81: 3 moon, on our solemn feast **d**.
84:10 For a **d** in Your courts is
86: 3 For I cry to You all **d** long.
86: 7 In the **d** of my trouble I will
88: 1 I have cried out **d** and night
88:17 They came around me all **d** long
89:16 Your name they rejoice all **d**
91: 5 of the arrow that flies by **d**,
92: A Song for the Sabbath **d**.
95: 8 As in the **d** of trial in the
96: 2 news of His salvation from **d**
96: 2 of His salvation from day to **d**.
102: 2 Your face from me in the **d** of
102: 2 In the **d** that I call, answer
102: 8 My enemies reproach me all **d**
110: 3 be volunteers In the **d** of
110: 5 kings in the **d** of His wrath.
118:24 This is the **d** the LORD has
119:91 They continue this **d** according
119:97 It is my meditation all the **d**.
119:164 Seven times a **d** I praise You,
121: 6 sun shall not strike you by **d**,
136: 8 The sun to rule by **d**,
137: 7 Edom The **d** of Jerusalem,
138: 3 In the **d** when I cried out, You
139:12 But the night shines as the **d**;
140: 7 my head in the **d** of battle.
145: 2 Every **d** I will bless You, And
146: 4 In that very **d** his plans
Prov 4:18 brighter unto the perfect **d**.
6:34 he will not spare in the **d** of
7:20 come home on the appointed **d**.
11: 4 profit in the **d** of wrath,
16: 4 even the wicked for the **d** of
21:26 He covets greedily all **d** long,
21:31 horse is prepared for the **d**
23:17 the fear of the LORD all the **d**;
24:10 If you faint in the **d** of
27: 1 For you do not know what a **d**
27:10 brother's house in the **d** of
27:15 dripping on a very rainy **d**
Eccl 7: 1 And the **d** of death than the
7: 1 the day of death than the **d** of
7:14 In the **d** of prosperity be
7:14 But in the **d** of adversity
8: 8 has power in the **d** of death.
8:16 though one sees no sleep **d** or

12: 3 In the **d** when the keepers of
Song 2:17 Until the **d** breaks And the
3:11 On the **d** of his wedding,
3:11 The **d** of the gladness of his
4: 6 Until the **d** breaks And the
8: 8 In the **d** when she is spoken
Isa 2:11 shall be exalted in that **d**.
2:12 For the **d** of the LORD of
2:17 alone will be exalted in that **d**,
2:20 In that **d** a man will cast away
3: 7 In that **d** he will protest,
3:18 In that **d** the Lord will take
4: 1 And in that **d** seven women shall
4: 2 In that **d** the Branch of the
4: 5 a cloud and smoke by **d** and the
5:30 In that **d** they will roar
7:17 have not come since the **d** that
7:18 it shall come to pass in that **d**
7:20 In the same **d** the Lord will
7:21 It shall be in that **d** That a
7:23 It shall happen in that **d**,
9: 4 As in the **d** of Midian.
9:14 branch and bulrush in one **d**.
10: 3 What will you do in the **d** of
10:17 thorns and his briers in one **d**.
10:20 it shall come to pass in that **d**
10:27 shall come to pass in that **d**
10:32 he will remain at Nob that **d**;
11:10 And in that **d** there shall be a
11:11 shall come to pass in that **d**
11:16 In the **d** that he came up
12: 1 And in that **d** you will say:
12: 4 And in that **d** you will say:
13: 6 for the **d** of the LORD is at
13: 9 the **d** of the LORD comes,
13:13 And in the **d** of His fierce
14: 3 come to pass in the **d** the LORD
16: 3 night in the middle of the **d**;
17: 4 In that **d** it shall come to pass
17: 7 In that **d** a man will look to
17: 9 In that **d** his strong cities
17:11 In the **d** you will make your
17:11 of ruins In the **d** of grief
19:16 In that **d** Egypt will be like
19:18 In that **d** five cities in the
19:19 In that **d** there will be an
19:21 will know the LORD in that **d**,
19:23 In that **d** there will be a
19:24 In that **d** Israel will be one of
20: 6 territory will say in that **d**,
22: 5 For it is a **d** of trouble and
22: 8 You looked in that **d** to the
22:12 And in that **d** the Lord GOD of
22:20 'Then it shall be in that **d**,
22:25 'In that **d**,' says the LORD
23:15 it shall come to pass in that **d**
24:21 shall come to pass in that **d**
25: 9 And it will be said in that **d**:
26: 1 In that **d** this song will be sung
27: 1 In that **d** the LORD with His
27: 2 In that **d** sing to her, "A
27: 3 hurt it, I keep it night and **d**.
27: 8 by His rough wind In the **d** of
27:12 it shall come to pass in that **d**
27:13 So it shall be in that **d**:
28: 5 In that **d** the LORD of hosts
28:19 And by **d** and by night; It
28:24 the plowman keep plowing all **d**
29:18 In that **d** the deaf shall hear
30:23 In that **d** your cattle will
30:25 In the **d** of the great
30:26 In the **d** that the LORD binds
31: 7 For in that **d** every man shall
34: 8 For it is the **d** of the
34:10 not be quenched night or **d**;
37: 3 This **d** is a day of trouble and
37: 3 This day is a **d** of trouble and
38:12 From **d** until night You make an
38:13 From **d** until night You make an
38:19 praise You, As I do this **d**;
39: 6 have accumulated until this **d**,
43:13 Indeed before the **d** was, I am
47: 9 to you In a moment, in one **d**:
48: 7 And before this **d** you have not
49: 8 And in the **d** of salvation I
51:13 have feared continually every **d**
52: 5 blasphemed continually every **d**.
52: 6 they shall know in that **d**
58: 3 in the **d** of your fast you find
58: 4 not fast as you do this **d**,
58: 5 A **d** for a man to afflict his
58: 5 And an acceptable **d** to the
58:13 your pleasure on My holy **d**,
58:13 The holy **d** of the LORD
60:11 They shall not be shut **d** or
60:19 no longer be your light by **d**,
61: 2 And the **d** of vengeance of our
62: 6 hold their peace **d** or night.
63: 4 For the **d** of vengeance is in
65: 2 stretched out My hands all **d**
65: 5 A fire that burns all the **d**.
66: 8 be made to give birth in one **d**?
Jer 1:10 I have this **d** set you over the
1:18 I have made you this **d** A
3:25 From our youth even to this **d**,
4: 9 it shall come to pass in that **d**,
6: 4 for the **d** goes away, For the
7:22 or command them in the **d** that I
7:25 Since the **d** that your fathers
7:25 the land of Egypt until this **d**,
9: 1 That I might weep **d** and night
11: 4 your fathers in the **d** I

11: 5 and honey,' as it is this **d**.
11: 7 fathers in the **d** I brought
11: 7 the land of Egypt, until this **d**,
12: 3 And prepare them for the **d** of
14:17 flow with tears night and **d**,
15: 9 gone down While it was yet **d**;
16:13 you shall serve other gods **d**
16:19 My refuge in the **d** of
17:16 have I desired the woeful **d**;
17:17 You are my hope in the **d** of
17:18 Bring on them the **d** of doom,
17:21 bear no burden on the Sabbath **d**,
17:22 of your houses on the Sabbath **d**,
17:22 work, but hallow the Sabbath **d**,
17:24 of this city on the Sabbath **d**,
17:24 day, but hallow the Sabbath **d**,
17:27 heed Me to hallow the Sabbath **d**,
17:27 of Jerusalem on the Sabbath **d**,
18:17 and not the face In the **d** of
20: 3 And it happened on the next **d**
20:14 Cursed be the **d** in which I
20:14 Let the **d** not be blessed
25: 3 king of Judah, even to this **d**,
25:18 and a curse, as it is this **d**;
25:33 And at that **d** the slain of the
27:22 they shall be until the **d** that
30: 7 Alas! For that **d** is great, So
30: 8 it shall come to pass in that **d**,
31: 6 For there shall be a **d** When
31:32 in the **d** that I took them
31:35 gives the sun for a light by **d**,
32:20 in the land of Egypt, to this **d**,
32:20 a name, as it is this **d**.
32:31 My anger and My fury from the **d**
32:31 they built it, even to this **d**;
33:20 break My covenant with the **d**
33:20 so that there will not be **d** and
33:25 If My covenant is not with **d**
34:13 with your fathers in the **d**
35:14 for to this **d** they drink none,
36: 2 from the **d** I spoke to you, from
36: 2 days of Josiah even to this **d**.
36: 6 house on the **d** of fasting.
36:30 cast out to the heat of the **d**
38:28 of the prison until the **d** that
39: 2 on the ninth **d** of the month,
39:16 shall be performed in that **d**
39:17 I will deliver you in that **d**,
40: 4 I free you this **d** from the
41: 4 on the second **d** after he had
42:19 I have admonished you this **d**.
42:21 And I have this **d** declared it
44: 2 this **d** they are a desolation,
44: 6 and desolate, as it is this **d**.
44:10 not been humbled, to this **d**,
44:22 inhabitant, as it is this **d**.
44:23 happened to you, as at this **d**.
46:10 For this is the **d** of the Lord
46:10 A **d** of vengeance, That He may
46:21 For the **d** of their calamity
47: 4 Because of the **d** that comes to
48:41 men's hearts in Moab on that **d**
49:22 mighty men of Edom in that **d**
49:26 war shall be cut off in that **d**,
50:27 For their **d** has come,
50:30 war shall be cut off in that **d**,
50:31 For your **d** has come, The time
51: 2 For in the **d** of doom They
52: 4 on the tenth **d** of the month,
52: 6 on the ninth **d** of the month,
52:11 till the **d** of his death.
52:12 on the tenth **d** of the month
52:31 on the twenty-fifth **d** of the
52:34 a portion for each **d** until the
52:34 for each day until the **d** of
Lam 1:12 In the **d** of His fierce anger.
1:13 desolate And faint all the **d**.
1:21 Bring on the **d** You have
2: 1 His footstool In the **d** of His
2: 7 of the LORD As on the **d** of a
2:16 the **d** we have waited for;
2:18 like a river **d** and night;
2:21 slain them in the **d** of Your
2:22 have invited as to a feast **d**
2:22 In the **d** of the LORD's anger
3: 3 and time again throughout the **d**.
3:14 taunting song all the **d**.
3:57 You drew near on the **d** I called
3:62 whispering against me all the **d**.
Ezek 1: 1 on the fifth **d** of the month,
1: 2 On the fifth **d** of the month,
1:28 rainbow in a cloud on a rainy **d**,
2: 3 against Me to this very **d**.
4: 6 I have laid on you a **d** for each
4:10 by weight, twenty shekels a **d**;
7: 7 A **d** of trouble is near, And
7:10 the **d**! Behold, it has come!
7:12 The **d** draws near. 'Let not
7:19 able to deliver them In the **d**
8: 1 on the fifth **d** of the month,
12: 3 and go into captivity by **d** in
12: 4 By **d** you shall bring out your
12: 7 brought out my belongings by **d**,
13: 5 to stand in battle on the **d** of
16: 4 on the **d** you were born your
16: 5 yourself were loathed on the **d**
20: 1 on the tenth **d** of the month,
20: 5 On the **d** when I chose Israel and
20: 6 On that **d** I raised My hand in an
20:29 name is called Bamah to this **d**.
20:31 all your idols, even to this **d**.
21:25 whose **d** has come, whose

21:29 the slain Whose **d** has come,
22:24 cleansed or rained on in the **d**
23:38 My sanctuary on the same **d** and
23:39 on the same **d** they came into My
24: 1 on the tenth **d** of the month,
24: 2 write down the name of the **d**,
24: 2 name of the day, this very **d**—
24: 2 against Jerusalem this very **d**.
24:25 will it not be in the **d** when
24:26 on that **d** one who escapes will
24:27 on that **d** your mouth will be
26: 1 on the first **d** of the month,
26:18 coastlands tremble on the **d** of
27:27 the seas on the **d** of your ruin.
28:13 Was prepared for you on the **d**
28:15 in your ways from the **d** you
29: 1 on the twelfth **d** of the month,
29:17 on the first **d** of the month,
29:21 In that **d** I will cause the horn
30: 2 'Wail, 'Woe to the **d**!'
30: 3 For the **d** is near, Even the
30: 3 Even the **d** of the LORD is
30: 3 It will be a **d** of clouds, the
30: 9 On that **d** messengers shall go
30: 9 As on the **d** of Egypt; For
30:18 At Tehaphnehes the **d** shall also
30:20 on the seventh **d** of the month,
31: 1 on the first **d** of the month,
31:15 In the **d** when it went down to
32: 1 on the first **d** of the month,
32:10 in the **d** of your fall.'
32:17 on the fifteenth **d** of the
33:12 in the **d** of his transgression;
33:12 because of it in the **d** that he
33:12 in the **d** that he sins.'
33:21 on the fifth **d** of the month,
34:12 seeks out his flock on the **d**
34:12 on a cloudy and dark **d**.
36:33 On the **d** that I cleanse you from
38:10 On that **d** it shall come to pass
38:14 On that **d** when My people Israel
38:19 Surely in that **d** there shall be
39: 8 This is the **d** of which I have
39:11 will come to pass in that **d**
39:13 on the **d** that I am glorified,"
39:22 the LORD their God from that **d**
40: 1 on the tenth **d** of the month,
40: 1 on the very same **d** the hand of
43:18 for the altar on the **d** when it
43:22 On the second **d** you shall offer
43:25 Every **d** for seven days you shall
43:27 on the eighth **d** and thereafter,
44:27 And on the **d** that he goes to the
45:18 on the first **d** of the month,
45:20 you shall do on the seventh **d**
45:21 on the fourteenth **d** of the
45:22 And on that **d** the prince shall
45:25 on the fifteenth **d** of the
46: 1 and on the **d** of the New Moon it
46: 4 to the LORD on the Sabbath **d**
46: 6 On the **d** of the New Moon it
46:12 as he did on the Sabbath **d**.
48:35 name of the city from that **d**
Dan 6:10 on his knees three times that **d**,
6:13 his petition three times a **d**.
9: 7 of face, as it is this **d**—
9:15 a name, as it is this **d**—
10: 4 Now on the twenty-fourth **d** of
10:12 for from the first **d** that you
Hos 1: 5 shall come to pass in that **d**
1:11 For great will be the **d** of
2: 3 as in the **d** she was born, And
2:15 As in the **d** when she came up
2:16 "And it shall be, in that **d**,
2:18 In that **d** I will make a
2:21 shall come to pass in that **d**
4: 5 you shall stumble in the **d**;
5: 9 shall be desolate in the **d** of
6: 2 On the third **d** He will raise
7: 5 In the **d** of our king Princes
9: 5 will you do in the appointed **d**,
9: 5 And in the **d** of the feast of
10:14 in the **d** of battle—A
Joel 1:15 Alas for the **d**! For the day of
1:15 For the **d** of the LORD is
2: 1 For the **d** of the LORD is
2: 2 A **d** of darkness and gloominess,
2: 2 A **d** of clouds and thick
2:11 For the **d** of the LORD is
2:31 of the great and awesome **d** of
3:14 For the **d** of the LORD is
3:18 it will come to pass in that **d**
Am 1:14 Amid shouting in the **d** of
1:14 And a tempest in the **d** of the
2:16 Shall flee naked in that **d**,
3:14 That in the **d** I punish Israel
5: 8 And makes the **d** dark as
5:18 Woe to you who desire the **d** of
5:18 For what good is the **d** of
5:20 Is not the **d** of the LORD
6: 3 to you who put far off the **d**
8: 3 Shall be wailing in that **d**,
8: 9 it shall come to pass in that **d**,
8:10 And its end like a bitter **d**.
8:13 In that **d** the fair virgins And
9:11 On that **d** I will raise up The
Ob 8 "Will I not in that **d**,
11 In the **d** that you stood on the
11 In the **d** that strangers carried
12 should not have gazed on the **d**
12 In the **d** of his captivity;
12 children of Judah In the **d** of
12 In the **d** of distress.
13 In the **d** of their calamity.
13 In the **d** of their calamity,
13 on their substance In the **d**
14 them who remained In the **d** of
15 For the **d** of the LORD upon all
Jon 4: 7 as morning dawned the next **d**
Mic 2: 4 In that **d** one shall take up a
3: 6 And the **d** shall be dark for
4: 6 In that **d**," says the LORD,
5:10 "And it shall be in that **d**,
7: 4 The **d** of your watchman and
7:11 In the **d** when your walls are
7:11 In that **d** the decree shall go
7:12 In that **d** they shall come to
Nah 1: 7 A stronghold in the **d** of
2: 3 In the **d** of his preparation,
3:17 camp in the hedges on a cold **d**;
Hab 3:16 That I might rest in the **d** of
Zeph 1: 7 For the **d** of the LORD is at
1: 8 In the **d** of the LORD's
1: 9 In the same **d** I will punish
1:10 "And there shall be on that **d**,
1:14 The great **d** of the LORD is
1:14 The noise of the **d** of the
1:15 That **d** is a day of wrath, A
1:15 That day is a **d** of wrath, A
1:15 A **d** of trouble and distress,
1:15 A **d** of devastation and
1:15 A **d** of darkness and
1:15 A **d** of clouds and thick
1:16 A **d** of trumpet and alarm
1:18 able to deliver them In the **d**
2: 2 Or the **d** passes like chaff,
2: 2 Before the **d** of the LORD's
2: 3 In the **d** of the LORD's anger.
3: 8 Until the **d** I rise up for
3:11 In that **d** you shall not be
3:16 In that **d** it shall be said to
Hag 1: 1 on the first **d** of the month,
1:15 on the twenty-fourth **d** of the
2:10 On the twenty-fourth **d** of the
2:15 carefully consider from this **d**
2:18 Consider now from this **d**
2:18 from the twenty-fourth **d** of the
2:18 from the **d** that the foundation
2:19 But from this **d** I will bless
2:20 Haggai on the twenty-fourth **d**
2:23 'In that **d**,' says the LORD
Zech 1: 7 On the twenty-fourth **d** of the
2:11 joined to the LORD in that **d**,
3: 9 iniquity of that land in one **d**.
3:10 In that **d**,' says the LORD
4:10 For who has despised the **d** of
6:10 and go the same **d** and enter the
7: 1 on the fourth **d** of the ninth
8: 9 Who spoke in the **d** the
9:16 God will save them in that **d**,
11:11 So it was broken on that **d**.
12: 3 And it shall happen in that **d**
12: 4 'In that **d**," says the LORD,
12: 6 In that **d** I will make the
12: 8 In that **d** the LORD will defend
12: 8 is feeble among them in that **d**
12: 9 It shall be in that **d** that I
12:11 In that **d** there shall be a great
13: 1 In that **d** a fountain shall be
13: 2 "It shall be in that **d**,
13: 4 And it shall be in that **d** that
14: 1 the **d** of the LORD is coming,
14: 3 As He fights in the **d** of
14: 4 And in that **d** His feet will
14: 6 shall come to pass in that **d**
14: 7 It shall be one **d** Which is
14: 7 Neither **d** nor night. But at
14: 8 And in that **d** it shall be
14: 9 In that **d** it shall be—"The
14:13 shall come to pass in that **d**
14:20 In that **d** "HOLINESS TO THE
14:21 In that **d** there shall no longer
Mal 3: 2 But who can endure the **d** of His
3:17 On the **d** that I make them My
4: 1 the **d** is coming, Burning like
4: 1 And the **d** which is coming
4: 3 On the **d** that I do this,"
4: 5 of the great and dreadful **d** of
Mt 6:11 Give us this **d** our daily bread.
6:34 Sufficient for the **d** is its
7:22 "Many will say to Me in that **d**,
10:15 Gomorrah in the **d** of judgment
11:22 for Tyre and Sidon in the **d** of
11:23 have remained until this **d**.
11:24 of Sodom in the **d** of judgment
12:36 give account of it in the **d** of
13: 1 On the same **d** Jesus went out of
16:21 and be raised the third **d**.
17:23 and the third **d** He will be
20: 2 the laborers for a denarius a **d**,
20: 6 been standing here idle all **d**?
20:12 burden and the heat of the **d**.
20:19 And the third **d** He will rise
22:23 The same **d** the Sadducees, who
22:46 nor from that **d** on did anyone
24:36 But of that **d** and hour no one
24:38 until the **d** that Noah entered
24:50 that servant will come on a **d**
25:13 for you know neither the **d** nor
26:17 Now on the first **d** of the
26:29 vine from now on until that **d**
27: 8 the Field of Blood to this **d**.
27:62 On the next **d**, which followed
27:62 which followed the *D* of
27:64 made secure until the third **d**,
28: 1 as the first **d** of the week
28:15 among the Jews until this **d**.
Mk 4:27 sleep by night and rise by **d**,
4:35 On the same **d**, when evening
5: 5 And always, night and **d**,
6:11 Sodom and Gomorrah in the **d** of
6:21 Then an opportune **d** came when
6:35 When the **d** was now far spent,
9:31 He will rise the third **d**.
10:34 And the third **d** He will rise
11:12 Now the next **d**, when they
13:32 But of that **d** and hour no one
14:12 Now on the first **d** of
14:25 fruit of the vine until that **d**
15:42 it was the Preparation *D*,
15:42 the **d** before the Sabbath,
16: 2 on the first **d** of the week,
16: 9 He rose early on the first **d**
Lk 1:20 speak until the **d** these things
1:59 So it was, on the eighth **d**,
1:80 the deserts till the **d** of his
2:11 there is born to you this **d** in
2:37 and prayers night and **d**.
4:16 the synagogue on the Sabbath **d**,
4:42 Now when it was **d**,
5:17 Now it happened on a certain **d**,
6:13 And when it was **d**, He called
6:23 Rejoice in that **d** and leap for
7:11 the **d** after, that He went into
8:22 it happened, on a certain **d**,
9:12 When the **d** began to wear away,
9:22 and be raised the third **d**.
9:37 Now it happened on the next **d**,
10:12 be more tolerable in that *D*
10:35 'On the next **d**, when he
11: 3 Give us **d** by day our daily
11: 3 Give us day by **d** our daily
12:46 that servant will come on a **d**
13:14 them, and not on the Sabbath **d**.
13:31 On that very **d** some Pharisees
13:32 and the third **d** I shall be
13:33 and the **d** following; for it
14: 5 pull him out on the Sabbath **d**?
16:19 and fared sumptuously every **d**.
17: 4 against you seven times in a **d**,
17: 4 and seven times in a **d** returns
17:24 the Son of Man will be in His **d**.
17:27 until the **d** that Noah entered
17:29 but on the **d** that Lot went out
17:30 Even so will it be in the **d** when
17:31 'In that **d**, he who is on the
18: 7 His own elect who cry out **d**
18:33 And the third **d** He will rise
19:42 you, especially in this your **d**,
21:34 and that *D* come on you
22: 7 Then came the *D* of Unleavened
22:34 rooster shall not crow this **d**
22:66 As soon as it was **d**,
23:12 That very **d** Pilate and Herod
23:54 That **d** was the Preparation, and
24: 1 Now on the first **d** of the week,
24: 7 and the third **d** rise again.'"
24:13 were traveling that same **d** to
24:21 today is the third **d** since
24:29 and the **d** is far spent."
24:46 rise from the dead the third **d**,
Jn 1:29 The next **d** John saw Jesus
1:35 Again, the next **d**,
1:39 and remained with Him that **d**
1:43 The following **d** Jesus wanted to
2: 1 On the third **d** there was a
5: 9 And that **d** was the Sabbath.
6:22 On the following **d**,
6:39 raise it up at the last **d**.
6:40 will raise him up at the last **d**.
6:44 will raise him up at the last **d**.
6:54 will raise him up at the last **d**.
7:37 On the last **d**, that great
7:37 that great **d** of the feast,
8:56 Abraham rejoiced to see My **d**,
9: 4 Him who sent Me while it is **d**;
11: 9 there not twelve hours in the **d**?
11: 9 If anyone walks in the **d**,
11:24 the resurrection at the last **d**.
11:53 from that **d** on, they plotted to
12: 7 this for the **d** of My burial.
12:12 The next **d** a great multitude
12:48 will judge him in the last **d**.
14:20 At that **d** you will know that I
16:23 And in that **d** you will ask Me
16:26 In that **d** you will ask in My
19:14 Now it was the Preparation *D* of
19:31 it was the Preparation *D*,
19:31 (for that Sabbath was a high **d**)
19:42 of the Jews' Preparation *D*,
20: 1 Now on the first **d** of the week
20:19 the same **d** at evening, being
20:19 being the first **d** of the week,
Acts 1: 2 until the **d** in which He was
1:22 the baptism of John to that **d**
2: 1 When the *D* of Pentecost had
2:15 only the third hour of the **d**.
2:20 the great and awesome **d**
2:29 his tomb is with us to this **d**.
2:41 and that **d** about three thousand
4: 3 in custody until the next **d**,
4: 5 it came to pass, on the next **d**,
4: 9 If we this **d** are judged for a
7: 8 circumcised him on the eighth **d**;
7:26 And the next **d** he appeared to
9:24 watched the gates **d** and night,

10: 3 About the ninth hour of the **d** he
10: 9 The next **d**, as they went on
10:23 On the next **d** Peter went away
10:24 And the following **d** they
10:40 God raised up on the third **d**,
12:18 Then, as soon as it was **d**,
12:21 So on a set **d** Herod, arrayed in
13:14 the synagogue on the Sabbath **d**
14:20 And the next **d** he departed with
16:11 and the next **d** came to
16:13 And on the Sabbath **d** we went out
16:35 And when it was **d**,
17:31 because He has appointed a **d** on
20: 7 Now on the first **d** of the
20: 7 ready to depart the next **d**,
20:15 and the next **d** came opposite
20:15 The following **d** we arrived at
20:15 The next **d** we came to Miletus.
20:16 on the **D** of Pentecost.
20:18 from the first **d** that I came to
20:26 I testify to you this **d** that I
20:31 to warn everyone night and **d**
21: 1 the following **d** to Rhodes, and
21: 7 and stayed with them one **d**.
21: 8 On the next **d** we who were
21:18 On the following **d** Paul went in
21:26 took the men, and the next **d**,
22:30 The next **d**, because he
23: 1 before God until this **d**.
23:12 And when it was **d**,
23:32 The next **d** they left the
24:21 I am being judged by you this **d**.
25: 6 to Caesarea. And the next **d**,
25:17 the next **d** I sat on the
25:23 So the next **d**, when Agrippa
26: 7 serving God night and **d**,
26:22 to this **d** I stand, witnessing
27: 3 And the next **d** we landed at
27:18 the next **d** they lightened the
27:19 On the third **d** we threw the
27:29 and prayed for **d** to come.
27:33 And as **d** was about to dawn, Paul
27:33 Today is the fourteenth **d** you
27:39 When it was **d**, they did not
28:13 And after one **d** the south wind
28:13 and the next **d** we came to
28:23 when they had appointed him a **d**,
Rom 2: 5 up for yourself wrath in the **d**
2:16 in the **d** when God will judge the
8:36 sake we are killed all **d**
10:21 All **d** long I have stretched
11: 8 not hear, To this very **d**.
13:12 the **d** is at hand. Therefore let
13:13 us walk properly, as in the **d**,
14: 5 One person esteems one **d** above
14: 5 another esteems every **d** alike.
14: 6 He who observes the **d**,
14: 6 he who does not observe the **d**,
1 Cor 1: 8 may be blameless in the **d** of
3:13 for the **D** will declare it,
5: 5 spirit may be saved in the **d**
10: 8 and in one **d** twenty-three
15: 4 that He rose again the third **d**
16: 2 On the first **d** of the week let
2 Cor 1:14 in the **d** of the Lord Jesus.
3:14 For until this **d** the same veil
3:15 But even to this **d**,
4:16 man is being renewed **d** by day.
4:16 man is being renewed day by **d**.
6: 2 And in the **d** of salvation I
6: 2 now is the **d** of salvation.
11:25 a night and a **d** I have been in
Eph 4:30 sealed for the **d** of redemption.
6:13 able to withstand in the evil **d**,
Phil 1: 5 in the gospel from the first **d**
1: 6 will complete it until the **d**
1:10 and without offense till the **d**
2:16 rejoice in the **d** of Christ
3: 5 circumcised the eighth **d**,
Col 1: 6 is also among you since the **d**
1: 9 since the **d** we heard it, do not
1 Th 2: 9 toil; for laboring night and **d**,
3:10 night and **d** praying exceedingly
5: 2 know perfectly that the **d** of
5: 4 so that this **D** should overtake
5: 5 sons of light and sons of the **d**.
5: 8 But let us who are of the **d** be
2 Th 1:10 when He comes, in that **D**,
2: 2 as though the **d** of Christ had
2: 3 for that **D** will not come
3: 8 with labor and toil night and **d**,
1 Tim 5: 5 and prayers night and **d**.
2 Tim 1: 3 you in my prayers night and **d**,
1:12 committed to Him until that **D**.
1:18 mercy from the Lord in that **D**—
4: 8 will give to me on that **D**,
Heb 3: 8 In the **d** of trial in
4: 4 place of the seventh **d** in
4: 4 rested on the seventh **d**
4: 7 again He designates a certain **d**,
4: 8 have spoken of another **d**.
8: 9 fathers in the **d** when
10:25 as you see the **D** approaching.
Jas 5: 5 hearts as in a **d** of slaughter.
1 Pe 2:12 glorify God in the **d** of
2 Pe 1:19 until the **d** dawns and the
2: 8 his righteous soul from **d** to
2: 8 righteous soul from day to **d**
2: 9 under punishment for the **d** of
3: 7 reserved for fire until the **d**
3: 8 that with the Lord one **d** is as
3: 8 and a thousand years as one **d**.
3:10 But the **d** of the Lord will come
3:12 hastening the coming of the **d**
1 Jn 4:17 we may have boldness in the **d**
Jude 6 for the judgment of the great **d**;
Rev 1:10 in the Spirit on the Lord's **D**,
4: 8 And they do not rest **d** or
6:17 For the great **d** of His wrath has
7:15 and serve Him **d** and night in
8:12 A third of the **d** did not shine,
9:15 prepared for the hour and **d**
12:10 before our God **d** and night,
14:11 and they have no rest **d** or
16:14 to the battle of that great **d**
18: 8 her plagues will come in one **d**—
20:10 And they will be tormented **d**
21:25 shall not be shut at all by **d**

DAY OF ATONEMENT (3/3)

Lev 23:27 seventh month shall be the **D**.
23:28 that same day, for it is the **D**,
25: 9 on the **D** you shall make the

DAY OF CHRIST (3/3)

Phil 1:10 and without offense till the **d**,
2:16 so that I may rejoice in the **d**
2 Th 2: 2 as though the **d** had come.

DAY OF THE LORD (26/24)

Isa 2:12 For the **d** of hosts Shall
13: 6 for the **d** is at hand! It will
13: 9 the **d** comes, Cruel, with both
58:13 The holy **d** honorable, And
Jer 46:10 For this is the **d** GOD of
Ezek 13: 5 to stand in battle on the **d**.
30: 3 Even the **d** is near; It will
Joel 1:15 Alas for the day! For the **d**
2: 1 For the **d** is coming, For it
2:11 For the **d** is great and very
2:31 of the great and awesome **d**.
3:14 valley of decision! For the **d**
Am 5:18 Woe to you who desire the **d**!
5:18 For what good is the **d** to
5:20 Is not the **d** darkness, and not
Ob 15 For the **d** upon all the nations
Zeph 1: 7 For the **d** is at hand, For
1:14 The great **d** is near; It is
1:14 The noise of the **d** is bitter;
Zech 14: 1 the **d** is coming, And your
Mal 4: 5 of the great and dreadful **d**.
Acts 2:20 the great and awesome **d**.
1 Cor 5: 5 spirit may be saved in the **d**
2 Cor 1:14 in the **d** Jesus.
1 Th 5: 2 know perfectly that the **d** so
2 Pe 3:10 But the **d** will come as a thief

DAY'S (7/6) DAY

Num 11:31 about a **d** journey on this side
11:31 and about a **d** journey
1 Ki 19: 4 But he himself went a **d** journey
1 Chr 16:37 as every **d** work required;
Jon 3: 4 the city on the first **d** walk.
Lk 2:44 they went a **d** journey, and
Acts 1:12 a Sabbath **d** journey.

DAYBREAK (3/3) DAY

2 Sam 2:32 and they came to Hebron at **d**.
Neh 4:21 men held the spears from **d**
Acts 20:11 a long while, even till **d**,

DAYLIGHT (3/3) DAY

Judg 16: 2 "In the morning, when it is **d**,
Am 8: 9 darken the earth in broad **d**;
Mk 1:35 risen a long while before **d**,

DAYS (854/782) DAY, DAYS'

Gen 1:14 and for **d** and years;
3:14 you shall eat dust All the **d**
3:17 shall eat of it All the **d** of
5: 4 the **d** of Adam were eight
5: 5 So all the **d** that Adam lived
5: 8 So all the **d** of Seth were nine
5:11 So all the **d** of Enosh were nine
5:14 So all the **d** of Cainan were nine
5:17 So all the **d** of Mahalalel were
5:20 So all the **d** of Jared were nine
5:23 So all the **d** of Enoch were three
5:27 So all the **d** of Methuselah were
5:31 So all the **d** of Lamech were
6: 3 yet his **d** shall be one hundred
6: 4 giants on the earth in those **d**,
7: 4 For after seven more **d** I will
7: 4 it to rain on the earth forty **d**
7:10 it came to pass after seven **d**
7:12 rain was on the earth forty **d**
7:17 flood was on the earth forty **d**.
7:24 earth one hundred and fifty **d**.
8: 3 end of the hundred and fifty **d**
8: 6 to pass, at the end of forty **d**,
8:10 he waited yet another seven **d**,
8:12 he waited yet another seven **d**
9:29 So all the **d** of Noah were nine
10:25 for in his **d** the earth was
11:32 So the **d** of Terah were two
14: 1 And it came to pass in the **d** of
17:12 He who is eight **d** old among you
21: 4 son Isaac when he was eight **d**
21:34 land of the Philistines many **d**.
24:55 woman stay with us a few **d**,
25:24 So when her **d** were fulfilled
26: 1 first famine that was in the **d**
26:15 servants had dug in the **d** of
26:18 which they had dug in the **d** of
27:41 The **d** of mourning for my father
27:44 "And stay with him a few **d**,
29:20 and they seemed only a few **d**
29:21 for my **d** are fulfilled, that I
30:14 Now Reuben went in the **d** of
35:28 Now the **d** of Isaac were one
35:29 being old and full of **d**.
37:34 and mourned for his son many **d**.
40:12 The three branches are three **d**.
40:13 Now within three **d** Pharaoh will
40:18 The three baskets are three **d**.
40:19 Within three **d** Pharaoh will lift
42:17 all together in prison three **d**.
47: 9 The **d** of the years of my
47: 9 few and evil have been the **d** of
47: 9 have not attained to the **d** of
47: 9 life of my fathers in the **d** of
49: 1 shall befall you in the last **d**:
50: 3 Forty **d** were required for him,
50: 3 for such are the **d** required for
50: 3 mourned for him seventy **d**.
50: 4 And when the **d** of his mourning
50:10 He observed seven **d** of mourning
Ex 2:11 Now it came to pass in those **d**,
7:25 And seven **d** passed after the
10:22 all the land of Egypt three **d**.
10:23 rise from his place for three **d**.
12:15 Seven **d** you shall eat unleavened
12:19 For seven **d** no leaven shall be
13: 6 Seven **d** you shall eat unleavened
13: 7 bread shall be eaten seven **d**.
15:22 And they went three **d** in the
16:26 Six **d** you shall gather it, but
16:29 the sixth day bread for two **d**.
20: 9 Six **d** you shall labor and do all
20:11 For in six **d** the LORD made the
20:12 that your **d** may be long upon
22:30 be with its mother seven **d**;
23:12 Six **d** you shall do your work,
23:15 eat unleavened bread seven **d**,
23:26 fulfill the number of your **d**.
24:16 and the cloud covered it six **d**.
24:18 was on the mountain forty **d**
29:30 shall put them on for seven **d**,
29:35 Seven **d** you shall consecrate
29:37 Seven **d** you shall make atonement
31:15 'Work shall be done for six **d**,
31:17 for in six **d** the LORD made
34:18 Seven **d** you shall eat
34:21 Six **d** you shall work, but on
34:28 there with the LORD forty **d**
35: 2 "Work shall be done for six **d**,
Lev 8:33 of meeting for seven **d**,
8:33 until the **d** of your
8:33 For seven **d** he shall consecrate
8:35 day and night for seven **d**,
12: 2 she shall be unclean seven **d**;
12: 2 as in the **d** of her customary
12: 4 purification thirty-three **d**.
12: 4 into the sanctuary until the **d**
12: 5 her purification sixty-six **d**.
12: 6 When the **d** of her purification
13: 4 one who has the sore seven **d**.
13: 5 isolate him another seven **d**.
13:21 shall isolate him seven **d**;
13:26 shall isolate him seven **d**.
13:31 who has the scale seven **d**.
13:33 has the scale another seven **d**.
13:46 All the **d** he has the sore he
13:50 which has the plague seven **d**.
13:54 isolate it another seven **d**.
14: 8 stay outside his tent seven **d**.
14:38 and shut up the house seven **d**.
15:13 count for himself seven **d** for
15:19 she shall be set apart seven **d**;
15:24 he shall be unclean seven **d**;
15:25 a discharge of blood for many **d**,
15:25 all the **d** of her unclean
15:25 discharge shall be as the **d** of
15:26 on which she lies all the **d** of
15:28 shall count for herself seven **d**,
22:27 it shall be seven **d** with its
23: 3 Six **d** shall work be done, but
23: 6 seven **d** you must eat unleavened
23: 8 fire to the LORD for seven **d**.
23:16 Count fifty **d** to the day after
23:34 of Tabernacles for seven **d** to
23:36 For seven **d** you shall offer an
23:39 feast of the LORD for seven **d**;
23:40 the LORD your God for seven **d**.
23:41 feast to the LORD for seven **d**
23:42 dwell in booths for seven **d**.
Num 6: 4 All the **d** of his separation he
6: 5 All the **d** of the vow of his
6: 5 until the **d** are fulfilled for
6: 6 All the **d** that he separates
6: 8 All the **d** of his separation he
6:12 consecrate to the LORD the **d**
6:12 but the former **d** shall be lost,
6:13 When the **d** of his separation
9:19 many **d** above the tabernacle,
9:20 above the tabernacle a few **d**:
9:22 Whether it was two **d**,
10:33 LORD on a journey of three **d**;
11:19 eat, not one day, nor two **d**,
11:19 day, nor two days, nor five **d**,

11:19 days, nor five days, nor ten **d**,
11:19 nor ten days, nor twenty **d**,
12:14 would she not be shamed seven **d**?
12:14 be shut out of the camp seven **d**,
12:15 shut out of the camp seven **d**,
13:25 out the land after forty **d**.
14:34 to the number of the **d** in
14:34 you spied out the land, forty **d**,
19:11 anyone shall be unclean seven **d**.
19:14 tent shall be unclean seven **d**;
19:16 grave, shall be unclean seven **d**.
20:29 mourned for Aaron thirty **d**.
24:14 to your people in the latter **d**.
28:17 shall be eaten for seven **d**.
28:24 made by fire daily for seven **d**,
29:12 a feast to the LORD seven **d**.
31:19 remain outside the camp seven **d**;
Deut 1:46 you remained in Kadesh many **d**,
1:46 according to the **d** that you
2: 1 skirted Mount Seir for many **d**.
4: 9 from your heart all the **d** of
4:10 may learn to fear Me all the **d**
4:26 you will not prolong your **d** in
4:30 come upon you in the latter **d**,
4:32 For ask now concerning the **d**
4:40 that you may prolong your **d**
5:13 Six **d** you shall labor and do all
5:16 that your **d** may be long, and
5:33 that you may prolong your **d**
6: 2 all the **d** of your life, and
6: 2 and that your **d** may be
9: 9 stayed on the mountain forty **d**
9:11 at the end of forty **d** and forty
9:18 forty **d** and forty nights;
9:25 forty **d** and forty nights I kept
10:10 stayed in the mountain forty **d**
11: 9 that you may prolong your **d**
11:21 that your **d** and the days of your
11:21 that your days and the **d** of your
11:21 like the **d** of the heavens above
12: 1 all the **d** that you live on the
16: 3 seven **d** you shall eat
16: 3 of the land of Egypt all the **d**
16: 4 all your territory for seven **d**,
16: 8 Six **d** you shall eat unleavened
16:13 Feast of Tabernacles seven **d**,
16:15 Seven **d** you shall keep a sacred
17: 9 to the judge there in those **d**,
17:19 and he shall read it all the **d**
17:20 and that he may prolong his **d**
19:17 the judges who serve in those **d**.
22: 7 that you may prolong your **d**.
22:19 he cannot divorce her all his **d**.
22:29 to divorce her all his **d**.
23: 6 nor their prosperity all your **d**
25:15 that your **d** may be lengthened
26: 3 one who is priest in those **d**,
30:18 you shall not prolong your **d**
30:20 life and the length of your **d**;
31:14 the **d** approach when you must
31:29 will befall you in the latter **d**,
32: 7 Remember the **d** of old, Consider
32:47 word you shall prolong your **d**
33:25 As your **d**, so shall your
34: 8 in the plains of Moab thirty **d**.
34: 8 So the **d** of weeping and
Josh 1: 5 to stand before you all the **d**
1:11 for within three **d** you will
2:16 meet you. Hide there three **d**,
2:22 and stayed there three **d** until
3: 2 So it was, after three **d**,
4:14 all the **d** of his life.
6: 3 once. This you shall do six **d**.
6:14 to the camp. So they did six **d**.
9:16 happened at the end of three **d**,
20: 6 who is high priest in those **d**.
22: 3 left your brethren these many **d**,
24:31 served the LORD all the **d** of
24:31 and all the **d** of the elders who
Judg 2: 7 served the LORD all the **d** of
2: 7 and all the **d** of the elders who
2:18 of their enemies all the **d** of
5: 6 In the **d** of Shamgar, son of
5: 6 In the **d** of Jael, The
8:28 quiet for forty years in the **d**
11:40 of Israel went four **d** each
14:12 it to me within the seven **d** of
14:14 Now for three **d** they could not
14:17 she had wept on him the seven **d**
15:20 Israel twenty years in the **d**
17: 6 In those **d** there was no king
18: 1 In those **d** there was no king
18: 1 And in those **d** the tribe of the
19: 1 And it came to pass in those **d**,
19: 4 and he stayed with him three **d**.
20:27 of God was there in those **d**,
20:28 stood before it in those **d**),
21:25 In those **d** there was no king
Ruth 1: 1 in the **d** when the judges ruled,
1 Sam 1:11 him to the LORD all the **d** of
2:31 the **d** are coming that I will
3: 1 the LORD was rare in those **d**;
7:13 the Philistines all the **d** of
7:15 Samuel judged Israel all the **d**
9:20 donkeys that were lost three **d**
10: 8 Seven **d** you shall wait, till I
11: 3 to him, "Hold off for seven **d**,
13: 8 Then he waited seven **d**,
13:11 you did not come within the **d**
14:52 with the Philistines all the **d**
17:12 in the **d** of Saul.
17:16 and presented himself forty **d**,
18:26 Now the **d** had not expired;
20:19 when you have stayed three **d**,
21: 5 kept from us about three **d**
25:28 found in you throughout your **d**.
25:38 came about, after about ten **d**,
28: 1 Now it happened in those **d** that
29: 3 who has been with me these **d**,
30:12 nor drunk water for three **d**
30:13 because three **d** ago I fell
31:13 at Jabesh, and fasted seven **d**.
2 Sam 1: 1 and David had stayed two **d** in
7:12 When your **d** are fulfilled and
16:23 which he gave in those **d**,
20: 4 of Judah for me within three **d**,
21: 1 there was a famine in the **d** of
21: 9 and were put to death in the **d**
21: 9 of harvest, in the first **d**,
24: 8 end of nine months and twenty **d**.
1 Ki 2: 1 Now the **d** of David drew near
2:38 dwelt in Jerusalem many **d**.
3: 2 name of the LORD until those **d**.
3:13 you among the kings all your **d**.
3:14 then I will lengthen your **d**.
4:21 and served Solomon all the **d**
4:25 all the **d** of Solomon.
8:40 they may fear You all the **d**
8:65 seven **d** and seven more
8:65 seven days and seven more **d**—
8:65 and seven more days—fourteen **d**.
10:21 accounted as nothing in the **d**
11:12 I will not do it in your **d**,
11:25 adversary of Israel all the **d**
11:34 I have made him ruler all the **d**
12: 5 to them, "Depart for three **d**,
14:30 and Jeroboam all their **d**.
15: 5 He commanded him all the **d** of
15: 6 and Jeroboam all the **d** of his
15:14 loyal to the LORD all his **d**.
15:16 king of Israel all their **d**.
15:32 king of Israel all their **d**.
16:15 had reigned in Tirzah seven **d**.
16:34 In his **d** Hiel of Bethel built
17:15 her household ate for many **d**.
18: 1 it came to pass after many **d**
19: 8 strength of that food forty **d**
20:29 opposite each other for seven **d**.
21:29 not bring the calamity in his **d**.
21:29 In the **d** of his son I will
22:46 who remained in the **d** of his
2 Ki 2:17 and they searched for three **d**
3: 9 that roundabout route seven **d**;
8:20 In his **d** Edom revolted against
10:32 In those **d** the LORD began to
12: 2 sight of the LORD all the **d**
13: 3 the son of Hazael, all their **d**.
13:22 oppressed Israel all the **d** of
15:18 he did not depart all his **d**
15:29 In the **d** of Pekah king of
15:37 In those **d** the LORD began to
18: 4 for until those **d** the children
20: 1 In those **d** Hezekiah was sick and
20: 6 And I will add to your **d** fifteen
20:17 the **d** are coming when all that
20:19 and truth at least in my **d**?
23:22 never been held since the **d** of
23:22 nor in all the **d** of the kings
23:29 In his **d** Pharaoh Necho king of
24: 1 In his **d** Nebuchadnezzar king of
25:29 before the king all the **d** of
25:30 all the **d** of his life.
1 Chr 1:19 for in his **d** the earth was
4:41 recorded by name came in the **d**
5:10 Now in the **d** of Saul they made
5:17 by genealogies in the **d** of
5:17 and in the **d** of Jeroboam king
7: 2 their number in the **d** of David
7:22 their father mourned many **d**,
9:25 from time to time for seven **d**.
10:12 at Jabesh, and fasted seven **d**.
12:39 were there with David three **d**,
13: 3 not inquired at it since the **d**
17:11 when your **d** are fulfilled, when
21:12 or else for three **d** the sword
22: 9 quietness to Israel in his **d**.
23: 1 David was old and full of **d**,
29:15 Our **d** on earth are as a
29:28 full of **d** and riches and honor;
2 Chr 7: 8 Solomon kept the feast seven **d**,
7: 9 dedication of the altar seven **d**,
7: 9 days, and the feast seven **d**.
9:20 accounted as nothing in the **d**
10: 5 "Come back to me after three **d**.
12:15 and Jeroboam all their **d**.
13:20 strength again in the **d** of
14: 1 In his **d** the land was quiet for
15:17 of Asa was loyal all his **d**.
20:25 and they were three **d** gathering
21: 8 In his **d** the Edomites revolted
24: 2 sight of the LORD all the **d**
24:14 LORD continually all the **d** of
24:15 grew old and was full of **d**,
26: 5 He sought God in the **d** of
29:17 house of the LORD in eight **d**,
30:21 of Unleavened Bread seven **d**
30:22 throughout the feast seven **d**,
30:23 the feast another seven **d**,
30:23 they kept it another seven **d**
32:24 In those **d** Hezekiah was sick
32:26 not come upon them in the **d** of
34:33 All his **d** they did not depart
35:17 of Unleavened Bread for seven **d**.
35:18 in Israel like that since the **d**
36: 9 three months and ten **d**.
Ezra 4: 2 sacrificed to Him since the **d**
4: 5 their purpose all the **d** of
4: 7 In the **d** of Artaxerxes also,
6:22 of Unleavened Bread seven **d**
8:15 and we camped there three **d**.
8:32 and stayed there three **d**.
9: 7 Since the **d** of our fathers to
10: 8 would not come within three **d**,
10: 9 at Jerusalem within three **d**.
10:13 this the work of one or two **d**,
Neh 1: 4 wept, and mourned for many **d**;
2:11 Jerusalem and was there three **d**.
5:18 and once every ten **d** an
6:15 day of Elul, in fifty-two **d**.
6:17 Also in those **d** the nobles of
8:17 for since the **d** of Joshua the
8:18 And they kept the feast seven **d**;
9:32 from the **d** of the kings of
12: 7 and their brethren in the **d** of
12:12 Now in the **d** of Joiakim, the
12:22 fathers' houses in the **d** of
12:23 fathers' houses until the **d**
12:26 These lived in the **d** of Joiakim
12:26 and in the **d** of Nehemiah the
12:46 For in the **d** of David and Asaph
12:47 In the **d** of Zerubbabel and in
12:47 of Zerubbabel and in the **d** of
13: 6 Then after certain **d** I obtained
13:15 In those **d** I saw people in
13:23 In those **d** I also saw Jews who
Esth 1: 1 Now it came to pass in the **d** of
1: 2 in those **d** when King Ahasuerus
1: 4 excellent majesty for many **d**,
1: 4 one hundred and eighty **d** in
1: 5 And when these **d** were completed,
1: 5 made a feast lasting seven **d**
2:12 for thus were the **d** of their
2:21 In those **d**, while Mordecai
4:11 in to the king these thirty **d**.
4:16 eat nor drink for three **d**,
9:21 the fourteenth and fifteenth **d**
9:22 as the **d** on which the Jews had
9:22 that they should make them **d** of
9:26 So they called these **d** Purim,
9:27 should celebrate these two **d**
9:28 that these **d** should be
9:28 that these **d** of Purim should
9:31 to confirm these **d** of Purim at
Job 1: 5 when the **d** of feasting had run
2:13 with him on the ground seven **d**
3: 6 it not rejoice among the **d** of
7: 1 Are not his **d** also like the
7: 1 not his days also like the **d**
7: 6 My **d** are swifter than a weaver's
7:16 For my **d** are but a breath.
8: 9 Because our **d** on earth are a
9:25 Now my **d** are swifter than a
10: 5 Are Your **d** like the days of a
10: 5 Are Your days like the **d** of a
10: 5 Are Your years like the **d** of
10:20 Are not my **d** few? Cease!
12:12 aged men, And with length of **d**,
14: 1 is born of woman Is of few **d**
14: 5 Since his **d** are determined,
14:14 All the **d** of my hard service I
15:20 writhes with pain all his **d**,
17: 1 My **d** are extinguished, The
17:11 My **d** are past, My purposes are
21:13 They spend their **d** in wealth,
24: 1 who know Him see not His **d**?
29: 2 As in the **d** when God watched
29: 4 Just as I was in the **d** of my
29:18 And multiply my **d** as the
30:16 The **d** of affliction take hold
30:27 **D** of affliction confront me.
33:25 He shall return to the **d** of
36:11 They shall spend their **d** in
38:12 the morning since your **d**
38:21 because the number of your **d**
42:12 LORD blessed the latter **d** of
42:17 So Job died, old and full of **d**.
Ps 21: 4 Length of **d** forever and ever.
23: 6 shall follow me All the **d** of
27: 4 house of the LORD All the **d**
34:12 life, And loves many **d**,
37:18 The LORD knows the **d** of the
37:19 And in the **d** of famine they
39: 4 what is the measure of my **d**,
39: 5 You have made my **d** as
44: 1 in their **d**, In days of old:
44: 1 In **d** of old:
49: 5 Why should I fear in the **d** of
55:23 shall not live out half their **d**;
72: 7 In His **d** the righteous shall
77: 5 I have considered the **d** of old,
78:33 Therefore their **d** He consumed
89:29 And his throne as the **d** of
89:45 The **d** of his youth You have
90: 9 For all our **d** have passed away
90:10 The **d** of our lives are seventy
90:12 So teach us to number our **d**,
90:14 rejoice and be glad all our **d**!
90:15 us glad according to the **d** in
94:13 may give him rest from the **d**
102: 3 For my **d** are consumed like
102:11 My **d** are like a shadow that
102:23 in the way; He shortened my **d**.
102:24 me away in the midst of my **d**;
103:15 his **d** are like grass; As a
109: 8 Let his **d** be few, And let
119:84 How many are the **d** of Your

128: 5 good of Jerusalem All the ***d***
139:16 The ***d*** fashioned for me, When
143: 5 I remember the ***d*** of old;
144: 4 His ***d*** are like a passing
Prov 3: 2 For length of ***d*** and long life
3:16 Length of ***d*** is in her right
9:11 For by me your ***d*** will be
10:27 fear of the LORD prolongs ***d***,
15:15 All the ***d*** of the afflicted are
19:20 may be wise in your latter ***d***.
28:16 will prolong his ***d***.
31:12 good and not evil All the ***d***
Eccl 2: 3 to do under heaven all the ***d***
2:16 is will be forgotten in the ***d***
2:23 For all his ***d*** are sorrowful,
5:17 All his ***d*** he also eats in
5:18 toils under the sun all the ***d***
5:20 will not dwell unduly on the ***d***
6: 3 so that the ***d*** of his years are
6:12 all the ***d*** of his vain life
7:10 Why were the former ***d*** better
7:15 I have seen everything in my ***d***
8:12 and his ***d*** are prolonged, yet I
8:13 nor will he prolong his ***d***,
8:15 him in his labor all the ***d*** of
9: 9 wife whom you love all the ***d***
9: 9 all your ***d*** of vanity; for that
11: 1 you will find it after many ***d***.
11: 8 Yet let him remember the ***d*** of
11: 9 your heart cheer you in the ***d***
12: 1 now your Creator in the ***d*** of
12: 1 Before the difficult ***d*** come,
Isa 1: 1 Judah and Jerusalem in the ***d***
2: 2 come to pass in the latter ***d***
7: 1 Now it came to pass in the ***d*** of
7:17 ***d*** that have not come since the
13:22 And her ***d*** will not be
23: 7 antiquity is from ancient ***d***,
23:15 according to the ***d*** of one king.
24:22 After many ***d*** they will be
30:26 As the light of seven ***d***,
32:10 In a year and some ***d*** You will
38: 1 In those ***d*** Hezekiah was sick and
38: 5 surely I will add to your ***d***
38:20 instruments All the ***d*** of our
39: 6 the ***d*** are coming when all that
39: 8 will be peace and truth in my ***d***.
51: 9 Awake as in the ancient ***d***,
53:10 seed, He shall prolong His ***d***,
60:20 And the ***d*** of your mourning
63: 9 and carried them All the ***d*** of
63:11 Then he remembered the ***d*** of
65:20 from there live but a few ***d***,
65:20 man who has not fulfilled his ***d***;
65:22 For as the ***d*** of a tree, so
65:22 so shall be the ***d*** of My
Jer 1: 2 of the LORD came in the ***d*** of
1: 3 It came also in the ***d*** of
2:32 My people have forgotten Me ***d***
3: 6 LORD said also to me in the ***d***
3:16 in the land in those ***d***,
3:18 In those ***d*** the house of Judah
5:18 "Nevertheless in those ***d***,
6:11 with him who is full of ***d***.
7:32 the ***d*** are coming," says the
9:25 the ***d*** are coming," says the
13: 6 it came to pass after many ***d***
16: 9 before your eyes and in your ***d***,
16:14 the ***d*** are coming," says the
17:11 leave him in the midst of his ***d***,
19: 6 the ***d*** are coming," says the
20:18 That my ***d*** should be consumed
22:30 who shall not prosper in his ***d***;
23: 5 the ***d*** are coming," says the
23: 6 In His ***d*** Judah will be saved,
23: 7 the ***d*** are coming," says the
23:20 In the latter ***d*** you will
25:34 For the ***d*** of your slaughter
26:18 Moresheth prophesied in the ***d***
30: 3 the ***d*** are coming,' says the
30:24 In the latter ***d*** you will
31:27 the ***d*** are coming, says the
31:29 In those ***d*** they shall say no
31:31 the ***d*** are coming, says the
31:33 house of Israel after those ***d***,
31:38 the ***d*** are coming, says the
32:14 that they may last many ***d***.
33:14 the ***d*** are coming,' says the
33:15 In those ***d*** and at that time I
33:16 In those ***d*** Judah will be saved,
35: 1 from the LORD in the ***d*** of
35: 7 but all your ***d*** you shall dwell
35: 7 that you may live many ***d*** in the
35: 8 us, to drink no wine all our ***d***,
36: 2 from the ***d*** of Josiah even to
37:16 had remained there many ***d***,
42: 7 And it happened after ten ***d***
46:26 shall be inhabited as in the ***d***
48:12 the ***d*** are coming," says the
48:47 of Moab In the latter ***d***,
49: 2 the ***d*** are coming," says the
49:39 come to pass in the latter ***d***:
50: 4 In those ***d*** and in that time,"
50:20 In those ***d*** and in that time,"
51:47 the ***d*** are coming That I will
51:52 the ***d*** are coming," says the
52:33 before the king all the ***d*** of
52:34 all the ***d*** of his life.
Lam 1: 7 In the ***d*** of her affliction and
1: 7 things That she had in the ***d***
2:17 word Which He commanded in ***d***
4:18 Our ***d*** were over, For our end
5:21 Renew our ***d*** as of old,
Ezek 3:15 astonished among them seven ***d***.
3:16 to pass at the end of seven ***d***
4: 4 to the number of the ***d*** that
4: 5 to the number of the ***d***,
4: 5 three hundred and ninety ***d***;
4: 6 of the house of Judah forty ***d***.
4: 8 till you have ended the ***d*** of
4: 9 During the number of ***d*** that
4: 9 three hundred and ninety ***d***,
5: 2 when the ***d*** of the siege are
12:22 The ***d*** are prolonged, and every
12:23 The ***d*** are at hand, and the
12:25 be postponed; for in your ***d***,
12:27 that he sees is for many ***d***
16:22 you did not remember the ***d*** of
16:43 you did not remember the ***d*** of
16:56 a byword in your mouth in the ***d***
16:60 My covenant with you in the ***d***
22: 4 You have caused your ***d*** to draw
22:14 in the ***d*** when I shall deal with
23:19 calling to remembrance the ***d***
36:38 at Jerusalem on its feast ***d***,
38: 8 After many ***d*** you will be
38:16 It will be in the latter ***d*** that
38:17 whom I have spoken in former ***d***
38:17 for years in those ***d*** that I
43:25 Every day for seven ***d*** you shall
43:26 Seven ***d*** they shall make
43:27 When these ***d*** are over it shall
44:26 they shall count seven ***d*** for
45:21 Passover, a feast of seven ***d***;
45:23 On the seven ***d*** of the feast he
45:23 blemish, daily for seven ***d***,
45:25 shall do likewise for seven ***d***,
46: 1 shall be shut the six working ***d***;
46: 9 LORD on the appointed feast ***d***,
46:11 and the appointed feast ***d*** the
Dan 1:12 test your servants for ten ***d***,
1:14 matter, and tested them ten ***d***.
1:15 And at the end of ten ***d*** their
1:18 Now at the end of the ***d***,
2:28 what will be in the latter ***d***.
2:44 And in the ***d*** of these kings the
5:11 And in the ***d*** of your father,
6: 7 any god or man for thirty ***d***,
6:10 as was his custom since early ***d***.
6:12 any god or man within thirty ***d***,
7: 9 And the Ancient of ***D*** was
7:13 He came to the Ancient of ***D***,
7:22 until the Ancient of ***D*** came, and
8:14 two thousand three hundred ***d***;
8:26 For it refers to many ***d*** in
8:27 fainted and was sick for ***d***;
10: 2 In those ***d*** I, Daniel, was
10:13 withstood me twenty-one ***d***;
10:14 to your people in the latter ***d***,
10:14 the vision refers to many ***d***
11:20 but within a few ***d*** he shall be
11:33 yet for many ***d*** they shall
12:11 two hundred and ninety ***d***.
12:12 three hundred and thirty-five ***d***.
12:13 inheritance at the end of the ***d***.
Hos 1: 1 in the ***d*** of Uzziah, Jotham,
1: 1 and in the ***d*** of Jeroboam the
2:11 mirth to cease, Her feast ***d***,
2:13 I will punish her For the ***d*** of
2:15 As in the ***d*** of her youth, As
3: 3 "You shall stay with me many ***d***;
3: 4 of Israel shall abide many ***d***
3: 5 His goodness in the latter ***d***.
6: 2 After two ***d*** He will revive us;
9: 7 The ***d*** of punishment have come;
9: 7 The ***d*** of recompense have come.
9: 9 As in the ***d*** of Gibeah.
10: 9 you have sinned from the ***d*** of
12: 9 As in the ***d*** of the appointed
Joel 1: 2 like this happened in your ***d***,
1: 2 Or even in the ***d*** of your
2:29 pour out My Spirit in those ***d***.
3: 1 in those ***d*** and at that time,
Am 1: 1 saw concerning Israel in the ***d***
1: 1 and in the ***d*** of Jeroboam the
4: 2 the ***d*** shall come upon you When
4: 4 Your tithes every three ***d***.
5:21 hate, I despise your feast ***d***,
8:11 the ***d*** are coming," says the
9:11 And rebuild it as in the ***d*** of
9:13 the ***d*** are coming," says the
Jon 1:17 the belly of the fish three ***d***
3: 4 out and said, "Yet forty ***d***,
Mic 1: 1 to Micah of Moresheth in the ***d***
4: 1 come to pass in the latter ***d***
7:14 As in ***d*** of old.
7:15 As in the ***d*** when you came out of
7:20 sworn to our fathers From ***d***
Hab 1: 5 I will work a work in your ***d***
Zeph 1: 1 in the ***d*** of Josiah the son of
Hag 2:16 'since those ***d***, when one
Zech 8: 6 of this people in these ***d***,
8: 9 have been hearing in these ***d***
8:10 For before these ***d*** There
8:11 this people as in the former ***d***,
8:15 So again in these ***d*** I am
8:23 In those ***d*** ten men from every
14: 5 from the earthquake In the ***d***
Mal 3: 4 As in the ***d*** of old, As in
3: 7 Yet from the ***d*** of your fathers
Mt 2: 1 in Bethlehem of Judea in the ***d***
3: 1 In those ***d*** John the Baptist came
4: 2 And when He had fasted forty ***d***
9:15 But the ***d*** will come when the
11:12 And from the ***d*** of John the
12:40 For as Jonah was three ***d*** and
12:40 will the Son of Man be three ***d***
15:32 now continued with Me three ***d***
17: 1 Now after six ***d*** Jesus took
23:30 If we had lived in the ***d*** of our
24:19 are nursing babies in those ***d***!
24:22 And unless those ***d*** were
24:22 for the elect's sake those ***d***
24:29 the tribulation of those ***d*** the
24:37 But as the ***d*** of Noah were, so
24:38 For as in the ***d*** before the
26: 2 You know that after two ***d*** is the
26:61 God and to build it in three ***d***.
27:40 temple and build it in three ***d***,
27:63 After three ***d*** I will rise.'
Mk 1: 9 It came to pass in those ***d***
1:13 there in the wilderness forty ***d***,
2: 1 entered Capernaum after some ***d***,
2:20 But the ***d*** will come when the
2:20 then they will fast in those ***d***.
2:26 the house of God in the ***d***
8: 1 In those ***d***, the multitude
8: 2 now continued with Me three ***d***
8:31 and after three ***d*** rise again.
9: 2 Now after six ***d*** Jesus took
13:17 are nursing babies in those ***d***!
13:19 For in those ***d*** there will be
13:20 the Lord had shortened those ***d***,
13:20 He chose, He shortened the ***d***.
13:24 But in those ***d***, after that
14: 1 After two ***d*** it was the Passover
14:58 and within three ***d*** I will build
15:29 temple and build it in three ***d***,
Lk 1: 5 There was in the ***d*** of Herod,
1:23 as soon as the ***d*** of his service
1:24 Now after those ***d*** his wife
1:25 in the ***d*** when He looked on me,
1:39 Now Mary arose in those ***d*** and
1:75 before Him all the ***d*** of our
2: 1 And it came to pass in those ***d***
2: 6 the ***d*** were completed for her to
2:21 And when eight ***d*** were completed
2:22 Now when the ***d*** of her
2:43 When they had finished the ***d***,
2:46 so it was that after three ***d***
4: 2 being tempted for forty ***d*** by the
4: 2 And in those ***d*** He ate nothing,
4:25 widows were in Israel in the ***d***
5:35 But the ***d*** will come when the
5:35 then they will fast in those ***d***.
6:12 Now it came to pass in those ***d***
9:28 about eight ***d*** after these
9:36 and told no one in those ***d*** any
13:14 There are six ***d*** on which men
15:13 And not many ***d*** after, the
17:22 The ***d*** will come when you will
17:22 desire to see one of the ***d*** of
17:26 And as it was in the ***d*** of Noah,
17:26 so it will be also in the ***d*** of
17:28 as it was also in the ***d*** of Lot:
19:43 For ***d*** will come upon you when
20: 1 it happened on one of those ***d***,
21: 6 the ***d*** will come in which not
21:22 For these are the ***d*** of
21:23 are nursing babies in those ***d***!
23:29 For indeed the ***d*** are coming in
24:18 which happened there in these ***d***?
Jn 2:12 they did not stay there many ***d***.
2:19 and in three ***d*** I will raise it
2:20 will You raise it up in three ***d***?
4:40 them; and He stayed there two ***d***.
4:43 Now after the two ***d*** He departed
11: 6 He stayed two more ***d*** in the
11:17 already been in the tomb four ***d***.
11:39 for he has been dead four ***d***.
12: 1 six ***d*** before the Passover,
20:26 And after eight ***d*** His disciples
Acts 1: 3 seen by them during forty ***d***
1: 5 with the Holy Spirit not many ***d***
1:15 And in those ***d*** Peter stood up
2:17 to pass in the last ***d***,
2:18 out My Spirit in those ***d***;
3:24 have also foretold these ***d***.
5:37 of Galilee rose up in the ***d*** of
6: 1 Now in those ***d***, when the number
7:41 they made a calf in those ***d***,
7:45 of our fathers until the ***d*** of
9: 9 And he was three ***d*** without
9:19 Then Saul spent some ***d*** with the
9:23 Now after many ***d*** were past, the
9:37 But it happened in those ***d*** that
9:43 So it was that he stayed many ***d***
10:30 Four ***d*** ago I was fasting until
10:48 they asked him to stay a few ***d***.
11:27 And in these ***d*** prophets came
11:28 which also happened in the ***d*** of
12: 3 Now it was during the ***D*** of
13:31 He was seen for many ***d*** by those
13:41 I work a work in your ***d***,
15:36 Then after some ***d*** Paul said to
16:12 staying in that city for some ***d***.
16:18 And this she did for many ***d***.
20: 6 away from Philippi after the ***D***
20: 6 and in five ***d*** joined them at
20: 6 Troas, where we stayed seven ***d***.
21: 4 we stayed there seven ***d***.
21: 5 had come to the end of those ***d***,
21:10 And as we stayed many ***d***,
21:15 And after those ***d*** we packed and
21:26 the expiration of the ***d*** of
21:27 Now when the seven ***d*** were almost

24: 1 Now after five **d** Ananias the
24:11 it is no more than twelve **d**
24:24 And after some **d**,
25: 1 after three **d** he went up from
25: 6 among them more than ten **d**,
25:13 And after some **d** King Agrippa
25:14 When they had been there many **d**,
27: 7 we had sailed slowly many **d**,
27:20 nor stars appeared for many **d**,
28: 7 us courteously for three **d**.
28:12 at Syracuse, we stayed three **d**.
28:14 to stay with them seven **d**.
28:17 it came to pass after three **d**
Gal 1:18 and remained with him fifteen **d**.
4:10 You observe **d** and months and
Eph 5:16 because the **d** are evil.
2 Tim 3: 1 that in the last **d** perilous
Heb 1: 2 has in these last **d** spoken to us
5: 7 in the **d** of His flesh, when He
7: 3 having neither beginning of **d**
8: 8 the **d** are coming, says
8:10 of Israel after those **d**,
10:16 with them after those **d**,
10:32 But recall the former **d** in
11:30 they were encircled for seven **d**.
12:10 For they indeed for a few **d**
Jas 5: 3 up treasure in the last **d**.
1 Pe 3:10 love life And see good **d**,
3:20 longsuffering waited in the **d**
2 Pe 3: 3 will come in the last **d**,
Rev 2:10 you will have tribulation ten **d**.
2:13 deny My faith even in the **d** in
9: 6 In those **d** men will seek death
10: 7 but in the **d** of the sounding of
11: 3 two hundred and sixty **d**,
11: 6 so that no rain falls in the **d**
11: 9 dead bodies three-and-a-half **d**,
11:11 after the three-and-a-half **d**
12: 6 two hundred and sixty **d**.

DAYS' (9/9) DAYS

Gen 30:36 Then he put three **d** journey
31:23 him and pursued him for seven **d**
Ex 3:18 let us go three **d** journey into
5: 3 let us go three **d** journey into
8:27 We will go three **d** journey into
Num 10:33 before them for the three **d**
33: 8 went three **d** journey in the
Deut 1: 2 It is eleven **d** journey from
2 Sam 24:13 Or shall there be three **d**

DAYSMAN (KJV) See MEDIATOR

DAYSPRING (1/1) DAY

Lk 1:78 With which the ***D*** from on high

DAYTIME (9/9) DAY

Job 5:14 meet with darkness in the **d**,
24:16 marked for themselves in the **d**;
Ps 22: 2 O My God, I cry in the **d**,
42: 8 His lovingkindness in the **d**,
78:14 In the **d** also He led them with
Isa 4: 6 a tabernacle for shade in the **d**
21: 8 on the watchtower in the **d**;
Lk 21:37 And in the **d** He was teaching in
2 Pe 2:13 it pleasure to carouse in the **d**.

DEACONS (5/5)

Phil 1: 1 with the bishops and **d**:
1 Tim 3: 8 Likewise **d** must be reverent,
3:10 then let them serve as **d**,
3:12 Let **d** be the husbands of one
3:13 those who have served well as **d**

DEAD (320/288) DEADLY, DEADNESS, DIE

Gen 20: 3 Indeed you are a **d** man because
23: 3 stood up from before his **d**,
23: 4 that I may bury my **d** out of my
23: 6 bury your **d** in the choicest of
23: 6 place, that you may bury your **d**.
23: 8 is your wish that I bury my **d**
23:11 it to you. Bury your **d**!"
23:13 from me and I will bury my **d**
23:15 you and me? So bury your **d**.
42:38 with you, for his brother is **d**,
44:20 is young; his brother is **d**,
50:15 saw that their father was **d**,
Ex 4:19 men who sought your life are **d**.
9: 7 of the Israelites was **d**.
12:30 where there was not one **d**.
12:33 said, "We shall all be **d**.
14:30 and Israel saw the Egyptians **d**
21:34 but the **d** animal shall be his.
21:35 and the **d** ox they shall also
21:36 and the **d** animal shall be his
Lev 11:31 touches them when they are **d**
11:32 when they are **d** shall be
19:28 in your flesh for the **d**,
21: 1 shall defile himself for the **d**
21:11 nor shall he go near any **d** body,
Num 6: 6 he shall not go near a **d** body.
12:12 do not let her be as one **d**,
16:48 And he stood between the **d** and
19:11 He who touches the **d** body of
19:18 a bone, the slain, the **d**,
20:29 saw that Aaron was **d**,
Deut 14: 1 front of your head for the **d**.
14: 8 or touch their **d** carcasses.
18:11 or one who calls up the **d**.
25: 5 the widow of the **d** man shall
25: 6 succeed to the name of his **d**
26:14 nor given any of it for the **d**.
Josh 1: 2 "Moses My servant is **d**.
Judg 2:19 to pass, when the judge was **d**,
3:25 fallen **d** on the floor.
4: 1 When Ehud was **d**, the children
4:22 **d** with the peg in his temple.
5:27 Where he sank, there he fell **d**.
8:33 it was, as soon as Gideon was **d**,
9:55 Israel saw that Abimelech was **d**,
16:24 the one who multiplied our **d**.
16:30 So the **d** that he killed at his
Ruth 1: 8 as you have dealt with the **d**
2:20 to the living and the **d**!"
4: 5 Moabitess, the wife of the **d**,
4: 5 to perpetuate the name of the **d**
4:10 to perpetuate the name of the **d**
4:10 that the name of the **d** may not
1 Sam 4:17 Hophni and Phinehas, are **d**;
4:19 and her husband were **d**,
17:51 saw that their champion was **d**,
24:14 A **d** dog? A flea?
25:39 David heard that Nabal was **d**,
31: 5 armorbearer saw that Saul was **d**,
31: 7 that Saul and his sons were **d**,
2 Sam 1: 4 of the people are fallen and **d**,
1: 4 Saul and Jonathan his son are **d**
1: 5 Saul and Jonathan his son are **d**?
2: 7 for your master Saul is **d**,
4:10 me, saying, 'Look, Saul is **d**,
9: 8 should look upon such a **d** dog
11:21 servant Uriah the Hittite is **d**
11:24 of the king's servants are **d**,
11:24 servant Uriah the Hittite is **d**
11:26 that Uriah her husband was **d**,
12:18 tell him that the child was **d**.
12:18 we tell him that the child is **d**?
12:19 perceived that the child was **d**.
12:19 his servants, "Is the child **d**?
12:19 And they said, "He is **d**.
12:23 "But now he is **d**;
13:32 sons, for only Amnon is **d**.
13:33 that all the king's sons are **d**.
13:33 are dead. For only Amnon is **d**.
13:39 Amnon, because he was **d**.
14: 2 mourning a long time for the **d**.
14: 5 I am a widow, my husband is **d**.
16: 9 Why should this **d** dog curse my
18:20 because the king's son is **d**.
19:28 my father's house were but **d**
1 Ki 3:20 and laid her **d** child in my
3:21 nurse my son, there he was, **d**.
3:22 and the **d** one is your son."
3:22 But the **d** one is your son,
3:23 and your son is the **d** one';
3:23 But your son is the **d** one,
11:21 the commander of the army was **d**,
13:31 his sons, saying, "When I am **d**,
21:14 has been stoned and is **d**.
21:15 had been stoned and was **d**,
21:15 for Naboth is not alive, but **d**.
21:16 Ahab heard that Naboth was **d**,
2 Ki 4: 1 "Your servant my husband is **d**,
4:32 lying **d** on his bed.
8: 5 king how he had restored the **d**
11: 1 Ahaziah saw that her son was **d**,
19:35 there were the corpses—all **d**.
1 Chr 5:22 for many fell **d**,
10: 5 armorbearer saw that Saul was **d**,
10: 7 that Saul and his sons were **d**,
2 Chr 20:24 and there were their **d** bodies,
20:25 of valuables on the **d** bodies,
22:10 Ahaziah saw that her son was **d**,
Job 1:19 young people, and they are **d**;
26: 5 The **d** tremble, Those under the
Ps 31:12 I am forgotten like a **d** man,
76: 6 and horse were cast into a **d**
79: 2 The **d** bodies of Your servants
88: 5 Adrift among the **d**,
88:10 You work wonders for the **d**?
88:10 Shall the **d** arise and praise
106:28 ate sacrifices made to the **d**.
110: 6 the places with **d** bodies,
115:17 The **d** do not praise the LORD,
143: 3 those who have long been **d**.
Prov 2:18 death, And her paths to the **d**;
9:18 he does not know that the **d**
21:16 rest in the assembly of the **d**.
Eccl 4: 2 Therefore I praised the **d** who
4: 2 the dead who were already **d**,
9: 3 after that they go to the **d**.
9: 4 dog is better than a **d** lion.
9: 5 But the **d** know nothing, And
10: 1 ***D*** flies putrefy the perfumer's
Isa 8:19 Should they seek the **d** on
14: 9 It stirs up the **d** for you,
22: 2 Nor **d** in battle.
26:14 They are **d**, they will not
26:19 Your **d** shall live; Together
26:19 Together with my **d** body they
26:19 the earth shall cast out the **d**.
37:36 there were the corpses—all **d**.
59:10 We are as **d** men in desolate
Jer 16: 7 them, to comfort them for the **d**;
22:10 Weep not for the **d**,
26:23 the sword and cast his **d** body
31:40 And the whole valley of the **d**
33: 5 to fill their places with the **d**
34:20 Their **d** bodies shall be for
36:30 and his **d** body shall be cast
41: 9 Ishmael had cast all the **d**
Lam 3: 6 Like the **d** of long ago.
Ezek 24:17 make no mourning for the **d**;
44:25 by coming near a **d** person.
Am 6:10 And when a relative of the **d**,
8: 3 Many **d** bodies everywhere, They
Hag 2:13 is unclean because of a **d**
Mt 2:19 But when Herod was **d**,
2:20 the young Child's life are **d**.
8:22 and let the **d** bury their own
8:22 let the dead bury their own **d**.
9:24 room, for the girl is not **d**,
10: 8 cleanse the lepers, raise the **d**,
11: 5 the **d** are raised up and the
14: 2 he is risen from the **d**,
17: 9 Son of Man is risen from the **d**.
22:31 the resurrection of the **d**,
22:32 God is not the God of the **d**,
23:27 but inside are full of **d** men's
27:64 'He has risen from the **d**.
28: 4 and became like **d** men.
28: 7 that He is risen from the **d**,
Mk 5:35 who said, "Your daughter is **d**.
5:39 and weep? The child is not **d**,
6:14 the Baptist is risen from the **d**,
6:16 he has been raised from the **d**!
9: 9 Son of Man had risen from the **d**.
9:10 what the rising from the **d**
9:26 of him. And he became as one **d**,
9:26 so that many said, "He is **d**.
12:25 "For when they rise from the **d**,
12:26 "But concerning the **d**,
12:27 "He is not the God of the **d**,
15:44 marveled that He was already **d**;
15:44 He had been **d** for some time.
Lk 7:12 a **d** man was being carried out,
7:15 So he who was **d** sat up and began
7:22 the **d** are raised, the poor
8:49 to him, "Your daughter is **d**.
8:52 "Do not weep; she is not **d**,
8:53 Him, knowing that she was **d**.
9: 7 that John had risen from the **d**,
9:60 Let the **d** bury their own dead,
9:60 "Let the dead bury their own **d**,
10:30 departed, leaving him half **d**.
15:24 for this my son was **d** and is
15:32 for your brother was **d** and is
16:30 if one goes to them from the **d**,
16:31 though one rise from the **d**.
20:35 and the resurrection from the **d**,
20:37 bush passage that the **d** are
20:38 He is not the God of the **d**
24: 5 you seek the living among the **d**?
24:46 suffer and to rise from the **d**
Jn 2:22 when He had risen from the **d**,
5:21 as the Father raises the **d**
5:25 when the **d** will hear the voice
6:49 in the wilderness, and are **d**.
6:58 ate the manna, and are **d**.
8:52 You have a demon! Abraham is **d**,
8:53 our father Abraham, who is **d**?
8:53 is dead? And the prophets are **d**.
11:14 to them plainly, "Lazarus is **d**.
11:39 the sister of him who was **d**,
11:39 for he has been **d** four days."
11:41 the place where the **d** man
12: 1 Lazarus was who had been **d**,
12: 1 whom He had raised from the **d**.
12: 9 whom He had raised from the **d**.
12:17 tomb and raised him from the **d**,
19:33 and saw that He was already **d**,
20: 9 He must rise again from the **d**.
21:14 after He was raised from the **d**.
Acts 2:29 that he is both **d** and buried,
3:15 whom God raised from the **d**,
4: 2 the resurrection from the **d**.
4:10 whom God raised from the **d**,
5:10 men came in and found her **d**,
7: 4 there, when his father was **d**,
10:41 Him after He arose from the **d**.
10:42 Judge of the living and the **d**.
13:30 "But God raised Him from the **d**.
13:34 that He raised Him from the **d**,
14:19 the city, supposing him to be **d**.
17: 3 and rise again from the **d**,
17:31 all by raising Him from the **d**.
17:32 of the resurrection of the **d**,
20: 9 third story and was taken up **d**.
23: 6 hope and resurrection of the **d**
24:15 be a resurrection of the **d**,
24:21 the resurrection of the **d** I am
26: 8 by you that God raises the **d**?
26:23 be the first to rise from the **d**,
28: 6 up or suddenly fall down **d**.
Rom 1: 4 by the resurrection from the **d**.
4:17 who gives life to the **d** and
4:19 already **d** (since he was about a
4:24 up Jesus our Lord from the **d**,
6: 4 as Christ was raised from the **d**
6: 9 having been raised from the **d**,
6:11 reckon yourselves to be **d**
6:13 God as being alive from the **d**,
7: 4 you also have become **d** to the
7: 4 Him who was raised from the **d**,
7: 8 apart from the law sin was **d**.
8:10 the body is **d** because of sin,
8:11 Him who raised Jesus from the **d**
8:11 He who raised Christ from the **d**
10: 7 to bring Christ up from the **d**).
10: 9 God has raised Him from the **d**,
11:15 be but life from the **d**?

14: 9 He might be Lord of both the **d**
1 Cor 15:12 He has been raised from the **d**,
15:12 is no resurrection of the **d**?
15:13 is no resurrection of the **d**,
15:15 if in fact the **d** do not rise.
15:16 For if the **d** do not rise, then
15:20 now Christ is risen from the **d**,
15:21 came the resurrection of the **d**.
15:29 do who are baptized for the **d**,
15:29 if the **d** do not rise at all?
15:29 are they baptized for the **d**?
15:32 If the **d** do not rise, "Let
15:35 'How are the **d** raised up?
15:42 is the resurrection of the **d**.
15:52 and the **d** will be raised
2 Cor 1: 9 but in God who raises the **d**,
Gal 1: 1 who raised Him from the **d**),
Eph 1:20 when He raised Him from the **d**
2: 1 who were **d** in trespasses and
2: 5 even when we were **d** in
5:14 who sleep, Arise from the **d**,
Phil 3:11 to the resurrection from the **d**.
Col 1:18 the firstborn from the **d**,
2:12 God, who raised Him from the **d**.
2:13 being **d** in your trespasses and
1 Th 1:10 whom He raised from the **d**,
4:16 And the **d** in Christ will rise
1 Tim 5: 6 she who lives in pleasure is **d**
2 Tim 2: 8 was raised from the **d** according
4: 1 judge the living and the **d** at
Heb 6: 1 of repentance from **d** works and
6: 2 hands, of resurrection of the **d**,
9:14 your conscience from **d** works
9:17 is in force after men are **d**,
11: 4 and through it he being **d** still
11:12 one man, and him as good as **d**,
11:19 raise him up, even from the **d**,
11:35 Women received their **d** raised to
13:20 up our Lord Jesus from the **d**,
Jas 2:17 if it does not have works, is **d**.
2:20 that faith without works is **d**?
2:26 body without the spirit is **d**,
2:26 so faith without works is **d**
1 Pe 1: 3 of Jesus Christ from the **d**,
1:21 who raised Him from the **d** and
4: 5 to judge the living and the **d**.
4: 6 also to those who are **d**,
Jude 12 trees without fruit, twice **d**,
Rev 1: 5 the firstborn from the **d**,
1:17 Him, I fell at His feet as **d**.
1:18 "I am He who lives, and was **d**,
2: 8 First and the Last, who was **d**,
3: 1 you are alive, but you are **d**.
11: 8 And their **d** bodies will lie in
11: 9 and nations will see their **d**
11: 9 and not allow their **d** bodies to
11:18 come, And the time of the **d**,
14:13 Blessed are the **d** who die in
16: 3 became blood as of a **d** man;
20: 5 But the rest of the **d** did not
20:12 And I saw the **d**, small and
20:12 And the **d** were judged according
20:13 The sea gave up the **d** who were
20:13 and Hades delivered up the **d**

DEADLY (8/8) DEAD

1 Sam 5:11 For there was a **d** destruction
Ps 17: 9 From my **d** enemies who
144:10 David His servant From the **d**
Ezek 9: 1 each with a **d** weapon in his
Mk 16:18 and if they drink anything **d**,
Jas 3: 8 full of **d** poison.
Rev 13: 3 and his **d** wound was healed.
13:12 whose **d** wound was healed.

DEADNESS (1/1) DEAD

Rom 4:19 and the **d** of Sarah's womb.

DEAF (15/15)

Ex 4:11 Or who makes the mute, the **d**,
Lev 19:14 'You shall not curse the **d**,
Ps 38:13 like a **d** man, do not hear;
58: 4 They are like the **d** cobra
Isa 29:18 In that day the **d** shall hear
35: 5 And the ears of the **d** shall be
42:18 Hear, you **d**; And look,
42:19 Or **d** as My messenger whom I
43: 8 And the **d** who have ears.
Mic 7:16 mouth; Their ears shall be **d**.
Mt 11: 5 are cleansed and the **d** hear;
Mk 7:32 brought to Him one who was **d**
7:37 He makes both the **d** to hear and
9:25 **D** and dumb spirit, I command
Lk 7:22 the **d** hear, the dead are

DEAL (50/49) DEALER, DEALING, DEALS, DEALT

Gen 19: 9 now we will **d** worse with you
21:23 that you will not **d** falsely
24:49 Now if you will **d** kindly and
32: 9 and I will **d** well with you':
43: 6 Why did you **d** so wrongfully
47:29 and **d** kindly and truly with me.
Ex 1:10 let us **d** shrewdly with them,
8:29 Pharaoh not **d** deceitfully
12:38 a great **d** of livestock.
21: 9 he shall **d** with her according
Lev 19:11 nor **d** falsely, nor lie to one
Deut 7: 5 But thus you shall **d** with them:
32: 6 Do you thus **d** with the LORD,
Josh 2:14 that we will **d** kindly and truly
Ruth 1: 8 The LORD **d** kindly with you, as
1 Sam 20: 8 Therefore you shall **d** kindly
2 Sam 18: 5 **D** gently for my sake with the
2 Ki 22: 7 because they **d** faithfully."
2 Chr 2: 3 so **d** with me.
Job 42: 8 lest I **d** with you according
Ps 25: 3 ashamed who **d** treacherously
75: 4 Do not **d** boastfully,' And to
83: 9 **D** with them as with Midian,
105:25 To **d** craftily with His
109:21 **D** with me for Your name's
119:17 **D** bountifully with Your
119:124 **D** with Your servant according
142: 7 For You shall **d** bountifully
Prov 12:22 But those who **d** truthfully
Isa 26:10 uprightness he will **d** unjustly,
33: 1 And you who **d** treacherously,
33: 1 They will **d** treacherously with
48: 8 For I knew that you would **d** very
52:13 My Servant shall **d** prudently;
Jer 9: 7 For how shall I **d** with the
12: 1 Why are those happy who **d** so
18:23 **D** thus with them In the time
21: 2 Perhaps the LORD will **d** with
Ezek 16:59 I will **d** with you as you have
22:14 in the days when I shall **d** with
23:25 And they shall **d** furiously
23:29 They will **d** hatefully with you,
31:11 and he shall surely **d** with it;
Dan 1:13 so **d** with your servants."
11: 7 and **d** with them and prevail.
Hab 1:13 Why do You look on those who **d**
Zeph 3:19 at that time I will **d** with all
Mal 2:10 Why do we **d** treacherously with
2:15 And let none **d** treacherously
2:16 do not **d** treacherously."

DEALER (1/1) DEAL, DEALERS

Isa 21: 2 The treacherous **d** deals

DEALERS (2/1) DEALER

Isa 24:16 Woe to me! The treacherous **d**
24:16 the treacherous **d** have dealt

DEALING (3/3) DEAL, DEALINGS

Ex 5:15 Why are you **d** thus with your
Ps 7:16 And his violent **d** shall come
Isa 33: 1 When you make an end of **d**

DEALINGS (2/2) DEALING

1 Sam 2:23 For I hear of your evil **d** from
Jn 4: 9 For Jews have no **d** with

DEALS (5/5) DEAL

Ps 112: 5 A good man **d** graciously and
Isa 21: 2 The treacherous dealer **d**
Jer 6:13 Everyone **d** falsely.
8:10 even to the priest Everyone **d**
Heb 12: 7 God **d** with you as with sons;

DEALT (44/43) DEAL

Gen 16: 6 And when Sarai **d** harshly with
33:11 because God has **d** graciously
Ex 1:20 Therefore God **d** well with the
14:11 Why have you so **d** with us, to
21: 8 since he has **d** deceitfully with
Judg 9:16 and if you have **d** well with
9:23 and the men of Shechem **d**
Ruth 1: 8 as you have **d** with the dead and
1:20 for the Almighty has **d** very
1 Sam 14:33 You have **d** treacherously; roll a
24:18 shown this day how you have **d**
25:31 But when the LORD has **d** well
2 Sam 18:13 Otherwise I would have **d** falsely
2 Ki 12:15 for they **d** faithfully.
2 Chr 2: 3 As you have **d** with David my
11:23 He **d** wisely, and dispersed some
Neh 9:33 For You have **d** faithfully,
Job 6:15 My brothers have **d** deceitfully
Ps 13: 6 Because He has **d** bountifully
44:17 Nor have we **d** falsely with
103:10 He has not **d** with us according
116: 7 For the LORD has **d**
119:65 You have **d** well with Your
147:20 He has not **d** thus with any
Isa 24:16 The treacherous dealers have **d**
24:16 the treacherous dealers have **d**
33: 1 though they have not **d**
Jer 3:20 So have you **d** treacherously
5:11 and the house of Judah Have **d**
12: 6 Even they have **d** treacherously
Lam 1: 2 All her friends have **d**
Ezek 20:44 when I have **d** with you for My
25:15 Because the Philistines **d**
39:24 their transgressions I have **d**
Hos 5: 7 They have **d** treacherously with
6: 7 There they **d** treacherously
Joel 2:26 Who has **d** wondrously with you;
Zech 1: 6 So He has **d** with us.'" '"
Mal 2:11 Judah has **d** treacherously, And
2:14 With whom you have **d**
Lk 1:25 Thus the Lord has **d** with me, in
16: 8 unjust steward because he had **d**
Acts 7:19 This man **d** treacherously with
Rom 12: 3 as God has **d** to each one a

DEAR (6/6) DEARLY

Jer 31:20 Is Ephraim My **d** son? Is he
Lk 7: 2 who was **d** to him, was sick and
Acts 20:24 nor do I count my life **d** to
Eph 5: 1 be imitators of God as **d**
Col 1: 7 our **d** fellow servant, who is a
1 Th 2: 8 because you had become **d** to us.

DEARLY (2/2) DEAR

Jer 12: 7 I have given the **d** beloved of
Hos 4:18 Her rulers **d** love dishonor.

DEARTH (KJV) See DROUGHTS, FAMINE

DEATH (395/360) DEATHS, DIE

Gen 21:16 Let me not see the **d** of the
24:67 comforted after his mother's **d**.
25:11 after the **d** of Abraham, that
26:11 wife shall surely be put to **d**.
26:18 stopped them up after the **d** of
27: 2 I do not know the day of my **d**.
27: 7 of the LORD before my **d**.
27:10 he may bless you before his **d**.
Ex 10:17 He may take away from me this **d**
19:12 shall surely be put to **d**.
21:12 dies shall surely be put to **d**.
21:15 mother shall surely be put to **d**.
21:16 hand, shall surely be put to **d**.
21:17 mother shall surely be put to **d**.
21:28 ox gores a man or a woman to **d**,
21:29 owner also shall be put to **d**.
22:19 animal shall surely be put to **d**.
31:14 it shall surely be put to **d**;
31:15 he shall surely be put to **d**.
35: 2 work on it shall be put to **d**.
Lev 16: 1 spoke to Moses after the **d** of
19:20 but they shall not be put to **d**,
20: 2 he shall surely be put to **d**.
20: 9 mother shall surely be put to **d**.
20:10 shall surely be put to **d**.
20:11 them shall surely be put to **d**.
20:12 them shall surely be put to **d**.
20:13 They shall surely be put to **d**.
20:15 he shall surely be put to **d**,
20:16 They shall surely be put to **d**.
20:27 shall surely be put to **d**;
24:16 LORD shall surely be put to **d**.
24:16 LORD, he shall be put to **d**.
24:17 man shall surely be put to **d**.
24:21 kills a man shall be put to **d**.
27:29 but shall surely be put to **d**.
Num 1:51 comes near shall be put to **d**.
3:10 comes near shall be put to **d**.
3:38 came near was to be put to **d**.
15:35 man must surely be put to **d**;
18: 7 comes near shall be put to **d**.
23:10 Let me die the **d** of the
35:16 shall surely be put to **d**.
35:17 shall surely be put to **d**.
35:18 shall surely be put to **d**.
35:19 shall put the murderer to **d**;
35:19 him, he shall put him to **d**.
35:21 him shall surely be put to **d**.
35:21 shall put the murderer to **d**
35:25 shall remain there until the **d**
35:28 his city of refuge until the **d**
35:28 But after the **d** of the high
35:30 the murderer shall be put to **d**
35:30 a person for the **d** penalty.
35:31 a murderer who is guilty of **d**,
35:31 but he shall surely be put to **d**.
35:32 dwell in the land before the **d**
Deut 13: 5 of dreams shall be put to **d**,
13: 9 against him to put him to **d**,
17: 5 and shall stone to **d** that man
17: 6 Whoever is deserving of **d** shall
17: 6 of death shall be put to **d** on
17: 6 he shall not be put to **d** on the
17: 7 against him to put him to **d**,
19: 6 he was not deserving of **d**,
21:21 his city shall stone him to **d**
21:22 committed a sin deserving of **d**,
21:22 of death, and he is put to **d**,
22:21 her city shall stone her to **d**
22:24 and you shall stone them to **d**
22:26 woman no sin deserving of **d**,
24:16 Fathers shall not be put to **d**
24:16 shall the children be put to **d**
24:16 a person shall be put to **d** for
30:15 life and good, **d** and evil,
30:19 have set before you life and **d**,
31:27 then how much more after my **d**?
31:29 For I know that after my **d** you
33: 1 children of Israel before his **d**.
Josh 1: 1 After the **d** of Moses the
1:18 command him, shall be put to **d**.
2:13 and deliver our lives from **d**.
20: 6 and until the **d** of the one who
Judg 1: 1 Now after the **d** of Joshua it
5:18 their lives to the point of **d**,
6:31 plead for him be put to **d** by
13: 7 the womb to the day of his **d**.
16:16 that his soul was vexed to **d**,
16:30 dead that he killed at his **d**
20:13 that we may put them to **d** and
21: 5 "He shall surely be put to **d**.
Ruth 1:17 If anything but **d** parts you

2:11 your mother-in-law since the ***d***
1 Sam 4:20 And about the time of her ***d*** the
11:12 men, that we may put them to ***d***.
11:13 Not a man shall be put to ***d*** this
15:32 Surely the bitterness of ***d*** is
15:35 see Saul until the day of his ***d***.
20: 3 is but a step between me and ***d***.
22:22 I have caused the ***d*** of all
2 Sam 1: 1 it came to pass after the ***d*** of
1:23 And in their ***d*** they were not
6:23 no children to the day of her ***d***.
8: 2 off those to be put to ***d***,
15:21 whether in ***d*** or life, even
19:21 Shall not Shimei be put to ***d*** for
19:22 Shall any man be put to ***d*** today
20: 3 shut up to the day of their ***d***,
21: 9 and were put to ***d*** in the days
22: 5 When the waves of ***d*** surrounded
22: 6 The snares of ***d*** confronted me.
1 Ki 1:51 will not put his servant to ***d***
2: 8 I will not put you to ***d*** with the
2:24 Adonijah shall be put to ***d***
2:26 for you are deserving of ***d***;
2:26 but I will not put you to ***d*** at
11:40 and was in Egypt until the ***d*** of
2 Ki 1: 1 against Israel after the ***d*** of
2:21 it there shall be no more ***d*** or
4:40 there is ***d*** in the pot!"
11: 8 range, let him be put to ***d***.
14: 6 Fathers shall not be put to ***d***
14: 6 nor shall children be put to ***d***
14: 6 but a person shall be put to ***d***
14:17 fifteen years after the ***d*** of
15: 5 a leper until the day of his ***d***;
20: 1 Hezekiah was sick and near ***d***.
25:21 struck them and put them to ***d***
1 Chr 22: 5 preparations before his ***d***.
2 Chr 15:13 of Israel was to be put to ***d***,
22: 4 his counselors after the ***d*** of
23: 7 the house, let him be put to ***d***.
24:17 Now after the ***d*** of Jehoiada the
25: 4 fathers shall not be put to ***d***
25: 4 shall the children be put to ***d***
25:25 fifteen years after the ***d*** of
26:21 a leper until the day of his ***d***.
32:24 Hezekiah was sick and near ***d***,
32:33 Jerusalem honored him at his ***d***.
Ezra 7:26 on him, whether it be ***d***,
Esth 4:11 has but one law: put all to ***d***,
Job 3: 5 darkness and the shadow of ***d***
3:21 Who long for ***d***, but it does
5:20 He shall redeem you from ***d***,
7:15 strangling And ***d*** rather than
10:21 of darkness and the shadow of ***d***,
10:22 itself, As the shadow of ***d***,
12:22 And brings the shadow of ***d*** to
16:16 my eyelids is the shadow of ***d***;
18:13 The firstborn of ***d*** devours his
24:17 same to them as the shadow of ***d***;
24:17 the terrors of the shadow of ***d***.
27:15 him shall be buried in ***d***,
28: 3 darkness and the shadow of ***d***.
28:22 Destruction and ***D*** say, 'We
30:23 that You will bring me to ***d***,
34:22 is no darkness nor shadow of ***d***
38:17 Have the gates of ***d*** been
38:17 the doors of the shadow of ***d***?
Ps 6: 5 For in ***d*** there is no
7:13 for Himself instruments of ***d***;
9: ***D*** of the Son." A Psalm of
9:13 lift me up from the gates of ***d***,
13: 3 Lest I sleep the sleep of ***d***;
18: 4 The pangs of ***d*** surrounded me,
18: 5 The snares of ***d*** confronted me.
22:15 brought Me to the dust of ***d***.
23: 4 the valley of the shadow of ***d***,
33:19 To deliver their soul from ***d***,
44:19 covered us with the shadow of ***d***.
48:14 will be our guide Even to ***d***.
49:14 ***D*** shall feed on them;
55: 4 And the terrors of ***d*** have
55:15 Let ***d*** seize them; Let them go
56:13 have delivered my soul from ***d***.
68:20 the Lord belong escapes from ***d***.
73: 4 there are no pangs in their ***d***,
78:50 did not spare their soul from ***d***,
89:48 man can live and not see ***d***?
102:20 release those appointed to ***d***,
107:10 darkness and in the shadow of ***d***,
107:14 of darkness and the shadow of ***d***,
107:18 drew near to the gates of ***d***.
116: 3 The pains of ***d*** surrounded me,
116: 8 have delivered my soul from ***d***,
116:15 sight of the LORD Is the ***d***
118:18 He has not given me over to ***d***.
Prov 2:18 For her house leads down to ***d***,
5: 5 Her feet go down to ***d***,
7:27 to the chambers of ***d***.
8:36 All those who hate me love ***d***.
10: 2 righteousness delivers from ***d***.
11: 4 righteousness delivers from ***d***.
11:19 evil pursues it to his own ***d***.
12:28 in its pathway there is no ***d***.
13:14 one away from the snares of ***d***.
14:12 But its end is the way of ***d***.
14:27 one away from the snares of ***d***.
14:32 righteous has a refuge in his ***d***.
16:14 As messengers of ***d*** is the
16:25 But its end is the way of ***d***.
18:21 ***D*** and life are in the power of
21: 6 fantasy of those who seek ***d***.
24:11 those who are drawn toward ***d***,

26:18 firebrands, arrows, and ***d***,
Eccl 7: 1 And the day of ***d*** than the day
7:26 And I find more bitter than ***d***
8: 8 one has power in the day of ***d***.
Song 8: 6 For love is as strong as ***d***,
Isa 9: 2 in the land of the shadow of ***d***,
22:14 for you, Even to your ***d***,
25: 8 He will swallow up ***d*** forever,
28:15 have made a covenant with ***d***,
28:18 Your covenant with ***d*** will be
38: 1 Hezekiah was sick and near ***d***.
38:18 ***D*** cannot praise You; Those
53: 9 with the rich at His ***d***,
53:12 He poured out His soul unto ***d***,
Jer 2: 6 of drought and the shadow of ***d***,
8: 3 Then ***d*** shall be chosen rather
9:21 For ***d*** has come through our
13:16 turns it into the shadow of ***d***
15: 2 LORD: "Such as are for ***d***,
15: 2 as are for death, to ***d***;
18:21 Let their men be put to ***d***,
21: 8 way of life and the way of ***d***.
26:15 certain that if you put me to ***d***,
26:19 and all Judah ever put him to ***d***?
26:21 the king sought to put him to ***d***;
26:24 of the people to put him to ***d***.
38: 4 let this man be put to ***d***,
38:15 will you not surely put me to ***d***?
38:16 souls, I will not put you to ***d***,
38:25 and we will not put you to ***d***,
43: 3 that they may put us to ***d*** or
43:11 of Egypt and deliver to ***d***
43:11 death those appointed for ***d***,
52:11 in prison till the day of his ***d***.
52:27 struck them and put them to ***d***.
52:34 each day until the day of his ***d***,
Lam 1:20 At home it is like ***d***.
Ezek 18:32 I have no pleasure in the ***d*** of
28: 8 And you shall die the ***d*** of the
28:10 You shall die the ***d*** of the
31:14 have all been delivered to ***d***,
33:11 I have no pleasure in the ***d*** of
Hos 13:14 I will redeem them from ***d***.
13:14 O ***D***, I will be your plagues!
Am 5: 8 He turns the shadow of ***d*** into
Jon 4: 8 Then he wished ***d*** for himself,
4: 9 to be angry, even to ***d***!"
Hab 2: 5 as hell, And he is like ***d***,
Mt 2:15 and was there until the ***d*** of
2:16 and he sent forth and put to ***d***
4:16 region and shadow of ***d***
10:21 will deliver up brother to ***d***,
10:21 and cause them to be put to ***d***.
14: 5 he wanted to put him to ***d***,
15: 4 let him be put to ***d***.
16:28 here who shall not taste ***d***
20:18 and they will condemn Him to ***d***,
26:38 sorrowful, even to ***d***.
26:59 against Jesus to put Him to ***d***,
26:66 said, "He is deserving of ***d***.
27: 1 against Jesus to put Him to ***d***.
Mk 5:23 daughter lies at the point of ***d***.
7:10 let him be put to ***d***.
9: 1 here who will not taste ***d*** till
10:33 and they will condemn Him to ***d***
13:12 will betray brother to ***d***,
13:12 and cause them to be put to ***d***.
14: 1 by trickery and put Him to ***d***.
14:34 sorrowful, even to ***d***.
14:55 against Jesus to put Him to ***d***,
14:64 Him to be deserving of ***d***.
Lk 1:79 in darkness and the shadow of ***d***,
2:26 Spirit that he would not see ***d***
9:27 here who shall not taste ***d***
21:16 they will put some of you to ***d***.
22:33 You, both to prison and to ***d***.
23:15 indeed nothing deserving of ***d***
23:22 I have found no reason for ***d*** in
23:32 led with Him to be put to ***d***.
24:20 Him to be condemned to ***d***,
Jn 4:47 for he was at the point of ***d***.
5:24 but has passed from ***d*** into
8:51 My word he shall never see ***d***.
8:52 My word he shall never taste ***d***.
11: 4 "This sickness is not unto ***d***,
11:13 However, Jesus spoke of his ***d***,
11:53 they plotted to put Him to ***d***.
12:10 plotted to put Lazarus to ***d***
12:33 signifying by what ***d*** He would
18:31 for us to put anyone to ***d***,
18:32 signifying by what ***d*** He would
21:19 signifying by what ***d*** he would
Acts 2:23 have crucified, and put to ***d***;
2:24 having loosed the pains of ***d***,
8: 1 Saul was consenting to his ***d***.
12:19 that they should be put to ***d***.
13:28 they found no cause for ***d*** in
13:28 that He should be put to ***d***.
22: 4 persecuted this Way to the ***d***,
22:20 standing by consenting to his ***d***,
23:29 against him deserving of ***d*** or
25:11 anything deserving of ***d***,
25:25 nothing deserving of ***d***,
26:10 and when they were put to ***d***,
26:31 is doing nothing deserving of ***d***
28:18 no cause for putting me to ***d***.
Rom 1:32 such things are deserving of ***d***,
5:10 to God through the ***d*** of His
5:12 and ***d*** through sin, and thus
5:12 and thus ***d*** spread to all men,
5:14 Nevertheless ***d*** reigned from Adam
5:17 one man's offense ***d*** reigned

5:21 so that as sin reigned in ***d***,
6: 3 Jesus were baptized into His ***d***?
6: 4 with Him through baptism into ***d***,
6: 5 in the likeness of His ***d***,
6: 9 ***D*** no longer has dominion over
6:10 For the ***d*** that He died, He
6:16 whether of sin leading to ***d***,
6:21 the end of those things is ***d***.
6:23 For the wages of sin is ***d***,
7: 5 our members to bear fruit to ***d***.
7:10 life, I found to bring ***d***.
7:13 then what is good become ***d*** to
7:13 was producing ***d*** in me through
7:24 deliver me from this body of ***d***?
8: 2 free from the law of sin and ***d***.
8: 6 For to be carnally minded is ***d***,
8:13 if by the Spirit you put to ***d***
8:38 that neither ***d*** nor life, nor
1 Cor 3:22 or the world or life or ***d***,
4: 9 last, as men condemned to ***d***;
11:26 you proclaim the Lord's ***d*** till
15:21 For since by man came ***d***,
15:26 that will be destroyed is ***d***.
15:54 ***D*** is swallowed up in
15:55 'O ***D***, where is your
15:56 The sting of ***d*** is sin, and the
2 Cor 1: 9 we had the sentence of ***d*** in
1:10 delivered us from so great a ***d***,
2:16 the one we are the aroma of ***d***
2:16 aroma of death leading to ***d***,
3: 7 But if the ministry of ***d***,
4:11 live are always delivered to ***d***
4:12 So then ***d*** is working in us, but
7:10 sorrow of the world produces ***d***.
Eph 2:16 thereby putting to ***d*** the
Phil 1:20 body, whether by life or by ***d***.
2: 8 obedient to the point of ***d***,
2: 8 even the ***d*** of the cross.
2:27 he was sick almost unto ***d***;
2:30 of Christ he came close to ***d***,
3:10 being conformed to His ***d***,
Col 1:22 the body of His flesh through ***d***,
3: 5 Therefore put to ***d*** your members
2 Tim 1:10 who has abolished ***d*** and
Heb 2: 9 for the suffering of ***d*** crowned
2: 9 might taste ***d*** for everyone.
2:14 that through ***d*** He might destroy
2:14 him who had the power of ***d***,
2:15 those who through fear of ***d***
5: 7 who was able to save Him from ***d***,
7:23 they were prevented by ***d*** from
9:15 the new covenant, by means of ***d***,
9:16 also of necessity be the ***d*** of
11: 5 away so that he did not see ***d***,
Jas 1:15 is full-grown, brings forth ***d***.
5:20 his way will save a soul from ***d***
1 Pe 3:18 being put to ***d*** in the flesh but
1 Jn 3:14 that we have passed from ***d*** to
3:14 love his brother abides in ***d***.
5:16 sin which does not lead to ***d***,
5:16 commit sin not leading to ***d***.
5:16 There is sin leading to ***d***.
5:17 there is sin not leading to ***d***.
Rev 1:18 have the keys of Hades and of ***D***.
2:10 ten days. Be faithful until ***d***,
2:11 not be hurt by the second ***d***.
2:23 will kill her children with ***d***,
6: 8 name of him who sat on it was ***D***,
6: 8 with sword, with hunger, with ***d***,
9: 6 In those days men will seek ***d***
9: 6 and ***d*** will flee from them.
12:11 not love their lives to the ***d***.
18: 8 —***d*** and mourning and famine.
20: 6 Over such the second ***d*** has no
20:13 and ***D*** and Hades delivered up
20:14 Then ***D*** and Hades were cast into
20:14 of fire. This is the second ***d***.
21: 4 eyes; there shall be no more ***d***,
21: 8 which is the second ***d***.

DEATHS (2/2) DEATH

Jer 16: 4 "They shall die gruesome ***d***;
2 Cor 11:23 more frequently, in ***d*** often.

DEBAR (4/4)

2 Sam 9: 4 the son of Ammiel, in Lo ***D***.
9: 5 the son of Ammiel, from Lo ***D***.
17:27 the son of Ammiel from Lo ***D***,
Am 6:13 You who rejoice over Lo ***D***,

DEBASE (KJV) See DESCENDED

DEBASED (1/1) DEBASES

Rom 1:28 God gave them over to a ***d*** mind,

DEBASES (1/1) DEBASED

Eccl 7: 7 And a bribe ***d*** the heart.

DEBATE (2/2)

Prov 25: 9 ***D*** your case with your neighbor,
Isa 58: 4 you fast for strife and ***d***,

DEBIR (14/12)

Josh 10: 3 and ***D*** king of Eglon, saying,
10:38 and all Israel with him, to ***D***;
10:39 so he did to ***D*** and its king, as

11:21 mountains: from Hebron, from **D**,
12:13 the king of **D**, one;
13:26 Mahanaim to the border of **D**,
15: 7 the border went up toward **D**
15:15 there to the inhabitants of **D**
15:15 Debir (formerly the name of **D**
15:49 Kirjath Sannah (which is **D**),
21:15 **D** with its common-land,
Judg 1:11 against the inhabitants of **D**.
1:11 (The name of **D** was formerly
1 Chr 6:58 **D** with its common-lands,

DEBORAH (10/10)

Gen 35: 8 Now **D**, Rebekah's nurse,
Judg 4: 4 Now **D**, a prophetess,
4: 5 sit under the palm tree of **D**
4: 9 Then **D** arose and went with
4:10 and **D** went up with him.
4:14 Then **D** said to Barak, "Up! For
5: 1 Then **D** and Barak the son of
5: 7 ceased in Israel, Until I, **D**,
5:12 **D**! Awake, awake, sing a song!
5:15 of Issachar were with **D**;

DEBRIS (1/1)

2 Chr 29:16 and brought out all the **d** that

DEBT (7/7) DEBTOR, DEBTS

1 Sam 22: 2 everyone who was in **d**,
2 Ki 4: 7 sell the oil and pay your **d**;
Neh 10:31 and the exacting of every **d**.
Mt 18:27 him, and forgave him the **d**.
18:30 prison till he should pay the **d**.
18:32 I forgave you all that **d**
Rom 4: 4 not counted as grace but as **d**.

DEBTOR (4/4) DEBT, DEBTORS

Isa 24: 2 the creditor, so with the **d**.
Ezek 18: 7 But has restored to the **d** his
Rom 1:14 I am a **d** both to Greeks and to
Gal 5: 3 circumcised that he is a **d** to

DEBTORS (5/5) DEBTOR

Mt 6:12 our debts, As we forgive our **d**.
Lk 7:41 certain creditor who had two **d**.
16: 5 every one of his master's **d** to
Rom 8:12 Therefore, brethren, we are **d**—
15:27 indeed, and they are their **d**.

DEBTS (3/3) DEBT

Deut 15: 1 shall grant a release of **d**.
Prov 22:26 of those who is surety for **d**;
Mt 6:12 And forgive us our **d**,

DECAPOLIS (3/3)

Mt 4:25 Him—from Galilee, and from **D**,
Mk 5:20 and began to proclaim in **D** all
7:31 the midst of the region of **D**

DECAYS (2/2)

Job 13:28 Man **d** like a rotten thing,
Eccl 10:18 of laziness the building **d**,

DECEASE (2/2) DECEASED

Lk 9:31 in glory and spoke of His **d**
2 Pe 1:15 of these things after my **d**.

DECEASED (1/1) DECEASE

Isa 26:14 They are **d**, they will not

DECEIT (41/40) DECEITFUL, DECEITS, DECEIVE

Gen 27:35 Your brother came with **d** and has
Job 15:35 Their womb prepares **d**.
27: 4 Nor my tongue utter **d**.
31: 5 if my foot has hastened to **d**,
Ps 10: 7 mouth is full of cursing and **d**
32: 2 in whose spirit there is no **d**.
34:13 And your lips from speaking **d**.
36: 3 his mouth are wickedness and **d**;
50:19 evil, And your tongue frames **d**.
55:11 Oppression and **d** do not depart
101: 7 He who works **d** shall not dwell
119:118 For their **d** is falsehood.
Prov 12:17 But a false witness, **d**.
12:20 **D** is in the heart of those who
14: 8 But the folly of fools is **d**.
20:17 Bread gained by **d** is sweet to
26:24 And lays up **d** within himself;
26:26 his hatred is covered by **d**,
Isa 53: 9 Nor was any **d** in His mouth.
Jer 5:27 So their houses are full of **d**.
8: 5 They hold fast to **d**,
9: 6 place is in the midst of **d**;
9: 6 Through **d** they refuse to know
9: 8 an arrow shot out; It speaks **d**;
14:14 and the **d** of their heart.
23:26 they are prophets of the **d**
Dan 8:25 his cunning He shall cause **d**
Hos 11:12 And the house of Israel with **d**;
Am 8: 5 Falsifying the scales by **d**,
Zeph 1: 9 houses with violence and **d**.
Mk 7:22 covetousness, wickedness, **d**,
Jn 1:47 in whom is no **d**!"
Acts 13:10 O full of all **d** and all fraud,
Rom 1:29 full of envy, murder, strife, **d**,
3:13 they have practiced **d**";
Col 2: 8 through philosophy and empty **d**,
1 Th 2: 3 uncleanness, nor was it in **d**.
1 Pe 2: 1 laying aside all malice, all **d**,
2:22 Nor was **d** found in His
3:10 his lips from speaking **d**.
Rev 14: 5 in their mouth was found no **d**,

DECEITFUL (24/24) DECEIT, DECEITFULLY, DECEITFULNESS

Job 11:11 For He knows **d** men; He sees
Ps 5: 6 abhors the bloodthirsty and **d**
17: 1 my prayer which is not from **d**
35:20 But they devise **d** matters
43: 1 deliver me from the **d** and
52: 4 words, You **d** tongue.
55:23 Bloodthirsty and **d** men shall
78:57 were turned aside like a **d** bow.
109: 2 wicked and the mouth of the **d**
120: 2 from lying lips And from a **d**
Prov 4:24 Put away from you a **d** mouth,
12: 5 counsels of the wicked are **d**.
14:25 But a **d** witness speaks lies.
17:20 He who has a **d** heart finds no
27: 6 the kisses of an enemy are **d**.
31:30 Charm is **d** and beauty is
Jer 17: 9 The heart is **d** above all
Hos 12: 7 A cunning Canaanite! **D** scales
Mic 6:11 And with the bag of **d** weights?
6:12 And their tongue is **d** in their
Zeph 3:13 Nor shall a **d** tongue be found
2 Cor 11:13 **d** workers, transforming
Eph 4:14 in the cunning craftiness of **d**
4:22 corrupt according to the **d**

DECEITFULLY (10/10) DECEITFUL

Gen 34:13 Hamor his father, and spoke **d**,
Ex 8:29 But let Pharaoh not deal **d**
21: 8 since he has dealt **d** with her.
Job 6:15 My brothers have dealt **d** like a
13: 7 And talk **d** for Him?
Ps 24: 4 soul to an idol, Nor sworn **d**.
52: 2 Like a sharp razor, working **d**.
Jer 48:10 does the work of the LORD **d**,
Dan 11:23 made with him he shall act **d**,
2 Cor 4: 2 nor handling the word of God **d**,

DECEITFULNESS (3/3) DECEITFUL

Mt 13:22 cares of this world and the **d**
Mk 4:19 the **d** of riches, and the
Heb 3:13 you be hardened through the **d**

DECEITS (1/1) DECEIT

Isa 30:10 to us smooth things, prophesy **d**.

DECEIVE (28/28) DECEIT, DECEIVED, DECEIVER, DECEIVES, DECEIVING, DECEPTION, DECEPTIVE

2 Sam 3:25 Abner the son of Ner came to **d**
2 Ki 4:28 I not say, 'Do not **d** me'?"
18:29 Do not let Hezekiah **d** you, for
19:10 your God in whom you trust **d**
2 Chr 32:15 do not let Hezekiah **d** you or
Prov 24:28 For would you **d** with your
Isa 36:14 Do not let Hezekiah **d** you, for
37:10 your God in whom you trust **d**
Jer 9: 5 Everyone will **d** his neighbor,
29: 8 who are in your midst **d** you,
37: 9 Do not **d** yourselves, saying,
Ob 7 men at peace with you Shall **d**
Zech 13: 4 wear a robe of coarse hair to **d**.
Mt 24: 5 the Christ,' and will **d** many.
24:11 prophets will rise up and **d**
24:24 great signs and wonders to **d**,
Mk 13: 6 'I am He,' and will **d** many.
13:22 and show signs and wonders to **d**,
Rom 16:18 words and flattering speech **d**
1 Cor 3:18 Let no one **d** himself. If anyone
Eph 5: 6 Let no one **d** you with empty
Col 2: 4 I say lest anyone should **d** you
2 Th 2: 3 Let no one **d** you by any means;
1 Jn 1: 8 we **d** ourselves, and the truth
2:26 those who try to **d** you.
3: 7 children, let no one **d** you.
Rev 20: 3 so that he should **d** the nations
20: 8 and will go out to **d** the nations

DECEIVED (32/31) DECEIVE

Gen 3:13 The serpent **d** me, and I ate."
29:25 Why then have you **d** me?"
31: 7 Yet your father has **d** me and
Deut 11:16 lest your heart be **d**,
Josh 7:11 and have both stolen and **d**;
9:22 Why have you **d** us, saying, 'We
1 Sam 19:17 Why have you **d** me like this, and
28:12 Why have you **d** me? For you are
2 Sam 19:26 my servant **d** me. For your
Job 12:16 The **d** and the deceiver are
Isa 19:13 The princes of Noph are **d**;
44:20 A **d** heart has turned him
Jer 4:10 Surely You have greatly **d**
49:16 Your fierceness has **d** you, The
Lam 1:19 But they **d** me; My priests
Ob 3 The pride of your heart has **d**
Mt 2:16 when he saw that he was **d** by
Lk 21: 8 "Take heed that you not be **d**.
Jn 7:47 answered them, "Are you also **d**?
Rom 7:11 **d** me, and by it killed me.
1 Cor 6: 9 the kingdom of God? Do not be **d**.
15:33 Do not be **d**: "Evil company
2 Cor 11: 3 as the serpent **d** Eve by his
Gal 6: 7 Do not be **d**, God is not
1 Tim 2:14 And Adam was not **d**,
2:14 deceived, but the woman being **d**,
2 Tim 3:13 worse, deceiving and being **d**.
Titus 3: 3 once foolish, disobedient, **d**,
Jas 1:16 Do not be **d**, my beloved
Rev 18:23 sorcery all the nations were **d**.
19:20 by which he **d** those who
20:10 who **d** them, was cast into the

DECEIVER (5/5) DECEIVE, DECEIVERS

Gen 27:12 and I shall seem to be a **d** to
Job 12:16 The deceived and the **d** are
Mal 1:14 But cursed be the **d** Who has in
Mt 27:63 how that **d** said, 'After three
2 Jn 7 This is a **d** and an antichrist.

DECEIVERS (3/3) DECEIVE

2 Cor 6: 8 as **d**, and yet true;
Titus 1:10 both idle talkers and **d**,
2 Jn 7 For many **d** have gone out into

DECEIVES (8/8)

Prov 26:19 Is the man who **d** his
Mt 24: 4 Take heed that no one **d** you.
Mk 13: 5 Take heed that no one **d** you.
Jn 7:12 He **d** the people."
Gal 6: 3 he is nothing, he **d** himself.
Jas 1:26 not bridle his tongue but **d**
Rev 12: 9 who **d** the whole world; he was
13:14 And he **d** those who dwell on the

DECEIVING (4/4) DECEIVE

Job 15:31 **d** himself, For futility will
1 Tim 4: 1 giving heed to **d** spirits and
2 Tim 3:13 **d** and being deceived.
Jas 1:22 hearers only, **d** yourselves.

DECENTLY (1/1)

1 Cor 14:40 Let all things be done **d** and in

DECEPTION (3/3) DECEIVE, DECEPTIONS

Ps 38:12 And plan **d** all the day long.
Mt 27:64 So the last **d** will be worse
2 Th 2:10 and with all unrighteous **d** among

DECEPTIONS (1/1) DECEPTION

2 Pe 2:13 carousing in their own **d** while

DECEPTIVE (4/4) DECEIVE, DECEPTIVELY

Prov 11:18 The wicked man does **d** work,
23: 3 For they are **d** food.
Lam 2:14 have seen for you False and **d**
2 Pe 2: 3 they will exploit you with **d**

DECEPTIVELY (1/1) DECEPTIVE

2 Ki 10:19 But Jehu acted **d**, with the

DECIDE (2/2) DECIDED

Isa 11: 3 Nor **d** by the hearing of His
11: 4 And **d** with equity for the meek

DECIDED (7/7)

1 Ki 20:40 you yourself have **d** it."
Acts 20: 3 he **d** to return through
20:16 For Paul had **d** to sail past
21:25 we have written and **d** that
25:25 I **d** to send him.
27: 1 And when it was **d** that we should
Titus 3:12 for I have **d** to spend the

DECISION (12/11) DECIDE

2 Sam 15: 2 came to the king for a **d**,
Prov 16:33 But its every **d** is from the
Dan 2: 5 My **d** is firm: if you do not make
2: 8 because you see that my **d** is
2:15 Then Arioch made the **d** known
2:17 and made the **d** known to
4:17 This **d** is by the decree of the
Joel 3:14 multitudes in the valley of **d**!
3:14 is near in the valley of **d**.
Lk 23:51 He had not consented to their **d**
Acts 24:22 I will make a **d** on your case."
25:21 to be reserved for the **d** of

DECKED (1/1) DECKS

Hos 2:13 She **d** herself with her

DECKEDST, DECKEST (KJV) See ADORN, ADORNED

DECKS (2/2) DECKED
Gen 6:16 lower, second, and third **d**.
Isa 61:10 As a bridegroom **d** himself

DECLARATION (1/1) DECLARE
Job 13:17 And to my **d** with your ears.

DECLARE (90/90) DECLARATION, DECLARED, DECLARES, DECLARING
Deut 5: 5 to **d** to you the word of the
26: 3 I **d** today to the LORD your God
1 Chr 16:24 **D** His glory among the nations,
Job 15:17 What I have seen I will **d**,
22:28 You will also **d** a thing, And
31:37 I would **d** to Him the number of
32: 6 And dared not **d** my opinion to
32:10 I also will **d** my opinion.'
32:17 I too will **d** my opinion.
Ps 2: 7 I will **d** the decree: The LORD
9:11 **D** His deeds among the people.
19: 1 The heavens **d** the glory of God;
22:22 I will **d** Your name to My
22:31 They will come and **d** His
30: 9 Will it **d** Your truth?
38:18 For I will **d** my iniquity;
40: 5 If I would **d** and speak of
50: 6 Let the heavens **d** His
50:16 What right have you to **d** My
64: 9 And shall **d** the work of God;
66:16 And I will **d** what He has done
71:17 And to this day I **d** Your
71:18 Until I **d** Your strength to
73:28 That I may **d** all Your works.
75: 1 For Your wondrous works **d**
75: 9 But I will **d** forever, I will
78: 6 they may arise and **d** them
92: 2 To **d** Your lovingkindness in the
92:15 To **d** that the LORD is upright;
96: 3 **D** His glory among the nations,
97: 6 heavens **d** His righteousness,
102:21 To **d** the name of the LORD in
106: 2 Who can **d** all His praise?
107:22 And **d** His works with
118:17 And **d** the works of the LORD.
142: 2 I **d** before Him my trouble.
145: 4 And shall **d** Your mighty acts.
145: 6 And I will **d** Your greatness.
Eccl 9: 1 so that I could **d** it all: that
Isa 3: 9 And they **d** their sin as Sodom;
12: 4 **D** His deeds among the peoples,
21: 6 Let him **d** what he sees."
41:22 Or **d** to us things to come.
42: 9 to pass, And new things I **d**;
42:12 And **d** His praise in the
43: 9 Who among them can **d** this,
43:21 They shall **d** My praise.
44: 7 Then let him **d** it and set it
45:19 I **d** things that are right.
48: 6 And will you not **d** it?
48:20 With a voice of singing, **D**,
53: 8 And who will **d** His generation?
57:12 I will **d** your righteousness
66:19 And they shall **d** My glory among
Jer 4: 5 **D** in Judah and proclaim in
5:20 **D** this in the house of Jacob
9:12 that he may **d** it? Why does the
31:10 And **d** it in the isles afar
38:15 If I **d** it to you, will you not
38:25 **D** to us now what you have said
42: 4 I will **d** it to you. I will
42:20 so **d** to us and we will do it.'
46:14 **D** in Egypt, and proclaim in
50: 2 **D** among the nations, Proclaim,
51:10 Come and let us **d** in Zion the
Ezek 12:16 that they may **d** all their
23:36 Then **d** to them their
40: 4 **D** to the house of Israel
Dan 2:27 and the soothsayers cannot **d** to
4: 2 I thought it good to **d** the signs
4:18 **d** its interpretation, since all
Mic 3: 8 To **d** to Jacob his
Zech 9:12 Even today I **d** That I will
Mt 7:23 And then I will **d** to them, 'I
12:18 And He will **d** justice to
Jn 16:14 take of what is Mine and **d** it
16:15 He will take of Mine and **d** it
17:26 and will **d** it, that the love
Acts 8:33 And who will **d** His
13:32 And we **d** to you glad
13:41 Though one were to **d** it
20:27 For I have not shunned to **d** to
1 Cor 3:13 for the Day will **d** it, because
15: 1 I **d** to you the gospel which I
1 Th 1: 9 For they themselves **d** concerning
Heb 2:12 I will **d** Your name to My
11:14 who say such things **d** plainly
1 Jn 1: 2 and **d** to you that eternal life
1: 3 we have seen and heard we **d** to
1: 5 heard from Him and **d** to you,

DECLARED (39/39) DECLARE
Ex 9:16 and that My name may be **d** in
Lev 23:44 So Moses **d** to the children of
Deut 4:13 So He **d** to you His covenant
2 Sam 19: 6 For you have **d** today that you
1 Ki 22:23 and the LORD has **d** disaster
2 Chr 18:22 and the LORD has **d** disaster
Neh 8:12 the words that were **d** to them.
Job 26: 3 And how have you **d** sound
28:27 Then He saw wisdom and **d** it;
Ps 40:10 I have **d** Your faithfulness and
77:14 You have **d** Your strength among
88:11 Your lovingkindness be **d** in
111: 6 He has **d** to His people the
119:13 With my lips I have **d** All the
119:26 I have **d** my ways, and You
Prov 30: 1 This man **d** to Ithiel—to Ithiel
Isa 21: 2 A distressing vision is **d** to
21:10 I have **d** to you.
41:26 Who has **d** from the beginning,
43:12 I have **d** and saved, I have
44: 8 from that time, and **d** it?
45:21 Who has **d** this from ancient
48: 3 I have **d** the former things from
48: 5 from the beginning I have **d**
48:14 Who among them has **d** these
Jer 36:13 Then Michaiah **d** to them all the
42:21 And I have this day **d** it to
Lk 8:47 she **d** to Him in the presence of
Jn 1:18 of the Father, He has **d** Him.
17:26 And I have **d** to them Your name,
Acts 9:27 And he **d** to them how he had
12:17 he **d** to them how the Lord had
15:14 Simon has **d** how God at the first
26:20 but **d** first to those in Damascus
Rom 1: 4 and **d** to be the Son of God
9:17 that My name may be **d**
1 Cor 1:11 For it has been **d** to me
Col 1: 8 who also **d** to us your love in
Rev 10: 7 as He **d** to His servants the

DECLARES (8/8) DECLARE
Josh 20: 4 and **d** his case in the hearing
Job 36:33 His thunder **d** it, The cattle
Ps 147:19 He **d** His word to Jacob, His
Prov 12:17 speaks truth **d** righteousness,
Isa 41:26 Surely there is no one who **d**,
Jer 4:15 For a voice **d** from Dan And
50:28 from the land of Babylon **D** in
Am 4:13 Who **d** to man what his thought

DECLARING (3/3) DECLARE
Isa 46:10 **D** the end from the beginning,
Acts 15:12 to Barnabas and Paul **d** how
1 Cor 2: 1 of speech or of wisdom **d** to

DECLINE (1/1)
2 Chr 28:19 for he had encouraged moral **d**

DECORATE (1/1) DECORATED
Jer 10: 4 They **d** it with silver and gold;

DECORATED (1/1) DECORATE
2 Chr 3: 6 And he **d** the house with precious

DECREASE (2/2) DECREASED
Ps 107:38 He does not let their cattle **d**.
Jn 3:30 must increase, but I must **d**.

DECREASED (2/2) DECREASE
Gen 8: 3 and fifty days the waters **d**.
8: 5 And the waters **d** continually

DECREE (50/49) DECREED, DECREES
Ezra 5:13 King Cyrus issued a **d** to build
5:17 whether it is so that a **d** was
6: 1 Then King Darius issued a **d**,
6: 3 King Cyrus issued a **d**
6: 8 Moreover I issue a **d** as to
6:11 Also I issue a **d** that whoever
6:12 Jerusalem. I Darius issue a **d**;
7:13 I issue a **d** that all those of
7:21 issue a **d** to all the treasurers
Esth 1:19 let a royal **d** go out from him,
1:20 When the king's **d** which he will
2: 8 when the king's command and **d**
3: 9 let a **d** be written that they
3:12 and a **d** was written according
3:15 and the **d** was proclaimed in
4: 3 where the king's command and **d**
4: 8 him a copy of the written **d**
8: 8 You yourselves write a **d**
8:13 was to be issued as a **d** in
8:14 And the **d** was issued in Shushan
8:17 the king's command and **d** came,
9: 1 the king's command and his **d**
9:13 tomorrow according to today's **d**,
9:14 the **d** was issued in Shushan,
9:32 So the **d** of Esther confirmed
Ps 2: 7 "I will declare the **d**:
148: 6 He made a **d** which shall not
Prov 8:15 And rulers **d** justice.
Isa 10: 1 Woe to those who **d** unrighteous
Jer 5:22 of the sea, By a perpetual **d**,
Dan 2: 9 there is only one **d** for you!
2:13 So the **d** went out, and they
2:15 Why is the **d** from the king so
3:10 have made a **d** that everyone who
3:29 Therefore I make a **d** that any
4: 6 Therefore I issued a **d** to bring
4:17 This decision is by the **d** of
4:24 and this is the **d** of the Most
6: 7 statute and to make a firm **d**,
6: 8 establish the **d** and sign the
6: 9 Darius signed the written **d**.
6:12 spoke concerning the king's **d**:
6:12 Have you not signed a **d** that
6:13 or for the **d** that you have
6:15 Medes and Persians that no **d**
6:26 I make a **d** that in every
Jon 3: 7 throughout Nineveh by the **d** of
Mic 7:11 In that day the **d** shall go
Zeph 2: 2 Before the **d** is issued, Or
Lk 2: 1 to pass in those days that a **d**

DECREED (4/4) DECREE
Esth 2: 1 and what had been **d** against
9:31 and as they had **d** for
Isa 10:22 The destruction **d** shall
Nah 2: 7 It is **d**: She shall be led

DECREES (3/3) DECREE
Isa 10: 1 those who decree unrighteous **d**,
Acts 16: 4 they delivered to them the **d** to
17: 7 all acting contrary to the **d**

DEDAN (11/10) DEDANITES
Gen 10: 7 of Raamah were Sheba and **D**.
25: 3 Jokshan begot Sheba and **D**.
25: 3 And the sons of **D** were
1 Chr 1: 9 sons of Raama were Sheba and **D**.
1:32 of Jokshan were Sheba and **D**.
Jer 25:23 **D**, Tema, Buz, and all who
49: 8 O inhabitants of **D**! For I will
Ezek 25:13 **D** shall fall by the sword.
27:15 The men of **D** were your traders;
27:20 **D** was your merchant in
38:13 'Sheba, **D**, the merchants of

DEDANITES (1/1) DEDAN
Isa 21:13 O you traveling companies of **D**.

DEDICATE (5/5) DEDICATED, DEDICATION
Lev 22: 2 My holy name by what they **d**
22: 3 which the children of Israel **d**
27:26 firstborn, no man shall **d**;
Deut 20: 5 in the battle and another man **d**
2 Chr 2: 4 to **d** it to Him, to burn before

DEDICATED (28/23) DEDICATE
Lev 27:15 If he who **d** it wants to redeem
Deut 20: 5 a new house and has not **d** it?
Judg 17: 3 I had wholly **d** the silver from
2 Sam 8:11 King David also **d** these to the
8:11 silver and gold that he had **d**
1 Ki 7:51 which his father David had **d**:
8:63 all the children of Israel **d**
15:15 things which his father had **d**,
15:15 things which he himself had **d**:
2 Ki 12: 4 All the money of the **d** gifts
12:18 Ahaziah, kings of Judah, had **d**,
23:11 that the kings of Judah had **d**
1 Chr 18:11 King David also **d** these to the
26:20 over the treasuries of the **d**
26:26 all the treasuries of the **d**
26:26 the captains of the army, had **d**.
26:27 spoils won in battles they **d**
26:28 Joab the son of Zeruiah had **d**,
26:28 every **d** thing, was under the
28:12 and of the treasuries for the **d**
2 Chr 5: 1 which his father David had **d**:
7: 5 the king and all the people **d**
15:18 things that his father had **d**
15:18 and that he himself had **d**:
24: 7 had also presented all the **d**
31:12 and the **d** things; Cononiah the
Ezek 44:29 every **d** thing in Israel shall
Heb 9:18 even the first covenant was **d**

DEDICATES (6/6)
Lev 27:14 And when a man **d** his house to
27:16 If a man **d** to the LORD part
27:17 If he **d** his field from the Year
27:18 But if he **d** his field after the
27:19 And if he who **d** the field ever
27:22 And if a man **d** to the LORD a

DEDICATION (13/12) DEDICATE
Num 7:10 Now the leaders offered the **d**
7:11 for the **d** of the altar."
7:84 This was the **d** offering for
7:88 This was the **d** offering for
2 Chr 7: 9 for they observed the **d** of the
Ezra 6:16 celebrated the **d** of this house
6:17 offered sacrifices at the **d** of
Neh 12:27 Now at the **d** of the wall of
12:27 to Jerusalem to celebrate the **d**
Ps 30: A Song at the **d** of the house of
Dan 3: 2 to come to the **d** of the image
3: 3 gathered together for the **d** of
Jn 10:22 Now it was the Feast of **D** in

DEDUCTED (1/1)

Lev 27:18 and it shall be **d** from your

DEED (27/25) DEEDED, DEEDS

Gen 44:15 What **d** is this you have done?
Judg 19:30 No such **d** has been done or seen
20: 3 how did this wicked **d** happen?"
1 Sam 20:19 you hid on the day of the **d**;
2 Sam 12:14 because by this **d** you have
Job 33:17 order to turn man from his **d**,
Jer 32:10 And I signed the **d** and sealed
32:11 "So I took the purchase **d**,
32:12 and I gave the purchase **d** to
32:12 who signed the purchase **d**,
32:14 both this purchase **d** which is
32:14 deed which is sealed and this **d**
32:16 I had delivered the purchase **d**
Mt 6: 2 when you do a charitable **d**,
6: 3 when you do a charitable **d**,
6: 4 that your charitable **d** may be in
Lk 23:51 to their decision and **d**.
24:19 who was a Prophet mighty in **d**
Acts 4: 9 day are judged for a good **d**
Rom 15:18 through me, in word and **d**,
1 Cor 5: 2 that he who has done this **d**
5: 3 him who has so done this **d**.
2 Cor 10:11 such we will also be in **d**
Col 3:17 whatever you do in word or **d**,
Titus 2:14 redeem us from every lawless **d**
Phm 1:14 that your good **d** might not be
1 Jn 3:18 but in **d** and in truth.

DEEDED (2/2) DEED

Gen 23:17 surrounding borders, were **d**
23:20 the cave that is in it were **d**

DEEDS (79/79) DEED

Gen 20: 9 You have done **d** to me that
Deut 3:24 Your works and Your mighty **d**?
2 Sam 7:23 for Youself great and awesome **d**
23:20 Kabzeel, who had done many **d**.
2 Ki 23:19 to them according to all the **d**
1 Chr 11:22 Kabzeel, who had done many **d**.
16: 8 Make known His **d** among the
17:21 a name by great and awesome **d**,
2 Chr 32: 1 After these **d** of faithfulness,
35:27 and his **d** from first to last,
Ezra 9:13 has come upon us for our evil **d**
Neh 6:19 Also they reported his good **d**
13:14 and do not wipe out my good **d**
Ps 9:11 dwells in Zion! Declare His **d**
28: 4 Give them according to their **d**,
44: 1 The **d** You did in their days,
65: 5 By awesome **d** in righteousness
77:12 Your work, And talk of Your **d**.
99: 8 You took vengeance on their **d**.
105: 1 Make known His **d** among the
106:29 Him to anger with their **d**,
106:39 the harlot by their own **d**.
141: 5 my prayer is against the **d** of
Prov 20:11 Even a child is known by his **d**,
24:12 to each man according to his **d**?
Isa 12: 4 Declare His **d** among the
59:18 According to their **d**,
Jer 5:28 they surpass the **d** of the
11:15 Having done lewd **d** with many?
25:14 them according to their **d** and
32:14 God of Israel: "Take these **d**,
32:44 sign **d** and seal them, and take
Ezek 9:10 but I will recompense their **d**
11:21 I will recompense their **d** on
16:30 the **d** of a brazen harlot.
16:43 I will also recompense your **d**
22:31 and I have recompensed their **d**
24:14 ways And according to your **d**
36:17 it by their own ways and **d**;
36:19 to their ways and their **d**.
36:31 your evil ways and your **d** that
Dan 9:18 You because of our righteous **d**,
Hos 4: 9 And reward them for their **d**.
5: 4 They do not direct their **d**
7: 2 Now their own **d** have
9:15 of the evil of their **d** I will
12: 2 According to his **d** He will
Mic 3: 4 they have been evil in their **d**.
7:13 And for the fruit of their **d**.
Zeph 3: 7 early and corrupted all their **d**.
3:11 not be shamed for any of your **d**
Zech 1: 4 your evil ways and your evil **d**.
1: 6 our ways and according to our **d**,
Mt 6: 1 you do not do your charitable **d**
Lk 11:48 witness that you approve the **d**
23:41 receive the due reward of our **d**;
Jn 3:19 because their **d** were evil.
3:20 lest his **d** should be exposed.
3:21 that his **d** may be clearly seen,
8:41 You do the **d** of your father."
Acts 7:22 and was mighty in words and **d**.
9:36 of good works and charitable **d**
19:18 confessing and telling their **d**.
Rom 2: 6 one according to his **d**":
3:20 Therefore by the **d** of the law no
3:28 by faith apart from the **d** of
4: 7 are those whose lawless **d**
8:13 Spirit you put to death the **d**
2 Cor 12:12 signs and wonders and mighty **d**.
Col 3: 9 put off the old man with his **d**,
Heb 8:12 sins and their lawless **d**
10:17 sins and their lawless **d**
2 Pe 2: 8 and hearing their lawless **d**)—
2 Jn 11 greets him shares in his evil **d**.
3 Jn 10 I will call to mind his **d** which
Jude 15 them of all their ungodly **d**
Rev 2: 6 that you hate the **d** of the
2:22 unless they repent of their **d**.
16:11 and did not repent of their **d**.

DEEP (74/72) DEEPER, DEEPLY

Gen 1: 2 was on the face of the **d**.
2:21 And the LORD God caused a **d**
7:11 the fountains of the great **d**
8: 2 The fountains of the **d** and the
15:12 a **d** sleep fell upon Abram; and
49:25 Blessings of the **d** that lies
50:11 This is a **d** mourning of the
Lev 14:37 which appear to be **d** in the
Deut 33:13 And the **d** lying beneath,
1 Sam 26:12 because a **d** sleep from the
2 Ki 4:27 for her soul is in **d** distress,
Neh 9:11 You threw into the **d**,
Job 4:13 When **d** sleep falls on men,
11: 7 Can you search out the **d** things
12:22 He uncovers **d** things out of
22:13 Can He judge through the **d**
23:17 And He did not hide **d**
28:14 The **d** says, 'It is not in
33:15 When **d** sleep falls upon men,
38:30 And the surface of the **d** is
41:31 He makes the **d** boil like a pot;
41:32 One would think the **d** had
Ps 2: 5 And distress them in His **d**
33: 7 He lays up the **d** in
36: 6 Your judgments are a great **d**;
42: 7 ***D*** calls unto deep at the noise
42: 7 Deep calls unto **d** at the noise
64: 6 and the heart of man are **d**.
69: 2 I sink in **d** mire, Where there
69: 2 I have come into **d** waters,
69:14 And out of the **d** waters.
69:15 Nor let the **d** swallow me up;
80: 9 And caused it to take **d** root,
92: 5 Your thoughts are very **d**.
95: 4 In His hand are the **d** places
104: 6 You covered it with the **d** as
107:24 And His wonders in the **d**.
135: 6 In the seas and in all **d**
140:10 Into **d** pits, that they rise
Prov 8:27 a circle on the face of the **d**,
8:28 the fountains of the **d**,
18: 4 words of a man's mouth are **d**
19:15 Laziness casts one into a **d**
20: 5 in the heart of man is like **d**
20:20 His lamp will be put out in **d**
22:14 of an immoral woman is a **d**
23:27 For a harlot is a **d** pit, And
Eccl 7:24 is far off and exceedingly **d**,
Isa 29:10 out on you The spirit of **d**
29:15 Woe to those who seek **d** to
30:33 He has made it **d** and large;
44:27 Who says to the **d**,
51:10 sea, The waters of the great **d**;
60: 2 And **d** darkness the people;
63:13 Who led them through the **d**,
Ezek 23:32 The **d** and wide one; You shall
26:19 when I bring the **d** upon you,
31:15 I covered the **d** because of it.
47: 5 for the water was too **d**,
Dan 2:22 He reveals **d** and secret things;
8:18 I was in a **d** sleep with my face
10: 9 sound of his words I was in a **d**
Am 7: 4 and it consumed the great **d** and
Jon 2: 3 For You cast me into the **d**,
2: 5 The **d** closed around me; Weeds
Hab 3:10 The **d** uttered its voice, And
Lk 5: 4 Launch out into the **d** and let
6:48 who dug **d** and laid the
Jn 4:11 to draw with, and the well is **d**.
Acts 20: 9 who was sinking into a **d** sleep.
1 Cor 2:10 the **d** things of God.
2 Cor 8: 2 of their joy and their **d**
11:25 and a day I have been in the **d**;
11:28 my **d** concern for all the

DEEPER (11/11) DEEP

Lev 13: 3 and the sore appears to be **d**
13: 4 and does not appear to be **d**
13:20 it indeed appears **d** than the
13:21 and it is not **d** than the skin,
13:25 and it appears **d** than the skin,
13:26 and it is not **d** than the skin,
13:30 and indeed if it appears **d** than
13:31 and indeed it does not appear **d**
13:32 and the scale does not appear **d**
13:34 and does not appear **d** than the
Job 11: 8 ***D*** than Sheol—what can you

DEEPLY (14/14) DEEP

1 Sam 28:15 I am **d** distressed; for the
2 Sam 18:33 Then the king was **d** moved, and
Neh 2:10 they were **d** disturbed that a
Esth 4: 4 and the queen was **d** distressed.
Ps 38: 2 For Your arrows pierce me **d**,
Song 5: 1 O friends! Drink, yes, drink **d**,
Isa 31: 6 the children of Israel have **d**
66:11 That you may drink **d** and be
Jer 50:12 Your mother shall be **d** ashamed;
Hos 5: 2 The revolters are **d** involved in
9: 9 They are **d** corrupted, As in
Mt 26:37 be sorrowful and **d** distressed.
Mk 8:12 But He sighed **d** in His spirit,
14:33 be troubled and **d** distressed.

DEER (17/16) DEER'S

Gen 49:21 Naphtali is a **d** let loose; He
Deut 12:15 of the gazelle and the **d** alike.
12:22 Just as the gazelle and the **d**
14: 5 'the **d**, the gazelle,
14: 5 deer, the gazelle, the roe **d**,
15:22 if it were a gazelle or a **d**.
2 Sam 22:34 my feet like the feet of **d**,
1 Ki 4:23 one hundred sheep, besides **d**,
Job 39: 1 Or can you mark when the **d**
Ps 18:33 my feet like the feet of **d**,
22: The ***D*** of the Dawn." A Psalm of
29: 9 voice of the LORD makes the **d**
42: 1 As the **d** pants for the water
Prov 5:19 As a loving **d** and a graceful
Isa 35: 6 the lame shall leap like a **d**,
Jer 14: 5 the **d** also gave birth in the
Lam 1: 6 Her princes have become like **d**

DEER'S (1/1) DEER

Hab 3:19 will make my feet like **d** feet,

DEFAME (1/1) DEFAMED

1 Pe 3:16 that when they **d** you as

DEFAMED (1/1) DEFAME

1 Cor 4:13 being **d**, we entreat.

DEFEAT (7/7) DEFEATED, DEFEATS

Gen 14:17 after his return from the **d** of
Ex 32:18 Nor the noise of the cry of **d**,
Num 22: 6 Perhaps I shall be able to **d**
Deut 7:23 and will inflict **d** upon them
Judg 6:16 and you shall **d** the Midianites
2 Sam 15:34 then you may **d** the counsel of
17:14 For the LORD had purposed to **d**

DEFEATED (61/60) DEFEAT

Ex 17:13 So Joshua **d** Amalek and his
Lev 26:17 and you shall be **d** by your
Num 14:42 lest you be **d** by your enemies,
21:24 Then Israel **d** him with the edge
21:35 So they **d** him, his sons, and all
32: 4 the country which the LORD **d**
Deut 1:42 lest you be **d** before your
2:33 so we **d** him, his sons, and all
4:46 and the children of Israel **d**
28: 7 who rise against you to be **d**
28:25 LORD will cause you to be **d**
Josh 11: 8 who **d** them and chased them to
12: 1 whom the children of Israel **d**,
13:12 for Moses had **d** and cast out
Judg 1: 5 and they **d** the Canaanites and
3:13 went and **d** Israel, and took
11:21 and they **d** them. Thus Israel
11:33 And he **d** them from Aroer as far
12: 4 And the men of Gilead **d**
20:32 They are **d** before us, as at
20:35 The LORD **d** Benjamin before
20:36 Benjamin saw that they were **d**.
20:39 Surely they are **d** before us, as
1 Sam 4: 2 Israel was **d** by the
4: 3 Why has the LORD **d** us today
4:10 fought, and Israel was **d**,
2 Sam 5:20 and David **d** them there; and he
8: 2 Then he **d** Moab. Forcing them
8: 3 David also **d** Hadadezer the son
8: 9 Hamath heard that David had **d**
8:10 fought against Hadadezer and **d**
10:15 saw that they had been **d** by
10:19 Hadadezer saw that they were **d**
1 Ki 8:33 Your people Israel are **d**
2 Ki 13:25 Three times Joash **d** him and
14:10 You have indeed **d** Edom, and your
14:12 And Judah was **d** by Israel, and
1 Chr 4:43 And they **d** the rest of the
14:11 and David **d** them there. Then
18: 2 Then he **d** Moab, and the Moabites
18: 3 And David **d** Hadadezer king of
18: 9 Hamath heard that David had **d**
18:10 fought against Hadadezer and **d**
19:16 saw that they had been **d** by
19:19 Hadadezer saw that they were **d**
20: 1 And Joab **d** Rabbah and overthrew
21:12 or three months to be **d** by your
2 Chr 6:24 if Your people Israel are **d**
14:14 Then they **d** all the cities
20:22 against Judah; and they were **d**.
25:19 you say that you have **d**
25:22 And Judah was **d** by Israel, and
27: 5 the king of the Ammonites and **d**
28: 5 They **d** him, and carried away a
28: 5 who **d** him with a great
28:23 gods of Damascus which had **d**
Esth 9: 5 Thus the Jews **d** all their
Ps 135:10 He **d** many nations And slew
Isa 10:20 again depend on him who **d** them,
Jer 37:10 For though you had **d** the whole
46: 2 king of Babylon **d** in the

DEFEATS (1/1) DEFEAT
2 Sam 5: 8 by way of the water shaft and **d**

DEFECT (13/11) DEFECTED, DEFECTING, DEFECTORS, DEFECTS
Lev 21:17 generations, who has any **d**,
21:18 For any man who has a **d** shall
21:20 or a man who has a **d** in his
21:21 Aaron the priest, who has a **d**,
21:21 fire to the LORD. He has a **d**;
21:23 the altar, because he has a **d**,
22:20 'Whatever has a **d**,
22:21 there shall be no **d** in it.
Num 19: 2 in which there is no **d** and on
Deut 15:21 But if there is a **d** in it, if
15:21 or blind or has any serious **d**,
17: 1 which has any blemish or **d**,
1 Chr 12:19 He may **d** to his master Saul and

DEFECTED (7/6) DEFECT
1 Sam 29: 3 no fault in him since he **d** to
1 Ki 2:28 for Joab had **d** to Adonijah,
2:28 though he had not **d** to Absalom.
1 Chr 12:19 And some from Manasseh **d** to
12:20 those of Manasseh who **d** to him
Jer 38:19 afraid of the Jews who have **d**
39: 9 in the city and those who **d** to

DEFECTING (2/2) DEFECT
Jer 37:13 You are **d** to the Chaldeans!"
37:14 False! I am not **d** to the

DEFECTORS (2/2) DEFECT
2 Ki 25:11 remained in the city and the **d**
Jer 52:15 the **d** who had deserted to the

DEFECTS (2/2) DEFECT
Lev 22:25 and **d** are in them. They shall
Jer 21: 9 but he who goes out and **d** to

DEFEND (15/15) DEFENDED, DEFENDER, DEFENDING, DEFENSE
2 Ki 19:34 For I will **d** this city, to save
20: 6 and I will **d** this city for My
Job 13:15 I will **d** my own ways before
Ps 5:11 because You **d** them; Let those
20: 1 the name of the God of Jacob **d**
59: 1 ***D*** me from those who rise up
82: 3 ***D*** the poor and fatherless
Isa 1:17 ***D*** the fatherless, Plead for
1:23 They do not **d** the fatherless,
31: 5 So will the LORD of hosts **d**
37:35 For I will **d** this city, to save
38: 6 and I will **d** this city." '
Jer 5:28 of the needy they do not **d**.
Zech 9:15 The LORD of hosts will **d** them;
12: 8 In that day the LORD will **d** the

DEFENDED (3/3) DEFEND
2 Sam 23:12 **d** it, and killed the
1 Chr 11:14 **d** it, and killed the
Acts 7:24 he **d** and avenged him who was

DEFENDER (1/1) DEFEND
Ps 68: 5 a **d** of widows, Is God in His

DEFENDING (2/2) DEFEND
2 Ki 9:14 (Now Joram had been **d** Ramoth
Isa 31: 5 ***D***, He will also deliver it;

DEFENSE (25/24) DEFEND, DEFENSES
2 Ki 19:24 dried up All the brooks of **d**.
2 Chr 11: 5 and built cities for **d** in
Ps 7:10 My **d** is of God, Who saves the
31: 2 A fortress of **d** to save me.
59: 9 his Strength; For God is my **d**;
59:16 For You have been my **d** And
59:17 sing praises; For God is my **d**,
62: 2 and my salvation; He is my **d**;
62: 6 and my salvation; He is my **d**;
94:22 But the LORD has been my **d**,
Eccl 7:12 For wisdom is a **d** as money
7:12 is a defense as money is a **d**,
Isa 19: 6 The brooks of **d** will be
33:16 His place of **d** will be the
37:25 dried up All the brooks of **d**.
Ezek 26: 8 and raise a **d** against you.
Nah 2: 5 And the **d** is prepared.
Acts 19:33 and wanted to make his **d** to the
22: 1 hear my **d** before you now."
26:24 Now as he thus made his **d**,
1 Cor 9: 3 My **d** to those who examine me is
Phil 1: 7 both in my chains and in the **d**
1:17 that I am appointed for the **d**
2 Tim 4:16 At my first **d** no one stood with
1 Pe 3:15 always be ready to give a **d**

DEFENSES (2/1) DEFENSE
Job 13:12 Your **d** are defenses of clay.
13:12 Your defenses are **d** of clay.

DEFER (1/1) DEFERRED
Isa 48: 9 For My name's sake I will **d** My

DEFERRED (1/1) DEFER
Prov 13:12 Hope **d** makes the heart sick,

DEFIANT (1/1) DEFIANTLY, DEFY
Jer 5:23 But this people has a **d** and

DEFIANTLY (2/2) DEFIANT
Job 15:25 And acts **d** against the
36: 9 they have acted **d**.

DEFIED (5/5) DEFY
1 Sam 17:36 seeing he has **d** the armies of
17:45 of Israel, whom you have **d**.
2 Sam 21:21 So when he **d** Israel, Jonathan
23: 9 men with David when they **d** the
1 Chr 20: 7 So when he **d** Israel, Jonathan

DEFILE (47/42) DEFILED, DEFILES, DEFILING, UNDEFILED
Lev 11:44 Neither shall you **d** yourselves
15:31 their uncleanness when they **d**
18:20 to **d** yourself with her.
18:23 to **d** yourself with it.
18:24 Do not **d** yourselves with any of
18:28 vomit you out also when you **d**
18:30 and that you do not **d**
20: 3 to **d** My sanctuary and profane
21: 1 None shall **d** himself for the
21: 3 for her he may **d** himself.
21: 4 Otherwise he shall not **d**
21:11 nor **d** himself for his father or
22: 8 to **d** himself with it: I am the
Num 5: 3 that they may not **d** their camps
35:34 Therefore do not **d** the land
Deut 21:23 so that you do not **d** the land
Song 5: 3 How can I **d** them?
Isa 30:22 You will also **d** the covering of
Jer 32:34 by My name, to **d** it.
Ezek 7:21 And they shall **d** it.
7:22 And they will **d** My secret
7:22 robbers shall enter it and **d**
9: 7 ***D*** the temple, and fill the
20: 7 and do not **d** yourselves with
20:18 nor **d** yourselves with their
20:31 you **d** yourselves with all your
22: 3 makes idols within herself to **d**
22:16 You shall **d** yourself in the
28: 7 And **d** your splendor.
33:26 and you **d** one another's wives.
37:23 They shall not **d** themselves
43: 7 shall the house of Israel **d** My
44: 7 to be in My sanctuary to **d**
44:25 They shall not **d** themselves by
44:25 or unmarried sister may they **d**
Dan 1: 8 his heart that he would not **d**
1: 8 the eunuchs that he might not **d**
11:31 and they shall **d** the sanctuary
Am 2: 7 To **d** My holy name.
Mt 15:18 and they **d** a man.
15:20 are the things which **d**
15:20 with unwashed hands does not **d**
Mk 7:15 a man from outside which can **d**
7:15 those are the things that **d** a
7:18 a man from outside cannot **d**
7:23 things come from within and **d**
Jude 8 Likewise also these dreamers **d**

DEFILED (84/80) DEFILE
Gen 34: 5 And Jacob heard that he had **d**
34:13 because he had **d** Dinah their
34:27 because their sister had been **d**.
49: 4 Then you **d** it—He went up to
Lev 5: 3 with which a man may be **d**,
11:43 lest you be **d** by them.
18:24 by all these the nations are **d**,
18:25 'For the land is **d**;
18:27 you, and thus the land is **d**),
19:31 to be **d** by them: I am the
21: 7 a wife who is a harlot or a **d**
21:14 or a divorced woman or a **d**
Num 5: 2 and whoever becomes **d** by a
5:13 it is concealed that she has **d**
5:14 who has **d** herself; or if the
5:14 although she has not **d** herself—
5:20 and if you have **d** yourself and
5:27 if she has **d** herself and
5:28 But if the woman has not **d**
6:12 because his separation was **d**.
9: 6 were certain men who were **d**
9: 7 We became **d** by a human corpse.
19:20 because he has **d** the sanctuary
Deut 22: 9 the fruit of your vineyard be **d**.
24: 4 his wife after she has been **d**;
2 Ki 23: 8 and **d** the high places where the
23:10 And he **d** Topheth, which is in
23:13 Then the king **d** the high places
23:16 and **d** it according to the word
1 Chr 5: 1 but because he **d** his father's
2 Chr 36:14 and **d** the house of the LORD
Ezra 2:62 from the priesthood as **d**.
Neh 7:64 from the priesthood as **d**.
13:29 because they have **d** the
Ps 74: 7 They have **d** the dwelling place
79: 1 Your holy temple they have **d**;
106:39 Thus they were **d** by their own
Isa 24: 5 The earth is also **d** under its
59: 3 For your hands are **d** with
Jer 2: 7 you **d** My land And made My
3: 9 that she **d** the land and
16:18 because they have **d** My land;
19:13 the kings of Judah shall be **d**
Lam 4:14 They have **d** themselves with
Ezek 4:13 children of Israel eat their **d**
4:14 Indeed I have never **d** myself
5:11 because you have **d** My sanctuary
7:24 their holy places shall be **d**.
18: 6 Nor **d** his neighbor's wife,
18:11 Or **d** his neighbor's wife;
18:15 Nor **d** his neighbor's wife;
20:13 and they greatly **d** My Sabbaths.
20:43 doings with which you were **d**;
22: 4 and have **d** yourself with the
23: 7 their idols, she **d** herself.
23:13 Then I saw that she was **d**;
23:17 And they **d** her with their
23:17 So she was **d** by them, and
23:30 because you have become **d** by
23:38 They have **d** My sanctuary on the
28:18 You **d** your sanctuaries By the
36:17 they **d** it by their own ways and
36:18 idols with which they had **d**
43: 8 they **d** My holy name by the
Hos 5: 3 commit harlotry; Israel is **d**.
6: 8 And **d** with blood.
6:10 of Ephraim; Israel is **d**.
9: 4 All who eat it shall be **d**.
Am 7:17 You shall die in a **d** land;
Mic 2:10 your rest; Because it is **d**,
4:11 you, Who say, "Let her be **d**,
Mal 1: 7 You offer **d** food on My altar.
1: 7 'In what way have we **d** You?'
1:12 'The table of the LORD is **d**;
Mk 7: 2 His disciples eat bread with **d**,
Jn 18:28 lest they should be **d**,
Acts 21:28 into the temple and has **d** this
1 Cor 8: 7 conscience, being weak, is **d**.
Titus 1:15 but to those who are **d** and
1:15 their mind and conscience are **d**.
Heb 12:15 and by this many become **d**;
Jude 23 hating even the garment **d** by
Rev 3: 4 even in Sardis who have not **d**
14: 4 are the ones who were not **d**

DEFILES (11/10) DEFILE
Num 5:29 goes astray and **d** herself,
6: 9 and he **d** his consecrated head,
19:13 **d** the tabernacle of the LORD.
35:33 for blood **d** the land, and no
Ezek 22:11 another lewdly **d** his
Mt 15:11 what goes into the mouth **d**
15:11 the mouth, this **d** a man."
Mk 7:20 of a man, that **d** a man.
1 Cor 3:17 If anyone **d** the temple of God,
Jas 3: 6 set among our members that it **d**
Rev 21:27 means enter it anything that **d**,

DEFILING (3/3) DEFILE
Isa 56: 2 Who keeps from **d** the Sabbath,
56: 6 Everyone who keeps from **d** the
Ezek 20:30 Are you **d** yourselves in the

DEFRAUD (2/2)
Mk 10:19 false witness,' 'Do not **d**,
1 Th 4: 6 should take advantage of and **d**

DEFY (3/3) DEFIANT, DEFIED
1 Sam 17:10 I **d** the armies of Israel this
17:25 Surely he has come up to **d**
17:26 that he should **d** the armies of

DEGENERATE (2/2)
Jer 2:21 turned before Me Into the **d**
Ezek 16:30 How **d** is your heart!" says the

DEGREE (4/3) DEGREES
1 Chr 17:17 to the rank of a man of high **d**,
Ps 62: 9 Surely men of low **d** are a
62: 9 Men of high **d** are a lie;
Phil 3:16 to the **d** that we have already

DEGREES (8/5) DEGREE
Deut 17: 8 between **d** of guilt for
2 Ki 20: 9 the shadow go forward ten **d** or
20: 9 degrees or go backward ten **d**?
20:10 for the shadow to go down ten **d**;
20:10 the shadow go backward ten **d**.
20:11 and He brought the shadow ten **d**
Isa 38: 8 ten **d** backward." So the sun
38: 8 So the sun returned ten **d** on

DEHAVITES (1/1)
Ezra 4: 9 and Babylon and Shushan, the ***D***,

DEITIES (1/1)
Jer 3:13 your charms To alien **d** under

DEKAR (KJV) See BEN-DEKER

DELAIAH (7/7)

1 Chr 3:24 Pelaiah, Akkub, Johanan, **D**,
24:18 the twenty-third to **D**,
Ezra 2:60 the sons of **D**, the sons of
Neh 6:10 house of Shemaiah the son of **D**,
7:62 the sons of **D**, the sons of
Jer 36:12 **D** the son of Shemaiah, Elnathan
36:25 Nevertheless Elnathan, **D**,

DELAY (14/14) DELAYED, DELAYING

Gen 34:19 So the young man did not **d** to do
Ex 22:29 You shall not **d** to offer the
Deut 23:21 you shall not **d** to pay it;
1 Sam 20:38 do not **d**!" So Jonathan's lad
2 Ki 9: 3 the door and flee, and do not **d**.
Ps 40:17 and my deliverer; Do not **d**,
70: 5 deliverer; O LORD, do not **d**.
119:60 and did not **d** To keep Your
Eccl 5: 4 do not **d** to pay it; For He
Jer 4: 6 Take refuge! Do not **d**! For I
Dan 9:19 listen and act! Do not **d** for
Acts 9:38 imploring him not to **d** in
25:17 come together, without any **d**,
Rev 10: 6 that there should be **d** no

DELAYED (6/6) DELAY

Ex 32: 1 the people saw that Moses **d**
Judg 3:26 Ehud had escaped while they **d**,
19: 8 So they **d** until afternoon;
2 Sam 20: 5 But he **d** longer than the set
Mt 25: 5 while the bridegroom was **d**,
1 Tim 3:15 but if I am **d**, I write

DELAYING (2/2) DELAY

Mt 24:48 My master is **d** his coming,'
Lk 12:45 'My master is **d** his coming,'

DELEGATE (1/1) DELEGATION

Ezek 23:24 I will **d** judgment to them, And

DELEGATION (2/2) DELEGATE

Lk 14:32 he sends a **d** and asks
19:14 and sent a **d** after him, saying,

DELICACIES (11/11)

Ps 141: 4 do not let me eat of their **d**.
Prov 23: 3 Do not desire his **d**,
23: 6 of a miser, Nor desire his **d**;
Jer 51:34 filled his stomach with my **d**,
Lam 4: 5 Those who ate **d** Are desolate
Dan 1: 5 provision of the king's **d** and
1: 8 the portion of the king's **d**,
1:13 eat the portion of the king's **d**;
1:15 ate the portion of the king's **d**.
1:16 took away their portion of **d**
11:26 who eat of the portion of his **d**

DELICATE (4/4) DELICATENESS

Gen 29:17 Leah's eyes were **d**,
Deut 28:56 The tender and **d** woman among
Isa 47: 1 no more be called Tender and **d**.
Jer 6: 2 of Zion To a lovely and **d**

DELICATENESS (1/1) DELICATE

Deut 28:56 on the ground because of her **d**

DELIGHT (62/60) DELIGHTED, DELIGHTFUL, DELIGHTS

Deut 21:14 if you have no **d** in her, then
1 Sam 15:22 Has the LORD as great **d** in
18:22 the king has **d** in you, and all
2 Sam 15:26 I have no **d** in you,' here I am,
2 Chr 17: 6 And his heart took **d** in the ways
Esth 6: 6 Whom would the king **d** to honor
Job 22:26 For then you will have your **d**
27:10 Will he **d** himself in the
33:26 and He will **d** in him, He shall
34: 9 a man nothing That he should **d**
Ps 1: 2 But his **d** is in the law of the
16: 3 ones, in whom is all my **d**.
37: 4 **D** yourself also in the LORD,
37:11 And shall **d** themselves in the
40: 8 I **d** to do Your will, O my God,
51:16 You do not **d** in burnt
62: 4 They **d** in lies; They bless
68:30 Scatter the peoples who **d** in
94:19 Your comforts **d** my soul.
109:17 As he did not **d** in blessing,
119:16 I will **d** myself in Your
119:24 testimonies also are my **d**
119:35 For I **d** in it.
119:47 And I will **d** myself in Your
119:70 But I **d** in Your law.
119:77 For Your law is my **d**.
119:92 Your law had been my **d**,
119:174 O LORD, And Your law is my **d**.
147:10 He does not **d** in the strength
Prov 1:22 For scorners **d** in their
2:14 And **d** in the perversity of
7:18 Let us **d** ourselves with love.
8:30 And I was daily His **d**,
8:31 And my **d** was with the sons of
11: 1 But a just weight is His **d**.
11:20 in their ways are His **d**.
12:22 who deal truthfully are His **d**.
15: 8 prayer of the upright is His **d**.
16:13 Righteous lips are the **d** of
18: 2 A fool has no **d** in
23:24 begets a wise child will **d** in
24:25 rebuke the wicked will have **d**,
27: 9 Ointment and perfume **d** the
27: 9 of a man's friend gives **d** by
29:17 he will give **d** to your soul.
Song 2: 3 down in his shade with great **d**,
Isa 1:11 I do not **d** in the blood of
11: 3 His **d** is in the fear of the
13:17 they will not **d** in it.
55: 2 And let your soul **d** itself in
58: 2 And **d** to know My ways, As a
58: 2 They take **d** in approaching
58:13 day, And call the Sabbath a **d**,
58:14 Then you shall **d** yourself in
65:12 chose that in which I do not **d**.
66: 4 chose that in which I do not **d**.
Jer 6:10 They have no **d** in it.
9:24 in the earth. For in these I **d**,
Ezek 24:21 the **d** of your soul; and your
Mal 3: 1 of the covenant, In whom you **d**.
Rom 7:22 For I **d** in the law of God
Col 2:18 taking **d** in false humility and

DELIGHTED (10/10) DELIGHT

Gen 34:19 because he **d** in Jacob's
Deut 10:15 The LORD **d** only in your
1 Sam 19: 1 **d** greatly in David.
2 Sam 22:20 He delivered me because He **d**
1 Ki 10: 9 who **d** in you, setting you on
2 Chr 9: 8 who **d** in you, setting you on
Neh 9:25 And **d** themselves in Your great
Esth 2:14 king again unless the king **d**
Ps 18:19 He delivered me because He **d**
Isa 66:11 you may drink deeply and be **d**

DELIGHTFUL (1/1) DELIGHT

Mal 3:12 For you will be a **d** land,"

DELIGHTS (18/17) DELIGHT

Num 14: 8 If the LORD **d** in us, then He
Esth 6: 6 for the man whom the king **d** to
6: 7 For the man whom the king **d** to
6: 9 array the man whom the king **d**
6: 9 to the man whom the king **d** to
6:11 to the man whom the king **d** to
Ps 22: 8 since He **d** in Him!"
37:23 And He **d** in his way.
112: 1 Who **d** greatly in His
119:143 Your commandments are my **d**.
Prov 3:12 a father the son in whom he **d**.
Eccl 2: 8 the **d** of the sons of men, and
Song 7: 6 O love, with your **d**!
Isa 42: 1 Elect One in whom My soul **d**!
62: 4 For the LORD **d** in you, And
66: 3 And their soul **d** in their
Mic 7:18 Because He **d** in mercy.
Mal 2:17 And He **d** in them,"

DELILAH (6/6)

Judg 16: 4 of Sorek, whose name was **D**.
16: 6 So **D** said to Samson, "Please
16:10 Then **D** said to Samson, "Look,
16:12 Therefore **D** took new ropes and
16:13 **D** said to Samson, "Until now
16:18 When **D** saw that he had told her

DELIVER (264/253) DELIVERANCE, DELIVERED, DELIVERER, DELIVERING, DELIVERS, DELIVERY

Gen 32:11 **D** me, I pray, from the hand of
37:22 that he might **d** him out of their
Ex 3: 8 So I have come down to **d** them
5:18 yet you shall **d** the quota of
23:31 For I will **d** the inhabitants of
Num 21: 2 If You will indeed **d** this people
35:25 So the congregation shall **d** the
Deut 1:27 the land of Egypt to **d** us
2:30 that He might **d** him into your
7:23 LORD your God will **d** them
7:24 And He will **d** their kings into
19:12 and **d** him over to the hand of
23:14 to **d** you and give your enemies
32:39 Nor is there any who can **d**
Josh 2:13 and **d** our lives from death."
7: 7 to **d** us into the hand of the
8: 7 the LORD your God will **d** it
11: 6 about this time I will **d** all
20: 5 they shall not **d** the slayer
Judg 2:23 nor did He **d** them into the hand
4: 7 and I will **d** him into your
7: 7 and **d** the Midianites into your
10:11 Did I not **d** you from the
10:13 Therefore I will **d** you no more.
10:14 let them **d** you in your time of
10:15 only **d** us this day, we pray."
11:30 If You will indeed **d** the people
12: 2 you did not **d** me out of their
12: 3 I saw that you would not **d** me,
13: 5 and he shall begin to **d** Israel
15:12 that we may **d** you into the hand
15:13 tie you securely and **d** you
20:13 **d** up the men, the perverted men
20:28 for tomorrow I will **d** them into
1 Sam 4: 8 Woe to us! Who will **d** us from
7: 3 and He will **d** you from the hand
12:10 but now **d** us from the hand of
12:21 things which cannot profit or **d**,
14:37 Will You **d** them into the hand
17:37 He will **d** me from the hand of
17:46 This day the LORD will **d** you
23: 4 For I will **d** the Philistines
23:11 Will the men of Keilah **d** me into
23:12 Will the men of Keilah **d** me and
23:12 They will **d** you."
23:14 but God did not **d** him into his
23:20 our part shall be to **d** him
24: 4 I will **d** your enemy into your
24:15 and **d** me out of your hand."
26:24 and let Him **d** me out of all
28:19 the LORD will also **d**
28:19 The LORD will also **d** the army
30:15 will neither kill me nor **d** me
2 Sam 5:19 Will You **d** them into my hand?"
5:19 for I will doubtless **d** the
14: 7 **D** him who struck his brother,
14:16 For the king will hear and **d** his
20:21 **D** him only, and I will depart
1 Ki 8:46 angry with them and **d** them
20: 5 You shall **d** to me your silver
20:13 I will **d** it into your hand
20:28 therefore I will **d** all this
22: 6 for the Lord will **d** it into
22:12 for the LORD will **d** it into
22:15 for the LORD will **d** it into
2 Ki 3:10 three kings together to **d** them
3:13 kings together to **d** them
3:18 He will also **d** the Moabites
12: 7 but **d** it for repairing the
17:39 and He will **d** you from the hand
18:29 he shall not be able to **d** you
18:30 'The LORD will surely **d** us;
18:32 The LORD will **d** us."
18:35 that the LORD should **d**
20: 6 I will **d** you and this city from
21:14 of My inheritance and **d** them
22: 5 And let them **d** it into the hand
1 Chr 14:10 Will You **d** them into my hand?"
14:10 for I will **d** them into your
16:35 and **d** us from the Gentiles, To
2 Chr 6:36 angry with them and **d** them
18: 5 for God will **d** it into the
18:11 for the LORD will **d** it into
32:11 The LORD our God will **d** us from
32:13 able to **d** their lands
32:14 destroyed that could **d** his
32:14 your God should be able to **d**
32:15 or kingdom was able to **d** his
32:15 How much less will your God **d**
32:17 Hezekiah will not **d** His people
Ezra 7:19 **d** in full before the God of
Job 5:19 He shall **d** you in six troubles,
6:23 **D** me from the enemy's hand'?
10: 7 there is no one who can **d**
22:30 He will even **d** one who is not
33:24 **D** him from going down to the
39: 3 They **d** their offspring.
Ps 6: 4 **d** me! Oh, save me for Your
7: 1 who persecute me; And **d** me,
7: 2 while there is none to **d**.
17:13 **D** my life from the wicked with
22: 8 Let Him **d** Him, since He
22:20 **D** Me from the sword, My
25:20 and **d** me; Let me not be
27:12 Do not **d** me to the will of my
31: 1 **D** me in Your righteousness.
31: 2 **D** me speedily; Be my rock of
31:15 **D** me from the hand of my
33:17 Neither shall it **d** any by its
33:19 To **d** their soul from death,
37:40 shall help them and **d** them;
37:40 He shall **d** them from the
39: 8 **D** me from all my transgressions
40:13 to **d** me; O LORD, make haste
41: 1 The LORD will **d** him in time
41: 2 You will not **d** him to the will
43: 1 **d** me from the deceitful and
50:15 I will **d** you, and you shall
50:22 And there be none to **d**:
51:14 **D** me from the guilt of
59: 1 **D** me from my enemies, O my God
59: 2 **D** me from the workers of
69:14 **D** me out of the mire, And let
69:18 **D** me because of my enemies.
70: 1 haste, O God, to **d** me!
71: 2 **D** me in Your righteousness, and
71: 4 **D** me, O my God, out of the hand
71:11 for there is none to **d**
72:12 For He will **d** the needy when he
74:19 do not **d** the life of Your
76: 9 To **d** all the oppressed of the
79: 9 And **d** us, and provide
82: 4 **D** the poor and needy
89:48 Can he **d** his life from the
91: 3 Surely He shall **d** you from the
91:14 therefore I will **d** him; I will
91:15 I will **d** him and honor him.
109:21 mercy is good, **d** me.
116: 4 implore You, **d** my soul!"
119:153 Consider my affliction and **d**
119:170 **D** me according to Your word.
120: 2 **D** my soul, O LORD, from lying
140: 1 **D** me, O LORD, from evil men
142: 6 **D** me from my persecutors, For

143: 9 **D** me, O LORD, from my enemies
144: 7 Rescue me and **d** me out of
144:11 Rescue me and **d** me from the
Prov 2:12 To **d** you from the way of evil,
2:16 To **d** you from the immoral
4: 9 A crown of glory she will **d** to
6: 3 and **d** yourself; For you have
6: 5 **D** yourself like a gazelle from
11: 6 of the upright will **d** them,
12: 6 the mouth of the upright will **d**
23:14 And **d** his soul from hell.
24:11 **D** those who are drawn toward
Eccl 8: 8 And wickedness will not **d**
Isa 5:29 away safely, And no one will **d**.
19:20 and He will **d** them.
29:11 which men **d** to one who is
31: 5 He will also **d** it; Passing
36:14 for he will not be able to **d**
36:15 'The LORD will surely **d** us;
36:18 The LORD will **d** us." Has any
36:20 that the LORD should **d**
38: 6 I will **d** you and this city from
43:13 there is no one who can **d**
44:17 **D** me, for you are my god!"
44:20 And he cannot **d** his soul, Nor
46: 2 They could not **d** the burden,
46: 4 and will **d** you.
47:14 They shall not **d** themselves
50: 2 Or have I no power to **d**?
57:13 your collection of idols **d**
Jer 1: 8 For I am with you to **d** you,"
1:19 says the LORD, "to **d** you."
15: 9 the remnant of them I will **d**
15:20 to save you And **d** you,"
15:21 I will **d** you from the hand of
18:21 Therefore **d** up their children
20: 5 Moreover I will **d** all the wealth
21: 7 I will **d** Zedekiah king of Judah,
21:12 And **d** him who is plundered
22: 3 and **d** the plundered out of the
24: 9 I will **d** them to trouble into
29:18 and I will **d** them to trouble
29:21 I will **d** them into the hand of
34:17 and to famine! And I will **d** you
38:19 lest they **d** me into their hand,
38:20 'They shall not **d** you.
39:17 But I will **d** you in that day,"
39:18 For I will surely **d** you, and you
42:11 to save you and **d** you from his
43: 3 to **d** us into the hand of the
43:11 the land of Egypt and **d** to
46:26 And I will **d** them into the hand
51:45 And let everyone **d** himself
Lam 5: 8 There is none to **d** us from
Ezek 7:19 gold will not be able to **d**
11: 9 and **d** you into the hands of
13:21 your veils and **d** My people
13:23 for I will **d** My people out of
14:14 they would **d** only themselves
14:16 they would **d** neither sons nor
14:18 they would **d** neither sons nor
14:20 they would **d** neither son nor
14:20 they would **d** only themselves
21:31 And **d** you into the hands of
23:28 Surely I will **d** you into the
25: 4 I will **d** you as a possession to
31:11 therefore I will **d** it into the
33:12 the righteous man shall not **d**
34:10 for I will **d** My flock from
34:12 seek out My sheep and **d** them
36:29 I will **d** you from all your
37:23 but I will **d** them from all
Dan 3:15 And who is the god who will **d**
3:17 God whom we serve is able to **d**
3:17 and He will **d** us from your
3:29 is no other God who can **d** like
6:14 set his heart on Daniel to **d**
6:14 the going down of the sun to **d**
6:16 continually, He will **d** you."
6:20 been able to **d** you from the
8: 4 was there any that could **d**
8: 7 there was no one that could **d**
Hos 2:10 And no one shall **d** her from My
Am 1: 6 the whole captivity To **d**
2:14 Nor shall the mighty **d**
2:15 who rides a horse **d** himself.
6: 8 Therefore I will **d** up the
Jon 4: 6 be shade for his head to **d** him
Mic 5: 6 Thus He shall **d** us from the
5: 8 in pieces, And none can **d**.
Zeph 1:18 their gold Shall be able to **d**
Zech 11: 6 and I will not **d** them from
Mt 5:25 lest your adversary **d** you to
6:13 But **d** us from the evil one.
10:17 for they will **d** you up to
10:19 But when they **d** you up, do not
10:21 Now brother will **d** up brother to
20:19 and **d** Him to the Gentiles to
24: 9 Then they will **d** you up to
26:15 you willing to give me if I **d**
27:43 let Him **d** Him now if He will
Mk 10:33 condemn Him to death and **d** Him
13: 9 for they will **d** you up to
13:11 when they arrest you and **d**
Lk 11: 4 But **d** us from the evil one."
12:58 the judge **d** you to the officer,
20:20 in order to **d** Him to the power
Acts 7:25 understood that God would **d**
7:34 and have come down to **d**
21:11 and **d** him into the hands of
25:11 no one can **d** me to them.
25:16 the custom of the Romans to **d**
26:17 I will **d** you from the Jewish
Rom 7:24 man that I am! Who will **d** me
1 Cor 5: 5 **d** such a one to Satan for the
2 Cor 1:10 and does **d** us; in whom we trust
1:10 we trust that He will still **d**
Gal 1: 4 that He might **d** us from this
2 Tim 4:18 And the Lord will **d** me from
2 Pe 2: 9 then the Lord knows how to **d**

DELIVERANCE (17/16) DELIVER

Gen 45: 7 to save your lives by a great **d**.
Judg 15:18 You have given this great **d** by
1 Sam 14:45 has accomplished this great **d**
19: 5 LORD brought about a great **d**
2 Ki 13:17 The arrow of the LORD's **d** and
13:17 deliverance and the arrow of **d**
2 Chr 12: 7 but I will grant them some **d**.
Ezra 9:13 and have given us such **d** as
Esth 4:14 relief and **d** will arise for the
Ps 18:50 Great **d** He gives to His king,
32: 7 surround me with songs of **d**.
Prov 21:31 But **d** is of the LORD.
Isa 26:18 have not accomplished any **d** in
Joel 2:32 in Jerusalem there shall be **d**,
Ob 17 on Mount Zion there shall be **d**,
Phil 1:19 this will turn out for my **d**
Heb 11:35 were tortured, not accepting **d**,

DELIVERED (246/244) DELIVER

Gen 14:20 Who has **d** your enemies into
32:16 Then he **d** them to the hand of
37:21 and he **d** him out of their
Ex 2:19 An Egyptian **d** us from the hand
5:23 neither have You **d** Your people
12:27 He struck the Egyptians and **d**
18: 4 and **d** me from the sword of
18: 8 and how the LORD had **d** them.
18: 9 whom He had **d** out of the hand
18:10 who has **d** you out of the hand
18:10 and who has **d** the people from
21:13 but God **d** him into his hand,
Lev 6: 2 his neighbor about what was **d**
6: 4 or what was **d** to him for
26:25 and you shall be **d** into the
Num 21: 3 to the voice of Israel and **d**
21:34 for I have **d** him into your
Deut 2:33 And the LORD our God **d** him over
2:36 the LORD our God **d** all to us.
3: 2 for I have **d** him and all his
3: 3 So the LORD our God also **d** into
9:10 Then the LORD **d** to me two
31: 9 So Moses wrote this law and **d**
Josh 2:24 Truly the LORD has **d** all the
9:26 and **d** them out of the hand of
10: 8 for I have **d** them into your
10:12 in the day when the LORD **d** up
10:19 for the LORD your God has **d**
10:30 And the LORD also **d** it and its
10:32 And the LORD **d** Lachish into the
11: 8 And the LORD **d** them into the
21:44 the LORD **d** all their enemies
22:31 Now you have **d** the children of
24:10 So I **d** you out of his hand.
24:11 But I **d** them into your hand.
Judg 1: 2 Indeed I have **d** the land into
1: 4 and the LORD **d** the Canaanites
2:14 So He **d** them into the hands of
2:16 LORD raised up judges who **d**
2:18 LORD was with the judge and **d**
3: 9 who **d** them: Othniel the son of
3:10 LORD **d** Cushan-Rishathaim
3:28 for the LORD has **d** your
3:31 and he also **d** Israel.
4:14 day in which the LORD has **d**
6: 1 So the LORD **d** them into the
6: 9 and I **d** you out of the hand of
6:13 LORD has forsaken us and **d** us
7: 9 for I have **d** it into your hand.
7:14 Into his hand God has **d** Midian
7:15 for the LORD has **d** the camp of
8: 3 God has **d** into your hands the
8: 7 when the LORD has **d** Zebah and
8:22 for you have **d** us from the hand
8:34 who had **d** them from the hands
9:17 and **d** you out of the hand of
10:12 and I **d** you from their hand.
11:21 And the LORD God of Israel **d**
11:32 and the LORD **d** them into his
12: 3 and the LORD **d** them into my
13: 1 and the LORD **d** them into the
16:23 Our god has **d** into our hands
16:24 Our god has **d** into our hands our
1 Sam 4:19 was with child, due to be **d**;
10:18 and **d** you from the hand of the
12:11 and **d** you out of the hand of
14:10 For the LORD has **d** them into
14:12 for the LORD has **d** them into
14:48 and **d** Israel from the hands of
17:35 and **d** the lamb from its
17:37 who **d** me from the paw of the
23: 7 God has **d** him into my hand, for
24:10 have seen that the LORD **d** you
24:18 for when the LORD **d** me into
26: 8 God has **d** your enemy into your
26:23 for the LORD **d** you into my
30:23 who has preserved us and **d** into
2 Sam 3: 8 and have not **d** you into the
12: 7 and I **d** you from the hand of
16: 8 and the LORD has **d** the kingdom
18:28 who has **d** up the men who raised
19: 9 he **d** us from the hand of the
21: 6 men of his descendants be **d** to
21: 9 and he **d** them into the hands of
22: 1 on the day when the LORD had **d**
22:18 He **d** me from my strong enemy,
22:20 He **d** me because He delighted
22:44 You have also **d** me from the
22:49 You have **d** me from the violent
1 Ki 13:26 Therefore the LORD has **d** him
15:18 and **d** them into the hand of his
2 Ki 12:15 the men into whose hand they **d**
13: 3 and He **d** them into the hand of
17:20 and **d** them into the hand of
18:33 gods of the nations at all **d**
18:34 have they **d** Samaria from my
18:35 the gods of the lands have **d**
19:11 them; and shall you be **d**?
19:12 'Have the gods of the nations **d**
22: 7 made with them of the money **d**
22: 9 and have **d** it into the hand of
1 Chr 5:20 and the Hagrites were **d** into
16: 7 On that day David first **d** this
2 Chr 13:16 and God **d** them into their hand.
16: 8 He **d** them into your hand.
18:14 and they shall be **d** into your
24:24 but the LORD **d** a very great
28: 5 Therefore the LORD his God **d**
28: 5 Then he was also **d** into the
28: 9 He has **d** them into your hand;
32:17 of other lands have not **d**
34: 9 they **d** the money that was
34:17 and have **d** it into the hand of
Ezra 8:31 and He **d** us from the hand of
8:36 And they **d** the king's orders to
9: 7 and our priests have been **d**
Neh 9:27 Therefore You **d** them into the
9:28 And many times You **d** them
Esth 6: 9 let this robe and horse be **d**
Job 16:11 God has **d** me to the ungodly,
22:30 he will be **d** by the purity of
23: 7 And I would be **d** forever from
29:12 Because I **d** the poor who cried
Ps 18: on the day that the LORD **d**
18:17 He **d** me from my strong enemy,
18:19 He **d** me because He delighted
18:43 You have **d** me from the
18:48 You have **d** me from the violent
22: 4 trusted, and You **d** them.
22: 5 They cried to You, and were **d**;
33:16 A mighty man is not **d** by great
34: 4 And **d** me from all my fears.
54: 7 For He has **d** me out of all
56:13 For You have **d** my soul from
60: 5 That Your beloved may be **d**,
69:14 Let me be **d** from those who
78:61 And **d** His strength into
81: 7 and I **d** you; I answered you in
86:13 And You have **d** my soul from
106:43 Many times He **d** them; But they
107: 6 And He **d** them out of their
107:20 And **d** them from their
108: 6 That Your beloved may be **d**,
116: 8 For You have **d** my soul from
Prov 11: 8 The righteous is **d** from
11: 9 the righteous will be **d**.
11:21 of the righteous will be **d**.
28:26 whoever walks wisely will be **d**.
Eccl 9:15 and he by his wisdom **d** the
Isa 20: 6 we flee for help to be **d** from
29:12 Then the book is **d** to one who is
36:18 of the gods of the nations **d**
36:19 have they **d** Samaria from my
36:20 the gods of these lands have **d**
37:11 them; and shall you be **d**?
37:12 'Have the gods of the nations **d**
38:17 But You have lovingly **d** my
49:24 captives of the righteous be **d**?
49:25 the prey of the terrible be **d**;
66: 7 She **d** a male child.
Jer 7:10 We are **d** to do all these
20:13 For He has **d** the life of the
32: 4 but shall surely be **d** into the
32:16 Now when I had **d** the purchase
32:36 It shall be **d** into the hand of
34: 3 surely be taken and **d** into his
37:17 You shall be **d** into the hand of
46:24 She shall be **d** into the hand
Lam 1:14 The Lord **d** me into the hands
Ezek 3:19 but you have **d** your soul.
3:21 also you will have **d** your
14:16 daughters; only they would be **d**,
14:18 only they themselves would be **d**.
17:15 break a covenant and still be **d**?
23: 9 Therefore I have **d** her Into the
31:14 For they have all been **d** to
32:20 She is **d** to the sword,
33: 9 but you have **d** your soul.
34:27 bands of their yoke and **d** them
Dan 3:28 who sent His Angel and **d** His
6:27 Who has **d** Daniel from the
12: 1 time your people shall be **d**,
Am 1: 9 Because they **d** up the whole
9: 1 from them shall not be **d**.
Ob 14 Nor should you have **d** up those
Mic 4:10 shall go. There you shall be **d**;
Hab 2: 9 That he may be **d** from the
Mt 11:27 All things have been **d** to Me by
18:34 and **d** him to the torturers
25:14 servants and **d** his goods
25:20 you **d** to me five talents; look,
25:22 you **d** to me two talents; look,
26: 2 and the Son of Man will be **d** up

27: 2 they led Him away and ***d*** Him to
27:26 he ***d*** Him to be crucified.
Mk 15: 1 and ***d*** Him to Pilate.
15:15 and he ***d*** Jesus, after he had
Lk 1: 2 ministers of the word ***d*** them
1:57 full time came for her to be ***d***,
1:74 Being ***d*** from the hand of our
2: 6 were completed for her to be ***d***.
4: 6 for this has been ***d*** to me, and
10:22 All things have been ***d*** to Me by
18:32 For He will be ***d*** to the Gentiles
19:13 ***d*** to them ten minas, and said
23:25 but he ***d*** Jesus to their will.
24: 7 The Son of Man must be ***d*** into
24:20 chief priests and our rulers ***d***
Jn 18:30 we would not have ***d*** Him up to
18:35 and the chief priests have ***d***
18:36 so that I should not be ***d*** to
19:11 Therefore the one who ***d*** Me to
19:16 Then he ***d*** Him to them to be
Acts 2:23 being ***d*** by the determined
3:13 whom you ***d*** up and denied in the
6:14 the customs which Moses ***d*** to
7:10 and ***d*** him out of all his
12: 4 and ***d*** him to four squads of
12:11 and has ***d*** me from the hand of
15:30 they ***d*** the letter.
16: 4 they ***d*** to them the decrees to
23:33 came to Caesarea and had ***d*** the
27: 1 they ***d*** Paul and some other
28:16 the centurion ***d*** the prisoners
28:17 yet I was ***d*** as a prisoner from
Rom 4:25 who was ***d*** up because of our
6:17 of doctrine to which you were ***d***.
7: 6 But now we have been ***d*** from the
8:21 creation itself also will be ***d***
8:32 but ***d*** Him up for us all, how
15:31 that I may be ***d*** from those in
1 Cor 11: 2 traditions just as I ***d*** them
11:23 the Lord that which I also ***d***
15: 3 For I ***d*** to you first of all that
2 Cor 1:10 who ***d*** us from so great a death,
4:11 For we who live are always ***d*** to
Col 1:13 He has ***d*** us from the power of
2 Th 3: 2 and that we may be ***d*** from
1 Tim 1:20 whom I ***d*** to Satan that they may
2 Tim 3:11 out of them all the Lord ***d*** me.
4:17 And I was ***d*** out of the mouth of
2 Pe 2: 4 them down to hell and ***d*** them
2: 7 and ***d*** righteous Lot, who was
2:21 from the holy commandment ***d*** to
Jude 3 faith which was once for all ***d***
Rev 20:13 and Death and Hades ***d*** up the

DELIVERER (12/12) DELIVER, DELIVERERS

Judg 3: 9 the LORD raised up a ***d*** for the
3:15 the LORD raised up a ***d*** for
18:28 There was no ***d***,
2 Sam 22: 2 rock and my fortress and my ***d***;
2 Ki 13: 5 Then the LORD gave Israel a ***d***,
Job 5: 4 the gate, And there is no ***d***.
Ps 18: 2 rock and my fortress and my ***d***;
40:17 You are my help and my ***d***;
70: 5 You are my help and my ***d***;
144: 2 My high tower and my ***d***,
Acts 7:35 sent to be a ruler and a ***d***
Rom 11:26 The ***D*** will come out of

DELIVERERS (1/1) DELIVERER

Neh 9:27 mercies You gave them ***d*** who

DELIVERING (4/4) DELIVER

1 Ki 18: 9 that you are ***d*** your servant
Ps 35:10 ***D*** the poor from him who is too
Lk 21:12 ***d*** you up to the synagogues and
Acts 22: 4 binding and ***d*** into prisons both

DELIVERS (22/22) DELIVER

Ex 22: 7 If a man ***d*** to his neighbor
22:10 If a man ***d*** to his neighbor a
Deut 7: 2 and when the LORD your God ***d***
7:16 whom the LORD your God ***d*** over
20:13 And when the LORD your God ***d*** it
21:10 and the LORD your God ***d*** them
Judg 11: 9 and the LORD ***d*** them to me,
2 Sam 22:49 He ***d*** me from my enemies.
Job 36:15 He ***d*** the poor in their
Ps 18:48 He ***d*** me from my enemies.
34: 7 who fear Him, And ***d*** them.
34:17 And ***d*** them out of all their
34:19 But the LORD ***d*** him out of
97:10 He ***d*** them out of the hand of
144:10 Who ***d*** David His servant From
Prov 10: 2 But righteousness ***d*** from
11: 4 But righteousness ***d*** from
14:25 A true witness ***d*** souls, But a
Isa 42:22 are for prey, and no one ***d***;
Dan 6:27 He ***d*** and rescues, And He works
1 Cor 15:24 when He ***d*** the kingdom to God
1 Th 1:10 even Jesus who ***d*** us from the

DELIVERY (3/2) DELIVER

Isa 26:17 draws near the time of her ***d***,
66: 9 time of birth, and not cause ***d***?
66: 9 Shall I who cause ***d*** shut up the

DELUDED (1/1) DELUSION

Isa 19:13 They have also ***d*** Egypt,

DELUSION (2/2) DELUDED, DELUSIONS

Zech 10: 2 For the idols speak ***d***;
2 Th 2:11 God will send them strong ***d***,

DELUSIONS (2/2) DELUSION

Isa 66: 4 So will I choose their ***d***,
Lam 2:14 for you false prophecies and ***d***.

DEMAND (3/3) DEMANDED, DEMANDING, DEMANDS

Gen 9: 5 for your lifeblood I will ***d*** a
Neh 5:18 in spite of this I did not ***d***
Dan 2:23 made known to us the king's ***d***.

DEMANDED (1/1) DEMAND

Dan 2:27 secret which the king has ***d***,

DEMANDING (1/1) DEMAND

Lk 23:23 ***d*** with loud voices that He be

DEMANDS (2/2) DEMAND

1 Sam 10: 7 that you do as the occasion ***d***;
1 Th 2: 6 when we might have made ***d*** as

DEMAS (3/3)

Col 4:14 the beloved physician and ***D***
2 Tim 4:10 for ***D*** has forsaken me, having
Phm 1:24 as do Mark, Aristarchus, ***D***,

DEMENTED (1/1)

Jer 29:26 LORD over every man who is ***d***

DEMETRIUS (3/3)

Acts 19:24 For a certain man named ***D***,
19:38 if ***D*** and his fellow craftsmen
3 Jn 12 ***D*** has a good testimony from

DEMOLISH (1/1)

Num 33:52 and ***d*** all their high places;

DEMOLISHED (1/1)

Judg 9:45 and he ***d*** the city and sowed it

DEMON (20/18) DEMON-POSSESSED, DEMONIC, DEMONS

Mt 9:33 And when the ***d*** was cast out, the
11:18 and they say, 'He has a ***d***.
17:18 And Jesus rebuked the ***d***,
Mk 7:26 kept asking Him to cast the ***d***
7:29 the ***d*** has gone out of your
7:30 she found the ***d*** gone out, and
Lk 4:33 had a spirit of an unclean ***d***.
4:35 And when the ***d*** had thrown
7:33 wine, and you say, 'He has a ***d***.
8:29 bonds and was driven by the ***d***
9:42 the ***d*** threw him down and
11:14 And He was casting out a ***d***,
11:14 when the ***d*** had gone out, that
Jn 7:20 and said, "You have a ***d***.
8:48 are a Samaritan and have a ***d***?
8:49 answered, "I do not have a ***d***;
8:52 Now we know that You have a ***d***!
10:20 He has a ***d*** and is mad. Why do
10:21 the words of one who has a ***d***.
10:21 Can a ***d*** open the eyes of the

DEMON-POSSESSED (12/12) DEMON

Mt 4:24 torments, and those who were ***d***,
8:16 brought to Him many who were ***d***.
8:28 there met Him two ***d*** men,
8:33 what had happened to the ***d***
9:32 to Him a man, mute and ***d***.
12:22 was brought to Him who was ***d***,
15:22 My daughter is severely ***d***.
Mk 1:32 were sick and those who were ***d***.
5:15 saw the one who had been ***d***
5:16 to him who had been ***d***,
5:18 he who had been ***d*** begged Him
Lk 8:36 by what means he who had been ***d***

DEMONIC (1/1) DEMON

Jas 3:15 but is earthly, sensual, ***d***.

DEMONS (49/42) DEMON

Lev 17: 7 offer their sacrifices to ***d***,
Deut 32:17 They sacrificed to ***d***,
2 Chr 11:15 for the high places, for the ***d***,
Ps 106:37 sons And their daughters to ***d***,
Mt 7:22 cast out ***d*** in Your name, and
8:31 So the ***d*** begged Him, saying,
9:34 He casts out ***d*** by the ruler of
9:34 demons by the ruler of the ***d***.
10: 8 raise the dead, cast out ***d***.
12:24 fellow does not cast out ***d***
12:24 Beelzebub, the ruler of the ***d***.
12:27 And if I cast out ***d*** by
12:28 But if I cast out ***d*** by the
Mk 1:34 diseases, and cast out many ***d***;
1:34 and He did not allow the ***d*** to
1:39 all Galilee, and casting out ***d***.
3:15 sicknesses and to cast out ***d***:
3:22 By the ruler of the ***d*** He casts
3:22 of the demons He casts out ***d***.
5:12 So all the ***d*** begged Him, saying,
6:13 And they cast out many ***d***,
9:38 not follow us casting out ***d*** in
16: 9 out of whom He had cast seven ***d***.
16:17 In My name they will cast out ***d***;
Lk 4:41 And ***d*** also came out of many,
8: 2 out of whom had come seven ***d***,
8:27 man from the city who had ***d***
8:30 because many ***d*** had entered
8:33 Then the ***d*** went out of the man
8:35 found the man from whom the ***d***
8:38 Now the man from whom the ***d*** had
9: 1 power and authority over all ***d***,
9:49 we saw someone casting out ***d*** in
10:17 even the ***d*** are subject to us in
11:15 He casts out ***d*** by Beelzebub, the
11:15 Beelzebub, the ruler of the ***d***.
11:18 Because you say I cast out ***d*** by
11:19 And if I cast out ***d*** by
11:20 But if I cast out ***d*** with the
13:32 I cast out ***d*** and perform cures
1 Cor 10:20 sacrifice they sacrifice to ***d***
10:20 you to have fellowship with ***d***.
10:21 of the Lord and the cup of ***d***;
10:21 table and of the table of ***d***.
1 Tim 4: 1 spirits and doctrines of ***d***,
Jas 2:19 Even the ***d*** believe—and tremble!
Rev 9:20 that they should not worship ***d***,
16:14 For they are spirits of ***d***,
18: 2 become a dwelling place of ***d***,

DEMONSTRATE (2/2) DEMONSTRATES, DEMONSTRATING, DEMONSTRATION

Rom 3:25 to ***d*** His righteousness, because
3:26 to ***d*** at the present time His

DEMONSTRATES (2/2) DEMONSTRATE

Rom 3: 5 But if our unrighteousness ***d*** the
5: 8 But God ***d*** His own love toward

DEMONSTRATING (1/1) DEMONSTRATE

Acts 17: 3 explaining and ***d*** that the Christ

DEMONSTRATION (1/1) DEMONSTRATE

1 Cor 2: 4 but in ***d*** of the Spirit and of

DEN (19/17) DENS

Ps 10: 9 secretly, as a lion in his ***d***;
Isa 11: 8 put his hand in the viper's ***d***.
Jer 7:11 become a ***d*** of thieves in your
9:11 a ***d*** of jackals. I will make
10:22 desolate, a ***d*** of jackals.
Dan 6: 7 shall be cast into the ***d*** of
6:12 shall be cast into the ***d*** of
6:16 and cast him into the ***d*** of
6:17 and laid on the mouth of the ***d***,
6:19 and went in haste to the ***d*** of
6:20 And when he came to the ***d***,
6:23 take Daniel up out of the ***d***.
6:23 was taken up out of the ***d***,
6:24 and they cast them into the ***d***
6:24 came to the bottom of the ***d***.
Am 3: 4 a young lion cry out of his ***d***,
Mt 21:13 ***d*** of thieves.'"
Mk 11:17 ***d*** of thieves.'"
Lk 19:46 ***d*** of thieves.'"

DENARII (7/7) DENARIUS

Mt 18:28 who owed him a hundred ***d***;
Mk 6:37 we go and buy two hundred ***d***
14: 5 for more than three hundred ***d***
Lk 7:41 One owed five hundred ***d***,
10:35 he departed, he took out two ***d***,
Jn 6: 7 Two hundred ***d*** worth of bread is
12: 5 not sold for three hundred ***d***

DENARIUS (9/8) DENARII

Mt 20: 2 with the laborers for a ***d*** a
20: 9 hour, they each received a ***d***.
20:10 they likewise received each a ***d***.
20:13 you not agree with me for a ***d***?
22:19 So they brought Him a ***d***.
Mk 12:15 Bring Me a ***d*** that I may see
Lk 20:24 'Show Me a ***d***. Whose image
Rev 6: 6 "A quart of wheat for a ***d***,
6: 6 three quarts of barley for a ***d***;

DENIED (17/17) DENY

Gen 18:15 But Sarah ***d*** it, saying, "I did
Job 31:28 For I would have ***d*** God who
Mt 26:70 But he ***d*** it before them all,
26:72 But again he ***d*** with an oath, "I

Mk 14:68 But he **d** it, saying, “I neither
14:70 But he **d** it again. And a little
Lk 8:45 When all **d** it, Peter and
12: 9 denies Me before men will be **d**
22:57 But he **d** Him, saying, “Woman, I
Jn 13:38 shall not crow till you have **d**
18:25 He **d** it and said, “I am
18:27 Peter then **d** again;
Acts 3:13 whom you delivered up and **d** in
3:14 But you **d** the Holy One and the
19:36 since these things cannot be **d**,
1 Tim 5: 8 he has **d** the faith and is worse
Rev 3: 8 and have not **d** My name.

DENIES (5/4) DENY

Mt 10:33 But whoever **d** Me before men, him
Lk 12: 9 But he who **d** Me before men will
1 Jn 2:22 Who is a liar but he who **d** that
2:22 He is antichrist who **d** the
2:23 Whoever **d** the Son does not have

DENOUNCE (2/2) DENOUNCED

Num 23: 7 And come, **d** Israel!’
23: 8 And how shall I **d** whom the

DENOUNCED (1/1) DENOUNCE

Num 23: 8 whom the LORD has not **d**?

DENS (7/7) DEN

Judg 6: 2 made for themselves the **d**,
Job 37: 8 The beasts go into **d**,
38:40 When they crouch in their **d**,
Ps 104:22 And lie down in their **d**.
Song 4: 8 and Hermon, From the lions’ **d**,
Nah 2:12 And his **d** with flesh.
Heb 11:38 in **d** and caves of the earth.

DENSE (2/2)

Jer 13:16 And makes it **d** darkness.
Ezek 19:11 seen in her height amid the **d**

DENY (26/25) DENIED, DENIES, DENYING

Josh 24:27 lest you **d** your God.”
1 Ki 2:16 do not **d** me.” And she said to
20: 7 and I did not **d** him.”
Job 8:18 Then it will **d** him, saying,
Prov 30: 9 Lest I be full and **d** You, And
Mt 10:33 him I will also **d** before My
16:24 let him **d** himself, and take up
26:34 you will **d** Me three times.”
26:35 I will not **d** You!” And so said
26:75 you will **d** Me three times.”
Mk 8:34 let him **d** himself, and take up
14:30 you will **d** Me three times.”
14:31 I will not **d** You!” And they
14:72 you will **d** Me three times.”
Lk 9:23 let him **d** himself, and take up
20:27 who **d** that there is a
22:34 crow this day before you will **d**
22:61 you will **d** Me three times.”
Jn 1:20 He confessed, and did not **d**,
Acts 4:16 and we cannot **d** it.
2 Tim 2:12 If we **d** Him, He also will
2:12 He also will **d** us.
2:13 He cannot **d** Himself.
Titus 1:16 but in works they **d** Him, being
Jude 4 of our God into lewdness and **d**
Rev 2:13 and did not **d** My faith even in

DENYING (3/3) DENY

2 Tim 3: 5 a form of godliness but **d** its
Titus 2:12 **d** ungodliness and worldly
2 Pe 2: 1 even **d** the Lord who bought

DEPART (125/122) DEPARTED, DEPARTING, DEPARTS, DEPARTURE

Gen 45:17 this: Load your animals and **d**;
49:10 The scepter shall not **d** from
Ex 8:11 And the frogs shall **d** from you,
8:29 the swarms of flies may **d**
18:27 Moses let his father-in-law **d**,
33: 1 **D** and go up from here, you and
33:11 did not **d** from the tabernacle.
Lev 25:41 And then he shall **d** from you—he
Num 10:30 but I will **d** to my own land
16:26 **D** now from the tents of these
Deut 4: 9 and lest they **d** from your heart
Josh 1: 8 Book of the Law shall not **d**
24:28 So Joshua let the people **d**,
Judg 6:18 Do not **d** from here, I pray,
7: 3 let him turn and **d** at once from
19: 5 the morning, and he stood to **d**;
19: 7 And when the man stood to **d**,
19: 8 morning on the fifth day to **d**,
19: 9 And when the man stood to **d**—
1 Sam 6: 6 people go, that they might **d**?
15: 6 said to the Kenites, “Go, **d**,
16:23 the distressing spirit would **d**
22: 5 not stay in the stronghold; **d**,
29:10 the morning and have light, **d**.
29:11 and his men rose early to **d** in
30:22 they may lead them away and **d**.
2 Sam 7:15 But My mercy shall not **d** from
11:12 and tomorrow I will let you **d**.
12:10 the sword shall never **d** from
15:14 from Absalom. Make haste to **d**,
20:21 and I will **d** from the city.”
22:23 I did not **d** from them.
1 Ki 11:21 said to Pharaoh, “Let me **d**,
12: 5 **D** for three days, then come
20:36 as soon as you **d** from me, a
2 Ki 3: 3 he did not **d** from them.
10:31 for he did not **d** from the sins
13: 2 He did not **d** from them.
13: 6 Nevertheless they did not **d** from
13:11 He did not **d** from all the sins
14:24 he did not **d** from all the sins
15: 9 he did not **d** from the sins of
15:18 he did not **d** all his days from
15:24 he did not **d** from the sins of
15:28 he did not **d** from the sins of
17:22 they did not **d** from them,
18: 6 he did not **d** from following
2 Chr 8:15 They did not **d** from the command
34:33 All his days they did not **d**
Neh 9:19 pillar of the cloud did not **d**
Job 15:30 He will not **d** from darkness;
20:28 increase of his house will **d**,
21:14 **D** from us, For we do not desire
22:17 **D** from us! What can the
28:28 And to **d** from evil is
39: 4 They **d** and do not return to
Ps 6: 8 **D** from me, all you workers of
34:14 **D** from evil and do good
37:27 **D** from evil, and do good
55:11 and deceit do not **d** from its
101: 4 A perverse heart shall **d** from
119:115 **D** from me, you evildoers, For
139:19 O God! **D** from me, therefore,
Prov 3: 7 Fear the LORD and **d** from
3:21 let them not **d** from your
4:21 Do not let them **d** from your
5: 7 And do not **d** from the words of
13:19 an abomination to fools to **d**
16:17 of the upright is to **d** from
17:13 Evil will not **d** from his
22: 6 when he is old he will not **d**
27:22 his foolishness will not **d**
Isa 11:13 the envy of Ephraim shall **d**,
52:11 **D**! Depart! Go out from there,
52:11 Depart! **D**! Go out from there,
54:10 For the mountains shall **d** And
54:10 But My kindness shall not **d**
59:21 shall not **d** from your mouth,
Jer 6: 8 Lest My soul **d** from you;
17:13 Those who **d** from Me Shall be
31:36 If those ordinances **d** From
32:40 hearts so that they will not **d**
37: 9 The Chaldeans will surely **d** from
37: 9 from us,” for they will not **d**.
50: 3 They shall move, they shall **d**,
Ezek 16:42 and My jealousy shall **d** from
Hos 9:12 woe to them when I **d** from them!
Mic 2:10 ‘Arise and **d**, For this is
Zech 10:11 the scepter of Egypt shall **d**.
13: 2 and the unclean spirit to **d**
Mt 7:23 **d** from Me, you who practice
8:18 He gave a command to **d** to the
8:34 they begged Him to **d** from
10:14 when you **d** from that house or
25:41 **D** from Me, you cursed, into the
Mk 5:17 began to plead with Him to **d**
6:10 stay there till you **d** from that
6:11 when you **d** from there, shake
Lk 2:29 You are letting Your servant **d**
2:37 who did not **d** from the temple,
5: 8 **D** from me, for I am a sinful
8:37 of the Gadarenes asked Him to **d**
9: 4 stay there, and from there **d**.
12:59 you shall not **d** from there till
13:27 **D** from Me, all you workers of
13:31 Get out and **d** from here, for
21:21 who are in the midst of her **d**,
Jn 7: 3 **D** from here and go into Judea,
13: 1 hour had come that He should **d**
16: 7 not come to you; but if I **d**,
Acts 1: 4 He commanded them not to **d** from
16:36 to let you go. Now therefore **d**,
16:39 and asked them to **d** from the
18: 2 had commanded all the Jews to **d**
20: 7 ready to **d** the next day, spoke
22:21 “Then He said to me, ‘**D**,
23:22 commander let the young man **d**,
1 Cor 7:10 A wife is not to **d** from her
7:11 But even if she does **d**,
7:15 unbeliever departs, let him **d**;
2 Cor 12: 8 three times that it might **d**
Phil 1:23 having a desire to **d** and be
1 Tim 4: 1 in latter times some will **d**
2 Tim 2:19 who names the name of Christ **d**
Jas 2:16 **D** in peace, be warmed and

DEPARTED (195/194) DEPART

Gen 12: 4 So Abram **d** as the LORD had
12: 4 years old when he **d** from Haran.
12: 5 and they **d** to go to the land of
14:12 in Sodom, and his goods, and **d**.
21:14 Then she **d** and wandered in the
24:10 of his master's camels and **d**,
24:61 the servant took Rebekah and **d**.
26:17 Then Isaac **d** from there and
26:31 and they **d** from him in peace.
31:40 and my sleep **d** from my eyes.
31:55 Then Laban **d** and returned to
37:17 They have **d** from here, for I
38: 1 pass at that time that Judah **d**
42:26 donkeys with the grain and **d**
45:24 his brothers away, and they **d**;
Ex 16: 1 the second month after they **d**
19: 2 For they had **d** from Rephidim,
35:20 of the children of Israel **d**
Num 10:33 So they **d** from the mountain of
12: 9 aroused against them, and He **d**.
12:10 And when the cloud **d** from above
13:26 Now they **d** and came back to
14: 9 their protection has **d** from
14:44 of the LORD nor Moses **d** from
22: 7 Moab and the elders of Midian **d**
24:25 So Balaam rose and **d** and
33: 3 They **d** from Rameses in the first
33: 6 They **d** from Succoth and camped
33: 8 They **d** from before Hahiroth and
33:13 They **d** from Dophkah and camped
33:15 They **d** from Rephidim and camped
33:17 They **d** from Kibroth Hattaavah
33:18 They **d** from Hazeroth and camped
33:19 They **d** from Rithmah and camped
33:20 They **d** from Rimmon Perez and
33:27 They **d** from Tahath and camped at
33:30 They **d** from Hashmonah and
33:31 They **d** from Moseroth and camped
33:35 They **d** from Abronah and camped
33:41 So they **d** from Mount Hor and
33:42 They **d** from Zalmonah and camped
33:43 They **d** from Punon and camped at
33:44 They **d** from Oboth and camped at
33:45 They **d** from Ijim and camped at
33:48 They **d** from the mountains of
Deut 1:19 So we **d** from Horeb, and went
1:24 And they **d** and went up into the
9: 7 From the day that you **d** from
24: 2 when she has **d** from his house,
Josh 2:21 she sent them away, and they **d**.
2:22 They **d** and went to the
9:12 our houses on the day we **d** to
22: 9 and **d** from the children of
Judg 6:21 And the Angel of the LORD **d**
9:55 that Abimelech was dead, they **d**,
16:20 not know that the LORD had **d**
17: 8 The man **d** from the city of
18: 7 So the five men **d** and went to
18:21 Then they turned and **d**,
19:10 that night; so he rose and **d**,
21:24 So the children of Israel **d** from
1 Sam 4:21 The glory has **d** from Israel!”
4:22 The glory has **d** from Israel, for
10: 2 When you have **d** from me today,
15: 6 So the Kenites **d** from among
16:14 But the Spirit of the LORD **d**
18:12 but had **d** from Saul.
20:42 So he arose and **d**,
22: 1 David therefore **d** from there and
22: 5 So David **d** and went into the
23:13 arose and **d** from Keilah and
28:15 and God has **d** from me and does
28:16 seeing the LORD has **d** from you
2 Sam 6:19 of raisins. So all the people **d**,
11: 8 So Uriah **d** from the king's
12:15 Then Nathan **d** to his house.
17:21 came to pass, after they had **d**,
19:24 from the day the king **d** until
22:22 And have not wickedly **d** from my
1 Ki 12: 5 back to me.” And the people **d**.
12:16 So Israel **d** to their tents.
14:17 Jeroboam's wife arose and **d**,
19:19 So he **d** from there, and found
20: 9 And the messengers **d** and
20:38 Then the prophet **d** and waited
2 Ki 1: 4 surely die.’” So Elijah **d**.
3:27 So they **d** from him and returned
4:25 And so she **d**, and went to
5: 5 So he **d** and took with him ten
5:19 So he **d** from him a short
5:24 he let the men go, and they **d**.
8:14 Then he **d** from Elisha, and came
10:12 And he arose and **d** and went to
10:15 Now when he **d** from there, he
19: 8 for he heard that he had **d** from
19:36 Sennacherib king of Assyria **d**
1 Chr 16:43 Then all the people **d**,
21: 4 Therefore Joab **d** and went
2 Chr 10: 5 three days.” And the people **d**.
10:16 So all Israel **d** to their tents.
21:20 and, to no one's sorrow, **d**.
Ezra 8:31 Then we **d** from the river of
Job 23:12 I have not **d** from the
Ps 18:21 And have not wickedly **d** from
34: who drove him away, and he **d**.
44:18 Nor have our steps **d** from Your
105:38 Egypt was glad when they **d**,
119:102 I have not **d** from Your
Isa 7:17 since the day that Ephraim **d**
37: 8 for he heard that he had **d** from
37:37 Sennacherib king of Assyria **d**
Jer 5:23 They have revolted and **d**.
29: 2 and the smiths had **d** from
37: 5 they **d** from Jerusalem.
41:10 them away captive and **d** to go
41:17 And they **d** and dwelt in the
Lam 1: 6 of Zion All her splendor has **d**.
Ezek 6: 9 adulterous heart which has **d**
10:18 Then the glory of the LORD **d**
Dan 4:31 the kingdom has **d** from you!
9:11 and has **d** so as not to obey
Hos 10: 5 Because its glory has **d** from
Mal 2: 8 But you have **d** from the way;

Mt 2: 9 they heard the king, they ***d***;
2:12 they ***d*** for their own country
2:13 Now when they had ***d***,
2:14 and His mother by night and ***d***
4:12 He ***d*** to Galilee.
9: 7 And he arose and ***d*** to his house.
9:27 When Jesus ***d*** from there, two
9:31 But when they had ***d***,
11: 1 that He ***d*** from there to teach
11: 7 As they ***d***, Jesus began to
12: 9 Now when He had ***d*** from there,
13:53 that He ***d*** from there.
14:13 He ***d*** from there by boat to a
15:21 went out from there and ***d*** to
15:29 Jesus ***d*** from there, skirted the
16: 4 And He left them and ***d***.
19: 1 that He ***d*** from Galilee and
19:15 laid His hands on them and ***d***
24: 1 Then Jesus went out and ***d*** from
27: 5 of silver in the temple and ***d***,
27:60 the door of the tomb, and ***d***.
Mk 1:35 He went out and ***d*** to a solitary
5:20 And he ***d*** and began to proclaim
6:32 So they ***d*** to a deserted place in
6:46 He ***d*** to the mountain to pray.
8:13 ***d*** to the other side.
9:30 Then they ***d*** from there and
Lk 1:23 that he ***d*** to his own house.
1:38 And the angel ***d*** from her.
4:13 he ***d*** from Him until an
4:42 He ***d*** and went into a deserted
5:25 and ***d*** to his own house,
7:24 the messengers of John had ***d***,
8:35 man from whom the demons had ***d***,
8:38 man from whom the demons had ***d***
9: 6 So they ***d*** and went through the
10:30 clothing, wounded him, and ***d***,
10:35 "On the next day, when he ***d***,
24:12 lying by themselves; and he ***d***,
Jn 4: 3 He left Judea and ***d*** again to
4:43 Now after the two days He ***d***
5:15 The man ***d*** and told the Jews that
6:15 He ***d*** again to the mountain by
12:36 These things Jesus spoke, and ***d***,
Acts 5:41 So they ***d*** from the presence of
10: 7 angel who spoke to him had ***d***,
11:25 Then Barnabas ***d*** for Tarsus to
12:10 and immediately the angel ***d***
12:17 And he ***d*** and went to another
13:14 But when they ***d*** from Perga, they
14:20 And the next day he ***d*** with
15:38 with them the one who had ***d***
15:40 but Paul chose Silas and ***d***,
16:40 they encouraged them and ***d***.
17:15 to him with all speed, they ***d***.
17:33 So Paul ***d*** from among them.
18: 1 After these things Paul ***d*** from
18: 7 And he ***d*** from there and entered
18:23 he ***d*** and went over the region
19: 9 he ***d*** from them and withdrew the
20: 1 and ***d*** to go to Macedonia.
20:11 while, even till daybreak, he ***d***.
21: 1 that when we had ***d*** from them
21: 5 we ***d*** and went on our way; and
21: 8 we who were Paul's companions ***d***
28:10 us in many ways; and when we ***d***,
28:25 they ***d*** after Paul had said one
28:29 the Jews ***d*** and had a great
2 Cor 2:13 I ***d*** for Macedonia.
Phil 4:15 when I ***d*** from Macedonia, no
2 Tim 4:10 present world, and has ***d*** for
Phm 1:15 For perhaps he ***d*** for a while for

DEPARTING (8/8) DEPART

Gen 35:18 as her soul was ***d*** (for she
Isa 59:13 And ***d*** from our God, Speaking
Dan 9: 5 even by ***d*** from Your precepts
Hos 1: 2 great harlotry By ***d*** from
Mk 6:33 But the multitudes saw them ***d***,
7:31 ***d*** from the region of Tyre and
Acts 13:13 ***d*** from them, returned to
Heb 3:12 an evil heart of unbelief in ***d***

DEPARTS (10/10) DEPART

Ps 146: 4 His spirit ***d***, he returns
Prov 14:16 A wise man fears and ***d*** from
16: 6 by the fear of the LORD one ***d***
Eccl 6: 4 for it comes in vanity and ***d*** in
Isa 59:15 And he who ***d*** from evil makes
Jer 3:20 as a wife treacherously ***d*** from
17: 5 Whose heart ***d*** from the LORD.
Nah 3: 1 Its victim never ***d***.
Lk 9:39 and it ***d*** from him with great
1 Cor 7:15 But if the unbeliever ***d***,

DEPARTURE (4/4) DEPART

Ezek 26:18 the sea are troubled at your ***d***.
Acts 20:29 that after my ***d*** savage wolves
2 Tim 4: 6 and the time of my ***d*** is at
Heb 11:22 made mention of the ***d*** of the

DEPEND (2/1) DEPENDS

Isa 10:20 Will never again ***d*** on him who
10:20 But will ***d*** on the LORD, the

DEPENDS (1/1) DEPEND

Rom 12:18 as much as ***d*** on you, live

DEPLETE (1/1)

Gen 41:30 and the famine will ***d*** the land.

DEPLOY (2/2) DEPLOYED

Judg 4: 6 Go and ***d*** troops at Mount Tabor;
4: 7 and against you I will ***d*** Sisera,

DEPLOYED (4/4) DEPLOY

Judg 15: 9 and ***d*** themselves against Lehi.
2 Sam 5:18 The Philistines also went and ***d***
5:22 went up once again and ***d***
Isa 7: 2 Syria's forces are ***d*** in

DEPOSED (2/2)

2 Chr 36: 3 Now the king of Egypt ***d*** him at
Dan 5:20 he was ***d*** from his kingly

DEPOSIT (3/3) DEPOSITED

Ezra 6: 5 and ***d*** them in the house of
Lk 19:21 You collect what you did not ***d***,
19:22 collecting what I did not ***d*** and

DEPOSITED (1/1) DEPOSIT

Mt 25:27 So you ought to have ***d*** my money

DEPRESSION (1/1)

Prov 12:25 in the heart of man causes ***d***,

DEPRIVE (3/3) DEPRIVED, DEPRIVES

Prov 30: 7 (***D*** me not before I die):
Eccl 4: 8 For whom do I toil and ***d*** myself
1 Cor 7: 5 Do not ***d*** one another except with

DEPRIVED (4/4) DEPRIVE

Job 39:17 Because God ***d*** her of wisdom,
Ps 78:30 They were not ***d*** of their
Isa 38:10 I am ***d*** of the remainder of my
Hos 13: 8 I will meet them like a bear ***d***

DEPRIVES (1/1) DEPRIVE

Job 12:20 He ***d*** the trusted ones of

DEPTH (9/9)

Ex 14:27 the sea returned to its full ***d***,
Prov 25: 3 for height and the earth for ***d***,
Isa 7:11 ask it either in the ***d*** or in
Mt 13: 5 up because they had no ***d*** of
18: 6 and he were drowned in the ***d*** of
Mk 4: 5 sprang up because it had no ***d***
Rom 8:39 nor height nor ***d***, nor any
11:33 the ***d*** of the riches both of the
Eph 3:18 is the width and length and ***d***

DEPTHS (31/31) DEPTH

Ex 15: 5 The ***d*** have covered them; They
15: 8 The ***d*** congealed in the heart
Job 36:30 And covers the ***d*** of the sea.
38:16 you walked in search of the ***d***?
Ps 68:22 bring them back from the ***d*** of
71:20 bring me up again from the ***d***
77:16 The ***d*** also trembled.
78:15 drink in abundance like the ***d***.
86:13 delivered my soul from the ***d***
88: 6 pit, In darkness, in the ***d***.
106: 9 So He led them through the ***d***,
107:26 They go down again to the ***d***;
130: 1 Out of the ***d*** I have cried to
148: 7 sea creatures and all the ***d***;
Prov 3:20 By His knowledge the ***d*** were
8:24 When there were no ***d*** I was
9:18 her guests are in the ***d*** of
20:27 Searching all the inner ***d*** of
20:30 As do stripes the inner ***d*** of
Isa 14:15 To the lowest ***d*** of the Pit.
51:10 That made the ***d*** of the sea a
Jer 49: 8 turn back, dwell in the ***d***,
49:30 get far away! Dwell in the ***d***,
Ezek 27:34 broken by the seas in the ***d*** of
31:14 To the ***d*** of the earth, Among
31:16 were comforted in the ***d*** of the
31:18 the trees of Eden to the ***d*** of
32:18 And cast them down to the ***d*** of
Mic 7:19 cast all our sins Into the ***d***
Zech 10:11 All the ***d*** of the River shall
Rev 2:24 who have not known the ***d*** of

DEPUTED (KJV) See DEPUTY

DEPUTIES (2/2) DEPUTY

1 Ki 5:16 from the chiefs of Solomon's ***d***,
Jer 51:57 wise men, Her governors, her ***d***,

DEPUTY (3/3) DEPUTIES

2 Sam 15: 3 but there is no ***d*** of the king
1 Ki 22:47 only a ***d*** of the king.
Neh 11:24 was the king's ***d*** in all

DERANGED (1/1)

Jer 51: 7 Therefore the nations are ***d***.

DERBE (4/4)

Acts 14: 6 of it and fled to Lystra and ***D***,
14:20 he departed with Barnabas to ***D***.
16: 1 Then he came to ***D*** and Lystra.
20: 4 Thessalonians, and Gaius of ***D***,

DERIDE (2/2) DERIDED, DERISION

Ps 102: 8 Those who ***d*** me swear an oath
Hab 1:10 They ***d*** every stronghold, For

DERIDED (1/1) DERIDE

Lk 16:14 these things, and they ***d*** Him.

DERISION (12/12) DERIDE

Ps 2: 4 The LORD shall hold them in ***d***.
44:13 A scorn and a ***d*** to those all
59: 8 shall have all the nations in ***d***.
79: 4 A scorn and ***d*** to those who are
119:51 The proud have me in great ***d***,
Jer 20: 7 I am in ***d*** daily; Everyone
20: 8 made to me A reproach and a ***d***
48:26 And he shall also be in ***d***.
48:27 For was not Israel a ***d*** to you?
48:39 So Moab shall be a ***d*** And
Ezek 23:32 laughed to scorn And held in ***d***;
Hos 7:16 This shall be their ***d*** in the

DERIVED (1/1)

Heb 7: 6 but he whose genealogy is not ***d***

DESCEND (10/10) DESCENDANT, DESCENDED, DESCENDING, DESCENT

2 Ki 20:18 some of your sons who will ***d***
Ps 49:17 His glory shall not ***d*** after
Isa 5:14 shall ***d*** into it.
39: 7 some of your sons who will ***d***
Ezek 26:20 you down with those who ***d*** into
31:16 hell together with those who ***d***
Mk 15:32 ***d*** now from the cross, that we
Rom 10: 7 Who will ***d*** into the abyss?'
1 Th 4:16 For the Lord Himself will ***d*** from
Jas 3:15 This wisdom does not ***d*** from

DESCENDANT (4/4) DESCEND, DESCENDANTS

Gen 17:12 any foreigner who is not your ***d***.
Num 16:40 who is not a ***d*** of Aaron,
1 Ki 11:14 he was a ***d*** of the king in
Neh 10:38 the ***d*** of Aaron, shall be with

DESCENDANTS (157/143) DESCENDANT, DESCENDANTS'

Gen 9: 9 with you and with your ***d*** after
12: 7 To your ***d*** I will give this
13:15 see I give to you and your ***d***
13:16 And I will make your ***d*** as the
13:16 then your ***d*** also could be
15: 5 So shall your ***d*** be."
15:13 Know certainly that your ***d*** will
15:18 To your ***d*** I have given this
16:10 I will multiply your ***d***
17: 7 between Me and you and your ***d***
17: 7 to be God to you and your ***d***
17: 8 Also I give to you and your ***d***
17: 9 you and your ***d*** after you
17:10 between Me and you and your ***d***
17:19 and with his ***d*** after him.
22:17 I will multiply your ***d*** as the
22:17 and your ***d*** shall possess the
24: 7 'To your ***d*** I give this land,'
24:60 And may your ***d*** possess The
26: 3 for to you and your ***d*** I give
26: 4 And I will make your ***d*** multiply
26: 4 I will give to your ***d*** all these
26:24 bless you and multiply your ***d***
28: 4 To you and your ***d*** with you,
28:13 I will give to you and your ***d***.
28:14 Also your ***d*** shall be as the dust
32:12 and make your ***d*** as the sand of
35:12 and to your ***d*** after you I give
46: 6 Jacob and all his ***d*** with him.
46: 7 and all his ***d*** he brought with
48: 4 and give this land to your ***d***
48:19 and his ***d*** shall become a
Ex 1: 5 All those who were ***d*** of Jacob
28:43 forever to him and his ***d*** after
30:21 to him and his ***d*** throughout
32:13 I will multiply your ***d*** as the
32:13 have spoken of I give to your ***d***,
33: 1 To your ***d*** I will give it.'
Lev 18:21 you shall not let any of your ***d***
20: 2 who gives any of his ***d*** to
20: 3 he has given some of his ***d*** to
20: 4 when he gives some of his ***d*** to
21:17 No man of your ***d*** in succeeding
21:21 No man of the ***d*** of Aaron the
22: 3 Whoever of all your ***d*** throughout
22: 4 Whatever man of the ***d*** of Aaron,
Num 13:22 the ***d*** of Anak, were there.
13:28 moreover we saw the ***d*** of Anak
13:33 the giants (the ***d*** of Anak
14:24 and his ***d*** shall inherit it.
18:19 the LORD with you and your ***d***

25:13 it shall be to him and his **d**
Deut 1: 8 to give to them and their **d**
2: 4 the **d** of Esau, who live in
2: 8 the **d** of Esau who dwell in
2: 9 I have given Ar to the **d** of
2:12 but the **d** of Esau dispossessed
2:19 I have given it to the **d** of
2:22 just as He had done for the **d** of
2:29 just as the **d** of Esau who dwell
4:37 therefore He chose their **d**
9: 2 the **d** of the Anakim, whom you
9: 2 Who can stand before the **d** of
10:15 and He chose their **d** after
11: 9 fathers, to them and their **d**,
23: 2 none of his **d** shall enter
23: 3 none of his **d** shall enter
28:46 and on your **d** forever.
28:59 will bring upon you and your **d**
30: 6 heart and the heart of your **d**,
30:19 that both you and your **d** may
31:21 in the mouths of their **d**,
34: 4 'I will give it to your **d**.
Josh 22:24 In time to come your **d** may speak
22:24 descendants may speak to our **d**,
22:25 So your **d** would make our
22:25 would make our **d** cease
22:27 that your **d** may not say to our
22:27 may not say to our **d** in time
24: 3 and multiplied his **d** and gave
1 Sam 2:20 The LORD give you **d** from this
2:33 And all the **d** of your house
20:42 and between your **d** and my
20:42 your descendants and my **d**,
24:21 that you will not cut off my **d**
2 Sam 4: 8 king this day of Saul and his **d**.
21: 6 let seven men of his **d** be
22:51 To David and his **d**
1 Ki 2:33 Joab and upon the head of his **d**
2:33 But upon David and his **d**,
9:21 their **d** who were left in the
11:39 And I will afflict the **d** of
2 Ki 5:27 shall cling to you and your **d**
17:20 the LORD rejected all the **d**
1 Chr 2:42 The **d** of Caleb the brother of
2:50 These were the **d** of Caleb: The
2:52 father of Kirjath Jearim had **d**:
7:14 The **d** of Manasseh: his Syrian
7:17 These were the **d** of Gilead
9: 4 of the **d** of Perez, the son of
23:17 Of the **d** of Eliezer, Rehabiah
26:21 the **d** of the Gershonites of
2 Chr 8: 8 their **d** who were left in the
20: 7 and gave it to the **d** of Abraham
Ezra 4: 1 and Benjamin heard that the **d**
6:16 Levites and the rest of the **d**
6:19 And the **d** of the captivity kept
6:20 Passover lambs for all the **d**
10: 7 and Jerusalem to all the **d** of
10:16 Then the **d** of the captivity did
Neh 9: 8 give it to his **d**.
11: 3 and **d** of Solomon's servants.)
Esth 9:27 it upon themselves and their **d**
9:28 should not perish among their **d**.
9:31 for themselves and their **d**
Job 5:25 that your **d** shall be many,
21: 8 Their **d** are established with
Ps 18:50 To David and his **d**
21:10 And their **d** from among the
22:23 praise Him! All you **d** of
25:13 And his **d** shall inherit the
37:25 Nor his **d** begging bread.
37:26 And his **d** are blessed.
37:28 But the **d** of the wicked shall
69:36 the **d** of His servants shall
102:28 And their **d** will be
106:27 To overthrow their **d** among the
112: 2 His **d** will be mighty on earth;
Isa 41: 8 The **d** of Abraham My friend.
43: 5 I will bring your **d** from the
44: 3 will pour My Spirit on your **d**,
45:25 In the LORD all the **d** of
48:19 Your **d** also would have been
54: 3 And your **d** will inherit the
59:21 your **d**, descendants"
59:21 mouth of your descendants' **d**,
61: 9 Their **d** shall be known among
65: 9 I will bring forth **d** from
65:23 For they shall be the **d** of
66:22 So shall your **d** and your name
Jer 22:28 are they cast out, he and his **d**,
22:30 For none of his **d** shall
23: 8 who brought up and led the **d**
33:22 so will I multiply the **d** of
33:26 then I will cast away the **d** of
33:26 I will not take any of his **d**
33:26 to be rulers over the **d** of
49:10 His **d** are plundered, His
Ezek 20: 5 My hand in an oath to the **d** of
44:22 but take virgins of the **d** of
Dan 1: 3 and some of the king's **d** and
Mal 2: 3 I will rebuke your **d** And
Jn 8:33 Him, "We are Abraham's **d**,
8:37 know that you are Abraham's **d**,
Acts 7: 5 and to his **d** after him.
7: 6 that his **d** would dwell in a
Rom 4:18 So shall your **d** be."

DESCENDANTS' (1/1) DESCENDANTS

Isa 59:21 mouth of your **d** descendants,"

DESCENDED (19/18) DESCEND

Gen 36:18 These were the chiefs who **d**
Ex 19:18 because the LORD **d** upon it in
33: 9 that the pillar of cloud **d** and
34: 5 Now the LORD **d** in the cloud and
Deut 9:21 its dust into the brook that **d**
Josh 2:23 **d** from the mountain, and
17: 9 And the border **d** to the Brook
18:13 and the border **d** to Ataroth
18:16 **d** to the Valley of Hinnom, to
18:16 and **d** to En Rogel.
18:17 and **d** to the stone of Bohan the
Prov 30: 4 has ascended into heaven, or **d**?
Isa 57: 9 And even **d** to Sheol.
Mt 7:25 "and the rain **d**,
7:27 "and the rain **d**,
28: 2 for an angel of the Lord **d** from
Lk 3:22 And the Holy Spirit **d** in bodily
Eph 4: 9 mean but that He also first **d**
4:10 He who **d** is also the One who

DESCENDING (11/11) DESCEND

Gen 28:12 of God were ascending and **d** on
Ps 133: 3 ***D*** upon the mountains of Zion;
Prov 7:27 ***D*** to the chambers of death.
Mt 3:16 and He saw the Spirit of God **d**
Mk 1:10 parting and the Spirit **d** upon
Jn 1:32 I saw the Spirit **d** from heaven
1:33 'Upon whom you see the Spirit **d**,
1:51 angels of God ascending and **d**
Acts 10:11 **d** to him and let down to the
11: 5 an object **d** like a great sheet,
Rev 21:10 **d** out of heaven from God,

DESCENT (6/6) DESCEND

Josh 7: 5 and struck them down on the **d**;
10:11 Israel and were on the **d** of
Esth 6:13 begun to fall, is of Jewish **d**,
Isa 30:30 And show the **d** of His arm,
Jer 48: 5 For in the **d** of Horonaim the
Lk 19:37 He was now drawing near the **d**

DESCRIBE (1/1) DESCRIBES, DESCRIBING

Ezek 43:10 **d** the temple to the house of

DESCRIBES (1/1) DESCRIBE

Rom 4: 6 just as David also **d** the

DESCRIBING (1/1) DESCRIBE

Acts 15: 3 **d** the conversion of the

DESCRY (KJV) See SPY (OUT)

DESERT (28/28) DESERTED, DESERTS

Ex 3: 1 the flock to the back of the **d**,
5: 3 three days' journey into the **d**
23:31 and from the **d** to the River.
Deut 32:10 He found him in a **d** land And in
2 Chr 26:10 Also he built towers in the **d**.
Job 24: 5 like wild donkeys in the **d**,
Ps 73:27 destroyed all those who **d** You
78:40 And grieved Him in the **d**!
102: 6 I am like an owl of the **d**.
106:14 And tested God in the **d**.
Isa 13:21 But wild beasts of the **d** will
21: 1 So it comes from the **d**,
23:13 it for wild beasts of the **d**.
34:14 The wild beasts of the **d** shall
35: 1 And the **d** shall rejoice and
35: 6 And streams in the **d**.
40: 3 Make straight in the **d** A
41:19 I will set in the **d** the
43:19 And rivers in the **d**.
43:20 And rivers in the **d**,
51: 3 And her **d** like the garden of
Jer 17: 6 shall be like a shrub in the **d**,
25:24 multitude who dwell in the **d**;
50:12 wilderness, A dry land and a **d**.
50:39 Therefore the wild **d** beasts
Mt 24:26 He is in the **d**!' do not go out;
Jn 6:31 fathers ate the manna in the **d**;
Acts 8:26 Jerusalem to Gaza." This is **d**.

DESERTED (15/15) DESERT

Judg 5: 6 of Jael, The highways were **d**,
2 Sam 20: 2 So every man of Israel **d** David,
2 Ki 25:11 and the defectors who had **d** to
Isa 32:14 The bustling city will be **d**.
Jer 49:25 is the city of praise not **d**,
52:15 the defectors who had **d** to the
Mt 14:13 from there by boat to a **d**
14:15 This is a **d** place, and the hour
Mk 1:45 but was outside in **d** places;
6:31 aside by yourselves to a **d**
6:32 So they departed to a **d** place in
6:35 This is a **d** place, and already
Lk 4:42 He departed and went into a **d**
9:10 went aside privately into a **d**
9:12 for we are in a **d** place here."

DESERTS (6/6) DESERT

Isa 48:21 When He led them through the **d**;
Jer 2: 6 Through a land of **d** and pits,
5: 6 A wolf of the **d** shall destroy
Ezek 13: 4 are like foxes in the **d**.
Lk 1:80 and was in the **d** till the day
Heb 11:38 They wandered in **d** and

DESERVE (5/5)

1 Sam 26:16 you **d** to die, because you have
Ezra 9:13 us less than our iniquities **d**,
Ps 28: 4 Render to them what they **d**.
Jer 26:16 'This man does not **d** to die.
Ezek 7:27 And according to what they **d**

DESERVES (4/4)

Deut 25: 2 if the wicked man **d** to be
Judg 9:16 and have done to him as he **d**—
Job 11: 6 Less than your iniquity **d**.
Jer 26:11 This man **d** to die! For he has

DESERVING (17/17) DESERVE

Deut 17: 6 Whoever is **d** of death shall be
19: 6 though he was not **d** of death,
21:22 a man has committed a sin **d** of
22:26 in the young woman no sin **d**
1 Ki 2:26 for you are **d** of death; but I
Job 31:11 it would be iniquity **d** of
31:28 would be an iniquity **d** of
Mt 26:66 He is **d** of death."
Mk 14:64 condemned Him to be **d** of death.
Lk 7: 4 whom He should do this was **d**,
12:48 yet committed things **d** of
23:15 and indeed nothing **d** of death
Acts 23:29 against him **d** of death
25:11 or have committed anything **d** of
25:25 he had committed nothing **d** of
26:31 This man is doing nothing **d** of
Rom 1:32 such things are **d** of death,

DESIGN (11/9) DESIGNER, DESIGNS

Ex 26:31 be woven with an artistic **d** of
31: 4 to **d** artistic works, to work in
35:32 to **d** artistic works, to work in
35:35 those who **d** artistic works.
36:35 was worked with an artistic **d**
1 Ki 7:28 And this was the **d** of the
2 Ki 16:10 to Urijah the priest the **d** of
2 Chr 4: 7 of gold according to their **d**,
Ezek 43:11 make known to them the **d** of the
43:11 its entire **d** and all its
43:11 that they may keep its whole **d**

DESIGNATED (6/6) DESIGNATES

Josh 21: 9 these cities which are **d** by
1 Chr 12:31 who were **d** by name to come and
16:41 who were **d** by name, to give
2 Chr 28:15 Then the men who were **d** by name
31:19 there were men who were **d** by
Ezra 8:20 All of them were **d** by name.

DESIGNATES (1/1) DESIGNATED

Heb 4: 7 again He **d** a certain day, saying

DESIGNER (2/2) DESIGN

Ex 35:35 work of the engraver and the **d**
38:23 tribe of Dan, an engraver and **d**,

DESIGNS (3/3) DESIGN

Ex 26: 1 with artistic **d** of cherubim you
36: 8 with artistic **d** of cherubim
39: 3 fine linen, into artistic **d**.

DESIRABLE (9/9) DESIRE

Gen 3: 6 and a tree **d** to make one wise,
2 Chr 32:27 and for all kinds of **d** items;
Prov 21:20 There is **d** treasure, And oil
Ezek 23: 6 All of them **d** young men,
23:12 All of them **d** young men.
23:23 All of them **d** young men,
Hos 13:15 the treasury of every **d** prize.
Nah 2: 9 Or wealth of every **d** prize.
Acts 6: 2 It is not **d** that we should leave

DESIRE (122/121) DESIRABLE, DESIRED, DESIRES, DESIRING, UNDESIRABLE

Gen 3:16 Your **d** shall be for your
4: 7 And its **d** is for you, but you
Ex 15: 9 My **d** shall be satisfied on
Deut 5:21 and you shall not **d** your
18: 6 and comes with all the **d** of his
21:11 and **d** her and would take her
1 Sam 9:20 And on whom is all the **d** of
18:25 The king does not **d** any dowry
20: 4 "Whatever you yourself **d**,
23:20 down according to all the **d** of
2 Sam 23: 5 all my salvation and all my **d**;
24: 3 lord the king **d** this thing?"
1 Ki 2:20 I **d** one small petition of you;
5: 8 and I will do all you **d**
5: 9 And you shall fulfill my **d** by
5:10 logs according to all his **d**.
9: 1 and all Solomon's **d** which he
Neh 1:11 Your servants who **d** to fear
Job 13: 3 And I **d** to reason with God.

D

14:15 You shall **d** the work of Your
21:14 For we do not **d** the knowledge
31:16 kept the poor from their **d**,
33:32 for I **d** to justify you.
36:20 Do not **d** the night, When
Ps 10: 3 wicked boasts of his heart's **d**;
10:17 You have heard the **d** of the
20: 4 according to your heart's **d**,
21: 2 have given him his heart's **d**,
38: 9 all my **d** is before You; And
40: 6 and offering You did not **d**;
45:11 So the King will greatly **d** your
51: 6 You **d** truth in the inward
51:16 For You do not **d** sacrifice, or
54: 7 And my eye has seen its **d**
59:10 God shall let me see my **d** on
70: 2 back and confused Who **d** my
73:25 is none upon earth that I **d**
78:29 For He gave them their own **d**.
92:11 My eye also has seen my **d** on
92:11 My ears hear my **d** on the
112: 8 Until he sees his **d** upon his
112:10 The **d** of the wicked shall
118: 7 Therefore I shall see my **d**
145:16 And satisfy the **d** of every
145:19 He will fulfill the **d** of those
Prov 3:15 And all the things you may **d**
8:11 And all the things one may **d**
10: 3 But He casts away the **d** of the
10:24 And the **d** of the righteous
11:23 The **d** of the righteous is only
13:12 But when the **d** comes, it is
13:19 A **d** accomplished is sweet to
18: 1 himself seeks his own **d**;
21:25 The **d** of the lazy man kills
23: 3 Do not **d** his delicacies, For
23: 6 Nor **d** his delicacies;
24: 1 Nor **d** to be with them;
Eccl 6: 9 eyes than the wandering of **d**.
12: 5 And **d** fails. For man goes to
Song 7:10 And his **d** is toward me.
Isa 26: 8 The **d** of our soul is for
53: 2 beauty that we should **d** Him.
Jer 2:24 sniffs at the wind in her **d**;
22:27 to the land to which they **d** to
42:22 in the place where you **d** to go
44:14 to which they **d** to return and
Ezek 11:21 whose hearts follow the **d** for
24:16 I take away from you the **d** of
24:21 the **d** of your eyes, the delight
24:25 the **d** of their eyes, and that
Dan 11:37 fathers nor the **d** of women,
Hos 6: 6 For I **d** mercy and not
10:10 When it is My **d**,
Am 5:18 Woe to you who **d** the day of
Mic 7: 3 great man utters his evil **d**;
Hab 2: 5 Because he enlarges his **d** as
Hag 2: 7 and they shall come to the ***D*** of
Mt 9:13 I **d** mercy and not
12: 7 I **d** mercy and not
15:28 Let it be to you as you **d**.
Mk 12:38 who **d** to go around in long
Lk 17:22 when you will **d** to see one
20:46 who **d** to go around in long
22:15 With fervent **d** I have desired
Jn 15: 7 in you, you will ask what you **d**,
17:24 I **d** that they also whom You
Acts 27:13 that they had obtained their **d**,
28:22 But we **d** to hear from you what
Rom 7: 8 in me all manner of evil **d**.
10: 1 my heart's **d** and prayer to God
11:25 For I do not **d**, brethren,
15:23 and having a great **d** these many
1 Cor 10:27 and you **d** to go, eat whatever
12:31 But earnestly **d** the best gifts.
14: 1 and **d** spiritual gifts, but
14:39 **d** earnestly to prophesy, and do
2 Cor 7: 7 he told us of your earnest **d**,
7:11 what fear, what vehement **d**,
8:11 as there was a readiness to **d**
11:12 opportunity from those who **d**
12: 6 For though I might **d** to boast, I
Gal 4: 9 to which you **d** again to be in
4:21 you who **d** to be under the law,
6:12 As many as **d** to make a good
6:13 but they **d** to have you
Phil 1:23 having a **d** to depart and be
Col 3: 5 uncleanness, passion, evil **d**,
1 Th 2:17 to see your face with great **d**.
1 Tim 2: 8 I **d** therefore that the men pray
5:11 they **d** to marry,
5:14 Therefore I **d** that the younger
6: 9 But those who **d** to be rich fall
2 Tim 3:12 and all who **d** to live godly in
Heb 6:11 And we **d** that each one of you
10: 5 offering You did not **d**,
10: 8 for sin You did not **d**,
11:16 But now they **d** a better, that
Jas 1:15 when **d** has conceived, it gives
1 Pe 1:12 things which angels **d** to look
2: 2 **d** the pure milk of the word,
Rev 9: 6 they will **d** to die, and death
11: 6 all plagues, as often as they **d**.

DESIRED (28/28) DESIRE

Ex 10:11 LORD, for that is what you **d**.
Deut 18:16 according to all you **d** of the
Judg 13:23 If the LORD had **d** to kill us,
1 Sam 2:25 because the LORD **d** to kill
12:13 chosen and whom you have **d**.
1 Ki 9:11 and gold, as much as he **d**),
9:19 and whatever Solomon **d** to build
10:13 the queen of Sheba all she **d**,
2 Chr 8: 6 and all that Solomon **d** to build
9:12 to the queen of Sheba all she **d**,
Esth 2:13 she was given whatever she **d**
Ps 19:10 More to be **d** are they than
27: 4 One thing I have **d** of the
107:30 guides them to their **d** haven.
132:13 He has **d** it for His dwelling
132:14 will dwell, for I have **d** it.
Prov 19:22 What is **d** in a man is kindness,
Eccl 2:10 Whatever my eyes **d** I did not
Isa 1:29 trees Which you have **d**;
26: 9 With my soul I have **d** You in
Jer 17:16 Nor have I **d** the woeful day;
Mt 13:17 and righteous men **d** to see
Lk 10:24 and kings have **d** to see
22:15 With fervent desire I have **d** to
23: 8 for he had **d** for a long time
Jn 16:19 Now Jesus knew that they **d** to
Acts 18:27 And when he **d** to cross to
Gal 2:10 They **d** only that we should

DESIRES (43/41) DESIRE

Deut 12:15 gates, whatever your heart **d**,
12:20 as much meat as your heart **d**.
12:21 gates as much as your heart **d**.
14:26 money for whatever your heart **d**:
14:26 for whatever your heart **d**;
1 Sam 2:16 take as much as your heart **d**,
2 Sam 3:21 over all that your heart **d**.
1 Ki 11:37 reign over all your heart **d**,
Job 7: 2 a servant who earnestly **d** the
20:20 He will not save anything he **d**.
23:13 And whatever His soul **d**,
Ps 34:12 Who is the man who **d** life,
37: 4 And He shall give you the **d** of
68:16 mountain which God **d** to dwell
140: 8 the **d** of the wicked; Do not
Prov 13: 4 The soul of a lazy man **d**,
21:10 The soul of the wicked **d** evil;
Eccl 6: 2 nothing for himself of all he **d**;
Mic 7: 1 fruit which my soul **d**.
Mt 16:24 If anyone **d** to come after Me,
16:25 For whoever **d** to save his life
20:26 but whoever **d** to become great
20:27 And whoever **d** to be first among
Mk 4:19 and the **d** for other things
8:34 Whoever **d** to come after Me, let
8:35 For whoever **d** to save his life
9:35 If anyone **d** to be first, he
10:43 but whoever **d** to become great
10:44 And whoever of you **d** to be first
Lk 5:39 immediately **d** new; for he says,
9:23 If anyone **d** to come after Me,
9:24 For whoever **d** to save his life
Jn 8:44 and the **d** of your father you
Gal 5:24 flesh with its passions and **d**.
Eph 2: 3 fulfilling the **d** of the flesh
1 Tim 2: 4 who **d** all men to be saved and to
3: 1 If a man **d** the position of a
3: 1 he **d** a good work.
2 Tim 4: 3 but according to their own **d**,
Jas 1:14 he is drawn away by his own **d**
3: 4 rudder wherever the pilot **d**.
4: 1 Do they not come from your **d**
Rev 22:17 him who thirsts come. Whoever **d**,

DESIRING (9/9) DESIRE

Lk 8:20 outside, **d** to see You."
16:21 **d** to be fed with the crumbs
2 Cor 5: 2 earnestly **d** to be clothed with
8:10 what you began and were **d** to
11:32 a garrison, **d** to arrest me;
1 Th 3: 6 greatly **d** to see us, as we also
1 Tim 1: 7 **d** to be teachers of the law,
2 Tim 1: 4 greatly **d** to see you, being
Heb 13:18 in all things **d** to live

DESISTED (1/1)

Jer 41: 8 So he **d** and did not kill them

DESOLATE (147/132) DESOLATED, DESOLATION

Gen 47:19 die, that the land may not be **d**.
Ex 23:29 lest the land become **d** and the
Lev 26:22 and your highways shall be **d**.
26:33 your land shall be **d** and your
26:34 sabbaths as long as it lies **d**
26:35 As long as it lies **d** it shall
26:43 its sabbaths while it lies **d**
Num 23: 3 So he went to a **d** height.
2 Sam 13:20 So Tamar remained **d** in her
2 Chr 36:21 As long as she lay **d** she kept
Job 15:28 He dwells in **d** cities, In
16: 7 You have made **d** all my
30: 3 the wilderness, **d** and waste,
38:27 To satisfy the **d** waste, And
Ps 25:16 For I am **d** and afflicted.
69:25 Let their dwelling place be **d**;
107: 4 in the wilderness in a **d** way;
109:10 their bread also from their **d**
Isa 1: 7 Your country is **d**,
1: 7 your presence; And it is **d**,
3:26 And she being **d** shall sit on
5: 9 many houses shall be **d**,
6:11 a man, The land is utterly **d**,
7:19 all of them will rest In the **d**
13: 9 anger, To lay the land **d**;
15: 6 the waters of Nimrim will be **d**,
24: 6 those who dwell in it are **d**.
27:10 the fortified city will be **d**,
41:18 I will open rivers in **d**
49: 8 To cause them to inherit the **d**
49: 9 pastures shall be on all **d**
49:19 For your waste and **d** places,
49:21 have lost my children and am **d**,
54: 1 more are the children of the **d**
54: 3 And make the **d** cities
59:10 We are as dead men in **d**
62: 4 your land any more be termed ***D***;
Jer 2:12 be horribly afraid; Be very **d**,
3: 2 Lift up your eyes to the **d**
3:21 A voice was heard on the **d**
4: 7 his place To make your land **d**.
4:11 A dry wind of the **d** heights
4:27 "The whole land shall be **d**;
6: 8 from you; Lest I make you **d**,
7:29 take up a lamentation on the **d**
7:34 bride. For the land shall be **d**.
9:11 will make the cities of Judah **d**,
10:22 To make the cities of Judah **d**,
10:25 And made his dwelling place **d**.
12:10 made My pleasant portion a **d**
12:11 **d**; Desolate, it mourns to Me;
12:11 ***D***, it mourns to Me;
12:11 The whole land is made **d**,
12:12 have come On all the **d**
14: 6 the wild donkeys stood in the **d**
18:16 To make their land **d** and a
19: 8 I will make this city **d** and a
25:38 For their land is **d** Because
26: 9 and this city shall be **d**,
32:43 of which you say, "It is **d**,
33:10 which you say, "It is **d**,
33:10 streets of Jerusalem that are **d**,
33:12 'In this place which is **d**,
44: 6 and they are wasted and **d**,
46:19 For Noph shall be waste and **d**,
48: 9 For her cities shall be **d**,
48:34 of Nimrim also shall be **d**.
49: 2 It shall be a **d** mound, And
49:20 make their dwelling places **d**
50: 3 Which shall make her land **d**,
50:13 But she shall be wholly **d**.
50:45 make their dwelling place **d**
51:26 But you shall be **d** forever,"
51:41 How Babylon has become **d**
51:62 but it shall be **d** forever.'
Lam 1: 4 All her gates are **d**;
1:13 He has made me **d** And faint
1:16 My children are **d** Because the
3:11 me in pieces; He has made me **d**.
4: 5 who ate delicacies Are **d** in
5:18 of Mount Zion which is **d**,
Ezek 6: 4 "Then your altars shall be **d**,
6: 6 and the high places shall be **d**,
6: 6 may be laid waste and made **d**,
6:14 them and make the land **d**,
6:14 more **d** than the wilderness
12:20 and the land shall become **d**;
14:15 and make it so **d** that no man
14:16 and the land would be **d**.
15: 8 'Thus I will make the land **d**,
19: 7 He knew their **d** places, And
20:26 that I might make them **d** and
25: 3 land of Israel when it was **d**,
25:13 and make it **d** from Teman; Dedan
26:19 When I make you a **d** city, like
26:20 in places **d** from antiquity,
29: 9 land of Egypt shall become **d**
29:10 of Egypt utterly waste and **d**,
29:12 will make the land of Egypt **d**
29:12 of the countries that are **d**;
29:12 her cities shall be **d** forty
30: 7 They shall be **d** in the midst of
30: 7 the midst of the **d** countries,
30:14 I will make Pathros **d**,
32:15 I make the land of Egypt **d**,
33:28 I will make the land most **d**,
33:28 of Israel shall be so **d** that
33:29 I have made the land most **d**
35: 3 you, And make you most **d**;
35: 4 waste, And you shall be **d**.
35: 7 I will make Mount Seir most **d**,
35: 9 "I will make you perpetually **d**,
35:12 of Israel, saying, 'They are **d**;
35:14 will rejoice when I make you **d**.
35:15 of the house of Israel was **d**,
35:15 will do to you; you shall be **d**,
36: 3 Because they made you **d** and
36: 4 the **d** wastes, and the cities
36:34 The **d** land shall be tilled
36:34 be tilled instead of lying **d**
36:35 This land that was **d** has become
36:35 of Eden; and the wasted, **d**,
36:36 places and planted what was **d**.
38: 8 Israel, which had long been **d**;
Dan 9:17 on Your sanctuary, which is **d**.
9:27 shall be one who makes **d**,
9:27 Is poured out on the **d**.
Hos 5: 9 Ephraim shall be **d** in the day
Joel 2: 3 And behind them a **d**
2:20 him away into a barren and **d**
3:19 And Edom a **d** wilderness,
Am 7: 9 high places of Isaac shall be **d**,
Mic 1: 7 All her idols I will lay **d**,
6:13 By making you **d** because of
7:13 Yet the land shall be **d**
Nah 2:10 She is empty, **d**,

Zeph 2: 4 be forsaken, And Ashkelon ***d***;
3: 6 I have made their streets ***d***,
Zech 7:14 Thus the land became ***d*** after
7:14 they made the pleasant land ***d***.
Mal 1: 4 and build the ***d*** places,"
Mt 23:38 Your house is left to you ***d***;
Lk 13:35 Your house is left to you ***d***;
Acts 1:20 his dwelling place be ***d***,
Gal 4:27 not in labor! For the ***d***
Rev 17:16 harlot, make her ***d*** and naked,
18:19 For in one hour she is made ***d***.

DESOLATED (1/1) DESOLATE

Ezek 19: 7 land with its fullness was ***d***

DESOLATION (45/45) DESOLATE, DESOLATIONS

Lev 26:31 and bring your sanctuaries to ***d***,
26:32 I will bring the land to ***d***,
Josh 8:28 a ***d*** to this day.
2 Ki 22:19 that they would become a ***d*** and
2 Chr 29: 8 given them up to trouble, to ***d***,
30: 7 so that He gave them up to ***d***,
Ps 73:19 Oh, how they are brought to ***d***,
Isa 10: 3 And in the ***d*** which will come
17: 9 of Israel; And there will be ***d***.
24:12 In the city ***d*** is left, And the
47:11 And ***d*** shall come upon you
51:19 ***D*** and destruction, famine and
64:10 is a wilderness, Jerusalem a ***d***.
Jer 22: 5 this house shall become a ***d***.
25:11 this whole land shall be a ***d***
25:12 I will make it a perpetual ***d***.
25:18 its princes, to make them a ***d***,
34:22 make the cities of Judah a ***d***
44: 2 behold, this day they are a ***d***,
44:22 Therefore your land is a ***d***,
49:13 "that Bozrah shall become a ***d***,
49:33 a ***d*** forever; No one shall
50:23 How Babylon has become a ***d***
51:29 make the land of Babylon a ***d***
51:43 Her cities are a ***d***,
Lam 3:47 ***D*** and destruction.
Ezek 7:27 prince will be clothed with ***d***,
23:33 The cup of horror and ***d***,
Dan 8:13 and the transgression of ***d***,
11:31 there the abomination of ***d***.
12:11 and the abomination of ***d*** is set
Hos 12: 1 He daily increases lies and ***d***.
Joel 3:19 "Egypt shall be a ***d***,
Mic 6:16 That I may make you a ***d***,
Zeph 1:13 booty, And their houses a ***d***;
1:15 A day of devastation and ***d***,
2: 9 saltpits, And a perpetual ***d***.
2:13 Assyria, And make Nineveh a ***d***,
2:14 ***D*** shall be at the threshold;
2:15 How has she become a ***d***,
Mt 12:25 against itself is brought to ***d***,
24:15 see the 'abomination of ***d***,
Mk 13:14 see the 'abomination of ***d***,
Lk 11:17 against itself is brought to ***d***,
21:20 then know that its ***d*** is near.

DESOLATIONS (8/7) DESOLATION

Ps 46: 8 Who has made ***d*** in the earth.
74: 3 up Your feet to the perpetual ***d***.
Isa 61: 4 shall raise up the former ***d***,
61: 4 The ***d*** of many generations.
Jer 25: 9 a hissing, and perpetual ***d***.
Dan 9: 2 seventy years in the ***d*** of
9:18 open Your eyes and see our ***d***,
9:26 And till the end of the war ***d***

DESPAIR (3/3) DESPAIRED, DESPERATE

1 Sam 27: 1 and Saul will ***d*** of me, to seek
Jer 19: 9 lives shall drive them to ***d***.
2 Cor 4: 8 are perplexed, but not in ***d***;

DESPAIRED (2/2) DESPAIR

Eccl 2:20 I turned my heart and ***d*** of all
2 Cor 1: 8 so that we ***d*** even of life.

DESPERATE (5/5) DESPAIR, DESPERATELY, DESPERATION

Deut 28:53 in the siege and ***d*** straits in
28:55 left in the siege and ***d*** straits
28:57 in the siege and ***d*** straits
Job 6:26 And the speeches of a ***d*** one,
Isa 17:11 day of grief and ***d*** sorrow.

DESPERATELY (2/2) DESPERATE

Job 27:22 He flees ***d*** from its power.
Jer 17: 9 And ***d*** wicked; Who can know

DESPERATION (1/1) DESPERATE

Jer 19: 9 in the siege and in the ***d*** with

DESPISE (40/40) DESPISED, DESPISERS, DESPISES, DESPISING

Lev 26:15 and if you ***d*** My statutes, or if
1 Sam 2:30 and those who ***d*** Me shall be
2 Sam 19:43 Why then do you ***d*** us—were we
Esth 1:17 so that they will ***d*** their
Job 5:17 Therefore do not ***d*** the
9:21 know myself; I ***d*** my life.
10: 3 That You should ***d*** the work of
19:18 Even young children ***d*** me;
Ps 51:17 O God, You will not ***d***.
69:33 And does not ***d*** His prisoners.
73:20 You shall ***d*** their image.
102:17 And shall not ***d*** their prayer.
Prov 1: 7 But fools ***d*** wisdom and
3:11 do not ***d*** the chastening of the
6:30 People do not ***d*** a thief If he
23: 9 For he will ***d*** the wisdom of
23:22 And do not ***d*** your mother when
Isa 30:12 Because you ***d*** this word, And
Jer 4:30 Your lovers will ***d*** you; They
23:17 say to those who ***d*** Me,
Lam 1: 8 All who honored her ***d*** her
Ezek 16:57 who ***d*** you everywhere.
28:24 who ***d*** them. Then they shall
28:26 those around them who ***d*** them.
Am 5:21 I ***d*** your feast days, And I do
Mal 1: 6 To you priests who ***d*** My name.
Mt 6:24 to the one and ***d*** the other.
18:10 Take heed that you do not ***d*** one
Lk 16:13 to the one and ***d*** the other.
Rom 2: 4 Or do you ***d*** the riches of His
14: 3 Let not him who eats ***d*** him who
1 Cor 11:22 Or do you ***d*** the church of God
16:11 Therefore let no one ***d*** him.
Gal 4:14 you did not ***d*** or reject,
1 Th 5:20 Do not ***d*** prophecies.
1 Tim 4:12 Let no one ***d*** your youth, but be
6: 2 let them not ***d*** them because
Titus 2:15 Let no one ***d*** you.
Heb 12: 5 do not ***d*** the chastening
2 Pe 2:10 uncleanness and ***d*** authority.

DESPISED (58/57) DESPISE

Gen 16: 4 her mistress became ***d*** in her
16: 5 I became ***d*** in her eyes.
25:34 Thus Esau ***d*** his birthright.
Lev 26:43 because they ***d*** My judgments and
Num 11:20 because you have ***d*** the LORD
14:31 know the land which you have ***d***.
15:31 Because he has ***d*** the word of the
Judg 9:38 not these the people whom you ***d***?
1 Sam 10:27 So they ***d*** him, and brought
15: 9 But everything ***d*** and worthless,
2 Sam 6:16 and she ***d*** him in her heart.
12: 9 Why have you ***d*** the commandment
12:10 because you have ***d*** Me, and have
2 Ki 19:21 Has ***d*** you, laughed you to
1 Chr 15:29 and she ***d*** him in her heart.
2 Chr 36:16 ***d*** His words, and scoffed at His
Neh 2:19 they laughed at us and ***d*** us,
4: 4 Hear, O our God, for we are ***d***;
Job 12: 5 A lamp is ***d*** in the thought of
31:13 If I have ***d*** the cause of my male
Ps 15: 4 whose eyes a vile person is ***d***,
22: 6 and ***d*** by the people.
22:24 For He has not ***d*** nor abhorred
53: 5 Because God has ***d*** them.
106:24 Then they ***d*** the pleasant land;
107:11 And ***d*** the counsel of the Most
119:141 I am small and ***d***,
Prov 1:30 none of my counsel And ***d*** my
5:12 And my heart ***d*** correction!
12: 8 of a perverse heart will be ***d***.
Eccl 9:16 the poor man's wisdom is ***d***,
Song 8: 1 kiss you; I would not be ***d***.
8: 7 house, It would be utterly ***d***.
Isa 5:24 And ***d*** the word of the Holy One
16:14 the glory of Moab will be ***d***
33: 8 He has ***d*** the cities, He
37:22 Has ***d*** you, laughed you to
53: 3 He is ***d*** and rejected by men, A
53: 3 our faces from Him; He was ***d***,
60:14 And all those who ***d*** you shall
Jer 22:28 "Is this man Coniah a ***d***,
33:24 Thus they have ***d*** My people, as
49:15 among nations, ***D*** among men.
Ezek 16:59 who ***d*** the oath by breaking the
17:16 whose oath he ***d*** and whose
17:18 Since he ***d*** the oath by breaking
17:19 live, surely My oath which he ***d***,
20:13 they ***d*** My judgments, 'which,
20:16 because they ***d*** My judgments and
20:24 but had ***d*** My statutes, profaned
22: 8 You have ***d*** My holy things and
Am 2: 4 Because they have ***d*** the law of
Ob 2 You shall be greatly ***d***.
Zech 4:10 For who has ***d*** the day of small
Mal 1: 6 In what way have we ***d*** Your
Lk 18: 9 righteous, and ***d*** others:
Acts 19:27 great goddess Diana may be ***d***
1 Cor 1:28 and the things which are ***d*** God

DESPISERS (2/2) DESPISE

Acts 13:41 "Behold, you ***d***,
2 Tim 3: 3 brutal, ***d*** of good,

DESPISES (12/12) DESPISE

Job 36: 5 is mighty, but ***d*** no one;
Prov 11:12 devoid of wisdom ***d*** his
13:13 He who ***d*** the word will be
14: 2 is perverse in his ways ***d*** Him.
14:21 He who ***d*** his neighbor sins;
15: 5 A fool ***d*** his father's
15:20 But a foolish man ***d*** his
15:32 disdains instruction ***d*** his own
Isa 33:15 He who ***d*** the gain of
49: 7 Holy One, To Him whom man ***d***,
Ezek 21:10 It ***d*** the scepter of My Son,
21:13 And what if the sword ***d*** even

DESPISING (1/1) DESPISE

Heb 12: 2 ***d*** the shame, and has sat down

DESPITE (3/3)

1 Sam 2:32 ***d*** all the good which God does
Ezek 32:29 Who ***d*** their might Are laid
Zeph 3: 7 ***D*** everything for which I

DESPOILED (1/1)

Judg 2:14 of plunderers who ***d*** them;

DESTINED (2/2) DESTINY

Job 15:28 Which are ***d*** to become ruins.
Lk 2:34 this Child is ***d*** for the fall

DESTINY (1/1) DESTINED

Lam 1: 9 She did not consider her ***d***;

DESTITUTE (7/7)

Ps 102:17 regard the prayer of the ***d***,
141: 8 refuge; Do not leave my soul ***d***.
Prov 15:21 is joy to him who is ***d*** of
Ezek 32:15 And the country is ***d*** of all
1 Tim 6: 5 of men of corrupt minds and ***d***
Heb 11:37 and goatskins, being ***d***,
Jas 2:15 or sister is naked and ***d*** of

DESTROY (270/252) DESTROYED, DESTROYER, DESTROYING, DESTROYS, DESTRUCTION, DESTRUCTIVE

Gen 6: 7 I will ***d*** man whom I have created
6:13 I will ***d*** them with the earth.
6:17 to ***d*** from under heaven all
7: 4 and I will ***d*** from the face of
8:21 nor will I again ***d*** every living
9:11 shall there be a flood to ***d***
9:15 again become a flood to ***d*** all
18:23 Would You also ***d*** the righteous
18:24 would You also ***d*** the place and
18:28 would You ***d*** all of the city for
18:28 I will not ***d*** it."
18:31 I will not ***d*** it for the sake of
18:32 I will not ***d*** it for the sake of
19:13 For we will ***d*** this place,
19:13 and the LORD has sent us to ***d***
19:14 for the LORD will ***d*** this
Ex 8: 9 to ***d*** the frogs from you and
12:13 shall not be on you to ***d*** you
15: 9 My hand shall ***d*** them.'
34:13 But you shall ***d*** their altars,
Lev 23:30 that person I will ***d*** from among
26:22 ***d*** your livestock, and make you
26:30 I will ***d*** your high places, cut
26:44 to utterly ***d*** them and break My
Num 21: 2 then I will utterly ***d*** their
24:17 And ***d*** all the sons of tumult.
24:19 And ***d*** the remains of the
32:15 and you will ***d*** all these
33:52 ***d*** all their engraved stones,
33:52 ***d*** all their molded images, and
Deut 1:27 the Amorites, to ***d*** us.
2:15 to ***d*** them from the midst of the
4:31 not forsake you nor ***d*** you,
6:15 aroused against you and ***d*** you
7: 2 them and utterly ***d*** them.
7: 4 aroused against you and ***d*** you
7: 5 you shall ***d*** their altars, and
7:10 to ***d*** them. He will not be slack
7:16 And you shall ***d*** all the peoples
7:22 you will be unable to ***d*** them at
7:24 and you will ***d*** their name from
9: 3 He will ***d*** them and bring them
9: 3 drive them out and ***d*** them
9:14 that I may ***d*** them and blot out
9:19 to ***d*** you. But the LORD
9:25 the LORD had said He would ***d***
9:26 do not ***d*** Your people and Your
10:10 and the LORD chose not to ***d***
12: 2 You shall utterly ***d*** all the
12: 3 And you shall ***d*** their altars,
12: 3 their gods and ***d*** their names
20:17 but you shall utterly ***d*** them:
20:19 you shall not ***d*** its trees by
20:20 not trees for food you may ***d***
28:63 will rejoice over you to ***d*** you
31: 3 He will ***d*** these nations from
32:25 The sword shall ***d*** outside;
33:27 And will say, '***D***!'
Josh 7: 7 of the Amorites, to ***d*** us?
7:12 unless you ***d*** the accursed from
9:24 and to ***d*** all the inhabitants of
11:20 that He might utterly ***d*** them,
11:20 but that He might ***d*** them, as
22:33 to ***d*** the land where the
Judg 6: 4 encamp against them and ***d*** the
6: 5 they would enter the land to ***d***
21:11 You shall utterly ***d*** every male,
1 Sam 15: 3 and utterly ***d*** all that they
15: 6 lest I ***d*** you with them. For you
15: 9 unwilling to utterly ***d*** them.

D

15:18 and utterly **d** the sinners, the
23:10 seeks to come to Keilah to **d**
24:21 and that you will not **d** my name
26: 9 Do not **d** him; for who can
26:15 one of the people came in to **d**
2 Sam 1:14 to put forth your hand to **d**
14: 7 and we will **d** the heir also.'
14:11 the avenger of blood to **d**
14:11 lest they **d** my son." And he
14:16 hand of the man who would **d**
20:19 You seek to **d** a city and a
20:20 that I should swallow up or **d**!
24:16 His hand over Jerusalem to **d**
1 Ki 9:21 Israel had not been able to **d**
13:34 so as to exterminate and **d** it
2 Ki 8:19 Yet the LORD would not **d** Judah,
13:23 and would not yet **d** them or
18:25 LORD against this place to **d**
18:25 this land, and **d** it.'
24: 2 He sent them against Judah to **d**
1 Chr 21:15 an angel to Jerusalem to **d** it.
2 Chr 8: 8 children of Israel did not **d**—
12: 7 therefore I will not **d** them,
12:12 so as not to **d** him completely;
20:10 turned from them and did not **d**
20:23 to utterly kill and **d** them.
20:23 they helped to **d** one another.
21: 7 Yet the LORD would not **d** the
25:16 that God has determined to **d**
35:21 with me, lest He **d** you."
Ezra 6:12 His name to dwell there **d** any
6:12 or to **d** this house of God which
Esth 3: 6 Haman sought to **d** all the Jews
3:13 all the king's provinces, to **d**,
4: 7 the king's treasuries to **d** the
8:11 and protect their lives—to **d**,
9:24 to consume them and **d** them;
Job 2: 3 to **d** him without cause."
10: 8 Yet You would **d** me.
14:19 So You **d** the hope of man.
Ps 5: 6 You shall **d** those who speak
21:10 Their offspring You shall **d**
28: 5 He shall **d** them And not build
40:14 confusion Who seek to **d** my
52: 5 God shall likewise **d** you
55: 9 ***D***, O Lord, and divide their
57: Set to "Do Not ***D***."
58: Set to "Do Not ***D***."
59: Set to "Do Not ***D***."
63: 9 to **d** it, Shall go into the
69: 4 They are mighty who would **d**
74: 8 Let us **d** them altogether."
74:11 of Your bosom and **d** them.
75: Musician. Set to "Do Not ***D***.
78:38 And did not **d** them. Yes,
101: 5 his neighbor, Him I will **d**;
101: 8 Early I will **d** all the wicked
106:23 He said that He would **d** them,
106:23 lest He **d** them.
106:34 They did not **d** the peoples,
118:10 the name of the LORD I will **d**
118:11 the name of the LORD I will **d**
118:12 the name of the LORD I will **d**
119:95 The wicked wait for me to **d** me,
143:12 And **d** all those who afflict my
144: 6 out Your arrows and **d** them.
145:20 But all the wicked He will **d**.
Prov 1:32 the complacency of fools will **d**
11: 3 of the unfaithful will **d** them.
15:25 The LORD will **d** the house of
21: 7 violence of the wicked will **d**
Eccl 5: 6 at your excuse and **d** the work
7:16 Why should you **d** yourself?
Isa 3:12 And **d** the way of your paths."
10: 7 But it is in his heart to **d**,
11: 9 They shall not hurt nor **d** in
11:15 The LORD will utterly **d** the
13: 5 To **d** the whole land.
13: 9 And He will **d** its sinners from
19: 3 I will **d** their counsel, And
23:11 against Canaan To **d** its
25: 7 And He will **d** on this mountain
32: 7 He devises wicked plans To **d**
36:10 LORD against this land to **d**
36:10 this land, and **d** it.'
51:13 When he has prepared to **d**.
54:16 I have created the spoiler to **d**.
65: 8 Do not **d** it, For a blessing is
65: 8 That I may not **d** them all.
65:25 They shall not hurt nor **d** in
Jer 1:10 To **d** and to throw down, To
5: 6 A wolf of the deserts shall **d**
5:10 "Go up on her walls and **d**,
5:17 They shall **d** your fortified
6: 5 And let us **d** her palaces."
11:19 Let us **d** the tree with its
12:17 pluck up and **d** that nation,"
13:14 but will **d** them." '"
15: 3 of the earth to devour and **d**.
15: 6 My hand against you and **d** you;
15: 7 I will **d** My people, Since
17:18 And **d** them with double
18: 7 to pull down, and to **d** it,
23: 1 Woe to the shepherds who **d** and
25: 9 and will utterly **d** them, and
31:28 break down, to throw down, to **d**,
36:29 will certainly come and **d** this
46: 8 I will **d** the city and its
49: 9 Would they not **d** until they
49:38 And will **d** from there the king
50:21 Waste and utterly **d** them,"
50:26 And **d** her utterly; Let
51: 3 Utterly **d** all her army.
51:11 is against Babylon to **d** it,
51:20 With you I will **d** kingdoms;
Lam 2: 8 The LORD has purposed to **d**
3:66 Pursue and **d** them From under
Ezek 5:16 which I will send to **d** you, I
6: 3 and I will **d** your high places.
9: 8 Lord GOD! Will You **d** all the
14: 9 My hand against him and **d** him
21:31 men who are skillful to **d**.
22:27 to **d** people, and to get
22:30 that I should not **d** it; but I
25: 7 I will **d** you, and you shall
25:15 to **d** because of the old
25:16 **d** the remnant of the seacoast.
26: 4 And they shall **d** the walls of
26:12 down your walls and **d** your
30:11 Shall be brought to **d** the
30:13 I will also **d** the idols, And
32:13 Also I will **d** all its animals
34:16 but I will **d** the fat and the
43: 3 which I saw when I came to **d**
Dan 2:12 and gave a command to **d** all the
2:24 the king had appointed to **d**
2:24 Do not **d** the wise men of
4:23 Chop down the tree and **d** it, but
7:26 To consume and **d** it forever.
8:24 He shall **d** fearfully, And
8:24 He shall **d** the mighty, and
8:25 He shall **d** many in their
9:26 prince who is to come Shall **d**
11:17 the daughter of women to **d** it;
11:26 of his delicacies shall **d** him;
11:44 go out with great fury to **d**
Hos 2:12 And I will **d** her vines and her
4: 5 And I will **d** your mother.
11: 9 I will not again **d** Ephraim.
Am 3:15 I will **d** the winter house along
9: 8 And I will **d** it from the face
9: 8 Yet I will not utterly **d** the
Ob 8 Even **d** the wise men from Edom,
Mic 2:10 it is defiled, it shall **d**,
5:10 And **d** your chariots.
5:14 Thus I will **d** your cities.
Zeph 2: 5 I will **d** you; So there shall be
2:13 ***D*** Assyria, And make Nineveh a
Hag 2:22 I will **d** the strength of the
Zech 9: 4 He will **d** her power in the
12: 9 day that I will seek to **d** all
Mal 3:11 So that he will not **d** the
Mt 2:13 will seek the young Child to **d**
5:17 not think that I came to **d**
5:17 I did not come to **d** but to
6:19 where moth and rust **d** and where
10:28 fear Him who is able to **d** both
12:14 how they might **d** Him.
21:41 He will **d** those wicked men
26:61 I am able to **d** the temple of God
27:20 ask for Barabbas and **d** Jesus.
27:40 You who **d** the temple and build
Mk 1:24 Did You come to **d** us? I know
3: 6 how they might **d** Him.
9:22 fire and into the water to **d**
11:18 it and sought how they might **d**
12: 9 He will come and **d** the
14:58 I will **d** this temple made with
15:29 Aha! You who **d** the temple and
Lk 4:34 Did You come to **d** us? I know
6: 9 do evil, to save life or to **d**?
9:56 Son of Man did not come to **d**
19:47 of the people sought to **d** Him,
20:16 He will come and **d** those
Jn 2:19 ***D*** this temple, and in three days
10:10 to steal, and to kill, and to **d**.
Acts 6:14 this Jesus of Nazareth will **d**
Rom 14:15 Do not **d** with your food the one
14:20 Do not **d** the work of God for the
1 Cor 1:19 I will **d** the wisdom of the
3:17 God will **d** him. For the temple
6:13 but God will **d** both it and
Gal 1:13 measure and tried to **d** it.
1:23 which he once tried to **d**.
2 Th 2: 8 breath of His mouth and **d** with
Heb 2:14 through death He might **d** him
Jas 4:12 who is able to save and to **d**.
1 Jn 3: 8 that He might **d** the works of
Rev 11:18 And should **d** those who destroy
11:18 should destroy those who **d** the

DESTROYED (171/166) DESTROY

Gen 7:23 So He **d** all living things which
7:23 They were **d** from the earth.
13:10 (before the LORD **d** Sodom and
19:17 to the mountains, lest you be **d**.
19:29 when God **d** the cities of the
34:30 I shall be **d**, my household
Ex 10: 7 not yet know that Egypt is **d**?
22:20 only, he shall be utterly **d**.
Num 21: 3 and they utterly **d** them and
Deut 2:12 of Esau dispossessed them and **d**
2:21 But the LORD **d** them before
2:22 when He **d** the Horites from
2:23 **d** them and dwelt in their
2:34 and we utterly **d** the men,
3: 6 And we utterly **d** them, as we did
4: 3 for the LORD your God has **d**
4:26 in it, but will be utterly **d**.
7:20 hide themselves from you, are **d**.
7:23 upon them until they are **d**.
7:24 against you until you have **d**
9: 8 enough with you to have **d** you.
9:20 with Aaron and would have **d**
11: 4 and how the LORD has **d** them
12:30 after they are **d** from before
28:20 until you are **d** and until you
28:24 down on you until you are **d**.
28:45 overtake you, until you are **d**,
28:48 on your neck until He has **d**
28:51 of your land, until you are **d**;
28:51 until they have **d** you.
28:61 bring upon you until you are **d**.
31: 4 their land, when He **d** them.
Josh 2:10 and Og, whom you utterly **d**.
6:21 And they utterly **d** all that was
8:26 until he had utterly **d** all the
10: 1 had taken Ai and had utterly **d**
10:28 He utterly **d** them—all the
10:35 who were in it he utterly **d**
10:37 but utterly **d** it and all the
10:39 of the sword and utterly **d** all
10:40 but utterly **d** all that
11:12 He utterly **d** them, as Moses the
11:14 of the sword until they had **d**
11:21 Joshua utterly **d** them with
23:15 until He has **d** you from this
24: 8 and I **d** them from before you.
Judg 1:17 and utterly **d** it. So the name
4:24 until they had **d** Jabin king of
20:35 And the children of Israel **d**
20:42 came out of the cities they **d**
21:16 women of Benjamin have been **d**?
21:17 that a tribe may not be **d** from
1 Sam 15: 8 and utterly **d** all the people
15: 9 worthless, that they utterly **d**.
15:15 and the rest we have utterly **d**.
15:20 I have utterly **d** the
15:21 should have been utterly **d**,
2 Sam 11: 1 and they **d** the people of Ammon
21: 5 that we should be **d** from
22:38 have pursued my enemies and **d**
22:38 back again till they were **d**.
22:39 And I have **d** them and wounded
22:41 So that I **d** those who hated
1 Ki 15:29 until he had **d** him, according
16:12 Thus Zimri **d** all the household
22:11 the Syrians until they are **d**.
2 Ki 3:25 Then they **d** the cities, and each
10:17 till he had **d** them, according
10:28 Thus Jehu **d** Baal from Israel.
11: 1 she arose and **d** all the royal
13: 7 for the king of Syria had **d**
13:17 at Aphek till you have **d** them.
13:19 struck Syria till you had **d**
19:12 those whom my fathers have **d**,
19:18 Therefore they **d** them.
21: 3 which Hezekiah his father had **d**;
21: 9 nations whom the LORD had **d**
1 Chr 4:41 and utterly **d** them, as it is to
5:25 whom God had **d** before them.
2 Chr 15: 6 So nation was **d** by nation, and
18:10 the Syrians until they are **d**.
20:37 the LORD has **d** your works."
22:10 she arose and **d** all the royal
24:23 and **d** all the leaders of the
31: 1 until they had utterly **d** them
32:14 that my fathers utterly **d** that
33: 9 nations whom the LORD had **d**
34:11 which the kings of Judah had **d**.
36:19 and **d** all its precious
Ezra 4:15 for which cause this city was **d**.
5:12 who **d** this temple and carried
Esth 3: 9 be written that they be **d**,
7: 4 sold, my people and I, to be **d**,
9: 6 Jews killed and **d** five hundred
9:12 The Jews have killed and **d** five
Job 8:18 If he is **d** from his place,
19:26 And after my skin is **d**,
Ps 9: 5 You have **d** the wicked; You
9: 6 And you have **d** cities;
11: 3 If the foundations are **d**,
18:37 back again till they were **d**.
18:40 So that I **d** those who hated
37:38 the transgressors shall be **d**
73:27 You have **d** all those who
78:45 And frogs, which **d** them.
78:47 He **d** their vines with hail,
78:51 And **d** all the firstborn in
92: 7 It is that they may be **d**
105:16 He **d** all the provision of
105:36 He also **d** all the firstborn in
135: 8 He **d** the firstborn of Egypt,
137: 8 of Babylon, who are to be **d**,
Prov 13:13 who despises the word will be **d**,
13:20 companion of fools will be **d**.
29: 1 his neck, Will suddenly be **d**,
Isa 9:16 who are led by them are **d**.
10:27 And the yoke will be **d** because
14:17 world as a wilderness And **d**
14:20 Because you have **d** your land
15: 1 of Moab is laid waste And **d**,
15: 1 of Moab is laid waste And **d**,
26:14 You have punished and **d** them,
34: 2 He has utterly **d** them, He has
37:12 those whom my fathers have **d**,
37:19 Therefore they have **d** them.
48:19 Nor **d** from before Me."
Jer 12:10 Many rulers have **d** My vineyard,
22:20 For all your lovers are **d**.
48: 4 'Moab is **d**; Her little ones
48: 8 And the plain shall be **d**,
48:18 He has **d** your strongholds.
48:42 And Moab shall be **d** as a
51: 8 has suddenly fallen and been **d**.

Lam 2: 5 He has ***d*** her strongholds, And
2: 6 He has ***d*** His place of
2: 9 He has ***d*** and broken her bars.
2:22 brought up My enemies have ***d***.
Ezek 27:32 ***D*** in the midst of the sea?
28:16 And I ***d*** you, O covering
30: 8 And all her helpers are ***d***.
32:12 all its multitude shall be ***d***.
Dan 2:44 kingdom which shall never be ***d***;
6:26 the one which shall not be ***d***,
7:11 and its body ***d*** and given to the
7:14 the one Which shall not be ***d***.
11:20 within a few days he shall be ***d***,
Hos 4: 6 My people are ***d*** for lack of
10: 8 the sin of Israel, Shall be ***d***.
13: 9 "O Israel, you are ***d***,
Am 2: 9 Yet it was I who ***d*** the
2: 9 Yet I ***d*** his fruit above And
Mic 2: 4 We are utterly ***d***! He has
Zeph 3: 6 passing by. Their cities are ***d***;
Mt 22: 7 ***d*** those murderers, and burned
Lk 9:25 and is himself ***d*** or lost?
17:27 and the flood came and ***d*** them
17:29 from heaven and ***d*** them all.
Acts 3:23 shall be utterly ***d*** from
9:21 Is this not he who ***d*** those who
13:19 And when He had ***d*** seven nations
19:27 despised and her magnificence ***d***,
1 Cor 10: 9 and were ***d*** by serpents;
10:10 and were ***d*** by the destroyer.
15:26 The last enemy that will be ***d***
2 Cor 4: 9 struck down, but not ***d***—
5: 1 earthly house, this tent, is ***d***,
Gal 2:18 again those things which I ***d***,
Heb 11:28 lest he who ***d*** the firstborn
2 Pe 2:12 beasts made to be caught and ***d***,
Jude 5 afterward ***d*** those who did not
Rev 8: 9 and a third of the ships were ***d***.

DESTROYER (8/8) DESTROY, DESTROYERS

Ex 12:23 the door and not allow the ***d***
Judg 16:24 The ***d*** of our land, And the
Job 15:21 In prosperity the ***d*** comes upon
Ps 17: 4 away from the paths of the ***d***.
Prov 18: 9 brother to him who is a great ***d***.
28:24 The same is companion to a ***d***.
Jer 4: 7 And the ***d*** of nations is on his
1 Cor 10:10 and were destroyed by the ***d***.

DESTROYERS (3/3) DESTROYER

Isa 49:17 Your ***d*** and those who laid you
Jer 22: 7 I will prepare ***d*** against you,
50:11 You ***d*** of My heritage, Because

DESTROYING (16/15) DESTROY

Lev 11:22 the ***d*** locust after its kind,
Deut 3: 6 utterly ***d*** the men, women, and
13:15 utterly ***d*** it, all that is in it
Josh 11:11 utterly ***d*** them. There was none
2 Sam 24:16 the angel who was ***d*** the people,
2 Ki 10:19 with the intent of ***d*** the
19:11 done to all lands by utterly ***d***
1 Chr 21:12 angel of the LORD ***d*** throughout
21:15 to destroy it. As he was ***d***,
21:15 and said to the angel who was ***d***,
Isa 28: 2 tempest of hail and a ***d*** storm,
37:11 all lands by utterly ***d*** them;
Jer 2:30 your prophets Like a ***d*** lion.
51: 1 Leb Kamai, A ***d*** wind.
51:25 O ***d*** mountain, Who destroys all
Lam 2: 8 not withdrawn His hand from ***d***;

DESTROYS (13/13) DESTROY

Ex 21:26 and ***d*** it, he shall let him go
Deut 8:20 the nations which the LORD ***d***
Job 9:22 He ***d*** the blameless and the
12:23 and ***d*** them; He enlarges
30:24 If they cry out when He ***d*** it.
Prov 6:32 He who does so ***d*** his own
11: 9 his mouth ***d*** his neighbor,
31: 3 ways to that which ***d*** kings.
Eccl 7: 7 Surely oppression ***d*** a wise
9:18 But one sinner ***d*** much good."
Jer 51:25 Who ***d*** all the earth," says
Mt 6:20 where neither moth nor rust ***d***
Lk 12:33 no thief approaches nor moth ***d***.

DESTRUCTION (108/106) DESTROY, DESTRUCTIONS

Lev 27:29 who may become doomed to ***d***
Deut 7:26 lest you be doomed to ***d*** like
32:24 by pestilence and bitter ***d***;
Josh 6:17 be doomed by the LORD to ***d***,
7:12 they have become doomed to ***d***.
1 Sam 5: 9 the city with a very great ***d***;
5:11 For there was a deadly ***d***
2 Sam 24:16 the LORD relented from the ***d***,
1 Ki 20:42 man whom I appointed to utter ***d***,
2 Chr 22: 4 death of his father, to his ***d***.
26:16 heart was lifted up, to his ***d***,
Esth 4: 8 the written decree for their ***d***,
8: 6 how can I endure to see the ***d***
9: 5 the sword, with slaughter and ***d***,
Job 5:21 you shall not be afraid of ***d***
5:22 You shall laugh at ***d*** and
18:12 And ***d*** is ready at his side.
21:17 How often does their ***d*** come
21:20 Let his eyes see his ***d***,
26: 6 And ***D*** has no covering.
28:22 ***D*** and Death say, 'We have
30:12 against me their ways of ***d***.
31: 3 Is it not ***d*** for the wicked,
31:12 be a fire that consumes to ***d***,
31:23 For ***d*** from God is a terror to
31:29 If I have rejoiced at the ***d*** of
Ps 5: 9 Their inward part is ***d***;
35: 8 Let ***d*** come upon him
35: 8 Into that very ***d*** let him fall.
38:12 who seek my hurt speak of ***d***,
52: 2 Your tongue devises ***d***,
55:11 ***D*** is in its midst
55:23 bring them down to the pit of ***d***;
73:18 You cast them down to ***d***.
78:49 By sending angels of ***d*** among
88:11 faithfulness in the place of ***d***?
90: 3 You turn man to ***d***,
91: 6 Nor of the ***d*** that lays waste
103: 4 Who redeems your life from ***d***,
Prov 1:27 And your ***d*** comes like a
10:14 mouth of the foolish is near ***d***.
10:15 The ***d*** of the poor is their
10:29 But ***d*** will come to the
13: 3 wide his lips shall have ***d***.
15:11 Hell and ***D*** are before the
16:18 Pride goes before ***d***,
17:19 he who exalts his gate seeks ***d***.
18: 7 A fool's mouth is his ***d***,
18:12 Before ***d*** the heart of a man is
19:18 do not set your heart on his ***d***.
21:15 But ***d*** will come to the
27:20 Hell and ***D*** are never full;
Isa 1:28 The ***d*** of transgressors and of
10:22 The ***d*** decreed shall overflow
10:25 as will My anger in their ***d***.
13: 6 is at hand! It will come as ***d***
14:23 sweep it with the broom of ***d***,
15: 5 They will raise up a cry of ***d***,
19:18 will be called the City of ***D***.
24:12 the gate is stricken with ***d***.
28:22 A ***d*** determined even upon the
49:19 places, And the land of your ***d***,
51:19 for you?—Desolation and ***d***,
59: 7 Wasting and ***d*** are in their
60:18 Neither wasting nor ***d*** within
Jer 4: 6 from the north, And great ***d***.
4:20 ***D*** upon destruction is cried,
4:20 Destruction upon ***d*** is cried,
6: 1 out of the north, And great ***d***.
15: 3 over them four forms of ***d***,
17:18 destroy them with double ***d***!
46:20 But ***d*** comes, it comes from
48: 3 Plundering and great ***d***!'
48: 5 enemies have heard a cry of ***d***.
50:22 in the land, And of great ***d***.
51:54 And great ***d*** from the land of
Lam 2:11 on the ground Because of the ***d***
3:47 come upon us, Desolation and ***d***.
3:48 rivers of water For the ***d*** of
4:10 became food for them In the ***d***
Ezek 5:16 of famine which shall be for ***d***,
7:25 ***D*** comes; They will seek
20:17 My eye spared them from ***d***.
32: 9 when I bring your ***d*** among the
Dan 11:16 in the Glorious Land with ***d*** in
Hos 7:13 ***D*** to them, Because they
9: 6 they are gone because of ***d***.
13:14 I will be your ***d***! Pity is
Joel 1:15 It shall come as ***d*** from the
Am 3:14 I will also visit ***d*** on the
Ob 12 of Judah In the day of their ***d***;
Mic 2:10 destroy, Yes, with utter ***d***.
Zech 14:11 longer shall there be utter ***d***,
Mt 7:13 is the way that leads to ***d***,
Acts 25:16 Romans to deliver any man to ***d***
Rom 3:16 ***D*** and misery are in their
9:22 vessels of wrath prepared for ***d***,
1 Cor 5: 5 such a one to Satan for the ***d***
2 Cor 10: 8 edification and not for your ***d***,
13:10 for edification and not for ***d***.
Phil 3:19 whose end is ***d***,
1 Th 5: 3 then sudden ***d*** comes upon
2 Th 1: 9 be punished with everlasting ***d***
1 Tim 6: 9 lusts which drown men in ***d*** and
2 Pe 2: 1 bring on themselves swift ***d***.
2: 3 and their ***d*** does not slumber.
2: 6 ashes, condemned them to ***d***,
3:16 people twist to their own ***d***,

DESTRUCTIONS (3/3) DESTRUCTION

Ps 9: 6 ***d*** are finished forever!
35:17 Rescue me from their ***d***,
107:20 delivered them from their ***d***.

DESTRUCTIVE (2/2) DESTROY

2 Pe 2: 1 secretly bring in ***d*** heresies,
2: 2 will follow their ***d*** ways,

DETACHMENT (2/2)

Jn 18: 3 having received a ***d*** of
18:12 Then the ***d*** of troops and the

DETAIL (2/2) DETAILS

Acts 21:19 he told in ***d*** those things which
Heb 9: 5 things we cannot now speak in ***d***.

DETAILS (1/1) DETAIL

1 Ki 6:38 was finished in all its ***d*** and

DETAIN (2/2) DETAINED

Judg 13:15 Please let us ***d*** You, and we will
13:16 Though you ***d*** Me, I will not eat

DETAINED (2/2) DETAIN

Judg 19: 4 ***d*** him; and he stayed with him
1 Sam 21: 7 ***d*** before the LORD. And his

DETERMINATE (KJV) See DETERMINED

DETERMINATION (1/1) DETERMINE

Zeph 3: 8 My ***d*** is to gather the nations

DETERMINE (5/5) DETERMINATION, DETERMINED, DETERMING

Gen 38:25 Please ***d*** whose these are—the
Ex 21:22 he shall pay as the judges ***d***.
Esth 3: 7 before Haman to ***d*** the day and
Mic 2: 5 you will have no one to ***d***
Mk 15:24 casting lots for them to ***d*** what

DETERMINED (41/41) DETERMINE

Josh 17:12 but the Canaanites were ***d*** to
Judg 1:27 for the Canaanites were ***d*** to
1:35 and the Amorites were ***d*** to dwell
Ruth 1:18 When she saw that she was ***d*** to
1 Sam 20: 7 then be sure that evil is ***d*** by
20: 9 knew certainly that evil was ***d***
20:33 Jonathan knew that it was ***d*** by
25:17 for harm is ***d*** against our
2 Sam 13:32 of Absalom this has been ***d***
1 Ki 7:47 weight of the bronze was not ***d***.
2 Chr 2: 1 Then Solomon ***d*** to build a temple
4:18 weight of the bronze was not ***d***.
25:16 I know that God has ***d*** to destroy
Esth 7: 7 that evil was ***d*** against
Job 14: 5 Since his days are ***d***,
38: 5 Who ***d*** its measurements?
Isa 10:23 Will make a ***d*** end In the
19:17 which He has ***d*** against it.
28:22 A destruction ***d*** even upon the
Dan 9:24 Seventy weeks are ***d*** For your
9:26 of the war desolations are ***d***.
9:27 the consummation, which is ***d***,
11:36 for what has been ***d*** shall be
Zech 1: 6 Just as the LORD of hosts ***d*** to
8:14 Just as I ***d*** to punish you When
8:15 again in these days I am ***d*** to
Mt 2: 7 ***d*** from them what time the star
2:16 to the time which he had ***d***
Lk 22:22 of Man goes as it has been ***d***,
Acts 2:23 being delivered by the ***d***
3:13 when he was ***d*** to let Him go.
4:28 Your hand and Your purpose ***d***
11:29 ***d*** to send relief to the
15: 2 they ***d*** that Paul and Barnabas
15:37 Now Barnabas was ***d*** to take with
16: 4 which were ***d*** by the apostles
17:26 and has ***d*** their preappointed
19:39 it shall be ***d*** in the lawful
1 Cor 2: 2 For I ***d*** not to know anything
7:37 and has so ***d*** in his heart that
2 Cor 2: 1 But I ***d*** this within myself, that

DETERMINING (1/1) DETERMINE

Heb 6:17 ***d*** to show more abundantly to

DETEST (2/2) DETESTABLE, DETESTS

Deut 7:26 You shall utterly ***d*** it and
Prov 3:11 Nor ***d*** His correction;

DETESTABLE (7/7) DETEST

Deut 14: 3 You shall not eat any ***d*** thing.
Jer 16:18 with the carcasses of their ***d*** and
Ezek 5:11 with all your ***d*** things and
7:20 Their ***d*** things; Therefore I
11:18 take away all its ***d*** things
11:21 the desire for their ***d*** things
37:23 nor with their ***d*** things, nor

DETESTS (3/3) DETEST

Deut 22:13 in to her, and ***d*** her,
22:16 as wife, and he ***d*** her.
24: 3 if the latter husband ***d*** her and

DEUEL (4/4) REUEL

Num 1:14 Gad, Eliasaph the son of ***D***;
7:42 sixth day Eliasaph the son of ***D***,
7:47 of Eliasaph the son of ***D***.
10:20 Gad was Eliasaph the son of ***D***.

DEVASTATE (1/1) DEVASTED, DEVASTATION

Jer 49:28 And ***d*** the men of the East!

DEVASTATED (1/1) DEVASTATE
Zeph 3: 6 Their fortresses are ***d***;

DEVASTATION (2/2) DEVASTATE
Isa 16: 4 ***D*** ceases, The oppressors are
Zeph 1:15 A day of ***d*** and desolation, A

DEVELOPS (1/1)
Lev 13:18 If the body ***d*** a boil in the

DEVICE (1/1) DEVICES
Eccl 9:10 for there is no work or ***d*** or

DEVICES (3/3) DEVICE
2 Chr 26:15 And he made ***d*** in Jerusalem,
Job 5:12 He frustrates the ***d*** of the
2 Cor 2:11 we are not ignorant of his ***d***.

DEVIL (35/33)
Mt 4: 1 to be tempted by the ***d***.
4: 5 Then the ***d*** took Him up into the
4: 8 the ***d*** took Him up on an
4:11 Then the ***d*** left Him, and behold,
13:39 enemy who sowed them is the ***d***,
25:41 fire prepared for the ***d*** and
Lk 4: 2 tempted for forty days by the ***d***.
4: 3 And the ***d*** said to Him, "If You
4: 5 Then the ***d***, taking Him up on
4: 6 And the ***d*** said to Him, "All
4:13 Now when the ***d*** had ended every
8:12 then the ***d*** comes and takes away
Jn 6:70 twelve, and one of you is a ***d***?
8:44 "You are of your father the ***d***,
13: 2 the ***d*** having already put it
Acts 10:38 all who were oppressed by the ***d***,
13:10 all fraud, you son of the ***d***,
Eph 4:27 nor give place to the ***d***.
6:11 against the wiles of the ***d***.
1 Tim 3: 6 the same condemnation as the ***d***.
3: 7 reproach and the snare of the ***d***.
2 Tim 2:26 and escape the snare of the ***d***,
Heb 2:14 power of death, that is, the ***d***,
Jas 4: 7 Resist the ***d*** and he will flee
1 Pe 5: 8 because your adversary the ***d***
1 Jn 3: 8 He who sins is of the ***d***,
3: 8 for the ***d*** has sinned from the
3: 8 destroy the works of the ***d***.
3:10 God and the children of the ***d***
Jude 9 in contending with the ***d***,
Rev 2:10 the ***d*** is about to throw some
12: 9 called the ***D*** and Satan, who
12:12 earth and the sea! For the ***d***
20: 2 who is the ***D*** and Satan, and
20:10 The ***d***, who deceived them,

DEVILS (KJV) See DEMONS

DEVIOUS (3/3) DEVISE
2 Sam 22:27 And with the ***d*** You will show
Ps 18:26 And with the ***d*** You will show
Prov 2:15 And who are ***d*** in their

DEVISE (15/14) DEVIOUS, DEVISED, DEVISES, DEVISING
Ps 35:20 But they ***d*** deceitful matters
41: 7 Against me they ***d*** my hurt.
64: 6 They ***d*** iniquities: "We have
Prov 3:29 Do not ***d*** evil against your
12:20 is in the heart of those who ***d***
14:22 Do they not go astray who ***d***
14:22 truth belong to those who ***d***
16:30 He winks his eye to ***d*** perverse
Isa 30: 1 And who ***d*** plans, but not of My
Jer 18:18 Come and let us ***d*** plans against
Ezek 11: 2 these are the men who ***d***
Dan 11:24 and he shall ***d*** his plans
11:25 for they shall ***d*** plans against
Hos 7:15 Yet they ***d*** evil against Me;
Mic 2: 1 Woe to those who ***d*** iniquity,

DEVISED (11/11) DEVISE
1 Ki 12:33 in the month which he had ***d*** in
Esth 8: 3 and the scheme which he had ***d***
8: 5 to revoke the letters ***d*** by
9:25 wicked plot which Haman had ***d***
Ps 10: 2 in the plots which they have ***d***.
21:11 They ***d*** a plot which they are
Prov 30:32 Or if you have ***d*** evil, put
Jer 11:19 I did not know that they had ***d***
48: 2 In Heshbon they have ***d*** evil
51:12 For the LORD has both ***d*** and
2 Pe 1:16 we did not follow cunningly ***d***

DEVISES (9/9) DEVISE
2 Sam 14:14 but He ***d*** means, so that His
Ps 36: 4 He ***d*** wickedness on his bed;
52: 2 Your tongue ***d*** destruction,
94:20 which ***d*** evil by law, Have
Prov 6:14 He ***d*** evil continually, He
6:18 A heart that ***d*** wicked plans,
24: 2 For their heart ***d*** violence,
Isa 32: 7 He ***d*** wicked plans To destroy
32: 8 But a generous man ***d*** generous

DEVISING (4/4) DEVISE
Prov 24: 9 The ***d*** of foolishness is sin,
Jer 18:11 am fashioning a disaster and ***d***
Mic 2: 3 against this family I am ***d***
Acts 17:29 shaped by art and man's ***d***.

DEVOID (6/6)
Prov 7: 7 A young man ***d*** of
10:13 for the back of him who is ***d***
11:12 He who is ***d*** of wisdom despises
12:11 he who follows frivolity is ***d***
17:18 A man ***d*** of understanding shakes
24:30 by the vineyard of the man ***d***

DEVOTE (3/3) DEVOTED, DEVOUT
Lev 27:28 offering that a man may ***d*** to
2 Chr 31: 4 that they might ***d*** themselves to
Prov 20:25 It is a snare for a man to ***d***

DEVOTED (7/6) DEVOTE
Lev 27:21 as a ***d*** field; it shall be the
27:28 Nevertheless no ***d*** offering
27:28 every ***d*** offering is most holy
Num 18:14 Every ***d*** thing in Israel shall be
18:16 And those redeemed of the ***d***
Ps 119:38 Who is ***d*** to fearing You.
1 Cor 16:15 and that they have ***d***

DEVOUR (66/65) DEVOURED, DEVOURER, DEVOURING, DEVOURS
Gen 49:27 In the morning he shall ***d*** the
Deut 32:42 And My sword shall ***d*** flesh,
Judg 9:15 come out of the bramble And ***d***
9:20 fire come from Abimelech and ***d***
9:20 and from Beth Millo and ***d***
2 Sam 2:26 'Shall the sword ***d*** forever?
2 Chr 7:13 or command the locusts to ***d*** the
Ps 21: 9 And the fire shall ***d*** them.
50: 3 A fire shall ***d*** before Him,
Prov 30:14 To ***d*** the poor from off the
Isa 1: 7 Strangers ***d*** your land in your
9:12 And they shall ***d*** Israel with
9:18 It shall ***d*** the briers and
9:20 He shall ***d*** on the left hand
9:21 Manasseh shall ***d*** Ephraim, and
10:17 It will burn and ***d*** His thorns
26:11 fire of Your enemies shall ***d***
31: 8 a sword not of mankind shall ***d***
33:11 as fire, shall ***d*** you.
56: 9 beasts of the field, come to ***d***,
Jer 2: 3 All that ***d*** him will offend;
5:14 And it shall ***d*** them.
12: 9 Bring them to ***d***!
12:12 the sword of the LORD shall ***d***
15: 3 the beasts of the earth to ***d***
17:27 and it shall ***d*** the palaces of
21:14 And it shall ***d*** all things
30:16 Therefore all those who ***d*** you
46:10 adversaries. The sword shall ***d***;
48:45 And shall ***d*** the brow of Moab,
50:32 And it will ***d*** all around
Ezek 7:15 Famine and pestilence will ***d***
15: 7 but another fire shall ***d*** them.
20:47 and it shall ***d*** every green tree
23:37 through the fire, to ***d*** them.
34:28 nor shall beasts of the land ***d***
36:13 You ***d*** men and bereave your
36:14 therefore you shall ***d*** men no
Dan 7: 5 'Arise, ***d*** much flesh!'
7:23 And shall ***d*** the whole earth,
Hos 5: 7 Now a New Moon shall ***d*** them
8:14 And it shall ***d*** his palaces."
11: 6 ***D*** his districts, And consume
13: 8 And there I will ***d*** them like a
Am 1: 4 Which shall ***d*** the palaces of
1: 7 Which shall ***d*** its palaces.
1:10 Which shall ***d*** its palaces."
1:12 Which shall ***d*** the palaces of
1:14 And it shall ***d*** its palaces,
2: 2 And it shall ***d*** the palaces of
2: 5 And it shall ***d*** the palaces of
5: 6 And ***d*** it, With no one to
Ob 18 They shall kindle them and ***d***
Nah 2:13 and the sword shall ***d*** your
3:13 Fire shall ***d*** the bars of your
3:15 There the fire will ***d*** you, The
Zech 9:15 They shall ***d*** and subdue with
11: 1 That fire may ***d*** your cedars.
12: 6 they shall ***d*** all the
Mt 23:14 For you ***d*** widows' houses,
Mk 12:40 who ***d*** widows' houses, and for a
Lk 20:47 who ***d*** widows' houses, and for a
Gal 5:15 But if you bite and ***d*** one
Heb 10:27 fiery indignation which will ***d***
1 Pe 5: 8 lion, seeking whom he may ***d***.
Rev 12: 4 to ***d*** her Child as soon as it

DEVOURED (50/49) DEVOUR
Gen 37:20 'Some wild beast has ***d*** him.'
37:33 A wild beast has ***d*** him. Without
41: 7 And the seven thin heads ***d*** the
41:24 And the thin heads ***d*** the seven
Lev 10: 2 went out from the LORD and ***d***
Num 26:10 when the fire ***d*** two hundred and
Deut 31:17 from them, and they shall be ***d***.
32:24 ***D*** by pestilence and bitter
2 Sam 18: 8 and the woods ***d*** more people
18: 8 that day than the sword ***d***.
Ps 78:45 which ***d*** them, And frogs, which
79: 7 For they have ***d*** Jacob, And
105:35 And ***d*** the fruit of their
Isa 1:20 You shall be ***d*** by the sword";
24: 6 Therefore the curse has ***d*** the
Jer 2:30 Your sword has ***d*** your prophets
3:24 For shame has ***d*** The labor of
8:16 For they have come and ***d*** the
10:25 ***D*** him and consumed him, And
30:16 those who devour you shall be ***d***;
50: 7 All who found them have ***d*** them;
50:17 First the king of Assyria ***d***
51:34 the king of Babylon Has ***d*** me,
Lam 4:11 And it has ***d*** its foundations.
Ezek 15: 5 any work when the fire has ***d***
16:20 you sacrificed to them to be ***d***.
19: 3 catch prey, And he ***d*** men.
19: 6 catch prey; He ***d*** men.
19:14 a rod of her branches And ***d***
22:25 they have ***d*** people; they have
23:25 And your remnant shall be ***d*** by
28:18 It ***d*** you, And I turned you to
33:27 will give to the beasts to be ***d***,
39: 4 the beasts of the field to be ***d***.
Dan 7:19 its nails of bronze, which ***d***,
Hos 7: 7 And have ***d*** their judges;
7: 9 Aliens have ***d*** his strength,
Joel 1:19 For fire has ***d*** the open
1:20 And fire has ***d*** the open
Am 4: 9 The locust ***d*** them; Yet you
7: 4 consumed the great deep and ***d***
Nah 1:10 They shall be ***d*** like stubble
Zeph 1:18 But the whole land shall be ***d***
3: 8 All the earth shall be ***d*** With
Zech 9: 4 And she will be ***d*** by fire.
Mt 13: 4 and the birds came and ***d*** them.
Mk 4: 4 birds of the air came and ***d*** it.
Lk 8: 5 and the birds of the air ***d*** it.
15:30 who has ***d*** your livelihood with
Rev 20: 9 from God out of heaven and ***d***

DEVOURER (1/1) DEVOUR
Mal 3:11 And I will rebuke the ***d*** for your

DEVOURING (9/9) DEVOUR
2 Sam 22: 9 And ***d*** fire from His mouth;
Ps 18: 8 And ***d*** fire from His mouth;
52: 4 You love all ***d*** words, You
Isa 29: 6 and tempest And the flame of ***d***
30:27 And His tongue like a ***d*** fire.
30:30 anger And the flame of a ***d***
33:14 us shall dwell with the ***d*** fire?
Lam 2: 3 Jacob like a flaming fire ***D***
Dan 7: 7 had huge iron teeth; it was ***d***,

DEVOURS (16/15) DEVOUR
Num 13:32 as spies is a land that ***d*** its
23:24 shall not lie down until it ***d***
2 Sam 11:25 for the sword ***d*** one as well as
Job 18:13 It ***d*** patches of his skin;
18:13 The firstborn of death ***d*** his
39:24 He ***d*** the distance with
Ps 80:13 the wild beast of the field ***d***
Prov 19:28 And the mouth of the wicked ***d***
Isa 5:24 as the fire ***d*** the stubble, And
Jer 46:14 For the sword ***d*** all around
Ezek 15: 4 the fire ***d*** both ends of it, and
Joel 2: 3 A fire ***d*** before them, And
2: 5 noise of a flaming fire that ***d***
Hab 1:13 Your tongue when the wicked ***d***
2 Cor 11:20 if one ***d*** you, if one takes
Rev 11: 5 from their mouth and ***d*** their

DEVOUT (9/9) DEVOTE, DEVOUTLY
Lk 2:25 and this man was just and ***d***,
Acts 2: 5 ***d*** men, from every nation under
8: 2 And ***d*** men carried Stephen to
10: 2 a ***d*** man and one who feared God
10: 7 his household servants and a ***d***
13:43 many of the Jews and ***d***
13:50 But the Jews stirred up the ***d***
17: 4 and a great multitude of the ***d***
22:12 a ***d*** man according to the law,

DEVOUTLY (1/1) DEVOUT
1 Th 2:10 how ***d*** and justly and

DEW (37/36)
Gen 27:28 may God give you Of the ***d*** of
27:39 And of the ***d*** of heaven from
Ex 16:13 and in the morning the ***d*** lay
16:14 And when the layer of ***d*** lifted,
Num 11: 9 And when the ***d*** fell on the camp
Deut 32: 2 My speech distill as the ***d***,
33:13 things of heaven, with the ***d***,
33:28 His heavens shall also drop ***d***.
Judg 6:37 if there is ***d*** on the fleece
6:38 he wrung the ***d*** out of the
6:39 all the ground let there be ***d***.
6:40 but there was ***d*** on all the
2 Sam 1:21 Let there be no ***d*** nor rain
17:12 we will fall on him as the ***d***
1 Ki 17: 1 there shall not be ***d*** nor rain
Job 29:19 And the ***d*** lies all night on my

29:22 speech settled on them as d.
38:28 who has begotten the drops of d?
Ps 110: 3 You have the d of Your youth.
133: 3 It is like the d of Hermon,
Prov 3:20 up, And clouds drop down the d.
19:12 But his favor is like d on
Song 5: 2 For my head is covered with d,
Isa 18: 4 Like a cloud of d in the heat
26:19 For your d is like the dew
26:19 For your dew is like the d
Dan 4:15 Let it be wet with the d of
4:23 let it be wet with the d of
4:25 They shall wet you with the d
4:33 his body was wet with the d of
5:21 his body was wet with the d of
Hos 6: 4 And like the early d it goes
13: 3 cloud And like the early d
14: 5 I will be like the d to Israel;
Mic 5: 7 Like d from the LORD, Like
Hag 1:10 above you withhold the d,
Zech 8:12 the heavens shall give their d—

DIADEM (2/2) DIADEMS

Isa 28: 5 For a crown of glory and a d
62: 3 And a royal d In the hand of

DIADEMS (1/1) DIADEM

Rev 12: 3 and seven d on his heads.

DIAL (1/1)

Isa 38: 8 returned ten degrees on the d

DIAMETER (2/1)

1 Ki 7:31 at the top was one cubit in d;
7:31 and a half cubits in outside d;

DIAMOND (4/4)

Ex 28:18 turquoise, a sapphire, and a d;
39:11 turquoise, a sapphire, and a d;
Jer 17: 1 With the point of a d it is
Ezek 28:13 The sardius, topaz, and d,

DIANA (5/5)

Acts 19:24 who made silver shrines of D,
19:27 temple of the great goddess D
19:28 Great is D of the Ephesians!"
19:34 Great is D of the Ephesians!"
19:35 guardian of the great goddess D,

DIBLAH (1/1)

Ezek 6:14 than the wilderness toward D,

DIBLAIM (1/1)

Hos 1: 3 took Gomer the daughter of D,

DIBLATH (KJV) See DIBLAH

DIBON (11/11) DIMON

Num 21:30 has perished as far as D.
32: 3 'Ataroth, D, Jazer, Nimrah,
32:34 And the children of Gad built D
33:45 from Ijim and camped at D Gad.
33:46 They moved from D Gad and
Josh 13: 9 the plain of Medeba as far as D;
13:17 the plain: D, Bamoth Baal,
Neh 11:25 D and its villages, Jekabzeel
Isa 15: 2 has gone up to the temple and D,
Jer 48:18 "O daughter inhabiting D,
48:22 On D and Nebo and Beth

DIBRI (1/1)

Lev 24:11 Shelomith the daughter of D,

DICTATES (9/9)

Deut 29:19 even though I follow the d of
Jer 3:17 No more shall they follow the d
7:24 the counsels and the d of
9:14 have walked according to the d
11: 8 but everyone followed the d of
13:10 who follow the d of their
16:12 each one follows the d of his
18:12 we will every one obey the d
23:17 who walks according to the d

DID (1309/1170)

Gen 4: 5 but He d not respect Cain and
6:22 Thus Noah d; according to
6:22 that God commanded him, so he d.
7: 5 And Noah d according to all that
8:12 which d not return again to him
9:23 and they d not see their
12:18 Why d you not tell me that she
12:19 Why d you say, 'She is my
15:10 but he d not cut the birds in
18:13 Why d Sarah laugh, saying,
18:15 I d not laugh," for she was
18:15 but you d laugh!"
19:33 and he d not know when she lay
19:35 and he d not know when she lay
20: 5 D he not say to me, 'She is my
20: 6 I know that you d this in the
20: 6 therefore I d not let you touch
20:10 What d you have in view, that
21: 1 and the LORD d for Sarah as He
21:26 you d not tell me, nor had I
26:22 and they d not quarrel over it.
27:23 And he d not recognize him,
28: 8 of Canaan d not please
28:16 and I d not know it."
29:28 Then Jacob d so and fulfilled
30:40 themselves and d not put them
30:42 he d not put them in; so the
31: 7 but God d not allow him to hurt
31:20 in that he d not tell him that
31:27 Why d you flee away secretly,
31:28 And you d not allow me to kiss
31:30 but why d you steal my gods?"
31:32 For Jacob d not know that
31:33 but he d not find them.
31:34 all about the tent but d not
31:35 And he searched but d not
31:39 torn by beasts I d not bring
32:25 Now when He saw that He d not
34:19 So the young man d not delay to
35: 5 and they d not pursue the sons
38:10 And the thing which he d
38:16 for he d not know that she was
38:20 but he d not find her.
38:26 because I d not give her to
38:29 'How d you break through?
39: 3 that the LORD made all he d
39: 6 and he d not know what he had
39:10 that he d not heed her, to lie
39:19 Your servant d to me after this
39:22 whatever they d there, it was
39:23 The keeper of the prison d not
39:23 was with him; and whatever he d,
40:23 Yet the chief butler d not
42: 4 But Jacob d not send Joseph's
42: 8 but they d not recognize him.
42:20 And they d so.
42:22 D I not speak to you, saying,
42:23 But they d not know that Joseph
42:25 Thus he d for them.
43: 6 Why d you deal so wrongfully
43:17 Then the man d as Joseph
44: 2 So he d according to the word
44:15 D you not know that such a man
45:21 Then the sons of Israel d so;
45:26 because he d not believe them.
47:22 of the priests he d not buy;
47:22 therefore they d not sell their
47:26 which d not become Pharaoh's.
50:12 So his sons d for him just as
50:15 us for all the evil which we d
50:17 for they d evil to you." '
Ex 1: 8 who d not know Joseph.
1:17 and d not do as the king of
2:13 to the one who d the wrong,
4:30 Then he d the signs in the
6: 9 but they d not heed Moses,
7: 6 Then Moses and Aaron d so; just
7: 6 LORD commanded them, so they d.
7:10 and they d so, just as the
7:11 they also d in like manner with
7:13 and he d not heed them, as the
7:20 And Moses and Aaron d so, just
7:22 Then the magicians of Egypt d so
7:22 and he d not heed them, as the
8: 7 And the magicians d so with
8:13 So the LORD d according to the
8:15 he hardened his heart and d not
8:17 And they d so. For Aaron
8:19 and he d not heed them, just as
8:24 And the LORD d so. Thick swarms
8:31 And the LORD d according to the
9: 6 So the LORD d this thing on the
9: 7 and he d not let the people go.
9:12 and he d not heed them, just as
9:21 But he who d not regard the word
10:20 and he d not let the children
10:23 They d not see one another;
10:23 nor d anyone rise from his
11:10 So Moses and Aaron d all these
11:10 and he d not let the children
12:28 of Israel went away and d so;
12:28 Moses and Aaron, so they d.
12:50 all the children of Israel d;
12:50 Moses and Aaron, so they d.
13: 8 because of what the LORD d
13:17 that God d not lead them by
13:22 He d not take away the pillar of
14: 4 And they d so.
14:20 so that the one d not come near
16:15 For they d not know what it
16:17 Then the children of Israel d so
16:20 Notwithstanding they d not heed
16:24 and it d not stink, nor were
17: 6 And Moses d so in the sight
17:10 So Joshua d as Moses said to
18:14 saw all that he d for the
18:24 of his father-in-law and d all
19: 4 You have seen what I d to the
21:13 if he d not lie in wait, but
24:11 Israel He d not lay His hand.
32:21 What d this people do to you
32:28 So the sons of Levi d according
32:35 people because of what they d
33:11 d not depart from the
34:29 that Moses d not know that the
36:11 likewise he d on the outer edge
39:32 And the children of Israel d
39:32 had commanded Moses; so they d.
39:42 so the children of Israel d all
40:16 Thus Moses d; according to
40:16 had commanded him, so he d.
40:37 then they d not journey till
Lev 4:20 shall do with the bull as he d
5:18 he erred and d not know it,
8: 4 So Moses d as the LORD
8:36 So Aaron and his sons d all the
10: 7 And they d according to the
16:15 do with that blood as he d with
16:34 And he d as the LORD
24:23 So the children of Israel d as
26:35 for the time it d not rest on
Num 1:54 Thus the children of Israel d;
1:54 commanded Moses, so they d.
2:34 children of Israel d according
5: 4 And the children of Israel d so,
5: 4 so the children of Israel d.
8: 3 And Aaron d so; he arranged the
8:20 of the children of Israel d to
8:20 so the children of Israel d to
8:22 so they d to them.
9: 5 so the children of Israel d.
9:13 because he d not bring the
9:19 the LORD and d not journey.
11:12 D I conceive all these people?
11:12 D I beget them, that You should
11:20 Why d we ever come up out of
11:25 although they never d so
12:15 and the people d not journey
14:22 glory and the signs which I d
15:26 because all the people d it
17:11 Thus d Moses; just as the LORD
17:11 had commanded him, so he d.
20:12 Because you d not believe Me, to
20:27 So Moses d just as the LORD
21:34 do to him as you d to Sihon
22:34 for I d not know You stood in
22:37 D I not earnestly send to you,
22:37 Why d you not come to me? Am I
23: 2 And Balak d just as Balaam had
23:26 D I not tell you, saying, 'All
23:30 And Balak d as Balaam had said,
24: 1 he d not go as at other times,
24:12 D I not also speak to your
25:11 so that I d not consume the
26:11 the children of Korah d not
27:22 So Moses d as the LORD
30:11 to her and d not overrule her,
31:31 Eleazar the priest d as the
32: 8 Thus your fathers d when I sent
32: 9 so that they d not go into the
36:10 so d the daughters of
Deut 1:30 according to all He d for you
1:32 you d not believe the LORD
2:12 just as Israel d to the land of
2:29 who dwell in Ar d for me,
2:37 Only you d not go near the land
3: 2 you shall do to him as you d to
3: 4 not a city which we d not take
3: 6 as we d to Sihon king of
4: 3 have seen what the LORD d at
4:33 D any people ever hear the
4:34 Or d God ever try to go and
4:34 all that the LORD your God d
5: 3 The LORD d not make this
5: 5 and you d not go up the
6:10 cities which you d not build,
6:11 which you d not fill, hewn-out
6:11 wells which you d not dig,
6:11 which you d not plant—when
7: 7 The LORD d not set His love on
7:18 LORD your God d to Pharaoh
8: 3 manna which you d not know
8: 3 nor d your fathers know,
8: 4 Your garments d not wear out on
8: 4 nor d your foot swell these
8:16 which your fathers d not know,
9:23 and you d not believe Him nor
11: 3 acts which He d in the midst
11: 4 what He d to the army of Egypt,
11: 5 what He d for you in the
11: 6 and what He d to Dathan and
11: 7 act of the LORD which He d.
12:30 How d these nations serve their
22:24 woman because she d not cry
23: 4 because they d not meet you with
24: 9 what the LORD your God d to
25:17 Remember what Amalek d to you
25:18 and he d not fear God.
28:45 because you d not obey the
28:47 Because you d not serve the
29: 2 have seen all that the LORD d
29:26 gods that they d not know and
31: 4 do to them as He d to Sihon
32:17 To gods they d not know, To
32:17 That your fathers d not fear.
32:51 because you d not hallow Me in
33: 9 Nor d he acknowledge his
34: 9 and d as the LORD had
Josh 2: 4 but I d not know where they
2:10 and what you d to the two kings
2:11 neither d there remain any more
2:22 but d not find them.
4: 8 the children of Israel d so,
4:23 as the LORD your God d to the
5: 6 because they d not obey the
5:15 And Joshua d so.
6:14 So they d six days.
8: 2 its king as you d to Jericho
8:14 But he d not know that there
8:17 in Ai or Bethel who d not go
8:26 For Joshua d not draw back his

8:35 had commanded which Joshua **d**
9: 9 and all that He **d** in Egypt,
9:10 and all that He **d** to the two
9:14 but they **d** not ask counsel of
9:18 children of Israel **d** not attack
9:26 So he **d** to them, and delivered
9:26 so that they **d** not kill them.
10:13 and **d** not hasten to go down
10:23 And they **d** so, and brought out
10:28 He also **d** to the king of
10:30 but **d** to its king as he had
10:39 so he **d** to Debir and its king,
11: 9 So Joshua **d** to them as the LORD
11:15 Joshua, and so Joshua **d**.
13:13 the children of Israel **d** not
14: 5 so the children of Israel **d**;
16:10 And they **d** not drive out the
17:13 but **d** not utterly drive them
20: 5 but **d** not hate him beforehand.
22:20 ***D*** not Achan the son of Zerah
22:20 And that man **d** not perish alone
24: 5 according to what I **d** among
24: 7 And your eyes saw what I **d** in
24:13 land for which you **d** not labor,
24:13 which you **d** not build,
24:13 groves which you **d** not plant.'
24:17 who **d** those great signs in our

Judg 1:21 of Benjamin **d** not drive
1:27 Manasseh **d** not drive out the
1:28 but **d** not completely drive them
1:29 Nor **d** Ephraim drive out the
1:30 Nor **d** Zebulun drive out the
1:31 Nor **d** Asher drive out the
1:32 for they **d** not drive them out.
1:33 Nor **d** Naphtali drive out the
2:10 after them who **d** not know
2:11 the children of Israel **d** evil
2:17 they **d** not do so.
2:19 They **d** not cease from their own
2:23 nor **d** He deliver them into the
3: 7 the children of Israel **d** evil
3:12 of Israel again **d** evil
3:22 for he **d** not draw the dagger
3:28 and **d** not allow anyone to cross
4: 1 of Israel again **d** evil
5:16 Why **d** you sit among the
5:17 And why **d** Dan remain on ships?
5:23 Because they **d** not come to the
6: 1 the children of Israel **d** evil
6:13 ***D*** not the LORD bring us up from
6:20 out the broth." And he **d** so.
6:27 servants and **d** as the LORD
6:27 he **d** it by night.
6:40 And God **d** so that night. It was
8:34 of Israel **d** not remember
8:35 nor **d** they show kindness to the
10: 6 children of Israel again **d** evil
10: 6 the LORD and **d** not serve
10:11 ***D*** I not deliver you from the
11: 7 ***D*** you not hate me, and expel me
11:15 Israel **d** not take away the land
11:18 But they **d** not enter the border
11:20 But Sihon **d** not trust Israel to
11:25 ***D*** he ever strive against
11:25 ***D*** he ever fight against them?
11:26 why **d** you not recover them
11:28 people of Ammon **d** not heed
12: 1 Why **d** you cross over to fight
12: 1 and **d** not call us to go with
12: 2 you **d** not deliver me out of
13: 1 children of Israel **d** evil
13: 6 but I **d** not ask Him where He
13: 6 and He **d** not tell me His name.
13:16 (For Manoah **d** not know He
13:19 And He **d** a wondrous thing while
14: 4 father and mother **d** not know
14: 6 But he **d** not tell his father or
14: 9 But he **d** not tell them that he
15:11 As they **d** to me, so I have done
16:20 But he **d** not know that the
17: 6 everyone **d** what was right in
18: 4 'Thus and so Micah **d** for me.
20: 3 how **d** this wicked deed
20:34 But the Benjamites **d** not know
21: 5 tribes of Israel who **d** not come
21: 8 tribes of Israel who **d** not come
21:22 because we **d** not take a wife
21:23 the children of Benjamin **d** so;
21:25 everyone **d** what was right in

Ruth 2:11 a people whom you **d** not know
2:19 And where **d** you work? Blessed
3: 6 floor and **d** according to all
3:10 in that you **d** not go after

1 Sam 1: 7 she wept and **d** not eat.
1:22 But Hannah **d** not go up, for she
2:12 they **d** not know the LORD.
2:14 So they **d** in Shiloh to all the
2:22 he heard everything his sons **d**
2:25 Nevertheless they **d** not heed
2:27 ***D*** I not clearly reveal Myself to
2:28 ***D*** I not choose him out of all
2:28 And **d** I not give to the house
3: 5 I **d** not call; lie down again."
3: 6 I **d** not call, my son; lie down
3: 7 (Now Samuel **d** not yet know the
3: 8 for you **d** call me." Then Eli
3:13 and he **d** not restrain them.
4:20 But she **d** not answer, nor did
4:20 nor **d** she regard it.
5:12 And the men who **d** not die were
6: 6 When He **d** mighty things among
6: 6 **d** they not let the people go,
6:10 Then the men **d** so; they took
6:12 and **d** not turn aside to the
7:13 and they **d** not come anymore
8: 3 But his sons **d** not walk in his
9: 4 but they **d** not find them.
9: 4 but they **d** not find them.
10:14 Where **d** you go?" So he said,
10:16 he **d** not tell him what Samuel
12: 7 acts of the LORD which He **d**
13: 8 But Samuel **d** not come to
13:11 and that you **d** not come within
14: 1 But he **d** not tell his father.
14: 3 But the people **d** not know that
14:37 But He **d** not answer him that
14:45 Jonathan, and he **d** not die.
15: 2 punish Amalek for what he **d**
15:17 And **d** not the LORD anoint you
15:19 Why then **d** you not obey the
15:19 Why **d** you swoop down on the
16: 4 So Samuel **d** what the LORD said,
17:28 'Why **d** you come down here?
17:30 him as the first ones **d**.
20:26 Nevertheless Saul **d** not say
20:39 But the lad **d** not know anything.
21:11 ***D*** they not sing of him to one
22:15 ***D*** I then begin to inquire of God
22:17 when he fled and **d** not tell
23:14 but God **d** not deliver him into
24: 7 and **d** not allow them to rise
24:11 and **d** not kill you, know and
24:18 your hand, you **d** not kill me.
25: 7 and we **d** not hurt them, nor was
25:15 nor **d** we miss anything as long
25:19 But she **d** not tell her
25:25 **d** not see the young men of my
27:11 on us, saying, 'Thus David **d**.
28: 6 the LORD **d** not answer him,
28:13 What **d** you see?" And the woman
28:18 Because you **d** not obey the voice
30: 2 they **d** not kill anyone, but
30:22 Because they **d** not go with us,

2 Sam 1: 4 How **d** the matter go? Please tell
1:11 and so **d** all the men who
1:22 The bow of Jonathan **d** not turn
1:22 And the sword of Saul **d** not
2:19 and in going he **d** not turn to
2:28 stood still and **d** not pursue
2:28 nor **d** they fight anymore.
3:26 But David **d** not know it.
3:36 since whatever the king **d**
5:25 And David **d** so, as the LORD
11: 9 and **d** not go down to his house.
11:10 Uriah **d** not go down to his
11:10 ***D*** you not come from a journey?
11:10 Why **d** you not go down to your
11:13 but he **d** not go down to his
11:20 Why **d** you approach so near to
11:20 ***D*** you not know that they would
11:21 Why **d** you go near the
12: 6 because he **d** this thing and
12:12 For you **d** it secretly, but I
12:17 nor **d** he eat food with them.
12:31 So he **d** to all the cities of
13:16 than the other that you **d** to
13:29 So the servants of Absalom **d** to
14:24 but **d** not see the king's face.
14:28 but **d** not see the king's face.
15:11 innocently and **d** not know
16:17 Why **d** you not go with your
18:11 And why **d** you not strike him
18:29 but I **d** not know what it was
19:19 what wrong your servant **d** on
19:25 Why **d** you not go with me,
20: 3 but **d** not go in to them.
20:10 But Amasa **d** not notice the sword
20:10 and he **d** not strike him again.
21:10 And she **d** not allow the birds
22:23 I **d** not depart from them.
22:37 So my feet **d** not slip.
22:38 Neither **d** I turn back again
22:42 but He **d** not answer them.
23:19 he **d** not attain to the first
23:22 Benaiah the son of Jehoiada **d**,
23:23 but he **d** not attain to the

1 Ki 1: 4 but the king **d** not know her.
1:10 But he **d** not invite Nathan the
1:13 ***D*** you not, my lord, O king,
1:16 Bathsheba bowed and **d** homage
2: 5 what Joab the son of Zeruiah **d**
2: 5 and what he **d** to the two
2:32 father David **d** not know it.
2:42 ***D*** I not make you swear by the
2:44 all the wickedness that you **d**
7:14 King Solomon and **d** all his
7:18 and thus he **d** for the other
7:47 And Solomon **d** not weigh all the
8:18 you **d** well that it was in your
9:12 but they **d** not please him.
9:23 over the people who **d** the work.
10: 7 However I **d** not believe the
11: 6 Solomon **d** evil in the sight of
11: 6 and **d** not fully follow the
11: 6 as **d** his father David.
11: 8 And he **d** likewise for all his
11:10 but he **d** not keep what the
11:33 as **d** his father David.
11:38 as My servant David **d**,
11:41 acts of Solomon, all that he **d**,
12:15 So the king **d** not listen to the
12:16 saw that the king **d** not listen
12:32 So he **d** at Bethel, sacrificing
13:10 another way and **d** not return
13:12 Which way **d** he go?" For his
13:33 this event Jeroboam **d** not turn
14: 4 And Jeroboam's wife **d** so;
14:22 Now Judah **d** evil in the sight of
14:24 They **d** according to all the
14:29 of Rehoboam, and all that he **d**,
15: 5 because David **d** what was right
15: 7 of Abijam, and all that he **d**,
15:11 Asa **d** what was right in the
15:11 as **d** his father David.
15:23 all his might, all that he **d**,
15:26 And he **d** evil in the sight of
15:29 He **d** not leave to Jeroboam
15:31 of Nadab, and all that he **d**,
15:34 He **d** evil in the sight of the
16: 5 the acts of Baasha, what he **d**,
16: 7 of all the evil that he **d** in
16:11 he **d** not leave him one male,
16:14 acts of Elah, and all that he **d**,
16:25 Omri **d** evil in the eyes of the
16:25 and **d** worse than all who were
16:27 of the acts of Omri which he **d**,
16:30 Now Ahab the son of Omri **d** evil
16:33 Ahab **d** more to provoke the
17: 5 So he went and **d** according to
17:15 So she went away and **d** according
17:16 nor **d** the jar of oil run dry,
18:13 reported to my lord what I **d**
18:34 and they **d** it a second time;
18:34 and they **d** it a third time.
20: 7 and I **d** not deny him."
20:25 their voice and **d** so.
20:34 as my father **d** in Samaria."
21:11 **d** as Jezebel had sent to them,
22:18 ***D*** I not tell you he would not
22:24 Which way **d** the spirit from the
22:39 acts of Ahab, and all that he **d**,
22:43 He **d** not turn aside from them,
22:52 He **d** evil in the sight of the

2 Ki 1:18 the acts of Ahaziah which he **d**,
2:17 searched for three days but **d**
2:18 ***D*** I not say to you, 'Do not
3: 2 And he **d** evil in the sight of
3: 3 he **d** not depart from them.
4:28 ***D*** I ask a son of my lord? Did I
4:28 ***D*** I not say, 'Do not deceive
4:39 though they **d** not know what
5:25 'Where **d** you go, Gehazi?"
5:25 Your servant **d** not go
5:26 ***D*** not my heart go with you
6: 6 Where **d** it fall?" And he showed
8: 2 arose and **d** according to
8:14 What **d** Elisha say to you?" And
8:18 and he **d** evil in the sight of
8:23 of Joram, and all that he **d**,
8:27 and **d** evil in the sight of the
9:11 Why **d** this madman come to
10:21 not a man left who **d** not come.
10:29 However Jehu **d** not turn away
10:31 for he **d** not depart from the
10:34 the acts of Jehu, all that he **d**,
11: 9 the hundreds **d** according to
12: 2 Jehoash **d** what was right in
12:11 hands of those who **d** the work,
12:15 Moreover they **d** not require an
12:19 of Joash, and all that he **d**,
13: 2 And he **d** evil in the sight of
13: 2 He **d** not depart from them.
13: 6 Nevertheless they **d** not depart
13: 8 acts of Jehoahaz, all that he **d**,
13:11 And he **d** evil in the sight of
13:11 He **d** not depart from all the
13:12 acts of Joash, all that he **d**,
14: 3 And he **d** what was right in the
14: 3 he **d** everything as his father
14: 6 the murderers he **d** not execute,
14:15 the acts of Jehoash which he **d**—
14:24 And he **d** evil in the sight of
14:24 he **d** not depart from all the
14:27 And the LORD **d** not say that He
14:28 of Jeroboam, and all that he **d**—
15: 3 And he **d** what was right in the
15: 6 of Azariah, and all that he **d**,
15: 9 And he **d** evil in the sight of
15: 9 he **d** not depart from the sins
15:16 Because they **d** not surrender,
15:18 And he **d** evil in the sight of
15:18 he **d** not depart all his days
15:20 and **d** not stay there in the
15:21 of Menahem, and all that he **d**,
15:24 And he **d** evil in the sight of
15:24 he **d** not depart from the sins
15:26 of Pekahiah, and all that he **d**,
15:28 And he **d** evil in the sight of
15:28 he **d** not depart from the sins
15:31 of Pekah, and all that he **d**,
15:34 And he **d** what was right in the
15:34 he **d** according to all that his
15:36 of Jotham, and all that he **d**,
16: 2 and he **d** not do what was
16:16 Thus **d** Urijah the priest,
16:19 of the acts of Ahaz which he **d**,
17: 2 And he **d** evil in the sight of
17: 9 of Israel secretly **d** against
17:11 and they **d** wicked things to
17:14 who **d** not believe in the LORD
17:19 Also Judah **d** not keep the
17:22 the sins of Jeroboam which he **d**;
17:22 they **d** not depart from them,
17:25 that they **d** not fear the

17:40 However they ***d*** not obey, but
17:41 doing as their fathers ***d***.
18: 3 And he ***d*** what was right in the
18: 6 he ***d*** not depart from following
18: 7 Assyria and ***d*** not serve him.
18:12 because they ***d*** not obey the
19:25 ***D*** you not hear long ago How I
20:13 that Hezekiah ***d*** not show them.
20:14 What ***d*** these men say, and from
20:14 and from where ***d*** they come to
21: 2 And he ***d*** evil in the sight of
21: 6 He ***d*** much evil in the sight of
21:17 acts of Manasseh—all that he ***d***,
21:20 And he ***d*** evil in the sight of
21:22 and ***d*** not walk in the way of
21:25 of the acts of Amon which he ***d***,
22: 2 And he ***d*** what was right in the
22: 2 he ***d*** not turn aside to the
23: 9 priests of the high places ***d***
23:19 and he ***d*** to them according to
23:25 nor after him ***d*** any arise like
23:26 Nevertheless the LORD ***d*** not
23:28 of Josiah, and all that he ***d***,
23:32 And he ***d*** evil in the sight of
23:37 And he ***d*** evil in the sight of
24: 5 of Jehoiakim, and all that he ***d***,
24: 7 And the king of Egypt ***d*** not come
24: 9 And he ***d*** evil in the sight of
24:19 He also ***d*** evil in the sight of
1 Chr 4:27 but his brothers ***d*** not have
4:27 nor ***d*** any of their families
10:13 because he ***d*** not keep the word
10:14 But he ***d*** not inquire of the
11:21 However he ***d*** not attain to the
11:24 Benaiah the son of Jehoiada ***d***,
11:25 but he ***d*** not attain to the
12:19 but they ***d*** not help them, for
14:16 So David ***d*** as God commanded him,
15:13 For because you ***d*** not do it
15:13 because we ***d*** not consult Him
19: 3 ***D*** his servants not come to you
20: 3 So David ***d*** to all the cities of
21: 6 But he ***d*** not count Levi and
23:11 But Jeush and Beriah ***d*** not have
23:24 who ***d*** the work for the service
24:31 brothers the sons of Aaron ***d***,
24:31 The chief fathers ***d*** just as
27:23 But David ***d*** not take the number
27:24 but he ***d*** not finish, for wrath
27:26 was over those who ***d*** the work
2 Chr 6: 5 nor ***d*** I choose any man to be a
6: 8 you ***d*** well in that it was in
8: 8 whom the children of Israel ***d***
8: 9 But Solomon ***d*** not make the
8:15 They ***d*** not depart from the
9: 6 However I ***d*** not believe their
10:15 So the king ***d*** not listen to the
10:16 that the king ***d*** not listen
12:14 And he ***d*** evil, because he did
12:14 because he ***d*** not prepare his
13:20 So Jeroboam ***d*** not recover
14: 2 Asa ***d*** what was good and right
16:12 in his disease he ***d*** not seek
17: 3 he ***d*** not seek the Baals,
17:10 so that they ***d*** not make war
18:17 ***D*** I not tell you he would not
18:23 Which way ***d*** the spirit from the
20:10 from them and ***d*** not destroy
20:32 and ***d*** not turn aside from it,
21: 6 and he ***d*** evil in the sight of
22: 4 Therefore he ***d*** evil in the sight
22:11 Athaliah so that she ***d*** not kill
23: 8 and all Judah ***d*** according to
24: 2 Joash ***d*** what was right in the
24: 5 However the Levites ***d*** not do
24:11 Thus they ***d*** day by day, and
24:12 to those who ***d*** the work
24:22 the king ***d*** not remember
24:25 but they ***d*** not bury him in the
25: 2 And he ***d*** what was right in the
25: 4 However he ***d*** not execute their
25: 4 but ***d*** as it is written in
26: 4 And he ***d*** what was right in the
27: 2 And he ***d*** what was right in the
27: 2 (although he ***d*** not enter the
28: 1 and he ***d*** not do what was
28:20 and ***d*** not assist him.
28:21 but he ***d*** not help him.
28:27 but they ***d*** not bring him into
29: 2 And he ***d*** what was right in the
31:20 Thus Hezekiah ***d*** throughout all
31:20 and he ***d*** what was good and
31:21 he ***d*** it with all his heart.
32:25 But Hezekiah ***d*** not repay
32:26 wrath of the LORD ***d*** not come
33: 2 But he ***d*** evil in the sight of
33: 6 He ***d*** much evil in the sight of
33:22 But he ***d*** evil in the sight of
33:23 And he ***d*** not humble himself
34: 2 And he ***d*** what was right in the
34: 2 he ***d*** not turn aside to the
34: 6 And so he ***d*** in the cities of
34:12 And the men ***d*** the work
34:13 overseers of all who ***d*** work
34:32 of Jerusalem ***d*** according to
34:33 All his days they ***d*** not depart
35:12 And so they ***d*** with the
35:15 they ***d*** not have to leave their
35:22 and ***d*** not heed the words of
36: 5 And he ***d*** evil in the sight of
36: 8 the abominations which he ***d***,
36: 9 And he ***d*** evil in the sight of
36:12 He ***d*** evil in the sight of the
36:12 and ***d*** not humble himself
Ezra 6:13 diligently ***d*** according to
9: 9 Yet our God ***d*** not forsake us in
10:16 of the captivity ***d*** so.
Neh 2:16 And the officials ***d*** not know
2:16 or the others who ***d*** the work.
3: 5 but their nobles ***d*** not put
5:13 Then the people ***d*** according to
5:15 but I ***d*** not do so, because of
5:16 and we ***d*** not buy any land. All
5:18 of this I ***d*** not demand
9:16 And ***d*** not heed Your
9:17 wonders That You ***d*** among
9:17 And ***d*** not forsake them.
9:19 mercies You ***d*** not forsake
9:19 of the cloud ***d*** not depart
9:20 And ***d*** not withhold Your manna
9:21 Their clothes ***d*** not wear out
9:21 And their feet ***d*** not swell.
9:28 They again ***d*** evil before You.
9:29 And ***d*** not heed Your
9:31 You ***d*** not utterly consume
9:35 Nor ***d*** they turn from their
11:12 Their brethren who ***d*** the work of
13:10 the singers who ***d*** the work
13:18 ***D*** not your fathers do thus, and
13:18 and ***d*** not our God bring all
13:26 ***D*** not Solomon king of Israel sin
Esth 1:15 because she ***d*** not obey the
1:17 but she ***d*** not come.'
1:21 and the king ***d*** according to the
2: 4 the king, and he ***d*** so.
3: 5 saw that Mordecai ***d*** not bow
4:17 went his way and ***d*** according
5: 9 and that he ***d*** not stand or
9: 5 and ***d*** what they pleased with
9:10 but they ***d*** not lay a hand on
9:15 but they ***d*** not lay a hand on
9:16 but they ***d*** not lay a hand on
Job 1: 5 Thus Job ***d*** regularly.
1:22 In all this Job ***d*** not sin nor
2:10 In all this Job ***d*** not sin
2:12 and ***d*** not recognize him, they
3:10 Because it ***d*** not shut up the
3:11 'Why ***d*** I not die at birth?
3:11 Why ***d*** I not perish when I
3:12 Why ***d*** the knees receive me?
6:22 ***D*** I ever say, 'Bring something
10:10 ***D*** you not pour me out like
20:19 house which he ***d*** not build.
23:17 And He ***d*** not hide deep
29:16 the case that I ***d*** not know.
29:22 After my words they ***d*** not speak
29:24 they ***d*** not believe it, And
29:24 countenance they ***d*** not cast
31:15 ***D*** not He who made me in the
31:15 ***D*** not the same One fashion us
31:34 kept silence And ***d*** not go out
32:16 because they ***d*** not speak,
33:27 And it ***d*** not profit me.'
39:17 And ***d*** not endow her with
42: 3 what I ***d*** not understand,
42: 3 which I ***d*** not know.
42: 9 the Naamathite went and ***d*** as
Ps 18:22 And I ***d*** not put away His
18:36 So my feet ***d*** not slip.
18:37 Neither ***d*** I turn back again
18:41 but He ***d*** not answer them.
35:15 And I ***d*** not know it; They
35:15 tore at me and ***d*** not cease;
39: 9 I ***d*** not open my mouth, Because
39: 9 Because it was You who ***d*** it.
40: 6 and offering You ***d*** not desire;
40: 6 offering You ***d*** not require.
44: 1 The deeds You ***d*** in their days,
44: 3 For they ***d*** not gain possession
44: 3 Nor ***d*** their own arm save them;
52: 7 Here is the man who ***d*** not make
60:10 who ***d*** not go out with our
78: 8 A generation that ***d*** not set
78:10 They ***d*** not keep the covenant of
78:12 Marvelous things He ***d*** in the
78:22 Because they ***d*** not believe in
78:22 And ***d*** not trust in His
78:32 AND ***d*** not believe in His
78:38 And ***d*** not destroy them.
78:38 And ***d*** not stir up all His
78:42 They ***d*** not remember His power:
78:50 He ***d*** not spare their soul from
78:53 so that they ***d*** not fear;
78:56 And ***d*** not keep His
78:67 And ***d*** not choose the tribe of
81: 5 language I ***d*** not understand.
105:28 And they ***d*** not rebel against
106: 7 in Egypt ***d*** not understand
106: 7 They ***d*** not remember the
106:13 They ***d*** not wait for His
106:24 They ***d*** not believe His word,
106:25 And ***d*** not heed the voice of
106:34 They ***d*** not destroy the peoples,
108:11 who ***d*** not go out with our
109:16 Because he ***d*** not remember to
109:17 As he ***d*** not delight in
119:60 and ***d*** not delay To keep Your
119:87 But I ***d*** not forsake Your
Prov 1:29 And ***d*** not choose the fear
7:23 He ***d*** not know it would cost
23:35 but I ***d*** not feel it.
24:12 Surely we ***d*** not know this,"
Eccl 2:10 my eyes desired I ***d*** not keep
2:10 I ***d*** not withhold my heart from
Song 3: 1 but I ***d*** not find him.
3: 2 but I ***d*** not find him.
Isa 5: 4 ***D*** it bring forth wild grapes?
14:17 Who ***d*** not open the house of
20: 2 And he ***d*** so, walking naked
22:11 But you ***d*** not look to its
22:11 Nor ***d*** you have respect for Him
29:16 He ***d*** not make me"? Or shall
37:26 ***D*** you not hear long ago How I
39: 2 that Hezekiah ***d*** not show
39: 3 What ***d*** these men say, and from
39: 3 and from where ***d*** they come to
40:14 With whom ***d*** He take counsel,
42:16 by a way they ***d*** not know;
42:25 Yet he ***d*** not know; And it
42:25 Yet he ***d*** not take it to
45:18 Who ***d*** not create it in vain,
45:19 I ***d*** not say to the seed of
47: 7 So that you ***d*** not take these
48: 3 Suddenly I ***d*** them, and they
48: 6 and you ***d*** not know them.
48: 8 Surely you ***d*** not hear, Surely
48: 8 Surely you ***d*** not know; Surely
48:21 And they ***d*** not thirst When He
50: 5 Nor ***d*** I turn away.
50: 6 I ***d*** not hide My face from
53: 3 and we ***d*** not esteem Him.
57:10 Yet you ***d*** not say, 'There is
58: 2 that ***d*** righteousness,
58: 2 And ***d*** not forsake the
64: 3 When You ***d*** awesome things for
64: 3 for which we ***d*** not look,
65: 1 by those who ***d*** not ask
65: 1 by those who ***d*** not seek
65:12 you ***d*** not answer; When I
65:12 you ***d*** not hear, But did evil
65:12 But ***d*** evil before My eyes,
66: 4 When I spoke they ***d*** not hear;
66: 4 But they ***d*** evil before My
Jer 2: 6 Neither ***d*** they say, 'Where is
2: 8 The priests ***d*** not say, 'Where
2: 8 who handle the law ***d*** not know
3: 7 But she ***d*** not return. And her
3: 8 sister Judah ***d*** not fear,
6:15 Nor ***d*** they know how to blush.
7:12 and see what I ***d*** to it because
7:13 but you ***d*** not hear, and I
7:13 but you ***d*** not answer,
7:22 For I ***d*** not speak to your
7:24 Yet they ***d*** not obey or incline
7:26 Yet they ***d*** not obey Me or
7:26 They ***d*** worse than their
7:31 which I ***d*** not command, nor did
7:31 nor ***d*** it come into My heart.
8:12 Nor ***d*** they know how to blush.
11: 8 Yet they ***d*** not obey or incline
11:19 and I ***d*** not know that they had
14:15 whom I ***d*** not send, and who say,
15: 4 for what he ***d*** in Jerusalem.
15:17 I ***d*** not sit in the assembly of
15:17 Nor ***d*** I rejoice; I sat alone
17:23 But they ***d*** not obey nor incline
19: 5 which I ***d*** not command or speak,
19: 5 nor ***d*** it come into My mind),
20:16 and ***d*** not relent; Let him hear
20:17 Because he ***d*** not kill me from
20:18 Why ***d*** I come forth from the
22:15 ***D*** not your father eat and
22:21 That you ***d*** not obey My voice.
23:32 Yet I ***d*** not send them or
26:19 ***D*** Hezekiah king of Judah and all
26:19 ***D*** he not fear the LORD and
27:20 king of Babylon ***d*** not take,
32:35 which I ***d*** not command them, nor
32:35 nor ***d*** it come into My mind that
34:14 But your fathers ***d*** not obey
34:15 you recently turned and ***d*** what
35:14 you ***d*** not obey Me.
36: 8 son of Neriah ***d*** according to
36:17 how ***d*** you write all these
36:24 nor ***d*** they tear their garments,
36:31 but they ***d*** not heed." '"
37:14 But he ***d*** not listen to him.
38:12 And Jeremiah ***d*** so.
40:14 son of Ahikam ***d*** not believe
41: 8 So he desisted and ***d*** not kill
43: 7 for they ***d*** not obey the voice
44: 3 gods whom they ***d*** not know,
44: 5 But they ***d*** not listen or incline
44:19 ***d*** we make cakes for her, to
44:21 ***d*** not the LORD remember them,
44:21 and ***d*** it not come into His
46: 5 And ***d*** not look back, For
46:15 They ***d*** not stand Because the
46:21 They ***d*** not stand, For the day
52: 2 He also ***d*** evil in the sight of
Lam 1: 9 She ***d*** not consider her
2: 1 And ***d*** not remember His
Ezek 1: 9 The creatures ***d*** not turn when
1:12 and they ***d*** not turn when they
1:17 they ***d*** not turn aside when they
3:20 because you ***d*** not give him
10:11 they ***d*** not turn aside when they
10:11 They ***d*** not turn aside when they
10:16 the same wheels also ***d*** not turn
12: 7 So I ***d*** as I was commanded.
16:22 harlotry you ***d*** not remember
16:43 Because you ***d*** not remember the
16:47 You ***d*** not walk in their ways nor
16:49 neither ***d*** she strengthen the
16:51 Samaria ***d*** not commit half of
16:54 be disgraced by all that you ***d***

D

17:18 and still ***d*** all these things,
18:18 And ***d*** what is not good among
20: 8 They ***d*** not all cast away the
20: 8 nor ***d*** they forsake the idols of
20:13 they ***d*** not walk in My statutes;
20:16 judgments and ***d*** not walk
20:17 I ***d*** not make an end of them in
20:21 they ***d*** not walk in My statutes,
24: 7 She ***d*** not pour it on the
24:18 and the next morning I ***d*** as I
25:12 Because of what Edom ***d*** against
33: 5 but ***d*** not take warning; his
34: 8 nor ***d*** My shepherds search for
34: 8 fed themselves and ***d*** not feed
42: 6 three stories and ***d*** not have
46:12 his peace offerings as he ***d*** on
48:11 who ***d*** not go astray when the
Dan 3:24 ***D*** we not cast three men bound
4: 7 but they ***d*** not make known to me
8: 4 but he ***d*** according to his will
8:12 He ***d*** all this and prospered.
10: 3 nor ***d*** I anoint myself at all,
10: 7 who were with me ***d*** not see
11:38 which his fathers ***d*** not know
12: 8 I ***d*** not understand. Then I
Hos 2: 8 For she ***d*** not know That I gave
7:14 They ***d*** not cry out to Me with
8: 4 but I ***d*** not acknowledge them.
9:17 Because they ***d*** not obey Him;
10: 3 Because we ***d*** not fear the
10: 9 iniquity ***D*** not overtake
11: 3 But they ***d*** not know that I
Am 1: 9 And ***d*** not remember the
4: 7 And where it ***d*** not rain the
5:25 ***D*** you offer Me sacrifices and
9: 7 ***D*** I not bring up Israel from the
Jon 3:10 and He ***d*** not do it.
Hag 2:17 yet you ***d*** not turn to Me,'
Zech 1: 4 But they ***d*** not hear nor
1: 6 ***D*** they not overtake your
7: 5 ***d*** you really fast for Me—for
Mal 2:15 But ***d*** He not make them one,
Mt 1:24 ***d*** as the angel of the Lord
1:25 and ***d*** not know her till she had
5:17 I ***d*** not come to destroy but to
7:25 and it ***d*** not fall, for it was
9:13 For I ***d*** not come to call the
9:19 and so ***d*** His disciples.
10:34 I ***d*** not come to bring peace but
11: 7 What ***d*** you go out into the
11: 8 'But what ***d*** you go out to see?
11: 9 'But what ***d*** you go out to see?
11:17 And you ***d*** not dance;
11:17 And you ***d*** not lament.'
11:20 because they ***d*** not repent:
12: 3 you not read what David ***d***
13: 5 where they ***d*** not have much
13:17 and ***d*** not see it, and to hear
13:17 and ***d*** not hear it.
13:27 ***d*** you not sow good seed in your
13:34 a parable He ***d*** not speak
13:54 Where ***d*** this Man get this
13:56 Where then ***d*** this Man get all
13:58 Now He ***d*** not do many mighty
14:31 why ***d*** you doubt?"
15: 7 Hypocrites! Well ***d*** Isaiah
16:11 understand that I ***d*** not speak
16:12 understood that He ***d*** not tell
17:12 and they ***d*** not know him but did
17:12 they did not know him but ***d*** to
18:13 ninety-nine that ***d*** not go
19: 7 Why then ***d*** Moses command to give
20: 5 ninth hour, and ***d*** likewise.
20:13 ***D*** you not agree with me for a
20:28 the Son of Man ***d*** not come to
21: 6 So the disciples went and ***d*** as
21:15 the wonderful things that He ***d***,
21:20 How ***d*** the fig tree wither away
21:25 Why then ***d*** you not believe him?'
21:30 but he ***d*** not go.
21:31 Which of the two ***d*** the will of
21:32 and you ***d*** not believe him; but
21:32 you ***d*** not afterward relent and
21:36 and they ***d*** likewise to them.
22:11 man there who ***d*** not have
22:12 how ***d*** you come in here without
22:46 nor from that day on ***d*** anyone
24:39 and ***d*** not know until the flood
25:37 when ***d*** we see You hungry and
25:38 When ***d*** we see You a stranger and
25:39 Or when ***d*** we see You sick, or in
25:40 inasmuch as you ***d*** it to one of
25:40 you ***d*** it to Me.'
25:43 stranger and you ***d*** not take Me
25:43 naked and you ***d*** not clothe Me,
25:43 in prison and you ***d*** not visit
25:44 when ***d*** we see You hungry or
25:44 and ***d*** not minister to You?'
25:45 inasmuch as you ***d*** not do it to
25:45 you ***d*** not do it to Me.'
26:12 she ***d*** it for My burial.
26:19 So the disciples ***d*** as Jesus had
26:55 and you ***d*** not seize Me.
28:15 So they took the money and ***d*** as
Mk 1:24 ***D*** You come to destroy us?
1:34 and He ***d*** not allow the demons
2:17 I ***d*** not come to call the
2:25 you never read what David ***d***
4: 5 where it ***d*** not have much earth;
4:34 a parable He ***d*** not speak
5:19 Jesus ***d*** not permit him, but
6: 2 Where ***d*** this Man get these
6:20 he ***d*** many things, and heard him
6:26 he ***d*** not want to refuse her.
6:31 and they ***d*** not even have time
7: 6 Well ***d*** Isaiah prophesy of you
8:14 and they ***d*** not have more than
8:19 full of fragments ***d*** you take
8:20 full of fragments ***d*** you take
9: 6 because he ***d*** not know what to
9:13 and they ***d*** to him whatever they
9:30 and He ***d*** not want anyone to
9:32 But they ***d*** not understand this
10: 3 What ***d*** Moses command you?"
10:45 the Son of Man ***d*** not come to
11:31 Why then ***d*** you not believe him?'
12:21 nor ***d*** he leave any offspring.
14:40 and they ***d*** not know what to
14:49 and you ***d*** not seize Me. But the
14:56 testimonies ***d*** not agree.
14:59 But not even then ***d*** their
15:23 but He ***d*** not take it.
16:11 they ***d*** not believe.
16:13 but they ***d*** not believe them
16:14 because they ***d*** not believe
Lk 1:20 because you ***d*** not believe my
2:37 who ***d*** not depart from the
2:43 and His mother ***d*** not know
2:45 So when they ***d*** not find Him,
2:49 Why ***d*** you seek Me? Did you not
2:49 ***D*** you not know that I must be
2:50 But they ***d*** not understand the
4:34 ***D*** You come to destroy us? I
4:35 out of him and ***d*** not hurt
4:41 ***d*** not allow them to speak, for
6: 3 what David ***d*** when he was
6:10 And he ***d*** so, and his hand was
6:23 their fathers ***d*** to the
6:26 For so ***d*** their fathers to the
6:49 But he who heard and ***d*** nothing
7: 7 Therefore I ***d*** not even think
7:24 What ***d*** you go out into the
7:25 'But what ***d*** you go out to see?
7:26 'But what ***d*** you go out to see?
7:32 And you ***d*** not dance;
7:32 And you ***d*** not weep.'
7:46 You ***d*** not anoint My head with
8:27 nor ***d*** he live in a house but in
9:15 And they ***d*** so, and made them all
9:43 at all the things which Jesus ***d***,
9:45 But they ***d*** not understand this
9:45 so that they ***d*** not perceive
9:53 But they ***d*** not receive Him,
9:54 consume them, just as Elijah ***d***?
9:56 For the Son of Man ***d*** not come to
11:40 Foolish ones! ***D*** not He who made
11:52 You ***d*** not enter in yourselves,
12:47 and ***d*** not prepare himself or
12:48 But he who ***d*** not know, yet
17: 9 that servant because he ***d*** the
18: 2 city a judge who ***d*** not fear
18:34 and they ***d*** not know the things
19:21 what you ***d*** not deposit,
19:21 and reap what you ***d*** not sow.'
19:22 collecting what I ***d*** not deposit
19:22 reaping what I ***d*** not sow.
19:23 Why then ***d*** you not put my money
19:27 who ***d*** not want me to reign over
19:44 because you ***d*** not know the time
20: 5 Why then ***d*** you not believe him?'
20: 7 answered that they ***d*** not know
22:35 ***d*** you lack anything?" So they
22:53 you ***d*** not try to seize Me.
23:15 neither ***d*** Herod, for I sent you
24: 3 Then they went in and ***d*** not find
24:11 and they ***d*** not believe them.
24:16 so that they ***d*** not know Him.
24:23 When they ***d*** not find His body,
24:24 but Him they ***d*** not see."
24:32 ***D*** not our heart burn within us
24:41 they still ***d*** not believe
Jn 1: 5 darkness ***d*** not comprehend
1:10 and the world ***d*** not know Him.
1:11 and His own ***d*** not receive Him.
1:20 and ***d*** not deny, but confessed,
1:31 I ***d*** not know Him; but that He
1:33 I ***d*** not know Him, but He who
2: 9 and ***d*** not know where it came
2:11 beginning of signs Jesus ***d*** in
2:12 and they ***d*** not stay there many
2:23 they saw the signs which He ***d***.
2:24 But Jesus ***d*** not commit Himself
3:17 For God ***d*** not send His Son into
4: 2 Jesus Himself ***d*** not baptize,
4:29 me all things that I ever ***d***.
4:39 "He told me all that I ever ***d***.
4:45 seen all the things He ***d*** in
4:54 is the second sign Jesus ***d***
5:13 one who was healed ***d*** not know
6:14 had seen the sign that Jesus ***d***,
6:25 when ***d*** You come here?"
6:32 Moses ***d*** not give you the bread
6:64 they were who ***d*** not believe,
6:70 ***D*** I not choose you, the twelve,
7: 1 for He ***d*** not want to walk in
7: 5 His brothers ***d*** not believe
7:19 ***D*** not Moses give you the law,
7:21 I ***d*** one work, and you all
8: 6 as though He ***d*** not hear.
8:27 They ***d*** not understand that He
8:40 Abraham ***d*** not do this.
9:18 But the Jews ***d*** not believe
9:26 What ***d*** He do to you? How did He
9:26 How ***d*** He open your eyes?"
9:27 and you ***d*** not listen. Why do
10: 6 but they ***d*** not understand the
10: 8 but the sheep ***d*** not hear them.
11:40 ***D*** I not say to you that if you
11:45 and had seen the things Jesus ***d***,
11:46 told them the things Jesus ***d***.
11:51 Now this he ***d*** not say on his own
12:16 His disciples ***d*** not understand
12:30 This voice ***d*** not come because of
12:37 they ***d*** not believe in Him,
12:42 they ***d*** not confess Him,
12:47 for I ***d*** not come to judge the
15:16 You ***d*** not choose Me, but I chose
15:24 the works which no one else ***d***,
16: 4 And these things I ***d*** not say to
18:15 and so ***d*** another disciple.
18:26 ***D*** I not see you in the garden
18:28 But they themselves ***d*** not go
18:34 or ***d*** others tell you this
19:24 Therefore the soldiers ***d*** these
19:33 they ***d*** not break His legs.
20: 5 yet he ***d*** not go in.
20: 9 For as yet they ***d*** not know the
20:14 and ***d*** not know that it was
20:30 And truly Jesus ***d*** many other
21: 4 yet the disciples ***d*** not know
21:23 Yet Jesus ***d*** not say to him that
21:25 many other things that Jesus ***d***,
Acts 2:22 and signs which God ***d*** through
2:31 nor ***d*** His flesh see corruption.
2:34 For David ***d*** not ascend into the
3:17 I know that you ***d*** it in
3:17 as ***d*** also your rulers.
4:25 Why ***d*** the nations rage,
4:32 neither ***d*** anyone say that any
5:22 officers came and ***d*** not find
5:28 ***D*** we not strictly command you
5:42 they ***d*** not cease teaching and
6: 8 ***d*** great wonders and signs among
7:18 king arose who ***d*** not know
7:25 but they ***d*** not understand.
7:27 But he who ***d*** his neighbor wrong
7:28 to kill me as you ***d*** the
7:42 ***D*** you offer Me slaughtered
7:51 Holy Spirit; as your fathers ***d***,
7:52 Which of the prophets ***d*** your
8: 6 seeing the miracles which he ***d***.
9:26 and ***d*** not believe that he was a
9:36 charitable deeds which she ***d***.
10:39 of all things which He ***d*** both
11:30 This they also ***d***,
12: 8 on your sandals"; and so he ***d***.
12: 9 and ***d*** not know that what was
12:14 she ***d*** not open the gate,
12:23 because he ***d*** not give glory to
13:27 because they ***d*** not know Him,
14:17 Nevertheless He ***d*** not leave
14:17 in that He ***d*** good, gave us rain
15: 8 just as He ***d*** to us,
16: 7 but the Spirit ***d*** not permit
16:18 And this she ***d*** for many days.
17: 6 But when they ***d*** not find them,
18:20 he ***d*** not consent,
19: 2 ***D*** you receive the Holy Spirit
19: 9 hardened and ***d*** not believe,
19:14 chief priest, who ***d*** so.
19:32 and most of them ***d*** not know why
20:31 for three years I ***d*** not cease
22: 9 but they ***d*** not hear the voice
23: 5 I ***d*** not know, brethren, that he
26:10 This I also ***d*** in Jerusalem, and
27:39 they ***d*** not recognize the land;
28:25 So when they ***d*** not agree among
Rom 1:21 they ***d*** not glorify Him as God,
1:28 And even as they ***d*** not like to
3: 3 For what if some ***d*** not believe?
4:17 do not exist as though they ***d***;
4:19 he ***d*** not consider his own body,
4:20 He ***d*** not waver at the promise of
6:21 What fruit ***d*** you have then in
8: 3 God ***d*** by sending His own Son
8:15 For you ***d*** not receive the spirit
8:32 He who ***d*** not spare His own Son,
9:30 who ***d*** not pursue righteousness,
9:32 Because they ***d*** not seek it
10:19 I say, ***d*** Israel not know?
10:20 by those who ***d*** not seek
10:20 to those who ***d*** not ask
11:21 For if God ***d*** not spare the
15: 3 For even Christ ***d*** not please
1 Cor 1:17 For Christ ***d*** not send me to
1:21 through wisdom ***d*** not know God,
2: 1 ***d*** not come with excellence of
4: 7 have that you ***d*** not receive?
4: 7 Now if you ***d*** indeed receive
4: 8 could wish you ***d*** reign,
5:10 Yet I certainly ***d*** not mean
7:30 weep as though they ***d*** not weep,
7:30 as though they ***d*** not rejoice,
7:30 as though they ***d*** not possess,
10: 8 immorality, as some of them ***d***,
14:36 Or ***d*** the word of God come
15:15 whom He ***d*** not raise up—if in
2 Cor 1:17 this, ***d*** I do it lightly?
2:13 because I ***d*** not find Titus my
7: 8 though I ***d*** regret it. For I
7:12 I ***d*** not do it for the sake
10:14 our authority ***d*** not extend
11: 7 ***D*** I commit sin in humbling
12:16 I ***d*** not burden you.
12:17 ***D*** I take advantage of you by any
12:18 ***D*** Titus take advantage of you?

12:18 ***D*** we not walk in the same
12:18 ***D*** we not walk in the same
Gal 1:16 I **d** not immediately confer with
1:17 nor **d** I go up to Jerusalem to
2: 5 to whom we **d** not yield
3: 2 ***D*** you receive the Spirit by the
4: 8 when you **d** not know God, you
4:14 in my flesh you **d** not despise
Phil 2: 6 **d** not consider it robbery to be
4:10 though you surely **d** care, but
1 Th 1: 5 For our gospel **d** not come to you
2: 3 For our exhortation **d** not come
2: 5 For neither at any time **d** we use
2: 6 Nor **d** we seek glory from men,
2:14 just as they **d** from the
4: 7 For God **d** not call us to
5: 9 For God **d** not appoint us to
2 Th 2:10 because they **d** not receive the
2:12 be condemned who **d** not believe
3: 8 nor **d** we eat anyone's bread free
1 Tim 1:13 obtained mercy because I **d** it
2 Tim 1: 3 as my forefathers **d**,
4:14 the coppersmith **d** me much harm.
Heb 1: 5 For to which of the angels **d** He
3:18 And to whom **d** He swear that they
3:18 but to those who **d** not obey?
4: 2 which they heard **d** not profit
4: 6 was first preached **d** not enter
4:10 from his works as God **d** from
5: 5 So also Christ **d** not glorify
7:27 for this He **d** once for all when
8: 9 they **d** not continue
10: 5 offering You **d** not desire,
10: 8 for sin You **d** not desire,
11: 5 so that he **d** not see death,
11:31 the harlot Rahab **d** not perish
11:31 with those who **d** not believe,
11:39 **d** not receive the promise,
12:25 For if they **d** not escape who
Jas 5:17 and it **d** not rain on the land
1 Pe 2:23 **d** not revile in return; when He
2:23 He **d** not threaten, but
2 Pe 1:16 For we **d** not follow cunningly
2: 4 For if God **d** not spare the
2: 5 and **d** not spare the ancient
1 Jn 3: 1 because it **d** not know Him.
3:12 And why **d** he murder him?
2 Jn 12 I **d** not wish to do so with
Jude 5 those who **d** not believe.
6 And the angels who **d** not keep
Rev 2:13 and **d** not deny My faith even in
2:21 and she **d** not repent.
7:13 and where **d** they come from?"
8:12 A third of the day **d** not shine,
9:20 **d** not repent of the works of
9:21 And they **d** not repent of their
12: 8 but they **d** not prevail, nor was
12:11 and they **d** not love their lives
16: 9 and they **d** not repent and give
16:11 and **d** not repent of their
17: 7 Why **d** you marvel? I will tell
20: 5 rest of the dead **d** not live

DIE (290/271) DEAD, DEATH, DIED, DIES

Gen 2:17 eat of it you shall surely **d**.
3: 3 shall you touch it, lest you **d**.
3: 4 woman, "You will not surely **d**.
6:17 that is on the earth shall **d**.
19:19 some evil overtake me and I **d**.
20: 7 know that you shall surely **d**,
25:32 said, "Look, I am about to **d**;
26: 9 Lest I **d** on account of her.'"
27: 4 soul may bless you before I **d**.
30: 1 children, or else I **d**!"
33:13 one day, all the flock will **d**.
38:11 Lest he also **d** like his
42: 2 that we may live and not **d**.
42:20 verified, and you shall not **d**.
43: 8 go, that we may live and not **d**,
44: 9 servants it is found, let him **d**,
44:22 father, his father would **d**.
44:31 not with us, that he will **d**.
45:28 will go and see him before I **d**.
46:30 said to Joseph, "Now let me **d**,
47:15 for why should we **d** in your
47:19 Why should we **d** before your
47:19 that we may live and not **d**,
47:29 drew near that Israel must **d**,
Ex 7:18 that are in the river shall **d**,
9: 4 So nothing shall **d** of all that
9:19 brought home; and they shall **d**.
10:28 you see my face you shall **d**!"
11: 5 in the land of Egypt shall **d**,
14:11 have you taken us away to **d** in
14:12 than that we should **d** in the
20:19 God speak with us, lest we **d**.
21:14 from My altar, that he may **d**.
21:18 and he does not **d** but is
28:35 he comes out, that he may not **d**.
28:43 do not incur iniquity and **d**.
30:20 wash with water, lest they **d**.
30:21 and their feet, lest they **d**.
Lev 8:35 LORD, so that you may not **d**;
10: 6 tear your clothes, lest you **d**,
10: 7 of meeting, lest you **d**,
10: 9 of meeting, lest you **d**.
15:31 lest they **d** in their
16: 2 which is on the ark, lest he **d**;
16:13 is on the Testimony, lest he **d**.
20:20 they shall **d** childless.
22: 9 lest they bear sin for it and **d**
Num 4:15 any holy thing, lest they **d**.
4:19 that they may live and not **d**
4:20 are being covered, lest they **d**.
6: 7 or his sister, when they **d**,
14:35 and there they shall **d**.
16:29 If these men **d** naturally like
17:10 away from Me, lest they **d**.
17:12 to Moses, saying, "Surely we **d**,
17:13 tabernacle of the LORD must **d**.
17:13 Shall we all utterly **d**?"
18: 3 and the altar, lest they **d**—
18:22 lest they bear sin and **d**.
18:32 children of Israel, lest you **d**.
20: 4 we and our animals should **d**
20:26 to his people and **d** there.
21: 5 us up out of Egypt to **d** in the
23:10 Let me **d** the death of the
26:11 the children of Korah did not **d**.
26:65 They shall surely **d** in the
35:12 that the manslayer may not **d**
35:17 the hand, by which one could **d**,
35:17 one could die, and he does **d**,
35:18 weapon, by which one could **d**,
35:18 one could die, and he does **d**,
35:23 a stone, by which a man could **d**,
Deut 4:22 But I must **d** in this land, I
5:25 'Now therefore, why should we **d**?
5:25 God anymore, then we shall **d**.
17:12 or the judge, that man shall **d**.
18:16 great fire anymore, lest I **d**.
18:20 gods, that prophet shall **d**.
19:12 avenger of blood, that he may **d**.
20: 5 lest he **d** in the battle and
20: 6 lest he **d** in the battle and
20: 7 lest he **d** in the battle and
22:22 then both of them shall **d**—
22:25 man who lay with her shall **d**.
24: 7 then that kidnapper shall **d**;
31:14 days approach when you must **d**;
32:50 and **d** on the mountain which you
33: 6 "Let Reuben live, and not **d**,
Josh 20: 9 and not **d** by the hand of the
Judg 6:23 do not fear, you shall not **d**.
6:30 out your son, that he may **d**,
13:22 his wife, "We shall surely **d**,
15:18 and now shall I **d** of thirst and
16:30 Let me **d** with the Philistines!"
Ruth 1:17 Where you **d**, I will die,
1:17 Where you die, I will **d**,
1 Sam 2:33 of your house shall **d** in the
2:34 in one day they shall **d**,
5:12 And the men who did not **d** were
12:19 your God, that we may not **d**;
14:39 my son, he shall surely **d**.
14:43 So now I must **d**!"
14:44 also; for you shall surely **d**,
14:45 to Saul, "Shall Jonathan **d**,
14:45 Jonathan, and he did not **d**.
20: 2 By no means! You shall not **d**!
20:14 I still live, that I may not **d**;
20:31 to me, for he shall surely **d**.
22:16 king said, "You shall surely **d**,
26:10 him, or his day shall come to **d**,
26:16 LORD lives, you deserve to **d**,
28: 9 for my life, to cause me to **d**?
2 Sam 3:33 Should Abner **d** as a fool dies?
11:15 he may be struck down and **d**.
12: 5 has done this shall surely **d**!
12:13 away your sin; you shall not **d**.
12:14 is born to you shall surely **d**.
14:14 For we will surely **d** and become
18: 3 about us; nor if half of us **d**,
19:23 to Shimei, "You shall not **d**.
19:37 that I may **d** in my own city,
1 Ki 1:52 is found in him, he shall **d**.
2: 1 drew near that he should **d**,
2:30 but I will **d** here."
2:37 for certain you shall surely **d**;
2:42 anywhere, you shall surely **d**'?
14:12 the city, the child shall **d**.
17:12 son, that we may eat it, and **d**.
19: 4 And he prayed that he might **d**,
21:10 and stone him, that he may **d**.
2 Ki 1: 4 gone up, but you shall surely **d**.
1: 6 gone up, but you shall surely **d**.
1:16 gone up, but you shall surely **d**.
7: 3 are we sitting here until we **d**?
7: 4 and we shall **d** there. And if we
7: 4 if we sit here, we **d** also.
7: 4 they kill us, we shall only **d**.
8:10 shown me that he will really **d**.
13:14 the illness of which he would **d**.
18:32 that you may live and not **d**.
20: 1 house in order, for you shall **d**,
2 Chr 25: 4 but a person shall **d** for his
32:11 to give yourselves over to **d**
Job 2: 9 Curse God and **d**!"
3:11 'Why did I not **d** at birth?
4:21 They **d**, even without wisdom.'
12: 2 And wisdom will **d** with you!
14: 8 And its stump may **d** in the
27: 5 Till I **d** I will not put away
29:18 I shall **d** in my nest, And
34:20 In a moment they **d**,
36:12 And they shall **d** without
36:14 They **d** in youth, And their
Ps 41: 5 evil of me: "When will he **d**,
49:10 For he sees wise men **d**;
79:11 those who are appointed to **d**;
82: 7 But you shall **d** like men, And
88:15 been afflicted and ready to **d**
104:29 they **d** and return to their
118:17 I shall not **d**,
Prov 5:23 He shall **d** for lack of
10:21 But fools **d** for lack of
15:10 he who hates correction will **d**.
19:16 is careless of his ways will **d**.
23:13 him with a rod, he will not **d**.
30: 7 (Deprive me not before I **d**):
31: 8 of all who are appointed to **d**.
Eccl 2:16 And how does a wise man **d**?
3: 2 to be born, And a time to **d**;
7:17 Why should you **d** before your
9: 5 living know that they will **d**;
Isa 22:13 for tomorrow we **d**!"
22:18 country; There you shall **d**,
38: 1 for you shall **d** and not live.'
50: 2 And **d** of thirst.
51: 6 those who dwell in it will **d**
51:12 be afraid Of a man who will **d**,
51:14 That he should not **d** in the
65:20 For the child shall **d** one
66:24 For their worm does not **d**,
Jer 11:21 lest you **d** by our hand'—
11:22 The young men shall **d** by the
11:22 and their daughters shall **d** by
16: 4 They shall **d** gruesome deaths;
16: 6 great and the small shall **d** in
20: 6 Babylon, and there you shall **d**,
21: 6 they shall **d** of a great
21: 9 remains in this city shall **d**
22:12 but he shall **d** in the place
22:26 not born; and there you shall **d**.
26: 8 You will surely **d**!
26:11 This man deserves to **d**! For he
26:16 'This man does not deserve to **d**.
27:13 "Why will you **d**,
28:16 This year you shall **d**,
31:30 But every one shall **d** for his
34: 4 You shall not **d** by the sword.
34: 5 You shall **d** in peace; as in the
37:20 lest I **d** there."
38: 2 remains in this city shall **d**
38: 9 and he is likely to **d** from
38:24 words, and you shall not **d**.
38:26 to Jonathan's house to **d** there.
42:16 Egypt; and there you shall **d**.
42:17 They shall **d** by the sword, by
42:22 certainly that you shall **d** by
44:12 They shall **d**, from the least
Lam 4: 9 better off Than those who **d**
Ezek 3:18 the wicked, 'You shall surely **d**,
3:18 that same wicked man shall **d**
3:19 he shall **d** in his iniquity; but
3:20 block before him, he shall **d**;
3:20 he shall **d** in his sin, and his
5:12 One-third of you shall **d** of the
6:12 He who is far off shall **d** by the
6:12 and is besieged shall **d** by the
7:15 is in the field Will **d** by
12:13 though he shall **d** there.
13:19 killing people who should not **d**,
17:16 the midst of Babylon he shall **d**.
18: 4 The soul who sins shall **d**.
18:13 He shall surely **d**;
18:17 He shall not **d** for the iniquity
18:18 he shall **d** for his iniquity.
18:20 "The soul who sins shall **d**.
18:21 surely live; he shall not **d**.
18:23 at all that the wicked should **d**?
18:24 because of them he shall **d**.
18:28 surely live; he shall not **d**.
18:31 For why should you **d**,
28: 8 And you shall **d** the death of
28:10 You shall **d** the death of the
33: 8 you shall surely **d**!' and you do
33: 8 that wicked man shall **d** in his
33: 9 he shall **d** in his iniquity; but
33:11 For why should you **d**,
33:13 he has committed, he shall **d**.
33:14 the wicked, 'You shall surely **d**,
33:15 surely live; he shall not **d**.
33:18 he shall **d** because of it.
33:27 strongholds and caves shall **d**
Am 2: 2 Moab shall **d** with tumult,
6: 9 in one house, they shall **d**.
7:11 Jeroboam shall **d** by the sword,
7:17 You shall **d** in a defiled land;
9:10 sinners of My people shall **d**
Jon 4: 3 for it is better for me to **d**
4: 8 It is better for me to **d** than
Hab 1:12 my Holy One? We shall not **d**.
Zech 11: 9 feed you. Let what is dying **d**,
13: 8 in it shall be cut off and **d**,
Mt 26:35 Even if I have to **d** with You, I
Mk 9:44 'Their worm does not **d**,
9:46 'Their worm does not **d**,
9:48 'Their worm does not **d**,
14:31 If I have to **d** with You, I will
Lk 7: 2 to him, was sick and ready to **d**.
20:36 nor can they **d** anymore, for they
Jn 6:50 one may eat of it and not **d**.
8:21 and will **d** in your sin. Where I
8:24 I said to you that you will **d**
8:24 you will **d** in your sins."
11:16 that we may **d** with Him."
11:25 believes in Me, though he may **d**,
11:26 believes in Me shall never **d**.
11:50 for us that one man should **d**
11:51 prophesied that Jesus would **d**
12:33 by what death He would **d**.
18:14 that one man should **d** for the
18:32 by what death He would **d**.
19: 7 to our law He ought to **d**,

21:23 that this disciple would not **d**.
21:23 say to him that he would not **d**,
Acts 21:13 but also to **d** at Jerusalem for
Rom 5: 7 for a righteous man will one **d**;
5: 7 someone would even dare to **d**.
8:13 to the flesh you will **d**;
14: 8 and if we **d**, we die to
14: 8 we **d** to the Lord.
14: 8 Therefore, whether we live or **d**,
1 Cor 9:15 would be better for me to **d**
15:22 For as in Adam all **d**,
15:31 Jesus our Lord, I **d** daily.
15:32 for tomorrow we **d**!"
2 Cor 7: 3 to **d** together and to live
Phil 1:21 and to **d** is gain.
Heb 9:27 as it is appointed for men to **d**
Rev 3: 2 remain, that are ready to **d**,
9: 6 find it; they will desire to **d**,
14:13 Blessed are the dead who **d** in

DIED (229/216) DIE

Gen 5: 5 and thirty years; and he **d**.
5: 8 and twelve years; and he **d**.
5:11 and five years; and he **d**.
5:14 hundred and ten years; and he **d**.
5:17 and ninety-five years; and he **d**.
5:20 and sixty-two years; and he **d**.
5:27 and sixty-nine years; and he **d**.
5:31 seventy-seven years; and he **d**.
7:21 And all flesh **d** that moved on
7:22 that was on the dry land, **d**.
9:29 and fifty years; and he **d**.
11:28 And Haran **d** before his father
11:32 and Terah **d** in Haran.
23: 2 So Sarah **d** in Kirjath Arba
25: 8 breathed his last and **d** in a
25:17 and he breathed his last and **d**,
25:18 He **d** in the presence of all
35: 8 Deborah, Rebekah's nurse, **d**,
35:18 soul was departing (for she **d**),
35:19 So Rachel **d** and was buried on
35:29 Isaac breathed his last and **d**,
36:33 And when Bela **d**,
36:34 When Jobab **d**, Husham
36:35 And when Husham **d**,
36:36 When Hadad **d**, Samlah
36:37 And when Samlah **d**,
36:38 When Saul **d**, Baal-Hanan
36:39 Baal-Hanan the son of Achbor **d**,
38:12 of Shua, Judah's wife, **d**;
46:12 and Zerah (but Er and Onan **d** in
48: 7 Rachel **d** beside me in the land
50:16 Before your father **d** he
50:26 So Joseph **d**, being one hundred
Ex 1: 6 And Joseph **d**, all his
2:23 time that the king of Egypt **d**.
7:21 fish that were in the river **d**,
8:13 And the frogs **d** out of the
9: 6 all the livestock of Egypt **d**;
9: 6 children of Israel, not one **d**.
16: 3 that we had **d** by the hand of
Lev 10: 2 and they **d** before the LORD.
16: 1 fire before the LORD, and **d**;
17:15 every person who eats what **d**
Num 3: 4 Nadab and Abihu had **d** before the
14: 2 If only we had **d** in the land of
14: 2 of Egypt! Or if only we had **d**
14:37 **d** by the plague before the
15:36 him with stones, and he **d**.
16:49 Now those who **d** in the plague
16:49 besides those who **d** in the
19:13 the body of anyone who has **d**,
19:16 slain by a sword or who has **d**,
20: 1 and Miriam **d** there and was
20: 3 If only we had **d** when our
20: 3 we had died when our brethren **d**
20:28 and Aaron **d** there on the top of
21: 6 many of the people of Israel **d**.
25: 9 And those who **d** in the plague
26:10 with Korah when that company **d**,
26:19 and Er and Onan **d** in the land
26:61 And Nadab and Abihu **d** when they
27: 3 Our father **d** in the wilderness;
27: 3 but he **d** in his own sin; and he
33:38 and **d** there in the fortieth
33:39 years old when he **d** on Mount
Deut 10: 6 to Moserah, where Aaron **d**,
32:50 just as Aaron your brother **d** on
34: 5 the servant of the LORD **d**
34: 7 and twenty years old when he **d**.
Josh 5: 4 had **d** in the wilderness on the
10:11 as far as Azekah, and they **d**.
10:11 There were more who **d** from
24:29 the servant of the LORD, **d**,
24:33 And Eleazar the son of Aaron **d**.
Judg 1: 7 to Jerusalem, and there he **d**.
2: 8 **d** when he was one hundred
2:21 which Joshua left when he **d**,
3:11 Then Othniel the son of Kenaz **d**.
4:21 fast asleep and weary. So he **d**.
8:32 Now Gideon the son of Joash **d** at
9:49 of the tower of Shechem **d**,
9:54 thrust him through, and he **d**.
10: 2 and he **d** and was buried in
10: 5 And Jair **d** and was buried in
12: 7 Then Jephthah the Gileadite **d**
12:10 Then Ibzan **d** and was buried at
12:12 And Elon the Zebulunite **d** and
12:15 son of Hillel the Pirathonite **d**
20: 5 my concubine so that she **d**.
Ruth 1: 3 Elimelech, Naomi's husband, **d**;
1: 5 both Mahlon and Chilion also **d**;
1 Sam 4:11 of Eli, Hophni and Phinehas, **d**.
4:18 his neck was broken and he **d**,
25: 1 Then Samuel **d**; and the
25:37 that his heart **d** within him,
25:38 LORD struck Nabal, and he **d**.
28: 3 Now Samuel had **d**,
31: 5 his sword, and **d** with him.
31: 6 and all his men **d** together that
2 Sam 1:15 And he struck him so that he **d**.
2:23 and he fell down there and **d** on
2:23 where Asahel fell down and **d**,
2:31 hundred and sixty men who **d**.
3:27 so that he **d** for the blood of
4: 1 son heard that Abner had **d** in
6: 7 and he **d** there by the ark of
10: 1 king of the people of Ammon **d**,
10:18 their army, who **d** there.
11:17 and Uriah the Hittite **d** also.
11:21 so that he **d** in Thebez?
12:18 came to pass that the child **d**.
12:21 alive, but when the child **d**,
17:23 and hanged himself, and **d**;
18:33 —if only I had **d** in your place!
19: 6 had lived and all of us had **d**
19:10 has **d** in battle. Now therefore,
20:10 strike him again. Thus he **d**.
24:15 thousand men of the people **d**.
1 Ki 2:25 he struck him down, and he **d**.
2:46 and struck him down, and he **d**.
3:19 And this woman's son **d** in the
12:18 him with stones, and he **d**.
14:17 of the house, the child **d**.
16:18 upon himself with fire, and **d**,
16:22 So Tibni **d** and Omri reigned.
21:13 him with stones, so that he **d**.
22:35 the Syrians, and **d** at evening.
22:37 So the king **d**, and was
2 Ki 1:17 So Ahaziah **d** according to the
3: 5 But it happened, when Ahab **d**,
4:20 knees till noon, and then **d**.
7:17 him in the gate, and he **d**,
7:20 him in the gate, and he **d**.
8:15 it over his face so that he **d**;
9:27 fled to Megiddo, and **d** there.
12:21 servants, struck him. So he **d**,
13:20 Then Elisha **d**, and they
13:24 Now Hazael king of Syria **d**.
23:34 to Egypt, and he **d** there.
1 Chr 1:44 And when Bela **d**,
1:45 When Jobab **d**, Husham of the
1:46 And when Husham **d**,
1:47 When Hadad **d**, Samlah of
1:48 And when Samlah **d**,
1:49 When Saul **d**, Baal-Hanan
1:50 And when Baal-Hanan **d**,
1:51 Hadad **d** also. And the chiefs of
2:19 When Azubah **d**, Caleb took
2:24 After Hezron **d** in Caleb
2:30 Seled **d** without children.
2:32 Jether **d** without children.
10: 5 he also fell on his sword and **d**.
10: 6 So Saul and his three sons **d**,
10: 6 and all his house **d** together.
10:13 So Saul **d** for his
13:10 and he **d** there before God.
19: 1 king of the people of Ammon **d**,
23:22 Eleazar **d**, and had no sons,
24: 2 And Nadab and Abihu **d** before
29:28 So he **d** in a good old age, full
2 Chr 10:18 him with stones, and he **d**.
13:20 the LORD struck him, and he **d**.
16:13 he **d** in the forty-first year of
18:34 about the time of sunset he **d**.
21:19 so he **d** in severe pain. And his
24:15 and was full of days, and he **d**;
24:15 and thirty years old when he **d**.
24:22 but killed his son; and as he **d**,
24:25 killed him on his bed. So he **d**.
35:24 him to Jerusalem. So he **d**,
Esth 2: 7 When her father and mother **d**,
Job 42:17 So Job **d**, old and full of
Isa 6: 1 In the year that King Uzziah **d**,
14:28 in the year that King Ahaz **d**.
Jer 28:17 So Hananiah the prophet **d** the
Ezek 4:14 I have never eaten what **d** of
11:13 Pelatiah the son of Benaiah **d**.
24:18 and at evening my wife **d**;
44:31 that **d** naturally or was torn
Hos 13: 1 through Baal worship, he **d**.
Mt 9:18 "My daughter has just **d**,
22:25 The first **d** after he had
22:27 Last of all the woman **d** also.
Mk 12:21 the second took her, and he **d**;
12:22 Last of all the woman **d** also.
Lk 16:22 "So it was that the beggar **d**,
16:22 The rich man also **d** and was
20:29 and **d** without children.
20:30 and he **d** childless.
20:31 they left no children, and **d**.
20:32 Last of all the woman **d** also.
Jn 11:21 my brother would not have **d**.
11:32 my brother would not have **d**.
11:44 And he who had **d** came out bound
Acts 7:15 went down to Egypt; and he **d**,
9:37 days that she became sick and **d**.
12:23 And he was eaten by worms and **d**.
25:19 a certain Jesus, who had **d**,
Rom 5: 6 in due time Christ **d** for the
5: 8 sinners, Christ **d** for us.
5:15 by the one man's offense many **d**,
6: 2 How shall we who **d** to sin
6: 7 For he who has **d** has been freed
6: 8 Now if we **d** with Christ, we
6:10 For the death that He **d**,
6:10 He **d** to sin once for all;
7: 6 having **d** to what we were held
7: 9 came, sin revived and I **d**.
8:34 It is Christ who **d**,
14: 9 For to this end Christ **d** and
14:15 food the one for whom Christ **d**.
1 Cor 8:11 perish, for whom Christ **d**?
15: 3 that Christ **d** for our sins
2 Cor 5:14 that if One **d** for all, then all
5:14 if One died for all, then all **d**;
5:15 and He **d** for all, that those who
5:15 but for Him who **d** for them and
Gal 2:19 For I through the law **d** to the
2:21 then Christ **d** in vain."
Col 2:20 if you **d** with Christ from the
3: 3 For you **d**, and your life
1 Th 4:14 For if we believe that Jesus **d**
5:10 who **d** for us, that whether we
2 Tim 2:11 For if we **d** with Him, We
Heb 11:13 These all **d** in faith, not
1 Pe 2:24 having **d** to sins, might live
Rev 8: 9 living creatures in the sea **d**,
8:11 and many men **d** from the water,
16: 3 living creature in the sea **d**.

DIES (56/49) DIE

Ex 21:12 who strikes a man so that he **d**
21:20 so that he **d** under his hand, he
21:35 hurts another's, so that it **d**,
22: 2 and he is struck so that he **d**,
22:10 or any animal to keep, and it **d**,
22:14 and it becomes injured or **d**,
Lev 7:24 the fat of an animal that **d**
11:39 any animal which you may eat **d**,
22: 8 Whatever **d** naturally or is torn
Num 6: 9 And if anyone **d** very suddenly
19:14 'This is the law when a man **d**
27: 8 If a man **d** and has no son, then
35:16 an iron implement, so that he **d**,
35:20 something at him so that he **d**,
35:21 him with his hand so that he **d**,
35:23 seeing him, so that he **d**,
Deut 13:10 him with stones until he **d**,
14:21 shall not eat anything that **d**
19: 5 his neighbor so that he **d**—
19:11 him mortally, so that he **d**,
24: 3 or if the latter husband **d** who
25: 5 and one of them **d** and has no
2 Sam 3:33 Abner die as a fool **d**?
1 Ki 14:11 belongs to Jeroboam and **d** in
14:11 of the air shall eat whoever **d**
16: 4 belongs to Baasha and **d** in the
16: 4 of the air shall eat whoever **d**
21:24 whoever belongs to Ahab and **d**
21:24 of the air shall eat whoever **d**
Job 14:10 But man **d** and is laid away;
14:14 If a man **d**, shall he live
21:23 One **d** in his full strength,
21:25 Another man **d** in the bitterness
Ps 49:17 For when he **d** he shall carry
Prov 11: 7 When a wicked man **d**,
Eccl 3:19 as one **d**, so dies the other.
3:19 as one dies, so **d** the other.
Isa 59: 5 He who eats of their eggs **d**,
Jer 38:10 out of the dungeon before he **d**.
Ezek 18:26 and **d** in it, it is because of
18:26 which he has done that he **d**.
18:32 in the death of one who **d**,
Mt 22:24 Moses said that if a man **d**,
Mk 12:19 to us that if a man's brother **d**,
Lk 20:28 us that if a man's brother **d**,
20:28 and he **d** without children, his
Jn 4:49 come down before my child **d**!"
12:24 falls into the ground and **d**,
12:24 it remains alone; but if it **d**,
Rom 6: 9 **d** no more. Death no longer has
7: 2 he lives. But if the husband **d**,
7: 3 but if her husband **d**,
14: 7 and no one **d** to himself.
1 Cor 7:39 lives; but if her husband **d**,
15:36 is not made alive unless it **d**.
Heb 10:28 who has rejected Moses' law **d**

DIFFER (2/2) DIFFERENCE, DIFFERENT, DIFFERING, DIFFERS

1 Cor 4: 7 For who makes you **d** from
Gal 4: 1 does not **d** at all from a slave,

DIFFERENCE (8/8) DIFFER, DIFFERENCES

Ex 8:23 I will make a **d** between My
9: 4 And the LORD will make a **d**
11: 7 that the LORD does make a **d**
Ezek 22:26 have they made known the **d**
44:23 shall teach My people the **d**
Rom 3:22 who believe. For there is no **d**;
1 Cor 7:34 There is a **d** between a wife and
Gal 2: 6 it makes no **d** to me; God shows

DIFFERENCES (1/1) DIFFERENCE

1 Cor 12: 5 There are **d** of ministries, but

DIFFERENT (15/14) DIFFER

Num 14:24 because he has a **d** spirit in

Deut 22: 9 vineyard with **d** kinds of seed,
22:11 not wear a garment of **d** sorts,
Esth 1: 7 each vessel being **d** from the
3: 8 their laws are **d** from all
Eccl 10:11 The babbler is no **d**.
Dan 7: 3 each **d** from the other.
7: 7 It was **d** from all the beasts
7:19 which was **d** from all the
7:23 Which shall be **d** from all
7:24 He shall be **d** from the first
1 Cor 12:10 to another **d** kinds of tongues,
2 Cor 11: 4 or if you receive a **d** spirit
11: 4 or a **d** gospel which you have
Gal 1: 6 of Christ, to a **d** gospel,

DIFFERING (3/3) DIFFER

Deut 25:13 in your bag **d** weights,
25:14 in your house **d** measures,
Rom 12: 6 Having then gifts **d** according to

DIFFERS (1/1) DIFFER

1 Cor 15:41 for one star **d** from another

DIFFICULT (5/5) DIFFICULTY

1 Ki 10: 3 there was nothing so **d** for the
2 Chr 9: 2 there was nothing so **d** for
Eccl 12: 1 Before the **d** days come, And
Dan 2:11 It is a **d** thing that the king
Mt 7:14 narrow is the gate and **d** is

DIFFICULTIES (1/1) DIFFICULTY

Ex 18:19 so that you may bring the **d** to

DIFFICULTY (7/7) DIFFICULT, DIFFICULTIES

Ex 14:25 so that they drove them with **d**;
18:16 "When they have a **d**,
24:14 with you. If any man has a **d**,
Lk 9:39 departs from him with great **d**,
Acts 27: 7 and arrived with **d** off Cnidus,
27: 8 Passing it with **d**,
27:16 we secured the skiff with **d**.

DIFFUSED (1/1) DIFFUSES

Job 38:24 By what way is light **d**,

DIFFUSES (1/1) DIFFUSED

2 Cor 2:14 and through us **d** the fragrance

DIG (11/11) DIGS, DUG

Deut 6:11 wells which you did not **d**,
8: 9 out of whose hills you can **d**
23:13 you shall **d** with it and turn
Job 11:18 you would **d** around you, and
Ezek 8: 8 **d** into the wall"; and when I
12: 5 **D** through the wall in their
12:12 They shall **d** through the wall
Am 9: 2 Though they **d** into hell, From
Nah 1:14 I will **d** your grave, For you
Lk 13: 8 until I **d** around it and
16: 3 away from me. I cannot **d**;

DIGNITARIES (2/2) DIGNITY

2 Pe 2:10 not afraid to speak evil of **d**,
Jude 8 authority, and speak evil of **d**.

DIGNITY (4/4) DIGNITARIES

Gen 49: 3 The excellency of **d** and the
Esth 6: 3 What honor or **d** has been
Eccl 10: 6 Folly is set in great **d**,
Hab 1: 7 Their judgment and their **d**

DIGS (4/4) DIG

Ex 21:33 or if a man **d** a pit and does
Prov 16:27 An ungodly man **d** up evil, And
26:27 Whoever **d** a pit will fall into
Eccl 10: 8 He who **d** a pit will fall into

DIKLAH (2/2)

Gen 10:27 Hadoram, Uzal, **D**,
1 Chr 1:21 Hadoram, Uzal, **D**,

DILAPIDATION (1/1)

2 Ki 12: 5 wherever any **d** is found."

DILEAN (1/1)

Josh 15:38 **D**, Mizpah, Joktheel,

DILIGENCE (9/9) DILIGENT

Prov 4:23 Keep your heart with all **d**,
12:27 But **d** is man's precious
Rom 12: 8 he who leads, with **d**;
12:11 not lagging in **d**, fervent in
2 Cor 7:11 What **d** it produced in you,
8: 7 speech, in knowledge, in all **d**,
8: 8 of your love by the **d** of
Heb 6:11 one of you show the same **d** to
2 Pe 1: 5 this very reason, giving all **d**,

DILIGENT (17/16) DILIGENCE, DILIGENTLY

2 Chr 29:34 for the Levites were more **d** in
Ps 77: 6 And my spirit makes **d** search.
Prov 10: 4 But the hand of the **d** makes
12:24 The hand of the **d** will rule,
13: 4 But the soul of the **d** shall be
21: 5 The plans of the **d** lead surely
27:23 Be **d** to know the state of your
2 Cor 8:17 exhortation, but being more **d**,
8:22 whom we have often proved **d** in
8:22 things, but now much more **d**,
2 Tim 2:15 Be **d** to present yourself
4: 9 Be **d** to come to me quickly;
Titus 3:12 be **d** to come to me at
Heb 4:11 Let us therefore be **d** to enter
2 Pe 1:10 be even more **d** to make your
3:14 be **d** to be found by Him in
Jude 3 while I was very **d** to write to

DILIGENTLY (23/23) DILIGENT

Ex 15:26 If you **d** heed the voice of the
Deut 4: 9 and **d** keep yourself, lest you
6: 7 You shall teach them **d** to your
6:17 You shall **d** keep the
13:14 inquire, search out, and ask **d**.
17: 4 it, then you shall inquire **d**.
28: 1 if you **d** obey the voice of the
2 Chr 34:33 who were present in Israel **d**
Ezra 5: 8 and this work goes on **d** and
6:12 a decree; let it be done **d**.
6:13 and their companions **d** did
7:21 of you, let it be done **d**,
7:23 let it **d** be done for the house
Job 7:21 dust, And You will seek me **d**,
Ps 119: 4 us To keep Your precepts **d**.
Prov 1:28 answer; They will seek me **d**,
7:15 **D** to seek your face, And I
8:17 And those who seek me **d** will
Jer 2:10 Send to Kedar and consider **d**,
Zech 6:15 shall come to pass if you **d**
1 Tim 5:10 if she has **d** followed every
Heb 11: 6 He is a rewarder of those who **d**
12:17 though he sought it **d** with

DIM (10/10) DIMLY

Gen 27: 1 was old and his eyes were so **d**
48:10 Now the eyes of Israel were **d**
Deut 34: 7 His eyes were not **d** nor his
1 Sam 3: 2 his eyes had begun to grow so **d**
4:15 and his eyes were so **d** that he
Job 17: 7 My eye has also grown **d** because
Eccl 12: 3 look through the windows grow **d**;
Isa 32: 3 of those who see will not be **d**,
Lam 4: 1 How the gold has become **d**!
5:17 these things our eyes grow **d**;

DIMINISH (9/9) DIMINISHED

Ex 21:10 he shall not **d** her food, her
Lev 25:16 number of years you shall **d**
Jer 26: 2 Do not **d** a word.
30:19 them, and they shall not **d**;
Ezek 5:11 therefore I will also **d** you;
29:15 for I will **d** them so that they
Joel 2:10 And the stars **d** their
3:15 And the stars will **d** their
Zech 14: 6 be no light; The lights will **d**.

DIMINISHED (8/8) DIMINISH

Deut 34: 7 not dim nor his natural vigor **d**.
Ezra 4:13 the king's treasury will be **d**.
Ps 107:39 When they are **d** and brought low
Prov 13:11 by dishonesty will be **d**,
Isa 21:17 the people of Kedar, will be **d**;
25: 5 of the terrible ones will be **d**.
Jer 29: 6 be increased there, and not **d**.
Ezek 16:27 **d** your allotment, and gave you

DIMLY (1/1) DIM

1 Cor 13:12 For now we see in a mirror, **d**,

DIMNAH (1/1)

Josh 21:35 **D** with its common-land, and

DIMON (2/1) DIBON, DIMONAH

Isa 15: 9 For the waters of **D** will be
15: 9 I will bring more upon **D**,

DIMONAH (1/1) DIMON

Josh 15:22 Kinah, **D**, Adadah,

DINAH (7/7) DINAH'S

Gen 30:21 daughter, and called her name **D**.
34: 1 Now **D** the daughter of Leah, whom
34: 3 was strongly attracted to **D**
34: 5 heard that he had defiled **D**
34:13 because he had defiled **D** their
34:26 and took **D** from Shechem's
46:15 Padan Aram, with his daughter **D**.

DINAH'S (1/1) DINAH

Gen 34:25 **D** brothers, each took his sword

DINAITES (1/1)

Ezra 4: 9 representatives of the **D**,

DINE (4/4) DINING

Gen 43:16 for these men will **d** with me
Esth 7: 1 So the king and Haman went to **d**
Lk 11:37 Pharisee asked Him to **d** with
Rev 3:20 I will come in to him and **d**

DINHABAH (2/2)

Gen 36:32 and the name of his city was **D**.
1 Chr 1:43 and the name of his city was **D**.

DINING (1/1) DINE

Mk 2:15 as He was **d** in Levi's house,

DINNER (5/5)

Prov 15:17 Better is a **d** of herbs where
Mt 22: 4 "See, I have prepared my **d**;
Lk 11:38 had not first washed before **d**.
14:12 When you give a **d** or a supper,
1 Cor 10:27 not believe invites you to **d**,

DIONYSIUS (1/1)

Acts 17:34 among them **D** the Areopagite, a

DIOTREPHES (1/1)

3 Jn 9 but **D**, who loves to have

DIP (10/10) DIPPED, DIPS

Ex 12:22 **d** it in the blood that is in
Lev 4: 6 The priest shall **d** his finger in
4:17 Then the priest shall **d** his
14: 6 and **d** them and the living bird
14:16 Then the priest shall **d** his
14:51 and **d** them in the blood of the
Num 19:18 take hyssop and **d** it in the
Deut 33:24 And let him **d** his foot in oil.
Ruth 2:14 and **d** your piece of bread in
Lk 16:24 may **d** the tip of his finger

DIPHATH (1/1)

1 Chr 1: 6 sons of Gomer were Ashkenaz, **D**,

DIPPED (10/9) DIP

Gen 37:31 and **d** the tunic in the blood.
Lev 9: 9 And he **d** his finger in the
Josh 3:15 priests who bore the ark **d** in
1 Sam 14:27 that was in his hand and **d** it
2 Ki 5:14 So he went down and **d** seven
8:15 took a thick cloth and **d** it
Mt 26:23 He who **d** his hand with Me in
Jn 13:26 a piece of bread when I have **d**
13:26 And having **d** the bread, He
Rev 19:13 He was clothed with a robe **d** in

DIPS (1/1) DIP

Mk 14:20 who **d** with Me in the dish.

DIRE (2/2)

Job 36:16 brought you out of **d** distress,
Lam 1: 3 overtake her in **d** straits.

DIRECT (12/12) DIRECTED, DIRECTING, DIRECTION, DIRECTLY, DIRECTOR, DIRECTS

1 Chr 15:21 to **d** with harps on the
Ps 5: 3 In the morning I will **d** it to
119:133 **D** my steps by Your word, And
Prov 3: 6 And He shall **d** your paths.
11: 5 of the blameless will **d** his
Isa 45:13 And I will **d** all his ways;
61: 8 I will **d** their work in truth,
Jer 10:23 walks to **d** his own steps.
Ezek 26: 9 He will **d** his battering rams
Hos 5: 4 They do not **d** their deeds
1 Th 3:11 **d** our way to you.
2 Th 3: 5 Now may the Lord **d** your hearts

DIRECTED (9/9) DIRECT

1 Sam 21: 2 And I have **d** my young men to
1 Ki 12:12 third day, as the king had **d**,
2 Chr 10:12 third day, as the king had **d**,
20:33 for as yet the people had not **d**
Job 32:14 Now he has not **d** his words
Ps 119: 5 that my ways were **d** To keep
Isa 40:13 Who has **d** the Spirit of the
Mt 26:19 disciples did as Jesus had **d**
27:10 as the LORD **d** me."

DIRECTING (1/1) DIRECT

Num 10: 2 the congregation and for **d** the

DIRECTION (11/11) DIRECT, DIRECTIONS

Num 34: 8 then the **d** of the border shall
Judg 20:42 the men of Israel in the **d** of
2 Ki 7:14 the king sent them in the **d** of

1 Chr 25: 2 of Asaph were under the ***d*** of
25: 3 under the ***d*** of their father
25: 6 All these were under the ***d*** of
Ezek 9: 2 six men came from the ***d*** of the
10:11 but followed in the ***d*** the head
48: 1 in the ***d*** of Hamath, there
Mk 1:45 they came to Him from every ***d***.
Acts 7:53 have received the law by the ***d***

DIRECTIONS (3/3) DIRECTION

1 Chr 9:24 were assigned to the four ***d***:
Ezek 1:17 went toward any one of four ***d***;
10:11 toward any of their four ***d***;

DIRECTLY (2/2) DIRECT

Num 19: 4 of its blood seven times ***d*** in
Ezek 42:12 the way ***d*** in front of the wall

DIRECTOR (1/1) DIRECT

Neh 12:42 loudly with Jezrahiah the ***d***.

DIRECTS (1/1) DIRECT

Prov 16: 9 But the LORD ***d*** his steps.

DIRT (4/4)

1 Sam 4:12 with his clothes torn and ***d*** on
2 Sam 22:43 I trod them like ***d*** in the
Ps 18:42 I cast them out like ***d*** in the
Isa 57:20 waters cast up mire and ***d***.

DISALLOW (KJV) See OVERRULES

DISANNUL, DISANNULLED (KJV) See ANNUL, ANNULLED

DISAPPEAR (1/1) DISAPPEARED, DISAPPEARS

Ps 12: 1 man ceases! For the faithful ***d***

DISAPPEARED (1/1) DISAPPEAR

Lev 13:58 if the plague has ***d*** from it,

DISAPPEARS (2/2) DISAPPEAR

Job 7: 9 As the cloud ***d*** and vanishes
14:11 As water ***d*** from the sea, And

DISAPPOINT (1/1) DISAPPOINTED

Rom 5: 5 Now hope does not ***d***,

DISAPPOINTED (1/1) DISAPPOINT

Job 6:20 They are ***d*** because they were

DISAPPROVED (1/1)

2 Tim 3: 8 ***d*** concerning the faith;

DISARMED (1/1) DISARMS

Col 2:15 Having ***d*** principalities and

DISARMS (1/1) DISARMED

Job 12:21 And ***d*** the mighty.

DISASTER (39/37) DISASTERS

Judg 20:34 did not know that ***d*** was upon
20:41 for they saw that ***d*** had come
2 Sam 15:14 us suddenly and bring ***d*** upon
17:14 that the LORD might bring ***d***
1 Ki 14:10 I will bring ***d*** on the
22:23 and the LORD has declared ***d***
1 Chr 21:15 looked and relented of the ***d***,
2 Chr 18:22 and the LORD has declared ***d***
20: 9 If ***d*** comes upon us—sword,
Neh 13:18 bring all this ***d*** on us
Job 31: 3 And ***d*** for the workers of
Isa 31: 2 also is wise and will bring ***d***,
Jer 2: 3 ***D*** will come upon them," says
4: 6 For I will bring ***d*** from the
6: 1 For ***d*** appears out of the
16:10 pronounced all this great ***d***
18: 8 I will relent of the ***d*** that I
18:11 I am fashioning a ***d*** and
23:12 For I will bring ***d*** on them,
25:32 ***d*** shall go forth From nation
28: 8 of war and ***d*** and pestilence.
42:10 For I relent concerning the ***d***
42:17 remain or escape from the ***d***
49:37 I will bring ***d*** upon them, My
Ezek 7: 5 'A ***d***, a singular disaster;
7: 5 'A disaster, a singular ***d***;
7:26 ***D*** will come upon disaster, And
7:26 Disaster will come upon ***d***,
14:22 be comforted concerning the ***d***
Dan 9:12 by bringing upon us a great ***d***;
9:13 all this ***d*** has come upon us;
9:14 the LORD has kept the ***d*** in
Jon 3:10 and God relented from the ***d***
Mic 1:12 But ***d*** came down from the LORD
2: 3 this family I am devising ***d***,
Hab 2: 9 delivered from the power of ***d***!

Zeph 3:15 You shall see ***d*** no more.
Acts 27:10 this voyage will end with ***d***
27:21 from Crete and incurred this ***d***

DISASTERS (1/1) DISASTER

Deut 32:23 I will heap ***d*** on them; I will

DISAVOW (1/1)

Job 34:33 Just because you ***d*** it?

DISBELIEVED (1/1)

Acts 28:24 which were spoken, and some ***d***.

DISC (1/1)

Zech 5: 7 Here is a lead ***d*** lifted up, and

DISCERN (15/13) DISCERNED, DISCERNER, DISCERNING, DISCERNMENT, DISCERNS, UNDISCERNING

2 Sam 19:35 Can I ***d*** between the good and
1 Ki 3: 9 that I may ***d*** between good and
3:11 for yourself understanding to ***d***
Ezra 3:13 so that the people could not ***d***
Job 4:16 But I could not ***d*** its
6:30 Cannot my taste ***d*** the
Prov 19:25 and he will ***d*** knowledge.
Ezek 44:23 and cause them to ***d*** between the
Jon 4:11 thousand persons who cannot ***d***
Mal 3:18 Then you shall again ***d*** Between
Mt 16: 3 Hypocrites! You know how to ***d***
16: 3 but you cannot ***d*** the signs of
Lk 12:56 Hypocrites! You can ***d*** the face
12:56 but how is it you do not ***d***
Heb 5:14 their senses exercised to ***d***

DISCERNED (1/1) DISCERN

1 Cor 2:14 because they are spiritually ***d***.

DISCERNER (1/1) DISCERN

Heb 4:12 and is a ***d*** of the thoughts and

DISCERNING (7/7) DISCERN

Gen 41:33 let Pharaoh select a ***d*** and wise
41:39 there is no one as ***d*** and wise
Ex 23: 8 for a bribe blinds the ***d*** and
2 Sam 14:17 so is my lord the king in ***d***
Prov 28: 7 Whoever keeps the law is a ***d***
1 Cor 11:29 not ***d*** the Lord's body.
12:10 to another ***d*** of spirits, to

DISCERNMENT (4/4) DISCERN

Job 12:20 And takes away the ***d*** of the
Prov 2: 3 Yes, if you cry out for ***d***,
15:21 him who is destitute of ***d***,
Phil 1: 9 and more in knowledge and all ***d***,

DISCERNS (1/1) DISCERN

Eccl 8: 5 And a wise man's heart ***d*** both

DISCHARGE (27/21) DISCHARGED

Lev 15: 2 When any man has a ***d*** from his
15: 2 his ***d*** is unclean.
15: 3 uncleanness in regard to his ***d***—
15: 3 his body runs with his ***d***,
15: 3 his body is stopped up by his ***d***,
15: 4 on which he who has the ***d*** lies,
15: 6 on which he who has the ***d*** sat
15: 7 the body of him who has the ***d***
15: 8 If he who has the ***d*** spits on him
15: 9 on which he who has the ***d***
15:11 whomever the one who has the ***d***
15:12 of earth that he who has the ***d***
15:13 And when he who has a ***d*** is
15:13 discharge is cleansed of his ***d***,
15:15 the LORD because of his ***d***.
15:19 'If a woman has a ***d***,
15:19 and the ***d*** from her body is
15:25 If a woman has a ***d*** of blood for
15:25 all the days of her unclean ***d***
15:26 she lies all the days of her ***d***
15:28 if she is cleansed of her ***d***,
15:30 her before the LORD for the ***d***
15:32 is the law for one who has a ***d***,
15:33 and for one who has a ***d***,
22: 4 who is a leper or has a ***d***,
Num 5: 2 leper, everyone who has a ***d***,
2 Sam 3:29 house of Joab one who has a ***d***

DISCHARGED (2/2) DISCHARGE

2 Chr 25:10 So Amaziah ***d*** the troops that had
25:13 of the army which Amaziah had ***d***,

DISCIPLE (29/27) DISCIPLES, DISCIPLINE

Mt 10:24 A ***d*** is not above his teacher,
10:25 It is enough for a ***d*** that he be
10:42 cold water in the name of a ***d***,
27:57 himself had also become a ***d*** of
Lk 6:40 A ***d*** is not above his teacher,
14:26 life also, he cannot be My ***d***.
14:27 come after Me cannot be My ***d***.
14:33 all that he has cannot be My ***d***.
Jn 9:28 him and said, "You are His ***d***,
18:15 Jesus, and so did another ***d***.
18:15 Now that ***d*** was known to the
18:16 Then the other ***d***, who was
19:26 and the ***d*** whom He loved
19:27 Then He said to the ***d***,
19:27 And from that hour that ***d*** took
19:38 being a ***d*** of Jesus, but
20: 2 Simon Peter, and to the other ***d***,
20: 3 went out, and the other ***d***,
20: 4 and the other ***d*** outran Peter
20: 8 Then the other ***d***,
21: 7 Therefore that ***d*** whom Jesus
21:20 saw the ***d*** whom Jesus loved
21:23 that this ***d*** would not die.
21:24 This is the ***d*** who testifies of
Acts 9:10 Now there was a certain ***d*** at
9:26 did not believe that he was a ***d***.
9:36 At Joppa there was a certain ***d***
16: 1 a certain ***d*** was there, named
21:16 Mnason of Cyprus, an early ***d***,

DISCIPLES (245/234) DISCIPLE, DISCIPLES'

Isa 8:16 Seal the law among my ***d***.
Mt 5: 1 when He was seated His ***d*** came
8:21 Then another of His ***d*** said to
8:23 His ***d*** followed Him.
8:25 Then His ***d*** came to Him and
9:10 and sat down with Him and His ***d***.
9:11 saw it, they said to His ***d***,
9:14 Then the ***d*** of John came to Him,
9:14 but Your ***d*** do not fast?"
9:19 followed him, and so did His ***d***.
9:37 Then He said to His ***d***,
10: 1 He had called His twelve ***d*** to
11: 1 commanding His twelve ***d***,
11: 2 he sent two of his ***d***
12: 1 And His ***d*** were hungry, and
12: 2 Your ***d*** are doing what is not
12:49 out His hand toward His ***d*** and
13:10 And the ***d*** came and said to Him,
13:36 And His ***d*** came to Him, saying,
14:12 Then his ***d*** came and took away
14:15 His ***d*** came to Him, saying,
14:19 and gave the loaves to the ***d***;
14:19 and the ***d*** gave to the
14:22 made His ***d*** get into the boat
14:26 And when the ***d*** saw Him walking
15: 2 Why do Your ***d*** transgress the
15:12 Then His ***d*** came and said to Him,
15:23 And His ***d*** came and urged Him,
15:32 Now Jesus called His ***d*** to
15:33 Then His ***d*** said to Him, "Where
15:36 them and gave them to His ***d***;
15:36 and the ***d*** gave to the
16: 5 Now when His ***d*** had come to the
16:13 Philippi, He asked His ***d***,
16:20 Then He commanded His ***d*** that
16:21 Jesus began to show to His ***d***
16:24 Then Jesus said to His ***d***,
17: 6 And when the ***d*** heard it, they
17:10 And His ***d*** asked Him, saying,
17:13 Then the ***d*** understood that He
17:16 "So I brought him to Your ***d***,
17:19 Then the ***d*** came to Jesus
18: 1 At that time the ***d*** came to
19:10 His ***d*** said to Him, "If such is
19:13 but the ***d*** rebuked them.
19:23 Then Jesus said to His ***d***,
19:25 When His ***d*** heard it, they were
20:17 took the twelve ***d*** aside on the
21: 1 Olives, then Jesus sent two ***d***,
21: 6 So the ***d*** went and did as Jesus
21:20 And when the ***d*** saw it, they
22:16 And they sent to Him their ***d***
23: 1 to the multitudes and to His ***d***,
24: 1 and His ***d*** came up to show Him
24: 3 the ***d*** came to Him privately,
26: 1 sayings, that He said to His ***d***,
26: 8 But when His ***d*** saw it, they
26:17 Unleavened Bread the ***d*** came
26:18 at your house with My ***d***.
26:19 So the ***d*** did as Jesus had
26:26 and gave it to the ***d*** and said,
26:35 And so said all the ***d***.
26:36 Gethsemane, and said to the ***d***,
26:40 Then He came to the ***d*** and found
26:45 Then He came to His ***d*** and said
26:56 Then all the ***d*** forsook Him
27:64 lest His ***d*** come by night and
28: 7 And go quickly and tell His ***d***
28: 8 and ran to bring His ***d*** word.
28: 9 And as they went to tell His ***d***,
28:13 His ***d*** came at night and stole
28:16 Then the eleven ***d*** went away
28:19 Go therefore and make ***d*** of all
Mk 2:15 together with Jesus and His ***d***;
2:16 and sinners, they said to His ***d***,
2:18 The ***d*** of John and of the
2:18 Why do the ***d*** of John and of the
2:18 but Your ***d*** do not fast?"
2:23 and as they went His ***d*** began to
3: 7 But Jesus withdrew with His ***d***
3: 9 So He told His ***d*** that a small
4:34 explained all things to His ***d***.
5:31 But His ***d*** said to Him, "You see
6: 1 and His ***d*** followed Him.
6:29 When his ***d*** heard of it, they

6:35 His **d** came to Him and said,
6:41 and gave them to His **d** to set
6:45 Immediately He made His **d** get
7: 2 Now when they saw some of His **d**
7: 5 Why do Your **d** not walk according
7:17 His **d** asked Him concerning the
8: 1 Jesus called His **d** to Him and
8: 4 Then His **d** answered Him, "How
8: 6 them and gave them to His **d**
8:10 got into the boat with His **d**,
8:14 Now the **d** had forgotten to take
8:27 Now Jesus and His **d** went out to
8:27 and on the road He asked His **d**,
8:33 around and looked at His **d**,
8:34 with His **d** also, He said to
9:14 And when He came to the **d**,
9:18 So I spoke to Your **d**,
9:28 His **d** asked Him privately,
9:31 For He taught His **d** and said to
10:10 In the house His **d** also asked
10:13 but the **d** rebuked those who
10:23 looked around and said to His **d**,
10:24 And the **d** were astonished at His
10:46 went out of Jericho with His **d**
11: 1 of Olives, He sent two of His **d**;
11:14 And His **d** heard it.
12:43 So He called His **d** to Himself
13: 1 one of His **d** said to Him,
14:12 His **d** said to Him, "Where do
14:13 And He sent out two of His **d** and
14:14 may eat the Passover with My **d**?
14:16 So His **d** went out, and came into
14:32 and He said to His **d**,
16: 7 "But go, tell His **d**—
Lk 5:30 complained against His **d**,
5:33 Why do the **d** of John fast often
6: 1 And His **d** plucked the heads of
6:13 He called His **d** to Himself;
6:17 place with a crowd of His **d**
6:20 lifted up His eyes toward His **d**,
7:11 and many of His **d** went with
7:18 Then the **d** of John reported to
7:19 calling two of his **d** to him,
8: 9 Then His **d** asked Him, saying,
8:22 He got into a boat with His **d**.
9: 1 Then He called His twelve **d**
9:14 Then He said to His **d**,
9:16 and gave them to the **d** to set
9:18 that His **d** joined Him, and He
9:40 So I implored Your **d** to cast it
9:43 Jesus did, He said to His **d**,
9:54 And when His **d** James and John
10:23 Then He turned to His **d** and
11: 1 that one of His **d** said to Him,
11: 1 pray, as John also taught his **d**.
12: 1 He began to say to His **d** first
12:22 Then He said to His **d**,
16: 1 He also said to His **d**:
17: 1 Then He said to the **d**,
17:22 Then He said to the **d**,
18:15 but when the **d** saw it, they
19:29 that He sent two of His **d**,
19:37 the whole multitude of the **d**
19:39 crowd, "Teacher, rebuke Your **d**.
20:45 the people, He said to His **d**,
22:11 may eat the Passover with My **d**?
22:39 and His **d** also followed Him.
22:45 prayer, and had come to His **d**,
Jn 1:35 John stood with two of his **d**.
1:37 The two **d** heard him speak, and
2: 2 Now both Jesus and His **d** were
2:11 and His **d** believed in Him.
2:12 mother, His brothers, and His **d**;
2:17 Then His **d** remembered that it
2:22 His **d** remembered that He had
3:22 these things Jesus and His **d**
3:25 between some of John's **d** and
4: 1 Jesus made and baptized more **d**
4: 2 did not baptize, but His **d**),
4: 8 For His **d** had gone away into the
4:27 And at this point His **d** came,
4:31 In the meantime His **d** urged Him,
4:33 Therefore the **d** said to one
6: 3 and there He sat with His **d**.
6: 8 One of His **d**, Andrew,
6:11 He distributed them to the **d**,
6:11 and the **d** to those sitting
6:12 were filled, He said to His **d**,
6:16 His **d** went down to the sea,
6:22 except that one which His **d** had
6:22 not entered the boat with His **d**,
6:22 but His **d** had gone away alone—
6:24 Jesus was not there, nor His **d**,
6:60 Therefore many of His **d**,
6:61 knew in Himself that His **d**
6:66 From that time many of His **d**
7: 3 that Your **d** also may see the
8:31 you are My **d** indeed.
9: 2 And His **d** asked Him, saying,
9:27 you also want to become His **d**?
9:28 disciple, but we are Moses' **d**.
11: 7 after this He said to the **d**,
11: 8 The **d** said to Him, "Rabbi,
11:12 Then His **d** said, "Lord, if he
11:16 the Twin, said to his fellow **d**,
11:54 and there remained with His **d**.
12: 4 Then one of His **d**,
12:16 His **d** did not understand these
13:22 Then the **d** looked at one
13:23 on Jesus' bosom one of His **d**,
13:35 all will know that you are My **d**,
15: 8 much fruit; so you will be My **d**.
16:17 Then some of His **d** said among
16:29 His **d** said to Him, "See, now
18: 1 He went out with His **d** over the
18: 1 which He and His **d** entered.
18: 2 often met there with His **d**.
18:17 not also one of this Man's **d**,
18:19 then asked Jesus about His **d**
18:25 are not also one of His **d**,
20:10 Then the **d** went away again to
20:18 Magdalene came and told the **d**
20:19 the doors were shut where the **d**
20:20 Then the **d** were glad when they
20:25 The other **d** therefore said to
20:26 And after eight days His **d** were
20:30 signs in the presence of His **d**,
21: 1 showed Himself again to the **d**
21: 2 and two others of His **d** were
21: 4 yet the **d** did not know that it
21: 8 But the other **d** came in the
21:12 Yet none of the **d** dared ask
21:14 Jesus showed Himself to His **d**
Acts 1:15 stood up in the midst of the **d**
6: 1 when the number of the **d** was
6: 2 the multitude of the **d** and
6: 7 and the number of the **d**
9: 1 and murder against the **d** of
9:19 spent some days with the **d** at
9:25 Then the **d** took him by night and
9:26 he tried to join the **d**;
9:38 and the **d** had heard that Peter
11:26 And the **d** were first called
11:29 Then the **d**, each according to
13:52 And the **d** were filled with joy
14:20 when the **d** gathered around him,
14:21 to that city and made many **d**,
14:22 the souls of the **d**,
14:28 there a long time with the **d**.
15:10 a yoke on the neck of the **d**
18:23 order, strengthening all the **d**.
18:27 exhorting the **d** to receive him;
19: 1 And finding some **d**
19: 9 from them and withdrew the **d**,
19:30 the **d** would not allow him.
20: 1 Paul called the **d** to himself,
20: 7 when the **d** came together to
20:30 to draw away the **d** after
21: 4 finding **d**, we stayed there
21:16 Also some of the **d** from Caesarea

DISCIPLES' (1/1) DISCIPLES

Jn 13: 5 began to wash the **d** feet,

DISCIPLINE (2/2) DISCIPLE, DISCIPLINED, DISCIPLINES

Prov 15:10 Harsh **d** is for him who
1 Cor 9:27 But I **d** my body and bring it

DISCIPLINED (1/1) DISCIPLINE

Hos 7:15 Though I **d** and strengthened

DISCIPLINES (1/1) DISCIPLINE

Prov 13:24 But he who loves him **d** him

DISCLOSE (3/3)

Ps 49: 4 I will **d** my dark saying on the
Prov 25: 9 And do not **d** the secret to
Isa 26:21 The earth will also **d** her

DISCOMFITED, DISCOMFITURE (KJV)

See DEFEATED, FORCED (LABOR), ROUTED

DISCONTENTED (1/1)

1 Sam 22: 2 and everyone who was **d**

DISCONTINUED (1/1)

Ezra 4:24 and it was **d** until the second

DISCORD (2/2)

Prov 6:14 evil continually, He sows **d**.
6:19 And one who sows **d** among

DISCOURAGE (2/2) DISCOURAGED

Num 32: 7 Now why will you **d** the heart of
Ezra 4: 4 people of the land tried to **d**

DISCOURAGED (8/8) DISCOURAGE

Num 21: 4 of the people became very **d** on
32: 9 they **d** the heart of the
Deut 1:21 to you; do not fear or be **d**.
1:28 Our brethren have **d** our hearts,
Isa 42: 4 He will not fail nor be **d**,
Col 3:21 children, lest they become **d**.
Heb 12: 3 lest you become weary and **d** in
12: 5 Nor be **d** when you are

DISCOURSE (2/2)

Job 27: 1 Moreover Job continued his **d**,
29: 1 Job further continued his **d**,

DISCOVER (1/1) DISCOVERED

Eccl 8:17 For though a man labors to **d**

DISCOVERED (4/4) DISCOVER

1 Sam 22: 6 who were with him had been **d**—
Neh 13: 7 and I came to Jerusalem and **d**
Job 8: 8 And consider the things **d** by
36:26 the number of His years be **d**.

DISCREET (1/1) DISCRETION

Titus 2: 5 to be **d**, chaste,

DISCRETION (9/9) DISCREET

Ps 112: 5 will guide his affairs with **d**.
Prov 1: 4 the young man knowledge and **d**—
2:11 ***D*** will preserve you
3:21 Keep sound wisdom and **d**;
5: 2 That you may preserve **d**,
8:12 And find out knowledge and **d**.
11:22 is a lovely woman who lacks **d**.
19:11 The **d** of a man makes him slow
Jer 10:12 out the heavens at His **d**.

DISCUSSED (2/2) DISCUSSING, DISCUSSION

Lk 1:65 and all these sayings were **d**
6:11 and **d** with one another what

DISCUSSING (1/1) DISCUSSED

Mk 9:16 What are you **d** with them?"

DISCUSSION (1/1) DISCUSSED

Heb 6: 1 leaving the **d** of the elementary

DISDAIN (2/2) DISDAINED, DISDAINS

Prov 8:33 And do not **d** it.
Ezek 25: 6 in heart with all your **d** for

DISDAINED (4/4) DISDAIN

1 Sam 17:42 saw David, he **d** him;
Esth 3: 6 But he **d** to lay hands on
Job 30: 1 Whose fathers I **d** to put with
Prov 1:25 Because you **d** all my counsel,

DISDAINS (2/2) DISDAIN

Prov 13:18 shame will come to him who **d**
15:32 He who **d** instruction despises

DISEASE (11/11) DISEASED, DISEASES

Lev 26:16 wasting **d** and fever which shall
2 Ki 8: 8 'Shall I recover from this **d**?
8: 9 'Shall I recover from this **d**?
2 Chr 16:12 yet in his **d** he did not seek
21:15 become very sick with a **d** of
21:18 intestines with an incurable **d**.
Ps 41: 8 'An evil **d**,' they say,
Mt 4:23 of sickness and all kinds of **d**
9:35 every sickness and every **d**
10: 1 of sickness and all kinds of **d**.
Jn 5: 4 made well of whatever **d** he had.

DISEASED (3/3) DISEASE

1 Ki 15:23 time of his old age he was **d**
2 Chr 16:12 Asa became **d** in his feet, and
Jn 6: 2 performed on those who were **d**.

DISEASES (11/11) DISEASE

Ex 15:26 I will put none of the **d** on you
Deut 7:15 with none of the terrible **d** of
28:60 bring back on you all the **d** of
Ps 103: 3 Who heals all your **d**,
Mt 4:24 were afflicted with various **d**
Mk 1:34 who were sick with various **d**,
Lk 4:40 that were sick with various **d**
6:17 Him and be healed of their **d**,
9: 1 over all demons, and to cure **d**.
Acts 19:12 and the **d** left them and the
28: 9 island who had **d** also came

DISFIGURE (2/2) DISFIGURED, DISFIGUREMENT

Lev 19:27 nor shall you **d** the edges of
Mt 6:16 For they **d** their faces that

DISFIGURED (1/1) DISFIGURE

Job 30:18 By great force my garment is **d**;

DISFIGUREMENT (2/2) DISFIGURE

Lev 24:19 If a man causes **d** of his
24:20 as he has caused **d** of a man, so

DISGRACE (4/4) DISGRACED, DISGRACEFUL

Job 10:15 up my head. I am full of **d**;
19: 5 And plead my **d** against me,
Ps 109:29 themselves with their own **d** as
Jer 14:21 Do not **d** the throne of Your

DISGRACED (9/9) DISGRACE

2 Sam 19: 5 Today you have ***d*** all your
Isa 24:23 Then the moon will be ***d*** And
41:11 you Shall be ashamed and ***d***;
45:16 shall be ashamed And also ***d***,
45:17 You shall not be ashamed or ***d***
50: 7 Therefore I will not be ***d***;
54: 4 not be ashamed; Neither be ***d***,
Ezek 16:52 be ***d*** also, and bear your own
16:54 bear your own shame and be ***d***

DISGRACEFUL (5/5) DISGRACE

Gen 34: 7 because he had done a ***d*** thing
Deut 22:21 because she has done a ***d*** thing
Josh 7:15 he has done a ***d*** thing
2 Sam 13:12 Do not do this ***d*** thing!
Jer 29:23 because they have done ***d*** things

DISGUISE (3/3) DISGUISED, DISGUISES

1 Ki 14: 2 and ***d*** yourself, that they may
22:30 I will ***d*** myself and go into
2 Chr 18:29 I will ***d*** myself and go into

DISGUISED (5/5) DISGUISE

1 Sam 28: 8 So Saul ***d*** himself and put on
1 Ki 20:38 and ***d*** himself with a bandage
22:30 king of Israel ***d*** himself
2 Chr 18:29 king of Israel ***d*** himself,
35:22 but ***d*** himself so that he might

DISGUISES (2/2) DISGUISE

Job 24:15 And he ***d*** his face.
Prov 26:24 ***d*** it with his lips, And lays

DISGUSTED (1/1)

Ps 119:158 see the treacherous, and am ***d***,

DISH (6/6) DISHES

2 Ki 21:13 Jerusalem as one wipes a ***d***,
Mt 23:25 the outside of the cup and ***d***,
23:26 the inside of the cup and ***d***,
26:23 his hand with Me in the ***d***
Mk 14:20 who dips with Me in the ***d***.
Lk 11:39 the outside of the cup and ***d***

DISHAN (5/5) DISHON

Gen 36:21 Dishon, Ezer, and ***D***.
36:28 These were the sons of ***D***:
36:30 Dishon, Chief Ezer, and Chief ***D***.
1 Chr 1:38 Anah, Dishon, Ezer, and ***D***.
1:42 The sons of ***D*** were Uz and

DISHEARTENED (1/1)

Neh 6:16 that they were very ***d*** in their

DISHES (3/3) DISH

Ex 25:29 "You shall make its ***d***,
37:16 on the table: its ***d***, its cups,
Num 4: 7 blue cloth, and put on it the ***d***,

DISHON (7/6) DISHAN

Gen 36:21 ***D***, Ezer, and Dishan.
36:25 ***D*** and Aholibamah the daughter
36:26 These were the sons of ***D***:
36:30 Chief ***D***, Chief Ezer, and
1 Chr 1:38 Lotan, Shobal, Zibeon, Anah, ***D***,
1:41 The son of Anah was ***D***.
1:41 The sons of ***D*** were Hamran,

DISHONEST (7/7) DISHONESTY

1 Sam 8: 3 they turned aside after ***d*** gain,
Prov 11: 1 ***D*** scales are an abomination to
20:23 And ***d*** scales are not good.
Ezek 22:13 I beat My fists at the ***d*** profit
22:27 and to get ***d*** gain.
Titus 1:11 for the sake of ***d*** gain.
1 Pe 5: 2 not for ***d*** gain but eagerly;

DISHONESTY (1/1) DISHONEST

Prov 13:11 Wealth gained by ***d*** will be

DISHONOR (19/19) DISHONORED, DISHONORS

Ezra 4:14 for us to see the king's ***d***;
Ps 35: 4 put to shame and brought to ***d***
35:26 be clothed with shame and ***d***
40:14 backward and brought to ***d*** Who
44:15 My ***d*** is continually before me,
69:19 my reproach, my shame, and my ***d***;
71:13 be covered with reproach and ***d***
Prov 6:33 Wounds and ***d*** he will get,
18: 3 And with ***d*** comes reproach.
Isa 23: 9 To bring to ***d*** the pride of all
Hos 4:18 Her rulers dearly love ***d***.
Jn 8:49 My Father, and you ***d*** Me.
Rom 1:24 to ***d*** their bodies among
2:23 do you ***d*** God through breaking
9:21 for honor and another for ***d***?
1 Cor 11:14 it is a ***d*** to him?
15:43 It is sown in ***d***, it is raised
2 Cor 6: 8 by honor and ***d***, by evil report
2 Tim 2:20 some for honor and some for ***d***.

DISHONORED (2/2) DISHONOR

1 Cor 4:10 but we are ***d***!
Jas 2: 6 But you have ***d*** the poor man.

DISHONORS (3/3) DISHONOR

Mic 7: 6 For son ***d*** father, Daughter
1 Cor 11: 4 head covered, ***d*** his head.
11: 5 with her head uncovered ***d*** her

DISINHERIT (1/1)

Num 14:12 with the pestilence and ***d*** them,

DISLOCATED (1/1)

Heb 12:13 that what is lame may not be ***d***,

DISMAY (3/3) DISMAYED

Jer 1:17 Lest I ***d*** you before them.
48:39 shall be a derision And a ***d***
Ezek 8:14 the LORD's house; and to my ***d***,

DISMAYED (36/34) DISMAY

Gen 45: 3 for they were ***d*** in his
Ex 15:15 the chiefs of Edom will be ***d***;
Deut 31: 8 do not fear nor be ***d***."
Josh 1: 9 do not be afraid, nor be ***d***,
8: 1 "Do not be afraid, nor be ***d***;
10:25 "Do not be afraid, nor be ***d***;
1 Sam 17:11 they were ***d*** and greatly afraid.
2 Ki 19:26 They were ***d*** and confounded;
1 Chr 22:13 courage; do not fear nor be ***d***.
28:20 do it; do not fear nor be ***d***,
2 Chr 20:15 Do not be afraid nor ***d*** because
20:17 Do not fear or be ***d***;
32: 7 do not be afraid nor ***d*** before
Job 32:15 They are ***d*** and answer no more;
Ps 83:17 Let them be confounded and ***d***
Isa 21: 3 I was ***d*** when I saw it.
37:27 They were ***d*** and confounded;
41:10 Be not ***d***, for I am your God.
41:23 That we may be ***d*** and see it
Jer 1:17 Do not be ***d*** before their
8: 9 They are ***d*** and taken.
10: 2 Do not be ***d*** at the signs of
10: 2 For the Gentiles are ***d*** at
17:18 Let them be ***d***, But do not
17:18 But do not let me be ***d***.
23: 4 shall fear no more, nor be ***d***,
30:10 says the LORD, 'Nor be ***d***,
46: 5 Why have I seen them ***d*** and
46:27 servant Jacob, And do not be ***d***,
48: 1 high stronghold is shamed and ***d***—
49:37 For I will cause Elam to be ***d***
50:36 mighty men, and they will be ***d***.
Ezek 2: 6 be afraid of their words or ***d***
3: 9 nor be ***d*** at their looks, though
4:17 and be ***d*** with one another, and
Ob 9 mighty men, O Teman, shall be ***d***,

DISMISS (2/2) DISMISSED

1 Ki 20:24 ***D*** the kings, each from his
Mk 10: 4 of divorce, and to ***d*** her."

DISMISSED (4/4) DISMISS

Judg 2: 6 And when Joshua had ***d*** the
2 Chr 23: 8 Jehoiada the priest had not ***d***
Zech 11: 8 I ***d*** the three shepherds in one
Acts 19:41 he ***d*** the assembly.

DISMOUNT (1/1) DISMOUNTED

1 Sam 25:23 she hastened to ***d*** from the

DISMOUNTED (3/3) DISMOUNT

Gen 24:64 and when she saw Isaac she ***d***
Josh 15:18 So she ***d*** from her donkey, and
Judg 1:14 And she ***d*** from her donkey, and

DISOBEDIENCE (11/11) DISOBEDIENT

Ezek 5: 7 'Because you have multiplied ***d***
Rom 5:19 For as by one man's ***d*** many were
11:30 obtained mercy through their ***d***,
11:32 God has committed them all to ***d***,
2 Cor 10: 6 and being ready to punish all ***d***
Eph 2: 2 who now works in the sons of ***d***,
5: 6 of God comes upon the sons of ***d***.
Col 3: 6 is coming upon the sons of ***d***,
Heb 2: 2 and every transgression and ***d***
4: 6 did not enter because of ***d***,
4:11 to the same example of ***d***.

DISOBEDIENT (14/14) DISOBEDIENCE, DISOBEYED

1 Ki 13:26 is the man of God who was ***d***
Neh 9:26 Nevertheless they were ***d*** And
Lk 1:17 and the ***d*** to the wisdom of the
Acts 26:19 I was not ***d*** to the heavenly
Rom 1:30 evil things, ***d*** to parents,
10:21 out My hands To a ***d***
11:30 For as you were once ***d*** to God,
11:31 so these also have now been ***d***,
2 Tim 3: 2 ***d*** to parents, unthankful,
Titus 1:16 deny Him, being abominable, ***d***,
3: 3 were also once foolish, ***d***,
1 Pe 2: 7 but to those who are ***d***,
2: 8 being ***d*** to the word, to which
3:20 who formerly were ***d***,

DISOBEYED (1/1) DISOBEDIENT, DISOBEYING

1 Ki 13:21 Because you have ***d*** the word of

DISOBEYING (1/1) DISOBEYED

Jer 42:13 ***d*** the voice of the LORD your

DISORDERLY (4/4)

Acts 19:40 account for this ***d*** gathering."
2 Th 3: 6 from every brother who walks ***d***
3: 7 for we were not ***d*** among you;
3:11 walk among you in a ***d*** manner,

DISPATCHES (1/1)

Job 37:15 Do you know when God ***d*** them,

DISPENSATION (2/2)

Eph 1:10 that in the ***d*** of the fullness of
3: 2 indeed you have heard of the ***d***

DISPERSE (10/10) DISPERSED, DISPERSION

1 Sam 14:34 ***D*** yourselves among the people,
Job 40:11 ***D*** the rage of your wrath
Prov 15: 7 The lips of the wise ***d***
Ezek 12:15 among the nations and ***d*** them
20:23 among the Gentiles and ***d*** them
22:15 ***d*** you throughout the countries,
29:12 among the nations and ***d*** them
30:23 and ***d*** them throughout the
30:26 among the nations and ***d*** them
Dan 11:24 he shall ***d*** among them the

DISPERSED (10/10) DISPERSE

Gen 10:18 of the Canaanites were ***d***.
2 Chr 11:23 and ***d*** some of his sons
Esth 3: 8 certain people scattered and ***d***
Ps 112: 9 He has ***d*** abroad, He has given
Prov 5:16 Should your fountains be ***d***
Isa 11:12 And gather together the ***d*** of
Ezek 36:19 and they were ***d*** throughout the
Zeph 3:10 The daughter of My ***d*** ones,
Acts 5:37 and all who obeyed him were ***d***.
2 Cor 9: 9 He has ***d*** abroad, He has

DISPERSION (2/2) DISPERSE, DISPERSIONS

Jn 7:35 Does He intend to go to the ***D***
1 Pe 1: 1 To the pilgrims of the ***D*** in

DISPERSIONS (1/1) DISPERSION

Jer 25:34 of your slaughter and your ***d***

DISPLACE (1/1)

Deut 12:29 and you ***d*** them and dwell in

DISPLAYED (2/2)

Ps 60: 4 That it may be ***d*** because of
1 Cor 4: 9 For I think that God has ***d*** us,

DISPLEASE (4/4) DISPLEASED, DISPLEASES, DISPLEASING, DISPLEASURE

Gen 31:35 Let it not ***d*** my lord that I
1 Sam 29: 7 that you may not ***d*** the lords of
2 Sam 11:25 Do not let this thing ***d*** you, for
Prov 24:18 and it ***d*** Him, And He turn away

DISPLEASED (18/18) DISPLEASE

Gen 38:10 And the thing which he did ***d*** the
48:17 it ***d*** him; so he took hold of
Num 11: 1 complained, it ***d*** the LORD;
11:10 aroused; Moses also was ***d***.
1 Sam 8: 6 But the thing ***d*** Samuel when
18: 8 and the saying ***d*** him; and he
2 Sam 11:27 the thing that David had done ***d***
1 Ki 20:43 went to his house sullen and ***d***,
21: 4 into his house sullen and ***d***
1 Chr 21: 7 And God was ***d*** with this thing;
Ps 60: 1 us down; You have been ***d***;
Isa 59:15 and it ***d*** Him That there was
Dan 6:14 was greatly ***d*** with himself, and
Jon 4: 1 But it ***d*** Jonah exceedingly, and
Hab 3: 8 were You ***d*** with the rivers,
Mt 20:24 they were greatly ***d*** with the
Mk 10:14 He was greatly ***d*** and said to
10:41 they began to be greatly ***d*** with

DISPLEASES (1/1) DISPLEASE

Num 22:34 if it ***d*** You, I will turn

DISPLEASING (3/3) DISPLEASE
Gen 21:11 And the matter was very ***d*** in
21:12 Do not let it be ***d*** in your sight
Jer 42: 6 "Whether it is pleasing or ***d***,

DISPLEASURE (4/4) DISPLEASE
Deut 9:19 afraid of the anger and hot ***d***
Ps 2: 5 distress them in His deep ***d***:
6: 1 Nor chasten me in Your hot ***d***.
38: 1 Nor chasten me in Your hot ***d***!

DISPOSED (1/1) DISPOSSESS
Num 22:30 Was I ever ***d*** to do this to

DISPOSSESS (9/9) DISPOSED, DISPOSSESSED, DISPOSSESSING
Num 33:53 you shall ***d*** the inhabitants
Deut 7:17 how can I ***d*** them?'—
9: 1 and go in to ***d*** nations greater
11:23 and you will ***d*** greater and
12: 2 the nations which you shall ***d***
12:29 the nations which you go to ***d***,
18:14 these nations which you will ***d***
19: 1 and you ***d*** them and dwell in
31: 3 and you shall ***d*** them.

DISPOSSESSED (5/5) DISPOSSESS
Num 32:39 ***d*** the Amorites who were in it.
Deut 2:12 but the descendants of Esau ***d***
2:21 and they ***d*** them and dwelt in
2:22 They ***d*** them and dwelt in their
Judg 11:23 the LORD God of Israel has ***d***

DISPOSSESSING (1/1) DISPOSSESS
Ezek 45: 9 and stop ***d*** My people," says

DISPUTE (13/13) DISPUTED, DISPUTER, DISPUTES, DISPUTING
Ex 23: 2 nor shall you testify in a ***d*** so
23: 3 to a poor man in his ***d***.
23: 6 judgment of your poor in his ***d***.
Deut 25: 1 If there is a ***d*** between men, and
2 Sam 19: 9 Now all the people were in a ***d***
Mk 8:11 came out and began to ***d*** with
Lk 9:46 Then a ***d*** arose among them as to
22:24 Now there was also a ***d*** among
Jn 3:25 Then there arose a ***d*** between
Acts 15: 2 had no small dissension and ***d***
15: 7 And when there had been much ***d***,
28:29 Jews departed and had a great ***d***
Heb 6:16 is for them an end of all ***d***.

DISPUTED (4/4) DISPUTE
Mk 9:33 What was it you ***d*** among
9:34 they had ***d*** among themselves
Acts 9:29 the Lord Jesus and ***d*** against
Jude 9 when he ***d*** about the body of

DISPUTER (1/1) DISPUTE
1 Cor 1:20 Where is the ***d*** of this age?

DISPUTES (6/6) DISPUTE
2 Sam 20:18 Abel,' and so they would end ***d***.
Rom 14: 1 but not to ***d*** over doubtful
1 Tim 1: 4 which cause ***d*** rather than godly
6: 4 but is obsessed with ***d*** and
2 Tim 2:23 avoid foolish and ignorant ***d***,
Titus 3: 9 But avoid foolish ***d***,

DISPUTING (4/4) DISPUTE
Mk 9:14 and scribes ***d*** with them.
Acts 6: 9 and Asia), ***d*** with Stephen.
24:12 found me in the temple ***d*** with
Phil 2:14 without complaining and ***d***,

DISQUALIFIED (5/5)
1 Cor 9:27 I myself should become ***d***.
2 Cor 13: 5 in you?—unless indeed you are ***d***.
13: 6 you will know that we are not ***d***.
13: 7 honorable, though we may seem ***d***.
Titus 1:16 and ***d*** for every good work.

DISQUIET (1/1) DISQUIETED, DISQUIETING
Jer 50:34 And ***d*** the inhabitants of

DISQUIETED (3/3) DISQUIET
Ps 42: 5 And why are you ***d*** within me?
42:11 And why are you ***d*** within me?
43: 5 And why are you ***d*** within me?

DISQUIETING (1/1) DISQUIET
Job 4:13 In ***d*** thoughts from the visions

DISREGARDED (1/1)
Heb 8: 9 and I ***d*** them, says the

DISREPUTABLE (1/1) DISREPUTE
Prov 19:28 A ***d*** witness scorns justice,

DISREPUTE (1/1) DISREPUTABLE
Acts 19:27 in danger of falling into ***d***,

DISSEMBLED, DISSIMULATION (KJV)
See DECEIVED, HYPOCRISY, HYPOCRITES

DISSENSION (4/4) DISSENSIONS
Acts 15: 2 and Barnabas had no small ***d***
23: 7 a ***d*** arose between the Pharisees
23:10 Now when there arose a great ***d***,
24: 5 a creator of ***d*** among all the

DISSENSIONS (1/1) DISSENSION
Gal 5:20 of wrath, selfish ambitions, ***d***,

DISSIPATION (3/3)
Eph 5:18 drunk with wine, in which is ***d***;
Titus 1: 6 children not accused of ***d*** or
1 Pe 4: 4 them in the same flood of ***d***,

DISSOLVE (3/1) DISSOLVED
Zech 14:12 Their flesh shall ***d*** while they
14:12 Their eyes shall ***d*** in their
14:12 And their tongues shall ***d*** in

DISSOLVED (6/6) DISSOLVE
Ps 75: 3 and all its inhabitants are ***d***;
Isa 14:31 All you of Philistia are ***d***;
34: 4 the host of heaven shall be ***d***,
Nah 2: 6 opened, And the palace is ***d***.
2 Pe 3:11 all these things will be ***d***,
3:12 of which the heavens will be ***d***,

DISTAFF (1/1)
Prov 31:19 out her hands to the ***d***,

DISTANCE (19/19)
Gen 21:16 down across from him at a ***d***
32:16 and put some ***d*** between
35:16 when there was but a little ***d***
48: 7 there was but a little ***d*** to
Num 2: 2 they shall camp some ***d*** from the
16:37 and scatter the fire some ***d***
Deut 21: 2 go out and measure the ***d***
1 Sam 26:13 a great ***d*** being between them.
2 Ki 2: 7 and stood facing them at a ***d***,
5:19 he departed from him a short ***d***.
Job 39:24 He devours the ***d*** with
Ezek 42: 4 at a ***d*** of one cubit; and their
Mt 26:58 But Peter followed Him at a ***d*** to
Mk 14:54 But Peter followed Him at a ***d***,
Lk 22:54 But Peter followed at a ***d***.
23:49 Him from Galilee, stood at a ***d***,
Rev 18:10 standing at a ***d*** for fear of her
18:15 will stand at a ***d*** for fear of
18:17 on the sea, stood at a ***d***

DISTANT (1/1)
Ps 56: 'The Silent Dove in ***D*** Lands."

DISTILL (2/2)
Deut 32: 2 My speech ***d*** as the dew,
Job 36:27 Which ***d*** as rain from the mist,

DISTINCTION (4/4) DISTINCTLY, DISTINGUISH
Acts 15: 9 and made no ***d*** between us and
Rom 10:12 For there is no ***d*** between Jew
1 Cor 14: 7 unless they make a ***d*** in the
Jude 22 have compassion, making a ***d***;

DISTINCTLY (1/1) DISTINCTION
Neh 8: 8 So they read ***d*** from the book, in

DISTINGUISH (4/4) DINTINCTION, DISTINGUISHED
Lev 10:10 that you may ***d*** between holy and
11:47 to ***d*** between the unclean and the
20:25 You shall therefore ***d*** between
2 Chr 12: 8 that they may ***d*** My service from

DISTINGUISHED (3/3) DISTINGUISH
Ezek 22:26 they have not ***d*** between the
Dan 6: 3 Then this Daniel ***d*** himself above
1 Cor 4:10 You are ***d***, but we are

DISTORTS (1/1)
Isa 24: 1 ***D*** its surface And scatters

DISTRACTED (1/1) DISTRACTION
Lk 10:40 But Martha was ***d*** with much

DISTRACTION (1/1) DISTRACTED
1 Cor 7:35 may serve the Lord without ***d***.

DISTRAUGHT (1/1)
Ps 88:15 I suffer Your terrors; I am ***d***.

DISTRESS (44/44) DISTRESSED, DISTRESSES, DISTRESSING
Gen 35: 3 answered me in the day of my ***d***
42:21 therefore this ***d*** has come upon
Deut 4:30 "When you are in ***d***,
28:53 in which your enemy shall ***d***
28:55 in which your enemy shall ***d***
28:57 in which your enemy shall ***d***
Judg 10:14 deliver you in your time of ***d***.
11: 7 to me now when you are in ***d***?
1 Sam 22: 2 And everyone who was in ***d***,
2 Sam 22: 7 In my ***d*** I called upon the
24:14 said to Gad, "I am in great ***d***.
1 Ki 1:29 redeemed my life from every ***d***,
2 Ki 4:27 for her soul is in deep ***d***,
1 Chr 21:13 said to Gad, "I am in great ***d***.
2 Chr 28:22 Now in the time of his ***d*** King
Neh 1: 3 province are there in great ***d***
2:17 You see the ***d*** that we are in,
9:37 And we are in great ***d***.
Job 20:22 he will be in ***d***; Every hand
36:16 have brought you out of dire ***d***,
36:19 mighty forces, Keep you from ***d***?
Ps 2: 5 And ***d*** them in His deep
4: 1 You have relieved me in my ***d***;
18: 6 In my ***d*** I called upon the
118: 5 I called on the LORD in ***d***;
120: 1 In my ***d*** I cried to the LORD,
Prov 1:27 When ***d*** and anguish come upon
Isa 21:15 and from the ***d*** of war.
25: 4 strength to the needy in his ***d***,
29: 2 Yet I will ***d*** Ariel;
29: 7 And ***d*** her, Shall be as a
Jer 10:18 And will ***d*** them, That they
Lam 1:20 O LORD, that I am in ***d***;
Ezek 30:16 And Noph shall be in ***d***
Ob 12 spoken proudly In the day of ***d***.
14 who remained In the day of ***d***.
Zeph 1:15 wrath, A day of trouble and ***d***,
1:17 'I will bring ***d*** upon men,
Lk 21:23 For there will be great ***d*** in
21:25 and on the earth ***d*** of nations,
Rom 8:35 Shall tribulation, or ***d***,
1 Cor 7:26 good because of the present ***d***—
Phil 4:14 well that you shared in my ***d***.
1 Th 3: 7 in all our affliction and ***d*** we

DISTRESSED (18/18) DISTRESS
Gen 32: 7 Jacob was greatly afraid and ***d***;
Judg 2:15 And they were greatly ***d***.
10: 9 so that Israel was severely ***d***.
1 Sam 13: 6 danger (for the people were ***d***),
14:24 And the men of Israel were ***d***
28:15 Saul answered, "I am deeply ***d***;
30: 6 Now David was greatly ***d***,
2 Sam 1:26 I am ***d*** for you, my brother
13: 2 Amnon was so ***d*** over his sister
2 Chr 28:20 came to him and ***d*** him,
Esth 4: 4 her, and the queen was deeply ***d***.
Ps 143: 4 My heart within me is ***d***.
Isa 9: 1 not be upon her who is ***d***,
21: 3 I was ***d*** when I heard it;
Mt 26:37 to be sorrowful and deeply ***d***.
Mk 14:33 to be troubled and deeply ***d***.
Lk 12:50 and how ***d*** I am till it is
Phil 2:26 and was ***d*** because you had heard

DISTRESSES (7/7) DISTRESS
Ps 25:17 Bring me out of my ***d***!
107: 6 delivered them out of their ***d***.
107:13 He saved them out of their ***d***.
107:19 He saved them out of their ***d***.
107:28 He brings them out of their ***d***.
2 Cor 6: 4 in tribulations, in needs, in ***d***,
12:10 in needs, in persecutions, in ***d***,

DISTRESSING (8/8) DISTRESS
1 Sam 16:14 and a ***d*** spirit from the LORD
16:15 a ***d*** spirit from God is
16:16 it with his hand when the ***d***
16:23 and the ***d*** spirit would depart
18:10 on the next day that the ***d***
19: 9 Now the ***d*** spirit from the LORD
Eccl 2:17 was done under the sun was ***d***
Isa 21: 2 A ***d*** vision is declared to me;

DISTRIBUTE (5/5) DISTRIBUTED, DISTRIBUTES, DISTRIBUTING, DISTRIBUTION
2 Chr 31:14 to ***d*** the offerings of the LORD
31:15 to ***d*** allotments to their
31:19 by name to ***d*** portions
Neh 13:13 and their task was to ***d*** to
Lk 18:22 Sell all that you have and ***d*** to

DISTRIBUTED (9/9) DISTRIBUTE
Josh 13:32 the areas which Moses had ***d***
14: 1 of the children of Israel ***d*** as
2 Sam 6:19 Then he ***d*** among all the people,

1 Chr 16: 3 Then he ***d*** to everyone of Israel,
2 Chr 31:16 they ***d*** to everyone who entered
Jn 6:11 when He had given thanks He ***d***
Acts 4:35 and they ***d*** to each as anyone
13:19 He ***d*** their land to them by
1 Cor 7:17 But as God has ***d*** to each one,

DISTRIBUTES (1/1) DISTRIBUTE
Job 21:17 The sorrows God ***d*** in His

DISTRIBUTING (2/2) DISTRIBUTE
Rom 12:13 ***d*** to the needs of the saints,
1 Cor 12:11 ***d*** to each one individually as

DISTRIBUTION (1/1) DISTRIBUTE
Acts 6: 1 were neglected in the daily ***d***.

DISTRICT (24/18) DISTRICTS
Neh 3: 9 leader of half the ***d*** of
3:12 leader of half the ***d*** of
3:14 leader of the ***d*** of Beth
3:15 leader of the ***d*** of Mizpah,
3:16 leader of half the ***d*** of Beth
3:17 leader of half the ***d*** of Keilah,
3:17 Keilah, made repairs for his ***d***.
3:18 of the other half of the ***d*** of
Ezek 45: 1 you shall set apart a ***d*** for the
45: 3 So this is the ***d*** you shall
45: 6 adjacent to the ***d*** of the holy
45: 7 and the other of the holy ***d***
45: 7 and bordering on the holy ***d*** and
48: 8 shall be the ***d*** which you shall
48: 9 The ***d*** that you shall set apart
48:10 the holy ***d*** shall belong: on the
48:12 And this ***d*** of land that is set
48:18 alongside the ***d*** of the holy
48:18 It shall be adjacent to the ***d***
48:20 The entire ***d*** shall be
48:20 You shall set apart the holy ***d***
48:21 and on the other of the holy ***d***
48:21 cubits of the holy ***d*** as far
48:21 It shall be the holy ***d***,

DISTRICTS (3/3) DISTRICT
Neh 9:22 And divided them into ***d***.
Hos 11: 6 in his cities, Devour his ***d***,
Mt 2:16 in Bethlehem and in all its ***d***,

DISTURBED (6/6) DISTURBS
1 Sam 28:15 Why have you ***d*** me by bringing me
Neh 2:10 they were deeply ***d*** that a man
Job 40:23 may rage, Yet he is not ***d***;
Isa 31: 4 of their voice Nor be ***d*** by
Acts 4: 2 being greatly ***d*** that they taught
21:30 And all the city was ***d***;

DISTURBS (1/1) DISBURBED
Jer 31:35 Who ***d*** the sea, And its waves

DITCH (3/3) DITCHES
Ps 7:15 And has fallen into the ***d***
Mt 15:14 blind, both will fall into a ***d***.
Lk 6:39 they not both fall into the ***d***?

DITCHES (1/1) DITCH
2 Ki 3:16 'Make this valley full of ***d***.

DIVERS (KJV) See DIFFERENT, MANY, SOME, VARIOUS

DIVERSE (3/2) DIVERSITIES
Prov 20:10 ***D*** weights and diverse
20:10 Diverse weights and ***d***
20:23 ***D*** weights are an abomination

DIVERSITIES (2/2) DIVERSE
1 Cor 12: 4 There are ***d*** of gifts, but the
12: 6 And there are ***d*** of activities,

DIVERTED (1/1)
2 Chr 18:31 and God ***d*** them from him.

DIVERTING (1/1)
Am 5:12 ***D*** the poor from justice at

DIVIDE (45/43) DIVIDED, DIVIDER, DIVIDES, DIVIDING, DIVISION, DIVISIVE
Gen 1: 6 and let it ***d*** the waters from
1:14 firmament of the heavens to ***d***
1:18 and to ***d*** the light from the
49: 7 I will ***d*** them in Jacob
49:27 And at night he shall ***d*** the
Ex 14:16 hand over the sea and ***d*** it.
15: 9 I will ***d*** the spoil; My desire
21:35 the live ox and ***d*** the money
21:35 the dead ox they shall also ***d***.
Lev 1:17 but shall not ***d*** it
5: 8 but shall not ***d*** it completely.
Num 31:27 and ***d*** the plunder into two
33:54 And you shall ***d*** the land by lot
34:17 names of the men who shall ***d***
34:18 one leader of every tribe to ***d***
34:29 ones the LORD commanded to ***d***
Deut 19: 3 and ***d*** into three parts the
Josh 1: 6 for to this people you shall ***d***
13: 6 only ***d*** it by lot to Israel as
13: 7 ***d*** this land as an inheritance
18: 5 And they shall ***d*** it into seven
22: 8 ***D*** the spoil of your enemies
2 Sam 19:29 You and Ziba ***d*** the land.'"
1 Ki 3:25 ***D*** the living child in two, and
3:26 mine nor yours, but ***d*** him."
Job 27:17 And the innocent will ***d*** the
Ps 22:18 They ***d*** My garments among them,
55: 9 and ***d*** their tongues, For I
60: 6 I will ***d*** Shechem And measure
108: 7 I will ***d*** Shechem And measure
Prov 16:19 Than to ***d*** the spoil with the
Isa 9: 3 when they ***d*** the spoil.
18: 2 down, Whose land the rivers ***d***.
18: 7 down, Whose land the rivers ***d***—
53:12 Therefore I will ***d*** Him a
53:12 And He shall ***d*** the spoil with
Ezek 5: 1 take scales to weigh and ***d*** the
45: 1 when you ***d*** the land by lot into
47:13 which you shall ***d*** the land
47:21 Thus you shall ***d*** this land
47:22 It shall be that you will ***d*** it
48:29 is the land which you shall ***d***
Dan 11:39 and ***d*** the land for gain.
Lk 12:13 tell my brother to ***d*** the
22:17 Take this and ***d*** it among

DIVIDED (72/69) DIVIDE
Gen 1: 4 and God ***d*** the light from the
1: 7 and ***d*** the waters which were
10:25 for in his days the earth was ***d***;
10:32 from these the nations were ***d***
14:15 He ***d*** his forces against them by
32: 7 and he ***d*** the people that were
33: 1 So he ***d*** the children among
Ex 14:21 land, and the waters were ***d***.
Num 26:53 To these the land shall be ***d*** as
26:55 But the land shall be ***d*** by lot;
26:56 their inheritance shall be ***d***
Deut 32: 8 When the Most High ***d*** their
Josh 14: 5 and they ***d*** the land.
18:10 and there Joshua ***d*** the land to
19:51 of the children of Israel ***d*** as
23: 4 I have ***d*** to you by lot these
Judg 7:16 Then he ***d*** the three hundred men
9:43 ***d*** them into three companies,
19:29 and ***d*** her into twelve pieces,
2 Sam 1:23 in their death they were not ***d***;
1 Ki 16:21 the people of Israel were ***d***
18: 6 So they ***d*** the land between them
2 Ki 2: 8 and it was ***d*** this way and that,
2:14 it was ***d*** this way and that;
1 Chr 1:19 for in his days the earth was ***d***;
24: 3 ***d*** them according to the
24: 4 Ithamar, and thus they were ***d***.
24: 5 Thus they were ***d*** by lot, one
2 Chr 35:13 and ***d*** them quickly among all
Neh 9:11 And You ***d*** the sea before them,
9:22 And ***d*** them into districts.
Job 38:25 Who has ***d*** a channel for the
Ps 74:13 You ***d*** the sea by Your strength;
78:13 He ***d*** the sea and caused them to
136:13 To Him who ***d*** the Red Sea in
Isa 33:23 the prey of great plunder is ***d***;
34:17 And His hand has ***d*** it among
51:15 Who ***d*** the sea whose waves
Ezek 37:22 nor shall they ever be ***d*** into
Dan 2:41 of iron, the kingdom shall be ***d***;
5:28 Your kingdom has been ***d***,
11: 4 shall be broken up and ***d***
Hos 10: 2 Their heart is ***d***; Now they are
Joel 3: 2 They have also ***d*** up My land.
Am 7:17 Your land shall be ***d*** by
Mic 2: 4 To a turncoat He has ***d*** our
Hab 3: 9 Selah You ***d*** the earth with
Zech 14: 1 And your spoil will be ***d*** in
Mt 12:25 Every kingdom ***d*** against itself
12:25 and every city or house ***d***
12:26 he is ***d*** against himself.
27:35 and ***d*** His garments, casting
27:35 They ***d*** My garments among
Mk 3:24 If a kingdom is ***d*** against
3:25 And if a house is ***d*** against
3:26 up against himself, and is ***d***,
6:41 and the two fish He ***d*** among
15:24 they ***d*** His garments, casting
Lk 11:17 Every kingdom ***d*** against itself
11:17 and a house ***d*** against a house
11:18 If Satan also is ***d*** against
12:52 on five in one house will be ***d***:
12:53 Father will be ***d*** against son and
15:12 So he ***d*** to them his
23:34 And they ***d*** His garments and
Jn 19:24 They ***d*** My garments among
Acts 2: 3 appeared to them ***d*** tongues,
2:45 and ***d*** them among all, as anyone
14: 4 the multitude of the city was ***d***:
23: 7 and the assembly was ***d***.
1 Cor 1:13 Is Christ ***d***? Was Paul crucified
Rev 16:19 Now the great city was ***d*** into

DIVIDER (1/1) DIVIDE
Ex 26:33 The veil shall be a ***d*** for you

DIVIDES (7/7) DIVIDE
Lev 11: 3 whatever ***d*** the hoof, having
11: 7 though it ***d*** the hoof, having
11:26 any animal which ***d*** the foot,
Ps 29: 7 The voice of the LORD ***d*** the
68:12 remains at home ***d*** the spoil.
Mt 25:32 as a shepherd ***d*** his sheep from
Lk 11:22 and ***d*** his spoils.

DIVIDING (5/5) DIVIDE
Josh 19:49 they had made an end of ***d*** the
19:51 So they made an end of ***d*** the
Judg 5:30 Are they not finding and ***d*** the
Isa 63:12 ***D*** the water before them To
2 Tim 2:15 rightly ***d*** the word of truth.

DIVINATION (15/15) DIVIDE
Gen 44: 5 which he indeed practices ***d***?
44:15 as I can certainly practice ***d***?
Lev 19:26 nor shall you practice ***d*** or
Num 23:23 Nor any ***d*** against Israel.
Prov 16:10 ***D*** is on the lips of the king;
Jer 14:14 to you a false vision, ***d***,
Ezek 12:24 false vision or flattering ***d***
13: 6 envisioned futility and false ***d***,
13: 7 and have you not spoken false ***d***?
13:23 futility nor practice ***d***;
21:21 fork of the two roads, to use ***d***:
21:22 In his right hand is the ***d*** for
21:23 will be to them like a false ***d***
Mic 3: 6 shall have darkness without ***d***;
Acts 16:16 possessed with a spirit of ***d***

DIVINE (9/9) DIVINATION, DIVINELY, DIVINER, DIVINING
Ezek 13: 9 futility and who ***d*** lies;
21:29 While they ***d*** a lie to you, To
Mic 3:11 And her prophets ***d*** for money.
Acts 17:29 to think that the ***D*** Nature
Rom 11: 4 But what does the ***d*** response say
Heb 9: 1 had ordinances of ***d*** service
1 Pe 3:20 when once the ***D*** longsuffering
2 Pe 1: 3 as His ***d*** power has given to us
1: 4 partakers of the ***d*** nature,

DIVINELY (4/4) DIVINE
Mt 2:12 being ***d*** warned in a dream that
Acts 10:22 was ***d*** instructed by a holy
Heb 8: 5 as Moses was ***d*** instructed when
11: 7 being ***d*** warned of things not

DIVINER (1/1) DIVINE, DIVINER'S, DIVINERS
Isa 3: 2 And the ***d*** and the elder;

DIVINER'S (1/1) DIVINER
Num 22: 7 departed with the ***d*** fee

DIVINERS (7/7) DIVINER, DIVINERS'
Deut 18:14 listened to soothsayers and ***d***;
1 Sam 6: 2 for the priests and the ***d***,
Isa 44:25 And drives ***d*** mad; Who turns
Jer 27: 9 listen to your prophets, your ***d***,
29: 8 let your prophets and your ***d***
Mic 3: 7 And the ***d*** abashed; Indeed
Zech 10: 2 The ***d*** envision lies, And tell

DIVINERS' (1/1) DIVINERS
Judg 9:37 from the ***D*** Terebinth Tree."

DIVINING (1/1) DIVINE
Ezek 22:28 and ***d*** lies for them, saying,

DIVISION (27/24) DIVIDE, DIVISIONS
1 Chr 27: 1 each ***d*** having twenty-four
27: 2 Over the first ***d*** for the first
27: 2 and in his ***d*** were twenty-four
27: 4 Over the ***d*** of the second month
27: 4 and of his ***d*** Mikloth also was
27: 4 in his ***d*** were twenty-four
27: 5 in his ***d*** were twenty-four
27: 6 in his ***d*** was Ammizabad his
27: 7 in his ***d*** were twenty-four
27: 8 in his ***d*** were twenty-four
27: 9 in his ***d*** were twenty-four
27:10 in his ***d*** were twenty-four
27:11 in his ***d*** were twenty-four
27:12 in his ***d*** were twenty-four
27:13 in his ***d*** were twenty-four
27:14 in his ***d*** were twenty-four
27:15 in his ***d*** were twenty-four
28:13 also for the ***d*** of the priests
2 Chr 31:16 work of his service, by his ***d***,
35: 5 and according to the ***d*** of the
Lk 1: 5 of the ***d*** of Abijah. His wife
1: 8 God in the order of his ***d***,
12:51 you, not at all, but rather ***d***.
Jn 7:43 So there was a ***d*** among the
9:16 And there was a ***d*** among them.
10:19 Therefore there was a ***d*** again
Heb 4:12 piercing even to the ***d*** of soul

DIVISIONS (41/37) DIVISION

Num 1:16 heads of the ***d*** in Israel.
10: 4 the heads of the ***d*** of Israel,
31: 5 were recruited from the ***d*** of
Josh 11:23 to Israel according to their ***d***
12: 7 possession according to their ***d***,
18:10 of Israel according to their ***d***.
22:14 of his father among the ***d*** of
22:21 and said to the heads of the ***d***
22:30 the heads of the ***d*** of Israel
Judg 5:15 Among the ***d*** of Reuben There
5:16 The ***d*** of Reuben have great
1 Chr 12:23 were the numbers of the ***d***
23: 6 David separated them into ***d***
24: 1 Now these are the ***d*** of the
26: 1 Concerning the ***d*** of the
26:12 Among these were the ***d*** of the
26:19 These were the ***d*** of the
27: 1 every matter of the military ***d***.
27: 1 These ***d*** came in and went out
28: 1 and the captains of the ***d*** who
28:21 Here are the ***d*** of the priests
2 Chr 5:11 without keeping to their ***d***),
8:14 he appointed the ***d*** of the
8:14 and the gatekeepers by their ***d***
23: 8 priest had not dismissed the ***d***.
31: 2 And Hezekiah appointed the ***d*** of
31: 2 Levites according to their ***d***,
31:15 to their brethren by ***d***,
31:17 to their work, by their ***d***,
35: 4 houses, according to your ***d***,
35: 5 holy place according to the ***d***
35:10 and the Levites in their ***d***,
35:12 they might give them to the ***d***
Ezra 6:18 the priests to their ***d*** and the
6:18 and the Levites to their ***d***,
Neh 11:36 Some of the Judean ***d*** of Levites
Rom 16:17 note those who cause ***d*** and
1 Cor 1:10 and that there be no ***d*** among
3: 3 envy, strife, and ***d*** among you,
11:18 I hear that there are ***d*** among
Jude 19 sensual persons, who cause ***d***,

DIVISIVE (1/1) DIVIDE

Titus 3:10 Reject a ***d*** man after the first

DIVORCE (16/16) DIVORCED, DIVORCES

Deut 22:19 he cannot ***d*** her all his days.
22:29 he shall not be permitted to ***d***
24: 1 writes her a certificate of ***d***,
24: 3 writes her a certificate of ***d***,
Isa 50: 1 certificate of your mother's ***d***,
Jer 3: 8 given her a certificate of ***d***;
Mal 2:16 of Israel says That He hates ***d***,
Mt 5:31 him give her a certificate of ***d***.
19: 3 Is it lawful for a man to ***d*** his
19: 7 to give a certificate of ***d***,
19: 8 permitted you to ***d*** your wives,
Mk 10: 2 Is it lawful for a man to ***d*** his
10: 4 to write a certificate of ***d***,
1 Cor 7:11 And a husband is not to ***d*** his
7:12 let him not ***d*** her.
7:13 let her not ***d*** him.

DIVORCED (9/9) DIVORCE

Lev 21: 7 nor shall they take a woman ***d***
21:14 A widow or a ***d*** woman or a
22:13 daughter is a widow or ***d***,
Num 30: 9 vow of a widow or a ***d*** woman,
Deut 24: 4 her former husband who ***d***
Ezek 44:22 as wife a widow or a ***d*** woman,
Mt 5:32 marries a woman who is ***d***
19: 9 whoever marries her who is ***d***
Lk 16:18 whoever marries her who is ***d***

DIVORCES (7/7) DIVORCE

Jer 3: 1 If a man ***d*** his wife, And she
Mt 5:31 Whoever ***d*** his wife, let him give
5:32 I say to you that whoever ***d***
19: 9 whoever ***d*** his wife, except for
Mk 10:11 Whoever ***d*** his wife and marries
10:12 And if a woman ***d*** her husband and
Lk 16:18 Whoever ***d*** his wife and marries

DIZAHAB (1/1)

Deut 1: 1 Tophel, Laban, Hazeroth, and ***D***.

DO (2574/2243) DOER, DOERS, DOES, DOING, DOINGS, DONE

Gen 4: 7 If you ***d*** well, will you not be
4: 7 And if you ***d*** not do well, sin
4: 7 And if you do not ***d*** well, sin
4: 9 I ***d*** not know. Am I my brother's
11: 6 this is what they begin to ***d***;
11: 6 nothing that they propose to ***d***
15: 1 '***D*** not be afraid, Abram.
16: 6 ***d*** to her as you please."
18: 3 ***d*** not pass on by Your servant.
18: 5 ***D*** as you have said."
18:19 to ***d*** righteousness and justice,
18:25 Far be it from You to ***d*** such a
18:25 of all the earth ***d*** right?"
18:29 I will not ***d*** it for the sake of
18:30 I will not ***d*** it if I find
19: 7 ***d*** not do so wickedly!
19: 7 do not ***d*** so wickedly!
19: 8 and you may ***d*** to them as you
19: 8 only ***d*** nothing to these men,
19:17 ***D*** not look behind you nor stay
19:22 For I cannot ***d*** anything until
20: 7 But if you ***d*** not restore her,
20:13 kindness that you should ***d*** for
21:12 ***D*** not let it be displeasing in
21:22 is with you in all that you ***d***.
21:23 you will ***d*** to me and to the
21:26 I ***d*** not know who has done this
22:12 ***D*** not lay your hand on the lad,
22:12 the lad, or ***d*** anything to him;
24: 6 Beware that you ***d*** not take my
24: 8 only ***d*** not take my son back
24:31 Why ***d*** you stand outside?
24:56 ***D*** not hinder me, since the LORD
26: 2 ***D*** not go down to Egypt; live in
26:24 ***d*** not fear, for I am with you.
26:29 that you will ***d*** us no harm,
27: 2 I ***d*** not know the day of my
27:37 What shall I ***d*** now for you, my
29: 5 ***D*** you know Laban the son of
30:31 If you will ***d*** this thing for
31:16 has said to you, ***d*** it."
31:29 It is in my power to ***d*** you harm,
31:32 your gods, ***d*** not let him live.
31:43 But what can I ***d*** this day to
32:17 To whom ***d*** you belong, and where
32:32 children of Israel ***d*** not eat
33: 8 What ***d*** you mean by all this
34:14 We cannot ***d*** this thing, to give
34:19 did not delay to ***d*** the thing,
35:17 ***D*** not fear; you will have this
37:22 and ***d*** not lay a hand on
37:32 ***D*** you know whether it is your
39: 9 How then can I ***d*** this great
39:11 went into the house to ***d*** his
40: 7 Why ***d*** you look so sad today?"
40: 8 ***D*** not interpretations belong to
41:25 Pharaoh what He is about to ***d***:
41:28 Pharaoh what He is about to ***d***.
41:34 Let Pharaoh ***d*** this, and let him
41:55 whatever he says to you, ***d***.
42: 1 Why ***d*** you look at one another?"
42: 7 'Where ***d*** you come from?"
42:18 ***D*** this and live, for I fear
42:22 '***D*** not sin against the boy';
42:37 Kill my two sons if I ***d*** not
43: 9 If I ***d*** not bring him back to
43:11 then ***d*** this: Take some of the
43:22 We ***d*** not know who put our money
43:23 be with you, ***d*** not be afraid.
44: 7 servants should ***d*** such a thing.
44:17 from me that I should ***d*** so;
44:18 and ***d*** not let your anger burn
44:32 If I ***d*** not bring him back to
45: 5 ***d*** not therefore be grieved or
45: 9 down to me, ***d*** not tarry.
45:17 ***D*** this: Load your animals and
45:19 ***d*** this: Take carts out of the
45:20 Also ***d*** not be concerned about
45:24 See that you ***d*** not become
46: 3 ***d*** not fear to go down to Egypt,
47:29 Please ***d*** not bury me in Egypt,
47:30 I will ***d*** as you have said."
50:19 ***D*** not be afraid, for am I in
50:21 ***d*** not be afraid; I will provide
Ex 1:16 When you ***d*** the duties of a
1:17 and did not ***d*** as the king of
2:14 ***D*** you intend to kill me as you
3: 5 '***D*** not draw near this place.
3:20 all My wonders which I will ***d***
4: 8 if they ***d*** not believe you, nor
4: 9 if they ***d*** not believe even
4:15 will teach you what you shall ***d***.
4:17 with which you shall ***d*** the
4:21 see that you ***d*** all those
5: 2 I ***d*** not know the LORD, nor
5: 4 why ***d*** you take the people from
6: 1 you shall see what I will ***d*** to
8:26 It is not right to ***d*** so, for we
9: 5 Tomorrow the LORD will ***d*** this
10: 7 ***D*** you not yet know that Egypt
10:26 and even we ***d*** not know with
12: 9 ***D*** not eat it raw, nor boiled at
12:26 What ***d*** you mean by this
14:13 ***D*** not be afraid. Stand still,
14:15 Why ***d*** you cry to Me? Tell the
15:26 your God and ***d*** what is right
16:28 How long ***d*** you refuse to keep My
17: 2 'Why ***d*** you contend with me?
17: 2 Why ***d*** you tempt the LORD?"
17: 4 What shall I ***d*** with this people?
18:14 Why ***d*** you alone sit, and all
18:17 The thing that you ***d*** is not
18:20 walk and the work they must ***d***.
18:23 If you ***d*** this thing, and God so
19: 8 the LORD has spoken we will ***d***.
19:12 yourselves that you ***d*** not go
19:15 ***d*** not come near your wives."
19:24 But ***d*** not let the priests and
20: 9 labor and ***d*** all your work,
20:10 In it you shall ***d*** no work:
20:20 ***D*** not fear; for God has come to
21: 7 not go out as the male slaves ***d***.
21:11 And if he does not ***d*** these three
22:30 Likewise you shall ***d*** with your
23: 1 ***D*** not put your hand with the
23: 2 not follow a crowd to ***d*** evil;
23: 7 ***d*** not kill the innocent and
23:11 In like manner you shall ***d*** with
23:12 Six days you shall ***d*** your work,
23:21 ***d*** not provoke Him, for He will
23:22 indeed obey His voice and ***d*** all
23:24 nor ***d*** according to their works;
24: 3 the LORD has said we will ***d***.
24: 7 the LORD has said we will ***d***,
26: 4 and likewise you shall ***d*** on the
28:43 that they ***d*** not incur iniquity
29: 1 And this is what you shall ***d*** to
29:35 Thus you shall ***d*** to Aaron and
31:11 have commanded you they shall ***d***.
32: 1 we ***d*** not know what has become
32:14 harm which He said He would ***d***
32:21 What did this people ***d*** to you
32:22 ***D*** not let the anger of my lord
32:23 we ***d*** not know what has become
33: 5 that I may know what to ***d*** to
33:15 ***d*** not bring us up from here.
33:17 I will also ***d*** this thing that
34:10 your people I will ***d*** marvels
34:10 an awesome thing that I will ***d***
35: 1 LORD has commanded you to ***d***:
35:35 has filled them with skill to ***d***
35:35 those who ***d*** every work and those
36: 1 to know how to ***d*** all manner of
36: 1 shall ***d*** according to all that
36: 2 to come and ***d*** the work.
36: 5 the LORD commanded us to ***d***.
36: 6 Let neither man nor woman ***d*** any
Lev 4:20 And he shall ***d*** with the bull as
4:20 thus he shall ***d*** with it. So the
5: 4 to ***d*** evil or to do good,
5: 4 his lips to do evil or to ***d***
6: 3 these things that a man may ***d***
8:34 the LORD has commanded to ***d***,
9: 6 the LORD commanded you to ***d***,
10: 6 ***D*** not uncover your heads nor
10: 9 ***D*** not drink wine or intoxicating
11:10 that ***d*** not have fins and
16:15 ***d*** with that blood as he did
16:16 and so he shall ***d*** for the
16:29 and ***d*** no work at all, whether
18: 3 you dwelt, you shall not ***d***;
18: 3 bringing you, you shall not ***d***;
18:24 ***D*** not defile yourselves with
18:30 so that you ***d*** not commit any
18:30 and that you ***d*** not defile
19: 4 ***D*** not turn to idols, nor make
19:15 You shall ***d*** no injustice in
19:29 ***D*** not prostitute your daughter,
19:31 ***d*** not seek after them, to be
19:35 You shall ***d*** no injustice in
20: 4 and they ***d*** not kill him,
22: 2 and that they ***d*** not profane My
22:28 ***d*** not kill both her and her
23: 3 You shall ***d*** no work on it;
23: 7 you shall ***d*** no customary work
23: 8 you shall ***d*** no customary work
23:21 You shall ***d*** no customary work
23:25 You shall ***d*** no customary work
23:28 And you shall ***d*** no work on that
23:31 You shall ***d*** no manner of work;
23:35 You shall ***d*** no customary work
23:36 and you shall ***d*** no customary
26:14 But if you ***d*** not obey Me, and
26:14 and ***d*** not observe all these
26:15 so that you ***d*** not perform all
26:16 I also will ***d*** this to you:
26:18 if you ***d*** not obey Me, then I
26:27 if you ***d*** not obey Me, but walk
27:11 animal which they ***d*** not offer
Num 3: 7 to ***d*** the work of the
3: 8 to ***d*** the work of the
4: 3 the service to ***d*** the work
4:18 ***D*** not cut off the tribe of the
4:19 but ***d*** this in regard to them,
4:23 to ***d*** the work in the tabernacle
4:30 the service to ***d*** the work
4:47 everyone who came to ***d*** the work
6:21 so he must ***d*** according to the
8: 7 Thus you shall ***d*** to them to
8:19 to ***d*** the work for the children
8:22 Levites went in to ***d*** their
8:26 but they themselves shall ***d*** no
8:26 Thus you shall ***d*** to the Levites
9:14 he must ***d*** so according to the
10:31 Please ***d*** not leave, inasmuch as
10:32 whatever good the LORD will ***d***
10:32 the same we will ***d*** to you."
11:15 and ***d*** not let me see my
12:11 my lord! Please ***d*** not lay this
12:12 Please ***d*** not let her be as one
14: 9 Only ***d*** not rebel against the
14: 9 ***D*** not fear them."
14:28 so I will ***d*** to you:
14:35 I will surely ***d*** so to all this
14:41 Now why ***d*** you transgress the
14:42 ***D*** not go up, lest you be
15:12 so you shall ***d*** with everyone
15:13 native-born shall ***d*** these
15:14 to the LORD, just as you ***d***,
15:14 just as you do, so shall he ***d***.
15:22 and ***d*** not observe all these
15:39 of the LORD and ***d*** them,
15:40 that you may remember and ***d***
16: 3 Why then ***d*** you exalt yourselves
16: 6 ***D*** this: Take censers, Korah and
16: 9 to ***d*** the work of the tabernacle
16:15 '***D*** not respect their offering.
16:28 the LORD has sent me to ***d*** all
18: 6 to ***d*** the work of the tabernacle
21:34 ***D*** not fear him, for I have
21:34 and you shall ***d*** to him as you

22:17 and I will **d** whatever you say
22:18 to **d** less or more.
22:20 I speak to you—that you shall **d**.
22:30 Was I ever disposed to **d** this
23:19 Has He said, and will He not **d**?
23:26 LORD speaks, that I must **d**'?
24:13 to **d** good or bad of my own
24:14 you what this people will **d** to
28:18 You shall **d** no customary work.
28:25 You shall **d** no customary work.
28:26 You shall **d** no customary work.
29: 1 You shall **d** no customary work.
29: 7 you shall not **d** any work.
29:12 You shall **d** no customary work,
29:35 You shall **d** no customary work.
30: 2 he shall **d** according to all
32: 5 **D** not take us over the
32:20 If you **d** this thing, if you arm
32:23 But if you **d** not do so, then
32:23 But if you do not **d** so, then
32:24 and **d** what has proceeded out of
32:25 Your servants will **d** as my lord
32:30 But if they **d** not cross over
32:31 to your servants, so we will **d**.
33:55 But if you **d** not drive out the
33:56 it shall be that I will **d** to
33:56 do to you as I thought to **d** to
35:34 Therefore **d** not defile the land
Deut 1:14 which you have told us to **d**
1:18 the things which you should **d**.
1:21 **d** not fear or be discouraged.'
1:29 **D** not be terrified, or afraid of
1:42 **D** not go up nor fight, for I am
1:44 you and chased you as bees **d**,
2: 5 **D** not meddle with them, for I
2: 9 **D** not harass Moab, nor contend
2:19 **d** not harass them or meddle
3: 2 **D** not fear him, for I have
3: 2 you shall **d** to him as you did
3:21 so will the LORD **d** to all the
3:24 on earth who can **d** anything
4:25 and **d** evil in the sight of the
5:13 labor and **d** all your work,
5:14 In it you shall **d** no work:
5:27 and we will hear and **d** it.'
5:32 you shall be careful to **d** as
6:18 And you shall **d** what is right
7:12 and keep and **d** them, that the
7:19 So shall the LORD your God **d**
8:11 Beware that you **d** not forget
8:16 to **d** you good in the end—
9: 4 **D** not think in your heart, after
9: 7 **D** not forget how you provoked
9:26 **d** not destroy Your people and
9:27 **d** not look on the stubbornness
11: 2 Know today that I **d** not speak
11:22 which I command you to **d**—
11:28 if you **d** not obey the
12: 8 You shall not at all **d** as we are
12:13 that you **d** not offer your
12:14 and there you shall **d** all that
12:19 **d** not forsake the Levite
12:23 Only be sure that you **d** not eat
12:25 when you **d** what is right in
12:28 when you **d** what is good and
12:30 and that you **d** not inquire
12:30 I also will **d** likewise.'
13:11 and not again **d** such wickedness
13:18 to **d** what is right in the
14: 7 for they chew the cud but **d** not
14:29 work of your hand which you **d**.
15:17 servant you shall **d** likewise.
15:18 bless you in all that you **d**.
15:19 you shall **d** no work with the
16: 8 You shall **d** no work on it.
17:10 You shall **d** according to the
17:10 be careful to **d** according to
17:11 they tell you, you shall **d**;
18: 7 all his brethren the Levites **d**,
18:12 For all who **d** these things are
19: 9 commandments and **d** them,
19:19 then you shall **d** to him as he
20: 1 **d** not be afraid of them;
20: 3 **D** not let your heart faint,
20: 3 **d** not be afraid, and do not
20: 3 and **d** not tremble or be
20:15 Thus you shall **d** to all the
20:18 they teach you to **d** according
20:19 **d** not cut them down to use in
21: 8 and **d** not lay innocent blood to
21: 9 when you **d** what is right
21:23 so that you **d** not defile the
22: 2 or if you **d** not know him, then
22: 3 You shall **d** the same with his
22: 3 and so shall you **d** with his
22: 3 you shall **d** likewise; you must
22: 5 for all who **d** so are an
22:26 But you shall **d** nothing to the
24: 8 you carefully observe and **d**
24: 8 so you shall be careful to **d**.
24:18 I command you to **d** this
24:22 I command you to **d** this
25: 8 I **d** not want to take her,'
25:16 For all who **d** such things, all
28:15 if you **d** not obey the voice of
28:20 all that you set your hand to **d**,
28:58 If you **d** not carefully observe
28:63 rejoiced over you to **d** you good
29: 9 and **d** them, that you may
29: 9 may prosper in all that you **d**.
29:29 that we may **d** all the words of

30: 8 the voice of the LORD and **d** all
30:12 that we may hear it and **d** it?'
30:13 that we may hear it and **d** it?'
30:14 that you may **d** it.
30:17 away so that you **d** not hear,
31: 4 And the LORD will **d** to them as
31: 5 that you may **d** to them
31: 6 **d** not fear nor be afraid of
31: 8 **d** not fear nor be dismayed."
31:29 because you will **d** evil in the
32: 6 **D** you thus deal with the LORD,
34:11 which the LORD sent him to **d**
Josh 1: 7 that you may observe to **d**
1: 7 **d** not turn from it to the right
1: 8 that you may observe to **d**
1: 9 **d** not be afraid, nor be
1:16 that you command us we will **d**,
2: 5 Where the men went I **d** not
3: 4 **D** not come near it, that you
3: 5 the LORD will **d** wonders
4: 6 What **d** these stones mean to
6: 3 This you shall **d** six days.
7: 3 **D** not let all the people go up,
7: 3 **D** not weary all the people
7: 9 Then what will You **d** for Your
7:10 Get up! Why **d** you lie thus on
7:19 **d** not hide it from me."
8: 1 **D** not be afraid, nor be
8: 2 And you shall **d** to Ai and its
8: 4 **D** not go very far from the
8: 8 of the LORD you shall **d**.
9: 8 and where **d** you come from?"
9:20 'This we will **d** to them:
9:25 **d** with us as it seems good and
9:25 as it seems good and right to **d**
10: 6 **D** not forsake your servants;
10: 8 **D** not fear them, for I have
10:19 And **d** not stay there
10:19 **D** not allow them to enter their
10:25 **D** not be afraid, nor be
10:25 for thus the LORD will **d** to
11: 6 **D** not be afraid because of them,
15:18 What **d** you wish?"
22: 5 But take careful heed to **d** the
22:19 but **d** not rebel against the
22:22 **d** not save us this day.
22:24 What have you to **d** with the
23: 6 to keep and to **d** all that is
23:12 if indeed you **d** go back, and
24:20 then He will turn and **d** you
Judg 1:14 What **d** you wish?"
2:17 they did not **d** so.
4:18 aside to me; **d** not fear."
6:10 **d** not fear the gods of the
6:18 **D** not depart from here, I pray,
6:23 **d** not fear, you shall not
6:27 men of the city too much to **d**
6:39 **D** not be angry with me, but let
7:17 Look at me and **d** likewise;
7:17 you shall **d** as I do:
7:17 of the camp you shall do as I **d**:
8: 3 And what was I able to **d** in
9:33 you may then **d** to them as you
9:48 'What you have seen me **d**,
9:48 make haste and **d** as I have
10:15 We have sinned! **D** to us whatever
11:10 if we **d** not do according to
11:10 if we do not **d** according to
11:12 What **d** you have against me, that
11:36 **d** to me according to what has
13: 8 and teach us what we shall **d**
13:18 Why **d** you ask My name, seeing it
14:10 for young men used to **d** so.
14:16 You only hate me! You **d** not love
15: 7 Since you would **d** a thing like
15:10 to **d** to him as he has done to
15:11 **D** you not know that the
17: 9 Where **d** you come from?" So he
18: 3 What **d** you have here?"
18: 9 Would you **d** nothing? Do not
18: 9 **D** not hesitate to go, and
18:14 **D** you know that there are in
18:14 consider what you should **d**.
18:24 Now what more **d** I have? How can
18:25 **D** not let your voice be heard
19:17 and where **d** you come from?"
19:20 only **d** not spend the night in
19:23 **d** not act so wickedly!
19:23 **d** not commit this outrage.
19:24 and **d** with them as you please;
19:24 but to this man **d** not do such a
19:24 but to this man do not **d** such a
20: 9 is the thing which we will **d**
21: 7 What shall we **d** for wives for
21:11 is the thing that you shall **d**:
21:16 What shall we **d** for wives for
Ruth 1:17 The LORD **d** so to me, and more
1:20 **D** not call me Naomi; call me
1:21 Why **d** you call me Naomi, since
2: 8 **D** not go to glean in another
2:15 and **d** not reproach her.
2:16 and **d** not rebuke her."
2:22 and that people **d** not meet you
3: 3 but **d** not make yourself known
3: 4 will tell you what you should **d**.
3: 5 that you say to me I will **d**.
3:11 **d** not fear. I will do for you
3:11 I will **d** for you all that you
3:13 let him **d** it. But if he does
3:14 **D** not let it be known that the
3:17 **D** not go empty-handed to your
1 Sam 1: 8 why **d** you weep? Why do you not

1: 8 Why **d** you not eat? And why is
1:16 **D** not consider your maidservant
1:23 '**D** what seems best to you;
2:23 Why **d** you do such things? For I
2:23 Why do you **d** such things? For I
2:29 Why **d** you kick at My sacrifice
2:33 your men whom I **d** not cut off
2:35 priest who shall **d** according
3:11 I will **d** something in Israel at
3:17 Please **d** not hide it from me.
3:17 God **d** so to you, and more also,
3:18 Let Him **d** what seems good to
4: 9 that you **d** not become servants
4:20 **D** not fear, for you have borne a
5: 8 What shall we **d** with the ark of
6: 2 What shall we **d** with the ark of
6: 3 **d** not send it empty; but by all
6: 6 Why then **d** you harden your
7: 8 **D** not cease to cry out to the
8: 5 and your sons **d** not walk in
9: 7 What **d** we have?"
9:20 **d** not be anxious about them,
9:21 Why then **d** you speak like this
10: 2 What shall I **d** about my son?" '
10: 7 that you **d** as the occasion
10: 8 and show you what you should **d**.
10:24 **D** you see him whom the LORD has
11:10 and you may **d** with us whatever
12:14 and **d** not rebel against the
12:15 if you **d** not obey the voice of
12:16 thing which the LORD will **d**
12:20 **D** not fear. You have done all
12:20 yet **d** not turn aside from
12:21 And **d** not turn aside; for then
12:25 But if you still **d** wickedly, you
14: 7 '**D** all that is in your heart.
14:34 and **d** not sin against the LORD
14:36 **D** whatever seems good to you."
14:40 **D** what seems good to you."
14:44 God **d** so and more also; for you
15: 3 and **d** not spare them. But kill
15:19 and **d** evil in the sight of the
16: 3 will show you what you shall **d**;
16: 4 **D** you come peaceably?"
16: 7 **D** not look at his appearance or
17:55 O king, I **d** not know."
19:11 If you **d** not save your life
20: 2 my father will **d** nothing either
20: 3 **D** not let Jonathan know this,
20: 4 I will **d** it for you."
20:12 and I **d** not send to you and
20:13 may the LORD **d** so and much more
20:13 my father to **d** you evil,
20:30 rebellious woman! **D** I not know
20:38 hurry, **d** not delay!"
21: 2 **D** not let anyone know anything
22: 3 till I know what God will **d** for
22: 5 **D** not stay in the stronghold;
22:23 **d** not fear. For he who seeks my
23:17 **D** not fear, for the hand of Saul
24: 4 that you may **d** to him as it
24: 6 LORD forbid that I should **d**
24: 9 Why **d** you listen to the words of
24:14 Whom **d** you pursue? A dead dog?
25:11 to men when I **d** not know
25:17 and consider what you will **d**,
25:22 May God **d** so, and more also, to
26: 9 **D** not destroy him; for who can
26:14 '**D** you not answer, Abner?"
26:20 **d** not let my blood fall to the
26:25 You shall both **d** great things
28: 2 know what your servant can **d**.
28: 9 Why then **d** you lay a snare for
28:13 **D** not be afraid. What did you
28:15 reveal to me what I should **d**.
28:16 Why then **d** you ask me, seeing
29: 4 and **d** not let him go down with
29: 6 the lords **d** not favor you.
30:13 To whom **d** you belong, and where
30:23 you shall not **d** so with what
2 Sam 1: 5 How **d** you know that Saul and
2:26 **D** you not know that it will be
3: 9 May God **d** so to Abner, and more
3: 9 if I **d** not do for David as the
3: 9 if I do not **d** for David as the
3:18 **d** it! For the LORD has spoken
3:35 God **d** so to me, and more also,
3:38 **D** you not know that a prince and
7: 3 **d** all that is in your heart,
7:23 and to **d** for Youself great and
7:25 establish it forever and **d** as
9: 7 **D** not fear, for I will surely
9:11 servant, so will your servant **d**.
10: 3 **D** you think that David really
10:12 And may the LORD **d** what is
11:11 I will not **d** this thing."
11:25 **D** not let this thing displease
12: 9 to **d** evil in His sight?
12:12 but I will **d** this thing before
12:18 He may **d** some harm!"
13: 2 for Amnon to **d** anything
13:12 **d** not force me, for no such
13:12 **D** not do this disgraceful
13:12 Do not **d** this disgraceful
13:20 **d** not take this thing to
13:28 **D** not be afraid. Have I not
14: 2 **d** not anoint yourself with oil,
14:11 and **d** not permit the avenger of
14:18 Please **d** not hide from me
14:24 but **d** not let him see my
15:15 ready to **d** whatever my lord

15:26 let Him ***d*** to me as seems good
15:35 And ***d*** you not have Zadok and
16: 2 What ***d*** you mean to do with
16: 2 What do you mean to ***d*** with
16:10 What have I to ***d*** with you, you
16:20 counsel as to what we should ***d***.
17: 6 Shall we ***d*** as he says? If not,
17:16 ***D*** not spend this night in the
18: 4 seems best to you I will ***d***.
18:32 all who rise against you to ***d***
19: 7 if you ***d*** not go out, not one
19:10 why ***d*** you say nothing about
19:13 God ***d*** so to me, and more also,
19:18 and to ***d*** what he thought good.
19:19 ***D*** not let my lord impute
19:22 What have I to ***d*** with you, you
19:22 For ***d*** I not know that today I
19:27 Therefore ***d*** what is good in
19:29 Why ***d*** you speak anymore of your
19:37 and ***d*** for him what seems good
19:38 and I will ***d*** for him what seems
19:38 I will ***d*** for you."
19:43 Why then ***d*** you despise us—were
20: 1 Nor ***d*** we have inheritance in
20: 6 Sheba the son of Bichri will ***d***
21: 3 What shall I ***d*** for you? And with
21: 4 I will ***d*** for you."
23:17 O LORD, that I should ***d*** this!
24:12 that I may ***d*** it to you.' "
24:14 but ***d*** not let me fall into the
1 Ki 1:18 you ***d*** not know about it.
1:30 so I certainly will ***d*** this
2: 3 may prosper in all that you ***d***
2: 6 Therefore ***d*** according to your
2: 6 and ***d*** not let his gray hair go
2: 9 ***d*** not hold him guiltless, for
2: 9 and know what you ought to ***d***
2:13 ***D*** you come peaceably?" And he
2:16 ***d*** not deny me." And she said
2:20 ***d*** not refuse me." And the king
2:22 Now why ***d*** you ask Abishag the
2:23 May God ***d*** so to me, and more
2:31 ***D*** as he has said, and strike him
2:36 and ***d*** not go out from there
2:38 said, so your servant will ***d***.
3: 7 I ***d*** not know how to go out or
5: 8 and I will ***d*** all you desire
7:40 all the work that he was to ***d***
8:43 and ***d*** according to all for
8:43 as ***d*** Your people Israel, and
9: 1 desire which he wanted to ***d***,
9: 4 to ***d*** according to all that I
9: 6 and ***d*** not keep My commandments
10: 9 to ***d*** justice and
11:12 Nevertheless I will not ***d*** it in
11:22 but ***d*** let me go anyway."
11:33 have not walked in My ways to ***d***
11:38 and ***d*** what is right in My
12: 6 How ***d*** you advise me to answer
12: 9 'What advice ***d*** you give?
14: 6 Why ***d*** you pretend to be
14: 8 to ***d*** only what was right in
17:12 I ***d*** not have bread, only a
17:13 ***D*** not fear; go and do as you
17:13 go and ***d*** as you have said, but
17:18 What have I to ***d*** with you, O man
18:12 to a place I ***d*** not know;
18:34 ***D*** it a second time," and they
18:34 ***D*** it a third time," and they
18:40 ***D*** not let one of them escape!"
19: 2 So let the gods ***d*** to me, and
19: 2 if I ***d*** not make your life as
20: 8 ***D*** not listen or consent."
20: 9 servant the first time I will ***d***,
20: 9 do, but this thing I cannot ***d***.
20:10 The gods ***d*** so to me, and more
20:22 note, and see what you should ***d***,
20:24 So ***d*** this thing: Dismiss the
21:20 have sold yourself to ***d*** evil
21:25 sold himself to ***d*** wickedness
22: 3 ***D*** you know that Ramoth in Gilead
22:22 Go out and ***d*** so.'
2 Ki 1:15 ***d*** not be afraid of him." So he
2: 3 ***D*** you know that the LORD will
2: 5 ***D*** you know that the LORD will
2: 9 Ask! What may I ***d*** for you,
2:18 say to you, '***D*** not go'?"
3:13 What have I to ***d*** with you? Go to
4: 2 What shall I ***d*** for you? Tell me,
4: 2 what ***d*** you have in the house?"
4: 3 ***d*** not gather just a few.
4:13 What can I ***d*** for you? Do you
4:13 ***D*** you want me to speak on your
4:16 ***d*** not lie to your
4:24 ***d*** not slacken the pace for me
4:28 ***D*** not deceive me'?"
4:29 ***d*** not greet him; and if anyone
4:29 ***d*** not answer him; but lay my
5:13 the prophet had told you to ***d***
6: 9 Beware that you ***d*** not pass this
6:15 my master! What shall we ***d***?
6:16 ***D*** not fear, for those who are
6:31 God ***d*** so to me and more also, if
6:32 ***D*** you see how this son of a
8:12 I know the evil that you will ***d***
8:13 that he should ***d*** this gross
9: 3 and ***d*** not delay."
9:18 What have you to ***d*** with peace?
9:19 What have you to ***d*** with peace?
10: 5 we will ***d*** all you tell us;
10: 5 ***D*** what is good in your
11: 5 "This is what you shall ***d***:
11:15 ***D*** not let her be killed in the
12: 7 ***d*** not take more money from
16: 2 and he did not ***d*** what was
17:12 You shall not ***d*** this thing."
17:15 they should not ***d*** like them.
17:17 and sold themselves to ***d*** evil
17:26 in the cities of Samaria ***d*** not
17:26 killing them because they ***d*** not
17:34 they ***d*** not fear the LORD, nor
17:34 nor ***d*** they follow their
18:12 they would neither hear nor ***d***
18:20 And in whom ***d*** you trust, that
18:26 and ***d*** not speak to us in Hebrew
18:29 ***D*** not let Hezekiah deceive you,
18:31 '***D*** not listen to Hezekiah;
18:32 But ***d*** not listen to Hezekiah,
18:36 ***D*** not answer him."
19: 6 ***D*** not be afraid of the words
19:10 ***D*** not let your God in whom you
19:31 of the LORD of hosts will ***d***
20: 9 that the LORD will ***d*** the thing
21: 8 —only if they are careful to ***d***
21: 9 seduced them to ***d*** more evil
22: 9 hand of those who ***d*** the work,
22:13 to ***d*** according to all that is
25:24 ***D*** not be afraid of the servants
1 Chr 11:19 my God, that I should ***d*** this!
12:32 to know what Israel ought to ***d***,
13: 4 said that they would ***d*** so,
15:13 For because you did not ***d*** it
16:21 He permitted no man to ***d*** them
16:22 ***D*** not touch My anointed ones,
16:22 And ***d*** My prophets no harm."
16:40 and to ***d*** according to all
17: 2 ***D*** all that is in your heart,
17:23 and ***d*** as You have said.
19: 3 ***D*** you think that David really
19:13 And may the LORD ***d*** what is
21:10 that I may ***d*** it to you.' "
21:13 but ***d*** not let me fall into the
21:23 let my lord the king ***d*** what
22:13 ***d*** not fear nor be dismayed.
28:10 be strong, and ***d*** it."
28:20 and ***d*** it; do not fear nor be
28:20 ***d*** not fear nor be dismayed, for
29:19 to ***d*** all these things, and to
2 Chr 4:11 the work that he was to ***d*** for
6:33 and ***d*** according to all for
6:33 as ***d*** Your people Israel, and
6:42 ***d*** not turn away the face of
7:17 and ***d*** according to all that I
9: 8 to ***d*** justice and
10: 6 How ***d*** you advise me to answer
10: 9 'What advice ***d*** you give?
13:12 ***d*** not fight against the LORD
14:11 ***d*** not let man prevail against
15: 7 be strong and ***d*** not let your
18:21 go out and ***d*** so.'
19: 6 for you ***d*** not judge for man but
19: 7 take care and ***d*** it, for there
19:10 ***D*** this, and you will not be
20: 6 and ***d*** You not rule over all
20:12 nor ***d*** we know what to do,
20:12 us; nor do we know what to ***d***,
20:15 ***D*** not be afraid nor dismayed
20:17 ***D*** not fear or be dismayed;
22: 3 advised him to ***d*** wickedly.
23: 4 "This is what you shall ***d***:
23:14 ***D*** not kill her in the house of
24: 5 and see that you ***d*** it
24: 5 the Levites did not ***d*** it
24:20 Why ***d*** you transgress the
25: 7 ***d*** not let the army of Israel go
25: 9 But what shall we ***d*** about the
28: 1 and he did not ***d*** what was
29:11 ***d*** not be negligent now, for the
30: 7 And ***d*** not be like your fathers
30: 8 Now ***d*** not be stiffnecked, as
32: 7 ***d*** not be afraid nor dismayed
32:10 In what ***d*** you trust, that you
32:13 ***D*** you not know what I and my
32:15 ***d*** not let Hezekiah deceive you
32:15 and ***d*** not believe him; for no
33: 8 if they are careful to ***d*** all
33: 9 of Jerusalem to ***d*** more evil
34:21 to ***d*** according to all that is
35: 6 that they may ***d*** according to
35:21 What have I to ***d*** with you, king
Ezra 4: 2 for we seek your God as you ***d***;
4: 3 You may ***d*** nothing with us to
4:22 you ***d*** not fail to do this.
4:22 now that you do not fail to ***d***
6: 8 as to what you shall ***d*** for
7:10 and to ***d*** it, and to teach
7:18 brethren to ***d*** with the rest
7:18 ***d*** it according to the will of
7:25 and teach those who ***d*** not know
9:12 ***d*** not give your daughters as
10: 4 of good courage, and ***d*** it."
10: 5 swear an oath that they would ***d***
10:11 your fathers, and ***d*** His will;
10:12 As you have said, so we must ***d***.
Neh 1: 9 and keep My commandments and ***d***
2: 4 What ***d*** you request?" So I
2:12 my God had put in my heart to ***d***
4: 5 ***D*** not cover their iniquity, and
4: 5 and ***d*** not let their sin be
4:14 ***D*** not be afraid of them.
5:12 we will ***d*** as you say." Then I
5:12 from them that they would ***d***
5:15 but I did not ***d*** so, because of
6: 2 But they thought to ***d*** me
7: 3 ***D*** not let the gates of Jerusalem
8: 9 ***d*** not mourn nor weep." For all
8:10 ***D*** not sorrow, for the joy of
8:11 ***d*** not be grieved."
9:24 That they might ***d*** with them as
9:32 ***D*** not let all the trouble seem
10:29 and to observe and ***d*** all the
13:14 and ***d*** not wipe out my good
13:17 evil thing is this that you ***d***,
13:18 Did not your fathers ***d*** thus, and
13:21 Why ***d*** you spend the night around
13:21 If you ***d*** so again, I will lay
Esth 1: 8 that they should ***d*** according to
1:15 What shall we ***d*** to Queen
3: 3 Why ***d*** you transgress the king's
3: 8 and they ***d*** not keep the king's
3: 9 into the hands of those who ***d***
3:11 to ***d*** with them as seems good to
4:13 ***D*** not think in your heart that
5: 3 What ***d*** you wish, Queen Esther?
5: 5 that he may ***d*** as Esther has
5: 8 and tomorrow I will ***d*** as the
6:10 and ***d*** so for Mordecai the Jew
7: 5 presume in his heart to ***d*** such
9:13 Jews who are in Shushan to ***d*** again
Job 1: 7 'From where ***d*** you come?"
1:12 only ***d*** not lay a hand on his
2: 2 'From where ***d*** you come?"
2: 9 ***D*** you still hold fast to your
3:18 They ***d*** not hear the voice of
5:17 Therefore ***d*** not despise the
6:11 What strength ***d*** I have, that I
6:26 ***D*** you intend to rebuke my
7:21 Why then ***d*** You not pardon my
9: 5 and they ***d*** not know When He
9:11 I ***d*** not see Him; If He moves
9:11 I ***d*** not perceive Him;
9:21 yet I ***d*** not know myself;
9:29 Why then ***d*** I labor in vain?
9:34 And ***d*** not let dread of Him
10: 2 ***D*** not condemn me; Show me why
10: 4 ***D*** You have eyes of flesh
10: 4 Or ***d*** You see as man sees?
11: 8 than heaven—what can you ***d***?
13:14 Why ***d*** I take my flesh in my
13:20 Only two things ***d*** not do to
13:20 Only two things do not ***d*** to
13:24 Why ***d*** You hide Your face,
14: 3 And ***d*** You open Your eyes on
14:16 But ***d*** not watch over my sin.
15: 3 by speeches with which he can ***d***
15: 8 ***D*** you limit wisdom to
15: 9 What ***d*** you know that we do not
15: 9 What do you know that we ***d*** not
15: 9 What ***d*** you understand that
15:12 And what ***d*** your eyes wink at,
16: 4 I also could speak as you ***d***,
16:18 ***d*** not cover my blood, And let
19:22 Why ***d*** you persecute me as God
20: 4 ***D*** you not know this of old,
21: 7 Why ***d*** the wicked live and
21:14 For we ***d*** not desire the
21:15 And what profit ***d*** we have if
21:29 And ***d*** you not know their
22:17 What can the Almighty ***d*** to
24: 1 Why ***d*** those who know Him see
24:13 They ***d*** not know its ways Nor
24:16 They ***d*** not know the light.
24:21 the barren who ***d*** not bear,
27:12 Why then ***d*** you behave with
30:10 They ***d*** not hesitate to spit in
30:20 but You ***d*** not answer me;
31:14 What then shall I ***d*** when God
32: 9 Nor ***d*** the aged always
32:22 For I ***d*** not know how to
33:13 Why ***d*** you contend with Him?
34:10 Far be it from God to ***d*** wickedness,
34:12 God will never ***d*** wickedly,
34:32 Teach me what I ***d*** not see;
34:32 I will ***d*** no more'?
35: 2 '***D*** you think this is right?
35: 2 ***D*** you say, 'My righteousness
35: 6 what ***d*** you accomplish against
35: 6 what ***d*** you do to Him?
35: 6 what do you ***d*** to Him?
35: 7 what ***d*** you give Him? Or what
35:14 Although you say you ***d*** not see
36:12 But if they ***d*** not obey, They
36:13 They ***d*** not cry for help when
36:20 ***D*** not desire the night, When
36:21 ***d*** not turn to iniquity, For
36:26 and we ***d*** not know Him; Nor
37:12 That they may ***d*** whatever He
37:15 ***D*** you know when God dispatches
37:16 ***D*** you know how the clouds are
38:21 ***D*** you know it, because you
38:33 ***D*** you know the ordinances of
39: 1 ***D*** you know the time when the
39: 2 Or ***d*** you know the time when
39: 4 They depart and ***d*** not return
41: 8 Never ***d*** it again!
42: 2 I know that You can ***d***
Ps 2: 1 Why ***d*** the nations rage, And
4: 4 Be angry, and ***d*** not sin.
6: 1 ***d*** not rebuke me in Your anger,
9:19 ***D*** not let man prevail;
10: 1 Why ***d*** You stand afar off,
10: 1 Why ***d*** You hide in times of
10:12 ***D*** not forget the humble.

10:13 Why ***d*** the wicked renounce God?
10:18 To ***d*** justice to the fatherless
11: 3 What can the righteous ***d***?
14: 4 And ***d*** not call on the LORD?
22: 2 but You ***d*** not hear; And in the
22:19 ***d*** not be far from Me; O My
25: 7 ***D*** not remember the sins of my
26: 9 ***D*** not gather my soul with
27: 9 ***D*** not hide Your face from me
27: 9 ***D*** not turn Your servant away
27: 9 ***D*** not leave me nor forsake me,
27:12 ***D*** not deliver me to the will of
28: 1 ***D*** not be silent to me, Lest,
28: 3 ***D*** not take me away with the
28: 5 Because they ***d*** not regard the
31:17 ***D*** not let me be ashamed,
32: 9 ***D*** not be like the horse or
34:14 Depart from evil and ***d*** good;
34:16 LORD is against those who ***d***
35:11 They ask me things that I ***d***
35:20 For they ***d*** not speak peace,
35:22 ***D*** not keep silence. O Lord,
35:22 ***d*** not be far from me.
36: 3 to be wise and to ***d*** good.
37: 1 ***D*** not fret because of
37: 3 Trust in the LORD, and ***d*** good;
37: 7 ***D*** not fret because of him who
37: 8 ***D*** not fret—it only causes
37:27 Depart from evil, and ***d*** good;
38: 1 ***d*** not rebuke me in Your wrath,
38:13 like a deaf man, ***d*** not hear;
38:21 ***D*** not forsake me, O LORD
39: 7 what ***d*** I wait for? My hope is
39: 8 ***D*** not make me the reproach of
39:12 ***D*** not be silent at my tears;
40: 8 I delight to ***d*** Your will, O my
40: 9 I ***d*** not restrain my lips,
40:11 ***D*** not withhold Your tender
40:17 ***D*** not delay, O my God.
42: 9 Why ***d*** I go mourning because of
43: 2 Why ***d*** You cast me off? Why do
43: 2 Why ***d*** I go mourning because of
44: 9 And You ***d*** not go out with our
44:23 Awake! Why ***d*** You sleep, O Lord?
44:23 Arise! ***D*** not cast us off
44:24 Why ***d*** You hide Your face,
49:16 ***D*** not be afraid when one
49:18 praise you when you ***d*** well
51:11 ***D*** not cast me away from Your
51:11 And ***d*** not take Your Holy
51:16 For You ***d*** not desire sacrifice,
51:16 You ***d*** not delight in burnt
51:18 ***D*** good in Your good pleasure to
52: 1 Why ***d*** you boast in evil,
53: 4 And ***d*** not call upon God?
55: 1 And ***d*** not hide Yourself from
55:11 Oppression and deceit ***d*** not
55:19 Because they ***d*** not change,
55:19 Therefore they ***d*** not fear God.
56: 4 What can flesh ***d*** to me?
56:11 What can man ***d*** to me?
57: ***D*** Not Destroy." A Michtam of
58: ***D*** Not Destroy." A Michtam of
58: 1 ***D*** you indeed speak
58: 1 ***D*** you judge uprightly, you
59: ***D*** Not Destroy." A Michtam of
59: 5 ***D*** not be merciful to any
59:11 ***D*** not slay them, lest my people
60:12 God we will ***d*** valiantly,
62:10 ***D*** not trust in oppression,
62:10 ***D*** not set your heart on
64: 4 they shoot at him and ***d*** not
66: 7 ***D*** not let the rebellious exalt
68:16 Why ***d*** you fume with envy, you
69:17 And ***d*** not hide Your face from
69:23 so that they ***d*** not see;
70: 5 O LORD, ***d*** not delay.
71: 9 ***D*** not cast me off in the time
71: 9 ***D*** not forsake me when my
71:12 ***d*** not be far from me; O my
71:15 For I ***d*** not know their
71:18 ***d*** not forsake me, Until I
74: 9 We ***d*** not see our signs;
74:11 Why ***d*** You withdraw Your hand,
74:19 ***d*** not deliver the life of Your
74:19 ***D*** not forget the life of
74:21 ***d*** not let the oppressed return
74:23 ***D*** not forget the voice of Your
75: ***D*** Not Destroy." A Psalm of
75: 4 ***D*** not deal boastfully,' And to
75: 4 ***D*** not lift up the horn.
75: 5 ***D*** not lift up your horn on high
75: 5 ***D*** not speak with a stiff
79: 6 nations that ***d*** not know
79: 6 And on the kingdoms that ***d*** not
79: 8 ***d*** not remember former
82: 3 ***D*** justice to the afflicted and
82: 5 They ***d*** not know, nor do they
82: 5 nor ***d*** they understand;
83: 1 ***D*** not keep silent, O God!
83: 1 O God! ***D*** not hold Your peace,
83: 1 And ***d*** not be still, O God!
86:10 and ***d*** wondrous things;
88:14 why ***d*** You cast off my soul?
88:14 Why ***d*** You hide Your face from
89:30 forsake My law And ***d*** not walk
89:31 My statutes And ***d*** not keep
95: 8 ***D*** not harden your hearts, as in
95:10 And they ***d*** not know My ways.'
102: 2 ***D*** not hide Your face from me in
102:24 ***D*** not take me away in the
103:18 remember His commandments to ***d***
103:20 who ***d*** His word, Heeding the
103:21 who ***d*** His pleasure.
105:14 He permitted no one to ***d*** them
105:15 ***D*** not touch My anointed ones,
105:15 And ***d*** My prophets no harm."
107:23 Who ***d*** business on great
108:13 Through God we will ***d***
109: 1 ***D*** not keep silent, O God of my
111:10 have all those who ***d*** His
115: 5 mouths, but they ***d*** not speak;
115: 5 but they ***d*** not see;
115: 6 ears, but they ***d*** not hear;
115: 6 but they ***d*** not smell;
115: 7 hands, but they ***d*** not handle;
115: 7 but they ***d*** not walk;
115: 7 Nor ***d*** they mutter through
115:17 The dead ***d*** not praise the
118: 6 What can man ***d*** to me?
119: 3 They also ***d*** no iniquity;
119: 8 ***d*** not forsake me utterly!
119:19 ***D*** not hide Your commandments
119:31 ***d*** not put me to shame!
119:51 Yet I ***d*** not turn aside from
119:68 You are good, and ***d*** good;
119:83 Yet I ***d*** not forget Your
119:109 Yet I ***d*** not forget Your law.
119:116 And ***d*** not let me be ashamed of
119:121 ***D*** not leave me to my
119:122 ***D*** not let the proud oppress
119:136 Because men ***d*** not keep Your
119:141 Yet I ***d*** not forget Your
119:153 For I ***d*** not forget Your law.
119:155 For they ***d*** not seek Your
119:157 Yet I ***d*** not turn from Your
119:158 Because they ***d*** not keep Your
119:166 And I ***d*** Your commandments.
119:176 For I ***d*** not forget Your
125: 4 ***D*** good, O LORD, to those who
130: 5 And in His word I ***d*** hope.
131: 1 Neither ***d*** I concern myself
132:10 ***D*** not turn away the face of
135:16 mouths, but they ***d*** not speak;
135:16 but they ***d*** not see;
135:17 ears, but they ***d*** not hear;
137: 6 If I ***d*** not remember you, Let
137: 6 If I ***d*** not exalt Jerusalem
138: 8 ***D*** not forsake the works of
139:21 ***D*** I not hate them, O LORD, who
139:21 And ***d*** I not loathe those who
140: 8 ***D*** not grant, O LORD, the
140: 8 ***D*** not further his wicked
141: 4 ***D*** not incline my heart to any
141: 4 And ***d*** not let me eat of their
141: 8 ***D*** not leave my soul destitute.
143: 2 ***D*** not enter into judgment with
143: 7 My spirit fails! ***D*** not hide
143: 8 For in You ***d*** I trust;
143:10 Teach me to ***d*** Your will,
146: 3 ***D*** not put your trust in

Prov 1: 8 And ***d*** not forsake the law of
1:10 ***D*** not consent.
1:15 ***d*** not walk in the way with
2:19 Nor ***d*** they regain the paths of
3: 1 ***d*** not forget my law, But let
3: 7 ***D*** not be wise in your own
3:11 ***d*** not despise the chastening of
3:25 ***D*** not be afraid of sudden
3:27 ***D*** not withhold good from those
3:27 power of your hand to ***d*** so.
3:28 ***D*** not say to your neighbor,
3:29 ***D*** not devise evil against your
3:30 ***D*** not strive with a man without
3:31 ***D*** not envy the oppressor,
4: 2 ***D*** not forsake my law.
4: 5 ***D*** not forget, nor turn
4: 6 ***D*** not forsake her, and she will
4:13 ***d*** not let go; Keep her, for
4:14 ***D*** not enter the path of the
4:14 And ***d*** not walk in the way of
4:15 ***d*** not travel on it; Turn away
4:16 For they ***d*** not sleep unless
4:19 They ***d*** not know what makes
4:21 ***D*** not let them depart from your
4:27 ***D*** not turn to the right or the
5: 6 You ***d*** not know them.
5: 7 And ***d*** not depart from the
5: 8 And ***d*** not go near the door of
6: 3 So ***d*** this, my son, and deliver
6:20 And ***d*** not forsake the law of
6:25 ***D*** not lust after her beauty in
6:30 People ***d*** not despise a thief
7:25 ***D*** not let your heart turn aside
7:25 ***D*** not stray into her paths;
8:33 And ***d*** not disdain it.
9: 8 ***D*** not correct a scoffer, lest
10:23 To ***d*** evil is like sport to a
11: 4 Riches ***d*** not profit in the day
14: 7 When you ***d*** not perceive in
14:22 ***D*** they not go astray who devise
15: 7 heart of the fool does not ***d***
19: 7 How much more ***d*** his friends go
19:18 And ***d*** not set your heart on
19:19 you will have to ***d*** it again.
20:13 ***D*** not love sleep, lest you come
20:19 Therefore ***d*** not associate with
20:22 ***D*** not say, "I will recompense
20:30 As ***d*** stripes the inner depths
21: 3 To ***d*** righteousness and justice
21: 7 they refuse to ***d*** justice.
21:15 joy for the just to ***d*** justice,
22:22 ***D*** not rob the poor because he
22:24 And with a furious man ***d*** not
22:26 ***D*** not be one of those who
22:28 ***D*** not remove the ancient
22:29 ***D*** you see a man who excels in
23: 3 ***D*** not desire his delicacies,
23: 4 ***D*** not overwork to be rich
23: 6 ***D*** not eat the bread of a miser,
23: 9 ***D*** not speak in the hearing of a
23:10 ***D*** not remove the ancient
23:13 ***D*** not withhold correction from
23:17 ***D*** not let your heart envy
23:20 ***D*** not mix with winebibbers,
23:22 And ***d*** not despise your mother
23:23 and ***d*** not sell it, Also
23:31 ***D*** not look on the wine when it
24: 1 ***D*** not be envious of evil men,
24: 8 He who plots to ***d*** evil Will be
24:15 ***D*** not lie in wait, O wicked
24:15 ***D*** not plunder his resting
24:17 ***D*** not rejoice when your enemy
24:17 And ***d*** not let your heart be
24:19 ***D*** not fret because of
24:21 ***D*** not associate with those
24:28 ***D*** not be a witness against your
24:29 ***D*** not say, "I will do to him
24:29 I will ***d*** to him just as he has
25: 6 ***D*** not exalt yourself in the
25: 6 And ***d*** not stand in the place
25: 8 ***D*** not go hastily to court
25: 8 For what will you ***d*** in the
25: 9 And ***d*** not disclose the secret
26: 4 ***D*** not answer a fool according
26:12 ***D*** you see a man wise in his own
26:25 ***d*** not believe him, For there
27: 1 ***D*** not boast about tomorrow,
27: 1 For you ***d*** not know what a day
27:10 ***D*** not forsake your own friend
28: 5 Evil men ***d*** not understand
29:20 ***D*** you see a man hasty in his
30: 2 And ***d*** not have the
30: 6 ***D*** not add to His words, Lest
30:10 ***D*** not malign a servant to his
30:18 four which I ***d*** not understand:
31: 3 ***D*** not give your strength to

Eccl 2: 3 good for the sons of men to ***d*** under
2:12 For what can the man ***d*** who
3:12 and to ***d*** good in their lives,
4: 8 For whom ***d*** I toil and deprive
5: 1 ***d*** not know that they do evil.
5: 1 they do not know that they ***d***
5: 4 ***d*** not delay to pay it; For He
5: 6 ***D*** not let your mouth cause your
5: 8 ***d*** not marvel at the matter;
6: 6 ***D*** not all go to one place?
7: 9 ***D*** not hasten in your spirit to
7:10 ***D*** not say, "Why were the
7:10 For you ***d*** not inquire wisely
7:16 ***D*** not be overly righteous, Nor
7:17 ***D*** not be overly wicked, Nor be
7:21 Also ***d*** not take to heart
8: 3 ***D*** not be hasty to go from his
8: 3 ***D*** not take your stand for an
8:11 fully set in them to ***d*** evil.
9:10 Whatever your hand finds to ***d***,
9:10 ***d*** it with your might;
10: 4 ***D*** not leave your post;
10:15 For they ***d*** not even know how
10:20 ***D*** not curse the king, even in
10:20 ***D*** not curse the rich, even in
11: 2 For you ***d*** not know what evil
11: 5 As you ***d*** not know what is the
11: 5 So you ***d*** not know the works of
11: 6 And in the evening ***d*** not
11: 6 For you ***d*** not know which will
12: 2 And the clouds ***d*** not return

Song 1: 4 Rightly ***d*** they love you.
1: 6 ***D*** not look upon me, because I
1: 8 If you ***d*** not know, O fairest
2: 7 ***D*** not stir up nor awaken love
3: 5 ***D*** not stir up nor awaken love
8: 4 ***D*** not stir up nor awaken love
8: 8 What shall we ***d*** for our sister

Isa 1: 3 My people ***d*** not consider."
1:11 I ***d*** not delight in the blood
1:16 My eyes. Cease to ***d*** evil,
1:17 Learn to ***d*** good; Seek justice,
1:23 They ***d*** not defend the
2: 9 Therefore ***d*** not forgive them.
3: 7 ***D*** not make me a ruler of the
3: 9 They ***d*** not hide it. Woe to
3:15 What ***d*** you mean by crushing My
5: 5 let Me tell you what I will ***d***
5:12 But they ***d*** not regard the work
6: 9 but ***d*** not understand; Keep on
6: 9 but ***d*** not perceive.'
7: 4 ***d*** not fear or be fainthearted
8:12 ***D*** not say, 'A conspiracy,'
8:20 If they ***d*** not speak according
9:13 For the people ***d*** not turn to
9:13 Nor ***d*** they seek the LORD of
10: 3 What will you ***d*** in the day of
10:11 Shall I not ***d*** also to
10:24 ***d*** not be afraid of the
14:29 ***D*** not rejoice, all you of
16: 3 ***D*** not betray him who escapes.
19:11 How ***d*** you say to Pharaoh, "I
19:15 Palm branch or bulrush, may ***d***.
22: 4 ***D*** not labor to comfort me
23: 4 I ***d*** not labor, nor bring forth
23: 4 Neither ***d*** I rear young men,
28:21 That He may ***d*** His work, His
28:22 ***d*** not be mockers, Lest your

29:14 I will again **d** a marvelous work
30:10 to the seers, "**D** not see,"
30:10 **D** not prophesy to us right
31: 1 But who **d** not look to the Holy
35: 4 **d** not fear! Behold, your God
36: 5 Now in whom **d** you trust, that
36:11 and **d** not speak to us in Hebrew
36:14 **D** not let Hezekiah deceive you,
36:16 '**D** not listen to Hezekiah;
36:21 **D** not answer him."
37: 6 **D** not be afraid of the words
37:10 **D** not let your God in whom you
37:32 of the LORD of hosts will **d**
38: 7 that the LORD will **d** this
38:19 As I **d** this day; The father
40:27 Why **d** you say, O Jacob, And
41:23 **d** good or do evil, That we may
41:23 do good or **d** evil, That we may
42:16 These things I will **d** for
42:20 but you **d** not observe; Opening
43: 6 **D** not keep them back!' Bring My
43:18 **D** not remember the former
43:19 I will **d** a new thing, Now it
44: 7 And who can proclaim as I **d**?
44: 8 **D** not fear, nor be afraid
44:18 They **d** not know nor
45: 7 **d** all these things.'
46:10 And I will **d** all My pleasure,'
46:11 I will also **d** it.
48: 9 So that I **d** not cut you off.
48:11 I will **d** it; For how should
48:14 He shall **d** His pleasure on
51: 7 **D** not fear the reproach of
54: 2 **D** not spare; Lengthen your
54: 4 **D** not fear, for you will not be
55: 2 Why **d** you spend money for what
55: 5 call a nation you **d** not know,
55: 5 And nations who **d** not know
55:10 And **d** not return there,
56: 1 and **d** righteousness, For My
56: 3 **D** not let the son of the
57: 4 Whom **d** you ridicule?
57: 4 Against whom **d** you make a wide
57:11 peace from of old That you **d**
58: 4 You will not fast as you **d**
58:11 whose waters **d** not fail.
62: 6 **d** not keep silent,
64: 9 **D** not be furious, O LORD,
65: 5 **D** not come near me, For I am
65: 8 **D** not destroy it, For a
65: 8 So will I **d** for My servants'
65:12 And chose that in which I **d**
66: 4 And chose that in which I **d**
Jer 1: 7 '**D** not say, 'I am a youth,'
1: 8 **D** not be afraid of their faces,
1:11 what **d** you see?" And I said,
1:13 What **d** you see?" And I said,
1:17 **D** not be dismayed before their
2: 8 things that **d** not profit.
2:31 Why **d** My people say, 'We are
2:33 Why **d** you beautify your way to
2:36 Why **d** you gad about so much to
3:22 'Indeed we **d** come to You,
4: 3 And **d** not sow among thorns.
4: 6 Take refuge! **D** not delay!
4:22 They are wise to **d** evil,
4:22 But to **d** good they have no
4:30 plundered, What will you **d**?
5: 4 For they **d** not know the way of
5:10 But **d** not make a complete end.
5:15 whose language you **d** not know,
5:19 Why does the LORD our God **d** all
5:22 **D** you not fear Me
5:24 They **d** not say in their heart,
5:28 They **d** not plead the cause,
5:28 the needy they **d** not defend.
5:31 But what will you **d** in the
6:25 **D** not go out into the field,
7: 4 **D** not trust in these lying
7: 6 if you **d** not oppress the
7: 6 and **d** not shed innocent blood
7: 9 gods whom you **d** not know,
7:10 We are delivered to **d** all these
7:14 therefore I will **d** to the house
7:16 Therefore **d** not pray for this
7:17 **D** you not see what they do in
7:17 Do you not see what they **d** in
7:19 **D** they provoke Me to anger?"
7:19 **D** they not provoke
8: 6 But they **d** not speak aright.
8: 7 But My people **d** not know the
8: 9 So what wisdom **d** they have?
8:14 Why **d** we sit still? Assemble
9: 3 And they **d** not know Me,"
9: 4 And **d** not trust any brother;
10: 2 **D** not learn the way of the
10: 2 **D** not be dismayed at the signs
10: 5 **D** not be afraid of them,
10: 5 For they cannot **d** evil,
10: 5 Nor can they **d** any good."
10:25 Gentiles, who **d** not know You,
10:25 And on the families who **d** not
11: 4 and **d** according to all that I
11: 6 of this covenant and **d** them.
11: 8 which I commanded them to **d**,
11:14 So **d** not pray for this people,
11:15 What has My beloved to **d** in My
11:15 When you **d** evil, then you
11:21 **D** not prophesy in the name of
12: 5 Then how will you **d** in the
12: 6 **D** not believe them, Even
12:13 to pain but **d** not profit.
12:17 But if they **d** not obey, I will
13: 1 but **d** not put it in water."
13:12 **D** we not certainly know that
13:15 **D** not be proud, For the LORD
13:23 Then may you also **d** good who
13:23 who are accustomed to **d** evil.
14: 7 **D** it for Your name's sake;
14: 9 **D** not leave us!
14:11 **D** not pray for this people, for
14:18 go about in a land they **d** not
14:21 **D** not abhor us, for Your
14:21 **D** not disgrace the throne of
14:21 **d** not break Your covenant with
15: 7 Since they **d** not return from
15:14 Into a land which you **d** not
15:15 **d** not take me away. Know that
16: 5 **D** not enter the house of
16:13 a land that you **d** not know,
17: 4 land which you **d** not know;
17:17 **D** not be a terror to me
17:18 But **d** not let me be put to
17:18 But **d** not let me be dismayed.
17:22 nor **d** any work, but hallow the
17:24 to **d** no work in it,
18: 6 can I not **d** with you as this
19:12 Thus I will **d** to this place,"
22: 3 **D** no wrong and do no violence
22: 3 Do no wrong and **d** no violence
22: 4 For if you indeed **d** this thing,
22:15 And **d** justice and
22:28 a land which they **d** not know?
23:16 **D** not listen to the words of the
23:24 **D** I not fill heaven and earth?"
23:38 **D** not say, 'The oracle of the
24: 3 'What **d** you see, Jeremiah?"
25: 6 **D** not go after other gods to
25: 6 and **d** not provoke Me to anger
26: 2 **D** not diminish a word.
26:14 **d** with me as seems good and
27: 9 Therefore **d** not listen to your
27:14 Therefore **d** not listen to the
27:16 **D** not listen to the words of
27:17 **D** not listen to them
27:18 **d** not go to Babylon.'
28: 6 Amen! The LORD **d** so; the LORD
29: 8 **D** not let your prophets and
29:32 he see the good that I will **d**
30: 6 So why **d** I see every man with
30:10 Therefore **d** not fear, O My
30:14 They **d** not seek you; For I
30:15 Why **d** you cry about your
32: 3 Why **d** you prophesy and say,
32:23 that You commanded them to **d**;
32:35 My mind that they should **d** this
32:41 over them to **d** them good,
33: 3 which you **d** not know.'
33: 9 hear all the good that I **d** to
35: 9 nor **d** we have vineyard, field,
35:15 and **d** not go after other gods
37: 9 **D** not deceive yourselves,
37:20 and **d** not make me return to the
38: 5 For the king can **d** nothing
38:18 But if you **d** not surrender to
38:25 **d** not hide it from us, and we
39:12 and **d** him no harm; but do to
39:12 but **d** to him just as he says to
40: 9 **D** not be afraid to serve the
40:14 **D** you certainly know that Baalis
40:16 You shall not **d** this thing, for
41: 8 **D** not kill us, for we have
42: 3 walk and the thing we should **d**.
42: 5 if we **d** not do according to
42: 5 if we do not **d** according to
42:11 **D** not be afraid of the king of
42:11 **d** not be afraid of him,' says
42:19 '**D** not go to Egypt!'
42:20 declare to us and we will **d** it.'
43: 2 **D** not go to Egypt to dwell
44: 4 **d** not do this abominable thing
44: 4 do not **d** this abominable thing
44: 7 Why **d** you commit this great
44:17 But we will certainly **d** whatever
45: 5 And **d** you seek great things for
45: 5 **D** not seek them; for behold, I
46: 6 **D** not let the swift flee away,
46:27 But **d** not fear, O My servant
46:27 And **d** not be dismayed,
46:28 **D** not fear, O Jacob My
49: 4 Why **d** you boast in the valleys,
50: 2 **d** not conceal it—Say, 'Babylon
50:15 she has done, so **d** to her.
50:21 And **d** according to all that I
50:29 **d** to her; For she has been
51: 3 **D** not spare her young men;
51: 6 **D** not be cut off in her
51:50 Get away! **D** not stand still!
Lam 1:22 And **d** to them as You have done
3:49 My eyes flow and **d** not cease,
3:56 **D** not hide Your ear From my
3:57 And said, "**D** not fear!"
4:15 **D** not touch us!" When they
4:16 The people **d** not respect the
5:20 Why **d** You forget us forever,
Ezek 2: 6 **d** not be afraid of them nor be
2: 6 **d** not be afraid of their words
2: 8 **D** not be rebellious like that
3: 9 **d** not be afraid of them, nor be
5: 9 And I will **d** among you what I
5: 9 which I will never **d** again,
7:27 I will **d** to them according to
8: 6 **d** you see what they are doing,
8:12 of the house of Israel **d** in
9: 5 **d** not let your eye spare, nor
9: 6 but **d** not come near anyone on
11:20 keep My judgments and **d** them;
16: 5 to **d** any of these things for
16:30 seeing you **d** all these things,
17:12 **D** you not know what these
17:17 and great company **d** anything
18: 2 What **d** you mean when you use
18:14 but does not **d** likewise;
18:23 **D** I have any pleasure at all
20: 7 and **d** not defile yourselves
20:18 **D** not walk in the statutes of
20:19 My judgments, and **d** them;
21:14 let the sword **d** double damage.
22:14 have spoken, and will **d** it.
23:30 I will **d** these things to you
24:14 and I will **d** it; I will not
24:17 **d** not cover your lips, and do
24:17 and **d** not eat man's bread of
24:22 And you shall **d** as I have done;
24:24 that he has done you shall **d**;
25:14 that they may **d** in Edom
32:19 Whom **d** you surpass in beauty?
32:27 They **d** not lie with the mighty
33: 8 you **d** not speak to warn
33:31 they come to you as people **d**,
33:31 but they **d** not do them;
33:31 but they do not **d** them;
33:32 but they **d** not do them.
33:32 but they do not **d** them.
34: 3 but you **d** not feed the flock.
35:11 I will **d** according to your anger
35:15 so I will **d** to you; you shall
36:11 and **d** better for you than at
36:22 I **d** not do this for your sake,
36:22 I do not **d** this for your sake,
36:27 keep My judgments and **d** them.
36:32 Not for your sake **d** I do
36:32 Not for your sake do I **d**
36:36 and I will **d** it."
36:37 of Israel inquire of Me to **d**
37:24 My statutes, and **d** them.
45:20 And so you shall **d** on the
45:25 he shall **d** likewise for seven
46:20 so that they **d** not bring them
Dan 2: 5 if you **d** not make known the
2: 9 if you **d** not make known the
2:24 **D** not destroy the wise men of
3:12 They **d** not serve your gods or
3:14 that you **d** not serve my gods
3:15 But if you **d** not worship,
3:18 that we **d** not serve your gods,
4:19 **d** not let the dream or its
5:10 **D** not let your thoughts
5:23 which **d** not see or hear or
9:18 for we **d** not present our
9:19 **D** not delay for Your own
10:12 **D** not fear, Daniel, for from the
10:20 **D** you know why I have come to
11: 3 and **d** according to his will.
11:16 against him shall **d** according
11:17 ones with him; thus shall he **d**.
11:24 and he shall **d** what his
11:28 so he shall **d** damage and
11:30 holy covenant, and **d** damage.
11:32 Those who **d** wickedly against the
11:36 Then the king shall **d** according
12:10 but the wicked shall **d**
Hos 4:14 Therefore people who **d** not
4:15 **D** not come up to Gilgal, Nor
5: 4 They **d** not direct their deeds
5: 4 And they **d** not know the LORD.
6: 4 what shall I **d** to you?
6: 4 what shall I **d** to you?
7: 2 They **d** not consider in their
7:10 But they **d** not return to the
9: 1 **D** not rejoice, O Israel, with
9: 5 What will you **d** in the
10: 3 what would he **d** for us?"
14: 8 What have I to **d** anymore with
Joel 2: 7 And they **d** not break ranks.
2: 8 They **d** not push one another;
2:17 And **d** not give Your heritage
2:22 **D** not be afraid, you beasts of
3: 4 what have you to **d** with Me,
Am 2:12 saying, '**D** not prophesy!'
3:10 For they **d** not know to do
3:10 For they do not know to **d**
4:12 Therefore thus will I **d** to you,
4:12 Because I will **d** this to you,
5: 5 But **d** not seek Bethel, Nor
5:21 And I **d** not savor your sacred
6:12 **D** horses run on rocks?
7: 8 what **d** you see?" And I said,
7:16 **D** not prophesy against Israel,
7:16 And **d** not spout against the
8: 2 what **d** you see?" So I said,
Jon 1: 6 'What **d** you mean, sleeper?
1: 8 And where **d** you come from?
1:11 What shall we **d** to you that the
1:14 please **d** not let us perish for
1:14 and **d** not charge us with
3: 7 **d** not let them eat, or drink
3:10 and He did not **d** it.
Mic 2: 6 **D** not prattle," you say to
2: 7 **D** not My words do good To him
2: 7 Do not My words **d** good To him
4: 9 Now why **d** you cry aloud?
4:12 But they **d** not know the
4:12 Nor **d** they understand His
6: 8 LORD require of you But to **d**
6:14 And what you **d** rescue I will

7: 3 That they may successfully ***d***
7: 5 ***D*** not trust in a friend
7: 5 ***D*** not put your confidence in a
7: 8 ***D*** not rejoice over me, my
Nah 1: 9 What ***d*** you conspire against
Hab 1: 3 Why ***d*** You show me iniquity,
1:13 Why ***d*** You look on those who
1:14 Why ***d*** You make men like fish
Zeph 1:12 The LORD will not ***d*** good, Nor
1:12 Nor will He ***d*** evil.'
3: 5 He will ***d*** no unrighteousness.
3:13 The remnant of Israel shall ***d***
3:16 ***D*** not fear; Zion, let not your
Hag 1: 6 but ***d*** not have enough;
2: 3 And how ***d*** you see it now?
2: 5 among you; ***d*** not fear!'
Zech 1: 4 ***D*** not be like your fathers, to
1: 5 ***d*** they live forever?
1: 6 LORD of hosts determined to ***d***
1:21 "What are these coming to ***d***?
4: 2 What ***d*** you see?" So I said, "I
4: 5 ***D*** you not know what these are?"
4:13 ***D*** you not know what these
5: 2 What ***d*** you see?" So I answered,
7: 6 ***d*** you not eat and drink for
7:10 ***D*** not oppress the widow or the
8:13 ***D*** not fear, Let your hands be
8:15 I am determined to ***d*** good
8:15 house of Judah. ***D*** not fear.
8:16 are the things you shall ***d***:
8:17 And ***d*** not love a false oath.
11: 5 and their shepherds ***d*** not pity
14:17 families of the earth ***d*** not
14:18 strikes the nations who ***d*** not
14:19 of all the nations that ***d*** not
Mal 2: 2 Because you ***d*** not take it to
2:10 Why ***d*** we deal treacherously
2:13 this is the second thing you ***d***:
2:16 That you ***d*** not deal
3: 5 Because they ***d*** not fear Me,"
3: 6 I ***d*** not change; Therefore you
3:15 For those who ***d*** wickedness are
4: 1 all who ***d*** wickedly will be
4: 3 On the day that I ***d*** this,"
Mt 1:20 ***d*** not be afraid to take to you
3: 9 and ***d*** not think to say to
5:15 Nor ***d*** they light a lamp and put
5:17 ***D*** not think that I came to
5:34 ***d*** not swear at all: neither by
5:42 from you ***d*** not turn away.
5:44 ***d*** good to those who hate you,
5:46 ***D*** not even the tax collectors
5:46 the tax collectors ***d*** the same?
5:47 what ***d*** you do more than
5:47 what do you ***d*** more than
5:47 ***D*** not even the tax collectors
5:47 even the tax collectors ***d*** so?
6: 1 Take heed that you ***d*** not do your
6: 1 Take heed that you do not ***d*** your
6: 2 when you ***d*** a charitable deed,
6: 2 ***d*** not sound a trumpet before
6: 2 before you as the hypocrites ***d***
6: 3 But when you ***d*** a charitable
6: 3 ***d*** not let your left hand know
6: 7 ***d*** not use vain repetitions as
6: 7 repetitions as the heathen ***d***.
6: 8 Therefore ***d*** not be like them.
6:13 And ***d*** not lead us into
6:15 But if you ***d*** not forgive men
6:16 ***d*** not be like the hypocrites,
6:18 so that you ***d*** not appear to men
6:19 ***D*** not lay up for yourselves
6:20 where thieves ***d*** not break in
6:25 ***d*** not worry about your life,
6:28 So why ***d*** you worry about
6:31 Therefore ***d*** not worry, saying,
6:34 Therefore ***d*** not worry about
7: 3 And why ***d*** you look at the speck
7: 3 but ***d*** not consider the plank in
7: 6 ***D*** not give what is holy to the
7:12 whatever you want men to ***d*** to
7:12 ***d*** also to them, for this is the
7:16 ***D*** men gather grapes from
7:26 and does not ***d*** them, will be
8: 9 ***D*** this,' and he does it."
8:29 What have we to ***d*** with You,
9: 4 Why ***d*** you think evil in your
9:14 Why ***d*** we and the Pharisees fast
9:14 but Your disciples ***d*** not
9:17 Nor ***d*** they put new wine into old
9:28 ***D*** you believe that I am able to
9:28 that I am able to ***d*** this?"
10: 5 ***D*** not go into the way of the
10: 5 and ***d*** not enter a city of the
10:19 ***d*** not worry about how or what
10:26 'Therefore ***d*** not fear them.
10:28 And ***d*** not fear those who kill
10:31 ***D*** not fear therefore; you are of
10:34 ***D*** not think that I came to
11: 3 or ***d*** we look for another?"
12: 2 doing what is not lawful to ***d***
12:12 it is lawful to ***d*** good
12:27 by whom ***d*** your sons cast them
13:10 Why ***d*** You speak to them in
13:13 because seeing they ***d*** not see,
13:13 and hearing they ***d*** not hear,
13:13 nor ***d*** they understand.
13:28 ***D*** you want us then to go and
13:58 Now He did not ***d*** many mighty
14:16 'They ***d*** not need to go away.
14:27 ***d*** not be afraid."
15: 2 Why ***d*** Your disciples transgress
15: 2 For they ***d*** not wash their hands
15: 3 Why ***d*** you also transgress the
15:12 ***D*** You know that the Pharisees
15:17 ***D*** you not yet understand that
15:32 And I ***d*** not want to send them
15:34 How many loaves ***d*** you have?"
16: 8 why ***d*** you reason among
16: 9 ***D*** you not yet understand, or
16:11 How is it you ***d*** not understand
16:13 Who ***d*** men say that I, the Son of
16:15 But who ***d*** you say that I am?"
17: 7 and ***d*** not be afraid."
17:10 Why then ***d*** the scribes say that
17:25 'What ***d*** you think, Simon?
17:25 From whom ***d*** the kings of the
18:10 Take heed that you ***d*** not
18:12 What ***d*** you think? If a man has a
18:22 I ***d*** not say to you, up to seven
18:35 My heavenly Father also will ***d*** to
19:14 and ***d*** not forbid them; for of
19:16 what good thing shall I ***d*** that
19:17 Why ***d*** you call Me good? No one
19:20 What ***d*** I still lack?"
20:15 'Is it not lawful for me to ***d*** what
20:21 What ***d*** you wish?" She said to
20:22 'You ***d*** not know what you ask.
20:32 What ***d*** you want Me to do for
20:32 What do you want Me to ***d*** for
21:16 ***D*** You hear what these are
21:21 if you have faith and ***d*** not
21:21 you will not only ***d*** what was
21:24 authority I ***d*** these things:
21:27 We ***d*** not know." And He said to
21:27 authority I ***d*** these things.
21:28 But what ***d*** you think? A man had
21:40 what will he ***d*** to those
22:16 nor ***d*** You care about anyone,
22:16 for You ***d*** not regard the person
22:17 what ***d*** You think? Is it lawful
22:18 Why ***d*** you test Me, you
22:42 What ***d*** you think about the
23: 3 to observe, that observe and ***d***,
23: 3 but ***d*** not do according to their
23: 3 but do not ***d*** according to their
23: 3 for they say, and ***d*** not do.
23: 3 for they say, and do not ***d***.
23: 5 But all their works they ***d*** to be
23: 8 ***d*** not be called 'Rabbi';
23: 9 ***D*** not call anyone on earth your
23:10 And ***d*** not be called teachers;
23:13 nor ***d*** you allow those who are
24: 2 ***D*** you not see all these things?
24:23 There!' ***d*** not believe it.
24:26 He is in the desert!' ***d*** not go
24:26 inner rooms!' ***d*** not believe
24:42 for you ***d*** not know what hour
24:44 at an hour you ***d*** not expect.
25:12 I ***d*** not know you.'
25:45 inasmuch as you did not ***d*** it
25:45 you did not ***d*** it to Me.'
26:10 'Why ***d*** you trouble the woman?
26:11 but Me you ***d*** not have always.
26:17 Where ***d*** You want us to prepare
26:53 Or ***d*** you think that I cannot now
26:62 ***D*** You answer nothing? What is
26:65 What further need ***d*** we have
26:66 What ***d*** you think?" They
26:70 I ***d*** not know what you are
26:72 I ***d*** not know the Man!"
26:74 I ***d*** not know the Man!"
27:13 ***D*** You not hear how many things
27:17 Whom ***d*** you want me to release to
27:19 Have nothing to ***d*** with that just
27:21 Which of the two ***d*** you want me
27:22 What then shall I ***d*** with Jesus
28: 5 ***D*** not be afraid, for I know that
28:10 ***D*** not be afraid. Go and tell My
Mk 1:24 What have we to ***d*** with You,
2: 8 Why ***d*** you reason about these
2:18 Why ***d*** the disciples of John and
2:18 but Your disciples ***d*** not
2:24 why ***d*** they do what is not
2:24 why do they ***d*** what is not
3: 4 on the Sabbath to ***d*** good
3: 4 to do good or to ***d*** evil,
4:13 ***D*** you not understand this
4:38 ***d*** You not care that we are
5: 7 What have I to ***d*** with You,
5: 7 that You ***d*** not torment me."
5:36 ***D*** not be afraid; only believe."
6: 5 Now He could ***d*** no mighty work
6:38 'How many loaves ***d*** you have?
6:50 ***d*** not be afraid."
7: 3 all the Jews ***d*** not eat
7: 4 they ***d*** not eat unless they
7: 5 Why ***d*** Your disciples not walk
7: 8 many other such things you ***d***.
7:12 no longer let him ***d*** anything
7:13 And many such things you ***d***.
7:18 ***D*** you not perceive that
8: 5 How many loaves ***d*** you have?"
8:17 Why ***d*** you reason because you
8:17 ***D*** you not yet perceive nor
8:18 'Having eyes, ***d*** you not see?
8:18 having ears, ***d*** you not hear?
8:18 And ***d*** you not remember?
8:21 How is it you ***d*** not
8:27 Who ***d*** men say that I am?"
8:29 But who ***d*** you say that I am?"
9:11 Why ***d*** the scribes say that
9:22 But if You can ***d*** anything, have
9:39 ***D*** not forbid him, for no one who
10:14 and ***d*** not forbid them; for of
10:17 what shall I ***d*** that I may
10:18 Why ***d*** you call Me good? No one
10:19 '***D*** not commit adultery,'
10:19 ***D*** not murder,' 'Do not
10:19 ***D*** not steal,' 'Do not bear
10:19 ***D*** not bear false witness,'
10:19 ***D*** not defraud,' 'Honor your
10:35 we want You to ***d*** for us
10:36 What ***d*** you want Me to do for
10:36 What do you want Me to ***d*** for
10:38 'You ***d*** not know what you ask.
10:51 What ***d*** you want Me to do for
10:51 What do you want Me to ***d*** for
11:26 But if you ***d*** not forgive,
11:28 authority to ***d*** these things?"
11:29 by what authority I ***d*** these
11:33 We ***d*** not know." And Jesus
11:33 by what authority I ***d*** these
12: 9 the owner of the vineyard ***d***?
12:14 for You ***d*** not regard the person
12:15 Why ***d*** you test Me? Bring Me a
12:24 because you ***d*** not know the
13: 2 ***D*** you see these great buildings?
13: 7 ***d*** not be troubled; for such
13:11 ***d*** not worry beforehand, or
13:21 He is there!' ***d*** not believe
13:33 for you ***d*** not know when the
13:35 for you ***d*** not know when the
14: 6 Why ***d*** you trouble her? She has
14: 7 you wish you may ***d*** them good;
14: 7 but Me you ***d*** not have always.
14:12 Where ***d*** You want us to go and
14:60 ***D*** You answer nothing? What is
14:63 What further need ***d*** we have of
14:64 What ***d*** you think?"
14:71 I ***d*** not know this Man of whom
15: 4 ***D*** You answer nothing? See how
15: 8 began to ask him to ***d*** just
15: 9 ***D*** you want me to release to you
15:12 What then ***d*** you want me to do
15:12 What then do you want me to ***d***
16: 6 ***D*** not be alarmed. You seek Jesus
Lk 1:13 ***D*** not be afraid, Zacharias, for
1:30 ***D*** not be afraid, Mary, for you
1:34 since I ***d*** not know a man?"
2:10 ***D*** not be afraid, for behold, I
2:27 to ***d*** for Him according to the
3: 8 and ***d*** not begin to say to
3:10 What shall we ***d*** then?"
3:11 let him ***d*** likewise."
3:12 'Teacher, what shall we ***d***?"
3:14 saying, "And what shall we ***d***?
3:14 ***D*** not intimidate anyone or
4:23 ***d*** also here in Your country.'
4:34 What have we to ***d*** with You,
5:10 ***D*** not be afraid. From now on you
5:30 Why ***d*** You eat and drink with tax
5:33 Why ***d*** the disciples of John fast
6: 2 doing what is not lawful to ***d***
6: 9 on the Sabbath to ***d*** good
6: 9 to do good or to ***d*** evil,
6:11 one another what they might ***d***
6:27 ***d*** good to those who hate you,
6:29 ***d*** not withhold your tunic
6:30 takes away your goods ***d*** not ask
6:31 And just as you want men to ***d*** to
6:31 you also ***d*** to them likewise.
6:33 'And if you ***d*** good to those who
6:33 do good to those who ***d*** good
6:33 For even sinners ***d*** the same.
6:35 ***d*** good, and lend, hoping for
6:41 And why ***d*** you look at the speck
6:41 but ***d*** not perceive the plank in
6:42 when you yourself ***d*** not see
6:44 For men ***d*** not gather figs from
6:44 nor ***d*** they gather grapes from a
6:46 But why ***d*** you call Me 'Lord,
6:46 and ***d*** not do the things which
6:46 and do not ***d*** the things which
7: 4 the one for whom He should ***d***
7: 6 ***d*** not trouble Yourself, for I
7: 8 ***D*** this,' and he does it."
7:13 said to her, "***D*** not weep."
7:19 or ***d*** we look for another?"
7:20 or ***d*** we look for another?'"
7:44 ***D*** you see this woman? I entered
8:21 hear the word of God and ***d*** it."
8:28 What have I to ***d*** with You,
8:28 ***d*** not torment me!"
8:49 ***D*** not trouble the Teacher."
8:50 ***D*** not be afraid; only believe,
8:52 ***D*** not weep; she is not dead, but
9: 3 and ***d*** not have two tunics
9:18 Who ***d*** the crowds say that I
9:20 But who ***d*** you say that I am?"
9:50 ***D*** not forbid him, for he who is
9:54 ***d*** You want us to command fire
9:55 You ***d*** not know what manner of
10: 7 ***D*** not go from house to house.
10:10 and they ***d*** not receive you, go
10:20 Nevertheless ***d*** not rejoice in
10:25 what shall I ***d*** to inherit
10:28 ***d*** this and you will live."
10:36 So which of these three ***d*** you
10:37 Go and ***d*** likewise."
10:40 ***d*** You not care that my sister
11: 4 And ***d*** not lead us into
11: 7 ***D*** not trouble me; the door is
11:19 by whom ***d*** your sons cast them
11:46 and you yourselves ***d*** not touch
12: 4 ***d*** not be afraid of those who

12: 4 have no more that they can ***d***.
12: 7 ***D*** not fear therefore; you are
12:11 ***d*** not worry about how or what
12:17 saying, 'What shall I ***d***,
12:18 I will ***d*** this: I will pull down
12:22 ***d*** not worry about your life,
12:26 are not able to ***d*** the least,
12:29 And ***d*** not seek what you should
12:32 ***D*** not fear, little flock, for it
12:33 money bags which ***d*** not grow
12:40 at an hour you ***d*** not expect."
12:41 ***d*** You speak this parable only
12:47 did not prepare himself or ***d***
12:51 ***D*** you suppose that I came to
12:56 but how is it you ***d*** not
12:57 ***d*** you not judge what is right?
13: 2 ***D*** you suppose that these
13: 4 ***d*** you think that they were
13:25 I ***d*** not know you, where you are
13:27 I tell you I ***d*** not know you,
14: 8 ***d*** not sit down in the best
14:12 ***d*** not ask your friends, your
16: 3 within himself, 'What shall I ***d***?
16: 4 'I have resolved what to ***d***,
16: 5 How much ***d*** you owe my master?'
16: 7 And how much ***d*** you owe?' So he
16:31 If they ***d*** not hear Moses and the
17: 1 through whom they ***d*** come!
17:10 done what was our duty to ***d***.
17:23 ***D*** not go after them
18: 4 Though I ***d*** not fear God nor
18:16 and ***d*** not forbid them; for of
18:18 what shall I ***d*** to inherit
18:19 Why ***d*** you call Me good? No one
18:20 '***D*** not commit adultery,'
18:20 ***D*** not murder,' 'Do not
18:20 ***D*** not steal,' 'Do not bear
18:20 ***D*** not bear false witness,'
18:41 What ***d*** you want Me to do for
18:41 What do you want Me to ***d*** for
19:13 ***D*** business till I come.'
19:48 and were unable to ***d*** anything;
20: 8 authority I ***d*** these things."
20:13 vineyard said, 'What shall I ***d***?
20:15 the owner of the vineyard ***d*** to
20:21 and You ***d*** not show personal
20:23 Why ***d*** you test Me?
21: 8 Therefore ***d*** not go after them.
21: 9 ***d*** not be terrified; for these
22: 9 Where ***d*** You want us to
22:19 ***d*** this in remembrance of Me."
22:23 who would ***d*** this thing.
22:46 Why ***d*** you sleep? Rise and pray,
22:57 I ***d*** not know Him."
22:60 I ***d*** not know what you are
22:71 What further testimony ***d*** we
23:28 ***d*** not weep for Me, but weep for
23:31 For if they ***d*** these things in
23:34 for they ***d*** not know what they
23:34 they do not know what they ***d***.
23:40 ***D*** you not even fear God, seeing
24: 5 Why ***d*** you seek the living among
24:38 And why ***d*** doubts arise in your
Jn 1:22 What ***d*** you say about
1:25 Why then ***d*** you baptize if you
1:26 One among you whom you ***d*** not
1:38 What ***d*** you seek?" They said to
1:48 How ***d*** You know me?" Jesus
1:50 ***d*** you believe? You will see
2: 4 concern have to ***d*** with Me?
2: 5 says to you, ***d*** it."
2:16 ***D*** not make My Father's house
2:18 What sign ***d*** You show to us,
2:18 since You ***d*** these things?"
3: 2 for no one can ***d*** these signs
3: 2 can do these signs that You ***d***
3: 7 ***D*** not marvel that I said to you,
3:10 and ***d*** not know these things?
3:11 and you ***d*** not receive Our
3:12 things and you ***d*** not believe,
4:11 Where then ***d*** You get that
4:22 You worship what you ***d*** not know;
4:27 What ***d*** You seek?" or, "Why are
4:32 food to eat of which you ***d*** not
4:34 My food is to ***d*** the will of Him
4:35 ***D*** you not say, 'There are still
5: 6 ***D*** you want to be made well?"
5:19 the Son can ***d*** nothing of
5:19 but what He sees the Father ***d***;
5:28 ***D*** not marvel at this; for the
5:30 I can of Myself ***d*** nothing. As I
5:30 because I ***d*** not seek My own
5:34 Yet I ***d*** not receive testimony
5:36 finish—the very works that I ***d***—
5:38 But you ***d*** not have His word
5:38 Him you ***d*** not believe.
5:41 I ***d*** not receive honor from men.
5:42 that you ***d*** not have the love of
5:43 and you ***d*** not receive Me;
5:44 and ***d*** not seek the honor that
5:45 ***D*** not think that I shall accuse
5:47 But if you ***d*** not believe his
6: 6 He Himself knew what He would ***d***.
6:20 ***d*** not be afraid."
6:27 ***D*** not labor for the food which
6:28 said to Him, "What shall we ***d***,
6:30 What work will You ***d***?
6:36 you have seen Me and yet ***d*** not
6:38 not to ***d*** My own will, but the
6:43 ***D*** not murmur among yourselves.
6:64 of you who ***d*** not believe."
6:67 ***D*** you also want to go away?"
7: 4 If You ***d*** these things, show
7:17 If anyone wants to ***d*** His will,
7:19 Why ***d*** you seek to kill Me?"
7:24 ***D*** not judge according to
7:26 ***D*** the rulers know indeed that
7:28 whom you ***d*** not know.
7:31 will He ***d*** more signs than these
8: 5 But what ***d*** You say?"
8:11 Neither ***d*** I condemn you; go and
8:14 but you ***d*** not know where I come
8:16 And yet if I ***d*** judge, My
8:24 for if you ***d*** not believe that I
8:28 and that I ***d*** nothing of
8:29 for I always ***d*** those things
8:38 and you ***d*** what you have seen
8:39 you would ***d*** the works of
8:40 Abraham did not ***d*** this.
8:41 You ***d*** the deeds of your
8:43 Why ***d*** you not understand My
8:44 of your father you want to ***d***.
8:45 you ***d*** not believe Me.
8:46 why ***d*** you not believe Me?
8:47 therefore you ***d*** not hear,
8:48 ***D*** we not say rightly that You
8:49 I ***d*** not have a demon; but I
8:50 And I ***d*** not seek My own glory;
8:53 Whom ***d*** You make Yourself out to
8:55 I ***d*** not know Him,' I shall be a
8:55 but I ***d*** know Him and keep His
9:12 He said, "I ***d*** not know."
9:16 who is a sinner ***d*** such signs?"
9:17 What ***d*** you say about Him because
9:21 he now sees we ***d*** not know,
9:21 or who opened his eyes we ***d*** not
9:25 sinner or not I ***d*** not know.
9:26 What did He ***d*** to you? How did He
9:27 Why ***d*** you want to hear it
9:27 ***D*** you also want to become His
9:29 we ***d*** not know where He is
9:30 that you ***d*** not know where He is
9:33 He could ***d*** nothing."
9:35 ***D*** you believe in the Son of
9:39 that those who ***d*** not see may
10: 5 for they ***d*** not know the voice
10:20 Why ***d*** you listen to Him?"
10:24 How long ***d*** You keep us in doubt?
10:25 and you ***d*** not believe.
10:25 The works that I ***d*** in My
10:26 But you ***d*** not believe, because
10:32 For which of those works ***d*** you
10:33 For a good work we ***d*** not stone
10:36 ***d*** you say of Him whom the Father
10:37 If I ***d*** not do the works of My
10:37 If I do not ***d*** the works of My
10:37 ***d*** not believe Me;
10:38 'but if I ***d***, though you do not
10:38 though you ***d*** not believe Me,
11:26 ***D*** you believe this?"
11:47 and said, "What shall we ***d***?
11:50 nor ***d*** you consider that it is
11:56 What ***d*** you think—that He will
12: 8 but Me you ***d*** not have always."
12:47 I ***d*** not judge him; for I did
13: 7 What I am doing you ***d*** not
13: 8 If I ***d*** not wash you, you have no
13:12 ***D*** you know what I have done to
13:15 that you should ***d*** as I have
13:17 blessed are you if you ***d*** them.
13:18 I ***d*** not speak concerning all of
13:27 'What you ***d***, do quickly.'
13:27 'What you do, ***d*** quickly.'
14: 5 we ***d*** not know where You are
14:10 ***D*** you not believe that I am in
14:10 I ***d*** not speak on My own
14:12 the works that I ***d*** he will do
14:12 the works that I do he will ***d***
14:12 works than these he will ***d***,
14:13 ask in My name, that I will ***d***,
14:14 My name, I will ***d*** it.
14:27 not as the world gives ***d*** I give
14:31 gave Me commandment, so I ***d***.
15: 5 without Me you can ***d*** nothing.
15:14 You are My friends if you ***d***
15:15 No longer ***d*** I call you servants,
15:21 all these things they will ***d***
15:21 because they ***d*** not know Him who
16: 3 And these things they will ***d*** to
16: 7 for if I ***d*** not go away, the
16: 9 because they ***d*** not believe in
16:18 We ***d*** not know what He is
16:26 and I ***d*** not say to you that I
16:31 ***D*** you now believe?
17: 4 which You have given Me to ***d***.
17: 9 I ***d*** not pray for the world but
17:15 I ***d*** not pray that You should
17:20 I ***d*** not pray for these alone,
18:21 Why ***d*** you ask Me? Ask those who
18:22 ***D*** You answer the high priest
18:23 why ***d*** you strike Me?"
18:29 What accusation ***d*** you bring
18:39 ***D*** you therefore want me to
19:10 ***D*** You not know that I have
19:21 ***D*** not write, 'The King of the
20: 2 and we ***d*** not know where they
20:13 and I ***d*** not know where they
20:17 ***D*** not cling to Me, for I have
20:27 ***D*** not be unbelieving, but
21:15 ***d*** you love Me more than
21:16 ***d*** you love Me?" He said to
21:17 ***d*** you love Me?" Peter was
21:17 ***D*** you love Me?" And he said to
21:18 carry you where you ***d*** not
Acts 1: 1 began both to ***d*** and teach,
1:11 why ***d*** you stand gazing up into
2:37 and brethren, what shall we ***d***?
3: 6 Silver and gold I ***d*** not have,
3: 6 but what I ***d*** have I give you:
3:12 why ***d*** you marvel at this?
4:16 What shall we ***d*** to these men?
4:28 to ***d*** whatever Your hand and Your
5:35 what you intend to ***d*** regarding
7:26 why ***d*** you wrong one another?'
7:28 ***D*** you want to kill me as
7:40 we ***d*** not know what has
7:51 your fathers did, so ***d*** you.
7:60 ***d*** not charge them with this
8:30 ***D*** you understand what you are
9: 6 what ***d*** You want me to do?"
9: 6 what do You want me to ***d***?
9: 6 will be told what you must ***d***.
10: 6 will tell you what you must ***d***.
13:22 who will ***d*** all My will.'
13:25 Who ***d*** you think I am? I am not
15:10 why ***d*** you test God by putting a
15:29 you will ***d*** well. Farewell.
16:28 ***D*** yourself no harm, for we are
16:30 what must I ***d*** to be saved?"
16:37 And now ***d*** they put us out
18: 9 ***D*** not be afraid, but speak, and
18: 9 and ***d*** not keep silent;
18:15 for I ***d*** not want to be a judge
19:36 be quiet and ***d*** nothing
20:10 ***D*** not trouble yourselves, for
20:24 nor ***d*** I count my life dear to
21:13 What ***d*** you mean by weeping and
21:23 Therefore ***d*** what we tell you: We
22:10 "So I said, 'What shall I ***d***,
22:10 are appointed for you to ***d***.
22:26 saying, "Take care what you ***d***,
23: 3 and ***d*** you command me to be
23: 4 ***D*** you revile God's high
23:21 But ***d*** not yield to them, for
24:10 I ***d*** the more cheerfully answer
24:27 wanting to ***d*** the Jews a favor,
25: 9 wanting to ***d*** the Jews a favor,
25:11 I ***d*** not object to dying; but if
26: 3 which have to ***d*** with the Jews.
26: 9 I myself thought I must ***d*** many
26:20 and ***d*** works befitting
26:27 ***d*** you believe the prophets?
26:27 I know that you ***d*** believe."
27:24 ***D*** not be afraid, Paul; you must
Rom 1:13 Now I ***d*** not want you to be
1:28 to ***d*** those things which are not
1:32 not only ***d*** the same but also
2: 3 And ***d*** you think this, O man, you
2: 4 Or ***d*** you despise the riches of
2: 8 who are self-seeking and ***d*** not
2:14 who ***d*** not have the law, by
2:14 by nature ***d*** the things in the
2:21 ***d*** you not teach yourself?
2:21 should not steal, ***d*** you steal?
2:22 ***D*** not commit adultery," do you
2:22 ***d*** you commit adultery?
2:22 ***d*** you rob temples?
2:23 ***d*** you dishonor God through
3: 8 Let us ***d*** evil that good may
3:31 ***D*** we then make void the law
4:17 things which ***d*** not exist as
6: 3 Or ***d*** you not know that as many
6:12 Therefore ***d*** not let sin reign in
6:13 And ***d*** not present your members
6:16 ***D*** you not know that to whom you
7: 1 Or ***d*** you not know, brethren
7:15 I ***d*** not understand. For what I
7:15 For what I will to ***d***,
7:15 to do, that I ***d*** not practice;
7:15 but what I hate, that I ***d***.
7:16 I ***d*** what I will not to do,
7:16 then, I do what I will not to ***d***,
7:17 it is no longer I who ***d*** it,
7:18 what is good I ***d*** not find.
7:19 For the good that I will to ***d***,
7:19 I ***d*** not do; but the evil I will
7:19 that I will to do, I do not ***d***;
7:19 but the evil I will not to ***d***,
7:20 Now if I ***d*** what I will not to
7:20 if I do what I will not to ***d***,
7:20 it is no longer I who ***d*** it, but
7:21 the one who wills to ***d*** good.
8: 1 who ***d*** not walk according to the
8: 3 For what the law could not ***d*** in
8: 4 might be fulfilled in us who ***d***
8:25 But if we hope for what we ***d*** not
8:26 For we ***d*** not know what we
10: 6 ***D*** not say in your heart,
11: 2 Or ***d*** you not know what the
11:10 so that they ***d*** not see,
11:18 ***d*** not boast against the
11:18 But if you ***d*** boast, remember
11:18 remember that you ***d*** not
11:20 ***D*** not be haughty, but fear.
11:23 if they ***d*** not continue in
11:25 For I ***d*** not desire, brethren,
12: 2 And ***d*** not be conformed to this
12: 4 but all the members ***d*** not have
12:14 bless and ***d*** not curse.
12:16 ***D*** not set your mind on high
12:16 ***D*** not be wise in your own
12:19 ***d*** not avenge yourselves, but
12:21 ***D*** not be overcome by evil, but
13: 3 ***D*** you want to be unafraid of
13: 3 ***D*** what is good, and you will

D

13: 4 But if you ***d*** evil, be afraid;
13:11 And ***d*** this, knowing the time,
14:10 But why ***d*** you judge your
14:10 Or why ***d*** you show contempt for
14:15 ***D*** not destroy with your food
14:16 Therefore ***d*** not let your good be
14:20 ***D*** not destroy the work of God
14:21 nor drink wine nor ***d*** anything
14:22 ***D*** you have faith? Have it to
15:31 from those in Judea who ***d*** not
16:18 For those who are such ***d*** not
1 Cor 1:16 I ***d*** not know whether I baptized
3:16 ***D*** you not know that you are the
4: 3 I ***d*** not even judge myself.
4: 7 And what ***d*** you have that you
4: 7 why ***d*** you boast as if you had
4:14 I ***d*** not write these things to
4:15 yet you ***d*** not have many
4:21 What ***d*** you want? Shall I come to
5: 6 ***D*** you not know that a little
5:12 For what have I to ***d*** with
5:12 ***D*** you not judge those who are
6: 2 ***D*** you not know that the saints
6: 3 ***D*** you not know that we shall
6: 4 ***d*** you appoint those who are
6: 7 Why ***d*** you not rather accept
6: 7 Why ***d*** you not rather let
6: 8 you yourselves ***d*** wrong and
6: 8 and you ***d*** these things to
6: 9 ***D*** you not know that the
6: 9 ***D*** not be deceived. Neither
6:15 ***D*** you not know that your bodies
6:16 Or ***d*** you not know that he who is
6:19 Or ***d*** you not know that your body
7: 5 ***D*** not deprive one another except
7:16 For how ***d*** you know, O wife,
7:16 Or how ***d*** you know, O husband,
7:21 ***D*** not be concerned about it;
7:23 ***d*** not become slaves of men.
7:27 ***D*** not seek to be loosed.
7:27 ***D*** not seek a wife.
7:28 But even if you ***d*** marry, you
7:36 let him ***d*** what he wishes.
8: 8 nor if we ***d*** not eat are we the
9: 4 ***D*** we have no right to eat and
9: 5 ***D*** we have no right to take along
9: 5 as ***d*** also the other apostles,
9: 8 ***D*** I say these things as a mere
9:13 ***D*** you not know that those who
9:16 woe is me if I ***d*** not preach the
9:17 For if I ***d*** this willingly,
9:23 Now this I ***d*** for the gospel's
9:24 ***D*** you not know that those who
9:25 Now they ***d*** it to obtain a
10: 1 I ***d*** not want you to be unaware
10: 7 And ***d*** not become idolaters as
10:20 and I ***d*** not want you to have
10:22 Or ***d*** we provoke the Lord to
10:27 If any of those who ***d*** not
10:28 ***d*** not eat it for the sake of
10:31 eat or drink, or whatever you ***d***,
10:31 ***d*** all to the glory of God.
11:16 nor ***d*** the churches of God.
11:17 I ***d*** not praise you, since
11:22 What! ***D*** you not have houses to
11:22 Or ***d*** you despise the church of
11:22 I ***d*** not praise you.
11:24 ***d*** this in remembrance of Me."
11:25 This ***d***, as often as you drink
12: 1 I ***d*** not want you to be
12:30 ***D*** all have gifts of healings?
12:30 ***D*** all speak with tongues?
12:30 ***D*** all interpret?
14:11 if I ***d*** not know the meaning of
14:20 ***d*** not be children in
14:39 and ***d*** not forbid to speak with
15:12 how ***d*** some among you say that
15:15 if in fact the dead ***d*** not rise.
15:16 For if the dead ***d*** not rise,
15:29 what will they ***d*** who are
15:29 if the dead ***d*** not rise at all?
15:30 And why ***d*** we stand in jeopardy
15:32 If the dead ***d*** not rise, "Let
15:33 ***D*** not be deceived: "Evil
15:34 and ***d*** not sin; for some do not
15:34 for some ***d*** not have the
15:35 And with what body ***d*** they
15:37 you ***d*** not sow that body that
16: 1 so you must ***d*** also:
16: 7 For I ***d*** not wish to see you now
16:10 work of the Lord, as I also ***d***.
16:14 Let all that you ***d*** be done
2 Cor 1: 8 For we ***d*** not want you to be
1:17 did I ***d*** it lightly? Or the
1:17 ***d*** I plan according to the
3: 1 ***D*** we begin again to commend
3: 1 Or ***d*** we need, as some others,
4: 1 we ***d*** not lose heart.
4: 4 who ***d*** not believe, lest the
4: 5 For we ***d*** not preach ourselves,
4:16 Therefore we ***d*** not lose heart.
4:18 while we ***d*** not look at the
5:12 For we ***d*** not commend ourselves
6:14 ***D*** not be unequally yoked
6:17 ***D*** not touch what is
7: 3 I ***d*** not say this to condemn;
7: 8 I ***d*** not regret it; though I did
7:12 I did not ***d*** it for the sake
8:10 desiring to ***d*** a year ago;
8:13 For I ***d*** not mean that others
10: 3 we ***d*** not war according to the
10: 7 ***D*** you look at things according
11: 1 and indeed you ***d*** bear with me.
11:11 Because I ***d*** not love you?
11:12 But what I ***d***, I will also
11:12 I will also continue to ***d***,
11:29 and I ***d*** not burn with
12: 2 whether in the body I ***d*** not
12: 2 out of the body I ***d*** not know,
12: 3 out of the body I ***d*** not know,
12:14 for I ***d*** not seek yours, but
12:19 ***d*** you think that we excuse
12:19 But we ***d*** all things, beloved,
12:20 such as you ***d*** not wish;
13: 5 ***D*** you not know yourselves, that
13: 7 Now I pray to God that you ***d*** no
13: 7 but that you should ***d*** what is
13: 8 For we can ***d*** nothing against the
Gal 1:10 For ***d*** I now persuade men, or
1:10 Or ***d*** I seek to please men?
1:20 before God, I ***d*** not lie.)
2:10 which I also was eager to ***d***.
2:14 why ***d*** you compel Gentiles to
2:21 I ***d*** not set aside the grace of
3: 5 does He ***d*** it by the works
3:10 of the law, to ***d*** them."
4:21 ***d*** you not hear the law?
4:27 You who ***d*** not bear!
5: 1 and ***d*** not be entangled again
5:11 why ***d*** I still suffer
5:13 only ***d*** not use liberty as an
5:17 so that you ***d*** not do the things
5:17 so that you do not ***d*** the things
6: 7 ***D*** not be deceived, God is not
6: 9 season we shall reap if we ***d***
6:10 let us ***d*** good to all,
Eph 1:16 ***d*** not cease to give thanks for
3:13 Therefore I ask that you ***d*** not
3:20 Now to Him who is able to ***d***
4:26 and ***d*** not sin": do not let
4:26 ***d*** not let the sun go down on
4:30 And ***d*** not grieve the Holy Spirit
5: 7 Therefore ***d*** not be partakers
5:17 Therefore ***d*** not be unwise, but
5:18 And ***d*** not be drunk with wine,
6: 4 ***d*** not provoke your children to
6: 9 ***d*** the same things to them,
6:12 For we ***d*** not wrestle against
Phil 2:13 in you both to will and to ***d***
2:14 ***D*** all things without complaining
3:13 I ***d*** not count myself to have
3:13 but one thing I ***d***,
4: 9 heard and saw in me, these ***d***,
4:13 I can ***d*** all things through
Col 1: 9 ***d*** not cease to pray for you,
2:20 ***d*** you subject yourselves to
2:21 ***D*** not touch, do not taste, do
2:21 ***d*** not taste, do not handle,"
2:21 ***d*** not handle,"
3: 9 ***D*** not lie to one another, since
3:13 you, so you also must ***d***.
3:17 And whatever you ***d*** in word or
3:17 ***d*** all in the name of the Lord
3:19 love your wives and ***d*** not be
3:21 ***d*** not provoke your children,
3:23 And whatever you ***d***,
3:23 ***d*** it heartily, as to the Lord
1 Th 1: 8 so that we ***d*** not need to say
2:15 and they ***d*** not please God and
3:12 just as we ***d*** to you,
4: 5 like the Gentiles who ***d*** not
4:10 and indeed you ***d*** so toward all
4:13 But I ***d*** not want you to be
5: 6 let us not sleep, as others ***d***,
5:19 ***D*** not quench the Spirit.
5:20 ***D*** not despise prophecies.
5:24 who also will ***d*** it.
2 Th 1: 8 vengeance on those who ***d*** not
1: 8 and on those who ***d*** not obey the
2: 5 ***D*** you not remember that when I
2: 7 He who now restrains will ***d***
3: 4 both that you ***d*** and will do the
3: 4 both that you do and will ***d*** the
3: 9 not because we ***d*** not have
3:13 ***d*** not grow weary in doing
3:14 note that person and ***d*** not keep
3:15 Yet ***d*** not count him as an
1 Tim 2:12 And I ***d*** not permit a woman to
4:14 ***D*** not neglect the gift that is
5: 1 ***D*** not rebuke an older man, but
5: 9 ***D*** not let a widow under sixty
5:16 and ***d*** not let the church be
5:19 ***D*** not receive an accusation
5:22 ***D*** not lay hands on anyone
6:18 Let them ***d*** good, that they be
2 Tim 1: 8 Therefore ***d*** not be ashamed of
2:26 taken captive by him to ***d*** his
3: 8 so ***d*** these also resist the
4: 5 ***d*** the work of an evangelist,
4:21 ***D*** your utmost to come before
Phm 1:14 I wanted to ***d*** nothing,
1:21 knowing that you will ***d*** even
1:24 as ***d*** Mark, Aristarchus, Demas,
Heb 2: 8 But now we ***d*** not yet see all
3: 8 ***D*** not harden your hearts
3:15 ***D*** not harden your hearts
4: 3 For we who have believed ***d*** enter
4: 7 ***D*** not harden your
4:15 For we ***d*** not have a High Priest
6: 3 And this we will ***d*** if God
6:10 to the saints, and ***d*** minister.
6:12 that you ***d*** not become sluggish,
10: 7 To ***d*** Your will, O God.'
10: 9 I have come to ***d*** Your
10:29 ***d*** you suppose, will he be
10:35 Therefore ***d*** not cast away your
11:29 attempting to ***d*** so, were
12: 5 ***d*** not despise the
12:25 See that you ***d*** not refuse Him
13: 2 ***D*** not forget to entertain
13: 6 What can man ***d*** to me?"
13: 9 ***D*** not be carried about with
13:16 But ***d*** not forget to do good and
13:16 But do not forget to ***d*** good and
13:17 Let them ***d*** so with joy and not
13:19 But I especially urge you to ***d***
13:21 in every good work to ***d*** His
Jas 1:16 ***D*** not be deceived, my beloved
2: 1 ***d*** not hold the faith of our
2: 6 ***D*** not the rich oppress you and
2: 7 ***D*** they not blaspheme that noble
2: 8 as yourself," you ***d*** well;
2:11 ***D*** not commit adultery," also
2:11 ***D*** not murder." Now if you do
2:11 Now if you ***d*** not commit
2:11 but you ***d*** murder, you have
2:12 So speak and so ***d*** as those who
2:16 but you ***d*** not give them the
2:19 You ***d*** well. Even the demons
2:20 But ***d*** you want to know,
2:22 ***D*** you see that faith was working
3:14 ***d*** not boast and lie against the
4: 1 Where ***d*** wars and fights come
4: 1 ***D*** they not come from your
4: 2 You lust and ***d*** not have.
4: 2 Yet you ***d*** not have because you
4: 2 have because you ***d*** not ask.
4: 3 You ask and ***d*** not receive,
4: 4 ***D*** you not know that friendship
4: 5 Or ***d*** you think that the
4:11 ***D*** not speak evil of one
4:14 whereas you ***d*** not know what
4:15 we shall live and ***d*** this or
4:17 to him who knows to ***d*** good and
4:17 to do good and does not ***d*** it,
5: 9 ***D*** not grumble against one
5:12 ***d*** not swear, either by heaven
1 Pe 1: 8 Though now you ***d*** not see Him,
2:14 praise of those who ***d*** good.
2:20 But when you ***d*** good and suffer,
3: 1 that even if some ***d*** not obey
3: 3 ***D*** not let your adornment be
3: 6 you are if you ***d*** good and
3:11 away from evil and ***d*** good;
3:12 those who ***d*** evil."
3:14 And ***d*** not be afraid of
4: 4 strange that you ***d*** not run
4:11 let him ***d*** it as with the
4:12 ***d*** not think it strange
4:17 be the end of those who ***d*** not
2 Pe 1:10 for if you ***d*** these things you
1:19 which you ***d*** well to heed as a
2:11 ***d*** not bring a reviling
2:12 evil of the things they ***d*** not
3: 8 ***d*** not forget this one thing,
3:16 as they ***d*** also the rest of
1 Jn 1: 6 we lie and ***d*** not practice the
2:15 ***D*** not love the world or the
2:21 you ***d*** not know the truth,
2:27 and you ***d*** not need that anyone
3:13 ***D*** not marvel, my brethren, if
3:22 His commandments and ***d*** those
4: 1 ***d*** not believe every spirit, but
5:16 I ***d*** not say that he should pray
2 Jn 7 out into the world who ***d*** not
8 that we ***d*** not lose those things
10 ***d*** not receive him into your
12 I did not wish to ***d*** so with
3 Jn 5 you ***d*** faithfully whatever you
5 do faithfully whatever you ***d***
6 you will ***d*** well,
11 ***d*** not imitate what is evil, but
13 but I ***d*** not wish to write to
Jude 10 speak evil of whatever they ***d***
Rev 1:17 ***D*** not be afraid; I am the First
2: 5 repent and ***d*** the first works,
2:10 ***D*** not fear any of those things
2:24 as many as ***d*** not have this
3:17 and ***d*** not know that you are
4: 8 And they ***d*** not rest day or
5: 5 ***D*** not weep. Behold, the Lion of
6: 6 and ***d*** not harm the oil and the
7: 3 ***D*** not harm the earth, the sea,
9: 4 but only those men who ***d*** not
9:19 and with them they ***d*** harm.
10: 4 and ***d*** not write them."
11: 2 and ***d*** not measure it, for it
13:14 which he was granted to ***d*** in
19:10 See that you ***d*** not do that!
19:10 See that you do not ***d*** that!
22: 9 See that you ***d*** not do that.
22: 9 See that you do not ***d*** that.
22:10 ***D*** not seal the words of the
22:14 Blessed are those who ***d*** His

DOCILE (1/1)

Jer 11:19 But I was like a ***d*** lamb brought

DOCTRINE (37/36) DOCTRINES

Job 11: 4 My ***d*** is pure, And I am clean
Prov 4: 2 For I give you good ***d***:
Isa 29:24 who complained will learn ***d***.
Jer 10: 8 wooden idol is a worthless ***d***.
Mt 16:12 but of the ***d*** of the Pharisees

Mk 1:27 What new **d** is this? For with
Jn 7:16 My **d** is not Mine, but His who
7:17 he shall know concerning the **d**,
18:19 about His disciples and His **d**.
Acts 2:42 steadfastly in the apostles' **d**
5:28 filled Jerusalem with your **d**,
17:19 May we know what this new **d** is
Rom 6:17 from the heart that form of **d**
16:17 contrary to the **d** which you
Eph 4:14 about with every wind of **d**,
1 Tim 1: 3 some that they teach no other **d**,
1:10 that is contrary to sound **d**,
4: 6 of faith and of the good **d**
4:13 reading, to exhortation, to **d**.
4:16 heed to yourself and to the **d**.
5:17 who labor in the word and **d**.
6: 1 the name of God and His **d** may
6: 3 and to the **d** which accords with
2 Tim 3:10 have carefully followed my **d**,
3:16 God, and is profitable for **d**,
4: 3 they will not endure sound **d**,
Titus 1: 9 that he may be able, by sound **d**,
2: 1 which are proper for sound **d**:
2: 7 in **d** showing integrity,
2:10 that they may adorn the **d** of
Heb 6: 2 of the **d** of baptisms, of laying
2 Jn 9 and does not abide in the **d** of
9 He who abides in the **d** of
10 you and does not bring this **d**,
Rev 2:14 there those who hold the **d** of
2:15 also have those who hold the **d**
2:24 as many as do not have this **d**,

DOCTRINES (5/5) DOCTRINE

Mt 15: 9 Teaching as **d** the
Mk 7: 7 Teaching as **d** the
Col 2:22 to the commandments and **d** of
1 Tim 4: 1 to deceiving spirits and **d** of
Heb 13: 9 with various and strange **d**.

DOCUMENT (3/3)

Neh 10: 1 placed their seal on the **d**
Esth 3:14 A copy of the **d** was to be issued
8:13 A copy of the **d** was to be issued

DODAI (1/1) DODO

1 Chr 27: 4 of the second month was **D** an

DODANIM (1/1) RODANIM

Gen 10: 4 Tarshish, Kittim, and **D**.

DODAVAH (1/1)

2 Chr 20:37 But Eliezer the son of **D** of

DODO (5/5) DODAI

Judg 10: 1 the son of Puah, the son of **D**,
2 Sam 23: 9 him was Eleazar the son of **D**,
23:24 Elhanan the son of **D** of
1 Chr 11:12 him was Eleazar the son of **D**,
11:26 Elhanan the son of **D** of

DOE (1/1)

Prov 5:19 a loving deer and a graceful **d**,

DOEG (6/5)

1 Sam 21: 7 the LORD. And his name was **D**,
22: 9 Then answered **D** the Edomite,
22:18 And the king said to **D**,
22:18 So **D** the Edomite turned and
22:22 when **D** the Edomite was there,
Ps 52: A Contemplation of David when **D**

DOER (3/3) DO, DOERS, DOINGS

Jas 1:23 hearer of the word and not a **d**,
1:25 not a forgetful hearer but a **d**
4:11 you are not a **d** of the law but

DOERS (2/2) DO, DOER

Rom 2:13 but the **d** of the law will be
Jas 1:22 But be **d** of the word, and not

DOES (558/509) DO

Gen 39: 8 my master **d** not know what is
44: 7 Why **d** my lord say these words?
45: 3 **d** my father still live?"
Ex 3: 3 why the bush **d** not burn."
11: 7 the LORD **d** make a difference
21: 8 If she **d** not please her master,
21:11 And if he **d** not do these three
21:18 and he **d** not die but is
21:33 digs a pit and **d** not cover
28:28 breastplate **d** not come loose
28:32 so that it **d** not tear.
31:14 for whoever **d** any work on it,
31:15 Whoever **d** any work on the
32:11 why **d** Your wrath burn hot
33:15 If Your Presence **d** not go with
35: 2 Whoever **d** any work on it shall
Lev 4: 2 and **d** any of them,
5: 1 if he **d** not tell it, he bears
5:17 though he **d** not know it, yet
11: 4 chews the cud but **d** not have
11: 5 chews the cud but **d** not have
11: 6 chews the cud but **d** not have
11: 7 yet **d** not chew the cud, is
11:12 Whatever in the water **d** not have
11:26 cloven-hoofed or **d** not chew
13: 4 and **d** not appear to be deeper
13:31 and indeed it **d** not appear
13:32 and the scale **d** not appear
13:34 and **d** not appear deeper than
17: 4 and **d** not bring it to the door
17: 9 and **d** not bring it to the door
17:16 But if he **d** not wash them or
18: 5 My judgments, which if a man **d**,
23:30 And any person who **d** any work on
27:20 But if he **d** not want to redeem
Num 15:30 But the person who **d** anything
19:12 But if he **d** not purify himself
19:13 and **d** not purify himself,
19:20 unclean and **d** not purify
24:18 While Israel **d** valiantly.
24:23 Who shall live when God **d** this?
30:15 But if he **d** make them void after
35:17 and he **d** die, he is a
35:18 and he **d** die, he is a
Deut 10:12 what **d** the LORD your God
14: 8 yet **d** not chew the cud;
14:10 And whatever **d** not have fins and
18:22 if the thing **d** not happen or
25: 7 But if the man **d** not want to
27:26 Cursed is the one who **d** not
28:50 which **d** not respect the elderly
29:23 nor **d** it bear, nor does any
29:23 nor **d** any grass grow there,
29:24 What **d** the heat of this great
Josh 1:18 against your command and **d** not
5:14 What **d** my Lord say to His
Ruth 3:13 But if he **d** not want to perform
1 Sam 2:32 all the good which God **d** for
4: 6 What **d** the sound of this great
4:14 What **d** the sound of this tumult
5:11 so that it **d** not kill us and
11: 7 Whoever **d** not go out with Saul
16: 7 For the LORD **d** not see as
17:47 the LORD **d** not save
18:23 **D** it seem to you a light thing
18:25 The king **d** not desire any dowry
26:18 Why **d** my lord thus pursue his
28:15 departed from me and **d** not
2 Sam 14:13 in that the king **d** not bring
14:14 Yet God **d** not take away a life;
24: 3 But why **d** my lord the king
1 Ki 1:11 and David our lord **d** not know
8:46 no one who **d** not sin),
22: 8 because he **d** not prophesy good
2 Ki 6:27 If the LORD **d** not help you,
1 Chr 21: 3 Why then **d** my lord require this
2 Chr 6:36 no one who **d** not sin),
32:11 **D** not Hezekiah persuade you to
Neh 5:13 who **d** not perform this promise.
9:29 judgments, 'Which if a man **d**,
Job 1: 9 **D** Job fear God for nothing?
3:21 but it **d** not come, And search
4:21 **D** not their own excellence go
5: 6 For affliction **d** not come from
5: 6 Nor **d** trouble spring from the
5: 9 Who **d** great things, and
6: 5 **D** the wild donkey bray when it
6: 5 Or **d** the ox low over its
6:25 But what **d** your arguing
7: 9 to the grave **d** not come up.
8: 3 **D** God subvert judgment
8: 3 Or **d** the Almighty pervert
8:15 but it **d** not stand. He holds
8:15 but it **d** not endure.
9: 7 and it **d** not rise; He seals
9:10 He **d** great things past finding
10: 3 **D** it seem good to You that
12: 3 who **d** not know such things as
12: 9 Who among all these **d** not know
12:11 **D** not the ear test words And
14: 2 a shadow and **d** not continue.
14:12 So man lies down and **d** not
14:21 and he **d** not know it;
14:21 and he **d** not perceive it.
15:12 Why **d** your heart carry you
15:22 He **d** not believe that he will
16:13 He pierces my heart and **d** not
17: 2 And **d** not my eye dwell on
18: 5 flame of his fire **d** not shine.
18:21 him who **d** not know God."
19:22 do you persecute me as God **d**,
20:13 Though he spares it and **d** not
21:17 How often **d** their
21:21 For what **d** he care about his
22:13 What **d** God know? Can He judge
23:13 His soul desires, that He **d**.
24:12 Yet God **d** not charge them
24:21 And **d** no good for the widow.
25: 3 Upon whom **d** His light not
25: 5 If even the moon **d** not shine,
27:22 It hurls against him and **d** not
28:13 Man **d** not know its value, Nor
28:20 From where then **d** wisdom come?
31: 4 **D** He not see my ways, And
33:13 For He **d** not give an
33:14 Yet man **d** not perceive it.
34:19 Nor **d** He regard the rich more
35: 7 Or what **d** He receive from your
35:12 but He **d** not answer, Because
36: 6 He **d** not preserve the life of
36: 7 He **d** not withdraw His eyes from
37: 4 And He **d** not restrain them
37: 5 He **d** great things which we
37:23 He **d** not oppress.
39: 7 He **d** not heed the shouts of
39:22 Nor **d** he turn back from the
39:24 Nor **d** he come to a halt
39:26 **D** the hawk fly by your wisdom,
39:27 **D** the eagle mount up at your
41:26 Nor **d** spear, dart, or javelin.
Ps 1: 3 And whatever he **d** shall
7:12 If he **d** not turn back, He will
9:12 He **d** not forget the cry of the
10: 4 in his proud countenance **d** not
14: 1 There is none who **d** good.
14: 3 There is none who **d** good,
15: 3 He who **d** not backbite with his
15: 3 Nor **d** evil to his neighbor,
15: 3 Nor **d** he take up a reproach
15: 4 his own hurt and **d** not change;
15: 5 He who **d** not put out his money
15: 5 Nor **d** he take a bribe against
15: 5 He who **d** these things shall
32: 2 the LORD **d** not impute
36: 4 He **d** not abhor evil.
37:21 The wicked borrows and **d** not
37:28 And **d** not forsake His saints;
38:13 who **d** not open his mouth.
38:14 Thus I am like a man who **d** not
39: 6 And **d** not know who will gather
40: 4 And **d** not respect the proud,
41:11 Because my enemy **d** not triumph
49:12 in honor, **d** not remain;
49:20 yet **d** not understand, Is like
53: 1 There is none who **d** good.
53: 3 There is none who **d** good,
66: 9 And **d** not allow our feet to be
69:33 And **d** not despise His
72:18 Who only **d** wondrous things!
73:11 How **d** God know? And is there
74: 1 Why **d** Your anger smoke
77:14 You are the God who **d** wonders;
78:39 passes away and **d** not come
92: 6 A senseless man **d** not know,
92: 6 Nor **d** a fool understand this.
94: 7 The LORD **d** not see, Nor does
94: 7 Nor **d** the God of Jacob
106: 3 And he who **d** righteousness at
107:38 And He **d** not let their cattle
115: 3 He **d** whatever He pleases.
118:15 hand of the LORD **d** valiantly.
118:16 hand of the LORD **d** valiantly.
129: 7 With which the reaper **d** not
135: 6 the LORD pleases He **d**,
136: 4 To Him who alone **d** great
147:10 He **d** not delight in the
Prov 6:32 He who **d** so destroys his own
8: 1 **D** not wisdom cry out, And
9:18 But he **d** not know that the dead
11:17 The merciful man **d** good for his
11:18 The wicked man **d** deceptive
12:27 The lazy man **d** not roast what
13: 1 But a scoffer **d** not listen to
13: 8 But the poor **d** not hear
14: 5 A faithful witness **d** not lie,
14: 6 seeks wisdom and **d** not find
14:10 And a stranger **d** not share its
15: 7 of the fool **d** not do so.
15:12 A scoffer **d** not love one who
17:21 He who begets a scoffer **d** so
17:22 A merry heart **d** good, like
20:11 Whether what he **d** is pure and
21:26 the righteous gives and **d** not
24: 7 He **d** not open his mouth in the
24:12 **D** not He who weighs the
24:12 **d** He not know it? And will
26:14 So **d** the lazy man on his
27:24 Nor **d** a crown endure to all
28:22 And **d** not consider that
29: 7 But the wicked **d** not
30:11 And **d** not bless its mother.
30:30 among beasts And **d** not turn
31:12 She **d** him good and not evil
31:18 And her lamp **d** not go out by
31:27 And **d** not eat the bread of
Eccl 2: 2 What **d** it accomplish?"
2:16 And how **d** a wise man die?
3:11 find out the work that God **d**
3:14 I know that whatever God **d**,
3:14 God **d** it, that men should
6: 2 yet God **d** not give him power to
6: 8 What **d** the poor man have, Who
7:20 man on earth who **d** good
7:20 who does good And **d** not sin.
8: 3 for he **d** whatever pleases
8: 7 For he **d** not know what will
8:12 Though a sinner **d** evil a hundred
8:13 because he **d** not fear before
9: 2 and him who **d** not sacrifice.
9:12 For man also **d** not know his
10: 1 So **d** a little folly to one
10:10 And one **d** not sharpen the
Song 2: 7 By the gazelles or by the **d** of
3: 5 By the gazelles or by the **d** of
Isa 1: 3 But Israel **d** not know, My
1:23 Nor **d** the cause of the widow
10: 7 Yet he **d** not mean so, Nor does
10: 7 Nor **d** his heart think so;
28:24 **D** the plowman keep plowing all
28:24 **D** he keep turning his soil and
28:25 **D** he not sow the black cummin
28:28 Therefore he **d** not thresh it
42:20 but he **d** not hear."
49:18 them on you as a bride **d**.
55: 2 And your wages for what **d** not

56: 2 Blessed is the man who ***d***
59: 4 Nor ***d*** any plead for truth.
59: 9 Nor ***d*** righteousness overtake
63:16 And Israel ***d*** not acknowledge
64: 5 rejoices and ***d*** righteousness,
66:24 For their worm ***d*** not die, And
Jer 2:11 For what ***d*** not profit.
5:19 Why ***d*** the LORD our God do all
7:28 This is a nation that ***d*** not
9:12 Why ***d*** the land perish and burn
11: 3 Cursed is the man who ***d*** not
12: 1 Why ***d*** the way of the wicked
14:10 Therefore the LORD ***d*** not
17:11 that broods but ***d*** not hatch,
18:10 if it ***d*** evil in My sight so that
18:10 My sight so that it ***d*** not obey
26:16 This man ***d*** not deserve to die.
31:10 And keep him as a shepherd ***d***
38: 4 For this man ***d*** not seek the
48:10 Cursed is he who ***d*** the work of
49: 1 Why then ***d*** Milcom inherit
Lam 3:33 For He ***d*** not afflict willingly,
3:36 The Lord ***d*** not approve.
Ezek 3:19 and he ***d*** not turn from his
3:21 and he ***d*** not sin, he shall
8:12 The LORD ***d*** not see us, the
9: 9 and the LORD ***d*** not see!'
12: 2 which has eyes to see but ***d*** not
12: 2 and ears to hear but ***d*** not
13:22 so that he ***d*** not turn from his
17:15 Will he who ***d*** such things
18: 5 is just And ***d*** what is lawful
18:10 Who ***d*** any of these things
18:11 And ***d*** none of those duties,
18:14 And considers but ***d*** not do
18:21 and ***d*** what is lawful and right,
18:24 and ***d*** according to all the
18:24 that the wicked man ***d***,
18:27 and ***d*** what is lawful and right,
20:11 judgments, 'which, if a man ***d***,
20:13 judgments, 'which, if a man ***d***,
20:21 judgments, 'which, if a man ***d***,
20:49 ***D*** he not speak parables?'"
21:10 As it ***d*** all wood.
33: 4 trumpet and ***d*** not take warning,
33: 6 sword coming and ***d*** not blow
33: 9 and he ***d*** not turn from his way,
33:14 his sin and ***d*** what is lawful
33:19 from his wickedness and ***d*** what
Dan 2:43 just as iron ***d*** not mix with
3: 6 and whoever ***d*** not fall down and
3:11 and whoever ***d*** not fall down and
4:35 He ***d*** according to His will in
6: 8 which ***d*** not alter."
6:12 which ***d*** not alter."
6:13 ***d*** not show due regard for you,
9:14 in all the works which He ***d***,
Hos 7: 9 But he ***d*** not know it;
7: 9 Yet he ***d*** not know it.
8:13 But the LORD ***d*** not accept
Am 3: 7 Surely the Lord GOD ***d*** nothing,
6:12 ***D*** one plow there with oxen?
9:12 Says the LORD who ***d*** this
Mic 1:11 The inhabitant of Zaanan ***d*** not
6: 8 And what ***d*** the LORD require
7:18 He ***d*** not retain His anger
Hab 2: 5 And he ***d*** not stay at home.
Mal 2:12 man who ***d*** this, being awake
2:13 So He ***d*** not regard the
2:17 Everyone who ***d*** evil Is good in
3:18 one who ***d*** not serve Him.
Mt 3:10 every tree which ***d*** not bear
5:19 but whoever ***d*** and teaches
7:19 Every tree that ***d*** not bear good
7:21 but he who ***d*** the will of My
7:24 and ***d*** them, I will liken him to
7:26 and ***d*** not do them, will be like
8: 9 'Do this,' and he ***d*** it."
9:11 Why ***d*** your Teacher eat with tax
10:38 And he who ***d*** not take his cross
11:27 Nor ***d*** anyone know the Father
12:24 This fellow ***d*** not cast out
12:30 and he who ***d*** not gather with Me
12:50 For whoever ***d*** the will of My
13:12 but whoever ***d*** not have, even
13:19 and ***d*** not understand it, then
13:27 How then ***d*** it have tares?'
15:20 unwashed hands ***d*** not defile
17:21 this kind ***d*** not go out except
17:24 ***D*** your Teacher not pay the
18:12 ***d*** he not leave the ninety-nine
18:35 ***d*** not forgive his brother his
22:43 How then ***d*** David in the Spirit
25:29 but from him who ***d*** not have,
Mk 2: 7 Why ***d*** this Man speak
3:35 For whoever ***d*** the will of God is
4:25 but whoever ***d*** not have, even
4:27 he himself ***d*** not know how.
7:19 because it ***d*** not enter his heart
8:12 Why ***d*** this generation seek a
9:38 we saw someone who ***d*** not follow
9:38 because he ***d*** not follow us."
9:44 Their worm ***d*** not die, And
9:46 Their worm ***d*** not die, And
9:48 Their worm ***d*** not die, And
10:15 whoever ***d*** not receive the
11:23 and ***d*** not doubt in his heart,
16:16 but he who ***d*** not believe will
Lk 3: 9 every tree which ***d*** not bear
5:36 out of the new ***d*** not match
6:43 For a good tree ***d*** not bear bad
6:43 nor ***d*** a bad tree bear good
6:47 hears My sayings and ***d*** them,
7: 8 'Do this,' and he ***d*** it."
8: 9 What ***d*** this parable mean?"
8:18 and whoever ***d*** not have, even
9:49 and we forbade him because he ***d***
11:23 and he who ***d*** not gather with Me
12:15 for one's life ***d*** not consist in
12:33 the heavens that ***d*** not fail,
13: 7 why ***d*** it use up the ground?'
13:15 Hypocrite! ***D*** not each one of you
14:26 If anyone comes to Me and ***d*** not
14:27 And whoever ***d*** not bear his cross
14:28 ***d*** not sit down first and count
14:31 ***d*** not sit down first and
14:33 whoever of you ***d*** not forsake
15: 4 ***d*** not leave the ninety-nine in
15: 8 ***d*** not light a lamp, sweep the
17: 9 ***D*** he thank that servant because
17:20 The kingdom of God ***d*** not come
18:17 whoever ***d*** not receive the
19:26 and from him who ***d*** not have,
20:24 image and inscription ***d*** it
20:33 whose wife ***d*** she become?
24:39 for a spirit ***d*** not have flesh
Jn 2: 4 what ***d*** your concern have to do
3:18 but he who ***d*** not believe is
3:20 evil hates the light and ***d*** not
3:21 But he who ***d*** the truth comes to
3:34 for God ***d*** not give the Spirit
3:36 and he who ***d*** not believe the
5:19 for whatever He ***d***, the Son
5:19 the Son also ***d*** in like manner.
5:20 all things that He Himself ***d***;
5:23 He who ***d*** not honor the Son does
5:23 He who does not honor the Son ***d***
6:61 ***D*** this offend you?
7: 4 For no one ***d*** anything in secret
7:15 How ***d*** this Man know letters,
7:35 Where ***d*** He intend to go that we
7:35 ***D*** He intend to go to the
7:49 But this crowd that ***d*** not know
7:51 ***D*** our law judge a man before it
8:35 And a slave ***d*** not abide in the
8:44 and ***d*** not stand in the truth,
9:16 because He ***d*** not keep the
9:19 How then ***d*** he now see?"
9:31 Now we know that God ***d*** not hear
9:31 is a worshiper of God and ***d*** His
10: 1 he who ***d*** not enter the
10:10 The thief ***d*** not come except to
10:12 one who ***d*** not own the sheep,
10:13 he is a hireling and ***d*** not care
11: 9 he ***d*** not stumble, because he
12:35 he who walks in darkness ***d*** not
12:47 My words and ***d*** not believe,
12:48 and ***d*** not receive My words, has
13:19 that when it ***d*** come to pass,
14:10 who dwells in Me ***d*** the works.
14:24 He who ***d*** not love Me does not
14:24 He who does not love Me ***d*** not
14:29 that when it ***d*** come to pass,
15: 2 Every branch in Me that ***d*** not
15: 6 If anyone ***d*** not abide in Me, he
15:15 for a servant ***d*** not know what
Acts 6:13 This man ***d*** not cease to speak
7:48 the Most High ***d*** not dwell in
8:34 of whom ***d*** the prophet say this,
15:17 Says the LORD who ***d*** all
17:18 What ***d*** this babbler want to
17:24 ***d*** not dwell in temples made
19:35 what man is there who ***d*** not
28: 4 yet justice ***d*** not allow to
Rom 2: 9 soul of man who ***d*** evil,
3:12 There is none who ***d*** good,
4: 3 For what ***d*** the Scripture say?
4: 5 But to him who ***d*** not work but
4: 9 ***D*** this blessedness then come
5: 5 Now hope ***d*** not disappoint,
8: 9 Now if anyone ***d*** not have the
8:24 for why ***d*** one still hope for
9:19 'Why ***d*** He still find fault?
9:21 ***D*** not the potter have power over
10: 5 The man who ***d*** those things
10: 8 But what ***d*** it say? "The word
11: 4 But what ***d*** the divine response
13: 4 for he ***d*** not bear the sword in
13:10 Love ***d*** no harm to a neighbor;
14: 3 despise him who ***d*** not eat,
14: 3 and let not him who ***d*** not eat
14: 6 and he who ***d*** not observe the
14: 6 to the Lord he ***d*** not observe
14: 6 and he who ***d*** not eat, to the
14: 6 to the Lord he ***d*** not eat, and
14:22 Happy is he who ***d*** not condemn
14:23 because he ***d*** not eat from
1 Cor 2:14 But the natural man ***d*** not
6:18 Every sin that a man ***d*** is
7: 4 The wife ***d*** not have authority
7: 4 own body, but the husband ***d***.
7: 4 And likewise the husband ***d*** not
7: 4 his own body, but the wife ***d***.
7: 5 so that Satan ***d*** not tempt
7:11 But even if she ***d*** depart, let
7:12 a wife who ***d*** not believe,
7:13 a husband who ***d*** not believe,
7:36 He ***d*** not sin; let them marry.
7:37 keep his virgin, ***d*** well.
7:38 gives her in marriage ***d*** well,
7:38 but he who ***d*** not give her in
7:38 give her in marriage ***d*** better.
8: 8 But food ***d*** not commend us to
9: 7 Who plants a vineyard and ***d*** not
9: 7 Or who tends a flock and ***d*** not
9: 8 Or ***d*** not the law say the same
9:10 Or ***d*** He say it altogether for
11:14 ***D*** not even nature itself teach
13: 4 love ***d*** not envy; love does not
13: 4 love ***d*** not parade itself, is
13: 5 ***d*** not behave rudely, does not
13: 5 ***d*** not seek its own, is not
13: 6 ***d*** not rejoice in iniquity,
14: 2 speaks in a tongue ***d*** not
14:16 since he ***d*** not understand what
15:50 nor ***d*** corruption inherit
16:10 for he ***d*** the work of the Lord,
16:22 If anyone ***d*** not love the Lord
2 Cor 1:10 and ***d*** deliver us; in whom we
8:12 not according to what he ***d*** not
Gal 3: 5 ***d*** He do it by the works of
3:10 who ***d*** not continue in
3:12 the man who ***d*** them shall
3:16 He ***d*** not say, "And to seeds,"
3:19 What purpose then ***d*** the law
3:20 Now a mediator ***d*** not mediate
4: 1 ***d*** not differ at all from a
4:30 Nevertheless what ***d*** the
5: 8 This persuasion ***d*** not come from
Eph 4: 9 what ***d*** it mean but that He also
4:16 every part ***d*** its share,
5:29 just as the Lord ***d*** the church.
6: 8 that whatever good anyone ***d***,
Col 3:25 But he who ***d*** wrong will be
1 Th 2:11 as a father ***d*** his own
4: 8 he who rejects this ***d*** not
2 Th 3:14 And if anyone ***d*** not obey our
1 Tim 3: 5 (for if a man ***d*** not know how to
5: 8 But if anyone ***d*** not provide for
6: 3 teaches otherwise and ***d*** not
2 Tim 2:15 a worker who ***d*** not need to be
Heb 2:16 For indeed He ***d*** not give aid to
2:16 but He ***d*** give aid to the seed
7:27 who ***d*** not need daily, as those
12: 7 whom a father ***d*** not chasten?
Jas 1:13 nor ***d*** He Himself tempt anyone.
1:20 for the wrath of man ***d*** not
1:25 will be blessed in what he ***d***.
1:26 and ***d*** not bridle his tongue but
2:14 What ***d*** it profit, my
2:14 says he has faith but ***d*** not
2:16 what ***d*** it profit?
2:17 if it ***d*** not have works, is
3: 2 If anyone ***d*** not stumble in
3:11 ***D*** a spring send forth fresh
3:15 This wisdom ***d*** not descend from
4:17 him who knows to do good and ***d***
5: 6 he ***d*** not resist you.
1 Pe 1: 4 and undefiled and that ***d*** not
5: 4 the crown of glory that ***d*** not
5:13 and so ***d*** Mark my son.
2 Pe 2: 3 and their destruction ***d*** not
1 Jn 2: 4 and ***d*** not keep His
2:11 and ***d*** not know where he is
2:17 but he who ***d*** the will of God
2:23 Whoever denies the Son ***d*** not
3: 1 the world ***d*** not know us,
3: 6 Whoever abides in Him ***d*** not sin.
3: 9 has been born of God ***d*** not sin,
3:10 Whoever ***d*** not practice
3:10 nor is he who ***d*** not love his
3:14 He who ***d*** not love his brother
3:17 how ***d*** the love of God abide in
3:21 if our heart ***d*** not condemn us,
4: 3 and every spirit that ***d*** not
4: 6 he who is not of God ***d*** not hear
4: 8 He who ***d*** not love does not know
4: 8 He who does not love ***d*** not know
4:20 for he who ***d*** not love his
5:10 he who ***d*** not believe God has
5:12 he who ***d*** not have the Son of
5:12 Son of God ***d*** not have life.
5:16 sinning a sin which ***d*** not
5:18 is born of God ***d*** not sin;
5:18 and the wicked one ***d*** not touch
2 Jn 9 Whoever transgresses and ***d*** not
9 of Christ ***d*** not have God.
10 If anyone comes to you and ***d*** not
3 Jn 9 ***d*** not receive us.
10 to mind his deeds which he ***d***,
10 he himself ***d*** not receive the
11 He who ***d*** good is of God, but he
11 but he who ***d*** evil has not seen

DOG (15/15)

Ex 11: 7 shall a ***d*** move its tongue,
Deut 23:18 of a harlot or the price of a ***d***
Judg 7: 5 as a ***d*** laps, you shall set
1 Sam 17:43 said to David, "Am I a ***d***,
24:14 Whom do you pursue? A dead ***d***?
2 Sam 9: 8 should look upon such a dead ***d***
16: 9 Why should this dead ***d*** curse my
2 Ki 8:13 "But what is your servant—a ***d***,
Ps 22:20 life from the power of the ***d***.
59: 6 return, They growl like a ***d***,
59:14 return, They growl like a ***d***,
Prov 26:11 As a ***d*** returns to his own
26:17 Is like one who takes a ***d***
Eccl 9: 4 for a living ***d*** is better than a
2 Pe 2:22 A ***d*** returns to his own

DOG'S (2/2) DOG

2 Sam 3: 8 Am I a ***d*** head that belongs to
Isa 66: 3 as if he breaks a ***d*** neck;

DOGS (24/23) DOG

Ex 22:31 you shall throw it to the **d**.
1 Ki 14:11 The **d** shall eat whoever belongs
16: 4 The **d** shall eat whoever belongs
21:19 In the place where **d** licked the
21:19 **d** shall lick your blood, even
21:23 The **d** shall eat Jezebel by the
21:24 The **d** shall eat whoever belongs
22:38 and the **d** licked up his blood
2 Ki 9:10 The **d** shall eat Jezebel on the
9:36 **d** shall eat the flesh of
Job 30: 1 I disdained to put with the **d**
Ps 22:16 For **d** have surrounded Me;
68:23 And the tongues of your **d** may
Isa 56:10 ignorant; They are all dumb **d**,
56:11 they are greedy **d** Which
Jer 15: 3 the **d** to drag, the birds of the
Mt 7: 6 not give what is holy to the **d**;
15:26 and throw it to the little **d**.
15:27 yet even the little **d** eat the
Mk 7:27 and throw it to the little **d**.
7:28 yet even the little **d** under the
Lk 16:21 Moreover the **d** came and licked
Phil 3: 2 Beware of **d**, beware of evil
Rev 22:15 But outside are **d** and sorcerers

DOING (104/98) DO

Gen 18:17 I hide from Abraham what I am **d**,
31:12 I have seen all that Laban is **d**
31:28 have done foolishly in so **d**.
39:22 they did there, it was his **d**.
44: 5 You have done evil in so **d**.
Ex 15:11 in praises, **d** wonders?
18:14 is this thing that you are **d**
36: 4 all the craftsmen who were **d**
36: 4 each from the work he was **d**,
Lev 4:27 sins unintentionally by **d**
Num 7: 5 that they may be used in **d** the
Deut 9:18 you committed in **d** wickedly
12: 8 not at all do as we are **d** here
12: 8 every man **d** whatever is right
Judg 18: 3 What are you **d** in this place?
18:18 said to them, "What are you **d**?
1 Sam 8: 8 so they are **d** to you also.
29: 3 What are these Hebrews **d**
2 Sam 3:25 and to know all that you are **d**.
11: 7 him, David asked how Joab was **d**,
11: 7 and how the people were **d**,
1 Ki 7:40 So Huram finished **d** all the
16:19 he had committed in **d** evil
19: 9 What are you **d** here, Elijah?"
19:13 What are you **d** here, Elijah?"
22:43 **d** what was right in the eyes
2 Ki 7: 9 We are not **d** right. This day is
10:30 you have done well in **d** what
17:41 children have continued **d** as
21:16 in **d** evil in the sight of the
22: 5 hand of those **d** the work,
22: 5 house of the LORD **d** the work,
2 Chr 4:11 So Huram finished **d** the work
19: 6 "Take heed to what you are **d**,
20:32 **d** what was right in the sight
34:16 to your servants they are **d**.
Neh 2:19 is this thing that you are **d**?
4: 2 "What are these feeble Jews **d**?
5: 9 What you are **d** is not good.
6: 3 I am **d** a great work, so that I
13:27 your **d** all this great evil,
Esth 9: 3 and all those **d** the king's
Job 9:12 can say to Him, 'What are You **d**?
Ps 64: 9 shall wisely consider His **d**.
66: 5 He is awesome in His **d**
118:23 This was the LORD's **d**;
Prov 2:14 Who rejoice in **d** evil, And
Eccl 8: 4 say to him, "What are you **d**?
Isa 56: 2 And keeps his hand from **d** any
58:13 From **d** your pleasure on My
58:13 not **d** your own ways, Nor
Jer 15: 5 turn aside to ask how you are **d**?
26:19 But we are **d** great evil against
32:40 turn away from **d** them good;
Ezek 5: 6 judgments by **d** wickedness
8: 6 man, do you see what they are **d**,
8: 9 abominations which they are **d**
8:13 abominations that they are **d**.
12: 9 said to you, 'What are you **d**?
Joel 2:13 And He relents from **d** harm.
Jon 4: 2 One who relents from **d** harm.
Mt 6: 3 know what your right hand is **d**,
12: 2 Your disciples are **d** what is
20:13 I am **d** you no wrong. Did you
21:23 what authority are You **d** these
21:42 This was the LORD's **d**,
24:46 when he comes, will find so **d**.
Mk 3: 8 heard how many things He was **d**,
11: 3 Why are you **d** this?' say, 'The
11: 5 said to them, "What are you **d**,
11:28 what authority are You **d** these
12:11 This was the LORD's **d**,
Lk 6: 2 Why are you **d** what is not lawful
12:43 find so **d** when he comes.
20: 2 what authority are You **d** these
Jn 2:14 the moneychangers **d** business.
7: 3 see the works that You are **d**.
7:51 him and knows what he is **d**?
13: 7 What I am **d** you do not
15:15 not know what his master is **d**;
Acts 10:38 who went about **d** good and
14:15 why are you **d** these things?
15:36 Lord, and see how they are **d**.
26:31 This man is **d** nothing deserving
Rom 2: 3 and **d** the same, that you will
2: 7 patient continuance in **d** good
7:15 For what I am **d**,
12:20 For in so **d** you will
2 Cor 8:10 not only to be **d** what you began
8:11 you also must complete the **d**
Gal 6: 9 not grow weary while **d** good,
Eph 6: 6 **d** the will of God from the
6: 7 with goodwill **d** service, as to
6:21 know my affairs and how I am **d**,
1 Th 5:11 another, just as you also are **d**.
2 Th 3:13 do not grow weary in **d** good.
1 Tim 4:16 for in **d** this you will save
5:21 **d** nothing with partiality.
Heb 13: 2 for by so **d** some have
1 Pe 2:15 that by **d** good you may put to
3:17 to suffer for **d** good than for
3:17 for doing good than for **d** evil.
4: 3 of our past lifetime in **d** the
4:19 their souls to Him in **d** good,

DOINGS (31/30) DO, DOER

Lev 18: 3 According to the **d** of the land
18: 3 and according to the **d** of the
Deut 28:20 of the wickedness of your **d** in
Judg 2:19 did not cease from their own **d**
1 Sam 25: 3 was harsh and evil in his **d**.
Isa 1:16 Put away the evil of your **d**
3: 8 their tongue and their **d** Are
3:10 shall eat the fruit of their **d**.
Jer 4: 4 Because of the evil of your **d**.
4:18 Your ways and your **d** Have
7: 3 "Amend your ways and your **d**,
7: 5 amend your ways and your **d**,
11:18 for You showed me their **d**.
17:10 to the fruit of his **d**.
18:11 and make your ways and your **d**
21:12 Because of the evil of your **d**.
21:14 to the fruit of your **d**,
23: 2 to you for the evil of your **d**,
23:22 And from the evil of their **d**.
25: 5 of his evil way and his evil **d**,
26: 3 because of the evil of their **d**.
26:13 amend your ways and your **d**,
32:19 according to the fruit of his **d**.
35:15 from his evil way, amend your **d**,
44:22 because of the evil of your **d**
Ezek 14:22 will see their ways and their **d**.
14:23 you see their ways and their **d**;
20:43 your ways and all your **d** with
20:44 nor according to your corrupt **d**,
21:24 so that in all your **d** your sins
Mic 2: 7 Are these His **d**?

DOLEFUL (KJV) See BITTER

DOMAIN (1/1) DOMINION

Jude 6 who did not keep their proper **d**,

DOMINION (56/50) DOMAIN, DOMINIONS

Gen 1:26 let them have **d** over the fish
1:28 have **d** over the fish of the
37: 8 Or shall you indeed have **d** over
Num 24:19 Out of Jacob One shall have **d**,
Judg 14: 4 that time the Philistines had **d**
1 Ki 4:24 For he had **d** over all the
9:19 and in all the land of his **d**.
2 Ki 20:13 in his house or in all his **d**
2 Chr 8: 6 and in all the land of his **d**.
13: 5 LORD God of Israel gave the **d**
Ezra 4:16 will be that you will have no **d**
Neh 9:28 So that they had **d** over them;
9:37 Also they have **d** over our
Job 25: 2 '**D** and fear belong to Him;
38:33 Can you set their **d** over the
Ps 8: 6 You have made him to have **d**
19:13 Let them not have **d** over me.
49:14 The upright shall have **d** over
72: 8 He shall have **d** also from sea
103:22 works, In all places of His **d**.
114: 2 sanctuary, And Israel His **d**.
119:133 And let no iniquity have **d**
145:13 And Your **d** endures throughout
Isa 26:13 besides You Have had **d** over
39: 2 in his house or in all his **d**
Jer 34: 1 of the earth under his **d**,
51:28 rulers, All the land of his **d**.
Dan 4: 3 And His **d** is from generation
4:22 and your **d** to the end of the
4:34 For His **d** is an everlasting
4:34 dominion is an everlasting **d**,
6:26 I make a decree that in every **d**
6:26 And His **d** shall endure to
7: 6 and **d** was given to it.
7:12 they had their **d** taken away,
7:14 Then to Him was given **d** and
7:14 His **d** is an everlasting
7:14 dominion is an everlasting **d**,
7:26 And they shall take away his **d**,
7:27 Then the kingdom and **d**,
11: 3 who shall rule with great **d**,
11: 4 nor according to his **d** with
11: 5 gain power over him and have **d**.
11: 5 His **d** shall be a great
11: 5 dominion shall be a great **d**.
Mic 4: 8 Even the former **d** shall come,
Zech 9:10 His **d** shall be 'from sea to
Rom 6: 9 Death no longer has **d** over Him.
6:14 For sin shall not have **d** over
7: 1 that the law has **d** over a man
2 Cor 1:24 Not that we have **d** over your
Eph 1:21 and power and might and **d**,
1 Pe 4:11 whom belong the glory and the **d**
5:11 To Him be the glory and the **d**
Jude 25 **D** and power, Both now and
Rev 1: 6 to Him be glory and **d** forever

DOMINIONS (2/2) DOMINION

Dan 7:27 And all **d** shall serve and obey
Col 1:16 whether thrones or **d** or

DONATIONS (1/1)

Lk 21: 5 with beautiful stones and **d**,

DONE (558/522) DO

Gen 2: 2 ended His work which He had **d**,
2: 2 all His work which He had **d**.
3:13 "What is this you have **d**?
3:14 Because you have **d** this, You
4:10 And He said, "What have you **d**?
8:21 every living thing as I have **d**.
9:24 what his younger son had **d** to
12:18 What is this you have **d** to me?
18:21 now and see whether they have **d**
20: 5 innocence of my hands I have **d**
20: 9 What have you **d** to us? How have
20: 9 You have **d** deeds to me that
20: 9 to me that ought not to be **d**.
20:10 that you have **d** this thing?"
21:23 to the kindness that I have **d**
21:26 I do not know who has **d** this
22:16 because you have **d** this thing,
24:66 all the things that he had **d**.
26:10 What is this you have **d** to us?
26:29 and since we have **d** nothing to
27:19 I have **d** just as you told me;
27:45 and he forgets what you have **d**
28:15 until I have **d** what I have
29:25 What is this you have **d** to me?
29:26 It must not be **d** so in our
30:26 know my service which I have **d**
31:26 to Jacob: "What have you **d**,
31:28 Now you have **d** foolishly in so
34: 7 because he had **d** a disgraceful
34: 7 a thing which ought not to be **d**.
40:15 and also I have **d** nothing here
42:28 What is this that God has **d** to
44: 5 You have **d** evil in so doing.'
44:15 "What deed is this you have **d**?
Ex 1:18 Why have you **d** this thing, and
2: 4 to know what would be **d** to him.
3:16 you and seen what is **d** to you
5:23 he has **d** evil to this people;
10: 2 son the mighty things I have **d**
10: 2 and My signs which I have **d**
12:16 No manner of work shall be **d** on
12:35 the children of Israel had **d**
13: 8 This is **d** because of what the
14: 5 Why have we **d** this, that we have
14:31 work which the LORD had **d** in
18: 1 heard of all that God had **d** for
18: 8 all that the LORD had **d** to
18: 9 the good which the LORD had **d**
21:31 to this judgment it shall be **d**
31:15 Work shall be **d** for six days,
34:10 such as have not been **d** in all
35: 2 Work shall be **d** for six days,
35:29 of Moses, had commanded to be **d**.
36: 7 for all the work to be **d**—
39:43 and indeed they had **d** it;
39:43 just so they had **d** it.
Lev 4: 2 which ought not to be **d**,
4:13 and they have **d** something
4:13 anything which should not be **d**,
4:22 and **d** something
4:22 anything which should not be **d**,
4:27 which ought not to be **d**,
5:16 for the harm that he has **d** in
5:17 which are forbidden to be **d** by
6: 7 things that he may have **d** in
8: 5 the LORD commanded to be **d**.
8:34 As he has **d** this day, so the
11:32 in which any work is **d**,
18:27 the men of the land have **d**,
23: 3 'Six days shall work be **d**,
24:19 of his neighbor, as he has **d**,
24:19 so shall it be **d** to him—
24:20 so shall it be **d** to him.
Num 12:11 in which we have **d** foolishly
15:11 Thus it shall be **d** for each
15:34 explained what should be **d** to
16:28 for I have not **d** them of my
22: 2 saw all that Israel had **d** to
22:28 What have I **d** to you, that you
23:11 What have you **d** to me? I took
23:23 'Oh, what God has **d**!'
32:13 generation that had **d** evil
Deut 2:22 just as He had **d** for the
3:21 that the LORD your God has **d**
10:21 who has **d** for you these great
12:31 which He hates they have **d** to
19:19 to him as he thought to have **d**
20:18 abominations which they have **d**
22:21 because she has **d** a disgraceful
25: 9 So shall it be **d** to the man who
26:14 and have **d** according to all

29:24 Why has the LORD **d** so to this
31:18 all the evil which they have **d**,
32:27 the LORD who has **d** all this."
Josh 7:15 he has **d** a disgraceful thing
7:19 and tell me now what you have **d**;
7:20 and this is what I have **d**:
9: 3 Gibeon heard what Joshua had **d**
9:24 and have **d** this thing.
10: 1 as he had **d** to Jericho and its
10: 1 so he had **d** to Ai and its
10:28 king of Makkedah as he had **d**
10:30 did to its king as he had **d** to
10:32 according to all that he had **d**
10:35 according to all that he had **d**
10:37 according to all that he had **d**
10:39 as he had **d** to Hebron, so he
10:39 as he had **d** also to Libnah and
22:24 But in fact we have **d** it for
23: 3 that the LORD your God has **d**
23: 8 as you have **d** to this day.
24:20 after He has **d** you good."
24:31 of the LORD which He had **d**
Judg 1: 7 under my table; as I have **d**,
2: 2 Why have you **d** this?
2: 7 of the LORD which He had **d**
2:10 nor the work which He had **d**
3:12 because they had **d** evil in the
6:29 'Who has **d** this thing?"
6:29 the son of Joash has **d** this
8: 1 Why have you **d** this to us by not
8: 2 What have I **d** now in comparison
8:35 with the good he had **d** for
9:16 and have **d** to him as he
9:24 that the crime **d** to the seventy
9:48 haste and do as I have **d**.
9:56 which he had **d** to his father by
11:37 'Let this thing be **d** for me:
14: 6 or his mother what he had **d**.
15: 6 Who has **d** this?" And they
15:10 to do to him as he has **d** to
15:11 What is this you have **d** to
15:11 so I have **d** to them."
19:30 No such deed has been **d** or seen
20:10 the vileness that they have **d**
Ruth 2:11 all that you have **d** for your
3:16 her all that the man had **d** for
1 Sam 6: 9 then He has **d** us this great
8: 8 all the works which they have **d**
11: 7 so it shall be **d** to his oxen."
12:17 which you have **d** in the sight
12:20 You have **d** all this wickedness;
12:24 what great things He has **d** for
13:11 Samuel said, "What have you **d**?
13:13 You have **d** foolishly. You have
14:43 "Tell me what you have **d**.
17:26 What shall be **d** for the man who
17:27 So shall it be **d** for the man who
17:29 What have I **d** now? Is there
19:18 told him all that Saul had **d**
20: 1 to Jonathan, "What have I **d**?
20:32 he be killed? What has he **d**?
24:19 with good for what you have **d**
25:30 when the LORD has **d** for my
26:16 This thing that you have **d** is
26:18 his servant? For what have I **d**,
28: 9 you know what Saul has **d**,
28:17 And the LORD has **d** for Himself
28:18 therefore the LORD has **d** this
29: 8 to Achish, "But what have I **d**?
31:11 what the Philistines had **d** to
2 Sam 2: 6 because you have **d** this thing.
3:24 and said, "What have you **d**?
7:21 You have **d** all these great
11:27 But the thing that David had **d**
12: 5 the man who has **d** this shall
12:21 "What is this that you have **d**?
13:12 for no such thing should be **d**
14:20 your servant Joab has **d** this
16:10 Why have you **d** so?'"
21:11 the concubine of Saul, had **d**.
23:17 These things were **d** by the
23:20 who had **d** many deeds. He had
24:10 sinned greatly in what I have **d**;
24:10 for I have **d** very foolishly."
24:17 and I have **d** wickedly; but
24:17 these sheep, what have they **d**?
1 Ki 1: 6 Why have you **d** so?" He was
1:27 Has this thing been **d** by my lord
3:12 I have **d** according to your
7:51 work that King Solomon had **d**
8:47 We have sinned and **d** wrong, we
8:66 the good that the LORD had **d**
9: 8 Why has the LORD **d** thus to this
11:11 Because you have **d** this, and
13:11 that the man of God had **d** that
14: 9 but you have **d** more evil than
14:22 all that their fathers had **d**.
15: 3 which he had **d** before him;
18:36 and that I have **d** all these
19: 1 Jezebel all that Elijah had **d**,
19:20 for what have I **d** to you?"
21:26 to all that the Amorites had **d**,
22:53 to all that his father had **d**.
2 Ki 4:14 What then is to be **d** for her?"
5:13 would you not have **d** it?
7:12 you what the Syrians have **d** to
8: 4 the great things Elisha has **d**.
8:18 just as the house of Ahab had **d**,
10:10 for the LORD has **d** what He
10:30 Because you have **d** well in doing
10:30 and have **d** to the house of
14: 3 as his father Joash had **d**.
15: 3 that his father Amaziah had **d**,
15: 9 the LORD, as his fathers had **d**;
15:34 that his father Uzziah had **d**.
16: 2 as his father David had **d**.
17: 4 as he had **d** year by year.
18: 3 all that his father David had **d**.
18:14 I have **d** wrong; turn away from
19:11 the kings of Assyria have **d** to
20: 3 and have **d** what was good in
21: 3 as Ahab king of Israel had **d**;
21:11 Manasseh king of Judah has **d**
21:15 because they have **d** evil in My
21:20 as his father Manasseh had **d**.
23:17 these things which you have **d**
23:19 to all the deeds he had **d** in
23:32 to all that his fathers had **d**.
23:37 to all that his fathers had **d**.
24: 3 according to all that he had **d**,
24: 9 to all that his father had **d**.
24:19 to all that Jehoiakim had **d**.
1 Chr 10:11 all that the Philistines had **d**
11:19 These things were **d** by the
11:22 who had **d** many deeds. He had
16:12 marvelous works which He has **d**,
17:19 You have **d** all this greatness,
21: 8 because I have **d** this thing;
21: 8 for I have **d** very foolishly."
21:17 one who has sinned and **d** evil
21:17 these sheep, what have they **d**?
29: 5 all kinds of work to be **d**
2 Chr 5: 1 all the work that Solomon had **d**
6:37 we have **d** wrong, and have
7:10 the good that the LORD had **d**
7:21 Why has the LORD **d** thus to this
16: 9 In this you have **d** foolishly;
21: 6 just as the house of Ahab had **d**,
24:16 because he had **d** good in
24:22 Jehoiada his father had **d** to
25:16 because you have **d** this and
26: 4 that his father Amaziah had **d**.
27: 2 that his father Uzziah had **d**
28: 1 as his father David had **d**.
29: 2 all that his father David had **d**.
29: 6 have trespassed and **d** evil
30: 5 since they had not **d** it for a
32:13 what I and my fathers have **d**
32:31 about the wonder that was **d**
33:22 as his father Manasseh had **d**;
Ezra 6:12 let it be **d** diligently.
7:21 let it be **d** diligently,
7:23 let it diligently be **d** for the
9: 1 When these things were **d**,
10: 3 and let it be **d** according to
Neh 2:16 I had gone or what I had **d**;
5:19 to all that I have **d** for this
6: 8 things as you say are being **d**,
6: 9 the work, and it will not be **d**.
6:16 perceived that this work was **d**
8:17 of Israel had not **d** so.
9:33 But we have **d** wickedly.
13: 7 the evil that Eliashib had **d**
13:14 out my good deeds that I have **d**
Esth 2: 1 Vashti, what she had **d**,
5: 6 It shall be **d**!"
6: 3 Nothing has been **d** for him."
6: 6 What shall be **d** for the man whom
6: 9 Thus shall it be **d** to the man
6:11 Thus shall it be **d** to the man
7: 2 It shall be **d**!"
9:12 What have they **d** in the rest of
9:12 further request? It shall be **d**.
9:14 the king commanded this to be **d**;
Job 7:20 What have I **d** to You,
12: 9 hand of the LORD has **d** this,
21:31 repays him for what he has **d**?
34:32 If I have **d** iniquity, I will
36:23 You have **d** wrong'?
Ps 7: 3 my God, if I have **d** this:
14: 1 They have **d** abominable works,
22:31 That He has **d** this.
33: 4 And all His work is **d** in
33: 9 For He spoke, and it was **d**;
40: 5 works Which You have **d**;
50:21 These things you have **d**,
51: 4 And **d** this evil in Your
52: 9 Because You have **d** it;
53: 1 and have **d** abominable iniquity;
66:16 I will declare what He has **d**
68:28 what You have **d** for us.
71:19 You who have **d** great things;
78: 4 wonderful works that He has **d**.
98: 1 For He has **d** marvelous
105: 5 marvelous works which He has **d**,
106: 6 We have **d** wickedly.
106:21 Who had **d** great things in
109:27 That You, LORD, have **d** it!
111: 8 And are **d** in truth and
119:121 I have **d** justice and
120: 3 Or what shall be **d** to you,
126: 2 The LORD has **d** great things for
126: 3 The LORD has **d** great things
Prov 3:30 If he has **d** you no harm.
4:16 sleep unless they have **d** evil;
24:29 do to him just as he has **d** to
30:20 I have **d** no wickedness."
31:29 Many daughters have **d** well, But
Eccl 1: 9 That which is **d** is what will
1: 9 is done is what will be **d**,
1:13 concerning all that is **d** under
1:14 seen all the works that are **d**
2:11 the works that my hands had **d**
2:12 what he has already **d**.
2:17 because the work that was **d**
4: 1 all the oppression that is **d**
4: 3 seen the evil work that is **d**
8: 9 heart to every work that is **d**
8:10 in the city where they had so **d**.
8:16 to see the business that is **d**
8:17 find out the work that is **d**
9: 3 is an evil in all that is **d**
9: 6 have a share In anything **d**
Isa 5: 4 What more could have been **d** to
5: 4 My vineyard That I have not **d**
10:11 As I have **d** to Samaria and her
10:13 strength of my hand I have **d**
12: 5 For He has **d** excellent things;
24:13 of grapes when the vintage is **d**.
25: 1 For You have **d** wonderful
26:12 For You have also **d** all our
33:13 are afar off, what I have **d**;
37:11 the kings of Assyria have **d** to
38: 3 and have **d** what is good in
38:15 And He Himself has **d** it.
41: 4 Who has performed and **d** it,
41:20 the hand of the LORD has **d**
44:23 for the LORD has **d** it!
46:10 things that are not yet **d**,
48: 5 My idol has **d** them, And my
53: 9 Because He had **d** no violence,
Jer 2:23 Know what you have **d**:
3: 5 you have spoken and **d** evil
3: 6 what backsliding Israel has **d**?
3: 7 after she had **d** all these
5:13 Thus shall it be **d** to them."
7:13 because you have **d** all these
7:14 as I have **d** to Shiloh.
7:30 children of Judah have **d** evil
8: 6 Saying, 'What have I **d**?
11: 8 do, but which they have not **d**.
11:15 Having **d** lewd deeds with many?
11:17 which they have **d** against
16:12 And you have **d** worse than your
18:13 The virgin of Israel has **d** a
22: 8 Why has the LORD **d** so to this
29:23 because they have **d** disgraceful
30:15 I have **d** these things to you.
30:24 not return until He has **d** it,
31:37 For all that they have **d**,
32:23 They have **d** nothing of all that
32:30 of Judah have **d** only evil
32:32 which they have **d** to provoke Me
35:10 and have obeyed and **d** according
35:18 and **d** according to all that he
38: 9 these men have **d** evil in all
38: 9 evil in all that they have **d**
40: 3 and has **d** just as He said.
41:11 the son of Nethaniah had **d**,
44:17 offerings to her, as we have **d**,
50:15 vengeance on her. As she has **d**,
50:29 According to all she has **d**,
51:12 LORD has both devised and **d**
51:24 For all the evil they have **d**
51:35 Let the violence **d** to me and
52: 2 to all that Jehoiakim had **d**.
Lam 1:21 are glad that You have **d** it.
1:22 And do to them as You have **d**
2: 6 He has **d** violence to His
2:17 The LORD has **d** what He
2:20 To whom have You **d** this?
Ezek 3:20 righteousness which he has **d**
5: 7 nor even **d** according to the
5: 9 among you what I have never **d**,
9: 4 all the abominations that are **d**
9:11 I have **d** as You commanded me."
11:12 but have **d** according to the
12:11 As I have **d**, so shall it be
12:11 so shall it be **d** to them;
12:28 word which I speak will be **d**,
14:23 know that I have **d** nothing
14:23 without cause that I have **d** in
16:48 Sodom nor her daughters have **d**
16:48 you and your daughters have **d**.
16:51 abominations which you have **d**.
16:59 deal with you as you have **d**,
16:63 an atonement for all you have **d**,
17:24 have spoken and have **d** it."
18:13 If he has **d** any of these
18:14 the sins which his father has **d**,
18:19 Because the son has **d** what is
18:22 righteousness which he has **d**,
18:24 righteousness which he has **d**
18:26 of the iniquity which he has **d**
23:38 Moreover they have **d** this to Me:
23:39 and indeed thus they have **d** in
24:22 'And you shall do as I have **d**;
24:24 according to all that he has **d**
33:16 he has **d** what is lawful and
39: 8 it is coming, and it shall be **d**,
43:11 ashamed of all that they have **d**,
44:14 and for all that has to be **d** in
Dan 4:35 say to Him, "What have You **d**?
6:22 I have **d** no wrong before you."
9: 5 we have **d** wickedly and
9:12 heaven such has never been **d**
9:12 been done as what has been **d**
9:15 we have **d** wickedly!
11:24 do what his fathers have not **d**,
11:36 has been determined shall be **d**.
Hos 10:15 Thus it shall be **d** to you,
Joel 2:20 Because he has **d** monstrous
2:21 For the LORD has **d** marvelous
Am 3: 6 will not the LORD have **d** it?
Ob 15 As you have **d**, it shall be
15 it shall be **d** to you;

Jon 1:10 'Why have you **d** this?"
1:14 have **d** as it pleased You."
Mic 6: 3 what have I **d** to you?
6:16 works of Ahab's house are **d**;
Hab 2:17 For the violence **d** to Lebanon
Zeph 3: 4 They have **d** violence to the
Zech 7: 3 month and fast as I have **d** for
Mal 1: 9 While this is being **d** by
Mt 1:22 So all this was **d** that it might
6:10 Your will be **d** On earth as
7:22 and **d** many wonders in Your
8:13 so let it be **d** for you."
11:20 of His mighty works had been **d**,
11:21 the mighty works which were **d**
11:21 were done in you had been **d** in
11:23 the mighty works which were **d**
11:23 were done in you had been **d** in
13:28 'An enemy has **d** this.'
18:19 it will be **d** for them by My
18:31 servants saw what had been **d**,
18:31 master all that had been **d**.
21: 4 All this was **d** that it might be
21:21 will not only do what was **d** to
21:21 into the sea,' it will be **d**.
23:23 These you ought to have **d**,
25:21 lord said to him, 'Well **d**,
25:23 lord said to him, 'Well **d**,
26:10 For she has **d** a good work for
26:13 what this woman has **d** will also
26:42 I drink it, Your will be **d**.
26:56 But all this was **d** that the
27:23 said, "Why, what evil has He **d**?
Mk 5:19 great things the Lord has **d**
5:20 Decapolis all that Jesus had **d**
5:32 her who had **d** this thing.
6:30 both what they had **d** and what
7:37 'He has **d** all things well.
11:23 those things he says will be **d**,
14: 6 She has **d** a good work for Me.
14: 8 'She has **d** what she could.
14: 9 what this woman has **d** will also
15: 8 to do just as he had always **d**
15:14 'Why, what evil has He **d**?"
Lk 1:49 He who is mighty has **d** great
2:48 why have You **d** this to us?
3:19 all the evils which Herod had **d**,
4:23 Whatever we have heard **d** in
5: 6 And when they had **d** this, they
8:39 what great things God has **d**
8:39 what great things Jesus had **d**
9: 7 heard of all that was **d** by Him;
9:10 told Him all that they had **d**.
10:13 the mighty works which were **d**
10:13 were done in you had been **d** in
11: 2 Your will be **d** On earth as
11:42 These you ought to have **d**,
13:17 glorious things that were **d** by
14:22 it is **d** as you commanded, and
17:10 when you have **d** all those
17:10 We have **d** what was our duty to
19:17 "And he said to him, 'Well **d**,
22:42 not My will, but Yours, be **d**.
23: 8 he hoped to see some miracle **d**
23:15 deserving of death has been **d**
23:22 'Why, what evil has He **d**?
23:31 what will be **d** in the dry?"
23:41 but this Man has **d** nothing
23:48 sight, seeing what had been **d**,
Jn 1:28 These things were **d** in Bethabara
3:21 that they have been **d** in God."
5:16 because He had **d** these things
5:29 those who have **d** good, to the
5:29 and those who have **d** evil, to
7:31 these which this Man has **d**?
12:16 about Him and that they had **d**
12:18 they heard that He had **d** this
12:37 But although He had **d** so many
13:12 Do you know what I have **d** to
13:15 that you should do as I have **d**
15: 7 and it shall be **d** for you.
15:24 If I had not **d** among them the
18:35 You to me. What have You **d**?
19:36 For these things were **d** that the
Acts 2:43 many wonders and signs were **d**
4: 7 by what name have you **d** this?"
4: 9 are judged for a good deed **d**
4:16 a notable miracle has been **d**
4:21 God for what had been **d**.
4:28 determined before to be **d**.
4:30 that signs and wonders may be **d**
5:12 many signs and wonders were **d**
8:13 miracles and signs which were **d**.
9:13 how much harm he has **d** to Your
10:16 This was **d** three times.
10:33 and you have **d** well to come.
11:10 Now this was **d** three times, and
12: 9 did not know that what was **d**
13:12 when he saw what had been **d**,
14: 3 signs and wonders to be **d** by
14:11 the people saw what Paul had **d**,
14:27 reported all that God had **d**
15: 4 all things that God had **d** with
21:14 "The will of the Lord be **d**.
21:19 those things which God had **d**
21:33 who he was and what he had **d**.
25:10 To the Jews I have **d** no wrong,
26:26 since this thing was not **d** in a
28: 9 So when this was **d**,
28:17 though I have **d** nothing against
Rom 6: 6 that the body of sin might be **d**
9:11 nor having **d** any good or evil,
1 Cor 5: 2 that he who has **d** this deed
5: 3 who has so **d** this deed.
9:15 things that it should be **d** so
13:10 that which is in part will be **d**
14:26 Let all things be **d** for
14:40 Let all things be **d** decently and
16:14 Let all that you do be **d** with
2 Cor 5:10 one may receive the things **d**
5:10 according to what he has **d**,
7:12 of him who had **d** the wrong,
Eph 5:12 of those things which are **d** by
6:13 and having **d** all, to stand.
Phil 2: 3 Let nothing be **d** through
4:14 Nevertheless you have **d** well
Col 3:25 be repaid for what he has **d**,
Titus 3: 5 righteousness which we have **d**,
Heb 10:36 so that after you have **d** the
Jas 3:13 that his works are **d** in the
Rev 16:17 throne, saying, "It is **d**!"
21: 6 It is **d**! I am the Alpha and the

DONKEY (84/75) DONKEY'S, DONKEYS

Gen 22: 3 the morning and saddled his **d**,
22: 5 'Stay here with the **d**;
42:27 opened his sack to give his **d**
44:13 and each man loaded his **d** and
49:11 Binding his **d** to the vine,
49:14 "Issachar is a strong **d**,
Ex 4:20 his sons and set them on a **d**,
13:13 But every firstborn of a **d** you
20:17 servant, nor his ox, nor his **d**,
21:33 and an ox or a **d** falls in it,
22: 4 whether it is an ox or **d** or
22: 9 it concerns an ox, a **d**,
22:10 delivers to his neighbor a **d**,
23: 4 meet your enemy's ox or his **d**
23: 5 If you see the **d** of one who
23:12 that your ox and your **d** may
34:20 But the firstborn of a **d** you
Num 16:15 I have not taken one **d** from
22:21 in the morning, saddled his **d**,
22:22 And he was riding on his **d**,
22:23 Now the **d** saw the Angel of the
22:23 and the **d** turned aside out of
22:23 So Balaam struck the **d** to turn
22:25 And when the **d** saw the Angel of
22:27 And when the **d** saw the Angel of
22:27 and he struck the **d** with his
22:28 LORD opened the mouth of the **d**,
22:29 And Balaam said to the **d**,
22:30 So the **d** said to Balaam, "Am I
22:30 Am I not your **d** on which you
22:32 Why have you struck your **d** these
22:33 The **d** saw Me and turned aside
Deut 5:14 nor your ox, nor your **d**,
5:21 female servant, his ox, his **d**,
22: 3 shall do the same with his **d**,
22: 4 shall not see your brother's **d**
22:10 not plow with an ox and a **d**
28:31 your **d** shall be violently
Josh 6:21 and old, ox and sheep and **d**,
15:18 So she dismounted from her **d**,
Judg 1:14 And she dismounted from her **d**,
6: 4 neither sheep nor ox nor **d**.
15:15 He found a fresh jawbone of a **d**,
15:16 "With the jawbone of a **d**,
15:16 With the jawbone of a **d** I
19:28 the man lifted her onto the **d**;
1 Sam 12: 3 or whose **d** have I taken, or
15: 3 ox and sheep, camel and **d**.
16:20 And Jesse took a **d** loaded with
25:20 it was, as she rode on the **d**,
25:23 hastened to dismount from the **d**,
25:42 rose in haste and rode on a **d**,
2 Sam 17:23 not followed, he saddled a **d**,
19:26 I will saddle a **d** for myself,
1 Ki 2:40 So Shimei arose, saddled his **d**,
13:13 'Saddle the **d** for me.'
13:13 So they saddled the **d** for
13:23 that he saddled the **d** for him,
13:24 and the **d** stood by it.
13:27 'Saddle the **d** for me.'
13:28 and the **d** and the lion standing
13:28 eaten the corpse nor torn the **d**.
13:29 man of God, laid it on the **d**,
2 Ki 4:24 Then she saddled a **d**,
Job 6: 5 Does the wild **d** bray when it
24: 3 They drive away the **d** of the
39: 5 'Who set the wild **d** free?
Prov 26: 3 the horse, A bridle for the **d**,
Isa 1: 3 And the **d** its master's crib;
32:20 the feet of the ox and the **d**.
Jer 2:24 A wild **d** used to the
22:19 buried with the burial of a **d**,
Hos 8: 9 Like a wild **d** alone by
Zech 9: 9 Lowly and riding on a **d**,
9: 9 A colt, the foal of a **d**.
14:15 mule, On the camel and the **d**,
Mt 21: 2 immediately you will find a **d**
21: 5 and sitting on a **d**,
21: 5 A colt, the foal of a **d**.
21: 7 They brought the **d** and the colt,
Lk 13:15 the Sabbath loose his ox or **d**
14: 5 having a **d** or an ox that has
Jn 12:14 when He had found a young **d**,
2 Pe 2:16 a dumb **d** speaking with a man's

DONKEY'S (4/4) DONKEY

Gen 49:11 And his **d** colt to the choice
2 Ki 6:25 besieged it until a **d** head
Job 11:12 When a wild **d** colt is born a
Jn 12:15 Sitting on a **d** colt."

DONKEYS (66/62) DONKEY

Gen 12:16 He had sheep, oxen, male **d**,
12:16 and female servants, female **d**,
24:35 servants, and camels and **d**.
30:43 male servants, and camels and **d**.
32: 5 "I have oxen, **d**,
32:15 twenty female **d** and ten foals.
34:28 sheep, their oxen, and their **d**,
36:24 as he pastured the **d** of his
42:26 So they loaded their **d** with the
43:18 to take us as slaves with our **d**.
43:24 and he gave their **d** feed.
44: 3 sent away, they and their **d**.
45:23 ten **d** loaded with the good
45:23 and ten female **d** loaded with
47:17 of the herds, and for the **d**.
Ex 9: 3 field, on the horses, on the **d**,
Num 31:28 the persons, the cattle, the **d**,
31:30 the persons, the cattle, the **d**,
31:34 sixty-one thousand **d**,
31:39 The **d** were thirty thousand five
31:45 thirty thousand five hundred **d**,
Josh 7:24 his daughters, his oxen, his **d**,
9: 4 they took old sacks on their **d**,
Judg 5:10 you who ride on white **d**,
10: 4 sons who rode on thirty **d**;
12:14 who rode on seventy young **d**.
19: 3 his servant and a couple of **d**
19:10 With him were the two saddled **d**;
19:19 both straw and fodder for our **d**,
19:21 house, and gave fodder to the **d**.
1 Sam 8:16 finest young men, and your **d**,
9: 3 Now the **d** of Kish, Saul's
9: 3 arise, go and look for the **d**.
9: 5 cease caring about the **d** and
9:20 But as for your **d** that were lost
10: 2 The **d** which you went to look for
10: 2 has ceased caring about the **d**
10:14 So he said, "To look for the **d**.
10:16 He told us plainly that the **d**
22:19 oxen and **d** and sheep—with the
25:18 of figs, and loaded them on **d**.
27: 9 away the sheep, the oxen, the **d**,
2 Sam 16: 1 him with a couple of saddled **d**,
16: 2 The **d** are for the king's
2 Ki 4:22 the young men and one of the **d**,
7: 7 their horses, and their **d**—
7:10 only horses and **d** tied, and the
1 Chr 5:21 and two thousand of their **d**—
12:40 were bringing food on **d** and
27:30 the Meronothite was over the **d**,
2 Chr 28:15 all the feeble ones ride on **d**.
Ezra 2:67 and their **d** six thousand seven
Neh 7:69 and **d** six thousand seven
13:15 and loading **d** with wine,
Job 1: 3 of oxen, five hundred female **d**,
1:14 oxen were plowing and the **d**
24: 5 like wild **d** in the desert,
42:12 oxen, and one thousand female **d**.
Ps 104:11 The wild **d** quench their
Isa 21: 7 of horsemen, A chariot of **d**,
30: 6 riches on the backs of young **d**,
30:24 the oxen and the young **d** that
32:14 lairs forever, A joy of wild **d**,
Jer 14: 6 And the wild **d** stood in the
Ezek 23:20 flesh is like the flesh of **d**,
Dan 5:21 dwelling was with the wild **d**.

DOOM (15/15) DOOMED

Job 21:30 are reserved for the day of **d**;
Prov 16: 4 the wicked for the day of **d**.
Jer 11:17 has pronounced **d** against you
17:17 are my hope in the day of **d**.
17:18 Bring on them the day of **d**,
19:15 all the **d** that I have
26:13 will relent concerning the **d**
26:19 Lord relented concerning the **d**
35:17 of Jerusalem all the **d** that I
36:31 on the men of Judah all the **d**
40: 2 your God has pronounced this **d**
51: 2 For in the day of **d** They
Ezek 7: 7 ***D*** has come to you, you who
7:10 it has come! ***D*** has gone out;
Am 6: 3 who put far off the day of **d**,

DOOMED (4/4) DOOM

Lev 27:29 who may become **d** to destruction
Deut 7:26 lest you be **d** to destruction
Josh 6:17 Now the city shall be **d** by the
7:12 because they have become **d** to

DOOR (163/155) DOORKEEPER, DOORPOST, DOORS, DOORWAY

Gen 4: 7 not do well, sin lies at the **d**.
6:16 and set the **d** of the ark in its
18: 1 as he was sitting in the tent **d**
18: 2 he ran from the tent **d** to meet
18:10 was listening in the tent **d**
19: 6 shut the **d** behind him,
19: 9 came near to break down the **d**.
19:10 house with them, and shut the **d**.
19:11 weary trying to find the **d**.
43:19 they talked with him at the **d**
Ex 12:22 of you shall go out of the **d**
12:23 the LORD will pass over the **d**

21: 6 shall also bring him to the **d**,
26:36 shall make a screen for the **d**
29: 4 sons you shall bring to the **d**
29:11 by the **d** of the tabernacle of
29:32 by the **d** of the tabernacle of
29:42 your generations at the **d** of
33: 8 each man stood at his tent **d**
33: 9 descended and stood at the **d**
33:10 standing at the tabernacle **d**,
33:10 each man in his tent **d**.
35:15 and the screen for the **d** at the
36:37 a screen for the tabernacle **d**,
38: 8 women who assembled at the **d**
38:30 he made the sockets for the **d**
39:38 the screen for the tabernacle **d**;
40: 5 put up the screen for the **d** of
40: 6 burnt offering before the **d** of
40:12 Aaron and his sons to the **d** of
40:28 He hung up the screen at the **d**
40:29 of burnt offering before the **d**
Lev 1: 3 of his own free will at the **d**
1: 5 on the altar that is by the **d**
3: 2 and kill it at the **d** of the
4: 4 shall bring the bull to the **d**
4: 7 which is at the **d** of the
4:18 which is at the **d** of the
8: 3 congregation together at the **d**
8: 4 was gathered together at the **d**
8:31 Boil the flesh at the **d** of the
8:33 you shall not go outside the **d**
8:35 you shall stay at the **d** of
10: 7 shall not go out from the **d** of
12: 6 to the **d** of the tabernacle of
14:11 at the **d** of the tabernacle of
14:23 to the **d** of the tabernacle of
14:38 to the **d** of the house, and shut
15:14 to the **d** of the tabernacle of
15:29 to the **d** of the tabernacle of
16: 7 before the LORD at the **d** of
17: 4 does not bring it to the **d**
17: 5 them to the LORD at the **d** of
17: 6 altar of the LORD at the **d**
17: 9 'and does not bring it to the **d**
19:21 to the **d** of the tabernacle of
Num 3:25 the screen for the **d** of the
3:26 the screen for the **d** of the
4:25 the screen for the **d** of the
4:26 the screen for the **d** of the gate
6:10 to the **d** of the tabernacle of
6:13 he shall be brought to the **d** of
6:18 his consecrated head at the **d**
10: 3 gather before you at the **d** of
11:10 everyone at the **d** of his tent;
12: 5 of cloud and stood in the **d**
16:18 and stood at the **d** of the
16:19 against them at the **d** of the
16:27 came out and stood at the **d** of
16:50 returned to Moses at the **d** of
20: 6 of the assembly to the **d** of
25: 6 who were weeping at the **d** of
Deut 15:17 it through his ear to the **d**,
22:21 out the young woman to the **d**
31:15 of cloud stood above the **d** of
Josh 19:51 at the **d** of the tabernacle of
Judg 4:20 'Stand at the **d** of the tent,
9:52 and he drew near the **d** of the
19:22 the house and beat on the **d**.
19:26 and fell down at the **d** of the
19:27 fallen at the **d** of the house
1 Sam 2:22 women who assembled at the **d**
2 Sam 11: 9 But Uriah slept at the **d** of the
13:17 and bolt the **d** behind her."
13:18 put her out and bolted the **d**
1 Ki 6:33 So for the **d** of the sanctuary he
6:34 panels comprised one folding **d**,
6:34 comprised the other folding **d**.
14: 6 as she came through the **d**,
2 Ki 4: 4 you shall shut the **d** behind you
4: 5 went from him and shut the **d**
4:21 shut the **d** upon him, and went
4:33 shut the **d** behind the two of
5: 9 and he stood at the **d** of
6:32 the messenger comes, shut the **d**,
6:32 and hold him fast at the **d**.
9: 3 Then open the **d** and flee,
9:10 And he opened the **d** and fled.
12: 9 and the priests who kept the **d**
1 Chr 9:21 was keeper of the **d** of the
Neh 3:20 from the buttress to the **d** of
3:21 from the **d** of the house of
Job 31: 9 have lurked at my neighbor's **d**,
31:34 And did not go out of the **d**—
Ps 141: 3 Keep watch over the **d** of my
Prov 5: 8 And do not go near the **d** of
9:14 For she sits at the **d** of her
26:14 As a **d** turns on its hinges,
Song 5: 4 By the latch of the **d**,
8: 9 of silver; And if she is a **d**,
Isa 6: 4 And the posts of the **d** were
Jer 35: 4 of Shallum, the keeper of the **d**.
Ezek 8: 3 to the **d** of the north gate of
8: 7 So He brought me to the **d** of
8: 8 into the wall, there was a **d**.
8:14 So He brought me to the **d** of the
8:16 at the **d** of the temple of the
10:19 and they stood at the **d** of the
11: 1 and there at the **d** of the gate
40:13 cubits, as **d** faces door.
40:13 cubits, as door faces **d**.
41:11 one **d** toward the north and
41:17 from the space above the **d**,
41:20 floor to the space above the **d**,
41:24 two panels for one **d** and two
41:24 and two panels for the other **d**.
42: 2 fifty cubits), was the north **d**.
42:12 there was a **d** in front of the
47: 1 he brought me back to the **d** of
Hos 2:15 the Valley of Achor as a **d** of
Mt 6: 6 and when you have shut your **d**,
25:10 and the **d** was shut.
27:60 a large stone against the **d** of
28: 2 back the stone from the **d**,
Mk 1:33 was gathered together at the **d**.
2: 2 them, not even near the **d**.
11: 4 found the colt tied by the **d**
15:46 rolled a stone against the **d**
16: 3 roll away the stone from the **d**
Lk 11: 7 the **d** is now shut, and my
13:25 has risen up and shut the **d**,
13:25 outside and knock at the **d**,
Jn 10: 1 enter the sheepfold by the **d**,
10: 2 But he who enters by the **d** is
10: 7 I am the **d** of the sheep.
10: 9 'I am the **d**. If anyone
18:16 But Peter stood at the **d**
18:16 and spoke to her who kept the **d**,
18:17 the servant girl who kept the **d**
Acts 5: 9 your husband are at the **d**,
12: 6 and the guards before the **d**
12:13 And as Peter knocked at the **d** of
12:16 and when they opened the **d**
14:27 and that He had opened the **d** of
18: 7 whose house was next **d** to the
1 Cor 16: 9 For a great and effective **d** has
2 Cor 2:12 and a **d** was opened to me by the
Col 4: 3 that God would open to us a **d**
Jas 5: 9 the Judge is standing at the **d**!
Rev 3: 8 I have set before you an open **d**,
3:20 I stand at the **d** and knock.
3:20 hears My voice and opens the **d**,
4: 1 a **d** standing open in heaven.

DOORKEEPER (3/3) DOOR, DOORKEEPERS

Ps 84:10 I would rather be a **d** in the
Mk 13:34 and commanded the **d** to watch.
Jn 10: 3 To him the **d** opens, and the

DOORKEEPERS (8/8) DOORKEEPER

2 Ki 22: 4 which the **d** have gathered from
23: 4 of the second order, and the **d**,
25:18 second priest, and the three **d**.
1 Chr 15:23 Berechiah and Elkanah were **d**
15:24 and Jehiah, **d** for the ark.
Esth 2:21 eunuchs, Bigthan and Teresh, **d**,
6: 2 the **d** who had sought to lay
Jer 52:24 second priest, and the three **d**.

DOORPOST (4/3) DOOR, DOORPOSTS

Ex 21: 6 him to the door, or to the **d**,
1 Sam 1: 9 sitting on the seat by the **d**
Ezek 43: 8 and their **d** by My doorpost,
43: 8 and their doorpost by My **d**,

DOORPOSTS (17/17) DOORPOST

Ex 12: 7 blood and put it on the two **d**
12:22 the lintel and the two **d** with
12:23 on the lintel and on the two **d**,
Deut 6: 9 You shall write them on the **d** of
11:20 you shall write them on the **d**
1 Ki 6:31 the lintel and **d** were
6:33 of the sanctuary he also made **d**
7: 5 And all the doorways and **d** had
2 Chr 3: 7 the house—the beams and **d**,
Ezek 40:48 the temple and measured the **d**
40:49 there were pillars by the **d**,
41: 1 sanctuary and measured the **d**,
41: 3 went inside and measured the **d**,
41:16 their **d** and the beveled window
41:21 The **d** of the temple were
45:19 offering and put it on the **d**
Am 9: 1 and He said: "Strike the **d**,

DOORS (70/67) DOOR

Josh 2:19 whoever goes outside the **d** of
Judg 3:23 the porch and shut the **d** of
3:24 the **d** of the upper room were
3:25 still he had not opened the **d**
11:31 whatever comes out of the **d** of
16: 3 took hold of the **d** of the gate
19:27 and opened the **d** of the house
1 Sam 3:15 and opened the **d** of the house
21:13 scratched on the **d** of the gate,
1 Ki 6:31 the inner sanctuary he made **d**
6:32 The two **d** were of olive wood;
6:34 And the two **d** were of cypress
7:50 both for the **d** of the inner
7:50 the **d** of the main hall
2 Ki 18:16 the gold from the **d** of the
1 Chr 22: 3 for the nails of the **d** of the
2 Chr 3: 7 and doorposts, its walls and **d**—
4: 9 and the great court and **d** for
4: 9 and he overlaid these **d** with
4:22 its inner **d** to the Most Holy
4:22 and the **d** of the main hall of
23: 4 be keeping watch over the **d**;
28:24 shut up the **d** of the house of
29: 3 he opened the **d** of the house of
29: 7 They have also shut up the **d** of
34: 9 the Levites who kept the **d** had
Neh 3: 1 consecrated it and hung its **d**.
3: 3 laid its beams and hung its **d**
3: 6 laid its beams and hung its **d**,
3:13 hung its **d** with its bolts and
3:14 he built it and hung its **d** with
3:15 hung its **d** with its bolts and
6: 1 that time I had not hung the **d**
6:10 and let us close the **d** of the
7: 1 was built and I had hung the **d**,
7: 3 let them shut and bar the **d**;
Job 3:10 it did not shut up the **d** of my
31:32 For I have opened my **d** to the
38: 8 who shut in the sea with **d**,
38:10 for it, And set bars and **d**;
38:17 Or have you seen the **d** of the
41:14 Who can open the **d** of his face,
Ps 24: 7 lifted up, you everlasting **d**!
24: 9 Lift up, you everlasting **d**!
78:23 And opened the **d** of heaven,
Prov 8: 3 At the entrance of the **d**:
8:34 Waiting at the posts of my **d**.
Eccl 12: 4 When the **d** are shut in the
Isa 26:20 And shut your **d** behind you;
45: 1 open before him the double **d**,
57: 8 Also behind the **d** and their
Ezek 33:30 beside the walls and in the **d**
41:11 The **d** of the side chambers
41:23 and the sanctuary had two **d**.
41:24 The **d** had two panels apiece,
41:25 trees were carved on the **d** of
42: 4 and their **d** faced north.
42:12 And corresponding to the **d** of
Mic 7: 5 Guard the **d** of your mouth
Zech 11: 1 Open your **d**, O Lebanon,
Mal 1:10 among you who would shut the **d**,
Mt 24:33 it is near—at the **d**!
Mk 13:29 it is near—at the **d**!
Jn 20:19 when the **d** were shut where the
20:26 the **d** being shut, and stood in
Acts 5:19 of the Lord opened the prison **d**
5:23 standing outside before the **d**;
16:26 and immediately all the **d** were
16:27 sleep and seeing the prison **d**
21:30 and immediately the **d** were

DOORWAY (7/7) DOOR, DOORWAYS

Gen 19: 6 went out to them through the **d**,
19:11 the men who were at the **d** of
Num 27: 2 by the **d** of the tabernacle of
1 Ki 6: 8 The **d** for the middle story was
14:27 who guarded the **d** of the king's
2 Ki 4:15 called her, she stood in the **d**.
2 Chr 12:10 who guarded the **d** of the king's

DOORWAYS (1/1) DOORWAY

1 Ki 7: 5 And all the **d** and doorposts had

DOPHKAH (2/2)

Num 33:12 of Sin and camped at ***D***.
33:13 They departed from ***D*** and camped

DOR (7/6)

Josh 11: 2 and in the heights of ***D*** on the
12:23 the king of ***D*** in the heights of
12:23 king of Dor in the heights of ***D***,
17:11 the inhabitants of ***D*** and its
Judg 1:27 or the inhabitants of ***D*** and its
1 Ki 4:11 in all the regions of ***D***;
1 Chr 7:29 ***D*** and its towns. In these dwelt

DORCAS (2/2) TABITHA

Acts 9:36 Tabitha, which is translated ***D***.
9:39 and garments which ***D*** had made

DOTED (KJV) See LUSTED

DOTHAN (3/2)

Gen 37:17 heard them say, 'Let us go to ***D***.
37:17 brothers and found them in ***D***.
2 Ki 6:13 saying, "Surely he is in ***D***.

DOUBLE (24/22) DOUBLED, DOUBLING

Gen 43:12 'Take **d** money in your hand,
43:15 and they took **d** money in their
Ex 22: 4 or sheep, he shall restore **d**.
22: 7 thief is found, he shall pay **d**.
22: 9 the judges condemn shall pay **d**
26: 9 and you shall **d** over the sixth
Deut 15:18 for he has been worth a **d** hired
21:17 giving him a **d** portion of all
1 Sam 1: 5 he would give a **d** portion,
2 Ki 2: 9 Please let a **d** portion of your
Job 11: 6 they would **d** your prudence.
41:13 approach him with a **d** bridle?
Ps 12: 2 flattering lips and a **d** heart
Isa 40: 2 from the LORD's hand ***D*** for
45: 1 open before him the **d** doors,
61: 7 you shall have **d** honor,
61: 7 their land they shall possess **d**;
Jer 16:18 And first I will repay **d** for
17:18 them with **d** destruction!
Ezek 21:14 third time let the sword do **d**

Zech 9:12 That I will restore **d** to you.
1 Tim 5:17 counted worthy of **d** honor,
Rev 18: 6 and repay her **d** according to
18: 6 has mixed, mix **d** for her.

DOUBLE-EDGED (1/1)

Judg 3:16 himself a dagger (it was **d** and

DOUBLE-MINDED (3/3)

Ps 119:113 I hate the **d**,
Jas 1: 8 he is a **d** man, unstable in all
4: 8 and purify your hearts, you **d**.

DOUBLE-TONGUED (1/1)

1 Tim 3: 8 must be reverent, not **d**,

DOUBLED (2/2) DOUBLE

Ex 28:16 'It shall be **d** into a square:
39: 9 and a span its width when **d**.

DOUBLING (1/1) DOUBLE

Ex 39: 9 the breastplate square by **d** it;

DOUBT (9/9) DOUBTED, DOUBTFUL, DOUBTING, DOUBTLESS, DOUBTS

Gen 37:33 Without **d** Joseph is torn to
Deut 28:66 Your life shall hang in **d** before
Job 12: 2 'No **d** you are the people,
Mt 14:31 of little faith, why did you **d**?
21:21 if you have faith and do not **d**,
Mk 11:23 and does not **d** in his heart,
Jn 10:24 "How long do You keep us in **d**?
Acts 28: 4 No **d** this man is a murderer,
1 Cor 9:10 For our sakes, no **d**,

DOUBTED (1/1) DOUBT

Mt 28:17 they worshiped Him; but some **d**.

DOUBTFUL (1/1) DOUBT

Rom 14: 1 not to disputes over **d** things.

DOUBTING (4/4) DOUBT

Acts 10:20 go with them, **d** nothing;
11:12 go with them, **d** nothing.
1 Tim 2: 8 holy hands, without wrath and **d**;
Jas 1: 6 let him ask in faith, with no **d**,

DOUBTLESS (5/5) DOUBT

2 Sam 5:19 for I will **d** deliver the
Ps 126: 6 Shall **d** come again with
Isa 63:16 ***D*** You are our Father, Though
1 Cor 9: 2 to others, yet **d** I am to you.
2 Cor 12: 1 It is **d** not profitable for me to

DOUBTS (4/4) DOUBT

Lk 24:38 And why do **d** arise in your
Rom 14:23 But he who **d** is condemned if he
Gal 4:20 for I have **d** about you.
Jas 1: 6 for he who **d** is like a wave of

DOUGH (5/5)

Ex 12:34 So the people took their **d**
12:39 baked unleavened cakes of the **d**
Neh 10:37 bring the firstfruits of our **d**,
Jer 7:18 the fire, and the women knead **d**,
Hos 7: 4 the fire after kneading the **d**,

DOVE (20/20) DOVE'S, DOVES

Gen 8: 8 also sent out from himself a **d**,
8: 9 But the **d** found no resting place
8:10 and again he sent the **d** out
8:11 Then the **d** came to him in the
8:12 seven days and sent out the **d**,
2 Ki 6:25 and one-fourth of a kab of **d**
Ps 55: 6 that I had wings like a **d**!
56: The Silent ***D*** in Distant Lands."
68:13 will be like the wings of a **d**
Song 2:14 'O my **d**, in the clefts of the
5: 2 me, my sister, my love, My **d**,
6: 9 My **d**, my perfect one,
Isa 38:14 I mourned like a **d**;
Jer 48:28 And be like the **d** which makes
Hos 7:11 also is like a silly **d**,
11:11 Like a **d** from the land of
Mt 3:16 of God descending like a **d** and
Mk 1:10 descending upon Him like a **d**.
Lk 3:22 in bodily form like a **d** upon
Jn 1:32 descending from heaven like a **d**,

DOVE'S (2/2) DOVE

Song 1:15 You have **d** eyes.
4: 1 You have **d** eyes behind

DOVES (10/10) DOVE

Song 5:12 His eyes are like **d** By the
Isa 59:11 And moan sadly like **d**;
60: 8 And like **d** to their roosts?
Ezek 7:16 be on the mountains Like **d** of

Nah 2: 7 her as with the voice of **d**,
Mt 10:16 as serpents and harmless as **d**.
21:12 the seats of those who sold **d**.
Mk 11:15 the seats of those who sold **d**.
Jn 2:14 who sold oxen and sheep and **d**,
2:16 And He said to those who sold **d**,

DOWN (1142/1058) See APPENDIX

DOWNCAST (1/1)

2 Cor 7: 6 God, who comforts the **d**,

DOWNFALL (3/3)

2 Chr 22: 7 God's occasion for Ahaziah's **d**;
Prov 14:28 in the lack of people is the **d**
Lam 1: 7 saw her And mocked at her **d**.

DOWNSITTING (KJV) See SITTING (DOWN)

DOWNWARD (4/4)

2 Ki 19:30 Judah Shall again take root **d**,
Isa 37:31 Judah Shall again take root **d**,
Ezek 1:27 appearance of His waist and **d**
8: 2 appearance of His waist and **d**,

DOWRY (3/3)

Gen 34:12 Ask me ever so much **d** and gift,
1 Sam 18:25 'The king does not desire any **d**
1 Ki 9:16 and had given it as a **d** to his

DRACHMAS (5/5)

Ezra 2:69 work sixty-one thousand gold **d**,
8:27 gold basins worth a thousand **d**,
Neh 7:70 treasury one thousand gold **d**,
7:71 the work twenty thousand gold **d**,
7:72 was twenty thousand gold **d**,

DRAG (3/3) DRAGGED, DRAGGING

Jer 15: 3 sword to slay, the dogs to **d**,
Lk 12:58 lest he **d** you to the judge,
Jas 2: 6 oppress you and **d** you into

DRAGGED (6/6) DRAG

Jer 22:19 ***D*** and cast out beyond the
Jn 21:11 Simon Peter went up and **d** the
Acts 14:19 they stoned Paul and **d** him
16:19 Paul and Silas and **d** them
17: 6 they **d** Jason and some brethren
21:30 and **d** him out of the temple;

DRAGGING (2/2) DRAG

Jn 21: 8 **d** the net with fish.
Acts 8: 3 and **d** off men and women,

DRAGNET (3/3)

Hab 1:15 And gather them in their **d**.
1:16 And burn incense to their **d**;
Mt 13:47 kingdom of heaven is like a **d**

DRAGON (13/12)

Rev 12: 3 fiery red **d** having seven heads
12: 4 And the **d** stood before the
12: 7 his angels fought with the **d**;
12: 7 and the **d** and his angels
12: 9 So the great **d** was cast out,
12:13 Now when the **d** saw that he had
12:16 up the flood which the **d** had
12:17 And the **d** was enraged with the
13: 2 The **d** gave him his power,
13: 4 So they worshiped the **d** who gave
13:11 like a lamb and spoke like a **d**.
16:13 out of the mouth of the **d**,
20: 2 He laid hold of the **d**,

DRAGONS (KJV) See JACKALS, SERPENTS

DRAIN (2/2) DRAINED, DRAINS

Ps 75: 8 all the wicked of the earth ***D***
Ezek 23:34 You shall drink and **d** it,

DRAINED (6/6) DRAIN

Lev 1:15 its blood shall be **d** out at the
5: 9 rest of the blood shall be **d**
Ps 73:10 waters of a full cup are **d** by
Isa 51:17 And **d** it out.
Joel 2: 6 All faces are **d** of color.
Nah 2:10 And all their faces are **d** of

DRAINS (1/1) DRAIN

Zech 4:12 from which the golden oil **d**?

DRAMS (KJV) See DARICS, DRACHMAS

DRANK (47/46) DRINK

Gen 9:21 Then he **d** of the wine and was
24:46 I **d**, and she gave the camels
24:54 who were with him ate and **d**
25:34 of lentils; then he ate and **d**,
26:30 a feast, and they ate and **d**.
27:25 he brought him wine, and he **d**.
43:34 So they **d** and were merry with
Ex 24:11 saw God, and they ate and **d**.
34:28 he neither ate bread nor **d**
Num 20:11 and their animals **d**.
Deut 9: 9 I neither ate bread nor **d**
9:18 I neither ate bread nor **d**
32:14 And you **d** wine, the blood of
32:38 And **d** the wine of their drink
Judg 9:27 of their god, and ate and **d**,
15:19 and water came out, and he **d**;
19: 4 So they ate and **d** and lodged
19: 6 and the two of them ate and **d**
19:21 their feet, and ate and **d**.
2 Sam 11:13 he ate and **d** before him;
12: 3 It ate of his own food and **d**
1 Ki 13:19 in his house, and **d** water.
13:22 and **d** water in the place of
17: 6 and he **d** from the brook.
19: 6 So he ate and **d**, and lay down
19: 8 So he arose, and ate and **d**;
2 Ki 6:23 and after they ate and **d**,
7: 8 into one tent and ate and **d**,
9:34 he had gone in, he ate and **d**.
1 Chr 29:22 So they ate and **d** before the
Ezra 10: 6 he ate no bread and **d** no water,
Jer 51: 7 The nations **d** her wine;
Dan 1: 5 and of the wine which he **d**,
1: 8 nor with the wine which he **d**;
5: 1 and **d** wine in the presence of
5: 3 and his concubines **d** from them.
5: 4 They **d** wine, and praised the
Ob 16 For as you **d** on my holy
Mk 14:23 and they all **d** from it.
Lk 13:26 We ate and **d** in Your presence,
17:27 "They ate, they **d**,
17:28 days of Lot: They ate, they **d**,
Jn 4:12 and **d** from it himself, as well
Acts 9: 9 sight, and neither ate nor **d**.
10:41 even to us who ate and **d** with
1 Cor 10: 4 and all **d** the same spiritual
10: 4 For they **d** of that spiritual

DRAUGHT (KJV) See CATCH, REFUSE

DRAW (65/64) DRAWING, DRAWN, DRAWS, DREW

Gen 24:11 the time when women go out to **d**
24:13 of the city are coming out to **d**
24:19 I will **d** water for your camels
24:20 ran back to the well to **d**
24:43 when the virgin comes out to **d**
24:44 and I will **d** for your camels
Ex 3: 5 'Do not **d** near this place.
15: 9 I will **d** my sword, My hand
Lev 26:33 among the nations and **d** out
Deut 32:13 He made him **d** honey from the
Josh 8:26 For Joshua did not **d** back his
Judg 3:22 for he did not **d** the dagger out
8:20 But the youth would not **d** his
9:54 '***D*** your sword and kill me,
19:13 let us **d** near to one of these
20:23 Shall I again **d** near for battle
20:32 Let us flee and **d** them away from
1 Sam 9:11 some young women going out to **d**
14:36 Let us **d** near to God here."
31: 4 ***D*** your sword, and thrust me
1 Chr 10: 4 ***D*** your sword, and thrust me
Job 41: 1 Can you **d** out Leviathan with a
Ps 35: 3 Also **d** out the spear, And stop
69:18 ***D*** near to my soul, and redeem
73:28 But it is good for me to **d**
119:150 They **d** near who follow after
Prov 20: 5 a man of understanding will **d**
Eccl 5: 1 and **d** near to hear rather than
12: 1 And the years **d** near when you
Song 1: 4 ***D*** me away! We will run after
Isa 5:18 Woe to those who **d** iniquity
5:19 of the Holy One of Israel **d**
12: 3 Therefore with joy you will **d**
29:13 Inasmuch as these people **d** near
45:20 ***D*** near together, You who
66:19 who **d** the bow, and Tubal and
Jer 30:21 Then I will cause him to **d**
46: 3 And **d** near to battle!
49:20 the least of the flock shall **d**
50:45 the least of the flock shall **d**
Ezek 5: 2 I will **d** out a sword after
5:12 and I will **d** out a sword after
9: 1 who have charge over the city **d**
12:14 and I will **d** out the sword
21: 3 and I will **d** My sword out of
22: 4 You have caused your days to **d**
28: 7 And they shall **d** their swords
30:11 They shall **d** their swords
32: 3 And they will **d** you up in My
Joel 3: 9 Let all the men of war **d** near,
Nah 3:14 ***D*** your water for the siege!
Hag 2:16 one came to the wine vat to **d**
Mt 15: 8 These people **d** near to Me
Jn 2: 8 ***D*** some out now, and take it to
4: 7 A woman of Samaria came to **d**
4:11 You have nothing to **d** with, and
4:15 not thirst, nor come here to **d**.
12:32 will **d** all peoples to
21: 6 now they were not able to **d** it
Acts 20:30 to **d** away the disciples after
Heb 7:19 through which we **d** near to God.

D

10:22 let us **d** near with a true heart
10:39 But we are not of those who **d**
Jas 4: 8 **D** near to God and He will draw
4: 8 Draw near to God and He will **d**

DRAWING (6/6) DRAW

Judg 19: 9 the day is now **d** toward
1 Sam 17:41 and began **d** near to David, and
Ezek 32:20 **D** her and all her multitudes.
Lk 19:37 as He was now **d** near the
Jn 6:19 walking on the sea and **d** near
Acts 27:27 sensed that they were **d** near

DRAWN (28/28) DRAW

Num 22:23 in the way with His **d** sword
22:31 in the way with His **d** sword
31:30 **d** from the persons, the cattle,
31:47 **d** from man and beast, and gave
Deut 30:17 and are **d** away, and worship
Josh 5:13 opposite him with His sword **d**
8: 6 out after us till we have **d**
8:16 they pursued Joshua and were **d**
Judg 20:31 and were **d** away from the city.
Ruth 2: 9 from what the young men have **d**.
1 Sam 17:21 and the Philistines had **d** up
1 Chr 21:16 having in his hand a **d** sword
Job 20:25 It is **d**, and comes out of
Ps 37:14 The wicked have **d** the sword
55:21 Yet they were **d** swords.
Prov 24:11 Deliver those who are **d**
Isa 21:15 from the **d** sword, From the
28: 9 Those just **d** from the
Jer 6:29 For the wicked are not **d** off.
31: 3 with lovingkindness I have **d**
Lam 2: 3 He has **d** back His right hand
Ezek 21: 5 have **d** My sword out of its
21:28 'A sword, a sword is **d**,
Zeph 3: 2 She has not **d** near to her God.
Lk 21: 8 'The time has **d** near.'
Jn 2: 9 (but the servants who had **d**
Acts 11:10 and all were **d** up again into
Jas 1:14 one is tempted when he is **d**

DRAWS (12/12) DRAW

Deut 25:11 and the wife of one **d** near to
29:11 cuts your wood to the one who **d**
Job 24:22 But God **d** the mighty away with
33:22 his soul **d** near the Pit,
36:27 For He **d** up drops of water,
Ps 10: 9 He catches the poor when he **d**
88: 3 And my life **d** near to the
Isa 26:17 When she **d** near the time of
Ezek 7:12 The day **d** near. 'Let not the
Lk 21:28 because your redemption **d**
Jn 6:44 the Father who sent Me **d** him;
Heb 10:38 But if anyone **d** back,

DREAD (14/14) DREADED, DREADFUL

Gen 9: 2 fear of you and the **d** of you
Ex 1:12 And they were in **d** of the
15:16 Fear and **d** will fall on them;
Num 22: 3 and Moab was sick with **d**
Deut 2:25 day I will begin to put the **d**
11:25 LORD your God will put the **d**
Job 9:34 And do not let **d** of Him
13:11 And the **d** of Him fall upon
13:21 And let not the **d** of You make
Ps 119:39 away my reproach which I **d**,
Isa 7:16 the land that you **d** will be
8:13 And let Him be your **d**.
Ezek 4:16 water by measure and with **d**,
12:19 and drink their water with **d**,

DREADED (2/2) DREAD

Job 3:25 And what I **d** has happened to
31:34 And **d** the contempt of

DREADFUL (6/6) DREAD, DREADFULLY

Job 15:21 **D** sounds are in his ears
Ezek 21:10 to make a **d** slaughter,
Dan 7: 7 **d** and terrible, exceedingly
7:19 all the others, exceedingly **d**,
Hab 1: 7 They are terrible and **d**;
Mal 4: 5 coming of the great and **d** day

DREADFULLY (4/4) DREADFUL

1 Sam 17:24 from him and were **d** afraid.
28:20 and was **d** afraid because of the
Neh 2: 2 So I became **d** afraid,
Mt 8: 6 paralyzed, **d** tormented."

DREAM (72/59) DREAMED, DREAMER, DREAMS

Gen 20: 3 God came to Abimelech in a **d**
20: 6 And God said to him in a **d**,
31:10 I lifted my eyes and saw in a **d**,
31:11 Angel of God spoke to me in a **d**,
31:24 to Laban the Syrian in a **d** by
37: 5 Now Joseph had a **d**,
37: 6 Please hear this **d** which I have
37: 9 he dreamed still another **d** and
37: 9 I have dreamed another **d**.
37:10 What is this **d** that you have
40: 5 confined in the prison, had a **d**,
40: 5 each man's **d** in one night and
40: 5 in one night and each man's **d**
40: 8 to him, "We each have had a **d**,
40: 9 the chief butler told his **d** to
40: 9 in my **d** a vine was before me,
40:16 'I also was in my **d**,
41: 1 years, that Pharaoh had a **d**;
41: 7 awoke, and indeed, it was a **d**.
41:11 'we each had a **d** in one night,
41:11 interpretation of his own **d**.
41:12 according to his own **d**.
41:15 to Joseph, "I have had a **d**,
41:15 that you can understand a **d**,
41:17 in my **d** I stood on the bank of
41:22 "Also I saw in my **d**,
41:32 And the **d** was repeated to
Num 12: 6 I speak to him in a **d**.
Judg 7:13 there was a man telling a **d** to
7:13 He said, "I have had a **d**:
7:15 heard the telling of the **d** and
1 Ki 3: 5 appeared to Solomon in a **d** by
3:15 and indeed it had been a **d**.
Job 20: 8 He will fly away like a **d**,
33:15 In a **d**, in a vision of the
Ps 73:20 As a **d** when one awakes,
126: 1 We were like those who **d**.
Eccl 5: 3 For a **d** comes through much
Isa 29: 7 Shall be as a **d** of a night
Jer 23:28 "The prophet who has a **d**,
23:28 has a dream, let him tell a **d**;
Dan 2: 3 said to them, "I have had a **d**,
2: 3 spirit is anxious to know the **d**.
2: 4 Tell your servants the **d**,
2: 5 if you do not make known the **d**
2: 6 if you tell the **d** and its
2: 6 Therefore tell me the **d** and its
2: 7 king tell his servants the **d**,
2: 9 you do not make known the **d**
2: 9 Therefore tell me the **d**,
2:26 able to make known to me the **d**
2:28 Your **d**, and the visions of
2:36 This is the **d**.
2:45 The **d** is certain, and its
4: 5 I saw a **d** which made me afraid,
4: 6 me the interpretation of the **d**.
4: 7 came in, and I told them the **d**;
4: 8 and I told the **d** before him,
4: 9 to me the visions of my **d** that
4:18 This **d** I, King Nebuchadnezzar,
4:19 do not let the **d** or its
4:19 may the **d** concern those who
7: 1 Daniel had a **d** and visions of
7: 1 Then he wrote down the **d**,
Joel 2:28 Your old men shall **d** dreams,
Mt 1:20 the Lord appeared to him in a **d**,
2:12 being divinely warned in a **d**
2:13 Lord appeared to Joseph in a **d**,
2:19 of the Lord appeared in a **d** to
2:22 And being warned by God in a **d**,
27:19 many things today in a **d**
Acts 2:17 Your old men shall **d**

DREAMED (11/9) DREAM

Gen 28:12 Then he **d**, and behold, a
37: 6 hear this dream which I have **d**:
37: 9 Then he **d** still another dream
37: 9 I have **d** another dream.
37:10 is this dream that you have **d**?
41: 5 He slept and **d** a second time;
41:11 Each of us **d** according to the
42: 9 the dreams which he had **d**
Jer 23:25 'I have **d**, I have dreamed!'
23:25 'I have dreamed, I have **d**!'
29: 8 dreams which you cause to be **d**.

DREAMER (4/4) DREAM, DREAMERS

Gen 37:19 this **d** is coming!
Deut 13: 1 among you a prophet or a **d** of
13: 3 of that prophet or that **d** of
13: 5 But that prophet or that **d** of

DREAMERS (2/2) DREAMER

Jer 27: 9 prophets, your diviners, your **d**,
Jude 8 Likewise also these **d** defile the

DREAMS (26/25) DREAM

Gen 37: 8 hated him even more for his **d**
37:20 see what will become of his **d**!
41: 8 And Pharaoh told them his **d**,
41:12 and he interpreted our **d** for
41:25 'The **d** of Pharaoh are one;
41:26 seven years; the **d** are one.
42: 9 Then Joseph remembered the **d**
Deut 13: 1 you a prophet or a dreamer of **d**,
13: 3 prophet or that dreamer of **d**
13: 5 prophet or that dreamer of **d**
1 Sam 28: 6 either by **d** or by Urim or by
28:15 neither by prophets nor by **d**.
Job 7:14 Then You scare me with **d** And
Eccl 5: 7 For in the multitude of **d** and
Isa 29: 8 even be as when a hungry man **d**,
29: 8 Or as when a thirsty man **d**,
Jer 23:27 forget My name by their **d**
23:32 those who prophesy false **d**,
29: 8 nor listen to your **d** which you
Dan 1:17 in all visions and **d**.
2: 1 reign, Nebuchadnezzar had **d**;
2: 2 to tell the king his **d**.
5:12 understanding, interpreting **d**,
Joel 2:28 Your old men shall dream **d**,
Zech 10: 2 lies, And tell false **d**;
Acts 2:17 old men shall dream **d**.

DREGS (4/4)

Ps 75: 8 Surely its **d** shall all the
Isa 51:17 You have drunk the **d** of the
51:22 The **d** of the cup of My fury;
Jer 48:11 He has settled on his **d**,

DRENCH (2/2)

Ps 6: 6 I **d** my couch with my tears.
Isa 16: 9 I will **d** you with my tears,

DRESS (1/1)

Jer 6:26 **D** in sackcloth And roll about

DRESSED (3/3) DRESSING

1 Sam 25:18 of wine, five sheep already **d**,
2 Sam 20: 8 Now Joab was **d** in battle armor;
2 Chr 28:15 **d** them and gave them sandals,

DRESSING (1/1) DRESSED

Joel 2:16 And the bride from her **d** room.

DREW (78/77) DRAW

Gen 8: 9 and **d** her into the ark to
24:20 and **d** for all his camels.
24:45 she went down to the well and **d**
38:29 as he **d** back his hand, that his
43:19 When they **d** near to the steward
47:29 When the time **d** near that Israel
49:33 he **d** his feet up into the bed
Ex 2:10 Because I **d** him out of the
2:16 And they came and **d** water, and
2:19 and he also **d** enough water for
4: 7 and **d** it out of his bosom, and
14:10 And when Pharaoh **d** near, the
20:21 but Moses **d** near the thick
Lev 9: 5 And all the congregation **d** near
Josh 8:11 were with him went up and **d**
10:24 And they **d** near and put their
Judg 8:10 and twenty thousand men who **d**
9:52 and he **d** near the door of the
20: 2 thousand foot soldiers who **d**
20:15 twenty-six thousand men who **d**
20:17 hundred thousand men who **d** the
20:25 all these **d** the sword.
20:35 all these **d** the sword.
20:46 twenty-five thousand men who **d**
1 Sam 7: 6 **d** water, and poured it out
7:10 the Philistines **d** near to
9:18 Then Saul **d** near to Samuel in
17: 2 and **d** up in battle array
17:16 And the Philistine **d** near and
17:40 And he **d** near to the
17:48 arose and came and **d** near to
17:51 took his sword and **d** it out of
2 Sam 10:13 the people who were with him **d**
18:25 And he came rapidly and **d**
22:17 He **d** me out of many waters.
23:16 **d** water from the well of
24: 9 thousand valiant men who **d** the
1 Ki 2: 1 Now the days of David **d** near
22:34 Now a certain man **d** a bow at
2 Ki 3:26 him seven hundred men who **d**
9:24 Now Jehu **d** his bow with full
1 Chr 11:18 **d** water from the well of
19:14 the people who were with him **d**
21: 5 one hundred thousand men who **d**
21: 5 and seventy thousand men who **d**
2 Chr 13: 3 Jeroboam also **d** up in battle
14: 8 men who carried shields and **d**
18:33 Now a certain man **d** a bow at
Job 26:10 He **d** a circular horizon on the
Ps 18:16 He **d** me out of many waters.
107:18 And they **d** near to the gates
Prov 8:27 When He **d** a circle on the face
Isa 41: 5 They **d** near and came.
Lam 3:57 You **d** near on the day I called
Hos 11: 4 I **d** them with gentle cords,
Mt 13:48 they **d** to shore; and they sat
21: 1 Now when they **d** near Jerusalem,
21:34 Now when vintage-time **d** near, he
26:51 stretched out his hand and **d**
Mk 11: 1 Now when they **d** near Jerusalem,
14:47 And one of those who stood by **d**
Lk 15: 1 collectors and the sinners **d**
15:25 And as he came and **d** near to
19:41 Now as He **d** near, He saw the
22: 1 the Feast of Unleavened Bread **d**
22:47 went before them and **d** near to
23:54 and the Sabbath **d** near.
24:15 that Jesus Himself **d** near and
24:28 Then they **d** near to the village
Jn 18: 6 they **d** back and fell to the
18:10 **d** it and struck the high
Acts 5:37 and **d** away many people after
7:17 when the time of the promise **d**
7:31 and as he **d** near to observe,
10: 9 went on their journey and **d**
16:27 **d** his sword and was about to
19:33 And they **d** Alexander out of the
Rev 12: 4 His tail **d** a third of the stars

DRIED (36/35) DRY

Gen 8: 7 and fro until the waters had **d**
8:13 that the waters were **d** up from
8:14 of the month, the earth was **d**.
Num 11: 6 but now our whole being is **d**
Josh 2:10 we have heard how the LORD **d**
4:23 for the LORD your God **d** up the
4:23 which He **d** up before us until
5: 1 heard that the LORD had **d** up
Judg 16: 7 fresh bowstrings, not yet **d**,
16: 8 fresh bowstrings, not yet **d**,
1 Sam 17:17 an ephah of this **d** grain
1 Ki 17: 7 after a while that the brook **d**
2 Ki 19:24 the soles of my feet I have **d**
Job 18:16 His roots are **d** out below,
Ps 22:15 My strength is **d** up like a
74:15 You **d** up mighty rivers.
106: 9 Red Sea also, and it **d** up;
Isa 5:13 And their multitude **d** up with
19: 5 the river will be wasted and **d**
19: 6 defense will be emptied and **d**
37:25 the soles of my feet I have **d**
51:10 Are You not the One who **d** up
Jer 23:10 places of the wilderness are **d**
50:38 and they will be **d** up.
Ezek 17:24 **d** up the green tree and made
19:12 And the east wind **d** her fruit.
Hos 9:16 Their root is **d** up;
13:15 And his fountain shall be **d**
Joel 1:10 The new wine is **d** up, The oil
1:12 The vine has **d** up, And the fig
1:20 For the water brooks are **d** up,
Nah 1:10 devoured like stubble fully **d**.
Zech 9: 5 for He **d** up her expectation.
Mk 5:29 fountain of her blood was **d** up,
11:20 they saw the fig tree **d** up from
Rev 16:12 and its water was **d** up, so that

DRIES (3/3) DRY

Job 14:11 a river becomes parched and **d**
Prov 17:22 But a broken spirit **d** the
Nah 1: 4 And **d** up all the rivers.

DRIFT (1/1)

Heb 2: 1 lest we **d** away.

DRINK (347/307) DRANK, DRINKERS, DRINKING, DRINKS, DRUNK

Gen 19:32 let us make our father **d** wine,
19:33 So they made their father **d** wine
19:34 let us make him **d** wine tonight
19:35 Then they made their father **d**
21:19 water, and gave the lad a **d**.
24:14 down your pitcher that I may **d**,
24:14 she says, '**D**, and I will
24:14 will also give your camels a **d**'
24:17 Please let me **d** a little water
24:18 So she said, "**D**, my lord."
24:18 to her hand, and gave him a **d**.
24:19 she had finished giving him a **d**,
24:43 water from your pitcher to **d**,
24:44 to me, "**D**, and I will draw
24:45 I said to her, 'Please let me **d**.
24:46 and said, '**D**, and I will
24:46 and I will give your camels a **d**
24:46 and she gave the camels a **d**
30:38 where the flocks came to **d**,
30:38 conceive when they came to **d**.
35:14 and he poured a **d** offering on
Ex 7:18 the Egyptians will loathe to **d**
7:21 and the Egyptians could not **d**
7:24 around the river for water to **d**,
7:24 because they could not **d** the
15:23 they could not **d** the waters of
15:24 saying, "What shall we **d**?
17: 1 no water for the people to **d**.
17: 2 "Give us water, that we may **d**.
17: 6 of it, that the people may **d**.
29:40 of a hin of wine as a **d**
29:41 it the grain offering and the **d**
30: 9 nor shall you pour a **d** offering
32: 6 people sat down to eat and **d**,
32:20 made the children of Israel **d**
Lev 10: 9 Do not **d** wine or intoxicating
10: 9 drink wine or intoxicating **d**,
11:34 and any **d** that may be drunk
23:13 and its **d** offering shall be
23:18 grain offering and their **d**
23:37 a sacrifice and **d** offerings,
Num 5:24 And he shall make the woman **d**
5:26 and afterward make the woman **d**
5:27 When he has made her **d** the
6: 3 from wine and similar **d**;
6: 3 he shall **d** neither vinegar made
6: 3 vinegar made from similar **d**;
6: 3 neither shall he **d** any grape
6:15 grain offering with their **d**
6:17 its grain offering and its **d**
6:20 After that the Nazirite may **d**
15: 5 of a HIN of wine as a **d**
15: 7 and as a **d** offering you shall
15:10 and you shall bring as the **d**
15:24 its grain offering and its **d**
20: 5 nor is there any water to **d**.
20: 8 and give **d** to the congregation
20:17 nor will we **d** water from wells;
20:19 and if I or my livestock **d** any
21:22 we will not **d** water from wells.
28: 7 And its **d** offering shall be
28: 7 you shall pour out the **d** to
28: 8 grain offering and its **d**
28: 9 with its **d** offering—
28:10 burnt offering with its **d**
28:14 Their **d** offering shall be half a
28:15 burnt offering and its **d**
28:24 burnt offering and its **d**
28:31 present them with their **d**
29: 6 and their **d** offerings,
29:11 and their **d** offerings.
29:16 and its **d** offering.
29:18 grain offering and their **d**
29:19 and their **d** offerings.
29:21 grain offering and their **d**
29:22 and its **d** offering.
29:24 grain offering and their **d**
29:25 and its **d** offering.
29:27 grain offering and their **d**
29:28 and its **d** offering.
29:30 grain offering and their **d**
29:31 and its **d** offering.
29:33 grain offering and their **d**
29:34 and its **d** offering.
29:37 grain offering and their **d**
29:38 and its **d** offering.
29:39 as your **d** offerings and your
33:14 no water for the people to **d**.
Deut 2: 6 them with money, that you may **d**.
2:28 water for money, that I may **d**;
14:26 or sheep, for wine or similar **d**,
28:39 but you shall neither **d** of the
29: 6 you drunk wine or similar **d**,
32:38 And drank the wine of their **d**
Judg 4:19 give me a little water to **d**,
4:19 a jug of milk, gave him a **d**,
7: 5 who gets down on his knees to **d**.
7: 6 got down on their knees to **d**
13: 4 please be careful not to **d** wine
13: 4 not to drink wine or similar **d**,
13: 7 Now **d** no wine or similar
13: 7 Now drink no wine or similar **d**,
13:14 nor may she **d** wine or similar
13:14 she drink wine or similar **d**,
Ruth 2: 9 go to the vessels and **d** from
1 Sam 1:15 neither wine nor intoxicating **d**,
30:11 and they let him **d** water.
2 Sam 11:11 go to my house to eat and **d**,
16: 2 faint in the wilderness to **d**.
19:35 taste what I eat or what I **d**?
23:15 that someone would give me a **d**
23:16 Nevertheless he would not **d** it,
23:17 Therefore he would not **d** it.
1 Ki 13: 8 nor would I eat bread nor **d**
13: 9 nor **d** water, nor return by the
13:16 neither can I eat bread nor **d**
13:17 You shall not eat bread nor **d**
13:18 that he may eat bread and **d**
13:22 Eat no bread and **d** no water,"
17: 4 it will be that you shall **d**
17:10 water in a cup, that I may **d**.
18:41 to Ahab, "Go up, eat and **d**;
18:42 So Ahab went up to eat and **d**.
2 Ki 3:17 cattle, and your animals may **d**.
6:22 that they may eat and **d** and go
16:13 and he poured his **d** offering
16:15 and their **d** offerings;
18:27 who will eat and **d** their own
18:31 and every one of you **d** the
1 Chr 11:17 that someone would give me a **d**
11:18 Nevertheless David would not **d**
11:19 Shall I **d** the blood of
11:19 Therefore he would not **d** it.
29:21 with their **d** offerings,
2 Chr 28:15 sandals, gave them food and **d**,
29:35 peace offerings and with the **d**
Ezra 3: 7 and the carpenters, and food, **d**,
7:17 grain offerings and their **d**
Neh 8:10 **d** the sweet, and send portions
8:12 went their way to eat and **d**,
Esth 3:15 king and Haman sat down to **d**,
4:16 neither eat nor **d** for three
Job 1: 4 three sisters to eat and **d**
21:20 And let him **d** of the wrath of
22: 7 not given the weary water to **d**,
Ps 16: 4 Their **d** offerings of blood I
36: 8 And You give them **d** from the
50:13 Or **d** the blood of goats?
60: 3 You have made us **d** the wine of
69:21 they gave me vinegar to **d**.
75: 8 Drain and **d** down.
78:15 And gave them **d** in abundance
78:44 streams, that they could not **d**.
80: 5 And given them tears to **d** in
102: 9 And mingled my **d** with weeping,
104:11 They give **d** to every beast of
110: 7 He shall **d** of the brook by the
Prov 4:17 And **d** the wine of violence.
5:15 **D** water from your own cistern,
9: 5 eat of my bread And **d** of the
20: 1 Strong **d** is a brawler,
23: 7 Eat and **d**!" he says to you,
23:35 that I may seek another **d**?
25:21 is thirsty, give him water to **d**;
31: 4 It is not for kings to **d**
31: 4 Nor for princes intoxicating **d**;
31: 5 Lest they **d** and forget the law,
31: 6 Give strong **d** to him who is
31: 7 Let him **d** and forget his
Eccl 2:24 than that he should eat and **d**,
3:13 every man should eat and **d** and
5:18 fitting for one to eat and **d**,
8:15 under the sun than to eat, **d**,
9: 7 And **d** your wine with a merry
Song 5: 1 Eat, O friends! **D**, yes,
5: 1 **d** deeply, O beloved ones!
8: 2 I would cause you to **d** of
Isa 5:11 they may follow intoxicating **d**;
5:22 for mixing intoxicating **d**,
21: 5 in the tower, Eat and **d**.
22:13 wine: "Let us eat and **d**,
24: 9 They shall not **d** wine with a
24: 9 Strong **d** is bitter to those
24: 9 drink is bitter to those who **d**
28: 7 And through intoxicating **d** are
28: 7 erred through intoxicating **d**,
28: 7 the way through intoxicating **d**;
29: 9 but not with intoxicating **d**.
32: 6 And he will cause the **d** of the
36:12 who will eat and **d** their own
36:16 and every one of you **d** the
43:20 To give **d** to My people,
51:22 You shall no longer **d** it.
56:12 ourselves with intoxicating **d**;
57: 6 to them you have poured a **d**
60:16 You shall **d** the milk of the
62: 8 of the foreigner shall not **d**
62: 9 brought it together shall **d** it
65:11 And who furnish a **d** offering
65:13 Behold, My servants shall **d**,
66:11 That you may **d** deeply and be
Jer 2:18 To **d** the waters of Sihor?
2:18 To **d** the waters of the River?
7:18 and they pour out **d** offerings
8:14 given us water of gall to **d**,
9:15 give them water of gall to **d**.
16: 7 the cup of consolation to **d**
16: 8 to sit with them, to eat and **d**.
19:13 and poured out **d** offerings to
22:15 Did not your father eat and **d**,
23:15 And make them **d** the water of
25:15 I send you, to **d** it.
25:16 And they will **d** and stagger and
25:17 and made all the nations **d**,
25:26 the king of Sheshach shall **d**
25:27 '**D**, be drunk, and vomit!
25:28 the cup from your hand to **d**,
25:28 You shall certainly **d**!
32:29 to Baal and poured out **d**
35: 2 and give them wine to **d**.
35: 5 said to them, "**D** wine."
35: 6 We will **d** no wine, for Jonadab
35: 6 You shall **d** no wine, you nor
35: 8 to **d** no wine all our days,
35:14 not to **d** wine, are performed;
35:14 for to this day they **d** none,
44:17 queen of heaven and pour out **d**
44:18 of heaven and pouring out **d**
44:19 of heaven and poured out **d**
44:19 and pour out **d** offerings to her
44:25 queen of heaven and pour out **d**
49:12 whose judgment was not to **d**
49:12 but you shall surely **d** of it.
Lam 3:15 He has made me **d** wormwood.
5: 4 We pay for the water we **d**,
Ezek 4:11 You shall also **d** water by
4:11 from time to time you shall **d**.
4:16 and shall **d** water by measure
12:18 and **d** your water with trembling
12:19 and **d** their water with dread,
20:28 aroma and poured out their **d**
23:32 You shall **d** of your sister's
23:34 You shall **d** and drain it,
25: 4 and they shall **d** your milk.
31:16 all that **d** water, were
34:19 and they **d** what you have fouled
39:17 That you may eat flesh and **d**
39:18 **D** the blood of the princes of
39:19 And **d** blood till you are
44:21 No priest shall **d** wine when he
45:17 and **d** offerings, at the feasts,
Dan 1:10 has appointed your food and **d**.
1:12 to eat and water to **d**.
1:16 the wine that they were to **d**,
5: 2 and his concubines might **d** from
Hos 2: 5 and my linen, My oil and my **d**.
4:18 Their **d** is rebellion,
Joel 1: 9 The grain offering and the **d**
1:13 the grain offering and the **d**
2:14 A grain offering and a **d**
3: 3 girl for wine, that they may **d**.
Am 2: 8 And **d** the wine of the
2:12 gave the Nazirites wine to **d**,
4: 1 'Bring wine, let us **d**!"
4: 8 wandered to another city to **d**
5:11 But you shall not **d** wine from
6: 6 Who **d** wine from bowls,
9:14 shall plant vineyards and **d**
Ob 16 So shall all the nations **d**
16 Yes, they shall **d**,
Jon 3: 7 let them eat, or **d** water.
Mic 2:11 prophesy to you of wine and **d**,
6:15 but not **d** wine.
Hab 2:15 Woe to him who gives **d** to his
2:16 You also—**d**! And be exposed
Zeph 1:13 but not **d** their wine."
Hag 1: 6 You **d**, but you are not
1: 6 but you are not filled with **d**;
Zech 7: 6 'When you eat and when you **d**,
7: 6 do you not eat and **d** for
9:15 They shall **d** and roar as if
Mt 6:25 you will eat or what you will **d**;
6:31 we eat?' or 'What shall we **d**?
20:22 Are you able to **d** the cup that

20:22 the cup that I am about to **d**,
20:23 You will indeed **d** My cup, and be
24:49 and to eat and **d** with the
25:35 I was thirsty and you gave Me **d**;
25:37 or thirsty and give You **d**?
25:42 thirsty and you gave Me no **d**;
26:27 ***D*** from it, all of you.
26:29 I will not **d** of this fruit of
26:29 now on until that day when I **d**
26:42 pass away from Me unless I **d**
27:34 wine mingled with gall to **d**.
27:34 had tasted it, He would not **d**.
27:48 and offered it to Him to **d**.
Mk 9:41 gives you a cup of water to **d**
10:38 Are you able to **d** the cup that
10:38 able to drink the cup that I **d**,
10:39 You will indeed **d** the cup that I
10:39 indeed drink the cup that I **d**,
14:25 I will no longer **d** of the fruit
14:25 vine until that day when I **d**
15:23 wine mingled with myrrh to **d**,
15:36 and offered it to Him to **d**,
16:18 and if they **d** anything deadly,
Lk 1:15 and shall **d** neither wine nor
1:15 drink neither wine nor strong **d**.
5:30 Why do You eat and **d** with tax
5:33 Pharisees, but Yours eat and **d**?
12:19 take your ease; eat, **d**,
12:29 should eat or what you should **d**,
12:45 and to eat and **d** and be drunk,
17: 8 afterward you will eat and **d**'?
22:18 I will not **d** of the fruit of
22:30 that you may eat and **d** at My
Jn 4: 7 said to her, "Give Me a **d**.
4: 9 ask a **d** from me, a Samaritan
4:10 who says to you, 'Give Me a **d**,
6:53 flesh of the Son of Man and **d**
6:55 and My blood is **d** indeed.
7:37 let him come to Me and **d**.
18:11 Shall I not **d** the cup which My
Acts 23:12 they would neither eat nor **d**
23:21 they will neither eat nor **d**
Rom 12:20 is thirsty, give him a **d**;
14:21 good neither to eat meat nor **d**
1 Cor 9: 4 we have no right to eat and **d**?
9: 7 tends a flock and does not **d**
10: 4 all drank the same spiritual **d**.
10: 7 sat down to eat and **d**,
10:21 You cannot **d** the cup of the Lord
10:31 Therefore, whether you eat or **d**,
11:22 not have houses to eat and **d**
11:25 as often as you **d** it, in
11:26 as you eat this bread and **d**
11:28 let him eat of the bread and **d**
12:13 and have all been made to **d** into
15:32 'Let us eat and **d**,
Phil 2:17 I am being poured out as a **d**
Col 2:16 one judge you in food or in **d**,
1 Tim 5:23 No longer **d** only water, but use
2 Tim 4: 6 already being poured out as a **d**
Rev 14: 8 she has made all nations **d** of
14:10 he himself shall also **d** of the
16: 6 You have given them blood to **d**.

DRINKERS (1/1) DRINK

Joel 1: 5 And wail, all you **d** of wine,

DRINKING (25/25) DRINK

Gen 24:19 until they have finished **d**.
24:22 when the camels had finished **d**,
Ruth 3: 3 he has finished eating and **d**.
1 Sam 1: 9 they had finished eating and **d**
30:16 eating and **d** and dancing,
1 Ki 1:25 They are eating and **d** before
4:20 eating and **d** and rejoicing.
10:21 All King Solomon's **d** vessels
16: 9 him as he was in Tirzah **d**
20:12 as he and the kings were **d** at
1 Chr 12:39 David three days, eating and **d**,
2 Chr 9:20 All King Solomon's **d** vessels
Esth 1: 8 the **d** was not compulsory;
Job 1:13 daughters were eating and **d**
1:18 daughters were eating and **d**
Isa 5:22 Woe to men mighty at **d** wine,
22:13 Eating meat and **d** wine: "Let
Mt 11:18 John came neither eating nor **d**,
11:19 Son of Man came eating and **d**,
24:38 flood, they were eating and **d**,
Lk 7:33 came neither eating bread nor **d**
7:34 of Man has come eating and **d**,
10: 7 eating and **d** such things as
Rom 14:17 of God is not eating and **d**,
1 Pe 4: 3 **d** parties, and abominable

DRINKS (21/20) DRINK

Gen 44: 5 the one from which my lord **d**,
Num 23:24 And **d** the blood of the
Deut 11:11 which **d** water from the rain of
Esth 1: 7 And they served **d** in golden
Job 6: 4 My spirit **d** in their poison;
15:16 Who **d** iniquity like water!
34: 7 Who **d** scorn like water,
Prov 26: 6 Cuts off his own feet and **d**
Isa 29: 8 man dreams, And look—he **d**;
44:12 He **d** no water and is faint.
Ezek 31:14 that no tree which **d** water may
Mk 2:16 is it that He eats and **d**
Jn 4:13 Whoever **d** of this water will
4:14 but whoever **d** of the water that
6:54 Whoever eats My flesh and **d** My
6:56 He who eats My flesh and **d** My
1 Cor 11:27 whoever eats this bread or **d**
11:29 For he who eats and **d** in an
11:29 an unworthy manner eats and **d**
Heb 6: 7 For the earth which **d** in the
9:10 only with foods and **d**,

DRIP (6/6) DRIPPED, DRIPPING

Ps 65:11 And Your paths **d** with
Prov 5: 3 the lips of an immoral woman **d**
Song 4:11 ***D*** as the honeycomb; Honey and
Joel 3:18 That the mountains shall **d**
Am 9:13 The mountains shall **d** with
Zech 4:12 two olive branches that **d**

DRIPPED (1/1) DRIP

Song 5: 5 And my hands **d** with myrrh,

DRIPPING (4/4) DRIP

1 Sam 14:26 woods, there was the honey, **d**;
Prov 19:13 of a wife are a continual **d**.
27:15 A continual **d** on a very rainy
Song 5:13 ***D*** liquid myrrh.

DRIVE (59/59) DRIVEN, DRIVER, DRIVES, DRIVING, DROVE, WELL-DRIVEN

Gen 33:13 And if the men should **d** them
Ex 6: 1 with a strong hand he will **d**
11: 1 he will surely **d** you out of
23:28 which shall **d** out the Hivite,
23:29 I will not **d** them out from
23:30 Little by little I will **d** them
23:31 and you shall **d** them out before
33: 2 and I will **d** out the Canaanite
Num 22: 6 be able to defeat them and **d**
22:11 be able to overpower them and **d**
33:52 then you shall **d** out all the
33:55 But if you do not **d** out the
Deut 4:27 nations where the LORD will **d**
7:22 And the LORD your God will **d**
9: 3 so you shall **d** them out and
11:23 then the LORD will **d** out all
28:37 nations where the LORD will **d**
Josh 3:10 that He will without fail **d**
13: 6 them I will **d** out from before
13:13 children of Israel did not **d**
14:12 and I shall be able to **d** them
15:63 children of Judah could not **d**
16:10 And they did not **d** out the
17:12 of Manasseh could not **d** out
17:13 but did not utterly **d** them out.
17:18 for you shall **d** out the
23: 5 them from before you and **d**
23:13 your God will no longer **d** out
Judg 1:19 but they could not **d** out the
1:21 children of Benjamin did not **d**
1:27 Manasseh did not **d** out the
1:28 but did not completely **d** them
1:29 Nor did Ephraim **d** out the
1:30 Nor did Zebulun **d** out the
1:31 Nor did Asher **d** out the
1:32 for they did not **d** them out.
1:33 Nor did Naphtali **d** out the
2: 3 I will not **d** them out before
2:21 I also will no longer **d** out
2 Ki 4:24 '***D***, and go forward;
Job 18:11 And **d** him to his feet.
24: 3 They **d** away the donkey of the
Ps 36:11 not the hand of the wicked **d**
68: 2 So **d** them away; As wax melts
Prov 22:15 The rod of correction will **d**
Isa 22:19 So I will **d** you out of your
Jer 19: 9 who seek their lives shall **d**
24: 9 in all places where I shall **d**
27:10 and I will **d** you out, and you
27:15 that I may **d** you out, and that
Ezek 4:13 where I will **d** them."
Dan 4:25 They shall **d** you from men, your
4:32 And they shall **d** you from men,
Hos 9:15 evil of their deeds I will **d**
Joel 2:20 And will **d** him away into a
Zeph 2: 4 They shall **d** out Ashdod at
Mk 11:15 into the temple and began to **d**
Lk 19:45 into the temple and began to **d**
Acts 27:15 into the wind, we let her **d**.

DRIVEN (47/47) DRIVE

Gen 4:14 Surely You have **d** me out this
Ex 10:11 And they were **d** out from
12:39 because they were **d** out of
22:10 or **d** away, no one seeing it,
Num 32:21 the LORD until He has **d** out
Deut 4:19 you feel **d** to worship them and
28:34 So you shall be **d** mad because of
30: 4 If any of you are **d** out to the
Josh 23: 9 For the LORD has **d** out from
1 Sam 14:31 Now they had **d** back the
26:19 for they have **d** me out this day
30:20 the flocks and herds they had **d**
Job 6:13 And is success **d** from me?
13:25 Will You frighten a leaf **d** to
18:18 He is **d** from light into
30: 5 They were **d** out from among
Ps 40:14 Let them be **d** backward and
68: 2 As smoke is **d** away, So drive
Isa 8:22 and they will be **d** into
19: 7 be **d** away, and be no more.
41: 2 As **d** stubble to his bow?
Jer 8: 3 all the places where I have **d**
16:15 all the lands where He had **d**
23: 2 **d** them away, and not attended
23: 3 of all countries where I have **d**
23: 8 all the countries where I had **d**
23:12 the darkness they shall be **d**
29:14 all the places where I have **d**
29:18 all the nations where I have **d**
32:37 of all countries where I have **d**
40:12 places where they had been **d**,
43: 5 nations where they had been **d**—
46:28 the nations To which I have **d**
49: 5 You shall be **d** out, everyone
50:17 The lions have **d** him away.
Ezek 31:11 I have **d** it out for its
34: 4 nor brought back what was **d**
34:16 lost and bring back what was **d**
Dan 4:33 he was **d** from men and ate grass
5:21 Then he was **d** from the sons of
9: 7 countries to which You have **d**
Zeph 3:19 And gather those who were **d**
Lk 8:29 he broke the bonds and was **d**
Acts 27:17 they struck sail and so were **d**.
27:27 as we were **d** up and down in the
Jas 1: 6 is like a wave of the sea **d**
3: 4 they are so large and are **d** by

DRIVER (3/3) DRIVE

1 Ki 22:34 So he said to the **d** of his
2 Chr 18:33 So he said to the **d** of his
Job 39: 7 not heed the shouts of the **d**.

DRIVES (7/7) DRIVE

Deut 9: 5 that the LORD your God **d**
18:12 the LORD your God **d** them out
30: 1 where the LORD your God **d** you,
2 Ki 9:20 for he **d** furiously!"
Ps 1: 4 like the chaff which the wind **d**
Prov 16:26 For his hungry mouth **d** him
Isa 44:25 And **d** diviners mad;

DRIVING (9/8) DRIVE

Ex 34:11 I am **d** out from before you the
Deut 4:38 **d** out from before you nations
9: 4 nations that the LORD is **d**
Judg 2:23 without **d** them out immediately;
2 Ki 9:20 and the **d** is like the driving
9:20 is like the **d** of Jehu
1 Chr 17:21 by **d** out nations from before
Prov 28: 3 the poor Is like a **d** rain
Acts 26:24 Much learning is **d** you mad!"

DROMEDARIES (1/1) DROMEDARY

Isa 60: 6 The **d** of Midian and Ephah;

DROMEDARY (1/1) DROMEDARIES

Jer 2:23 You are a swift **d** breaking

DROP (7/7) DROPPED, DROPPINGS, DROPS

Deut 28:40 for your olives shall **d** off.
32: 2 Let my teaching **d** as the rain,
33:28 His heavens shall also **d** dew.
Job 36:28 Which the clouds **d** down And
Ps 65:12 They **d** on the pastures of the
Prov 3:20 And clouds **d** down the dew.
Isa 40:15 the nations are as a **d** in a

DROPPED (3/3) DROP

Judg 9:53 But a certain woman **d** an upper
Ps 68: 8 The heavens also **d** rain at
Acts 27:29 they **d** four anchors from the

DROPPINGS (1/1) DROP

2 Ki 6:25 one-fourth of a kab of dove **d**

DROPS (5/5) DROP

Job 36:27 For He draws up **d** of water,
38:28 Or who has begotten the **d** of
Song 5: 2 My locks with the **d** of the
Lk 22:44 His sweat became like great **d**
Rev 6:13 as a fig tree **d** its late figs

DROPSY (1/1)

Lk 14: 2 man before Him who had **d**.

DROSS (8/7)

Ps 119:119 the wicked of the earth like **d**;
Prov 25: 4 Take away the **d** from silver,
26:23 covered with silver **d**.
Isa 1:22 Your silver has become **d**,
1:25 thoroughly purge away your **d**,
Ezek 22:18 house of Israel has become **d**
22:18 they have become **d** from silver.
22:19 'Because you have all become **d**,

DROUGHT (9/9) DROUGHTS

Gen 31:40 In the day the **d** consumed
Job 24:19 As **d** and heat consume the snow

Ps 32: 4 vitality was turned into the **d**
Isa 58:11 And satisfy your soul in **d**,
Jer 2: 6 Through a land of **d** and the
17: 8 not be anxious in the year of **d**,
50:38 A **d** is against her waters, and
Hos 13: 5 In the land of great **d**.
Hag 1:11 For I called for a **d** on the land

DROUGHTS (1/1) DROUGHT

Jer 14: 1 to Jeremiah concerning the **d**.

DROVE (37/37) DRIVE, DROVES

Gen 3:24 So He **d** out the man; and He
15:11 Abram **d** them away.
32:16 every **d** by itself, and said to
Ex 2:17 Then the shepherds came and **d**
14:25 so that they **d** them with
Num 14:45 and **d** them back as far as
21:32 they took its villages and **d**
Deut 1:44 and **d** you back from Seir to
Josh 15:14 Caleb **d** out the three sons of
24:12 the hornet before you which **d**
24:18 And the LORD **d** out from before
Judg 1:19 And they **d** out the
4:21 and went softly to him and **d**
6: 9 and **d** them out before you and
9:41 and Zebul **d** out Gaal and his
11: 2 they **d** Jephthah out, and said
1 Sam 7:11 and **d** them back as far as below
19:10 and he **d** the spear into the
2 Sam 5:25 and he **d** back the Philistines
6: 3 **d** the new cart.
11:23 then we **d** them back as far as
2 Ki 16: 6 and **d** the men of Judah from
17:21 Then Jeroboam **d** Israel from
1 Chr 8:13 who **d** out the inhabitants of
13: 7 and Uzza and Ahio **d** the cart.
14:16 and they **d** back the army of the
2 Chr 20: 7 who **d** out the inhabitants of
Neh 13:28 therefore I **d** him from me.
Ps 34: who **d** him away, and he
44: 2 You **d** out the nations with Your
78:55 He also **d** out the nations
Jer 46:15 Because the LORD **d** them
Mt 21:12 into the temple of God and **d**
Mk 1:12 Immediately the Spirit **d** Him
Jn 2:15 He **d** them all out of the
Acts 7:45 whom God **d** out before the face
18:16 And he **d** them from the judgment

DROVES (2/2) DROVE

Gen 32:16 distance between successive **d**.
32:19 and all who followed the **d**,

DROWN (2/2) DROWNED

Song 8: 7 Nor can the floods **d** it.
1 Tim 6: 9 and harmful lusts which **d** men

DROWNED (5/5) DROWN

Ex 15: 4 chosen captains also are **d** in
Mt 18: 6 and he were **d** in the depth of
Mk 5:13 and **d** in the sea.
Lk 8:33 steep place into the lake and **d**.
Heb 11:29 attempting to do so, were **d**.

DROWSINESS (1/1)

Prov 23:21 And **d** will clothe a man with

DRUNK (48/46) DRINK, DRUNKARD, DRUNKEN

Gen 9:21 he drank of the wine and was **d**,
Lev 11:34 and any drink that may be **d**
Deut 29: 6 nor have you **d** wine or similar
32:42 I will make My arrows **d** with
Ruth 3: 7 And after Boaz had eaten and **d**,
1 Sam 1:13 Therefore Eli thought she was **d**.
1:14 'How long will you be **d**?
1:15 I have **d** neither wine nor
25:36 within him, for he was very **d**;
30:12 for he had eaten no bread nor **d**
2 Sam 11:13 before him; and he made him **d**.
1 Ki 13:23 eaten bread and after he had **d**,
16: 9 in Tirzah drinking himself **d**
20:16 helping him were getting **d** at
2 Ki 19:24 I have dug and **d** strange water,
Song 5: 1 I have **d** my wine with my milk.
Isa 29: 9 They are **d**, but not with
37:25 I have dug and **d** water,
49:26 And they shall be **d** with their
51:17 You who have **d** at the hand of
51:17 You have **d** the dregs of the
51:21 And **d** but not with wine.
63: 6 Made them **d** in My fury,
Jer 25:27 'Drink, be **d**, and vomit!
46:10 shall be satiated and made **d**
48:26 Make him **d**, Because he
49:12 of the cup have assuredly **d**.
51: 7 That made all the earth **d**.
51:39 I will make them **d**,
51:57 And I will make **d** Her princes
Lam 4:21 to you And you shall become **d**
Ezek 34:18 and to have **d** of the clear
39:19 And drink blood till you are **d**,
Dan 5:23 have **d** wine from them.
Nah 3:11 You also will be **d**;
Hab 2:15 bottle, Even to make him **d**,
Lk 5:39 having **d** old wine, immediately
12:45 and to eat and drink and be **d**,
17: 8 me till I have eaten and **d**,
Jn 2:10 when the guests have well **d**,
Acts 2:15 "For these are not **d**,
1 Cor 11:21 one is hungry and another is **d**.
Eph 5:18 And do not be **d** with wine,
1 Th 5: 7 and those who get **d** are drunk
5: 7 and those who get drunk are **d**
Rev 17: 2 of the earth were made **d** with
17: 6 **d** with the blood of the saints
18: 3 For all the nations have **d** of

DRUNKARD (6/6) DRUNK, DRUNKARDS

Deut 21:20 he is a glutton and a **d**.'
29:19 as though the **d** could be
Prov 23:21 For the **d** and the glutton will
26: 9 goes into the hand of a **d** Is
Isa 24:20 shall reel to and fro like a **d**,
1 Cor 5:11 idolater, or a reviler, or a **d**,

DRUNKARDS (7/7) DRUNKARD

Ps 69:12 And I am the song of the **d**.
Isa 28: 1 to the **d** of Ephraim, Whose
28: 3 the **d** of Ephraim, Will be
Joel 1: 5 Awake, you **d**, and weep;
Nah 1:10 And while drunken like **d**,
Mt 24:49 and to eat and drink with the **d**,
1 Cor 6:10 thieves, nor covetous, nor **d**,

DRUNKEN (5/5) DRUNK, DRUNKENNESS

Job 12:25 stagger like a **d** man.
Ps 107:27 and stagger like a **d** man,
Isa 19:14 As a **d** man staggers in his
Jer 23: 9 I am like a **d** man, And like a
Nah 1:10 And while **d** like drunkards,

DRUNKENNESS (8/8) DRUNKEN

Eccl 10:17 For strength and not for **d**!
Jer 13:13 of Jerusalem—with **d**!
Ezek 23:33 You will be filled with **d** and
Zech 12: 2 will make Jerusalem a cup of **d**
Lk 21:34 weighed down with carousing, **d**,
Rom 13:13 the day, not in revelry and **d**,
Gal 5:21 envy, murders, **d**,
1 Pe 4: 3 we walked in lewdness, lusts, **d**,

DRUSILLA (1/1)

Acts 24:24 when Felix came with his wife ***D***,

DRY (75/70) DRIED, DRIES, DRYSHOD

Gen 1: 9 and let the **d** land appear";
1:10 And God called the **d** land
7:22 all that was on the **d** land,
8:13 the surface of the ground was **d**.
Ex 4: 9 and pour it on the **d** land.
4: 9 become blood on the **d** land."
14:16 shall go on **d** ground
14:21 and made the sea into **d** land,
14:22 the sea on the **d** ground,
14:29 Israel had walked on **d** land
15:19 children of Israel went on **d**
Lev 7:10 whether mixed with oil, or **d**,
Josh 3:17 stood firm on **d** ground
3:17 crossed over on **d** ground,
4:18 feet touched the **d** land,
4:22 over this Jordan on **d** land';
9: 5 bread of their provision was **d**
9:12 it is **d** and moldy.
Judg 6:37 and it is **d** on all the
6:39 let it now be **d** only on the
6:40 It was **d** on the fleece only,
1 Ki 17:14 nor shall the jar of oil run **d**,
17:16 nor did the jar of oil run **d**,
2 Ki 2: 8 crossed over on **d** ground.
Neh 9:11 of the sea on the **d** land;
Job 12:15 the waters, they **d** up;
13:25 And will You pursue **d** stubble?
15:30 The flame will **d** out his
24:24 They **d** out like the heads of
Ps 63: 1 In a **d** and thirsty land
66: 6 He turned the sea into **d** land;
68: 6 rebellious dwell in a **d** land.
69: 3 with my crying; My throat is **d**;
95: 5 His hands formed the **d** land.
105:41 It ran in the **d** places like a
107:33 watersprings into **d** ground;
107:35 And **d** land into watersprings.
Prov 17: 1 Better is a **d** morsel with
Isa 25: 5 As heat in a **d** place;
32: 2 rivers of water in a **d** place,
41:18 And the **d** land springs of
42:15 And **d** up all their vegetation;
42:15 And I will **d** up the pools.
44: 3 And floods on the **d** ground; I
44:27 says to the deep, 'Be **d**!
44:27 And I will **d** up your rivers';
50: 2 Indeed with My rebuke I **d** up
53: 2 And as a root out of **d** ground.
56: 3 'Here I am, a **d** tree."
Jer 4:11 A **d** wind of the desolate heights
50:12 A **d** land and a desert.
51:36 I will **d** up her sea and make
51:36 her sea and make her springs **d**.
51:43 A **d** land and a wilderness,
Lam 4: 8 It has become as **d** as wood.
Ezek 17:24 and made the **d** tree flourish;
19:13 In a **d** and thirsty land.
20:47 and every **d** tree in you;
30:12 I will make the rivers **d**,
37: 2 and indeed they were very **d**.
37: 4 O **d** bones, hear the word of the
37:11 indeed say, 'Our bones are **d**,
Hos 2: 3 And set her like a **d** land,
9:14 womb And **d** breasts!
13:15 Then his spring shall become **d**,
Jon 1: 9 the sea and the **d** land."
2:10 vomited Jonah onto **d** land.
Nah 1: 4 rebukes the sea and makes it **d**,
Zeph 2:13 As **d** as the wilderness.
Hag 2: 6 the sea and **d** land;
Zech 10:11 depths of the River shall **d** up.
Mt 12:43 he goes through **d** places,
Lk 11:24 he goes through **d** places,
23:31 what will be done in the **d**?
Heb 11:29 the Red Sea as by **d** land,

DRYSHOD (1/1) DRY

Isa 11:15 And make men cross over **d**.

DUE (38/35)

Lev 10:13 because it is your **d** and your
10:13 is your due and your sons' **d**,
10:14 for they are your **d** and your
10:14 are your due and your sons' **d**,
27:18 shall reckon to him the money **d**
Num 18:29 up every heave offering **d** to
Deut 18: 3 this shall be the priest's **d**
24:17 shall not pervert justice **d**
27:19 one who perverts the justice **d**
32:35 Their foot shall slip in **d**
1 Sam 4:19 **d** to be delivered; and when
1 Chr 16:29 to the LORD the glory **d** His
Job 36:17 are filled with the judgment **d**
Ps 29: 2 unto the LORD the glory **d** to
96: 8 to the LORD the glory **d** His
104:27 may give them their food in **d**
145:15 You give them their food in **d**
Prov 3:27 good from those to whom it is **d**,
15:23 And a word spoken in **d**
Jer 10: 7 For this is Your rightful **d**.
Lam 3:35 To turn aside the justice **d** a
Dan 3:12 have not paid **d** regard to you.
6:13 does not show **d** regard for you,
Mt 18:34 he should pay all that was **d**
24:45 to give them food in **d** season?
Lk 12:42 their portion of food in **d**
23:41 for we receive the **d** reward of
Rom 1:27 of their error which was **d**.
5: 6 in **d** time Christ died for the
13: 7 Render therefore to all their **d**:
13: 7 taxes to whom taxes are **d**,
1 Cor 7: 3 to his wife the affection **d**
15: 8 as by one born out of **d** time.
Gal 6: 9 for in **d** season we shall reap
1 Tim 2: 6 to be testified in **d** time,
Titus 1: 3 but has in **d** time manifested His
1 Pe 5: 6 that He may exalt you in **d**
Rev 16: 6 For it is their just **d**."

DUG (34/33) DIG

Gen 21:30 may be my witness that I have **d**
26:15 his father's servants had **d** in
26:18 And Isaac **d** again the wells of
26:18 of water which they had **d** in
26:19 Also Isaac's servants **d** in the
26:21 Then they **d** another well, and
26:22 And he moved from there and **d**
26:25 and there Isaac's servants **d** a
26:32 about the well which they had **d**,
50: 5 in my grave which I **d** for
Ex 7:24 So all the Egyptians **d** all
Num 21:18 ***D*** by the nation's nobles,
2 Ki 19:24 I have **d** and drunk strange
2 Chr 26:10 He **d** many wells, for he had
Neh 9:25 all goods, Cisterns already **d**,
Ps 7:15 He made a pit and **d** it out,
35: 7 Which they have **d** without
57: 6 They have **d** a pit before me;
94:13 Until the pit is **d** for the
119:85 The proud have **d** pits for me,
Isa 5: 2 He **d** it up and cleared out its
5: 6 It shall not be pruned or **d**,
7:25 to any hill which could be **d**
37:25 I have **d** and drunk water,
51: 1 the pit from which you were **d**.
Jer 13: 7 I went to the Euphrates and **d**,
18:20 For they have **d** a pit for my
18:22 For they have **d** a pit to take
Ezek 8: 8 and when I **d** into the wall,
12: 7 and at evening I **d** through the
Mt 21:33 **d** a winepress in it and built a
25:18 had received one went and **d** in
Mk 12: 1 **d** a place for the wine vat
Lk 6:48 who **d** deep and laid the

DUKE, DUKES (KJV) See CHIEF, CHIEFS, PRINCES

DULCIMER (KJV) See LYRE

DULL (6/6) DULL-HEARTED

Lev 13:39 skin of the body are **d** white,
Eccl 10:10 If the ax is **d**, And one does
Isa 6:10 the heart of this people **d**,
Mt 13:15 this people have grown **d**.
Acts 28:27 this people have grown **d**.
Heb 5:11 since you have become **d** of

DULL-HEARTED (4/4) DULL

Jer 10: 8 But they are altogether **d** and
10:14 Everyone is **d**, without
10:21 the shepherds have become **d**,
51:17 Everyone is **d**, without

DUMAH (4/4)

Gen 25:14 Mishma, ***D***, Massa,
Josh 15:52 Arab, ***D***, Eshean,
1 Chr 1:30 Mishma, ***D***, Massa, Hadad,
Isa 21:11 The burden against ***D***.

DUMB (5/5)

Isa 35: 6 And the tongue of the **d** sing.
56:10 They are all **d** dogs,
Mk 9:25 Deaf and **d** spirit, I command
1 Cor 12: 2 carried away to these **d** idols,
2 Pe 2:16 a **d** donkey speaking with a

DUMP (1/1)

2 Ki 10:27 of Baal and made it a refuse **d**

DUNG (1/1)

Ezek 4:15 I am giving you cow **d** instead

DUNGEON (11/10)

Gen 40:15 they should put me into the **d**.
41:14 him quickly out of the **d**;
Ex 12:29 the captive who was in the **d**,
Jer 37:16 When Jeremiah entered the **d** and
38: 6 and cast him into the **d** of
38: 6 And in the **d** there was no
38: 7 they had put Jeremiah in the **d**.
38: 9 whom they have cast into the **d**,
38:10 the prophet out of the **d**
38:11 them down by ropes into the **d**
38:13 and lifted him out of the **d**.

DUNGHILL (1/1)

Lk 14:35 fit for the land nor for the **d**,

DURA (1/1)

Dan 3: 1 He set it up in the plain of ***D***,

DURETH (KJV) See ENDURES

DURING (19/19)

Gen 41:36 that the land may not perish **d**
Lev 15:20 Everything that she lies on **d**
20:18 If a man lies with a woman **d** her
Num 27:14 **d** the strife of the
Josh 3:15 overflows all its banks **d** the
Neh 8:14 should dwell in booths **d** the
12:22 ***D*** the reign of Darius the
13: 6 But **d** all this I was not in
Prov 20: 4 He will beg **d** harvest and
Ezek 4: 9 ***D*** the number of days that you
18: 6 Nor approached a woman **d** her
22:10 women who are set apart **d**
Zech 7: 5 the fifth and seventh months **d**
Mt 26: 5 Not **d** the feast, lest there be
Mk 14: 2 Not **d** the feast, lest there be
Jn 2:23 **d** the feast, many believed in
Acts 1: 3 being seen by them **d** forty days
7:42 animals and sacrifices **d**
12: 3 Now it was **d** the Days of

DURST (KJV) See DARE, DARED

DUST (114/107)

Gen 2: 7 LORD God formed man of the **d**
3:14 And you shall eat **d** All the
3:19 For **d** you are, And to dust
3:19 And to **d** you shall return."
13:16 make your descendants as the **d**
13:16 if a man could number the **d** of
18:27 I who am but **d** and ashes have
28:14 descendants shall be as the **d**
Ex 8:16 and strike the **d** of the land,
8:17 with his rod and struck the **d**
8:17 All the **d** of the land became
9: 9 And it will become fine **d** in all
Lev 14:41 and the **d** that they scrape off
17:13 its blood and cover it with **d**;
Num 5:17 and take some of the **d** that is
23:10 Who can count the **d** of Jacob,
Deut 9:21 until it was as fine as **d**;
9:21 and I threw its **d** into the
28:24 of your land to powder and **d**;
32:24 the poison of serpents of the **d**.
Josh 7: 6 and they put **d** on their heads.
1 Sam 2: 8 He raises the poor from the **d**
2 Sam 1: 2 with his clothes torn and **d** on
15:32 him with his robe torn and **d**
16:13 stones at him and kicked up **d**.
22:43 I beat them as fine as the **d**
1 Ki 16: 2 as I lifted you out of the **d**
18:38 wood and the stones and the **d**,
20:10 if enough **d** is left of Samaria
2 Ki 13: 7 them and made them like the **d**
23:12 and threw their **d** into the
2 Chr 1: 9 king over a people like the **d**
34: 4 and made **d** of them and
Neh 9: 1 and with **d** on their heads.
Job 2:12 tore his robe and sprinkled **d**
4:19 Whose foundation is in the **d**,
5: 6 does not come from the **d**,
7: 5 flesh is caked with worms and **d**,
7:21 now I will lie down in the **d**,
10: 9 And will You turn me into **d**
16:15 And laid my head in the **d**.
17:16 have rest together in the **d**?
20:11 will lie down with him in the **d**.
21:26 They lie down alike in the **d**,
22:24 you will lay your gold in the **d**,
27:16 he heaps up silver like **d**,
28: 6 And it contains gold **d**.
30:19 And I have become like **d** and
34:15 And man would return to **d**.
38:38 When the **d** hardens in clumps,
39:14 And warms them in the **d**;
40:13 Hide them in the **d** together,
42: 6 And repent in **d** and ashes."
Ps 7: 5 And lay my honor in the **d**.
18:42 I beat them as fine as the **d**
22:15 You have brought Me to the **d**
22:29 All those who go down to the **d**
30: 9 Will the **d** praise You?
44:25 our soul is bowed down to the **d**;
72: 9 His enemies will lick the **d**.
78:27 rained meat on them like the **d**,
83:13 make them like the whirling **d**,
102:14 And show favor to her **d**.
103:14 He remembers that we are **d**.
104:29 they die and return to their **d**.
113: 7 raises the poor out of the **d**,
119:25 My soul clings to the **d**;
Prov 8:26 Or the primeval **d** of the
Eccl 3:20 one place: all are from the **d**,
3:20 the dust, and all return to **d**.
12: 7 Then the **d** will return to the
Isa 2:10 the rock, and hide in the **d**,
5:24 blossom will ascend like **d**;
25:12 to the ground, down to the **d**.
26: 5 He brings it down to the **d**.
26:19 and sing, you who dwell in **d**;
27: 9 that are beaten to **d**,
29: 4 shall be low, out of the **d**;
29: 4 shall whisper out of the **d**.
29: 5 your foes Shall be like fine **d**,
34: 7 And their **d** saturated with
34: 9 And its **d** into brimstone;
40:12 a span And calculated the **d**
40:15 are counted as the small **d** on
41: 2 Who gave them as the **d** to
47: 1 "Come down and sit in the **d**,
49:23 And lick up the **d** of your
52: 2 Shake yourself from the **d**,
65:25 And **d** shall be the serpent's
Lam 2:10 They throw **d** on their heads
3:29 Let him put his mouth in the **d**—
Ezek 24: 7 the ground, To cover it with **d**.
26: 4 I will also scrape her **d** from
26:10 their **d** will cover you;
27:30 will cry bitterly and cast **d**
Dan 12: 2 of those who sleep in the **d** of
Am 2: 7 They pant after the **d** of the
Mic 1:10 Aphrah Roll yourself in the **d**.
7:17 They shall lick the **d** like a
Nah 1: 3 And the clouds are the **d** of
3:18 Your nobles rest in the **d**.
Zeph 1:17 shall be poured out like **d**,
Zech 9: 3 Heaped up silver like the **d**,
Mt 10:14 shake off the **d** from your feet.
Mk 6:11 shake off the **d** under your feet
Lk 9: 5 shake off the very **d** from your
10:11 The very **d** of your city which
Acts 13:51 But they shook off the **d** from
22:23 off their clothes and threw **d**
1 Cor 15:47 was of the earth, made of **d**;
15:48 As was the man of **d**,
15:48 are those who are made of **d**;
15:49 the image of the man of **d**,
Rev 18:19 They threw **d** on their heads and

DUTIES (15/14) DUTY

Ex 1:16 When you do the **d** of a midwife
Num 3:25 The **d** of the children of Gershon
4:28 And their **d** shall be under
8:26 the Levites regarding their **d**.
18: 5 And you shall attend to the **d** of
18: 5 of the sanctuary and the **d** of
1 Chr 9:33 and were free from other **d**;
26:12 having **d** just like their
26:29 and his sons performed **d** as
2 Chr 8:14 the Levites for their **d** (to
13:10 the Levites attend to their **d**.
35: 2 he set the priests in their **d**
Neh 12: 9 across from them in their **d**.
13:30 I also assigned **d** to the
Ezek 18:11 And does none of those **d**,

DUTY (20/16) DUTIES

Num 3:31 Their **d** included the ark, the
3:36 And the appointed **d** of the
4:16 The appointed **d** of Eleazar the
4:27 them all their tasks as their **d**.
Deut 25: 5 and perform the **d** of a
25: 7 he will not perform the **d** of my
Ruth 3:13 that if he will perform the **d**
3:13 does not want to perform the **d**
3:13 then I will perform the **d** for
2 Ki 11: 5 One-third of you who come on **d**
11: 7 of you who go off **d** on the
11: 9 his men who were to be on **d** on
11: 9 those who were going off **d** on
1 Chr 23:28 because their **d** was to help the
25: 8 And they cast lots for their **d**,
2 Chr 8:14 as the **d** of each day
23: 8 his men who were to be on **d** on
23: 8 those who were going off **d**
Lk 17:10 We have done what was our **d** to
Rom 15:27 their **d** is also to minister to

DWARF (1/1)

Lev 21:20 'or is a hunchback or a **d**,

DWELL (369/343) DWELLERS, DWELLING, DWELLS, DWELT

Gen 4:20 was the father of those who **d**
9:27 And may he **d** in the tents of
12:10 Abram went down to Egypt to **d**
13: 6 that they might **d** together,
13: 6 so great that they could not **d**
16:12 And he shall **d** in the presence
19:30 for he was afraid to **d** in Zoar.
20:15 **d** where it pleases you."
24: 3 the Canaanites, among whom I **d**;
24:37 Canaanites, in whose land I **d**;
26: 3 ***D*** in this land, and I will be
30:20 now my husband will **d** with me,
34:10 So you shall **d** with us, and the
34:10 ***D*** and trade in it, and acquire
34:16 and we will **d** with you, and we
34:21 Therefore let them **d** in the
34:22 will the men consent to **d** with
34:23 and they will **d** with us."
35: 1 go up to Bethel and **d** there;
36: 7 were too great for them to **d**
45:10 You shall **d** in the land of
46:34 that you may **d** in the land of
47: 4 We have come to **d** in the land,
47: 4 please let your servants **d** in
47: 6 your father and brothers **d** in
47: 6 let them **d** in the land of
49:13 Zebulun shall **d** by the haven of
Ex 8:22 of Goshen, in which My people **d**,
23:33 They shall not **d** in your land,
25: 8 that I may **d** among them.
29:45 I will **d** among the children of
29:46 that I may **d** among them.
Lev 13:46 and he shall **d** alone;
17: 8 or of the strangers who **d** among
17:10 or of the strangers who **d** among
17:13 or of the strangers who **d** among
20: 2 or of the strangers who **d** in
20:22 where I am bringing you to **d**
23:42 You shall **d** in booths for seven
23:42 are native Israelites shall **d**
23:43 I made the children of Israel **d**
25:18 and you will **d** in the land in
25:19 and **d** there in safety.
25:45 of the strangers who **d** among
26: 5 and **d** in your land safely.
26:32 and your enemies who **d** in it
Num 5: 3 camps in the midst of which I **d**.
13:18 whether the people who **d** in it
13:19 whether the land they **d** in is
13:28 Nevertheless the people who **d** in
13:29 The Amalekites **d** in the land of
13:29 and the Amorites **d** in the
13:29 and the Canaanites **d** by the sea
14:25 and the Canaanites **d** in the
14:30 I swore I would make you **d** in.
32:17 and our little ones will **d** in
33:53 of the land and **d** in it,
33:55 you in the land where you **d**.
35: 2 give the Levites cities to **d**
35: 3 shall have the cities to **d** in;
35:32 that he may return to **d** in the
35:34 in the midst of which I **d**;
35:34 for I the LORD **d** among the
Deut 2: 8 the descendants of Esau who **d**
2:29 the descendants of Esau who **d**
2:29 in Seir and the Moabites who **d**
8:12 built beautiful houses and **d**
11:30 land of the Canaanites who **d**
11:31 and you will possess it and **d**
12:10 cross over the Jordan and **d** in
12:10 so that you **d** in safety,
12:29 and you displace them and **d** in
13:12 LORD your God gives you to **d**
17:14 and possess it and **d** in it, and
19: 1 and you dispossess them and **d**
23:16 He may **d** with you in your midst,
25: 5 If brothers **d** together, and one
26: 1 and you possess it and **d** in it,
28:30 but you shall not **d** in it;
30:20 and that you may **d** in the land
33:12 beloved of the LORD shall **d**
33:12 And he shall **d** between His
33:28 Then Israel shall **d** in safety,
Josh 9: 7 'Perhaps you **d** among us;
9:22 when you **d** near us?

10: 6 kings of the Amorites who ***d*** in
13:13 and the Maachathites ***d*** among
14: 4 except cities to ***d*** in, with
15:63 but the Jebusites ***d*** with the
16:10 but the Canaanites ***d*** among the
17:12 were determined to ***d*** in that
17:16 and all the Canaanites who ***d*** in
20: 4 that he may ***d*** among them.
20: 6 And he shall ***d*** in that city
21: 2 Moses to give us cities to ***d***
24:13 not build, and you ***d*** in them;
24:15 Amorites, in whose land you ***d***.
Judg 1:21 so the Jebusites ***d*** with the
1:27 were determined to ***d*** in that
1:35 Amorites were determined to ***d***
6:10 Amorites, in whose land you ***d***.
8:11 up by the road of those who ***d***
9:41 so that they would not ***d*** in
17:10 ***D*** with me, and be a father and a
17:11 the Levite was content to ***d***
18: 1 an inheritance for itself to ***d***
Ruth 1: 1 went to ***d*** in the country of
1 Sam 12: 8 out of Egypt and made them ***d***
27: 5 that I may ***d*** there. For why
27: 5 For why should your servant ***d***
2 Sam 7: 2 I ***d*** in a house of cedar,
7: 5 you build a house for Me to ***d***
7:10 that they may ***d*** in a place of
1 Ki 2:36 a house in Jerusalem and ***d***
3:17 this woman and I ***d*** in the same
6:13 And I will ***d*** among the children
8:12 The LORD said He would ***d*** in the
8:13 And a place for You to ***d*** in
8:27 But will God indeed ***d*** on the
17: 9 to Sidon, and ***d*** there.
2 Ki 4:13 I ***d*** among my own people."
6: 1 the place where we ***d*** with you
6: 2 there a place where we may ***d***.
16: 6 and ***d*** there to this day.
17:27 let him go and ***d*** there, and let
25:24 ***D*** in the land and serve the
1 Chr 4:23 the potters and those who ***d*** at
17: 1 I ***d*** in a house of cedar,
17: 4 not build Me a house to ***d*** in.
17: 9 that they may ***d*** in a place of
23:25 that they may ***d*** in Jerusalem
2 Chr 2: 3 to build himself a house to ***d***
6: 1 The LORD said He would ***d*** in the
6: 2 And a place for You to ***d*** in
6:18 But will God indeed ***d*** with men
8:11 My wife shall not ***d*** in the house
19:10 to you from your brethren who ***d***
20: 8 And they ***d*** in it, and have built
Ezra 4:17 rest of their companions who ***d***
6:12 God who causes His name to ***d***
Neh 8:14 children of Israel should ***d*** in
11: 1 to bring one out of ten to ***d***
11: 1 and nine-tenths were to ***d*** in
11: 2 offered themselves to ***d*** at
Job 4:19 How much more those who ***d*** in
11:14 would not let wickedness ***d*** in
17: 2 And does not my eye ***d*** on their
18:15 They ***d*** in his tent who are
19:15 Those who ***d*** in my house, and my
Ps 4: 8 make me ***d*** in safety.
5: 4 Nor shall evil ***d*** with You.
15: 1 Who may ***d*** in Your holy hill?
23: 6 And I will ***d*** in the house of
24: 1 The world and those who ***d***
25:13 He himself shall ***d*** in
27: 4 That I may ***d*** in the house of
37: 3 ***D*** in the land, and feed on His
37:27 And ***d*** forevermore.
37:29 And ***d*** in it forever.
65: 4 That he may ***d*** in Your courts.
65: 8 They also who ***d*** in the farthest
68: 6 But the rebellious ***d*** in a dry
68:16 which God desires to ***d*** in;
68:16 the LORD will ***d*** in it
68:18 That the LORD God might ***d***
69:35 That they may ***d*** there and
69:36 who love His name shall ***d*** in
72: 9 Those who ***d*** in the wilderness
78:55 made the tribes of Israel ***d*** in
80: 1 You who ***d*** between the
84: 4 Blessed are those who ***d*** in
84:10 in the house of my God Than ***d***
85: 9 That glory may ***d*** in our land.
98: 7 The world and those who ***d*** in
101: 6 That they may ***d*** with me;
101: 7 who works deceit shall not ***d***
107: 4 They found no city to ***d*** in.
107:34 the wickedness of those who ***d***
107:36 There He makes the hungry ***d***,
120: 5 that I ***d*** in Meshech, That I
120: 5 That I ***d*** among the tents of
123: 1 O You who ***d*** in the heavens.
132:14 Here I will ***d***, for I have
133: 1 it is For brethren to ***d***
139: 9 And ***d*** in the uttermost parts
140:13 The upright shall ***d*** in Your
143: 3 He has made me ***d*** in darkness,
Prov 1:33 whoever listens to me will ***d***
2:21 For the upright will ***d*** in the
8:12 I, wisdom, ***d*** with prudence,
21: 9 Better to ***d*** in a corner of a
21:19 Better to ***d*** in the wilderness,
25:24 It is better to ***d*** in a corner
Eccl 5:20 For he will not ***d*** unduly on the
Song 8:13 You who ***d*** in the gardens,
Isa 5: 8 is no place Where they may ***d***
6: 5 And I ***d*** in the midst of a
10:24 who ***d*** in Zion, do not be afraid
11: 6 The wolf also shall ***d*** with the
13:21 Ostriches will ***d*** there,
16: 4 Let My outcasts ***d*** with you,
23: 7 feet carried her far off to ***d***?
23:18 gain will be for those who ***d***
24: 6 And those who ***d*** in it are
26: 5 He brings down those who ***d*** on
26:19 and sing, you who ***d*** in dust;
30:19 For the people shall ***d*** in Zion
32:16 Then justice will ***d*** in the
32:18 My people will ***d*** in a peaceful
33:14 Who among us shall ***d*** with the
33:14 Who among us shall ***d*** with
33:16 He will ***d*** on high; His place
33:24 The people who ***d*** in it will
34:11 the owl and the raven shall ***d***
34:17 to generation they shall ***d*** in
40:22 them out like a tent to ***d*** in.
47: 8 Who ***d*** securely, Who say in
49:20 Give me a place where I may ***d***.
51: 6 And those who ***d*** in it will die
52: 4 down at first Into Egypt to ***d***
57:15 I ***d*** in the high and holy place,
58:12 The Restorer of Streets to ***D***
65: 9 And My servants shall ***d*** there.
Jer 4:29 And not a man shall ***d*** in it.
7: 3 and I will cause you to ***d*** in
7: 7 then I will cause you to ***d*** in
8:16 The city and those who ***d*** in
9:26 who ***d*** in the wilderness.
12: 4 the wickedness of those who ***d***
20: 6 and all who ***d*** in your house,
23: 6 And Israel will ***d*** safely;
23: 8 And they shall ***d*** in their own
24: 8 and those who ***d*** in the land of
25: 5 and ***d*** in the land that the
25:24 of the mixed multitude who ***d***
27:11 and they shall till it and ***d*** in
29: 5 Build houses and ***d*** in them;
29:16 all the people who ***d*** in this
29:28 build houses and ***d*** in them,
29:32 he shall not have anyone to ***d***
31:24 And there shall ***d*** in Judah
32:37 and I will cause them to ***d***
33:16 And Jerusalem will ***d*** safely.
35: 7 but all your days you shall ***d***
35: 9 to build ourselves houses to ***d***
35:11 So we ***d*** at Jerusalem."
35:15 then you will ***d*** in the land
40: 5 and ***d*** with him among the
40: 9 ***D*** in the land and serve the
40:10 I will indeed ***d*** at Mizpah and
40:10 and ***d*** in your cities that you
42:13 We will not ***d*** in this land,'
42:14 for bread, and there we will ***d***'—
42:15 and go to ***d*** there,
42:17 their faces to go to Egypt to ***d***
42:22 where you desire to go to ***d***.
43: 2 Do not go to Egypt to ***d*** there.'
43: 5 of Judah who had returned to ***d***
44: 1 concerning all the Jews who ***d***
44: 1 who ***d*** at Migdol, at Tahpanhes,
44: 8 Egypt where you have gone to ***d***,
44:12 go into the land of Egypt to ***d***
44:13 For I will punish those who ***d*** in
44:14 into the land of Egypt to ***d***
44:14 they desire to return and ***d***.
44:26 all Judah who ***d*** in the land of
44:28 gone to the land of Egypt to ***d***
47: 2 The city and those who ***d***
48: 9 Without any to ***d*** in them.
48:28 You who ***d*** in Moab, Leave the
48:28 Leave the cities and ***d*** in the
49: 1 And his people ***d*** in its
49: 8 turn back, ***d*** in the depths,
49:16 O you who ***d*** in the clefts of
49:18 Nor shall a son of man ***d*** in
49:30 ***D*** in the depths, O inhabitants
49:33 Nor son of man ***d*** in it."
50: 3 And no one shall ***d*** therein.
50:39 the wild desert beasts shall ***d***
50:39 And the ostriches shall ***d*** in
50:40 Nor son of man ***d*** in it.
51: 1 Against those who ***d*** in Leb
51:13 O you who ***d*** by many waters,
Lam 4:15 They shall no longer ***d*** here."
4:21 You who ***d*** in the land of Uz!
Ezek 2: 6 thorns are with you and you ***d***
7: 7 you who ***d*** in the land;
12: 2 you ***d*** in the midst of a
12:19 violence of all those who ***d*** in
14: 7 or of the strangers who ***d*** in
17:23 Under it will ***d*** birds of every
17:23 of its branches they will ***d***.
20:38 out of the country where they ***d***,
26:20 and I will make you ***d*** in the
28:25 then they will ***d*** in their own
28:26 And they will ***d*** safely there,
28:26 they will ***d*** securely, when I
32:15 When I strike all who ***d*** in it,
34:25 and they will ***d*** safely in the
34:28 but they shall ***d*** safely, and no
36:28 Then you shall ***d*** in the land
36:33 I will also enable you to ***d*** in
37:25 Then they shall ***d*** in the land
37:25 and they shall ***d*** there, they,
38: 8 and now all of them ***d*** safely.
38:11 who ***d*** safely, all of them
38:12 who ***d*** in the midst of the land.
38:14 day when My people Israel ***d***
39: 9 Then those who ***d*** in the cities
43: 7 where I will ***d*** in the midst of
43: 9 and I will ***d*** in their midst
47:22 and for the strangers who ***d***
Dan 2:38 wherever the children of men ***d***,
4: 1 and languages that ***d*** in all the
6:25 and languages that ***d*** in all the
Hos 9: 3 They shall not ***d*** in the
11:11 And I will let them ***d*** in their
12: 9 I will again make you ***d*** in
14: 7 Those who ***d*** under his shadow
Am 3:12 of Israel be taken out Who ***d***
5:11 Yet you shall not ***d*** in them;
9: 5 And all who ***d*** there mourn;
Ob 3 You who ***d*** in the clefts of
Mic 4:10 You shall ***d*** in the field,
7:13 Because of those who ***d*** in it,
7:14 Who ***d*** solitarily in a
Nah 1: 5 the world and all who ***d*** in it.
Hab 2: 8 And of all who ***d*** in it.
2:17 And of all who ***d*** in it.
Zeph 1:18 riddance Of all those who ***d***
Hag 1: 4 time for you yourselves to ***d***
Zech 2: 7 you who ***d*** with the daughter of
2:10 I am coming and I will ***d*** in
2:11 And I will ***d*** in your midst.
8: 3 And ***d*** in the midst of
8: 8 And they shall ***d*** in the midst
14:11 The people shall ***d*** in it;
Mt 12:45 and they enter and ***d*** there;
Lk 11:26 and they enter and ***d*** there;
21:35 as a snare on all those who ***d***
Acts 2:14 Men of Judea and all who ***d*** in
4:16 them is evident to all who ***d***
7: 4 to this land in which you now ***d***.
7: 6 that his descendants would ***d*** in
7:48 the Most High does not ***d*** in
13:27 For those who ***d*** in Jerusalem,
17:24 does not ***d*** in temples made with
17:26 blood every nation of men to ***d***
28:16 but Paul was permitted to ***d*** by
2 Cor 6:16 I will ***d*** in them And walk
Eph 3:17 that Christ may ***d*** in your hearts
Col 1:19 Him all the fullness should ***d***,
3:16 Let the word of Christ ***d*** in you
1 Pe 3: 7 likewise, ***d*** with them
Rev 2:13 your works, and where you ***d***,
3:10 to test those who ***d*** on the
6:10 our blood on those who ***d*** on
7:15 who sits on the throne will ***d***
11:10 And those who ***d*** on the earth
11:10 prophets tormented those who ***d***
12:12 and you who ***d*** in them!
13: 6 and those who ***d*** in heaven.
13: 8 All who ***d*** on the earth will
13:12 the earth and those who ***d*** in
13:14 And he deceives those who ***d*** on
13:14 telling those who ***d*** on the
14: 6 to preach to those who ***d*** on
17: 8 And those who ***d*** on the earth
21: 3 and He will ***d*** with them,

DWELLER (1/1) DWELL

Acts 7:29 Moses fled and became a ***d*** in

DWELLERS (1/1) DWELL

Isa 18: 3 inhabitants of the world and ***d***

DWELLING (109/109) DWELL, DWELLINGS

Gen 10:30 And their ***d*** place was from Mesha
25:27 was a mild man, ***d*** in tents.
27:39 your ***d*** shall be of the fatness
36:43 according to their ***d*** places in
49: 5 of cruelty are in their ***d***
Ex 15:17 You have made For Your own ***d***,
Lev 13:46 his ***d*** shall be outside the
Num 21:15 brooks That reaches to the ***d***
23: 9 There! A people ***d*** alone,
24:21 Firm is your ***d*** place, And your
Deut 12: 5 to put His name for His ***d***
Josh 13:21 who were princes of Sihon ***d*** in
1 Sam 2:29 I have commanded in My ***d***
2:32 you will see an enemy in My ***d***
2 Sam 7: 1 to pass when the king was ***d*** in
11:11 ark and Israel and Judah are ***d***
15:25 and show me both it and His ***d***
1 Ki 8:30 Hear in heaven Your ***d*** place;
8:39 then hear in heaven Your ***d***
8:43 'hear in heaven Your ***d*** place,
8:49 then hear in heaven Your ***d*** place
12: 2 of King Solomon and had been ***d***
21: 8 and the nobles who were ***d*** in
2 Ki 17:25 at the beginning of their ***d***
19:27 But I know your ***d*** place,
1 Chr 4:33 These were their ***d*** places,
6:32 with music before the ***d*** place
6:54 Now these are their ***d*** places
7:28 Now their possessions and ***d***
17: 1 when David was ***d*** in his house,
2 Chr 6:21 Hear from heaven Your ***d*** place,
6:30 then hear from heaven Your ***d***
6:33 then hear from heaven Your ***d***
6:39 then hear from heaven Your ***d***
29: 6 their faces away from the ***d***
30:27 prayer came up to His holy ***d***
36:15 on His people and on His ***d***
Ezra 7:15 whose ***d*** is in Jerusalem;
Neh 1: 9 which I have chosen as a ***d*** for
3:30 made repairs in front of his ***d***.

Job 5: 3 But suddenly I cursed his ***d***
5:24 You shall visit your ***d*** and
8: 6 And prosper your rightful ***d***
8:22 And the ***d*** place of the wicked
18:15 is scattered on his ***d***.
21:28 The ***d*** place of the wicked?'
38:19 Where is the way to the ***d*** of
39: 6 And the barren land his ***d***?
Ps 33:14 From the place of His ***d*** He
49:11 Their ***d*** places to all
49:14 in the grave, far from their ***d***.
52: 5 and pluck you out of your ***d***
69:25 Let their ***d*** place be desolate;
74: 7 They have defiled the ***d*** place
76: 2 And His ***d*** place in Zion.
79: 7 And laid waste his ***d*** place.
90: 1 You have been our ***d*** place in
91: 9 the Most High, your ***d*** place,
91:10 any plague come near your ***d***;
107: 7 they might go to a city for a ***d***
107:36 may establish a city for a ***d***
132: 5 A ***d*** place for the Mighty One
132:13 He has desired it for His ***d***
Prov 21:20 And oil in the ***d*** of the wise,
24:15 against the ***d*** of the righteous;
Isa 4: 5 LORD will create above every ***d***
18: 4 And I will look from My ***d***
37:28 'But I know your ***d*** place,
Jer 9: 6 Your ***d*** place is in the midst
9:10 And for the ***d*** places of the
10:25 And made his ***d*** place
30:18 And have mercy on his ***d***
33:12 there shall again be a ***d*** place
46:19 O you daughter ***d*** in Egypt,
49:19 of the Jordan Against the ***d***
49:20 Surely He shall make their ***d***
49:31 gates nor bars, ***D*** alone.
49:33 Hazor shall be a ***d*** for jackals,
50:44 of the Jordan Against the ***d***
50:45 Surely He will make their ***d***
51:30 They have burned her ***d*** places,
51:37 A ***d*** place for jackals,
Lam 2: 2 and has not pitied All the ***d***
Ezek 6: 6 In all your ***d*** places the cities
6:14 in all their ***d*** places.
37:23 deliver them from all their ***d***
38:11 all of them ***d*** without walls,
Dan 2:11 whose ***d*** is not with flesh."
4:25 your ***d*** shall be with the beasts
4:30 I have built for a royal ***d*** by
4:32 and your ***d*** shall be with the
5:21 and his ***d*** was with the wild
Joel 3:17 ***D*** in Zion My holy mountain.
Nah 2:11 Where is the ***d*** of the lions,
Hab 1: 6 To possess ***d*** places that are
Zeph 3: 7 So that her ***d*** would not be cut
Mk 5: 3 who had his ***d*** among the tombs;
Acts 1:19 it became known to all those ***d***
1:20 Let his ***d*** place be
2: 5 And there were ***d*** in Jerusalem
2: 9 those ***d*** in Mesopotamia, Judea
7:46 God and asked to find a ***d*** for
11:29 send relief to the brethren ***d***
19:17 both to all Jews and Greeks ***d***
Eph 2:22 being built together for a ***d***
1 Tim 6:16 ***d*** in unapproachable light, whom
Heb 11: 9 ***d*** in tents with Isaac and
2 Pe 2: 8 ***d*** among them, tormented his
Rev 18: 2 and has become a ***d*** place of

DWELLINGS (25/25) DWELLING

Ex 10:23 of Israel had light in their ***d***.
12:20 in all your ***d*** you shall eat
35: 3 no fire throughout your ***d*** on
Lev 3:17 your generations in all your ***d***:
7:26 eat any blood in any of your ***d***,
23: 3 of the LORD in all your ***d***.
23:14 your generations in all your ***d***.
23:17 You shall bring from your ***d*** two
23:21 a statute forever in all your ***d***
23:31 your generations in all your ***d***.
Num 24: 5 Your ***d***, O Israel!
35:29 your generations in all your ***d***.
Job 18:19 Nor any remaining in his ***d***.
18:21 Surely such are the ***d*** of the
Ps 55:15 For wickedness is in their ***d***
78:28 their camp, All around their ***d***.
87: 2 of Zion More than all the ***d***
Isa 32:18 habitation, In secure ***d***,
54: 2 out the curtains of your ***d***;
Jer 9:19 we have been cast out of our ***d***.
21:13 Or who shall enter our ***d***?'
25:37 And the peaceful ***d*** are cut down
Ezek 25: 4 among you and make their ***d***
48:15 for ***d*** and common-land;
Acts 17:26 and the boundaries of their ***d***,

DWELLS (68/66) DWELL

Ex 3:22 of her who ***d*** near her house,
12:48 And when a stranger ***d*** with you
12:49 and for the stranger who ***d***
Lev 16:29 own country or a stranger who ***d***
17:12 nor shall any stranger who ***d***
18:26 nation or any stranger who ***d***
19:33 And if a stranger ***d*** with you in
19:34 The stranger who ***d*** among you
22:10 one who ***d*** with the priest,
25: 6 and the stranger who ***d*** with
25:39 one of your brethren who ***d***
25:47 one of your brethren who ***d***
Num 9:14 'And if a stranger ***d*** among you,
15:14 And if a stranger ***d*** with you, or
15:15 and for the stranger who ***d***
15:16 you and for the stranger who ***d***
15:26 Israel and the stranger who ***d***
15:29 and for the stranger who ***d***
19:10 and to the stranger who ***d***
Deut 18: 6 from where he ***d*** among all
33:20 He ***d*** as a lion, And tears the
Josh 6:25 So she ***d*** in Israel to this day,
1 Sam 4: 4 who ***d*** between the cherubim.
2 Sam 6: 2 who ***d*** between the cherubim.
7: 2 but the ark of God ***d*** inside
2 Ki 19:15 the One who ***d*** between the
1 Chr 13: 6 who ***d*** between the cherubim,
Ezra 1: 4 is left in any place where he ***d***,
Job 15:28 He ***d*** in desolate cities,
39:28 On the rocks it ***d*** and resides,
41:22 Strength ***d*** in his neck,
Ps 9:11 to the LORD, who ***d*** in Zion!
26: 8 the place where Your glory ***d***.
91: 1 He who ***d*** in the secret place of
99: 1 He ***d*** between the cherubim;
113: 5 our God, Who ***d*** on high,
135:21 Who ***d*** in Jerusalem!
Prov 3:29 For he ***d*** by you for safety's
Isa 8:18 Who ***d*** in Mount Zion.
33: 5 for He ***d*** on high;
37:16 the One who ***d*** between the
Jer 44: 2 and no one ***d*** in them,
49:31 up to the wealthy nation that ***d***
51:43 A land where no one ***d***,
Lam 1: 3 She ***d*** among the nations,
Ezek 16:46 who ***d*** with her daughters to the
16:46 who ***d*** to the south of you,
17:16 in the place where the king ***d***
47:23 whatever tribe the stranger ***d***,
Dan 2:22 And light ***d*** with Him.
Hos 4: 3 And everyone who ***d*** there will
Joel 3:21 For the LORD ***d*** in Zion."
Am 8: 8 And everyone mourn who ***d*** in
Mt 23:21 swears by it and by Him who ***d***
Jn 14:10 but the Father who ***d*** in Me does
14:17 for He ***d*** with you and will be
Rom 7:17 but sin that ***d*** in me.
7:18 is, in my flesh) nothing good ***d***;
7:20 but sin that ***d*** in me.
8: 9 if indeed the Spirit of God ***d***
8:11 raised Jesus from the dead ***d***
8:11 through His Spirit who ***d*** in
1 Cor 3:16 and that the Spirit of God ***d***
Col 2: 9 For in Him ***d*** all the fullness of
2 Tim 1:14 keep by the Holy Spirit who ***d***
Jas 4: 5 The Spirit who ***d*** in us yearns
2 Pe 3:13 earth in which righteousness ***d***.
Rev 2:13 killed among you, where Satan ***d***.

DWELT (220/212) DWELL

Gen 4:16 presence of the LORD and ***d*** in
11: 2 and they ***d*** there.
11:31 and they came to Haran and ***d***
13: 7 and the Perizzites then ***d*** in
13:12 Abram ***d*** in the land of Canaan,
13:12 and Lot ***d*** in the cities of the
13:18 and went and ***d*** by the terebinth
14: 7 and also the Amorites who ***d*** in
14:12 Abram's brother's son who ***d*** in
14:13 for he ***d*** by the terebinth trees
16: 3 after Abram had ***d*** ten years in
19:29 the cities in which Lot had ***d***.
19:30 Lot went up out of Zoar and ***d***
19:30 And he and his two daughters ***d***
20: 1 and ***d*** between Kadesh and Shur,
21:20 and he grew and ***d*** in the
21:21 He ***d*** in the Wilderness of Paran;
21:23 to the land in which you have ***d***.
22:19 and Abraham ***d*** at Beersheba.
23:10 Now Ephron ***d*** among the sons of
24:62 for he ***d*** in the South.
25:11 And Isaac ***d*** at Beer Lahai Roi.
25:18 (They ***d*** from Havilah as far as
26: 6 So Isaac ***d*** in Gerar.
26:17 Valley of Gerar, and ***d*** there.
32: 4 I have ***d*** with Laban and stayed
35:22 when Israel ***d*** in that land,
35:27 where Abraham and Isaac had ***d***.
36: 8 So Esau ***d*** in Mount Seir.
37: 1 Now Jacob ***d*** in the land where
38:11 And Tamar went and ***d*** in her
47:27 So Israel ***d*** in the land of
50:22 So Joseph ***d*** in Egypt, he and
Ex 2:15 from the face of Pharaoh and ***d***
Lev 18: 3 the land of Egypt, where you ***d***,
26:35 on your sabbaths when you ***d*** in
Num 14:45 and the Canaanites who ***d*** in
20:15 and we ***d*** in Egypt a long time,
21: 1 who ***d*** in the South, heard that
21:25 and Israel ***d*** in all the cities
21:31 Thus Israel ***d*** in the land of the
21:34 who ***d*** at Heshbon."
31:10 all the cities where they ***d***,
32:40 Manasseh, and he ***d*** in it.
33:40 who ***d*** in the South in the land
Deut 1: 4 who ***d*** in Heshbon, and Og king
1: 4 who ***d*** at Ashtaroth in Edrei.
1: 6 You have ***d*** long enough at this
1:44 And the Amorites who ***d*** in that
2:10 (The Emim had ***d*** there in times
2:12 The Horites formerly ***d*** in Seir,
2:12 and ***d*** in their place, just as
2:20 giants formerly ***d*** there.
2:21 they dispossessed them and ***d***
2:22 who ***d*** in Seir, when He
2:22 They dispossessed them and ***d*** in
2:23 who ***d*** in villages as far as
2:23 destroyed them and ***d*** in their
3: 2 who ***d*** at Heshbon.'
4:46 who ***d*** at Heshbon, whom Moses
26: 5 and he went down to Egypt and ***d***
29:16 (for you know that we ***d*** in the
33:16 And the favor of Him who ***d*** in
Josh 2:15 she ***d*** on the wall.
7: 7 and ***d*** on the other side of the
9:16 were their neighbors who ***d***
12: 2 who ***d*** in Heshbon and ruled
12: 4 who ***d*** at Ashtaroth and at
16:10 drive out the Canaanites who ***d***
19:47 possession of it, and ***d*** in it.
19:50 and he built the city and ***d*** in
20: 9 and for the stranger who ***d***
21:43 took possession of it and ***d*** in
22:33 children of Reuben and Gad ***d***.
24: 2 ***d*** on the other side of the
24: 7 Then you ***d*** in the wilderness a
24: 8 who ***d*** on the other side of the
24:18 including the Amorites who ***d*** in
Judg 1: 9 against the Canaanites who ***d***
1:10 against the Canaanites who ***d***
1:16 and they went and ***d*** among the
1:29 drive out the Canaanites who ***d***
1:29 so the Canaanites ***d*** in Gezer
1:30 so the Canaanites ***d*** among them,
1:32 So the Asherites ***d*** among the
1:33 but they ***d*** among the
3: 3 and the Hivites who ***d*** in Mount
3: 5 Thus the children of Israel ***d***
4: 2 who ***d*** in Harosheth Hagoyim.
8:29 the son of Joash went and ***d*** in
9:21 and he went to Beer and ***d***
9:41 Then Abimelech ***d*** at Arumah,
10: 1 and he ***d*** in Shamir in the
11: 3 fled from his brothers and ***d***
11:26 While Israel ***d*** in Heshbon and
15: 8 then he went down and ***d*** in the
18: 7 how they ***d*** safely, in the
18:28 So they rebuilt the city and ***d***
21:23 they rebuilt the cities and ***d***
Ruth 1: 4 And they ***d*** there about ten
2:23 and she ***d*** with her
1 Sam 12:11 and you ***d*** in safety.
22: 4 and they ***d*** with him all the
23:29 David went up from there and ***d***
27: 3 So David ***d*** with Achish at Gath,
27: 7 Now the time that David ***d*** in the
27:11 his behavior all the time he ***d***
31: 7 and the Philistines came and ***d***
2 Sam 2: 3 So they ***d*** in the cities of
5: 9 Then David ***d*** in the stronghold,
7: 6 For I have not ***d*** in a house
9:12 And all who ***d*** in the house of
9:13 So Mephibosheth ***d*** in Jerusalem,
14:28 And Absalom ***d*** two full years in
15: 8 servant took a vow while I ***d***
1 Ki 2:38 So Shimei ***d*** in Jerusalem many
4:25 And Judah and Israel ***d*** safely,
7: 8 And the house where he ***d*** had
9:16 killed the Canaanites who ***d*** in
11:24 And they went to Damascus and ***d***
12:17 the children of Israel who ***d***
12:25 of Ephraim, and ***d*** there.
13:11 Now an old prophet ***d*** in Bethel,
13:25 city where the old prophet ***d***.
15:18 who ***d*** in Damascus, saying,
2 Ki 8: 2 went with her household and ***d***
13: 5 and the children of Israel ***d*** in
15: 5 so he ***d*** in an isolated house.
17:24 possession of Samaria and ***d*** in
17:28 away from Samaria came and ***d***
17:29 in the cities where they ***d***.
22:14 (She ***d*** in Jerusalem in the
1 Chr 2:55 families of the scribes who ***d***
4:23 there they ***d*** with the king for
4:28 They ***d*** at Beersheba, Moladah,
4:41 So they ***d*** in their place,
4:43 They have ***d*** there to this day.
5: 8 who ***d*** in Aroer, as far as Nebo
5:10 and they ***d*** in their tents
5:11 And the children of Gad ***d*** next
5:16 And the Gadites ***d*** in Gilead,
5:22 And they ***d*** in their place until
5:23 of the half-tribe of Manasseh ***d***
7:29 In these ***d*** the children of
8:28 These ***d*** in Jerusalem.
8:29 was Maacah, ***d*** at Gibeon.
8:32 They also ***d*** alongside their
9: 2 the first inhabitants who ***d***
9: 3 the children of Judah ***d***,
9:34 They ***d*** at Jerusalem.
9:35 was Maacah, ***d*** at Gibeon.
9:38 They also ***d*** alongside their
10: 7 the Philistines came and ***d*** in
11: 7 Then David ***d*** in the stronghold;
17: 5 For I have not ***d*** in a house
2 Chr 10:17 the children of Israel who ***d***
11: 5 So Rehoboam ***d*** in Jerusalem,
15: 9 and those who ***d*** with them from
16: 2 who ***d*** in Damascus, saying,
19: 4 So Jehoshaphat ***d*** at Jerusalem;
26:21 He ***d*** in an isolated house,
28:18 and they ***d*** there.
30:25 and those who ***d*** in Judah.
31: 4 he commanded the people who ***d***
31: 6 who ***d*** in the cities of Judah,

34:22 (She ***d*** in Jerusalem in the
Ezra 2:70 ***d*** in their cities, and all
Neh 3:26 Moreover the Nethinim who ***d*** in
4:12 when the Jews who ***d*** near them
7:73 and all Israel ***d*** in their
11: 1 the leaders of the people ***d*** at
11: 3 heads of the province who ***d*** in
11: 3 the cities of Judah everyone ***d***
11: 4 Also in Jerusalem ***d*** some of the
11: 6 All the sons of Perez who ***d*** at
11:21 But the Nethinim ***d*** in Ophel.
11:25 of the children of Judah ***d*** in
11:30 They ***d*** from Beersheba to the
11:31 of Benjamin from Geba ***d*** in
13:16 Men of Tyre ***d*** there also,
Esth 9:19 the Jews of the villages who ***d***
Job 22: 8 And the honorable man ***d*** in it.
29:25 So I ***d*** as a king in the army,
Ps 68:10 Your congregation ***d*** in it;
74: 2 Mount Zion where You have ***d***.
105:23 And Jacob ***d*** in the land of
120: 6 My soul has ***d*** too long With
Isa 9: 2 Those who ***d*** in the land of the
29: 1 the city where David ***d***!
Jer 2: 6 one crossed And where no one ***d***?
35:10 But we have ***d*** in tents, and have
39:14 So he ***d*** among the people.
40: 6 and ***d*** with him among the people
41:17 And they departed and ***d*** in the
44:15 and all the people who ***d*** in the
50:39 Nor shall it be ***d*** in from
Ezek 3:15 who ***d*** by the River Chebar;
31:17 who were its strong arm ***d***
36:17 when the house of Israel ***d*** in
37:25 servant, where your fathers ***d***;
39:26 when they ***d*** safely in their
Dan 4:12 The birds of the heavens ***d*** in
4:21 which the beasts of the field ***d***,
Zeph 2:15 is the rejoicing city That ***d***
Mt 2:23 And he came and ***d*** in a city
4:13 He came and ***d*** in Capernaum,
Lk 1:65 Then fear came on all who ***d***
13: 4 than all other men who ***d*** in
Jn 1:14 the Word became flesh and ***d***
Acts 7: 2 before he ***d*** in Haran,
7: 4 land of the Chaldeans and ***d*** in
9:22 and confounded the Jews who ***d***
9:32 came down to the saints who ***d***
9:35 So all who ***d*** at Lydda and Sharon
13:17 exalted the people when they ***d***
19:10 so that all who ***d*** in Asia heard
22:12 with all the Jews who ***d*** there,
28:30 Then Paul ***d*** two whole years in
2 Tim 1: 5 which ***d*** first in your
Heb 11: 9 By faith he ***d*** in the land of

DYED (9/7) DYING

Ex 25: 5 ram skins ***d*** red, badger skins,
26:14 make a covering of ram skins ***d***
35: 7 ram skins ***d*** red, badger skins,
36:19 for the tent of ram skins ***d***
39:34 the covering of ram skins ***d*** red,
Judg 5:30 plunder of ***d*** garments,
5:30 of garments embroidered and ***d***,
5:30 Two pieces of ***d*** embroidery for
Isa 63: 1 With ***d*** garments from Bozrah,

DYING (13/13) DYED

Gen 48:21 to Joseph, "Behold, I am ***d***,
50: 5 swear, saying, "Behold, I am ***d***;
50:24 said to his brethren, "I am ***d***;
Job 24:12 The ***d*** groan in the city,
Zech 11: 9 Let what is ***d*** die, and what is
Mk 12:20 The first took a wife; and ***d***,
Lk 8:42 years of age, and she was ***d***.
Jn 11:37 also have kept this man from ***d***?
Acts 25:11 of death, I do not object to ***d***;
2 Cor 4:10 about in the body the ***d*** of the
6: 9 as ***d***, and behold we live;
Heb 11:21 By faith Jacob, when he was ***d***,
11:22 By faith Joseph, when he was ***d***,

DYSENTERY (1/1)

Acts 28: 8 lay sick of a fever and ***d***.

E

EACH (360/316)

Gen 1:24 ***e*** according to its kind";
2:19 called ***e*** living creature,
7: 2 shall take with you seven ***e*** of
7: 2 two ***e*** of animals that are
7: 3 also seven ***e*** of birds of the
13:11 they separated from ***e*** other.
15:10 and placed ***e*** piece opposite the
34:25 ***e*** took his sword and came
40: 5 ***e*** man's dream in one night and
40: 5 one night and ***e*** man's dream
40: 8 We ***e*** have had a dream, and
41:11 we ***e*** had a dream in one night,
41:11 ***E*** of us dreamed according to
41:12 to ***e*** man he interpreted
42:35 that surprisingly ***e*** man's
43:21 ***e*** man's money was in the
44: 1 and put ***e*** man's money in the
44:11 Then ***e*** man speedily let down his
44:11 and ***e*** opened his sack.
44:13 and ***e*** man loaded his donkey and
45:22 to ***e*** man, changes of garments;
49:28 he blessed ***e*** one according to
Ex 1: 1 ***e*** man and his household came
12: 4 according to ***e*** man's need you
16:16 according to ***e*** one's need,
16:16 one omer for ***e*** person,
16:18 according to ***e*** one's need.
16:22 two omers for ***e*** one.
18: 7 And they asked ***e*** other about
21:18 If men contend with ***e*** other,
25:34 ***e*** with its ornamental knob
26: 2 The length of ***e*** curtain shall
26: 2 and the width of ***e*** curtain four
26: 8 The length of ***e*** curtain shall
26: 8 and the width of ***e*** curtain four
26:16 be the width of ***e*** board.
26:17 Two tenons shall be in ***e*** board
26:19 two sockets under ***e*** of the
26:21 two sockets under ***e*** of the
26:25 two sockets under ***e*** board.
28:21 ***e*** one with its own name;
30:34 shall be equal amounts of ***e***.
33: 8 and ***e*** man stood at his tent
33:10 ***e*** man in his tent door.
36: 4 ***e*** from the work he was doing,
36: 9 The length of ***e*** curtain was
36: 9 and the width of ***e*** curtain four
36:15 The length of ***e*** curtain was
36:15 and the width of ***e*** curtain four
36:21 The length of ***e*** board was ten
36:21 and the width of ***e*** board a
36:22 ***E*** board had two tenons for
36:24 two sockets under ***e*** of the
36:26 two sockets under ***e*** of the
36:30 two sockets under ***e*** of the
37:20 ***e*** with its ornamental knob
38:26 a bekah for ***e*** man (that is,
38:27 one talent for ***e*** socket.
39:14 ***e*** one with its own name
Lev 7:14 offer one cake from ***e*** offering
10: 1 ***e*** took his censer and put fire
24: 5 ephah shall be in ***e*** cake.
24: 7 frankincense on ***e*** row,
24:10 man of Israel fought ***e*** other
25:10 and ***e*** of you shall return to
25:10 and ***e*** of you shall return to
25:13 ***e*** of you shall return to his
Num 1: 4 ***e*** one the head of his father's
1:18 ***e*** one individually.
1:44 ***e*** one representing his father's
2:34 ***e*** one by his family, according
3:47 shall take five shekels for ***e***
4:19 go in and appoint ***e*** of them
4:32 shall assign to ***e*** man
4:49 ***e*** according to his service and
7: 3 and for ***e*** one an ox; and they
7:11 one leader ***e*** day, for the
7:85 ***E*** silver platter weighed one
7:85 and thirty shekels and ***e*** bowl
13: 2 from ***e*** tribe of their fathers
14:34 for ***e*** day you shall bear your
15: 5 the sacrifice, for ***e*** lamb.
15:11 be done for ***e*** young bull,
15:11 for ***e*** ram, or for each lamb or
15:11 or for ***e*** lamb or young goat.
16:17 Let ***e*** take his censer and put
16:17 and ***e*** of you bring his censer
16:17 ***e*** with his censer."
17: 2 rod from ***e*** father's house,
17: 2 Write ***e*** man's name on his rod.
17: 3 the head of ***e*** father's house.
17: 6 and ***e*** of their leaders gave him
17: 6 for ***e*** leader according to their
17: 9 and ***e*** man took his rod.
23: 2 a bull and a ram on ***e*** altar.
23: 4 and I have offered on ***e*** altar
23:14 a bull and a ram on ***e*** altar.
26:54 ***E*** shall be given its
28: 7 of a hin for ***e*** lamb;
28:12 for ***e*** bull; two-tenths of an
28:13 as a grain offering for ***e*** lamb,
28:14 burnt offering for ***e*** month
28:21 one-tenth of an ephah for ***e***
28:28 of an ephah for ***e*** bull,
28:29 and one-tenth for ***e*** of the seven
29: 4 and one-tenth for ***e*** of the seven
29:10 and one-tenth for ***e*** of the seven
29:14 of an ephah for ***e*** of the
29:14 two-tenths for ***e*** of the two
29:15 and one-tenth for ***e*** of the
31: 4 A thousand from ***e*** tribe of all
31: 5 one thousand from ***e*** tribe,
31: 6 one thousand from ***e*** tribe;
35: 8 ***E*** shall give some of its cities
35: 8 inheritance that ***e*** receives."
36: 8 that the children of Israel ***e***
Deut 1:23 one man from ***e*** tribe.
3:20 Then ***e*** of you may return to his
24:15 ***E*** day you shall give him his
Josh 4: 5 and ***e*** one of you take up a
18: 4 three men for ***e*** tribe,
22:14 one ruler ***e*** from the chief
22:14 and ***e*** one was the head of the
24:28 ***e*** to his own inheritance.
Judg 2: 6 the children of Israel went ***e***
8:18 ***e*** one resembled the son of a
8:24 that ***e*** of you would give me the
8:25 and ***e*** man threw into it the
9:49 So ***e*** of the people likewise cut
11:40 of Israel went four days ***e***
15: 4 and put a torch between ***e*** pair
Ruth 1: 8 return ***e*** to her mother's house.
1: 9 ***e*** in the house of her
1 Sam 13:20 to sharpen ***e*** man's plowshare,
25:10 nowadays who break away ***e*** one
27: 3 ***e*** man with his household, and
2 Sam 2:16 And ***e*** one grasped his opponent
13:29 and ***e*** one got on his mule and
14: 6 and the two fought with ***e*** other
21:20 who had six fingers on ***e*** hand
21:20 and six toes on ***e*** foot,
1 Ki 1:49 and ***e*** one went his way.
4: 7 ***e*** one made provision for one
4:25 ***e*** man under his vine and his
4:27 ***e*** man in his month, provided
4:28 ***e*** man according to his charge.
6:10 ***e*** five cubits high; they were
6:23 ***e*** ten cubits high.
6:27 And their wings touched ***e*** other
7:15 ***e*** one eighteen cubits high, and
7:15 measured the circumference of ***e***.
7:20 such pomegranates in rows on ***e***
7:27 was the length of ***e*** cart,
7:30 bronze beside ***e*** wreath.
7:34 at the four corners of ***e*** cart;
7:36 there was a clear space on ***e***,
7:38 ***e*** laver contained forty baths,
7:38 and ***e*** laver was four cubits.
7:38 On ***e*** of the ten carts was a
7:42 pomegranates for ***e*** network,
8:38 when ***e*** one knows the plague of
8:59 as ***e*** day may require,
10:16 gold went into ***e*** shield.
10:17 gold went into ***e*** shield.
10:20 one on ***e*** side of the six steps;
10:25 ***E*** man brought his present:
20:10 handful for ***e*** of the people
20:20 And ***e*** one killed his man;
20:24 ***e*** from his position, and put
20:29 encamped opposite ***e*** other
22:10 sat ***e*** on his throne, at a
22:17 Let ***e*** return to his house in
2 Ki 3:25 and ***e*** man threw a stone on
9:13 Then ***e*** man hastened to take his
9:21 ***e*** in his chariot; and they went
11: 9 ***E*** of them took his men who were
12: 4 ***e*** man's census money, each man's
12: 4 ***e*** man's assessment money—and
12: 5 ***e*** from his constituency;
15:20 from ***e*** man fifty shekels of
25:30 a portion for ***e*** day, all the
1 Chr 20: 6 six on ***e*** hand and six on
20: 6 and six on ***e*** foot;
26:13 And they cast lots for ***e*** gate,
26:17 on the north four ***e*** day, on the
26:17 on the south four ***e*** day, and
27: 1 ***e*** division having twenty-four
28:15 by weight for ***e*** lampstand and
28:15 the use of ***e*** lampstand.
28:16 for ***e*** table, and silver for the
2 Chr 3:15 that was on the top of ***e*** of
4:13 pomegranates for ***e*** network,
6:29 when ***e*** one knows his own burden
8:14 duty of ***e*** day required,
8:14 by their divisions at ***e*** gate;
9:15 gold went into ***e*** shield.
9:16 gold went into ***e*** shield.
9:19 one on ***e*** side of the six steps;
9:24 ***E*** man brought his present:
18: 9 sat ***e*** on his throne; and they
18:16 Let ***e*** return to his house in
23: 8 And ***e*** man took his men who were
31: 2 ***e*** man according to his service,
35:15 gatekeepers were at ***e*** gate;
Ezra 3: 4 by ordinance for ***e*** day,
6: 5 ***e*** to its place; and deposit
10:16 ***e*** of them by name; and they sat
Neh 3:28 ***e*** in front of his own house.
4:22 Let ***e*** man and his servant stay
5: 7 ***E*** of you is exacting usury from
5:13 So may God shake out ***e*** man from
8:16 ***e*** one on the roof of his house,
12:47 a portion for ***e*** day. They also
13:10 for ***e*** of the Levites and the
13:30 ***e*** to his service,
Esth 1: 7 ***e*** vessel being different from
1: 8 according to ***e*** man's pleasure.
1:22 to ***e*** province in its own
1:22 that ***e*** man should be master in
2:12 ***E*** young woman's turn came to go
2:13 ***e*** young woman went to the
3:12 who were over ***e*** province,
Job 1: 4 ***e*** on his appointed day, and
2:11 ***e*** one came from his own
2:12 and ***e*** one tore his robe and
42:11 ***E*** one gave him a piece of
42:11 him a piece of silver and ***e*** a
Ps 62:12 For You render to ***e*** one
84: 7 ***E*** one appears before God in
Prov 20: 6 Most men will proclaim ***e*** his
24:12 And will He not render to ***e***
Isa 2: 9 And ***e*** man humbles himself;
2:20 ***e*** for himself to worship, To
5:15 ***E*** man shall be humbled, And
6: 2 ***e*** one had six wings: with two
35: 7 where ***e*** lay, There shall be
47:15 They shall wander ***e*** one to his
49:11 I will make ***e*** of My mountains a
57: 2 ***E*** one walking in his
Jer 1:15 They shall come and ***e*** one set
6: 3 ***E*** one shall pasture in his own

E

16:12 *e* one follows the dictates of
52:34 a portion for *e* day until the
Ezek 1: 6 *E* one had four faces, and each
1: 6 and *e* one had four wings.
1: 8 and *e* of the four had faces and
1: 9 but *e* one went straight
1:10 *e* had the face of a man;
1:10 *e* of the four had the face of a
1:10 *e* of the four had the face of
1:10 and *e* of the four had the face
1:11 two wings of *e* one touched one
1:12 And *e* one went straight forward;
1:15 beside *e* living creature
1:23 *E* one had two which covered one
1:23 and *e* one had two which covered
4: 6 laid on you a day for *e* year.
7:16 *E* for his iniquity.
8:11 *E* man had a censer in his hand,
9: 1 *e* with a deadly weapon in his
9: 2 *e* with his battle-ax in his
10: 9 wheel by *e* other cherub;
10:14 *E* one had four faces:
10:21 *E* one had four faces and each
10:21 and *e* one four wings,
10:22 They *e* went straight forward.
20: 7 *E* of you, throw away the
22: 6 *e* one has used his power to
40: 5 *e* being a cubit and a
40: 7 *E* gate chamber was one rod long
40:16 And on *e* gatepost were palm
41: 5 The width of *e* side chamber all
41: 6 thirty chambers in *e* story;
41:18 *E* cherub had two faces,
45:24 one ephah for *e* bull
45:24 and one ephah for *e* ram,
45:24 with a hin of oil for *e* ephah.
Dan 5: 6 knees knocked against *e* other.
5:26 interpretation of *e* word.
7: 3 *e* different from the other.
Am 4: 3 *E* one straight ahead of her,
Mic 4: 5 For all people walk *e* in the
Zeph 2:11 *E* one from his place, Indeed
Zech 8: 4 *E* one with his staff in his
8:16 Speak *e* man the truth to his
11: 9 left eat *e* other's flesh."
13: 9 And *e* one will say, 'The LORD
Mt 16:27 and then He will reward *e*
18:35 also will do to you if *e* of
20: 9 they *e* received a denarius.
20:10 and they likewise received *e* a
25:15 to *e* according to his own
26:22 and *e* of them began to say to
Mk 13:34 and to *e* his work, and
Lk 13:15 Hypocrite! Does not *e* one of you
23:12 became friends with *e* other,
23:12 at enmity with *e* other.
Jn 16:32 *e* to his own, and will leave Me
19:23 to *e* soldier a part, and also
Acts 2: 3 and one sat upon *e* of them.
2: 8 *e* in our own language in which
4:35 and they distributed to *e* as
11:29 *e* according to his ability,
17:27 though He is not far from *e* one
21:26 should be made for *e* one
Rom 2: 6 will render to *e* one
12: 3 as God has dealt to *e* one a
14: 5 Let *e* be fully convinced in his
14:12 So then *e* of us shall give
15: 2 Let *e* of us please his neighbor
1 Cor 1:12 that *e* of you says, "I am of
3: 5 as the Lord gave to *e* one?
3: 8 and *e* one will receive his own
3:10 But let *e* one take heed how he
3:13 *e* one's work will become clear;
3:13 and the fire will test *e* one's
4: 5 Then *e* one's praise will come
7: 2 let *e* man have his own wife,
7: 2 and let *e* woman have her own
7: 7 But *e* one has his own gift from
7:17 has distributed to *e* one,
7:17 as the Lord has called *e* one,
7:20 Let *e* one remain in the same
7:24 let *e* one remain with God in
10:24 but *e* one the other's
11:21 *e* one takes his own supper
12: 7 Spirit is given to *e* one
12:11 distributing to *e* one
12:18 *e* one of them, in the body just
14:26 *e* of you has a psalm, has a
14:27 *e* in turn, and let one
15:23 But *e* one in his own order:
15:38 and to *e* seed its own body.
16: 2 day of the week let *e* one
2 Cor 5:10 that *e* one may receive the
9: 7 So let *e* one give as he
Gal 6: 4 But let *e* one examine his own
6: 5 For *e* one shall bear his own
Eph 4: 7 But to *e* one of us grace was
4:25 Let *e* one of you speak
5:33 Nevertheless let *e* one of you in
Phil 2: 3 of mind let *e* esteem
2: 4 Let *e* of you look out not only
Col 4: 6 how you ought to answer *e* one.
1 Th 4: 4 that *e* of you should know how to
5:11 Therefore comfort *e* other and
2 Th 1: 3 all abounds toward *e* other,
Heb 6:11 And we desire that *e* one of you
11:21 blessed *e* of the sons of
Jas 1:14 But *e* one is tempted when he is
1 Pe 1:17 judges according to *e* one's
4:10 As *e* one has received a gift,
Rev 2:23 And I will give to *e* one of you
4: 8 *e* having six wings, were full
5: 8 *e* having a harp, and golden
6:11 a white robe was given to *e* of
16:21 *e* hailstone about the weight
20:13 *e* one according to his works.
21:21 *e* individual gate was of one
22: 2 *e* tree yielding its fruit

EAGER (3/3) EAGERLY

Ps 17:12 As a lion is *e* to tear his
Zech 6: 7 *e* to go, that they might walk
Gal 2:10 very thing which I also was *e*

EAGERLY (12/12) EAGER

Job 7: 2 a hired man who *e* looks
Prov 17: 4 A liar listens *e* to a spiteful
Rom 8:19 creation *e* waits for the
8:23 *e* waiting for the adoption, the
8:25 we *e* wait for it with
1 Cor 1: 7 *e* waiting for the revelation of
Gal 5: 5 For we through the Spirit *e* wait
Phil 2:28 Therefore I sent him the more *e*,
3:20 from which we also *e* wait for
1 Th 2:17 endeavored more *e* to see your
Heb 9:28 To those who *e* wait for Him He
1 Pe 5: 2 not for dishonest gain but *e*;

EAGLE (21/21) EAGLE'S, EAGLES

Lev 11:13 they are an abomination: the *e*,
Deut 14:12 these you shall not eat: the *e*,
28:49 as swift as the *e* flies, a
32:11 As an *e* stirs up its nest,
Job 9:26 Like an *e* swooping on its
39:27 Does the *e* mount up at your
Prov 23: 5 They fly away like an *e*
30:19 The way of an *e* in the air,
Jer 48:40 one shall fly like an *e*,
49:16 make your nest as high as the *e*,
49:22 come up and fly like the *e*,
Ezek 1:10 the four had the face of an *e*.
10:14 and the fourth the face of an *e*.
17: 3 A great *e* with large wings and
17: 7 there was another great *e*
Hos 8: 1 He shall come like an *e*
Ob 4 you ascend as high as the *e*,
Mic 1:16 your baldness like an *e*,
Hab 1: 8 They fly as the *e* that
Rev 4: 7 creature was like a flying *e*.
12:14 given two wings of a great *e*,

EAGLE'S (2/2) EAGLE

Ps 103: 5 youth is renewed like the *e*.
Dan 7: 4 and had *e* wings. I watched till

EAGLES (7/7) EAGLE, EAGLES'

2 Sam 1:23 They were swifter than *e*,
Prov 30:17 And the young *e* will eat it.
Isa 40:31 mount up with wings like *e*,
Jer 4:13 His horses are swifter than *e*.
Lam 4:19 were swifter Than the *e* of
Mt 24:28 there the *e* will be gathered
Lk 17:37 there the *e* will be gathered

EAGLES' (2/2) EAGLES

Ex 19: 4 and how I bore you on *e* wings
Dan 4:33 had grown like *e* feathers

EAR (112/111) EARS

Ex 15:26 give *e* to His commandments and
21: 6 his master shall pierce his *e*
29:20 it on the tip of the right *e*
29:20 and on the tip of the right *e*
Lev 8:23 on the tip of Aaron's right *e*,
14:14 it on the tip of the right *e*
14:17 on the tip of the right *e* of
14:25 it on the tip of the right *e*
14:28 hand on the tip of the right *e*
Deut 1:45 to your voice nor give *e* to
15:17 and thrust it through his *e*
32: 1 'Give *e*, O heavens,
Judg 5: 3 "Hear, O kings! Give *e*,
1 Sam 9:15 LORD had told Samuel in his *e*
2 Ki 19:16 'Incline Your *e*, O LORD,
Neh 1: 6 please let Your *e* be attentive
1:11 please let Your *e* be attentive
Job 4:12 And my *e* received a whisper of
12:11 Does not the *e* test words And
13: 1 My *e* has heard and understood
29:11 When the *e* heard, then it
33:31 'Give *e*, Job, listen to
34: 2 Give *e* to me, you who have
34: 3 For the *e* tests words As the
36:10 He also opens their *e* to
42: 5 of You by the hearing of the *e*,
Ps 5: 1 Give *e* to my words, O LORD,
10:17 You will cause Your *e* to hear,
17: 1 Give *e* to my prayer which is
17: 6 Incline Your *e* to me, and
31: 2 Bow down Your *e* to me, Deliver
39:12 And give *e* to my cry; Do not
45:10 Consider and incline your *e*;
49: 1 Give *e*, all inhabitants
49: 4 I will incline my *e* to a
54: 2 Give *e* to the words of my
55: 1 Give *e* to my prayer, O God,
58: 4 deaf cobra that stops its *e*,
71: 2 Incline Your *e* to me, and save
77: 1 And He gave *e* to me.
78: 1 Give *e*, O my people,
80: 1 Give *e*, O Shepherd
84: 8 hosts, hear my prayer; Give *e*,
86: 1 Bow down Your *e*,
86: 6 Give *e*, O LORD, to my
88: 2 Incline Your *e* to my cry.
94: 9 He who planted the *e*,
102: 2 Incline Your *e* to me; In the
116: 2 Because He has inclined His *e*
141: 1 Give *e* to my voice when
143: 1 Give *e* to my supplications!
Prov 2: 2 So that you incline your *e* to
4:20 Incline your *e* to my sayings.
5: 1 Lend your *e* to my
5:13 Nor inclined my *e* to those who
15:31 The *e* that hears the rebukes of
18:15 And the *e* of the wise seeks
20:12 The hearing *e* and the seeing
22:17 Incline your *e* and hear the
25:12 a wise rebuker to an obedient *e*.
28: 9 One who turns away his *e* from
Eccl 1: 8 Nor the *e* filled with hearing.
12:13 Fe God and keep His
Isa 1: 2 Hear, O heavens, and give *e*,
1:10 Give *e* to the law of our God,
8: 9 Give *e*, all you from far
28:23 Give *e* and hear my voice,
32: 9 Give *e* to my speech.
37:17 'Incline Your *e*, O LORD,
42:23 Who among you will give *e* to
48: 8 Surely from long ago your *e*
50: 4 He awakens My *e* To hear as
50: 5 The Lord GOD has opened My *e*;
51: 4 And give *e* to Me, O My nation:
55: 3 Incline your *e*, and come
59: 1 Nor His *e* heavy, That it
64: 4 heard nor perceived by the *e*,
Jer 6:10 Indeed their *e* is
7:24 did not obey or incline their *e*,
7:26 not obey Me or incline their *e*,
9:20 And let your *e* receive the
11: 8 did not obey or incline their *e*,
13:15 Hear and give *e*:
17:23 not obey nor incline their *e*,
25: 4 listened nor inclined your *e*
34:14 not obey Me nor incline their *e*.
35:15 you have not inclined your *e*,
44: 5 not listen or incline their *e*
Lam 3:56 Do not hide Your *e* From my
Dan 9:18 incline Your *e* and hear;
Hos 4: 1 He the word of the LORD, You
5: 1 O house of Israel! Give *e*,
Joel 1: 2 this, you elders, And give *e*,
Am 3:12 Two legs or a piece of an *e*,
Mt 10:27 and what you hear in the *e*,
26:51 high priest, and cut off his *e*.
Mk 14:47 high priest, and cut off his *e*.
Lk 12: 3 what you have spoken in the *e*
22:50 priest and cut off his right *e*.
22:51 And He touched his *e* and
Jn 18:10 and cut off his right *e*.
18:26 a relative of him whose *e*
1 Cor 2: 9 nor *e* heard, Nor have
12:16 And if the *e* should say,
Rev 2: 7 "He who has an *e*,
2:11 "He who has an *e*,
2:17 "He who has an *e*,
2:29 "He who has an *e*,
3: 6 "He who has an *e*,
3:13 "He who has an *e*,
3:22 "He who has an *e*,
13: 9 If anyone has an *e*,

EARED, EARING (KJV) See PLOWING, WORKED

EARLY (83/82)

Gen 19: 2 then you may rise *e* and go on
19:27 And Abraham went *e* in the
20: 8 So Abimelech rose *e* in the
21:14 So Abraham rose *e* in the
22: 3 So Abraham rose *e* in the
26:31 Then they arose *e* in the morning
28:18 Then Jacob rose *e* in the
31:55 And *e* in the morning Laban
Ex 8:20 Rise *e* in the morning and stand
9:13 Rise *e* in the morning and stand
24: 4 And he rose *e* in the morning,
32: 6 Then they rose *e* on the next
34: 4 Then Moses rose *e* in the
Num 14:40 And they rose *e* in the morning
Deut 11:14 the *e* rain and the latter rain,
Josh 3: 1 Then Joshua rose *e* in the
6:12 And Joshua rose *e* in the
6:15 seventh day that they rose *e*,
7:16 So Joshua rose *e* in the morning
8:10 Then Joshua rose up *e* in the
8:14 of the city hurried and rose *e*
Judg 6:28 the men of the city arose *e* in
6:38 When he rose *e* the next morning
7: 1 who were with him rose *e* and
9:33 that you shall rise *e* and rush
19: 5 fourth day that they arose *e*
19: 8 Then he arose *e* in the morning
19: 9 Tomorrow go your way *e*,
21: 4 that the people rose *e* and
1 Sam 1:19 Then they rose *e* in the morning
5: 3 the people of Ashdod arose *e*

5: 4 And when they arose *e* the next
9:26 They arose *e*; and it was
15:12 So when Samuel rose *e* in the
17:20 So David rose *e* in the morning,
29:10 rise *e* in the morning with your
29:10 And as soon as you are up *e* in
29:11 So David and his men rose *e* to
2 Sam 15: 2 Now Absalom would rise *e* and
2 Ki 3:22 Then they rose up *e* in the
6:15 of the man of God arose *e* and
19:35 and when people arose *e* in the
2 Chr 20:20 So they rose *e* in the morning
29:20 Then King Hezekiah rose *e*,
36:15 rising up *e* and sending them,
Job 1: 5 and he would rise *e* in the
Ps 63: 1 *E* will I seek You; My soul
90:14 satisfy us *e* with Your mercy,
101: 8 *E* I will destroy all the wicked
127: 2 is vain for you to rise up *e*,
Prov 27:14 rising *e* in the morning, It
Song 7:12 Let us get up *e* to the
Isa 5:11 Woe to those who rise *e* in the
26: 9 within me I will seek You *e*;
37:36 and when people arose *e* in the
Jer 7:13 rising up *e* and speaking, but
7:25 daily rising up *e* and sending
11: 7 rising *e* and exhorting, saying,
25: 3 rising *e* and speaking, but you
25: 4 rising *e* and sending them, but
26: 5 both rising up *e* and sending
29:19 rising up *e* and sending them;
32:33 rising up *e* and teaching them,
35:14 rising *e* and speaking, you did
35:15 rising up *e* and sending them,
44: 4 rising *e* and sending them,
Dan 6:10 as was his custom since *e* days.
6:19 Then the king arose very *e* in
Hos 6: 4 And like the *e* dew it goes
13: 3 morning cloud And like the *e*
Zeph 3: 7 But they rose *e* and corrupted
Mt 20: 1 a landowner who went out *e* in
Mk 16: 2 Very *e* in the morning, on the
16: 9 Now when He rose *e* on the
Lk 21:38 Then *e* in the morning all the
24: 1 very *e* in the morning, they,
24:22 who arrived at the tomb *e*,
Jn 8: 2 Now *e* in the morning He came
18:28 and it was *e* morning. But they
20: 1 Magdalene went to the tomb *e*,
Acts 5:21 they entered the temple *e* in
21:16 an *e* disciple, with whom we
Jas 5: 7 for it until it receives the *e*

EARNED (2/2) EARNS

Lk 19:16 your mina has *e* ten minas.'
19:18 your mina has *e* five minas.'

EARNERS (1/1) EARNS

Mal 3: 5 those who exploit wage *e* and

EARNEST (5/5) EARNESTLY

Rom 8:19 For the *e* expectation of the
2 Cor 7: 7 told us of your *e* desire,
8:16 God who puts the same *e* care
Phil 1:20 according to my *e* expectation
Heb 2: 1 we must give the more *e* heed

EARNESTLY (24/24) EARNEST

Num 22:37 Did I not *e* send to you, calling
Deut 11:13 'And it shall be that if you *e*
1 Sam 20: 6 David *e* asked permission of me
20:28 David *e* asked permission of me
Job 7: 2 Like a servant who *e* desires
8: 5 If you would *e* seek God And
Ps 78:34 they returned and sought *e* for
Prov 11:27 He who *e* seeks good finds
Isa 21: 7 And he listened *e* with great
Jer 11: 7 For I *e* exhorted your fathers in
31:20 I *e* remember him still;
Hos 5:15 their affliction they will *e*
Mk 5:10 Also he begged Him *e* that He
5:23 and begged Him *e*,
Lk 7: 4 to Jesus, they begged Him *e*,
22:44 in agony, He prayed more *e*.
Acts 23: 1 looking *e* at the council, said,
26: 7 *e* serving God night and day,
1 Cor 12:31 But *e* desire the best gifts.
14:39 desire *e* to prophesy, and do
2 Cor 5: 2 *e* desiring to be clothed with
Col 4: 2 Continue *e* in prayer, being
Jas 5:17 and he prayed *e* that it would
Jude 3 you exhorting you to contend *e*

EARNS (2/1) EARNED, EARNERS

Hag 1: 6 And he who *e* wages, Earns
1: 6 *E* wages to put into a bag

EARRING (1/1) EARRINGS

Prov 25:12 Like an *e* of gold and an

EARRINGS (11/10) EARRING

Gen 35: 4 and the *e* which were in their
Ex 32: 2 Break off the golden *e* which
32: 3 people broke off the golden *e*
35:22 and brought *e* and nose rings,
Num 31:50 and signet rings and *e* and
Judg 8:24 each of you would give me the *e*
8:24 For they had gold *e*,
8:25 each man threw into it the *e*
8:26 Now the weight of the gold *e*
Ezek 16:12 *e* in your ears, and a beautiful
Hos 2:13 She decked herself with her *e*

EARS (86/83) EAR

Gen 35: 4 earrings which were in their *e*;
Ex 32: 2 earrings which are in the *e*
32: 3 earrings which were in their *e*,
Lev 8:24 on the tips of their right *e*,
Deut 29: 4 perceive and eyes to see and *e*
Judg 17: 2 a curse, even saying it in my *e*—
1 Sam 3:11 in Israel at which both *e* of
15:14 bleating of the sheep in my *e*,
25:24 maidservant speak in your *e*,
2 Sam 7:22 that we have heard with our *e*.
22: 7 And my cry entered His *e*.
2 Ki 19:28 tumult Have come up to My *e*,
21:12 both his *e* will tingle.
1 Chr 17:20 that we have heard with our *e*.
2 Chr 6:40 eyes be open and let Your *e*
7:15 My eyes will be open and My *e*
Neh 8: 3 and the *e* of all the people
Job 13:17 to my declaration with your *e*.
15:21 Dreadful sounds are in his *e*;
28:22 a report about it with our *e*.
33:16 Then He opens the *e* of men,
36:15 And opens their *e* in
Ps 18: 6 came before Him, even to His *e*.
34:15 And His *e* are open to their
40: 6 My *e* You have opened.
44: 1 We have heard with our *e*,
78: 1 Incline your *e* to the words of
92:11 My *e* hear my desire on the
115: 6 They have *e*, but they do
130: 2 Let Your *e* be attentive
135:17 They have *e*, but they do
Prov 21:13 Whoever shuts his *e* to the cry
23:12 And your *e* to words of
26:17 one who takes a dog by the *e*.
Isa 6:10 And their *e* heavy, And shut
6:10 And hear with their *e*,
11: 3 decide by the hearing of His *e*;
30:21 Your *e* shall hear a word behind
32: 3 And the *e* of those who hear
33:15 Who stops his *e* from hearing
35: 5 And the *e* of the deaf shall be
37:29 tumult Have come up to My *e*,
42:20 Opening the *e*, but he does
43: 8 And the deaf who have *e*.
49:20 Will say again in your *e*,
Jer 5:21 And who have *e* and hear not:
19: 3 his *e* will tingle.
26:11 as you have heard with your *e*.
Ezek 3:10 to you, and hear with your *e*.
8:18 and though they cry in My *e*
12: 2 and *e* to hear but does not
16:12 your nose, earrings in your *e*,
23:25 remove your nose and your *e*,
24:26 let you hear it with your *e*;
40: 4 your eyes and hear with your *e*,
44: 5 your eyes and hear with your *e*,
Mic 7:16 Their *e* shall be deaf.
Zech 7:11 and stopped their *e* so that
Mt 11:15 He who has *e* to hear, let him
13: 9 He who has *e* to hear, let him
13:15 Their *e* are hard of
13:15 and hear with their *e*,
13:16 and your *e* for they hear;
13:43 He who has *e* to hear, let him
28:14 this comes to the governor's *e*,
Mk 4: 9 He who has *e* to hear, let him
4:23 If anyone has *e* to hear, let him
7:16 If anyone has *e* to hear, let him
7:33 and put His fingers in his *e*,
7:35 Immediately his *e* were opened,
8:18 having *e*, do you not hear?
Lk 1:44 your greeting sounded in my *e*,
8: 8 He who has *e* to hear, let him
9:44 words sink down into your *e*,
14:35 He who has *e* to hear, let him
Acts 7:51 uncircumcised in heart and *e*!
7:57 a loud voice, stopped their *e*,
11:22 of these things came to the *e*
17:20 some strange things to our *e*.
28:27 Their *e* are hard of
28:27 and hear with their *e*,
Rom 11: 8 should not see And *e*
2 Tim 4: 3 because they have itching *e*,
4: 4 and they will turn their *e* away
Jas 5: 4 the reapers have reached the *e*
1 Pe 3:12 And His *e* are open to

EARTH (941/863) EARTHEN, EARTHLY, EARTHQUAKE

Gen 1: 1 created the heavens and the *e*.
1: 2 The *e* was without form, and
1:10 And God called the dry land *E*,
1:11 Let the *e* bring forth grass, the
1:11 is in itself, on the *e*";
1:12 And the *e* brought forth grass,
1:15 heavens to give light on the *e*'
1:17 heavens to give light on the *e*,
1:20 and let birds fly above the *e*
1:22 and let birds multiply on the *e*.
1:24 Let the *e* bring forth the living
1:24 thing and beast of the *e*,
1:25 And God made the beast of the *e*
1:25 that creeps on the *e* according
1:26 over all the *e* and over every
1:26 thing that creeps on the *e*.
1:28 fill the *e* and subdue it;
1:28 thing that moves on the *e*.
1:29 is on the face of all the *e*,
1:30 "Also, to every beast of the *e*,
1:30 everything that creeps on the *e*,
2: 1 Thus the heavens and the *e*,
2: 4 of the heavens and the *e* when
2: 4 that the LORD God made the *e*
2: 5 of the field was in the *e* and
2: 5 not caused it to rain on the *e*,
2: 6 but a mist went up from the *e*
4:11 now you are cursed from the *e*,
4:12 vagabond you shall be on the *e*.
4:14 and a vagabond on the *e*,
6: 1 multiply on the face of the *e*,
6: 4 There were giants on the *e* in
6: 5 of man was great in the *e*,
6: 6 that He had made man on the *e*,
6: 7 created from the face of the *e*,
6:11 The *e* also was corrupt before
6:11 and the *e* was filled with
6:12 So God looked upon the *e*,
6:12 corrupted their way on the *e*.
6:13 for the *e* is filled with
6:13 I will destroy them with the *e*.
6:17 bringing floodwaters on the *e*,
6:17 everything that is on the *e*
6:20 every creeping thing of the *e*
7: 3 alive on the face of all the *e*.
7: 4 will cause it to rain on the *e*
7: 4 destroy from the face of the *e*
7: 6 the floodwaters were on the *e*.
7: 8 everything that creeps on the *e*,
7:10 of the flood were on the *e*.
7:12 And the rain was on the *e* forty
7:14 thing that creeps on the *e*
7:17 Now the flood was on the *e*
7:17 and it rose high above the *e*.
7:18 and greatly increased on the *e*,
7:19 prevailed exceedingly on the *e*,
7:21 flesh died that moved on the *e*:
7:21 thing that creeps on the *e*,
7:23 They were destroyed from the *e*.
7:24 the waters prevailed on the *e*
8: 1 made a wind to pass over the *e*,
8: 3 receded continually from the *e*.
8: 7 waters had dried up from the *e*.
8: 9 on the face of the whole *e*.
8:11 waters had receded from the *e*.
8:13 waters were dried up from the *e*;
8:14 the month, the *e* was dried.
8:17 thing that creeps on the *e*,
8:17 that they may abound on the *e*,
8:17 fruitful and multiply on the *e*.
8:19 and whatever creeps on the *e*,
8:22 While the *e* remains, Seedtime
9: 1 and multiply, and fill the *e*.
9: 2 be on every beast of the *e*,
9: 2 air, on all that move on the *e*,
9: 7 forth abundantly in the *e* And
9:10 and every beast of the *e* with
9:10 the ark, every beast of the *e*.
9:11 be a flood to destroy the *e*.
9:13 covenant between Me and the *e*.
9:14 when I bring a cloud over the *e*,
9:16 of all flesh that is on the *e*.
9:17 and all flesh that is on the *e*.
9:19 and from these the whole *e* was
10: 8 to be a mighty one on the *e*.
10:25 for in his days the *e* was
10:32 nations were divided on the *e*
11: 1 Now the whole *e* had one language
11: 4 over the face of the whole *e*.
11: 8 over the face of all the *e*,
11: 9 the language of all the *e*;
11: 9 over the face of all the *e*.
12: 3 you all the families of the *e*
13:16 as the dust of the *e*;
13:16 could number the dust of the *e*,
14:19 Possessor of heaven and *e*;
14:22 the Possessor of heaven and *e*,
18:18 and all the nations of the *e*
18:25 not the Judge of all the *e* do
19:23 The sun had risen upon the *e*
19:31 and there is no man on the *e*
19:31 as is the custom of all the *e*.
22:18 seed all the nations of the *e*
24: 3 of heaven and the God of the *e*,
24:52 bowing himself to the *e*.
26: 4 seed all the nations of the *e*
26:15 and they had filled them with *e*.
27:28 Of the fatness of the *e*,
27:39 be of the fatness of the *e*,
28:12 a ladder was set up on the *e*,
28:14 shall be as the dust of the *e*;
28:14 seed all the families of the *e*
37:10 come to bow down to the *e*
41:56 was over all the face of the *e*,
42: 6 him with their faces to the *e*.
43:26 bowed down before him to the *e*.
45: 7 a posterity for you in the *e*,
48:12 down with his face to the *e*.
48:16 multitude in the midst of the *e*.
Ex 8:17 and struck the dust of the *e*,
9:14 is none like Me in all the *e*.
9:15 have been cut off from the *e*.
9:16 may be declared in all the *e*.
9:29 that you may know that the *e*
9:33 rain was not poured on the *e*.

E

10: 5 shall cover the face of the *e*,
10: 5 one will be able to see the *e*;
10: 6 day that they were on the *e* to
10:15 covered the face of the whole *e*,
15:12 The *e* swallowed them.
19: 5 for all the *e* is Mine.
20: 4 or that is in the *e* beneath,
20: 4 is in the water under the *e*;
20:11 made the heavens and the *e*,
20:24 An altar of *e* you shall make for
31:17 made the heavens and the *e*,
32:12 them from the face of the *e*'?
33:16 who are upon the face of the *e*.
34: 8 and bowed his head toward the *e*,
34:10 have not been done in all the *e*,
Lev 11: 2 the animals that are on the *e*:
11:21 with which to leap on the *e*.
11:29 things that creep on the *e*:
11:41 thing that creeps on the *e*
11:42 things that creep on the *e*—
11:44 thing that creeps on the *e*.
11:46 creature that creeps on the *e*,
15:12 The vessel of *e* that he who has
26:19 heavens like iron and your *e*
Num 12: 3 who were on the face of the *e*.
14:21 all the *e* shall be filled with
16:30 and the *e* opens its mouth and
16:32 and the *e* opened its mouth and
16:33 the *e* closed over them, and
16:34 Lest the *e* swallow us up
22: 5 they cover the face of the *e*,
22:11 they cover the face of the *e*.
26:10 and the *e* opened its mouth and
Deut 3:24 is there in heaven or on *e*
4:10 all the days they live on the *e*,
4:17 of any animal that is on the *e*
4:18 is in the water beneath the *e*.
4:26 I call heaven and *e* to witness
4:32 that God created man on the *e*,
4:36 on *e* He showed you His great
4:39 in heaven above and on the *e*
5: 8 or that is in the *e* beneath,
5: 8 is in the water under the *e*;
6:15 you from the face of the *e*.
7: 6 peoples on the face of the *e*.
10:14 also the *e* with all that is
11: 6 how the *e* opened its mouth and
11:21 days of the heavens above the *e*.
12: 1 the days that you live on the *e*.
12:16 you shall pour it on the *e* like
12:24 you shall pour it on the *e* like
13: 7 from one end of the *e* to the
13: 7 to the other end of the *e*,
14: 2 who are on the face of the *e*.
28: 1 high above all nations of the *e*.
28:10 Then all peoples of the *e* shall
28:23 and the *e* which is under you
28:25 to all the kingdoms of the *e*.
28:26 the air and the beasts of the *e*,
28:49 afar, from the end of the *e*,
28:64 from one end of the *e* to the
30:19 I call heaven and *e* as witnesses
31:28 hearing and call heaven and *e*
32: 1 And hear, O *e*, the words
32:13 ride in the heights of the *e*,
32:22 It shall consume the *e* with
33:16 the precious things of the *e*
33:17 peoples To the ends of the *e*;
Josh 2:11 God in heaven above and on *e*
3:11 of the Lord of all the *e* is
3:13 LORD, the Lord of all the *e*,
4:24 that all the peoples of the *e*
5:14 fell on his face to the *e* and
7: 6 and fell to the *e* on his face
7: 9 and cut off our name from the *e*.
7:21 hidden in the *e* in the midst of
23:14 am going the way of all the *e*.
Judg 5: 4 The *e* trembled and the heavens
6: 4 destroy the produce of the *e*
18:10 of anything that is on the *e*.
1 Sam 2: 8 For the pillars of the *e* are
2:10 will judge the ends of the *e*.
4: 5 shouted so loudly that the *e*
5: 3 fallen on its face to the *e*
14:15 and the *e* quaked, so that it
17:46 and the wild beasts of the *e*,
17:46 that all the *e* may know that
17:49 he fell on his face to the *e*.
20:15 of David from the face of the *e*.
20:31 the son of Jesse lives on the *e*,
24: 8 stooped with his face to the *e*,
25:41 arose, bowed her face to the *e*,
26: 8 with the spear, right to the *e*;
26:20 not let my blood fall to the *e*
28:13 a spirit ascending out of the *e*.
2 Sam 4:11 hand and remove you from the *e*?
7: 9 the great men who are on the *e*.
7:23 the one nation on the *e* whom
14: 7 name nor remnant on the *e*.
14:20 everything that is in the *e*.
18: 9 hanging between heaven and *e*.
18:28 down with his face to the *e*
22: 8 Then the *e* shook and trembled;
22:43 as fine as the dust of the *e*;
23: 4 grass springing out of the *e*,
1 Ki 1:31 bowed with her face to the *e*,
1:40 so that the *e* seemed to split
1:52 hair of him shall fall to the *e*;
2: 2 "I go the way of all the *e*;
4:34 from all the kings of the *e* who
8:23 no God in heaven above or on *e*
8:27 will God indeed dwell on the *e*?
8:43 that all peoples of the *e* may
8:53 among all the peoples of the *e*
8:60 that all the peoples of the *e*
10:23 all the kings of the *e* in
10:24 Now all the *e* sought the
13:34 it from the face of the *e*.
17:14 the LORD sends rain on the *e*.
18: 1 and I will send rain on the *e*.
2 Ki 5:15 there is no God in all the *e*,
5:17 be given two mule-loads of *e*;
10:10 nothing shall fall to the *e* of
19:15 of all the kingdoms of the *e*.
19:15 You have made heaven and *e*.
19:19 that all the kingdoms of the *e*
1 Chr 1:10 to be a mighty one on the *e*.
1:19 for in his days the *e* was
16:14 judgments are in all the *e*.
16:23 Sing to the LORD, all the *e*;
16:30 Tremble before Him, all the *e*.
16:31 and let the *e* be glad; And let
16:33 He is coming to judge the *e*.
17: 8 the great men who are on the *e*.
17:21 the one nation on the *e* whom
21:16 of the LORD standing between *e*
22: 8 have shed much blood on the *e*
29:11 that is in heaven and in *e*
29:15 Our days on *e* are as a
2 Chr 1: 9 a people like the dust of the *e*
2:12 Israel, who made heaven and *e*,
6:14 is no God in heaven or on *e*
6:18 indeed dwell with men on the *e*?
6:33 that all peoples of the *e* may
9:22 all the kings of the *e* in
9:23 And all the kings of the *e*
16: 9 and fro throughout the whole *e*,
20:24 dead bodies, fallen on the *e*.
32:19 the gods of the people of the *e*—
36:23 All the kingdoms of the *e* the
Ezra 1: 2 All the kingdoms of the *e* the
5:11 of the God of heaven and *e*,
Neh 9: 6 The *e* and everything on it,
Job 1: 7 going to and fro on the *e*,
1: 8 is none like him on the *e*,
2: 2 going to and fro on the *e*,
2: 3 is none like him on the *e*,
3:14 kings and counselors of the *e*,
5:10 He gives rain on the *e*,
5:22 afraid of the beasts of the *e*.
5:25 like the grass of the *e*.
7: 1 of hard service for man on *e*?
8: 9 Because our days on *e* are a
8:19 And out of the *e* others will
9: 6 He shakes the *e* out of its
9:24 The *e* is given into the hand of
11: 9 measure is longer than the *e*
12: 8 Or speak to the *e*,
12:15 them out, they overwhelm the *e*.
12:24 chiefs of the people of the *e*,
14: 8 its root may grow old in the *e*,
14:19 wash away the soil of the *e*;
15:29 possessions overspread the *e*.
16:18 O *e*, do not cover my
18: 4 Shall the *e* be forsaken for
18:17 of him perishes from the *e*,
19:25 He shall stand at last on the *e*;
20: 4 old, Since man was placed on *e*,
20:27 And the *e* will rise up against
24:18 should be cursed in the *e*,
26: 7 He hangs the *e* on nothing.
28: 2 Iron is taken from the *e*,
28: 5 As for the *e*, from it
28:24 He looks to the ends of the *e*,
30: 6 In caves of the *e* and the
34:13 Who gave Him charge over the *e*?
35:11 more than the beasts of the *e*,
37: 3 lightning to the ends of the *e*.
37: 6 to the snow, 'Fall on the *e*';
37:12 On the face of the whole *e*.
37:17 When He quiets the *e* by the
38: 4 I laid the foundations of the *e*?
38:13 take hold of the ends of the *e*,
38:18 the breadth of the *e*?
38:24 east wind scattered over the *e*?
38:33 set their dominion over the *e*?
41:33 On *e* there is nothing like him,
Ps 2: 2 The kings of the *e* set
2: 8 And the ends of the *e* for
2:10 instructed, you judges of the *e*.
7: 5 him trample my life to the *e*,
8: 1 is Your name in all the *e*,
8: 9 is Your name in all the *e*!
10:18 That the man of the *e* may
12: 6 silver tried in a furnace of *e*,
16: 3 the saints who are on the *e*,
17:11 eyes, crouching down to the *e*,
18: 7 Then the *e* shook and trembled;
19: 4 has gone out through all the *e*,
21:10 You shall destroy from the *e*,
22:29 All the prosperous of the *e*
24: 1 The *e* is the LORD's, and all
25:13 descendants shall inherit the *e*.
33: 5 The *e* is full of the goodness
33: 8 Let all the *e* fear the LORD;
33:14 all the inhabitants of the *e*;
34:16 remembrance of them from the *e*.
37: 9 They shall inherit the *e*.
37:11 the meek shall inherit the *e*,
37:22 by Him shall inherit the *e*,
41: 2 he will be blessed on the *e*;
45:16 shall make princes in all the *e*.
46: 2 Even though the *e* be removed,
46: 6 His voice, the *e* melted.
46: 8 has made desolations in the *e*.
46: 9 wars cease to the end of the *e*;
46:10 I will be exalted in the *e*!
47: 2 is a great King over all the *e*.
47: 7 God is the King of all the *e*;
47: 9 For the shields of the *e*
48: 2 The joy of the whole *e*,
48:10 praise to the ends of the *e*;
50: 1 Has spoken and called the *e*
50: 4 from above, And to the *e*,
57: 5 Your glory be above all the *e*.
57:11 Your glory be above all the *e*.
58: 2 violence of your hands in the *e*.
58:11 He is God who judges in the *e*.
59:13 in Jacob To the ends of the *e*.
60: 2 You have made the *e* tremble;
61: 2 From the end of the *e* I will
63: 9 into the lower parts of the *e*.
65: 5 of all the ends of the *e*,
65: 9 You visit the *e* and water it,
66: 1 shout to God, all the *e*!
66: 4 All the *e* shall worship You
67: 2 Your way may be known on *e*,
67: 4 And govern the nations on *e*.
67: 6 Then the *e* shall yield her
67: 7 And all the ends of the *e*
68: 8 The *e* shook; The heavens also
68:32 to God, you kingdoms of the *e*;
69:34 Let heaven and *e* praise Him,
71:20 again from the depths of the *e*.
72: 6 Like showers that water the *e*.
72: 8 the River to the ends of the *e*.
72:16 an abundance of grain in the *e*,
72:16 flourish like grass of the *e*.
72:19 let the whole *e* be filled
73: 9 tongue walks through the *e*.
73:25 And there is none upon *e*
74:12 salvation in the midst of the *e*.
74:17 set all the borders of the *e*;
74:20 For the dark places of the *e*
75: 3 The *e* and all its inhabitants
75: 8 shall all the wicked of the *e*
76: 8 The *e* feared and was still,
76: 9 all the oppressed of the *e*.
76:12 awesome to the kings of the *e*.
77:18 The *e* trembled and shook.
78:69 Like the *e* which He has
79: 2 saints to the beasts of the *e*.
82: 5 All the foundations of the *e*
82: 8 Arise, O God, judge the *e*;
83:10 became as refuse on the *e*.
83:18 the Most High over all the *e*.
85:11 shall spring out of the *e*,
89:11 the *e* also is Yours;
89:27 highest of the kings of the *e*.
90: 2 Or ever You had formed the *e*
94: 2 Rise up, O Judge of the *e*;
95: 4 are the deep places of the *e*;
96: 1 Sing to the LORD, all the *e*.
96: 9 Tremble before Him, all the *e*.
96:11 and let the *e* be glad; Let the
96:13 for He is coming to judge the *e*.
97: 1 Let the *e* rejoice; Let the
97: 4 The *e* sees and trembles.
97: 5 of the Lord of the whole *e*.
97: 9 are most high above all the *e*;
98: 3 All the ends of the *e* have
98: 4 to the LORD, all the *e*;
98: 9 He is coming to judge the *e*.
99: 1 Let the *e* be moved!
102:15 And all the kings of the *e*
102:19 heaven the LORD viewed the *e*,
102:25 laid the foundation of the *e*,
103:11 heavens are high above the *e*,
104: 5 laid the foundations of the *e*,
104: 9 may not return to cover the *e*.
104:13 The *e* is satisfied with the
104:14 may bring forth food from the *e*,
104:24 The *e* is full of Your
104:30 You renew the face of the *e*.
104:32 He looks on the *e*,
104:35 sinners be consumed from the *e*,
105: 7 judgments are in all the *e*.
106:17 The *e* opened up and swallowed
108: 5 And Your glory above all the *e*;
109:15 the memory of them from the *e*;
112: 2 descendants will be mighty on *e*;
113: 6 in the heavens and in the *e*?
114: 7 Tremble, O *e*, at the
115:15 LORD, Who made heaven and *e*.
115:16 But the *e* He has given to the
119:19 I am a stranger in the *e*;
119:64 The *e*, O LORD, is full of
119:87 almost made an end of me on *e*,
119:90 You established the *e*,
119:119 away all the wicked of the *e*
121: 2 LORD, Who made heaven and *e*.
124: 8 LORD, Who made heaven and *e*.
134: 3 LORD who made heaven and *e*
135: 6 He does, In heaven and in *e*,
135: 7 ascend from the ends of the *e*;
136: 6 To Him who laid out the *e* above
138: 4 All the kings of the *e* shall
139:15 in the lowest parts of the *e*.
140:11 be established in the *e*;
141: 7 one plows and breaks up the *e*.
146: 4 departs, he returns to his *e*;
146: 6 Who made heaven and *e*,
147: 8 Who prepares rain for the *e*,
147:15 out His command to the *e*;
148: 7 Praise the LORD from the *e*,
148:11 Kings of the *e* and all peoples;

148:11 and all judges of the **e**;
148:13 His glory is above the **e** and
Prov 2:22 will be cut off from the **e**,
3:19 LORD by wisdom founded the **e**;
8:16 All the judges of the **e**.
8:23 before there was ever an **e**.
8:26 as yet He had not made the **e**
8:29 out the foundations of the **e**,
10:30 wicked will not inhabit the **e**.
11:31 will be recompensed on the **e**,
17:24 fool are on the ends of the **e**.
25: 3 heavens for height and the **e**
30: 4 all the ends of the **e**?
30:14 devour the poor from off the **e**,
30:16 The **e** that is not satisfied
30:21 For three things the **e** is
30:24 which are little on the **e**,
Eccl 1: 4 But the **e** abides forever.
3:21 which goes down to the **e**?
5: 2 God is in heaven, and you on **e**;
7:20 there is not a just man on **e**
8:14 is a vanity which occurs on **e**,
8:16 the business that is done on **e**,
11: 2 know what evil will be on the **e**.
11: 3 empty themselves upon the **e**;
12: 7 the dust will return to the **e**
Song 2:12 The flowers appear on the **e**;
Isa 1: 2 and give ear, O **e**!
2:19 And into the caves of the **e**,
2:19 When He arises to shake the **e**
2:21 When He arises to shake the **e**
4: 2 And the fruit of the **e** shall
5:26 to them from the end of the **e**;
6: 3 The whole **e** is full of His
8:22 Then they will look to the **e**,
10:14 I have gathered all the **e**;
11: 4 equity for the meek of the **e**;
11: 4 He shall strike the **e** with the
11: 9 For the **e** shall be full of the
11:12 From the four corners of the **e**.
12: 5 This is known in all the **e**.
13:13 And the **e** will move out of her
14: 7 The whole **e** is at rest and
14: 9 All the chief ones of the **e**;
14:16 this the man who made the **e**
14:26 is purposed against the whole **e**,
18: 3 the world and dwellers on the **e**:
18: 6 And for the beasts of the **e**;
18: 6 And all the beasts of the **e**
23: 8 are the honorable of the **e**?
23: 9 all the honorable of the **e**.
23:17 the world on the face of the **e**.
24: 1 the LORD makes the **e** empty and
24: 4 The **e** mourns and fades away,
24: 4 The haughty people of the **e**
24: 5 The **e** is also defiled under its
24: 6 the curse has devoured the **e**,
24: 6 the inhabitants of the **e** are
24:16 From the ends of the **e** we have
24:17 upon you, O inhabitant of the **e**.
24:18 And the foundations of the **e**
24:19 The **e** is violently broken, The
24:19 The **e** is split open, The
24:19 The **e** is shaken exceedingly.
24:20 The **e** shall reel to and fro
24:21 And on the **e** the kings of the
24:21 on the earth the kings of the **e**.
25: 8 will take away from all the **e**;
26: 9 Your judgments are in the **e**,
26:18 any deliverance in the **e**,
26:19 And the **e** shall cast out the
26:21 the inhabitants of the **e** for
26:21 The **e** will also disclose her
28: 2 will bring them down to the **e**
28:22 even upon the whole **e**.
30:23 bread of the increase of the **e**;
33: 9 The **e** mourns and languishes,
34: 1 you people! Let the **e** hear,
37:16 of all the kingdoms of the **e**.
37:16 You have made heaven and **e**.
37:20 that all the kingdoms of the **e**
40:12 calculated the dust of the **e**
40:21 from the foundations of the **e**?
40:22 sits above the circle of the **e**,
40:23 He makes the judges of the **e**
40:24 their stock take root in the **e**,
40:28 Creator of the ends of the **e**,
41: 5 The ends of the **e** were afraid;
41: 9 taken from the ends of the **e**,
42: 4 established justice in the **e**;
42: 5 Who spread forth the **e** and
42:10 praise from the ends of the **e**,
43: 6 from the ends of the **e**—
44:23 you lower parts of the **e**;
44:24 Who spreads abroad the **e** by
45: 8 Let the **e** open, let them bring
45: 9 with the potsherds of the **e**!
45:12 I have made the **e**,
45:18 Who formed the **e** and made it,
45:19 In a dark place of the **e**;
45:22 All you ends of the **e**! For I
48:13 laid the foundation of the **e**,
48:20 Utter it to the end of the **e**;
49: 6 salvation to the ends of the **e**.
49: 8 the people, To restore the **e**,
49:13 Be joyful, O **e**!
49:23 you with their faces to the **e**,
51: 6 And look on the **e** beneath.
51: 6 The **e** will grow old like a
51:13 laid the foundations of the **e**;
51:16 Lay the foundations of the **e**,
52:10 And all the ends of the **e**
54: 5 called the God of the whole **e**.
54: 9 would no longer cover the **e**,
55: 9 heavens are higher than the **e**,
55:10 return there, But water the **e**,
58:14 ride on the high hills of the **e**,
60: 2 the darkness shall cover the **e**,
61:11 For as the **e** brings forth its
62: 7 Jerusalem a praise in the **e**.
63: 6 down their strength to the **e**.
65:16 he who blesses himself in the **e**
65:16 And he who swears in the **e**
65:17 create new heavens and a new **e**;
66: 1 And **e** is My footstool.
66: 8 Shall the **e** be made to give
66:22 the new heavens and the new **e**
Jer 4:23 I beheld the **e**,
4:28 For this shall the **e** mourn,
6:19 Hear, O **e**! Behold, I will
6:22 the farthest parts of the **e**.
7:33 and for the beasts of the **e**.
8: 2 refuse on the face of the **e**.
9: 3 valiant for the truth on the **e**.
9:24 and righteousness in the **e**.
10:10 At His wrath the **e** will
10:11 not made the heavens and the **e**
10:11 earth shall perish from the **e**
10:12 He has made the **e** by His
10:13 ascend from the ends of the **e**.
15: 3 and the beasts of the **e** to
15: 4 to all kingdoms of the **e**,
15:10 of contention to the whole **e**!
16: 4 refuse on the face of the **e**.
16: 4 and for the beasts of the **e**.
16:19 to You From the ends of the **e**
17:13 Me Shall be written in the **e**,
19: 7 and for the beasts of the **e**.
22:29 O **e**, earth, earth,
22:29 O earth, **e**, earth,
22:29 O earth, earth, **e**,
23: 5 and righteousness in the **e**.
23:24 "Do I not fill heaven and **e**?
24: 9 into all the kingdoms of the **e**,
25:26 which are on the face of the **e**.
25:29 on all the inhabitants of the **e**,
25:30 all the inhabitants of the **e**.
25:31 will come to the ends of the **e**—
25:32 the farthest parts of the **e**.
25:33 be from one end of the **e** even
25:33 even to the other end of the **e**.
26: 6 to all the nations of the **e**.
27: 5 'I have made the **e**,
28:16 cast you from the face of the **e**.
29:18 among all the kingdoms of the **e**—
31: 8 them from the ends of the **e**,
31:22 created a new thing in the **e**—
31:37 And the foundations of the **e**
32:17 made the heavens and the **e** by
33: 9 before all nations of the **e**,
33:15 and righteousness in the **e**.
33:25 the ordinances of heaven and **e**,
34: 1 all the kingdoms of the **e** under
34:17 among all the kingdoms of the **e**.
34:20 heaven and the beasts of the **e**.
44: 8 among all the nations of the **e**?
46: 8 'I will go up and cover the **e**,
49:21 The **e** shakes at the noise of
50:23 How the hammer of the whole **e**
50:41 up from the ends of the **e**.
50:46 The **e** trembles, And the
51: 7 That made all the **e** drunk.
51:15 He has made the **e** by His
51:16 ascend from the ends of the **e**;
51:25 Who destroys all the **e**,
51:41 how the praise of the whole **e**
51:48 Then the heavens and the **e** and
51:49 Babylon the slain of all the **e**
Lam 2: 1 cast down from heaven to the **e**
2:15 The joy of the whole **e**'?
3:34 All the prisoners of the **e**,
4:12 The kings of the **e**,
Ezek 1:15 a wheel was on the **e** beside
1:19 were lifted up from the **e**,
1:21 those were lifted up from the **e**,
7:21 And to the wicked of the **e** as
8: 3 Spirit lifted me up between **e**
10:16 wings to mount up from the **e**,
10:19 and mounted up from the **e** in
26:20 in the lowest part of the **e**,
27:33 enriched the kings of the **e**
28:18 turned you to ashes upon the **e**
31:12 and all the peoples of the **e**
31:14 death, To the depths of the **e**,
31:16 in the depths of the **e**.
31:18 of Eden to the depths of the **e**;
32: 4 fill the beasts of the whole **e**.
32:18 down to the depths of the **e**,
32:24 to the lower parts of the **e**,
34: 6 over the whole face of the **e**,
34:27 and the **e** shall yield her
35:14 The whole **e** will rejoice when I
38:20 things that creep on the **e**,
38:20 who are on the face of the **e**
39:18 blood of the princes of the **e**,
43: 2 and the **e** shone with His glory.
Dan 2:10 There is not a man on **e** who can
2:35 mountain and filled the whole **e**.
2:39 which shall rule over all the **e**.
4: 1 that dwell in all the **e**:
4:10 A tree in the midst of the **e**,
4:11 seen to the ends of all the **e**.
4:15 the stump and roots in the **e**,
4:15 beasts On the grass of the **e**.
4:20 could be seen by all the **e**,
4:22 dominion to the end of the **e**.
4:23 its stump and roots in the **e**,
4:35 All the inhabitants of the **e**
4:35 among the inhabitants of the **e**.
6:25 that dwell in all the **e**:
6:27 and wonders In heaven and on **e**,
7: 4 and it was lifted up from the **e**
7:17 kings which arise out of the **e**.
7:23 shall be A fourth kingdom on **e**,
7:23 And shall devour the whole **e**,
8: 5 the surface of the whole **e**,
12: 2 who sleep in the dust of the **e**
Hos 2:18 I will shatter from the **e**,
2:21 And they shall answer the **e**.
2:22 The **e** shall answer With grain,
2:23 sow her for Myself in the **e**,
6: 3 and former rain to the **e**.
Joel 2:10 The **e** quakes before them, The
2:30 in the heavens and in the **e**:
3:16 The heavens and **e** will shake;
Am 2: 7 pant after the dust of the **e**
3: 2 of all the families of the **e**;
3: 5 bird fall into a snare on the **e**,
3: 5 a snare spring up from the **e**,
4:13 treads the high places of the **e**—
5: 7 righteousness to rest in the **e**!
5: 8 them out on the face of the **e**;
8: 9 And I will darken the **e** in
9: 5 He who touches the **e** and it
9: 6 has founded His strata in the **e**;
9: 6 them out on the face of the **e**—
9: 8 it from the face of the **e**;
Jon 2: 6 The **e** with its bars closed
Mic 1: 2 Listen, O **e**, and all that
1: 3 on the high places of the **e**.
4:13 to the Lord of the whole **e**.
5: 4 be great To the ends of the **e**;
6: 2 you strong foundations of the **e**;
7: 2 man has perished from the **e**,
7:17 holes like snakes of the **e**.
Nah 1: 5 And the **e** heaves at His
2:13 cut off your prey from the **e**,
Hab 1: 6 through the breadth of the **e**,
2:14 For the **e** will be filled With
2:20 Let all the **e** keep silence
3: 3 And the **e** was full of His
3: 6 He stood and measured the **e**;
3: 9 Selah You divided the **e** with
Zeph 2: 3 LORD, all you meek of the **e**,
2:11 nothing all the gods of the **e**;
3: 8 All the **e** shall be devoured
3:20 Among all the peoples of the **e**,
Hag 1:10 and the **e** withholds its fruit.
2: 6 I will shake heaven and **e**,
2:21 'I will shake heaven and **e**.
Zech 1:10 to and fro throughout the **e**.
1:11 to and fro throughout the **e**,
1:11 all the **e** is resting quietly."
4:10 and fro throughout the whole **e**.
4:14 beside the Lord of the whole **e**.
5: 3 over the face of the whole **e**:
5: 6 resemblance throughout the **e**:
5: 9 lifted up the basket between **e**
6: 5 before the Lord of all the **e**.
6: 7 to and fro throughout the **e**.
6: 7 to and fro throughout the **e**.
6: 7 to and fro throughout the **e**.
9:10 the River to the ends of the **e**.
12: 1 lays the foundation of the **e**,
12: 3 though all nations of the **e** are
14: 9 shall be King over all the **e**.
14:17 of the families of the **e** do
Mal 4: 6 Lest I come and strike the **e**
Mt 5: 5 For they shall inherit the **e**.
5:13 "You are the salt of the **e**;
5:18 till heaven and **e** pass away,
5:35 "nor by the **e**,
6:10 Your will be done On **e** as it
6:19 for yourselves treasures on **e**,
9: 6 the Son of Man has power on **e**
10:34 that I came to bring peace on **e**.
11:25 Father, Lord of heaven and **e**,
12:40 nights in the heart of the **e**.
12:42 came from the ends of the **e** to
13: 5 where they did not have much **e**;
13: 5 because they had no depth of **e**.
16:19 and whatever you bind on **e** will
16:19 and whatever you loose on **e**
17:25 From whom do the kings of the **e**
18:18 whatever you bind on **e** will be
18:18 and whatever you loose on **e**
18:19 that if two of you agree on **e**
23: 9 Do not call anyone on **e** your
23:35 righteous blood shed on the **e**,
24:30 then all the tribes of the **e**
24:35 Heaven and **e** will pass away, but
27:51 and the **e** quaked, and the rocks
28:18 given to Me in heaven and on **e**.
Mk 2:10 the Son of Man has power on **e**
4: 5 where it did not have much **e**;
4: 5 up because it had no depth of **e**.
4:28 For the **e** yields crops by
4:31 smaller than all the seeds on **e**;
9: 3 such as no launderer on **e** can
13:27 from the farthest part of **e** to
13:31 Heaven and **e** will pass away, but
Lk 2:14 And on **e** peace, goodwill
5:24 the Son of Man has power on **e**
6:49 man who built a house on the **e**
10:21 Father, Lord of heaven and **e**,
11: 2 Your will be done On **e** as it

11:31 came from the ends of the *e* to
12:49 "I came to send fire on the *e*,
12:51 that I came to give peace on *e*?
12:56 face of the sky and of the *e*,
16:17 it is easier for heaven and *e*
18: 8 He really find faith on the *e*?
21:25 and on the *e* distress of
21:26 which are coming on the *e*,
21:33 Heaven and *e* will pass away, but
21:35 on the face of the whole *e*.
23:44 was darkness over all the *e*
24: 5 and bowed their faces to the *e*,
Jn 3:31 he who is of the *e* is earthly
3:31 is earthly and speaks of the *e*.
12:32 I, if I am lifted up from the *e*,
17: 4 "I have glorified You on the *e*.
Acts 1: 8 and to the end of the *e*.
2:19 above And signs in the *e*
3:25 all the families of the *e*
4:24 who made heaven and *e* and the
4:26 The kings of the *e* took
7:49 And *e* is My footstool.
8:33 life is taken from the *e*.
10:11 to him and let down to the *e*.
10:12 of four-footed animals of the *e*,
11: 6 four-footed animals of the *e*,
13:47 to the ends of the *e*.
14:15 God, who made the heaven, the *e*,
17:24 He is Lord of heaven and *e*,
17:26 dwell on all the face of the *e*,
22:22 with such a fellow from the *e*,
Rom 9:17 be declared in all the *e*.
9:28 a short work upon the *e*.
10:18 gone out to all the *e*,
1 Cor 8: 5 whether in heaven or on *e* (as
10:26 the *e* is the LORD's, and
10:28 the *e* is the LORD's, and
15:47 The first man was of the *e*,
Eph 1:10 in heaven and which are on *e*—
3:15 whole family in heaven and *e*
4: 9 into the lower parts of the *e*?
6: 3 may live long on the *e*.
Phil 2:10 in heaven, and of those on *e*,
2:10 earth, and of those under the *e*,
Col 1:16 are in heaven and that are on *e*,
1:20 whether things on *e* or things
3: 2 above, not on things on the *e*.
3: 5 your members which are on the *e*:
Heb 1:10 the foundation of the *e*,
6: 7 For the *e* which drinks in the
8: 4 For if He were on *e*,
11:13 strangers and pilgrims on the *e*.
11:38 in dens and caves of the *e*.
12:25 who refused Him who spoke on *e*,
12:26 whose voice then shook the *e*;
12:26 I shake not only the *e*,
Jas 5: 5 You have lived on the *e* in
5: 7 for the precious fruit of the *e*,
5:12 either by heaven or by *e* or
5:18 and the *e* produced its fruit.
2 Pe 3: 5 and the *e* standing out of water
3: 7 But the heavens and the *e* which
3:10 both the *e* and the works that
3:13 for new heavens and a new *e* in
1 Jn 5: 8 three that bear witness on *e*:
Rev 1: 5 ruler over the kings of the *e*.
1: 7 And all the tribes of the *e*
3:10 test those who dwell on the *e*.
5: 3 no one in heaven or on the *e*
5: 3 or on the earth or under the *e*
5: 6 of God sent out into all the *e*.
5:10 And we shall reign on the *e*.
5:13 is in heaven and on the *e* and
5:13 on the earth and under the *e*
6: 4 on it to take peace from the *e*,
6: 8 to them over a fourth of the *e*,
6: 8 and by the beasts of the *e*.
6:10 on those who dwell on the *e*?
6:13 stars of heaven fell to the *e*,
6:15 And the kings of the *e*,
7: 1 at the four corners of the *e*,
7: 1 holding the four winds of the *e*,
7: 1 wind should not blow on the *e*,
7: 2 it was granted to harm the *e*
7: 3 saying, "Do not harm the *e*,
8: 5 altar, and threw it to the *e*.
8: 7 and they were thrown to the *e*.
8:13 woe to the inhabitants of the *e*,
9: 1 fallen from heaven to the *e*.
9: 3 smoke locusts came upon the *e*.
9: 3 as the scorpions of the *e* have
9: 4 not to harm the grass of the *e*,
10: 6 the *e* and the things that are
10: 8 stands on the sea and on the *e*.
11: 4 before the God of the *e*.
11: 6 and to strike the *e* with all
11:10 And those who dwell on the *e*
11:10 those who dwell on the *e*.
11:18 destroy those who destroy the *e*.
12: 4 heaven and threw them to the *e*.
12: 9 world; he was cast to the *e*,
12:12 Woe to the inhabitants of the *e*
12:13 that he had been cast to the *e*,
12:16 But the *e* helped the woman, and
12:16 and the *e* opened its mouth and
13: 8 All who dwell on the *e* will
13:11 beast coming up out of the *e*,
13:12 and causes the *e* and those who
13:13 come down from heaven on the *e*
13:14 those who dwell on the *e* by
13:14 those who dwell on the *e* to
14: 3 who were redeemed from the *e*.
14: 6 to those who dwell on the *e*—
14: 7 Him who made heaven and *e*,
14:15 for the harvest of the *e* is
14:16 thrust in His sickle on the *e*,
14:16 and the *e* was reaped.
14:18 clusters of the vine of the *e*,
14:19 thrust his sickle into the *e*
14:19 and gathered the vine of the *e*,
16: 1 of the wrath of God on the *e*.
16: 2 poured out his bowl upon the *e*,
16:14 go out to the kings of the *e*
16:18 since men were on the *e*.
17: 2 with whom the kings of the *e*
17: 2 and the inhabitants of the *e*
17: 5 ABOMINATIONS OF THE *E*.
17: 8 And those who dwell on the *e*
17:18 reigns over the kings of the *e*.
18: 1 and the *e* was illuminated with
18: 3 the kings of the *e* have
18: 3 and the merchants of the *e* have
18: 9 The kings of the *e* who
18:11 And the merchants of the *e* will
18:23 were the great men of the *e*,
18:24 of all who were slain on the *e*.
19: 2 harlot who corrupted the *e*
19:19 the beast, the kings of the *e*,
20: 8 in the four corners of the *e*,
20: 9 up on the breadth of the *e* and
20:11 from whose face the *e* and the
21: 1 I saw a new heaven and a new *e*,
21: 1 first heaven and the first *e*
21:24 and the kings of the *e* bring

EARTHEN (10/10) EARTH, EARTHENWARE

Lev 6:28 But the *e* vessel in which it is
11:33 Any *e* vessel into which any of
14: 5 birds be killed in an *e* vessel
14:50 the birds in an *e* vessel
Num 5:17 holy water in an *e* vessel,
2 Sam 17:28 *e* vessels and wheat, barley and
Jer 19: 1 Go and get a potter's *e* flask,
32:14 and put them in an *e* vessel,
Hab 1:10 For they heap up *e* mounds and
2 Cor 4: 7 this treasure in *e* vessels,

EARTHENWARE (1/1) EARTHEN

Prov 26:23 a wicked heart Are like *e*

EARTHLY (6/6) EARTH

Jn 3:12 If I have told you *e* things and
3:31 he who is of the earth is *e* and
2 Cor 5: 1 For we know that if our *e* house,
Phil 3:19 who set their mind on *e* things.
Heb 9: 1 of divine service and the *e*
Jas 3:15 descend from above, but is *e*,

EARTHQUAKE (17/14) EARTH, EARTHQUAKES

1 Ki 19:11 and after the wind an *e*,
19:11 the LORD was not in the *e*;
19:12 and after the *e* a fire, but the
Isa 29: 6 of hosts With thunder and *e*
Ezek 38:19 day there shall be a great *e*
Am 1: 1 Israel, two years before the *e*.
Zech 14: 5 flee As you fled from the *e*
Mt 27:54 saw the *e* and the things that
28: 2 And behold, there was a great *e*;
Acts 16:26 Suddenly there was a great *e*,
Rev 6:12 and behold, there was a great *e*;
8: 5 lightnings, and an *e*.
11:13 same hour there was a great *e*,
11:13 In the *e* seven thousand people
11:19 noises, thunderings, an *e*,
16:18 and there was a great *e*,
16:18 such a mighty and great *e* as

EARTHQUAKES (3/3) EARTHQUAKE

Mt 24: 7 and *e* in various places.
Mk 13: 8 And there will be *e* in various
Lk 21:11 And there will be great *e* in

EASE (14/14)

Job 3:26 I am not at *e*, nor am I
7:13 My couch will *e* my complaint,'
12: 5 the thought of one who is at *e*;
16:12 I was at *e*, but He has
21:23 Being wholly at *e* and secure;
Ps 73:12 ungodly, Who are always at *e*;
123: 4 the scorn of those who are at *e*,
Isa 32: 9 up, you women who are at *e*,
32:11 you women who are at *e*;
Jer 46:27 return, have rest and be at *e*;
48:11 Moab has been at *e* from his
Am 6: 1 Woe to you who are at *e* in
Zech 1:15 angry with the nations at *e*;
Lk 12:19 up for many years; take your *e*;

EASED (2/2)

Job 16: 6 if I remain silent, how am I *e*?
2 Cor 8:13 mean that others should be *e*

EASIER (8/8) EASY

Ex 18:22 So it will be *e* for you, for
Mt 9: 5 'For which is *e*, to say,
19:24 it is *e* for a camel to go
Mk 2: 9 'Which is *e*, to say to the
10:25 It is *e* for a camel to go
Lk 5:23 'Which is *e*, to say,
16:17 And it is *e* for heaven and earth
18:25 For it is *e* for a camel to go

EASILY (2/2) EASY

Judg 20:43 and *e* trampled them down as
Heb 12: 1 and the sin which so *e* ensnares

EAST (169/161) EASTERN, EASTWARD

Gen 2:14 one which goes toward the *e* of
3:24 He placed cherubim at the *e* of
4:16 in the land of Nod on the *e* of
10:30 Sephar, the mountain of the *e*.
11: 2 as they journeyed from the *e*,
12: 8 from there to the mountain *e*
12: 8 on the west and Ai on the *e*;
13:11 of Jordan, and Lot journeyed *e*.
25: 6 son, to the country of the *e*.
25:18 which is *e* of Egypt as you go
28:14 abroad to the west and the *e*,
29: 1 the land of the people of the *E*.
41: 6 blighted by the *e* wind, sprang
41:23 and blighted by the *e* wind,
41:27 empty heads blighted by the *e*
Ex 10:13 and the LORD brought an *e* wind
10:13 the *e* wind brought the locusts.
14:21 sea to go back by a strong *e*
27:13 width of the court on the *e*
38:13 For the *e* side the hangings
Lev 1:16 it beside the altar on the *e*
16:14 on the mercy seat on the *e*
Num 2: 3 On the *e* side, toward the rising
3:38 before the tabernacle on the *e*,
10: 5 the camps that lie on the *e*
21:11 in the wilderness which is *e*
23: 7 From the mountains of the *e*.
33: 7 which is *e* of Baal Zephon;
34:11 from Shepham to Riblah on the *e*
35: 5 outside the city on the *e* side
Deut 3:17 from Chinnereth as far as the *e*
3:27 the north, the south, and the *e*;
4:49 and all the plain on the *e* side
Josh 4:19 they camped in Gilgal on the *e*
7: 2 on the *e* side of Bethel, and
11: 3 to the Canaanites in the *e* and
13: 3 which is *e* of Egypt, as far as
15: 5 The *e* border was the Salt Sea
16: 1 the waters of Jericho on the *e*,
16: 5 of their inheritance on the *e*
16: 6 and passed by it on the *e* of
17: 7 that lies *e* of Shechem;
17:10 the north and Issachar on the *e*.
18: 7 beyond the Jordan on the *e*,
18:20 Jordan was its border on the *e*
19:11 along the brook that is *e* of
19:13 there it passed along on the *e*
Judg 6: 3 and the people of the *E* would
6:33 Amalekites, the people of the *E*,
7:12 all the people of the *E*,
8:10 the army of the people of the *E*;
8:11 who dwell in tents on the *e* of
11:18 came to the *e* side of the land
20:43 front of Gibeah toward the *e*.
21:19 on the *e* side of the highway
1 Sam 13: 5 to the *e* of Beth Aven.
15: 7 which is *e* of Egypt.
1 Ki 4:30 wisdom of all the men of the *E*
7:25 and three looking toward the *e*;
11: 7 on the hill that is *e* of
2 Ki 13:17 Open the *e* window"; and he
23:13 the high places that were *e*
1 Chr 4:39 as far as the *e* side of the
5:10 throughout the entire area *e*
6:78 on the *e* side of the Jordan,
7:28 to the *e* Naaran, to the west
9:18 at the King's Gate on the *e*.
9:24 to the four directions: the *e*,
12:15 to the *e* and to the west.
26:14 The lot for the *E* Gate fell to
26:17 On the *e* were six Levites, on
2 Chr 4: 4 and three looking toward the *e*;
5:12 stood at the *e* end of the
29: 4 and gathered them in the *E*
31:14 the keeper of the *E* Gate, was
Neh 3:26 of the Water Gate toward the *e*,
3:29 the keeper of the *E* Gate, made
Job 1: 3 of all the people of the *E*.
15: 2 And fill himself with the *e*
18:20 As those in the *e* are
27:21 The *e* wind carries him away,
38:24 Or the *e* wind scattered over
Ps 48: 7 ships of Tarshish With an *e*
75: 6 comes neither from the *e* Nor
78:26 He caused an *e* wind to blow in
103:12 As far as the *e* is from the
107: 3 From the *e* and from the west,
Isa 11:14 plunder the people of the *E*;
27: 8 wind In the day of the *e* wind.
41: 2 "Who raised up one from the *e*?
43: 5 your descendants from the *e*,
46:11 a bird of prey from the *e*,
Jer 18:17 will scatter them as with an *e*
31:40 of the Horse Gate toward the *e*,
49:28 devastate the men of the *E*!
Ezek 8:16 and their faces toward the *e*,
8:16 worshiping the sun toward the *e*.

10:19 they stood at the door of the e
11: 1 me up and brought me to the E
11:23 which is on the e side of the
17:10 not utterly wither when the e
19:12 And the e wind dried her
25: 4 possession to the men of the E,
25:10 To the men of the E I will give
27:26 But the e wind broke you in
39:11 valley of those who pass by e
40: 6 to the gateway which faced e;
40:19 one hundred cubits toward the e
40:22 as the gateway facing e;
40:32 into the inner court facing e;
42: 9 was the entrance on the e
42:10 wall of the court toward the e,
42:12 front of the wall toward the e.
42:15 gateway that faces toward the e,
42:16 He measured the e side with the
43: 1 gate that faces toward the e.
43: 2 came from the way of the e.
43: 4 gate which faces toward the e.
43:17 and its steps face toward the e.
44: 1 which faces toward the e,
45: 7 west side and eastward on the e
45: 7 from the west border to the e
46: 1 court that faces toward the e
46:12 gate that faces toward the e
47: 1 of the temple toward the e,
47: 1 the front of the temple faced e;
47: 2 the outer gateway that faces e;
47: 3 when the man went out to the e
47:18 On the e side you shall mark out
47:18 This is the e side.
48: 1 section for Dan from its e
48: 2 from the e side to the west,
48: 3 from the e side to the west,
48: 4 from the e side to the west,
48: 5 from the e side to the west,
48: 6 from the e side to the west,
48: 7 from the e side to the west,
48: 8 from the e side to the west,
48: 8 from the e side to the west,
48:10 on the e ten thousand in width,
48:16 the e side four thousand five
48:17 to the e two hundred and fifty,
48:18 ten thousand cubits to the e
48:23 from the e side to the west,
48:24 from the e side to the west,
48:25 from the e side to the west,
48:26 from the e side to the west,
48:27 from the e side to the west,
48:32 on the e side, four thousand
Dan 8: 9 toward the south, toward the e,
11:44 But news from the e and the
Hos 12: 1 And pursues the e wind;
13:15 An e wind shall come;
Am 8:12 to sea, And from north to e;
Jon 4: 5 of the city and sat on the e
4: 8 that God prepared a vehement e
Hab 1: 9 faces are set like the e wind.
Zech 8: 7 people from the land of the e
14: 4 Which faces Jerusalem on the e.
14: 4 From e to west, Making a
Mt 2: 1 wise men from the E came to
2: 2 we have seen His star in the E
2: 9 which they had seen in the E
8:11 you that many will come from e
24:27 the lightning comes from the e
Lk 13:29 They will come from the e and
Rev 7: 2 angel ascending from the e,
16:12 the way of the kings from the e
21:13 three gates on the e,

EASTER (KJV) See PASSOVER

EASTERN (14/14) EAST

Num 32:19 to us on this e side
34:10 mark out your e border
34:11 and reach to the e side
Josh 12: 1 and all the e Jordan plain:
12: 3 and the e Jordan plain from the
Isa 2: 6 they are filled with e ways;
Ezek 40:10 In the e gateway were three
40:23 just as the e gateway; and he
41:14 also the width of the e face of
47: 8 flows toward the e region,
47:18 and along the e side of the
48:21 as far as the e border,
Joel 2:20 With his face toward the e sea
Zech 14: 8 Half of them toward the e sea

EASTWARD (18/18) EAST

Gen 2: 8 LORD God planted a garden e
13:14 you are—northward, southward, e,
25: 6 was still living he sent them e,
Num 34: 3 southern border shall extend e
34:15 Jordan, across from Jericho e,
Josh 11: 8 and to the Valley of Mizpah e;
13: 8 given them, beyond the Jordan e,
13:27 the other side of the Jordan e.
13:32 of the Jordan, by Jericho e.
16: 6 then the border went around e
19:12 Then from Sarid it went e toward
20: 8 of the Jordan, by Jericho e,
1 Ki 17: 3 "Get away from here and turn e,
2 Ki 10:33 from the Jordan e:
1 Chr 5: 9 E they settled as far as the
Neh 12:37 as far as the Water Gate e.
Ezek 11: 1 LORD's house, which faces e;
45: 7 on the west side and e on the

EASY (4/4) EASIER, EASILY

2 Ki 20:10 It is an e thing for the shadow
Prov 14: 6 But knowledge is e to him who
Mt 11:30 For My yoke is e and My burden
1 Cor 14: 9 utter by the tongue words e to

EAT (554/494) ATE, EATEN, EATER, EATING, EATS

Gen 2:16 of the garden you may freely e;
2:17 good and evil you shall not e,
2:17 for in the day that you e of it
3: 1 You shall not e of every tree of
3: 2 We may e the fruit of the trees
3: 3 You shall not e it, nor shall
3: 5 knows that in the day you e of
3:11 you that you should not e?
3:14 And you shall e dust All the
3:17 You shall not e of it':
3:17 In toil you shall e of it
3:18 And you shall e the herb of
3:19 sweat of your face you shall e
3:22 also of the tree of life, and e,
9: 4 But you shall not e flesh with
24:33 Food was set before him to e,
24:33 I will not e until I have told
27: 4 bring it to me that I may e,
27: 7 that I may e it and bless you
27:10 that he may e it, and that he
27:19 sit and e of my game, that your
27:25 and I will e of my son's game,
27:31 Let my father arise and e of his
28:20 and give me bread to e and
31:54 and called his brethren to e
32:32 the children of Israel do not e
37:25 And they sat down to e a meal.
40:19 and the birds will e your flesh
43:25 they heard that they would e
43:32 the Egyptians could not e food
45:18 and you will e the fat of the
Ex 2:20 that he may e bread."
10: 5 and they shall e the residue of
10: 5 and they shall e every tree
10:12 and e every herb of the
12: 7 of the houses where they e it.
12: 8 Then they shall e the flesh on
12: 8 bitter herbs they shall e it.
12: 9 Do not e it raw, nor boiled at
12:11 'And thus you shall e it:
12:11 So you shall e it in haste.
12:15 Seven days you shall e
12:16 but that which everyone must e—
12:18 you shall e unleavened bread,
12:20 You shall e nothing leavened; in
12:20 all your dwellings you shall e
12:43 No foreigner shall e it.
12:44 then he may e it.
12:45 a hired servant shall not e it.
12:48 no uncircumcised person shall e
13: 6 Seven days you shall e
16: 8 the LORD gives you meat to e
16:12 At twilight you shall e meat,
16:15 the LORD has given you to e.
16:25 E that today, for today is a
18:12 all the elders of Israel to e
22:31 you shall not e meat torn by
23:11 the poor of your people may e;
23:11 the beasts of the field may e.
23:15 Unleavened Bread (you shall e
29:32 Aaron and his sons shall e the
29:33 They shall e those things with
29:33 but an outsider shall not e
32: 6 and the people sat down to e
34:15 them invites you and you e of
34:18 Seven days you shall e
Lev 3:17 you shall e neither fat nor
6:16 it Aaron and his sons shall e;
6:16 of meeting they shall e it.
6:18 the children of Aaron may e it.
6:26 who offers it for sin shall e
6:29 males among the priests may e
7: 6 male among the priests may e
7:19 all who are clean may e of it.
7:23 You shall not e any fat, of ox
7:24 but you shall by no means e it.
7:26 Moreover you shall not e any
8:31 and e it there with the bread
8:31 Aaron and his sons shall e it.'
10:12 and e it without leaven beside
10:13 You shall e it in a holy place,
10:14 the heave offering you shall e
11: 2 the animals which you may e
11: 3 chewing the cud—that you may e.
11: 4 these you shall not e among
11: 8 'Their flesh you shall not e,
11: 9 These you may e of all that
11: 9 or in the rivers—that you may e.
11:11 you shall not e their flesh,
11:21 Yet these you may e of every
11:22 'These you may e:
11:39 if any animal which you may e
11:42 the earth—these you shall not e,
17:12 No one among you shall e blood,
17:12 who dwells among you e blood.
17:14 You shall not e the blood of any
19:25 in the fifth year you may e
19:26 You shall not e anything with
21:22 He may e the bread of his God,
22: 4 shall not e the holy offerings
22: 6 and shall not e the holy
22: 7 and afterward he may e the holy
22: 8 torn by beasts he shall not e,
22:10 No outsider shall e the holy
22:10 shall not e the holy thing.
22:11 he may e it; and one who is
22:11 who is born in his house may e
22:12 she may not e of the holy
22:13 she may e her father's food;
22:13 but no outsider shall e it.
22:16 guilt of trespass when they e
23: 6 seven days you must e
23:14 You shall e neither bread nor
24: 9 and they shall e it in a holy
25:12 you shall e its produce from
25:19 and you will e your fill, and
25:20 What shall we e in the seventh
25:22 and e old produce until the
25:22 you shall e of the old
26: 5 you shall e your bread to the
26:10 You shall e the old harvest, and
26:16 for your enemies shall e it.
26:26 and you shall e and not be
26:29 You shall e the flesh of your
26:29 and you shall e the flesh of
26:38 land of your enemies shall e
Num 6: 3 nor e fresh grapes or raisins.
6: 4 of his separation he shall e
9:11 They shall e it with unleavened
11: 4 "Who will give us meat to e?
11:13 'Give us meat, that we may e.
11:18 and you shall e meat; for you
11:18 "Who will give us meat to e?
11:18 give you meat, and you shall e.
11:19 'You shall e, not one day,
11:21 that they may e for a whole
15:19 when you e of the bread of the
18:10 a most holy place you shall e
18:10 every male shall e it.
18:11 is clean in your house may e
18:13 is clean in your house may e
18:31 You may e it in any place, you
Deut 2: 6 them with money, that you may e;
2:28 me food for money, that I may e,
4:28 neither see nor hear nor e nor
8: 9 a land in which you will e bread
11:15 that you may e and be filled.'
12: 7 And there you shall e before the
12:15 you may slaughter and e meat
12:15 unclean and the clean may e of
12:16 Only you shall not e the blood;
12:17 You may not e within your gates
12:18 But you must e them before the
12:20 Let me e meat,' because you long
12:20 because you long to e meat,
12:20 you may e as much meat as your
12:21 and you may e within your gates
12:22 so you may e them; the unclean
12:22 and the clean alike may e them.
12:23 be sure that you do not e
12:23 you may not e the life with the
12:24 You shall not e it; you shall
12:25 You shall not e it, that it may
12:27 and you shall e the meat.
14: 3 You shall not e any detestable
14: 4 the animals which you may e:
14: 6 And you may e every animal with
14: 7 cloven hooves, you shall not e,
14: 8 you shall not e their flesh or
14: 9 These you may e of all that
14: 9 you may e all that have fins
14:10 fins and scales you shall not e;
14:11 "All clean birds you may e.
14:12 "But these you shall not e:
14:20 You may e all clean birds.
14:21 You shall not e anything that
14:21 that he may e it, or you may
14:23 And you shall e before the LORD
14:26 you shall e there before the
14:29 may come and e and be
15:20 and your household shall e
15:22 You may e it within your gates;
15:22 the clean person alike may e
15:23 Only you shall not e its blood;
16: 3 You shall e no leavened bread
16: 3 seven days you shall e
16: 7 And you shall roast and e it in
16: 8 Six days you shall e unleavened
18: 1 they shall e the offerings of
18: 8 shall have equal portions to e,
20: 6 in the battle and another man e
20:14 and you shall e the enemies'
20:19 if you can e of them, do not
23:24 you may e your fill of grapes
26:12 so that they may e within your
27: 7 and shall e there, and rejoice
28:31 but you shall not e of it; your
28:33 you have not known shall e the
28:39 for the worms shall e them.
28:51 And they shall e the increase of
28:53 You shall e the fruit of your
28:55 of his children whom he will e,
28:57 for she will e them secretly
32:13 That he might e the produce of
Josh 24:13 you e of the vineyards and
Judg 13: 4 and not to e anything unclean.
13: 7 nor e anything unclean, for the
13:14 She may not e anything that
13:14 nor e anything unclean.
13:16 I will not e your food.
14:14 the eater came something to e,
Ruth 2:14 and e of the bread, and dip
1 Sam 1: 7 she wept and did not e.
1: 8 do you weep? Why do you not e?

2:36 that I may *e* a piece of
9:13 goes up to the high place to *e*.
9:13 For the people will not *e* until
9:13 those who are invited will *e*.
9:19 for you shall *e* with me today;
9:24 *E*; for until this time it
14:34 slaughter them here, and *e*;
20: 5 fail to sit with the king to *e*.
20:24 the king sat down to *e* the
20:27 the son of Jesse not come to *e*,
28:22 and *e*, that you may have
28:23 and said, "I will not *e*.
2 Sam 3:35 came to persuade David to *e*
9: 7 and you shall *e* bread at my
9:10 master's son may have food to *e*.
9:10 your master's son shall *e*
9:11 he shall *e* at my table like one
11:11 I then go to my house to *e* and
12:17 nor did he *e* food with them.
13: 5 that I may see it and *e* it
13: 6 that I may *e* from her hand."
13: 9 before him, but he refused to *e*.
13:10 that I may *e* from your hand."
13:11 had brought them to him to *e*,
16: 2 fruit for the young men to *e*,
17:29 people who were with him to *e*.
19:28 your servant among those who *e*
19:35 your servant taste what I *e* or
1 Ki 2: 7 let them be among those who *e*
13: 8 nor would I *e* bread nor drink
13: 9 You shall not *e* bread, nor drink
13:15 Come home with me and *e* bread."
13:16 neither can I *e* bread nor drink
13:17 You shall not *e* bread nor drink
13:18 that he may *e* bread and drink
13:22 *E* no bread and drink no water,"
14:11 The dogs shall *e* whoever belongs
14:11 the birds of the air shall *e*
16: 4 The dogs shall *e* whoever belongs
16: 4 the birds of the air shall *e*
17:12 that we may *e* it, and die."
18:19 who *e* at Jezebel's table."
18:41 'Go up, *e* and drink;
18:42 So Ahab went up to *e* and drink.
19: 5 and said to him, "Arise and *e*.
19: 7 and said, "Arise and *e*,
21: 4 and would *e* no food.
21: 5 spirit so sullen that you *e* no
21: 7 *e* food, and let your heart be
21:23 The dogs shall *e* Jezebel by the
21:24 The dogs shall *e* whoever belongs
21:24 the birds of the air shall *e*
2 Ki 4: 8 and she persuaded him to *e* some
4: 8 he would turn in there to *e*
4:40 they served it to the men to *e*.
4:40 And they could not *e* it.
4:41 to the people, that they may *e*.
4:42 to the people, that they may *e*.
4:43 to the people, that they may *e*;
4:43 They shall *e* and have some left
6:22 that they may *e* and drink and
6:28 that we may *e* him today, and we
6:28 and we will *e* my son tomorrow.'
6:29 that we may *e* him'; but she has
7: 2 but you shall not *e* of it."
7:19 but you shall not *e* of it."
9:10 The dogs shall *e* Jezebel on the
9:36 at Jezreel dogs shall *e* the
18:27 who will *e* and drink their own
18:31 and every one of you *e* from his
19:29 You shall *e* this year such as
19:29 Plant vineyards and *e* the
2 Chr 31:10 we have had enough to *e* and
Ezra 2:63 to them that they should not *e*
9:12 that you may be strong and *e*
Neh 5: 2 that we may *e* and live."
7:65 to them that they should not *e*
8:10 *e* the fat, drink the sweet, and
8:12 the people went their way to *e*
9:36 To *e* its fruit and its bounty,
Esth 4:16 neither *e* nor drink for three
Job 1: 4 their three sisters to *e* and
3:24 my sighing comes before I *e*,
5: 5 Because the hungry *e* up his
20:21 Nothing is left for him to *e*;
31: 8 let me sow, and another *e*;
31:17 the fatherless could not *e* of
Ps 14: 4 Who *e* up my people as they
14: 4 eat up my people as they *e*
22:26 The poor shall *e* and be
22:29 of the earth Shall *e* and
27: 2 wicked came against me To *e*
50:13 Will I *e* the flesh of bulls,
53: 4 Who *e* up my people as they
53: 4 eat up my people as they *e*
78:24 rained down manna on them to *e*,
102: 4 So that I forget to *e* my
127: 2 To *e* the bread of sorrows;
128: 2 When you *e* the labor of your
141: 4 And do not let me *e* of their
Prov 1:31 Therefore they shall *e* the
4:17 For they *e* the bread of
9: 5 *e* of my bread And drink of the
13: 2 A man shall *e* well by the fruit
18:21 And those who love it will *e*
23: 1 When you sit down to *e* with a
23: 6 Do not *e* the bread of a miser,
23: 7 *E* and drink!" he says to you,
24:13 *e* honey because it is good,
25:16 *E* only as much as you need,
25:21 is hungry, give him bread to *e*;
25:27 It is not good to *e* much

27:18 keeps the fig tree will *e* its
30:17 And the young eagles will *e*
31:27 And does not *e* the bread of
Eccl 2:24 a man than that he should *e*
2:25 For who can *e*, or who can
3:13 also that every man should *e*
5:11 They increase who *e* them; So
5:18 and fitting for one to *e* and
5:19 and given him power to *e* of it,
6: 2 does not give him power to *e*
8:15 better under the sun than to *e*,
9: 7 *e* your bread with joy, And
Song 4:16 come to his garden And *e* its
5: 1 *E*, O friends! Drink, yes,
Isa 1:19 You shall *e* the good of the
3:10 For they shall *e* the fruit of
4: 1 We will *e* our own food and wear
5:17 the fat ones strangers shall *e*.
7:15 "Curds and honey He shall *e*,
7:22 That he will *e* curds;
7:22 and honey everyone will *e* who
9:20 Every man shall *e* the flesh of
11: 7 And the lion shall *e* straw
21: 5 *E* and drink. Arise, you
22:13 Let us *e* and drink, for tomorrow
23:18 to *e* sufficiently, and for fine
30:24 that work the ground Will *e*
36:12 who will *e* and drink their own
36:16 and every one of you *e* from his
37:30 You shall *e* this year such as
37:30 Plant vineyards and *e* the
50: 9 The moth will *e* them up.
51: 8 For the moth will *e* them up
51: 8 And the worm will *e* them like
55: 1 have no money, Come, buy and *e*.
55: 2 and *e* what is good, And let
61: 6 You shall *e* the riches of the
62: 9 who have gathered it shall *e*
65: 4 Who *e* swine's flesh, And the
65:13 "Behold, My servants shall *e*,
65:21 shall plant vineyards and *e*
65:22 shall not plant and another *e*;
65:25 The lion shall *e* straw like
Jer 2: 7 To *e* its fruit and its
5:17 And they shall *e* up your
5:17 sons and daughters should *e*.
5:17 They shall *e* up your flocks
5:17 They shall *e* up your vines and
7:21 to your sacrifices and *e* meat.
16: 8 with them, to *e* and drink."
19: 9 And I will cause them to *e* the
19: 9 and everyone shall *e* the flesh
22:15 Did not your father *e* and
22:22 The wind shall *e* up all your
29: 5 plant gardens and *e* their
29:28 and plant gardens and *e* their
31: 5 The planters shall plant and *e*
Lam 2:20 Should the women *e* their
Ezek 2: 8 open your mouth and *e* what I
3: 1 *e* what you find; eat this
3: 1 *e* this scroll, and go, speak to
3: 2 and He caused me to *e* that
4: 9 ninety days, you shall *e* it.
4:10 And your food which you *e* shall
4:10 from time to time you shall *e*
4:12 And you shall *e* it as barley
4:13 shall the children of Israel *e*
4:16 they shall *e* bread by weight
5:10 Therefore fathers shall *e* their
5:10 and sons shall *e* their fathers;
12:18 *e* your bread with quaking, and
12:19 They shall *e* their bread with
22: 9 in you are those who *e* on the
24:17 and do not *e* man's bread of
24:22 not cover your lips nor *e*
25: 4 they shall *e* your fruit, and
33:25 You *e* meat with blood, you lift
34: 3 You *e* the fat and clothe
34:19 they *e* what you have trampled
39:17 That you may *e* flesh and drink
39:18 You shall *e* the flesh of the
39:19 You shall *e* fat till you are
42:13 who approach the LORD shall *e*
44: 3 he may sit in it to *e* bread
44:29 They shall *e* the grain offering,
44:31 The priests shall not *e*
Dan 1:12 them give us vegetables to *e*
1:13 of the young men who *e* the
4:25 and they shall make you *e* grass
4:32 They shall make you *e* grass
11:26 those who *e* of the portion of
Hos 2:12 the beasts of the field shall *e*
4: 8 They *e* up the sin of My people;
4:10 For they shall *e*,
8:13 they sacrifice flesh and *e* it,
9: 3 And shall *e* unclean things in
9: 4 All who *e* it shall be defiled.
Joel 2:26 You shall *e* in plenty and be
Am 6: 4 *E* lambs from the flock And
7:12 There *e* bread, And there
9:14 shall also make gardens and *e*
Ob 7 Those who *e* your bread
Jon 3: 7 do not let them *e*,
Mic 3: 3 Who also *e* the flesh of My
6:14 You shall *e*, but not be
7: 1 There is no cluster to *e*
Nah 3:15 It will *e* you up like a
Hab 1: 8 as the eagle that hastens to *e*.
Hag 1: 6 You *e*, but do not have
Zech 7: 6 When you *e* and when you drink,
7: 6 do you not *e* and drink for
11: 9 Let those that are left *e* each

11:16 But he will *e* the flesh of the
Mt 6:25 what you will *e* or what you
6:31 worry, saying, 'What shall we *e*?
9:11 Why does your Teacher *e* with tax
12: 1 pluck heads of grain and to *e*.
12: 4 was not lawful for him to *e*,
14:16 You give them something to *e*.
15: 2 wash their hands when they *e*
15:20 but to *e* with unwashed hands
15:27 yet even the little dogs *e* the
15:32 days and have nothing to *e*.
24:49 and to *e* and drink with the
26:17 us to prepare for You to *e* the
26:26 disciples and said, "Take, *e*;
Mk 2:26 which is not lawful to *e*,
3:20 they could not so much as *e*
5:43 should be given her to *e*.
6:31 did not even have time to *e*.
6:36 for they have nothing to *e*.
6:37 "You give them something to *e*.
6:37 and give them something to *e*?
7: 2 saw some of His disciples *e*
7: 3 and all the Jews do not *e*
7: 4 they do not *e* unless they wash.
7: 5 but *e* bread with unwashed
7:28 little dogs under the table *e*
8: 1 great and having nothing to *e*,
8: 2 days and have nothing to *e*.
11:14 Let no one *e* fruit from you ever
14:12 that You may *e* the Passover?"
14:14 the guest room in which I may *e*
14:22 it to them and said, "Take, *e*;
Lk 5:30 Why do You *e* and drink with tax
5:33 but Yours *e* and drink?"
6: 4 for any but the priests to *e*?
7:36 of the Pharisees asked Him to *e*
7:36 house, and sat down to *e*.
8:55 she be given something to *e*.
9:13 "You give them something to *e*.
10: 8 *e* such things as are set before
11:37 So He went in and sat down to *e*.
12:19 *e*, drink, and be merry."
12:22 your life, what you will *e*;
12:29 do not seek what you should *e*
12:37 and have them sit down to *e*,
12:45 and to *e* and drink and be
14: 1 rulers of the Pharisees to *e*
14:15 Blessed is he who shall *e* bread
15:23 and let us *e* and be merry;
17: 7 at once and sit down to *e*?
17: 8 and afterward you will *e* and
22: 8 Passover for us, that we may *e*.
22:11 is the guest room where I may *e*
22:15 desire I have desired to *e*
22:16 I will no longer *e* of it until
22:30 that you may *e* and drink at My
Jn 4:31 urged Him, saying, "Rabbi, *e*.
4:32 I have food to *e* of which you do
4:33 brought Him anything to *e*?
6: 5 we buy bread, that these may *e*?
6:31 bread from heaven to *e*.
6:50 that one may *e* of it and not
6:52 Man give us His flesh to *e*?
6:53 unless you *e* the flesh of the
18:28 but that they might *e* the
21:12 'Come and *e* breakfast."
Acts 10:10 very hungry and wanted to *e*;
10:13 him, "Rise, Peter; kill and *e*.
11: 7 to me, 'Rise, Peter; kill and *e*.
23:12 that they would neither *e* nor
23:14 a great oath that we will *e*
23:21 oath that they will neither *e*
27:35 he had broken it he began to *e*.
Rom 14: 2 For one believes he may *e* all
14: 3 eats despise him who does not *e*,
14: 3 and let not him who does not *e*
14: 6 thanks; and he who does not *e*,
14: 6 eat, to the Lord he does not *e*,
14:21 It is good neither to *e* meat
14:23 because he does not *e* from
1 Cor 5:11 not even to *e* with such a
8: 7 until now *e* it as a thing
8: 8 for neither if we *e* are we the
8: 8 nor if we do not *e* are we the
8:10 who is weak be emboldened to *e*
8:13 I will never again *e* meat, lest
9: 4 Do we have no right to *e* and
9: 7 a vineyard and does not *e* of
9:13 who minister the holy things *e*
10: 7 The people sat down to *e*
10:18 Are not those who *e* of the
10:25 *E* whatever is sold in the meat
10:27 *e* whatever is set before you,
10:28 do not *e* it for the sake of
10:31 whether you *e* or drink, or
11:20 it is not to *e* the Lord's
11:22 Do you not have houses to *e*
11:24 broke it and said, "Take, *e*;
11:26 For as often as you *e* this bread
11:28 and so let him *e* of the bread
11:33 when you come together to *e*,
11:34 let him *e* at home, lest you
15:32 Let us *e* and drink, for
Gal 2:12 he would *e* with the Gentiles;
2 Th 3: 8 nor did we *e* anyone's bread free
3:10 not work, neither shall he *e*.
3:12 they work in quietness and *e*
Heb 13:10 tabernacle have no right to *e*.
Jas 5: 3 witness against you and will *e*
Rev 2: 7 who overcomes I will give to *e*
2:14 to *e* things sacrificed to
2:17 some of the hidden manna to *e*.

2:20 commit sexual immorality and *e*
10: 9 Take and *e* it; and it will make
17:16 *e* her flesh and burn her with
19:18 that you may *e* the flesh of

EATEN (96/90) EAT

Gen 3:11 Have you *e* from the tree of
3:17 and have *e* from the tree of
6:21 yourself of all food that is *e*,
14:24 only what the young men have *e*,
31:38 and I have not *e* the rams of
41:21 When they had *e* them up, no one
41:21 have known that they had *e*
43: 2 when they had *e* up the grain
Ex 12:46 "In one house it shall be *e*;
13: 3 No leavened bread shall be *e*.
13: 7 Unleavened bread shall be *e*
21:28 and its flesh shall not be *e*;
29:34 with fire. It shall not be *e*,
Lev 6:16 unleavened bread it shall be *e*
6:23 It shall not be *e*."
6:26 In a holy place it shall be *e*,
6:30 in the holy place, shall be *e*.
7: 6 It shall be *e* in a holy place.
7:15 for thanksgiving shall be *e*
7:16 it shall be *e* the same day that
7:16 remainder of it also may be *e*;
7:18 of his peace offering is *e* at
7:19 unclean thing shall not be *e*.
10:17 Why have you not *e* the sin
10:18 indeed you should have *e* it in
10:19 I had *e* the sin offering
11:13 the birds; they shall not be *e*,
11:41 It shall not be *e*.
11:47 the animal that may be *e* and
11:47 the animal that may not be *e*.
17:13 animal or bird that may be *e*,
19: 6 It shall be *e* the same day you
19: 7 And if it is *e* at all on the
19:23 to you. It shall not be *e*.
22:30 "On the same day it shall be *e*;
Num 28:17 unleavened bread shall be *e* for
Deut 6:11 when you have *e* and are full—
8:10 When you have *e* and are full,
8:12 when you have *e* and are full,
12:22 the gazelle and the deer are *e*,
14:19 for you; they shall not be *e*.
20: 6 a vineyard and has not *e* of it?
26:14 I have not *e* any of it when in
29: 6 You have not *e* bread, nor have
31:20 and they have *e* and filled
Josh 5:12 on the day after they had *e*
Ruth 3: 7 And after Boaz had *e* and drunk,
1 Sam 14:30 much better if the people had *e*
28:20 for he had *e* no food all day or
30:12 of raisins. So when he had *e*,
30:12 for he had *e* no bread nor drunk
2 Sam 19:42 Have we ever *e* at the king's
1 Ki 13:23 after he had *e* bread and after
13:28 The lion had not *e* the corpse
Job 6: 6 Can flavorless food be *e*
21:25 Never having *e* with pleasure.
31:17 Or *e* my morsel by myself, So
31:39 If I have *e* its fruit without
Ps 69: 9 zeal for Your house has *e* me
102: 9 For I have *e* ashes like bread,
Prov 9:17 And bread *e* in secret is
23: 8 The morsel you have *e*,
Song 5: 1 I have *e* my honeycomb with my
Isa 3:14 For you have *e* up the vineyard;
44:19 I have roasted meat and *e* it;
Jer 10:25 For they have *e* up Jacob,
24: 2 bad figs which could not be *e*,
24: 3 very bad, which cannot be *e*,
24: 8 the bad figs which cannot be *e*,
29:17 rotten figs that cannot be *e*,
31:29 The fathers have *e* sour grapes,
Ezek 4:14 I have never *e* what died of
18: 2 The fathers have *e* sour grapes,
18: 6 If he has not *e* on the
18:11 But has *e* on the mountains Or
18:15 Who has not *e* on the
34:18 too little for you to have *e*
45:21 unleavened bread shall be *e*.
Hos 10:13 You have *e* the fruit of lies,
Joel 1: 4 left, the swarming locust has *e*;
1: 4 left, the crawling locust has *e*;
1: 4 the consuming locust has *e*.
2:25 that the swarming locust has *e*,
Mt 14:21 Now those who had *e* were about
Mk 6:44 Now those who had *e* the loaves
8: 9 Now those who had *e* were about
Lk 17: 8 and serve me till I have *e* and
Jn 2:17 for Your house has *e*
6:13 left over by those who had *e*.
21:15 So when they had *e* breakfast,
Acts 10:14 I have never *e* anything
12:23 And he was *e* by worms and died.
20:11 come up, had broken bread and *e*,
27:33 without food, and *e* nothing.
27:38 So when they had *e* enough, they
Rev 10:10 But when I had *e* it, my stomach

EATER (3/3) EAT

Judg 14:14 Out of the *e* came something to
Isa 55:10 the sower And bread to the *e*,
Nah 3:12 fall into the mouth of the *e*.

EATERS (1/1)

Prov 23:20 Or with gluttonous *e* of meat;

EATING (32/32) EAT

Lev 13:55 it continues *e* away, whether
Judg 14: 9 in his hands and went along, *e*.
Ruth 3: 3 the man until he has finished *e*
1 Sam 1: 9 after they had finished *e* and
14:33 sinning against the LORD by *e*
14:34 not sin against the LORD by *e*
30:16 *e* and drinking and dancing,
1 Ki 1:25 They are *e* and drinking
1:41 heard it as they finished *e*.
4:20 *e* and drinking and rejoicing.
2 Ki 4:40 as they were *e* the stew, that
1 Chr 12:39 *e* and drinking, for their
Job 1:13 his sons and daughters were *e*
1:18 sons and daughters were *e* and
20:23 rain it on him while he is *e*.
Isa 22:13 *E* meat and drinking wine:
66:17 *E* swine's flesh and the
Am 7: 2 when they had finished *e* the
Mt 11:18 For John came neither *e* nor
11:19 The Son of Man came *e* and
24:38 they were *e* and drinking,
26:21 Now as they were *e*,
26:26 And as they were *e*,
Mk 2:16 and Pharisees saw Him *e* with
14:22 And as they were *e*,
Lk 7:33 John the Baptist came neither *e*
7:34 The Son of Man has come *e* and
10: 7 *e* and drinking such things as
Rom 14:17 for the kingdom of God is not *e*
1 Cor 8: 4 Therefore concerning the *e* of
8:10 sees you who have knowledge *e*
11:21 For in *e*, each one takes

EATS (47/42) EAT

Ex 12:15 For whoever *e* leavened bread
12:19 since whoever *e* what is
Lev 7:18 and the person who *e* of it
7:20 But the person who *e* the flesh
7:21 and who *e* the flesh of the
7:25 For whoever *e* the fat of the
7:25 the person who *e* it shall be
7:27 Whoever *e* any blood, that person
11:40 He who *e* of its carcass shall
14:47 and he who *e* in the house shall
17:10 who *e* any blood, I will set My
17:10 face against that person who *e*
17:14 Whoever *e* it shall be cut off.'
17:15 And every person who *e* what
19: 8 Therefore everyone who *e* it
22:14 And if a man *e* the holy
1 Sam 14:24 Cursed is the man who *e* any
14:28 Cursed is the man who *e* food
Job 40:15 He *e* grass like an ox.
Ps 106:20 Into the image of an ox that *e*
Prov 13:25 The righteous *e* to the
30:20 She *e* and wipes her mouth,
Eccl 5:12 Whether he *e* little or much;
5:17 All his days he also *e* in
Isa 28: 4 He *e* it up while it is still
29: 8 man dreams, And look—he *e*;
44:16 With this half he *e* meat;
59: 5 He who *e* of their eggs dies,
Jer 31:30 every man who *e* the sour
Mk 2:16 How is it that He *e* and drinks
14:18 one of you who *e* with Me will
Lk 15: 2 Man receives sinners and *e*
Jn 6:51 If anyone *e* of this bread, he
6:54 Whoever *e* My flesh and drinks My
6:56 He who *e* My flesh and drinks My
6:58 He who *e* this bread will live
13:18 He who *e* bread with Me has
Rom 14: 2 but he who is weak *e* only
14: 3 Let not him who *e* despise him
14: 3 does not eat judge him who *e*;
14: 6 He who *e*, eats to the Lord,
14: 6 *e* to the Lord, for he gives God
14:20 it is evil for the man who *e*
14:23 who doubts is condemned if he *e*,
1 Cor 11:27 Therefore whoever *e* this bread
11:29 For he who *e* and drinks in an
11:29 drinks in an unworthy manner *e*

EAVES (1/1)

1 Ki 7: 9 from the foundation to the *e*,

EBAL (8/8)

Gen 36:23 of Shobal: Alvan, Manahath, *E*,
Deut 11:29 and the curse on Mount *E*.
27: 4 that on Mount *E* you shall set
27:13 these shall stand on Mount *E*
Josh 8:30 LORD God of Israel in Mount *E*,
8:33 of them in front of Mount *E*,
1 Chr 1:22 *E*, Abimael, Sheba,
1:40 Shobal were Alian, Manahath, *E*,

EBED (6/6)

Judg 9:26 Now Gaal the son of *E* came with
9:28 Then Gaal the son of *E* said,
9:30 the words of Gaal the son of *E*,
9:31 Take note! Gaal the son of *E* and
9:35 When Gaal the son of *E* went out
Ezra 8: 6 *E* the son of Jonathan, and with

EBED-MELECH (6/6)

Jer 38: 7 Now *E* the Ethiopian, one of the
38: 8 *E* went out of the king's house
38:10 Then the king commanded *E* the
38:11 So *E* took the men with him and
38:12 Then *E* the Ethiopian said to
39:16 Go and speak to *E* the Ethiopian,

EBENEZER (3/3)

1 Sam 4: 1 and encamped beside *E*;
5: 1 of God and brought it from *E*
7:12 and Shen, and called its name *E*,

EBER (16/16)

Gen 10:21 father of all the children of *E*,
10:24 begot Salah, and Salah begot *E*.
10:25 To *E* were born two sons:
11:14 lived thirty years, and begot *E*.
11:15 After he begot *E*,
11:16 *E* lived thirty-four years, and
11:17 *E* lived four hundred and thirty
Num 24:24 afflict Asshur and afflict *E*,
1 Chr 1:18 Shelah, and Shelah begot *E*.
1:19 To *E* were born two sons:
1:25 *E*, Peleg, Reu,
5:13 Jorai, Jachan, Zia, and *E*—
8:12 The sons of Elpaal were *E*,
8:22 Ishpan, *E*, Eliel,
Neh 12:20 of Sallai, Kallai; of Amok, *E*;
Lk 3:35 son of Peleg, the son of *E*,

EBIASAPH (3/3)

1 Chr 6:23 *E* his son, Assir his son,
6:37 the son of Assir, the son of *E*,
9:19 the son of Kore, the son of *E*,

EBONY (1/1)

Ezek 27:15 brought you ivory tusks and *e*

EBRON (1/1)

Josh 19:28 including *E*, Rehob,

ECZEMA (2/2)

Lev 21:20 or *e* or scab, or is a eunuch.
22:22 or have an ulcer or *e* or scabs,

ED (KJV) See WITNESS

EDEN (19/18)

Gen 2: 8 planted a garden eastward in *E*,
2:10 Now a river went out of *E* to
2:15 and put him in the garden of *E*
3:23 him out of the garden of *E* to
3:24 at the east of the garden of *E*,
4:16 land of Nod on the east of *E*.
2 Ki 19:12 and the people of *E* who were
2 Chr 29:12 Joah the son of Zimmah and *E*
31:15 And under him were *E*,
Isa 37:12 and the people of *E* who were
51: 3 will make her wilderness like *E*,
Ezek 27:23 "Haran, Canneh, *E*,
28:13 You were in *E*, the garden
31: 9 So that all the trees of *E*
31:16 the Pit; and all the trees of *E*,
31:18 To which of the trees in *E* will
31:18 down with the trees of *E* to
36:35 has become like the garden of *E*;
Joel 2: 3 land is like the Garden of *E*

EDER (5/5)

Gen 35:21 his tent beyond the tower of *E*.
Josh 15:21 in the South, were Kabzeel, *E*,
1 Chr 8:15 Zebadiah, Arad, *E*,
23:23 sons of Mushi were Mahli, *E*,
24:30 sons of Mushi were Mahli, *E*,

EDGE (69/62) EDGES

Gen 34:26 and Shechem his son with the *e*
Ex 13:20 and camped in Etham at the *e*
17:13 and his people with the *e* of
26: 4 loops of blue yarn on the *e*
26: 4 you shall do on the outer *e* of
26: 5 loops you shall make on the *e*
26:10 make fifty loops on the *e* of
26:10 and fifty loops on the *e* of the
28:26 on the *e* of it, which is on the
36:11 loops of blue yarn on the *e*
36:11 likewise he did on the outer *e*
36:12 fifty loops he made on the *e*
36:17 he made fifty loops on the *e*
36:17 fifty loops he made on the *e*
39:19 on the *e* of it, which was on
Num 20:16 a city on the *e* of your border.
21:24 Israel defeated him with the *e*
33: 6 which is on the *e* of the
Deut 13:15 of that city with the *e* of the
13:15 with the *e* of the sword.
20:13 every male in it with the *e* of
Josh 3: 8 When you have come to the *e* of
3:15 bore the ark dipped in the *e*
6:21 with the *e* of the sword.
8:24 they all had fallen by the *e*
8:24 to Ai and struck it with the *e*

10:28 it and its king with the *e* of
10:30 who were in it with the *e* of
10:32 who were in it with the *e* of
10:35 day and struck it with the *e*
10:37 it and struck it with the *e* of
10:39 they struck them with the *e* of
11:11 who were in it with the *e* of
11:12 took and struck with the *e* of
11:14 struck every man with the *e* of
13:27 as far as the *e* of the Sea of
19:47 and they struck it with the *e*
Judg 1: 8 they struck it with the *e* of
1:25 struck the city with the *e* of
4:15 and all his army with the *e*
4:16 army of Sisera fell by the *e*
7:17 and when I come to the *e* of the
18:27 they struck them with the *e* of
20:37 the whole city with the *e* of
20:48 struck them down with the *e* of
21:10 of Jabesh Gilead with the *e* of
1 Sam 15: 8 all the people with the *e* of
15:27 Saul seized the *e* of his robe,
22:19 he struck with the *e* of the
22:19 with the *e* of the sword.
2 Sam 15:14 and strike the city with the *e*
2 Ki 10:25 they killed them with the *e* of
Job 1:15 killed the servants with the *e*
1:17 killed the servants with the *e*
Ps 89:43 have also turned back the *e* of
133: 2 Running down on the *e* of his
Eccl 10:10 And one does not sharpen the *e*,
Jer 21: 7 he shall strike them with the *e*
31:29 children's teeth are set on *e*.
31:30 his teeth shall be set on *e*.
Ezek 5: 3 of them and bind them in the *e*
18: 2 children's teeth are set on *e*'?
21:16 Wherever your *e* is ordered!
43:13 with a rim all around its *e* of
48:15 along the *e* of the twenty-five
Am 3:12 corner of a bed and on the *e*
Hag 2:12 and with the *e* he touches bread
Lk 21:24 And they will fall by the *e* of
Heb 11:34 escaped the *e* of the sword, out

EDGES (5/5) EDGE

Ex 28: 7 straps joined at its two *e*,
39: 4 coupled together at its two *e*.
Lev 19:27 nor shall you disfigure the *e*
21: 5 nor shall they shave the *e* of
Job 26:14 Indeed these are the mere *e* of

EDIBLE (1/1)

Lev 11:34 any *e* food upon which water

EDICT (1/1)

Ezra 6:11 that whoever alters this *e*,

EDIFICATION (10/10) EDIFY

Rom 15: 2 for his good, leading to *e*.
1 Cor 14: 3 But he who prophesies speaks *e*
14: 5 that the church may receive *e*.
14:12 let it be for the *e* of the
14:26 Let all things be done for *e*.
2 Cor 10: 8 which the Lord gave us for *e*
12:19 all things, beloved, for your *e*.
13:10 the Lord has given me for *e*
Eph 4:29 what is good for necessary *e*,
1 Tim 1: 4 disputes rather than godly *e*

EDIFIED (2/2) EDIFY

Acts 9:31 Samaria had peace and were *e*.
1 Cor 14:17 well, but the other is not *e*.

EDIFIES (3/2) EDIFY

1 Cor 8: 1 Knowledge puffs up, but love *e*.
14: 4 He who speaks in a tongue *e*
14: 4 but he who prophesies *e* the

EDIFY (3/3) EDIFICATION, EDIFIED, EDIFIES, EDIFYING

Rom 14:19 the things by which one may *e*
1 Cor 10:23 for me, but not all things *e*.
1 Th 5:11 comfort each other and *e* one

EDIFYING (2/2) EDIFY

Eph 4:12 for the *e* of the body of
4:16 growth of the body for the *e*

EDOM (89/85) EDOMITE, ESAU, IDUMEA, OBED-EDOM

Gen 25:30 Therefore his name was called *E*.
32: 3 land of Seir, the country of *E*.
36: 1 the genealogy of Esau, who is *E*.
36: 8 dwelt in Mount Seir. Esau is *E*.
36:16 of Eliphaz in the land of *E*.
36:17 of Reuel in the land of *E*.
36:19 the sons of Esau, who is *E*,
36:21 sons of Seir, in the land of *E*.
36:31 who reigned in the land of *E*
36:32 the son of Beor reigned in *E*,
36:43 These were the chiefs of *E*,
Ex 15:15 Then the chiefs of *E* will be
Num 20:14 from Kadesh to the king of *E*.
20:18 Then *E* said to him, "You shall
20:20 So *E* came out against them
20:21 Thus *E* refused to give Israel
20:23 by the border of the land of *E*,
21: 4 to go around the land of *E*;
24:18 And *E* shall be a possession;
33:37 the boundary of the land of *E*.
34: 3 of Zin along the border of *E*;
Josh 15: 1 The border of *E* at the
15:21 toward the border of *E* in the
Judg 5: 4 You marched from the field of *E*,
11:17 messengers to the king of *E*,
11:17 But the king of *E* would not
11:18 and bypassed the land of *E* and
1 Sam 14:47 the people of Ammon, against *E*,
2 Sam 8:14 He also put garrisons in *E*;
8:14 throughout all *E* he put
1 Ki 9:26 the Red Sea, in the land of *E*.
11:14 a descendant of the king in *E*.
11:15 happened, when David was in *E*,
11:15 he had killed every male in *E*
11:16 had cut down every male in *E*),
22:47 There was then no king in *E*,
2 Ki 3: 8 "By way of the Wilderness of *E*.
3: 9 king of Judah and the king of *E*,
3:12 Jehoshaphat and the king of *E*
3:20 suddenly water came by way of *E*,
3:26 break through to the king of *E*,
8:20 In his days *E* revolted against
8:22 Thus *E* has been in revolt
14:10 "You have indeed defeated *E*,
1 Chr 1:43 who reigned in the land of *E*
1:51 And the chiefs of *E* were Chief
1:54 These were the chiefs of *E*.
18:11 from all these nations—from *E*,
18:13 He also put garrisons in *E*,
2 Chr 8:17 the seacoast, in the land of *E*.
21:10 Thus *E* has been in revolt
25:20 they sought the gods of *E*.
Ps 60: 8 Over *E* I will cast My shoe;
60: 9 Who will lead me to *E*?
83: 6 The tents of *E* and the
108: 9 Over *E* I will cast My shoe;
108:10 Who will lead me to *E*?
137: 7 against the sons of *E* The day
Isa 11:14 shall lay their hand on *E* and
34: 5 Indeed it shall come down on *E*,
34: 6 slaughter in the land of *E*.
63: 1 Who is this who comes from *E*,
Jer 9:26 'Egypt, Judah, *E*, the people
25:21 *E*, Moab, and the people
27: 3 'and send them to the king of *E*,
40:11 Moab, among the Ammonites, in *E*,
49: 7 Against *E*. Thus says
49:17 *E* also shall be an astonishment;
49:20 that He has taken against *E*,
49:22 heart of the mighty men of *E*
Lam 4:21 and be glad, O daughter of *E*,
4:22 your iniquity, O daughter of *E*;
Ezek 25:12 Because of what *E* did against
25:13 stretch out My hand against *E*,
25:14 I will lay My vengeance on *E* by
25:14 that they may do in *E* according
32:29 There is *E*, Her kings
35:15 Mount Seir, as well as all of *E*—
36: 5 the nations and against all *E*,
Dan 11:41 shall escape from his hand: *E*,
Joel 3:19 And *E* a desolate wilderness,
Am 1: 6 To deliver them up to *E*.
1: 9 up the whole captivity to *E*,
1:11 three transgressions of *E*,
2: 1 the bones of the king of *E* to
9:12 may possess the remnant of *E*,
Ob 1 says the Lord GOD concerning *E*
8 destroy the wise men from *E*,
Mal 1: 4 Even though *E* has said,

EDOMITE (7/7) EDOM, EDOMITES

Deut 23: 7 "You shall not abhor an *E*,
1 Sam 21: 7 And his name was Doeg, an *E*,
22: 9 Then answered Doeg the *E*,
22:18 So Doeg the *E* turned and
22:22 when Doeg the *E* was there,
1 Ki 11:14 against Solomon, Hadad the *E*;
Ps 52: of David when Doeg the *E* went

EDOMITES (16/16) EDOMITE

Gen 36: 9 of Esau the father of the *E* in
36:43 Esau was the father of the *E*.
2 Sam 8:14 and all the *E* became David's
1 Ki 11: 1 of the Moabites, Ammonites, *E*,
11:17 he and certain *E* of his
2 Ki 8:21 by night and attacked the *E*
14: 7 He killed ten thousand *E* in the
16: 6 Then the *E* went to Elath, and
1 Chr 18:12 killed eighteen thousand *E* in
18:13 and all the *E* became David's
2 Chr 21: 8 In his days the *E* revolted
21: 9 by night and attacked the *E*
25:14 from the slaughter of the *E*,
25:19 that you have defeated the *E*,
28:17 For again the *E* had come,
Ps 60: and killed twelve thousand *E*

EDREI (8/8)

Num 21:33 all his people, to battle at *E*.
Deut 1: 4 who dwelt at Ashtaroth in *E*.
3: 1 all his people, to battle at *E*.
3:10 Bashan, as far as Salcah and *E*,
Josh 12: 4 who dwelt at Ashtaroth and at *E*,
13:12 who reigned in Ashtaroth and *E*,
13:31 of Gilead, and Ashtaroth and *E*,
19:37 Kedesh, *E*, En Hazor,

EFFECT (11/11) EFFECTIVE

1 Sam 21: 5 and the bread is in *e*
2 Chr 34:22 they spoke to her to that *e*.
Ps 33:10 plans of the peoples of no *e*.
Isa 32:17 And the *e* of righteousness,
Mt 15: 6 the commandment of God of no *e*
Mk 7:13 the word of God of no *e*
Rom 3: 3 faithfulness of God without *e*?
4:14 and the promise made of no *e*,
9: 6 the word of God has taken no *e*.
1 Cor 1:17 Christ should be made of no *e*.
Gal 3:17 should make the promise of no *e*.

EFFECTIVE (7/7) EFFECT, EFFECTIVELY

Prov 17:10 Rebuke is more *e* for a wise
1 Cor 16: 9 For a great and *e* door has
2 Cor 1: 6 which is *e* for enduring the
Eph 3: 7 given to me by the *e* working
4:16 according to the *e* working by
Phm 1: 6 of your faith may become *e* by
Jas 5:16 The *e*, fervent prayer of a

EFFECTIVELY (3/2) EFFECTIVE

Gal 2: 8 (for He who worked *e* in Peter
2: 8 the circumcised also worked *e*
1 Th 2:13 which also *e* works in you who

EFFEMINATE (KJV) See HOMOSEXUALS

EFFORT (1/1)

Lk 12:58 make every *e* along the way to

EGG (2/2) EGGS

Job 6: 6 any taste in the white of an *e*?
Lk 11:12 "Or if he asks for an *e*,

EGGS (7/5) EGG

Deut 22: 6 ground, with young ones or *e*,
22: 6 on the young or on the *e*,
Job 39:14 For she leaves her *e* on the
Isa 10:14 And as one gathers *e* that
34:15 shall make her nest and lay *e*
59: 5 They hatch vipers' *e* and weave
59: 5 He who eats of their *e* dies,

EGLAH (2/2)

2 Sam 3: 5 Ithream, by David's wife *E*.
1 Chr 3: 3 sixth, Ithream, by his wife *E*.

EGLAIM (1/1)

Isa 15: 8 Its wailing to *E* And its

EGLON (13/12)

Josh 10: 3 of Lachish, and Debir king of *E*,
10: 5 of Lachish, and the king of *E*,
10:23 of Lachish, and the king of *E*.
10:34 Lachish Joshua passed to *E*,
10:36 So Joshua went up from *E*,
10:37 to all that he had done to *E*,
12:12 the king of *E*, one;
15:39 Lachish, Bozkath, *E*,
Judg 3:12 So the LORD strengthened *E*
3:14 the children of Israel served *E*
3:15 of Israel sent tribute to *E*
3:17 So he brought the tribute to *E*
3:17 (Now *E* was a very fat man.)

EGLON'S (1/1)

Judg 3:24 *E* servants came to look, and

EGYPT (612/559) EGYPTIAN, GOSHEN, MIZRAIM

Gen 12:10 and Abram went down to *E* to
12:11 when he was close to entering *E*,
12:14 it was, when Abram came into *E*,
13: 1 Then Abram went up from *E*,
13:10 like the land of *E* as you go
15:18 from the river of *E* to the
21:21 wife for him from the land of *E*.
25:18 which is east of *E* as you go
26: 2 and said: "Do not go down to *E*;
37:25 way to carry them down to *E*.
37:28 And they took Joseph to *E*.
37:36 Midianites had sold him in *E*
39: 1 Joseph had been taken down to *E*.
40: 1 and the baker of the king of *E*
40: 1 their lord, the king of *E*.
40: 5 and the baker of the king of *E*,
41: 8 for all the magicians of *E* and
41:19 never seen in all the land of *E*.
41:29 throughout all the land of *E*;
41:30 be forgotten in the land of *E*;
41:33 and set him over the land of *E*.
41:34 the produce of the land of *E*
41:36 which shall be in the land of *E*,
41:41 set you over all the land of *E*.

41:43 set him over all the land of E.
41:44 or foot in all the land of E.
41:45 out over all the land of E.
41:46 stood before Pharaoh king of E.
41:46 throughout all the land of E.
41:48 which were in the land of E,
41:53 which were in the land of E
41:54 but in all the land of E there
41:55 So when all the land of E was
41:56 became severe in the land of E.
41:57 countries came to Joseph in E
42: 1 saw that there was grain in E,
42: 2 heard that there is grain in E;
42: 3 went down to buy grain in E.
43: 2 which they had brought from E,
43:15 and arose and went down to E;
45: 4 brother, whom you sold into E.
45: 8 throughout all the land of E.
45: 9 "God has made me lord of all E;
45:13 my father of all my glory in E,
45:18 you the best of the land of E,
45:19 carts out of the land of E for
45:20 the best of all the land of E
45:23 with the good things of E,
45:25 Then they went up out of E,
45:26 governor over all the land of E.
46: 3 do not fear to go down to E,
46: 4 "I will go down with you to E,
46: 6 land of Canaan, and went to E,
46: 7 he brought with him to E.
46: 8 and his sons, who went to E:
46:20 And to Joseph in the land of E
46:26 who went with Jacob to E,
46:27 who were born to him in E
46:27 house of Jacob who went to E
47: 6 The land of E is before you.
47:11 a possession in the land of E,
47:13 so that the land of E and the
47:14 was found in the land of E and
47:15 money failed in the land of E
47:20 bought all the land of E for
47:21 one end of the borders of E
47:26 it a law over the land of E to
47:27 Israel dwelt in the land of E,
47:28 Jacob lived in the land of E
47:29 me. Please do not bury me in E,
47:30 you shall carry me out of E and
48: 5 born to you in the land of E
48: 5 Egypt before I came to you in E,
50: 7 all the elders of the land of E,
50:14 father, Joseph returned to E,
50:22 So Joseph dwelt in E,
50:26 and he was put in a coffin in E.
Ex 1: 1 of Israel who came to E;
1: 5 persons (for Joseph was in E
1: 8 there arose a new king over E,
1:15 Then the king of E spoke to the
1:17 and did not do as the king of E
1:18 So the king of E called for the
2:23 of time that the king of E
3: 7 of My people who are in E,
3:10 children of Israel, out of E.
3:11 the children of Israel out of E?
3:12 brought the people out of E,
3:16 seen what is done to you in E;
3:17 up out of the affliction of E
3:18 of Israel, to the king of E;
3:19 I am sure that the king of E
3:20 out My hand and strike E with
4:18 to my brethren who are in E,
4:19 in Midian, "Go, return to E;
4:20 he returned to the land of E.
4:21 Moses, "When you go back to E,
5: 4 Then the king of E said to them,
5:12 throughout all the land of E
6:11 tell Pharaoh king of E to let
6:13 and for Pharaoh king of E,
6:13 of Israel out of the land of E.
6:26 of Israel from the land of E
6:27 who spoke to Pharaoh king of E,
6:27 the children of Israel from E.
6:28 spoke to Moses in the land of E,
6:29 Speak to Pharaoh king of E all
7: 3 and My wonders in the land of E.
7: 4 so that I may lay My hand on E
7: 4 out of the land of E by great
7: 5 I stretch out My hand on E and
7:11 so the magicians of E,
7:19 your hand over the waters of E,
7:19 throughout all the land of E,
7:21 throughout all the land of E.
7:22 Then the magicians of E did so
8: 5 to come up on the land of E.
8: 6 his hand over the waters of E,
8: 6 up and covered the land of E.
8: 7 up frogs on the land of E.
8:16 throughout all the land of E.
8:17 throughout all the land of E.
8:24 and into all the land of E.
9: 4 Israel and the livestock of E.
9: 6 and all the livestock of E
9: 9 fine dust in all the land of E,
9: 9 throughout all the land of E.
9:18 such as has not been in E since
9:22 be hail in all the land of E—
9:22 field, throughout the land of E.
9:23 rained hail on the land of E.
9:24 like it in all the land of E
9:25 throughout the whole land of E,
10: 2 mighty things I have done in E,
10: 7 Do you not yet know that E is
10:12 your hand over the land of E
10:12 may come upon the land of E,
10:13 out his rod over the land of E,
10:14 went up over all the land of E
10:14 on all the territory of E.
10:15 throughout all the land of E.
10:19 in all the territory of E.
10:21 be darkness over the land of E,
10:22 darkness in all the land of E
11: 1 plague on Pharaoh and on E.
11: 3 very great in the land of E,
11: 4 will go out into the midst of E;
11: 5 the firstborn in the land of E
11: 6 throughout all the land of E,
11: 9 be multiplied in the land of E.
12: 1 and Aaron in the land of E,
12:12 pass through the land of E on
12:12 the firstborn in the land of E,
12:12 and against all the gods of E
12:13 when I strike the land of E.
12:17 armies out of the land of E.
12:27 of the children of Israel in E
12:29 the firstborn in the land of E,
12:30 and there was a great cry in E,
12:39 which they had brought out of E;
12:39 they were driven out of E and
12:40 of Israel who lived in E was
12:41 went out from the land of E.
12:42 them out of the land of E.
12:51 of Israel out of the land of E
13: 3 day in which you went out of E,
13: 8 for me when I came up from E.
13: 9 LORD has brought you out of E.
13:14 the LORD brought us out of E,
13:15 the firstborn in the land of E,
13:16 the LORD brought us out of E.
13:17 they see war, and return to E.
13:18 ranks out of the land of E.
14: 5 Now it was told the king of E
14: 7 and all the chariots of E with
14: 8 the heart of Pharaoh king of E,
14:11 there were no graves in E,
14:11 us, to bring us up out of E?
14:12 the word that we told you in E,
14:31 which the LORD had done in E;
16: 1 departed from the land of E.
16: 3 of the LORD in the land of E,
16: 6 you out of the land of E.
16:32 you out of the land of E.
17: 3 you have brought us up out of E,
18: 1 had brought Israel out of E.
19: 1 had gone out of the land of E,
20: 2 you out of the land of E,
22:21 were strangers in the land of E.
23: 9 were strangers in the land of E.
23:15 for in it you came out of E;
29:46 them up out of the land of E,
32: 1 us up out of the land of E,
32: 4 you out of the land of E!"
32: 7 brought out of the land of E
32: 8 you out of the land of E!'"
32:11 brought out of the land of E
32:23 brought us out of the land of E,
33: 1 brought out of the land of E,
34:18 of Abib you came out from E.
Lev 11:45 you up out of the land of E,
18: 3 to the doings of the land of E,
19:34 were strangers in the land of E:
19:36 you out of the land of E.
22:33 you out of the land of E,
23:43 them out of the land of E:
25:38 you out of the land of E,
25:42 I brought out of the land of E;
25:55 I brought out of the land of E:
26:13 you out of the land of E,
26:45 I brought out of the land of E
Num 1: 1 had come out of the land of E,
3:13 the firstborn in the land of E,
8:17 the firstborn in the land of E
9: 1 had come out of the land of E,
11: 5 fish which we ate freely in E,
11:18 For it was well with us in E.
11:20 did we ever come up out of E?
13:22 seven years before Zoan in E.
14: 2 we had died in the land of E!
14: 3 be better for us to return to E?
14: 4 select a leader and return to E.
14:19 from E even until now."
14:22 and the signs which I did in E
15:41 you out of the land of E,
20: 5 you made us come up out of E,
20:15 'how our fathers went down to E,
20:15 and we dwelt in E a long time,
20:16 and brought us up out of E;
21: 5 you brought us up out of E to
22: 5 a people has come from E.
22:11 a people has come out of E,
23:22 God brings them out of E;
24: 8 "God brings him out of E;
26: 4 who came out of the land of E.
26:59 Levi, who was born to Levi in E;
32:11 of the men who came up from E,
33: 1 who went out of the land of E
33:38 had come out of the land of E,
34: 5 from Azmon to the Brook of E,
Deut 1:27 us out of the land of E to
1:30 to all He did for you in E
4:20 of the iron furnace, out of E,
4:34 LORD your God did for you in E
4:37 and He brought you out of E
4:45 Israel after they came out of E,
4:46 after they came out of E.
5: 6 you out of the land of E,
5:15 were a slave in the land of E,
6:12 you out of the land of E,
6:21 'We were slaves of Pharaoh in E,
6:21 the LORD brought us out of E
6:22 great and severe, against E,
7: 8 the hand of Pharaoh king of E.
7:15 of the terrible diseases of E
7:18 God did to Pharaoh and to all E:
8:14 you out of the land of E,
9: 7 you departed from the land of E
9:12 whom you brought out of E have
9:26 whom You have brought out of E
10:19 were strangers in the land of E.
10:22 Your fathers went down to E with
11: 3 which He did in the midst of E,
11: 3 of Egypt, to Pharaoh king of E,
11: 4 "what He did to the army of E,
11:10 is not like the land of E
13: 5 you out of the land of E and
13:10 you out of the land of E,
15:15 were a slave in the land of E,
16: 1 your God brought you out of E
16: 3 you came out of the land of E
16: 3 you came out of the land of E
16: 6 at the time you came out of E.
16:12 that you were a slave in E,
17:16 the people to return to E to
20: 1 you up from the land of E.
23: 4 the road when you came out of E,
24: 9 the way when you came out of E.
24:18 that you were a slave in E,
24:22 were a slave in the land of E;
25:17 way as you were coming out of E,
26: 5 and he went down to E and dwelt
26: 8 the LORD brought us out of E
28:27 strike you with the boils of E,
28:60 on you all the diseases of E,
28:68 LORD will take you back to E
29: 2 your eyes in the land of E,
29:16 that we dwelt in the land of E
29:25 them out of the land of E;
34:11 sent him to do in the land of E,
Josh 2:10 for you when you came out of E,
5: 4 the people who came out of E
5: 4 after they had come out of E.
5: 5 the way as they came out of E,
5: 6 men of war, who came out of E,
5: 9 rolled away the reproach of E
9: 9 fame, and all that He did in E,
13: 3 Sihor, which is east of E,
15: 4 and went out to the Brook of E;
15:47 as far as the Brook of E and the
24: 4 and his children went down to E.
24: 5 and Aaron, and I plagued E,
24: 6 I brought your fathers out of E,
24: 7 your eyes saw what I did in E.
24:14 side of the River and in E.
24:17 fathers up out of the land of E,
24:32 Israel had brought up out of E,
Judg 2: 1 I led you up from E and brought
2:12 them out of the land of E;
6: 8 I brought you up from E and
6:13 the LORD bring us up from E?
11:13 land when they came up out of E,
11:16 'for when Israel came up from E,
19:30 came up from the land of E
1 Sam 2:27 father when they were in E in
8: 8 that I brought them up out of E,
10:18 'I brought up Israel out of E,
12: 6 fathers up from the land of E.
12: 8 "When Jacob had gone into E,
12: 8 brought your fathers out of E
15: 2 the way when he came up from E.
15: 6 when they came up out of E.
15: 7 way to Shur, which is east of E.
27: 8 even as far as the land of E.
30:13 "I am a young man from E,
2 Sam 7: 6 children of Israel up from E,
7:23 redeemed for Yourself from E,
1 Ki 3: 1 a treaty with Pharaoh king of E,
4:21 as far as the border of E.
4:30 East and all the wisdom of E.
6: 1 had come out of the land of E,
8: 9 they came out of the land of E.
8:16 My people Israel out of E,
8:21 them out of the land of E.
8:51 whom You brought out of E,
8:53 brought our fathers out of E,
8:65 of Hamath to the Brook of E,
9: 9 fathers out of the land of E,
9:16 (Pharaoh king of E had gone up
10:28 had horses imported from E and
10:29 that was imported from E cost
11:17 that Hadad fled to go to E,
11:18 them from Paran and came to E,
11:18 to Egypt, to Pharaoh king of E,
11:21 So when Hadad heard in E that
11:40 Jeroboam arose and fled to E,
11:40 to Egypt, to Shishak king of E,
11:40 and was in E until the death of
12: 2 heard it (he was still in E,
12: 2 and had been dwelling in E),
12:28 you up from the land of E!"
14:25 that Shishak king of E came
2 Ki 17: 4 messengers to So, king of E,
17: 7 them up out of the land of E,
17: 7 the hand of Pharaoh king of E;
17:36 you up from the land of E with
18:21 broken reed, E, on which
18:21 So is Pharaoh king of E to all
18:24 and put your trust in E for
21:15 day their fathers came out of E,

23:29 days Pharaoh Necho king of **E**
23:34 took Jehoahaz and went to **E**,
24: 7 And the king of **E** did not come
24: 7 that belonged to the king of **E**
24: 7 of Egypt from the Brook of **E**
25:26 the armies, arose and went to **E**;
1 Chr 13: 5 from Shihor in **E** to as far as
17:21 people whom You redeemed from **E**?
2 Chr 1:16 had horses imported from **E** and
1:17 acquired and imported from **E** a
5:10 when they had come out of **E**.
6: 5 My people out of the land of **E**,
7: 8 of Hamath to the Brook of **E**.
7:22 them out of the land of **E**,
9:26 as far as the border of **E**.
9:28 horses to Solomon from **E** and
10: 2 of Nebat heard it (he was in **E**,
10: 2 that Jeroboam returned from **E**.
12: 2 that Shishak king of **E** came up
12: 3 who came with him out of **E**—
12: 9 So Shishak king of **E** came up
20:10 they came out of the land of **E**,
26: 8 as far as the entrance of **E**,
35:20 Necho king of **E** came up to
36: 3 Now the king of **E** deposed him at
36: 4 Then the king of **E** made
36: 4 and carried him off to **E**.
Neh 9: 9 affliction of our fathers in **E**,
9:18 That brought you up out of **E**,
Ps 68:31 Envoys will come out of **E**;
78:12 fathers, In the land of **E**,
78:43 When He worked His signs in **E**,
78:51 all the firstborn in **E**,
80: 8 have brought a vine out of **E**;
81: 5 went throughout the land of **E**,
81:10 you out of the land of **E**;
105:23 Israel also came into **E**,
105:38 **E** was glad when they departed,
106: 7 Our fathers in **E** did not
106:21 Who had done great things in **E**,
114: 1 When Israel went out of **E**,
135: 8 destroyed the firstborn of **E**,
135: 9 into the midst of you, O **E**,
136:10 To Him who struck **E** in their
Isa 7:18 part of the rivers of **E**,
10:24 against you, in the manner of **E**.
10:26 lift it up in the manner of **E**.
11:11 are left, From Assyria and **E**,
11:15 the tongue of the Sea of **E**;
11:16 he came up from the land of **E**.
19: 1 The burden against **E**.
19: 1 cloud, And will come into **E**;
19: 1 The idols of **E** will totter at
19: 1 And the heart of **E** will melt
19: 3 The spirit of **E** will fail in
19:12 of hosts has purposed against **E**.
19:13 They have also deluded **E**,
19:14 And they have caused **E** to err
19:15 will there be any work for **E**,
19:16 In that day **E** will be like
19:17 of Judah will be a terror to **E**;
19:18 five cities in the land of **E**
19:19 in the midst of the land of **E**,
19:20 LORD of hosts in the land of **E**;
19:21 the LORD will be known to **E**,
19:22 And the LORD will strike **E**,
19:23 there will be a highway from **E**
19:23 the Assyrian will come into **E**
19:24 will be one of three with **E**
19:25 Blessed is **E** My people, and
20: 3 a sign and a wonder against **E**
20: 4 uncovered, to the shame of **E**.
20: 5 their expectation and **E** their
23: 5 When the report reaches **E**,
27:12 of the River to the Brook of **E**;
27:13 are outcasts in the land of **E**,
30: 2 Who walk to go down to **E**,
30: 2 to trust in the shadow of **E**!
30: 3 And trust in the shadow of **E**
31: 1 Woe to those who go down to **E**
36: 6 staff of this broken reed, **E**,
36: 6 So is Pharaoh king of **E** to all
36: 9 and put your trust in **E** for
43: 3 I gave **E** for your ransom,
45:14 The labor of **E** and merchandise
52: 4 went down at first Into **E** to
Jer 2: 6 us up out of the land of **E**,
2:18 And now why take the road to **E**,
2:36 you shall be ashamed of **E** as
7:22 them out of the land of **E**,
7:25 came out of the land of **E**,
9:26 '**E**, Judah, Edom, the people
11: 4 them out of the land of **E**,
11: 7 them up out of the land of **E**,
16:14 of Israel from the land of **E**,
23: 7 of Israel from the land of **E**,
24: 8 who dwell in the land of **E**.
25:19 Pharaoh king of **E**,
26:21 afraid and fled, and went to **E**.
26:22 the king sent men to **E**:
26:22 men who went with him to **E**.
26:23 And they brought Urijah from **E**
31:32 lead them out of the land of **E**,
32:20 and wonders in the land of **E**,
32:21 Israel out of the land of **E**
34:13 them out of the land of **E**,
37: 5 Pharaoh's army came up from **E**;
37: 7 up to help you will return to **E**,
41:17 as they went on their way to **E**,
42:14 but we will go to the land of **E**
42:15 set your faces to enter **E**,
42:16 you there in the land of **E**;
42:16 close after you there in **E**;
42:17 who set their faces to go to **E**
42:18 out on you when you enter **E**.
42:19 Do not go to **E**!' Know certainly
43: 2 Do not go to **E** to dwell there.'
43: 7 So they went to the land of **E**,
43:11 he shall strike the land of **E**
43:12 in the houses of the gods of **E**,
43:12 himself with the land of **E**,
43:13 that are in the land of **E**;
44: 1 Jews who dwell in the land of **E**,
44: 8 to other gods in the land of **E**
44:12 faces to go into the land of **E**
44:12 and fall in the land of **E**.
44:13 who dwell in the land of **E**,
44:14 have gone into the land of **E**
44:15 who dwelt in the land of **E**,
44:24 who are in the land of **E**!
44:26 who dwell in the land of **E**:
44:26 of Judah in all the land of **E**,
44:27 Judah who are in the land of **E**
44:28 return from the land of **E** to
44:28 who have gone to the land of **E**
44:30 give Pharaoh Hophra king of **E**
46: 2 Against **E**. Concerning the army
46: 2 of Pharaoh Necho, king of **E**,
46: 8 **E** rises up like a flood,
46:11 O virgin, the daughter of **E**;
46:13 come and strike the land of **E**.
46:14 'Declare in **E**, and proclaim
46:17 there, 'Pharaoh, king of **E**,
46:19 O you daughter dwelling in **E**,
46:20 **E** is a very pretty heifer,
46:24 The daughter of **E** shall be
46:25 Amon of No, and Pharaoh and **E**,
Ezek 17:15 by sending his ambassadors to **E**,
19: 4 with chains to the land of **E**.
20: 5 known to them in the land of **E**,
20: 6 them out of the land of **E** into
20: 7 yourselves with the idols of **E**.
20: 8 did they forsake the idols of **E**.
20: 8 in the midst of the land of **E**.
20: 9 bring them out of the land of **E**.
20:10 them go out of the land of **E**
20:36 the wilderness of the land of **E**,
23: 3 They committed harlotry in **E**,
23: 8 up her harlotry brought from **E**,
23:19 the harlot in the land of **E**.
23:27 Brought from the land of **E**,
23:27 Nor remember **E** anymore.'
27: 7 Fine embroidered linen from **E**
29: 2 face against Pharaoh king of **E**,
29: 2 against him, and against all **E**.
29: 3 you, O Pharaoh king of **E**,
29: 6 Then all the inhabitants of **E**
29: 9 And the land of **E** shall become
29:10 and I will make the land of **E**
29:12 I will make the land of **E**
29:14 bring back the captives of **E**
29:19 I will give the land of **E** to
29:20 'I have given him the land of **E**
30: 4 The sword shall come upon **E**,
30: 4 When the slain fall in **E**,
30: 6 Those who uphold **E** shall fall,
30: 8 When I have set a fire in **E**
30: 9 upon them, As on the day of **E**;
30:10 also make a multitude of **E** to
30:11 draw their swords against **E**,
30:13 be princes from the land of **E**;
30:13 will put fear in the land of **E**.
30:15 fury on Sin, the strength of **E**;
30:16 And set a fire in **E**;
30:18 When I break the yokes of **E**
30:19 I will execute judgments on **E**,
30:21 the arm of Pharaoh king of **E**;
30:22 I am against Pharaoh king of **E**,
30:25 it out against the land of **E**.
31: 2 say to Pharaoh king of **E** and to
32: 2 for Pharaoh king of **E**,
32:12 shall plunder the pomp of **E**,
32:15 When I make the land of **E**
32:16 shall lament for her, for **E**,
32:18 wail over the multitude of **E**,
Dan 9:15 people out of the land of **E**
11: 8 carry their gods captive to **E**,
11:42 and the land of **E** shall not
11:43 all the precious things of **E**;
Hos 2:15 she came up from the land of **E**.
7:11 They call to **E**, They go to
7:16 their derision in the land of **E**.
8:13 They shall return to **E**.
9: 3 But Ephraim shall return to **E**,
9: 6 **E** shall gather them up;
11: 1 And out of **E** I called My son.
11: 5 not return to the land of **E**;
11:11 trembling like a bird from **E**,
12: 1 And oil is carried to **E**.
12: 9 God, Ever since the land of **E**;
12:13 LORD brought Israel out of **E**,
13: 4 God Ever since the land of **E**,
Joel 3:19 **E** shall be a desolation, And
Am 2:10 you up from the land of **E**,
3: 1 I brought up from the land of **E**,
3: 9 in the palaces in the land of **E**,
4:10 a plague after the manner of **E**;
8: 8 subside Like the River of **E**.
9: 5 subside like the River of **E**.
9: 7 up Israel from the land of **E**,
Mic 6: 4 you up from the land of **E**,
7:15 you came out of the land of **E**,
Nah 3: 9 Ethiopia and **E** were her
Hag 2: 5 with you when you came out of **E**,
Zech 10:10 them back from the land of **E**,
10:11 And the scepter of **E** shall
14:18 If the family of **E** will not come
14:19 shall be the punishment of **E**
Mt 2:13 Child and His mother, flee to **E**,
2:14 by night and departed for **E**,
2:15 Out of **E** I called My
2:19 in a dream to Joseph in **E**,
Acts 2:10 **E** and the parts of Libya
7: 9 envious, sold Joseph into **E**.
7:10 presence of Pharaoh, king of **E**;
7:10 and he made him governor over **E**
7:11 came over all the land of **E**
7:12 heard that there was grain in **E**,
7:15 "So Jacob went down to **E**;
7:17 grew and multiplied in **E**
7:34 my people who are in **E**;
7:34 I will send you to **E**.
7:36 and signs in the land of **E**,
7:39 hearts they turned back to **E**,
7:40 us out of the land of **E**,
13:17 as strangers in the land of **E**,
Heb 3:16 it not all who came out of **E**,
8: 9 out of the land of **E**;
11:26 riches than the treasures in **E**;
11:27 By faith he forsook **E**,
Jude 5 the people out of the land of **E**,
Rev 11: 8 is called Sodom and **E**,

EGYPTIAN (23/22) EGYPT, EGYPTIANS

Gen 16: 1 And she had an **E** maidservant
16: 3 took Hagar her maid, the **E**,
21: 9 saw the son of Hagar the **E**,
25:12 Abraham's son, whom Hagar the **E**,
39: 1 captain of the guard, an **E**,
39: 2 the house of his master the **E**.
Ex 1:19 women are not like the **E**
2:11 And he saw an **E** beating a
2:12 he killed the **E** and hid him in
2:14 to kill me as you killed the **E**?
2:19 An **E** delivered us from the hand
Lev 24:10 woman, whose father was an **E**,
Deut 23: 7 You shall not abhor an **E**,
1 Sam 30:11 Then they found an **E** in the
2 Sam 23:21 And he killed an **E**,
23:21 The **E** had a spear in his hand;
1 Chr 2:34 And Sheshan had an **E** servant
11:23 And he killed an **E**,
Prov 7:16 Colored coverings of **E** linen.
Isa 19:23 will come into Egypt and the **E**
Acts 7:24 and struck down the **E**.
7:28 kill me as you did the **E**
21:38 Are you not the **E** who some time

EGYPTIAN'S (4/3)

Gen 39: 5 the LORD blessed the **E** house
2 Sam 23:21 the spear out of the **E** hand,
1 Chr 11:23 In the **E** hand there was a
11:23 the spear out of the **E** hand,

EGYPTIANS (97/86) EGYPTIAN

Gen 12:12 when the **E** see you, that they
12:14 that the **E** saw the woman, that
41:55 Then Pharaoh said to all the **E**,
41:56 storehouses and sold to the **E**.
43:32 and the **E** who ate with him by
43:32 because the **E** could not eat
43:32 is an abomination to the **E**.
45: 2 and the **E** and the house of
46:34 is an abomination to the **E**.
47:15 all the **E** came to Joseph and
47:20 for every man of the **E** sold his
50: 3 and the **E** mourned for him
50:11 is a deep mourning of the **E**.
Ex 1:13 So the **E** made the children of
3: 8 them out of the hand of the **E**,
3: 9 the oppression with which the **E**
3:21 favor in the sight of the **E**;
3:22 So you shall plunder the **E**.
6: 5 children of Israel whom the **E**
6: 6 from under the burdens of the **E**,
6: 7 from under the burdens of the **E**.
7: 5 And the **E** shall know that I am
7:18 and the **E** will loathe to drink
7:21 and the **E** could not drink the
7:24 So all the **E** dug all around the
8:21 The houses of the **E** shall be
8:26 the abomination of the **E** to
8:26 the abomination of the **E**
9:11 the magicians and on all the **E**.
10: 6 and the houses of all the **E**—
11: 3 favor in the sight of the **E**.
11: 7 a difference between the **E** and
12:23 pass through to strike the **E**;
12:27 in Egypt when He struck the **E**
12:30 all his servants, and all the **E**;
12:33 And the **E** urged the people, that
12:35 and they had asked from the **E**
12:36 favor in the sight of the **E**,
12:36 Thus they plundered the **E**.
14: 4 that the **E** may know that I am
14: 9 So the **E** pursued them, all the
14:10 the **E** marched after them.
14:12 alone that we may serve the **E**?
14:12 better for us to serve the **E**
14:13 For the **E** whom you see today,
14:17 will harden the hearts of the **E**,
14:18 Then the **E** shall know that I am
14:20 came between the camp of the **E**

14:23 And the *E* pursued and went after
14:24 down upon the army of the *E*
14:24 He troubled the army of the *E*.
14:25 and the *E* said, "Let us flee
14:25 fights for them against the *E*.
14:26 waters may come back upon the *E*,
14:27 while the *E* were fleeing into
14:27 So the LORD overthrew the *E* in
14:30 day out of the hand of the *E*,
14:30 and Israel saw the *E* dead on
15:26 which I have brought on the *E*.
18: 8 done to Pharaoh and to the *E*
18: 9 out of the hand of the *E*.
18:10 you out of the hand of the *E*
18:10 from under the hand of the *E*.
19: 4 have seen what I did to the *E*,
32:12 Why should the *E* speak, and say,
Num 14:13 Then the *E* will hear it, for by
20:15 and the *E* afflicted us and our
33: 3 in the sight of all the *E*.
33: 4 For the *E* were burying all
Deut 26: 6 But the *E* mistreated us,
Josh 24: 6 and the *E* pursued your fathers
24: 7 darkness between you and the *E*,
Judg 6: 9 you out of the hand of the *E*
10:11 I not deliver you from the *E*
1 Sam 4: 8 are the gods who struck the *E*
6: 6 you harden your hearts as the *E*
10:18 you from the hand of the *E*
2 Ki 7: 6 and the kings of the *E* to
Ezra 9: 1 Ammonites, the Moabites, the *E*,
Isa 19: 2 I will set *E* against Egyptians;
19: 2 will set Egyptians against *E*;
19: 4 And the *E* I will give Into the
19:21 and the *E* will know the LORD
19:23 and the *E* will serve with the
20: 4 of Assyria lead away the *E* as
30: 7 For the *E* shall help in vain
31: 3 Now the *E* are men, and not
Jer 43:13 houses of the gods of the *E* he
Lam 5: 6 have given our hand to the *E*
Ezek 16:26 committed harlotry with the *E*,
23:21 When the *E* pressed your bosom
29:12 and I will scatter the *E* among
29:13 years I will gather the *E* from
30:23 I will scatter the *E* among the
30:26 I will scatter the *E* among the
Acts 7:22 in all the wisdom of the *E*,
Heb 11:29 as by dry land, whereas the *E*,

EHI (1/1)

Gen 46:21 Becher, Ashbel, Gera, Naaman, *E*,

EHUD (10/9)

Judg 3:15 *E* the son of Gera, the
3:16 Now *E* made himself a dagger
3:20 And *E* came to him (now he was
3:20 Then *E* said, "I have a message
3:21 Then *E* reached with his left
3:23 Then *E* went out through the
3:26 But *E* had escaped while they
4: 1 When *E* was dead, the children of
1 Chr 7:10 Bilhan were Jeush, Benjamin, *E*,
8: 6 These are the sons of *E*,

EIGHT (53/53) EIGHTH

Gen 5: 4 the days of Adam were *e* hundred
5: 7 Seth lived *e* hundred and seven
5:10 Enosh lived *e* hundred and
5:13 Cainan lived *e* hundred and
5:16 Mahalalel lived *e* hundred and
5:17 the days of Mahalalel were *e*
5:19 Jared lived *e* hundred years,
17:12 He who is *e* days old among you
21: 4 his son Isaac when he was *e*
22:23 These *e* Milcah bore to Nahor,
Ex 26:25 So there shall be *e* boards with
36:30 So there were *e* boards and their
Num 2:24 one hundred and *e* thousand one
3:28 there were *e* thousand six
4:48 those who were numbered were *e*
7: 8 and four carts and *e* oxen he
29:29 On the sixth day present *e*
Judg 3: 8 served Cushan-Rishathaim *e*
12:14 He judged Israel *e* years.
1 Sam 17:12 and who had *e* sons. And the man
2 Sam 23: 8 because he had killed *e* hundred
24: 9 And there were in Israel *e*
1 Ki 7:10 some ten cubits and some *e*
2 Ki 8:17 and he reigned *e* years in
22: 1 Josiah was *e* years old when he
1 Chr 12:24 six thousand *e* hundred armed
12:30 of Ephraim twenty thousand *e*
24: 4 and *e* heads of their fathers'
2 Chr 13: 3 formation against him with *e*
21: 5 and he reigned *e* years in
21:20 He reigned in Jerusalem *e* years
29:17 the house of the LORD in *e*
34: 1 Josiah was *e* years old when he
36: 9 Jehoiachin was *e* years old
Ezra 2: 6 two thousand *e* hundred and
Neh 7:11 two thousand *e* hundred and
7:13 *e* hundred and forty-five;
11:12 the work of the house were *e*
Eccl 11: 2 serving to seven, and also to *e*,
Jer 41:15 escaped from Johanan with *e*
52:29 away captive from Jerusalem *e*
Ezek 40: 9 *e* cubits; and the gateposts,
40:31 and going up to it were *e*
40:34 and going up to it were *e*
40:37 and going up to it were *e*
40:41 *e* tables on which they
Mic 5: 5 him Seven shepherds and *e*
Lk 2:21 And when *e* days were completed
9:28 about *e* days after these
Jn 20:26 And after *e* days His disciples
Acts 9:33 who had been bedridden *e* years
1 Pe 3:20 *e* souls, were saved through
2 Pe 2: 5 one of *e* people, a preacher

EIGHT-STRINGED (2/2)

Ps 6: On an *e* harp. A Psalm of David.
12: On an *e* harp. A Psalm of David.

EIGHTEEN (22/22) EIGHTEENTH

Gen 14:14 armed his three hundred and *e*
Judg 3:14 served Eglon king of Moab *e*
10: 8 the children of Israel for *e*
20:25 and cut down to the ground *e*
20:44 And *e* thousand men of Benjamin
2 Sam 8:13 when he returned from killing *e*
1 Ki 7:15 each one *e* cubits high, and a
2 Ki 24: 8 Jehoiachin was *e* years old
25:17 The height of one pillar was *e*
1 Chr 12:31 of the half-tribe of Manasseh *e*
18:12 the son of Zeruiah killed *e*
26: 9 and brethren, *e* able men.
29: 7 *e* thousand talents of bronze,
2 Chr 11:21 for he took *e* wives and sixty
Ezra 8: 9 and with him two hundred and *e*
8:18 sons and brothers, *e* men;
Neh 7:11 thousand eight hundred and *e*;
Jer 52:21 the height of one pillar was *e*
Ezek 48:35 the way around shall be *e*
Lk 13: 4 Or those *e* on whom the tower in
13:11 who had a spirit of infirmity *e*
13:16 for *e* years, be loosed from this

EIGHTEENTH (11/11) EIGHTEEN

1 Ki 15: 1 In the *e* year of King Jeroboam
2 Ki 3: 1 over Israel at Samaria in the *e*
22: 3 in the *e* year of King Josiah,
23:23 But in the *e* year of King Josiah
1 Chr 24:15 the *e* to Happizzez,
25:25 the *e* for Hanani, his sons and
2 Chr 13: 1 In the *e* year of King Jeroboam,
34: 8 In the *e* year of his reign,
35:19 In the *e* year of the reign of
Jer 32: 1 which was the *e* year of
52:29 in the *e* year of Nebuchadnezzar

EIGHTH (36/35) EIGHT

Ex 22:30 on the *e* day you shall give it
Lev 9: 1 It came to pass on the *e* day
12: 3 And on the *e* day the flesh of
14:10 And on the *e* day he shall take
14:23 them to the priest on the *e*
15:14 On the *e* day he shall take for
15:29 And on the *e* day she shall take
22:27 and from the *e* day and
23:36 On the *e* day you shall have a
23:39 and on the *e* day a
25:22 And you shall sow in the *e* year,
Num 6:10 Then on the *e* day he shall bring
7:54 On the *e* day Gamaliel the son
29:35 On the *e* day you shall have a
1 Ki 6:38 which is the *e* month, the house
8:66 On the *e* day he sent the people
12:32 on the fifteenth day of the *e*
12:33 on the fifteenth day of the *e*
2 Ki 24:12 in the *e* year of his reign,
1 Chr 12:12 Johanan the *e*,
24:10 to Hakkoz, the *e* to Abijah,
25:15 the *e* for Jeshaiah, his sons and
26: 5 the seventh, Peulthai the *e*;
27:11 The *e* captain for the eighth
27:11 The eighth captain for the *e*
2 Chr 7: 9 And on the *e* day they held a
29:17 and on the *e* day of the month
34: 3 For in the *e* year of his reign,
Neh 8:18 and on the *e* day there was a
Ezek 43:27 on the *e* day and thereafter,
Zech 1: 1 In the *e* month of the second
Lk 1:59 on the *e* day, that they came to
Acts 7: 8 and circumcised him on the *e*
Phil 3: 5 circumcised the *e* day, of the
Rev 17:11 is not, is himself also the *e*,
21:20 the *e* beryl, the ninth topaz,

EIGHTIETH (1/1)

1 Ki 6: 1 pass in the four hundred and *e*

EIGHTY (24/24)

Gen 35:28 of Isaac were one hundred and *e*
Ex 7: 7 And Moses was *e* years old and
Num 4:48 thousand five hundred and *e*.
Judg 3:30 And the land had rest for *e*
2 Sam 19:32 *e* years old. And he had
19:35 I am today *e* years old. Can I
1 Ki 5:15 and *e* thousand who quarried
12:21 one hundred and *e* thousand
2 Ki 6:25 a donkey's head was sold for *e*
10:24 had appointed for himself *e*
1 Chr 15: 9 and *e* of his brethren;
2 Chr 2: 2 *e* thousand to quarry stone in
2:18 *e* thousand stonecutters in the
11: 1 and Benjamin one hundred and *e*
14: 8 from Benjamin two hundred and *e*
17:15 and with him two hundred and *e*
17:18 and with him one hundred and *e*
26:17 and with him were *e* priests of
Ezra 8: 8 and with him *e* males;
Esth 1: 4 one hundred and *e* days in
Ps 90:10 of strength they are *e* years,
Song 6: 8 There are sixty queens And *e*
Jer 41: 5 *e* men with their beards shaved
Lk 16: 7 'Take your bill, and write *e*.

EIGHTY-EIGHT (2/2)

1 Chr 25: 7 was two hundred and *e*.
Neh 7:26 and Netophah, one hundred and *e*;

E

EIGHTY-FIVE (4/4)

Josh 14:10 I am this day, *e* years old.
1 Sam 22:18 and killed on that day *e* men
2 Ki 19:35 the Assyrians one hundred and *e*
Isa 37:36 the Assyrians one hundred and *e*

EIGHTY-FOUR (2/2)

Neh 11:18 city were two hundred and *e*.
Lk 2:37 woman was a widow of about *e*

EIGHTY-SEVEN (2/2)

Gen 5:25 lived one hundred and *e* years,
1 Chr 7: 5 *e* thousand in all.

EIGHTY-SIX (2/2)

Gen 16:16 Abram was *e* years old when
Num 2: 9 one hundred and *e* thousand four

EIGHTY-THREE (1/1)

Ex 7: 7 eighty years old and Aaron *e*

EIGHTY-TWO (2/2)

Gen 5:26 lived seven hundred and *e*
5:28 lived one hundred and *e* years,

EITHER (43/43)

Gen 24:50 we cannot speak to you *e* bad or
Lev 13:51 *e* in the warp or in the woof,
13:53 *e* in the warp or in the woof,
13:57 *e* in the warp or in the woof,
13:58 *e* warp or woof, or whatever is
13:59 *e* in the warp or woof, or in
15:33 *e* man or woman, and for him who
18:26 *e* any of your own nation or
22:23 *E* a bull or a lamb that has any
Num 6: 2 When *e* a man or woman
22:26 there was no way to turn *e* to
Deut 17: 3 *e* the sun or moon or any of the
Josh 8:33 stood on *e* side of the ark
1 Sam 20: 2 my father will do nothing *e*
20:27 *e* yesterday or today?"
25:31 *e* that you have shed blood
28: 6 *e* by dreams or by Urim or by
30:19 *e* small or great, sons or
1 Ki 10:19 there were armrests on *e* side
18:27 *e* he is meditating, or he is
2 Ki 5:17 servant will no longer offer *e*
7:13 they may *e* become like all
1 Chr 21:12 *e* three years of famine, or
2 Chr 9:18 there were armrests on *e* side
Eccl 11: 6 *E* this or that, Or whether
Isa 7:11 ask it *e* in the depth or in the
Mt 6:24 for *e* he will hate the one and
12:32 *e* in this age or in the age to
12:33 *E* make the tree good and its
Mk 16:13 they did not believe them *e*.
Lk 6:29 do not withhold your tunic *e*.
16:13 for *e* he will hate the one and
Jn 19:18 one on *e* side, and Jesus in the
Acts 17:21 time in nothing else but *e* to
24:12 *e* in the synagogues or in the
Rom 11:21 He may not spare you *e*.
1 Cor 10:32 *e* to the Jews or to the Greeks
14: 6 you unless I speak to you *e* by
1 Th 2: 6 *e* from you or from others, when
2 Th 2: 2 *e* by spirit or by word or by
Jas 5:12 *e* by heaven or by earth or with
1 Jn 2:23 Son does not have the Father *e*;
Rev 22: 2 and on *e* side of the river,

EKER (1/1)

1 Chr 2:27 were Maaz, Jamin, and *E*.

EKRON (22/20)

Josh 13: 3 as far as the border of *E*
15:11 went out to the side of *E*
15:45 *E*, with its towns
15:46 from *E* to the sea, all that lay
19:43 Elon, Timnah, *E*,
Judg 1:18 and *E* with its territory.
1 Sam 5:10 they sent the ark of God to *E*.
5:10 as the ark of God came to *E*,
6:16 they returned to *E* the same
6:17 one for Gath, one for *E*;
7:14 from *E* to Gath; and Israel

17:52 valley and to the gates of ***E***.
17:52 even as far as Gath and ***E***.
2 Ki 1: 2 of Baal-Zebub, the god of ***E***,
1: 3 of Baal-Zebub, the god of ***E***?
1: 6 of Baal-Zebub, the god of ***E***?
1:16 of Baal-Zebub, the god of ***E***,
Jer 25:20 (namely, Ashkelon, Gaza, ***E***,
Am 1: 8 I will turn My hand against ***E***,
Zeph 2: 4 And ***E*** shall be uprooted.
Zech 9: 5 shall be very sorrowful; And ***E***,
9: 7 And ***E*** like a Jebusite.

EKRONITES (2/2)

Josh 13: 3 the Gittites, and the ***E***;
1 Sam 5:10 that the ***E*** cried out, saying,

EL BETHEL (1/1) BETHEL

Gen 35: 7 there and called the place ***E***,

EL ELOHE ISRAEL (1/1)

Gen 33:20 an altar there and called it ***E***.

EL PARAN (1/1)

Gen 14: 6 mountain of Seir, as far as ***E***,

ELABORATE (2/2)

Zech 6:11 make an ***e*** crown, and set it on
6:14 Now the ***e*** crown shall be for a

ELADAH (1/1)

1 Chr 7:20 ***E*** his son, Tahath his son,

ELAH (17/16)

Gen 36:41 Chief Aholibamah, Chief ***E***,
1 Sam 17: 2 encamped in the Valley of ***E***,
17:19 Israel were in the Valley of ***E***,
21: 9 you killed in the Valley of ***E***,
1 Ki 4:18 Shimei the son of ***E***,
16: 6 Then ***E*** his son reigned in his
16: 8 ***E*** the son of Baasha became king
16:13 of Baasha and the sins of ***E***
16:14 Now the rest of the acts of ***E***,
2 Ki 15:30 Then Hoshea the son of ***E*** led a
17: 1 Hoshea the son of ***E*** became king
18: 1 year of Hoshea the son of ***E***,
18: 9 year of Hoshea the son of ***E***,
1 Chr 1:52 Chief Aholibamah, Chief ***E***,
4:15 son of Jephunneh were Iru, ***E***,
4:15 The son of ***E*** was Kenaz.
9: 8 ***E*** the son of Uzzi, the son of

ELAM (28/27) ELAMITES, PERSIA

Gen 10:22 The sons of Shem were ***E***,
14: 1 Ellasar, Chedorlaomer king of ***E***,
14: 9 against Chedorlaomer king of ***E***,
1 Chr 1:17 The sons of Shem were ***E***,
8:24 Hananiah, ***E***, Antothijah,
26: 3 ***E*** the fifth, Jehohanan the
Ezra 2: 7 people of ***E***, one thousand
2:31 the people of the other ***E***,
8: 7 of the sons of ***E***,
10: 2 Jehiel, one of the sons of ***E***,
10:26 of the sons of ***E***:
Neh 7:12 the sons of ***E***, one thousand
7:34 the sons of the other ***E***,
10:14 people: Parosh, Pahath-Moab, ***E***,
12:42 Uzzi, Jehohanan, Malchijah, ***E***,
Isa 11:11 From ***E*** and Shinar, From
21: 2 O ***E***! Besiege, O Media!
22: 6 ***E*** bore the quiver With
Jer 25:25 of Zimri, all the kings of ***E***,
49:34 Jeremiah the prophet against ***E***,
49:35 I will break the bow of ***E***,
49:36 Against ***E*** I will bring the four
49:36 where the outcasts of ***E*** will
49:37 For I will cause ***E*** to be
49:38 I will set My throne in ***E***,
49:39 bring back the captives of ***E***,
Ezek 32:24 There is ***E*** and all her
Dan 8: 2 which is in the province of ***E***;

ELAMITES (2/2) ELAM, PERSIAN

Ezra 4: 9 Shushan, the Dehavites, the ***E***,
Acts 2: 9 "Parthians and Medes and ***E***,

ELASAH (2/2)

Ezra 10:22 Nethanel, Jozabad, and ***E***.
Jer 29: 3 was sent by the hand of ***E***

ELATH (8/6)

Deut 2: 8 away from ***E*** and Ezion Geber, we
1 Ki 9:26 which is near ***E*** on the shore
2 Ki 14:22 He built ***E*** and restored it to
16: 6 Rezin king of Syria captured ***E***
16: 6 drove the men of Judah from ***E***.
16: 6 Then the Edomites went to ***E***,
2 Chr 8:17 went to Ezion Geber and ***E*** on
26: 2 He built ***E*** and restored it to

ELDAAH (2/2)

Gen 25: 4 Epher, Hanoch, Abidah, and ***E***.
1 Chr 1:33 Epher, Hanoch, Abida, and ***E***.

ELDAD (2/2)

Num 11:26 camp: the name of one was ***E***,
11:27 ***E*** and Medad are prophesying in

ELDER (12/12) ELDERLY, ELDERS, ELDEST

Gen 10:21 the brother of Japheth the ***e***.
27:15 the choice clothes of her ***e***
29:16 the name of the ***e*** was Leah,
Isa 3: 2 And the diviner and the ***e***;
3: 5 will be insolent toward the ***e***,
9:15 The ***e*** and honorable, he is the
Ezek 16:46 Your ***e*** sister is Samaria, who
23: 4 Oholah the ***e*** and Oholibah her
1 Tim 5:19 an accusation against an ***e***
1 Pe 5: 1 I who am a fellow ***e*** and a
2 Jn 1 The ***E***, To the elect lady
3 Jn 1 The ***E***, To the beloved

ELDERLY (2/2) ELDER

Deut 28:50 which does not respect the ***e***
Isa 47: 6 On the ***e*** you laid your yoke

ELDERS (199/194) ELDER

Gen 50: 7 the ***e*** of his house, and all the
50: 7 and all the ***e*** of the land of
Ex 3:16 Go and gather the ***e*** of Israel
3:18 you and the ***e*** of Israel, to the
4:29 gathered together all the ***e*** of
12:21 Moses called for all the ***e*** of
17: 5 take with you some of the ***e*** of
17: 6 did so in the sight of the ***e***
18:12 And Aaron came with all the ***e***
19: 7 came and called for the ***e*** of
24: 1 and seventy of the ***e*** of Israel,
24: 9 and seventy of the ***e*** of Israel,
24:14 And he said to the ***e***,
Lev 4:15 And the ***e*** of the congregation
9: 1 Aaron and his sons and the ***e***
Num 11:16 to Me seventy men of the ***e*** of
11:16 whom you know to be the ***e*** of
11:24 the seventy men of the ***e*** of
11:25 the same upon the seventy ***e***;
11:30 both he and the ***e*** of Israel.
16:25 and the ***e*** of Israel followed
22: 4 So Moab said to the ***e*** of Midian,
22: 7 So the ***e*** of Moab and the elders
22: 7 the elders of Moab and the ***e***
Deut 5:23 heads of your tribes and your ***e***.
19:12 then the ***e*** of his city shall
21: 2 then your ***e*** and your judges
21: 3 And it shall be that the ***e*** of
21: 4 The ***e*** of that city shall bring
21: 6 And all the ***e*** of that city
21:19 him and bring him out to the ***e***
21:20 And they shall say to the ***e*** of
22:15 woman's virginity to the ***e*** of
22:16 father shall say to the ***e***,
22:17 spread the cloth before the ***e***
22:18 Then the ***e*** of that city shall
25: 7 wife go up to the gate to the ***e***,
25: 8 Then the ***e*** of his city shall
25: 9 to him in the presence of the ***e***,
27: 1 with the ***e*** of Israel, commanded
29:10 and your tribes and your ***e*** and
31: 9 and to all the ***e*** of Israel.
31:28 Gather to me all the ***e*** of your
32: 7 and he will show you; Your ***e***,
Josh 7: 6 he and the ***e*** of Israel; and
8:10 he and the ***e*** of Israel, before
8:33 with their ***e*** and officers and
9:11 Therefore our ***e*** and all the
20: 4 case in the hearing of the ***e***
23: 2 for all Israel, for their ***e***,
24: 1 to Shechem and called for the ***e***
24:31 and all the days of the ***e*** who
Judg 2: 7 and all the days of the ***e*** who
8:14 leaders of Succoth and its ***e***,
8:16 And he took the ***e*** of the city,
11: 5 that the ***e*** of Gilead went to
11: 7 So Jephthah said to the ***e*** of
11: 8 And the ***e*** of Gilead said to
11: 9 So Jephthah said to the ***e*** of
11:10 And the ***e*** of Gilead said to
11:11 Then Jephthah went with the ***e*** of
21:16 Then the ***e*** of the congregation
Ruth 4: 2 And he took ten men of the ***e*** of
4: 4 of the inhabitants and the ***e***
4: 9 And Boaz said to the ***e*** and all
4:11 were at the gate, and the ***e***,
1 Sam 4: 3 the ***e*** of Israel said, "Why has
8: 4 Then all the ***e*** of Israel
11: 3 Then the ***e*** of Jabesh said to
15:30 before the ***e*** of my people and
16: 4 And the ***e*** of the town trembled
30:26 some of the spoil to the ***e*** of
2 Sam 3:17 had communicated with the ***e*** of
5: 3 Therefore all the ***e*** of Israel
12:17 So the ***e*** of his house arose and
17: 4 pleased Absalom and all the ***e***
17:15 advised Absalom and the ***e*** of
19:11 Speak to the ***e*** of Judah, saying,
1 Ki 8: 1 Now Solomon assembled the ***e*** of
8: 3 So all the ***e*** of Israel came, and
12: 6 King Rehoboam consulted the ***e***
12: 8 the advice which the ***e*** had
12:13 the advice which the ***e*** had
20: 7 of Israel called all the ***e*** of
20: 8 And all the ***e*** and all the people
21: 8 and sent the letters to the ***e***
21:11 the ***e*** and nobles who were
2 Ki 6:32 and the ***e*** were sitting with
6:32 came to him, he said to the ***e***,
10: 1 the rulers of Jezreel, to the ***e***,
10: 5 the ***e*** also, and those who
19: 2 and the ***e*** of the priests,
23: 1 sent them to gather all the ***e***
1 Chr 11: 3 Therefore all the ***e*** of Israel
15:25 the ***e*** of Israel, and the
21:16 Jerusalem. So David and the ***e***,
2 Chr 5: 2 Now Solomon assembled the ***e*** of
5: 4 So all the ***e*** of Israel came, and
10: 6 King Rehoboam consulted the ***e***
10: 8 the advice which the ***e*** had
10:13 rejected the advice of the ***e***,
34:29 sent and gathered all the ***e*** of
Ezra 5: 5 of their God was upon the ***e*** of
5: 9 Then we asked those ***e***,
6: 7 governor of the Jews and the ***e***
6: 8 what you shall do for the ***e*** of
6:14 So the ***e*** of the Jews built, and
10: 8 of the leaders and ***e***,
10:14 together with the ***e*** and judges
Job 12:20 away the discernment of the ***e***.
Ps 105:22 And teach his ***e*** wisdom.
107:32 Him in the company of the ***e***.
Prov 31:23 When he sits among the ***e*** of
Isa 3:14 into judgment With the ***e*** of
24:23 in Jerusalem And before His ***e***,
37: 2 and the ***e*** of the priests,
Jer 19: 1 and take some of the ***e*** of the
19: 1 of the people and some of the ***e***
26:17 Then certain of the ***e*** of the
29: 1 to the remainder of the ***e*** who
Lam 1:19 My priests and my ***e*** Breathed
2:10 The ***e*** of the daughter of Zion
4:16 Nor show favor to the ***e***.
5:12 And ***e*** were not respected.
5:14 The ***e*** have ceased gathering
Ezek 7:26 priest, And counsel from the ***e***.
8: 1 as I sat in my house with the ***e***
8:11 them seventy men of the ***e*** of
8:12 have you seen what the ***e*** of the
9: 6 So they began with the ***e*** who
14: 1 Now some of the ***e*** of Israel came
20: 1 that certain of the ***e*** of
20: 3 speak to the ***e*** of Israel, and
27: 9 ***E*** of Gebal and its wise men
Joel 1: 2 Hear this, you ***e***,
1:14 Gather the ***e*** And all the
2:16 congregation, Assemble the ***e***,
Mt 15: 2 the tradition of the ***e***?
16:21 suffer many things from the ***e***
21:23 the chief priests and the ***e*** of
26: 3 and the ***e*** of the people
26:47 from the chief priests and ***e***
26:57 where the scribes and the ***e***
26:59 Now the chief priests, the ***e***,
27: 1 all the chief priests and ***e*** of
27: 3 to the chief priests and ***e***,
27:12 by the chief priests and ***e***,
27:20 But the chief priests and ***e***
27:41 mocking with the scribes and ***e***,
28:12 they had assembled with the ***e***
Mk 7: 3 holding the tradition of the ***e***.
7: 5 to the tradition of the ***e***,
8:31 and be rejected by the ***e*** and
11:27 and the ***e*** came to Him.
14:43 and the scribes and the ***e***.
14:53 all the chief priests, the ***e***,
15: 1 held a consultation with the ***e***
Lk 7: 3 he sent ***e*** of the Jews to Him,
9:22 and be rejected by the ***e*** and
20: 1 scribes, together with the ***e***,
22:52 and the ***e*** who had come to Him,
22:66 the ***e*** of the people, both chief
Acts 4: 5 next day, that their rulers, ***e***,
4: 8 Rulers of the people and ***e*** of
4:23 that the chief priests and ***e***
5:21 with all the ***e*** of the children
6:12 stirred up the people, the ***e***,
11:30 and sent it to the ***e*** by the
14:23 So when they had appointed ***e*** in
15: 2 to the apostles and ***e***,
15: 4 and the apostles and the ***e***;
15: 6 Now the apostles and ***e*** came
15:22 it pleased the apostles and ***e***,
15:23 by them: The apostles, the ***e***,
16: 4 by the apostles and ***e*** at
20:17 to Ephesus and called for the ***e***
21:18 and all the ***e*** were present.
22: 5 and all the council of the ***e***,
23:14 came to the chief priests and ***e***,
24: 1 priest came down with the ***e***
25:15 the chief priests and the ***e*** of
1 Tim 5:17 Let the ***e*** who rule well be
Titus 1: 5 and appoint ***e*** in every city as
Heb 11: 2 For by it the ***e*** obtained a good
Jas 5:14 Let him call for the ***e*** of the
1 Pe 5: 1 The ***e*** who are among you I
5: 5 submit yourselves to your ***e***.
Rev 4: 4 the thrones I saw twenty-four ***e***
4:10 the twenty-four ***e*** fall down
5: 5 But one of the ***e*** said to me,
5: 6 and in the midst of the ***e***,
5: 8 and the twenty-four ***e*** fell

5:11 the living creatures, and the *e*;
5:14 And the twenty-four *e* fell
7:11 around the throne and the *e*
7:13 Then one of the *e* answered,
11:16 And the twenty-four *e* who sat
14: 3 living creatures, and the *e*;
19: 4 And the twenty-four *e* and the

ELDERSHIP (1/1)

1 Tim 4:14 laying on of the hands of the *e*.

ELDEST (1/1) ELDER, OLD

2 Ki 3:27 Then he took his *e* son who would

ELEAD (1/1)

1 Chr 7:21 his son, and Ezer and *E*.

ELEALEH (5/5)

Num 32: 3 Jazer, Nimrah, Heshbon, *E*,
32:37 of Reuben built Heshbon and *E*
Isa 15: 4 Heshbon and *E* will cry out,
16: 9 with my tears, O Heshbon and *E*;
Jer 48:34 From the cry of Heshbon to *E*

ELEASAH (4/4)

1 Chr 2:39 begot Helez, and Helez begot *E*;
2:40 *E* begot Sismai, and Sismai begot
8:37 *E* his son, and Azel his son.
9:43 *E* his son, and Azel his son.

ELEAZAR (74/71)

Ex 6:23 she bore him Nadab, Abihu, *E*,
6:25 *E*, Aaron's son,
28: 1 Aaron's sons: Nadab, Abihu, *E*,
Lev 10: 6 and to *E* and Ithamar, his sons,
10:12 and to *E* and Ithamar, his sons
10:16 And he was angry with *E* and
Num 3: 2 the firstborn, and Abihu, *E*,
3: 4 So *E* and Ithamar ministered as
3:32 And *E* the son of Aaron the
4:16 The appointed duty of *E* the son
16:37 'Tell *E*, the son of Aaron
16:39 So *E* the priest took the bronze
19: 3 You shall give it to *E* the
19: 4 and *E* the priest shall take some
20:25 Take Aaron and *E* his son, and
20:26 his garments and put them on *E*
20:28 his garments and put them on *E*
20:28 Then Moses and *E* came down from
25: 7 Now when Phinehas the son of *E*,
25:11 "Phinehas the son of *E*,
26: 1 the LORD spoke to Moses and *E*
26: 3 So Moses and *E* the priest spoke
26:60 and Abihu, *E* and Ithamar.
26:63 were numbered by Moses and *E*
27: 2 before *E* the priest, and before
27:19 set him before *E* the priest and
27:21 He shall stand before *E* the
27:22 Joshua and set him before *E*
31: 6 war with Phinehas the son of *E*
31:12 to *E* the priest, and to the
31:13 *E* the priest, and all the
31:21 Then *E* the priest said to the
31:26 you and *E* the priest and the
31:29 and give it to *E* the priest as
31:31 So Moses and *E* the priest did as
31:41 the LORD's heave offering to *E*
31:51 So Moses and *E* the priest
31:54 And Moses and *E* the priest
32: 2 to *E* the priest, and to the
32:28 command concerning them to *E*
34:17 *E* the priest and Joshua the son
Deut 10: 6 and *E* his son ministered as
Josh 14: 1 which *E* the priest, Joshua the
17: 4 And they came near before *E* the
19:51 were the inheritances which *E*
21: 1 of the Levites came near to *E*
22:13 sent Phinehas the son of *E* the
22:31 Then Phinehas the son of *E* the
22:32 And Phinehas the son of *E* the
24:33 And *E* the son of Aaron died.
Judg 20:28 and Phinehas the son of *E*,
1 Sam 7: 1 and consecrated *E* his son to
2 Sam 23: 9 And after him was *E* the son of
1 Chr 6: 3 of Aaron were Nadab, Abihu, *E*,
6: 4 *E* begot Phinehas, and Phinehas
6:50 *E* his son, Phinehas his son,
9:20 And Phinehas the son of *E* had
11:12 After him was *E* the son of
23:21 The sons of Mahli were *E* and
23:22 And *E* died, and had no sons, but
24: 1 of Aaron were Nadab, Abihu, *E*,
24: 2 therefore *E* and Ithamar
24: 3 with Zadok of the sons of *E*,
24: 4 leaders found of the sons of *E*
24: 4 Among the sons of *E* were
24: 5 from the sons of *E* and from the
24: 6 one father's house taken for *E*
24:28 Of Mahli: *E*, who had no
Ezra 7: 5 son of Phinehas, the son of *E*,
8:33 and with him was *E* the son of
10:25 Jeziah, Malchiah, Mijamin, *E*,
Neh 12:42 also Maaseiah, Shemaiah, *E*,
Mt 1:15 Eliud begot *E*, Eleazar begot
1:15 *E* begot Matthan, and Matthan

ELECT (20/20) ELECT'S, ELECTION

Isa 42: 1 My *E* One in whom My soul
45: 4 sake, And Israel My *e*,
65: 9 My *e* shall inherit it, And My
65:22 And My *e* shall long enjoy the
Mt 24:24 if possible, even the *e*.
24:31 they will gather together His *e*
Mk 13:22 if possible, even the *e*.
13:27 and gather together His *e* from
Lk 18: 7 shall God not avenge His own *e*
Rom 8:33 bring a charge against God's *e*?
11: 7 but the *e* have obtained it, and
Col 3:12 as the *e* of God, holy and
1 Tim 5:21 the Lord Jesus Christ and the *e*
2 Tim 2:10 things for the sake of the *e*,
Titus 1: 1 to the faith of God's *e* and
1 Pe 1: 2 *e* according to the foreknowledge
2: 6 A chief cornerstone, *e*,
5:13 *e* together with you, greets
2 Jn 1 To the *e* lady and her
13 The children of your *e* sister

ELECT'S (2/2) ELECT

Mt 24:22 but for the *e* sake those days
Mk 13:20 but for the *e* sake, whom He

ELECTION (5/5) ELECT

Rom 9:11 purpose of God according to *e*
11: 5 is a remnant according to the *e*
11:28 but concerning the *e* they are
1 Th 1: 4 brethren, your *e* by God.
2 Pe 1:10 to make your call and *e* sure,

ELEMENTARY (1/1)

Heb 6: 1 leaving the discussion of the *e*

ELEMENTS (4/4)

Gal 4: 3 were in bondage under the *e* of
4: 9 to the weak and beggarly *e*,
2 Pe 3:10 and the *e* will melt with
3:12 and the *e* will melt with

ELEPH (1/1)

Josh 18:28 Zelah, *E*, Jebus

ELEVATED (1/1)

Isa 49:11 And My highways shall be *e*.

ELEVATION (2/2)

Ps 48: 2 Beautiful in *e*, The joy of
Ezek 41: 8 I also saw an *e* all around the

ELEVEN (24/24) ELEVENTH

Gen 32:22 and his *e* sons, and crossed
37: 9 and the *e* stars bowed down to
Ex 26: 7 You shall make *e* curtains.
26: 8 and the *e* curtains shall all
36:14 he made *e* curtains.
36:15 the *e* curtains were the same
Num 29:20 On the third day present *e*
Deut 1: 2 It is *e* days' journey from
Josh 15:51 *e* cities with their villages;
Judg 16: 5 every one of us will give you *e*
17: 2 The *e* hundred shekels of silver
17: 3 So when he had returned the *e*
2 Ki 23:36 and he reigned *e* years in
24:18 and he reigned *e* years in
2 Chr 36: 5 and he reigned *e* years in
36:11 and he reigned *e* years in
Jer 52: 1 and he reigned *e* years in
Ezek 40:49 and the width *e* cubits;
Mt 28:16 Then the *e* disciples went away
Mk 16:14 Later He appeared to the *e* as
Lk 24: 9 told all these things to the *e*
24:33 and found the *e* and those who
Acts 1:26 And he was numbered with the *e*
2:14 Peter, standing up with the *e*,

ELEVENTH (20/19) ELEVEN

Num 7:72 On the *e* day Pagiel the son of
Deut 1: 3 in the *e* month, on the first
1 Ki 6:38 And in the *e* year, in the month
2 Ki 9:29 In the *e* year of Joram the son
25: 2 city was besieged until the *e*
1 Chr 12:13 the tenth, and Machbanai the *e*.
24:12 the *e* to Eliashib, the twelfth
25:18 the *e* for Azarel, his sons and
27:14 The *e* captain for the eleventh
27:14 The eleventh captain for the *e*
Jer 1: 3 until the end of the *e* year of
39: 2 In the *e* year of Zedekiah, in
52: 5 city was besieged until the *e*
Ezek 26: 1 And it came to pass in the *e*
30:20 And it came to pass in the *e*
31: 1 Now it came to pass in the *e*
Zech 1: 7 the twenty-fourth day of the *e*
Mt 20: 6 And about the *e* hour he went out
20: 9 who were hired about the *e*
Rev 21:20 the *e* jacinth, and the twelfth

ELHANAN (4/4)

2 Sam 21:19 where *E* the son of Jaare-Oregim
23:24 *E* the son of Dodo of Bethlehem,
1 Chr 11:26 *E* the son of Dodo of Bethlehem,
20: 5 and *E* the son of Jair killed

ELI (35/32) ELOI

1 Sam 1: 3 Also the two sons of *E*,
1: 9 Now *E* the priest was sitting on
1:12 that *E* watched her mouth.
1:13 Therefore *E* thought she was
1:14 So *E* said to her, "How long
1:17 Then *E* answered and said, "Go
1:25 and brought the child to *E*.
2:11 to the LORD before *E* the
2:12 Now the sons of *E* were
2:20 And *E* would bless Elkanah and
2:22 Now *E* was very old; and he
2:27 Then a man of God came to *E* and
3: 1 to the LORD before *E*.
3: 2 while *E* was lying down in his
3: 5 So he ran to *E* and said, "Here
3: 6 So Samuel arose and went to *E*,
3: 8 Then he arose and went to *E*,
3: 8 Then *E* perceived that the
3: 9 Therefore *E* said to Samuel,
3:12 day I will perform against *E*
3:14 I have sworn to the house of *E*
3:15 And Samuel was afraid to tell *E*
3:16 Then *E* called Samuel and said,
4: 4 And the two sons of *E*,
4:11 and the two sons of *E*,
4:13 Now when he came, there was *E*,
4:14 When *E* heard the noise of the
4:14 the man came quickly and told *E*.
4:15 *E* was ninety-eight years old,
4:16 Then the man said to *E*,
4:18 that *E* fell off the seat
14: 3 son of Phinehas, the son of *E*,
1 Ki 2:27 concerning the house of *E* at
Mt 27:46 with a loud voice, saying, "*E*,
27:46 a loud voice, saying, "Eli, *E*,

ELI'S (1/1)

1 Sam 3:14 of Eli that the iniquity of *E*

ELIAB (19/19)

Num 1: 9 *E* the son of Helon;
2: 7 and *E* the son of Helon shall
7:24 On the third day *E* the son of
7:29 This was the offering of *E* the
10:16 the children of Zebulun was *E*
16: 1 Dathan and Abiram the sons of *E*,
16:12 Dathan and Abiram the sons of *E*,
26: 8 And the son of Pallu was *E*.
26: 9 The sons of *E* were Nemuel,
Deut 11: 6 Dathan and Abiram the sons of *E*,
1 Sam 16: 6 that he looked at *E* and said,
17:13 who went to the battle were *E*
17:28 Now *E* his oldest brother heard
1 Chr 2:13 Jesse begot *E* his firstborn,
6:27 *E* his son, Jeroham his son, and
12: 9 the second, *E* the third,
15:18 Shemiramoth, Jehiel, Unni, *E*,
15:20 Shemiramoth, Jehiel, Unni, *E*,
16: 5 Jehiel, Mattithiah, *E*,

ELIAB'S (1/1)

1 Sam 17:28 and *E* anger was aroused against

ELIADA (3/3)

2 Sam 5:16 Elishama, *E*, and Eliphelet.
1 Chr 3: 8 Elishama, *E*, and Eliphelet—nine
2 Chr 17:17 *E* a mighty man of valor, and

ELIADAH (1/1)

1 Ki 11:23 against him, Rezon the son of *E*,

ELIAH (2/2)

2 Chr 11:18 of Abihail the daughter of *E*
Ezra 10:26 Jehiel, Abdi, Jeremoth, and *E*;

ELIAHBA (2/2)

2 Sam 23:32 *E* the Shaalbonite (of the sons
1 Chr 11:33 *E* the Shaalbonite,

ELIAKIM (15/14) JEHOIAKIM

2 Ki 18:18 *E* the son of Hilkiah, who was
18:26 Then *E* the son of Hilkiah,
18:37 Then *E* the son of Hilkiah, who
19: 2 Then he sent *E*, who was over
23:34 Then Pharaoh Necho made *E* the
2 Chr 36: 4 made Jehoahaz's brother *E*
Neh 12:41 and the priests, *E*,
Isa 22:20 That I will call My servant *E*
36: 3 And *E* the son of Hilkiah, who
36:11 Then *E*, Shebna, and Joah
36:22 Then *E* the son of Hilkiah, who
37: 2 Then he sent *E*, who was
Mt 1:13 begot Abiud, Abiud begot *E*,
1:13 and *E* begot Azor.
Lk 3:30 son of Jonan, the son of *E*,

E

ELIAM (2/2)

2 Sam 11: 3 Bathsheba, the daughter of *E*,
23:34 *E* the son of Ahithophel the

ELIAS (KJV) See ELIJAH

ELIASAPH (6/6)

Num 1:14 *E* the son of Deuel;
2:14 children of Gad shall be *E*
3:24 of the Gershonites was *E* the
7:42 On the sixth day *E* the son of
7:47 This was the offering of *E* the
10:20 of the children of Gad was *E*

ELIASHIB (18/16)

1 Chr 3:24 of Elioenai were Hodaviah, *E*,
24:12 the eleventh to *E*,
Ezra 10: 6 of Jehohanan the son of *E*;
10:24 Also of the singers: *E*;
10:27 the sons of Zattu: Elioenai, *E*,
10:36 Vaniah, Meremoth, *E*,
Neh 3: 1 Then *E* the high priest rose up
3: 2 Next to *E* the men of Jericho
3:20 to the door of the house of *E*
3:21 the door of the house of *E* to
3:21 to the end of the house of *E*.
12:10 begot Joiakim, Joiakim begot *E*,
12:10 *E* begot Joiada,
12:22 houses in the days of *E*,
12:23 days of Johanan the son of *E*,
13: 4 *E* the priest, having authority
13: 7 and discovered the evil that *E*
13:28 the son of *E* the high priest,

ELIATHAH (2/2)

1 Chr 25: 4 Jerimoth, Hananiah, Hanani, *E*,
25:27 the twentieth for *E*,

ELIDAD (1/1)

Num 34:21 *E* the son of Chislon;

ELIEHOENAI (2/2) ELIOENAI

1 Chr 26: 3 the sixth, *E* the seventh.
Ezra 8: 4 *E* the son of Zerahiah, and with

ELIEL (10/10)

1 Chr 5:24 fathers' houses: Epher, Ishi, *E*,
6:34 son of Jeroham, the son of *E*,
8:20 Elienai, Zillethai, *E*,
8:22 Ishpan, Eber, *E*,
11:46 *E* the Mahavite, Jeribai and
11:47 *E*, Obed, and Jaasiel
12:11 *E* the seventh,
15: 9 *E* the chief, and eighty of his
15:11 Asaiah, Joel, Shemaiah, *E*,
2 Chr 31:13 Asahel, Jerimoth, Jozabad, *E*,

ELIENAI (1/1)

1 Chr 8:20 *E*, Zillethai, Eliel,

ELIEZER (15/14)

Gen 15: 2 and the heir of my house is *E*
Ex 18: 4 the name of the other was *E*
1 Chr 7: 8 Becher were Zemirah, Joash, *E*,
15:24 Zechariah, Benaiah, and *E*,
23:15 of Moses were Gershon and *E*.
23:17 Of the descendants of *E*,
23:17 And *E* had no other sons, but
26:25 And his brethren by *E* were
27:16 over the Reubenites was *E* the
2 Chr 20:37 But *E* the son of Dodavah of
Ezra 8:16 Then I sent for *E*,
10:18 and his brothers: Maaseiah, *E*,
10:23 Pethahiah, Judah, and *E*.
10:31 of the sons of Harim: *E*,
Lk 3:29 son of Jose, the son of *E*,

ELIHOREPH (1/1)

1 Ki 4: 3 *E* and Ahijah, the sons of

ELIHU (11/11)

1 Sam 1: 1 son of Jeroham, the son of *E*,
1 Chr 12:20 Jediael, Michael, Jozabad, *E*,
26: 7 whose brothers *E* and Semachiah
27:18 over Judah, *E*, one of
Job 32: 2 Then the wrath of *E*,
32: 4 *E* had waited to speak to Job.
32: 5 When *E* saw that there was no
32: 6 So *E*, the son of Barachel
34: 1 *E* further answered and said:
35: 1 Moreover *E* answered and said:
36: 1 *E* also proceeded and said:

ELIJAH (100/94)

1 Ki 17: 1 And *E* the Tishbite, of the
17:13 And *E* said to her, "Do not
17:15 did according to the word of *E*;
17:16 the LORD which He spoke by *E*.
17:18 So she said to *E*,
17:22 the LORD heard the voice of *E*;
17:23 And *E* took the child and brought
17:23 And *E* said, "See, your son
17:24 Then the woman said to *E*,
18: 1 the word of the LORD came to *E*,
18: 2 So *E* went to present himself to
18: 7 suddenly *E* met him; and he
18: 7 said, "Is that you, my lord *E*?
18: 8 your master, '*E* is here.'
18:11 your master, "*E* is here"
18:14 *E* is here." ' He will kill
18:15 Then *E* said, "As the LORD of
18:16 him; and Ahab went to meet *E*.
18:17 it happened, when Ahab saw *E*,
18:21 And *E* came to all the people,
18:22 Then *E* said to the people, "I
18:25 Now *E* said to the prophets of
18:27 that *E* mocked them and said,
18:30 Then *E* said to all the people,
18:31 And *E* took twelve stones,
18:36 that *E* the prophet came near
18:40 And *E* said to them, "Seize the
18:40 and *E* brought them down to the
18:41 Then *E* said to Ahab, "Go up,
18:42 And *E* went up to the top of
18:46 hand of the LORD came upon *E*;
19: 1 Ahab told Jezebel all that *E*
19: 2 Jezebel sent a messenger to *E*,
19: 9 "What are you doing here, *E*?
19:13 when *E* heard it, that he
19:13 "What are you doing here, *E*?
19:19 Then *E* passed by him and threw
19:20 left the oxen and ran after *E*,
19:21 Then he arose and followed *E*,
21:17 the word of the LORD came to *E*
21:20 So Ahab said to *E*,
21:28 the word of the LORD came to *E*
2 Ki 1: 3 angel of the LORD said to *E*
1: 4 So *E* departed.
1: 8 It is *E* the Tishbite."
1:10 So *E* answered and said to the
1:12 So *E* answered and said to them,
1:13 and fell on his knees before *E*,
1:15 angel of the LORD said to *E*,
1:17 the word of the LORD which *E*
2: 1 LORD was about to take up *E*
2: 1 that *E* went with Elisha from
2: 2 Then *E* said to Elisha, "Stay
2: 4 Then *E* said to him, "Elisha,
2: 6 Then *E* said to him, "Stay here,
2: 8 Now *E* took his mantle, rolled
2: 9 that *E* said to Elisha, "Ask!
2:11 and *E* went up by a whirlwind
2:13 He also took up the mantle of *E*
2:14 Then he took the mantle of *E*
2:14 "Where is the LORD God of *E*?
2:15 The spirit of *E* rests on
3:11 poured water on the hands of *E*.
9:36 He spoke by His servant *E* the
10:10 what He spoke by His servant *E*.
10:17 the LORD which He spoke to *E*.
1 Chr 8:27 Jaareshiah, *E*, and Zichri
2 Chr 21:12 a letter came to him from *E*
Ezra 10:21 the sons of Harim: Maaseiah, *E*,
Mal 4: 5 I will send you *E* the prophet
Mt 11:14 he is *E* who is to come.
16:14 say John the Baptist, some *E*,
17: 3 Moses and *E* appeared to them,
17: 4 one for Moses, and one for *E*."
17:10 then do the scribes say that *E*
17:11 *E* is coming first and will
17:12 But I say to you that *E* has come
27:47 This Man is calling for *E*!"
27:49 let us see if *E* will come to
Mk 6:15 Others said, "It is *E*.
8:28 the Baptist; but some say, *E*;
9: 4 And *E* appeared to them with
9: 5 for Moses, and one for *E*"—
9:11 Why do the scribes say that *E*
9:12 *E* is coming first and restores
9:13 But I say to you that *E* has also
15:35 He is calling for *E*!"
15:36 let us see if *E* will come to
Lk 1:17 in the spirit and power of *E*,
4:25 were in Israel in the days of *E*,
4:26 but to none of them was *E* sent
9: 8 and by some that *E* had appeared,
9:19 the Baptist, but some say *E*;
9:30 with Him, who were Moses and *E*,
9:33 and one for *E*"—not knowing
9:54 them, just as *E* did?"
Jn 1:21 him, "What then? Are you *E*?
1:25 you are not the Christ, nor *E*,
Rom 11: 2 what the Scripture says of *E*,
Jas 5:17 *E* was a man with a nature like

ELIKA (1/1)

2 Sam 23:25 *E* the Harodite,

ELIM (7/5)

Ex 15:27 Then they came to *E*,
16: 1 And they journeyed from *E*,
16: 1 which is between *E* and Sinai,
Num 33: 9 moved from Marah and came to *E*.
33: 9 At *E* were twelve springs of
33:10 They moved from *E* and camped by
Isa 15: 8 And its wailing to Beer *E*.

ELIMELECH (5/5)

Ruth 1: 2 The name of the man was *E*,
1: 3 Then *E*, Naomi's husband,
2: 1 wealth, of the family of *E*.
2: 3 who was of the family of *E*.
4: 3 belonged to our brother *E*.

ELIMELECH'S (1/1)

Ruth 4: 9 I have bought all that was *E*,

ELIMINATED (2/2)

Mt 15:17 goes into the stomach and is *e*?
Mk 7:19 heart but his stomach, and is *e*,

ELIOENAI (7/7)

1 Chr 3:23 The sons of Neariah were *E*,
3:24 The sons of *E* were Hodaviah,
4:36 *E*, Jaakobah, Jeshohaiah,
7: 8 Zemirah, Joash, Eliezer, *E*,
Ezra 10:22 of the sons of Pashhur: *E*,
10:27 of the sons of Zattu: *E*,
Neh 12:41 Maaseiah, Minjamin, Michaiah, *E*,

ELIPHAL (1/1)

1 Chr 11:35 *E* the son of Ur,

ELIPHAZ (15/14)

Gen 36: 4 Now Adah bore *E* to Esau, and
36:10 *E* the son of Adah the wife of
36:11 And the sons of *E* were Teman,
36:12 Timna was the concubine of *E*,
36:12 son, and she bore Amalek to *E*.
36:15 the sons of Esau. The sons of *E*,
36:16 These were the chiefs of *E* in
1 Chr 1:35 The sons of Esau were *E*,
1:36 And the sons of *E* were Teman,
Job 2:11 *E* the Temanite, Bildad the
4: 1 Then *E* the Temanite answered and
15: 1 Then *E* the Temanite answered and
22: 1 Then *E* the Temanite answered and
42: 7 that the LORD said to *E* the
42: 9 So *E* the Temanite and Bildad the

ELIPHELEH (2/2)

1 Chr 15:18 Maaseiah, Mattithiah, *E*,
15:21 Mattithiah, *E*, Mikneiah,

ELIPHELET (8/8)

2 Sam 5:16 Elishama, Eliada, and *E*.
23:34 *E* the son of Ahasbai, the son of
1 Chr 3: 6 there were Ibhar, Elishama, *E*,
3: 8 Elishama, Eliada, and *E*—
8:39 and *E* the third.
14: 7 Elishama, Beeliada, and *E*.
Ezra 8:13 whose names are these—*E*,
10:33 Mattenai, Mattattah, Zabad, *E*,

ELISABETH (KJV) See ELIZABETH

ELISEUS (KJV) See ELISHA

ELISHA (59/53) ELISHA'S

1 Ki 19:16 And *E* the son of Shaphat of
19:17 sword of Jehu, *E* will kill.
19:19 and found *E* the son of Shaphat,
19:21 So *E* turned back from him, and
2 Ki 2: 1 that Elijah went with *E* from
2: 2 Then Elijah said to *E*,
2: 2 But *E* said, "As the LORD
2: 3 were at Bethel came out to *E*,
2: 4 Then Elijah said to him, "*E*,
2: 5 who were at Jericho came to *E*
2: 9 over, that Elijah said to *E*,
2: 9 *E* said, "Please let a double
2:12 And *E* saw it, and he cried
2:14 and *E* crossed over.
2:15 spirit of Elijah rests on *E*.
2:19 the men of the city said to *E*,
2:22 according to the word of *E*
3:11 *E* the son of Shaphat is here,
3:13 Then *E* said to the king of
3:14 And *E* said, "As the LORD of
4: 1 of the prophets cried out to *E*,
4: 2 So *E* said to her, "What shall I
4: 8 Now it happened one day that *E*
4:17 of which *E* had told her.
4:32 When *E* came into the house,
4:38 And *E* returned to Gilgal, and
5: 8 when *E* the man of God heard
5:10 And *E* sent a messenger to him,
5:20 the servant of *E* the man of
5:25 *E* said to him, "Where did
6: 1 sons of the prophets said to *E*,
6:12 "None, my lord, O king; but *E*,
6:17 And *E* prayed, and said, "LORD,
6:17 chariots of fire all around *E*.
6:18 *E* prayed to the LORD, and
6:18 according to the word of *E*.
6:19 Now *E* said to them, "This is
6:20 that *E* said, "LORD, open the
6:21 Israel saw them, he said to *E*,
6:31 if the head of *E* the son of
6:32 But *E* was sitting in his house,
7: 1 Then *E* said, "Hear the word of

8: 1 Then **E** spoke to the woman whose
8: 4 all the great things **E** has
8: 5 and this is her son whom **E**
8: 7 Then **E** went to Damascus, and
8:10 And **E** said to him, "Go, say to
8:13 And **E** answered, "The LORD
8:14 Then he departed from **E**,
8:14 What did **E** say to you?" And he
9: 1 And **E** the prophet called one of
13:14 **E** had become sick with the
13:15 And **E** said to him, "Take a bow
13:16 and **E** put his hands on the
13:17 Then **E** said, "Shoot"; and he
13:20 Then **E** died, and they buried
13:21 put the man in the tomb of **E**;
13:21 down and touched the bones of **E**,
Lk 4:27 in Israel in the time of **E** the

ELISHA'S (1/1)

2 Ki 5: 9 stood at the door of **E** house.

ELISHAH (3/3)

Gen 10: 4 The sons of Javan were **E**,
1 Chr 1: 7 The sons of Javan were **E**,
Ezek 27: 7 and purple from the coasts of **E**

ELISHAMA (17/17)

Num 1:10 **E** the son of Ammihud; from
2:18 of Ephraim shall be **E** the
7:48 On the seventh day **E** the son of
7:53 This was the offering of **E** the
10:22 over their army was **E** the son
2 Sam 5:16 **E**, Eliada, and Eliphelet.
2 Ki 25:25 son of Nethaniah, the son of **E**,
1 Chr 2:41 Jekamiah, and Jekamiah begot **E**.
3: 6 Also there were Ibhar, **E**,
3: 8 **E**, Eliada, and Eliphelet—nine
7:26 **E** his son,
14: 7 **E**, Beeliada, and Eliphelet.
2 Chr 17: 8 and with them **E** and Jehoram,
Jer 36:12 **E** the scribe, Delaiah the son of
36:20 the scroll in the chamber of **E**
36:21 and he took it from **E** the
41: 1 son of Nethaniah, the son of **E**,

ELISHAPHAT (1/1)

2 Chr 23: 1 and **E** the son of Zichri.

ELISHEBA (1/1)

Ex 6:23 Aaron took to himself **E**,

ELISHUA (2/2)

2 Sam 5:15 Ibhar, **E**, Nepheg, Japhia,
1 Chr 14: 5 Ibhar, **E**, Elpelet,

ELIUD (2/2)

Mt 1:14 begot Achim, and Achim begot **E**.
1:15 **E** begot Eleazar, Eleazar begot

ELIZABETH (8/7)

Lk 1: 5 of Aaron, and her name was **E**.
1: 7 because **E** was barren, and they
1:13 and your wife **E** will bear you a
1:24 Now after those days his wife **E**
1:36 **E** your relative has also
1:40 of Zacharias and greeted **E**.
1:41 when **E** heard the greeting of
1:41 and **E** was filled with the Holy

ELIZABETH'S (1/1)

Lk 1:57 Now **E** full time came for her to

ELIZAPHAN (4/4)

Num 3:30 of the Kohathites was **E** the
34:25 **E** the son of Parnach;
1 Chr 15: 8 of the sons of **E**, Shemaiah
2 Chr 29:13 of the sons of **E**, Shimri

ELIZUR (5/5)

Num 1: 5 **E** the son of Shedeur;
2:10 of Reuben shall be **E** the son
7:30 On the fourth day **E** the son of
7:35 This was the offering of **E** the
10:18 over their army was **E** the son

ELKANAH (21/20)

Ex 6:24 sons of Korah were Assir, **E**,
1 Sam 1: 1 and his name was **E** the son of
1: 4 whenever the time came for **E**
1: 8 Then **E** her husband said to her,
1:19 And **E** knew Hannah his wife, and
1:21 Now the man **E** and all his house
1:23 And **E** her husband said to her,
2:11 Then **E** went to his house at
2:20 And Eli would bless **E** and his
1 Chr 6:23 **E** his son, Ebiasaph his son,
6:25 The sons of **E** were Amasai and
6:26 As for **E**, the sons of
6:26 the sons of **E** were Zophai his
6:27 and **E** his son.
6:34 the son of **E**, the son of
6:35 the son of Zuph, the son of **E**,
6:36 the son of **E**, the son of
9:16 the son of Asa, the son of **E**,
12: 6 **E**, Jisshiah, Azarel, Joezer,
15:23 Berechiah and **E** were
2 Chr 28: 7 and **E** who was second to the

ELKOSHITE (1/1)

Nah 1: 1 of the vision of Nahum the **E**.

ELLASAR (2/2)

Gen 14: 1 of Shinar, Arioch king of **E**,
14: 9 of Shinar, and Arioch king of **E**—

ELMODAM (1/1)

Lk 3:28 son of Cosam, the son of **E**,

ELNAAM (1/1)

1 Chr 11:46 and Joshaviah the sons of **E**,

ELNATHAN (7/5)

2 Ki 24: 8 Nehushta the daughter of **E** of
Ezra 8:16 for Eliezer, Ariel, Shemaiah, **E**,
8:16 Shemaiah, Elnathan, Jarib, **E**,
8:16 leaders; also for Joiarib and **E**,
Jer 26:22 **E** the son of Achbor, and other
36:12 **E** the son of Achbor, Gemariah
36:25 Nevertheless **E**, Delaiah, and

ELOI (2/1) ELI

Mk 15:34 with a loud voice, saying, "**E**,
15:34 a loud voice, saying, "Eloi, **E**,

ELON (7/7)

Gen 26:34 and Basemath the daughter of **E**
36: 2 Adah the daughter of **E** the
46:14 sons of Zebulun were Sered, **E**,
Num 26:26 family of the Sardites; of **E**,
Josh 19:43 **E**, Timnah, Ekron,
Judg 12:11 **E** the Zebulunite judged Israel.
12:12 And **E** the Zebulunite died and

ELON BETH HANAN (1/1)

1 Ki 4: 9 Shaalbim, Beth Shemesh, and **E**;

ELONITES (1/1)

Num 26:26 of Elon, the family of the **E**;

ELOQUENT (2/2)

Ex 4:10 LORD, "O my Lord, I am not **e**,
Acts 18:24 an **e** man and mighty in the

ELOTH (KJV) See ELATH

ELPAAL (3/3)

1 Chr 8:11 by Hushim he begot Abitub and **E**.
8:12 The sons of **E** were Eber,
8:18 and Jobab were the sons of **E**.

ELPELET (1/1)

1 Chr 14: 5 Ibhar, Elishua, **E**,

ELSE (36/36)

Gen 19:12 Have you anyone **e** here?
30: 1 me children, or **e** I die!"
42:16 is any truth in you; or **e**,
Ex 4:13 by the hand of whomever **e** You
8:21 'Or **e**, if you will not let
10: 4 'Or **e**, if you refuse to
Num 6:21 whatever **e** his hand is able to
Josh 23:12 "Or **e**,
Judg 7:14 This is nothing **e** but the sword
14:15 or **e** we will burn you and your
2 Sam 3:35 if I taste bread or anything **e**
1 Ki 20:39 or **e** you shall pay a talent of
21: 6 your vineyard for money; or **e**,
1 Chr 21:12 or **e** for three days the sword
Job 9:24 not He, who **e** could it be?
32:22 **E** my Maker would soon take me
Ps 32: 9 **E** they will not come near you.
51:16 or **e** I would give it; You do
Isa 47: 8 and there is no one **e** besides
47:10 and there is no one **e** besides
Mt 6:24 or **e** he will be loyal to the
9:17 or **e** the wineskins break, the
12:33 or **e** make the tree bad and its
Mk 2:21 or **e** the new piece pulls away
2:22 or **e** the new wine bursts the
Lk 5:37 or **e** the new wine will burst
14:32 'Or **e**, while the other
16:13 or **e** he will be loyal to the
Jn 14:11 or **e** believe Me for the sake of
15:24 them the works which no one **e**
Acts 17:21 spent their time in nothing **e**
24:20 Or **e** let those who are here
Rom 2:15 their thoughts accusing or **e**
Phil 3: 4 If anyone **e** thinks he may have
Rev 2: 5 or **e** I will come to you quickly
2:16 or **e** I will come to you quickly

ELSEWHERE (2/2)

Lev 18: 9 whether born at home or **e**,
Judg 12: 9 in thirty daughters from **e** for

ELTEKEH (2/2)

Josh 19:44 **E**, Gibbethon, Baalath,
21:23 **E** with its common-land,

ELTEKON (1/1)

Josh 15:59 Maarath, Beth Anoth, and **E**:

ELTOLAD (2/2)

Josh 15:30 **E**, Chesil, Hormah,
19: 4 **E**, Bethul, Hormah,

ELUL (1/1)

Neh 6:15 on the twenty-fifth day of **E**,

ELUZAI (1/1)

1 Chr 12: 5 **E**, Jerimoth, Bealiah,

ELYMAS (1/1)

Acts 13: 8 But **E** the sorcerer (for so his

ELZABAD (2/2)

1 Chr 12:12 the eighth, **E** the ninth,
26: 7 Othni, Rephael, Obed, and **E**,

ELZAPHAN (2/2)

Ex 6:22 sons of Uzziel were Mishael, **E**,
Lev 10: 4 And Moses called Mishael and **E**,

EMASCULATED (1/1)

Deut 23: 1 He who is **e** by crushing or

EMBALM (1/1) EMBALMED

Gen 50: 2 servants the physicians to **e**

EMBALMED (3/3) EMBALM

Gen 50: 2 So the physicians **e** Israel.
50: 3 required for those who are **e**;
50:26 and they **e** him, and he was put

EMBANKMENT (1/1)

Lk 19:43 your enemies will build an **e**

EMBARRASSED (2/2)

Judg 3:25 So they waited till they were **e**,
Isa 1:29 And you shall be **e** because of

EMBELLISHED (1/1)

Hos 10: 1 of his land They have **e** his

EMBER (1/1)

2 Sam 14: 7 So they would extinguish my **e**

EMBLEMS (1/1)

Num 2: 2 beside the **e** of his father's

EMBOLDENED (1/1)

1 Cor 8:10 of him who is weak be **e** to eat

EMBOSSED (1/1)

Job 15:26 With his strong, **e** shield.

EMBRACE (5/5) EMBRACED, EMBRACES, EMBRACING

Gen 16: 5 I gave my maid into your **e**;
2 Ki 4:16 time next year you shall **e** a
Prov 4: 8 you honor, when you **e** her.
Eccl 3: 5 to gather stones; A time to **e**,
Lam 4: 5 were brought up in scarlet **E**

EMBRACED (9/9) EMBRACE

Gen 29:13 and **e** him and kissed him, and
33: 4 and **e** him, and fell on his neck
48:10 and he kissed them and **e** them.
1 Ki 9: 9 and have **e** other gods, and
2 Chr 7:22 and **e** other gods, and worshiped
Prov 5:20 And be **e** in the arms of a
Ezek 23: 3 Their breasts were there **e**,
Acts 20: 1 **e** them, and departed to go to
Heb 11:13 **e** them and confessed that they

EMBRACES (2/2) EMBRACE

Song 2: 6 And his right hand **e** me.
8: 3 And his right hand **e** me.

EMBRACING (2/2) EMBRACE

Eccl 3: 5 And a time to refrain from **e**;
Acts 20:10 and **e** him said, "Do not

EMBROIDERED (7/7) EMBROIDERY

Judg 5:30 Plunder of garments *e* and
Ezek 16:10 I clothed you in *e* cloth and
16:13 and *e* cloth. You ate pastry
16:18 You took your *e* garments and
26:16 and take off their *e* garments;
27: 7 Fine *e* linen from Egypt was
27:24 in *e* garments, in chests of

EMBROIDERY (2/2) EMBROIDERED

Judg 5:30 Two pieces of dyed *e* for the
Ezek 27:16 your wares emeralds, purple, *e*,

EMEK KEZIZ (1/1)

Josh 18:21 were Jericho, Beth Hoglah, *E*,

EMERALD (5/5)

Ex 28:17 a sardius, a topaz, and an *e*;
39:10 and an *e* was the first row;
Ezek 28:13 turquoise, and *e* with gold.
Rev 4: 3 throne, in appearance like an *e*.
21:19 third chalcedony, the fourth *e*,

EMERALDS (1/1)

Ezek 27:16 They gave you for your wares *e*,

EMIM (3/3)

Gen 14: 5 the *E* in Shaveh Kiriathaim,
Deut 2:10 (The *E* had dwelt there in times
2:11 but the Moabites call them *E*.

EMINENT (2/2)

2 Cor 11: 5 at all inferior to the most *e*
12:11 nothing was I behind the most *e*

EMISSION (3/3) EMITS

Lev 15:16 If any man has an *e* of semen,
15:18 and there is an *e* of semen,
22: 4 or a man who has had an *e* of

EMITS (1/1) EMISSION, EMITTED

Lev 15:32 and for him who *e* semen and

EMITTED (1/1) EMITS

Gen 38: 9 that he *e* on the ground, lest

EMMANUEL (KJV) See IMMANUEL

EMMAUS (1/1)

Lk 24:13 same day to a village called *E*,

EMMOR (KJV) See HAMOR

EMPIRE (1/1)

Esth 1:20 throughout all his *e* (for it

EMPLOYED (2/2)

1 Chr 9:33 for they were *e* in that work
Ezek 39:14 will set apart men regularly *e*,

EMPTIED (9/9) EMPTY

Gen 24:20 Then she quickly *e* her pitcher
42:35 Then it happened as they *e*
2 Chr 24:11 priest's officer came and *e*
Neh 5:13 thus may he be shaken out and *e*.
Isa 19: 6 brooks of defense will be *e*
24: 3 The land shall be entirely *e*
Jer 48:11 And has not been *e* from vessel
Ezek 12:19 so that her land may be *e* of
Nah 2: 2 For the emptiers have *e* them

EMPTIERS (1/1)

Nah 2: 2 For the *e* have emptied them

EMPTIES (1/1)

Hos 10: 1 Israel *e* his vine; He brings

EMPTINESS (2/2) EMPTY

Isa 34:11 confusion and the stones of *e*.
2 Pe 2:18 great swelling words of *e*,

EMPTY (39/38) EMPTIED, EMPTINESS, EMPTY-HANDED, EMPTY-HEADED

Gen 37:24 into a pit. And the pit was *e*;
41:27 and the seven *e* heads blighted
Ex 23:15 none shall appear before Me *e*);
Lev 14:36 shall command that they *e* the
26:43 The land also shall be left *e* by
Judg 7:16 with *e* pitchers, and torches
Ruth 1:21 has brought me home again *e*.
1 Sam 6: 3 God of Israel, do not send it *e*;
12:21 then you would go after *e*
20:18 because your seat will be *e*.
20:25 side, but David's place was *e*.
20:27 month, that David's place was *e*.
2 Sam 1:22 sword of Saul did not return *e*.
2 Ki 4: 3 *e* vessels; do not gather just a
Job 11: 3 Should your *e* talk make men
15: 2 a wise man answer with *e*
21:34 then can you comfort me with *e*
22: 9 You have sent widows away *e*,
26: 7 stretches out the north over *e*
35:13 God will not listen to *e* talk,
Eccl 11: 3 They *e* themselves upon the
Isa 24: 1 the LORD makes the earth *e* and
29: 8 awakes, and his soul is still *e*;
29:21 And turn aside the just by *e*
59: 4 They trust in *e* words and
Jer 14: 3 returned with their vessels *e*;
48:12 Who will tip him over And *e*
51: 2 Who shall winnow her and *e* her
51:34 He has made me an *e* vessel,
Ezek 14:15 and they *e* it, and make it so
24:11 Then set the pot *e* on the coals,
Nah 2:10 She is *e*, desolate, and
Hab 1:17 Shall they therefore *e* their
Mt 12:44 when he comes, he finds it *e*,
Lk 1:53 the rich He has sent away *e*.
1 Cor 15:14 then our preaching is *e* and
15:14 empty and your faith is also *e*.
Eph 5: 6 Let no one deceive you with *e*
Col 2: 8 you through philosophy and *e*

EMPTY-HANDED (9/9) EMPTY

Gen 31:42 you would have sent me away *e*.
Ex 3:21 you go, that you shall not go *e*.
34:20 none shall appear before Me *e*.
Deut 15:13 you shall not let him go away *e*;
16:16 not appear before the LORD *e*.
Ruth 3:17 Do not go *e* to your
Mk 12: 3 beat him and sent him away *e*.
Lk 20:10 beat him and sent him away *e*.
20:11 and sent him away *e*.

EMPTY-HEADED (1/1) EMPTY

Job 11:12 For an *e* man will be wise,

EMULATION (KJV) See JEALOUSY

EN DOR (3/3)

Josh 17:11 the inhabitants of *E* and
1 Sam 28: 7 who is a medium at *E*."
Ps 83:10 Who perished at *E*

EN EGLAIM (1/1)

Ezek 47:10 stand by it from En Gedi to *E*;

EN GANNIM (3/3)

Josh 15:34 Zanoah, *E*, Tappuah, Enam,
19:21 Remeth, *E*, En Haddah, and Beth
21:29 and *E* with its common-land:

EN GEDI (6/6)

Josh 15:62 the City of Salt, and *E*:
1 Sam 23:29 and dwelt in strongholds at *E*.
24: 1 is in the Wilderness of *E*.
2 Chr 20: 2 Hazazon Tamar" (which is *E*).
Song 1:14 blooms In the vineyards of *E*.
Ezek 47:10 will stand by it from *E* to En

EN HADDAH (1/1)

Josh 19:21 Remeth, En Gannim, *E*,

EN HAKKORE (1/1)

Judg 15:19 Therefore he called its name *E*,

EN HAZOR (1/1)

Josh 19:37 Kedesh, Edrei, *E*,

EN MISHPAT (1/1)

Gen 14: 7 they turned back and came to *E*

EN RIMMON (1/1)

Neh 11:29 in *E*, Zorah, Jarmuth,

EN ROGEL (4/4)

Josh 15: 7 of En Shemesh and ended at *E*.
18:16 the south, and descended to *E*.
2 Sam 17:17 and Ahimaaz stayed at *E*,
1 Ki 1: 9 of Zoheleth, which is by *E*;

EN SHEMESH (2/2)

Josh 15: 7 toward the waters of *E* and
18:17 from the north, went out to *E*,

EN TAPPUAH (1/1)

Josh 17: 7 south to the inhabitants of *E*.

ENABLE (1/1)

Ezek 36:33 I will also *e* you to dwell in

ENABLED (1/1)

1 Tim 1:12 Jesus our Lord who has *e* me,

ENAM (1/1)

Josh 15:34 Zanoah, En Gannim, Tappuah, *E*,

ENAN (5/5)

Num 1:15 Naphtali, Ahira the son of *E*.
2:29 shall be Ahira the son of *E*.
7:78 twelfth day Ahira the son of *E*,
7:83 offering of Ahira the son of *E*.
10:27 was Ahira the son of *E*.

ENCAMP (6/6) CAMP, ENCAMPED, ENCAMPMENT, ENCAMPS

Judg 6: 4 Then they would *e* against them
2 Sam 12:28 of the people together and *e*
Job 19:12 They *e* all around my tent.
Ps 27: 3 Though an army may *e* against
Isa 29: 3 I will *e* against you all
Jer 50:29 *e* against it all around;

ENCAMPED (44/40) ENCAMP

Ex 18: 5 where he was *e* at the mountain
Num 9:18 the tabernacle they remained *e*.
9:20 the LORD they would remain *e*,
9:22 of Israel would remain *e* and
9:23 of the LORD they remained *e*,
24: 2 and saw Israel *e* according to
Josh 10:31 and they *e* against it and
10:34 and they *e* against it and
Judg 6:33 and they crossed over and *e* in
7: 1 were with him rose early and *e*
9:50 and he *e* against Thebez and
10:17 Ammon gathered together and *e*
10:17 assembled together and *e* in
11:18 and *e* on the other side of the
11:20 *e* in Jahaz, and fought against
15: 9 *e* in Judah, and deployed
18:12 Then they went up and *e* in
20:19 rose in the morning and *e*
1 Sam 4: 1 and *e* beside Ebenezer; and the
4: 1 and the Philistines *e* in Aphek.
11: 1 the Ammonite came up and *e*
13: 5 And they came up and *e* in
13:16 But the Philistines *e* in
17: 1 they *e* between Sochoh and
17: 2 and they *e* in the Valley of
26: 3 And Saul *e* in the hill of
26: 5 to the place where Saul had *e*.
26: 5 with the people *e* all around
28: 4 and came and *e* at Shunem.
28: 4 and they *e* at Gilboa.
29: 1 and the Israelites *e* by a
2 Sam 11:11 the servants of my lord are *e*
17:26 So Israel and Absalom *e* in the
23:13 And the troop of Philistines *e*
1 Ki 16:15 And the people were *e* against
16:16 Now the people who were *e*
20:27 Now the children of Israel *e*
20:29 And they *e* opposite each other
2 Ki 25: 1 came against Jerusalem and *e*
25: 4 the Chaldeans were still *e*
1 Chr 11:15 the army of the Philistines *e*
19: 7 who came and *e* before Medeba.
2 Chr 32: 1 he *e* against the fortified
Jer 52: 4 came against Jerusalem and *e*

ENCAMPMENT (3/3) ENCAMP

Gen 42:27 give his donkey feed at the *e*,
43:21 happened, when we came to the *e*,
Ex 4:24 to pass on the way, at the *e*,

ENCAMPMENTS (1/1)

Ezek 25: 4 and they shall set their *e*

ENCAMPS (2/2) ENCAMP

Ps 34: 7 The angel of the LORD *e* all
53: 5 the bones of him who *e* against

ENCHANTER (1/1) ENCHANTMENTS

Isa 3: 3 artisan, And the expert *e*.

ENCHANTMENTS (6/6) ENCHANTER

Ex 7:11 did in like manner with their *e*.
7:22 of Egypt did so with their *e*;
8: 7 magicians did so with their *e*,
8:18 so worked with their *e* to
Isa 47: 9 the great abundance of your *e*.
47:12 Stand now with your *e* And the

ENCIRCLE (1/1)

Isa 50:11 Who *e* yourselves with sparks:

ENCIRCLED (4/4)

Deut 32:10 He *e* him, He instructed him,
Ps 22:12 bulls of Bashan have *e* Me.
Hos 11:12 Ephraim has *e* Me with lies,
Heb 11:30 fell down after they were *e*

ENCIRCLING (3/3)

1 Sam 23:26 for Saul and his men were *e*
1 Ki 7:24 brim were ornamental buds *e*
2 Chr 4: 3 it was the likeness of oxen *e*

ENCLOSE (2/2) ENCLOSED
Song 8: 9 We will *e* her With boards of
Jer 22:15 Shall you reign because you *e*

ENCLOSED (7/7) ENCLOSE
Ex 39: 6 *e* in settings of gold; they
39:13 They were *e* in settings of
1 Ki 7:12 The great court was *e* with
2 Chr 33:14 and it *e* Ophel, and he raised
Ps 22:16 of the wicked has *e* Me.
Song 4:12 A garden *e* Is my sister, my
Ezek 46:22 corners of the court were *e*

ENCLOSING (1/1)
Josh 19:33 *e* the territory from the

ENCLOSURES (1/1)
2 Chr 14:15 also attacked the livestock *e*,

ENCOMPASS (1/1)
Jer 31:22 A woman shall *e* a man."

ENCOUNTERED (1/1)
Acts 17:18 and Stoic philosophers *e* him.

ENCOURAGE (7/7) ENCOURAGED, ENCOURAGEMENT
Deut 1:38 *E* him, for he shall cause
3:28 and *e* him and strengthen him;
2 Sam 11:25 overthrow it.' So *e* him."
1 Ki 22:13 the prophets with one accord *e*
2 Chr 18:12 the prophets with one accord *e*
Ps 64: 5 They *e* themselves in an evil
1 Th 3: 2 to establish you and *e* you

ENCOURAGED (14/14) ENCOURAGE
Judg 20:22 *e* themselves and again formed
2 Chr 28:19 for he had *e* moral decline in
35: 2 priests in their duties and *e*
Ezra 1: 6 those who were around them *e*
7:28 mighty princes. So I was *e*,
Isa 41: 7 So the craftsman *e* the
Acts 11:23 and *e* them all that with
16:40 they *e* them and departed.
20: 2 had gone over that region and *e*
27:36 Then they were all *e*,
Rom 1:12 that I may be *e* together with
1 Cor 14:31 all may learn and all may be *e*.
Phil 2:19 that I also may be *e* when I
Col 2: 2 that their hearts may be *e*,

ENCOURAGEMENT (6/6) ENCOURAGE
1 Ki 22:13 of one of them, and speak *e*.
2 Chr 18:12 of one of them, and speak *e*.
30:22 And Hezekiah gave *e* to all the
32: 6 the city gate, and gave them *e*,
Acts 4:36 (which is translated Son of *E*),
15:31 it, they rejoiced over its *e*.

END (256/239) ENDED, ENDLESS, ENDS
Gen 6:13 The *e* of all flesh has come
8: 3 At the *e* of the hundred and
8: 6 at the *e* of forty days, that
23: 9 which is at the *e* of his
41: 1 at the *e* of two full years,
47:21 from one *e* of the borders of
47:21 of Egypt to the other *e*.
Ex 12:41 And it came to pass at the *e* of
23:16 Feast of Ingathering at the *e*
25:19 "Make one cherub at one *e*,
25:19 the other cherub at the other *e*;
26: 5 the curtain that is on the *e*
26:28 the midst of the boards from *e*
26:28 of the boards from end to *e*.
28:22 for the breastplate at the *e*,
31:18 And when He had made an *e* of
34:22 of Ingathering at the year's *e*.
36:12 edge of the curtain on the *e*
36:33 through the boards from one *e*
37: 8 one cherub at one *e* on this
37: 8 other cherub at the other *e*
Lev 16:20 And when he has made an *e* of
17: 5 to the *e* that the children of
Num 23:10 And let my *e* be like his!"
34: 3 shall extend eastward to the *e*
34: 5 and it shall *e* at the Sea.
34: 9 and it shall *e* at Hazar Enan.
34:12 and it shall *e* at the Salt Sea.
Deut 4:32 and ask from one *e* of heaven
8:16 you, to do you good in the *e*—
9:11 at the *e* of forty days and
11:12 of the year to the very *e* of
13: 7 from one *e* of the earth to the
13: 7 of the earth to the other *e*
14:28 At the *e* of every third year
15: 1 At the *e* of every seven years
28:49 from the *e* of the earth, as
28:64 from one *e* of the earth to the
31:10 At the *e* of every seven years,
32:20 I will see what their *e* will
32:29 would consider their latter *e*!
Josh 8:24 pass when Israel had made an *e*
9:16 And it happened at the *e* of
10:20 children of Israel made an *e*
15: 8 which is at the *e* of the
18:15 The south side began at the *e*
18:16 the border came down to the *e*
18:19 at the south *e* of the Jordan.
19:49 When they had made an *e* of
19:51 So they made an *e* of dividing
Judg 6:21 of the LORD put out the *e* of
11:39 And it was so at the *e* of two
19: 9 See, the day is coming to an *e*;
Ruth 2:23 to glean until the *e* of barley
3: 7 he went to lie down at the *e* of
3:10 shown more kindness at the *e*
1 Sam 3:12 his house, from beginning to *e*.
14:27 he stretched out the *e* of the
14:43 a little honey with the *e* of
2 Sam 2:23 in the stomach with the blunt *e*
2:26 will be bitter in the latter *e*?
14:26 at the *e* of every year he cut
20:18 and so they would *e* disputes.
24: 8 came to Jerusalem at the *e* of
1 Ki 2:39 Now it happened at the *e* of
9:10 Now it happened at the *e* of
2 Ki 8: 3 at the *e* of seven years, that
10:21 of Baal was full from one *e* to
10:25 as soon as he had made an *e* of
18:10 And at the *e* of three years they
21:16 filled Jerusalem from one *e* to
2 Chr 5:12 stood at the east *e* of the
8: 1 It came to pass at the *e* of
20:16 you will find them at the *e* of
20:23 And when they had made an *e* of
21:19 after the *e* of two years, that
Ezra 9:11 have filled it from one *e* to
Neh 3:21 the house of Eliashib to the *e*
Job 6:11 should hope? And what is my *e*,
8: 7 Yet your latter *e* would
16: 3 Shall words of wind have an *e*?
18: 2 How long till you put an *e* to
22: 5 And your iniquity without *e*?
28: 3 Man puts an *e* to darkness,
Ps 7: 9 of the wicked come to an *e*,
19: 4 And their words to the *e* of
19: 6 Its rising is from one *e* of
19: 6 And its circuit to the other *e*;
30:12 To the *e* that my glory may
39: 4 "LORD, make me to know my *e*,
46: 9 He makes wars cease to the *e* of
61: 2 From the *e* of the earth I will
73:17 Then I understood their *e*.
102:27 And Your years will have no *e*.
107:27 man, And are at their wits' *e*.
119:33 And I shall keep it to the *e*.
119:87 They almost made an *e* of me on
119:112 Forever, to the very *e*.
Prov 5: 4 But in the *e* she is bitter as
14:12 But its *e* is the way of
14:13 And the *e* of mirth may be
16:25 But its *e* is the way of
20:21 Will not be blessed at the *e*.
25: 8 For what will you do in the *e*,
29:21 have him as a son in the *e*.
Eccl 3:11 God does from beginning to *e*.
4: 8 Yet there is no *e* to all his
4:16 There was no *e* of all the
7: 2 For that is the *e* of all men;
7: 8 The *e* of a thing is better
10:13 And the *e* of his talk is
12:12 many books there is no *e*,
Isa 2: 7 And there is no *e* to their
2: 7 And there is no *e* to their
5:26 whistle to them from the *e* of
7: 3 at the *e* of the aqueduct from
9: 7 peace There will be no *e*,
10:23 Will make a determined *e* In
13: 5 From the *e* of heaven—The
16: 4 For the extortioner is at an *e*,
23:15 At the *e* of seventy years it
23:17 at the *e* of seventy years, that
33: 1 When you make an *e* of dealing
38:12 day until night You make an *e*
38:13 day until night You make an *e*
41:22 And know the latter *e* of them;
46:10 Declaring the *e* from the
47: 7 Nor remember the latter *e* of
48:20 Utter it to the *e* of the
62:11 LORD has proclaimed To the *e*
Jer 1: 3 until the *e* of the eleventh
3: 5 Will He keep it to the *e*?
4:27 Yet I will not make a full *e*.
5:10 But do not make a complete *e*.
5:18 I will not make a complete *e* of
5:31 But what will you do in the *e*?
12: 4 "He will not see our final *e*.
12:12 shall devour From one *e* of
12:12 of the land to the other *e* of
17:11 And at his *e* he will be a
25:33 the LORD shall be from one *e*
25:33 the earth even to the other *e*
26: 8 when Jeremiah had made an *e* of
30:11 Though I make a full *e* of all
30:11 I will not make a complete *e*
34:14 At the *e* of seven years let
44:27 until there is an *e* to them.
46:28 For I will make a complete *e*
46:28 I will not make a complete *e*
51:13 Your *e* has come, The measure
Lam 4:18 Our *e* was near; Our days were
4:18 For our *e* had come.
Ezek 3:16 Now it came to pass at the *e* of
7: 2 An *e*! The end has come upon the
7: 2 An end! The *e* has come upon the
7: 3 Now the *e* has come upon you,
7: 6 An *e* has come, The end has
7: 6 The *e* has come; It has dawned
11:13 Will You make a complete *e* of
20:17 I did not make an *e* of them in
21:25 come, whose iniquity shall *e*,
21:29 come, Whose iniquity shall *e*.
22: 4 and have come to the *e* of
26:13 I will put an *e* to the sound of
29:13 At the *e* of forty years I will
35: 5 their iniquity came to an *e*,
39:14 At the *e* of seven months they
41:12 courtyard at its western *e*
46:19 at their extreme western *e*.
Dan 1: 5 so that at the *e* of that time
1:15 And at the *e* of ten days their
1:18 Now at the *e* of the days, when
4:22 and your dominion to the *e* of
4:29 At the *e* of the twelve months he
4:34 And at the *e* of the time I,
6:26 shall endure to the *e*.
7:28 This is the *e* of the account.
8:17 refers to the time of the *e*.
8:19 for at the appointed time the *e*
9:24 To make an *e* of sins, To make
9:26 The *e* of it shall be with a
9:26 And till the *e* of the war
9:27 the week He shall bring an *e*
11: 6 And at the *e* of some years they
11:13 shall certainly come at the *e*
11:18 reproach against them to an *e*;
11:27 for the *e* will still be at
11:35 white, until the time of the *e*;
11:40 At the time of the *e* the king
11:45 yet he shall come to his *e*,
12: 4 book until the time of the *e*;
12: 8 what shall be the *e* of these
12: 9 sealed till the time of the *e*.
12:13 you, go your way till the *e*;
12:13 to your inheritance at the *e*
Hos 1: 4 And bring an *e* to the kingdom
Am 3:15 great houses shall have an *e*,
8: 2 The *e* has come upon My people
8:10 And its *e* like a bitter day.
Ob 9 To the *e* that everyone from
Nah 1: 8 flood He will make an utter *e*
1: 9 He will make an utter *e* of
2: 9 of gold! There is no *e* of
Hab 2: 3 But at the *e* it will speak,
Mt 10:22 But he who endures to the *e*
13:39 the harvest is the *e* of the
13:40 so it will be at the *e* of this
13:49 So it will be at the *e* of the
24: 3 and of the *e* of the age?"
24: 6 but the *e* is not yet.
24:13 But he who endures to the *e*
24:14 and then the *e* will come.
24:31 from one *e* of heaven to the
26:58 with the servants to see the *e*.
28:20 even to the *e* of the age."
Mk 3:26 he cannot stand, but has an *e*.
13: 7 but the *e* is not yet.
13:13 But he who endures to the *e*
Lk 1:33 His kingdom there will be no *e*.
21: 9 but the *e* will not come
22:37 things concerning Me have an *e*.
Jn 13: 1 world, He loved them to the *e*.
Acts 1: 8 and to the *e* of the earth."
21: 5 When we had come to the *e* of
27:10 that this voyage will *e* with
Rom 6:21 For the *e* of those things is
6:22 fruit to holiness, and the *e*,
10: 4 For Christ is the *e* of the law
14: 9 For to this *e* Christ died and
1 Cor 1: 8 will also confirm you to the *e*,
15:24 Then comes the *e*, when He
15:24 when He puts an *e* to all rule
2 Cor 1:13 understand, even to the *e*
2: 9 For to this *e* I also wrote, that
3:13 not look steadily at the *e* of
11:15 whose *e* will be according to
Eph 6:18 being watchful to this *e* with
Phil 3:19 whose *e* is destruction, whose
Col 1:29 To this *e* I also labor,
1 Tim 4:10 For to this *e* we both labor and
Heb 3: 6 of the hope firm to the *e*.
3:14 confidence steadfast to the *e*,
6: 8 whose *e* is to be burned.
6:11 assurance of hope until the *e*,
6:16 confirmation is for them an *e*
7: 3 beginning of days nor *e* of
9:26 once at the *e* of the ages, He
Jas 5:11 of Job and seen the *e*
1 Pe 1: 9 receiving the *e* of your
4: 7 But the *e* of all things is at
4:17 what will be the *e* of those
2 Pe 2:20 the latter *e* is worse for them
Rev 1: 8 the Beginning and the *E*,
2:26 and keeps My works until the *e*,
21: 6 Omega, the Beginning and the *E*.
22:13 the Beginning and the *E*,

ENDANGER (2/2)
1 Chr 12:19 to his master Saul and *e* our
Dan 1:10 Then you would *e* my head before

ENDANGERED (1/1)
Eccl 10: 9 he who splits wood may be *e* by

ENDEARMENT (1/1)

Gen 26: 8 showing *e* to Rebekah his wife.

ENDEAVORED (1/1) ENDEAVORING

1 Th 2:17 *e* more eagerly to see your face

ENDEAVORING (1/1) ENDEAVORED

Eph 4: 3 *e* to keep the unity of the

ENDEAVORS (1/1)

Ps 28: 4 to the wickedness of their *e*;

ENDEAVOUR (KJV) See (CAREFUL TO) ENSURE

ENDED (33/33) END

Gen 2: 2 And on the seventh day God *e* His
41:53 were in the land of Egypt *e*,
47:18 When that year had *e*,
Lev 8:33 days of your consecration are *e*.
Deut 31:30 of this song until they were *e*:
34: 8 and mourning for Moses *e*.
Josh 15: 4 and the border *e* at the sea.
15: 7 the waters of En Shemesh and *e*
15:11 and the border *e* at the sea.
16: 3 and it *e* at the sea.
16: 8 and it *e* at the sea. This was
17: 9 and it *e* at the sea.
18:12 it *e* at the Wilderness of Beth
18:14 and it *e* at Kirjath Baal
18:19 then the border *e* at the north
19:14 and it *e* in the Valley of
19:22 their border *e* at the Jordan:
19:29 and *e* at the sea by the region
19:33 it *e* at the Jordan.
19:34 and *e* at Judah by the Jordan
2 Chr 29:34 them until the work was *e* and
Job 7: 4 I arise, And the night be *e*?
31:40 The words of Job are *e*.
Ps 72:20 of David the son of Jesse are *e*.
Isa 40: 2 to her, That her warfare is *e*,
60:20 of your mourning shall be *e*.
Jer 8:20 is past, The summer is *e*,
Ezek 4: 8 to another till you have *e* the
Mt 7:28 when Jesus had *e* these sayings,
Lk 4: 2 and afterward, when they had *e*,
4:13 Now when the devil had *e* every
Jn 13: 2 And supper being *e*,
Acts 21:27 the seven days were almost *e*,

ENDLESS (2/2) END

1 Tim 1: 4 to fables and *e* genealogies,
Heb 7:16 to the power of an *e* life.

ENDLESSLY (1/1)

Prov 21:28 man who hears him will speak *e*.

ENDOW (1/1)

Job 39:17 And did not *e* her with

ENDOWED (3/3)

Gen 30:20 God has *e* me with a good
2 Chr 2:12 *e* with prudence and
2:13 *e* with understanding, Huram my

ENDOWMENT (1/1)

Gen 30:20 has endowed me with a good *e*;

ENDS (57/57) END

Ex 25:18 shall make them at the two *e*
25:19 make the cherubim at the two *e*
28:23 put the two rings on the two *e*
28:24 two rings which are on the *e*
28:25 and the other two *e* of the two
28:26 and put them on the two *e* of
37: 7 them of one piece at the two *e*
37: 8 made the cherubim at the two *e*
39:15 for the breastplate at the *e*,
39:16 put the two rings on the two *e*
39:17 gold in the two rings on the *e*
39:18 The two *e* of the two braided
39:19 and put them on the two *e* of
Deut 33:17 push the peoples To the *e* of
1 Sam 2:10 The LORD will judge the *e* of
1 Ki 8: 8 poles extended so that the *e*
2 Chr 5: 9 poles extended so that the *e*
Job 28:24 For He looks to the *e* of the
36:14 And their life *e* among the
37: 3 His lightning to the *e* of the
38:13 it might take hold of the *e* of
Ps 2: 8 And the *e* of the earth for
22:27 All the *e* of the world Shall
48:10 So is Your praise to the *e* of
59:13 God rules in Jacob To the *e*
65: 5 the confidence of all the *e* of
67: 7 And all the *e* of the earth
72: 8 And from the River to the *e* of
98: 3 All the *e* of the earth have
135: 7 vapors to ascend from the *e* of
Prov 17:24 eyes of a fool are on the *e*
30: 4 Who has established all the *e*
Isa 24: 8 The noise of the jubilant *e*,
24:16 From the *e* of the earth we have
40:28 The Creator of the *e* of the
41: 5 The *e* of the earth were
41: 9 whom I have taken from the *e*
42:10 And His praise from the *e* of
43: 6 And My daughters from the *e* of
45:22 All you *e* of the earth! For I
49: 6 be My salvation to the *e* of
52:10 And all the *e* of the earth
Jer 10:13 vapors to ascend from the *e* of
16:19 shall come to You From the *e*
25:31 A noise will come to the *e* of
31: 8 And gather them from the *e* of
50:41 Shall be raised up from the *e*
51:16 vapors to ascend from the *e* of
Ezek 15: 4 the fire devours both *e* of it,
Dan 4:11 And it could be seen to the *e*
Mic 5: 4 He shall be great To the *e* of
Zech 9:10 And from the River to the *e* of
Mt 12:42 for she came from the *e* of the
Lk 11:31 for she came from the *e* of the
Acts 13:47 be for salvation to the *e*
Rom 10:18 their words to the *e* of
1 Cor 10:11 upon whom the *e* of the ages

ENDUED (1/1)

Lk 24:49 of Jerusalem until you are *e*

ENDURANCE (2/2) ENDURE

Heb 10:36 For you have need of *e*,
12: 1 and let us run with *e* the race

ENDURE (42/40) ENDURANCE, ENDURED, ENDURES, ENDURING

Gen 33:14 and the children, are able to *e*,
Ex 18:23 you, then you will be able to *e*,
Num 31:23 everything that can *e* fire, you
31:23 But all that cannot *e* fire you
Judg 10:16 And His soul could no longer *e*
Esth 8: 6 For how can I *e* to see the evil
8: 6 Or how can I *e* to see the
Job 8:15 it fast, but it does not *e*.
31:23 of His magnificence I cannot *e*.
Ps 9: 7 But the LORD shall *e* forever;
30: 5 Weeping may *e* for a night,
72: 5 As long as the sun and moon *e*,
72:17 His name shall *e* forever;
81:15 But their fate would *e*
89:29 seed also I will make to *e*
89:36 His seed shall *e* forever, And
101: 5 proud heart, Him I will not *e*.
102:12 shall *e* forever, And the
102:26 will perish, but You will *e*;
104:31 May the glory of the LORD *e*
Prov 27:24 Nor does a crown *e* to all
Isa 1:13 I cannot *e* iniquity and the
Jer 10:10 nations will not be able to *e*
Ezek 22:14 'Can your heart *e*, or can
Dan 6:26 And His dominion shall *e* to
Joel 2:11 very terrible; Who can *e* it?
Nah 1: 6 And who can *e* the fierceness
Mal 3: 2 But who can *e* the day of His
Mk 4:17 and so *e* only for a time.
1 Cor 4:12 being persecuted, we *e*;
9:12 but *e* all things lest we hinder
1 Th 3: 1 when we could no longer *e* it,
3: 5 when I could no longer *e* it, I
2 Th 1: 4 and tribulations that you *e*,
2 Tim 2: 3 You therefore must *e* hardship as
2:10 Therefore I *e* all things for the
2:12 If we *e*, We shall also
4: 3 will come when they will not *e*
4: 5 *e* afflictions, do the work of
Heb 12: 7 If you *e* chastening, God deals
12:20 (For they could not *e* what was
Jas 5:11 we count them blessed who *e*.

ENDURED (7/7) ENDURE

Rom 9:22 *e* with much longsuffering the
2 Tim 3:11 at Lystra—what persecutions I *e*.
Heb 6:15 so, after he had patiently *e*,
10:32 you *e* a great struggle with
11:27 for he *e* as seeing Him who is
12: 2 joy that was set before Him *e*
12: 3 For consider Him who *e* such

ENDURES (64/64) ENDURE

1 Chr 16:34 He is good! For His mercy *e*
16:41 because His mercy *e* forever;
2 Chr 5:13 For His mercy *e* forever,"
7: 3 For His mercy *e* forever."
7: 6 For His mercy *e* forever,"
20:21 For His mercy *e* forever."
Ezra 3:11 For His mercy *e* forever
Ps 52: 1 The goodness of God *e*
100: 5 And His truth *e* to all
106: 1 He is good! For His mercy *e*
107: 1 He is good! For His mercy *e*
111: 3 And His righteousness *e*
111:10 His praise *e* forever.
112: 3 And his righteousness *e*
112: 9 His righteousness *e* forever;
117: 2 And the truth of the LORD *e*
118: 1 He is good! For His mercy *e*
118: 2 His mercy *e* forever."
118: 3 His mercy *e* forever."
118: 4 His mercy *e* forever."
118:29 He is good! For His mercy *e*
119:90 Your faithfulness *e* to all
119:160 of Your righteous judgments *e*
135:13 *e* forever, Your fame, O
136: 1 He is good! For His mercy *e*
136: 2 God of gods! For His mercy *e*
136: 3 of lords! For His mercy *e*
136: 4 For His mercy *e* forever;
136: 5 For His mercy *e* forever;
136: 6 For His mercy *e* forever;
136: 7 For His mercy *e* forever—
136: 8 For His mercy *e* forever;
136: 9 For His mercy *e* forever.
136:10 For His mercy *e* forever;
136:11 For His mercy *e* forever;
136:12 For His mercy *e* forever;
136:13 For His mercy *e* forever;
136:14 For His mercy *e* forever;
136:15 For His mercy *e* forever;
136:16 For His mercy *e* forever;
136:17 For His mercy *e* forever;
136:18 For His mercy *e* forever—
136:19 For His mercy *e* forever;
136:20 For His mercy *e* forever—
136:21 For His mercy *e* forever;
136:22 For His mercy *e* forever.
136:23 For His mercy *e* forever;
136:24 For His mercy *e* forever;
136:25 For His mercy *e* forever.
136:26 of heaven! For His mercy *e*
138: 8 *e* forever; Do not forsake the
145:13 And Your dominion *e*
Jer 33:11 His mercy *e* forever"—and
Mt 10:22 But he who *e* to the end will be
13:21 but *e* only for a while. For
24:13 But he who *e* to the end shall be
Mk 13:13 But he who *e* to the end shall
Jn 6:27 but for the food which *e* to
1 Cor 3:14 which he has built on it *e*,
13: 7 all things, *e* all things.
2 Cor 9: 9 His righteousness *e*
Jas 1:12 Blessed is the man who *e*
1 Pe 1:25 the word of the LORD *e*
2:19 of conscience toward God one *e*

ENDURING (7/7) ENDURE

1 Sam 25:28 make for my lord an *e* house,
1 Ki 11:38 with you and build for you an *e*
Ps 19: 9 *e* forever; The judgments of
Prov 8:18 *E* riches and righteousness.
Jer 15:15 In Your *e* patience, do not
2 Cor 1: 6 which is effective for *e* the
Heb 10:34 that you have a better and an *e*

ENEMIES (267/260) ENEMY

Gen 14:20 Who has delivered your *e* into
22:17 possess the gate of their *e*.
49: 8 be on the neck of your *e*;
Ex 1:10 that they also join our *e* and
23:22 I will be an enemy to your *e*
23:27 and will make all your *e* turn
32:25 to their shame among their *e*),
Lev 26: 7 You will chase your *e*,
26: 8 your *e* shall fall by the sword
26:16 for your *e* shall eat it.
26:17 you shall be defeated by your *e*.
26:32 and your *e* who dwell in it
26:36 hearts in the lands of their *e*;
26:37 power to stand before your *e*.
26:38 and the land of your *e* shall
26:41 them into the land of their *e*;
26:44 they are in the land of their *e*,
Num 10: 9 you will be saved from your *e*.
10:35 O LORD! Let Your *e* be
14:42 lest you be defeated by your *e*,
23:11 to me? I took you to curse my *e*,
24: 8 consume the nations, his *e*;
24:10 "I called you to curse my *e*,
24:18 a possession; Seir also, his *e*,
32:21 until He has driven out His *e*
Deut 1:42 you be defeated before your *e*.
6:19 to cast out all your *e* from
12:10 gives you rest from all your *e*
20: 1 go out to battle against your *e*,
20: 3 the verge of battle with your *e*.
20: 4 to fight for you against your *e*,
21:10 go out to war against your *e*,
23: 9 army goes out against your *e*,
23:14 to deliver you and give your *e*
25:19 has given you rest from your *e*
28: 7 The LORD will cause your *e* who
28:25 to be defeated before your *e*;
28:31 shall be given to your *e*,
28:48 you shall serve your *e*,
28:68 be offered for sale to your *e*
30: 7 put all these curses on your *e*
32:31 Even our *e* themselves being
32:41 will render vengeance to My *e*,
33: 7 may You be a help against his *e*.
33:29 sword of your majesty! Your *e*
Josh 7: 8 turns its back before its *e*?
7:12 could not stand before their *e*,
7:12 their backs before their *e*,
7:13 you cannot stand before your *e*
10:13 had revenge Upon their *e*.
10:19 yourselves, but pursue your *e*,
10:25 the LORD will do to all your *e*
21:44 And not a man of all their *e*
21:44 the LORD delivered all their *e*

22: 8 Divide the spoil of your ***e*** with
23: 1 rest to Israel from all their ***e***
Judg 2:14 them into the hands of their ***e***
2:14 no longer stand before their ***e***.
2:18 out of the hand of their ***e*** all
3:28 the LORD has delivered your ***e***
5:31 'Thus let all Your ***e*** perish,
8:34 from the hands of all their ***e***
11:36 LORD has avenged you of your ***e***,
1 Sam 2: 1 in the LORD. I smile at my ***e***,
4: 3 save us from the hand of our ***e***.
12:10 us from the hand of our ***e***,
12:11 you out of the hand of your ***e***
14:24 I have taken vengeance on my ***e***.
14:30 today of the spoil of their ***e***
14:47 and fought against all his ***e*** on
18:25 take vengeance on the king's ***e***.
20:15 has cut off every one of the ***e***
20:16 it at the hand of David's ***e***.
25:22 to the ***e*** of David, if I leave
25:26 let your ***e*** and those who seek
25:29 and the lives of your ***e*** He
29: 8 not go and fight against the ***e***
30:26 you from the spoil of the ***e*** of
2 Sam 3:18 and the hand of all their ***e***.
5:20 LORD has broken through my ***e***
7: 1 given him rest from all his ***e***
7: 9 and have cut off all your ***e***
7:11 you to rest from all your ***e***.
12:14 given great occasion to the ***e***
18:19 LORD has avenged him of his ***e***.
18:32 May the ***e*** of my lord the king,
19: 6 in that you love your ***e*** and hate
19: 9 saved us from the hand of our ***e***,
22: 1 him from the hand of all his ***e***,
22: 4 So shall I be saved from my ***e***.
22:38 I have pursued my ***e*** and
22:41 also given me the necks of my ***e***,
22:49 He delivers me from my ***e***.
24:13 flee three months before your ***e***,
1 Ki 3:11 have asked the life of your ***e***,
8:48 soul in the land of their ***e***
2 Ki 17:39 you from the hand of all your ***e***.
21:14 them into the hand of their ***e***;
21:14 of plunder to all their ***e***,
1 Chr 12:17 but if to betray me to my ***e***,
14:11 God has broken through my ***e*** by
17: 8 and have cut off all your ***e***
17:10 Also I will subdue all your ***e***.
21:12 foes with the sword of your ***e***
22: 9 give him rest from all his ***e***
2 Chr 1:11 or honor or the life of your ***e***,
6:28 when their ***e*** besiege them in
6:34 out to battle against their ***e***,
20:27 made them rejoice over their ***e***.
20:29 LORD had fought against the ***e***
25:20 into the hand of their ***e***,
Neh 4:15 when our ***e*** heard that it was
5: 9 reproach of the nations, our ***e***?
6: 1 and the rest of our ***e*** heard
6:16 when all our ***e*** heard of it,
9:27 them into the hand of their ***e***,
9:27 them From the hand of their ***e***.
9:28 them in the hand of their ***e***,
Esth 8:13 to avenge themselves on their ***e***.
9: 1 On the day that the ***e*** of the
9: 5 the Jews defeated all their ***e***
9:16 lives, had rest from their ***e***,
9:16 thousand of their ***e***;
9:22 the Jews had rest from their ***e***,
Job 19:11 He counts me as one of His ***e***.
Ps 3: 7 For You have struck all my ***e***
5: 8 righteousness because of my ***e***;
6: 7 grows old because of all my ***e***.
6:10 Let all my ***e*** be ashamed and
7: 6 up because of the rage of my ***e***;
8: 2 strength, Because of Your ***e***,
9: 3 When my ***e*** turn back, They
10: 5 his sight; As for all his ***e***,
17: 9 From my deadly ***e*** who surround
18: him from the hand of all his ***e***
18: 3 So shall I be saved from my ***e***.
18:37 I have pursued my ***e*** and
18:40 also given me the necks of my ***e***,
18:48 He delivers me from my ***e***.
21: 8 Your hand will find all Your ***e***;
23: 5 me in the presence of my ***e***;
25: 2 Let not my ***e*** triumph over me.
25:19 Consider my ***e***, for they
27: 2 My ***e*** and foes, They stumbled
27: 6 shall be lifted up above my ***e***
27:11 a smooth path, because of my ***e***.
31:11 I am a reproach among all my ***e***,
31:15 me from the hand of my ***e***,
35:19 over me who are wrongfully my ***e***;
37:20 And the ***e*** of the LORD, Like
38:19 But my ***e*** are vigorous, and
41: 2 him to the will of his ***e***.
41: 5 My ***e*** speak evil of me:
42:10 My ***e*** reproach me, While they
44: 5 You we will push down our ***e***;
44: 7 You have saved us from our ***e***,
45: 5 in the heart of the King's ***e***;
54: 5 He will repay my ***e*** for their
54: 7 has seen its desire upon my ***e***.
56: 2 My ***e*** would hound me all day,
56: 9 Then my ***e*** will turn back;
59: 1 Deliver me from my ***e***,
59:10 let me see my desire on my ***e***.
60:12 He who shall tread down our ***e***.
66: 3 of Your power Your ***e*** shall
68: 1 Let His ***e*** be scattered;
68:21 will wound the head of His ***e***,
68:23 their portion from your ***e***.
69: 4 Being my ***e*** wrongfully;
69:18 Deliver me because of my ***e***.
71:10 For my ***e*** speak against me;
72: 9 And His ***e*** will lick the dust.
74: 4 Your ***e*** roar in the midst of
74:23 not forget the voice of Your ***e***;
78:53 the sea overwhelmed their ***e***.
78:66 And He beat back His ***e***;
80: 6 And our ***e*** laugh among
81:14 I would soon subdue their ***e***,
83: 2 Your ***e*** make a tumult;
89:10 You have scattered Your ***e*** with
89:42 You have made all his ***e***
89:51 With which Your ***e*** have
92: 9 For behold, Your ***e***,
92: 9 Your ***e*** shall perish; All the
92:11 has seen my desire on my ***e***;
97: 3 And burns up His ***e*** round
102: 8 My ***e*** reproach me all day long,
105:24 made them stronger than their ***e***.
106:11 The waters covered their ***e***;
106:42 Their ***e*** also oppressed them,
108:13 He who shall tread down our ***e***.
110: 1 Till I make Your ***e*** Your
110: 2 Rule in the midst of Your ***e***!
112: 8 he sees his desire upon his ***e***.
119:98 make me wiser than my ***e***;
119:139 Because my ***e*** have forgotten
119:157 are my persecutors and my ***e***,
127: 5 But shall speak with their ***e***
132:18 His ***e*** I will clothe with shame,
136:24 And rescued us from our ***e***,
138: 7 hand Against the wrath of my ***e***,
139:20 Your ***e*** take Your name in
139:22 I count them my ***e***.
143: 9 Deliver me, O LORD, from my ***e***;
143:12 In Your mercy cut off my ***e***,
Prov 16: 7 He makes even his ***e*** to be at
Isa 1:24 And take vengeance on My ***e***.
9:11 And spur his ***e*** on,
26:11 the fire of Your ***e*** shall devour
42:13 He shall prevail against His ***e***.
59:18 Recompense to His ***e***;
62: 8 your grain As food for your ***e***;
66: 6 Who fully repays His ***e***!
66:14 And His indignation to His ***e***.
Jer 12: 7 My soul into the hand of her ***e***.
15: 9 to the sword Before their ***e***,
15:14 you cross over with your ***e***
17: 4 will cause you to serve your ***e***
19: 7 by the sword before their ***e***
19: 9 desperation with which their ***e***
20: 4 fall by the sword of their ***e***,
20: 5 give into the hand of their ***e***,
21: 7 into the hand of their ***e***,
34:20 them into the hand of their ***e***
34:21 into the hand of their ***e***,
44:30 of Egypt into the hand of his ***e***
48: 5 the descent of Horonaim the ***e***
49:37 to be dismayed before their ***e***
Lam 1: 2 They have become her ***e***.
1: 5 Her ***e*** prosper; For the LORD
1:21 All my ***e*** have heard of my
2:16 All your ***e*** have opened their
2:22 have borne and brought up My ***e***
3:46 All our ***e*** Have opened their
3:52 My ***e*** without cause Hunted me
3:62 The lips of my ***e*** And their
Ezek 39:23 them into the hand of their ***e***,
Dan 4:19 interpretation concern your ***e***!
Am 9: 4 into captivity before their ***e***,
Mic 4:10 you From the hand of your ***e***.
5: 9 And all your ***e*** shall be cut
7: 6 A man's ***e*** are the men of his
Nah 1: 2 He reserves wrath for His ***e***;
1: 8 And darkness will pursue His ***e***.
3:13 land are wide open for your ***e***;
Zech 10: 5 Who tread down their ***e*** In
Mt 5:44 "But I say to you, love your ***e***,
10:36 a man's ***e*** will be those of
22:44 Till I make Your ***e*** Your
Mk 12:36 Till I make Your ***e*** Your
Lk 1:71 we should be saved from our ***e***
1:74 from the hand of our ***e***,
6:27 to you who hear: Love your ***e***,
6:35 'But love your ***e***, do good,
19:27 But bring here those ***e*** of mine,
19:43 will come upon you when your ***e***
20:43 Till I make Your ***e*** Your
Acts 2:35 Till I make Your ***e*** Your
Rom 5:10 For if when we were ***e*** we were
11:28 the gospel they are ***e*** for
1 Cor 15:25 reign till He has put all ***e***
Phil 3:18 that they are the ***e*** of the
Col 1:21 who once were alienated and ***e***
Heb 1:13 Till I make Your ***e*** Your
10:13 that time waiting till His ***e***
Rev 11: 5 their mouth and devours their ***e***.
11:12 and their ***e*** saw them.

ENEMIES' (4/4)

Lev 26:34 and you are in your ***e*** land;
26:39 in their iniquity in your ***e***
Deut 20:14 and you shall eat the ***e*** plunder
Ezek 39:27 gathered them out of their ***e***

ENEMY (110/109) ENEMIES, ENEMY'S

Ex 15: 6 has dashed the ***e*** in pieces.
15: 9 The ***e*** said, 'I will pursue, I
23:22 then I will be an ***e*** to your
Lev 26:25 into the hand of the ***e***.
Num 10: 9 war in your land against the ***e***
35:23 while he was not his ***e*** or
Deut 28:53 straits in which your ***e*** shall
28:55 straits in which your ***e*** shall
28:57 straits in which your ***e*** shall
32:27 I not feared the wrath of the ***e***,
32:42 heads of the leaders of the ***e***.
33:27 He will thrust out the ***e*** from
Judg 16:23 into our hands Samson our ***e***!
16:24 delivered into our hands our ***e***,
1 Sam 2:32 And you will see an ***e*** in My
18:29 So Saul became David's ***e***
19:17 and sent my ***e*** away, so that he
24: 4 I will deliver your ***e*** into your
24:19 "For if a man finds his ***e***,
26: 8 God has delivered your ***e*** into
28:16 from you and has become your ***e***?
2 Sam 4: 8 the son of Saul your ***e***,
22:18 delivered me from my strong ***e***,
1 Ki 8:33 Israel are defeated before an ***e***
8:37 when their ***e*** besieges them in
8:44 out to battle against their ***e***,
8:46 them and deliver them to the ***e***,
8:46 captive to the land of the ***e***,
21:20 "Have you found me, O my ***e***?
2 Chr 6:24 Israel are defeated before an ***e***
6:36 them and deliver them to the ***e***,
25: 8 make you fall before the ***e***;
26:13 to help the king against the ***e***.
Ezra 8:22 to help us against the ***e*** on
8:31 us from the hand of the ***e*** and
Esth 3:10 the ***e*** of the Jews.
7: 4 although the ***e*** could never
7: 6 The adversary and ***e*** is this
8: 1 the ***e*** of the Jews. And Mordecai
9:10 the ***e*** of the Jews—they killed;
9:24 the ***e*** of all the Jews, had
Job 13:24 face, And regard me as Your ***e***?
27: 7 May my ***e*** be like the wicked,
33:10 me, He counts me as His ***e***;
Ps 7: 4 Or have plundered my ***e*** without
7: 5 Let the ***e*** pursue me and
8: 2 That You may silence the ***e*** and
9: 6 O ***e***, destructions are
13: 2 How long will my ***e*** be exalted
13: 4 Lest my ***e*** say, "I have
18:17 delivered me from my strong ***e***,
31: 8 me up into the hand of the ***e***;
41:11 Because my ***e*** does not triumph
42: 9 of the oppression of the ***e***?
43: 2 of the oppression of the ***e***?
44:10 make us turn back from the ***e***,
44:16 Because of the ***e*** and the
55: 3 Because of the voice of the ***e***,
55:12 For it is not an ***e*** who
61: 3 me, A strong tower from the ***e***.
64: 1 my life from fear of the ***e***.
74: 3 The ***e*** has damaged everything
74:10 Will the ***e*** blaspheme Your name
74:18 that the ***e*** has reproached,
78:42 He redeemed them from the ***e***,
89:22 The ***e*** shall not outwit him,
106:10 them from the hand of the ***e***.
107: 2 redeemed from the hand of the ***e***,
143: 3 For the ***e*** has persecuted my
Prov 24:17 Do not rejoice when your ***e***
25:21 If your ***e*** is hungry, give him
27: 6 But the kisses of an ***e*** are
Isa 59:19 When the ***e*** comes in like a
63:10 Himself against them as an ***e***,
Jer 6:25 Because of the sword of the ***e***,
15:11 Surely I will cause the ***e*** to
18:17 with an east wind before the ***e***;
30:14 you with the wound of an ***e***,
31:16 back from the land of the ***e***.
44:30 his ***e*** who sought his life.'"
Lam 1: 5 into captivity before the ***e***.
1: 7 fell into the hand of the ***e***,
1: 9 For the ***e*** is exalted!"
1:16 are desolate Because the ***e***
2: 3 right hand From before the ***e***.
2: 4 Standing like an ***e***, He has
2: 5 The Lord was like an ***e***.
2: 7 palaces Into the hand of the ***e***.
2:17 And He has caused an ***e*** to
4:12 That the adversary and the ***e***
Ezek 36: 2 Because the ***e*** has said of you,
Dan 11:11 given into the hand of his ***e***.
Hos 8: 3 The ***e*** will pursue him.
Mic 2: 8 My people have risen up as an ***e***—
7: 8 Do not rejoice over me, my ***e***;
7:10 Then she who is my ***e*** will
Nah 3:11 will seek refuge from the ***e***.
Zeph 3:15 He has cast out your ***e***.
Zech 8:10 was no peace from the ***e*** for
Mt 5:43 your neighbor and hate your ***e***.
13:25 his ***e*** came and sowed tares
13:28 'An ***e*** has done this.'
13:39 The ***e*** who sowed them is the
Lk 10:19 and over all the power of the ***e***,
Acts 13:10 you ***e*** of all righteousness,
Rom 12:20 If your ***e*** is hungry, feed
1 Cor 15:26 The last ***e*** that will be
Gal 4:16 Have I therefore become your ***e***
2 Th 3:15 Yet do not count him as an ***e***,
Jas 4: 4 of the world makes himself an ***e***

ENEMY'S (3/3) ENEMY

Ex 23: 4 If you meet your *e* ox or his
Job 6:23 Deliver me from the *e* hand'?
Ps 78:61 And His glory into the *e* hand.

ENGAGE (1/1)

Deut 2:24 and *e* him in battle.

ENGAGED (1/1)

2 Tim 2: 4 No one *e* in warfare entangles

ENGRAFTED (KJV) See IMPLANTED

ENGRAVE (5/5) ENGRAVED, ENGRAVER, ENGRAVING

Ex 28: 9 take two onyx stones and *e* on
28:11 you shall *e* the two stones with
28:36 a plate of pure gold and *e* on
2 Chr 2: 7 who has skill to *e* with the
Zech 3: 9 I will *e* its inscription,'

ENGRAVED (11/10) ENGRAVE

Ex 32:16 was the writing of God *e* on
39: 6 settings of gold; they were *e*,
39: 6 were engraved, as signets are *e*,
39:14 *e* like a signet, each one
Lev 26: 1 nor shall you set up an *e* stone
Num 33:52 destroy all their *e* stones,
1 Ki 7:36 flanges and on its panels he *e*
Job 19:24 That they were *e* on a rock
Jer 17: 1 point of a diamond it is *e*
Zech 14:20 TO THE LORD" shall be *e* on
2 Cor 3: 7 written and *e* on stones, was

ENGRAVER (3/3) ENGRAVE

Ex 28:11 With the work of an *e* in stone,
35:35 do all manner of work of the *e*
38:23 an *e* and designer, a weaver of

ENGRAVING (4/4) ENGRAVE

Ex 28:36 like the *e* of a signet:
32: 4 and he fashioned it with an *e*
39:30 it an inscription like the *e*
2 Chr 2:14 and to make any *e* and to

ENGRAVINGS (3/3)

Ex 28:11 like the *e* of a signet, you
28:21 like the *e* of a signet, each
1 Ki 7:31 and also on the opening were *e*,

ENGULFED (1/1)

Ps 88:17 They *e* me altogether.

ENGULFING (1/1)

Ezek 1: 4 great cloud with raging fire *e*

ENIGMA (1/1) ENIGMAS

Prov 1: 6 understand a proverb and an *e*,

ENIGMAS (2/2) ENIGMA

Dan 5:12 and explaining *e* were found in
5:16 interpretations and explain *e*.

ENJOIN, ENJOINED (KJV) See ASSIGNED, COMMAND, PRESCRIBED

ENJOY (13/12) ENJOYED, ENJOYMENT

Lev 26:34 Then the land shall *e* its
26:34 then the land shall rest and *e*
26:43 and will *e* its sabbaths while
Josh 1:15 land of your possession and *e*
Eccl 2: 1 therefore *e* pleasure";
2:24 and that his soul should *e*
3:13 man should eat and drink and *e*
5:18 and to *e* the good of all his
Isa 65:22 And My elect shall long *e* the
Acts 24: 2 Seeing that through you we *e*
Rom 15:24 if first I may *e* your company
1 Tim 6:17 gives us richly all things to *e*.
Heb 11:25 the people of God than to *e*

ENJOYED (2/2) ENJOY

2 Chr 36:21 until the land had *e* her
Gal 4:15 then was the blessing you *e*?

ENJOYING (1/1)

Judg 19:22 As they were *e* themselves,

ENJOYMENT (3/3) ENJOY

Job 20:18 of business He will get no *e*.
Eccl 2:25 who can eat, or who can have *e*,
8:15 So I commended *e*, because

ENLARGE (9/9) ENLARGED, ENLARGES

Gen 9:27 May God *e* Japheth, And may he
Ex 34:24 the nations before you and *e*
1 Chr 4:10 and *e* my territory, that Your
Ps 119:32 For You shall *e* my heart.
Isa 54: 2 *E* the place of your tent, And
Jer 4:30 Though you *e* your eyes with
Am 1:13 That they might *e* their
Mic 1:16 *E* your baldness like an eagle,
Mt 23: 5 their phylacteries broad and *e*

ENLARGED (7/7) ENLARGE

2 Sam 22:37 You *e* my path under me; So my
Ps 18:36 You *e* my path under me, So my
25:17 troubles of my heart have *e*;
Isa 5:14 Therefore Sheol has *e* itself
57: 8 You have *e* your bed And made
Jer 20:17 And her womb always *e* with
2 Cor 10:15 we shall be greatly *e* by you in

ENLARGES (5/5) ENLARGE

Deut 12:20 When the LORD your God *e* your
19: 8 Now if the LORD your God *e* your
33:20 'Blessed is he who *e* Gad;
Job 12:23 He *e* nations, and guides them.
Hab 2: 5 Because he *e* his desire as

ENLIGHTEN (4/4) ENLIGHTENED, ENLIGHTENING

2 Sam 22:29 The LORD shall *e* my darkness.
Ezra 9: 8 that our God may *e* our eyes and
Ps 13: 3 *E* my eyes, Lest I sleep the
18:28 The LORD my God will *e* my

ENLIGHTENED (3/3) ENLIGHTEN

Job 33:30 That he may be *e* with the
Eph 1:18 of your understanding being *e*;
Heb 6: 4 for those who were once *e*,

ENLIGHTENING (1/1) ENLIGHTEN

Ps 19: 8 LORD is pure, *e* the eyes;

ENLISTED (1/1)

2 Tim 2: 4 that he may please him who *e*

ENMITY (10/10)

Gen 3:15 And I will put *e* Between you
Num 35:21 or in *e* he strikes him with his
35:22 pushes him suddenly without *e*,
Hos 9: 7 of your iniquity and great *e*.
9: 8 *E* in the house of his God.
Lk 23:12 previously they had been at *e*
Rom 8: 7 Because the carnal mind is *e*
Eph 2:15 abolished in His flesh the *e*,
2:16 thereby putting to death the *e*.
Jas 4: 4 friendship with the world is *e*

ENOCH (13/12)

Gen 4:17 and she conceived and bore *E*.
4:17 after the name of his son—*E*.
4:18 To *E* was born Irad; and Irad
5:18 sixty-two years, and begot *E*.
5:19 After he begot *E*,
5:21 *E* lived sixty-five years, and
5:22 *E* walked with God three hundred
5:23 So all the days of *E* were three
5:24 And *E* walked with God; and he
1 Chr 1: 3 *E*, Methuselah, Lamech,
Lk 3:37 of Methuselah, the son of *E*,
Heb 11: 5 By faith *E* was taken away so
Jude 14 Now *E*, the seventh from

ENOS (1/1)

Lk 3:38 the son of *E*, the son of

ENOSH (7/7)

Gen 4:26 was born; and he named him *E*.
5: 6 and five years, and begot *E*.
5: 7 After he begot *E*, Seth lived
5: 9 *E* lived ninety years, and begot
5:10 *E* lived eight hundred and
5:11 So all the days of *E* were nine
1 Chr 1: 1 Adam, Seth, *E*,

ENOUGH (53/52)

Gen 19:20 this city is near *e* to flee
24:25 "We have both straw and feed *e*,
33: 9 But Esau said, "I have *e*,
33:11 with me, and because I have *e*.
34:21 For indeed the land is large *e*
45:28 Then Israel said, "It is *e*.
Ex 2:19 and he also drew *e* water for us
9:28 and hail, for it is *e*.
36: 5 people bring much more than *e*
Lev 25:21 it will bring forth produce *e*
Num 11:22 to provide *e* for them? Or shall
11:22 to provide *e* for them?"
Deut 1: 6 You have dwelt long *e* at this
2: 3 skirted this mountain long *e*;
3:26 *E* of that! Speak no more to Me
9: 8 so that the LORD was angry *e*
Josh 17:16 The mountain country is not *e*
22:17 'Is the iniquity of Peor not *e*
Judg 21:14 and yet they had not found *e*
21:23 they took *e* wives for their
2 Sam 8: 4 except that he spared *e* of
24:16 the people, "It is *e*;
1 Ki 18:32 around the altar large *e* to
19: 4 It is *e*! Now, LORD, take my
20:10 if *e* dust is left of Samaria
1 Chr 18: 4 except that he spared *e* of them
21:15 who was destroying, "It is *e*;
2 Chr 31:10 we have had *e* to eat and have
Prov 27:27 You shall have *e* goats' milk
28:19 frivolity will have poverty *e*!
30:15 Four never say, "*E*!":
30:16 fire never says, "*E*!"
Isa 1:11 I have had *e* of burnt offerings
56:11 dogs Which never have *e*.
Jer 49: 9 not destroy until they have *e*?
Ezek 30:21 to make it strong *e* to hold a
31:14 water may ever be high *e* to
45: 9 'Thus says the Lord GOD: "*E*,
Hos 4:10 they shall eat, but not have *e*;
Ob 5 not have stolen till they had *e*?
Nah 2:12 The lion tore in pieces *e* for
Hag 1: 6 You eat, but do not have *e*;
Mal 3:10 there will not be room *e*
Mt 10:25 It is *e* for a disciple that he
15:33 Where could we get *e* bread in
25: 9 lest there should not be *e* for
Mk 14:41 It is *e*! The hour has come;
Lk 14:28 whether he has *e* to finish
15:17 hired servants have bread *e*
22:38 And He said to them, "It is *e*.
Acts 7: 5 not even *e* to set his foot on.
27:38 So when they had eaten *e*,
1 Pe 4: 3 For we have spent *e* of our

ENQUIRE, ENQUIRED, ENQUIREST, ENQUIRY (KJV) See DETERMINED, INQUIRE, INQUIRES, INQUIRING, INQUIRY, QUESTION, SEEK

ENRAGED (5/5)

2 Sam 17: 8 and they are *e* in their minds,
2 Chr 16:10 for he was *e* at him because
Isa 8:21 that they will be *e* and curse
Acts 26:11 and being exceedingly *e* against
Rev 12:17 And the dragon was *e* with the

ENRAPTURED (2/2)

Prov 5:19 And always be *e* with her love.
5:20 be *e* by an immoral woman, And

ENRICH (2/2)

1 Sam 17:25 who kills him the king will *e*
Ps 65: 9 You greatly *e* it; The river

ENRICHED (4/4)

Ps 44:12 And are not *e* by selling them.
Ezek 27:33 You *e* the kings of the earth
1 Cor 1: 5 that you were *e* in everything by
2 Cor 9:11 while you are *e* in everything

ENSAMPLE (KJV) See EXAMPLE, PATTERN

ENSLAVE (2/2)

Jer 30: 8 Foreigners shall no more *e*
Hos 4:11 and new wine *e* the heart.

ENSLAVED (1/1)

Ezek 34:27 from the hand of those who *e*

ENSNARED (3/3)

Deut 12:30 to yourself that you are not *e*
Job 34:30 reign, Lest the people be *e*.
Prov 12:13 The wicked is *e* by the

ENSNARES (1/1)

Heb 12: 1 and the sin which so easily *e*

ENSUE (KJV) See PURSUE

ENSURE (1/1)

2 Pe 1:15 I will be careful to *e* that

ENTANGLE (1/1) ENTANGLED, ENTANGLES

Mt 22:15 and plotted how they might *e*

ENTANGLED (2/2) ENTANGLE

Gal 5: 1 and do not be *e* again with a
2 Pe 2:20 they are again *e* in them and

ENTANGLES (1/1) ENTANGLE

2 Tim 2: 4 No one engaged in warfare *e*

ENTER (155/149) ENTERED, ENTERING, ENTERS, ENTRY

Gen 49: 6 Let not my soul *e* their
Ex 40:35 And Moses was not able to *e* the

Num 4: 3 all who *e* the service to do the
4:23 all who *e* to perform the
5:24 that brings the curse shall *e*
5:27 that brings a curse will *e* her
8:24 years old and above one may *e*
14:30 you shall by no means *e* the
20:24 for he shall not *e* the land
Deut 4:21 and that I would not *e* the good
23: 1 or mutilation shall not *e* the
23: 2 illegitimate birth shall not *e*
23: 2 of his descendants shall *e*
23: 3 or Moabite shall not *e* the
23: 3 of his descendants shall *e*
23: 8 generation born to them may *e*
27: 3 that you may *e* the land which
29:12 that you may *e* into covenant
Josh 10:19 Do not allow them to *e* their
Judg 6: 5 and they would *e* the land to
11:18 But they did not *e* the border
18: 9 and *e* to possess the land.
1 Ki 14:12 When your feet *e* the city, the
2 Ki 7: 4 We will *e* the city,' the famine
19:23 I will *e* the extremity of its
2 Chr 7: 2 And the priests could not *e* the
23:19 in any way unclean should *e*.
27: 2 had done (although he did not *e*
30: 8 and *e* His sanctuary, which He
Esth 4: 2 for no one might *e* the king's
Ps 37:15 Their sword shall *e* their own
45:15 They shall *e* the King's
95:11 They shall not *e* My rest.'"
100: 4 *E* into His gates with
109:18 So let it *e* his body like
118:20 which the righteous shall *e*.
143: 2 Do not *e* into judgment with
Prov 4:14 Do not *e* the path of the
18: 6 A fool's lips *e* into
23:10 Nor *e* the fields of the
Isa 2:10 *E* into the rock, and hide in
3:14 The LORD will *e* into judgment
13: 2 that they may *e* the gates of
26: 2 which keeps the truth may *e* in.
26:20 *e* your chambers, And shut your
37:24 I will *e* its farthest height,
57: 2 He shall *e* into peace;
59:14 street, And equity cannot *e*.
Jer 7: 2 all you of Judah who *e* in at
8:14 And let us *e* the fortified
14:18 with the sword! And if I *e*
16: 5 Do not *e* the house of mourning,
17:20 who *e* by these gates.
17:25 then shall *e* the gates of this
21:13 Or who shall *e* our dwellings?'
22: 2 servants and your people who *e*
22: 4 then shall *e* the gates of this
42:15 you wholly set your faces to *e*
42:18 be poured out on you when you *e*
Lam 1:10 she has seen the nations *e* her
1:10 whom You commanded Not to *e*
4:12 and the enemy Could *e* the
Ezek 7:22 For robbers shall *e* it and
13: 9 nor shall they *e* into the land
20:38 but they shall not *e* the land
26:10 as men *e* a city that has been
37: 5 I will cause breath to *e* into
42:14 When the priests *e* them, they
44: 2 and no man shall *e* by it,
44: 3 he shall *e* by way of the
44: 5 Mark well who may *e* the house
44: 9 shall *e* My sanctuary, including
44:16 They shall *e* My sanctuary, and
44:17 whenever they *e* the gates of
46: 2 The prince shall *e* by way of the
Dan 11: 7 *e* the fortress of the king of
11:17 shall also set his face to *e*
11:24 He shall *e* peaceably, even into
11:40 and he shall *e* the countries,
11:41 He shall also *e* the Glorious
Joel 2: 9 They *e* at the windows like a
3: 2 And I will *e* into judgment
Am 5: 5 Nor *e* Gilgal, Nor pass over
Jon 3: 4 And Jonah began to *e* the city on
Zech 5: 4 It shall *e* the house of the
6:10 and go the same day and *e* the
14:18 of Egypt will not come up and *e*
Mt 5:20 you will by no means *e* the
7:13 *E* by the narrow gate; for wide
7:21 shall *e* the kingdom of heaven,
10: 5 and do not *e* a city of the
10:11 whatever city or town you *e*,
12:29 Or how can one *e* a strong man's
12:45 and they *e* and dwell there; and
18: 3 you will by no means *e* the
18: 8 It is better for you to *e* into
18: 9 It is better for you to *e* into
19:17 But if you want to *e* into life,
19:23 it is hard for a rich man to *e*
19:24 than for a rich man to *e* the
21:31 tax collectors and harlots *e*
25:21 *E* into the joy of your lord.'
25:23 *E* into the joy of your lord.'
26:41 lest you *e* into temptation.
Mk 1:45 Jesus could no longer openly *e*
3:27 No one can *e* a strong man's
5:12 that we may *e* them."
6:10 In whatever place you *e* a house,
7:19 because it does not *e* his heart
9:25 come out of him and *e* him no
9:43 It is better for you to *e* into
9:45 It is better for you to *e* life
9:47 It is better for you to *e* the
10:15 child will by no means *e* it.
10:23 for those who have riches to *e*
10:24 those who trust in riches to *e*
10:25 than for a rich man to *e* the
13:15 nor *e* to take anything out of
14:38 lest you *e* into temptation.
Lk 7: 6 am not worthy that You should *e*
8:16 that those who *e* may see the
8:32 that He would permit them to *e*
9: 4 "Whatever house you *e*,
10: 5 "But whatever house you *e*,
10: 8 "Whatever city you *e*,
10:10 "But whatever city you *e*,
11:26 and they *e* and dwell there;
11:52 You did not *e* in yourselves,
13:24 Strive to *e* through the narrow
13:24 will seek to *e* and will not be
18:17 child will by no means *e* it.
18:24 for those who have riches to *e*
18:25 than for a rich man to *e* the
19:30 where as you *e* you will find a
21:21 those who are in the country *e*
22:40 Pray that you may not *e* into
22:46 lest you *e* into temptation."
24:26 suffered these things and to *e*
Jn 3: 4 Can he *e* a second time into his
3: 5 he cannot *e* the kingdom of God.
10: 1 he who does not *e* the sheepfold
Acts 14:22 through many tribulations *e*
Heb 3:11 They shall not *e* My rest.'
3:18 He swear that they would not *e*
3:19 we see that they could not *e*
4: 3 For we who have believed do *e*
4: 3 They shall not *e* My rest,'
4: 5 They shall not *e* My rest."
4: 6 it remains that some must *e*
4: 6 it was first preached did not *e*
4:11 us therefore be diligent to *e*
10:19 having boldness to *e* the
Rev 15: 8 and no one was able to *e* the
21:27 But there shall by no means *e* it
22:14 and may *e* through the gates

ENTERED (99/98) ENTER

Gen 7:13 sons with them, *e* the ark—
7:16 So those that *e*,
19: 3 so they turned in to him and *e*
19:23 upon the earth when Lot *e* Zoar.
23:10 all who *e* at the gate of his
31:33 went out of Leah's tent and *e*
Ex 33: 9 when Moses *e* the tabernacle,
Num 4:35 everyone who *e* the service for
4:39 everyone who *e* the service for
4:43 everyone who *e* the service for
Josh 2: 3 who have *e* your house, for they
8:19 and they *e* the city and took
10:20 that those who escaped *e*
Judg 9:46 they *e* the stronghold of the
19:29 When he *e* his house he took a
2 Sam 10:14 and *e* the city. So Joab
22: 7 And my cry *e* His ears.
1 Ki 14:28 And whenever the king *e* the
2 Ki 3:24 and they *e* their land, killing
7: 8 then they came back and *e*
9:31 as Jehu *e* at the gate, she
1 Chr 19:15 and *e* the city. So Joab went to
2 Chr 12:11 And whenever the king *e* the
15:12 Then they *e* into a covenant to
31:16 distributed to everyone who *e*
32: 1 king of Assyria came and *e*
Neh 2:15 then I turned back and *e* by the
10:29 and *e* into a curse and an oath
Esth 6: 4 Now Haman had just *e* the
Job 38:16 Have you *e* the springs of the
38:22 Have you *e* the treasury of snow,
Jer 2: 7 its goodness. But when you *e*,
9:21 Has *e* our palaces, To kill
34:10 who had *e* into the covenant,
37:16 When Jeremiah *e* the dungeon and
Ezek 2: 2 Then the Spirit *e* me when He
3:24 Then the Spirit *e* me and set me
16: 8 I swore an oath to you and *e*
44: 2 the LORD God of Israel has *e*
Ob 11 When foreigners *e* his gates
13 You should not have *e* the gate
Hab 3:16 Rottenness *e* my bones; And I
Mt 8: 5 Now when Jesus had *e* Capernaum,
12: 4 how he *e* the house of God and
24:38 until the day that Noah *e* the
Mk 1:21 on the Sabbath He *e* the
1:29 they *e* the house of Simon and
2: 1 And again He *e* Capernaum after
3: 1 And He *e* the synagogue again,
5:13 unclean spirits went out and *e*
5:40 and *e* where the child was
6:56 Wherever He *e* into villages,
7:17 When He had *e* a house away from
7:24 And He *e* a house and wanted no
11: 2 and as soon as you have *e* it
Lk 1:40 and *e* the house of Zacharias and
4:38 arose from the synagogue and *e*
6: 6 that He *e* the synagogue and
7: 1 the people, He *e* Capernaum.
7:44 I *e* your house; you gave Me no
8:30 because many demons had *e*
8:33 went out of the man and *e* the
9:34 and they were fearful as they *e*
9:52 they *e* a village of the
10:38 as they went that He *e* a
17:12 Then as He *e* a certain village,
17:27 until the day that Noah *e* the
19: 1 Then Jesus *e* and passed through
22: 3 Then Satan *e* Judas, surnamed
22:10 when you have *e* the city, a man
Jn 4:38 and you have *e* into their
6:22 one which His disciples had *e*,
6:22 and that Jesus had not *e* the
13:27 Satan *e* him. Then Jesus said to
18: 1 which He and His disciples *e*.
18:33 Then Pilate *e* the Praetorium
Acts 1:13 And when they had *e*,
3: 2 to ask alms from those who *e*
3: 8 stood and walked and *e* the
5:21 they *e* the temple early in the
9:17 And Ananias went his way and *e*
10:24 And the following day they *e*
11: 8 or unclean has at any time *e*
11:12 and we *e* the man's house.
16:40 went out of the prison and *e*
18: 7 he departed from there and *e*
18:19 but he himself *e* the synagogue
21: 8 and *e* the house of Philip the
21:26 *e* the temple to announce the
23:16 he went and *e* the barracks and
25:23 and had *e* the auditorium with
Rom 5:12 just as through one man sin *e*
5:20 Moreover the law *e* that the
1 Cor 2: 9 Nor have *e* into the
Heb 4:10 For he who has *e* His rest has
6:20 where the forerunner has *e* for
9:12 but with His own blood He *e* the
9:24 For Christ has not *e* the holy
Rev 11:11 the breath of life from God *e*

ENTERING (15/15) ENTER

Gen 12:11 when he was close to *e* Egypt,
Deut 23:20 in the land which you are *e* to
Judg 18:17 *E* there, they took the carved
1 Sam 23: 7 he has shut himself in by *e* a
2 Chr 23: 4 One-third of you *e* on the
26:16 against the LORD his God by *e*
Ezra 9:11 The land which you are *e* to
Jer 17:27 as not carrying a burden when *e*
Mt 23:13 do you allow those who are *e*
Mk 4:19 the desires for other things *e*
16: 5 And *e* the tomb, they saw a young
Lk 11:52 and those who were *e* in you
Acts 8: 3 *e* every house, and dragging off
27: 2 *e* a ship of Adramyttium, we put
Heb 4: 1 since a promise remains of *e*

ENTERS (20/19) ENTER

Ex 29:30 when he *e* the tabernacle of
Num 4:30 everyone who *e* the service to
Job 22: 4 And *e* into judgment with you?
Prov 2:10 When wisdom *e* your heart, And
Ezek 21:14 That *e* their private chambers.
26:10 when he *e* your gates, as men
42:12 as one *e* them, there was a
44:21 shall drink wine when he *e* the
46: 8 "When the prince *e*,
46: 9 whoever *e* by way of the north
46: 9 and whoever *e* by way of the
47: 8 and *e* the sea. When it
Mt 15:17 yet understand that whatever *e*
Mk 7:15 There is nothing that *e* a man
7:18 not perceive that whatever *e* a
Lk 22:10 him into the house which he *e*.
Jn 10: 2 But he who *e* by the door is the
10: 9 If anyone *e* by Me, he will be
Heb 6:19 and which *e* the Presence
9:25 as the high priest *e* the Most

ENTERTAIN (1/1) ENTERTAINED

Heb 13: 2 Do not forget to *e* strangers,

ENTERTAINED (2/2) ENTERTAIN

Acts 28: 7 who received us and *e* us
Heb 13: 2 doing some have unwittingly *e*

ENTHRONED (2/2) INHABIT

Ps 22: 3 *E* in the praises of Israel.
29:10 The LORD sat *e* at the Flood,

ENTICE (5/5) ENTICED, ENTICES, ENTICING

Deut 13: 5 to *e* you from the way in which
13:10 because he sought to *e* you away
Judg 14:15 *E* your husband, that he may
16: 5 *E* him, and find out where his
Prov 1:10 if sinners *e* you, Do not

ENTICED (4/4) ENTICE

Deut 13:13 gone out from among you and *e*
Job 31: 9 If my heart has been *e* by a
31:27 my heart has been secretly *e*,
Jas 1:14 away by his own desires and *e*.

ENTICES (3/3) ENTICE

Ex 22:16 If a man *e* a virgin who is not
Deut 13: 6 secretly *e* you, saying, 'Let us
Prov 16:29 A violent man *e* his neighbor,

ENTICING (2/2) ENTICE

Prov 7:21 With her *e* speech she caused
2 Pe 2:14 *e* unstable souls. They have a

ENTIRE (12/12) ENTIRELY, ENTIRETY

Num 14:29 according to your *e* number,
1 Ki 6:10 side chambers against the *e*
6:22 he overlaid with gold the *e*
1 Chr 5:10 in their tents throughout the *e*
2 Chr 26:14 for the *e* army, shields,
Ezra 10:14 let the leaders of our *e*
Neh 4: 6 and the *e* wall was joined
Ezek 27:27 And the *e* company which is in
27:34 Your merchandise and the *e*
43:11 its *e* design and all its
48:13 its *e* length shall be
48:20 The *e* district shall be

ENTIRELY (4/4) ENTIRE

Num 3: 9 they are given *e* to him from
4: 6 spread over that a cloth *e* of
Isa 24: 3 The land shall be *e* emptied and
1 Tim 4:15 give yourself *e* to them, that

ENTIRETY (2/2) ENTIRE

Ps 119:160 The *e* of Your word is truth,
Ezek 11:15 the house of Israel in its *e*,

ENTRAILS (24/20)

Ex 12: 9 head with its legs and its *e*.
29:13 all the fat that covers the *e*,
29:17 wash its *e* and its legs, and
29:22 tail, the fat that covers the *e*,
Lev 1: 9 but he shall wash its *e* and its
1:13 but he shall wash the *e* and the
3: 3 The fat that covers the *e* and
3: 3 all the fat that is on the *e*,
3: 9 And the fat that covers the *e*
3: 9 all the fat that is on the *e*,
3:14 The fat that covers the *e* and
3:14 all the fat that is on the *e*,
4: 8 The fat that covers the *e* and
4: 8 all the fat which is on the *e*,
4:11 its *e* and offal—
7: 3 and the fat that covers the *e*,
8:16 all the fat that was on the *e*,
8:21 Then he washed the *e* and the
8:25 all the fat that was on the *e*,
9:14 And he washed the *e* and the
9:19 what covers the *e* and the
Judg 3:22 and his *e* came out.
2 Sam 20:10 and his *e* poured out on the
Acts 1:18 in the middle and all his *e*

ENTRANCE (63/61)

Ex 32:26 then Moses stood in the *e* of the
32:27 and go in and out from *e* to
32:27 in and out from entrance to *e*
35:15 screen for the door at the *e*
Num 13:21 near the *e* of Hamath.
34: 8 out your border to the *e* of
Josh 8:29 cast it at the *e* of the gate of
13: 5 Mount Hermon as far as the *e*
20: 4 and stands at the *e* of the gate
Judg 1:24 Please show us the *e* to the
1:25 So he showed them the *e* to the
3: 3 Mount Baal Hermon to the *e* of
9:35 went out and stood in the *e* to
9:40 to the very *e* of the gate.
9:44 forward and stood at the *e* of
18:16 stood by the *e* of the gate.
18:17 The priest stood at the *e* of
1 Sam 17:52 Philistines as far as the *e* of
2 Sam 10: 8 in battle array at the *e* of
11:23 them back as far as the *e* of
1 Ki 6:31 For the *e* of the inner
8:65 a great assembly from the *e* of
18:46 and ran ahead of Ahab to the *e*
19:13 went out and stood in the *e* of
22:10 at a threshing floor at the *e*
2 Ki 7: 3 were four leprous men at the *e*
10: 8 them in two heaps at the *e*
11:16 went by way of the horses' *e*
14:25 territory of Israel from the *e*
16:18 he removed the king's outer *e*
23: 8 the gates which were at the *e*
23:11 at the *e* to the house of the
1 Chr 4:39 So they went to the *e* of Gedor,
5: 9 they settled as far as the *e*
9:19 had been keepers of the *e* to
13: 5 in Egypt to as far as the *e* of
2 Chr 7: 8 very great assembly from the *e*
18: 9 at a threshing floor at the *e*
23:13 standing by his pillar at the *e*;
23:15 and she went by way of the *e* of
26: 8 fame spread as far as the *e* of
33:14 as far as the *e* of the Fish
Esth 5: 1 facing the *e* of the house.
Ps 119:130 The *e* of Your words gives
Prov 8: 3 At the *e* of the doors:
Jer 1:15 one set his throne At the *e*
38:14 brought to him at the third *e*
43: 9 courtyard which is at the *e*
Ezek 8: 5 this image of jealousy in the *e*.
27: 3 You who are situated at the *e* of
40:11 He measured the width of the *e*
40:15 From the front of the *e* gate to
40:38 was a chamber and its *e* by
40:40 as one goes up to the *e* of the
41: 2 and the side walls of the *e*
41: 3 two cubits; and the *e*,
41: 3 and the width of the *e*,
42: 9 the lower chambers was the *e*
46: 3 land shall worship at the *e* to
46:19 he brought me through the *e*,
48: 1 the road to Hethlon at the *e*
Am 6:14 will afflict you from the *e* of
2 Pe 1:11 for so an *e* will be supplied to

ENTRANCES (3/3)

Ezek 42:11 and all their exits and *e* were
43:11 its exits and its *e*,
Mic 5: 6 the land of Nimrod at its *e*;

ENTRAP (1/1)

Prov 5:22 His own iniquities *e* the wicked

ENTREAT (9/9) ENTREATED

Ex 8: 8 *E* the LORD that He may take
8:29 and I will *e* the LORD, that
9:28 *E* the LORD, that there may be
10:17 and *e* the LORD your God, that
Ruth 1:16 *E* me not to leave you, Or to
1 Ki 13: 6 Please *e* the favor of the LORD
Prov 19: 6 Many *e* the favor of the
Mal 1: 9 But now *e* God's favor, That He
1 Cor 4:13 being defamed, we *e*.

ENTREATED (6/6) ENTREAT

Ex 8:30 went out from Pharaoh and *e*
10:18 he went out from Pharaoh and *e*
1 Ki 13: 6 So the man of God *e* the
Ezra 8:23 So we fasted and *e* our God for
Ps 119:58 I *e* Your favor with my whole
Isa 19:22 and He will be *e* by them and

ENTREATIES (1/1)

Prov 18:23 The poor man uses *e*,

ENTREATY (2/2)

2 Chr 33:13 to Him; and He received his *e*,
33:19 and how God received his *e*,

ENTRIES, ENTRY (KJV) See ENTRANCE

ENTRUSTED (3/3)

1 Cor 9:17 I have been *e* with a
1 Th 2: 4 been approved by God to be *e*
1 Pe 5: 3 as being lords over those *e* to

ENTRY (6/6) ENTER

2 Chr 4:22 As for the *e* of the sanctuary,
Prov 8: 3 at the *e* of the city, At the
Jer 19: 2 which is by the *e* of the
26:10 LORD and sat down in the *e* of
36:10 in the upper court at the *e* of
1 Th 1: 9 concerning us what manner of *e*

ENTRYWAY (3/3)

1 Ki 10: 5 and his *e* by which he went up
2 Chr 9: 4 and his *e* by which he went up
Ezek 41: 2 The width of the *e* was ten

ENVIED (6/6) ENVY

Gen 26:14 So the Philistines *e* him.
30: 1 Rachel *e* her sister, and said
37:11 And his brothers *e* him, but his
Ps 106:16 When they *e* Moses in the camp,
Eccl 4: 4 every skillful work a man is *e*
Ezek 31: 9 that all the trees of Eden *e*

ENVIOUS (6/6) ENVY

Ps 37: 1 Nor be *e* of the workers of
73: 3 For I was *e* of the boastful,
Prov 24: 1 Do not be *e* of evil men, Nor
24:19 Nor be *e* of the wicked;
Acts 7: 9 the patriarchs, becoming *e*,
17: 5 were not persuaded, becoming *e*,

ENVISION (3/3)

Ezek 13: 9 be against the prophets who *e*
13:23 you shall no longer *e* futility
Zech 10: 2 The diviners *e* lies, And tell

ENVISIONED (3/3)

Lam 2:14 But have *e* for you false
Ezek 13: 6 They have *e* futility and false
13: 8 you have spoken nonsense and *e*

ENVOYS (1/1)

Ps 68:31 *E* will come out of Egypt

ENVY (24/23) ENVIED, ENVIOUS, ENVYING

Job 5: 2 And *e* slays a simple one.
Ps 68:16 Why do you fume with *e*,
Prov 3:31 Do not *e* the oppressor, And
14:30 But *e* is rottenness to the
23:17 Do not let your heart *e*
Eccl 9: 6 and their *e* have now perished;
Isa 11:13 Also the *e* of Ephraim shall
11:13 Ephraim shall not *e* Judah,
26:11 and be ashamed For their *e*
Ezek 35:11 anger and according to the *e*
Mt 27:18 handed Him over because of *e*.
Mk 15:10 handed Him over because of *e*.
Acts 13:45 they were filled with *e*;
Rom 1:29 maliciousness; full of *e*,
13:13 and lust, not in strife and *e*.
1 Cor 3: 3 For where there are *e*,
13: 4 and is kind; love does not *e*;
Gal 5:21 *e*, murders, drunkenness,
Phil 1:15 preach Christ even from *e* and
1 Tim 6: 4 over words, from which come *e*,
Titus 3: 3 living in malice and *e*,
Jas 3:14 But if you have bitter *e* and
3:16 For where *e* and self-seeking
1 Pe 2: 1 all deceit, hypocrisy, *e*,

ENVYING (1/1) ENVY

Gal 5:26 one another, *e* one another.

EPAENETUS (1/1)

Rom 16: 5 their house. Greet my beloved *E*,

EPAPHRAS (3/3)

Col 1: 7 as you also learned from *E*,
4:12 *E*, who is one of you,
Phm 1:23 *E*, my fellow prisoner

EPAPHRODITUS (2/2)

Phil 2:25 it necessary to send to you *E*,
4:18 having received from *E* the

EPHAH (53/43) EPHAHS

Gen 25: 4 And the sons of Midian were *E*,
Ex 16:36 an omer is one-tenth of an *e*.
29:40 shall be one-tenth of an *e*
Lev 5:11 his offering one-tenth of an *e*
6:20 one-tenth of an *e* of fine flour
14:10 three-tenths of an *e* of fine
14:21 one-tenth of an *e* of fine
19:36 honest weights, an honest *e*,
23:13 be two-tenths of an *e* of
23:17 of two-tenths of an *e*.
24: 5 Two-tenths of an *e* shall be
Num 5:15 one-tenth of an *e* of barley
15: 4 of one-tenth of an *e* of
15: 6 offering two-tenths of an *e*
15: 9 of three-tenths of an *e* of
28: 5 and one-tenth of an *e* of fine
28: 9 and two-tenths of an *e* of fine
28:12 three-tenths of an *e* of fine
28:12 two-tenths of an *e* of fine
28:13 and one-tenth of an *e* of fine
28:20 three-tenths of an *e* you
28:21 offer one-tenth of an *e* for
28:28 three-tenths of an *e* for
29: 3 three-tenths of an *e* for the
29: 9 three-tenths of an *e* for the
29:14 three-tenths of an *e* for
Judg 6:19 and unleavened bread from an *e*
Ruth 2:17 and it was about an *e* of
1 Sam 1:24 one *e* of flour, and a skin of
17:17 now for your brothers an *e* of
1 Chr 1:33 The sons of Midian were *E*,
2:46 *E*, Caleb's concubine, bore
2:47 Regem, Jotham, Geshan, Pelet, *E*,
Isa 5:10 homer of seed shall yield one *e*.
60: 6 dromedaries of Midian and *E*;
Ezek 45:10 have honest scales, an honest *e*,
45:11 The *e* and the bath shall be of
45:11 and the *e* one-tenth of a homer;
45:13 shall give one-sixth of an *e*
45:13 and one-sixth of an *e* from a
45:24 a grain offering of one *e* for
45:24 ephah for each bull and one *e*
45:24 with a hin of oil for each *e*.
46: 5 offering shall be one *e* for
46: 5 as a hin of oil with every *e*.
46: 7 a grain offering of an *e* for a
46: 7 an *e* for a ram, as much as he
46: 7 and a hin of oil with every *e*.
46:11 grain offering shall be an *e*
46:11 an *e* for a ram, as much as he
46:11 and a hin of oil with every *e*.
46:14 every morning, a sixth of an *e*,
Am 8: 5 Making the *e* small and the

EPHAHS (3/3) EPHAH

Ruth 3:15 he measured six *e* of barley,
3:17 These six *e* of barley he gave
Hag 2:16 one came to a heap of twenty *e*,

EPHAI (1/1)

Jer 40: 8 the sons of *E* the Netophathite,

EPHER (4/4)

Gen 25: 4 sons of Midian were Ephah, *E*,
1 Chr 1:33 sons of Midian were Ephah, *E*,
4:17 of Ezrah were Jether, Mered, *E*,
5:24 of their fathers' houses: *E*,

EPHES DAMMIM (1/1)

1 Sam 17: 1 between Sochoh and Azekah, in *E*.

EPHESIAN (1/1)

Acts 21:29 seen Trophimus the *E* with him

EPHESIANS (3/3) EPHESUS

Acts 19:28 Great is Diana of the *E*!"
19:34 Great is Diana of the *E*!"
19:35 know that the city of the *E* is

EPHESUS (17/17) EPHESIANS

Acts 18:19 And he came to *E*, and left
18:21 And he sailed from *E*.
18:24 in the Scriptures, came to *E*.
19: 1 the upper regions, came to *E*.
19:17 Jews and Greeks dwelling in *E*;
19:26 see and hear that not only at *E*,
19:35 the crowd, he said: "Men of *E*,
20:16 Paul had decided to sail past *E*,
20:17 From Miletus he sent to *E* and
1 Cor 15:32 I have fought with beasts at *E*,
16: 8 But I will tarry in *E* until
Eph 1: 1 To the saints who are in *E*,
1 Tim 1: 3 remain in *E* that you may charge
2 Tim 1:18 ways he ministered to me at *E*.
4:12 And Tychicus I have sent to *E*.
Rev 1:11 which are in Asia: to *E*,
2: 1 the angel of the church of *E*

EPHLAL (2/1)

1 Chr 2:37 Zabad begot *E*, and Ephlal
2:37 and *E* begot Obed;

EPHOD (53/42)

Ex 25: 7 and stones to be set in the *e*
28: 4 shall make: a breastplate, an *e*,
28: 6 and they shall make the *e* of
28: 8 intricately woven band of the *e*,
28:12 on the shoulders of the *e* as
28:15 to the workmanship of the *e*
28:25 on the shoulder straps of the *e*
28:26 is on the inner side of the *e*.
28:27 underneath the *e* toward its
28:27 intricately woven band of the *e*.
28:28 its rings to the rings of the *e*,
28:28 intricately woven band of the *e*,
28:28 does not come loose from the *e*.
28:31 shall make the robe of the *e*
29: 5 on Aaron, and the robe of the *e*,
29: 5 the robe of the ephod, the *e*,
29: 5 intricately woven band of the *e*.
35: 9 and stones to be set in the *e*
35:27 the stones to be set in the *e*
39: 2 He made the *e* of gold, blue,
39: 5 woven band of his *e* that was
39: 7 them on the shoulders of the *e*
39: 8 like the workmanship of the *e*,
39:18 on the shoulder straps of the *e*
39:19 on the inward side of the *e*.
39:20 underneath the *e* toward its
39:20 intricately woven band of the *e*.
39:21 its rings to the rings of the *e*
39:21 intricately woven band of the *e*,
39:21 would not come loose from the *e*,
39:22 He made the robe of the *e* of
Lev 8: 7 and put the *e* on him; and he
8: 7 intricately woven band of the *e*,
8: 7 and with it tied the *e* on
Num 34:23 Manasseh, Hanniel the son of *E*,
Judg 8:27 Then Gideon made it into an *e*
17: 5 and made an *e* and household
18:14 there are in these houses an *e*,
18:17 took the carved image, the *e*,
18:18 took the carved image, the *e*,
18:20 was glad; and he took the *e*,
1 Sam 2:18 as a child, wearing a linen *e*.
2:28 and to wear an *e* before Me?
14: 3 in Shiloh, was wearing an *e*.
21: 9 wrapped in a cloth behind the *e*.
22:18 men who wore a linen *e*.
23: 6 that he went down with an *e*
23: 9 Bring the *e* here."
30: 7 Please bring the *e* here to me."
30: 7 And Abiathar brought the *e* to
2 Sam 6:14 David was wearing a linen *e*.
1 Chr 15:27 David also wore a linen *e*.
Hos 3: 4 without *e* or teraphim.

EPHPHATHA (1/1)

Mk 7:34 He sighed, and said to him, "*E*,

EPHRAIM (172/159) EPHRAIM'S, EPHRAIMITE

Gen 41:52 name of the second he called *E*:
46:20 Egypt were born Manasseh and *E*,
48: 1 his two sons, Manasseh and *E*.
48: 5 *E* and Manasseh, who were born
48:13 *E* with his right hand toward
48:17 his right hand on the head of *E*,
48:20 May God make you as *E* and as
48:20 And thus he set *E* before
Num 1:10 the sons of Joseph: from *E*,
1:32 of Joseph, the children of *E*,
1:33 were numbered of the tribe of *E*
2:18 standard of the forces with *E*
2:18 the leader of the children of *E*
2:24 armies of the forces with *E*,
7:48 leader of the children of *E*,
10:22 the camp of the children of *E*
13: 8 from the tribe of *E*,
26:28 families, by Manasseh and *E*,
26:35 These are the sons of *E*
26:37 the families of the sons of *E*
34:24 the tribe of the children of *E*,
Deut 33:17 are the ten thousands of *E*,
34: 2 all Naphtali and the land of *E*
Josh 14: 4 were two tribes: Manasseh and *E*.
16: 4 of Joseph, Manasseh and *E*,
16: 5 border of the children of *E*,
16: 8 the tribe of the children of *E*
16: 9 cities for the children of *E*
17: 8 belonged to the children of *E*.
17: 9 These cities of *E* are among
17:15 since the mountains of *E* are
17:17 to *E* and Manasseh—saying, "You
19:50 Serah in the mountains of *E*;
20: 7 Shechem in the mountains of *E*,
21: 5 the families of the tribe of *E*,
21:20 their lot from the tribe of *E*.
21:21 in the mountains of *E* (a city
24:30 which is in the mountains of *E*,
24:33 to him in the mountains of *E*.
Judg 1:29 Nor did *E* drive out the
2: 9 Heres, in the mountains of *E*,
3:27 trumpet in the mountains of *E*,
4: 5 Bethel in the mountains of *E*.
5:14 From *E* were those whose roots
7:24 all the mountains of *E*,
7:24 Then all the men of *E*
8: 1 Now the men of *E* said to him,
8: 2 gleaning of the grapes of *E*
10: 1 in Shamir in the mountains of *E*.
10: 9 and against the house of *E*,
12: 1 Then the men of *E* gathered
12: 4 of Gilead and fought against *E*.
12: 4 the men of Gilead defeated *E*,
12: 4 Gileadites are fugitives of *E*
12:15 in Pirathon in the land of *E*,
17: 1 a man from the mountains of *E*,
17: 8 he came to the mountains of *E*,
18: 2 they went to the mountains of *E*,
18:13 there to the mountains of *E*,
19: 1 in the remote mountains of *E*.
19:16 was from the mountains of *E*;
19:18 the remote mountains of *E*;
1 Sam 1: 1 Zophim, of the mountains of *E*,
9: 4 through the mountains of *E* and
14:22 hidden in the mountains of *E*,
2 Sam 2: 9 Ashurites, over Jezreel, over *E*,
13:23 in Baal Hazor, which is near *E*;
18: 6 battle was in the woods of *E*.
20:21 a man from the mountains of *E*,
1 Ki 4: 8 Ben-Hur, in the mountains of *E*;
12:25 Shechem in the mountains of *E*,
2 Ki 5:22 to me from the mountains of *E*.
14:13 of Jerusalem from the Gate of *E*
1 Chr 6:66 territory from the tribe of *E*.
6:67 in the mountains of *E*,
7:20 The sons of *E* were Shuthelah,
7:22 Then *E* their father mourned many
9: 3 and of the children of *E* and
12:30 of the sons of *E* twenty thousand
27:10 Pelonite, of the children of *E*;
27:14 of the children of *E*;
27:20 over the children of *E*,
2 Chr 13: 4 which is in the mountains of *E*,
15: 8 had taken in the mountains of *E*;
15: 9 who dwelt with them from *E*,
17: 2 of Judah and in the cities of *E*
19: 4 Beersheba to the mountains of *E*,
25: 7 with any of the children of *E*.
25:10 that had come to him from *E*,
25:23 of Jerusalem from the Gate of *E*
28: 7 Zichri, a mighty man of *E*,
28:12 the heads of the children of *E*,
30: 1 and also wrote letters to *E* and
30:10 city through the country of *E*
30:18 of the people, many from *E*,
31: 1 all Judah, Benjamin, *E*,
34: 6 in the cities of Manasseh, *E*,
34: 9 from the hand of Manasseh and *E*,
Neh 8:16 open square of the Gate of *E*.
12:39 and above the Gate of *E*,
Ps 60: 7 *E* also is the helmet for My
78: 9 The children of *E*,
78:67 did not choose the tribe of *E*,
80: 2 Before *E*, Benjamin,
108: 8 *E* also is the helmet for My
Isa 7: 2 forces are deployed in *E*.
7: 5 'Because Syria, *E*,
7: 8 Within sixty-five years *E* will
7: 9 The head of *E* is Samaria, And
7:17 not come since the day that *E*
9: 9 *E* and the inhabitant of
9:21 Manasseh shall devour *E*,
9:21 and *E* Manasseh; Together they
11:13 Also the envy of *E* shall
11:13 *E* shall not envy Judah, And
11:13 And Judah shall not harass *E*.
17: 3 fortress also will cease from *E*,
28: 1 of pride, to the drunkards of *E*,
28: 3 of pride, the drunkards of *E*,
Jer 4:15 affliction from Mount *E*:
7:15 whole posterity of *E*.
31: 6 watchmen will cry on Mount *E*,
31: 9 And *E* is My firstborn.
31:18 I have surely heard *E* bemoaning
31:20 Is *E* My dear son? Is he a
50:19 shall be satisfied on Mount *E*
Ezek 37:16 it, 'For Joseph, the stick of *E*,
37:19 which is in the hand of *E*,
48: 5 the west, one section for *E*;
48: 6 "by the border of *E*,
Hos 4:17 *E* is joined to idols, Let him
5: 3 I know *E*, And Israel is not
5: 3 hidden from Me; For now, O *E*,
5: 5 Therefore Israel and *E* stumble
5: 9 *E* shall be desolate in the day
5:11 *E* is oppressed and broken in
5:12 Therefore I will be to *E* like
5:13 When *E* saw his sickness, And
5:13 Then *E* went to Assyria And
5:14 I will be like a lion to *E*,
6: 4 O *E*, what shall I
6:10 There is the harlotry of *E*;
7: 1 Then the iniquity of *E* was
7: 8 *E* has mixed himself among the
7: 8 *E* is a cake unturned.
7:11 *E* also is like a silly dove,
8: 9 *E* has hired lovers.
8:11 Because *E* has made many altars
9: 3 But *E* shall return to Egypt,
9: 8 The watchman of *E* is with my
9:11 As for *E*, their glory
9:13 Just as I saw *E* like Tyre,
9:13 So *E* will bring out his
9:16 *E* is stricken, Their root is
10: 6 *E* shall receive shame, And
10:11 *E* is a trained heifer That
10:11 I will make *E* pull a plow.
11: 3 I taught *E* to walk, Taking them
11: 8 "How can I give you up, *E*?
11: 9 I will not again destroy *E*.
11:12 *E* has encircled Me with lies,
12: 1 *E* feeds on the wind, And
12: 8 And *E* said, 'Surely I have
12:14 *E* provoked Him to anger most
13: 1 When *E* spoke, trembling, He
13:12 The iniquity of *E* is bound up;
14: 8 *E* shall say, 'What have I to
Ob 19 shall possess the fields of *E*
Zech 9:10 will cut off the chariot from *E*
9:13 My bow, Fitted the bow with *E*,
10: 7 Those of *E* shall be like a
Jn 11:54 wilderness, to a city called *E*,

E

EPHRAIM'S (4/4) EPHRAIM

Gen 48:14 right hand and laid it on *E*
48:17 hand to remove it from *E* head
50:23 Joseph saw *E* children to the
Josh 17:10 Southward it was *E*,

EPHRAIMITE (4/3) EPHRAIM

Judg 12: 5 And when any *E* who escaped
12: 5 say to him, "Are you an *E*?
1 Sam 1: 1 of Tohu, the son of Zuph, an *E*.
1 Ki 11:26 an *E* from Zereda, whose

EPHRAIMITES (4/4)

Josh 16:10 Canaanites dwell among the *E*
Judg 12: 4 of Ephraim among the *E* and
12: 5 of the Jordan before the *E*
12: 6 that time forty-two thousand *E*.

EPHRAIN (1/1)

2 Chr 13:19 and *E* with its villages.

EPHRATH (5/4) EPHRATHAH, EPHRATHITE

Gen 35:16 a little distance to go to *E*,
35:19 and was buried on the way to *E*
48: 7 a little distance to go to *E*;
48: 7 her there on the way to *E*
1 Chr 2:19 Caleb took *E* as his wife, who

EPHRATHAH (5/5) EPHRATH

Ruth 4:11 and may you prosper in *E* and be
1 Chr 2:50 sons of Hur, the firstborn of *E*,
4: 4 the firstborn of *E* the father
Ps 132: 6 Behold, we heard of it in *E*;
Mic 5: 2 "But you, Bethlehem *E*,

EPHRATHITE (1/1) EPHRATH, EPHRATHITES

1 Sam 17:12 David was the son of that *E*

EPHRATHITES (1/1) EPHRATHITE

Ruth 1: 2 *E* of Bethlehem, Judah. And they

EPHRON (13/11)

Gen 23: 8 and meet with *E* the son of
23:10 Now *E* dwelt among the sons of
23:10 and *E* the Hittite answered
23:13 and he spoke to *E* in the hearing
23:14 And *E* answered Abraham, saying
23:16 And Abraham listened to *E*;
23:16 weighed out the silver for *E*
23:17 So the field of *E* which was in
25: 9 in the field of *E* the son of
49:29 that is in the field of *E* the

49:30 bought with the field of E the
50:13 bought with the field from E
Josh 15: 9 to the cities of Mount E.

EPICUREAN (1/1)

Acts 17:18 Then certain E and Stoic

EPILEPTIC (1/1) EPILEPTICS

Mt 17:15 for he is an e and suffers

EPILEPTICS (1/1) EPILEPTIC

Mt 4:24 who were demon-possessed, e,

EPISTLE (12/11) EPISTLES

Rom 16:22 I, Tertius, who wrote this e,
1 Cor 5: 9 I wrote to you in my e not to
2 Cor 3: 2 You are our e written in our
3: 3 clearly you are an e of
7: 8 For I perceive that the same e
Col 4:16 Now when this e is read among
4:16 that you likewise read the e
1 Th 5:27 you by the Lord that this e be
2 Th 2:15 whether by word or our e.
3:14 not obey our word in this e,
3:17 which is a sign in every e;
2 Pe 3: 1 now write to you this second e

EPISTLES (2/2) EPISTLE

2 Cor 3: 1 e of commendation to you or
2 Pe 3:16 as also in all his e,

EQUAL (12/12) EQUITY, UNEQUALLY

Ex 30:34 there shall be e amounts of
Deut 18: 8 They shall have e portions to
Job 28:17 gold nor crystal can e it,
28:19 topaz of Ethiopia cannot e it,
Ps 55:13 But it was you, a man my e,
Isa 40:25 Me, Or to whom shall I be e?
46: 5 and make Me e And compare Me,
Mt 20:12 and you made them e to us who
Lk 20:36 for they are e to the angels
Jn 5:18 making Himself e with God.
Phil 2: 6 not consider it robbery to be e
Rev 21:16 breadth, and height are e.

EQUALITY (2/1)

2 Cor 8:14 but by an e, that now at
8:14 your lack—that there may be e.

EQUALLY (1/1)

Ezek 47:14 You shall inherit it e with one

EQUIPMENT (6/6) EQUIPPED

Deut 23:13 have an implement among your e,
1 Sam 8:12 make his weapons of war and e
10:22 he is, hidden among the e.
1 Ki 19:21 their flesh, using the oxen's e,
Isa 10:28 he has attended to his e.
Dan 11:13 with a great army and much e.

EQUIPPED (2/2) EQUIPMENT, EQUIPPING

1 Chr 12:23 of the divisions that were e
2 Tim 3:17 thoroughly e for every good

EQUIPPING (1/1) EQUIPPED

Eph 4:12 for the e of the saints for the

EQUITY (8/8) EQUAL

Ps 98: 9 world, And the peoples with e.
99: 4 You have established e;
Prov 1: 3 Justice, judgment, and e;
2: 9 E and every good path.
Isa 11: 4 And decide with e for the meek
59:14 And e cannot enter.
Mic 3: 9 justice And pervert all e,
Mal 2: 6 walked with Me in peace and e,

ER (11/8)

Gen 38: 3 a son, and he called his name E.
38: 6 Then Judah took a wife for E his
38: 7 But E, Judah's firstborn,
46:12 The sons of Judah were E,
46:12 and Zerah (but E and Onan died
Num 26:19 The sons of Judah were E and
26:19 and E and Onan died in the land
1 Chr 2: 3 The sons of Judah were E,
2: 3 of Shua, the Canaanitess. E,
4:21 the son of Judah were E the
Lk 3:28 son of Elmodam, the son of E,

ERAN (1/1)

Num 26:36 the sons of Shuthelah: of E,

ERANITES (1/1)

Num 26:36 of Eran, the family of the E.

ERASTUS (3/3)

Acts 19:22 to him, Timothy and E,
Rom 16:23 the whole church, greets you. E,
2 Tim 4:20 E stayed in Corinth, but

ERECH (2/2)

Gen 10:10 of his kingdom was Babel, E,
Ezra 4: 9 the people of Persia and E and

ERECT (3/3)

2 Sam 24:18 e an altar to the LORD on the
1 Chr 21:18 that David should go and e an
Ezra 2:68 to e it in its place:

ERECTED (6/6)

Gen 33:20 Then he e an altar there and
2 Sam 6:17 the tabernacle that David had e
1 Chr 16: 1 the tabernacle that David had e
Ezra 6:11 be pulled from his house and e,
Ezek 16:31 You e your shrine at the head
Heb 8: 2 tabernacle which the Lord e,

ERI (2/2)

Gen 46:16 Ziphion, Haggi, Shuni, Ezbon, E,
Num 26:16 family of the Oznites; of E,

ERITES (1/1)

Num 26:16 of Eri, the family of the E;

ERR (7/7) ERRED, ERROR

Isa 3:12 who lead you cause you to e,
9:16 of this people cause them to e,
19:14 they have caused Egypt to e in
28: 7 They e in vision, they stumble
30:28 the people, Causing them to e.
Jer 23:13 caused My people Israel to e.
23:32 and cause My people to e by

ERRAND (1/1)

Gen 24:33 until I have told about my e.

ERRED (7/6) ERR

Lev 5:18 his ignorance in which he e
1 Sam 26:21 I have played the fool and e
Job 6:24 to understand wherein I have e.
19: 4 And if indeed I have e,
Isa 28: 7 But they also have e through
28: 7 priest and the prophet have e
29:24 These also who e in spirit will

ERROR (14/14) ERR, ERRORS

2 Sam 6: 7 God struck him there for his e;
Job 4:18 He charges His angels with e,
19: 4 My e remains with me.
Eccl 5: 6 of God that it was an e.
10: 5 As an e proceeding from the
Isa 32: 6 To utter e against the LORD,
Dan 6: 4 nor was there any e or fault
Rom 1:27 the penalty of their e which
1 Th 2: 3 did not come from e or
Jas 5:20 who turns a sinner from the e
2 Pe 2:18 from those who live in e.
3:17 being led away with the e of
1 Jn 4: 6 of truth and the spirit of e.
Jude 11 have run greedily in the e of

ERRORS (3/3) ERROR

Ps 19:12 Who can understand his e?
Jer 10:15 They are futile, a work of e;
51:18 They are futile, a work of e;

ESAIAS (KJV) See ISAIAH

ESARHADDON (3/3)

2 Ki 19:37 Then E his son reigned in his
Ezra 4: 2 to Him since the days of E
Isa 37:38 Then E his son reigned in his

ESAU (92/82) EDOM, ESAU'S

Gen 25:25 so they called his name E.
25:27 And E was a skillful hunter, a
25:28 And Isaac loved E because he ate
25:29 and E came in from the field,
25:30 And E said to Jacob, "Please
25:32 And E said, "Look, I am about
25:34 And Jacob gave E bread and stew
25:34 Thus E despised his
26:34 When E was forty years old, he
27: 1 that he called E his older son
27: 5 when Isaac spoke to E his son.
27: 5 And E went to the field to hunt
27: 6 I heard your father speak to E
27:11 E my brother is a hairy man,
27:15 clothes of her elder son E,
27:19 I am E your firstborn; I have
27:21 you are really my son E or
27:22 the hands are the hands of E.
27:24 "Are you really my son E?
27:30 that E his brother came in from
27:32 am your son, your firstborn, E.
27:34 When E heard the words of his
27:36 And E said, "Is he not rightly
27:37 Isaac answered and said to E,
27:38 And E said to his father, "Have
27:38 O my father!" And E lifted up
27:41 So E hated Jacob because of the
27:41 and E said in his heart, "The
27:42 And the words of E her older son
27:42 Surely your brother E comforts
28: 5 the mother of Jacob and E.
28: 6 E saw that Isaac had blessed
28: 8 Also E saw that the daughters of
28: 9 So E went to Ishmael and took
32: 3 messengers before him to E his
32: 4 "Speak thus to my lord E,
32: 6 "We came to your brother E,
32: 8 If E comes to the one company
32:11 my brother, from the hand of E;
32:13 to his hand as a present for E
32:17 When E my brother meets you and
32:18 is a present sent to my lord E;
32:19 manner you shall speak to E
33: 1 E was coming, and with him were
33: 4 But E ran to meet him, and
33: 8 Then E said, "What do you
33: 9 But E said, "I have enough, my
33:12 Then E said, "Let us take our
33:15 And E said, "Now let me leave
33:16 So E returned that day on his
35: 1 you fled from the face of E
35:29 And his sons E and Jacob buried
36: 1 Now this is the genealogy of E,
36: 2 E took his wives from the
36: 4 Now Adah bore Eliphaz to E,
36: 5 These were the sons of E who
36: 6 Then E took his wives, his sons,
36: 8 So E dwelt in Mount Seir. Esau
36: 8 in Mount Seir. E is Edom.
36: 9 this is the genealogy of E
36:10 the son of Adah the wife of E,
36:10 son of Basemath the wife of E.
36:14 of Zibeon. And she bore to E:
36:15 the chiefs of the sons of E.
36:15 the firstborn son of E,
36:19 These were the sons of E,
36:40 the names of the chiefs of E,
36:43 E was the father of the
Deut 2: 4 brethren, the descendants of E,
2: 5 I have given Mount Seir to E
2: 8 the descendants of E who dwell
2:12 but the descendants of E
2:22 done for the descendants of E,
2:29 just as the descendants of E who
Josh 24: 4 'To Isaac I gave Jacob and E.
24: 4 To E I gave the mountains of
1 Chr 1:34 The sons of Isaac were E and
1:35 The sons of E were Eliphaz,
Jer 49: 8 I will bring the calamity of E
49:10 But I have made E bare; I have
Ob 6 how E shall be searched out!
8 from the mountains of E?
9 from the mountains of E May
18 But the house of E shall be
18 shall remain of the house of E,
19 possess the mountains of E,
21 To judge the mountains of E,
Mal 1: 2 Was not E Jacob's brother?"
1: 3 But E I have hated, And laid
Rom 9:13 but E I have hated."
Heb 11:20 faith Isaac blessed Jacob and E
12:16 or profane person like E,

ESAU'S (11/8) ESAU

Gen 25:26 and his hand took hold of E
27:23 were hairy like his brother E
36:10 These were the names of E sons:
36:12 E son, and she bore Amalek to
36:12 the sons of Adah, E wife.
36:13 sons of Basemath, E wife.
36:14 E wife, the daughter of Anah,
36:17 E son: Chief Nahath, Chief
36:17 sons of Basemath, E wife.
36:18 E wife: Chief Jeush, Chief
36:18 E wife, the daughter of Anah.

ESCAPE (65/61) ESCAPED, ESCAPES

Gen 19:17 E for your life! Do not look
19:17 E to the mountains, lest you be
19:19 but I cannot e to the
19:20 please let me e there (is it
19:22 e there. For I cannot do
32: 8 company which is left will e.
Josh 8:22 let none of them remain or e.
1 Sam 23:28 called that place the Rock of E.
27: 1 than that I should speedily e
27: 1 So I shall e out of his hand."
2 Sam 15:14 or we shall not e from Absalom.
20: 6 fortified cities, and e us."
1 Ki 18:40 Baal! Do not let one of them e!
2 Ki 9:15 let no one leave or e from the
10:24 escapes, whoever lets him e,
19:31 And those who e from Mount
Ezra 9: 8 God, to leave us a remnant to e,
Esth 4:13 in your heart that you will e
Job 11:20 fail, And they shall not e,
32:15 no more; Words e them.
Ps 55: 8 I would hasten my e From the
56: 7 Shall they e by iniquity?
71: 2 and cause me to e;
141:10 While I e safely.
Prov 19: 5 he who speaks lies will not e.
Eccl 7:18 For he who fears God will e
7:26 He who pleases God shall e
Isa 20: 6 of Assyria; and how shall we e?

37:32 And those who ***e*** from Mount
66:19 and those among them who ***e*** I
Jer 11:11 they will not be able to ***e***;
25:35 the leaders of the flock to ***e***.
32: 4 king of Judah shall not ***e*** from
34: 3 And you shall not ***e*** from his
38:18 and you shall not ***e*** from their
38:23 You shall not ***e*** from their
42:17 none of them shall remain or ***e***
44:14 of Egypt to dwell there shall ***e***
44:14 shall return except those who ***e***.
44:28 Yet a small number who ***e*** the
46: 6 away, Nor the mighty man ***e***;
48: 8 every city; No one shall ***e***.
50:28 voice of those who flee and ***e***
50:29 all around; Let none of them ***e***.
Ezek 6: 8 that you may have some who ***e***
6: 9 Then those of you who ***e*** will
7:16 Those who survive will ***e*** and be
17:15 Will he who does such things ***e***?
17:18 these things, he shall not ***e***.
Dan 11:41 but these shall ***e*** from his
11:42 the land of Egypt shall not ***e***.
Joel 2: 3 Surely nothing shall ***e*** them.
Am 2:15 The swift of foot shall not ***e***,
Zech 2: 7 'Up, Zion! ***E***, you who dwell
Mt 23:33 brood of vipers! How can you ***e***
Lk 21:36 you may be counted worthy to ***e***
Acts 27:30 the sailors were seeking to ***e***
27:42 of them should swim away and ***e***.
Rom 2: 3 that you will ***e*** the judgment of
1 Cor 10:13 will also make the way of ***e***,
1 Th 5: 3 And they shall not ***e***.
2 Tim 2:26 come to their senses and ***e***
Heb 2: 3 how shall we ***e*** if we neglect so
12:25 For if they did not ***e*** who
12:25 much more shall we not ***e*** if

ESCAPED (56/54) ESCAPE

Gen 14:13 Then one who had ***e*** came and
Deut 23:15 his master the slave who has ***e***
Josh 10:20 that those who ***e*** entered
Judg 3:26 But Ehud had ***e*** while they
3:26 beyond the stone images and ***e***
3:29 stout men of valor; not a man ***e***.
12: 5 And when any Ephraimite who ***e***
1 Sam 14:41 were taken, but the people ***e***.
18:11 to the wall!" But David ***e*** his
19:10 So David fled and ***e*** that night.
19:12 And he went and fled and ***e***.
19:17 my enemy away, so that he has ***e***?
19:18 So David fled and ***e***,
22: 1 departed from there and ***e*** to
22:20 ***e*** and fled after David.
23:13 was told Saul that David had ***e***
30:17 next day. Not a man of them ***e***,
2 Sam 1: 3 I have ***e*** from the camp of
4: 6 Rechab and Baanah his brother ***e***.
1 Ki 20:20 Ben-Hadad the king of Syria ***e***
2 Ki 13: 5 so that they ***e*** from under the
19:30 And the remnant who have ***e*** of
19:37 and they ***e*** into the land of
1 Chr 4:43 of the Amalekites who had ***e***.
2 Chr 16: 7 army of the king of Syria has ***e***
20:24 on the earth. No one had ***e***.
30: 6 the remnant of you who have ***e***
36:20 And those who ***e*** from the sword
Neh 1: 2 concerning the Jews who had ***e***,
Job 1:15 and I alone have ***e*** to tell
1:16 and I alone have ***e*** to tell
1:17 and I alone have ***e*** to tell
1:19 and I alone have ***e*** to tell
19:20 And I have ***e*** by the skin of my
Ps 124: 7 Our soul has ***e*** as a bird from
124: 7 snare is broken, and we have ***e***.
Isa 4: 2 For those of Israel who have ***e***.
10:20 And such as have ***e*** of the
37:31 And the remnant who have ***e*** of
37:38 and they ***e*** into the land of
45:20 You who have ***e*** from the
Jer 41:15 Ishmael the son of Nethaniah ***e***
51:50 You who have ***e*** the sword, Get
Ezek 24:27 will be opened to him who has ***e***;
33:21 that one who had ***e*** from
33:22 before the man came who had ***e***.
Ob 14 cut off those among them who ***e***;
Jn 10:39 but He ***e*** out of their hand.
Acts 27:44 And so it was that they all ***e***
28: 1 Now when they had ***e***,
28: 4 though he has ***e*** the sea, yet
2 Cor 11:33 and ***e*** from his hands.
Heb 11:34 ***e*** the edge of the sword, out of
2 Pe 1: 4 having ***e*** the corruption that
2:18 the ones who have actually ***e***
2:20 after they have ***e*** the

ESCAPES (10/9) ESCAPE

1 Ki 19:17 It shall be that whoever ***e*** the
19:17 and whoever ***e*** the sword of
2 Ki 10:24 have brought into your hands ***e***,
Ps 68:20 And to GOD the Lord belong ***e***
Isa 15: 9 Lions upon him who ***e*** from
16: 3 Do not betray him who ***e***.
Jer 48:19 him who flees And her who ***e***;
Ezek 24:26 on that day one who ***e*** will come
Am 9: 1 And he who ***e*** from them shall
Acts 26:26 that none of these things ***e***

ESCAPING (1/1)

2 Sam 4: 7 and were all night ***e*** through

ESCHEW (KJV) See TURN (AWAY)

ESCORT (3/3)

2 Sam 19:15 to ***e*** the king across the
19:31 to ***e*** him across the Jordan.
Ezra 8:22 to request of the king an ***e*** of

ESCORTED (1/1)

2 Sam 19:40 And all the people of Judah ***e***

ESCORTS (6/5)

2 Ki 11: 4 the bodyguards and the ***e***—
11: 6 at the gate behind the ***e***.
11:11 Then the ***e*** stood, every man with
11:13 heard the noise of the ***e*** and
11:19 hundreds, the bodyguards, the ***e***,
11:19 by way of the gate of the ***e*** to

ESEK (1/1)

Gen 26:20 called the name of the well ***E***,

ESH-BAAL (2/2) ISHBOSHETH

1 Chr 8:33 Malchishua, Abinadab, and ***E***.
9:39 Malchishua, Abinadab, and ***E***.

ESHBAN (2/2)

Gen 36:26 the sons of Dishon: Hemdan, ***E***,
1 Chr 1:41 sons of Dishon were Hamran, ***E***,

ESHCOL (6/6)

Gen 14:13 brother of ***E*** and brother of
14:24 men who went with me: Aner, ***E***,
Num 13:23 they came to the Valley of ***E***,
13:24 was called the Valley of ***E***,
32: 9 went up to the Valley of ***E*** and
Deut 1:24 and came to the Valley of ***E***,

ESHEAN (1/1)

Josh 15:52 Arab, Dumah, ***E***,

ESHEK (1/1)

1 Chr 8:39 And the sons of ***E*** his brother

ESHKALONITES (KJV) See ASHKELONITES

ESHTAOL (7/7)

Josh 15:33 In the lowland: ***E***, Zorah,
19:41 their inheritance was Zorah, ***E***,
Judg 13:25 Mahaneh Dan between Zorah and ***E***.
16:31 buried him between Zorah and ***E***
18: 2 men of valor from Zorah and ***E***,
18: 8 their brethren at Zorah and ***E***,
18:11 from there, from Zorah and ***E***,

ESHTAOLITES (1/1)

1 Chr 2:53 came the Zorathites and the ***E***.

ESHTEMOA (5/5)

Josh 21:14 ***E*** with its common-land,
1 Sam 30:28 Siphmoth, those who were in ***E***,
1 Chr 4:17 and Ishbah the father of ***E***.
4:19 of Keilah the Garmite and of ***E***
6:57 ***E*** with its common-lands,

ESHTEMOH (1/1)

Josh 15:50 Anab, ***E***, Anim,

ESHTERAH (1/1)

Josh 21:27 and Be ***E*** with its common-land:

ESHTON (2/2)

1 Chr 4:11 Mehir, who was the father of ***E***.
4:12 And ***E*** begot Beth-Rapha, Paseah,

ESLI (1/1)

Lk 3:25 son of Nahum, the son of ***E***,

ESPECIALLY (18/18)

Deut 4:10 ***e*** concerning the day you stood
Josh 2: 1 ***e*** Jericho." So they went, and
Ps 31:11 But ***e*** among my neighbors,
Lk 19:42 ***e*** in this your day, the things
Acts 25:26 and ***e*** before you, King Agrippa,
26: 3 ***e*** because you are expert in all
1 Cor 14: 1 but ***e*** that you may prophesy.
2 Cor 10:13 a sphere which ***e*** includes you.
Gal 6:10 ***e*** to those who are of the
Phil 4:22 but ***e*** those who are of Caesar's
1 Tim 4:10 ***e*** of those who believe.
5: 8 and ***e*** for those of his
5:17 ***e*** those who labor in the word
2 Tim 4:13 the books, ***e*** the parchments.
Titus 1:10 ***e*** those of the circumcision,
Phm 1:16 ***e*** to me but how much more to
Heb 13:19 But I ***e*** urge you to do this,
2 Pe 2:10 and ***e*** those who walk according

ESPIED, ESPY (KJV) See SAW, SEARCHED, SPY, WATCH

ESPOUSALS, ESPOUSED (KJV) See BETROTHAL, BETROTHED, WEDDING

ESROM (KJV) See HEZRON

ESTABLISH (56/55) ESTABLISHED, ESTABLISHES

Gen 6:18 But I will ***e*** My covenant with
9: 9 I ***e*** My covenant with you and
9:11 Thus I ***e*** My covenant with you:
17: 7 And I will ***e*** My covenant between
17:19 I will ***e*** My covenant with him
17:21 But My covenant I will ***e*** with
Deut 8:18 that He may ***e*** His covenant
28: 9 The LORD will ***e*** you as a holy
29:13 that He may ***e*** you today as a
1 Sam 1:23 Only let the LORD ***e*** His
2 Sam 7:12 and I will ***e*** his kingdom.
7:13 and I will ***e*** the throne of his
7:25 ***e*** it forever and do as You
1 Ki 9: 5 then I will ***e*** the throne of your
1 Chr 17:11 and I will ***e*** his kingdom.
17:12 and I will ***e*** his throne
17:14 And I will ***e*** him in My house and
18: 3 as he went to ***e*** his power by
22:10 and I will ***e*** the throne of his
28: 7 Moreover I will ***e*** his kingdom
2 Chr 7:18 then I will ***e*** the throne of your
9: 8 to ***e*** them forever, therefore He
Esth 9:21 to ***e*** among them that they should
Job 28:25 To ***e*** a weight for the wind,
Ps 7: 9 But ***e*** the just; For the
48: 8 God will ***e*** it forever. Selah
87: 5 the Most High Himself shall ***e***
89: 2 Your faithfulness You shall ***e***
89: 4 Your seed I will ***e*** forever, And
90:17 And ***e*** the work of our hands
90:17 ***e*** the work of our hands.
107:36 That they may ***e*** a city for a
119:38 ***E*** Your word to Your servant,
Prov 15:25 But He will ***e*** the boundary of
Isa 9: 7 To order it and ***e*** it with
26:12 You will ***e*** peace for us, For
Jer 11: 5 that I may ***e*** the oath which I
33: 2 the LORD who formed it to ***e*** it
Ezek 16:60 and I will ***e*** an everlasting
16:62 And I will ***e*** My covenant with
26:20 and I shall ***e*** glory in the land
34:23 I will ***e*** one shepherd over them,
37:26 I will ***e*** them and multiply
Dan 6: 7 have consulted together to ***e*** a
6: 8 ***e*** the decree and sign the
Am 5:15 ***E*** justice in the gate. It may
Rom 3:31 we ***e*** the law.
10: 3 and seeking to ***e*** their own
16:25 Now to Him who is able to ***e*** you
1 Th 3: 2 to ***e*** you and encourage you
3:13 so that He may ***e*** your hearts
2 Th 2:17 comfort your hearts and ***e*** you in
3: 3 who will ***e*** you and guard you
Heb 10: 9 away the first that He may ***e***
Jas 5: 8 ***E*** your hearts, for the coming
1 Pe 5:10 suffered a while, perfect, ***e***,

ESTABLISHED (89/87) CONFIRMED, ESTABLISH

Gen 9:17 of the covenant which I have ***e***
41:32 twice because the thing is ***e***
Ex 6: 4 I have also ***e*** My covenant with
15:17 LORD, which Your hands have ***e***.
Deut 19:15 witnesses the matter shall be ***e***.
32: 6 Has He not made you and ***e*** you?
1 Sam 3:20 knew that Samuel had been ***e***
13:13 For now the LORD would have ***e***
14:47 So Saul ***e*** his sovereignty over
20:31 the earth, you shall not be ***e***,
24:20 kingdom of Israel shall be ***e***
2 Sam 5:12 knew that the LORD had ***e*** him
7:16 and your kingdom shall be ***e***
7:16 Your throne shall be ***e***
7:26 of Your servant David be ***e***
1 Ki 2:12 and his kingdom was firmly ***e***.
2:24 and who has ***e*** a house for me,
2:45 the throne of David shall be ***e***
2:46 Thus the kingdom was ***e*** in the
2 Ki 14: 5 as soon as the kingdom was ***e*** in
1 Chr 14: 2 knew that the LORD had ***e*** him
16:30 The world also is firmly ***e***,
17:14 and his throne shall be ***e***
17:23 let it be ***e*** forever, and do
17:24 'So let it be ***e***, that Your
17:24 of Your servant David be ***e***
2 Chr 1: 9 promise to David my father be ***e***,
12: 1 when Rehoboam had ***e*** the kingdom
17: 5 Therefore the LORD ***e*** the
20:20 your God, and you shall be ***e***;
21: 4 Now when Jehoram was ***e*** over the
23:18 as it was ***e*** by David.
25: 3 as soon as the kingdom was ***e***
Esth 9:27 the Jews ***e*** and imposed it upon

E

Job 21: 8 Their descendants are *e* with
22:28 And it will be *e* for you; So
Ps 24: 2 And *e* it upon the waters.
40: 2 And *e* my steps.
65: 6 Who *e* the mountains by His
78: 5 For He *e* a testimony in Jacob,
78:69 Like the earth which He has *e*
81: 5 This He *e* in Joseph as a
89:21 With whom My hand shall be *e*;
89:37 It shall be *e* forever like the
93: 1 Surely the world is *e*,
93: 2 Your throne is *e* from of old;
96:10 The world also is firmly *e*,
99: 4 You have *e* equity; You have
102:28 their descendants will be *e*
103:19 The LORD has *e* His throne in
112: 8 His heart is *e*;
119:90 You *e* the earth, and it
140:11 Let not a slanderer be *e* in the
148: 6 He also *e* them forever and
Prov 3:19 By understanding He *e* the
4:26 And let all your ways be *e*.
8:23 I have been *e* from everlasting,
8:28 When He *e* the clouds above,
12: 3 A man is not *e* by wickedness,
12:19 The truthful lip shall be *e*
15:22 of counselors they are *e*.
16: 3 And your thoughts will be *e*.
16:12 For a throne is *e* by
20:18 Plans are *e* by counsel;
24: 3 And by understanding it is *e*;
25: 5 And his throne will be *e* in
29:14 His throne will be *e* forever.
30: 4 Who has *e* all the ends of the
Isa 2: 2 the LORD's house Shall be *e*
7: 9 Surely you shall not be *e*.
16: 5 In mercy the throne will be *e*;
30:33 For Tophet was *e* of old, Yes,
42: 4 Till He has *e* justice in the
45:18 Who has *e* it, Who did not
54:14 righteousness you shall be *e*;
Jer 10:12 He has *e* the world by His
12:16 then they shall be *e* in the
30:20 their congregation shall be *e*
51:15 He has *e* the world by His
Ezek 28:14 I *e* you; You were on the holy
Hos 6: 3 His going forth is *e* as the
Mic 4: 1 the LORD's house Shall be *e*
Mt 18:16 every word may be *e*.
Rom 1:11 gift, so that you may be *e*—
2 Cor 13: 1 every word shall be *e*.
Col 2: 7 and built up in Him and *e* in
Heb 8: 6 which was *e* on better promises.
13: 9 is good that the heart be *e*
2 Pe 1:12 though you know and are *e* in

ESTABLISHES (6/6) ESTABLISH

Prov 21:29 the upright, he *e* his way.
29: 4 The king *e* the land by justice,
Isa 62: 7 And give Him no rest till He *e*
Dan 6:15 or statute which the king *e*
Hab 2:12 Who *e* a city by iniquity!
2 Cor 1:21 Now He who *e* us with you in

ESTABLISHING (1/1)

1 Ki 15: 4 up his son after him and by *e*

ESTATE (1/1)

Acts 28: 7 In that region there was an *e* of

ESTEEM (6/6) ESTEEMED, ESTEEMING, ESTEEMS

Prov 3: 4 And so find favor and high *e*
18:11 like a high wall in his own *e*.
Isa 53: 3 and we did not *e* Him.
Phil 2: 3 in lowliness of mind let each *e*
2:29 and hold such men in *e*;
1 Th 5:13 and to *e* them very highly in

ESTEEMED (11/11) ESTEEM

Deut 32:15 And scornfully *e* the Rock of
1 Sam 2:30 despise Me shall be lightly *e*.
18:23 I am a poor and lightly *e* man?
18:30 that his name became highly *e*.
Isa 9: 1 As when at first He lightly *e*
29:16 Shall the potter be *e* as
29:17 And the fruitful field be *e* as
53: 4 Yet we *e* Him stricken,
Lk 16:15 For what is highly *e* among men
Acts 5:13 but the people *e* them highly.
1 Cor 6: 4 appoint those who are least *e*

ESTEEMING (1/1) ESTEEM

Heb 11:26 *e* the reproach of Christ greater

ESTEEMS (2/1) ESTEEM

Rom 14: 5 One person *e* one day above
14: 5 another *e* every day alike.

ESTHER (53/43) ESTHER'S, HADASSAH

Esth 2: 7 up Hadassah, that is, *E*,
2: 8 that *E* also was taken to the
2:10 *E* had not revealed her people or
2:15 Now when the turn came for *E*
2:15 And *E* obtained favor in the
2:16 So *E* was taken to King
2:17 The king loved *E* more than all
2:18 a great feast, the Feast of *E*,
2:20 Now *E* had not revealed her
2:20 for *E* obeyed the command of
2:22 to Mordecai, who told Queen *E*,
2:22 and *E* informed the king in
4: 5 Then *E* called Hathach, one of
4: 8 that he might show it to *E* and
4: 9 So Hathach returned and told *E*
4:10 Then *E* spoke to Hathach, and
4:13 Mordecai told them to answer *E*:
4:15 Then *E* told them to reply to
4:17 and did according to all that *E*
5: 1 on the third day that *E* put on
5: 2 when the king saw Queen *E*
5: 2 and the king held out to *E* the
5: 2 Then *E* went near and touched
5: 3 "What do you wish, Queen *E*?
5: 4 So *E* answered, "If it pleases
5: 5 that he may do as *E* has said."
5: 5 went to the banquet that *E* had
5: 6 of wine the king said to *E*,
5: 7 Then *E* answered and said, "My
5:12 Queen *E* invited no one but me
6:14 Haman to the banquet which *E*
7: 1 Haman went to dine with Queen *E*.
7: 2 wine, the king again said to *E*,
7: 2 is your petition, Queen *E*?
7: 3 Then Queen *E* answered and said,
7: 5 answered and said to Queen *E*,
7: 6 And *E* said, "The adversary and
7: 7 but Haman stood before Queen *E*,
7: 8 across the couch where *E* was.
8: 1 day King Ahasuerus gave Queen *E*
8: 1 for *E* had told how he was
8: 2 and *E* appointed Mordecai over
8: 3 Now *E* spoke again to the king,
8: 4 out the golden scepter toward *E*.
8: 4 So *E* arose and stood before the
8: 7 King Ahasuerus said to Queen *E*
8: 7 I have given *E* the house of
9:12 And the king said to Queen *E*,
9:13 Then *E* said, "If it pleases the
9:25 but when *E* came before the
9:29 Then Queen *E*, the daughter
9:31 as Mordecai the Jew and Queen *E*
9:32 So the decree of *E* confirmed

ESTHER'S (3/3) ESTHER

Esth 2:11 to learn of *E* welfare and what
4: 4 So *E* maids and eunuchs came and
4:12 So they told Mordecai *E* words.

ESTRANGED (4/4)

Job 19:13 acquaintances are completely *e*
Ps 58: 3 The wicked are *e* from the womb;
Ezek 14: 5 because they are all *e* from Me
Gal 5: 4 You have become *e* from Christ,

ETAM (5/5)

Judg 15: 8 in the cleft of the rock of *E*.
15:11 to the cleft of the rock of *E*,
1 Chr 4: 3 the sons of the father of *E*:
4:32 And their villages were *E*,
2 Chr 11: 6 And he built Bethlehem, *E*,

ETERNAL (50/50) ETERNALLY, ETERNITY

Deut 33:27 The *e* God is your refuge,
Eccl 12: 5 For man goes to his *e* home,
Isa 60:15 I will make you an *e*
Mt 19:16 shall I do that I may have *e*
19:29 and inherit *e* life.
25:46 but the righteous into *e*
Mk 3:29 but is subject to *e*
10:17 I do that I may inherit *e* life?
10:30 the age to come, *e* life.
Lk 10:25 what shall I do to inherit *e*
18:18 what shall I do to inherit *e*
18:30 and in the age to come *e*
Jn 3:15 should not perish but have *e*
4:36 and gathers fruit for *e* life,
5:39 in them you think you have *e*
6:54 and drinks My blood has *e* life,
6:68 You have the words of *e* life.
10:28 And I give them *e* life, and they
12:25 this world will keep it for *e*
17: 2 that He should give *e* life to
17: 3 And this is *e* life, that they
Acts 13:48 many as had been appointed to *e*
Rom 1:20 even His *e* power and Godhead,
2: 7 *e* life to those who by patient
5:21 through righteousness to *e*
6:23 but the gift of God is *e* life
2 Cor 4:17 us a far more exceeding and *e*
4:18 which are not seen are *e*.
5: 1 with hands, *e* in the heavens.
Eph 3:11 according to the *e* purpose which
1 Tim 1:17 Now to the King *e*,
6:12 lay hold on *e* life, to which
6:19 that they may lay hold on *e*
2 Tim 2:10 which is in Christ Jesus with *e*
Titus 1: 2 in hope of *e* life which God, who
3: 7 according to the hope of *e*
Heb 5: 9 He became the author of *e*
6: 2 and of *e* judgment.
9:12 having obtained *e* redemption.
9:14 who through the *e* Spirit
9:15 receive the promise of the *e*
1 Pe 5:10 who called us to His *e* glory by
1 Jn 1: 2 and declare to you that *e* life
2:25 has promised us—*e* life.
3:15 you know that no murderer has *e*
5:11 that God has given us *e* life,
5:13 you may know that you have *e*
5:20 This is the true God and *e*
Jude 7 suffering the vengeance of *e*
21 of our Lord Jesus Christ unto *e*

ETERNALLY (2/2) ETERNAL

Ps 49: 9 he should continue to live *e*,
Rom 9: 5 the *e* blessed God. Amen.

ETERNITY (3/3) ETERNAL

Eccl 3:11 Also He has put *e* in their
Isa 57:15 and Lofty One Who inhabits *e*,
Acts 15:18 Known to God from *e* are all His

ETH KAZIN (1/1)

Josh 19:13 east of Gath Hepher, toward *E*,

ETHAM (4/4)

Ex 13:20 from Succoth and camped in *E*
Num 33: 6 from Succoth and camped at *E*,
33: 7 They moved from *E* and turned
33: 8 journey in the Wilderness of *E*,

ETHAN (8/8)

1 Ki 4:31 than *E* the Ezrahite, and Heman,
1 Chr 2: 6 sons of Zerah were Zimri, *E*,
2: 8 The son of *E* was Azariah.
6:42 the son of *E*, the son of
6:44 were *E* the son of Kishi, the
15:17 *E* the son of Kushaiah;
15:19 singers, Heman, Asaph, and *E*,
Ps 89: A Contemplation of *E* the

ETHANIM (1/1)

1 Ki 8: 2 at the feast in the month of *E*,

ETHBAAL (1/1)

1 Ki 16:31 wife Jezebel the daughter of *E*,

ETHER (2/2)

Josh 15:42 Libnah, *E*,
19: 7 Ain, Rimmon, *E*,

ETHIOPIA (19/19) CUSH, ETHIOPIAN

2 Ki 19: 9 concerning Tirhakah king of *E*,
Esth 1: 1 provinces, from India to *E*),
8: 9 the provinces from India to *E*,
Job 28:19 The topaz of *E* cannot equal it,
Ps 68:31 *E* will quickly stretch out her
87: 4 O Philistia and Tyre, with *E*:
Isa 18: 1 is beyond the rivers of *E*,
20: 3 a wonder against Egypt and *E*,
20: 5 be afraid and ashamed of *E*
37: 9 concerning Tirhakah king of *E*,
43: 3 *E* and Seba in your place.
Ezek 29:10 as far as the border of *E*.
30: 4 great anguish shall be in *E*,
30: 5 '*E*, Libya, Lydia, all the
38: 5 'Persia, *E*, and Libya
Am 9: 7 you not like the people of *E*
Nah 3: 9 *E* and Egypt were her strength,
Zeph 3:10 From beyond the rivers of *E* My
Acts 8:27 And behold, a man of *E*,

ETHIOPIAN (8/7) ETHIOPIA, ETHIOPIANS

Num 12: 1 against Moses because of the *E*
12: 1 for he had married an *E* woman.
2 Chr 14: 9 Then Zerah the *E* came out
Jer 13:23 Can the *E* change his skin or
38: 7 Now Ebed-Melech the *E*,
38:10 commanded Ebed-Melech the *E*,
38:12 Then Ebed-Melech the *E* said to
39:16 and speak to Ebed-Melech the *E*,

ETHIOPIANS (12/11) ETHIOPIAN

2 Chr 12: 3 Lubim and the Sukkiim and the *E*.
14:12 So the LORD struck the *E*
14:12 and the *E* fled.
14:13 So the *E* were overthrown, and
16: 8 Were the *E* and the Lubim not a
21:16 Arabians who were near the *E*.
Isa 20: 4 as prisoners and the *E* as
Jer 46: 9 The *E* and the Libyans who
Ezek 30: 9 ships To make the careless *E*
Dan 11:43 also the Libyans and *E* shall
Zeph 2:12 You *E* also, You shall be slain
Acts 8:27 Candace the queen of the *E*,

ETHNAN (1/1)

1 Chr 4: 7 were Zereth, Zohar, and *E*;

ETHNI (1/1)

1 Chr 6:41 the son of *E*, the son of

EUBULUS (1/1)
2 Tim 4:21 *E* greets you, as well as

EUNICE (1/1)
2 Tim 1: 5 Lois and your mother *E*,

EUNUCH (10/10) EUNUCHS
Lev 21:20 or eczema or scab, or is a *e*.
Esth 2: 3 custody of Hegai the king's *e*,
2:14 the king's *e* who kept the
2:15 but what Hegai the king's *e*,
Isa 56: 3 Nor let the *e* say, "Here I
Acts 8:27 a *e* of great authority under
8:34 So the *e* answered Philip and
8:36 And the *e* said, "See, here
8:38 And both Philip and the *e* went
8:39 so that the *e* saw him no more;

EUNUCHS (29/25) EUNUCH
2 Ki 9:32 So two or three *e* looked out
20:18 and they shall be *e* in the
Esth 1:10 seven *e* who served in the
1:12 command brought by his *e*;
1:15 brought to her by the *e*?
2:21 gate, two of the king's *e*,
4: 4 So Esther's maids and *e* came
4: 5 one of the king's *e* whom he
6: 2 and Teresh, two of the king's *e*,
6:14 the king's *e* came, and hastened
7: 9 Now Harbonah, one of the *e*,
Isa 39: 7 and they shall be *e* in the
56: 4 To the *e* who keep My Sabbaths,
Jer 29: 2 king, the queen mother, the *e*,
34:19 the princes of Jerusalem, the *e*,
38: 7 the Ethiopian, one of the *e*,
41:16 and the children and the *e*,
Dan 1: 3 Ashpenaz, the master of his *e*,
1: 7 To them the chief of the *e* gave
1: 8 of the chief of the *e* that he
1: 9 goodwill of the chief of the *e*.
1:10 And the chief of the *e* said to
1:11 whom the chief of the *e* had
1:18 the chief of the *e* brought them
Mt 19:12 For there are *e* who were born
19:12 and there are *e* who were made
19:12 are eunuchs who were made *e* by
19:12 and there are *e* who have made
19:12 who have made themselves *e* for

EUODIA (1/1)
Phil 4: 2 I implore *E* and I implore

EUPHRATES (21/21)
Gen 2:14 The fourth river is the *E*.
15:18 to the great river, the River *E*—
Deut 1: 7 as the great river, the River *E*.
11:24 from the river, the River *E*,
Josh 1: 4 as the great river, the River *E*,
2 Sam 8: 3 his territory at the River *E*.
2 Ki 23:29 king of Assyria, to the River *E*;
24: 7 Brook of Egypt to the River *E*.
1 Chr 5: 9 this side of the River *E*,
18: 3 his power by the River *E*.
2 Chr 35:20 against Carchemish by the *E*;
Jer 13: 4 waist, and arise, go to the *E*,
13: 5 So I went and hid it by the *E*,
13: 6 to me, "Arise, go to the *E*,
13: 7 Then I went to the *E* and dug,
46: 2 which was by the River *E* in
46: 6 the north, by the River *E*.
46:10 north country by the River *E*.
51:63 it and throw it out into the *E*.
Rev 9:14 are bound at the great river *E*.
16:12 his bowl on the great river *E*,

EUROCLYDON (1/1)
Acts 27:14 head wind arose, called *E*.

EUTYCHUS (1/1)
Acts 20: 9 sat a certain young man named *E*,

EVANGELIST (2/2) EVANGELISTS
Acts 21: 8 the house of Philip the *e*,
2 Tim 4: 5 do the work of an *e*,

EVANGELISTS (1/1) EVANGELIST
Eph 4:11 apostles, some prophets, some *e*,

EVE (4/4)
Gen 3:20 Adam called his wife's name *E*,
4: 1 Now Adam knew *E* his wife, and
2 Cor 11: 3 as the serpent deceived *E* by
1 Tim 2:13 Adam was formed first, then *E*.

EVEN (478/467)
Gen 4:23 *E* a young man for hurting me.
9: 3 *e* as the green herbs.
13:12 plain and pitched his tent *e*
20: 5 *e* she herself said, 'He is my
34:29 and they plundered *e* all that
37: 5 and they hated him *e* more.
37: 8 So they hated him *e* more for
37:18 *e* before he came near them,
44:18 for you are *e* like Pharaoh.
46:34 from our youth *e* till now,
Ex 3:19 not *e* by a mighty hand.
4: 9 if they do not believe *e* these
9: 7 not *e* one of the livestock of
10:21 darkness which may *e* be
10:26 and *e* we do not know with what
11: 5 *e* to the firstborn of the
34: 9 *e* though we are a stiff-necked
Lev 26:16 I will *e* appoint terror over
26:28 *e* I, will chastise you seven
Num 4: 3 *e* to fifty years old, all who
4:23 *e* to fifty years old, you shall
4:30 *e* to fifty years old, you shall
4:35 *e* to fifty years old, everyone
4:39 *e* to fifty years old, everyone
4:43 *e* to fifty years old, everyone
4:47 *e* to fifty years old, everyone
6: 7 not make himself unclean *e* for
9:19 *E* when the cloud continued long,
12: 8 *E* plainly, and not in dark
14:19 from Egypt *e* until now."
17:13 Whoever *e* comes near the
Deut 1:37 *E* you shall not go in there;
2:22 their place, *e* to this day.
4:48 *e* to Mount Sion (that is,
11:24 *e* to the Western Sea, shall be
12:31 for they burn *e* their sons and
22:26 *e* so is this matter.
23: 2 *e* to the tenth generation none
23: 3 *e* to the tenth generation none
29:19 *e* though I follow the dictates
31:21 *e* before I have brought them to
32:31 *E* our enemies themselves
32:39 *e* I, am He, And there is
Josh 7:11 For they have *e* taken some of
9:27 would choose, *e* to this day.
10:41 *e* as far as Gibeon.
11:17 *e* as far as Baal Gad in the
12: 2 *e* as far as the River Jabbok,
21:20 *e* they had the cities of their
Judg 3:22 *E* the hilt went in after the
5: 3 *e* I, will sing to the LORD;
17: 2 *e* saying it in my ears—here is
Ruth 2:15 Let her glean *e* among the
1 Sam 2: 5 *E* the barren has borne seven,
2:18 *e* as a child, wearing a linen
6:18 *e* as far as the large stone
8: 8 *e* to this day—with which they
17:52 *e* as far as Gath and Ekron.
18: 4 *e* to his sword and his bow and
21: 5 *e* though it was sanctified in
23:17 *E* my father Saul knows that."
27: 8 *e* as far as the land of Egypt.
2 Sam 6:22 And I will be *e* more undignified
7: 6 *e* to this day, but have moved
15:21 *e* there also your servant will
17:10 And *e* he who is valiant, whose
22:42 *E* to the LORD, but He did
1 Ki 1:37 *e* so may He be with Solomon,
4:24 of the River from Tiphsah *e* to
4:33 the cedar tree of Lebanon *e* to
14:14 What? *E* now!
18:26 the name of Baal from morning *e*
21:19 your blood, *e* yours."
2 Ki 17:41 fathers did, *e* to this day.
21: 7 He *e* set a carved image of
21:15 of Egypt, *e* to this day."
25: 4 *e* though the Chaldeans were
1 Chr 11: 2 *e* when Saul was king, you were
17: 5 *e* to this day, but have gone
2 Chr 25: 8 Be strong in battle! *E* so,
33: 7 He *e* set a carved image, the
Ezra 4: 5 *e* until the reign of Darius
5:16 but from that time *e* until now
7:21 *e* I, Artaxerxes the king,
Neh 3:24 *e* as far as the corner.
4: 3 if *e* a fox goes up on it, he
5: 8 will you *e* sell your brethren?
5:11 *e* this day, their lands, their
5:13 *E* thus may he be shaken out and
5:15 *e* their servants bore rule over
9:18 *E* when they made a molded calf
13:26 pagan women caused *e* him to
Job 4: 8 *E* as I have seen, Those who
4:21 They die, *e* without wisdom.'
5: 5 Taking it *e* from the thorns,
6:14 *E* though he forsakes the fear
10:15 *E* if I am righteous, I cannot
10:22 Where *e* the light is like
13:15 *E* so, I will defend my own
16:19 Surely *e* now my witness is in
17: 5 *E* the eyes of his children
17:11 *E* the thoughts of my heart.
19:18 *E* young children despise me
21: 6 *E* when I remember I am
22:30 He will *e* deliver one who is
23: 2 *E* today my complaint is bitter;
25: 5 If *e* the moon does not shine,
37:21 *E* now men cannot look at the
41:24 *E* as hard as the lower
Ps 8: 7 *E* the beasts of the field,
9: 6 *E* their memory has perished.
18: 6 before Him, *e* to His ears.
18:41 *E* to the LORD, but He did
22:29 *E* he who cannot keep himself
26:12 My foot stands in an *e* place;
39: 2 I held my peace *e* from good;
41: 9 *E* my own familiar friend in
46: 2 *E* though the earth be removed,
48:14 He will be our guide *E* to
55:19 *E* He who abides from of old.
59:12 Let them *e* be taken in their
68:17 *E* thousands of thousands;
68:18 *E* from the rebellious, That
74:11 *e* Your right hand? Take it
78:17 But they sinned *e* more against
84: 2 *e* faints For the courts of the
84: 3 *E* the sparrow has found a home,
84: 3 *E* Your altars, O LORD of
89:37 *E* like the faithful witness
90: 2 *E* from everlasting to
91: 9 *E* the Most High, your
105:30 *E* in the chambers of their
106:37 They *e* sacrificed their sons
108: 1 give praise, *e* with my glory.
109:16 That he might *e* slay the
115:16 *e* the heavens, are the
121: 8 time forth, and *e* forevermore.
139:10 *E* there Your hand shall lead
139:11 *E* the night shall be light
Prov 14:13 *E* in laughter the heart may
14:20 The poor man is hated *e* by his
16: 4 *e* the wicked for the day of
16: 7 He makes *e* his enemies to be
17:28 *E* a fool is counted wise when
20:11 *E* a child is known by his
22:19 instructed you today, *e* you.
28: 9 *E* his prayer is an
Eccl 2:23 *e* in the night his heart takes
5: 9 *e* the king is served from the
6: 6 *e* if he lives a thousand years
7:22 own heart has known That *e*
7:25 *E* of foolishness and madness.
8:16 *e* though one sees no sleep day
10: 3 *E* when a fool walks along the
10:15 For they do not *e* know how to
10:20 *e* in your thought; Do not
10:20 *e* in your bedroom; For a bird
Song 6:12 Before I was *e* aware, My soul
Isa 1: 6 From the sole of the foot *e* to
1:15 *E* though you make many
9: 7 *e* forever. The zeal of the
10:14 Nor opened his mouth with *e*
18: 2 *E* in vessels of reed on the
22:14 *E* to your death," says the
28:22 A destruction determined *e*
29: 7 *E* all who fight against her
29: 8 It shall *e* be as when a hungry
32: 7 *E* when the needy speaks
35: 2 *E* with joy and singing.
40:30 *E* the youths shall faint and be
43:11 *e* I, am the LORD, And
43:19 I will *e* make a road in the
43:25 *e* I, am He who blots out your
44:12 *E* so, he is hungry, and his
44:16 He *e* warms himself and says,
45: 4 I have *e* called you by your
46: 4 *E* to your old age, I am He,
46: 4 And *e* to gray hairs I will
46: 4 *E* I will carry, and will
48: 5 *E* from the beginning I have
48: 6 *E* hidden things, and you did
48:15 *e* I, have spoken; Yes, I have
49:10 *E* by the springs of water He
49:19 Will *e* now be too small for
49:25 *E* the captives of the mighty
51:12 *e* I, am He who comforts you.
56: 5 *E* to them I will give in My
56: 7 *E* them I will bring to My holy
57: 6 are your lot! *E* to them you
57: 7 *E* there you went up To offer
57: 9 And *e* descended to Sheol.
65: 6 *E* repay into their bosom—
Jer 3:25 From our youth *e* to this day,
6:11 For *e* the husband shall be
6:13 from the least of them *e* to
6:13 And from the prophet *e* to the
7:11 *e* I, have seen it," says the
7:25 I have *e* sent to you all My
8: 7 *E* the stork in the heavens
8:10 Because from the least *e* to
8:10 From the prophet *e* to the
9:22 *E* the carcasses of men shall
11:23 *e* the year of their
12: 6 For *e* your brothers, the house
12: 6 *E* they have dealt
12: 6 *E* though they speak smooth
13:13 *e* the kings who sit on David's
13:14 *e* the fathers and the sons
15: 1 *E* if Moses and Samuel stood
17: 4 *e* yourself, Shall let go of
17:10 *E* to give every man according
19:11 *E* so I will break this people
21: 5 *e* in anger and fury and great
23:33 I will *e* forsake you," says
23:34 oracle of the LORD!' I will *e*
23:39 *e* I, will utterly forget you
25: 3 *e* to this day, this is the
25:33 be from one end of the earth *e*
28:11 *E* so I will break the yoke of
31:19 *e* humiliated, Because I bore
32:31 *e* to this day; so I will remove
36: 2 from the days of Josiah *e* to
42: 8 the people from the least *e* to
52: 7 *e* though the Chaldeans were
Lam 3: 8 *E* when I cry and shout, He
4: 3 *E* the jackals present their
Ezek 5: 7 nor *e* done according to the
5: 8 *e* I, am against you and will
6: 3 *e* I, will bring a sword
10: 5 of the cherubim was heard *e*
14:14 *E* if these three men, Noah,

E

14:16 **e** though these three men were
14:18 **e** though these three men were
14:20 **e** though Noah, Daniel, and Job
16:29 and **e** then you were not
20:31 **e** to this day. So shall I be
21:13 what if the sword despises **e**
23: 5 Oholah played the harlot **e**
23:37 and **e** sacrificed their sons
30: 3 **E** the day of the LORD is
32: 6 **E** to the mountains; And the
41:17 **e** to the inner room, as well as
Dan 7:18 **e** forever and ever.'
8:11 He **e** exalted himself as high as
8:25 He shall **e** rise against the
9: 5 **e** by departing from Your
9:25 **E** in troublesome times.
9:27 **E** until the consummation,
11: 1 **e** I, stood up to confirm and
11: 4 **e** for others besides these.
11:15 **E** his choice troops shall
11:24 **e** into the richest places of
12: 1 **E** to that time. And at that
Hos 4: 3 **E** the fish of the sea will be
5:14 **e** I, will tear them and go
8: 6 For from Israel is **e** this: A
11:12 **E** with the Holy One who is
Joel 1: 2 Or **e** in the days of your
1:18 **E** the flocks of sheep suffer
2: 2 **E** for many successive
Am 8: 6 **E** sell the bad wheat?"
Ob 8 **E** destroy the wise men from
11 **E** you were as one of them.
Jon 2: 5 **e** to my soul; The deep closed
4: 9 me to be angry, **e** to death!"
Mic 2:11 **E** he would be the prattler of
3: 4 He will **e** hide His face from
4: 7 From now on, **e** forever.
4: 8 **E** the former dominion shall
Hab 1: 2 **E** cry out to You,
2:15 **E** to make him drunk, That
Zeph 3:20 **E** at the time I gather you;
Zech 6:15 **E** those from afar shall come and
9: 7 **e** he shall be for our God,
9:12 **E** today I declare That I
Mal 1: 4 **E** though Edom has said, "We
1:10 Who is there **e** among you who
1:11 **e** to its going down, My name
3: 1 **E** the Messenger of the
3: 9 **E** this whole nation.
3:15 They **e** tempt God and go free.'
Mt 3:10 And **e** now the ax is laid to the
5:46 Do not **e** the tax collectors do
5:47 Do not **e** the tax collectors do
6:29 and yet I say to you that **e**
7:17 **E** so, every good tree bears good
8:10 not **e** in Israel!
8:27 that **e** the winds and the sea
11:26 **E** so, Father, for so it seemed
12: 8 For the Son of Man is Lord **e** of
13:12 **e** what he has will be taken
15:27 yet **e** the little dogs eat the
18:14 **E** so it is not the will of your
18:17 But if he refuses **e** to hear the
22:26 the third, **e** to the seventh.
23:28 **E** so you also outwardly appear
24:24 if possible, **e** the elect.
24:36 not **e** the angels of heaven, but
25:29 **e** what he has will be taken
26:33 **E** if all are made to stumble
26:35 **E** if I have to die with You, I
26:38 **e** to death. Stay here and watch
26:60 **E** though many false witnesses
27:44 **E** the robbers who were crucified
28:20 **e** to the end of the age."
Mk 1:27 with authority He commands **e**
2: 2 not **e** near the door. And He
4:25 **e** what he has will be taken
4:41 that **e** the wind and the sea
5: 3 bind him, not **e** with chains,
6:31 and they did not **e** have time to
7:28 yet **e** the little dogs under the
10:45 For **e** the Son of Man did not
12:10 Have you not **e** read this
13:22 if possible, **e** the elect.
13:32 not **e** the angels in heaven,
14:29 **E** if all are made to stumble,
14:30 **e** this night, before the
14:34 **e** to death. Stay here and
14:59 But not **e** then did their
15:32 **E** those who were crucified
Lk 1:15 **e** from his mother's womb.
3: 9 And **e** now the ax is laid to the
6: 3 Have you not **e** read this, what
6:32 For **e** sinners love those who
6:33 For **e** sinners do the same.
6:34 For **e** sinners lend to sinners
7: 7 Therefore I did not **e** think
7: 9 not **e** in Israel!"
7:29 **e** the tax collectors justified
7:49 Who is this who **e** forgives
8:18 **e** what he seems to have will be
8:25 For He commands **e** the winds and
10:17 **e** the demons are subject to us
10:21 **E** so, Father, for so it seemed
12:27 **e** Solomon in all his glory was
12:57 **e** of yourselves, do you not
17:30 **E** so will it be in the day when
18:11 or **e** as this tax collector.
19:26 **e** what he has will be taken
19:42 **e** you, especially in this your
20:37 But **e** Moses showed in the
21:16 You will be betrayed **e** by
22:51 Permit **e** this." And He touched
23:35 But **e** the rulers with them
23:40 Do you not **e** fear God, seeing
Jn 3:14 **e** so must the Son of Man be
5:21 **e** so the Son gives life to whom
7: 5 For **e** His brothers did not
8: 9 beginning with the oldest **e** to
8:14 **E** if I bear witness of Myself,
10:15 **e** so I know the Father; and I
11:22 But **e** now I know that whatever
12:42 Nevertheless **e** among the rulers
21:25 I suppose that **e** the world
Acts 5:39 lest you **e** be found to fight
7: 5 not **e** enough to set his foot
7: 5 But **e** when Abraham had no
10:41 **e** to us who ate and drank with
13:27 nor **e** the voices of the
15:17 **E** all the Gentiles who
17:23 I **e** found an altar with this
19:12 so that **e** handkerchiefs or
20:11 **e** till daybreak, he departed.
22: 5 Damascus to bring in chains **e**
24: 6 He **e** tried to profane the
26:11 I persecuted them **e** to foreign
Rom 1:20 **e** His eternal power and
1:26 For **e** their women exchanged the
1:28 And **e** as they did not like to
2:27 **e** with your written code and
3:22 **e** the righteousness of God,
5: 7 for a good man someone would **e**
5:14 **e** over those who had not sinned
5:18 **e** so through one Man's
5:21 **e** so grace might reign through
6: 4 **e** so we also should walk in
8:23 **e** we ourselves groan within
8:34 who is **e** at the right hand of
9:10 **e** by our father Isaac
9:24 **e** us whom He called, not of the
9:30 **e** the righteousness of faith;
11: 5 **E** so then, at this present time
11:31 **e** so these also have now been
15: 3 For **e** Christ did not please
1 Cor 1: 6 **e** as the testimony of Christ was
2:11 **E** so no one knows the things of
3: 2 and **e** now you are still not
4: 3 I do not **e** judge myself.
5: 1 sexual immorality as is not **e**
5:11 not **e** to eat with such a person.
6: 5 not **e** one, who will be able to
7: 7 For I wish that all men were **e**
7: 8 good for them if they remain **e**
7:11 But **e** if she does depart, let
7:28 But **e** if you do marry, you have
7:29 so that from now on **e** those who
8: 5 For **e** if there are so-called
9:12 are we not **e** more?
9:14 **E** so the Lord has commanded that
11:12 **e** so man also comes through
11:14 Does not **e** nature itself teach
14: 5 but **e** more that you prophesied;
14: 7 **E** things without life, whether
14:12 **E** so you, since you are zealous
15:22 **e** so in Christ all shall be
16: 6 or **e** spend the winter with you,
2 Cor 1: 8 so that we despaired **e** of life.
1:13 will understand, **e** to the end
3:10 For **e** what was made glorious had
3:15 But **e** to this day, when Moses is
4: 3 But **e** if our gospel is veiled,
4:16 **E** though our outward man is
5:16 **E** though we have known Christ
7: 7 so that I rejoiced **e** more.
7: 8 For **e** if I made you sorry with
7:14 **e** so our boasting to Titus was
10: 7 **e** so we are Christ's.
10: 8 For **e** if I should boast somewhat
11: 6 **E** though I am untrained in
Gal 1: 8 But **e** if we, or an angel from
2: 3 Yet not **e** Titus who was with
2: 5 we did not yield submission **e**
2:13 so that **e** Barnabas was carried
2:16 **e** we have believed in Christ
4: 3 **E** so we, when we were children,
4:14 **e** as Christ Jesus.
4:29 the Spirit, **e** so it is now.
5:12 those who trouble you would **e**
5:14 **e** in this: "You shall love
6:13 For not **e** those who are
Eph 2: 5 **e** when we were dead in
5: 3 let it not **e** be named among
5:12 For it is shameful **e** to speak of
Phil 1:15 Some indeed preach Christ **e** from
2: 8 **e** the death of the cross.
3:15 God will reveal **e** this to you.
3:18 and now tell you **e** weeping,
3:21 working by which He is able **e**
4:16 For **e** in Thessalonica you sent
Col 3:13 **e** as Christ forgave you, so you
1 Th 1:10 **e** Jesus who delivers us from
2: 2 But **e** after we had suffered
2: 4 **e** so we speak, not as pleasing
2:18 **e** I, Paul, time and again—but
2:19 Is it not **e** you in the
4:14 **e** so God will bring with Him
2 Th 3:10 For **e** when we were with you, we
1 Tim 6: 3 **e** the words of our Lord Jesus
2 Tim 2: 9 **e** to the point of chains;
Titus 1:15 but **e** their mind and conscience
Phm 1:19 to you that you owe me **e** your
1:21 knowing that you will do **e** more
Heb 4:12 piercing **e** to the division of
6:20 **e** Jesus, having become High
7: 4 to whom **e** the patriarch Abraham
7: 9 **E** Levi, who receives tithes,
9: 1 **e** the first covenant had
9:18 Therefore not **e** the first
11:19 **e** from the dead, from which he
Jas 2:19 **E** the demons believe—and
3: 5 **E** so the tongue is a little
4:14 It is **e** a vapor that appears
1 Pe 3: 1 that **e** if some do not obey the
3:14 But **e** if you should suffer for
2 Pe 1: 9 **e** to blindness, and has
1:10 be **e** more diligent to make your
2: 1 **e** as there will be false
2: 1 **e** denying the Lord who bought
1 Jn 2:18 **e** now many antichrists have
Jude 23 hating **e** the garment defiled by
Rev 1: 7 **e** they who pierced Him. And all
1: 7 **E** so, Amen.
2:13 and did not deny My faith **e** in
3: 4 You have a few names **e** in Sardis
13:13 so that he **e** makes fire come
16: 7 **E** so, Lord God Almighty, true
22:20 **E** so, come, Lord Jesus!

EVENING (136/129) EVENINGS

Gen 1: 5 So the **e** and the morning were
1: 8 So the **e** and the morning were
1:13 So the **e** and the morning were
1:19 So the **e** and the morning were
1:23 So the **e** and the morning were
1:31 So the **e** and the morning were
8:11 the dove came to him in the **e**,
19: 1 angels came to Sodom in the **e**,
24:11 city by a well of water at **e**
24:63 meditate in the field in the **e**;
29:23 Now it came to pass in the **e**,
30:16 came out of the field in the **e**,
Ex 12:18 day of the month at **e**,
12:18 day of the month at **e**.
16: 6 At **e** you shall know that the
16: 8 gives you meat to eat in the **e**,
16:13 it was that quails came up at **e**
18:13 Moses from morning until **e**.
18:14 before you from morning until **e**?
27:21 his sons shall tend it from **e**
Lev 11:24 them shall be unclean until **e**;
11:25 clothes and be unclean until **e**:
11:27 shall be unclean until **e**.
11:28 clothes and be unclean until **e**.
11:31 dead shall be unclean until **e**.
11:32 And it shall be unclean until **e**;
11:39 shall be unclean until **e**.
11:40 clothes and be unclean until **e**.
11:40 clothes and be unclean until **e**.
14:46 up shall be unclean until **e**.
15: 5 water, and be unclean until **e**.
15: 6 water, and be unclean until **e**.
15: 7 water, and be unclean until **e**.
15: 8 water, and be unclean until **e**.
15:10 him shall be unclean until **e**.
15:10 water, and be unclean until **e**.
15:11 water, and be unclean until **e**.
15:16 water, and be unclean until **e**.
15:17 water, and be unclean until **e**.
15:18 water, and be unclean until **e**.
15:19 her shall be unclean until **e**.
15:21 water, and be unclean until **e**.
15:22 water, and be unclean until **e**.
15:23 it, he shall be unclean until **e**.
15:27 water, and be unclean until **e**.
17:15 water, and be unclean until **e**.
22: 6 thing shall be unclean until **e**,
23:32 ninth day of the month at **e**,
23:32 from **e** to evening, you shall
23:32 at evening, from evening to **e**,
24: 3 shall be in charge of it from **e**
Num 9:15 from **e** until morning it was
9:21 the cloud remained only from **e**
19: 7 priest shall be unclean until **e**.
19: 8 and shall be unclean until **e**.
19:10 clothes, and be unclean until **e**.
19:19 and at **e** he shall be clean.
19:21 shall be unclean until **e**.
19:22 it shall be unclean until **e**.
28: 4 lamb you shall offer in the **e**,
28: 8 lamb you shall offer in the **e**;
Deut 23:11 when **e** comes, that he shall
28:67 that it were **e**!' And at evening
28:67 it were evening!' And at **e** you
Josh 7: 6 the ark of the LORD until **e**,
8:29 Ai he hanged on a tree until **e**.
10:26 hanging on the trees until **e**.
Judg 19: 9 the day is now drawing toward **e**;
19:16 from his work in the field at **e**,
20:23 wept before the LORD until **e**,
20:26 and fasted that day until **e**;
21: 2 there before God till **e**.
Ruth 2:17 gleaned in the field until **e**,
1 Sam 14:24 man who eats any food until **e**,
17:16 forty days, morning and **e**.
20: 5 field until the third day at **e**.
30:17 them from twilight until the **e**
2 Sam 1:12 and wept and fasted until **e**
11: 2 Then it happened one **e** that
11:13 And at **e** he went out to lie on
1 Ki 17: 6 and bread and meat in the **e**;
18:29 time of the offering of the **e**
18:36 of the offering of the **e**
22:35 the Syrians, and died at **e**.
2 Ki 16:15 the **e** grain offering, the
1 Chr 16:40 regularly morning and **e**,

23:30 the LORD, and likewise at *e*;
2 Chr 2: 4 burnt offerings morning and *e*,
13:11 LORD every morning and every *e*
13:11 with its lamps to burn every *e*;
18:34 facing the Syrians until *e*;
31: 3 for the morning and *e* burnt
Ezra 3: 3 both the morning and *e* burnt
9: 4 I sat astonished until the *e*
9: 5 At the *e* sacrifice I arose from
Esth 2:14 In the *e* she went, and in the
Job 4:20 in pieces from morning till *e*;
Ps 55:17 *E* and morning and at noon I
59: 6 At *e* they return, They growl
59:14 And at *e* they return, They
65: 8 outgoings of the morning and *e*
90: 6 In the *e* it is cut down and
104:23 And to his labor until the *e*.
141: 2 up of my hands as the *e*
Prov 7: 9 In the twilight, in the *e*,
Eccl 11: 6 And in the *e* do not withhold
Jer 6: 4 For the shadows of the *e* are
Ezek 12: 4 and at *e* you shall go in their
12: 7 and at *e* I dug through the wall
24:18 and at *e* my wife died; and the
33:22 LORD had been upon me the *e*
46: 2 gate shall not be shut until *e*.
Dan 9:21 me about the time of the *e*
Hab 1: 8 And more fierce than *e* wolves.
Zeph 2: 7 they shall lie down at *e*.
3: 3 Her judges are *e* wolves That
Zech 14: 7 But at *e* time it shall happen
Mt 8:16 When *e* had come, they brought
14:15 When it was *e*, His disciples
14:23 Now when *e* came, He was alone
16: 2 When it is *e* you say, 'It will
20: 8 So when *e* had come, the owner of
26:20 When *e* had come, He sat down
27:57 Now when *e* had come, there came
Mk 1:32 At *e*, when the sun had set,
4:35 when *e* had come, He said to
6:47 Now when *e* came, the boat was in
11:19 When *e* had come, He went out of
13:35 of the house is coming—in the *e*,
14:17 In the *e* He came with the
15:42 Now when *e* had come, because it
Lk 24:29 with us, for it is toward *e*,
Jn 6:16 Now when *e* came, His disciples
20:19 Then, the same day at *e*,
Acts 4: 3 next day, for it was already *e*.
28:23 Prophets, from morning till *e*.

EVENINGS (1/1) EVENING

Dan 8:26 And the vision of the *e* and

EVENLY (1/1)

1 Ki 6:35 them with gold applied *e* on

EVENT (4/4)

Ex 1:10 in the *e* of war, that they also
1 Ki 13:33 After this *e* Jeroboam did not
Eccl 2:14 perceived That the same *e*
9: 2 One *e* happens to the righteous

EVENTIDE (1/1)

Isa 17:14 Then behold, at *e*,

EVENTS (4/4)

1 Ki 12:15 for the turn of *e* was from
1 Chr 29:30 and the *e* that happened to him,
2 Chr 10:15 for the turn of *e* was from
29:36 since the *e* took place so

EVER (105/101) ALWAYS

Gen 34:12 Ask me *e* so much dowry and gift,
Ex 15:18 LORD shall reign forever and *e*.
22:26 If you *e* take your neighbor's
Lev 27:19 if he who dedicates the field *e*
Num 11:20 Why did we *e* come up out of
22:30 *e* since I became yours, to
22:30 Was I *e* disposed to do this to
Deut 4:33 Did any people *e* hear the
4:34 Or did God *e* try to go and
Josh 14:10 *e* since the LORD spoke this
Judg 11:25 Did he *e* strive against Israel?
11:25 Did he *e* fight against them?
16:17 No razor has *e* come upon my
2 Sam 7: 7 have I *e* spoken a word to
19:42 Have we *e* eaten at the king's
1 Ki 22:28 If you *e* return in peace, the
1 Chr 17: 6 have I *e* spoken a word to any
29:10 our Father, forever and *e*.
2 Chr 18:27 If you *e* return in peace, the
Neh 9: 5 LORD your God Forever and *e*!
13: 1 no Ammonite or Moabite should *e*
Job 4: 7 who *e* perished being innocent?
4: 7 Or where were the upright *e*
6:22 Did I *e* say, 'Bring something
10:17 Changes and war are *e* with
Ps 5:11 Let them *e* shout for joy,
9: 5 out their name forever and *e*.
10:16 LORD is King forever and *e*;
21: 4 of days forever and *e*.
25:15 My eyes are *e* toward the
37:26 He is *e* merciful, and lends;
45: 6 O God, is forever and *e*;
45:17 shall praise You forever and *e*.
48:14 is God, Our God forever and *e*;
52: 8 the mercy of God forever and *e*.
58: 5 Charming *e* so skillfully.
90: 2 Or *e* You had formed the earth
111: 5 He will *e* be mindful of His
111: 8 They stand fast forever and *e*,
119:44 law continually, Forever and *e*.
119:98 For they are *e* with me.
145: 1 bless Your name forever and *e*.
145: 2 praise Your name forever and *e*.
145:21 His holy name Forever and *e*.
148: 6 established them forever and *e*;
Prov 4:18 That shines *e* brighter unto
8:23 before there was *e* an earth.
Isa 30: 8 time to come, Forever and *e*:
33:20 Not one of its stakes will *e*
34:10 pass through it forever and *e*.
45:17 or disgraced Forever and *e*.
Jer 7: 7 to your fathers forever and *e*.
25: 5 and your fathers forever and *e*.
26:19 king of Judah and all Judah *e*
30: 6 Whether a man is *e* in labor
Ezek 4:14 nor has abominable flesh *e* come
31:14 no trees by the waters may *e*
31:14 tree which drinks water may *e*
37:22 nor shall they *e* be divided
Dan 2:10 or ruler has *e* asked such
2:20 the name of God forever and *e*,
6:24 bones in pieces before they *e*
7:18 forever, even forever and *e*.
12: 3 Like the stars forever and *e*.
Hos 12: 9 *E* since the land of Egypt; I
13: 4 I am the LORD your God *E*
Joel 2: 2 Nor will there *e* be any such
3:17 And no aliens shall *e* pass
Mic 4: 5 LORD our God Forever and *e*.
Mt 21:19 Let no fruit grow on you *e*
24:21 this time, no, nor *e* shall be.
Mk 11:14 no one eat fruit from you *e*
13:19 this time, nor *e* shall be.
Lk 19:30 on which no one has *e* sat.
23:53 where no one had *e* lain before.
Jn 4:29 who told me all things that I *e*
4:39 He told me all that I *e* did."
7:46 No man *e* spoke like this Man!"
10: 8 All who *e* came before Me are
1 Cor 9: 7 Who *e* goes to war at his own
Gal 1: 5 to whom be glory forever and *e*.
Eph 3:21 all generations, forever and *e*.
5:29 For no one *e* hated his own
Phil 4:20 Father be glory forever and *e*.
1 Tim 1:17 honor and glory forever and *e*.
2 Tim 4:18 To Him be glory forever and *e*.
Heb 1: 5 to which of the angels did He *e*
1: 8 O God, is forever and *e*;
1:13 to which of the angels has He *e*
13:21 to whom be glory forever and *e*.
1 Pe 4:11 and the dominion forever and *e*.
5:11 and the dominion forever and *e*.
Rev 1: 6 and dominion forever and *e*.
4: 9 throne, who lives forever and *e*,
4:10 Him who lives forever and *e*,
5:13 to the Lamb, forever and *e*!"
5:14 Him who lives forever and *e*.
7:12 Be to our God forever and *e*.
10: 6 by Him who lives forever and *e*,
11:15 He shall reign forever and *e*!
14:11 torment ascends forever and *e*;
15: 7 of God who lives forever and *e*.
19: 3 smoke rises up forever and *e*!
20:10 day and night forever and *e*.
22: 5 they shall reign forever and *e*.

EVERLASTING (100/93) ETERNAL

Gen 9:16 look on it to remember the *e*
17: 7 for an *e* covenant, to be God to
17: 8 as an *e* possession; and I will
17:13 shall be in your flesh for an *e*
17:19 My covenant with him for an *e*
21:33 name of the LORD, the *E* God.
48: 4 descendants after you as an *e*
49:26 to the utmost bound of the *e*
Ex 12:14 keep it as a feast by an *e*
12:17 your generations as an *e*
40:15 anointing shall surely be an *e*
Lev 16:34 This shall be an *e* statute for
24: 8 the children of Israel by an *e*
Num 25:13 after him a covenant of an *e*
Deut 33:15 the precious things of the *e*
33:27 And underneath are the *e*
2 Sam 23: 5 Yet He has made with me an *e*
1 Chr 16:17 To Israel for an *e* covenant,
16:36 LORD God of Israel From *e* to
16:36 Israel From everlasting to *e*!
Ps 24: 7 you *e* doors! And the King of
24: 9 you *e* doors! And the King of
41:13 LORD God of Israel From *e* to
41:13 Israel From everlasting to *e*!
90: 2 Even from *e* to everlasting,
90: 2 Even from everlasting to *e*,
93: 2 from of old; You are from *e*.
100: 5 is good; His mercy is *e*,
103:17 mercy of the LORD is from *e*
103:17 is from everlasting to *e* On
105:10 To Israel as an *e* covenant,
106:48 LORD God of Israel From *e* to
106:48 Israel From everlasting to *e*!
112: 6 The righteous will be in *e*
119:142 Your righteousness is an *e*
119:144 of Your testimonies is *e*;
139:24 me, And lead me in the way *e*.
145:13 Your kingdom is an *e* kingdom,
Prov 8:23 I have been established from *e*,
10:25 But the righteous has an *e*
Isa 9: 6 *E* Father, Prince of Peace.
24: 5 Broken the *e* covenant.
26: 4 the LORD, is *e* strength.
33:14 among us shall dwell with *e*
35:10 With *e* joy on their heads.
40:28 The *e* God, the LORD, The
45:17 saved by the LORD With an *e*
51:11 With *e* joy on their heads.
54: 8 But with *e* kindness I will
55: 3 And I will make an *e* covenant
55:13 For an *e* sign that shall not
56: 5 I will give them an *e* name
60:19 the LORD will be to you an *e*
60:20 For the LORD will be your *e*
61: 7 *E* joy shall be theirs.
61: 8 And will make with them an *e*
63:12 them To make for Himself an *e*
63:16 Our Redeemer from *E* is Your
Jer 10:10 is the living God and the *e*
20:11 Their *e* confusion will never
23:40 And I will bring an *e* reproach
31: 3 I have loved you with an *e*
32:40 And I will make an *e* covenant
Ezek 16:60 and I will establish an *e*
37:26 and it shall be an *e* covenant
Dan 4: 3 wonders! His kingdom is an *e*
4:34 For His dominion is an *e*
7:14 His dominion is an *e*
7:27 His kingdom is an *e* kingdom,
9:24 To bring in *e* righteousness,
12: 2 Some to *e* life, Some to shame
12: 2 Some to shame and *e* contempt.
Mic 5: 2 forth are from of old, From *e*.
Hab 1:12 Are You not from *e*,
3: 6 And the *e* mountains were
3: 6 hills bowed. His ways are *e*.
Mt 18: 8 to be cast into the *e* fire.
25:41 into the *e* fire prepared for
25:46 And these will go away into *e*
Lk 16: 9 they may receive you into an *e*
Jn 3:16 should not perish but have *e*
3:36 who believes in the Son has *e*
4:14 of water springing up into *e*
5:24 in Him who sent Me has *e* life,
6:27 for the food which endures to *e*
6:40 and believes in Him may have *e*
6:47 he who believes in Me has *e*
12:50 I know that His command is *e*
Acts 13:46 judge yourselves unworthy of *e*
Rom 6:22 and the end, *e* life.
16:26 to the commandment of the *e*
Gal 6: 8 will of the Spirit reap *e* life.
2 Th 1: 9 These shall be punished with *e*
2:16 has loved us and given us *e*
1 Tim 1:16 going to believe on Him for *e*
6:16 to whom be honor and *e* power.
Heb 13:20 through the blood of the *e*
2 Pe 1:11 to you abundantly into the *e*
Jude 6 He has reserved in *e* chains
Rev 14: 6 having the *e* gospel to preach

EVERMORE (2/2)

1 Chr 16:11 Seek His face *e*!
Ps 105: 4 Seek His face *e*!

EVERY (770/656)

Gen 1:21 great sea creatures and *e*
1:21 and *e* winged bird according to
1:26 over all the earth and over *e*
1:28 and over *e* living thing that
1:29 I have given you *e* herb that
1:29 and *e* tree whose fruit yields
1:30 to *e* beast of the earth, to
1:30 to *e* bird of the air, and to
1:30 I have given *e* green herb
2: 9 the ground the LORD God made *e*
2:16 Of *e* tree of the garden you may
2:19 ground the LORD God formed *e*
2:19 every beast of the field and *e*
2:20 and to *e* beast of the field.
3: 1 You shall not eat of *e* tree of
3:14 And more than *e* beast of the
3:24 a flaming sword which turned *e*
4:22 an instructor of *e* craftsman in
6: 5 and that *e* intent of the
6:19 And of *e* living thing of all
6:19 flesh you shall bring two of *e*
6:20 and of *e* creeping thing of the
6:20 two of *e* kind will come to you
7: 2 take with you seven each of *e*
7:14 they and *e* beast after its kind,
7:14 *e* creeping thing that creeps on
7:14 and *e* bird after its kind,
7:14 *e* bird of every sort.
7:14 every bird of *e* sort.
7:21 and cattle and beasts and *e*
7:21 on the earth, and *e* man.
8: 1 and *e* living thing, and all the
8:17 Bring out with you *e* living
8:17 birds and cattle and *e* creeping
8:19 *E* animal, every creeping thing,
8:19 *e* creeping thing, every bird,
8:19 *e* bird, and whatever creeps on
8:20 and took of *e* clean animal and
8:20 of every clean animal and of *e*
8:21 nor will I again destroy *e*
9: 2 the dread of you shall be on *e*

	9: 2	on *e* bird of the air, on all
	9: 3	*E* moving thing that lives shall
	9: 5	from the hand of *e* beast I will
	9: 5	From the hand of *e* man's
	9:10	and with *e* living creature that
	9:10	and *e* beast of the earth with
	9:10	*e* beast of the earth.
	9:12	and *e* living creature that is
	9:15	is between Me and you and *e*
	9:16	covenant between God and *e*
	16:12	His hand shall be against *e*
	16:12	And *e* man's hand against him.
	17:10	*E* male child among you shall be
	17:12	*e* male child in your
	17:23	*e* male among the men of
	19: 4	all the people from *e* quarter,
	20:13	in *e* place, wherever we go, say
	30:33	*e* one that is not speckled and
	30:35	*e* one that had some white in
	32:16	*e* drove by itself, and said to
	34:15	if *e* male of you is
	34:22	if *e* male among us is
	34:23	and *e* animal of theirs be
	34:24	*e* male was circumcised, all who
	41:48	he laid up in *e* city the food
	42:25	to restore *e* man's money to his
	46:34	for *e* shepherd is an
	47:20	for *e* man of the Egyptians sold
Ex	1:22	*E* son who is born you shall cast
	1:22	and *e* daughter you shall save
	3:22	But *e* woman shall ask of her
	7:12	For *e* man threw down his rod,
	9:19	the hail shall come down on *e*
	9:19	come down on every man and *e*
	9:22	and on *e* herb of the field,
	9:25	and the hail struck *e* herb of
	9:25	herb of the field and broke *e*
	10: 5	and they shall eat *e* tree which
	10:12	and eat *e* herb of the land—all
	10:15	and they ate *e* herb of the land
	11: 2	and let *e* man ask from his
	11: 2	man ask from his neighbor and *e*
	12: 3	the tenth day of this month *e*
	12:44	But *e* man's servant who is
	13:12	*e* firstborn that comes from an
	13:13	But *e* firstborn of a donkey you
	14: 7	of Egypt with captains over *e*
	16: 4	and gather a certain quota *e*
	16:16	Let *e* man gather it according to
	16:16	let *e* man take for those who
	16:18	*E* man had gathered according to
	16:21	So they gathered it *e* morning,
	16:21	*e* man according to his need.
	16:29	Let *e* man remain in his place;
	18:22	Then it will be that *e* great
	18:22	but *e* small matter they
	18:26	but they judged *e* small case
	20:24	In *e* place where I record My
	26: 2	And *e* one of the curtains shall
	29:36	And you shall offer a bull *e* day
	30: 7	burn on it sweet incense *e*
	30:12	then *e* man shall give a ransom
	32:27	Let *e* man put his sword on his
	32:27	and let *e* man kill his brother,
	32:27	*e* man his companion, and every
	32:27	and *e* man his neighbor.'"
	32:29	for *e* man has opposed his son
	34:19	and *e* male firstborn among your
	35:22	*e* man who made an offering of
	35:23	And *e* man, with whom was found
	35:35	those who do *e* work and those
	36: 1	and *e* gifted artisan in whom
	36: 2	and *e* gifted artisan in whose
	36: 3	to him freewill offerings *e*
Lev	2:13	And *e* offering of your grain
	6:12	priest shall burn wood on it *e*
	6:23	For *e* grain offering for the
	7: 6	*E* male among the priests may eat
	7: 9	Also *e* grain offering that is
	7:10	*E* grain offering, whether mixed
	11:15	*e* raven after its kind,
	11:21	Yet these you may eat of *e*
	11:41	And *e* creeping thing that
	11:46	the animals and the birds and *e*
	11:46	and of *e* creature that creeps
	15: 4	*E* bed is unclean on which he who
	15:12	and *e* vessel of wood shall be
	15:24	and *e* bed on which he lies
	15:26	*E* bed on which she lies all the
	17:15	And *e* person who eats what died
	19: 3	*E* one of you shall revere his
	19:10	nor shall you gather *e* grape
	24: 8	*E* Sabbath he shall set it in
	27:28	*e* devoted offering is most
Num	1: 2	*e* male individually,
	1: 4	you there shall be a man from *e*
	1:20	*e* male individually, from
	1:22	*e* male individually, from
	3:12	children of Israel instead of *e*
	3:15	you shall number *e* male from a
	5: 2	that they put out of the camp *e*
	5: 9	*E* offering of all the holy
	5:10	And *e* man's holy things shall be
	7: 3	a cart for *e* two of the
	7: 5	to *e* man according to his
	13: 2	*e* one a leader among them."
	16: 3	*e* one of them, and the LORD
	16:18	So *e* man took his censer, put
	18: 9	*e* offering of theirs, every
	18: 9	*e* grain offering and every sin
	18: 9	every grain offering and *e* sin
	18: 9	and every sin offering and *e*
	18:10	*e* male shall eat it. It shall
	18:14	*E* devoted thing in Israel shall
	18:29	your gifts you shall offer up *e*
	19:15	and *e* open vessel, which has no
	23:30	offered a bull and a ram on *e*
	25: 5	*E* one of you kill his men who
	26:62	*e* male from a month old and
	28:10	is the burnt offering for *e*
	30: 4	and *e* agreement with which she
	30:11	and *e* agreement by which she
	30:13	*E* vow and every binding oath to
	30:13	Every vow and *e* binding oath to
	31:17	kill *e* male among the little
	31:17	and kill *e* woman who has known
	31:20	Purify *e* garment, everything
	31:28	one of *e* five hundred of the
	31:30	half you shall take one of *e*
	31:47	half Moses took one of *e* fifty,
	31:50	what *e* man found of ornaments
	31:53	*e* man for himself.)
	32:18	not return to our homes until *e*
	32:27	*e* man armed for war, before the
	32:29	*e* man armed for battle before
	34:18	you shall take one leader of *e*
	36: 7	for *e* one of the children of
	36: 8	And *e* daughter who possesses an
	36: 9	but *e* tribe of the children of
Deut	2:34	and little ones of *e* city; we
	3: 6	and children of *e* city.
	4: 4	alive today, *e* one of you.
	8: 1	*E* commandment which I command
	8: 3	but man lives by *e* word that
	11: 7	but your eyes have seen *e* great
	11: 8	Therefore you shall keep *e*
	11:24	*E* place on which the sole of
	12: 2	and on the hills and under *e*
	12: 8	*e* man doing whatever is right
	12:13	offer your burnt offerings in *e*
	12:31	for *e* abomination to the LORD
	14: 6	And you may eat *e* animal with
	14:14	*e* raven after its kind;
	14:19	Also *e* creeping thing that flies
	14:28	At the end of *e* third year you
	15: 1	At the end of *e* seven years you
	15: 2	*E* creditor who has lent
	16:17	*E* man shall give as he is
	20:13	you shall strike *e* male in it
	21: 5	by their word *e* controversy and
	21: 5	word every controversy and *e*
	23: 9	then keep yourself from *e*
	26:11	So you shall rejoice in *e* good
	28:61	Also *e* sickness and every
	28:61	Also every sickness and *e*
	29:20	and *e* curse that is written in
	29:27	to bring on it *e* curse that is
	31: 5	may do to them according to *e*
	31:10	At the end of *e* seven years, at
Josh	1: 3	*E* place that the sole of your
	3:12	one man from *e* tribe.
	4: 2	one man from *e* tribe,
	4: 4	one man from *e* tribe;
	6: 5	And the people shall go up *e*
	6:20	*e* man straight before him, and
	11:14	but they struck *e* man with the
	21:42	*E* one of these cities had its
	22:14	each from the chief house of *e*
Judg	5:30	To *e* man a girl or two;
	7: 7	*e* man to his place."
	7: 8	*e* man to his tent, and retained
	7:16	and he put a trumpet into *e*
	7:18	you also blow the trumpets on *e*
	7:21	And *e* man stood in his place all
	7:22	the LORD set *e* man's sword
	8:34	of all their enemies on *e* side;
	9:55	*e* man to his place.
	16: 5	and *e* one of us will give you
	20:10	will take ten men out of *e*
	20:10	a hundred out of *e* thousand,
	20:10	and a thousand out of *e* ten
	20:16	*e* one could sling a stone at a
	20:48	from *e* city, men and beasts,
	21:11	You shall utterly destroy *e*
	21:11	and *e* woman who has known a man
	21:21	and *e* man catch a wife for
	21:24	*e* man to his tribe and family;
	21:24	*e* man to his inheritance.
1 Sam	4:10	and *e* man fled to his tent.
	8:22	*E* man go to his city."
	10:25	*e* man to his house.
	12:11	the hand of your enemies on *e*
	13: 2	*e* man to his tent.
	14:20	and indeed *e* man's sword was
	14:34	Bring me here *e* man's ox and
	14:34	me here every man's ox and *e*
	14:34	" So *e* one of the people
	14:47	against all his enemies on *e*
	20:15	when the LORD has cut off *e*
	22: 7	Will the son of Jesse give *e*
	23:14	Saul sought him *e* day, but God
	25:13	'*E* man gird on his sword."
	25:13	So *e* man girded on his sword,
	26:23	May the LORD repay *e* man for
	30: 6	*e* man for his sons and his
	30:22	except for *e* man's wife and
2 Sam	2: 3	*e* man with his household.
	13:37	David mourned for his son *e*
	14:26	at the end of *e* year he cut it
	20: 1	*E* man to his tents,
	20: 2	So *e* man of Israel deserted
	20:22	*e* man to his tent. So Joab
1 Ki	1:29	who has redeemed my life from *e*
	2:26	because you were afflicted *e*
	4:24	and he had peace on *e* side all
	5: 3	were fought against him on *e*
	5: 4	my God has given me rest on *e*
	7:30	*E* cart had four bronze wheels
	10:22	Once *e* three years the merchant
	11:15	after he had killed *e* male in
	11:16	until he had cut down *e* male in
	12:24	Let *e* man return to his house,
	12:31	and made priests from *e* class
	13:33	again he made priests from *e*
	14:10	will cut off from Jeroboam *e*
	14:23	and wooden images on *e* high
	14:23	on every high hill and under *e*
	19:18	and *e* mouth that has not kissed
	21:21	and will cut off from Ahab *e*
	22:36	*E* man to his city, and every man
	22:36	and *e* man to his own country!"
2 Ki	3:19	Also you shall attack *e*
	3:19	every fortified city and *e*
	3:19	and shall cut down *e* good tree,
	3:19	and stop up *e* spring of water,
	3:19	and ruin *e* good piece of land
	3:25	and each man threw a stone on *e*
	6: 2	and let *e* man take a beam from
	8: 9	of *e* good thing of Damascus,
	11: 8	*e* man with his weapons in his
	11:11	*e* man with his weapons in his
	14:12	and *e* man fled to his tent.
	16: 4	and under *e* green tree.
	17:10	pillars and wooden images on *e*
	17:10	on every high hill and under *e*
	17:13	*e* seer, saying, "Turn from
	17:29	However *e* nation continued to
	17:29	*e* nation in the cities where
	17:32	and from *e* class they appointed
	18:31	and *e* one of you eat from his
	18:31	you eat from his own vine and *e*
	18:31	and *e* one of you drink the
	23:35	from *e* one according to his
1 Chr	6:48	were appointed to *e* kind of
	9:27	in charge of opening it *e*
	9:32	preparing the showbread for *e*
	12:37	armed for battle with *e* kind
	13: 1	and with *e* leader.
	16:37	as *e* day's work required;
	16:43	*e* man to his house; and David
	22:15	all types of skillful men for *e*
	22:18	has He not given you rest on *e*
	23:30	to stand *e* morning to thank and
	23:31	and at *e* presentation of a burnt
	26:28	*e* dedicated thing, was under
	26:32	for *e* matter pertaining to God
	27: 1	served the king in *e* matter of
	28:14	for all articles used in *e* kind
	28:14	for all articles used in *e* kind
	28:17	gave gold by weight for *e*
	28:17	silver by weight for *e* bowl;
	28:21	and *e* willing craftsman will
	28:21	for *e* kind of service; also the
2 Chr	1: 2	and to *e* leader in all Israel,
	9:21	Once *e* three years the merchant
	10:16	*E* man to your tents, O Israel!
	11: 4	against your brethren! Let *e*
	11:12	Also in *e* city he put shields
	11:23	to *e* fortified city; and he
	13:11	And they burn to the LORD *e*
	13:11	the LORD every morning and *e*
	13:11	gold with its lamps to burn *e*
	14: 7	and He has given us rest on *e*
	15: 6	for God troubled them with *e*
	20:27	*e* man of Judah and Jerusalem,
	23: 7	*e* man with his weapons in his
	23:10	*e* man with his weapon in his
	25:22	and *e* man fled to his tent.
	28: 4	and under *e* green tree.
	28:24	made for himself altars in *e*
	28:25	And in *e* single city of Judah he
	29:35	the drink offerings for *e*
	31: 1	*e* man to his possession.
	31:19	in *e* single city, there were
	31:21	And in *e* work that he began in
	32:21	sent an angel who cut down *e*
	32:22	and guided them on *e* side.
Neh	4:18	*E* one of the builders had his
	5:18	and once *e* ten days an
	10:31	produce and the exacting of *e*
Esth	1:22	and to *e* people in their own
	2:11	And *e* day Mordecai paced in
	3:12	to *e* province according to its
	3:12	and to *e* people in their
	3:14	was to be issued as law in *e*
	4: 3	And in *e* province where the
	8: 9	to *e* province in its own
	8: 9	to *e* people in their own
	8:11	the Jews who were in *e* city
	8:13	to be issued as a decree in *e*
	8:17	And in *e* province and city,
	9:27	celebrate these two days *e*
	9:28	and kept throughout *e*
	9:28	*e* family, every province, and
	9:28	*e* province, and every city,
	9:28	and *e* city, that these days of
Job	1:10	and around all that he has on *e*
	7:18	That You should visit him *e*
	7:18	And test him *e* moment?
	12:10	whose hand is the life of *e*
	18:11	Terrors frighten him on *e* side,
	19:10	He breaks me down on *e* side,
	20:22	*E* hand of misery will come

28: 3 And searches *e* recess For ore
28:10 And his eye sees *e* precious
37: 7 He seals the hand of *e* man,
39: 8 And he searches after *e* green
41:34 He beholds *e* high thing;
Ps 7:11 is angry with the wicked *e*
12: 8 The wicked prowl on *e* side,
31:13 Fear is on *e* side; While
39: 5 Certainly *e* man at his best
39: 6 Surely *e* man walks about like a
39:11 Surely *e* man is vapor. Selah
50:10 For *e* beast of the forest is
53: 3 *E* one of them has turned aside
65:12 the little hills rejoice on *e*
71:21 And comfort me on *e* side.
73:14 And chastened *e* morning.
92: 2 And Your faithfulness *e* night,
104:11 They give drink to *e* beast of
119:101 have restrained my feet from *e*
119:104 Therefore I hate *e* false way.
119:128 I hate *e* false way.
119:160 And *e* one of Your righteous
128: 1 Blessed is *e* one who fears the
145: 2 *E* day I will bless You, And I
145:16 And satisfy the desire of *e*
Prov 1:30 my counsel And despised my *e*
2: 9 Equity and *e* good path.
7:12 Lurking at *e* corner.
13:16 *E* prudent man acts with
14:15 The simple believes *e* word,
15: 3 eyes of the LORD are in *e*
16:33 But its *e* decision is from
19: 6 And *e* man is a friend to one
21: 2 *E* way of a man is right in his
27: 7 But to a hungry soul *e* bitter
30: 5 *E* word of God is pure;
Eccl 3: 1 A time for *e* purpose under
3:13 and also that *e* man should eat
3:17 there is a time there for *e*
3:17 for every purpose and for *e*
4: 4 I saw that for all toil and *e*
5:19 As for *e* man to whom God has
8: 6 Because for *e* matter there is a
8: 9 and applied my heart to *e* work
12:14 For God will bring *e* work into
12:14 Including *e* secret thing,
Song 3: 8 *E* man has his sword on his
4: 2 *E* one of which bears twins,
6: 6 *E* one bears twins, And none
Isa 2:15 Upon *e* high tower, And upon
2:15 And upon *e* fortified wall;
3: 5 *E* one by another and every one
3: 5 Every one by another and *e* one
4: 5 the LORD will create above *e*
9: 5 For *e* warrior's sandal from the
9:17 And *e* mouth speaks folly.
9:20 *E* man shall eat the flesh of
13: 7 *E* man's heart will melt,
13:14 *E* man will turn to his own
15: 2 And *e* beard cut off.
21: 8 I have sat at my post *e* night.
24:10 *E* house is shut up, so that
27: 3 I water it *e* moment; Lest any
30:25 There will be on *e* high
30:25 every high mountain And on *e*
30:32 And in *e* place where the staff
31: 7 For in that day *e* man shall
33: 2 Be their arm *e* morning, Our
34:15 *E* one with her mate.
36:16 and *e* one of you eat from his
36:16 you eat from his own vine and *e*
36:16 and *e* one of you drink the
40: 4 *E* valley shall be exalted And
40: 4 valley shall be exalted And *e*
44:23 and *e* tree in it! For the
45:23 That to Me *e* knee shall bow,
45:23 *E* tongue shall take an oath.
51:13 You have feared continually *e*
52: 5 is blasphemed continually *e*
53: 6 *e* one, to his own way; And the
54:17 And *e* tongue which rises
56:11 *E* one for his own gain, From
57: 5 yourselves with gods under *e*
58: 6 And that you break *e* yoke?
Jer 2:20 When on *e* high hill and under
2:20 on every high hill and under *e*
3: 6 She has gone up on *e* high
3: 6 every high mountain and under *e*
3:13 To alien deities under *e*
4:29 *E* city shall be forsaken,
5: 8 *E* one neighed after his
6:25 Fear is on *e* side.
9: 4 For *e* brother will utterly
9: 4 And *e* neighbor will walk with
10:14 *E* metalsmith is put to shame
12: 4 And the herbs of *e* field
13:12 *E* bottle shall be filled with
13:12 we not certainly know that *e*
15:10 *E* one of them curses me.
16:16 and they shall hunt them from *e*
16:16 them from every mountain and *e*
17:10 Even to give *e* man according
18:11 Return now *e* one from his evil
18:12 and we will *e* one obey the
20:10 Fear on *e* side!" "Report,"
23:30 who steal My words *e* one from
23:35 Thus *e* one of you shall say to
23:35 and *e* one to his brother, 'What
23:36 For *e* man's word will be his
29:26 the house of the LORD over *e*
30: 6 So why do I see *e* man with
30:16 *e* one of them, shall go into
31:25 and I have replenished *e*
31:30 But *e* one shall die for his own
31:30 *e* man who eats the sour grapes,
31:34 No more shall *e* man teach his
31:34 and *e* man his brother, saying,
34: 9 that *e* man should set free his
34:14 the end of seven years let *e*
34:15 *e* man proclaiming liberty to his
34:16 and *e* one of you brought back
34:17 *e* one to his brother and every
34:17 every one to his brother and *e*
37:10 *e* man in his tent, and burn the
43: 6 and *e* person whom Nebuzaradan
47: 4 cut off from Tyre and Sidon *e*
48: 8 plunderer shall come against *e*
48:37 For *e* head shall be bald, and
48:37 and *e* beard clipped; On all
49:29 Fear is on *e* side!'
51: 6 And *e* one save his life!
51:17 *E* metalsmith is put to shame
51:29 For *e* purpose of the LORD
51:56 *E* one of their bows is broken;
Lam 2: 3 has cut off in fierce anger *E*
2:19 from hunger at the head of *e*
3:23 They are new *e* morning;
4: 1 are scattered At the head of *e*
Ezek 6:13 on *e* high hill, on all the
6:13 under *e* green tree, and under
6:13 and under *e* thick oak, wherever
7:17 *E* hand will be feeble, And
7:17 And *e* knee will be as weak
7:18 Shame will be on *e* face,
8:10 *e* sort of creeping thing,
8:12 *e* man in the room of his idols?
12:14 I will scatter to *e* wind all who
12:22 and *e* vision fails'?
12:23 and the fulfillment of *e*
13:18 for the heads of people of *e*
16:24 a high place for yourself in *e*
16:25 high places at the head of *e*
16:31 your shrine at the head of *e*
16:31 and built your high place in *e*
17:21 remain shall be scattered to *e*
17:23 Under it will dwell birds of *e*
18:30 *e* one according to his ways,"
19: 8 him from the provinces on *e*
20:39 serve *e* one of you his
20:47 and it shall devour *e* green
20:47 devour every green tree and *e*
21: 7 *e* heart will melt, all hands
21: 7 *e* spirit will faint, and all
23:22 bring them against you from *e*
24: 4 *E* good piece, The thigh and
26:16 tremble *e* moment, and be
28:13 *E* precious stone was your
28:23 By the sword against her on *e*
29:18 *e* head was made bald, and
29:18 and *e* shoulder rubbed raw;
32:10 and they shall tremble *e*
32:10 *e* man for his own life, in the
33:20 I will judge *e* one of you
34: 6 and on *e* high hill; yes, My
34: 8 and My flock became food for *e*
36: 3 and swallowed you up on *e* side,
37:21 and will gather them from *e*
38:20 and *e* wall shall fall to the
38:21 *E* man's sword will be against
39: 4 give you to birds of prey of *e*
39:17 Speak to *e* sort of bird and to
39:17 to every sort of bird and to *e*
41: 5 temple was four cubits on *e*
41:10 all around the temple on *e*
41:17 and on *e* wall all around,
43:25 *E* day for seven days you shall
44:29 *e* dedicated thing in Israel
44:30 and *e* sacrifice of any kind
46: 5 as well as a hin of oil with *e*
46: 7 and a hin of oil with *e* ephah.
46:11 and a hin of oil with *e* ephah.
46:13 you shall prepare it *e* morning.
46:14 a grain offering with it *e*
46:15 as a regular burnt offering *e*
46:21 in *e* corner of the court there
47: 9 And it shall be that *e* living
47:12 They will bear fruit *e* month,
Dan 6:12 you not signed a decree that *e*
6:26 I make a decree that in *e*
11:36 and magnify himself above *e*
12: 1 *E* one who is found written in
Hos 9: 1 have made love for hire on *e*
13:15 shall plunder the treasury of *e*
Joel 2: 7 *E* one marches in formation,
2: 8 *E* one marches in his own
Am 2: 8 They lie down by *e* altar on
4: 4 Bring your sacrifices *e*
4: 4 Your tithes *e* three days.
8:10 I will bring sackcloth on *e*
8:10 And baldness on *e* head;
Jon 1: 5 and *e* man cried out to his god,
3: 8 let *e* one turn from his evil
Mic 7: 2 *E* man hunts his brother with a
Nah 2: 9 Or wealth of *e* desirable
2:10 Much pain is in *e* side, And
3:10 to pieces At the head of *e*
Hab 1:10 They deride *e* stronghold, For
Zeph 1: 4 I will cut off *e* trace of Baal
2:14 *E* beast of the nation.
3: 5 *E* morning He brings His
3:19 them for praise and fame In *e*
Hag 1: 9 while *e* one of you runs to his
2:14 and so is *e* work of their hands;
2:22 *E* one by the sword of his
Zech 5: 3 *E* thief shall be expelled,'
5: 3 *E* perjurer shall be expelled,'
8:23 In those days ten men from *e*
10: 4 From him *e* ruler together.
12: 4 I will strike *e* horse with
12: 4 and will strike *e* horse of the
12:12 *e* family by itself: the family
12:14 *e* family by itself, and their
13: 4 it shall be in that day that *e*
14:21 *e* pot in Jerusalem and Judah
Mal 1:11 In *e* place incense shall be
Mt 3:10 Therefore *e* tree which does not
4: 4 but by *e* word that
7:17 *e* good tree bears good fruit,
7:19 *E* tree that does not bear good
9:35 and healing *e* sickness and
9:35 healing every sickness and *e*
12:25 *E* kingdom divided against itself
12:25 and *e* city or house divided
12:31 *e* sin and blasphemy will be
12:36 But I say to you that for *e* idle
13:47 the sea and gathered some of *e*
13:52 Therefore *e* scribe instructed
15:13 *E* plant which My heavenly Father
18:16 two or three witnesses *e*
Mk 1:45 and they came to Him from *e*
9:49 and *e* sacrifice will be
15:24 for them to determine what *e*
16:15 and preach the gospel to *e*
Lk 2:23 *E* male who opens the womb
2:41 parents went to Jerusalem *e*
3: 5 *E* valley shall be filled
3: 5 shall be filled And *e*
3: 9 Therefore *e* tree which does not
4: 4 but by *e* word of God.'"
4:13 Now when the devil had ended *e*
4:37 about Him went out into *e*
4:40 and He laid His hands on *e* one
5:17 who had come out of *e* town of
6:44 For *e* tree is known by its own
8: 1 that He went through *e* city and
8: 4 and they had come to Him from *e*
10: 1 by two before His face into *e*
11:17 *E* kingdom divided against itself
12:58 make *e* effort along the way to
16: 5 So he called *e* one of his
16:19 linen and fared sumptuously *e*
19:15 that he might know how much *e*
19:43 you and close you in on *e* side,
Jn 1: 9 Light which gives light to *e*
2:10 *E* man at the beginning sets out
6: 7 that *e* one of them may have a
15: 2 *E* branch in Me that does not
15: 2 and *e* branch that bears fruit
Acts 2: 5 from *e* nation under heaven.
2:38 and let *e* one of you be
2:43 Then fear came upon *e* soul, and
3:23 And it shall be that *e*
3:26 in turning away *e* one of you
5:42 and in *e* house, they did not
8: 3 entering *e* house, and dragging
10:35 But in *e* nation whoever fears
13:27 the Prophets which are read *e*
14:23 they had appointed elders in *e*
15:21 those who preach him in *e* city,
15:21 being read in the synagogues *e*
15:36 and visit our brethren in *e*
17:26 He has made from one blood *e*
18: 4 he reasoned in the synagogue *e*
20:23 the Holy Spirit testifies in *e*
20:35 I have shown you in *e* way, by
22:19 they know that in *e* synagogue I
26:11 I punished them often in *e*
Rom 2: 9 on *e* soul of man who does evil,
3: 2 Much in *e* way! Chiefly because
3: 4 let God be true but *e* man a
3:19 that *e* mouth may be stopped,
13: 1 Let *e* soul be subject to the
14: 5 another esteems *e* day alike.
14:11 *E* knee shall bow to Me,
14:11 And *e* tongue shall
1 Cor 1: 2 with all who in *e* place call on
4:17 as I teach everywhere in *e*
6:18 *E* sin that a man does is
11: 3 you to know that the head of *e*
11: 4 *E* man praying or prophesying,
11: 5 But *e* woman who prays or
15:30 why do we stand in jeopardy *e*
2 Cor 2:14 of His knowledge in *e* place.
4: 2 truth commending ourselves to *e*
4: 8 We are hard pressed on *e* side,
7: 5 but we were troubled on *e* side.
9: 8 may have an abundance for *e*
10: 5 casting down arguments and *e*
10: 5 bringing *e* thought into
13: 1 two or three witnesses *e*
Gal 5: 3 And I testify again to *e* man who
Eph 1: 3 who has blessed us with *e*
1:21 and *e* name that is named, not
4:14 fro and carried about with *e*
4:16 and knit together by what *e*
4:16 effective working by which *e*
Phil 1: 3 I thank my God upon *e*
1: 4 always in *e* prayer of mine
1:18 Only that in *e* way, whether in
2: 9 Him the name which is above *e*
2:10 that at the name of Jesus *e* knee
2:11 and that *e* tongue should
4:21 Greet *e* saint in Christ Jesus.
Col 1:10 being fruitful in *e* good work
1:23 which was preached to *e*
1:28 warning *e* man and teaching

1:28 every man and teaching *e* man
1:28 that we may present *e* man
1 Th 1: 8 but also in *e* place. Your faith
2:11 and charged *e* one of you, as a
5:22 Abstain from *e* form of evil.
2 Th 1: 3 and the love of *e* one of you
2:17 hearts and establish you in *e*
3: 6 that you withdraw from *e*
3:16 give you peace always in *e* way.
3:17 which is a sign in *e* epistle;
1 Tim 4: 4 For *e* creature of God is good,
5:10 she has diligently followed *e*
2 Tim 2:21 prepared for *e* good work.
3:17 thoroughly equipped for *e* good
4:18 the Lord will deliver me from *e*
Titus 1: 5 and appoint elders in *e* city as
1:16 and disqualified for *e* good
2:14 that He might redeem us from *e*
3: 1 to be ready for *e* good work,
Phm 1: 6 by the acknowledgment of *e*
Heb 2: 2 and *e* transgression and
3: 4 For *e* house is built by someone,
5: 1 For *e* high priest taken from
8: 3 For *e* high priest is appointed
9:19 For when Moses had spoken *e*
9:25 enters the Most Holy Place *e*
10: 3 is a reminder of sins *e* year.
10:11 And *e* priest stands ministering
12: 1 let us lay aside *e* weight, and
12: 6 And scourges *e* son whom
13:21 make you complete in *e* good work
Jas 1:17 *E* good gift and every perfect
1:17 Every good gift and *e* perfect
1:19 let *e* man be swift to hear,
3: 7 For *e* kind of beast and bird, of
3:16 confusion and *e* evil thing are
1 Pe 2:13 submit yourselves to *e*
1 Jn 4: 1 do not believe *e* spirit, but
4: 2 *E* spirit that confesses that
4: 3 and *e* spirit that does not
Rev 1: 7 and *e* eye will see Him, even
5: 9 to God by Your blood Out of *e*
5:13 And *e* creature which is in
6:14 and *e* mountain and island was
6:15 *e* slave and every free man, hid
6:15 every slave and *e* free man, hid
7:17 And God will wipe away *e* tear
13: 7 authority was given him over *e*
14: 6 to *e* nation, tribe, tongue, and
16: 3 and *e* living creature in the
16:20 Then *e* island fled away, and the
18: 2 a prison for *e* foul spirit, and
18: 2 and a cage for *e* unclean and
18:12 *e* kind of citron wood, every
18:12 *e* kind of object of ivory,
18:12 *e* kind of object of most
18:17 *E* shipmaster, all who travel
21: 4 And God will wipe away *e* tear
22: 2 each tree yielding its fruit *e*
22:12 to give to *e* one according to

EVERYBODY (1/1)

Gen 20:16 who are with you and before *e*.

EVERYONE (211/197)

Gen 10: 5 *e* according to his language,
27:29 Cursed be *e* who curses you,
45: 1 'Make *e* go out from me!'
Ex 12:16 but that which *e* must eat—that
25: 2 From *e* who gives it willingly
30:13 This is what *e* among those who
30:14 *E* included among those who are
31:14 *E* who profanes it shall surely
33: 7 And it came to pass that *e* who
35:21 Then *e* came whose heart was
35:21 and *e* whose spirit was willing,
35:24 *E* who offered an offering of
35:24 And *e* with whom was found
36: 2 *e* whose heart was stirred, to
38:26 for *e* included in the numbering
Lev 6:18 *E* who touches them must be
6:27 *E* who touches its flesh must be
11:26 *E* who touches it shall be
19: 8 Therefore *e* who eats it shall
20: 9 For *e* who curses his father or
Num 1:52 *e* by his own camp, everyone by
1:52 *e* by his own standard,
2: 2 *E* of the children of Israel
2:17 *e* in his place, by their
4:30 *e* who enters the service to do
4:35 *e* who entered the service for
4:39 *e* who entered the service for
4:43 *e* who entered the service for
4:47 *e* who came to do the work of
5: 2 *e* who has a discharge, and
11:10 *e* at the door of his tent;
15:12 so you shall do with *e*
18:11 *E* who is clean in your house
18:13 *E* who is clean in your house
21: 8 and it shall be that *e* who is
Deut 1:22 And *e* of you came near to me and
1:41 And when *e* of you had girded
33: 3 *E* receives Your words.
Judg 7: 5 *E* who laps from the water with
7: 5 likewise *e* who gets down on his
17: 6 *e* did what was right in his
21:25 *e* did what was right in his
1 Sam 2:36 it shall come to pass that *e*
3:11 Israel at which both ears of *e*
22: 2 And *e* who was in distress,
22: 2 *e* who was in debt, and
22: 2 and *e* who was discontented
2 Sam 6:19 to *e* a loaf of bread, a piece
6:19 *e* to his house.
13: 9 'Have *e* go out from me."
15: 4 and *e* who has any suit or cause
18:17 Israel fled, *e* to his tent.
19: 8 For *e* of Israel had fled to his
20:12 when he saw that *e* who came
1 Ki 8:39 and give to *e* according to all
9: 8 *e* who passes by it will be
1 Chr 16: 3 Then he distributed to *e* of
16: 3 to *e* a loaf of bread, a piece
2 Chr 6:30 and give to *e* according to all
7:21 *e* who passes by it will be
30:17 of the Passover lambs for *e*
30:18 LORD provide atonement for *e*
31:16 they distributed to *e* who
Ezra 2: 1 *e* to his own city.
3: 5 and those of *e* who willingly
9: 4 Then *e* who trembled at the words
Neh 4:15 *e* to his work.
4:23 except that *e* took them off
7: 6 *e* to his city.
10:28 *e* who had knowledge and
11: 3 (But in the cities of Judah *e*
11:20 *e* in his inheritance.
Job 21:33 *E* shall follow him, As
36:25 *E* has seen it
40:11 Look on *e* who is proud, and
40:12 Look on *e* who is proud, and
Ps 12: 2 They speak idly *e* with his
29: 9 And in His temple *e* says,
32: 6 For this cause *e* who is godly
63:11 *E* who swears by Him shall
68:30 Till *e* submits himself with
71:18 Your power to *e* who is to
115: 8 So is *e* who trusts in them.
135:18 So is *e* who trusts in them.
Prov 1:19 So are the ways of *e* who is
16: 5 *E* proud in heart is an
21: 5 But those of *e* who is
Eccl 10: 3 And he shows *e* that he is a
Song 8:11 *E* was to bring for its fruit
Isa 1:23 *E* loves bribes, And follows
4: 3 *e* who is recorded among the
7:22 For curds and honey *e* will eat
9:17 For *e* is a hypocrite and an
13:14 And *e* will flee to his own
13:15 *E* who is found will be thrust
13:15 And *e* who is captured will
14:18 *E* in his own house;
15: 3 And in their streets *E* will
16: 7 *E* shall wail. For the
19: 2 *E* will fight against his
19: 2 And *e* against his neighbor,
19:17 *e* who makes mention of it will
41: 6 *E* helped his neighbor, And
43: 7 *E* who is called by My name,
55: 1 Ho! *E* who thirsts, Come to the
56: 6 *E* who keeps from defiling the
Jer 5: 6 *E* who goes out from there
6:13 *E* is given to covetousness;
6:13 *E* deals falsely.
8: 6 *E* turned to his own course,
8:10 *E* is given to covetousness;
8:10 *E* deals falsely.
9: 4 *E* take heed to his neighbor,
9: 5 *E* will deceive his neighbor,
9:20 And *e* her neighbor a
10:14 *E* is dull-hearted, without
11: 8 but *e* followed the dictates of
12:15 *e* to his heritage and everyone
12:15 everyone to his heritage and *e*
18:16 *E* who passes by it will be
19: 8 *e* who passes by it will be
19: 9 and *e* shall eat the flesh of
20: 7 derision daily; *E* mocks me.
22: 7 *E* with his weapons; They
22: 8 and *e* will say to his neighbor,
23:17 And to *e* who walks according
23:27 My name by their dreams which *e*
25: 5 Repent now *e* of his evil way and
26: 3 Perhaps *e* will listen and turn
32:19 to give *e* according to his ways
34:10 heard that *e* should set free
35:15 Turn now *e* from his evil way,
36: 3 that *e* may turn from his evil
36: 7 and *e* will turn from his evil
49: 5 *e* headlong, And no one will
49:17 *E* who goes by it will be
50:13 *E* who goes by Babylon shall be
50:16 *E* shall turn to his own
50:16 And *e* shall flee to his own
51: 9 and let us go *e* to his own
51:17 *E* is dull-hearted, without
51:45 of the midst of her! And let *e*
Ezek 7:14 blown the trumpet and made *e*
14: 4 *E* of the house of Israel who
16:15 poured out your harlotry on *e*
16:25 You offered yourself to *e* who
16:44 Indeed *e* who quotes proverbs
33:30 *e* saying to his brother,
45:20 day of the month for *e* who
Dan 3:10 have made a decree that *e* who
Hos 4: 3 And *e* who dwells there will
Am 8: 8 And *e* mourn who dwells in it?
Ob 9 To the end that *e* from the
Mic 4: 4 But *e* shall sit under his vine
Zeph 2:15 for beasts to lie down! *E* who
Zech 3:10 *E* will invite his neighbor
7: 9 Show mercy and compassion *E*
8:10 came in; For I set all men, *e*,
10: 1 rain, Grass in the field for *e*.
11: 6 But indeed I will give *e* into
14:13 *E* will seize the hand of his
14:16 it shall come to pass that *e*
14:21 *E* who sacrifices shall come and
Mal 2:17 *E* who does evil Is good in the
Mt 7: 8 For *e* who asks receives, and he
7:21 Not *e* who says to Me, 'Lord,
7:26 But *e* who hears these sayings of
19:29 And *e* who has left houses or
25:29 For to *e* who has, more will be
Mk 1:37 *E* is looking for You."
7:14 He said to them, "Hear Me, *e*,
8:25 And he was restored and saw *e*
9:49 For *e* will be seasoned with
Lk 2: 3 *e* to his own city.
6:30 Give to *e* who asks of you. And
6:40 but *e* who is perfectly trained
9:43 But while *e* marveled at all the
11: 4 For we also forgive *e* who is
11:10 For *e* who asks receives, and he
12:48 For *e* to whom much is given,
16:16 and *e* is pressing into it.
18:14 for *e* who exalts himself will
19:26 that to *e* who has will be
Jn 3: 8 So is *e* who is born of the
3:20 For *e* practicing evil hates the
6:40 that *e* who sees the Son and
6:45 Therefore *e* who has heard and
7:53 And *e* went to his own house.
11:48 *e* will believe in Him, and the
18:37 *E* who is of the truth hears My
Acts 2: 6 because *e* heard them speak in
13:39 and by Him *e* who believes is
20:31 years I did not cease to warn *e*
Rom 1:16 of God to salvation for *e* who
2:10 and peace to *e* who works what
10: 4 the law for righteousness to *e*
12: 3 to *e* who is among you, not to
1 Cor 8: 7 there is not in *e* that
9:25 And *e* who competes for the
16:16 and to *e* who works and labors
Gal 3:10 Cursed is *e* who does not
3:13 Cursed is *e* who hangs on a
2 Tim 2:19 Let *e* who names the name of
Heb 2: 9 of God, might taste death for *e*.
5:13 For *e* who partakes only of milk
1 Pe 3:15 ready to give a defense to *e*
1 Jn 2:29 you know that *e* who practices
3: 3 And *e* who has this hope in Him
4: 7 and *e* who loves is born of God
5: 1 and *e* who loves Him who begot
Rev 22:18 For I testify to *e* who hears

EVERYONE'S (2/2)

Num 33:54 there *e* inheritance shall be
Acts 16:26 all the doors were opened and *e*

EVERYTHING (70/65)

Gen 1:25 and *e* that creeps on the earth
1:30 and to *e* that creeps on the
1:31 Then God saw *e* that He had made,
6:17 *e* that is on the earth shall
7: 8 and of *e* that creeps on the
Ex 25:22 about *e* which I will give you
Lev 11:35 And *e* on which a part of any
15: 4 and *e* on which he sits shall be
15:20 *E* that she lies on during her
15:20 also *e* that she sits on shall
23:37 offerings, *e* on its day—
Num 18: 7 to your priesthood for *e* at
18:15 *E* that first opens the womb of
22: 4 this company will lick up *e*
29:40 told the children of Israel *e*,
31:20 *e* made of leather, everything
31:20 *e* woven of goats' hair, and
31:20 and *e* made of wood."
31:23 *e* that can endure fire, you
Deut 28:47 heart, for the abundance of *e*,
28:48 in nakedness, and in need of *e*;
28:57 them secretly for lack of *e* in
Josh 4:10 the midst of the Jordan until *e*
1 Sam 2:22 and he heard *e* his sons did to
3:18 Then Samuel told him *e*,
15: 9 But *e* despised and worthless,
2 Sam 14:20 to know *e* that is in the
15:36 and by them you shall send me *e*
1 Ki 14:26 king's house; he took away *e*.
2 Ki 14: 3 he did *e* as his father Joash
2 Chr 12: 9 of the king's house; he took *e*.
31: 5 in abundantly the tithe of *e*.
Ezra 8:34 the number and weight of *e*.
Neh 9: 6 The earth and *e* on it, The
13:30 Thus I cleansed them of *e*
Esth 5:11 *e* in which the king had
6:13 Zeresh and all his friends *e*
Job 41:11 *E* under heaven is Mine.
42: 2 "I know that You can do *e*,
Ps 69:34 The seas and *e* that moves in
74: 3 The enemy has damaged *e* in the
150: 6 Let *e* that has breath praise
Prov 26:10 The great God who formed *e*
Eccl 3: 1 To *e* there is a season, A
3:11 He has made *e* beautiful in its
7:15 I have seen *e* in my days of
7:21 Also do not take to heart *e*
10:19 But money answers *e*.
11: 5 the works of God who makes *e*.
Isa 2:12 of hosts Shall come upon *e*

2:12 Upon *e* lifted up—And it shall
19: 7 And *e* sown by the River, Will
Jer 42: 5 if we do not do according to *e*
44:18 we have lacked *e* and have been
Ezek 40: 4 and fix your mind on *e* I show
40: 4 to the house of Israel *e* you
47: 9 and *e* will live wherever the
Dan 2:40 breaks in pieces and shatters *e*;
Zeph 1: 2 I will utterly consume *e* From
3: 7 Despite *e* for which I
Mt 8:33 away into the city and told *e*,
Acts 17:24 who made the world and *e* in it,
1 Cor 1: 5 that you were enriched in *e* by
2 Cor 7:16 I have confidence in you in *e*.
8: 7 But as you abound in *e*—
9:11 while you are enriched in *e*
11: 9 And in *e* I kept myself from
Eph 5:24 be to their own husbands in *e*.
Phil 4: 6 but in *e* by prayer and
1 Th 5:18 in *e* give thanks; for this is

EVERYWHERE (14/14)

Gen 13:10 that it was well watered *e*
2 Ki 4: 3 "Go, borrow vessels from *e*,
1 Chr 13: 2 us send out to our brethren *e*
Ezek 16:57 Philistines, who despise you *e*.
Am 8: 3 Lord GOD—"Many dead bodies *e*,
Mk 16:20 they went out and preached *e*,
Lk 9: 6 the gospel and healing *e*.
Acts 8: 4 those who were scattered went *e*
17:30 but now commands all men *e* to
21:28 the man who teaches all men *e*
28:22 that it is spoken against *e*.
1 Cor 4:17 as I teach *e* in every church.
Phil 4:12 *E* and in all things I have
1 Tim 2: 8 therefore that the men pray *e*,

EVI (2/2)

Num 31: 8 of those who were killed—*E*,
Josh 13:21 with the princes of Midian: *E*,

EVICTING (1/1)

Ezek 46:18 the people's inheritance by *e*

EVIDENCE (6/6) EVIDENCES, EVIDENT

Ex 22:13 then he shall bring it as *e*,
Deut 22:15 take and bring out the *e* of
Job 16:19 And my *e* is on high.
Acts 24: 1 These gave *e* to the governor
2 Th 1: 5 which is manifest *e* of the
Heb 11: 1 the *e* of things not seen.

EVIDENCES (2/2) EVIDENCE

Deut 22:17 and yet these are the *e*
22:20 and *e* of virginity are not

EVIDENT (10/10) EVIDENCE

Acts 4:16 been done through them is *e*
1 Cor 15:27 it is *e* that He who put all
Gal 3:11 law in the sight of God is *e*,
5:19 the works of the flesh are *e*,
Phil 1:13 so that it has become *e* to the
1 Tim 4:15 that your progress may be *e* to
5:24 Some men's sins are clearly *e*,
5:25 works of some are clearly *e*,
Heb 7:14 For it is *e* that our Lord
7:15 And it is yet far more *e* if, in

EVIL (482/454) EVILDOER, EVILDOERS, EVILS

Gen 2: 9 of the knowledge of good and *e*.
2:17 of the knowledge of good and *e*
3: 5 be like God, knowing good and *e*.
3:22 one of Us, to know good and *e*.
6: 5 of his heart was only *e*
8:21 of man's heart is *e* from his
19:19 lest some *e* overtake me and I
44: 4 Why have you repaid *e* for good?
44: 5 You have done *e* in so doing.'
44:34 lest perhaps I see the *e* that
47: 9 few and *e* have been the days of
48:16 who has redeemed me from all *e*,
50:15 repay us for all the *e* which
50:17 for they did *e* to you."
50:20 you meant *e* against me; but
Ex 5:23 he has done *e* to this people;
10:10 for *e* is ahead of you.
23: 2 not follow a crowd to do *e*;
32:22 that they are set on *e*.
Lev 5: 4 with his lips to do *e* or to
26: 6 I will rid the land of *e*
Num 14:27 shall I bear with this *e*
14:35 will surely do so to all this *e*
14:37 very men who brought the *e*
20: 5 to bring us to this *e* place?
32:13 the generation that had done *e*
Deut 1:35 not one of these men of this *e*
1:39 have no knowledge of good and *e*,
4:25 and do *e* in the sight of the
13: 5 So you shall put away the *e*
15: 9 and your eye be *e* against your
17: 7 So you shall put away the *e*
17:12 So you shall put away the *e*
19:19 so you shall put away the *e*
19:20 shall not again commit such *e*
21:21 so you shall put away the *e*
22:21 So you shall put away the *e*
22:22 so you shall put away the *e*
22:24 so you shall put away the *e*
24: 7 and you shall put away the *e*
30:15 life and good, death and *e*,
31:18 that day because of all the *e*
31:29 and *e* will befall you in the
31:29 because you will do *e* in the
Josh 24:15 And if it seems *e* to you to
Judg 2:11 the children of Israel did *e*
3: 7 the children of Israel did *e*
3:12 children of Israel again did *e*
3:12 because they had done *e* in the
4: 1 children of Israel again did *e*
6: 1 the children of Israel did *e*
9:57 And all the *e* of the men of
10: 6 children of Israel again did *e*
13: 1 the children of Israel did *e*
20:13 them to death and remove the *e*
1 Sam 2:23 For I hear of your *e* dealings
6: 9 He has done us this great *e*.
12:19 added to all our sins the *e* of
15:19 and do *e* in the sight of the
20: 7 then be sure that *e* is
20: 9 For if I knew certainly that *e*
20:13 pleases my father to do you *e*,
23: 9 David knew that Saul plotted *e*
24:11 see that there is neither *e*
24:17 I have rewarded you with *e*.
25: 3 but the man was harsh and *e* in
25:21 And he has repaid me *e* for
25:28 and *e* is not found in you
25:39 has kept His servant from *e*!
26:18 or what *e* is in my hand?
29: 6 to this day I have not found *e*
2 Sam 12: 9 to do *e* in His sight? You have
13:16 This *e* of sending me
14:17 king in discerning good and *e*.
16: 8 you are caught in your own *e*,
19: 7 be worse for you than all the *e*
1 Ki 3: 9 may discern between good and *e*.
5: 4 is neither adversary nor *e*
11: 6 Solomon did *e* in the sight of
13:33 did not turn from his *e* way,
14: 9 but you have done more *e* than
14:22 Now Judah did *e* in the sight of
15:26 And he did *e* in the sight of the
15:34 He did *e* in the sight of the
16: 7 because of all the *e* that he
16:19 he had committed in doing *e* in
16:25 Omri did *e* in the eyes of the
16:30 Now Ahab the son of Omri did *e*
21:20 you have sold yourself to do *e*
22: 8 good concerning me, but *e*.
22:18 good concerning me, but *e*?
22:52 He did *e* in the sight of the
2 Ki 3: 2 And he did *e* in the sight of the
8:12 Because I know the *e* that you
8:18 and he did *e* in the sight of
8:27 and did *e* in the sight of the
13: 2 And he did *e* in the sight of the
13:11 And he did *e* in the sight of the
14:24 And he did *e* in the sight of the
15: 9 And he did *e* in the sight of the
15:18 And he did *e* in the sight of the
15:24 And he did *e* in the sight of the
15:28 And he did *e* in the sight of the
17: 2 And he did *e* in the sight of the
17:13 Turn from your *e* ways, and keep
17:17 and sold themselves to do *e* in
21: 2 And he did *e* in the sight of the
21: 6 He did much *e* in the sight of
21: 9 seduced them to do more *e* than
21:15 because they have done *e* in My
21:16 in doing *e* in the sight of the
21:20 And he did *e* in the sight of the
23:32 And he did *e* in the sight of the
23:37 And he did *e* in the sight of the
24: 9 And he did *e* in the sight of the
24:19 He also did *e* in the sight of
1 Chr 4:10 that You would keep me from *e*,
21:17 one who has sinned and done *e*
2 Chr 12:14 And he did *e*, because he did
18: 7 concerning me, but always *e*.
18:17 good concerning me, but *e*?
21: 6 and he did *e* in the sight of
22: 4 Therefore he did *e* in the sight
29: 6 have trespassed and done *e* in
33: 2 But he did *e* in the sight of the
33: 6 He did much *e* in the sight of
33: 9 of Jerusalem to do more *e* than
33:22 But he did *e* in the sight of the
36: 5 And he did *e* in the sight of
36: 9 And he did *e* in the sight of
36:12 He did *e* in the sight of the
Ezra 4:12 building the rebellious and *e*
9:13 that has come upon us for our *e*
Neh 6:13 they might have cause for an *e*
9:28 They again did *e* before You.
13: 7 Jerusalem and discovered the *e*
13:17 What *e* thing is this that you
13:27 of your doing all this great *e*,
Esth 7: 7 for he saw that *e* was
8: 3 with tears to counteract the *e*
8: 6 how can I endure to see the *e*
Job 1: 1 who feared God and shunned *e*.
1: 8 one who fears God and shuns *e*?
2: 3 one who fears God and shuns *e*?
5:19 in seven no *e* shall touch you.
20:12 Though *e* is sweet in his mouth,
28:28 And to depart from *e* is
30:26 *e* came to me; And when I
31:29 Or lifted myself up when *e*
35:12 Because of the pride of *e* men.
Ps 5: 4 Nor shall *e* dwell with You.
7: 4 If I have repaid *e* to him who
10:15 the arm of the wicked and the *e*
15: 3 Nor does *e* to his neighbor,
21:11 For they intended *e* against
23: 4 of death, I will fear no *e*;
28: 3 But *e* is in their hearts.
34:13 Keep your tongue from *e*,
34:14 Depart from *e* and do good;
34:16 is against those who do *e*,
34:21 *E* shall slay the wicked, And
35:12 They reward me *e* for good, To
36: 4 not good; He does not abhor *e*.
37:19 shall not be ashamed in the *e*
37:27 Depart from *e*, and do good;
38:20 Those also who render *e* for
40:14 to dishonor Who wish me *e*.
41: 5 My enemies speak *e* of me:
41: 8 An *e* disease," they say,
49: 5 should I fear in the days of *e*,
50:19 You give your mouth to *e*,
51: 4 And done this *e* in Your
52: 1 Why do you boast in *e*,
52: 3 You love *e* more than good,
54: 5 repay my enemies for their *e*.
56: 5 thoughts are against me for *e*.
64: 5 encourage themselves in an *e*
90:15 years in which we have seen *e*.
91:10 No *e* shall befall you, Nor
94:20 which devises *e* by law, Have
97:10 hate *e*! He preserves the souls
109: 5 Thus they have rewarded me *e*
109:20 And to those who speak *e*
112: 7 He will not be afraid of *e*
119:101 my feet from every *e* way,
121: 7 shall preserve you from all *e*;
140: 1 from *e* men; Preserve me from
140: 2 Who plan *e* things in their
140: 9 Let the *e* of their lips cover
140:11 Let *e* hunt the violent man to
141: 4 not incline my heart to any *e*
Prov 1:16 For their feet run to *e*,
1:33 be secure, without fear of *e*.
2:12 deliver you from the way of *e*,
2:14 Who rejoice in doing *e*,
3: 7 the LORD and depart from *e*.
3:29 Do not devise *e* against your
4:14 do not walk in the way of *e*.
4:16 sleep unless they have done *e*;
4:27 left; Remove your foot from *e*.
6:14 He devises *e* continually, He
6:18 that are swift in running to *e*,
6:24 To keep you from the *e* woman,
8:13 fear of the LORD is to hate *e*;
8:13 Pride and arrogance and the *e*
10:23 To do *e* is like sport to a
11:19 So he who pursues *e* pursues
11:27 will come to him who seeks *e*.
12:12 wicked covet the catch of *e*
12:20 the heart of those who devise *e*,
12:21 wicked shall be filled with *e*.
13:19 to fools to depart from *e*.
13:21 *E* pursues sinners, But to the
14:16 man fears and departs from *e*,
14:19 The *e* will bow before the good,
14:22 they not go astray who devise *e*?
15: 3 Keeping watch on the *e* and the
15:15 days of the afflicted are *e*,
15:28 of the wicked pours forth *e*.
16: 6 the LORD one departs from *e*.
16:17 upright is to depart from *e*;
16:27 An ungodly man digs up *e*,
16:30 his lips and brings about *e*.
17:11 An *e* man seeks only rebellion;
17:13 Whoever rewards *e* for good,
17:13 *E* will not depart from his
17:20 a perverse tongue falls into *e*.
19:23 He will not be visited with *e*.
20: 8 of judgment Scatters all *e*
20:22 I will recompense *e*"; Wait for
20:30 Blows that hurt cleanse away *e*,
21:10 soul of the wicked desires *e*;
22: 3 A prudent man foresees *e* and
24: 1 Do not be envious of *e* men,
24: 8 He who plots to do *e* Will be
24:20 will be no prospect for the *e*
27:12 A prudent man foresees *e* and
28: 5 *E* men do not understand
28:10 upright to go astray in an *e*
28:22 A man with an *e* eye hastens
29: 6 By transgression an *e* man is
30:32 Or if you have devised *e*,
31:12 She does him good and not *e*
Eccl 2:21 also is vanity and a great *e*.
4: 3 Who has not seen the *e* work
5: 1 they do not know that they do *e*.
5:13 There is a severe *e* which I
5:16 And this also is a severe *e*—
6: 1 There is an *e* which I have seen
6: 2 and it is an *e* affliction.
8: 3 Do not take your stand for an *e*
8:11 the sentence against an *e* work
8:11 is fully set in them to do *e*.
8:12 Though a sinner does *e* a hundred
9: 3 This is an *e* in all that is
9: 3 the sons of men are full of *e*;
9:12 sons of men are snared in an *e*
10: 5 There is an *e* I have seen
11: 2 For you do not know what *e*
11:10 And put away *e* from your

12:14 thing, Whether good or *e*.
Isa 1:16 Put away the *e* of your doings
1:16 before My eyes. Cease to do *e*,
3: 9 soul! For they have brought *e*
5:20 Woe to those who call *e* good,
5:20 who call evil good, and good *e*;
7: 5 son of Remaliah have plotted *e*
7:15 He may know to refuse the *e*
7:16 shall know to refuse the *e* and
13:11 punish the world for its *e*,
32: 7 schemes of the schemer are *e*;
33:15 shuts his eyes from seeing *e*:
41:23 Yes, do good or do *e*,
47:11 Therefore *e* shall come upon
56: 2 keeps his hand from doing any *e*.
57: 1 righteous is taken away from *e*.
59: 4 They conceive *e* and bring
59: 7 Their feet run to *e*,
59:15 And he who departs from *e*
65:12 But did *e* before My eyes, And
66: 4 But they did *e* before My eyes,
Jer 2:19 and see that it is an *e* and
3: 5 you have spoken and done *e*
3:17 follow the dictates of their *e*
4: 4 Because of the *e* of your
4:14 How long shall your *e* thoughts
4:22 They are wise to do *e*,
5:12 Neither will *e* come upon us,
7:24 and the dictates of their *e*
7:30 children of Judah have done *e*
8: 3 of those who remain of this *e*
9: 3 For they proceed from *e* to
9: 3 they proceed from evil to *e*,
10: 5 of them, For they cannot do *e*,
11: 8 followed the dictates of his *e*
11:15 passed from you. When you do *e*,
11:17 doom against you for the *e* of
12:14 Against all My *e* neighbors who
13:10 This *e* people, who refuse to
13:23 good who are accustomed to do *e*.
16:12 the dictates of his own *e*
18: 8 I have spoken turns from its *e*,
18:10 if it does *e* in My sight so that
18:11 now every one from his *e* way,
18:12 one obey the dictates of his *e*
18:20 Shall *e* be repaid for good?
21:12 Because of the *e* of your
23: 2 I will attend to you for the *e*
23:10 Their course of life is *e*,
23:17 No *e* shall come upon you.'"
23:22 have turned them from their *e*
23:22 their evil way And from the *e*
25: 5 Repent now everyone of his *e* way
25: 5 of his evil way and his *e*
26: 3 listen and turn from his *e* way,
26: 3 bring on them because of the *e*
26:19 But we are doing great *e*
29:11 thoughts of peace and not of *e*,
32:30 of Judah have done only *e*
32:32 because of all the *e* of the
35:15 Turn now everyone from his *e*
36: 3 everyone may turn from his *e*
36: 7 everyone will turn from his *e*
38: 9 these men have done *e* in all
41:11 with him heard of all the *e*
44: 7 do you commit this great *e*
44:22 because of the *e* of your doings
48: 2 In Heshbon they have devised *e*
51:24 of Chaldea For all the *e* they
51:60 wrote in a book all the *e* that
52: 2 He also did *e* in the sight of
Ezek 6:11 for all the *e* abominations of
33:11 turn from your *e* ways! For why
36:31 Then you will remember your *e*
38:10 and you will make an *e* plan:
Dan 11:27 hearts shall be bent on *e*,
Hos 7:15 Yet they devise *e* against Me;
9:15 Because of the *e* of their
Am 5:13 For it is an *e* time.
5:14 Seek good and not *e*,
5:15 Hate *e*, love good;
Jon 3: 8 let every one turn from his *e*
3:10 that they turned from their *e*
Mic 2: 1 And work out *e* on their beds!
2: 3 For this is an *e* time.
3: 2 You who hate good and love *e*;
3: 4 Because they have been *e* in
7: 3 they may successfully do *e*
7: 3 the great man utters his *e*
Nah 1:11 comes forth one Who plots *e*
Hab 1:13 of purer eyes than to behold *e*,
2: 9 Woe to him who covets *e* gain
Zeph 1:12 not do good, Nor will He do *e*.
Zech 1: 4 Turn now from your *e* ways and
1: 4 from your evil ways and your *e*
1:15 but with *e* intent.'
7:10 Let none of you plan *e* in his
8:17 Let none of you think *e* in your
Mal 1: 8 as a sacrifice, Is it not *e*?
1: 8 lame and sick, Is it not *e*?
2:17 Everyone who does *e* Is good in
Mt 5:11 and say all kinds of *e* against
5:37 more than these is from the *e*
5:39 I tell you not to resist an *e*
5:45 He makes His sun rise on the *e*
6:13 But deliver us from the *e* one.
7:11 "If you then, being *e*,
9: 4 Why do you think *e* in your
12:34 of vipers! How can you, being *e*,
12:35 and an *e* man out of the evil
12:35 and an evil man out of the *e*
12:35 evil treasure brings forth *e*
12:39 An *e* and adulterous generation
15:19 out of the heart proceed *e*
20:15 Or is your eye *e* because I am
24:48 But if that *e* servant says in
27:23 what *e* has He done?" But they
Mk 3: 4 Sabbath to do good or to do *e*,
7:21 proceed *e* thoughts, adulteries,
7:22 an *e* eye, blasphemy, pride,
7:23 All these *e* things come from
9:39 can soon afterward speak *e* of
15:14 what *e* has He done?" But they
Lk 6: 9 Sabbath to do good or to do *e*,
6:22 and cast out your name as *e*,
6:35 is kind to the unthankful and *e*.
6:45 and an *e* man out of the evil
6:45 and an evil man out of the *e*
6:45 of his heart brings forth *e*.
7:21 and *e* spirits; and to many
8: 2 women who had been healed of *e*
11: 4 But deliver us from the *e*
11:13 "If you then, being *e*,
11:29 'This is an *e* generation.
16:25 and likewise Lazarus *e* things;
23:22 what *e* has He done? I have
Jn 3:19 because their deeds were *e*.
3:20 For everyone practicing *e* hates
5:29 life, and those who have done *e*,
7: 7 of it that its works are *e*.
17:15 You should keep them from the *e*
18:23 him, "If I have spoken *e*,
18:23 evil, bear witness of the *e*;
Acts 17: 5 took some of the *e* men from the
19: 9 but spoke *e* of the Way before
19:12 diseases left them and the *e*
19:13 Lord Jesus over those who had *e*
19:15 And the *e* spirit answered and
19:16 Then the man in whom the *e*
23: 5 You shall not speak *e* of a
23: 9 We find no *e* in this man; but if
28:21 came reported or spoken any *e*
Rom 1:30 inventors of *e* things,
2: 9 on every soul of man who does *e*,
3: 8 Let us do *e* that good may
7: 8 in me all manner of *e*
7:19 but the *e* I will not to do,
7:21 that *e* is present with me, the
9:11 nor having done any good or *e*,
12: 9 Abhor what is *e*.
12:17 Repay no one *e* for evil.
12:17 Repay no one evil for *e*.
12:21 Do not be overcome by *e*,
12:21 but overcome *e* with good.
13: 3 terror to good works, but to *e*.
13: 4 you for good. But if you do *e*,
13: 4 wrath on him who practices *e*.
14:16 let your good be spoken of as *e*;
14:20 but it is *e* for the man who
16:19 good, and simple concerning *e*.
1 Cor 5:13 away from yourselves the *e*
10: 6 that we should not lust after *e*
10:30 why am I *e* spoken of for the
13: 5 is not provoked, thinks no *e*;
15:33 *E* company corrupts good
2 Cor 6: 8 by *e* report and good report; as
13: 7 I pray to God that you do no *e*,
Gal 1: 4 deliver us from this present *e*
Eph 4:31 and *e* speaking be put away from
5:16 time, because the days are *e*.
6:13 be able to withstand in the *e*
Phil 3: 2 beware of *e* workers, beware of
Col 3: 5 *e* desire, and covetousness,
1 Th 5:15 See that no one renders *e* for
5:15 that no one renders evil for *e*,
5:22 Abstain from every form of *e*.
2 Th 3: 3 you and guard you from the *e*
1 Tim 6: 4 reviling, *e* suspicions,
6:10 is a root of all kinds of *e*,
2 Tim 3:13 But *e* men and impostors will
4:18 will deliver me from every *e*
Titus 1:12 *e* beasts, lazy gluttons."
2: 8 having nothing *e* to say of you.
3: 2 to speak *e* of no one, to be
Heb 3:12 there be in any of you an *e*
5:14 to discern both good and *e*.
10:22 our hearts sprinkled from an *e*
Jas 1:13 for God cannot be tempted by *e*,
2: 4 and become judges with *e*
3: 8 the tongue. It is an unruly *e*,
3:16 confusion and every *e* thing
4:11 Do not speak *e* of one another,
4:11 He who speaks *e* of a brother
4:11 speaks *e* of the law and judges
4:16 All such boasting is *e*.
1 Pe 2: 1 and all *e* speaking,
3: 9 not returning *e* for evil or
3: 9 not returning evil for *e* or
3:10 refrain his tongue from *e*,
3:11 him turn away from *e* and
3:12 is against those who do *e*.
3:17 for doing good than for doing *e*.
4: 4 speaking *e* of you.
2 Pe 2:10 They are not afraid to speak *e*
2:12 speak *e* of the things they do
1 Jn 3:12 Because his works were *e* and
2 Jn 11 who greets him shares in his *e*
3 Jn 11 do not imitate what is *e*,
11 but he who does *e* has not seen
Jude 8 and speak *e* of dignitaries.
10 But these speak *e* of whatever
Rev 2: 2 you cannot bear those who are *e*.

EVIL-MERODACH (2/2)

2 Ki 25:27 that *E* king of Babylon, in the
Jer 52:31 that *E* king of Babylon, in the

EVIL-MINDEDNESS (1/1)

Rom 1:29 envy, murder, strife, deceit, *e*;

EVILDOER (6/6) EVIL, EVILDOERS

2 Sam 3:39 The LORD shall repay the *e*
Prov 17: 4 An *e* gives heed to false lips;
Isa 9:17 is a hypocrite and an *e*,
Jn 18:30 to him, "If He were not an *e*,
2 Tim 2: 9 which I suffer trouble as an *e*,
1 Pe 4:15 as a murderer, a thief, an *e*,

EVILDOERS (17/17) EVILDOER

Job 8:20 Nor will He uphold the *e*.
Ps 26: 5 I have hated the assembly of *e*,
37: 1 Do not fret because of *e*,
37: 9 For *e* shall be cut off;
94:16 rise up for me against the *e*?
101: 8 That I may cut off all the *e*
119:115 Depart from me, you *e*,
Prov 24:19 Do not fret because of *e*,
Isa 1: 4 with iniquity, A brood of *e*,
14:20 The brood of *e* shall never be
31: 2 arise against the house of *e*,
Jer 20:13 of the poor From the hand of *e*.
23:14 also strengthen the hands of *e*,
Hos 6: 8 Gilead is a city of *e*,
1 Pe 2:12 they speak against you as *e*,
2:14 by him for the punishment of *e*
3:16 that when they defame you as *e*,

EVILS (8/7) EVIL

Deut 31:17 And many *e* and troubles shall
31:17 Have not these *e* come upon us
31:21 when many *e* and troubles have
Ps 40:12 For innumerable *e* have
Jer 2:13 My people have committed two *e*:
Ezek 6: 9 loathe themselves for the *e*
20:43 own sight because of all the *e*
Lk 3:19 and for all the *e* which Herod

EWE (7/7)

Gen 21:28 And Abraham set seven *e* lambs of
21:29 the meaning of these seven *e*
21:30 You will take these seven *e*
Lev 14:10 one *e* lamb of the first year
22:28 "Whether it is a cow or *e*,
Num 6:14 one *e* lamb in its first year
2 Sam 12: 3 except one little *e* lamb which

EWES (3/3)

Gen 31:38 your *e* and your female goats
32:14 two hundred *e* and twenty rams,
Ps 78:71 From following the *e* that had

EXACT (1/1)

Neh 10:32 to *e* from ourselves yearly

EXACTED (4/4)

2 Ki 15:20 And Menahem *e* the money from
23:35 he *e* the silver and gold from
Ezek 18: 8 If he has not *e* usury Nor
18:13 If he has *e* usury Or taken

EXACTING (2/2)

Neh 5: 7 Each of you is *e* usury from his
10:31 year's produce and the *e* of

EXACTLY (1/1)

Eccl 5:16 Just *e* as he came, so shall he

EXACTS (1/1)

Job 11: 6 Know therefore that God *e* from

EXALT (34/34) EXALTATION, EXALTED, EXALTS, MAGNIFY

Ex 9:17 As yet you *e* yourself against My
15: 2 and I will *e* Him.
Num 16: 3 Why then do you *e* yourselves
Josh 3: 7 This day I will begin to *e* you
1 Sam 2:10 And *e* the horn of His
1 Chr 25: 5 to *e* his horn. For God gave
Job 7:17 that You should *e* him, That
17: 4 Therefore You will not *e*
19: 5 If indeed you *e* yourselves
Ps 34: 3 And let us *e* His name
35:26 with shame and dishonor Who *e*
37:34 And He shall *e* you to inherit
38:16 they *e* themselves against
66: 7 Do not let the rebellious *e*
99: 5 *E* the LORD our God, And
99: 9 *E* the LORD our God, And
107:32 Let them *e* Him also in the
118:28 I will *e* You.
137: 6 If I do not *e* Jerusalem Above
Prov 4: 8 *E* her, and she will promote you
25: 6 Do not *e* yourself in the
Isa 10:15 Or shall the saw *e* itself

14:13 I will *e* my throne above the
25: 1 I will *e* You, I will praise
42:21 He will *e* the law and make it
Ezek 21:26 *E* the humble, and humble the
29:15 it shall never again *e* itself
31:14 by the waters may ever again *e*
Dan 8:25 And he shall *e* himself in his
11:14 men of your people shall *e*
11:36 he shall *e* and magnify himself
11:37 for he shall *e* himself above
Hos 11: 7 None at all *e* Him.
1 Pe 5: 6 that He may *e* you in due time,

EXALTATION (4/4) EXALT

Job 22:29 *E* will come!' Then He will
Ps 75: 6 For *e* comes neither from the
Isa 13: 3 who rejoice in My *e*.
Jas 1: 9 lowly brother glory in his *e*,

EXALTED (81/79) EXALT

Num 24: 7 And his kingdom shall be *e*.
Josh 4:14 On that day the LORD *e* Joshua
1 Sam 2: 1 My horn is *e* in the LORD.
2 Sam 5:12 and that He had *e* His kingdom
22:47 be my Rock! Let God be *e*,
1 Ki 1: 5 Adonijah the son of Haggith *e*
8:13 I have surely built You an *e*
9: 8 for this house, which is *e*,
14: 7 Because I *e* you from among the
1 Chr 14: 2 for his kingdom was highly *e*
29:11 And You are *e* as head over
29:25 So the LORD *e* Solomon
2 Chr 1: 1 his God was with him and *e*
6: 2 I have surely built You an *e*
7:21 as for this house, which is *e*,
32:23 so that he was *e* in the sight
Neh 9: 5 Which is *e* above all blessing
Job 10:16 If my head is *e*,
24:24 They are *e* for a little while,
36: 7 them forever, And they are *e*.
36:22 God is *e* by His power;
Ps 12: 8 When vileness is *e* among the
13: 2 How long will my enemy be *e*
18:46 the God of my salvation be *e*.
21:13 Be *e*, O LORD, in Your own
46:10 I will be *e* among the nations,
46:10 I will be *e* in the earth!
47: 9 to God; He is greatly *e*.
55:12 it one who hates me who has *e*
57: 5 Be *e*, O God, above the
57:11 Be *e*, O God, above the
75:10 of the righteous shall be *e*.
89:16 Your righteousness they are *e*.
89:17 in Your favor our horn is *e*.
89:19 I have *e* one chosen from the
89:24 in My name his horn shall be *e*.
89:42 You have *e* the right hand of
92:10 But my horn You have *e* like a
97: 9 You are *e* far above all gods.
108: 5 Be *e*, O God, above the
112: 9 His horn will be *e* with honor.
118:16 right hand of the LORD is *e*;
140: 8 scheme, Lest they be *e*.
148:13 LORD, For His name alone is *e*;
148:14 And He has *e* the horn of His
Prov 11:11 of the upright the city is *e*,
Isa 2: 2 And shall be *e* above the
2:11 the LORD alone shall be *e* in
2:17 The LORD alone will be *e* in
5:16 the LORD of hosts shall be *e*
12: 4 mention that His name is *e*.
24:21 punish on high the host of *e*
30:18 And therefore He will be *e*,
33: 5 The LORD is *e*,
33:10 the LORD; "Now I will be *e*,
40: 4 Every valley shall be *e* And
52:13 He shall be *e* and extolled and
Jer 48:26 Because he *e* himself against
48:42 Because he *e* himself against
Lam 1: 9 For the enemy is *e*!"
2:17 He has *e* the horn of your
Ezek 17:24 down the high tree and *e* the
21:26 the humble, and humble the *e*.
31: 5 Therefore its height was *e* above
Dan 8:11 He even *e* himself as high as
Hos 13: 1 He *e* himself in Israel;
13: 6 filled and their heart was *e*;
Mic 4: 1 And shall be *e* above the
Mt 11:23 who are *e* to heaven, will be
23:12 who humbles himself will be *e*.
Lk 1:52 And *e* the lowly.
10:15 who are *e* to heaven, will be
14:11 who humbles himself will be *e*.
18:14 who humbles himself will be *e*.
Acts 2:33 Therefore being *e* to the right
5:31 Him God has *e* to His right hand
13:17 and *e* the people when they
2 Cor 11: 7 myself that you might be *e*,
12: 7 And lest I should be *e* above
12: 7 lest I be *e* above measure.
Phil 2: 9 God also has highly *e* Him and

EXALTING (1/1)

Prov 30:32 have been foolish in *e* yourself,

EXALTS (10/10) EXALT

Ps 75: 7 puts down one, And *e* another.
Prov 14:29 But he who is impulsive *e*
14:34 Righteousness *e* a nation, But
17:19 And he who *e* his gate seeks
Mt 23:12 And whoever *e* himself will be
Lk 14:11 For whoever *e* himself will be
18:14 for everyone who *e* himself will
2 Cor 10: 5 and every high thing that *e*
11:20 if one *e* himself, if one
2 Th 2: 4 who opposes and *e* himself above

EXAMINATION (1/1)

Acts 25:26 so that after the *e* has taken

EXAMINE (29/27) EXAMINED, EXAMINES, LOOK

Lev 13: 3 The priest shall *e* the sore on
13: 3 Then the priest shall *e* him,
13: 5 And the priest shall *e* him on
13: 6 Then the priest shall *e* him
13:10 And the priest shall *e* him; and
13:15 And the priest shall *e* the raw
13:17 And the priest shall *e* him; and
13:25 then the priest shall *e* it; and
13:27 And the priest shall *e* him on
13:30 then the priest shall *e* the
13:32 seventh day the priest shall *e*
13:34 seventh day the priest shall *e*
13:36 'then the priest shall *e* him;
13:43 Then the priest shall *e* it; and
13:50 The priest shall *e* the plague
13:51 And he shall *e* the plague on the
13:55 Then the priest shall *e* the
14: 3 and the priest shall *e* him;
14:36 the priest goes into it to *e*
14:36 the priest shall go in to *e*
14:37 And he shall *e* the plague; and
Ezra 10:16 day of the tenth month to *e*
Ps 26: 2 *E* me, O LORD, and prove me
Lam 3:40 Let us search out and *e* our
Acts 22:29 those who were about to *e* him
1 Cor 9: 3 My defense to those who *e* me is
11:28 But let a man *e* himself, and so
2 Cor 13: 5 *E* yourselves as to whether you
Gal 6: 4 But let each one *e* his own work,

EXAMINED (7/7) EXAMINE

1 Ki 3:21 But when I had *e* him in the
Dan 1:13 Then let our appearance be *e*
1:20 about which the king *e* them,
Lk 23:14 having *e* Him in your presence,
Acts 12:19 he *e* the guards and commanded
22:24 and said that he should be *e*
28:18 when they had *e* me, wanted to

EXAMINES (7/7) EXAMINE

Lev 13:21 But if the priest *e* it, and
13:26 But if the priest *e* it, and
13:31 But if the priest *e* the scaly
13:53 But if the priest *e* it, and
13:56 If the priest *e* it, and indeed
14:48 if the priest comes in and *e*
Prov 18:17 his neighbor comes and *e* him.

EXAMINING (1/1)

Acts 24: 8 By *e* him yourself you may

EXAMPLE (10/10) EXAMPLES

Mt 1:19 wanting to make her a public *e*,
Jn 13:15 "For I have given you an *e*,
Phil 3:17 join in following my *e*,
2 Th 3: 9 but to make ourselves an *e* of
1 Tim 4:12 but be an *e* to the believers in
Heb 4:11 fall according to the same *e*
Jas 5:10 as an *e* of suffering and
1 Pe 2:21 for us, leaving us an *e*,
2 Pe 2: 6 making them an *e* to those who
Jude 7 flesh, are set forth as an *e*,

EXAMPLES (4/4) EXAMPLE

1 Cor 10: 6 Now these things became our *e*,
10:11 things happened to them as *e*,
1 Th 1: 7 so that you became *e* to all in
1 Pe 5: 3 but being *e* to the flock;

EXCEED (3/3) EXCEEDING, EXCEEDS

Deut 25: 3 lest he should *e* this and beat
1 Ki 10: 7 Your wisdom and prosperity *e*
2 Chr 9: 6 You *e* the fame of which I

EXCEEDING (7/7) EXCEED, EXCEEDINGLY

Ps 43: 4 To God my *e* joy; And on the
2 Cor 4:17 is working for us a far more *e*
9:14 for you because of the *e* grace
Eph 1:19 and what is the *e* greatness of
2: 7 come He might show the *e* riches
1 Pe 4:13 you may also be glad with *e* joy.
Jude 24 of His glory with *e* joy,

EXCEEDINGLY (77/77) EXCEEDING

Gen 7:19 And the waters prevailed *e* on
13:13 But the men of Sodom were *e*
15: 1 your *e* great reward."
16:10 multiply your descendants *e*,
17: 2 you, and will multiply you *e*.
17: 6 'I will make you *e* fruitful;
17:20 and will multiply him *e*.
27:33 Then Isaac trembled *e*,
27:34 he cried with an *e* great and
30:43 Thus the man became *e*
47:27 there and grew and multiplied *e*.
Ex 1: 7 multiplied and grew *e* mighty;
Num 14: 7 through to spy out is an *e*
22: 3 And Moab was *e* afraid of the
1 Sam 26:21 played the fool and erred *e*.
2 Sam 12: 2 The rich man had *e* many flocks
13:15 Then Amnon hated her *e*,
1 Ki 4:29 God gave Solomon wisdom and *e*
2 Ki 10: 4 But they were *e* afraid, and
1 Chr 22: 5 built for the LORD must be *e*
29:25 So the LORD exalted Solomon *e*
2 Chr 1: 1 was with him and exalted him *e*.
14:14 for there was *e* much spoil in
26: 8 for he became *e* strong.
Job 3:22 Who rejoice *e*, And are glad
Ps 21: 6 You have made him *e* glad with
68: 3 Yes, let them rejoice *e*.
106:14 But lusted *e* in the wilderness,
119:96 But Your commandment is *e*
119:167 testimonies, And I love them *e*.
123: 3 have mercy on us! For we are *e*
123: 4 Our soul is *e* filled With the
Prov 30:24 But they are *e* wise:
Eccl 7:24 for that which is far off and *e*
Isa 24:19 open, The earth is shaken *e*.
Jer 48:29 the pride of Moab (He is *e*
Ezek 9: 9 house of Israel and Judah is *e*
16:13 You were *e* beautiful, and
37:10 their feet, an *e* great army.
47:10 of the Great Sea, *e* many.
Dan 3:22 and the furnace *e* hot, the
6:23 Then the king was *e* glad for
7: 7 *e* strong. It had huge iron
7:19 *e* dreadful, with its teeth of
8: 9 came a little horn which grew *e*
Jon 1:10 Then the men were *e* afraid, and
1:16 Then the men feared the LORD *e*,
3: 3 Now Nineveh was an *e* great
4: 1 But it displeased Jonah *e*,
Zech 1:15 I am *e* angry with the nations
Mt 2:10 they rejoiced with *e* great joy.
2:16 was *e* angry; and he sent forth
4: 8 the devil took Him up on an *e*
5:12 Rejoice and be *e* glad, for great
8:28 *e* fierce, so that no one could
17:23 And they were *e* sorrowful.
26:22 And they were *e* sorrowful, and
26:38 My soul is *e* sorrowful, even to
Mk 4:41 And they feared *e*,
6:26 And the king was *e* sorry;
9: 3 *e* white, like snow, such as no
14:34 My soul is *e* sorrowful, even to
Lk 23: 8 he was *e* glad; for he had
Acts 16:20 *e* trouble our city;
26:11 and being *e* enraged against
27:18 And because we were *e*
Rom 7:13 the commandment might become *e*
2 Cor 7: 4 I am *e* joyful in all our
7:13 And we rejoiced *e* more for the
Gal 1:14 being more *e* zealous for the
Eph 3:20 Now to Him who is able to do *e*
1 Th 3:10 night and day praying *e* that we
2 Th 1: 3 because your faith grows *e*,
1 Tim 1:14 And the grace of our Lord was *e*
Heb 12:21 I am *e* afraid and
2 Pe 1: 4 which have been given to us *e*
Rev 16:21 since that plague was *e* great.

EXCEEDS (2/2) EXCEED

Mt 5:20 unless your righteousness *e*
2 Cor 3: 9 the ministry of righteousness *e*

EXCEL (4/4) EXCELLED, EXCELS

Gen 49: 4 as water, you shall not *e*,
Ps 103:20 Who *e* in strength, who do His
Prov 31:29 But you *e* them all."
1 Cor 14:12 the church that you seek to *e*.

EXCELLED (4/4) EXCEL

Gen 49:26 of your father Have *e* the
1 Ki 4:30 Thus Solomon's wisdom *e* the
Eccl 2: 9 So I became great and *e* more
Isa 10:10 Whose carved images *e* those of

EXCELLENCE (13/12) EXCELLENT

Ex 15: 7 And in the greatness of Your *e*
Job 4:21 Does not their own *e* go away?
13:11 Will not His *e* make you afraid,
Ps 47: 4 The *e* of Jacob whom He loves.
68:34 His *e* is over Israel, And
Eccl 7:12 But the *e* of knowledge is
Isa 35: 2 The *e* of Carmel and Sharon.
60:15 I will make you an eternal *e*,
Nah 2: 2 the LORD will restore the *e*
2: 2 of Jacob Like the *e* of Israel,
1 Cor 2: 1 did not come with *e* of speech
2 Cor 4: 7 that the *e* of the power may be
Phil 3: 8 all things loss for the *e* of

EXCELLENCY (4/3)

Gen 49: 3 The *e* of dignity and the
49: 3 of dignity and the *e* of power.

Deut 33:26 And in His *e* on the clouds.
Isa 35: 2 The *e* of our God.

EXCELLENT (30/30) EXCELLENCE

Esth 1: 4 and the splendor of his *e*
Job 37:23 He is *e* in power, In
Ps 8: 1 How *e* is Your name in all the
8: 9 How *e* is Your name in all the
16: 3 They are the *e* ones, in whom is
76: 4 You are more glorious and *e*
141: 5 It shall be as *e* oil;
150: 2 Praise Him according to His *e*
Prov 8: 6 for I will speak of *e* things,
12: 4 An *e* wife is the crown of her
17: 7 *E* speech is not becoming to a
22:20 Have I not written to you *e*
Song 5:15 *E* as the cedars.
Isa 4: 2 of the earth shall be *e* and
12: 5 For He has done *e* things;
28:29 is wonderful in counsel and *e*
Dan 2:31 image, whose splendor was *e*,
4:36 and *e* majesty was added to me.
5:12 Inasmuch as an *e* spirit,
5:14 light and understanding and *e*
6: 3 because an *e* spirit was in
Lk 1: 3 most *e* Theophilus,
Acts 23:26 to the most *e* governor Felix:
Rom 2:18 approve the things that are *e*,
1 Cor 12:31 And yet I show you a more *e*
Phil 1:10 approve the things that are *e*,
Heb 1: 4 inheritance obtained a more *e*
8: 6 now He has obtained a more *e*
11: 4 Abel offered to God a more *e*
2 Pe 1:17 a voice came to Him from the *E*

EXCELS (4/3) EXCEL

Prov 22:29 Do you see a man who *e* in his
Eccl 2:13 Then I saw that wisdom *e* folly
2:13 wisdom excels folly As light *e*
2 Cor 3:10 because of the glory that *e*.

EXCEPT (100/95)

Gen 14:24 *e* only what the young men have
39: 6 he did not know what he had *e*
47:26 *e* for the land of the priests
Ex 22:20 *e* to the LORD only, he shall
33:16 *e* You go with us? So we shall
Lev 21: 2 *e* for his relatives who are
Num 11: 6 there is nothing at all *e*
14:30 *E* for Caleb the son of Jephunneh
26:65 *e* Caleb the son of Jephunneh
32:12 *e* Caleb the son of Jephunneh,
35:33 *e* by the blood of him who shed
Deut 1:36 *e* Caleb the son of Jephunneh
15: 4 *e* when there may be no poor
Josh 11:13 *e* Hazor only, which Joshua
11:19 *e* the Hivites, the inhabitants
14: 4 *e* cities to dwell in, with
1 Sam 21: 9 For there is no other *e* that
30:17 *e* four hundred young men who
30:22 *e* for every man's wife and
2 Sam 8: 4 *e* that he spared enough of
12: 3 *e* one little ewe lamb which he
17: 3 When all return *e* the man whom
22:32 *e* the LORD? And who is a
22:32 who is a rock, *e* our God?
1 Ki 3: 3 *e* that he sacrificed and burned
3:18 *e* the two of us in the house.
8: 9 Nothing was in the ark *e* the
15: 5 *e* in the matter of Uriah the
17: 1 *e* at my word."
2 Ki 5:15 *e* in Israel; now therefore,
15: 4 *e* that the high places were not
24:14 None remained *e* the poorest
1 Chr 18: 4 *e* that he spared enough of them
2 Chr 2: 6 *e* to burn sacrifice before Him?
5:10 Nothing was in the ark *e* the two
21:17 was not a son left to him *e*
23: 6 into the house of the LORD *e*
Neh 2:12 *e* the one on which I rode.
4:23 *e* that everyone took them off
Esth 4:11 *e* the one to whom the king
Ps 18:31 *e* the LORD? And who is a
18:31 who is a rock, *e* our God?
Eccl 3:11 *e* that no one can find out the
5:11 the owners *E* to see them
Jer 44:14 For none shall return *e* those
Dan 2:11 who can tell it to the king *e*
3:28 not serve nor worship any god *e*
6: 7 *e* you, O king, shall be cast
6:12 *e* you, O king, shall be cast
10:21 *e* Michael your prince.
Mt 5:32 his wife for any reason *e*
11:27 and no one knows the Son *e* the
11:27 does anyone know the Father *e*
12:24 does not cast out demons *e* by
12:39 no sign will be given to it *e*
13:57 prophet is not without honor *e*
15:24 I was not sent *e* to the lost
16: 4 no sign shall be given to it *e*
17:21 this kind does not go out *e* by
19: 9 *e* for sexual immorality, and
Mk 2:26 *e* for the priests, and also
5:37 no one to follow Him *e* Peter,
6: 4 prophet is not without honor *e*
6: 5 *e* that He laid His hands on a
6: 8 take nothing for the journey *e*
Lk 4:26 none of them was Elijah sent *e*
4:27 and none of them was cleansed *e*
8:51 He permitted no one to go in *e*
10:22 no one knows who the Son is *e*
10:22 and who the Father is *e* the
11:29 no sign will be given to it *e*
17:18 to give glory to God *e* this
Jn 6:22 *e* that one which His disciples
6:46 *e* He who is from God; He has
10:10 The thief does not come *e* to
14: 6 No one comes to the Father *e*
17:12 and none of them is lost *e* the
Acts 8: 1 and Samaria, *e* the apostles.
20:23 *e* that the Holy Spirit testifies
21:25 *e* that they should keep
26:29 *e* for these chains."
Rom 7: 7 I would not have known sin *e*
13: 1 For there is no authority *e*
13: 8 Owe no one anything *e* to love
1 Cor 1:14 that I baptized none of you *e*
2: 2 to know anything among you *e*
2:11 man knows the things of a man *e*
2:11 one knows the things of God *e*
7: 5 Do not deprive one another *e*
10:13 temptation has overtaken you *e*
12: 3 can say that Jesus is Lord *e*
2 Cor 12: 5 *e* in my infirmities.
12:13 *e* that I myself was not
Gal 1:19 none of the other apostles *e*
6:14 forbid that I should boast *e*
1 Tim 5:19 accusation against an elder *e*
Rev 2:17 written which no one knows *e*
13:17 that no one may buy or sell *e*
14: 3 no one could learn that song *e*
19:12 name written that no one knew *e*

EXCEPTED (1/1)

1 Cor 15:27 put all things under Him is *e*.

EXCESS (1/1)

Num 3:48 with which the *e* number of them

EXCESSIVE (1/1)

Esth 1:18 Thus there will be *e*

EXCHANGE (8/7) EXCHANGED, EXCHANGING

Gen 47:17 Joseph gave them bread in *e*
47:17 he fed them with bread in *e*
Lev 27:10 shall not substitute it or *e*
27:33 nor shall he *e* it; and if he
Deut 14:25 then you shall *e* it for money,
Ezek 48:14 And they shall not sell or *e* any
Mt 16:26 Or what will a man give in *e*
Mk 8:37 Or what will a man give in *e* for

EXCHANGED (5/5) EXCHANGE

Lev 27:10 then both it and the one *e* for
27:33 then both it and the one *e* for
Job 28:17 Nor can it be *e* for jewelry of
Rom 1:25 who *e* the truth of God for the
1:26 For even their women *e* the

EXCHANGES (2/2)

Lev 27:10 and if he at all *e* animal for
27:33 and if he *e* it at all, then

EXCHANGING (1/1) EXCHANGE

Ruth 4: 7 concerning redeeming and *e*,

EXCITED (2/2)

Ruth 1:19 that all the city was *e* because
Isa 14: 9 Hell from beneath is *e* about

EXCITEMENT (1/1)

Jer 51:39 In their *e* I will prepare their

EXCLUDE (2/2) EXCLUDED

Lk 6:22 And when they *e* you, And
Gal 4:17 they want to *e* you, that you

EXCLUDED (3/3) EXCLUDE

Ezra 2:62 therefore they were *e* from
Neh 7:64 therefore they were *e* from the
Rom 3:27 is boasting then? It is *e*.

EXCUSE (4/4) EXCUSING

Eccl 5: 6 should God be angry at your *e*
Jn 15:22 but now they have no *e* for
Rom 1:20 so that they are without *e*,
2 Cor 12:19 do you think that we *e*

EXCUSED (2/2)

Lk 14:18 see it. I ask you to have me *e*.
14:19 I ask you to have me *e*.'

EXCUSES (1/1)

Lk 14:18 one accord began to make *e*.

EXCUSING (1/1) EXCUSE

Rom 2:15 thoughts accusing or else *e*

EXECRATION (KJV) See OATH

EXECUTE (40/40) EXECUTED, EXECUTES, EXECUTIONER

Ex 12:12 all the gods of Egypt I will *e*
Lev 26:25 a sword against you that will *e*
Num 5:30 and the priest shall *e* all this
1 Sam 28:18 the voice of the LORD nor *e*
2 Sam 1:15 and *e* him!" And he struck him
14: 7 that we may *e* him for the life
14:32 in me, let him *e* me."
1 Ki 6:12 *e* My judgments, keep all My
2 Ki 14: 6 of the murderers he did not *e*,
2 Chr 25: 4 However he did not *e* their
Ps 110: 5 He shall *e* kings in the day of
110: 6 He shall *e* the heads of many
119:84 When will You *e* judgment on
149: 7 To *e* vengeance on the nations,
149: 9 To *e* on them the written
Isa 16: 3 *e* judgment; Make your shadow
Jer 7: 5 if you thoroughly *e* judgment
21:12 '*E* judgment in the morning;
22: 3 *E* judgment and righteousness,
23: 5 And *e* judgment and
33:15 He shall *e* judgment and
Ezek 5: 8 am against you and will *e*
5:10 and I will *e* judgments among
5:15 when I *e* judgments among you in
11: 9 and *e* judgments on you.
16:41 and *e* judgments on you in the
23:47 stone them with stones and *e*
25:11 And I will *e* judgments upon
25:17 I will *e* great vengeance on them
28:22 When I *e* judgments in her and
28:26 when I *e* judgments on all those
30:14 And *e* judgments in No.
30:19 Thus I will *e* judgments on
45: 9 *e* justice and righteousness,
Hos 11: 9 I will not *e* the fierceness of
Mic 5:15 And I will *e* vengeance in anger
Zech 7: 9 *E* true justice, Show mercy and
Jn 5:27 has given Him authority to *e*
Rom 13: 4 an avenger to *e* wrath on him
Jude 15 to *e* judgment on all, to convict

EXECUTED (23/23) EXECUTE

Num 33: 4 on their gods the LORD had *e*
2 Sam 4:10 I arrested him and had him *e* in
4:12 and they *e* them, cut off their
1 Ki 18:40 down to the Brook Kishon and *e*
19: 1 also how he had *e* all the
2 Ki 14: 5 that he *e* his servants who had
21:24 But the people of the land *e* all
23:20 He *e* all the priests of the high
2 Chr 24:24 So they *e* judgment against
25: 3 that he *e* his servants who had
33:25 But the people of the land *e* all
Ezra 7:26 let judgment be *e* speedily on
Esth 9: 1 command and his decree to be *e*.
Ps 99: 4 You have *e* justice and
Eccl 8:11 against an evil work is not *e*
Jer 23:20 not turn back Until He has *e*
Ezek 11:12 walked in My statutes nor *e* My
18: 8 his hand from iniquity And *e*
18:17 But has *e* My judgments And
20:24 because they had not *e* My
23:10 For they had *e* judgment on
39:21 see My judgment which I have *e*,
Dan 5:19 Whomever he wished, he *e*;

EXECUTES (7/7) EXECUTE

Ps 9:16 is known by the judgment He *e*;
103: 6 The LORD *e* righteousness And
146: 7 Who *e* justice for the
Isa 46:11 The man who *e* My counsel, from
Jer 5: 1 If there is anyone who *e*
Joel 2:11 strong is the One who *e* His
Mic 7: 9 Until He pleads my case And *e*

EXECUTING (1/1)

2 Chr 22: 8 when Jehu was *e* judgment on the

EXECUTIONER (1/1) EXECUTE, EXECUTIONERS

Mk 6:27 Immediately the king sent an *e*

EXECUTIONERS (1/1) EXECUTIONER

Job 33:22 the Pit, And his life to the *e*.

EXEMPTED (1/1)

1 Ki 15:22 all Judah; none was *e*.

EXEMPTION (1/1)

1 Sam 17:25 and give his father's house *e*

EXERCISE (8/7) EXERCISED, EXERCISES, EXERCISING

1 Ki 21: 7 You now *e* authority over Israel!
Mt 20:25 and those who are great *e*
Mk 10:42 and their great ones *e*

Lk 22:25 The kings of the Gentiles *e*
22:25 and those who *e* authority over
1 Cor 7: 9 but if they cannot *e*
1 Tim 4: 7 and *e* yourself toward
4: 8 For bodily *e* profits a little,

EXERCISED (2/2) EXERCISE

Eccl 1:13 of man, by which they may be *e*.
Heb 5:14 of use have their senses *e* to

EXERCISES (1/1) EXERCISE

Rev 13:12 And he *e* all the authority of

EXERCISING (1/1) EXERCISE

Jer 9:24 *e* lovingkindness, judgment, and

EXHAUSTED (2/2)

Judg 8: 4 *e* but still in pursuit.
8: 5 who follow me, for they are *e*,

EXHAUSTION (1/1)

Jer 48:45 shadow of Heshbon Because of *e*.

EXHORT (14/14) EXHORTATION, EXHORTED, EXHORTING, EXHORTS

2 Cor 9: 5 I thought it necessary to *e*
1 Th 4: 1 we urge and *e* in the Lord Jesus
5:14 Now we *e* you, brethren, warn
2 Th 3:12 who are such we command and *e*
1 Tim 2: 1 Therefore I *e* first of all that
5: 1 but *e* him as a father, younger
6: 2 Teach and *e* these things.
2 Tim 4: 2 of season. Convince, rebuke, *e*,
Titus 1: 9 both to *e* and convict those who
2: 6 Likewise *e* the young men to be
2: 9 *E* bondservants to be obedient
2:15 Speak these things, *e*,
Heb 3:13 but *e* one another daily, while
1 Pe 5: 1 elders who are among you I *e*,

EXHORTATION (8/8) EXHORT

Acts 13:15 if you have any word of *e* for
Rom 12: 8 he who exhorts, in *e*;
1 Cor 14: 3 speaks edification and *e* and
2 Cor 8:17 For he not only accepted the *e*,
1 Th 2: 3 For our *e* did not come from
1 Tim 4:13 give attention to reading, to *e*,
Heb 12: 5 And you have forgotten the *e*
13:22 bear with the word of *e*,

EXHORTATIONS (1/1)

Lk 3:18 And with many other *e* he

EXHORTED (4/4) EXHORT

Jer 11: 7 For I earnestly *e* your fathers
Acts 2:40 other words he testified and *e*
15:32 *e* and strengthened the brethren
1 Th 2:11 as you know how we *e*,

EXHORTING (6/6) EXHORT

Jer 11: 7 this day, rising early and *e*,
Acts 14:22 *e* them to continue in the
18:27 *e* the disciples to receive him;
Heb 10:25 but *e* one another, and so
1 Pe 5:12 *e* and testifying that this is
Jude 3 it necessary to write to you *e*

EXHORTS (1/1) EXHORT

Rom 12: 8 he who *e*, in exhortation;

EXILE (2/2)

2 Sam 15:19 are a foreigner and also an *e*
Isa 51:14 The captive *e* hastens, that he

EXILES (1/1)

Isa 45:13 build My city And let My *e* go

EXIST (5/5) EXISTED

Isa 66: 2 made, And all those things *e*,
Rom 4:17 those things which do not *e* as
13: 1 and the authorities that *e* are
Jas 3:16 where envy and self-seeking *e*,
Rev 4:11 And by Your will they *e* and

EXISTED (2/2) EXIST

Eccl 4: 3 both is he who has never *e*,
2 Pe 3: 6 by which the world that then *e*

EXITS (3/3)

Ezek 42:11 and all their *e* and entrances
43:11 its *e* and its entrances, its
48:30 These are the *e* of the city.

EXORCISE (1/1)

Acts 19:13 We *e* you by the Jesus whom Paul

EXORCISTS (1/1)

Acts 19:13 some of the itinerant Jewish *e*

EXPAND (1/1)

Isa 54: 3 For you shall *e* to the right

EXPANDED (1/1)

Isa 26:15 You have *e* all the borders of

EXPECT (2/2) EXPECTANTLY, EXPECTATION, EXPECTED, EXPECTING, UNEXPECTEDLY

Mt 24:44 coming at an hour you do not *e*.
Lk 12:40 coming at an hour you do not *e*.

EXPECTANTLY (1/1) EXPECT

Ps 145:15 The eyes of all look *e* to You,

EXPECTATION (14/14) EXPECT

Ps 9:18 The *e* of the poor shall not
62: 5 For my *e* is from Him.
Prov 10:28 But the *e* of the wicked will
11: 7 his *e* will perish, And the
11:23 But the *e* of the wicked is
Isa 20: 5 and ashamed of Ethiopia their *e*
20: 6 day, 'Surely such is our *e*,
Zech 9: 5 Ekron, for He dried up her *e*.
Lk 3:15 Now as the people were in *e*,
21:26 them from fear and the *e* of
Acts 12:11 of Herod and from all the *e*
Rom 8:19 For the earnest *e* of the
Phil 1:20 according to my earnest *e* and
Heb 10:27 but a certain fearful *e* of

EXPECTATIONS (1/1)

1 Ki 2:15 and all Israel had set their *e*

EXPECTED (2/2) EXPECT

Isa 5: 2 So He *e* it to bring forth
5: 4 when I *e* it to bring forth

EXPECTING (2/2) EXPECT

Acts 3: 5 *e* to receive something from
28: 6 they were *e* that he would swell

EXPEDIENT (2/2)

Jn 11:50 do you consider that it is *e*
18:14 advised the Jews that it was *e*

EXPEDITION (1/1)

1 Sam 23:13 from Keilah; so he halted the *e*.

EXPEL (2/2)

Josh 23: 5 And the LORD your God will *e*
Judg 11: 7 and *e* me from my father's

EXPELLED (5/4)

Judg 1:20 Then he *e* from there the three
2 Sam 14:14 His banished ones are not *e*
Zech 5: 3 'Every thief shall be *e*,'
5: 3 and, 'Every perjurer shall be *e*,
Acts 13:50 and *e* them from their region.

EXPENDED (1/1)

Ezek 29:18 for the labor which they *e* on

EXPENSE (3/3) EXPENSES

2 Sam 19:42 we ever eaten at the king's *e*?
Ezra 6: 8 cost be paid at the king's *e*
1 Cor 9: 7 ever goes to war at his own *e*?

EXPENSES (2/2) EXPENSE

Ezra 6: 4 Let the *e* be paid from the
Acts 21:24 and pay their *e* so that they

EXPERIENCE (2/2) EXPERIENCED

Gen 30:27 for I have learned by *e* that
Eccl 8: 5 who keeps his command will *e*

EXPERIENCED (1/1) EXPERIENCE

1 Pe 5: 9 that the same sufferings are *e*

EXPERT (6/6)

1 Chr 12:33 *e* in war with all weapons of
Ezra 7:11 *e* in the words of the
Song 3: 8 Being *e* in war. Every man
Isa 3: 3 And the *e* enchanter.
Jer 50: 9 shall be like those of an *e*
Acts 26: 3 especially because you are *e* in

EXPIRATION (1/1)

Acts 21:26 the temple to announce the *e*

EXPIRED (2/2)

1 Sam 18:26 Now the days had not *e*;
Rev 20: 7 when the thousand years have *e*,

EXPLAIN (16/16) EXPLAINED, EXPLAINING

Gen 41:24 there was no one who could *e*
Deut 1: 5 Moses began to *e* this law,
Judg 14:12 you can correctly solve and *e*
14:13 But if you cannot *e* it to me,
14:14 for three days they could not *e*
14:15 that he may *e* the riddle to us,
14:16 so should I *e* it to you?"
1 Ki 10: 3 the king that he could not *e*
2 Chr 9: 2 Solomon that he could not *e* it
Esth 4: 8 might show it to Esther and *e*
Job 12: 8 the fish of the sea will *e* to
Dan 4: 9 *e* to me the visions of my dream
5:16 can give interpretations and *e*
Mt 13:36 *E* to us the parable of the tares
15:15 *E* this parable to us."
Heb 5:11 have much to say, and hard to *e*,

E

EXPLAINED (11/10) EXPLAIN

Num 15:34 because it had not been *e* what
Judg 14:16 but you have not *e* it to me."
14:16 I have not *e* it to my father
14:17 Then she *e* the riddle to the
14:19 clothing to those who had *e*
1 Sam 10:25 Then Samuel *e* to the people the
Mk 4:34 He *e* all things to His
Acts 10: 8 So when he had *e* all these
11: 4 But Peter *e* it to them in order
18:26 they took him aside and *e* to
28:23 to whom he *e* and solemnly

EXPLAINING (2/2) EXPLAIN

Dan 5:12 and *e* enigmas were found in
Acts 17: 3 *e* and demonstrating that the

EXPLOIT (3/3) EXPLOITS

Isa 58: 3 And *e* all your laborers.
Mal 3: 5 Against those who *e* wage
2 Pe 2: 3 By covetousness they will *e* you

EXPLOITS (1/1) EXPLOIT

Dan 11:32 strong, and carry out great *e*.

EXPLORE (1/1)

1 Ki 18: 6 the land between them to *e* it;

EXPORTED (2/2)

1 Ki 10:29 they *e* them to all the kings
2 Chr 1:17 they *e* them to all the kings of

EXPOSE (4/4) EXPOSED

Prov 25:10 Lest he who hears it *e* your
Hos 2: 3 Lest I strip her naked And *e*
Acts 7:19 making them *e* their babies, so
Eph 5:11 but rather *e* them.

EXPOSED (6/6) EXPOSE

Gen 30:37 and *e* the white which was in
Ex 20:26 your nakedness may not be *e* on
Lev 20:18 he has *e* her flow, and she has
Hab 2:16 And be *e* as uncircumcised!
Jn 3:20 lest his deeds should be *e*.
Eph 5:13 But all things that are *e* are

EXPOUNDED (1/1)

Lk 24:27 He *e* to them in all the

EXPRESS (2/2) EXPRESSION, EXPRESSLY

Eccl 1: 8 Man cannot *e* it. The eye is
Heb 1: 3 of His glory and the *e* image

EXPRESSING (1/1)

Prov 18: 2 But in *e* his own heart.

EXPRESSION (1/1) EXPRESS

Dan 3:19 and the *e* on his face changed

EXPRESSLY (3/3) EXPRESS

1 Sam 20:21 If I *e* say to him, 'Look, the
Ezek 1: 3 the word of the LORD came *e* to
1 Tim 4: 1 Now the Spirit *e* says that in

EXQUISITE (1/1)

Ex 39:28 *e* hats of fine linen, short

EXTEND (8/8) EXTENDED, EXTENDING, EXTENDS, EXTENT

Ex 25:35 to the six branches that *e*
Num 34: 3 your southern border shall *e*
35: 4 give the Levites shall *e*
Ps 109:12 Let there be none to *e* mercy to
Isa 58:10 If you *e* your soul to the

66:12 I will *e* peace to her like a
Jer 31:39 surveyor's line shall again *e*
2 Cor 10:14 our authority did not *e* to

EXTENDED (14/14) EXTEND

Josh 15: 9 and *e* to the cities of Mount
15:11 and *e* to Jabneel; and the
18:14 Then the border *e* around the
18:15 and the border *e* on the west
18:17 and *e* toward Geliloth, which is
19:11 and *e* along the brook that is
19:13 and *e* to Rimmon, which borders
19:34 From Heleph the border *e*
1 Ki 6: 3 the width of the vestible *e*
8: 8 The poles *e* so that the ends of
2 Chr 5: 9 And the poles *e* so that the ends
Ezra 7:28 and has *e* mercy to me before the
9: 9 but He *e* mercy to us in the
Ezek 40:14 all around the gateway *e* to

EXTENDING (3/3) EXTEND

Ex 37:21 to the six branches *e* from it.
Ezek 43:15 with four horns *e* upward from
45: 7 *e* westward on the west side and

EXTENDS (2/2) EXTEND

Num 21:13 is in the wilderness that *e*
Prov 31:20 She *e* her hand to the poor,

EXTENSIVE (1/1) EXTENT

Neh 4:19 "The work is great and *e*,

EXTENSIVELY (1/1)

2 Chr 27: 3 and he built *e* on the wall of

EXTENT (5/5) EXTEND, EXTENSIVE

Num 22:41 there he might observe the *e*
Josh 17:18 and its farthest *e* shall be
Jon 3: 3 a three-day journey in *e*.
2 Cor 2: 5 me, but all of you to some *e*—
1 Pe 4:13 but rejoice to the *e* that you

EXTERIOR (1/1)

Ezek 40:19 the front of the inner court *e*,

EXTERMINATE (1/1)

1 Ki 13:34 so as to *e* and destroy it from

EXTINCT (KJV) See EXTINGUISHED

EXTINGUISH (1/1) EXTINGUISHED

2 Sam 14: 7 So they would *e* my ember that

EXTINGUISHED (2/2) EXTINGUISH

Job 17: 1 is broken, My days are *e*,
Isa 43:17 shall not rise; They are *e*,

EXTOL (4/4) EXTOLLED

Ps 30: 1 I will *e* You, O LORD, for You
68: 4 *E* Him who rides on the clouds,
145: 1 I will *e* You, my God, O King;
Dan 4:37 praise and *e* and honor the King

EXTOLLED (2/2) EXTOL

Ps 66:17 And He was *e* with my tongue.
Isa 52:13 He shall be exalted and *e* and

EXTORTED (2/2)

Lev 6: 2 or if he has *e* from his
6: 4 or the thing which he has *e*,

EXTORTION (3/3) EXTORTIONER

Prov 28: 8 his possessions by usury and *e*
Ezek 22:12 profit from your neighbors by *e*,
Mt 23:25 but inside they are full of *e*

EXTORTIONER (2/2) EXTORTION, EXTORTIONERS

Isa 16: 4 For the *e* is at an end,
1 Cor 5:11 reviler, or a drunkard, or an *e*—

EXTORTIONERS (3/3) EXTORTIONER

Lk 18:11 that I am not like other men—*e*,
1 Cor 5:10 or with the covetous, or *e*,
6:10 nor *e* will inherit the kingdom

EXTRAORDINARY (1/1)

Deut 28:59 upon you and your descendants *e*

EXTREME (2/2)

Josh 15: 1 of Zin southward was the *e*
Ezek 46:19 place was situated at their *e*

EXTREMITY (1/1)

2 Ki 19:23 I will enter the *e* of its

EXULT (1/1)

Job 6:10 Though in anguish, I would *e*,

EYE (108/85) EYED, EYELIDS, EYES, EYESERVICE

Ex 21:24 *e* for eye, tooth for tooth, hand
21:24 'eye for *e*, tooth for tooth,
21:26 If a man strikes the *e* of his
21:26 go free for the sake of his *e*.
Lev 21:20 man who has a defect in his *e*,
24:20 *e* for eye, tooth for tooth;
24:20 for fracture, eye for *e*,
Deut 7:16 your *e* shall have no pity on
13: 8 nor shall your *e* pity him, nor
15: 9 and your *e* be evil against
19:13 Your *e* shall not pity him, but
19:21 'Your *e* shall not pity:
19:21 *e* for eye, tooth for tooth,
19:21 shall be for life, eye for *e*,
25:12 your *e* shall not pity her.
32:10 kept him as the apple of His *e*.
1 Sam 24:10 But my *e* spared you, and I
Ezra 5: 5 But the *e* of their God was upon
Job 7: 7 my life is a breath! My *e*
7: 8 The *e* of him who sees me will
10:18 that I had perished and no *e*
13: 1 my *e* has seen all this, My
17: 2 And does not my *e* dwell on
17: 7 My *e* has also grown dim because
20: 9 The *e* that saw him will see
24:15 The *e* of the adulterer waits
24:15 No *e* will see me'; And he
28: 7 Nor has the falcon's *e* seen
28:10 And his *e* sees every precious
29:11 And when the *e* saw, then it
42: 5 But now my *e* sees You.
Ps 6: 7 My *e* wastes away because of
17: 8 Keep me as the apple of Your *e*;
31: 9 My *e* wastes away with grief,
32: 8 I will guide you with My *e*.
33:18 the *e* of the LORD is on those
35:19 Nor let them wink with the *e*
54: 7 And my *e* has seen its desire
88: 9 My *e* wastes away because of
92:11 My *e* also has seen my desire
94: 9 not hear? He who formed the *e*,
Prov 7: 2 my law as the apple of your *e*.
10:10 He who winks with the *e* causes
16:30 He winks his *e* to devise
20:12 hearing ear and the seeing *e*,
22: 9 He who has a generous *e* will be
28:22 A man with an evil *e* hastens
30:17 The *e* that mocks his father,
Eccl 1: 8 The *e* is not satisfied with
4: 8 Nor is his *e* satisfied with
Isa 13:18 Their *e* will not spare
52: 8 For they shall see *e* to eye
52: 8 For they shall see eye to *e*
64: 4 Nor has the *e* seen any God
Jer 32: 4 and see him *e* to eye;
32: 4 to face, and see him eye to *e*;
Lam 1:16 these things I weep; My *e*,
1:16 my *e* overflows with water;
2: 4 who were pleasing to His *e*;
Ezek 5:11 My *e* will not spare, nor will I
7: 4 My *e* will not spare you, Nor
7: 9 My *e* will not spare, Nor will I
8:18 My *e* will not spare nor will I
9: 5 do not let your *e* spare, nor
9:10 My *e* will neither spare, nor
16: 5 No *e* pitied you, to do any of
20:17 Nevertheless My *e* spared them
Mic 4:11 And let our *e* look upon
Zech 2: 8 you touches the apple of His *e*.
11:17 arm And against his right *e*;
11:17 And his right *e* shall be
Mt 5:29 If your right *e* causes you to
5:38 An *e* for an eye and a
5:38 An eye for an *e* and a
6:22 lamp of the body is the *e*.
6:22 If therefore your *e* is good,
6:23 But if your *e* is bad, your whole
7: 3 the speck in your brother's *e*,
7: 3 the plank in your own *e*?
7: 4 remove the speck from your *e*';
7: 4 look, a plank is in your own *e*?
7: 5 the plank from your own *e*,
7: 5 the speck from your brother's *e*.
18: 9 And if your *e* causes you to sin,
18: 9 to enter into life with one *e*,
19:24 a camel to go through the *e* of
20:15 Or is your *e* evil because I am
Mk 7:22 deceit, lewdness, an evil *e*,
9:47 And if your *e* causes you to sin,
9:47 the kingdom of God with one *e*,
10:25 a camel to go through the *e* of
Lk 6:41 the speck in your brother's *e*,
6:41 the plank in your own *e*?
6:42 the speck that is in your *e*,
6:42 plank that is in your own *e*?
6:42 the plank from your own *e*,
6:42 that is in your brother's *e*.
11:34 "The lamp of the body is the *e*.
11:34 when your *e* is good, your whole
11:34 But when your *e* is bad, your
18:25 a camel to go through the *e* of
1 Cor 2: 9 *E* has not seen, nor ear
12:16 say, "Because I am not an *e*,
12:17 If the whole body were an *e*,
12:21 And the *e* cannot say to the
15:52 in the twinkling of an *e*,
Rev 1: 7 and every *e* will see Him, even
3:18 and anoint your eyes with *e*

EYEBROWS (1/1)

Lev 14: 9 head and his beard and his *e*—

EYED (1/1) EYE

1 Sam 18: 9 So Saul *e* David from that day

EYELIDS (10/10) EYE

Job 16:16 And on my *e* is the shadow of
41:18 And his eyes are like the *e*
Ps 11: 4 His *e* test the sons of men.
77: 4 You hold my *e* open; I am so
132: 4 to my eyes Or slumber to my *e*,
Prov 4:25 And your *e* look right before
6: 4 eyes, Nor slumber to your *e*.
6:25 let her allure you with her *e*.
30:13 are their eyes! And their *e*
Jer 9:18 And our *e* gush with water.

EYES (501/481) EYE

Gen 3: 5 in the day you eat of it your *e*
3: 6 that it was pleasant to the *e*,
3: 7 Then the *e* of both of them were
6: 8 But Noah found grace in the *e* of
13:10 And Lot lifted his *e* and saw all
13:14 Lift your *e* now and look from
16: 4 became despised in her *e*.
16: 5 I became despised in her *e*.
18: 2 So he lifted his *e* and looked,
21:19 Then God opened her *e*,
22: 4 third day Abraham lifted his *e*
22:13 Then Abraham lifted his *e* and
24:63 and he lifted his *e* and looked,
24:64 Then Rebekah lifted her *e*,
27: 1 when Isaac was old and his *e*
29:17 Leah's *e* were delicate, but
30:27 if I have found favor in your *e*,
30:41 placed the rods before the *e*
31:10 that I lifted my *e* and saw in a
31:12 Lift your *e* now and see, all the
31:40 and my sleep departed from my *e*.
33: 1 Now Jacob lifted his *e* and
33: 5 And he lifted his *e* and saw the
34:11 "Let me find favor in your *e*,
37:25 Then they lifted their *e* and
39: 7 master's wife cast longing *e*
41:37 the advice was good in the *e*
41:37 eyes of Pharaoh and in the *e*
42:24 and bound him before their *e*.
43:29 Then he lifted his *e* and saw his
44:21 that I may set my *e* on him.'
45:12 your *e* and the eyes of my
45:12 your eyes and the *e* of my
46: 4 will put his hand on your *e*.
47:19 should we die before your *e*,
48:10 Now the *e* of Israel were dim
49:12 His *e* are darker than wine,
50: 4 I have found favor in your *e*,
Ex 8:26 of the Egyptians before their *e*,
13: 9 as a memorial between your *e*,
13:16 and as frontlets between your *e*,
14:10 of Israel lifted their *e*,
24:17 top of the mountain in the *e*
Lev 4:13 the thing is hidden from the *e*
20: 4 should in any way hide their *e*
26:16 which shall consume the *e* and
Num 5:13 and it is hidden from the *e* of
10:31 and you can be our *e*.
11: 6 this manna before our *e*!"
15:39 your own heart and your own *e*
16:14 Will you put out the *e* of these
20: 8 to the rock before their *e*,
20:12 to hallow Me in the *e* of the
22:31 the LORD opened Balaam's *e*,
24: 2 And Balaam raised his *e*,
24: 3 utterance of the man whose *e*
24: 4 falls down, with *e* wide open:
24:15 utterance of the man whose *e*
24:16 falls down, with *e* wide open:
27:14 Me at the waters before their *e*.
33:55 shall be irritants in your *e*
Deut 1:30 for you in Egypt before your *e*,
3:21 Your *e* have seen all that the
3:27 and lift your *e* toward the
3:27 behold it with your *e*,
4: 3 Your *e* have seen what the LORD
4: 9 you forget the things your *e*
4:19 lest you lift your *e* to heaven,
4:34 for you in Egypt before your *e*?
6: 8 be as frontlets between your *e*.
6:22 signs and wonders before our *e*,
7:19 the great trials which your *e*
9:17 and broke them before your *e*.
10:21 and awesome things which your *e*
11: 7 but your *e* have seen every great
11:12 the *e* of the LORD your God
11:18 be as frontlets between your *e*.
12: 8 whatever is right in his own *e*—
13:18 to do what is right in the *e*
16:19 for a bribe blinds the *e* of the
21: 7 nor have our *e* seen it.
24: 1 she finds no favor in his *e*
28:31 be slaughtered before your *e*,
28:32 and your *e* shall look and fail
28:34 of the sight which your *e* see.

28:65 a trembling heart, failing **e**,
28:67 of the sight which your **e** see.
29: 2 the LORD did before your **e** in
29: 3 the great trials which your **e**
29: 4 you a heart to perceive and **e**
34: 4 you to see it with your **e**,
34: 7 His **e** were not dim nor his
Josh 5:13 that he lifted his **e** and
23:13 your sides and thorns in your **e**,
24: 7 And your **e** saw what I did in
Judg 16:21 took him and put out his **e**,
16:28 on the Philistines for my two **e**!
17: 6 what was right in his own **e**.
19:17 And when he raised his **e**,
21:25 what was right in his own **e**.
Ruth 2: 9 Let your **e** be on the field
2:10 have I found favor in your **e**,
1 Sam 2:33 My altar shall consume your **e**
3: 2 and when his **e** had begun to
4:15 and his **e** were so dim that he
6:13 and they lifted their **e** and saw
11: 2 I may put out all your right **e**,
12: 3 bribe with which to blind my **e**?
12:16 the LORD will do before your **e**:
15:17 you were little in your own **e**,
16:12 he was ruddy, with bright **e**,
20: 3 I have found favor in your **e**,
20:29 if I have found favor in your **e**,
24:10 this day your **e** have seen that
25: 8 young men find favor in your **e**,
26:21 my life was precious in your **e**
26:24 valued much this day in my **e**,
26:24 my life be valued much in the **e**
27: 5 have now found favor in your **e**,
2 Sam 6:20 himself today in the **e** of the
12:11 take your wives before your **e**
13:34 was keeping watch lifted his **e**
15:25 If I find favor in the **e** of the
18:24 lifted his **e** and looked, and
19:27 do what is good in your **e**.
22:25 to my cleanness in His **e**.
22:28 But Your **e** are on the
24: 3 and may the **e** of my lord the
1 Ki 1:20 the **e** of all Israel are on
1:48 while my **e** see it!'"
8:29 that Your **e** may be open toward
8:52 that Your **e** may be open to the
9: 3 and My **e** and My heart will be
10: 7 I came and saw with my own **e**;
11:33 to do what is right in My **e**
14: 4 for his **e** were glazed by reason
14: 8 only what was right in My **e**;
15: 5 did what was right in the **e**
15:11 did what was right in the **e**
16:25 Omri did evil in the **e** of the
20: 6 whatever is pleasant in your **e**,
20:38 with a bandage over his **e**.
20:41 the bandage away from his **e**;
22:43 what was right in the **e** of
2 Ki 4:34 his **e** on his eyes, and his
4:34 on his mouth, his eyes on his **e**,
4:35 and the child opened his **e**.
5: 1 and honorable man in the **e** of
6:17 open his **e** that he may see."
6:17 Then the LORD opened the **e**
6:20 open the **e** of these men, that
6:20 And the LORD opened their **e**,
7: 2 you shall see it with your **e**,
7:19 you shall see it with your **e**,
9:30 and she put paint on her **e** and
19:16 O LORD, and hear; open Your **e**,
19:22 And lifted up your **e** on high?
22:20 and your **e** shall not see all
25: 7 sons of Zedekiah before his **e**,
25: 7 put out the **e** of Zedekiah,
1 Chr 13: 4 the thing was right in the **e**
21:16 Then David lifted his **e** and saw
21:23 king do what is good in his **e**.
2 Chr 6:20 that Your **e** may be open toward
6:40 let Your **e** be open and let
7:15 Now My **e** will be open and My
7:16 and My **e** and My heart will be
9: 6 I came and saw with my own **e**;
14: 2 was good and right in the **e**
16: 9 For the **e** of the LORD run to
20:12 but our **e** are upon You."
29: 6 and done evil in the **e** of the
29: 8 jeering, as you see with your **e**.
34:28 and your **e** shall not see all
Ezra 3:12 temple was laid before their **e**.
9: 8 our God may enlighten our **e**
Neh 1: 6 ear be attentive and Your **e**
6:16 disheartened in their own **e**;
Esth 1:17 their husbands in their **e**,
8: 5 king and I am pleasing in his **e**,
Job 2:12 And when they raised their **e**
3:10 Nor hide sorrow from my **e**.
4:16 A form was before my **e**;
7: 8 While your **e** are upon me, I
10: 4 Do You have **e** of flesh? Or do
11: 4 pure, And I am clean in your **e**.
11:20 But the **e** of the wicked will
14: 3 And do You open Your **e** on such
15:12 And what do your **e** wink at,
16:20 My **e** pour out tears to God.
17: 5 Even the **e** of his children
19:27 And my **e** shall behold, and not
21: 8 their offspring before their **e**.
21:20 Let his **e** see his destruction,
24:23 Yet His **e** are on their ways.
27:19 gathered up; He opens his **e**,
28:21 It is hidden from the **e** of all
29:15 I was **e** to the blind, And I
31: 1 have made a covenant with my **e**;
31: 7 Or my heart walked after my **e**,
31:16 Or caused the **e** of the widow
32: 1 he was righteous in his own **e**.
34:21 For His **e** are on the ways of
36: 7 He does not withdraw His **e** from
39:29 Its **e** observe from afar.
40:24 Though he takes it in his **e**,
41:18 And his **e** are like the
Ps 10: 8 His **e** are secretly fixed on
11: 4 His **e** behold, His eyelids
13: 3 O LORD my God; Enlighten my **e**,
15: 4 In whose **e** a vile person is
17: 2 Let Your **e** look on the things
17:11 steps; They have set their **e**,
19: 8 is pure, enlightening the **e**;
25:15 My **e** are ever toward the
26: 3 lovingkindness is before my **e**,
31:22 am cut off from before Your **e**'
34:15 The **e** of the LORD are on the
35:21 aha! Our **e** have seen it."
36: 1 is no fear of God before his **e**.
36: 2 flatters himself in his own **e**,
38:10 As for the light of my **e**,
50:21 them in order before your **e**.
66: 7 His **e** observe the nations; Do
69: 3 My **e** fail while I wait for my
69:23 Let their **e** be darkened, so
73: 7 Their **e** bulge with abundance;
91: 8 Only with your **e** shall you
101: 3 set nothing wicked before my **e**;
101: 6 My **e** shall be on the faithful
115: 5 ***E*** they have, but they do not
116: 8 My **e** from tears, And my feet
118:23 It is marvelous in our **e**.
119:18 Open my **e**, that I may see
119:37 Turn away my **e** from looking at
119:82 My **e** fail from searching Your
119:123 My **e** fail from seeking Your
119:136 of water run down from my **e**,
119:148 My **e** are awake through the
121: 1 I will lift up my **e** to the
123: 1 Unto You I lift up my **e**,
123: 2 as the **e** of servants look to
123: 2 As the **e** of a maid to the hand
123: 2 So our **e** look to the LORD
131: 1 Nor my **e** lofty. Neither do I
132: 4 I will not give sleep to my **e**
135:16 ***E*** they have, but they do not
139:16 Your **e** saw my substance, being
141: 8 But my **e** are upon You, O GOD
145:15 The **e** of all look expectantly
146: 8 The LORD opens the **e** of the
Prov 3: 7 Do not be wise in your own **e**;
3:21 let them not depart from your **e**—
4:21 not let them depart from your **e**;
4:25 Let your **e** look straight ahead,
5:21 ways of man are before the **e**
6: 4 Give no sleep to your **e**,
6:13 He winks with his **e**,
10:26 to the teeth and smoke to the **e**,
12:15 a fool is right in his own **e**,
15: 3 The **e** of the LORD are in
15:30 The light of the **e** rejoices the
16: 2 of a man are pure in his own **e**,
17: 8 is a precious stone in the **e**
17:24 But the **e** of a fool are on
20: 8 Scatters all evil with his **e**.
20:13 come to poverty; Open your **e**,
21: 2 of a man is right in his own **e**,
21:10 finds no favor in his **e**.
22:12 The **e** of the LORD preserve
23: 5 Will you set your **e** on that
23:26 And let your **e** observe my
23:29 Who has redness of **e**?
23:33 Your **e** will see strange things,
25: 7 Whom your **e** have seen.
26: 5 Lest he be wise in his own **e**.
26:12 you see a man wise in his own **e**?
26:16 man is wiser in his own **e**
27:20 So the **e** of man are never
28:11 rich man is wise in his own **e**,
28:27 But he who hides his **e** will
29:13 LORD gives light to the **e** of
30:12 that is pure in its own **e**,
30:13 how lofty are their **e**! And
Eccl 2:10 Whatever my **e** desired I did not
2:14 The wise man's **e** are in his
5:11 to see them with their **e**?
6: 9 Better is the sight of the **e**
11: 7 it is pleasant for the **e** to
11: 9 And in the sight of your **e**;
Song 1:15 are fair! You have dove's **e**.
4: 1 are fair! You have dove's **e**
4: 9 heart With one look of your **e**,
5:12 His **e** are like doves By the
6: 5 Turn your **e** away from me, For
7: 4 Your **e** like the pools in
8:10 Then I became in his **e** As one
Isa 1:15 I will hide My **e** from you;
1:16 of your doings from before My **e**.
3: 8 To provoke the **e** of His glory.
3:16 necks And wanton **e**,
5:15 And the **e** of the lofty shall
5:21 who are wise in their own **e**,
6: 5 For my **e** have seen the King,
6:10 ears heavy, And shut their **e**;
6:10 Lest they see with their **e**,
11: 3 not judge by the sight of His **e**,
13:16 dashed to pieces before their **e**;
17: 7 And his **e** will have respect
29:10 sleep, And has closed your **e**,
29:18 And the **e** of the blind shall
30:20 But your **e** shall see your
32: 3 The **e** of those who see will not
33:15 And shuts his **e** from seeing
33:17 Your **e** will see the King in
33:20 Your **e** will see Jerusalem, a
35: 5 Then the **e** of the blind shall
37:17 O LORD, and hear; open Your **e**,
37:23 And lifted up your **e** on high?
38:14 My **e** fail from looking
40:26 Lift up your **e** on high, And
42: 7 To open blind **e**, To bring
43: 8 out the blind people who have **e**,
44:18 For He has shut their **e**,
49: 5 I shall be glorious in the **e**
49:18 Lift up your **e**,
51: 6 Lift up your **e** to the heavens,
52:10 bare His holy arm In the **e** of
59:10 we grope as if we had no **e**;
60: 4 Lift up your **e** all around, and
65:12 hear, But did evil before My **e**,
65:16 they are hidden from My **e**.
66: 4 But they did evil before My **e**,
Jer 3: 2 Lift up your **e** to the desolate
4:30 Though you enlarge your **e** with
5: 3 are not Your **e** on the truth?
5:21 Who have **e** and see not, And
7:11 a den of thieves in your **e**?
9: 1 And my **e** a fountain of tears,
9:18 That our **e** may run with tears,
13:17 My **e** will weep bitterly And
13:20 Lift up your **e** and see Those
14: 6 Their **e** failed because there
14:17 Let my **e** flow with tears night
16: 9 before your **e** and in your days,
16:17 For My **e** are on all their ways;
16:17 their iniquity hidden from My **e**.
20: 4 and your **e** shall see it.
22:17 Yet your **e** and your heart are
24: 6 For I will set My **e** on them for
29:21 shall slay them before your **e**.
31:16 And your **e** from tears;
32:19 for your **e** are open to all the
34: 3 your **e** shall see the eyes of
34: 3 your eyes shall see the **e** of
39: 6 sons of Zedekiah before his **e**
39: 7 he put out Zedekiah's **e**,
52:10 sons of Zedekiah before his **e**.
52:11 He also put out the **e** of
Lam 2:11 My **e** fail with tears, My
2:18 Give your **e** no rest.
3:48 My **e** overflow with rivers of
3:49 My **e** flow and do not cease,
3:51 My **e** bring suffering to my soul
4:17 Still our **e** failed us,
5:17 of these things our **e** grow
Ezek 1:18 and their rims were full of **e**,
6: 9 and by their **e** which play the
8: 5 lift your **e** now toward the
8: 5 So I lifted my **e** toward the
10:12 were full of **e** all around.
12: 2 which has **e** to see but does not
12:12 see the ground with his **e**.
18: 6 Nor lifted up his **e** to the
18:12 Lifted his **e** to the idols,
18:15 Nor lifted his **e** to the idols
20: 7 which are before his **e**,
20: 8 which were before their **e**,
20:24 and their **e** were fixed on their
21: 6 with bitterness before their **e**.
21:23 a false divination in the **e** of
22:26 and they have hidden their **e**
23:16 As soon as her **e** saw them, She
23:27 that you will not lift your **e**
23:40 for them, painted your **e**,
24:16 from you the desire of your **e**
24:21 boast, the desire of your **e**,
24:25 glory, the desire of their **e**,
33:25 you lift up your **e** toward your
36:23 hallowed in you before their **e**.
37:20 be in your hand before their **e**.
38:16 in you, O Gog, before their **e**.
38:23 and I will be known in the **e** of
40: 4 look with your **e** and hear with
44: 5 see with your **e** and hear with
Dan 4:34 lifted my **e** to heaven, and my
7: 8 were **e** like the eyes of a man,
7: 8 were eyes like the **e** of a man,
7:20 that horn which had **e** and a
8: 3 Then I lifted my **e** and saw, and
8: 5 a notable horn between his **e**.
8:21 horn that is between its **e**
9:18 open Your **e** and see our
10: 5 I lifted my **e** and looked, and
10: 6 his **e** like torches of fire, his
Hos 13:14 Pity is hidden from My **e**.
Joel 1:16 the food cut off before our **e**,
Am 9: 4 I will set My **e** on them for
9: 8 the **e** of the Lord GOD are on
Mic 7:10 My **e** will see her; Now she
Hab 1:13 You are of purer **e** than to
Zeph 3:20 your captives before your **e**,
Hag 2: 3 is this not in your **e** as
Zech 1:18 Then I raised my **e** and looked,
2: 1 Then I raised my **e** and looked,
3: 9 Upon the stone are seven **e**.
4:10 They are the **e** of the LORD,
5: 1 Then I turned and raised my **e**,
5: 5 Lift your **e** now, and see what
5: 9 Then I raised my **e** and looked,
6: 1 Then I turned and raised my **e**

8: 6 If it is marvelous in the *e* of
8: 6 it also be marvelous in My *e*?
9: 1 its resting place (For the *e*
9: 8 For now I have seen with My *e*.
12: 4 I will open My *e* on the house
14:12 Their *e* shall dissolve in
Mal 1: 5 Your *e* shall see, And you
Mt 9:29 Then He touched their *e*,
9:30 And their *e* were opened.
13:15 And their *e* they have
13:15 should see with their *e*
13:16 But blessed are your *e* for they
17: 8 When they had lifted up their *e*,
18: 9 eye, rather than having two *e*,
20:33 that our *e* may be opened."
20:34 compassion and touched their *e*.
20:34 And immediately their *e*
21:42 it is marvelous in our *e*'
26:43 for their *e* were heavy.
Mk 8:18 'Having *e*, do you not see?
8:23 And when He had spit on his *e*
8:25 Then He put His hands on his *e*
9:47 eye, rather than having two *e*,
12:11 it is marvelous in our *e*'
14:40 for their *e* were heavy;
Lk 2:30 For my *e* have seen Your
4:20 And the *e* of all who were in
6:20 Then He lifted up His *e* toward
10:23 Blessed are the *e* which see the
16:23 he lifted up his *e* and saw
18:13 not so much as raise his *e* to
19:42 now they are hidden from your *e*.
24:16 But their *e* were restrained, so
24:31 Then their *e* were opened and
Jn 4:35 lift up your *e* and look at the
6: 5 Then Jesus lifted up His *e*,
9: 6 and He anointed the *e* of the
9:10 How were your *e* opened?"
9:11 made clay and anointed my *e*
9:14 made the clay and opened his *e*.
9:15 to them, "He put clay on my *e*,
9:17 Him because He opened your *e*?
9:21 or who opened his *e* we do not
9:26 to you? How did He open your *e*?
9:30 yet He has opened my *e*!
9:32 of that anyone opened the *e* of
10:21 Can a demon open the *e* of the
11:37 who opened the *e* of the blind,
11:41 And Jesus lifted up His *e* and
12:40 He has blinded their *e* and
12:40 should see with their *e*,
17: 1 lifted up His *e* to heaven, and
Acts 3: 4 And fixing his *e* on him, with
9: 8 and when his *e* were opened he
9:18 there fell from his *e*
9:40 And she opened her *e*,
26:18 'to open their *e*, in order to
28:27 And their *e* they have
28:27 should see with their *e*
Rom 3:18 of God before their *e*.
11: 8 *E* that they should not
11:10 Let their *e* be darkened,
Gal 3: 1 before whose *e* Jesus Christ was
4:15 have plucked out your own *e*
Eph 1:18 the *e* of your understanding
Heb 4:13 are naked and open to the *e*
1 Pe 3:12 For the *e* of the LORD
2 Pe 2:14 having *e* full of adultery and
1 Jn 1: 1 which we have seen with our *e*,
2:11 the darkness has blinded his *e*.
2:16 of the flesh, the lust of the *e*,
Rev 1:14 and His *e* like a flame of fire;
2:18 who has *e* like a flame of fire,
3:18 and anoint your *e* with eye
4: 6 living creatures full of *e* in
4: 8 were full of *e* around and
5: 6 having seven horns and seven *e*,
7:17 away every tear from their *e*.
19:12 His *e* were like a flame of
21: 4 away every tear from their *e*;

EYES OF THE LORD (20/20)

Gen 6: 8 But Noah found grace in the *e*.
Deut 11:12 the *e* your God are always on
13:18 to do what is right in the *e*
1 Sam 26:24 my life be valued much in the *e*,
2 Sam 15:25 If I find favor in the *e*,
1 Ki 15: 5 did what was right in the *e*,
15:11 did what was right in the *e*,
16:25 Omri did evil in the *e*,
22:43 doing what was right in the *e*.
2 Chr 14: 2 was good and right in the *e*
16: 9 For the *e* run to and fro
29: 6 and done evil in the *e* our God;
Ps 34:15 The *e* are on the righteous,
Prov 5:21 ways of man are before the *e*,
15: 3 The *e* are in every place,
22:12 The *e* preserve knowledge, But
Isa 49: 5 I shall be glorious in the *e*,
Am 9: 8 the *e* GOD are on the sinful
Zech 4:10 of Zerubbabel. They are the *e*,
1 Pe 3:12 For the *e* are on the

EYESERVICE (2/2) EYE

Eph 6: 6 not with *e*, as men-pleasers,
Col 3:22 to the flesh, not with *e*,

EYEWITNESSES (2/2) WITNESS

Lk 1: 2 who from the beginning were *e*
2 Pe 1:16 but were *e* of His majesty.

EZBAI (1/1)

1 Chr 11:37 Carmelite, Naarai the son of *E*,

EZBON (2/2)

Gen 46:16 were Ziphion, Haggi, Shuni, *E*,
1 Chr 7: 7 The sons of Bela were *E*,

EZEKIAS (KJV) See HEZEKIAH

EZEKIEL (2/2)

Ezek 1: 3 the LORD came expressly to *E*
24:24 Thus *E* is a sign to you;

EZEL (1/1)

1 Sam 20:19 and remain by the stone *E*.

EZEM (3/3)

Josh 15:29 Baalah, Ijim, *E*,
19: 3 Hazar Shual, Balah, *E*,
1 Chr 4:29 Bilhah, *E*, Tolad,

EZER (10/10)

Gen 36:21 Dishon, *E*, and Dishan.
36:27 These were the sons of *E*:
36:30 Chief Dishon, Chief *E*,
1 Chr 1:38 Shobal, Zibeon, Anah, Dishon, *E*,
1:42 The sons of *E* were Bilhan,
4: 4 and *E* was the father of
7:21 and *E* and Elead. The men of
12: 9 *E* the first, Obadiah the second,
Neh 3:19 And next to him *E* the son of
12:42 Malchijah, Elam, and *E*.

EZION GEBER (7/7)

Num 33:35 from Abronah and camped at *E*.
33:36 They moved from *E* and camped in
Deut 2: 8 plain, away from Elath and *E*,
1 Ki 9:26 built a fleet of ships at *E*,
22:48 for the ships were wrecked at *E*.
2 Chr 8:17 Then Solomon went to *E* and
20:36 and they made the ships in *E*.

EZNITE (1/1)

2 Sam 23: 8 He was called Adino the *E*,

EZRA (26/26) AZARIAH

Ezra 7: 1 *E* the son of Seraiah, the son
7: 6 this *E* came up from Babylon;
7: 8 And *E* came to Jerusalem in the
7:10 For *E* had prepared his heart to
7:11 that King Artaxerxes gave *E*
7:12 To *E* the priest, a scribe of
7:21 that whatever *E* the priest, the
7:25 And you, *E*, according to
10: 1 Now while *E* was praying, and
10: 2 of Elam, spoke up and said to *E*,
10: 5 Then *E* arose, and made the
10: 6 Then *E* rose up from before the
10:10 Then *E* the priest stood up and
10:16 And *E* the priest, with certain
Neh 8: 1 and they told *E* the scribe to
8: 2 So *E* the priest brought the Law
8: 4 So *E* the scribe stood on a
8: 5 And *E* opened the book in the
8: 6 And *E* blessed the LORD, the
8: 9 *E* the priest and scribe, and
8:13 were gathered to *E* the scribe,
12: 1 Jeshua: Seraiah, Jeremiah, *E*,
12:13 of *E*, Meshullam;
12:26 and of *E* the priest, the
12:33 and Azariah, *E*, Meshullam,
12:36 *E* the scribe went before them.

EZRAH (1/1)

1 Chr 4:17 The sons of *E* were Jether,

EZRAHITE (3/3)

1 Ki 4:31 than all men—than Ethan the *E*,
Ps 88: A Contemplation of Heman the *E*.
89: A Contemplation of Ethan the *E*.

EZRI (1/1)

1 Chr 27:26 *E* the son of Chelub was over

F

FABLES (5/5)

1 Tim 1: 4 nor give heed to *f* and endless
4: 7 reject profane and old wives' *f*,
2 Tim 4: 4 truth, and be turned aside to *f*.
Titus 1:14 not giving heed to Jewish *f* and
2 Pe 1:16 not follow cunningly devised *f*

FABRIC (1/1)

Isa 19: 9 And those who weave fine *f*

FACE (390/351) FACED, FACES, FACING

Gen 1: 2 and darkness was on the *f* of
1: 2 of God was hovering over the *f*
1:20 above the earth across the *f*
1:29 yields seed which is on the *f*
2: 6 earth and watered the whole *f*
3:19 In the sweat of your *f* you
4:14 me out this day from the *f* of
4:14 I shall be hidden from Your *f*;
6: 1 men began to multiply on the *f*
6: 7 whom I have created from the *f*
7: 3 the species alive on the *f* of
7: 4 and I will destroy from the *f*
7:23 things which were on the *f* of
8: 8 waters had receded from the *f*
8: 9 for the waters were on the *f*
11: 4 be scattered abroad over the *f*
11: 8 abroad from there over the *f*
11: 9 them abroad over the *f* of all
17: 3 Then Abram fell on his *f*,
17:17 Then Abraham fell on his *f* and
19: 1 and he bowed himself with his *f*
19:13 has grown great before the *f*
30:40 and made the flocks *f* toward
32:20 and afterward I will see his *f*;
32:30 For I have seen God *f* to face,
32:30 "For I have seen God face to *f*,
33:10 inasmuch as I have seen your *f*
33:10 as though I had seen the *f* of
35: 1 to you when you fled from the *f*
35: 7 to him when he fled from the *f*
38:15 because she had covered her *f*.
41:56 The famine was over all the *f* of
43: 3 You shall not see my *f* unless
43: 5 You shall not see my *f* unless
43:31 Then he washed his *f* and came
44:23 you shall see my *f* no more.'
44:26 for we may not see the man's *f*
46:30 die, since I have seen your *f*,
48:11 had not thought to see your *f*;
48:12 and he bowed down with his *f* to
50: 1 Joseph fell on his father's *f*,
50:18 went and fell down before his *f*,
Ex 2:15 But Moses fled from the *f* of
3: 6 of Jacob." And Moses hid his *f*,
10: 5 And they shall cover the *f* of
10:15 For they covered the *f* of the
10:28 heed to yourself and see my *f*
10:28 For in the day you see my *f*
10:29 I will never see your *f*
14:25 Let us flee from the *f* of
25:20 and they shall *f* one another;
32:12 and to consume them from the *f*
33:11 So the LORD spoke to Moses *f* to
33:11 LORD spoke to Moses face to *f*,
33:16 the people who are upon the *f*
33:20 He said, "You cannot see My *f*;
33:23 but My *f* shall not be seen."
34:29 not know that the skin of his *f*
34:30 the skin of his *f* shone, and
34:33 them, he put a veil on his *f*.
34:35 children of Israel saw the *f*
34:35 that the skin of Moses' *f*
34:35 would put the veil on his *f*
Lev 17:10 I will set My *f* against that
20: 3 I will set My *f* against that
20: 5 then I will set My *f* against
20: 6 I will set My *f* against that
21:18 who has a marred *f* or any
26:17 I will set My *f* against you, and
Num 6:25 The LORD make His *f* shine upon
8: 3 he arranged the lamps to *f*
12: 3 all men who were on the *f* of
12: 8 I speak with him *f* to face,
12: 8 I speak with him face to *f*,
12:14 father had but spit in her *f*,
14:14 are seen *f* to face and Your
14:14 are seen face to *f* and Your
16: 4 heard it, he fell on his *f*;
22: 5 they cover the *f* of the earth,
22:11 and they cover the *f* of the
22:31 his head and fell flat on his *f*.
24: 1 but he set his *f* toward the
Deut 5: 4 The LORD talked with you *f* to
5: 4 talked with you face to *f* on
6:15 you and destroy you from the *f*
7: 6 above all the peoples on the *f*
7:10 those who hate Him to their *f*,
7:10 He will repay him to his *f*.
14: 2 the peoples who are on the *f*
25: 9 from his foot, spit in his *f*,
28: 7 to be defeated before your *f*;
31:17 and I will hide My *f* from them,
31:18 And I will surely hide My *f* in
32:20 I will hide My *f* from them, I
34:10 whom the LORD knew *f* to face,
34:10 whom the LORD knew face to *f*,
Josh 5:14 And Joshua fell on his *f* to
7: 6 and fell to the earth on his *f*
7:10 Why do you lie thus on your *f*?
Judg 6:22 seen the Angel of the LORD *f*
6:22 Angel of the LORD face to *f*.
Ruth 2:10 So she fell on her *f*,
1 Sam 1:18 and her *f* was no longer sad.
5: 3 fallen on its *f* to the earth
5: 4 fallen on its *f* to the ground
17:49 and he fell on his *f* to the
20:15 enemies of David from the *f* of
20:41 fell on his *f* to the ground,
24: 8 David stooped with his *f* to the
25:23 fell on her *f* before David, and

25:41 bowed her *f* to the earth, and
26:20 fall to the earth before the *f*
28:14 and he stooped with his *f* to
2 Sam 2:22 How then could I *f* your brother
3:13 you shall not see my *f* unless
3:13 when you come to see my *f*.
9: 6 he fell on his *f* and prostrated
14: 4 she fell on her *f* to the ground
14:22 fell to the ground on his *f*
14:24 but do not let him see my *f*.
14:24 but did not see the king's *f*.
14:28 but did not see the king's *f*.
14:32 let me see the king's *f*;
14:33 and bowed himself on his *f* to
18: 8 there was scattered over the *f*
18:28 Then he bowed down with his *f*
19: 4 But the king covered his *f*,
24:20 before the king with his *f* to
1 Ki 1:23 before the king with his *f* to
1:31 Bathsheba bowed with her *f* to
13:34 and destroy it from the *f* of
18: 7 him, and fell on his *f*,
18:42 and put his *f* between his
19:13 that he wrapped his *f* in his
21: 4 his bed, and turned away his *f*,
2 Ki 4:29 but lay my staff on the *f* of
4:31 and laid the staff on the *f* of
8:15 and spread it over his *f* so
12:17 then Hazael set his *f* to go up
13:14 to him, and wept over his *f*,
14: 8 let us *f* one another in
20: 2 Then he turned his *f* toward the
1 Chr 16:11 Seek His *f* evermore!
21:21 bowed before David with his *f*
2 Chr 6:42 do not turn away the *f* of Your
7:14 and pray and seek My *f*,
20:18 bowed his head with his *f* to
25:17 let us *f* one another in
30: 9 and will not turn His *f* from
35:22 Josiah would not turn his *f*
Ezra 9: 6 and humiliated to lift up my *f*
Neh 2: 2 Why is your *f* sad, since you
2: 3 live forever! Why should my *f*
Esth 7: 8 mouth, they covered Haman's *f*.
Job 1:11 surely curse You to Your *f*!"
2: 5 surely curse You to Your *f*!"
4:15 a spirit passed before my *f*;
6:28 I would never lie to your *f*.
9:27 I will put off my sad *f* and
11:15 surely you could lift up your *f*
13:24 Why do You hide Your *f*,
15:27 Though he has covered his *f* with
16: 8 me And bears witness to my *f*.
16:16 My *f* is flushed from weeping,
17: 6 I have become one in whose *f*
17:12 in the *f* of darkness.
21:31 Who condemns his way to his *f*?
22:26 And lift up your *f* to God.
23:17 hide deep darkness from my *f*.
24:15 And he disguises his *f*.
24:18 should be swift on the *f* of
26: 9 He covers the *f* of His throne,
26:10 a circular horizon on the *f* of
30:10 do not hesitate to spit in my *f*.
33:26 He shall see His *f* with joy,
34:29 And when He hides His *f*,
37:12 He commands them On the *f* of
41:14 can open the doors of his *f*,
Ps 5: 8 Your way straight before my *f*.
10:11 has forgotten; He hides His *f*;
13: 1 How long will You hide Your *f*
17:15 I will see Your *f* in
22:24 Nor has He hidden His *f* from
24: 6 who seek Him, Who seek Your *f*.
27: 8 When You said, "Seek My *f*,
27: 8 My heart said to You, "Your *f*,
27: 9 Do not hide Your *f* from me;
30: 7 stand strong; You hid Your *f*,
31:16 Make Your *f* shine upon Your
34:16 The *f* of the LORD is against
41:12 And set me before Your *f*
44:15 And the shame of my *f* has
44:24 Why do You hide Your *f*,
51: 9 Hide Your *f* from my sins, And
67: 1 And cause His *f* to shine upon
69: 7 Shame has covered my *f*.
69:17 And do not hide Your *f* from
80: 3 Cause Your *f* to shine, And we
80: 7 Cause Your *f* to shine, And we
80:19 Cause Your *f* to shine, And we
84: 9 And look upon the *f* of Your
88:14 Why do You hide Your *f* from
89:14 and truth go before Your *f*.
89:23 beat down his foes before his *f*,
102: 2 Do not hide Your *f* from me in
104:15 Oil to make his *f* shine, And
104:29 You hide Your *f*,
104:30 And You renew the *f* of the
105: 4 Seek His *f* evermore!
119:135 Make Your *f* shine upon Your
132:10 Do not turn away the *f* of Your
143: 7 Do not hide Your *f* from
Prov 7:13 With an impudent *f* she said to
7:15 you, Diligently to seek your *f*,
8:27 He drew a circle on the *f* of
16:15 In the light of the king's *f*
21:29 A wicked man hardens his *f*,
27:19 As in water *f* reflects face,
27:19 As in water face reflects *f*,
Eccl 8: 1 A man's wisdom makes his *f*
8: 1 And the sternness of his *f* is
Song 2:14 the cliff, Let me see your *f*,
2:14 And your *f* is lovely."
Isa 6: 2 with two he covered his *f*,
8:17 Who hides His *f* from the house
14:21 And fill the *f* of the world
16: 4 a shelter to them from the *f*
23:17 kingdoms of the world on the *f*
27: 6 And fill the *f* of the world
29:22 Nor shall his *f* now grow pale;
38: 2 Then Hezekiah turned his *f*
50: 6 I did not hide My *f* from shame
50: 7 Therefore I have set My *f* like
54: 8 a little wrath I hid My *f* from
59: 2 your sins have hidden His *f*
64: 7 For You have hidden Your *f*
65: 3 Me to anger continually to My *f*;
Jer 2:27 back to Me, and not their *f*.
8: 2 shall be like refuse on the *f*
13:26 uncover your skirts over your *f*,
16: 4 shall be like refuse on the *f*
16:17 they are not hidden from My *f*,
18:17 them the back and not the *f*
21:10 For I have set My *f* against this
22:25 the hand of those whose *f*
25:26 the world which are on the *f*
28:16 I will cast you from the *f* of
32: 4 and shall speak with him *f* to
32: 4 shall speak with him face to *f*,
32:31 remove it from before My *f*
32:33 to Me the back, and not the *f*;
33: 5 wickedness I have hidden My *f*
34: 3 he shall speak with you *f* to
34: 3 shall speak with you face to *f*,
44:11 I will set My *f* against you for
Lam 2:19 heart like water before the *f*
3:35 due a man Before the *f* of
4:16 The *f* of the LORD scattered
Ezek 1:10 each had the *f* of a man; each
1:10 each of the four had the *f* of a
1:10 each of the four had the *f* of
1:10 and each of the four had the *f*
1:28 when I saw it, I fell on my *f*,
3: 8 I have made your *f* strong
3:23 and I fell on my *f*.
4: 3 Set your *f* against it, and it
4: 7 you shall set your *f*
6: 2 set your *f* toward the mountains
7:18 Shame will be on every *f*,
7:22 I will turn My *f* from them,
9: 8 and I fell on my *f* and cried
10:14 the first *f* was the face of a
10:14 the first face was the *f* of a
10:14 the second *f* the face of a man,
10:14 the second face the *f* of a man,
10:14 the third the *f* of a lion, and
10:14 and the fourth the *f* of an
11:13 Then I fell on my *f* and cried
12: 6 you shall cover your *f*,
12:12 He shall cover his *f*,
13:17 set your *f* against the
14: 8 I will set My *f* against that man
15: 7 and I will set My *f* against
15: 7 when I set My *f* against them.
20:35 I will plead My case with you *f*
20:35 My case with you face to *f*.
20:46 set your *f* toward the south;
21: 2 set your *f* toward Jerusalem,
25: 2 set your *f* against the
28:21 set your *f* toward Sidon, and
29: 2 set your *f* against Pharaoh king
34: 6 was scattered over the whole *f*
35: 2 set your *f* against Mount Seir
38: 2 set your *f* against Gog, of the
38:18 My fury will show in My *f*.
38:20 and all men who are on the *f*
39:23 therefore I hid My *f* from them.
39:24 and hidden My *f* from them." '
39:29 And I will not hide My *f* from
41:14 the width of the eastern *f* of
41:19 so that the *f* of a man was
41:19 and the *f* of a young lion
43: 3 and I fell on my *f*.
43:17 and its steps *f* toward the
44: 4 the LORD; and I fell on my *f*.
46:19 of the priests which *f* toward
Dan 2:46 Nebuchadnezzar fell on his *f*,
3:19 and the expression on his *f*
8:17 I was afraid and fell on my *f*;
8:18 I was in a deep sleep with my *f*
9: 3 Then I set my *f* toward the Lord
9: 7 to You, but to us shame of *f*,
9: 8 Lord, to us belongs shame of *f*,
9:17 the Lord's sake cause Your *f*
10: 6 his *f* like the appearance of
10: 9 I was in a deep sleep on my *f*,
10: 9 with my *f* to the ground.
10:15 I turned my *f* toward the ground
11:17 He shall also set his *f* to enter
11:18 this he shall turn his *f*
11:19 Then he shall turn his *f* toward
Hos 5: 5 of Israel testifies to his *f*;
5:15 Then they will seek My *f*;
7: 2 They are before My *f*.
7:10 of Israel testifies to his *f*,
Joel 2:20 With his *f* toward the eastern
Am 5: 8 And pours them out on the *f*
9: 6 And pours them out on the *f* of
9: 8 I will destroy it from the *f*
Mic 3: 4 He will even hide His *f* from
Nah 2: 1 has come up before your *f*.
3: 5 lift your skirts over your *f*,
Zeph 1: 2 consume everything From the *f*
1: 3 I will cut off man from the *f*
Zech 5: 3 curse that goes out over the *f*
Mt 6:17 your head and wash your *f*,
11:10 My messenger before Your *f*,
16: 3 You know how to discern the *f*
17: 2 His *f* shone like the sun, and
18:10 their angels always see the *f*
26:39 farther and fell on His *f*,
26:67 Then they spat in His *f* and beat
Mk 1: 2 My messenger before Your *f*,
Lk 1:76 For you will go before the *f*
2:31 You have prepared before the *f*
5:12 and he fell on his *f* and
7:27 My messenger before Your *f*,
9:29 the appearance of His *f* was
9:51 that He steadfastly set His *f*
9:52 sent messengers before His *f*.
9:53 because His *f* was set for the
10: 1 them two by two before His *f*
12:56 You can discern the *f* of the
17:16 and fell down on his *f* at His
21:35 on all those who dwell on the *f*
22:64 they struck Him on the *f* and
Jn 11:44 and his *f* was wrapped with a
Acts 2:25 LORD always before my *f*,
6:15 saw his *f* as the face of an
6:15 saw his face as the *f* of an
7:45 God drove out before the *f* of
17:26 of men to dwell on all the *f*
20:25 will see my *f* no more.
20:38 that they would see his *f* no
25:16 accused meets the accusers *f*
25:16 meets the accusers face to *f*,
1 Cor 13:12 but then *f* to face. Now I know
13:12 dimly, but then face to *f*.
14:25 and so, falling down on his *f*,
2 Cor 3: 7 not look steadily at the *f* of
3:13 who put a veil over his *f* so
3:18 But we all, with unveiled *f*,
4: 6 of the glory of God in the *f*
11:20 if one strikes you on the *f*.
Gal 1:22 And I was unknown by *f* to the
2:11 I withstood him to his *f*,
Col 2: 1 as many as have not seen my *f*
1 Th 2:17 more eagerly to see your *f*
3:10 that we may see your *f* and
Jas 1:23 a man observing his natural *f*
1 Pe 3:12 But the *f* of the LORD
2 Jn 12 to come to you and speak *f* to
12 come to you and speak face to *f*,
3 Jn 14 and we shall speak *f* to face.
14 and we shall speak face to *f*.
Rev 4: 7 third living creature had a *f*
6:16 on us and hide us from the *f*
10: 1 his *f* was like the sun, and
20:11 from whose *f* the earth and the
22: 4 They shall see His *f*,

FACE TO FACE (14/14)

Gen 32:30 Peniel: "For I have seen God *f*,
Ex 33:11 So the LORD spoke to Moses *f*,
Num 12: 8 I speak with him *f*,
14:14 are seen *f* and Your cloud
Deut 5: 4 The LORD talked with you *f* on
34:10 Moses, whom the LORD knew *f*,
Judg 6:22 seen the Angel of the LORD *f*.
Jer 32: 4 and shall speak with him *f*,
34: 3 he shall speak with you *f*,
Ezek 20:35 I will plead My case with you *f*.
Acts 25:16 accused meets the accusers *f*,
1 Cor 13:12 in a mirror, dimly, but then *f*.
2 Jn 12 hope to come to you and speak *f*,
3 Jn 14 shortly, and we shall speak *f*.

FACED (13/13) FACE

Ex 37: 9 They *f* one another; the faces
1 Sam 14: 5 The front of one *f* northward
2 Ki 14:11 he and Amaziah king of Judah *f*
2 Chr 3:13 and they *f* inward.
25:21 he and Amaziah king of Judah *f*
Ezek 40: 6 he went to the gateway which *f*
40:17 thirty chambers *f* the pavement.
40:31 Its archways *f* the outer court,
40:34 Its archways *f* the outer court,
40:37 Its gateposts *f* the outer court,
41:12 The building that *f* the
42: 4 and their doors *f* north.
47: 1 for the front of the temple *f*

FACES (78/75) FACE

Gen 9:23 Their *f* were turned away, and
42: 6 down before him with their *f*
Ex 25:20 the *f* of the cherubim shall
37: 9 the *f* of the cherubim were
Lev 9:24 shouted and fell on their *f*.
Num 14: 5 Moses and Aaron fell on their *f*
16:22 Then they fell on their *f*,
16:45 And they fell on their *f*.
20: 6 and they fell on their *f*.
Josh 15: 2 from the bay that *f* southward.
Judg 13:20 they fell on their *f* to the
16: 3 to the top of the hill that *f*
1 Ki 18:39 saw it, they fell on their *f*;
1 Chr 12: 8 whose *f* were like the faces
12: 8 whose faces were like the *f*
21:16 in sackcloth, fell on their *f*.
2 Chr 7: 3 they bowed their *f* to the
29: 6 have turned their *f* away from
Neh 8: 6 the LORD with their *f* to the
Job 9:24 He covers the *f* of its judges.

40:13 Bind their *f* in hidden
Ps 21:12 on Your string toward their *f*.
34: 5 And their *f* were not ashamed.
83:16 Fill their *f* with shame, That
Isa 3:15 My people And grinding the *f*
13: 8 Their *f* will be like
25: 8 will wipe away tears from all *f*;
49:23 bow down to you with their *f*
53: 3 our *f* from Him; He was
Jer 1: 8 Do not be afraid of their *f*,
1:17 not be dismayed before their *f*,
5: 3 They have made their *f* harder
7:19 to the shame of their own *f*?
30: 6 And all *f* turned pale?
42:15 If you wholly set your *f* to
42:17 all the men who set their *f* to
44:12 of Judah who have set their *f*
50: 5 With their *f* toward it,
51:51 Shame has covered our *f*,
Ezek 1: 6 Each one had four *f*,
1: 8 and each of the four had *f* and
1:10 As for the likeness of their *f*,
1:11 Thus were their *f*.
1:15 living creature with its four *f*.
3: 8 face strong against their *f*,
8:16 temple of the LORD and their *f*
9: 2 which *f* north, each with his
10:14 Each one had four *f*:
10:21 Each one had four *f* and each one
10:22 And the likeness of their *f* was
10:22 faces was the same as the *f*
11: 1 which *f* eastward; and there at
14: 6 and turn your *f* away from all
20:47 and all *f* from the south to the
40:13 as door *f* door.
40:45 This chamber which *f* south is
40:46 The chamber which *f* north is
41:18 cherub. Each cherub had two *f*,
42:15 out through the gateway that *f*
43: 1 the gate that *f* toward the
43: 4 by way of the gate which *f*
44: 1 gate of the sanctuary which *f*
46: 1 of the inner court that *f*
46:12 the gate that *f* toward the east
47: 2 to the outer gateway that *f*
Dan 1:10 For why should he see your *f*
Joel 2: 6 All *f* are drained of color.
Nah 2:10 And all their *f* are drained of
Hab 1: 9 Their *f* are set like the east
Zech 14: 4 Which *f* Jerusalem on the east.
Mal 2: 3 And spread refuse on your *f*,
Mt 6:16 For they disfigure their *f* that
17: 6 they fell on their *f* and were
Lk 24: 5 were afraid and bowed their *f*
Rev 7:11 and fell on their *f* before the
9: 7 and their *f* were like the
9: 7 their faces were like the *f*
11:16 their thrones fell on their *f*

FACING (18/17) FACE

1 Ki 22:35 *f* the Syrians, and died at
2 Ki 2: 7 the prophets went and stood *f*
2 Chr 18:34 himself up in his chariot *f*
Esth 5: 1 *f* the entrance of the house.
Jer 1:13 and it is *f* away from the
Ezek 10:11 in the direction the head was *f*.
40:20 court was also a gateway *f*
40:22 measurements as the gateway *f*
40:24 and there a gateway was *f*
40:27 *f* south; and he measured from
40:32 me into the inner court *f* east;
40:44 one *f* south at the side of the
40:44 and the other *f* north at the
41:15 *f* the separating courtyard,
42: 2 *F* the length, which was one
42: 8 whereas that *f* the temple was
42:12 of the chambers that were *f*
Mk 4: 1 multitude was on the land *f*

FACT (21/21) FACTS

Gen 42:13 in the land of Canaan; and in *f*,
48:11 to see your face; but in *f*,
Ex 22:12 'But if, in *f*, it is stolen
Num 24:11 greatly honor you, but in *f*,
Josh 22:24 But in *f* we have done it for
Judg 21: 8 to the LORD?" And, in *f*,
21:19 Then they said, "In *f*,
Ruth 3: 2 is he not our relative? In *f*,
1 Sam 28: 7 servants said to him, "In *f*,
2 Sam 15:20 'In *f*, you came only
2 Ki 7: 2 thing be?" And he said, "In *f*,
7:19 And he had said, "In *f*,
Job 33:29 these things, Twice, in *f*,
Isa 58: 3 You take no notice?' "In *f*,
Ezek 17:18 and in *f* gave his hand and
46:21 corners of the court; and in *f*,
Lk 11:48 'In *f*, you bear witness
1 Cor 4: 3 you or by a human court. In *f*,
12:14 For in *f* the body is not one
15:15 if in *f* the dead do not rise.
1 Th 3: 4 For, in *f*, we told you

FACTION (1/1)

Ps 106:17 And covered the *f* of Abiram.

FACTIONS (1/1)

1 Cor 11:19 For there must also be *f* among

FACTS (1/1) FACT

Dan 7: 1 the dream, telling the main *f*.

FADE (7/7) FADES

2 Sam 22:46 The foreigners *f* away, And
Ps 18:45 The foreigners *f* away, And
Isa 64: 6 We all *f* as a leaf, And our
Jer 8:13 fig tree, And the leaf shall *f*;
Jas 1:11 So the rich man also will *f*
1 Pe 1: 4 undefiled and that does not *f*
5: 4 crown of glory that does not *f*

FADED (5/5)

Lev 13: 6 and indeed if the sore has *f*,
13:21 deeper than the skin, but has *f*,
13:26 deeper than the skin, but has *f*,
13:28 spread on the skin, but has *f*,
13:56 and indeed the plague has *f*

FADES (6/5) FADE

Job 14: 2 forth like a flower and *f* away;
Isa 1:30 be as a terebinth whose leaf *f*,
24: 4 The earth mourns and *f* away,
24: 4 The world languishes and *f*
40: 7 grass withers, the flower *f*,
40: 8 grass withers, the flower *f*,

FADING (2/2)

Isa 28: 1 glorious beauty is a *f* flower
28: 4 glorious beauty is a *f* flower

FAIL (52/52) FAILED, FAILING, FAILS, FAILURE

Deut 28:32 and your eyes shall look and *f*
Josh 3:10 and that He will without *f*
1 Sam 17:32 Let no man's heart *f* because of
20: 5 and I should not *f* to sit with
30: 8 overtake them and without *f*
2 Sam 3:29 and let there never *f* to be in
1 Ki 8:25 You shall not *f* to have a man
9: 5 You shall not *f* to have a man on
2 Chr 6:16 You shall not *f* to have a man
7:18 You shall not *f* to have a man
Ezra 4:22 heed now that you do not *f* to
6: 9 given them day by day without *f*,
Esth 9:27 that without *f* they should
9:28 days of Purim should not *f* to
Job 11:20 the eyes of the wicked will *f*,
17: 5 the eyes of his children will *f*.
31:16 the eyes of the widow to *f*,
Ps 69: 3 My eyes *f* while I wait for my
73:26 My flesh and my heart *f*;
89:33 Nor allow My faithfulness to *f*.
119:82 My eyes *f* from searching Your
119:123 My eyes *f* from seeking Your
Prov 22: 8 the rod of his anger will *f*.
Isa 19: 3 The spirit of Egypt will *f* in
19: 5 The waters will *f* from the
21:16 all the glory of Kedar will *f*;
32: 6 the drink of the thirsty to *f*.
32:10 For the vintage will *f*,
34:16 Not one of these shall *f*;
38:14 My eyes *f* from looking
41:17 Their tongues *f* for thirst.
42: 4 He will not *f* nor be
51:14 that his bread should not *f*.
57:16 For the spirit would *f* before
58:11 of water, whose waters do not *f*.
Jer 15:18 stream, As waters that *f*?
48:33 I have caused wine to *f* from
Lam 1:14 my neck. He made my strength *f*;
2:11 My eyes *f* with tears, My
3:22 Because His compassions *f* not.
Ezek 47:12 and their fruit will not *f*.
Hos 9: 2 And the new wine shall *f* in
Am 8: 4 make the poor of the land *f*,
Hab 3:17 the labor of the olive may *f*,
Mal 3:11 Nor shall the vine *f* to bear
Lk 12:33 in the heavens that does not *f*,
16: 9 mammon, that when you *f*,
16:17 for one tittle of the law to *f*.
22:32 that your faith should not *f*;
1 Cor 13: 8 are prophecies, they will *f*;
Heb 1:12 Your years will not *f*.
11:32 For the time would *f* me to tell

FAILED (14/12) FAIL

Gen 42:28 my sack!" Then their hearts *f*
47:15 So when the money *f* in the land
47:15 presence? For the money has *f*.
Josh 3:16 of the Arabah, the Salt Sea, *f*,
21:45 Not a word *f* of any good thing
23:14 souls that not one thing has *f* of
23:14 not one word of them has *f*.
1 Ki 8:56 There has not *f* one word of all
Job 19:14 My relatives have *f*,
Ps 77: 8 Has His promise *f*
142: 4 Refuge has *f* me; No one cares
Jer 14: 6 Their eyes *f* because there
51:30 strongholds; Their might has *f*,
Lam 4:17 Still our eyes *f* us, Watching

FAILING (3/3) FAIL

Deut 28:65 *f* eyes, and anguish of soul.
Neh 4:10 strength of the laborers is *f*,
Lk 21:26 men's hearts *f* them from fear

FAILS (14/14) FAIL

Ps 31:10 My strength *f* because of my
38:10 my strength *f* me; As for the
40:12 Therefore my heart *f* me.
71: 9 forsake me when my strength *f*.
143: 7 My spirit *f*! Do not hide Your
Eccl 12: 5 is a burden, And desire *f*.
Isa 15: 6 has withered away; The grass *f*,
24: 7 The new wine *f*, the vine
44:12 is hungry, and his strength *f*;
59:15 So truth *f*, And he who
Ezek 12:22 prolonged, and every vision *f*?
Joel 1:10 wine is dried up, The oil *f*.
Zeph 3: 5 justice to light; He never *f*,
1 Cor 13: 8 Love never *f*.

FAILURE (3/3) FAIL

Job 21:10 Their bull breeds without *f*;
Rom 11:12 and their *f* riches for the
1 Cor 6: 7 it is already an utter *f* for

FAIN (KJV) See DESPERATELY, GLADLY

FAINT (23/23) FAINTED, FAINTHEARTED, FAINTS

Deut 20: 3 Do not let your heart *f*,
20: 8 the heart of his brethren *f*
1 Sam 14:28 And the people were *f*.
14:31 So the people were very *f*.
2 Sam 16: 2 the wine for those who are *f*
21:15 and David grew *f*.
Prov 24:10 If you *f* in the day of
Isa 29: 8 he awakes, and indeed he is *f*,
40:30 Even the youths shall *f* and be
40:31 They shall walk and not *f*.
44:12 He drinks no water and is *f*.
Jer 8:18 My heart is *f* in me.
51:46 And lest your heart *f*,
Lam 1:13 has made me desolate And *f*
1:22 are many, And my heart is *f*.
2:11 children and the infants *F* in
2:19 Who *f* from hunger at the head
5:17 Because of this our heart is *f*;
Ezek 21: 7 be feeble, every spirit will *f*,
Am 8:13 And strong young men Shall *f*
Jon 4: 8 Jonah's head, so that he grew *f*.
Mt 15:32 lest they *f* on the way."
Mk 8: 3 they will *f* on the way;

FAINTED (5/5) FAINT

Ps 107: 5 Their soul *f* in them.
Isa 51:20 Your sons have *f*,
Jer 45: 3 I *f* in my sighing, and I find
Dan 8:27 *f* and was sick for days;
Jon 2: 7 When my soul *f* within me, I

FAINTHEARTED (6/6) FAINT

Deut 20: 8 there who is fearful and *f*?
Josh 2: 9 inhabitants of the land are *f*
2:24 of the country are *f* because
Isa 7: 4 do not fear or be *f* for these
Jer 49:23 heard bad news. They are *f*
1 Th 5:14 who are unruly, comfort the *f*,

FAINTNESS (1/1)

Lev 26:36 I will send *f* into their hearts

FAINTS (4/4) FAINT

Ps 84: 2 even *f* For the courts of the
119:81 My soul *f* for Your salvation,
Isa 1: 5 is sick, And the whole heart *f*.
40:28 Neither *f* nor is weary.

FAIR (25/18) FAIR-MINDED, FAIRER, FAIREST

Song 1:15 Behold, you are *f*,
1:15 you are *f*! You have dove's
2:10 my *f* one, And come away.
2:13 my *f* one, And come away!
4: 1 Behold, you are *f*,
4: 1 you are *f*! You have dove's
4: 7 You are all *f*, my love,
4:10 How *f* is your love, My sister,
6:10 *F* as the moon, Clear as the
7: 6 How *f* and how pleasant you are,
Jer 4:30 vain you will make yourself *f*;
Ezek 18:25 'The way of the Lord is not *f*.'
18:25 is it not My way which is *f*,
18:25 and your ways which are not *f*?
18:29 'The way of the Lord is not *f*.'
18:29 is it not My ways which are *f*,
18:29 and your ways which are not *f*?
33:17 'The way of the LORD is not *f*.'
33:17 it is their way which is not *f*!
33:20 'The way of the LORD is not *f*.'
Hos 10:11 But I harnessed her *f* neck, I
Am 8:13 In that day the *f* virgins And
Mt 16: 2 It will be *f* weather, for the
Acts 27: 8 we came to a place called *F*
Col 4: 1 bondservants what is just and *f*,

FAIR-MINDED (1/1) FAIR

Acts 17:11 These were more *f* than those in

FAIRER (1/1) FAIR

Ps 45: 2 You are *f* than the sons of men;

FAIREST (3/3) FAIR

Song 1: 8 O *f* among women, Follow in the
5: 9 O *f* among women? What is
6: 1 O *f* among women? Where has

FAIRS (KJV) See WARES

FAITH (245/229) FAITHFUL, FAITHLESS

Deut 32:20 Children in whom is no *f*.
Hab 2: 4 the just shall live by his *f*.
Mt 6:30 clothe you, O you of little *f*?
8:10 I have not found such great *f*,
8:26 you fearful, O you of little *f*?
9: 2 a bed. When Jesus saw their *f*,
9:22 your *f* has made you well."
9:29 According to your *f* let it be to
14:31 to him, "O you of little *f*,
15:28 great is your *f*! Let it be to
16: 8 to them, "O you of little *f*,
17:20 if you have *f* as a mustard
21:21 if you have *f* and do not doubt,
23:23 law: justice and mercy and *f*.
Mk 2: 5 When Jesus saw their *f*,
4:40 How is it that you have no *f*?
5:34 your *f* has made you well. Go in
10:52 your *f* has made you well."
11:22 Have *f* in God.
Lk 5:20 When He saw their *f*,
7: 9 I have not found such great *f*,
7:50 Your *f* has saved you. Go in
8:25 said to them, "Where is your *f*?
8:48 your *f* has made you well. Go in
12:28 clothe you, O you of little *f*?
17: 5 to the Lord, "Increase our *f*.
17: 6 If you have *f* as a mustard seed,
17:19 Your *f* has made you well."
18: 8 will He really find *f* on the
18:42 your *f* has made you well."
22:32 that your *f* should not fail;
Acts 3:16 through *f* in His name, has made
3:16 the *f* which comes through Him
6: 5 a man full of *f* and the Holy
6: 7 priests were obedient to the *f*.
6: 8 full of *f* and power, did great
11:24 of the Holy Spirit and of *f*.
13: 8 the proconsul away from the *f*.
14: 9 and seeing that he had *f* to be
14:22 them to continue in the *f*,
14:27 He had opened the door of *f* to
15: 9 purifying their hearts by *f*.
16: 5 were strengthened in the *f*,
20:21 repentance toward God and *f*
24:24 and heard him concerning the *f*
26:18 those who are sanctified by *f*
Rom 1: 5 for obedience to the *f* among
1: 8 that your *f* is spoken of
1:12 with you by the mutual *f* both
1:17 of God is revealed from *f* to
1:17 God is revealed from faith to *f*;
1:17 just shall live by *f*.
3:22 through *f* in Jesus Christ, to
3:25 by His blood, through *f*,
3:26 justifier of the one who has *f*
3:27 works? No, but by the law of *f*.
3:28 that a man is justified by *f*
3:30 justify the circumcised by *f*
3:30 and the uncircumcised through *f*.
3:31 make void the law through *f*?
4: 5 his *f* is accounted for
4: 9 For we say that *f* was accounted
4:11 of the righteousness of the *f*
4:12 also walk in the steps of the *f*
4:13 through the righteousness of *f*.
4:14 *f* is made void and the promise
4:16 Therefore it is of *f* that it
4:16 also to those who are of the *f*
4:19 And not being weak in *f*,
4:20 but was strengthened in *f*,
5: 1 having been justified by *f*,
5: 2 whom also we have access by *f*
9:30 even the righteousness of *f*;
9:32 they did not seek it by *f*,
10: 6 But the righteousness of *f*
10: 8 the word of *f* which we preach):
10:17 So then *f* comes by hearing, and
11:20 broken off, and you stand by *f*.
12: 3 to each one a measure of *f*.
12: 6 in proportion to our *f*;
14: 1 one who is weak in the *f*,
14:22 Do you have *f*?
14:23 he does not eat from *f*;
14:23 for whatever is not from *f* is
16:26 God, for obedience to the *f*—
1 Cor 2: 5 that your *f* should not be in the
12: 9 to another *f* by the same Spirit,
13: 2 and though I have all *f*,
13:13 And now abide *f*, hope, love,
15:14 preaching is empty and your *f*
15:17 your *f* is futile; you are
16:13 Watch, stand fast in the *f*,
2 Cor 1:24 we have dominion over your *f*,
1:24 for by *f* you stand.
4:13 we have the same spirit of *f*,
5: 7 For we walk by *f*, not by
8: 7 you abound in everything—in *f*,
10:15 that as your *f* is increased,
13: 5 to whether you are in the *f*.
Gal 1:23 us now preaches the *f* which he
2:16 the works of the law but by *f*
2:16 we might be justified by *f* in
2:20 live in the flesh I live by *f*
3: 2 the law, or by the hearing of *f*?
3: 5 the law, or by the hearing of *f*?
3: 7 that only those who are of *f*
3: 8 would justify the Gentiles by *f*,
3: 9 So then those who are of *f* are
3:11 just shall live by *f*.
3:12 Yet the law is not of *f*,
3:14 promise of the Spirit through *f*.
3:22 that the promise by *f* in Jesus
3:23 But before *f* came, we were kept
3:23 kept for the *f* which would
3:24 that we might be justified by *f*.
3:25 But after *f* has come, we are no
3:26 are all sons of God through *f*
5: 5 the hope of righteousness by *f*.
5: 6 but *f* working through love.
6:10 who are of the household of *f*.
Eph 1:15 after I heard of your *f* in the
2: 8 you have been saved through *f*,
3:12 with confidence through *f* in
3:17 dwell in your hearts through *f*;
4: 5 one Lord, one *f*, one baptism;
4:13 all come to the unity of the *f*
6:16 taking the shield of *f* with
6:23 the brethren, and love with *f*,
Phil 1:25 for your progress and joy of *f*,
1:27 striving together for the *f* of
2:17 sacrifice and service of your *f*,
3: 9 but that which is through *f* in
3: 9 which is from God by *f*;
Col 1: 4 since we heard of your *f* in
1:23 if indeed you continue in the *f*,
2: 5 the steadfastness of your *f* in
2: 7 in Him and established in the *f*,
2:12 raised with Him through *f* in
1 Th 1: 3 without ceasing your work of *f*,
1: 8 Your *f* toward God has gone out,
3: 2 encourage you concerning your *f*,
3: 5 it, I sent to know your *f*,
3: 6 brought us good news of your *f*
3: 7 concerning you by your *f*.
3:10 what is lacking in your *f*?
5: 8 on the breastplate of *f* and
2 Th 1: 3 because your *f* grows
1: 4 of God for your patience and *f*
1:11 His goodness and the work of *f*
3: 2 wicked men; for not all have *f*.
1 Tim 1: 2 To Timothy, a true son in the *f*:
1: 4 godly edification which is in *f*.
1: 5 conscience, and from sincere *f*,
1:14 with *f* and love which are in
1:19 having *f* and a good conscience,
1:19 concerning the *f* have suffered
2: 7 teacher of the Gentiles in *f*
2:15 if they continue in *f*,
3: 9 holding the mystery of the *f*
3:13 and great boldness in the *f*
4: 1 some will depart from the *f*,
4: 6 nourished in the words of *f* and
4:12 in love, in spirit, in *f*,
5: 8 he has denied the *f* and is
5:12 have cast off their first *f*.
6:10 some have strayed from the *f*
6:11 righteousness, godliness, *f*,
6:12 Fight the good fight of *f*,
6:21 have strayed concerning the *f*.
2 Tim 1: 5 to remembrance the genuine *f*
1:13 in *f* and love which are in
2:18 and they overthrow the *f* of
2:22 but pursue righteousness, *f*,
3: 8 disapproved concerning the *f*;
3:10 manner of life, purpose, *f*,
3:15 wise for salvation through *f*
4: 7 the race, I have kept the *f*.
Titus 1: 1 according to the *f* of God's
1: 4 a true son in our common *f*:
1:13 that they may be sound in the *f*,
2: 2 reverent, temperate, sound in *f*,
3:15 those who love us in the *f*.
Phm 1: 5 hearing of your love and *f* which
1: 6 that the sharing of your *f* may
Heb 4: 2 not being mixed with *f* in those
6: 1 from dead works and of *f*
6:12 but imitate those who through *f*
10:22 heart in full assurance of *f*,
10:38 the just shall live by *f*;
11: 1 Now *f* is the substance of things
11: 3 By *f* we understand that the
11: 4 By *f* Abel offered to God a more
11: 5 By *f* Enoch was taken away so
11: 6 But without *f* it is impossible
11: 7 By *f* Noah, being divinely warned
11: 7 which is according to *f*.
11: 8 By *f* Abraham obeyed when he was
11: 9 By *f* he dwelt in the land of
11:11 By *f* Sarah herself also received
11:13 These all died in *f*,
11:17 By *f* Abraham, when he was
11:20 By *f* Isaac blessed Jacob and
11:21 By *f* Jacob, when he was dying,
11:22 By *f* Joseph, when he was dying,
11:23 By *f* Moses, when he was born,
11:24 By *f* Moses, when he became of
11:27 By *f* he forsook Egypt, not
11:28 By *f* he kept the Passover and
11:29 By *f* they passed through the Red
11:30 By *f* the walls of Jericho fell
11:31 By *f* the harlot Rahab did not
11:33 who through *f* subdued kingdoms,
11:39 a good testimony through *f*,
12: 2 author and finisher of our *f*,
13: 7 whose *f* follow, considering the
Jas 1: 3 that the testing of your *f*
1: 6 But let him ask in *f*,
2: 1 do not hold the *f* of our Lord
2: 5 of this world to be rich in *f*
2:14 if someone says he has *f* but
2:14 Can *f* save him?
2:17 Thus also *f* by itself, if it
2:18 someone will say, "You have *f*,
2:18 Show me your *f* without your
2:18 and I will show you my *f* by my
2:20 that *f* without works is dead?
2:22 Do you see that *f* was working
2:22 and by works *f* was made
2:24 and not by *f* only.
2:26 so *f* without works is dead
5:15 And the prayer of *f* will save
1 Pe 1: 5 by the power of God through *f*
1: 7 that the genuineness of your *f*,
1: 9 receiving the end of your *f*—
1:21 so that your *f* and hope are in
5: 9 Resist him, steadfast in the *f*,
2 Pe 1: 1 have obtained like precious *f*
1: 5 add to your *f* virtue, to virtue
1 Jn 5: 4 has overcome the world—our *f*.
Jude 3 to contend earnestly for the *f*
20 up on your most holy *f*,
Rev 2:13 and did not deny My *f* even in
2:19 your works, love, service, *f*,
13:10 Here is the patience and the *f*
14:12 commandments of God and the *f*

F

FAITHFUL (85/81) FAITH, FAITHFULLY, FAITHFULNESS, UNFAITHFUL

Num 12: 7 He is *f* in all My house.
Deut 7: 9 the *f* God who keeps covenant
1 Sam 2:35 I will raise up for Myself a *f*
22:14 all your servants is as *f* as
2 Sam 20:19 among the peaceable and *f*
2 Chr 31:15 his *f* assistants in the cities
Neh 7: 2 for he was a *f* man and feared
9: 8 You found his heart *f* before
13:13 for they were considered *f*,
Ps 12: 1 godly man ceases! For the *f*
31:23 For the LORD preserves the *f*,
78: 8 And whose spirit was not *f* to
78:37 Nor were they *f* in His
89:37 Even like the *f* witness in
101: 6 My eyes shall be on the *f* of
119:86 All Your commandments are *f*;
119:138 Are righteous and very *f*.
Prov 11:13 But he who is of a *f* spirit
13:17 But a *f* ambassador brings
14: 5 A *f* witness does not lie, But
20: 6 But who can find a *f* man?
25:13 in time of harvest Is a *f*
27: 6 *F* are the wounds of a friend,
28:20 A *f* man will abound with
Isa 1:21 How the *f* city has become a
1:26 the *f* city."
8: 2 And I will take for Myself *f*
49: 7 Because of the LORD who is *f*,
Jer 42: 5 Let the LORD be a true and *f*
Dan 6: 4 or fault, because he was *f*;
Hos 11:12 with the Holy One who is *f*.
Mic 7: 2 The *f* man has perished from
Mt 24:45 Who then is a *f* and wise
25:21 good and *f* servant; you were
25:21 you were *f* over a few things, I
25:23 good and *f* servant; you have
25:23 you have been *f* over a few
Lk 12:42 Who then is that *f* and wise
16:10 He who is *f* in what is least
16:10 in what is least is *f* also
16:11 if you have not been *f* in the
16:12 And if you have not been *f* in
19:17 because you were *f* in a very
Acts 16:15 If you have judged me to be *f* to
1 Cor 1: 9 God is *f*, by whom you were
4: 2 in stewards that one be found *f*.
4:17 who is my beloved and *f* son in
10:13 is common to man; but God is *f*,
2 Cor 1:18 But as God is *f*,
Eph 1: 1 and *f* in Christ Jesus:
6:21 a beloved brother and *f*
Col 1: 2 To the saints and *f* brethren in
1: 7 who is a *f* minister of Christ
4: 7 *f* minister, and fellow servant
4: 9 a *f* and beloved brother, who is
1 Th 5:24 He who calls you is *f*,
2 Th 3: 3 But the Lord is *f*, who will
1 Tim 1:12 me, because He counted me *f*,
1:15 This is a *f* saying and worthy
3: 1 This is a *f* saying: If a man
3:11 temperate, *f* in all things.
4: 9 This is a *f* saying and worthy
2 Tim 2: 2 commit these to *f* men who will
2:11 This is a *f* saying: For if
2:13 we are faithless, He remains *f*;
Titus 1: 6 having *f* children not accused
1: 9 holding fast the *f* word as he
3: 8 This is a *f* saying, and these
Heb 2:17 He might be a merciful and *f*

3: 2 who was *f* to Him who appointed
3: 2 as Moses also was *f* in all
3: 5 And Moses indeed was *f* in all
10:23 for He who promised is *f*.
11:11 because she judged Him *f* who
1 Pe 4:19 as to a *f* Creator.
5:12 our *f* brother as I consider
1 Jn 1: 9 He is *f* and just to forgive us
Rev 1: 5 the *f* witness, the firstborn
2:10 Be *f* until death, and I will
2:13 days in which Antipas was My *f*
3:14 the *F* and True Witness, the
17:14 Him are called, chosen, and *f*.
19:11 He who sat on him was called *F*
21: 5 for these words are true and *f*.
22: 6 These words are *f* and true."

FAITHFULLY (10/10) FAITHFUL

2 Ki 12:15 to workmen, for they dealt *f*.
22: 7 their hand, because they deal *f*.
2 Chr 19: 9 *f* and with a loyal heart:
31:12 Then they *f* brought in the
34:12 And the men did the work *f*.
Neh 9:33 us; For You have dealt *f*,
Jer 23:28 word, let him speak My word *f*.
Ezek 18: 9 And kept My judgments *f*—
Joel 2:23 has given you the former rain *f*,
3 Jn 5 you do *f* whatever you do for

FAITHFULNESS (27/27) FAITHFUL

1 Sam 26:23 his righteousness and his *f*;
2 Chr 31:18 for in their *f* they sanctified
32: 1 After these deeds of *f*,
Ps 5: 9 For there is no *f* in their
36: 5 Your *f* reaches to the clouds.
37: 3 in the land, and feed on His *f*.
40:10 I have declared Your *f* and
71:22 I will praise you—And Your *f*,
88:11 Or Your *f* in the place of
89: 1 mouth will I make known Your *f*
89: 2 Your *f* You shall establish in
89: 5 Your *f* also in the assembly of
89: 8 Your *f* also surrounds You.
89:24 But My *f* and My mercy shall be
89:33 Nor allow My *f* to fail.
92: 2 And Your *f* every night,
98: 3 remembered His mercy and His *f*
119:75 And that in *f* You have
119:90 Your *f* endures to all
143: 1 to my supplications! In Your *f*
Isa 11: 5 And *f* the belt of His waist.
25: 1 Your counsels of old are *f*
Lam 3:23 Great is Your *f*.
Hos 2:20 I will betroth you to Me in *f*,
6: 4 For your *f* is like a morning
Rom 3: 3 Will their unbelief make the *f*
Gal 5:22 kindness, goodness, *f*,

FAITHLESS (5/5) FAITH

Prov 22:12 overthrows the words of the *f*.
Mt 17:17 O *f* and perverse generation, how
Mk 9:19 O *f* generation, how long shall I
Lk 9:41 O *f* and perverse generation, how
2 Tim 2:13 If we are *f*, He remains

FALCON (2/2)

Lev 11:14 and the *f* after its kind;
Deut 14:13 "the red kite, the *f*,

FALCON'S (1/1)

Job 28: 7 Nor has the *f* eye seen it.

FALL (225/213) FALLEN, FALLING, FALLS, FELL

Gen 2:21 God caused a deep sleep to *f*
43:18 make a case against us and *f*
49:17 So that its rider shall *f*
Ex 5: 3 lest He *f* upon us with
15:16 Fear and dread will *f* on them;
Lev 19:29 lest the land *f* into harlotry,
26: 7 and they shall *f* by the sword
26: 8 your enemies shall *f* by the
26:36 and they shall *f* when no one
Num 14: 3 brought us to this land to *f*
14:29 complained against Me shall *f*
14:32 your carcasses shall *f* in this
14:43 and you shall *f* by the sword;
34: 2 this is the land that shall *f*
Deut 22: 4 brother's donkey or his ox *f*
Josh 6: 5 the wall of the city will *f*
Judg 15:18 now shall I die of thirst and *f*
18:25 lest angry men *f* upon you, and
Ruth 2:16 let grain from the bundles *f*
1 Sam 3:19 and let none of his words *f* to
14:45 one hair of his head shall *f*
18:25 Saul thought to make David *f*
21:13 and let his saliva *f* down on
26:20 do not let my blood *f* to the
2 Sam 14:11 one hair of your son shall *f*
17:12 and we will *f* on him as the dew
24:14 Please let us *f* into the hand
24:14 but do not let me *f* into the
1 Ki 1:52 not one hair of him shall *f* to
22:20 that he may *f* at Ramoth
2 Ki 6: 6 of God said, "Where did it *f*?
10:10 Know now that nothing shall *f* to
14:10 with trouble so that you *f*—
19: 7 and I will cause him to *f* by
1 Chr 21:13 Please let me *f* into the hand
21:13 but do not let me *f* into the
2 Chr 18:19 that he may *f* at Ramoth
25: 8 God shall make you *f* before the
25:19 with trouble, that you should *f*—
Esth 6:13 before whom you have begun to *f*,
6:13 against him but will surely *f*
Job 13:11 And the dread of Him *f* upon
31:22 Then let my arm *f* from my
37: 6 *F* on the earth'; Likewise to
Ps 5:10 O God! Let them *f* by their own
9: 3 They shall *f* and perish at
10:10 That the helpless may *f* by his
35: 8 that very destruction let him *f*.
37:24 Though he *f*, he shall not
38:17 For I am ready to *f*,
45: 5 The peoples *f* under You.
63:10 They shall *f* by the sword;
72:11 all kings shall *f* down before
78:28 And He let them *f* in the midst
82: 7 And *f* like one of the
91: 7 A thousand may *f* at your side,
101: 3 I hate the work of those who *f*
118:13 me violently, that I might *f*,
139:11 Surely the darkness shall *f* on
140:10 Let burning coals *f* upon them;
141:10 Let the wicked *f* into their own
145:14 The LORD upholds all who *f*,
Prov 4:16 unless they make someone *f*.
10: 8 But a prating fool will *f*.
10:10 But a prating fool will *f*.
11: 5 But the wicked will *f* by his
11:14 is no counsel, the people *f*;
11:28 who trusts in his riches will *f*,
16:18 a haughty spirit before a *f*.
22:14 is abhorred by the LORD will *f*
24:16 For a righteous man may *f*
24:16 But the wicked shall *f* by
26:27 Whoever digs a pit will *f* into
28:10 He himself will *f* into his own
28:14 he who hardens his heart will *f*
28:18 in his ways will suddenly *f*.
29:16 the righteous will see their *f*.
Eccl 4:10 For if they *f*, one will lift
10: 8 He who digs a pit will *f* into
Isa 3:25 Your men shall *f* by the sword,
8:15 They shall *f* and be broken,
10: 4 And they shall *f* among the
10:34 And Lebanon will *f* by the
13:15 who is captured will *f* by the
22:25 removed and be cut down and *f*,
24:18 the noise of the fear Shall *f*
24:20 heavy upon it, And it will *f*,
28:13 That they might go and *f*
30:13 you Like a breach ready to *f*,
30:25 slaughter, When the towers *f*.
31: 3 hand, Both he who helps will *f*,
31: 3 And he who is helped will *f*
31: 8 Then Assyria shall *f* by a sword
34: 4 All their host shall *f* down
37: 7 and I will cause him to *f* by
40:30 the young men shall utterly *f*,
44:19 Shall I *f* down before a block
47:11 And trouble shall *f* upon you;
54:15 assembles against you shall *f*
60:14 those who despised you shall *f*
Jer 3:12 will not cause My anger to *f*
6:15 Therefore they shall *f* among
6:15 shall fall among those who *f*;
6:21 and the sons together shall *f*
8: 4 'Will they *f* and not rise?
8:12 Therefore they shall *f* among
8:12 shall fall among those who *f*;
9:22 the carcasses of men shall *f*
15: 8 cause anguish and terror to *f*
19: 7 and I will cause them to *f* by
20: 4 and they shall *f* by the sword
23:12 they shall be driven on And *f*
23:19 violent whirlwind! It will *f*
25:27 and vomit! *F* and rise no more,
25:34 You shall *f* like a precious
30:23 It will *f* violently on the
39:18 and you shall not *f* by the
44:12 shall all be consumed and *f*
46: 6 They will stumble and *f*
46:16 He made many *f*;
48:44 who flees from the fear shall *f*
49:21 shakes at the noise of their *f*;
49:26 her young men shall *f* in her
50:30 her young men shall *f* in the
50:32 most proud shall stumble and *f*,
51: 4 Thus the slain shall *f* in the
51:44 the wall of Babylon shall *f*.
51:47 And all her slain shall *f* in
51:49 the slain of Israel to *f*,
51:49 slain of all the earth shall *f*.
Ezek 5:12 and one-third shall *f* by the
6: 7 The slain shall *f* in your midst,
6:11 of Israel! For they shall *f* by
6:12 he who is near shall *f* by the
11:10 You shall *f* by the sword. I will
13:11 mortar, that it will *f*.
13:11 O great hailstones, shall *f*;
13:14 will be uncovered; it will *f*,
17:21 with all his troops shall *f* by
23:25 And your remnant shall *f* by
24:21 whom you left behind shall *f*
25:13 Dedan shall *f* by the sword.
26:11 and your strong pillars will *f*
26:15 shake at the sound of your *f*,
26:18 tremble on the day of your *f*;
27:27 Will *f* into the midst of the
27:34 and the entire company will *f*
29: 5 You shall *f* on the open field;
30: 4 When the slain *f* in Egypt,
30: 5 shall *f* with them by the
30: 6 who uphold Egypt shall *f*,
30: 6 Those within her shall *f* by
30:17 of Aven and Pi Beseth shall *f*
30:22 and I will make the sword *f* out
30:25 but the arms of Pharaoh shall *f*
31:16 shake at the sound of its *f*,
32:10 own life, in the day of your *f*.
32:12 will cause your multitude to *f*.
32:20 They shall *f* in the midst of
33:12 he shall not *f* because of it in
33:27 who are in the ruins shall *f*
35: 8 are slain by the sword shall *f*.
38:20 down, the steep places shall *f*,
38:20 and every wall shall *f* to the
39: 3 and cause the arrows to *f* out
39: 4 You shall *f* upon the mountains
39: 5 You shall *f* on the open field;
44:12 the house of Israel to *f* into
47:14 and this land shall *f* to you as
Dan 3: 5 you shall *f* down and worship
3: 6 and whoever does not *f* down and
3:10 shall *f* down and worship the
3:11 and whoever does not *f* down and
3:15 and you *f* down and worship the
11:14 of the vision, but they shall *f*.
11:19 but he shall stumble and *f*,
11:26 and many shall *f* down slain.
11:33 for many days they shall *f*
11:34 "Now when they *f*,
11:35 those of understanding shall *f*,
Hos 7:16 Their princes shall *f* by the
10: 8 And to the hills, "*F* on us!"
13:16 They shall *f* by the sword,
Am 3: 5 Will a bird *f* into a snare on
3:14 altar shall be cut off And *f*
7:17 sons and daughters shall *f* by
8:14 They shall *f* and
9: 9 not the smallest grain shall *f*
Mic 7: 8 over me, my enemy; When I *f*,
Nah 3:12 They *f* into the mouth of the
Mt 4: 9 I will give You if You will *f*
7:25 on that house; and it did not *f*,
7:27 it fell. And great was its *f*.
15:14 both will *f* into a ditch."
15:27 dogs eat the crumbs which *f*
24:29 the stars will *f* from heaven,
Mk 13:25 "the stars of heaven will *f*,
Lk 2:34 Child is destined for the *f*
6:39 Will they not both *f* into the
8:13 and in time of temptation *f*
10:18 I saw Satan *f* like lightning
21:24 And they will *f* by the edge of
23:30 *F* on us!" and to the
Acts 5:15 of Peter passing by might *f* on
27:32 of the skiff and let it *f* off.
27:34 since not a hair will *f* from
28: 6 he would swell up or suddenly *f*
Rom 3:23 for all have sinned and *f* short
11:11 stumbled that they should *f*?
11:11 But through their *f*,
11:12 Now if their *f* is riches for
14:13 block or a cause to *f* in our
1 Cor 10:12 he stands take heed lest he *f*.
1 Tim 3: 6 puffed up with pride he *f* into
3: 7 lest he *f* into reproach and the
6: 9 those who desire to be rich *f*
Heb 4:11 lest anyone *f* according to the
6: 6 if they *f* away, to renew them
10:31 It is a fearful thing to *f* into
12:15 carefully lest anyone *f* short
Jas 1: 2 count it all joy when you *f*
5:12 lest you *f* into judgment.
2 Pe 3:17 beware lest you also *f* from
Rev 4:10 the twenty-four elders *f* down
6:16 *F* on us and hide us from the

FALLEN (80/77) FALL

Gen 4: 6 And why has your countenance *f*?
Lev 13:40 for the man whose hair has *f*
13:41 He whose hair has *f* from his
Num 32:19 because our inheritance has *f*
Josh 2: 9 that the terror of you has *f* on
8:24 and when they all had *f* by the
Judg 3:25 *f* dead on the floor.
8:10 men who drew the sword had *f*.
18: 1 the tribes of Israel had not *f*
19:27 *f* at the door of the house
1 Sam 5: 3 *f* on its face to the earth
5: 4 *f* on its face to the ground
26:12 sleep from the LORD had *f* on
31: 8 Saul and his three sons *f* on
2 Sam 1: 4 many of the people are *f* and
1:10 could not live after he had *f*.
1:12 because they had *f* by the
1:19 How the mighty have *f*!
1:25 How the mighty have *f* in the
1:27 "How the mighty have *f*,
3:38 a prince and a great man has *f*
22:39 They have *f* under my feet.
2 Ki 2:13 the mantle of Elijah that had *f*
2:14 the mantle of Elijah that had *f*
1 Chr 10: 8 they found Saul and his sons *f*
2 Chr 20:24 *f* on the earth. No one had
29: 9 of this our fathers have *f* by
Esth 7: 8 Haman had *f* across the couch
Ps 7:15 And has *f* into the ditch

16: 6 The lines have *f* to me in
18:38 They have *f* under my feet.
20: 8 They have bowed down and *f*;
36:12 the workers of iniquity have *f*;
55: 4 the terrors of death have *f*
57: 6 of it they themselves have *f*.
69: 9 those who reproach You have *f*
105:38 For the fear of them had *f*
Isa 3: 8 stumbled, And Judah is *f*,
9: 8 And it has *f* on Israel.
9:10 The bricks have *f* down, But we
14:12 How you are *f* from heaven,
16: 9 For battle cries have *f* Over
21: 9 and said, "Babylon is *f*,
21: 9 is *f*! And all the carved
26:18 the inhabitants of the world *f*.
59:14 For truth is *f* in the street,
Jer 46:12 They both have *f* together."
48:32 The plunderer has *f* on your
50:15 hand, Her foundations have *f*,
51: 8 Babylon has suddenly *f* and been
Lam 2:21 and my young men Have *f* by
5:16 The crown has *f* from our head.
Ezek 13:12 "Surely, when the wall has *f*,
24: 6 piece, On which no lot has *f*.
31:12 its branches have *f* on the
32:22 them slain, *f* by the sword.
32:23 *f* by the sword, Who caused
32:24 *f* by the sword, Who have gone
32:27 with the mighty Who are *f*
Hos 7: 7 All their kings have *f*.
Am 5: 2 The virgin of Israel has *f*;
9:11 which has *f* down, And repair
Zech 11: 2 O cypress, for the cedar has *f*,
Mt 27:52 bodies of the saints who had *f*
Lk 14: 5 a donkey or an ox that has *f*
Acts 8:16 For as yet He had *f* upon none of
15:16 which has *f* down; I will
26:14 And when we all had *f* to the
1 Cor 15: 6 but some have *f* asleep.
15:18 Then also those who have *f*
15:20 of those who have *f* asleep.
Gal 5: 4 you have *f* from grace.
1 Th 4:13 concerning those who have *f*
Rev 2: 5 therefore from where you have *f*;
9: 1 And I saw a star *f* from heaven
14: 8 saying, "Babylon is *f*,
14: 8 "Babylon is fallen, is *f*,
17:10 also seven kings. Five have *f*,
18: 2 "Babylon the great is *f*,
18: 2 the great is fallen, is *f*,

FALLING (10/10) FALL

Ps 56:13 You not kept my feet from *f*,
116: 8 tears, And my feet from *f*.
Isa 34: 4 And as fruit *f* from a fig
Lk 8:47 and *f* down before Him, she
22:44 like great drops of blood *f*
Acts 1:18 and *f* headlong, he burst open
19:27 trade of ours in danger of *f*
28: 2 because of the rain that was *f*
1 Cor 14:25 *f* down on his face, he will
2 Th 2: 3 will not come unless the *f*

FALLOW (4/4)

Ex 23:11 you shall let it rest and lie *f*,
Prov 13:23 Much food is in the *f* ground
Jer 4: 3 Break up your *f* ground, And do
Hos 10:12 Break up your *f* ground, For

FALLOWDEER (KJV) See GAZELLES

FALLS (43/40) FALL

Ex 21:33 and an ox or a donkey *f* in it,
Lev 11:32 on which any of them *f*,
11:33 into which any of them *f* you
11:34 edible food upon which water *f*
11:35 part of any such carcass *f*
11:37 a part of any such carcass *f*
11:38 part of any such carcass *f*
25:35 and *f* into poverty among you,
Num 24: 4 Who *f* down, with eyes wide
24:16 Who *f* down, with eyes wide
33:54 shall be whatever *f* to him by
Deut 22: 8 on your household if anyone *f*
2 Sam 3:29 who leans on a staff or *f* by
3:34 As a man *f* before wicked men,
17:12 will fall on him as the dew *f*
Job 4:13 When deep sleep *f* on men,
14:18 But as a mountain *f* and
30:30 My skin grows black and *f* from
33:15 When deep sleep *f* upon men,
Prov 13:17 A wicked messenger *f* into
17:20 he who has a perverse tongue *f*
24:17 not rejoice when your enemy *f*,
Eccl 4:10 to him who is alone when he *f*,
9:12 When it *f* suddenly upon them.
11: 3 And if a tree *f* to the south
11: 3 In the place where the tree *f*,
Isa 34: 4 shall fall down As the leaf *f*
44:15 and *f* down to it.
44:17 He *f* down before it and
Mt 10:29 And not one of them *f* to the
12:11 and if it *f* into a pit on the
17:15 for he often *f* into the fire
21:44 And whoever *f* on this stone will
21:44 be broken; but on whomever it *f*,
Lk 11:17 divided against a house *f*.
15:12 me the portion of goods that *f*
20:18 Whoever *f* on that stone will be
20:18 be broken; but on whomever it *f*,
Jn 12:24 unless a grain of wheat *f* into
Rom 14: 4 his own master he stands or *f*.
Jas 1:11 withers the grass; its flower *f*,
1 Pe 1:24 And its flower *f* away,
Rev 11: 6 so that no rain *f* in the days

FALSE (68/63) FALSEHOOD, FALSELY, FALSIFYING

Ex 5: 9 and let them not regard *f*
20:16 You shall not bear *f* witness
23: 1 You shall not circulate a *f*
23: 7 Keep yourself far from a *f*
Deut 5:20 You shall not bear *f* witness
19:16 If a *f* witness rises against any
19:18 if the witness is a *f*
Job 36: 4 For truly my words are not *f*;
41: 9 hope of overcoming him is *f*;
Ps 27:12 For *f* witnesses have risen
119:104 Therefore I hate every *f* way.
119:128 I hate every *f* way.
120: 3 You *f* tongue?
Prov 6:19 A *f* witness who speaks lies,
12:17 But a *f* witness, deceit.
14: 5 But a *f* witness will utter
17: 4 An evildoer gives heed to *f*
19: 5 A *f* witness will not go
19: 9 A *f* witness will not go
21:28 A *f* witness shall perish, But
25:18 A man who bears *f* witness
Jer 8: 8 the *f* pen of the scribe
14:14 they prophesy to you a *f*
23:32 against those who prophesy *f*
37:14 *F*! I am not defecting to the
Lam 2:14 prophets have seen for you *F*
2:14 But have envisioned for you *f*
Ezek 12:24 no more shall there be any *f*
13: 6 have envisioned futility and *f*
13: 7 and have you not spoken *f*
21:23 it will be to them like a *f*
21:29 While they see *f* visions for
22:28 seeing *f* visions, and divining
Mic 2:11 If a man should walk in a *f*
Zech 8:17 And do not love a *f* oath.
10: 2 And tell *f* dreams; They
Mt 7:15 Beware of *f* prophets, who come
15:19 *f* witness, blasphemies.
19:18 You shall not bear *f*
24:11 Then many *f* prophets will rise
24:24 For *f* christs and false prophets
24:24 For false christs and *f* prophets
26:59 and all the council sought *f*
26:60 Even though many *f* witnesses
26:60 But at last two *f* witnesses
Mk 10:19 'Do not bear *f* witness,'
13:22 For *f* christs and false prophets
13:22 For false christs and *f* prophets
14:56 For many bore *f* witness against
14:57 Then some rose up and bore *f*
Lk 6:26 so did their fathers to the *f*
18:20 Do not bear *f* witness,'
19: 8 taken anything from anyone by *f*
Acts 6:13 They also set up *f* witnesses who
13: 6 a *f* prophet, a Jew whose name
Rom 13: 9 You shall not bear *f*
1 Cor 15:15 and we are found *f* witnesses of
2 Cor 11:13 For such are *f* apostles,
11:26 in perils among *f* brethren;
Gal 2: 4 this occurred because of *f*
Col 2:18 taking delight in *f* humility
2:23 *f* humility, and neglect of the
2 Pe 2: 1 But there were also *f* prophets
2: 1 even as there will be *f*
1 Jn 4: 1 because many *f* prophets have
Rev 16:13 and out of the mouth of the *f*
19:20 and with him the *f* prophet who
20:10 where the beast and the *f*

FALSEHOOD (17/17) FALSE

Job 21:34 Since *f* remains in your
31: 5 "If I have walked with *f*,
Ps 4: 2 love worthlessness And seek *f*?
5: 6 shall destroy those who speak *f*;
7:14 trouble and brings forth *f*.
119:78 treated me wrongfully with *f*;
119:118 For their deceit is *f*.
144: 8 hand is a right hand of *f*.
144:11 hand is a right hand of *f*—
Prov 30: 8 Remove *f* and lies far from me;
Isa 28:15 And under *f* we have hidden
57: 4 transgression, Offspring of *f*,
59:13 from the heart words of *f*.
Jer 8: 8 of the scribe certainly works *f*.
10:14 For his molded image is *f*,
13:25 forgotten Me And trusted in *f*.
51:17 For his molded image is *f*,

FALSELY (23/23) FALSE

Gen 21:23 by God that you will not deal *f*
Lev 6: 3 concerning it, and swears *f*—
6: 5 that about which he has sworn *f*.
19:11 shall not steal, nor deal *f*,
19:12 shall not swear by My name *f*,
Deut 19:18 who has testified *f* against his
2 Sam 18:13 I would have dealt *f*
Ps 44:17 Nor have we dealt *f* with Your
Prov 25:14 Whoever *f* boasts of giving Is
Jer 5: 2 lives,' Surely they swear *f*.
5:31 The prophets prophesy *f*,
6:13 the priest, Everyone deals *f*.
7: 9 commit adultery, swear *f*,
8:10 to the priest Everyone deals *f*.
29: 9 For they prophesy *f* to you in My
40:16 for you speak *f* concerning
43: 2 You speak *f*! The LORD our God
Hos 10: 4 Swearing *f* in making a
Zech 5: 4 house of the one who swears *f*
Mt 5:11 all kinds of evil against you *f*
5:33 of old, 'You shall not swear *f*,
Lk 3:14 intimidate anyone or accuse *f*,
1 Tim 6:20 and contradictions of what is *f*

FALSIFYING (1/1) FALSE

Am 8: 5 *F* the scales by deceit,

FALTER (1/1) FALTERS

1 Ki 18:21 How long will you *f* between two

FALTERS (1/1) FALTER

Prov 25:26 A righteous man who *f* before

FAME (20/20) FAMOUS

Num 14:15 which have heard of Your *f*
Josh 6:27 and his *f* spread throughout all
9: 9 for we have heard of His *f*,
1 Ki 4:31 and his *f* was in all the
10: 1 queen of Sheba heard of the *f*
10: 7 and prosperity exceed the *f* of
1 Chr 14:17 Then the *f* of David went out
2 Chr 9: 1 queen of Sheba heard of the *f*
9: 6 You exceed the *f* of which I
26: 8 His *f* spread as far as the
26:15 So his *f* spread far and wide,
Esth 9: 4 and his *f* spread throughout all
Ps 135:13 endures forever, Your *f*,
Isa 66:19 off who have not heard My *f*
Ezek 16:14 Your *f* went out among the
16:15 the harlot because of your *f*,
Zeph 3:19 appoint them for praise and *f*
3:20 For I will give you *f* and
Mt 4:24 Then His *f* went throughout all
Mk 1:28 And immediately His *f* spread

FAMILIAR (4/4) UNFAMILIAR

Lev 19:31 no regard to mediums and *f*
20: 6 who turns to mediums and *f*
20:27 or who has *f* spirits, shall
Ps 41: 9 Even my own *f* friend in whom I

FAMILIES (176/167) FAMILY

Gen 8:19 the earth, according to their *f*,
10: 5 language, according to their *f*,
10:18 Afterward the *f* of the
10:20 of Ham, according to their *f*,
10:31 of Shem, according to their *f*,
10:32 These were the *f* of the sons
12: 3 And in you all the *f* of the
28:14 you and in your seed all the *f*
36:40 according to their *f* and their
47:12 to the number in their *f*.
Ex 6:14 These are the *f* of Reuben.
6:15 These are the *f* of Simeon.
6:17 and Shimi according to their *f*.
6:19 These are the *f* of Levi
6:24 These are the *f* of the
6:25 Levites according to their *f*.
12:21 yourselves according to your *f*,
Lev 25:45 and their *f* who are with you,
Num 1: 2 children of Israel, by their *f*,
1:18 recited their ancestry by *f*,
1:20 their genealogies by their *f*,
1:22 their genealogies by their *f*,
1:24 their genealogies by their *f*,
1:26 their genealogies by their *f*,
1:28 their genealogies by their *f*,
1:30 their genealogies by their *f*,
1:32 their genealogies by their *f*,
1:34 their genealogies by their *f*,
1:36 their genealogies by their *f*,
1:38 their genealogies by their *f*,
1:40 their genealogies by their *f*,
1:42 their genealogies by their *f*,
3:15 fathers' houses, by their *f*;
3:18 the sons of Gershon by their *f*:
3:19 the sons of Kohath by their *f*:
3:20 the sons of Merari by their *f*:
3:20 These are the *f* of the Levites
3:21 these were the *f* of the
3:23 The *f* of the Gershonites were to
3:27 these were the *f* of the
3:29 The *f* of the children of Kohath
3:30 of the fathers' house of the *f*
3:33 these were the *f* of Merari.
3:35 of the fathers' house of the *f*
3:39 of the LORD, by their *f*,
4: 2 children of Levi, by their *f*,
4:18 not cut off the tribe of the *f*
4:22 fathers' house, by their *f*.
4:24 This is the service of the *f* of
4:28 This is the service of the *f* of
4:29 shall number them by their *f*
4:33 This is the service of the *f* of
4:34 of the Kohathites by their *f*
4:36 who were numbered by their *f*
4:37 who were numbered of the *f* of

4:38 by their *f* and by their
4:40 who were numbered by their *f*,
4:41 who were numbered of the *f* of
4:42 Those of the *f* of the sons of
4:42 who were numbered, by their *f*,
4:44 who were numbered by their *f*
4:45 who were numbered of the *f* of
4:46 by their *f* and by their
11:10 weeping throughout their *f*,
26: 7 These are the *f* of the
26:12 of Simeon according to their *f*
26:14 These are the *f* of the
26:15 of Gad according to their *f*
26:18 These are the *f* of the sons of
26:20 of Judah according to their *f*
26:22 These are the *f* of Judah
26:23 Issachar according to their *f*
26:25 These are the *f* of Issachar
26:26 of Zebulun according to their *f*
26:27 These are the *f* of the
26:28 of Joseph according to their *f*,
26:34 These are the *f* of Manasseh;
26:35 of Ephraim according to their *f*:
26:37 These are the *f* of the sons of
26:37 of Joseph according to their *f*.
26:38 Benjamin according to their *f*:
26:41 Benjamin according to their *f*;
26:42 of Dan according to their *f*:
26:42 These are the *f* of Dan
26:42 of Dan according to their *f*.
26:43 All the *f* of the Shuhamites,
26:44 of Asher according to their *f*
26:47 These are the *f* of the sons of
26:48 Naphtali according to their *f*
26:50 These are the *f* of Naphtali
26:50 Naphtali according to their *f*;
26:57 Levites according to their *f*:
26:58 These are the *f* of the Levites:
27: 1 from the *f* of Manasseh the son
33:54 as an inheritance among your *f*;
36: 1 Now the chief fathers of the *f*
36: 1 of the *f* of the sons of Joseph,
36:12 They were married into the *f* of
Josh 7:14 takes shall come according to *f*;
13:15 according to their *f*.
13:23 of Reuben according to their *f*,
13:24 of Gad according to their *f*.
13:28 of Gad according to their *f*,
13:29 Manasseh according to their *f*:
13:31 of Machir according to their *f*.
15: 1 of Judah according to their *f*:
15:12 all around according to their *f*.
15:20 of Judah according to their *f*:
16: 5 Ephraim, according to their *f*,
16: 8 of Ephraim according to their *f*.
17: 2 Manasseh according to their *f*:
17: 2 of Joseph according to their *f*.
18:11 came up according to their *f*,
18:20 around, according to their *f*.
18:21 Benjamin, according to their *f*,
18:28 Benjamin according to their *f*.
19: 1 of Simeon according to their *f*.
19: 8 of Simeon according to their *f*.
19:10 of Zebulun according to their *f*,
19:16 of Zebulun according to their *f*,
19:17 Issachar according to their *f*.
19:23 Issachar according to their *f*,
19:24 of Asher according to their *f*.
19:31 of Asher according to their *f*,
19:32 Naphtali according to their *f*.
19:39 Naphtali according to their *f*,
19:40 of Dan according to their *f*.
19:48 of Dan according to their *f*,
21: 4 Now the lot came out for the *f*
21: 5 ten cities by lot from the *f*
21: 6 cities by lot from the *f* of
21: 7 of Merari according to their *f*
21:10 one of the *f* of the Kohathites,
21:20 And the *f* of the children of
21:26 were for the rest of the *f* of
21:27 of the *f* of the Levites, from
21:33 according to their *f* were
21:34 And to the *f* of the children of
21:40 of Merari according to their *f*,
21:40 the rest of the *f* of the
1 Sam 9:21 family the least of all the *f*
10:21 to come near by their *f*,
1 Chr 2:52 and half of the *f* of
2:53 The *f* of Kirjath Jearim were
2:55 And the *f* of the scribes who
4: 2 These were the *f* of the
4: 8 and the *f* of Aharhel the son of
4:21 and the *f* of the house of the
4:27 nor did any of their *f* multiply
4:38 name were leaders in their *f*,
5: 7 And his brethren by their *f*,
6:19 Now these are the *f* of the
6:60 All their cities among their *f*
6:62 of Gershon, throughout their *f*,
6:63 of Merari, throughout their *f*,
6:66 Now some of the *f* of the sons
7: 5 their brethren among all the *f*
16:28 O *f* of the peoples, Give to
Neh 4:13 the people according to their *f*,
Job 31:34 And dreaded the contempt of *f*,
Ps 22:27 And all the *f* of the nations
68: 6 God sets the solitary in *f*;
96: 7 O *f* of the peoples, Give to
107:41 And makes their *f* like a
Jer 1:15 I am calling All the *f* of the
2: 4 O house of Jacob and all the *f*
10:25 And on the *f* who do not call
25: 9 I will send and take all the *f*
31: 1 will be the God of all the *f*
33:24 The two *f* which the LORD has
Ezek 20:32 like the *f* in other countries,
Am 3: 2 only have I known of all the *f*
Nah 3: 4 And *f* through her sorceries.
Zech 12:14 all the *f* that remain, every
14:17 be that whichever of the *f* of
Acts 3:25 in your seed all the *f*

FAMILY (145/99) FAMILIES

Gen 12: 1 From your *f* And from your
24: 4 go to my country and to my *f*,
24: 7 house and from the land of my *f*,
24:38 my father's house and to my *f*,
24:40 a wife for my son from my *f*
24:41 oath when you arrive among my *f*;
31: 3 of your fathers and to your *f*,
31:13 return to the land of your *f*.
32: 9 to your country and to your *f*,
43: 7 about ourselves and our *f*,
Lev 20: 5 that man and against his *f*;
25:10 of you shall return to his *f*.
25:41 shall return to his own *f*.
25:47 to a member of the stranger's *f*,
25:49 is near of kin to him in his *f*
Num 2:34 broke camp, each one by his *f*,
3:21 From Gershon came the *f* of the
3:21 of the Libnites and the *f* of
3:27 From Kohath came the *f* of the
3:27 the *f* of the Izharites, the
3:27 the *f* of the Hebronites, and
3:27 and the *f* of the Uzzielites;
3:33 From Merari came the *f* of the
3:33 of the Mahlites and the *f* of
26: 5 the *f* of the Hanochites; of
26: 5 the *f* of the Palluites;
26: 6 the *f* of the Hezronites; of
26: 6 the *f* of the Carmites.
26:12 the *f* of the Nemuelites; of
26:12 the *f* of the Jaminites; of
26:12 the *f* of the Jachinites;
26:13 the *f* of the Zarhites; of
26:13 the *f* of the Shaulites.
26:15 the *f* of the Zephonites; of
26:15 the *f* of the Haggites; of
26:15 the *f* of the Shunites;
26:16 the *f* of the Oznites; of Eri,
26:16 the *f* of the Erites;
26:17 the *f* of the Arodites; of
26:17 the *f* of the Arelites.
26:20 the *f* of the Shelanites; of
26:20 the *f* of the Parzites; of
26:20 the *f* of the Zarhites.
26:21 the *f* of the Hezronites; of
26:21 the *f* of the Hamulites.
26:23 the *f* of the Tolaites; of Puah,
26:23 the *f* of the Punites;
26:24 the *f* of the Jashubites; of
26:24 the *f* of the Shimronites.
26:26 the *f* of the Sardites; of Elon,
26:26 the *f* of the Elonites; of
26:26 the *f* of the Jahleelites.
26:29 the *f* of the Machirites; and
26:29 the *f* of the Gileadites.
26:30 the *f* of the Jeezerites; of
26:30 the *f* of the Helekites;
26:31 the *f* of the Asrielites; of
26:31 the *f* of the Shechemites;
26:32 the *f* of the Shemidaites; of
26:32 the *f* of the Hepherites.
26:35 the *f* of the Shuthalhites; of
26:35 the *f* of the Bachrites; of
26:35 the *f* of the Tahanites.
26:36 the *f* of the Eranites.
26:38 the *f* of the Belaites; of
26:38 the *f* of the Ashbelites; of
26:38 the *f* of the Ahiramites;
26:39 the *f* of the Shuphamites; of
26:39 the *f* of the Huphamites.
26:40 the *f* of the Ardites; of
26:40 the *f* of the Naamites.
26:42 the *f* of the Shuhamites. These
26:44 the *f* of the Jimnites; of
26:44 the *f* of the Jesuites; of
26:44 the *f* of the Beriites.
26:45 the *f* of the Heberites; of
26:45 the *f* of the Malchielites.
26:48 the *f* of the Jahzeelites; of
26:48 the *f* of the Gunites;
26:49 the *f* of the Jezerites; of
26:49 the *f* of the Shillemites.
26:57 the *f* of the Gershonites; of
26:57 the *f* of the Kohathites; of
26:57 the *f* of the Merarites.
26:58 the *f* of the Libnites, the
26:58 the *f* of the Hebronites, the
26:58 the *f* of the Mahlites, the
26:58 the *f* of the Mushites, and the
26:58 and the *f* of the Korathites.
27: 4 be removed from among his *f*
27:11 relative closest him in his *f*,
36: 6 may marry only within the *f* of
36: 8 be the wife of one of the *f* of
36:12 the tribe of their father's *f*.
Deut 25: 5 to a stranger outside the *f*;
29:18 be among you man or woman or *f*
Josh 7:14 and the *f* which the LORD takes
7:17 and he took the *f* of the
7:17 and he brought the *f* of the
Judg 1:25 they let the man and all his *f*
9: 1 with them and with all the *f*
13: 2 of the *f* of the Danites, whose
17: 7 of the *f* of Judah; he was a
18: 2 of Dan sent five men of their *f*
18:11 And six hundred men of the *f* of
18:19 be a priest to a tribe and a *f*
21:24 every man to his tribe and *f*;
Ruth 2: 1 of the *f* of Elimelech. His name
2: 3 who was of the *f* of Elimelech.
1 Sam 9:21 and my *f* the least of all the
10:21 the *f* of Matri was chosen.
18:18 is my life or my father's *f*
20: 6 sacrifice there for all the *f*.
20:29 for our *f* has a sacrifice in
2 Sam 14: 7 And now the whole *f* has risen up
16: 5 there was a man from the *f* of
2 Ki 25:25 son of Elishama, of the royal *f*,
1 Chr 6:54 of the *f* of the Kohathites:
6:61 To the rest of the *f* of the
6:70 for the rest of the *f* of the
6:71 From the *f* of the half-tribe of
13:14 ark of God remained with the *f*
Esth 2:10 not revealed her people or *f*,
2:20 Esther had not revealed her *f*
9:28 every generation, every *f*,
Job 32: 2 of the *f* of Ram, was aroused
Jer 3:14 from a city and two from a *f*,
8: 3 those who remain of this evil *f*,
29:32 the Nehelamite and his *f*:
36:31 "I will punish him, his *f*,
41: 1 of the royal *f* and of the
Am 3: 1 against the whole *f* which I
Mic 2: 3 against this *f* I am devising
Zech 12:12 every *f* by itself: the family
12:12 the *f* of the house of David by
12:12 the *f* of the house of Nathan by
12:13 the *f* of the house of Levi by
12:13 the *f* of Shimei by itself, and
12:14 every *f* by itself, and their
14:18 If the *f* of Egypt will not come
Acts 4: 6 and as many as were of the *f* of
7:13 and Joseph's *f* became known to
13:26 sons of the *f* of Abraham, and
16:33 immediately he and all his *f*
Eph 3:15 from whom the whole *f* in heaven

FAMINE (103/90) FAMINES

Gen 12:10 Now there was a *f* in the land,
12:10 for the *f* was severe in the
26: 1 There was a *f* in the land,
26: 1 besides the first *f* that was in
41:27 east wind are seven years of *f*.
41:30 after them seven years of *f*
41:30 and the *f* will deplete the
41:31 in the land because of the *f*
41:36 land for the seven years of *f*
41:36 may not perish during the *f*.
41:50 two sons before the years of *f*
41:54 and the seven years of *f* began
41:54 The *f* was in all lands, but in
41:56 The *f* was over all the face of
41:56 And the *f* became severe in the
41:57 because the *f* was severe in all
42: 5 for the *f* was in the land of
42:19 go and carry grain for the *f* of
42:33 take food for the *f* of your
43: 1 Now the *f* was severe in the
45: 6 For these two years the *f* has
45:11 are still five years of *f*.
47: 4 for the *f* is severe in the
47:13 for the *f* was very severe, so
47:13 languished because of the *f*.
47:20 because the *f* was severe upon
Ruth 1: 1 that there was a *f* in the land.
2 Sam 21: 1 Now there was a *f* in the days of
24:13 Shall seven years of *f* come to
1 Ki 8:37 When there is *f* in the land,
18: 2 and there was a severe *f* in
2 Ki 4:38 and there was a *f* in the
6:25 And there was a great *f* in
7: 4 the *f* is in the city, and we
8: 1 the LORD has called for a *f*,
25: 3 of the fourth month the *f* had
1 Chr 21:12 'either three years of *f*,
2 Chr 6:28 When there is *f* in the land,
20: 9 judgment, pestilence, or *f*—
32:11 yourselves over to die by *f*
Neh 5: 3 buy grain because of the *f*.
Job 5:20 In *f* He shall redeem you from
5:22 laugh at destruction and *f*,
30: 3 are gaunt from want and *f*,
Ps 33:19 And to keep them alive in *f*.
37:19 And in the days of *f* they
105:16 Moreover He called for a *f* in
Isa 14:30 I will kill your roots with *f*,
51:19 *f* and sword—By whom will I
Jer 5:12 Nor shall we see sword or *f*.
11:22 their daughters shall die by *f*;
14:12 them by the sword, by the *f*,
14:13 the sword, nor shall you have *f*,
14:15 Sword and *f* shall not be in this
14:15 By sword and *f* those prophets
14:16 of Jerusalem because of the *f*
14:18 those sick from *f*! Yes, both
15: 2 And such as are for the *f*,
15: 2 are for the famine, to the *f*;
16: 4 consumed by the sword and by *f*,
18:21 up their children to the *f*,
21: 7 and the sword and the *f*,
21: 9 shall die by the sword, by *f*,
24:10 I will send the sword, the *f*,

27: 8 LORD, 'with the sword, the *f*,
27:13 people, by the sword, by the *f*,
29:17 send on them the sword, the *f*,
29:18 them with the sword, with *f*,
32:24 because of the sword and *f* and
32:36 Babylon by the sword, by the *f*,
34:17 and to *f*! And I will deliver
38: 2 shall die by the sword, by *f*,
42:16 the *f* of which you were afraid
42:17 shall die by the sword, by *f*,
42:22 shall die by the sword, by *f*,
44:12 consumed by the sword and by *f*.
44:12 greatest, by the sword and by *f*;
44:13 Jerusalem, by the sword, by *f*,
44:18 consumed by the sword and by *f*.
44:27 consumed by the sword and by *f*,
52: 6 the *f* had become so severe in
Lam 5:10 Because of the fever of *f*.
Ezek 5:12 and be consumed with *f* in your
5:16 them the terrible arrows of *f*
5:16 I will increase the *f* upon you
5:17 So I will send against you *f* and
6:11 shall fall by the sword, by *f*,
6:12 is besieged shall die by the *f*.
7:15 And the pestilence and *f*
7:15 *F* and pestilence will devour
12:16 men from the sword, from *f*,
14:13 send *f* on it, and cut off man
14:21 the sword and *f* and wild beasts
36:29 and bring no *f* upon you.
36:30 again bear the reproach of *f*
Am 8:11 That I will send a *f* on the
8:11 Not a *f* of bread, Nor a
Lk 4:25 and there was a great *f*
15:14 there arose a severe *f* in that
Acts 7:11 Now a *f* and great trouble came
11:28 there was going to be a great *f*
Rom 8:35 distress, or persecution, or *f*,
Rev 18: 8 day—death and mourning and *f*.

FAMINES (3/3) FAMINE

Mt 24: 7 And there will be *f*,
Mk 13: 8 and there will be *f* and
Lk 21:11 and *f* and pestilences;

FAMISH (1/1)

Prov 10: 3 allow the righteous soul to *f*,

FAMISHED (2/2)

Gen 41:55 all the land of Egypt was *f*,
Isa 5:13 Their honorable men are *f*,

FAMOUS (7/7) FAME

Ruth 4:11 prosper in Ephrathah and be *f*
4:14 and may his name be *f* in
1 Chr 5:24 *f* men, and heads of their
12:30 *f* men throughout their father's
22: 5 *f* and glorious throughout all
Ps 136:18 And slew *f* kings, For His
Ezek 32:18 Her and the daughters of the *f*

FAN (5/5) UNFANNED

Isa 30:24 winnowed with the shovel and *f*.
Jer 4:11 Not to *f* or to cleanse—
15: 7 winnow them with a winnowing *f*
Mt 3:12 His winnowing *f* is in His hand,
Lk 3:17 His winnowing *f* is in His hand,

FANCIES (1/1)

Prov 1:31 to the full with their own *f*.

FANCY (1/1)

Ps 78:18 asking for the food of their *f*.

FANGS (4/4)

Job 29:17 I broke the *f* of the wicked,
Ps 58: 6 O God! Break out the *f* of the
Prov 30:14 And whose *f* are like knives,
Joel 1: 6 And he has the *f* of a fierce

FANNERS (KJV) See WINNOWERS

FANTASY (1/1)

Prov 21: 6 tongue Is the fleeting *f* of

FAR (293/280)

Gen 10:19 as *f* as Gaza; then as you go
10:19 as *f* as Lasha.
12: 6 as *f* as the terebinth tree of
13: 3 journey from the South as *f* as
13:12 pitched his tent even as *f* as
14: 6 as *f* as El Paran, which is by
14:14 and went in pursuit as *f* as
14:15 them and pursued them as *f* as
18:25 *F* be it from You to do such a
18:25 *f* be it from You! Shall not the
25:18 (They dwelt from Havilah as *f* as
44: 4 and were not yet *f* off,
44: 7 *F* be it from us that your
44:17 *F* be it from me that I should do
Ex 8:28 only you shall not go very *f*
23: 7 Keep yourself *f* from a false
26:22 For the *f* side of the
26:27 for the *f* side westward.
33: 7 *f* from the camp, and called it
36:32 of the tabernacle on the *f*
Num 9:10 or is *f* away on a journey, he
13:21 the Wilderness of Zin as *f* as
14:45 and drove them back as *f* as
21:24 as *f* as the people of Ammon;
21:26 his land from his hand as *f* as
21:30 Heshbon has perished as *f* as
21:30 Then we laid waste as *f* as
33:49 from Beth Jesimoth as *f* as the
Deut 1: 7 as *f* as the great river, the
2:23 who dwelt in villages as *f* as
2:36 as *f* as Gilead, there was not
3:10 as *f* as Salcah and Edrei,
3:14 as *f* as the border of the
3:16 I gave from Gilead as *f* as the
3:16 as *f* as the River Jabbok, the
3:17 from Chinnereth as *f* as the
4:49 east side of the Jordan as *f*
12:21 to put His name is too *f* from
13: 7 near to you or *f* off from you,
14:24 to put His name is too *f* from
20:15 the cities which are very *f*
29:22 foreigner who comes from a *f*
30:11 for you, nor is it *f* off.
34: 1 all the land of Gilead as *f* as
34: 2 all the land of Judah as *f* as
34: 3 of palm trees, as *f* as Zoar.
Josh 1: 4 and this Lebanon as *f* as the
3:16 and rose in a heap very *f* away
7: 5 from before the gate as *f* as
8: 4 Do not go very *f* from the city,
9: 6 We have come from a *f* country;
9: 9 From a very *f* country your
9:22 We are very *f* from you,' when
10:10 and struck them down as *f* as
10:11 from heaven on them as *f* as
10:41 them from Kadesh Barnea as *f*
10:41 even as *f* as Gibeon.
11:17 even as *f* as Baal Gad in the
12: 2 even as *f* as the River Jabbok,
12: 3 the Sea of Chinneroth as *f* as
12: 5 as *f* as the border of the
12: 7 in the Valley of Lebanon as *f*
13: 3 as *f* as the border of Ekron
13: 4 belongs to the Sidonians as *f*
13: 5 Gad below Mount Hermon as *f* as
13: 6 mountains from Lebanon as *f* as
13: 9 all the plain of Medeba as *f*
13:10 as *f* as the border of the
13:11 and all Bashan as *f* as Salcah;
13:25 the land of the Ammonites as *f*
13:27 as *f* as the edge of the Sea of
15: 5 border was the Salt Sea as *f*
15:47 as *f* as the Brook of Egypt and
16: 3 as *f* as the boundary of Lower
16: 5 side was Ataroth Addar as *f* as
19: 8 all around these cities as *f*
19:10 of their inheritance was as *f*
19:28 as *f* as Greater Sidon.
19:33 as *f* as Lakkum; it ended at the
22:29 *F* be it from us that we should
23: 4 as *f* as the Great Sea westward.
24:16 *F* be it from us that we should
Judg 4:16 the chariots and the army as *f*
5:11 *F* from the noise of the
6: 4 the produce of the earth as *f*
7:22 as *f* as the border of Abel
7:24 them the watering places as *f*
7:24 the watering places as *f* as
9:52 So Abimelech came as *f* as the
11:13 from the Arnon as *f* as the
11:16 through the wilderness as *f* as
11:33 defeated them from Aroer as *f*
18: 7 They were *f* from the
18:28 because it was *f* from Sidon,
19:11 and the day was *f* spent; and
20:43 easily trampled them down as *f*
1 Sam 2:30 *F* be it from Me; for those who
6:18 even as *f* as the large stone
7:11 and drove them back as *f* as
7:12 Thus *f* the LORD has helped
12:23 *f* be it from me that I should
17:52 pursued the Philistines as *f*
17:52 even as *f* as Gath and Ekron.
20: 9 *F* be it from you! For if I knew
22:15 *F* be it from me! Let not the
27: 8 even as *f* as the land of Egypt.
2 Sam 5:25 the Philistines from Geba as *f*
7:18 that You have brought me this *f*?
11:23 then we drove them back as *f* as
20: 2 from the Jordan as *f* as
20:20 *F* be it, far be it from me, that
20:20 *f* be it from me, that I should
23:17 *F* be it from me, O LORD, that I
24: 7 went out to South Judah as *f*
1 Ki 4:12 as *f* as the other side of
4:21 as *f* as the border of Egypt.
4:25 from Dan as *f* as Beersheba, all
8:41 but has come from a *f* country
8:46 land of the enemy, *f* or near;
12:30 worship before the one as *f*
19: 8 days and forty nights as *f* as
2 Ki 18: 8 as *f* as Gaza and its territory,
20:14 They came from a *f* country, from
1 Chr 4:33 were around these cities as *f*
4:39 as *f* as the east side of the
5: 8 as *f* as Nebo and Baal Meon.
5: 9 Eastward they settled as *f* as
5:11 in the land of Bashan as *f* as
7:28 as *f* as Ayyah and its towns;
11:19 *F* be it from me, O my God, that
12:40 from as *f* away as Issachar and
13: 5 from Shihor in Egypt to as *f* as
14:16 Philistines from Gibeon as *f*
17:16 that You have brought me this *f*?
18: 3 Hadadezer king of Zobah as *f*
2 Chr 6:32 but who comes from a *f* country
6:36 take them captive to a land *f*
9:26 as *f* as the border of Egypt.
26: 8 His fame spread as *f* as the
26:15 So his fame spread *f* and wide,
30:10 as *f* as Zebulun; but they
33:14 as *f* as the entrance of the
34: 6 as *f* as Naphtali and all
Ezra 6: 6 keep yourselves *f* from there.
Neh 3: 1 They built as *f* as the Tower of
3: 1 then as *f* as the Tower of
3: 8 they fortified Jerusalem as *f*
3:13 cubits of the wall as *f* as the
3:15 as *f* as the stairs that go down
3:16 made repairs as *f* as the
3:16 and as *f* as the House of the
3:24 even as *f* as the corner.
3:26 in Ophel made repairs as *f*
3:27 and as *f* as the wall of Ophel.
3:31 made repairs as *f* as the house
3:31 and as *f* as the upper room at
3:32 as *f* as the Sheep Gate, the
4:19 and we are separated *f* from one
12:37 as *f* as the Water Gate
12:38 the Tower of the Ovens as *f* as
12:39 as *f* as the Sheep Gate; and
Esth 4: 2 He went as *f* as the front of the
9:20 to all the Jews, near and *f*,
Job 5: 4 His sons are *f* from safety,
11:14 and you put it *f* away, And
13:21 Withdraw Your hand *f* from me,
19:13 He has removed my brothers *f*
21:16 The counsel of the wicked is *f*
22:18 the counsel of the wicked is *f*
22:23 You will remove iniquity *f*
27: 5 *F* be it from me That I should
28: 4 forgotten by feet They hang *f*
30:10 they keep *f* from me; They do
34:10 *F* be it from God to do
38:11 This *f* you may come, but no
Ps 10: 5 Your judgments are *f* above,
22: 1 Why are You so *f* from
22:11 Be not *f* from Me, For trouble
22:19 do not be *f* from Me; O My
35:22 O Lord, do not be *f* from me.
38:21 my God, be not *f* from me!
49:14 *f* from their dwelling.
55: 7 I would wander *f* off, And
71:12 do not be *f* from me; O my God,
73:27 those who are *f* from You shall
88: 8 put away my acquaintances *f*
88:18 one and friend You have put *f*
97: 9 You are exalted *f* above all
103:12 As *f* as the east is from the
103:12 So *f* has He removed our
107:41 *f* from affliction, And makes
109:17 so let it be *f* from him.
119:150 They are *f* from Your law.
119:155 Salvation is *f* from the
Prov 4:24 And put perverse lips *f* from
5: 8 Remove your way *f* from her,
15:29 The LORD is *f* from the
19: 7 much more do his friends go *f*
22: 5 who guards his soul will be *f*
22:15 of correction will drive it *f*
25:25 So is good news from a *f*
27:10 nearby than a brother *f* away.
30: 8 Remove falsehood and lies *f*
31:10 For her worth is *f* above
Eccl 7:23 But it was *f* from me.
7:24 As for that which is *f* off and
Isa 6:12 The LORD has removed men *f*
8: 9 all you from *f* countries.
10:30 Cause it to be heard as *f* as
13: 5 They come from a *f* country,
15: 4 voice shall be heard as *f* as
17:13 them and they will flee *f* away,
23: 7 Whose feet carried her *f* off
29:13 have removed their hearts *f*
29:15 deep to hide their counsel *f*
33:17 see the land that is very *f*
39: 3 They came to me from a *f*
46:11 from a *f* country. Indeed I
46:12 Who are *f* from righteousness:
46:13 it shall not be *f* off;
49:19 who swallowed you up will be *f*
54:14 You shall be *f* from
57: 9 You sent your messengers *f*
57:19 peace to him who is *f* off
59: 9 Therefore justice is *f* from
59:11 but it is *f* from us.
Jer 2: 5 That they have gone *f* from Me,
4:16 That watchers come from a *f*
6:20 And sweet cane from a *f*
8:19 of my people From a *f* country:
12: 2 are near in their mouth But *f*
25:26 *f* and near, one with another;
27:10 to remove you *f* from your land;
31:40 and all the fields as *f* as the
43: 7 And they went as *f* as
48:24 land of Moab, *F* or near.
48:47 Thus *f* is the judgment of
49:30 get *f* away! Dwell in the
51:64 Thus *f* are the words of
Lam 1:16 Is *f* from me. My children are
3:17 You have moved my soul *f* from

F

Ezek 6:12 He who is *f* off shall die by the
8: 6 to make Me go *f* away from My
11:15 'Get *f* away from the LORD;
11:16 Although I have cast them *f* off
12:27 and he prophesies of times *f*
16:29 your acts of harlotry as *f* as
22: 5 Those near and those *f* from
29:10 as *f* as the border of Ethiopia.
38: 6 house of Togarmah from the *f*
38:15 from your place out of the *f*
39: 2 bringing you up from the *f*
43: 9 the carcasses of their kings *f*
44:10 And the Levites who went *f* from
48:21 of the holy district as *f* as
48:21 the twenty-five thousand as *f*
Dan 9: 7 those near and those *f* off in
11: 2 and the fourth shall be *f*
Joel 2:20 But I will remove *f* from you the
3: 6 That you may remove them *f*
3: 8 To a people *f* off; For the
Am 6: 3 Woe to you who put *f* off the
Ob 20 land of the Canaanites As *f*
Mic 7:11 that day the decree shall go *f*
Zech 10: 9 they shall remember Me in *f*
Mt 15: 8 But their heart is *f*
16:22 '*F* be it from You, Lord;
21:33 vinedressers and went into a *f*
25:14 is like a man traveling to a *f*
Mk 6:35 When the day was now *f* spent,
7: 6 But their heart is *f*
12: 1 vinedressers and went into a *f*
12:34 You are not *f* from the kingdom
13:34 is like a man going to a *f*
Lk 7: 6 And when He was already not *f*
15:13 journeyed to a *f* country, and
19:12 certain nobleman went into a *f*
20: 9 and went into a *f* country for a
24:29 and the day is *f* spent."
24:50 And He led them out as *f* as
Jn 21: 8 boat (for they were not *f* from
Acts 11:19 over Stephen traveled as *f* as
11:22 sent out Barnabas to go as *f*
17:27 though He is not *f* from each
22:21 for I will send you *f* from here
28:15 they came to meet us as *f* as
Rom 13:12 The night is *f* spent, the day is
2 Cor 4:17 is working for us a *f* more
Eph 1:21 *f* above all principality and
2:13 Jesus you who once were *f* off
4:10 is also the One who ascended *f*
Phil 1:23 which is *f* better.
Heb 7:15 And it is yet *f* more evident if,

FAR-OFF (1/1)

Ps 65: 5 And of the *f* seas;

FARE (2/2) FARED

1 Sam 17:18 and see how your brothers *f*,
Jon 1: 3 to Tarshish; so he paid the *f*,

FARED (1/1) FARE

Lk 16:19 in purple and fine linen and *f*

FAREWELL (4/4)

Lk 9:61 let me first go and bid them *f*
Acts 15:29 from these, you will do well. *F*.
23:30 you the charges against him. *F*.
2 Cor 13:11 Finally, brethren, *f*.

FARM (1/1)

Mt 22: 5 their ways, one to his own *f*,

FARMER (6/6)

Gen 9:20 And Noah began to be a *f*,
Jer 51:23 I will break in pieces the *f*
Am 5:16 They shall call the *f* to
Zech 13: 5 'I am no prophet, I am a *f*;
2 Tim 2: 6 The hard-working *f* must be first
Jas 5: 7 See how the *f* waits for the

FARMERS (5/5)

2 Ki 25:12 the land as vinedressers and *f*.
2 Chr 26:10 he also had *f* and
Jer 31:24 *f* and those going out with
52:16 the land as vinedressers and *f*.
Joel 1:11 Be ashamed, you *f*,

FARMING (1/1)

Neh 10:37 receive the tithes in all our *f*

FARTHER (6/6)

Job 38:11 far you may come, but no *f*,
Mt 26:39 He went a little *f* and fell on
Mk 1:19 When He had gone a little *f* from
14:35 He went a little *f*, and fell
Lk 24:28 that He would have gone *f*.
Acts 27:28 when they had gone a little *f*,

FARTHEST (16/15)

Deut 30: 4 of you are driven out to the *f*
Josh 17:18 and its *f* extent shall be
Neh 1: 9 of you were cast out to the *f*
Ps 65: 8 They also who dwell in the *f*
Isa 7:18 for the fly That is in the *f*
14:13 of the congregation On the *f*
37:24 I will enter its *f* height, To
41: 9 And called from its *f* regions,
Jer 6:22 will be raised from the *f*
9:26 and all who are in the *f*
25:23 and all who are in the *f*
25:32 shall be raised up From the *f*
49:32 to all winds those in the *f*
50:26 Come against her from the *f*
Mk 13:27 from the *f* part of earth to the
13:27 part of earth to the *f* part of

FARTHING (KJV) See (COPPER) COIN, PENNY, QUADRANS

FASHION (2/2) FASHIONED, FASHIONS

Ezra 4: 8 to King Artaxerxes in this *f*:
Job 31:15 Did not the same One *f* us in

FASHIONED (7/7) FASHION

Ex 32: 4 and he *f* it with an engraving
Num 31:51 all the *f* ornaments.
2 Chr 3:10 *f* by carving, and overlaid them
Job 10: 8 Your hands have made me and *f*
Ps 119:73 hands have made me and *f* me;
139:16 The days *f* for me, When as
Isa 22:11 you have respect for Him who *f*

FASHIONING (1/1)

Jer 18:11 I am *f* a disaster and devising

FASHIONS (3/3) FASHION

Ps 33:15 He *f* their hearts individually;
Isa 44:12 *F* it with hammers, And works
44:13 He *f* it with a plane, He

FAST (81/72) FASTED, FASTEN, FASTING

Deut 4: 4 But you who held *f* to the LORD
10:20 and to Him you shall hold *f*,
11:22 and to hold *f* to Him—
13: 4 you shall serve Him and hold *f*
Josh 22: 5 to hold *f* to Him, and to serve
23: 8 but you shall hold *f* to the
Judg 4:21 for he was *f* asleep and weary.
2 Sam 12:23 now he is dead; why should I *f*?
1 Ki 21: 9 letters, saying, Proclaim a *f*,
21:12 They proclaimed a *f*,
2 Ki 6:32 and hold him *f* at the door. Is
18: 6 For he held *f* to the LORD;
2 Chr 20: 3 and proclaimed a *f* throughout
Ezra 8:21 Then I proclaimed a *f* there at
Esth 4:16 and *f* for me; neither eat nor
4:16 My maids and I will *f* likewise.
Job 2: 3 And still he holds *f* to his
2: 9 Do you still hold *f* to your
8:15 does not stand. He holds it *f*,
23:11 My foot has held *f* to His
27: 6 My righteousness I hold *f*,
Ps 33: 9 He commanded, and it stood *f*.
111: 8 They stand *f* forever and ever,
Isa 56: 4 And hold *f* My covenant,
56: 6 And holds *f* My covenant—
58: 3 in the day of your *f* you find
58: 4 Indeed you *f* for strife and
58: 4 You will not *f* as you do
58: 5 Is it a *f* that I have chosen,
58: 5 Would you call this a *f*,
58: 6 Is this not the *f* that I have
Jer 8: 5 They hold *f* to deceit, They
14:12 'When they *f*, I will not
36: 9 that they proclaimed a *f*
46:14 Stand *f* and prepare yourselves,
50:33 them captive have held them *f*;
Joel 1:14 Consecrate a *f*, Call a
2:15 in Zion, Consecrate a *f*,
Jon 1: 5 lain down, and was *f* asleep.
3: 5 believed God, proclaimed a *f*,
Zech 7: 3 I weep in the fifth month and *f*
7: 5 did you really *f* for Me—for Me?
8:19 The *f* of the fourth month, The
8:19 The *f* of the fifth, The fast
8:19 The *f* of the seventh, And the
8:19 And the *f* of the tenth, Shall
Mt 6:16 "Moreover, when you *f*,
6:17 "But you, when you *f*,
9:14 Why do we and the Pharisees *f*
9:14 but Your disciples do not *f*?
9:15 from them, and then they will *f*.
Mk 2:18 of John and of the Pharisees *f*,
2:18 but Your disciples do not *f*?
2:19 the friends of the bridegroom *f*
2:19 with them they cannot *f*.
2:20 and then they will *f* in those
Lk 5:33 do the disciples of John *f*
5:34 the friends of the bridegroom *f*
5:35 then they will *f* in those
18:12 I *f* twice a week; I give tithes
Acts 27: 9 was now dangerous because the *F*
27:41 and the prow stuck *f* and
1 Cor 15: 2 if you hold *f* that word which I
16:13 stand *f* in the faith, be brave,
Gal 5: 1 Stand *f* therefore in the liberty
Phil 1:27 that you stand *f* in one spirit,
2:16 holding *f* the word of life, so
4: 1 so stand *f* in the Lord,
Col 2:19 and not holding *f* to the Head,
1 Th 3: 8 if you stand *f* in the Lord.
5:21 hold *f* what is good.
2 Th 2:15 stand *f* and hold the traditions
2 Tim 1:13 Hold *f* the pattern of sound
Titus 1: 9 holding *f* the faithful word as
Heb 3: 6 house we are if we hold *f* the
4:14 let us hold *f* our confession.
10:23 Let us hold *f* the confession of
Rev 2:13 And you hold *f* to My name, and
2:25 But hold *f* what you have till I
3: 3 hold *f* and repent. Therefore if
3:11 I am coming quickly! Hold *f*

FASTED (15/15) FAST

Judg 20:26 there before the LORD and *f*
1 Sam 7: 6 And they *f* that day, and said
31:13 and *f* seven days.
2 Sam 1:12 And they mourned and wept and *f*
12:16 and David *f* and went in and lay
12:21 You *f* and wept for the child
12:22 I *f* and wept; for I said, 'Who
1 Ki 21:27 and *f* and lay in sackcloth, and
1 Chr 10:12 and *f* seven days.
Ezra 8:23 So we *f* and entreated our God
Isa 58: 3 'Why have we *f*,' they say,
Zech 7: 5 When you *f* and mourned in the
Mt 4: 2 And when He had *f* forty days and
Acts 13: 2 ministered to the Lord and *f*,
13: 3 having *f* and prayed, and laid

FASTEN (5/5)

Ex 28:14 and *f* the braided chains to the
28:25 braided chains you shall *f* to
39:31 to *f* it above on the turban,
Isa 22:23 I will *f* him as a peg in a
Jer 10: 4 They *f* it with nails and

FASTENED (18/18) FAST

Ex 39:18 the two braided chains they *f*
40:18 *f* its sockets, set up its
Num 19:15 which has no cover *f* on it, is
Judg 3:16 and a cubit in length) and *f*
1 Sam 17:39 David *f* his sword to his armor
31:10 and they *f* his body to the wall
2 Sam 20: 8 it was a belt with a sword *f*
1 Ki 6: 6 support beams would not be *f*
1 Chr 10:10 and *f* his head in the temple of
2 Chr 9:18 which were *f* to the throne;
Esth 1: 6 and blue linen curtains *f*
Job 38: 6 To what were its foundations *f*?
Isa 22:25 the peg that is *f* in the secure
41: 7 Then he *f* it with pegs, That
Ezek 40:43 *f* all around; and the flesh of
41: 6 but not *f* to the wall of the
Acts 16:24 into the inner prison and *f*
28: 3 and *f* on his hand.

FASTING (20/20) FAST, FASTINGS

Ezra 9: 5 sacrifice I arose from my *f*;
Neh 1: 4 I was *f* and praying before the
9: 1 of Israel were assembled with *f*,
Esth 4: 3 mourning among the Jews, with *f*,
9:31 concerning matters of their *f*
Ps 35:13 I humbled myself with *f*;
69:10 and chastened my soul with *f*,
109:24 My knees are weak through *f*,
Jer 36: 6 LORD's house on the day of *f*.
Dan 6:18 palace and spent the night *f*;
9: 3 and supplications, with *f*,
Joel 2:12 Me with all your heart, With *f*,
Mt 6:16 they may appear to men to be *f*.
6:18 do not appear to men to be *f*,
17:21 go out except by prayer and *f*.
Mk 2:18 and of the Pharisees were *f*.
9:29 out by nothing but prayer and *f*.
Acts 10:30 Four days ago I was *f* until this
14:23 every church, and prayed with *f*,
1 Cor 7: 5 you may give yourselves to *f*

FASTINGS (3/3) FASTING

Lk 2:37 but served God with *f* and
2 Cor 6: 5 labors, in sleeplessness, in *f*;
11:27 in *f* often, in cold and

FAT (110/85) FATNESS, FATTED, FATTENED, FATTER, FATTY

Gen 4: 4 of his flock and of their *f*.
41: 2 seven cows, fine looking and *f*;
41: 4 up the seven fine looking and *f*
41:18 the river, fine looking and *f*;
41:20 the first seven, the *f* cows.
45:18 and you will eat the *f* of the
Ex 23:18 nor shall the *f* of My sacrifice
29:13 And you shall take all the *f*
29:13 and the two kidneys and the *f*
29:22 Also you shall take the *f* of the
29:22 the *f* tail, the fat that covers
29:22 the *f* that covers the entrails,
29:22 the two kidneys and the *f* on
Lev 1: 8 and the *f* in order on the wood
1:12 pieces, with its head and its *f*;
3: 3 The *f* that covers the entrails
3: 3 the entrails and all the *f*
3: 4 the two kidneys and the *f* that
3: 9 its *f* and the whole fat tail
3: 9 its fat and the whole *f* tail
3: 9 And the *f* that covers the
3: 9 the entrails and all the *f*

3:10 the two kidneys and the *f* that
3:14 The *f* that covers the entrails
3:14 the entrails and all the *f*
3:15 the two kidneys and the *f* that
3:16 all the *f* is the LORD's.
3:17 you shall eat neither *f* nor
4: 8 shall take from it all the *f*
4: 8 The *f* that covers the entrails
4: 8 the entrails and all the *f*
4: 9 the two kidneys and the *f* that
4:19 He shall take all the *f* from it
4:26 And he shall burn all its *f* on
4:26 like the *f* of the sacrifice of
4:31 'He shall remove all its *f*,
4:31 as *f* is removed from the
4:35 'He shall remove all its *f*,
4:35 as the *f* of the lamb is removed
6:12 and he shall burn on it the *f*
7: 3 shall offer from it all its *f*.
7: 3 The *f* tail and the fat that
7: 3 The fat tail and the *f* that
7: 4 the two kidneys and the *f* that
7:23 'You shall not eat any *f*,
7:24 And the *f* of an animal that dies
7:24 and the *f* of what is torn by
7:25 For whoever eats the *f* of the
7:30 The *f* with the breast he shall
7:31 the priest shall burn the *f* on
7:33 of the peace offering and the *f*,
8:16 Then he took all the *f* that was
8:16 the two kidneys with their *f*,
8:20 the head, the pieces, and the *f*.
8:25 Then he took the *f* and the fat
8:25 Then he took the fat and the *f*
8:25 all the *f* that was on the
8:25 the two kidneys and their *f*,
8:26 and put them on the *f* and on
9:10 But the *f*, the kidneys, and
9:19 and the *f* from the bull and the
9:20 and they put the *f* on the
9:20 Then he burned the *f* on the
9:24 the burnt offering and the *f*
10:15 bring with the offerings of *f*
16:25 The *f* of the sin offering he
17: 6 and burn the *f* for a sweet
Num 18:17 and burn their *f* as an
Deut 31:20 filled themselves and grown *f*,
32:14 With *f* of lambs; And rams of
32:15 But Jeshurun grew *f* and kicked;
32:15 fat and kicked; You grew *f*,
32:38 Who ate the *f* of their
Judg 3:17 (Now Eglon was a very *f* man.)
3:22 and the *f* closed over the
1 Sam 2:15 Also, before they burned the *f*,
2:16 They should really burn the *f*
2:29 to make yourselves *f* with the
15:22 And to heed than the *f* of
2 Sam 1:22 From the *f* of the mighty,
1 Ki 8:64 and the *f* of the peace
8:64 and the *f* of the peace
2 Chr 7: 7 burnt offerings and the *f* of
7: 7 the grain offerings, and the *f*.
29:35 with the *f* of the peace
35:14 offering burnt offerings and *f*
Neh 8:10 them, "Go your way, eat the *f*,
9:25 ate and were filled and grew *f*,
Job 15:27 made his waist heavy with *f*,
Ps 17:10 They have closed up their *f*
66:15 offer You burnt sacrifices of *f*
119:70 Their heart is as *f* as grease,
Isa 1:11 offerings of rams And the *f*
5:17 in the waste places of the *f*
10:16 send leanness among his *f* ones;
25: 6 Of *f* things full of marrow,
30:23 It will be *f* and plentiful.
34: 6 With the *f* of the kidneys of
43:24 you satisfied Me with the *f* of
Jer 5:28 They have grown *f*,
46:21 are in her midst like *f* bulls,
50:11 Because you have grown *f* like
Ezek 34: 3 You eat the *f* and clothe
34:16 but I will destroy the *f* and
34:20 will judge between the *f* and
39:19 You shall eat *f* till you are
44: 7 the *f* and the blood, then they
44:15 before Me to offer to Me the *f*
Zech 11:16 he will eat the flesh of the *f*
Mal 4: 2 you shall go out And grow *f*

FATE (2/2)

Num 16:29 are visited by the common *f* of
Ps 81:15 But their *f* would endure

FATFLESHED (KJV) See FAT (LOOKING)

FATHER (943/820) FATHER-IN-LAW, FATHER'S, FATHERED, FATHERLESS, FATHERS, GRANDFATHER

Gen 2:24 a man shall leave his *f* and
4:20 He was the *f* of those who dwell
4:21 He was the *f* of all those who
9:18 And Ham was the *f* of Canaan.
9:22 the *f* of Canaan, saw the
9:22 saw the nakedness of his *f*,
9:23 the nakedness of their *f*.
10:21 the *f* of all the children of
11:28 And Haran died before his *f*
11:29 the daughter of Haran the *f* of
11:29 the father of Milcah and the *f*
17: 4 and you shall be a *f* of many
17: 5 for I have made you a *f* of many
19:31 Our *f* is old, and there is no
19:32 let us make our *f* drink wine,
19:32 preserve the lineage of our *f*.
19:33 So they made their *f* drink wine
19:33 went in and lay with her *f*,
19:34 Indeed I lay with my *f* last
19:34 preserve the lineage of our *f*.
19:35 Then they made their *f* drink
19:36 Lot were with child by their *f*.
19:37 he is the *f* of the Moabites to
19:38 he is the *f* of the people of
20:12 She is the daughter of my *f*,
22: 7 Isaac spoke to Abraham his *f*
22: 7 My *f*!" And he said, "Here I
22:21 Kemuel the *f* of Aram,
26: 3 which I swore to Abraham your *f*.
26:15 in the days of Abraham his *f*,
26:18 in the days of Abraham his *f*,
26:18 them by the names which his *f*
26:24 I am the God of your *f* Abraham;
27: 6 Indeed I heard your *f* speak to
27: 9 food from them for your *f*,
27:10 you shall take it to your *f*,
27:12 Perhaps my *f* will feel me, and I
27:14 such as his *f* loved.
27:18 So he went to his *f* and said,
27:18 to his father and said, "My *f*."
27:19 Jacob said to his *f*,
27:22 Jacob went near to Isaac his *f*,
27:26 Then his *f* Isaac said to him,
27:30 the presence of Isaac his *f*,
27:31 food, and brought it to his *f*,
27:31 his father, and said to his *f*,
27:31 Let my *f* arise and eat of his
27:32 And his *f* Isaac said to him,
27:34 Esau heard the words of his *f*,
27:34 bitter cry, and said to his *f*,
27:34 'Bless me—me also, O my *f*!"
27:38 And Esau said to his *f*,
27:38 you only one blessing, my *f*?
27:38 O my *f*!" And Esau lifted up
27:39 Then Isaac his *f* answered and
27:41 the blessing with which his *f*
27:41 The days of mourning for my *f*
28: 2 of Bethuel your mother's *f*;
28: 7 and that Jacob had obeyed his *f*
28: 8 of Canaan did not please his *f*
28:13 the LORD God of Abraham your *f*
29:12 So she ran and told her *f*.
31: 5 but the God of my *f* has been
31: 6 my might I have served your *f*.
31: 7 Yet your *f* has deceived me and
31: 9 away the livestock of your *f*
31:16 which God has taken from our *f*
31:18 to go to his *f* Isaac in the
31:29 but the God of your *f* spoke to
31:35 And she said to her *f*,
31:42 "Unless the God of my *f*,
31:53 and the God of their *f* judge
31:53 swore by the Fear of his *f*
32: 9 O God of my *f* Abraham and God of
32: 9 father Abraham and God of my *f*
33:19 children of Hamor, Shechem's *f*,
34: 4 So Shechem spoke to his *f* Hamor,
34: 6 Then Hamor the *f* of Shechem went
34:11 Then Shechem said to her *f* and
34:13 Shechem and Hamor his *f*,
34:19 than all the household of his *f*.
35:18 but his *f* called him Benjamin.
35:27 Then Jacob came to his *f* Isaac
36: 9 the genealogy of Esau the *f* of
36:24 pastured the donkeys of his *f*
36:43 Esau was the *f* of the
37: 1 dwelt in the land where his *f*
37: 2 a bad report of them to his *f*.
37: 4 his brothers saw that their *f*
37:10 So he told it to his *f* and his
37:10 and his *f* rebuked him and said
37:11 but his *f* kept the matter in
37:22 and bring him back to his *f*.
37:32 and they brought it to their *f*
37:35 Thus his *f* wept for him.
42:13 the youngest is with our *f*
42:29 they went to Jacob their *f* in
42:32 twelve brothers, sons of our *f*;
42:32 and the youngest is with our *f*
42:35 and when they and their *f* saw
42:36 And Jacob their *f* said to them,
42:37 Then Reuben spoke to his *f*,
43: 2 that their *f* said to them, "Go
43: 7 Is your *f* still alive? Have you
43: 8 Judah said to Israel his *f*,
43:11 And their *f* Israel said to them,
43:23 Your God and the God of your *f*
43:27 Is your *f* well, the old man of
43:28 Your servant our *f* is in good
44:17 you, go up in peace to your *f*.
44:19 Have you a *f* or a brother?'
44:20 said to my lord, 'We have a *f*,
44:20 and his *f* loves him.'
44:22 'The lad cannot leave his *f*,
44:22 for if he should leave his *f*,
44:22 his *f* would die.'
44:24 we went up to your servant my *f*,
44:25 And our *f* said, 'Go back and
44:27 Then your servant my *f* said to
44:30 I come to your servant my *f*,
44:31 gray hair of your servant our *f*
44:32 surety for the lad to my *f*,
44:32 bear the blame before my *f*
44:34 For how shall I go up to my *f* if
44:34 evil that would come upon my *f*?
45: 3 does my *f* still live?" But his
45: 8 and He has made me a *f* to
45: 9 "Hurry and go up to my *f*,
45:13 So you shall tell my *f* of all my
45:13 you shall hurry and bring my *f*
45:18 Bring your *f* and your households
45:19 bring your *f* and come.
45:23 And he sent to his *f* these
45:23 and food for his *f* for the
45:25 land of Canaan to Jacob their *f*.
45:27 the spirit of Jacob their *f*
46: 1 sacrifices to the God of his *f*
46: 3 "I am God, the God of your *f*;
46: 5 sons of Israel carried their *f*
46:29 went up to Goshen to meet his *f*
47: 1 My *f* and my brothers, their
47: 5 Your *f* and your brothers have
47: 6 Have your *f* and brothers dwell
47: 7 Then Joseph brought in his *f*
47:11 And Joseph situated his *f* and
47:12 Then Joseph provided his *f*,
48: 1 Indeed your *f* is sick"; and he
48: 9 And Joseph said to his *f*,
48:17 Now when Joseph saw that his *f*
48:18 And Joseph said to his *f*,
48:18 to his father, "Not so, my *f*,
48:19 But his *f* refused and said, "I
49: 2 And listen to Israel your *f*.
49:25 By the God of your *f* who will
49:26 The blessings of your *f* Have
49:28 and this is what their *f* spoke
50: 2 the physicians to embalm his *f*.
50: 5 My *f* made me swear, saying,
50: 5 let me go up and bury my *f*,
50: 6 said, "Go up and bury your *f*,
50: 7 Joseph went up to bury his *f*;
50:10 days of mourning for his *f*.
50:14 And after he had buried his *f*,
50:14 went up with him to bury his *f*.
50:15 brothers saw that their *f* was
50:16 Before your *f* died he commanded,
50:17 servants of the God of your *f*.
Ex 2:18 When they came to Reuel their *f*,
3: 6 said, "I am the God of your *f*—
12: 3 to the house of his *f*,
18: 4 The God of my *f* was my help,
20:12 Honor your *f* and your mother,
21:15 And he who strikes his *f* or his
21:17 And he who curses his *f* or his
22:17 If her *f* utterly refuses to give
40:15 them, as you anointed their *f*,
Lev 18: 7 The nakedness of your *f* or the
18: 9 sister, the daughter of your *f*,
18:11 daughter, begotten by your *f*—
18:12 she is near of kin to your *f*.
19: 3 revere his mother and his *f*,
20: 9 For everyone who curses his *f* or
20: 9 He has cursed his *f* or his
21: 2 to him: his mother, his *f*,
21: 9 the harlot, she profanes her *f*.
21:11 nor defile himself for his *f* or
24:10 whose *f* was an Egyptian, went
Num 3: 4 the presence of Aaron their *f*.
6: 7 himself unclean even for his *f*
12:14 If her *f* had but spit in her
18: 2 of Levi, the tribe of your *f*,
27: 3 Our *f* died in the wilderness;
27: 4 Why should the name of our *f* be
27: 7 the inheritance of their *f* to
27:11 And if his *f* has no brothers,
30: 4 and her *f* hears her vow and the
30: 4 and her *f* holds his peace, then
30: 5 But if her *f* overrules her on
30: 5 because her *f* overruled her.
30:16 and between a *f* and his
Deut 5:16 Honor your *f* and your mother,
21:13 and mourn her *f* and her mother
21:18 not obey the voice of his *f* or
21:19 then his *f* and his mother shall
22:15 then the *f* and mother of the
22:16 And the young woman's *f* shall
22:19 silver and give them to the *f*
22:29 give to the young woman's *f*
26: 5 My *f* was a Syrian, about to
27:16 is the one who treats his *f*
27:22 the daughter of his *f* or the
32: 6 people? Is He not your *F*,
32: 7 many generations. Ask your *f*,
33: 9 Who says of his *f* and mother,
Josh 2:13 'and spare my *f*, my mother,
2:18 and unless you bring your *f*,
6:23 in and brought out Rahab, her *f*,
15:13 is Hebron (Arba was the *f*
15:18 she persuaded him to ask her *f*
17: 1 the *f* of Gilead, because he was
19:47 after the name of Dan their *f*
21:11 Kirjath Arba (Arba was the *f*
22:14 the head of the house of his *f*
24: 2 the *f* of Abraham and the father
24: 2 father of Abraham and the *f* of
24: 3 Then I took your *f* Abraham from
24:32 from the sons of Hamor the *f*
Judg 1:14 she urged him to ask her *f* for
6:25 the altar of Baal that your *f*
8:32 in the tomb of Joash his *f*,
9: 1 of the house of his mother's *f*,
9:17 for my *f* fought for you, risked
9:28 Serve the men of Hamor the *f* of
9:56 which he had done to his *f* by

11:36 So she said to him, "My *f*,
11:37 Then she said to her *f*,
11:39 that she returned to her *f*,
14: 2 So he went up and told his *f* and
14: 3 Then his *f* and mother said to
14: 3 And Samson said to his *f*,
14: 4 But his *f* and mother did not
14: 5 went down to Timnah with his *f*
14: 6 But he did not tell his *f* or
14: 9 When he came to his *f* and
14:10 So his *f* went down to the
14:16 have not explained it to my *f*
15: 1 But her *f* would not permit
15: 2 Her *f* said, "I really thought
15: 6 up and burned her and her *f*
16:31 Eshtaol in the tomb of his *f*
17:10 and be a *f* and a priest to me,
18:19 be a *f* and a priest to us. Is
18:29 after the name of Dan their *f*,
19: 3 and when the *f* of the young
19: 4 the young woman's *f*,
19: 5 but the young woman's *f* said to
19: 6 Then the young woman's *f* said
19: 8 but the young woman's *f* said,
19: 9 the young woman's *f*,
Ruth 2:11 and how you have left your *f*
4:17 He is the *f* of Jesse, the
4:17 of Jesse, the *f* of David.
1 Sam 2:25 not heed the voice of their *f*,
2:27 Myself to the house of your *f*
2:28 not give to the house of your *f*
2:30 house and the house of your *f*
9: 3 the donkeys of Kish, Saul's *f*,
9: 5 lest my *f* cease caring about
10: 2 And now your *f* has ceased
10:12 and said, "But who is their *f*?
14: 1 But he did not tell his *f*.
14:27 Jonathan had not heard his *f*
14:28 Your *f* strictly charged the
14:29 'My *f* has troubled the land.
14:51 Kish was the *f* of Saul, and Ner
14:51 and Ner the *f* of Abner was the
19: 2 My *f* Saul seeks to kill you.
19: 3 go out and stand beside my *f*
19: 3 and I will speak with my *f*
19: 4 well of David to Saul his *f*,
20: 1 what is my sin before your *f*,
20: 2 my *f* will do nothing either
20: 2 And why should my *f* hide this
20: 3 Your *f* certainly knows that I
20: 6 If your *f* misses me at all, then
20: 8 should you bring me to your *f*?
20: 9 evil was determined by my *f* to
20:10 or what if your *f* answers you
20:12 When I have sounded out my *f*
20:13 But if it pleases my *f* to do
20:13 you as He has been with my *f*.
20:32 Jonathan answered Saul his *f*,
20:33 it was determined by his *f* to
20:34 because his *f* had treated him
22: 3 Please let my *f* and mother come
22:15 or to any in the house of my *f*.
23:17 for the hand of Saul my *f* shall
23:17 Even my *f* Saul knows that."
24:11 'Moreover, my *f*, see!
2 Sam 3: 8 to the house of Saul your *f*,
6:21 who chose me instead of your *f*
7:14 'I will be his *F*, and he
10: 2 as his *f* showed kindness to
10: 2 to comfort him concerning his *f*.
10: 3 that David really honors your *f*
13: 5 And when your *f* comes to see
16: 3 restore the kingdom of my *f* to
16:21 that you are abhorred by your *f*.
17: 8 you know your *f* and his men,
17: 8 and your *f* is a man of war,
17:10 all Israel knows that your *f*
19:37 near the grave of my *f* and
21:14 in the tomb of Kish his *f*.
1 Ki 1: 6 (And his *f* had not rebuked him
2:12 sat on the throne of his *f*
2:24 me on the throne of David my *f*,
2:26 of the Lord GOD before my *f*
2:26 were afflicted every time my *f*
2:31 me and from the house of my *f*
2:32 though my *f* David did not know
2:44 that you did to my *f* David;
3: 3 in the statutes of his *f* David,
3: 6 to Your servant David my *f*,
3: 7 servant king instead of my *f*
3:14 as your *f* David walked, then I
5: 1 him king in place of his *f*,
5: 3 You know how my *f* David could
5: 5 as the LORD spoke to my *f*
6:12 which I spoke to your *f* David.
7:14 and his *f* was a man of Tyre, a
7:51 in the things which his *f*
8:15 spoke with His mouth to my *f*
8:17 it was in the heart of my *f*
8:18 But the LORD said to my *f*
8:20 filled the position of my *f*
8:24 Your servant David my *f*;
8:25 Your servant David my *f*,
8:26 to Your servant David my *f*.
9: 4 if you walk before Me as your *f*
9: 5 as I promised David your *f*,
11: 4 as was the heart of his *f*
11: 6 as did his *f* David.
11:12 for the sake of your *f* David; I
11:27 to the City of David his *f*.
11:33 as did his *f* David.
11:43 in the City of David his *f*.
12: 4 Your *f* made our yoke heavy; now
12: 4 burdensome service of your *f*,
12: 6 elders who stood before his *f*
12: 9 Lighten the yoke which your *f*
12:10 Your *f* made our yoke heavy, but
12:11 whereas my *f* put a heavy yoke
12:11 my *f* chastised you with whips,
12:14 My *f* made your yoke heavy, but I
12:14 my *f* chastised you with whips,
13:11 they also told their *f* the
13:12 And their *f* said to them,
15: 3 walked in all the sins of his *f*,
15: 3 as was the heart of his *f*
15:11 as did his *f* David.
15:15 LORD the things which his *f*
15:19 as there was between my *f* and
15:19 between my father and your *f*.
15:24 in the City of David his *f*.
15:26 and walked in the way of his *f*,
19:20 Please let me kiss my *f* and my
20:34 The cities which my *f* took from
20:34 my father took from your *f* I
20:34 as my *f* did in Samaria."
22:43 in all the ways of his *f* Asa.
22:46 remained in the days of his *f*
22:50 in the City of David his *f*.
22:52 and walked in the way of his *f*
22:53 according to all that his *f* had
2 Ki 2:12 it, and he cried out, "My *f*,
2:12 he cried out, "My father, my *f*,
3: 2 but not like his *f* and mother;
3: 2 pillar of Baal that his *f* had
3:13 Go to the prophets of your *f*
4:18 day that he went out to his *f*,
4:19 And he said to his *f*,
5:13 spoke to him, and said, "My *f*,
6:21 them, he said to Elisha, "My *f*,
9:25 together behind Ahab his *f*,
13:14 his face, and said, "O my *f*,
13:14 and said, "O my father, my *f*,
13:25 of the hand of Jehoahaz his *f*
14: 3 yet not like his *f* David; he
14: 3 he did everything as his *f*
14: 5 who had murdered his *f* the
14:21 made him king instead of his *f*
15: 3 according to all that his *f*
15:34 did according to all that his *f*
15:38 in the City of David his *f*.
16: 2 as his *f* David had done.
18: 3 according to all that his *f*
20: 5 LORD, the God of David your *f*:
21: 3 places which Hezekiah his *f*
21:20 as his *f* Manasseh had done.
21:21 in all the ways that his *f* had
21:21 he served the idols that his *f*
22: 2 in all the ways of his *f* David;
23:34 Josiah king in place of his *f*
24: 9 according to all that his *f* had
1 Chr 2:17 and the *f* of Amasa was Jether
2:21 to the daughter of Machir the *f*
2:23 to the sons of Machir the *f*
2:24 Abijah bore him Ashhur the *f*
2:42 who was the *f* of Ziph, and the
2:42 and the sons of Mareshah the *f*
2:44 Shema begot Raham the *f* of
2:45 and Maon was the *f* of Beth
2:49 She also bore Shaaph the *f* of
2:49 Sheva the *f* of Machbenah and
2:49 father of Machbenah and the *f*
2:50 were Shobal the *f* of Kirjath
2:51 Salma the *f* of Bethlehem, and
2:51 and Hareph the *f* of Beth
2:52 And Shobal the *f* of Kirjath
2:55 the *f* of the house of Rechab.
4: 3 were the sons of the *f* of
4: 4 and Penuel was the *f* of Gedor,
4: 4 and Ezer was the *f* of Hushah.
4: 4 firstborn of Ephrathah the *f*
4: 5 And Ashhur the *f* of Tekoa had
4:11 who was the *f* of Eshton.
4:12 and Tehinnah the *f* of
4:14 Seraiah begot Joab the *f* of Ge
4:17 and Ishbah the *f* of Eshtemoa.
4:18 Jehudijah bore Jered the *f* of
4:18 Heber the *f* of Sochoh, and
4:18 and Jekuthiel the *f* of Zanoah.)
4:21 son of Judah were Er the *f* of
4:21 Laadah the *f* of Mareshah, and
7:14 bore him Machir the *f* of
7:14 Gilead, the *f* of Asriel.
7:22 Then Ephraim their *f* mourned
7:31 who was the *f* of Birzaith.
8:29 Now the *f* of Gibeon, whose
9:35 Jeiel the *f* of Gibeon, whose
17:13 'I will be his *F*, and he
19: 2 because his *f* showed kindness
19: 2 to comfort him concerning his *f*.
19: 3 that David really honors your *f*
22:10 My son, and I will be his *F*;
24: 2 and Abihu died before their *f*,
24:19 by the hand of Aaron their *f*,
25: 3 under the direction of their *f*
25: 6 under the direction of their *f*
26:10 his *f* made him the first),
28: 4 me above all the house of my *f*
28: 4 of Judah, the house of my *f*,
28: 4 and among the sons of my *f*,
28: 6 be My son, and I will be his *F*.
28: 9 Solomon, know the God of your *f*,
29:10 You, LORD God of Israel, our *F*,
29:23 as king instead of David his *f*,
2 Chr 1: 8 shown great mercy to David my *f*,
1: 9 let Your promise to David my *f*
2: 3 you have dealt with David my *f*,
2: 7 whom David my *f* provided.
2:14 and his *f* was a man of Tyre),
2:14 men of my lord David your *f*.
2:17 the census in which David his *f*
3: 1 LORD had appeared to his *f*
5: 1 in the things which his *f*
6: 4 He spoke with His mouth to my *f*
6: 7 it was in the heart of my *f*
6: 8 But the LORD said to my *f*
6:10 filled the position of my *f*
6:15 Your servant David my *f*;
6:16 Your servant David my *f*,
7:17 if you walk before Me as your *f*
7:18 I covenanted with David your *f*,
8:14 to the order of David his *f*,
9:31 in the City of David his *f*.
10: 4 Your *f* made our yoke heavy; now
10: 4 burdensome service of your *f*
10: 6 elders who stood before his *f*
10: 9 Lighten the yoke which your *f*
10:10 Your *f* made our yoke heavy, but
10:11 whereas my *f* put a heavy yoke
10:11 my *f* chastised you with whips,
10:14 My *f* made your yoke heavy, but I
10:14 my *f* chastised you with whips,
15:18 of God the things that his *f*
16: 3 as there was between my *f* and
16: 3 between my father and your *f*.
17: 2 of Ephraim which Asa his *f* had
17: 3 in the former ways of his *f*
17: 4 but sought the God of his *f*,
20:32 he walked in the way of his *f*
21: 3 Their *f* gave them great gifts of
21: 4 over the kingdom of his *f*,
21:12 says the LORD God of your *f*
21:12 the ways of Jehoshaphat your *f*,
22: 4 after the death of his *f*,
24:22 kindness which Jehoiada his *f*
25: 3 who had murdered his *f* the
26: 1 made him king instead of his *f*
26: 4 according to all that his *f*
27: 2 according to all that his *f*
28: 1 as his *f* David had done.
29: 2 according to all that his *f*
33: 3 places which Hezekiah his *f*
33:22 as his *f* Manasseh had done; for
33:22 the carved images which his *f*
33:23 as his *f* Manasseh had humbled
34: 2 and walked in the ways of his *f*
34: 3 began to seek the God of his *f*
Esth 2: 7 for she had neither *f* nor
2: 7 When her *f* and mother died,
Job 15:10 us, Much older than your *f*.
17:14 to corruption, 'You are my *f*,
29:16 I was a *f* to the poor, And I
31:18 my youth I reared him as a *f*,
38:28 Has the rain a *f*?
42:15 and their *f* gave them an
Ps 27:10 When my *f* and my mother forsake
68: 5 A *f* of the fatherless, a
89:26 shall cry to Me, 'You are my *F*,
103:13 As a *f* pities his children,
Prov 1: 8 hear the instruction of your *f*,
3:12 Just as a *f* the son in whom
4: 1 the instruction of a *f*,
10: 1 A wise son makes a glad *f*,
15:20 A wise son makes a *f* glad, But
17: 6 glory of children is their *f*.
17:21 And the *f* of a fool has no
17:25 son is a grief to his *f*,
19:13 son is the ruin of his *f*,
19:26 He who mistreats his *f* and
20:20 Whoever curses his *f* or his
23:22 Listen to your *f* who begot you,
23:24 The *f* of the righteous will
23:25 Let your *f* and your mother be
28: 7 of gluttons shames his *f*.
28:24 Whoever robs his *f* or his
29: 3 loves wisdom makes his *f*
30:11 a generation that curses its *f*,
30:17 The eye that mocks his *f*,
Isa 3: 6 brother In the house of his *f*,
8: 4 'My *f*' and 'My mother,' the
9: 6 Mighty God, Everlasting *F*,
22:21 He shall be a *f* to the
38: 5 LORD, the God of David your *f*:
38:19 The *f* shall make known Your
43:27 Your first *f* sinned, And your
45:10 Woe to him who says to his *f*,
51: 2 Look to Abraham your *f*,
58:14 the heritage of Jacob your *f*.
63:16 Doubtless You are our *F*,
63:16 You, O LORD, are our *F*;
64: 8 now, O LORD, You are our *F*;
Jer 2:27 to a tree, 'You are my *f*,
3: 4 this time cry to Me, 'My *f*,
3:19 'You shall call Me, "My *F*,"
12: 6 brothers, the house of your *f*,
16: 7 to drink for their *f* or their
20:15 Who brought news to my *f*,
22:11 reigned instead of Josiah his *f*,
22:15 Did not your *f* eat and drink,
31: 9 For I am a *F* to Israel, And
35: 6 the son of Rechab, our *f*,
35: 8 the son of Rechab, our *f*,
35:10 to all that Jonadab our *f*
35:16 the commandment of their *f*,
35:18 commandment of Jonadab your *f*,
Ezek 16: 3 your *f* was an Amorite and your
16:45 was a Hittite and your *f* an

18: 4 The soul of the *f* As well as
18:14 sees all the sins which his *f*
18:17 die for the iniquity of his *f*;
18:18 "As for his *f*,
18:19 son not bear the guilt of the *f*?
18:20 not bear the guilt of the *f*,
18:20 nor the *f* bear the guilt of the
22: 7 you they have made light of *f*
44:25 Only for *f* or mother, for son
Dan 5: 2 and silver vessels which his *f*
5:11 And in the days of your *f*,
5:11 and King Nebuchadnezzar your *f*—
5:11 your *f* the king—made him chief
5:13 whom my *f* the king brought from
5:18 God gave Nebuchadnezzar your *f*
Am 2: 7 A man and his *f* go in to the
Mic 7: 6 For son dishonors *f*,
Zech 13: 3 then his *f* and mother who begot
13: 3 And his *f* and mother who begot
Mal 1: 6 "A son honors his *f*,
1: 6 If then I am the *F*, Where
2:10 Have we not all one *F*?
Mt 2:22 over Judea instead of his *f*
3: 9 'We have Abraham as our *f*.
4:21 the boat with Zebedee their *f*,
4:22 they left the boat and their *f*,
5:16 good works and glorify your *F*
5:45 you may be sons of your *F*
5:48 just as your *F* in heaven is
6: 1 you have no reward from your *F*
6: 4 and your *F* who sees in secret
6: 6 pray to your *F* who is in the
6: 6 and your *F* who sees in secret
6: 8 For your *F* knows the things you
6: 9 Our *F* in heaven, Hallowed be
6:14 your heavenly *F* will also
6:15 neither will your *F* forgive
6:18 but to your *F* who is in the
6:18 and your *F* who sees in secret
6:26 yet your heavenly *F* feeds them.
6:32 For your heavenly *F* knows that
7:11 how much more will your *F* who
7:21 he who does the will of My *F*
8:21 let me first go and bury my *f*.
10:20 but the Spirit of your *F* who
10:21 and a *f* his child; and
10:32 I will also confess before My *F*
10:33 I will also deny before My *F*
10:35 'set a man against his *f*,
10:37 He who loves *f* or mother more
11:25 and said, "I thank You, *F*,
11:26 'Even so, *F*, for so it
11:27 been delivered to Me by My *F*,
11:27 one knows the Son except the *F*.
11:27 Nor does anyone know the *F*
12:50 whoever does the will of My *F*
13:43 sun in the kingdom of their *F*.
15: 4 Honor your *f* and your
15: 4 He who curses *f* or mother,
15: 5 Whoever says to his *f* or mother,
15: 6 then he need not honor his *f* or
15:13 plant which My heavenly *F* has
16:17 but My *F* who is in heaven.
16:27 will come in the glory of His *F*
18:10 always see the face of My *F*
18:14 so it is not the will of your *F*
18:19 will be done for them by My *F*
18:35 So My heavenly *F* also will do to
19: 5 a man shall leave his *f*
19:19 Honor your *f* and your
19:29 or brothers or sisters or *f* or
20:23 for whom it is prepared by My *F*.
21:31 the two did the will of his *f*?
23: 9 not call anyone on earth your *f*;
23: 9 your father; for One is your *F*,
24:36 of heaven, but My *F* only.
25:34 'Come, you blessed of My *F*,
26:39 and prayed, saying, "O My *F*,
26:42 and prayed, saying, "O My *F*,
26:53 that I cannot now pray to My *F*,
28:19 them in the name of the *F* and
Mk 1:20 and they left their *f* Zebedee
5:40 He took the *f* and the mother of
7:10 Honor your *f* and your
7:10 He who curses *f* or mother,
7:11 If a man says to his *f* or
7:12 let him do anything for his *f*
8:38 He comes in the glory of His *F*
9:21 So He asked his *f*, "How long
9:24 Immediately the *f* of the child
10: 7 a man shall leave his *f*
10:19 Honor your *f* and your
10:29 or brothers or sisters or *f* or
11:10 is the kingdom of our *f* David
11:25 that your *F* in heaven may also
11:26 neither will your *F* in heaven
13:12 and a *f* his child;
13:32 nor the Son, but only the *F*.
14:36 And He said, "Abba, *F*,
15:21 the *f* of Alexander and Rufus,
Lk 1:32 give Him the throne of His *f*
1:59 called him by the name of his *f*,
1:62 So they made signs to his *f*—
1:67 Now his *f* Zacharias was filled
1:73 oath which He swore to our *f*
2:48 Your *f* and I have sought You
3: 8 'We have Abraham as our *f*.
6:36 just as your *F* also is
8:51 and the *f* and mother of the
9:42 and gave him back to his *f*.
9:59 let me first go and bury my *f*.
10:21 and said, "I thank You, *F*,
10:21 them to babes. Even so, *F*,
10:22 been delivered to Me by My *F*,
10:22 who the Son is except the *F*,
10:22 and who the *F* is except the
11: 2 Our *F* in heaven, Hallowed be
11:11 a son asks for bread from any *f*
11:13 much more will your heavenly *F*
12:30 and your *F* knows that you need
12:53 *F* will be divided against son
12:53 against son and son against *f*,
14:26 to Me and does not hate his *f*
15:12 younger of them said to his *f*,
15:12 of them said to his father, '*F*,
15:18 'I will arise and go to my *f*,
15:18 and will say to him, "*F*,
15:20 he arose and came to his *f*.
15:20 his *f* saw him and had
15:21 "And the son said to him, '*F*,
15:22 But the *f* said to his servants,
15:27 your *f* has killed the fatted
15:28 Therefore his *f* came out and
15:29 he answered and said to his *f*,
16:24 *F* Abraham, have mercy on me, and
16:27 said, 'I beg you therefore, *f*,
16:30 *f* Abraham; but if one goes to
18:20 Honor your *f* and your
22:29 just as My *F* bestowed one upon
22:42 saying, "*F*, if it is Your
23:34 Then Jesus said, "*F*, forgive
23:46 with a loud voice, He said, "*F*,
24:49 I send the Promise of My *F* upon
Jn 1:14 of the only begotten of the *F*,
1:18 who is in the bosom of the *F*,
3:35 The *F* loves the Son, and has
4:12 Are You greater than our *f*
4:21 nor in Jerusalem, worship the *F*.
4:23 worshipers will worship the *F*
4:23 for the *F* is seeking such to
4:53 So the *f* knew that it was at
5:17 My *F* has been working until now,
5:18 also said that God was His *F*,
5:19 but what He sees the *F* do; for
5:20 For the *F* loves the Son, and
5:21 For as the *F* raises the dead and
5:22 For the *F* judges no one, but has
5:23 Son just as they honor the *F*.
5:23 the Son does not honor the *F*
5:26 For as the *F* has life in
5:30 own will but the will of the *F*
5:36 for the works which the *F* has
5:36 that the *F* has sent Me.
5:37 And the *F* Himself, who sent Me,
5:45 I shall accuse you to the *F*;
6:27 because God the *F* has set His
6:32 but My *F* gives you the true
6:37 All that the *F* gives Me will
6:39 This is the will of the *F* who
6:42 whose *f* and mother we know? How
6:44 one can come to Me unless the *F*
6:45 heard and learned from the *F*
6:46 that anyone has seen the *F*,
6:46 is from God; He has seen the *F*.
6:57 As the living *F* sent Me, and I
6:57 Me, and I live because of the *F*,
6:65 has been granted to him by My *F*.
8:16 but I am with the *F* who sent
8:18 and the *F* who sent Me bears
8:19 said to Him, "Where is Your *F*?
8:19 "You know neither Me nor My *F*.
8:19 you would have known My *F*
8:27 that He spoke to them of the *F*.
8:28 but as My *F* taught Me, I speak
8:29 The *F* has not left Me alone,
8:38 what I have seen with My *F*,
8:38 what you have seen with your *f*.
8:39 said to Him, "Abraham is our *f*.
8:41 "You do the deeds of your *f*.
8:41 of fornication; we have one *F*—
8:42 to them, "If God were your *F*,
8:44 You are of your *f* the devil,
8:44 and the desires of your *f* you
8:44 for he is a liar and the *f* of
8:49 have a demon; but I honor My *F*,
8:53 Are You greater than our *f*
8:54 It is My *F* who honors Me, of
8:56 Your *f* Abraham rejoiced to see
10:15 As the *F* knows Me, even so I
10:15 knows Me, even so I know the *F*;
10:17 Therefore My *F* loves Me, because
10:18 I have received from My *F*.
10:29 'My *F*, who has given them
10:30 I and My *F* are one."
10:32 I have shown you from My *F*.
10:36 do you say of Him whom the *F*
10:37 I do not do the works of My *F*,
10:38 may know and believe that the *F*
11:41 up His eyes and said, "*F*,
12:26 him My *F* will honor.
12:27 and what shall I say? '*F*,
12:28 '*F*, glorify Your name."
12:49 but the *F* who sent Me gave Me a
12:50 just as the *F* has told Me, so I
13: 1 depart from this world to the *F*,
13: 3 knowing that the *F* had given
14: 6 No one comes to the *F* except
14: 7 you would have known My *F* also;
14: 8 to Him, "Lord, show us the *F*,
14: 9 who has seen Me has seen the *F*;
14: 9 can you say, 'Show us the *F*'?
14:10 not believe that I am in the *F*,
14:10 and the *F* in Me? The words that
14:10 but the *F* who dwells in Me does
14:11 Me that I am in the *F*
14:11 I am in the Father and the *F*
14:12 will do, because I go to My *F*.
14:13 that the *F* may be glorified in
14:16 "And I will pray the *F*,
14:20 will know that I am in My *F*,
14:21 loves Me will be loved by My *F*,
14:23 and My *F* will love him, and We
14:26 whom the *F* will send in My
14:28 I said, 'I am going to the *F*,
14:28 for My *F* is greater than I.
14:31 may know that I love the *F*,
14:31 and as the *F* gave Me
15: 1 and My *F* is the vinedresser.
15: 8 By this My *F* is glorified, that
15: 9 As the *F* loved Me, I also have
15:15 things that I heard from My *F*
15:16 that whatever you ask the *F* in
15:23 He who hates Me hates My *F* also.
15:24 and also hated both Me and My *F*.
15:26 I shall send to you from the *F*,
15:26 truth who proceeds from the *F*,
16: 3 they have not known the *F* nor
16:10 because I go to My *F* and you
16:15 All things that the *F* has are
16:16 see Me, because I go to the *F*.
16:17 and, 'because I go to the *F*'?
16:23 whatever you ask the *F* in My
16:25 tell you plainly about the *F*.
16:26 to you that I shall pray the *F*
16:27 for the *F* Himself loves you,
16:28 I came forth from the *F* and have
16:28 leave the world and go to the *F*.
16:32 because the *F* is with Me.
17: 1 eyes to heaven, and said: "*F*,
17: 5 'And now, O *F*, glorify Me
17:11 and I come to You. Holy *F*,
17:21 they all may be one, as You, *F*,
17:24 '*F*, I desire that they
17:25 O righteous *F*! The world has not
18:11 I not drink the cup which My *F*
20:17 I have not yet ascended to My *F*;
20:17 I am ascending to My *F* and your
20:17 to My Father and your *F*,
20:21 Peace to you! As the *F* has sent
Acts 1: 4 wait for the Promise of the *F*,
1: 7 times or seasons which the *F*
2:33 and having received from the *F*
7: 2 God of glory appeared to our *f*
7: 4 when his *f* was dead, He moved
7:14 Joseph sent and called his *f*
7:16 the *f* of Shechem.
16: 1 but his *f* was Greek.
16: 3 for they all knew that his *f*
28: 8 And it happened that the *f* of
Rom 1: 7 to you and peace from God our *F*
4: 1 we say that Abraham our *f* has
4:11 that he might be the *f* of all
4:12 and the *f* of circumcision to
4:12 steps of the faith which our *f*
4:16 who is the *f* of us all
4:17 I have made you a *f* of
4:18 so that he became the *f* of many
6: 4 the dead by the glory of the *F*,
8:15 by whom we cry out, "Abba, *F*."
9:10 even by our *f* Isaac
15: 6 mouth glorify the God and *F* of
1 Cor 1: 3 to you and peace from God our *F*
8: 6 us there is one God, the *F*,
15:24 the kingdom to God the *F*,
2 Cor 1: 2 to you and peace from God our *F*
1: 3 Blessed be the God and *F* of
1: 3 the *F* of mercies and God of all
6:18 I will be a *F* to you, And you
11:31 The God and *F* of our Lord Jesus
Gal 1: 1 Jesus Christ and God the *F* who
1: 3 to you and peace from God the *F*
1: 4 to the will of our God and *F*,
4: 2 the time appointed by the *f*.
4: 6 crying out, "Abba, *F*!"
Eph 1: 2 to you and peace from God our *F*
1: 3 Blessed be the God and *F* of
1:17 the *F* of glory, may give to you
2:18 access by one Spirit to the *F*.
3:14 reason I bow my knees to the *F*
4: 6 one God and *F* of all, who is
5:20 for all things to God the *F* in
5:31 a man shall leave his *f*
6: 2 Honor your *f* and mother,"
6:23 from God the *F* and the Lord
Phil 1: 2 to you and peace from God our *F*
2:11 Lord, to the glory of God the *F*.
2:22 that as a son with his *f* he
4:20 Now to our God and *F* be glory
Col 1: 2 to you and peace from God our *F*
1: 3 give thanks to the God and *F*
1:12 giving thanks to the *F* who has
1:19 For it pleased the *F* that in
2: 2 both of the *F* and of Christ,
3:17 giving thanks to God the *F*
1 Th 1: 1 the Thessalonians in God the *F*
1: 1 to you and peace from God our *F*
1: 3 in the sight of our God and *F*,
2:11 as a *f* does his own children,
3:11 Now may our God and *F* Himself,
3:13 holiness before our God and *F*
2 Th 1: 1 the Thessalonians in God our *F*
1: 2 to you and peace from God our *F*
2:16 Himself, and our God and *F*,
1 Tim 1: 2 and peace from God our *F* and
5: 1 man, but exhort him as a *f*,
2 Tim 1: 2 and peace from God the *F* and

Titus 1: 4 and peace from God the *F* and
Phm 1: 3 to you and peace from God our *F*
Heb 1: 5 "I will be to Him a *F*,
7: 3 without *f*, without mother,
7:10 was still in the loins of his *f*
12: 7 for what son is there whom a *f*
12: 9 be in subjection to the *F* of
Jas 1:17 and comes down from the *F* of
1:27 religion before God and the *F*
2:21 Was not Abraham our *f* justified
3: 9 With it we bless our God and *F*,
1 Pe 1: 2 the foreknowledge of God the *F*,
1: 3 Blessed be the God and *F* of
1:17 And if you call on the *F*,
2 Pe 1:17 For He received from God the *F*
1 Jn 1: 2 life which was with the *F* and
1: 3 our fellowship is with the *F*
2: 1 we have an Advocate with the *F*,
2:13 Because you have known the *F*.
2:15 the love of the *F* is not in
2:16 is not of the *F* but is of the
2:22 is antichrist who denies the *F*
2:23 the Son does not have the *F*
2:23 acknowledges the Son has the *F*
2:24 abide in the Son and in the *F*.
3: 1 what manner of love the *F* has
4:14 seen and testify that the *F*
5: 7 bear witness in heaven: the *F*,
2 Jn 3 be with you from God the *F* and
3 Jesus Christ, the Son of the *F*,
4 received commandment from the *F*.
9 of Christ has both the *F* and
Jude 1 called, sanctified by God the *F*,
Rev 1: 6 and priests to His God and *F*,
2:27 I also have received from My *F*;
3: 5 confess his name before My *F*
3:21 and sat down with My *F* on His

FATHER-IN-LAW (26/25) FATHER

Gen 38:13 your *f* is going up to Timnah to
38:25 brought out, she sent to her *f*,
Ex 3: 1 the flock of Jethro his *f*,
4:18 and returned to Jethro his *f*,
18: 1 the priest of Midian, Moses' *f*,
18: 2 Then Jethro, Moses' *f*,
18: 5 and Jethro, Moses' *f*,
18: 6 your *f* Jethro, am coming to you
18: 7 Moses went out to meet his *f*,
18: 8 And Moses told his *f* all that
18:12 Then Jethro, Moses' *f*,
18:12 to eat bread with Moses' *f*
18:14 So when Moses' *f* saw all that he
18:15 And Moses said to his *f*,
18:17 So Moses' *f* said to him,
18:24 heeded the voice of his *f* and
18:27 Then Moses let his *f* depart, and
Num 10:29 Reuel the Midianite, Moses' *f*,
Judg 1:16 of the Kenite, Moses' *f*,
4:11 of the children of Hobab the *f*
19: 4 Now his *f*, the young woman's
19: 7 his *f* urged him; so he lodged
19: 9 concubine and his servant—his *f*,
1 Sam 4:19 and that her *f* and her husband
4:21 captured and because of her *f*
Jn 18:13 for he was the *f* of Caiaphas

FATHER'S (166/157) FATHER

Gen 9:23 and they did not see their *f*
12: 1 your family And from your *f*
20:13 caused me to wander from my *f*
24: 7 who took me from my *f* house and
24:23 is there room in your *f* house
24:38 but you shall go to my *f* house
24:40 from my family and from my *f*
26:15 up all the wells which his *f*
28:21 so that I come back to my *f*
29: 9 Rachel came with her *f* sheep,
29:12 told Rachel that he was her *f*
31: 1 taken away all that was our *f*,
31: 1 and from what was our *f* he has
31: 5 I see your *f* countenance, that
31:14 or inheritance for us in our *f*
31:19 household idols that were her *f*.
31:30 you greatly long for your *f*
35:22 went and lay with Bilhah his *f*
37: 2 his *f* wives; and Joseph brought
37:12 brothers went to feed their *f*
38:11 Remain a widow in your *f* house
38:11 Tamar went and dwelt in her *f*
41:51 all my toil and all my *f* house.
46:31 to his brothers and to his *f*
46:31 My brothers and those of my *f*
47:12 and all his *f* household with
48:17 so he took hold of his *f* hand
49: 4 Because you went up to your *f*
49: 8 Your *f* children shall bow down
50: 1 Then Joseph fell on his *f* face,
50: 8 and his *f* house. Only their
50:22 he and his *f* household.
Ex 2:16 the troughs to water their *f*
6:20 his *f* sister, as wife; and she
15: 2 My *f* God, and I will exalt
Lev 16:32 to minister as priest in his *f*
18: 8 The nakedness of your *f* wife you
18: 8 it is your *f* nakedness.
18:11 The nakedness of your *f* wife's
18:12 the nakedness of your *f* sister;
18:14 uncover the nakedness of your *f*
20:11 The man who lies with his *f* wife
20:11 wife has uncovered his *f*
20:17 his *f* daughter or his mother's
20:19 mother's sister nor of your *f*
22:13 and has returned to her *f* house
22:13 she may eat her *f* food; but no
Num 1: 4 each one the head of his *f*
1:44 each one representing his *f*
2: 2 beside the emblems of his *f*
17: 2 get from them a rod from each *f*
17: 3 one rod for the head of each *f*
18: 1 You and your sons and your *f*
25:14 a leader of a *f* house among the
25:15 was head of the people of a *f*
27: 4 us a possession among our *f*
27: 7 of inheritance among their *f*
27:10 give his inheritance to his *f*
30: 3 some agreement while in her *f*
30:16 daughter in her youth in her *f*
32:14 You have risen in your *f* place,
36: 6 within the family of their *f*
36: 8 of one of the family of her *f*
36:11 married to the sons of their *f*
36:12 in the tribe of their *f* family.
Deut 22:21 woman to the door of her *f*
22:21 to play the harlot in her *f*
22:30 A man shall not take his *f*
22:30 nor uncover his *f* bed.
27:20 is the one who lies with his *f*
27:20 because he has uncovered his *f*
Josh 2:12 also will show kindness to my *f*
2:18 and all your *f* household to
6:25 her *f* household, and all that
17: 4 an inheritance among their *f*
Judg 6:15 and I am the least in my *f*
6:25 Take your *f* young bull, the
6:27 But because he feared his *f*
9: 5 Then he went to his *f* house at
9:18 you have risen up against my *f*
11: 2 have no inheritance in our *f*
11: 7 and expel me from my *f* house?
14:15 we will burn you and your *f*
14:19 and he went back up to his *f*
16:31 And his brothers and all his *f*
19: 2 and went away from him to her *f*
19: 3 So she brought him into her *f*
1 Sam 2:31 your arm and the arm of your *f*
9:20 not on you and on all your *f*
17:15 from Saul to feed his *f* sheep
17:25 and give his *f* house exemption
17:34 servant used to keep his *f*
18: 2 not let him go home to his *f*
18:18 and what is my life or my *f*
22: 1 when his brothers and all his *f*
22:11 and all his *f* house, the
22:16 you and all your *f* house!"
22:22 of all the persons of your *f*
24:21 not destroy my name from my *f*
2 Sam 2:32 Asahel and buried him in his *f*
3: 7 Why have you gone in to my *f*
3:29 head of Joab and on all his *f*
9: 7 kindness for Jonathan your *f*
14: 9 iniquity be on me and on my *f*
15:34 as I was your *f* servant
16:19 As I have served in your *f*
16:21 Go in to your *f* concubines, whom
16:22 and Absalom went in to his *f*
17:23 and he was buried in his *f*
19:28 For all my *f* house were but dead
24:17 be against me and against my *f*
1 Ki 11:17 and certain Edomites of his *f*
12:10 shall be thicker than my *f*
18:18 but you and your *f* house have,
2 Ki 10: 3 set him on his *f* throne, and
23:30 and made him king in his *f*
1 Chr 4:38 and their *f* house increased
5: 1 but because he defiled his *f*
5:13 and their brethren of their *f*
5:15 was chief of their *f* house.
7: 2 heads of their *f* house.
9: 9 these men were heads of a *f*
9:19 from his *f* house, the
12:28 and from his *f* house twenty-two
12:30 famous men throughout their *f*
21:17 be against me and my *f* house,
23:11 they were assigned as one *f*
24: 6 one *f* house taken for Eleazar
26:13 according to their *f* house.
2 Chr 10:10 shall be thicker than my *f*
21:13 those of your *f* household, who
31:17 genealogy according to their *f*
35: 5 to the division of the *f*
36: 1 and made him king in his *f*
Ezra 2:59 they could not identify their *f*
Neh 1: 6 Both my *f* house and I have
7:61 they could not identify their *f*
Esth 4:14 but you and your *f* house will
Ps 45:10 and your *f* house;
Prov 4: 3 When I was my *f* son, Tender
6:20 keep your *f* command, And do
13: 1 A wise son heeds his *f*
15: 5 A fool despises his *f*
27:10 your own friend or your *f*
Isa 7:17 you and your people and your *f*
22:23 a glorious throne to his *f*
22:24 on him all the glory of his *f*
Jer 35:14 and obey their *f* commandment.
Ezek 22:11 his sister, his *f* daughter.
Mt 10:29 to the ground apart from your *F*
26:29 I drink it new with you in My *F*
Lk 2:49 know that I must be about My *F*
9:26 His own glory, and in His *F*,
12:32 for it is your *F* good pleasure
15:17 How many of my *f* hired servants
16:27 that you would send him to my *f*
Jn 2:16 things away! Do not make My *F*
5:43 I have come in My *F* name, and
10:25 The works that I do in My *F*
10:29 to snatch them out of My *F*
14: 2 In My *F* house are many mansions;
14:24 you hear is not Mine but the *F*
15:10 just as I have kept My *F*
Acts 7:20 and he was brought up in his *f*
1 Cor 5: 1 that a man has his *f* wife!
Rev 14: 1 having His *F* name written on

FATHERED (1/1) FATHER

Deut 32:18 forgotten the God who *f* you.

FATHERLESS (40/40) FATHER

Ex 22:22 not afflict any widow or *f*
22:24 be widows, and your children *f*.
Deut 10:18 administers justice for the *f*
14:29 and the stranger and the *f* and
16:11 the stranger and the *f* and the
16:14 the stranger and the *f* and the
24:17 due the stranger or the *f*,
24:19 be for the stranger, the *f*,
24:20 be for the stranger, the *f*,
24:21 be for the stranger, the *f*,
26:12 the Levite, the stranger, the *f*,
26:13 the Levite, the stranger, the *f*,
27:19 justice due the stranger, the *f*,
Job 6:27 Yes, you overwhelm the *f*,
22: 9 And the strength of the *f* was
24: 3 drive away the donkey of the *f*;
24: 9 Some snatch the *f* from the
29:12 The *f* and the one who had
31:17 So that the *f* could not eat of
31:21 raised my hand against the *f*,
Ps 10:14 You are the helper of the *f*.
10:18 To do justice to the *f* and the
68: 5 A father of the *f*,
82: 3 Defend the poor and *f*;
94: 6 the stranger, And murder the *f*.
109: 9 Let his children be *f*,
109:12 let there be any to favor his *f*
146: 9 He relieves the *f* and widow;
Prov 23:10 Nor enter the fields of the *f*;
Isa 1:17 the oppressor; Defend the *f*,
1:23 They do not defend the *f*,
9:17 Nor have mercy on their *f* and
10: 2 And that they may rob the *f*.
Jer 5:28 the cause, The cause of the *f*;
7: 6 not oppress the stranger, the *f*,
22: 3 violence to the stranger, the *f*,
49:11 Leave your *f* children, I will
Ezek 22: 7 you they have mistreated the *f*
Hos 14: 3 For in You the *f* finds
Zech 7:10 not oppress the widow or the *f*,

FATHERS (435/411) FATHER, FATHERS', FOREFATHERS

Gen 15:15 you shall go to your *f* in
31: 3 Return to the land of your *f* and
46:34 now, both we and also our *f*,
47: 3 both we and also our *f*,
47: 9 the years of the life of my *f*
47:30 "but let me lie with my *f*;
48:15 before whom my *f* Abraham and
48:16 And the name of my *f* Abraham
48:21 you back to the land of your *f*.
49:29 bury me with my *f* in the cave
Ex 3:13 The God of your *f* has sent me to
3:15 'The LORD God of your *f*,
3:16 them, 'The LORD God of your *f*,
4: 5 that the LORD God of their *f*,
10: 6 which neither your *f* nor your
10: 6 fathers nor your fathers' *f*
13: 5 which He swore to your *f* to
13:11 as He swore to you and your *f*,
20: 5 visiting the iniquity of the *f*
34: 7 visiting the iniquity of the *f*
Lev 25:41 to the possession of his *f*.
26:40 and the iniquity of their *f*,
Num 11:12 land which You swore to their *f*?
13: 2 from each tribe of their *f* you
14:18 visiting the iniquity of the *f*
14:23 of which I swore to their *f*,
20:15 how our *f* went down to Egypt,
20:15 afflicted us and our *f*.
26:55 names of the tribes of their *f*.
31:26 the priest and the chief *f* of
32: 8 Thus your *f* did when I sent them
32:28 and to the chief *f* of the
33:54 to the tribes of your *f*.
34:14 to the house of their *f*,
34:14 to the house of their *f*,
36: 1 Now the chief *f* of the families
36: 1 the chief *f* of the children of
36: 3 from the inheritance of our *f*,
36: 4 of the tribe of our *f*.
36: 7 of the tribe of his *f*.
36: 8 the inheritance of his *f*.
Deut 1: 8 which the LORD swore to your *f*—
1:11 May the LORD God of your *f* make
1:21 as the LORD God of your *f* has
1:35 which I swore to give to your *f*,
4: 1 which the LORD God of your *f*
4:31 forget the covenant of your *f*
4:37 "And because He loved your *f*,
5: 3 make this covenant with our *f*,
5: 9 visiting the iniquity of the *f*

6: 3 as the LORD God of your *f* has
6:10 of which He swore to your *f*,
6:18 which the LORD swore to your *f*,
6:23 land of which He swore to our *f*.
7: 8 oath which He swore to your *f*,
7:12 mercy which He swore to your *f*.
7:13 of which He swore to your *f* to
8: 1 which the LORD swore to your *f*.
8: 3 you did not know nor did your *f*
8:16 which your *f* did not know, that
8:18 which He swore to your *f*,
9: 5 which the LORD swore to your *f*,
10:11 land which I swore to their *f*
10:15 LORD delighted only in your *f*,
10:22 Your *f* went down to Egypt with
11: 9 the LORD swore to give your *f*,
11:21 the LORD swore to your *f* to
12: 1 which the LORD God of your *f*
13: 6 known, neither you nor your *f*,
13:17 you, just as He swore to your *f*,
19: 8 as He swore to your *f*,
19: 8 He promised to give to your *f*,
24:16 *F* shall not be put to death for
24:16 be put to death for their *f*;
26: 3 which the LORD swore to our *f*
26: 7 out to the LORD God of our *f*,
26:15 us, just as You swore to our *f*,
27: 3 just as the LORD God of your *f*
28:11 the LORD swore to your *f* to
28:36 which neither you nor your *f*
28:64 which neither you nor your *f*
29:13 just as He has sworn to your *f*,
29:25 of the LORD God of their *f*,
30: 5 you to the land which your *f*
30: 5 multiply you more than your *f*.
30: 9 good as He rejoiced over your *f*,
30:20 which the LORD swore to your *f*,
31: 7 the LORD has sworn to their *f*
31:16 you will rest with your *f*;
31:20 of which I swore to their *f*,
32:17 new arrivals That your *f* did
Josh 1: 6 land which I swore to their *f*
4:21 your children ask their *f*
5: 6 the LORD had sworn to their *f*
14: 1 and the heads of the *f* of the
18: 3 which the LORD God of your *f*
19:51 and the heads of the *f* of the
21:43 He had sworn to give to their *f*,
21:44 that He had sworn to their *f*,
22:28 altar of the LORD which our *f*
24: 2 LORD God of Israel: 'Your *f*,
24: 6 Then I brought your *f* out of
24: 6 the Egyptians pursued your *f*
24:14 put away the gods which your *f*
24:15 whether the gods which your *f*
24:17 He who brought us and our *f* up
Judg 2: 1 land of which I swore to your *f*;
2:10 had been gathered to their *f*,
2:12 the LORD God of their *f*,
2:17 from the way in which their *f*
2:19 more corruptly than their *f*,
2:20 which I commanded their *f*,
2:22 to walk in them as their *f* kept
3: 4 which He had commanded their *f*
6:13 all His miracles which our *f*
21:22 when their *f* or their brothers
1 Sam 12: 6 and who brought your *f* up from
12: 7 which He did to you and your *f*:
12: 8 and your *f* cried out to the
12: 8 who brought your *f* out of Egypt
12:15 you, as it was against your *f*.
2 Sam 7:12 and you rest with your *f*,
1 Ki 1:21 lord the king rests with his *f*,
2:10 So David rested with his *f*,
8: 1 the chief *f* of the children of
8:21 LORD which He made with our *f*,
8:34 land which You gave to their *f*.
8:40 land which You gave to our *f*.
8:48 land which You gave to their *f*,
8:53 when You brought our *f* out of
8:57 with us, as He was with our *f*.
8:58 which He commanded our *f*.
9: 9 who brought their *f* out of the
11:21 that David rested with his *f*,
11:43 Then Solomon rested with his *f*,
13:22 not come to the tomb of your *f*.
14:15 land which He gave to their *f*,
14:20 So he rested with his *f*.
14:22 more than all that their *f* had
14:31 So Rehoboam rested with his *f*,
14:31 and was buried with his *f* in
15: 8 So Abijam rested with his *f*,
15:12 all the idols that his *f* had
15:24 So Asa rested with his *f*,
15:24 and was buried with his *f* in
16: 6 So Baasha rested with his *f* and
16:28 So Omri rested with his *f* and
19: 4 for I am no better than my *f*!
21: 3 give the inheritance of my *f*
21: 4 you the inheritance of my *f*.
22:40 So Ahab rested with his *f*.
22:50 Jehoshaphat rested with his *f*,
22:50 and was buried with his *f* in
2 Ki 8:24 So Joram rested with his *f*,
8:24 and was buried with his *f* in
9:28 him in his tomb with his *f* in
10:35 So Jehu rested with his *f*,
12:18 the sacred things that his *f*,
12:21 and they buried him with his *f*
13: 9 So Jehoahaz rested with his *f*,
13:13 So Joash rested with his *f*.
14: 6 *F* shall not be put to death for
14: 6 be put to death for their *f*;
14:16 So Jehoash rested with his *f*,
14:20 buried at Jerusalem with his *f*
14:22 the king rested with his *f*.
14:29 So Jeroboam rested with his *f*,
15: 7 So Azariah rested with his *f*,
15: 7 and they buried him with his *f*
15: 9 as his *f* had done; he did not
15:22 So Menahem rested with his *f*.
15:38 So Jotham rested with his *f*,
15:38 and was buried with his *f* in
16:20 So Ahaz rested with his *f*,
16:20 and was buried with his *f* in
17:13 law which I commanded your *f*,
17:14 like the necks of their *f*,
17:15 that He had made with their *f*,
17:41 continued doing as their *f* did,
19:12 delivered those whom my *f* have
20:17 and what your *f* have
20:21 So Hezekiah rested with his *f*.
21: 8 the land which I gave their *f*—
21:15 to anger since the day their *f*
21:18 So Manasseh rested with his *f*,
21:22 forsook the LORD God of his *f*,
22:13 because our *f* have not obeyed
22:20 I will gather you to your *f*,
23:32 according to all that his *f* had
23:37 according to all that his *f* had
24: 6 So Jehoiakim rested with his *f*.
1 Chr 4:19 were the *f* of Keilah the
5:25 to the God of their *f*,
6:19 Levites according to their *f*:
9:19 Their *f* had been keepers of the
12:17 may the God of our *f* look and
17:11 you must go to be with your *f*,
24:31 The chief *f* did just as their
26:31 to his genealogy of the *f*.
29:15 before You, As were all our *f*;
29:18 Isaac, and Israel, our *f*,
29:20 the LORD God of their *f*,
2 Chr 5: 2 the chief *f* of the children of
6:25 You gave to them and their *f*.
6:31 land which You gave to our *f*.
6:38 land which You gave to their *f*,
7:22 the LORD God of their *f*,
9:31 Then Solomon rested with his *f*,
11:16 to the LORD God of their *f*.
12:16 So Rehoboam rested with his *f*,
13:12 against the LORD God of your *f*,
13:18 on the LORD God of their *f*.
14: 1 So Abijah rested with his *f*,
14: 4 seek the LORD God of their *f*,
15:12 seek the LORD God of their *f*
16:13 So Asa rested with his *f*;
19: 4 to the LORD God of their *f*.
19: 8 and some of the chief *f* of
20: 6 said: "O LORD God of our *f*,
20:33 hearts to the God of their *f*.
21: 1 Jehoshaphat rested with his *f*,
21: 1 and was buried with his *f* in
21:10 forsaken the LORD God of his *f*.
21:19 him, like the burning for his *f*.
23: 2 and the chief *f* of Israel, and
24:18 of the LORD God of their *f*,
24:24 the LORD God of their *f*.
25: 4 The *f* shall not be put to death
25: 4 be put to death for their *f*;
25:28 and buried him with his *f* in
26: 2 the king rested with his *f*.
26:23 So Uzziah rested with his *f*,
26:23 and they buried him with his *f*
27: 9 So Jotham rested with his *f*,
28: 6 the LORD God of their *f*.
28: 9 the LORD God of your *f* was
28:25 to anger the LORD God of his *f*.
28:27 So Ahaz rested with his *f*,
29: 5 of the LORD God of your *f*,
29: 6 For our *f* have trespassed and
29: 9 because of this our *f* have
30: 7 And do not be like your *f* and
30: 7 the LORD God of their *f*,
30: 8 as your *f* were, but yield
30:19 God, the LORD God of his *f*,
30:22 to the LORD God of their *f*.
32:13 you not know what I and my *f*
32:14 gods of those nations that my *f*
32:15 my hand or the hand of my *f*.
32:33 So Hezekiah rested with his *f*,
33: 8 I have appointed for your *f*—
33:12 greatly before the God of his *f*,
33:20 So Manasseh rested with his *f*,
34:21 because our *f* have not kept the
34:28 I will gather you to your *f*,
34:32 of God, the God of their *f*.
34:33 the LORD God of their *f*.
35:24 in one of the tombs of his *f*.
36:15 And the LORD God of their *f*
Ezra 4:15 book of the records of your *f*.
5:12 But because our *f* provoked the
7:27 be the LORD God of our *f*,
8:28 to the LORD God of your *f*.
9: 7 Since the days of our *f* to this
10:11 to the LORD God of your *f*,
Neh 9: 2 and the iniquities of their *f*.
9: 9 saw the affliction of our *f* in
9:16 But they and our *f* acted
9:23 Which You had told their *f*
9:32 Our *f* and on all Your people,
9:34 princes, Our priests nor our *f*,
9:36 the land that You gave to our *f*,
13:18 Did not your *f* do thus, and did
Job 8: 8 things discovered by their *f*;
15:18 received from their *f*,
30: 1 Whose *f* I disdained to put
Ps 22: 4 Our *f* trusted in You; They
39:12 as all my *f* were.
44: 1 Our *f* have told us, The deeds
45:16 Instead of Your *f* shall be Your
49:19 go to the generation of his *f*;
78: 3 And our *f* have told us.
78: 5 Which He commanded our *f*,
78: 8 And may not be like their *f*,
78:12 He did in the sight of their *f*,
78:57 acted unfaithfully like their *f*;
95: 9 When your *f* tested Me;
106: 6 We have sinned with our *f*,
106: 7 Our *f* in Egypt did not
109:14 Let the iniquity of his *f* be
Prov 19:14 are an inheritance from *f*,
22:28 ancient landmark Which your *f*
Isa 14:21 of the iniquity of their *f*,
37:12 delivered those whom my *f* have
39: 6 and what your *f* have
49:23 Kings shall be your foster *f*,
64:11 Where our *f* praised You, Is
65: 7 and the iniquities of your *f*
Jer 2: 5 What injustice have your *f* found
3:18 as an inheritance to your *f*.
3:24 devoured The labor of our *f*
3:25 LORD our God, We and our *f*,
6:21 And the *f* and the sons
7: 7 the land that I gave to your *f*
7:14 which I gave to you and your *f*,
7:18 the *f* kindle the fire, and the
7:22 "For I did not speak to your *f*,
7:25 Since the day that your *f* came
7:26 They did worse than their *f*.
9:14 which their *f* taught them,"
9:16 whom neither they nor their *f*
11: 4 which I commanded your *f* in the
11: 5 which I have sworn to your *f*,
11: 7 I earnestly exhorted your *f* in
11:10 which I made with their *f*.
13:14 even the *f* and the sons
14:20 And the iniquity of our *f*,
16: 3 who bore them and their *f* who
16:11 Because your *f* have forsaken
16:12 you have done worse than your *f*,
16:13 know, neither you nor your *f*;
16:15 land which I gave to their *f*.
16:19 Surely our *f* have inherited
17:22 day, as I commanded your *f*.
19: 4 gods whom neither they, their *f*,
23:27 as their *f* forgot My name for
23:39 city that I gave you and your *f*,
24:10 that I gave to them and their *f*.
25: 5 has given to you and your *f*
30: 3 the land that I gave to their *f*,
31:29 The *f* have eaten sour grapes,
31:32 that I made with their *f* in
32:18 and repay the iniquity of the *f*
32:22 of which You swore to their *f*
34: 5 as in the ceremonies of your *f*,
34:13 I made a covenant with your *f* in
34:14 But your *f* did not obey Me
35:15 I have given you and your *f*.
44: 3 know, they nor you nor your *f*.
44: 9 the wickedness of your *f*,
44:10 I set before you and your *f*.
44:17 as we have done, we and our *f*,
44:21 of Jerusalem, you and your *f*,
47: 3 The *f* will not look back for
50: 7 The LORD, the hope of their *f*.
Lam 5: 7 Our *f* sinned and are no more,
Ezek 2: 3 they and their *f* have
5:10 Therefore *f* shall eat their
5:10 and sons shall eat their *f*;
18: 2 The *f* have eaten sour grapes,
20: 4 the abominations of their *f*.
20:18 walk in the statutes of your *f*,
20:27 In this too your *f* have
20:30 in the manner of your *f*,
20:36 I pleaded My case with your *f*
20:42 in an oath to give to your *f*.
36:28 the land that I gave to your *f*;
37:25 where your *f* dwelt; and they
47:14 in an oath to give it to your *f*,
Dan 2:23 and praise You, O God of my *f*;
9: 6 to our *f* and all the people of
9: 8 kings, our princes, and our *f*,
9:16 and for the iniquities of our *f*,
11:24 and he shall do what his *f*
11:37 neither the God of his *f* nor
11:38 and a god which his *f* did not
Hos 9:10 I saw your *f* As the
Joel 1: 2 Or even in the days of your *f*?
Am 2: 4 Lies which their *f* followed.
Mic 7:20 Which You have sworn to our *f*
Zech 1: 2 has been very angry with your *f*.
1: 4 "Do not be like your *f*,
1: 5 'Your *f*, where are they?
1: 6 Did they not overtake your *f*?
8:14 to punish you When your *f*
Mal 2:10 profaning the covenant of the *f*?
3: 7 Yet from the days of your *f*
4: 6 will turn The hearts of the *f*
4: 6 of the children to their *f*,
Mt 23:30 had lived in the days of our *f*,
Lk 1:17 turn the hearts of the *f*
1:55 As He spoke to our *f*,
1:72 the mercy promised to our *f*
6:23 For in like manner their *f* did
6:26 For so did their *f* to the
11:47 and your *f* killed them.

11:48 you approve the deeds of your *f*;
Jn 4:20 Our *f* worshiped on this
6:31 Our *f* ate the manna in the
6:49 Your *f* ate the manna in the
6:58 not as your *f* ate the manna, and
7:22 is from Moses, but from the *f*),
Acts 3:13 and Jacob, the God of our *f*,
3:22 "For Moses truly said to the *f*,
3:25 which God made with our *f*,
5:30 The God of our *f* raised up Jesus
7: 2 And he said, "Brethren and *f*,
7:11 and our *f* found no sustenance.
7:12 he sent out our *f* first.
7:15 and he died, he and our *f*.
7:32 'I am the God of your *f*—
7:38 on Mount Sinai, and with our *f*,
7:39 whom our *f* would not obey, but
7:44 Our *f* had the tabernacle of
7:45 'which our *f*, having
7:45 out before the face of our *f*
7:51 as your *f* did, so do you.
7:52 of the prophets did your *f* not
13:17 this people Israel chose our *f*,
13:32 promise which was made to the *f*.
13:36 asleep, was buried with his *f*,
15:10 disciples which neither our *f*
22: 1 'Brethren and *f*, hear my
22:14 The God of our *f* has chosen you
24:14 so I worship the God of my *f*,
26: 6 promise made by God to our *f*.
28:17 people or the customs of our *f*,
28:25 Isaiah the prophet to our *f*,
Rom 9: 5 of whom are the *f* and from
11:28 beloved for the sake of the *f*.
15: 8 the promises made to the *f*,
1 Cor 4:15 yet you do not have many *f*;
10: 1 to be unaware that all our *f*
Gal 1:14 for the traditions of my *f*.
Eph 6: 4 And you, *f*, do not provoke
Col 3:21 *F*, do not provoke your
1 Tim 1: 9 for murderers of *f* and
Heb 1: 1 spoke in time past to the *f* by
3: 9 Where your *f* tested Me,
8: 9 that I made with their *f*
12: 9 we have had human *f* who
1 Pe 1:18 by tradition from your *f*,
2 Pe 3: 4 For since the *f* fell asleep,
1 Jn 2:13 I write to you, *f*,
2:14 I have written to you, *f*,

FATHERS' (101/96) FATHERS

Ex 6:14 are the heads of their *f*
6:25 These are the heads of the *f*
10: 6 neither your fathers nor your *f*
Lev 26:39 also in their *f* iniquities,
Num 1: 2 by their *f* houses, according to
1:16 leaders of their *f* tribes,
1:18 by their *f* houses, according to
1:20 by their *f* house, according to
1:22 by their *f* house, of those who
1:24 by their *f* house, according to
1:26 by their *f* house, according to
1:28 by their *f* house, according to
1:30 by their *f* house, according to
1:32 by their *f* house, according to
1:34 by their *f* house, according to
1:36 by their *f* house, according to
1:38 by their *f* house, according to
1:40 by their *f* house, according to
1:42 by their *f* house, according to
1:45 by their *f* houses, from twenty
1:47 numbered among them by their *f*
2:32 children of Israel by their *f*
2:34 according to their *f* houses.
3:15 the children of Levi by their *f*
3:20 of the Levites by their *f*
3:24 And the leader of the *f* house of
3:30 And the leader of the *f* house of
3:35 The leader of the *f* house of the
4: 2 by their *f* house,
4:22 by their *f* house, by their
4:29 their families and by their *f*
4:34 their families and by their *f*
4:38 their families and by their *f*
4:40 by their *f* house, were two
4:42 by their *f* house,
4:46 their families and by their *f*
7: 2 the heads of their *f* houses,
17: 2 leaders according to their *f*
17: 6 leader according to their *f*
26: 2 by their *f* houses, all who are
Josh 21: 1 Then the heads of the *f* houses
21: 1 and to the heads of the *f*
1 Chr 5:24 were the heads of their *f*
5:24 and heads of their *f* houses.
7: 4 according to their *f* houses,
7: 7 They were heads of their *f*
7: 9 heads of their *f* houses, twenty
7:11 Jediael were heads of their *f*
7:40 heads of their *f* houses,
8: 6 who were the heads of the *f*
8:10 heads of their *f* houses.
8:13 who were heads of their *f*
8:28 These were heads of the *f*
9: 9 of a father's house in their *f*
9:13 heads of their *f* houses—one
9:33 heads of the *f* houses of the
9:34 These heads of the *f* houses of
15:12 You are the heads of the *f*
23: 9 These were the heads of the *f*
23:24 the sons of Levi by their *f*
23:24 the heads of the *f* houses as
24: 4 were sixteen heads of their *f*
24: 4 and eight heads of their *f*
24: 6 and the heads of the *f* houses
24:30 Levites according to their *f*
24:31 and the heads of the *f* houses
26: 6 sons born who governed their *f*
26:21 heads of their *f* houses, of
26:26 King David and the heads of *f*
26:32 heads of *f* houses, whom King
27: 1 the heads of *f* houses, the
29: 6 Then the leaders of the *f*
2 Chr 1: 2 the heads of the *f* houses.
17:14 according to their *f* houses. Of
25: 5 according to their *f* houses,
35: 4 according to your *f* houses,
35: 5 to the divisions of the *f*
35:12 them to the divisions of the *f*
Ezra 1: 5 Then the heads of the *f* houses
2:68 Some of the heads of the *f*
3:12 and Levites and heads of the *f*
4: 2 and the heads of the *f* houses,
4: 3 the rest of the heads of the *f*
8: 1 These are the heads of their *f*
8:29 the Levites and heads of the *f*
10:16 with certain heads of the *f*
10:16 were set apart by the *f*
Neh 2: 3 the place of my *f* tombs, lies
2: 5 to the city of my *f* tombs, that
7:70 And some of the heads of the *f*
7:71 Some of the heads of the *f*
8:13 second day the heads of the *f*
10:34 according to our *f* houses, at
11:13 heads of the *f* houses, were
12:12 the heads of the *f* houses
12:22 had been heads of their *f*
12:23 the heads of the *f* houses
Ezek 20:24 eyes were fixed on their *f*
22:10 In you men uncover their *f*
Mt 23:32 the measure of your *f* guilt.
Acts 22: 3 to the strictness of our *f* law,

FATHOMS (2/1)

Acts 27:28 and found it to be twenty *f*;
27:28 and found it to be fifteen *f*.

FATLING (1/1) FATLINGS

Isa 11: 6 and the young lion and the *f*

FATLINGS (3/3) FATLING

1 Sam 15: 9 of the sheep, the oxen, the *f*,
Ezek 34: 3 the wool; you slaughter the *f*,
39:18 All of them *f* of Bashan.

FATNESS (9/9) FAT

Gen 27:28 Of the *f* of the earth, And
27:39 dwelling shall be of the *f* of
Job 15:27 has covered his face with his *f*,
Ps 63: 5 satisfied as with marrow and *f*,
109:24 flesh is feeble from lack of *f*.
Isa 17: 4 And the *f* of his flesh grow
34: 6 It is made overflowing with *f*,
34: 7 their dust saturated with *f*.
Rom 11:17 a partaker of the root and *f*

FATTED (9/8) FAT

1 Sam 28:24 Now the woman had a *f* calf in
2 Sam 6:13 that he sacrificed oxen and *f*
1 Ki 4:23 ten *f* oxen, twenty oxen from the
4:23 roebucks, and *f* fowl.
Prov 15:17 Than a *f* calf with hatred.
Mt 22: 4 my oxen and *f* cattle are
Lk 15:23 And bring the *f* calf here and
15:27 your father has killed the *f*
15:30 you killed the *f* calf for him.'

FATTENED (5/5) FAT

1 Ki 1: 9 sheep and oxen and *f* cattle by
1:19 He has sacrificed oxen and *f*
1:25 and has sacrificed oxen and *f*
Am 5:22 Nor will I regard your *f* peace
Jas 5: 5 you have *f* your hearts as in a

FATTER (1/1) FAT

Dan 1:15 features appeared better and *f*

FATTY (12/11) FAT

Ex 29:13 the *f* lobe attached to the
29:22 the *f* lobe attached to the
Lev 3: 4 and the *f* lobe attached to the
3:10 and the *f* lobe attached to the
3:15 and the *f* lobe attached to the
4: 9 and the *f* lobe attached to the
7: 4 and the *f* lobe attached to the
8:16 the *f* lobe attached to the
8:25 the *f* lobe attached to the
9:10 and the *f* lobe from the liver
9:19 the *f* tail, what covers the
9:19 and the *f* lobe attached to

FAULT (18/17) FAULTLESS, FAULTS

Ex 5:16 but the *f* is in your own
1 Sam 29: 3 to this day I have found no *f*
2 Sam 3: 8 you charge me today with a *f*
Ps 59: 4 themselves through no *f* of
Dan 6: 4 they could find no charge or *f*,
6: 4 nor was there any error or *f*
Mt 18:15 go and tell him his *f* between
Mk 7: 2 unwashed hands, they found *f*.
Lk 23: 4 I find no *f* in this Man."
23:14 I have found no *f* in this Man
Jn 18:38 I find no *f* in Him at all.
19: 4 you may know that I find no *f*
19: 6 for I find no *f* in Him."
Acts 25: 5 to see if there is any *f* in
Rom 9:19 "Why does He still find *f*?
Phil 2:15 children of God without *f* in
Heb 8: 8 Because finding *f* with them, He
Rev 14: 5 for they are without *f* before

FAULTLESS (2/2) FAULT

Heb 8: 7 that first covenant had been *f*,
Jude 24 And to present you *f* Before

FAULTS (3/3) FAULT

Gen 41: 9 I remember my *f* this day.
Ps 19:12 Cleanse me from secret *f*.
1 Pe 2:20 when you are beaten for your *f*,

FAVOR (96/96) FAVORABLE, FAVORED, FAVORITE

Gen 18: 3 if I have now found *f* in Your
19:19 your servant has found *f* in
30:27 if I have found *f* in your eyes,
32: 5 that I may find *f* in your
33: 8 These are to find *f* in the
33:10 if I have now found *f* in your
33:15 Let me find *f* in the sight of
34:11 Let me find *f* in your eyes, and
39: 4 So Joseph found *f* in his sight,
39:21 and He gave him *f* in the sight
47:25 let us find *f* in the sight of
47:29 Now if I have found *f* in your
50: 4 If now I have found *f* in your
Ex 3:21 And I will give this people *f* in
11: 3 the LORD gave the people *f* in
12:36 LORD had given the people *f*
Num 11:11 And why have I not found *f* in
11:15 if I have found *f* in Your
32: 5 If we have found *f* in your
Deut 24: 1 it happens that she finds no *f*
28:50 respect the elderly nor show *f*
33:16 And the *f* of Him who dwelt in
33:23 "O Naphtali, satisfied with *f*,
Judg 6:17 If now I have found *f* in Your
Ruth 2: 2 in whose sight I may find *f*.
2:10 Why have I found *f* in your eyes,
2:13 Let me find *f* in your sight, my
1 Sam 1:18 Let your maidservant find *f* in
2:26 and in *f* both with the LORD
16:22 for he has found *f* in my
20: 3 knows that I have found *f* in
20:29 if I have found *f* in your eyes,
25: 8 let my young men find *f* in
27: 5 If I have now found *f* in your
29: 6 the lords do not *f* you.
2 Sam 14:22 knows that I have found *f* in
15:25 If I find *f* in the eyes of the
16: 4 that I may find *f* in your
1 Ki 11:19 And Hadad found great *f* in the
13: 6 Please entreat the *f* of the
2 Chr 32:25 not repay according to the *f*
Neh 2: 5 if your servant has found *f* in
Esth 2: 9 him, and she obtained his *f*;
2:15 And Esther obtained *f* in the
2:17 and she obtained grace and *f* in
5: 2 that she found *f* in his sight,
5: 8 If I have found *f* in the sight
7: 3 If I have found *f* in your sight,
8: 5 and if I have found *f* in his
Job 10:12 You have granted me life and *f*,
11:19 Yes, many would court your *f*.
20:10 His children will seek the *f* of
Ps 5:12 With *f* You will surround him
30: 5 His *f* is for life;
30: 7 by Your *f* You have made my
35:27 Who *f* my righteous cause;
45:12 the people will seek your *f*.
89:17 And in Your *f* our horn is
102:13 For the time to *f* her, Yes,
102:14 And show *f* to her dust.
106: 4 with the *f* You have toward
109:12 Nor let there be any to *f* his
119:58 I entreated Your *f* with my
Prov 3: 4 And so find *f* and high esteem
8:35 And obtains *f* from the LORD;
11:27 earnestly seeks good finds *f*,
12: 2 A good man obtains *f* from the
13:15 Good understanding gains *f*,
14: 9 among the upright there is *f*.
14:35 The king's *f* is toward a wise
16:15 And his *f* is like a cloud of
18:22 And obtains *f* from the LORD.
19: 6 Many entreat the *f* of the
19:12 But his *f* is like dew on the
21:10 His neighbor finds no *f* in his
22: 1 Loving *f* rather than silver
28:23 rebukes a man will find more *f*
29:26 Many seek the ruler's *f*,
Eccl 9:11 Nor *f* to men of skill;
Isa 27:11 formed them will show them no *f*.
60:10 But in My *f* I have had mercy
Jer 16:13 where I will not show you *f*.

26:19 LORD and seek the LORD's *f*?
Lam 4:16 the priests Nor show *f* to the
Dan 1: 9 had brought Daniel into the *f*
7:22 and a judgment was made in *f*
Hos 12: 4 and sought *f* from Him.
Mal 1: 9 "But now entreat God's *f*,
Lk 1:30 for you have found *f* with God.
2:52 and in *f* with God and men.
Acts 2:47 praising God and having *f* with
7:10 and gave him *f* and wisdom in
7:46 who found *f* before God and asked
24:27 wanting to do the Jews a *f*,
25: 3 asking a *f* against him, that he
25: 9 wanting to do the Jews a *f*,

FAVORABLE (5/5) FAVOR, FAVORABLY

Gen 31: 2 and indeed it was not *f*
31: 5 that it is not *f* toward me as
Ps 77: 7 And will He be *f* no more?
85: 1 You have been *f* to Your land;
Jer 15: 1 My mind would not be *f* toward

FAVORABLY (3/3) FAVORABLE

Lev 26: 9 For I will look on you *f* and
Mal 1: 8 Would he accept you *f*?"
1: 9 hands, Will He accept you *f*?

FAVORED (4/4) FAVOR

Gen 19:21 I have *f* you concerning this
Deut 33:24 Let him be *f* by his brothers,
Ps 44: 3 Because You *f* them.
Lk 1:28 highly *f* one, the Lord is

FAVORITE (1/1) FAVOR, FAVORITISM

Song 6: 9 The *f* of the one who bore her.

FAVORITISM (2/2) FAVORITE

Lk 20:21 and You do not show personal *f*,
Gal 2: 6 God shows personal *f* to no

FAVORS (1/1)

2 Sam 20:11 Whoever *f* Joab and whoever is

FAWNS (2/2)

Song 4: 5 two breasts are like two *f*,
7: 3 two breasts are like two *f*,

FEAR (366/353) FEARED, FEARFUL, FEARING, FEARS

Gen 9: 2 And the *f* of you and the dread
20:11 surely the *f* of God is not in
21:17 *F* not, for God has heard the
22:12 for now I know that you *f* God,
26:24 your father Abraham; do not *f*,
31:42 the God of Abraham and the *F* of
31:53 And Jacob swore by the *F* of
32:11 for I *f* him, lest he come and
35:17 midwife said to her, "Do not *f*;
42:18 this and live, for I *f* God:
46: 3 do not *f* to go down to Egypt,
Ex 9:30 I know that you will not yet *f*
15:16 *F* and dread will fall on them
18:21 such as *f* God, men of truth,
20:20 said to the people, "Do not *f*;
20:20 and that His *f* may be before
23:27 I will send My *f* before you, I
Lev 19:14 but shall *f* your God: I am the
19:32 and *f* your God: I am the
25:17 but you shall *f* your God; for I
25:36 but *f* your God, that your
25:43 but you shall *f* your God.
Num 14: 9 nor *f* the people of the land,
14: 9 Do not *f* them."
21:34 Do not *f* him, for I have
Deut 1:21 do not *f* or be discouraged.'
2:25 begin to put the dread and *f*
3: 2 Do not *f* him, for I have
3:22 You must not *f* them, for the
4:10 that they may learn to *f* Me all
5:29 in them that they would *f* Me
6: 2 that you may *f* the LORD your
6:13 You shall *f* the LORD your God
6:24 to *f* the LORD our God, for our
8: 6 to walk in His ways and to *f*
10:12 but to *f* the LORD your God, to
10:20 You shall *f* the LORD your God;
11:25 put the dread of you and the *f*
13: 4 after the LORD your God and *f*
13:11 all Israel shall hear and *f*,
14:23 that you may learn to *f* the
17:13 all the people shall hear and *f*,
17:19 that he may learn to *f* the
19:20 who remain shall hear and *f*,
21:21 and all Israel shall hear and *f*.
25:18 and he did not *f* God.
28:58 that you may *f* this glorious
28:66 you shall *f* day and night, and
28:67 were morning!' because of the *f*
31: 6 do not *f* nor be afraid of them;
31: 8 do not *f* nor be dismayed."
31:12 and that they may learn to *f*
31:13 may hear and learn to *f* the
32:17 That your fathers did not *f*.
Josh 4:24 that you may *f* the LORD your
10: 8 Do not *f* them, for I have

22:24 in fact we have done it for *f*,
24:14 *f* the LORD, serve Him in
Judg 4:18 turn aside to me; do not *f*.
6:10 do not *f* the gods of the
6:23 "Peace be with you; do not *f*,
9:21 for *f* of Abimelech his brother.
Ruth 3:11 now, my daughter, do not *f*.
1 Sam 4:20 by her said to her, "Do not *f*,
11: 7 And the *f* of the LORD fell
12:14 If you *f* the LORD and serve Him
12:20 said to the people, "Do not *f*.
12:24 Only *f* the LORD, and serve Him
22:23 "Stay with me; do not *f*.
23:17 And he said to him, "Do not *f*,
2 Sam 9: 7 David said to him, "Do not *f*,
23: 3 Ruling in the *f* of God.
1 Ki 8:40 that they may *f* You all the days
8:43 earth may know Your name and *f*
17:13 Elijah said to her, "Do not *f*;
2 Ki 6:16 So he answered, "Do not *f*,
17:25 that they did not *f* the LORD;
17:28 taught them how they should *f*
17:34 they do not *f* the LORD, nor do
17:35 You shall not *f* other gods, nor
17:36 arm, Him you shall *f*,
17:37 you shall not *f* other gods.
17:38 nor shall you *f* other gods.
17:39 the LORD your God you shall *f*;
1 Chr 14:17 and the LORD brought the *f* of
22:13 do not *f* nor be dismayed.
28:20 do not *f* nor be dismayed, for
2 Chr 6:31 that they may *f* You, to walk in
6:33 earth may know Your name and *f*
14:14 for the *f* of the LORD came
17:10 And the *f* of the LORD fell on
19: 7 let the *f* of the LORD be upon
19: 9 Thus you shall act in the *f* of
20:17 Judah and Jerusalem!' Do not *f*
20:29 And the *f* of God was on all the
Ezra 3: 3 Though *f* had come upon them
Neh 1:11 Your servants who desire to *f*
5: 9 Should you not walk in the *f* of
5:15 because of the *f* of God.
Esth 8:17 because *f* of the Jews fell upon
9: 2 because *f* of them fell upon all
9: 3 because the *f* of Mordecai fell
Job 1: 9 Does Job *f* God for nothing?
4:14 *F* came upon me, and trembling,
6:14 Even though he forsakes the *f*
9:35 Then I would speak and not *f*
11:15 could be steadfast, and not *f*;
15: 4 Yes, you cast off *f*,
21: 9 Their houses are safe from *f*,
22: 4 Is it because of your *f* of Him
22:10 And sudden *f* troubles you,
25: 2 Dominion and *f* belong to Him;
28:28 the *f* of the Lord, that is
33: 7 Surely no *f* of me will terrify
37:24 Therefore men *f* Him; He shows
39:22 He mocks at *f*, and is not
41:33 him, Which is made without *f*.
Ps 2:11 Serve the LORD with *f*,
5: 7 In *f* of You I will worship
9:20 Put them in *f*, O LORD,
14: 5 There they are in great *f*,
15: 4 But he honors those who *f* the
19: 9 The *f* of the LORD is clean,
22:23 You who *f* the LORD, praise
22:23 And *f* Him, all you offspring
22:25 pay My vows before those who *f*
23: 4 I will *f* no evil; For You
25:14 the LORD is with those who *f*
27: 1 my salvation; Whom shall I *f*?
27: 3 me, My heart shall not *f*;
31:13 *F* is on every side;
31:19 have laid up for those who *f*
33: 8 Let all the earth *f* the LORD;
33:18 of the LORD is on those who *f*
34: 7 encamps all around those who *f*
34: 9 *f* the LORD, you His saints!
34: 9 is no want to those who *f* Him.
34:11 I will teach you the *f* of the
36: 1 There is no *f* of God before
40: 3 Many will see it and *f*,
46: 2 Therefore we will not *f*,
48: 6 *F* took hold of them there,
49: 5 Why should I *f* in the days of
52: 6 righteous also shall see and *f*,
53: 5 There they are in great *f*
53: 5 are in great fear Where no *f*
55:19 Therefore they do not *f* God.
56: 4 put my trust; I will not *f*.
60: 4 given a banner to those who *f*
61: 5 me the heritage of those who *f*
64: 1 Preserve my life from *f* of the
64: 4 they shoot at him and do not *f*.
64: 9 All men shall *f*, And shall
66:16 all you who *f* God, And I will
67: 7 the ends of the earth shall *f*
72: 5 They shall *f* You As long as
78:33 futility, And their years in *f*.
78:53 safely, so that they did not *f*;
85: 9 is near to those who *f* Him,
86:11 Unite my heart to *f* Your name.
90:11 For as the *f* of You, so is
102:15 So the nations shall *f* the name
103:11 is His mercy toward those who *f*
103:13 the LORD pities those who *f*
103:17 to everlasting On those who *f*
105:38 For the *f* of them had fallen
111: 5 has given food to those who *f*
111:10 The *f* of the LORD is the

115:11 You who *f* the LORD, trust in
115:13 He will bless those who *f* the
118: 4 Let those who *f* the LORD now
118: 6 is on my side; I will not *f*.
119:63 I am a companion of all who *f*
119:74 Those who *f* You will be glad
119:79 Let those who *f* You turn to me,
119:120 My flesh trembles for *f* of You,
135:20 O house of Levi! You who *f* the
145:19 the desire of those who *f* Him;
147:11 takes pleasure in those who *f*
Prov 1: 7 The *f* of the LORD is the
1:29 And did not choose the *f* of
1:33 without *f* of evil."
2: 5 you will understand the *f* of
3: 7 *F* the LORD and depart from
8:13 The *f* of the LORD is to hate
9:10 The *f* of the LORD is the
10:24 The *f* of the wicked will come
10:27 The *f* of the LORD prolongs
14:26 In the *f* of the LORD there
14:27 The *f* of the LORD is a
15:16 is a little with the *f* of the
15:33 The *f* of the LORD is the
16: 6 And by the *f* of the LORD one
19:23 The *f* of the LORD leads to
22: 4 By humility and the *f* of the
23:17 But be zealous for the *f* of
24:21 *f* the LORD and the king;
29:25 The *f* of man brings a snare,
Eccl 3:14 that men should *f* before Him.
5: 7 is also vanity. But *f* God.
8:12 will be well with those who *f*
8:12 who *f* before Him.
8:13 because he does not *f* before
Song 3: 8 on his thigh Because of *f* in
Isa 7: 4 do not *f* or be fainthearted for
7:25 You will not go there for *f* of
8:13 Let Him be your *f*,
11: 2 of knowledge and of the *f* of
11: 3 His delight is in the *f* of the
14: 3 and from your *f* and the hard
19:16 and will be afraid and *f*
21: 4 I longed He turned into *f* for
24:17 *F* and the pit and the snare
24:18 flees from the noise of the *f*
25: 3 of the terrible nations will *f*
29:13 And their *f* toward Me is
29:23 And *f* the God of Israel.
31: 9 over to his stronghold for *f*,
33: 6 The *f* of the LORD is His
35: 4 do not *f*! Behold, your God
41:10 *F* not, for I am with you
41:13 *F* not, I will help you.'
41:14 *F* not, you worm Jacob, You men
43: 1 *F* not, for I have redeemed you;
43: 5 *F* not, for I am with you
44: 2 '*F* not, O Jacob My servant;
44: 8 Do not *f*, nor be afraid;
44:11 stand up; Yet they shall *f*,
51: 7 Do not *f* the reproach of men,
54: 4 Do not *f*, for you will not be
54:14 oppression, for you shall not *f*;
57:11 from of old That you do not *f*
59:19 So shall they *f* The name of
63:17 hardened our heart from Your *f*?
Jer 2:19 And the *f* of Me is not in
3: 8 sister Judah did not *f*,
5:22 Do you not *f* Me?' says the
5:24 Let us now *f* the LORD our God,
6:25 *F* is on every side.
10: 7 Who would not *f* You, O King of
17: 8 And will not *f* when heat
20:10 '*F* on every side!"
22:25 of those whose face you *f*—
23: 4 and they shall *f* no more, nor
26:19 Did he not *f* the LORD and seek
30: 5 a voice of trembling, Of *f*,
30:10 'Therefore do not *f*,
32:39 that they may *f* Me forever, for
32:40 but I will put My *f* in their
33: 9 they shall *f* and tremble for
35:11 let us go to Jerusalem for *f* of
35:11 of the Chaldeans and for *f* of
36:16 that they looked in *f* from one
37:11 the siege of Jerusalem for *f*
41: 9 Asa the king had made for *f* of
46: 5 For *f* was all around," says
46:27 "But do not *f*,
46:28 Do not *f*, O Jacob My
48:43 *F* and the pit and the snare
48:44 He who flees from the *f* shall
49: 5 I will bring *f* upon you,"
49:24 And *f* has seized her.
49:29 *F* is on every side!'
50:16 For *f* of the oppressing sword
51:46 And you *f* for the rumor that
Lam 3:47 *F* and a snare have come upon
3:57 And said, "Do not *f*!"
Ezek 30:13 I will put *f* in the land of
Dan 1:10 I *f* my lord the king, who has
6:26 men must tremble and *f*
10:12 Then he said to me, "Do not *f*,
10:19 *f* not! Peace be to you; be
Hos 3: 5 They shall *f* the LORD and His
10: 3 Because we did not *f* the
10: 5 The inhabitants of Samaria *f*
Joel 2:21 *F* not, O land; Be glad and
Am 3: 8 has roared! Who will not *f*?
Jon 1: 9 and I *f* the LORD, the God of
Mic 7:17 And shall *f* because of You.
Zeph 3: 7 Surely you will *f* Me, You will

3:16 said to Jerusalem: "Do not *f*;
Hag 2: 5 among you; do not *f*!'
Zech 8:13 shall be a blessing. Do not *f*,
8:15 the house of Judah. Do not *f*.
9: 5 Ashkelon shall see it and *f*;
Mal 2: 5 them to him that he might *f*
3: 5 Because they do not *f* Me,"
3:16 before Him For those who *f*
4: 2 But to you who *f* My name The
Mt 10:26 'Therefore do not *f* them.
10:28 And do not *f* those who kill the
10:28 But rather *f* Him who is able to
10:31 Do not *f* therefore; you are of
14:26 And they cried out for *f*.
21:26 we *f* the multitude, for all
28: 4 And the guards shook for *f* of
28: 8 quickly from the tomb with *f*
Lk 1:12 and *f* fell upon him.
1:50 His mercy is on those who *f*
1:65 Then *f* came on all who dwelt
1:74 Might serve Him without *f*,
5:26 God and were filled with *f*,
7:16 Then *f* came upon all, and they
8:37 they were seized with great *f*.
12: 5 will show you whom you should *f*:
12: 5 *F* Him who, after He has killed,
12: 5 yes, I say to you, *f* Him!
12: 7 Do not *f* therefore; you are of
12:32 'Do not *f*, little flock,
18: 2 city a judge who did not *f* God
18: 4 Though I do not *f* God nor regard
21:26 hearts failing them from *f* and
23:40 Do you not even *f* God, seeing
Jn 7:13 one spoke openly of Him for *f*
12:15 *F* not, daughter of Zion;
19:38 for *f* of the Jews, asked Pilate
20:19 for *f* of the Jews, Jesus came
Acts 2:43 Then *f* came upon every soul, and
5: 5 So great *f* came upon all those
5:11 So great *f* came upon all the
9:31 And walking in the *f* of the
13:16 and you who *f* God, listen:
13:26 and those among you who *f* God,
19:17 and *f* fell on them all, and the
Rom 3:18 There is no *f* of God
8:15 spirit of bondage again to *f*,
11:20 Do not be haughty, but *f*.
13: 7 *f* to whom fear, honor to whom
13: 7 to whom customs, fear to whom *f*,
1 Cor 2: 3 was with you in weakness, in *f*,
16:10 he may be with you without *f*;
2 Cor 7: 1 perfecting holiness in the *f* of
7:11 what indignation, what *f*,
7:15 how with *f* and trembling you
11: 3 But I *f*, lest somehow,
12:20 For I *f* lest, when I come, I
Eph 5:21 to one another in the *f* of God.
6: 5 with *f* and trembling, in
Phil 1:14 to speak the word without *f*.
2:12 out your own salvation with *f*
1 Tim 5:20 all, that the rest also may *f*.
2 Tim 1: 7 has not given us a spirit of *f*,
Heb 2:15 release those who through *f* of
4: 1 let us *f* lest any of you seem
5: 7 heard because of His godly *f*,
11: 7 yet seen, moved with godly *f*,
12:28 with reverence and godly *f*.
13: 6 my helper; I will not *f*.
1 Pe 1:17 time of your stay here in *f*;
2:17 *F* God. Honor the king.
2:18 to your masters with all *f*,
3: 2 conduct accompanied by *f*.
3:15 is in you, with meekness and *f*;
1 Jn 4:18 There is no *f* in love;
4:18 but perfect love casts out *f*,
4:18 because *f* involves torment.
Jude 12 they feast with you without *f*,
23 but others save with *f*,
Rev 2:10 Do not *f* any of those things
11:11 and great *f* fell on those who
11:18 And those who *f* Your name,
14: 7 *F* God and give glory to Him, for
15: 4 Who shall not *f* You, O Lord,
18:10 standing at a distance for *f* of
18:15 will stand at a distance for *f*
19: 5 His servants and those who *f*

FEAR OF THE LORD (27/27)

1 Sam 11: 7 And the *f* fell on the people,
2 Chr 14:14 for the *f* came upon them;
17:10 And the *f* fell on all the
19: 7 let the *f* be upon you;
19: 9 "Thus you shall act in the *f*,
Job 28:28 to man He said, 'Behold, the *f*,
Ps 19: 9 The *f* is clean, enduring
34:11 to me; I will teach you the *f*.
111:10 The *f* is the beginning of
Prov 1: 7 The *f* is the beginning of
1:29 And did not choose the *f*,
2: 5 Then you will understand the *f*,
8:13 The *f* is to hate evil;
9:10 The *f* is the beginning of
10:27 The *f* prolongs days, But the
14:26 In the *f* there is strong
14:27 The *f* is a fountain of life,
15:16 Better is a little with the *f*,
15:33 The *f* is the instruction of
16: 6 And by the *f* one departs from
19:23 The *f* leads to life, And he
22: 4 By humility and the *f* Are
23:17 But be zealous for the *f* all
Isa 11: 2 of knowledge and of the *f*.
11: 3 His delight is in the *f*,
33: 6 The *f* is His treasure.
Acts 9:31 And walking in the *f* and in the

FEARED (60/59) FEAR

Ex 1:17 But the midwives *f* God, and did
1:21 because the midwives *f* God,
2:14 So Moses *f* and said, "Surely
9:20 He who *f* the word of the LORD
14:31 so the people *f* the LORD, and
Deut 32:27 Had I not *f* the wrath of the
Josh 4:14 and they *f* him, as they had
4:14 as they had *f* Moses, all the
10: 2 that they *f* greatly, because
Judg 6:27 But because he *f* his father's
1 Sam 12:18 and all the people greatly *f*
14:26 for the people *f* the oath.
15:24 because I *f* the people and
2 Sam 3:11 because he *f* him.
1 Ki 3:28 and they *f* the king, for they
18: 3 (Now Obadiah *f* the LORD
18:12 But I your servant have *f* the
2 Ki 4: 1 you know that your servant *f*
17: 7 and they had *f* other gods,
17:32 So they *f* the LORD, and from
17:33 They *f* the LORD, yet served
17:41 So these nations *f* the LORD,
1 Chr 16:25 He is also to be *f* above all
2 Chr 20: 3 And Jehoshaphat *f*,
Neh 7: 2 he was a faithful man and *f*
Job 1: 1 and one who *f* God and shunned
3:25 For the thing I greatly *f* has
31:34 Because I *f* the great
Ps 76: 7 You, Yourself, are to be *f*;
76: 8 The earth *f* and was still,
76:11 to Him who ought to be *f*.
89: 7 God is greatly to be *f* in the
96: 4 He is to be *f* above all gods.
130: 4 with You, That You may be *f*.
Isa 41: 5 The coastlands saw it and *f*,
51:13 You have *f* continually every
57:11 whom have you been afraid, or *f*,
Jer 42:16 be that the sword which you *f*
44:10 to this day, nor have they *f*;
Ezek 11: 8 You have *f* the sword; and I will
Dan 5:19 and languages trembled and *f*
Jon 1:16 Then the men *f* the LORD
Hag 1:12 and the people *f* the presence
Mal 1:14 And My name is to be *f* among
2: 5 So he *f* Me And was reverent
3:16 Then those who *f* the LORD
Mt 14: 5 he *f* the multitude, because
21:46 they *f* the multitudes, because
27:54 they *f* greatly, saying, "Truly
Mk 4:41 And they *f* exceedingly, and said
6:20 for Herod *f* John, knowing that
11:18 for they *f* Him, because all the
11:32 they *f* the people, for all
12:12 but *f* the multitude, for they
Lk 19:21 For I *f* you, because you are an
20:19 but they *f* the people—for they
22: 2 for they *f* the people.
Jn 9:22 these things because they *f*
Acts 5:26 for they *f* the people, lest
10: 2 a devout man and one who *f* God

FEARFUL (9/9) FEAR, FEARFULLY

Ex 15:11 *F* in praises, doing wonders?
Deut 20: 8 'What man is there who is *f*
Judg 7: 3 Whoever is *f* and afraid, let
Mt 8:26 said to them, "Why are you *f*,
Mk 4:40 to them, "Why are you so *f*?
Lk 9:34 and they were *f* as they entered
21:11 and there will be *f* sights and
Heb 10:27 but a certain *f* expectation of
10:31 It is a *f* thing to fall into the

FEARFUL-HEARTED (1/1)

Isa 35: 4 Say to those who are *f*,

FEARFULLY (2/2) FEARFUL

Ps 139:14 for I am *f* and wonderfully
Dan 8:24 own power; He shall destroy *f*,

FEARFULNESS (3/3)

Ps 55: 5 *F* and trembling have come upon
Isa 21: 4 *f* frightened me; The night for
33:14 *F* has seized the hypocrites:

FEARING (9/9) FEAR

Josh 22:25 make our descendants cease *f*
Ps 119:38 Who is devoted to *f* You.
Mk 5:33 *f* and trembling, knowing what
Acts 23:10 *f* lest Paul might be pulled to
27:17 and *f* lest they should run
27:29 *f* lest we should run aground on
Gal 2:12 *f* those who were of the
Col 3:22 in sincerity of heart, *f* God.
Heb 11:27 not *f* the wrath of the king;

FEARS (19/19) FEAR

Job 1: 8 one who *f* God and shuns evil?"
2: 3 one who *f* God and shuns evil?
Ps 25:12 Who is the man that *f* the
34: 4 And delivered me from all my *f*.
112: 1 Blessed is the man who *f*
128: 1 Blessed is every one who *f* the
128: 4 the man be blessed Who *f* the
Prov 13:13 But he who *f* the commandment
14: 2 who walks in his uprightness *f*
14:16 A wise man *f* and departs from
31:30 But a woman who *f* the LORD,
Eccl 7:18 For he who *f* God will escape
9: 2 who takes an oath as he who *f*
Isa 50:10 Who among you *f* the LORD?
66: 4 And bring their *f* on them;
Acts 10:22 one who *f* God and has a good
10:35 But in every nation whoever *f*
2 Cor 7: 5 were conflicts, inside were *f*.
1 Jn 4:18 But he who *f* has not been made

FEAST (136/122) FEASTING, FEASTS

Gen 19: 3 Then he made them a *f*,
21: 8 And Abraham made a great *f* on
26:30 So he made them a *f*,
29:22 men of the place and made a *f*.
40:20 that he made a *f* for all his
Ex 5: 1 that they may hold a *f* to Me in
10: 9 for we must hold a *f* to the
12:14 and you shall keep it as a *f* to
12:14 You shall keep it as a *f* by an
12:17 So you shall observe the *F* of
13: 6 day there shall be a *f* to
23:14 times you shall keep a *f* to Me
23:15 You shall keep the *F* of
23:16 and the *F* of Harvest, the
23:16 and the *F* of Ingathering at the
32: 5 Tomorrow is a *f* to the LORD."
34:18 The *F* of Unleavened Bread you
34:22 And you shall observe the *F* of
34:22 and the *F* of Ingathering at the
34:25 shall the sacrifice of the *F*
Lev 23: 6 of the same month is the *F* of
23:34 seventh month shall be the *F*
23:39 you shall keep the *f* of the
23:41 You shall keep it as a *f* to the
Num 28:17 day of this month is the *f*;
28:26 to the LORD at your *F* of
29:12 and you shall keep a *f* to the
Deut 16:10 Then you shall keep the *F* of
16:13 You shall observe the *F* of
16:14 you shall rejoice in your *f*,
16:15 days you shall keep a sacred *f*
16:16 at the *F* of Unleavened Bread,
16:16 at the *F* of Weeks, and at the
16:16 and at the *F* of Tabernacles;
31:10 at the *F* of Tabernacles,
Judg 14:10 And Samson gave a *f* there, for
14:12 within the seven days of the *f*,
14:17 the seven days while their *f*
21:19 there is a yearly *f* of the
1 Sam 20:24 the king sat down to eat the *f*.
25: 8 for we come on a *f* day. Please
25:36 holding a *f* in his house, like
25:36 like the *f* of a king.
2 Sam 3:20 And David made a *f* for Abner
1 Ki 3:15 and made a *f* for all his
8: 2 with King Solomon at the *f* in
8:65 At that time Solomon held a *f*,
12:32 Jeroboam ordained a *f* on the
12:32 like the *f* that was in Judah,
12:33 And he ordained a *f* for the
2 Ki 6:23 Then he prepared a great *f* for
2 Chr 5: 3 with the king at the *f*,
7: 8 that time Solomon kept the *f*
7: 9 and the *f* seven days.
8:13 the *F* of Unleavened Bread, the
8:13 the *F* of Weeks, and the Feast
8:13 and the *F* of Tabernacles.
30:13 at Jerusalem to keep the *F* of
30:21 at Jerusalem kept the *F* of
30:22 and they ate throughout the *f*
30:23 agreed to keep the *f* another
35:17 and the *F* of Unleavened Bread
Ezra 3: 4 They also kept the *F* of
6:22 And they kept the *F* of
Neh 8:14 dwell in booths during the *f*
8:18 And they kept the *f* seven days;
Esth 1: 3 year of his reign he made a *f*
1: 5 the king made a *f* lasting seven
1: 9 Queen Vashti also made a *f* for
2:18 Then the king made a great *f*,
2:18 the *F* of Esther, for all his
8:17 a *f* and a holiday. Then many of
Job 1: 4 And his sons would go and *f* in
Ps 42: 4 multitude that kept a pilgrim *f*.
81: 3 on our solemn *f* day.
Prov 15:15 merry heart has a continual *f*.
Eccl 10:16 And your princes *f* in the
10:17 And your princes *f* at the
10:19 A *f* is made for laughter, And
Isa 25: 6 will make for all people A *f*
25: 6 A *f* of wines on the lees,
Lam 2: 7 LORD As on the day of a set *f*.
2:22 You have invited as to a *f* day
Ezek 36:38 the flock at Jerusalem on its *f*
45:21 a *f* of seven days; unleavened
45:23 On the seven days of the *f* he
45:25 day of the month, at the *f*,
46: 9 the LORD on the appointed *f*
46:11 festivals and the appointed *f*
Dan 5: 1 the king made a great *f* for a
Hos 2:11 Her *f* days, Her New Moons,
9: 5 And in the day of the *f* of the
12: 9 in the days of the appointed *f*.
Am 5:21 I despise your *f* days, And I

Zech 14:16 and to keep the *F* of
14:18 do not come up to keep the *F*
14:19 do not come up to keep the *F*
Mt 26: 5 they said, "Not during the *f*,
26:17 on the first day of the *F*
27:15 Now at the *f* the governor was
Mk 6:21 Herod on his birthday gave a *f*
14: 1 it was the Passover and the *F*
14: 2 they said, "Not during the *f*,
15: 6 Now at the *f* he was accustomed
Lk 2:41 Jerusalem every year at the *F*
2:42 to the custom of the *f*.
5:29 Then Levi gave Him a great *f* in
14: 8 by anyone to a wedding *f*,
14:13 "But when you give a *f*,
22: 1 Now the *F* of Unleavened Bread
23:17 release one to them at the *f*).
Jn 2: 8 take it to the master of the *f*.
2: 9 When the master of the *f* had
2: 9 the master of the *f* called the
2:23 at the Passover, during the *f*,
4:45 He did in Jerusalem at the *f*;
4:45 for they also had gone to the *f*.
5: 1 After this there was a *f* of the
6: 4 a *f* of the Jews, was near.
7: 2 Now the Jews' *F* of Tabernacles
7: 8 "You go up to this *f*.
7: 8 I am not yet going up to this *f*,
7:10 then He also went up to the *f*,
7:11 the Jews sought Him at the *f*,
7:14 Now about the middle of the *f*
7:37 day, that great day of the *f*,
10:22 Now it was the *F* of Dedication
11:56 He will not come to the *f*?
12:12 that had come to the *f*,
12:20 who came up to worship at the *f*.
13: 1 Now before the *f* of the
13:29 things we need for the *f*,
Acts 18:21 by all means keep this coming *f*
1 Cor 5: 8 Therefore let us keep the *f*,
2 Pe 2:13 own deceptions while they *f*
Jude 12 while they *f* with you without

FEASTING (9/9) FEAST

Esth 9:17 rested and made it a day of *f*
9:18 and made it a day of *f* and
9:19 of Adar with gladness and *f*,
9:22 should make them days of *f* and
Job 1: 5 when the days of *f* had run
Prov 17: 1 Than a house full of *f* with
Eccl 7: 2 Than to go to the house of *f*,
Jer 16: 8 not go into the house of *f* to
Hab 3:14 Their rejoicing was like *f* on

FEASTS (32/31) FEAST

Lev 23: 2 The *f* of the LORD, which you
23: 2 convocations, these are My *f*.
23: 4 These are the *f* of the LORD,
23:37 These are the *f* of the LORD
23:44 to the children of Israel the *f*
Num 10:10 gladness, in your appointed *f*,
15: 3 offering or in your appointed *f*,
29:39 the LORD at your appointed *f*
1 Chr 23:31 the New Moons and on the set *f*,
2 Chr 2: 4 and on the set *f* of the LORD
8:13 the three appointed yearly *f*—
31: 3 and the New Moons and the set *f*,
Ezra 3: 5 and for all the appointed *f* of
Neh 10:33 the New Moons, and the set *f*;
Ps 35:16 With ungodly mockers at *f* They
Isa 1:14 New Moons and your appointed *f*
5:12 flute, And wine are in their *f*;
29: 1 Let *f* come around.
33:20 the city of our appointed *f*;
Jer 51:39 I will prepare their *f*;
Lam 1: 4 no one comes to the set *f*.
2: 6 has caused The appointed *f*
Ezek 45:17 and drink offerings, at the *f*,
Hos 2:11 Sabbaths—All her appointed *f*.
Am 8:10 I will turn your *f* into
Nah 1:15 O Judah, keep your appointed *f*,
Zech 8:19 joy and gladness and cheerful *f*
Mal 2: 3 The refuse of your solemn *f*;
Mt 23: 6 love the best places at *f*,
Mk 12:39 and the best places at *f*,
Lk 20:46 and the best places at *f*,
Jude 12 These are spots in your love *f*,

FEATHERED (1/1)

Ps 78:27 *F* fowl like the sand of the

FEATHERS (6/6)

Lev 1:16 remove its crop with its *f* and
Ps 68:13 And her *f* with yellow gold."
91: 4 He shall cover you with His *f*,
Ezek 17: 3 Full of *f* of various colors,
17: 7 with large wings and many *f*;
Dan 4:33 hair had grown like eagles' *f*

FEATURES (2/2)

Dan 1:15 at the end of ten days their *f*
8:23 shall arise, Having fierce *f*,

FED (26/25) FEED

Gen 30:36 and Jacob *f* the rest of Laban's
41: 2 and they *f* in the meadow.
41:18 and they *f* in the meadow.
47:17 Thus he *f* them with bread in
48:15 The God who has *f* me all my
Ex 16:32 see the bread with which I *f*
Deut 8: 3 and *f* you with manna which you
8:16 who *f* you in the wilderness with
1 Ki 18: 4 and had *f* them with bread and
18:13 and *f* them with bread and
1 Chr 27:29 was over the herds that *f* in
Ps 80: 5 You have *f* them with the bread
81:16 He would have *f* them also with
Isa 1:11 of rams And the fat of *f*
Jer 5: 7 When I had *f* them to the full,
Ezek 16:19 and honey which I *f* you—you
34: 8 but the shepherds *f* themselves
Dan 4:12 And all flesh was *f* from it.
5:21 They *f* him with grass like
Hos 11: 4 I stooped and *f* them.
Zech 11: 7 So I *f* the flock for slaughter,
11: 7 and I *f* the flock.
Mk 5:14 So those who *f* the swine fled,
Lk 8:34 When those who *f* them saw what
16:21 desiring to be *f* with the crumbs
1 Cor 3: 2 I *f* you with milk and not with

FEE (1/1)

Num 22: 7 departed with the diviner's *f*

FEEBLE (18/18)

Gen 30:42 But when the flocks were *f*,
1 Sam 2: 5 has many children has become *f*.
2 Chr 28:15 and they let all the *f* ones
Neh 4: 2 What are these *f* Jews doing?
Job 4: 4 you have strengthened the *f*
Ps 38: 8 I am *f* and severely broken;
105:37 And there was none *f* among
109:24 And my flesh is *f* from lack of
Prov 30:26 The rock badgers are a *f* folk,
Isa 16:14 will be very small and *f*.
35: 3 And make firm the *f* knees.
Jer 6:24 report of it; Our hands grow *f*.
49:24 Damascus has grown *f*;
50:43 them, And his hands grow *f*;
Ezek 7:17 Every hand will be *f*,
21: 7 will melt, all hands will be *f*,
Zech 12: 8 the one who is *f* among them in
Heb 12:12 hang down, and the *f* knees,

FEEBLEMINDED (KJV) See FAINTHEARTED

FEEBLER (1/1)

Gen 30:42 so the *f* were Laban's and the

FEED (71/68) FED, FEEDING, FEEDS, WELL-FED

Gen 24:25 We have both straw and *f* enough,
24:32 and provided straw and *f* for
25:30 Please *f* me with that same red
29: 7 and go and *f* them."
30:31 I will again *f* and keep your
37:12 Then his brothers went to *f*
42:27 his sack to give his donkey *f*
43:24 and he gave their donkeys *f*.
46:32 their occupation has been to *f*
Ex 34: 3 let neither flocks nor herds *f*
1 Sam 17:15 and returned from Saul to *f*
1 Ki 17: 4 have commanded the ravens to *f*
22:27 and *f* him with bread of
2 Chr 18:26 and *f* him with bread of
Job 24: 2 seize flocks violently and *f*
24:20 The worm should *f* sweetly on
Ps 37: 3 and *f* on His faithfulness.
49:14 Death shall *f* on them;
Prov 10:21 The lips of the righteous *f*
30: 8 *F* me with the food allotted to
Song 1: 7 Where you *f* your flock,
1: 8 And *f* your little goats
4: 5 Which *f* among the lilies.
6: 2 To *f* his flock in the
Isa 5:17 Then the lambs shall *f* in their
14:30 firstborn of the poor will *f*,
27:10 There the calf will *f*,
30:23 In that day your cattle will *f*
40:11 He will *f* His flock like a
49: 9 They shall *f* along the roads,
49:26 I will *f* those who oppress you
58:14 And *f* you with the heritage of
61: 5 Strangers shall stand and *f*
65:25 The wolf and the lamb shall *f*
66:11 That you may *f* and be satisfied
66:12 Then you shall *f*;
Jer 3:15 who will *f* you with knowledge
9:15 I will *f* them, this people,
23: 2 against the shepherds who *f* My
23: 4 shepherds over them who will *f*
23:15 I will *f* them with wormwood,
50:19 And he shall *f* on Carmel and
Ezek 3: 3 *f* your belly, and fill your
34: 2 the shepherds of Israel who *f*
34: 2 Should not the shepherds *f* the
34: 3 but you do not *f* the flock.
34: 8 fed themselves and did not *f*
34:10 and the shepherds shall *f*
34:13 I will *f* them on the mountains
34:14 I will *f* them in good pasture,
34:14 lie down in a good fold and *f*
34:15 I will *f* My flock, and I will
34:16 and *f* them in judgment."
34:23 and he shall *f* them—My servant
34:23 He shall *f* them and be their
Hos 9: 2 and the winepress Shall not *f*
Mic 5: 4 And He shall stand and *f* His
7:14 Let them *f* in Bashan and
Hab 2:13 That the peoples labor to *f*
Zeph 2: 7 They shall *f* their flocks
3:13 For they shall *f* their flocks
Zech 11: 4 *F* the flock for slaughter,
11: 9 I will not *f* you. Let what is
11:16 nor *f* those that still stand.
Mt 25:37 did we see You hungry and *f*
Lk 15:15 sent him into his fields to *f*
Jn 21:15 He said to him, "*F* My lambs."
21:17 Jesus said to him, "*F* My
Rom 12:20 *f* him; If he is thirsty,
1 Cor 13: 3 I bestow all my goods to *f*
Rev 12: 6 that they should *f* her there

FEEDING (9/9) FEED

Gen 37: 2 was *f* the flock with his
37:13 Are not your brothers *f* the
37:16 Please tell me where they are *f*
Job 1:14 were plowing and the donkeys *f*
Ezek 34:10 I will cause them to cease *f*
Nah 2:11 And the *f* place of the young
Mt 8:30 was a herd of many swine *f*.
Mk 5:11 Now a large herd of swine was *f*
Lk 8:32 Now a herd of many swine was *f*

FEEDS (10/10) FEED

Ex 22: 5 and it *f* in another man's
Prov 13: 2 the soul of the unfaithful *f*
15:14 But the mouth of fools *f* on
Song 2:16 He *f* his flock among the
6: 3 He *f* his flock among the
Isa 44:20 He *f* on ashes; A deceived
Hos 12: 1 Ephraim *f* on the wind, And
Mt 6:26 yet your heavenly Father *f*
Lk 12:24 and God *f* them. Of how much
Jn 6:57 so he who *f* on Me will live

FEEL (7/7) FEELING, FEELINGS, FELT

Gen 27:12 Perhaps my father will *f* me, and
27:21 that I may *f* you, my son,
Deut 4:19 you *f* driven to worship them
Judg 16:26 Let me *f* the pillars which
Ps 58: 9 Before your pots can *f* the
Prov 23:35 but I did not *f* it.
Zech 11: 5 owners slaughter them and *f* no

FEELING (1/1) FEEL

Eph 4:19 who, being past *f*,

FEELINGS (1/1) FEEL

Prov 29:11 A fool vents all his *f*,

FEET (243/227) FOOT

Gen 18: 4 be brought, and wash your *f*,
19: 2 the night, and wash your *f*;
24:32 and water to wash his *f* and the
24:32 to wash his feet and the *f* of
43:24 water, and they washed their *f*;
49:10 a lawgiver from between his *f*,
49:33 he drew his *f* up into the bed
Ex 3: 5 Take your sandals off your *f*,
4:25 son and cast it at Moses' *f*,
12:11 waist, your sandals on your *f*,
24:10 And there was under His *f* as
30:19 wash their hands and their *f*
30:21 wash their hands and their *f*,
40:31 wash their hands and their *f*
Lev 8:24 the big toes of their right *f*.
11:21 have jointed legs above their *f*
11:23 insects which have four *f*
11:42 or whatever has many *f* among
Deut 28:57 comes out from between her *f*
29: 5 have not worn out on your *f*.
33: 3 They sit down at Your *f*;
Josh 3:13 as soon as the soles of the *f*
3:15 and the *f* of the priests who
4: 3 the place where the priests' *f*
4: 9 in the place where the *f* of the
4:18 the soles of the priests' *f*
9: 5 and patched sandals on their *f*,
10:24 put your *f* on the necks of
10:24 they drew near and put their *f*
Judg 5:27 At her *f* he sank, he fell, he
5:27 At her *f* he sank, he fell;
19:21 And they washed their *f*,
Ruth 3: 4 you shall go in, uncover his *f*,
3: 7 came softly, uncovered his *f*,
3: 8 a woman was lying at his *f*.
3:14 So she lay at his *f* until
1 Sam 2: 9 He will guard the *f* of His
25:24 So she fell at his *f* and said:
25:41 a servant to wash the *f* of the
2 Sam 3:34 were not bound Nor your *f* put
4: 4 a son who was lame in his *f*.
4:12 them, cut off their hands and *f*,
9: 3 who is lame in his *f*.
9:13 And he was lame in both his *f*.
11: 8 to your house and wash your *f*.
19:24 And he had not cared for his *f*,
22:10 down With darkness under His *f*.
22:34 He makes my *f* like the feet of
22:34 He makes my feet like the *f* of

22:37 So my *f* did not slip.
22:39 They have fallen under my *f*.
1 Ki 2: 5 his sandals that were on his *f*.
5: 3 foes under the soles of his *f*.
7:30 and its four *f* had supports.
14:12 When your *f* enter the city, the
15:23 age he was diseased in his *f*.
2 Ki 4:27 hill, she caught him by the *f*,
4:37 So she went in, fell at his *f*,
6:32 not the sound of his master's *f*
9:35 of her than the skull and the *f*
13:21 he revived and stood on his *f*.
19:24 And with the soles of my *f* I
21: 8 and I will not make the *f* of
1 Chr 28: 2 Then King David rose to his *f*
2 Chr 3:13 overall. They stood on their *f*,
16:12 Asa became diseased in his *f*,
Neh 9:21 did not wear out And their *f*
Esth 8: 3 to the king, fell down at his *f*,
Job 12: 5 made ready for those whose *f*
13:27 You put my *f* in the stocks,
13:27 a limit for the soles of my *f*.
18: 8 is cast into a net by his own *f*,
18:11 side, And drive him to his *f*.
28: 4 In places forgotten by *f*
29:15 And I was *f* to the lame.
30:12 They push away my *f*,
33:11 He puts my *f* in the stocks, He
Ps 8: 6 put all things under his *f*,
18: 9 down With darkness under His *f*.
18:33 He makes my *f* like the feet
18:33 He makes my feet like the *f*
18:36 So my *f* did not slip.
18:38 They have fallen under my *f*.
22:16 They pierced My hands and My *f*;
25:15 For He shall pluck my *f* out of
31: 8 You have set my *f* in a wide
40: 2 And set my *f* upon a rock,
47: 3 And the nations under our *f*.
56:13 Have You not kept my *f* from
58:10 He shall wash his *f* in the
66: 9 And does not allow our *f* to be
73: 2 my *f* had almost stumbled;
74: 3 Lift up Your *f* to the perpetual
105:18 They hurt his *f* with fetters,
115: 7 *F* they have, but they do not
116: 8 And my *f* from falling.
119:59 And turned my *f* to Your
119:101 I have restrained my *f* from
119:105 Your word is a lamp to my *f*
122: 2 Our *f* have been standing
Prov 1:16 For their *f* run to evil, And
4:26 Ponder the path of your *f*,
5: 5 Her *f* go down to death, Her
6:13 his eyes, He shuffles his *f*,
6:18 *F* that are swift in running to
6:28 And his *f* not be seared?
7:11 Her *f* would not stay at home.
19: 2 he sins who hastens with his *f*.
26: 6 of a fool Cuts off his own *f*
29: 5 Spreads a net for his *f*.
Song 5: 3 on again? I have washed my *f*;
7: 1 How beautiful are your *f* in
Isa 3:16 Making a jingling with their *f*,
6: 2 face, with two he covered his *f*,
20: 2 take your sandals off your *f*.
23: 7 Whose *f* carried her far off to
26: 6 The *f* of the poor And the
32:20 Who send out freely the *f* of
37:25 And with the soles of my *f* I
41: 2 called him to His *f*?
41: 3 he had not gone with his *f*?
49:23 And lick up the dust of your *f*.
52: 7 upon the mountains Are the *f*
59: 7 Their *f* run to evil, And they
60:13 I will make the place of My *f*
60:14 at the soles of your *f*;
Jer 13:16 And before your *f* stumble On
14:10 have not restrained their *f*.
18:22 me, And hidden snares for my *f*.
38:22 Your *f* have sunk in the mire,
Lam 1:13 He has spread a net for my *f*
3:34 To crush under one's *f* All the
Ezek 1: 7 and the soles of their *f* were
1: 7 like the soles of calves' *f*.
2: 1 "Son of man, stand on your *f*,
2: 2 spoke to me, and set me on my *f*;
3:24 entered me and set me on my *f*,
6:11 your fists and stamp your *f*,
24:17 and put your sandals on your *f*;
24:23 and your sandals on your *f*;
25: 6 your hands, stamped your *f*,
32: 2 the waters with your *f*,
34:18 you must tread down with your *f*
34:18 foul the residue with your *f*?
34:19 you have trampled with your *f*,
34:19 you have fouled with your *f*.
37:10 lived, and stood upon their *f*,
43: 7 the place of the soles of My *f*,
Dan 2:33 its *f* partly of iron and partly
2:34 struck the image on its *f* of
2:41 Whereas you saw the *f* and toes,
2:42 And as the toes of the *f* were
7: 4 and made to stand on two *f*
7: 7 the residue with its *f*.
7:19 trampled the residue with its *f*;
10: 6 his arms and *f* like burnished
Nah 1: 3 clouds are the dust of His *f*.
1:15 on the mountains The *f* of him
Hab 3: 5 And fever followed at His *f*.
3:19 He will make my *f* like deer's
3:19 make my feet like deer's *f*,
Zech 14: 4 And in that day His *f* will
14:12 while they stand on their *f*,
Mal 4: 3 under the soles of your *f* On
Mt 7: 6 they trample them under their *f*,
10:14 shake off the dust from your *f*.
15:30 they laid them down at Jesus' *f*,
18: 8 than having two hands or two *f*,
18:29 servant fell down at his *f* and
28: 9 came and held Him by the *f* and
Mk 5:22 he fell at His *f*
6:11 off the dust under your *f* as a
7:25 and she came and fell at His *f*.
9:45 lame, rather than having two *f*,
Lk 1:79 To guide our *f* into the way of
7:38 and stood at His *f* behind Him
7:38 and she began to wash His *f*
7:38 and she kissed His *f* and
7:44 you gave Me no water for My *f*,
7:44 but she has washed My *f* with
7:45 has not ceased to kiss My *f*
7:46 this woman has anointed My *f*
8:35 sitting at the *f* of Jesus,
8:41 And he fell down at Jesus' *f*
9: 5 off the very dust from your *f*
10:39 who also sat at Jesus' *f* and
15:22 his hand and sandals on his *f*.
17:16 fell down on his face at His *f*,
24:39 "Behold My hands and My *f*,
24:40 showed them His hands and His *f*.
Jn 11: 2 fragrant oil and wiped His *f*
11:32 saw Him, she fell down at His *f*,
12: 3 anointed the *f* of Jesus, and
12: 3 and wiped His *f* with her hair.
13: 5 began to wash the disciples' *f*,
13: 6 "Lord, are You washing my *f*?
13: 8 You shall never wash my *f*!"
13: 9 not my *f* only, but also my
13:10 needs only to wash his *f*,
13:12 So when He had washed their *f*,
13:14 and Teacher, have washed your *f*,
13:14 ought to wash one another's *f*.
20:12 the head and the other at the *f*,
Acts 3: 7 and immediately his *f* and ankle
4:35 laid them at the apostles' *f*;
4:37 and laid it at the apostles' *f*.
5: 2 and laid it at the apostles' *f*.
5: 9 the *f* of those who have buried
5:10 she fell down at his *f* and
7:33 your sandals off your *f*,
7:58 down their clothes at the *f* of
10:25 met him and fell down at his *f*
13:25 the sandals of whose *f* I am not
13:51 shook off the dust from their *f*
14: 8 man without strength in his *f*
14:10 Stand up straight on your *f*!"
16:24 prison and fastened their *f* in
21:11 bound his own hands and *f*,
22: 3 up in this city at the *f* of
26:16 'But rise and stand on your *f*;
Rom 3:15 Their *f* are swift to shed
10:15 How beautiful are the *f* of
16:20 will crush Satan under your *f*
1 Cor 12:21 nor again the head to the *f*,
15:25 has put all enemies under His *f*.
15:27 all things under His *f*.
Eph 1:22 He put all things under His *f*,
6:15 and having shod your *f* with the
1 Tim 5:10 if she has washed the saints' *f*,
Heb 2: 8 in subjection under his *f*.
12:13 make straight paths for your *f*,
Rev 1:13 with a garment down to the *f*
1:15 His *f* were like fine brass, as
1:17 I fell at His *f* as dead. But He
2:18 and His *f* like fine brass:
3: 9 come and worship before your *f*,
10: 1 and his *f* like pillars of fire.
11:11 them, and they stood on their *f*,
12: 1 sun, with the moon under her *f*,
13: 2 his *f* were like the feet of
13: 2 his feet were like the *f* of
19:10 And I fell at his *f* to worship
22: 8 down to worship before the *f*

FEIGNED (1/1)

1 Sam 21:13 *f* madness in their hands,

FELIX (9/8)

Acts 23:24 and bring him safely to *F* the
23:26 the most excellent governor *F*:
24: 3 and in all places, most noble *F*,
24:22 But when *F* heard these things,
24:24 when *F* came with his wife
24:25 *F* was afraid and answered, "Go
24:27 Porcius Festus succeeded *F*;
24:27 Festus succeeded Felix; and *F*,
25:14 man left a prisoner by *F*,

FELL (211/205) FALL

Gen 4: 5 angry, and his countenance *f*.
14:10 some *f* there, and the
15:12 a deep sleep *f* upon Abram;
15:12 horror and great darkness *f*
17: 3 Then Abram *f* on his face, and
17:17 Then Abraham *f* on his face and
33: 4 and *f* on his neck and kissed
44:14 and they *f* before him on the
45:14 Then he *f* on his brother
46:29 and *f* on his neck and wept on
50: 1 Then Joseph *f* on his father's
50:18 his brothers also went and *f*
Ex 32:28 thousand men of the people *f*
Lev 9:24 they shouted and *f* on their
16: 9 goat on which the LORD's lot *f*,
16:10 the goat on which the lot *f* to
Num 11: 9 And when the dew *f* on the camp
11: 9 the manna *f* on it.
14: 5 Then Moses and Aaron *f* on their
16: 4 he *f* on his face;
16:22 Then they *f* on their faces, and
16:45 And they *f* on their faces.
20: 6 and they *f* on their faces.
22:31 and he bowed his head and *f*
Deut 9:18 And I *f* down before the LORD,
Josh 5:14 And Joshua *f* on his face to
6:20 that the wall *f* down flat.
7: 6 and *f* to the earth on his face
8:25 So it was that all who *f* that
16: 1 The lot *f* to the children of
17: 5 Ten shares *f* to Manasseh,
22:20 and wrath *f* on all the
Judg 4:16 and all the army of Sisera *f* by
5:27 At her feet he sank, he *f*,
5:27 At her feet he sank, he *f*;
5:27 there he *f* dead.
7:13 and struck it so that it *f* and
9:40 and many *f* wounded, to the
12: 6 There *f* at that time forty-two
13:20 they *f* on their faces to the
16:30 and the temple *f* on the lords
19:26 and *f* down at the door of the
20:44 thousand men of Benjamin *f*;
20:46 So all who *f* of Benjamin that
Ruth 2:10 So she *f* on her face, bowed down
1 Sam 4:10 and there *f* of Israel thirty
4:18 that Eli *f* off the seat
11: 7 And the fear of the LORD *f*
14:13 and they *f* before Jonathan.
17:49 and he *f* on his face to the
17:52 wounded of the Philistines *f*
20:41 *f* on his face to the ground,
25:23 *f* on her face before David, and
25:24 So she *f* at his feet and said:
28:20 Then immediately Saul *f* full
30:13 because three days ago I *f*
31: 1 and *f* slain on Mount Gilboa.
31: 4 Saul took a sword and *f* on it.
31: 5 he also *f* on his sword, and
2 Sam 1: 2 that he *f* to the ground and
2:16 so they *f* down together.
2:23 and he *f* down there and died on
2:23 to the place where Asahel *f*
3:34 before wicked men, so you *f*.
4: 4 that he *f* and became lame.
9: 6 he *f* on his face and prostrated
11:17 of the servants of David *f*;
14: 4 she *f* on her face to the ground
14:22 Then Joab *f* to the ground on his
19:18 Now Shimei the son of Gera *f*
20: 8 was going forward, it *f* out.
21: 9 before the LORD. So they *f*,
21:22 and *f* by the hand of David and
1 Ki 1:53 And he came and *f* down before
18: 7 and *f* on his face, and said,
18:38 Then the fire of the LORD *f* and
18:39 they *f* on their faces; and they
20:30 then a wall *f* on twenty-seven
2 Ki 1: 2 Now Ahaziah *f* through the
1:13 and came and *f* on his knees
4:37 *f* at his feet, and bowed to the
6: 5 the iron ax head *f* into the
1 Chr 5:10 who *f* by their hand; and they
5:22 for many *f* dead, because the war
10: 1 and *f* slain on Mount Gilboa.
10: 4 Saul took a sword and *f* on it.
10: 5 he also *f* on his sword and
20: 8 and they *f* by the hand of David
21:14 thousand men of Israel *f*.
21:16 *f* on their faces.
24: 7 Now the first lot *f* to
26:14 The lot for the East Gate *f* to
2 Chr 13:17 choice men of Israel *f* slain.
17:10 And the fear of the LORD *f* on
29: 8 the wrath of the LORD *f* upon
Ezra 9: 5 I *f* on my knees and spread out
Esth 3: 7 until it *f* on the twelfth
8: 3 *f* down at his feet, and
8:17 because fear of the Jews *f* upon
9: 2 because fear of them *f* upon all
9: 3 because the fear of Mordecai *f*
Job 1:16 The fire of God *f* from heaven
1:19 and it *f* on the young people,
1:20 and he *f* to the ground and
Ps 27: 2 and foes, They stumbled and *f*.
78:64 Their priests *f* by the sword,
107:12 They *f* down, and there was
Jer 46:16 one *f* upon another. And they
Lam 1: 7 When her people *f* into the
Ezek 1:28 I *f* on my face, and I heard a
3:23 and I *f* on my face.
8: 1 the hand of the Lord GOD *f*
9: 8 and I *f* on my face and cried
11: 5 the Spirit of the LORD *f* upon
11:13 Then I *f* on my face and cried
39:23 and they all *f* by the sword.
43: 3 and I *f* on my face.
44: 4 and I *f* on my face.
Dan 2:46 Then King Nebuchadnezzar *f* on
3: 7 and languages *f* down and
3:23 *f* down bound into the midst of
4:31 a voice *f* from heaven: "King
7:20 came up, before which three *f*,

8:17 he came I was afraid and *f* on
10: 7 but a great terror *f* upon them,
Jon 1: 7 and the lot *f* on Jonah.
Mt 2:11 and *f* down and worshiped Him.
7:27 beat on that house; and it *f*.
13: 4 some seed *f* by the wayside;
13: 5 Some *f* on stony places, where
13: 7 And some *f* among thorns, and the
13: 8 But others *f* on good ground and
17: 6 they *f* on their faces and were
18:26 The servant therefore *f* down
18:29 So his fellow servant *f* down at
26:39 He went a little farther and *f*
Mk 3:11 *f* down before Him and cried
4: 4 that some seed *f* by the
4: 5 Some *f* on stony ground, where it
4: 7 And some seed *f* among thorns;
4: 8 But other seed *f* on good ground
5:22 he *f* at His feet
5:33 came and *f* down before Him and
7:25 and she came and *f* at His feet.
9:20 and he *f* on the ground and
14:35 and *f* on the ground, and prayed
Lk 1: 9 his lot *f* to burn incense when
1:12 and fear *f* upon him.
5: 8 he *f* down at Jesus' knees,
5:12 and he *f* on his face and
6:49 and immediately it *f*.
8: 5 some *f* by the wayside; and it
8: 6 Some *f* on rock; and as soon as
8: 7 And some *f* among thorns, and the
8: 8 But others *f* on good ground,
8:14 Now the ones that *f* among
8:15 But the ones that *f* on the good
8:23 But as they sailed He *f* asleep.
8:28 *f* down before Him, and with a
8:41 And he *f* down at Jesus' feet
10:30 and *f* among thieves, who
10:36 think was neighbor to him who *f*
13: 4 on whom the tower in Siloam *f*
15:20 and ran and *f* on his neck and
16:21 be fed with the crumbs which *f*
17:16 and *f* down on his face at His
Jn 11:32 she *f* down at His feet, saying
18: 6 they drew back and *f* to the
Acts 1:25 which Judas by transgression *f*,
1:26 and the lot *f* on Matthias.
5: 5 *f* down and breathed his last.
5:10 Then immediately she *f* down at
7:60 he had said this, he *f* asleep.
9: 4 Then he *f* to the ground, and
9:18 Immediately there *f* from his
10:10 he *f* into a trance
10:25 Cornelius met him and *f* down at
10:44 the Holy Spirit *f* upon all
11:15 the Holy Spirit *f* upon them, as
12: 7 quickly!" And his chains *f*
13:11 And immediately a dark mist *f*
13:36 *f* asleep, was buried with his
16:29 and *f* down trembling before
19:17 and fear *f* on them all, and the
19:35 and of the image which *f* down
20: 9 he *f* down from the third story
20:10 *f* on him, and embracing him
20:37 and *f* on Paul's neck and kissed
22: 7 And I *f* to the ground and heard
Rom 11:22 severity of God: on those who *f*,
15: 3 who reproached You *f* on
1 Cor 10: 8 one day twenty-three thousand *f*;
1 Tim 2:14 *f* into transgression.
Heb 3:17 whose corpses *f* in the
11:30 faith the walls of Jericho *f*
2 Pe 3: 4 For since the fathers *f* asleep,
Rev 1:17 I *f* at His feet as dead. But He
5: 8 and the twenty-four elders *f*
5:14 And the twenty-four elders *f*
6:13 And the stars of heaven *f* to the
7:11 and *f* on their faces before the
8:10 And a great star *f* from heaven,
8:10 and it *f* on a third of the
11:11 and great fear *f* on those who
11:13 and a tenth of the city *f*.
11:16 before God on their thrones *f*
16:19 and the cities of the nations *f*.
16:21 And great hail from heaven *f*
19: 4 and the four living creatures *f*
19:10 And I *f* at his feet to worship
22: 8 I *f* down to worship before the

FELLER (KJV) See WOODSMAN

FELLOW (48/46) FELLOWS, FELLOWSHIP

1 Sam 21:15 that you have brought this *f*
21:15 Shall this *f* come into my
25:21 protected all that this *f* has
29: 4 Make this *f* return, that he may
1 Ki 22:27 Put this *f* in prison, and feed
2 Chr 18:26 Put this *f* in prison, and feed
Mt 12:24 This *f* does not cast out demons
18:28 went out and found one of his *f*
18:29 So his *f* servant fell down at
18:31 So when his *f* servants saw what
18:33 have had compassion on your *f*
24:49 and begins to beat his *f*
26:61 This *f* said, 'I am able to
26:71 This *f* also was with Jesus of
Mk 15: 7 who was chained with his *f*
Lk 22:59 Surely this *f* also was with
23: 2 We found this *f* perverting the
Jn 9:29 to Moses; as for this *f*,
11:16 said to his *f* disciples, "Let
Acts 18:13 This *f* persuades men to worship
19:38 if Demetrius and his *f*
22:22 Away with such a *f* from the
Rom 16: 3 my *f* workers in Christ Jesus,
16: 7 my countrymen and my *f*
16: 9 our *f* worker in Christ, and
16:21 my *f* worker, and Lucius, Jason,
1 Cor 3: 9 For we are God's *f* workers;
2 Cor 1:24 but are *f* workers for your joy;
8:23 he is my partner and *f* worker
Eph 2:19 but *f* citizens with the saints
3: 6 that the Gentiles should be *f*
Phil 2:25 *f* worker, and fellow soldier,
2:25 and *f* soldier, but your
4: 3 and the rest of my *f* workers,
Col 1: 7 our dear *f* servant, who is a
4: 7 and *f* servant in the Lord, will
4:10 Aristarchus my *f* prisoner greets
4:11 These are my only *f* workers
1 Th 3: 2 and our *f* laborer in the gospel
Phm 1: 1 our beloved friend and *f*
1: 2 Archippus our *f* soldier, and to
1:23 my *f* prisoner in Christ Jesus,
1:24 Demas, Luke, my *f* laborers.
1 Pe 5: 1 I who am a *f* elder and a
3 Jn 8 that we may become *f* workers
Rev 6:11 both the number of their *f*
19:10 do not do that! I am your *f*
22: 9 For I am your *f* servant, and of

FELLOWCITIZENS (KJV) See (FELLOW) CITIZENS

FELLOWLABOURER (KJV) See (FELLOW) LABORER

FELLOWPRISONER (KJV) See (FELLOW) PRISONER

FELLOWS (2/2) FELLOW

2 Sam 6:20 as one of the base *f*
Dan 7:20 was greater than his *f*.

FELLOWSERVANT (KJV) See (FELLOW) SERVANT

FELLOWSHIP (16/15) FELLOW

Ps 94:20 Have *f* with You?
Acts 2:42 in the apostles' doctrine and *f*,
1 Cor 1: 9 you were called into the *f* of
10:20 and I do not want you to have *f*
2 Cor 6:14 For what *f* has righteousness
8: 4 receive the gift and the *f* of
Gal 2: 9 Barnabas the right hand of *f*,
Eph 3: 9 to make all see what is the *f*
5:11 And have no *f* with the
Phil 1: 5 for your *f* in the gospel from
2: 1 if any *f* of the Spirit, if any
3:10 and the *f* of His sufferings,
1 Jn 1: 3 that you also may have *f* with
1: 3 and truly our *f* is with the
1: 6 If we say that we have *f* with
1: 7 we have *f* with one another, and

FELLOWSOLDIER (KJV) See (FELLOW) SOLDIER

FELT (5/5) FEEL

Gen 27:22 and he *f* him and said, "The
Ex 10:21 darkness which may even be *f*.
Judg 8:11 the army while the camp *f*
1 Sam 13:12 Therefore I *f* compelled, and
Mk 5:29 and she *f* in her body that she

FEMALE (83/77) MAIDSERVANT

Gen 1:27 male and *f* He created them.
5: 2 He created them male and *f*,
6:19 they shall be male and *f*.
7: 2 clean animal, a male and his *f*;
7: 2 are unclean, a male and his *f*;
7: 3 of birds of the air, male and *f*,
7: 9 the ark to Noah, male and *f*,
7:16 male and *f* of all flesh, went
12:16 male and *f* servants, female
12:16 *f* donkeys, and camels.
15: 9 a three-year-old *f* goat, a
20:14 and male and *f* servants, and
20:17 and his *f* servants. Then they
24:35 male and *f* servants, and camels
30:35 all the *f* goats that were
30:43 *f* and male servants, and camels
31:38 your ewes and your *f* goats have
32: 5 and male and *f* servants; and I
32:14 two hundred *f* goats and twenty
32:15 twenty *f* donkeys and ten foals.
32:22 his two *f* servants, and his
45:23 and ten *f* donkeys loaded with
Ex 11: 5 even to the firstborn of the *f*
20:10 nor your *f* servant, nor your
20:17 nor his *f* servant, nor his ox,
21: 7 sells his daughter to be a *f*
21:20 if a man beats his male or *f*
21:26 the eye of his male or *f*
21:27 out the tooth of his male or *f*
21:32 If the ox gores a male or *f*
23:12 and the son of your *f* servant
Lev 3: 1 of the herd, whether male or *f*,
3: 6 the flock, whether male or *f*,
4:28 a *f* without blemish, for his
4:32 he shall bring a *f* without
5: 6 a *f* from the flock, a lamb or a
12: 5 But if she bears a *f* child, then
12: 7 her who has borne a male or a *f*.
25: 6 your male and *f* servants, your
25:44 And as for your male and *f*
25:44 them you may buy male and *f*
27: 4 it is a *f*, then your valuation
27: 5 and for a *f* ten shekels;
27: 6 and for a *f* your valuation
27: 7 and for a *f* ten shekels.
Num 5: 3 shall put out both male and *f*;
15:27 then he shall bring a *f* goat in
Deut 4:16 the likeness of male or *f*,
5:14 nor your *f* servant, nor your
5:14 your male servant and your *f*
5:21 his *f* servant, his ox, his
7:14 there shall not be a male or *f*
12:12 your male and *f* servants, and
12:18 your male servant and your *f*
15:17 Also to your *f* servant you
16:11 your male servant and your *f*
16:14 your male servant and your *f*
28:68 to your enemies as male and *f*
Judg 9:18 the son of his *f* servant, king
19:19 for your *f* servant, and for the
1 Sam 8:16 your *f* servants, your finest
2 Sam 17:17 so a *f* servant would come and
2 Ki 2:24 And two *f* bears came out of the
5:26 male and *f* servants?
2 Chr 28:10 to be your male and *f* slaves;
Ezra 2:65 besides their male and *f*
Neh 7:67 besides their male and *f*
Esth 7: 4 Had we been sold as male and *f*
Job 1: 3 five hundred *f* donkeys, and a
31:13 the cause of my male or *f*
42:12 and one thousand *f* donkeys.
Eccl 2: 7 I acquired male and *f* servants,
2: 8 I acquired male and *f* singers,
Jer 34: 9 should set free his male and *f*
34:10 should set free his male and *f*
34:11 minds and made the male and *f*
34:11 into subjection as male and *f*
34:16 you brought back his male and *f*
34:16 to be your male and *f* slaves.'
Mt 19: 4 'made them male and *f*,
Mk 10: 6 God 'made them male and *f*.
Lk 12:45 begins to beat the male and *f*
Gal 3:28 there is neither male nor *f*;

FENCE (1/1) FENCED

Ps 62: 3 leaning wall and a tottering *f*.

FENCED (1/1) FENCE

Job 19: 8 He has *f* up my way, so that I

FERRYBOAT (1/1)

2 Sam 19:18 Then a *f* went across to carry

FERTILE (1/1)

Ezek 17: 5 the land And planted it in a *f*

FERTILIZE (1/1)

Lk 13: 8 until I dig around it and *f*

FERVENT (8/8) FERVENTLY

Prov 26:23 *F* lips with a wicked heart
Lk 22:15 With *f* desire I have desired to
Acts 18:25 and being *f* in spirit, he spoke
Rom 12:11 *f* in spirit, serving the Lord;
Jas 5:16 *f* prayer of a righteous man
1 Pe 4: 8 And above all things have *f* love
2 Pe 3:10 the elements will melt with *f*
3:12 the elements will melt with *f*

FERVENTLY (2/2) FERVENT

Col 4:12 always laboring *f* for you in
1 Pe 1:22 love one another *f* with a pure

FERVOR (1/1)

Zech 8: 2 With great *f* I am zealous for

FESTAL (1/1)

Isa 3:22 the *f* apparel, and the mantles;

FESTERING (1/1)

Ps 38: 5 My wounds are foul and *f*

FESTIVAL (2/2)

Isa 30:29 in the night when a holy *f* is
Col 2:16 or regarding a *f* or a new moon

FESTIVALS (1/1)

Ezek 46:11 At the *f* and the appointed feast

FESTUS (12/12)

Acts 24:27 But after two years Porcius *F*

F

25: 1 Now when *F* had come to the
25: 4 But *F* answered that Paul should
25: 9 But *F*, wanting to do the Jews
25:12 Then *F*, when he had conferred
25:13 came to Caesarea to greet *F*.
25:14 *F* laid Paul's case before the
25:22 Then Agrippa said to *F*,
25:24 And *F* said: "King Agrippa and
26:24 *F* said with a loud voice,
26:25 "I am not mad, most noble *F*,
26:32 Then Agrippa said to *F*,

FESTUS' (1/1)

Acts 25:23 at *F* command Paul was brought

FETCH (1/1)

Job 36: 3 I will *f* my knowledge from

FETCHED (KJV) See BROUGHT, TOOK

FETTERS (11/11)

Judg 16:21 They bound him with bronze *f*,
2 Sam 3:34 bound Nor your feet put into *f*;
2 Ki 25: 7 bound him with bronze *f*,
2 Chr 33:11 hooks, bound him with bronze *f*,
36: 6 and bound him in bronze *f* to
Job 36: 8 And if they are bound in *f*,
Ps 105:18 They hurt his feet with *f*,
149: 8 And their nobles with *f* of
Eccl 7:26 and nets, Whose hands are *f*.
Jer 39: 7 and bound him with bronze *f* to
52:11 Babylon bound him in bronze *f*,

FEVER (14/13)

Lev 26:16 wasting disease and *f* which
Deut 28:22 you with consumption, with *f*,
28:22 with severe burning *f*,
Job 30:30 from me; My bones burn with *f*.
Lam 5:10 Because of the *f* of famine.
Hab 3: 5 And *f* followed at His feet.
Mt 8:14 mother lying sick with a *f*.
8:15 and the *f* left her. And she
Mk 1:30 wife's mother lay sick with a *f*,
1:31 and immediately the *f* left her.
Lk 4:38 mother was sick with a high *f*,
4:39 over her and rebuked the *f*,
Jn 4:52 at the seventh hour the *f* left
Acts 28: 8 of Publius lay sick of a *f* and

FEW (61/59)

Gen 24:55 young woman stay with us a *f*
27:44 And stay with him a *f* days,
29:20 and they seemed only a *f* days
34:30 and since I am *f* in number,
47: 9 *f* and evil have been the days
Lev 25:52 And if there remain but a *f*
26:22 and make you *f* in number; and
Num 9:20 was above the tabernacle a *f*
13:18 are strong or weak, *f* or many;
35: 8 the smaller you shall give *f*.
Deut 4:27 and you will be left *f* in
26: 5 *f* in number; and there he
28:62 You shall be left *f* in number,
33: 6 not die, Nor let his men be *f*.
Josh 7: 3 for the people of Ai are *f*.
1 Sam 14: 6 from saving by many or by *f*.
17:28 with whom have you left those *f*
2 Ki 4: 3 vessels; do not gather just a *f*.
1 Chr 16:19 When you were *f* in number,
16:19 few in number, Indeed very *f*,
2 Chr 29:34 But the priests were too *f*,
Neh 2:12 I and a *f* men with me; I told
7: 4 but the people in it were *f*,
Job 10:20 Are not my days *f*?
14: 1 who is born of woman Is of *f*
16:22 For when a *f* years are
Ps 105:12 When they were *f* in number,
105:12 few in number, Indeed very *f*,
109: 8 Let his days be *f*,
Eccl 5: 2 Therefore let your words be *f*.
9:14 was a little city with *f* men
12: 3 cease because they are *f*,
Isa 10: 7 And cut off not a *f* nations.
10:19 of his forest Will be so *f* in
24: 6 And *f* men are left.
65:20 from there live but a *f*
Jer 42: 2 (since we are left but a *f* of
Ezek 12:16 But I will spare a *f* of their
Dan 11:20 but within a *f* days he shall be
Mt 7:14 and there are *f* who find it.
9:37 but the laborers are *f*.
15:34 and a *f* little fish."
20:16 many are called, but *f* chosen."
22:14 but *f* are chosen."
25:21 you were faithful over a *f*
25:23 you have been faithful over a *f*
Mk 6: 5 that He laid His hands on a *f*
8: 7 They also had a *f* small fish;
Lk 10: 2 great, but the laborers are *f*;
12:48 stripes, shall be beaten with *f*.
13:23 are there *f* who are saved?"
Acts 10:48 Then they asked him to stay a *f*
17: 4 and not a *f* of the leading
17:12 and also not a *f* of the Greeks,
24: 4 a *f* words from us.
Heb 12:10 For they indeed for a *f* days
13:22 for I have written to you in *f*
1 Pe 3:20 being prepared, in which a *f*,
Rev 2:14 But I have a *f* things against
2:20 Nevertheless I have a *f* things
3: 4 You have a *f* names even in

FEWER (1/1)

Lev 25:16 and according to the *f* number

FIDELITY (1/1)

Titus 2:10 but showing all good *f*,

FIELD (290/263) FIELDS

Gen 2: 5 before any plant of the *f* was in
2: 5 and before any herb of the *f*
2:19 God formed every beast of the *f*
2:20 and to every beast of the *f*.
3: 1 than any beast of the *f* which
3:14 more than every beast of the *f*;
3:18 you shall eat the herb of the *f*.
4: 8 pass, when they were in the *f*,
23: 9 which is at the end of his *f*.
23:11 I give you the *f* and the cave
23:13 I will give you money for the *f*;
23:17 So the *f* of Ephron which was
23:17 the *f* and the cave which was
23:17 the trees that were in the *f*,
23:19 his wife in the cave of the *f*
23:20 So the *f* and the cave that is
24:63 went out to meditate in the *f*
24:65 is this man walking in the *f*
25: 9 in the *f* of Ephron the son of
25:10 the *f* which Abraham purchased
25:27 skillful hunter, a man of the *f*;
25:29 and Esau came in from the *f*,
27: 3 and go out to the *f* and hunt
27: 5 And Esau went to the *f* to hunt
27:27 son Is like the smell of a *f*
29: 2 looked, and saw a well in the *f*;
30:14 and found mandrakes in the *f*,
30:16 When Jacob came out of the *f* in
31: 4 called Rachel and Leah to the *f*,
34: 5 with his livestock in the *f*;
34: 7 of Jacob came in from the *f*
34:28 the city and what was in the *f*,
36:35 who attacked Midian in the *f* of
37: 7 were, binding sheaves in the *f*.
37:15 he was, wandering in the *f*.
39: 5 had in the house and in the *f*.
47:20 man of the Egyptians sold his *f*,
47:24 as seed for the *f* and for your
49:29 in the cave that is in the *f*
49:30 in the cave that is in the *f* of
49:30 Abraham bought with the *f* of
49:32 The *f* and the cave that is
50:13 him in the cave of the *f* of
50:13 Abraham bought with the *f* from
Ex 1:14 all manner of service in the *f*.
9: 3 will be on your cattle in the *f*,
9:19 and all that you have in the *f*,
9:19 animal which is found in the *f*
9:21 and his livestock in the *f*.
9:22 and on every herb of the *f*,
9:25 Egypt, all that was in the *f*,
9:25 struck every herb of the *f* and
9:25 and broke every tree of the *f*.
10: 5 grows up for you out of the *f*.
10:15 trees or on the plants of the *f*
16:25 you will not find it in the *f*.
22: 5 If a man causes a *f* or vineyard
22: 5 and it feeds in another man's *f*,
22: 5 from the best of his own *f* and
22: 6 or the *f* is consumed, he who
22:31 meat torn by beasts in the *f*;
23:11 the beasts of the *f* may eat.
23:16 which you have sown in the *f*;
23:16 of your labors from the *f*.
23:29 and the beast of the *f* become
Lev 14: 7 living bird loose in the open *f*.
14:53 outside the city in the open *f*,
17: 5 which they offer in the open *f*,
19: 9 reap the corners of your *f*,
19:19 You shall not sow your *f* with
23:22 reap the corners of your *f*
25: 3 'Six years you shall sow your *f*,
25: 4 You shall neither sow your *f*
25:12 eat its produce from the *f*.
25:34 But the *f* of the common-land of
26: 4 and the trees of the *f* shall
27:16 to the LORD part of a *f* of
27:17 If he dedicates his *f* from the
27:18 But if he dedicates his *f* after
27:19 And if he who dedicates the *f*
27:20 does not want to redeem the *f*,
27:20 or if he has sold the *f* to
27:21 'but the *f*, when it is released
27:21 to the LORD, as a devoted *f*;
27:22 man dedicates to the LORD a *f*
27:22 which is not the *f* of his
27:24 In the Year of Jubilee the *f*
27:28 or the *f* of his possession,
Num 19:16 Whoever in the open *f* touches
22: 4 ox licks up the grass of the *f*.
22:23 of the way and went into the *f*.
23:14 So he brought him to the *f* of
Deut 5:21 your neighbor's house, his *f*,
7:22 lest the beasts of the *f* become
14:22 of your grain that the *f*
20:19 for the tree of the *f* is man's
21: 1 lying in the *f* in the land
24:19 you reap your harvest in your *f*,
24:19 and forget a sheaf in the *f*,
28:38 carry much seed out to the *f*
Josh 8:24 the inhabitants of Ai in the *f*,
15:18 him to ask her father for a *f*.
Judg 1:14 him to ask her father for a *f*.
5: 4 When You marched from the *f* of
9:32 you, and lie in wait in the *f*.
9:42 the people went out into the *f*,
9:43 and lay in wait in the *f*.
13: 9 as she was sitting in the *f*;
19:16 came in from his work in the *f*
20:31 other to Gibeah) and in the *f*,
Ruth 2: 2 "Please let me go to the *f*,
2: 3 and went and gleaned in the *f*
2: 3 to come to the part of the *f*
2: 8 Do not go to glean in another *f*,
2: 9 Let your eyes be on the *f*
2:17 So she gleaned in the *f* until
2:22 do not meet you in any other *f*.
4: 5 On the day you buy the *f* from
1 Sam 4: 2 men of the army in the *f*.
6:14 Then the cart came into the *f* of
6:18 remains to this day in the *f*
11: 5 behind the herd from the *f*;
14:15 trembling in the camp, in the *f*,
17:44 air and the beasts of the *f*!"
19: 3 stand beside my father in the *f*
20: 5 that I may hide in the *f* until
20:11 and let us go out into the *f*.
20:11 of them went out into the *f*.
20:24 Then David hid in the *f*.
20:35 Jonathan went out into the *f*
30:11 they found an Egyptian in the *f*,
2 Sam 2:16 that place was called the *F* of
10: 8 were by themselves in the *f*.
11:23 us and came out to us in the *f*;
14: 6 fought with each other in the *f*,
14:30 Joab's *f* is near mine, and he
14:30 Absalom's servants set the *f*
14:31 have your servants set my *f* on
17: 8 robbed of her cubs in the *f*;
18: 6 the people went out into the *f*
20:12 from the highway to the *f* and
21:10 by day nor the beasts of the *f*
23:12 himself in the middle of the *f*,
1 Ki 11:29 the two were alone in the *f*.
14:11 shall eat whoever dies in the *f*;
21:24 shall eat whoever dies in the *f*.
2 Ki 4:39 So one went out into the *f* to
7:12 to hide themselves in the *f*,
8: 6 and all the proceeds of the *f*
9:25 him into the tract of the *f* of
9:37 refuse on the surface of the *f*,
18:17 the highway to the Fuller's *F*.
19:26 were as the grass of the *f*
1 Chr 1:46 who attacked Midian in the *f* of
11:14 in the middle of that *f*,
16:32 Let the *f* rejoice, and all
19: 9 were by themselves in the *f*.
27:25 over the storehouses in the *f*,
27:26 who did the work of the *f* for
2 Chr 26:23 him with his fathers in the *f*
31: 5 and of all the produce of the *f*;
Neh 13:10 the work had gone back to his *f*.
Job 5:23 with the stones of the *f*,
5:23 And the beasts of the *f* shall
24: 6 gather their fodder in the *f*
40:20 And all the beasts of the *f*
Ps 8: 7 oxen—Even the beasts of the *f*,
50:11 And the wild beasts of the *f*
78:12 in the *f* of Zoan.
78:43 And His wonders in the *f* of
80:13 And the wild beast of the *f*
96:12 Let the *f* be joyful, and all
103:15 grass; As a flower of the *f*,
104:11 drink to every beast of the *f*;
Prov 24:27 it fit for yourself in the *f*;
24:30 I went by the *f* of the lazy
27:26 And the goats the price of a *f*;
31:16 She considers a *f* and buys it;
Eccl 5: 9 the king is served from the *f*.
Song 2: 7 or by the does of the *f*,
3: 5 or by the does of the *f*,
7:11 Let us go forth to the *f*;
Isa 5: 8 They add *f* to field, Till
5: 8 to house; They add field to *f*,
7: 3 the highway to the Fuller's *F*,
10:18 forest and of his fruitful *f*,
16:10 And joy from the plentiful *f*;
29:17 be turned into a fruitful *f*,
29:17 And the fruitful *f* be esteemed
32:15 wilderness becomes a fruitful *f*,
32:15 And the fruitful *f* is counted
32:16 remain in the fruitful *f*.
36: 2 the highway to the Fuller's *F*.
37:27 were as the grass of the *f*
40: 6 is like the flower of the *f*.
43:20 The beast of the *f* will honor
55:12 And all the trees of the *f*
56: 9 All you beasts of the *f*,
Jer 4:17 Like keepers of a *f* they are
6:25 Do not go out into the *f*,
7:20 on the trees of the *f* and on
9:22 fall as refuse on the open *f*,
12: 4 And the herbs of every *f*
12: 9 all the beasts of the *f*,
14: 5 deer also gave birth in the *f*,
14:18 If I go out to the *f*,
17: 3 O My mountain in the *f*,
18:14 comes from the rock of the *f*?
26:18 shall be plowed like a *f*,

27: 6 and the beasts of the *f* I have
28:14 given him the beasts of the *f*
32: 7 Buy my *f* which is in Anathoth,
32: 8 Please buy my *f* that is in
32: 9 So I bought the *f* from Hanamel,
32:25 Buy the *f* for money, and take
35: 9 in; nor do we have vineyard, *f*,
41: 8 barley, oil, and honey in the *f*
48:33 are taken From the plentiful *f*
Lam 4: 9 lack of the fruits of the *f*.
Ezek 7:15 Whoever is in the *f* Will die
16: 5 were thrown out into the open *f*,
16: 7 thrive like a plant in the *f*;
17: 5 And planted it in a fertile *f*;
17:24 And all the trees of the *f* shall
29: 5 You shall fall on the open *f*;
29: 5 as food To the beasts of the *f*
31: 4 to all the trees of the *f*.
31: 5 above all the trees of the *f*;
31: 6 all the beasts of the *f*
31:13 And all the beasts of the *f*
31:15 and all the trees of the *f*
33:27 the one who is in the open *f*
34: 5 for all the beasts of the *f*
34: 8 food for every beast of the *f*,
34:27 Then the trees of the *f* shall
38:20 heavens, the beasts of the *f*,
39: 4 and to the beasts of the *f* to
39: 5 "You shall fall on the open *f*;
39:10 will not take wood from the *f*
39:17 and to every beast of the *f*:
Dan 2:38 or the beasts of the *f* and the
4:12 The beasts of the *f* found
4:15 In the tender grass of the *f*.
4:21 under which the beasts of the *f*
4:23 in the tender grass of the *f*;
4:23 graze with the beasts of the *f*,
4:25 be with the beasts of the *f*,
4:32 be with the beasts of the *f*.
Hos 2:12 And the beasts of the *f* shall
2:18 them With the beasts of the *f*,
4: 3 away With the beasts of the *f*
10: 4 hemlock in the furrows of the *f*.
12:11 heaps in the furrows of the *f*.
Joel 1:10 The *f* is wasted, The land
1:11 Because the harvest of the *f*
1:12 All the trees of the *f* are
1:19 burned all the trees of the *f*.
1:20 The beasts of the *f* also cry
2:22 be afraid, you beasts of the *f*;
Mic 1: 6 a heap of ruins in the *f*,
3:12 Zion shall be plowed like a *f*,
4:10 city, You shall dwell in the *f*,
Zech 10: 1 Grass in the *f* for everyone.
Mal 3:11 to bear fruit for you in the *f*,
Mt 6:28 Consider the lilies of the *f*,
6:30 so clothes the grass of the *f*,
13:24 who sowed good seed in his *f*;
13:27 you not sow good seed in your *f*?
13:31 a man took and sowed in his *f*,
13:36 parable of the tares of the *f*.
13:38 The *f* is the world, the good
13:44 is like treasure hidden in a *f*,
13:44 all that he has and buys that *f*.
24:18 And let him who is in the *f* not
24:40 two men will be in the *f*:
27: 7 bought with them the potter's *f*,
27: 8 Therefore that *f* has been called
27: 8 field has been called the *F* of
27:10 them for the potter's *f*,
Mk 13:16 And let him who is in the *f* not
Lk 12:28 which today is in the *f* and
15:25 his older son was in the *f*.
17: 7 when he has come in from the *f*,
17:31 the one who is in the *f*,
17:36 "Two men will be in the *f*:
Acts 1:18 (Now this man purchased a *f* with
1:19 so that *f* is called in their
1:19 that is, *F* of Blood.)
1 Cor 3: 9 fellow workers; you are God's *f*,
Jas 1:10 because as a flower of the *f* he

FIELDS (57/56) FIELD

Gen 41:48 in every city the food of the *f*
Ex 8:13 courtyards, and out of the *f*.
Lev 25:31 them shall be counted as the *f*
Num 16:14 nor given us inheritance of *f*
20:17 We will not pass through *f* or
21:22 We will not turn aside into *f*
Deut 11:15 I will send grass in your *f*
32:13 might eat the produce of the *f*;
32:32 vine of Sodom And of the *f* of
Josh 21:12 But the *f* of the city and its
Judg 9:27 So they went out into the *f*,
9:44 upon all who were in the *f*
1 Sam 8:14 he will take the best of your *f*,
22: 7 Jesse give every one of you *f*
25:15 them, when we were in the *f*.
2 Sam 1:21 Nor *f* of offerings. For the
11:11 lord are encamped in the open *f*.
1 Ki 2:26 "Go to Anathoth, to your own *f*,
16: 4 shall eat whoever dies in the *f*.
2 Ki 23: 4 outside Jerusalem in the *f* of
1 Chr 6:56 But the *f* of the city and its
2 Chr 31:19 who were in the *f* of the
Neh 11:25 for the villages with their *f*,
11:30 villages; in Lachish and its *f*;
12:29 and from the *f* of Geba and
12:44 to gather into them from the *f*
Job 5:10 And sends waters on the *f*.
Ps 107:37 And sow *f* and plant vineyards,
132: 6 We found it in the *f* of the
144:13 And ten thousands in our *f*;
Prov 8:26 had not made the earth or the *f*,
23:10 Nor enter the *f* of the
Isa 16: 8 For the *f* of Heshbon languish,
32:12 breasts For the pleasant *f*,
Jer 6:12 *F* and wives together; For I
8:10 And their *f* to those who will
13:27 on the hills in the *f*.
31:40 and all the *f* as far as the
32:15 Houses and *f* and vineyards shall
32:43 And *f* will be bought in this
32:44 Men will buy *f* for money, sign
39:10 and gave them vineyards and *f*
40: 7 the armies who were in the *f*,
40:13 the forces that were in the *f*
Ezek 26: 6 villages which are in the *f*
26: 8 daughter villages in the *f*;
32: 4 will cast you out on the open *f*,
36:30 and the increase of your *f*,
Ob 19 They shall possess the *f* of
19 fields of Ephraim And the *f*
Mic 2: 2 They covet *f* and take them by
2: 4 a turncoat He has divided our *f*.
Hab 3:17 And the *f* yield no food;
Lk 2: 8 shepherds living out in the *f*,
15:15 and he sent him into his *f* to
Jn 4:35 up your eyes and look at the *f*,
Jas 5: 4 the laborers who mowed your *f*,

FIERCE (49/49) FIERCENESS

Gen 49: 7 be their anger, for it is *f*;
Ex 32:12 Turn from Your *f* wrath, and
Num 25: 4 that the *f* anger of the LORD
32:14 to increase still more the *f*
Deut 28:50 a nation of *f* countenance, which
Judg 20:34 Gibeah, and the battle was *f*.
1 Sam 14:52 Now there was *f* war with the
20:34 arose from the table in *f*
28:18 of the LORD nor execute His *f*
31: 3 The battle became *f* against
2 Sam 2:17 So there was a very *f* battle
2 Ki 3:26 saw that the battle was too *f*
1 Chr 10: 3 The battle became *f* against
2 Chr 28:11 for the *f* wrath of the LORD
28:13 and there is *f* wrath against
29:10 that His *f* wrath may turn away
Ezra 10:14 until the *f* wrath of our God is
Job 4:10 The voice of the *f* lion, And
10:16 You hunt me like a *f* lion,
28: 8 Nor has the *f* lion passed over
41:10 No one is so *f* that he would
Ps 35:11 *F* witnesses rise up
88:16 Your *f* wrath has gone over me;
Prov 26:13 is a lion in the road! A *f*
Isa 7: 4 for the *f* anger of Rezin and
13: 9 with both wrath and *f* anger,
13:13 hosts And in the day of His *f*
19: 4 And a *f* king will rule over
33:19 You will not see a *f* people, A
Jer 4: 8 For the *f* anger of the LORD
4:26 By His *f* anger.
12:13 your harvest Because of the *f*
25:37 are cut down Because of the *f*
25:38 And because of His *f* anger."
30:24 The *f* anger of the LORD will
49:37 My *f* anger,' says the LORD;
51:45 deliver himself from the *f*
Lam 1:12 inflicted In the day of His *f*
2: 3 He has cut off in *f* anger
4:11 He has poured out His *f* anger.
Dan 8:23 Having *f* features, Who
Joel 1: 6 And he has the fangs of a *f*
Jon 3: 9 and turn away from His *f* anger,
Hab 1: 8 And more *f* than evening
Zeph 2: 2 Before the LORD's *f* anger
3: 8 All my *f* anger; All the earth
Mt 8:28 out of the tombs, exceedingly *f*,
Lk 23: 5 But they were the more *f*,
Jas 3: 4 so large and are driven by *f*

FIERCELY (1/1)

Jer 6:29 The bellows blow *f*,

FIERCENESS (13/13) FIERCE

Deut 13:17 the LORD may turn from the *f*
Josh 7:26 So the LORD turned from the *f*
2 Ki 23:26 LORD did not turn from the *f*
2 Chr 30: 8 that the *f* of His wrath may
Job 39:24 He devours the distance with *f*
Ps 78:49 He cast on them the *f* of His
85: 3 You have turned from the *f* of
Jer 25:38 is desolate Because of the *f*
49:16 Your *f* has deceived you, The
Hos 11: 9 I will not execute the *f* of My
Nah 1: 6 And who can endure the *f* of
Rev 16:19 the cup of the wine of the *f*
19:15 treads the winepress of the *f*

FIERCER (1/1)

2 Sam 19:43 of the men of Judah were *f*

FIERY (28/28) FIRE

Num 21: 6 So the LORD sent *f* serpents
21: 8 Make a *f* serpent, and set it on
Deut 8:15 in which were *f* serpents and
33: 2 His right hand Came a *f* law
Ps 7:13 makes His arrows into *f* shafts.
21: 9 You shall make them as a *f* oven
78:48 their flocks to *f* lightning.
Isa 14:29 will be a *f* flying serpent.
30: 6 The viper and *f* flying
Ezek 28:14 forth in the midst of *f* stones.
28:16 the midst of the *f* stones.
Dan 3: 6 midst of a burning *f* furnace."
3:11 midst of a burning *f* furnace.
3:15 midst of a burning *f* furnace.
3:17 us from the burning *f* furnace,
3:20 into the burning *f* furnace.
3:21 midst of the burning *f* furnace.
3:23 midst of the burning *f* furnace.
3:26 mouth of the burning *f* furnace
7: 9 His throne was a *f* flame,
7:10 A *f* stream issued And came
Zech 12: 6 and like a *f* torch in the
Eph 6:16 able to quench all the *f* darts
Heb 10:27 and *f* indignation which will
1 Pe 4:12 strange concerning the *f* trial
Rev 6: 4 *f* red, went out. And it was
9:17 had breastplates of *f* red,
12: 3 *f* red dragon having seven heads

F

FIFTEEN (19/19) FIFTEENTH

Gen 5:10 Enosh lived eight hundred and *f*
7:20 The waters prevailed *f* cubits
Ex 27:14 of the gate shall be *f*
27:15 side shall be hangings of *f*
38:14 one side of the gate were *f*
38:15 and that were hangings of *f*
Lev 27: 7 then your valuation shall be *f*
Judg 8:10 about *f* thousand, all who were
2 Sam 9:10 Now Ziba had *f* sons and
19:17 and his *f* sons and his twenty
1 Ki 7: 3 forty-five pillars, *f* to a
2 Ki 14:17 lived *f* years after the death
20: 6 And I will add to your days *f*
2 Chr 25:25 lived *f* years after the death
Isa 38: 5 I will add to your days *f*
Ezek 45:12 and *f* shekels shall be your
Hos 3: 2 I bought her for myself for *f*
Acts 27:28 again and found it to be *f*
Gal 1:18 and remained with him *f* days.

FIFTEENTH (18/18) FIFTEEN

Ex 16: 1 on the *f* day of the second
Lev 23: 6 And on the *f* day of the same
23:34 The *f* day of this seventh month
23:39 Also on the *f* day of the
Num 28:17 And on the *f* day of this month
29:12 On the *f* day of the seventh
33: 3 on the *f* day of the first
1 Ki 12:32 ordained a feast on the *f* day
12:33 he had made at Bethel on the *f*
2 Ki 14:23 In the *f* year of Amaziah the
1 Chr 24:14 the *f* to Bilgah, the sixteenth
25:22 the *f* for Jeremoth, his sons and
2 Chr 15:10 in the *f* year of the reign of
Esth 9:18 and on the *f* of the month
9:21 yearly the fourteenth and *f*
Ezek 32:17 on the *f* day of the month,
45:25 on the *f* day of the month, at
Lk 3: 1 Now in the *f* year of the reign

FIFTH (43/41) FIVE

Gen 1:23 and the morning were the *f* day.
30:17 conceived and bore Jacob a *f*
Lev 19:25 And in the *f* year you may eat
Num 7:36 On the *f* day Shelumiel the son
29:26 On the *f* day present nine
33:38 on the first day of the *f*
Josh 19:24 The *f* lot came out for the
Judg 19: 8 early in the morning on the *f*
2 Sam 3: 4 the son of Haggith; the *f*,
1 Ki 14:25 It happened in the *f* year of
2 Ki 8:16 Now in the *f* year of Joram the
25: 8 And in the *f* month, on the
1 Chr 2:14 the fourth, Raddai the *f*,
3: 3 the *f*, Shephatiah, by Abital;
8: 2 the fourth, and Rapha the *f*.
12:10 the fourth, Jeremiah the *f*,
24: 9 the *f* to Malchijah, the sixth to
25:12 the *f* for Nethaniah, his sons
26: 3 Elam the *f*, Jehohanan the
26: 4 the fourth, Nethanel the *f*,
27: 8 The *f* captain for the fifth
27: 8 The fifth captain for the *f*
2 Chr 12: 2 And it happened in the *f* year
Ezra 7: 8 Ezra came to Jerusalem in the *f*
7: 9 and on the first day of the *f*
Neh 6: 5 the *f* time, with an open letter
Jer 1: 3 of Jerusalem captive in the *f*
28: 1 the fourth year and in the *f*
36: 9 Now it came to pass in the *f*
52:12 Now in the *f* month, on the
Ezek 1: 1 on the *f* day of the month, as
1: 2 On the *f* day of the month,
1: 2 which was in the *f* year of
8: 1 on the *f* day of the month, as
20: 1 in the *f* month, on the tenth
33:21 on the *f* day of the month,
Zech 7: 3 Should I weep in the *f* month and
7: 5 you fasted and mourned in the *f*
8:19 month, The fast of the *f*
Rev 6: 9 When He opened the *f* seal, I
9: 1 Then the *f* angel sounded: And I
16:10 Then the *f* angel poured out his
21:20 the *f* sardonyx, the sixth

FIFTIES (7/6) FIFTY

Ex 18:21 rulers of hundreds, rulers of *f*,
18:25 rulers of hundreds, rulers of *f*,
Deut 1:15 of hundreds, leaders of *f*,
1 Sam 8:12 and captains over his *f*,
2 Ki 1:14 up the first two captains of *f*
1:14 of fifties with their *f*.
Mk 6:40 in ranks, in hundreds and in *f*.

FIFTIETH (3/3) FIFTY

Lev 25:10 'And you shall consecrate the *f*
25:11 That *f* year shall be a Jubilee
2 Ki 15:23 In the *f* year of Azariah king

FIFTY (123/105) FIFTIES, FIFTIETH

Gen 6:15 its width *f* cubits, and its
7:24 on the earth one hundred and *f*
8: 3 At the end of the hundred and *f*
9:28 the flood three hundred and *f*
9:29 of Noah were nine hundred and *f*
18:24 Suppose there were *f* righteous
18:24 and not spare it for the *f*
18:26 If I find in Sodom *f* righteous
18:28 there were five less than the *f*
Ex 26: 5 *F* loops you shall make in the
26: 5 and *f* loops you shall make on
26: 6 And you shall make *f* clasps of
26:10 You shall make *f* loops on the
26:10 and *f* loops on the edge of the
26:11 And you shall make *f* bronze
27:12 side shall be hangings of *f*
27:13 on the east side shall be *f*
27:18 the width *f* throughout, and the
30:23 cinnamon (two hundred and *f*
30:23 two hundred and *f* shekels of
36:12 *F* loops he made on one curtain,
36:12 and *f* loops he made on the edge
36:13 And he made *f* clasps of gold,
36:17 And he made *f* loops on the edge
36:17 and *f* loops he made on the edge
36:18 He also made *f* bronze clasps to
38:12 side there were hangings of *f*
38:13 side the hangings were *f*
38:26 five hundred and *f* men.
Lev 23:16 Count *f* days to the day after
27: 3 then your valuation shall be *f*
27:16 seed shall be valued at *f*
Num 1:25 thousand six hundred and *f*.
1:46 thousand five hundred and *f*.
2:15 thousand six hundred and *f*.
2:16 thousand four hundred and *f*—
2:32 thousand five hundred and *f*.
4: 3 even to *f* years old, all who
4:23 even to *f* years old, you shall
4:30 even to *f* years old, you shall
4:35 even to *f* years old, everyone
4:36 thousand seven hundred and *f*.
4:39 even to *f* years old, everyone
4:43 even to *f* years old, everyone
4:47 even to *f* years old, everyone
8:25 and at the age of *f* years they
16: 2 two hundred and *f* leaders of
16:17 two hundred and *f* censers;
16:35 consumed the two hundred and *f*
26:10 devoured two hundred and *f* men;
31:30 you shall take one of every *f*,
31:47 half Moses took one of every *f*,
31:52 thousand seven hundred and *f*
Deut 22:29 to the young woman's father *f*
Josh 7:21 and a wedge of gold weighing *f*
1 Sam 6:19 He struck *f* thousand and
2 Sam 15: 1 and *f* men to run before him.
24:24 floor and the oxen for *f*
1 Ki 1: 5 and *f* men to run before him.
7: 2 its width *f* cubits, and its
7: 6 its length was *f* cubits, and
9:23 work: five hundred and *f*,
10:29 and a horse one hundred and *f*;
18: 4 *f* to a cave, and had fed them
18:13 *f* to a cave, and fed them with
18:19 the four hundred and *f* prophets
18:22 are four hundred and *f* men.
2 Ki 1: 9 king sent to him a captain of *f*
1: 9 a captain of fifty with his *f*
1:10 and said to the captain of *f*,
1:10 and consume you and your *f* men.
1:10 and consumed him and his *f*.
1:11 to him another captain of *f*
1:11 captain of fifty with his *f*
1:12 and consume you and your *f* men.
1:12 and consumed him and his *f*.
1:13 he sent a third captain of *f*
1:13 captain of fifty with his *f*
1:13 And the third captain of *f* went
1:13 my life and the life of these *f*
2: 7 And *f* men of the sons of the
2:16 there are *f* strong men with
2:17 Therefore they sent *f* men,
13: 7 of the army of Jehoahaz only *f*
15:20 from each man *f* shekels of
15:25 and with him were *f* men of
1 Chr 5:21 *f* thousand of their camels, two
5:21 two hundred and *f* thousand of
8:40 one hundred and *f* in all.
12:33 of Zebulun there were *f* thousand
2 Chr 1:17 a horse for one hundred and *f*;
3: 9 The weight of the nails was *f*
8:10 King Solomon: two hundred and *f*,
8:18 and acquired four hundred and *f*
Ezra 8: 3 him were one hundred and *f*
8: 6 and with him *f* males;
8:26 their hand six hundred and *f*
Neh 5:17 table were one hundred and *f*
7:70 *f* basins, and five hundred and
Esth 5:14 *f* cubits high, and in the
7: 9 *f* cubits high, which Haman made
Isa 3: 3 The captain of *f* and the
Ezek 40:15 of the inner gate was *f*
40:21 its length was *f* cubits and
40:25 its length was *f* cubits and
40:29 it was *f* cubits long and
40:33 it was *f* cubits long and
40:36 its length was *f* cubits and
42: 2 hundred cubits (the width was *f*
42: 7 its length was *f* cubits.
42: 8 toward the outer court was *f*
45: 2 with *f* cubits around it for an
48:17 to the north two hundred and *f*
48:17 to the south two hundred and *f*,
48:17 to the east two hundred and *f*,
48:17 to the west two hundred and *f*.
Hag 2:16 to the wine vat to draw out *f*
Lk 7:41 denarii, and the other *f*.
9:14 them sit down in groups of *f*.
16: 6 sit down quickly and write *f*.
Jn 8:57 You are not yet *f* years old, and
Acts 13:20 for about four hundred and *f*
19:19 and it totaled *f* thousand

FIFTY-FIVE (3/3)

2 Ki 21: 1 and he reigned *f* years in
2 Chr 33: 1 and he reigned *f* years in
Neh 7:20 sons of Adin, six hundred and *f*;

FIFTY-FOUR (7/7)

Num 1:29 the tribe of Issachar were *f*
2: 6 And his army was numbered at *f*
Ezra 2: 7 one thousand two hundred and *f*;
2:15 of Adin, four hundred and *f*;
2:31 one thousand two hundred and *f*;
Neh 7:12 one thousand two hundred and *f*;
7:34 one thousand two hundred and *f*;

FIFTY-NINE (2/2)

Num 1:23 of the tribe of Simeon were *f*
2:13 And his army was numbered at *f*

FIFTY-ONE (1/1)

Num 2:16 one hundred and *f* thousand four

FIFTY-SECOND (1/1)

2 Ki 15:27 In the *f* year of Azariah king

FIFTY-SEVEN (3/3)

Num 1:31 of the tribe of Zebulun were *f*
2: 8 And his army was numbered at *f*
2:31 one hundred and *f* thousand six

FIFTY-SIX (4/4)

1 Chr 9: 9 generations—nine hundred and *f*.
Ezra 2:14 of Bigvai, two thousand and *f*;
2:22 the men of Netophah, *f*;
2:30 of Magbish, one hundred and *f*;

FIFTY-THREE (5/5)

Num 1:43 the tribe of Naphtali were *f*
2:30 And his army was numbered at *f*
26:47 *f* thousand four hundred.
2 Chr 2:17 found to be one hundred and *f*
Jn 21:11 large fish, one hundred and *f*;

FIFTY-TWO (10/10)

Num 26:34 were numbered of them were *f*
2 Ki 15: 2 and he reigned *f* years in
2 Chr 26: 3 and he reigned *f* years in
Ezra 2:29 the people of Nebo, *f*;
2:37 of Immer, one thousand and *f*;
2:60 of Nekoda, six hundred and *f*;
Neh 6:15 day of Elul, in *f* days.
7:10 sons of Arah, six hundred and *f*;
7:33 the men of the other Nebo, *f*;
7:40 of Immer, one thousand and *f*;

FIG (40/39) FIGS

Gen 3: 7 and they sewed *f* leaves
Deut 8: 8 of vines and *f* trees and
Judg 9:10 Then the trees said to the *f*
9:11 But the *f* tree said to them,
1 Ki 4:25 man under his vine and his *f*
2 Ki 18:31 and every one from his own *f*
Ps 105:33 and their *f* trees, And
Prov 27:18 Whoever keeps the *f* tree will
Song 2:13 The *f* tree puts forth her green
Isa 34: 4 And as fruit falling from a *f*
36:16 and every one from his own *f*
Jer 5:17 eat up your vines and your *f*
8:13 Nor figs on the *f* tree, And
Hos 2:12 destroy her vines and her *f*
9:10 As the firstfruits on the *f*
Joel 1: 7 And ruined My *f* tree; He has
1:12 And the *f* tree has withered;
2:22 The *f* tree and the vine yield
Am 4: 9 Your *f* trees, And your olive
Mic 4: 4 under his vine and under his *f*
Nah 3:12 All your strongholds are *f*
Hab 3:17 Though the *f* tree may not
Hag 2:19 the *f* tree, the pomegranate,
Zech 3:10 his vine and under his *f* tree.
Mt 21:19 And seeing a *f* tree by the road,
21:19 Immediately the *f* tree
21:20 How did the *f* tree wither away
21:21 only do what was done to the *f*
24:32 learn this parable from the *f*
Mk 11:13 And seeing from afar a *f* tree
11:20 they saw the *f* tree dried up
11:21 The *f* tree which You
13:28 learn this parable from the *f*
Lk 13: 6 A certain man had a *f* tree
13: 7 come seeking fruit on this *f*
21:29 Look at the *f* tree, and all the
Jn 1:48 when you were under the *f* tree,
1:50 I saw you under the *f* tree,' do
Jas 3:12 Can a *f* tree, my brethren, bear
Rev 6:13 as a *f* tree drops its late figs

FIGHT (102/98) FIGHTING, FIGHTS, FOUGHT

Ex 1:10 also join our enemies and *f*
14:14 The LORD will *f* for you, and
17: 9 *f* with Amalek. Tomorrow I will
21:22 If men *f*, and hurt a woman
Deut 1:30 He will *f* for you, according to
1:41 the LORD; we will go up and *f*,
1:42 them, "Do not go up nor *f*,
2:32 came out against us to *f* at
20: 4 to *f* for you against your
20:10 When you go near a city to *f*
25:11 If two men *f* together, and the
Josh 9: 2 they gathered together to *f*
10:25 your enemies against whom you *f*.
11: 5 at the waters of Merom to *f*
19:47 children of Dan went up to *f*
Judg 1: 1 us against the Canaanites to *f*
1: 3 that we may *f* against the
1: 9 of Judah went down to *f*
8: 1 calling us when you went to *f*
9:38 and *f* with them now."
10: 9 crossed over the Jordan to *f*
10:18 the man who will begin the *f*
11: 6 that we may *f* against the
11: 8 that you may go with us and *f*
11: 9 If you take me back home to *f*
11:12 that you have come to *f* against
11:25 Did he ever *f* against them?
11:32 toward the people of Ammon to *f*
12: 1 Why did you cross over to *f*
12: 3 you come up to me this day to *f*
20:20 in battle array to *f* against
1 Sam 4: 9 yourselves like men, and *f*!"
8:20 us and go out before us and *f*
13: 5 gathered together to *f* with
15:18 and *f* against them until they
17: 9 If he is able to *f* with me and
17:10 that we may *f* together."
17:20 the army was going out to the *f*
17:32 your servant will go and *f* with
17:33 go against this Philistine to *f*
18:17 and *f* the LORD's battles."
28: 1 to *f* with Israel. And Achish
29: 8 that I may not go and *f* against
2 Sam 2:28 nor did they *f* anymore.
1 Ki 12:21 to *f* against the house of
12:24 You shall not go up nor *f*
20:23 but if we *f* against them in the
20:25 Then we will *f* against them in
20:26 and went up to Aphek to *f*
22: 4 Will you go with me to *f* at
22: 6 I go against Ramoth Gilead to *f*,
22:31 *F* with no one small or great,
22:32 they turned aside to *f* against
2 Ki 3: 7 Will you go with me to *f*
3:21 that the kings had come up to *f*
10: 3 and *f* for your master's house.
2 Chr 11: 1 to *f* against Israel, that he
11: 4 You shall not go up or *f* against
13:12 do not *f* against the LORD God
18:30 *F* with no one small or great,
20:17 You will not need to *f* in this
32: 8 to help us and to *f* our
35:20 king of Egypt came up to *f*
35:22 himself so that he might *f*
35:22 So he came to *f* in the Valley
Neh 4:14 and *f* for your brethren, your
4:20 Our God will *f* for us."
Ps 35: 1 *F* against those who fight
35: 1 Fight against those who *f*
56: 2 For there are many who *f*
Isa 19: 2 Everyone will *f* against his
29: 7 of all the nations who *f*
29: 7 Even all who *f* against her and
29: 8 Who *f* against Mount Zion."
30:32 of brandishing He will *f* with
31: 4 of hosts will come down To *f*
Jer 1:19 They will *f* against you, But
15:20 And they will *f* against you,
21: 4 with which you *f* against the
21: 5 I Myself will *f* against you with
32: 5 though you *f* with the Chaldeans,
32:24 the hand of the Chaldeans who *f*
32:29 And the Chaldeans who *f* against
33: 5 They come to *f* with the
34:22 They will *f* against it and take
37: 8 shall come back and *f* against
37:10 army of the Chaldeans who *f*

41:12 took all the men and went to *f*
Dan 10:20 And now I must return to *f* with
11:11 and go out and *f* with him, with
Zech 10: 5 They shall *f* because the LORD
14: 3 the LORD will go forth And *f*
14:14 Judah also will *f* at Jerusalem.
Jn 18:36 this world, My servants would *f*,
Acts 5:39 lest you even be found to *f*
23: 9 let us not *f* against God."
1 Cor 9:26 not with uncertainty. Thus I *f*:
1 Tim 6:12 *F* the good fight of faith, lay
6:12 Fight the good *f* of faith, lay
2 Tim 4: 7 I have fought the good *f*,
Jas 4: 2 You *f* and war. Yet you do not
Rev 2:16 come to you quickly and will *f*

FIGHTING (8/8) FIGHT

Ex 2:13 behold, two Hebrew men were *f*,
Judg 11:27 but you wronged me by *f* against
1 Sam 17:19 *f* with the Philistines.
23: 1 the Philistines are *f* against
2 Chr 26:11 Uzziah had an army of *f* men
Ps 56: 1 *F* all day he oppresses me.
Jer 51:30 men of Babylon have ceased *f*,
Acts 7:26 to two of them as they were *f*,

FIGHTS (6/6) FIGHT

Ex 14:25 for the LORD *f* for them
Deut 3:22 the LORD your God Himself *f*
Josh 23:10 the LORD your God is He who *f*
1 Sam 25:28 because my lord *f* the battles
Zech 14: 3 As He *f* in the day of battle.
Jas 4: 1 Where do wars and *f* come from

FIGS (25/22) FIG

Num 13:23 some of the pomegranates and *f*.
20: 5 is not a place of grain or *f*
1 Sam 25:18 and two hundred cakes of *f*,
30:12 him a piece of a cake of *f* and
2 Ki 20: 7 Isaiah said, "Take a lump of *f*.
1 Chr 12:40 of flour and cakes of *f* and
Neh 13:15 donkeys with wine, grapes, *f*,
Song 2:13 fig tree puts forth her green *f*,
Isa 38:21 "Let them take a lump of *f*,
Jer 8:13 Nor *f* on the fig tree, And
24: 1 and there were two baskets of *f*
24: 2 One basket had very good *f*,
24: 2 like the *f* that are first
24: 2 other basket had very bad *f*
24: 3 And I said, "*F*,
24: 3 And I said, "Figs, the good *f*,
24: 5 of Israel: 'Like these good *f*,
24: 8 And as the bad *f* which cannot
29:17 will make them like rotten *f*
Nah 3:12 are fig trees with ripened *f*:
Mt 7:16 grapes from thornbushes or *f*
Mk 11:13 for it was not the season for *f*.
Lk 6:44 For men do not gather *f* from
Jas 3:12 olives, or a grapevine bear *f*?
Rev 6:13 as a fig tree drops its late *f*

FIGURATIVE (3/2) FIGURE

Jn 16:25 I have spoken to you in *f*
16:25 no longer speak to you in *f*
Heb 11:19 he also received him in a *f*

FIGURATIVELY (1/1)

1 Cor 4: 6 I have *f* transferred to myself

FIGURE (3/3) FIGURATIVE, FIGUREHEAD

Deut 4:16 image in the form of any *f*:
Isa 44:13 And makes it like the *f* of a
Jn 16:29 and using no *f* of speech!

FIGUREHEAD (1/1) FIGURE

Acts 28:11 in an Alexandrian ship whose *f*

FIGURES (2/2)

1 Ki 6:29 with carved *f* of cherubim, palm
6:32 and he carved on them *f* of

FILL (52/52) FILLED, FILLING, FILLS, FULL

Gen 1:22 and *f* the waters in the seas,
1:28 *f* the earth and subdue it; have
9: 1 and *f* the earth.
42:25 Joseph gave a command to *f*
44: 1 *F* the men's sacks with food, as
Ex 10: 6 They shall *f* your houses, the
16:32 *F* an omer with it, to be kept
Lev 25:19 fruit, and you will eat your *f*,
Deut 6:11 things, which you did not *f*,
23:24 you may eat your *f* of grapes at
1 Sam 16: 1 *F* your horn with oil, and go;
1 Ki 18:33 *F* four waterpots with water, and
Job 7: 4 For I have had my *f* of
8:21 He will yet *f* your mouth with
15: 2 And *f* himself with the east
20:23 When he is about to *f* his
23: 4 And *f* my mouth with arguments.
41: 7 Can you *f* his skin with
Ps 17:14 And whose belly You *f* with
81:10 and I will *f* it.
83:16 *F* their faces with shame, That
110: 6 He shall *f* the places with
129: 7 which the reaper does not *f*
Prov 1:13 We shall *f* our houses with
7:18 let us take our *f* of love until
8:21 That I may *f* their treasuries.
Isa 8: 8 out of his wings Will *f* the
14:21 And *f* the face of the world
27: 6 And *f* the face of the world
56:12 And we will *f* ourselves with
Jer 13:13 I will *f* all the inhabitants of
23:24 Do I not *f* heaven and earth?"
33: 5 but only to *f* their places
51:14 Surely I will *f* you with men, as
Ezek 3: 3 and *f* your stomach with this
7:19 Nor *f* their stomachs, Because
9: 7 and *f* the courts with the
10: 2 *f* your hands with coals of fire
24: 4 *F* it with choice cuts;
30:11 And *f* the land with the slain.
32: 4 And with you I will *f* the
32: 5 And *f* the valleys with your
35: 8 And I will *f* its mountains with
Zeph 1: 9 Who *f* their masters' houses
Hag 2: 7 and I will *f* this temple with
Mt 15:33 bread in the wilderness to *f*
23:32 *F* up, then, the measure of your
Jn 2: 7 *F* the waterpots with water."
Rom 15:13 Now may the God of hope *f* you
Eph 4:10 that He might *f* all things.)
Col 1:24 and *f* up in my flesh what is
1 Th 2:16 so as always to *f* up the

FILLED (159/157) FILL

Gen 6:11 and the earth was *f* with
6:13 for the earth is *f* with
21:19 And she went and *f* the skin
24:16 *f* her pitcher, and came up.
26:15 and they had *f* them with earth.
Ex 1: 7 and the land was *f* with them.
2:16 and they *f* the troughs to water
16:12 in the morning you shall be *f*
28: 3 whom I have *f* with the spirit
31: 3 And I have *f* him with the Spirit
35:31 and He has *f* him with the Spirit
35:35 He has *f* them with skill to do
40:34 and the glory of the LORD *f*
40:35 and the glory of the LORD *f*
Num 14:21 all the earth shall be *f* with
Deut 11:15 that you may eat and be *f*.
26:12 eat within your gates and be *f*,
31:20 and they have eaten and *f*
Josh 9:13 these wineskins which we *f*
1 Ki 7:14 he was *f* with wisdom and
8:10 that the cloud *f* the house of
8:11 for the glory of the LORD *f*
8:20 and I have *f* the position of my
18:35 and he also *f* the trench with
20:27 while the Syrians *f* the
2 Ki 3:17 yet that valley shall be *f* with
3:20 and the land was *f* with water.
3:25 every good piece of land and *f*
21:16 till he had *f* Jerusalem from
23:14 and *f* their places with the
24: 4 for he had *f* Jerusalem with
2 Chr 5:13 was *f* with a cloud,
5:14 for the glory of the LORD *f*
6:10 and I have *f* the position of my
7: 1 and the glory of the LORD *f*
7: 2 the glory of the LORD had *f*
16:14 laid him in the bed which was *f*
Ezra 9:11 abominations which have *f* it
Neh 9:25 So they ate and were *f* and
Esth 3: 5 Haman was *f* with wrath.
5: 9 he was *f* with indignation
Job 3:15 Who *f* their houses with
22:18 Yet He *f* their houses with good
36:17 But you are *f* with the judgment
Ps 71: 8 Let my mouth be *f* with Your
72:19 And let the whole earth be *f*
78:29 So they ate and were well *f*,
80: 9 And it *f* the land.
104:28 they are *f* with good.
123: 3 For we are exceedingly *f* with
123: 4 Our soul is exceedingly *f* With
126: 2 Then our mouth was *f* with
Prov 1:31 And be *f* to the full with
3:10 So your barns will be *f* with
5:10 Lest aliens be *f* with your
12:21 But the wicked shall be *f* with
14:14 backslider in heart will be *f*
18:20 of his lips he shall be *f*.
20:17 afterward his mouth will be *f*
24: 4 By knowledge the rooms are *f*
25:16 Lest you be *f* with it and
30:22 A fool when he is *f* with food,
Eccl 1: 8 Nor the ear *f* with hearing.
Isa 2: 6 Because they are *f* with
6: 1 and the train of His robe *f*
6: 4 and the house was *f* with smoke.
21: 3 Therefore my loins are *f* with
23: 2 those who cross the sea have *f*.
33: 5 He has *f* Zion with justice and
34: 6 The sword of the LORD is *f*
Jer 13:12 Every bottle shall be *f* with
13:12 that every bottle will be *f*
15:17 For You have *f* me with
16:18 they have *f* My inheritance with
19: 4 and have *f* this place with the
41: 9 Ishmael the son of Nethaniah *f*
46:12 And your cry has *f* the land;
51: 5 Though their land was *f* with
51:34 He has *f* his stomach with my
Lam 3:15 He has *f* me with bitterness,
Ezek 7:23 For the land is *f* with crimes
8:17 For they have *f* the land with
10: 3 and the cloud *f* the inner
10: 4 and the house was *f* with the
11: 6 and you have *f* its streets with
23:33 You will be *f* with drunkenness
26: 2 turned over to me; I shall be *f*;
27:25 You were *f* and very glorious
28:16 of your trading You became *f*
32:15 is destitute of all that once *f*
36:38 so shall the ruined cities be *f*
39:20 You shall be *f* at My table
43: 5 the glory of the LORD *f* the
44: 4 the glory of the LORD *f* the
Dan 2:35 became a great mountain and *f*
Hos 13: 6 they had pasture, they were *f*;
13: 6 They were *f* and their heart
Nah 2:12 *F* his caves with prey, And
Hab 2:14 For the earth will be *f* With
2:16 You are *f* with shame instead of
Hag 1: 6 but you are not *f* with drink;
Zech 9:15 They shall be *f* with blood
Mt 5: 6 For they shall be *f*.
14:20 So they all ate and were *f*,
15:37 So they all ate and were *f*,
22:10 And the wedding hall was *f*
27:48 *f* it with sour wine and put
Mk 6:42 So they all ate and were *f*.
7:27 Let the children be *f* first, for
8: 8 So they ate and were *f*,
15:36 Then someone ran and *f* a sponge
Lk 1:15 He will also be *f* with the Holy
1:41 and Elizabeth was *f* with the
1:53 He has *f* the hungry with good
1:67 Now his father Zacharias was *f*
2:40 *f* with wisdom; and the grace of
3: 5 Every valley shall be *f*
4: 1 being *f* with the Holy Spirit,
4:28 were *f* with wrath,
5: 7 And they came and *f* both the
5:26 they glorified God and were *f*
6:11 But they were *f* with rage, and
6:21 hunger now, For you shall be *f*.
9:17 So they all ate and were *f*,
14:23 come in, that my house may be *f*.
15:16 And he would gladly have *f* his
Jn 2: 7 And they *f* them up to the
6:12 So when they were *f*,
6:13 and *f* twelve baskets with the
6:26 ate of the loaves and were *f*.
12: 3 And the house was *f* with the
16: 6 sorrow has *f* your heart.
19:29 and they *f* a sponge with sour
Acts 2: 2 and it *f* the whole house where
2: 4 And they were all *f* with the
3:10 and they were *f* with wonder and
4: 8 *f* with the Holy Spirit, said to
4:31 and they were all *f* with the
5: 3 why has Satan *f* your heart to
5:17 and they were *f* with
5:28 you have *f* Jerusalem with your
9:17 may receive your sight and be *f*
13: 9 *f* with the Holy Spirit, looked
13:45 they were *f* with envy;
13:52 And the disciples were *f* with
19:29 So the whole city was *f* with
Rom 1:29 being *f* with all
15:14 *f* with all knowledge, able also
2 Cor 7: 4 I am *f* with comfort. I am
Eph 3:19 that you may be *f* with all the
5:18 but be *f* with the Spirit,
Phil 1:11 being *f* with the fruits of
Col 1: 9 and to ask that you may be *f*
2 Tim 1: 4 that I may be *f* with joy,
Jas 2:16 in peace, be warmed and *f*,
Rev 8: 5 *f* it with fire from the altar,
15: 8 The temple was *f* with smoke from
19:21 And all the birds were *f* with
21: 9 who had the seven bowls *f* with

FILLET, FILLETED (KJV) See BANDS, (MEASURING) LINE

FILLING (3/3) FILL

Mk 4:37 boat, so that it was already *f*.
Lk 8:23 and they were *f* with water,
Acts 14:17 *f* our hearts with food and

FILLS (4/4) FILL

Job 9:18 But *f* me with bitterness.
Ps 107: 9 And *f* the hungry soul with
147:14 And *f* you with the finest
Eph 1:23 the fullness of Him who *f* all

FILLY (1/1)

Song 1: 9 To my *f* among Pharaoh's

FILTH (6/6) FILTHY

Ezra 6:21 themselves from the *f* of the
Isa 4: 4 the Lord has washed away the *f*
28: 8 tables are full of vomit and *f*;
Nah 3: 6 I will cast abominable *f* upon
1 Cor 4:13 We have been made as the *f* of
1 Pe 3:21 (not the removal of the *f* of

F

FILTHINESS (11/10) FILTHY

Prov 30:12 Yet is not washed from its *f*.
Ezek 16:36 Because your *f* was poured out
22:15 and remove your *f* completely
24:11 That its *f* may be melted in
24:13 In your *f* is lewdness.
24:13 will not be cleansed of your *f*
36:25 cleanse you from all your *f*
2 Cor 7: 1 us cleanse ourselves from all *f*
Eph 5: 4 neither *f*, nor foolish talking,
Jas 1:21 Therefore lay aside all *f* and
Rev 17: 4 full of abominations and the *f*

FILTHY (9/8) FILTH, FILTHINESS

Job 15:16 man, who is abominable and *f*,
Isa 64: 6 our righteousnesses are like *f*
Zech 3: 3 was clothed with *f* garments,
3: 4 Take away the *f* garments from
Col 3: 8 *f* language out of your mouth.
Jas 2: 2 come in a poor man in *f* clothes,
2 Pe 2: 7 oppressed by the *f* conduct
Rev 22:11 be unjust still; he who is *f*,
22:11 let him be *f* still; he who is

FINAL (1/1) FINALLY

Jer 12: 4 He will not see our *f* end."

FINALLY (12/12) FINAL

Deut 2:16 when all the men of war had *f*
2 Ki 24:20 that He *f* cast them out from
Jer 52: 3 till He *f* cast them out from
Acts 27:20 would be saved was *f* given up.
2 Cor 13:11 *F*, brethren, farewell.
Eph 6:10 *F*, my brethren, be strong
Phil 3: 1 *F*, my brethren, rejoice
4: 8 *F*, brethren, whatever things
1 Th 4: 1 *F* then, brethren, we urge and
2 Th 3: 1 *F*, brethren, pray for us,
2 Tim 4: 8 *F*, there is laid up for me
1 Pe 3: 8 *F*, all of you be of one

FIND (171/164) FINDING, FINDS, FOUND

Gen 18:26 If I *f* in Sodom fifty righteous
18:28 If I *f* there forty-five, I will
18:30 I will not do it if I *f* thirty
19:11 they became weary trying to *f*
31:32 With whomever you *f* your gods,
31:33 but he did not *f* them. Then he
31:34 about the tent but did not *f*
31:35 And he searched but did not *f*
32: 5 that I may *f* favor in your
32:19 shall speak to Esau when you *f*
33: 8 These are to *f* favor in the
33:15 Let me *f* favor in the sight of
34:11 Let me *f* favor in your eyes, and
38:20 but he did not *f* her.
38:22 I cannot *f* her. Also, the men of
41:38 Can we *f* such a one as this,
47:25 let us *f* favor in the sight of
Ex 5:11 straw where you can *f* it;
16:25 today you will not *f* it in the
33:13 I may know You and that I may *f*
Num 32:23 and be sure your sin will *f* you
Deut 4:29 and you will *f* Him if you seek
28:65 those nations you shall *f* no
Josh 2:22 but did not *f* them.
Judg 9:33 may then do to them as you *f*
16: 5 and *f* out where his great
17: 8 to stay wherever he could *f* a
17: 9 and I am on my way to *f* a
Ruth 1: 9 LORD grant that you may *f*
2: 2 him in whose sight I may *f*
2:13 Let me *f* favor in your sight, my
1 Sam 1:18 Let your maidservant *f* favor in
9: 4 but they did not *f* them.
9: 4 but they did not *f* them.
9:13 you will surely *f* him before he
9:13 for about this time you will *f*
10: 2 you will *f* two men by Rachel's
20:21 *f* the arrows.' If I expressly
20:36 *f* the arrows which I shoot."
23:17 of Saul my father shall not *f*
23:22 Please go and *f* out for sure,
25: 8 Therefore let my young men *f*
28: 7 *F* me a woman who is a medium,
2 Sam 15:25 If I *f* favor in the eyes of the
16: 4 that I may *f* favor in your
17:20 had searched and could not *f*
20: 6 lest he *f* for himself fortified
1 Ki 18: 5 perhaps we may *f* grass to keep
18:10 or nation that they could not *f*
18:12 and he cannot *f* you, he will
2 Ki 2:17 for three days but did not *f*
6:27 where can I *f* help for you?
2 Chr 20:16 and you will *f* them at the end
32: 4 the kings of Assyria come and *f*
Ezra 4:15 And you will *f* in the book of
7:16 silver and gold that you may *f*
Job 3:22 And are glad when they can *f*
5:24 shall visit your dwelling and *f*
11: 7 Can you *f* out the limits of
17:10 For I shall not *f* one wise
23: 3 that I knew where I might *f*
32:20 that I may *f* relief; I must
34:11 And makes man to *f* a reward
37:23 we cannot *f* Him; He is
Ps 10:15 out his wickedness until You *f*
21: 8 Your hand will *f* all Your
21: 8 Your right hand will *f* those
132: 5 Until I *f* a place for the
Prov 1:13 We shall *f* all kinds of
1:28 but they will not *f* me.
2: 5 And *f* the knowledge of God.
3: 4 And so *f* favor and high esteem
4:22 they are life to those who *f*
8: 9 And right to those who *f*
8:12 And *f* out knowledge and
8:17 who seek me diligently will *f*
14: 6 seeks wisdom and does not *f*
16:20 heeds the word wisely will *f*
19: 8 who keeps understanding will *f*
20: 6 But who can *f* a faithful man?
28:23 He who rebukes a man will *f*
31:10 Who can *f* a virtuous wife?
Eccl 3:11 except that no one can *f* out
7:14 So that man can *f* out nothing
7:24 Who can *f* it out?
7:26 And I *f* more bitter than death
7:27 one thing to the other to *f*
7:28 soul still seeks but I cannot *f*:
8:17 that a man cannot *f* out the
8:17 yet he will not *f* it;
8:17 he will not be able to *f* it.
11: 1 For you will *f* it after many
12:10 The Preacher sought to *f*
Song 3: 1 but I did not *f* him.
3: 2 but I did not *f* him.
5: 6 but I could not *f* him;
5: 8 If you *f* my beloved, That you
8: 1 If I should *f* you
Isa 34:14 And *f* for herself a place of
41:12 You shall seek them and not *f*
58: 3 in the day of your fast you *f*
Jer 2:24 In her month they will *f* her.
5: 1 her open places If you can *f*
6:16 Then you will *f* rest for your
10:18 That they may *f* it so."
29:13 And you will seek Me and *f* Me,
45: 3 and I *f* no rest." '
Lam 1: 6 have become like deer That *f*
2: 9 And her prophets *f* no vision
Ezek 3: 1 "Son of man, eat what you *f*;
Dan 6: 4 and satraps sought to *f* some
6: 4 but they could *f* no charge or
6: 5 We shall not *f* any charge
6: 5 this Daniel unless we *f* it
Hos 2: 6 So that she cannot *f* her
2: 7 but not *f* them. Then she will
5: 6 But they will not *f* Him;
12: 8 all my labors They shall *f* in
Am 8:12 But shall not *f* it.
Mt 7: 7 to you; seek, and you will *f*;
7:14 and there are few who *f* it.
10:39 his life for My sake will *f* it.
11:29 and you will *f* rest for your
16:25 his life for My sake will *f* it.
17:27 you will *f* a piece of money;
18:13 And if he should *f* it,
21: 2 and immediately you will *f* a
22: 9 highways, and as many as you *f*,
24:46 will *f* so doing.
Mk 11: 2 you have entered it you will *f*
11:13 to see if perhaps He would *f*
13:36 he *f* you sleeping.
Lk 2:12 You will *f* a Babe wrapped in
2:45 So when they did not *f* Him, they
5:19 And when they could not *f* how
6: 7 that they might *f* an accusation
11: 9 to you; seek, and you will *f*;
12:37 will *f* watching. Assuredly, I
12:38 and *f* them so, blessed are
12:43 servant whom his master will *f*
13: 7 fruit on this fig tree and *f*
18: 8 will He really *f* faith on the
19:30 where as you enter you will *f*
23: 4 I *f* no fault in this Man."
24: 3 they went in and did not *f* the
24:23 When they did not *f* His body,
Jn 7:34 You will seek Me and not *f* Me,
7:35 to go that we shall not *f* Him?
7:36 You will seek Me and not *f* Me,
10: 9 and will go in and out and *f*
18:38 I *f* no fault in Him at all.
19: 4 that you may know that I *f* no
19: 6 for I *f* no fault in Him."
21: 6 and you will *f* some." So they
Acts 5:22 the officers came and did not *f*
7:46 before God and asked to *f* a
17: 6 But when they did not *f* them,
17:11 the Scriptures daily to *f*
17:27 they might grope for Him and *f*
23: 9 We *f* no evil in this man; but if
Rom 1:10 now at last I may *f* a way in
7:18 perform what is good I do not *f*.
7:21 I *f* then a law, that evil is
9:19 'Why does He still *f* fault?
2 Cor 2:13 because I did not *f* Titus my
9: 4 Macedonians come with me and *f*
12:20 I shall not *f* you such as I
2 Tim 1:18 Lord grant to him that he may *f*
Heb 4:16 that we may obtain mercy and *f*
Rev 9: 6 will seek death and will not *f*
18:14 and you shall *f* them no more at

FINDING (12/12) FIND

Gen 4:15 lest anyone *f* him should kill
Judg 5:30 Are they not *f* and dividing the
Job 9:10 He does great things past *f*
Isa 58:13 Nor *f* your own pleasure, Nor
Lk 11:24 and *f* none, he says, 'I will
Acts 4:21 *f* no way of punishing them,
19: 1 And *f* some disciples
21: 2 And *f* a ship sailing over to
21: 4 And *f* disciples, we stayed there
Rom 11:33 judgments and His ways past *f*
Eph 5:10 *f* out what is acceptable to the
Heb 8: 8 Because *f* fault with them, He

FINDS (30/28) FIND

Gen 4:14 will happen that anyone who *f*
Num 35:27 and the avenger of blood *f* him
Deut 22:23 and a man *f* her in the city and
22:25 But if a man *f* a betrothed
22:28 If a man *f* a young woman who
24: 1 and it happens that she *f* no
1 Sam 24:19 For if a man *f* his enemy, will
Job 33:10 Yet He *f* occasions against me,
Ps 36: 2 When he *f* out his iniquity
119:162 at Your word As one who *f*
Prov 3:13 Happy is the man who *f*
8:35 For whoever *f* me finds life,
8:35 For whoever finds me *f* life,
11:27 He who earnestly seeks good *f*
17:20 who has a deceitful heart *f* no
18:22 He who *f* a wife finds a good
18:22 He who finds a wife *f* a good
21:10 His neighbor *f* no favor in his
21:21 righteousness and mercy *F*
Eccl 9:10 Whatever your hand *f* to do, do
Lam 1: 3 She *f* no rest; All her
Hos 14: 3 For in You the fatherless *f*
Mt 7: 8 receives, and he who seeks *f*,
10:39 He who *f* his life will lose it,
12:43 seeking rest, and *f* none.
12:44 he *f* it empty, swept, and put
Lk 11:10 receives, and he who seeks *f*,
11:25 he *f* it swept and put in
15: 4 one which is lost until he *f*
15: 8 search carefully until she *f*

FINE (140/133) FINEST

Gen 18: 6 three measures of *f* meal;
41: 2 *f* looking and fat; and they fed
41: 4 ate up the seven *f* looking
41:18 *f* looking and fat; and they fed
41:42 him in garments of *f* linen
Ex 9: 9 And it will become *f* dust in all
16:14 as *f* as frost on the ground.
25: 4 *f* linen, and goats' hair;
26: 1 with ten curtains of *f* woven
26:31 and *f* woven linen. It shall be
26:36 and *f* woven linen, made by a
27: 9 court made of *f* woven linen,
27:16 and *f* woven linen, made by a
27:18 made of *f* woven linen, and
28: 5 scarlet thread, and *f* linen,
28: 6 and *f* woven linen, artistically
28: 8 thread, and *f* woven linen.
28:15 and *f* woven linen, you shall
28:39 weave the tunic of *f* linen
28:39 make the turban of *f* linen,
30:36 shall beat some of it very *f*,
35: 6 *f* linen, and goats' hair;
35:23 *f* linen, and goats' hair, red
35:25 and scarlet, and *f* linen.
35:35 and *f* linen, and of the
36: 8 curtains woven of *f* linen,
36:35 and *f* woven linen; it was
36:37 and *f* woven linen, made by a
38: 9 of the court were of *f* woven
38:16 around were of *f* woven linen.
38:18 and of *f* woven linen. The
38:23 thread, and of *f* linen.
39: 2 and of *f* woven linen.
39: 3 thread and the *f* linen,
39: 5 and of *f* woven linen, as the
39: 8 and of *f* woven linen.
39:24 and of *f* woven linen.
39:27 artistically woven of *f* linen,
39:28 a turban of *f* linen, exquisite
39:28 exquisite hats of *f* linen,
39:28 short trousers of *f* woven
39:29 and a sash of *f* woven linen with
Lev 2: 1 offering shall be of *f* flour.
2: 2 from it his handful of *f* flour
2: 4 unleavened cakes of *f* flour
2: 5 it shall be of *f* flour,
2: 7 it shall be made of *f* flour
5:11 of an ephah of *f* flour
6:15 his handful of the *f* flour
6:20 of an ephah of *f* flour
14:10 of an ephah of *f* flour
14:21 of an ephah of *f* flour
16:12 full of sweet incense beaten *f*,
23:13 of an ephah of *f* flour
23:17 They shall be of *f* flour;
24: 5 And you shall take *f* flour and
Num 6:15 cakes of *f* flour mixed with
7:13 both of them full of *f* flour
7:19 both of them full of *f* flour
7:25 both of them full of *f* flour
7:31 both of them full of *f* flour
7:37 both of them full of *f* flour
7:43 both of them full of *f* flour
7:49 both of them full of *f* flour
7:55 both of them full of *f* flour
7:61 both of them full of *f* flour
7:67 both of them full of *f* flour

7:73 both of them full of *f* flour
7:79 both of them full of *f* flour
8: 8 its grain offering of *f* flour
15: 4 of an ephah of *f* flour
15: 6 of an ephah of *f* flour
15: 9 of an ephah of *f* flour
28: 5 of an ephah of *f* flour
28: 9 of an ephah of *f* flour
28:12 of an ephah of *f* flour as a
28:12 of an ephah of *f* flour
28:13 of an ephah of *f* flour,
28:20 offering shall be of *f* flour
28:28 their grain offering of *f* flour
29: 3 offering shall be *f* flour
29: 9 offering shall be of *f* flour
29:14 grain offering shall be of *f*
Deut 9:21 until it was as *f* as dust;
22:19 and they shall *f* him one hundred
2 Sam 22:43 Then I beat them as *f* as the
1 Ki 4:22 was thirty kors of *f* flour,
2 Ki 7: 1 this time a seah of *f* flour
7:16 So a seah of *f* flour was sold
7:18 and a seah of *f* flour for a
1 Chr 9:29 and over the *f* flour and the
15:27 clothed with a robe of *f* linen,
23:29 the showbread and the *f* flour
2 Chr 2:14 *f* linen and crimson, and to
3: 5 which he overlaid with *f* gold,
3: 8 six hundred talents of *f* gold.
3:14 and *f* linen, and wove cherubim
Ezra 8:27 and two vessels of *f* polished
Esth 1: 6 fastened with cords of *f* linen
8:15 and a garment of *f* linen
Job 28:17 exchanged for jewelry of *f* gold.
31:24 Or said to *f* gold, 'You are
Ps 18:42 Then I beat them as *f* as the
19:10 than much *f* gold; Sweeter also
119:127 than gold, yes, than *f* gold!
Prov 3:14 And her gain than *f* gold.
8:19 than *f* gold, And my revenue
25:12 and an ornament of *f* gold
31:22 Her clothing is *f* linen and
Song 5:15 Set on bases of *f* gold.
Isa 3:23 The *f* linen, the turbans, and
13:12 mortal more rare than *f* gold,
19: 9 those who work in *f* flax
19: 9 And those who weave *f* fabric
23:18 and for *f* clothing.
29: 5 Shall be like *f* dust,
Lam 4: 1 dim! How changed the *f* gold!
4: 2 Valuable as *f* gold, How they
Ezek 16:10 I clothed you with *f* linen and
16:13 clothing was of *f* linen,
16:13 You ate pastry of *f* flour,
16:19 the pastry of *f* flour, oil, and
27: 7 *F* embroidered linen from Egypt
27:16 *f* linen, corals, and rubies.
31: 3 With *f* branches that shaded
46:14 oil to moisten the *f* flour.
Dan 2:32 image's head was of *f* gold,
Mk 15:46 Then he bought *f* linen, took Him
Lk 16:19 clothed in purple and *f* linen
Jas 2: 2 in *f* apparel, and there should
2: 3 the one wearing the *f* clothes
1 Pe 3: 3 or putting on *f* apparel—
Rev 1:15 His feet were like *f* brass, as
2:18 and His feet like *f* brass:
18:12 *f* linen and purple, silk and
18:13 *f* flour and wheat, cattle and
18:16 that was clothed in *f* linen,
19: 8 to be arrayed in *f* linen,
19: 8 for the *f* linen is the
19:14 clothed in *f* linen, white and

FINER (KJV) See JEWELRY

FINERY (1/1)

Isa 3:18 the Lord will take away the *f*:

FINEST (4/4) FINE

1 Sam 8:16 your *f* young men, and your
Ps 81:16 have fed them also with the *f*
147:14 And fills you with the *f*
Song 5:11 His head is like the *f* gold;

FINGER (26/24) FINGERS

Ex 8:19 'This is the *f* of God."
29:12 horns of the altar with your *f*,
31:18 written with the *f* of God.
Lev 4: 6 The priest shall dip his *f* in
4:17 the priest shall dip his *f* in
4:25 of the sin offering with his *f*,
4:30 some of its blood with his *f*,
4:34 of the sin offering with his *f*,
8:15 the altar all around with his *f*,
9: 9 And he dipped his *f* in the
14:16 priest shall dip his right *f*
14:16 some of the oil with his *f*
14:27 shall sprinkle with his right *f*
16:14 and sprinkle it with his *f* on
16:14 some of the blood with his *f*
16:19 of the blood on it with his *f*
Num 19: 4 some of its blood with his *f*,
Deut 9:10 of stone written with the *f* of
1 Ki 12:10 My little *f* shall be thicker
2 Chr 10:10 My little *f* shall be thicker
Isa 58: 9 midst, The pointing of the *f*,
Lk 11:20 if I cast out demons with the *f*
16:24 he may dip the tip of his *f* in
Jn 8: 6 wrote on the ground with His *f*,
20:25 and put my *f* into the print of
20:27 Reach your *f* here, and look at

FINGERS (16/16) FINGER

2 Sam 21:20 who had six *f* on each hand and
1 Chr 20: 6 with twenty-four *f* and toes,
Ps 8: 3 heavens, the work of Your *f*,
144: 1 And my *f* for battle—
Prov 6:13 his feet, He points with his *f*;
7: 3 Bind them on your *f*;
Song 5: 5 My *f* with liquid myrrh, On
Isa 2: 8 That which their own *f* have
17: 8 He will not respect what his *f*
59: 3 And your *f* with iniquity;
Jer 52:21 and its thickness was four *f*;
Dan 5: 5 In the same hour the *f* of a
5:24 Then the *f* of the hand were sent
Mt 23: 4 move them with one of their *f*.
Mk 7:33 and put His *f* in his ears, and
Lk 11:46 the burdens with one of your *f*.

FINING POT (KJV) See REFINING POT

FINISH (15/15) FINISHED, FINISHER, FINISHING

Gen 6:16 and you shall *f* it to a cubit
1 Chr 27:24 a census, but he did not *f*,
Ezra 5: 3 you to build this temple and *f*
5: 9 to build this temple and to *f*
Ps 90: 9 We *f* our years like a sigh.
Dan 9:24 To *f* the transgression, To
Zech 4: 9 His hands shall also *f* it.
Lk 14:28 whether he has enough to *f*
14:29 and is not able to *f*,
14:30 to build and was not able to *f*.
Jn 4:34 and to *f* His work.
5:36 the Father has given Me to *f*—
Acts 20:24 so that I may *f* my race with
Rom 9:28 For He will *f* the work
Rev 11: 7 When they *f* their testimony,

FINISHED (90/89) FINISH

Gen 2: 1 all the host of them, were *f*.
17:22 Then He *f* talking with him, and
18:33 His way as soon as He had *f*
24:15 before he had *f* speaking, that
24:19 And when she had *f* giving him a
24:19 until they have *f* drinking."
24:22 when the camels had *f* drinking,
24:45 But before I had *f* speaking in
27:30 as soon as Isaac had *f* blessing
49:33 And when Jacob had *f* commanding
Ex 34:33 And when Moses had *f* speaking
39:32 of the tent of meeting was *f*.
40:33 So Moses *f* the work.
Num 4:15 when Aaron and his sons have *f*
7: 1 when Moses had *f* setting up the
16:31 as he *f* speaking all these
Deut 20: 9 when the officers have *f*
26:12 When you have *f* laying aside
31:24 law in a book, when they were *f*,
32:45 Moses *f* speaking all these words
Josh 4:10 Jordan until everything was *f*
5: 8 when they had *f* circumcising
10:20 slaughter, till they had *f*,
Judg 3:18 And when he had *f* presenting the
15:17 when he had *f* speaking, that he
Ruth 2:21 my young men until they have *f*
3: 3 known to the man until he has *f*
1 Sam 1: 9 Hannah arose after they had *f*
10:13 And when he had *f* prophesying,
13:10 as soon as he had *f* presenting
18: 1 Now when he had *f* speaking to
24:16 when David had *f* speaking these
2 Sam 6:18 And when David had *f* offering
11:19 When you have *f* telling the
13:36 as soon as he had *f* speaking,
15:24 up until all the people had *f*
1 Ki 1:41 with him heard it as they *f*
3: 1 City of David until he had *f*
6: 7 was built with stone *f* at the
6: 9 So he built the temple and *f* it,
6:14 Solomon built the temple and *f*
6:22 until he had *f* all the temple;
6:38 the house was *f* in all its
7: 1 so he *f* all his house.
7:22 the work of the pillars was *f*.
7:40 So Huram *f* doing all the work
7:51 the house of the LORD was *f*;
8:54 when Solomon had *f* praying all
9: 1 when Solomon had *f* building the
9:25 So he *f* the temple.
1 Chr 16: 2 And when David had *f* offering
28:20 until you have *f* all the work
2 Chr 4:11 So Huram *f* doing the work that
5: 1 the house of the LORD was *f*;
7: 1 When Solomon had *f* praying, fire
7:11 Thus Solomon *f* the house of the
8:16 of the LORD until it was *f*.
24:14 When they had *f*, they brought
29:17 day of the first month they *f*.
29:28 until the burnt offering was *f*.
29:29 And when they had *f* offering,
31: 1 Now when all this was *f*,
31: 7 and they *f* in the seventh
Ezra 5:16 construction, and it is not *f*.
6:14 And they built and *f* it,
6:15 Now the temple was *f* on the
10:17 day of the first month they *f*
Neh 6:15 So the wall was *f* on the
Job 16:22 For when a few years are *f*,
Ps 9: 6 destructions are *f* forever!
Jer 51:63 when you have *f* reading this
Ezek 5: 2 the days of the siege are *f*;
42:15 Now when he had *f* measuring the
43:23 When you have *f* cleansing it,
Dan 5:26 your kingdom, and *f* it;
12: 7 all these things shall be *f*.
Am 7: 2 when they had *f* eating the
Mt 11: 1 when Jesus *f* commanding His
13:53 when Jesus had *f* these
19: 1 when Jesus had *f* these sayings,
26: 1 when Jesus had *f* all these
Lk 2:43 When they had *f* the days, as
Jn 17: 4 I have *f* the work which You
19:30 It is *f*!" And bowing His head,
Acts 21: 7 And when we had *f* our voyage
2 Tim 4: 7 I have *f* the race, I have kept
Heb 4: 3 although the works were *f* from
Rev 10: 7 the mystery of God would be *f*,
20: 3 till the thousand years were *f*.
20: 5 until the thousand years were *f*.

FINISHER (1/1) FINISH

Heb 12: 2 the author and *f* of our faith,

FINISHES (1/1)

Job 14: 6 Till like a hired man he *f* his

FINISHING (2/2) FINISH

Ezra 4:12 and are *f* its walls and
Acts 13:25 And as John was *f* his course, he

FINS (5/5)

Lev 11: 9 whatever in the water has *f* and
11:10 the rivers that do not have *f*
11:12 in the water does not have *f*
Deut 14: 9 you may eat all that have *f* and
14:10 And whatever does not have *f* and

FIR (5/5)

2 Sam 6: 5 all kinds of instruments of *f*
Ps 104:17 stork has her home in the *f*
Song 1:17 cedar, And our rafters of *f*.
Ezek 27: 5 made all your planks of *f*
31: 8 The *f* trees were not like its

FIRE (543/503) FIERY, FIREBRAND

Gen 19:24 LORD rained brimstone and *f*
22: 6 and he took the *f* in his hand,
22: 7 the *f* and the wood, but where
Ex 3: 2 to him in a flame of *f* from
3: 2 the bush was burning with *f*,
9:23 and *f* darted to the ground.
9:24 and *f* mingled with the hail, so
12: 8 on that night; roasted in *f*,
12: 9 with water, but roasted in *f*—
12:10 morning you shall burn with *f*.
13:21 and by night in a pillar of *f*
13:22 by day or the pillar of *f* by
14:24 through the pillar of *f* and
19:18 LORD descended upon it in *f*.
22: 6 If *f* breaks out and catches in
22: 6 he who kindled the *f* shall
24:17 LORD was like a consuming *f*
29:14 you shall burn with *f* outside
29:18 an offering made by *f* to the
29:25 It is an offering made by *f* to
29:34 shall burn the remainder with *f*.
29:41 an offering made by *f* to the
30:20 to burn an offering made by *f*
32:20 had made, burned it in the *f*,
32:24 to me, and I cast it into the *f*,
35: 3 You shall kindle no *f* throughout
40:38 and *f* was over it by night, in
Lev 1: 7 of Aaron the priest shall put *f*
1: 7 lay the wood in order on the *f*.
1: 8 on the wood that is on the *f*
1: 9 an offering made by *f*,
1:12 on the wood that is on the *f*
1:13 an offering made by *f*,
1:17 on the wood that is on the *f*.
1:17 an offering made by *f*,
2: 2 altar, an offering made by *f*,
2: 3 to the LORD made by *f*.
2: 9 It is an offering made by *f*,
2:10 to the LORD made by *f*.
2:11 offering to the LORD made by *f*.
2:14 heads of grain roasted on the *f*,
2:16 as an offering made by *f* to the
3: 3 offering an offering made by *f*
3: 5 on the wood that is on the *f*,
3: 5 fire, as an offering made by *f*,
3: 9 as an offering made by *f* to the
3:11 an offering made by *f* to the
3:14 as an offering made by *f* to the
3:16 an offering made by *f* for a
4:12 out, and burn it on wood with *f*;
4:35 to the offerings made by *f* to
5:12 to the offerings made by *f* to
6: 9 and the *f* of the altar shall be
6:10 the burnt offering which the *f*
6:12 And the *f* on the altar shall be
6:13 A *f* shall always be burning on
6:17 of My offerings made by *f*;

6:18 the offerings made by *f* to the
6:30 It shall be burned in the *f*.
7: 5 as an offering made by *f* to
7:17 third day must be burned with *f*.
7:19 It shall be burned with *f*.
7:25 offer an offering made by *f* to
7:30 bring the offerings made by *f*
7:35 from the offerings made by *f* to
8:17 he burned with *f* outside the
8:21 an offering made by *f* to the
8:28 was an offering made by *f* to
8:32 the bread you shall burn with *f*.
9:11 and the hide he burned with *f*
9:24 and *f* came out from before the
10: 1 each took his censer and put *f*
10: 1 and offered profane *f* before
10: 2 So *f* went out from the LORD and
10:12 of the offerings made by *f* to
10:13 of the sacrifices made by *f* to
10:15 the offerings of fat made by *f*,
13:24 a burn on its skin by *f*,
13:52 shall be burned in the *f*.
13:55 and you shall burn it in the *f*;
13:57 you shall burn with *f* that in
16: 1 when they offered profane *f*
16:12 full of burning coals of *f*
16:13 shall put the incense on the *f*
16:27 And they shall burn in the *f*
18:21 pass through the *f* to Molech,
19: 6 it shall be burned in the *f*.
20:14 They shall be burned with *f*,
21: 6 of the LORD made by *f*,
21: 9 She shall be burned with *f*.
21:21 offer the offerings made by *f*
22:22 nor make an offering by *f* of
22:27 as an offering made by *f* to
23: 8 offer an offering made by *f* to
23:13 an offering made by *f* to the
23:18 an offering made by *f* for a
23:25 offer an offering made by *f* to
23:27 offer an offering made by *f* to
23:36 offer an offering made by *f* to
23:36 offer an offering made by *f* to
23:37 to offer an offering made by *f*
24: 7 an offering made by *f* to the
24: 9 of the LORD made by *f*,
Num 3: 4 when they offered profane *f*
6:18 head and put it on the *f*
9:15 like the appearance of *f*.
9:16 and the appearance of *f* by
11: 1 So the *f* of the LORD burned
11: 2 the *f* was quenched.
11: 3 because the *f* of the LORD had
14:14 by day and in a pillar of *f* by
15: 3 and you make an offering by *f* to
15:10 wine as an offering made by *f*,
15:13 an offering made by *f*,
15:14 present an offering made by *f*,
15:25 an offering made by *f* to the
16: 7 put *f* in them and put incense in
16:18 put *f* in it, laid incense on
16:35 And a *f* came out from the LORD
16:37 and scatter the *f* some distance
16:46 Take a censer and put *f* in it
18: 9 things reserved from the *f*:
18:17 fat as an offering made by *f*
19: 6 them into the midst of the *f*
21:28 'For *f* went out from Heshbon,
26:10 when the *f* devoured two hundred
26:61 when they offered profane *f*
28: 2 for My offerings made by *f* as
28: 3 is the offering made by *f*
28: 6 an offering made by *f* to the
28: 8 it as an offering made by *f*,
28:13 an offering made by *f* to the
28:19 present an offering made by *f*
28:24 food of the offering made by *f*
29: 6 an offering made by *f* to the
29:13 an offering made by *f* as a
29:36 an offering made by *f* as a
31:10 They also burned with *f* all the
31:23 "everything that can endure *f*,
31:23 you shall put through the *f*,
31:23 But all that cannot endure *f*
Deut 1:33 in the *f* by night and in the
4:11 and the mountain burned with *f*
4:12 you out of the midst of the *f*.
4:15 Horeb out of the midst of the *f*,
4:24 your God is a consuming *f*,
4:33 out of the midst of the *f*,
4:36 earth He showed you His great *f*,
4:36 words out of the midst of the *f*.
5: 4 from the midst of the *f*.
5: 5 were afraid because of the *f*,
5:22 from the midst of the *f*,
5:23 the mountain was burning with *f*,
5:24 voice from the midst of the *f*.
5:25 For this great *f* will consume
5:26 from the midst of the *f*,
7: 5 burn their carved images with *f*.
7:25 images of their gods with *f*;
9: 3 before you as a consuming *f*.
9:10 from the midst of the *f* in the
9:15 and the mountain burned with *f*;
9:21 and burned it with *f* and
10: 4 from the midst of the *f* in the
12: 3 burn their wooden images with *f*;
12:31 sons and daughters in the *f* to
13:16 and completely burn with *f* the
18: 1 of the LORD made by *f*,
18:10 his daughter pass through the *f*,
18:16 nor let me see this great *f*
32:22 For a *f* is kindled by my anger,
32:22 And set on *f* the foundations
Josh 6:24 and all that was in it with *f*.
7:15 thing shall be burned with *f*,
7:25 and they burned them with *f*
8: 8 you shall set the city on *f*.
8:19 hurried to set the city on *f*.
11: 6 and burn their chariots with *f*.
11: 9 burned their chariots with *f*.
11:11 Then he burned Hazor with *f*.
13:14 LORD God of Israel made by *f*
Judg 1: 8 the sword and set the city on *f*.
6:21 and *f* rose out of the rock and
9:15 let *f* come out of the bramble
9:20 let *f* come from Abimelech and
9:20 and let *f* come from the men of
9:49 and set the stronghold on *f*
9:52 of the tower to burn it with *f*.
12: 1 your house down on you with *f*!
14:15 and your father's house with *f*.
15: 5 he had set the torches on *f*,
15: 6 her and her father with *f*.
15:14 like flax that is burned with *f*,
16: 9 yarn breaks when it touches *f*.
18:27 and burned the city with *f*.
20:48 They also set *f* to all the
1 Sam 2:28 children of Israel made by *f*?
30: 1 Ziklag and burned it with *f*,
30: 3 and there it was, burned with *f*;
30:14 and we burned Ziklag with *f*.
2 Sam 14:30 there; go and set it on *f*.
14:30 servants set the field on *f*.
14:31 your servants set my field on *f*?
22: 9 And devouring *f* from His
22:13 before Him Coals of *f* were
23: 7 shall be utterly burned with *f*
1 Ki 9:16 Gezer and burned it with *f*,
16:18 house down upon himself with *f*,
18:23 but put no *f* under it; and I
18:23 but put no *f* under it.
18:24 and the God who answers by *f*,
18:25 but put no *f* under it."
18:38 Then the *f* of the LORD fell and
19:12 and after the earthquake a *f*,
19:12 the LORD was not in the *f*;
19:12 and after the *f* a still small
2 Ki 1:10 then let *f* come down from
1:10 And *f* came down from heaven
1:12 let *f* come down from heaven and
1:12 And the *f* of God came down
1:14 *f* has come down from heaven and
2:11 that suddenly a chariot of *f*
2:11 fire appeared with horses of *f*,
6:17 of horses and chariots of *f*
8:12 strongholds you will set on *f*,
16: 3 made his son pass through the *f*,
17:17 daughters to pass through the *f*,
17:31 burned their children in *f* to
19:18 have cast their gods into the *f*;
21: 6 made his son pass through the *f*,
23:10 daughter pass through the *f* to
23:11 the chariots of the sun with *f*.
25: 9 of the great, he burned with *f*.
1 Chr 14:12 and they were burned with *f*.
21:26 answered him from heaven by *f*
2 Chr 7: 1 *f* came down from heaven and
7: 3 of Israel saw how the *f* came
28: 3 burned his children in the *f*,
33: 6 his sons to pass through the *f*
35:13 the Passover offerings with *f*
36:19 burned all its palaces with *f*,
Neh 1: 3 its gates are burned with *f*.
2: 3 and its gates are burned with *f*?
2:13 gates which were burned with *f*.
2:17 and its gates are burned with *f*.
9:12 by night with a pillar of *f*,
9:19 Nor the pillar of *f* by night,
Job 1:16 The *f* of God fell from heaven
15:34 And *f* will consume the tents
18: 5 And the flame of his *f* does
20:26 An unfanned *f* will consume
22:20 And the *f* consumes their
28: 5 it is turned up as by *f*;
31:12 For that would be a *f* that
41:19 Sparks of *f* shoot out.
Ps 11: 6 *F* and brimstone and a burning
18: 8 And devouring *f* from His
18:12 with hailstones and coals of *f*.
18:13 Hailstones and coals of *f*.
21: 9 And the *f* shall devour them.
29: 7 LORD divides the flames of *f*.
39: 3 the *f* burned. Then I spoke
46: 9 He burns the chariot in the *f*.
50: 3 A *f* shall devour before Him,
57: 4 sons of men Who are set on *f*,
66:12 We went through *f* and through
68: 2 As wax melts before the *f*,
74: 7 They have set *f* to Your
78:14 all the night with a light of *f*.
78:21 So a *f* was kindled against
78:63 The *f* consumed their young men,
79: 5 Will Your jealousy burn like *f*?
80:16 It is burned with *f*,
83:14 As the *f* burns the woods,
83:14 flame sets the mountains on *f*,
89:46 Will Your wrath burn like *f*?
97: 3 A *f* goes before Him, And burns
104: 4 His ministers a flame of *f*.
105:32 And flaming *f* in their land.
105:39 And *f* to give light in the
106:18 A *f* was kindled in their
118:12 They were quenched like a *f* of
140:10 Let them be cast into the *f*,
148: 8 *F* and hail, snow and clouds
Prov 6:27 Can a man take *f* to his bosom,
16:27 on his lips like a burning *f*.
25:22 so you will heap coals of *f*
26:20 the *f* goes out; And where
26:21 to burning coals, and wood to *f*,
30:16 And the *f* never says,
Song 8: 6 Its flames are flames of *f*,
Isa 1: 7 Your cities are burned with *f*;
4: 5 and the shining of a flaming *f*
5:24 as the *f* devours the stubble,
9: 5 used for burning and fuel of *f*.
9:18 For wickedness burns as the *f*;
9:19 shall be as fuel for the *f*;
10:16 Like the burning of a *f*.
10:17 Light of Israel will be for a *f*,
26:11 the *f* of Your enemies shall
27:11 women come and set them on *f*.
29: 6 And the flame of devouring *f*.
30:14 fragments A shard to take *f*
30:27 His tongue like a devouring *f*.
30:30 And the flame of a devouring *f*,
30:33 Its pyre is *f* with much wood;
31: 9 Whose *f* is in Zion And whose
33:11 Your breath, as *f*,
33:12 they shall be burned in the *f*.
33:14 dwell with the devouring *f*?
37:19 have cast their gods into the *f*;
42:25 It has set him on *f* all
43: 2 When you walk through the *f*,
44:16 He burns half of it in the *f*;
44:16 I am warm, I have seen the *f*.
44:19 have burned half of it in the *f*,
47:14 The *f* shall burn them;
47:14 Nor a *f* to sit before!
50:11 Look, all you who kindle a *f*,
50:11 Walk in the light of your *f*
54:16 Who blows the coals in the *f*,
64: 2 As *f* burns brushwood, As fire
64: 2 As *f* causes water to boil—To
64:11 You, Is burned up with *f*;
65: 5 A *f* that burns all the day.
66:15 the LORD will come with *f* And
66:15 His rebuke with flames of *f*.
66:16 For by *f* and by His sword
66:24 And their *f* is not quenched.
Jer 4: 4 Lest My fury come forth like *f*,
5:14 make My words in your mouth *f*,
6:29 The lead is consumed by the *f*;
7:18 wood, the fathers kindle the *f*,
7:31 and their daughters in the *f*,
11:16 great tumult He has kindled *f*
15:14 For a *f* is kindled in My
17: 4 For you have kindled a *f* in My
17:27 then I will kindle a *f* in its
19: 5 to burn their sons with *f* for
20: 9 in my heart like a burning *f*
21:10 and he shall burn it with *f*.
21:12 Lest My fury go forth like *f*
21:14 I will kindle a *f* in its forest,
22: 7 And cast them into the *f*.
23:29 "Is not My word like a *f*?
29:22 of Babylon roasted in the *f*";
32:29 this city shall come and set *f*
32:35 to pass through the *f* to
34: 2 and he shall burn it with *f*.
34:22 and take it and burn it with *f*;
36:22 with a *f* burning on the
36:23 knife and cast it into the *f*
36:23 scroll was consumed in the *f*
36:32 of Judah had burned in the *f*.
37: 8 and take it and burn it with *f*.
37:10 tent, and burn the city with *f*.
38:17 city shall not be burned with *f*,
38:18 they shall burn it with *f*,
38:23 this city to be burned with *f*.
39: 8 the houses of the people with *f*,
43:12 I will kindle a *f* in the houses
43:13 Egyptians he shall burn with *f*.
48:45 But a *f* shall come out of
49: 2 villages shall be burned with *f*.
49:27 I will kindle a *f* in the wall of
50:32 I will kindle a *f* in his
51:32 reeds they have burned with *f*,
51:58 gates shall be burned with *f*;
51:58 the nations, because of the *f*;
52:13 of the great, he burned with *f*.
Lam 1:13 From above He has sent *f* into my
2: 3 against Jacob like a flaming *f*
2: 4 has poured out His fury like *f*.
4:11 He kindled a *f* in Zion,
Ezek 1: 4 a great cloud with raging *f*
1: 4 out of the midst of the *f*.
1:13 was like burning coals of *f*,
1:13 The *f* was bright, and out of
1:13 and out of the *f* went
1:27 amber with the appearance of *f*
1:27 the appearance of *f* with
5: 2 You shall burn with *f* one-third
5: 4 them into the midst of the *f*,
5: 4 fire, and burn them in the *f*.
5: 4 From there a *f* will go out into
8: 2 like the appearance of *f*—
8: 2 of His waist and downward, *f*;
10: 2 fill your hands with coals of *f*
10: 6 Take *f* from among the wheels,
10: 7 among the cherubim to the *f*
15: 4 it is thrown into the *f* for
15: 4 the *f* devours both ends of it,
15: 5 for any work when the *f* has
15: 6 which I have given to the *f* for

15: 7 They will go out from one *f*,
15: 7 but another *f* shall devour
16:21 them to pass through the *f*?
16:41 shall burn your houses with *f*,
19:12 The *f* consumed them.
19:14 *F* has come out from a rod of
20:26 to pass through the *f*,
20:31 your sons pass through the *f*,
20:47 I will kindle a *f* in you, and
21:31 blow against you with the *f* of
21:32 You shall be fuel for the *f*;
22:20 to blow *f* on it, to melt it;
22:21 you and blow on you with the *f*
22:31 I have consumed them with the *f*
23:25 remnant shall be devoured by *f*.
23:37 passing them through the *f*,
23:47 and burn their houses with *f*.
24:10 on the wood, Kindle the *f*;
24:12 Let her scum be in the *f*!
28:18 Therefore I brought *f* from
30: 8 When I have set a *f* in Egypt
30:14 Set *f* to Zoan, And execute
30:16 And set a *f* in Egypt;
38:19 in My jealousy and in the *f*
38:22 rain, great hailstones, *f*,
39: 6 And I will send *f* on Magog and
39: 9 will go out and set on *f* and
Dan 3:22 the flame of the *f* killed those
3:24 bound into the midst of the *f*?
3:25 walking in the midst of the *f*;
3:26 came from the midst of the *f*.
3:27 men on whose bodies the *f* had
3:27 and the smell of *f* was not on
7: 9 flame, Its wheels a burning *f*;
10: 6 his eyes like torches of *f*,
Hos 7: 4 He ceases stirring the *f*
7: 6 it burns like a flaming *f*.
8:14 But I will send *f* upon his
Joel 1:19 For *f* has devoured the open
1:20 And *f* has devoured the open
2: 3 A *f* devours before them,
2: 5 Like the noise of a flaming *f*
2:30 Blood and *f* and pillars of
Am 1: 4 But I will send a *f* into the
1: 7 But I will send a *f* upon the
1:10 But I will send a *f* upon the
1:12 But I will send a *f* upon Teman,
1:14 But I will kindle a *f* in the
2: 2 But I will send a *f* upon Moab,
2: 5 But I will send a *f* upon Judah,
5: 6 Lest He break out like *f* in
7: 4 GOD called for conflict by *f*,
Ob 18 house of Jacob shall be a *f*,
Mic 1: 4 split Like wax before the *f*,
1: 7 shall be burned with the *f*;
Nah 1: 6 His fury is poured out like *f*,
3:13 *F* shall devour the bars of
3:15 There the *f* will devour you,
Hab 2:13 the peoples labor to feed the *f*,
Zeph 1:18 shall be devoured By the *f* of
3: 8 shall be devoured With the *f*
Zech 2: 5 will be a wall of *f* all around
3: 2 not a brand plucked from the *f*?
9: 4 And she will be devoured by *f*.
11: 1 That *f* may devour your cedars.
13: 9 the one-third through the *f*,
Mal 1:10 So that you would not kindle *f*
3: 2 For He is like a refiner's *f*
Mt 3:10 cut down and thrown into the *f*.
3:11 you with the Holy Spirit and *f*.
3:12 the chaff with unquenchable *f*.
5:22 shall be in danger of hell *f*.
7:19 cut down and thrown into the *f*.
13:40 gathered and burned in the *f*,
13:42 cast them into the furnace of *f*.
13:50 cast them into the furnace of *f*.
17:15 for he often falls into the *f*
18: 8 be cast into the everlasting *f*.
18: 9 eyes, to be cast into hell *f*.
25:41 into the everlasting *f* prepared
Mk 9:22 has thrown him both into the *f*
9:43 into the *f* that shall never be
9:44 And the *f* is not
9:45 into the *f* that shall never be
9:46 And the *f* is not
9:47 eyes, to be cast into hell *f*—
9:48 And the *f* is not
9:49 will be seasoned with *f*,
14:54 and warmed himself at the *f*.
Lk 3: 9 cut down and thrown into the *f*.
3:16 you with the Holy Spirit and *f*.
3:17 will burn with unquenchable *f*.
9:54 do You want us to command *f* to
12:49 I came to send *f* on the earth,
17:29 went out of Sodom it rained *f*
22:55 Now when they had kindled a *f* in
22:56 seeing him as he sat by the *f*,
Jn 15: 6 them and throw them into the *f*,
18:18 and officers who had made a *f*
21: 9 they saw a *f* of coals there,
Acts 2: 3 them divided tongues, as of *f*,
2:19 Blood and *f* and vapor of
7:30 to him in a flame of *f* in a
28: 2 for they kindled a *f* and made
28: 3 sticks and laid them on the *f*,
28: 5 off the creature into the *f*
Rom 12:20 you will heap coals of *f*
1 Cor 3:13 it will be revealed by *f*;
3:13 and the *f* will test each one's
3:15 be saved, yet so as through *f*.
2 Th 1: 8 in flaming *f* taking vengeance on
Heb 1: 7 ministers a flame of *f*.
11:34 quenched the violence of *f*,
12:18 touched and that burned with *f*,
12:29 For our God is a consuming *f*.
Jas 3: 5 how great a forest a little *f*
3: 6 And the tongue is a *f*,
3: 6 and sets on *f* the course of
3: 6 and it is set on *f* by hell.
5: 3 and will eat your flesh like *f*.
1 Pe 1: 7 though it is tested by *f*,
2 Pe 3: 7 are reserved for *f* until the
3:12 will be dissolved, being on *f*,
Jude 7 the vengeance of eternal *f*.
23 pulling them out of the *f*,
Rev 1:14 and His eyes like a flame of *f*;
2:18 who has eyes like a flame of *f*,
3:18 from Me gold refined in the *f*,
4: 5 Seven lamps of *f* were burning
8: 5 filled it with *f* from the
8: 7 And hail and *f* followed,
8: 8 a great mountain burning with *f*
9:17 and out of their mouths came *f*,
9:18 by the *f* and the smoke and the
10: 1 and his feet like pillars of *f*.
11: 5 *f* proceeds from their mouth and
13:13 so that he even makes *f* come
14:10 He shall be tormented with *f*
14:18 the altar, who had power over *f*,
15: 2 a sea of glass mingled with *f*,
16: 8 to him to scorch men with *f*.
17:16 her flesh and burn her with *f*.
18: 8 will be utterly burned with *f*,
19:12 eyes were like a flame of *f*,
19:20 cast alive into the lake of *f*
20: 9 And *f* came down from God out of
20:10 was cast into the lake of *f* and
20:14 were cast into the lake of *f*.
20:15 was cast into the lake of *f*.
21: 8 in the lake which burns with *f*

FIREBRAND (1/1) FIRE, FIREBRANDS
Am 4:11 And you were like a *f* plucked

FIREBRANDS (2/2) FIREBRAND
Prov 26:18 Like a madman who throws *f*,
Isa 7: 4 these two stubs of smoking *f*,

FIREPAN (1/1)
Zech 12: 6 governors of Judah like a *f* in

FIREPANS (5/5)
Ex 27: 3 basins and its forks and its *f*;
38: 3 basins, the forks, and the *f*;
Num 4:14 which they minister there—the *f*,
2 Ki 25:15 The *f* and the basins, the things
Jer 52:19 The basins, the *f*,

FIRES (2/2)
Ezek 39: 9 and they will make *f* with them
39:10 because they will make *f* with

FIRKINS (KJV) See GALLONS

FIRM (13/13) FIRMLY
Num 24:21 '*F* is your dwelling place,
Deut 25: 8 But if he stands *f* and says,
Josh 3:17 covenant of the LORD stood *f*
4: 3 where the priests' feet stood *f*.
Job 41:23 They are *f* on him and cannot
Ps 73: 4 But their strength is *f*.
89:28 And My covenant shall stand *f*
Prov 4:13 Take *f* hold of instruction, do
Isa 35: 3 And make *f* the feeble knees.
Dan 2: 5 Chaldeans, "My decision is *f*:
2: 8 you see that my decision is *f*:
6: 7 a royal statute and to make a *f*
Heb 3: 6 the rejoicing of the hope *f* to

FIRMAMENT (17/15)
Gen 1: 6 Let there be a *f* in the midst of
1: 7 Thus God made the *f*,
1: 7 waters which were under the *f*
1: 7 waters which were above the *f*;
1: 8 And God called the *f* Heaven.
1:14 Let there be lights in the *f* of
1:15 them be for lights in the *f* of
1:17 God set them in the *f* of the
1:20 earth across the face of the *f*
Ps 19: 1 And the *f* shows His handiwork.
150: 1 Praise Him in His mighty *f*!
Ezek 1:22 The likeness of the *f* above the
1:23 And under the *f* their wings
1:25 A voice came from above the *f*
1:26 And above the *f* over their
10: 1 and there in the *f* that was
Dan 12: 3 Like the brightness of the *f*,

FIRMLY (5/5) FIRM
1 Ki 2:12 his kingdom was *f* established.
1 Chr 16:30 world also is *f* established,
Ezra 6: 3 foundations of it be *f* laid,
Ps 75: 3 I set up its pillars *f*.
96:10 world also is *f* established,

FIRST (443/415) FIRSTBORN, FIRSTFRUIT, FIRSTLING
Gen 1: 5 and the morning were the *f* day.
2:11 The name of the *f* is Pishon;
8: 5 on the *f* day of the month, the
8:13 pass in the six hundred and *f*
8:13 in the *f* month, the first day
8:13 the *f* day of the month, that
13: 4 which he had made there at *f*.
25:25 And the *f* came out red. He was
26: 1 besides the *f* famine that was
32:17 And he commanded the *f* one,
38:28 saying, "This one came out *f*.
41:20 and ugly cows ate up the *f*
43:18 was returned in our sacks the *f*
43:20 we indeed came down the *f* time
Ex 4: 8 nor heed the message of the *f*
12: 2 it shall be the *f* month of
12: 5 a male of the *f* year. You may
12:15 On the *f* day you shall remove
12:15 eats leavened bread from the *f*
12:16 On the *f* day there shall be a
12:18 In the *f* month, on the
22:29 not delay to offer the *f* of
23:19 The *f* of the firstfruits of your
25:35 shall be a knob under the *f*
28:17 The *f* row shall be a
28:17 this shall be the *f* row;
29:38 two lambs of the *f* year, day by
34: 1 two tablets of stone like the *f*
34: 1 the words that were on the *f*
34: 4 two tablets of stone like the *f*
34:26 The *f* of the firstfruits of your
37:21 was a knob under the *f* two
39:10 and an emerald was the *f* row;
40: 2 On the *f* day of the first month
40: 2 On the first day of the *f* month
40:17 And it came to pass in the *f*
40:17 on the *f* day of the month,
Lev 4:21 and burn it as he burned the *f*
5: 8 is for the sin offering *f*,
9: 3 both of the *f* year, without
9:15 like the *f* one.
12: 6 to the priest a lamb of the *f*
14:10 one ewe lamb of the *f* year
23: 5 the fourteenth day of the *f*
23: 7 On the *f* day you shall have a
23:12 a male lamb of the *f* year,
23:18 the bread seven lambs of the *f*
23:19 and two male lambs of the *f*
23:24 on the *f* day of the month, you
23:35 On the *f* day there shall be a
23:39 on the *f* day there shall be
23:40 take for yourselves on the *f*
Num 1: 1 on the *f* day of the second
1:18 congregation together on the *f*
2: 9 shall break camp *f*.
6:12 and bring a male lamb in its *f*
6:14 one male lamb in its *f* year
6:14 one ewe lamb in its *f* year
7:12 offered his offering on the *f*
7:15 and one male lamb in its *f*
7:17 and five male lambs in their *f*
7:21 and one male lamb in its *f*
7:23 and five male lambs in their *f*
7:27 and one male lamb in its *f*
7:29 and five male lambs in their *f*
7:33 and one male lamb in its *f*
7:35 and five male lambs in their *f*
7:39 and one male lamb in its *f*
7:41 and five male lambs in their *f*
7:45 and one male lamb in its *f*
7:47 and five male lambs in their *f*
7:51 and one male lamb in its *f*
7:53 and five male lambs in their *f*
7:57 and one male lamb in its *f*
7:59 and five male lambs in their *f*
7:63 and one male lamb in its *f*
7:65 and five male lambs in their *f*
7:69 and one male lamb in its *f*
7:71 and five male lambs in their *f*
7:75 and one male lamb in its *f*
7:77 and five male lambs in their *f*
7:81 and one male lamb in its *f*
7:83 and five male lambs in their *f*
7:87 the male lambs in their *f* year
7:88 and the lambs in their *f* year
9: 1 in the *f* month of the second
9: 5 on the fourteenth day of the *f*
10:13 So they started out for the *f*
10:14 the children of Judah set out *f*
13:20 time was the season of the *f*
15:20 shall offer up a cake of the *f*
15:21 Of the *f* of your ground meal you
15:27 bring a female goat in its *f*
18:13 Whatever *f* ripe fruit is in
18:15 Everything that *f* opens the womb
20: 1 the Wilderness of Zin in the *f*
24:20 Amalek was *f* among the nations,
28: 3 two male lambs in their *f* year
28: 9 day two lambs in their *f* year,
28:11 and seven lambs in their *f*
28:16 the fourteenth day of the *f*
28:18 On the *f* day you shall have a
28:19 and seven lambs in their *f*
28:27 and seven lambs in their *f*
29: 1 on the *f* day of the month, you
29: 2 and seven lambs in their *f*
29: 8 and seven lambs in their *f*
29:13 and fourteen lambs in their *f*

29:17 fourteen lambs in their *f* year
29:20 fourteen lambs in their *f* year
29:23 and fourteen lambs in their *f*
29:26 and fourteen lambs in their *f*
29:29 and fourteen lambs in their *f*
29:32 and fourteen lambs in their *f*
29:36 seven lambs in their *f* year
33: 3 departed from Rameses in the *f*
33: 3 on the fifteenth day of the *f*
33:38 on the *f* day of the fifth
Deut 1: 3 on the *f* day of the month,
9:18 before the LORD, as at the *f*,
10: 1 two tablets of stone like the *f*,
10: 2 the words that were on the *f*
10: 3 two tablets of stone like the *f*,
10: 4 the tablets according to the *f*
10:10 As at the *f* time, I stayed in
13: 9 your hand shall be *f* against
16: 4 meat which you sacrifice the *f*
17: 7 of the witnesses shall be the *f*
18: 4 and the *f* of the fleece of your
26: 2 you shall take some of the *f*
33:21 He provided the *f* part for
Josh 4:19 on the tenth day of the *f*
8: 5 come out against us as at the *f*,
8: 6 fleeing before us as at the *f*.
21:10 Levi; for the lot was theirs *f*.
Judg 1: 1 Who shall be *f* to go up for us
20:18 Which of us shall go up *f* to
20:18 The LORD said, "Judah *f*!"
20:22 themselves in array on the *f*
20:32 defeated before us, as at *f*.
20:39 as in the *f* battle."
1 Sam 2:16 should really burn the fat *f*;
14:14 That *f* slaughter which Jonathan
14:35 This was the *f* altar that he
17:30 people answered him as the *f*
20: 2 either great or small without *f*
2 Sam 3:13 not see my face unless you *f*
17: 9 of them are overthrown at the *f*,
18:27 I think the running of the *f* is
19:20 the *f* to come today of all the
19:43 were we not the *f* to advise
21: 9 in the *f* days, in the
23:19 he did not attain to the *f*
23:23 but he did not attain to the *f*
1 Ki 3:22 And the *f* woman said, "No!
3:27 Give the *f* woman the living
17:13 make me a small cake from it *f*,
18:25 yourselves and prepare it *f*,
20: 9 sent for to your servant the *f*
20:17 of the provinces went out *f*.
2 Ki 1:14 heaven and burned up the *f* two
1 Chr 9: 2 And the *f* inhabitants who dwelt
11: 6 attacks the Jebusites *f* shall
11: 6 the son of Zeruiah went up *f*,
11:21 he did not attain to the *f*
11:25 but he did not attain to the *f*
12: 9 Ezer the *f*, Obadiah the second,
12:15 who crossed the Jordan in the *f*
15:13 you did not do it the *f*
16: 7 On that day David *f* delivered
23: 8 the *f* Jehiel, then Zetham and
23:11 Jahath was the *f* and Zizah the
23:16 of Gershon, Shebuel was the *f*.
23:17 of Eliezer, Rehabiah was the *f*.
23:18 of Izhar, Shelomith was the *f*.
23:19 of Hebron, Jeriah was the *f*,
23:20 Michah was the *f* and Jesshiah
24: 7 Now the *f* lot fell to
24:21 the *f* was Isshiah.
24:23 Hebron, Jeriah was the *f*,
25: 9 Now the *f* lot for Asaph came
26:10 Shimri the *f* (for though he
26:10 his father made him the *f*),
27: 2 Over the *f* division for the
27: 2 the first division for the *f*
27: 3 captains of the army for the *f*
29:29 *f* and last, indeed they are
2 Chr 9:29 *f* and last, are they not
12:15 *f* and last, are they not
16:11 *f* and last, are indeed written
20:34 *f* and last, indeed they are
25:26 from *f* to last, indeed are
26:22 from *f* to last, the prophet
28:26 from *f* to last, indeed they
29: 3 In the *f* year of his reign, in
29: 3 in the *f* month, he opened the
29:17 they began to sanctify on the *f*
29:17 on the first day of the *f*
29:17 on the sixteenth day of the *f*
35: 1 on the fourteenth day of the *f*
35:27 and his deeds from *f* to last,
36:22 Now in the *f* year of Cyrus king
Ezra 1: 1 Now in the *f* year of Cyrus king
3: 6 From the *f* day of the seventh
3:12 old men who had seen the *f*
5:13 in the *f* year of Cyrus king of
6: 3 In the *f* year of King Cyrus,
6:19 on the fourteenth day of the *f*
7: 9 On the *f* day of the first month
7: 9 On the first day of the *f* month
7: 9 and on the *f* day of the fifth
8:31 on the twelfth day of the *f*
10:16 and they sat down on the *f* day
10:17 By the *f* day of the first month
10:17 By the first day of the *f* month
Neh 7: 5 those who had come up in the *f*
8: 2 with understanding on the *f*
8:18 from the *f* day until the last
Esth 3: 7 In the *f* month, which is the
3:12 on the thirteenth day of the *f*

Job 15: 7 Are you the *f* man who was
40:19 He is the *f* of the ways of
42:14 And he called the name of the *f*
Ps 78:51 The *f* of their strength in
105:36 The *f* of all their strength.
Prov 18:17 The *f* one to plead his cause
Isa 1:26 restore your judges as at the *f*,
9: 1 As when at *f* He lightly
28: 4 Like the *f* fruit before the
41: 4 'I, the LORD, am the *f*;
41:27 The *f* time I said to Zion,
43:27 Your *f* father sinned, And your
44: 6 I am the *F* and I am the Last;
48:12 I am He, I am the *F*,
52: 4 My people went down at *f* Into
60: 9 ships of Tarshish will come *f*,
Jer 4:31 of her who brings forth her *f*
7:12 where I set My name at the *f*,
16:18 And *f* I will repay double for
24: 2 like the figs that are *f*
25: 1 king of Judah (which was the *f*
33: 7 those places as at the *f*.
33:11 the land to return as at the *f*,
36:28 former words that were in the *f*
50:17 *F* the king of Assyria devoured
52:31 in the *f* year of his reign,
Ezek 10:14 the *f* face was the face of a
26: 1 on the *f* day of the month,
29:17 in the *f* month, on the first
29:17 on the *f* day of the month,
30:20 in the *f* month, on the seventh
31: 1 on the *f* day of the month,
32: 1 on the *f* day of the month,
40:21 the same measurements as the *f*
44:30 shall give to the priest the *f*
45:18 In the *f* month, on the first
45:18 on the *f* day of the month, you
45:21 In the *f* month, on the
46:13 the LORD of a lamb of the *f*
Dan 1:21 Daniel continued until the *f*
7: 1 In the *f* year of Belshazzar king
7: 4 The *f* was like a lion, and had
7: 8 before whom three of the *f*
7:24 shall be different from the *f*
8: 1 one that appeared to me the *f*
8:21 is between its eyes is the *f*
9: 1 In the *f* year of Darius the son
9: 2 in the *f* year of his reign I,
10: 4 the twenty-fourth day of the *f*
10:12 for from the *f* day that you set
11: 1 Also in the *f* year of Darius the
Hos 2: 7 I will go and return to my *f*
9:10 on the fig tree in its *f*
Joel 2:23 And the latter rain in the *f*
Am 6: 7 shall now go captive as the *f*
Jon 3: 4 to enter the city on the *f*
Hag 1: 1 on the *f* day of the month, the
Zech 6: 2 With the *f* chariot were red
12: 7 will save the tents of Judah *f*,
14:10 Gate to the place of the *F*
Mt 5:24 *F* be reconciled to your
6:33 But seek *f* the kingdom of God
7: 5 Hypocrite! *F* remove the plank
8:21 let me *f* go and bury my
10: 2 twelve apostles are these: *f*,
12:29 unless he *f* binds the strong
12:45 of that man is worse than the *f*.
13:30 *F* gather together the tares and
17:10 say that Elijah must come *f*?
17:11 Elijah is coming *f* and will
17:27 take the fish that comes up *f*.
19:30 But many who are *f* will be
19:30 will be last, and the last *f*.
20: 8 with the last to the *f*.
20:10 But when the *f* came, they
20:16 "So the last will be *f*,
20:16 and the *f* last. For many are
20:27 And whoever desires to be *f*
21:28 and he came to the *f* and said,
21:31 They said to Him, "The *f*."
21:36 other servants, more than the *f*,
22:25 The *f* died after he had
22:38 This is the *f* and great
23:26 *f* cleanse the inside of the cup
26:17 Now on the *f* day of the Feast
27:64 will be worse than the *f*.
28: 1 as the *f* day of the week began
Mk 3:27 unless he *f* binds the strong
4:28 *f* the blade, then the head,
7:27 "Let the children be filled *f*,
9:11 say that Elijah must come *f*?
9:12 Elijah is coming *f* and restores
9:35 "If anyone desires to be *f*,
10:31 But many who are *f* will be
10:31 will be last, and the last *f*.
10:44 whoever of you desires to be *f*
12:20 The *f* took a wife; and dying,
12:28 Which is the *f* commandment of
12:29 The *f* of all the commandments
12:30 This is the *f* commandment.
13:10 And the gospel must *f* be
14:12 Now on the *f* day of Unleavened
16: 2 on the *f* day of the week, they
16: 9 when He rose early on the *f*
16: 9 He appeared *f* to Mary
Lk 1: 3 of all things from the very *f*,
2: 2 This census *f* took place while
6: 1 the second Sabbath after the *f*
6:42 Hypocrite! *F* remove the plank
9:59 let me *f* go and bury my
9:61 but let me *f* go and bid them
10: 5 *f* say, 'Peace to this house.'

11:26 of that man is worse than the *f*.
11:38 he marveled that He had not *f*
12: 1 to say to His disciples *f* of
13:30 there are last who will be *f*,
13:30 and there are *f* who will be
14:18 The *f* said to him, 'I have
14:28 does not sit down *f* and count
14:31 does not sit down *f* and
16: 5 to him, and said to the *f*,
17:25 But *f* He must suffer many things
19:16 "Then came the *f*,
20:29 And the *f* took a wife, and died
21: 9 things must come to pass *f*,
24: 1 Now on the *f* day of the week,
Jn 1:41 He *f* found his own brother
5: 4 then whoever stepped in *f*,
8: 7 let him throw a stone at her *f*.
10:40 where John was baptizing at *f*,
12:16 understand these things at *f*;
18:13 they led Him away to Annas *f*,
19:32 and broke the legs of the *f*
19:39 who at *f* came to Jesus by
20: 1 Now on the *f* day of the week
20: 4 Peter and came to the tomb *f*.
20: 8 who came to the tomb *f*,
20:19 being the *f* day of the week,
Acts 3:26 'To you *f*, God, having raised
7:12 he sent out our fathers *f*.
11:26 And the disciples were *f* called
12:10 When they were past the *f* and
13:24 after John had *f* preached,
13:46 God should be spoken to you *f*;
15:14 has declared how God at the *f*
20: 7 Now on the *f* day of the week,
20:18 from the *f* day that I came to
26: 5 "They knew me from the *f*,
26:20 but declared *f* to those in
26:23 that He would be the *f* to rise
27:43 swim should jump overboard *f*
Rom 1: 8 *F*, I thank my God through
1:16 for the Jew *f* and also for the
2: 9 of the Jew *f* and also of the
2:10 to the Jew *f* and also to the
10:19 *F* Moses says: "I will
11:35 Or who has *f* given to Him
13:11 is nearer than when we *f*
15:24 if *f* I may enjoy your company
1 Cor 11:18 For *f* of all, when you come
12:28 *f* apostles, second prophets,
14:30 let the *f* keep silent.
15: 3 For I delivered to you *f* of all
15:45 The *f* man Adam became a
15:46 However, the spiritual is not *f*,
15:47 The *f* man was of the earth,
16: 2 On the *f* day of the week let
2 Cor 8: 5 but they *f* gave themselves to
8:12 For if there is *f* a willing
Gal 4:13 the gospel to you at the *f*.
Eph 1:12 that we who *f* trusted in Christ
4: 9 does it mean but that He also *f*
6: 2 which is the *f* commandment
Phil 1: 5 in the gospel from the *f* day
1 Th 4:16 the dead in Christ will rise *f*.
2 Th 2: 3 unless the falling away comes *f*,
1 Tim 1:16 that in me *f* Jesus Christ might
2: 1 Therefore I exhort *f* of all that
2:13 For Adam was formed *f*,
3:10 But let these also *f* be tested;
5: 4 let them *f* learn to show piety
5:12 they have cast off their *f*
2 Tim 1: 5 which dwelt *f* in your
2: 6 hard-working farmer must be *f*
4:16 At my *f* defense no one stood
Titus 3:10 a divisive man after the *f* and
Heb 2: 3 which at the *f* began to be
4: 6 and those to whom it was *f*
5:12 to teach you again the *f*
7: 2 *f* being translated "king of
7:27 *f* for His own sins and then for
8: 7 For if that *f* covenant had
8:13 He has made the *f* obsolete.
9: 1 even the *f* covenant had
9: 2 the *f* part, in which was the
9: 6 priests always went into the *f*
9: 8 yet made manifest while the *f*
9:15 the transgressions under the *f*
9:18 Therefore not even the *f*
10: 9 He takes away the *f* that He
Jas 3:17 wisdom that is from above is *f*
1 Pe 4:17 and if it begins with us *f*,
2 Pe 1:20 knowing this *f*, that no
3: 3 knowing this *f*: that scoffers
1 Jn 4:19 We love Him because He *f* loved
Rev 1:11 the *F* and the Last," and,
1:17 I am the *F* and the Last.
2: 4 that you have left your *f* love.
2: 5 repent and do the *f* works, or
2: 8 These things says the *F* and the
2:19 the last are more than the *f*.
4: 1 And the *f* voice which I heard
4: 7 The *f* living creature was like
8: 7 The *f* angel sounded: And hail
13:12 all the authority of the *f*
13:12 dwell in it to worship the *f*
16: 2 So the *f* went and poured out
20: 5 This is the *f* resurrection.
20: 6 is he who has part in the *f*
21: 1 for the *f* heaven and the first
21: 1 for the first heaven and the *f*
21:19 the *f* foundation was jasper,

22:13 the *F* and the Last."

FIRST-RIPE (1/1)

Mic 7: 1 no cluster to eat Of the *f*

FIRSTBORN (141/114) FIRST

Gen 4: 4 Abel also brought of the *f* of
10:15 Canaan begot Sidon his *f*,
19:31 Now the *f* said to the younger,
19:33 And the *f* went in and lay with
19:34 on the next day that the *f*
19:37 The *f* bore a son and called his
22:21 'Huz his *f*, Buz his brother,
25:13 The *f* of Ishmael, Nebajoth;
27:19 his father, "I am Esau your *f*;
27:32 said, "I am your son, your *f*,
29:26 give the younger before the *f*.
35:23 of Leah were Reuben, Jacob's *f*,
36:15 the *f* son of Esau, were Chief
38: 6 Judah took a wife for Er his *f*,
38: 7 But Er, Judah's *f*,
41:51 Joseph called the name of the *f*
43:33 the *f* according to his
46: 8 to Egypt: Reuben was Jacob's *f*.
48:14 for Manasseh was the *f*.
48:18 father, for this one is the *f*;
49: 3 "Reuben, you are my *f*,
Ex 4:22 "Israel is My son, My *f*.
4:23 I will kill your son, your *f*.
6:14 the *f* of Israel, were Hanoch,
11: 5 and all the *f* in the land of
11: 5 from the *f* of Pharaoh who sits
11: 5 even to the *f* of the female
11: 5 and all the *f* of the animals.
12:12 and will strike all the *f* in
12:29 the LORD struck all the *f* in
12:29 from the *f* of Pharaoh who sat
12:29 who sat on his throne to the *f*
12:29 and all the *f* of livestock.
13: 2 "Consecrate to Me all the *f*,
13:12 every *f* that comes from an
13:13 But every *f* of a donkey you
13:13 And all the *f* of man among your
13:15 the LORD killed all the *f* in
13:15 both the *f* of man and the
13:15 the firstborn of man and the *f*
13:15 but all the *f* of my sons I
22:29 The *f* of your sons you shall
34:19 and every male *f* among your
34:20 But the *f* of a donkey you shall
34:20 All the *f* of your sons you
Lev 27:26 But the *f* of the animals, which
27:26 which should be the LORD's *f*,
Num 3: 2 the sons of Aaron: Nadab, the *f*,
3:12 of Israel instead of every *f*
3:13 'because all the *f* are Mine.
3:13 day that I struck all the *f* in
3:13 sanctified to Myself all the *f*
3:40 Number all the *f* males of the
3:41 instead of all the *f* among the
3:41 Levites instead of all the *f*
3:42 So Moses numbered all the *f*
3:43 And all the *f* males, according
3:45 Levites instead of all the *f*
3:46 and seventy-three of the *f* of
3:50 From the *f* of the children of
8:16 the *f* of all the children of
8:17 For all the *f* among the children
8:17 day that I struck all the *f* in
8:18 Levites instead of all the *f*
18:15 nevertheless the *f* of man you
18:15 and the *f* of unclean animals
18:17 But the *f* of a cow, the
18:17 the *f* of a sheep, or the
18:17 or the *f* of a goat you shall
26: 5 Reuben was the *f* of Israel.
33: 4 were burying all their *f*,
Deut 12: 6 and the *f* of your herds and
12:17 of the *f* of your herd or your
14:23 of the *f* of your herds and your
15:19 All the *f* males that come from
15:19 shall do no work with the *f* of
15:19 nor shear the *f* of your flock.
21:15 and if the *f* son is of her who
21:16 that he must not bestow *f*
21:16 son of the unloved, the true *f*.
21:17 of the unloved wife as the *f*
21:17 the right of the *f* is his.
25: 6 And it shall be that the *f* son
33:17 His glory is like a *f* bull,
Josh 6:26 lay its foundation with his *f*,
17: 1 for he was the *f* of Joseph:
17: 1 namely for Machir the *f* of
Judg 8:20 And he said to Jether his *f*,
1 Sam 8: 2 The name of his *f* was Joel,
14:49 the name of the *f* Merab, and
17:13 to the battle were Eliab the *f*,
2 Sam 3: 2 His *f* was Amnon by Ahinoam the
1 Ki 16:34 foundation with Abiram his *f*,
1 Chr 1:13 Canaan begot Sidon, his *f*,
1:29 The *f* of Ishmael was Nebajoth;
2: 3 the *f* of Judah, was wicked in
2:13 Jesse begot Eliab his *f*,
2:25 the *f* of Hezron, were Ram,
2:25 of Hezron, were Ram, the *f*,
2:27 the *f* of Jerahmeel, were Maaz,
2:42 of Jerahmeel were Mesha, his *f*,
2:50 the *f* of Ephrathah, were
3: 1 The *f* was Amnon, by Ahinoam
3:15 of Josiah were Johanan the *f*,
4: 4 the *f* of Ephrathah the father
5: 1 Now the sons of Reuben the *f* of
5: 1 of Israel—he was indeed the *f*,
5: 3 the sons of Reuben the *f* of
6:28 of Samuel were Joel the *f*,
8: 1 Now Benjamin begot Bela his *f*,
8:30 And his *f* son was Abdon, then
8:39 his brother were Ulam his *f*,
9: 5 Asaiah the *f* and his sons.
9:31 the *f* of Shallum the Korahite,
9:36 His *f* son was Abdon, then Zur,
26: 2 were Zechariah the *f*,
26: 4 Obed-Edom were Shemaiah the *f*,
26:10 (for though he was not the *f*,
2 Chr 21: 3 Jehoram, because he was the *f*.
Neh 10:36 to bring the *f* of our sons and
10:36 and the *f* of our herds and our
Job 18:13 The *f* of death devours his
Ps 78:51 And destroyed all the *f* in
89:27 Also I will make him My *f*,
105:36 He also destroyed all the *f* in
135: 8 He destroyed the *f* of Egypt,
136:10 Him who struck Egypt in their *f*,
Isa 14:30 The *f* of the poor will feed,
Jer 31: 9 Israel, And Ephraim is My *f*.
Ezek 20:26 in that they caused all their *f*
Mic 6: 7 Shall I give my *f* for my
Zech 12:10 for Him as one grieves for a *f*.
Mt 1:25 she had brought forth her *f*
Lk 2: 7 And she brought forth her *f* Son,
Rom 8:29 that He might be the *f* among
Col 1:15 the *f* over all creation.
1:18 the *f* from the dead, that in
Heb 1: 6 But when He again brings the *f*
11:28 lest he who destroyed the *f*
12:23 assembly and church of the *f*
Rev 1: 5 the *f* from the dead, and the

FIRSTFRUIT (1/1) FIRST, FIRSTFRUITS

Rom 11:16 For if the *f* is holy, the lump

FIRSTFRUITS (33/31) FIRSTFRUIT

Ex 23:16 the *f* of your labors which you
23:19 The first of the *f* of your land
34:22 of the *f* of wheat harvest,
34:26 The first of the *f* of your land
Lev 2:12 'As for the offering of the *f*,
2:14 a grain offering of your *f* to
2:14 the grain offering of your *f*
23:10 shall bring a sheaf of the *f*
23:17 They are the *f* to the LORD.
23:20 them with the bread of the *f*
Num 18:12 their *f* which they offer to the
28:26 'Also on the day of the *f*,
Deut 18: 4 The *f* of your grain and your new
26:10 I have brought the *f* of the
2 Ki 4:42 the man of God bread of the *f*,
2 Chr 31: 5 brought in abundance the *f* of
Neh 10:35 ordinances to bring the *f* of
10:35 of our ground and the *f* of all
10:37 to bring the *f* of our dough,
12:44 for the offerings, the *f*,
13:31 the wood offering and the *f* at
Prov 3: 9 And with the *f* of all your
Jer 2: 3 The *f* of His increase.
Ezek 20:40 your offerings and the *f* of
44:30 The best of all *f* of any kind,
Hos 9:10 I saw your fathers As the *f*
Rom 8:23 but we also who have the *f* of
16: 5 who is the *f* of Achaia to
1 Cor 15:20 and has become the *f* of those
15:23 in his own order: Christ the *f*,
16:15 that it is the *f* of Achaia,
Jas 1:18 that we might be a kind of *f* of
Rev 14: 4 being *f* to God and to the

FIRSTLING (KJV) See FIRSTBORN

FIRST BEGOTTEN (KJV) See FIRSTBORN

FISH (61/56) FISH'S, FISHHOOKS, FISHING

Gen 1:26 them have dominion over the *f*
1:28 have dominion over the *f* of the
9: 2 and on all the *f* of the sea.
Ex 7:18 And the *f* that are in the river
7:21 The *f* that were in the river
Num 11: 5 We remember the *f* which we ate
11:22 Or shall all the *f* of the sea
Deut 4:18 or the likeness of any *f* that
1 Ki 4:33 of creeping things, and of *f*.
2 Chr 33:14 as far as the entrance of the *F*
Neh 3: 3 sons of Hassenaah built the *F*
12:39 above the *F* Gate, the Tower of
13:16 who brought in *f* and all kinds
Job 12: 8 And the *f* of the sea will
Ps 8: 8 And the *f* of the sea That
105:29 into blood, And killed their *f*.
Eccl 9:12 Like *f* taken in a cruel net,
Isa 50: 2 Their *f* stink because there
Jer 16:16 'and they shall *f* them;
Ezek 29: 4 And cause the *f* of your rivers
29: 4 And all the *f* in your rivers
29: 5 You and all the *f* of your
38:20 so that the *f* of the sea, the
47: 9 be a very great multitude of *f*,
47:10 Their *f* will be of the same
47:10 be of the same kinds as the *f*
Hos 4: 3 Even the *f* of the sea will be
Jon 1:17 LORD had prepared a great *f*
1:17 Jonah was in the belly of the *f*
2:10 So the LORD spoke to the *f*,
Hab 1:14 Why do You make men like *f* of
Zeph 1: 3 The *f* of the sea, And the
1:10 of a mournful cry from the *F*
Mt 7:10 "Or if he asks for a *f*,
12:40 in the belly of the great *f*,
14:17 here only five loaves and two *f*.
14:19 the five loaves and the two *f*,
15:34 "Seven, and a few little *f*.
15:36 the seven loaves and the *f* and
17:27 and take the *f* that comes up
Mk 6:38 they said, "Five, and two *f*.
6:41 the five loaves and the two *f*,
6:41 and the two *f* He divided among
6:43 full of fragments and of the *f*.
8: 7 They also had a few small *f*;
Lk 5: 6 they caught a great number of *f*,
5: 9 astonished at the catch of *f*
9:13 more than five loaves and two *f*,
9:16 the five loaves and the two *f*,
11:11 Or if he asks for a *f*,
11:11 him a serpent instead of a *f*?
24:42 Him a piece of a broiled *f* and
Jn 6: 9 barley loaves and two small *f*,
6:11 down; and likewise of the *f*,
21: 6 because of the multitude of *f*.
21: 8 dragging the net with *f*.
21: 9 and *f* laid on it, and bread.
21:10 Bring some of the *f* which you
21:11 net to land, full of large *f*,
21:13 it to them, and likewise the *f*.
1 Cor 15:39 flesh of animals, another of *f*,

FISH'S (1/1) FISH

Jon 2: 1 LORD his God from the *f* belly.

FISHER (2/2)

Lev 11:17 the *f* owl, and the screech owl;
Deut 14:17 carrion vulture, the *f* owl,

FISHERMEN (6/6) FISHERS

Isa 19: 8 The *f* also will mourn;
Jer 16:16 I will send for many *f*,
Ezek 47:10 It shall be that *f* will stand
Mt 4:18 into the sea; for they were *f*.
Mk 1:16 into the sea; for they were *f*.
Lk 5: 2 but the *f* had gone from them

FISHERS (2/2) FISHERMEN

Mt 4:19 and I will make you *f* of men."
Mk 1:17 and I will make you become *f* of

FISHHOOKS (2/1) FISH

Am 4: 2 He will take you away with *f*,
4: 2 And your posterity with *f*.

FISHING (2/2) FISH

Job 41: 7 Or his head with *f* spears?
Jn 21: 3 said to them, "I am going *f*.

FISHPOOLS (KJV) See POOLS

FIST (5/5) FISTS

Ex 21:18 with a stone or with his *f*,
Isa 10:32 He will shake his *f* at the
11:15 wind He will shake His *f* over
58: 4 And to strike with the *f* of
Zeph 2:15 Shall hiss and shake his *f*.

FISTS (4/4) FIST

Prov 30: 4 has gathered the wind in His *f*?
Ezek 6:11 Pound your *f* and stamp your
21:17 I also will beat My *f* together,
22:13 I beat My *f* at the dishonest

FIT (11/11) FITLY, FITTING

2 Ki 24:16 all who were strong and *f*
1 Chr 7:11 hundred mighty men of valor *f*
7:40 by genealogies among the army *f*
12:25 mighty men of valor *f* for war,
Prov 24:27 Make it *f* for yourself in the
Ezek 16:50 I took them away as I saw *f*.
Dan 1:13 delicacies; and as you see *f*,
Lk 9:62 is *f* for the kingdom of God."
14:35 It is neither *f* for the land nor
Acts 22:22 for he is not *f* to live!"
25:24 crying out that he was not *f* to

FITCHES (KJV) See CUMMIN, SPELT

FITLY (2/2) FIT

Prov 25:11 A word *f* spoken is like
Song 5:12 Washed with milk, And *f* set.

FITTED (1/1)

Zech 9:13 *F* the bow with Ephraim,

FITTING (15/15) FIT

Esth 3: 8 Therefore it is not *f* for the
Job 34:18 Is it *f* to say to a king,
Prov 19:10 Luxury is not *f* for a fool,
26: 1 So honor is not *f* for a fool.
Eccl 5:18 It is good and *f* for one to
Mt 3:15 for thus it is *f* for us to
Rom 1:28 do those things which are not *f*;
1 Cor 16: 4 But if it is *f* that I go also,
Eph 5: 3 as is *f* for saints;
5: 4 coarse jesting, which are not *f*,
Col 3:18 as is *f* in the Lord.
2 Th 1: 3 for you, brethren, as it is *f*,
Phm 1: 8 Christ to command you what is *f*,
Heb 2:10 For it was *f* for Him, for whom
7:26 For such a High Priest was *f* for

FIVE (256/194) FIFTH

Gen 5: 6 Seth lived one hundred and *f*
5:11 Enosh were nine hundred and *f*
5:30 Lamech lived *f* hundred and
5:32 And Noah was *f* hundred years
11:11 Shem lived *f* hundred years,
11:32 of Terah were two hundred and *f*
14: 9 of Ellasar—four kings against *f*.
18:28 Suppose there were *f* less than
18:28 all of the city for lack of *f*?
43:34 but Benjamin's serving was *f*
45: 6 and there are still *f* years
45:11 for there are still *f* years
45:22 hundred pieces of silver and *f*
47: 2 And he took *f* men from among his
Ex 22: 1 he shall restore *f* oxen for an
26: 3 *F* curtains shall be coupled to
26: 3 and the other *f* curtains
26: 9 And you shall couple *f* curtains
26:26 *f* for the boards on one side of
26:27 *f* bars for the boards on the
26:27 and *f* bars for the boards of
26:37 you shall make for the screen *f*
26:37 and you shall cast *f* sockets of
27: 1 *f* cubits long and five cubits
27: 1 five cubits long and *f* cubits
27:18 and the height *f* cubits, made
30:23 *f* hundred shekels of liquid
30:24 *f* hundred shekels of cassia,
36:10 And he coupled *f* curtains to one
36:10 and the other *f* curtains he
36:16 He coupled *f* curtains by
36:31 *f* for the boards on one side of
36:32 *f* bars for the boards on the
36:32 and *f* bars for the boards of
36:38 and its *f* pillars with their
36:38 but their *f* sockets were
38: 1 *f* cubits was its length and
38: 1 cubits was its length and *f*
38:18 height along its width was *f*
38:26 *f* hundred and fifty men.
Lev 26: 8 *F* of you shall chase a hundred,
27: 5 and if from *f* years old up to
27: 6 if from a month old up to *f*
27: 6 for a male shall be *f* shekels
Num 1:21 were forty-six thousand *f*
1:33 Ephraim were forty thousand *f*
1:41 were forty-one thousand *f*
1:46 hundred and three thousand *f*
2:11 at forty-six thousand *f*
2:19 numbered at forty thousand *f*
2:28 at forty-one thousand *f*
2:32 hundred and three thousand *f*
3:22 there were seven thousand *f*
3:47 you shall take *f* shekels for
4:48 numbered were eight thousand *f*
7:17 *f* rams, five male goats, and
7:17 *f* male goats, and five male
7:17 and *f* male lambs in their first
7:23 *f* rams, five male goats, and
7:23 *f* male goats, and five male
7:23 and *f* male lambs in their first
7:29 *f* rams, five male goats, and
7:29 *f* male goats, and five male
7:29 and *f* male lambs in their first
7:35 *f* rams, five male goats, and
7:35 *f* male goats, and five male
7:35 and *f* male lambs in their first
7:41 *f* rams, five male goats, and
7:41 *f* male goats, and five male
7:41 and *f* male lambs in their first
7:47 *f* rams, five male goats, and
7:47 *f* male goats, and five male
7:47 and *f* male lambs in their first
7:53 *f* rams, five male goats, and
7:53 *f* male goats, and five male
7:53 and *f* male lambs in their first
7:59 *f* rams, five male goats, and
7:59 *f* male goats, and five male
7:59 and *f* male lambs in their first
7:65 *f* rams, five male goats, and
7:65 *f* male goats, and five male
7:65 and *f* male lambs in their first
7:71 *f* rams, five male goats, and
7:71 *f* male goats, and five male
7:71 and *f* male lambs in their first
7:77 *f* rams, five male goats, and
7:77 *f* male goats, and five male
7:77 and *f* male lambs in their first
7:83 *f* rams, five male goats, and
7:83 *f* male goats, and five male
7:83 and *f* male lambs in their first
11:19 nor *f* days, nor ten days, nor
18:16 for *f* shekels of silver,
26:18 forty thousand *f* hundred.
26:22 seventy-six thousand *f* hundred.
26:27 sixty thousand *f* hundred.
26:37 thirty-two thousand *f* hundred.
31: 8 the *f* kings of Midian.
31:28 one of every *f* hundred of the
31:36 and thirty-seven thousand *f*
31:39 donkeys were thirty thousand *f*
31:43 and thirty-seven thousand *f*
31:45 thirty thousand *f* hundred
Josh 8:12 So he took about *f* thousand men
10: 5 Therefore the *f* kings of the
10:16 But these *f* kings had fled and
10:17 The *f* kings have been found
10:22 and bring out those *f* kings to
10:23 and brought out those *f* kings
10:26 and hanged them on *f* trees;
13: 3 the *f* lords of the
Judg 3: 3 *f* lords of the Philistines, all
18: 2 So the children of Dan sent *f*
18: 7 So the *f* men departed and went
18:14 Then the *f* men who had gone to
18:17 Then the *f* men who had gone to
20:45 and they cut down *f* thousand of
1 Sam 6: 4 *F* golden tumors and five golden
6: 4 Five golden tumors and *f* golden
6:16 So when the *f* lords of the
6:18 belonging to the *f* lords,
17: 5 the weight of the coat was *f*
17:40 and he chose for himself *f*
21: 3 Give me *f* loaves of bread in
25:18 *f* sheep already dressed, five
25:18 *f* seahs of roasted grain, one
25:42 attended by *f* of her maidens;
2 Sam 4: 4 He was *f* years old when the
21: 8 and the *f* sons of Michal the
24: 9 and the men of Judah were *f*
1 Ki 4:32 songs were one thousand and *f*.
6: 6 The lowest chamber was *f* cubits
6:10 each *f* cubits high; they were
6:24 One wing of the cherub was *f*
6:24 the other wing of the cherub *f*
7:16 height of one capital was *f*
7:16 of the other capital was *f*
7:23 Its height was *f* cubits, and a
7:39 And he put *f* carts on the right
7:39 and *f* on the left side of the
7:49 *f* on the right side and five
7:49 five on the right side and *f*
9:23 *f* hundred and fifty, who ruled
2 Ki 6:25 a kab of dove droppings for *f*
7:13 let several men take *f* of the
13:19 You should have struck *f* or six
25:19 *f* men of the king's close
1 Chr 2: 4 All the sons of Judah were *f*.
2: 6 *f* of them in all.
3:20 and Jushab-Hesed—*f* in all.
4:32 Tochen, and Ashan—*f* cities—
4:42 *f* hundred men of the sons of
7: 3 All *f* of them were chief men.
7: 7 *f* in all. They were heads of
11:23 *f* cubits tall. In the
29: 7 the work of the house of God *f*
2 Chr 3:11 of the one cherub was *f*
3:11 and the other wing was *f*
3:12 wing of the other cherub was *f*
3:12 and the other wing also was *f*
3:15 the top of each of them was *f*
4: 2 Its height was *f* cubits, and a
4: 6 and put *f* on the right side and
4: 6 five on the right side and *f*
4: 7 *f* on the right side and five on
4: 7 five on the right side and *f* on
4: 8 *f* on the right side and five on
4: 8 five on the right side and *f* on
6:13 had made a bronze platform *f*
6:13 *f* cubits wide, and three cubits
13:17 so *f* hundred thousand choice
26:13 hundred and seven thousand *f*
35: 9 for Passover offerings *f*
35: 9 from the flock and *f*
Ezra 1:11 of gold and silver were *f*
2:69 *f* thousand minas of silver, and
Neh 7:70 and *f* hundred and thirty
Esth 9: 6 the Jews killed and destroyed *f*
9:12 have killed and destroyed *f*
Job 1: 3 *f* hundred yoke of oxen, five
1: 3 *f* hundred female donkeys, and a
Isa 17: 6 Four or *f* in its most
19:18 In that day *f* cities in the
30:17 At the threat of *f* you shall
Jer 52:22 height of one capital was *f*
Ezek 40: 7 chambers was a space of *f*
40:30 twenty-five cubits long and *f*
40:48 *f* cubits on this side and five
40:48 five cubits on this side and *f*
41: 2 walls of the entrance were *f*
41: 2 five cubits on this side and *f*
41: 9 of the side chambers was *f*
41:11 the width of the terrace was *f*
41:12 the wall of the building was *f*
42:16 *f* hundred rods by the measuring
42:17 *f* hundred rods by the measuring
42:18 *f* hundred rods by the measuring
42:19 the west side and measured *f*
42:20 *f* hundred cubits long and five
42:20 five hundred cubits long and *f*
45: 2 *f* hundred by five hundred
45: 2 five hundred by *f* hundred
45: 6 of the city an area *f*
48:15 The *f* thousand cubits in width
48:16 the north side four thousand *f*
48:16 the south side four thousand *f*
48:16 the east side four thousand *f*
48:16 the west side four thousand *f*
48:30 measuring four thousand *f*
48:32 four thousand *f* hundred
48:33 measuring four thousand *f*
48:34 four thousand *f* hundred cubits
Mt 14:17 We have here only *f* loaves and
14:19 And He took the *f* loaves and
14:21 who had eaten were about *f*
16: 9 or remember the *f* loaves of the
16: 9 the five loaves of the *f*
25: 2 'Now *f* of them were wise,
25: 2 and *f* were foolish.
25:15 'And to one he gave *f* talents,
25:16 he who had received the *f*
25:16 and made another *f* talents.
25:20 So he who had received *f* talents
25:20 five talents came and brought *f*
25:20 you delivered to me *f* talents;
25:20 I have gained *f* more talents
Mk 6:38 they found out they said, "*F*,
6:41 And when He had taken the *f*
6:44 eaten the loaves were about *f*
8:19 When I broke the *f* loaves for
8:19 broke the five loaves for the *f*
Lk 1:24 and she hid herself *f* months,
7:41 One owed *f* hundred denarii,
9:13 We have no more than *f* loaves
9:14 For there were about *f* thousand
9:16 Then He took the *f* loaves and
12: 6 Are not *f* sparrows sold for two
12:52 For from now on *f* in one house
14:19 I have bought *f* yoke of oxen,
16:28 for I have *f* brothers, that he
19:18 your mina has earned *f* minas.'
19:19 You also be over *f* cities.'
Jn 4:18 'for you have had *f* husbands,
5: 2 having *f* porches.
6: 9 There is a lad here who has *f*
6:10 in number about *f* thousand.
6:13 with the fragments of the *f*
Acts 4: 4 of the men came to be about *f*
20: 6 and in *f* days joined them at
24: 1 Now after *f* days Ananias the
1 Cor 14:19 church I would rather speak *f*
15: 6 that He was seen by over *f*
2 Cor 11:24 From the Jews *f* times I received
Rev 9: 5 but to torment them for *f*
9:10 Their power was to hurt men *f*
17:10 *F* have fallen, one is, and the

FIX (2/2) FIXED, FIXING

1 Chr 29:18 and *f* their heart toward You.
Ezek 40: 4 and *f* your mind on everything I

FIXED (6/6) FIX

Job 38:10 When I *f* My limit for it,
Ps 10: 8 His eyes are secretly *f* on the
Prov 22:18 Let them all be *f* upon your
Ezek 20:24 and their eyes were *f* on their
Lk 4:20 were in the synagogue were *f*
16:26 and you there is a great gulf *f*,

FIXING (1/1) FIX

Acts 3: 4 And *f* his eyes on him, with

FLAG (KJV) See PAPYRUS

FLAME (32/31) FLAMES, FLAMING

Ex 3: 2 LORD appeared to him in a *f*
Num 21:28 A *f* from the city of Sihon;
Judg 13:20 it happened as the *f* went up
13:20 of the LORD ascended in the *f*
Job 15:30 The *f* will dry out his
18: 5 And the *f* of his fire does not
41:21 And a *f* goes out of his mouth.
Ps 83:14 And as the *f* sets the
104: 4 His ministers a *f* of fire.
106:18 The *f* burned up the wicked.
Song 8: 6 of fire, A most vehement *f*.
Isa 5:24 And the *f* consumes the chaff,
10:17 fire, And his Holy One for a *f*;
29: 6 storm and tempest And the *f*
30:30 of His anger And the *f* of a
43: 2 Nor shall the *f* scorch you.
47:14 From the power of the *f*;
Jer 48:45 A *f* from the midst of Sihon,
Ezek 20:47 the blazing *f* shall not be
Dan 3:22 the *f* of the fire killed those
7: 9 His throne was a fiery *f*,
7:11 and given to the burning *f*.
11:33 they shall fall by sword and *f*,
Joel 1:19 And a *f* has burned all the
2: 3 And behind them a *f* burns;
Ob 18 And the house of Joseph a *f*;
Lk 16:24 for I am tormented in this *f*.
Acts 7:30 Lord appeared to him in a *f* of
Heb 1: 7 And His ministers a *f*
Rev 1:14 and His eyes like a *f* of fire;
2:18 who has eyes like a *f* of fire,
19:12 His eyes were like a *f* of fire,

FLAMES (5/4) FLAME

Ps 29: 7 of the LORD divides the *f* of
Song 8: 6 Its *f* are flames of fire,

8: 6 Its flames are *f* of fire,
Isa 13: 8 Their faces will be like *f*.
66:15 And His rebuke with *f* of fire.

FLAMING (8/8) FLAME

Gen 3:24 and a *f* sword which turned
Ps 105:32 And *f* fire in their land.
Isa 4: 5 and the shining of a *f* fire
Lam 2: 3 against Jacob like a *f* fire
Hos 7: 6 morning it burns like a *f* fire.
Joel 2: 5 Like the noise of a *f* fire
Nah 2: 3 chariots come with *f* torches
2 Th 1: 8 in *f* fire taking vengeance on

FLANGES (2/2)

1 Ki 7:35 its *f* and its panels were of
7:36 On the plates of its *f* and on

FLANKS (6/6)

Lev 3: 4 fat that is on them by the *f*,
3:10 fat that is on them by the *f*,
3:15 fat that is on them by the *f*,
4: 9 fat that is on them by the *f*,
7: 4 fat that is on them by the *f*,
Nah 2: 1 the road! Strengthen your *f*!

FLASH (4/4) FLASHED, FLASHES

Job 41:18 His sneezings *f* forth light,
Ps 144: 6 *F* forth lightning and scatter
Ezek 1:14 in appearance like a *f* of
21:10 Polished to *f* like lightning!

FLASHED (1/1) FLASH

Ps 77:17 Your arrows also *f* about.

FLASHES (3/3) FLASH

Ex 20:18 thunderings, the lightning *f*,
Mt 24:27 comes from the east and *f* to
Lk 17:24 For as the lightning that *f* out

FLASHING (3/3)

Ezek 21:28 For consuming, for *f*—
Hab 3: 4 He had rays *f* from His hand,
Zech 10: 1 The LORD will make *f* clouds;

FLASK (9/8)

1 Sam 10: 1 Then Samuel took a *f* of oil and
2 Ki 9: 1 take this *f* of oil in your
9: 3 Then take the *f* of oil, and pour
Jer 19: 1 and get a potter's earthen *f*,
19:10 Then you shall break the *f* in
Mt 26: 7 to Him having an alabaster *f*
Mk 14: 3 came having an alabaster *f* of
14: 3 Then she broke the *f* and poured
Lk 7:37 brought an alabaster *f* of

FLAT (3/3)

Num 22:31 he bowed his head and fell *f*
Josh 6: 5 of the city will fall down *f*.
6:20 that the wall fell down *f*.

FLATTER (3/3) FLATTERED, FLATTERING, FLATTERS, FLATTERY

Job 32:21 Nor let me *f* any man.
32:22 For I do not know how to *f*,
Ps 5: 9 They *f* with their tongue.

FLATTERED (1/1) FLATTER

Ps 78:36 Nevertheless they *f* Him with

FLATTERING (9/9) FLATTER

Ps 12: 2 With *f* lips and a double
12: 3 May the LORD cut off all *f*
Prov 6:24 From the *f* tongue of a
7:21 With her *f* lips she seduced
26:28 And a *f* mouth works ruin.
Ezek 12:24 there be any false vision or *f*
Rom 16:18 and by smooth words and *f*
1 Th 2: 5 at any time did we use *f* words,
Jude 16 *f* people to gain advantage.

FLATTERS (6/6) FLATTER

Ps 36: 2 For he *f* himself in his own
Prov 2:16 From the seductress who *f*
7: 5 From the seductress who *f*
20:19 do not associate with one who *f*
28:23 favor afterward Than he who *f*
29: 5 A man who *f* his neighbor

FLATTERY (2/2) FLATTER

Job 17: 5 He who speaks *f* to his
Dan 11:32 he shall corrupt with *f*;

FLAVOR (3/3) FLAVORLESS

Mt 5:13 but if the salt loses its *f*,
Mk 9:50 but if the salt loses its *f*,
Lk 14:34 but if the salt has lost its *f*,

FLAVORLESS (1/1) FLAVOR

Job 6: 6 Can *f* food be eaten without

FLAX (9/8)

Ex 9:31 Now the *f* and the barley were
9:31 was in the head and the *f*
Josh 2: 6 them with the stalks of *f*,
Judg 15:14 on his arms became like *f* that
Prov 31:13 She seeks wool and *f*,
Isa 19: 9 those who work in fine *f* And
42: 3 And smoking *f* He will not
Ezek 40: 3 He had a line of *f* and a
Mt 12:20 And smoking *f* He will

FLAY (1/1)

Mic 3: 3 *F* their skin from them, Break

FLEA (2/2)

1 Sam 24:14 do you pursue? A dead dog? A *f*?
26:20 Israel has come out to seek a *f*,

FLED (145/138) FLEE

Gen 14:10 kings of Sodom and Gomorrah *f*;
14:10 and the remainder *f* to the
16: 6 she *f* from her presence.
31:21 So he *f* with all that he had.
31:22 the third day that Jacob had *f*.
35: 1 who appeared to you when you *f*
35: 7 God appeared to him when he *f*
39:12 and *f* and ran outside.
39:13 his garment in her hand and *f*
39:15 and *f* and went outside."
39:18 left his garment with me and *f*
Ex 2:15 But Moses *f* from the face of
4: 3 and Moses *f* from it.
14: 5 of Egypt that the people had *f*,
Num 16:34 Israel who were around them *f*
35:25 city of refuge where he had *f*,
35:26 the city of refuge where he *f*,
35:32 no ransom for him who has *f* to
Josh 7: 4 but they *f* before the men of
8:15 and *f* by the way of the
8:20 and the people who had *f* to the
10:11 as they *f* before Israel and
10:16 But these five kings had *f* and
20: 6 to the city from which he *f*.
Judg 1: 6 Then Adoni-Bezek *f*,
4:15 from his chariot and *f* away
4:17 Sisera had *f* away on foot to
7:21 army ran and cried out and *f*.
7:22 and the army *f* to Beth Acacia,
8:12 When Zebah and Zalmunna *f*,
9:21 And Jotham ran away and *f*;
9:40 and he *f* from him; and many
9:51 *f* there and shut themselves in;
11: 3 Then Jephthah *f* from his
20:45 Then they turned and *f* toward
20:47 six hundred men turned and *f*
1 Sam 4:10 and every man *f* to his tent.
4:16 And I *f* today from the battle
4:17 Israel has *f* before the
14:22 heard that the Philistines *f*,
17:24 *f* from him and were dreadfully
17:51 their champion was dead, they *f*.
19: 8 and they *f* from him.
19:10 So David *f* and escaped that
19:12 And he went and *f* and escaped.
19:18 So David *f* and escaped,
20: 1 Then David *f* from Naioth in
21:10 Then David arose and *f* that day
22:17 and because they knew when he *f*
22:20 escaped and *f* after David.
23: 6 the son of Ahimelech *f* to
27: 4 was told Saul that David had *f*
30:17 men who rode on camels and *f*.
31: 1 and the men of Israel *f* from
31: 7 that the men of Israel had *f*
31: 7 they forsook the cities and *f*;
2 Sam 1: 4 The people have *f* from the
4: 3 because the Beerothites *f* to
4: 4 and his nurse took him up and *f*.
10:13 and they *f* before him.
10:14 they also *f* before Abishai,
10:18 Then the Syrians *f* before
13:29 each one got on his mule and *f*.
13:34 Then Absalom *f*.
13:37 But Absalom *f* and went to Talmai
13:38 So Absalom *f* and went to Geshur,
18:17 over him. Then all Israel *f*,
19: 8 For everyone of Israel had *f* to
19: 9 and now he has *f* from the land
23:11 Then the people *f* from the
1 Ki 2: 7 for so they came to me when I *f*
2:28 So Joab *f* to the tabernacle of
2:29 Joab has *f* to the tabernacle of
11:17 that Hadad *f* to go to Egypt, he
11:23 who had *f* from his lord,
11:40 But Jeroboam arose and *f* to
12: 2 for he had *f* from the presence
20:20 his man; so the Syrians *f*,
20:30 But the rest *f* to Aphek, into
20:30 And Ben-Hadad *f* and went into
2 Ki 3:24 so that they *f* before them;
7: 7 Therefore they arose and *f* at
7: 7 and they *f* for their lives.
8:21 and the troops *f* to their
9:10 And he opened the door and *f*.
9:23 Then Joram turned around and *f*,
9:27 he *f* by the road to Beth
9:27 Then he *f* to Megiddo, and died
14:12 and every man *f* to his tent.
14:19 and he *f* to Lachish; but they
25: 4 and all the men of war *f* at
1 Chr 10: 1 and the men of Israel *f* from
10: 7 the valley saw that they had *f*
10: 7 they forsook their cities and *f*;
11:13 And the people *f* from the
19:14 and they *f* before him.
19:15 they also *f* before Abishai his
19:18 Then the Syrians *f* before
2 Chr 10: 2 where he had *f* from the
13:16 And the children of Israel *f*
14:12 and Judah, and the Ethiopians *f*.
25:22 and every man *f* to his tent.
25:27 and he *f* to Lachish; but they
Ps 3: A Psalm of David when he *f* from
57: A Michtam of David when he *f*
104: 7 At Your rebuke they *f*;
114: 3 The sea saw it and *f*;
114: 5 ails you, O sea, that you *f*?
Isa 10:29 afraid, Gibeah of Saul has *f*.
10:31 Madmenah has *f*,
21:14 their bread they met him who *f*.
21:15 For they *f* from the swords,
22: 3 All your rulers have *f*
22: 3 They have *f* from afar.
Jer 4:25 the birds of the heavens had *f*.
9:10 heavens and the beasts have *f*;
26:21 heard it, he was afraid and *f*,
39: 4 that they *f* and went out of the
46: 5 They have speedily *f*,
46:21 They have *f* away together.
48:45 Those who *f* stood under the
52: 7 and all the men of war *f* and
Lam 4:15 not touch us!" When they *f*
Dan 10: 7 so that they *f* to hide
Hos 7:13 for they have *f* from Me!
12:12 Jacob *f* to the country of
Am 5:19 It will be as though a man *f*
Jon 1:10 For the men knew that he *f*
4: 2 Therefore I *f* previously to
Zech 14: 5 you shall flee As you *f* from
Mt 8:33 Then those who kept them *f*;
26:56 the disciples forsook Him and *f*.
Mk 5:14 So those who fed the swine *f*,
14:50 Then they all forsook Him and *f*.
14:52 he left the linen cloth and *f*
16: 8 So they went out quickly and *f*
Lk 8:34 they *f* and told it in the city
Acts 7:29 Moses *f* and became a dweller in
14: 6 they became aware of it and *f* to
16:27 supposing the prisoners had *f*,
19:16 so that they *f* out of that
Heb 6:18 who have *f* for refuge to lay
Rev 12: 6 Then the woman *f* into the
16:20 Then every island *f* away,
20:11 face the earth and the heaven *f*

FLEE (100/95) FLED, FLEEING, FLEES

Gen 19:20 city is near enough to *f* to,
27:43 *f* to my brother Laban in Haran.
31:20 tell him that he intended to *f*.
31:27 'Why did you *f* away secretly,
Ex 9:20 servants and his livestock *f*
14:25 Let us *f* from the face of
21:13 for you a place where he may *f*.
Lev 26:17 and you shall *f* when no one
26:36 leaf shall cause them to *f*;
26:36 they shall *f* as though fleeing
Num 10:35 And let those who hate You *f*
24:11 *f* to your place. I said I would
35: 6 to which a manslayer may *f*.
35:11 any person accidentally may *f*
35:15 a person accidentally may *f*
Deut 4:42 that the manslayer might *f*
19: 3 that any manslayer may *f* there.
19: 5 he shall *f* to one of these
28: 7 out against you one way and *f*
28:25 out one way against them and *f*
Josh 8: 5 that we shall *f* before them.
8: 6 Therefore we will *f* before
8:20 So they had no power to *f* this
20: 3 or unintentionally may *f*
20: 9 a person accidentally might *f*
Judg 20:32 Let us *f* and draw them away from
2 Sam 4: 4 as she made haste to *f*,
15:14 "Arise, and let us *f*;
17: 2 people who are with him will *f*,
18: 3 shall not go out! For if we *f*
19: 3 ashamed steal away when they *f*
24:13 Or shall you *f* three months
1 Ki 12:18 his chariot in haste to *f* to
2 Ki 9: 3 Then open the door and *f*,
2 Chr 10:18 his chariot in haste to *f* to
Neh 6:11 "Should such a man as I *f*?
Job 9:25 They *f* away, they see no good.
20:24 He will *f* from the iron weapon;
41:28 The arrow cannot make him *f*;
Ps 11: 1 *F* as a bird to your mountain"?
31:11 Those who see me outside *f*
64: 8 All who see them shall *f* away.
68: 1 Let those also who hate Him *f*
68:12 "Kings of armies *f*,
68:12 "Kings of armies flee, they *f*,
139: 7 Or where can I *f* from Your
Prov 28: 1 The wicked *f* when no one
28:17 burdened with bloodshed will *f*
Song 2:17 day breaks And the shadows *f*

F

4: 6 day breaks And the shadows *f*
Isa 10: 3 To whom will you *f* for help?
13:14 And everyone will *f* to his own
15: 5 His fugitives shall *f* to
17:13 rebuke them and they will *f*
20: 6 wherever we *f* for help to be
30:16 for we will *f* on
30:16 Therefore you shall *f*!
30:17 One thousand shall *f* at the
30:17 the threat of five you shall *f*,
31: 8 But he shall *f* from the sword,
33: 3 the tumult the people shall *f*;
35:10 And sorrow and sighing shall *f*
48:20 Go forth from Babylon! *F* from
51:11 Sorrow and sighing shall *f*
Jer 4:29 The whole city shall *f* from the
6: 1 Gather yourselves to *f* from
25:35 shepherds will have no way to *f*,
46: 6 Do not let the swift *f* away,
48: 6 *F*, save your lives!
48: 9 That she may *f* and get away;
49: 8 *F*, turn back, dwell in the
49:24 grown feeble; She turns to *f*,
49:30 '*F*, get far away!
50:16 And everyone shall *f* to his
50:28 The voice of those who *f* and
51: 6 *F* from the midst of Babylon,
Lam 1: 6 That *f* without strength
Am 2:16 men of might Shall *f* naked in
7:12 you seer! *F* to the land of
Jon 1: 3 But Jonah arose to *f* to Tarshish
Nah 2: 8 Now they *f* away. "Halt!
3: 7 all who look upon you Will *f*
3:17 When the sun rises they *f*
Zech 2: 6 *F* from the land of the
14: 5 Then you shall *f* through My
14: 5 you shall *f* As you fled from
Mt 2:13 *f* to Egypt, and stay there
3: 7 of vipers! Who warned you to *f*
10:23 *f* to another. For assuredly, I
24:16 let those who are in Judea *f*
Mk 13:14 let those who are in Judea *f*
Lk 3: 7 of vipers! Who warned you to *f*
21:21 let those who are in Judea *f*
Jn 10: 5 but will *f* from him, for they
1 Cor 6:18 *F* sexual immorality. Every sin
10:14 *f* from idolatry.
1 Tim 6:11 *f* these things and pursue
2 Tim 2:22 *F* also youthful lusts;
Jas 4: 7 Resist the devil and he will *f*
Rev 9: 6 and death will *f* from them.

FLEECE (9/6)

Deut 18: 4 and the first of the *f* of your
Judg 6:37 I shall put a *f* of wool on the
6:37 if there is dew on the *f* only,
6:38 next morning and squeezed the *f*
6:38 he wrung the dew out of the *f*,
6:39 pray, just once more with the *f*;
6:39 let it now be dry only on the *f*,
6:40 It was dry on the *f* only,
Job 31:20 he was not warmed with the *f*

FLEEING (10/10) FLEE

Gen 16: 8 I am *f* from the presence of my
Ex 14:27 while the Egyptians were *f* into
Lev 26:36 they shall flee as though *f*
Deut 4:42 and that by *f* to one of these
Josh 8: 6 They are *f* before us as at the
2 Sam 10:14 saw that the Syrians were *f*,
1 Chr 19:15 saw that the Syrians were *f*,
Job 26:13 His hand pierced the *f*
30: 3 *F* late to the wilderness,
Isa 27: 1 Will punish Leviathan the *f*

FLEES (11/11) FLEE

Deut 19: 4 the case of the manslayer who *f*
19:11 and he *f* to one of these
Josh 20: 4 And when he *f* to one of those
Job 14: 2 He *f* like a shadow and does
27:22 He *f* desperately from its
Isa 24:18 it shall be That he who *f*
Jer 48:19 Ask him who *f* And her who
48:44 He who *f* from the fear shall
Am 9: 1 He who *f* from them shall not
Jn 10:12 and leaves the sheep and *f*;
10:13 The hireling *f* because he is a

FLEET (4/4)

2 Sam 2:18 And Asahel was as *f* of foot
1 Ki 9:26 King Solomon also built a *f* of
9:27 sent his servants with the *f*,
10:22 ships at sea with the *f* of

FLEETING (1/1)

Prov 21: 6 a lying tongue Is the *f* fantasy

FLESH (337/300) FLESHHOOK, FLESHLY

Gen 2:21 and closed up the *f* in its
2:23 now bone of my bones And *f* of
2:23 of my bones And flesh of my *f*;
2:24 and they shall become one *f*.
6: 3 forever, for he is indeed *f*;
6:12 for all *f* had corrupted their
6:13 The end of all *f* has come before
6:17 from under heaven all *f* in
6:19 of every living thing of all *f*
7:15 of all *f* in which is the
7:16 male and female of all *f*,
7:21 And all *f* died that moved on the
8:17 you every living thing of all *f*
9: 4 But you shall not eat *f* with its
9:11 Never again shall all *f* be cut
9:15 every living creature of all *f*;
9:15 become a flood to destroy all *f*.
9:16 every living creature of all *f*
9:17 between Me and all *f* that is
17:11 shall be circumcised in the *f*
17:13 My covenant shall be in your *f*
17:14 is not circumcised in the *f* of
17:23 and circumcised the *f* of their
17:24 he was circumcised in the *f* of
17:25 he was circumcised in the *f* of
29:14 you are my bone and my *f*.
37:27 he is our brother and our *f*.
40:19 and the birds will eat your *f*
Ex 4: 7 was restored like his other *f*.
12: 8 Then they shall eat the *f* on
12:46 shall not carry any of the *f*
21:28 and its *f* shall not be eaten;
29:14 But the *f* of the bull, with its
29:31 consecration and boil its *f* in
29:32 and his sons shall eat the *f*
29:34 And if any of the *f* of the
30:32 shall not be poured on man's *f*;
Lev 4:11 the bull's hide and all its *f*,
6:27 Everyone who touches its *f* must
7:15 The *f* of the sacrifice of his
7:17 the remainder of the *f* of the
7:18 And if any of the *f* of the
7:19 The *f* that touches any unclean
7:19 And as for the clean *f*,
7:20 But the person who eats the *f* of
7:21 and who eats the *f* of the
8:17 But the bull, its hide, its *f*,
8:31 Boil the *f* at the door of the
8:32 What remains of the *f* and of the
9:11 The *f* and the hide he burned
11: 8 Their *f* you shall not eat, and
11:11 you shall not eat their *f*,
12: 3 And on the eighth day the *f* of
13:10 and there is a spot of raw *f*
13:14 But when raw *f* appears on him,
13:15 priest shall examine the raw *f*
13:15 for the raw *f* is unclean.
13:16 Or if the raw *f* changes and
13:24 and the raw *f* of the burn
16:27 the fire their skins, their *f*,
17:11 For the life of the *f* is in the
17:14 "for it is the life of all *f*.
17:14 not eat the blood of any *f*,
17:14 for the life of all *f* is its
19:28 not make any cuttings in your *f*
21: 5 make any cuttings in their *f*.
26:29 You shall eat the *f* of your
26:29 and you shall eat the *f* of your
Num 12:12 whose *f* is half consumed when
16:22 the God of the spirits of all *f*,
18:15 first opens the womb of all *f*,
18:18 And their *f* shall be yours, just
19: 5 in his sight: its hide, its *f*,
27:16 the God of the spirits of all *f*,
Deut 5:26 For who is there of all *f* who
14: 8 you shall not eat their *f* or
28:53 the *f* of your sons and your
28:55 not give any of them the *f* of
32:42 And My sword shall devour *f*,
Judg 8: 7 then I will tear your *f* with
9: 2 Remember that I am your own *f*
1 Sam 17:44 and I will give your *f* to the
2 Sam 5: 1 we are your bone and your *f*.
19:12 you are my bone and my *f*.
19:13 'Are you not my bone and my *f*?
1 Ki 19:21 them and boiled their *f*,
2 Ki 4:34 and the *f* of the child became
5:10 and your *f* shall be restored to
5:14 and his *f* was restored like the
5:14 flesh was restored like the *f*
9:36 at Jezreel dogs shall eat the *f*
1 Chr 11: 1 we are your bone and your *f*.
2 Chr 32: 8 "With him is an arm of *f*;
Neh 5: 5 Yet now our *f* is as the flesh
5: 5 now our flesh is as the *f*
Job 2: 5 and touch his bone and his *f*,
6:12 Or is my *f* bronze?
7: 5 My *f* is caked with worms and
10: 4 Do You have eyes of *f*?
10:11 Clothe me with skin and *f*,
13:14 Why do I take my *f* in my teeth,
14:22 But his *f* will be in pain over
19:20 clings to my skin and to my *f*,
19:22 are not satisfied with my *f*?
19:26 That in my *f* I shall see God,
21: 6 trembling takes hold of my *f*.
33:21 His *f* wastes away from sight,
33:25 His *f* shall be young like a
34:15 All *f* would perish together,
41:23 The folds of his *f* are joined
Ps 16: 9 My *f* also will rest in hope.
27: 2 came against me To eat up my *f*,
38: 3 is no soundness in my *f*
38: 7 there is no soundness in my *f*.
50:13 Will I eat the *f* of bulls,
56: 4 What can *f* do to me?
63: 1 My *f* longs for You In a dry
65: 2 To You all *f* will come.
73:26 My *f* and my heart fail;
78:39 that they were but *f*,
79: 2 The *f* of Your saints to the
84: 2 My heart and my *f* cry out for
109:24 And my *f* is feeble from lack
119:120 My *f* trembles for fear of You,
136:25 Who gives food to all *f*,
145:21 And all *f* shall bless His holy
Prov 3: 8 It will be health to your *f*,
4:22 And health to all their *f*.
5:11 When your *f* and your body are
11:17 is cruel troubles his own *f*.
Eccl 2: 3 my heart how to gratify my *f*
4: 5 hands And consumes his own *f*.
5: 6 let your mouth cause your *f* to
11:10 And put away evil from your *f*,
12:12 study is wearisome to the *f*.
Isa 9:20 Every man shall eat the *f* of
17: 4 And the fatness of his *f* grow
31: 3 And their horses are *f*,
40: 5 And all *f* shall see it
40: 6 All *f* is grass, And all its
49:26 oppress you with their own *f*,
49:26 All *f* shall know That I, the
58: 7 hide yourself from your own *f*?
65: 4 the tombs; Who eat swine's *f*,
66:16 The LORD will judge all *f*;
66:17 Eating swine's *f* and the
66:23 All *f* shall come to worship
66:24 shall be an abhorrence to all *f*.
Jer 11:15 And the holy *f* has passed from
12:12 No *f* shall have peace.
17: 5 who trusts in man And makes *f*
19: 9 I will cause them to eat the *f*
19: 9 flesh of their sons and the *f*
19: 9 and everyone shall eat the *f* of
25:31 will plead His case with all *f*.
32:27 am the LORD, the God of all *f*.
45: 5 I will bring adversity on all *f*,
51:35 violence done to me and my *f*
Lam 3: 4 He has aged my *f* and my skin,
Ezek 4:14 nor has abominable *f* ever come
11:19 the stony heart out of their *f*,
11:19 and give them a heart of *f*,
20:48 All *f* shall see that I, the
21: 4 out of its sheath against all *f*
21: 5 that all *f* may know that I, the
23:20 Whose *f* is like the flesh of
23:20 Whose flesh is like the *f* of
32: 5 I will lay your *f* on the
36:26 heart of stone out of your *f*
36:26 flesh and give you a heart of *f*.
37: 6 put sinews on you and bring *f*
37: 8 the sinews and the *f* came upon
39:17 That you may eat *f* and drink
39:18 You shall eat the *f* of the
40:43 and the *f* of the sacrifices
44: 7 in heart and uncircumcised in *f*,
44: 9 in heart or uncircumcised in *f*,
Dan 1:15 better and fatter in *f* than
2:11 whose dwelling is not with *f*.
4:12 And all *f* was fed from it.
7: 5 'Arise, devour much *f*!'
Hos 8:13 My offerings they sacrifice *f*
Joel 2:28 pour out My Spirit on all *f*;
Mic 3: 2 And the *f* from their bones;
3: 3 Who also eat the *f* of My
3: 3 Like *f* in the caldron."
Nah 2:12 with prey, And his dens with *f*.
Zeph 1:17 And their *f* like refuse."
Zech 2:13 "Be silent, all *f*,
11: 9 are left eat each other's *f*.
11:16 But he will eat the *f* of the
14:12 Their *f* shall dissolve while
Mt 16:17 for *f* and blood has not
19: 5 two shall become one *f*'?
19: 6 are no longer two but one *f*.
24:22 no *f* would be saved; but for
26:41 but the *f* is weak."
Mk 10: 8 two shall become one *f*';
10: 8 are no longer two, but one *f*.
13:20 no *f* would be saved; but for
14:38 but the *f* is weak."
Lk 3: 6 And all *f* shall see the
24:39 for a spirit does not have *f*
Jn 1:13 blood, nor of the will of the *f*,
1:14 And the Word became *f* and dwelt
3: 6 That which is born of the *f* is
3: 6 which is born of the flesh is *f*,
6:51 bread that I shall give is My *f*,
6:52 can this Man give us His *f*
6:53 unless you eat the *f* of the Son
6:54 Whoever eats My *f* and drinks My
6:55 For My *f* is food indeed, and My
6:56 He who eats My *f* and drinks My
6:63 the *f* profits nothing.
8:15 "You judge according to the *f*;
17: 2 given Him authority over all *f*,
Acts 2:17 of My Spirit on all *f*;
2:26 Moreover my *f* also will
2:30 of his body, according to the *f*,
2:31 nor did His *f* see corruption.
Rom 1: 3 of David according to the *f*,
2:28 that which is outward in the *f*;
3:20 by the deeds of the law no *f*
4: 1 has found according to the *f*?
6:19 of the weakness of your *f*.
7: 5 For when we were in the *f*,
7:18 in my *f*) nothing good dwells;
7:25 but with the *f* the law of sin.
8: 1 do not walk according to the *f*,
8: 3 that it was weak through the *f*,
8: 3 Son in the likeness of sinful *f*,
8: 3 He condemned sin in the *f*,
8: 4 do not walk according to the *f*

8: 5 who live according to the *f*
8: 5 minds on the things of the *f*,
8: 8 those who are in the *f* cannot
8: 9 But you are not in the *f* but in
8:12 we are debtors—not to the *f*,
8:12 to live according to the *f*.
8:13 if you live according to the *f*
9: 3 countrymen according to the *f*,
9: 5 from whom, according to the *f*,
9: 8 who are the children of the *f*,
11:14 jealousy those who are my *f*
13:14 and make no provision for the *f*,
1 Cor 1:26 many wise according to the *f*,
1:29 that no *f* should glory in His
5: 5 for the destruction of the *f*,
6:16 says, "shall become one *f*.
7:28 such will have trouble in the *f*,
10:18 Observe Israel after the *f*:
15:39 All *f* is not the same flesh,
15:39 All flesh is not the same *f*,
15:39 but there is one kind of *f*
15:39 another *f* of animals, another
15:50 that *f* and blood cannot inherit
2 Cor 1:17 do I plan according to the *f*,
3: 3 of stone but on tablets of *f*,
4:11 be manifested in our mortal *f*.
5:16 no one according to the *f*.
5:16 known Christ according to the *f*,
7: 1 from all filthiness of the *f*
10: 2 if we walked according to the *f*.
10: 3 For though we walk in the *f*,
10: 3 do not war according to the *f*.
11:18 many boast according to the *f*,
12: 7 a thorn in the *f* was given to
Gal 1:16 not immediately confer with *f*
2:16 by the works of the law no *f*
2:20 which I now live in the *f* I
3: 3 now being made perfect by the *f*?
4:14 And my trial which was in my *f*
4:23 was born according to the *f*,
4:29 who was born according to the *f*
5:13 as an opportunity for the *f*,
5:16 not fulfill the lust of the *f*.
5:17 For the *f* lusts against the
5:17 and the Spirit against the *f*;
5:19 Now the works of the *f* are
5:24 Christ's have crucified the *f*
6: 8 For he who sows to his *f* will of
6: 8 sows to his flesh will of the *f*
6:12 to make a good showing in the *f*,
6:13 that they may boast in your *f*.
Eph 2: 3 ourselves in the lusts of our *f*,
2: 3 the desires of the *f* and of
2:11 you, once Gentiles in the *f*—
2:11 the Circumcision made in the *f*
2:15 having abolished in His *f* the
5:29 For no one ever hated his own *f*,
5:30 of His *f* and of His bones.
5:31 two shall become one *f*.
6: 5 your masters according to the *f*,
6:12 For we do not wrestle against *f*
Phil 1:22 But if I live on in the *f*,
1:24 to remain in the *f* is more
3: 3 and have no confidence in the *f*,
3: 4 might have confidence in the *f*.
3: 4 he may have confidence in the *f*,
Col 1:22 in the body of His *f* through
1:24 and fill up in my *f* what is
2: 1 have not seen my face in the *f*,
2: 5 For though I am absent in the *f*,
2:11 the body of the sins of the *f*,
2:13 the uncircumcision of your *f*,
2:23 against the indulgence of the *f*.
3:22 your masters according to the *f*,
1 Tim 3:16 God was manifested in the *f*,
Phm 1:16 both in the *f* and in the Lord.
Heb 2:14 the children have partaken of *f*
5: 7 who, in the days of His *f*,
9:13 for the purifying of the *f*,
10:20 the veil, that is, His *f*,
Jas 5: 3 you and will eat your *f* like
1 Pe 1:24 'All *f* is as grass,
3:18 being put to death in the *f* but
3:21 removal of the filth of the *f*,
4: 1 Christ suffered for us in the *f*,
4: 1 he who has suffered in the *f*
4: 2 the rest of his time in the *f*
4: 6 according to men in the *f*,
2 Pe 2:10 who walk according to the *f* in
2:18 through the lusts of the *f*,
1 Jn 2:16 in the world—the lust of the *f*,
4: 2 Jesus Christ has come in the *f*
4: 3 Jesus Christ has come in the *f*
2 Jn 7 Christ as coming in the *f*.
Jude 7 and gone after strange *f*,
8 these dreamers defile the *f*,
23 the garment defiled by the *f*.
Rev 17:16 eat her *f* and burn her with
19:18 that you may eat the *f* of kings,
19:18 the *f* of captains, the flesh of
19:18 the *f* of mighty men, the flesh
19:18 the *f* of horses and of those
19:18 and the *f* of all people, free
19:21 birds were filled with their *f*.

FLESHHOOK (2/2) FLESH

1 Sam 2:13 come with a three-pronged *f* in
2:14 take for himself all that the *f*

FLESHLY (6/6) FLESH

Ezek 16:26 your very *f* neighbors, and
2 Cor 1:12 not with *f* wisdom but by the
Col 2:18 vainly puffed up by his *f* mind,
Heb 7:16 to the law of a *f* commandment,
9:10 and *f* ordinances imposed until
1 Pe 2:11 abstain from *f* lusts which war

FLEW (5/4) FLY

2 Sam 22:11 He rode upon a cherub, and *f*;
Ps 18:10 He rode upon a cherub, and *f*;
18:10 He *f* upon the wings of the
Isa 6: 2 his feet, and with two he *f*.
6: 6 Then one of the seraphim *f* to

FLIES (15/13) FLY

Ex 8:21 I will send swarms of *f* on
8:21 shall be full of swarms of *f*,
8:22 that no swarms of *f* shall be
8:24 Thick swarms of *f* came into
8:24 because of the swarms of *f*.
8:29 that the swarms of *f* may
8:31 He removed the swarms of *f*
Deut 4:17 of any winged bird that *f* in
14:19 every creeping thing that *f* is
28:49 as swift as the eagle *f*,
Ps 78:45 He sent swarms of *f* among them,
91: 5 Nor of the arrow that *f* by
105:31 and there came swarms of *f*,
Eccl 10: 1 Dead *f* putrefy the perfumer's
Nah 3:16 The locust plunders and *f*

FLIGHT (9/9) FLY

Lev 26: 8 you shall put ten thousand to *f*;
Deut 32:30 And two put ten thousand to *f*,
1 Chr 12:15 and they put to *f* all those in
Eccl 10:20 And a bird in *f* may tell the
Isa 52:12 go out with haste, Nor go by *f*;
Am 2:14 Therefore *f* shall perish from
Mt 24:20 And pray that your *f* may not be
Mk 13:18 And pray that your *f* may not be
Heb 11:34 turned to *f* the armies of the

FLINT (8/8) FLINTY

Josh 5: 2 'Make *f* knives for yourself,
5: 3 So Joshua made *f* knives for
Job 28: 9 He puts his hand on the *f*;
Ps 114: 8 The *f* into a fountain of
Isa 5:28 horses' hooves will seem like *f*,
50: 7 I have set My face like a *f*,
Ezek 3: 9 adamant stone, harder than *f*,
Zech 7:12 they made their hearts like *f*,

FLINTY (2/2) FLINT

Deut 8:15 water for you out of the *f*
32:13 And oil from the *f* rock;

FLITTING (1/1)

Prov 26: 2 Like a *f* sparrow, like a flying

FLOAT (2/2)

1 Ki 5: 9 I will *f* them in rafts by sea
2 Ki 6: 6 and he made the iron *f*.

FLOCK (121/108) FLOCKS

Gen 4: 4 of the firstborn of his *f* and
21:28 set seven ewe lambs of the *f*
27: 9 Go now to the *f* and bring me
29:10 and watered the *f* of Laban his
30:32 me pass through all your *f*
30:40 and all the brown in the *f* of
30:40 did not put them with Laban's *f*.
31: 4 and Leah to the field, to his *f*,
31:38 not eaten the rams of your *f*.
31:41 and six years for your *f*,
31:43 and this *f* is my flock;
31:43 and this flock is my *f*;
33:13 all the *f* will die.
37: 2 was feeding the *f* with his
37:12 went to feed their father's *f*
37:13 your brothers feeding the *f*
38:17 send a young goat from the *f*.
Ex 2:16 to water their father's *f*.
2:17 them, and watered their *f*.
2:19 water for us and watered the *f*.
3: 1 Now Moses was tending the *f* of
3: 1 And he led the *f* to the back of
Lev 1: 2 the herd and of the *f*.
3: 6 to the LORD is of the *f*,
5: 6 committed, a female from the *f*,
5:18 ram without blemish from the *f*,
6: 6 ram without blemish from the *f*,
27:32 the tithe of the herd or the *f*,
Num 15: 3 LORD, from the herd or the *f*,
Deut 7:13 and the offspring of your *f*,
12:17 of your herd or your *f*,
12:21 from your herd and from your *f*
15:14 him liberally from your *f*,
15:19 come from your herd and your *f*
15:19 shear the firstborn of your *f*.
16: 2 from the *f* and the herd, in the
32:14 the cattle, and milk of the *f*,
1 Sam 17:34 and took a lamb out of the *f*,
2 Sam 12: 4 refused to take from his own *f*
2 Chr 35: 7 and young goats from the *f*,
35: 8 six hundred from the *f*,
35: 9 five thousand from the *f*
Ezra 10:19 presented a ram of the *f* as
Job 21:11 their little ones like a *f*,
30: 1 to put with the dogs of my *f*.
Ps 77:20 You led Your people like a *f*
78:52 them in the wilderness like a *f*;
80: 1 You who lead Joseph like a *f*;
107:41 makes their families like a *f*.
Song 1: 7 Where you feed your *f*,
1: 8 in the footsteps of the *f*,
2:16 He feeds his *f* among the
4: 1 Your hair is like a *f* of
4: 2 Your teeth are like a *f* of
6: 2 To feed his *f* in the
6: 3 He feeds his *f* among the
6: 5 Your hair is like a *f* of
6: 6 Your teeth are like a *f* of
Isa 40:11 He will feed His *f* like a
63:11 With the shepherd of His *f*?
Jer 13:17 Because the LORD's *f* has been
13:20 Where is the *f* that was
23: 2 "You have scattered My *f*,
23: 3 gather the remnant of My *f* out
25:34 You leaders of the *f*! For the
25:35 Nor the leaders of the *f* to
25:36 of the leaders to the *f* will
31:10 him as a shepherd does his *f*.
31:12 For the young of the *f* and the
49:20 Surely the least of the *f*
50:45 Surely the least of the *f*
51:23 pieces the shepherd and his *f*;
Ezek 24: 5 Take the choice of the *f*.
34: 3 but you do not feed the *f*.
34: 6 My *f* was scattered over the
34: 8 surely because My *f* became a
34: 8 and My *f* became food for every
34: 8 My shepherds search for My *f*,
34: 8 and did not feed My *f*"—
34:10 and I will require My *f* at
34:10 for I will deliver My *f* from
34:12 As a shepherd seeks out his *f* on
34:15 "I will feed My *f*,
34:17 'And as for you, O My *f*,
34:19 "And as for My *f*,
34:22 "therefore I will save My *f*,
34:31 "You are My *f*,
34:31 the *f* of My pasture; you are
36:37 increase their men like a *f*.
36:38 Like a *f* offered as holy
36:38 like the *f* at Jerusalem on its
43:23 and a ram from the *f* without
43:25 young bull and a ram from the *f*,
45:15 lamb shall be given from a *f*
Am 6: 4 Eat lambs from the *f* And
7:15 took me as I followed the *f*,
Jon 3: 7 man nor beast, herd nor *f*,
Mic 2:12 Like a *f* in the midst of their
4: 8 And you, O tower of the *f*,
5: 4 He shall stand and feed His *f*
7:14 The *f* of Your heritage,
Hab 3:17 Though the *f* may be cut off
Zech 9:16 As the *f* of His people.
10: 3 LORD of hosts will visit His *f*,
11: 4 Feed the *f* for slaughter,
11: 7 So I fed the *f* for slaughter,
11: 7 in particular the poor of the *f*.
11: 7 I called Bonds; and I fed the *f*.
11:11 Thus the poor of the *f*,
11:17 Who leaves the *f*! A sword
Mal 1:14 the deceiver Who has in his *f*
Mt 26:31 And the sheep of the *f*
Lk 2: 8 keeping watch over their *f* by
12:32 "Do not fear, little *f*,
Jn 10:16 and there will be one *f* and
Acts 20:28 to yourselves and to all the *f*,
20:29 in among you, not sparing the *f*.
1 Cor 9: 7 Or who tends a *f* and does not
9: 7 not drink of the milk of the *f*?
1 Pe 5: 2 Shepherd the *f* of God which is
5: 3 but being examples to the *f*;

FLOCKS (89/83) FLOCK

Gen 13: 5 had *f* and herds and tents.
24:35 and He has given him *f* and
26:14 for he had possessions of *f* and
29: 2 there were three *f* of sheep
29: 2 of that well they watered the *f*.
29: 3 Now all the *f* would be gathered
29: 8 We cannot until all the *f* are
30:31 will again feed and keep your *f*:
30:36 Jacob fed the rest of Laban's *f*.
30:38 he set before the *f* in the
30:38 watering troughs where the *f*
30:39 So the *f* conceived before the
30:39 and the *f* brought forth
30:40 and made the *f* face toward the
30:40 but he put his own *f* by
30:42 But when the *f* were feeble, he
30:43 prosperous, and had large *f*,
31: 8 then all the *f* bore speckled.
31: 8 then all the *f* bore streaked.
31:10 at the time when the *f*
31:10 rams which leaped upon the *f*
31:12 the rams which leap on the *f*
32: 5 "I have oxen, donkeys, *f*,
32: 7 and the *f* and herds and camels,
33:13 and the *f* and herds which are
37:14 brothers and well with the *f*,
37:16 they are feeding their *f*.

F

45:10 your *f* and your herds, and all
46:32 and they have brought their *f*,
47: 1 their *f* and their herds and all
47: 4 have no pasture for their *f*,
47:17 exchange for the horses, the *f*,
50: 8 Only their little ones, their *f*,
Ex 10: 9 with our *f* and our herds we
10:24 only let your *f* and your herds
12:32 Also take your *f* and your herds,
12:38 and *f* and herds—a great deal of
34: 3 let neither *f* nor herds feed
Lev 1:10 'If his offering is of the *f*—
5:15 ram without blemish from the *f*,
Num 11:22 Shall *f* and herds be slaughtered
31: 9 all their cattle, all their *f*,
32:26 little ones, our wives, our *f*,
Deut 8:13 when your herds and your *f*
12: 6 firstborn of your herds and *f*.
14:23 of your herds and your *f*,
28: 4 and the offspring of your *f*.
28:18 and the offspring of your *f*.
28:51 or the offspring of your *f*,
Judg 5:16 To hear the pipings for the *f*?
1 Sam 30:20 Then David took all the *f* and
2 Sam 12: 2 man had exceedingly many *f*
1 Ki 20:27 before them like two little *f*
1 Chr 4:39 to seek pasture for their *f*.
4:41 was pasture for their *f* there.
27:31 the Hagrite was over the *f*.
2 Chr 17:11 and the Arabians brought him *f*,
32:28 of livestock, and folds for *f*.
32:29 and possessions of *f* and herds
Neh 10:36 of our herds and our *f*,
Job 24: 2 They seize *f* violently and
Ps 65:13 pastures are clothed with *f*;
78:48 And their *f* to fiery
Prov 27:23 to know the state of your *f*,
Eccl 2: 7 possessions of herds and *f*
Song 1: 7 who veils herself By the *f* of
Isa 17: 2 They will be for *f* Which lie
32:14 of wild donkeys, a pasture of *f*—
60: 7 All the *f* of Kedar shall be
61: 5 shall stand and feed your *f*,
65:10 Sharon shall be a fold of *f*,
Jer 3:24 Their *f* and their herds,
5:17 They shall eat up your *f* and
6: 3 The shepherds with their *f*
10:21 And all their *f* shall be
31:24 and those going out with *f*.
33:12 of shepherds causing their *f*
33:13 the *f* shall again pass under
49:29 Their tents and their *f* they
50: 8 be like the rams before the *f*.
Ezek 25: 5 and Ammon a resting place for *f*.
34: 2 not the shepherds feed the *f*?
36:38 ruined cities be filled with *f*
Hos 5: 6 With their *f* and herds They
Joel 1:18 Even the *f* of sheep suffer
Mic 5: 8 Like a young lion among *f* of
Zeph 2: 6 for shepherds and folds for *f*.
2: 7 They shall feed their *f*
3:13 For they shall feed their *f*

FLOOD (33/31) FLOODED, FLOODING, FLOODPLAIN, FLOODS, FLOODWATERS

Gen 7: 7 because of the waters of the *f*.
7:10 days that the waters of the *f*
7:17 Now the *f* was on the earth
9:11 cut off by the waters of the *f*;
9:11 never again shall there be a *f*
9:15 shall never again become a *f*
9:28 And Noah lived after the *f*
10: 1 were born to them after the *f*.
10:32 on the earth after the *f*.
11:10 Arphaxad two years after the *f*.
Job 22:16 were swept away by a *f*?
27:20 Terrors overtake him like a *f*;
Ps 29:10 LORD sat enthroned at the *F*,
32: 6 Surely in a *f* of great waters
74:15 open the fountain and the *f*;
90: 5 You carry them away like a *f*;
Isa 28: 2 Like a *f* of mighty waters
59:19 the enemy comes in like a *f*,
Jer 46: 7 is this coming up like a *f*,
46: 8 Egypt rises up like a *f*,
47: 2 And shall be an overflowing *f*;
Dan 9:26 end of it shall be with a *f*,
11:22 With the force of a *f* they shall
Nah 1: 8 But with an overflowing *f* He
Mt 24:38 as in the days before the *f*,
24:39 and did not know until the *f*
Lk 6:48 And when the *f* arose, the
17:27 and the *f* came and destroyed
1 Pe 4: 4 run with them in the same *f*
2 Pe 2: 5 bringing in the *f* on the world
Rev 12:15 water out of his mouth like a *f*
12:15 her to be carried away by the *f*.
12:16 mouth and swallowed up the *f*

FLOODED (2/2) FLOOD

Joel 3:18 the brooks of Judah shall be *f*
2 Pe 3: 6 being *f* with water.

FLOODING (3/3) FLOOD

Ezek 13:11 There will be *f* rain, and you,
13:13 and there shall be a *f* rain in
38:22 *f* rain, great hailstones, fire,

FLOODPLAIN (3/3) FLOOD

Jer 12: 5 Then how will you do in the *f*
49:19 come up like a lion from the *f*
50:44 come up like a lion from the *f*

FLOODS (12/10) FLOOD

Ex 15: 8 The *f* stood upright like a
2 Sam 22: 5 The *f* of ungodliness made me
Ps 18: 4 And the *f* of ungodliness made
69: 2 Where the *f* overflow me.
93: 3 The *f* have lifted up, O LORD,
93: 3 The *f* have lifted up their
93: 3 The *f* lift up their waves.
Song 8: 7 Nor can the *f* drown it. If a
Isa 44: 3 And *f* on the dry ground;
Jon 2: 3 And the *f* surrounded me;
Mt 7:25 the *f* came, and the winds blew
7:27 the *f* came, and the winds blew

FLOODWATER (1/1)

Ps 69:15 Let not the *f* overflow me, Nor

FLOODWATERS (2/2) FLOOD

Gen 6:17 I Myself am bringing *f* on the
7: 6 hundred years old when the *f*

FLOOR (10/9) FLOORS

Judg 3:25 master, fallen dead on the *f*.
1 Ki 6:15 from the *f* of the temple to the
6:15 and he covered the *f* of the
6:16 from *f* to ceiling, with cedar
6:30 And the *f* of the temple he
7: 7 was paneled with cedar from *f*
22:35 out from the wound onto the *f*
2 Chr 34:11 and to *f* the houses which the
Isa 21:10 and the grain of my *f*!
Ezek 41:20 From the *f* to the space above

FLOORS (3/3) FLOOR

1 Sam 23: 1 are robbing the threshing *f*.
Dan 2:35 from the summer threshing *f*;
Joel 2:24 The threshing *f* shall be full

FLOUR (64/63)

Ex 29: 2 shall make them of wheat *f*).
29:40 one-tenth of an ephah of *f*
Lev 2: 1 offering shall be of fine *f*.
2: 2 from it his handful of fine *f*
2: 4 be unleavened cakes of fine *f*
2: 5 pan, it shall be of fine *f*,
2: 7 it shall be made of fine *f*
5:11 of an ephah of fine *f* as a sin
6:15 it his handful of the fine *f*
6:20 of an ephah of fine *f* as a
7:12 or cakes of blended *f* mixed
14:10 of an ephah of fine *f* mixed
14:21 of an ephah of fine *f* mixed
23:13 of an ephah of fine *f* mixed
23:17 ephah. They shall be of fine *f*;
24: 5 And you shall take fine *f* and
Num 6:15 cakes of fine *f* mixed with oil,
7:13 both of them full of fine *f*
7:19 both of them full of fine *f*
7:25 both of them full of fine *f*
7:31 both of them full of fine *f*
7:37 both of them full of fine *f*
7:43 both of them full of fine *f*
7:49 both of them full of fine *f*
7:55 both of them full of fine *f*
7:61 both of them full of fine *f*
7:67 both of them full of fine *f*
7:73 both of them full of fine *f*
7:79 both of them full of fine *f*
8: 8 its grain offering of fine *f*
15: 4 of an ephah of fine *f* mixed
15: 6 of an ephah of fine *f* mixed
15: 9 of an ephah of fine *f* mixed
28: 5 of an ephah of fine *f* as a
28: 9 of an ephah of fine *f* as a
28:12 of an ephah of fine *f* as a
28:12 of an ephah of fine *f* as a
28:13 of an ephah of fine *f*,
28:20 offering shall be of fine *f*
28:28 their grain offering of fine *f*
29: 3 offering shall be fine *f*
29: 9 offering shall be of fine *f*
29:14 offering shall be of fine *f*
Judg 6:19 bread from an ephah of *f*.
1 Sam 1:24 three bulls, one ephah of *f*,
28:24 And she took *f* and kneaded it,
2 Sam 13: 8 Then she took *f* and kneaded
17:28 vessels and wheat, barley and *f*,
1 Ki 4:22 day was thirty kors of fine *f*,
17:12 only a handful of *f* in a bin,
17:14 The bin of *f* shall not be used
17:16 The bin of *f* was not used up,
2 Ki 4:41 So he said, "Then bring some *f*.
7: 1 this time a seah of fine *f*
7:16 So a seah of fine *f* was sold
7:18 and a seah of fine *f* for a
1 Chr 9:29 and over the fine *f* and the
12:40 provisions of *f* and cakes of
23:29 the showbread and the fine *f*
Isa 28:28 Bread *f* must be ground;
Ezek 16:13 You ate pastry of fine *f*,
16:19 I gave you—the pastry of fine *f*,
46:14 of oil to moisten the fine *f*.
Rev 18:13 fine *f* and wheat, cattle and

FLOURISH (12/12) FLOURISHED, FLOURISHES, FLOURISHING

Job 8:11 Can the reeds *f* without water?
Ps 72: 7 His days the righteous shall *f*,
72:16 And those of the city shall *f*
92: 7 all the workers of iniquity *f*,
92:12 The righteous shall *f* like a
92:13 house of the LORD Shall *f* in
132:18 upon Himself His crown shall *f*.
Prov 11:28 But the righteous will *f* like
14:11 the tent of the upright will *f*.
Isa 17:11 you will make your seed to *f*;
66:14 And your bones shall *f* like
Ezek 17:24 tree and made the dry tree *f*;

FLOURISHED (1/1) FLOURISH

Phil 4:10 at last your care for me has *f*

FLOURISHES (2/2) FLOURISH

Ps 90: 6 In the morning it *f* and grows
103:15 a flower of the field, so he *f*.

FLOURISHING (2/2) FLOURISH

Ps 92:14 They shall be fresh and *f*,
Dan 4: 4 and *f* in my palace.

FLOW (26/24) FLOWED, FLOWING, FLOWS

Lev 12: 7 she shall be clean from the *f*
20:18 nakedness, he has exposed her *f*,
20:18 and she has uncovered the *f* of
Deut 8: 7 that *f* out of valleys and
Job 6:17 it is warm, they cease to *f*;
20:28 And his goods will *f* away
Ps 58: 7 Let them *f* away as waters
104:10 They *f* among the hills.
147:18 wind to blow, and the waters *f*.
Song 4:16 That its spices may *f* out.
Isa 2: 2 And all nations shall *f* to it.
8: 6 The waters of Shiloah that *f*
48:21 He caused the waters to *f* from
Jer 14:17 Let my eyes *f* with tears night
Lam 3:49 My eyes *f* and do not cease,
Ezek 32: 6 also water the land with the *f*
Joel 3:18 The hills shall *f* with milk,
3:18 A fountain shall *f* from the
Am 9:13 And all the hills shall *f*
Mic 4: 1 And peoples shall *f* to it.
Zech 14: 8 That living waters shall *f* from
Mt 9:20 a woman who had a *f* of blood
Mk 5:25 Now a certain woman had a *f* of
Lk 8:43 having a *f* of blood for twelve
8:44 And immediately her *f* of blood
Jn 7:38 out of his heart will *f* rivers

FLOWED (1/1) FLOW

Lam 3:54 The waters *f* over my head;

FLOWER (21/18) FLOWERS

Ex 25:33 an ornamental knob and a *f*,
25:33 an ornamental knob and a *f*—
25:34 its ornamental knob and *f*.
37:19 an ornamental knob and a *f*,
37:19 an ornamental knob and a *f*—
37:20 its ornamental knob and *f*.
1 Sam 2:33 your house shall die in the *f*
Job 14: 2 He comes forth like a *f* and
Ps 103:15 As a *f* of the field, so he
Isa 18: 5 sour grape is ripening in the *f*,
28: 1 glorious beauty is a fading *f*
28: 4 glorious beauty is a fading *f*
40: 6 its loveliness is like the *f*
40: 7 the *f* fades, Because the
40: 8 the *f* fades, But the word of
Nah 1: 4 And the *f* of Lebanon wilts.
1 Cor 7:36 if she is past the *f* of youth,
Jas 1:10 because as a *f* of the field he
1:11 its *f* falls, and its beautiful
1 Pe 1:24 glory of man as the *f*
1:24 And its *f* falls away,

FLOWERS (10/10) FLOWER

Ex 25:31 and *f* shall be of one piece.
37:17 and its *f* were of the same
Num 8: 4 from its shaft to its *f* it was
1 Ki 6:18 with ornamental buds and open *f*.
6:29 palm trees, and open *f*.
6:32 palm trees, and open *f*,
6:35 and open *f* on them, and
7:49 with the *f* and the lamps and
2 Chr 4:21 with the *f* and the lamps and the
Song 2:12 The *f* appear on the earth;

FLOWING (27/26) FLOW

Ex 3: 8 to a land *f* with milk and
3:17 to a land *f* with milk and
13: 5 a land *f* with milk and honey,
33: 3 Go up to a land *f* with milk
Lev 20:24 a land *f* with milk and honey."
Num 16:13 a land *f* with milk and honey,
16:14 a land *f* with milk and honey,

Deut 6: 3 a land *f* with milk and honey.'
11: 9 a land *f* with milk and honey.'
21: 4 down to a valley with *f* water,
26: 9 a land *f* with milk and honey";
26:15 a land *f* with milk and honey."
27: 3 a land *f* with milk and honey,'
31:20 the land *f* with milk and honey,
Josh 5: 6 a land *f* with milk and honey."
Job 20:17 The rivers *f* with honey and
Prov 18: 4 of wisdom is a *f* brook.
Isa 66:12 the Gentiles like a *f* stream.
Jer 11: 5 a land *f* with milk and honey,'
18:14 Will the cold *f* waters be
32:22 a land *f* with milk and honey."
49: 4 Your *f* valley, O backsliding
Ezek 20: 6 *f* with milk and honey,' the
20:15 *f* with milk and honey,' the
23:15 *F* turbans on their heads,
47: 1 *f* from under the threshold of
47: 1 the water was *f* from under the

FLOWS (7/7) FLOW

Num 13:27 It truly *f* with milk and honey,
14: 8 a land which *f* with milk and
1 Ki 17: 3 which *f* into the Jordan.
17: 5 which *f* into the Jordan.
Ezra 8:15 them by the river that *f* to
Ezek 47: 8 This water *f* toward the eastern
47:12 because their water *f* from the

FLUSHED (1/1)

Job 16:16 My face is *f* from weeping,

FLUTE (14/14) FLUTES

Gen 4:21 those who play the harp and *f*.
1 Sam 10: 5 instrument, a tambourine, a *f*,
Job 21:12 rejoice to the sound of the *f*.
30:31 And my *f* to the voice of those
Isa 5:12 strings, The tambourine and *f*,
30:29 heart as when one goes with a *f*,
Dan 3: 5 hear the sound of the horn, *f*,
3: 7 heard the sound of the horn, *f*,
3:10 hears the sound of the horn, *f*,
3:15 hear the sound of the horn, *f*,
Mt 9:23 and saw the *f* players and the
11:17 'We played the *f* for you,
Lk 7:32 'We played the *f* for you,
1 Cor 14: 7 whether *f* or harp, when they

FLUTES (5/4) FLUTE

1 Ki 1:40 and the people played the *f* and
Ps 5: To the Chief Musician. With *f*.
150: 4 stringed instruments and *f*!
Jer 48:36 My heart shall wail like *f* for
48:36 And like *f* My heart shall wail

FLUTISTS (1/1)

Rev 18:22 sound of harpists, musicians, *f*,

FLUTTERING (1/1)

Num 11:31 from the sea and left them *f*

FLUX (KJV) See DYSENTERY

FLY (17/17) FLEW, FLIES, FLIGHT, FLYING

Gen 1:20 and let birds *f* above the earth
Job 5: 7 As the sparks *f* upward.
20: 8 He will *f* away like a dream,
39:26 Does the hawk *f* by your wisdom,
Ps 55: 6 wings like a dove! I would *f*
90:10 soon cut off, and we *f* away.
Prov 23: 5 They *f* away like an eagle
Isa 7:18 LORD will whistle for the *f*
11:14 But they shall *f* down upon the
60: 8 Who are these who *f* like a
Jer 48:40 one shall *f* like an eagle,
49:22 He shall come up and *f* like the
Dan 9:21 being caused to *f* swiftly,
Hos 9:11 their glory shall *f* away like a
Hab 1: 8 They *f* as the eagle that
Rev 12:14 that she might *f* into the
19:17 saying to all the birds that *f*

FLYING (13/13) FLY

Lev 11:20 All *f* insects that creep on
11:21 these you may eat of every *f*
11:23 But all other *f* insects which
Ps 148:10 Creeping things and *f* fowl;
Prov 26: 2 like a *f* swallow, So a curse
Isa 14:29 offspring will be a fiery *f*
30: 6 The viper and fiery *f* serpent,
31: 5 Like birds *f* about, So will
Zech 5: 1 and saw there a *f* scroll.
5: 2 I see a *f* scroll. Its length is
Rev 4: 7 living creature was like a *f*
8:13 and I heard an angel *f* through
14: 6 Then I saw another angel *f* in

FOAL (2/2) FOALS

Zech 9: 9 the *f* of a donkey.
Mt 21: 5 the *f* of a donkey.' "

FOALS (1/1)

Gen 32:15 twenty female donkeys and ten *f*.

FOAMING (2/2) FOAMS

Mk 9:20 *f* at the mouth.
Jude 13 *f* up their own shame; wandering

FOAMS (2/2) FOAMING

Mk 9:18 he *f* at the mouth, gnashes his
Lk 9:39 it convulses him so that he *f*

FODDER (5/5)

Judg 19:19 we have both straw and *f* for
19:21 and gave *f* to the donkeys.
Job 6: 5 Or does the ox low over its *f*?
24: 6 They gather their *f* in the
Isa 30:24 the ground Will eat cured *f*,

FOE (1/1) FOES

Ps 18:14 His arrows and scattered the *f*,

FOES (6/6) FOE

1 Ki 5: 3 until the LORD put his *f*
1 Chr 21:12 to be defeated by your *f* with
Ps 27: 2 up my flesh, My enemies and *f*,
30: 1 And have not let my *f* rejoice
89:23 I will beat down his *f* before
Isa 29: 5 the multitude of your *f* Shall

FOLD (10/9) FOLDED, FOLDING, FOLDS

Neh 5:13 Then I shook out the *f* of my
Isa 65:10 Sharon shall be a *f* of flocks,
Jer 25:30 roar mightily against His *f*.
Ezek 34:14 and their *f* shall be on the
34:14 shall lie down in a good *f* and
Mic 2:12 together like sheep of the *f*,
Hab 3:17 flock may be cut off from the *f*,
Hag 2:12 one carries holy meat in the *f*
Jn 10:16 I have which are not of this *f*;
Heb 1:12 Like a cloak You will *f*

FOLDED (1/1) FOLD

Jn 20: 7 but *f* together in a place by

FOLDING (5/4) FOLD

1 Ki 6:34 two panels comprised one *f*
6:34 panels comprised the other *f*
Prov 6:10 A little *f* of the hands to
24:33 A little *f* of the hands to
Ezek 41:24 two *f* panels: two panels for

FOLDS (8/8) FOLD

Num 32:24 for your little ones and *f* for
32:36 and *f* for sheep.
2 Chr 32:28 and *f* for flocks.
Job 41:23 The *f* of his flesh are joined
Ps 50: 9 Nor goats out of your *f*.
Eccl 4: 5 The fool *f* his hands And
Jer 23: 3 and bring them back to their *f*;
Zeph 2: 6 shelters for shepherds and *f*

FOLIAGE (2/2)

Prov 11:28 righteous will flourish like *f*.
Ezek 19:11 in her height amid the dense *f*.

FOLK (1/1)

Prov 30:26 rock badgers are a feeble *f*,

FOLLOW (95/92) FOLLOWED, FOLLOWERS, FOLLOWING, FOLLOWS

Gen 24: 5 woman will not be willing to *f*
24: 8 the woman is not willing to *f*
24:39 Perhaps the woman will not *f*
44: 4 *f* the men; and when you
Ex 11: 8 and all the people who *f* you!'
14:17 and they shall *f* them. So I
23: 2 You shall not *f* a crowd to do
Num 15:39 and that you may not *f* the
Deut 8:19 and *f* other gods, and serve
12:30 that you are not ensnared to *f*
16:20 You shall *f* what is altogether
18: 9 you shall not learn to *f* the
29:19 even though I *f* the dictates of
Judg 3:28 *F* me, for the LORD has
8: 5 of bread to the people who *f*
9: 3 their heart was inclined to *f*
1 Sam 17:13 sons of Jesse had gone to *f*
25:27 be given to the young men who *f*
30:21 so weary that they could not *f*
2 Sam 17: 9 among the people who *f* Absalom.
20:11 whoever is for David—*f* Joab!"
1 Ki 11: 6 and did not fully *f* the LORD,
18:21 *f* Him; but if Baal, follow
18:21 *f* him." But the people
19:20 and then I will *f* you."
20:10 for each of the people who *f*
2 Ki 6:19 *F* me, and I will bring you to
9:18 Turn around and *f* me." So the
9:19 Turn around and *f* me."
17:34 nor do they *f* their statutes or
23: 3 to *f* the LORD and to keep His
2 Chr 34:31 to *f* the LORD, and to keep His
Job 21:33 Everyone shall *f* him, As
Ps 23: 6 goodness and mercy shall *f* me
38:20 because I *f* what is good.
45:14 her companions who *f* her, shall
94:15 the upright in heart will *f* it.
119:150 They draw near who *f* after
Song 1: 8 *F* in the footsteps of the
Isa 5:11 That they may *f* intoxicating
51: 1 you who *f* after righteousness,
Jer 3:17 No more shall they *f* the
13:10 who *f* the dictates of their
42:16 which you were afraid shall *f*
Ezek 11:21 as for those whose hearts *f*
13: 3 who *f* their own spirit and have
29:16 iniquity when they turned to *f*
Dan 11:43 and Ethiopians shall *f* at
Mt 4:19 *F* Me, and I will make you
8:19 I will *f* You wherever You go."
8:22 *F* Me, and let the dead bury
9: 9 *F* Me." So he arose and followed
10:38 does not take his cross and *f*
16:24 take up his cross, and *f* Me.
19:21 and come, *f* Me."
Mk 1:17 *F* Me, and I will make you become
2:14 *F* Me." So he arose and followed
5:37 And He permitted no one to *f* Him
8:34 take up his cross, and *f* Me.
9:38 we saw someone who does not *f*
9:38 him because he does not *f* us.
10:21 take up the cross, and *f* Me."
14:13 a pitcher of water; *f* him.
16:17 And these signs will *f* those who
Lk 5:27 And He said to him, "*F* Me."
9:23 up his cross daily, and *f* Me.
9:49 him because he does not *f* with
9:57 I will *f* You wherever You go."
9:59 *F* Me." But he said, "Lord, let
9:61 I will *f* You, but let me first
17:23 Do not go after them or *f*
18:22 and come, *f* Me."
22:10 *f* him into the house which he
Jn 1:43 and said to him, "*F* Me."
10: 4 and the sheep *f* him, for they
10: 5 Yet they will by no means *f* a
10:27 I know them, and they *f* Me.
12:26 let him *f* Me; and where I am,
13:36 Where I am going you cannot *f* Me
13:36 but you shall *f* Me afterward."
13:37 why can I not *f* You now? I will
21:19 He said to him, "*F* Me."
21:22 is that to you? You *f* Me."
Acts 3:24 from Samuel and those who *f*,
12: 8 Put on your garment and *f* me."
2 Th 3: 7 know how you ought to *f* us,
3: 9 an example of how you should *f*
1 Tim 5:24 but those of some men *f* later.
Heb 13: 7 of God to you, whose faith *f*,
1 Pe 1:11 and the glories that would *f*.
2:21 that you should *f* His steps:
2 Pe 1:16 For we did not *f* cunningly
2: 2 And many will *f* their
Rev 14: 4 These are the ones who *f* the
14:13 and their works *f* them."

FOLLOWED (117/115) FOLLOW

Gen 24:61 they rode on the camels and *f*
32:19 and all who *f* the droves,
Num 14:24 spirit in him and has *f* Me
16:25 and the elders of Israel *f* him.
32:11 because they have not wholly *f*
32:12 for they have wholly *f* the
Deut 1:36 because he wholly *f* the LORD.'
4: 3 among you all the men who *f*
Josh 6: 8 of the covenant of the LORD *f*
14: 8 but I wholly *f* the LORD my
14: 9 because you have wholly *f* the
14:14 because he wholly *f* the LORD
Judg 2:12 and they *f* other gods from
9: 4 and they *f* him.
9:49 cut down his own bough and *f*
13:11 So Manoah arose and *f* his wife.
1 Sam 13: 7 and all the people *f* him
14:22 they also *f* hard after them in
17:14 And the three oldest *f* Saul.
25:42 and she *f* the messengers of
31: 2 Then the Philistines *f* hard
2 Sam 1: 6 the chariots and horsemen *f*
2:10 Only the house of Judah *f*
3:31 And King David *f* the coffin.
11: 8 gift of food from the king *f*
15:18 six hundred men who had *f* him
17:23 saw that his advice was not *f*,
20: 2 and *f* Sheba the son of Bichri.
1 Ki 1: 7 and they *f* and helped Adonijah.
12:20 There was none who *f* the house
14: 8 kept My commandments and who *f*
16:21 half of the people *f* Tibni the
16:21 and half *f* Omri.
16:22 But the people who *f* Omri
16:22 over the people who *f* Tibni
18:18 of the LORD and have *f* the
19:21 Then he arose and *f* Elijah, and
20:19 the city with the army which *f*
2 Ki 3: 9 nor for the animals that *f*
4:30 So he arose and *f* her.
13: 2 and *f* the sins of Jeroboam the
17:15 they *f* idols, became idolaters,
17:40 but they *f* their former
1 Chr 10: 2 Then the Philistines *f* hard

F

2 Chr 22: 5 He also *f* their advice, and went
Neh 4:23 nor the men of the guard who *f*
Ps 68:25 the players on instruments *f*
Jer 2: 5 Have *f* idols, And have become
7:24 but *f* the counsels and the
11: 8 but everyone *f* the dictates of
Ezek 10:11 but *f* in the direction the head
Am 2: 4 Lies which their fathers *f*.
7:15 Then the LORD took me as I *f*
Hab 3: 5 And fever *f* at His feet.
Mt 4:20 left their nets and *f* Him.
4:22 and their father, and *f* Him.
4:25 Great multitudes *f* Him—from
8: 1 great multitudes *f* Him.
8:10 and said to those who *f*,
8:23 His disciples *f* Him.
9: 9 So he arose and *f* Him.
9:19 So Jesus arose and *f* him, and so
9:27 two blind men *f* Him, crying out
12:15 And great multitudes *f* Him, and
14:13 they *f* Him on foot from the
19: 2 And great multitudes *f* Him, and
19:27 we have left all and *f* You.
19:28 you who have *f* Me will also sit
20:29 a great multitude *f* Him.
20:34 and they *f* Him.
21: 9 who went before and those who *f*
26:58 But Peter *f* Him at a distance to
27:55 And many women who *f* Jesus from
27:62 which *f* the Day of Preparation,
Mk 1:18 left their nets and *f* Him.
2:14 So he arose and *f* Him.
2:15 and they *f* Him.
3: 7 great multitude from Galilee *f*
5:24 and a great multitude *f* Him and
6: 1 and His disciples *f* Him.
10:28 we have left all and *f* You."
10:32 And as they *f* they were afraid.
10:52 he received his sight and *f*
11: 9 who went before and those who *f*
14:51 Now a certain young man *f* Him,
14:54 But Peter *f* Him at a distance,
15:41 who also *f* Him and ministered to
Lk 5:11 they forsook all and *f* Him.
5:28 he left all, rose up, and *f* Him.
7: 9 and said to the crowd that *f*
9:11 they *f* Him; and He received
18:28 we have left all and *f* You."
18:43 and *f* Him, glorifying God.
22:39 and His disciples also *f* Him.
22:54 But Peter *f* at a distance.
23:27 multitude of the people *f* Him,
23:49 and the women who *f* Him from
23:55 come with Him from Galilee *f*
Jn 1:37 and they *f* Jesus.
1:40 and *f* Him, was Andrew, Simon
6: 2 Then a great multitude *f* Him,
11:31 *f* her, saying, "She is going
18:15 And Simon Peter *f* Jesus, and so
Acts 12: 9 So he went out and *f* him, and
13:43 Jews and devout proselytes *f*
16:17 This girl *f* Paul and us, and
21:36 the multitude of the people *f*
1 Cor 10: 4 of that spiritual Rock that *f*
1 Tim 4: 6 which you have carefully *f*.
5:10 if she has diligently *f* every
2 Tim 3:10 But you have carefully *f* my
Rev 6: 8 and Hades *f* with him. And power
8: 7 And hail and fire *f*,
13: 3 all the world marveled and *f*
14: 8 And another angel *f*,
14: 9 Then a third angel *f* them,
19:14 *f* Him on white horses.

FOLLOWERS (3/3) FOLLOW

2 Sam 2:15 *f* of Ishbosheth the son of
1 Th 1: 6 And you became *f* of us and of
1 Pe 3:13 will harm you if you become *f*

FOLLOWING (45/45) FOLLOW

Gen 41:31 land because of the famine *f*,
Num 32:15 For if you turn away from *f* Him,
Deut 7: 4 turn your sons away from *f* Me,
Josh 22:16 to turn away this day from *f*
22:18 must turn away this day from *f*
22:23 an altar to turn from *f* the
22:29 and turn from *f* the LORD this
Judg 2:19 by *f* other gods, to serve them
4:14 Tabor with ten thousand men *f*
Ruth 1:16 Or to turn back from *f* after
1 Sam 12:14 over you will continue *f* the
12:20 yet do not turn aside from *f*
15:11 for he has turned back from *f*
24: 1 when Saul had returned from *f*
2 Sam 2:19 hand or to the left from *f*
2:21 would not turn aside from *f*
2:22 Turn aside from *f* me. Why should
7: 8 from *f* the sheep, to be ruler
1 Ki 9: 6 or your sons at all turn from *f*
21:26 he behaved very abominably in *f*
2 Ki 17:21 Jeroboam drove Israel from *f*
18: 6 he did not depart from *f* Him,
1 Chr 17: 7 from *f* the sheep, to be ruler
2 Chr 25:27 Amaziah turned away from *f* the
34:33 they did not depart from *f* the
35: 4 *f* the written instruction of
Ezra 10:18 had taken pagan wives the *f*
Ps 48:13 tell it to the generation *f*.
78:71 From *f* the ewes that had young
109:13 And in the generation *f* let
Zeph 1: 6 who have turned back from *f*
Lk 13:33 today, tomorrow, and the day *f*;
Jn 1:38 Jesus turned, and seeing them *f*,
1:43 The *f* day Jesus wanted to go to
6:22 On the *f* day, when the people
20: 6 *f* him, and went into the tomb;
21:20 the disciple whom Jesus loved *f*,
Acts 10:24 And the *f* day they entered
20:15 The *f* day we arrived at Samos
21: 1 the *f* day to Rhodes, and from
21:18 On the *f* day Paul went in with
23:11 But the *f* night the Lord stood
23:25 He wrote a letter in the *f*
Phil 3:17 join in *f* my example, and note
2 Pe 2:15 *f* the way of Balaam the son of

FOLLOWS (14/14) FOLLOW

Ex 21:22 prematurely, yet no harm *f*,
21:23 "But if any harm *f*,
2 Ki 11:15 slay with the sword whoever *f*
2 Chr 23:14 slay with the sword whoever *f*
Ps 63: 8 My soul *f* close behind You;
Prov 12:11 But he who *f* frivolity is
15: 9 But He loves him who *f*
21:21 He who *f* righteousness and
28:19 But he who *f* frivolity will
Isa 1:23 And *f* after rewards. They do
Jer 16:12 each one *f* the dictates of his
17:16 from being a shepherd who *f*
Mt 1:18 birth of Jesus Christ was as *f*:
Jn 8:12 He who *f* Me shall not walk in

FOLLY (28/28) FOOL

1 Sam 25:25 and *f* is with him. But I, your
Job 35:15 Nor taken much notice of *f*,
42: 8 with you according to your *f*;
Ps 85: 8 let them not turn back to *f*.
Prov 5:23 And in the greatness of his *f*
13:16 But a fool lays open his *f*.
14: 8 But the *f* of fools is deceit.
14:18 The simple inherit *f*,
14:24 the foolishness of fools is *f*.
14:29 he who is impulsive exalts *f*.
15:21 *F* is joy to him who is
16:22 the correction of fools is *f*.
17:12 Rather than a fool in his *f*.
18:13 It is *f* and shame to him.
26: 4 a fool according to his *f*,
26: 5 a fool according to his *f*,
26:11 So a fool repeats his *f*.
Eccl 1:17 and to know madness and *f*.
2: 3 and how to lay hold on *f*,
2:12 wisdom and madness and *f*;
2:13 I saw that wisdom excels *f* As
7:25 To know the wickedness of *f*,
10: 1 So does a little *f* to one
10: 6 *F* is set in great dignity,
Isa 9:17 And every mouth speaks *f*.
Jer 23:13 And I have seen *f* in the
2 Cor 11: 1 bear with me in a little *f*—
2 Tim 3: 9 for their *f* will be manifest to

FOOD (212/196) FOODS

Gen 1:29 to you it shall be for *f*.
1:30 given every green herb for *f*
2: 9 to the sight and good for *f*.
3: 6 that the tree was good for *f*,
6:21 take for yourself of all *f*
6:21 and it shall be *f* for you and
9: 3 thing that lives shall be *f*
24:33 *F* was set before him to eat,
27: 4 "And make me savory *f*,
27: 7 me game and make savory *f* for
27: 9 and I will make savory *f* from
27:14 and his mother made savory *f*,
27:17 Then she gave the savory *f* and
27:31 He also had made savory *f*,
41:35 And let them gather all the *f* of
41:35 and let them keep *f* in the
41:36 Then that *f* shall be as a
41:48 So he gathered up all the *f* of
41:48 and laid up the *f* in the
41:48 he laid up in every city the *f*
42: 7 the land of Canaan to buy *f*.
42:10 servants have come to buy *f*.
42:33 take *f* for the famine of your
43: 2 "Go back, buy us a little *f*.
43: 4 we will go down and buy you *f*.
43:20 down the first time to buy *f*;
43:22 money in our hands to buy *f*.
43:32 the Egyptians could not eat *f*
44: 1 "Fill the men's sacks with *f*,
44:25 'Go back and buy us a little *f*.
45:23 and *f* for his father for the
47:24 for the field and for your *f*,
47:24 of your households and as *f*
Ex 21:10 he shall not diminish her *f*,
Lev 3:11 burn them on the altar as *f*,
3:16 burn them on the altar as *f*,
11:34 any edible *f* upon which water
19:23 all kinds of trees for *f*,
22: 7 because it is his *f*.
22:11 born in his house may eat his *f*.
22:13 she may eat her father's *f*;
25: 6 of the land shall be *f* for you:
25: 7 its produce shall be for *f*.
25:37 nor lend him your *f* at a
Num 21: 5 For there is no *f* and no
28: 2 My *f* for My offerings made by
28:24 manner you shall offer the *f*
Deut 2: 6 You shall buy *f* from them with
2:28 You shall sell me *f* for money,
10:18 giving him *f* and clothing.
20:19 tree of the field is man's *f*.
20:20 you know are not trees for *f*
23:19 interest on money or *f* or
28:26 Your carcasses shall be *f* for
Josh 5:12 but they ate the *f* of the land
Judg 13:16 Me, I will not eat your *f*.
1 Sam 14:24 is the man who eats any *f*
14:24 So none of the people tasted *f*.
14:28 Cursed is the man who eats *f*
20:34 and ate no *f* the second day of
28:20 for he had eaten no *f* all day
2 Sam 3:35 came to persuade David to eat *f*
9:10 your master's son may have *f*
11: 8 and a gift of *f* from the king
12: 3 It ate of his own *f* and drank
12:17 nor did he eat *f* with them.
12:20 they set *f* before him, and he
12:21 child died, you arose and ate *f*.
13: 5 sister Tamar come and give me *f*,
13: 5 and prepare the *f* in my sight,
13: 7 and prepare *f* for him."
13:10 Bring the *f* into the bedroom,
1 Ki 4: 7 who provided *f* for the king and
4:27 provided *f* for King Solomon and
5: 9 fulfill my desire by giving *f*
5:11 thousand kors of wheat as *f*
10: 5 the *f* on his table, the seating
11:18 apportioned *f* for him, and gave
19: 8 went in the strength of that *f*
21: 4 his face, and would eat no *f*.
21: 5 so sullen that you eat no *f*?
21: 7 over Israel! Arise, eat *f*,
2 Ki 4: 8 she persuaded him to eat some *f*.
4: 8 turn in there to eat some *f*.
6:22 Set *f* and water before them,
25: 3 in the city that there was no *f*
1 Chr 12:40 were bringing *f* on donkeys and
2 Chr 9: 4 the *f* on his table, the seating
11:11 in them, and stores of *f*,
28:15 gave them *f* and drink, and
Ezra 3: 7 and the carpenters, and *f*,
Job 6: 6 Can flavorless *f* be eaten
6: 7 They are as loathsome *f* to
12:11 And the mouth taste its *f*?
20:14 Yet his *f* in his stomach turns
23:12 More than my necessary *f*.
24: 5 to their work, searching for *f*.
24: 5 The wilderness yields *f* for
30: 4 broom tree roots for their *f*.
33:20 And his soul succulent *f*.
34: 3 As the palate tastes *f*.
36:31 He gives *f* in abundance.
38:41 Who provides *f* for the raven,
38:41 And wander about for lack of *f*?
40:20 Surely the mountains yield *f*
42:11 came to him and ate *f* with him
Ps 42: 3 My tears have been my *f* day and
44:11 up like sheep intended for *f*,
59:15 They wander up and down for *f*,
69:21 also gave me gall for my *f*,
74:14 And gave him as *f* to the
78:18 heart By asking for the *f* of
78:25 Men ate angels' *f*;
78:25 He sent them *f* to the full.
78:30 But while their *f* was still
79: 2 They have given as *f* for the
104:14 That he may bring forth *f* from
104:21 And seek their *f* from God.
104:27 You may give them their *f* in
107:18 soul abhorred all manner of *f*,
111: 5 He has given *f* to those who
136:25 Who gives *f* to all flesh,
145:15 And You give them their *f* in
146: 7 Who gives *f* to the hungry.
147: 9 He gives to the beast its *f*,
Prov 6: 8 And gathers her *f* in the
13:23 Much *f* is in the fallow
23: 3 For they are deceptive *f*.
27:27 enough goats' milk for your *f*,
27:27 For the *f* of your household,
28: 3 driving rain which leaves no *f*.
30: 8 Feed me with the *f* allotted to
30:22 fool when he is filled with *f*,
30:25 Yet they prepare their *f* in
31:14 She brings her *f* from afar.
31:15 And provides *f* for her
Isa 3: 7 For in my house is neither *f*
4: 1 We will eat our own *f* and wear
62: 8 longer give your grain As *f*
65:25 dust shall be the serpent's *f*.
Jer 7:33 of this people will be *f* for
31: 5 and eat them as ordinary *f*.
44:17 For then we had plenty of *f*,
52: 6 in the city that there was no *f*
Lam 1:11 given their valuables for *f* to
1:19 While they sought *f* To
4:10 They became *f* for them In the
Ezek 4:10 And your *f* which you eat shall
16:19 Also My *f* which I gave you—the
16:49 had pride, fullness of *f*,
29: 5 I have given you as *f* To the
34: 5 and they became *f* for all the
34: 8 and My flock became *f* for every
34:10 that they may no longer be *f*
44: 7 house—and when you offered My *f*,
47:12 all kinds of trees used for *f*;
47:12 Their fruit will be for *f*,
48:18 and its produce shall be *f* for

Dan 1:10 who has appointed your *f* and
4:12 And in it was *f* for all.
4:21 in which was *f* for all, under
10: 3 I ate no pleasant *f*,
Joel 1:16 Is not the *f* cut off before our
Hab 1:16 is sumptuous And their *f*
3:17 And the fields yield no *f*;
Hag 2:12 or stew, wine or oil, or any *f*,
Mal 1: 7 You offer defiled *f* on My
1:12 And its fruit, its *f*,
3:10 That there may be *f* in My
Mt 3: 4 and his *f* was locusts and wild
6:25 Is not life more than *f* and the
10:10 for a worker is worthy of his *f*.
14:15 villages and buy themselves *f*.
24:45 to give them *f* in due season?
25:35 I was hungry and you gave Me *f*;
25:42 was hungry and you gave Me no *f*;
Lk 3:11 who has none; and he who has *f*,
9:13 unless we go and buy *f* for all
12:23 "Life is more than *f*,
12:42 give them their portion of *f*
24:41 Have you any *f* here?"
Jn 4: 8 away into the city to buy *f*.
4:32 I have *f* to eat of which you do
4:34 My *f* is to do the will of Him
6:27 Do not labor for the *f* which
6:27 but for the *f* which endures to
6:55 For My flesh is *f* indeed, and My
21: 5 "Children, have you any *f*?
Acts 2:46 they ate their *f* with gladness
9:19 So when he had received *f*,
12:20 country was supplied with *f* by
14:17 filling our hearts with *f* and
16:34 he set *f* before them; and he
27:21 after long abstinence from *f*,
27:33 implored them all to take *f*,
27:33 waited and continued without *f*,
27:36 and also took *f* themselves.
Rom 14:15 is grieved because of your *f*,
14:15 Do not destroy with your *f* the
14:20 work of God for the sake of *f*.
1 Cor 3: 2 with milk and not with solid *f*;
8: 8 But *f* does not commend us to
8:13 if *f* makes my brother stumble,
10: 3 all ate the same spiritual *f*,
10:30 am I evil spoken of for the *f*
2 Cor 9:10 to the sower, and bread for *f*,
Col 2:16 So let no one judge you in *f* or
1 Tim 6: 8 And having *f* and clothing, with
Heb 5:12 to need milk and not solid *f*.
5:14 But solid *f* belongs to those who
12:16 who for one morsel of *f* sold
Jas 2:15 naked and destitute of daily *f*,

FOODS (6/5) FOOD

Mk 7:19 thus purifying all *f*?
1 Cor 6:13 *F* for the stomach and the
6:13 stomach and the stomach for *f*,
1 Tim 4: 3 commanding to abstain from *f*
Heb 9:10 concerned only with *f* and
13: 9 not with *f* which have not

FOOL (68/65) FOLLY, FOOL'S, FOOLISH, FOOLS

1 Sam 26:21 Indeed I have played the *f* and
2 Sam 3:33 Should Abner die as a *f* dies?
Ps 14: 1 The *f* has said in his heart,
49:10 Likewise the *f* and the
53: 1 The *f* has said in his heart,
92: 6 Nor does a *f* understand this.
Prov 7:22 Or as a *f* to the correction of
10: 8 But a prating *f* will fall.
10:10 But a prating *f* will fall.
10:18 whoever spreads slander is a *f*.
10:23 do evil is like sport to a *f*,
11:29 And the *f* will be servant to
12:15 The way of a *f* is right in his
13:16 But a *f* lays open his folly.
14: 3 In the mouth of a *f* is a rod
14:16 But a *f* rages and is
15: 5 A *f* despises his father's
15: 7 But the heart of the *f* does
17: 7 speech is not becoming to a *f*,
17:10 Than a hundred blows on a *f*.
17:12 Rather than a *f* in his folly.
17:16 is there in the hand of a *f*
17:21 And the father of a *f* has no
17:24 But the eyes of a *f* are on
17:28 Even a *f* is counted wise when
18: 2 A *f* has no delight in
19: 1 in his lips, and is a *f*.
19:10 Luxury is not fitting for a *f*,
20: 3 Since any *f* can start a
23: 9 not speak in the hearing of a *f*,
24: 7 Wisdom is too lofty for a *f*;
26: 1 honor is not fitting for a *f*.
26: 4 Do not answer a *f* according to
26: 5 Answer a *f* according to his
26: 6 a message by the hand of a *f*
26: 8 Is he who gives honor to a *f*.
26:10 formed everything Gives the *f*
26:11 So a *f* repeats his folly.
26:12 There is more hope for a *f*
27:22 Though you grind a *f* in a
28:26 trusts in his own heart is a *f*,
29: 9 Whether the *f* rages or
29:11 A *f* vents all his feelings,
29:20 There is more hope for a *f*
30:22 A *f* when he is filled with
Eccl 2:14 But the *f* walks in darkness.
2:15 "As it happens to the *f*,
2:16 of the wise than of the *f*
2:16 a wise man die? As the *f*!
2:19 whether he will be wise or a *f*?
4: 5 The *f* folds his hands And
6: 8 has the wise man than the *f*?
7: 6 So is the laughter of the *f*.
10: 3 Even when a *f* walks along the
10: 3 shows everyone that he is a *f*.
10:12 But the lips of a *f* shall
10:14 A *f* also multiplies words.
Isa 35: 8 walks the road, although a *f*,
Jer 17:11 And at his end he will be a *f*.
Hos 9: 7 The prophet is a *f*,
Mt 5:22 You *f*!' shall be in danger of
Lk 12:20 *F*! This night your soul will be
1 Cor 3:18 let him become a *f* that he may
2 Cor 11:16 again, let no one think me a *f*.
11:16 at least receive me as a *f*,
11:23 of Christ?—I speak as a *f*—
12: 6 to boast, I will not be a *f*;
12:11 I have become a *f* in boasting;

FOOL'S (7/7) FOOL

Prov 12:16 A *f* wrath is known at once,
18: 6 A *f* lips enter into contention,
18: 7 A *f* mouth is his destruction,
26: 3 And a rod for the *f* back.
27: 3 But a *f* wrath is heavier than
Eccl 5: 3 And a *f* voice is known by
10: 2 But a *f* heart at his left.

FOOLISH (54/53) FOOL, FOOLISHLY, FOOLISHNESS

Deut 32: 6 O *f* and unwise people? Is He
32:21 moved Me to anger by their *f*
32:21 will move them to anger by a *f*
Job 2:10 You speak as one of the *f* women
5: 2 For wrath kills a *f* man, And
5: 3 I have seen the *f* taking root,
Ps 39: 8 make me the reproach of the *f*.
49:13 is the way of those who are *f*,
73:22 I was so *f* and ignorant;
74:18 And that a *f* people has
74:22 Remember how the *f* man
Prov 9:13 A *f* woman is clamorous;
10: 1 But a *f* son is the grief of
10:14 But the mouth of the *f* is
14: 1 But the *f* pulls it down with
14: 7 Go from the presence of a *f*
15:20 But a *f* man despises his
17:25 A *f* son is a grief to his
19:13 A *f* son is the ruin of his
21:20 But a *f* man squanders it.
29: 9 a wise man contends with a *f*
30:32 If you have been *f* in exalting
Eccl 4:13 wise youth Than an old and *f*
7:17 not be overly wicked, Nor be *f*:
Isa 19:11 wise counselors give *f* counsel.
32: 5 The *f* person will no longer be
32: 6 For the *f* person will speak
Jer 4:22 "For My people are *f*,
5: 4 these are poor. They are *f*;
5:21 O *f* people, Without
10: 8 altogether dull-hearted and *f*;
Ezek 13: 3 Woe to the *f* prophets, who
Zech 11:15 yourself the implements of a *f*
Mt 7:26 will be like a *f* man who built
25: 2 were wise, and five were *f*.
25: 3 Those who were *f* took their
25: 8 And the *f* said to the wise,
Lk 11:40 *F* ones! Did not He who made the
24:25 O *f* ones, and slow of heart to
Rom 1:21 and their *f* hearts were
2:20 an instructor of the *f*,
10:19 move you to anger by a *f*
1 Cor 1:20 Has not God made *f* the wisdom
1:27 But God has chosen the *f* things
15:36 *F* one, what you sow is not made
Gal 3: 1 O *f* Galatians! Who has bewitched
3: 3 Are you so *f*? Having begun
Eph 5: 4 nor *f* talking, nor coarse
1 Tim 6: 9 and into many *f* and harmful
2 Tim 2:23 But avoid *f* and ignorant
Titus 3: 3 we ourselves were also once *f*,
3: 9 But avoid *f* disputes,
Jas 2:20 O *f* man, that faith without
1 Pe 2:15 to silence the ignorance of *f*

FOOLISHLY (9/9) FOOLISH

Gen 31:28 Now you have done *f* in so
Num 12:11 in which we have done *f* and in
1 Sam 13:13 said to Saul, "You have done *f*.
2 Sam 24:10 servant, for I have done very *f*.
1 Chr 21: 8 servant, for I have done very *f*.
2 Chr 16: 9 to Him. In this you have done *f*;
Prov 14:17 A quick-tempered man acts *f*,
2 Cor 11:17 to the Lord, but as it were, *f*,
11:21 anyone is bold—I speak *f*—

FOOLISHNESS (23/23) FOOLISH

2 Sam 15:31 counsel of Ahithophel into *f*!
Ps 38: 5 and festering Because of my *f*.
69: 5 O God, You know my *f*;
Prov 9: 6 Forsake *f* and live, And go in
12:23 the heart of fools proclaims *f*.
14:24 But the *f* of fools is folly.
15: 2 mouth of fools pours forth *f*.
15:14 the mouth of fools feeds on *f*.
19: 3 The *f* of a man twists his way,
22:15 *F* is bound up in the heart of
24: 9 The devising of *f* is sin,
27:22 Yet his *f* will not depart
Eccl 7:25 Even of *f* and madness.
10:13 words of his mouth begin with *f*,
Isa 32: 6 the foolish person will speak *f*,
44:25 And makes their knowledge *f*;
Mk 7:22 evil eye, blasphemy, pride, *f*.
1 Cor 1:18 the message of the cross is *f*
1:21 it pleased God through the *f* of
1:23 block and to the Greeks *f*,
1:25 Because the *f* of God is wiser
2:14 for they are *f* to him; nor can
3:19 the wisdom of this world is *f*

FOOLS (40/40) FOOL

2 Sam 13:13 you would be like one of the *f*
Job 12:17 And makes *f* of the judges.
30: 8 They were sons of *f*,
Ps 94: 8 among the people; And you *f*,
107:17 *F*, because of their
Prov 1: 7 But *f* despise wisdom and
1:22 And *f* hate knowledge.
1:32 And the complacency of *f* will
3:35 shame shall be the legacy of *f*.
8: 5 understand prudence, And you *f*,
10:21 But *f* die for lack of wisdom.
12:23 But the heart of *f* proclaims
13:19 it is an abomination to *f* to
13:20 But the companion of *f* will be
14: 8 But the folly of *f* is deceit.
14: 9 *F* mock at sin, But among the
14:24 But the foolishness of *f* is
14:33 what is in the heart of *f* is
15: 2 But the mouth of *f* pours forth
15:14 But the mouth of *f* feeds on
16:22 But the correction of *f* is
19:29 beatings for the backs of *f*.
26: 7 a proverb in the mouth of *f*.
26: 9 a proverb in the mouth of *f*.
Eccl 5: 1 than to give the sacrifice of *f*,
5: 4 For He has no pleasure in *f*.
7: 4 But the heart of *f* is in the
7: 5 for a man to hear the song of *f*.
7: 9 anger rests in the bosom of *f*.
9:17 than the shout of a ruler of *f*.
10:15 The labor of *f* wearies them,
Isa 19:11 the princes of Zoan are *f*;
19:13 princes of Zoan have become *f*;
Jer 50:36 soothsayers, and they will be *f*.
Mt 23:17 *F* and blind! For which is
23:19 *F* and blind! For which is
Rom 1:22 to be wise, they became *f*,
1 Cor 4:10 We are *f* for Christ's sake, but
2 Cor 11:19 For you put up with *f* gladly,
Eph 5:15 not as *f* but as wise,

FOOT (93/89) FEET, FOOTSTEP, FOOTSTOOL, FOUR-FOOTED

Gen 8: 9 place for the sole of her *f*,
41:44 no man may lift his hand or *f*
Ex 12:37 six hundred thousand men on *f*,
19:17 and they stood at the *f* of the
21:24 hand for hand, *f* for
21:24 hand for hand, foot for *f*,
24: 4 and built an altar at the *f* of
29:20 on the big toe of their right *f*,
32:19 hands and broke them at the *f*
Lev 8:23 on the big toe of his right *f*.
11:26 any animal which divides the *f*,
13:12 sore, from his head to his *f*,
14:14 on the big toe of his right *f*.
14:17 on the big toe of his right *f*,
14:25 on the big toe of his right *f*.
14:28 on the big toe of his right *f*,
21:19 a man who has a broken *f* or
Num 11:21 six hundred thousand men on *f*;
20:19 let me only pass through on *f*,
22:25 the wall and crushed Balaam's *f*
Deut 2:28 only let me pass through on *f*,
4:11 came near and stood at the *f*
8: 4 nor did your *f* swell these
11:10 your seed and watered it by *f*,
11:24 on which the sole of your *f*
19:21 hand for hand, *f* for foot.
19:21 hand for hand, foot for *f*.
25: 9 remove his sandal from his *f*,
28:35 and from the sole of your *f* to
28:56 to set the sole of her *f* on
28:65 nor shall the sole of your *f*
32:35 Their *f* shall slip in due
33:24 And let him dip his *f* in oil.
Josh 1: 3 place that the sole of your *f*
5:15 "Take your sandal off your *f*,
14: 9 Surely the land where your *f* has
Judg 4:15 his chariot and fled away on *f*.
4:17 Sisera had fled away on *f* to
20: 2 four hundred thousand *f*
1 Sam 4:10 of Israel thirty thousand *f*
15: 4 two hundred thousand *f* soldiers
2 Sam 2:18 And Asahel was as fleet of *f*
8: 4 and twenty thousand *f* soldiers.
10: 6 twenty thousand *f* soldiers; and
14:25 From the sole of his *f* to the
21:20 hand and six toes on each *f*,
1 Ki 20:29 killed one hundred thousand *f*
2 Ki 13: 7 and ten thousand *f* soldiers;

1 Chr 18: 4 and twenty thousand *f* soldiers.
19:18 and forty thousand *f* soldiers
20: 6 hand and six on each *f*;
2 Chr 33: 8 I will not again remove the *f*
Job 2: 7 boils from the sole of his *f*
23:11 My *f* has held fast to His
31: 5 Or if my *f* has hastened to
39:15 She forgets that a *f* may crush
Ps 9:15 their own *f* is caught.
26:12 My *f* stands in an even place;
36:11 Let not the *f* of pride come
38:16 when my *f* slips, they exalt
66: 6 went through the river on *f*.
68:23 That your *f* may crush them in
91:12 Lest you dash your *f* against a
94:18 'My *f* slips," Your mercy,
121: 3 He will not allow your *f* to be
Prov 1:15 Keep your *f* from their path;
3:23 And your *f* will not stumble.
3:26 And will keep your *f* from
4:27 Remove your *f* from evil.
25:17 Seldom set *f* in your neighbor's
25:19 Is like a bad tooth and a *f*
Isa 1: 6 From the sole of the *f* even to
26: 6 The *f* shall tread it down—The
58:13 If you turn away your *f* from
Jer 2:25 Withhold your *f* from being
Ezek 29:11 Neither *f* of man shall pass
29:11 shall pass through it nor *f* of
32:13 The *f* of man shall muddy them
Dan 8:13 the host to be trampled under *f*?
Am 2:15 The swift of *f* shall not
Mt 4: 6 Lest you dash your *f*
14:13 they followed Him on *f* from the
18: 8 If your hand or *f* causes you to
22:13 servants, 'Bind him hand and *f*,
Mk 6:33 knew Him and ran there on *f*
9:45 And if your *f* causes you to sin,
Lk 4:11 Lest you dash your *f*
Jn 11:44 died came out bound hand and *f*
Acts 7: 5 not even enough to set his *f*
20:13 intending himself to go on *f*.
1 Cor 12:15 If the *f* should say, "Because I
Rev 10: 2 And he set his right *f* on the
10: 2 on the sea and his left *f* on

FOOTMEN (1/1)

Jer 12: 5 "If you have run with the *f*,

FOOTSTEP (1/1) FOOT, FOOTSTEPS

Deut 2: 5 land, no, not so much as one *f*,

FOOTSTEPS (6/6) FOOTSTEP

1 Ki 14: 6 heard the sound of her *f* as
Ps 17: 5 That my *f* may not slip.
77:19 And Your *f* were not known.
85:13 And shall make His *f* our
89:51 they have reproached the *f* of
Song 1: 8 Follow in the *f* of the flock,

FOOTSTOOL (16/16) FOOT

1 Chr 28: 2 and for the *f* of our God, and
2 Chr 9:18 with a *f* of gold, which were
Ps 99: 5 our God, And worship at His *f*—
110: 1 I make Your enemies Your *f*.
132: 7 Let us worship at His *f*.
Isa 66: 1 My throne, And earth is My *f*.
Lam 2: 1 And did not remember His *f* In
Mt 5:35 by the earth, for it is His *f*;
22:44 make Your enemies Your *f*'
Mk 12:36 make Your enemies Your *f*.
Lk 20:43 make Your enemies Your *f*.
Acts 2:35 make Your enemies Your *f*.
7:49 And earth is My *f*.
Heb 1:13 make Your enemies Your *f*'
10:13 till His enemies are made His *f*.
Jas 2: 3 there," or, "Sit here at my *f*,

FOR (8893/7172) See APPENDIX

FORAGE (1/1)

Hos 4:16 Now the LORD will let them *f*

FORBAD (KJV) See FORBADE, FORBIDDEN, PREVENT

FORBADE (2/2)

Mk 9:38 and we *f* him because he does
Lk 9:49 and we *f* him because he does

FORBEARANCE (3/3)

Prov 25:15 By long *f* a ruler is persuaded,
Rom 2: 4 the riches of His goodness, *f*,
3:25 because in His *f* God had passed

FORBID (13/13) FORBIDDEN, FORBIDDING

Num 11:28 'Moses my lord, *f* them!"
1 Sam 24: 6 The LORD *f* that I should do
26:11 The LORD *f* that I should
1 Ki 21: 3 The LORD *f* that I should give
Mt 19:14 and do not *f* them; for of such
Mk 9:39 Do not *f* him, for no one who
10:14 and do not *f* them; for of such
Lk 9:50 Do not *f* him, for he who is not
18:16 and do not *f* them; for of such
Acts 10:47 Can anyone *f* water, that these
24:23 and told him not to *f* any of
1 Cor 14:39 and do not *f* to speak with
Gal 6:14 But God *f* that I should boast

FORBIDDEN (4/4) FORBID

Lev 5:17 of these things which are *f* to
Deut 2:37 the LORD our God had *f* us.
4:23 which the LORD your God has *f*
Acts 16: 6 they were *f* by the Holy Spirit

FORBIDDING (4/4) FORBID

Lk 23: 2 and *f* to pay taxes to Caesar,
Acts 28:31 all confidence, no one *f* him.
1 Th 2:16 *f* us to speak to the Gentiles
1 Tim 4: 3 *f* to marry, and commanding to

FORBIDS (1/1)

3 Jn 10 and *f* those who wish to,

FORCE (20/19) FORCED, FORCES, FORCING

Gen 31:31 your daughters from me by *f*.
1 Sam 2:16 if not, I will take it by *f*.
2 Sam 13:12 do not *f* me, for no such thing
1 Ki 4: 6 son of Abda, over the labor *f*.
5:13 Solomon raised up a labor *f*
5:13 and the labor *f* was thirty
5:14 was in charge of the labor *f*.
9:15 is the reason for the labor *f*
11:28 officer over all the labor *f*
2 Chr 28:10 And now you propose to *f* the
Ezra 4:23 and by *f* of arms made them
Job 30:18 By great *f* my garment is
Jer 18:21 out their blood By the *f* of
Ezek 34: 4 but with *f* and cruelty you have
Dan 11:22 With the *f* of a flood they shall
Ob 7 in your confederacy Shall *f*
Mt 11:12 and the violent take it by *f*.
Jn 6:15 to come and take Him by *f* to
Acts 23:10 to go down and take him by *f*
Heb 9:17 For a testament is in *f* after

FORCED (17/17) FORCE

Ex 5:13 And the taskmasters *f* them to
Josh 16:10 to this day and have become *f*
17:13 they put the Canaanites to *f*
Judg 1:34 And the Amorites *f* the children
2 Sam 13:14 he *f* her and lay with her.
13:22 because he had *f* his sister
13:32 from the day that he *f* his
1 Ki 8:31 and is *f* to take an oath, and
9:21 from these Solomon raised *f*
9:22 of Israel Solomon made no *f*
1 Chr 8: 6 and who *f* them to move to
8: 7 and Gera who *f* them to move.
2 Chr 6:22 and is *f* to take an oath, and
8: 8 from these Solomon raised *f*
Job 24: 4 the poor of the land are *f* to
Prov 12:24 the lazy man will be put to *f*
Isa 31: 8 his young men shall become *f*

FORCEFUL (1/1)

Job 6:25 How *f* are right words!

FORCES (32/32) FORCE

Gen 14:15 He divided his *f* against them by
Num 2: 3 those of the standard of the *f*
2: 9 to their armies of the *f* with
2:10 be the standard of the *f* with
2:16 to their armies of the *f* with
2:18 be the standard of the *f* with
2:24 to their armies of the *f* with
2:25 The standard of the *f* with Dan
2:31 who were numbered of the *f*
2:32 to their armies of the *f* were
Deut 22:25 and the man *f* her and lies with
1 Ki 20: 1 of Syria gathered all his *f*
1 Chr 20: 1 that Joab led out the armed *f*
2 Chr 32: 9 (but he and all the *f* with him
Esth 8:11 and annihilate all the *f* of any
Job 36:19 riches, Or all the mighty *f*,
Prov 11:21 Though they join *f*,
16: 5 Though they join *f*,
Isa 7: 2 Syria's *f* are deployed in
Jer 40:13 and all the captains of the *f*
41:11 and all the captains of the *f*
41:13 and all the captains of the *f*
41:16 and all the captains of the *f*
42: 1 Now all the captains of the *f*,
42: 8 all the captains of the *f* which
43: 4 all the captains of the *f*,
43: 5 and all the captains of the *f*
Dan 11: 6 some years they shall join *f*,
11:10 assemble a multitude of great *f*;
11:15 and the *f* of the South shall
11:31 And *f* shall be mustered by him,
Ob 11 strangers carried captive his *f*,

FORCING (3/3) FORCE

2 Sam 8: 2 *F* them down to the ground, he
Neh 5: 5 and indeed we are *f* our sons
Prov 30:33 So the *f* of wrath produces

FORD (1/1) FORDS

Gen 32:22 and crossed over the *f* of

FORDS (5/5) FORD

Josh 2: 7 road to the Jordan, to the *f*.
Judg 3:28 seized the *f* of the Jordan
12: 5 The Gileadites seized the *f* of
12: 6 take him and kill him at the *f*
Isa 16: 2 the daughters of Moab at the *f*

FORECAST (KJV) See DEVISE

FOREFATHERS (4/4) FATHERS

Jer 11:10 to the iniquities of their *f*
Dan 11:24 have not done, nor his *f*:
Acts 7:19 our people, and oppressed our *f*,
2 Tim 1: 3 as my *f* did, as without

FOREFRONT (2/2)

Ex 26: 9 the sixth curtain at the *f* of
2 Sam 11:15 Set Uriah in the *f* of the

FOREGO (1/1)

Neh 10:31 and we would *f* the seventh

FOREHEAD (16/12) FOREHEADS

Ex 28:38 "So it shall be on Aaron's *f*,
28:38 and it shall always be on his *f*,
Lev 13:41 hair has fallen from his *f*,
13:41 forehead, he is bald on the *f*,
13:42 is on the bald head or bald *f*
13:42 on his bald head or his bald *f*.
13:43 his bald head or on his bald *f*,
1 Sam 17:49 struck the Philistine in his *f*,
17:49 that the stone sank into his *f*,
2 Chr 26:19 leprosy broke out on his *f*,
26:20 at him, and there, on his *f*,
Jer 3: 3 You have had a harlot's *f*;
Ezek 3: 8 and your *f* strong against their
3: 9 than flint, I have made your *f*;
Rev 14: 9 receives his mark on his *f* or
17: 5 And on her *f* a name was

FOREHEADS (8/8) FOREHEAD

Ezek 3: 8 forehead strong against their *f*.
9: 4 and put a mark on the *f* of the
Rev 7: 3 servants of our God on their *f*.
9: 4 have the seal of God on their *f*.
13:16 their right hand or on their *f*,
14: 1 name written on their *f*.
20: 4 received his mark on their *f*
22: 4 His name shall be on their *f*.

FOREIGN (30/29) FOREIGNER

Gen 35: 2 Put away the *f* gods that are
35: 4 So they gave Jacob all the *f*
Ex 2:22 I have been a stranger in a *f*
18: 3 I have been a stranger in a *f*
21: 8 no right to sell her to a *f*
Deut 32:12 And there was no *f* god with
32:16 Him to jealousy with *f* gods;
Josh 24:20 forsake the LORD and serve *f*
24:23 put away the *f* gods which are
Judg 10:16 So they put away the *f* gods from
1 Sam 7: 3 then put away the *f* gods and
1 Ki 11: 1 But King Solomon loved many *f*
11: 8 he did likewise for all his *f*
2 Chr 14: 3 he removed the altars of the *f*
33:15 He took away the *f* gods and the
Ps 44:20 stretched out our hands to a *f*
81: 9 There shall be no *f* god among
81: 9 Nor shall you worship any *f*
137: 4 sing the LORD's song In a *f*
Isa 17:10 pleasant plants And set out *f*
43:12 And there was no *f* god
Jer 5:19 have forsaken Me and served *f*
8:19 With *f* idols?"
Dan 11:39 strongest fortresses with a *f*
Zeph 1: 8 all such as are clothed with *f*
Mal 2:11 has married the daughter of a *f*
Acts 7: 6 descendants would dwell in a *f*
17:18 seems to be a proclaimer of *f*
26:11 I persecuted them even to *f*
Heb 11: 9 the land of promise as in a *f*

FOREIGNER (26/24) FOREIGN, FOREIGNERS

Gen 17:12 or bought with money from any *f*
17:27 or bought with money from a *f*,
23: 4 I am a *f* and a visitor among
Ex 12:43 No *f* shall eat it.
Deut 14:21 it, or you may sell it to a *f*;
15: 3 'Of a *f* you may require it;
17:15 you may not set a *f* over you,
23:20 To a *f* you may charge interest,
29:22 and the *f* who comes from a far
Ruth 2:10 notice of me, since I am a *f*?
2 Sam 15:19 For you are a *f* and also an
1 Ki 8:41 "Moreover, concerning a *f*,
8:43 to all for which the *f* calls
2 Chr 6:32 "Moreover, concerning a *f*,
6:33 to all for which the *f* calls
Prov 5:10 labors go to the house of a *f*;
Eccl 6: 2 but a *f* consumes it. This is

Isa 56: 3 Do not let the son of the *f*
56: 6 Also the sons of the *f* Who
61: 5 And the sons of the *f* Shall
62: 8 And the sons of the *f* shall
Ezek 44: 9 says the Lord GOD: "No *f*,
44: 9 including any *f* who is among
Lk 17:18 give glory to God except this *f*?
1 Cor 14:11 I shall be a *f* to him who
14:11 he who speaks will be a *f* to

FOREIGNER'S (1/1)

Lev 22:25 Nor from a *f* hand shall you

FOREIGNERS (18/18) FOREIGNER

Deut 31:16 harlot with the gods of the *f*
Judg 19:12 aside here into a city of *f*,
2 Sam 22:45 The *f* submit to me; As soon as
22:46 The *f* fade away, And come
Neh 9: 2 separated themselves from all *f*;
Ps 18:44 The *f* submit to me.
18:45 The *f* fade away, And come
144: 7 waters, From the hand of *f*,
144:11 deliver me from the hand of *f*,
Isa 2: 6 pleased with the children of *f*.
25: 2 A palace of *f* to be a city no
60:10 The sons of *f* shall build up
Jer 30: 8 *F* shall no more enslave them.
Lam 5: 2 to aliens, And our houses to *f*.
Ezek 44: 7 "When you brought in *f*,
Ob 11 When *f* entered his gates And
Acts 17:21 For all the Athenians and the *f*
Eph 2:19 are no longer strangers and *f*,

FOREKNEW (2/2) FOREKNOWLEDGE

Rom 8:29 For whom He *f*,
11: 2 cast away His people whom He *f*.

FOREKNOW (KJV) See FOREKNEW

FOREKNOWLEDGE (2/2) FOREKNEW

Acts 2:23 by the determined purpose and *f*
1 Pe 1: 2 elect according to the *f* of God

FOREMEN (1/1)

2 Chr 34:10 put it in the hand of the *f*

FOREMOST (3/3)

Ezra 9: 2 leaders and rulers has been *f*
Jer 49:35 The *f* of their might.
Acts 16:12 which is the *f* city of that

FOREORDAINED (1/1)

1 Pe 1:20 He indeed was *f* before the

FOREPART (KJV) See FRONT, INNER, PROW

FORERUNNER (1/1)

Heb 6:20 where the *f* has entered for us,

FORESAW (1/1) FORESEES

Acts 2:25 I *f* the LORD always before

FORESEEING (2/2) FORESEES

Acts 2:31 *f* this, spoke concerning the
Gal 3: 8 *f* that God would justify the

FORESEES (2/2) FORESAW, FORESEEING

Prov 22: 3 A prudent man *f* evil and hides
27:12 A prudent man *f* evil and

FORESEETH (KJV) See FORESEES

FORESHIP (KJV) See PROW

FORESIGHT (1/1)

Acts 24: 2 to this nation by your *f*,

FORESKIN (6/6) FORESKINS

Gen 17:14 in the flesh of his *f*,
17:24 in the flesh of his *f*.
17:25 in the flesh of his *f*.
Ex 4:25 a sharp stone and cut off the *f*
Lev 12: 3 eighth day the flesh of his *f*
Deut 10:16 Therefore circumcise the *f* of

FORESKINS (7/7) FORESKIN

Gen 17:11 in the flesh of your *f*,
17:23 the flesh of their *f* that very
Josh 5: 3 of Israel at the hill of the *f*.
1 Sam 18:25 any dowry but one hundred *f* of
18:27 And David brought their *f*,
2 Sam 3:14 to myself for a hundred *f* of
Jer 4: 4 And take away the *f* of your

FOREST (43/43) FORESTS

Josh 17:15 then go up to the *f* country
1 Sam 14:25 people of the land came to a *f*;
22: 5 departed and went into the *f*
23:15 the Wilderness of Ziph in a *f*.
1 Ki 7: 2 also built the House of the *F*
10:17 put them in the House of the *F*
10:21 vessels of the House of the *F*
2 Ki 19:23 borders, To its fruitful *f*.
2 Chr 9:16 put them in the House of the *F*
9:20 vessels of the House of the *F*
Neh 2: 8 the keeper of the king's *f*,
Ps 50:10 For every beast of the *f* is
104:20 which all the beasts of the *f*
Isa 9:18 kindle in the thickets of the *f*;
10:18 consume the glory of his *f* and
10:19 the rest of the trees of his *f*
10:34 cut down the thickets of the *f*
21:13 In the *f* in Arabia you will
22: 8 the armor of the House of the *F*;
29:17 field be esteemed as a *f*?
32:15 field is counted as a *f*.
32:19 hail comes down on the *f*,
37:24 height, To its fruitful *f*.
44:14 among the trees of the *f*.
44:23 singing, you mountains, O *f*,
56: 9 All you beasts in the *f*.
Jer 5: 6 Therefore a lion from the *f*
10: 3 one cuts a tree from the *f*,
12: 8 is to Me like a lion in the *f*;
21:14 will kindle a fire in its *f*,
26:18 Like the bare hills of the *f*.
46:23 "They shall cut down her *f*,
Ezek 15: 2 is among the trees of the *f*?
15: 6 vine among the trees of the *f*,
20:46 and prophesy against the *f*
20:47 and say to the *f* of the South,
31: 3 fine branches that shaded the *f*,
Hos 2:12 So I will make them a *f*,
Am 3: 4 Will a lion roar in the *f*,
Mic 3:12 Like the bare hills of the *f*.
5: 8 lion among the beasts of the *f*,
Zech 11: 2 For the thick *f* has come down.
Jas 3: 5 See how great a *f* a little fire

FORESTS (4/4) FOREST

Num 13:20 and whether there are *f* there
2 Chr 27: 4 and in the *f* he built
Ps 29: 9 And strips the *f* bare; And in
Ezek 39:10 nor cut down any from the *f*,

FORETELL (1/1) FORETOLD

2 Cor 13: 2 and *f* as if I were present the

FORETOLD (3/3) FORETELL

Acts 3:18 But those things which God *f* by
3:24 have also *f* these days.
7:52 And they killed those who *f* the

FOREVER (393/382) FOREVERMORE

Gen 3:22 and eat, and live *f*"—
6: 3 shall not strive with man *f*,
13:15 to you and your descendants *f*.
43: 9 then let me bear the blame *f*.
44:32 the blame before my father *f*.
Ex 3:15 me to you. This is My name *f*,
12:24 for you and your sons *f*.
14:13 you shall see again no more *f*.
15:18 The LORD shall reign *f* and
19: 9 with you, and believe you *f*.
21: 6 and he shall serve him *f*.
27:21 It shall be a statute *f* to
28:43 It shall be a statute *f* to
29:28 and his sons by a statute *f*.
30:21 And it shall be a statute *f* to
31:17 Me and the children of Israel *f*;
32:13 and they shall inherit it *f*.
Lev 6:18 It shall be a statute *f* in
6:22 It is a statute *f* to the
7:34 of Israel by a statute *f*.
7:36 by a statute *f* throughout
10: 9 It shall be a statute *f*
10:15 sons' with you, by a statute *f*,
16:29 This shall be a statute *f* for
16:31 your souls. It is a statute *f*.
17: 7 This shall be a statute *f* for
23:14 it shall be a statute *f*
23:21 it shall be a statute *f* in
23:31 it shall be a statute *f*
23:41 It shall be a statute *f* in
24: 3 it shall be a statute *f* in
Num 10: 8 be to you as an ordinance *f*
15:15 an ordinance *f* throughout your
18: 8 your sons, as an ordinance *f*.
18:11 with you, as an ordinance *f*.
18:19 with you as an ordinance *f*;
18:19 it is a covenant of salt *f*
18:23 it shall be a statute *f*,
19:10 It shall be a statute *f* to the
Deut 5:29 them and with their children *f*!
12:28 and your children after you *f*,
13:16 your God. It shall be a heap *f*;
15:17 and he shall be your servant *f*.
18: 5 the LORD, him and his sons *f*.
23: 3 the assembly of the LORD *f*,
23: 6 prosperity all your days *f*.
28:46 and on your descendants *f*.
29:29 to us and to our children *f*,
32:40 And say, "As I live *f*,
Josh 4: 7 to the children of Israel *f*.
4:24 may fear the LORD your God *f*.
8:28 burned Ai and made it a heap *f*,
14: 9 and your children's *f*,
1 Sam 1:22 the LORD and remain there *f*.
2:30 father would walk before Me *f*.
2:32 be an old man in your house *f*.
2:35 shall walk before My anointed *f*.
3:13 that I will judge his house *f*
3:14 for by sacrifice or offering *f*.
13:13 your kingdom over Israel *f*.
20:15 your kindness from my house *f*,
20:23 LORD be between you and me *f*.
20:42 and my descendants, *f*.
27:12 he will be my servant *f*.
28: 2 you one of my chief guardians *f*.
2 Sam 2:26 "Shall the sword devour *f*?
3:28 guiltless before the LORD *f*
7:13 the throne of his kingdom *f*.
7:16 kingdom shall be established *f*
7:16 throne shall be established *f*.
7:24 Israel Your very own people *f*;
7:25 establish it *f* and do as You
7:26 let Your name be magnified *f*,
7:29 that it may continue *f* before
7:29 of Your servant be blessed *f*.
1 Ki 1:31 Let my lord King David live *f*!"
2:33 the head of his descendants *f*.
2:33 there shall be peace *f* from the
2:45 established before the LORD *f*.
8:13 a place for You to dwell in *f*.
9: 3 built to put My name there *f*,
9: 5 of your kingdom over Israel *f*,
10: 9 the LORD has loved Israel *f*,
11:39 because of this, but not *f*.
12: 7 they will be your servants *f*.
2 Ki 5:27 to you and your descendants *f*.
8:19 a lamp to him and his sons *f*.
17:37 shall be careful to observe *f*;
21: 7 of Israel, I will put My name *f*;
1 Chr 15: 2 and to minister before Him *f*.
16:15 Remember His covenant *f*,
16:34 For His mercy endures *f*.
16:41 because His mercy endures *f*;
17:12 I will establish his throne *f*.
17:14 in My house and in My kingdom *f*;
17:14 throne shall be established *f*.
17:22 Israel Your very own people *f*;
17:23 let it be established *f*,
17:24 Your name may be magnified *f*,
17:27 it may continue before You *f*;
17:27 and it shall be blessed *f*.
22:10 of his kingdom over Israel *f*.
23:13 set apart, he and his sons *f*,
23:13 give the blessing in His name *f*.
23:25 they may dwell in Jerusalem *f*
28: 4 father to be king over Israel *f*,
28: 7 I will establish his kingdom *f*,
28: 8 for your children after you *f*.
28: 9 Him, He will cast you off *f*.
29:10 our Father, *f* and ever.
29:18 keep this *f* in the intent of
2 Chr 2: 4 This is an ordinance *f* to
5:13 good, For His mercy endures *f*,
6: 2 a place for You to dwell in *f*.
7: 3 good, For His mercy endures *f*.
7: 6 "For His mercy endures *f*,
7:16 that My name may be there *f*;
9: 8 Israel, to establish them *f*,
10: 7 they will be your servants *f*.
13: 5 dominion over Israel to David *f*,
20: 7 of Abraham Your friend *f*?
20:21 For His mercy endures *f*.
21: 7 a lamp to him and to his sons *f*.
30: 8 which He has sanctified *f*,
33: 4 Jerusalem shall My name be *f*.
33: 7 of Israel, I will put My name *f*;
Ezra 3:11 For His mercy endures *f*
9:12 inheritance to your children *f*.
Neh 2: 3 May the king live *f*! Why should
9: 5 bless the LORD your God *F*
Job 4:20 till evening; They perish *f*,
7:16 my life; I would not live *f*.
14:20 You prevail *f* against him, and
19:24 With an iron pen and lead, *f*!
20: 7 Yet he will perish *f* like his
23: 7 And I would be delivered *f*
36: 7 For He has seated them *f*,
41: 4 you take him as a servant *f*?
Ps 9: 5 have blotted out their name *f*
9: 6 destructions are finished *f*!
9: 7 But the LORD shall endure *f*;
9:18 of the poor shall not perish *f*.
10:16 The LORD is King *f* and ever;
12: 7 them from this generation *f*.
13: 1 O LORD? Will You forget me *f*?
19: 9 the LORD is clean, enduring *f*;
21: 4 Length of days *f* and ever.
21: 6 have made him most blessed *f*;
22:26 Let your heart live *f*!
23: 6 in the house of the LORD *F*.
28: 9 them also, And bear them up *f*.
29:10 And the LORD sits as King *f*.
30:12 I will give thanks to You *f*.
33:11 counsel of the LORD stands *f*,
37:18 their inheritance shall be *f*.
37:28 saints; They are preserved *f*,
37:29 the land, And dwell in it *f*.
41:12 And set me before Your face *f*.
44: 8 And praise Your name *f*.

44:23 Arise! Do not cast us off *f*.
45: 2 God has blessed You *f*.
45: 6 is *f* and ever; A scepter of
45:17 the people shall praise You *f*
48: 8 God: God will establish it *f*.
48:14 Our God *f* and ever; He will
49: 8 costly, And it shall cease *f*—
49:11 their houses will last *f*,
52: 5 shall likewise destroy you *f*;
52: 8 I trust in the mercy of God *f*
52: 9 I will praise You *f*,
61: 4 will abide in Your tabernacle *f*;
61: 7 He shall abide before God *f*.
61: 8 will sing praise to Your name *f*,
66: 7 He rules by His power *f*;
68:16 the LORD will dwell in it *f*.
72:17 His name shall endure *f*;
72:19 be His glorious name *f*!
73:26 of my heart and my portion *f*.
74: 1 why have You cast us off *f*?
74:10 the enemy blaspheme Your name *f*?
74:19 forget the life of Your poor *f*.
75: 9 But I will declare *f*,
77: 7 Will the Lord cast off *f*?
77: 8 Has His mercy ceased *f*?
78:69 which He has established *f*.
79: 5 Will You be angry *f*?
79:13 Will give You thanks *f*;
81:15 But their fate would endure *f*.
83:17 be confounded and dismayed *f*;
85: 5 Will You be angry with us *f*?
89: 1 of the mercies of the LORD *f*;
89: 2 "Mercy shall be built up *f*;
89: 4 'Your seed I will establish *f*,
89:28 My mercy I will keep for him *f*,
89:29 also I will make to endure *f*,
89:36 His seed shall endure *f*,
89:37 It shall be established *f* like
89:46 Will You hide Yourself *f*?
92: 7 that they may be destroyed *f*.
93: 5 adorns Your house, O LORD, *f*.
102:12 You, O LORD, shall endure *f*,
103: 9 Nor will He keep His anger *f*.
104: 5 that it should not be moved *f*,
104:31 the glory of the LORD endure *f*;
105: 8 He remembers His covenant *f*,
106: 1 For His mercy endures *f*.
107: 1 For His mercy endures *f*.
110: 4 You are a priest *f* According
111: 3 His righteousness endures *f*.
111: 8 They stand fast *f* and ever,
111: 9 has commanded His covenant *f*:
111:10 His praise endures *f*.
112: 3 his righteousness endures *f*.
112: 9 His righteousness endures *f*;
117: 2 truth of the LORD endures *f*.
118: 1 For His mercy endures *f*.
118: 2 say, "His mercy endures *f*.
118: 3 say, "His mercy endures *f*.
118: 4 say, "His mercy endures *f*.
118:29 For His mercy endures *f*.
119:44 law continually, *F* and ever.
119:89 *F*, O LORD, Your word is
119:111 I have taken as a heritage *f*,
119:112 to perform Your statutes *F*,
119:152 that You have founded them *f*.
119:160 righteous judgments endures *f*.
125: 1 cannot be moved, but abides *f*.
125: 2 From this time forth and *f*.
131: 3 From this time forth and *f*.
132:14 "This is My resting place *f*;
135:13 Your name, O LORD, endures *f*,
136: 1 For His mercy endures *f*.
136: 2 For His mercy endures *f*.
136: 3 For His mercy endures *f*:
136: 4 For His mercy endures *f*;
136: 5 For His mercy endures *f*;
136: 6 For His mercy endures *f*;
136: 7 For His mercy endures *f*—
136: 8 day, For His mercy endures *f*;
136: 9 For His mercy endures *f*.
136:10 For His mercy endures *f*;
136:11 them, For His mercy endures *f*;
136:12 arm, For His mercy endures *f*;
136:13 two, For His mercy endures *f*;
136:14 it, For His mercy endures *f*;
136:15 Sea, For His mercy endures *f*;
136:16 For His mercy endures *f*.
136:17 For His mercy endures *f*;
136:18 For His mercy endures *f*—
136:19 For His mercy endures *f*;
136:20 For His mercy endures *f*—
136:21 For His mercy endures *f*;
136:22 For His mercy endures *f*.
136:23 For His mercy endures *f*;
136:24 For His mercy endures *f*;
136:25 For His mercy endures *f*.
136:26 For His mercy endures *f*.
138: 8 mercy, O LORD, endures *f*;
145: 1 And I will bless Your name *f*
145: 2 And I will praise Your name *f*
145:21 shall bless His holy name *F*
146: 6 is in them; Who keeps truth *f*,
146:10 The LORD shall reign *f*—
148: 6 He also established them *f* and
Prov 12:19 lip shall be established *f*,
27:24 For riches are not *f*,
29:14 throne will be established *f*.
Eccl 1: 4 But the earth abides *f*.
2:16 of the wise than of the fool *f*,
3:14 God does, It shall be *f*.
Isa 9: 7 From that time forward, even *f*.
25: 8 He will swallow up death *f*,
26: 4 Trust in the LORD *f*,
28:28 he does not thresh it *f*,
30: 8 for time to come, *F* and ever:
32:14 and towers will become lairs *f*,
32:17 quietness and assurance *f*.
34:10 Its smoke shall ascend *f*.
34:10 No one shall pass through it *f*
34:17 line. They shall possess it *f*;
40: 8 the word of our God stands *f*.
45:17 not be ashamed or disgraced *F*
47: 7 you said, 'I shall be a lady *f*,
51: 6 But My salvation will be *f*,
51: 8 But My righteousness will be *f*,
57:16 For I will not contend *f*,
60:21 They shall inherit the land *f*,
64: 9 LORD, Nor remember iniquity *f*;
65:18 But be glad and rejoice *f* in
Jer 3: 5 Will He remain angry *f*?
3:12 'I will not remain angry *f*.
7: 7 that I gave to your fathers *f*
17: 4 in My anger which shall burn *f*.
17:25 and this city shall remain *f*.
25: 5 to you and your fathers *f* and
31:36 being a nation before Me *f*.
31:40 up or thrown down anymore *f*.
32:39 way, that they may fear Me *f*,
33:11 For His mercy endures
35: 6 no wine, you nor your sons, *f*.
35:19 lack a man to stand before Me *f*.
49:33 for jackals, a desolation *f*;
50:39 shall be inhabited no more *f*,
51:26 But you shall be desolate *f*,
51:62 but it shall be desolate *f*.
Lam 3:31 the Lord will not cast off *f*.
5:19 You, O LORD, remain *f*;
5:20 Why do You forget us *f*,
Ezek 27:36 a horror, and be no more *f*.
28:19 And shall be no more *f*.
37:25 their children's children, *f*;
37:25 David shall be their prince *f*.
43: 7 of the children of Israel *f*.
43: 9 I will dwell in their midst *f*.
Dan 2: 4 live *f*! Tell your servants the
2:20 Blessed be the name of God *f* and
2:44 kingdoms, and it shall stand *f*.
3: 9 'O king, live *f*!
4:34 and honored Him who lives *f*:
5:10 live *f*! Do not let your
6: 6 'King Darius, live *f*!
6:21 'O king, live *f*!
6:26 living God, And steadfast *f*;
7:18 and possess the kingdom *f*,
7:18 even *f* and ever.'
7:26 To consume and destroy it *f*.
12: 3 Like the stars *f* and ever.
12: 7 and swore by Him who lives *f*,
Hos 2:19 "I will betroth you to Me *f*;
Joel 3:20 But Judah shall abide *f*,
Am 1:11 And he kept his wrath *f*.
Ob 10 And you shall be cut off *f*.
Jon 2: 6 its bars closed behind me *f*;
Mic 2: 9 You have taken away My glory *f*.
4: 5 name of the LORD our God *F*
4: 7 Mount Zion From now on, even *f*.
7:18 He does not retain His anger *f*,
Zech 1: 5 the prophets, do they live *f*?
Mal 1: 4 LORD will have indignation *f*.
Mt 6:13 and the power and the glory *f*.
Lk 1:33 reign over the house of Jacob *f*,
1:55 To Abraham and to his seed *f*.
Jn 6:51 of this bread, he will live *f*;
6:58 who eats this bread will live *f*.
8:35 does not abide in the house *f*,
8:35 forever, but a son abides *f*.
12:34 law that the Christ remains *f*;
14:16 that He may abide with you *f*—
Rom 1:25 the Creator, who is blessed *f*.
11:36 all things, to whom be glory *f*.
16:27 glory through Jesus Christ *f*.
2 Cor 9: 9 righteousness endures *f*.
11:31 Jesus Christ, who is blessed *f*,
Gal 1: 5 to whom be glory *f* and ever.
Eph 3:21 *f* and ever. Amen.
Phil 4:20 our God and Father be glory *f*
1 Tim 1:17 be honor and glory *f* and ever.
2 Tim 4:18 To Him be glory *f* and ever.
Phm 1:15 that you might receive him *f*,
Heb 1: 8 is *f* and ever; A scepter
5: 6 You are a priest *f*
6:20 having become High Priest *f*
7:17 You are a priest *f*
7:21 You are a priest *f*
7:24 But He, because He continues *f*,
7:28 Son who has been perfected *f*.
10:12 one sacrifice for sins *f*,
10:14 one offering He has perfected *f*
13: 8 same yesterday, today, and *f*.
13:21 to whom be glory *f* and ever.
1 Pe 1:23 of God which lives and abides *f*,
1:25 of the LORD endures *f*.
4:11 the glory and the dominion *f*
5:11 the glory and the dominion *f*
2 Pe 2:17 the blackness of darkness *f*.
3:18 be the glory both now and *f*.
1 Jn 2:17 does the will of God abides *f*.
2 Jn 2 in us and will be with us *f*:
Jude 13 the blackness of darkness *f*.
25 and power, Both now and *f*.
Rev 1: 6 to Him be glory and dominion *f*
4: 9 who lives *f* and ever,
4:10 and worship Him who lives *f*
5:13 to the Lamb, *f* and ever!"
5:14 and worshiped Him who lives *f*
7:12 Be to our God *f* and ever.
10: 6 and swore by Him who lives *f* and
11:15 and He shall reign *f* and
14:11 of their torment ascends *f* and
15: 7 of the wrath of God who lives *f*
19: 3 Her smoke rises up *f*
20:10 be tormented day and night *f*
22: 5 And they shall reign *f* and

FOREVERMORE (18/18) FOREVER

2 Sam 22:51 To David and his descendants *f*.
Ps 16:11 right hand are pleasures *f*.
18:50 To David and his descendants *f*.
37:27 evil, and do good; And dwell *f*.
77: 8 Has His promise failed *f*?
86:12 And I will glorify Your name *f*.
89:52 Blessed be the LORD *f*! Amen
92: 8 But You, LORD, are on high *f*.
106:31 To all generations *f*.
113: 2 From this time forth and *f*!
115:18 From this time forth and *f*.
121: 8 this time forth, and even *f*.
132:12 shall sit upon your throne *f*.
133: 3 commanded the blessing—Life *f*.
Isa 59:21 LORD, "from this time and *f*.
Ezek 37:26 My sanctuary in their midst *f*.
37:28 sanctuary is in their midst *f*.
Rev 1:18 dead, and behold, I am alive *f*.

FOREWARN (1/1)

1 Sam 8: 9 you shall solemnly *f* them, and

FOREWARNED (1/1)

1 Th 4: 6 as we also *f* you and testified.

FORGAT (KJV) See FORGOT, FORGOTTEN

FORGAVE (8/8) FORGIVE

Ps 32: 5 And You *f* the iniquity of my
78:38 *f* their iniquity, And did not
Mt 18:27 and *f* him the debt.
18:32 You wicked servant! I *f* you all
Lk 7:42 he freely *f* them both. Tell Me,
7:43 I suppose the one whom he *f*
Eph 4:32 just as God in Christ *f* you.
Col 3:13 even as Christ *f* you, so you

FORGED (1/1)

Ps 119:69 The proud have *f* a lie against

FORGERS (1/1)

Job 13: 4 But you *f* of lies, You are

FORGET (60/57) FORGETFULNESS, FORGETS, FORGETTING, FORGOT, FORGOTTEN

Gen 41:51 For God has made me *f* all my
Deut 4: 9 lest you *f* the things your eyes
4:23 lest you *f* the covenant of the
4:31 nor *f* the covenant of your
6:12 lest you *f* the LORD who
8:11 Beware that you do not *f* the
8:14 and you *f* the LORD your God
8:19 if you by any means *f* the LORD
9: 7 Do not *f* how you provoked the
24:19 and *f* a sheaf in the field, you
25:19 under heaven. You shall not *f*.
1 Sam 1:11 and not *f* Your maidservant, but
2 Ki 17:38 made with you, you shall not *f*,
Job 8:13 So are the paths of all who *f*
9:27 I will *f* my complaint, I will
11:16 Because you would *f* your
24:20 The womb should *f* him,
Ps 9:12 He does not *f* the cry of the
9:17 And all the nations that *f*
10:12 lift up Your hand! Do not *f*
13: 1 Will You *f* me forever?
44:24 And *f* our affliction and our
45:10 *F* your own people also, and
50:22 you who *f* God, Lest I tear
59:11 not slay them, lest my people *f*;
74:19 to the wild beast! Do not *f*
74:23 Do not *f* the voice of Your
78: 7 And not *f* the works of God,
102: 4 So that I *f* to eat my bread.
103: 2 And *f* not all His benefits:
119:16 I will not *f* Your word.
119:83 Yet I do not *f* Your statutes.
119:93 I will never *f* Your precepts,
119:109 Yet I do not *f* Your law.
119:141 Yet I do not *f* Your precepts.
119:153 For I do not *f* Your law.
119:176 For I do not *f* Your
137: 5 If I *f* you, O Jerusalem, Let
137: 5 Let my right hand *f* its
Prov 3: 1 do not *f* my law, But let your
4: 5 Get understanding! Do not *f*,
31: 5 Lest they drink and *f* the law,
31: 7 Let him drink and *f* his
Isa 49:15 Can a woman *f* her nursing child,
49:15 of her womb? Surely they may *f*,
49:15 Yet I will not *f* you.

51:13 And you *f* the LORD your Maker,
54: 4 For you will *f* the shame of
65:11 Who *f* My holy mountain, Who
Jer 2:32 Can a virgin *f* her ornaments,
23:27 who try to make My people *f* My
23:39 will utterly *f* you and forsake
Lam 5:20 Why do You *f* us forever,
Hos 4: 6 I also will *f* your children.
Am 8: 7 Surely I will never *f* any of
Heb 6:10 For God is not unjust to *f* your
13: 2 Do not *f* to entertain strangers,
13:16 But do not *f* to do good and to
2 Pe 3: 5 For this they willfully *f*:
3: 8 do not *f* this one thing, that

FORGETFUL (1/1)

Jas 1:25 and is not a *f* hearer but a

FORGETFULNESS (1/1) FORGET

Ps 88:12 righteousness in the land of *f*?

FORGETS (4/4) FORGET

Gen 27:45 and he *f* what you have done to
Job 39:15 She *f* that a foot may crush
Prov 2:17 And *f* the covenant of her God.
Jas 1:24 and immediately *f* what kind of

FORGETTING (1/1) FORGET

Phil 3:13 *f* those things which are behind

FORGIVE (53/45) FORGAVE, FORGIVEN, FORGIVES, FORGIVING, UNFORGIVING

Gen 50:17 please *f* the trespass of your
50:17 *f* the trespass of the servants
Ex 10:17 please *f* my sin only this once,
32:32 if You will *f* their sin—but if
Josh 24:19 He will not *f* your
1 Sam 25:28 Please *f* the trespass of your
1 Ki 8:30 and when You hear, *f*.
8:34 and *f* the sin of Your people
8:36 and *f* the sin of Your servants,
8:39 Your dwelling place, and *f*,
8:50 and *f* Your people who have
2 Chr 6:21 place, and when You hear, *f*.
6:25 then hear from heaven and *f* the
6:27 and *f* the sin of Your servants,
6:30 Your dwelling place, and *f*,
6:39 and *f* Your people who have
7:14 and will *f* their sin and heal
Ps 25:18 And *f* all my sins.
86: 5 Lord, are good, and ready to *f*,
Isa 2: 9 Therefore do not *f* them.
Jer 31:34 For I will *f* their iniquity,
36: 3 that I may *f* their iniquity and
Dan 9:19 *f*! O Lord, listen and act!
Am 7: 2 that I said: "O Lord GOD, *f*,
Mt 6:12 And *f* us our debts, As we
6:12 As we *f* our debtors.
6:14 For if you *f* men their
6:14 heavenly Father will also *f*
6:15 But if you do not *f* men their
6:15 neither will your Father *f* your
9: 6 of Man has power on earth to *f*
18:21 and I *f* him? Up to seven
18:35 does not *f* his brother his
Mk 2: 7 Who can *f* sins but God alone?"
2:10 of Man has power on earth to *f*
11:25 *f* him, that your Father in
11:25 Father in heaven may also *f*
11:26 "But if you do not *f*,
11:26 will your Father in heaven *f*
Lk 5:21 Who can *f* sins but God alone?"
5:24 of Man has power on earth to *f*
6:37 you shall not be condemned. *F*,
11: 4 And *f* us our sins, For we also
11: 4 For we also *f* everyone who is
17: 3 and if he repents, *f* him.
17: 4 you shall *f* him."
23:34 *f* them, for they do not know
Jn 20:23 If you *f* the sins of any, they
2 Cor 2: 7 you ought rather to *f* and
2:10 Now whom you *f* anything, I also
2:10 you forgive anything, I also *f*.
12:13 *F* me this wrong!
1 Jn 1: 9 He is faithful and just to *f* us

FORGIVEN (43/38) FORGIVE, FORGIVENESS

Lev 4:20 and it shall be *f* them.
4:26 and it shall be *f* him.
4:31 and it shall be *f* him.
4:35 and it shall be *f* him.
5:10 and it shall be *f* him.
5:13 and it shall be *f* him.
5:16 and it shall be *f* him.
5:18 and it shall be *f* him.
6: 7 and he shall be *f* for any one
19:22 he has committed shall be *f*
Num 14:19 just as You have *f* this people,
15:25 and it shall be *f* them, for it
15:26 It shall be *f* the whole
15:28 and it shall be *f* him.
Ps 32: 1 he whose transgression is *f*,
85: 2 You have *f* the iniquity of Your
Isa 33:24 who dwell in it will be *f*
Mt 9: 2 your sins are *f* you."
9: 5 Your sins are *f* you,' or to
12:31 sin and blasphemy will be *f*
12:31 the Spirit will not be *f* men.
12:32 it will be *f* him; but whoever
12:32 it will not be *f* him, either in
Mk 2: 5 your sins are *f* you."
2: 9 Your sins are *f* you,' or to
3:28 all sins will be *f* the sons of
4:12 And their sins be *f*
Lk 5:20 your sins are *f* you."
5:23 Your sins are *f* you,' or to say,
6:37 Forgive, and you will be *f*.
7:47 sins, which are many, are *f*,
7:47 But to whom little is *f*,
7:48 said to her, "Your sins are *f*.
12:10 it will be *f* him; but to him
12:10 Holy Spirit, it will not be *f*.
Jn 20:23 they are *f* them; if you retain
Acts 8:22 thought of your heart may be *f*
Rom 4: 7 whose lawless deeds are *f*,
2 Cor 2:10 For if indeed I have *f*
2:10 I have *f* that one for your
Col 2:13 having *f* you all trespasses,
Jas 5:15 committed sins, he will be *f*.
1 Jn 2:12 Because your sins are *f* you

FORGIVENESS (8/8) FORGIVEN

Ps 130: 4 But there is *f* with You,
Dan 9: 9 our God belong mercy and *f*,
Mk 3:29 the Holy Spirit never has *f*,
Acts 5:31 repentance to Israel and *f* of
13:38 Man is preached to you the *f*
26:18 that they may receive *f* of sins
Eph 1: 7 the *f* of sins, according to the
Col 1:14 His blood, the *f* of sins.

FORGIVES (2/2) FORGIVE

Ps 103: 3 Who *f* all your iniquities,
Lk 7:49 Who is this who even *f* sins?"

FORGIVING (4/4) FORGIVE

Ex 34: 7 *f* iniquity and transgression
Num 14:18 *f* iniquity and transgression;
Eph 4:32 *f* one another, just as God in
Col 3:13 and *f* one another, if anyone

FORGOT (9/9) FORGET

Gen 40:23 remember Joseph, but *f* him.
Judg 3: 7 They *f* the LORD their God, and
1 Sam 12: 9 And when they *f* the LORD their
Ps 78:11 And *f* His works And His
106:13 They soon *f* His works;
106:21 They *f* God their Savior,
Jer 23:27 as their fathers *f* My name for
Hos 2:13 after her lovers; But Me she *f*,
13: 6 Therefore they *f* Me.

FORGOTTEN (45/45) FORGET

Gen 41:30 and all the plenty will be *f* in
Deut 26:13 nor have I *f* them.
31:21 for it will not be *f* in the
32:18 And have *f* the God who
Job 19:14 And my close friends have *f*
28: 4 In places *f* by feet They
Ps 9:18 the needy shall not always be *f*;
10:11 said in his heart, "God has *f*;
31:12 I am *f* like a dead man, out of
42: 9 Why have You *f* me? Why do I go
44:17 But we have not *f* You,
44:20 If we had *f* the name of our
77: 9 Has God *f* to be gracious?
119:61 But I have not *f* Your law.
119:139 Because my enemies have *f* Your
Eccl 2:16 all that now is will be *f* in
8:10 and they were *f* in the city
9: 5 For the memory of them is *f*.
Isa 17:10 Because you have *f* the God of
23:15 in that day that Tyre will be *f*
23:16 You *f* harlot; Make sweet
44:21 you will not be *f* by Me!
49:14 And my Lord has *f* me."
65:16 the former troubles are *f*,
Jer 2:32 Yet My people have *f* Me days
3:21 They have *f* the LORD their
13:25 Because you have *f* Me And
18:15 Because My people have *f* Me,
20:11 confusion will never be *f*.
23:40 shame, which shall not be *f*.
30:14 All your lovers have *f* you;
44: 9 Have you *f* the wickedness of
50: 5 covenant That will not be *f*.
50: 6 They have *f* their resting
Lam 2: 6 feasts and Sabbaths to be *f* in
3:17 I have *f* prosperity.
Ezek 22:12 and have *f* Me," says the Lord
23:35 Because you have *f* Me and cast
Hos 4: 6 Because you have *f* the law of
8:14 'For Israel has *f* his Maker,
Mt 16: 5 they had *f* to take bread.
Mk 8:14 Now the disciples had *f* to take
Lk 12: 6 And not one of them is *f* before
Heb 12: 5 And you have *f* the exhortation
2 Pe 1: 9 and has *f* that he was cleansed

FORK (1/1)

Ezek 21:21 at the *f* of the two roads,

FORKS (6/6)

Ex 27: 3 and its basins and its *f* and
38: 3 the shovels, the basins, the *f*,
Num 4:14 there—the firepans, the *f*,
1 Sam 13:21 plowshares, the mattocks, the *f*,
1 Chr 28:17 also pure gold for the *f*,
2 Chr 4:16 the pots, the shovels, the *f*—

FORM (33/33) FORMED, FORMS, UNFORMED

Gen 1: 2 The earth was without *f*,
29:17 but Rachel was beautiful of *f*
39: 6 Now Joseph was handsome in *f*
Num 12: 8 And he sees the *f* of the
Deut 4:12 of the words, but saw no *f*;
4:15 for you saw no *f* when the LORD
4:16 a carved image in the *f* of any
4:23 a carved image in the *f* of
4:25 make a carved image in the *f*
15: 2 And this is the *f* of the
1 Sam 28:14 said to her, "What is his *f*?
Job 4:16 A *f* was before my eyes;
38:14 It takes on *f* like clay under
Ps 83: 5 They *f* a confederacy against
Isa 44:10 Who would *f* a god or mold an
45: 7 I *f* the light and create
52:14 And His *f* more than the sons
53: 2 He has no *f* or comeliness;
Jer 4:23 and indeed it was without *f*,
Ezek 8: 3 He stretched out the *f* of a
10: 8 appeared to have the *f* of a
Dan 2:31 and its *f* was awesome.
3:25 and the *f* of the fourth is like
Mk 16:12 He appeared in another *f* to two
Lk 3:22 Spirit descended in bodily *f*
Jn 5:37 at any time, nor seen His *f*.
Rom 2:20 having the *f* of knowledge and
6:17 obeyed from the heart that *f*
1 Cor 7:31 For the *f* of this world is
Phil 2: 6 being in the *f* of God, did not
2: 7 taking the *f* of a bondservant,
1 Th 5:22 Abstain from every *f* of evil.
2 Tim 3: 5 having a *f* of godliness but

F

FORMATION (4/4)

1 Chr 12:35 Danites who could keep battle *f*,
12:36 to war, able to keep battle *f*,
2 Chr 13: 3 also drew up in battle *f*
Joel 2: 7 of war; Every one marches in *f*,

FORMED (38/35) FORM

Gen 2: 7 And the LORD God *f* man of the
2: 8 He put the man whom He had *f*.
2:19 of the ground the LORD God *f*
Judg 20:22 themselves and again *f* the
2 Ki 12:20 And his servants arose and *f* a
14:19 And they *f* a conspiracy against
19:25 From ancient times that I *f*
Job 1:17 The Chaldeans *f* three bands,
33: 6 I also have been *f* out of
Ps 90: 2 Or ever You had *f* the earth
94: 9 He who *f* the eye, shall He not
95: 5 And His hands *f* the dry land.
139:13 For You *f* my inward parts;
Prov 26:10 The great God who *f* everything
Isa 27:11 And He who *f* them will show
29:16 Or shall the thing *f* say of
29:16 thing formed say of him who *f*
37:26 From ancient times that I *f*
43: 1 And He who *f* you, O Israel:
43: 7 I have *f* him, yes, I have made
43:10 Before Me there was no God *f*,
43:21 This people I have *f* for
44: 2 the LORD who made you And *f*
44:21 I have *f* you, you are My
44:24 And He who *f* you from the
45:18 Who *f* the earth and made it,
45:18 Who *f* it to be inhabited:
49: 5 Who *f* Me from the womb to be
54:17 No weapon *f* against you shall
Jer 1: 5 Before I *f* you in the womb I
33: 2 the LORD who *f* it to establish
Ezek 16: 7 Your breasts were *f*,
Am 7: 1 He *f* locust swarms at the
Acts 23:13 were more than forty who had *f*
Rom 9:20 Will the thing *f* say to him who
9:20 thing formed say to him who *f*
Gal 4:19 birth again until Christ is *f*
1 Tim 2:13 For Adam was *f* first, then Eve.

FORMER (60/57) FORMERLY

Gen 40:13 in his hand according to the *f*
Num 6:12 but the *f* days shall be lost,
21:26 who had fought against the *f*
Deut 24: 4 then her *f* husband who divorced
Ruth 4: 7 this was the custom in *f*
2 Sam 20:18 They used to talk in *f* times,
2 Ki 17:34 they continue practicing the *f*
17:40 but they followed their *f*
2 Chr 3: 3 (by cubits according to the *f*
17: 3 because he walked in the *f* ways
Ezra 4:15 sedition within the city in *f*
4:19 was found that this city in *f*
5:15 of God be rebuilt on its *f*
Neh 5:15 But the *f* governors who were
Job 8: 8 of the *f* age, And consider the
Ps 79: 8 do not remember *f* iniquities

89:49 are Your *f* lovingkindnesses,
Eccl 1:11 There is no remembrance of *f*
7:10 Why were the *f* days better than
Isa 41:22 Let them show the *f* things,
41:26 And *f* times, that we may say,
42: 9 the *f* things have come to pass,
43: 9 And show us *f* things?
43:18 Do not remember the *f* things,
46: 9 Remember the *f* things of old,
48: 3 I have declared the *f* things
61: 4 They shall raise up the *f*
65: 7 I will measure their *f* work
65:16 Because the *f* troubles are
65:17 And the *f* shall not be
Jer 5:24 both the *f* and the latter, in
34: 5 the *f* kings who were before
36:28 and write on it all the *f* words
Ezek 16:55 return to their *f* state, and
16:55 her daughters return to their *f*
16:55 will return to your *f* state.
36:11 will make you inhabited as in *f*
38:17 he of whom I have spoken in *f*
Dan 11:13 a multitude greater than the *f*,
11:29 but it shall not be like the *f*
Hos 6: 3 Like the latter and *f* rain to
Joel 2:23 For He has given you the *f*
2:23 The *f* rain, And the latter
Mic 4: 8 Even the *f* dominion shall
Hag 2: 3 who saw this temple in its *f*
2: 9 shall be greater than the *f*,
Zech 1: 4 to whom the *f* prophets
7: 7 LORD proclaimed through the *f*
7:12 by His Spirit through the *f*
8:11 of this people as in the *f*
Mal 3: 4 As in *f* years.
Acts 1: 1 The *f* account I made,
Gal 1:13 you have heard of my *f* conduct
Eph 4:22 concerning your *f* conduct,
Phil 1:16 The *f* preach Christ from selfish
Heb 7:18 annulling of the *f* commandment
10:32 But recall the *f* days in which,
1 Pe 1:14 yourselves to the *f* lusts,
3: 5 in *f* times, the holy women who
Rev 21: 4 for the *f* things have passed

FORMERLY (18/17) FORMER

Deut 2:12 The Horites *f* dwelt in Seir,
2:20 giants *f* dwelt there. But the
Josh 11:10 for Hazor was *f* the head of all
14:15 And the name of Hebron *f* was
15:15 inhabitants of Debir (*f* the
Judg 1:10 Hebron was *f* Kirjath Arba.)
1:11 Debir was *f* Kirjath Sepher.)
1:23 name of the city was *f* Luz.)
3: 2 those who had not *f* known it),
18:29 the name of the city *f* was
1 Sam 9: 9 (*F* in Israel, when a man went to
9: 9 prophet was *f* called a seer.)
10:11 when all who knew him *f* saw
1 Chr 4:40 for some Hamites *f* lived there.
Jn 9:13 They brought him who *f* was
Gal 1:23 He who *f* persecuted us now
1 Tim 1:13 although I was *f* a blasphemer,
1 Pe 3:20 who *f* were disobedient, when

FORMS (6/6) FORM

Lev 26:30 carcasses on the lifeless *f* of
Isa 45: 9 the clay say to him who *f* it,
Jer 15: 3 I will appoint over them four *f*
Ezek 43:11 all its *f* and all its laws.
Am 4:13 He who *f* mountains, And
Zech 12: 1 and *f* the spirit of man within

FORNICATION (14/12) FORNICATIONS, FORNICATOR

Isa 23:17 and commit *f* with all the
Jn 8:41 to Him, "We were not born of *f*;
2 Cor 12:21 repented of the uncleanness, *f*,
Gal 5:19 evident, which are: adultery, *f*,
Eph 5: 3 But *f* and all uncleanness or
Col 3: 5 which are on the earth: *f*,
Rev 14: 8 the wine of the wrath of her *f*.
17: 2 kings of the earth committed *f*,
17: 2 drunk with the wine of her *f*.
17: 4 and the filthiness of her *f*.
18: 3 the wine of the wrath of her *f*,
18: 3 of the earth have committed *f*
18: 9 of the earth who committed *f*
19: 2 corrupted the earth with her *f*;

FORNICATIONS (2/2) FORNICATION

Mt 15:19 murders, adulteries, *f*,
Mk 7:21 evil thoughts, adulteries, *f*,

FORNICATOR (2/2) FORNICATION, FORNICATORS

Eph 5: 5 For this you know, that no *f*,
Heb 12:16 lest there be any *f* or profane

FORNICATORS (3/3) FORNICATOR

1 Cor 6: 9 Do not be deceived. Neither *f*,
1 Tim 1:10 for *f*, for sodomites,
Heb 13: 4 but *f* and adulterers God will

FORSAKE (64/63) FORSAKEN, FORSAKES, FORSAKING, FORSOOK

Deut 4:31 He will not *f* you nor destroy
12:19 to yourself that you do not *f*
14:27 You shall not *f* the Levite who
31: 6 He will not leave you nor *f*
31: 8 He will not leave you nor *f*
31:16 and they will *f* Me and break My
31:17 and I will *f* them, and I will
Josh 1: 5 I will not leave you nor *f* you.
10: 6 Do not *f* your servants; come up
24:16 be it from us that we should *f*
24:20 If you *f* the LORD and serve
1 Sam 12:22 For the LORD will not *f* His
1 Ki 6:13 and will not *f* My people
8:57 May He not leave us nor *f* us,
2 Ki 21:14 So I will *f* the remnant of My
1 Chr 28: 9 but if you *f* Him, He will cast
28:20 He will not leave you nor *f*
2 Chr 7:19 But if you turn away and *f* My
15: 2 but if you *f* Him, He will
15: 2 He will *f* you.
Ezra 8:22 are against all those who *f*
9: 9 Yet our God did not *f* us in our
Neh 9:17 And did not *f* them.
9:19 mercies You did not *f* them in
9:31 not utterly consume them nor *f*
Job 20:13 he spares it and does not *f* it,
Ps 27: 9 Do not leave me nor *f* me,
27:10 my father and my mother *f* me,
37: 8 and *f* wrath; Do not fret—it
37:28 And does not *f* His saints;
38:21 Do not *f* me, O LORD; O my
71: 9 Do not *f* me when my strength
71:18 do not *f* me, Until I declare
89:30 If his sons *f* My law And do not
94:14 Nor will He *f* His inheritance.
119: 8 do not *f* me utterly!
119:53 of the wicked, who *f* Your law.
119:87 But I did not *f* Your precepts.
138: 8 Do not *f* the works of Your
Prov 1: 8 And do not *f* the law of your
3: 3 Let not mercy and truth *f* you;
4: 2 Do not *f* my law.
4: 6 Do not *f* her, and she will
6:20 And do not *f* the law of your
9: 6 *F* foolishness and live, And go
27:10 Do not *f* your own friend or
28: 4 Those who *f* the law praise the
Isa 1:28 And those who *f* the LORD
41:17 will not *f* them.
42:16 And not *f* them.
55: 7 Let the wicked *f* his way,
58: 2 And did not *f* the ordinance of
65:11 But you are those who *f* the
Jer 17:13 All who *f* You shall be
23:33 I will even *f* you," says the
23:39 will utterly forget you and *f*
51: 9 *F* her, and let us go everyone
Lam 5:20 And *f* us for so long a time?
Ezek 20: 8 nor did they *f* the idols of
Dan 11:30 and show regard for those who *f*
Jon 2: 8 who regard worthless idols *F*
Lk 14:33 whoever of you does not *f* all
Acts 21:21 who are among the Gentiles to *f*
Heb 13: 5 never leave you nor *f*

FORSAKEN (75/73) FORSAKE

Gen 24:27 who has not *f* His mercy and His
Deut 28:20 doings in which you have *f* Me.
29:25 Because they have *f* the covenant
Judg 6:13 But now the LORD has *f* us and
10:10 because we have both *f* our God
10:13 Yet you have *f* Me and served
Ruth 2:20 who has not *f* His kindness to
1 Sam 8: 8 with which they have *f* Me and
12:10 because we have *f* the LORD and
1 Ki 11:33 because they have *f* Me, and
18:18 in that you have *f* the
19:10 the children of Israel have *f*
19:14 the children of Israel have *f*
2 Ki 22:17 because they have *f* Me and
2 Chr 12: 5 You have *f* Me, and therefore I
13:10 and we have not *f* Him; and the
13:11 but you have *f* Him.
21:10 because he had *f* the LORD God
24:20 Because you have *f* the LORD,
24:20 He also has *f* you.'"
24:24 because they had *f* the LORD
28: 6 because they had *f* the LORD
29: 6 they have *f* Him, have turned
34:25 because they have *f* Me and
Ezra 9:10 For we have *f* Your
Neh 13:11 "Why is the house of God *f*?
Job 18: 4 Shall the earth be *f* for you?
20:19 For he has oppressed and *f* the
Ps 9:10 have not *f* those who seek You.
22: 1 why have You *f* Me? Why are
37:25 I have not seen the righteous *f*,
71:11 God has *f* him; Pursue and take
Isa 1: 4 are corrupters! They have *f*
2: 6 For You have *f* Your people, the
6:12 And the *f* places are many in
7:16 land that you dread will be *f*
17: 2 The cities of Aroer are *f*;
17: 9 strong cities will be as a *f*
27:10 The habitation *f* and left like
32:14 Because the palaces will be *f*,
49:14 The LORD has *f* me, And my Lord
54: 6 has called you Like a woman *f*
54: 7 For a mere moment I have *f* you,
60:15 Whereas you have been *f* and
62: 4 shall no longer be termed *F*,
62:12 Sought Out, A City Not *F*.
Jer 1:16 Because they have *f* Me,
2:13 They have *f* Me, the fountain
2:17 In that you have *f* the LORD
2:19 bitter thing That you have *f*
4:29 Every city shall be *f*,
5: 7 Your children have *f* Me And
5:19 Just as you have *f* Me and served
7:29 the LORD has rejected and *f*
9:13 Because they have *f* My law which
9:19 Because we have *f* the land,
12: 7 I have *f* My house, I have left
15: 6 You have *f* Me," says the
16:11 Because your fathers have *f* Me,'
16:11 and have *f* Me and not kept My
17:13 Because they have *f* the LORD,
18:14 the cold flowing waters be *f*
19: 4 Because they have *f* Me and made
22: 9 Because they have *f* the covenant
51: 5 For Israel is not *f*,
Ezek 8:12 the LORD has *f* the land.'"
9: 9 The LORD has *f* the land, and
36: 4 and the cities that have been *f*,
Am 5: 2 She lies *f* on her land;
Zeph 2: 4 For Gaza shall be *f*,
Mt 27:46 why have You *f* Me?"
Mk 15:34 why have You *f* Me?"
2 Cor 4: 9 persecuted, but not *f*;
2 Tim 4:10 for Demas has *f* me, having loved
2 Pe 2:15 They have *f* the right way and

FORSAKES (4/4) FORSAKE

Job 6:14 Even though he *f* the fear of
Prov 2:17 Who *f* the companion of her
15:10 discipline is for him who *f*
28:13 But whoever confesses and *f*

FORSAKING (1/1) FORSAKE

Heb 10:25 not *f* the assembling of

FORSOMUCH (KJV) See BECAUSE

FORSOOK (16/16) FORSAKE

Deut 32:15 You are obese! Then he *f* God
Judg 2:12 and they *f* the LORD God of
2:13 They *f* the LORD and served Baal
10: 6 and they *f* the LORD and did
1 Sam 31: 7 they *f* the cities and fled;
1 Ki 9: 9 Because they *f* the LORD their
2 Ki 21:22 He *f* the LORD God of his
1 Chr 10: 7 they *f* their cities and fled;
2 Chr 7:22 Because they *f* the LORD God of
12: 1 that he *f* the law of the LORD,
Ps 78:60 So that He *f* the tabernacle of
Mt 26:56 Then all the disciples *f* Him
Mk 14:50 Then they all *f* Him and fled.
Lk 5:11 they *f* all and followed Him.
2 Tim 4:16 but all *f* me. May it not be
Heb 11:27 By faith he *f* Egypt, not fearing

FORSWEAR (KJV) See SWEAR (FALSELY)

FORT (2/2) FORTIFY, FORTRESS, FORTS

Isa 25:12 The fortress of the high *f* of
Nah 2: 1 Man the *f*! Watch the road!

FORTH (222/209)

Gen 1:11 Let the earth bring *f* grass, the
1:12 And the earth brought *f* grass,
1:24 Let the earth bring *f* the living
3:16 In pain you shall bring *f*
3:18 and thistles it shall bring *f*
9: 7 Bring *f* abundantly in the
30:39 and the flocks brought *f*
40:10 it budded, its blossoms shot *f*,
40:10 and its clusters brought *f* ripe
41:47 years the ground brought *f*
Ex 8: 3 So the river shall bring *f* frogs
8:18 their enchantments to bring *f*
15: 7 You; You sent *f* Your wrath;
15:13 You in Your mercy have led *f*
Lev 25:21 and it will bring *f* produce
Num 17: 8 had sprouted and put *f* buds,
Deut 33: 2 He shone *f* from Mount Paran,
Judg 9: 8 The trees once went *f* to anoint
20:33 Israel's men in ambush burst *f*
2 Sam 1:14 it you were not afraid to put *f*
2 Ki 4:35 returned and walked back and *f*
19: 3 is no strength to bring them *f*.
Ezra 4:10 beyond the River—and so *f*.
4:11 beyond the River, and so *f*:
4:17 the River: Peace, and so *f*.
7:12 Perfect peace, and so *f*.
Job 1: 7 and from walking back and *f* on
2: 2 and from walking back and *f* on
14: 2 He comes *f* like a flower and
14: 9 water it will bud And bring *f*
15:35 conceive trouble and bring *f*
21:11 They send *f* their little ones
23:10 I shall come *f* as gold.
28:11 What is hidden he brings *f*
37: 3 He sends it *f* under the whole

38: 8 When it burst *f* and issued
38:27 And cause to spring *f* the
39: 3 They bring *f* their young,
41:18 His sneezings flash *f* light,
Ps 1: 3 That brings *f* its fruit in its
7:14 the wicked brings *f* iniquity;
7:14 conceives trouble and brings *f*
37: 6 He shall bring *f* your
50: 2 of beauty, God will shine *f*.
51: 5 I was brought *f* in iniquity,
51:15 And my mouth shall show *f* Your
55:20 He has put *f* his hands against
57: 3 Selah God shall send *f* His
78:52 He made His own people go *f*
79:13 We will show *f* Your praise to
80: 1 between the cherubim, shine *f*!
90: 2 the mountains were brought *f*,
94: 1 vengeance belongs, shine *f*!
98: 4 Break *f* in song, rejoice, and
104:14 That he may bring *f* food from
104:30 You send *f* Your Spirit, they
107: 7 And He led them *f* by the right
113: 2 of the LORD From this time *f*
115:18 the LORD From this time *f*
121: 8 coming in From this time *f*,
125: 2 His people From this time *f*
126: 6 He who continually goes *f*
131: 3 in the LORD From this time *f*
144: 6 Flash *f* lightning and scatter
144:13 That our sheep may bring *f*
Prov 8:24 were no depths I was brought *f*,
8:25 the hills, I was brought *f*;
10:31 mouth of the righteous brings *f*
15: 2 But the mouth of fools pours *f*
15:28 the mouth of the wicked pours *f*
25:23 The north wind brings *f* rain,
27: 1 not know what a day may bring *f*.
Song 1: 3 name is ointment poured *f*;
1:12 My spikenard sends *f* its
2:13 The fig tree puts *f* her green
3:11 Go *f*, O daughters of Zion,
6:10 Who is she who looks *f* as the
7:11 Let us go *f* to the field;
8: 5 your mother brought you *f*;
8: 5 who bore you brought you *f*.
Isa 2: 3 For out of Zion shall go *f*
5: 2 So He expected it to bring *f*
5: 2 But it brought *f* wild grapes.
5: 4 when I expected it to bring *f*
5: 4 Did it bring *f* wild grapes?
11: 1 There shall come *f* a Rod from
13:10 will be darkened in its going *f*,
14: 7 They break *f* into singing.
14:29 serpent's roots will come *f* a
23: 4 nor bring *f* children;
26:18 brought *f* wind; We have not
33:11 You shall bring *f* stubble;
34: 1 and all things that come *f*
35: 6 For waters shall burst *f* in
37: 3 is no strength to bring them *f*.
41:21 Bring *f* your strong reasons,"
41:22 Let them bring *f* and show us
42: 1 He will bring *f* justice to the
42: 3 He will bring *f* justice for
42: 5 Who spread *f* the earth and
42: 9 Before they spring *f* I tell
42:13 The LORD shall go *f* like a
43:17 Who brings *f* the chariot and
43:19 thing, Now it shall spring *f*;
44:23 Break *f* into singing, you
45: 8 let them bring *f* salvation,
45:10 woman, 'What have you brought *f*?
45:21 Tell and bring *f* your case;
48: 1 And have come *f* from the
48: 3 They went *f* from My mouth,
48:20 Go *f* from Babylon! Flee from
49: 9 may say to the prisoners, 'Go *f*,
51: 5 near, My salvation has gone *f*,
51:18 all the sons she has brought *f*;
52: 9 Break *f* into joy, sing
54: 1 who have not borne! Break *f*
54:16 Who brings *f* an instrument for
55:10 And make it bring *f* and bud,
55:11 shall My word be that goes *f*
55:12 and the hills Shall break *f*
58: 8 Then your light shall break *f*
58: 8 Your healing shall spring *f*
59: 4 They conceive evil and bring *f*
61:11 For as the earth brings *f* its
61:11 that are sown in it to spring *f*,
61:11 and praise to spring *f* before
62: 1 her righteousness goes *f* as
65: 9 I will bring *f* descendants from
65:23 Nor bring *f* children for
66:24 And they shall go *f* and look
Jer 1: 9 Then the LORD put *f* His hand
1:14 north calamity shall break *f*
2:37 Indeed you will go *f* from him
4: 4 Lest My fury come *f* like fire,
4: 7 He has gone *f* from his place
4:24 all the hills moved back and *f*.
4:31 anguish as of her who brings *f*
15: 1 of My sight, and let them go *f*.
20:18 Why did I come *f* from the womb
21:12 Lest My fury go *f* like fire
23:19 of the LORD has gone *f* in
25:32 disaster shall go *f* From
30:23 whirlwind of the LORD Goes *f*
31: 4 And shall go *f* in the dances
46: 4 you horsemen! Stand *f* with
46: 9 And let the mighty men come *f*:
48: 7 And Chemosh shall go *f* into
Ezek 1:13 of torches going back and *f*
1:14 living creatures ran back and *f*,
13:13 cause a stormy wind to break *f*
17: 6 Brought *f* branches, And put
17: 6 And put *f* shoots.
17: 8 To bring *f* branches, bear
17:23 and it will bring *f* boughs,
27:19 wares, traversing back and *f*.
28:14 You walked back and *f* in the
29:21 the house of Israel to spring *f*,
30: 9 that day messengers shall go *f*
31: 6 beasts of the field brought *f*
32: 2 Bursting *f* in your rivers,
36: 8 you shall shoot *f* your branches
Dan 7:10 stream issued And came *f* from
9:22 I have now come *f* to give you
9:25 That from the going *f* of the
10:20 and when I have gone *f*,
Hos 6: 3 His going *f* is established as
6: 5 are like light that goes *f*.
10: 1 He brings *f* fruit for himself.
Mic 4: 2 out of Zion the law shall go *f*,
4:10 in pain, and labor to bring *f*,
4:10 For now you shall go *f* from
5: 2 Yet out of you shall come *f*
5: 2 Whose goings *f* are from of
7: 9 He will bring me *f* to the
Nah 1:11 From you comes *f* one Who
Hab 1: 4 And justice never goes *f*.
3:13 You went *f* for the salvation of
Hag 1:11 on whatever the ground brings *f*,
Zech 3: 8 I am bringing *f* My Servant the
4: 7 a plain! And he shall bring *f*
5: 5 see what this is that goes *f*.
5: 6 is a basket that is going *f*.
9:14 And His arrow will go *f* like
14: 3 Then the LORD will go *f* And
Mt 1:21 'And she will bring *f* a Son,
1:25 her till she had brought *f* her
2:16 and he sent *f* and put to death
12:20 Till He sends *f* justice
12:35 treasure of his heart brings *f*
12:35 of the evil treasure brings *f*
13:24 Another parable He put *f* to
13:31 Another parable He put *f* to
13:43 the righteous will shine *f* as
13:49 the age. The angels will come *f*,
24:32 become tender and puts *f*
Mk 1:38 for this purpose I have come *f*.
13:28 and puts *f* leaves, you know
Lk 1:31 in your womb and bring *f* a Son,
1:57 and she brought *f* a son.
2: 7 And she brought *f* her firstborn
6:45 treasure of his heart brings *f*
6:45 treasure of his heart brings *f*
Jn 5:29 'and come *f*—those who have
8:42 for I proceeded *f* and came from
11:43 'Lazarus, come *f*!"
16:27 and have believed that I came *f*
16:28 I came *f* from the Father and
16:30 this we believe that You came *f*
17: 8 have known surely that I came *f*
Rom 3:25 whom God set *f* as a
Gal 4: 4 God sent *f* His Son, born of a
4: 6 God has sent *f* the Spirit of
4:27 who do not bear! Break *f*
Col 1: 6 and is bringing *f* fruit, as it
1 Th 1: 8 word of the Lord has sounded *f*,
Heb 1:14 all ministering spirits sent *f*
13:13 Therefore let us go *f* to Him,
Jas 1:15 is full-grown, brings *f* death.
1:18 Of His own will He brought us *f*
3:11 Does a spring send *f* fresh
3 Jn 7 because they went *f* for His
Jude 7 are set *f* as an example,

FORTHWITH (KJV) See IMMEDIATELY, (AT) ONCE

FORTIETH (3/3) FORTY

Num 33:38 and died there in the *f* year
Deut 1: 3 Now it came to pass in the *f*
1 Chr 26:31 In the *f* year of the reign of

FORTIFIED (51/51) FORTIFY

Num 13:28 the cities are *f* and very
21:24 of the people of Ammon was *f*.
32:17 little ones will dwell in the *f*
32:36 *f* cities, and folds for sheep.
Deut 1:28 the cities are great and *f* up
3: 5 All these cities were *f* with
9: 1 cities great and *f* up to
28:52 gates until your high and *f*
Josh 10:20 those who escaped entered *f*
14:12 the cities were great and *f*.
19:29 turned to Ramah and to the *f*
19:35 And the *f* cities are Ziddim,
1 Sam 6:18 both *f* cities and country
2 Sam 20: 6 lest he find for himself *f*
2 Ki 3:19 Also you shall attack every *f*
10: 2 a *f* city also, and weapons,
17: 9 from watchtower to *f* city.
18: 8 from watchtower to *f* city.
18:13 came up against all the *f*
19:25 you should be For crushing *f*
2 Chr 8: 5 *f* cities with walls, gates,
11:10 Judah and Benjamin, *f* cities.
11:11 And he *f* the strongholds, and
11:23 to every *f* city; and he gave
12: 4 And he took the *f* cities of
14: 6 And he built *f* cities in Judah,
17: 2 he placed troops in all the *f*
17:19 those the king put in the *f*
19: 5 the land throughout all the *f*
21: 3 with *f* cities in Judah; but he
26: 9 of the wall; then he *f* them.
32: 1 he encamped against the *f*
33:14 military captains in all the *f*
Neh 3: 8 and they *f* Jerusalem as far as
Isa 2:15 And upon every *f* wall;
25: 2 A *f* city a ruin, A palace of
27:10 Yet the *f* city will be
36: 1 came up against all the *f*
37:26 you should be For crushing *f*
Jer 1:18 I have made you this day A *f*
4: 5 And let us go into the *f*
5:17 They shall destroy your *f*
8:14 And let us enter the *f* cities,
15:20 make you to this people a *f*
34: 7 for only these *f* cities
Ezek 21:20 into *f* Jerusalem.
36:35 and ruined cities are now *f*
Dan 11:15 and take a *f* city; and the
Hos 8:14 Judah also has multiplied *f*
Mic 7:12 to you From Assyria and the *f*
Zeph 1:16 and alarm Against the *f*

FORTIFY (6/6) FORT, FORTIFIED, FORTIFYING

Neh 4: 2 Will they *f* themselves? Will
Isa 22:10 the houses you broke down To *f*
Jer 33: 4 have been pulled down to *f*
51:53 And though she were to *f* the
Nah 2: 1 *F* your power mightily.
3:14 *F* your strongholds!

FORTIFYING (1/1) FORTIFY

Judg 9:31 *f* the city against you.

FORTRESS (20/20) FORT, FORTRESSES

2 Sam 22: 2 LORD is my rock and my *f*
Ps 18: 2 The LORD is my rock and my *f*
31: 2 A *f* of defense to save me.
31: 3 For You are my rock and my *f*;
71: 3 For You are my rock and my *f*.
91: 2 "He is my refuge and my *f*;
144: 2 My lovingkindness and my *f*,
Isa 17: 3 The *f* also will cease from
25:12 The *f* of the high fort of your
29: 7 who fight against her and her *f*,
33:16 of defense will be the *f* of
Jer 6:27 set you as an assayer and a *f*
10:17 land, O inhabitant of the *f*!
16:19 LORD, my strength and my *f*,
Dan 11: 7 enter the *f* of the king of the
11:10 then he shall return to his *f*
11:19 turn his face toward the *f* of
11:31 shall defile the sanctuary *f*;
Am 5: 9 So that fury comes upon the *f*.
Mic 7:12 From the *f* to the River,

FORTRESSES (8/8) FORTRESS

1 Chr 27:25 in the villages, and in the *f*.
2 Chr 17:12 and he built *f* and storage
27: 4 and in the forests he built *f*
Isa 34:13 Nettles and brambles in its *f*;
Dan 11:38 place he shall honor a god of *f*;
11:39 act against the strongest *f*
Hos 10:14 And all your *f* shall be
Zeph 3: 6 Their *f* are devastated;

FORTS (2/2) FORT

Num 31:10 they dwelt, and all their *f*.
Isa 32:14 The *f* and towers will become

FORTUNATUS (1/1)

1 Cor 16:17 the coming of Stephanas, *F*,

FORTUNE-TELLING (1/1)

Acts 16:16 her masters much profit by *f*.

FORTY (104/91) FORTIETH

Gen 5:13 lived eight hundred and *f*
7: 4 it to rain on the earth *f* days
7: 4 on the earth forty days and *f*
7:12 And the rain was on the earth *f*
7:12 on the earth forty days and *f*
7:17 the flood was on the earth *f*
8: 6 at the end of *f* days, that Noah
18:29 Suppose there should be *f* found
18:29 not do it for the sake of *f*.
25:20 Isaac was *f* years old when he
26:34 When Esau was *f* years old, he
32:15 *f* cows and ten bulls, twenty
50: 3 *F* days were required for him,
Ex 16:35 children of Israel ate manna *f*
24:18 And Moses was on the mountain *f*
24:18 the mountain forty days and *f*
26:19 You shall make *f* sockets of
26:21 and their *f* sockets of silver:
34:28 he was there with the LORD *f*
34:28 with the LORD forty days and *f*
36:24 *F* sockets of silver he made to
36:26 and their *f* sockets of silver:
Num 1:33 of the tribe of Ephraim were *f*

2:19 And his army was numbered at *f*
13:25 spying out the land after *f*
14:33 shepherds in the wilderness *f*
14:34 *f* days, for each day you shall
14:34 namely *f* years, and you shall
26:18 *f* thousand five hundred.
32:13 them wander in the wilderness *f*
Deut 2: 7 These *f* years the LORD your
8: 2 God led you all the way these *f*
8: 4 nor did your foot swell these *f*
9: 9 then I stayed on the mountain *f*
9: 9 the mountain forty days and *f*
9:11 at the end of *f* days and forty
9:11 at the end of forty days and *f*
9:18 *f* days and forty nights;
9:18 forty days and *f* nights;
9:25 *f* days and forty nights I kept
9:25 forty days and *f* nights I kept
10:10 I stayed in the mountain *f* days
10:10 the mountain forty days and *f*
25: 3 *F* blows he may give him and no
29: 5 And I have led you *f* years in
Josh 4:13 About *f* thousand prepared for
5: 6 the children of Israel walked *f*
14: 7 I was *f* years old when Moses
Judg 3:11 So the land had rest for *f*
5: 8 or spear was seen among *f*
5:31 So the land had rest for *f*
8:28 And the country was quiet for *f*
12:14 He had *f* sons and thirty
13: 1 hand of the Philistines for *f*
1 Sam 4:18 And he had judged Israel *f*
17:16 near and presented himself *f*
2 Sam 2:10 was *f* years old when he began
5: 4 and he reigned *f* years.
10:18 seven hundred charioteers and *f*
15: 7 Now it came to pass after *f*
1 Ki 2:11 reigned over Israel was *f*
4:26 Solomon had *f* thousand stalls
6:17 it the temple sanctuary was *f*
7:38 each laver contained *f* baths,
11:42 over all Israel was *f* years.
19: 8 in the strength of that food *f*
19: 8 of that food forty days and *f*
2 Ki 8: 9 *f* camel-loads; and he came and
12: 1 and he reigned *f* years in
1 Chr 12:36 battle formation, *f* thousand;
19:18 thousand charioteers and *f*
29:27 he reigned over Israel was *f*
2 Chr 9:30 in Jerusalem over all Israel *f*
24: 1 and he reigned *f* years in
Neh 5:15 besides *f* shekels of silver.
9:21 *F* years You sustained them in
Job 42:16 Job lived one hundred and *f*
Ps 95:10 For *f* years I was grieved with
Ezek 4: 6 of the house of Judah *f* days.
29:11 and it shall be uninhabited *f*
29:12 her cities shall be desolate *f*
29:13 At the end of *f* years I will
41: 2 *f* cubits, and its width, twenty
46:22 *f* cubits long and thirty wide;
Am 2:10 And led you *f* years through
5:25 offerings In the wilderness *f*
Jon 3: 4 Yet *f* days, and Nineveh shall be
Mt 4: 2 And when He had fasted *f* days
4: 2 He had fasted forty days and *f*
Mk 1:13 was there in the wilderness *f*
Lk 4: 2 being tempted for *f* days by the
Acts 1: 3 being seen by them during *f*
4:22 For the man was over *f* years old
7:23 Now when he was *f* years old, it
7:30 And when *f* years had passed, an
7:36 and in the wilderness *f* years.
7:42 and sacrifices during *f*
13:18 Now for a time of about *f* years
13:21 tribe of Benjamin, for *f* years.
23:13 Now there were more than *f* who
23:21 for more than *f* of them lie in
2 Cor 11:24 Jews five times I received *f*
Heb 3: 9 And saw My works *f*
3:17 Now with whom was He angry *f*

FORTY-EIGHT (4/4)

Num 35: 7 to the Levites shall be *f*;
Josh 21:41 the children of Israel were *f*
Neh 7:15 of Binnui, six hundred and *f*;
7:44 of Asaph, one hundred and *f*.

FORTY-FIRST (1/1)

2 Chr 16:13 he died in the *f* year of his

FORTY-FIVE (15/15)

Gen 18:28 So He said, "If I find there *f*,
Num 1:25 of the tribe of Gad were *f*
2:15 And his army was numbered at *f*
26:41 were numbered of them were *f*
26:50 were numbered of them were *f*
Josh 14:10 these *f* years, ever since the
1 Ki 7: 3 above the beams that were on *f*
Ezra 2: 8 of Zattu, nine hundred and *f*;
2:34 of Jericho, three hundred and *f*;
2:66 their mules two hundred and *f*,
Neh 7:13 of Zattu, eight hundred and *f*;
7:36 of Jericho, three hundred and *f*;
7:67 and they had two hundred and *f*
7:68 their mules two hundred and *f*,
Jer 52:30 of the Jews seven hundred and *f*

FORTY-FOUR (5/5)

1 Chr 5:18 the tribe of Manasseh had *f*
Rev 7: 4 One hundred and *f* thousand of
14: 1 and with Him one hundred and *f*
14: 3 song except the hundred and *f*
21:17 one hundred and *f* cubits,

FORTY-NINE (1/1)

Lev 25: 8 of years shall be to you *f*

FORTY-ONE (6/6)

Num 1:41 of the tribe of Asher were *f*
2:28 And his army was numbered at *f*
1 Ki 14:21 Rehoboam was *f* years old when
15:10 And he reigned *f* years in
2 Ki 14:23 and reigned *f* years.
2 Chr 12:13 Now Rehoboam was *f* years old

FORTY-SEVEN (3/3)

Gen 47:28 life was one hundred and *f*
Ezra 2:38 one thousand two hundred and *f*;
Neh 7:41 one thousand two hundred and *f*;

FORTY-SIX (3/3)

Num 1:21 of the tribe of Reuben were *f*
2:11 And his army was numbered at *f*
Jn 2:20 It has taken *f* years to build

FORTY-THREE (3/3)

Num 26: 7 were numbered of them were *f*
Ezra 2:25 Beeroth, seven hundred and *f*;
Neh 7:29 Beeroth, seven hundred and *f*;

FORTY-TWO (14/14)

Num 35: 6 And to these you shall add *f*
Judg 12: 6 There fell at that time *f*
2 Ki 2:24 out of the woods and mauled *f*
10:14 *f* men; and he left none of
2 Chr 22: 2 Ahaziah was *f* years old when he
Ezra 2:10 of Bani, six hundred and *f*;
2:24 the people of Azmaveth, *f*;
2:64 whole assembly together was *f*
Neh 7:28 the men of Beth Azmaveth, *f*;
7:62 of Nekoda, six hundred and *f*;
7:66 the whole assembly was *f*
11:13 were two hundred and *f*;
Rev 11: 2 the holy city underfoot for *f*
13: 5 authority to continue for *f*

FORUM (1/1)

Acts 28:15 to meet us as far as Appii *F*

FORWARD (32/31)

Ex 14:15 the children of Israel to go *f*.
Num 1:51 when the tabernacle is to go *f*,
12: 5 And they both went *f*.
Judg 9:44 that was with him rushed *f*
1 Sam 10: 3 Then you shall go on *f* from
16:13 came upon David from that day *f*.
18: 9 Saul eyed David from that day *f*.
30:25 So it was, from that day *f*;
2 Sam 20: 8 his hips; and as he was going *f*,
1 Ki 22:21 Then a spirit came *f* and stood
2 Ki 4:24 her servant, "Drive, and go *f*;
20: 9 shall the shadow go *f* ten
2 Chr 18:20 Then a spirit came *f* and stood
Job 23: 8 "Look, I go *f*,
Isa 9: 7 and justice From that time *f*,
Jer 7:24 and went backward and not *f*.
31:39 shall again extend straight *f*
Ezek 1: 9 but each one went straight *f*.
1:12 And each one went straight *f*;
10:22 They each went straight *f*.
39:22 LORD their God from that day *f*.
Dan 3: 8 time certain Chaldeans came *f*
Hag 2:15 consider from this day *f*:
2:18 'Consider now from this day *f*,
Mt 26:60 many false witnesses came *f*,
26:60 two false witnesses came *f*
Mk 3: 3 had the withered hand, "Step *f*.
Jn 18: 4 went *f* and said to them, "Whom
Acts 19:33 the Jews putting him *f*.
Phil 3:13 are behind and reaching *f* to
2 Pe 3:14 looking *f* to these things, be
3 Jn 6 If you send them *f* on their

FORWARDNESS (KJV) See DILIGENCE, WILLINGNESS

FOSTER (1/1)

Isa 49:23 Kings shall be your *f* fathers,

FOSTERED (1/1)

Ezra 4:19 and sedition have been *f* in it.

FOUGHT (67/64) FIGHT

Ex 17: 8 Now Amalek came and *f* with
17:10 and *f* with Amalek. And Moses,
Lev 24:10 son and a man of Israel *f* each
Num 21: 1 then he *f* against Israel and
21:23 and he came to Jahaz and *f*
21:26 who had *f* against the former
31:42 separated from the men who *f*—
Josh 10:14 for the LORD *f* for Israel.
10:29 and they *f* against Libnah.
10:31 they encamped against it and *f*
10:34 they encamped against it and *f*
10:36 and they *f* against it.
10:38 and they *f* against it.
10:42 the LORD God of Israel *f* for
23: 3 your God is He who has *f* for
24: 8 and they *f* with you. But I gave
24:11 And the men of Jericho *f*
Judg 1: 5 and *f* against him; and they
1: 8 Now the children of Judah *f*
5:19 "The kings came and *f*,
5:19 Then the kings of Canaan *f* In
5:20 They *f* from the heavens;
5:20 The stars from their courses *f*
9:17 for my father *f* for you, risked
9:39 and *f* with Abimelech.
9:45 So Abimelech *f* against the city
9:52 came as far as the tower and *f*
11:20 and *f* against Israel.
12: 4 all the men of Gilead and *f*
1 Sam 4:10 So the Philistines *f*,
12: 9 and they *f* against them.
14:47 and *f* against all his enemies
19: 8 and David went out and *f* with
23: 5 his men went to Keilah and *f*
31: 1 Now the Philistines *f* against
2 Sam 8:10 because he had *f* against
10:17 array against David and *f* with
11:17 men of the city came out and *f*
11:20 so near to the city when you *f*?
12:26 Now Joab *f* against Rabbah of
12:27 I have *f* against Rabbah, and I
12:29 *f* against it, and took it.
14: 6 and the two *f* with each other
21:15 with him went down and *f*
1 Ki 5: 3 of the wars which were *f*
2 Ki 8:29 when he *f* against Hazael king
9:15 had inflicted on him when he *f*
12:17 king of Syria went up and *f*
13:12 and his might with which he *f*
14:15 and how he *f* with Amaziah king
1 Chr 10: 1 Now the Philistines *f* against
18:10 because he had *f* against
19:17 they *f* with him.
2 Chr 20:29 they heard that the LORD had *f*
22: 6 when he *f* against Hazael king
27: 5 He also *f* with the king of the
Ps 60: When he *f* against Mesopotamia
109: 3 And *f* against me without a
Isa 20: 1 and he *f* against Ashdod and
63:10 And He *f* against them.
Jer 34: 1 *f* against Jerusalem and all its
34: 7 the king of Babylon's army *f*
Zech 14:12 strike all the people who *f*
1 Cor 15:32 I have *f* with beasts at
2 Tim 4: 7 I have *f* the good fight, I have
Rev 12: 7 Michael and his angels *f* with
12: 7 and the dragon and his angels *f*,

FOUL (8/8)

Ps 38: 5 My wounds are *f* and festering
Eccl 10: 1 And cause it to give off a *f*
Isa 19: 6 The rivers will turn *f*;
Ezek 34:18 that you must *f* the residue
Joel 2:20 And his *f* odor will rise,
Mt 16: 3 It will be *f* weather today,
Rev 16: 2 and a *f* and loathsome sore came
18: 2 a prison for every *f* spirit,

FOULED (1/1)

Ezek 34:19 and they drink what you have *f*

FOULING (1/1)

Ezek 32: 2 And *f* their rivers.'

FOUND (398/384) FIND, FOUNDED, FOUNDING

Gen 2:20 But for Adam there was not *f* a
6: 8 But Noah *f* grace in the eyes of
8: 9 But the dove *f* no resting place
11: 2 that they *f* a plain in the land
16: 7 Now the Angel of the LORD *f*
18: 3 if I have now *f* favor in Your
18:29 there should be forty *f* there?
18:30 Suppose thirty should be *f*
18:31 Suppose twenty should be *f*
18:32 Suppose ten should be *f*
19:19 your servant has *f* favor in
26:19 and *f* a well of running water
26:32 We have *f* water."
27:20 How is it that you have *f* it
30:14 the days of wheat harvest and *f*
30:27 if I have *f* favor in your eyes,
31:37 household things have you *f*?
33:10 if I have now *f* favor in your
36:24 This was the Anah who *f* the
37:15 Now a certain man *f* him, and
37:17 went after his brothers and *f*
37:32 We have *f* this. Do you know
38:23 young goat and you have not *f*
39: 4 So Joseph *f* favor in his sight,
44: 8 of Canaan the money which we *f*
44: 9 of your servants it is *f*,
44:10 he with whom it is *f* shall be

44:12 and the cup was *f* in Benjamin's
44:16 God has *f* out the iniquity of
44:16 also with whom the cup was *f*.
44:17 man in whose hand the cup was *f*,
47:14 up all the money that was *f* in
47:29 Now if I have *f* favor in your
50: 4 If now I have *f* favor in your
Ex 9:19 and every animal which is *f* in
12:19 days no leaven shall be *f* in
15:22 days in the wilderness and *f*
16:27 but they *f* none.
21:16 or if he is *f* in his hand,
22: 2 If the thief is *f* breaking in,
22: 4 If the theft is certainly *f*
22: 7 man's house, if the thief is *f*,
22: 8 "If the thief is not *f*,
33:12 and you have also *f* grace in My
33:13 if I have *f* grace in Your
33:16 that Your people and I have *f*
33:17 for you have *f* grace in My
34: 9 If now I have *f* grace in Your
35:23 with whom was *f* blue, purple,
35:24 And everyone with whom was *f*
Lev 6: 3 or if he has *f* what was lost and
6: 4 or the lost thing which he *f*,
Num 11:11 And why have I not *f* favor in
11:15 if I have *f* favor in Your
15:32 they *f* a man gathering sticks
15:33 And those who *f* him gathering
31:50 what every man *f* of ornaments
32: 5 If we have *f* favor in your
Deut 17: 2 If there is *f* among you, within
18:10 There shall not be *f* among you
20:11 all the people who are *f* in
21: 1 If anyone is *f* slain, lying in
22: 3 he has lost and you have *f*,
22:14 and when I came to her I *f* she
22:17 I *f* your daughter was not a
22:20 of virginity are not *f* for
22:22 If a man is *f* lying with a
22:27 For he *f* her in the countryside,
22:28 and they are *f* out,
24: 1 in his eyes because he has *f*
24: 7 If a man is *f* kidnapping any of
32:10 'He *f* him in a desert land
Josh 10:17 The five kings have been *f*
Judg 1: 5 And they *f* Adoni-Bezek in Bezek,
6:17 If now I have *f* favor in Your
15:15 He *f* a fresh jawbone of a
20:48 men and beasts, all who were *f*.
21:12 So they *f* among the inhabitants
21:14 and yet they had not *f* enough
Ruth 2:10 Why have I *f* favor in your eyes,
1 Sam 9:20 them, for they have been *f*.
10: 2 went to look for have been *f*.
10:14 they were nowhere to be *f*,
10:16 that the donkeys had been *f*.
10:21 sought him, he could not be *f*.
12: 5 that you have not *f* anything in
13:19 there was no blacksmith to be *f*
13:22 was neither sword nor spear *f*
13:22 But they were *f* with Saul and
14:30 of their enemies which they *f*!
16:22 for he has *f* favor in my
20: 3 certainly knows that I have *f*
20:29 if I have *f* favor in your eyes,
21: 3 my hand, or whatever can be *f*.
25:28 and evil is not *f* in you
27: 5 If I have now *f* favor in your
29: 3 And to this day I have *f* no
29: 6 For to this day I have not *f*
29: 8 to this day what have you *f* in
30:11 Then they *f* an Egyptian in the
31: 8 that they *f* Saul and his three
2 Sam 7:27 Therefore Your servant has *f*
14:22 servant knows that I have *f*
17:12 in some place where he may be *f*,
17:13 there is not one small stone *f*
1 Ki 1: 3 and *f* Abishag the Shunammite,
1:52 but if wickedness is *f* in him,
11:19 And Hadad *f* great favor in the
13:14 and *f* him sitting under an oak.
13:28 Then he went and *f* his corpse
14:13 because in him there is *f*
19:19 and *f* Elisha the son of
20:36 a lion *f* him and killed him.
20:37 And he *f* another man, and said,
21:20 'Have you *f* me, O my enemy?"
21:20 I have *f* you, because you have
2 Ki 4:39 and *f* a wild vine, and gathered
9:35 but they *f* no more of her than
12: 5 wherever any dilapidation is *f*.
12:10 counted the money that was *f*
12:18 and all the gold *f* in the
14:14 all the articles that were *f* in
16: 8 the silver and gold that was *f*
18:15 him all the silver that was *f*
19: 8 the Rabshakeh returned and *f*
20:13 all that was *f* among his
22: 8 I have *f* the Book of the Law in
22: 9 gathered the money that was *f*
22:13 of this book that has been *f*;
23: 2 the Covenant which had been *f*
23:24 book that Hilkiah the priest *f*
25:19 close associates who were *f* in
25:19 of the land who were *f* in
1 Chr 4:40 And they *f* rich, good pasture,
4:41 and the Meunites who were *f*
10: 8 that they *f* Saul and his sons
17:25 Therefore Your servant has *f* it
20: 2 and *f* it to weigh a talent of
24: 4 There were more leaders *f* of the
26:31 and there were *f* among them
28: 9 He will be *f* by you; but if you
2 Chr 2:17 and there were *f* to be one
15: 2 He will be *f* by you; but if you
15: 4 He was *f* by them.
15:15 and He was *f* by them, and the
19: 3 good things are *f*
20:25 they *f* among them an abundance
21:17 the possessions that were *f* in
22: 8 and *f* the princes of Judah and
25: 5 and *f* them to be three hundred
25:24 all the articles that were *f* in
29:16 out all the debris that they *f*
34:14 Hilkiah the priest *f* the Book
34:15 I have *f* the Book of the Law in
34:17 gathered the money that was *f*
34:21 the words of the book that is *f*;
34:30 the Covenant which had been *f*
36: 8 and what was *f* against him,
Ezra 2:62 genealogy, but they were not *f*;
4:19 and it was *f* that this city in
6: 2 of Media, a scroll was *f*,
8:15 and *f* none of the sons of Levi
10:18 wives the following were *f*
Neh 2: 5 and if your servant has *f* favor
5: 8 Then they were silenced and *f*
7: 5 And I *f* a register of the
7: 5 and *f* written in it:
7:64 by genealogy, but it was not *f*;
8:14 And they *f* written in the Law,
9: 8 You *f* his heart faithful before
13: 1 and in it was *f* written that no
Esth 5: 2 that she *f* favor in his sight,
5: 8 If I have *f* favor in the sight
6: 2 And it was *f* written that
7: 3 If I have *f* favor in your sight,
8: 5 and if I have *f* favor in his
Job 19:28 the root of the matter is *f* in
20: 8 away like a dream, and not be *f*;
28:12 "But where can wisdom be *f*?
28:13 Nor is it *f* in the land of the
31:29 lifted myself up when evil *f*
32: 3 because they had *f* no answer,
32:13 We have *f* wisdom'; God will
33:24 I have *f* a ransom';
42:15 In all the land were *f* no women
Ps 17: 3 You have tried me and have *f*
32: 6 In a time when You may be *f*;
37:36 him, but he could not be *f*.
51: 4 That You may be *f* just when You
69:20 for comforters, but I *f* none.
76: 5 none of the mighty men have *f*
84: 3 Even the sparrow has *f* a home,
89:20 I have *f* My servant David;
107: 4 They *f* no city to dwell in.
109: 7 let him be *f* guilty, And let
116: 3 I *f* trouble and sorrow.
132: 6 We *f* it in the fields of the
Prov 6:31 Yet when he is *f*,
7:15 And I have *f* you.
10:13 Wisdom is *f* on the lips of him
16:31 If it is *f* in the way of
24:14 If you have *f* it, there is a
25:16 Have you *f* honey? Eat only as
30: 6 and you be *f* a liar.
30:10 and you be *f* guilty.
Eccl 7:27 "Here is what I have *f*,
7:28 man among a thousand I have *f*,
7:28 among all these I have not *f*.
7:29 Truly, this only I have *f*:
9:15 Now there was *f* in it a poor
Song 3: 3 who go about the city *f* me;
3: 4 When I *f* the one I love.
5: 7 who went about the city *f* me.
8:10 in his eyes As one who *f*
Isa 10:10 As my hand has *f* the kingdoms
10:14 My hand has *f* like a nest the
13:15 Everyone who is *f* will be
22: 3 All who are *f* in you are bound
30:14 So there shall not be *f* among
35: 9 it; It shall not be *f* there.
37: 8 and *f* the king of Assyria
39: 2 all that was *f* among his
51: 3 Joy and gladness will be *f* in
55: 6 the LORD while He may be *f*,
57:10 You have *f* the life of your
65: 1 I was *f* by those who did not
65: 8 As the new wine is *f* in the
Jer 2: 5 injustice have your fathers *f*
2:26 thief is ashamed when he is *f*
2:34 Also on your skirts is *f* The
2:34 I have not *f* it by secret
5:26 For among My people are *f* wicked
11: 9 A conspiracy has been *f* among
14: 3 went to the cisterns and *f* no
15:16 Your words were *f*,
23:11 in My house I have *f* their
29:14 I will be *f* by you, says the
31: 2 who survived the sword *F*
41: 3 and the Chaldeans who were *f*
41: 8 But ten men were *f* among them
41:12 and they *f* him by the great
48:27 Was he *f* among thieves?
50: 7 All who *f* them have devoured
50:20 Judah, but they shall not be *f*;
50:24 You have been *f* and also
52:25 close associates who were *f* in
52:25 people of the land who were *f*
Lam 2:16 We have *f* it, we have seen
Ezek 22:30 destroy it; but I *f* no one.
26:21 you will never be *f* again,'
28:15 Till iniquity was *f* in you.
Dan 1:19 and among them all none was *f*
1:20 he *f* them ten times better than
2:25 I have *f* a man of the captives
2:35 so that no trace of them was *f*.
4:12 The beasts of the field *f*
5:11 were *f* in him; and King
5:12 and explaining enigmas were *f*
5:14 and excellent wisdom are *f* in
5:27 in the balances, and *f* wanting;
6: 4 was there any error or fault *f*
6:11 Then these men assembled and *f*
6:22 because I was *f* innocent before
6:23 and no injury whatever was *f* on
11:19 stumble and fall, and not be *f*.
12: 1 Every one who is *f* written in
Hos 9:10 I *f* Israel Like grapes in the
12: 4 He *f* Him in Bethel,
12: 8 I have *f* wealth for myself;
14: 8 Your fruit is *f* in Me."
Jon 1: 3 and *f* a ship going to Tarshish;
Mic 1:13 of Israel were *f* in you.
Zeph 3:13 shall a deceitful tongue be *f*
Zech 10:10 Until no more room is *f* for
Mal 2: 6 And injustice was not *f* on his
Mt 1:18 she was *f* with child of the
2: 8 and when you have *f* Him, bring
8:10 I have not *f* such great faith,
13:44 which a man *f* and hid; and for
13:46 when he had *f* one pearl of
18:28 that servant went out and *f*
20: 6 hour he went out and *f* others
21:19 He came to it and *f* nothing on
22:10 together all whom they *f*,
26:40 He came to the disciples and *f*
26:43 And He came and *f* them asleep
26:60 but *f* none. Even though many
26:60 they *f* none. But at last two
27:32 they *f* a man of Cyrene, Simon
Mk 1:37 When they *f* Him, they said to
6:38 And when they *f* out they
7: 2 unwashed hands, they *f* fault.
7:30 she *f* the demon gone out, and
11: 4 and *f* the colt tied by the door
11:13 He *f* nothing but leaves, for it
14:16 and *f* it just as He had said to
14:37 Then He came and *f* them
14:40 He *f* them asleep again, for
14:55 put Him to death, but *f* none.
15:45 So when he *f* out from the
Lk 1:30 for you have *f* favor with God.
2:16 And they came with haste and *f*
2:46 that after three days they *f*
4:17 He *f* the place where it was
7: 9 I have not *f* such great faith,
7:10 *f* the servant well who had been
8:35 and *f* the man from whom the
9:36 Jesus was *f* alone. But they
13: 6 came seeking fruit on it and *f*
15: 5 And when he has *f* it, he lays
15: 6 for I have *f* my sheep which was
15: 9 And when she has *f* it, she
15: 9 for I have *f* the piece which I
15:24 he was lost and is *f*.'
15:32 again, and was lost and is *f*.
17:18 Were there not any *f* who
19:32 were sent went their way and *f*
22:13 So they went and *f* it just as He
22:45 He *f* them sleeping from sorrow.
23: 2 We *f* this fellow perverting the
23:14 I have *f* no fault in this Man
23:22 I have *f* no reason for death in
24: 2 But they *f* the stone rolled away
24:24 with us went to the tomb and *f*
24:33 and *f* the eleven and those who
Jn 1:41 He first *f* his own brother
1:41 We have *f* the Messiah" (which
1:43 and He *f* Philip and said to
1:45 Philip *f* Nathanael and said to
1:45 We have *f* Him of whom Moses in
2:14 And He *f* in the temple those who
5:14 Afterward Jesus *f* him in the
6:25 And when they *f* Him on the other
9:35 and when He had *f* him, He said
11:17 He *f* that he had already been
12:14 when He had *f* a young donkey,
Acts 5:10 And the young men came in and *f*
5:23 Indeed we *f* the prison shut
5:23 we *f* no one inside!"
5:39 lest you even be *f* to fight
7:11 and our fathers *f* no
7:46 who *f* favor before God and asked
8:40 But Philip was *f* at Azotus.
9: 2 so that if he *f* any who were of
9:30 When the brethren *f* out, they
9:33 There he *f* a certain man named
10:27 he went in and *f* many who had
11:26 And when he had *f* him, he
12:19 had searched for him and not *f*
13: 6 they *f* a certain sorcerer,
13:22 I have *f* David the son of
13:28 And though they *f* no cause for
17:23 I even *f* an altar with this
18: 2 And he *f* a certain Jew named
19:34 But when they *f* out that he was
22:29 was also afraid after he *f* out
23:29 I *f* out that he was accused
24: 5 For we have *f* this man a plague,
24:12 And they neither *f* me in the
24:18 of which some Jews from Asia *f*
24:20 here themselves say if they *f*
25:25 But when I *f* that he had
27: 6 There the centurion *f* an

27:28 And they took soundings and *f*
27:28 took soundings again and *f* it
28: 1 they then *f* out that the island
28:14 where we *f* brethren, and were
Rom 4: 1 that Abraham our father has *f*
7:10 I *f* to bring death.
10:20 I was *f* by those who did
1 Cor 4: 2 in stewards that one be *f*
15:15 and we are *f* false witnesses of
2 Cor 5: 3 we shall not be *f* naked.
7:14 so our boasting to Titus was *f*
12:20 and that I shall be *f* by you
Gal 2:17 we ourselves also are *f*
Phil 2: 8 And being *f* in appearance as a
3: 9 and be *f* in Him, not having my
1 Tim 3:10 being *f* blameless.
2 Tim 1:17 me out very zealously and *f*
Heb 11: 5 see death, "and was not *f*,
12:17 for he *f* no place for
1 Pe 1: 7 may be *f* to praise, honor, and
2:22 Nor was deceit *f* in His
2 Pe 3:14 be diligent to be *f* by Him in
2 Jn 4 rejoiced greatly that I have *f*
Jude 3 I *f* it necessary to write to
Rev 2: 2 and have *f* them liars;
3: 2 for I have not *f* your works
5: 4 because no one was *f* worthy to
12: 8 nor was a place *f* for them in
14: 5 And in their mouth was *f* no
16:20 and the mountains were not *f*.
18:21 and shall not be *f* anymore.
18:22 of any craft shall be *f* in you
18:24 And in her was *f* the blood of
20:11 And there was *f* no place for
20:15 And anyone not *f* written in the

FOUNDATION (56/55) FOUNDATIONS

Josh 6:26 he shall lay its *f* with his
1 Ki 5:17 to lay the *f* of the temple.
6:37 In the fourth year the *f* of the
7: 9 from the *f* to the eaves, and
7:10 The *f* was of costly stones,
16:34 He laid its *f* with Abiram his
2 Chr 3: 3 This is the *f* which Solomon
8:16 from the day of the *f* of the
23: 5 one-third at the Gate of the *F*.
Ezra 3: 6 although the *f* of the temple of
3:10 When the builders laid the *f* of
3:11 because the *f* of the house of
3:12 with a loud voice when the *f*
5:16 came and laid the *f* of the
Job 4:19 Whose *f* is in the dust, Who
Ps 87: 1 His *f* is in the holy
89:14 and justice are the *f* of Your
97: 2 and justice are the *f* of His
102:25 Of old You laid the *f* of the
137: 7 To its very *f*!"
Prov 10:25 righteous has an everlasting *f*.
Isa 28:16 I lay in Zion a stone for a *f*,
28:16 precious cornerstone, a sure *f*;
44:28 Your *f* shall be laid." '
48:13 Indeed My hand has laid the *f*
Jer 51:26 a corner Nor a stone for a *f*,
Ezek 13:14 so that its *f* will be
41: 8 it was the *f* of the side
Hab 3:13 By laying bare from *f* to neck.
Hag 2:18 from the day that the *f* of the
Zech 4: 9 of Zerubbabel Have laid the *f*
8: 9 Who spoke in the day the *f*
12: 1 lays the *f* of the earth, and
Mt 13:35 kept secret from the *f*
25:34 prepared for you from the *f* of
Lk 6:48 who dug deep and laid the *f* on
6:49 house on the earth without a *f*,
11:50 which was shed from the *f* of
14:29 "lest, after he has laid the *f*,
Jn 17:24 for You loved Me before the *f*
Rom 15:20 should build on another man's *f*,
1 Cor 3:10 builder I have laid the *f*,
3:11 For no other *f* can anyone lay
3:12 Now if anyone builds on this *f*
Eph 1: 4 He chose us in Him before the *f*
2:20 having been built on the *f* of
1 Tim 6:19 up for themselves a good *f* for
2 Tim 2:19 Nevertheless the solid *f* of God
Heb 1:10 the beginning laid the *f*
4: 3 works were finished from the *f*
6: 1 not laying again the *f* of
9:26 to suffer often since the *f* of
1 Pe 1:20 was foreordained before the *f*
Rev 13: 8 of the Lamb slain from the *f*
17: 8 in the Book of Life from the *f*
21:19 the first *f* was jasper, the

FOUNDATIONS (32/32) FOUNDATION

Deut 32:22 And set on fire the *f* of the
2 Sam 22: 8 The *f* of heaven quaked and
22:16 The *f* of the world were
Ezra 4:12 its walls and repairing the *f*.
6: 3 and let the *f* of it be firmly
Job 22:16 Whose *f* were swept away by a
38: 4 were you when I laid the *f* of
38: 6 To what were its *f* fastened?
Ps 11: 3 If the *f* are destroyed,
18: 7 The *f* of the hills also quaked
18:15 The *f* of the world were
82: 5 All the *f* of the earth are
104: 5 You who laid the *f* of the
Prov 8:29 When He marked out the *f* of
Isa 16: 7 For the *f* of Kir Hareseth you
19:10 And its *f* will be broken.
24:18 And the *f* of the earth are
40:21 you not understood from the *f*
51:13 the heavens And laid the *f* of
51:16 Lay the *f* of the earth,
54:11 And lay your *f* with sapphires.
58:12 You shall raise up the *f* of
Jer 31:37 And the *f* of the earth
50:15 Her *f* have fallen, Her walls
Lam 4:11 And it has devoured its *f*.
Ezek 30: 4 And her *f* are broken down.
Mic 1: 6 And I will uncover her *f*.
6: 2 And you strong *f* of the earth;
Acts 16:26 so that the *f* of the prison
Heb 11:10 waited for the city which has *f*,
Rev 21:14 wall of the city had twelve *f*,
21:19 The *f* of the wall of the city

FOUNDED (10/10) FOUND

Ps 24: 2 For He has *f* it upon the seas,
89:11 You have *f* them.
104: 8 To the place which You *f* for
119:152 known of old that You have *f*
Prov 3:19 The LORD by wisdom *f* the
Isa 14:32 That the LORD has *f* Zion,
23:13 Assyria *f* it for wild beasts
Am 9: 6 And has *f* His strata in the
Mt 7:25 for it was *f* on the rock.
Lk 6:48 for it was *f* on the rock.

FOUNDING (1/1) FOUND

Ex 9:18 not been in Egypt since its *f*

FOUNTAIN (26/26) FOUNTAINS

Deut 33:28 The *f* of Jacob alone, In a
Josh 15: 9 the top of the hill to the *f*
1 Sam 29: 1 the Israelites encamped by a *f*
Neh 2:14 Then I went on to the *F* Gate and
3:15 repaired the *F* Gate; he built
12:37 By the *F* Gate, in front of them,
Ps 36: 9 For with You is the *f* of life;
68:26 from the *f* of Israel.
74:15 You broke open the *f* and the
114: 8 The flint into a *f* of waters.
Prov 5:18 Let your *f* be blessed,
13:14 The law of the wise is a *f* of
14:27 The fear of the LORD is a *f*
Eccl 12: 6 the pitcher shattered at the *f*,
Song 4:12 spring shut up, A *f* sealed.
4:15 A *f* of gardens, A well of
Jer 2:13 the *f* of living waters,
6: 7 As a *f* wells up with water,
9: 1 And my eyes a *f* of tears,
17:13 The *f* of living waters."
Hos 13:15 And his *f* shall be dried up.
Joel 3:18 A *f* shall flow from the house
Zech 13: 1 In that day a *f* shall be opened
Mk 5:29 Immediately the *f* of her blood
Jn 4:14 him will become in him a *f* of
Rev 21: 6 I will give of the *f* of the

FOUNTAINS (8/8) FOUNTAIN

Gen 7:11 on that day all the *f* of the
8: 2 The *f* of the deep and the
Deut 8: 7 of *f* and springs, that flow out
Prov 5:16 Should your *f* be dispersed
8:24 When there were no *f*
8:28 When He strengthened the *f* of
Isa 41:18 And *f* in the midst of the
Rev 7:17 them and lead them to living *f*

FOUR (269/232) FOUR-FOOTED, FOURS, FOURTH

Gen 2:10 there it parted and became *f*
11:13 Arphaxad lived *f* hundred and
11:15 Salah lived *f* hundred and three
11:17 Eber lived *f* hundred and thirty
14: 9 *f* kings against five.
15:13 and they will afflict them *f*
23:15 the land is worth *f* hundred
23:16 *f* hundred shekels of silver,
32: 6 and *f* hundred men are with
33: 1 and with him were *f* hundred
Ex 12:40 who lived in Egypt was *f*
12:41 to pass at the end of the *f*
22: 1 five oxen for an ox and *f*
25:12 You shall cast *f* rings of gold
25:12 and put them in its *f* corners;
25:26 And you shall make for it *f*
25:26 and put the rings on the *f*
25:26 four corners that are at its *f*
25:34 On the lampstand itself *f* bowls
26: 2 and the width of each curtain *f*
26: 8 and the width of each curtain *f*
26:32 You shall hang it upon the *f*
26:32 upon *f* sockets of silver.
27: 2 shall make its horns on its *f*
27: 4 on the network you shall make *f*
27: 4 make four bronze rings at its *f*
27:16 It shall have *f* pillars and
27:16 shall have four pillars and *f*
28:17 *f* rows of stones: The first
36: 9 and the width of each curtain *f*
36:15 and the width of each curtain *f*
36:36 He made for it *f* pillars of
36:36 and he cast *f* sockets of silver
37: 3 And he cast for it *f* rings of
37: 3 of gold to be set in its *f*
37:13 And he cast for it *f* rings of
37:13 and put the rings on the *f*
37:13 corners that were at its *f*
37:20 on the lampstand itself were *f*
38: 2 He made its horns on its *f*
38: 5 He cast *f* rings for the four
38: 5 He cast four rings for the *f*
38:19 And there were *f* pillars with
38:19 four pillars with their *f*
38:29 talents and two thousand *f*
39:10 And they set in it *f* rows of
Lev 11:23 flying insects which have *f*
Num 1:29 were fifty-four thousand *f*
1:31 were fifty-seven thousand *f*
1:37 were thirty-five thousand *f*
1:43 were fifty-three thousand *f*
2: 6 at fifty-four thousand *f*
2: 8 at fifty-seven thousand *f*
2: 9 and eighty-six thousand *f*
2:16 and fifty-one thousand *f*
2:23 at thirty-five thousand *f*
2:30 at fifty-three thousand *f*
7: 7 Two carts and *f* oxen he gave to
7: 8 and *f* carts and eight oxen he
7:85 vessels weighed two thousand *f*
26:43 were sixty-four thousand *f*
26:47 fifty-three thousand *f* hundred.
26:50 were forty-five thousand *f*
Deut 3:11 cubits is its length and *f*
22:12 shall make tassels on the *f*
Josh 19: 7 *f* cities and their villages;
21:18 its common-land: *f* cities.
21:22 its common-land: *f* cities;
21:24 its common-land: *f* cities;
21:29 its common-land: *f* cities;
21:31 its common-land: *f* cities;
21:35 its common-land: *f* cities;
21:37 its common-land: *f* cities;
21:39 its common-land: *f* cities
Judg 9:34 in wait against Shechem in *f*
11:40 the daughters of Israel went *f*
19: 2 and was there *f* whole months.
20: 2 *f* hundred thousand foot
20:17 the men of Israel numbered *f*
20:47 at the rock of Rimmon for *f*
21:12 inhabitants of Jabesh Gilead *f*
1 Sam 4: 2 who killed about *f* thousand men
22: 2 And there were about *f* hundred
25:13 And about *f* hundred men went
27: 7 was one full year and *f* months.
30:10 he and *f* hundred men; for two
30:17 except *f* hundred young men who
2 Sam 21:22 These *f* were born to the giant
1 Ki 6: 1 And it came to pass in the *f*
7: 2 with *f* rows of cedar pillars,
7:19 the shape of lilies, *f* cubits.
7:27 *f* cubits was the length of
7:27 *f* cubits its width, and three
7:30 Every cart had *f* bronze wheels
7:30 and its *f* feet had supports.
7:32 Under the panels were the *f*
7:34 And there were *f* supports at
7:34 were four supports at the *f*
7:38 and each laver was *f* cubits.
7:42 *f* hundred pomegranates for the
9:28 and acquired *f* hundred and
10:26 he had one thousand *f* hundred
18:19 the *f* hundred and fifty
18:19 and the *f* hundred prophets of
18:22 but Baal's prophets are *f*
18:33 'Fill *f* waterpots with water,
22: 6 about *f* hundred men, and said
2 Ki 7: 3 Now there were *f* leprous men at
14:13 *f* hundred cubits.
1 Chr 3: 5 *f* by Bathshua the daughter of
7: 1 and Shimron—*f* in all.
9:24 were assigned to the *f*
9:26 in this trusted office were *f*
12:26 of the sons of Levi *f* thousand
21: 5 and Judah had *f* hundred and
21:20 and his *f* sons who were with
23: 5 *f* thousand were gatekeepers,
23: 5 and *f* thousand praised the
23:10 These were the *f* sons of
23:12 and Uzziel—*f* in all.
26:17 on the north *f* each day, on the
26:17 on the south *f* each day,
26:18 there were *f* on the highway
2 Chr 1:14 he had one thousand *f* hundred
4:13 *f* hundred pomegranates for the
8:18 and acquired *f* hundred and
9:25 Solomon had *f* thousand stalls
13: 3 *f* hundred thousand choice men.
18: 5 *f* hundred men, and said to
25:23 *f* hundred cubits.
Ezra 1:10 *f* hundred and ten silver basins
1:11 silver were five thousand *f*
2:15 *f* hundred and fifty-four;
2:67 their camels *f* hundred and
6:17 *f* hundred lambs, and as a sin
Neh 6: 4 But they sent me this message *f*
7:69 their camels *f* hundred and
11: 6 who dwelt at Jerusalem were *f*
Job 1:19 the wilderness and struck the *f*
42:16 and grandchildren for *f*
Prov 30:15 *F* never say, "Enough!":
30:18 *f* which I do not understand:
30:21 for *f* it cannot bear up:
30:24 There are *f* things which are
30:29 *f* which are stately in walk:
Isa 11:12 dispersed of Judah From the *f*

17: 6 *F* or five in its most
Jer 15: 3 I will appoint over them *f*
36:23 when Jehudi had read three or *f*
49:36 Elam I will bring the *f* winds
49:36 the four winds From the *f*
52:21 and its thickness was *f*
52:30 All the persons were *f*
Ezek 1: 5 it came the likeness of *f*
1: 6 Each one had *f* faces, and each
1: 6 and each one had *f* wings.
1: 8 under their wings on their *f*
1: 8 and each of the *f* had faces and
1:10 each of the *f* had the face of a
1:10 each of the *f* had the face of
1:10 and each of the *f* had the face
1:15 each living creature with its *f*
1:16 and all *f* had the same
1:17 they went toward any one of *f*
1:18 all around the *f* of them.
7: 2 The end has come upon the *f*
10: 9 there were *f* wheels by the
10:10 all *f* looked alike—as it were,
10:11 went toward any of their *f*
10:12 and the wheels that the *f* had,
10:14 Each one had *f* faces: the first
10:21 Each one had *f* faces and each
10:21 had four faces and each one *f*
14:21 it shall be when I send My *f*
37: 9 Come from the *f* winds, O breath,
40:41 *F* tables were on this side and
40:41 tables were on this side and *f*
40:42 There were also *f* tables of
41: 5 all around the temple was *f*
42:20 He measured it on the *f* sides;
43:14 *f* cubits; and the width of the
43:15 The altar hearth is *f* cubits
43:15 with *f* horns extending upward
43:16 square at its *f* corners;
43:17 long and fourteen wide on its *f*
43:20 its blood and put it on the *f*
43:20 on the *f* corners of the ledge,
45:19 on the *f* corners of the ledge
46:21 and caused me to pass by the *f*
46:22 In the *f* corners of the court
46:22 all *f* corners were the same
46:23 all around the *f* of them;
48:16 the north side *f* thousand five
48:16 the south side *f* thousand five
48:16 the east side *f* thousand five
48:16 and the west side *f* thousand
48:30 measuring *f* thousand five
48:32 *f* thousand five hundred
48:33 measuring *f* thousand five
48:34 *f* thousand five hundred cubits
Dan 1:17 As for these *f* young men, God
3:25 I see *f* men loose, walking in
7: 2 the *f* winds of heaven were
7: 3 And *f* great beasts came up from
7: 6 which had on its back *f* wings
7: 6 The beast also had *f* heads,
7:17 great beasts, which are *f*,
7:17 are *f* kings which arise out
8: 8 and in place of it *f* notable
8: 8 ones came up toward the *f*
8:22 for the broken horn and the *f*
8:22 *f* kingdoms shall arise out of
11: 4 up and divided toward the *f*
Am 1: 3 of Damascus, and for *f*,
1: 6 of Gaza, and for *f*,
1: 9 of Tyre, and for *f*,
1:11 of Edom, and for *f*,
1:13 the people of Ammon, and for *f*,
2: 1 of Moab, and for *f*,
2: 4 of Judah, and for *f*,
2: 6 of Israel, and for *f*,
Zech 1:18 and there were *f* horns.
1:20 Then the LORD showed me *f*
2: 6 spread you abroad like the *f*
6: 1 *f* chariots were coming from
6: 5 These are *f* spirits of heaven,
Mt 15:38 Now those who ate were *f*
16:10 Nor the seven loaves of the *f*
24:31 together His elect from the *f*
Mk 2: 3 paralytic who was carried by *f*
8: 9 who had eaten were about *f*
8:20 I broke the seven for the *f*
13:27 together His elect from the *f*
Jn 4:35 There are still *f* months and
6:19 they had rowed about three or *f*
11:17 had already been in the tomb *f*
11:39 for he has been dead *f* days."
19:23 took His garments and made *f*
Acts 5:36 about *f* hundred, joined him.
7: 6 bondage and oppress them *f*
10:11 a great sheet bound at the *f*
10:30 *F* days ago I was fasting until
11: 5 let down from heaven by *f*
12: 4 and delivered him to *f* squads
13:20 gave them judges for about *f*
21: 9 Now this man had *f* virgin
21:23 We have *f* men who have taken a
21:38 up a rebellion and led the *f*
27:29 they dropped *f* anchors from the
Gal 3:17 which was *f* hundred and thirty
Rev 4: 6 were *f* living creatures full
4: 8 The *f* living creatures, each
5: 6 of the throne and of the *f*
5: 8 the *f* living creatures and the
5:14 Then the *f* living creatures
6: 1 and I heard one of the *f* living
6: 6 a voice in the midst of the *f*
7: 1 After these things I saw *f*
7: 1 four angels standing at the *f*
7: 1 holding the *f* winds of the
7: 2 with a loud voice to the *f*
7:11 throne and the elders and the *f*
9:13 And I heard a voice from the *f*
9:14 Release the *f* angels who are
9:15 So the *f* angels, who had been
14: 3 before the *f* living creatures,
15: 7 Then one of the *f* living
19: 4 twenty-four elders and the *f*
20: 8 the nations which are in the *f*

FOUR-FIFTHS (1/1)

Gen 47:24 *F* shall be your own, as seed

FOUR-FOOTED (3/3) FOOT, FOUR

Acts 10:12 In it were all kinds of *f*
11: 6 I saw *f* animals of the earth,
Rom 1:23 and birds and *f* animals and

FOURFOLD (2/2)

2 Sam 12: 6 And he shall restore *f* for the
Lk 19: 8 false accusation, I restore *f*.

FOURS (4/4) FOUR

Lev 11:20 insects that creep on all *f*
11:21 insect that creeps on all *f*:
11:27 of animals that go on all *f*,
11:42 belly, whatever goes on all *f*,

FOURSCORE (KJV) See EIGHT (HUNDRED), EIGHTY

FOURSQUARE (2/2)

Ezek 40:47 and one hundred cubits wide, *f*.
48:20 twenty-five thousand cubits, *f*.

FOURTEEN (24/21) FOURTEENTH

Gen 31:41 I served you *f* years for your
46:22 *f* persons in all.
Num 16:49 who died in the plague were *f*
29:13 and *f* lambs in their first
29:15 one-tenth for each of the *f*
29:17 *f* lambs in their first year
29:20 *f* lambs in their first year
29:23 and *f* lambs in their first
29:26 and *f* lambs in their first
29:29 and *f* lambs in their first
29:32 and *f* lambs in their first
Josh 15:36 *f* cities with their villages;
18:28 *f* cities with their villages.
1 Ki 8:65 seven more days—*f* days.
1 Chr 25: 5 For God gave Heman *f* sons and
2 Chr 13:21 married *f* wives, and begot
Job 42:12 for he had *f* thousand sheep,
Ezek 43:17 *f* cubits long and fourteen
43:17 fourteen cubits long and *f*
Mt 1:17 from Abraham to David are *f*
1:17 the captivity in Babylon are *f*
1:17 Babylon until the Christ are *f*
2 Cor 12: 2 I know a man in Christ who *f*
Gal 2: 1 Then after *f* years I went up

FOURTEENTH (25/25) FOURTEEN

Gen 14: 5 In the *f* year Chedorlaomer and
Ex 12: 6 you shall keep it until the *f*
12:18 on the *f* day of the month at
Lev 23: 5 On the *f* day of the first month
Num 9: 3 'On the *f* day of this month,
9: 5 kept the Passover on the *f* day
9:11 On the *f* day of the second
28:16 On the *f* day of the first month
Josh 5:10 and kept the Passover on the *f*
2 Ki 18:13 And in the *f* year of King
1 Chr 24:13 the *f* to Jeshebeab,
25:21 the *f* for Mattithiah, his sons
2 Chr 30:15 the Passover lambs on the *f*
35: 1 the Passover lambs on the *f*
Ezra 6:19 kept the Passover on the *f*
Esth 9:15 together again on the *f* day of
9:17 And on the *f* day of the month
9:18 day, as well as on the *f*;
9:19 towns celebrated the *f* day of
9:21 should celebrate yearly the *f*
Isa 36: 1 Now it came to pass in the *f*
Ezek 40: 1 in the *f* year after the city
45:21 on the *f* day of the month, you
Acts 27:27 Now when the *f* night had come,
27:33 Today is the *f* day you have

FOURTH (71/67) FOUR

Gen 1:19 and the morning were the *f* day.
2:14 The *f* river is the Euphrates.
15:16 But in the *f* generation they
Ex 20: 5 the children to the third and *f*
28:20 and the *f* row, a beryl, an onyx,
34: 7 children to the third and the *f*
39:13 the *f* row, a beryl, an onyx, and
Lev 19:24 But in the *f* year all its fruit
Num 7:30 On the *f* day Elizur the son of
14:18 the children to the third and *f*
29:23 On the *f* day present ten
Deut 5: 9 the children to the third and *f*
Josh 19:17 The *f* lot came out to Issachar,
Judg 19: 5 Then it came to pass on the *f*
1 Sam 9: 8 I have here at hand one *f* of a
2 Sam 3: 4 the *f*, Adonijah the son
1 Ki 6: 1 in the *f* year of Solomon's
6:37 In the *f* year the foundation of
22:41 king over Judah in the *f* year
2 Ki 10:30 the throne of Israel to the *f*
15:12 the throne of Israel to the *f*
18: 9 Now it came to pass in the *f*
25: 3 By the ninth day of the *f*
1 Chr 2:14 Nethanel the *f*, Raddai the
3: 2 Talmai, king of Geshur; the *f*,
3:15 and the *f* Shallum.
8: 2 Nohah the *f*, and Rapha the
12:10 Mishmannah the *f*,
23:19 the third, and Jekameam the *f*.
24: 8 the *f* to Seorim,
24:23 the third, and Jekameam the *f*.
25:11 the *f* for Jizri, his sons and
26: 2 the third, Jathniel the *f*,
26: 4 Joah the third, Sacar the *f*,
26:11 the third, Zechariah the *f*;
27: 7 The *f* captain for the fourth
27: 7 The fourth captain for the *f*
2 Chr 3: 2 of the second month in the *f*
20:26 And on the *f* day they assembled
Ezra 8:33 Now on the *f* day the silver and
Neh 9: 3 and for another *f* they
Jer 25: 1 in the *f* year of Jehoiakim the
28: 1 in the *f* year and in the fifth
36: 1 Now it came to pass in the *f*
39: 2 in the *f* month, on the ninth
45: 1 in the *f* year of Jehoiakim the
46: 2 of Babylon defeated in the *f*
51:59 of Judah to Babylon in the *f*
52: 6 By the *f* month, on the ninth day
Ezek 1: 1 in the *f* month, on the fifth
10:14 and the *f* the face of an eagle.
Dan 2:40 And the *f* kingdom shall be as
3:25 and the form of the *f* is like
7: 7 a *f* beast, dreadful and
7:19 to know the truth about the *f*
7:23 The *f* beast shall be A fourth
7:23 fourth beast shall be A *f*
11: 2 and the *f* shall be far richer
Zech 6: 3 and with the *f* chariot dappled
7: 1 Now in the *f* year of King Darius
7: 1 on the *f* day of the ninth
8:19 'The fast of the *f* month,
Mt 14:25 Now in the *f* watch of the night
Mk 6:48 Now about the *f* watch of the
Rev 4: 7 and the *f* living creature was
6: 7 When He opened the *f* seal,
6: 7 I heard the voice of the *f*
6: 8 was given to them over a *f* of
8:12 Then the *f* angel sounded: And a
16: 8 Then the *f* angel poured out his
21:19 chalcedony, the *f* emerald,

FOWL (4/4) FOWLER

1 Ki 4:23 roebucks, and fatted *f*.
Neh 5:18 Also *f* were prepared for me,
Ps 78:27 Feathered *f* like the sand of
148:10 Creeping things and flying *f*;

FOWLER (2/2) FOWL, FOWLER'S, FOWLERS

Ps 91: 3 you from the snare of the *f*
Prov 6: 5 a bird from the hand of the *f*.

FOWLER'S (1/1) FOWLER

Hos 9: 8 But the prophet is a *f* snare

FOWLERS (1/1) FOWLER

Ps 124: 7 a bird from the snare of the *f*;

FOWLS (KJV) See BIRDS, FOWL, VULTURES

FOX (2/2) FOXES

Neh 4: 3 if even a *f* goes up on it, he
Lk 13:32 said to them, "Go, tell that *f*,

FOXES (9/7) FOX

Judg 15: 4 went and caught three hundred *f*;
15: 4 turned the *f* tail to tail,
15: 5 he let the *f* go into the
Song 2:15 Catch us the *f*,
2:15 The little *f* that spoil the
Lam 5:18 With *f* walking about on it.
Ezek 13: 4 your prophets are like *f* in the
Mt 8:20 *F* have holes and birds of the
Lk 9:58 *F* have holes and birds of the

FRACTURE (2/1)

Lev 24:20 *f* for fracture, eye for eye,
24:20 'fracture for *f*,

FRAGILE (1/1)

Dan 2:42 be partly strong and partly *f*.

FRAGMENTS (10/10)

Isa 30:14 shall not be found among its *f*
Mt 14:20 up twelve baskets full of the *f*
15:37 large baskets full of the *f*

Mk 6:43 up twelve baskets full of *f*
8: 8 large baskets of leftover *f*.
8:19 how many baskets full of *f* did
8:20 many large baskets full of *f*
Lk 9:17 baskets of the leftover *f* were
Jn 6:12 'Gather up the *f* that remain,
6:13 twelve baskets with the *f* of

FRAGRANCE (11/10) FRAGRANT

Lev 26:31 and I will not smell the *f* of
Song 1: 3 Because of the *f* of your good
1:12 My spikenard sends forth its *f*.
4:11 And the *f* of your garments
4:11 your garments Is like the *f*
7: 8 The *f* of your breath like
7:13 The mandrakes give off a *f*,
Hos 14: 6 And his *f* like Lebanon.
Jn 12: 3 house was filled with the *f* of
2 Cor 2:14 and through us diffuses the *f*
2:15 For we are to God the *f* of

FRAGRANT (13/13) FRAGRANCE

Song 3: 6 With all the merchant's *f*
4:13 *F* henna with spikenard,
Mt 26: 7 flask of very costly *f* oil,
26: 9 For this *f* oil might have been
26:12 For in pouring this *f* oil on My
Mk 14: 4 Why was this *f* oil wasted?
Lk 7:37 an alabaster flask of *f* oil,
7:38 and anointed them with the *f*
7:46 has anointed My feet with *f*
23:56 and prepared spices and *f* oils.
Jn 11: 2 who anointed the Lord with *f*
12: 5 Why was this *f* oil not sold for
Rev 18:13 *f* oil and frankincense, wine

FRAIL (1/1) FRAILTY

Ps 39: 4 That I may know how *f* I am.

FRAILTY (1/1) FRAIL

Dan 10: 8 for my vigor was turned to *f* in

FRAME (8/6) FRAMED, FRAMES

Ex 25:25 You shall make for it a *f* of a
25:25 make a gold molding for the *f*
25:27 rings shall be close to the *f*
37:12 Also he made a *f* of a
37:12 a molding of gold for the *f*
37:14 The rings were close to the *f*,
Ps 103:14 For He knows our *f*;
139:15 My *f* was not hidden from You,

FRAMED (1/1) FRAME

Heb 11: 3 that the worlds were *f* by the

FRAMES (10/9) FRAME

1 Ki 6: 4 house windows with beveled *f*.
7: 4 windows with beveled *f* in
7: 5 doorposts had rectangular *f*;
7:28 and the panels were between *f*;
7:29 that were between the *f* were
7:29 And on the *f* was a pedestal on
Ps 50:19 And your tongue *f* deceit.
Ezek 40:16 There were beveled window *f*
41:16 and the beveled window *f*.
41:26 There were beveled window *f*

FRANKINCENSE (17/17)

Ex 30:34 and pure *f* with these sweet
Lev 2: 1 and put *f* on it.
2: 2 flour and oil with all the *f*.
2:15 and lay *f* on it. It is a grain
2:16 of its oil, with all the *f*,
5:11 nor shall he put *f* on it,
6:15 and all the *f* which is on the
24: 7 And you shall put pure *f* on
Num 5:15 pour no oil on it and put no *f*
Neh 13: 5 the grain offerings, the *f*,
13: 9 the grain offering and the *f*.
Song 3: 6 Perfumed with myrrh and *f*,
4: 6 of myrrh And to the hill of *f*.
4:14 cinnamon, With all trees of *f*,
Jer 6:20 what purpose to Me Comes *f*
Mt 2:11 presented gifts to Him: gold, *f*,
Rev 18:13 and incense, fragrant oil and *f*,

FRAUD (3/3)

Hos 7: 1 For they have committed *f*;
Acts 13:10 full of all deceit and all *f*,
Jas 5: 4 which you kept back by *f*,

FRECKLED (KJV) See WHITE

FREE (73/71) FREED, FREEDMAN, FREEDOM, FREELY, FREEWILL, FREEWOMAN

Ex 21: 2 the seventh he shall go out *f*
21: 5 I will not go out *f*,'
21:11 her, then she shall go out *f*,
21:26 he shall let him go *f* for the
21:27 he shall let him go *f* for the
Lev 1: 3 he shall offer it of his own *f*
19: 5 shall offer it of your own *f*
19:20 to death, because she was not *f*.
22:19 shall offer of your own *f*
22:29 offer it of your own *f* will.
Num 5:19 be *f* from this bitter water
5:28 then she shall be *f* and may
5:31 Then the man shall be *f* from
Deut 15:12 year you shall let him go *f*
15:13 And when you send him away *f*
15:18 to you when you send him away *f*
21:14 her, then you shall set her *f*,
24: 5 he shall be *f* at home one year,
32:36 no one remaining, bond or *f*.
Josh 2:20 then we will be *f* from your
Judg 16:20 and shake myself *f*!" But he
1 Ki 14:10 male in Israel, bond and *f*;
21:21 male in Israel, both bond and *f*.
2 Ki 9: 8 in Israel, both bond and *f*.
14:26 and whether bond or *f*,
1 Chr 9:33 and were *f* from other
Job 3:19 And the servant is *f* from his
10: 1 I will give *f* course to my
39: 5 "Who set the wild donkey *f*?
Ps 82: 4 *F* them from the hand of the
105:20 of the people let him go *f*.
Isa 45:13 My city And let My exiles go *f*,
58: 6 To let the oppressed go *f*,
Jer 34: 9 that every man should set *f* his
34:10 that everyone should set *f* his
34:11 return, whom they had set *f*,
34:14 years let every man set *f* his
34:14 you shall let him go *f* from
40: 4 I *f* you this day from the
Zech 9:11 I will set your prisoners *f*
Mal 3:15 They even tempt God and go *f*.
Mt 17:26 to him, "Then the sons are *f*.
Jn 8:32 and the truth shall make you *f*.
8:33 you say, 'You will be made *f*'?
8:36 if the Son makes you *f*,
8:36 you shall be *f* indeed.
Acts 26:32 man might have been set *f*
Rom 5:15 But the *f* gift is not like the
5:16 but the *f* gift which came
5:18 one Man's righteous act the *f*
6:18 And having been set *f* from sin,
6:20 you were *f* in regard to
6:22 But now having been set *f* from
7: 3 she is *f* from that law, so that
8: 2 in Christ Jesus has made me *f*
1 Cor 7:21 but if you can be made *f*,
7:22 he who is called while *f* is
9: 1 Am I not an apostle? Am I not *f*?
9:19 For though I am *f* from all
12:13 or Greeks, whether slaves or *f*—
2 Cor 11: 7 the gospel of God to you *f* of
Gal 3:28 there is neither slave nor *f*,
4:26 but the Jerusalem above is *f*,
4:31 of the bondwoman but of the *f*.
5: 1 by which Christ has made us *f*,
Eph 6: 8 whether he is a slave or *f*.
Col 3:11 Scythian, slave nor *f*,
2 Th 3: 8 did we eat anyone's bread *f* of
Heb 13:23 brother Timothy has been set *f*,
1 Pe 2:16 as *f*, yet not using liberty
Rev 6:15 every slave and every *f* man,
13:16 *f* and slave, to receive a mark
19:18 *f* and slave, both small and

FREED (3/3) FREE

Josh 9:23 and none of you shall be *f* from
Ps 81: 6 His hands were *f* from the
Rom 6: 7 For he who has died has been *f*

FREEDMAN (1/1) FREE, FREEDMEN

1 Cor 7:22 while a slave is the Lord's *f*.

FREEDMEN (1/1) FREEDMAN

Acts 6: 9 called the Synagogue of the *F*

FREEDOM (2/2) FREE

Lev 19:20 been redeemed nor given her *f*,
Ps 146: 7 The LORD gives *f* to the

FREELY (22/21) FREE

Gen 2:16 tree of the garden you may *f*
Num 11: 5 the fish which we ate *f* in
1 Sam 14:30 if the people had eaten *f*
Ezra 2:68 offered *f* for the house of God,
7:15 king and his counselors have *f*
7:16 are to be *f* offered for the
Ps 54: 6 I will *f* sacrifice to You;
Isa 32:20 Who send out *f* the feet of the
Hos 14: 4 I will love them *f*,
Mt 10: 8 *F* you have received, freely
10: 8 you have received, *f* give.
Mk 1:45 out and began to proclaim it *f*,
Lk 7:42 he *f* forgave them both.
Acts 2:29 let me speak *f* to you of the
20:37 Then they all wept *f*,
26:26 before whom I also speak *f*,
Rom 3:24 being justified *f* by His grace
8:32 shall He not with Him also *f*
1 Cor 2:12 the things that have been *f*
2 Cor 8: 3 they were *f* willing,
Rev 21: 6 of the water of life *f* to him
22:17 him take the water of life *f*.

FREEMAN (KJV) See FREEDMAN

FREEWILL (18/18) FREE

Ex 35:29 children of Israel brought a *f*
36: 3 continued bringing to him *f*
Lev 22:18 of his vows or for any of his *f*
22:21 or a *f* offering from the cattle
22:23 too short you may offer as a *f*
23:38 and besides all your *f*
Num 15: 3 to fulfill a vow or as a *f*
29:39 your vowed offerings and your *f*
Deut 12: 6 your *f* offerings, and the
12:17 of your *f* offerings, or of the
16:10 God with the tribute of a *f*
2 Chr 31:14 was over the *f* offerings to
Ezra 1: 4 besides the *f* offerings for the
3: 5 who willingly offered a *f*
7:16 along with the *f* offering of
8:28 silver and the gold are a *f*
Ps 119:108 the *f* offerings of my mouth,
Am 4: 5 Proclaim and announce the *f*

FREEWOMAN (3/3) FREE

Gal 4:22 a bondwoman, the other by a *f*.
4:23 and he of the *f* through
4:30 with the son of the *f*.

FREQUENT (1/1) FREQUENTLY

1 Tim 5:23 your stomach's sake and your *f*

FREQUENTLY (1/1) FREQUENT

2 Cor 11:23 measure, in prisons more *f*,

FRESH (10/10) FRESHLY

Lev 23:14 bread nor parched grain nor *f*
Num 6: 3 nor eat *f* grapes or raisins.
Judg 15:15 He found a *f* jawbone of a
16: 7 If they bind me with seven *f*
16: 8 brought up to her seven *f*
Job 29:20 My glory is *f* within me,
Ps 92:10 I have been anointed with *f*
92:14 They shall be *f* and
Jas 3:11 Does a spring send forth *f*
3:12 yields both salt water and *f*.

FRESHLY (1/1) FRESH

Gen 8:11 a *f* plucked olive leaf was in

FRET (4/4)

Ps 37: 1 Do not *f* because of evildoers,
37: 7 Do not *f* because of him who
37: 8 and forsake wrath; Do not *f*—
Prov 24:19 Do not *f* because of evildoers,

FRETS (1/1)

Prov 19: 3 And his heart *f* against the

FRIEND (55/51) FRIENDLY, FRIENDS, FRIENDSHIP

Gen 38:12 he and his *f* Hirah the
38:20 goat by the hand of his *f* the
Ex 33:11 face, as a man speaks to his *f*.
Deut 13: 6 or your *f* who is as your own
Ruth 4: 1 So Boaz said, "Come aside, *f*,
2 Sam 13: 3 But Amnon had a *f* whose name
15:37 So Hushai, David's *f*,
16:16 Hushai the Archite, David's *f*,
16:17 this your loyalty to your *f*?
16:17 Why did you not go with your *f*?
1 Ki 4: 5 a priest and the king's *f*;
2 Chr 20: 7 descendants of Abraham Your *f*
Job 6:14 should be shown by his *f*,
6:27 And you undermine your *f*.
Ps 15: 3 up a reproach against his *f*;
35:14 about as though he were my *f*
41: 9 Even my own familiar *f* in whom
88:18 Loved one and *f* You have put
Prov 6: 1 if you become surety for your *f*,
6: 3 come into the hand of your *f*:
6: 3 Plead with your *f*.
17:17 A *f* loves at all times, And a
17:18 And becomes surety for his *f*.
18:24 But there is a *f* who sticks
19: 4 poor is separated from his *f*.
19: 6 And every man is a *f* to one
22:11 The king will be his *f*.
27: 6 are the wounds of a *f*,
27: 9 And the sweetness of a man's *f*
27:10 Do not forsake your own *f* or
27:10 own friend or your father's *f*,
27:14 He who blesses his *f* with a
27:17 the countenance of his *f*.
Song 5:16 my beloved, And this is my *f*,
Isa 41: 8 descendants of Abraham My *f*.
Jer 6:21 The neighbor and his *f* shall
19: 9 shall eat the flesh of his *f*
Mic 7: 5 Do not trust in a *f*;
Mt 11:19 a *f* of tax collectors and
20:13 one of them and said, '*F*,
22:12 "So he said to him, '*F*,
26:50 But Jesus said to him, "*F*,
Lk 7:34 a *f* of tax collectors and
11: 5 "Which of you shall have a *f*,
11: 5 at midnight and say to him, '*F*,
11: 6 for a *f* of mine has come to me
11: 8 give to him because he is his *f*,

14:10 you comes he may say to you, '*F*,
Jn 3:29 but the *f* of the bridegroom,
11:11 Our *f* Lazarus sleeps, but I go
19:12 Man go, you are not Caesar's *f*.
Acts 12:20 king's personal aide their *f*,
Phm 1: 1 To Philemon our beloved *f* and
Jas 2:23 And he was called the *f* of
4: 4 therefore wants to be a *f* of

FRIENDLY (2/2) FRIEND

Job 29: 4 When the *f* counsel of God was
Prov 18:24 has friends must himself be *f*,

FRIENDS (56/55) FRIEND

Gen 26:26 with Ahuzzath, one of his *f*,
Judg 11:37 my virginity, my *f* and I."
11:38 and she went with her *f*,
1 Sam 30:26 the elders of Judah, to his *f*,
2 Sam 3: 8 to his brothers, and to his *f*,
19: 6 your enemies and hate your *f*.
1 Ki 16:11 of his relatives nor of his *f*.
Esth 5:10 he sent and called for his *f*
5:14 his wife Zeresh and all his *f*
6:13 his wife Zeresh and all his *f*
Job 2:11 Now when Job's three *f* heard of
12: 4 "I am one mocked by his *f*,
16:20 My *f* scorn me; My eyes pour
17: 5 who speaks flattery to his *f*,
19:14 And my close *f* have forgotten
19:19 All my close *f* abhor me,
19:21 me, have pity on me, O you my *f*,
32: 3 Also against his three *f* his
42: 7 against you and your two *f*,
42:10 losses when he prayed for his *f*.
Ps 38:11 My loved ones and my *f* stand
Prov 12:26 righteous should choose his *f*
14:20 But the rich has many *f*.
16:28 separates the best of *f*.
17: 9 repeats a matter separates *f*.
18:24 A man who has *f* must himself
19: 4 Wealth makes many *f*,
19: 7 How much more do his *f* go far
Song 5: 1 O *f*! Drink, yes, drink deeply,
Jer 20: 4 to yourself and to all your *f*;
20: 6 there, you and all your *f*,
38:22 Your close *f* have set upon you
Lam 1: 2 All her *f* have dealt
Zech 13: 6 wounded in the house of my *f*.
Mt 9:15 Can the *f* of the bridegroom
Mk 2:19 Can the *f* of the bridegroom fast
5:19 to him, "Go home to your *f*,
Lk 5:34 Can you make the *f* of the
7: 6 the centurion sent *f* to Him,
12: 4 "And I say to you, My *f*,
14:12 or a supper, do not ask your *f*,
15: 6 he calls together his *f* and
15: 9 she calls her *f* and neighbors
15:29 I might make merry with my *f*.
16: 9 make *f* for yourselves by
21:16 and brothers, relatives and *f*;
23:12 day Pilate and Herod became *f*
Jn 15:13 lay down one's life for his *f*.
15:14 You are My *f* if you do whatever
15:15 but I have called you *f*,
Acts 10:24 his relatives and close *f*.
19:31 of Asia, who were his *f*,
24:23 him not to forbid any of his *f*
27: 3 him liberty to go to his *f*
3 Jn 14 Our *f* greet you. Greet the
14 Greet the *f* by name.

FRIENDSHIP (2/2) FRIEND

Prov 22:24 Make no *f* with an angry man,
Jas 4: 4 Do you not know that *f* with

FRIGHTEN (8/8) FRIGHTENED

Deut 28:26 and no one shall *f* them away.
2 Chr 32:18 to *f* them and trouble them,
Neh 6:19 Tobiah sent letters to *f* me.
Job 13:25 Will You *f* a leaf driven to and
18:11 Terrors *f* him on every side,
39:20 Can you *f* him like a locust?
Ps 83:15 And *f* them with Your storm.
Jer 7:33 And no one will *f* them away.

FRIGHTENED (6/6) FRIGHTEN

2 Sam 22:46 And come *f* from their
Job 18:20 As those in the east are *f*.
39:22 He mocks at fear, and is not *f*;
Ps 18:45 And come *f* from their
Isa 21: 4 fearfulness *f* me; The night
Lk 24:37 But they were terrified and *f*,

FRIVOLITY (2/2)

Prov 12:11 But he who follows *f* is
28:19 But he who follows *f* will have

FRO (23/21)

Gen 8: 7 which kept going to and *f* until
2 Chr 16: 9 eyes of the LORD run to and *f*
Job 1: 7 From going to and *f* on the
2: 2 From going to and *f* on the
13:25 frighten a leaf driven to and *f*?
28: 4 from men; They swing to and *f*.
Ps 107:27 They reel to and *f*,
Isa 24:20 The earth shall reel to and *f*
33: 4 As the running to and *f* of
49:21 captive, and wandering to and *f*?
Jer 5: 1 Run to and *f* through the streets
5:22 though its waves toss to and *f*,
49: 3 Lament and run to and *f* by
Dan 12: 4 many shall run to and *f*,
Joel 2: 9 They run to and *f* in the city,
Am 8:12 They shall run to and *f*,
Zech 1:10 LORD has sent to walk to and *f*
1:11 We have walked to and *f*
4:10 Which scan to and *f* throughout
6: 7 that they might walk to and *f*
6: 7 walk to and *f* throughout the
6: 7 So they walked to and *f*
Eph 4:14 tossed to and *f* and carried

FROGS (14/14)

Ex 8: 2 smite all your territory with *f*.
8: 3 the river shall bring forth *f*
8: 4 And the *f* shall come up on you,
8: 5 and cause *f* to come up on the
8: 6 and the *f* came up and covered
8: 7 and brought up *f* on the land of
8: 8 that He may take away the *f*
8: 9 to destroy the *f* from you and
8:11 And the *f* shall depart from you,
8:12 to the LORD concerning the *f*
8:13 And the *f* died out of the
Ps 78:45 which devoured them, And *f*,
105:30 Their land abounded with *f*,
Rev 16:13 three unclean spirits like *f*

FROM (5170/4336) See APPENDIX

FRONT (76/70)

Gen 32:17 Whose are these in *f* of you?'
33: 2 and their children in *f*,
Ex 25:37 so that they give light in *f*
28:25 straps of the ephod in the *f*.
28:27 the ephod toward its *f*,
28:37 it shall be on the *f* of the
39:18 straps of the ephod in the *f*.
39:20 the ephod toward its *f*,
40:26 the tabernacle of meeting in *f*
Lev 4: 6 in *f* of the veil of the
4:17 in *f* of the veil.
8: 9 Also on the turban, on its *f*,
Num 8: 2 lamps shall give light in *f* of
8: 3 the lamps to face toward the *f*
19: 4 seven times directly in *f* of
Deut 14: 1 cut yourselves nor shave the *f*
Josh 8:33 Half of them were in *f* of
8:33 Gerizim and half of them in *f*
Judg 18:21 and the goods in *f* of them.
20:43 them down as far as the *f* of
1 Sam 14: 5 The *f* of one faced northward
2 Sam 5:23 and come upon them in *f* of the
1 Ki 6: 3 The vestibule in *f* of the
6: 3 ten cubits from the *f* of the
6:17 And in *f* of it the temple
6:21 gold chains across the *f* of
7: 6 and in *f* of them was a portico
7: 6 and a canopy was in *f* of them.
7:49 and five on the left in *f* of
8: 8 in *f* of the inner sanctuary;
8:64 of the court that was in *f* of
2 Ki 15:10 and struck and killed him in *f*
16:14 from the *f* of the temple—from
1 Chr 14:14 and come upon them in *f* of the
2 Chr 3: 4 the vestibule that was in *f*
3:15 Also he made in *f* of the temple
4:20 in the prescribed manner in *f*
5: 9 in *f* of the inner sanctuary;
7: 7 of the court that was in *f* of
13:13 so they were in *f* of Judah, and
13:14 the battle line was at both *f*
20:27 with Jehoshaphat in *f* of them,
Neh 3:10 of Harumaph made repairs in *f*
3:16 as far as the place in *f* of
3:19 repaired another section in *f*
3:26 as far as the place in *f* of
3:28 each in *f* of his own house.
3:29 son of Immer made repairs in *f*
3:30 of Berechiah made repairs in *f*
3:31 in *f* of the Miphkad Gate, and
7: 3 watch station and another in *f*
8: 1 the open square that was in *f*
8: 3 the open square that was in *f*
12:37 in *f* of them, they went up the
Esth 2:11 every day Mordecai paced in *f*
4: 2 He went as far as the *f* of the
4: 6 the city square that was in *f*
Ezek 40:12 There was a space in *f* of the
40:15 From the *f* of the entrance gate
40:15 of the entrance gate to the *f*
40:19 measured the width from the *f*
40:19 of the lower gateway to the *f*
40:22 and its archway was in *f* of
40:26 and its archway was in *f* of
40:47 The altar was in *f* of the
41:21 as was the *f* of the
41:25 A wooden canopy was on the *f*
42: 4 In *f* of the chambers, toward the
42: 7 at the *f* of the chambers,
42:11 There was a walk in *f* of them
42:12 there was a door in *f* of the
42:12 the way directly in *f* of the
44: 4 way of the north gate to the *f*
47: 1 for the *f* of the temple faced
Acts 14:13 whose temple was in *f* of their
Rev 4: 6 creatures full of eyes in *f*

FRONTIER (2/2)

Josh 22:11 have built an altar on the *f*
Ezek 25: 9 cities, of the cities on its *f*,

FRONTLETS (3/3)

Ex 13:16 as a sign on your hand and as *f*
Deut 6: 8 and they shall be as *f* between
11:18 and they shall be as *f* between

FROST (6/6)

Gen 31:40 and the *f* by night, and my
Ex 16:14 as fine as *f* on the ground.
Job 38:29 And the *f* of heaven, who gives
Ps 78:47 their sycamore trees with *f*.
147:16 He scatters the *f* like ashes;
Jer 36:30 the heat of the day and the *f*

FROWARD (KJV) See CUNNING, DEVIOUS, HARSH, PERVERSE

FROZEN (2/2)

Job 37:10 And the broad waters are *f*.
38:30 the surface of the deep is *f*.

FRUIT (189/175) FRUITFUL, FRUITS

Gen 1:11 and the *f* tree that yields
1:11 the fruit tree that yields *f*
1:12 and the tree that yields *f*,
1:29 and every tree whose *f* yields
3: 2 We may eat the *f* of the trees of
3: 3 but of the *f* of the tree which
3: 6 she took of its *f* and ate.
4: 3 brought an offering of the *f*
30: 2 has withheld from you the *f* of
Ex 10:15 herb of the land and all the *f*
23:16 you have gathered in the *f*
Lev 19:23 then you shall count their *f* as
19:24 in the fourth year all its *f*
19:25 fifth year you may eat its *f*,
23:39 you have gathered in the *f* of
23:40 on the first day the *f* of
25: 3 your vineyard, and gather its *f*;
25:19 'Then the land will yield its *f*,
26: 4 the field shall yield their *f*.
26:20 trees of the land yield their *f*.
27:30 seed of the land or of the *f*
Num 13:20 And bring some of the *f* of the
13:26 and showed them the *f* of the
13:27 and honey, and this is its *f*.
18:13 Whatever first ripe *f* is in
Deut 1:25 They also took some of the *f* of
7:13 He will also bless the *f* of
7:13 fruit of your womb and the *f*
22: 9 which you have sown and the *f*
28: 4 Blessed shall be the *f* of your
28:11 in the *f* of your body, in the
28:18 Cursed shall be the *f* of your
28:33 have not known shall eat the *f*
28:53 You shall eat the *f* of your own
30: 9 in the *f* of your body, in the
Judg 9:11 my sweetness and my good *f*,
2 Sam 16: 2 the bread and summer *f* for the
2 Ki 19:29 Plant vineyards and eat the *f*
19:30 And bear *f* upward.
Neh 9:25 And *f* trees in abundance.
9:36 To eat its *f* and its bounty,
10:35 and the firstfruits of all *f*
10:37 the *f* from all kinds of trees,
Job 31:39 If I have eaten its *f* without
Ps 1: 3 That brings forth its *f* in its
72:16 Its *f* shall wave like Lebanon;
80:12 pass by the way pluck her *f*?
92:14 They shall still bear *f* in old
104:13 earth is satisfied with the *f*
105:35 And devoured the *f* of their
127: 3 The *f* of the womb is a
132:11 set upon your throne the *f* of
Prov 1:31 they shall eat the *f* of their
8:19 My *f* is better than gold, yes,
11:30 The *f* of the righteous is a
12:12 root of the righteous yields *f*.
12:14 be satisifed with good by the *f*
13: 2 A man shall eat well by the *f*
18:20 shall be satisfied from the *f*
18:21 who love it will eat its *f*.
27:18 the fig tree will eat its *f*;
31:31 Give her of the *f* of her hands,
Eccl 2: 5 and I planted all kinds of *f*
Song 2: 3 And his *f* was sweet to my
8:11 was to bring for its *f* A
8:12 And those who tend its *f* two
Isa 3:10 For they shall eat the *f* of
4: 2 And the *f* of the earth shall
10:12 I will punish the *f* of the
13:18 will have no pity on the *f* of
27: 6 the face of the world with *f*.
27: 9 And this is all the *f* of
28: 4 Like the first *f* before the
34: 4 And as *f* falling from a fig
37:30 Plant vineyards and eat the *f*
37:31 And bear *f* upward.
57:19 I create the *f* of the lips:
65:21 plant vineyards and eat their *f*.

Jer 2: 7 To eat its *f* and its goodness.
6:19 The *f* of their thoughts,
7:20 of the field and on the *f* of
11:16 Tree, Lovely and of Good *F*.
11:19 us destroy the tree with its *f*,
12: 2 They grow, yes, they bear *f*.
17: 8 Nor will cease from yielding *f*.
17:10 According to the *f* of his
21:14 punish you according to the *f*
29: 5 plant gardens and eat their *f*.
29:28 plant gardens and eat their *f*.
32:19 ways and according to the *f* of
40:10 gather wine and summer *f* and
40:12 and gathered wine and summer *f*
48:32 has fallen on your summer *f*
Ezek 17: 8 bring forth branches, bear *f*,
17: 9 up its roots, Cut off its *f*,
17:23 bring forth boughs, and bear *f*,
19:12 And the east wind dried her *f*.
19:14 branches And devoured her *f*,
25: 4 they shall eat your *f*,
34:27 the field shall yield their *f*,
36: 8 your branches and yield your *f*
36:30 And I will multiply the *f* of
47:12 and their *f* will not fail.
47:12 They will bear *f* every month,
47:12 Their *f* will be for food, and
Dan 4:12 Its *f* abundant, And in it
4:14 its leaves and scatter its *f*.
4:21 leaves were lovely and its *f*
Hos 9:16 dried up; They shall bear no *f*.
10: 1 He brings forth *f* for himself.
10: 1 to the multitude of his *f* He
10:13 You have eaten the *f* of lies,
14: 8 Your *f* is found in Me."
Joel 2:22 And the tree bears its *f*;
Am 2: 9 Yet I destroyed his *f* above
6:12 And the *f* of righteousness
7:14 And a tender of sycamore *f*.
8: 1 Behold, a basket of summer *f*.
8: 2 I said, "A basket of summer *f*."
9:14 also make gardens and eat *f*
Mic 6: 7 The *f* of my body for the sin
7: 1 to eat Of the first-ripe *f*
7:13 And for the *f* of their deeds.
Hab 3:17 Nor *f* be on the vines;
Hag 1:10 and the earth withholds its *f*.
2:19 olive tree have not yielded *f*.
Zech 8:12 The vine shall give its *f*,
Mal 1:12 LORD is defiled; And its *f*,
3:11 that he will not destroy the *f*
3:11 shall the vine fail to bear *f*
Mt 3:10 which does not bear good *f* is
7:17 every good tree bears good *f*,
7:17 but a bad tree bears bad *f*.
7:18 "A good tree cannot bear bad *f*,
7:18 nor can a bad tree bear good *f*.
7:19 tree that does not bear good *f*
12:33 make the tree good and its *f*
12:33 make the tree bad and its *f*
12:33 for a tree is known by its *f*.
13:23 who indeed bears *f* and
21:19 Let no *f* grow on you ever
21:34 that they might receive its *f*.
26:29 I will not drink of this *f* of
Mk 4:20 word, accept it, and bear *f*:
11:14 Let no one eat *f* from you ever
12: 2 he might receive some of the *f*
14:25 I will no longer drink of the *f*
Lk 1:42 and blessed is the *f* of your
3: 9 which does not bear good *f* is
6:43 a good tree does not bear bad *f*,
6:43 nor does a bad tree bear good *f*.
6:44 tree is known by its own *f*.
8:14 and bring no *f* to maturity.
8:15 keep it and bear *f* with
13: 6 and he came seeking *f* on it and
13: 7 years I have come seeking *f* on
13: 9 'And if it bears *f*,
20:10 might give him some of the *f*
22:18 I will not drink of the *f* of
Jn 4:36 and gathers *f* for eternal life,
15: 2 in Me that does not bear *f* He
15: 2 and every branch that bears *f*
15: 2 prunes, that it may bear more *f*.
15: 4 As the branch cannot bear *f* of
15: 5 Me, and I in him, bears much *f*;
15: 8 glorified, that you bear much *f*;
15:16 that you should go and bear *f*,
15:16 and that your *f* should remain,
Acts 2:30 an oath to him that of the *f*
Rom 1:13 that I might have some *f* among
6:21 What *f* did you have then in the
6:22 you have your *f* to holiness,
7: 4 that we should bear *f* to God.
7: 5 work in our members to bear *f*
15:28 and have sealed to them this *f*,
1 Cor 9: 7 and does not eat of its *f*?
Gal 5:22 But the *f* of the Spirit is love,
Eph 5: 9 (for the *f* of the Spirit is in
Phil 1:22 this will mean *f* from my
4:17 but I seek the *f* that abounds
Col 1: 6 world, and is bringing forth *f*,
Heb 12:11 it yields the peaceable *f* of
13:15 the *f* of our lips, giving
Jas 3:18 Now the *f* of righteousness is
5: 7 waits for the precious *f* of
5:18 and the earth produced its *f*.
Jude 12 late autumn trees without *f*,
Rev 18:14 The *f* that your soul longed for
22: 2 each tree yielding its *f* every

FRUITFUL (37/34) FRUIT, UNFRUITFUL

Gen 1:22 Be *f* and multiply, and fill the
1:28 Be *f* and multiply; fill the
8:17 and be *f* and multiply on the
9: 1 Be *f* and multiply, and fill the
9: 7 be *f* and multiply; Bring forth
17: 6 "I will make you exceedingly *f*;
17:20 him, and will make him *f*,
26:22 and we shall be *f* in the
28: 3 And make you *f* and multiply
35:11 Be *f* and multiply; a nation and
41:52 For God has caused me to be *f* in
48: 4 I will make you *f* and multiply
49:22 'Joseph is a *f* bough,
49:22 A *f* bough by a well;
Ex 1: 7 the children of Israel were *f*
Lev 26: 9 on you favorably and make you *f*,
2 Ki 19:23 To its *f* forest.
Ps 107:34 A *f* land into barrenness,
107:37 That they may yield a *f*
128: 3 Your wife shall be like a *f*
148: 9 *F* trees and all cedars;
Isa 5: 1 has a vineyard On a very *f*
10:18 of his forest and of his *f*
17: 6 Four or five in its most *f*
29:17 shall be turned into a *f* field,
29:17 And the *f* field be esteemed as
32:12 for the *f* vine.
32:15 And the wilderness becomes a *f*
32:15 And the *f* field is counted as
32:16 righteousness remain in the *f*
37:24 To its *f* forest.
Jer 4:26 and indeed the *f* land was a
23: 3 and they shall be *f* and
Ezek 19:10 *F* and full of branches
Hos 13:15 Though he is *f* among his
Acts 14:17 gave us rain from heaven and *f*
Col 1:10 being *f* in every good work and

FRUITS (20/20) FRUIT

Gen 43:11 Take some of the best *f* of the
Deut 33:14 With the precious *f* of the sun,
2 Sam 16: 1 raisins, one hundred summer *f*,
Song 4:13 pomegranates With pleasant *f*,
4:16 garden And eat its pleasant *f*.
7:13 at our gates are pleasant *f*,
Isa 16: 9 fallen Over your summer *f* and
33: 9 and Carmel shake off their *f*.
Lam 4: 9 Stricken for lack of the *f*
Mic 7: 1 like those who gather summer *f*,
Mt 3: 8 Therefore bear *f* worthy of
7:16 "You will know them by their *f*.
7:20 Therefore by their *f* you will
21:41 who will render to him the *f*
21:43 to a nation bearing the *f* of
Lk 3: 8 Therefore bear *f* worthy of
2 Cor 9:10 have sown and increase the *f*
Phil 1:11 being filled with the *f* of
Jas 3:17 yield, full of mercy and good *f*,
Rev 22: 2 of life, which bore twelve *f*,

FRUSTRATE (1/1)

Ezra 4: 5 counselors against them to *f*

FRUSTRATED (1/1)

Dan 3:28 and they have *f* the king's

FRUSTRATES (2/2)

Job 5:12 He *f* the devices of the crafty,
Isa 44:25 Who *f* the signs of the

FRYINGPAN (KJV) See (COVERED) PAN

FUEL (7/7)

Isa 9: 5 be used for burning and *f* of
9:19 And the people shall be as *f*
Ezek 4:12 and bake it using *f* of human
15: 4 is thrown into the fire for *f*;
15: 6 I have given to the fire for *f*,
21:32 You shall be *f* for the fire;
24: 5 Also pile *f* bones under it,

FUGITIVE (3/3)

Gen 4:12 A *f* and a vagabond you shall be
4:14 I shall be a *f* and a vagabond
1 Chr 12: 1 Ziklag while he was still a *f*

FUGITIVES (5/5)

Num 21:29 He has given his sons as *f*,
Judg 12: 4 You Gileadites are *f* of Ephraim
Isa 15: 5 His *f* shall flee to Zoar,
43:14 And bring them all down as *f*—
Ezek 17:21 All his *f* with all his troops

FULFILL (34/33) FULFILLED, FULFILLING, FULFILLMENT, FULFILLS

Gen 29:27 *F* her week, and we will give you
Ex 5:13 *F* your work, your daily quota,
23:26 I will *f* the number of your
Lev 22:21 to *f* his vow, or a freewill
Num 15: 3 to *f* a vow or as a freewill
15: 8 or as a sacrifice to *f* a vow,
Deut 9: 5 and that He may *f* the word
1 Ki 2: 4 that the LORD may *f* His word
2:27 that he might *f* the word of the
5: 9 And you shall *f* my desire by
12:15 that He might *f* His word, which
1 Chr 22:13 if you take care to *f* the
2 Chr 10:15 that the LORD might *f* His
36:21 to *f* the word of the LORD by
36:21 to *f* seventy years.
Esth 5: 8 to grant my petition and *f* my
Job 39: 2 number the months that they *f*?
Ps 20: 4 And *f* all your purpose.
20: 5 our banners! May the LORD *f*
145:19 He will *f* the desire of those
Ezek 20: 8 pour out My fury on them and *f*
20:21 pour out My fury on them and *f*
Mt 3:15 thus it is fitting for us to *f*
5:17 not come to destroy but to *f*.
Rom 13:14 to *f* its lusts.
Gal 5:16 and you shall not *f* the lust of
6: 2 and so *f* the law of Christ.
Phil 2: 2 *f* my joy by being like-minded,
Col 1:25 to *f* the word of God,
4:17 that you may *f* it."
2 Th 1:11 and *f* all the good pleasure of
2 Tim 4: 5 *f* your ministry.
Jas 2: 8 If you really *f* the royal law
Rev 17:17 put it into their hearts to *f*

FULFILLED (75/75) FULFILL

Gen 25:24 So when her days were *f* for
29:21 me my wife, for my days are *f*,
29:28 Then Jacob did so and *f* her
Ex 5:14 Why have you not *f* your task in
Lev 12: 4 days of her purification are *f*.
12: 6 days of her purification are *f*,
Num 6: 5 until the days are *f* for which
6:13 days of his separation are *f*,
2 Sam 7:12 When your days are *f* and you
14:22 in that the king has *f* the
1 Ki 8:15 and with His hand has *f* it,
8:20 So the LORD has *f* His word
8:24 spoken with Your mouth and *f*
1 Chr 17:11 shall be, when your days are *f*,
2 Chr 6: 4 who has *f* with His hands what
6:10 So the LORD has *f* His word
6:15 spoken with Your mouth and *f*
36:22 mouth of Jeremiah might be *f*,
Ezra 1: 1 mouth of Jeremiah might be *f*,
Isa 65:20 Nor an old man who has not *f*
Jer 25:34 and your dispersions are *f*;
44:25 spoken with your mouths and *f*
Lam 2:17 He has *f* His word Which He
4:11 The LORD has *f* His fury,
Dan 4:33 That very hour the word was *f*
10: 3 till three whole weeks were *f*.
Mt 1:22 was done that it might be *f*
2:15 that it might be *f* which was
2:17 Then was *f* what was spoken by
2:23 that it might be *f* which was
4:14 that it might be *f* which was
5:18 pass from the law till all is *f*.
8:17 that it might be *f* which was
12:17 that it might be *f* which was
13:14 the prophecy of Isaiah is *f*,
13:35 that it might be *f* which was
21: 4 was done that it might be *f*
26:54 then could the Scriptures be *f*,
26:56 of the prophets might be *f*.
27: 9 Then was *f* what was spoken by
27:35 that it might be *f* which was
Mk 1:15 and saying, "The time is *f*,
13: 4 when all these things will be *f*?
14:49 But the Scriptures must be *f*.
15:28 So the Scripture was *f* which
Lk 1: 1 those things which have been *f*
1:20 my words which will be *f* in
4:21 Today this Scripture is *f* in
21:22 which are written may be *f*.
21:24 the times of the Gentiles are *f*.
22:16 longer eat of it until it is *f*
24:44 that all things must be *f* which
Jn 3:29 Therefore this joy of mine is *f*.
12:38 Isaiah the prophet might be *f*,
13:18 but that the Scripture may be *f*,
15:25 that the word might be *f* which
17:12 that the Scripture might be *f*.
17:13 that they may have My joy *f* in
18: 9 that the saying might be *f* which
18:32 the saying of Jesus might be *f*
19:24 that the Scripture might be *f*
19:28 that the Scripture might be *f*,
19:36 that the Scripture should be *f*,
Acts 1:16 this Scripture had to be *f*,
3:18 would suffer, He has thus *f*.
12:25 from Jerusalem when they had *f*
13:27 have *f* them in condemning
13:29 Now when they had *f* all that was
13:33 God has *f* this for us their
Rom 8: 4 of the law might be *f* in us
13: 8 for he who loves another has *f*
2 Cor 10: 6 when your obedience is *f*.
Gal 5:14 For all the law is *f* in one
Jas 2:23 And the Scripture was *f* which
Rev 17:17 until the words of God are *f*.

FULFILLING (2/2) FULFILL

Ps 148: 8 Stormy wind, *f* His word;
Eph 2: 3 *f* the desires of the flesh and

FULFILLMENT (6/6) FULFILL

Ps 66:12 You brought us out to rich *f*.
Ezek 12:23 and the *f* of every vision.
Dan 11:14 shall exalt themselves in *f* of
12: 6 How long shall the *f* of these
Lk 1:45 for there will be a *f* of the
Rom 13:10 therefore love is the *f* of the

FULFILLS (1/1) FULFILL

Rom 2:27 if he *f* the law, judge you who,

FULL (242/234) FILL, FULL-GROWN, FULLNESS, FULLY

Gen 14:10 the Valley of Siddim was *f*
23: 9 Let him give it to me at the *f*
25: 8 an old man and *f* of years,
35:29 being old and *f* of days.
41: 1 at the end of two *f* years, that
41: 7 devoured the seven plump and *f*
41:22 up on one stalk, *f* and good.
43:21 our money in *f* weight; so we
Ex 8:21 of the Egyptians shall be *f* of
14:27 the sea returned to its *f*
16: 3 when we ate bread to the *f*!
16: 8 in the morning bread to the *f*;
22: 3 He should make *f* restitution;
Lev 2:14 grain beaten from *f* heads.
6: 5 He shall restore its *f* value,
16:12 Then he shall take a censer *f* of
16:12 with his hands *f* of sweet
19:29 and the land become *f* of
25:29 within a *f* year he may redeem
25:30 within the space of a *f* year,
26: 5 shall eat your bread to the *f*,
Num 5: 7 for his trespass in *f*,
7:13 both of them *f* of fine flour
7:14 of ten shekels, *f* of incense;
7:19 both of them *f* of fine flour
7:20 of ten shekels, *f* of incense;
7:25 both of them *f* of fine flour
7:26 of ten shekels, *f* of incense;
7:31 both of them *f* of fine flour
7:32 of ten shekels, *f* of incense;
7:37 both of them *f* of fine flour
7:38 of ten shekels, *f* of incense;
7:43 both of them *f* of fine flour
7:44 of ten shekels, *f* of incense;
7:49 both of them *f* of fine flour
7:50 of ten shekels, *f* of incense;
7:55 both of them *f* of fine flour
7:56 of ten shekels, *f* of incense;
7:61 both of them *f* of fine flour
7:62 of ten shekels, *f* of incense;
7:67 both of them *f* of fine flour
7:68 of ten shekels, *f* of incense;
7:73 both of them *f* of fine flour
7:74 of ten shekels, *f* of incense;
7:79 both of them *f* of fine flour
7:80 of ten shekels, *f* of incense;
7:86 The twelve gold pans *f* of
22:18 were to give me his house *f* of
24:13 were to give me his house *f* of
Deut 6:11 houses *f* of all good things,
6:11 you have eaten and are *f*—
8:10 "When you have eaten and are *f*,
8:12 you have eaten and are *f*,
21:13 her father and her mother a *f*
33:23 And *f* of the blessing of the
34: 9 Joshua the son of Nun was *f* of
Judg 5:31 the sun When it comes out in *f*
16:27 Now the temple was *f* of men and
Ruth 1:21 'I went out *f*, and the LORD
2:12 and a *f* reward be given you by
1 Sam 2: 5 Those who were *f* have hired
18:27 and they gave them in *f* count
27: 7 of the Philistines was one *f*
28:20 Then immediately Saul fell *f*
2 Sam 8: 2 and with one *f* line those to be
13:23 after two *f* years, that Absalom
14:28 And Absalom dwelt two *f* years
23:11 there was a piece of ground *f*
2 Ki 3:16 Make this valley *f* of ditches.'
4: 4 and set aside the *f* ones."
4: 6 pass, when the vessels were *f*,
6:17 the mountain was *f* of horses
7:15 and indeed all the road was *f*
9:24 Now Jehu drew his bow with *f*
10:21 and the temple of Baal was *f*
15:13 and he reigned a *f* month in
1 Chr 11:13 there was a piece of ground *f*
21:22 shall grant it to me at the *f*
21:24 I will surely buy it for the *f*
23: 1 So when David was old and *f* of
29:28 *f* of days and riches and honor;
2 Chr 24:15 Jehoiada grew old and was *f* of
Ezra 7:19 deliver in *f* before the God of
Neh 9:25 And possessed houses *f* of all
Esth 9:29 wrote with *f* authority to
Job 5:26 shall come to the grave at a *f*
10:15 I am *f* of disgrace; See my
11: 2 And should a man *f* of talk be
14: 1 of woman Is of few days and *f*
20:11 His bones are *f* of his youthful
21:23 One dies in his *f* strength,
21:24 His pails are *f* of milk,
32:18 For I am *f* of words;
36:16 set on your table would be *f*
42:17 old and *f* of days.
Ps 10: 7 His mouth is *f* of cursing and
26:10 And whose right hand is *f* of
29: 4 The voice of the LORD is *f*
33: 5 The earth is *f* of the goodness
38: 7 For my loins are *f* of
48:10 Your right hand is *f* of
65: 9 The river of God is *f* of
69:20 And I am *f* of heaviness;
73:10 And waters of a *f* cup are
74:20 dark places of the earth are *f*
78:25 He sent them food to the *f*.
78:38 being *f* of compassion, forgave
81: 3 At the *f* moon, on our solemn
86:15 are a God *f* of compassion, and
88: 3 For my soul is *f* of troubles,
104:16 The trees of the LORD are *f*
104:24 The earth is *f* of Your
111: 4 The LORD is gracious and *f*
112: 4 and *f* of compassion, and
119:64 is *f* of Your mercy; Teach me
127: 5 the man who has his quiver *f*
144:13 That our barns may be *f*,
145: 8 The LORD is gracious and *f* of
Prov 1:31 And be filled to the *f* with
17: 1 Than a house *f* of feasting
27:20 and Destruction are never *f*;
30: 9 Lest I be *f* and deny You,
Eccl 1: 7 the sea, Yet the sea is not *f*;
1: 8 All things are *f* of labor;
4: 6 quietness Than both hands *f*,
9: 3 of the sons of men are *f* of
11: 3 If the clouds are *f* of rain,
Isa 1:15 Your hands are *f* of blood.
1:21 has become a harlot! It was *f*
2: 7 Their land is also *f* of silver
2: 7 Their land is also *f* of
2: 8 Their land is also *f* of idols;
6: 3 The whole earth is *f* of His
11: 9 For the earth shall be *f* of
13:21 And their houses will be *f* of
15: 9 the waters of Dimon will be *f*
22: 2 You who are *f* of noise,
22: 7 choicest valleys Shall be *f*
25: 6 Of fat things *f* of marrow,
28: 8 For all tables are *f* of vomit
30:27 His lips are *f* of indignation,
51:20 They are *f* of the fury of the
Jer 4:27 Yet I will not make a *f* end.
5: 7 When I had fed them to the *f*,
5:27 As a cage is *f* of birds,
5:27 So their houses are *f* of
6: 6 She is *f* of oppression in her
6:11 Therefore I am *f* of the fury of
6:11 The aged with him who is *f*
23:10 For the land is *f* of
28: 3 Within two *f* years I will bring
28:11 within the space of two *f*
30:11 Though I make a *f* end of all
35: 5 of the Rechabites bowls *f* of
Lam 1: 1 sits the city That was *f* of
3:30 And be *f* of reproach.
Ezek 1:18 and their rims were *f* of eyes,
7:23 And the city is *f* of violence.
9: 9 and the land is *f* of bloodshed,
9: 9 and the city *f* of perversity;
10: 4 and the court was *f* of the
10:12 were *f* of eyes all around.
17: 3 *F* of feathers of various
19:10 Fruitful and *f* of branches
22: 5 mock you as infamous and *f* of
28:12 *F* of wisdom and perfect in
32: 6 And the riverbeds will be *f* of
37: 1 and it was *f* of bones.
39:19 shall eat fat till you are *f*,
41: 8 a *f* rod, that is, six cubits
Dan 3:19 Then Nebuchadnezzar was *f* of
10: 2 was mourning three *f* weeks.
Joel 2:24 threshing floors shall be *f* of
3:13 For the winepress is *f*,
Am 2:13 As a cart *f* of sheaves is
Mic 3: 8 But truly I am *f* of power by
6:12 For her rich men are *f* of
Nah 3: 1 the bloody city! It is all *f*
Hab 3: 3 And the earth was *f* of His
Zech 8: 5 of the city Shall be *f* of
Mt 6:22 your whole body will be *f* of
6:23 your whole body will be *f* of
13:48 "which, when it was *f*,
14:20 they took up twelve baskets *f*
15:37 took up seven large baskets *f*
23:25 but inside they are *f* of
23:27 but inside are *f* of dead men's
23:28 but inside you are *f* of
Mk 4:28 after that the *f* grain in the
6:43 they took up twelve baskets *f*
8:19 how many baskets *f* of fragments
8:20 how many large baskets *f* of
15:36 ran and filled a sponge *f* of
Lk 1:57 Now Elizabeth's *f* time came for
5:12 a man who was *f* of leprosy saw
6:25 Woe to you who are *f*,
11:34 your whole body also is *f* of
11:34 your body also is *f* of
11:36 If then your whole body is *f* of
11:36 the whole body will be *f* of
11:39 but your inward part is *f* of
16:20 *f* of sores, who was laid at his
Jn 1:14 *f* of grace and truth.
15:11 and that your joy may be *f*.
16:24 receive, that your joy may be *f*.
19:29 Now a vessel *f* of sour wine was
21:11 *f* of large fish, one hundred
Acts 2:13 They are *f* of new wine."
2:28 You will make me *f* of
6: 3 *f* of the Holy Spirit and
6: 5 a man *f* of faith and the Holy
6: 8 *f* of faith and power, did great
7:55 being *f* of the Holy Spirit,
9:36 This woman was *f* of good works
11:24 *f* of the Holy Spirit and of
13:10 O *f* of all deceit and all fraud,
19:28 they were *f* of wrath and cried
Rom 1:29 *f* of envy, murder, strife,
3:14 Whose mouth is *f* of cursing
15:14 that you also are *f* of
1 Cor 4: 8 You are already *f*! You are
Phil 4:12 I have learned both to be *f*
4:18 I have all and abound. I am *f*,
Col 2: 2 to all riches of the *f*
Heb 5:14 belongs to those who are of *f*
6:11 the same diligence to the *f*
10:22 near with a true heart in *f*
Jas 3: 8 *f* of deadly poison.
3:17 *f* of mercy and good fruits,
1 Pe 1: 8 with joy inexpressible and *f*
2 Pe 2:14 having eyes *f* of adultery and
1 Jn 1: 4 to you that your joy may be *f*.
2 Jn 8 but that we may receive a *f*
12 to face, that our joy may be *f*.
Rev 4: 6 were four living creatures *f*
4: 8 were *f* of eyes around and
5: 8 and golden bowls *f* of incense,
14:10 which is poured out *f* strength
15: 7 angels seven golden bowls *f* of
16:10 and his kingdom became *f* of
17: 3 a scarlet beast which was *f*
17: 4 in her hand a golden cup *f* of

FULL-GROWN (1/1) FULL, GROW

Jas 1:15 to sin; and sin, when it is *f*,

FULLER (KJV) See LAUNDERER

FULLER'S (3/3)

2 Ki 18:17 was on the highway to the ***F***
Isa 7: 3 on the highway to the ***F*** Field,
36: 2 on the highway to the ***F*** Field.

FULLNESS (27/27) FULL

Num 18:27 threshing floor and as the *f*
Deut 33:16 things of the earth and its *f*,
1 Chr 16:32 the sea roar, and all its *f*;
Ps 16:11 In Your presence is *f* of joy;
24: 1 is the LORD's, and all its *f*,
36: 8 satisfied with the *f* of Your
50:12 world is Mine, and all its *f*.
89:11 The world and all its *f*,
96:11 the sea roar, and all its *f*;
98: 7 the sea roar, and all its *f*,
Isa 47: 9 shall come upon you in their *f*
Ezek 16:49 *f* of food, and abundance of
19: 7 The land with its *f* was
Dan 8:23 have reached their *f*,
Jn 1:16 And of His *f* we have all
Rom 11:12 how much more their *f*!
11:25 happened to Israel until the *f*
15:29 I shall come in the *f* of the
1 Cor 10:26 LORD's, and all its *f*.
10:28 LORD's, and all its *f*.
Gal 4: 4 But when the *f* of the time had
Eph 1:10 in the dispensation of the *f*
1:23 the *f* of Him who fills all in
3:19 may be filled with all the *f*
4:13 of the stature of the *f* of
Col 1:19 Father that in Him all the *f*
2: 9 For in Him dwells all the *f* of

FULLY (23/23) FULL

Num 14:24 in him and has followed Me *f*,
Ruth 2:11 It has been *f* reported to me,
2 Sam 17:11 I advise that all Israel be *f*
1 Ki 11: 6 and did not *f* follow the LORD,
Job 6: 2 that my grief were *f* weighed,
Ps 31:23 And *f* repays the proud person.
75: 8 It is *f* mixed, and He pours it
Eccl 8:11 heart of the sons of men is *f*
Isa 59:18 The coastlands He will *f*
66: 6 Who *f* repays His enemies!
Nah 1:10 be devoured like stubble *f*
Lk 9:32 and when they were *f* awake,
11:21 *f* armed, guards his own palace,
Jn 7: 8 for My time has not yet *f*
Acts 2: 1 When the Day of Pentecost had *f*
23:20 were going to inquire more *f*
Rom 4:21 and being *f* convinced that what
14: 5 Let each be *f* convinced in his
15:19 about to Illyricum I have *f*
Col 1:10 *f* pleasing Him, being fruitful
2 Tim 4:17 the message might be preached *f*
1 Pe 1:13 and rest your hope *f* upon the
Rev 14:18 for her grapes are *f* ripe."

FUME (1/1)

Ps 68:16 Why do you *f* with envy, you

FUNCTION (1/1)

Rom 12: 4 members do not have the same *f*,

FURBISHED (KJV) See POLISHED

FURIOUS (19/19) FURIOUSLY, FURY

2 Ki 5:11 But Naaman became *f*,
2 Chr 26:19 Then Uzziah became *f*;
Neh 4: 1 that he was *f* and very
Esth 1:12 therefore the king was *f*,
2:21 became *f* and sought to lay
Ps 78:21 the LORD heard this and was *f*;
78:59 When God heard this, He was *f*,
78:62 And was *f* with His
89:38 You have been *f* with Your
Prov 22:24 And with a *f* man do not go,
29:22 And a *f* man abounds in
Isa 64: 9 Do not be *f*, O LORD,
Ezek 5:15 in anger and in fury and in *f*
25:17 great vengeance on them with *f*
Dan 2:12 the king was angry and very *f*,
8: 6 and ran at him with *f* power.
Nah 1: 2 The LORD avenges and is *f*.
Mt 22: 7 king heard about it, he was *f*.
Acts 5:33 they were *f* and plotted to kill

FURIOUSLY (2/2) FURIOUS

2 Ki 9:20 for he drives *f*!"
Ezek 23:25 And they shall deal *f* with

FURLONGS (2/2)

Rev 14:20 for one thousand six hundred *f*.
21:16 the reed: twelve thousand *f*.

FURNACE (29/29)

Gen 19:28 went up like the smoke of a *f*.
Ex 9: 8 handfuls of ashes from a *f*,
9:10 they took ashes from the *f* and
19:18 ascended like the smoke of a *f*,
Deut 4:20 brought you out of the iron *f*,
1 Ki 8:51 of Egypt, out of the iron *f*),
Ps 12: 6 Like silver tried in a *f* of
Prov 17: 3 pot is for silver and the *f*
27:21 pot is for silver and the *f*
Isa 31: 9 fire is in Zion And whose *f*
48:10 I have tested you in the *f* of
Jer 11: 4 land of Egypt, from the iron *f*,
Ezek 22:18 and lead, in the midst of a *f*;
22:20 and tin into the midst of a *f*,
22:22 is melted in the midst of a *f*,
Dan 3: 6 the midst of a burning fiery *f*.
3:11 the midst of a burning fiery *f*.
3:15 the midst of a burning fiery *f*.
3:17 us from the burning fiery *f*,
3:19 commanded that they heat the *f*
3:20 them into the burning fiery *f*.
3:21 midst of the burning fiery *f*.
3:22 and the *f* exceedingly hot,
3:23 midst of the burning fiery *f*.
3:26 mouth of the burning fiery *f*
Mt 13:42 and will cast them into the *f* of
13:50 and cast them into the *f* of
Rev 1:15 brass, as if refined in a *f*,
9: 2 pit like the smoke of a great *f*.

FURNISH (1/1)

Isa 65:11 And who *f* a drink offering for

FURNISHED (3/3) FURNISHINGS

Prov 9: 2 She has also *f* her table.
Mk 14:15 *f* and prepared; there make
Lk 22:12 *f* upper room; there make

FURNISHINGS (17/16) FURNISHED, FURNITURE

Ex 25: 9 and the pattern of all its *f*,
39:33 Moses, the tent and all its *f*:
Num 1:50 the Testimony, over all its *f*,
1:50 the tabernacle and all its *f*;
3: 8 they shall attend to all the *f*
4:15 the sanctuary and all the *f* of
4:16 with the sanctuary and its *f*.
4:26 all the *f* for their service and
4:32 with all their *f* and all their
7: 1 consecrated it and all its *f*,
1 Ki 7:48 Thus Solomon had all the *f* made
7:51 silver and the gold and the *f*.
8: 4 and all the holy *f* that were
1 Chr 9:29 were appointed over the *f* and
2 Chr 4:19 Thus Solomon had all the *f* made
5: 1 and the gold and all the *f*.
5: 5 and all the holy *f* that were

FURNITURE (1/1) FURNISHINGS

Ex 31: 7 and all the *f* of the

FURROW (1/1)

Job 39:10 you bind the wild ox in the *f*

FURROWS (5/5)

Job 31:38 And its *f* weep together;
Ps 65:10 abundantly, You settle its *f*;
129: 3 They made their *f* long."
Hos 10: 4 up like hemlock in the *f* of
12:11 shall be heaps in the *f* of

FURTHER (24/24)

Num 22:26 the Angel of the LORD went *f*,
Deut 20: 8 The officers shall speak *f* to
1 Sam 10:22 they inquired of the LORD *f*,
2 Sam 19:35 then should your servant be a *f*
Esth 9:12 Or what is your *f* request?
Job 29: 1 Job *f* continued his discourse,
34: 1 Elihu *f* answered and said:
34:23 For He need not *f* consider a
40: 5 twice, but I will proceed no *f*.
Ps 140: 8 Do not *f* his wicked scheme,
Eccl 12:12 And *f*, my son, be admonished
Zech 4:12 And I *f* answered and said to
Mt 26:65 has spoken blasphemy! What *f*
Mk 5:35 Why trouble the Teacher any *f*?
14:63 What *f* need do we have of
Lk 22:71 'What *f* testimony do we need?
Acts 4:17 But so that it spreads no *f*
4:21 So when they had *f* threatened
12: 3 he proceeded *f* to seize Peter
23:15 though you were going to make *f*
24: 4 not to be tedious to you any *f*,
2 Cor 5: 4 but *f* clothed, that mortality
2 Tim 3: 9 but they will progress no *f*,
Heb 7:11 what *f* need was there that

FURTHERANCE (1/1)

Phil 1:12 actually turned out for the *f*

FURTHERMORE (22/22)

Gen 38:24 *f* she is with child by
Ex 4: 6 *F* the LORD said to him, "Now
Deut 4:21 *F* the LORD was angry with me
9:13 *F* the LORD spoke to me,
1 Sam 26:10 David said *f*, "As the LORD
2 Sam 16:19 '*F*, whom should I serve?
2 Ki 8: 1 has called for a famine, and *f*,
1 Chr 17:10 *F* I tell you that the LORD
27:16 *F*, over the tribes of Israel:
29: 1 *F* King David said to all the
2 Chr 4: 9 *F* he made the court of the
7: 7 *F* Solomon consecrated the
32:16 *F*, his servants spoke against
Neh 2: 7 *F* I said to the king, "If it
Ezek 8: 6 *F* He said to me, "Son of man,
20:45 *F* the word of the LORD came to
23:40 *F* you sent for men to come from
Mt 5:31 *F* it has been said, 'Whoever
Acts 21:28 and *f* he also brought Greeks
Rom 8:34 and *f* is also risen, who is
2 Cor 2:12 *F*, when I came to
Heb 12: 9 *F*, we have had human fathers

FURY (70/66) FURIOUS

Gen 27:44 until your brother's *f* turns
Lev 26:28 will walk contrary to you in *f*;
Job 20:23 God will cast on him the *f* of
Prov 6:34 For jealousy is a husband's *f*;
Isa 27: 4 *F* is not in Me
34: 2 And His *f* against all their
42:25 He has poured on him the *f* of
51:13 every day Because of the *f* of
51:13 And where is the *f* of the
51:17 of the LORD The cup of His *f*;
51:20 They are full of the *f* of the
51:22 The dregs of the cup of My *f*;
59:18 *F* to His adversaries,
63: 3 And trampled them in My *f*;
63: 5 salvation for Me; And My own *f*,
63: 6 anger, Made them drunk in My *f*,
66:15 To render His anger with *f*,
Jer 4: 4 Lest My *f* come forth like
6:11 Therefore I am full of the *f* of
7:20 My anger and My *f* will be
10:25 Pour out Your *f* on the
21: 5 even in anger and *f* and great
21:12 Lest My *f* go forth like fire
23:19 the LORD has gone forth in *f*—
25:15 Take this wine cup of *f* from My
30:23 of the LORD Goes forth with *f*,
32:31 of My anger and My *f* from the
32:37 them in My anger, in My *f*,
33: 5 will slay in My anger and My *f*,
36: 7 great is the anger and the *f*
42:18 As My anger and My *f* have been
42:18 so will My *f* be poured out on
44: 6 So My *f* and My anger were poured
Lam 2: 4 He has poured out His *f* like
4:11 The LORD has fulfilled His *f*,
Ezek 5:13 and I will cause My *f* to rest
5:13 when I have spent My *f* upon
5:15 among you in anger and in *f*
6:12 Thus will I spend My *f* upon
7: 8 you I will soon pour out My *f*,
8:18 I also will act in *f*.
9: 8 of Israel in pouring out Your *f*
13:13 wind to break forth in My *f*;
13:13 and great hailstones in *f* to
14:19 that land and pour out My *f* on
16:38 will bring blood upon you in *f*
16:42 So I will lay to rest My *f*
19:12 But she was plucked up in *f*,
20: 8 I will pour out My *f* on them and
20:13 I said I would pour out My *f*
20:21 I said I would pour out My *f*
20:33 and with *f* poured out, I will
20:34 and with *f* poured out.
21:17 And I will cause My *f* to rest;
22:20 you in My anger and in My *f*,
22:22 have poured out My *f* on you.'
24: 8 That it may raise up *f* and take
24:13 Till I have caused My *f* to
25:14 My anger and according to My *f*;
30:15 I will pour My *f* on Sin,
36: 6 spoken in My jealousy and My *f*,
36:18 Therefore I poured out My *f* on
38:18 that My *f* will show in My face.
Dan 3:13 Nebuchadnezzar, in rage and *f*,
3:19 Nebuchadnezzar was full of *f*,
9:16 let Your anger and Your *f* be
11:44 he shall go out with great *f*
Am 5: 9 So that *f* comes upon the
Mic 5:15 vengeance in anger and *f* On
Nah 1: 6 His *f* is poured out like fire,

FUTILE (11/11) FUTILITY

Deut 32:47 For it is not a *f* thing for
Job 15:31 Let him not trust in *f* things,
Ps 94:11 of man, That they are *f*.
Isa 1:13 Bring no more *f* sacrifices;
Jer 10: 3 customs of the peoples are *f*;
10:15 They are *f*, a work of errors;
51:18 They are *f*, a work of errors;
Ezek 13: 7 Have you not seen a *f* vision,
Rom 1:21 but became *f* in their thoughts,
1 Cor 3:20 the wise, that they are *f*.
15:17 is not risen, your faith is *f*;

FUTILITY (11/11) FUTILE

Job 7: 3 have been allotted months of *f*,
15:31 For *f* will be his reward.
15:35 trouble and bring forth *f*;
Ps 78:33 their days He consumed in *f*,
89:47 For what *f* have You created
Isa 30:28 the nations with the sieve of *f*;
Ezek 13: 6 They have envisioned *f* and false
13: 9 the prophets who envision *f*
13:23 you shall no longer envision *f*
Rom 8:20 the creation was subjected to *f*,
Eph 4:17 in the *f* of their mind,

FUTURE (5/5)

Ps 37:37 For the *f* of that man is
37:38 The *f* of the wicked shall be
Jer 29:11 to give you a *f* and a hope.
31:17 There is hope in your *f*,
Dan 8:26 to many days in the *f*.

G

GAAL (9/9)

Judg 9:26 Now *G* the son of Ebed came with
9:28 Then *G* the son of Ebed said,
9:30 heard the words of *G* the son of
9:31 Take note! *G* the son of Ebed and
9:35 When *G* the son of Ebed went out
9:36 And when *G* saw the people, he
9:37 So *G* spoke again and said,
9:39 So *G* went out, leading the men
9:41 and Zebul drove out *G* and his

GAASH (4/4)

Josh 24:30 on the north side of Mount *G*.
Judg 2: 9 on the north side of Mount *G*.
2 Sam 23:30 Hiddai from the brooks of *G*,
1 Chr 11:32 Hurai of the brooks of *G*,

GABA (1/1)

Josh 18:24 Chephar Haammoni, Ophni, and *G*:

GABBAI (1/1)

Neh 11: 8 and after him *G* and Sallai,

GABBATHA (1/1)

Jn 19:13 The Pavement, but in Hebrew, *G*.

GABRIEL (4/4)

Dan 8:16 Ulai, who called, and said, "*G*,
9:21 speaking in prayer, the man *G*,
Lk 1:19 and said to him, "I am *G*,
1:26 in the sixth month the angel *G*

GAD (78/75)

Gen 30:11 So she called his name *G*.
35:26 were *G* and Asher. These were
46:16 The sons of *G* were Ziphion,
49:19 '*G*, a troop shall tramp upon
Ex 1: 4 Dan, Naphtali, *G*,
Num 1:14 'from *G*, Eliasaph the son of
1:24 From the children of *G*,
1:25 were numbered of the tribe of *G*
2:14 "Then comes the tribe of *G*,
2:14 the leader of the children of *G*
7:42 leader of the children of *G*,
10:20 the tribe of the children of *G*
13:15 from the tribe of *G*,
26:15 The sons of *G* according to
26:18 the families of the sons of *G*

32: 1 of Reuben and the children of ***G***
32: 2 the children of ***G*** and the
32: 6 said to the children of ***G*** and
32:25 And the children of ***G*** and the
32:29 If the children of ***G*** and the
32:31 Then the children of ***G*** and the
32:33 Moses gave to the children of ***G***,
32:34 And the children of ***G*** built
33:45 from Ijim and camped at Dibon ***G***.
33:46 They moved from Dibon ***G*** and
34:14 the tribe of the children of ***G***
Deut 27:13 Mount Ebal to curse: Reuben, ***G***,
33:20 And of ***G*** he said: "Blessed
33:20 is he who enlarges ***G***;
Josh 4:12 the men of Reuben, the men of ***G***,
13:24 inheritance to the tribe of ***G***,
13:24 to the children of ***G*** according
13:28 of the children of ***G*** according
18: 7 is their inheritance. And ***G***,
20: 8 in Gilead, from the tribe of ***G***,
21: 7 of Reuben, from the tribe of ***G***,
21:38 and from the tribe of ***G***,
22: 9 of Reuben, the children of ***G***,
22:10 of Reuben, the children of ***G***,
22:11 of Reuben, the children of ***G***,
22:13 of Reuben, to the children of ***G***,
22:15 of Reuben, to the children of ***G***,
22:21 of Reuben, the children of ***G***,
22:25 of Reuben and children of ***G***.
22:30 of Reuben, the children of ***G***,
22:31 of Reuben, the children of ***G***,
22:32 of Reuben and the children of ***G***,
22:33 the children of Reuben and ***G***
22:34 of Reuben and the children of ***G***
1 Sam 13: 7 the Jordan to the land of ***G***
22: 5 Now the prophet ***G*** said to David,
2 Sam 24: 5 in the midst of the ravine of ***G***,
24:11 the LORD came to the prophet ***G***,
24:13 So ***G*** came to David and told him;
24:14 And David said to ***G***,
24:18 And ***G*** came that day to David
24:19 according to the word of ***G***,
2 Ki 10:33 all the land of Gilead—***G***,
1 Chr 2: 2 Joseph, Benjamin, Naphtali, ***G***,
5:11 And the children of ***G*** dwelt
6:63 of Reuben, from the tribe of ***G***,
6:80 And from the tribe of ***G***:
12:14 These were from the sons of ***G***,
21: 9 And the LORD spoke to ***G***,
21:11 So ***G*** came to David and said to
21:13 And David said to ***G***,
21:18 angel of the LORD commanded ***G***
21:19 David went up at the word of ***G***,
29:29 and in the book of ***G*** the seer,
2 Chr 29:25 of ***G*** the king's seer, and of
Isa 65:11 Who prepare a table for ***G***,
Jer 2:36 Why do you ***g*** about so much to
31:22 How long will you ***g*** about,
49: 1 then does Milcom inherit ***G***,
Ezek 48:27 ***G*** shall have one section;
48:28 "by the border of ***G***,
48:34 three gates: one gate for ***G***,
Rev 7: 5 of the tribe of ***G*** twelve

GADARENES (3/3)

Mk 5: 1 sea, to the country of the ***G***.
Lk 8:26 sailed to the country of the ***G***,
8:37 the surrounding region of the ***G***

GADDEST (KJV) See GAD

GADDI (1/1)

Num 13:11 ***G*** the son of Susi;

GADDIEL (1/1)

Num 13:10 ***G*** the son of Sodi;

GADI (2/2)

2 Ki 15:14 For Menahem the son of ***G*** went up
15:17 Menahem the son of ***G*** became

GADITE (1/1)

2 Sam 23:36 of Nathan of Zobah, Bani the ***G***,

GADITES (14/14)

Deut 3:12 to the Reubenites and the ***G***.
3:16 to the Reubenites and the ***G*** I
4:43 Ramoth in Gilead for the ***G***,
29: 8 to the Reubenites, to the ***G***,
Josh 1:12 And to the Reubenites, the ***G***,
12: 6 to the Reubenites, the ***G***,
13: 8 tribe the Reubenites and the ***G***
22: 1 called the Reubenites, the ***G***,
1 Chr 5:16 And the ***G*** dwelt in Gilead,
5:18 The sons of Reuben, the ***G***,
5:26 carried the Reubenites, the ***G***,
12: 8 Some ***G*** joined David at the
12:37 of the Reubenites and the ***G*** and
26:32 over the Reubenites, the ***G***,

GAHAM (1/1)

Gen 22:24 was Reumah, also bore Tebah, ***G***,

GAHAR (2/2)

Ezra 2:47 sons of Giddel, the sons of ***G***,
Neh 7:49 sons of Giddel, the sons of ***G***,

GAIN (33/32) GAINED, GAINS

Ex 14: 4 and I will ***g*** honor over Pharaoh
14:17 So I will ***g*** honor over Pharaoh
1 Sam 8: 3 turned aside after dishonest ***g***,
Job 18: 2 ***G*** understanding, and afterward
22: 3 Or is it ***g*** to Him that you
27: 8 Though he may ***g*** much, If God
Ps 44: 3 For they did not ***g*** possession
90:12 That we may ***g*** a heart of
Prov 1:19 of everyone who is greedy for ***g***;
3:14 And her ***g*** than fine gold.
15:27 He who is greedy for ***g*** troubles
31:11 So he will have no lack of ***g***.
Eccl 3: 6 A time to ***g***, And a time to
Isa 23:18 Her ***g*** and her pay will be set
23:18 for her ***g*** will be for those who
33:15 He who despises the ***g*** of
56:11 Every one for his own ***g***,
Ezek 22:27 people, and to get dishonest ***g***.
33:31 hearts pursue their own ***g***.
39:13 and they will ***g*** renown for it
Dan 2: 8 for certain that you would ***g***
11: 5 and he shall ***g*** power over him
11:39 many, and divide the land for ***g***.
Mic 4:13 I will consecrate their ***g*** to
Hab 2: 9 Woe to him who covets evil ***g***
Phil 1:21 is Christ, and to die is ***g***.
3: 7 But what things were ***g*** to me,
3: 8 that I may ***g*** Christ
1 Tim 6: 5 godliness is a means of ***g***.
6: 6 with contentment is great ***g***.
Titus 1:11 for the sake of dishonest ***g***.
1 Pe 5: 2 not for dishonest ***g*** but
Jude 16 flattering people to ***g***

GAINED (19/18) GAIN

Gen 31:18 his possessions which he had ***g***,
31:18 livestock which he had ***g*** in
36: 6 all his goods which he had ***g***
Ex 14:18 when I have ***g*** honor for Myself
Deut 8:17 the might of my hand have ***g*** me
Judg 11:21 Thus Israel ***g*** possession of all
Job 31:25 And because my hand had ***g***
Ps 98: 1 hand and His holy arm have ***g***
Prov 13:11 Wealth ***g*** by dishonesty will
20:17 Bread ***g*** by deceit is sweet to
20:21 An inheritance ***g*** hastily at the
Eccl 1:16 and have ***g*** more wisdom than all
Isa 15: 7 the abundance they have ***g***,
Ezek 28: 4 your understanding You have ***g***
Mt 18:15 you have ***g*** your brother.
25:17 he who had received two ***g***
25:20 I have ***g*** five more talents
25:22 I have ***g*** two more talents
Lk 19:15 know how much every man had ***g***

GAINS (5/5) GAIN

Prov 3:13 And the man who ***g***
13:15 Good understanding ***g*** favor,
Mt 16:26 profit is it to a man if he ***g***
Mk 8:36 will it profit a man if he ***g***
Lk 9:25 profit is it to a man if he ***g***

GAINSAY, GAINSAYERS (KJV) See CONTRADICT

GAINSAYING (KJV) See CONTRARY, OBJECTION, REBELLION

GAIUS (5/5)

Acts 19:29 having seized ***G*** and
20: 4 and ***G*** of Derbe, and Timothy,
Rom 16:23 ***G***, my host and the
1 Cor 1:14 of you except Crispus and ***G***,
3 Jn 1 The Elder, To the beloved ***G***,

GALAL (3/3)

1 Chr 9:15 Bakbakkar, Heresh, ***G***,
9:16 son of Shemaiah, the son of ***G***,
Neh 11:17 son of Shammua, the son of ***G***,

GALATIA (6/6) GALATIANS

Acts 16: 6 Phrygia and the region of ***G***,
18:23 and went over the region of ***G***
1 Cor 16: 1 orders to the churches of ***G***,
Gal 1: 2 with me, To the churches of ***G***:
2 Tim 4:10 for Thessalonica—Crescens for ***G***,
1 Pe 1: 1 of the Dispersion in Pontus, ***G***,

GALATIANS (1/1) GALATIA

Gal 3: 1 O foolish ***G***! Who has bewitched

GALBANUM (1/1)

Ex 30:34 spices, stacte and onycha and ***g***,

GALEED (2/2)

Gen 31:47 but Jacob called it ***G***.
31:48 Therefore its name was called ***G***,

GALILEAN (3/3) GALILEANS, GALILEE

Mk 14:70 one of them; for you are a ***G***,
Lk 22:59 was with Him, for he is a ***G***.
23: 6 he asked if the Man were a ***G***.

GALILEANS (5/4) GALILEAN

Lk 13: 1 some who told Him about the ***G***
13: 2 Do you suppose that these ***G*** were
13: 2 worse sinners than all other ***G***,
Jn 4:45 the ***G*** received Him, having seen
Acts 2: 7 are not all these who speak ***G***?

GALILEE (72/71) GALILEAN

Josh 20: 7 So they appointed Kedesh in ***G***,
21:32 Kedesh in ***G*** with its
1 Ki 9:11 twenty cities in the land of ***G***.
2 Ki 15:29 Kedesh, Hazor, Gilead, and ***G***,
1 Chr 6:76 Kedesh in ***G*** with its
Isa 9: 1 In ***G*** of the Gentiles.
Mt 2:22 aside into the region of ***G***.
3:13 Then Jesus came from ***G*** to John
4:12 put in prison, He departed to ***G***.
4:15 ***G*** of the Gentiles:
4:18 Jesus, walking by the Sea of ***G***,
4:23 And Jesus went about all ***G***,
4:25 multitudes followed Him—from ***G***,
15:29 there, skirted the Sea of ***G***,
17:22 while they were staying in ***G***,
19: 1 that He departed from ***G*** and
21:11 the prophet from Nazareth of ***G***.
26:32 I will go before you to ***G***.
26:69 "You also were with Jesus of ***G***.
27:55 women who followed Jesus from ***G***,
28: 7 He is going before you into ***G***;
28:10 tell My brethren to go to ***G***,
28:16 disciples went away into ***G***,
Mk 1: 9 Jesus came from Nazareth of ***G***,
1:14 put in prison, Jesus came to ***G***,
1:16 as He walked by the Sea of ***G***,
1:28 all the region around ***G***.
1:39 synagogues throughout all ***G***,
3: 7 And a great multitude from ***G***
6:21 and the chief men of ***G***.
7:31 of Decapolis to the Sea of ***G***.
9:30 from there and passed through ***G***,
14:28 I will go before you to ***G***.
15:41 to Him when He was in ***G***,
16: 7 He is going before you into ***G***;
Lk 1:26 was sent by God to a city of ***G***
2: 4 Joseph also went up from ***G***,
2:39 of the Lord, they returned to ***G***,
3: 1 Herod being tetrarch of ***G***,
4:14 in the power of the Spirit to ***G***,
4:31 down to Capernaum, a city of ***G***,
4:44 in the synagogues of ***G***.
5:17 had come out of every town of ***G***,
8:26 Gadarenes, which is opposite ***G***.
17:11 the midst of Samaria and ***G***.
23: 5 beginning from ***G*** to this
23: 6 When Pilate heard of ***G***,
23:49 women who followed Him from ***G***,
23:55 who had come with Him from ***G***
24: 6 to you when He was still in ***G***,
Jn 1:43 day Jesus wanted to go to ***G***,
2: 1 was a wedding in Cana of ***G***,
2:11 of signs Jesus did in Cana of ***G***,
4: 3 Judea and departed again to ***G***.
4:43 from there and went to ***G***.
4:45 So when He came to ***G***,
4:46 Jesus came again to Cana of ***G***
4:47 had come out of Judea into ***G***,
4:54 He had come out of Judea into ***G***.
6: 1 Jesus went over the Sea of ***G***,
7: 1 these things Jesus walked in ***G***;
7: 9 to them, He remained in ***G***.
7:41 "Will the Christ come out of ***G***?
7:52 to him, "Are you also from ***G***?
7:52 no prophet has arisen out of ***G***.
12:21 who was from Bethsaida of ***G***,
21: 2 Twin, Nathanael of Cana in ***G***,
Acts 1:11 who also said, "Men of ***G***,
5:37 Judas of ***G*** rose up in the days
9:31 throughout all Judea, ***G***,
10:37 and began from ***G*** after the
13:31 who came up with Him from ***G*** to

GALL (10/10)

Deut 32:32 Their grapes are grapes of ***g***,
Job 16:13 He pours out my ***g*** on the
20:25 point comes out of his ***g***,
Ps 69:21 They also gave me ***g*** for my
Jer 8:14 And given us water of ***g*** to
9:15 and give them water of ***g*** to
23:15 make them drink the water of ***g***;
Lam 3:19 The wormwood and the ***g***.
Am 6:12 you have turned justice into ***g***,
Mt 27:34 Him sour wine mingled with ***g***

GALLERIES (3/3)

Ezek 41:15 with its ***g*** on the one side and
41:16 And the ***g*** all around their
42: 5 because the ***g*** took away space

GALLERY (2/1)

Ezek 42: 3 was ***g*** against gallery in three
42: 3 was gallery against ***g*** in three

GALLEY (1/1)

Isa 33:21 In which no ***g*** with oars will

G

GALLIM (2/2)

1 Sam 25:44 son of Laish, who was from *G*.
Isa 10:30 O daughter of *G*! Cause it to

GALLIO (3/3)

Acts 18:12 When *G* was proconsul of Achaia,
18:14 *G* said to the Jews, "If it
18:17 But *G* took no notice of these

GALLONS (1/1)

Jn 2: 6 containing twenty or thirty *g*

GALLOPING (3/2)

Judg 5:22 horses' hooves pounded, The *g*,
5:22 *g* of his steeds.
Nah 3: 2 Of *g* horses, Of clattering

GALLOPS (1/1)

Job 39:21 He *g* into the clash of arms.

GALLOWS (9/8)

Esth 2:23 and both were hanged on a *g*;
5:14 Let a *g* be made, fifty cubits
5:14 so he had the *g* made.
6: 4 the king hang Mordecai on the *g*
7: 9 said to the king, "Look! The *g*,
7:10 So they hanged Haman on the *g*
8: 7 they have hanged him on the *g*
9:13 ten sons be hanged on the *g*.
9:25 sons should be hanged on the *g*.

GAMALIEL (7/7)

Num 1:10 *G* the son of Pedahzur;
2:20 of Manasseh shall be *G* the
7:54 On the eighth day *G* the son of
7:59 This was the offering of *G* the
10:23 the children of Manasseh was *G*
Acts 5:34 stood up, a Pharisee named *G*,
22: 3 in this city at the feet of *G*,

GAME (8/8)

Gen 25:28 Esau because he ate of his *g*,
27: 3 go out to the field and hunt *g*
27: 5 went to the field to hunt *g*
27: 7 Bring me *g* and make savory food
27:19 arise, sit and eat of my *g*,
27:25 and I will eat of my son's *g*,
27:31 arise and eat of his son's *g*,
27:33 Where is the one who hunted *g*

GAMMAD (1/1)

Ezek 27:11 And the men of *G* were in your

GAMUL (1/1)

1 Chr 24:17 Jachin, the twenty-second to *G*,

GAP (2/2) GAPS

Isa 7: 6 and let us make a *g* in its wall
Ezek 22:30 and stand in the *g* before Me on

GAPE (2/2)

Job 16:10 They *g* at me with their mouth,
Ps 22:13 They *g* at Me with their

GAPS (2/2) GAP

Neh 4: 7 were being restored and the *g*
Ezek 13: 5 have not gone up into the *g* to

GARDEN (54/49) GARDENER, GARDENS

Gen 2: 8 The LORD God planted a *g*
2: 9 was also in the midst of the *g*,
2:10 went out of Eden to water the *g*,
2:15 the man and put him in the *g*
2:16 Of every tree of the *g* you may
3: 1 not eat of every tree of the *g*'
3: 2 the fruit of the trees of the *g*;
3: 3 which is in the midst of the *g*,
3: 8 the LORD God walking in the *g*
3: 8 God among the trees of the *g*.
3:10 "I heard Your voice in the *g*,
3:23 God sent him out of the *g* of
3:24 cherubim at the east of the *g*
13:10 Sodom and Gomorrah) like the *g*
Deut 11:10 it by foot, as a vegetable *g*;
1 Ki 21: 2 I may have it for a vegetable *g*,
2 Ki 21:18 and was buried in the *g* of his
21:18 in the *g* of Uzza. Then his son
21:26 buried in his tomb in the *g* of
25: 4 which was by the king's *g*,
Neh 3:15 Pool of Shelah by the King's *G*,
Esth 1: 5 in the court of the *g* of the
7: 7 and went into the palace *g*;
7: 8 returned from the palace *g* to
Job 8:16 branches spread out in his *g*.
Song 4:12 A *g* enclosed Is my sister,
4:16 come, O south! Blow upon my *g*,
4:16 Let my beloved come to his *g*
5: 1 I have come to my *g*,
6: 2 My beloved has gone to his *g*,
6:11 I went down to the *g* of nuts
Isa 1: 8 As a hut in a *g* of cucumbers,
1:30 And as a *g* that has no water.
51: 3 And her desert like the *g* of
58:11 You shall be like a watered *g*,
61:11 As the *g* causes the things
Jer 31:12 shall be like a well-watered *g*,
39: 4 night, by way of the king's *g*,
52: 7 which was by the king's *g*,
Lam 2: 6 As if it were a *g*;
Ezek 17: 7 From the *g* terrace where it
17:10 It will wither in the *g*
28:13 the *g* of God; Every precious
31: 8 The cedars in the *g* of God
31: 8 No tree in the *g* of God was
31: 9 That were in the *g* of God.'
34:29 I will raise up for them a *g* of
36:35 desolate has become like the *g*
Joel 2: 3 The land is like the *G* of
Lk 13:19 a man took and put in his *g*;
Jn 18: 1 Kidron, where there was a *g*,
18:26 Did I not see you in the *g* with
19:41 He was crucified there was a *g*,
19:41 and in the *g* a new tomb in

GARDENER (1/1) GARDEN

Jn 20:15 She, supposing Him to be the *g*,

GARDENS (12/12) GARDEN

Num 24: 6 Like *g* by the riverside,
Eccl 2: 5 I made myself *g* and orchards,
Song 4:15 A fountain of *g*,
6: 2 To feed his flock in the *g*,
8:13 You who dwell in the *g*,
Isa 1:29 be embarrassed because of the *g*
65: 3 to My face; Who sacrifice in *g*,
66:17 To go to the *g* After an
Jer 29: 5 plant *g* and eat their fruit.
29:28 and plant *g* and eat their
Am 4: 9 When your *g* increased,
9:14 They shall also make *g* and eat

GAREB (3/3)

2 Sam 23:38 Ira the Ithrite, *G* the Ithrite,
1 Chr 11:40 Ira the Ithrite, *G* the Ithrite,
Jer 31:39 forward over the hill *G*;

GARLAND (1/1)

Rev 12: 1 and on her head a *g* of twelve

GARLANDS (1/1)

Acts 14:13 brought oxen and *g* to the

GARLIC (1/1)

Num 11: 5 leeks, the onions, and the *g*;

GARMENT (90/85) GARMENTS

Gen 9:23 But Shem and Japheth took a *g*,
25:25 He was like a hairy *g* all
39:12 that she caught him by his *g*,
39:12 But he left his *g* in her
39:13 she saw that he had left his *g*
39:15 that he left his *g* with me,
39:16 So she kept his *g* with her until
39:18 that he left his *g* with me and
Ex 22:26 ever take your neighbor's *g* as
22:27 it is his *g* for his skin.
Lev 6:10 priest shall put on his linen *g*,
6:27 its blood is sprinkled on any *g*,
13:47 if a *g* has a leprous plague in
13:47 whether it is a woolen *g* or
13:47 a woolen garment or a linen *g*,
13:49 is greenish or reddish in the *g*
13:51 the plague has spread in the *g*,
13:52 shall therefore burn that *g*
13:52 the *g* shall be burned in the
13:53 plague has not spread in the *g*,
13:56 he shall tear it out of the *g*,
13:57 if it appears again in the *g*,
13:58 "And if you wash the *g*,
13:59 of the leprous plague in a *g*
14:55 for the leprosy of a *g* and of a
15:17 And any *g* and any leather on
19:19 Nor shall a *g* of mixed linen
Num 31:20 "Purify every *g*,
Deut 22: 3 and so shall you do with his *g*;
22: 5 shall a man put on a woman's *g*,
22:11 You shall not wear a *g* of
24:13 that he may sleep in his own *g*
24:17 nor take a widow's *g* as a
Josh 7:21 spoils a beautiful Babylonian *g*,
7:24 son of Zerah, the silver, the *g*,
Judg 8:25 And they spread out a *g*,
Ruth 3: 3 put on your best *g* and go down
2 Sam 20:12 to the field and threw a *g*
1 Ki 11:29 clothed himself with a new *g*,
11:30 Ahijah took hold of the new *g*
2 Ki 9:13 man hastened to take his *g* and
Ezra 9: 3 I tore my *g* and my robe,
9: 5 and having torn my *g* and my
Neh 5:13 I shook out the fold of my *g*
Esth 8:15 a great crown of gold and a *g*
Job 13:28 Like a *g* that is moth-eaten.
30:18 By great force my *g* is
38: 9 When I made the clouds its *g*,
38:14 And stands out like a *g*.
Ps 69:11 I also made sackcloth my *g*;
73: 6 Violence covers them like a *g*.
102:26 they will all grow old like a *g*;
104: 2 with light as with a *g*,
104: 6 it with the deep as with a *g*;
109:18 with cursing as with his *g*,
109:19 Let it be to him like the *g*
Prov 20:16 Take the *g* of one who is surety
25:20 Like one who takes away a *g* in
27:13 Take the *g* of him who is surety
30: 4 has bound the waters in a *g*?
Isa 14:19 Like the *g* of those who are
50: 9 they will all grow old like a *g*;
51: 6 earth will grow old like a *g*,
51: 8 moth will eat them up like a *g*,
61: 3 The *g* of praise for the spirit
Jer 43:12 as a shepherd puts on his *g*,
Ezek 5: 3 them in the edge of your *g*.
Dan 7: 9 His *g* was white as snow,
Mic 2: 8 pull off the robe with the *g*
Hag 2:12 holy meat in the fold of his *g*,
Mal 2:16 For it covers one's *g* with
Mt 9:16 of unshrunk cloth on an old *g*;
9:16 the patch pulls away from the *g*,
9:20 and touched the hem of His *g*.
9:21 "If only I may touch His *g*,
14:36 only touch the hem of His *g*.
22:11 who did not have on a wedding *g*.
22:12 in here without a wedding *g*?
Mk 2:21 of unshrunk cloth on an old *g*;
5:27 in the crowd and touched His *g*.
6:56 just touch the hem of His *g*.
10:50 And throwing aside his *g*,
Lk 5:36 one puts a piece from a new *g*
8:44 and touched the border of His *g*.
22:36 let him sell his *g* and buy one.
Jn 21: 7 he put on his outer *g* (for he
Acts 12: 8 Put on your *g* and follow me."
Heb 1:11 all grow old like a *g*;
Jude 23 hating even the *g* defiled by
Rev 1:13 clothed with a *g* down to the

GARMENTS (118/97) GARMENT

Gen 35: 2 yourselves, and change your *g*.
38:14 So she took off her widow's *g*,
38:19 her veil and put on the *g* of
41:42 and he clothed him in *g* of fine
45:22 them, to each man, changes of *g*;
45:22 of silver and five changes of *g*.
49:11 He washed his *g* in wine,
Ex 28: 2 And you shall make holy *g* for
28: 3 that they may make Aaron's *g*,
28: 4 And these are the *g* which they
28: 4 So they shall make holy *g* for
29: 5 "Then you shall take the *g*,
29:21 it on Aaron and on his *g*,
29:21 on his sons and on the *g* of his
29:21 and he and his *g* shall be
29:21 and his sons and his sons' *g*
29:29 And the holy *g* of Aaron shall
31:10 the *g* of ministry, the holy
31:10 the holy *g* for Aaron the priest
31:10 for Aaron the priest and the *g*
35:19 the *g* of ministry, for
35:19 the holy *g* for Aaron the priest
35:19 for Aaron the priest and the *g*
35:21 its service, and for the holy *g*.
39: 1 scarlet thread they made *g* of
39: 1 and made the holy *g* for Aaron,
39:41 and the *g* of ministry, to
39:41 the holy *g* for Aaron the
39:41 the priest, and his sons' *g*,
40:13 You shall put the holy *g* on
Lev 6:11 'Then he shall take off his *g*,
6:11 his garments, put on other *g*,
8: 2 his sons with him, and the *g*,
8:30 it on Aaron, on his *g*,
8:30 and on the *g* of his sons with
8:30 and he consecrated Aaron, his *g*,
8:30 and the *g* of his sons with him.
16: 4 be attired. These are holy *g*.
16:23 shall take off the linen *g*
16:24 in a holy place, put on his *g*,
16:32 the linen clothes, the holy *g*;
21:10 is consecrated to wear the *g*,
Num 15:38 on the corners of their *g*
20:26 and strip Aaron of his *g* and put
20:28 Moses stripped Aaron of his *g*
Deut 8: 4 Your *g* did not wear out on you,
Josh 9: 5 and old *g* on themselves;
9:13 and these our *g* and our sandals
Judg 5:30 For Sisera, plunder of dyed *g*,
5:30 Plunder of *g* embroidered and
14:12 I will give you thirty linen *g*
14:13 shall give me thirty linen *g*
2 Sam 10: 4 cut off their *g* in the middle,
13:31 the king arose and tore his *g*
1 Ki 10:25 articles of silver and gold, *g*,
2 Ki 5:22 of silver and two changes of *g*.
5:23 two bags, with two changes of *g*,
7:15 all the road was full of *g*
25:29 changed from his prison *g*,
1 Chr 19: 4 and cut off their *g* in the
2 Chr 9:24 articles of silver and gold, *g*,
Ezra 2:69 and one hundred priestly *g*.
Neh 7:70 hundred and thirty priestly *g*.
7:72 and sixty-seven priestly *g*.
Esth 4: 4 Then she sent *g* to clothe
Job 37:17 Why are your *g* hot, When He
Ps 22:18 They divide My *g* among them,
45: 8 All Your *g* are scented with
133: 2 down on the edge of his *g*.

Prov 31:24 She makes linen **g** and sells
Eccl 9: 8 Let your **g** always be white,
Song 4:11 And the fragrance of your **g**
Isa 3:22 and the mantles; The outer **g**,
9: 5 And **g** rolled in blood, Will
52: 1 Put on your beautiful **g**,
59: 6 Their webs will not become **g**,
59:17 He put on the **g** of vengeance
61:10 He has clothed me with the **g**
63: 1 With dyed **g** from Bozrah,
63: 2 And Your **g** like one who treads
63: 3 blood is sprinkled upon My **g**,
Jer 36:24 nor did they tear their **g**,
52:33 changed from his prison **g**,
Lam 4:14 that no one would touch their **g**.
Ezek 16:16 You took some of your **g** and
16:18 You took your embroidered **g** and
26:16 take off their embroidered **g**;
27:24 clothes, in embroidered **g**,
42:14 they shall leave their **g** in
42:14 holy. They shall put on other **g**;
44:17 that they shall put on linen **g**;
44:19 they shall take off their **g** in
44:19 chambers, and put on other **g**;
44:19 and in their holy **g** they shall
Dan 3:21 turbans, and their other **g**,
3:27 was not singed nor were their **g**
Joel 2:13 rend your heart, and not your **g**;
Zech 3: 3 was clothed with filthy **g**,
3: 4 Take away the filthy **g** from
Mt 11: 8 to see? A man clothed in soft **g**?
23: 5 enlarge the borders of their **g**.
27:35 Him, and divided His **g**,
27:35 They divided My **g** among
Mk 15:24 Him, they divided His **g**,
Lk 7:25 to see? A man clothed in soft **g**?
23:34 And they divided His **g** and
24: 4 men stood by them in shining **g**.
Jn 13: 4 supper and laid aside His **g**,
13:12 washed their feet, taken His **g**,
19:23 took His **g** and made four parts,
19:24 They divided My **g** among
Acts 9:39 showing the tunics and **g** which
18: 6 he shook his **g** and said to
Jas 5: 2 and your **g** are moth-eaten.
Rev 3: 4 who have not defiled their **g**;
3: 5 shall be clothed in white **g**,
3:18 you may be rich; and white **g**,
16:15 he who watches, and keeps his **g**,

GARMITE (1/1)

1 Chr 4:19 the fathers of Keilah the **G**

GARNER, GARNERS (KJV) See BARN, BARNS

GARRISON (16/16) GARRISONS

1 Sam 10: 5 of God where the Philistine **g**
13: 3 And Jonathan attacked the **g** of
13: 4 that Saul had attacked a **g** of
13:23 And the **g** of the Philistines
14: 1 go over to the Philistines' **g**
14: 4 go over to the Philistines' **g**,
14: 6 let us go over to the **g** of
14:11 showed themselves to the **g** of
14:12 Then the men of the **g** called to
14:15 The **g** and the raiders also
2 Sam 23:14 and the **g** of the Philistines
1 Chr 11:16 and the **g** of the Philistines
Mt 27:27 and gathered the whole **g**
Mk 15:16 called together the whole **g**.
Acts 21:31 came to the commander of the **g**
2 Cor 11:32 city of the Damascenes with a **g**,

GARRISONS (6/5) GARRISON

2 Sam 8: 6 Then David put **g** in Syria of
8:14 He also put **g** in Edom;
8:14 throughout all Edom he put **g**,
1 Chr 18: 6 Then David put **g** in Syria of
18:13 He also put **g** in Edom, and all
2 Chr 17: 2 and set **g** in the land of Judah

GASP (1/1)

Isa 42:14 I will pant and **g** at once.

GAT (KJV) See RETURNED, STOLE (BACK), TAKE, WENT

GATAM (3/3)

Gen 36:11 were Teman, Omar, Zepho, **G**,
36:16 Chief Korah, Chief **G**,
1 Chr 1:36 were Teman, Omar, Zephi, **G**,

GATE (252/207) GATEKEEPER, GATEPOST, GATES

Gen 19: 1 and Lot was sitting in the **g** of
22:17 shall possess the **g** of their
23:10 all who entered at the **g** of his
23:18 all who went in at the **g** of
28:17 and this is the **g** of heaven!"
34:20 Shechem his son came to the **g**
34:24 And all who went out of the **g** of
34:24 all who went out of the **g** of
Ex 27:14 on one side of the **g**
27:16 For the **g** of the court there
35:17 and the screen for the **g** of the
38:14 of one side of the **g** were
38:15 the other side of the court **g**;
38:18 The screen for the **g** of the
38:31 the bases for the court **g**,
39:40 the screen for the court **g**,
40: 8 up the screen at the court **g**.
40:33 up the screen of the court **g**.
Num 4:26 screen for the door of the **g**
Deut 21:19 to the **g** of his city.
22:15 the elders of the city at the **g**.
22:24 bring them both out to the **g**
25: 7 brother's wife go up to the **g**
Josh 2: 5 And it happened as the **g** was
2: 7 had gone out, they shut the **g**.
7: 5 chased them from before the **g**
8:29 it at the entrance of the **g** of
20: 4 at the entrance of the **g** of
Judg 9:35 in the entrance to the city **g**,
9:40 to the very entrance of the **g**.
9:44 stood at the entrance of the **g**
16: 2 for him all night at the **g** of
16: 3 hold of the doors of the **g** of
18:16 stood by the entrance of the **g**.
18:17 stood at the entrance of the **g**
Ruth 4: 1 Now Boaz went up to the **g** and
4:10 and from his position at the **g**.
4:11 the people who were at the **g**,
1 Sam 4:18 backward by the side of the **g**;
9:18 drew near to Samuel in the **g**,
21:13 scratched on the doors of the **g**,
2 Sam 3:27 Joab took him aside in the **g** to
10: 8 array at the entrance of the **g**.
11:23 as far as the entrance of the **g**.
15: 2 stand beside the way to the **g**.
18: 4 So the king stood beside the **g**,
18:24 went up to the roof over the **g**,
18:33 up to the chamber over the **g**,
19: 8 the king arose and sat in the **g**.
19: 8 is the king, sitting in the **g**.
23:15 which is by the **g**!"
23:16 of Bethlehem that was by the **g**,
1 Ki 17:10 And when he came to the **g** of
22:10 floor at the entrance of the **g**
2 Ki 7: 1 at the **g** of Samaria.'"
7: 3 men at the entrance of the **g**;
7:17 leaned to have charge of the **g**.
7:17 people trampled him in the **g**,
7:18 about this time in the **g** of
7:20 people trampled him in the **g**,
9:31 Then, as Jehu entered at the **g**,
10: 8 heaps at the entrance of the **g**
11: 6 one-third shall be at the **g** of
11: 6 and one-third at the **g** behind
11:19 and went by way of the **g** of the
14:13 wall of Jerusalem from the **G**
14:13 Gate of Ephraim to the Corner **G**—
15:35 He built the Upper **G** of the
23: 8 were at the entrance of the **G**
23: 8 were to the left of the city **g**.
25: 4 fled at night by way of the **g**
1 Chr 9:18 of Levi at the King's **G** on the
11:17 which is by the **g**!"
11:18 of Bethlehem that was by the **g**,
19: 9 in battle array before the **g**
26:13 And they cast lots for each **g**,
26:14 The lot for the East **G** fell to
26:14 lot came out for the North **G**;
26:15 to Obed-Edom the South **G**,
26:16 lot came out for the West **G**,
26:16 with the Shallecheth **G** on the
2 Chr 8:14 by their divisions at each **g**;
18: 9 floor at the entrance of the **g**
23: 5 and one-third at the **G** of the
23:15 of the entrance of the Horse **G**
23:20 they went through the Upper **G**
24: 8 and set it outside at the **g** of
25:23 wall of Jerusalem from the **G**
25:23 Gate of Ephraim to the Corner **G**—
26: 9 in Jerusalem at the Corner **G**,
26: 9 Corner Gate, at the Valley **G**,
27: 3 He built the Upper **G** of the
31:14 the keeper of the East **G**,
32: 6 the open square of the city **g**,
33:14 as the entrance of the Fish **G**;
35:15 the gatekeepers were at each **g**;
Neh 2:13 by night through the Valley **G**
2:13 Serpent Well and the Refuse **G**,
2:14 I went on to the Fountain **G**
2:15 and entered by the Valley **G**,
3: 1 priests and built the Sheep **G**;
3: 3 of Hassenaah built the Fish **G**;
3: 6 of Besodeiah repaired the Old **G**;
3:13 of Zanoah repaired the Valley **G**.
3:13 the wall as far as the Refuse **G**.
3:14 Haccerem, repaired the Refuse **G**;
3:15 Mizpah, repaired the Fountain **G**;
3:26 place in front of the Water **G**
3:28 Beyond the Horse **G** the priests
3:29 the keeper of the East **G**,
3:31 in front of the Miphkad **G**,
3:32 corner, as far as the Sheep **G**,
8: 1 was in front of the Water **G**;
8: 3 was in front of the Water **G**
8:16 the open square of the Water **G**
8:16 in the open square of the **G** of
12:31 on the wall toward the Refuse **G**.
12:37 By the Fountain **G**,
12:37 as far as the Water **G** eastward.
12:39 and above the **G** of Ephraim,
12:39 of Ephraim, above the Old **G**,
12:39 the Old Gate, above the Fish **G**,
12:39 Hundred, as far as the Sheep **G**;
12:39 and they stopped by the **G** of
Esth 2:19 sat within the king's **g**.
2:21 sat within the king's **g**,
3: 2 who were within the king's **g**
3: 3 who were within the king's **g**
4: 2 as the front of the king's **g**,
4: 2 one might enter the king's **g**
4: 6 was in front of the king's **g**.
5: 9 saw Mordecai in the king's **g**,
5:13 the Jew sitting at the king's **g**.
6:10 who sits within the king's **g**!
6:12 went back to the king's **g**.
Job 5: 4 They are crushed in the **g**,
29: 7 When I went out to the **g** by the
31:21 When I saw I had help in the **g**;
Ps 69:12 Those who sit in the **g** speak
118:20 This is the **g** of the LORD,
127: 5 with their enemies in the **g**.
Prov 17:19 And he who exalts his **g** seeks
22:22 oppress the afflicted at the **g**;
24: 7 not open his mouth in the **g**
Song 7: 4 the pools in Heshbon By the **g**
Isa 14:31 O **g**! Cry, O city! All you of
22: 7 themselves in array at the **g**.
24:12 And the **g** is stricken with
28: 6 turn back the battle at the **g**.
29:21 for him who reproves in the **g**,
Jer 7: 2 Stand in the **g** of the LORD's
17:19 Go and stand in the **g** of the
19: 2 by the entry of the Potsherd **G**;
20: 2 that were in the high **g** of
26:10 down in the entry of the New **G**
31:38 of Hananel to the Corner **G**.
31:40 to the corner of the Horse **G**
36:10 at the entry of the New **G** of
37:13 And when he was in the **G** of
38: 7 the king was sitting at the **G**
39: 3 came in and sat in the Middle **G**:
39: 4 by the **g** between the two walls.
51:30 The bars of her **g** are broken.
52: 7 city at night by way of the **g**
Lam 5:14 ceased gathering at the **g**,
Ezek 8: 3 to the door of the north **g** of
8: 5 and there, north of the altar **g**,
8:14 me to the door of the north **g**
9: 2 the direction of the upper **g**,
10:19 at the door of the east **g** of
11: 1 up and brought me to the East **G**
11: 1 and there at the door of the **g**
40: 7 Each **g** chamber was one rod long
40: 7 between the **g** chambers was a
40: 7 the vestibule of the inside **g**
40: 8 the vestibule of the inside **g**,
40: 9 The vestibule of the **g** was on
40:10 eastern gateway were three **g**
40:11 and the length of the **g**,
40:12 was a space in front of the **g**
40:12 the **g** chambers were six cubits
40:13 gateway from the roof of one **g**
40:15 the front of the entrance **g** to
40:15 of the vestibule of the inner **g**
40:16 beveled window frames in the **g**
40:21 Its **g** chambers, three on this
40:21 measurements as the first **g**;
40:23 A **g** of the inner court was
40:29 Also its **g** chambers, its
40:33 Also its **g** chambers, its
40:36 also its **g** chambers, its
40:44 Outside the inner **g** were the
43: 1 he brought me to the **g**,
43: 1 the **g** that faces toward the
43: 4 into the temple by way of the **g**
44: 1 brought me back to the outer **g**
44: 2 This **g** shall be shut; it shall
44: 4 me by way of the north **g** to
45:19 and on the gateposts of the **g**
46: 2 at the threshold of the **g**.
46: 2 but the **g** shall not be shut
46: 9 enters by way of the north **g**
46: 9 go out by way of the south **g**;
46: 9 enters by way of the south **g**
46: 9 go out by way of the north **g**.
46: 9 not return by way of the **g**
46: 9 go out through the opposite **g**.
46:12 the **g** that faces toward the
46:12 and after he goes out the **g**
46:19 which was at the side of the **g**,
47: 2 me out by way of the north **g**,
48:31 one **g** for Reuben, one gate for
48:31 one **g** for Judah, and one gate
48:31 and one **g** for Levi;
48:32 one **g** for Joseph, one gate for
48:32 one **g** for Benjamin, and one
48:32 and one **g** for Dan;
48:33 one **g** for Simeon, one gate for
48:33 one **g** for Issachar, and one
48:33 and one **g** for Zebulun;
48:34 one **g** for Gad, one gate for
48:34 one **g** for Asher, and one gate
48:34 and one **g** for Naphtali.
Dan 2:49 but Daniel sat in the **g** of the
Am 1: 5 I will also break the **g** bar of
5:10 the one who rebukes in the **g**,
5:12 poor from justice at the **g**.
5:15 Establish justice in the **g**.
Ob 13 should not have entered the **g**
Mic 1: 9 It has come to the **g** of My
1:12 down from the LORD To the **g**
2:13 break out, Pass through the **g**,
Zeph 1:10 a mournful cry from the Fish **G**,
Zech 14:10 in her place from Benjamin's **G**
14:10 to the place of the First **G**

14:10 the First Gate and the Corner **G**,
Mt 7:13 "Enter by the narrow **g**;
7:13 for wide is the **g** and broad
7:14 Because narrow is the **g** and
Lk 7:12 And when He came near the **g** of
13:24 to enter through the narrow **g**,
16:20 of sores, who was laid at his **g**,
Jn 5: 2 in Jerusalem by the Sheep **G** a
Acts 3: 2 whom they laid daily at the **g**
3:10 alms at the Beautiful **G** of the
10:17 house, and stood before the **g**.
12:10 they came to the iron **g** that
12:13 knocked at the door of the **g**,
12:14 gladness she did not open the **g**,
12:14 that Peter stood before the **g**.
Heb 13:12 blood, suffered outside the **g**.
Rev 21:21 each individual **g** was of one

GATE-BARS (1/1)

1 Ki 4:13 cities with walls and bronze **g**;

GATEKEEPER (1/1) GATE, GATEKEEPERS

2 Sam 18:26 the watchman called to the **g**

GATEKEEPERS (35/35) GATEKEEPER

2 Ki 7:10 they went and called to the **g**
7:11 And the **g** called out, and they
1 Chr 9:17 And the **g** were Shallum, Akkub,
9:18 Until then they had been **g**
9:19 **g** of the tabernacle.
9:22 All those chosen as **g** were two
9:24 The **g** were assigned to the four
9:26 office were four chief **g**;
15:18 Obed-Edom, and Jeiel, the **g**;
16:38 Jeduthun, and Hosah, to be **g**;
16:42 the sons of Jeduthun were **g**.
23: 5 four thousand were **g**,
26: 1 the divisions of the **g**:
26:12 were the divisions of the **g**,
26:19 were the divisions of the **g**
2 Chr 8:14 and the **g** by their divisions at
23:19 And he set the **g** at the gates of
34:13 were scribes, officers, and **g**.
35:15 Also the **g** were at each gate;
Ezra 2:42 The sons of the **g**:
2:70 the people, the singers, the **g**,
7: 7 the Levites, the singers, the **g**,
7:24 priests, Levites, singers, **g**,
10:24 singers: Eliashib; and of the **g**:
Neh 7: 1 had hung the doors, when the **g**,
7:45 The **g**: the sons of Shallum,
7:73 the priests, the Levites, the **g**,
10:28 priests, the Levites, the **g**,
10:39 priests who minister and the **g**
11:19 Moreover the **g**, Akkub, Talmon,
12:25 and Akkub were **g** keeping the
12:45 Both the singers and the **g** kept
12:47 for the singers and the **g**,
13: 5 the Levites and singers and **g**,
Ezek 44:11 as **g** of the house and

GATEPOST (3/3) GATE, GATEPOSTS

Ezek 40:14 the gateway extended to the **g**.
40:16 And on each **g** were palm trees.
46: 2 the outside, and stand by the **g**.

GATEPOSTS (16/15) GATEPOST

Judg 16: 3 gate of the city and the two **g**,
Ezek 40: 9 eight cubits; and the **g**,
40:10 also the **g** were of the same
40:14 He measured the **g**,
40:21 its **g** and its archways, had the
40:24 and he measured its **g** and
40:26 and it had palm trees on its **g**,
40:29 Also its gate chambers, its **g**,
40:31 palm trees were on its **g**,
40:33 Also its gate chambers, its **g**,
40:34 and palm trees were on its **g**
40:36 also its gate chambers, its **g**,
40:37 Its **g** faced the outer court,
40:37 palm trees were on its **g** on
40:38 and its entrance by the **g** of
45:19 and on the **g** of the gate of the

GATES (139/128) GATE

Gen 24:60 descendants possess The **g** of
Ex 20:10 stranger who is within your **g**.
Deut 3: 5 fortified with high walls, **g**,
5:14 stranger who is within your **g**,
6: 9 of your house and on your **g**.
11:20 of your house and on your **g**,
12:12 Levite who is within your **g**,
12:15 and eat meat within all your **g**,
12:17 You may not eat within your **g**
12:18 Levite who is within your **g**;
12:21 and you may eat within your **g**
14:21 the alien who is within your **g**,
14:27 Levite who is within your **g**,
14:28 and store it up within your **g**.
14:29 widow who are within your **g**,
15: 7 within any of the **g** in your
15:22 "You may eat it within your **g**;
16: 5 Passover within any of your **g**
16:11 Levite who is within your **g**,
16:14 widow, who are within your **g**.
16:18 and officers in all your **g**,
17: 2 within any of your **g** which the
17: 5 you shall bring out to your **g**
17: 8 of controversy within your **g**,
18: 6 Levite comes from any of your **g**,
23:16 he chooses within one of your **g**,
24:14 is in your land within your **g**.
26:12 they may eat within your **g** and
28:52 shall besiege you at all your **g**
28:52 shall besiege you at all your **g**
28:55 distress you at all your **g**.
28:57 distress you at all your **g**.
31:12 stranger who is within your **g**,
Josh 6:26 youngest he shall set up its **g**.
Judg 5: 8 Then there was war in the **g**;
5:11 LORD shall go down to the **g**.
1 Sam 17:52 of the valley and to the **g** of
23: 7 by entering a town that has **g**
2 Sam 18:24 was sitting between the two **g**.
1 Ki 16:34 son Segub he set up its **g**,
2 Ki 23: 8 down the high places at the **g**
1 Chr 9:23 were in charge of the **g** of
22: 3 the nails of the doors of the **g**
2 Chr 8: 5 fortified cities with walls, **g**,
14: 7 around them, and towers, **g**,
23:19 he set the gatekeepers at the **g**
31: 2 and to praise in the **g** of the
Neh 1: 3 and its **g** are burned with
2: 3 and its **g** are burned with
2: 8 timber to make beams for the **g**
2:13 were broken down and its **g**
2:17 and its **g** are burned with fire.
6: 1 not hung the doors in the **g**),
7: 3 Do not let the **g** of Jerusalem be
11:19 their brethren who kept the **g**,
12:25 at the storerooms of the **g**.
12:30 and purified the people, the **g**,
13:19 at the **g** of Jerusalem, as it
13:19 that I commanded the **g** to be
13:19 some of my servants at the **g**,
13:22 they should go and guard the **g**,
Job 17:16 Will they go down to the **g** of
38:17 Have the **g** of death been
Ps 9:13 You who lift me up from the **g**
9:14 of all Your praise In the **g**
24: 7 O you **g**! And be lifted up, you
24: 9 O you **g**! Lift up, you
87: 2 The LORD loves the **g** of Zion
100: 4 Enter into His **g** with
107:16 For He has broken the **g** of
107:18 And they drew near to the **g** of
118:19 Open to me the **g** of
122: 2 been standing Within your **g**,
147:13 strengthened the bars of your **g**;
Prov 1:21 At the openings of the **g** in
8: 3 She cries out by the **g**,
8:34 to me, Watching daily at my **g**,
14:19 And the wicked at the **g** of the
31:23 Her husband is known in the **g**,
31:31 own works praise her in the **g**.
Song 7:13 And at our **g** are pleasant
Isa 3:26 Her **g** shall lament and mourn,
13: 2 that they may enter the **g** of
26: 2 Open the **g**, That the
38:10 of my life I shall go to the **g**
45: 1 So that the **g** will not be
45: 2 I will break in pieces the **g**
54:12 Your **g** of crystal, And all
60:11 Therefore your **g** shall be open
60:18 And your **g** Praise.
62:10 Go through the **g**! Prepare the
Jer 1:15 At the entrance of the **g** of
7: 2 Judah who enter in at these **g**
14: 2 And her **g** languish;
15: 7 with a winnowing fan in the **g**
17:19 and in all the **g** of Jerusalem;
17:20 Jerusalem, who enter by these **g**.
17:21 nor bring it in by the **g** of
17:24 bring no burden through the **g**
17:25 then shall enter the **g** of this
17:27 a burden when entering the **g**
17:27 I will kindle a fire in its **g**,
22: 2 your people who enter these **g**!
22: 4 then shall enter the **g** of this
22:19 and cast out beyond the **g** of
49:31 Which has neither **g** nor bars,
51:58 And her high **g** shall be burned
Lam 1: 4 All her **g** are desolate;
2: 9 Her **g** have sunk into the
4:12 the enemy Could enter the **g**
Ezek 21:15 the sword against all their **g**,
21:22 battering rams against the **g**,
26:10 chariots, when he enters your **g**,
38:11 and having neither bars nor **g**'—
44:17 whenever they enter the **g** of
44:17 they minister within the **g** of
48:31 (the **g** of the city shall be
48:31 the three **g** northward: one gate
48:32 five hundred cubits, three **g**:
48:33 five hundred cubits, three **g**:
48:34 cubits with their three **g**:
Ob 11 When foreigners entered his **g**
Nah 2: 6 The **g** of the rivers are opened,
3:13 your midst are women! The **g**
3:13 devour the bars of your **g**.
Zech 8:16 Give judgment in your **g** for
Mt 16:18 and the **g** of Hades shall not
Acts 9:24 And they watched the **g** day and
14:13 oxen and garlands to the **g**,
Rev 21:12 and high wall with twelve **g**,
21:12 and twelve angels at the **g**,
21:13 three **g** on the east, three gates
21:13 three **g** on the north, three
21:13 three **g** on the south, and three
21:13 and three **g** on the west.
21:15 reed to measure the city, its **g**,
21:21 The twelve **g** were twelve
21:25 Its **g** shall not be shut at all
22:14 and may enter through the **g**

GATEWAY (42/33)

Ezek 26: 2 She is broken who was the **g**
40: 3 his hand, and he stood in the **g**.
40: 6 Then he went to the **g** which
40: 6 measured the threshold of the **g**,
40: 7 and the threshold of the **g** by
40: 9 measured the vestibule of the **g**,
40:10 In the eastern **g** were three
40:11 width of the entrance to the **g**,
40:13 Then he measured the **g** from the
40:14 and the court all around the **g**
40:16 on the inside of the **g** all
40:19 from the front of the lower **g**
40:20 the outer court was also a **g**
40:22 the same measurements as the **g**
40:23 was opposite the northern **g**,
40:23 gateway, just as the eastern **g**;
40:23 and he measured from **g** to
40:23 he measured from gateway to **g**,
40:24 and there a **g** was facing south;
40:27 There was also a **g** on the
40:27 and he measured from **g** to
40:27 he measured from gateway to **g**
40:28 court through the southern **g**;
40:28 he measured the southern **g**
40:32 he measured the **g** according to
40:35 he brought me to the north **g**
40:38 by the gateposts of the **g**,
40:39 In the vestibule of the **g** were
40:40 the entrance of the northern **g**,
40:40 side of the vestibule of the **g**
40:41 that side, by the side of the **g**,
40:44 at the side of the northern **g**,
40:44 at the side of the southern **g**.
40:48 and the width of the **g** was
42:15 he brought me out through the **g**
44: 3 way of the vestibule of the **g**,
46: 1 The **g** of the inner court that
46: 2 way of the vestibule of the **g**
46: 3 at the entrance to this **g**
46: 8 way of the vestibule of the **g**,
47: 2 on the outside to the outer **g**
Mt 26:71 when he had gone out to the **g**,

GATEWAYS (2/1)

Ezek 40:18 was by the side of the **g**,
40:18 to the length of the **g**;

GATH (36/34) GITTITE, MORESHETH GATH

Josh 11:22 remained only in Gaza, in **G**,
1 Sam 5: 8 of Israel be carried away to **G**.
6:17 one for Ashkelon, one for **G**,
7:14 to Israel, from Ekron to **G**;
17: 4 named Goliath, from **G**,
17:23 champion, the Philistine of **G**,
17:52 even as far as **G** and Ekron.
21:10 went to Achish the king of **G**.
21:12 afraid of Achish the king of **G**.
27: 2 the son of Maoch, king of **G**.
27: 3 So David dwelt with Achish at **G**,
27: 4 Saul that David had fled to **G**;
27:11 alive, to bring news to **G**,
2 Sam 1:20 Tell it not in **G**,
15:18 men who had followed him from **G**,
21:20 Yet again there was war at **G**,
21:22 were born to the giant in **G**,
1 Ki 2:39 the son of Maachah, king of **G**.
2:39 your slaves are in **G**!"
2:40 and went to Achish at **G** to seek
2:40 and brought his slaves from **G**.
2:41 had gone from Jerusalem to **G**
2 Ki 12:17 went up and fought against **G**,
1 Chr 7:21 The men of **G** who were born in
8:13 drove out the inhabitants of **G**.
18: 1 and took **G** and its towns from
20: 6 Yet again there was war at **G**,
20: 8 were born to the giant in **G**,
2 Chr 11: 8 **G**, Mareshah, Ziph,
26: 6 and broke down the wall of **G**,
Ps 8: On the instrument of **G**.
56: Philistines captured him in **G**.
81: On an instrument of **G**.
84: On an instrument of **G**.
Am 6: 2 Then go down to **G** of the
Mic 1:10 Tell it not in **G**,

GATH HEPHER (2/2) GATH

Josh 19:13 passed along on the east of **G**,
2 Ki 14:25 the prophet who was from **G**.

GATH RIMMON (4/4)

Josh 19:45 Jehud, Bene Berak, **G**,
21:24 and **G** with its common-land:
21:25 with its common-land and **G**
1 Chr 6:69 and **G** with its common-lands.

GATHER (168/162) GATHERED, GATHERING, GATHERS

Gen 6:21 and you shall **g** it to

31:46 G stones." And they took stones
34:30 they will g themselves together
41:35 And let them g all the food of
49: 1 G together, that I may tell you
49: 2 G together and hear, you sons of
Ex 3:16 Go and g the elders of Israel
5: 7 Let them go and g straw for
5:12 all the land of Egypt to g
9:19 Therefore send now and g your
16: 4 the people shall go out and g
16: 5 be twice as much as they g
16:16 Let every man g it according to
16:26 Six days you shall g it, but on
16:27 out on the seventh day to g,
23:10 you shall sow your land and g
Lev 8: 3 and g all the congregation
19: 9 nor shall you g the gleanings
19:10 nor shall you g every grape of
23:22 nor shall you g any gleaning
25: 3 and g its fruit;
25: 5 nor g the grapes of your
25:11 nor g the grapes of your
25:20 since we shall not sow nor g in
Num 8: 9 and you shall g together the
10: 3 all the congregation shall g
10: 4 shall g to you.
11:16 G to Me seventy men of the
19: 9 a man who is clean shall g
20: 8 you and your brother Aaron g
21:16 G the people together, and I
Deut 4:10 G the people to Me, and I will
11:14 that you may g in your grain,
13:16 And you shall g all its plunder
24:21 When you g the grapes of your
28:30 but shall not g its grapes.
28:38 seed out to the field but g
28:39 drink of the wine nor g the
30: 3 and g you again from all the
30: 4 the LORD your God will g you,
31:12 G the people together, men and
31:28 G to me all the elders of your
Judg 1: 7 and big toes cut off used to g
Ruth 2: 7 Please let me glean and g after
1 Sam 7: 5 G all Israel to Mizpah, and I
2 Sam 3:21 and g all Israel to my lord the
12:28 g the rest of the people
1 Ki 18:19 send and g all Israel to me on
2 Ki 4: 3 do not g just a few.
4:39 went out into the field to g
22:20 I will g you to your fathers,
23: 1 Now the king sent them to g all
1 Chr 13: 2 that they may g together to us;
16:35 G us together, and deliver us
22: 2 So David commanded to g the
2 Chr 24: 5 and g from all Israel money to
34:28 Surely I will g you to your
Ezra 10: 7 that they must g at Jerusalem,
Neh 1: 9 yet I will g them from there,
7: 5 God put it into my heart to g
12:44 to g into them from the fields
Esth 2: 3 that they may g all the
4:16 g all the Jews who are present
8:11 who were in every city to g
Job 16:10 They g together against me.
24: 6 They g their fodder in the
34:14 If He should g to Himself His
39:12 And g it to your threshing
Ps 26: 9 Do not g my soul with sinners,
39: 6 And does not know who will g
50: 5 G My saints together to Me,
56: 6 They g together, They hide,
59: 3 The mighty g against me,
94:21 They g together against the
104:22 they g together And lie down
104:28 What You give them they g in;
106:47 And g us from among the
140: 2 They continually g together
Eccl 3: 5 And a time to g stones;
Song 6: 2 And to g lilies.
Isa 11:12 And g together the dispersed
34:15 and g them under her shadow;
40:11 He will g the lambs with His
43: 5 And g you from the west;
49:18 All these g together and come
54: 7 with great mercies I will g
56: 8 Yet I will g to him Others
60: 4 They all g together, they come
66:18 It shall be that I will g all
Jer 4: 5 G together,' And say, 'Assemble
6: 1 G yourselves to flee from the
7:18 The children g wood, the fathers
9:22 And no one shall g them.'"
10:17 G up your wares from the land,
23: 3 But I will g the remnant of My
29:14 I will g you from all the
31: 8 And g them from the ends of
31:10 who scattered Israel will g
32:37 I will g them out of all
40:10 g wine and summer fruit and
49: 5 And no one will g those who
49:14 G together, come against her,
51:11 Make the arrows bright! G the
Ezek 11:17 I will g you from the peoples,
16:37 I will g all your lovers with
16:37 I will g them from all around
20:34 you out from the peoples and g
20:41 you out from the peoples and g
22:19 I will g you into the midst of
22:20 As men g silver, bronze, iron,
22:20 so I will g you in My anger
22:21 I will g you and blow on you
24: 4 G pieces of meat in it,
29:13 the end of forty years I will g
34:13 them out from the peoples and g
36:24 g you out of all countries,
37:21 and will g them from every side
39:17 G together from all sides to
Dan 3: 2 Nebuchadnezzar sent word to g
Hos 8:10 Now I will g them; And they
9: 6 Egypt shall g them up;
Joel 1:14 G the elders And all the
2:16 G the people, Sanctify the
2:16 G the children and nursing
3: 2 I will also g all nations,
3:11 And g together all around.
Mic 2:12 I will surely g the remnant of
4: 6 I will g the outcast
4:12 For He will g them like
5: 1 Now g yourself in troops,
7: 1 For I am like those who g summer
Hab 1: 9 They g captives like sand.
1:15 And g them in their dragnet.
Zeph 2: 1 G yourselves together, yes,
2: 1 g together, O undesirable
3: 8 My determination is to g the
3:18 I will g those who sorrow over
3:19 And g those who were driven
3:20 Even at the time I g you;
Zech 10: 8 I will whistle for them and g
10:10 And g them from Assyria.
14: 2 For I will g all the nations to
Mt 3:12 and g His wheat into the barn;
6:26 they neither sow nor reap nor g
7:16 Do men g grapes from
12:30 and he who does not g with Me
13:28 you want us then to go and g
13:29 lest while you g up the tares
13:30 First g together the tares and
13:30 but g the wheat into my barn."
13:41 and they will g out of His
23:37 to her! How often I wanted to g
24:31 and they will g together His
25:26 and g where I have not
Mk 13:27 and g together His elect from
Lk 3:17 and g the wheat into His barn;
6:44 For men do not g figs from
6:44 nor do they g grapes from a
11:23 and he who does not g with Me
13:34 to her! How often I wanted to g
Jn 6:12 G up the fragments that remain,
11:52 but also that He would g
15: 6 and they g them and throw them
Eph 1:10 of the times He might g
Rev 14:18 in your sharp sickle and g the
16:14 to g them to the battle of that
19:17 Come and g together for the
20: 8 to g them together to battle,

GATHERED (259/248) GATHER

Gen 1: 9 waters under the heavens be g
12: 5 possessions that they had g,
25: 8 and was g to his people.
25:17 and was g to his people.
29: 3 Now all the flocks would be g
29: 7 not time for the cattle to be g
29: 8 until all the flocks are g
29:22 And Laban g together all the men
35:29 and was g to his people, being
41:48 So he g up all the food of the
41:49 Joseph g very much grain, as the
47:14 And Joseph g up all the money
49:29 'I am to be g to my people;
49:33 and was g to his people.
Ex 4:29 Then Moses and Aaron went and g
8:14 They g them together in heaps,
15: 8 nostrils The waters were g
16:17 children of Israel did so and g,
16:18 he who g much had nothing left
16:18 and he who g little had no
16:18 Every man had g according to
16:21 So they g it every morning,
16:22 that they g twice as much
23:16 when you have g in the fruit
32: 1 the people g together to Aaron,
32:26 And all the sons of Levi g
35: 1 Then Moses g all the
Lev 8: 4 And the congregation was g
23:39 when you have g in the fruit of
26:25 when you are g together within
Num 10: 7 when the assembly is to be g
11: 8 The people went about and g it,
11:22 all the fish of the sea be g
11:24 and he g the seventy men of the
11:32 and g the quail (he who
11:32 gathered the quail (he who g
11:32 quail (he who gathered least g
14:35 evil congregation who are g
16: 3 They g together against Moses
16:11 you and all your company are g
16:19 And Korah g all the congregation
16:42 when the congregation had g
20: 2 so they g together against
20:10 And Moses and Aaron g the
20:24 Aaron shall be g to his people,
20:26 for Aaron shall be g to his
21:23 So Sihon g all his people
27: 3 in the company of those who g
27:13 you also shall be g to your
27:13 as Aaron your brother was g.
31: 2 Afterward you shall be g to
Deut 16:13 when you have g from your
32:50 and be g to your people, just
32:50 died on Mount Hor and was g to
33: 5 leaders of the people were g,
Josh 9: 2 that they g together to fight
10: 5 g together and went up, they
10: 6 dwell in the mountains have g
22:12 of the children of Israel g
24: 1 Then Joshua g all the tribes of
Judg 2:10 all that generation had been g
3:13 Then he g to himself the people
4:13 So Sisera g together all his
6:33 g together; and they crossed
6:34 and the Abiezrites g behind
6:35 who also g behind him. He also
7:23 And the men of Israel g together
7:24 Then all the men of Ephraim g
9: 6 And all the men of Shechem g
9:27 and g grapes from their
9:47 of the tower of Shechem were g
10:17 Then the people of Ammon g
11:20 So Sihon g all his people
12: 1 Then the men of Ephraim g
12: 4 Now Jephthah g together all the
16:23 the lords of the Philistines g
18:22 the houses near Micah's house g
18:23 that you have g such a
20: 1 and the congregation g together
20:11 So all the men of Israel were g
20:14 the children of Benjamin g
1 Sam 5: 8 Therefore they sent and g to
5:11 So they sent and g together all
7: 6 So they g together at Mizpah,
7: 7 the children of Israel had g
8: 4 Then all the elders of Israel g
13: 5 Then the Philistines g together
13:11 and that the Philistines g
14:48 And he g an army and attacked
15: 4 So Saul g the people together
17: 1 Now the Philistines g their
17: 1 and were g together at Sochoh,
17: 2 and the men of Israel were g
20:38 So Jonathan's lad g up
22: 2 who was discontented g to
25: 1 and the Israelites g together
28: 1 days that the Philistines g
28: 4 Then the Philistines g together,
28: 4 So Saul g all Israel together,
29: 1 Then the Philistines g together
2 Sam 2:25 Now the children of Benjamin g
2:30 And when he had g all the
6: 1 Again David g all the choice
10:15 they g together.
10:17 he g all Israel, crossed over
12:29 So David g all the people
14:14 which cannot be g up again.
17:11 that all Israel be fully g to
20:14 So they were g together and
21:13 and they g the bones of those
23: 9 the Philistines who were g
23:11 The Philistines had g together
1 Ki 10:26 And Solomon g chariots and
11:24 So he g men to him and became
18:20 and g the prophets together on
20: 1 Ben-Hadad the king of Syria g
22: 6 Then the king of Israel g the
2 Ki 3:21 to bear arms and older were g;
4:39 and g from it a lapful of wild
6:24 that Ben-Hadad king of Syria g
10:18 Then Jehu g all the people
22: 4 which the doorkeepers have g
22: 9 Your servants have g the money
22:20 and you shall be g to your
1 Chr 11:13 there the Philistines were g
13: 5 So David g all Israel together,
15: 3 And David g all Israel together
19: 7 Also the people of Ammon g
19:17 he g all Israel, crossed over
23: 2 And he g together all the
2 Chr 1:14 And Solomon g chariots and
12: 5 who were g together in
13: 7 Then worthless rogues g to him,
15: 9 Then he g all Judah and
15:10 So they g together at Jerusalem
18: 5 Then the king of Israel g the
20: 4 So Judah g together to ask help
23: 2 went throughout Judah and g
24: 5 Then he g the priests and the
24:11 and g money in abundance.
25: 5 Moreover Amaziah g Judah
28:24 So Ahaz g the articles of the
29: 4 and g them in the East Square,
29:15 And they g their brethren,
29:20 g the rulers of the city,
30: 3 nor had the people g together
30:13 g at Jerusalem to keep the
32: 4 Thus many people g together who
32: 6 g them together to him in the
34: 9 who kept the doors had g from
34:17 And they have g the money that
34:28 and you shall be g to your
34:29 Then the king sent and g all
Ezra 3: 1 the people g together as one
7:28 and I g leading men of Israel
8:15 Now I g them by the river that
10: 1 and children g to him from
10: 9 men of Judah and Benjamin g at
Neh 5:16 All my servants were g there
8: 1 Now all the people g together as
8:13 were g to Ezra the scribe, in
12:28 And the sons of the singers g
13:11 And I g them together and set
Esth 2: 8 when many young women were g
2:19 When virgins were g together a
9: 2 The Jews g together in their

G

9:15 the Jews who were in Shushan *g*
9:16 Jews in the king's provinces *g*
Job 27:19 But not be *g* up; He opens
Ps 35:15 adversity they rejoiced And *g*
35:15 Attackers *g* against me, And I
47:9 princes of the people have *g*
102:22 When the peoples are *g*
107:3 And *g* out of the lands, From
Prov 27:25 herbs of the mountains are *g*
30:4 Who has *g* the wind in His
Eccl 2:8 I also *g* for myself silver and
Song 5:1 I have *g* my myrrh with my
Isa 10:14 I have *g* all the earth;
13:4 of the kingdoms of nations *g*
22:9 And you *g* together the waters
24:22 They will be *g* together,
24:22 As prisoners are *g* in the
27:12 And you will be *g* one by one,
33:4 And Your plunder shall be *g*
34:15 also shall the hawks be *g*,
34:16 and His Spirit has *g* them.
43:9 Let all the nations be *g*
44:11 Let them all be *g* together,
49:5 So that Israel is *g* to Him
56:8 besides those who are *g* to him.
60:7 the flocks of Kedar shall be *g*
62:9 But those who have *g* it shall
Jer 3:17 and all the nations shall be *g*
8:2 They shall not be *g* nor buried;
25:33 shall not be lamented, or *g*,
26:9 And all the people were *g*
40:12 and *g* wine and summer fruit in
40:15 so that all the Jews who are *g*
Ezek 28:4 And *g* gold and silver into
28:25 When I have *g* the house of
29:5 shall not be picked up or *g*.
38:7 all your companies that are *g*
38:8 back from the sword and *g*
38:12 and against a people *g* from the
38:13 Have you *g* your army to take
39:27 back from the peoples and *g*
Dan 3:3 officials of the provinces *g*
3:27 and the king's counselors *g*
Hos 1:11 children of Israel Shall be *g*
10:10 Peoples shall be *g* against
Mic 1:7 For she *g* it from the pay of
4:11 Now also many nations have *g*
Zech 12:3 all nations of the earth are *g*
14:14 nations Shall be *g* together:
Mt 2:4 And when he had *g* all the chief
13:2 And great multitudes were *g*
13:40 Therefore as the tares are *g* and
13:47 was cast into the sea and *g*
13:48 and they sat down and *g* the
18:20 For where two or three are *g*
22:10 out into the highways and *g*
22:34 they *g* together.
22:41 While the Pharisees were *g*
24:28 there the eagles will be *g*
25:32 All the nations will be *g* before
27:17 when they had *g* together,
27:27 into the Praetorium and *g* the
27:62 chief priests and Pharisees *g*
Mk 1:33 And the whole city was *g*
2:2 Immediately many *g* together, so
4:1 And a great multitude was *g* to
5:21 a great multitude *g* to Him;
6:30 Then the apostles *g* to Jesus
10:1 And multitudes *g* to Him again,
Lk 8:4 when a great multitude had *g*,
11:29 while the crowds were thickly *g*
12:1 multitude of people had *g*
15:13 the younger son *g* all together,
17:37 there the eagles will be *g*
24:33 those who were with them *g*
Jn 6:13 Therefore they *g* them up, and
11:47 priests and the Pharisees *g* a
Acts 4:6 were *g* together at Jerusalem.
4:26 And the rulers were *g*
4:27 were *g* together
5:16 Also a multitude *g* from the
12:12 where many were *g* together
14:20 when the disciples *g* around
14:27 Now when they had come and *g* the
15:30 and when they had *g* the
20:8 upper room where they were *g*
28:3 But when Paul had *g* a bundle of
1 Cor 5:4 when you are *g* together, along
2 Cor 8:15 He who *g* much had nothing
8:15 and he who *g* little had
Rev 14:19 his sickle into the earth and *g*
16:16 And they *g* them together to the
19:19 *g* together to make war against

GATHERING (15/15) GATHER

Gen 1:10 and the *g* together of the
50:9 and it was a very great *g*.
Num 15:32 they found a man *g* sticks on
15:33 And those who found him *g* sticks
1 Ki 17:10 indeed a widow was there *g*
17:12 I am *g* a couple of sticks that
2 Chr 20:25 and they were three days *g* the
Eccl 2:26 sinner He gives the work of *g*
Isa 32:10 The *g* will not come.
33:4 shall be gathered Like the *g*
Lam 5:14 The elders have ceased *g* at
Mt 25:24 and *g* where you have not
Acts 17:5 and *g* a mob, set all the city
19:40 account for this disorderly *g*.
2 Th 2:1 our Lord Jesus Christ and our *g*

GATHERS (18/17) GATHER

Num 19:10 And the one who *g* the ashes of
Job 11:10 and *g* to judgment, Then who
Ps 33:7 He *g* the waters of the sea
41:6 His heart *g* iniquity to
147:2 He *g* together the outcasts of
Prov 6:8 And *g* her food in the
10:5 He who *g* in summer is a wise
13:11 But he who *g* by labor will
28:8 by usury and extortion *G* it
Isa 10:14 And as one *g* eggs that are
17:5 be as when the harvester *g* the
17:5 It shall be as he who *g* heads
56:8 who *g* the outcasts of Israel,
Nah 3:18 And no one *g* them.
Hab 2:5 He *g* to himself all nations
Mt 23:37 as a hen *g* her chicks under
Lk 13:34 as a hen *g* her brood under
Jn 4:36 and *g* fruit for eternal life,

GAUNT (5/5)

Gen 41:3 out of the river, ugly and *g*,
41:4 And the ugly and *g* cows ate up
41:19 them, poor and very ugly and *g*,
41:20 And the *g* and ugly cows ate up
Job 30:3 They are *g* from want and

GAVE (496/463) GIVE

Gen 2:20 So Adam *g* names to all cattle,
3:6 She also *g* to her husband with
3:12 The woman whom You *g* to be
3:12 she *g* me of the tree, and I
14:20 And he *g* him a tithe of all.
16:3 and *g* her to her husband Abram
16:5 My wrong be upon you! I *g* my
18:7 *g* it to a young man, and he
20:14 and *g* them to Abraham; and he
21:14 he *g* it and the boy to Hagar,
21:19 and *g* the lad a drink.
21:27 took sheep and oxen and *g* them
24:18 and *g* him a drink.
24:46 and she *g* the camels a drink
24:53 and *g* them to Rebekah. He also
24:53 He also *g* precious things to
25:5 And Abraham *g* all that he had to
25:6 But Abraham *g* gifts to the sons
25:34 And Jacob *g* Esau bread and stew
27:17 Then she *g* the savory food and
28:4 Which God *g* to Abraham."
28:6 that as he blessed him he *g*
29:24 And Laban *g* his maid Zilpah to
29:28 So he *g* him his daughter Rachel
29:29 And Laban *g* his maid Bilhah to
30:4 Then she *g* him Bilhah her maid
30:9 she took Zilpah her maid and *g*
30:35 and *g* them into the hand of
35:4 So they *g* Jacob all the foreign
35:12 The land which I *g* Abraham and
38:18 Then he *g* them to her, and
39:21 and He *g* him favor in the sight
41:45 And he *g* him as a wife Asenath,
42:25 Then Joseph *g* a command to fill
43:24 men into Joseph's house and *g*
43:24 and he *g* their donkeys feed.
45:21 and Joseph *g* them carts,
45:21 and he *g* them provisions for
45:22 He *g* to all of them, to each
45:22 but to Benjamin he *g* three
46:18 whom Laban *g* to Leah his
46:25 whom Laban *g* to Rachel his
47:11 and *g* them a possession in the
47:17 and Joseph *g* them bread in
47:22 their rations which Pharaoh *g*
Ex 2:21 and he *g* Zipporah his daughter
6:13 and *g* them a command for the
11:3 And the LORD *g* the people favor
14:20 and it *g* light by night to
31:18 He *g* Moses two tablets of the
32:24 So they *g* it to me, and I
34:32 and he *g* them as commandments
36:6 So Moses *g* a commandment,
Num 3:51 And Moses *g* their redemption
7:6 and *g* them to the Levites.
7:7 Two carts and four oxen he *g* to
7:8 four carts and eight oxen he *g*
7:9 But to the sons of Kohath he *g*
13:32 And they *g* the children of
15:23 from the day the LORD *g*
17:6 and each of their leaders *g* him
31:41 So Moses *g* the tribute which
31:47 and *g* them to the Levites, who
32:28 So Moses *g* command concerning
32:33 So Moses *g* to the children of
32:38 and they *g* other names to the
32:40 So Moses *g* Gilead to Machir the
Deut 2:12 possession which the LORD *g*
3:12 I *g* to the Reubenites and the
3:13 I *g* to half the tribe of
3:15 Also I *g* Gilead to Machir.
3:16 Reubenites and the Gadites I *g*
5:22 on two tablets of stone and *g*
9:11 that the LORD *g* me the two
10:4 and the LORD *g* them to me.
22:16 I *g* my daughter to this man as
29:8 We took their land and *g* it as
Josh 1:14 in the land which Moses *g* you
1:15 as He *g* you, and they also
1:15 Moses the LORD's servant *g*
11:23 and Joshua *g* it as an
12:7 which Joshua *g* to the tribes of
14:4 And they *g* no part to the
14:13 and *g* Hebron to Caleb the son
15:13 the son of Jephunneh he *g* a
15:17 and he *g* him Achsah his
15:19 So he *g* her the upper springs
17:4 he *g* them an inheritance among
18:7 the servant of the LORD *g*
19:49 the children of Israel *g* an
19:50 to the word of the LORD they *g*
21:3 So the children of Israel *g* to
21:8 And the children of Israel *g*
21:9 So they *g* from the tribe of the
21:11 And they *g* them Kirjath Arba
21:12 city and its villages they *g*
21:13 of Aaron the priest they *g*
21:21 For they *g* them Shechem with its
21:27 they *g* Golan in Bashan with
21:43 So the LORD *g* to Israel all
21:44 The LORD *g* them rest all
22:4 the servant of the LORD *g* you
22:7 the other half of it Joshua *g*
24:3 his descendants and *g* him
24:4 'To Isaac I *g* Jacob and Esau.
24:4 To Esau I *g* the mountains of
24:8 But I *g* them into your hand,
Judg 1:13 so he *g* him his daughter Achsah
1:15 And Caleb *g* her the upper
1:20 And they *g* Hebron to Caleb, as
3:6 and *g* their daughters to their
4:19 *g* him a drink, and covered him.
5:25 she *g* milk; She brought out
6:9 them out before you and *g* you
9:4 So they *g* him seventy shekels
12:9 And he *g* away thirty daughters
14:9 he *g* some to them, and they
14:10 And Samson *g* a feast there, for
14:19 and *g* the changes of clothing
15:2 therefore I *g* her to your
17:4 shekels of silver and *g* them
19:21 and *g* fodder to the donkeys.
21:14 and they *g* them the women whom
Ruth 2:18 So she brought out and *g* to her
3:17 six ephahs of barley he *g* me;
4:7 man took off his sandal and *g*
4:13 the LORD *g* her conception, and
4:17 Also the neighbor women *g* him a
1 Sam 4:19 she bowed herself and *g* birth,
9:23 Bring the portion which I *g* you,
10:9 that God *g* him another heart;
18:4 robe that was on him and *g* it
18:27 and they *g* them in full count
18:27 Then Saul *g* him Michal his
20:40 Then Jonathan *g* his weapons to
21:6 So the priest *g* him holy bread;
22:10 *g* him provisions, and gave him
22:10 and *g* him the sword of Goliath
27:6 So Achish *g* him Ziklag that day.
30:11 and they *g* him bread and he
30:12 And they *g* him a piece of a cake
2 Sam 12:8 I *g* you your master's house and
12:8 and *g* you the house of Israel
16:23 which he *g* in those days, was
18:5 people heard when the king *g*
24:9 Then Joab *g* the sum of the
1 Ki 2:43 and the commandment that I *g*
3:17 and I *g* birth while she was in
3:18 that this woman also *g* birth.
4:29 And God *g* Solomon wisdom and
5:10 Then Hiram *g* Solomon cedar and
5:11 And Solomon *g* Hiram twenty
5:11 Thus Solomon *g* to Hiram year by
5:12 So the LORD *g* Solomon wisdom,
8:34 back to the land which You *g*
8:40 live in the land which You *g*
8:48 toward their land which You *g*
9:11 that King Solomon then *g* Hiram
10:10 Then she *g* the king one hundred
10:10 spices as the queen of Sheba *g*
10:13 Now King Solomon *g* the queen of
11:18 who *g* him a house, apportioned
11:18 and *g* him land.
11:19 so that he *g* him as wife the
13:3 And he *g* a sign the same day,
14:8 and *g* it to you; and yet you
14:15 from this good land which He *g*
15:4 sake the LORD his God *g* him a
17:23 and *g* him to his mother.
19:21 and *g* it to the people, and
2 Ki 10:15 So he *g* him his hand, and he
11:10 And the priest *g* the captains of
11:12 and *g* him the Testimony;
12:11 Then they *g* the money, which had
12:14 But they *g* that to the workmen,
13:5 Then the LORD *g* Israel a
15:19 and Menahem *g* Pul a thousand
18:15 So Hezekiah *g* him all the
18:16 and *g* it to the king of
21:8 from the land which I *g* their
22:8 And Hilkiah *g* the book to
23:35 So Jehoiakim *g* the silver and
25:28 and *g* him a more prominent seat
1 Chr 2:35 Sheshan *g* his daughter to Jarha
6:55 They *g* them Hebron in the land
6:56 city and its villages they *g*
6:57 And to the sons of Aaron they *g*
6:61 of the Kohathites they *g* by
6:62 they *g* thirteen cities from
6:63 they *g* twelve cities from the
6:64 So the children of Israel *g*
6:65 And they *g* by lot from the tribe
6:67 And they *g* them one of the

14:12 David *g* a commandment, and they
21: 5 Then Joab *g* the sum of the
21:25 So David *g* Ornan six hundred
25: 5 For God *g* Heman fourteen sons
28:11 Then David *g* his son Solomon
28:14 He *g* gold by weight for
28:16 And by weight he *g* gold for
28:17 he *g* gold by weight for every
29: 7 They *g* for the work of the house
29: 8 whoever had precious stones *g*
2 Chr 6:25 back to the land which You *g*
6:31 live in the land which You *g*
6:38 toward their land which You *g*
9: 9 And she *g* the king one hundred
9: 9 as those the queen of Sheba *g*
9:12 Now King Solomon *g* to the queen
11:23 and he *g* them provisions in
13: 5 that the LORD God of Israel *g*
13:15 Then the men of Judah *g* a shout;
15:15 and the LORD *g* them rest all
17: 5 and all Judah *g* presents to
20: 7 and *g* it to the descendants of
20:30 for his God *g* him rest all
21: 3 Their father *g* them great gifts
21: 3 but he *g* the kingdom to
23: 9 And Jehoiada the priest *g* to the
23:11 *g* him the Testimony, and made
24:12 The king and Jehoiada *g* it to
27: 5 And the people of Ammon *g* him
28:15 dressed them and *g* them
28:15 *g* them food and drink, and
28:21 and he *g* it to the king of
30: 7 so that He *g* them up to
30:22 And Hezekiah *g* encouragement to
30:24 For Hezekiah king of Judah *g* to
30:24 and the leaders *g* to the
32: 6 and *g* them encouragement,
32:24 and He spoke to him and *g* him a
34:10 and they *g* it to the workmen
34:11 They *g* it to the craftsmen and
34:15 And Hilkiah *g* the book to
35: 7 Then Josiah *g* the lay people
35: 8 And his leaders *g* willingly to
35: 8 *g* to the priests for the
35: 9 *g* to the Levites for Passover
36:17 He *g* them all into his hand.
Ezra 2:69 they *g* to the treasury for the
3: 7 They also *g* money to the masons
4:19 And I *g* the command, and a
5:12 He *g* them into the hand of
7:11 letter that King Artaxerxes *g*
8:17 And I *g* them a command for Iddo
8:36 So they *g* support to the people
10:15 and Shabbethai the Levite *g*
10:19 And they *g* their promise that
Neh 2: 1 that I took the wine and *g* it
2: 9 and *g* them the king's letters.
7: 2 that I *g* the charge of Jerusalem
7:70 heads of the fathers' houses *g*
7:70 The governor *g* to the treasury
7:71 of the fathers' houses *g* to
7:72 which the rest of the people *g*
8: 8 and they *g* the sense, and
9: 7 And *g* him the name Abraham;
9:13 And *g* them just ordinances and
9:15 You *g* them bread from heaven
9:20 You also *g* Your good Spirit to
9:20 And *g* them water for their
9:22 Moreover You *g* them kingdoms and
9:24 And *g* them into their hands,
9:27 to Your abundant mercies You *g*
9:30 Therefore You *g* them into the
9:35 many good things that You *g*
9:36 And the land that You *g* to
12:47 days of Nehemiah all Israel *g*
Esth 2: 9 so he readily *g* beauty
2:18 holiday in the provinces and *g*
3:10 ring from his hand and *g* it to
4: 5 and she *g* him a command
4: 8 He also *g* him a copy of the
4:10 and *g* him a command for
8: 1 On that day King Ahasuerus *g*
8: 2 and *g* it to Mordecai;
Job 1:21 I return there. The LORD *g*,
34:13 Who *g* Him charge over the
42:10 Indeed the LORD *g* Job twice as
42:11 Each one *g* him a piece of
42:15 and their father *g* them an
Ps 21: 4 and You *g* it to him—Length
68:11 The Lord *g* the word;
69:21 They also *g* me gall for my
69:21 And for my thirst they *g* me
74:14 And *g* him as food to the
77: 1 And He *g* ear to me.
78:15 And *g* them drink in abundance
78:29 For He *g* them their own
78:46 He also *g* their crops to the
78:48 He also *g* up their cattle to
78:50 But *g* their life over to the
78:62 He also *g* His people over to
81:12 So I *g* them over to their own
99: 7 and the ordinance He *g* them.
105:32 He *g* them hail for rain,
105:44 He *g* them the lands of the
106:15 And He *g* them their request,
106:41 And He *g* them into the hand of
135:12 And *g* their land as a
136:21 And *g* their land as a heritage,
Eccl 12: 7 will return to God who *g* it.
Song 5: 6 but he *g* me no answer.
Isa 41: 2 Who *g* the nations before him,
41: 2 Who *g* them as the dust to
42:24 Who *g* Jacob for plunder, and
43: 3 I *g* Egypt for your ransom,
50: 6 I *g* My back to those who struck
66: 7 she *g* birth; Before her pain
66: 8 She *g* birth to her children.
Jer 2:27 You *g* birth to me.' For they
7: 7 in the land that I *g* to your
7:14 and to this place which I *g* to
11:18 Now the LORD *g* me knowledge
14: 5 the deer also *g* birth in the
16:15 back into their land which I *g*
17: 4 go of your heritage which I *g*
23:39 and the city that I *g* you and
24:10 from the land that I *g* to them
30: 3 to return to the land that I *g*
32:12 and I *g* the purchase deed to
36:32 took another scroll and *g* it
37: 2 nor the people of the land *g*
39:10 and *g* them vineyards and fields
39:11 king of Babylon *g* charge
40: 5 So the captain of the guard *g*
44:30 as I *g* Zedekiah king of Judah
52:32 he spoke kindly to him and *g*
Ezek 16:10 you in embroidered cloth and *g*
16:19 Also My food which I *g* you—the
16:27 and *g* you up to the will of
16:34 In that you *g* payment but no
16:36 of your children which you *g*
17:18 and in fact *g* his hand and
20:11 And I *g* them My statutes and
20:12 Moreover I also *g* them My
20:25 Therefore I also *g* them up to
27:10 They *g* splendor to you.
27:12 They *g* you silver, iron, tin,
27:16 They *g* you for your wares
28:25 in their own land which I *g* to
31: 4 Underground waters *g* it
36: 5 who *g* My land to themselves as
36:28 dwell in the land that I *g* to
39:23 I *g* them into the hand of their
Dan 1: 2 And the Lord *g* Jehoiakim king of
1: 7 them the chief of the eunuchs *g*
1: 7 he *g* Daniel the name
1:16 and *g* them vegetables.
1:17 God *g* them knowledge and skill
2: 2 Then the king *g* the command to
2:12 and *g* a command to destroy all
2:48 the king promoted Daniel and *g*
3:13 *g* the command to bring
4:26 And inasmuch as they *g* the
5: 2 Belshazzar *g* the command to
5:18 the Most High God *g*
5:19 of the majesty that He *g* him,
5:29 Then Belshazzar *g* the command,
6: 3 and the king *g* thought to
6:10 and prayed and *g* thanks before
6:16 So the king *g* the command, and
6:24 And the king *g* the command, and
Hos 2: 8 she did not know That I *g* her
13:11 I *g* you a king in My anger,
Am 2:12 But you *g* the Nazirites wine to
4: 6 Also I *g* you cleanness of teeth
Mal 2: 5 And I *g* them to him that he
Mt 8:18 He *g* a command to depart to the
10: 1 He *g* them power over unclean
14:19 He blessed and broke and *g* the
14:19 and the disciples *g* to the
15:36 seven loaves and the fish and *g*
15:36 broke them and *g* them to His
15:36 and the disciples *g* to the
21:23 And who *g* You this authority?"
25:15 And to one he *g* five talents, to
25:35 for I was hungry and you *g* Me
25:35 I was thirsty and you *g* Me
25:42 for I was hungry and you *g* Me no
25:42 I was thirsty and you *g* Me no
26:26 and *g* it to the disciples and
26:27 and *g* thanks, and gave it to
26:27 and *g* it to them, saying,
27:10 and *g* them for the potter's
27:34 they *g* Him sour wine mingled
28:12 they *g* a large sum of money to
Mk 2:26 and also *g* some to those who
3:16 to whom He *g* the name Peter;
3:17 to whom He *g* the name
5:13 And at once Jesus *g* them
6: 7 and *g* them power over unclean
6:21 when Herod on his birthday *g* a
6:28 and *g* it to the girl; and the
6:28 and the girl *g* it to her
6:41 and *g* them to His disciples to
8: 6 He took the seven loaves and *g*
8: 6 broke them and *g* them to His
11:28 And who *g* You this authority to
13:34 who left his house and *g*
14:22 and *g* it to them and said,
14:23 when He had given thanks He *g*
15:23 Then they *g* Him wine mingled
Lk 2:38 coming in that instant she *g*
4:20 and *g* it back to the attendant
5:29 Then Levi *g* Him a great feast in
6: 4 and also *g* some to those with
7:21 and to many blind He *g* sight.
7:44 you *g* Me no water for My feet,
7:45 You *g* Me no kiss, but this woman
9: 1 disciples together and *g* them
9:16 and *g* them to the disciples to
9:42 and *g* him back to his father.
10:35 *g* them to the innkeeper, and
14:16 A certain man *g* a great supper
15:16 and no one *g* him anything.
15:29 and yet you never *g* me a young
18:43 *g* praise to God.
20: 2 Or who is he who *g* You this
22:17 and *g* thanks, and said, "Take
22:19 *g* thanks and broke it, and
22:19 and *g* it to them, saying,
23:24 So Pilate *g* sentence that it
24:30 and *g* it to them.
24:42 So they *g* Him a piece of a
Jn 1:12 to them He *g* the right to
3:16 so loved the world that He *g*
4: 5 plot of ground that Jacob *g* to
4:12 who *g* us the well, and drank
6:31 He *g* them bread from heaven
7:22 Moses therefore *g* you
12:49 but the Father who sent Me *g* Me
13:26 He *g* it to Judas Iscariot,
14:31 and as the Father *g* Me
17: 6 You *g* them to Me, and they have
17:12 Those whom You *g* Me I have
17:22 And the glory which You *g* Me I
17:24 that they also whom You *g* Me
18: 9 Of those whom You *g* Me I have
19: 9 But Jesus *g* him no answer.
19:30 He *g* up His spirit.
19:38 and Pilate *g* him permission.
21:13 came and took the bread and *g*
Acts 2: 4 as the Spirit *g* them utterance.
3: 5 So he *g* them his attention,
4:33 with great power the apostles *g*
7: 5 And God *g* him no inheritance in
7: 8 Then He *g* him the covenant of
7:10 and *g* him favor and wisdom in
7:42 Then God turned and *g* them up to
8:10 to whom they all *g* heed, from
9:41 Then he *g* her his hand and
10: 2 who *g* alms generously to the
11:17 If therefore God *g* them the same
11:17 them the same gift as He *g*
12:21 sat on his throne and *g* an
13:20 After that He *g* them judges for
13:21 so God *g* them Saul the son of
13:22 to whom also He *g* testimony and
14:17 *g* us rain from heaven and
15:24 to whom we *g* no such
24: 1 These *g* evidence to the
27: 3 treated Paul kindly and *g* him
27:35 he took bread and *g* thanks to
Rom 1:24 Therefore God also *g* them up to
1:26 For this reason God *g* them up to
1:28 God *g* them over to a debased
1 Cor 3: 5 as the Lord *g* to each one?
3: 6 but God *g* the increase.
2 Cor 8: 5 but they first *g* themselves to
10: 8 which the Lord *g* us for
Gal 1: 4 who *g* Himself for our sins, that
2: 9 they *g* me and Barnabas the
2:20 who loved me and *g* Himself for
3:18 but God *g* it to Abraham by
Eph 1:22 and *g* Him to be head over all
4: 8 And *g* gifts to men."
4:11 And He Himself *g* some to be
5:25 also loved the church and *g*
1 Th 4: 2 you know what commandments we *g*
1 Tim 2: 6 who *g* Himself a ransom for all,
Titus 2:14 who *g* Himself for us, that He
Heb 7: 2 to whom also Abraham *g* a tenth
7: 4 even the patriarch Abraham *g* a
11:22 and *g* instructions concerning
Jas 5:18 and the heaven *g* rain, and the
1 Pe 1:21 raised Him from the dead and *g*
1 Jn 3:23 as He *g* us commandment.
Rev 1: 1 which God *g* Him to show His
2:21 And I *g* her time to repent of
11:13 and the rest were afraid and *g*
12:13 he persecuted the woman who *g*
13: 2 The dragon *g* him his power, his
13: 4 they worshiped the dragon who *g*
15: 7 of the four living creatures *g*
20:13 The sea *g* up the dead who were

GAY (KJV) See FINE

GAZA (21/20)

Gen 10:19 go toward Gerar, as far as *G*;
Deut 2:23 dwelt in villages as far as *G*—
Josh 10:41 from Kadesh Barnea as far as *G*,
11:22 they remained only in *G*,
15:47 *G* with its towns and
Judg 1:18 Also Judah took *G* with its
6: 4 of the earth as far as *G*,
16: 1 Now Samson went to *G* and saw a
16:21 eyes, and brought him down to *G*.
1 Sam 6:17 one for Ashdod, one for *G*,
1 Ki 4:24 River from Tiphsah even to *G*,
2 Ki 18: 8 as far as *G* and its territory,
Jer 25:20 (namely, Ashkelon, *G*,
47: 1 before Pharaoh attacked *G*.
47: 5 Baldness has come upon *G*,
Am 1: 6 three transgressions of *G*,
1: 7 send a fire upon the wall of *G*,
Zeph 2: 4 For *G* shall be forsaken,
Zech 9: 5 *G* also shall be very
9: 5 The king shall perish from *G*,
Acts 8:26 goes down from Jerusalem to *G*.

GAZATHITES (KJV) See GAZITES

GAZE (5/5) GAZED, GAZING

Ex 19:21 lest they break through to *g* at

Job 16: 9 My adversary sharpens His **g** on
Ps 39:13 Remove Your **g** from me, that I
Isa 14:16 Those who see you will **g** at you,
Ezek 28:17 That they might **g** at you.

GAZED (3/3) GAZE

Ob 12 But you should not have **g** on
13 you should not have **g** on their
Acts 7:55 **g** into heaven and saw the glory

GAZELLE (12/12) GAZELLES

Deut 12:15 of the **g** and the deer alike.
12:22 Just as the **g** and the deer are
14: 5 "the deer, the **g**,
15:22 as if it were a **g** or a deer.
2 Sam 2:18 as fleet of foot as a wild **g**.
Prov 6: 5 Deliver yourself like a **g** from
Song 2: 9 My beloved is like a **g** or a
2:17 And be like a **g** Or a young
4: 5 like two fawns, Twins of a **g**,
7: 3 like two fawns, Twins of a **g**.
8:14 And be like a **g** Or a young
Isa 13:14 It shall be as the hunted **g**,

GAZELLES (4/4) GAZELLE

1 Ki 4:23 hundred sheep, besides deer, **g**,
1 Chr 12: 8 and were as swift as **g** on the
Song 2: 7 By the **g** or by the does of the
3: 5 By the **g** or by the does of the

GAZER (KJV) See GEZER

GAZEZ (2/1)

1 Chr 2:46 bore Haran, Moza, and **G**;
2:46 and Gazez; and Haran begot **G**.

GAZING (2/2) GAZE

Song 2: 9 **G** through the lattice.
Acts 1:11 why do you stand **g** up into

GAZINGSTOCK (KJV) See SPECTACLE

GAZITES (2/2)

Josh 13: 3 lords of the Philistines—the **G**,
Judg 16: 2 When the **G** were told,

GAZZAM (2/2)

Ezra 2:48 sons of Nekoda, the sons of **G**,
Neh 7:51 the sons of **G**, the sons of

GE HARASHIM (1/1)

1 Chr 4:14 begot Joab the father of **G**,

GEBA (15/15) GIBEAH, GIBEON

Josh 21:17 **G** with its common-land,
Judg 20:33 position in the plain of **G**.
1 Sam 13: 3 the Philistines that was in **G**,
2 Sam 5:25 back the Philistines from **G** as
1 Ki 15:22 and with them King Asa built **G**
2 Ki 23: 8 from **G** to Beersheba; also he
1 Chr 6:60 **G** with its common-lands,
8: 6 houses of the inhabitants of **G**,
2 Chr 16: 6 and with them he built **G** and
Ezra 2:26 the people of Ramah and **G**,
Neh 7:30 the men of Ramah and **G**,
11:31 the children of Benjamin from **G**
12:29 and from the fields of **G** and
Isa 10:29 have taken up lodging at **G**.
Zech 14:10 be turned into a plain from **G**

GEBAL (2/2)

Ps 83: 7 **G**, Ammon, and Amalek;
Ezek 27: 9 Elders of **G** and its wise men

GEBALITES (2/2)

Josh 13: 5 "the land of the **G**,
1 Ki 5:18 and the **G** quarried them;

GEBER (1/1)

1 Ki 4:19 **G** the son of Uri, in the land of

GEBIM (1/1)

Isa 10:31 The inhabitants of **G** seek

GECKO (1/1)

Lev 11:30 'the **g**, the monitor lizard,

GEDALIAH (32/31)

2 Ki 25:22 Then he made **G** the son of
25:23 the king of Babylon had made **G**
25:23 they came to **G** at
25:24 And **G** took an oath before them
25:25 ten men and struck and killed **G**,
1 Chr 25: 3 the sons of Jeduthun: **G**,
25: 9 for Joseph; the second for **G**,
Ezra 10:18 Maaseiah, Eliezer, Jarib, and **G**.
Jer 38: 1 **G** the son of Pashhur, Jucal the
39:14 and committed him to **G** the son
40: 5 Go back to **G** the son of Ahikam,
40: 6 Then Jeremiah went to **G** the son
40: 7 the king of Babylon had made **G**
40: 8 then they came to **G** at
40: 9 And **G** the son of Ahikam, the son
40:11 and that he had set over them **G**
40:12 to **G** at Mizpah, and gathered
40:13 were in the fields came to **G**
40:14 But **G** the son of Ahikam did
40:15 of Kareah spoke secretly to **G**
40:16 But **G** the son of Ahikam said to
41: 1 came with ten men to **G** the son
41: 2 arose and struck **G** the son of
41: 3 with **G** at Mizpah, and the
41: 4 day after he had killed **G**,
41: 6 Come to **G** the son of Ahikam!"
41: 9 whom he had slain, because of **G**,
41:10 of the guard had committed to **G**
41:16 after he had murdered **G** the
41:18 son of Nethaniah had murdered **G**
43: 6 of the guard had left with **G**
Zeph 1: 1 the son of Cushi, the son of **G**,

GEDEON (KJV) See GIDEON

GEDER (1/1)

Josh 12:13 of Debir, one; the king of **G**,

GEDERAH (2/2)

Josh 15:36 Sharaim, Adithaim, **G**,
1 Chr 4:23 those who dwell at Netaim and **G**;

GEDERATHITE (1/1)

1 Chr 12: 4 Johanan, and Jozabad the **G**;

GEDERITE (1/1)

1 Chr 27:28 Baal-Hanan the **G** was over the

GEDEROTH (2/2)

Josh 15:41 **G**, Beth Dagon, Naamah,
2 Chr 28:18 taken Beth Shemesh, Aijalon, **G**,

GEDEROTHAIM (1/1)

Josh 15:36 Adithaim, Gederah, and **G**:

GEDOR (7/7)

Josh 15:58 Halhul, Beth Zur, **G**,
1 Chr 4: 4 and Penuel was the father of **G**,
4:18 bore Jered the father of **G**,
4:39 they went to the entrance of **G**,
8:31 **G**, Ahio, Zecher,
9:37 **G**, Ahio, Zechariah, and Mikloth.
12: 7 the sons of Jeroham of **G**.

GEHAZI (12/12)

2 Ki 4:12 Then he said to **G** his servant,
4:14 And **G** answered, "Actually,
4:25 that he said to his servant **G**,
4:27 but **G** came near to push her
4:29 Then he said to **G**,
4:31 Now **G** went on ahead of them, and
4:36 And he called **G** and said, "Call
5:20 But **G**, the servant of Elisha
5:21 So **G** pursued Naaman. When
5:25 him, "Where did you go, **G**?
8: 4 Then the king talked with **G**,
8: 5 And **G** said, "My lord, O king,

GELILOTH (1/1)

Josh 18:17 Shemesh, and extended toward **G**,

GEMALLI (1/1)

Num 13:12 of Dan, Ammiel the son of **G**;

GEMARIAH (5/5)

Jer 29: 3 and **G** the son of Hilkiah, whom
36:10 in the chamber of **G** the son of
36:11 When Michaiah the son of **G**,
36:12 **G** the son of Shaphan, Zedekiah
36:25 and **G** implored the king not to

GEMS (1/1)

Isa 54:11 lay your stones with colorful **g**,

GENDER (KJV) See GENERATE, KIND

GENEALOGIES (22/22) GENEALOGY

Num 1:20 their **g** by their families, by
1:22 their **g** by their families, by
1:24 their **g** by their families, by
1:26 their **g** by their families, by
1:28 their **g** by their families, by
1:30 their **g** by their families, by
1:32 their **g** by their families, by
1:34 their **g** by their families, by
1:36 their **g** by their families, by
1:38 their **g** by their families, by
1:40 their **g** by their families, by
1:42 their **g** by their families, by
1 Chr 1:29 These are their **g**:
5:17 All these were registered by **g**
7: 5 men of valor, listed by their **g**,
7: 7 and they were listed by their **g**,
7:40 And they were recorded by **g**
9: 1 So all Israel was recorded by **g**,
2 Chr 12:15 of Iddo the seer concerning **g**?
31:19 and to all who were listed by **g**
1 Tim 1: 4 heed to fables and endless **g**,
Titus 3: 9 But avoid foolish disputes, **g**,

GENEALOGY (28/27) GENEALOGIES

Gen 5: 1 This is the book of the **g** of
6: 9 This is the **g** of Noah. Noah was
10: 1 Now this is the **g** of the sons
11:10 This is the **g** of Shem: Shem
11:27 This is the **g** of Terah: Terah
25:12 Now this is the **g** of Ishmael,
25:19 This is the **g** of Isaac,
36: 1 Now this is the **g** of Esau, who
36: 9 And this is the **g** of Esau the
Ruth 4:18 Now this is the **g** of Perez:
1 Chr 4:33 and they maintained their **g**:
5: 1 so that the **g** is not listed
5: 7 when the **g** of their generations
7: 9 And they were recorded by **g**
9:22 They were recorded by their **g**,
26:31 Hebronites according to his **g**
2 Chr 31:16 up who were written in the **g**,
31:17 who were written in the **g**
31:18 all who were written in the **g**—
Ezra 2:59 their father's house or their **g**,
2:62 those who were registered by **g**,
8: 1 and this is the **g** of those
Neh 7: 5 they might be registered by **g**.
7: 5 I found a register of the **g** of
7:64 those who were registered by **g**,
Mt 1: 1 The book of the **g** of Jesus
Heb 7: 3 without mother, without **g**,
7: 6 but he whose **g** is not derived

GENERAL (5/5)

1 Chr 27:34 And the **g** of the king's army
Jer 48:38 A **g** lamentation On all the
51:27 Appoint a **g** against her;
Ezek 48:15 shall be for **g** use by the city,
Heb 12:23 to the **g** assembly and church of

GENERALS (1/1)

Nah 3:17 And your **g** like great

GENERATE (1/1)

2 Tim 2:23 knowing that they **g** strife.

GENERATION (100/85) GENERATIONS

Gen 7: 1 righteous before Me in this **g**.
15:16 But in the fourth **g** they shall
50:23 children to the third **g**.
Ex 1: 6 his brothers, and all that **g**.
17:16 have war with Amalek from **g**
17:16 Amalek from generation to **g**.
34: 7 to the third and the fourth **g**.
Num 14:18 to the third and fourth **g**.
32:13 until all the **g** that had done
Deut 1:35 one of these men of this evil **g**
2:14 until all the **g** of the men of
23: 2 even to the tenth **g** none of his
23: 3 even to the tenth **g** none of his
23: 8 The children of the third **g** born
29:22 so that the coming **g** of your
32: 5 A perverse and crooked **g**.
32:20 For they are a perverse **g**,
Judg 2:10 When all that **g** had been
2:10 another **g** arose after them who
2 Ki 10:30 of Israel to the fourth **g**.
15:12 of Israel to the fourth **g**.
Esth 9:28 and kept throughout every **g**,
Ps 12: 7 shall preserve them from this **g**
14: 5 For God is with the **g** of the
22:30 of the Lord to the next **g**,
24: 6 the **g** of those who seek Him,
48:13 That you may tell it to the **g**
49:19 He shall go to the **g** of his
71:18 Your strength to this **g**,
73:15 have been untrue to the **g** of
78: 4 Telling to the **g** to come the
78: 6 That the **g** to come might know
78: 8 A stubborn and rebellious **g**,
78: 8 A **g** that did not set its
95:10 I was grieved with that **g**,
102:18 will be written for the **g** to
109:13 And in the **g** following let
112: 2 The **g** of the upright will be
145: 4 One **g** shall praise Your works
Prov 30:11 There is a **g** that curses its
30:12 There is a **g** that is pure
30:13 There is a **g**—
30:14 There is a **g** whose teeth are
Eccl 1: 4 One **g** passes away, and
1: 4 and another **g** comes; But the
Isa 13:20 Nor will it be settled from **g**
13:20 be settled from generation to **g**;
34:10 From **g** to generation it shall
34:10 From generation to **g** it shall
34:17 From **g** to generation they
34:17 From generation to **g** they
51: 8 And My salvation from **g** to
51: 8 salvation from generation to **g**.
53: 8 And who will declare His **g**?

Jer 2:31 'O **g**, see the word of the
7:29 rejected and forsaken the **g** of
50:39 shall it be dwelt in from **g** to
50:39 dwelt in from generation to **g**.
Lam 5:19 Your throne from **g** to
5:19 throne from generation to **g**.
Dan 4: 3 And His dominion is from **g** to
4: 3 is from generation to **g**.
4:34 And His kingdom is from **g** to
4:34 is from generation to **g**.
Joel 1: 3 And their children another **g**.
3:20 And Jerusalem from **g** to
3:20 Jerusalem from generation to **g**.
Mt 11:16 to what shall I liken this **g**?
12:39 An evil and adulterous **g** seeks
12:41 up in the judgment with this **g**
12:42 up in the judgment with this **g**
12:45 it also be with this wicked **g**.
16: 4 A wicked and adulterous **g** seeks
17:17 "O faithless and perverse **g**,
23:36 things will come upon this **g**.
24:34 this **g** will by no means pass
Mk 8:12 Why does this **g** seek a sign?
8:12 sign shall be given to this **g**.
8:38 in this adulterous and sinful **g**,
9:19 him and said, "O faithless **g**,
13:30 this **g** will by no means pass
Lk 1:50 on those who fear Him From **g**
1:50 fear Him From generation to **g**.
7:31 shall I liken the men of this **g**,
9:41 "O faithless and perverse **g**,
11:29 to say, "This is an evil **g**.
11:30 Son of Man will be to this **g**.
11:31 with the men of this **g** and
11:32 up in the judgment with this **g**
11:50 world may be required of this **g**,
11:51 it shall be required of this **g**.
16: 8 are more shrewd in their **g**
17:25 and be rejected by this **g**.
21:32 this **g** will by no means pass
Acts 2:40 "Be saved from this perverse **g**.
8:33 who will declare His **g**?
13:36 after he had served his own **g**
Phil 2:15 of a crooked and perverse **g**,
Heb 3:10 I was angry with that **g**,
1 Pe 2: 9 But you are a chosen **g**,

GENERATIONS (97/94) GENERATION

Gen 6: 9 a just man, perfect in his **g**.
9:12 is with you, for perpetual **g**:
10:32 of Noah, according to their **g**,
17: 7 after you in their **g**,
17: 9 after you throughout their **g**.
17:12 every male child in your **g**,
25:13 names, according to their **g**:
Ex 3:15 this is My memorial to all **g**.
6:16 of Levi according to their **g**:
6:19 of Levi according to their **g**.
12:14 to the LORD throughout your **g**.
12:17 this day throughout your **g** as
12:42 of Israel throughout their **g**.
16:32 with it, to be kept for your **g**,
16:33 LORD, to be kept for your **g**.
20: 5 to the third and fourth **g** of
27:21 a statute forever to their **g**
29:42 offering throughout your **g** at
30: 8 the LORD throughout your **g**.
30:10 upon it throughout your **g**.
30:21 descendants throughout their **g**.
30:31 oil to Me throughout your **g**.
31:13 Me and you throughout your **g**,
31:16 the Sabbath throughout their **g**
40:15 priesthood throughout their **g**.
Lev 3:17 statute throughout your **g** in
6:18 be a statute forever in your **g**
7:36 forever throughout their **g**.
10: 9 forever throughout your **g**,
17: 7 for them throughout their **g**.
21:17 descendants in succeeding **g**,
22: 3 descendants throughout your **g**,
23:14 forever throughout your **g** in
23:21 dwellings throughout your **g**.
23:31 forever throughout your **g** in
23:41 be a statute forever in your **g**.
23:43 that your **g** may know that I made
24: 3 be a statute forever in your **g**.
25:30 who bought it, throughout his **g**.
Num 10: 8 forever throughout your **g**.
15:14 is among you throughout your **g**,
15:15 forever throughout your **g**;
15:21 offering throughout your **g**.
15:23 and onward throughout your **g**—
15:38 garments throughout their **g**,
18:23 forever, throughout your **g**,
35:29 to you throughout your **g** in
Deut 5: 9 to the third and fourth **g** of
7: 9 and mercy for a thousand **g**
32: 7 Consider the years of many **g**.
Josh 22:27 between you and us and our **g**
22:28 say this to us or to our **g** in
Judg 3: 2 (this was only so that the **g**
1 Chr 5: 7 when the genealogy of their **g**
7: 2 mighty men of valor in their **g**;
7: 4 And with them, by their **g**,
7: 9 genealogy according to their **g**,
8:28 the fathers' houses by their **g**,
9: 9 brethren, according to their **g**—
9:34 were heads throughout their **g**.
16:15 He commanded, for a thousand **g**,
Job 42:16 and grandchildren for four **g**.
Ps 33:11 plans of His heart to all **g**.
45:17 name to be remembered in all **g**;
49:11 Their dwelling places to all **g**;
61: 6 His years as many **g**.
72: 5 moon endure, Throughout all **g**.
79:13 show forth Your praise to all **g**.
85: 5 You prolong Your anger to all **g**?
89: 1 Your faithfulness to all **g**.
89: 4 build up your throne to all **g**.
90: 1 our dwelling place in all **g**.
100: 5 His truth endures to all **g**.
102:12 of Your name to all **g**.
102:24 years are throughout all **g**.
105: 8 He commanded, for a thousand **g**,
106:31 him for righteousness To all **g**
119:90 faithfulness endures to all **g**;
135:13 fame, O LORD, throughout all **g**.
145:13 endures throughout all **g**.
146:10 God, O Zion, to all **g**.
Prov 27:24 does a crown endure to all **g**.
Isa 41: 4 Calling the **g** from the
51: 9 In the **g** of old. Are You not
58:12 up the foundations of many **g**;
60:15 excellence, A joy of many **g**.
61: 4 The desolations of many **g**.
Joel 2: 2 Even for many successive **g**.
Mt 1:17 So all the **g** from Abraham to
1:17 to David are fourteen **g**,
1:17 in Babylon are fourteen **g**,
1:17 the Christ are fourteen **g**.
Lk 1:48 henceforth all **g** will call me
Acts 14:16 who in bygone **g** allowed all
15:21 Moses has had throughout many **g**
Eph 3:21 church by Christ Jesus to all **g**,
Col 1:26 hidden from ages and from **g**,

GENEROSITY (5/5) GENEROUS

1 Ki 10:13 her according to the royal **g**.
Esth 1: 7 according to the **g** of the king.
2:18 gave gifts according to the **g**
Isa 32: 8 And by **g** he shall stand.
2 Cor 9: 5 be ready as a matter of **g**

GENEROUS (7/6) GENEROSITY, GENEROUSLY

Ps 51:12 And uphold me by Your **g**
Prov 11:25 The **g** soul will be made rich,
22: 9 He who has a **g** eye will be
Isa 32: 5 will no longer be called **g**,
32: 8 But a **g** man devises generous
32: 8 But a generous man devises **g**
2 Cor 9: 5 and prepare your **g** gift

GENEROUSLY (1/1) GENEROUS

Acts 10: 2 who gave alms **g** to the people,

GENITALS (1/1)

Deut 25:11 hand and seizes him by the **g**,

GENNESARET (3/3) CHINNERETH

Mt 14:34 they came to the land of **G**.
Mk 6:53 they came to the land of **G** and
Lk 5: 1 that He stood by the Lake of **G**,

GENTILE (2/2) GENTILES

Hag 2:22 destroy the strength of the **G**
Acts 17:17 with the Jews and with the **G**

GENTILES (149/141) GENTILE

Gen 10: 5 the coastland peoples of the **G**
Deut 32:43 "Rejoice, O **G**,
2 Sam 22:50 to You, O LORD, among the **G**,
1 Chr 16:35 and deliver us from the **G**,
Ps 18:49 to You, O LORD, among the **G**,
105:44 gave them the lands of the **G**,
106:35 But they mingled with the **G**
106:41 them into the hand of the **G**,
106:47 And gather us from among the **G**,
115: 2 Why should the **G** say, "So
117: 1 all you **G**! Laud Him, all you
Isa 9: 1 Jordan, In Galilee of the **G**.
11:10 For the **G** shall seek Him,
42: 1 bring forth justice to the **G**.
42: 6 people, As a light to the **G**,
49: 6 give You as a light to the **G**,
60: 3 The **G** shall come to your light,
60: 5 The wealth of the **G** shall come
60:11 to you the wealth of the **G**,
60:16 shall drink the milk of the **G**,
61: 6 shall eat the riches of the **G**,
61: 9 shall be known among the **G**,
62: 2 The **G** shall see your
66:12 And the glory of the **G** like a
66:19 declare My glory among the **G**.
Jer 9:16 scatter them also among the **G**,
10: 2 not learn the way of the **G**;
10: 2 For the **G** are dismayed at
10:25 Pour out Your fury on the **G**,
16:19 The **G** shall come to You
18:13 LORD: "Ask now among the **G**,
Ezek 4:13 their defiled bread among the **G**,
7:24 I will bring the worst of the **G**,
11:12 to the customs of the **G** which
11:16 cast them far off among the **G**,
12:16 their abominations among the **G**
20: 9 not be profaned before the **G**
20:14 not be profaned before the **G**,
20:22 profaned in the sight of the **G**,
20:23 would scatter them among the **G**
20:32 you say, 'We will be like the **G**,
20:41 be hallowed in you before the **G**.
23:30 gone as a harlot after the **G**,
28:25 in them in the sight of the **G**,
30: 3 of clouds, the time of the **G**.
34:29 nor bear the shame of the **G**
39:23 The **G** shall know that the house
Hos 8: 8 Now they are among the **G** Like
Am 9:12 And all the **G** who are called
Mic 5: 8 of Jacob Shall be among the **G**,
Mal 1:11 shall be great among the **G**;
Mt 4:15 Jordan, Galilee of the **G**:
6:32 after all these things the **G**
10: 5 not go into the way of the **G**,
10:18 testimony to them and to the **G**.
12:18 declare justice to the **G**.
12:21 And in His name **G** will
20:19 and deliver Him to the **G** to mock
20:25 know that the rulers of the **G**
Mk 10:33 death and deliver Him to the **G**;
10:42 considered rulers over the **G**
Lk 2:32 to bring revelation to the **G**,
18:32 He will be delivered to the **G**
21:24 will be trampled by **G** until
21:24 until the times of the **G** are
22:25 The kings of the **G** exercise
Acts 4:27 with the **G** and the people of
7:45 the land possessed by the **G**,
9:15 Mine to bear My name before **G**,
10:45 had been poured out on the **G**
11: 1 were in Judea heard that the **G**
11:18 God has also granted to the **G**
13:42 the **G** begged that these words
13:46 life, behold, we turn to the **G**.
13:47 you as a light to the **G**,
13:48 Now when the **G** heard this, they
14: 2 Jews stirred up the **G** and
14: 5 attempt was made by both the **G**
14:27 the door of faith to the **G**.
15: 3 the conversion of the **G**;
15: 7 that by my mouth the **G** should
15:12 worked through them among the **G**.
15:14 God at the first visited the **G**
15:17 Even all the **G** who are
15:19 trouble those from among the **G**
15:23 the brethren who are of the **G**
18: 6 From now on I will go to the **G**.
21:11 him into the hands of the **G**.
21:19 which God had done among the **G**
21:21 the Jews who are among the **G**
21:25 But concerning the **G** who
22:21 send you far from here to the **G**.
26:17 people, as well as from the **G**,
26:20 of Judea, and then to the **G**,
26:23 the Jewish people and to the **G**.
28:28 of God has been sent to the **G**,
Rom 1:13 also, just as among the other **G**.
2:14 for when **G**, who do not have
2:24 is blasphemed among the **G**
3:29 He not also the God of the **G**?
3:29 Yes, of the **G** also,
9:24 Jews only, but also of the **G**?
9:30 What shall we say then? That **G**,
11:11 salvation has come to the **G**.
11:12 their failure riches for the **G**,
11:13 For I speak to you **G**;
11:13 as I am an apostle to the **G**,
11:25 until the fullness of the **G**
15: 9 and that the **G** might glorify God
15: 9 to You among the **G**,
15:10 he says: "Rejoice, O **G**,
15:11 all you **G**! Laud Him, all
15:12 rise to reign over the **G**,
15:12 In Him the **G** shall
15:16 of Jesus Christ to the **G**,
15:16 that the offering of the **G**
15:18 to make the **G** obedient—
15:27 For if the **G** have been
16: 4 also all the churches of the **G**.
1 Cor 5: 1 is not even named among the **G**—
10:20 that the things which the **G**
12: 2 You know that you were **G**,
2 Cor 11:26 countrymen, in perils of the **G**,
Gal 1:16 I might preach Him among the **G**,
2: 2 which I preach among the **G**,
2: 8 effectively in me toward the **G**)
2: 9 that we should go to the **G**
2:12 James, he would eat with the **G**;
2:14 live in the manner of **G** and not
2:14 why do you compel **G** to live as
2:15 and not sinners of the **G**,
3: 8 that God would justify the **G**
3:14 Abraham might come upon the **G**
Eph 2:11 once **G** in the flesh—who are
3: 1 of Christ Jesus for you **G**—
3: 6 that the **G** should be fellow
3: 8 I should preach among the **G**
4:17 walk as the rest of the **G** walk,
Col 1:27 of this mystery among the **G**:
1 Th 2:16 us to speak to the **G** that they
4: 5 like the **G** who do not know God;
1 Tim 2: 7 a teacher of the **G** in faith and
3:16 angels, Preached among the **G**,
2 Tim 1:11 apostle, and a teacher of the **G**.
4:17 and that all the **G** might hear.
1 Pe 2:12 conduct honorable among the **G**,
4: 3 in doing the will of the **G**—
3 Jn 7 sake, taking nothing from the **G**.
Rev 11: 2 for it has been given to the **G**.

GENTLE (11/11) GENTLENESS, GENTLY

Job 37: 6 Likewise to the *g* rain and the
Prov 25:15 And a *g* tongue breaks a bone.
Hos 11: 4 I drew them with *g* cords,
Mt 11:29 for I am *g* and lowly in heart,
1 Th 2: 7 But we were *g* among you, just as
1 Tim 3: 3 not greedy for money, but *g*,
2 Tim 2:24 Lord must not quarrel but be *g*
Titus 3: 2 of no one, to be peaceable, *g*,
Jas 3:17 first pure, then peaceable, *g*,
1 Pe 2:18 not only to the good and *g*,
3: 4 incorruptible beauty of a *g*

GENTLENESS (9/9) GENTLE

2 Sam 22:36 Your *g* has made me great.
Ps 18:35 Your *g* has made me great.
1 Cor 4:21 or in love and a spirit of *g*?
2 Cor 10: 1 with you by the meekness and *g*
Gal 5:23 *g*, self-control.
6: 1 such a one in a spirit of *g*,
Eph 4: 2 with all lowliness and *g*,
Phil 4: 5 Let your *g* be known to all men.
1 Tim 6:11 faith, love, patience, *g*.

GENTLY (4/4) GENTLE

2 Sam 18: 5 Deal *g* for my sake with the
Job 15:11 And the word spoken *g* with
Song 7: 9 Moving *g* the lips of sleepers.
Isa 40:11 And *g* lead those who are with

GENUBATH (2/1)

1 Ki 11:20 sister of Tahpenes bore him *G*
11:20 And *G* was in Pharaoh's

GENUINE (1/1) GENUINENESS

2 Tim 1: 5 I call to remembrance the *g*

GENUINENESS (1/1) GENUINE

1 Pe 1: 7 that the *g* of your faith, being

GERA (9/9)

Gen 46:21 were Belah, Becher, Ashbel, *G*,
Judg 3:15 for them: Ehud the son of *G*,
2 Sam 16: 5 name was Shimei the son of *G*,
19:16 And Shimei the son of *G*,
19:18 Now Shimei the son of *G* fell
1 Ki 2: 8 with you Shimei the son of *G*,
1 Chr 8: 3 The sons of Bela were Addar, *G*,
8: 5 *G*, Shephuphan, and Huram.
8: 7 and *G* who forced them to move.

GERAHS (5/5)

Ex 30:13 (a shekel is twenty *g*).
Lev 27:25 twenty *g* to the shekel.
Num 3:47 the shekel of twenty *g*.
18:16 sanctuary, which is twenty *g*.
Ezek 45:12 shekel shall be twenty *g*;

GERAR (10/10)

Gen 10:19 from Sidon as you go toward *G*,
20: 1 and Shur, and stayed in *G*.
20: 2 And Abimelech king of *G* sent
26: 1 king of the Philistines, in *G*.
26: 6 So Isaac dwelt in *G*.
26:17 his tent in the Valley of *G*,
26:20 But the herdsmen of *G* quarreled
26:26 Abimelech came to him from *G*
2 Chr 14:13 with him pursued them to *G*.
14:14 all the cities around *G*,

GERGESENES (1/1)

Mt 8:28 side, to the country of the *G*,

GERIZIM (4/4)

Deut 11:29 put the blessing on Mount *G*
27:12 These shall stand on Mount *G* to
Josh 8:33 them were in front of Mount *G*
Judg 9: 7 and stood on top of Mount *G*,

GERSHOM (6/6) GERSHON

Ex 2:22 a son, and he called his name *G*;
18: 3 of whom the name of one was *G*
Judg 18:30 and Jonathan the son of *G*,
1 Chr 15: 7 of the sons of *G*,
26:24 Shebuel the son of *G*,
Ezra 8: 2 of the sons of Phinehas, *G*;

GERSHON (26/26) GERSHOM

Gen 46:11 The sons of Levi were *G*,
Ex 6:16 to their generations: *G*,
6:17 The sons of *G* were Libni and
Num 3:17 sons of Levi by their names: *G*,
3:18 the names of the sons of *G* by
3:21 From *G* came the family of the
3:25 duties of the children of *G* in
4:22 take a census of the sons of *G*,
4:28 the families of the sons of *G*
4:38 were numbered of the sons of *G*,
4:41 the families of the sons of *G*,
7: 7 oxen he gave to the sons of *G*,
10:17 and the sons of *G* and the sons
26:57 to their families: of *G*,
Josh 21: 6 And the children of *G* had
21:27 Also to the children of *G*,
1 Chr 6: 1 The sons of Levi were *G*,
6:16 The sons of Levi were *G*,
6:17 are the names of the sons of *G*:
6:20 Of *G* were Libni his son, Jahath
6:43 the son of Jahath, the son of *G*,
6:62 And to the sons of *G*,
6:71 of Manasseh the sons of *G*
23: 6 among the sons of Levi: *G*,
23:15 The sons of Moses were *G* and
23:16 Of the sons of *G*,

GERSHONITE (2/2)

1 Chr 26:21 houses, of Laadan the *G*:
29: 8 into the hand of Jehiel the *G*.

GERSHONITES (10/10)

Num 3:21 were the families of the *G*.
3:23 The families of the *G* were to
3:24 of the fathers' house of the *G*
4:24 of the families of the *G*,
4:27 service of the sons of the *G*,
26:57 of Gershon, the family of the *G*;
Josh 21:33 All the cities of the *G*
1 Chr 23: 7 Of the *G*: Laadan and Shimei.
26:21 the descendants of the *G* of
2 Chr 29:12 the son of Jehallelel; of the *G*,

GESHAN (1/1)

1 Chr 2:47 Jahdai were Regem, Jotham, *G*,

GESHEM (4/4)

Neh 2:19 and *G* the Arab heard of it,
6: 1 *G* the Arab, and the rest of our
6: 2 that Sanballat and *G* sent to me,
6: 6 and *G* says, that you and the

GESHUR (8/8)

2 Sam 3: 3 daughter of Talmai, king of *G*;
13:37 the son of Ammihud, king of *G*.
13:38 So Absalom fled and went to *G*,
14:23 So Joab arose and went to *G*,
14:32 say, "Why have I come from *G*?
15: 8 took a vow while I dwelt at *G*
1 Chr 2:23 (*G* and Syria took from them the
3: 2 daughter of Talmai, king of *G*;

GESHURITES (7/6)

Deut 3:14 as far as the border of the *G*
Josh 12: 5 as far as the border of the *G*
13: 2 and all that of the *G*,
13:11 and the border of the *G* and
13:13 Israel did not drive out the *G*
13:13 but the *G* and the Maachathites
1 Sam 27: 8 men went up and raided the *G*,

GESTURES (1/1)

Isa 33:15 Who *g* with his hands, refusing

GET (103/98) GETS, GETTING, GOT

Gen 12: 1 '*G* out of your country,
19:14 '*G* up, get out of this place;
19:14 *g* out of this place; for the
27:13 *g* them for me."
31:13 *g* out of this land, and return
34: 4 *G* me this young woman as a
40:14 and *g* me out of this house.
44: 4 *G* up, follow the men; and when
Ex 2: 5 she sent her maid to *g* it.
5: 4 *G* back to your labor."
5:11 *g* yourselves straw where you
10:28 *G* away from me! Take heed to
11: 8 *G* out, and all the people who
19:24 Away! *G* down and then come up,
32: 7 *g* down! For your people whom
Num 11:13 Where am I to *g* meat to give to
16:24 *G* away from the tents of Korah,
16:45 *G* away from among this
17: 2 and *g* from them a rod from each
Deut 8:18 is He who gives you power to *g*
24:10 not go into his house to *g* his
24:19 you shall not go back to *g* it;
Josh 2:16 *G* to the mountain, lest the
7:10 *G* up! Why do you lie thus on
7:13 *G* up, sanctify the people, and
Judg 9:32 *g* up by night, you and the
11: 5 the elders of Gilead went to *g*
14: 2 *g* her for me as a wife."
14: 3 that you must go and *g* a wife
14: 3 *G* her for me, for she pleases me
14: 8 when he returned to *g* her, he
19: 9 so that you may *g* home."
19:28 '*G* up and let us be going."
1 Sam 9:26 *G* up, that I may send you on
15: 6 *g* down from among the
20:21 *g* them and come'—then, as the
20:29 please let me *g* away and see my
23:26 So David made haste to *g* away
24:19 will he let him *g* away safely?
26:22 the young men come over and *g*
2 Sam 4: 6 as though to *g* wheat, and
1 Ki 1: 1 but he could not *g* warm.
17: 3 *G* away from here and turn
17:11 And as she was going to *g* it,
20:12 *G* ready." And they got ready to
2 Ki 4:29 *G* yourself ready, and take my
6:13 that I may send and *g* him."
7:12 and *g* into the city.'"
9: 1 *G* yourself ready, take this
9:17 *G* a horseman and send him to
2 Chr 26:18 *G* out of the sanctuary, for you
26:20 Indeed he also hurried to *g*
Neh 5: 2 therefore let us *g* grain, that
Job 20:18 of business He will *g* no
Ps 88: 8 and I cannot *g* out;
119:104 Through Your precepts I *g*
Prov 4: 5 *G* wisdom! Get understanding!
4: 5 Get wisdom! *G* understanding!
4: 7 Therefore *g* wisdom. And in
4: 7 *g* understanding.
6:33 Wounds and dishonor he will *g*,
16:16 How much better to *g* wisdom
16:16 get wisdom than gold! And to *g*
Song 7:12 Let us *g* up early to the
Isa 30:11 *G* out of the way, Turn aside
30:22 You will say to them, "*G* away!"
40: 9 *G* up into the high mountain;
Jer 13: 1 Go and *g* yourself a linen sash,
19: 1 Go and *g* a potter's earthen
48: 9 That she may flee and *g* away;
49:30 *g* far away! Dwell in the
51:50 *G* away! Do not stand still!
Lam 3: 7 me in so that I cannot *g* out;
5: 9 We *g* our bread at the risk
Ezek 3:11 *g* to the captives, to the
11:15 '*G* far away from the LORD;
18:31 and *g* yourselves a new heart
22:27 and to *g* dishonest gain.
Dan 4:14 Let the beasts *g* out from
Am 9: 1 who flees from them shall not *g*
Mt 5:26 you will by no means *g* out of
13:54 Where did this Man *g* this
13:56 Where then did this Man *g* all
14:22 Jesus made His disciples *g*
15:33 Where could we *g* enough bread in
16:23 *G* behind Me, Satan! You are an
24:18 in the field not go back to *g*
Mk 6: 2 Where did this Man *g* these
6:45 He made His disciples *g* into
8:33 *G* behind Me, Satan! For you are
13:16 in the field not go back to *g*
Lk 4: 8 *G* behind Me, Satan! For it is
9:12 and lodge and *g* provisions;
13:31 '*G* out and depart from here,
18: 3 *G* justice for me from my
Jn 4:11 Where then do You *g* that living
11:12 if he sleeps he will *g* well."
Acts 7: 3 *G* out of your country and
16:37 Let them come themselves and *g*
22:18 Make haste and *g* out of
27:43 jump overboard first and *g* to
1 Th 5: 7 and those who *g* drunk are drunk
2 Tim 4:11 *G* Mark and bring him with you,

GETHER (2/2)

Gen 10:23 sons of Aram were Uz, Hul, *G*,
1 Chr 1:17 Arphaxad, Lud, Aram, Uz, Hul, *G*,

GETHSEMANE (2/2)

Mt 26:36 with them to a place called *G*,
Mk 14:32 to a place which was named *G*;

GETS (6/6) GET

Judg 7: 5 likewise everyone who *g* down on
Prov 9: 7 He who corrects a scoffer *g*
15:32 But he who heeds rebuke *g*
19: 8 He who *g* wisdom loves his own
Jer 17:11 So is he who *g* riches, but
48:44 And he who *g* out of the pit

GETTING (4/4) GET

1 Ki 20:16 kings helping him were *g* drunk
Prov 4: 7 get wisdom. And in all your *g*,
21: 6 *G* treasures by a lying tongue
Mk 8:13 and *g* into the boat again,

GEUEL (1/1)

Num 13:15 *G* the son of Machi.

GEZER (15/14)

Josh 10:33 Then Horam king of *G* came up to
12:12 of Eglon, one; the king of *G*,
16: 3 of Lower Beth Horon to *G*;
16:10 the Canaanites who dwelt in *G*;
21:21 *G* with its common-land,
Judg 1:29 the Canaanites who dwelt in *G*;
1:29 so the Canaanites dwelt in *G*
2 Sam 5:25 from Geba as far as *G*.
1 Ki 9:15 Hazor, Megiddo, and *G*.
9:16 Egypt had gone up and taken *G*
9:17 And Solomon built *G*,
1 Chr 6:67 also *G* with its common-lands,
7:28 to the west *G* and its towns,
14:16 from Gibeon as far as *G*.
20: 4 that war broke out at *G* with

GEZRITES (KJV) See GESHURITES

GHOST (2/2)
Mt 14:26 It is a *g*!" And they cried out
Mk 6:49 sea, they supposed it was a *g*,

GIAH (1/1)
2 Sam 2:24 which is before *G* by the road

GIANT (7/7) GIANTS
2 Sam 21:16 was one of the sons of the *g*,
21:18 was one of the sons of the *g*.
21:20 and he also was born to the *g*.
21:22 These four were born to the *g* in
1 Chr 20: 4 was one of the sons of the *g*.
20: 6 and he also was born to the *g*.
20: 8 These were born to the *g* in

GIANTS (11/9) GIANT
Gen 6: 4 There were *g* on the earth in
Num 13:33 There we saw the *g* (the
13:33 of Anak came from the *g*);
Deut 2:11 They were also regarded as *g*,
2:20 also regarded as a land of *g*;
2:20 *g* formerly dwelt there. But the
3:11 of the remnant of the *g*.
3:13 was called the land of the *g*.
Josh 12: 4 was of the remnant of the *g*,
13:12 of the remnant of the *g*;
17:15 of the Perizzites and the *g*,

GIBBAR (1/1)
Ezra 2:20 the people of *G*,

GIBBETHON (6/5)
Josh 19:44 Eltekeh, *G*, Baalath,
21:23 *G* with its common-land,
1 Ki 15:27 And Baasha killed him at *G*,
15:27 and all Israel laid siege to *G*.
16:15 people were encamped against *G*,
16:17 Israel with him went up from *G*,

GIBEA (1/1)
1 Chr 2:49 Machbenah and the father of *G*.

GIBEAH (45/44) GEBA, GIBEON
Josh 15:57 Kain, *G*, and Timnah:
Judg 19:12 of Israel; we will go on to *G*.
19:13 and spend the night in *G* or in
19:14 sun went down on them near *G*,
19:15 there to go in to lodge in *G*.
19:16 of Ephraim; he was staying in *G*,
20: 4 concubine and I went into *G*,
20: 5 And the men of *G* rose against
20: 9 the thing which we will do to *G*:
20:10 that when they come to *G* in
20:13 the perverted men who are in *G*,
20:14 together from their cities to *G*,
20:15 besides the inhabitants of *G*,
20:19 morning and encamped against *G*.
20:20 to fight against them at *G*.
20:21 of Benjamin came out of *G*,
20:25 went out against them from *G*
20:29 set men in ambush all around *G*.
20:30 in battle array against *G* as
20:31 to Bethel and the other to *G*)
20:34 from all Israel came against *G*,
20:36 whom they had set against *G*.
20:37 in ambush quickly rushed upon *G*;
20:43 down as far as the front of *G*
1 Sam 10:26 And Saul also went home to *G*;
11: 4 So the messengers came to *G* of
13: 2 were with Jonathan in *G* of
13:15 and went up from Gilgal to *G*
13:16 with them remained in *G* of
14: 2 sitting in the outskirts of *G*
14: 5 the other southward opposite *G*.
14:16 Now the watchmen of Saul in *G* of
15:34 Saul went up to his house at *G*
22: 6 now Saul was staying in *G* under
23:19 Ziphites came up to Saul at *G*,
26: 1 the Ziphites came to Saul at *G*,
2 Sam 21: 6 them before the LORD in *G* of
23:29 Ittai the son of Ribai from *G*
1 Chr 11:31 Ithai the son of Ribai of *G*,
2 Chr 13: 2 the daughter of Uriel of *G*.
Isa 10:29 *G* of Saul has fled.
Hos 5: 8 "Blow the ram's horn in *G*,
9: 9 corrupted, As in the days of *G*.
10: 9 have sinned from the days of *G*;
10: 9 The battle in *G* against the

GIBEATH (1/1)
Josh 18:28 Jebus (which is Jerusalem), *G*,

GIBEATHITE (1/1)
1 Chr 12: 3 the sons of Shemaah the *G*;

GIBEON (37/35) GEBA, GIBEAH, GIBEONITES
Josh 9: 3 But when the inhabitants of *G*
9:17 Now their cities were *G*,
10: 1 and how the inhabitants of *G* had
10: 2 because *G* was a great city,
10: 4 help me, that we may attack *G*,
10: 5 and camped before *G* and made
10: 6 And the men of *G* sent to Joshua
10:10 with a great slaughter at *G*,
10:12 "Sun, stand still over *G*;
10:41 of Goshen, even as far as *G*.
11:19 Hivites, the inhabitants of *G*.
18:25 *G*, Ramah, Beeroth,
21:17 *G* with its common-land, Geba
2 Sam 2:12 went out from Mahanaim to *G*.
2:13 and met them by the pool of *G*.
2:16 of Sharp Swords, which is in *G*.
2:24 the road to the Wilderness of *G*.
3:30 their brother Asahel at *G* in
20: 8 the large stone which is in *G*,
1 Ki 3: 4 Now the king went to *G* to
3: 5 At *G* the LORD appeared to
9: 2 as He had appeared to him at *G*.
1 Chr 8:29 Now the father of *G*,
8:29 name was Maacah, dwelt at *G*.
9:35 Jeiel the father of *G*,
9:35 name was Maacah, dwelt at *G*.
14:16 army of the Philistines from *G*
16:39 the high place that was at *G*,
21:29 time at the high place in *G*.
2 Chr 1: 3 the high place that was at *G*;
1:13 the high place that was at *G*,
Neh 3: 7 the men of *G* and Mizpah,
7:25 the sons of *G*, ninety-five;
Isa 28:21 be angry as in the Valley of *G*—
Jer 28: 1 the prophet, who was from *G*,
41:12 by the great pool that is in *G*.
41:16 whom he had brought back from *G*.

GIBEONITE (2/2)
1 Chr 12: 4 Ishmaiah the *G*, a mighty man
Neh 3: 7 And next to them Melatiah the *G*,

GIBEONITES (6/5)
2 Sam 21: 1 house, because he killed the *G*.
21: 2 So the king called the *G* and
21: 2 Now the *G* were not of the
21: 3 Therefore David said to the *G*,
21: 4 And the *G* said to him, "We will
21: 9 them into the hands of the *G*,

GIBLITES (KJV) See GEBALITES

GIDDALTI (2/2)
1 Chr 25: 4 Hananiah, Hanani, Eliathah, *G*,
25:29 the twenty-second for *G*,

GIDDEL (4/4)
Ezra 2:47 the sons of *G*, the sons of
2:56 sons of Darkon, the sons of *G*,
Neh 7:49 sons of Hanan, the sons of *G*,
7:58 sons of Darkon, the sons of *G*,

GIDEON (40/38) JERUBBAAL
Judg 6:11 while his son *G* threshed wheat
6:13 *G* said to Him, "O my lord, if
6:19 So *G* went in and prepared a
6:22 Now *G* perceived that He was the
6:22 So *G* said, "Alas, O Lord GOD!
6:24 So *G* built an altar there to the
6:27 So *G* took ten men from among his
6:29 *G* the son of Joash has done this
6:34 Spirit of the LORD came upon *G*;
6:36 So *G* said to God, "If You will
6:39 Then *G* said to God, "Do not be
7: 1 *G*) and all the people who were
7: 2 And the LORD said to *G*,
7: 4 But the LORD said to *G*,
7: 5 water. And the LORD said to *G*,
7: 7 Then the LORD said to *G*,
7:13 And when *G* had come, there was a
7:14 else but the sword of *G* the
7:15 when *G* heard the telling of the
7:18 sword of the LORD and of *G*!
7:19 So *G* and the hundred men who
7:20 sword of the LORD and of *G*!"
7:24 Then *G* sent messengers
7:25 heads of Oreb and Zeeb to *G* on
8: 4 When *G* came to the Jordan, he
8: 7 So *G* said, "For this cause,
8:11 Then *G* went up by the road of
8:13 Then *G* the son of Joash
8:21 So *G* arose and killed Zebah
8:22 the men of Israel said to *G*,
8:23 But *G* said to them, "I will not
8:24 Then *G* said to them, "I would
8:27 Then *G* made it into an ephod and
8:27 It became a snare to *G* and to
8:28 forty years in the days of *G*.
8:30 *G* had seventy sons who were his
8:32 Now *G* the son of Joash died at a
8:33 as soon as *G* was dead, that the
8:35 to the house of Jerubbaal (*G*)
Heb 11:32 would fail me to tell of *G* and

GIDEONI (5/5)
Num 1:11 Benjamin, Abidan the son of *G*;
2:22 shall be Abidan the son of *G*.
7:60 ninth day Abidan the son of *G*,
7:65 offering of Abidan the son of *G*.
10:24 was Abidan the son of *G*.

GIDOM (1/1)
Judg 20:45 them relentlessly up to *G*,

GIER (KJV) See (CARRION) VULTURE

GIFT (59/54) GIFTED, GIFTS, GIVE
Gen 34:12 me ever so much dowry and *g*,
Num 8:19 I have given the Levites as a *g*
18: 6 they are a *g* to you, given by
18: 7 priesthood to you as a *g* for
18:11 the heave offering of their *g*,
2 Sam 11: 8 and a *g* of food from the king
19:42 Or has he given us any *g*?
2 Ki 5:15 please take a *g* from your
Ps 45:12 of Tyre will come with a *g*;
Prov 18:16 A man's *g* makes room for him,
21:14 A *g* in secret pacifies anger,
Eccl 3:13 it is the *g* of God.
5:19 this is the *g* of God.
Jer 40: 5 guard gave him rations and a *g*
Ezek 46:16 If the prince gives a *g* of
46:17 But if he gives a *g* of some of
Zech 6:10 Receive the *g* from the
Mt 5:23 Therefore if you bring your *g* to
5:24 leave your *g* there before the
5:24 and then come and offer your *g*.
8: 4 and offer the *g* that Moses
15: 5 have received from me is a *g*
23:18 but whoever swears by the *g*
23:19 the *g* or the altar that
23:19 the altar that sanctifies the *g*?
Mk 7:11 (that is, a *g* to God),
Jn 4:10 If you knew the *g* of God, and
Acts 2:38 and you shall receive the *g* of
8:20 because you thought that the *g*
10:45 because the *g* of the Holy
11:17 God gave them the same *g* as
Rom 1:11 impart to you some spiritual *g*,
5:15 But the free *g* is not like the
5:15 the grace of God and the *g* by
5:16 And the *g* is not like that
5:16 but the free *g* which came
5:17 of grace and of the *g* of
5:18 righteous act the free *g*
6:23 but the *g* of God is eternal
1 Cor 1: 7 so that you come short in no *g*,
7: 7 But each one has his own *g* from
13: 2 And though I have the *g* of
16: 3 I will send to bear your *g* to
2 Cor 1:11 persons on our behalf for the *g*
8: 4 that we would receive the *g*
8:19 to travel with us with this *g*,
8:20 blame us in this lavish *g*
9: 5 and prepare your generous *g*
9:15 to God for His indescribable *g*!
Eph 2: 8 it is the *g* of God,
3: 7 a minister according to the *g*
4: 7 to the measure of Christ's *g*.
Phil 4:17 Not that I seek the *g*,
1 Tim 4:14 Do not neglect the *g* that is in
2 Tim 1: 6 I remind you to stir up the *g*
Heb 6: 4 and have tasted the heavenly *g*,
Jas 1:17 Every good *g* and every perfect
1:17 good gift and every perfect *g*
1 Pe 4:10 As each one has received a *g*,

GIFTED (8/8) GIFT
Ex 28: 3 shall speak to all who are *g*
31: 6 in the hearts of all who are *g*
35:10 All who are *g* artisans among
35:25 All the women who were *g*
36: 1 and every *g* artisan in whom the
36: 2 and every *g* artisan in whose
36: 8 Then all the *g* artisans among
Dan 1: 4 *g* in all wisdom, possessing

GIFTS (44/44) GIFT
Gen 25: 6 But Abraham gave *g* to the sons
Ex 28:38 hallow in all their holy *g*;
Lev 23:38 of the LORD, besides your *g*,
Num 18: 8 all the holy *g* of the children
18:29 Of all your *g* you shall offer up
18:32 shall not profane the holy *g*
2 Ki 12: 4 the money of the dedicated *g*
2 Chr 21: 3 Their father gave them great *g*
32:23 And many brought *g* to the LORD
Esth 2:18 in the provinces and gave *g*
9:22 presents to one another and *g*
Ps 68:18 You have received *g* among men,
72:10 of Sheba and Seba Will offer *g*.
Prov 6:35 appeased though you give many *g*.
19: 6 is a friend to one who gives *g*.
Ezek 20:26 because of their ritual *g*,
20:31 For when you offer your *g* and
20:39 holy name no more with your *g*
Dan 2: 6 you shall receive from me *g*,
2:48 and gave him many great *g*;
5:17 Let your *g* be for yourself, and
Mic 7: 3 hands—The prince asks for *g*,
Mt 2:11 they presented *g* to Him: gold,
7:11 know how to give good *g* to your
Lk 11:13 know how to give good *g* to your
21: 1 saw the rich putting their *g*
Rom 11:29 For the *g* and the calling of God
12: 6 Having then *g* differing
1 Cor 12: 1 Now concerning spiritual *g*,
12: 4 There are diversities of *g*,
12: 9 to another *g* of healings by the

G

12:28 then **g** of healings, helps,
12:30 Do all have **g** of healings?
12:31 But earnestly desire the best **g**.
14: 1 love, and desire spiritual **g**,
14:12 are zealous for spiritual **g**,
Eph 4: 8 And gave **g** to men."
Heb 2: 4 and **g** of the Holy Spirit,
5: 1 that he may offer both **g** and
8: 3 is appointed to offer both **g**
8: 4 are priests who offer the **g**
9: 9 present time in which both **g**
11: 4 God testifying of his **g**;
Rev 11:10 and send **g** to one another,

GIHON (6/6)

Gen 2:13 name of the second river is **G**;
1 Ki 1:33 mule, and take him down to **G**.
1:38 David's mule, and took him to **G**.
1:45 have anointed him king at **G**;
2 Chr 32:30 the water outlet of Upper **G**,
33:14 of David on the west side of **G**,

GILALAI (1/1)

Neh 12:36 Shemaiah, Azarel, Milalai, **G**,

GILBOA (8/8)

1 Sam 28: 4 and they encamped at **G**.
31: 1 and fell slain on Mount **G**.
31: 8 three sons fallen on Mount **G**.
2 Sam 1: 6 by chance to be on Mount **G**,
1:21 "O mountains of **G**,
21:12 had struck down Saul in **G**.
1 Chr 10: 1 and fell slain on Mount **G**.
10: 8 and his sons fallen on Mount **G**.

GILEAD (132/123) GILEADITE, JABESH GILEAD, RAMOTH GILEAD

Gen 31:21 toward the mountains of **G**.
31:23 him in the mountains of **G**.
31:25 pitched in the mountains of **G**.
37:25 coming from **G** with their
Num 26:29 Machirites; and Machir begot **G**;
26:29 and Machir begot Gilead; of **G**,
26:30 These are the sons of **G**:
27: 1 the son of Hepher, the son of **G**,
32: 1 land of Jazer and the land of **G**,
32:26 be there in the cities of **G**;
32:29 shall give them the land of **G**
32:39 the son of Manasseh went to **G**
32:40 So Moses gave **G** to Machir the
36: 1 families of the children of **G**
Deut 2:36 is in the ravine, as far as **G**,
3:10 the cities of the plain, all **G**,
3:12 and half the mountains of **G** and
3:13 "The rest of **G**,
3:15 Also I gave **G** to Machir.
3:16 and the Gadites I gave from **G**
4:43 Ramoth in **G** for the Gadites,
34: 1 showed him all the land of **G**
Josh 12: 2 in Heshbon and ruled half of **G**,
12: 5 and over half of **G** to the
13:11 **G**, and the border of the
13:25 Jazer, and all the cities of **G**,
13:31 half of **G**, and Ashtaroth
17: 1 of Manasseh, the father of **G**,
17: 1 therefore he was given **G** and
17: 3 the son of Hepher, the son of **G**,
17: 5 besides the land of **G** and
17: 6 sons had the land of **G**.
20: 8 tribe of Reuben, Ramoth in **G**,
21:38 Ramoth in **G** with its
22: 9 to go to the country of **G**,
22:13 of Manasseh, into the land of **G**,
22:15 of Manasseh, to the land of **G**,
22:32 from the land of **G** to the land
Judg 5:17 **G** stayed beyond the Jordan,
7: 3 and depart at once from Mount **G**.
10: 4 which are in the land of **G**.
10: 8 the land of the Amorites, in **G**.
10:17 together and encamped in **G**.
10:18 the people, the leaders of **G**,
10:18 over all the inhabitants of **G**.
11: 1 and **G** begot Jephthah.
11: 5 that the elders of **G** went to
11: 7 said to the elders of **G**,
11: 8 And the elders of **G** said to
11: 8 over all the inhabitants of **G**.
11: 9 said to the elders of **G**,
11:10 And the elders of **G** said to
11:11 went with the elders of **G**,
11:29 and he passed through **G** and
11:29 and passed through Mizpah of **G**;
11:29 and from Mizpah of **G** he
12: 4 together all the men of **G** and
12: 4 And the men of **G** defeated
12: 5 the men of **G** would say to
12: 7 buried in among the cities of **G**.
20: 1 as well as from the land of **G**,
1 Sam 13: 7 Jordan to the land of Gad and **G**.
2 Sam 2: 9 and he made him king over **G**,
17:26 encamped in the land of **G**.
24: 6 Then they came to **G** and to the
1 Ki 4:13 Ben-Geber, in Ramoth **G**;
4:13 Jair the son of Manasseh, in **G**;
4:19 son of Uri, in the land of **G**,
17: 1 of the inhabitants of **G**,
22: 3 Do you know that Ramoth in **G** is
22: 4 go with me to fight at Ramoth **G**?
22: 6 Shall I go against Ramoth **G** to
22:12 Go up to Ramoth **G** and prosper,
22:15 we go to war against Ramoth **G**,
22:20 that he may fall at Ramoth **G**?
22:29 of Judah went up to Ramoth **G**.
2 Ki 8:28 king of Syria at Ramoth **G**;
9: 1 your hand, and go to Ramoth **G**.
9: 4 the prophet, went to Ramoth **G**.
9:14 had been defending Ramoth **G**,
10:33 eastward: all the land of **G**—
10:33 including **G** and Bashan.
15:25 with him were fifty men of **G**.
15:29 Janoah, Kedesh, Hazor, **G**,
1 Chr 2:21 of Machir the father of **G**,
2:22 cities in the land of **G**.
2:23 sons of Machir the father of **G**.
5: 9 had multiplied in the land of **G**.
5:10 the entire area east of **G**.
5:14 the son of Jaroah, the son of **G**,
5:16 And the Gadites dwelt in **G**,
6:80 Ramoth in **G** with its
7:14 bore him Machir the father of **G**,
7:17 were the descendants of **G** the
26:31 them capable men at Jazer of **G**.
27:21 half-tribe of Manasseh in **G**,
2 Chr 18: 2 to go up with him to Ramoth **G**.
18: 3 go with me against Ramoth **G**?
18: 5 we go to war against Ramoth **G**,
18:11 Go up to Ramoth **G** and prosper,
18:14 we go to war against Ramoth **G**,
18:19 that he may fall at Ramoth **G**?
18:28 of Judah went up to Ramoth **G**.
22: 5 king of Syria at Ramoth **G**;
Ps 60: 7 **G** is Mine, and Manasseh is
108: 8 **G** is Mine; Manasseh is Mine;
Song 4: 1 goats, Going down from Mount **G**.
6: 5 of goats Going down from **G**.
Jer 8:22 Is there no balm in **G**,
22: 6 You are **G** to Me, The head of
46:11 'Go up to **G** and take balm,
50:19 on Mount Ephraim and **G**.
Ezek 47:18 and between **G** and the land of
Hos 6: 8 **G** is a city of evildoers,
12:11 Though **G** has idols—Surely
Am 1: 3 Because they have threshed **G**
1:13 open the women with child in **G**,
Ob 19 Benjamin shall possess **G**.
Mic 7:14 Let them feed in Bashan and **G**,
Zech 10:10 bring them into the land of **G**

GILEAD'S (2/2)

Judg 11: 2 **G** wife bore sons; and when his
1 Chr 7:15 The name of **G** grandson was

GILEADITE (9/9) GILEAD

Judg 10: 3 After him arose Jair, a **G**;
11: 1 Now Jephthah the **G** was a mighty
11:40 the daughter of Jephthah the **G**.
12: 7 Then Jephthah the **G** died and
2 Sam 17:27 and Barzillai the **G** from
19:31 And Barzillai the **G** came down
1 Ki 2: 7 to the sons of Barzillai the **G**,
Ezra 2:61 daughters of Barzillai the **G**,
Neh 7:63 daughters of Barzillai the **G**,

GILEADITES (3/3)

Num 26:29 of Gilead, the family of the **G**.
Judg 12: 4 You **G** are fugitives of Ephraim
12: 5 The **G** seized the fords of the

GILGAL (41/39)

Deut 11:30 dwell in the plain opposite **G**,
Josh 4:19 and they camped in **G** on the
4:20 the Jordan, Joshua set up in **G**.
5: 9 name of the place is called **G**
5:10 children of Israel camped in **G**,
9: 6 to Joshua, to the camp at **G**,
10: 6 sent to Joshua at the camp at **G**,
10: 7 So Joshua ascended from **G**,
10: 9 having marched all night from **G**.
10:15 with him, to the camp at **G**.
10:43 with him, to the camp at **G**.
12:23 the king of the people of **G**,
14: 6 of Judah came to Joshua in **G**.
15: 7 it turned northward toward **G**,
Judg 2: 1 of the LORD came up from **G** to
3:19 stone images that were at **G**,
1 Sam 7:16 year on a circuit to Bethel, **G**,
10: 8 shall go down before me to **G**;
11:14 let us go to **G** and renew the
11:15 So all the people went to **G**,
11:15 Saul king before the LORD in **G**.
13: 4 called together to Saul at **G**.
13: 7 As for Saul, he was still in **G**,
13: 8 But Samuel did not come to **G**;
13:12 will now come down on me at **G**,
13:15 arose and went up from **G** to
15:12 passed by, and gone down to **G**.
15:21 to the LORD your God in **G**.
15:33 in pieces before the LORD in **G**.
2 Sam 19:15 the Jordan. And Judah came to **G**,
19:40 Now the king went on to **G**,
2 Ki 2: 1 Elijah went with Elisha from **G**.
4:38 And Elisha returned to **G**,
Neh 12:29 from the house of **G**,
Hos 4:15 Do not come up to **G**,
9:15 their wickedness is in **G**,
12:11 they sacrifice bulls in **G**,
Am 4: 4 At **G** multiply transgression;
5: 5 not seek Bethel, Nor enter **G**,
5: 5 For **G** shall surely go into
Mic 6: 5 From Acacia Grove to **G**,

GILOH (2/2)

Josh 15:51 Goshen, Holon, and **G**:
2 Sam 15:12 counselor, from his city—from **G**—

GILONITE (2/2)

2 Sam 15:12 sent for Ahithophel the **G**,
23:34 the son of Ahithophel the **G**,

GIMZO (1/1)

2 Chr 28:18 and **G** with its villages;

GIN (KJV) See NET, TRAP

GINATH (2/2)

1 Ki 16:21 followed Tibni the son of **G**,
16:22 who followed Tibni the son of **G**.

GINNETHOI (1/1)

Neh 12: 4 Iddo, **G**, Abijah,

GINNETHON (2/2)

Neh 10: 6 Daniel, **G**, Baruch,
12:16 of Iddo, Zechariah; of **G**,

GIRD (19/18) GIRDED, GIRDS

Ex 29: 5 and **g** him with the intricately
29: 9 And you shall **g** them with
1 Sam 25:13 'Every man **g** on his sword."
2 Sam 3:31 **g** yourselves with sackcloth,
Ps 45: 3 **G** Your sword upon Your thigh,
76:10 remainder of wrath You shall **g**
Isa 8: 9 **G** yourselves, but be broken in
8: 9 **G** yourselves, but be broken in
32:11 And **g** sackcloth on your
45: 5 I will **g** you, though you have
Jer 49: 3 **G** yourselves with sackcloth!
Lam 2:10 dust on their heads And **g**
Ezek 27:31 **G** themselves with sackcloth,
Joel 1:13 **G** yourselves and lament,
Lk 12:37 I say to you that he will **g**
17: 8 and **g** yourself and serve me
Jn 21:18 and another will **g** you and
Acts 12: 8 **G** yourself and tie on your
1 Pe 1:13 Therefore **g** up the loins of

GIRDED (22/20) GIRD

Lev 8: 7 **g** him with the sash, clothed
8: 7 and he **g** him with the
8:13 **g** them with sashes, and put
16: 4 he shall be **g** with a linen
Deut 1:41 And when everyone of you had **g**
1 Sam 2: 4 And those who stumbled are **g**
25:13 So every man **g** on his sword,
25:13 and David also **g** on his sword.
1 Ki 18:46 and he **g** up his loins and ran
Neh 4:18 of the builders had his sword **g**
Ps 93: 1 He has **g** Himself with
Ezek 7:18 They will also be **g** with
23:15 **G** with belts around their
Dan 10: 5 whose waist was **g** with gold of
Joel 1: 8 Lament like a virgin **g** with
Lk 12:35 Let your waist be **g** and your
Jn 13: 4 took a towel and **g** Himself.
13: 5 the towel with which He was **g**.
21:18 you **g** yourself and walked where
Eph 6:14 having **g** your waist with truth,
Rev 1:13 garment down to the feet and **g**
15: 6 and having their chests **g** with

GIRDING (2/2)

Isa 3:24 a **g** of sackcloth; And branding
22:12 For baldness and for **g** with

GIRDS (2/2) GIRD

Ps 109:19 And for a belt with which he **g**
Prov 31:17 She **g** herself with strength,

GIRGASHITE (2/2) GIRGASHITES

Gen 10:16 the Amorite, and the **G**;
1 Chr 1:14 the Amorite, and the **G**;

GIRGASHITES (5/5) GIRGASHITE

Gen 15:21 Amorites, the Canaanites, the **G**,
Deut 7: 1 the Hittites and the **G** and the
Josh 3:10 and the Perizzites and the **G**
24:11 Canaanites, the Hittites, the **G**,
Neh 9: 8 the Jebusites, And the **G**—

GIRGASITE (KJV) See GIRGASHITE

GIRL (23/22) GIRLS

Judg 5:30 To every man a **g** or two;
2 Ki 5: 2 brought back captive a young **g**
5: 4 Thus and thus said the **g** who is
Joel 3: 3 And sold a **g** for wine, that

Am 2: 7 his father go in to the same *g*,
Mt 9:24 for the *g* is not dead, but
9:25 and the *g* arose.
14:11 on a platter and given to the *g*,
26:69 And a servant *g* came to him,
26:71 another *g* saw him and said to
Mk 5:41 which is translated, "Little *g*,
5:42 Immediately the *g* arose and
6:22 him, the king said to the *g*,
6:28 a platter, and gave it to the *g*;
6:28 and the *g* gave it to her
14:69 And the servant *g* saw him again,
Lk 8:51 the father and mother of the *g*.
8:54 and called, saying, "Little *g*,
22:56 And a certain servant *g*,
Jn 18:17 Then the servant *g* who kept the
Acts 12:13 a *g* named Rhoda came to answer.
16:16 that a certain slave *g*
16:17 This *g* followed Paul and us, and

GIRLS (3/3) GIRL

Num 31:18 for yourselves all the young *g*
Zech 8: 5 Shall be full of boys and *g*
Mk 14:66 one of the servant *g* of the

GIRZITES (1/1)

1 Sam 27: 8 raided the Geshurites, the *G*,

GISHPA (1/1)

Neh 11:21 And Ziha and *G* were over the

GITTAIM (2/2)

2 Sam 4: 3 the Beerothites fled to *G* and
Neh 11:33 in Hazor, Ramah, *G*;

GITTITE (8/8) GATH, GITTITES

2 Sam 6:10 the house of Obed-Edom the *G*.
6:11 in the house of Obed-Edom the *G*
15:19 the king said to Ittai the *G*,
15:22 Then Ittai the *G* and all his
18: 2 under the hand of Ittai the *G*.
21:19 the brother of Goliath the *G*,
1 Chr 13:13 the house of Obed-Edom the *G*.
20: 5 the brother of Goliath the *G*,

GITTITES (2/2) GITTITE

Josh 13: 3 the Ashkelonites, the *G*,
2 Sam 15:18 the Pelethites, and all the *G*,

GIVE (865/795) GAVE, GIFT, GIVEN, GIVER, GIVES, GIVING

Gen 1:15 firmament of the heavens to *g*
1:17 firmament of the heavens to *g*
12: 7 To your descendants I will *g*
13:15 all the land which you see I *g*
13:17 for I *g* it to you."
14:21 *G* me the persons, and take the
15: 2 what will You *g* me, seeing I go
15: 7 to *g* you this land to inherit
17: 8 Also I *g* to you and your
17:16 I will bless her and also *g*
23: 4 *G* me property for a burial
23: 9 that he may *g* me the cave of
23: 9 Let him *g* it to me at the full
23:11 I *g* you the field and the cave
23:11 I *g* it to you in the presence
23:11 I *g* it to you. Bury your
23:13 If you will *g* it, please hear
23:13 I will *g* you money for the
24: 7 To your descendants I *g* this
24:12 please *g* me success this day,
24:14 and I will also *g* your camels a
24:41 for if they will not *g* her to
24:43 Please *g* me a little water from
24:46 and I will *g* your camels a
25:24 were fulfilled for her to *g*
26: 3 to you and your descendants I *g*
26: 4 I will *g* to your descendants
27:28 Therefore may God *g* you Of the
28: 4 And *g* you the blessing of
28:13 land on which you lie I will *g*
28:20 and *g* me bread to eat and
28:22 and of all that You *g* me I will
28:22 You give me I will surely *g* a
29:19 It is better that I *g* her to
29:19 her to you than that I should *g*
29:21 *G* me my wife, for my days are
29:26 to *g* the younger before the
29:27 and we will *g* you this one also
30: 1 *G* me children, or else I die!"
30:14 Please *g* me some of your son's
30:26 *G* me my wives and my children
30:28 and I will *g* it."
30:31 What shall I *g* you?" And Jacob
30:31 'You shall not *g* me anything.
34: 8 Please *g* her to him as a wife.
34: 9 *g* your daughters to us, and
34:11 whatever you say to me I will *g*.
34:12 and I will *g* according to what
34:12 but *g* me the young woman as a
34:14 to *g* our sister to one who is
34:16 then we will *g* our daughters to
34:21 and let us *g* them our
35:12 I gave Abraham and Isaac I *g*
35:12 your descendants after you I *g*
38: 9 lest he should *g* an heir to his
38:16 What will you *g* me, that you may
38:17 Will you *g* me a pledge till you
38:18 'What pledge shall I *g* you?"
38:26 because I did not *g* her to
41:16 God will *g* Pharaoh an answer of
42:25 and to *g* them provisions for
42:27 of them opened his sack to *g*
43:14 And may God Almighty *g* you mercy
45:18 I will *g* you the best of the
47:15 *G* us bread, for why should we
47:16 *G* your livestock, and I will
47:16 and I will *g* you bread for
47:19 *g* us seed, that we may live
47:24 in the harvest that you shall *g*
48: 4 and *g* this land to your
Ex 1:19 for they are lively and *g*
2: 9 and I will *g* you your wages."
3:21 And I will *g* this people favor
5: 7 You shall no longer *g* the people
5:10 I will not *g* you straw.
6: 4 to *g* them the land of Canaan,
6: 8 the land which I swore to *g* to
6: 8 and I will *g* it to you as a
10:25 You must also *g* us sacrifices
12:25 the land which the LORD will *g*
13: 5 He swore to your fathers to *g*
13:21 night in a pillar of fire to *g*
15:26 *g* ear to His commandments and
17: 2 *G* us water, that we may drink."
18:19 I will *g* you counsel, and God
21:23 then you shall *g* life for life,
21:32 he shall *g* to their master
21:34 he shall *g* money to their
22:17 her father utterly refuses to *g*
22:29 of your sons you shall *g* to Me.
22:30 on the eighth day you shall *g*
24:12 and I will *g* you tablets of
25:16 the Testimony which I will *g*
25:21 put the Testimony that I will *g*
25:22 everything which I will *g* you
25:37 its lamps so that they *g* light
30:12 then every man shall *g* a ransom
30:13 those who are numbered shall *g*:
30:14 shall *g* an offering to the
30:15 The rich shall not *g* more and
30:15 more and the poor shall not *g*
30:15 when you *g* an offering to the
32:13 land that I have spoken of I *g*
33: 1 To your descendants I will *g*
33:14 and I will *g* you rest."
Lev 5:16 add one-fifth to it and *g* it
6: 5 and *g* it to whomever it
7:32 the right thigh you shall *g* to
14:34 which I *g* you as a possession,
15:14 and *g* them to the priest.
19:31 *G* no regard to mediums and
20:24 and I will *g* it to you to
23:10 come into the land which I *g*
23:38 freewill offerings which you *g*
25: 2 come into the land which I *g*
25:38 to *g* you the land of Canaan
26: 4 then I will *g* you rain in its
26: 6 I will *g* peace in the land, and
27:23 and he shall *g* your valuation
Num 3: 9 And you shall *g* the Levites to
3:48 And you shall *g* the money, with
5: 7 and *g* it to the one he has
6:26 And *g* you peace." '
7: 5 and you shall *g* them to the
8: 2 the seven lamps shall *g* light
10:29 I will *g* it to you.' Come with
11: 4 Who will *g* us meat to eat?
11:13 Where am I to get meat to *g* to
11:13 *G* us meat, that we may eat.'
11:18 'Who will *g* us meat to eat?
11:18 Therefore the LORD will *g*
11:21 I will *g* them meat, that they
14: 8 bring us into this land and *g*
14:16 to the land which He swore to *g*
15:21 of your ground meal you shall *g*
18: 7 I *g* your priesthood to you as
18:28 and you shall *g* the LORD's
19: 3 You shall *g* it to Eleazar the
20: 8 and *g* drink to the congregation
20:21 Thus Edom refused to *g* Israel
21:16 and I will *g* them water."
22:13 for the LORD has refused to *g*
22:18 Though Balak were to *g* me his
24:13 If Balak were to *g* me his house
25:12 I *g* to him My covenant of
26:54 To a large tribe you shall *g* a
26:54 to a small tribe you shall *g*
27: 4 *G* us a possession among our
27: 7 you shall surely *g* them a
27: 9 then you shall *g* his
27:10 then you shall *g* his
27:11 then you shall *g* his
27:20 And you shall *g* some of your
31:29 and *g* it to Eleazar the priest
31:30 and *g* them to the Levites who
32:29 then you shall *g* them the land
33:54 to the larger you shall *g* a
33:54 and to the smaller you shall *g*
34:13 the LORD has commanded to *g*
35: 2 children of Israel that they *g*
35: 2 and you shall also *g* the
35: 4 of the cities which you shall *g*
35: 6 the cities which you will *g* to
35: 7 So all the cities you will *g* to
35: 7 these you shall *g* with their
35: 8 the cities which you will *g*
35: 8 the larger tribe you shall *g*
35: 8 from the smaller you shall *g*
35: 8 Each shall *g* some of its cities
35:13 'And of the cities which you *g*,
36: 2 commanded my lord Moses to *g*
36: 2 was commanded by the LORD to *g*
Deut 1: 8 to *g* to them and their
1:35 land of which I swore to *g* to
1:39 to them I will *g* it, and they
1:45 not listen to your voice nor *g*
2: 5 for I will not *g* you any of
2: 9 for I will not *g* you any of
2:19 for I will not *g* you any of
2:28 and *g* me water for money, that
2:31 I have begun to *g* Sihon and his
4:38 to *g* you their land as an
6:10 to *g* you large and beautiful
6:23 to *g* us the land of which He
7: 3 You shall not *g* your daughter
7:13 He swore to your fathers to *g*
10:11 I swore to their fathers to *g*
11: 9 land which the LORD swore to *g*
11:14 then I will *g* you the rain for
11:21 swore to your fathers to *g*
14:21 you may *g* it to the alien who
15: 3 but you shall *g* up your claim
15: 9 your poor brother and you *g*
15:10 You shall surely *g* to him, and
15:10 not be grieved when you *g* to
15:14 you shall *g* to him.
16:10 which you shall *g* as the LORD
16:17 Every man shall *g* as he is
18: 3 they shall *g* to the priest the
18: 4 you shall *g* him.
19: 8 land which He promised to *g* to
22:19 shekels of silver and *g* them
22:29 man who lay with her shall *g*
23:14 to deliver you and *g* your
23:15 You shall not *g* back to his
24:15 Each day you shall *g* him his
25: 3 Forty blows he may *g* him and no
26: 3 swore to our fathers to *g* us.
28:11 swore to your fathers to *g* you.
28:12 to *g* the rain to your land in
28:55 so that he will not *g* any of
28:65 but there the LORD will *g* you
30:20 Isaac, and Jacob, to *g* them."
31: 5 The LORD will *g* them over to
31: 7 has sworn to their fathers to *g*
31:21 land of which I swore to *g*
32: 1 *G* ear, O heavens, and I will
32:49 which I *g* to the children of
34: 4 the land of which I swore to *g*
34: 4 I will *g* it to your
Josh 1: 6 I swore to their fathers to *g*
2:12 and *g* me a true token,
5: 6 their fathers that He would *g*
7:19 *g* glory to the LORD God of
8:18 for I will *g* it into your
9:24 His servant Moses to *g* you all
14:12 *g* me this mountain of which the
15:16 to him I will *g* Achsah my
15:19 *G* me a blessing; since you have
15:19 *g* me also springs of water."
17: 4 LORD commanded Moses to *g*
20: 4 and *g* him a place, that he may
21: 2 commanded through Moses to *g*
21:43 of which He had sworn to *g* to
Judg 1:12 to him I will *g* my daughter
1:15 *G* me a blessing; since you have
1:15 *g* me also springs of water."
4:19 Please *g* me a little water to
5: 3 O kings! *G* ear, O princes!
7: 2 you are too many for Me to *g*
8: 5 Please *g* loaves of bread to the
8: 6 that we should *g* bread to your
8:15 that we should *g* bread to your
8:24 that each of you would *g* me the
8:25 'We will gladly *g* them."
14:12 then I will *g* you thirty linen
14:13 then you shall *g* me thirty
16: 5 and every one of us will *g* you
17:10 and I will *g* you ten shekels
20: 7 *g* your advice and counsel here
21: 1 None of us shall *g* his daughter
21: 7 by the LORD that we will not *g*
21:18 we cannot *g* them wives from our
Ruth 4:12 which the LORD will *g* you
1 Sam 1: 4 he would *g* portions to Peninnah
1: 5 But to Hannah he would *g* a
1:11 but will *g* Your maidservant a
1:11 then I will *g* him to the LORD
2:10 He will *g* strength to His king,
2:15 *G* meat for roasting to the
2:16 but you must *g* it now; and if
2:20 The LORD *g* you descendants from
2:28 And did I not *g* to the house of
6: 5 and you shall *g* glory to the
8: 6 '*G* us a king to judge us."
8:14 and *g* them to his servants.
8:15 and *g* it to his officers and
9: 8 I will *g* that to the man of
10: 4 And they will greet you and *g*
14:41 *G* a perfect lot." So Saul and
17:10 *g* me a man, that we may fight
17:25 will *g* him his daughter, and
17:25 and *g* his father's house
17:44 and I will *g* your flesh to the
17:46 And this day I will *g* the
17:47 and He will *g* you into our
18:17 I will *g* her to you as a wife.
18:21 I will *g* her to him, that she
21: 3 *G* me five loaves of bread in

21: 9 is none like it; **g** it to me."
22: 7 Will the son of Jesse **g** every
25: 8 Please **g** whatever comes to your
25:11 and **g** it to men when I do not
27: 5 let them **g** me a place in some
30:22 we will not **g** them any of the
2 Sam 3:14 **G** me my wife Michal, whom I
4:10 one who thought I would **g**
12:11 wives before your eyes and **g**
13: 5 let my sister Tamar come and **g**
14: 8 and I will **g** orders concerning
15: 4 then I would **g** him justice."
16:20 **G** counsel as to what we should
21: 6 I will **g** them."
22:50 Therefore I will **g** thanks to
23:15 that someone would **g** me a drink
1 Ki 1:12 let me now **g** you advice, that
2:17 that he may **g** me Abishag the
3: 5 Ask! What shall I **g** you?"
3: 9 Therefore **g** to Your servant an
3:25 and **g** half to one, and half to
3:26 **g** her the living child, and by
3:27 **G** the first woman the living
8:39 and **g** to everyone according to
11:11 kingdom away from you and **g** it
11:13 I will **g** one tribe to your son
11:31 the hand of Solomon and will **g**
11:35 out of his son's hand and **g** it
11:36 And to his son I will **g** one
11:38 and will **g** Israel to you.
12: 9 to them, "What advice do you **g**?
13: 7 and I will **g** you a reward."
13: 8 If you were to **g** me half your
14:16 And He will **g** Israel up because
17:19 **G** me your son." So he took him
18:23 Therefore let them **g** us two
21: 2 **G** me your vineyard, that I may
21: 2 and for it I will **g** you a
21: 2 I will **g** you its worth in
21: 3 LORD forbid that I should **g**
21: 4 I will not **g** you the inheritance
21: 6 '**G** me your vineyard for money;
21: 6 I will **g** you another vineyard
21: 6 I will not **g** you my vineyard.'
21: 7 I will **g** you the vineyard of
21:15 which he refused to **g** you for
2 Ki 4:42 **G** it to the people, that they
4:43 **G** it to the people, that they
5:22 Please **g** them a talent of
6:28 **G** your son, that we may eat him
6:29 **G** your son, that we may eat
8:19 as He promised him to **g** a lamp
10:15 **g** me your hand." So he gave
14: 9 **G** your daughter to my son as
15:20 to **g** to the king of Assyria.
18:23 **g** a pledge to my master the
18:23 and I will **g** you two thousand
22: 5 let them **g** it to those who are
23:35 but he taxed the land to **g**
23:35 to **g** it to Pharaoh Necho.
1 Chr 11:17 that someone would **g** me a drink
16: 8 **g** thanks to the LORD!
16:18 To you I will **g** the land of
16:28 **G** to the LORD, O families of
16:28 **G** to the LORD glory and
16:29 **G** to the LORD the glory due
16:34 **g** thanks to the LORD, for He
16:35 To **g** thanks to Your holy name,
16:41 to **g** thanks to the LORD,
21:23 I also **g** you the oxen for
21:23 grain offering; I **g** it all."
22: 9 and I will **g** him rest from all
22: 9 for I will **g** peace and
22:12 Only may the LORD **g** you wisdom
22:12 and **g** you charge concerning
23:13 and to **g** the blessing in His
25: 3 who prophesied with a harp to **g**
29:12 it is to make great And to **g**
29:19 And **g** my son Solomon a loyal
2 Chr 1: 7 Ask! What shall I **g** you?"
1:10 Now **g** me wisdom and knowledge,
1:12 and I will **g** you riches and
2:10 And indeed I will **g** to your
6:30 and **g** to everyone according to
10: 9 to them, "What advice do you **g**?
21: 7 and since He had promised to **g**
25: 9 The LORD is able to **g** you much
25:18 **G** your daughter to my son as
25:20 that He might **g** them into the
30:12 hand of God was on Judah to **g**
31: 2 to **g** thanks, and to praise in
32:11 not Hezekiah persuade you to **g**
35:12 offerings that they might **g**
Ezra 4:21 Now **g** the command to make these
9: 8 and to **g** us a peg in His holy
9: 8 may enlighten our eyes and **g**
9: 9 and to **g** us a wall in Judah and
9:12 do not **g** your daughters as
Neh 2: 8 that he must **g** me timber to
4: 4 and **g** them as plunder to a land
9: 8 made a covenant with him To **g**
9: 8 To **g** it to his descendants.
9:12 To **g** them light on the road
9:15 land Which You had sworn to **g**
10:30 We would not **g** our daughters as
12:24 to praise and **g** thanks, group
13:25 You shall not **g** your daughters
Esth 1:19 and let the king **g** her royal
Job 2: 4 all that a man has he will **g**
10: 1 I will **g** free course to my
33:13 For He does not **g** an
33:31 '**G** ear, Job, listen to me;

34: 2 **G** ear to me, you who have
35: 7 what do you **g** Him? Or what
Ps 2: 8 and I will **g** You The nations
5: 1 **G** ear to my words, O LORD,
5: 2 **G** heed to the voice of my cry,
6: 5 In the grave who will **g** You
17: 1 **G** ear to my prayer which is
18:49 Therefore I will **g** thanks to
28: 4 **G** them according to their
28: 4 **G** them according to the work
29: 1 **G** unto the LORD, O you mighty
29: 1 **G** unto the LORD glory and
29: 2 **G** unto the LORD the glory due
29: 9 of the LORD makes the deer **g**
29:11 The LORD will **g** strength to
30: 4 And **g** thanks at the
30:12 I will **g** thanks to You forever.
35:18 I will **g** You thanks in the
36: 8 And You **g** them drink from the
37: 4 And He shall **g** you the desires
39:12 And **g** ear to my cry; Do not
49: 1 **G** ear, all inhabitants of the
49: 3 of my heart shall **g**
49: 7 Nor **g** to God a ransom for him—
50:19 You **g** your mouth to evil,
51:16 or else I would **g** it; You do
54: 2 **G** ear to the words of my
55: 1 **G** ear to my prayer, O God,
57: 7 I will sing and **g** praise.
60:11 **G** us help from trouble,
72: 1 **G** the king Your judgments,
75: 1 We **g** thanks to You, O God, we
75: 1 we **g** thanks! For Your wondrous
78: 1 **G** ear, O my people, to my law
78:20 Can He **g** bread also? Can He
79:13 Will **g** You thanks forever;
80: 1 **G** ear, O Shepherd of Israel,
84: 8 **G** ear, O God of Jacob! Selah
84:11 The LORD will **g** grace and
85:12 the LORD will **g** what is
86: 6 **G** ear, O LORD, to my prayer
86:16 and have mercy on me! **G** Your
91:11 For He shall **g** His angels
92: 1 It is good to **g** thanks to the
94:13 That You may **g** him rest from
96: 7 **G** to the LORD, O families of
96: 7 **G** to the LORD glory and
96: 8 **G** to the LORD the glory due
97:12 And **g** thanks at the
104:11 They **g** drink to every beast of
104:27 That You may **g** them their
104:28 What You **g** them they gather
105: 1 **g** thanks to the LORD!
105:11 To you I will **g** the land of
105:39 And fire to **g** light in the
106: 1 **g** thanks to the LORD, for He
106:47 To **g** thanks to Your holy name,
107: 1 **g** thanks to the LORD, for He
107: 8 that men would **g** thanks to the
107:15 that men would **g** thanks to the
107:21 that men would **g** thanks to the
107:31 that men would **g** thanks to the
108: 1 I will sing and **g** praise, even
108:12 **G** us help from trouble,
109: 4 But I **g** myself to prayer.
115: 1 But to Your name **g** glory,
115:14 May the LORD **g** you increase
118: 1 **g** thanks to the LORD, for He
118:29 **g** thanks to the LORD, for He
119:34 **G** me understanding, and I shall
119:62 At midnight I will rise to **g**
119:73 **G** me understanding, that I may
119:125 **G** me understanding, That I
119:144 **G** me understanding, and I
119:169 **G** me understanding according
122: 4 To **g** thanks to the name of the
132: 4 I will not **g** sleep to my eyes
136: 1 **g** thanks to the LORD, for He
136: 2 **g** thanks to the God of gods!
136: 3 **g** thanks to the Lord of lords!
136:26 **g** thanks to the God of heaven!
140:13 Surely the righteous shall **g**
141: 1 Make haste to me! **G** ear to my
143: 1 **G** ear to my supplications!
145:15 And You **g** them their food in
Prov 1: 4 To **g** prudence to the simple,
3:28 And tomorrow I will **g** it,"
4: 1 And **g** attention to know
4: 2 For I **g** you good doctrine:
4:20 **g** attention to my words;
5: 9 Lest you **g** your honor to
6: 4 **G** no sleep to your eyes,
6:31 He may have to **g** up all the
6:35 he be appeased though you **g**
9: 9 **G** instruction to a wise man,
23:26 **g** me your heart, And let your
25:21 **g** him bread to eat; And if he
25:21 **g** him water to drink;
29:15 The rod and rebuke **g** wisdom,
29:17 and he will **g** you rest;
29:17 he will **g** delight to your soul.
30: 8 **G** me neither poverty nor
30:15 **G** and Give! There are three
30:15 Give and **G**! There are three
31: 3 Do not **g** your strength to
31: 6 **G** strong drink to him who is
31:31 **G** her of the fruit of her
Eccl 2:26 that he may **g** to him who is
5: 1 near to hear rather than to **g**
6: 2 yet God does not **g** him power to
10: 1 And cause it to **g** off a foul
11: 2 **G** a serving to seven, and also

Song 2:13 with the tender grapes **G** a
7:12 There I will **g** you my love.
7:13 The mandrakes **g** off a
8: 7 If a man would **g** for love All
Isa 1: 2 and **g** ear, O earth! For the
1:10 **G** ear to the law of our God,
3: 4 I will **g** children to be their
7:14 the Lord Himself will **g** you a
7:22 the abundance of milk they **g**,
8: 9 and be broken in pieces! **G**
10: 6 people of My wrath I will **g**
13:10 constellations Will not **g**
19: 4 And the Egyptians I will **g**
19:11 Pharaoh's wise counselors **g**
28:23 **G** ear and hear my voice,
30:23 Then He will **g** the rain for
32: 9 **G** ear to my speech.
36: 8 **g** a pledge to my master the
36: 8 and I will **g** you two thousand
41:27 there they are!' And I will **g**
42: 6 I will keep You and **g** You as a
42: 8 And My glory I will not **g** to
42:12 Let them **g** glory to the LORD,
42:23 Who among you will **g** ear to
43: 4 Therefore I will **g** men for
43: 6 **G** them up!' And to the south,
43:20 Because I **g** waters in the
43:20 To **g** drink to My people,
43:28 I will **g** Jacob to the curse,
45: 3 I will **g** you the treasures of
48:11 And I will not **g** My glory to
49: 6 I will also **g** You as a light
49: 8 I will preserve You and **g** You
49:20 **G** me a place where I may
51: 4 And **g** ear to Me, O My nation:
55:10 That it may **g** seed to the
56: 5 Even to them I will **g** in My
56: 5 I will **g** them an everlasting
60:19 for brightness shall the moon **g**
61: 3 To **g** them beauty for ashes,
62: 7 And **g** Him no rest till He
62: 8 Surely I will no longer **g** your
66: 8 Shall the earth be made to **g**
Jer 3:15 And I will **g** you shepherds
3:19 you among the children And **g**
6:10 To whom shall I speak and **g**
6:10 And they cannot **g** heed.
8:10 Therefore I will **g** their wives
9:15 and **g** them water of gall to
11: 5 to **g** them 'a land flowing with
13:15 Hear and **g** ear: Do not be
13:16 **G** glory to the LORD your God
14:13 but I will **g** you assured peace
14:22 Or can the heavens **g** showers?
15:13 and your treasures I will **g**
16: 7 nor shall men **g** them the cup
17: 3 I will **g** as plunder your
17:10 Even to **g** every man according
18:18 and let us not **g** heed to any of
18:19 **G** heed to me, O LORD,
19: 7 their corpses I will **g** as meat
20: 4 I will **g** all Judah into the
20: 5 of the kings of Judah I will **g**
22:25 and I will **g** you into the hand
24: 7 Then I will **g** them a heart to
24: 8 so will I **g** up Zedekiah the king
25:30 He will **g** a shout, as those
25:31 He will **g** those who are
26:24 so that they should not **g** him
29: 6 take wives for your sons and **g**
29:11 to **g** you a future and a hope.
31: 2 when I went to **g** him rest."
31: 7 **g** praise, and say, 'O LORD,
32: 3 I will **g** this city into the
32:19 to **g** everyone according to his
32:22 You swore to their fathers to **g**
32:28 I will **g** this city into the
32:39 then I will **g** them one heart and
34: 2 I will **g** this city into the
34:18 And I will **g** the men who have
34:20 I will **g** them into the hand of
34:21 And I will **g** Zedekiah king of
35: 2 and **g** them wine to drink."
37:21 and that they should **g** him
38:15 And if I **g** you advice, you will
38:16 nor will I **g** you into the hand
44:30 I will **g** Pharaoh Hophra king of
45: 5 But I will **g** your life to you as
48: 9 **G** wings to Moab, That she may
50:34 That He may **g** rest to the
Lam 2:18 **G** yourself no relief;
2:18 **G** your eyes no rest.
3:30 Let him **g** his cheek to the one
3:65 **G** them a veiled heart
Ezek 2: 8 your mouth and eat what I **g**
3: 3 with this scroll that I **g** you.
3:17 and **g** them warning from Me:
3:18 and you **g** him no warning,
3:20 because you did not **g** him
7:21 I will **g** it as plunder Into
11: 2 men who devise iniquity and **g**
11:17 and I will **g** you the land of
11:19 Then I will **g** them one heart,
11:19 and **g** them a heart of flesh,
15: 6 so I will **g** up the inhabitants
16:39 I will also **g** you into their
16:61 for I will **g** them to you for
17:15 that they might **g** him horses
20:28 raised My hand in an oath to **g**
20:42 raised My hand in an oath to **g**
21:27 And I will **g** it to Him." '
23:46 **g** them up to trouble and

25: 7 and **g** you as plunder to the
25:10 the men of the East I will **g**
29:19 Surely I will **g** the land of
32: 7 And the moon shall not **g** her
33:27 is in the open field I will **g**
36:26 I will **g** you a new heart and put
36:26 stone out of your flesh and **g**
39: 4 I will **g** you to birds of prey
39:11 in that day that I will **g** Gog
43:19 You shall **g** a young bull for a
44:28 You shall **g** them no possession
44:30 also you shall **g** to the priest
45: 8 but they shall **g** the rest of
45:13 you shall **g** one-sixth of an
45:16 the people of the land shall **g**
45:17 be the prince's part to **g**
46: 5 lambs, as much as he wants to **g**,
46: 7 as much as he wants to **g** for
46:11 as much as he wants to **g** for
47:14 raised My hand in an oath to **g**
47:23 there you shall **g** him his
Dan 1:12 and let them **g** us vegetables to
2: 4 and we will **g** the
2: 7 and we will **g** its
2: 9 I shall know that you can **g** me
2:16 in and asked the king to **g** him
5:12 and he will **g** the
5:15 but they could not **g** the
5:16 that you can **g** interpretations
5:17 and **g** your rewards to another;
6: 2 that the satraps might **g**
9:22 I have now come forth to **g** you
11:17 And he shall **g** him the daughter
11:21 to whom they will not **g** the
Hos 2: 5 Who **g** me my bread and my
2:15 I will **g** her her vineyards from
5: 1 O house of Israel! **G** ear,
9:14 **G** them, O LORD—What
9:14 O LORD—What will You **g**?
9:14 **G** them a miscarrying womb
11: 8 How can I **g** you up, Ephraim?
13:10 **G** me a king and princes'?
Joel 1: 2 And **g** ear, all you inhabitants
2:17 And do not **g** Your heritage to
Mic 1:14 Therefore you shall **g** presents
5: 3 Therefore He shall **g** them up,
6: 7 Shall I **g** my firstborn for my
6:14 what you do rescue I will **g**
7:20 You will **g** truth to Jacob
Hab 2:10 You **g** shameful counsel to your
Zeph 3:20 For I will **g** you fame and
Hag 2: 9 And in this place I will **g**
Zech 3: 7 I will **g** you places to walk
8:12 The vine shall **g** its fruit,
8:12 The ground shall **g** her
8:12 And the heavens shall **g** their
8:16 **G** judgment in your gates for
10: 1 He will **g** them showers of
11: 6 But indeed I will **g** everyone
11:12 **g** me my wages; and if not,
Mal 2: 2 To **g** glory to My name,"
Mt 4: 6 He shall **g** His angels
4: 9 All these things I will **g** You if
5:31 let him **g** her a certificate of
5:42 **G** to him who asks you, and from
6:11 **G** us this day our daily bread
7: 6 Do not **g** what is holy to the
7: 9 will **g** him a stone?
7:10 will he **g** him a serpent?
7:11 know how to **g** good gifts to
7:11 your Father who is in heaven **g**
10: 8 you have received, freely **g**.
11:28 and I will **g** you rest.
12:36 they will **g** account of it in
14: 7 he promised with an oath to **g**
14: 8 **G** me John the Baptist's head
14:16 You **g** them something to eat."
16:19 And I will **g** you the keys of the
16:26 Or what will a man **g** in
17:27 take that and **g** it to them for
19: 7 then did Moses command to **g** a
19:21 sell what you have and **g** to the
20: 4 and whatever is right I will **g**
20: 8 Call the laborers and **g** them
20:14 I wish to **g** to this last man
20:23 and on My left is not Mine to **g**,
20:28 and to **g** His life a ransom for
24:29 and the moon will not **g** its
24:45 to **g** them food in due season?
25: 8 **G** us some of your oil, for our
25:28 and **g** it to him who has ten
25:37 or thirsty and **g** You drink?
26:15 What are you willing to **g** me if
Mk 6:22 and I will **g** it to you."
6:23 I will **g** you, up to half of my
6:25 I want you to **g** me at once the
6:37 You **g** them something to eat."
6:37 denarii worth of bread and **g**
8:37 Or what will a man **g** in exchange
10:21 sell whatever you have and **g** to
10:40 and on My left is not Mine to **g**,
10:45 and to **g** His life a ransom for
12: 9 and **g** the vineyard to others.
13:24 and the moon will not **g** its
14:11 and promised to **g** him money.
Lk 1:32 and the Lord God will **g** Him the
1:77 To **g** knowledge of salvation to
1:79 To **g** light to those who sit in
3:11 let him **g** to him who has none;
4: 6 All this authority I will **g** You,
4: 6 and I **g** it to whomever I wish.
4:10 He shall **g** His angels
6:30 **G** to everyone who asks of you.
6:38 '**G**, and it will be given to
9:13 You **g** them something to eat."
10: 7 drinking such things as they **g**,
10:19 I **g** you the authority to
11: 3 **G** us day by day our daily bread
11: 7 I cannot rise and **g** to you'?
11: 8 though he will not rise and **g**
11: 8 persistence he will rise and **g**
11:11 will he **g** him a stone? Or if
11:11 will he **g** him a serpent instead
11:13 know how to **g** good gifts to
11:13 will your heavenly Father **g**
11:41 But rather **g** alms of such things
12:32 Father's good pleasure to **g**
12:33 Sell what you have and **g** alms;
12:42 to **g** them their portion of
12:51 you suppose that I came to **g**
14: 9 **G** place to this man,' and then
14:12 When you **g** a dinner or a supper,
14:13 But when you **g** a feast, invite
15:12 **g** me the portion of goods that
16: 2 **G** an account of your
16:12 who will **g** you what is your
17:18 not any found who returned to **g**
18:12 I **g** tithes of all that I
19: 8 I **g** half of my goods to the
19:24 and **g** it to him who has ten
20:10 that they might **g** him some of
20:16 those vinedressers and **g** the
21:15 for I will **g** you a mouth and
22: 5 and agreed to **g** him money.
Jn 1:22 that we may **g** an answer to
3:34 for God does not **g** the Spirit
4: 7 **G** Me a drink."
4:10 **G** Me a drink,' you would have
4:14 of the water that I shall **g**
4:14 But the water that I shall **g**
4:15 **g** me this water, that I may not
6:27 which the Son of Man will **g**
6:32 Moses did not **g** you the bread
6:34 **g** us this bread always."
6:51 and the bread that I shall **g** is
6:51 which I shall **g** for the life of
6:52 How can this Man **g** us His
7:19 Did not Moses **g** you the law, yet
9:24 **G** God the glory! We know that
10:28 And I **g** them eternal life, and
11:22 God will **g** You."
13:26 It is he to whom I shall **g** a
13:29 or that he should **g** something
13:34 A new commandment I **g** to you,
14:16 and He will **g** you another
14:27 My peace I **g** to you; not as the
14:27 not as the world gives do I **g**
15:16 the Father in My name He may **g**
16:23 the Father in My name He will **g**
17: 2 that He should **g** eternal life
Acts 3: 6 but what I do have I **g** you:
5:31 to **g** repentance to Israel and
6: 4 but we will **g** ourselves
7: 5 He promised to **g** it to him for
7:38 the living oracles to **g** to us,
8:19 **G** me this power also, that
12:23 because he did not **g** glory to
13:34 I will **g** you the sure
19:40 being no reason which we may **g**
20:32 is able to build you up and **g**
20:35 It is more blessed to **g** than to
Rom 8:11 from the dead will also **g** life
8:32 He not with Him also freely **g**
12:19 but rather **g** place to wrath;
12:20 **g** him a drink; For in
14:12 So then each of us shall **g**
16: 4 to whom not only I **g** thanks,
1 Cor 7: 5 that you may **g** yourselves to
7:25 yet I **g** judgment as one whom
7:38 but he who does not **g** her in
10:30 for the food over which I **g**
10:32 **G** no offense, either to the Jews
13: 3 and though I **g** my body to be
14:17 For you indeed **g** thanks well,
2 Cor 4: 6 has shone in our hearts to **g**
5:12 but **g** you opportunity to boast
6: 3 We **g** no offense in anything,
8:10 And in this I **g** advice: It is to
9: 7 So let each one **g** as he
Eph 1:16 do not cease to **g** thanks for
1:17 may **g** to you the spirit of
4:27 nor **g** place to the devil.
4:28 he may have something to **g** him
5:14 And Christ will **g** you
Col 1: 3 We **g** thanks to the God and
4: 1 **g** your bondservants what is
1 Th 1: 2 We **g** thanks to God always for
5:18 in everything **g** thanks; for this
2 Th 1: 7 and to **g** you who are troubled
2:13 But we are bound to **g** thanks to
3:16 may the Lord of peace Himself **g**
1 Tim 1: 4 nor **g** heed to fables and endless
4:13 **g** attention to reading, to
4:15 **g** yourself entirely to them,
5:14 **g** no opportunity to the
6:18 rich in good works, ready to **g**,
2 Tim 2: 7 and may the Lord **g** you
4: 8 will **g** to me on that Day, and
Heb 2: 1 Therefore we must **g** the more
2:16 For indeed He does not **g** aid to
2:16 but He does **g** aid to the seed
4:13 eyes of Him to whom we must **g**
13:17 as those who must **g** account.
Jas 2:16 but you do not **g** them the
1 Pe 3:15 and always be ready to **g** a
4: 5 They will **g** an account to Him
1 Jn 5:16 and He will **g** him life for
Rev 2: 7 To him who overcomes I will **g**
2:10 and I will **g** you the crown of
2:17 To him who overcomes I will **g**
2:17 And I will **g** him a white stone,
2:23 And I will **g** to each one of you
2:26 to him I will **g** power over the
2:28 and I will **g** him the morning
4: 9 the living creatures **g** glory
10: 9 **G** me the little book." And he
11: 3 And I will **g** power to my two
11:17 We **g** You thanks, O Lord God
12: 2 out in labor and in pain to **g**
12: 4 the woman who was ready to **g**
13:15 He was granted power to **g**
14: 7 Fear God and **g** glory to Him, for
16: 9 and they did not repent and **g**
16:19 to **g** her the cup of the wine of
17:13 and they will **g** their power and
17:17 and to **g** their kingdom to the
18: 7 in the same measure **g** her
19: 7 us be glad and rejoice and **g**
21: 6 I will **g** of the fountain of the
22:12 to **g** to every one according to

GIVEN (503/487) GIVE

Gen 1:29 I have **g** you every herb that
1:30 I have **g** every green herb
9: 2 They are **g** into your hand.
9: 3 I have **g** you all things, even
15: 3 You have **g** me no offspring;
15:18 To your descendants I have **g**
20:16 I have **g** your brother a
24:35 and He has **g** him flocks and
24:36 and to him he has **g** all that he
27:37 and all his brethren I have **g**
29:33 He has therefore **g** me this son
30: 6 has also heard my voice and **g**
30:18 God has **g** me my wages, because I
30:18 because I have **g** my maid to my
31: 9 livestock of your father and **g**
33: 5 whom God has graciously **g** your
38:14 and she was not **g** to him as a
43:23 the God of your father has **g**
48: 9 whom God has **g** me in this
48:22 Moreover I have **g** to you one
Ex 5:16 There is no straw **g** to your
5:18 for no straw shall be **g** you,
12:36 And the LORD had **g** the people
16:15 the bread which the LORD has **g**
16:29 See! For the LORD has **g** you the
21: 4 If his master has **g** him a wife,
Lev 6:17 I have **g** it as their portion
7:34 and I have **g** them to Aaron the
7:36 LORD commanded this to be **g**
10:14 which are **g** from the
10:17 and God has **g** it to you to
17:11 and I have **g** it to you upon the
19:20 not at all been redeemed nor **g**
20: 3 because he has **g** some of his
Num 3: 9 they are **g** entirely to him
8:16 For they are wholly **g** to Me
8:19 And I have **g** the Levites as a
16:14 nor **g** us inheritance of fields
18: 6 **g** by the LORD, to do the work
18: 8 I Myself have also **g** you charge
18: 8 I have **g** them as a portion to
18:11 I have **g** them to you, and your
18:12 I have **g** them to you.
18:19 I have **g** to you and your sons
18:21 I have **g** the children of Levi
18:24 I have **g** to the Levites as an
18:26 the tithes which I have **g** you
20:12 into the land which I have **g**
20:24 enter the land which I have **g**
21:29 O people of Chemosh! He has **g**
26:54 Each shall be **g** its inheritance
26:62 there was no inheritance **g** to
27:12 see the land which I have **g** to
32: 5 let this land be **g** to your
32: 7 the land which the LORD has **g**
32: 9 the land which the LORD had **g**
33:53 for I have **g** you the land to
Deut 1: 3 to all that the LORD had **g**
2: 5 because I have **g** Mount Seir to
2: 9 because I have **g** Ar to the
2:19 because I have **g** it to the
2:24 I have **g** into your hand Sihon
3:18 The LORD your God has **g** you
3:19 in your cities which I have **g**
3:20 until the LORD has **g** rest to
3:20 his possession which I have **g**
4:19 which the LORD your God has **g**
8:10 the good land which He has **g**
9:23 the land which I have **g** you,
12:15 LORD your God which He has **g**
12:21 flock which the LORD has **g**
16:17 LORD your God which He has **g**
25:19 when the LORD your God has **g**
26: 9 us to this place and has **g** us
26:10 have **g** me.' Then you shall set
26:11 which the LORD your God has **g**
26:12 and have **g** it to the Levite,
26:13 and also have **g** them to the
26:14 nor **g** any of it for the dead.
26:15 and the land which You have **g**
28:31 your sheep shall be **g** to your
28:32 your daughters shall be **g** to
28:52 which the LORD your God has **g**

28:53 whom the LORD your God has *g*
29: 4 Yet the LORD has not *g* you a
29:26 not know and that He had not *g*
Josh 1: 3 foot will tread upon I have *g*
1:15 until the LORD has *g* your
2: 9 I know that the LORD has *g* you
2:14 when the LORD has *g* us the
6: 2 See! I have *g* Jericho into your
6:16 for the LORD has *g* you the
8: 1 I have *g* into your hand the
12: 6 the servant of the LORD had *g*
13: 8 which Moses had *g* them, beyond
13: 8 the servant of the LORD had *g*
13:14 to the tribe of Levi he had *g*
13:15 And Moses had *g* to the tribe of
13:24 Moses also had *g* an
13:29 Moses also had *g* an
13:33 the tribe of Levi Moses had *g*
14: 3 For Moses had *g* the inheritance
14: 3 but to the Levites he had *g* no
15:19 since you have *g* me land in the
17: 1 therefore he was *g* Gilead and
17:14 Why have you *g* us only one lot
18: 3 God of your fathers has *g* you?
22: 4 now the LORD your God has *g*
22: 7 tribe of Manasseh Moses had *g*
23: 1 long time after the LORD had *g*
23:13 which the LORD your God has *g*
23:15 which the LORD your God has *g*
23:16 the good land which He has *g*
24:13 I have *g* you a land for which
24:33 which was *g* to him in the
Judg 1:15 since you have *g* me land in the
11:35 who trouble me! For I have *g*
11:36 if you have *g* your word to the
14:20 And Samson's wife was *g* to his
15: 6 he has taken his wife and *g*
15:18 You have *g* this great
18:10 For God has *g* it into your
20:36 The men of Israel had *g* ground
21:22 is not as though you have *g*
Ruth 2:12 and a full reward be *g* you by
1 Sam 2:20 woman for the loan that was *g*
15:28 and has *g* it to a neighbor of
18:19 should have been *g* to David,
18:19 that she was *g* to Adriel the
22:13 in that you have *g* him bread
25:27 let it be *g* to the young men
25:44 But Saul had *g* Michal his
28:17 kingdom out of your hand and *g*
30:23 do so with what the LORD has *g*
2 Sam 2:27 all the people would have *g* up
7: 1 and the LORD had *g* him rest
9: 9 I have *g* to your master's son
12: 8 I also would have *g* you much
12:14 by this deed you have *g* great
17: 7 advice that Ahithophel has *g*
18:11 I would have *g* you ten shekels
19:42 Or has he *g* us any gift?"
22:36 You have also *g* me the shield of
22:41 You have also *g* me the necks of
24:23 Araunah has *g* to the king."
1 Ki 1:48 who has *g* one to sit on my
2:21 Abishag the Shunammite be *g* to
3: 6 and You have *g* him a son to sit
3:12 I have *g* you a wise and
3:13 And I have also *g* you what you
3:18 the third day after I had *g*
5: 4 But now the LORD my God has *g*
5: 7 for He has *g* David a wise son
8:36 on Your land which You have *g*
8:56 who has *g* rest to His people
9: 7 from the land which I have *g*
9:12 the cities which Solomon had *g*
9:13 are these which you have *g* me,
9:16 and had *g* it as a dowry to his
10:13 besides what Solomon had *g* her
12: 8 advice which the elders had *g*
12:13 advice which the elders had *g*
13: 5 which the man of God had *g* by
18:26 they took the bull which was *g*
20:27 of Israel were mustered and *g*
2 Ki 5: 1 because by him the LORD had *g*
5:17 please let your servant be *g*
18:30 this city shall not be *g* into
19:10 Jerusalem shall not be *g* into
22:10 Hilkiah the priest has *g* me a
25:30 there was a regular ration *g*
1 Chr 5: 1 his birthright was *g* to the
6:54 for they were *g* by lot to the
6:66 of the sons of Kohath were *g*
6:71 the sons of Gershon were *g*
6:77 the children of Merari were *g*
6:78 they were *g* from the tribe
22:18 And has He not *g* you rest on
22:18 For He has *g* the inhabitants of
23:25 The LORD God of Israel has *g*
28: 5 my sons (for the LORD has *g*
29: 3 I have *g* to the house of my
29:14 And of Your own we have *g* You.
2 Chr 2:12 for He has *g* King David a wise
2:14 any plan which may be *g* to him,
6:27 on Your land which You have *g*
7:20 from My land which I have *g*
8: 2 the cities which Hiram had *g*
10: 8 advice which the elders had *g*
14: 6 because the LORD had *g* him
14: 7 and He has *g* us rest on every
20:11 possession which You have *g* us
24:10 into the chest until all had *g*.
25: 9 hundred talents which I have *g*
29: 8 and He has *g* them up to
32:29 for God had *g* him very much
34:14 of the Law of the LORD *g* by
34:18 Hilkiah the priest has *g* me a
36:23 the LORD God of heaven has *g*
Ezra 1: 2 the LORD God of heaven has *g*
4:21 be built until the command is *g*
5:14 and they were *g* to one named
6: 8 this is to be *g* immediately to
6: 9 let it be *g* them day by day
7: 6 the LORD God of Israel had *g*.
7:19 Also the articles that are *g* to
9:13 and have *g* us such deliverance
Neh 2: 7 let letters be *g* to me for the
10:29 which was *g* by Moses the
13: 5 were commanded to be *g* to
13:10 for the Levites had not been *g*
Esth 2: 3 let beauty preparations be *g*
2:13 and she was *g* whatever she
3:11 money and the people are *g* to
4: 8 which was *g* at Shushan, that he
5: 3 It shall be *g* to you—up to half
7: 3 let my life be *g* me at my
8: 7 I have *g* Esther the house of
Job 3:20 Why is light *g* to him who is in
3:23 Why is light *g* to a man
9:24 The earth is *g* into the hand of
15:19 To whom alone the land was *g*,
22: 7 You have not *g* the weary water
37:10 By the breath of God ice is *g*,
38:36 Or who has *g* understanding to
39:19 Have you *g* the horse strength?
Ps 16: 7 will bless the LORD who has *g*
18:35 You have also *g* me the shield
18:40 You have also *g* me the necks of
21: 2 You have *g* him his heart's
44:11 You have *g* us up like sheep
60: 4 You have *g* a banner to those
61: 5 You have *g* me the heritage of
71: 3 You have *g* the commandment to
72:15 the gold of Sheba will be *g* to
78:24 And *g* them of the bread of
78:63 And their maidens were not *g*
79: 2 of Your servants They have *g*
80: 5 And *g* them tears to drink in
89:19 I have *g* help to one who is
111: 5 He has *g* food to those who fear
112: 9 He has *g* to the poor;
115:16 But the earth He has *g* to the
118:18 But He has not *g* me over to
118:27 And He has *g* us light;
119:50 For Your word has *g* me life.
119:93 For by them You have *g* me
120: 3 What shall be *g* to you,
124: 6 Who has not *g* us as prey to
Prov 19:17 He will pay back what he has *g*.
23: 2 throat If you are a man *g* to
24:21 Do not associate with those *g*
Eccl 1:13 this burdensome task God has *g*
5:19 for every man to whom God has *g*
5:19 and *g* him power to eat of it,
6: 2 A man to whom God has *g* riches
8: 8 not deliver those who are *g* to
9: 9 your vain life which He has *g*
12:11 *g* by one Shepherd.
Isa 3:11 reward of his hands shall be *g*
8:18 children whom the LORD has *g*
9: 6 is born, Unto us a Son is *g*;
23:11 The LORD has *g* a commandment
33:16 Bread will be *g* him,
34: 2 He has *g* them over to the
35: 2 glory of Lebanon shall be *g* to
36:15 this city will not be *g* into
37:10 Jerusalem shall not be *g* into
47: 6 And *g* them into your hand.
47: 8 you who are *g* to pleasures,
50: 4 The Lord GOD has *g* Me
55: 4 Indeed I have *g* him as a
Jer 3: 8 I had put her away and *g* her a
3:18 to the land that I have *g* as
6:13 Everyone is *g* to
8:10 to the greatest Everyone is *g*
8:13 And the things I have *g* them
8:14 has put us to silence And *g*
12: 7 I have *g* the dearly beloved of
13:20 is the flock that was *g* to
21:10 It shall be *g* into the hand of
25: 5 the land that the LORD has *g*
27: 5 and have *g* it to whom it seemed
27: 6 And now I have *g* all these lands
27: 6 of the field I have also *g* him
28:14 I have *g* him the beasts of the
32:22 'You have *g* them this land,
32:24 and the city has been *g* into
32:25 yet the city has been *g* into the
32:43 it has been *g* into the hand of
35:15 in the land which I have *g* you
38: 3 This city shall surely be *g* into
38:18 then this city shall be *g* into
39:17 and you shall not be *g* into the
44:20 and all the people who had *g*
47: 7 Seeing the LORD has *g* it a
50:15 She has *g* her hand,
52:34 there was a regular ration *g*
Lam 1:11 They have *g* their valuables
2: 7 He has *g* up the walls of her
5: 6 We have *g* our hand to the
Ezek 11:15 this land has been *g* to us as a
15: 6 which I have *g* to the fire for
16:17 which I had *g* you, and made for
16:34 payment but no payment was *g*
18: 7 But has *g* his bread to the
18:16 But has *g* his bread to the
20:15 into the land which I had *g*
21:11 And He has *g* it to be polished,
21:11 and it is polished To be *g*
23: 8 She has never *g* up her harlotry
29: 5 I have *g* you as food To the
29:20 I have *g* him the land of Egypt
33:24 the land has been *g* to us as a
35:12 they are *g* to us to consume.'
37:25 in the land that I have *g* to
45:15 And one lamb shall be *g* from a
47:11 they will be *g* over to salt.
Dan 2:23 You have *g* me wisdom and
2:37 For the God of heaven has *g* you
2:38 He has *g* them into your hand,
4:16 Let him be *g* the heart of a
5:28 and *g* to the Medes and
7: 4 and a man's heart was *g* to it.
7: 6 and dominion was *g* to it.
7:11 and its body destroyed and *g* to
7:14 Then to Him was *g* dominion and
7:25 Then the saints shall be *g*
7:27 Shall be *g* to the people, the
8:12 an army was *g* over to the
11: 6 but she shall be *g* up, with
11:11 but the multitude shall be *g*
Hos 2: 9 *G* to cover her nakedness.
2:12 my wages that my lovers have *g*
12:10 I have *g* symbols through the
Joel 2:23 For He has *g* you the former
3: 3 Have *g* a boy as payment for
Am 9:15 up From the land I have *g*
Mic 5: 3 that she who is in labor has *g*
Nah 1:14 The LORD has *g* a command
Zech 6: 8 the north country have *g* rest
Mt 7: 7 and it will be *g* to you;
9: 8 who had *g* such power to men.
10:19 For it will be *g* to you in that
12:39 and no sign will be *g* to it
13:11 Because it has been *g* to you to
13:11 but to them it has not been *g*.
13:12 has, to him more will be *g*,
14: 9 he commanded it to be *g* to
14:11 was brought on a platter and *g*
16: 4 and no sign shall be *g* to it
19:11 those to whom it has been *g*:
21:43 will be taken from you and *g*
22:30 they neither marry nor are *g*
25:29 who has, more will be *g*,
26: 9 have been sold for much and *g*
26:48 Now His betrayer had *g* them a
27:58 commanded the body to be *g* to
28:18 All authority has been *g* to Me
Mk 4:11 To you it has been *g* to know the
4:24 to you who hear, more will be *g*.
4:25 has, to him more will be *g*;
5:43 that something should be *g*
6: 2 wisdom is this which is *g* to
8:12 no sign shall be *g* to this
12:25 they neither marry nor are *g* in
12:43 more than all those who have *g*
13:11 But whatever is *g* you in that
14: 5 three hundred denarii and *g* to
14:23 and when He had *g* thanks He
14:44 Now His betrayer had *g* them a
Lk 2:21 the name *g* by the angel before
6:38 and it will be *g* to you:
8:10 To you it has been *g* to know the
8:10 but to the rest it is *g* in
8:18 has, to him more will be *g*;
8:55 And He commanded that she be *g*
11: 9 and it will be *g* to you;
11:29 and no sign will be *g* to it
12:48 For everyone to whom much is *g*,
17:27 they were *g* in marriage, until
19:15 to whom he had *g* the money, to
19:26 to everyone who has will be *g*;
20:34 of this age marry and are *g* in
20:35 neither marry nor are *g* in
22:19 This is My body which is *g* for
Jn 1:17 For the law was *g* through Moses,
3:27 nothing unless it has been *g*
3:35 and has *g* all things into His
4:10 and He would have *g* you living
5:27 and has *g* Him authority to
5:36 works which the Father has *g*
6:11 and when He had *g* thanks He
6:23 ate bread after the Lord had *g*
6:39 that of all He has *g* Me I
7:39 the Holy Spirit was not yet *g*,
10:29 who has *g* them to Me, is
11:57 and the Pharisees had *g* a
12: 5 three hundred denarii and *g* to
13: 3 knowing that the Father had *g*
13:15 For I have *g* you an example,
16:21 but as soon as she has *g* birth
17: 2 as You have *g* Him authority over
17: 2 life to as many as You have *g*
17: 4 the work which You have *g* Me
17: 6 to the men whom You have *g* Me
17: 7 all things which You have *g* Me
17: 8 For I have *g* to them the words
17: 8 the words which You have *g* Me;
17: 9 but for those whom You have *g*
17:11 name those whom You have *g* Me,
17:14 I have *g* them Your word; and the
17:22 which You gave Me I have *g*
17:24 My glory which You have *g* Me;
18:11 the cup which My Father has *g*
19:11 Me unless it had been *g* you
Acts 1: 2 through the Holy Spirit had *g*
3:16 which comes through Him has *g*
4:12 is no other name under heaven *g*

5:32 the Holy Spirit whom God has **g**
8:18 hands the Holy Spirit was **g**,
17:16 when he saw that the city was **g**
17:31 He has **g** assurance of this to
20:13 for so he had **g** orders,
21:40 So when he had **g** him permission,
24:26 hoped that money would be **g**
27:20 we would be saved was finally **g**
Rom 5: 5 by the Holy Spirit who was **g**
11: 8 God has **g** them a spirit of
11:35 Or who has first **g** to Him
12: 3 through the grace **g** to me, to
12: 6 to the grace that is **g** to us,
12:13 **g** to hospitality.
15:15 because of the grace **g** to me by
1 Cor 1: 4 the grace of God which was **g**
2:12 things that have been freely **g**
3:10 to the grace of God which was **g**
11:15 for her hair is **g** to her for a
11:24 and when He had **g** thanks, He
12: 7 of the Spirit is **g** to each one
12: 8 for to one is **g** the word of
12:24 having **g** greater honor to that
16: 1 as I have **g** orders to the
2 Cor 1:11 that thanks may be **g** by many
1:22 who also has sealed us and **g** us
5: 5 who also has **g** us the Spirit as
5:18 and has **g** us the ministry of
9: 9 He has **g** to the poor;
12: 7 a thorn in the flesh was **g** to
13:10 authority which the Lord has **g**
Gal 2: 9 the grace that had been **g** to
3:21 For if there had been a law **g**
3:21 a law given which could have **g**
3:22 in Jesus Christ might be **g** to
4:15 out your own eyes and **g** them
Eph 3: 2 of the grace of God which was **g**
3: 7 the gift of the grace of God **g**
3: 8 the saints, this grace was **g**,
4: 7 to each one of us grace was **g**
4:19 have **g** themselves over to
5: 2 Christ also has loved us and **g**
6:19 that utterance may be **g** to me,
Phil 2: 9 has highly exalted Him and **g**
Col 1:25 from God which was **g** to me for
1 Th 4: 8 who has also **g** us His Holy
2 Th 2:16 who has loved us and **g** us
1 Tim 3: 3 not **g** to wine, not violent, not
3: 8 not **g** to much wine, not greedy
4:14 which was **g** to you by prophecy
2 Tim 1: 7 For God has not **g** us a spirit of
1: 9 purpose and grace which was **g**
3:16 All Scripture is **g** by
Titus 1: 7 not **g** to wine, not violent, not
2: 3 not **g** to much wine, teachers of
Heb 2:13 children whom God has **g**
4: 8 For if Joshua had **g** them rest,
Jas 1: 5 and it will be **g** to him.
2 Pe 1: 3 as His divine power has **g** to us
1: 4 by which have been **g** to us
3:15 according to the wisdom **g** to
1 Jn 3:24 by the Spirit whom He has **g** us.
4:13 because He has **g** us of His
5:10 the testimony that God has **g**
5:11 that God has **g** us eternal life,
5:20 Son of God has come and has **g**
Jude 7 having **g** themselves over to
Rev 6: 2 and a crown was **g** to him, and
6: 4 and there was **g** to him a great
6: 8 And power was **g** to them over a
6:11 Then a white robe was **g** to each
8: 2 and to them were **g** seven
8: 3 He was **g** much incense, that he
9: 1 To him was **g** the key to the
9: 3 And to them was **g** power, as the
9: 5 And they were not **g** authority
11: 1 Then I was **g** a reed like a
11: 2 for it has been **g** to the
12:14 But the woman was **g** two wings of
13: 5 And he was **g** a mouth speaking
13: 5 and he was **g** authority to
13: 7 And authority was **g** him over
16: 6 And You have **g** them blood to
16: 8 and power was **g** to him to

GIVER (1/1) GIVE

2 Cor 9: 7 for God loves a cheerful **g**.

GIVES (111/105) GIVE

Ex 13:11 and **g** it to you,
16: 8 be seen when the LORD **g** you
16:29 therefore He **g** you on the sixth
21:22 so that she **g** birth
25: 2 From everyone who **g** it
Lev 20: 2 who **g** any of his descendants
20: 4 when he **g** some of his
27: 9 all that anyone **g** to the LORD
Num 5:10 whatever any man **g** the priest
Deut 8:18 for it is He who **g** you power
12:10 and He **g** you rest from all your
13: 1 and he **g** you a sign or a
13:12 which the LORD your God **g** you
16: 5 which the LORD your God **g** you;
16:18 which the LORD your God **g** you,
17: 2 which the LORD your God **g** you,
19: 8 and **g** you the land which He
20:14 which the LORD your God **g** you.
20:16 which the LORD your God **g** you
Judg 11:24 whatever Chemosh your god **g**
21:18 Cursed be the one who **g** a wife
Job 5:10 He **g** rain on the earth,
19:16 but he **g** no answer; I beg him
24:23 He **g** them security, and they
32: 8 the breath of the Almighty **g**
33: 4 the breath of the Almighty **g**
34:29 When He **g** quietness, who then
35:10 Who **g** songs in the night,
36: 6 But **g** justice to the
36:31 He **g** food in abundance.
38:29 who **g** it birth?
39: 1 can you mark when the deer **g**
Ps 18:50 Great deliverance He **g** to His
37:21 the righteous shows mercy and **g**.
68:35 The God of Israel is He who **g**
119:130 The entrance of Your words **g**
119:130 It **g** understanding to the
127: 2 For so He **g** His beloved
136:25 Who **g** food to all flesh,
144:10 The One who **g** salvation to
146: 7 Who **g** food to the hungry.
146: 7 The LORD **g** freedom to the
147: 9 He **g** to the beast its food,
147:16 He **g** snow like wool;
Prov 2: 6 For the LORD **g** wisdom;
3:34 But **g** grace to the humble.
17: 4 An evildoer **g** heed to false
19: 6 man is a friend to one who **g**
21:26 But the righteous **g** and does
22: 9 For he **g** of his bread to the
22:16 And he who **g** to the rich,
24:26 He who **g** a right answer kisses
26: 8 stone in a sling Is he who **g**
26:10 God who formed everything **G**
27: 9 sweetness of a man's friend **g**
28:27 He who **g** to the poor will not
29:13 The LORD **g** light to the eyes
Eccl 2:26 For God **g** wisdom and knowledge
2:26 but to the sinner He **g** the work
5:18 days of his life which God **g**
7:12 of knowledge is that wisdom **g**
8:15 days of his life which God **g**
Isa 14: 3 to pass in the day the LORD **g**
30:20 And though the Lord **g** you The
40:29 He **g** power to the weak, And to
42: 5 Who **g** breath to the people on
Jer 5:24 Who **g** rain, both the former
22:13 service without wages And **g**
31:35 Who **g** the sun for a light by
Ezek 33:15 **g** back what he has stolen, and
46:16 If the prince **g** a gift of some
46:17 But if he **g** a gift of some of
Dan 2:21 He **g** wisdom to the wise And
4:17 **G** it to whomever He will,
4:25 and **g** it to whomever He
4:32 and **g** it to whomever He
Joel 2:11 The LORD **g** voice before His
Am 6:11 the LORD **g** a command: He will
Hab 2:15 Woe to him who **g** drink to his
Mt 5:15 and it **g** light to all who are
10:42 And whoever **g** one of these
Mk 9:41 For whoever **g** you a cup of water
Lk 11:36 the bright shining of a lamp **g**
Jn 1: 9 That was the true Light which **g**
5:21 Father raises the dead and **g**
5:21 even so the Son **g** life to whom
6:32 but My Father **g** you the true
6:33 comes down from heaven and **g**
6:37 All that the Father **g** Me will
6:63 'It is the Spirit who **g** life;
10:11 The good shepherd **g** His life
14:27 not as the world **g** do I give to
Acts 17:25 since He **g** to all life, breath,
Rom 4:17 who **g** life to the dead and
12: 8 in exhortation; he who **g**,
14: 6 for he **g** God thanks; and he who
14: 6 and **g** God thanks.
1 Cor 3: 7 but God who **g** the increase.
7:38 So then he who **g** her in
15:38 But God **g** it a body as He
15:57 who **g** us the victory through
2 Cor 3: 6 but the Spirit **g** life.
Gal 4:24 one from Mount Sinai which **g**
1 Tim 6:13 you in the sight of God who **g**
6:17 who **g** us richly all things to
Jas 1: 5 who **g** to all liberally and
1:15 it **g** birth to sin; and sin,
4: 6 But He **g** more grace.
4: 6 But **g** grace to the
1 Pe 5: 5 But **g** grace to the
Rev 22: 5 for the Lord God **g** them light.

GIVING (81/80) GIVE

Gen 24:19 And when she had finished **g** him
38:27 at the time for **g** birth, that
38:28 when she was **g** birth, that the
Ex 20:12 which the LORD your God is **g**
Num 13: 2 which I am **g** to the children of
15: 2 which I am **g** to you,
Deut 1:20 which the LORD our God is **g**
1:25 which the LORD our God is **g**
1:36 to him and his children I am **g**
2:29 which the LORD our God is **g**
3:20 which the LORD your God is **g**
4: 1 LORD God of your fathers is **g**
4:21 which the LORD your God is **g**
4:40 which the LORD your God is **g**
5:16 which the LORD your God is **g**
5:31 them in the land which I am **g**
9: 6 the LORD your God is not **g**
10:18 **g** him food and clothing.
11:17 good land which the LORD is **g**
11:31 which the LORD your God is **g**
12: 1 LORD God of your fathers is **g**
12: 9 which the LORD your God is **g**
12:10 which the LORD your God is **g**
15: 4 which the LORD your God is **g**
15: 7 which the LORD your God is **g**
16:20 which the LORD your God is **g**
17:14 which the LORD your God is **g**
18: 9 which the LORD your God is **g**
19: 1 land the LORD your God is **g**
19: 2 which the LORD your God is **g**
19: 3 which the LORD your God is **g**
19:10 which the LORD your God is **g**
19:14 that the LORD your God is **g**
21: 1 which the LORD your God is **g**
21:17 wife as the firstborn by **g**
21:23 which the LORD your God is **g**
24: 4 which the LORD your God is **g**
25:15 which the LORD your God is **g**
25:19 which the LORD your God is **g**
26: 1 which the LORD your God is **g**
26: 2 that the LORD your God is **g**
27: 2 which the LORD your God is **g**
27: 3 which the LORD your God is **g**
28: 8 which the LORD your God is **g**
32:52 into the land which I am **g** to
Josh 1: 2 to the land which I am **g** to
1:11 which the LORD your God is **g**
1:13 The LORD your God is **g** you rest
1:13 God is giving you rest and is **g**
1:15 which the LORD your God is **g**
Judg 9: 9 'Should I cease **g** my oil,
Ruth 1: 6 had visited His people by **g**
1 Ki 5: 9 shall fulfill my desire by **g**
8:32 justifying the righteous by **g**
1 Chr 23: 5 said David, "for **g** praise."
2 Chr 6:23 justifying the righteous by **g**
Ezra 3:11 praising and **g** thanks to the
Ps 111: 6 In **g** them the heritage of the
Prov 25:14 Whoever falsely boasts of **g**
Ezek 4:15 I am **g** you cow dung instead of
Dan 8:13 the **g** of both the sanctuary and
Mt 24:38 marrying and **g** in marriage,
Lk 17:16 **g** Him thanks. And he was a
Acts 15: 8 acknowledged them by **g** them the
Rom 4:20 in faith, **g** glory to God,
9: 4 the **g** of the law, the service
12:10 in honor **g** preference to one
1 Cor 11:17 Now in **g** these instructions I
14:16 Amen" at your **g** of thanks,
Eph 5: 4 but rather **g** of thanks.
5:20 **g** thanks always for all things
6: 9 **g** up threatening, knowing that
Phil 4:15 shared with me concerning **g**
Col 1:12 **g** thanks to the Father who has
3:17 **g** thanks to God the Father
1 Tim 2: 1 and **g** of thanks be made for
4: 1 **g** heed to deceiving spirits and
Titus 1:14 not **g** heed to Jewish fables and
Heb 13:15 **g** thanks to His name.
1 Pe 3: 7 **g** honor to the wife, as to the
2 Pe 1: 5 **g** all diligence, add to your

GIZONITE (1/1)

1 Chr 11:34 the sons of Hashem the **G**,

GLAD (91/91) GLADLY, GLADNESS

Ex 4:14 he will be **g** in his heart.
Judg 18:20 So the priest's heart was **g**;
19: 3 he was **g** to meet him.
1 Sam 11: 9 men of Jabesh, and they were **g**.
1 Ki 8:66 to their tents joyful and **g** of
1 Chr 16:31 rejoice, and let the earth be **g**;
2 Chr 7:10 joyful and **g** of heart for the
Esth 5: 9 that day joyful and with a **g**
8:15 of Shushan rejoiced and was **g**.
Job 3:22 And are **g** when they can find
22:19 righteous see it and are **g**,
Ps 9: 2 I will be **g** and rejoice in You;
14: 7 Jacob rejoice and Israel be **g**.
16: 9 Therefore my heart is **g**,
21: 6 have made him exceedingly **g**
31: 7 I will be **g** and rejoice in Your
32:11 Be **g** in the LORD and rejoice,
34: 2 shall hear of it and be **g**.
35:27 them shout for joy and be **g**,
40:16 who seek You rejoice and be **g**
45: 8 by which they have made You **g**.
46: 4 whose streams shall make **g** the
48:11 the daughters of Judah be **g**,
53: 6 Jacob rejoice and Israel be **g**.
64:10 The righteous shall be **g** in the
67: 4 let the nations be **g** and sing
68: 3 But let the righteous be **g**;
69:32 shall see this and be **g**;
70: 4 who seek You rejoice and be **g**
90:14 That we may rejoice and be **g**
90:15 Make us **g** according to the days
92: 4 have made me **g** through Your
96:11 rejoice, and let the earth be **g**;
97: 1 the multitude of isles be **g**!
97: 8 Zion hears and is **g**,
104:15 And wine that makes **g** the
104:34 I will be **g** in the LORD.
105:38 Egypt was **g** when they departed,
107:30 Then they are **g** because they
118:24 We will rejoice and be **g** in
119:74 Those who fear You will be **g**
122: 1 I was **g** when they said to me,
126: 3 things for us, And we are **g**.

Prov 10: 1 A wise son makes a *g* father,
12:25 But a good word makes it *g*.
15:20 A wise son makes a father *g*,
17: 5 He who is *g* at calamity will
23:25 father and your mother be *g*,
24:17 And do not let your heart be *g*
27:11 be wise, and make my heart *g*,
Song 1: 4 We will be *g* and rejoice
Isa 25: 9 We will be *g* and rejoice in
35: 1 and the wasteland shall be *g*
52: 7 Who brings *g* tidings of good
65:18 But be *g* and rejoice forever in
66:10 And be *g* with her, all you who
Jer 20:15 to you!" Making him very *g*.
41:13 with him, that they were *g*.
50:11 "Because you were *g*,
Lam 1:21 They are *g* that You have done
4:21 Rejoice and be *g*,
Dan 6:23 the king was exceedingly *g* for
Hos 7: 3 They make a king *g* with their
Joel 2:21 Be *g* and rejoice, For the
2:23 Be *g* then, you children of
Hab 1:15 they rejoice and are *g*.
Zeph 3:14 O Israel! Be *g* and rejoice
Zech 10: 7 children shall see it and be *g*;
Mt 5:12 "Rejoice and be exceedingly *g*,
Mk 14:11 they heard it, they were *g*,
Lk 1:19 to you and bring you these *g*
8: 1 preaching and bringing the *g*
15:32 we should make merry and be *g*,
22: 5 And they were *g*,
23: 8 saw Jesus, he was exceedingly *g*;
Jn 8:56 day, and he saw it and was *g*.
11:15 And I am *g* for your sakes that I
20:20 Then the disciples were *g* when
Acts 2:26 and my tongue was *g*;
11:23 seen the grace of God, he was *g*,
13:32 And we declare to you *g*
13:48 they were *g* and glorified the
Rom 10:15 Who bring *g* tidings of
16:19 Therefore I am *g* on your
1 Cor 16:17 I am *g* about the coming of
2 Cor 2: 2 then who is he who makes me *g*
13: 9 For we are *g* when we are weak
Phil 2:17 I am *g* and rejoice with you
2:18 the same reason you also be *g*
1 Pe 4:13 you may also be *g* with
Rev 19: 7 Let us be *g* and rejoice and give

GLADLY (9/9) GLAD

Judg 8:25 We will *g* give them." And they
Mk 6:20 many things, and heard him *g*.
12:37 the common people heard Him *g*.
Lk 15:16 And he would *g* have filled his
Acts 2:41 Then those who *g* received his
21:17 the brethren received us *g*.
2 Cor 11:19 For you put up with fools *g*,
12: 9 Therefore most *g* I will
12:15 And I will very *g* spend and be

GLADNESS (48/48) GLAD

Num 10:10 "Also in the day of your *g*,
Deut 28:47 LORD your God with joy and *g*
2 Sam 6:12 to the City of David with *g*.
1 Chr 16:27 Strength and *g* are in His
29:22 before the LORD with great *g*
2 Chr 29:30 So they sang praises with *g*,
30:21 Bread seven days with great *g*;
30:23 it another seven days with *g*.
Neh 8:17 And there was very great *g*.
12:27 celebrate the dedication with *g*,
Esth 8:16 The Jews had light and *g*,
8:17 came, the Jews had joy and *g*,
9:17 made it a day of feasting and *g*.
9:18 made it a day of feasting and *g*.
9:19 of the month of Adar with *g*
Ps 4: 7 You have put *g* in my heart,
30:11 sackcloth and clothed me with *g*,
45: 7 You With the oil of *g* more
45:15 With *g* and rejoicing they shall
51: 8 Make me hear joy and *g*,
97:11 And *g* for the upright in
100: 2 Serve the LORD with *g*;
105:43 joy, His chosen ones with *g*.
106: 5 That I may rejoice in the *g* of
Prov 10:28 of the righteous will be *g*,
Song 3:11 The day of the *g* of his heart.
Isa 16:10 *G* is taken away, And joy from
22:13 But instead, joy and *g*,
30:29 And *g* of heart as when one
35:10 They shall obtain joy and *g*,
51: 3 Joy and *g* will be found in it,
51:11 They shall obtain joy and *g*;
Jer 7:34 of mirth and the voice of *g*,
16: 9 of mirth and the voice of *g*,
25:10 of mirth and the voice of *g*,
31: 7 'Sing with *g* for Jacob,
33:11 voice of joy and the voice of *g*,
48:33 Joy and *g* are taken From the
Joel 1:16 Joy and *g* from the house of
Zeph 3:17 will rejoice over you with *g*,
Zech 8:19 Shall be joy and *g* and
Mk 4:16 immediately receive it with *g*;
Lk 1:14 "And you will have joy and *g*,
Acts 2:46 they ate their food with *g* and
12:14 because of her *g* she did not
14:17 our hearts with food and *g*.
Phil 2:29 in the Lord with all *g*,
Heb 1: 9 You With the oil of *g*

GLASS (5/4)

Rev 4: 6 throne there was a sea of *g*,
15: 2 saw something like a sea of *g*
15: 2 name, standing on the sea of *g*,
21:18 was pure gold, like clear *g*.
21:21 pure gold, like transparent *g*.

GLASSES (KJV) See MIRRORS

GLAZED (1/1)

1 Ki 14: 4 for his eyes were *g* by reason

GLEAN (12/11) GLEANED, GLEANING

Lev 19:10 And you shall not *g* your
Deut 24:21 you shall not *g* it afterward;
Ruth 2: 2 and *g* heads of grain after him
2: 7 Please let me *g* and gather after
2: 8 Do not go to *g* in another
2:15 And when she rose up to *g*,
2:15 Let her *g* even among the
2:16 leave it that she may *g*,
2:23 to *g* until the end of barley
Job 24: 6 fodder in the field And *g* in
Jer 6: 9 They shall thoroughly *g* as a
Mic 7: 1 Like those who *g* vintage

GLEANED (5/4) GLEAN

Ruth 2: 3 and went and *g* in the field
2:17 So she *g* in the field until
2:17 and beat out what she had *g*,
2:18 saw what she had *g*.
2:19 'Where have you *g* today?

GLEANING (5/5) GLEAN

Lev 23:22 nor shall you gather any *g* from
Judg 8: 2 Is not the *g* of the grapes
Isa 17: 6 Yet *g* grapes will be left in
24:13 Like the *g* of grapes when the
Jer 49: 9 Would they not leave some *g*

GLEANINGS (2/2)

Lev 19: 9 nor shall you gather the *g* of
Ob 5 they not have left some *g*?

GLISTENING (2/2)

1 Chr 29: 2 *g* stones of various colors, all
Lk 9:29 His robe became white and *g*.

GLITTERING (5/5)

Deut 32:41 If I whet My *g* sword, And My
Job 20:25 the *g* point comes out of his
39:23 The *g* spear and javelin.
Nah 3: 3 charge with bright sword and *g*
Hab 3:11 At the shining of Your *g*

GLOOM (3/3) GLOOMINESS

Isa 8:22 *g* of anguish; and they will
9: 1 Nevertheless the *g* will not
Jas 4: 9 to mourning and your joy to *g*.

GLOOMINESS (2/2) GLOOM

Joel 2: 2 A day of darkness and *g*,
Zeph 1:15 A day of darkness and *g*,

GLORIES (4/4) GLORY

Jer 9:24 But let him who *g* glory in
1 Cor 1:31 as it is written, "He who *g*,
2 Cor 10:17 But "he who *g*,
1 Pe 1:11 sufferings of Christ and the *g*

GLORIFIED (48/47) GLORIFY

Lev 10: 3 all the people I must be *g*.
Isa 26:15 the nation; You are *g*;
44:23 And *g* Himself in Israel.
49: 3 O Israel, In whom I will be *g*.
55: 5 For He has *g* you."
60: 9 Because He has *g* you.
60:21 of My hands, That I may be *g*.
61: 3 of the LORD, that He may be *g*.
66: 5 said, 'Let the LORD be *g*,
Ezek 28:22 I will be *g* in your midst;
39:13 for it on the day that I am *g*,
Dan 5:23 all your ways, you have not *g*.
Hag 1: 8 take pleasure in it and be *g*,
Mt 9: 8 they marveled and *g* God, who
15:31 and they *g* the God of Israel.
Mk 2:12 so that all were amazed and *g*
Lk 4:15 synagogues, being *g* by all.
5:26 and they *g* God and were filled
7:16 and they *g* God, saying,
13:13 was made straight, and *g* God.
17:15 and with a loud voice *g* God,
23:47 he *g* God, saying, "Certainly
Jn 7:39 because Jesus was not yet *g*.
11: 4 that the Son of God may be *g*
12:16 at first; but when Jesus was *g*,
12:23 that the Son of Man should be *g*.
12:28 I have both *g* it and will
13:31 said, "Now the Son of Man is *g*,
13:31 and God is *g* in Him.
13:32 If God is *g* in Him, God will
14:13 that the Father may be *g* in the
15: 8 "By this My Father is *g*,
17: 4 I have *g* You on the earth. I
17:10 and I am *g* in them.
Acts 3:13 *g* His Servant Jesus, whom you
4:21 since they all *g* God for what
11:18 and they *g* God, saying, "Then
13:48 they were glad and *g* the word
21:20 they *g* the Lord. And they said
Rom 8:17 that we may also be *g* together.
8:30 He justified, these He also *g*.
Gal 1:24 And they *g* God in me.
2 Th 1:10 to be *g* in His saints and to be
1:12 our Lord Jesus Christ may be *g*
3: 1 Lord may run swiftly and be *g*,
1 Pe 4:11 that in all things God may be *g*
4:14 but on your part He is *g*.
Rev 18: 7 In the measure that she *g*

GLORIFIES (1/1) GLORIFY

Ps 50:23 Whoever offers praise *g* Me;

GLORIFY (27/24) GLORIFIED, GLORIFIES, GLORIFYING, GLORY

Ps 22:23 *g* Him, And fear Him, all you
50:15 and you shall *g* Me."
86: 9 And shall *g* Your name.
86:12 And I will *g* Your name
Isa 24:15 Therefore *g* the LORD in the
25: 3 the strong people will *g* You;
60: 7 And I will *g* the house of My
Jer 30:19 I will also *g* them, and they
Mt 5:16 may see your good works and *g*
Jn 12:28 *g* Your name." Then a voice
12:28 both glorified it and will *g*
13:32 God will also *g* Him in Himself,
13:32 and *g* Him immediately.
16:14 He will *g* Me, for He will take
17: 1 *G* Your Son, that Your Son also
17: 1 that Your Son also may *g* You,
17: 5 *g* Me together with Yourself,
21:19 by what death he would *g* God.
Rom 1:21 they did not *g* Him as God, nor
15: 6 with one mind and one mouth *g*
15: 9 and that the Gentiles might *g*
1 Cor 6:20 therefore *g* God in your body
2 Cor 9:13 they *g* God for the obedience of
Heb 5: 5 So also Christ did not *g*
1 Pe 2:12 *g* God in the day of visitation.
4:16 but let him *g* God in this
Rev 15: 4 and *g* Your name? For You

GLORIFYING (3/3) GLORIFY

Lk 2:20 *g* and praising God for all the
5:25 to his own house, *g* God.
18:43 *g* God. And all the people, when

GLORIOUS (48/47) GLORIOUSLY, GLORY

Ex 15: 6 has become *g* in power;
15:11 *g* in holiness, Fearful in
Deut 28:58 that you may fear this *g* and
2 Sam 6:20 How *g* was the king of Israel
1 Chr 22: 5 famous and *g* throughout all
29:13 thank You And praise Your *g*
Neh 9: 5 'Blessed be Your *g* name,
Esth 1: 4 he showed the riches of his *g*
Ps 45:13 The royal daughter is all *g*
66: 2 of His name; Make His praise *g*.
72:19 And blessed be His *g* name
76: 4 You are more *g* and excellent
87: 3 *G* things are spoken of you,
111: 3 His work is honorable and *g*,
145: 5 I will meditate on the *g*
145:12 And the *g* majesty of His
Isa 4: 2 LORD shall be beautiful and *g*;
11:10 His resting place shall be *g*.
22:18 and there your *g* chariots
22:23 And he will become a *g* throne
28: 1 Whose *g* beauty is a fading
28: 4 And the *g* beauty is a fading
30:30 The LORD will cause His *g*
49: 5 to Him (For I shall be *g* in
60:13 make the place of My feet *g*.
63: 1 This One who is *g* in His
63:12 With His *g* arm, Dividing the
63:14 To make Yourself a *g* name.
63:15 Your habitation, holy and *g*.
Jer 17:12 A *g* high throne from the
Ezek 27:25 You were filled and very *g* in
Dan 8: 9 and toward the *G* Land.
11:16 He shall stand in the *G* Land
11:20 one who imposes taxes on the *g*
11:41 He shall also enter the *G* Land,
11:45 between the seas and the *g*
Lk 13:17 rejoiced for all the *g* things
Rom 8:21 of corruption into the *g*
2 Cor 3: 7 and engraved on stones, was *g*,
3: 8 of the Spirit not be more *g*?
3:10 For even what was made *g* had no
3:11 if what is passing away was *g*,
3:11 what remains is much more *g*.
Eph 5:27 present her to Himself a *g*
Phil 3:21 it may be conformed to His *g*
Col 1:11 according to His *g* power, for
1 Tim 1:11 according to the *g* gospel of the
Titus 2:13 for the blessed hope and *g*

GLORIOUSLY (3/3) GLORIOUS

Ex 15: 1 For He has triumphed **g**!
15:21 For He has triumphed **g**!
Isa 24:23 And before His elders, **g**.

GLORY (379/351) GLORIES, GLORIFY, GLORIOUS, GLORYING

Gen 45:13 tell my father of all my **g** in
Ex 16: 7 morning you shall see the **g** of
16:10 the **g** of the LORD appeared in
24:16 Now the **g** of the LORD rested on
24:17 The sight of the **g** of the LORD
28: 2 for **g** and for beauty.
28:40 for **g** and beauty.
29:43 shall be sanctified by My **g**.
33:18 said, "Please, show me Your **g**.
33:22 while My **g** passes by, that I
40:34 and the **g** of the LORD filled
40:35 and the **g** of the LORD filled
Lev 9: 6 and the **g** of the LORD will
9:23 Then the **g** of the LORD
Num 14:10 Now the **g** of the LORD appeared
14:21 shall be filled with the **g** of
14:22 these men who have seen My **g**
16:19 Then the **g** of the LORD
16:42 and the **g** of the LORD
20: 6 And the **g** of the LORD appeared
Deut 5:24 our God has shown us His **g** and
33:17 His **g** is like a firstborn
Josh 7:19 give **g** to the LORD God of
Judg 4: 9 there will be no **g** for you in
7: 2 lest Israel claim **g** for itself
1 Sam 2: 8 them inherit the throne of **g**.
4:21 The **g** has departed from
4:22 The **g** has departed from Israel,
6: 5 and you shall give **g** to the God
1 Ki 8:11 for the **g** of the LORD filled
2 Ki 14:10 **G** in that, and stay at home;
1 Chr 16:10 **G** in His holy name
16:24 Declare His **g** among the
16:28 Give to the LORD **g** and
16:29 Give to the LORD the **g** due
29:11 greatness, The power and the **g**,
2 Chr 5:14 for the **g** of the LORD filled
7: 1 and the **g** of the LORD filled
7: 2 because the **g** of the LORD had
7: 3 and the **g** of the LORD on the
Job 19: 9 He has stripped me of my **g**,
29:20 My **g** is fresh within me,
40:10 and array yourself with **g** and
Ps 3: 3 My **g** and the One who lifts up
4: 2 Will you turn my **g** to
8: 1 Who have set Your **g** above the
8: 5 You have crowned him with **g**
16: 9 and my **g** rejoices; My flesh
19: 1 The heavens declare the **g** of
21: 5 His **g** is great in Your
24: 7 And the King of **g** shall
24: 8 Who is this King of **g**?
24: 9 And the King of **g** shall
24:10 Who is this King of **g**?
24:10 of hosts, He is the King of **g**.
26: 8 And the place where Your **g**
29: 1 Give unto the LORD **g** and
29: 2 Give unto the LORD the **g** due
29: 3 The God of **g** thunders;
29: 9 temple everyone says, "**G**!"
30:12 To the end that my **g** may sing
45: 3 With Your **g** and Your majesty.
49:16 When the **g** of his house is
49:17 His **g** shall not descend after
57: 5 Let Your **g** be above all the
57: 8 my **g**! Awake, lute and harp!
57:11 Let Your **g** be above all the
62: 7 God is my salvation and my **g**;
63: 2 To see Your power and Your **g**.
63:11 who swears by Him shall **g**;
64:10 the upright in heart shall **g**.
71: 8 Your praise And with Your **g**
72:19 earth be filled with His **g**.
73:24 And afterward receive me to **g**.
78:61 And His **g** into the enemy's
79: 9 For the **g** of Your name;
84:11 LORD will give grace and **g**;
85: 9 That **g** may dwell in our land.
89:17 For You are the **g** of their
89:44 You have made his **g** cease,
90:16 And Your **g** to their children.
96: 3 Declare His **g** among the
96: 7 Give to the LORD **g** and
96: 8 Give to the LORD the **g** due
97: 6 And all the peoples see His **g**.
102:15 the kings of the earth Your **g**.
102:16 He shall appear in His **g**.
104:31 May the **g** of the LORD endure
105: 3 **G** in His holy name
106: 5 That I may **g** with Your
106:20 Thus they changed their **g** Into
108: 1 and give praise, even with my **g**.
108: 5 And Your **g** above all the
113: 4 His **g** above the heavens.
115: 1 But to Your name give **g**,
138: 5 For great is the **g** of the
145:11 They shall speak of the **g** of
148:13 His **g** is above the earth and
149: 5 Let the saints be joyful in **g**;
Prov 3:35 The wise shall inherit **g**,
4: 9 A crown of **g** she will deliver
16:31 head is a crown of **g**,
17: 6 And the **g** of children is
19:11 And his **g** is to overlook a
20:29 The **g** of young men is their
25: 2 It is the **g** of God to conceal
25: 2 But the **g** of kings is to
25:27 So to seek one's own **g** is
25:27 seek one's own glory is not **g**.
28:12 rejoice, there is great **g**;
Isa 2:10 terror of the LORD And the **g**
2:19 terror of the LORD And the **g**
2:21 terror of the LORD And the **g**
3: 8 To provoke the eyes of His **g**.
4: 5 For over all the **g** there will
5:14 Their **g** and their multitude
6: 3 whole earth is full of His **g**!
8: 7 king of Assyria and all his **g**;
10: 3 where will you leave your **g**?
10:12 and the **g** of his haughty
10:16 And under his **g** He will
10:18 And it will consume the **g** of
13:19 the **g** of kingdoms, The beauty
14:18 All of them, sleep in **g**,
16:14 the **g** of Moab will be despised
17: 3 They will be as the **g** of the
17: 4 come to pass That the **g** of
20: 5 expectation and Egypt their **g**.
21:16 all the **g** of Kedar will fail;
22:24 will hang on him all the **g** of
23: 9 to dishonor the pride of all **g**,
24:16 **G** to the righteous!" But I
28: 5 will be For a crown of **g** and
35: 2 The **g** of Lebanon shall be
35: 2 They shall see the **g** of the
40: 5 The **g** of the LORD shall be
41:16 And **g** in the Holy One of
42: 8 And My **g** I will not give to
42:12 Let them give **g** to the LORD,
43: 7 Whom I have created for My **g**;
45:25 be justified, and shall **g**.
46:13 in Zion, For Israel My **g**.
48:11 And I will not give My **g** to
58: 8 The **g** of the LORD shall be
59:19 And His **g** from the rising of
60: 1 light has come! And the **g** of
60: 2 And His **g** will be seen upon
60: 7 will glorify the house of My **g**.
60:13 The **g** of Lebanon shall come to
60:19 light, And your God your **g**.
61: 6 And in their **g** you shall
62: 2 And all kings your **g**.
62: 3 shall also be a crown of **g** In
66:11 With the abundance of her **g**.
66:12 And the **g** of the Gentiles like
66:18 they shall come and see My **g**.
66:19 not heard My fame nor seen My **g**.
66:19 And they shall declare My **g**
Jer 2:11 My people have changed their **G**
4: 2 And in Him they shall **g**."
9:23 Let not the wise man **g** in his
9:23 Let not the mighty man **g** in
9:23 Nor let the rich man **g** in his
9:24 But let him who glories **g** in
13:11 renown, for praise, and for **g**;
13:16 Give **g** to the LORD your God
13:18 collapse, the crown of your **g**.
14:21 disgrace the throne of Your **g**.
22:18 or 'Alas, his **g**!'
48:18 Dibon, Come down from your **g**,
Ezek 1:28 of the likeness of the **g** of
3:12 Blessed is the **g** of the LORD
3:23 the **g** of the LORD stood there,
3:23 like the **g** which I saw by the
8: 4 the **g** of the God of Israel was
9: 3 Now the **g** of the God of Israel
10: 4 Then the **g** of the LORD went up
10: 4 the brightness of the LORD's **g**.
10:18 Then the **g** of the LORD
10:19 and the **g** of the God of Israel
11:22 and the **g** of the God of Israel
11:23 And the **g** of the LORD went up
20: 6 the **g** of all lands.
20:15 the **g** of all lands,
24:25 their joy and their **g**,
25: 9 the **g** of the country, Beth
26:20 and I shall establish **g** in the
31:18 will you then be likened in **g**
39:21 I will set My **g** among the
43: 2 the **g** of the God of Israel came
43: 2 and the earth shone with His **g**.
43: 4 And the **g** of the LORD came into
43: 5 the **g** of the LORD filled the
44: 4 the **g** of the LORD filled the
Dan 2:37 kingdom, power, strength, and **g**;
4:36 and for the **g** of my kingdom, my
5:18 and majesty, **g** and honor.
5:20 and they took his **g** from him.
7:14 to Him was given dominion and **g**
11:39 and advance its **g**;
Hos 4: 7 I will change their **g** into
9:11 their **g** shall fly away like a
10: 5 Because its **g** has departed from
Mic 1:15 The **g** of Israel shall come to
2: 9 You have taken away My **g**
Hab 2:14 With the knowledge of the **g**
2:16 filled with shame instead of **g**.
2:16 utter shame will be on your **g**.
3: 3 Selah His **g** covered the
Hag 2: 3 saw this temple in its former **g**?
2: 7 I will fill this temple with **g**,
2: 9 The **g** of this latter temple
Zech 2: 5 and I will be the **g** in her
2: 8 of hosts: "He sent Me after **g**,
6:13 the LORD. He shall bear the **g**,
11: 3 shepherds! For their **g** is in
12: 7 so that the **g** of the house of
12: 7 of the house of David and the **g**
Mal 2: 2 To give **g** to My name,"
Mt 4: 8 of the world and their **g**.
6: 2 that they may have **g** from men.
6:13 kingdom and the power and the **g**
6:29 that even Solomon in all his **g**
16:27 Son of Man will come in the **g**
19:28 Man sits on the throne of His **g**,
24:30 heaven with power and great **g**.
25:31 the Son of Man comes in His **g**,
25:31 will sit on the throne of His **g**.
Mk 8:38 ashamed when He comes in the **g**
10:37 other on Your left, in Your **g**.
13:26 clouds with great power and **g**.
Lk 2: 9 and the **g** of the Lord shone
2:14 **G** to God in the highest, And on
2:32 And the **g** of Your people
4: 6 I will give You, and their **g**;
9:26 when He comes in His own **g**,
9:31 who appeared in **g** and spoke of
9:32 they saw His **g** and the two men
12:27 even Solomon in all his **g** was
14:10 Then you will have **g** in the
17:18 found who returned to give **g**
19:38 Peace in heaven and **g** in the
21:27 a cloud with power and great **g**.
24:26 things and to enter into His **g**?
Jn 1:14 among us, and we beheld His **g**,
1:14 the **g** as of the only begotten
2:11 Galilee, and manifested His **g**;
7:18 from himself seeks his own **g**;
7:18 but He who seeks the **g** of the
8:50 "And I do not seek My own **g**;
9:24 Give God the **g**! We know that
11: 4 but for the **g** of God, that the
11:40 believe you would see the **g** of
12:41 Isaiah said when he saw His **g**
17: 5 with the **g** which I had with You
17:22 And the **g** which You gave Me I
17:24 that they may behold My **g** which
Acts 7: 2 The God of **g** appeared to our
7:55 into heaven and saw the **g** of
12:23 because he did not give **g** to
22:11 I could not see for the **g** of
Rom 1:23 and changed the **g** of the
2: 7 in doing good seek for **g**,
2:10 but **g**, honor, and peace to
3: 7 through my lie to His **g**,
3:23 sinned and fall short of the **g**
4:20 giving **g** to God,
5: 2 and rejoice in hope of the **g** of
5: 3 but we also **g** in tribulations,
6: 4 raised from the dead by the **g**
8:18 to be compared with the **g**
9: 4 pertain the adoption, the **g**,
9:23 make known the riches of His **g**
9:23 had prepared beforehand for **g**,
11:36 to whom be **g** forever. Amen.
15: 7 received us, to the **g** of God.
15:17 Therefore I have reason to **g** in
16:27 be **g** through Jesus Christ
1 Cor 1:29 that no flesh should **g** in His
1:31 let him **g** in the LORD."
2: 7 before the ages for our **g**,
2: 8 have crucified the Lord of **g**.
10:31 do all to the **g** of God.
11: 7 since he is the image and **g** of
11: 7 but woman is the **g** of man.
11:15 it is a **g** to her; for her hair
15:40 but the **g** of the celestial is
15:40 and the **g** of the terrestrial
15:41 There is one **g** of the sun,
15:41 another **g** of the moon, and
15:41 and another **g** of the stars;
15:41 differs from another star in **g**.
15:43 in dishonor, it is raised in **g**.
2 Cor 1:20 to the **g** of God through us.
3: 7 face of Moses because of the **g**
3: 7 which **g** was passing away,
3: 9 ministry of condemnation had **g**,
3: 9 exceeds much more in **g**.
3:10 was made glorious had no **g** in
3:10 because of the **g** that excels.
3:18 beholding as in a mirror the **g**
3:18 into the same image from **g** to
3:18 the same image from glory to **g**,
4: 4 light of the gospel of the **g**
4: 6 of the knowledge of the **g** of
4:15 to abound to the **g** of God.
4:17 and eternal weight of **g**,
8:19 is administered by us to the **g**
8:23 the **g** of Christ.
10:17 let him **g** in the LORD."
Gal 1: 5 to whom be **g** forever and ever.
Eph 1: 6 to the praise of the **g** of His
1:12 be to the praise of His **g**.
1:14 to the praise of His **g**.
1:17 Jesus Christ, the Father of **g**,
1:18 what are the riches of the **g** of
3:13 for you, which is your **g**.
3:16 to the riches of His **g**,
3:21 to Him be **g** in the church by
Phil 1:11 to the **g** and praise of God.
2:11 to the **g** of God the Father.
3:19 and whose **g** is in their
4:19 according to His riches in **g**
4:20 Now to our God and Father be **g**
Col 1:27 what are the riches of the **g**
1:27 is Christ in you, the hope of **g**.
3: 4 also will appear with Him in **g**.

1 Th 2: 6 Nor did we seek **g** from men,
2:12 you into His own kingdom and **g**.
2:20 For you are our **g** and joy.
2 Th 1: 9 of the Lord and from the **g** of
2:14 for the obtaining of the **g** of
1 Tim 1:17 be honor and **g** forever and
3:16 in the world, Received up in **g**.
2 Tim 2:10 in Christ Jesus with eternal **g**.
4:18 To Him be **g** forever and ever.
Heb 1: 3 being the brightness of His **g**
2: 7 have crowned him with **g**
2: 9 of death crowned with **g** and
2:10 in bringing many sons to **g**,
3: 3 been counted worthy of more **g**
9: 5 above it were the cherubim of **g**
13:21 to whom be **g** forever and ever.
Jas 1: 9 Let the lowly brother **g** in his
2: 1 Jesus Christ, the Lord of **g**,
1 Pe 1: 7 and **g** at the revelation of
1: 8 joy inexpressible and full of **g**,
1:21 from the dead and gave Him **g**,
1:24 And all the **g** of man as
4:11 to whom belong the **g** and the
4:13 that when His **g** is revealed,
4:14 for the Spirit of **g** and of God
5: 1 and also a partaker of the **g**
5: 4 you will receive the crown of **g**
5:10 who called us to His eternal **g**
5:11 To Him be the **g** and the
2 Pe 1: 3 of Him who called us by **g** and
1:17 from God the Father honor and **g**
1:17 to Him from the Excellent **G**:
3:18 To Him be the **g** both now and
Jude 24 Before the presence of His **g**
25 Be **g** and majesty, Dominion
Rev 1: 6 to Him be **g** and dominion
4: 9 the living creatures give **g**
4:11 To receive **g** and honor and
5:12 And strength and honor and **g**
5:13 Blessing and honor and **g** and
7:12 Amen! Blessing and **g** and wisdom,
11:13 rest were afraid and gave **g** to
14: 7 Fear God and give **g** to Him, for
15: 8 filled with smoke from the **g**
16: 9 did not repent and give Him **g**.
18: 1 was illuminated with his **g**.
19: 1 Alleluia! Salvation and **g** and
19: 7 glad and rejoice and give Him **g**,
21:11 having the **g** of God. Her light
21:23 for the **g** of God illuminated
21:24 of the earth bring their **g** and
21:26 And they shall bring the **g** and

GLORYING (1/1) GLORY

1 Cor 5: 6 Your **g** is not good. Do you not

GLUTTON (4/4) GLUTTONOUS, GLUTTONS

Deut 21:20 he is a **g** and a drunkard.'
Prov 23:21 For the drunkard and the **g** will
Mt 11:19 a **g** and a winebibber, a friend
Lk 7:34 a **g** and a winebibber, a friend

GLUTTONOUS (1/1) GLUTTON

Prov 23:20 Or with **g** eaters of meat;

GLUTTONS (2/2) GLUTTON

Prov 28: 7 But a companion of **g** shames
Titus 1:12 liars, evil beasts, lazy **g**.

GNASH (2/2) GNASHED, GNASHES, GNASHING

Ps 112:10 He will **g** his teeth and melt
Lam 2:16 They hiss and **g** their teeth.

GNASHED (2/2) GNASH

Ps 35:16 mockers at feasts They **g** at
Acts 7:54 and they **g** at him with their

GNASHES (3/3) GNASH

Job 16: 9 He **g** at me with His teeth;
Ps 37:12 And **g** at him with his teeth.
Mk 9:18 **g** his teeth, and becomes rigid.

GNASHING (7/7) GNASH

Mt 8:12 There will be weeping and **g** of
13:42 There will be wailing and **g** of
13:50 There will be wailing and **g** of
22:13 there will be weeping and **g** of
24:51 There shall be weeping and **g** of
25:30 There will be weeping and **g** of
Lk 13:28 There will be weeping and **g** of

GNAT (1/1)

Mt 23:24 who strain out a **g** and swallow

GNAWED (1/1)

Rev 16:10 and they **g** their tongues

GNAWING (1/1)

Job 30:17 And my **g** pains take no rest.

GO (1487/1358)

Gen 3:14 On your belly you shall **g**,
6:18 and you shall **g** into the
8:16 **G** out of the ark, you and your
9:10 of all that **g** out of the ark,
10:19 was from Sidon as you **g** toward
10:19 then as you **g** toward Sodom,
10:30 place was from Mesha as you **g**
11: 7 let Us **g** down and there confuse
11:31 from Ur of the Chaldeans to **g**
12: 5 and they departed to **g** to the
12:19 take her and **g** your way."
13: 9 then I will **g** to the right;
13: 9 if you **g** to the right, then I
13: 9 then I will **g** to the left."
13:10 like the land of Egypt as you **g**
15: 2 seeing I **g** childless, and the
15:15 you shall **g** to your fathers in
16: 2 **g** in to my maid; perhaps I
18:21 I will **g** down now and see
19: 2 then you may rise early and **g**
19:34 and you **g** in and lie with him,
20:13 in every place, wherever we **g**,
22: 2 and **g** to the land of Moriah,
22: 5 the lad and I will **g** yonder and
24: 4 but you shall **g** to my country
24:11 the time when women **g** out to
24:38 but you shall **g** to my father's
24:42 prosper the way in which I **g**,
24:51 before you; take her and **g**,
24:55 least ten; after that she may **g**.
24:56 send me away so that I may **g** to
24:58 'Will you **g** with this man?"
24:58 And she said, "I will **g**."
25:18 is east of Egypt as you **g**
26: 2 Do not **g** down to Egypt; live in
26:16 **G** away from us, for you are much
27: 3 and **g** out to the field and hunt
27: 9 **G** now to the flock and bring me
27:13 only obey my voice, and **g**,
28: 2 **g** to Padan Aram, to the house
28:15 will keep you wherever you **g**,
29: 7 and **g** and feed them."
29:21 that I may **g** in to her."
30: 3 **g** in to her, and she will bear
30:25 that I may **g** to my own place
30:26 I have served you, and let me **g**;
31:18 to **g** to his father Isaac in the
32:26 And He said, "Let Me **g**,
32:26 I will not let You **g** unless You
33:12 us take our journey; let us **g**,
33:12 and I will **g** before you."
33:14 Please let my lord **g** on ahead
33:14 pace which the livestock that **g**
35: 1 **g** up to Bethel and dwell there;
35: 3 Then let us arise and **g** up to
35:16 was but a little distance to **g**
37:14 Please **g** and see if it is well
37:17 'Let us **g** to Dothan.'
37:30 and I, where shall I **g**?"
37:35 For I shall **g** down into the
38: 8 **G** in to your brother's wife and
41:55 **G** to Joseph; whatever he says to
42: 2 **g** down to that place and buy
42:19 **g** and carry grain for the
42:38 My son shall not **g** down with
42:38 along the way in which you **g**,
43: 2 **G** back, buy us a little food."
43: 4 we will **g** down and buy you
43: 5 we will not **g** down; for the man
43: 8 me, and we will arise and **g**,
43:13 **g** back to the man.
44:17 **g** up in peace to your father."
44:25 **G** back and buy us a little
44:26 We cannot **g** down; if our
44:26 then we will **g** down; for we may
44:33 and let the lad **g** up with his
44:34 For how shall I **g** up to my
45: 1 Make everyone **g** out from me!"
45: 9 Hurry and **g** up to my father, and
45:17 **g** to the land of Canaan.
45:28 I will **g** and see him before I
46: 3 do not fear to **g** down to Egypt,
46: 4 I will **g** down with you to Egypt,
46:31 I will **g** up and tell Pharaoh,
48: 7 but a little distance to **g** to
50: 5 please let me **g** up and bury my
50: 6 **G** up and bury your father, as he
Ex 1:10 and so **g** up out of the land."
2: 7 Shall I **g** and call a nurse for
2: 8 daughter said to her, "**G**.
3:11 Who am I that I should **g** to
3:16 **G** and gather the elders of
3:18 let us **g** three days' journey
3:19 of Egypt will not let you **g**,
3:20 after that he will let you **g**.
3:21 and it shall be, when you **g**,
3:21 that you shall not **g**
4:12 "Now therefore, **g**,
4:18 'Please let me **g** and return to
4:18 said to Moses, "**G** in peace."
4:19 said to Moses in Midian, "**G**,
4:21 When you **g** back to Egypt, see
4:21 he will not let the people **g**.
4:23 let My son **g** that he may serve
4:23 But if you refuse to let him **g**,
4:26 So He let him **g**.
4:27 **G** into the wilderness to meet
5: 1 God of Israel: 'Let My people **g**,
5: 2 obey His voice to let Israel **g**?
5: 2 LORD, nor will I let Israel **g**.
5: 3 let us **g** three days' journey
5: 7 Let them **g** and gather straw for
5: 8 Let us **g** and sacrifice to our
5:11 '**G**, get yourselves straw
5:17 Let us **g** and sacrifice to the
5:18 'Therefore **g** now and work;
6: 1 strong hand he will let them **g**,
6:11 **G** in, tell Pharaoh king of Egypt
6:11 to let the children of Israel **g**
7:14 he refuses to let the people **g**.
7:15 **G** to Pharaoh in the morning,
7:16 you, saying, "Let My people **g**,
8: 1 **G** to Pharaoh and say to him,
8: 1 the LORD: "Let My people **g**,
8: 2 if you refuse to let them **g**,
8: 3 which shall **g** up and come into
8: 8 and I will let the people **g**,
8:20 the LORD: "Let My people **g**,
8:21 if you will not let My people **g**,
8:25 Moses and Aaron, and said, "**G**,
8:27 We will **g** three days' journey
8:28 said, "I will let you **g**,
8:28 only you shall not **g** very far
8:29 in not letting the people **g** to
8:32 would he let the people **g**.
9: 1 **G** in to Pharaoh and tell him,
9: 1 the Hebrews: "Let My people **g**,
9: 2 if you refuse to let them **g**,
9: 7 and he did not let the people **g**.
9:13 the Hebrews: "Let My people **g**,
9:17 in that you will not let them **g**.
9:28 is enough. I will let you **g**,
9:35 he let the children of Israel **g**,
10: 1 **G** in to Pharaoh; for I have
10: 3 before Me? Let My people **g**,
10: 4 you refuse to let My people **g**,
10: 7 be a snare to us? Let the men **g**,
10: 8 and he said to them, "**G**,
10: 9 We will **g** with our young and our
10: 9 flocks and our herds we will **g**,
10:10 let you and your little ones **g**!
10:11 Not so! **G** now, you who are
10:20 let the children of Israel **g**.
10:24 called to Moses and said, "**G**,
10:24 Let your little ones also **g**
10:26 Our livestock also shall **g** with
10:27 and he would not let them **g**.
11: 1 Afterward he will let you **g**
11: 1 from here. When he lets you **g**,
11: 4 About midnight I will **g** out into
11: 8 After that I will **g** out."
11:10 let the children of Israel **g**
12:22 And none of you shall **g** out of
12:31 **g** out from among my people,
12:31 the children of Israel. And **g**,
13:15 was stubborn about letting us **g**,
13:17 Pharaoh had let the people **g**,
13:21 so as to **g** by day and night.
14: 5 that we have let Israel **g** from
14:15 the children of Israel to **g**
14:16 the children of Israel shall **g**
14:21 the LORD caused the sea to **g**
16: 4 And the people shall **g** out and
16:29 let no man **g** out of his place
17: 5 **G** on before the people, and take
17: 5 you struck the river, and **g**.
17: 9 Choose us some men and **g** out,
18:23 all this people will also **g** to
19:10 **G** to the people and consecrate
19:12 yourselves that you do not **g**
19:21 **G** down and warn the people, lest
20:26 Nor shall you **g** up by steps to
21: 2 and in the seventh he shall **g**
21: 3 he shall **g** out by himself;
21: 3 then his wife shall **g** out with
21: 4 and he shall **g** out by himself.
21: 5 I will not **g** out free,'
21: 7 she shall not **g** out as the male
21:11 then she shall **g** out free,
21:26 he shall let him **g** free for the
21:27 he shall let him **g** free for the
23:23 For My Angel will **g** before you
24: 2 nor shall the people **g** up with
24:14 let him **g** to them."
30:20 When they **g** into the tabernacle
32: 1 make us gods that shall **g**
32: 7 the LORD said to Moses, "**G**,
32:23 Make us gods that shall **g** before
32:27 and **g** in and out from entrance
32:30 So now I will **g** up to the
32:34 "Now therefore, **g**,
32:34 My Angel shall **g** before you.
33: 1 Depart and **g** up from here, you
33: 3 **G** up to a land flowing with
33: 3 for I will not **g** up in your
33:14 My Presence will **g** with you,
33:15 If Your Presence does not **g**
33:16 except You **g** with us? So we
34: 9 **g** among us, even though we are
34:24 man covet your land when you **g**
36:24 sockets of silver he made to **g**
40:36 the children of Israel would **g**
Lev 6:13 it shall never **g** out.
8:33 And you shall not **g** outside the
9: 7 **G** to the altar, offer your sin
10: 7 You shall not **g** out from the
10: 9 when you **g** into the tabernacle
11:27 all kinds of animals that **g** on
14: 3 And the priest shall **g** out of
14:36 afterward the priest shall **g**
14:38 then the priest shall **g** out of
16:10 and to let it **g** as the

16:18 And he shall **g** out to the altar
19:16 You shall not **g** about as a
21:11 nor shall he **g** near any dead
21:12 nor shall he **g** out of the
21:23 only he shall not **g** near the
26: 6 and the sword will not **g**
Num 1: 3 all who are able to **g** to war
1:20 all who were able to **g** to
1:22 all who were able to **g** to
1:24 all who were able to **g** to
1:26 all who were able to **g** to
1:28 all who were able to **g** to
1:30 all who were able to **g** to
1:32 all who were able to **g** to
1:34 all who were able to **g** to
1:36 all who were able to **g** to
1:38 all who were able to **g** to
1:40 all who were able to **g** to
1:42 all who were able to **g** to
1:45 all who were able to **g** to
1:51 when the tabernacle is to **g**
4:15 when the camp is set to **g**,
4:19 Aaron and his sons shall **g** in
4:20 But they shall not **g** in to watch
5: 8 for the wrong must **g** to the
5:22 water that causes the curse **g**
6: 6 to the LORD he shall not **g**
8:15 that the Levites shall **g**
10: 9 When you **g** to war in your land
10:30 he said to him, "I will not **g**,
10:32 if you **g** with us—indeed it
13:17 **G** up this way into the South,
13:17 and **g** up to the mountains,
13:30 Let us **g** up at once and take
13:31 We are not able to **g** up against
14:14 and You **g** before them in a
14:40 and we will **g** up to the place
14:42 Do not **g** up, lest you be
14:44 But they presumed to **g** up to the
16:30 and they **g** down alive into the
20:17 we will **g** along the King's
20:19 We will **g** by the Highway, and if
21: 4 to **g** around the land of Edom;
21:22 We will **g** by the King's Highway
22:12 'You shall not **g** with them;
22:13 **G** back to your land, for the
22:13 to give me permission to **g**
22:18 I could not **g** beyond the word
22:20 rise and **g** with them; but only
22:35 **G** with the men, but only the
23: 3 burnt offering, and I will **g**;
23:16 **G** back to Balak, and thus you
24: 1 he did not **g** as at other times,
24:13 I could not **g** beyond the word
26: 2 all who are able to **g** to war in
27:12 **G** up into this Mount Abarim, and
27:17 who may **g** out before them and go
27:17 may go out before them and **g**
27:21 At his word they shall **g** out,
31: 3 and let them **g** against the
32: 6 Shall your brethren **g** to war
32: 9 so that they did not **g** into the
32:17 ready to **g** before the
34: 4 then it shall **g** on to Hazar
34:11 the border shall **g** down from
34:11 the border shall **g** down and
34:12 the border shall **g** down along
Deut 1: 7 and **g** to the mountains of the
1: 8 **g** in and possess the land which
1:21 **g** up and possess it, as the
1:22 of the way by which we should **g**
1:26 Nevertheless you would not **g**
1:28 Where can we **g** up? Our brethren
1:33 show you the way you should **g**,
1:37 Even you shall not **g** in there;
1:38 he shall **g** in there.
1:39 they shall **g** in there; to them
1:41 we will **g** up and fight, just as
1:41 you were ready to **g** up into the
1:42 Do not **g** up nor fight, for I am
2:37 Only you did not **g** near the land
3:27 **G** up to the top of Pisgah, and
3:28 for he shall **g** over before this
4: 1 and **g** in and possess the land
4: 5 them in the land which you **g**
4:34 Or did God ever try to **g** and
4:40 that it may **g** well with you and
5: 5 and you did not **g** up the
5:27 You **g** near and hear all that the
5:30 **G** and say to them, "Return to
6:14 You shall not **g** after other
6:18 and that you may **g** in and
7: 1 you into the land which you **g**
8: 1 and **g** in and possess the land
9: 1 and **g** in to dispossess nations
9: 5 of your heart that you **g** in
9:12 **g** down quickly from here, for
9:23 **G** up and possess the land which
10:11 that they may **g** in and possess
11: 8 and **g** in and possess the land
11:10 For the land which you **g** to
11:28 to **g** after other gods which you
11:29 you into the land which you **g**
11:31 cross over the Jordan and **g** in
12: 5 and there you shall **g**.
12:25 that it may **g** well with you and
12:26 you shall take and **g** to the
12:28 that it may **g** well with you and
12:29 you the nations which you **g** to
13: 2 Let us **g** after other gods'—which
13: 6 Let us **g** and serve other gods,'
13:13 Let us **g** and serve other gods"
14:25 and **g** to the place which the
15:12 year you shall let him **g** free
15:13 you shall not let him **g** away
15:16 I will not **g** away from you,'
16: 7 morning you shall turn and **g**
17: 8 then you shall arise and **g** up
19:13 that it may **g** well with you.
20: 1 When you **g** out to battle against
20: 5 Let him **g** and return to his
20: 6 Let him **g** and return to his
20: 7 Let him **g** and return to his
20: 8 Let him **g** and return to his
20:10 When you **g** near a city to fight
21: 2 elders and your judges shall **g**
21:10 When you **g** out to war against
21:13 after that you may **g** in to her
22: 7 shall surely let the mother **g**,
23:10 then he shall **g** outside the
23:12 where you may **g** out;
24: 5 he shall not **g** out to war or be
24:10 you shall not **g** into his house
24:15 and not let the sun **g** down on
24:19 you shall not **g** back to get it;
24:20 you shall not **g** over the boughs
25: 5 her husband's brother shall **g**
25: 7 then let his brother's wife **g**
26: 2 and put it in a basket and **g**
26: 3 And you shall **g** to the one who
28: 6 shall you be when you **g** out.
28:14 to **g** after other gods to serve
28:19 shall you be when you **g** out.
28:25 you shall **g** out one way against
28:41 for they shall **g** into
28:63 from off the land which you **g**
29:18 to **g** and serve the gods of
30:13 Who will **g** over the sea for us
30:16 you in the land which you **g** to
30:18 you cross over the Jordan to **g**
31: 2 I can no longer **g** out and come
31: 7 for you must **g** with this people
31:16 where they **g** to be among
32:49 **G** up this mountain of the
32:52 though you shall not **g** there,
Josh 1: 2 **g** over this Jordan, you and all
1: 7 you may prosper wherever you **g**.
1: 9 God is with you wherever you **g**.
1:11 to **g** in to possess the land
1:16 wherever you send us we will **g**.
2: 1 to spy secretly, saying, "**G**,
2:16 Afterward you may **g** your way."
3: 3 set out from your place and **g**
3: 4 the way by which you must **g**,
6: 3 you shall **g** all around the city
6: 5 And the people shall **g** up every
6:22 **G** into the harlot's house, and
7: 2 **G** up and spy out the country."
7: 3 Do not let all the people **g** up,
7: 3 two or three thousand men **g** up
8: 1 **g** up to Ai. See, I have given
8: 3 to **g** up against Ai; and Joshua
8: 4 Do not **g** very far from the
8:17 in Ai or Bethel who did not **g**
9:11 and **g** to meet them, and say to
10:13 and did not hasten to **g** down
17:15 then **g** up to the forest
18: 3 long will you neglect to **g**
18: 4 they shall rise and **g** through
18: 8 Then the men arose to **g** away;
18: 8 to survey the land, saying, "**G**,
22: 4 return and **g** to your tents and
22: 9 to **g** to the country of Gilead,
22:12 together at Shiloh to **g** to war
23: 7 and lest you **g** among these
23:12 if indeed you do **g** back, and
23:12 and **g** in to them and they to
Judg 1: 1 Who shall be first to **g** up for
1: 2 Judah shall **g** up. Indeed I have
1: 3 and I will likewise **g** with you
1:25 the man and all his family **g**.
4: 6 **G** and deploy troops at Mount
4: 8 If you will **g** with me, then I
4: 8 will **g**; but if you will not go
4: 8 but if you will not **g** with me,
4: 8 with me, I will not **g**!"
4: 9 I will surely **g** with you;
5:11 the people of the LORD shall **g**
6:14 **G** in this might of yours, and
7: 4 This one shall **g** with you,' the
7: 4 the same shall **g** with you;
7: 4 This one shall not **g** with you,'
7: 4 with you,' the same shall not **g**.
7: 7 Let all the other people **g**,
7: 9 **g** down against the camp, for I
7:10 But if you are afraid to **g** down,
7:10 **g** down to the camp with Purah
7:11 shall be strengthened to **g**
9: 9 And **g** to sway over trees?'
9:11 And **g** to sway over trees?'
9:13 And **g** to sway over trees?'
9:38 **G** out, if you will, and fight
10:14 **G** and cry out to the gods which
11: 8 that you may **g** with us and
11:35 and I cannot **g** back on it."
11:37 that I may **g** and wander on the
11:38 So he said, "**G**." And he sent
12: 1 and did not call us to **g** with
14: 3 that you must **g** and get a wife
15: 1 Let me **g** in to my wife, into
15: 1 would not permit him to **g** in.
15: 5 he let the foxes **g** into the
16:20 I will **g** out as before, at other
18: 2 They said to them, "**G**,
18: 5 the journey on which we **g** will
18: 6 **G** in peace. The presence of the
18: 9 let us **g** up against them.
18: 9 Do not hesitate to **g**,
18:10 'When you **g**, you will come to
19: 5 and afterward **g** your way."
19: 9 Tomorrow **g** your way early, so
19:12 we will **g** on to Gibeah."
19:15 They turned aside there to **g** in
19:25 began to break, they let her **g**.
19:27 of the house and went out to **g**
20: 8 None of us will **g** to his tent,
20: 9 We will **g** up against it by
20:14 to **g** to battle against the
20:18 Which of us shall **g** up first to
20:23 **G** up against him."
20:28 Shall I yet again **g** out to
20:28 **G** up, for tomorrow I will
21:10 **G** and strike the inhabitants of
21:20 of Benjamin, saying, "**G**,
21:21 then **g** to the land of Benjamin.
Ruth 1: 8 her two daughters-in-law, "**G**,
1:11 why will you **g** with me?
1:12 "Turn back, my daughters, **g**—
1:16 after you; For wherever you **g**,
1:16 For wherever you go, I will **g**;
1:18 that she was determined to **g**
2: 2 Please let me **g** to the field,
2: 2 And she said to her, "**G**,
2: 8 Do not **g** to glean in another
2: 8 nor **g** from here, but stay close
2: 9 and **g** after them. Have I not
2: 9 **g** to the vessels and drink from
2:22 that you **g** out with his young
3: 3 put on your best garment and **g**
3: 4 and you shall **g** in, uncover his
3:10 in that you did not **g** after
3:17 Do not **g** empty-handed to your
1 Sam 1:17 **G** in peace, and the God of
1:22 But Hannah did not **g** up, for she
2:20 Then they would **g** to their
3: 9 Eli said to Samuel, "**G**,
5:11 and let it **g** back to its own
6: 6 did they not let the people **g**,
6: 8 Then send it away, and let it **g**.
6:20 And to whom shall it **g** up from
8:20 our king may judge us and **g**
8:22 Every man **g** to his city."
9: 3 **g** and look for the donkeys."
9: 6 So let us **g** there; perhaps he
9: 6 us the way that we should **g**.
9: 7 servant, "But look, if we **g**,
9: 9 let us **g** to the seer"; for he
9:10 "Well said; come, let us **g**.
9:13 **g** up, for about this time you
9:19 **G** up before me to the high
9:19 and tomorrow I will let you **g**
9:27 Tell the servant to **g** on ahead
10: 3 Then you shall **g** on forward from
10: 8 You shall **g** down before me to
10: 9 he had turned his back to **g**
10:14 his servant, "Where did you **g**?
11: 7 Whoever does not **g** out with Saul
11:14 let us **g** to Gilgal and renew
12:21 for then you would **g** after
13:20 But all the Israelites would **g**
14: 1 let us **g** over to the
14: 4 by which Jonathan sought to **g**
14: 6 let us **g** over to the garrison
14: 7 **G** then; here I am with you,
14: 9 still in our place and not **g**
14:10 then we will **g** up. For the
14:36 Let us **g** down after the
14:37 Shall I **g** down after the
15: 3 Now **g** and attack Amalek, and
15: 6 Saul said to the Kenites, "**G**,
15:18 you on a mission, and said, '**G**,
15:27 as Samuel turned around to **g**
16: 1 Fill your horn with oil, and **g**.
16: 2 And Samuel said, "How can I **g**?
17:32 your servant will **g** and fight
17:33 You are not able to **g** against
17:37 And Saul said to David, "**G**,
18: 2 and would not let him **g** home to
19: 3 And I will **g** out and stand
19:17 Let me **g**! Why should I kill
20: 5 the king to eat. But let me **g**,
20:11 and let us **g** out into the
20:13 that you may **g** in safety.
20:19 **g** down quickly and come to the
20:21 I will send a lad, saying, '**G**,
20:22 **g** your way, for the LORD has
20:28 asked permission of me to **g**
20:29 "And he said, 'Please let me **g**,
20:40 his lad, and said to him, "**G**,
20:42 **G** in peace, since we have both
22: 5 and **g** to the land of Judah."
23: 2 Shall I **g** and attack these
23: 2 **G** and attack the Philistines,
23: 3 How much more then if we **g** to
23: 4 **g** down to Keilah. For I will
23: 8 to **g** down to Keilah to besiege
23:13 and went wherever they could **g**.
23:22 Please **g** and find out for sure,
23:23 and I will **g** with you. And it
25: 5 **G** up to Carmel, go to Nabal, and
25: 5 **g** to Nabal, and greet him in my
25:19 **G** on before me; see, I am coming
25:35 **G** up in peace to your house.
26: 6 Who will **g** down with me to Saul
26: 6 I will **g** down with you."
26:10 or he shall **g** out to battle and

26:11 are by his head, and let us *g*.
26:19 of the LORD, saying, '*G*,
27: 8 as you *g* to Shur, even as far
28: 1 assuredly know that you will *g*
28: 7 that I may *g* to her and inquire
28:22 may have strength when you *g*
29: 4 that he may *g* back to the place
29: 4 and do not let him *g* down with
29: 7 and *g* in peace, that you may
29: 8 that I may not *g* and fight
29: 9 He shall not *g* up with us to the
30:22 Because they did not *g* with us,
2 Sam 1: 4 to him, "How did the matter *g*?
1:15 '*G* near, and execute him!"
2: 1 Shall I *g* up to any of the
2: 1 *G* up." David said, "Where
2: 1 Where shall I *g* up?" And He
3:16 So Abner said to him, "*G*,
3:21 to David, "I will arise and *g*,
5:19 Shall I *g* up against the
5:19 *G* up, for I will doubtless
5:23 'You shall not *g* up;
5:24 For then the LORD will *g* out
7: 3 Nathan said to the king, "*G*,
7: 5 *G* and tell My servant David,
11: 1 at the time when kings *g* out
11: 8 *G* down to your house and wash
11: 9 and did not *g* down to his
11:10 Uriah did not *g* down to his
11:10 Why did you not *g* down to your
11:11 Shall I then *g* to my house to
11:13 but he did not *g* down to his
11:21 Why did you *g* near the
12:23 I shall *g* to him, but he shall
13: 7 Now *g* to your brother Amnon's
13: 9 Have everyone *g* out from me."
13:24 let the king and his servants *g*
13:25 let us not all *g* now, lest we
13:25 urged him, but he would not *g*;
13:26 please let my brother Amnon *g*
13:26 Why should he *g* with you?"
13:27 and all the king's sons *g* with
13:39 And King David longed to *g* to
14: 3 *G* to the king and speak to him
14: 8 *G* to your house, and I will give
14:21 *G* therefore, bring back the
14:30 *g* and set it on fire."
15: 7 let me *g* to Hebron and pay the
15: 9 *G* in peace." So he arose and
15:20 since I *g* I know not where?
15:22 So David said to Ittai, "*G*,
15:33 If you *g* on with me, then you
16: 9 let me *g* over and take off his
16:17 Why did you not *g* with your
16:21 *G* in to your father's
17:11 and that you *g* to battle in
17:17 and they would *g* and tell King
18: 2 I also will surely *g* out with
18: 3 You shall not *g* out! For if we
18:21 Joab said to the Cushite, "*G*,
19: 7 *g* out and speak comfort to your
19: 7 if you do not *g* out, not one
19:15 to *g* to meet the king, to
19:20 of all the house of Joseph to *g*
19:25 Why did you not *g* with me,
19:26 that I may ride on it and *g* to
19:34 that I should *g* up with the
19:36 Your servant will *g* a little way
20: 3 but did not *g* in to them.
21:17 You shall *g* out no more with us
24: 1 David against them to say, "*G*,
24: 2 Now *g* throughout all the tribes
24:12 *G* and tell David, 'Thus says the
24:18 *G* up, erect an altar to the
1 Ki 1:13 *G* immediately to King David and
1:53 *G* to your house."
2: 2 'I *g* the way of all the earth;
2: 6 and do not let his gray hair *g*
2:26 *G* to Anathoth, to your own
2:29 son of Jehoiada, saying, "*G*,
2:36 and do not *g* out from there
2:37 on the day you *g* out and cross
2:42 certain that on the day you *g*
3: 7 I do not know how to *g* out or
8:44 When Your people *g* out to
9: 6 but *g* and serve other gods and
11:10 that he should not *g* after
11:17 that Hadad fled to *g* to Egypt,
11:21 that I may *g* to my own
11:22 that suddenly you seek to *g* to
11:22 but do let me *g* anyway."
12:24 You shall not *g* up nor fight
12:27 If these people *g* up to offer
12:27 and they will kill me and *g*
12:28 It is too much for you to *g* up
13: 8 I would not *g* in with you;
13:12 to them, "Which way did he *g*?
13:16 cannot return with you nor *g*
14: 2 and *g* to Shiloh. Indeed, Ahijah
14: 3 and *g* to him; he will tell you
14: 7 '*G*, tell Jeroboam, 'Thus says
14:12 *g* to your own house. When your
15:17 that he might let none *g* out or
17: 9 *g* to Zarephath, which belongs
17:12 a couple of sticks that I may *g*
17:13 *g* and do as you have said, but
18: 1 in the third year, saying, "*G*,
18: 5 *G* into the land to all the
18: 8 he answered him, "It is I. *G*,
18:11 "And now you say, '*G*,
18:12 so when I *g* and tell Ahab, and
18:14 "And now you say, '*G*,
18:41 *G* up, eat and drink; for there
18:43 *G* up now, look toward the sea."
18:43 he said, "*G* again."
18:44 *G* up, say to Ahab, 'Prepare
18:44 and *g* down before the rain
19:11 *G* out, and stand on the mountain
19:15 Then the LORD said to him: "*G*,
19:20 *G* back again, for what have I
20:22 of Israel and said to him, "*G*,
20:31 and *g* out to the king of
20:33 Ben-Hadad." So he said, "*G*,
20:42 therefore your life shall *g* for
21:18 *g* down to meet Ahab king of
22: 4 Will you *g* with me to fight at
22: 6 Shall I *g* against Ramoth Gilead
22: 6 *G* up, for the Lord will deliver
22:12 *G* up to Ramoth Gilead and
22:15 shall we *g* to war against
22:15 *G* and prosper, for the LORD
22:20 Who will persuade Ahab to *g* up,
22:22 I will *g* out and be a lying
22:22 *G* out and do so.'
22:24 did the spirit from the LORD *g*
22:25 see on that day when you *g*
22:30 I will disguise myself and *g*
22:48 made merchant ships to *g* to
22:49 Let my servants *g* with your
2 Ki 1: 2 and said to them, "*G*,
1: 3 *g* up to meet the messengers of
1: 6 to meet us, and said to us, '*G*,
1:15 *G* down with him; do not be
2:16 Please let them *g* and search
2:18 I not say to you, 'Do not *g*'?
2:23 *G* up, you baldhead! Go up, you
2:23 you baldhead! *G* up, you
3: 7 Will you *g* with me to fight
3: 7 I will *g* up; I am as you are,
3: 8 'Which way shall we *g* up?"
3:13 *G* to the prophets of your
4: 3 Then he said, "*G*,
4: 7 man of God. And he said, "*G*,
4:24 and *g* forward; do not slacken
5: 5 *G* now, and I will send a letter
5:10 *G* and wash in the Jordan seven
5:19 *G* in peace." So he departed
5:24 then he let the men *g*,
5:25 to him, "Where did you *g*,
5:25 Your servant did not *g*
5:26 Did not my heart *g* with you
6: 2 let us *g* to the Jordan, and let
6: 2 So he answered, "*G*."
6: 3 Please consent to *g* with your
6: 3 And he answered, "I will *g*.
6:13 *G* and see where he is, that I
6:22 they may eat and drink and *g*
7: 5 And they rose at twilight to *g*
7: 9 let us *g* and tell the king's
7:14 saying, "*G* and see."
8: 1 to life, saying, "Arise and *g*,
8: 8 and *g* to meet the man of God,
8:10 And Elisha said to him, "*G*,
9: 1 and *g* to Ramoth Gilead.
9: 2 and *g* in and make him rise up
9:15 or escape from the city to *g*
9:34 *G* now, see to this accursed
10:25 *G* in and kill them; let no one
11: 7 two contingents of you who *g*
12:17 then Hazael set his face to *g*
17:27 let him *g* and dwell there, and
18:21 it will *g* into his hand and
18:25 *G* up against this land, and
19:31 For out of Jerusalem shall *g* a
20: 5 On the third day you shall *g* up
20: 8 and that I shall *g* up to the
20: 9 shall the shadow *g* forward ten
20: 9 go forward ten degrees or *g*
20:10 easy thing for the shadow to *g*
20:10 but let the shadow *g* backward
22: 4 *G* up to Hilkiah the high priest,
22:13 '*G*, inquire of the LORD
1 Chr 7:11 mighty men of valor fit to *g*
12:36 those who could *g* out to war,
14:10 Shall I *g* up against the
14:10 *G* up, for I will deliver them
14:14 You shall not *g* up after them;
14:15 then you shall *g* out to battle,
17: 4 *G* and tell My servant David,
17:11 when you must *g* to be with
20: 1 at the time kings *g* out to
21: 2 the leaders of the people, "*G*,
21:10 *G* and tell David, saying, 'Thus
21:18 to David that David should *g*
21:30 But David could not *g* before it
2 Chr 1:10 that I may *g* out and come in
6:34 When Your people *g* out to
7:19 and *g* and serve other gods, and
11: 4 You shall not *g* up or fight
12:11 the guard would *g* and bring
13:13 Jeroboam caused an ambush to *g*
14:11 and in Your name we *g* against
16: 1 that he might let none *g* out or
18: 2 and persuaded him to *g* up with
18: 3 Will you *g* with me against
18: 5 Shall we *g* to war against Ramoth
18: 5 *G* up, for God will deliver it
18:11 *G* up to Ramoth Gilead and
18:14 shall we *g* to war against
18:14 *G* and prosper, and they shall be
18:19 Ahab king of Israel to *g* up,
18:21 I will *g* out and be a lying
18:21 *g* out and do so.'
18:23 did the spirit from the LORD *g*
18:24 see on that day when you *g*
18:29 I will disguise myself and *g*
20:16 Tomorrow *g* down against them.
20:17 tomorrow *g* out against them,
20:27 to *g* back to Jerusalem with
20:36 with him to make ships to *g* to
20:37 so that they were not able to *g*
23: 6 They may *g* in, for they are
24: 5 *G* out to the cities of Judah,
25: 5 able to *g* to war, who could
25: 7 do not let the army of Israel *g*
25: 8 'But if you *g*, be gone!
25:10 to *g* back home. Therefore their
25:13 so that they would not *g* with
34:21 '*G*, inquire of the LORD
36:23 and let him *g* up!
Ezra 1: 3 and let him *g* up to Jerusalem
1: 5 arose to *g* up and build the
5: 5 cease till a report could *g* to
5:15 to him, 'Take these articles; *g*,
7:13 who volunteer to *g* up to
7:13 to Jerusalem, may *g* with you.
7:28 leading men of Israel to *g* up
8:31 to *g* to Jerusalem. And the hand
Neh 3:15 as far as the stairs that *g*
6: 3 cease while I leave it and *g*
6:11 there such as I who would *g*
6:11 I will not *g* in!"
8:10 *G* your way, eat the fat, drink
8:15 *G* out to the mountain, and bring
9:15 And told them to *g* in to
9:19 And the way they should *g*.
9:23 had told their fathers To *g*
13:22 and that they should *g* and
Esth 1:19 let a royal decree *g* out from
2:12 young woman's turn came to *g*
2:14 She would not *g* in to the king
2:15 to *g* in to the king, she
4: 8 that he might command her to *g*
4:11 have not been called to *g* in
4:16 '*G*, gather all the Jews
4:16 And so I will *g* to the king,
5:14 then *g* merrily with the king to
Job 1: 4 And his sons would *g* and feast
4:21 not their own excellence *g*
6:18 They *g* nowhere and perish.
9:32 And that we should *g* to
10:21 Before I *g* to the place
15:13 And let such words *g* out of
15:30 breath of His mouth he will *g*
16:22 I shall *g* the way of no
17:16 Will they *g* down to the gates
20:26 It shall *g* ill with him who is
21:13 And in a moment *g* down to the
23: 8 I *g* forward, but He is not
24: 5 They *g* out to their work,
24:10 They cause the poor to *g*
27: 6 fast, and will not let it *g*;
30:28 I *g* about mourning, but not in
31:34 I kept silence And did not *g*
34:23 That he should *g* before God in
37: 8 The beasts *g* into dens,
38:35 out lightnings, that they may *g*,
41:19 Out of his mouth *g* burning
42: 8 *g* to My servant Job, and offer
Ps 22:29 All those who *g* down to the
26: 4 Nor will I *g* in with
26: 6 So I will *g* about Your altar,
28: 1 I become like those who *g* down
30: 3 that I should not *g* down to the
30: 9 When I *g* down to the pit?
32: 8 you in the way you should *g*;
38: 6 I *g* mourning all the day long.
39:13 Before I *g* away and am no
42: 4 For I used to *g* with the
42: 9 Why do I *g* mourning because of
43: 2 Why do I *g* mourning because of
43: 4 Then I will *g* to the altar of
44: 9 And You do not *g* out with our
48:12 And *g* all around her.
49:19 He shall *g* to the generation of
55:10 Day and night they *g* around it
55:15 Let them *g* down alive into
58: 3 They *g* astray as soon as they
59: 6 And *g* all around the city.
59:14 And *g* all around the city.
60:10 who did not *g* out with our
63: 9 Shall *g* into the lower parts
66:13 I will *g* into Your house with
71:16 I will *g* in the strength of the
78:52 But He made His own people *g*
84: 7 They *g* from strength to
85:13 Righteousness will *g* before
88: 4 I am counted with those who *g*
89:14 Mercy and truth *g* before Your
95:10 It is a people who *g* astray in
105:20 ruler of the people let him *g*
107: 7 That they might *g* to a city
107:23 Those who *g* down to the sea in
107:26 They *g* down again to the
108:11 who did not *g* out with our
115:17 Nor any who *g* down into
118:19 I will *g* through them, And I
122: 1 Let us *g* into the house of the
122: 4 Where the tribes *g* up,
132: 3 Surely I will not *g* into the
132: 3 Or *g* up to the comfort of my
132: 7 Let us *g* into His tabernacle;
139: 7 Where can I *g* from Your Spirit?
143: 7 Lest I be like those who *g*
Prov 1:12 like those who *g* down to the
2:19 None who *g* to her return, Nor

3:28 not say to your neighbor, "**G**,
4:13 of instruction, do not let **g**;
5: 5 Her feet **g** down to death,
5: 8 And do not **g** near the door of
5:10 And your labors **g** to the
5:23 of his folly he shall **g** astray.
6: 3 **G** and humble yourself;
6: 6 **G** to the ant, you sluggard!
9: 6 And **g** in the way of
9:15 Who **g** straight on their way:
11:21 the wicked will not **g**
14: 7 **G** from the presence of a
14:22 Do they not **g** astray who devise
15:12 Nor will he **g** to the wise.
15:22 plans **g** awry, But in the
16: 5 none will **g** unpunished.
17: 5 is glad at calamity will not **g**
18: 8 And they **g** down into the
19: 5 A false witness will not **g**
19: 7 much more do his friends **g** far
19: 9 A false witness will not **g**
22: 6 a child in the way he should **g**,
22:24 with a furious man do not **g**,
23:30 Those who **g** in search of mixed
25: 4 And it will **g** to the
25: 8 Do not **g** hastily to court;
26:22 And they **g** down into the
27:10 Nor **g** to your brother's house
28:10 causes the upright to **g** astray
28:20 hastens to be rich will not **g**
31:18 And her lamp does not **g** out by
Eccl 3:20 All **g** to one place: all are from
5: 1 Walk prudently when you **g** to the
5:15 To **g** as he came; And he shall
5:16 as he came, so shall he **g**.
6: 6 Do not all **g** to one place?
7: 2 Better to **g** to the house of
7: 2 house of mourning Than to **g**
8: 3 Do not be hasty to **g** from his
9: 3 and after that they **g** to the
9: 7 **G**, eat your bread with joy,
10:15 they do not even know how to **g**
12: 5 And the mourners **g** about the
Song 3: 2 And **g** about the city; In the
3: 3 The watchmen who **g** about the
3: 4 him and would not let him **g**,
3:11 **G** forth, O daughters of Zion,
4: 6 I will **g** my way to the
7: 8 'I will **g** up to the palm tree,
7:11 Let us **g** forth to the field;
Isa 2: 3 and let us **g** up to the mountain
2: 3 For out of Zion shall **g**
2:19 They shall **g** into the holes of
2:21 To **g** into the clefts of the
3:16 Walking and mincing as they **g**,
6: 8 And who will **g** for Us?"
6: 9 And He said, "**G**,
7: 3 **G** out now to meet Ahaz, you and
7: 6 Let us **g** up against Judah and
7:25 You will not **g** there for fear
8: 7 He will **g** up over all his
8: 7 up over all his channels And **g**
14:19 Who **g** down to the stones of
15: 5 Ascent of Luhith They will **g**
18: 2 on the waters, saying, "**G**,
20: 2 the son of Amoz, saying, "**G**,
21: 2 **G** up, O Elam! Besiege, O
21: 6 has the Lord said to me: "**G**,
22:15 the Lord GOD of hosts: "**G**,
23:16 **g** about the city, You
24:10 so that none may **g** in.
27: 4 I would **g** through them,
28:13 That they might **g** and fall
30: 2 Who walk to **g** down to Egypt,
30: 8 Now **g**, write it before them
31: 1 Woe to those who **g** down to
35: 8 Shall not **g** astray.
35: 9 shall any ravenous beast **g** up
36: 6 it will **g** into his hand and
36:10 **G** up against this land, and
37:32 For out of Jerusalem shall **g** a
38: 5 **G** and tell Hezekiah, 'Thus says
38:10 prime of my life I shall **g** to
38:18 Those who **g** down to the pit
38:22 is the sign that I shall **g** up
42:10 You who **g** down to the sea, and
42:13 The LORD shall **g** forth like a
45: 2 I will **g** before you And make
45:13 My city And let My exiles **g**
45:16 They shall **g** in confusion
47: 5 and **g** into darkness,
48:17 you by the way you should **g**.
48:20 **G** forth from Babylon!
49: 9 **G** forth,' To those who are in
49:17 who laid you waste Shall **g**
52:11 Depart! Depart! **G** out from
52:11 **G** out from the midst of her,
52:12 For you shall not **g** out with
52:12 Nor **g** by flight; For the
52:12 For the LORD will **g** before
55:12 For you shall **g** out with joy,
58: 6 To let the oppressed **g** free,
58: 8 And your righteousness shall **g**
60:20 Your sun shall no longer **g**
62:10 **G** through, Go through the
62:10 **G** through the gates!
66:17 To **g** to the gardens After
66:24 And they shall **g** forth and look
Jer 1: 7 For you shall **g** to all to
2: 2 **G** and cry in the hearing of
2:25 aliens, and after them I will **g**.
2:37 Indeed you will **g** forth from
3:12 **G** and proclaim these words
4: 5 And let us **g** into the
4:29 They shall **g** into thickets and
5: 5 I will **g** to the great men and
5:10 **G** up on her walls and destroy,
6: 4 and let us **g** up at noon.
6: 5 and let us **g** by night, And let
6:25 Do not **g** out into the field,
7:12 But **g** now to My place which
9: 2 And **g** from them! For they
10: 5 Because they cannot **g** by
11:12 of Jerusalem will **g** and cry
13: 1 **G** and get yourself a linen sash,
13: 4 **g** to the Euphrates, and hide it
13: 6 **g** to the Euphrates, and take
14:18 If I **g** out to the field,
14:18 both prophet and priest **g** about
15: 1 and let them **g** forth.
15: 2 say to you, 'Where should we **g**?
16: 5 nor **g** to lament or bemoan them;
16: 8 Also you shall not **g** into the
17: 4 Shall let **g** of your heritage
17:19 **G** and stand in the gate of the
17:19 come in and by which they **g**
18: 2 Arise and **g** down to the potter's
19: 1 **G** and get a potter's earthen
19: 2 And **g** out to the Valley of the
19:10 in the sight of the men who **g**
20: 6 shall **g** into captivity.
20: 6 You shall **g** to Babylon, and
21: 2 that the king may **g** away from
21:12 Lest My fury **g** forth like fire
22: 1 **G** down to the house of the king
22:20 **G** up to Lebanon, and cry out,
22:22 And your lovers shall **g** into
25: 6 Do not **g** after other gods to
25:16 will drink and stagger and **g**
25:32 disaster shall **g** forth From
27:18 do not **g** to Babylon.'
28:13 **G** and tell Hananiah, saying,
29:12 you will call upon Me and **g**
30:11 And will not let you **g**
30:16 shall **g** into captivity;
31: 4 And shall **g** forth in the
31: 6 and let us **g** up to Zion,
34: 2 **G** and speak to Zedekiah king of
34: 3 and you shall **g** to Babylon.'"
34:10 they obeyed and let them **g**.
34:14 you shall let him **g** free from
35: 2 **G** to the house of the
35:11 let us **g** to Jerusalem for fear
35:13 **G** and tell the men of Judah and
35:15 and do not **g** after other gods
36: 5 I cannot **g** into the house of
36: 6 'You **g**, therefore, and read
36:19 **G** and hide, you and Jeremiah;
37:12 went out of Jerusalem to **g**
39:16 **G** and speak to Ebed-Melech the
40: 1 of the guard had let him **g**
40: 4 and convenient for you to **g**,
40: 4 for you to go, **g** there."
40: 5 **G** back to Gedaliah the son of
40: 5 Or **g** wherever it seems
40: 5 seems convenient for you to **g**.
40: 5 and a gift and let him **g**.
40:15 in Mizpah, saying, "Let me **g**,
41:10 away captive and departed to **g**
42:14 but we will **g** to the land of
42:15 and **g** to dwell there,
42:17 men who set their faces to **g**
42:19 Do not **g** to Egypt!' Know
42:22 place where you desire to **g** to
43: 2 Do not **g** to Egypt to dwell
43:12 and he shall **g** out from there
44:12 who have set their faces to **g**
45: 5 in all places, wherever you **g**.
46: 8 I will **g** up and cover the
46:11 '**G** up to Gilead and take balm,
46:16 Arise! Let us **g** back to our own
46:19 Prepare yourself to **g** into
46:22 Her noise shall **g** like a
48: 7 And Chemosh shall **g** forth into
49: 3 For Milcom shall **g** into
49:12 the one who will altogether **g**
49:12 You shall not **g** unpunished, but
49:28 **g** up to Kedar, And devastate
49:31 **g** up to the wealthy nation that
49:36 the outcasts of Elam will not **g**.
50: 8 **G** out of the land of the
50:21 **G** up against the land of
50:27 Let them **g** down to the
50:33 have refused to let them **g**.
51: 9 and let us **g** everyone to his
51:45 **g** out of the midst of her!
Lam 4: 8 They **g** unrecognized in the
4:15 **G** away, unclean! Go away, go
4:15 unclean! **G** away, go away,
4:15 **g** away, Do not touch us!"
Ezek 1:12 wherever the spirit wanted to **g**,
1:20 Wherever the spirit wanted to **g**,
3: 1 eat this scroll, and **g**,
3: 4 **g** to the house of Israel and
3:11 'And **g**, get to the captives,
3:22 **g** out into the plain, and there
3:24 with me and said to me: "**G**,
3:25 so that you cannot **g** out among
5: 4 From there a fire will **g** out
8: 6 to make Me **g** far away from My
8: 9 **G** in, and see the wicked
9: 4 **G** through the midst of the city,
9: 5 **G** after him through the city and
9: 7 **G** out!" And they went out and
10: 2 **G** in among the wheels, under the
11:18 And they will **g** there, and they
12: 3 and **g** into captivity by day in
12: 3 You shall **g** from your place
12: 4 and at evening you shall **g** in
12: 4 like those who **g** into
12:12 shoulder at twilight and **g** out.
12:16 the Gentiles wherever they **g**.
13:20 your arms, and let the souls **g**,
14:17 **g** through the land,' and I cut
15: 7 They will **g** out from one fire,
20:10 Therefore I made them **g** out of
20:29 this high place to which you **g**?
20:39 thus says the Lord GOD: "**G**,
21: 4 therefore My sword shall **g** out
21:19 of the king of Babylon to **g**;
21:19 both of them shall **g** from the
21:20 a road for the sword to **g** to
23:44 as men **g** in to a woman who
26:20 with those who **g** down to the
30: 9 On that day messengers shall **g**
30:17 And these cities shall **g** into
30:18 And her daughters shall **g** into
31:14 the children of men who **g** down
32:18 With those who **g** down to the
32:19 **G** down, be placed with the
32:24 their shame with those who **g**
32:25 their shame With those who **g**
32:29 And with those who **g** down to
32:30 their shame with those who **g**
38:11 I will **g** up against a land of
38:11 I will **g** to a peaceful people,
39: 9 in the cities of Israel will **g**
42:14 they shall not **g** out of the
44: 3 and **g** out the same way."
44: 5 enter the house and all who **g**
44:19 When they **g** out to the outer
46: 2 Then he shall **g** out, but the
46: 8 he shall **g** in by way of the
46: 8 and **g** out the same way.
46: 9 north gate to worship shall **g**
46: 9 way of the south gate shall **g**
46: 9 but shall **g** out through the
46:10 When they **g** in, he shall go in;
46:10 he shall **g** in; and when they go
46:10 and when they **g** out, he shall
46:10 he shall **g** out.
46:12 Then he shall **g** out, and after
47: 9 moves, wherever the rivers **g**,
47: 9 because these waters **g** there;
48:11 who did not **g** astray when the
Dan 11: 6 the king of the South shall **g**
11:11 and **g** out and fight with him,
11:29 time he shall return and **g**
11:44 therefore he shall **g** out with
12: 9 **G** your way, Daniel, for the
12:13 **g** your way till the end;
Hos 1: 2 the LORD said to Hosea: "**G**,
2: 5 I will **g** after my lovers, Who
2: 7 I will **g** and return to my first
3: 1 **G** again, love a woman who is
4:14 For the men themselves **g**
4:15 Nor **g** up to Beth Aven,
5: 6 flocks and herds They shall **g**
5:14 will tear them and **g** away;
7:11 They **g** to Assyria.
7:12 Wherever they **g**,
Joel 2:16 Let the bridegroom **g** out from
3:11 Cause Your mighty ones to **g**
3:13 **g** down; For the winepress is
Am 1: 5 The people of Syria shall **g**
1:15 Their king shall **g** into
2: 7 A man and his father **g** in to
4: 3 You will **g** out through broken
5: 5 For Gilgal shall surely **g** into
6: 2 **G** over to Calneh and see
6: 2 And from there **g** to Hamath the
6: 2 Then **g** down to Gath of the
6: 7 Therefore they shall now **g**
7:12 Amaziah said to Amos: "**G**,
7:15 And the LORD said to me, '**G**,
8: 9 That I will make the sun **g** down
9: 4 Though they **g** into captivity
Jon 1: 2 **g** to Nineveh, that great city,
1: 3 to **g** with them to Tarshish from
3: 2 **g** to Nineveh, that great city,
Mic 1: 8 I will **g** stripped and naked;
1:11 of Zaanan does not **g** out.
1:16 For they shall **g** from you into
2:13 And **g** out by it; Their king
3: 6 The sun shall **g** down on the
4: 2 and let us **g** up to the mountain
4: 2 out of Zion the law shall **g**
4:10 For now you shall **g** forth from
4:10 And to Babylon you shall **g**.
7:11 that day the decree shall **g**
Nah 3:14 Fortify your strongholds! **G**
Hag 1: 8 **G** up to the mountains and bring
Zech 6: 5 who **g** out from their station
6: 7 steeds went out, eager to **g**,
6: 7 the earth. And He said, "**G**,
6: 8 those who **g** toward the north
6:10 and **g** the same day and enter the
8:21 of one city shall **g** to
8:21 Let us continue to **g** and pray
8:21 I myself will **g** also."
8:23 Let us **g** with you, for we have
9:14 And His arrow will **g** forth
9:14 And **g** with whirlwinds from the
14: 2 Half of the city shall **g** into
14: 3 Then the LORD will **g** forth
14:16 came against Jerusalem shall **g**

Mal 3:15 They even tempt God and **g**
4: 2 And you shall **g** out And grow
Mt 2: 8 **G** and search carefully for the
2:20 and **g** to the land of Israel,
2:22 he was afraid to **g** there.
5:24 and **g** your way. First be
5:41 And whoever compels you to **g** one
5:41 one mile, **g** with him two.
6: 6 **g** into your room, and when you
7:13 and there are many who **g** in by
8: 4 but **g** your way, show yourself
8: 9 And I say to this one, '**G**,'
8:13 **G** your way; and as you have
8:19 will follow You wherever You **g**.
8:21 let me first **g** and bury my
8:31 permit us to **g** away into the
8:32 And He said to them, "**G**.
9: 6 and **g** to your house."
9:13 But **g** and learn what this
10: 5 Do not **g** into the way of the
10: 6 But **g** rather to the lost sheep
10: 7 'And as you **g**, preach,
10:11 and stay there till you **g** out.
10:12 And when you **g** into a household,
11: 4 **G** and tell John the things which
11: 7 What did you **g** out into the
11: 8 'But what did you **g** out to see?
11: 9 'But what did you **g** out to see?
13:28 Do you want us then to **g** and
14:15 that they may **g** into the
14:16 'They do not need to **g** away.
14:22 get into the boat and **g** before
14:29 he walked on the water to **g** to
16:21 to His disciples that He must **g**
17:21 this kind does not **g** out except
17:27 **g** to the sea, cast in a hook,
18:12 leave the ninety-nine and **g** to
18:13 the ninety-nine that did not **g**
18:15 **g** and tell him his fault
19:21 "If you want to be perfect, **g**,
19:24 it is easier for a camel to **g**
20: 4 You also **g** into the vineyard,
20: 7 You also **g** into the vineyard,
20:14 Take what is yours and **g** your
21: 2 **G** into the village opposite you,
21:28 to the first and said, 'Son, **g**,
21:30 And he answered and said, 'I **g**,
21:30 'I go, sir,' but he did not **g**.
22: 9 Therefore **g** into the highways,
23:13 for you neither **g** in
23:13 those who are entering to **g** in.
24:17 who is on the housetop not **g**
24:18 him who is in the field not **g**
24:26 He is in the desert!' do not **g**
25: 6 **g** out to meet him!'
25: 9 but **g** rather to those who sell,
25:46 And these will **g** away into
26:18 **G** into the city to a certain
26:32 I will **g** before you to
26:36 Sit here while I **g** and pray over
27:65 **g** your way, make it as secure
28: 7 And **g** quickly and tell His
28:10 **G** and tell My brethren to go
28:10 Go and tell My brethren to **g**
28:19 **G** therefore and make disciples
Mk 1:38 Let us **g** into the next towns,
1:44 but **g** your way, show yourself
2:11 and **g** to your house."
5:19 **G** home to your friends, and tell
5:34 **G** in peace, and be healed of
6:36 that they may **g** into the
6:37 Shall we **g** and buy two hundred
6:38 **G** and see." And when they
6:45 get into the boat and **g** before
7:29 'For this saying **g** your way;
8:26 Neither **g** into the town, nor
9:43 to **g** to hell, into the fire
10:21 **G** your way, sell whatever you
10:25 It is easier for a camel to **g**
10:52 **G** your way; your faith has made
11: 2 **G** into the village opposite you;
11: 6 So they let them **g**.
12:38 who desire to **g** around in long
13:15 who is on the housetop not **g**
13:16 him who is in the field not **g**
14:12 Where do You want us to **g** and
14:13 **G** into the city, and a man will
14:28 I will **g** before you to
16: 7 'But **g**, tell His
16:15 **G** into all the world and preach
Lk 1:17 He will also **g** before Him in the
1:76 For you will **g** before the face
2:15 Let us now **g** to Bethlehem and
5:14 But **g** and show yourself to the
5:24 and **g** to your house."
7: 8 under me. And I say to one, '**G**,
7:22 **G** and tell John the things you
7:24 What did you **g** out into the
7:25 'But what did you **g** out to see?
7:26 'But what did you **g** out to see?
7:50 has saved you. **G** in peace."
8:14 **g** out and are choked with
8:31 He would not command them to **g**
8:48 made you well. **G** in peace."
8:51 He permitted no one to **g** in
9: 5 when you **g** out of that city,
9:12 that they may **g** into the
9:13 unless we **g** and buy food for
9:51 steadfastly set His face to **g**
9:57 will follow You wherever You **g**.
9:59 let me first **g** and bury my
9:60 but you **g** and preach the
9:61 but let me first **g** and bid
10: 1 where He Himself was about to **g**.
10: 3 **G** your way; behold, I send you
10: 7 Do not **g** from house to house.
10:10 **g** out into its streets and say,
10:37 **G** and do likewise."
11: 5 and **g** to him at midnight and
12:58 When you **g** with your adversary
13:32 And He said to them, "**G**,
14: 4 and healed him, and let him **g**.
14:10 **g** and sit down in the lowest
14:10 **g** up higher.' Then you will
14:18 and I must **g** and see it. I ask
14:21 **G** out quickly into the streets
14:23 **G** out into the highways and
15: 4 and **g** after the one which is
15:18 I will arise and **g** to my father,
15:28 he was angry and would not **g**
17:14 saw them, He said to them, "**G**,
17:19 **g** your way. Your faith has made
17:23 Look there!' Do not **g** after
18:25 it is easier for a camel to **g**
19:30 **G** into the village opposite
20:46 who desire to **g** around in long
21: 8 Therefore do not **g** after them.
22: 8 **G** and prepare the Passover for
22:33 I am ready to **g** with You, both
22:68 no means answer Me or let Me **g**.
23:22 chastise Him and let Him **g**.
Jn 1:43 day Jesus wanted to **g** to
4: 4 But He needed to **g** through
4:16 Jesus said to her, "**G**,
4:50 '**G** your way; your son lives."
6:67 Do you also want to **g** away?"
6:68 Him, "Lord, to whom shall we **g**?
7: 3 Depart from here and **g** into
7: 8 You **g** up to this feast. I am not
7:33 and then I **g** to Him who sent
7:35 Where does He intend to **g** that
7:35 Does He intend to **g** to the
8:11 **g** and sin no more."
8:21 Where I **g** you cannot come."
8:22 Where I **g** you cannot come'?"
9: 7 And He said to him, "**G**,
9:11 **G** to the pool of Siloam and
10: 9 and will **g** in and out and find
11: 7 Let us **g** to Judea again."
11:11 but I **g** that I may wake him
11:15 Nevertheless let us **g** to him."
11:16 disciples, "Let us also **g**,
11:44 "Loose him, and let him **g**.
14: 2 I **g** to prepare a place for you.
14: 3 And if I **g** and prepare a place
14: 4 And where I **g** you know, and the
14:12 because I **g** to My Father.
14:31 let us **g** from here.
15:16 you that you should **g** and bear
16: 5 But now I **g** away to Him who
16: 7 is to your advantage that I **g**
16: 7 for if I do not **g** away, the
16:10 because I **g** to My Father and
16:16 because I **g** to the Father."
16:17 because I **g** to the Father'?"
16:28 I leave the world and **g** to the
18: 8 let these **g** their way,"
18:28 But they themselves did not **g**
19:12 saying, "If you let this Man **g**,
20: 5 yet he did not **g** in.
20:17 but **g** to My brethren and say to
Acts 1:11 in like manner as you saw Him **g**
1:25 that he might **g** to his own
3: 3 Peter and John about to **g** into
3:13 he was determined to let Him **g**.
4:15 they had commanded them to **g**
4:21 them, they let them **g**,
4:23 And being let **g**, they went to
5:20 '**G**, stand in the temple
5:40 name of Jesus, and let them **g**.
7:40 Make us gods to **g** before
8:26 Arise and **g** toward the south
8:29 **G** near and overtake this
9: 6 Arise and **g** into the city, and
9:11 Arise and **g** to the street called
9:15 But the Lord said to him, "**G**,
10:20 **g** down and go with them,
10:20 go down and **g** with them,
10:28 man to keep company with or **g**
11:12 Then the Spirit told me to **g**
11:22 they sent out Barnabas to **g** as
12:17 of the prison. And he said, "**G**,
15: 2 others of them should **g** up to
15:36 Let us now **g** back and visit our
16: 3 Paul wanted to have him **g** on
16: 7 they tried to **g** into Bithynia,
16:10 immediately we sought to **g** to
16:35 saying, "Let those men **g**.
16:36 have sent to let you **g**.
16:36 and **g** in peace."
17: 9 and the rest, they let them **g**.
17:14 to **g** to the sea; but both Silas
18: 6 From now on I will **g** to the
19:21 to **g** to Jerusalem, saying,
19:30 And when Paul wanted to **g** in to
20: 1 and departed to **g** to Macedonia.
20:13 intending himself to **g** on foot.
20:22 now I **g** bound in the spirit to
21: 4 through the Spirit not to **g** up
21:12 pleaded with him not to **g** up
22:10 Arise and **g** into Damascus, and
23:10 commanded the soldiers to **g**
23:23 and two hundred spearmen to **g**
23:32 they left the horsemen to **g** on
24:25 **G** away for now; when I have a
25: 5 who have authority among you **g**
25: 9 Are you willing to **g** up to
25:12 To Caesar you shall **g**!"
25:20 whether he was willing to **g** to
27: 3 and gave him liberty to **g** to
27:40 And they let **g** the anchors and
28:18 me, wanted to let me **g**,
28:26 **G** to this people and say:
Rom 15:28 I shall **g** by way of you to
1 Cor 5:10 since then you would need to **g**
6: 1 **g** to law before the
6: 7 failure for you that you **g** to
10:27 dinner, and you desire to **g**,
16: 4 But if it is fitting that I **g**
16: 4 they will **g** with me.
16: 6 me on my journey, wherever I **g**.
2 Cor 9: 5 to exhort the brethren to **g** to
Gal 1:17 nor did I **g** up to Jerusalem to
2: 9 that we should **g** to the
Eph 4:26 do not let the sun **g** down on
Heb 3:10 They always **g** astray in
6: 1 let us **g** on to perfection, not
11: 8 obeyed when he was called to **g**
13:13 Therefore let us **g** forth to Him,
Jas 4:13 Today or tomorrow we will **g** to
Rev 3:12 and he shall **g** out no more.
10: 8 spoke to me again and said, "**G**,
13:10 leads into captivity shall **g**
16: 1 **G** and pour out the bowls of the
16:14 which **g** out to the kings of
17: 8 of the bottomless pit and **g** to
20: 8 and will **g** out to deceive the

GOAD (1/1) GOADS

Judg 3:31 of the Philistines with an ox **g**;

GOADS (4/4) GOAD

1 Sam 13:21 and to set the points of the **g**.
Eccl 12:11 words of the wise are like **g**,
Acts 9: 5 for you to kick against the **g**.
26:14 for you to kick against the **g**.

GOAL (1/1)

Phil 3:14 I press toward the **g** for the

GOAT (52/48) GOATS, GOATSKINS

Gen 15: 9 a three-year-old female **g**,
38:17 I will send a young **g** from the
38:20 And Judah sent the young **g** by
38:23 for I sent this young **g** and you
Ex 23:19 You shall not boil a young **g** in
34:26 You shall not boil a young **g** in
Lev 3:12 'And if his offering is a **g**,
4:24 his hand on the head of the **g**,
7:23 any fat, of ox or sheep or **g**.
9:15 offering, and took the **g**,
10:16 careful inquiry about the **g** of
16: 9 And Aaron shall bring the **g** on
16:10 But the **g** on which the lot fell
16:15 Then he shall kill the **g** of the
16:18 and some of the blood of the **g**,
16:20 he shall bring the live **g**.
16:21 hands on the head of the live **g**,
16:21 them on the head of the **g**,
16:22 The **g** shall bear on itself all
16:22 and he shall release the **g** in
16:26 And he who released the **g** as the
16:27 for the sin offering and the **g**
17: 3 who kills an ox or lamb or **g**
22:27 When a bull or a sheep or a **g** is
Num 15:11 or for each lamb or young **g**.
15:27 then he shall bring a female **g**
18:17 or the firstborn of a **g** you
28:22 also one **g** as a sin offering,
29:22 also one **g** as a sin offering,
29:28 also one **g** as a sin offering,
29:31 also one **g** as a sin offering,
29:34 also one **g** as a sin offering,
29:38 also one **g** as a sin offering,
Deut 14: 4 eat: the ox, the sheep, the **g**,
14: 5 the roe deer, the wild **g**,
14: 5 the wild goat, the mountain **g**,
14:21 You shall not boil a young **g** in
Judg 6:19 went in and prepared a young **g**,
13:15 and we will prepare a young **g**
13:19 So Manoah took the young **g** with
14: 6 would have torn apart a young **g**,
15: 1 visited his wife with a young **g**,
1 Sam 16:20 a skin of wine, and a young **g**,
Prov 30:31 A male **g** also, And a king
Isa 11: 6 shall lie down with the young **g**,
34:14 And the wild **g** shall bleat to
Ezek 43:25 days you shall prepare a **g**
Dan 8: 5 suddenly a male **g** came from the
8: 5 and the **g** had a notable horn
8: 8 Therefore the male **g** grew very
8:21 And the male **g** is the kingdom
Lk 15:29 yet you never gave me a young **g**,

GOATH (1/1)

Jer 31:39 then it shall turn toward **G**.

GOATHERDS (1/1)

Zech 10: 3 And I will punish the **g**.

GOATS (90/88) GOAT, GOATS'

Gen 27: 9 there two choice kids of the *g*,
27:16 the skins of the kids of the *g*
30:32 and speckled among the *g*;
30:33 and spotted among the *g*,
30:35 he removed that day the male *g*
30:35 all the female *g* that were
31:38 your ewes and your female *g*
32:14 two hundred female *g* and twenty
32:14 female goats and twenty male *g*,
37:31 tunic, killed a kid of the *g*,
Ex 12: 5 from the sheep or from the *g*.
Lev 1:10 flocks—of the sheep or of the *g*—
4:23 as his offering a kid of the *g*,
4:28 as his offering a kid of the *g*,
5: 6 a lamb or a kid of the *g* as a
9: 3 Take a kid of the *g* as a sin
16: 5 of Israel two kids of the *g* as
16: 7 He shall take the two *g* and
16: 8 shall cast lots for the two *g*:
22:19 from the sheep, or from the *g*.
23:19 sacrifice one kid of the *g* as
Num 7:16 one kid of the *g* as a sin
7:17 oxen, five rams, five male *g*,
7:22 one kid of the *g* as a sin
7:23 oxen, five rams, five male *g*,
7:28 one kid of the *g* as a sin
7:29 oxen, five rams, five male *g*,
7:34 one kid of the *g* as a sin
7:35 oxen, five rams, five male *g*,
7:40 one kid of the *g* as a sin
7:41 oxen, five rams, five male *g*,
7:46 one kid of the *g* as a sin
7:47 oxen, five rams, five male *g*,
7:52 one kid of the *g* as a sin
7:53 oxen, five rams, five male *g*,
7:58 one kid of the *g* as a sin
7:59 oxen, five rams, five male *g*,
7:64 one kid of the *g* as a sin
7:65 oxen, five rams, five male *g*,
7:70 one kid of the *g* as a sin
7:71 oxen, five rams, five male *g*,
7:76 one kid of the *g* as a sin
7:77 oxen, five rams, five male *g*,
7:82 one kid of the *g* as a sin
7:83 oxen, five rams, five male *g*,
7:87 and the kids of the *g* as a sin
7:88 the male *g* sixty, and the lambs
15:24 and one kid of the *g* as a sin
28:15 Also one kid of the *g* as a sin
28:30 'also one kid of the *g*,
29: 5 also one kid of the *g* as a sin
29:11 also one kid of the *g* as a sin
29:16 also one kid of the *g* as a sin
29:19 also one kid of the *g* as a sin
29:25 also one kid of the *g* as a sin
Deut 32:14 of the breed of Bashan, and *g*,
1 Sam 10: 3 you, one carrying three young *g*,
24: 2 men on the Rocks of the Wild *G*.
25: 2 thousand sheep and a thousand *g*.
1 Ki 20:27 like two little flocks of *g*,
2 Chr 17:11 thousand seven hundred male *g*.
29:21 and seven male *g* for a sin
29:23 they brought out the male *g*
35: 7 lay people lambs and young *g*
Ezra 6:17 for all Israel twelve male *g*,
8:35 and twelve male *g* as a sin
Job 39: 1 time when the wild mountain *g*
Ps 50: 9 Nor *g* out of your folds.
50:13 Or drink the blood of *g*?
66:15 I will offer bulls with *g*.
104:18 high hills are for the wild *g*;
Prov 27:26 And the *g* the price of a
Song 1: 8 And feed your little *g* Beside
4: 1 hair is like a flock of *g*,
6: 5 hair is like a flock of *g*
Isa 1:11 of bulls, Or of lambs or *g*.
13:21 And wild *g* will caper there.
34: 6 With the blood of lambs and *g*,
Jer 51:40 Like rams with male *g*.
Ezek 27:21 with you in lambs, rams, and *g*.
34:17 and sheep, between rams and *g*.
39:18 Of *g* and bulls, All of them
43:22 you shall offer a kid of the *g*
45:23 and a kid of the *g* daily for a
Mt 25:32 divides his sheep from the *g*.
25:33 but the *g* on the left.
Heb 9:12 Not with the blood of *g* and
9:13 For if the blood of bulls and *g*
9:19 took the blood of calves and *g*,
10: 4 that the blood of bulls and *g*

GOATS' (10/10) GOATS

Ex 25: 4 fine linen, and *g* hair;
26: 7 shall also make curtains of *g*
35: 6 fine linen, and *g* hair;
35:23 and *g* hair, red skins of rams,
35:26 with wisdom spun yarn of *g*
36:14 He made curtains of *g* hair for
Num 31:20 everything woven of *g* hair,
1 Sam 19:13 put a cover of *g* hair for his
19:16 with a cover of *g* hair for his
Prov 27:27 You shall have enough *g* milk

GOATSKINS (1/1) GOAT

Heb 11:37 about in sheepskins and *g*,

GOB (2/2)

2 Sam 21:18 with the Philistines at *G*.
21:19 Again there was war at *G* with

GOBLET (1/1)

Song 7: 2 Your navel is a rounded *g*;

GOD (4393/3841) GOD-GIVEN, GOD-WHO-FORGIVES, GOD'S, GODHEAD, GODLY, ONE, YAH, YOU-ARE-THE-GOD-WHO-SEES

Gen 1: 1 In the beginning *G* created the
1: 2 And the Spirit of *G* was
1: 3 Then *G* said, "Let there be
1: 4 And *G* saw the light, that it
1: 4 and *G* divided the light from
1: 5 *G* called the light Day, and the
1: 6 Then *G* said, "Let there be a
1: 7 Thus *G* made the firmament, and
1: 8 And *G* called the firmament
1: 9 Then *G* said, "Let the waters
1:10 And *G* called the dry land
1:10 And *G* saw that it was good.
1:11 Then *G* said, "Let the earth
1:12 And *G* saw that it was good.
1:14 Then *G* said, "Let there be
1:16 Then *G* made two great lights:
1:17 *G* set them in the firmament of
1:18 And *G* saw that it was good.
1:20 Then *G* said, "Let the waters
1:21 So *G* created great sea creatures
1:21 And *G* saw that it was good.
1:22 And *G* blessed them, saying, "Be
1:24 Then *G* said, "Let the earth
1:25 And *G* made the beast of the
1:25 And *G* saw that it was good.
1:26 Then *G* said, "Let Us make man
1:27 So *G* created man in His own
1:27 in the image of *G* He created
1:28 Then *G* blessed them, and God
1:28 and *G* said to them, "Be
1:29 And *G* said, "See, I have given
1:31 Then *G* saw everything that He
2: 2 And on the seventh day *G* ended
2: 3 Then *G* blessed the seventh day
2: 3 from all His work which *G* had
2: 4 in the day that the LORD *G*
2: 5 For the LORD *G* had not caused
2: 7 And the LORD *G* formed man of
2: 8 The LORD *G* planted a garden
2: 9 out of the ground the LORD *G*
2:15 Then the LORD *G* took the man
2:16 And the LORD *G* commanded the
2:18 And the LORD *G* said, "It is
2:19 Out of the ground the LORD *G*
2:21 And the LORD *G* caused a deep
2:22 Then the rib which the LORD *G*
3: 1 of the field which the LORD *G*
3: 1 Has *G* indeed said, 'You shall
3: 3 *G* has said, 'You shall not eat
3: 5 For *G* knows that in the day you
3: 5 opened, and you will be like *G*,
3: 8 heard the sound of the LORD *G*
3: 8 the presence of the LORD *G*
3: 9 Then the LORD *G* called to Adam
3:13 And the LORD *G* said to the
3:14 So the LORD *G* said to the
3:21 Adam and his wife the LORD *G*
3:22 Then the LORD *G* said,
3:23 therefore the LORD *G* sent him
4:25 For *G* has appointed another seed
5: 1 In the day that *G* created man,
5: 1 made him in the likeness of *G*.
5:22 Enoch walked with *G* three
5:24 And Enoch walked with *G*;
5:24 for *G* took him.
6: 2 that the sons of *G* saw the
6: 4 when the sons of *G* came in to
6: 9 generations. Noah walked with *G*.
6:11 earth also was corrupt before *G*,
6:12 So *G* looked upon the earth, and
6:13 And *G* said to Noah, "The end of
6:22 according to all that *G*
7: 9 as *G* had commanded Noah.
7:16 went in as *G* had commanded him;
8: 1 Then *G* remembered Noah, and
8: 1 And *G* made a wind to pass over
8:15 Then *G* spoke to Noah, saying,
9: 1 So *G* blessed Noah and his sons,
9: 6 For in the image of *G* He made
9: 8 Then *G* spoke to Noah and to his
9:12 And *G* said: "This is the sign
9:16 everlasting covenant between *G*
9:17 And *G* said to Noah, "This is
9:26 The *G* of Shem, And may Canaan
9:27 May *G* enlarge Japheth, And may
14:18 he was the priest of *G* Most
14:19 Blessed be Abram of *G* Most High,
14:20 And blessed be *G* Most High,
14:22 *G* Most High, the Possessor of
15: 2 But Abram said, "Lord *G*,
15: 8 And he said, "Lord *G*,
17: 1 said to him, "I am Almighty *G*;
17: 3 and *G* talked with him, saying:
17: 7 to be *G* to you and your
17: 8 and I will be their *G*.
17: 9 And *G* said to Abraham: "As for
17:15 Then *G* said to Abraham, "As
17:18 And Abraham said to *G*,
17:19 Then *G* said: "No, Sarah your
17:22 and *G* went up from Abraham.
17:23 as *G* had said to him.
19:29 when *G* destroyed the cities of
19:29 that *G* remembered Abraham, and
20: 3 But *G* came to Abimelech in a
20: 6 And *G* said to him in a dream,
20:11 surely the fear of *G* is not in
20:13 when *G* caused me to wander from
20:17 So Abraham prayed to *G*;
20:17 and *G* healed Abimelech, his
21: 2 at the set time of which *G* had
21: 4 as *G* had commanded him.
21: 6 *G* has made me laugh, and all
21:12 But *G* said to Abraham, "Do not
21:17 And *G* heard the voice of the
21:17 Then the angel of *G* called to
21:17 for *G* has heard the voice of
21:19 Then *G* opened her eyes, and she
21:20 So *G* was with the lad; and he
21:22 *G* is with you in all that you
21:23 swear to me by *G* that you will
21:33 of the LORD, the Everlasting *G*.
22: 1 pass after these things that *G*
22: 3 went to the place of which *G*
22: 8 *G* will provide for Himself the
22: 9 came to the place of which *G*
22:12 for now I know that you fear *G*,
24: 3 the *G* of heaven and the God of
24: 3 the God of heaven and the *G* of
24: 7 The LORD *G* of heaven, who took
24:12 O LORD *G* of my master Abraham,
24:27 Blessed be the LORD *G* of my
24:42 O LORD *G* of my master Abraham,
24:48 and blessed the LORD *G* of my
25:11 that *G* blessed his son Isaac.
26:24 I am the *G* of your father
27:20 Because the LORD your *G* brought
27:28 Therefore may *G* give you Of
28: 3 'May *G* Almighty bless you,
28: 4 Which *G* gave to Abraham."
28:12 and there the angels of *G* were
28:13 I am the LORD *G* of Abraham
28:13 Abraham your father and the *G*
28:17 none other than the house of *G*,
28:20 If *G* will be with me, and keep
28:21 then the LORD shall be my *G*.
30: 2 said, "Am I in the place of *G*,
30: 6 *G* has judged my case; and He has
30:17 And *G* listened to Leah, and she
30:18 *G* has given me my wages, because
30:20 *G* has endowed me with a good
30:22 Then *G* remembered Rachel, and
30:22 and *G* listened to her and
30:23 *G* has taken away my reproach."
31: 5 but the *G* of my father has been
31: 7 but *G* did not allow him to hurt
31: 9 So *G* has taken away the
31:11 Then the Angel of *G* spoke to me
31:13 I am the *G* of Bethel, where you
31:16 For all these riches which *G* has
31:16 whatever *G* has said to you, do
31:24 But *G* had come to Laban the
31:29 but the *G* of your father spoke
31:42 Unless the *G* of my father, the
31:42 the *G* of Abraham and the Fear
31:42 *G* has seen my affliction and
31:50 *G* is witness between you and
31:53 The *G* of Abraham, the God of
31:53 the *G* of Nahor, and the God of
31:53 and the *G* of their father judge
32: 1 and the angels of *G* met him.
32: 9 O *G* of my father Abraham and God
32: 9 God of my father Abraham and *G*
32:28 for you have struggled with *G*
32:30 For I have seen *G* face to face,
33: 5 The children whom *G* has
33:10 though I had seen the face of *G*,
33:11 because *G* has dealt graciously
35: 1 Then *G* said to Jacob, "Arise,
35: 1 and make an altar there to *G*,
35: 3 I will make an altar there to *G*,
35: 5 and the terror of *G* was upon
35: 7 because there *G* appeared to him
35: 9 Then *G* appeared to Jacob again,
35:10 And *G* said to him, "Your name
35:11 Also *G* said to him: "I am God
35:11 I am *G* Almighty. Be fruitful
35:13 Then *G* went up from him in the
35:15 the name of the place where *G*
39: 9 wickedness, and sin against *G*?
40: 8 not interpretations belong to *G*?
41:16 *G* will give Pharaoh an answer
41:25 *G* has shown Pharaoh what He is
41:28 *G* has shown Pharaoh what He is
41:32 the thing is established by *G*,
41:32 and *G* will shortly bring it to
41:38 man in whom is the Spirit of *G*?
41:39 Inasmuch as *G* has shown you all
41:51 For *G* has made me forget all my
41:52 For *G* has caused me to be
42:18 this and live, for I fear *G*:
42:28 What is this that *G* has done
43:14 And may *G* Almighty give you
43:23 Your *G* and the God of your
43:23 Your God and the *G* of your
43:29 *G* be gracious to you, my son."
44:16 *G* has found out the iniquity of
45: 5 for *G* sent me before you to
45: 7 And *G* sent me before you to
45: 8 you who sent me here, but *G*;
45: 9 *G* has made me lord of all Egypt;

G

46: 1 offered sacrifices to the **G** of
46: 2 Then **G** spoke to Israel in the
46: 3 So He said, "I am **G**,
46: 3 the **G** of your father; do not
48: 3 **G** Almighty appeared to me at Luz
48: 9 whom **G** has given me in this
48:11 **G** has also shown me your
48:15 blessed Joseph, and said: "**G**,
48:15 The **G** who has fed me all my
48:20 May **G** make you as Ephraim and as
48:21 but **G** will be with you and
49:24 By the hands of the Mighty **G**
49:25 By the **G** of your father who
50:17 of the servants of the **G** of
50:19 for am I in the place of **G**?
50:20 but **G** meant it for good, in
50:24 but **G** will surely visit you,
50:25 **G** will surely visit you, and you
Ex 1:17 But the midwives feared **G**,
1:20 Therefore **G** dealt well with the
1:21 because the midwives feared **G**,
2:23 and their cry came up to **G**
2:24 So **G** heard their groaning, and
2:24 and **G** remembered His covenant
2:25 And **G** looked upon the children
2:25 and **G** acknowledged them.
3: 1 to Horeb, the mountain of **G**.
3: 4 **G** called to him from the midst
3: 6 I am the **G** of your father—the
3: 6 the **G** of Abraham, the God of
3: 6 the **G** of Isaac, and the God of
3: 6 and the **G** of Jacob." And Moses
3: 6 he was afraid to look upon **G**.
3:11 But Moses said to **G**,
3:12 you shall serve **G** on this
3:13 Then Moses said to **G**,
3:13 The **G** of your fathers has sent
3:14 And **G** said to Moses, "I AM WHO
3:15 Moreover **G** said to Moses, "Thus
3:15 The LORD **G** of your fathers, the
3:15 the **G** of Abraham, the God of
3:15 the **G** of Isaac, and the God of
3:15 and the **G** of Jacob, has sent me
3:16 The LORD **G** of your fathers, the
3:16 the **G** of Abraham, of Isaac, and
3:18 The LORD **G** of the Hebrews has
3:18 sacrifice to the LORD our **G**.
4: 5 may believe that the LORD **G**
4: 5 the **G** of Abraham, the God of
4: 5 the **G** of Isaac, and the God of
4: 5 and the **G** of Jacob, has
4:16 and you shall be to him as **G**.
4:20 And Moses took the rod of **G** in
4:27 met him on the mountain of **G**,
5: 1 Thus says the LORD **G** of Israel:
5: 3 The **G** of the Hebrews has met
5: 3 sacrifice to the LORD our **G**,
5: 8 us go and sacrifice to our **G**.
6: 2 And **G** spoke to Moses and said
6: 3 as **G** Almighty, but by My name
6: 7 My people, and I will be your **G**.
6: 7 that I am the LORD your **G**
7: 1 I have made you as **G** to
7:16 The LORD **G** of the Hebrews has
8:10 is no one like the LORD our **G**.
8:19 "This is the finger of **G**.
8:25 sacrifice to your **G** in the
8:26 Egyptians to the LORD our **G**.
8:27 sacrifice to the LORD our **G**
8:28 sacrifice to the LORD your **G**
9: 1 Thus says the LORD **G** of the
9:13 Thus says the LORD **G** of the
9:30 will not yet fear the LORD **G**.
10: 3 Thus says the LORD **G** of the
10: 7 may serve the LORD their **G**.
10: 8 "Go, serve the LORD your **G**.
10:16 against the LORD your **G** and
10:17 and entreat the LORD your **G**,
10:25 sacrifice to the LORD our **G**.
10:26 them to serve the LORD our **G**,
13:17 that **G** did not lead them by
13:17 for **G** said, "Lest perhaps the
13:18 So **G** led the people around by
13:19 **G** will surely visit you, and you
14:19 And the Angel of **G**,
15: 2 my salvation; He is my **G**,
15: 2 will praise Him; My father's **G**,
15:26 the voice of the LORD your **G**
16:12 that I am the LORD your **G**.
17: 9 of the hill with the rod of **G**
18: 1 heard of all that **G** had done
18: 4 The **G** of my father was my help,
18: 5 encamped at the mountain of **G**.
18:12 sacrifices to offer to **G**.
18:12 Moses' father-in-law before **G**.
18:15 come to me to inquire of **G**.
18:16 I make known the statutes of **G**
18:19 and **G** will be with you:
18:19 Stand before **G** for the people,
18:19 may bring the difficulties to **G**.
18:21 people able men, such as fear **G**,
18:23 and **G** so commands you, then
19: 3 And Moses went up to **G**,
19:17 out of the camp to meet with **G**,
19:19 and **G** answered him by voice.
20: 1 And **G** spoke all these words,
20: 2 "I am the LORD your **G**,
20: 5 For I, the LORD your **G**,
20: 5 LORD your God, am a jealous **G**,
20: 7 the name of the LORD your **G**
20:10 the Sabbath of the LORD your **G**.
20:12 land which the LORD your **G** is
20:19 but let not **G** speak with us,
20:20 for **G** has come to test you, and
20:21 near the thick darkness where **G**
21:13 but **G** delivered him into his
22:20 "He who sacrifices to any **g**,
22:28 "You shall not revile **G**,
23:17 shall appear before the Lord **G**.
23:19 the house of the LORD your **G**.
23:25 shall serve the LORD your **G**,
24:10 and they saw the **G** of Israel.
24:11 not lay His hand. So they saw **G**,
24:13 went up to the mountain of **G**.
29:45 of Israel and will be their **G**.
29:46 that I am the LORD their **G**,
29:46 I am the LORD their **G**.
31: 3 filled him with the Spirit of **G**,
31:18 written with the finger of **G**.
32: 4 they said, "This is your **g**,
32: 8 it, and said, 'This is your **g**,
32:11 pleaded with the LORD his **G**,
32:16 the tablets were the work of **G**,
32:16 writing was the writing of **G**
32:27 Thus says the LORD **G** of Israel:
32:31 have made for themselves a **g**
34: 6 "The LORD, the LORD **G**,
34:14 you shall worship no other **g**,
34:14 is Jealous, is a jealous **G**),
34:23 the LORD **G** of Israel.
34:24 appear before the LORD your **G**
34:26 the house of the LORD your **G**.
35:31 filled him with the Spirit of **G**,
Lev 2:13 salt of the covenant of your **G**
4:22 of the LORD his **G** in
10:17 and **G** has given it to you to
11:44 'For I am the LORD your **G**.
11:45 the land of Egypt, to be your **G**.
18: 2 to them: 'I am the LORD your **G**.
18: 4 in them: I am the LORD your **G**.
18:21 you profane the name of your **G**:
18:30 by them: I am the LORD your **G**.
19: 2 for I the LORD your **G** am
19: 3 I am the LORD your **G**.
19: 4 I am the LORD your **G**.
19:10 I am the LORD your **G**.
19:12 you profane the name of your **G**:
19:14 blind, but shall fear your **G**:
19:25 I am the LORD your **G**.
19:31 by them: I am the LORD your **G**.
19:32 of an old man, and fear your **G**:
19:34 I am the LORD your **G**.
19:36 I am the LORD your **G**,
20: 7 for I am the LORD your **G**.
20:24 honey." I am the LORD your **G**,
21: 6 They shall be holy to their **G**
21: 6 not profane the name of their **G**,
21: 6 fire, and the bread of their **G**;
21: 7 the priest is holy to his **G**.
21: 8 he offers the bread of your **G**.
21:12 profane the sanctuary of his **G**;
21:12 of the anointing oil of his **G**
21:17 to offer the bread of his **G**.
21:21 to offer the bread of his **G**.
21:22 'He may eat the bread of his **G**,
22:25 of these as the bread of your **G**,
22:33 the land of Egypt, to be your **G**:
23:14 brought an offering to your **G**;
23:22 I am the LORD your **G**.
23:28 for you before the LORD your **G**.
23:40 before the LORD your **G** for
23:43 I am the LORD your **G**.'
24:15 Whoever curses his **G** shall bear
24:22 for I am the LORD your **G**.
25:17 but you shall fear your **G**;
25:17 for I am the LORD your **G**.
25:36 from him; but fear your **G**,
25:38 'I am the LORD your **G**,
25:38 of Canaan and to be your **G**.
25:43 but you shall fear your **G**.
25:55 I am the LORD your **G**.
26: 1 for I am the LORD your **G**.
26:12 walk among you and be your **G**,
26:13 I am the LORD your **G**,
26:44 for I am the LORD their **G**.
26:45 that I might be their **G**:
Num 6: 7 because his separation to **G** is
10: 9 before the LORD your **G**,
10:10 memorial for you before your **G**:
10:10 I am the LORD your **G**."
12:13 saying, "Please heal her, O **G**,
15:40 and be holy for your **G**.
15:41 "I am the LORD your **G**,
15:41 land of Egypt, to be your **G**:
15:41 I am the LORD your **G**."
16: 9 a small thing to you that the **G**
16:22 on their faces, and said, "O **G**,
16:22 the **G** of the spirits of all
21: 5 And the people spoke against **G**
22: 9 Then **G** came to Balaam and said,
22:10 So Balaam said to **G**,
22:12 And **G** said to Balaam, "You
22:18 the word of the LORD my **G**,
22:20 And **G** came to Balaam at night
22:38 The word that **G** puts in my
23: 4 And **G** met Balaam, and he said to
23: 8 How shall I curse whom **G** has not
23:19 **G** is not a man, that He should
23:21 The LORD his **G** is with him,
23:22 **G** brings them out of Egypt
23:23 what **G** has done!'
23:27 perhaps it will please **G** that
24: 2 and the Spirit of **G** came upon
24: 4 of him who hears the words of **G**,
24: 8 '**G** brings him out of Egypt;
24:16 of him who hears the words of **G**,
24:23 Alas! Who shall live when **G** does
25:13 he was zealous for his **G**,
27:16 the **G** of the spirits of all
Deut 1: 6 The LORD our **G** spoke to us in
1:10 The LORD your **G** has multiplied
1:11 May the LORD **G** of your fathers
1:19 as the LORD our **G** had
1:20 which the LORD our **G** is giving
1:21 the LORD your **G** has set the
1:21 as the LORD **G** of your fathers
1:25 land which the LORD our **G** is
1:26 the command of the LORD your **G**;
1:30 'The LORD your **G**,
1:31 you saw how the LORD your **G**
1:32 not believe the LORD your **G**,
1:41 just as the LORD our **G**
2: 7 For the LORD your **G** has blessed
2: 7 forty years the LORD your **G**
2:29 the land which the LORD our **G**
2:30 for the LORD your **G** hardened
2:33 And the LORD our **G** delivered
2:36 the LORD our **G** delivered all
2:37 or wherever the LORD our **G** had
3: 3 So the LORD our **G** also
3:18 The LORD your **G** has given you
3:20 land which the LORD your **G** is
3:21 seen all that the LORD your **G**
3:22 for the LORD your **G** Himself
3:24 'O Lord **G**, You have begun to
3:24 for what **g** is there in heaven
4: 1 the land which the LORD **G** of
4: 2 of the LORD your **G** which I
4: 3 for the LORD your **G** has
4: 4 held fast to the LORD your **G**
4: 5 just as the LORD my **G**
4: 7 nation is there that has **G**
4: 7 as the LORD our **G** is to us,
4:10 stood before the LORD your **G**
4:19 which the LORD your **G** has
4:21 land which the LORD your **G** is
4:23 covenant of the LORD your **G**
4:23 which the LORD your **G** has
4:24 For the LORD your **G** is a
4:24 a consuming fire, a jealous **G**.
4:25 the sight of the LORD your **G**
4:29 you will seek the LORD your **G**,
4:30 you turn to the LORD your **G**
4:31 (for the LORD your **G** is a
4:31 your God is a merciful **G**),
4:32 since the day that **G** created
4:33 ever hear the voice of **G**
4:34 Or did **G** ever try to go and
4:34 to all that the LORD your **G**
4:35 that the LORD Himself is **G**;
4:39 that the LORD Himself is **G** in
4:40 land which the LORD your **G** is
5: 2 The LORD our **G** made a covenant
5: 6 I am the LORD your **G** who
5: 9 For I, the LORD your **G**,
5: 9 LORD your God, am a jealous **G**,
5:11 the name of the LORD your **G**
5:12 as the LORD your **G** commanded
5:14 the Sabbath of the LORD your **G**.
5:15 and the LORD your **G** brought
5:15 therefore the LORD your **G**
5:16 as the LORD your **G** has
5:16 land which the LORD your **G** is
5:24 Surely the LORD our **G** has shown
5:24 We have seen this day that **G**
5:25 the voice of the LORD our **G**
5:26 heard the voice of the living **G**
5:27 hear all that the LORD our **G**
5:27 us all that the LORD our **G**
5:32 to do as the LORD your **G** has
5:33 the ways which the LORD your **G**
6: 1 which the LORD your **G** has
6: 2 you may fear the LORD your **G**,
6: 3 greatly as the LORD **G** of your
6: 4 O Israel: The LORD our **G**,
6: 5 shall love the LORD your **G**
6:10 when the LORD your **G** brings
6:13 shall fear the LORD your **G**
6:15 (for the LORD your **G** is a
6:15 LORD your God is a jealous **G**
6:15 the anger of the LORD your **G**
6:16 not tempt the LORD your **G** as
6:17 of the LORD your **G**,
6:20 which the LORD our **G** has
6:24 to fear the LORD our **G**,
6:25 before the LORD our **G**,
7: 1 When the LORD your **G** brings you
7: 2 and when the LORD your **G**
7: 6 holy people to the LORD your **G**;
7: 6 the LORD your **G** has chosen you
7: 9 know that the LORD your **G**,
7: 9 the LORD your God, He is **G**,
7: 9 the faithful **G** who keeps
7:12 that the LORD your **G** will keep
7:16 peoples whom the LORD your **G**
7:18 well what the LORD your **G** did
7:19 by which the LORD your **G**
7:19 So shall the LORD your **G** do to
7:20 Moreover the LORD your **G** will
7:21 of them; for the LORD your **G**,
7:21 God, the great and awesome **G**,
7:22 And the LORD your **G** will drive
7:23 But the LORD your **G** will
7:25 abomination to the LORD your **G**.
8: 2 remember that the LORD your **G**
8: 5 so the LORD your **G** chastens

8: 6 of the LORD your G,
8: 7 For the LORD your G is bringing
8:10 shall bless the LORD your G
8:11 do not forget the LORD your G
8:14 and you forget the LORD your G
8:18 shall remember the LORD your G,
8:19 means forget the LORD your G,
8:20 the voice of the LORD your G.
9: 3 today that the LORD your G
9: 4 after the LORD your G has cast
9: 5 nations that the LORD your G
9: 6 that the LORD your G is not
9: 7 you provoked the LORD your G
9:10 written with the finger of G,
9:16 sinned against the LORD your G—
9:23 commandment of the LORD your G,
9:26 the LORD, and said: 'O Lord G,
10: 9 just as the LORD your G
10:12 what does the LORD your G
10:12 but to fear the LORD your G,
10:12 to serve the LORD your G with
10:14 belong to the LORD your G,
10:17 For the LORD your G is God of
10:17 For the LORD your God is G of
10:17 and Lord of lords, the great G,
10:20 shall fear the LORD your G;
10:21 your praise, and He is your G,
10:22 and now the LORD your G has
11: 1 you shall love the LORD your G,
11: 2 chastening of the LORD your G,
11:12 land for which the LORD your G
11:12 the eyes of the LORD your G
11:13 to love the LORD your G and
11:22 to do—to love the LORD your G,
11:25 the LORD your G will put the
11:27 of the LORD your G which I
11:28 of the LORD your G,
11:29 when the LORD your G has
11:31 land which the LORD your G is
12: 1 in the land which the LORD G
12: 4 not worship the LORD your G
12: 5 place where the LORD your G
12: 7 eat before the LORD your G,
12: 7 in which the LORD your G has
12: 9 which the LORD your G is
12:10 land which the LORD your G is
12:11 place where the LORD your G
12:12 rejoice before the LORD your G,
12:15 blessing of the LORD your G
12:18 them before the LORD your G
12:18 place which the LORD your G
12:18 before the LORD your G in all
12:20 When the LORD your G enlarges
12:21 place where the LORD your G
12:27 the altar of the LORD your G;
12:27 the altar of the LORD your G,
12:28 the sight of the LORD your G.
12:29 When the LORD your G cuts off
12:31 not worship the LORD your G
13: 3 for the LORD your G is testing
13: 3 you love the LORD your G with
13: 4 walk after the LORD your G
13: 5 you away from the LORD your G,
13: 5 way in which the LORD your G
13:10 you away from the LORD your G,
13:12 which the LORD your G gives
13:16 plunder, for the LORD your G.
13:18 the voice of the LORD your G,
13:18 in the eyes of the LORD your G.
14: 1 children of the LORD your G;
14: 2 holy people to the LORD your G,
14:21 holy people to the LORD your G.
14:23 eat before the LORD your G,
14:23 learn to fear the LORD your G
14:24 place where the LORD your G
14:24 when the LORD your G has
14:25 place which the LORD your G
14:26 there before the LORD your G,
14:29 that the LORD your G may bless
15: 4 land which the LORD your G is
15: 5 the voice of the LORD your G,
15: 6 For the LORD your G will bless
15: 7 land which the LORD your G is
15:10 for this thing the LORD your G
15:15 and the LORD your G redeemed
15:18 Then the LORD your G will
15:19 sanctify to the LORD your G;
15:20 eat it before the LORD your G
15:21 it to the LORD your G.
16: 1 Passover to the LORD your G,
16: 1 month of Abib the LORD your G
16: 2 Passover to the LORD your G,
16: 5 gates which the LORD your G
16: 6 place where the LORD your G
16: 7 place which the LORD your G
16: 8 assembly to the LORD your G.
16:10 of Weeks to the LORD your G
16:10 shall give as the LORD your G
16:11 rejoice before the LORD your G,
16:11 place where the LORD your G
16:15 feast to the LORD your G in
16:15 because the LORD your G will
16:16 appear before the LORD your G
16:17 blessing of the LORD your G
16:18 which the LORD your G gives
16:20 land which the LORD your G is
16:21 yourself to the LORD your G.
16:22 which the LORD your G hates.
17: 1 sacrifice to the LORD your G
17: 1 abomination to the LORD your G.
17: 2 gates which the LORD your G
17: 2 the sight of the LORD your G,
17: 8 place which the LORD your G
17:12 there before the LORD your G,
17:14 land which the LORD your G is
17:15 over you whom the LORD your G
17:19 learn to fear the LORD his G
18: 5 For the LORD your G has chosen
18: 7 in the name of the LORD his G
18: 9 land which the LORD your G is
18:12 abominations the LORD your G
18:13 before the LORD your G.
18:14 the LORD your G has not
18:15 The LORD your G will raise up
18:16 desired of the LORD your G in
18:16 the voice of the LORD my G,
19: 1 When the LORD your G has cut
19: 1 whose land the LORD your G is
19: 2 land which the LORD your G is
19: 3 land which the LORD your G is
19: 8 Now if the LORD your G enlarges
19: 9 to love the LORD your G and to
19:10 land which the LORD your G is
19:14 the land that the LORD your G
20: 1 for the LORD your G is with
20: 4 for the LORD your G is He who
20:13 And when the LORD your G
20:14 plunder which the LORD your G
20:16 peoples which the LORD your G
20:17 just as the LORD your G has
20:18 sin against the LORD your G.
21: 1 land which the LORD your G is
21: 5 for the LORD your G has chosen
21:10 and the LORD your G delivers
21:23 land which the LORD your G is
21:23 who is hanged is accursed of G.
22: 5 abomination to the LORD your G.
23: 5 Nevertheless the LORD your G
23: 5 but the LORD your G turned the
23: 5 because the LORD your G loves
23:14 For the LORD your G walks in
23:18 the house of the LORD your G
23:18 abomination to the LORD your G.
23:20 that the LORD your G may bless
23:21 make a vow to the LORD your G,
23:21 for the LORD your G will
23:23 vowed to the LORD your G what
24: 4 land which the LORD your G is
24: 9 what the LORD your G
24:13 to you before the LORD your G.
24:18 and the LORD your G redeemed
24:19 that the LORD your G may bless
25:15 land which the LORD your G is
25:16 abomination to the LORD your G.
25:18 and he did not fear G.
25:19 when the LORD your G has given
25:19 land which the LORD your G is
26: 1 land which the LORD your G is
26: 2 land that the LORD your G is
26: 2 place where the LORD your G
26: 3 today to the LORD your G that
26: 4 the altar of the LORD your G.
26: 5 and say before the LORD your G:
26: 7 we cried out to the LORD G of
26:10 set it before the LORD your G,
26:10 worship before the LORD your G.
26:11 thing which the LORD your G
26:13 say before the LORD your G:
26:14 the voice of the LORD my G,
26:16 This day the LORD your G
26:17 the LORD to be your G,
26:19 holy people to the LORD your G,
27: 2 land which the LORD your G is
27: 3 land which the LORD your G is
27: 3 just as the LORD G of your
27: 5 an altar to the LORD your G,
27: 6 the altar of the LORD your G,
27: 6 on it to the LORD your G.
27: 7 rejoice before the LORD your G.
27: 9 the people of the LORD your G.
27:10 the voice of the LORD your G,
28: 1 the voice of the LORD your G,
28: 1 that the LORD your G will set
28: 2 the voice of the LORD your G:
28: 8 land which the LORD your G is
28: 9 of the LORD your G and walk
28:13 of the LORD your G,
28:15 the voice of the LORD your G,
28:45 the voice of the LORD your G,
28:47 did not serve the LORD your G
28:52 land which the LORD your G
28:53 whom the LORD your G has
28:58 name, THE LORD YOUR G,
28:62 the voice of the LORD your G.
29: 6 that I am the LORD your G.
29:10 today before the LORD your G:
29:12 covenant with the LORD your G,
29:12 which the LORD your G makes
29:13 and that He may be G to you,
29:15 us today before the LORD our G,
29:18 away today from the LORD our G,
29:25 the covenant of the LORD G of
29:29 belong to the LORD our G,
30: 1 nations where the LORD your G
30: 2 you return to the LORD your G
30: 3 that the LORD your G will bring
30: 3 nations where the LORD your G
30: 4 from there the LORD your G
30: 5 Then the LORD your G will bring
30: 6 And the LORD your G will
30: 6 to love the LORD your G with
30: 7 Also the LORD your G will put
30: 9 The LORD your G will make you
30:10 the voice of the LORD your G,
30:10 if you turn to the LORD your G
30:16 today to love the LORD your G,
30:16 and the LORD your G will bless
30:20 you may love the LORD your G,
31: 3 The LORD your G Himself crosses
31: 6 of them; for the LORD your G,
31:11 appear before the LORD your G
31:12 learn to fear the LORD your G
31:13 learn to fear the LORD your G
31:17 come upon us because our G is
31:26 covenant of the LORD your G,
32: 3 Ascribe greatness to our G.
32: 4 A G of truth and without
32:12 And there was no foreign g
32:15 are obese! Then he forsook G
32:17 sacrificed to demons, not to G,
32:18 And have forgotten the G who
32:21 to jealousy by what is not G;
32:39 And there is no G besides
33: 1 with which Moses the man of G
33:26 There is no one like the G of
33:27 The eternal G is your refuge,
Josh 1: 9 for the LORD your G is with
1:11 land which the LORD your G is
1:13 The LORD your G is giving you
1:15 land which the LORD your G is
1:17 Only the LORD your G be with
2:11 of you, for the LORD your G,
2:11 He is G in heaven above and on
3: 3 covenant of the LORD your G,
3: 9 the words of the LORD your G.
3:10 shall know that the living G
4: 5 the ark of the LORD your G
4:23 for the LORD your G dried up
4:23 as the LORD your G did to the
4:24 you may fear the LORD your G
7: 7 Joshua said, "Alas, Lord G,
7:13 because thus says the LORD G
7:19 give glory to the LORD G of
7:20 sinned against the LORD G of
8: 7 for the LORD your G will
8:30 built an altar to the LORD G
9: 9 of the name of the LORD your G;
9:18 sworn to them by the LORD G
9:19 sworn to them by the LORD G
9:23 carriers for the house of my G.
9:24 told that the LORD your G
10:19 for the LORD your G has
10:40 as the LORD G of Israel had
10:42 because the LORD G of Israel
13:14 the sacrifices of the LORD G
13:33 the LORD G of Israel was
14: 6 said to Moses the man of G
14: 8 wholly followed the LORD my G.
14: 9 wholly followed the LORD my G.
14:14 he wholly followed the LORD G
18: 3 the land which the LORD G of
18: 6 you here before the LORD our G.
22: 3 commandment of the LORD your G.
22: 4 And now the LORD your G has
22: 5 you, to love the LORD your G,
22:16 have committed against the G
22:19 the altar of the LORD our G.
22:22 The LORD G of gods, the LORD
22:22 the LORD G of gods, He knows,
22:24 you to do with the LORD G of
22:29 the altar of the LORD our G
22:33 children of Israel blessed G;
22:34 between us that the LORD is G.
23: 3 seen all that the LORD your G
23: 3 for the LORD your G is He who
23: 5 And the LORD your G will expel
23: 5 as the LORD your G promised
23: 8 hold fast to the LORD your G,
23:10 for the LORD your G is He who
23:11 that you love the LORD your G.
23:13 certain that the LORD your G
23:13 land which the LORD your G
23:14 things which the LORD your G
23:15 upon you which the LORD your G
23:15 land which the LORD your G
23:16 covenant of the LORD your G,
24: 1 presented themselves before G.
24: 2 Thus says the LORD G of Israel:
24:17 for the LORD our G is He who
24:18 the LORD, for He is our G.
24:19 the LORD, for He is a holy G.
24:19 a holy God. He is a jealous G;
24:23 your heart to the LORD G of
24:24 The LORD our G we will serve,
24:26 in the Book of the Law of G.
24:27 to you, lest you deny your G.
Judg 1: 7 so G has repaid me." Then they
2:12 and they forsook the LORD G of
3: 7 They forgot the LORD their G,
3:20 I have a message from G for
4: 6 Has not the LORD G of Israel
4:23 So on that day G subdued Jabin
5: 3 sing praise to the LORD G of
5: 5 before the LORD G of Israel.
6: 8 Thus says the LORD G of Israel:
6:10 you, "I am the LORD your G;
6:20 The Angel of G said to him,
6:22 O Lord G! For I have seen the
6:26 an altar to the LORD your G
6:31 death by morning! If he is a g,
6:36 So Gideon said to G,
6:39 Then Gideon said to G,
6:40 And G did so that night. It was
7:14 man of Israel! Into his hand G
8: 3 G has delivered into your hands
8:33 and made Baal-Berith their g.

G

8:34 not remember the LORD their **G**,
9: 7 That **G** may listen to you!
9: 9 With which they honor **G** and
9:13 Which cheers both **G** and men,
9:23 **G** sent a spirit of ill will
9:27 went into the house of their **g**,
9:46 of the temple of the **g** Berith.
9:56 Thus **G** repaid the wickedness of
9:57 evil of the men of Shechem **G**
10:10 we have both forsaken our **G**
11:21 And the LORD **G** of Israel
11:23 And now the LORD **G** of Israel
11:24 whatever Chemosh your **g** gives
11:24 So whatever the LORD our **G**
13: 5 child shall be a Nazirite to **G**
13: 6 A Man of **G** came to me, and His
13: 6 countenance of the Angel of **G**,
13: 7 child shall be a Nazirite to **G**
13: 8 please let the Man of **G** whom
13: 9 And **G** listened to the voice of
13: 9 and the Angel of **G** came to the
13:22 because we have seen **G**!"
15:19 So **G** split the hollow place that
16:17 I have been a Nazirite to **G**
16:23 sacrifice to Dagon their **g**,
16:23 Our **g** has delivered into our
16:24 saw him, they praised their **g**;
16:24 Our **g** has delivered into our
16:28 the LORD, saying, "O Lord **G**,
16:28 me, I pray, just this once, O **G**,
18: 5 to him, "Please inquire of **G**,
18:10 For **G** has given it into your
18:31 the time that the house of **G**
20: 2 the assembly of the people of **G**,
20:18 and went up to the house of **G**
20:18 house of God to inquire of **G**.
20:26 up and came to the house of **G**
20:27 (the ark of the covenant of **G**
21: 2 people came to the house of **G**,
21: 2 and remained there before **G**
21: 3 O LORD **G** of Israel, why has
Ruth 1:16 be my people, And your **G**,
1:16 my people, And your God, my **G**.
2:12 be given you by the LORD **G** of
1 Sam 1:17 and the **G** of Israel grant your
2: 2 is there any rock like our **G**.
2: 3 For the LORD is the **G** of
2:25 **G** will judge him. But if a man
2:27 Then a man of **G** came to Eli and
2:30 Therefore the LORD **G** of Israel
2:32 despite all the good which **G**
3: 3 and before the lamp of **G** went
3: 3 of the LORD where the ark of **G**
3:17 **G** do so to you, and more also,
4: 4 the ark of the covenant of **G**.
4: 7 '**G** has come into the camp!'
4:11 Also the ark of **G** was captured;
4:13 heart trembled for the ark of **G**.
4:17 and the ark of **G** has been
4:18 he made mention of the ark of **G**,
4:19 the news that the ark of **G** was
4:21 because the ark of **G** had
4:22 for the ark of **G** has been
5: 1 Philistines took the ark of **G**
5: 2 Philistines took the ark of **G**,
5: 7 The ark of the **G** of Israel must
5: 7 harsh toward us and Dagon our **g**.
5: 8 we do with the ark of the **G** of
5: 8 Let the ark of the **G** of Israel
5: 8 they carried the ark of the **G**
5:10 they sent the ark of **G** to
5:10 as the ark of **G** came to Ekron,
5:10 have brought the ark of the **G**
5:11 Send away the ark of the **G** of
5:11 the hand of **G** was very heavy
6: 3 you send away the ark of the **G**
6: 5 you shall give glory to the **G**
6:20 stand before this holy LORD **G**?
7: 8 to cry out to the LORD our **G**
9: 6 is in this city a man of **G**,
9: 7 to bring to the man of **G**.
9: 8 will give that to the man of **G**,
9: 9 when a man went to inquire of **G**,
9:10 to the city where the man of **G**
9:27 announce to you the word of **G**.
10: 3 There three men going up to **G**
10: 5 you shall come to the hill of **G**
10: 7 for **G** is with you.
10: 9 that **G** gave him another heart;
10:10 then the Spirit of **G** came upon
10:18 Thus says the LORD **G** of Israel:
10:19 you have today rejected your **G**,
10:26 whose hearts **G** had touched.
11: 6 Then the Spirit of **G** came upon
12: 9 they forgot the LORD their **G**,
12:12 when the LORD your **G** was
12:14 following the LORD your **G**.
12:19 servants to the LORD your **G**,
13:13 commandment of the LORD your **G**,
14:18 Bring the ark of **G** here" (for
14:18 (for at that time the ark of **G**
14:36 Let us draw near to **G** here."
14:37 So Saul asked counsel of **G**,
14:41 Saul said to the LORD **G** of
14:44 **G** do so and more also; for you
14:45 for he has worked with **G** this
15:15 sacrifice to the LORD your **G**;
15:21 sacrifice to the LORD your **G**
15:30 I may worship the LORD your **G**.
16:15 a distressing spirit from **G** is
16:16 the distressing spirit from **G**
16:23 whenever the spirit from **G** was

17:26 defy the armies of the living **G**?
17:36 the armies of the living **G**.
17:45 the **G** of the armies of Israel,
17:46 may know that there is a **G** in
18:10 the distressing spirit from **G**
19:20 the Spirit of **G** came upon the
19:23 Then the Spirit of **G** was upon
20:12 The LORD **G** of Israel is
22: 3 till I know what **G** will do for
22:13 and have inquired of **G** for him,
22:15 I then begin to inquire of **G**
23: 7 **G** has delivered him into my
23:10 O LORD **G** of Israel, Your
23:11 O LORD **G** of Israel, I pray,
23:14 but **G** did not deliver him into
23:16 and strengthened his hand in **G**.
25:22 May **G** do so, and more also, to
25:29 living with the LORD your **G**;
25:32 Blessed is the LORD **G** of
25:34 as the LORD **G** of Israel
26: 8 **G** has delivered your enemy into
28:15 and **G** has departed from me and
29: 9 in my sight as an angel of **G**;
30: 6 himself in the LORD his **G**.
30:15 Swear to me by **G** that you will
2 Sam 2:27 As **G** lives, unless you had
3: 9 May **G** do so to Abner, and more
3:35 **G** do so to me, and more also, if
5:10 and the LORD **G** of hosts was
6: 2 up from there the ark of **G**,
6: 3 So they set the ark of **G** on a
6: 4 hill, accompanying the ark of **G**;
6: 6 out his hand to the ark of **G**
6: 7 and **G** struck him there for his
6: 7 he died there by the ark of **G**.
6:12 to him, because of the ark of **G**.
6:12 and brought up the ark of **G**
7: 2 but the ark of **G** dwells inside
7:18 he said: "Who am I, O Lord **G**?
7:19 thing in Your sight, O Lord **G**;
7:19 the manner of man, O Lord **G**?
7:20 say to You? For You, Lord **G**,
7:22 You are great, O Lord **G**.
7:22 nor is there any **G** besides
7:23 one nation on the earth whom **G**
7:24 You, LORD, have become their **G**.
7:25 "Now, O LORD **G**,
7:26 The LORD of hosts is the **G**
7:27 **G** of Israel, have revealed
7:28 "And now, O Lord **G**,
7:28 now, O Lord GOD, You are **G**,
7:29 before You; for You, O Lord **G**,
9: 3 I may show the kindness of **G**?
10:12 and for the cities of our **G**.
12: 7 the man! Thus says the LORD **G**
12:16 David therefore pleaded with **G**
14:11 king remember the LORD your **G**,
14:13 a thing against the people of **G**?
14:14 Yet **G** does not take away a
14:16 from the inheritance of **G**.
14:17 for as the angel of **G**,
14:17 And may the LORD your **G** be
14:20 to the wisdom of the angel of **G**,
15:24 the ark of the covenant of **G**.
15:24 And they set down the ark of **G**,
15:25 Carry the ark of **G** back into the
15:29 Abiathar carried the ark of **G**
15:32 mountain, where he worshiped **G**—
16:23 had inquired at the oracle of **G**.
18:28 "Blessed be the LORD your **G**,
19:13 **G** do so to me, and more also,
19:27 king is like the angel of **G**.
21:14 And after that **G** heeded the
22: 3 The **G** of my strength, in whom I
22: 7 LORD, And cried out to my **G**;
22:22 not wickedly departed from my **G**.
22:30 By my **G** I can leap over a
22:31 As for **G**, His way is
22:32 "For who is **G**,
22:32 who is a rock, except our **G**?
22:33 **G** is my strength and power,
22:47 Blessed be my Rock! Let **G**
22:48 It is **G** who avenges me,
23: 1 The anointed of the **G** of
23: 3 The **G** of Israel said, The Rock
23: 3 Ruling in the fear of **G**.
23: 5 my house is not so with **G**,
24: 3 Now may the LORD your **G** add to
24:23 May the LORD your **G** accept
24:24 offerings to the LORD my **G**
1 Ki 1:17 you swore by the LORD your **G**
1:30 I swore to you by the LORD **G**
1:36 Amen! May the LORD **G** of my lord
1:47 May **G** make the name of Solomon
1:48 Blessed be the LORD **G** of
2: 3 the charge of the LORD your **G**:
2:23 May **G** do so to me, and more
2:26 carried the ark of the Lord **G**
3: 5 and **G** said, "Ask! What shall I
3: 7 "Now, O LORD my **G**,
3:11 Then **G** said to him: "Because
3:28 they saw that the wisdom of **G**
4:29 And **G** gave Solomon wisdom and
5: 3 for the name of the LORD his **G**
5: 4 But now the LORD my **G** has given
5: 5 for the name of the LORD my **G**,
8:15 Blessed be the LORD **G** of
8:17 for the name of the LORD **G** of
8:20 for the name of the LORD **G** of
8:23 LORD **G** of Israel, there is no
8:23 there is no **G** in heaven above
8:25 LORD **G** of Israel, now keep

8:26 O **G** of Israel, let Your word
8:27 But will **G** indeed dwell on the
8:28 his supplication, O LORD my **G**,
8:53 fathers out of Egypt, O Lord **G**.
8:57 May the LORD our **G** be with us,
8:59 be near the LORD our **G** day and
8:60 may know that the LORD is **G**;
8:61 be loyal to the LORD our **G**,
8:65 Egypt, before the LORD our **G**,
9: 9 they forsook the LORD their **G**,
10: 9 "Blessed be the LORD your **G**,
10:24 which **G** had put in his heart.
11: 4 not loyal to the LORD his **G**,
11: 9 had turned from the LORD **G** of
11:23 And **G** raised up another
11:31 the **G** of Israel: 'Behold, I
11:33 Chemosh the **g** of the Moabites,
11:33 and Milcom the **g** of the people
12:22 But the word of **G** came to
12:22 came to Shemaiah the man of **G**,
13: 1 a man of **G** went from Judah to
13: 4 the saying of the man of **G**,
13: 5 to the sign which the man of **G**
13: 6 and said to the man of **G**,
13: 6 the favor of the LORD your **G**,
13: 6 So the man of **G** entreated the
13: 7 the king said to the man of **G**,
13: 8 But the man of **G** said to the
13:11 all the works that the man of **G**
13:12 had seen which way the man of **G**
13:14 and went after the man of **G**,
13:14 Are you the man of **G** who came
13:21 he cried out to the man of **G**
13:21 which the LORD your **G**
13:26 It is the man of **G** who was
13:29 up the corpse of the man of **G**,
13:31 in the tomb where the man of **G**
14: 7 Thus says the LORD **G** of Israel:
14:13 good toward the LORD **G** of
15: 3 not loyal to the LORD his **G**,
15: 4 David's sake the LORD his **G**
15:30 he had provoked the LORD **G** of
16:13 in provoking the LORD **G** of
16:26 provoking the LORD **G** of Israel
16:33 more to provoke the LORD **G** of
17: 1 As the LORD **G** of Israel lives,
17:12 As the LORD your **G** lives, I do
17:14 For thus says the LORD **G** of
17:18 I to do with you, O man of **G**?
17:20 LORD and said, "O LORD my **G**,
17:21 LORD and said, "O LORD my **G**,
17:24 I know that you are a man of **G**,
18:10 As the LORD your **G** lives,
18:21 opinions? If the LORD is **G**,
18:24 and the **G** who answers by fire,
18:24 who answers by fire, He is **G**.
18:25 and call on the name of your **g**,
18:27 "Cry aloud, for he is a **g**;
18:36 LORD **G** of Abraham, Isaac, and
18:36 known this day that You are **G**
18:37 know that You are the LORD **G**,
18:39 He is **G**! The LORD, He is
18:39 The LORD, He is **G**!"
19: 8 far as Horeb, the mountain of **G**.
19:10 very zealous for the LORD **G**
19:14 very zealous for the LORD **G**
20:28 Then a man of **G** came and spoke
20:28 The LORD is **G** of the hills,
20:28 but He is not **G** of the
21:10 You have blasphemed **G** and the
21:13 Naboth has blasphemed **G** and the
22:53 and provoked the LORD **G** of
2 Ki 1: 2 the **g** of Ekron, whether I shall
1: 3 it because there is no **G** in
1: 3 the **g** of Ekron?'
1: 6 it because there is no **G** in
1: 6 the **g** of Ekron? Therefore you
1: 9 And he spoke to him: "Man of **G**,
1:10 of fifty, "If I am a man of **G**,
1:11 and said to him: "Man of **G**,
1:12 to them, "If I am a man of **G**,
1:12 And the fire of **G** came down
1:13 and said to him: "Man of **G**,
1:16 the **g** of Ekron, is it because
1:16 it because there is no **G** in
2:14 Where is the LORD **G** of
4: 7 she came and told the man of **G**.
4: 9 that this is a holy man of **G**,
4:16 said, "No, my lord. Man of **G**,
4:21 him on the bed of the man of **G**,
4:22 that I may run to the man of **G**
4:25 and went to the man of **G** at
4:25 when the man of **G** saw her afar
4:27 when she came to the man of **G**
4:27 But the man of **G** said, "Let
4:40 cried out and said, "Man of **G**,
4:42 and brought the man of **G** bread
5: 7 his clothes and said, "Am I **G**,
5: 8 when Elisha the man of **G** heard
5:11 on the name of the LORD his **G**,
5:14 to the saying of the man of **G**;
5:15 he returned to the man of **G**,
5:15 I know that there is no **G** in
5:20 servant of Elisha the man of **G**,
6: 6 So the man of **G** said, "Where
6: 9 And the man of **G** sent to the
6:10 the place of which the man of **G**
6:15 the servant of the man of **G**
6:31 **G** do so to me and more also, if
7: 2 leaned answered the man of **G**
7:17 just as the man of **G** had said,
7:18 happened just as the man of **G**

7:19 had answered the man of *G*,
8: 2 to the saying of the man of *G*,
8: 4 the servant of the man of *G*,
8: 7 The man of *G* has come here."
8: 8 and go to meet the man of *G*,
8:11 and the man of *G* wept.
9: 6 Thus says the LORD *G* of Israel:
10:31 walk in the law of the LORD *G*
13:19 And the man of *G* was angry with
14:25 to the word of the LORD *G* of
16: 2 in the sight of the LORD his *G*,
17: 7 against the LORD their *G*,
17: 9 did against the LORD their *G*
17:14 believe in the LORD their *G*.
17:16 of the LORD their *G*,
17:19 of the LORD their *G*,
17:26 not know the rituals of the *G*
17:26 not know the rituals of the *G*
17:27 them the rituals of the *G* of
17:39 But the LORD your *G* you shall
18: 5 He trusted in the LORD *G* of
18:12 the voice of the LORD their *G*,
18:22 'We trust in the LORD our *G*,
19: 4 may be that the LORD your *G*
19: 4 sent to reproach the living *G*,
19: 4 words which the LORD your *G*
19:10 Do not let your *G* in whom you
19:15 O LORD *G* of Israel, the One
19:15 the cherubim, You are *G*,
19:16 sent to reproach the living *G*.
19:19 "Now therefore, O LORD our *G*,
19:19 know that You are the LORD *G*,
19:20 Thus says the LORD *G* of Israel:
19:37 in the temple of Nisroch his *g*,
20: 5 the *G* of David your father:
21:12 thus says the LORD *G* of
21:22 He forsook the LORD *G* of his
22:15 Thus says the LORD *G* of Israel,
22:18 Thus says the LORD *G* of Israel:
23:16 of the LORD which the man of *G*
23:17 is the tomb of the man of *G*
23:21 Passover to the LORD your *G*,
1 Chr 4:10 And Jabez called on the *G* of
4:10 I may not cause pain!" So *G*
5:20 for they cried out to *G* in the
5:25 they were unfaithful to the *G*
5:25 whom *G* had destroyed before
5:26 So the *G* of Israel stirred up
6:48 tabernacle of the house of *G*.
6:49 all that Moses the servant of *G*
9:11 the officer over the house of *G*;
9:13 the service of the house of *G*.
9:26 treasuries of the house of *G*.
9:27 all around the house of *G*
11: 2 and the LORD your *G* said to
11:19 "Far be it from me, O my *G*,
12:17 may the *G* of our fathers look
12:18 to your helpers! For your *G*
12:22 great army, like the army of *G*.
13: 2 and if it is of the LORD our *G*,
13: 3 let us bring the ark of our *G*
13: 5 to bring the ark of *G* from
13: 6 up from there the ark of *G* the
13: 7 So they carried the ark of *G* on
13: 8 Israel played music before *G*
13:10 ark; and he died there before *G*.
13:12 David was afraid of *G* that day,
13:12 How can I bring the ark of *G* to
13:14 The ark of *G* remained with the
14:10 And David inquired of *G*,
14:11 *G* has broken through my enemies
14:14 David inquired again of *G*,
14:14 and *G* said to him, "You shall
14:15 for *G* has gone out before you
14:16 So David did as *G* commanded him,
15: 1 a place for the ark of *G*,
15: 2 No one may carry the ark of *G*
15: 2 them to carry the ark of *G* and
15:12 up the ark of the LORD *G* of
15:13 the LORD our *G* broke out
15:14 up the ark of the LORD *G* of
15:15 the Levites bore the ark of *G*
15:24 trumpets before the ark of *G*;
15:26 when *G* helped the Levites who
16: 1 So they brought the ark of *G*,
16: 1 and peace offerings before *G*.
16: 4 and to praise the LORD *G* of
16: 6 the ark of the covenant of *G*.
16:14 He is the LORD our *G*;
16:35 O *G* of our salvation;
16:36 Blessed be the LORD *G* of
16:42 the musical instruments of *G*.
17: 2 for *G* is with you."
17: 3 that night that the word of *G*
17:16 he said: "Who am I, O LORD *G*?
17:17 small thing in Your sight, O *G*;
17:17 a man of high degree, O LORD *G*.
17:20 nor is there any *G* besides
17:21 one nation on the earth whom *G*
17:22 You, LORD, have become their *G*.
17:24 the *G* of Israel, is Israel's
17:24 God of Israel, is Israel's *G*.
17:25 "For You, O my *G*,
17:26 "And now, LORD, You are *G*,
19:13 and for the cities of our *G*.
21: 7 And *G* was displeased with this
21: 8 So David said to *G*,
21:15 And *G* sent an angel to Jerusalem
21:17 And David said to *G*,
21:17 Your hand, I pray, O LORD my *G*,
21:30 go before it to inquire of *G*,
22: 1 is the house of the LORD *G*,
22: 2 stones to build the house of *G*.
22: 6 build a house for the LORD *G*
22: 7 to the name of the LORD my *G*;
22:11 the house of the LORD your *G*,
22:12 the law of the LORD your *G*.
22:18 Is not the LORD your *G* with
22:19 soul to seek the LORD your *G*.
22:19 the sanctuary of the LORD *G*,
22:19 and the holy articles of *G*
23:14 the sons of Moses the man of *G*
23:25 The LORD *G* of Israel has given
23:28 the service of the house of *G*,
24: 5 officials of the house of *G*,
24:19 as the LORD *G* of Israel had
25: 5 king's seer in the words of *G*,
25: 5 For *G* gave Heman fourteen sons
25: 6 the service of the house of *G*.
26: 5 for *G* blessed him.
26:20 treasuries of the house of *G*
26:32 every matter pertaining to *G*
28: 2 and for the footstool of our *G*,
28: 3 But *G* said to me, 'You shall not
28: 4 However the LORD *G* of Israel
28: 8 and in the hearing of our *G*,
28: 8 of the LORD your *G*,
28: 9 know the *G* of your father,
28:12 treasuries of the house of *G*,
28:20 be dismayed, for the LORD *G*—
28:20 for the LORD God—my *G*—
28:21 the service of the house of *G*;
29: 1 whom alone *G* has chosen, is
29: 1 not for man but for the LORD *G*.
29: 2 Now for the house of my *G* I have
29: 3 affection on the house of my *G*,
29: 3 have given to the house of my *G*,
29: 7 for the work of the house of *G*
29:10 LORD *G* of Israel, our Father,
29:13 "Now therefore, our *G*,
29:16 "O LORD our *G*,
29:17 "I know also, my *G*,
29:18 O LORD *G* of Abraham, Isaac, and
29:20 "Now bless the LORD your *G*."
29:20 assembly blessed the LORD *G*
2 Chr 1: 1 and the LORD his *G* was with
1: 3 tabernacle of meeting with *G*
1: 4 had brought up the ark of *G*
1: 7 On that night *G* appeared to
1: 8 And Solomon said to *G*:
1: 9 "Now, O LORD *G*,
1:11 And *G* said to Solomon: "Because
2: 4 for the name of the LORD my *G*,
2: 4 set feasts of the LORD our *G*.
2: 5 for our *G* is greater than all
2:12 Blessed be the LORD *G* of
3: 3 for building the house of *G*:
4:11 King Solomon for the house of *G*:
4:19 made for the house of *G*:
5: 1 treasuries of the house of *G*.
5:14 the LORD filled the house of *G*.
6: 4 Blessed be the LORD *G* of
6: 7 for the name of the LORD *G* of
6:10 for the name of the LORD *G* of
6:14 LORD *G* of Israel, there is no
6:14 there is no *G* in heaven or on
6:16 LORD *G* of Israel, now keep
6:17 O LORD *G* of Israel, let Your
6:18 But will *G* indeed dwell with
6:19 his supplication, O LORD my *G*,
6:40 'Now, my *G*, I pray, let Your
6:41 therefore, Arise, O LORD *G*,
6:41 Let Your priests, O LORD *G*,
6:42 'O LORD *G*, do not turn away
7: 5 people dedicated the house of *G*.
7:22 they forsook the LORD *G* of
8:14 for so David the man of *G* had
9: 8 "Blessed be the LORD your *G*,
9: 8 be king for the LORD your *G*!
9: 8 LORD your God! Because your *G*
9:23 which *G* had put in his heart.
10:15 the turn of events was from *G*,
11: 2 came to Shemaiah the man of *G*,
11:16 heart to seek the LORD *G* of
11:16 to sacrifice to the LORD *G* of
13: 5 you not know that the LORD *G*
13:10 as for us, the LORD is our *G*,
13:11 the command of the LORD our *G*,
13:12 *G* Himself is with us as our
13:12 not fight against the LORD *G*
13:15 it happened that *G* struck
13:16 and *G* delivered them into their
13:18 they relied on the LORD *G* of
14: 2 in the eyes of the LORD his *G*,
14: 4 Judah to seek the LORD *G* of
14: 7 we have sought the LORD our *G*;
14:11 cried out to the LORD his *G*,
14:11 help us, O LORD our *G*,
14:11 O LORD, You are our *G*;
15: 1 Now the Spirit of *G* came upon
15: 3 has been without the true *G*,
15: 4 they turned to the LORD *G* of
15: 6 for *G* troubled them with every
15: 9 they saw that the LORD his *G*
15:12 a covenant to seek the LORD *G*
15:13 would not seek the LORD *G* of
15:18 brought into the house of *G*
16: 7 not relied on the LORD your *G*,
17: 4 but sought the *G* of his father,
18: 5 for *G* will deliver it into the
18:13 whatever my *G* says, that I will
18:31 and *G* diverted them from him.
19: 3 prepared your heart to seek *G*.
19: 4 them back to the LORD *G* of
19: 7 iniquity with the LORD our *G*,
20: 6 O LORD *G* of our fathers, are
20: 6 are You not *G* in heaven, and
20: 7 "Are You not our *G*,
20:12 'O our *G*, will You not judge
20:19 stood up to praise the LORD *G*
20:20 Believe in the LORD your *G*,
20:29 And the fear of *G* was on all the
20:30 for his *G* gave him rest all
20:33 directed their hearts to the *G*
21:10 he had forsaken the LORD *G* of
21:12 Thus says the LORD *G* of your
22:12 with them in the house of *G*
23: 3 with the king in the house of *G*.
23: 9 that were in the temple of *G*.
24: 5 to repair the house of your *G*
24: 7 had broken into the house of *G*,
24: 9 that Moses the servant of *G*
24:13 they restored the house of *G* to
24:16 both toward *G* and His house.
24:18 left the house of the LORD *G*
24:20 Then the Spirit of *G* came upon
24:20 and said to them, "Thus says *G*:
24:24 they had forsaken the LORD *G*
24:27 the repairing of the house of *G*,
25: 7 But a man of *G* came to him,
25: 8 *G* shall make you fall before
25: 8 for *G* has power to help and to
25: 9 Amaziah said to the man of *G*,
25: 9 And the man of *G* answered,
25:16 I know that *G* has determined to
25:20 not heed, for it came from *G*,
25:24 were found in the house of *G*
26: 5 He sought *G* in the days of
26: 5 in the visions of *G*;
26: 5 *G* made him prosper.
26: 7 *G* helped him against the
26:16 against the LORD his *G* by
26:18 have no honor from the LORD *G*.
27: 6 his ways before the LORD his *G*.
28: 5 Therefore the LORD his *G*
28: 6 they had forsaken the LORD *G*
28: 9 because the LORD *G* of your
28:10 guilty before the LORD your *G*?
28:24 the articles of the house of *G*,
28:24 the articles of the house of *G*,
28:25 provoked to anger the LORD *G*
29: 5 the house of the LORD *G* of
29: 6 in the eyes of the LORD our *G*;
29: 7 in the holy place to the *G* of
29:10 a covenant with the LORD *G* of
29:36 all the people rejoiced that *G*
30: 1 the Passover to the LORD *G* of
30: 5 the Passover to the LORD *G* of
30: 6 return to the LORD *G* of
30: 7 trespassed against the LORD *G*
30: 8 and serve the LORD your *G*,
30: 9 for the LORD your *G* is
30:12 Also the hand of *G* was on Judah
30:16 the Law of Moses the man of *G*;
30:19 prepares his heart to seek *G*,
30:19 the LORD *G* of his fathers,
30:22 confession to the LORD *G* of
31: 6 to the LORD their *G* they laid
31:13 the ruler of the house of *G*.
31:14 the freewill offerings to *G*,
31:20 and true before the LORD his *G*.
31:21 the service of the house of *G*,
31:21 the commandment, to seek his *G*,
32: 8 but with us is the LORD our *G*,
32:11 The LORD our *G* will deliver us
32:14 that your *G* should be able to
32:15 for no *g* of any nation or
32:15 How much less will your *G*
32:16 spoke against the LORD *G* and
32:17 letters to revile the LORD *G*
32:17 so the *G* of Hezekiah will not
32:19 And they spoke against the *G* of
32:21 gone into the temple of his *g*,
32:29 for *G* had given him very much
32:31 *G* withdrew from him, in order
33: 7 he had made, in the house of *G*,
33: 7 of which *G* had said to David
33:12 he implored the LORD his *G*,
33:12 himself greatly before the *G*
33:13 knew that the LORD was *G*.
33:16 Judah to serve the LORD *G* of
33:17 but only to the LORD their *G*.
33:18 Manasseh, his prayer to his *G*,
33:18 him in the name of the LORD *G*
33:19 Also his prayer and how *G*
34: 3 he began to seek the *G* of his
34: 8 the house of the LORD his *G*.
34: 9 was brought into the house of *G*,
34:23 Thus says the LORD *G* of Israel,
34:26 Thus says the LORD *G* of Israel:
34:27 you humbled yourself before *G*
34:32 according to the covenant of *G*,
34:32 the *G* of their fathers.
34:33 serve the LORD their *G*.
34:33 from following the LORD *G* of
35: 3 Now serve the LORD your *G* and
35: 8 rulers of the house of *G*,
35:21 for *G* commanded me to make
35:21 Refrain from meddling with *G*,
35:22 of Necho from the mouth of *G*.
36: 5 in the sight of the LORD his *G*.
36:12 in the sight of the LORD his *G*,
36:13 made him swear an oath by *G*;
36:13 against turning to the LORD *G*
36:15 And the LORD *G* of their
36:16 they mocked the messengers of *G*,

36:18 articles from the house of G,
36:19 Then they burned the house of G,
36:23 of the earth the LORD G of
36:23 May the LORD his G be with
Ezra 1: 2 of the earth the LORD G of
1: 3 May his G be with him, and let
1: 3 build the house of the LORD G
1: 3 LORD God of Israel (He is G),
1: 4 offerings for the house of G
1: 5 with all whose spirits G had
2:68 freely for the house of G,
3: 2 and built the altar of the G
3: 2 the Law of Moses the man of G.
3: 8 their coming to the house of G
3: 9 those working on the house of G:
4: 1 the temple of the LORD G of
4: 2 for we seek your G as you do;
4: 3 us to build a house for our G;
4: 3 will build to the LORD G of
4:24 the work of the house of G
5: 1 in the name of the G of Israel,
5: 2 began to build the house of G
5: 2 and the prophets of G were
5: 5 But the eye of their G was upon
5: 8 to the temple of the great G,
5:11 We are the servants of the G of
5:12 our fathers provoked the G of
5:13 decree to build this house of G.
5:14 articles of the house of G,
5:15 and let the house of G be
5:16 foundation of the house of G
5:17 Cyrus to build this house of G
6: 3 concerning the house of G at
6: 5 articles of the house of G,
6: 5 them in the house of G"—
6: 7 Let the work of this house of G
6: 7 the Jews build this house of G
6: 8 the building of this house of G:
6: 9 the burnt offerings of the G
6:10 of sweet aroma to the G of
6:12 And may the G who causes His
6:12 or to destroy this house of G
6:14 to the commandment of the G of
6:16 dedication of this house of G
6:17 dedication of this house of G,
6:18 over the service of G in
6:21 in order to seek the LORD G
6:22 in the work of the house of G,
6:22 the G of Israel.
7: 6 which the LORD G of Israel had
7: 6 to the hand of the LORD his G
7: 9 to the good hand of his G upon
7:12 a scribe of the Law of the G of
7:14 regard to the Law of your G
7:15 have freely offered to the G
7:16 for the house of their G in
7:17 altar of the house of your G
7:18 according to the will of your G.
7:19 service of the house of your G,
7:19 deliver in full before the G of
7:20 needed for the house of your G,
7:21 the scribe of the Law of the G
7:23 Whatever is commanded by the G
7:23 be done for the house of the G
7:24 or servants of this house of G.
7:25 such as know the laws of your G;
7:26 not observe the law of your G
7:27 Blessed be the LORD G of our
7:28 as the hand of the LORD my G
8:17 servants for the house of our G.
8:18 by the good hand of our G upon
8:21 humble ourselves before our G,
8:22 The hand of our G is upon all
8:23 we fasted and entreated our G
8:25 for the house of our G which
8:28 offering to the LORD G of
8:30 Jerusalem to the house of our G.
8:31 And the hand of our G was upon
8:33 weighed in the house of our G
8:35 burnt offerings to the G of
8:36 the people and the house of G.
9: 4 trembled at the words of the G
9: 5 out my hands to the LORD my G.
9: 6 And I said: "O my G,
9: 6 to lift up my face to You, my G;
9: 8 shown from the LORD our G,
9: 8 that our G may enlighten our
9: 9 Yet our G did not forsake us in
9: 9 to repair the house of our G,
9:10 "And now, O our G,
9:13 since You our G have punished
9:15 O LORD G of Israel, You are
10: 1 down before the house of G,
10: 2 have trespassed against our G,
10: 3 us make a covenant with our G
10: 3 at the commandment of our G;
10: 6 up from before the house of G,
10: 9 open square of the house of G,
10:11 make confession to the LORD G
10:14 the fierce wrath of our G is
Neh 1: 4 and praying before the G of
1: 5 LORD G of heaven, O great and
1: 5 heaven, O great and awesome G,
2: 4 So I prayed to the G of
2: 8 to the good hand of my G upon
2:12 I told no one what my G had put
2:18 I told them of the hand of my G
2:20 The G of heaven Himself will
4: 4 Hear, O our G, for we are
4: 9 we made our prayer to our G,
4:15 and that G had brought their
4:20 Our G will fight for us."
5: 9 not walk in the fear of our G
5:13 So may G shake out each man from
5:15 do so, because of the fear of G.
5:19 Remember me, my G,
6: 9 Now therefore, O G,
6:10 meet together in the house of G,
6:12 Then I perceived that G had not
6:14 My G, remember Tobiah and
6:16 this work was done by our G.
7: 2 a faithful man and feared G
7: 5 Then my G put it into my heart
8: 6 blessed the LORD, the great G.
8: 8 from the book, in the Law of G;
8: 9 is holy to the LORD your G;
8:16 or the courts of the house of G,
8:18 from the Book of the Law of G.
9: 3 of the Law of the LORD their G
9: 3 and worshiped the LORD their G.
9: 4 loud voice to the LORD their G.
9: 5 up and bless the LORD your G
9: 7 "You are the LORD G,
9:17 their bondage. But You are G,
9:18 This is your g That brought
9:31 forsake them; For You are G,
9:32 "Now therefore, our G,
9:32 the mighty, and awesome G,
10:28 of the lands to the Law of G,
10:29 given by Moses the servant of G,
10:32 service of the house of our G:
10:33 the work of the house of our G.
10:34 into the house of our G,
10:34 on the altar of the LORD our G
10:36 flocks, to the house of our G,
10:36 minister in the house of our G;
10:37 of the house of our G;
10:38 tithes to the house of our G,
10:39 not neglect the house of our G.
11:11 the leader of the house of G.
11:16 outside of the house of G;
11:22 the service of the house of G.
12:24 command of David the man of G.
12:36 of David the man of G.
12:40 choirs stood in the house of G,
12:43 for G had made them rejoice
12:45 kept the charge of their G and
12:46 of praise and thanksgiving to G.
13: 1 come into the assembly of G,
13: 2 our G turned the curse into a
13: 4 of the house of our G,
13: 7 in the courts of the house of G.
13: 9 the articles of the house of G,
13:11 Why is the house of G
13:14 Remember me, O my G,
13:14 have done for the house of my G,
13:18 and did not our G bring all
13:22 Remember me, O my G,
13:25 hair, and made them swear by G,
13:26 him, who was beloved of his G;
13:26 and G made him king over all
13:27 transgressing against our G by
13:29 Remember them, O my G,
13:31 Remember me, O my G,
Job 1: 1 and one who feared G and
1: 5 sons have sinned and cursed G
1: 6 was a day when the sons of G
1: 8 one who fears G and shuns
1: 9 Does Job fear G for nothing?
1:16 The fire of G fell from heaven
1:22 Job did not sin nor charge G
2: 1 was a day when the sons of G
2: 3 one who fears G and shuns evil?
2: 9 Curse G and die!"
2:10 we indeed accept good from G,
3: 4 May G above not seek it,
3:23 And whom G has hedged in?
4: 9 By the blast of G they perish,
4:17 mortal be more righteous than G?
5: 8 as for me, I would seek G,
5: 8 And to G I would commit my
5:17 happy is the man whom G
6: 4 The terrors of G are arrayed
6: 8 That G would grant me the
6: 9 That it would please G to crush
8: 3 Does G subvert judgment?
8: 5 If you would earnestly seek G
8:13 the paths of all who forget G;
8:20 G will not cast away the
9: 2 can a man be righteous before G?
9: 4 G is wise in heart and mighty
9:13 G will not withdraw His anger,
10: 2 I will say to G,
11: 5 that G would speak, And open
11: 6 Know therefore that G exacts
11: 7 search out the deep things of G?
12: 4 his friends, Who called on G,
12: 6 And those who provoke G are
12: 6 In what G provides by His hand.
13: 3 And I desire to reason with G.
13: 7 Will you speak wickedly for G,
13: 8 Will you contend for G?
15: 4 And restrain prayer before G.
15: 8 you heard the counsel of G?
15:11 Are the consolations of G too
15:13 you turn your spirit against G,
15:15 If G puts no trust in His
15:25 out his hand against G,
16:11 G has delivered me to the
16:20 My eyes pour out tears to G.
16:21 might plead for a man with G,
18:21 of him who does not know G.
19: 6 Know then that G has wronged
19:21 For the hand of G has struck
19:22 Why do you persecute me as G
19:26 That in my flesh I shall see G,
20:15 G casts them out of his belly.
20:23 G will cast on him the fury
20:29 This is the portion from G for
20:29 heritage appointed to him by G.
21: 9 Neither is the rod of G upon
21:14 Yet they say to G,
21:17 The sorrows G distributes in
21:19 G lays up one's iniquity for his
21:22 Can anyone teach G knowledge,
22: 2 a man be profitable to G,
22:12 Is not G in the height of
22:13 What does G know? Can He judge
22:17 They said to G,
22:26 And lift up your face to G.
23:16 For G made my heart weak,
24:12 Yet G does not charge them
24:22 But G draws the mighty away
25: 4 can man be righteous before G?
27: 2 As G lives, who has taken away
27: 3 And the breath of G in my
27: 8 If G takes away his life?
27: 9 Will G hear his cry When
27:10 Will he always call on G?
27:11 teach you about the hand of G;
27:13 portion of a wicked man with G,
28:23 G understands its way, And He
29: 2 As in the days when G
29: 4 the friendly counsel of G was
31: 2 what is the allotment of G
31: 6 That G may know my integrity.
31:14 What then shall I do when G
31:23 For destruction from G is a
31:28 For I would have denied G who
32: 2 justified himself rather than G.
32:13 G will vanquish him, not man.
33: 4 The Spirit of G has made me,
33: 6 am as your spokesman before G;
33:12 For G is greater than man.
33:14 For G may speak in one way, or
33:26 He shall pray to G,
33:29 G works all these things,
34: 5 But G has taken away my
34: 9 That he should delight in G.
34:10 Far be it from G to do
34:12 Surely G will never do
34:23 That he should go before G in
34:31 "For has anyone said to G,
34:37 multiplies his words against G.
35:10 Where is G my Maker, Who gives
35:13 Surely G will not listen to
36: 5 G is mighty, but despises no
36:22 G is exalted by His power;
36:26 G is great, and we do not know
37: 5 G thunders marvelously with His
37:10 By the breath of G ice is
37:14 the wondrous works of G.
37:15 Do you know when G dispatches
37:22 With G is awesome majesty.
38: 7 And all the sons of G shouted
38:41 When its young ones cry to G,
39:17 Because G deprived her of
40: 2 correct Him? He who rebukes G,
40: 9 Have you an arm like G?
40:19 is the first of the ways of G;
Ps 3: 2 is no help for him in G.
3: 7 O my G! For You have struck
4: 1 O G of my righteousness!
5: 2 of my cry, My King and my G,
5: 4 For You are not a G who takes
5:10 O G! Let them fall by their
7: 1 O LORD my G, in You I put my
7: 3 O LORD my G, if I have done
7: 9 For the righteous G tests the
7:10 My defense is of G,
7:11 G is a just judge, And God is
7:11 And G is angry with the
9:17 all the nations that forget G.
10: 4 countenance does not seek G;
10: 4 G is in none of his thoughts.
10:11 G has forgotten; He hides His
10:12 Arise, O LORD! O G,
10:13 Why do the wicked renounce G?
13: 3 and hear me, O LORD my G;
14: 1 his heart, "There is no G.
14: 2 any who understand, who seek G.
14: 5 For G is with the generation
16: 1 Preserve me, O G,
16: 4 who hasten after another g;
17: 6 for You will hear me, O G;
18: 2 and my deliverer; My G,
18: 6 LORD, And cried out to my G;
18:21 not wickedly departed from my G.
18:28 The LORD my G will enlighten
18:29 By my G I can leap over a
18:30 As for G, His way is
18:31 For who is G, except the
18:31 who is a rock, except our G?
18:32 It is G who arms me with
18:46 be my Rock! Let the G of my
18:47 It is G who avenges me,
19: 1 heavens declare the glory of G;
20: 1 May the name of the G of Jacob
20: 5 And in the name of our G we
20: 7 the name of the LORD our G.
22: 1 My G, My God, why have You
22: 1 My God, My G, why have You
22: 2 O My G, I cry in the daytime,
22:10 womb You have been My G.
24: 5 And righteousness from the G
25: 2 O my G, I trust in You;

25: 5 For You are the **G** of my
25:22 Redeem Israel, O **G**,
27: 9 O **G** of my salvation.
29: 3 The **G** of glory thunders;
30: 2 O LORD my **G**, I cried out to
30:12 not be silent. O LORD my **G**,
31: 5 O LORD **G** of truth.
31:14 LORD; I say, "You are my **G**.
33:12 is the nation whose **G** is the
35:23 my **G** and my Lord.
35:24 Vindicate me, O LORD my **G**,
36: 1 There is no fear of **G** before
36: 7 O **G**! Therefore the children of
37:31 The law of his **G** is in his
38:15 You will hear, O Lord my **G**.
38:21 forsake me, O LORD; O my **G**,
40: 3 in my mouth—Praise to our **G**;
40: 5 Many, O LORD my **G**,
40: 8 delight to do Your will, O my **G**,
40:17 Do not delay, O my **G**.
41:13 Blessed be the LORD **G** of
42: 1 So pants my soul for You, O **G**.
42: 2 My soul thirsts for **G**,
42: 2 for God, for the living **G**.
42: 2 I come and appear before **G**?
42: 3 say to me, "Where is your **G**?
42: 4 with them to the house of **G**,
42: 5 within me? Hope in **G**,
42: 6 O my **G**, my soul is cast down
42: 8 A prayer to the **G** of my life.
42: 9 I will say to **G** my Rock, "Why
42:10 day long, "Where is your **G**?
42:11 within me? Hope in **G**;
42:11 help of my countenance and my **G**.
43: 1 Vindicate me, O **G**,
43: 2 For You are the **G** of my
43: 4 I will go to the altar of **G**,
43: 4 To **G** my exceeding joy; And on
43: 4 harp I will praise You, O **G**,
43: 4 I will praise You, O God, my **G**.
43: 5 within me? Hope in **G**;
43: 5 help of my countenance and my **G**.
44: 1 have heard with our ears, O **G**,
44: 4 You are my King, O **G**;
44: 8 In **G** we boast all day long,
44:20 had forgotten the name of our **G**,
44:20 out our hands to a foreign **g**,
44:21 Would not **G** search this out?
45: 2 Therefore **G** has blessed You
45: 6 Your throne, O **G**,
45: 7 hate wickedness; Therefore **G**,
45: 7 Therefore God, Your **G**,
46: 1 **G** is our refuge and strength,
46: 4 shall make glad the city of **G**,
46: 5 **G** is in the midst of her, she
46: 5 **G** shall help her, just at the
46: 7 The **G** of Jacob is our refuge.
46:10 still, and know that I am **G**;
46:11 The **G** of Jacob is our refuge.
47: 1 all you peoples! Shout to **G**
47: 5 **G** has gone up with a shout,
47: 6 Sing praises to **G**,
47: 7 For **G** is the King of all the
47: 8 **G** reigns over the nations
47: 8 **G** sits on His holy throne.
47: 9 The people of the **G** of
47: 9 of the earth belong to **G**;
48: 1 praised In the city of our **G**,
48: 3 **G** is in her palaces
48: 8 of hosts, In the city of our **G**:
48: 8 **G** will establish it forever.
48: 9 We have thought, O **G**,
48:10 According to Your name, O **G**,
48:14 For this is **G**,
48:14 Our **G** forever and ever;
49: 7 Nor give to **G** a ransom for
49:15 But **G** will redeem my soul from
50: 1 **G** the LORD, Has spoken and
50: 2 **G** will shine forth.
50: 3 Our **G** shall come, and shall not
50: 6 For **G** Himself is Judge. Selah
50: 7 testify against you; I am **G**,
50: 7 I am God, your **G**!
50:14 Offer to **G** thanksgiving, And
50:16 But to the wicked **G** says:
50:22 consider this, you who forget **G**,
50:23 I will show the salvation of **G**.
51: 1 Have mercy upon me, O **G**,
51:10 in me a clean heart, O **G**,
51:14 the guilt of bloodshed, O **G**,
51:14 The **G** of my salvation, And
51:17 The sacrifices of **G** are a
51:17 a contrite heart—These, O **G**,
52: 1 The goodness of **G** endures
52: 5 **G** shall likewise destroy you
52: 7 is the man who did not make **G**
52: 8 olive tree in the house of **G**;
52: 8 I trust in the mercy of **G**
53: 1 his heart, "There is no **G**.
53: 2 **G** looks down from heaven upon
53: 2 any who understand, who seek **G**.
53: 4 And do not call upon **G**?
53: 5 For **G** has scattered the bones
53: 5 Because **G** has despised them.
53: 6 would come out of Zion! When **G**
54: 1 Save me, O **G**, by Your name,
54: 2 Hear my prayer, O **G**;
54: 3 They have not set **G** before
54: 4 **G** is my helper; The Lord is
55: 1 Give ear to my prayer, O **G**,
55:14 And walked to the house of **G**
55:16 As for me, I will call upon **G**,
55:19 **G** will hear, and afflict them,
55:19 Therefore they do not fear **G**.
55:23 But You, O **G**, shall bring
56: 1 Be merciful to me, O **G**,
56: 4 In **G** (I will praise His word),
56: 4 In **G** I have put my trust;
56: 7 cast down the peoples, O **G**!
56: 9 because **G** is for me.
56:10 In **G** (I will praise His word),
56:11 In **G** I have put my trust;
56:12 You are binding upon me, O **G**;
56:13 That I may walk before **G** In
57: 1 Be merciful to me, O **G**,
57: 2 I will cry out to **G** Most High,
57: 2 To **G** who performs all things
57: 3 Selah **G** shall send forth His
57: 5 Be exalted, O **G**,
57: 7 My heart is steadfast, O **G**,
57:11 Be exalted, O **G**,
58: 6 O **G**! Break out the fangs of
58:11 Surely He is **G** who judges in
59: 1 me from my enemies, O my **G**;
59: 5 O LORD **G** of hosts, the God of
59: 5 the **G** of Israel, Awake to
59: 9 For **G** is my defense;
59:10 My **G** of mercy shall come to
59:10 **G** shall let me see my desire
59:13 And let them know that **G** rules
59:17 For **G** is my defense, My God
59:17 my defense, My **G** of mercy.
60: 1 O **G**, You have cast us off;
60: 6 **G** has spoken in His holiness
60:10 Is it not You, O **G**,
60:10 who cast us off? And You, O **G**,
60:12 Through **G** we will do valiantly,
61: 1 Hear my cry, O **G**;
61: 5 For You, O **G**, have heard my
61: 7 He shall abide before **G**
62: 1 my soul silently waits for **G**;
62: 5 wait silently for **G** alone,
62: 7 In **G** is my salvation and my
62: 7 And my refuge, is in **G**.
62: 8 **G** is a refuge for us. Selah
62:11 **G** has spoken once, Twice I
62:11 That power belongs to **G**.
63: 1 O **G**, You are my God;
63: 1 O God, You are my **G**;
63:11 the king shall rejoice in **G**;
64: 1 Hear my voice, O **G**,
64: 7 But **G** shall shoot at them with
64: 9 shall declare the work of **G**;
65: 1 Praise is awaiting You, O **G**,
65: 5 O **G** of our salvation, You
65: 9 The river of **G** is full of
66: 1 Make a joyful shout to **G**,
66: 3 Say to **G**, "How awesome are
66: 5 Come and see the works of **G**;
66: 8 Oh, bless our **G**, you peoples!
66:10 For You, O **G**, have tested us;
66:16 and hear, all you who fear **G**,
66:19 But certainly **G** has heard me;
66:20 Blessed be **G**, Who has not
67: 1 **G** be merciful to us and bless
67: 3 the peoples praise You, O **G**;
67: 5 the peoples praise You, O **G**;
67: 6 shall yield her increase; **G**,
67: 6 her increase; God, our own **G**,
67: 7 **G** shall bless us, And all the
68: 1 Let **G** arise, Let His enemies
68: 2 perish at the presence of **G**.
68: 3 Let them rejoice before **G**;
68: 4 Sing to **G**, sing praises to
68: 5 Is **G** in His holy habitation.
68: 6 **G** sets the solitary in families
68: 7 O **G**, when You went out before
68: 8 rain at the presence of **G**;
68: 8 moved at the presence of **G**,
68: 8 the **G** of Israel.
68: 9 You, O **G**, sent a plentiful
68:10 dwelt in it; You, O **G**,
68:15 A mountain of **G** is the
68:16 is the mountain which **G**
68:17 The chariots of **G** are twenty
68:18 That the LORD **G** might dwell
68:19 The **G** of our salvation! Selah
68:20 Our **G** is the God of salvation;
68:20 Our God is the **G** of salvation;
68:20 And to **G** the Lord belong
68:21 But **G** will wound the head of
68:24 have seen Your procession, O **G**,
68:24 O God, The procession of my **G**,
68:26 Bless **G** in the congregations,
68:28 Your **G** has commanded your
68:28 your strength; Strengthen, O **G**,
68:31 stretch out her hands to **G**.
68:32 Sing to **G**, you kingdoms of the
68:34 Ascribe strength to **G**;
68:35 O **G**, You are more awesome
68:35 The **G** of Israel is He who
68:35 Blessed be **G**!
69: 1 O **G**! For the waters have come
69: 3 eyes fail while I wait for my **G**.
69: 5 O **G**, You know my foolishness;
69: 6 O Lord **G** of hosts, be ashamed
69: 6 O **G** of Israel.
69:13 in the acceptable time; O **G**,
69:29 Let Your salvation, O **G**,
69:30 I will praise the name of **G**
69:32 be glad; And you who seek **G**,
69:35 For **G** will save Zion And build
70: 1 Make haste, O **G**,
70: 4 Let **G** be magnified!"
70: 5 O **G**! You are my help and my
71: 4 Deliver me, O my **G**,
71: 5 For You are my hope, O Lord **G**;
71:11 **G** has forsaken him; Pursue and
71:12 O **G**, do not be far from me;
71:12 do not be far from me; O my **G**,
71:16 in the strength of the Lord **G**;
71:17 O **G**, You have taught me
71:18 I am old and grayheaded, O **G**,
71:19 Also Your righteousness, O **G**,
71:19 have done great things; O **G**,
71:22 O my **G**! To You I will sing
72: 1 the king Your judgments, O **G**,
72:18 Blessed be the LORD **G**,
72:18 the **G** of Israel, Who only does
73: 1 Truly **G** is good to Israel,
73:11 How does **G** know? And is there
73:17 I went into the sanctuary of **G**;
73:26 But **G** is the strength of my
73:28 good for me to draw near to **G**;
73:28 put my trust in the Lord **G**,
74: 1 O **G**, why have You cast us off
74: 8 up all the meeting places of **G**
74:10 O **G**, how long will the
74:12 For **G** is my King from of old,
74:22 Arise, O **G**, plead Your own
75: 1 We give thanks to You, O **G**,
75: 7 But **G** is the Judge: He puts
75: 9 I will sing praises to the **G**
76: 1 In Judah **G** is known; His name
76: 6 O **G** of Jacob, Both the chariot
76: 9 When **G** arose to judgment,
76:11 Make vows to the LORD your **G**,
77: 1 I cried out to **G** with my
77: 1 To **G** with my voice; And He
77: 3 I remembered **G**, and was
77: 9 Has **G** forgotten to be gracious?
77:13 Your way, O **G**, is in the
77:13 Who is so great a **G** as our
77:13 is so great a God as our **G**?
77:14 You are the **G** who does
77:16 The waters saw You, O **G**;
78: 7 they may set their hope in **G**,
78: 7 And not forget the works of **G**,
78: 8 spirit was not faithful to **G**.
78:10 did not keep the covenant of **G**;
78:18 And they tested **G** in their
78:19 Yes, they spoke against **G**:
78:19 Can **G** prepare a table in the
78:22 they did not believe in **G**,
78:31 The wrath of **G** came against
78:34 and sought earnestly for **G**.
78:35 Then they remembered that **G**
78:35 And the Most High **G** their
78:41 again and again they tempted **G**,
78:56 and provoked the Most High **G**,
78:59 When **G** heard this, He was
79: 1 O **G**, the nations have come
79: 9 O **G** of our salvation, For the
79:10 say, "Where is their **G**?
80: 3 Restore us, O **G**;
80: 4 O LORD **G** of hosts, How long
80: 7 O **G** of hosts; Cause Your face
80:14 O **G** of hosts; Look down from
80:19 O LORD **G** of hosts; Cause Your
81: 1 Sing aloud to **G** our strength;
81: 1 Make a joyful shout to the **G**
81: 4 A law of the **G** of Jacob.
81: 9 There shall be no foreign **g**
81: 9 shall you worship any foreign **g**.
81:10 I am the LORD your **G**,
82: 1 **G** stands in the congregation of
82: 8 Arise, O **G**, judge the earth;
83: 1 O **G**! Do not hold Your peace,
83: 1 And do not be still, O **G**!
83:12 ourselves The pastures of **G**
83:13 O my **G**, make them like the
84: 2 flesh cry out for the living **G**.
84: 3 of hosts, My King and my **G**.
84: 7 Each one appears before **G** in
84: 8 O LORD **G** of hosts, hear my
84: 8 O **G** of Jacob! Selah
84: 9 O **G**, behold our shield,
84:10 in the house of my **G** Than
84:11 For the LORD **G** is a sun and
85: 4 O **G** of our salvation, And
85: 8 I will hear what **G** the LORD
86: 2 for I am holy; You are my **G**;
86:10 You alone are **G**.
86:12 I will praise You, O Lord my **G**,
86:14 O **G**, the proud have risen
86:15 are a **G** full of compassion,
87: 3 O city of **G**! Selah
88: 1 **G** of my salvation, I have
89: 7 **G** is greatly to be feared in
89: 8 O LORD **G** of hosts, Who is
89:26 Me, 'You are my Father, My **G**,
90: A Prayer of Moses the man of **G**.
90: 2 to everlasting, You are **G**.
90:17 the beauty of the LORD our **G**
91: 2 refuge and my fortress; My **G**,
92:13 flourish in the courts of our **G**.
94: 1 O LORD **G**, to whom vengeance
94: 1 to whom vengeance belongs—O **G**,
94: 7 Nor does the **G** of Jacob
94:22 And my **G** the rock of my
94:23 The LORD our **G** shall cut them
95: 3 For the LORD is the great **G**,
95: 7 For He is our **G**,
98: 3 seen the salvation of our **G**.
99: 5 Exalt the LORD our **G**,
99: 8 answered them, O LORD our **G**;

99: 9 Exalt the LORD our **G**,
99: 9 For the LORD our **G** is holy.
100: 3 Know that the LORD, He is **G**;
102:24 I said, "O my **G**,
104: 1 LORD, O my soul! O LORD my **G**,
104:21 And seek their food from **G**.
104:33 I will sing praise to my **G**
105: 7 He is the LORD our **G**;
106:14 And tested **G** in the desert.
106:21 They forgot **G** their Savior,
106:47 Save us, O LORD our **G**,
106:48 Blessed be the LORD **G** of
107:11 rebelled against the words of **G**,
108: 1 O **G**, my heart is steadfast;
108: 5 Be exalted, O **G**,
108: 7 **G** has spoken in His holiness
108:11 Is it not You, O **G**,
108:11 cast us off? And You, O **G**,
108:13 Through **G** we will do valiantly,
109: 1 O **G** of my praise!
109:21 O **G** the Lord, Deal with me
109:26 O LORD my **G**! Oh, save me
113: 5 Who is like the LORD our **G**,
114: 7 At the presence of the **G** of
115: 2 say, "So where is their **G**?
115: 3 But our **G** is in heaven;
116: 5 our **G** is merciful.
118:27 **G** is the LORD, And He has
118:28 You are my **G**,
118:28 praise You; You are my **G**,
119:115 keep the commandments of my **G**!
122: 9 of the house of the LORD our **G**
123: 2 eyes look to the LORD our **G**,
135: 2 courts of the house of our **G**,
136: 2 give thanks to the **G** of gods!
136:26 give thanks to the **G** of heaven!
139:17 O **G**! How great is the sum of
139:19 O **G**! Depart from me,
139:23 Search me, O **G**,
140: 6 to the LORD: "You are my **G**;
140: 7 O **G** the Lord, the strength of
141: 8 O **G** the Lord; In You I take
143:10 Your will, For You are my **G**;
144: 9 sing a new song to You, O **G**;
144:15 Happy are the people whose **G**
145: 1 I will extol You, my **G**,
146: 2 I will sing praises to my **G**
146: 5 Happy is he who has the **G** of
146: 5 hope is in the LORD his **G**,
146:10 shall reign forever—Your **G**,
147: 1 good to sing praises to our **G**;
147: 7 praises on the harp to our **G**,
147:12 O Jerusalem! Praise your **G**,
149: 6 Let the high praises of **G** be
150: 1 Praise the LORD! Praise **G** in
Prov 2: 5 And find the knowledge of **G**.
2:17 forgets the covenant of her **G**.
3: 4 high esteem In the sight of **G**
21:12 The righteous **G** wisely
25: 2 It is the glory of **G** to
26:10 The great **G** who formed
30: 5 Every word of **G** is pure;
30: 9 And profane the name of my **G**.
Eccl 1:13 this burdensome task **G** has
2:24 I saw, was from the hand of **G**.
2:26 For **G** gives wisdom and
2:26 to him who is good before **G**.
3:11 can find out the work that **G**
3:13 his labor—it is the gift of **G**.
3:14 I know that whatever **G** does,
3:14 **G** does it, that men should
3:15 And **G** requires an account of
3:17 **G** shall judge the righteous and
3:18 **G** tests them, that they may see
5: 1 when you go to the house of **G**;
5: 2 utter anything hastily before **G**.
5: 2 For **G** is in heaven, and you
5: 4 When you make a vow to **G**,
5: 6 say before the messenger of **G**
5: 6 Why should **G** be angry at your
5: 7 is also vanity. But fear **G**.
5:18 the days of his life which **G**
5:19 As for every man to whom **G** has
5:19 labor—this is the gift of **G**.
5:20 because **G** keeps him busy with
6: 2 A man to whom **G** has given riches
6: 2 yet **G** does not give him power
7:13 Consider the work of **G**;
7:14 Surely **G** has appointed the one
7:18 For he who fears **G** will escape
7:26 He who pleases **G** shall escape
7:29 That **G** made man upright,
8: 2 for the sake of your oath to **G**.
8:12 be well with those who fear **G**,
8:13 he does not fear before **G**.
8:15 the days of his life which **G**
8:17 then I saw all the work of **G**,
9: 1 works are in the hand of **G**.
9: 7 For **G** has already accepted
11: 5 you do not know the works of **G**
11: 9 But know that for all these **G**
12: 7 the spirit will return to **G**
12:13 Fear **G** and keep His
12:14 For **G** will bring every work
Isa 1:10 Give ear to the law of our **G**,
2: 3 To the house of the **G** of
3:15 Says the Lord **G** of hosts.
5:16 And **G** who is holy shall be
7: 7 'thus says the Lord **G**:
7:11 yourself from the LORD your **G**;
7:13 but will you weary my **G** also?
8:10 For **G** is with us."
8:19 not a people seek their **G**?
8:21 curse their king and their **G**,
9: 6 Wonderful, Counselor, Mighty **G**,
10:21 of Jacob, To the Mighty **G**.
10:23 For the Lord **G** of hosts Will
10:24 thus says the Lord **G** of hosts:
12: 2 **G** is my salvation, I will
13:19 Will be as when **G** overthrew
14:13 my throne above the stars of **G**;
17: 6 Says the LORD **G** of Israel.
17:10 you have forgotten the **G** of
17:13 But **G** will rebuke them and
21:10 The **G** of Israel, I have
21:17 for the LORD **G** of Israel has
22: 5 and perplexity By the Lord **G**
22:12 And in that day the Lord **G** of
22:14 says the Lord **G** of hosts.
22:15 Thus says the Lord **G** of hosts:
24:15 The name of the LORD **G** of
25: 1 O LORD, You are my **G**.
25: 8 And the Lord **G** will wipe away
25: 9 'Behold, this is our **G**;
26: 1 **G** will appoint salvation for
26:13 O LORD our **G**, masters besides
28:16 thus says the Lord **G**:
28:22 I have heard from the Lord **G**
28:26 His **G** teaches him.
29:23 And fear the **G** of Israel.
30:15 For thus says the Lord **G**,
30:18 For the LORD is a **G** of
31: 3 Egyptians are men, and not **G**;
35: 2 LORD, The excellency of our **G**.
35: 4 your **G** will come with
35: 4 With the recompense of **G**;
36: 7 'We trust in the LORD our **G**,
37: 4 may be that the LORD your **G**
37: 4 sent to reproach the living **G**,
37: 4 words which the LORD your **G**
37:10 Do not let your **G** in whom you
37:16 **G** of Israel, the One who
37:16 the cherubim, You are **G**,
37:17 sent to reproach the living **G**.
37:20 "Now therefore, O LORD our **G**,
37:21 Thus says the LORD **G** of Israel,
37:38 in the house of Nisroch his **g**,
38: 5 the **G** of David your father:
40: 1 My people!" Says your **G**.
40: 3 the desert A highway for our **G**.
40: 8 But the word of our **G** stands
40: 9 of Judah, "Behold your **G**!"
40:10 the Lord**G** shall come with a
40:18 To whom then will you liken **G**?
40:27 claim is passed over by my **G**"?
40:28 not heard? The everlasting **G**,
41:10 not dismayed, for I am your **G**.
41:13 For I, the LORD your **G**,
41:17 the **G** of Israel, will not
42: 5 Thus says **G** the LORD,
43: 3 For I am the LORD your **G**,
43:10 Before Me there was no **G**
43:12 And there was no foreign **g**
43:12 Says the LORD, "that I am **G**.
44: 6 Besides Me there is no **G**.
44: 8 Is there a **G** besides Me?
44:10 Who would form a **g** or mold an
44:15 Indeed he makes a **g** and
44:17 rest of it he makes into a **g**,
44:17 for you are my **g**!"
45: 3 Am the **G** of Israel.
45: 5 There is no **G** besides Me.
45:14 Surely **G** is in you, And there
45:14 There is no other **G**.'
45:15 Truly You are **G**,
45:15 O **G** of Israel, the Savior!
45:18 created the heavens, Who is **G**,
45:20 And pray to a **g** that cannot
45:21 And there is no other **G**
45:21 A just **G** and a Savior;
45:22 ends of the earth! For I am **G**,
46: 6 goldsmith, and he makes it a **g**;
46: 9 things of old, For I am **G**,
46: 9 there is no other; I am **G**,
48: 1 And make mention of the **G** of
48: 2 And lean on the **G** of Israel;
48:16 And now the Lord **G** and His
48:17 "I am the LORD your **G**,
49: 4 LORD, And my work with my **G**.
49: 5 And My **G** shall be My
49:22 Thus says the Lord **G**:
50: 4 The Lord **G** has given Me
50: 5 The Lord **G** has opened My ear;
50: 7 For the Lord **G** will help Me;
50: 9 Surely the Lord **G** will help
50:10 the LORD And rely upon his **G**.
51:15 But I am the LORD your **G**,
51:20 LORD, The rebuke of your **G**.
51:22 Lord, The LORD and your **G**,
52: 4 For thus says the Lord **G**:
52: 7 Your **G** reigns!"
52:10 see The salvation of our **G**.
52:12 And the **G** of Israel will be
53: 4 Him stricken, Smitten by **G**,
54: 5 He is called the **G** of the
54: 6 were refused," Says your **G**.
55: 5 Because of the LORD your **G**,
55: 7 mercy on him; And to our **G**,
56: 8 The Lord **G**, who gathers
57:21 is no peace," Says my **G**,
58: 2 the ordinance of their **G**.
58: 2 take delight in approaching **G**.
59: 2 have separated you from your **G**;
59:13 And departing from our **G**,
60: 9 the name of the LORD your **G**,
60:19 And your **G** your glory.
61: 1 The Spirit of the Lord **G** is
61: 2 the day of vengeance of our **G**;
61: 6 call you the servants of our **G**.
61:10 soul shall be joyful in my **G**;
61:11 So the Lord **G** will cause
62: 3 In the hand of your **G**.
62: 5 So shall your **G** rejoice over
64: 4 Nor has the eye seen any **G**
65:13 thus says the Lord **G**:
65:15 For the Lord **G** will slay you,
65:16 Shall bless himself in the **G**
65:16 earth Shall swear by the **G** of
66: 9 up the womb?" says your **G**.
Jer 1: 6 Lord **G**! Behold, I cannot
2:17 have forsaken the LORD your **G**
2:19 have forsaken the LORD your **G**,
2:19 Says the Lord **G** of hosts.
2:22 before Me," says the Lord **G**.
3:13 against the LORD your **G**,
3:21 forgotten the LORD their **G**.
3:22 For You are the LORD our **G**.
3:23 in the LORD our **G** Is the
3:25 sinned against the LORD our **G**,
3:25 the voice of the LORD our **G**.
4:10 Lord **G**! Surely You have
5: 4 LORD, The judgment of their **G**.
5: 5 LORD, The judgment of their **G**.
5:14 thus says the LORD **G** of hosts:
5:19 Why does the LORD our **G** do all
5:24 us now fear the LORD our **G**,
7: 3 the **G** of Israel: "Amend your
7:20 Therefore thus says the Lord **G**:
7:21 the **G** of Israel: "Add your
7:23 My voice, and I will be your **G**,
7:28 the voice of the LORD their **G**
8:14 For the LORD our **G** has put us
9:15 the **G** of Israel: "Behold, I
10:10 But the LORD is the true **G**;
10:10 He is the living **G** and the
11: 3 Thus says the LORD **G** of Israel:
11: 4 My people, and I will be your **G**,
13:12 Thus says the LORD **G** of Israel:
13:16 Give glory to the LORD your **G**
14:13 Lord **G**! Behold, the prophets
14:22 Are You not He, O LORD our **G**?
15:16 O LORD **G** of hosts.
16: 9 the **G** of Israel: "Behold, I
16:10 against the LORD our **G**?
19: 3 the **G** of Israel: "Behold, I
19:15 the **G** of Israel: 'Behold, I
21: 4 Thus says the LORD **G** of Israel:
22: 9 covenant of the LORD their **G**,
23: 2 thus says the LORD **G** of
23:23 Am I a **G** near at hand," says
23:23 And not a **G** afar off?
23:36 the words of the living **G**,
23:36 God, the LORD of hosts, our **G**.
24: 5 the **G** of Israel: 'Like these
24: 7 people, and I will be their **G**,
25:15 For thus says the LORD **G** of
25:27 the **G** of Israel: "Drink, be
26:13 the voice of the LORD your **G**;
26:16 in the name of the LORD our **G**.
27: 4 the **G** of Israel—thus you shall
27:21 the **G** of Israel, concerning the
28: 2 the **G** of Israel, saying: 'I
28:14 the **G** of Israel: "I have put a
29: 4 the **G** of Israel, to all who
29: 8 the **G** of Israel: Do not let
29:21 the **G** of Israel, concerning
29:25 the **G** of Israel, saying: You
30: 2 Thus speaks the LORD **G** of
30: 9 shall serve the LORD their **G**,
30:22 people, And I will be your **G**.
31: 1 I will be the **G** of all the
31: 6 to Zion, To the LORD our **G**.
31:18 For You are the LORD my **G**.
31:23 the **G** of Israel: "They shall
31:33 and I will be their **G**,
32:14 the **G** of Israel: "Take these
32:15 the **G** of Israel: "Houses and
32:17 Lord **G**! Behold, You have made
32:18 them—the Great, the Mighty **G**,
32:25 You have said to me, O Lord **G**,
32:27 the **G** of all flesh. Is there
32:36 the **G** of Israel, concerning
32:38 people, and I will be their **G**;
33: 4 the **G** of Israel, concerning the
34: 2 the **G** of Israel: 'Go and speak
34:13 the **G** of Israel: 'I made a
35: 4 the son of Igdaliah, a man of **G**,
35:13 the **G** of Israel: 'Go and tell
35:17 thus says the LORD **G** of hosts,
35:17 the **G** of Israel: 'Behold, I
35:18 the **G** of Israel: 'Because you
35:19 the **G** of Israel: "Jonadab the
37: 3 Pray now to the LORD our **G** for
37: 7 the **G** of Israel, 'Thus you
38:17 the **G** of hosts, the God of
38:17 the **G** of Israel: 'If you surely
39:16 the **G** of Israel: "Behold, I
40: 2 The LORD your **G** has pronounced
42: 2 pray for us to the LORD your **G**,
42: 3 that the LORD your **G** may show
42: 4 I will pray to the LORD your **G**
42: 5 which the LORD your **G** sends
42: 6 the voice of the LORD our **G**
42: 6 the voice of the LORD our **G**.
42: 9 the **G** of Israel, to whom you
42:13 the voice of the LORD your **G**,

42:15 the G of Israel: 'If you wholly
42:18 the G of Israel: 'As My anger
42:20 you sent me to the LORD your G,
42:20 'Pray for us to the LORD our G,
42:20 to all that the LORD your G
42:21 the voice of the LORD your G,
43: 1 the words of the LORD their G,
43: 1 for which the LORD their G had
43: 2 speak falsely! The LORD our G
43:10 the G of Israel: "Behold, I
44: 2 the G of Israel: 'You have seen
44: 7 the G of hosts, the God of
44: 7 the G of Israel: 'Why do you
44:11 the G of Israel: 'Behold, I
44:25 the G of Israel, saying: 'You
44:26 The Lord G lives."
45: 2 the G of Israel, to you,
46:10 is the day of the Lord G of
46:10 For the Lord G of hosts has a
46:25 the G of Israel, says:
48: 1 the G of Israel: "Woe to
49: 5 Says the Lord G of hosts,
50: 4 And seek the LORD their G.
50:18 the G of Israel: "Behold, I
50:25 is the work of the Lord G of
50:28 vengeance of the LORD our G,
50:31 says the Lord G of
50:40 As G overthrew Sodom and
51: 5 forsaken, nor Judah, By his G,
51:10 the work of the LORD our G.
51:33 the G of Israel: "The
51:56 For the LORD is the G of
Lam 3:28 Because G has laid it on
3:41 our hearts and hands To G in
Ezek 1: 1 opened and I saw visions of G.
2: 4 to them, 'Thus says the Lord G.
3:11 them, 'Thus says the Lord G,
3:27 to them, 'Thus says the Lord G.
4:14 Lord G! Indeed I have never
5: 5 "Thus says the Lord G:
5: 7 thus says the Lord G:
5: 8 thus says the Lord G:
5:11 as I live,' says the Lord G,
6: 3 hear the word of the Lord G!'
6: 3 GOD!' Thus says the Lord G
6:11 'Thus says the Lord G:
7: 2 thus says the Lord G to the
7: 5 "Thus says the Lord G:
8: 1 that the hand of the Lord G
8: 3 and brought me in visions of G
8: 4 the glory of the G of Israel
9: 3 Now the glory of the G of
9: 8 Lord G! Will You destroy all
10: 5 like the voice of Almighty G
10:19 and the glory of the G of
10:20 creature I saw under the G of
11: 7 thus says the Lord G:
11: 8 upon you," says the Lord G.
11:13 Lord G! Will You make a
11:16 say, 'Thus says the Lord G:
11:17 say, 'Thus says the Lord G:
11:20 people, and I will be their G.
11:21 own heads," says the Lord G.
11:22 and the glory of the G of
11:24 in a vision by the Spirit of G
12:10 to them, 'Thus says the Lord G:
12:19 Thus says the Lord G to the
12:23 'Thus says the Lord G:
12:25 perform it," says the Lord G.
12:28 to them, 'Thus says the Lord G:
12:28 be done," says the Lord G.
13: 3 Thus says the Lord G:
13: 8 thus says the Lord G:
13: 8 against you," says the Lord G.
13: 9 know that I am the Lord G.
13:13 Therefore thus says the Lord G:
13:16 no peace,'" says the Lord G.
13:18 say, 'Thus says the Lord G:
13:20 thus says the Lord G:
14: 4 to them, 'Thus says the Lord G:
14: 6 Israel, 'Thus says the Lord G:
14:11 My people and I may be their G,
14:11 their God," says the Lord G.
14:14 says the Lord G.
14:16 as I live," says the Lord G,
14:18 as I live," says the Lord G,
14:20 as I live," says the Lord G,
14:21 For thus says the Lord G:
14:23 done in it," says the LORD G.
15: 6 thus says the Lord G:
15: 8 says the Lord G.
16: 3 Thus says the Lord G to
16: 8 became Mine," says the Lord G.
16:14 on you," says the Lord G.
16:19 so it was," says the Lord G.
16:23 woe to you!' says the Lord G—
16:30 your heart!" says the Lord G,
16:36 'Thus says the Lord G:
16:43 own head," says the Lord G.
16:48 I live," says the Lord G,
16:59 'For thus says the Lord G:
16:63 have done," says the Lord G.
17: 3 say, 'Thus says the Lord G:
17: 9 "Say, 'Thus says the Lord G:
17:16 'As I live,' says the Lord G,
17:19 Therefore thus says the Lord G:
17:22 Thus says the Lord G:
18: 3 I live," says the Lord G,
18: 9 Says the Lord G.
18:23 should die?" says the Lord G,
18:30 to his ways," says the Lord G.
18:32 who dies," says the Lord G.
20: 3 to them, 'Thus says the Lord G:
20: 3 As I live," says the Lord G,
20: 5 to them, 'Thus says the Lord G:
20: 5 saying, 'I am the LORD your G.
20: 7 I am the LORD your G.'
20:19 'I am the LORD your G:
20:20 that I am the LORD your G.
20:27 to them, 'Thus says the Lord G:
20:30 Israel, 'Thus says the Lord G:
20:31 As I live," says the Lord G,
20:33 I live," says the Lord G,
20:36 with you," says the Lord G.
20:39 Israel," thus says the Lord G:
20:40 of Israel," says the Lord G,
20:44 of Israel," says the Lord G.
20:47 Thus says the Lord G:
20:49 Lord G! They say of me, 'Does
21: 7 to pass,' says the Lord G.
21:13 no more," says the Lord G.
21:24 thus says the Lord G:
21:26 'thus says the Lord G:
21:28 Thus says the Lord G concerning
22: 3 say, 'Thus says the Lord G:
22:12 Me," says the Lord G.
22:19 thus says the Lord G:
22:28 saying, 'Thus says the Lord G,
22:31 own heads," says the Lord G.
23:22 Oholibah, thus says the Lord G:
23:28 "For thus says the Lord G:
23:32 "Thus says the Lord G:
23:34 have spoken,' Says the Lord G.
23:35 thus says the Lord G:
23:46 "For thus says the Lord G:
23:49 know that I am the Lord G.
24: 3 to them, 'Thus says the Lord G:
24: 6 thus says the Lord G:
24: 9 thus says the Lord G:
24:14 judge you," Says the Lord G.
24:21 Israel, "Thus says the Lord G:
24:24 know that I am the Lord G.
25: 3 Hear the word of the Lord G!
25: 3 Thus says the Lord G:
25: 6 'For thus says the Lord G:
25: 8 'Thus says the Lord G:
25:12 'Thus says the Lord G:
25:13 thus says the Lord G:
25:14 vengeance," says the Lord G.
25:15 'Thus says the Lord G:
25:16 thus says the Lord G:
26: 3 thus says the Lord G:
26: 5 have spoken,' says the Lord G;
26: 7 "For thus says the Lord G:
26:14 have spoken,' says the Lord G.
26:15 Thus says the Lord G to Tyre:
26:19 "For thus says the Lord G:
26:21 found again,' says the Lord G.
27: 3 thus says the Lord G:
28: 2 of Tyre, 'Thus says the Lord G:
28: 2 And you say, 'I am a g,
28: 2 you are a man, and not a g,
28: 2 your heart as the heart of a g
28: 6 thus says the Lord G:
28: 6 your heart as the heart of a g,
28: 9 him who slays you, 'I am a g'?
28: 9 shall be a man, and not a g,
28:10 have spoken," says the Lord G.
28:12 to him, 'Thus says the Lord G:
28:13 were in Eden, the garden of G;
28:14 were on the holy mountain of G;
28:16 Out of the mountain of G;
28:22 say, 'Thus says the Lord G:
28:24 know that I am the Lord G.
28:25 'Thus says the Lord G:
28:26 that I am the LORD their G.
29: 3 and say, 'Thus says the Lord G:
29: 8 thus says the Lord G:
29:13 'Yet, thus says the Lord G:
29:16 know that I am the Lord G.
29:19 thus says the Lord G:
29:20 for Me,' says the Lord G.
30: 2 and say, 'Thus says the Lord G:
30: 6 the sword," Says the Lord G.
30:10 'Thus says the Lord G:
30:13 'Thus says the Lord G:
30:22 thus says the Lord G:
31: 8 The cedars in the garden of G
31: 8 No tree in the garden of G was
31: 9 That were in the garden of G.
31:10 thus says the Lord G:
31:15 "Thus says the Lord G:
31:18 multitude,' says the Lord G.
32: 3 "Thus says the Lord G:
32: 8 your land,' Says the Lord G.
32:11 "For thus says the Lord G:
32:14 like oil,' Says the Lord G.
32:16 multitude,' Says the Lord G.
32:31 the sword," Says the Lord G.
32:32 multitude," Says the Lord G.
33:11 'As I live,' says the Lord G,
33:25 to them, 'Thus says the Lord G:
33:27 to them, 'Thus says the Lord G:
34: 2 Thus says the Lord G to the
34: 8 I live," says the Lord G,
34:10 'Thus says the Lord G:
34:11 'For thus says the Lord G:
34:15 lie down," says the Lord G.
34:17 My flock, thus says the Lord G:
34:20 thus says the Lord G to them:
34:24 I, the LORD, will be their G,
34:30 know that I, the LORD their G,
34:30 My people," says the Lord G.
34:31 you are men, and I am your G,
34:31 your God," says the Lord G.
35: 3 to it, 'Thus says the Lord G:
35: 6 as I live," says the Lord G,
35:11 as I live," says the Lord G,
35:14 'Thus says the Lord G:
36: 2 'Thus says the Lord G:
36: 3 and say, 'Thus says the Lord G:
36: 4 hear the word of the Lord G!
36: 4 Thus says the Lord G to
36: 5 thus says the Lord G:
36: 6 valleys, 'Thus says the Lord G:
36: 7 thus says the Lord G:
36:13 'Thus says the Lord G:
36:14 anymore," says the Lord G.
36:15 anymore," says the Lord G.
36:22 Israel, 'Thus says the Lord G:
36:23 the LORD," says the Lord G,
36:28 My people, and I will be your G.
36:32 I do this," says the Lord G,
36:33 'Thus says the Lord G:
36:37 'Thus says the Lord G:
37: 3 So I answered, "O Lord G,
37: 5 Thus says the Lord G to these
37: 9 breath, 'Thus says the Lord G:
37:12 to them, 'Thus says the Lord G:
37:19 to them, 'Thus says the Lord G:
37:21 to them, 'Thus says the Lord G:
37:23 people, and I will be their G.
37:27 indeed I will be their G,
38: 3 say, 'Thus says the Lord G:
38:10 'Thus says the Lord G:
38:14 to Gog, 'Thus says the Lord G:
38:17 'Thus says the Lord G:
38:18 of Israel," says the Lord G,
38:21 mountains," says the Lord G.
39: 1 and say, 'Thus says the Lord G:
39: 5 have spoken," says the Lord G.
39: 8 be done," says the Lord G.
39:10 them," says the Lord G.
39:13 glorified," says the Lord G.
39:17 of man, thus says the Lord G,
39:20 men of war," says the Lord G.
39:22 that I am the LORD their G
39:25 thus says the Lord G:
39:28 that I am the LORD their G,
39:29 of Israel,' says the Lord G.
40: 2 In the visions of G He took me
43: 2 the glory of the G of Israel
43:18 of man, thus says the Lord G:
43:19 to Me,' says the Lord G.
43:27 accept you,' says the Lord G.
44: 2 because the LORD G of Israel
44: 6 Israel, 'Thus says the Lord G:
44: 9 'Thus says the Lord G:
44:12 them," says the Lord G,
44:15 the blood," says the Lord G.
44:27 inner court," says the Lord G.
45: 9 'Thus says the Lord G:
45: 9 My people," says the Lord G.
45:15 for them," says the Lord G.
45:18 'Thus says the Lord G:
46: 1 'Thus says the Lord G:
46:16 'Thus says the Lord G:
47:13 Thus says the Lord G:
47:23 inheritance," says the Lord G.
48:29 portions," says the Lord G.
Dan 1: 2 the articles of the house of G,
1: 2 of Shinar to the house of his g;
1: 2 the treasure house of his g.
1: 9 Now G had brought Daniel into
1:17 G gave them knowledge and skill
2:18 might seek mercies from the G
2:19 So Daniel blessed the G of
2:20 Blessed be the name of G forever
2:23 O G of my fathers; You have
2:28 But there is a G in heaven who
2:37 For the G of heaven has given
2:44 the days of these kings the G
2:45 the great G has made known to
2:47 Truly your G is the God of
2:47 Truly your God is the G of
3:15 And who is the g who will
3:17 our G whom we serve is able to
3:25 the fourth is like the Son of G.
3:26 servants of the Most High G,
3:28 Blessed be the G of Shadrach,
3:28 not serve nor worship any g
3:28 any god except their own G!
3:29 anything amiss against the G
3:29 because there is no other G who
4: 2 wonders that the Most High G
4: 8 according to the name of my g;
4: 8 is the Spirit of the Holy G),
4: 9 that the Spirit of the Holy G
4:18 for the Spirit of the Holy G
5: 3 the temple of the house of G
5:11 is the Spirit of the Holy G.
5:14 that the Spirit of G is in
5:18 the Most High G gave
5:21 he knew that the Most High G
5:23 and the G who holds your
5:26 G has numbered your kingdom,
6: 5 him concerning the law of his G.
6: 7 that whoever petitions any g or
6:10 and gave thanks before his G,
6:11 supplication before his G.
6:12 every man who petitions any g
6:16 saying to Daniel, "Your G,
6:20 servant of the living G,
6:20 of the living God, has your G,
6:22 My G sent His angel and shut the
6:23 because he believed in his G.

G

6:26 tremble and fear before the G
6:26 For He is the living G,
9: 3 I set my face toward the Lord G
9: 4 And I prayed to the LORD my G,
9: 4 "O Lord, great and awesome G,
9: 9 To the Lord our G belong mercy
9:10 the voice of the LORD our G,
9:11 Law of Moses the servant of G
9:13 prayer before the LORD our G,
9:14 for the LORD our G is
9:15 "And now, O Lord our G,
9:17 "Now therefore, our G,
9:18 'O my G, incline Your ear
9:19 delay for Your own sake, my G,
9:20 before the LORD my G for the
9:20 for the holy mountain of my G,
10:12 humble yourself before your G,
11:32 but the people who know their G
11:36 magnify himself above every g,
11:36 blasphemies against the G of
11:37 He shall regard neither the G of
11:37 of women, nor regard any g;
11:38 their place he shall honor a g
11:38 and a g which his fathers did
11:39 fortresses with a foreign g,
Hos 1: 6 Then G said to him: "Call
1: 7 save them by the LORD their G,
1: 9 Then G said: "Call his name
1: 9 And I will not be your G.
1:10 are sons of the living G.
2:23 You are my G!'"
3: 5 and seek the LORD their G and
4: 1 or mercy Or knowledge of G in
4: 6 forgotten the law of your G,
4:12 the harlot against their G.
5: 4 Toward turning to their G,
6: 6 And the knowledge of G more
7:10 not return to the LORD their G,
8: 2 Israel will cry to Me, 'My G,
8: 6 made it, and it is not G;
9: 1 the harlot against your G.
9: 8 of Ephraim is with my G;
9: 8 in the house of his G.
9:17 My G will cast them away,
11: 9 destroy Ephraim. For I am G,
11:12 But Judah still walks with G,
12: 3 strength he struggled with G.
12: 5 the LORD G of hosts.
12: 6 you, by the help of your G,
12: 6 And wait on your G
12: 9 "But I am the LORD your G,
13: 4 Yet I am the LORD your G
13: 4 And you shall know no G but
13:16 she has rebelled against her G.
14: 1 return to the LORD your G,
Joel 1:13 You who minister to my G;
1:13 from the house of your G.
1:14 the house of the LORD your G,
1:16 from the house of our G?
2:13 Return to the LORD your G,
2:14 offering For the LORD your G?
2:17 peoples, 'Where is their G?
2:23 rejoice in the LORD your G;
2:26 the name of the LORD your G,
2:27 I am the LORD your G And
3:17 that I am the LORD your G,
Am 1: 8 perish," Says the Lord G.
2: 8 in the house of their g.
3: 7 Surely the Lord G does
3: 8 The Lord G has spoken!
3:11 thus says the Lord G:
3:13 of Jacob," Says the Lord G,
3:13 the G of hosts,
4: 2 The Lord G has sworn by His
4: 5 of Israel!" Says the Lord G.
4:11 As G overthrew Sodom and
4:12 to you, Prepare to meet your G,
4:13 The LORD G of hosts is His
5: 3 For thus says the Lord G:
5:14 So the LORD G of hosts will
5:15 It may be that the LORD G of
5:16 Therefore the LORD G of hosts,
5:27 whose name is the G of hosts.
6: 8 The Lord G has sworn by
6: 8 The LORD G of hosts says:
6:14 Says the LORD G of hosts;
7: 1 Thus the Lord G showed me:
7: 2 that I said: "O Lord G,
7: 4 Thus the Lord G showed me:
7: 4 the Lord G called for conflict
7: 5 Then I said: "O Lord G,
7: 6 not be," said the Lord G.
8: 1 Thus the Lord G showed me:
8: 3 that day," Says the Lord G—
8: 9 in that day," says the Lord G,
8:11 are coming," says the Lord G,
8:14 'As your g lives, O Dan!'
9: 5 The Lord G of hosts, He who
9: 8 the eyes of the Lord G are on
9:15 them," Says the LORD your G.
Ob 1 Thus says the Lord G
Jon 1: 5 every man cried out to his g,
1: 6 Arise, call on your G;
1: 6 perhaps your G will consider
1: 9 the G of heaven, who made the
2: 1 prayed to the LORD his G from
2: 6 from the pit, O LORD, my G.
3: 5 people of Nineveh believed G,
3: 8 and cry mightily to G;
3: 9 Who can tell if G will turn and
3:10 Then G saw their works, that
3:10 and G relented from the

4: 2 are a gracious and merciful G,
4: 6 And the LORD G prepared a plant
4: 7 morning dawned the next day G
4: 8 that G prepared a vehement east
4: 9 Then G said to Jonah, "Is it
Mic 1: 2 is in it! Let the Lord G be
3: 7 there is no answer from G.
4: 2 To the house of the G of
4: 5 walk each in the name of his g,
4: 5 in the name of the LORD our G
5: 4 of the name of the LORD His G;
6: 6 bow myself before the High G?
6: 8 And to walk humbly with your G?
7: 7 I will wait for the G of my
7: 7 My G will hear me.
7:10 "Where is the LORD your G?
7:17 be afraid of the LORD our G,
7:18 Who is a G like You,
Nah 1: 2 G is jealous, and the LORD
Hab 1:11 Ascribing this power to his g.
1:12 from everlasting, O LORD my G,
3: 3 G came from Teman, The Holy
3:18 I will joy in the G of my
3:19 The LORD G is my strength;
Zeph 1: 7 in the presence of the Lord G;
2: 7 For the LORD their G will
2: 9 the G of Israel, "Surely Moab
3: 2 has not drawn near to her G.
3:17 The LORD your G in your midst,
Hag 1:12 the voice of the LORD their G,
1:12 as the LORD their G had sent
1:14 of the LORD of hosts, their G,
Zech 6:15 the voice of the LORD your G.
7: 2 and his men, to the house of G,
8: 8 people And I will be their G,
8:23 for we have heard that G is
9: 7 even he shall be for our G,
9:14 The Lord G will blow the
9:16 The LORD their G will save
10: 6 For I am the LORD their G,
11: 4 Thus says the LORD my G,
12: 5 in the LORD of hosts, their G.
12: 8 of David shall be like G,
13: 9 will say, 'The LORD is my G.
14: 5 Thus the LORD my G will come,
Mal 2:10 Has not one G created us?
2:11 the daughter of a foreign g.
2:16 For the LORD G of Israel says
2:17 Where is the G of justice?"
3: 8 "Will a man rob G?
3:14 'It is useless to serve G;
3:15 They even tempt G and go
3:18 Between one who serves G And
Mt 1:23 is translated, "G with us."
2:22 And being warned by G in a
3: 9 For I say to you that G is
3:16 and He saw the Spirit of G
4: 3 said, "If You are the Son of G,
4: 4 from the mouth of G.
4: 6 'If You are the Son of G,
4: 7 tempt the LORD your G.
4:10 worship the LORD your G,
5: 8 in heart, For they shall see G.
5: 9 they shall be called sons of G.
6:24 You cannot serve G and mammon.
6:30 Now if G so clothes the grass of
6:33 seek first the kingdom of G
8:29 with You, Jesus, You Son of G?
9: 8 they marveled and glorified G,
12: 4 how he entered the house of G
12:28 out demons by the Spirit of G,
12:28 surely the kingdom of G has
14:33 "Truly You are the Son of G.
15: 3 the commandment of G because
15: 4 For G commanded, saying, 'Honor
15: 5 from me is a gift to G"—
15: 6 have made the commandment of G
15:31 and they glorified the G of
16:16 Christ, the Son of the living G.
16:23 not mindful of the things of G,
19: 6 Therefore what G has joined
19:17 is good but One, that is, G.
19:24 man to enter the kingdom of G.
19:26 but with G all things are
21:12 went into the temple of G and
21:31 harlots enter the kingdom of G
21:43 the kingdom of G will be taken
22:16 and teach the way of G in
22:21 and to G the things that are
22:29 Scriptures nor the power of G.
22:30 but are like angels of G in
22:31 what was spoken to you by G,
22:32 I am the G of Abraham, the
22:32 the G of Isaac, and the
22:32 and the G of Jacob'?
22:32 G is not the God of the dead,
22:32 God is not the G of the dead,
22:37 love the LORD your G
23:22 swears by the throne of G and
26:61 to destroy the temple of G and
26:63 You under oath by the living G:
26:63 the Son of G!"
27:40 If You are the Son of G,
27:43 "He trusted in G;
27:43 for He said, 'I am the Son of G.
27:46 that is, "My G,
27:46 that is, "My God, My G,
27:54 Truly this was the Son of G!"
Mk 1: 1 of Jesus Christ, the Son of G.
1:14 the gospel of the kingdom of G,
1:15 and the kingdom of G is at
1:24 the Holy One of G!"

2: 7 Who can forgive sins but G
2:12 all were amazed and glorified G,
2:26 he went into the house of G
3:11 saying, "You are the Son of G.
3:35 whoever does the will of G
4:11 the mystery of the kingdom of G;
4:26 The kingdom of G is as if a man
4:30 shall we liken the kingdom of G?
5: 7 Jesus, Son of the Most High G?
5: 7 I implore You by G that You do
7: 8 aside the commandment of G,
7: 9 you reject the commandment of G,
7:11 (that is, a gift to G),
7:13 making the word of G of no
8:33 not mindful of the things of G,
9: 1 till they see the kingdom of G
9:47 you to enter the kingdom of G
10: 6 G 'made them male and
10: 9 Therefore what G has joined
10:14 for of such is the kingdom of G.
10:15 not receive the kingdom of G
10:18 is good but One, that is, G.
10:23 to enter the kingdom of G!"
10:24 to enter the kingdom of G!
10:25 man to enter the kingdom of G.
10:27 is impossible, but not with G;
10:27 for with G all things are
11:22 said to them, "Have faith in G.
12:14 but teach the way of G in
12:17 and to G the things that are
12:24 Scriptures nor the power of G?
12:26 how G spoke to him, saying, 'I
12:26 I am the G of Abraham, the
12:26 the G of Isaac, and the
12:26 and the G of Jacob'?
12:27 He is not the G of the dead, but
12:27 but the G of the living.
12:29 O Israel, the LORD our G,
12:30 love the LORD your G
12:32 the truth, for there is one G,
12:34 not far from the kingdom of G.
13:19 of the creation which G
14:25 it new in the kingdom of G.
15:34 which is translated, "My G,
15:34 translated, "My God, My G,
15:39 this Man was the Son of G!"
15:43 waiting for the kingdom of G,
16:19 sat down at the right hand of G.
Lk 1: 6 were both righteous before G,
1: 8 was serving as priest before G
1:16 of Israel to the Lord their G.
1:19 who stands in the presence of G,
1:26 angel Gabriel was sent by G to
1:30 for you have found favor with G.
1:32 and the Lord G will give Him
1:35 will be called the Son of G.
1:37 For with G nothing will be
1:47 my spirit has rejoiced in G my
1:64 and he spoke, praising G.
1:68 Blessed is the Lord G of
1:78 the tender mercy of our G,
2:13 of the heavenly host praising G
2:14 'Glory to G in the highest,
2:20 glorifying and praising G for
2:28 up in his arms and blessed G
2:37 but served G with fastings and
2:40 and the grace of G was upon
2:52 and in favor with G and men.
3: 2 the word of G came to John the
3: 6 see the salvation of G.
3: 8 For I say to you that G is
3:38 son of Adam, the son of G.
4: 3 Him, "If You are the Son of G,
4: 4 but by every word of G.
4: 8 worship the LORD your G,
4: 9 Him, "If You are the Son of G,
4:12 tempt the LORD your G.
4:34 the Holy One of G!"
4:41 the Son of G!" And He,
4:43 must preach the kingdom of G
5: 1 about Him to hear the word of G,
5:21 Who can forgive sins but G
5:25 to his own house, glorifying G.
5:26 and they glorified G and were
6: 4 he went into the house of G,
6:12 all night in prayer to G.
6:20 For yours is the kingdom of G.
7:16 upon all, and they glorified G,
7:16 G has visited His people."
7:28 is least in the kingdom of G
7:29 the tax collectors justified G,
7:30 lawyers rejected the will of G
8: 1 tidings of the kingdom of G.
8:10 mysteries of the kingdom of G,
8:11 The seed is the word of G.
8:21 these who hear the word of G
8:28 Jesus, Son of the Most High G?
8:39 and tell what great things G
9: 2 to preach the kingdom of G and
9:11 to them about the kingdom of G,
9:20 and said, "The Christ of G.
9:27 till they see the kingdom of G.
9:43 all amazed at the majesty of G.
9:60 go and preach the kingdom of G.
9:62 is fit for the kingdom of G.
10: 9 The kingdom of G has come near
10:11 that the kingdom of G has come
10:27 love the LORD your G
11:20 out demons with the finger of G,
11:20 surely the kingdom of G has
11:28 those who hear the word of G
11:42 by justice and the love of G.

11:49 Therefore the wisdom of ***G*** also
12: 6 of them is forgotten before ***G***.
12: 8 confess before the angels of ***G***.
12: 9 denied before the angels of ***G***.
12:20 'But ***G*** said to him, 'Fool!
12:21 and is not rich toward ***G***.
12:24 and ***G*** feeds them. Of how much
12:28 If then ***G*** so clothes the grass,
12:31 "But seek the kingdom of ***G***,
13:13 made straight, and glorified ***G***.
13:18 What is the kingdom of ***G*** like?
13:20 shall I liken the kingdom of ***G***?
13:28 prophets in the kingdom of ***G***,
13:29 sit down in the kingdom of ***G***.
14:15 eat bread in the kingdom of ***G***!
15:10 the presence of the angels of ***G***
16:13 You cannot serve ***G*** and
16:15 but ***G*** knows your hearts.
16:15 abomination in the sight of ***G***.
16:16 that time the kingdom of ***G*** has
17:15 with a loud voice glorified ***G***,
17:18 who returned to give glory to ***G***
17:20 when the kingdom of ***G*** would
17:20 The kingdom of ***G*** does not come
17:21 the kingdom of ***G*** is within
18: 2 a judge who did not fear ***G*** nor
18: 4 Though I do not fear ***G*** nor
18: 7 And shall ***G*** not avenge His own
18:11 prayed thus with himself, '***G***,
18:13 but beat his breast, saying, '***G***,
18:16 for of such is the kingdom of ***G***.
18:17 not receive the kingdom of ***G***
18:19 is good but One, that is, ***G***.
18:24 to enter the kingdom of ***G***!
18:25 man to enter the kingdom of ***G***.
18:27 with men are possible with ***G***.
18:29 the sake of the kingdom of ***G***,
18:43 and followed Him, glorifying ***G***.
18:43 they saw it, gave praise to ***G***.
19:11 they thought the kingdom of ***G***
19:37 began to rejoice and praise ***G***
20:21 but teach the way of ***G*** in
20:25 and to ***G*** the things that are
20:36 to the angels and are sons of ***G***,
20:37 the ***G*** of Abraham, the God
20:37 the ***G*** of Isaac, and the
20:37 and the ***G*** of Jacob.'
20:38 For He is not the ***G*** of the dead
21: 4 have put in offerings for ***G***,
21:31 know that the kingdom of ***G*** is
22:16 fulfilled in the kingdom of ***G***.
22:18 the vine until the kingdom of ***G***
22:69 right hand of the power of ***G***.
22:70 "Are You then the Son of ***G***?
23:35 is the Christ, the chosen of ***G***.
23:40 "Do you not even fear ***G***,
23:47 had happened, he glorified ***G***,
23:51 waiting for the kingdom of ***G***.
24:19 in deed and word before ***G*** and
24:53 temple praising and blessing ***G***.
Jn 1: 1 Word, and the Word was with ***G***,
1: 1 with God, and the Word was ***G***.
1: 2 He was in the beginning with ***G***.
1: 6 There was a man sent from ***G***,
1:12 right to become children of ***G***,
1:13 of the will of man, but of ***G***.
1:18 No one has seen ***G*** at any time.
1:29 Behold! The Lamb of ***G*** who takes
1:34 that this is the Son of ***G***.
1:36 Behold the Lamb of ***G***!"
1:49 You are the Son of ***G***! You are
1:51 and the angels of ***G*** ascending
3: 2 You are a teacher come from ***G***;
3: 2 signs that You do unless ***G*** is
3: 3 he cannot see the kingdom of ***G***.
3: 5 cannot enter the kingdom of ***G***.
3:16 For ***G*** so loved the world that He
3:17 For ***G*** did not send His Son into
3:18 of the only begotten Son of ***G***.
3:21 that they have been done in ***G***.
3:33 testimony has certified that ***G***
3:34 For He whom ***G*** has sent speaks
3:34 has sent speaks the words of ***G***,
3:34 for ***G*** does not give the Spirit
3:36 but the wrath of ***G*** abides on
4:10 "If you knew the gift of ***G***,
4:24 ***G*** is Spirit, and those who
5:18 but also said that ***G*** was His
5:18 making Himself equal with ***G***.
5:25 hear the voice of the Son of ***G***;
5:42 you do not have the love of ***G***
5:44 that comes from the only ***G***?
6:27 because ***G*** the Father has set
6:28 that we may work the works of ***G***?
6:29 them, "This is the work of ***G***,
6:33 For the bread of ***G*** is He who
6:45 shall all be taught by ***G***.
6:46 Father, except He who is from ***G***;
6:69 Christ, the Son of the living ***G***.
7:17 whether it is from ***G*** or
8:40 the truth which I heard from ***G***.
8:41 we have one Father—***G***.
8:42 If ***G*** were your Father, you would
8:42 proceeded forth and came from ***G***;
8:47 He who is of ***G*** hears God's
8:47 hear, because you are not of ***G***.
8:54 whom you say that He is your ***G***.
9: 3 but that the works of ***G*** should
9:16 said, "This Man is not from ***G***,
9:24 Give ***G*** the glory! We know that
9:29 We know that ***G*** spoke to Moses;
9:31 Now we know that ***G*** does not hear
9:31 if anyone is a worshiper of ***G***
9:33 "If this Man were not from ***G***,
9:35 you believe in the Son of ***G***?
10:33 being a Man, make Yourself ***G***.
10:35 to whom the word of ***G*** came (and
10:36 I said, 'I am the Son of ***G***'?
11: 4 death, but for the glory of ***G***,
11: 4 that the Son of ***G*** may be
11:22 know that whatever You ask of ***G***,
11:22 ***G*** will give You."
11:27 are the Christ, the Son of ***G***,
11:40 you would see the glory of ***G***?
11:52 in one the children of ***G*** who
12:43 men more than the praise of ***G***.
13: 3 and that He had come from ***G*** and
13: 3 from God and was going to ***G***,
13:31 and ***G*** is glorified in Him.
13:32 If ***G*** is glorified in Him, God
13:32 ***G*** will also glorify Him in
14: 1 be troubled; you believe in ***G***,
16: 2 you will think that he offers ***G***
16:27 that I came forth from ***G***.
16:30 that You came forth from ***G***.
17: 3 may know You, the only true ***G***,
19: 7 He made Himself the Son of ***G***.
20:17 and to My ***G*** and your God.'"
20:17 and to My God and your ***G***.
20:28 My Lord and my ***G***!"
20:31 is the Christ, the Son of ***G***,
21:19 what death he would glorify ***G***.
Acts 1: 3 pertaining to the kingdom of ***G***.
2:11 the wonderful works of ***G***.
2:17 in the last days, says ***G***,
2:22 a Man attested by ***G*** to you by
2:22 and signs which ***G*** did through
2:23 purpose and foreknowledge of ***G***,
2:24 whom ***G*** raised up, having loosed
2:30 and knowing that ***G*** had sworn
2:32 This Jesus ***G*** has raised up, of
2:33 exalted to the right hand of ***G***,
2:36 of Israel know assuredly that ***G***
2:39 as many as the Lord our ***G*** will
2:47 praising ***G*** and having favor with
3: 8 leaping, and praising ***G***.
3: 9 saw him walking and praising ***G***.
3:13 The ***G*** of Abraham, Isaac, and
3:13 the ***G*** of our fathers, glorified
3:15 whom ***G*** raised from the dead, of
3:18 But those things which ***G***
3:21 which ***G*** has spoken by the mouth
3:22 The LORD your ***G*** will raise
3:25 and of the covenant which ***G***
3:26 "To you first, ***G***,
4:10 whom ***G*** raised from the dead, by
4:19 it is right in the sight of ***G***
4:19 to listen to you more than to ***G***,
4:21 since they all glorified ***G*** for
4:24 they raised their voice to ***G***
4:24 and said: "Lord, You are ***G***,
4:31 and they spoke the word of ***G***
5: 4 have not lied to men but to ***G***.
5:29 We ought to obey ***G*** rather than
5:30 The ***G*** of our fathers raised up
5:31 Him ***G*** has exalted to His right
5:32 is the Holy Spirit whom ***G*** has
5:39 "but if it is of ***G***,
5:39 be found to fight against ***G***.
6: 2 we should leave the word of ***G***
6: 7 Then the word of ***G*** spread, and
6:11 words against Moses and ***G***.
7: 2 The ***G*** of glory appeared to our
7: 5 And ***G*** gave him no inheritance
7: 6 But ***G*** spoke in this way: that
7: 7 I will judge,' said ***G***,
7: 9 But ***G*** was with him
7:17 the promise drew near which ***G***
7:20 and was well pleasing to ***G***;
7:25 would have understood that ***G***
7:32 I am the ***G*** of your
7:32 the ***G*** of Abraham, the God
7:32 the ***G*** of Isaac, and the
7:32 and the ***G*** of Jacob.'
7:35 is the one ***G*** sent to be a
7:37 The LORD your ***G*** will raise
7:42 Then ***G*** turned and gave them up
7:43 And the star of your ***g***
7:45 whom ***G*** drove out before the
7:46 who found favor before ***G*** and
7:46 to find a dwelling for the ***G***
7:55 heaven and saw the glory of ***G***,
7:55 standing at the right hand of ***G***,
7:56 at the right hand of ***G***!"
7:59 as he was calling on ***G*** and
8:10 man is the great power of ***G***.
8:12 concerning the kingdom of ***G***
8:14 had received the word of ***G***,
8:20 you thought that the gift of ***G***
8:21 is not right in the sight of ***G***.
8:22 and pray ***G*** if perhaps the
8:37 Jesus Christ is the Son of ***G***.
9:20 that He is the Son of ***G***.
10: 2 man and one who feared ***G*** with
10: 2 and prayed to ***G*** always.
10: 3 in a vision an angel of ***G***
10: 4 come up for a memorial before ***G***.
10:15 What ***G*** has cleansed you must not
10:22 one who fears ***G*** and has a good
10:28 But ***G*** has shown me that I
10:31 remembered in the sight of ***G***.
10:33 we are all present before ***G***,
10:33 the things commanded you by ***G***.
10:34 In truth I perceive that ***G*** shows
10:36 The word which ***G*** sent to the
10:38 how ***G*** anointed Jesus of Nazareth
10:38 for ***G*** was with Him.
10:40 Him ***G*** raised up on the third
10:41 to witnesses chosen before by ***G***,
10:42 it is He who was ordained by ***G***
10:46 with tongues and magnify ***G***.
11: 1 had also received the word of ***G***.
11: 9 What ***G*** has cleansed you must not
11:17 If therefore ***G*** gave them the
11:17 was I that I could withstand ***G***?
11:18 silent; and they glorified ***G***,
11:18 Then ***G*** has also granted to the
11:23 and had seen the grace of ***G***,
12: 5 prayer was offered to ***G*** for
12:22 The voice of a ***g*** and not of a
12:23 he did not give glory to ***G***.
12:24 But the word of ***G*** grew and
13: 5 they preached the word of ***G*** in
13: 7 sought to hear the word of ***G***.
13:16 of Israel, and you who fear ***G***,
13:17 The ***G*** of this people Israel
13:21 so ***G*** gave them Saul the son of
13:23 ***G*** raised up for Israel a
13:26 and those among you who fear ***G***,
13:30 But ***G*** raised Him from the dead.
13:33 ***G*** has fulfilled this for us
13:36 own generation by the will of ***G***,
13:37 but He whom ***G*** raised up saw no
13:43 to continue in the grace of ***G***.
13:44 together to hear the word of ***G***.
13:46 necessary that the word of ***G***
14:15 useless things to the living ***G***,
14:22 enter the kingdom of ***G***.
14:26 commended to the grace of ***G***
14:27 they reported all that ***G*** had
15: 4 reported all things that ***G*** had
15: 7 know that a good while ago ***G***
15: 8 'So ***G***, who knows the heart,
15:10 why do you test ***G*** by putting a
15:12 how many miracles and wonders ***G***
15:14 Simon has declared how ***G*** at the
15:18 Known to ***G*** from eternity are all
15:19 Gentiles who are turning to ***G***,
15:40 the brethren to the grace of ***G***.
16:14 of Thyatira, who worshiped ***G***.
16:17 the servants of the Most High ***G***,
16:25 praying and singing hymns to ***G***,
16:34 having believed in ***G*** with all
17:13 learned that the word of ***G*** was
17:23 inscription: TO THE UNKNOWN ***G***.
17:24 '***G***, who made the world
17:29 since we are the offspring of ***G***,
17:30 these times of ignorance ***G***
18: 7 Justus, one who worshiped ***G***,
18:11 teaching the word of ***G*** among
18:13 persuades men to worship ***G***
18:21 ***G*** willing." And he sailed from
18:26 explained to him the way of ***G***
19: 8 the things of the kingdom of ***G***.
19:11 Now ***G*** worked unusual miracles
20:21 repentance toward ***G*** and faith
20:24 to the gospel of the grace of ***G***.
20:25 gone preaching the kingdom of ***G***,
20:27 to you the whole counsel of ***G***.
20:28 to shepherd the church of ***G***
20:32 I commend you to ***G*** and to the
21:19 in detail those things which ***G***
22: 3 and was zealous toward ***G*** as you
22:14 The ***G*** of our fathers has chosen
23: 1 in all good conscience before ***G***
23: 3 ***G*** will strike you, you
23: 9 him, let us not fight against ***G***.
24:14 so I worship the ***G*** of my
24:15 "I have hope in ***G***,
24:16 without offense toward ***G*** and
26: 6 hope of the promise made by ***G***
26: 7 earnestly serving ***G*** night and
26: 8 incredible by you that ***G***
26:18 from the power of Satan to ***G***,
26:20 they should repent, turn to ***G***,
26:22 having obtained help from ***G***,
26:29 I would to ***G*** that not only you,
27:23 me this night an angel of the ***G***
27:24 and indeed ***G*** has granted you
27:25 for I believe ***G*** that it will be
27:35 bread and gave thanks to ***G*** in
28: 6 minds and said that he was a ***g***.
28:15 he thanked ***G*** and took courage.
28:23 testified of the kingdom of ***G***,
28:28 to you that the salvation of ***G***
28:31 preaching the kingdom of ***G*** and
Rom 1: 1 separated to the gospel of ***G***
1: 4 declared to be the Son of ***G***
1: 7 who are in Rome, beloved of ***G***,
1: 7 Grace to you and peace from ***G***
1: 8 I thank my ***G*** through Jesus
1: 9 For ***G*** is my witness, whom I
1:10 find a way in the will of ***G*** to
1:16 for it is the power of ***G*** to
1:17 in it the righteousness of ***G***
1:18 For the wrath of ***G*** is revealed
1:19 because what may be known of ***G***
1:19 for ***G*** has shown it to them.
1:21 because, although they knew ***G***,
1:21 they did not glorify Him as ***G***,
1:23 glory of the incorruptible ***G***
1:24 Therefore ***G*** also gave them up to
1:25 who exchanged the truth of ***G*** for
1:26 For this reason ***G*** gave them up
1:28 they did not like to retain ***G***
1:28 ***G*** gave them over to a debased

1:30 backbiters, haters of **G**,
1:32 the righteous judgment of **G**,
2: 2 we know that the judgment of **G**
2: 3 will escape the judgment of **G**?
2: 4 knowing that the goodness of **G**
2: 5 of the righteous judgment of **G**,
2:11 there is no partiality with **G**.
2:13 law are just in the sight of **G**,
2:16 in the day when **G** will judge the
2:17 law, and make your boast in **G**,
2:23 do you dishonor **G** through
2:24 the name of **G** is blasphemed
2:29 is not from men but from **G**.
3: 2 were committed the oracles of **G**.
3: 3 make the faithfulness of **G**
3: 4 let **G** be true but every man a
3: 5 the righteousness of **G**,
3: 5 Is **G** unjust who inflicts
3: 6 For then how will **G** judge
3: 7 For if the truth of **G** has
3:11 is none who seeks after **G**.
3:18 There is no fear of **G**
3:19 may become guilty before **G**.
3:21 But now the righteousness of **G**
3:22 even the righteousness of **G**,
3:23 fall short of the glory of **G**,
3:25 whom **G** set forth as a
3:25 because in His forbearance **G**
3:29 Or is He the **G** of the Jews
3:29 Is He not also the **G** of the
3:30 since there is one **G** who will
4: 2 boast about, but not before **G**.
4: 3 'Abraham believed **G**,
4: 6 of the man to whom **G** imputes
4:17 of Him whom he believed—**G**,
4:20 not waver at the promise of **G**
4:20 in faith, giving glory to **G**,
5: 1 we have peace with **G** through
5: 2 in hope of the glory of **G**.
5: 5 because the love of **G** has been
5: 8 But **G** demonstrates His own love
5:10 enemies we were reconciled to **G**
5:11 but we also rejoice in **G**
5:15 much more the grace of **G** and
6:10 that He lives, He lives to **G**.
6:11 but alive to **G** in Christ Jesus
6:13 but present yourselves to **G** as
6:13 of righteousness to **G**.
6:17 But **G** be thanked that though
6:22 and having become slaves of **G**,
6:23 but the gift of **G** is eternal
7: 4 that we should bear fruit to **G**.
7:22 For I delight in the law of **G**
7:25 I thank **G**—through Jesus Christ
7:25 I myself serve the law of **G**,
8: 3 **G** did by sending His own Son
8: 7 mind is enmity against **G**;
8: 7 is not subject to the law of **G**,
8: 8 in the flesh cannot please **G**.
8: 9 if indeed the Spirit of **G**
8:14 as are led by the Spirit of **G**,
8:14 of God, these are sons of **G**.
8:16 that we are children of **G**,
8:17 heirs of **G** and joint heirs with
8:19 the revealing of the sons of **G**.
8:21 liberty of the children of **G**.
8:27 according to the will of **G**.
8:28 for good to those who love **G**,
8:31 If **G** is for us, who can be
8:33 It is **G** who justifies.
8:34 is even at the right hand of **G**,
8:39 separate us from the love of **G**
9: 4 of the law, the service of **G**,
9: 5 all, the eternally blessed **G**.
9: 6 it is not that the word of **G**
9: 8 are not the children of **G**;
9:11 that the purpose of **G** according
9:14 there unrighteousness with **G**?
9:16 but of **G** who shows mercy.
9:20 who are you to reply against **G**?
9:22 What if **G**, wanting to show
9:26 sons of the living **G**.
10: 1 heart's desire and prayer to **G**
10: 2 that they have a zeal for **G**,
10: 3 to the righteousness of **G**.
10: 9 believe in your heart that **G**
10:17 and hearing by the word of **G**.
11: 1 has **G** cast away His people?
11: 2 **G** has not cast away His people
11: 2 how he pleads with **G** against
11: 8 **G** has given them a spirit
11:21 For if **G** did not spare the
11:22 the goodness and severity of **G**:
11:23 for **G** is able to graft them in
11:29 the gifts and the calling of **G**
11:30 you were once disobedient to **G**,
11:32 For **G** has committed them all to
11:33 the wisdom and knowledge of **G**!
12: 1 brethren, by the mercies of **G**,
12: 1 holy, acceptable to **G**,
12: 2 and perfect will of **G**.
12: 3 as **G** has dealt to each one a
13: 1 is no authority except from **G**,
13: 1 that exist are appointed by **G**.
13: 2 resists the ordinance of **G**,
14: 3 for **G** has received him.
14: 4 for **G** is able to make him
14: 6 for he gives **G** thanks; and he
14: 6 and gives **G** thanks.
14:11 tongue shall confess to **G**.
14:12 give account of himself to **G**.
14:17 for the kingdom of **G** is not
14:18 things is acceptable to **G** and
14:20 Do not destroy the work of **G** for
14:22 Have it to yourself before **G**.
15: 5 Now may the **G** of patience and
15: 6 and one mouth glorify the **G**
15: 7 received us, to the glory of **G**.
15: 8 circumcision for the truth of **G**,
15: 9 the Gentiles might glorify **G**
15:13 Now may the **G** of hope fill you
15:15 of the grace given to me by **G**,
15:16 ministering the gospel of **G**,
15:17 the things which pertain to **G**.
15:19 by the power of the Spirit of **G**,
15:30 with me in prayers to **G** for me,
15:32 you with joy by the will of **G**,
15:33 Now the **G** of peace be with you
16:20 And the **G** of peace will crush
16:26 of the everlasting **G**,
16:27 to **G**, alone wise, be glory

1 Cor 1: 1 Christ through the will of **G**,
1: 2 To the church of **G** which is at
1: 3 Grace to you and peace from **G**
1: 4 I thank my **G** always concerning
1: 4 you for the grace of **G** which
1: 9 **G** is faithful, by whom you were
1:14 I thank **G** that I baptized none
1:18 saved it is the power of **G**.
1:20 Has not **G** made foolish the
1:21 For since, in the wisdom of **G**,
1:21 through wisdom did not know **G**,
1:21 it pleased **G** through the
1:24 Christ the power of **G** and the
1:24 of God and the wisdom of **G**.
1:25 Because the foolishness of **G** is
1:25 and the weakness of **G** is
1:27 But **G** has chosen the foolish
1:27 and **G** has chosen the weak
1:28 the things which are despised **G**
1:30 who became for us wisdom from **G**—
2: 1 to you the testimony of **G**.
2: 5 of men but in the power of **G**.
2: 7 But we speak the wisdom of **G** in
2: 7 the hidden wisdom which **G**
2: 9 man The things which **G**
2:10 But **G** has revealed them to us
2:10 yes, the deep things of **G**.
2:11 so no one knows the things of **G**
2:11 of God except the Spirit of **G**.
2:12 but the Spirit who is from **G**,
2:12 been freely given to us by **G**.
2:14 the things of the Spirit of **G**,
3: 6 but **G** gave the increase.
3: 7 but **G** who gives the increase.
3:10 According to the grace of **G**
3:16 that you are the temple of **G**
3:16 God and that the Spirit of **G**
3:17 anyone defiles the temple of **G**,
3:17 **G** will destroy him. For the
3:17 For the temple of **G** is holy,
3:19 world is foolishness with **G**.
4: 1 stewards of the mysteries of **G**.
4: 5 one's praise will come from **G**.
4: 9 For I think that **G** has displayed
4:20 For the kingdom of **G** is not in
5:13 But those who are outside **G**
6: 9 not inherit the kingdom of **G**?
6:10 will inherit the kingdom of **G**.
6:11 and by the Spirit of our **G**.
6:13 but **G** will destroy both it and
6:14 And **G** both raised up the Lord
6:19 in you, whom you have from **G**,
6:20 therefore glorify **G** in your
7: 7 one has his own gift from **G**,
7:15 But **G** has called us to peace.
7:17 But as **G** has distributed to
7:19 keeping the commandments of **G**
7:24 let each one remain with **G** in
7:40 I also have the Spirit of **G**.
8: 3 But if anyone loves **G**,
8: 4 and that there is no other **G**
8: 6 yet for us there is one **G**,
8: 8 food does not commend us to **G**;
9: 9 Is it oxen **G** is concerned
9:21 (not being without law toward **G**,
10: 5 But with most of them **G** was not
10:13 but **G** is faithful, who will
10:20 to demons and not to **G**,
10:31 do, do all to the glory of **G**.
10:32 Greeks or to the church of **G**,
11: 3 and the head of Christ is **G**.
11: 7 he is the image and glory of **G**;
11:12 but all things are from **G**.
11:13 for a woman to pray to **G** with
11:16 nor do the churches of **G**.
11:22 do you despise the church of **G**
12: 3 one speaking by the Spirit of **G**
12: 6 but it is the same **G** who works
12:18 But now **G** has set the members,
12:24 But **G** composed the body, having
12:28 And **G** has appointed these in the
14: 2 does not speak to men but to **G**,
14:18 I thank my **G** I speak with
14:25 he will worship **G** and report
14:25 worship God and report that **G**
14:28 him speak to himself and to **G**.
14:33 For **G** is not the author of
14:36 Or did the word of **G** come
15: 9 I persecuted the church of **G**.
15:10 But by the grace of **G** I am what
15:10 but the grace of **G** which was
15:15 are found false witnesses of **G**,
15:15 because we have testified of **G**
15:24 He delivers the kingdom to **G**
15:28 that **G** may be all in all.
15:34 do not have the knowledge of **G**.
15:38 But **G** gives it a body as He
15:50 cannot inherit the kingdom of **G**;
15:57 But thanks be to **G**,

2 Cor 1: 1 Jesus Christ by the will of **G**,
1: 1 To the church of **G** which is at
1: 2 Grace to you and peace from **G**
1: 3 Blessed be the **G** and Father of
1: 3 the Father of mercies and **G** of
1: 4 we ourselves are comforted by **G**.
1: 9 not trust in ourselves but in **G**
1:12 wisdom but by the grace of **G**,
1:18 But as **G** is faithful, our word
1:19 For the Son of **G**,
1:20 For all the promises of **G** in Him
1:20 to the glory of **G** through us.
1:21 and has anointed us is **G**,
1:23 Moreover I call **G** as witness
2:14 Now thanks be to **G** who always
2:15 For we are to **G** the fragrance of
2:17 so many, peddling the word of **G**;
2:17 as of sincerity, but as from **G**,
2:17 we speak in the sight of **G** in
3: 3 by the Spirit of the living **G**,
3: 4 trust through Christ toward **G**.
3: 5 but our sufficiency is from **G**,
4: 2 nor handling the word of **G**
4: 2 conscience in the sight of **G**.
4: 4 whose minds the **g** of this age
4: 4 Christ, who is the image of **G**,
4: 6 For it is the **G** who commanded
4: 6 knowledge of the glory of **G** in
4: 7 of the power may be of **G** and
4:15 to abound to the glory of **G**.
5: 1 we have a building from **G**,
5: 5 us for this very thing is **G**,
5:11 but we are well known to **G**,
5:13 beside ourselves, it is for **G**;
5:18 Now all things are of **G**,
5:19 that **G** was in Christ
5:20 as though **G** were pleading
5:20 behalf, be reconciled to **G**.
5:21 become the righteousness of **G**
6: 1 not to receive the grace of **G**
6: 4 ourselves as ministers of **G**:
6: 7 of truth, by the power of **G**,
6:16 agreement has the temple of **G**
6:16 are the temple of the living **G**.
6:16 As **G** has said: "I will
6:16 I will be their **G**,
7: 1 holiness in the fear of **G**.
7: 6 Nevertheless **G**, who comforts
7:12 care for you in the sight of **G**
8: 1 known to you the grace of **G**
8: 5 then to us by the will of **G**.
8:16 But thanks be to **G** who puts
9: 7 for **G** loves a cheerful giver.
9: 8 And **G** is able to make all grace
9:11 thanksgiving through us to **G**.
9:12 through many thanksgivings to **G**,
9:13 they glorify **G** for the
9:14 of the exceeding grace of **G** in
9:15 Thanks be to **G** for His
10: 4 not carnal but mighty in **G** for
10: 5 against the knowledge of **G**,
10:13 limits of the sphere which **G**
11: 7 I preached the gospel of **G** to
11:11 I do not love you? **G** knows!
11:31 The **G** and Father of our Lord
12: 2 **G** knows—such a one was caught
12: 3 I do not know, **G** knows—
12:19 We speak before **G** in Christ.
12:21 my **G** will humble me among you,
13: 4 yet He lives by the power of **G**.
13: 4 live with Him by the power of **G**
13: 7 Now I pray to **G** that you do no
13:11 and the **G** of love and peace
13:14 Jesus Christ, and the love of **G**,

Gal 1: 1 but through Jesus Christ and **G**
1: 3 Grace to you and peace from **G**
1: 4 according to the will of our **G**
1:10 For do I now persuade men, or **G**?
1:13 I persecuted the church of **G**
1:15 But when it pleased **G**,
1:20 write to you, indeed, before **G**,
1:24 And they glorified **G** in me.
2: 6 **G** shows personal favoritism to
2:19 the law that I might live to **G**.
2:20 I live by faith in the Son of **G**,
2:21 do not set aside the grace of **G**;
3: 6 just as Abraham "believed **G**,
3: 8 foreseeing that **G** would justify
3:11 by the law in the sight of **G**
3:17 that was confirmed before by **G**
3:18 but **G** gave it to Abraham by
3:20 for one only, but **G** is one.
3:21 then against the promises of **G**?
3:26 For you are all sons of **G**
4: 4 **G** sent forth His Son, born of a
4: 6 **G** has sent forth the Spirit of
4: 7 then an heir of **G** through
4: 8 indeed, when you did not know **G**,
4: 9 But now after you have known **G**,
4: 9 God, or rather are known by **G**,
4:14 received me as an angel of **G**,
5:21 not inherit the kingdom of **G**.
6: 7 **G** is not mocked; for whatever a
6:14 But **G** forbid that I should boast
6:16 them, and upon the Israel of **G**.

Eph 1: 1 Jesus Christ by the will of **G**,

1: 2 Grace to you and peace from G
1: 3 Blessed be the G and Father of
1:17 that the G of our Lord Jesus
2: 4 But G, who is rich in mercy,
2: 8 it is the gift of G,
2:10 which G prepared beforehand
2:12 having no hope and without G in
2:16 might reconcile them both to G
2:19 members of the household of G,
2:22 for a dwelling place of G in
3: 2 dispensation of the grace of G
3: 7 to the gift of the grace of G
3: 9 the ages has been hidden in G
3:10 now the manifold wisdom of G
3:19 with all the fullness of G.
4: 6 one G and Father of all, who is
4:13 the knowledge of the Son of G,
4:18 alienated from the life of G,
4:24 was created according to G,
4:30 not grieve the Holy Spirit of G,
4:32 just as G in Christ forgave
5: 1 Therefore be imitators of G as
5: 2 offering and a sacrifice to G
5: 5 in the kingdom of Christ and G.
5: 6 of these things the wrath of G
5:20 always for all things to G the
5:21 to one another in the fear of G.
6: 6 doing the will of G from the
6:11 Put on the whole armor of G,
6:13 take up the whole armor of G,
6:17 Spirit, which is the word of G;
6:23 from G the Father and the Lord
Phil 1: 2 Grace to you and peace from G
1: 3 I thank my G upon every
1: 8 For G is my witness, how greatly
1:11 to the glory and praise of G.
1:28 of salvation, and that from G.
2: 6 who, being in the form of G,
2: 6 it robbery to be equal with G,
2: 9 Therefore G also has highly
2:11 to the glory of G the Father.
2:13 for it is G who works in you
2:15 children of G without fault in
2:27 but G had mercy on him, and not
3: 3 who worship G in the Spirit,
3: 9 righteousness which is from G
3:14 prize of the upward call of G
3:15 G will reveal even this to you.
3:19 whose g is their belly, and
4: 6 requests be made known to G;
4: 7 and the peace of G,
4: 9 and the G of peace will be with
4:18 sacrifice, well pleasing to G.
4:19 And my G shall supply all your
4:20 Now to our G and Father be
Col 1: 1 Jesus Christ by the will of G,
1: 2 Grace to you and peace from G
1: 3 We give thanks to the G and
1: 6 heard and knew the grace of G
1:10 in the knowledge of G;
1:15 is the image of the invisible G,
1:25 to the stewardship from G
1:25 you, to fulfill the word of G,
1:27 To them G willed to make known
2: 2 knowledge of the mystery of G,
2:12 faith in the working of G,
2:19 the increase that is from G.
3: 1 sitting at the right hand of G.
3: 3 life is hidden with Christ in G.
3: 6 of these things the wrath of G
3:12 Therefore, as the elect of G,
3:15 And let the peace of G rule in
3:17 giving thanks to G the Father
3:22 sincerity of heart, fearing G.
4: 3 that G would open to us a door
4:11 workers for the kingdom of G
4:12 complete in all the will of G.
1 Th 1: 1 of the Thessalonians in G the
1: 1 Grace to you and peace from G
1: 2 We give thanks to G always for
1: 3 Christ in the sight of our G
1: 4 brethren, your election by G.
1: 8 Your faith toward G has gone
1: 9 and how you turned to G from
1: 9 to serve the living and true G,
2: 2 we were bold in our G to speak
2: 2 to speak to you the gospel of G
2: 4 as we have been approved by G
2: 4 but G who tests our hearts.
2: 5 covetousness—G is witness.
2: 8 to you not only the gospel of G,
2: 9 preached to you the gospel of G.
2:10 and G also, how devoutly and
2:12 you would walk worthy of G who
2:13 this reason we also thank G
2:13 when you received the word of G
2:13 it is in truth, the word of G,
2:14 imitators of the churches of G
2:15 and they do not please G and
3: 2 our brother and minister of G,
3: 9 what thanks can we render to G
3: 9 for your sake before our G,
3:11 Now may our G and Father
3:13 in holiness before our G and
4: 1 ought to walk and to please G;
4: 3 For this is the will of G,
4: 5 the Gentiles who do not know G;
4: 7 For G did not call us to
4: 8 does not reject man, but G,
4: 9 you yourselves are taught by G
4:14 even so G will bring with Him
4:16 and with the trumpet of G.
5: 9 For G did not appoint us to
5:18 for this is the will of G in
5:23 Now may the G of peace Himself
2 Th 1: 1 of the Thessalonians in G our
1: 2 Grace to you and peace from G
1: 3 We are bound to thank G always
1: 4 of you among the churches of G
1: 5 of the righteous judgment of G,
1: 5 worthy of the kingdom of G,
1: 6 is a righteous thing with G
1: 8 on those who do not know G,
1:11 pray always for you that our G
1:12 to the grace of our G and the
2: 4 above all that is called G or
2: 4 so that he sits as G in the
2: 4 sits as God in the temple of G,
2: 4 showing himself that he is G.
2:11 And for this reason G will send
2:13 are bound to give thanks to G
2:13 because G from the beginning
2:16 and our G and Father, who has
3: 5 your hearts into the love of G
1 Tim 1: 1 by the commandment of G our
1: 2 and peace from G our Father
1:11 gospel of the blessed G which
1:17 to G who alone is wise, be
2: 3 acceptable in the sight of G
2: 5 For there is one G and one
2: 5 God and one Mediator between G
3: 5 he take care of the church of G?
3:15 yourself in the house of G,
3:15 is the church of the living G,
3:16 Gd was manifested in the flesh,
4: 3 to abstain from foods which G
4: 4 For every creature of G is
4: 5 is sanctified by the word of G
4:10 we trust in the living G,
5: 4 is good and acceptable before G.
5: 5 trusts in G and continues in
5:21 I charge you before G and the
6: 1 so that the name of G and His
6:11 But you, O man of G,
6:13 I urge you in the sight of G who
6:17 riches but in the living G,
2 Tim 1: 1 Jesus Christ by the will of G,
1: 2 and peace from G the Father
1: 3 I thank G, whom I serve
1: 6 you to stir up the gift of G
1: 7 For G has not given us a spirit
1: 8 according to the power of G,
2: 9 but the word of G is not
2:15 present yourself approved to G,
2:19 the solid foundation of G
2:25 if G perhaps will grant them
3: 4 rather than lovers of G,
3:16 is given by inspiration of G,
3:17 that the man of G may be
4: 1 charge you therefore before G
Titus 1: 1 a bondservant of G and an
1: 2 in hope of eternal life which G,
1: 3 to the commandment of G our
1: 4 and peace from G the Father
1: 7 be blameless, as a steward of G,
1:16 They profess to know G,
2: 5 that the word of G may not be
2:10 may adorn the doctrine of G
2:11 For the grace of G that brings
2:13 appearing of our great G and
3: 4 the kindness and the love of G
3: 8 those who have believed in G
Phm 1: 3 Grace to you and peace from G
1: 4 I thank my G, making mention
Heb 1: 1 G, who at various times
1: 6 Let all the angels of G
1: 8 says: "Your throne, O G,
1: 9 lawlessness; Therefore G,
1: 9 Therefore God, Your G,
2: 4 G also bearing witness both with
2: 9 that He, by the grace of G,
2:13 I and the children whom G
2:17 in things pertaining to G,
3: 4 He who built all things is G.
3:12 in departing from the living G;
4: 4 And G rested on the seventh
4: 9 a rest for the people of G.
4:10 also ceased from his works as G
4:12 For the word of G is living and
4:14 the heavens, Jesus the Son of G,
5: 1 men in things pertaining to G,
5: 4 but he who is called by G,
5:10 called by G as High Priest
5:12 principles of the oracles of G;
6: 1 works and of faith toward G,
6: 3 And this we will do if G
6: 5 have tasted the good word of G
6: 6 for themselves the Son of G,
6: 7 receives blessing from G;
6:10 For G is not unjust to forget
6:13 For when G made a promise to
6:17 Thus G, determining to show
6:18 which it is impossible for G
7: 1 priest of the Most High G,
7: 3 but made like the Son of G,
7:19 through which we draw near to G.
7:25 uttermost those who come to G
8:10 and I will be their G,
9:14 Himself without spot to G,
9:14 works to serve the living G?
9:20 of the covenant which G
9:24 to appear in the presence of G
10: 7 Me—To do Your will, O G.
10: 9 to do Your will, O G.
10:12 sat down at the right hand of G,
10:21 High Priest over the house of G,
10:29 who has trampled the Son of G
10:31 into the hands of the living G.
10:36 you have done the will of G,
11: 3 were framed by the word of G,
11: 4 By faith Abel offered to G a
11: 4 G testifying of his gifts;
11: 5 because G had taken him";
11: 5 testimony, that he pleased G.
11: 6 for he who comes to G must
11:10 whose builder and maker is G.
11:16 Therefore G is not ashamed to
11:16 ashamed to be called their G,
11:19 concluding that G was able to
11:25 with the people of G than to
11:40 G having provided something
12: 2 right hand of the throne of G.
12: 7 G deals with you as with sons;
12:15 fall short of the grace of G;
12:22 and to the city of the living G,
12:23 to G the Judge of all, to the
12:28 by which we may serve G
12:29 For our G is a consuming fire.
13: 4 fornicators and adulterers G
13: 7 who have spoken the word of G
13:15 the sacrifice of praise to G,
13:16 for with such sacrifices G is
13:20 Now may the G of peace who
Jas 1: 1 a bondservant of G and of the
1: 5 lacks wisdom, let him ask of G,
1:13 I am tempted by G"; for God
1:13 for G cannot be tempted by
1:20 produce the righteousness of G.
1:27 and undefiled religion before G
2: 5 Has G not chosen the poor of
2:19 You believe that there is one G.
2:23 says, "Abraham believed G,
2:23 he was called the friend of G.
3: 9 With it we bless our G and
3: 9 made in the similitude of G.
4: 4 with the world is enmity with G?
4: 4 makes himself an enemy of G.
4: 6 'G resists the proud,
4: 7 Therefore submit to G.
4: 8 Draw near to G and He will draw
1 Pe 1: 2 to the foreknowledge of G the
1: 3 Blessed be the G and Father of
1: 5 who are kept by the power of G
1:21 who through Him believe in G,
1:21 your faith and hope are in G.
1:23 through the word of G which
2: 4 but chosen by G and precious,
2: 5 sacrifices acceptable to G
2:10 but are now the people of G,
2:12 glorify G in the day of
2:15 For this is the will of G,
2:16 vice, but as bondservants of G.
2:17 Love the brotherhood. Fear G.
2:19 because of conscience toward G
2:20 this is commendable before G.
3: 4 very precious in the sight of G.
3: 5 the holy women who trusted in G
3:15 But sanctify the Lord G in your
3:17 better, if it is the will of G,
3:18 that He might bring us to G,
3:21 of a good conscience toward G),
3:22 and is at the right hand of G,
4: 2 of men, but for the will of G.
4: 6 but live according to G in the
4:10 of the manifold grace of G.
4:11 him speak as the oracles of G.
4:11 it as with the ability which G
4:11 that in all things G may be
4:14 the Spirit of glory and of G
4:16 but let him glorify G in this
4:17 to begin at the house of G;
4:17 who do not obey the gospel of G?
4:19 according to the will of G
5: 2 Shepherd the flock of G which is
5: 5 'G resists the proud,
5: 6 under the mighty hand of G,
5:10 But may the G of all grace, who
5:12 this is the true grace of G in
2 Pe 1: 1 by the righteousness of our G
1: 2 to you in the knowledge of G
1:17 For He received from G the
1:21 but holy men of G spoke as
2: 4 For if G did not spare the
3: 5 that by the word of G the
3:12 the coming of the day of G,
1 Jn 1: 5 that G is light and in Him is
2: 5 truly the love of G is
2:14 and the word of G abides in
2:17 but he who does the will of G
3: 1 should be called children of G!
3: 2 now we are children of G;
3: 8 For this purpose the Son of G
3: 9 Whoever has been born of G does
3: 9 because he has been born of G.
3:10 In this the children of G and
3:10 righteousness is not of G,
3:17 how does the love of G abide in
3:20 G is greater than our heart,
3:21 us, we have confidence toward G.
4: 1 spirits, whether they are of G;
4: 2 this you know the Spirit of G:
4: 2 has come in the flesh is of G,
4: 3 come in the flesh is not of G.
4: 4 You are of G, little children,
4: 6 We are of G. He who knows God
4: 6 He who knows G hears us; he who

4: 6 he who is not of **G** does not
4: 7 one another, for love is of **G**;
4: 7 who loves is born of **G** and
4: 7 is born of God and knows **G**.
4: 8 does not love does not know **G**,
4: 8 not know God, for **G** is love.
4: 9 In this the love of **G** was
4: 9 that **G** has sent His only
4:10 is love, not that we loved **G**,
4:11 if **G** so loved us, we also ought
4:12 No one has seen **G** at any time.
4:12 **G** abides in us, and His love
4:15 that Jesus is the Son of **G**,
4:15 **G** abides in him, and he in God.
4:15 God abides in him, and he in **G**.
4:16 and believed the love that **G**
4:16 **G** is love, and he who abides in
4:16 who abides in love abides in **G**,
4:16 abides in God, and **G** in him.
4:20 If someone says, "I love **G**,
4:20 how can he love **G** whom he has
4:21 that he who loves **G** must love
5: 1 is the Christ is born of **G**,
5: 2 that we love the children of **G**,
5: 2 when we love **G** and keep His
5: 3 For this is the love of **G**,
5: 4 For whatever is born of **G**
5: 5 that Jesus is the Son of **G**?
5: 9 the witness of **G** is greater;
5: 9 for this is the witness of **G**
5:10 He who believes in the Son of **G**
5:10 he who does not believe **G** has
5:10 believed the testimony that **G**
5:11 that **G** has given us eternal
5:12 who does not have the Son of **G**
5:13 in the name of the Son of **G**,
5:13 in the name of the Son of **G**.
5:18 know that whoever is born of **G**
5:18 but he who has been born of **G**
5:19 We know that we are of **G**,
5:20 And we know that the Son of **G**
5:20 This is the true **G** and eternal
2 Jn 3 peace will be with you from **G**
9 of Christ does not have **G**.
3 Jn 6 journey in a manner worthy of **G**,
11 He who does good is of **G**,
11 he who does evil has not seen **G**.
Jude 1 sanctified by **G** the Father, and
4 who turn the grace of our **G**
4 and deny the only Lord **G** and
21 yourselves in the love of **G**,
25 To **G** our Savior, Who alone is
Rev 1: 1 which **G** gave Him to show His
1: 2 bore witness to the word of **G**,
1: 6 us kings and priests to His **G**
1: 9 Patmos for the word of **G** and
2: 7 the midst of the Paradise of **G**.
2:18 things says the Son of **G**,
3: 1 who has the seven Spirits of **G**
3: 2 your works perfect before **G**.
3:12 a pillar in the temple of My **G**,
3:12 write on him the name of My **G**
3:12 the name of the city of My **G**,
3:12 down out of heaven from My **G**.
3:14 Beginning of the creation of **G**:
4: 5 are the seven Spirits of **G**.
4: 8 Lord **G** Almighty, Who was and
5: 6 are the seven Spirits of **G**
5: 9 And have redeemed us to **G** by
5:10 us kings and priests to our **G**;
6: 9 been slain for the word of **G**
7: 2 having the seal of the living **G**.
7: 3 sealed the servants of our **G**
7:10 Salvation belongs to our **G** who
7:11 the throne and worshiped **G**,
7:12 Be to our **G** forever and ever.
7:15 they are before the throne of **G**,
7:17 And **G** will wipe away every tear
8: 2 seven angels who stand before **G**,
8: 4 ascended before **G** from the
9: 4 who do not have the seal of **G**
9:13 golden altar which is before **G**,
10: 7 the mystery of **G** would be
11: 1 and measure the temple of **G**,
11: 4 standing before the **G** of the
11:11 days the breath of life from **G**
11:13 afraid and gave glory to the **G**
11:16 elders who sat before **G** on
11:16 on their faces and worshiped **G**,
11:17 O Lord **G** Almighty, The One who
11:19 Then the temple of **G** was opened
12: 5 her Child was caught up to **G**
12: 6 she has a place prepared by **G**,
12:10 and the kingdom of our **G**,
12:10 who accused them before our **G**
12:17 who keep the commandments of **G**
13: 6 mouth in blasphemy against **G**,
14: 4 being firstfruits to **G** and to
14: 5 fault before the throne of **G**.
14: 7 Fear **G** and give glory to Him,
14:10 of the wine of the wrath of **G**,
14:12 who keep the commandments of **G**
14:19 winepress of the wrath of **G**.
15: 1 for in them the wrath of **G** is
15: 2 sea of glass, having harps of **G**.
15: 3 song of Moses, the servant of **G**,
15: 3 Lord **G** Almighty! Just and
15: 7 bowls full of the wrath of **G**
15: 8 with smoke from the glory of **G**
16: 1 the bowls of the wrath of **G** on
16: 7 Lord **G** Almighty, true and
16: 9 they blasphemed the name of **G**
16:11 They blasphemed the **G** of heaven
16:14 battle of that great day of **G**
16:19 Babylon was remembered before **G**,
16:21 Men blasphemed **G** because of the
17:17 For **G** has put it into their
17:17 until the words of **G** are
18: 5 and **G** has remembered her
18: 8 for strong is the Lord **G** who
18:20 for **G** has avenged you on her!"
19: 1 belong to the Lord our **G**!
19: 4 fell down and worshiped **G** who
19: 5 throne, saying, "Praise our **G**,
19: 6 Alleluia! For the Lord **G**
19: 9 are the true sayings of **G**.
19:10 Worship **G**! For the testimony of
19:13 name is called The Word of **G**.
19:15 and wrath of Almighty **G**.
19:17 for the supper of the great **G**,
20: 4 to Jesus and for the word of **G**,
20: 6 but they shall be priests of **G**
20: 9 And fire came down from **G** out
20:12 and great, standing before **G**,
21: 2 down out of heaven from **G**,
21: 3 the tabernacle of **G** is with
21: 3 **G** Himself will be with them
21: 3 be with them and be their **G**.
21: 4 And **G** will wipe away every tear
21: 7 and I will be his **G** and he
21:10 descending out of heaven from **G**,
21:11 having the glory of **G**.
21:22 for the Lord **G** Almighty and the
21:23 for the glory of **G** illuminated
22: 1 from the throne of **G** and of
22: 3 but the throne of **G** and of the
22: 5 for the Lord **G** gives them
22: 6 And the Lord **G** of the holy
22: 9 words of this book. Worship **G**.
22:18 **G** will add to him the plagues
22:19 **G** shall take away his part from

GOD-GIVEN (2/2) GOD

Ezra 7:25 according to your **G** wisdom, set
Eccl 3:10 I have seen the **G** task with

GOD-WARD (KJV) See TOWARD (GOD)

GOD-WHO-FORGIVES (1/1) GOD

Ps 99: 8 our God; You were to them **G**,

GOD'S (28/25) GOD

Gen 28:22 have set as a pillar shall be **G**
32: 2 This is **G** camp." And he called
Num 22:22 Then **G** anger was aroused
Deut 1:17 for the judgment is **G**.
1 Chr 5:22 dead, because the war was **G**.
2 Chr 20:15 the battle is not yours, but **G**.
22: 7 His going to Joram was **G**
Neh 10:29 curse and an oath to walk in **G**
Job 35: 2 righteousness is more than **G**'?
36: 2 are yet words to speak on **G**
Mal 1: 9 'But now entreat **G** favor,
Mt 5:34 for it is **G** throne;
22:21 to God the things that are **G**.
Mk 12:17 to God the things that are **G**.
Lk 20:25 to God the things that are **G**.
Jn 8:47 He who is of God hears **G** words;
Acts 23: 4 Do you revile **G** high priest?"
Rom 8:33 shall bring a charge against **G**
10: 3 For they being ignorant of **G**
13: 4 For he is **G** minister to you for
13: 4 for he is **G** minister, an
13: 6 for they are **G** ministers
1 Cor 3: 9 For we are **G** fellow workers;
3: 9 you are **G** field, you are
3: 9 you are **G** building.
3:23 are Christ's, and Christ is **G**.
6:20 and in your spirit, which are **G**.
Titus 1: 1 according to the faith of **G**

GODDESS (5/5)

1 Ki 11: 5 went after Ashtoreth the **g** of
11:33 and worshiped Ashtoreth the **g**
Acts 19:27 also the temple of the great **g**
19:35 temple guardian of the great **g**
19:37 nor blasphemers of your **g**.

GODHEAD (2/2) GOD

Rom 1:20 even His eternal power and **G**,
Col 2: 9 all the fullness of the **G**

GODLINESS (16/16) GODLY

Acts 3:12 as though by our own power or **g**
1 Tim 2: 2 and peaceable life in all **g**
2:10 proper for women professing **g**,
3:16 great is the mystery of **g**:
4: 7 and exercise yourself toward **g**.
4: 8 but **g** is profitable for all
6: 3 doctrine which accords with **g**,
6: 5 who suppose that **g** is a means
6: 6 Now **g** with contentment is great
6:11 and pursue righteousness, **g**,
2 Tim 3: 5 having a form of **g** but denying
Titus 1: 1 the truth which accords with **g**,
2 Pe 1: 3 that pertain to life and **g**,
1: 6 perseverance, to perseverance **g**,
1: 7 to **g** brotherly kindness, and to
3:11 you to be in holy conduct and **g**,

GODLY (16/16) GOD, GODLINESS, UNGODLY

Ps 4: 3 apart for Himself him who is **g**;
12: 1 for the **g** man ceases! For the
32: 6 this cause everyone who is **g**
Mal 2:15 He seeks **g** offspring.
2 Cor 1:12 the world in simplicity and **g**
7: 9 For you were made sorry in a **g**
7:10 For **g** sorrow produces repentance
7:11 that you sorrowed in a **g**
11: 2 For I am jealous for you with **g**
1 Tim 1: 4 cause disputes rather than **g**
2 Tim 3:12 and all who desire to live **g** in
Titus 2:12 and **g** in the present age,
Heb 5: 7 and was heard because of His **g**
11: 7 moved with **g** fear, prepared an
12:28 with reverence and **g** fear.
2 Pe 2: 9 knows how to deliver the **g** out

GODS (235/207)

Gen 31:30 but why did you steal my **g**?
31:32 "With whomever you find your **g**,
35: 2 Put away the foreign **g** that are
35: 4 gave Jacob all the foreign **g**
Ex 12:12 and against all the **g** of Egypt
15:11 like You, O LORD, among the **g**?
18:11 is greater than all the **g**;
20: 3 You shall have no other **g**
20:23 **g** of silver or gods of gold you
20:23 gods of silver or **g** of gold you
23:13 mention of the name of other **g**,
23:24 shall not bow down to their **g**,
23:32 with them, nor with their **g**.
23:33 For if you serve their **g**,
32: 1 make us **g** that shall go before
32:23 Make us **g** that shall go before
34:15 play the harlot with their **g**
34:15 and make sacrifice to their **g**,
34:16 play the harlot with their **g**
34:16 play the harlot with their **g**.
34:17 You shall make no molded **g** for
Lev 19: 4 make for yourselves molded **g**:
Num 25: 2 to the sacrifices of their **g**,
25: 2 ate and bowed down to their **g**.
33: 4 Also on their **g** the LORD had
Deut 4:28 "And there you will serve **g**,
5: 7 You shall have no other **g**
6:14 shall not go after other **g**,
6:14 the **g** of the peoples who are
7: 4 following Me, to serve other **g**;
7:16 nor shall you serve their **g**,
7:25 the carved images of their **g**
8:19 your God, and follow other **g**,
10:17 the LORD your God is God of **g**
11:16 turn aside and serve other **g**
11:28 to go after other **g** which you
12: 2 shall dispossess served their **g**,
12: 3 the carved images of their **g**
12:30 do not inquire after their **g**,
12:30 did these nations serve their **g**?
12:31 hates they have done to their **g**;
12:31 in the fire to their **g**.
13: 2 'Let us go after other **g**'—
13: 6 'Let us go and serve other **g**,
13: 7 of the **g** of the people which
13:13 Let us go and serve other **g**"
17: 3 has gone and served other **g**
18:20 speaks in the name of other **g**,
20:18 they have done for their **g**,
28:14 to go after other **g** to serve
28:36 there you shall serve other **g**—
28:64 there you shall serve other **g**,
29:18 to go and serve the **g** of these
29:26 they went and served other **g**
29:26 **g** that they did not know and
30:17 and worship other **g** and serve
31:16 and play the harlot with the **g**
31:18 they have turned to other **g**.
31:20 then they will turn to other **g**
32:16 Him to jealousy with foreign **g**;
32:17 To **g** they did not know,
32:17 they did not know, To new **g**,
32:37 will say: 'Where are their **g**,
Josh 22:22 "The LORD God of **g**,
22:22 God of gods, the LORD God of **g**,
23: 7 mention of the name of their **g**,
23:16 have gone and served other **g**,
24: 2 times; and they served other **g**.
24:14 and put away the **g** which your
24:15 whether the **g** which your
24:15 or the **g** of the Amorites, in
24:16 the LORD to serve other **g**;
24:20 the LORD and serve foreign **g**,
24:23 put away the foreign **g** which
Judg 2: 3 and their **g** shall be a snare to
2:12 and they followed other **g** from
2:12 other gods from among the **g**
2:17 played the harlot with other **g**,
2:19 fathers, by following other **g**,
3: 6 and they served their **g**.
5: 8 They chose new **g**;
6:10 do not fear the **g** of the
10: 6 the **g** of Syria, the gods of
10: 6 the **g** of Sidon, the gods of
10: 6 the **g** of Moab, the gods of the
10: 6 the **g** of the people of Ammon,
10: 6 and the **g** of the Philistines;
10:13 forsaken Me and served other **g**.

10:14 Go and cry out to the *g* which
10:16 So they put away the foreign *g*
18:24 You have taken away my *g* which I
Ruth 1:15 back to her people and to her *g*;
1 Sam 4: 8 from the hand of these mighty *g*?
4: 8 These are the *g* who struck the
6: 5 His hand from you, from your *g*,
7: 3 then put away the foreign *g*
8: 8 forsaken Me and served other *g*—
17:43 cursed David by his *g*.
26:19 saying, 'Go, serve other *g*.
2 Sam 7:23 Egypt, the nations, and their *g*?
1 Ki 9: 6 but go and serve other *g* and
9: 9 and have embraced other *g*,
11: 2 away your hearts after their *g*.
11: 4 turned his heart after other *g*;
11: 8 and sacrificed to their *g*.
11:10 he should not go after other *g*;
12:28 to Jerusalem. Here are your *g*,
14: 9 and made for yourself other *g*
18:24 you call on the name of your *g*,
19: 2 So let the *g* do to me, and
20:10 The *g* do so to me, and more
20:23 Their *g* are gods of the hills.
20:23 Their gods are *g* of the hills.
2 Ki 5:17 or sacrifice to other *g*,
17: 7 and they had feared other *g*,
17:29 nation continued to make *g* of
17:31 the *g* of Sepharvaim.
17:33 LORD, yet served their own *g*—
17:35 "You shall not fear other *g*,
17:37 you shall not fear other *g*.
17:38 nor shall you fear other *g*.
18:33 Has any of the *g* of the nations
18:34 Where are the *g* of Hamath and
18:34 Where are the *g* of Sepharvaim
18:35 Who among all the *g* of the lands
19:12 Have the *g* of the nations
19:18 and have cast their *g* into the
19:18 the fire; for they were not *g*,
22:17 and burned incense to other *g*,
23:24 the household *g* and idols, all
1 Chr 5:25 played the harlot after the *g*
10:10 armor in the temple of their *g*,
14:12 And when they left their *g*
16:25 also to be feared above all *g*.
16:26 For all the *g* of the peoples
2 Chr 2: 5 our God is greater than all *g*.
7:19 you, and go and serve other *g*,
7:22 of Egypt, and embraced other *g*,
13: 8 Jeroboam made for you as *g*.
13: 9 of things that are not *g*?
14: 3 the altars of the foreign *g*
25:14 that he brought the *g* of the
25:14 Seir, set them up to be his *g*,
25:15 Why have you sought the *g* of the
25:20 because they sought the *g* of
28:23 For he sacrificed to the *g* of
28:23 Because the *g* of the kings of
28:25 to burn incense to other *g*,
32:13 Were the *g* of the nations of
32:14 was there among all the *g* of
32:17 As the *g* of the nations of
32:19 as against the *g* of the people
33:15 He took away the foreign *g* and
34:25 and burned incense to other *g*,
Ezra 1: 7 and put in the temple of his *g*;
Ps 82: 1 He judges among the *g*.
82: 6 I said, "You are *g*,
86: 8 Among the *g* there is none
95: 3 And the great King above all *g*.
96: 4 is to be feared above all *g*.
96: 5 For all the *g* of the peoples
97: 7 Worship Him, all you *g*.
97: 9 are exalted far above all *g*.
135: 5 And our Lord is above all *g*.
136: 2 give thanks to the God of *g*!
138: 1 Before the *g* I will sing
Isa 21: 9 all the carved images of her *g*
36:18 Has any one of the *g* of the
36:19 Where are the *g* of Hamath and
36:19 Where are the *g* of Sepharvaim?
36:20 Who among all the *g* of these
37:12 Have the *g* of the nations
37:19 and have cast their *g* into the
37:19 the fire; for they were not *g*,
41:23 we may know that you are *g*;
42:17 molded images, 'You are our *g*.
57: 5 Inflaming yourselves with *g*
Jer 1:16 Burned incense to other *g*,
2:11 Has a nation changed its *g*,
2:11 its gods, Which are not *g*?
2:28 But where are your *g* that you
2:28 of your cities Are your *g*,
5: 7 by those that are not *g*.
5:19 Me and served foreign *g* in
7: 6 or walk after other *g* to your
7: 9 and walk after other *g* whom you
7:18 out drink offerings to other *g*,
10:11 The *g* that have not made the
11:10 they have gone after other *g*
11:12 will go and cry out to the *g*
11:13 of your cities were your *g*,
13:10 and walk after other *g* to serve
16:11 'they have walked after other *g*
16:13 there you shall serve other *g*
16:20 Will a man make *g* for himself,
16:20 for himself, Which are not *g*?
19: 4 incense in it to other *g* whom
19:13 out drink offerings to other *g*.
22: 9 and worshiped other *g* and
25: 6 Do not go after other *g* to serve
32:29 out drink offerings to other *g*,
35:15 and do not go after other *g* to
43:12 a fire in the houses of the *g*
43:13 and the houses of the *g* of the
44: 3 incense and to serve other *g*
44: 5 to burn no incense to other *g*.
44: 8 burning incense to other *g* in
44:15 had burned incense to other *g*,
46:25 with their *g* and their
48:35 And burns incense to his *g*.
Ezek 28: 2 a god, I sit in the seat of *g*,
Dan 2:11 it to the king except the *g*,
2:47 your God is the God of *g*,
3:12 They do not serve your *g* or
3:14 that you do not serve my *g* or
3:18 that we do not serve your *g*,
5: 4 and praised the *g* of gold and
5:11 like the wisdom of the *g*,
5:23 And you have praised the *g* of
11: 8 he shall also carry their *g*
11:36 against the God of *g*,
Hos 3: 1 who look to other *g* and love
14: 3 of our hands, 'You are our *g*.
Am 5:26 your idols, The star of your *g*,
Nah 1:14 Out of the house of your *g* I
Zeph 2:11 reduce to nothing all the *g* of
Jn 10:34 You are *g*" '?
10:35 "If He called them *g*,
Acts 7:40 Make us *g* to go before us;
14:11 The *g* have come down to us in
17:18 to be a proclaimer of foreign *g*,
19:26 saying that they are not *g*
1 Cor 8: 5 even if there are so-called *g*,
8: 5 on earth (as there are many *g*
Gal 4: 8 those which by nature are not *g*.

GOES (126/122)

Gen 2:13 it is the one which *g* around
2:14 it is the one which *g* toward
32:20 him with the present that *g*
Ex 7:15 when he *g* out to the water, and
22:26 it to him before the sun *g*
28:29 when he *g* into the holy place,
28:30 be over Aaron's heart when he *g*
28:35 sound will be heard when he *g*
Lev 11:27 And whatever *g* on its paws,
11:42 whatever *g* on all fours, or
14:36 before the priest *g* into it
14:46 Moreover he who *g* into the house
16:17 of meeting when he *g* in to
22: 3 who *g* near the holy things
22: 7 And when the sun *g* down he shall
Num 5:12 If any man's wife *g* astray and
5:29 *g* astray and defiles herself,
35:26 if the manslayer at any time *g*
Deut 1:30 who *g* before you, He will fight
9: 3 the LORD your God is He who *g*
19: 5 as when a man *g* to the woods
20: 4 the LORD your God is He who *g*
22:13 and *g* in to her, and detests
23: 9 When the army *g* out against
24: 2 and *g* and becomes another man's
24:13 to him again when the sun *g*
31: 6 He is the One who *g* with you.
31: 8 He is the one who *g* before
Josh 2:19 it shall be that whoever *g*
10:10 them along the road that *g* to
16: 1 to the wilderness that *g* up
Judg 20:31 in the highways (one of which *g*
21:19 side of the highway that *g* up
1 Sam 6: 9 if it *g* up the road to its own
9:13 surely find him before he *g* up
22:14 who *g* at your bidding, and is
30:24 But as his part is who *g* down
2 Sam 3:35 or anything else till the sun *g*
2 Ki 5:18 when my master *g* into the
11: 8 are to be with the king as he *g*
12:20 which *g* down to Silla.
2 Chr 23: 7 when he comes in and when he *g*
Ezra 5: 8 and this work *g* on diligently
Neh 4: 3 if even a fox *g* up on it, he
Esth 4:11 that any man or woman who *g*
Job 7: 9 So he who *g* down to the grave
9:11 If He *g* by me, I do not see
18: 5 light of the wicked indeed *g*
34: 8 Who *g* in company with the
41:20 Smoke *g* out of his nostrils,
41:21 And a flame *g* out of his
Ps 41: 6 When he *g* out, he tells it.
58: 8 snail which melts away as it *g*,
68:21 scalp of the one who still *g*
97: 3 A fire *g* before Him, And burns
104:23 Man *g* out to his work And to
126: 6 He who continually *g* forth
Prov 6:29 So is he who *g* in to his
7:22 as an ox *g* to the slaughter,
10:17 he who refuses correction *g*
11:10 When it *g* well with the
16:18 Pride *g* before destruction,
20:19 He who *g* about as a talebearer
26: 9 Like a thorn that *g* into the
26:20 the fire *g* out; And where
Eccl 1: 5 and the sun *g* down,
1: 6 The wind *g* toward the south,
3:21 which *g* upward, and the spirit
3:21 which *g* down to the earth?
12: 5 For man *g* to his eternal home,
Song 7: 9 THE SHULAMITE The wine *g*
Isa 28:19 As often as it *g* out it will
30:29 of heart as when one *g* with a
55:11 So shall My word be that *g*
62: 1 Until her righteousness *g*
63:14 As a beast *g* down into the
Jer 3: 1 And she *g* from him And
5: 6 Everyone who *g* out from there
6: 4 for the day *g* away, For the
21: 9 but he who *g* out and defects to
22:10 Weep bitterly for him who *g*
30:23 the whirlwind of the LORD *G*
38: 2 but he who *g* over to the
49:17 Everyone who *g* by it will be
50:13 Everyone who *g* by Babylon
Ezek 7:14 But no one *g* to battle;
40:40 as one *g* up to the entrance of
42: 9 as one *g* into them from the
44:27 And on the day that he *g* to the
46:12 and after he *g* out the gate
47: 8 *g* down into the valley, and
47: 9 will live wherever the river *g*.
47:15 as one *g* to Zedad,
Hos 6: 4 And like the early dew it *g*
6: 5 are like light that *g* forth.
Am 5: 3 The city that *g* out by a
5: 3 And that which *g* out by a
Hab 1: 4 And justice never *g* forth.
Zech 5: 3 This is the curse that *g* out
5: 5 and see what this is that *g*
Mt 8: 9 to this one, 'Go,' and he *g*;
12:43 When an unclean spirit *g* out of
12:43 he *g* through dry places,
12:45 Then he *g* and takes with him
13:44 and for joy over it he *g* and
15:11 Not what *g* into the mouth
15:17 whatever enters the mouth *g*
18:12 and one of them *g* astray, does
26:24 The Son of Man indeed *g* just as
Mk 14:14 Wherever he *g* in, say to the
14:21 The Son of Man indeed *g* just as
Lk 7: 8 I say to one, 'Go,' and he *g*;
11:24 When an unclean spirit *g* out of
11:24 he *g* through dry places,
11:26 Then he *g* and takes with him
16:30 but if one *g* to them from the
22:22 And truly the Son of Man *g* as it
Jn 3: 8 it comes from and where it *g*.
10: 4 he *g* before them; and the sheep
Acts 8:26 south along the road which *g*
1 Cor 6: 6 But brother *g* to law against
9: 7 Who ever *g* to war at his own
Phil 2:23 as soon as I see how it *g* with
Jas 1:24 *g* away, and immediately forgets
Rev 14: 4 follow the Lamb wherever He *g*.
19:15 Now out of His mouth *g* a sharp

GOG (12/10) HAMON GOG, MAGOG

1 Chr 5: 4 *G* his son, Shimei his son,
Ezek 38: 2 of man, set your face against *G*,
38: 3 I am against you, O *G*,
38:14 of man, prophesy and say to *G*,
38:16 when I am hallowed in you, O *G*,
38:18 when *G* comes against the land
38:21 will call for a sword against *G*
39: 1 son of man, prophesy against *G*,
39: 1 I am against you, O *G*,
39:11 will give *G* a burial place
39:11 because there they will bury *G*
Rev 20: 8 *G* and Magog, to gather them

GOING (144/137)

Gen 8: 7 which kept *g* to and fro until
12: 9 *g* on still toward the South.
15:12 Now when the sun was *g* down, a
16: 8 come from, and where are you *g*?
28:20 keep me in this way that I am *g*,
32:17 you belong, and where are you *g*?
38:13 your father-in-law is *g* up to
Ex 8:29 Indeed I am *g* out from you, and
10: 8 Who are the ones that are *g*?
13: 4 On this day you are *g* out, in
17:12 hands were steady until the *g*
23: 4 your enemy's ox or his donkey *g*
34:12 of the land where you are *g*,
Num 24:14 I am *g* to my people. Come, I
32: 7 the children of Israel from *g*
Deut 16: 6 at the *g* down of the sun, at
22: 1 brother's ox or his sheep *g*
28:21 from the land which you are *g*
33:18 in your *g* out, And Issachar in
Josh 1: 4 to the Great Sea toward the *g*
6:11 *g* around it once. Then they
10:27 So it was at the time of the *g*
14:11 both for *g* out and for coming
22:33 they spoke no more of *g* against
23:14 this day I am *g* the way of all
Judg 19:17 old man said, "Where are you *g*,
19:18 now I am *g* to the house of the
19:28 her, "Get up and let us be *g*.
20:40 and there was the whole city *g*
1 Sam 9:11 they met some young women *g* out
9:27 As they were *g* down to the
10: 3 There three men *g* up to God at
17:20 to the camp as the army was *g*
17:55 When Saul saw David *g* out
22: 9 I saw the son of Jesse *g* to Nob,
29: 6 and your *g* out and your coming
2 Sam 2:19 and in *g* he did not turn to the
2:24 And the sun was *g* down when
3:25 to know your *g* out and your
15:19 Why are you also *g* with us?
20: 8 and as he was *g* forward, it
1 Ki 13:17 nor return by *g* the way you

G

17:11 And as she was ***g*** to get it, he
22:36 as the sun was ***g*** down, a shout
2 Ki 1: 3 God in Israel that you are ***g***
2:23 and as he was ***g*** up the road,
4:23 'Why are you ***g*** to him today?
11: 9 with those who were ***g*** off duty
19:27 Your ***g*** out and your coming in,
1 Chr 12:19 to David when he was ***g*** with
2 Chr 22: 7 His ***g*** to Joram was God's
23: 8 with those who were ***g*** off
Neh 12:38 ***g*** past the Tower of the Ovens
Job 1: 7 From ***g*** to and fro on the earth,
2: 2 From ***g*** to and fro on the earth,
33:24 Deliver him from ***g*** down to the
33:28 He will redeem his soul from ***g***
Ps 50: 1 the rising of the sun to its ***g***
104:19 The sun knows its ***g*** down.
113: 3 the rising of the sun to its ***g***
121: 8 LORD shall preserve your ***g***
144:14 there be no breaking in or ***g***
Eccl 9:10 in the grave where you are ***g***.
Song 4: 1 ***G*** down from Mount Gilead.
6: 5 is like a flock of goats ***G***
Isa 13:10 sun will be darkened in its ***g***
37:28 Your ***g*** out and your coming in,
Jer 31:24 farmers and those ***g*** out with
37: 4 Now Jeremiah was coming and ***g***
Ezek 1:13 the appearance of torches ***g***
12: 4 as though ***g*** into captivity;
12: 7 as though ***g*** into captivity, and
40:31 and ***g*** up to it were eight
40:34 and ***g*** up to it were eight
40:37 and ***g*** up to it were eight
Dan 6:14 and he labored till the ***g*** down
9:25 That from the ***g*** forth of the
Hos 6: 3 His ***g*** forth is established as
Jon 1: 3 and found a ship ***g*** to Tarshish;
Zech 2: 2 So I said, "Where are you ***g***?
2: 3 ***g*** out; and another angel was
5: 6 It is a basket that is ***g***
6: 6 one with the black horses is ***g***
6: 6 the white are ***g*** after them, and
6: 6 and the dappled are ***g*** toward
Mal 1:11 even to its ***g*** down, My name
Mt 4:21 ***G*** on from there, He saw two
20:17 ***g*** up to Jerusalem, took the
20:18 we are ***g*** up to Jerusalem, and
25: 8 for our lamps are ***g*** out.'
26:46 "Rise, let us be ***g***.
28: 7 and indeed He is ***g*** before you
28:11 Now while they were ***g***,
Mk 6:31 there were many coming and ***g***,
10:17 Now as He was ***g*** out on the
10:32 ***g*** up to Jerusalem, and Jesus
10:32 and Jesus was ***g*** before them;
10:33 we are ***g*** up to Jerusalem, and
13:34 It is like a man ***g*** to a far
14:42 "Rise, let us be ***g***.
16: 7 that He is ***g*** before you into
Lk 8:46 for I perceived power ***g*** out
14:19 and I am ***g*** to test them. I ask
14:31 ***g*** to make war against another
18:31 we are ***g*** up to Jerusalem, and
19: 4 for He was ***g*** to pass that way.
19:28 ***g*** up to Jerusalem.
22:49 around Him saw what was ***g*** to
24:21 that it was He who was ***g*** to
24:28 the village where they were ***g***,
Jn 4:51 And as he was now ***g*** down, his
6:21 at the land where they were ***g***.
7: 8 I am not yet ***g*** up to this
8:14 I came from and where I am ***g***;
8:14 I come from and where I am ***g***.
8:21 I am ***g*** away, and you will seek
8:59 ***g*** through the midst of them,
11: 8 and are You ***g*** there again?"
11:31 She is ***g*** to the tomb to weep
12:35 does not know where he is ***g***.
13: 3 He had come from God and was ***g***
13:33 said to the Jews, 'Where I am ***g***,
13:36 to Him, "Lord, where are You ***g***?
13:36 Where I am ***g*** you cannot follow
14: 5 we do not know where You are ***g***,
14:28 I am ***g*** away and coming back to
14:28 I am ***g*** to the Father,' for My
16: 5 you asks Me, 'Where are You ***g***?
20: 3 and were ***g*** to the tomb.
21: 3 I am ***g*** fishing." They said to
21: 3 'We are ***g*** with you also."
Acts 9:28 coming in and ***g*** out.
11:28 by the Spirit that there was ***g***
20: 5 ***g*** ahead, waited for us at
23:15 as though you were ***g*** to make
23:20 as though they were ***g*** to
25: 4 and that he himself was ***g***
Rom 15:25 But now I am ***g*** to Jerusalem to
1 Tim 1:16 as a pattern to those who are ***g***
Heb 5: 2 on those who are ignorant and ***g***
11: 8 out, not knowing where he was ***g***.
1 Pe 2:25 For you were like sheep ***g***
1 Jn 2:11 and does not know where he is ***g***,
Rev 17:11 and is ***g*** to perdition.

GOINGS (1/1)

Mic 5: 2 Whose ***g*** forth are from of

GOLAN (4/4)

Deut 4:43 and ***G*** in Bashan for the
Josh 20: 8 and ***G*** in Bashan, from the tribe
21:27 they gave ***G*** in Bashan with
1 Chr 6:71 sons of Gershon were given ***G***

GOLD (452/394) GOLDEN, GOLDSMITH

Gen 2:11 of Havilah, where there is ***g***.
2:12 And the ***g*** of that land is good.
13: 2 livestock, in silver, and in ***g***.
24:22 weighing ten shekels of ***g***,
24:35 flocks and herds, silver and ***g***,
24:53 jewelry of silver, jewelry of ***g***,
41:42 of fine linen and put a ***g***
44: 8 then could we steal silver or ***g***
Ex 3:22 of silver, articles of ***g***,
11: 2 of silver and articles of ***g***.
12:35 of silver, articles of ***g***,
20:23 gods of silver or gods of ***g*** you
25: 3 you shall take from them: ***g***,
25:11 shall overlay it with pure ***g***,
25:11 make on it a molding of ***g*** all
25:12 shall cast four rings of ***g***
25:13 wood, and overlay them with ***g***.
25:17 make a mercy seat of pure ***g***;
25:18 shall make two cherubim of ***g***;
25:24 shall overlay it with pure ***g***,
25:24 and make a molding of ***g*** all
25:25 and you shall make a ***g*** molding
25:26 make for it four rings of ***g***,
25:28 wood, and overlay them with ***g***,
25:29 You shall make them of pure ***g***.
25:31 also make a lampstand of pure ***g***;
25:36 one hammered piece of pure ***g***.
25:38 trays shall be of pure ***g***.
25:39 be made of a talent of pure ***g***,
26: 6 shall make fifty clasps of ***g***,
26:29 shall overlay the boards with ***g***,
26:29 make their rings of ***g*** as
26:29 and overlay the bars with ***g***.
26:32 of acacia wood overlaid with ***g***.
26:32 Their hooks shall be ***g***,
26:37 wood, and overlay them with ***g***;
26:37 their hooks shall be of ***g***,
28: 5 "They shall take the ***g***,
28: 6 they shall make the ephod of ***g***,
28: 8 same workmanship, made of ***g***,
28:11 shall set them in settings of ***g***.
28:13 shall also make settings of ***g***,
28:14 make two chains of pure ***g*** like
28:15 ephod you shall make it: of ***g***,
28:20 They shall be set in ***g***
28:22 like braided cords of pure ***g***.
28:23 you shall make two rings of ***g***
28:24 the two braided chains of ***g***
28:26 shall make two rings of ***g***,
28:27 And two other rings of ***g*** you
28:33 and bells of ***g*** between them all
28:36 also make a plate of pure ***g***
30: 3 and its horns with pure ***g***;
30: 3 make for it a molding of ***g*** all
30: 4 Two ***g*** rings you shall make for
30: 5 wood, and overlay them with ***g***.
31: 4 artistic works, to work in ***g***,
31: 8 the pure ***g*** lampstand with all
32: 4 And he received the ***g*** from
32:24 to them, 'Whoever has any ***g***,
32:31 made for themselves a god of ***g***!
35: 5 as an offering to the LORD: ***g***,
35:22 and necklaces, all jewelry of ***g***,
35:22 man who made an offering of ***g***
35:32 to work in ***g*** and silver and
36:13 And he made fifty clasps of ***g***,
36:34 He overlaid the boards with ***g***,
36:34 made their rings of ***g*** to be
36:34 and overlaid the bars with ***g***.
36:36 wood, and overlaid them with ***g***,
36:36 gold, with their hooks of ***g***;
36:38 capitals and their rings with ***g***,
37: 2 He overlaid it with pure ***g***
37: 2 and made a molding of ***g*** all
37: 3 he cast for it four rings of ***g***
37: 4 wood, and overlaid them with ***g***.
37: 6 made the mercy seat of pure ***g***;
37: 7 made two cherubim of beaten ***g***;
37:11 And he overlaid it with pure ***g***,
37:11 and made a molding of ***g*** all
37:12 and made a molding of ***g*** for the
37:13 he cast for it four rings of ***g***,
37:15 table, and overlaid them with ***g***.
37:16 He made of pure ***g*** the utensils
37:17 made the lampstand of pure ***g***;
37:22 one hammered piece of pure ***g***.
37:23 and its trays of pure ***g***.
37:24 Of a talent of pure ***g*** he made
37:26 And he overlaid it with pure ***g***:
37:26 made for it a molding of ***g*** all
37:27 He made two rings of ***g*** for it
37:28 wood, and overlaid them with ***g***.
38:24 All the ***g*** that was used in all
38:24 the ***g*** of the offering, was
39: 2 He made the ephod of ***g***,
39: 3 And they beat the ***g*** into thin
39: 5 same workmanship, woven of ***g***,
39: 6 enclosed in settings of ***g***;
39: 8 workmanship of the ephod, of ***g***,
39:13 enclosed in settings of ***g*** in
39:15 like braided cords of pure ***g***.
39:16 also made two settings of ***g***
39:16 two settings of gold and two ***g***
39:17 the two braided chains of ***g*** in
39:19 And they made two rings of ***g*** and
39:20 They made two other ***g*** rings and
39:25 And they made bells of pure ***g***,
39:30 of the holy crown of pure ***g***,
39:37 the pure ***g*** lampstand with its
39:38 the ***g*** altar, the anointing oil,
40: 5 shall also set the altar of ***g***
40:26 He put the ***g*** altar in the
Lev 24: 4 of the lamps on the pure ***g***
24: 6 on the pure ***g*** table before the
Num 7:14 one ***g*** pan of ten shekels, full
7:20 one ***g*** pan of ten shekels, full
7:26 one ***g*** pan of ten shekels, full
7:32 one ***g*** pan of ten shekels, full
7:38 one ***g*** pan of ten shekels, full
7:44 one ***g*** pan of ten shekels, full
7:50 one ***g*** pan of ten shekels, full
7:56 one ***g*** pan of ten shekels, full
7:62 one ***g*** pan of ten shekels, full
7:68 one ***g*** pan of ten shekels, full
7:74 one ***g*** pan of ten shekels, full
7:80 one ***g*** pan of ten shekels, full
7:84 and twelve ***g*** pans.
7:86 The twelve ***g*** pans full of
7:86 all the ***g*** of the pans weighed
8: 4 the lampstand was hammered ***g***;
22:18 his house full of silver and ***g***,
24:13 his house full of silver and ***g***,
31:22 'Only the ***g***, the silver,
31:50 man found of ornaments of ***g***:
31:51 the priest received the ***g*** from
31:52 And all the ***g*** of the offering
31:54 the priest received the ***g*** from
Deut 7:25 shall not covet the silver or ***g***
8:13 and your silver and your ***g*** are
17:17 greatly multiply silver and ***g***
29:17 and stone and silver and ***g***);
Josh 6:19 "But all the silver and ***g***,
6:24 Only the silver and ***g***,
7:21 and a wedge of ***g*** weighing fifty
7:24 the garment, the wedge of ***g***,
22: 8 livestock, with silver, with ***g***,
Judg 8:24 For they had ***g*** earrings,
8:26 Now the weight of the ***g*** earrings
8:26 seven hundred shekels of ***g***,
1 Sam 6: 8 and put the articles of ***g*** which
6:11 and the chest with the ***g*** rats
6:15 which were the articles of ***g***,
2 Sam 1:24 Who put ornaments of ***g*** on your
8: 7 And David took the shields of ***g***
8:10 of silver, articles of ***g***,
8:11 along with the silver and ***g***
12:30 Its weight was a talent of ***g***,
21: 4 We will have no silver or ***g*** from
1 Ki 6:20 He overlaid it with pure ***g***,
6:21 of the temple with pure ***g***.
6:21 He stretched ***g*** chains across
6:21 and overlaid it with ***g***.
6:22 whole temple he overlaid with ***g***,
6:22 also he overlaid with ***g*** the
6:28 he overlaid the cherubim with ***g***.
6:30 the temple he overlaid with ***g***,
6:32 and overlaid them with ***g***;
6:32 and he spread ***g*** on the cherubim
6:35 and overlaid them with ***g***
7:48 of the LORD: the altar of ***g***,
7:48 and the table of ***g*** on which
7:49 the lampstands of pure ***g***,
7:49 and the wick-trimmers of ***g***;
7:50 and the censers of pure ***g***;
7:50 pure gold; and the hinges of ***g***,
7:51 the silver and the ***g*** and the
9:11 with cedar and cypress and ***g***,
9:14 hundred and twenty talents of ***g***.
9:28 and twenty talents of ***g*** from
10: 2 that bore spices, very much ***g***,
10:10 hundred and twenty talents of ***g***,
10:11 which brought ***g*** from Ophir,
10:14 The weight of ***g*** that came to
10:14 and sixty-six talents of ***g***,
10:16 large shields of hammered ***g***;
10:16 six hundred shekels of ***g*** went
10:17 hundred shields of hammered ***g***;
10:17 three minas of ***g*** went into each
10:18 and overlaid it with pure ***g***.
10:21 drinking vessels were ***g***,
10:21 Forest of Lebanon were pure ***g***.
10:22 merchant ships came bringing ***g***,
10:25 articles of silver and ***g***,
12:28 advice, made two calves of ***g***,
14:26 He also took away all the ***g***
15:15 silver and ***g*** and utensils.
15:18 Asa took all the silver and ***g***
15:19 you a present of silver and ***g***.
20: 3 Your silver and your ***g*** are
20: 5 to me your silver and your ***g***,
20: 7 children, my silver, and my ***g***;
22:48 ships to go to Ophir for ***g***;
2 Ki 5: 5 six thousand shekels of ***g***,
7: 8 carried from it silver and ***g***
12:13 any articles of ***g*** or articles
12:18 and all the ***g*** found in the
14:14 And he took all the ***g*** and
16: 8 And Ahaz took the silver and ***g***
18:14 silver and thirty talents of ***g***.
18:16 time Hezekiah stripped the ***g***
20:13 his treasures—the silver and ***g***,
23:33 of silver and a talent of ***g***.
23:35 gave the silver and ***g*** to
23:35 he exacted the silver and ***g***
24:13 in pieces all the articles of ***g***
25:15 the things of solid ***g*** and solid
1 Chr 18: 7 And David took the shields of ***g***
18:10 him all kinds of articles of ***g***,
18:11 along with the silver and ***g***
20: 2 found it to weigh a talent of ***g***,

21:25 Ornan six hundred shekels of **g**
22:14 hundred thousand talents of **g**
22:16 Of **g** and silver and bronze and
28:14 He gave **g** by weight for
28:14 gold by weight for things of **g**,
28:15 weight for the lampstands of **g**,
28:15 of gold, and their lamps of **g**,
28:16 And by weight he gave **g** for
28:17 also pure **g** for the forks, the
28:17 basins, the pitchers of pure **g**,
28:17 he gave **g** by weight for every
28:18 and refined **g** by weight for the
28:18 the **g** cherubim that spread
29: 2 **g** for things to be made of
29: 2 for things to be made of **g**
29: 3 my own special treasure of **g**
29: 4 "three thousand talents of **g**,
29: 4 of the **g** of Ophir, and seven
29: 5 the **g** for things of gold and
29: 5 the gold for things of **g** and
29: 7 and ten thousand darics of **g**,
2 Chr 1:15 the king made silver and **g** as
2: 7 a man skillful to work in **g**
2:14 skilled to work in **g** and
3: 4 overlaid the inside with pure **g**.
3: 5 which he overlaid with fine **g**,
3: 6 and the **g** was gold from
3: 6 and the gold was **g** from
3: 7 its walls and doors—with **g**;
3: 8 six hundred talents of fine **g**.
3: 9 nails was fifty shekels of **g**;
3: 9 overlaid the upper area with **g**.
3:10 and overlaid them with **g**.
4: 7 And he made ten lampstands of **g**
4: 8 he made one hundred bowls of **g**.
4:19 the altar of **g** and the tables
4:20 with their lamps of pure **g**,
4:21 and the wick-trimmers of **g**,
4:21 of gold, of purest **g**;
4:22 and the censers of pure **g**.
4:22 hall of the temple, were **g**.
5: 1 the silver and the **g** and all
8:18 hundred and fifty talents of **g**
9: 1 **g** in abundance, and precious
9: 9 hundred and twenty talents of **g**,
9:10 who brought **g** from Ophir,
9:13 The weight of **g** that came to
9:13 and sixty-six talents of **g**,
9:14 of the country brought **g** and
9:15 large shields of hammered **g**;
9:15 hundred shekels of hammered **g**
9:16 hundred shields of hammered **g**;
9:16 three hundred shekels of **g**
9:17 and overlaid it with pure **g**.
9:18 steps, with a footstool of **g**,
9:20 drinking vessels were **g**,
9:20 Forest of Lebanon were pure **g**.
9:21 merchant ships came, bringing **g**,
9:24 articles of silver and **g**,
12: 9 He also carried away the **g**
13: 8 and with you are the **g** calves
13:11 in order on the pure **g**
13:11 and the lampstand of **g** with its
15:18 silver and **g** and utensils.
16: 2 Then Asa brought silver and **g**
16: 3 I have sent you silver and **g**;
21: 3 great gifts of silver and **g**
24:14 spoons and vessels of **g** and
25:24 And he took all the **g** and
32:27 treasuries for silver, for **g**,
36: 3 of silver and a talent of **g**.
Ezra 1: 4 help him with silver and **g**,
1: 6 with articles of silver and **g**,
1: 9 thirty **g** platters, one thousand
1:10 thirty **g** basins, four hundred
1:11 All the articles of **g** and silver
2:69 the work sixty-one thousand **g**
5:14 the **g** and silver articles of
6: 5 Also let the **g** and silver
7:15 are to carry the silver and **g**
7:16 whereas all the silver and **g**
7:18 rest of the silver and the **g**,
8:25 out to them the silver, the **g**,
8:26 one hundred talents of **g**,
8:27 twenty **g** basins worth a
8:27 polished bronze, precious as **g**.
8:28 and the silver and the **g** are a
8:30 received the silver and the **g**
8:33 day the silver and the **g** and
Neh 7:70 to the treasury one thousand **g**
7:71 of the work twenty thousand **g**
7:72 gave was twenty thousand **g**
Esth 1: 6 and the couches were of **g**
8:15 with a great crown of **g** and a
Job 3:15 Or with princes who had **g**,
22:24 Then you will lay your **g** in the
22:24 And the **g** of Ophir among the
22:25 the Almighty will be your **g**
23:10 I shall come forth as **g**.
28: 1 And a place where **g** is
28: 6 And it contains **g** dust.
28:15 It cannot be purchased for **g**,
28:16 It cannot be valued in the **g** of
28:17 Neither **g** nor crystal can equal
28:17 exchanged for jewelry of fine **g**.
28:19 Nor can it be valued in pure **g**.
31:24 'If I have made **g** my hope,
31:24 my hope, Or said to fine **g**,
42:11 of silver and each a ring of **g**.
Ps 19:10 to be desired are they than **g**,
19:10 Yea, than much fine **g**;
21: 3 You set a crown of pure **g** upon
45: 9 hand stands the queen in **g**
45:13 Her clothing is woven with **g**.
68:13 And her feathers with yellow **g**.
72:15 And the **g** of Sheba will be
105:37 them out with silver and **g**,
115: 4 Their idols are silver and **g**,
119:72 thousands of coins of **g** and
119:127 Your commandments More than **g**,
119:127 than fine **g**!
135:15 the nations are silver and **g**,
Prov 3:14 And her gain than fine **g**.
8:10 knowledge rather than choice **g**;
8:19 My fruit is better than **g**,
8:19 than gold, yes, than fine **g**,
11:22 As a ring of **g** in a swine's
16:16 better to get wisdom than **g**!
17: 3 silver and the furnace for **g**,
20:15 There is **g** and a multitude of
22: 1 favor rather than silver and **g**.
25:11 spoken is like apples of **g**
25:12 Like an earring of **g** and an
25:12 gold and an ornament of fine **g**
27:21 silver and the furnace for **g**,
Eccl 2: 8 for myself silver and **g** and
Song 1:10 Your neck with chains of **g**.
1:11 will make you ornaments of **g**
3:10 of silver, Its support of **g**,
5:11 head is like the finest **g**;
5:14 His hands are rods of **g** Set
5:15 marble Set on bases of fine **g**.
Isa 2: 7 is also full of silver and **g**,
2:20 of silver And his idols of **g**,
13:12 a mortal more rare than fine **g**,
13:17 regard silver; And as for **g**,
30:22 of your molded images of **g**.
31: 7 of silver and his idols of **g**—
39: 2 his treasures—the silver and **g**,
40:19 goldsmith overspreads it with **g**,
46: 6 They lavish **g** out of the bag,
60: 6 They shall bring **g** and
60: 9 Their silver and their **g** with
60:17 of bronze I will bring **g**,
Jer 4:30 yourself with ornaments of **g**,
10: 4 decorate it with silver and **g**;
10: 9 And **g** from Uphaz, The work of
52:19 whatever was solid **g** and
Lam 4: 1 How the **g** has become dim!
4: 1 dim! How changed the fine **g**!
4: 2 of Zion, Valuable as fine **g**,
Ezek 7:19 And their **g** will be like
7:19 Their silver and their **g** will
16:13 Thus you were adorned with **g** and
16:17 beautiful jewelry from My **g**
27:22 kinds of precious stones, and **g**.
28: 4 And gathered **g** and silver into
28:13 turquoise, and emerald with **g**.
38:13 to carry away silver and **g**,
Dan 2:32 image's head was of fine **g**,
2:35 and the **g** were crushed
2:38 all—you are this head of **g**.
2:45 the clay, the silver, and the **g**—
3: 1 the king made an image of **g**,
3: 5 fall down and worship the **g**
3: 7 fell down and worshiped the **g**
3:10 fall down and worship the **g**
3:12 your gods or worship the **g**
3:14 serve my gods or worship the **g**
3:18 nor will we worship the **g** image
5: 2 the command to bring the **g** and
5: 3 Then they brought the **g** vessels
5: 4 and praised the gods of **g** and
5: 7 purple and have a chain of **g**
5:16 purple and have a chain of **g**
5:23 the gods of silver and **g**,
5:29 purple and put a chain of **g**
10: 5 whose waist was girded with **g**
11: 8 articles of silver and **g**;
11:38 not know he shall honor with **g**
11:43 power over the treasures of **g**
Hos 2: 8 multiplied her silver and **g**—
8: 4 From their silver and **g** They
Joel 3: 5 have taken My silver and My **g**,
Nah 2: 9 of silver! Take spoil of **g**!
Hab 2:19 it is overlaid with **g** and
Zeph 1:18 their silver nor their **g**
Hag 2: 8 and the **g** is Mine,' says the
Zech 4: 2 is a lampstand of solid **g**
4:12 the receptacles of the two **g**
6:11 "Take the silver and **g**,
9: 3 And **g** like the mire of the
13: 9 And test them as **g** is tested.
14:14 Shall be gathered together: **G**,
Mal 3: 3 And purge them as **g** and
Mt 2:11 they presented gifts to Him: **g**,
10: 9 Provide neither **g** nor silver nor
23:16 but whoever swears by the **g** of
23:17 the **g** or the temple that
23:17 temple that sanctifies the **g**?
Acts 3: 6 Silver and **g** I do not have, but
17:29 the Divine Nature is like **g** or
20:33 coveted no one's silver or **g**
1 Cor 3:12 on this foundation with **g**,
1 Tim 2: 9 not with braided hair or **g** or
2 Tim 2:20 are not only vessels of **g** and
Heb 9: 4 overlaid on all sides with **g**,
Jas 2: 2 into your assembly a man with **g**
5: 3 Your **g** and silver are corroded,
1 Pe 1: 7 much more precious than **g** that
1:18 things, like silver or **g**,
3: 3 the hair, wearing **g**,
Rev 3:18 counsel you to buy from Me **g**
4: 4 and they had crowns of **g** on
9: 7 were crowns of something like **g**,
9:20 worship demons, and idols of **g**,
17: 4 and adorned with **g** and precious
18:12 merchandise of **g** and silver,
18:16 and adorned with **g** and precious
21:15 he who talked with me had a **g**
21:18 and the city was pure **g**,
21:21 street of the city was pure **g**,

GOLDEN (37/33) GOLD

Gen 24:22 that the man took a **g** nose ring
Ex 28:34 'a **g** bell and a pomegranate,
28:34 a **g** bell and a pomegranate,
32: 2 Break off the **g** earrings which
32: 3 all the people broke off the **g**
Lev 8: 9 he put the **g** plate, the holy
Num 4:11 Over the **g** altar they shall
1 Sam 6: 4 Five **g** tumors and five golden
6: 4 Five golden tumors and five **g**
6:17 These are the **g** tumors which
6:18 and the **g** rats, according to
2 Ki 10:29 from the **g** calves that were at
1 Chr 28:17 and the **g** bowls—he gave gold
Esth 1: 7 And they served drinks in **g**
4:11 whom the king holds out the **g**
5: 2 king held out to Esther the **g**
8: 4 And the king held out the **g**
Job 37:22 He comes from the north as **g**
Eccl 12: 6 Or the **g** bowl is broken, Or
Isa 13:12 A man more than the **g** wedge of
14: 4 The **g** city ceased!
Jer 51: 7 Babylon was a **g** cup in the
Zech 4:12 two gold pipes from which the **g**
Heb 9: 4 which had the **g** censer and the
9: 4 in which were the **g** pot that
Rev 1:12 And having turned I saw seven **g**
1:13 about the chest with a **g** band.
1:20 and the seven **g** lampstands:
2: 1 in the midst of the seven **g**
5: 8 and **g** bowls full of incense,
8: 3 having a **g** censer, came and
8: 3 of all the saints upon the **g**
9:13 from the four horns of the **g**
14:14 having on His head a **g** crown,
15: 6 their chests girded with **g**
15: 7 to the seven angels seven **g**
17: 4 having in her hand a **g** cup full

GOLDSMITH (3/3) GOLD

Isa 40:19 The **g** overspreads it with
41: 7 the craftsman encouraged the **g**;
46: 6 on the scales; They hire a **g**,

GOLDSMITHS (3/3)

Neh 3: 8 son of Harhaiah, one of the **g**,
3:31 him Malchijah, one of the **g**,
3:32 the **g** and the merchants made

GOLGOTHA (3/3) CALVARY

Mt 27:33 had come to a place called **G**,
Mk 15:22 they brought Him to the place **G**,
Jn 19:17 which is called in Hebrew, **G**,

GOLIATH (6/6)

1 Sam 17: 4 of the Philistines, named **G**,
17:23 **G** by name, coming up from the
21: 9 The sword of **G** the Philistine,
22:10 and gave him the sword of **G** the
2 Sam 21:19 killed the brother of **G** the
1 Chr 20: 5 killed Lahmi the brother of **G**

GOMER (6/6)

Gen 10: 2 The sons of Japheth were **G**,
10: 3 The sons of **G** were Ashkenaz,
1 Chr 1: 5 The sons of Japheth were **G**,
1: 6 The sons of **G** were Ashkenaz,
Ezek 38: 6 **G** and all its troops; the house
Hos 1: 3 So he went and took **G** the

GOMORRAH (24/24)

Gen 10:19 then as you go toward Sodom, **G**,
13:10 LORD destroyed Sodom and **G**)
14: 2 king of Sodom, Birsha king of **G**,
14: 8 king of Sodom, the king of **G**,
14:10 and the kings of Sodom and **G**
14:11 all the goods of Sodom and **G**,
18:20 the outcry against Sodom and **G**
19:24 and fire on Sodom and **G**,
19:28 he looked toward Sodom and **G**,
Deut 29:23 the overthrow of Sodom and **G**,
32:32 Sodom And of the fields of **G**;
Isa 1: 9 We would have been made like **G**.
1:10 of our God, You people of **G**:
13:19 when God overthrew Sodom and **G**.
Jer 23:14 Me, And her inhabitants like **G**.
49:18 in the overthrow of Sodom and **G**
50:40 As God overthrew Sodom and **G**
Am 4:11 As God overthrew Sodom and **G**,
Zeph 2: 9 And the people of Ammon like **G**—
Mt 10:15 for the land of Sodom and **G** in
Mk 6:11 more tolerable for Sodom and **G**
Rom 9:29 have been made like **G**.
2 Pe 2: 6 the cities of Sodom and **G** into
Jude 7 as Sodom and **G**,

G

GONE (221/217)

Gen 27:30 and Jacob had scarcely *g* out
28: 7 and his mother and had *g* to
31:19 Now Laban had *g* to shear his
31:30 And now you have surely *g*
34:17 will take our daughter and be *g*.
35: 3 me in the way which I have *g*.
42:33 of your households, and be *g*.
44: 4 When they had *g* out of the city,
47:16 livestock, if the money is *g*.
47:18 my lord that our money is *g*;
49: 9 you have *g* up. He bows down,
Ex 9:29 As soon as I have *g* out of the
12:32 as you have said, and be *g*;
19: 1 the children of Israel had *g*
33: 8 watched Moses until he had *g*
Num 5:19 and if you have not *g* astray to
5:20 But if you have *g* astray while
11:26 but who had not *g* out to the
13:31 But the men who had *g* up with
13:32 land through which we have *g*
16:46 for wrath has *g* out from the
31:21 to the men of war who had *g* to
31:36 the portion for those who had *g*
32:13 in the sight of the LORD was *g*.
Deut 13:13 Corrupt men have *g* out from
17: 3 who has *g* and served other gods
23:23 That which has *g* from your lips
32:36 He sees that their power is *g*,
Josh 2: 7 as those who pursued them had *g*
23:16 and have *g* and served other
Judg 3:24 When he had *g* out, Eglon's
4:12 Barak the son of Abinoam had *g*
4:14 Has not the LORD *g* out before
11:36 to me according to what has *g*
18:14 Then the five men who had *g* to
18:17 Then the five men who had *g* to
18:24 and you have *g* away. Now what
20: 3 the children of Israel had *g*
Ruth 1:13 the hand of the LORD has *g*
1:15 your sister-in-law has *g* back
1 Sam 9: 7 bread in our vessels is all *g*,
12: 8 When Jacob had *g* into Egypt, and
14: 3 not know that Jonathan had *g*.
14:17 call the roll and see who has *g*
15:12 and he has *g* on around, passed
15:12 and *g* down to Gilgal."
15:20 and *g* on the mission on which
17:13 oldest sons of Jesse had *g* to
20:41 As soon as the lad had *g*,
23: 7 Saul was told that David had *g*
25:37 when the wine had *g* from Nabal,
2 Sam 3: 7 Why have you *g* in to my father's
3:22 and he had *g* in peace.
3:23 and he has *g* in peace."
3:24 him away, and he has already *g*?
3:26 And when Joab had *g* from David's
6:13 the ark of the LORD had *g* six
7: 9 with you wherever you have *g*,
13:15 said to her, "Arise, be *g*!"
17:20 They have *g* over the water
17:22 of them was left who had not *g*
17:25 who had *g* in to Abigail the
23:20 He also had *g* down and killed a
24: 8 So when they had *g* through all
1 Ki 1:25 For he has *g* down today, and has
1:45 and they have *g* up from there
1:47 the king's servants have *g* to
2:41 was told that Shimei had *g*
9:16 (Pharaoh king of Egypt had *g* up
11:15 commander of the army had *g* up
12: 1 for all Israel had *g* to Shechem
13:24 When he was *g*, a lion met
14: 9 for you have *g* and made for
14:10 away refuse until it is all *g*.
18:12 as soon as I am *g* from you,
20:40 busy here and there, he was *g*.
21:18 where he has *g* down to take
22:13 Then the messenger who had *g* to
2 Ki 1: 4 the bed to which you have *g* up,
1: 6 the bed to which you have *g* up,
1:16 the bed to which you have *g* up,
5: 2 And the Syrians had *g* out on
7:12 therefore they have *g* out of
9:34 And when he had *g* in, he ate and
20: 4 before Isaiah had *g* out into
20:11 by which it had *g* down on the
1 Chr 11:22 He also had *g* down and killed a
14:15 for God has *g* out before you to
17: 5 but have *g* from tent to tent,
17: 8 with you wherever you have *g*,
2 Chr 10: 1 for all Israel had *g* to Shechem
18:12 Then the messenger who had *g* to
25: 8 be *g*! Be strong in battle!
32:21 And when he had *g* into the
Neh 2:16 did not know where I had *g* or
13:10 singers who did the work had *g*
Job 19:10 down on every side, And I am *g*;
21:33 As countless have *g* before
24:24 little while, Then they are *g*.
27:21 carries him away, and he is *g*;
Ps 19: 4 Their line has *g* out through
38: 4 For my iniquities have *g* over
38:10 it also has *g* from me.
42: 7 Your waves and billows have *g*
47: 5 God has *g* up with a shout,
51: after he had *g* in to Bathsheba.
52: David has *g* to the house of
88:16 Your fierce wrath has *g* over
89:34 Nor alter the word that has *g*
103:16 passes over it, and it is *g*,
109:23 I am *g* like a shadow when it
119:176 I have *g* astray like a lost
124: 4 The stream would have *g* over
124: 5 swollen waters Would have *g*
Prov 7:19 He has *g* on a long journey;
20:14 But when he has *g* his way,
Eccl 8:10 who had come and *g* from the
Song 2:11 past, The rain is over and *g*.
5: 6 had turned away and was *g*.
6: 1 Where has your beloved *g*,
6: 2 My beloved has *g* to his garden,
Isa 5:13 Therefore my people have *g*
10:29 They have *g* along the ridge,
15: 2 He has *g* up to the temple and
15: 8 For the cry has *g* all around
16: 8 They are *g* over the sea.
22: 1 that you have all *g* up to the
24:11 The mirth of the land is *g*.
38: 8 which has *g* down with the sun
38: 8 on the dial by which it had *g*
38:12 My life span is *g*, Taken
41: 3 By the way that he had not *g*
45:23 The word has *g* out of My mouth
46: 2 But have themselves *g* into
51: 5 My salvation has *g* forth,
53: 6 All we like sheep have *g*
57: 8 And have *g* up to them;
Jer 2: 5 That they have *g* far from Me,
2:23 I have not *g* after the Baals'?
3: 6 She has *g* up on every high
4: 7 He has *g* forth from his place
9:10 beasts have fled; They are *g*.
10:20 My children have *g* from me,
11:10 and they have *g* after other
14: 2 the cry of Jerusalem has *g* up.
15: 6 'You have *g* backward.
15: 9 Her sun has *g* down While it
23:15 of Jerusalem Profaneness has *g*
23:19 a whirlwind of the LORD has *g*
29:16 your brethren who have not *g*
34:21 of Babylon's army which has *g*
37:21 all the bread in the city was *g*.
40: 5 while Jeremiah had not yet *g*
44: 8 land of Egypt where you have *g*
44:14 the remnant of Judah who have *g*
44:17 certainly do whatever has *g*
44:28 who have *g* to the land of Egypt
48:11 Nor has he *g* into captivity.
48:15 Moab is plundered and *g* up
48:15 Her chosen young men have *g*
48:32 Your plants have *g* over the
50: 6 They have *g* from mountain to
Lam 1: 3 Judah has *g* into captivity,
1: 5 Her children have *g* into
1:18 and my young men Have *g* into
Ezek 7:10 it has come! Doom has *g* out;
9: 3 of the God of Israel had *g* up
11:16 the countries where they have *g*.
13: 5 You have not *g* up into the gaps
23:30 to you because you have *g* as a
24: 6 And whose scum is not *g* from
24:12 And her great scum has not *g*
31:12 the peoples of the earth have *g*
32:21 They have *g* down, They lie with
32:24 Who have *g* down uncircumcised
32:27 Who have *g* down to hell with
32:30 Who have *g* down with the slain
36:20 and yet they have *g* out of His
37:21 nations, wherever they have *g*,
Dan 2:14 who had *g* out to kill the wise
10:20 and when I have *g* forth, indeed
Hos 8: 9 For they have *g* up to Assyria,
9: 6 For indeed they are *g* because
Jon 1: 5 But Jonah had *g* down into the
Mal 3: 7 of your fathers You have *g*
Mt 10:23 you will not have *g* through the
26:71 And when he had *g* out to the
Mk 1:19 When He had *g* a little farther
5:30 in Himself that power had *g*
7:29 the demon has *g* out of your
7:30 she found the demon *g* out, and
Lk 2:15 when the angels had *g* away from
5: 2 but the fishermen had *g* from
11:14 when the demon had *g* out, that
19: 7 He has *g* to be a guest with a
24:28 indicated that He would have *g*
Jn 4: 8 For His disciples had *g* away
4:45 for they also had *g* to the
6:22 but His disciples had *g* away
7:10 But when His brothers had *g* up,
12:19 the world has *g* after Him!"
13:31 when he had *g* out, Jesus said,
Acts 13: 6 Now when they had *g* through the
15:38 and had not *g* with them to the
16: 6 Now when they had *g* through
16:19 that their hope of profit was *g*,
18:22 and *g* up and greeted the
20: 2 Now when he had *g* over that
20:25 among whom I have *g* preaching
26:31 and when they had *g* aside, they
27:28 and when they had *g* a little
Rom 10:18 Their sound has *g* out to
1 Th 1: 8 Your faith toward God has *g*
1 Pe 3:22 who has *g* into heaven and is at
2 Pe 2:15 forsaken the right way and *g*
1 Jn 4: 1 many false prophets have *g* out
2 Jn 7 For many deceivers have *g* out
Jude 7 over to sexual immorality and *g*
11 Woe to them! For they have *g* in
Rev 18:14 that your soul longed for has *g*
18:14 are rich and splendid have *g*

GOOD (700/643) GOOD-LOOKING, GOODNESS

Gen 1: 4 saw the light, that it was *g*;
1:10 And God saw that it was *g*.
1:12 And God saw that it was *g*.
1:18 And God saw that it was *g*.
1:21 And God saw that it was *g*.
1:25 And God saw that it was *g*.
1:31 and indeed it was very *g*.
2: 9 is pleasant to the sight and *g*
2: 9 the tree of the knowledge of *g*
2:12 And the gold of that land is *g*.
2:17 the tree of the knowledge of *g*
2:18 It is not *g* that man should be
3: 5 God, knowing *g* and evil."
3: 6 woman saw that the tree was *g*
3:22 to know *g* and evil. And now,
15:15 you shall be buried at a *g* old
18: 7 took a tender and *g* calf, gave
24:50 speak to you either bad or *g*.
25: 8 his last and died in a *g* old
26:29 have done nothing to you but *g*
27:46 what *g* will my life be to me?"
30:20 God has endowed me with a *g*
31:24 you speak to Jacob neither *g*
31:29 you speak to Jacob neither *g*
40:16 that the interpretation was *g*,
41: 5 up on one stalk, plump and *g*.
41:22 up on one stalk, full and *g*.
41:24 thin heads devoured the seven *g*
41:26 The seven *g* cows are seven
41:26 and the seven *g* heads are
41:35 gather all the food of those *g*
41:37 So the advice was *g* in the eyes
43:28 servant our father is in *g*
44: 4 'Why have you repaid evil for *g*?
45:23 ten donkeys loaded with the *g*
46:29 neck and wept on his neck a *g*
49:15 He saw that rest was *g*,
50:20 but God meant it for *g*,
Ex 3: 8 them up from that land to a *g*
18: 9 Jethro rejoiced for all the *g*
18:17 thing that you do is not *g*.
21:34 of the pit shall make it *g*;
22:11 and he shall not make it *g*.
22:13 and he shall not make *g* what
22:14 it, he shall surely make it *g*.
22:15 it, he shall not make it *g*;
Lev 5: 4 his lips to do evil or to do *g*,
24:18 kills an animal shall make it *g*,
27:10 *g* for bad or bad for good;
27:10 it, good for bad or bad for *g*;
27:12 whether it is *g* or bad; as you,
27:14 whether it is *g* or bad; as the
27:33 not inquire whether it is *g* or
Num 10:29 for the LORD has promised *g*
10:32 that whatever *g* the LORD will
13:19 the land they dwell in is *g*
13:20 Be of *g* courage. And bring some
14: 7 to spy out is an exceedingly *g*
23:19 and will He not make it *g*?
24:13 to do *g* or bad of my own will.
Deut 1:14 you have told us to do is *g*.
1:25 It is a *g* land which the LORD
1:35 generation shall see that *g*
1:39 today have no knowledge of *g*
3:25 let me cross over and see the *g*
4:21 that I would not enter the *g*
4:22 cross over and possess that *g*
6:11 houses full of all *g* things,
6:18 shall do what is right and *g*
6:18 you may go in and possess the *g*
6:24 for our *g* always, that He might
8: 7 God is bringing you into a *g*
8:10 the LORD your God for the *g*
8:16 to do you *g* in the end—
9: 6 God is not giving you this *g*
10:13 I command you today for your *g*?
11:17 you perish quickly from the *g*
12:28 when you do what is *g* and
18:17 'What they have spoken is *g*.
26:11 you shall rejoice in every *g*
28:12 LORD will open to you His *g*
28:63 rejoiced over you to do you *g*
30: 9 the produce of your land for *g*.
30: 9 again rejoice over you for *g*
30:15 set before you today life and *g*,
31: 6 Be strong and of *g* courage, do
31: 7 Be strong and of *g* courage, for
31:23 'Be strong and of *g* courage;
Josh 1: 6 Be strong and of *g* courage, for
1: 8 and then you will have *g*
1: 9 Be strong and of *g* courage;
1:18 Only be strong and of *g*
9:25 do with us as it seems *g* and
10:25 be strong and of *g* courage, for
21:45 Not a word failed of any *g* thing
23:13 until you perish from this *g*
23:14 thing has failed of all the *g*
23:15 that as all the *g* things have
23:15 has destroyed you from this *g*
23:16 perish quickly from the *g* land
24:20 you, after He has done you *g*.
Judg 8:32 the son of Joash died at a *g*
8:35 in accordance with the *g* he
9:11 I cease my sweetness and my *g*
17:13 I know that the LORD will be *g*
18: 9 land, and indeed it is very *g*.
18:22 When they were a *g* way from the
Ruth 2:22 daughter-in-law, "It is *g*,

3:13 of a close relative for you—**g**;
1 Sam 2:24 my sons! For it is not a **g**
2:32 despite all the **g** which God
3:18 Let Him do what seems **g** to
11:10 do with us whatever seems **g** to
12:23 but I will teach you the **g** and
14:36 Do whatever seems **g** to you."
14:40 Do what seems **g** to you."
15: 9 the lambs, and all that was **g**,
19: 4 his works have been very **g**
20:12 and indeed there is **g** toward
24: 4 may do to him as it seems **g** to
24:17 for you have rewarded me with **g**,
24:19 may the LORD reward you with **g**
25: 3 And she was a woman of **g**
25:15 But the men were very **g** to us,
25:21 And he has repaid me evil for **g**.
25:30 my lord according to all the **g**
26:16 that you have done is not **g**.
29: 6 in with me in the army is **g**
29: 9 I know that you are as **g** in my
2 Sam 3:13 And David said, "**G**, I will
3:19 in Hebron all that seemed **g** to
4:10 thinking to have brought **g**
10:12 Be of **g** courage, and let us be
10:12 may the LORD do what is **g**
13:22 to his brother Amnon neither **g**
14:17 lord the king in discerning **g**
14:25 as much as Absalom for his **g**
15: 3 your case is **g** and right; but
15:26 let Him do to me as seems **g** to
16:12 the LORD will repay me with **g**
17: 7 Ahithophel has given is not **g**
17:14 had purposed to defeat the **g**
18:27 He is a **g** man, and comes with
18:27 man, and comes with **g** news."
18:31 There is **g** news, my lord the
19:18 and to do what he thought **g**.
19:27 Therefore do what is **g** in
19:35 Can I discern between the **g** and
19:37 and do for him what seems **g** to
19:38 I will do for him what seems **g**
24:22 and offer up whatever seems **g**
1 Ki 1:42 and bring **g** news."
2:38 to the king, "The saying is **g**.
2:42 'The word I have heard is **g**.
3: 9 that I may discern between **g**
8:36 that You may teach them the **g**
8:56 failed one word of all His **g**
8:66 and glad of heart for all the **g**
12: 7 and speak **g** words to them, then
14:13 him there is found something **g**
14:15 will uproot Israel from this **g**
21: 2 if it seems **g** to you, I will
22: 8 because he does not prophesy **g**
22:18 you he would not prophesy **g**
2 Ki 3:19 and shall cut down every **g**
3:19 and ruin every **g** piece of land
3:25 man threw a stone on every **g**
3:25 of water and cut down all the **g**
7: 9 This day is a day of **g** news,
8: 9 of every **g** thing of Damascus,
10: 5 Do what is **g** in your sight."
20: 3 and have done what was **g** in
20:19 which you have spoken is **g**!"
1 Chr 4:40 **g** pasture, and the land was
13: 2 If it seems **g** to you, and if
16:23 Proclaim the **g** news of His
16:34 for He is **g**! For His mercy
19:13 Be of **g** courage, and let us be
19:13 may the LORD do what is **g**
21:23 my lord the king do what is **g**
22:13 Be strong and of **g** courage;
28: 8 that you may possess this **g**
28:20 Be strong and of **g** courage, and
29:28 So he died in a **g** old age, full
2 Chr 5:13 saying: "For He is **g**,
6:27 that You may teach them the **g**
7: 3 saying: "For He is **g**,
7:10 and glad of heart for the **g**
10: 7 and speak **g** words to them, they
14: 2 Asa did what was **g** and right
18: 7 because he never prophesies **g**
18:17 you he would not prophesy **g**
19: 3 Nevertheless **g** things are found
19:11 the LORD will be with the **g**.
24:16 because he had done **g** in
30:18 May the **g** LORD provide
30:22 the Levites who taught the **g**
31:20 and he did what was **g** and
Ezra 3:11 to the LORD: "For He is **g**,
5:17 if it seems **g** to the king,
7: 9 according to the **g** hand of his
7:18 And whatever seems **g** to you and
8:18 by the **g** hand of our God upon
8:22 God is upon all those for **g**
9:12 may be strong and eat the **g** of
10: 4 Be of **g** courage, and do it."
Neh 2: 8 them to me according to the **g**
2:18 hand of my God which had been **g**
2:18 they set their hands to this **g**
5: 9 "What you are doing is not **g**.
5:19 Remember me, my God, for **g**,
6:19 Also they reported his **g** deeds
9:13 **G** statutes and commandments.
9:20 You also gave Your **g** Spirit to
9:35 Or in the many **g** things that
13:14 and do not wipe out my **g** deeds
13:31 Remember me, O my God, for **g**!
Esth 3:11 to do with them as seems **g** to
7: 9 who spoke **g** on the king's
10: 3 seeking the **g** of his people and

Job 2:10 Shall we indeed accept **g** from
7: 7 My eye will never again see **g**.
9:25 They flee away, they see no **g**.
10: 3 Does it seem **g** to You that
15: 3 with which he can do no **g**?
22:18 He filled their houses with **g**
22:21 Thereby **g** will come to you.
24:21 And does no **g** for the widow.
30:26 But when I looked for **g**,
34: 4 know among ourselves what is **g**.
Ps 4: 6 say, "Who will show us any **g**?
14: 1 There is none who does **g**.
14: 3 There is none who does **g**,
16: 6 I have a **g** inheritance.
25: 8 **G** and upright is the LORD
27:14 Be of **g** courage, And He shall
31:24 Be of **g** courage, And He shall
34: 8 and see that the LORD is **g**;
34:10 the LORD shall not lack any **g**
34:12 many days, that he may see **g**?
34:14 Depart from evil and do **g**;
35:12 They reward me evil for **g**,
36: 3 ceased to be wise and to do **g**.
36: 4 in a way that is not **g**;
37: 3 Trust in the LORD, and do **g**;
37:23 The steps of a **g** man are
37:27 Depart from evil, and do **g**;
38:20 also who render evil for **g**,
38:20 because I follow what is **g**.
39: 2 I held my peace even from **g**;
40: 9 I have proclaimed the **g** news of
45: 1 heart is overflowing with a **g**
51:18 Do **g** in Your good pleasure to
51:18 Do good in Your **g** pleasure to
52: 3 You love evil more than **g**,
52: 9 on Your name, for it is **g**.
53: 1 There is none who does **g**.
53: 3 There is none who does **g**,
54: 6 name, O LORD, for it is **g**.
69:16 for Your lovingkindness is **g**;
73: 1 Truly God is **g** to Israel,
73:28 But it is **g** for me to draw
84:11 No **g** thing will He withhold
85:12 the LORD will give what is **g**;
86: 5 For You, Lord, are **g**,
86:17 Show me a sign for **g**,
92: 1 It is **g** to give thanks to the
96: 2 Proclaim the **g** news of His
100: 5 For the LORD is **g**; His mercy
103: 5 satisfies your mouth with **g**
104:28 hand, they are filled with **g**.
106: 1 for He is **g**! For His mercy
107: 1 for He is **g**! For His mercy
109: 5 have rewarded me evil for **g**,
109:21 Because Your mercy is **g**,
111:10 A **g** understanding have all
112: 5 A **g** man deals graciously and
118: 1 for He is **g**! For His mercy
118:29 for He is **g**! For His mercy
119:39 For Your judgments are **g**.
119:66 Teach me **g** judgment and
119:68 You are **g**, and do good;
119:68 You are good, and do **g**;
119:71 It is **g** for me that I have
119:122 surety for Your servant for **g**;
122: 9 our God I will seek your **g**.
125: 4 Do **g**, O LORD, to those who
125: 4 O LORD, to those who are **g**,
128: 5 And may you see the **g** of
133: 1 how **g** and how pleasant it is
135: 3 the LORD, for the LORD is **g**;
136: 1 for He is **g**! For His mercy
143:10 are my God; Your Spirit is **g**.
145: 9 The LORD is **g** to all,
147: 1 the LORD! For it is **g** to
Prov 2: 9 Equity and every **g** path.
3:27 Do not withhold **g** from those
4: 2 For I give you **g** doctrine:
11:17 The merciful man does **g** for his
11:23 of the righteous is only **g**,
11:27 He who earnestly seeks **g** finds
12: 2 A **g** man obtains favor from the
12:14 A man will be satisifed with **g**
12:25 But a **g** word makes it glad.
13:15 **G** understanding gains favor,
13:21 **g** shall be repaid.
13:22 A **g** man leaves an inheritance
14:14 But a **g** man will be
14:19 The evil will bow before the **g**,
14:22 belong to those who devise **g**.
15: 3 watch on the evil and the **g**.
15:23 due season, how **g** it is!
15:30 And a **g** report makes the
16:20 the word wisely will find **g**,
16:29 him in a way that is not **g**.
17:13 Whoever rewards evil for **g**,
17:20 a deceitful heart finds no **g**,
17:22 A merry heart does **g**,
17:26 punish the righteous is not **g**,
18: 5 It is not **g** to show
18:22 who finds a wife finds a **g**
19: 2 Also it is not **g** for a soul
19: 8 keeps understanding will find **g**.
20:14 It is **g** for nothing," cries
20:23 dishonest scales are not **g**.
22: 1 A **g** name is to be chosen
24:13 eat honey because it is **g**,
24:23 It is not **g** to show
24:25 And a **g** blessing will come
25:25 So is **g** news from a far
25:27 It is not **g** to eat much
28:10 the blameless will inherit **g**.

28:21 To show partiality is not **g**,
31:12 She does him **g** and not evil
31:18 that her merchandise is **g**,
Eccl 2: 3 till I might see what was **g**
2:24 that his soul should enjoy **g**
2:26 and joy to a man who is **g** in
2:26 he may give to him who is **g**
3:12 and to do **g** in their lives,
3:13 eat and drink and enjoy the **g**
4: 8 I toil and deprive myself of **g**?
4: 9 Because they have a **g** reward
5:18 It is **g** and fitting for one
5:18 and to enjoy the **g** of all his
6:12 For who knows what is **g** for man
7: 1 A **g** name is better than
7:11 Wisdom is **g** with an
7:18 It is **g** that you grasp this,
7:20 a just man on earth who does **g**
9: 2 and the wicked; To the **g**,
9: 2 not sacrifice. As is the **g**,
9:18 But one sinner destroys much **g**.
11: 6 whether both alike will be **g**.
12:14 Whether **g** or evil.
Song 1: 3 of the fragrance of your **g**
2:13 the tender grapes Give a **g**
Isa 1:17 Learn to do **g**; Seek justice,
1:19 You shall eat the **g** of the
5: 2 expected it to bring forth **g**
5: 4 expected it to bring forth **g**
5:20 Woe to those who call evil **g**,
5:20 and **g** evil; Who put darkness
7:15 the evil and choose the **g**.
7:16 the evil and choose the **g**,
38: 3 and have done what is **g** in
39: 8 which you have spoken is **g**!"
40: 9 You who bring **g** tidings, Get
40: 9 You who bring **g** tidings, Lift
41: 6 brother, "Be of **g** courage!"
41:23 do **g** or do evil, That we may
41:27 to Jerusalem one who brings **g**
52: 7 the feet of him who brings **g**
52: 7 Who brings glad tidings of **g**
55: 2 to Me, and eat what is **g**,
61: 1 has anointed Me To preach **g**
65: 2 walk in a way that is not **g**,
Jer 4:22 But to do **g** they have no
5:25 And your sins have withheld **g**
6:16 where the **g** way is, And walk
8:15 but no **g** came; And for a time
10: 5 do evil, Nor can they do any **g**.
11:16 Lovely and of **G** Fruit.
13:23 Then may you also do **g** who
14:11 for this people, for their **g**.
14:19 for peace, but there was no **g**;
17: 6 And shall not see when **g**
18: 4 as it seemed **g** to the potter to
18:10 I will relent concerning the **g**
18:11 your ways and your doings **g**.
18:20 Shall evil be repaid for **g**?
18:20 I stood before You To speak **g**
21:10 for adversity and not for **g**,
24: 2 One basket had very **g** figs,
24: 3 the **g** figs, very good; and the
24: 3 "Figs, the good figs, very **g**;
24: 5 Like these **g** figs, so will I
24: 5 of this place for their own **g**,
24: 6 will set My eyes on them for **g**,
26:14 do with me as seems **g** and
29:10 will visit you and perform My **g**
29:32 nor shall he see the **g** that I
32:39 for the **g** of them and their
32:40 not turn away from doing them **g**;
32:41 rejoice over them to do them **g**,
32:42 I will bring on them all the **g**
33: 9 who shall hear all the **g** that I
33:11 of hosts, For the LORD is **g**,
33:14 that I will perform that **g** thing
39:16 for adversity and not for **g**,
40: 4 If it seems **g** to you to come
40: 4 wherever it seems **g** and
44:27 for adversity and not for **g**.
Lam 3:25 The LORD is **g** to those who
3:26 It is **g** that one should hope
3:27 It is **g** for a man to bear
Ezek 17: 8 It was planted in **g** soil by
18:18 And did what is not **g** among
20:25 to statutes that were not **g**,
24: 4 Every **g** piece, The thigh and
34:14 I will feed them in **g** pasture,
34:14 they shall lie down in a **g**
34:18 for you to have eaten up the **g**
36:31 and your deeds that were not **g**;
Dan 3:15 **g**! But if you do not worship,
4: 2 I thought it **g** to declare the
Hos 4:13 Because their shade is **g**.
8: 3 Israel has rejected the **g**;
Am 5:14 Seek **g** and not evil, That you
5:15 Hate evil, love **g**;
5:18 day of the LORD! For what **g**
9: 4 on them for harm and not for **g**.
Mic 1:12 of Maroth pined for **g**,
2: 7 Do not My words do **g** To him
3: 2 You who hate **g** and love evil;
6: 8 shown you, O man, what is **g**;
Nah 1: 7 The LORD is **g**,
1:15 The feet of him who brings **g**
Zeph 1:12 'The LORD will not do **g**,
Zech 1:13 with **g** and comforting words.
8:15 days I am determined to do **g**
Mal 2:17 Everyone who does evil Is **g** in
Mt 3:10 tree which does not bear **g**
5:13 It is then **g** for nothing but to

5:16 that they may see your **g** works
5:44 do **g** to those who hate you, and
5:45 rise on the evil and on the **g**,
6:22 If therefore your eye is **g**,
7:11 know how to give **g** gifts to
7:11 Father who is in heaven give **g**
7:17 every **g** tree bears good fruit,
7:17 every good tree bears **g** fruit,
7:18 A **g** tree cannot bear bad fruit,
7:18 nor can a bad tree bear **g**
7:19 tree that does not bear **g**
8:30 Now a **g** way off from them there
9: 2 be of **g** cheer; your sins are
9:22 'Be of **g** cheer, daughter;
11:26 for so it seemed **g** in Your
12:12 Therefore it is lawful to do **g**
12:33 Either make the tree **g** and its
12:33 the tree good and its fruit **g**,
12:34 speak **g** things? For out of the
12:35 A **g** man out of the good treasure
12:35 A good man out of the **g** treasure
12:35 of his heart brings forth **g**
13: 8 But others fell on **g** ground and
13:23 he who received seed on the **g**
13:24 is like a man who sowed **g** seed
13:27 did you not sow **g** seed in your
13:37 He who sows the **g** seed is the
13:38 the **g** seeds are the sons of the
13:48 sat down and gathered the **g**
14:27 Be of **g** cheer! It is I; do not
15:26 It is not **g** to take the
17: 4 it is **g** for us to be here;
19:16 **G** Teacher, what good thing shall
19:16 what **g** thing shall I do that I
19:17 to him, "Why do you call Me **g**?
19:17 No one is **g** but One, that
20:15 is your eye evil because I am **g**?
22:10 whom they found, both bad and **g**.
25:21 **g** and faithful servant;
25:23 **g** and faithful servant;
26:10 For she has done a **g** work for
26:24 betrayed! It would have been **g**
Mk 3: 4 lawful on the Sabbath to do **g**
4: 8 But other seed fell on **g** ground
4:20 these are the ones sown on **g**
6:50 Be of **g** cheer! It is I; do not
7:27 for it is not **g** to take the
9: 5 it is **g** for us to be here; and
9:50 'Salt is **g**, but if the salt
10:17 **G** Teacher, what shall I do that
10:18 to him, "Why do you call Me **g**?
10:18 No one is **g** but One, that
10:49 Be of **g** cheer. Rise, He is
14: 6 She has done a **g** work for Me.
14: 7 you wish you may do them **g**;
14:21 It would have been **g** for
Lk 1: 3 it seemed **g** to me also, having
1:53 has filled the hungry with **g**
2:10 I bring you **g** tidings of great
3: 9 tree which does not bear **g**
6: 9 lawful on the Sabbath to do **g**
6:27 do **g** to those who hate you,
6:33 And if you do **g** to those who do
6:33 you do good to those who do **g**
6:35 "But love your enemies, do **g**,
6:38 **g** measure, pressed down, shaken
6:43 For a **g** tree does not bear bad
6:43 nor does a bad tree bear **g**
6:45 A **g** man out of the good treasure
6:45 A good man out of the **g** treasure
6:45 of his heart brings forth **g**;
8: 8 But others fell on **g** ground,
8:15 the ones that fell on the **g**
8:15 the word with a noble and **g**
8:48 be of **g** cheer; your faith has
9:33 it is **g** for us to be here;
10:21 for so it seemed **g** in Your
10:42 and Mary has chosen that **g**
11:13 know how to give **g** gifts to
11:34 Therefore, when your eye is **g**,
12:32 for it is your Father's **g**
14:34 Salt is **g**; but if the
16:25 lifetime you received your **g**
18:18 **G** Teacher, what shall I do to
18:19 to him, "Why do you call Me **g**?
18:19 No one is **g** but One, that
19:17 **g** servant; because you were
23:50 member, a **g** and just man.
Jn 1:46 Can anything **g** come out of
2:10 at the beginning sets out the **g**
2:10 You have kept the **g** wine until
5:29 forth—those who have done **g**,
7:12 He is **g**"; others said, "No, on
10:11 I am the **g** shepherd. The good
10:11 The **g** shepherd gives His life
10:14 I am the **g** shepherd; and I know
10:32 Many **g** works I have shown you
10:33 For a **g** work we do not stone
16:33 but be of **g** cheer, I have
Acts 4: 9 we this day are judged for a **g**
6: 3 from among you seven men of **g**
9:36 This woman was full of **g** works
10:22 one who fears God and has a **g**
10:38 who went about doing **g** and
11:24 For he was a **g** man, full of the
14:17 witness, in that He did **g**,
15: 7 you know that a **g** while ago God
15:25 it seemed **g** to us, being
15:28 For it seemed **g** to the Holy
15:34 it seemed **g** to Silas to remain
18:18 So Paul still remained a **g**
22:12 having a **g** testimony with all
23: 1 I have lived in all **g**
23:11 Be of **g** cheer, Paul; for as you
Rom 2: 7 patient continuance in doing **g**
2:10 to everyone who works what is **g**,
3: 8 Let us do evil that **g** may
3:12 There is none who does **g**,
5: 7 yet perhaps for a **g** man someone
7:12 commandment holy and just and **g**.
7:13 Has then what is **g** become death
7:13 death in me through what is **g**,
7:16 with the law that it is **g**.
7:18 in my flesh) nothing **g** dwells;
7:18 but how to perform what is **g**
7:19 For the **g** that I will to do,
7:21 me, the one who wills to do **g**.
8:28 all things work together for **g**
9:11 nor having done any **g** or evil,
10:15 bring glad tidings of **g**
12: 2 you may prove what is that **g**
12: 9 is evil. Cling to what is **g**.
12:17 Have regard for **g** things in the
12:21 evil, but overcome evil with **g**.
13: 3 rulers are not a terror to **g**
13: 3 of the authority? Do what is **g**,
13: 4 is God's minister to you for **g**.
14:16 Therefore do not let your **g** be
14:21 It is **g** neither to eat meat
15: 2 please his neighbor for his **g**,
16:19 you to be wise in what is **g**,
1 Cor 5: 6 Your glorying is not **g**.
7: 1 It is **g** for a man not to
7: 8 It is **g** for them if they remain
7:26 therefore that this is **g**
7:26 that it is **g** for a man to
15:33 Evil company corrupts **g**
2 Cor 5:10 has done, whether **g** or bad.
6: 8 by evil report and **g** report;
9: 8 have an abundance for every **g**
13:11 Be of **g** comfort, be of one
Gal 4:17 court you, but for no **g**;
4:18 But it is **g** to be zealous in a
4:18 it is good to be zealous in a **g**
6: 6 taught the word share in all **g**
6: 9 us not grow weary while doing **g**,
6:10 let us do **g** to all, especially
6:12 As many as desire to make a **g**
Eph 1: 5 according to the **g** pleasure of
1: 9 according to His **g** pleasure
2:10 created in Christ Jesus for **g**
4:28 with his hands what is **g**,
4:29 but what is **g** for necessary
6: 8 knowing that whatever **g** anyone
Phil 1: 6 that He who has begun a **g** work
1:15 and some also from **g** will:
2:13 to will and to do for His **g**
4: 8 whatever things are of **g**
Col 1:10 being fruitful in every **g** work
2: 5 rejoicing to see your **g** order
1 Th 3: 1 we thought it **g** to be left in
3: 6 and brought us **g** news of your
3: 6 and that you always have **g**
5:15 but always pursue what is **g**
5:21 all things; hold fast what is **g**.
2 Th 1:11 and fulfill all the **g** pleasure
2:16 everlasting consolation and **g**
2:17 and establish you in every **g**
3:13 do not grow weary in doing **g**.
1 Tim 1: 5 from a **g** conscience, and from
1: 8 But we know that the law is **g**
1:18 that by them you may wage the **g**
1:19 having faith and a **g** conscience,
2: 3 For this is **g** and acceptable in
2:10 godliness, with **g** works.
3: 1 he desires a **g** work.
3: 2 of **g** behavior, hospitable, able
3: 7 Moreover he must have a **g**
3:13 obtain for themselves a **g**
4: 4 For every creature of God is **g**,
4: 6 you will be a **g** minister of
4: 6 the words of faith and of the **g**
5: 4 for this is **g** and acceptable
5:10 well reported for **g** works:
5:10 has diligently followed every **g**
5:25 the **g** works of some are
6:12 Fight the **g** fight of faith, lay
6:12 called and have confessed the **g**
6:13 Jesus who witnessed the **g**
6:18 Let them do **g**, that they be
6:18 that they be rich in **g** works,
6:19 storing up for themselves a **g**
2 Tim 1:14 That **g** thing which was committed
2: 3 must endure hardship as a **g**
2:21 prepared for every **g** work.
3: 3 brutal, despisers of **g**,
3:17 equipped for every **g** work.
4: 7 I have fought the **g** fight,
Titus 1: 8 a lover of what is **g**,
1:16 and disqualified for every **g**
2: 3 teachers of **g** things—
2: 5 discreet, chaste, homemakers, **g**,
2: 7 to be a pattern of **g** works;
2:10 but showing all **g** fidelity,
2:14 zealous for **g** works.
3: 1 to be ready for every **g** work,
3: 8 be careful to maintain **g** works.
3: 8 These things are **g** and
3:14 also learn to maintain **g** works,
Phm 1: 6 the acknowledgment of every **g**
1:14 that your **g** deed might not be
Heb 5:14 exercised to discern both **g**
6: 5 and have tasted the **g** word of
9:11 came as High Priest of the **g**
10: 1 having a shadow of the **g** things
10:24 in order to stir up love and **g**
11: 2 by it the elders obtained a **g**
11:12 and him as **g** as dead, were born
11:39 having obtained a **g** testimony
13: 9 For it is **g** that the heart be
13:16 But do not forget to do **g** and to
13:18 are confident that we have a **g**
13:21 make you complete in every **g**
Jas 1:17 Every **g** gift and every perfect
2: 3 You sit here in a **g** place," and
3:13 Let him show by **g** conduct that
3:17 full of mercy and **g** fruits,
4:17 to him who knows to do **g** and
1 Pe 2:12 by your **g** works which they
2:14 the praise of those who do **g**.
2:15 that by doing **g** you may put to
2:18 not only to the **g** and gentle,
2:20 But when you do **g** and suffer,
3: 6 daughters you are if you do **g**
3:10 love life And see **g**
3:11 away from evil and do **g**;
3:13 become followers of what is **g**?
3:16 having a **g** conscience, that when
3:16 those who revile your **g** conduct
3:17 to suffer for doing **g** than for
3:21 but the answer of a **g**
4:10 as **g** stewards of the manifold
4:19 their souls to Him in doing **g**,
3 Jn 11 what is evil, but what is **g**.
11 He who does **g** is of God, but he
12 Demetrius has a **g** testimony

GOODLIER, GOODLIEST, GOODLY (KJV) See BEAUTIFUL, FINEST, HANDSOME, LOVELIEST, PLEASANT

GOOD-LOOKING (4/4) GOOD

1 Sam 16:12 ruddy, with bright eyes, and **g**.
17:42 was only a youth, ruddy and **g**.
1 Ki 1: 6 done so?" He was also very **g**.
Dan 1: 4 there was no blemish, but **g**,

GOODMAN (KJV) See HUSBAND, LANDOWNER, MASTER

GOODNESS (45/42) GOOD

Ex 33:19 I will make all My **g** pass before
34: 6 and abounding in **g** and truth,
2 Sam 7:28 and You have promised this **g** to
1 Chr 17:26 and have promised this **g** to
2 Chr 6:41 let Your saints rejoice in **g**.
32:32 the acts of Hezekiah, and his **g**,
35:26 of the acts of Josiah and his **g**,
Neh 9:25 themselves in Your great **g**.
Ps 16: 2 My **g** is nothing apart from
21: 3 him with the blessings of **g**;
23: 6 Surely **g** and mercy shall follow
25: 7 For Your **g**' sake, O LORD.
27:13 That I would see the **g** of the
31:19 Oh, how great is Your **g**,
33: 5 The earth is full of the **g** of
52: 1 The **g** of God endures
65: 4 shall be satisfied with the **g**
65:11 You crown the year with Your **g**,
68:10 provided from Your **g** for the
107: 8 thanks to the LORD for His **g**,
107: 9 fills the hungry soul with **g**.
107:15 thanks to the LORD for His **g**,
107:21 thanks to the LORD for His **g**,
107:31 thanks to the LORD for His **g**,
145: 7 the memory of Your great **g**,
Prov 2:20 you may walk in the way of **g**,
20: 6 will proclaim each his own **g**,
Eccl 6: 3 soul is not satisfied with **g**,
6: 6 years twice—but has not seen **g**.
Isa 63: 7 And the great **g** toward the
Jer 2: 7 To eat its fruit and its **g**.
31:12 Streaming to the **g** of the
31:14 shall be satisfied with My **g**,
33: 9 fear and tremble for all the **g**
Hos 3: 5 shall fear the LORD and His **g**
Zech 9:17 For how great is its **g** And how
Rom 2: 4 you despise the riches of His **g**,
2: 4 not knowing that the **g** of God
11:22 Therefore consider the **g** and
11:22 severity; but toward you, **g**,
11:22 if you continue in His **g**.
15:14 that you also are full of **g**,
Gal 5:22 longsuffering, kindness, **g**,
Eph 5: 9 of the Spirit is in all **g**,
2 Th 1:11 all the good pleasure of His **g**

GOODS (48/46)

Gen 14:11 Then they took all the **g** of
14:12 who dwelt in Sodom, and his **g**,
14:16 So he brought back all the **g**,
14:16 back his brother Lot and his **g**,
14:21 and take the **g** for yourself."
24:10 for all his master's **g** were
36: 6 and all his **g** which he had
40:17 were all kinds of baked **g** for
45:20 not be concerned about your **g**,
46: 6 their livestock and their **g**,
Ex 22: 8 his hand into his neighbor's **g**.
22:11 his hand into his neighbor's **g**;

Num 16:32 with Korah, with all their **g**.
31: 9 their flocks, and all their **g**.
Deut 28:11 will grant you plenty of **g**,
Judg 18:21 and the **g** in front of them.
Ezra 1: 4 with **g** and livestock, besides
1: 6 with **g** and livestock, and with
7:26 or confiscation of **g**,
Neh 9:25 possessed houses full of all **g**,
13: 8 I threw all the household **g** of
13:16 in fish and all kinds of **g**,
Job 20:28 And his **g** will flow away in
Eccl 5:11 When **g** increase, They increase
Ezek 27:12 because of your many luxury **g**.
27:12 iron, tin, and lead for your **g**.
27:16 because of the abundance of **g**
27:18 because of the abundance of **g**
27:33 earth With your many luxury **g**
38:12 have acquired livestock and **g**,
38:13 to take away livestock and **g**,
Zeph 1:13 Therefore their **g** shall become
Mt 12:29 man's house and plunder his **g**,
24:47 make him ruler over all his **g**.
25:14 servants and delivered his **g**
Mk 3:27 man's house and plunder his **g**,
Lk 6:30 from him who takes away your **g**
11:21 his **g** are in peace.
12:18 store all my crops and my **g**.
12:19 you have many **g** laid up for
15:12 give me the portion of **g** that
16: 1 that this man was wasting his **g**.
17:31 and his **g** are in the house,
19: 8 I give half of my **g** to the
Acts 2:45 sold their possessions and **g**,
1 Cor 13: 3 And though I bestow all my **g** to
Heb 10:34 the plundering of your **g**,
1 Jn 3:17 But whoever has this world's **g**,

GOODWILL (4/4)

Dan 1: 9 Daniel into the favor and **g** of
Mal 2:13 Nor receive it with **g** from
Lk 2:14 earth peace, **g** toward men!"
Eph 6: 7 with **g** doing service, as to the

GOPHERWOOD (1/1)

Gen 6:14 "Make yourself an ark of **g**;

GORE (2/2)

1 Ki 22:11 With these you shall **g** the
2 Chr 18:10 With these you shall **g** the

GORED (2/1)

Ex 21:31 Whether it has **g** a son or gored
21:31 it has gored a son or **g** a

GORES (2/2)

Ex 21:28 If an ox **g** a man or a woman to
21:32 If the ox **g** a male or female

GORGEOUS (1/1) GORGEOUSLY

Lk 23:11 arrayed Him in a **g** robe,

GORGEOUSLY (2/2) GORGEOUS

Ezek 23:12 and rulers, Clothed most **g**,
Lk 7:25 Indeed those who are **g**

GOSHEN (15/14) EGYPT

Gen 45:10 shall dwell in the land of **G**,
46:28 out before him the way to **G**.
46:28 And they came to the land of **G**.
46:29 his chariot and went up to **G**
46:34 you may dwell in the land of **G**;
47: 1 they are in the land of **G**.
47: 4 servants dwell in the land of **G**.
47: 6 let them dwell in the land of **G**.
47:27 of Egypt, in the country of **G**;
50: 8 they left in the land of **G**.
Ex 8:22 I will set apart the land of **G**,
9:26 Only in the land of **G**,
Josh 10:41 Gaza, and all the country of **G**,
11:16 the South, all the land of **G**,
15:51 **G**, Holon, and Giloh:

GOSPEL (100/94) GOSPEL'S

Mt 4:23 preaching the **g** of the kingdom,
9:35 preaching the **g** of the kingdom,
11: 5 up and the poor have the **g**
24:14 And this **g** of the kingdom will
26:13 wherever this **g** is preached in
Mk 1: 1 The beginning of the **g** of Jesus
1:14 preaching the **g** of the kingdom
1:15 Repent, and believe in the **g**.
13:10 And the **g** must first be preached
14: 9 wherever this **g** is preached in
16:15 all the world and preach the **g**
Lk 4:18 Me To preach the **g** to
7:22 the poor have the **g** preached
9: 6 preaching the **g** and healing
20: 1 the temple and preached the **g**,
Acts 8:25 preaching the **g** in many
14: 7 And they were preaching the **g**
14:21 when they had preached the **g**
15: 7 should hear the word of the **g**
16:10 had called us to preach the **g**
20:24 to testify to the **g** of the
Rom 1: 1 separated to the **g** of God
1: 9 I serve with my spirit in the **g**
1:15 I am ready to preach the **g** to
1:16 For I am not ashamed of the **g**
2:16 Jesus Christ, according to my **g**.
10:15 of those who preach the **g**
10:16 they have not all obeyed the **g**.
11:28 Concerning the **g** they are
15:16 ministering the **g** of God, that
15:19 I have fully preached the **g** of
15:20 made it my aim to preach the **g**,
15:29 of the blessing of the **g** of
16:25 you according to my **g** and the
1 Cor 1:17 to baptize, but to preach the **g**,
4:15 have begotten you through the **g**.
9:12 things lest we hinder the **g** of
9:14 that those who preach the **g**
9:14 gospel should live from the **g**.
9:16 For if I preach the **g**,
9:16 is me if I do not preach the **g**!
9:18 That when I preach the **g**,
9:18 I may present the **g** of Christ
9:18 not abuse my authority in the **g**.
15: 1 I declare to you the **g** which I
2 Cor 2:12 to Troas to preach Christ's **g**,
4: 3 But even if our **g** is veiled, it
4: 4 lest the light of the **g** of the
8:18 whose praise is in the **g**
9:13 of your confession to the **g** of
10:14 to you that we came with the **g**
10:16 to preach the **g** in the regions
11: 4 or a different **g** which you have
11: 7 because I preached the **g** of God
Gal 1: 6 of Christ, to a different **g**,
1: 7 you and want to pervert the **g**
1: 8 preach any other **g** to you than
1: 9 if anyone preaches any other **g**
1:11 that the **g** which was preached
2: 2 and communicated to them that **g**
2: 5 that the truth of the **g** might
2: 7 when they saw that the **g** for
2: 7 as the **g** for the circumcised
2:14 about the truth of the **g**,
3: 8 preached the **g** to Abraham
4:13 infirmity I preached the **g** to
Eph 1:13 the **g** of your salvation;
3: 6 promise in Christ through the **g**,
6:15 with the preparation of the **g**
6:19 make known the mystery of the **g**,
Phil 1: 5 for your fellowship in the **g**
1: 7 and confirmation of the **g**,
1:12 for the furtherance of the **g**,
1:17 for the defense of the **g**.
1:27 conduct be worthy of the **g** of
1:27 together for the faith of the **g**,
2:22 he served with me in the **g**.
4: 3 who labored with me in the **g**,
4:15 that in the beginning of the **g**,
Col 1: 5 the word of the truth of the **g**,
1:23 away from the hope of the **g**
1 Th 1: 5 For our **g** did not come to you in
2: 2 our God to speak to you the **g**
2: 4 God to be entrusted with the **g**,
2: 8 to impart to you not only the **g**
2: 9 we preached to you the **g** of
3: 2 our fellow laborer in the **g** of
2 Th 1: 8 on those who do not obey the **g**
2:14 to which He called you by our **g**,
1 Tim 1:11 according to the glorious **g** of
2 Tim 1: 8 me in the sufferings for the **g**
1:10 to light through the **g**,
2: 8 from the dead according to my **g**,
Phm 1:13 to me in my chains for the **g**.
Heb 4: 2 For indeed the **g** was preached to
1 Pe 1:12 those who have preached the **g**
1:25 is the word which by the **g** was
4: 6 For this reason the **g** was
4:17 of those who do not obey the **g**
Rev 14: 6 having the everlasting **g** to

GOSPEL'S (3/3) GOSPEL

Mk 8:35 his life for My sake and the **g**
10:29 or lands, for My sake and the **g**,
1 Cor 9:23 Now this I do for the **g** sake,

GOSSIPS (1/1)

1 Tim 5:13 and not only idle but also **g**

GOT (26/26) GET

Gen 27:14 And he went and **g** them and
Num 16:27 So they **g** away from around the
Judg 7: 6 all the rest of the people **g**
19:28 and the man **g** up and went to
1 Sam 24: 7 And Saul **g** up from the cave and
26:12 and they **g** away; and no man saw
2 Sam 13:29 and each one **g** on his mule and
1 Ki 20:12 And they **g** ready to attack
21:16 that Ahab **g** up and went down to
2 Ki 5:21 he **g** down from the chariot to
Jer 13: 2 So I **g** a sash according to the
Mt 8:23 Now when He **g** into a boat, His
9: 1 So He **g** into a boat, crossed
13: 2 so that He **g** into a boat and
14:32 And when they **g** into the boat,
15:39 **g** into the boat, and came to
Mk 4: 1 so that He **g** into a boat and
5:18 And when He **g** into the boat, he
8:10 immediately **g** into the boat with
Lk 5: 3 Then He **g** into one of the boats,
8:22 that He **g** into a boat with His
8:37 And He **g** into the boat and
Jn 4:52 of them the hour when he **g**
6:17 **g** into the boat, and went over
6:24 they also **g** into boats and came
21: 3 They went out and immediately **g**

GOURD (KJV) See PLANT

GOURDS (1/1)

2 Ki 4:39 from it a lapful of wild **g**,

GOVERN (2/2)

Job 34:17 Should one who hates justice **g**?
Ps 67: 4 And **g** the nations on earth.

GOVERNED (1/1)

1 Chr 26: 6 his son were sons born who **g**

GOVERNING (3/3) GOVERNMENT, GOVERNOR

1 Chr 23:31 according to the ordinance **g**
Lk 2: 2 place while Quirinius was **g**
Rom 13: 1 every soul be subject to the **g**

GOVERNMENT (2/2) GOVERNING, GOVERNOR

Isa 9: 6 And the **g** will be upon His
9: 7 Of the increase of His **g** and

GOVERNMENTS (KJV) See ADMINISTRATIONS

GOVERNOR (53/52) GOVERNOR'S, GOVERNORS

Gen 42: 6 Now Joseph was **g** over the
45:26 and he is **g** over all the land
1 Ki 4:19 He was the only **g** who was in
22:26 and return him to Amon the **g** of
2 Ki 23: 8 of the Gate of Joshua the **g** of
25:22 **g** over the people who remained
25:23 of Babylon had made Gedaliah **g**,
2 Chr 18:25 and return him to Amon the **g** of
34: 8 Maaseiah the **g** of the city, and
Ezra 2:63 And the **g** said to them that they
5: 3 the same time Tattenai the **g**
5: 6 The **g** of the region beyond
5:14 Sheshbazzar, whom he had made **g**.
6: 6 **g** of the region beyond the
6: 7 let the **g** of the Jews and the
6:13 **g** of the region beyond the
Neh 3: 7 the residence of the **g** of
5:14 I was appointed to be their **g**
7:65 And the **g** said to them that they
7:70 The **g** gave to the treasury one
8: 9 And Nehemiah, who was the **g**,
10: 1 document were: Nehemiah the **g**,
12:26 in the days of Nehemiah the **g**,
Jer 20: 1 priest who was also chief **g**
30:21 And their **g** shall come from
40: 5 the king of Babylon has made **g**
40: 7 Gedaliah the son of Ahikam **g**
41: 2 the king of Babylon had made **g**
41:18 the king of Babylon had made **g**
Hag 1: 1 **g** of Judah, and to Joshua the
1:14 **g** of Judah, and the spirit of
2: 2 **g** of Judah, and to Joshua the
2:21 **g** of Judah, saying: 'I will
Mal 1: 8 Offer it then to your **g**!
Mt 27: 2 Him to Pontius Pilate the **g**.
27:11 Now Jesus stood before the **g**.
27:11 And the **g** asked Him, saying,
27:14 so that the **g** marveled greatly.
27:15 Now at the feast the **g** was
27:21 The **g** answered and said to them,
27:23 Then the **g** said, "Why, what
27:27 Then the soldiers of the **g** took
Lk 3: 1 Pontius Pilate being **g** of
20:20 and the authority of the **g**.
Acts 7:10 and he made him **g** over Egypt
23:24 him safely to Felix the **g**.
23:26 to the most excellent **g** Felix:
23:33 delivered the letter to the **g**,
23:34 And when the **g** had read it, he
24: 1 These gave evidence to the **g**
24:10 after the **g** had nodded to him
26:30 as well as the **g** and Bernice
2 Cor 11:32 In Damascus the **g**,

GOVERNOR'S (3/3) GOVERNOR

Neh 5:14 brothers ate the **g** provisions.
5:18 not demand the **g** provisions,
Mt 28:14 And if this comes to the **g** ears,

GOVERNORS (28/28) GOVERNOR

1 Ki 4: 7 And Solomon had twelve **g** over
4:27 And these **g**, each man in
10:15 and from the **g** of the country.
2 Chr 9:14 all the kings of Arabia and **g**
23:20 the **g** of the people, and all
Ezra 8:36 to the king's satraps and the **g**
Neh 2: 7 be given to me for the **g** of
2: 9 Then I went to the **g** in the
5:15 But the former **g** who were

Esth 3:12 to the ***g*** who were over each
8: 9 to the Jews, the satraps, the ***g***,
9: 3 provinces, the satraps, the ***g***,
Jer 51:23 you I will break in pieces ***g***
51:28 Its ***g*** and all its rulers,
51:57 princes and wise men, Her ***g***,
Ezek 23:23 ***G*** and rulers, Captains and
Dan 3: 2 the administrators, the ***g***,
3: 3 the administrators, the ***g***,
3:27 the satraps, administrators, ***g***,
6: 2 and over these, three ***g***,
6: 3 himself above the ***g*** and
6: 4 So the ***g*** and satraps sought to
6: 6 So these ***g*** and satraps thronged
6: 7 All the ***g*** of the kingdom, the
Zech 12: 5 And the ***g*** of Judah shall say in
12: 6 In that day I will make the ***g*** of
Mt 10:18 You will be brought before ***g*** and
1 Pe 2:14 or to ***g***, as to those who are

GOVERNS (1/1)

Lk 22:26 and he who ***g*** as he who serves.

GOZAN (5/5)

2 Ki 17: 6 by the Habor, the River of ***G***,
18:11 by the Habor, the River of ***G***,
19:12 ***G*** and Haran and Rezeph, and the
1 Chr 5:26 and the river of ***G*** to this day.
Isa 37:12 ***G*** and Haran and Rezeph, and the

GRACE (148/137) GRACEFUL, GRACIOUS

Gen 6: 8 But Noah found ***g*** in the eyes of
Ex 33:12 and you have also found ***g*** in My
33:13 if I have found ***g*** in Your
33:13 know You and that I may find ***g***
33:16 Your people and I have found ***g***
33:17 for you have found ***g*** in My
34: 9 If now I have found ***g*** in Your
Ezra 9: 8 And now for a little while ***g*** has
Esth 2:17 and she obtained ***g*** and favor in
Ps 45: 2 ***G*** is poured upon Your lips;
84:11 The LORD will give ***g*** and
Prov 3:22 be life to your soul And ***g*** to
3:34 But gives ***g*** to the humble.
4: 9 on your head an ornament of ***g***;
22:11 purity of heart And has ***g***
Isa 26:10 Let ***g*** be shown to the wicked,
Jer 31: 2 survived the sword Found ***g*** in
Zech 4: 7 capstone With shouts of "***G***,
4: 7 shouts of "Grace, ***g*** to it!" '"
12:10 of Jerusalem the Spirit of ***g*** and
Lk 2:40 and the ***g*** of God was upon Him.
Jn 1:14 full of ***g*** and truth.
1:16 received, and ***g*** for
1:16 all received, and grace for ***g***.
1:17 but ***g*** and truth came through
Acts 4:33 And great ***g*** was upon them all.
11:23 he came and had seen the ***g*** of
13:43 them to continue in the ***g*** of
14: 3 witness to the word of His ***g***,
14:26 had been commended to the ***g*** of
15:11 we believe that through the ***g***
15:40 by the brethren to the ***g*** of
18:27 who had believed through ***g***;
20:24 testify to the gospel of the ***g***
20:32 to God and to the word of His ***g***,
Rom 1: 5 Through Him we have received ***g***
1: 7 ***G*** to you and peace from God
3:24 being justified freely by His ***g***
4: 4 the wages are not counted as ***g***
4:16 it might be according to ***g***,
5: 2 access by faith into this ***g*** in
5:15 much more the ***g*** of God and the
5:15 of God and the gift by the ***g***
5:17 who receive abundance of ***g*** and
5:20 ***g*** abounded much more,
5:21 even so ***g*** might reign through
6: 1 we continue in sin that ***g*** may
6:14 are not under law but under ***g***.
6:15 are not under law but under ***g***?
11: 5 according to the election of ***g***.
11: 6 And if by ***g***, then it is no
11: 6 otherwise ***g*** is no longer grace.
11: 6 otherwise grace is no longer ***g***.
11: 6 is of works, it is no longer ***g***;
12: 3 through the ***g*** given to me, to
12: 6 differing according to the ***g***
15:15 because of the ***g*** given to me by
16:20 The ***g*** of our Lord Jesus Christ
16:24 The ***g*** of our Lord Jesus Christ
1 Cor 1: 3 ***G*** to you and peace from God our
1: 4 concerning you for the ***g*** of
3:10 According to the ***g*** of God which
15:10 But by the ***g*** of God I am what I
15:10 and His ***g*** toward me was not in
15:10 but the ***g*** of God which was
16:23 The ***g*** of our Lord Jesus Christ
2 Cor 1: 2 ***G*** to you and peace from God our
1:12 fleshly wisdom but by the ***g*** of
4:15 are for your sakes, that ***g***,
6: 1 with you not to receive the ***g***
8: 1 we make known to you the ***g*** of
8: 6 he would also complete this ***g***
8: 7 that you abound in this ***g***
8: 9 For you know the ***g*** of our Lord
9: 8 And God is able to make all ***g***
9:14 you because of the exceeding ***g***
12: 9 My ***g*** is sufficient for you, for
13:14 The ***g*** of the Lord Jesus Christ,
Gal 1: 3 ***G*** to you and peace from God the
1: 6 Him who called you in the ***g*** of
1:15 and called me through His ***g***,
2: 9 perceived the ***g*** that had been
2:21 I do not set aside the ***g*** of God;
5: 4 by law; you have fallen from ***g***.
6:18 the ***g*** of our Lord Jesus Christ
Eph 1: 2 ***G*** to you and peace from God our
1: 6 praise of the glory of His ***g***,
1: 7 to the riches of His ***g***
2: 5 together with Christ (by ***g*** you
2: 7 the exceeding riches of His ***g***
2: 8 For by ***g*** you have been saved
3: 2 of the dispensation of the ***g***
3: 7 according to the gift of the ***g***
3: 8 this ***g*** was given, that I should
4: 7 But to each one of us ***g*** was
4:29 that it may impart ***g*** to the
6:24 ***G*** be with all those who love
Phil 1: 2 ***G*** to you and peace from God our
1: 7 all are partakers with me of ***g***.
4:23 The ***g*** of our Lord Jesus Christ
Col 1: 2 ***G*** to you and peace from God
1: 6 day you heard and knew the ***g***
3:16 singing with ***g*** in your hearts
4: 6 your speech always be with ***g***,
4:18 ***G*** be with you. Amen.
1 Th 1: 1 ***G*** to you and peace from God
5:28 The ***g*** of our Lord Jesus Christ
2 Th 1: 2 ***G*** to you and peace from God our
1:12 according to the ***g*** of our God
2:16 consolation and good hope by ***g***,
3:18 The ***g*** of our Lord Jesus Christ
1 Tim 1: 2 a true son in the faith: ***G***,
1:14 And the ***g*** of our Lord was
6:21 ***G*** be with you. Amen.
2 Tim 1: 2 To Timothy, a beloved son: ***G***,
1: 9 to His own purpose and ***g*** which
2: 1 be strong in the ***g*** that is in
4:22 ***G*** be with you. Amen.
Titus 1: 4 son in our common faith: ***G***,
2:11 For the ***g*** of God that brings
3: 7 having been justified by His ***g***
3:15 ***G*** be with you all. Amen.
Phm 1: 3 ***G*** to you and peace from God our
1:25 The ***g*** of our Lord Jesus Christ
Heb 2: 9 by the ***g*** of God, might taste
4:16 come boldly to the throne of ***g***,
4:16 we may obtain mercy and find ***g***
10:29 and insulted the Spirit of ***g***?
12:15 anyone fall short of the ***g*** of
12:28 cannot be shaken, let us have ***g***,
13: 9 the heart be established by ***g***,
13:25 ***G*** be with you all. Amen.
Jas 4: 6 But He gives more ***g***.
4: 6 But gives ***g*** to the
1 Pe 1: 2 ***G*** to you and peace be
1:10 who prophesied of the ***g*** that
1:13 your hope fully upon the ***g***
3: 7 being heirs together of the ***g***
4:10 stewards of the manifold ***g*** of
5: 5 But gives ***g*** to the
5:10 But may the God of all ***g***,
5:12 that this is the true ***g*** of God
2 Pe 1: 2 ***G*** and peace be multiplied to you
3:18 but grow in the ***g*** and knowledge
2 Jn 3 ***G***, mercy, and peace will
Jude 4 who turn the ***g*** of our God into
Rev 1: 4 ***G*** to you and peace from Him
22:21 The ***g*** of our Lord Jesus Christ

GRACEFUL (3/3) GRACE

Job 41:12 or his ***g*** proportions.
Prov 1: 9 For they will be a ***g*** ornament
5:19 As a loving deer and a ***g*** doe,

GRACIOUS (32/31) GRACE, GRACIOUSLY

Gen 43:29 God be ***g*** to you, my son."
Ex 22:27 to Me, I will hear, for I am ***g***.
33:19 I will be ***g*** to whom I will be
33:19 be gracious to whom I will be ***g***,
34: 6 the LORD God, merciful and ***g***,
Num 6:25 upon you, And be ***g*** to you;
2 Sam 12:22 whether the LORD will be ***g***
2 Ki 13:23 But the LORD was ***g*** to them, had
2 Chr 30: 9 for the LORD your God is ***g***
Neh 9:17 ***G*** and merciful, Slow to
9:31 are God, ***g*** and merciful.
Job 33:24 Then He is ***g*** to him, and says,
Ps 77: 9 Has God forgotten to be ***g***?
86:15 a God full of compassion, and ***g***,
103: 8 The LORD is merciful and ***g***,
111: 4 The LORD is ***g*** and full of
112: 4 in the darkness; He is ***g***,
116: 5 ***G*** is the LORD, and righteous
145: 8 The LORD is ***g*** and full of
145:17 ***G*** in all His works.
Prov 11:16 A ***g*** woman retains honor, But
Eccl 10:12 of a wise man's mouth are ***g***,
Isa 30:18 that He may be ***g*** to you;
30:19 He will be very ***g*** to you at
33: 2 be ***g*** to us; We have waited for
Jer 22:23 How ***g*** will you be when pangs
Joel 2:13 For He is ***g*** and merciful,
Am 5:15 LORD God of hosts Will be ***g***
Jon 4: 2 for I know that You are a ***g***
Mal 1: 9 That He may be ***g*** to us.
Lk 4:22 and marveled at the ***g*** words
1 Pe 2: 3 have tasted that the Lord is ***g***.

GRACIOUSLY (5/5) GRACIOUS

Gen 33: 5 The children whom God has ***g***
33:11 because God has dealt ***g*** with
Ps 112: 5 A good man deals ***g*** and lends;
119:29 lying, And grant me Your law ***g***.
Hos 14: 2 all iniquity; Receive us ***g***,

GRAFT (1/1) GRAFTED

Rom 11:23 for God is able to ***g*** them in

GRAFTED (5/4) GRAFT

Rom 11:17 were ***g*** in among them, and with
11:19 broken off that I might be ***g***
11:23 will be ***g*** in, for God is able
11:24 and were ***g*** contrary to nature
11:24 be ***g*** into their own olive tree?

GRAIN (251/229) GRAINFIELDS, GRAINS

Gen 27:28 And plenty of ***g*** and wine.
27:37 with ***g*** and wine I have
41: 5 and suddenly seven heads of ***g***
41:35 and store up ***g*** under the
41:49 Joseph gathered very much ***g***,
41:57 to Joseph in Egypt to buy ***g***,
42: 1 Jacob saw that there was ***g*** in
42: 2 I have heard that there is ***g***
42: 3 brothers went down to buy ***g*** in
42: 5 sons of Israel went to buy ***g***
42:19 go and carry ***g*** for the famine
42:25 to fill their sacks with ***g***,
42:26 their donkeys with the ***g*** and
43: 2 when they had eaten up the ***g***
44: 2 and his ***g*** money." So he did
45:23 female donkeys loaded with ***g***,
47:14 for the ***g*** which they bought;
Ex 22: 6 in thorns, so that stacked ***g***,
22: 6 that stacked grain, standing ***g***,
29:41 you shall offer with it the ***g***
30: 9 or a ***g*** offering; nor shall you
40:29 it the burnt offering and the ***g***
Lev 2: 1 When anyone offers a ***g*** offering
2: 3 The rest of the ***g*** offering
2: 4 if you bring as an offering a ***g***
2: 5 But if your offering is a ***g***
2: 6 on it; it is a ***g*** offering.
2: 7 If your offering is a ***g***
2: 8 You shall bring the ***g*** offering
2: 9 priest shall take from the ***g***
2:10 And what is left of the ***g***
2:11 No ***g*** offering which you bring
2:13 And every offering of your ***g***
2:13 God to be lacking from your ***g***
2:14 If you offer a ***g*** offering of
2:14 you shall offer for the ***g***
2:14 firstfruits green heads of ***g***
2:14 ***g*** beaten from full heads.
2:15 It is a ***g*** offering.
2:16 part of its beaten ***g*** and part
5:13 shall be the priest's as a ***g***
6:14 This is the law of the ***g***
6:15 of the fine flour of the ***g***
6:15 which is on the ***g*** offering,
6:20 of fine flour as a daily ***g***
6:21 The baked pieces of the ***g***
6:23 For every ***g*** offering for the
7: 9 Also every ***g*** offering that is
7:10 Every ***g*** offering, whether mixed
7:37 the ***g*** offering, the sin
9: 4 and a ***g*** offering mixed with
9:17 Then he brought the ***g*** offering,
10:12 Take the ***g*** offering that remains
14:10 flour mixed with oil as a ***g***
14:20 the burnt offering and the ***g***
14:21 flour mixed with oil as a ***g***
14:31 with the ***g*** offering. So the
23:13 Its ***g*** offering shall be
23:14 eat neither bread nor parched ***g***
23:14 nor parched grain nor fresh ***g***
23:16 then you shall offer a new ***g***
23:18 with their ***g*** offering and their
23:37 a burnt offering and a ***g***
Num 4:16 the daily ***g*** offering, the
5:15 because it is a ***g*** offering of
5:18 which is the ***g*** offering of
5:25 the priest shall take the ***g***
6:15 and their ***g*** offering with their
6:17 priest shall also offer its ***g***
7:13 flour mixed with oil as a ***g***
7:19 flour mixed with oil as a ***g***
7:25 flour mixed with oil as a ***g***
7:31 flour mixed with oil as a ***g***
7:37 flour mixed with oil as a ***g***
7:43 flour mixed with oil as a ***g***
7:49 flour mixed with oil as a ***g***
7:55 flour mixed with oil as a ***g***
7:61 flour mixed with oil as a ***g***
7:67 flour mixed with oil as a ***g***
7:73 flour mixed with oil as a ***g***
7:79 flour mixed with oil as a ***g***
7:87 with their ***g*** offering, and the
8: 8 take a young bull with its ***g***
15: 4 to the LORD shall bring a ***g***
15: 6 a ram you shall prepare as a ***g***
15: 9 offered with the young bull a ***g***
15:24 with its ***g*** offering and its
18: 9 every ***g*** offering and every sin
18:12 best of the new wine and the ***g***,
18:27 you as though it were the ***g***

20: 5 It is not a place of **g** or figs
28: 5 an ephah of fine flour as a **g**
28: 8 as the morning **g** offering and
28: 9 an ephah of fine flour as a **g**
28:12 an ephah of fine flour as a **g**
28:12 an ephah of fine flour as a **g**
28:13 as a **g** offering for each lamb,
28:20 Their **g** offering shall be of
28:26 when you bring a new **g** offering
28:28 with their **g** offering of fine
28:31 burnt offering with its **g**
29: 3 Their **g** offering shall be fine
29: 6 the burnt offering with its **g**
29: 6 burnt offering with its **g**
29: 9 Their **g** offering shall be of
29:11 burnt offering with its **g**
29:14 Their **g** offering shall be of
29:16 its **g** offering, and its drink
29:18 and their **g** offering and their
29:19 burnt offering with its **g**
29:21 and their **g** offering and their
29:22 its **g** offering, and its drink
29:24 and their **g** offering and their
29:25 its **g** offering, and its drink
29:27 and their **g** offering and their
29:28 its **g** offering, and its drink
29:30 and their **g** offering and their
29:31 its **g** offering, and its drink
29:33 and their **g** offering and their
29:34 its **g** offering, and its drink
29:37 and their **g** offering and their
29:38 its **g** offering, and its drink
29:39 your burnt offerings and your **g**
Deut 7:13 your **g** and your new wine and
11:14 that you may gather in your **g**,
12:17 your gates the tithe of your **g**
14:22 all the increase of your **g**
14:23 the tithe of your **g** and your
16: 9 to put the sickle to the **g**.
18: 4 The firstfruits of your **g** and
23:25 into your neighbor's standing **g**,
23:25 on your neighbor's standing **g**.
25: 4 ox while it treads out the **g**.
28:51 they shall not leave you **g** or
33:28 In a land of **g** and new wine;
Josh 5:11 unleavened bread and parched **g**,
22:23 on it burnt offerings or **g**
22:29 for **g** offerings, or for
Judg 13:19 took the young goat with the **g**
13:23 a burnt offering and a **g**
15: 5 foxes go into the standing **g**
15: 5 the shocks and the standing **g**,
Ruth 2: 2 and glean heads of **g** after him
2:14 and he passed parched **g** to
2:16 Also let **g** from the bundles
3: 7 at the end of the heap of **g**;
1 Sam 8:15 will take a tenth of your **g**
17:17 an ephah of this dried **g** and
25:18 five seahs of roasted **g**,
2 Sam 17:19 and spread ground **g** on it;
17:28 parched **g** and beans, lentils
1 Ki 8:64 **g** offerings, and the fat of the
8:64 the **g** offerings, and the fat of
2 Ki 3:20 when the **g** offering was
4:42 and newly ripened **g** in his
16:13 his burnt offering and his **g**
16:15 the evening **g** offering, the
16:15 and his **g** offering, with the
16:15 their **g** offering, and their
18:32 a land of **g** and new wine, a
19:26 grass on the housetops And **g**
1 Chr 21:23 and the wheat for the **g**
23:29 and the fine flour for the **g**
2 Chr 7: 7 the **g** offerings, and the fat.
31: 5 abundance the firstfruits of **g**
32:28 for the harvest of **g**,
Ezra 7:17 with their **g** offerings and
Neh 5: 2 therefore let us get **g**,
5: 3 that we might buy **g** because of
5:10 am lending them money and **g**.
5:11 of the money and the **g**,
10:31 land brought wares or any **g** to
10:33 for the regular **g** offering, for
10:39 bring the offering of the **g**,
13: 5 they had stored the **g**
13: 5 the articles, the tithes of **g**,
13: 9 with the **g** offering and the
13:12 brought the tithe of the **g** and
Job 5:26 As a sheaf of **g** ripens in its
24:24 dry out like the heads of **g**.
39: 4 They grow strong with **g**;
39:12 trust him to bring home your **g**,
Ps 4: 7 in the season that their **g** and
65: 9 of water; You provide their **g**,
65:13 valleys also are covered with **g**;
72:16 will be an abundance of **g** in
Prov 11:26 will curse him who withholds **g**,
27:22 a pestle along with crushed **g**,
Isa 17: 5 the harvester gathers the **g**,
17: 5 be as he who gathers heads of **g**
21:10 my threshing and the **g** of my
23: 3 And on great waters the **g** of
36:17 a land of **g** and new wine, a
37:27 grass on the housetops And **g**
43:23 not caused you to serve with **g**
57: 6 You have offered a **g** offering.
62: 8 I will no longer give your **g**
66: 3 He who offers a **g** offering,
Jer 14:12 they offer burnt offering and **g**
17:26 **g** offerings and incense,
33:18 to kindle **g** offerings, and to
50:11 fat like a heifer threshing **g**,
Lam 2:12 Where is **g** and wine?" As they
Ezek 36:29 I will call for the **g** and
42:13 the **g** offering, the sin
44:29 They shall eat the **g** offering,
45:15 These shall be for **g** offerings,
45:17 **g** offerings, and drink
45:17 the **g** offering, the burnt
45:24 And he shall prepare a **g**
45:25 the **g** offering, and the oil."
46: 5 and the **g** offering shall be
46: 5 and the **g** offering for the
46: 7 He shall prepare a **g** offering of
46:11 the appointed feast days the **g**
46:14 And you shall prepare a **g**
46:14 This **g** offering is a perpetual
46:15 the **g** offering, and the oil,
46:20 where they shall bake the **g**
Hos 2: 8 did not know That I gave her **g**,
2: 9 return and take away My **g** in
2:22 The earth shall answer With **g**,
7:14 They assemble together for **g** and
10:11 heifer That loves to thresh **g**;
14: 7 They shall be revived like **g**,
Joel 1: 9 The **g** offering and the drink
1:10 For the **g** is ruined, The new
1:13 For the **g** offering and the
1:17 For the **g** has withered.
2:14 A **g** offering and a drink
2:19 I will send you **g** and new wine
Am 5:11 tread down the poor And take **g**
5:22 Me burnt offerings and your **g**
8: 5 be past, That we may sell **g**?
9: 9 As **g** is sifted in a sieve;
9: 9 Yet not the smallest **g** shall
Hag 1:11 on the **g** and the new wine and
Zech 9:17 And how great its beauty! **G**
Mt 12: 1 and began to pluck heads of **g**
13:26 But when the **g** had sprouted and
Mk 2:23 began to pluck the heads of **g**.
4:28 after that the full **g** in the
4:29 But when the **g** ripens,
Lk 6: 1 plucked the heads of **g** and ate
Jn 12:24 unless a **g** of wheat falls into
12:24 if it dies, it produces much **g**.
Acts 7:12 Jacob heard that there was **g**
1 Cor 9: 9 while it treads out the **g**.
15:37 body that shall be, but mere **g**—
15:37 wheat or some other **g**.
1 Tim 5:18 while it treads out the **g**,

GRAINFIELDS (3/3) GRAIN

Mt 12: 1 time Jesus went through the **g**
Mk 2:23 that He went through the **g** on
Lk 6: 1 that He went through the **g**.

GRAINS (1/1) GRAIN

Isa 48:19 of your body like the **g** of

GRANDCHILDREN (4/4) CHILDREN

Deut 4: 9 to your children and your **g**,
4:25 you beget children and **g**
Job 42:16 and saw his children and **g** for
1 Tim 5: 4 if any widow has children or **g**,

GRANDDAUGHTER (6/6) DAUGHTER

1 Ki 15: 2 name was Maachah the **g** of
15:10 name was Maachah the **g** of
2 Ki 8:26 name was Athaliah the **g** of
2 Chr 11:20 After her he took Maacah the **g**
11:21 Rehoboam loved Maachah the **g**
22: 2 name was Athaliah the **g** of

GRANDFATHER (1/1) FATHER

2 Sam 9: 7 you all the land of Saul your **g**;

GRANDMOTHER (2/2) MOTHER

1 Ki 15:13 Also he removed Maachah his **g**
2 Tim 1: 5 which dwelt first in your **g**

GRANDMOTHER'S (1/1)

1 Ki 15:10 His **g** name was Maachah the

GRANDSON (4/4) SON

Gen 11:31 took his son Abram and his **g**
Deut 6: 2 you and your son and your **g**,
Judg 8:22 and your **g** also; for you have
1 Chr 7:15 The name of Gilead's **g** was

GRANDSONS (2/2)

Judg 12:14 He had forty sons and thirty **g**,
1 Chr 8:40 They had many sons and **g**,

GRANT (27/26) GRANTED

Gen 42:34 I will **g** your brother to you,
Lev 25:24 of your possession you shall **g**
Deut 15: 1 every seven years you shall **g**
28:11 And the LORD will **g** you plenty
Ruth 1: 9 The LORD **g** that you may find
1 Sam 1:17 and the God of Israel **g** your
1 Ki 8:50 and **g** them compassion before
1 Chr 21:22 **G** me the place of this
21:22 You shall **g** it to me at the
2 Chr 12: 7 but I will **g** them some
Neh 1:11 and **g** him mercy in the sight of
Esth 5: 8 if it pleases the king to **g** my
Job 6: 8 That God would **g** me the thing
Ps 20: 4 May He **g** you according to your
85: 7 And **g** us Your salvation.
119:29 And **g** me Your law graciously.
140: 8 Do not **g**, O LORD, the desires
Mt 20:21 **G** that these two sons of mine
Mk 10:37 **G** us that we may sit, one on
Lk 1:74 To **g** us that we, Being
Acts 4:29 and **g** to Your servants that
Rom 15: 5 God of patience and comfort **g**
Eph 3:16 that He would **g** you, according
2 Tim 1:16 The Lord **g** mercy to the
1:18 The Lord **g** to him that he may
2:25 if God perhaps will **g** them
Rev 3:21 To him who overcomes I will **g** to

GRANTED (30/30) GRANT

Gen 25:21 and the LORD **g** his plea, and
Ex 12:36 so that they **g** them what they
1 Sam 1:27 and the LORD has **g** me my
2 Sam 14:21 I have **g** this thing.
1 Chr 4:10 may not cause pain!" So God **g**
2 Chr 1:12 wisdom and knowledge are **g** to
Ezra 7: 6 The king **g** him all his request,
Neh 2: 8 And the king **g** them to me
Esth 5: 6 It shall be **g** you. What is
7: 2 It shall be **g** you. And what is
9:12 It shall be **g** to you. Or what
9:13 let it be **g** to the Jews who
Job 10:12 You have **g** me life and favor,
Prov 10:24 of the righteous will be **g**.
Mk 15:45 he **g** the body to Joseph.
Lk 1:43 But why is this **g** to me, that
Jn 5:26 so He has **g** the Son to have
6:65 to Me unless it has been **g** to
Acts 3:14 asked for a murderer to be **g**
11:18 Then God has also **g** to the
27:24 and indeed God has **g** you all
2 Cor 1:11 on our behalf for the gift **g**
Phil 1:29 For to you it has been **g** on
Phm 1:22 your prayers I shall be **g** to
Rev 6: 4 And it was **g** to the one who sat
7: 2 four angels to whom it was **g**
13: 7 It was **g** to him to make war with
13:14 by those signs which he was **g**
13:15 He was **g** power to give breath
19: 8 And to her it was **g** to be

GRANTING (1/1)

Acts 14: 3 **g** signs and wonders to be done

GRANTS (1/1)

Ps 113: 9 He **g** the barren woman a home,

GRAPE (5/5) GRAPES, GRAPEVINE

Lev 19:10 nor shall you gather every **g**
Num 6: 3 neither shall he drink any **g**
Job 15:33 He will shake off his unripe **g**
Song 7:12 Whether the **g** blossoms are
Isa 18: 5 bud is perfect And the sour **g**

GRAPE-GATHERER (1/1)

Jer 6: 9 the remnant of Israel; As a **g**,

GRAPE-GATHERERS (2/2)

Jer 49: 9 If **g** came to you, Would they
Ob 5 If **g** had come to you, Would

GRAPES (38/35) GRAPE

Gen 40:10 clusters brought forth ripe **g**.
40:11 and I took the **g** and pressed
49:11 his clothes in the blood of **g**.
Lev 25: 5 nor gather the **g** of your
25:11 nor gather the **g** of your
Num 6: 3 nor eat fresh **g** or raisins.
13:20 the season of the first ripe **g**.
13:23 a branch with one cluster of **g**;
Deut 23:24 you may eat your fill of **g** at
24:21 When you gather the **g** of your
28:30 but shall not gather its **g**.
28:39 of the wine nor gather the **g**;
32:14 drank wine, the blood of the **g**.
32:32 Their **g** are grapes of gall,
32:32 Their grapes are **g** of gall,
Judg 8: 2 not the gleaning of the **g**
9:27 and gathered **g** from their
Neh 13:15 loading donkeys with wine, **g**,
Song 2:13 the vines with the tender **g**
2:15 For our vines have tender **g**.
Isa 5: 2 it to bring forth good **g**,
5: 2 But it brought forth wild **g**.
5: 4 it to bring forth good **g**,
5: 4 Did it bring forth wild **g**?
17: 6 Yet gleaning **g** will be left in
24:13 Like the gleaning of **g** when
Jer 8:13 No **g** shall be on the vine,
25:30 as those who tread the **g**,
31:29 fathers have eaten sour **g**,
31:30 every man who eats the sour **g**,
49: 9 they not leave some gleaning **g**?
Ezek 18: 2 fathers have eaten sour **g**,
Hos 9:10 I found Israel Like **g** in the
Am 9:13 And the treader of **g** him who
Mic 7: 1 Like those who glean vintage **g**;
Mt 7:16 Do men gather **g** from

Lk 6:44 nor do they gather ***g*** from a
Rev 14:18 for her ***g*** are fully ripe."

GRAPEVINE (2/2) GRAPE, VINE
Num 6: 4 that is produced by the ***g***,
Jas 3:12 or a ***g*** bear figs? Thus no

GRASP (2/2)
Eccl 7:18 It is good that you ***g*** this,
Zech 8:23 of the nations shall ***g*** the

GRASPED (3/3) GRASPING
2 Sam 2:16 And each one ***g*** his opponent by
1 Ki 20:33 and they quickly ***g*** at this
Ezek 21:15 It is ***g*** for slaughter:

GRASPING (9/9) GRASPED
Eccl 1:14 all is vanity and ***g*** for the
1:17 I perceived that this also is ***g***
2:11 indeed all was vanity and ***g***
2:17 for all is vanity and ***g*** for
2:26 This also is vanity and ***g*** for
4: 4 This also is vanity and ***g*** for
4: 6 together with toil and ***g*** for
4:16 this also is vanity and ***g*** for
6: 9 This also is vanity and ***g*** for

GRASPS (2/2)
Prov 27:16 And ***g*** oil with his right hand.
30:28 The spider skillfully ***g*** with

GRASS (63/56) GRASSHOPPER
Gen 1:11 "Let the earth bring forth ***g***,
1:12 And the earth brought forth ***g***,
Num 22: 4 as an ox licks up the ***g*** of the
Deut 11:15 And I will send ***g*** in your fields
29:23 nor does any ***g*** grow there, like
32: 2 herb, And as showers on the ***g***.
2 Sam 23: 4 Like the tender ***g*** springing
1 Ki 18: 5 perhaps we may find ***g*** to keep
2 Ki 19:26 They were as the ***g*** of the
19:26 As the ***g*** on the housetops
Job 5:25 And your offspring like the ***g***
6: 5 wild donkey bray when it has ***g***,
38:27 forth the growth of tender ***g***?
40:15 He eats ***g*** like an ox.
Ps 37: 2 soon be cut down like the ***g***,
72: 6 come down like rain upon the ***g***
72:16 the city shall flourish like ***g***
90: 5 In the morning they are like ***g***
92: 7 the wicked spring up like ***g***,
102: 4 is stricken and withered like ***g***,
102:11 And I wither away like ***g***.
103:15 for man, his days are like ***g***;
104:14 He causes the ***g*** to grow for the
106:20 the image of an ox that eats ***g***.
129: 6 Let them be as the ***g*** on the
147: 8 Who makes ***g*** to grow on the
Prov 19:12 his favor is like dew on the ***g***.
27:25 and the tender ***g*** shows itself,
Isa 15: 6 For the green ***g*** has withered
15: 6 The ***g*** fails, there is nothing
35: 7 There shall be ***g*** with reeds
37:27 They were as the ***g*** of the
37:27 As the ***g*** on the housetops
40: 6 I cry?" "All flesh is ***g***,
40: 7 The ***g*** withers, the flower
40: 7 Surely the people are ***g***.
40: 8 The ***g*** withers, the flower
44: 4 will spring up among the ***g***
51:12 a man who will be made like ***g***?
66:14 bones shall flourish like ***g***;
Jer 14: 5 left because there was no ***g***.
14: 6 failed because there was no ***g***.
Dan 4:15 In the tender ***g*** of the field.
4:15 with the beasts On the ***g*** of
4:23 and bronze in the tender ***g*** of
4:25 and they shall make you eat ***g***
4:32 They shall make you eat ***g*** like
4:33 was driven from men and ate ***g***
5:21 They fed him with ***g*** like oxen,
Am 7: 2 they had finished eating the ***g***
Mic 5: 7 LORD, Like showers on the ***g***,
Zech 10: 1 ***G*** in the field for everyone.
Mt 6:30 Now if God so clothes the ***g*** of
14:19 multitudes to sit down on the ***g***.
Mk 6:39 down in groups on the green ***g***.
Lk 12:28 "If then God so clothes the ***g***,
Jn 6:10 Now there was much ***g*** in the
Jas 1:11 heat than it withers the ***g***;
1 Pe 1:24 "All flesh is as ***g***,
1:24 as the flower of the ***g***.
1:24 The ***g*** withers, And its
Rev 8: 7 and all green ***g*** was burned up.
9: 4 commanded not to harm the ***g*** of

GRASSHOPPER (2/2) GRASS, GRASSHOPPERS
Lev 11:22 and the ***g*** after its kind.
Eccl 12: 5 The ***g*** is a burden, And desire

GRASSHOPPERS (6/6) GRASSHOPPER
Num 13:33 and we were like ***g*** in our own
1 Ki 8:37 or mildew, locusts or ***g***;
2 Chr 6:28 blight or mildew, locusts or ***g***;
Isa 40:22 its inhabitants are like ***g***,
Jer 46:23 And more numerous than ***g***.
Nah 3:17 And your generals like great ***g***,

GRATE (3/3)
Ex 27: 4 You shall make a ***g*** for it, a
38: 4 And he made a ***g*** of bronze
39:39 its ***g*** of bronze, its poles, and

GRATEFUL (1/1)
Jon 4: 6 So Jonah was very ***g*** for the

GRATIFY (2/2)
Eccl 2: 3 searched in my heart how to ***g***
Mk 15:15 wanting to ***g*** the crowd,

GRATING (3/3)
Ex 35:16 offering with its bronze ***g***,
38: 5 four corners of the bronze ***g***,
38:30 the bronze ***g*** for it, and all

GRAVE (53/50) GRAVECLOTHES, GRAVES
Gen 18:20 and because their sin is very ***g***,
35:20 And Jacob set a pillar on her ***g***,
35:20 is the pillar of Rachel's ***g***
37:35 I shall go down into the ***g***
42:38 gray hair with sorrow to the ***g***.
44:29 gray hair with sorrow to the ***g***.
44:31 our father with sorrow to the ***g***.
50: 5 in my ***g*** which I dug for myself
Num 19:16 or a bone of a man, or a ***g***,
19:18 the slain, the dead, or a ***g***.
Deut 34: 6 but no one knows his ***g*** to this
1 Sam 2: 6 He brings down to the ***g*** and
2 Sam 3:32 up his voice and wept at the ***g***
19:37 near the ***g*** of my father and
1 Ki 2: 6 his gray hair go down to the ***g***
2: 9 his gray hair down to the ***g***
14:13 who shall come to the ***g***,
2 Ki 22:20 shall be gathered to your ***g*** in
2 Chr 34:28 shall be gathered to your ***g*** in
Job 3:22 glad when they can find the ***g***?
5:26 You shall come to the ***g*** at a
7: 9 So he who goes down to the ***g***
10:19 carried from the womb to the ***g***.
14:13 that You would hide me in the ***g***,
17: 1 The ***g*** is ready for me.
17:13 If I wait for the ***g*** as my
21:13 in a moment go down to the ***g***.
21:32 he shall be brought to the ***g***,
24:19 So the ***g*** consumes those
Ps 6: 5 In the ***g*** who will give You
30: 3 brought my soul up from the ***g***;
31:17 Let them be silent in the ***g***.
49:14 sheep they are laid in the ***g***;
49:14 shall be consumed in the ***g***,
49:15 my soul from the power of the ***g***,
88: 3 my life draws near to the ***g***.
88: 5 the slain who lie in the ***g***,
88:11 be declared in the ***g***?
89:48 life from the power of the ***g***?
141: 7 scattered at the mouth of the ***g***,
Prov 12:21 No ***g*** trouble will overtake the
30:16 The ***g***, The barren womb,
Eccl 4: 8 This also is vanity and a ***g***
9:10 or knowledge or wisdom in the ***g***
Song 8: 6 Jealousy as cruel as the ***g***;
Isa 14:19 But you are cast out of your ***g***
53: 9 And they made His ***g*** with the
Jer 20:17 my mother might have been my ***g***,
Ezek 32:23 her company is all around her ***g***,
32:24 multitude, All around her ***g***,
Hos 13:14 them from the power of the ***g***;
13:14 I will be your plagues! O ***G***,
Nah 1:14 I will dig your ***g***,

GRAVECLOTHES (1/1) GRAVE
Jn 11:44 out bound hand and foot with ***g***,

GRAVED (KJV) See CARVED, ENGRAVED

GRAVEL (2/2)
Prov 20:17 his mouth will be filled with ***g***.
Lam 3:16 has also broken my teeth with ***g***,

GRAVELY (1/1)
Lam 1: 8 Jerusalem has sinned ***g***,

GRAVES (19/17) GRAVE
Ex 14:11 Because there were no ***g*** in
2 Ki 23: 6 and threw its ashes on the ***g*** of
2 Chr 34: 4 and scattered it on the ***g*** of
Isa 65: 4 Who sit among the ***g***,
Jer 8: 1 of Jerusalem, out of their ***g***.
26:23 cast his dead body into the ***g***
Ezek 32:22 With their ***g*** all around her,
32:23 Her ***g*** are set in the recesses
32:25 With her ***g*** all around it,
32:26 With all their ***g*** around it,
37:12 I will open your ***g*** and cause
37:12 you to come up from your ***g***,
37:13 when I have opened your ***g***,
37:13 and brought you up from your ***g***.
Mt 27:52 and the ***g*** were opened; and many
27:53 and coming out of the ***g*** after
Lk 11:44 For you are like ***g*** which
Jn 5:28 in which all who are in the ***g***
Rev 11: 9 dead bodies to be put into ***g***.

GRAVESTONE (1/1)
2 Ki 23:17 'What ***g*** is this that I see?"

GRAVITY (KJV) See REVERENCE

GRAY (10/10) GRAYHEADED
Gen 42:38 then you would bring down my ***g***
44:29 you shall bring down my ***g*** hair
44:31 servants will bring down the ***g***
Lev 19:32 You shall rise before the ***g***
Deut 32:25 child with the man of ***g*** hairs.
1 Ki 2: 6 and do not let his ***g*** hair go
2: 9 but bring his ***g*** hair down to
Prov 20:29 of old men is their ***g*** head.
Isa 46: 4 And even to ***g*** hairs I will
Hos 7: 9 ***g*** hairs are here and there on

GRAY-HAIRED (1/1)
Job 15:10 Both the ***g*** and the aged are

GRAY-SPOTTED (2/2)
Gen 31:10 were streaked, speckled, and ***g***.
31:12 are streaked, speckled, and ***g***;

GRAYHEADED (2/2) GRAY
1 Sam 12: 2 before you; and I am old and ***g***,
Ps 71:18 Now also when I am old and ***g***,

GRAZE (3/3)
Isa 11: 7 The cow and the bear shall ***g***;
Dan 4:15 And let him ***g*** with the beasts
4:23 and let him ***g*** with the beasts

GRAZED (1/1)
Ex 22: 5 a field or vineyard to be ***g***,

GREASE (1/1)
Ps 119:70 Their heart is as fat as ***g***,

GREAT (837/803) GREATER, GREATEST, GREATLY, GREATNESS
Gen 1:16 Then God made two ***g*** lights:
1:21 So God created ***g*** sea creatures
6: 5 the wickedness of man was ***g***
7:11 day all the fountains of the ***g***
12: 2 I will make you a ***g*** nation;
12: 2 bless you And make your name ***g***;
12:17 Pharaoh and his house with ***g***
13: 6 for their possessions were so ***g***
15: 1 your exceedingly ***g*** reward."
15:12 horror and ***g*** darkness fell
15:14 they shall come out with ***g***
15:18 the river of Egypt to the ***g***
17:20 and I will make him a ***g*** nation.
18:18 shall surely become a ***g*** and
18:20 against Sodom and Gomorrah is ***g***,
19:11 blindness, both small and ***g***,
19:13 outcry against them has grown ***g***
20: 9 on me and on my kingdom a ***g***
21: 8 And Abraham made a ***g*** feast on
21:18 for I will make him a ***g***
24:35 greatly, and he has become ***g***;
26:14 possessions of herds and a ***g***
27:34 he cried with an exceedingly ***g***
30: 8 With ***g*** wrestlings I have
30:30 and it has increased to a ***g***
36: 7 their possessions were too ***g***
39: 9 How then can I do this ***g***
41:29 Indeed seven years of ***g*** plenty
45: 7 and to save your lives by a ***g***
46: 3 for I will make of you a ***g***
48:19 people, and he also shall be ***g***;
50: 9 and it was a very ***g*** gathering.
50:10 and they mourned there with a ***g***
Ex 3: 3 now turn aside and see this ***g***
6: 6 an outstretched arm and with ***g***
7: 4 out of the land of Egypt by ***g***
11: 3 the man Moses was very ***g*** in
11: 6 Then there shall be a ***g*** cry
11: 8 he went out from Pharaoh in ***g***
12:30 and there was a ***g*** cry in Egypt,
12:38 a ***g*** deal of livestock.
14:31 Thus Israel saw the ***g*** work which
18:22 Then it will be that every ***g***
32:10 And I will make of you a ***g***
32:11 out of the land of Egypt with ***g***
32:21 that you have brought so ***g*** a
32:30 'You have committed a ***g*** sin.
32:31 people have committed a ***g*** sin,
Num 11:33 struck the people with a very ***g***
13:32 we saw in it are men of ***g***
14:17 let the power of my LORD be ***g***,
32: 1 children of Gad had a very ***g***
34: 6 you shall have the ***G*** Sea for a
34: 7 From the ***G*** Sea you shall mark

Deut 1: 7 as far as the *g* river, the
1:17 hear the small as well as the *g*;
1:19 and went through all that *g* and
1:28 the cities are *g* and fortified
2: 7 your trudging through this *g*
2:10 a people as *g* and numerous and
2:21 a people as *g* and numerous and
3: 5 besides a *g* many rural towns.
4: 6 Surely this *g* nation is a wise
4: 7 For what *g* nation is there
4: 8 And what *g* nation is there
4:32 whether any *g* thing like this
4:34 and by *g* terrors, according to
4:36 on earth He showed you His *g*
5:25 For this *g* fire will consume
6:22 *g* and severe, against Egypt,
7:19 the *g* trials which your eyes
7:21 the *g* and awesome God, is
8:15 who led you through that *g* and
9: 1 cities *g* and fortified up to
9: 2 a people *g* and tall, the
10:17 the *g* God, mighty and awesome,
10:21 who has done for you these *g*
11: 7 your eyes have seen every *g*
18:16 nor let me see this *g* fire
26: 5 and there he became a nation, *g*,
26: 8 with *g* terror and with signs
28:59 *g* and prolonged plagues—and
29: 3 'the *g* trials which your eyes
29: 3 the signs, and those *g* wonders.
29:24 What does the heat of this *g*
29:28 and in *g* indignation, and cast
34:12 that mighty power and all the *g*
Josh 1: 4 this Lebanon as far as the *g*
1: 4 and to the *G* Sea toward the
6: 5 the people shall shout with a *g*
6:20 and the people shouted with a *g*
7: 9 what will You do for Your *g*
7:26 Then they raised over him a *g*
8:29 and raise over it a *g* heap of
9: 1 and in all the coasts of the *G*
10: 2 because Gibeon was a *g* city,
10:10 killed them with a *g* slaughter
10:20 of slaying them with a very *g*
14:12 and that the cities were *g*
15:12 was the coastline of the *G*
15:47 as the Brook of Egypt and the *G*
17:14 since we are a *g* people,
17:15 If you are a *g* people, then go
17:17 You are a *g* people and have
17:17 are a great people and have *g*
22:10 altar there by the Jordan—a *g*,
23: 4 as far as the *G* Sea westward.
23: 9 driven out from before you *g*
24:17 who did those *g* signs in our
Judg 2: 7 who had seen all the *g* works of
5:15 of Reuben There were *g*
5:16 The divisions of Reuben have *g*
11:33 with a very *g* slaughter.
12: 2 My people and I were in a *g*
15: 8 them hip and thigh with a *g*
15:18 You have given this *g*
16: 5 and find out where his *g*
16: 6 Please tell me where your *g*
16:15 have not told me where your *g*
16:23 gathered together to offer a *g*
20:38 was that they would make a *g*
21: 5 For they had made a *g* oath
Ruth 2: 1 a man of *g* wealth, of the
1 Sam 2:17 sin of the young men was very *g*
4: 6 does the sound of this *g*
4:10 There was a very *g* slaughter,
4:17 and there has been a *g*
5: 9 against the city with a very *g*
5: 9 of the city, both small and *g*,
6: 9 then He has done us this *g*
6:19 had struck the people with a *g*
12:16 stand and see this *g* thing
12:17 see that your wickedness is *g*,
12:22 for His *g* name's sake, because
12:24 for consider what *g* things He
14:15 so that it was a very *g*
14:20 and there was very *g*
14:45 who has accomplished this *g*
15:22 Has the LORD as *g* delight in
17:25 him the king will enrich with *g*
19: 5 and the LORD brought about a *g*
19:22 and came to the *g* well that is
20: 2 will do nothing either *g* or
26:13 a *g* distance being between
26:25 son David! You shall both do *g*
30: 2 were there, from small to *g*;
30:16 because of all the *g* spoil
30:19 was lacking, either small or *g*,
2 Sam 3:38 not know that a prince and a *g*
5:10 So David went on and became *g*,
7: 9 and have made you a *g* name,
7: 9 like the name of the *g* men who
7:19 of Your servant's house for a *g*
7:21 You have done all these *g*
7:22 'Therefore You are *g*, O Lord
7:23 and to do for Youself *g* and
12:14 by this deed you have given *g*
12:30 out the spoil of the city in *g*
18: 7 and a *g* slaughter of twenty
18: 9 under the thick boughs of a *g*
18:29 I saw a *g* tumult, but I did not
21:20 where there was a man of *g*
22:36 Your gentleness has made me *g*.
23:10 The LORD brought about a *g*
23:12 And the LORD brought about a *g*
24:14 I am in *g* distress. Please let
24:14 LORD, for His mercies are *g*;
1 Ki 1:40 the flutes and rejoiced with *g*
3: 4 for that was the *g* high place:
3: 6 You have shown *g* mercy to Your
3: 6 You have continued this *g*
3: 8 a *g* people, too numerous to be
3: 9 For who is able to judge this *g*
4:29 wisdom and exceedingly *g*
5: 7 David a wise son over this *g*
7: 9 also on the outside to the *g*
7:12 The *g* court was enclosed with
8:42 (for they will hear of Your *g*
8:65 a *g* assembly from the entrance
10: 2 came to Jerusalem with a very *g*
10:10 spices in *g* quantity, and
10:11 brought *g* quantities of almug
10:18 Moreover the king made a *g*
11:19 And Hadad found *g* favor in the
19: 7 because the journey is too *g*
19:11 and a *g* and strong wind tore
20:13 Have you seen all this *g*
20:21 and killed the Syrians with a *g*
20:28 I will deliver all this *g*
22:31 "Fight with no one small or *g*,
2 Ki 3:27 and there was *g* indignation
5: 1 was a *g* and honorable man in
5:13 told you to do something *g*,
6:14 horses and chariots and a *g*
6:23 Then he prepared a *g* feast for
6:25 And there was a *g* famine in
7: 6 the noise of a *g* army; so they
8: 4 all the *g* things Elisha has
10: 6 were with the *g* men of the
10:11 and all his *g* men and his close
10:19 for I have a *g* sacrifice for
16:15 On the *g* new altar burn the
17:21 and made them commit a *g* sin.
17:36 from the land of Egypt with *g*
18:17 with a *g* army against
18:19 Thus says the *g* king, the king
18:28 Hear the word of the *g* king, the
22:13 for *g* is the wrath of the
23: 2 the people, both small and *g*.
23:26 from the fierceness of His *g*
25: 9 is, all the houses of the *g*,
25:26 And all the people, small and *g*,
1 Chr 11: 9 Then David went on and became *g*,
11:14 So the LORD brought about a *g*
11:23 a man of *g* height, five cubits
12:22 until it was a *g* army, like
16:25 For the LORD is *g* and greatly
17: 8 a name like the name of the *g*
17:17 of Your servant's house for a *g*
17:19 in making known all these *g*
17:21 make for Yourself a name by *g*
20: 2 out the spoil of the city in *g*
20: 6 where there was a man of *g*
21:13 I am in *g* distress. Please let
21:13 for His mercies are very *g*;
22: 8 shed much blood and have made *g*
25: 8 the small as well as the *g*,
26: 6 because they were men of *g*
26:13 the small as well as the *g*,
29: 1 and the work is *g*,
29:12 In Your hand it is to make *g*
29:22 drank before the LORD with *g*
2 Chr 1: 8 You have shown *g* mercy to David
1:10 for who can judge this *g* people
2: 5 which I build will be *g*,
2: 9 am about to build shall be *g*
4: 9 and the *g* court and doors for
4:18 these articles made in such *g*
6:32 country for the sake of Your *g*
7: 8 a very *g* assembly from the
9: 1 having a very *g* retinue,
9: 9 spices in *g* abundance, and
9:17 Moreover the king made a *g*
13: 8 and you are a *g* multitude, and
13:17 his people struck them with a *g*
15: 5 but *g* turmoil was on all the
15: 9 for they came over to him in *g*
15:13 to death, whether small or *g*,
16:14 They made a very *g* burning for
18:30 "Fight with no one small or *g*,
20: 2 A *g* multitude is coming against
20:12 we have no power against this *g*
20:15 nor dismayed because of this *g*
21: 3 Their father gave them *g* gifts
24:24 the LORD delivered a very *g*
25:10 and they returned home in *g*
28: 5 and carried away a *g* multitude
28: 5 who defeated him with a *g*
28:13 our guilt; for our guilt is *g*,
30:13 a very *g* assembly, gathered at
30:21 Bread seven days with *g*
30:24 and a *g* number of priests
30:26 So there was *g* joy in Jerusalem,
31:10 and what is left is this *g*
31:15 to the *g* as well as the small.
32:27 Hezekiah had very *g* riches and
33:14 and he raised it to a very *g*
34:21 for *g* is the wrath of the
34:30 *g* and small. And he read in
36:18 *g* and small, the treasures of
Ezra 3:11 all the people shouted with a *g*
4:10 rest of the nations whom the *g*
5: 8 to the temple of the *g* God,
5:11 which a *g* king of Israel built
9:13 our evil deeds and for our *g*
Neh 1: 3 in the province are there in *g*
1: 5 O *g* and awesome God, You who
1:10 You have redeemed by Your *g*
3:27 next to the *g* projecting tower,
4:14 *g* and awesome, and fight for
4:19 The work is *g* and extensive,
5: 1 And there was a *g* outcry of the
5: 7 So I called a *g* assembly
6: 3 I am doing a *g* work, so that I
8: 6 the *g* God. Then all the people
8:17 And there was very *g* gladness.
9:18 And worked *g* provocations,
9:25 delighted themselves in Your *g*
9:26 And they worked *g*
9:31 Nevertheless in Your *g* mercy
9:32 therefore, our God, The *g*,
9:37 And we are in *g* distress.
11:14 the son of one of the *g* men.
12:43 Also that day they offered *g*
12:43 had made them rejoice with *g*
13:27 hear of your doing all this *g*
Esth 1: 5 from *g* to small, in the court
1:20 all his empire (for it is *g*),
1:20 husbands, both *g* and small."
2:18 Then the king made a *g* feast,
4: 3 there was *g* mourning among
5:11 Then Haman told them of his *g*
8:15 with a *g* crown of gold and a
9: 4 For Mordecai was *g* in the
10: 3 and was *g* among the Jews and
Job 1:19 and suddenly a *g* wind came from
2:13 saw that his grief was very *g*.
3:19 The small and *g* are there,
5: 9 Who does *g* things, and
9:10 He does *g* things past finding
12:23 He makes nations *g*,
22: 5 Is not your wickedness *g*,
23: 6 He contend with me in His *g*
30:18 By *g* force my garment is
31:25 because my wealth was *g*,
31:34 Because I feared the *g*
32: 9 *G* men are not always wise,
36:26 'Behold, God is *g*, and we
37: 5 He does *g* things which we
38:21 the number of your days is *g*?
38:32 Or can you guide the *G* Bear
39:11 him because his strength is *g*?
Ps 14: 5 There they are in *g* fear,
18:35 Your gentleness has made me *g*.
18:50 *G* deliverance He gives to His
19:11 in keeping them there is *g*
19:13 And I shall be innocent of *g*
21: 5 His glory is *g* in Your
22:25 shall be of You in the *g*
25:11 my iniquity, for it is *g*.
31:19 how *g* is Your goodness, Which
32: 6 Surely in a flood of *g* waters
33:16 man is not delivered by *g*
33:17 shall it deliver any by its *g*
35:18 will give You thanks in the *g*
36: 6 righteousness is like the *g*
36: 6 Your judgments are a *g* deep;
37:35 I have seen the wicked in *g*
40: 9 news of righteousness In the *g*
40:10 and Your truth From the *g*
47: 2 He is a *g* King over all the
48: 1 *G* is the LORD, and greatly to
48: 2 The city of the *g* King.
53: 5 There they are in *g* fear
68:11 *G* was the company of those
71:19 You who have done *g* things;
71:20 who have shown me *g* and severe
76: 1 His name is *g* in Israel.
77:13 Who is so *g* a God as our
77:19 Your path in the *g* waters,
80: 5 given them tears to drink in *g*
86:10 For You are *g*, and do
86:13 For *g* is Your mercy toward me,
92: 5 how *g* are Your works! Your
95: 3 For the LORD is the *g* God,
95: 3 And the *g* King above all gods.
96: 4 For the LORD is *g* and greatly
99: 2 The LORD is *g* in Zion,
99: 3 Let them praise Your *g* and
103:11 So *g* is His mercy toward
104: 1 O LORD my God, You are very *g*:
104:25 This *g* and wide sea, In which
104:25 Living things both small and *g*.
106:21 Who had done *g* things in
107:23 Who do business on *g* waters,
108: 4 For Your mercy is *g* above the
111: 2 The works of the LORD are *g*,
115:13 the LORD, Both small and *g*.
117: 2 For His merciful kindness is *g*
119:51 The proud have me in *g*
119:156 *G* are Your tender mercies,
119:162 Your word As one who finds *g*
119:165 *G* peace have those who love
126: 2 The LORD has done *g* things for
126: 3 The LORD has done *g* things for
131: 1 do I concern myself with *g*
135: 5 I know that the LORD is *g*,
136: 4 To Him who alone does *g*
136: 7 To Him who made *g* lights,
136:17 To Him who struck down *g* kings,
138: 5 For *g* is the glory of the
139:17 O God! How *g* is the sum of
144: 7 me and deliver me out of *g*
145: 3 *G* is the LORD, and greatly to
145: 7 utter the memory of Your *g*
145: 8 Slow to anger and *g* in mercy.
147: 5 *G* is our Lord, and mighty in
148: 7 You *g* sea creatures and all
Prov 13: 7 poor, yet has *g* riches.
14:29 who is slow to wrath has *g*

15:16 Than **g** treasure with trouble.
18: 9 Is a brother to him who is a **g**
18:16 And brings him before **g** men.
19:19 A man of **g** wrath will suffer
22: 1 is to be chosen rather than **g**
25: 6 not stand in the place of the **g**;
26:10 The **g** God who formed
28:12 there is **g** glory; But when
28:16 who lacks understanding is a **g**
Eccl 1:16 My heart has understood **g**
2: 4 I made my works **g**, I built
2: 9 So I became **g** and excelled more
2:21 This also is vanity and a **g**
9:13 and it seemed **g** to me:
9:14 and a **g** king came against it,
9:14 and built **g** snares around it.
10: 4 For conciliation pacifies **g**
10: 6 Folly is set in **g** dignity,
Song 2: 3 I sat down in his shade with **g**
Isa 5: 9 **G** and beautiful ones, without
9: 2 in darkness Have seen a **g**
12: 6 For **g** is the Holy One of
16:14 be despised with all that **g**
21: 7 he listened earnestly with **g**
22: 9 city of David, That it was **g**;
23: 3 And on **g** waters the grain of
27: 1 **g** and strong, Will punish
27:13 The **g** trumpet will be blown;
29: 6 thunder and earthquake and **g**
30:25 In the day of the **g** slaughter,
32: 2 As the shadow of a **g** rock in a
33:23 Then the prey of **g** plunder is
34: 6 And a **g** slaughter in the land
36: 2 sent the Rabshakeh with a **g**
36: 4 Thus says the **g** king, the king
36:13 Hear the words of the **g** king,
38:17 my own peace That I had **g**
47: 9 For the **g** abundance of your
51:10 The waters of the **g** deep;
53:12 divide Him a portion with the **g**,
54: 7 But with **g** mercies I will
54:13 And **g** shall be the peace of
63: 7 And the **g** goodness toward the
Jer 4: 6 And **g** destruction."
5: 5 I will go to the **g** men and
5:27 Therefore they have become **g**
6: 1 And **g** destruction.
6:22 And a **g** nation will be raised
10: 6 like You, O LORD (You are **g**,
10: 6 and Your name is **g** in might),
10:22 And a **g** commotion out of the
11:16 With the noise of a **g** tumult
13: 9 the pride of Judah and the **g**
16: 6 Both the **g** and the small shall
16:10 the LORD pronounced all this **g**
21: 5 even in anger and fury and **g**
21: 6 they shall die of a **g**
22: 8 has the LORD done so to this **g**
25:14 (For many nations and **g** kings
25:32 And a **g** whirlwind shall be
26:19 But we are doing **g** evil against
27: 5 by My **g** power and by My
27: 7 and then many nations and **g**
28: 8 against many countries and **g**
30: 7 Alas! For that day is **g**,
31: 8 A **g** throng shall return there.
32:17 and the earth by Your **g** power
32:18 their children after them—the **G**,
32:19 You are **g** in counsel and
32:21 and with **g** terror;
32:37 and in **g** wrath; I will bring
32:42 as I have brought all this **g**
33: 3 and show you **g** and mighty
36: 7 For **g** is the anger and the
41:12 and they found him by the **g**
44: 7 Why do you commit this **g** evil
44:15 a **g** multitude, and all the
44:26 I have sworn by My **g** name,'
45: 5 And do you seek **g** things for
48: 3 Plundering and **g** destruction!'
50: 9 Babylon An assembly of **g**
50:22 And of **g** destruction.
50:41 And a **g** nation and many kings
51:54 And **g** destruction from the
51:55 Though her waves roar like **g**
52:13 is, all the houses of the **g**,
Lam 1: 1 Who was **g** among the nations!
3:23 **G** is Your faithfulness.
Ezek 1: 4 a **g** cloud with raging fire
3:12 and I heard behind me a **g**
3:13 and a **g** thunderous noise.
8: 6 the **g** abominations that the
9: 9 and Judah is exceedingly **g**,
13:11 O **g** hailstones, shall fall;
13:13 and **g** hailstones in fury to
17: 3 A **g** eagle with large wings and
17: 7 But there was another **g** eagle
17: 9 And no **g** power or many people
17:17 with his mighty army and **g**
21:14 The sword that slays the **g**
24: 9 I too will make the pyre **g**.
24:12 And her **g** scum has not gone
25:17 I will execute **g** vengeance on
26:19 and **g** waters cover you,
28: 5 By your **g** wisdom in trade you
29: 3 O **g** monster who lies in the
30: 4 And **g** anguish shall be in
30: 9 And **g** anguish shall come upon
30:16 Sin shall have **g** pain,
31: 6 And in its shadow all **g**
31:15 and the **g** waters were held
32:13 its animals From beside its **g**

36:23 And I will sanctify My **g** name,
37:10 an exceedingly **g** army.
38: 4 a **g** company with bucklers and
38:13 goods, to take **g** plunder?'
38:15 a **g** company and a mighty army.
38:19 in that day there shall be a **g**
38:22 **g** hailstones, fire, and
39:17 A **g** sacrificial meal on the
47: 9 There will be a very **g**
47:10 kinds as the fish of the **G** Sea,
47:15 from the **G** Sea, by the road to
47:19 along the brook to the **G** Sea.
47:20 west side shall be the **G**
48:28 along the brook to the **G** Sea.
Dan 2: 6 and **g** honor. Therefore tell me
2:31 a **g** image! This great image,
2:31 a great image! This **g** image,
2:35 struck the image became a **g**
2:45 the **g** God has made known to the
2:48 Daniel and gave him many **g**
4: 3 How **g** are His signs, And how
4:10 earth, And its height was **g**.
4:30 Is not this **g** Babylon, that I
5: 1 Belshazzar the king made a **g**
7: 2 heaven were stirring up the **G**
7: 3 And four **g** beasts came up from
7:17 Those **g** beasts, which are four,
8: 4 to his will and became **g**.
8: 8 the male goat grew very **g**;
8: 9 horn which grew exceedingly **g**
9: 4 **g** and awesome God, who keeps
9:12 by bringing upon us a **g**
9:18 but because of Your **g** mercies.
10: 4 as I was by the side of the **g**
10: 7 but a **g** terror fell upon them,
10: 8 left alone when I saw this **g**
11: 3 who shall rule with **g** dominion,
11: 5 His dominion shall be a **g**
11:10 and assemble a multitude of **g**
11:11 who shall muster a **g** multitude;
11:13 the end of some years with a **g**
11:25 the king of the South with a **g**
11:25 up to battle with a very **g** and
11:28 returning to his land with **g**
11:32 and carry out **g** exploits.
11:44 he shall go out with **g** fury to
12: 1 The **g** prince who stands watch
Hos 1: 2 For the land has committed **g**
1:11 For **g** will be the day of
8:12 I have written for him the **g**
9: 7 of your iniquity and **g** enmity.
10:15 Because of your **g** wickedness.
13: 5 In the land of **g** drought.
Joel 2: 2 **g** and strong, The like of whom
2:11 army, For His camp is very **g**;
2:11 the day of the LORD is **g** and
2:13 and of **g** kindness; And He
2:25 My **g** army which I sent among
2:31 Before the coming of the **g** and
3:13 their wickedness is **g**.
Am 3: 9 See **g** tumults in her midst,
3:15 And the **g** houses shall have an
6: 2 from there go to Hamath the **g**;
6:11 He will break the **g** house into
7: 4 and it consumed the **g** deep and
Jon 1: 2 that **g** city, and cry out
1: 4 But the LORD sent out a **g** wind
1:12 For I know that this **g** tempest
1:17 Now the LORD had prepared a **g**
3: 2 that **g** city, and preach to it
3: 3 Nineveh was an exceedingly **g**
4:11 that **g** city, in which are more
Mic 5: 4 For now He shall be **g** To the
7: 3 And the **g** man utters his evil
Nah 1: 3 LORD is slow to anger and **g**
3: 3 A **g** number of bodies,
3:10 And all her **g** men were bound
3:17 And your generals like **g**
Hab 3:15 Through the heap of **g** waters.
Zeph 1:14 The **g** day of the LORD is
Zech 1:14 Jerusalem And for Zion with **g**
4: 7 O **g** mountain? Before
7:12 Thus **g** wrath came from the
8: 2 I am zealous for Zion with **g**
8: 2 With **g** fervor I am zealous for
8: 4 in his hand Because of **g** age.
9:17 For how **g** is its goodness
9:17 is its goodness And how **g** its
12:11 that day there shall be a **g**
14:13 to pass in that day That a **g**
14:14 and apparel in **g** abundance.
Mal 1:11 My name shall be **g** among the
1:11 For My name shall be **g** among
1:14 For I am a **g** King," Says the
4: 5 Before the coming of the **g**
Mt 2:10 rejoiced with exceedingly **g**
2:18 and **g** mourning, Rachel
4:16 in darkness have seen a **g**
4:25 **G** multitudes followed Him—from
5:12 for **g** is your reward in
5:19 he shall be called **g** in the
5:35 for it is the city of the **g**
6:23 how **g** is that darkness!
7:27 And **g** was its fall."
8: 1 **g** multitudes followed Him.
8:10 I have not found such **g** faith,
8:18 And when Jesus saw **g** multitudes
8:24 And suddenly a **g** tempest arose
8:26 and there was a **g** calm.
12:15 And **g** multitudes followed Him,
12:40 nights in the belly of the **g**
13: 2 And **g** multitudes were gathered

13:46 he had found one pearl of **g**
14:14 when Jesus went out He saw a **g**
15:28 **g** is your faith! Let it be to
15:30 Then **g** multitudes came to Him,
15:33 the wilderness to fill such a **g**
19: 2 And **g** multitudes followed Him,
19:22 for he had **g** possessions.
20:25 and those who are **g** exercise
20:26 but whoever desires to become **g**
20:29 a **g** multitude followed Him.
21: 8 And a very **g** multitude spread
22:36 which is the **g** commandment in
22:38 This is the first and **g**
24:21 For then there will be **g**
24:24 prophets will rise and show **g**
24:30 of heaven with power and **g**
24:31 will send His angels with a **g**
26:47 with a **g** multitude with swords
28: 2 there was a **g** earthquake; for
28: 8 from the tomb with fear and **g**
Mk 3: 7 And a **g** multitude from Galilee
3: 8 a **g** multitude, when they heard
4: 1 And a **g** multitude was gathered
4:37 And a **g** windstorm arose, and the
4:39 wind ceased and there was a **g**
5:19 and tell them what **g** things the
5:21 a **g** multitude gathered to Him;
5:24 and a **g** multitude followed Him
5:42 And they were overcome with **g**
6:34 saw a **g** multitude and was moved
8: 1 the multitude being very **g** and
9:14 He saw a **g** multitude around
10:22 for he had **g** possessions.
10:42 and their **g** ones exercise
10:43 but whoever desires to become **g**
10:46 with His disciples and a **g**
13: 2 Do you see these **g** buildings?
13:26 Man coming in the clouds with **g**
14:43 with a **g** multitude with swords
Lk 1:15 For he will be **g** in the sight of
1:32 'He will be **g**, and will be
1:49 He who is mighty has done **g**
1:58 heard how the Lord had shown **g**
2:10 I bring you good tidings of **g**
2:36 She was of a **g** age, and had
4:25 and there was a **g** famine
5: 6 they caught a **g** number of fish,
5:15 and **g** multitudes came together
5:29 Then Levi gave Him a **g** feast in
5:29 And there were a **g** number of
6:17 crowd of His disciples and a **g**
6:23 For indeed your reward is **g**
6:35 and your reward will be **g**,
6:49 the ruin of that house was **g**.
7: 9 I have not found such **g** faith,
7:16 A **g** prophet has risen up among
8: 4 And when a **g** multitude had
8:37 for they were seized with **g**
8:39 and tell what **g** things God has
8:39 the whole city what **g** things
9:37 that a **g** multitude met Him.
9:39 and it departs from him with **g**
9:48 least among you all will be **g**.
10: 2 them, "The harvest truly is **g**,
14:16 A certain man gave a **g** supper
14:25 Now **g** multitudes went with Him.
14:32 while the other is still a **g**
15:20 But when he was still a **g** way
16:26 us and you there is a **g** gulf
21:11 And there will be **g** earthquakes
21:11 will be fearful sights and **g**
21:23 those days! For there will be **g**
21:27 in a cloud with power and **g**
22:44 Then His sweat became like **g**
23:27 And a **g** multitude of the people
24:52 returned to Jerusalem with **g**
Jn 5: 3 In these lay a **g** multitude of
6: 2 Then a **g** multitude followed Him,
6: 5 and seeing a **g** multitude coming
6:18 Then the sea arose because a **g**
7:37 that **g** day of the feast, Jesus
12: 9 Now a **g** many of the Jews knew
12:12 The next day a **g** multitude that
Acts 2:20 the coming of the **g** and
4:33 And with **g** power the apostles
4:33 And **g** grace was upon them all.
5: 5 So **g** fear came upon all those
5:11 So **g** fear came upon all the
6: 7 and a **g** many of the priests
6: 8 did **g** wonders and signs among
7:11 Now a famine and **g** trouble came
8: 1 At that time a **g** persecution
8: 2 and made **g** lamentation over
8: 8 And there was **g** joy in that
8: 9 claiming that he was someone **g**,
8:10 This man is the **g** power of
8:27 a eunuch of **g** authority under
10:11 opened and an object like a **g**
11: 5 an object descending like a **g**
11:21 and a **g** number believed and
11:24 And a **g** many people were added
11:26 with the church and taught a **g**
11:28 that there was going to be a **g**
14: 1 and so spoke that a **g** multitude
15: 3 and they caused **g** joy to all
16:26 Suddenly there was a **g**
17: 4 and a **g** multitude of the devout
19:23 about that time there arose a **g**
19:27 but also the temple of the **g**
19:28 **G** is Diana of the Ephesians!"
19:34 **G** is Diana of the Ephesians!"
19:35 is temple guardian of the **g**

21:40 And when there was a *g* silence,
22: 6 suddenly a *g* light from heaven
23:10 Now when there arose a *g*
23:14 have bound ourselves under a *g*
24: 2 that through you we enjoy *g*
24: 7 Lysias came by and with *g*
25:23 and Bernice had come with *g*
26:22 witnessing both to small and *g*,
28:29 the Jews departed and had a *g*
Rom 9: 2 that I have *g* sorrow and
15:23 and having a *g* desire these
1 Cor 9:11 is it a *g* thing if we reap
16: 9 For a *g* and effective door has
2 Cor 1:10 who delivered us from so *g* a
3:12 we use *g* boldness of speech—
7: 4 *G* is my boldness of speech
7: 4 *g* is my boasting on your
8: 2 that in a *g* trial of affliction
8:22 because of the *g* confidence
11:15 Therefore it is no *g* thing if
Eph 2: 4 because of His *g* love with
5:32 This is a *g* mystery, but I speak
Col 2: 1 For I want you to know what a *g*
4:13 him witness that he has a *g*
1 Th 2:17 to see your face with *g* desire.
1 Tim 3:13 a good standing and *g* boldness
3:16 And without controversy *g* is the
6: 6 with contentment is *g* gain.
2 Tim 2:20 But in a *g* house there are not
Titus 2:13 and glorious appearing of our *g*
Phm 1: 7 For we have *g* joy and
Heb 2: 3 we escape if we neglect so *g* a
4:14 Seeing then that we have a *g*
7: 4 Now consider how *g* this man
10:32 you endured a *g* struggle with
10:35 which has *g* reward.
12: 1 we are surrounded by so *g* a
13:20 that *g* Shepherd of the sheep,
Jas 3: 5 is a little member and boasts *g*
3: 5 See how *g* a forest a little
2 Pe 1: 4 been given to us exceedingly *g*
2:18 For when they speak *g* swelling
3:10 will pass away with a *g* noise,
Jude 6 for the judgment of the *g* day;
16 and they mouth *g* swelling
Rev 2:22 commit adultery with her into *g*
6: 4 and there was given to him a *g*
6:12 there was a *g* earthquake;
6:15 the *g* men, the rich men, the
6:17 For the *g* day of His wrath has
7: 9 a *g* multitude which no one
7:14 the ones who come out of the *g*
8: 8 And something like a *g*
8:10 And a *g* star fell from heaven,
9: 2 the pit like the smoke of a *g*
9:14 angels who are bound at the *g*
11: 8 lie in the street of the *g*
11:11 and *g* fear fell on those who
11:13 In the same hour there was a *g*
11:17 Because You have taken Your *g*
11:18 who fear Your name, small and *g*,
11:19 an earthquake, and *g* hail.
12: 1 Now a *g* sign appeared in heaven:
12: 3 appeared in heaven: behold, a *g*,
12: 9 So the *g* dragon was cast out,
12:12 having *g* wrath, because he
12:14 was given two wings of a *g*
13: 2 his throne, and *g* authority.
13: 5 he was given a mouth speaking *g*
13:13 He performs *g* signs, so that he
13:16 He causes all, both small and *g*,
14: 8 that *g* city, because she has
14:19 and threw it into the *g*
15: 1 *g* and marvelous: seven angels
15: 3 *G* and marvelous are Your works,
16: 9 And men were scorched with *g*
16:12 poured out his bowl on the *g*
16:14 them to the battle of that *g*
16:18 and there was a *g* earthquake,
16:18 such a mighty and *g* earthquake
16:19 Now the *g* city was divided into
16:19 And *g* Babylon was remembered
16:21 And *g* hail from heaven fell upon
16:21 that plague was exceedingly *g*.
17: 1 show you the judgment of the *g*
17: 5 MYSTERY, BABYLON THE *G*,
17: 6 I marveled with *g* amazement.
17:18 woman whom you saw is that *g*
18: 1 having *g* authority, and the
18: 2 Babylon the *g* is fallen, is
18:10 that *g* city Babylon, that
18:16 that *g* city that was clothed in
18:17 For in one hour such *g* riches
18:18 What is like this *g* city?'
18:19 that *g* city, in which all who
18:21 angel took up a stone like a *g*
18:21 Thus with violence the *g* city
18:23 For your merchants were the *g*
19: 1 I heard a loud voice of a *g*
19: 2 because He has judged the *g*
19: 5 fear Him, both small and *g*!"
19: 6 the voice of a *g* multitude, as
19:17 for the supper of the *g* God,
19:18 and slave, both small and *g*.
20: 1 to the bottomless pit and a *g*
20:11 Then I saw a *g* white throne and
20:12 And I saw the dead, small and *g*,
21:10 me away in the Spirit to a *g*
21:10 and showed me the *g* city, the
21:12 Also she had a *g* and high wall
21:16 its length is as *g* as its

GREATER (82/78) GREAT

Gen 1:16 the *g* light to rule the day,
4:13 My punishment is *g* than I can
39: 9 There is no one *g* in this
41:40 to the throne will I be *g* than
48:19 his younger brother shall be *g*
Ex 18:11 I know that the LORD is *g*
Num 14:12 I will make of you a nation *g*
Deut 1:28 The people are *g* and taller
4:38 out from before you nations *g*
7: 1 seven nations *g* and mightier
7:17 'These nations are *g* than I;
9: 1 go in to dispossess nations *g*
9:14 of you a nation mightier and *g*
11:23 and you will dispossess *g* and
Josh 10: 2 and because it was *g* than Ai,
11: 8 them and chased them to *G*
19:28 and Kanah, as far as *G* Sidon.
Judg 1:35 of the house of Joseph became *g*,
1 Sam 14:30 there not have been a much *g*
2 Sam 13:15 with which he hated her was *g*
1 Ki 1:37 and make his throne *g* than the
1:47 and may He make his throne *g*
2 Chr 2: 5 for our God is *g* than all gods.
Job 33:12 For God is *g* than man.
Eccl 2: 7 I had *g* possessions of herds
Lam 4: 6 the daughter of my people Is *g*
Ezek 8: 6 you will see *g* abominations."
8:13 you will see *g* abominations
8:15 you will see *g* abominations
Dan 7:20 whose appearance was *g* than
11:13 and muster a multitude *g* than
Am 6: 2 Or is their territory *g* than
Hag 2: 9 this latter temple shall be *g*
Zech 12: 7 of Jerusalem shall not become *g*
Mt 11:11 there has not risen one *g* than
11:11 in the kingdom of heaven is *g*
12: 6 in this place there is One *g*
12:41 and indeed a *g* than Jonah is
12:42 and indeed a *g* than Solomon is
13:32 but when it is grown it is *g*
23:14 Therefore you will receive *g*
23:17 and blind! For which is *g*,
23:19 and blind! For which is *g*,
Mk 4:32 it grows up and becomes *g* than
12:31 is no other commandment *g* than
12:40 These will receive *g*
Lk 7:28 born of women there is not a *g*
7:28 in the kingdom of God is *g*
11:31 and indeed a *g* than Solomon is
11:32 and indeed a *g* than Jonah is
12:18 pull down my barns and build *g*,
20:47 These will receive *g*
22:27 'For who is *g*, he who sits
Jn 1:50 You will see *g* things than
4:12 Are You *g* than our father Jacob,
5:20 and He will show Him *g* works
5:36 But I have a *g* witness than
8:53 Are You *g* than our father
10:29 is *g* than all; and no one is
13:16 a servant is not *g* than his
13:16 nor is he who is sent *g* than he
14:12 and *g* works than these he will
14:28 for My Father is *g* than I.
15:13 *G* love has no one than this,
15:20 A servant is not *g* than his
19:11 delivered Me to you has the *g*
Acts 15:28 to lay upon you no *g* burden
1 Cor 12:23 on these we bestow *g* honor;
12:23 our unpresentable parts have *g*
12:24 having given *g* honor to that
14: 5 for he who prophesies is *g*
15: 6 of whom the *g* part remain to
2 Cor 7:15 And his affections are *g* for you
Heb 6:13 He could swear by no one *g*,
6:16 For men indeed swear by the *g*,
9:11 with the *g* and more perfect
11:26 the reproach of Christ *g*
2 Pe 2:11 who are *g* in power and might,
1 Jn 3:20 God is *g* than our heart, and
4: 4 because He who is in you is *g*
5: 9 of men, the witness of God is *g*;
3 Jn 4 I have no *g* joy than to hear

GREATEST (21/21) GREAT

Josh 14:15 Kirjath Arba (Arba was the *g*
1 Chr 12:14 and the *g* was over a thousand.
12:29 thousand (until then the *g*
Job 1: 3 so that this man was the *g* of
Jer 6:13 least of them even to the *g* of
8:10 from the least even to the *g*
31:34 the least of them to the *g* of
42: 1 people, from the least to the *g*,
42: 8 from the least even to the *g*
44:12 die, from the least to the *g*,
Jon 3: 5 from the *g* to the least of
Mt 18: 1 Who then is *g* in the kingdom of
18: 4 as this little child is the *g*
23:11 But he who is *g* among you shall
Mk 9:34 who would be the *g*.
Lk 9:46 as to which of them would be *g*.
22:24 them should be considered the *g*.
22:26 he who is *g* among you, let him
Acts 8:10 heed, from the least to the *g*,
1 Cor 13:13 but the *g* of these is love.
Heb 8:11 least of them to the *g*

GREATLY (111/111) GREAT

Gen 3:16 I will *g* multiply your sorrow
7:18 The waters prevailed and *g*
24:35 LORD has blessed my master *g*,
31:30 have surely gone because you *g*
32: 7 So Jacob was *g* afraid and
Ex 19:18 and the whole mountain quaked *g*.
Num 11:10 the anger of the LORD was *g*
14:39 and the people mourned *g*.
22:17 I will certainly honor you *g*,
24:11 I said I would *g* honor you, but
Deut 6: 3 and that you may multiply *g* as
15: 4 for the LORD will *g* bless you
17:17 nor shall he *g* multiply silver
Josh 10: 2 that they feared *g*, because
Judg 2:15 And they were *g* distressed.
6: 6 So Israel was *g* impoverished
1 Sam 11: 6 and his anger was *g* aroused.
11:15 the men of Israel rejoiced *g*.
12:18 and all the people *g* feared the
15:11 I *g* regret that I have set up
16:21 before him. And he loved him *g*,
17:11 they were dismayed and *g*
19: 1 son, delighted *g* in David.
28: 5 and his heart trembled *g*.
30: 6 Now David was *g* distressed, for
31: 4 for he was *g* afraid. Therefore
2 Sam 10: 5 because the men were *g* ashamed.
12: 5 So David's anger was *g* aroused
24:10 I have sinned *g* in what I have
1 Ki 5: 7 that he rejoiced *g* and said,
18: 3 (Now Obadiah feared the LORD *g*.
2 Ki 6:11 of the king of Syria was *g*
1 Chr 4:38 father's house increased *g*.
10: 4 for he was *g* afraid.
16:25 For the LORD is great and *g*
19: 5 because the men were *g* ashamed.
21: 8 said to God, "I have sinned *g*,
29: 9 and King David also rejoiced *g*.
2 Chr 25:10 Therefore their anger was *g*
33:12 and humbled himself *g* before
Neh 8:12 to send portions and rejoice *g*,
Job 3:25 For the thing I *g* feared has
Ps 6: 3 My soul also is *g* troubled;
6:10 all my enemies be ashamed and *g*
21: 1 And in Your salvation how *g*
28: 7 Therefore my heart *g* rejoices,
38: 6 am troubled, I am bowed down *g*;
45:11 So the King will *g* desire your
47: 9 to God; He is *g* exalted.
48: 1 and *g* to be praised In the
62: 2 I shall not be *g* moved.
65: 9 You *g* enrich it; The river of
71:23 My lips shall *g* rejoice when I
78:59 And *g* abhorred Israel,
89: 7 God is *g* to be feared in the
96: 4 For the LORD is great and *g*
105:24 He increased His people *g*,
107:38 them, and they multiply *g*;
109:30 I will *g* praise the LORD with
112: 1 Who delights *g* in His
116:10 I spoke, "I am *g* afflicted."
145: 3 and *g* to be praised; And His
Prov 23:24 father of the righteous will *g*
Eccl 8: 6 the misery of man increases *g*.
Isa 42:17 They shall be *g* ashamed,
61:10 I will *g* rejoice in the LORD,
Jer 3: 1 Would not that land be *g*
4:10 Lord GOD! Surely You have *g*
9:19 we are plundered! We are *g*
20:11 They will be *g* ashamed, for
Ezek 20:13 and they *g* defiled My Sabbaths.
25:12 and has *g* offended by avenging
27:35 Their kings will be *g* afraid,
Dan 5: 9 Then King Belshazzar was *g*
6:14 was *g* displeased with himself,
7:28 my thoughts *g* troubled me, and
9:23 for you are *g* beloved;
10:11 man *g* beloved, understand the
10:19 'O man *g* beloved, fear not!
Ob 2 You shall be *g* despised.
Zech 9: 9 Rejoice *g*, O daughter
Mt 17: 6 fell on their faces and were *g*
19:25 they were *g* astonished, saying,
20:24 they were *g* displeased with the
27:14 so that the governor marveled *g*.
27:54 had happened, they feared *g*,
Mk 6:51 And they were *g* amazed in
9: 6 for they were *g* afraid.
9:15 all the people were *g* amazed,
9:26 cried out, convulsed him *g*,
10:14 He was *g* displeased and said to
10:26 And they were *g* astonished,
10:41 they began to be *g* displeased
12:27 You are therefore *g* mistaken."
Lk 2: 9 and they were *g* afraid.
24: 4 as they were *g* perplexed about
Jn 3:29 rejoices *g* because of the
Acts 3:11 called Solomon's, *g* amazed.
4: 2 being *g* disturbed that they
6: 7 of the disciples multiplied *g*
16:18 *g* annoyed, turned and said to
18:27 he *g* helped those who had
2 Cor 10:15 we shall be *g* enlarged by you
Phil 1: 8 how *g* I long for you all with
4:10 But I rejoiced in the Lord *g*
1 Th 3: 6 *g* desiring to see us, as we
2 Tim 1: 4 *g* desiring to see you, being
4:15 for he has *g* resisted our
1 Pe 1: 6 In this you *g* rejoice, though
2 Jn 4 I rejoiced *g* that I have found

G

3 Jn 3 For I rejoiced **g** when brethren

GREATNESS (31/31) GREAT

Ex 15: 7 And in the **g** of Your excellence
15:16 By the **g** of Your arm
Num 14:19 according to the **g** of Your
Deut 3:24 to show Your servant Your **g**
5:24 shown us His glory and His **g**,
9:26 have redeemed through Your **g**,
11: 2 His **g** and His mighty hand and
32: 3 Ascribe **g** to our God.
1 Chr 17:19 heart, You have done all this **g**,
29:11 Yours, O LORD, is the **g**,
2 Chr 9: 6 and indeed the half of the **g** of
Neh 13:22 spare me according to the **g** of
Esth 10: 2 and the account of the **g** of
Ps 66: 3 are Your works! Through the **g**
71:21 You shall increase my **g**,
79:11 According to the **g** of Your
145: 3 And His **g** is unsearchable.
145: 6 And I will declare Your **g**.
150: 2 according to His excellent **g**!
Prov 5:23 And in the **g** of his folly he
Eccl 1:16 "Look, I have attained **g**,
Isa 40:26 By the **g** of His might And the
63: 1 Traveling in the **g** of His
Jer 13:22 For the **g** of your iniquity
Ezek 31: 2 'Whom are you like in your **g**?
31: 7 Thus it was beautiful in **g** and
31:18 then be likened in glory and **g**?
Dan 4:22 for your **g** has grown and
7:27 And the **g** of the kingdoms
Hos 9: 7 Because of the **g** of your
Eph 1:19 and what is the exceeding **g** of

GRECIA, GRECIANS (KJV) See GREECE, HELLENISTS

GREECE (5/5) GREEK

Dan 8:21 male goat is the kingdom of **G**.
10:20 indeed the prince of **G** will
11: 2 up all against the realm of **G**.
Zech 9:13 O Zion, Against your sons, O **G**,
Acts 20: 2 many words, he came to **G**

GREED (1/1) GREEDILY, GREEDY

Lk 11:39 your inward part is full of **g**

GREEDILY (2/2) GREED

Prov 21:26 He covets **g** all day long,
Jude 11 have run **g** in the error of

GREEDINESS (2/2) GREEDY

Eph 4:19 to work all uncleanness with **g**.
1 Tim 6:10 from the faith in their **g**,

GREEDY (7/7) GREED, GREEDINESS

Ps 10: 3 He blesses the **g** and
Prov 1:19 the ways of everyone who is **g**
15:27 He who is **g** for gain troubles
Isa 56:11 they are **g** dogs Which never
1 Tim 3: 3 not **g** for money, but gentle,
3: 8 much wine, not **g** for money,
Titus 1: 7 not violent, not **g** for money,

GREEK (14/14) GREECE, GREEKS

Mk 7:26 The woman was a **G**,
Lk 23:38 over Him in letters of **G**,
Jn 19:20 and it was written in Hebrew, **G**,
Acts 16: 1 believed, but his father was **G**.
16: 3 all knew that his father was **G**.
21:37 He replied, "Can you speak **G**?
Rom 1:16 Jew first and also for the **G**.
2: 9 the Jew first and also of the **G**;
2:10 the Jew first and also to the **G**.
10:12 distinction between Jew and **G**,
Gal 2: 3 who was with me, being a **G**,
3:28 There is neither Jew nor **G**,
Col 3:11 where there is neither **G** nor
Rev 9:11 but in **G** he has the name

GREEKS (20/19) GREEK

Joel 3: 6 You have sold to the **G**,
Jn 7:35 to the Dispersion among the **G**
7:35 the Greeks and teach the **G**?
12:20 Now there were certain **G** among
Acts 14: 1 both of the Jews and of the **G**
17: 4 great multitude of the devout **G**,
17:12 and also not a few of the **G**,
18: 4 and persuaded both Jews and **G**.
18:17 Then all the **G** took Sosthenes,
19:10 the Lord Jesus, both Jews and **G**.
19:17 known both to all Jews and **G**
20:21 to Jews, and also to **G**,
21:28 furthermore he also brought **G**
Rom 1:14 I am a debtor both to **G** and to
3: 9 charged both Jews and **G** that
1 Cor 1:22 and **G** seek after wisdom;
1:23 a stumbling block and to the **G**
1:24 who are called, both Jews and **G**,
10:32 either to the Jews or to the **G**
12:13 into one body—whether Jews or **G**,

GREEN (39/38)

Gen 1:30 I have given every **g** herb
9: 3 even as the **g** herbs.
30:37 took for himself rods of **g**
Ex 10:15 So there remained nothing **g** on
Lev 2:14 offering of your firstfruits **g**
Deut 12: 2 on the hills and under every **g**
1 Ki 14:23 high hill and under every **g**
2 Ki 16: 4 and under every **g** tree.
17:10 high hill and under every **g**
19:26 grass of the field And the **g**
2 Chr 28: 4 and under every **g** tree.
Job 8:12 While it is yet **g** and not cut
8:16 He grows **g** in the sun, And his
15:32 And his branch will not be **g**.
39: 8 And he searches after every **g**
Ps 23: 2 He makes me to lie down in **g**
37: 2 And wither as the **g** herb.
37:35 himself like a native **g** tree.
52: 8 But I am like a **g** olive tree
Song 1:16 pleasant! Also our bed is **g**.
2:13 The fig tree puts forth her **g**
Isa 15: 6 For the **g** grass has withered
15: 6 grass fails, there is nothing **g**.
37:27 grass of the field And the **g**
57: 5 with gods under every **g** tree,
Jer 2:20 high hill and under every **g**
3: 6 high mountain and under every **g**
3:13 To alien deities under every **g**
11:16 **G** Olive Tree, Lovely and of
17: 2 their wooden images By the **g**
17: 8 But its leaf will be **g**,
Ezek 6:13 under every **g** tree, and under
17:24 dried up the **g** tree and made
20:47 and it shall devour every **g**
Hos 14: 8 I am like a **g** cypress tree;
Mk 6:39 all sit down in groups on the **g**
Lk 23:31 they do these things in the **g**
Rev 8: 7 and all **g** grass was burned up.
9: 4 or any **g** thing, or any tree,

GREENISH (2/2)

Lev 13:49 and if the plague is **g** or
14:37 **g** or reddish, which appear to

GREET (54/43) GREETED, GREETING, GREETS

1 Sam 10: 4 And they will **g** you and give you
13:10 that he might **g** him.
25: 5 and **g** him in my name.
25:14 from the wilderness to **g** our
2 Sam 8:10 to **g** him and bless him, because
2 Ki 4:29 do not **g** him; and if anyone
10:13 we have come down to **g** the sons
1 Chr 18:10 to **g** him and bless him, because
Mt 5:47 And if you **g** your brethren only,
10:12 a household, **g** it.
Lk 10: 4 and **g** no one along the road.
Acts 25:13 Bernice came to Caesarea to **g**
Rom 16: 3 **G** Priscilla and Aquila, my
16: 5 Likewise **g** the church that is
16: 5 **G** my beloved Epaenetus, who is
16: 6 **G** Mary, who labored much for us.
16: 7 **G** Andronicus and Junia, my
16: 8 **G** Amplias, my beloved in the
16: 9 **G** Urbanus, our fellow worker in
16:10 **G** Apelles, approved in Christ.
16:10 **G** those who are of the
16:11 **G** Herodion, my countryman.
16:11 **G** those who are of the
16:12 **G** Tryphena and Tryphosa, who
16:12 **G** the beloved Persis, who
16:13 **G** Rufus, chosen in the Lord, and
16:14 **G** Asyncritus, Phlegon, Hermas,
16:15 **G** Philologus and Julia, Nereus
16:16 **G** one another with a holy kiss.
16:16 The churches of Christ **g** you.
16:21 my countrymen, **g** you.
16:22 **g** you in the Lord.
1 Cor 16:19 The churches of Asia **g** you.
16:19 Aquila and Priscilla **g** you
16:20 All the brethren **g** you.
16:20 **G** one another with a holy kiss.
2 Cor 13:12 **G** one another with a holy kiss.
13:13 All the saints **g** you.
Phil 4:21 **G** every saint in Christ Jesus
4:21 The brethren who are with me **g**
4:22 All the saints **g** you, but
Col 4:14 beloved physician and Demas **g**.
4:15 **G** the brethren who are in
1 Th 5:26 **G** all the brethren with a holy
2 Tim 4:19 **G** Prisca and Aquila, and the
Titus 3:15 All who are with me **g** you.
3:15 **G** those who love us in the
Heb 13:24 **G** all those who rule over you,
13:24 Those from Italy **g** you.
1 Pe 5:14 **G** one another with a kiss of
2 Jn 10 him into your house nor **g** him;
13 of your elect sister **g** you.
3 Jn 14 Our friends **g** you. Greet the
14 **G** the friends by name.

GREETED (9/9) GREET

Judg 18:15 house of Micah—and **g** him.
1 Sam 17:22 and came and **g** his brothers.
30:21 near the people, he **g** them.
2 Ki 10:15 and he **g** him and said to him,
Mk 9:15 running to Him, **g** Him.
Lk 1:40 the house of Zacharias and **g**
Acts 18:22 and gone up and **g** the church,
21: 7 **g** the brethren, and stayed with
21:19 When he had **g** them, he told in

GREETING (3/3) GREET, GREETINGS

Lk 1:29 and considered what manner of **g**
1:41 when Elizabeth heard the **g** of
1:44 as soon as the voice of your **g**

GREETINGS (9/9) GREETING

Mt 23: 7 **g** in the marketplaces, and to be
26:49 went up to Jesus and said, "**G**,
Mk 12:38 love **g** in the marketplaces,
Lk 11:43 seats in the synagogues and **g**
20:46 love **g** in the marketplaces, the
Acts 15:23 Antioch, Syria, and Cilicia: **G**.
15:33 they were sent back with **g** from
23:26 excellent governor Felix: **G**.
Jas 1: 1 which are scattered abroad: **G**.

GREETS (9/8) GREET

2 Ki 4:29 and if anyone **g** you, do not
Rom 16:23 **g** you. Erastus, the treasurer
16:23 **g** you, and Quartus, a brother.
Col 4:10 my fellow prisoner **g** you,
4:12 **g** you, always laboring
2 Tim 4:21 Eubulus **g** you, as well as
Phm 1:23 in Christ Jesus, **g** you,
1 Pe 5:13 **g** you; and so does Mark my
2 Jn 11 for he who **g** him shares in his

GREW (51/47) GROW

Gen 19:25 and what **g** on the ground.
21: 8 So the child **g** and was weaned.
21:20 and he **g** and dwelt in the
25:27 So the boys **g**. And Esau was
47:27 had possessions there and **g**
Ex 1: 7 multiplied and **g** exceedingly
1:12 the more they multiplied and **g**.
1:20 and the people multiplied and **g**
2:10 And the child **g**, and she
7:13 And Pharaoh's heart **g** hard, and
7:22 and Pharaoh's heart **g** hard, and
8:19 But Pharaoh's heart **g** hard,
Deut 32:15 But Jeshurun **g** fat and kicked;
32:15 You **g** fat, you grew thick,
32:15 you **g** thick, You are obese!
Josh 17:13 when the children of Israel **g**
Judg 4:24 of the children of Israel **g**
11: 2 and when his wife's sons **g** up,
13:24 name Samson; and the child **g**,
1 Sam 2:21 Meanwhile the child Samuel **g**
2:26 And the child Samuel **g** in
3:19 So Samuel **g**, and the LORD
2 Sam 3: 1 But David **g** stronger and
3: 1 and the house of Saul **g** weaker
12: 3 and it **g** up together with him
15:12 And the conspiracy **g** strong,
21:15 and David **g** faint.
2 Ki 4:18 And the child **g**.
2 Chr 13:21 But Abijah **g** mighty, married
24:15 But Jehoiada **g** old and was full
Neh 9:25 they ate and were filled and **g**
Ps 32: 3 my bones **g** old Through my
Ezek 16: 7 a plant in the field; and you **g**,
16: 7 were formed, your hair **g**,
17: 6 And it **g** and became a spreading
17:10 the garden terrace where it **g**.
Dan 4:11 The tree **g** and became strong;
4:20 which **g** and became strong,
8: 8 Therefore the male goat **g** very
8: 9 them came a little horn which **g**
8:10 And it **g** up to the host of
Jon 4: 8 so that he **g** faint. Then he
Mk 4: 7 and the thorns **g** up and choked
5:26 no better, but rather **g** worse.
Lk 1:80 So the child **g** and became strong
2:40 And the Child **g** and became
13:19 and it **g** and became a large
Acts 7:17 the people **g** and multiplied in
12:24 But the word of God **g** and
13:46 Then Paul and Barnabas **g** bold
19:20 So the word of the Lord **g**

GREY, GREYHEADED (KJV) See GRAY, GRAYHEADED

GREYHOUND (1/1)

Prov 30:31 A **g**, A male goat also,

GRIEF (28/28) GRIEFS, GRIEVE

Gen 26:35 And they were a **g** of mind to
1 Sam 1:16 of my complaint and **g** I have
25:31 that this will be no **g** to you,
2 Chr 6:29 his own burden and his own **g**,
Job 2:13 for they saw that his **g** was
6: 2 that my **g** were fully weighed,
16: 5 my lips would relieve your **g**.
16: 6 my **g** is not relieved; And if
Ps 6: 7 eye wastes away because of **g**;
10:14 for You observe trouble and **g**,
31: 9 My eye wastes away with **g**,
31:10 For my life is spent with **g**,
69:26 And talk of the **g** of those You
Prov 10: 1 But a foolish son is the **g** of

14:13 the end of mirth may be **g**.
17:25 A foolish son is a **g** to his
Eccl 1:18 For in much wisdom is much **g**,
Isa 17:11 heap of ruins In the day of **g**
53: 3 sorrows and acquainted with **g**.
53:10 He has put Him to **g**.
65:14 And wail for **g** of spirit.
Jer 6: 7 Before Me continually are **g**
45: 3 For the LORD has added **g** to
Lam 3:32 Though He causes **g**, Yet He
Rom 9: 2 great sorrow and continual **g**
2 Cor 2: 5 But if anyone has caused **g**,
Heb 13:17 do so with joy and not with **g**,
1 Pe 2:19 toward God one endures **g**,

GRIEFS (1/1) GRIEF
Isa 53: 4 Surely He has borne our **g** And

GRIEVE (4/4) GRIEF, GRIEVED, GRIEVES
1 Sam 2:33 shall consume your eyes and **g**
Lam 3:33 Nor **g** the children of men.
Zech 12:10 and **g** for Him as one grieves
Eph 4:30 And do not **g** the Holy Spirit of

GRIEVED (34/34) GRIEVE
Gen 6: 6 and He was **g** in His heart.
34: 7 and the men were **g** and very
45: 5 do not therefore be **g** or angry
49:23 The archers have bitterly **g**
Deut 15:10 and your heart should not be **g**
Judg 21: 6 And the children of Israel **g** for
21:15 And the people **g** for Benjamin,
1 Sam 1: 8 And why is your heart **g**?
15:11 And it **g** Samuel, and he cried
20: 3 know this, lest he be **g**.
20:34 for he was **g** for David, because
30: 6 soul of all the people was **g**,
2 Sam 19: 2 The king is **g** for his son."
Neh 8:11 the day is holy; do not be **g**.
13: 8 And it **g** me bitterly; therefore
Job 30:25 Has not my soul **g** for the
Ps 73:21 Thus my heart was **g**, And I
78:40 And **g** Him in the desert!
95:10 For forty years I was **g** with
112:10 wicked will see it and be **g**;
Isa 54: 6 Like a woman forsaken and **g**
57:10 Therefore you were not **g**.
63:10 But they rebelled and **g** His
Jer 5: 3 But they have not **g**;
Dan 7:15 was **g** in my spirit within my
11:30 therefore he shall be **g**,
Am 6: 6 But are not **g** for the
Mt 18:31 had been done, they were very **g**,
Mk 3: 5 being **g** by the hardness of
Jn 21:17 Peter was **g** because He said
Rom 14:15 Yet if your brother is **g** because
2 Cor 2: 4 tears, not that you should be **g**,
2: 5 he has not **g** me, but all of you
1 Pe 1: 6 you have been **g** by various

GRIEVES (2/2) GRIEVE
Ruth 1:13 for it **g** me very much for your
Zech 12:10 and grieve for Him as one **g** for

GRIND (5/5) GRINDER, GRINDING
Job 31:10 Then let my wife **g** for
Prov 27:22 Though you **g** a fool in a mortar
Isa 47: 2 Take the millstones and **g** meal.
Mt 21:44 it will **g** him to powder."
Lk 20:18 it will **g** him to powder."

GRINDER (1/1) GRIND, GRINDERS
Judg 16:21 and he became a **g** in the

GRINDERS (1/1) GRINDER
Eccl 12: 3 When the **g** cease because they

GRINDING (4/4) GRIND
Eccl 12: 4 And the sound of **g** is low;
Isa 3:15 by crushing My people And **g**
Mt 24:41 Two women will be **g** at the
Lk 17:35 Two women will be **g** together:

GRIP (1/1)
Jer 15:21 I will redeem you from the **g**

GRISLED (KJV) See DAPPLED, GRAY-SPOTTED

GROAN (9/9) GROANED, GROANING, GROANS
Job 24:12 The dying **g** in the city,
Ps 38: 8 I **g** because of the turmoil of
Prov 29: 2 wicked man rules, the people **g**.
Jer 51:52 her land the wounded shall **g**.
Ezek 30:24 and he will **g** before him with
Joel 1:18 How the animals **g**! The herds
Rom 8:23 even we ourselves **g** within
2 Cor 5: 2 For in this we **g**, earnestly
5: 4 For we who are in this tent **g**,

GROANED (2/2) GROAN
Ex 2:23 Then the children of Israel **g**
Jn 11:33 He **g** in the spirit and was

GROANING (12/12) GROAN, GROANINGS
Ex 2:24 So God heard their **g**,
6: 5 And I have also heard the **g** of
Judg 2:18 was moved to pity by their **g**
Job 23: 2 is listless because of my **g**.
Ps 6: 6 I am weary with my **g**;
22: 1 And from the words of My **g**?
32: 3 my bones grew old Through my **g**
79:11 Let the **g** of the prisoner come
102: 5 Because of the sound of my **g**
102:20 To hear the **g** of the prisoner,
Jn 11:38 again **g** in Himself, came to the
Acts 7:34 I have heard their **g** and

GROANINGS (3/3) GROANING
Job 3:24 And my **g** pour out like water.
Ezek 30:24 groan before him with the **g** of
Rom 8:26 intercession for us with **g**

GROANS (1/1) GROAN
Rom 8:22 know that the whole creation **g**

GROPE (6/5)
Deut 28:29 And you shall **g** at noonday, as a
Job 5:14 And **g** at noontime as in the
12:25 They **g** in the dark without
Isa 59:10 We **g** for the wall like the
59:10 And we **g** as if we had no
Acts 17:27 in the hope that they might **g**

GROPES (1/1)
Deut 28:29 as a blind man **g** in darkness;

GROSS (1/1)
2 Ki 8:13 that he should do this **g** thing?"

GROUND (217/213) GROUNDED
Gen 2: 5 was no man to till the **g**;
2: 6 watered the whole face of the **g**.
2: 7 man of the dust of the **g**,
2: 9 And out of the **g** the LORD God
2:19 Out of the **g** the LORD God
3:17 Cursed is the **g** for your sake;
3:19 Till you return to the **g**,
3:23 garden of Eden to till the **g**
4: 2 but Cain was a tiller of the **g**.
4: 3 offering of the fruit of the **g**
4:10 cries out to Me from the **g**.
4:12 "When you till the **g**,
4:14 this day from the face of the **g**;
5:29 because of the **g** which the
7:23 which were on the face of the **g**:
8: 8 receded from the face of the **g**.
8:13 and indeed the surface of the **g**
8:21 will never again curse the **g**
18: 2 and bowed himself to the **g**,
19: 1 with his face toward the **g**.
19:25 cities, and what grew on the **g**.
33: 3 them and bowed himself to the **g**
38: 9 wife, that he emitted on the **g**,
41:47 the seven plentiful years the **g**
44:11 let down his sack to the **g**,
44:14 they fell before him on the **g**.
Ex 3: 5 where you stand is holy **g**.
4: 3 And He said, "Cast it on the **g**.
4: 3 So he cast it on the **g**,
8:21 and also the **g** on which they
9:23 hail, and fire darted to the **g**.
14:16 of Israel shall go on dry **g**
14:22 midst of the sea on the dry **g**,
16:14 as fine as frost on the **g**.
32:20 and **g** it to powder; and he
Lev 20:25 thing that creeps on the **g**,
Num 11: 8 **g** it on millstones or beat it
11:31 above the surface of the **g**.
15:20 a cake of the first of your **g**
15:21 Of the first of your **g** meal you
16:31 that the **g** split apart under
Deut 4:18 anything that creeps on the **g**
9:21 fire and crushed it and **g** it
15:23 you shall pour it on the **g** like
22: 6 way, in any tree or on the **g**,
26: 2 of all the produce of the **g**,
28: 4 the produce of your **g** and the
28:11 and in the produce of your **g**,
28:56 the sole of her foot on the **g**
Josh 3:17 the LORD stood firm on dry **g**
3:17 Israel crossed over on dry **g**,
24:32 in the plot of **g** which Jacob
Judg 4:21 and it went down into the **g**;
6:37 and it is dry on all the **g**,
6:39 but on all the **g** let there be
6:40 but there was dew on all the **g**.
13:20 fell on their faces to the **g**.
20:21 on that day cut down to the **g**
20:25 and cut down to the **g** eighteen
20:36 The men of Israel had given **g**
Ruth 2:10 her face, bowed down to the **g**,
1 Sam 3:19 none of his words fall to the **g**.
5: 4 fallen on its face to the **g**
8:12 will set some to plow his **g**
14:25 and there was honey on the **g**.
14:32 and slaughtered them on the **g**;
14:45 of his head shall fall to the **g**,
20:41 fell on his face to the **g**,
25:23 David, and bowed down to the **g**.
26: 7 with his spear stuck in the **g**
28:14 with his face to the **g** and
28:20 Saul fell full length on the **g**,
28:23 Then he arose from the **g** and
2 Sam 1: 2 that he fell to the **g** and
2:22 should I strike you to the **g**?
8: 2 Forcing them down to the **g**,
12:16 in and lay all night on the **g**.
12:17 him, to raise him up from the **g**.
12:20 So David arose from the **g**,
13:31 his garments and lay on the **g**,
14: 4 she fell on her face to the **g**
14:11 of your son shall fall to the **g**.
14:14 like water spilled on the **g**,
14:22 Then Joab fell to the **g** on his
14:33 himself on his face to the **g**
17:12 him as the dew falls on the **g**.
17:19 and spread **g** grain on it;
18:11 not strike him there to the **g**?
20:10 entrails poured out on the **g**;
23:11 where there was a piece of **g**
24:20 the king with his face to the **g**.
1 Ki 1:23 the king with his face to the **g**.
18:42 then he bowed down on the **g**,
2 Ki 2: 8 of them crossed over on dry **g**.
2:15 and bowed to the **g** before him.
2:19 is bad, and the **g** barren."
4:37 at his feet, and bowed to the **g**;
9:10 eat Jezebel on the plot of **g**
9:26 throw him on the plot of **g**,
9:36 On the plot of **g** at Jezreel
13:18 Strike the **g**"; so he struck
23: 6 it at the Brook Kidron and **g**
1 Chr 11:13 and there was a piece of **g** full
21:21 David with his face to the **g**.
27:26 of the field for tilling the **g**.
2 Chr 2:10 twenty thousand kors of **g**
7: 3 bowed their faces to the **g** on
20:18 head with his face to the **g**,
Neh 8: 6 with their faces to the **g**.
10:35 bring the firstfruits of our **g**
Job 1:20 and he fell to the **g** and
2:13 they sat down with him on the **g**
5: 6 does trouble spring from the **g**;
14: 8 And its stump may die in the **g**,
16:13 He pours out my gall on the **g**.
18:10 is hidden for him on the **g**,
39:14 she leaves her eggs on the **g**,
Ps 44:25 Our body clings to the **g**.
74: 7 place of Your name to the **g**.
89:39 crown by casting it to the **g**.
89:44 cast his throne down to the **g**.
105:35 devoured the fruit of their **g**.
107:33 the watersprings into dry **g**;
143: 3 has crushed my life to the **g**;
147: 6 casts the wicked down to the **g**.
Prov 13:23 food is in the fallow **g** of
Eccl 10: 7 While princes walk on the **g**
Isa 3:26 desolate shall sit on the **g**.
14:12 How you are cut down to the **g**,
21: 9 gods He has broken to the **g**.
25:12 lay low, And bring to the **g**,
26: 5 low, He lays it low to the **g**,
28:28 Bread flour must be **g**;
29: 4 You shall speak out of the **g**;
29: 4 like a medium's, out of the **g**;
30:23 seed With which you sow the **g**,
30:24 young donkeys that work the **g**
35: 7 The parched **g** shall become a
44: 3 And floods on the dry **g**;
47: 1 Sit on the **g** without a throne,
51:23 have laid your body like the **g**,
53: 2 And as a root out of dry **g**.
Jer 4: 3 "Break up your fallow **g**,
7:20 field and on the fruit of the **g**.
14: 4 Because the **g** is parched,
25:33 shall become refuse on the **g**.
27: 5 the beast that are on the **g**,
Lam 2: 2 has brought them down to the **g**;
2: 9 Her gates have sunk into the **g**;
2:10 daughter of Zion Sit on the **g**
2:10 Bow their heads to the **g**.
2:11 My bile is poured on the **g**
2:21 Young and old lie On the **g** in
5:13 Young men **g** at the millstones;
Ezek 12: 6 so that you cannot see the **g**,
12:12 so that he cannot see the **g**
13:14 and bring it down to the **g**,
19:12 She was cast down to the **g**,
24: 7 She did not pour it on the **g**,
26:11 pillars will fall to the **g**.
26:16 they will sit on the **g**,
28:17 I cast you to the **g**, I laid
38:20 every wall shall fall to the **g**.
39:14 those bodies remaining on the **g**,
41:16 paneled with wood from the **g**
42: 6 and middle levels from the **g**
43:14 from the base on the **g** to the
44:30 the priest the first of your **g**
Dan 8: 5 earth, without touching the **g**;
8: 7 but he cast him down to the **g**
8:10 and some of the stars to the **g**
8:12 and he cast truth down to the **g**.
8:18 sleep with my face to the **g**;
10: 9 my face, with my face to the **g**.
10:15 I turned my face toward the **g**

Hos 2:18 the creeping things of the **g**.
10:12 Break up your fallow **g**,
Am 3:14 be cut off And fall to the **g**.
9: 9 grain shall fall to the **g**.
Ob 3 will bring me down to the **g**?
Hag 1:11 on whatever the **g** brings forth,
Zech 8:12 The **g** shall give her increase,
Mal 3:11 not destroy the fruit of your **g**,
Mt 10:29 not one of them falls to the **g**
13: 8 But others fell on good **g** and
13:23 received seed on the good **g** is
15:35 multitude to sit down on the **g**.
25:18 one went and dug in the **g**,
25:25 and hid your talent in the **g**.
Mk 4: 5 "Some fell on stony **g**,
4: 8 other seed fell on good **g**
4:16 are the ones sown on stony **g**
4:20 are the ones sown on good **g**,
4:26 should scatter seed on the **g**,
4:31 which, when it is sown on the **g**,
8: 6 multitude to sit down on the **g**.
9:20 and he fell on the **g** and
14:35 farther, and fell on the **g**,
Lk 8: 8 "But others fell on good **g**,
8:15 ones that fell on the good **g**
12:16 The **g** of a certain rich man
13: 7 why does it use up the **g**?'
14:18 'I have bought a piece of **g**,
19:44 children within you, to the **g**;
22:44 of blood falling down to the **g**.
Jn 4: 5 near the plot of **g** that Jacob
8: 6 down and wrote on the **g** with
8: 8 stooped down and wrote on the **g**.
9: 6 He spat on the **g** and made clay
12:24 of wheat falls into the **g** and
18: 6 drew back and fell to the **g**.
Acts 7:33 where you stand is holy **g**.
9: 4 Then he fell to the **g**,
9: 8 Then Saul arose from the **g**,
22: 7 And I fell to the **g** and heard a
26:14 when we all had fallen to the **g**,
1 Tim 3:15 the pillar and **g** of the truth.

GROUNDED (2/2) GROUND

Eph 3:17 being rooted and **g** in love,
Col 1:23 **g** and steadfast, and are not

GROUP (6/5) GROUPS

1 Sam 10: 5 that you will meet a **g** of
10:10 there was a **g** of prophets to
19:20 And when they saw the **g** of
1 Chr 24: 5 one **g** as another, for there
Neh 12:24 **g** alternating with group,
12:24 group alternating with **g**,

GROUPS (2/2) GROUP

Mk 6:39 to make them all sit down in **g**
Lk 9:14 Make them sit down in **g** of

GROVE (7/7) GROVES

Ex 23:11 your vineyard and your olive **g**.
Num 25: 1 Now Israel remained in Acacia **G**,
Josh 2: 1 sent out two men from Acacia **G**
3: 1 and they set out from Acacia **G**
Eccl 2: 6 the growing trees of the **g**.
Mic 6: 5 From Acacia **G** to Gilgal,

GROVES (7/7) GROVE

Josh 24:13 of the vineyards and olive **g**
Judg 15: 5 as the vineyards and olive **g**.
1 Sam 8:14 vineyards, and your olive **g**,
2 Ki 5:26 olive **g** and vineyards, sheep
18:32 a land of olive **g** and honey,
Neh 5:11 their vineyards, their olive **g**,
9:25 dug, vineyards, olive **g**,

GROW (56/56) FULL-GROWN, GREW, GROWING, GROWN, GROWS, GROWTH

Gen 2: 9 the LORD God made every tree **g**
48:16 And let them **g** into a
Num 6: 5 locks of the hair of his head **g**.
Deut 29:23 nor does any grass **g** there,
Judg 16:22 the hair of his head began to **g**
1 Sam 3: 2 when his eyes had begun to **g**
Job 8:11 Can the papyrus **g** up without a
8:19 out of the earth others will **g**.
14: 8 Though its root may **g** old in
31:40 Then let thistles **g** instead of
39: 4 They **g** strong with grain;
Ps 92:12 He shall **g** like a cedar in
102:26 they will all **g** old like a
104:14 He causes the grass to **g** for
132:17 I will make the horn of David **g**;
147: 8 Who makes grass to **g** on the
Eccl 11: 5 Or how the bones **g** in the
12: 3 look through the windows **g** dim;
Isa 11: 1 And a Branch shall **g** out of
17: 4 And the fatness of his flesh **g**
17:11 you will make your plant to **g**,
29:22 Nor shall his face now **g** pale;
50: 9 Indeed they will all **g** old
51: 6 The earth will **g** old like a
53: 2 For He shall **g** up before Him as
Jer 6:24 Our hands **g** feeble.
12: 2 they have taken root; They **g**,
33:15 at that time I will cause to **g**
50:43 And his hands **g** feeble;
Lam 5:17 of these things our eyes **g**
Ezek 31: 4 The waters made it **g**;
44:20 heads nor let their hair **g**
47:12 will **g** all kinds of trees
Hos 10: 8 The thorn and thistle shall **g**
14: 5 He shall **g** like the lily,
14: 7 And **g** like a vine.
Joel 2:10 The sun and moon **g** dark,
3:15 The sun and moon will **g** dark,
Jon 1:13 for the sea continued to **g** more
4:10 have not labored, nor made it **g**,
Mal 4: 2 And you shall go out And **g**
Mt 6:28 lilies of the field, how they **g**:
13:30 Let both **g** together until the
21:19 Let no fruit **g** on you ever
24:12 the love of many will **g** cold.
Mk 4:27 the seed should sprout and **g**,
Lk 12:27 the lilies, how they **g**:
12:33 money bags which do not **g** old,
Gal 6: 9 And let us not **g** weary while
Eph 4:15 may **g** up in all things into Him
2 Th 3:13 do not **g** weary in doing good.
1 Tim 5:11 for when they have begun to **g**
2 Tim 3:13 evil men and impostors will **g**
Heb 1:11 And they will all **g** old
1 Pe 2: 2 that you may **g** thereby,
2 Pe 3:18 but **g** in the grace and knowledge

GROWING (3/3) GROW

Eccl 2: 6 pools from which to water the **g**
Jon 1:11 for the sea was **g** more
Heb 8:13 is becoming obsolete and **g** old

GROWL (4/4)

Ps 59: 6 They **g** like a dog, And go all
59:14 They **g** like a dog, And go all
Isa 59:11 We all **g** like bears, And moan
Jer 51:38 They shall **g** like lions'

GROWLED (1/1)

Jer 2:15 lions roared at him, and **g**;

GROWN (33/32) GROW

Gen 2: 5 any herb of the field had **g**.
18:12 After I have **g** old, shall I have
19:13 the outcry against them has **g**
38:11 house till my son Shelah is **g**.
38:14 for she saw that Shelah was **g**,
Ex 2:11 in those days, when Moses was **g**,
Lev 13:37 and there is black hair **g** up in
Deut 4:25 and grandchildren and have **g**
31:20 and filled themselves and **g**
Ruth 1:13 wait for them till they were **g**?
2 Sam 10: 5 until your beards have **g**,
1 Ki 12: 8 the young men who had **g** up
12:10 Then the young men who had **g** up
2 Ki 19:26 grain blighted before it is **g**.
1 Chr 19: 5 until your beards have **g**,
2 Chr 10: 8 the young men who had **g** up
10:10 Then the young men who had **g** up
Ezra 9: 6 and our guilt has **g** up to the
Job 17: 7 My eye has also **g** dim because
Ps 144:12 our sons may be as plants **g**
Isa 37:27 grain blighted before it is **g**.
Jer 5:27 they have become great and **g**
5:28 They have **g** fat, they are
49:24 Damascus has **g** feeble;
50:11 Because you have **g** fat like a
Ezek 23:43 concerning her who had **g**
24:12 She has **g** weary with lies,
Dan 4:22 who have **g** and become strong;
4:22 for your greatness has **g** and
4:33 of heaven till his hair had **g**
Mt 13:15 of this people have **g**
13:32 but when it is **g** it is greater
Acts 28:27 of this people have **g**

GROWS (17/17) GROW

Ex 10: 5 shall eat every tree which **g**
Lev 13:39 it is a white spot that **g** on
25: 5 What **g** of its own accord of your
25:11 neither sow nor reap what **g** of
2 Ki 19:29 shall eat this year such as **g**
Job 8:16 He **g** green in the sun, And his
30:30 My skin **g** black and falls from
Ps 6: 7 It **g** old because of all my
90: 5 they are like grass which **g**
90: 6 morning it flourishes and **g** up;
129: 6 Which withers before it **g** up,
Isa 37:30 shall eat this year such as **g**
Mk 4:32 it **g** up and becomes greater
Eph 2:21 **g** into a holy temple in the
4:22 the old man which **g** corrupt
Col 2:19 **g** with the increase that is
2 Th 1: 3 because your faith **g**

GROWTH (3/3) GROW

Job 38:27 cause to spring forth the **g** of
Ps 65:10 with showers, You bless its **g**.
Eph 4:16 causes **g** of the body for the

GRUDGE (1/1) GRUDGING, GRUDGINGLY

Lev 19:18 nor bear any **g** against the

GRUDGING (1/1) GRUDGE, GRUDGINGLY

2 Cor 9: 5 and not as a **g** obligation.

GRUDGINGLY (1/1) GRUDGE, GRUDGING

2 Cor 9: 7 not **g** or of necessity; for God

GRUESOME (1/1)

Jer 16: 4 'They shall die **g** deaths;

GRUMBLE (1/1) GRUMBLING

Jas 5: 9 Do not **g** against one another,

GRUMBLERS (1/1)

Jude 16 These are **g**, complainers,

GRUMBLING (1/1) GRUMBLE

1 Pe 4: 9 to one another without **g**.

GUARANTEE (3/3)

2 Cor 1:22 the Spirit in our hearts as a **g**.
5: 5 has given us the Spirit as a **g**.
Eph 1:14 who is the **g** of our inheritance

GUARD (74/74) GUARDED, GUARDIAN, GUARDING, GUARDROOM, GUARDS

Gen 3:24 to **g** the way to the tree of
37:36 Pharaoh and captain of the **g**.
39: 1 of Pharaoh, captain of the **g**,
40: 3 house of the captain of the **g**,
40: 4 And the captain of the **g** charged
41:10 house of the captain of the **g**,
41:12 servant of the captain of the **g**.
Num 10:25 children of Dan (the rear **g** of
15:34 They put him under **g**,
Josh 6: 9 and the rear **g** came after the
6:13 But the rear **g** came after the
8:13 and its rear **g** on the west of
10:18 and set men by it to **g** them.
10:19 and attack their rear **g**.
1 Sam 2: 9 He will **g** the feet of His
19: 2 Therefore please be on your **g**
2 Sam 23:23 David appointed him over his **g**.
1 Ki 14:27 hands of the captains of the **g**,
20:39 **G** this man; if by any means he
2 Ki 10:25 that Jehu said to the **g** and to
11:15 "Take her outside under **g**,
25: 8 the captain of the **g**,
25:10 with the captain of the **g**
25:11 the captain of the **g** carried
25:12 But the captain of the **g** left
25:15 the captain of the **g** took away.
25:18 And the captain of the **g** took
25:20 Nebuzaradan, captain of the **g**,
1 Chr 11:25 David appointed him over his **g**.
2 Chr 12:10 hands of the captains of the **g**,
12:11 the **g** would go and bring them
23:14 "Take her outside under **g**,
Neh 4:22 that they may be our **g** by night
4:23 nor the men of the **g** who
7: 3 is hot; and while they stand **g**,
13:22 and that they should go and **g**
Job 7:12 That You set a **g** over me?
Ps 39: 1 I will **g** my ways, Lest I sin
141: 3 Set a **g**, O LORD, over my
Isa 52:12 of Israel will be your rear **g**.
58: 8 the LORD shall be your rear **g**.
Jer 37:13 a captain of the **g** was there
39: 9 the captain of the **g** carried
39:10 the captain of the **g** left in
39:11 the captain of the **g**, saying,
39:13 the captain of the **g** sent
40: 1 the captain of the **g** had let
40: 2 And the captain of the **g** took
40: 5 So the captain of the **g** gave
41:10 the captain of the **g** had
43: 6 the captain of the **g** had left
51:12 Make the **g** strong, Set up the
52:12 the captain of the **g**,
52:14 were with the captain of the **g**
52:15 the captain of the **g** carried
52:16 the captain of the **g** left
52:19 the captain of the **g** took away.
52:24 The captain of the **g** took
52:26 the captain of the **g** took
52:30 the captain of the **g** carried
Ezek 38: 7 and be a **g** for them.
Dan 2:14 the captain of the king's **g**,
Mic 7: 5 **G** the doors of your mouth
Mt 27:65 said to them, "You have a **g**;
27:66 the stone and setting the **g**.
28:11 some of the **g** came into the
Lk 8:29 him, and he was kept under **g**,
Acts 12:10 past the first and the second **g**
28:16 to the captain of the **g**;
Gal 3:23 we were kept under **g** by the
Phil 1:13 evident to the whole palace **g**,
4: 7 will **g** your hearts and minds
2 Th 3: 3 who will establish you and **g**
1 Tim 6:20 O Timothy! **G** what was committed

GUARDED (5/5) GUARD
1 Sam 26:15 Why then have you not *g* your
26:16 because you have not *g* your
1 Ki 14:27 who *g* the doorway of the king's
2 Chr 12:10 who *g* the doorway of the king's
Acts 28:16 himself with the soldier who *g*

GUARDIAN (2/2) GUARD, GUARDIANS
Num 11:12 as a *g* carries a nursing
Acts 19:35 of the Ephesians is temple *g*

GUARDIANS (2/2) GUARDIAN
1 Sam 28: 2 will make you one of my chief *g*
Gal 4: 2 but is under *g* and stewards

GUARDING (3/3) GUARD
Mt 27:54 who were *g* Jesus, saw the
Acts 22:20 and *g* the clothes of those who
2 Cor 11:32 was *g* the city of the

GUARDROOM (2/2) GUARD
1 Ki 14:28 brought them back into the *g*.
2 Chr 12:11 would take them back into the *g*.

GUARDS (16/16) GUARD
1 Sam 22:17 Then the king said to the *g* who
1 Ki 14:28 the *g* carried them, then
2 Ki 10:25 then the *g* and the officers
Neh 7: 3 and appoint *g* from among the
Ps 34:20 He *g* all his bones; Not one of
127: 1 Unless the LORD *g* the city,
Prov 2: 8 He *g* the paths of justice,
13: 3 He who *g* his mouth preserves
13: 6 Righteousness *g* him whose way
21:23 Whoever *g* his mouth and tongue
22: 5 He who *g* his soul will be far
Mt 28: 4 And the *g* shook for fear of him,
Lk 11:21 *g* his own palace, his goods are
Acts 5:23 and the *g* standing outside
12: 6 and the *g* before the door were
12:19 he examined the *g* and commanded

GUDGODAH (2/1)
Deut 10: 7 From there they journeyed to *G*,
10: 7 and from *G* to Jotbathah, a land

GUEST (4/4) GUESTS
Mk 14:14 Where is the *g* room in which I
Lk 19: 7 He has gone to be a *g* with a man
22:11 Where is the *g* room where I may
Phm 1:22 also prepare a *g* room for me,

GUESTCHAMBER (KJV) See GUEST (ROOM)

GUESTS (7/7) GUEST
1 Ki 1:41 Now Adonijah and all the *g* who
1:49 So all the *g* who were with
Prov 9:18 That her *g* are in the depths
Zeph 1: 7 He has invited His *g*.
Mt 22:10 wedding hall was filled with *g*.
22:11 the king came in to see the *g*,
Jn 2:10 and when the *g* have well

GUIDANCE (4/4) GUIDE
2 Sam 20:18 They shall surely seek *g* at
1 Chr 10:13 he consulted a medium for *g*.
Job 37:12 about, being turned by His *g*,
Isa 28:29 in counsel and excellent in *g*.

GUIDE (16/16) GUIDANCE, GUIDED, GUIDES, GUIDING
Job 38:32 Or can you *g* the Great Bear
Ps 31: 3 Lead me and *g* me.
32: 8 I will *g* you with My eye.
48:14 He will be our *g* Even to
73:24 You will *g* me with Your
112: 5 He will *g* his affairs with
Prov 11: 3 of the upright will *g* them,
23:19 And *g* your heart in the way.
Isa 49:10 the springs of water He will *g*
51:18 There is no one to *g* her
58:11 The LORD will *g* you
Jer 3: 4 You are the *g* of my youth?
Lk 1:79 To *g* our feet into the way of
Jn 16:13 He will *g* you into all truth;
Acts 1:16 who became a *g* to those who
Rom 2:19 that you yourself are a *g* to

GUIDED (5/5) GUIDE
Ex 15:13 You have *g* them in Your
2 Chr 32:22 and *g* them on every side.
Job 31:18 And from my mother's womb I *g*
Ps 78:52 And *g* them in the wilderness
78:72 And *g* them by the skillfulness

GUIDES (6/6) GUIDE
Job 12:23 enlarges nations, and *g* them.
Ps 25: 9 The humble He *g* in justice,
107:30 So He *g* them to their desired
Mt 23:16 "Woe to you, blind *g*,
23:24 'Blind *g*, who strain out a
Acts 8:31 unless someone *g* me?" And he

GUIDING (2/2) GUIDE
Gen 48:14 *g* his hands knowingly, for
Eccl 2: 3 while *g* my heart with wisdom,

GUILE (KJV) See DECEIT, TREACHERY

GUILT (40/38) GUILTLESS, GUILTY
Gen 26:10 and you would have brought *g* on
Ex 22: 2 there shall be no *g* for his
22: 3 there shall be *g* for his
Lev 4: 3 bringing *g* on the people, then
5: 1 does not tell it, he bears *g*.
7:18 who eats of it shall bear *g*.
10:17 given it to you to bear the *g*
17: 4 the *g* of bloodshed shall be
17:16 body, then he shall bear his *g*.
20:17 nakedness. He shall bear his *g*.
20:19 of kin. They shall bear their *g*.
22:16 or allow them to bear the *g* of
26:41 and they accept their *g*—
26:43 they will accept their *g*,
Num 5:31 but that woman shall bear her *g*.
14:34 each day you shall bear your *g*
15:31 his *g* shall be upon him.' "
30:15 them, then he shall bear her *g*.
Deut 17: 8 between degrees of *g* for
19:10 and thus *g* of bloodshed be
19:13 but you shall put away the *g*
21: 9 So you shall put away the *g* of
22: 8 that you may not bring *g* of
25: 2 presence, according to his *g*,
1 Chr 21: 3 Why should he be a cause of *g*
2 Chr 28:13 to add to our sins and to our *g*;
28:13 for our *g* is great, and there
Ezra 9: 6 and our *g* has grown up to the
9:13 evil deeds and for our great *g*,
9:15 we are before You, in our *g*,
10: 6 he mourned because of the *g* of
10:10 adding to the *g* of Israel.
Ps 51:14 Deliver me from the *g* of
Ezek 18:19 should the son not bear the *g*
18:20 The son shall not bear the *g* of
18:20 nor the father bear the *g* of
Hos 12:14 his Lord will leave the *g* of
Joel 3:21 I will acquit them of the *g* of
Zech 11: 5 slaughter them and feel no *g*;
Mt 23:32 the measure of your fathers' *g*.

GUILTLESS (8/8) GUILT
Ex 20: 7 the LORD will not hold him *g*
Deut 5:11 the LORD will not hold him *g*
Josh 2:19 own head, and we will be *g*.
1 Sam 26: 9 the LORD's anointed, and be *g*?
2 Sam 3:28 My kingdom and I are *g* before
14: 9 the king and his throne be *g*.
1 Ki 2: 9 therefore, do not hold him *g*,
Mt 12: 7 would not have condemned the *g*.

GUILTY (32/32) GUILT
Gen 42:21 We are truly *g* concerning our
Ex 34: 7 by no means clearing the *g*,
Lev 4:13 should not be done, and are *g*;
4:22 should not be done, and is *g*,
4:27 ought not to be done, and is *g*,
5: 2 he also shall be unclean and *g*.
5: 3 it, then he shall be *g*.
5: 4 then he shall be *g* in any of
5: 5 when he is *g* in any of these
5:17 yet he is *g* and shall bear his
6: 4 because he has sinned and is *g*,
Num 5: 6 the LORD, and that person is *g*,
14:18 He by no means clears the *g*,
35:27 he shall not be *g* of blood,
35:31 life of a murderer who is *g*
Judg 21:22 making yourselves *g* of your
2 Sam 14:13 this thing as one who is *g*,
2 Chr 19:10 Do this, and you will not be *g*.
28:10 but are you not also *g* before
Ezra 9: 7 this day we have been very *g*,
10:19 away their wives; and being *g*,
Ps 5:10 Pronounce them *g*, O God!
109: 7 is judged, let him be found *g*,
Prov 21: 8 The way of a *g* man is
30:10 curse you, and you be found *g*.
Ezek 18:24 of which he is *g* and the sin
22: 4 You have become *g* by the blood
Hos 10: 2 Now they are held *g*.
13:16 Samaria is held *g*, For she
Rom 3:19 and all the world may become *g*
1 Cor 11:27 in an unworthy manner will be *g*
Jas 2:10 one point, he is *g* of all.

GULF (1/1)
Lk 16:26 us and you there is a great *g*

GULL (2/2)
Lev 11:16 the short-eared owl, the sea *g*,
Deut 14:15 short-eared owl, the sea *g*,

GULLIBLE (1/1)
2 Tim 3: 6 and make captives of *g* women

GUNI (4/4)
Gen 46:24 of Naphtali were Jahzeel, *G*,
Num 26:48 family of the Jahzeelites; of *G*,
1 Chr 5:15 the son of Abdiel, the son of *G*,
7:13 of Naphtali were Jahziel, *G*,

GUNITES (1/1)
Num 26:48 of Guni, the family of the *G*;

GUR (1/1)
2 Ki 9:27 shot him at the Ascent of *G*,

GUR BAAL (1/1)
2 Chr 26: 7 the Arabians who lived in *G*,

GUSH (1/1) GUSHED
Jer 9:18 And our eyelids *g* with water.

GUSHED (6/6) GUSH
Judg 5: 5 The mountains *g* before the
1 Ki 18:28 until the blood *g* out on them.
Ps 78:20 So that the waters *g* out,
105:41 and water *g* out; It ran in the
Isa 48:21 the rock, and the waters *g* o
Acts 1:18 middle and all his entrails *g*

GUSHES (1/1)
Job 40:23 though the Jordan *g* into his

GUTTERS (2/2)
Gen 30:38 set before the flocks in the *g*,
30:41 eyes of the livestock in the *g*,

H

HAAHASHTARI (1/1)
1 Chr 4: 6 Ahuzzam, Hepher, Temeni, and *H*.

HABAIAH (2/2)
Ezra 2:61 of the priests: the sons of *H*,
Neh 7:63 of the priests: the sons of *H*,

HABAKKUK (2/2)
Hab 1: 1 burden which the prophet *H* saw.
3: 1 A prayer of *H* the prophet, on

HABAZZINIAH (1/1)
Jer 35: 3 son of Jeremiah, the son of *H*,

HABERGEONS (KJV) See ARMOR

HABITATION (16/16) HOME
Ex 15:13 Your strength To Your holy *h*.
Deut 26:15 'Look down from Your holy *h*,
Ps 26: 8 I have loved the *h* of Your
68: 5 widows, Is God in His holy *h*.
Isa 27:10 The *h* forsaken and left like a
32:18 will dwell in a peaceful *h*,
34:13 It shall be a *h* of jackals,
35: 7 In the *h* of jackals, where
63:15 heaven, And see from Your *h*,
Jer 25:30 utter His voice from His holy *h*;
41:17 departed and dwelt in the *h* of
50: 7 the *h* of justice, The LORD,
Ob 3 Whose *h* is high; You who say
Hab 3:11 and moon stood still in their *h*;
Zech 2:13 He is aroused from His holy *h*!
2 Cor 5: 2 to be clothed with our *h* which

HABITS (1/1)
1 Cor 15:33 "Evil company corrupts good *h*.

HABOR (3/3)
2 Ki 17: 6 them in Halah and by the *H*,
18:11 put them in Halah and by the *H*,
1 Chr 5:26 He took them to Halah, *H*,

HACALIAH (1/1)
Neh 10: 1 the governor, the son of *H*,

HACHALIAH (1/1)
Neh 1: 1 words of Nehemiah the son of *H*.

HACHILAH (3/3)
1 Sam 23:19 in the woods, in the hill of *H*,
26: 1 not hiding in the hill of *H*,
26: 3 Saul encamped in the hill of *H*,

HACHMONI (1/1)
1 Chr 27:32 and Jehiel the son of *H* was

HACHMONITE (1/1)

1 Chr 11:11 Jashobeam the son of a ***H***,

HACKED (1/1)

1 Sam 15:33 And Samuel ***h*** Agag in pieces

HAD (420/395) See APPENDIX

Gen 5: 4 and he ***h*** sons and daughters.
5: 7 and ***h*** sons and daughters.
5:10 and ***h*** sons and daughters,
5:13 and ***h*** sons and daughters.
5:16 and ***h*** sons and daughters.
5:19 and ***h*** sons and daughters.
5:22 and ***h*** sons and daughters.
5:26 and ***h*** sons and daughters.
5:28 years, and ***h*** a son,
5:30 and ***h*** sons and daughters.
11: 1 Now the whole earth ***h*** one
11: 3 They ***h*** brick for stone, and
11: 3 and they ***h*** asphalt for mortar.
11: 5 tower which the sons of men ***h***
11:30 she ***h*** no child.
12:16 He ***h*** sheep, oxen, male donkeys,
12:20 with his wife and all that he ***h***
13: 1 and his wife and all that he ***h***
13: 5 ***h*** flocks and herds and tents.
16: 1 And she ***h*** an Egyptian
24: 2 who ruled over all that he ***h***,
24:29 Now Rebekah ***h*** a brother whose
25: 5 And Abraham gave all that he ***h***
25: 6 the concubines which Abraham ***h***;
26:14 for he ***h*** possessions of flocks
28: 9 in addition to the wives he ***h***
29:16 Now Laban ***h*** two daughters:
29:20 to him because of the love he ***h***
30:30 For what you ***h*** before I came
30:35 every one that ***h*** some white in
30:43 and ***h*** large flocks, female and
31:21 So he fled with all that he ***h***
32:23 brook, and sent over what he ***h***.
35:16 and she ***h*** hard labor.
37: 5 Now Joseph ***h*** a dream, and he
38:30 his brother came out who ***h*** the
39: 4 and all that he ***h*** made
39: 5 of his house and all that he ***h***,
39: 5 theLORD was on all that he ***h***
39: 6 Thus he left all that he ***h*** in
39: 6 and he did not know what he ***h***
40: 8 We each have ***h*** a dream,
41: 1 that Pharaoh ***h*** a dream;
41:11 We each ***h*** a dream in one night,
41:15 I have ***h*** a dream, and there is
41:43 And he ***h*** him ride in the second
41:43 the second chariot which he ***h***;
43:23 I ***h*** your money.' Then he
46: 1 his journey with all that he ***h***,
47:22 for the priests ***h*** rations
47:27 and they ***h*** possessions there
Ex 2:16 of Midian ***h*** seven daughters.
10:23 the children of Israel ***h*** light
16:18 he who gathered much ***h*** nothing
16:18 who gathered little ***h*** no lack.
36: 7 for the material they ***h*** was
36:22 Each board ***h*** two tenons for
Lev 14:32 for one who ***h*** a leprous sore,
Num 3: 4 and they ***h*** no children.
27: 3 and he ***h*** no sons.
27: 4 family because he ***h*** no son?
32: 1 and the children of Gad ***h*** a
Deut 5:29 that they ***h*** such a heart in
Josh 7:24 his tent, and all that he ***h***,
8:20 So they ***h*** no power to flee this
11:23 to all that the LORD ***h*** said
14:15 Then the land ***h*** rest from war.
17: 3 ***h*** no sons, but only daughters.
17: 6 of Manasseh's sons ***h*** the land
17: 8 Manasseh ***h*** the land of Tappuah,
17:11 Manasseh ***h*** Beth Shean and its
19: 2 They ***h*** in their inheritance
21:42 Every one of these cities ***h*** its
Judg 1:19 because they ***h*** chariots of
3: 2 at least those who ***h*** not
3:11 So the land ***h*** rest for forty
3:30 And the land ***h*** rest for eighty
4: 3 for Jabin ***h*** nine hundred
5:31 So the land ***h*** rest for forty
7:13 I have ***h*** a dream: To my
8:24 For they ***h*** gold earrings,
8:30 Gideon ***h*** seventy sons who were
8:30 for he ***h*** many wives.
10: 4 Now he ***h*** thirty sons who rode on
10: 4 they also ***h*** thirty towns, which
11:34 Besides her he ***h*** neither son
12: 9 He ***h*** thirty sons. And he gave
12:14 He ***h*** forty sons and thirty
14: 4 the Philistines ***h*** dominion
14: 6 though he ***h*** nothing in his
16:19 and called for a man and ***h*** him
17: 5 The man Micah ***h*** a shrine,
18: 7 and they ***h*** no ties with anyone.
18:28 and they ***h*** no ties with anyone.
21:15 because the LORD ***h*** made a void
1 Sam 1: 2 And he ***h*** two wives: the name of
1: 2 Peninnah ***h*** children, but Hannah
1: 2 but Hannah ***h*** no children.
9: 2 And he ***h*** a choice and handsome
17: 5 He ***h*** a bronze helmet on his
17: 6 And he ***h*** a bronze armor on his
17:12 and who ***h*** eight sons. And the
25: 2 He ***h*** three thousand sheep and a
28:24 Now the woman ***h*** a fatted calf in
30: 4 until they ***h*** no more power to
2 Sam 3: 7 And Saul ***h*** a concubine, whose
3:37 understood that day that it ***h***
4: 2 Now Saul's son ***h*** two men who
4: 4 ***h*** a son who was lame in his
6:23 daughter of Saul ***h*** no children
9:10 Now Ziba ***h*** fifteen sons and
9:12 Mephibosheth ***h*** a young son whose
12: 2 The rich man ***h*** exceedingly many
12: 3 But the poor man ***h*** nothing,
12: 6 and because he ***h*** no pity.'
13: 1 son of David ***h*** a lovely sister,
13: 3 But Amnon ***h*** a friend whose name
13:23 that Absalom ***h*** sheepshearers in
14: 6 Now your maidservant ***h*** two sons;
15: 2 whenever anyone who ***h*** a lawsuit
17:18 who ***h*** a well in his court;
21:20 who ***h*** six fingers on each hand
23: 8 of the mighty men whom David ***h***:
23:21 The Egyptian ***h*** a spear in his
1 Ki 1:38 the Pelethites went down and ***h***
2:19 his throne and ***h*** a throne set
4: 7 And Solomon ***h*** twelve governors
4:11 he ***h*** Taphath the daughter of
4:24 For he ***h*** dominion over all the
4:24 and he ***h*** peace on every side
4:26 Solomon ***h*** forty thousand stalls
5:15 Solomon ***h*** seventy thousand who
7: 5 the doorways and doorposts ***h***
7:20 pillars also ***h*** pomegranates
7:28 They ***h*** panels, and the panels
7:30 and its four feet ***h*** supports.
9:19 storage cities that Solomon ***h***,
10:19 The throne ***h*** six steps, and the
10:22 For the king ***h*** merchant ships at
10:26 he ***h*** one thousand four hundred
10:28 Also Solomon ***h*** horses imported
11: 3 And he ***h*** seven hundred wives,
21: 1 the Jezreelite ***h*** a vineyard
2 Ki 1:17 Because he ***h*** no son, Jehoram
4:44 and they ate and ***h*** some left
10: 1 Now Ahab ***h*** seventy sons in
10:16 So they ***h*** him ride in his
12:11 who ***h*** the oversight of the
13:23 ***h*** compassion on the,
1 Chr 2:18 the son of Hezron ***h*** children
2:22 who ***h*** twenty-three cities in
2:26 Jerahmeel ***h*** another wife,
2:34 Now Sheshan ***h*** no sons,
2:34 And Sheshan ***h*** an Egyptian
2:52 Kirjath Jearim ***h*** descendants:
4: 5 father of Tekoa ***h*** two wives,
4:27 Shimei ***h*** sixteen sons and six
5:18 half the tribe of Manasseh ***h***
7: 4 for they ***h*** many wives and sons.
8: 8 And Shaharaim ***h*** children in the
8:38 Azel ***h*** six sons whose names
8:40 They ***h*** many sons and
9:26 And they ***h*** charge over the
9:27 they ***h*** the responsibility,
9:31 ***h*** the trusted office over the
9:44 And Azel ***h*** six sons whose names
11:10 of the mighty men whom David ***h***,
11:11 of the mighty men whom David ***h***:
12:32 Issacher who ***h*** understanding
13:14 of Obed-Edom and all that he ***h***.
14: 4 of his children whom he ***h*** in
21: 5 All Israel ***h*** one million one
21: 5 and Judah ***h*** four hundred and
23:17 And Eliezer ***h*** no other sons,
23:22 and ***h*** no sons, but only
24: 2 and ***h*** no children; therefore
24:28 Eleazar, who ***h*** no sons.
26: 9 And Meshelemiah ***h*** sons and
26:10 ***h*** sons: Shimri the first (for
26:30 ***h*** the oversight of Israel on
28: 2 I ***h*** it in my heart to build a
28:12 the plans for all that he ***h*** by
29: 8 And whoever ***h*** precious stones
2 Chr 1:12 as none of the kings have ***h***
1:14 he ***h*** one thousand four hundred
1:16 And Solomon ***h*** horses imported
9:18 The throne ***h*** six steps, with a
9:25 Solomon ***h*** four thousand stalls
14: 6 for the land ***h*** rest, he had no
14: 6 he ***h*** no war in those years,
14: 8 And Asa ***h*** an army of three
17: 5 and he ***h*** riches and honor in
17: 9 and ***h*** the Book of the Law of
17:13 He ***h*** much property in the cities
18: 1 Jehoshaphat ***h*** riches and honor
21: 2 He ***h*** brothers, the sons of
21: 6 for he ***h*** the daughter of Ahab
22: 9 the house of Ahaziah ***h*** no one
26: 5 who ***h*** understanding in the
26:10 for he ***h*** much livestock,
26:10 he also ***h*** farmers and
26:11 Moreover Uzziah ***h*** an army of
26:19 and he ***h*** a censer in his hand
30:17 therefore the Levites ***h*** charge
31:10 we have ***h*** enough to eat and
31:12 Cononiah the Levite ***h*** charge of
32:27 Hezekiah ***h*** very great riches
34:10 foremen who ***h*** the oversight
35:24 in the second chariot that he ***h***,
36:15 because He ***h*** compassion on His
36:17 and ***h*** no compassion on young
Ezra 2:65 and they ***h*** two hundred men and
10:44 and some of them ***h*** wives by
10:44 by whom they ***h*** children.
Neh 4: 6 for the people ***h*** a mind to
4:18 one of the builders ***h*** his sword
7:67 and they ***h*** two hundred and
9:28 But after they ***h*** rest, They
9:28 So that they ***h*** dominion over
10:28 everyone who ***h*** knowledge and
11:16 ***h*** the oversight of the
Esth 1:14 who ***h*** access to the king's
2: 7 for she ***h*** neither father nor
2:15 who ***h*** taken her as his
8:16 The Jews ***h*** light and gladness,
8:17 the Jews ***h*** joy and gladness,
9:16 ***h*** rest from their enemies,
9:22 days on which the Jews ***h*** rest
Job 3:15 Or with princes who ***h*** gold,
29:12 and the one who ***h*** no helper.
31:21 When I saw I ***h*** help in the
31:35 that I ***h*** one to hear me
42:10 twice as much as he ***h*** before.
42:12 for he ***h*** fourteen thousand
42:13 He also ***h*** seven sons and three
Ps 55: 6 that I ***h*** wings like a dove
Eccl 2: 7 and ***h*** servants born in my
2: 7 I ***h*** greater possessions of
Song 8:11 Solomon ***h*** a vineyard at Baal
Isa 1:11 I have ***h*** enough of burnt
6: 2 each one ***h*** six wings: with two
37:27 inhabitants ***h*** little power;
59:10 we grope as if we WLh no eyes;
60:10 But in My favor I have ***h*** mercy
Jer 3: 3 have ***h*** a harlot's forehead;
4:23 the heavens, they ***h*** no light.
9: 2 that I ***h*** in the wilderness A
24: 2 One basket ***h*** very good figs,
24: 2 other basket ***h*** very bad figs
39:10 who ***h*** nothing, and gave them
Ezek 1: 6 Each one ***h*** four faces, and each
1: 6 and each one ***h*** four wings,
1: 8 and each of the four ***h*** faces
1:10 each ***h*** the face of a man;
1:16 and all four ***h*** the same
1:23 Each one ***h*** two which covered
1:23 and each one ***h*** two which
8:11 Each man ***h*** a censer in his
9: 3 who ***h*** in the writer's inkhorn at
9:11 who ***h*** the inkhorn at his side,
10:14 Each one ***h*** four faces: the first
10:21 Each one ***h*** four faces and each
16:49 She and her daughter ***h*** pride,
19:11 She ***h*** strong branches for
40:26 and it ***h*** palm trees on its
40:36 It ***h*** windows all around;
41:18 Each cherub ***h*** two faces,
41:23 The temple and the sanctuary ***h***
41:24 The doors ***h*** two panels apiece,
42:20 it ***h*** a wall all around, five
Dan 1:17 and Daniel ***h*** understanding in
2: 1 Nebuchadnezzar ***h*** dreams;
2:3 I have ***h*** a dream, and my spirit
4:21 of the heaven ***h*** their home—
7: 1 Daniel ***h*** a dream and visions of
7: 4 and ***h*** eagle's wings. I watched
7: 5 and ***h*** three ribs in its mouth
7: 6 which ***h*** on its back four wings
7: 6 The beast also ***h*** four heads,
7: 7 It ***h*** huge iron teeth: it was
7: 7 and it ***h*** ten horns.
7:20 that horn which ***h*** eyes and a
8: 3 was a ram which ***h*** two horns,
8: 5 and the goat ***h*** a notable horn
10: 1 and ***h*** understanding, of the
Hos 13: 6 When they ***h*** pasture, they were
Jon 4:10 You have ***h*** pity on the plant for
Nah 3: 8 That ***h*** the waters around her,
Zech 5: 9 for they ***h*** wings like the wings
Mt 9:20 a woman who ***h*** a flow of blood
12:10 a man who ***h*** a withered hand.
13: 5 up because they ***h*** no depth
13: 6 and because they ***h*** no root they
14:10 So he sent and ***h*** John beheaded
18:25 and children and all that he ***h***,
18:33 you not also have ***h*** compassion
18:33 just as I ***h*** pity on you?'
19:22 for he ***h*** great possessions.
20:34 So Jesus ***h*** compassion and
21:28 A man ***h*** two sons, and he came
22:28 For they all ***h*** her.'
27:16 they ***h*** a notorious prisoner
Mk 3: 1 was there who ***h*** a withered hand.
3: 3 man who ***h*** the withered hand,
3:10 that as many as ***h*** afflictions
4: 5 sprang up because it ***h*** no depth
4: 6 and because it ***h*** no root it
5: 4 because he ***h*** often been bound
5:15 and ***h*** the legion, sitting and
5:19 and how He has ***h*** compassion on
5:25 Now a certain woman ***h*** a flow of
5:26 She had spent all that she ***h***
7:25 a woman whose young daughter ***h***7.
7:32 was deaf and ***h*** an impediment
8: 7 They also ***h*** a few small fish;
10:22 for he ***h*** great possessions.
12:23 For all seven ***h*** her as wife.'
12:44 poverty put in all that she ***h***,
Lk 1: 3 having ***h*** perfect understanding
1: 7 But they ***h*** no child, because
4:33 there was a man who ***h*** a spirit
4:40 all those who ***h*** any that were
5: 9 the catch of fish which they ***h***
6: 8 man who ***h*** the withered hand,

7:13 He **h** compassion on her and said
7:41 creditor who **h** two debtors.
8:27 man from the city who **h** demons
8:42 for he **h** an only daughter about
8:43 who **h** spent all her livelihood
10:33 he saw him, he **h** compassion.
10:39 And she **h** a sister called Mary,
13: 6 A certain man **h** a fig tree
13:11 was a woman who **h** a spirit
14: 2 man before Him who **h** dropsy.
15:11 A certain man **h** two sons.
16: 1 rich man who **h** a steward,
20:33 For all seven **h** her as wife.'
21: 4 all the livelihood that sh **h**.
Jn 2:25 and **h** no need that anyone should
4:18 for you have **h** five husbands,
5: 4 well of whatever disease he **h**.
12: 6 and **h** the money box, and he
13:29 because Judas **h** the money box,
17: 5 with the glory which I **h** with
Acts 1:16 this Scripture **h** to be
2:45 as anyone **h** need.
4:14 And seeing the man who **h** been
4:32 but they **h** all things in
4:35 to each as anyone **h** need.
5:27 And when they **h** brought them,
5:40 and when they **h** called for the
6: 6 and when they **h** prayed, they
7: 5 even when Abraham **h** no child,
7:29 where he **h** two sons.
7:44 Our fathers **h** the tabernacle of
8:27 who **h** charge of all her
9:31 and Samaria **h** peace and were
9:33 who **h** been bedriddden eight
13: 5 They also **h** John as their
14: 9 and seeing that he **h** faith
15: 2 when Paul and Barnabas **h** no
15:21 For Moses has **h** throughout many
18:18 He **h** his hair cut off at
19:13 over those who **h** evil spirits,
21: 9 Now this man **h** four virgin
25:19 but **h** some questions against him
27: 9 Now when much time **h** been
28:19 not that I **h** anything of which
28:29 departed and **h** a great dispute
1 Cor 7:29 be as though they **h** none,
2 Cor 1: 9 we **h** the sentence of death in
2:13 I **h** no rest in my spirit,
3:10 was made glorious **h** no glory
7: 5 our bodies **h** no rest, but we
8:15 who gathered much **h** nothing
8:15 gathered little **h** no lack.'
Gal 4:22 that Abraham **h** two sons:
Phil 2:27 but God **h** mercy on him, and not
1 Th 1: 9 manner of entry we **h** to you,
2: 2 but even after we **h** suffered
Heb 2:14 destroy him who **h** the power
2:17 in all things He **h** to be made
7: 6 blessed him who **h** the promises.
9: 1 first covenant **h** ordinances
9: 4 which **h** the golden censer and
9: 4 golden pot that **h** the manna,
9:26 He then would have **h** to suffer
10: 2 would have **h** no more
10: 6 for sin You **h** no pleasure.
10: 8 nor **h** pleasure in them'
10:34 for you **h** compassion on me in my
11:15 they would have **h** opportunity
12: 9 we have **h** human fathers who
2 Jn 1: 5 but that which we have **h** from
3 Jn 1:13 I **h** many things to write, but I
Rev 1:16 He **h** in His right hand seven
4: 4 and they **h** crowns of gold on
4: 7 third living creature **h** a face
6: 2 He who sat on it **h** a bow; and a
6: 5 and he who sat on it **h** a pair
8: 6 So the seven angels who **h** the
9: 8 They **h** hair like women's hair,
9: 9 **h**And they **h** breastplates like
9:10 They **h** tails like scorpions,
9:10 And they **h** as king over them the
9:14 sixth angel who **h** the trumpet,
10: 2 He **h** a little book open in his
13:11 and he **h** two horns like a lamb
14:18 who **h** power over fire, and he
14:18 to him who **h** the sharp sickle,
15: 2 upon the men who **h** the mark
17: 1 one of the seven angels who **h**
18:19 in which all who **h** ships on the
19:12 He **h** a name written that no one
21: 9 one of the seven angels who **h**
21:12 Also she **h** a great and high wall
21:14 the city **h** twelve foundations,
21:15 talked with me **h** a gold reed
21:23 The city **h** no need of the sun or

HADAD (14/13)

Gen 36:35 **H** the son of Bedad, who
36:36 When **H** died, Samlah of Masrekah
1 Ki 11:14 **H** the Edomite; he was a
11:17 that **H** fled to go to Egypt, he
11:17 **H** was still a little child.
11:19 And **H** found great favor in the
11:21 So when **H** heard in Egypt that
11:21 **H** said to Pharaoh, "Let me
11:25 (besides the trouble that **H**
1 Chr 1:30 Mishma, Dumah, Massa, **H**,
1:46 **H** the son of Bedad, who
1:47 When **H** died, Samlah of Masrekah
1:50 **H** reigned in his place; and the
1:51 **H** died also. And the chiefs of

HADAD RIMMON (1/1)

Zech 12:11 like the mourning at **H** in the

HADADEZER (19/17)

2 Sam 8: 3 David also defeated **H** the son
8: 5 of Damascus came to help **H**
8: 7 belonged to the servants of **H**,
8: 8 and from Berothai, cities of **H**,
8: 9 had defeated all the army of **H**,
8:10 he had fought against **H** and
8:10 and defeated him (for **H** had
8:12 and from the spoil of **H** the son
10:16 Then **H** sent and brought out the
10:19 kings who were servants to **H**
1 Ki 11:23 his lord, **H** king of Zobah.
1 Chr 18: 3 And David defeated **H** king of
18: 5 of Damascus came to help **H**
18: 7 that were on the servants of **H**,
18: 8 and from Chun, cities of **H**,
18: 9 had defeated all the army of **H**
18:10 he had fought against **H** and
18:10 and defeated him (for **H** had
19:19 And when the servants of **H** saw

HADADEZER'S (2/2)

2 Sam 10:16 And Shobach the commander of **H**
1 Chr 19:16 and Shophach the commander of **H**

HADAR (2/2)

Gen 25:15 **H**, Tema, Jetur, Naphish, and
36:39 **H** reigned in his place; and the

HADASHAH (1/1)

Josh 15:37 Zenan, **H**, Migdal Gad,

HADASSAH (1/1) ESTHER

Esth 2: 7 And Mordecai had brought up **H**,

HADATTAH (1/1)

Josh 15:25 Hazor, **H**, Kerioth, Hezron

HADES (11/11)

Mt 11:23 will be brought down to **H**;
16:18 and the gates of **H** shall not
Lk 10:15 will be brought down to **H**.
16:23 "And being in torments in **H**,
Acts 2:27 not leave my soul in **H**,
2:31 that His soul was not left in **H**,
1 Cor 15:55 **H**, where is your sting?
Rev 1:18 And I have the keys of **H** and of
6: 8 and **H** followed with him.
20:13 and Death and **H** delivered up
20:14 Then Death and **H** were cast into

HADID (3/3)

Ezra 2:33 the people of Lod, **H**,
Neh 7:37 the sons of Lod, **H**, and Ono,
11:34 in **H**, Zeboim, Neballat;

HADLAI (1/1)

2 Chr 28:12 Shallum, and Amasa the son of **H**,

HADORAM (5/4)

Gen 10:27 **H**, Uzal, Diklah,
1 Chr 1:21 **H**, Uzal, Diklah,
18:10 he sent **H** his son to King David,
18:10 and **H** brought with him all
2 Chr 10:18 Then King Rehoboam sent **H**,

HADRACH (1/1)

Zech 9: 1 LORD Against the land of **H**,

HAFT (KJV) See HILT

HAGAB (1/1)

Ezra 2:46 the sons of **H**, the sons of

HAGABA (1/1)

Neh 7:48 sons of Lebana, the sons of **H**,

HAGABAH (1/1)

Ezra 2:45 sons of Lebanah, the sons of **H**,

HAGAR (14/12)

Gen 16: 1 maidservant whose name was **H**.
16: 3 took **H** her maid, the Egyptian,
16: 4 So he went in to **H**, and she
16: 8 And He said, "**H**, Sarai's
16:15 So **H** bore Abram a son; and
16:15 whom **H** bore, Ishmael.
16:16 eighty-six years old when **H**
21: 9 the son of **H** the Egyptian,
21:14 he gave it and the boy to **H**,
21:17 the angel of God called to **H**
21:17 said to her, "What ails you, **H**?
25:12 whom **H** the Egyptian, Sarah's
Gal 4:24 birth to bondage, which is **H**—
4:25 for this **H** is Mount Sinai in

HAGARENES (KJV) See HAGRITES

HAGARITES, HAGERITE (KJV) See HAGRITES

HAGGAI (11/11)

Ezra 5: 1 Then the prophet **H** and Zechariah
6:14 through the prophesying of **H**
Hag 1: 1 the word of the LORD came by **H**
1: 3 the word of the LORD came by **H**
1:12 and the words of **H** the prophet,
1:13 Then **H**, the LORD's messenger,
2: 1 the word of the LORD came by **H**
2:10 the word of the LORD came by **H**
2:13 And **H** said, "If one who is
2:14 Then **H** answered and said, "'So
2:20 word of the LORD came to **H** on

HAGGERI (KJV) See HAGRI

HAGGI (2/2)

Gen 46:16 sons of Gad were Ziphion, **H**,
Num 26:15 family of the Zephonites; of **H**,

HAGGIAH (1/1)

1 Chr 6:30 **H** his son, and Asaiah his son.

HAGGITES (1/1)

Num 26:15 of Haggi, the family of the **H**;

HAGGITH (5/5)

2 Sam 3: 4 fourth, Adonijah the son of **H**;
1 Ki 1: 5 Then Adonijah the son of **H**
1:11 that Adonijah the son of **H** has
2:13 Now Adonijah the son of **H** came
1 Chr 3: 2 fourth, Adonijah the son of **H**;

HAGRI (1/1)

1 Chr 11:38 of Nathan, Mibhar the son of **H**,

HAGRITE (1/1)

1 Chr 27:31 and Jaziz the **H** was over the

HAGRITES (4/4)

1 Chr 5:10 Saul they made war with the **H**,
5:19 They made war with the **H**,
5:20 and the **H** were delivered into
Ps 83: 6 Ishmaelites; Moab and the **H**;

HAHIROTH (1/1)

33: 8 They departed from before **H** and

HAI (KJV) See AI

HAIL (34/30) HAILSTONE

Ex 9:18 very heavy **h** to rain down,
9:19 for the **h** shall come down on
9:22 that there may be **h** in all the
9:23 the LORD sent thunder and **h**,
9:23 And the LORD rained **h** on the
9:24 So there was **h**, and fire
9:24 and fire mingled with the **h**,
9:25 And the **h** struck throughout the
9:25 and the **h** struck every herb of
9:26 of Israel were, there was no **h**.
9:28 more mighty thundering and **h**,
9:29 and there will be no more **h**,
9:33 then the thunder and the **h**
9:34 saw that the rain, the **h**,
10: 5 which remains to you from the **h**,
10:12 all that the **h** has left."
10:15 fruit of the trees which the **h**
Job 38:22 have you seen the treasury of **h**,
Ps 78:47 destroyed their vines with **h**,
78:48 gave up their cattle to tne **h**,
105:32 He gave them **h** for rain, And
147:17 His **h** like morsels;
148: 8 Fire and **h**, snow and clouds;
Isa 28: 2 Like a tempest of **h** and a
28:17 The **h** will sweep away the
32:19 Though **h** comes down on the
Hag 2:17 with blight and mildew and **h**
Mt 27:29 Him and mocked Him, saying, "**H**,
Mk 15:18 and began to salute Him, "**H**,
Jn 19: 3 '**H**, King of the Jews!"
Rev 8: 7 And **h** and fire followed,
11:19 an earthquake, and great **h**.
16:21 And great **h** from heaven fell
16:21 because of the plague of the **h**,

HAILSTONE (1/1) HAIL, HAILSTONES

Rev 16:21 each **h** about the weight of a

HAILSTONES (8/7) HAILSTONE

Josh 10:11 the LORD cast down large **h**
10:11 were more who died from the **h**
Ps 18:12 thick clouds passed with **h** and

18:13 ***H*** and coals of fire.
Isa 30:30 scattering, tempest, and ***h***.
Ezek 13:11 rain, and you, O great ***h***,
13:13 and great ***h*** in fury to consume
38:22 him, flooding rain, great ***h***,

HAIR (77/72) HAIR'S, HAIRS, HAIRY

Gen 42:38 you would bring down my gray ***h***
44:29 you shall bring down my gray ***h***
44:31 will bring down the gray ***h*** of
Ex 25: 4 fine linen, and goats' ***h***;
26: 7 also make curtains of goats' ***h***,
35: 6 fine linen, and goats' ***h***;
35:23 fine linen, and goats' ***h***,
35:26 wisdom spun yarn of goats' ***h***.
36:14 He made curtains of goats' ***h***
Lev 13: 3 and if the ***h*** on the sore has
13: 4 and its ***h*** has not turned white,
13:10 and it has turned the ***h*** white,
13:20 and its ***h*** has turned white, the
13:25 and indeed if the ***h*** of the
13:30 there is in it thin yellow ***h***,
13:31 and there is no black ***h*** in
13:32 and there is no yellow ***h*** in it,
13:36 need not seek for yellow ***h***.
13:37 and there is black ***h*** grown up
13:40 As for the man whose ***h*** has
13:41 He whose ***h*** has fallen from his
14: 8 clothes, shave off all his ***h***,
14: 9 day he shall shave all the ***h***
14: 9 —all his ***h*** he shall shave off.
Num 6: 5 he shall let the locks of the ***h***
6:18 and shall take the ***h*** from his
6:19 has shaved his consecrated ***h***,
31:20 everything woven of goats' ***h***,
Judg 16:22 the ***h*** of his head began to grow
1 Sam 14:45 not one ***h*** of his head shall
19:13 put a cover of goats' ***h*** for
19:16 with a cover of goats' ***h*** for
2 Sam 14:11 not one ***h*** of your son shall
14:26 And when he cut the ***h*** of his
14:26 he weighed the ***h*** of his head at
1 Ki 1:52 not one ***h*** of him shall fall to
2: 6 and do not let his gray ***h*** go
2: 9 but bring his gray ***h*** down to
Ezra 9: 3 and plucked out some of the ***h***
Neh 13:25 of them and pulled out their ***h***,
Job 4:15 The ***h*** on my body stood up.
41:32 think the deep had white ***h***.
Song 4: 1 Your ***h*** is like a flock of
6: 5 Your ***h*** is like a flock of
7: 5 And the ***h*** of your head is
Isa 3:24 a rope; Instead of well-set ***h***,
7:20 The head and the ***h*** of the
Jer 7:29 Cut off your ***h*** and cast it
Ezek 5: 1 to weigh and divide the ***h***.
8: 3 and took me by a lock of my ***h***;
16: 7 your ***h*** grew, but you were
44:20 their heads nor let their ***h***
44:20 but they shall keep their ***h***
Dan 3:27 the ***h*** of their head was not
4:33 the dew of heaven till his ***h***
7: 9 And the ***h*** of His head was
Mic 1:16 bald and cut off your ***h***,
Zech 13: 4 not wear a robe of coarse ***h*** to
Mt 3: 4 was clothed in camel's ***h***,
5:36 because you cannot make one ***h***
Mk 1: 6 was clothed with camel's ***h*** and
Lk 7:38 and wiped them with the ***h*** of
7:44 and wiped them with the ***h*** of
21:18 But not a ***h*** of your head shall
Jn 11: 2 and wiped His feet with her ***h***,
12: 3 and wiped His feet with her ***h***.
Acts 18:18 He had his ***h*** cut off at
27:34 since not a ***h*** will fall from
1 Cor 11:14 you that if a man has long ***h***,
11:15 But if a woman has long ***h***,
11:15 for her ***h*** is given to her for
1 Tim 2: 9 not with braided ***h*** or gold or
1 Pe 3: 3 merely outward—arranging the ***h***,
Rev 1:14 His head and ***h*** were white like
6:12 became black as sackcloth of ***h***,
9: 8 They had ***h*** like women's hair,
9: 8 They had hair like women's ***h***,

HAIR'S (1/1) HAIR

Judg 20:16 sling a stone at a ***h*** breadth

HAIRS (9/9) HAIR

Lev 13:21 indeed there are no white ***h***
13:26 indeed there are no white ***h***
Deut 32:25 child with the man of gray ***h***.
Ps 40:12 They are more than the ***h*** of my
69: 4 a cause Are more than the ***h***
Isa 46: 4 And even to gray ***h*** I will
Hos 7: 9 gray ***h*** are here and there on
Mt 10:30 But the very ***h*** of your head are
Lk 12: 7 But the very ***h*** of your head are

HAIRY (5/5) HAIR

Gen 25:25 He was like a ***h*** garment all
27:11 Esau my brother is a ***h*** man,
27:23 because his hands were ***h*** like
2 Ki 1: 8 A ***h*** man wearing a leather belt
Ps 68:21 The ***h*** scalp of the one who

HAKKATAN (1/1)

Ezra 8:12 of Azgad, Johanan the son of ***H***,

HAKKOZ (1/1)

1 Chr 24:10 the seventh to ***H***, the eighth

HAKUPHA (2/2)

Ezra 2:51 sons of Bakbuk, the sons of ***H***,
Neh 7:53 sons of Bakbuk, the sons of ***H***,

HALAH (3/3)

2 Ki 17: 6 and placed them in ***H*** and by the
18:11 and put them in ***H*** and by the
1 Chr 5:26 captivity. He took them to ***H***,

HALAK (2/2)

Josh 11:17 from Mount ***H*** and the ascent to
12: 7 of Lebanon as far as Mount ***H***

HALE (KJV) See DRAG

HALF (118/99)

Gen 24:22 ring weighing ***h*** a shekel,
Ex 24: 6 And Moses took ***h*** the blood and
24: 6 and ***h*** the blood he sprinkled on
25:10 two and a ***h*** cubits shall be
25:10 a cubit and a ***h*** its width, and
25:10 and a cubit and a ***h*** its height.
25:17 two and a ***h*** cubits shall be
25:17 a cubit and a ***h*** its width.
25:23 and a cubit and a ***h*** its height.
26:12 the ***h*** curtain that remains,
26:16 and a cubit and a ***h*** shall be
30:13 ***h*** a shekel according to the
30:15 give less than ***h*** a shekel,
30:23 ***h*** as much sweet-smelling
36:21 of each board a cubit and a ***h***.
37: 1 two and a ***h*** cubits was its
37: 1 a cubit and a ***h*** its width, and
37: 1 and a cubit and a ***h*** its height.
37: 6 two and a ***h*** cubits was its
37: 6 a cubit and a ***h*** its width.
37:10 and a cubit and a ***h*** its height.
38:26 ***h*** a shekel, according to the
Lev 6:20 ***h*** of it in the morning and half
6:20 and ***h*** of it at night.
Num 12:12 whose flesh is ***h*** consumed when
15: 9 mixed with ***h*** a HIN of oil;
15:10 ***h*** a hin of wine as an
28:14 shall be ***h*** a hin of wine
31:29 "take it from their ***h***,
31:30 the children of Israel's ***h*** you
31:36 And the ***h***, the portion for
31:42 from the children of Israel's ***h***,
31:43 now the ***h*** belonging to the
31:47 Israel's ***h*** Moses took
32:33 and to ***h*** the tribe of Manasseh
Deut 3:12 and ***h*** the mountains of Gilead
3:13 I gave to ***h*** the tribe of
29: 8 and to ***h*** the tribe of Manasseh.
Josh 1:12 and ***h*** the tribe of Manasseh
4:12 and ***h*** the tribe of Manasseh
8:33 ***H*** of them were in front of
8:33 and ***h*** of them in front of
12: 2 and ruled ***h*** of Gilead,
12: 5 and over ***h*** of Gilead to the
12: 6 and ***h*** the tribe of Manasseh.
13: 7 nine tribes and ***h*** the tribe
13: 8 With the other ***h*** tribe the
13:25 and ***h*** the land of the Ammonites
13:29 had given an inheritance to ***h***
13:29 it was for ***h*** the tribe of the
13:31 ***h*** of Gilead, and Ashtaroth and
13:31 for ***h*** of the children of Machir
18: 7 and ***h*** the tribe of Manasseh
22: 1 and ***h*** the tribe of Manasseh,
22: 7 Now to ***h*** the tribe of Manasseh
22: 7 but to the other ***h*** of it
22: 9 and ***h*** the tribe of Manasseh
22:10 and ***h*** the tribe of Manasseh
22:11 and ***h*** the tribe of Manasseh
22:13 and to ***h*** the tribe of Manasseh,
22:15 and to ***h*** the tribe of Manasseh,
22:21 and ***h*** the tribe of Manasseh
1 Sam 14:14 about ***h*** an acre of land.
2 Sam 10: 4 shaved off ***h*** of their beards,
18: 3 nor if ***h*** of us die, will they
19:40 and also ***h*** the people of
1 Ki 3:25 and give ***h*** to one, and half to
3:25 to one, and ***h*** to the other."
7:31 one and a ***h*** cubits in outside
7:32 was one and a ***h*** cubits.
7:35 at the height of ***h*** a cubit, it
10: 7 and indeed the ***h*** was not told
13: 8 were to give me ***h*** your house,
16: 9 commander of ***h*** his chariots,
16:21 ***h*** of the people followed Tibni
16:21 king, and ***h*** followed Omri.
1 Chr 2:52 and ***h*** of the families of
2:54 ***h*** of the Manahethites, and the
5:18 and ***h*** the tribe of Manasseh
6:61 ten cities from ***h*** the tribe
2 Chr 9: 6 the ***h*** of the greatness
Neh 3: 9 leader of ***h*** the district of
3:12 leader of ***h*** the district of
3:16 leader of ***h*** the district of
3:17 leader of ***h*** the district of
3:18 other ***h*** of the district
4: 6 up to ***h*** its height,
4:16 that ***h*** of my servants worked
4:16 while the other ***h*** held the
4:21 and ***h*** of the men held the
12:32 Hoshaiah and ***h*** of the leaders
12:38 them with ***h*** of the people
12:40 I and the ***h*** of the rulers
13:24 And ***h*** of their children spoke
Esth 5: 3 up to ***h*** the kingdom!"
5: 6 up to ***h*** the kingdom? It shall
7: 2 up to ***h*** the kingdom? It shall
Job 21:21 of his months is cut in ***h***?
Ps 55:23 not live out ***h*** their days;
Isa 44:16 He burns ***h*** of it in the fire;
44:16 With this ***h*** he eats meat;
44:19 I have burned ***h*** of it in the
Ezek 16:51 not commit ***h*** of your sins;
40:42 one cubit and a ***h*** long, one
40:42 one cubit and a ***h*** wide, and one
43:17 with a rim of ***h*** a cubit around
Dan 7:25 and times and ***h*** a time.
12: 7 and ***h*** a time; and when the
Zech 14: 2 ***H*** of the city shall go into
14: 4 ***H*** of the mountain shall move
14: 4 ***h*** of it toward the south.
14: 8 ***H*** of them toward the eastern
14: 8 And ***h*** of them toward the
Mk 6:23 up to ***h*** of my kingdom."
Lk 10:30 leaving him ***h*** dead.
19: 8 I give ***h*** of my goods to the
Rev 8: 1 heaven for about ***h*** an hour.
12:14 and times and ***h*** a time,

HALF-SHEKEL (1/1)

Ex 30:13 The ***h*** shall be an offering to

HALF-TRIBE (18/18)

Num 34:13 to the nine tribes and to the ***h***.
34:14 and the ***h*** of Manasseh has
34:15 The two tribes and the ***h*** have
Josh 14: 2 for the nine tribes and the ***h***.
14: 3 of the two tribes and the ***h*** on
21: 5 and from the ***h*** of Manasseh.
21: 6 and from the ***h*** of Manasseh in
21:25 and from the ***h*** of Manasseh,
21:27 from the other ***h*** of Manasseh,
1 Chr 5:23 So the children of the ***h*** of
5:26 and the ***h*** of Manasseh into
6:70 And from the ***h*** of Manasseh:
6:71 From the family of the ***h*** of
12:31 of the ***h*** of Manasseh eighteen
12:37 and the Gadites and the ***h*** of
26:32 and the ***h*** of Manasseh, for
27:20 over the ***h*** of Manasseh, Joel
27:21 over the ***h*** of Manasseh in

HALHUL (1/1)

Josh 15:58 ***H***, Beth Zur, Gedor,

HALI (1/1)

Josh 19:25 territory included Helkath, ***H***,

HALL (12/10)

1 Sam 9:22 and brought them into the ***h***,
1 Ki 7: 6 He also made the ***H*** of Pillars:
7: 7 Then he made a ***h*** for the throne,
7: 7 the ***H*** of Judgment, where he
7: 8 had another court inside the ***h***,
7: 8 also made a house like this ***h***
7:19 on top of the pillars in the ***h***
7:50 for the doors of the main ***h*** of
2 Chr 4:22 and the doors of the main ***h*** of
Dan 5:10 lords, came to the banquet ***h***.
Mt 22:10 And the wedding ***h*** was filled
Mk 15:16 led Him away into the ***h*** called

HALLOHESH (2/2)

Neh 3:12 to him was Shallum the son of ***H***,
10:24 ***H***, Pilha, Shobek,

HALLOW (14/13) HALLOWED

Ex 28:38 children of Israel ***h*** in all
29: 1 shall do to them to ***h*** them
40: 9 and you shall ***h*** it and all its
Num 20:12 to ***h*** Me in the eyes of the
27:14 against My command to ***h*** Me at
Deut 32:51 because you did not ***h*** Me in the
Isa 8:13 LORD of hosts, Him you shall ***h***;
29:23 They will ***h*** My name, And
29:23 And ***h*** the Holy One of Jacob,
Jer 17:22 but ***h*** the Sabbath day, as I
17:24 but ***h*** the Sabbath day, to do no
17:27 heed Me to ***h*** the Sabbath day,
Ezek 20:20 ***h*** My Sabbaths, and they will be
44:24 and they shall ***h*** My Sabbaths.

HALLOWED (15/15) HALLOW

Ex 20:11 the Sabbath day and ***h*** it.
29:21 he and his garments shall be ***h***,
Lev 12: 4 not touch any ***h*** thing,
19: 8 has profaned the ***h*** offering
22:32 but I will be ***h*** among the
Num 20:13 and He was ***h*** among them.

Isa 5:16 God who is holy shall be *h* in
Ezek 20:41 and I will be *h* in you before
28:22 judgments in her and am *h* in
28:25 and am *h* in them in the sight
36:23 when I am *h* in you before their
38:16 when I am *h* in you, O Gog,
39:27 and I am *h* in them in the sight
Mt 6: 9 in heaven, *H* be Your name.
Lk 11: 2 *H* be Your name. Your kingdom

HALOHESH (KJV) See HALLOHESH

HALT (4/3)

Job 39:24 Nor does he come to a *h*
Isa 13:11 I will *h* the arrogance of the
Nah 2: 8 *H*! Halt!" they cry; But no
2: 8 Halt! *H*!" they cry; But no

HALTED (2/2)

1 Sam 23:13 so he *h* the expedition.
2 Sam 20:12 everyone who came upon him *h*.

HAM (16/15)

Gen 5:32 old, and Noah begot Shem, *H*,
6:10 Noah begot three sons: Shem, *H*,
7:13 Noah and Noah's sons, Shem, *H*,
9:18 out of the ark were Shem, *H*,
9:18 And *H* was the father of
9:22 And *H*, the father of
10: 1 of the sons of Noah: Shem, *H*,
10: 6 The sons of *H* were Cush,
10:20 These were the sons of *H*,
14: 5 Karnaim, the Zuzim in *H*,
1 Chr 1: 4 Noah, Shem, *H*, and Japheth.
1: 8 The sons of *H* were Cush,
Ps 78:51 strength in the tents of *H*.
105:23 Jacob dwelt in the land of *H*.
105:27 And wonders in the land of *H*.
106:22 works in the land of *H*,

HAMAN (51/44) HAMAN'S

Esth 3: 1 King Ahasuerus promoted *H*,
3: 2 gate bowed and paid homage to *H*,
3: 4 them, that they told it to *H*,
3: 5 When *H* saw that Mordecai did not
3: 5 *H* was filled with wrath.
3: 6 *H* sought to destroy all the
3: 7 before *H* to determine the day
3: 8 Then *H* said to King Ahasuerus,
3:10 from his hand and gave it to *H*,
3:11 And the king said to *H*,
3:12 written according to all that *H*
3:15 So the king and *H* sat down to
4: 7 and the sum of money that *H* had
5: 4 let the king and *H* come today
5: 5 Bring *H* quickly, that he may do
5: 5 So the king and *H* went to the
5: 8 then let the king and *H* come to
5: 9 So *H* went out that day joyful
5: 9 but when *H* saw Mordecai in the
5:10 Nevertheless *H* restrained
5:11 Then *H* told them of his great
5:12 Moreover *H* said, "Besides,
5:14 And the thing pleased *H*;
6: 4 Now *H* had just entered the
6: 5 *H* is there, standing in the
6: 6 So *H* came in, and the king asked
6: 6 Now *H* thought in his heart,
6: 7 And *H* answered the king, "For
6:10 Then the king said to *H*,
6:11 So *H* took the robe and the
6:12 But *H* hurried to his house,
6:13 When *H* told his wife Zeresh and
6:14 and hastened to bring *H* to the
7: 1 So the king and *H* went to dine
7: 6 and enemy is this wicked *H*!"
7: 6 is this wicked Haman!" So *H*
7: 7 but *H* stood before Queen
7: 8 *H* had fallen across the couch
7: 9 which *H* made for Mordecai, who
7: 9 is standing at the house of *H*.
7:10 So they hanged *H* on the gallows
8: 1 Queen Esther the house of *H*,
8: 2 ring, which he had taken from *H*,
8: 2 Mordecai over the house of *H*.
8: 3 to counteract the evil of *H*
8: 5 revoke the letters devised by *H*,
8: 7 given Esther the house of *H*,
9:10 the ten sons of *H* the son of
9:12 citadel, and the ten sons of *H*.
9:24 because *H*, the son of
9:25 that this wicked plot which *H*

HAMAN'S (3/3) HAMAN

Esth 7: 8 they covered *H* face.
9:13 and let *H* ten sons be hanged on
9:14 and they hanged *H* ten sons.

HAMATH (36/35)

Num 13:21 Rehob, near the entrance of *H*.
34: 8 border to the entrance of *H*;
Josh 13: 5 as far as the entrance to *H*;
Judg 3: 3 Hermon to the entrance of *H*.
2 Sam 8: 9 When Toi king of *H* heard that
1 Ki 8:65 from the entrance of *H* to the
2 Ki 14:25 Israel from the entrance of *H*
14:28 for Israel, from Damascus and *H*,
17:24 from Babylon, Cuthah, Ava, *H*,
17:30 the men of *H* made Ashima,
18:34 Where are the gods of *H* and
19:13 'Where is the king of *H*,
23:33 at Riblah in the land of *H*,
25:21 at Riblah in the land of *H*.
1 Chr 13: 5 to as far as the entrance of *H*,
18: 3 king of Zobah as far as *H*,
18: 9 Now when Tou king of *H* heard
2 Chr 7: 8 from the entrance of *H* to the
8: 4 cities which he built in *H*.
Isa 10: 9 Is not *H* like Arpad? Is not
11:11 From *H* and the islands of the
36:19 Where are the gods of *H* and
37:13 'Where is the king of *H*,
Jer 39: 5 to Riblah in the land of *H*,
49:23 *H* and Arpad are shamed, For
52: 9 at Riblah in the land of *H*,
52:27 at Riblah in the land of *H*.
Ezek 47:16 '*H*, Berothah, Sibraim
47:16 Damascus and the border of *H*),
47:17 it is the border of *H*.
47:20 one comes to a point opposite *H*.
48: 1 to Hethlon at the entrance of *H*,
48: 1 in the direction of *H*,
Am 6: 2 And from there go to *H* the
6:14 you from the entrance of *H* To
Zech 9: 2 Also against *H*, which

HAMATH ZOBAH (1/1)

2 Chr 8: 3 And Solomon went to *H* and seized

HAMATHITE (2/2)

Gen 10:18 the Zemarite, and the *H*.
1 Chr 1:16 the Zemarite, and the *H*.

HAMITES (1/1)

1 Chr 4:40 for some *H* formerly lived

HAMMATH (2/2)

Josh 19:35 cities are Ziddim, Zer, *H*,
1 Chr 2:55 the Kenites who came from *H*,

HAMMEDATHA (5/5)

Esth 3: 1 the son of *H* the Agagite, and
3:10 the son of *H* the Agagite, the
8: 5 the son of *H* the Agagite, which
9:10 ten sons of Haman the son of *H*,
9:24 the son of *H* the Agagite, the

HAMMER (6/6) HAMMERED, HAMMERS

Judg 4:21 took a tent peg and took a *h* in
5:26 right hand to the workmen's *h*;
1 Ki 6: 7 so that no *h* or chisel or any
Isa 41: 7 He who smooths with the *h*
Jer 23:29 And like a *h* that breaks the
50:23 How the *h* of the whole earth

HAMMERED (15/13) HAMMER

Ex 25:18 of *h* work you shall make them
25:31 lampstand shall be of *h* work.
25:36 it shall be one *h* piece
37:17 of *h* work he made the
37:22 all of it was one *h* piece of
Num 8: 4 of the lampstand was *h* gold;
8: 4 its flowers it was *h* work.
10: 2 you shall make them of *h* work;
16:38 let them be made into *h* plates
16:39 and they were *h* out as a
1 Ki 10:16 large shields of *h* gold;
10:17 shields of *h* gold;
2 Chr 9:15 large shields of *h* gold;
9:15 six hundred shekels of *h* gold
9:16 shields of *h* gold;

HAMMERS (3/3) HAMMER

Ps 74: 6 all at once, With axes and *h*.
Isa 44:12 the coals, Fashions it with *h*,
Jer 10: 4 fasten it with nails and *h* So

HAMMOLEKETH (1/1)

1 Chr 7:18 His sister *H* bore Ishhod,

HAMMON (2/2)

Josh 19:28 including Ebron, Rehob, *H*,
1 Chr 6:76 *H* with its common-lands, and

HAMMOTH DOR (1/1)

Josh 21:32 *H* with its common-land, and

HAMON GOG (2/2)

Ezek 39:11 will call it the Valley of *H*.
39:15 buried it in the Valley of *H*.

HAMONAH (1/1)

Ezek 39:16 of the city will also be *H*.

HAMOR (13/13)

Gen 33:19 tent, from the children of *H*,
34: 2 And when Shechem the son of *H*
34: 4 Shechem spoke to his father *H*,
34: 6 Then *H* the father of Shechem
34: 8 But *H* spoke with them, saying,
34:13 of Jacob answered Shechem and *H*
34:18 And their words pleased *H* and
34:20 And *H* and Shechem his son came
34:24 the gate of his city heeded *H*
34:26 And they killed *H* and Shechem
Josh 24:32 had bought from the sons of *H*
Judg 9:28 Serve the men of *H* the father
Acts 7:16 sum of money from the sons of *H*,

HAMOR'S (1/1)

Gen 34:18 Hamor and Shechem, *H* son.

HAMRAN (1/1)

1 Chr 1:41 The sons of Dishon were *H*,

HAMSTRING (1/1) HAMSTRUNG

Josh 11: 6 You shall *h* their horses and

HAMSTRUNG (4/4) HAMSTRING

Gen 49: 6 And in their self-will they *h*
Josh 11: 9 he *h* their horses and burned
2 Sam 8: 4 Also David *h* all the chariot
1 Chr 18: 4 And David also *h* all the

HAMUEL (1/1)

1 Chr 4:26 And the sons of Mishma were *H*

HAMUL (3/3)

Gen 46:12 sons of Perez were Hezron and *H*.
Num 26:21 family of the Hezronites; of *H*,
1 Chr 2: 5 of Perez were Hezron and *H*.

HAMULITES (1/1)

Num 26:21 of Hamul, the family of the *H*.

HAMUTAL (3/3)

2 Ki 23:31 His mother's name was *H* the
24:18 His mother's name was *H* the
Jer 52: 1 His mother's name was *H* the

HANAMEL (4/4)

Jer 32: 7 *H* the son of Shallum your uncle
32: 8 Then *H* my uncle's son came to me
32: 9 "So I bought the field from *H*,
32:12 in the presence of *H* my uncle's

HANAN (13/13)

1 Chr 8:23 Abdon, Zichri, *H*,
8:38 Sheariah, Obadiah, and *H*.
9:44 Sheariah, Obadiah, and *H*;
11:43 *H* the son of Maachah, Joshaphat
Ezra 2:46 sons of Shalmai, the sons of *H*,
Neh 7:49 the sons of *H*, the sons of
8: 7 Kelita, Azariah, Jozabad, *H*,
10:10 Hodijah, Kelita, Pelaiah, *H*,
10:22 Pelatiah, *H*, Anaiah,
10:26 Ahijah, *H*, Anan,
13:13 and next to them was *H* the son
Jer 35: 4 the chamber of the sons of *H*

HANANEEL (1/1)

Zech 14:10 and from the Tower of *H* to the

HANANEL (3/3)

Neh 3: 1 then as far as the Tower of *H*.
12:39 the Fish Gate, the Tower of *H*,
Jer 31:38 the LORD from the Tower of *H*

HANANI (11/11)

1 Ki 16: 1 LORD came to Jehu the son of *H*,
16: 7 the prophet Jehu the son of *H*
1 Chr 25: 4 Shebuel, Jerimoth, Hananiah, *H*,
25:25 the eighteenth for *H*,
2 Chr 16: 7 And at that time *H* the seer
19: 2 And Jehu the son of *H* the seer
20:34 the book of Jehu the son of *H*,
Ezra 10:20 of Immer: *H* and Zebadiah;
Neh 1: 2 that *H* one of my brethren came
7: 2 of Jerusalem to my brother *H*,
12:36 Maai, Nethanel, Judah, and *H*,

HANANIAH (29/28) SHADRACH

1 Chr 3:19 Zerubbabel were Meshullam, *H*,
3:21 The sons of *H* were Pelatiah and
8:24 *H*, Elam, Antothijah,
25: 4 Uzziel, Shebuel, Jerimoth, *H*,
25:23 the sixteenth for *H*,
2 Chr 26:11 officer, under the hand of *H*,
Ezra 10:28 the sons of Bebai: Jehohanan, *H*,
Neh 3: 8 Also next to him *H*,
3:30 After him *H* the son of
7: 2 and *H* the leader of the
10:23 Hoshea, *H*, Hasshub,

12:12 Meraiah; of Jeremiah, **H**;
12:41 Elioenai, Zechariah, and **H**,
Jer 28: 1 that **H** the son of Azur the
28: 5 spoke to the prophet **H** in the
28:10 Then **H** the prophet took the
28:11 And **H** spoke in the presence of
28:12 after **H** the prophet had broken
28:13 'Go and tell **H**, saying,
28:15 the prophet Jeremiah said to **H**
28:15 the prophet, "Hear now, **H**,
28:17 So **H** the prophet died the same
36:12 Shaphan, Zedekiah the son of **H**,
37:13 son of Shelemiah, the son of **H**;
Dan 1: 6 sons of Judah were Daniel, **H**,
1: 7 the name Belteshazzar; to **H**,
1:11 eunuchs had set over Daniel, **H**,
1:19 none was found like Daniel, **H**,
2:17 made the decision known to **H**,

HAND (1367/1210) HANDED, HANDFUL, HANDIWORK, HANDS, MEANS

Gen 3:22 lest he put out his **h** and take
4:11 brother's blood from your **h**.
8: 9 So he put out his **h** and took
9: 2 They are given into your **h**.
9: 5 from the **h** of every beast I
9: 5 and from the **h** of man. From the
9: 5 From the **h** of every man's
14:20 your enemies into your **h**.
14:22 I have raised my **h** to the LORD,
16: 6 your maid is in your **h**;
16: 9 and submit yourself under her **h**.
16:12 His **h** shall be against every
16:12 And every man's **h** against him.
19:16 the men took hold of his **h**,
19:16 hold of his hand, his wife's **h**,
21:18 lad and hold him with your **h**,
21:30 seven ewe lambs from my **h**,
22: 6 and he took the fire in his **h**,
22:10 And Abraham stretched out his **h**
22:12 Do not lay your **h** on the lad, or
24: 2 put your **h** under my thigh,
24: 9 So the servant put his **h** under
24:10 master's goods were in his **h**.
24:18 let her pitcher down to her **h**,
24:49 that I may turn to the right **h**
25:26 and his **h** took hold of Esau's
27:17 into the **h** of her son Jacob.
27:41 mourning for my father are at **h**;
30:35 and gave them into the **h** of
31:39 You required it from my **h**,
32:11 from the **h** of my brother, from
32:11 from the **h** of Esau; for I fear
32:13 and took what came to his **h** as
32:16 he delivered them to the **h** of
33:10 receive my present from my **h**,
37:22 and do not lay a **h** on
37:27 and let not our **h** be upon him,
38:18 your staff that is in your **h**.
38:20 sent the young goat by the **h**
38:20 his pledge from the woman's **h**,
38:28 that the one put out his **h**;
38:28 thread and bound it on his **h**,
38:29 happened, as he drew back his **h**,
38:30 the scarlet thread on his **h**.
39: 3 all he did to prosper in his **h**.
39: 6 all that he had in Joseph's **h**,
39: 8 all that he has to my **h**.
39:12 he left his garment in her **h**,
39:13 had left his garment in her **h**
39:22 prison committed to Joseph's **h**
40:11 Pharaoh's cup was in my **h**;
40:11 placed the cup in Pharaoh's **h**.
40:13 will put Pharaoh's cup in his **h**
40:21 placed the cup in Pharaoh's **h**.
41:42 took his signet ring off his **h**
41:42 hand and put it on Joseph's **h**;
41:44 consent no man may lift his **h**
43: 9 from my **h** you shall require
43:12 "Take double money in your **h**,
43:12 and take back in your **h** the
43:15 took double money in their **h**,
43:21 have brought it back in our **h**.
43:26 present which was in their **h**
44:17 the man in whose **h** the cup was
46: 4 and Joseph will put his **h** on
47:29 please put your **h** under my
48:13 Ephraim with his right **h** toward
48:13 hand toward Israel's left **h**,
48:13 and Manasseh with his left **h**
48:13 hand toward Israel's right **h**,
48:14 stretched out his right **h** and
48:14 and his left **h** on Manasseh's
48:17 his father laid his right **h** on
48:17 he took hold of his father's **h**
48:18 put your right **h** on his head."
48:22 which I took from the **h** of the
49: 8 Your **h** shall be on the neck
Ex 2:19 delivered us from the **h** of the
3: 8 to deliver them out of the **h**
3:19 go, no, not even by a mighty **h**.
3:20 So I will stretch out My **h** and
4: 2 him, "What is that in your **h**?
4: 4 Reach out your **h** and take it by
4: 4 (and he reached out his **h** and
4: 4 and it became a rod in his **h**),
4: 6 Now put your **h** in your bosom."
4: 6 And he put his **h** in his
4: 6 his **h** was leprous, like snow.
4: 7 Put your **h** in your bosom
4: 7 So he put his **h** in his bosom
4:13 please send by the **h** of
4:17 shall take this rod in your **h**,
4:20 took the rod of God in his **h**.
4:21 which I have put in your **h**.
5:21 to put a sword in their **h** to
6: 1 For with a strong **h** he will let
6: 1 and with a strong **h** he will
7: 4 so that I may lay My **h** on Egypt
7: 5 when I stretch out My **h** on
7:15 you shall take in your **h**.
7:17 with the rod that is in my **h**,
7:19 your rod and stretch out your **h**
8: 5 Stretch out your **h** with your rod
8: 6 So Aaron stretched out his **h**
8:17 For Aaron stretched out his **h**
9: 3 the **h** of the LORD will be on
9:15 if I had stretched out My **h**
9:22 Stretch out your **h** toward
10:12 Stretch out your **h** over the land
10:21 Stretch out your **h** toward
10:22 So Moses stretched out his **h**
12:11 feet, and your staff in your **h**.
13: 3 for by strength of **h** the LORD
13: 9 be as a sign to you on your **h**
13: 9 for with a strong **h** the LORD
13:14 By strength of **h** the LORD
13:16 shall be as a sign on your **h**
13:16 for by strength of **h** the LORD
14:16 and stretch out your **h** over the
14:21 Moses stretched out his **h** over
14:22 a wall to them on their right **h**
14:26 Stretch out your **h** over the sea,
14:27 And Moses stretched out his **h**
14:29 a wall to them on their right **h**
14:30 Israel that day out of the **h**
15: 6 'Your right **h**, O LORD,
15: 6 in power; Your right **h**,
15: 9 My **h** shall destroy them.'
15:12 You stretched out Your right **h**;
15:20 took the timbrel in her **h**;
16: 3 that we had died by the **h** of
17: 5 Also take in your **h** your rod
17: 9 with the rod of God in my **h**.
17:11 was, when Moses held up his **h**,
17:11 and when he let down his **h**,
18: 9 He had delivered out of the **h**
18:10 has delivered you out of the **h**
18:10 the Egyptians and out of the **h**
18:10 the people from under the **h** of
19:13 Not a **h** shall touch him, but he
21:13 God delivered him into his **h**,
21:16 him, or if he is found in his **h**,
21:20 so that he dies under his **h**,
21:24 **h** for hand, foot for foot,
21:24 tooth for tooth, hand for **h**,
22: 4 certainly found alive in his **h**,
22: 8 see whether he has put his **h**
22:11 that he has not put his **h** into
23: 1 Do not put your **h** with the
23:31 of the land into your **h**,
24:11 of Israel He did not lay His **h**.
29:20 on the thumb of their right **h**
32: 4 the gold from their **h**,
32:11 great power and with a mighty **h**?
32:15 of the Testimony were in his **h**.
33:22 and will cover you with My **h**
33:23 "Then I will take away My **h**,
34: 4 and he took in his **h** the two
34:29 the Testimony were in Moses' **h**
35:29 by the **h** of Moses, had
38:21 by the **h** of Ithamar, son of
Lev 1: 4 Then he shall put his **h** on the
3: 2 And he shall lay his **h** on the
3: 8 And he shall lay his **h** on the
3:13 He shall lay his **h** on its head
4: 4 lay his **h** on the bull's head,
4:24 And he shall lay his **h** on the
4:29 And he shall lay his **h** on the
4:33 Then he shall lay his **h** on the
8:23 on the thumb of his right **h**,
8:36 LORD had commanded by the **h**
9:22 Then Aaron lifted his **h** toward
10:11 has spoken to them by the **h** of
14:14 on the thumb of his right **h**,
14:15 into the palm of his own left **h**.
14:16 the oil that is in his left **h**,
14:17 of the rest of the oil in his **h**,
14:17 on the thumb of his right **h**,
14:18 oil that is in the priest's **h**
14:25 on the thumb of his right **h**,
14:26 into the palm of his own left **h**.
14:27 the oil that is in his left **h**
14:28 of the oil that is in his **h**
14:28 on the thumb of the right **h**,
14:29 oil that is in the priest's **h**
16:21 into the wilderness by the **h**
21:19 has a broken foot or broken **h**,
22:25 Nor from a foreigner's **h** shall
25:14 or buy from your neighbor's **h**,
25:28 was sold shall remain in the **h**
26:25 shall be delivered into the **h**
26:46 Israel on Mount Sinai by the **h**
Num 4:37 of the LORD by the **h** of Moses.
4:45 the word of the LORD by the **h**
4:49 they were numbered by the **h** of
5:18 the priest shall have in his **h**
5:25 of jealousy from the woman's **h**,
6:21 whatever else his **h** is able to
9:23 command of the LORD by the **h**
10:13 command of the LORD by the **h**
15:23 has commanded you by the **h** of
20:11 Then Moses lifted his **h** and
20:17 not turn aside to the right **h**
20:20 many men and with a strong **h**.
21: 2 deliver this people into my **h**,
21:26 taken all his land from his **h**
21:34 have delivered him into your **h**,
22: 7 the diviner's fee in their **h**,
22:23 with His drawn sword in His **h**,
22:26 to turn either to the right **h**
22:29 wish there were a sword in my **h**,
22:31 with His drawn sword in His **h**;
25: 7 and took a javelin in his **h**;
27:18 and lay your **h** on him;
27:23 as the LORD commanded by the **h**
31: 6 the signal trumpets in his **h**.
33: 1 by their armies under the **h** of
35:17 him with a stone in the **h**,
35:18 he strikes him with a wooden **h**
35:21 he strikes him with his **h** so
35:25 the manslayer from the **h** of
36:13 children of Israel by the **h** of
Deut 1:27 Egypt to deliver us into the **h**
2: 7 you in all the work of your **h**.
2:15 For indeed the **h** of the LORD
2:24 I have given into your **h** Sihon
2:30 might deliver him into your **h**,
3: 2 people and his land into your **h**;
3: 8 we took the land from the **h** of
3:24 greatness and Your mighty **h**,
4:34 by a mighty **h** and an
5:15 out from there by a mighty **h**
5:32 not turn aside to the right **h**
6: 8 bind them as a sign on your **h**,
6:21 us out of Egypt with a mighty **h**;
7: 8 brought you out with a mighty **h**,
7: 8 from the **h** of Pharaoh king of
7:19 the mighty **h** and the
7:24 deliver their kings into your **h**,
8:17 'My power and the might of my **h**
9:26 out of Egypt with a mighty **h**.
10: 3 having the two tablets in my **h**.
11: 2 His greatness and His mighty **h**
11:18 bind them as a sign on your **h**,
12: 6 the heave offerings of your **h**,
12: 7 to which you have put your **h**,
12:11 the heave offerings of your **h**,
12:17 of the heave offering of your **h**.
13: 9 your **h** shall be first against
13: 9 and afterward the **h** of all the
13:17 things shall remain in your **h**,
14:25 money, take the money in your **h**,
14:29 you in all the work of your **h**
15: 7 your heart nor shut your **h**
15: 8 but you shall open your **h** wide
15: 9 the year of release, is at **h**,
15:10 in all to which you put your **h**.
15:11 You shall open your **h** wide to
16:10 a freewill offering from your **h**,
17:11 not turn aside to the right **h**
17:20 commandment to the right **h** or
19: 5 and his **h** swings a stroke with
19:12 and deliver him over to the **h**
19:21 **h** for hand, foot for foot.
19:21 tooth for tooth, hand for **h**,
21:10 God delivers them into your **h**,
23:20 in all to which you set your **h**
23:25 may pluck the heads with your **h**,
24: 1 of divorce, puts it in her **h**,
24: 3 of divorce, puts it in her **h**,
25:11 rescue her husband from the **h**
25:11 and puts out her **h** and seizes
25:12 "then you shall cut off her **h**;
26: 4 take the basket out of your **h**
26: 8 us out of Egypt with a mighty **h**
28: 8 in all to which you set your **h**,
28:12 to bless all the work of your **h**.
28:20 in all that you set your **h** to
28:32 be no strength in your **h**.
30: 9 in all the work of your **h**,
32:27 Our **h** is high; And it is not
32:35 day of their calamity is at **h**,
32:39 any who can deliver from My **h**.
32:40 For I raise My **h** to heaven,
32:41 And My **h** takes hold on
33: 2 From His right **h** Came a
33: 3 All His saints are in Your **h**;
Josh 1: 7 turn from it to the right **h** or
2:19 shall be on our head if a **h**
4:24 of the earth may know the **h** of
5:13 with His sword drawn in His **h**.
6: 2 have given Jericho into your **h**,
7: 7 to deliver us into the **h** of the
8: 1 I have given into your **h** the
8: 7 God will deliver it into your **h**.
8:18 the spear that is in your **h**
8:18 for I will give it into your **h**.
8:18 the spear that was in his **h**
8:19 as he had stretched out his **h**,
8:26 Joshua did not draw back his **h**,
9:26 delivered them out of the **h** of
10: 8 have delivered them into your **h**;
10:19 has delivered them into your **h**.
10:30 it and its king into the **h** of
10:32 delivered Lachish into the **h**
11: 8 delivered them into the **h** of
14: 2 LORD had commanded by the **h**
20: 5 deliver the slayer into his **h**,
20: 9 and not die by the **h** of the
21: 8 LORD had commanded by the **h**
21:44 all their enemies into their **h**.
22: 9 the word of the LORD by the **h**
22:31 of Israel out of the **h** of the

23: 6 aside from it to the right **h**
24: 8 But I gave them into your **h**,
24:10 So I delivered you out of his **h**.
24:11 I delivered them into your **h**.
Judg 1: 2 delivered the land into his **h**.
1: 4 and the Perizzites into their **h**;
2:15 the **h** of the LORD was against
2:16 delivered them out of the **h** of
2:18 delivered them out of the **h** of
2:23 did He deliver them into the **h**
3: 4 their fathers by the **h** of
3: 8 and He sold them into the **h** of
3:10 king of Mesopotamia into his **h**;
3:10 and his **h** prevailed over
3:21 Ehud reached with his left **h**,
3:28 the Moabites into your **h**.
3:30 subdued that day under the **h**
4: 2 the LORD sold them into the **h**
4: 7 I will deliver him into your **h**'
4: 9 will sell Sisera into the **h** of
4:14 delivered Sisera into your **h**.
4:21 peg and took a hammer in her **h**,
4:24 And the **h** of the children of
5:26 She stretched her **h** to the tent
5:26 Her right **h** to the workmen's
6: 1 delivered them into the **h** of
6: 2 and the **h** of Midian prevailed
6: 9 I delivered you out of the **h**
6: 9 the Egyptians and out of the **h**
6:14 shall save Israel from the **h**
6:21 of the staff that was in His **h**,
6:36 You will save Israel by my **h**
6:37 You will save Israel by my **h**,
7: 2 My own **h** has saved me.'
7: 6 putting their **h** to their
7: 7 the Midianites into your **h**.
7: 9 I have delivered it into your **h**.
7:14 a man of Israel! Into his **h** God
7:15 the camp of Midian into your **h**.
7:16 a trumpet into every man's **h**,
8: 6 and Zalmunna now in your **h**,
8: 7 Zebah and Zalmunna into my **h**,
8:15 and Zalmunna now in your **h**,
8:22 have delivered us from the **h**
9:17 and delivered you out of the **h**
9:48 Abimelech took an ax in his **h**
10:12 I delivered you from their **h**.
11:21 and all his people into the **h**
12: 3 LORD delivered them into my **h**.
13: 1 delivered them into the **h** of
13: 5 to deliver Israel out of the **h**
14: 6 he had nothing in his **h**.
15:12 we may deliver you into the **h**
15:13 and deliver you into their **h**;
15:15 reached out his **h** and took it,
15:17 he threw the jawbone from his **h**,
15:18 great deliverance by the **h** of
15:18 of thirst and fall into the **h**
16:18 brought the money in their **h**.
16:26 the lad who held him by the **h**,
17: 3 dedicated the silver from my **h**
18:19 put your **h** over your mouth, and
20:28 I will deliver them into your **h**.
Ruth 1:13 much for your sakes that the **h**
4: 5 you buy the field from the **h**
4: 9 from the **h** of Naomi.
1 Sam 2:13 fleshhook in his **h** while the
4: 3 us it may save us from the **h**
4: 8 Who will deliver us from the **h**
5: 6 But the **h** of the LORD was
5: 7 for His **h** is harsh toward us
5: 9 that the **h** of the LORD was
5:11 the **h** of God was very heavy
6: 3 will be known to you why His **h**
6: 5 perhaps He will lighten His **h**
6: 9 know that it is not His **h**
6:12 not turn aside to the right **h**
7: 3 He will deliver you from the **h**
7: 8 that He may save us from the **h**
7:13 And the **h** of the LORD was
9: 8 I have here at **h** one fourth of
9:16 may save My people from the **h**
10:18 and delivered you from the **h** of
10:18 the Egyptians and from the **h**
12: 3 or from whose **h** have I received
12: 4 taken anything from any man's **h**.
12: 5 have not found anything in my **h**.
12: 9 He sold them into the **h** of
12: 9 into the **h** of the Philistines,
12: 9 and into the **h** of the king of
12:10 but now deliver us from the **h**
12:11 and delivered you out of the **h**
12:15 then the **h** of the LORD will be
13:22 sword nor spear found in the **h**
14:10 has delivered them into our **h**,
14:12 has delivered them into the **h**
14:19 the priest, "Withdraw your **h**.
14:26 but no one put his **h** to his
14:27 of the rod that was in his **h**
14:27 and put his **h** to his mouth;
14:37 You deliver them into the **h** of
14:43 of the rod that was in my **h**.
16:16 that he will play it with his **h**
16:23 a harp and play it with his **h**.
17:22 left his supplies in the **h** of
17:37 He will deliver me from the **h**
17:40 he took his staff in his **h**;
17:40 had, and his sling was in his **h**.
17:46 will deliver you into my **h**,
17:49 Then David put his **h** in his bag
17:50 there was no sword in the **h**
17:57 head of the Philistine in his **h**.
18:10 David played music with his **h**,
18:10 there was a spear in Saul's **h**.
18:17 Let my **h** not be against him, but
18:17 him, but let the **h** of the
18:21 to him, and that the **h** of the
18:25 to make David fall by the **h** of
19: 9 house with his spear in his **h**.
19: 9 was playing music with his **h**.
20:16 the LORD require it at the **h**
21: 3 therefore, what have you on **h**?
21: 3 five loaves of bread in my **h**,
21: 4 is no common bread on **h**;
21: 8 Is there not here on **h** a spear
22: 6 Ramah, with his spear in his **h**,
22:17 because their **h** also is with
23: 4 the Philistines into your **h**.
23: 6 down with an ephod in his **h**.
23: 7 has delivered him into my **h**,
23:11 of Keilah deliver me into his **h**?
23:12 me and my men into the **h** of
23:14 did not deliver him into his **h**.
23:16 woods and strengthened his **h**
23:17 for the **h** of Saul my father
23:20 deliver him into the king's **h**.
24: 4 deliver your enemy into your **h**,
24: 6 to stretch out my **h** against
24:10 delivered you today into my **h**
24:10 I will not stretch out my **h**
24:11 corner of your robe in my **h**!
24:11 evil nor rebellion in my **h**,
24:12 But my **h** shall not be against
24:13 But my **h** shall not be against
24:15 and deliver me out of your **h**.
24:18 LORD delivered me into your **h**,
24:20 shall be established in your **h**.
25: 8 give whatever comes to your **h**
25:26 yourself with your own **h**,
25:33 avenging myself with my own **h**.
25:35 So David received from her **h**
25:39 of my reproach from the **h** of
26: 8 your enemy into your **h** this
26: 9 for who can stretch out his **h**
26:11 that I should stretch out my **h**
26:18 done, or what evil is in my **h**?
26:23 LORD delivered you into my **h**
26:23 I would not stretch out my **h**
27: 1 I shall perish someday by the **h**
27: 1 So I shall escape out of his **h**.
28:17 torn the kingdom out of your **h**
28:19 Israel with you into the **h** of
28:19 the army of Israel into the **h**
30:23 us and delivered into our **h**
2 Sam 1:14 not afraid to put forth your **h**
2:19 he did not turn to the right **h**
2:21 Turn aside to your right **h** or to
3: 8 not delivered you into the **h**
3:12 and indeed my **h** shall be with
3:18 By the **h** of My servant David, I
3:18 My people Israel from the **h** of
3:18 of the Philistines and the **h**
4:11 now require his blood at your **h**
5:19 Will You deliver them into my **h**?
5:19 the Philistines into your **h**.
6: 6 Uzzah put out his **h** to the
8: 1 took Metheg Ammah from the **h**
10: 2 So David sent by the **h** of his
11:14 to Joab and sent it by the **h**
12: 7 and I delivered you from the **h**
12:25 and He sent word by the **h** of
13: 5 see it and eat it from her **h**.
13: 6 that I may eat from her **h**.
13:10 that I may eat from your **h**.
13:19 and laid her **h** on her head and
14:16 his maidservant from the **h** of
14:19 Is the **h** of Joab with you in
14:19 no one can turn to the right **h**
15: 5 that he would put out his **h** and
16: 6 men were on his right **h** and
16: 8 the kingdom into the **h** of
18: 2 of the people under the **h** of
18: 2 one third under the **h** of
18: 2 and one third under the **h** of
18:12 shekels of silver in my **h**,
18:12 I would not raise my **h** against
18:14 he took three spears in his **h**
18:28 up the men who raised their **h**
19: 9 The king saved us from the **h** of
19: 9 he delivered us from the **h** of
20: 9 by the beard with his right **h**
20:10 the sword that was in Joab's **h**.
20:21 has raised his **h** against the
21:20 who had six fingers on each **h**
21:22 and fell by the **h** of David and
21:22 the hand of David and by the **h**
22: 1 had delivered him from the **h**
22: 1 and from the **h** of Saul.
23:10 the Philistines until his **h**
23:10 and his **h** stuck to the sword.
23:21 Egyptian had a spear in his **h**;
23:21 spear out of the Egyptian's **h**,
24:14 Please let us fall into the **h**
24:14 do not let me fall into the **h**
24:16 the angel stretched out His **h**
24:16 is enough; now restrain your **h**.
24:17 what have they done? Let Your **h**,
1 Ki 2:19 so she sat at his right **h**.
2:25 So King Solomon sent by the **h** of
2:46 was established in the **h** of
8:15 and with His **h** has fulfilled
8:24 and fulfilled it with Your **h**,
8:42 great name and Your strong **h**
11:12 I will tear it out of the **h** of
11:31 tear the kingdom out of the **h**
11:34 the whole kingdom out of his **h**,
11:35 the kingdom out of his son's **h**
13: 4 that he stretched out his **h**
13: 4 "Arrest him!" Then his **h**,
13: 6 that my **h** may be restored to
13: 6 and the king's **h** was restored
15:18 and delivered them into the **h**
17:11 me a morsel of bread in your **h**.
18: 9 your servant into the **h** of
18:44 a cloud, as small as a man's **h**,
18:46 Then the **h** of the LORD came
20:13 I will deliver it into your **h**
20:28 great multitude into your **h**,
20:42 have let slip out of your **h** a
22: 3 to take it out of the **h** of the
22: 6 will deliver it into the **h** of
22:12 deliver it into the king's **h**.
22:15 will deliver it into the **h** of
22:19 on His right **h** and on His left.
2 Ki 3:10 to deliver them into the **h** of
3:13 to deliver them into the **h** of
3:15 that the **h** of the LORD came
3:18 the Moabites into your **h**.
4:29 and take my staff in your **h**,
5:11 and wave his **h** over the place,
5:18 there, and he leans on my **h**,
5:24 he took them from their **h**,
6: 7 So he reached out his **h** and
7: 2 So an officer on whose **h** the
7:17 the officer on whose **h** he
8: 8 "Take a present in your **h**,
9: 1 this flask of oil in your **h**,
9: 7 LORD, at the **h** of Jezebel.
10:15 "If it is, give me your **h**.
10:15 So he gave him his **h**,
11: 8 man with his weapons in his **h**;
11:11 man with his weapons in his **h**,
12:15 from the men into whose **h** they
13: 3 He delivered them into the **h**
13: 3 and into the **h** of Ben-Hadad the
13: 5 they escaped from under the **h**
13:16 'Put your **h** on the bow."
13:16 So he put his **h** on it, and
13:25 Jehoahaz recaptured from the **h**
13:25 he had taken out of the **h** of
14: 5 was established in his **h**,
14:27 but He saved them by the **h** of
15:19 that his **h** might be with him to
16: 7 Come up and save me from the **h**
16: 7 king of Syria and from the **h**
17: 7 from under the **h** of Pharaoh
17:20 and delivered them into the **h**
17:39 He will deliver you from the **h**
18:21 it will go into his **h** and
18:29 able to deliver you from his **h**;
18:30 shall not be given into the **h**
18:33 delivered its land from the **h**
18:34 delivered Samaria from my **h**?
18:35 their countries from my **h**,
18:35 deliver Jerusalem from my **h**?
19:10 shall not be given into the **h**
19:14 received the letter from the **h**
19:19 God, I pray, save us from his **h**,
20: 6 you and this city from the **h**
21:14 and deliver them into the **h** of
22: 2 not turn aside to the right **h**
22: 5 let them deliver it into the **h**
22: 7 money delivered into their **h**,
22: 9 have delivered it into the **h**
1 Chr 4:10 that Your **h** would be with me,
5:10 Hagrites, who fell by their **h**;
5:20 were delivered into their **h**,
6:15 into captivity by the **h** of
6:39 Asaph, who stood at his right **h**,
6:44 sons of Merari, on the left **h**,
11:23 In the Egyptian's **h** there was
11:23 spear out of the Egyptian's **h**,
12: 2 using both the right **h** and the
13: 9 Uzza put out his **h** to hold the
13:10 him because he put his **h** to
14:10 Will You deliver them into my **h**?
14:10 I will deliver them into your **h**.
14:11 through my enemies by my **h**
16: 7 this psalm into the **h** of
18: 1 Gath and its towns from the **h**
20: 6 six on each **h** and six on
20: 8 and they fell by the **h** of David
20: 8 the hand of David and by the **h**
21:13 Please let me fall into the **h**
21:13 do not let me fall into the **h**
21:15 is enough; now restrain your **h**.
21:16 having in his **h** a drawn sword
21:17 what have they done? Let Your **h**,
22:18 of the land into my **h**,
24:19 to their ordinance by the **h** of
26:28 was under the **h** of Shelomith
28:19 by His **h** upon me, all the
29: 8 into the **h** of Jehiel the
29:12 In Your **h** is power and might;
29:12 In Your **h** it is to make
29:16 Your holy name is from Your **h**,
2 Chr 3:17 one on the right **h** and the
3:17 name of the one on the right **h**
6:15 and fulfilled it with Your **h**,
6:32 great name and Your mighty **h**
8:18 Hiram sent him ships by the **h**
10:15 which He had spoken by the **h** of
12: 5 I also have left you in the **h**
12: 7 out on Jerusalem by the **h** of
13: 8 which is in the **h** of the sons
13:16 God delivered them into their **h**.

16: 7 Syria has escaped from your ***h***.
16: 8 He delivered them into your ***h***.
17: 5 the kingdom in his ***h***;
18: 5 deliver it into the king's ***h***.
18:11 deliver it into the king's ***h***.
18:14 shall be delivered into your ***h***!
18:18 heaven standing on His right ***h***
20: 6 and in Your ***h*** is there not
23: 7 man with his weapons in his ***h***;
23:10 man with his weapon in his ***h***,
23:18 house of the LORD to the ***h*** of
24:11 to the king's official by the ***h***
24:24 a very great army into their ***h***,
25:15 their own people from your ***h***?
25:20 He might give them into the ***h***
26:11 under the ***h*** of Hananiah, one
26:19 and he had a censer in his ***h***
28: 5 God delivered him into the ***h***
28: 5 was also delivered into the ***h***
28: 9 has delivered them into your ***h***;
30: 6 who have escaped from the ***h*** of
30:12 Also the ***h*** of God was on Judah
30:16 the blood received from the ***h***
31:13 were overseers under the ***h*** of
32:11 God will deliver us from the ***h***
32:13 deliver their lands out of my ***h***?
32:14 deliver his people from my ***h***,
32:14 able to deliver you from my ***h***?
32:15 to deliver his people from my ***h***
32:15 people from my hand or the ***h***
32:15 your God deliver you from my ***h***?
32:17 their people from my ***h***,
32:17 deliver His people from my ***h***.
32:22 of Jerusalem from the ***h*** of
32:22 and from the ***h*** of all others,
33: 8 and the ordinances by the ***h*** of
34: 2 not turn aside to the right ***h***
34: 9 doors had gathered from the ***h***
34:10 Then they put it in the ***h*** of
34:17 have delivered it into the ***h***
35: 6 the word of the LORD by the ***h***
36:17 He gave them all into his ***h***.
Ezra 1: 8 brought them out by the ***h*** of
5:12 He gave them into the ***h*** of
6:12 king or people who put their ***h***
7: 6 according to the ***h*** of the LORD
7: 9 according to the good ***h*** of his
7:14 of your God which is in your ***h***;
7:28 as the ***h*** of the LORD my God
8:18 by the good ***h*** of our God upon
8:22 The ***h*** of our God is upon all
8:26 I weighed into their ***h*** six
8:31 And the ***h*** of our God was upon
8:31 and He delivered us from the ***h***
8:33 the house of our God by the ***h***
9: 2 the ***h*** of the leaders and rulers
9: 7 have been delivered into the ***h***
Neh 1:10 power, and by Your strong ***h***.
2: 8 to me according to the good ***h***
2:18 And I told them of the ***h*** of my
4:17 themselves so that with one ***h***
6: 5 with an open letter in his ***h***.
8: 4 and beside him, at his right ***h***,
8: 4 and at his left ***h*** Pedaiah,
9:14 By the ***h*** of Moses Your
9:27 You delivered them into the ***h***
9:27 who saved them From the ***h*** of
9:28 You left them in the ***h*** of
9:30 You gave them into the ***h*** of
12:31 One went to the right ***h*** on the
Esth 3:10 his signet ring from his ***h*** and
5: 2 scepter that was in his ***h***.
6: 9 horse be delivered to the ***h*** of
8: 7 he tried to lay his ***h*** on the
9:10 but they did not lay a ***h*** on the
9:15 but they did not lay a ***h*** on the
9:16 but they did not lay a ***h*** on the
Job 1:11 stretch out Your ***h*** and touch
1:12 only do not lay a ***h*** on his
2: 5 But stretch out Your ***h*** now, and
2: 6 "Behold, he is in your ***h***,
5:15 the mighty, And from their ***h***.
6: 9 That He would loose His ***h*** and
6:23 'Deliver me from the enemy's ***h***'?
6:23 Redeem me from the ***h*** of
9:24 The earth is given into the ***h***
9:33 Who may lay his ***h*** on us both.
10: 7 one who can deliver from Your ***h***?
11:14 If iniquity were in your ***h***,
12: 6 what God provides by His ***h***.
12: 9 does not know That the ***h*** of
12:10 In whose ***h*** is the life of
13:21 Withdraw Your ***h*** far from me,
15:23 of darkness is ready at his ***h***.
15:25 For he stretches out his ***h***
19:21 For the ***h*** of God has struck
20:22 Every ***h*** of misery will come
21: 5 Put your ***h*** over your mouth.
21:16 prosperity is not in their ***h***;
23: 2 My ***h*** is listless because of my
23: 9 When He works on the left ***h***,
23: 9 When He turns to the right ***h***,
26:13 His ***h*** pierced the fleeing
27:11 I will teach you about the ***h*** of
28: 9 He puts his ***h*** on the flint;
29: 9 And put their ***h*** on their
29:20 And my bow is renewed in my ***h***.
30:12 At my right ***h*** the rabble
30:21 With the strength of Your ***h***
30:24 He would not stretch out His ***h***
31:21 If I have raised my ***h*** against
31:25 And because my ***h*** had gained

31:27 And my mouth has kissed my ***h***;
33: 7 Nor will my ***h*** be heavy on you.
34:20 are taken away without a ***h***.
35: 7 does He receive from your ***h***?
37: 7 He seals the ***h*** of every man,
40: 4 I lay my ***h*** over my mouth.
40:14 to you That your own right ***h***
41: 8 Lay your ***h*** on him;
Ps 10:12 lift up Your ***h***! Do not forget
10:14 grief, To repay it by Your ***h***.
16: 8 Because He is at my right ***h***
16:11 At Your right ***h*** are pleasures
17: 7 lovingkindness by Your right ***h***,
17:14 With Your ***h*** from men, O LORD,
18: LORD delivered him from the ***h***
18: all his enemies and from the ***h***
18:35 Your right ***h*** has held me up,
20: 6 saving strength of His right ***h***.
21: 8 Your ***h*** will find all Your
21: 8 Your right ***h*** will find those
26:10 And whose right ***h*** is full of
31: 5 Into Your ***h*** I commit my spirit;
31: 8 have not shut me up into the ***h***
31:15 My times are in Your ***h***;
31:15 Deliver me from the ***h*** of my
32: 4 For day and night Your ***h*** was
36:11 And let not the ***h*** of the
37:24 LORD upholds him with His ***h***.
37:33 will not leave him in his ***h***,
38: 2 And Your ***h*** presses me down.
39:10 consumed by the blow of Your ***h***.
44: 2 out the nations with Your ***h***,
44: 3 But it was Your right ***h***,
45: 4 And Your right ***h*** shall teach
45: 9 At Your right ***h*** stands the
48:10 Your right ***h*** is full of
60: 5 Save with Your right ***h***,
63: 8 Your right ***h*** upholds me.
71: 4 out of the ***h*** of the wicked,
71: 4 Out of the ***h*** of the
73:23 You hold me by my right ***h***.
74:11 Why do You withdraw Your ***h***,
74:11 Your hand, even Your right ***h***?
75: 8 For in the ***h*** of the LORD
77: 2 My ***h*** was stretched out in the
77:10 the years of the right ***h*** of
77:20 people like a flock By the ***h***
78:54 mountain which His right ***h***
78:61 His glory into the enemy's ***h***.
80:15 the vineyard which Your right ***h***
80:17 Let Your ***h*** be upon the man of
80:17 be upon the man of Your right ***h***,
81:14 And turn My ***h*** against their
82: 4 Free them from the ***h*** of the
88: 5 who are cut off from Your ***h***.
89:13 a mighty arm; Strong is Your ***h***,
89:13 hand, and high is Your right ***h***.
89:21 With whom My ***h*** shall be
89:25 Also I will set his ***h*** over the
89:25 And his right ***h*** over the
89:42 You have exalted the right ***h*** of
91: 7 ten thousand at your right ***h***;
95: 4 In His ***h*** are the deep places
95: 7 And the sheep of His ***h***.
97:10 He delivers them out of the ***h***
98: 1 His right ***h*** and His holy arm
104:28 gather in; You open Your ***h***,
106:10 He saved them from the ***h*** of him
106:10 And redeemed them from the ***h***
106:26 Therefore He raised up His ***h***
106:41 And He gave them into the ***h*** of
106:42 into subjection under their ***h***.
107: 2 He has redeemed from the ***h*** of
108: 6 Save with Your right ***h***,
109: 6 an accuser stand at his right ***h***.
109:27 may know that this is Your ***h***—
109:31 He shall stand at the right ***h***
110: 1 my Lord, "Sit at My right ***h***,
110: 5 The Lord is at Your right ***h***;
118:15 The right ***h*** of the LORD does
118:16 The right ***h*** of the LORD is
118:16 The right ***h*** of the LORD does
119:109 life is continually in my ***h***,
119:173 Let Your ***h*** become my help, For
121: 5 is your shade at your right ***h***.
123: 2 of servants look to the ***h*** of
123: 2 the eyes of a maid to the ***h*** of
127: 4 Like arrows in the ***h*** of a
129: 7 the reaper does not fill his ***h***,
136:12 With a strong ***h***, and with
137: 5 Let my right ***h*** forget its
138: 7 You will stretch out Your ***h***
138: 7 And Your right ***h*** will save me.
139: 5 And laid Your ***h*** upon me.
139:10 Even there Your ***h*** shall lead
139:10 And Your right ***h*** shall hold
142: 4 Look on my right ***h*** and see,
144: 7 Stretch out Your ***h*** from above;
144: 7 From the ***h*** of foreigners,
144: 8 And whose right ***h*** is a right
144: 8 whose right hand is a right ***h***
144:11 me and deliver me from the ***h***
144:11 And whose right ***h*** is a right
144:11 whose right hand is a right ***h***
145:16 You open Your ***h*** And satisfy
149: 6 a two-edged sword in their ***h***,
Prov 1:24 I have stretched out my ***h*** and
3:16 of days is in her right ***h***,
3:16 In her left ***h*** riches and
3:27 it is in the power of your ***h***
6: 3 For you have come into the ***h***
6: 5 like a gazelle from the ***h*** of

6: 5 And like a bird from the ***h*** of
10: 4 He who has a slack ***h*** becomes
10: 4 But the ***h*** of the diligent
12:24 The ***h*** of the diligent will
17:16 Why is there in the ***h*** of a
19:24 A lazy man buries his ***h*** in the
21: 1 The king's heart is in the ***h***
26: 6 who sends a message by the ***h***
26: 9 a thorn that goes into the ***h***
26:15 The lazy man buries his ***h*** in
27:16 grasps oil with his right ***h***.
30:32 put your ***h*** on your mouth.
31:19 And her ***h*** holds the spindle.
31:20 She extends her ***h*** to the poor,
Eccl 2:24 was from the ***h*** of God.
5:14 there is nothing in his ***h***.
5:15 he may carry away in his ***h***.
7:18 And also not remove your ***h***
9: 1 and their works are in the ***h***
9:10 Whatever your ***h*** finds to do, do
10: 2 man's heart is at his right ***h***,
11: 6 evening do not withhold your ***h***;
Song 2: 6 His left ***h*** is under my head,
2: 6 And his right ***h*** embraces me.
5: 4 My beloved put his ***h*** By the
8: 3 His left ***h*** is under my head,
8: 3 And his right ***h*** embraces me.
Isa 1:12 has required this from your ***h***,
1:25 I will turn My ***h*** against you,
5:25 He has stretched out His ***h***
5:25 But His ***h*** is stretched out
6: 6 having in his ***h*** a live coal
8:11 thus to me with a strong ***h***,
9:12 But His ***h*** is stretched out
9:17 But His ***h*** is stretched out
9:20 he shall snatch on the right ***h***
9:20 He shall devour on the left ***h***
9:21 But His ***h*** is stretched out
10: 4 But His ***h*** is stretched out
10: 5 And the staff in whose ***h*** is
10:10 As my ***h*** has found the kingdoms
10:13 By the strength of my ***h*** I have
10:14 My ***h*** has found like a nest the
11: 8 weaned child shall put his ***h***
11:11 the LORD shall set His ***h***
11:14 They shall lay their ***h*** on Edom
13: 2 voice to them; Wave your ***h***,
13: 6 the day of the LORD is at ***h***!
14:26 And this is the ***h*** that is
14:27 His ***h*** is stretched out, And
19: 4 I will give Into the ***h*** of a
19:16 because of the waving of the ***h***
22:21 your responsibility into his ***h***.
23:11 He stretched out His ***h*** over the
25:10 For on this mountain the ***h*** of
26:11 when Your ***h*** is lifted up, they
28: 2 down to the earth with His ***h***.
28: 4 up while it is still in his ***h***.
30:21 you turn to the right ***h*** Or
31: 3 the LORD stretches out His ***h***,
34:17 And His ***h*** has divided it among
36: 6 it will go into his ***h*** and
36:15 will not be given into the ***h***
36:18 delivered its land from the ***h***
36:19 delivered Samaria from my ***h***?
36:20 their countries from my ***h***,
36:20 deliver Jerusalem from my ***h***?
37:10 shall not be given into the ***h***
37:14 received the letter from the ***h***
37:20 our God, save us from his ***h***,
38: 6 you and this city from the ***h***
40: 2 has received from the LORD's ***h***
40:10 shall come with a strong ***h***,
40:12 waters in the hollow of His ***h***,
41:10 you with My righteous right ***h***.
41:13 God, will hold your right ***h***,
41:20 That the ***h*** of the LORD has
42: 6 And will hold Your ***h***;
43:13 one who can deliver out of My ***h***;
44: 5 Another will write with his ***h***,
44:20 there not a lie in my right ***h***?
45: 1 whose right ***h*** I have held—To
47: 6 And given them into your ***h***.
48:13 Indeed My ***h*** has laid the
48:13 And My right ***h*** has stretched
49: 2 In the shadow of His ***h*** He has
49:22 I will lift My ***h*** in an oath to
50: 2 Is My ***h*** shortened at all that
50:11 you shall have from My ***h***:
51:16 you with the shadow of My ***h***,
51:17 You who have drunk at the ***h*** of
51:18 any who takes her by the ***h***
51:22 I have taken out of your ***h*** The
51:23 But I will put it into the ***h*** of
53:10 LORD shall prosper in His ***h***.
56: 2 And keeps his ***h*** from doing any
57:10 have found the life of your ***h***;
59: 1 the LORD's ***h*** is not shortened,
62: 3 be a crown of glory In the ***h***
62: 3 And a royal diadem In the ***h***
62: 8 LORD has sworn by His right ***h***
63:12 Who led them by the right ***h*** of
64: 8 all we are the work of Your ***h***.
66: 2 For all those things My ***h*** has
66:14 The ***h*** of the LORD shall be
Jer 1: 9 the LORD put forth His ***h*** and
6: 9 put your ***h*** back into the
6:12 For I will stretch out My ***h***
11:21 LORD, lest you die by our ***h***'—
12: 7 beloved of My soul into the ***h***
15: 4 I will ***h*** them over to trouble,
15: 6 I will stretch out My ***h***

15:17 I sat alone because of Your **h**,
15:21 I will deliver you from the **h** of
16:21 will cause them to know My **h**
18: 4 of clay was marred in the **h** of
18: 6 the clay is in the potter's **h**,
18: 6 hand, so are you in My **h**,
20: 4 will give all Judah into the **h**
20: 5 of Judah I will give into the **h**
20:13 life of the poor From the **h**
21: 5 you with an outstretched **h** and
21: 7 into the **h** of Nebuchadnezzar
21: 7 into the **h** of their enemies,
21: 7 and into the **h** of those who
21:10 It shall be given into the **h** of
21:12 is plundered Out of the **h** of
22: 3 the plundered out of the **h** of
22:24 were the signet on My right **h**,
22:25 I will give you into the **h**
22:25 and into the **h** of those whose
22:25 the **h** of Nebuchadnezzar king of
22:25 king of Babylon and the **h** of
23:23 "Am I a God near at **h**,
25:15 this wine cup of fury from My **h**,
25:17 took the cup from the LORD's **h**,
25:28 to take the cup from your **h** to
26:14 for me, here I am, in your **h**;
26:24 Nevertheless the **h** of Ahikam the
26:24 should not give him into the **h**
27: 3 by the **h** of the messengers who
27: 6 all these lands into the **h** of
27: 8 I have consumed them by his **h**.
29: 3 letter was sent by the **h** of
29:21 I will deliver them into the **h**
31:11 And ransomed him from the **h** of
31:32 day that I took them by the **h**
32: 3 will give this city into the **h**
32: 4 shall not escape from the **h** of
32: 4 surely be delivered into the **h**
32:21 with a strong **h** and an
32:24 city has been given into the **h**
32:25 city has been given into the **h**
32:28 will give this city into the **h**
32:28 into the **h** of Nebuchadnezzar
32:36 shall be delivered into the **h**
32:43 it has been given into the **h** of
34: 2 will give this city into the **h**
34: 3 you shall not escape from his **h**,
34: 3 taken and delivered into his **h**;
34:20 I will give them into the **h** of
34:20 of their enemies and into the **h**
34:21 and his princes into the **h** of
34:21 into the **h** of those who seek
34:21 and into the **h** of the king of
36:14 Take in your **h** the scroll from
36:14 took the scroll in his **h** and
37:17 shall be delivered into the **h**
38: 3 surely be given into the **h** of
38: 5 said, "Look, he is in your **h**.
38:16 nor will I give you into the **h**
38:18 city shall be given into the **h**
38:18 shall not escape from their **h**.
38:19 they deliver me into their **h**,
38:23 shall not escape from their **h**,
38:23 but shall be taken by the **h** of
39:17 shall not be given into the **h**
40: 4 the chains that were on your **h**.
41: 5 and incense in their **h**,
42:11 you and deliver you from his **h**.
43: 3 to deliver us into the **h** of the
43: 9 "Take large stones in your **h**,
44:30 king of Egypt into the **h** of
44:30 of his enemies and into the **h**
44:30 king of Judah into the **h** of
46:24 shall be delivered into the **h**
46:26 I will deliver them into the **h**
46:26 into the **h** of Nebuchadnezzar
46:26 king of Babylon and the **h** of
48:16 calamity of Moab is near at **h**,
50:15 She has given her **h**,
51: 7 a golden cup in the LORD's **h**,
51:25 And I will stretch out My **h**
Lam 1: 7 her people fell into the **h** of
1:10 The adversary has spread his **h**
2: 3 He has drawn back His right **h**
2: 4 bent His bow; With His right **h**,
2: 7 of her palaces Into the **h** of
2: 8 He has not withdrawn His **h**
3: 3 Surely He has turned His **h**
4: 6 With no **h** to help her!
5: 6 We have given our **h** to the
5: 8 to deliver us from their **h**.
Ezek 1: 3 and the **h** of the LORD was upon
2: 9 there was a **h** stretched out to
3:14 but the **h** of the LORD was
3:18 blood I will require at your **h**.
3:20 blood I will require at your **h**.
3:22 Then the **h** of the LORD was
6:14 So I will stretch out My **h**
7:17 Every **h** will be feeble, And
8: 1 that the **h** of the Lord GOD
8: 3 stretched out the form of a **h**,
8:11 Each man had a censer in his **h**,
9: 1 with a deadly weapon in his **h**.
9: 2 with his battle-ax in his **h**.
10: 7 the cherub stretched out his **h**
10: 8 to have the form of a man's **h**
12: 7 dug through the wall with my **h**.
12:23 to them, "The days are at **h**,
13: 9 My **h** will be against the
13:21 deliver My people out of your **h**,
13:21 no longer be as prey in your **h**.
13:23 deliver My people out of your **h**,
14: 9 and I will stretch out My **h**
14:13 I will stretch out My **h** against
16:27 I stretched out My **h** against
16:39 will also give you into their **h**,
16:49 did she strengthen the **h** of
17:18 and in fact gave his **h** and
18: 8 But has withdrawn his **h** from
18:17 Who has withdrawn his **h** from
20: 5 I chose Israel and raised My **h**
20: 5 I raised My **h** in an oath to
20: 6 On that day I raised My **h** in an
20:15 So I also raised My **h** in an oath
20:22 Nevertheless I withdrew My **h** and
20:23 Also I raised My **h** in an oath to
20:28 which I had raised My **h** in an
20:33 GOD, "surely with a mighty **h**,
20:34 are scattered, with a mighty **h**,
20:42 for which I raised My **h** in an
21:11 To be given into the **h** of the
21:22 In his right **h** is the divination
21:24 you shall be taken in **h**.
23: 9 have delivered her Into the **h**
23: 9 Into the **h** of the Assyrians,
23:28 I will deliver you into the **h**
23:28 into the **h** of those from whom
23:31 I will put her cup in your **h**.
25: 7 I will stretch out My **h** against
25:13 I will also stretch out My **h**
25:14 My vengeance on Edom by the **h**
25:16 I will stretch out My **h** against
27:15 were the market of your **h**.
28: 9 In the **h** of him who slays you.
28:10 of the uncircumcised By the **h**
29: 7 took hold of you with the **h**,
30:10 of Egypt to cease By the **h** of
30:12 And sell the land into the **h**
30:12 By the **h** of aliens. I, the
30:22 the sword fall out of his **h**.
30:24 and put My sword in his **h**;
30:25 when I put My sword into the **h**
31:11 I will deliver it into the **h**
33: 6 require at the watchman's **h**.
33: 8 blood I will require at your **h**.
33:22 Now the **h** of the LORD had been
34:10 require My flock at their **h**;
34:27 and delivered them from the **h**
35: 3 I will stretch out My **h**
36: 7 I have raised My **h** in an oath
37: 1 The **h** of the LORD came upon me
37:17 they will become one in your **h**.
37:19 which is in the **h** of Ephraim,
37:19 and they will be one in My **h**.
37:20 you write will be in your **h**
38:12 to stretch out your **h** against
39: 3 the bow out of your left **h**,
39: 3 to fall out of your right **h**.
39:21 and My **h** which I have laid on
39:23 I gave them into the **h** of their
40: 1 on the very same day the **h** of
40: 3 and a measuring rod in his **h**,
40: 5 In the man's **h** was a measuring
44:12 therefore I have raised My **h** in
47: 3 the east with the line in his **h**,
47:14 for I raised My **h** in an oath to
Dan 1: 2 king of Judah into his **h**,
2:38 He has given them into your **h**,
3:17 He will deliver us from your **h**,
4:35 No one can restrain His **h** Or
5: 5 hour the fingers of a man's **h**
5: 5 the king saw the part of the **h**
5:23 who holds your breath in His **h**
5:24 Then the fingers of the **h** were
7:25 shall be given into his **h** For
8: 4 that could deliver from his **h**,
8: 7 deliver the ram from his **h**.
9:15 land of Egypt with a mighty **h**,
10:10 a **h** touched me, which made me
11:11 shall be given into the **h** of
11:41 these shall escape from his **h**:
11:42 He shall stretch out his **h**
12: 7 when he held up his right **h** and
12: 7 his right hand and his left **h**
Hos 2:10 one shall deliver her from My **h**.
7: 5 He stretched out his **h** with
11: 8 How can I **h** you over, Israel?
12: 7 Deceitful scales are in his **h**;
Joel 1:15 the day of the LORD is at **h**;
2: 1 is coming, For it is at **h**:
3: 8 and your daughters Into the **h**
Am 1: 8 I will turn My **h** against
5:19 Leaned his **h** on the wall, And
7: 7 with a plumb line in His **h**.
9: 2 From there my **h** shall take
Jon 4:11 discern between their right **h**
Mic 2: 1 it is in the power of their **h**.
4:10 will redeem you From the **h** of
5: 9 Your **h** shall be lifted against
5:12 cut off sorceries from your **h**,
7:16 They shall put their **h** over
Hab 2:16 The cup of the LORD's right **h**
3: 4 had rays flashing from His **h**,
Zeph 1: 4 I will stretch out My **h** against
1: 7 the day of the LORD is at **h**,
2:13 And He will stretch out His **h**
Zech 2: 1 with a measuring line in his **h**.
2: 9 For surely I will shake My **h**
3: 1 Satan standing at his right **h**
4:10 to see The plumb line in the **h**
8: 4 one with his staff in his **h**
11: 6 everyone into his neighbor's **h**
11: 6 neighbor's hand and into the **h**
11: 6 not deliver them from their **h**.
12: 6 peoples on the right **h** and on
13: 7 Then I will turn My **h** against
14:13 Everyone will seize the **h** of
14:13 And raise his **h** against his
14:13 hand against his neighbor's **h**;
Mal 1:13 I accept this from your **h**?
Mt 3: 2 the kingdom of heaven is at **h**!
3:12 winnowing fan is in His **h**,
4:17 the kingdom of heaven is at **h**.
5:25 the judge **h** you over to the
5:30 And if your right **h** causes you
6: 3 do not let your left **h** know
6: 3 hand know what your right **h** is
8: 3 Then Jesus put out His **h** and
8:15 So He touched her **h**,
9:18 but come and lay Your **h** on her
9:25 went in and took her by the **h**,
10: 7 'The kingdom of heaven is at **h**.
12:10 was a man who had a withered **h**.
12:13 the man, "Stretch out your **h**.
12:49 And He stretched out His **h**
14:31 Jesus stretched out His **h** and
18: 8 If your **h** or foot causes you to
20:21 one on Your right **h** and the
20:23 but to sit on My right **h** and on
22:13 Bind him **h** and foot, take him
22:44 "Sit at My right **h**,
25:33 set the sheep on His right **h**,
25:34 say to those on His right **h**,
25:41 also say to those on the left **h**,
26:18 Teacher says, "My time is at **h**;
26:23 He who dipped his **h** with Me in
26:45 Behold, the hour is at **h**,
26:46 See, My betrayer is at **h**."
26:51 Jesus stretched out his **h** and
26:64 of Man sitting at the right **h**
27:29 head, and a reed in His right **h**.
Mk 1:15 and the kingdom of God is at **h**.
1:31 He came and took her by the **h**
1:41 stretched out His **h** and
3: 1 was there who had a withered **h**.
3: 3 the man who had the withered **h**,
3: 5 the man, "Stretch out your **h**.
3: 5 and his **h** was restored as whole
5:41 Then He took the child by the **h**,
7:32 they begged Him to put His **h**
8:23 He took the blind man by the **h**
9:27 But Jesus took him by the **h** and
9:43 If your **h** causes you to sin, cut
10:37 one on Your right **h** and the
10:40 but to sit on My right **h** and on
12:36 "Sit at My right **h**,
14:42 See, My betrayer is at **h**."
14:62 of Man sitting at the right **h**
16:19 and sat down at the right **h** of
Lk 1: 1 as many have taken in **h** to set
1:66 And the **h** of the Lord was
1:71 our enemies And from the **h** of
1:74 Being delivered from the **h** of
3:17 winnowing fan is in His **h**,
5:13 Then He put out His **h** and
6: 6 a man was there whose right **h**
6: 8 the man who had the withered **h**,
6:10 the man, "Stretch out your **h**.
6:10 and his **h** was restored as whole
8:54 took her by the **h** and called,
9:62 having put his **h** to the plow,
15:22 and put a ring on his **h** and
20:42 "Sit at My right **h**,
22:21 the **h** of My betrayer is with
22:69 of Man will sit on the right **h**
23:33 one on the right **h** and the
Jn 2:13 Passover of the Jews was at **h**,
3:35 has given all things into His **h**.
7: 2 Feast of Tabernacles was at **h**.
7:30 but no one laid a **h** on Him,
10:28 anyone snatch them out of My **h**.
10:29 them out of My Father's **h**.
10:39 but He escaped out of their **h**.
11:44 who had died came out bound **h**
18:22 Jesus with the palm of his **h**,
20:25 and put my **h** into His side, I
20:27 and reach your **h** here, and put
Acts 2:25 For He is at my right **h**,
2:33 being exalted to the right **h**
2:34 "Sit at My right **h**,
3: 7 And he took him by the right **h**
4:28 to do whatever Your **h** and Your
4:30 by stretching out Your **h** to
5:31 God has exalted to His right **h**
7:25 God would deliver them by his **h**,
7:35 ruler and a deliverer by the **h**
7:50 Has My **h** not made all
7:55 Jesus standing at the right **h**
7:56 of Man standing at the right **h**
9: 8 But they led him by the **h** and
9:12 coming in and putting his **h**
9:41 Then he gave her his **h** and
11:21 And the **h** of the Lord was with
12: 1 the king stretched out his **h**
12:11 has delivered me from the **h** of
12:17 motioning to them with his **h**
13:11 the **h** of the Lord is upon you,
13:11 someone to lead him by the **h**.
13:16 and motioning with his **h** said,
19:33 Alexander motioned with his **h**,
21:40 stairs and motioned with his **h**
22:11 being led by the **h** of those who
23:19 the commander took him by the **h**,
26: 1 So Paul stretched out his **h**
28: 3 the heat, and fastened on his **h**.
28: 4 the creature hanging from his **h**,

Rom 8:34 who is even at the right **h** of
13:12 is far spent, the day is at **h**.
1 Cor 12:15 say, "Because I am not a **h**,
12:21 And the eye cannot say to the **h**,
16:21 The salutation with my own **h**—
2 Cor 6: 7 of righteousness on the right **h**
Gal 2: 9 me and Barnabas the right **h** of
3:19 through angels by the **h** of a
6:11 written to you with my own **h**!
Eph 1:20 and seated Him at His right **h**
Phil 4: 5 to all men. The Lord is at **h**.
Col 3: 1 sitting at the right **h** of God.
4:18 This salutation by my own **h**—
2 Th 3:17 of Paul with my own **h**,
2 Tim 4: 6 time of my departure is at **h**.
Phm 1:19 Paul, am writing with my own **h**.
Heb 1: 3 sat down at the right **h** of the
1:13 "Sit at My right **h**,
7:18 For on the one **h** there is an
7:19 nothing perfect; on the other **h**,
8: 1 who is seated at the right **h** of
8: 9 I took them by the **h** to
10:12 sat down at the right **h** of God,
12: 2 has sat down at the right **h** of
Jas 5: 8 the coming of the Lord is at **h**.
1 Pe 3:22 heaven and is at the right **h**
4: 7 the end of all things is at **h**;
5: 6 yourselves under the mighty **h**
Rev 1:16 He had in His right **h** seven
1:17 But He laid His right **h** on me,
1:20 which you saw in My right **h**,
2: 1 the seven stars in His right **h**,
5: 1 And I saw in the right **h** of Him
5: 7 the scroll out of the right **h**
6: 5 had a pair of scales in his **h**.
8: 4 before God from the angel's **h**.
10: 2 had a little book open in his **h**.
10: 5 on the land raised up his **h** to
10: 8 book which is open in the **h** of
10:10 book out of the angel's **h** and
13:16 a mark on their right **h** or on
14: 9 on his forehead or on his **h**,
14:14 and in His **h** a sharp sickle.
17: 4 having in her **h** a golden cup
20: 1 pit and a great chain in his **h**.
22:10 this book, for the time is at **h**.

HANDBREADTH (7/7)
HANDBREADTHS

Ex 25:25 make for it a frame of a **h** all
37:12 Also he made a frame of a **h** all
1 Ki 7:26 It was a **h** thick; and its brim
2 Chr 4: 5 It was a **h** thick; and its brim
Ezek 40: 5 each being a cubit and a **h**;
40:43 a **h** wide, fastened all around;
43:13 cubit is one cubit and a **h**):

HANDBREADTHS (1/1)
HANDBREADTH

Ps 39: 5 You have made my days as **h**,

HANDED (5/5) HAND

2 Ki 5:23 and **h** them to two of his
Mt 27:18 For he knew that they had **h** Him
Mk 7:13 your tradition which you have **h**
15:10 that the chief priests had **h**
Lk 4:17 And He was **h** the book of the

HANDFUL (8/8) HAND

Lev 2: 2 whom shall take from it his **h**
5:12 the priest shall take his **h** of
6:15 He shall take from it his **h** of
9:17 took a **h** of it, and burned it
Num 5:26 and the priest shall take a **h** of
1 Ki 17:12 only a **h** of flour in a bin, and
20:10 is left of Samaria for a **h** for
Eccl 4: 6 Better a **h** with quietness

HANDFULS (2/2)

Ex 9: 8 Take for yourselves **h** of ashes
Ezek 13:19 Me among My people for **h** of

HANDIWORK (2/2) HAND

Ps 19: 1 And the firmament shows His **h**.
Isa 45: 9 Or shall your **h** say, 'He has

HANDKERCHIEF (2/2)
HANDKERCHIEFS

Lk 19:20 I have kept put away in a **h**.
Jn 20: 7 and the **h** that had been around

HANDKERCHIEFS (1/1)
HANDKERCHIEF

Acts 19:12 so that even **h** or aprons were

HANDLE (11/10) HANDLED

Deut 19: 5 and the head slips from the **h**
1 Chr 12: 8 who could **h** shield and spear,
2 Chr 25: 5 who could **h** spear and shield.
Ps 115: 7 have hands, but they do not **h**;
Jer 2: 8 And those who **h** the law did
46: 9 and the Libyans who **h** the
46: 9 and the Lydians who **h** and
Ezek 27:29 All who **h** the oar, The

Zeph 1:11 All those who **h** money are cut
Lk 24:39 **H** Me and see, for a spirit does
Col 2:21 touch, do not taste, do not **h**,

HANDLED (2/2) HANDLE

Ezek 21:11 be polished, That it may be **h**;
1 Jn 1: 1 upon, and our hands have **h**,

HANDLES (3/3)

Song 5: 5 On the **h** of the lock.
Jer 50:16 And him who **h** the sickle at
Am 2:15 He shall not stand who **h** the

HANDLING (2/2)

Ezek 38: 4 all of them **h** swords.
2 Cor 4: 2 not walking in craftiness nor **h**

HANDMAID (KJV) See MAIDSERVANT, (FEMALE) SERVANT

HANDMILL (1/1)

Ex 11: 5 servant who is behind the **h**,

HANDS (456/434) ARMS, HAND

Gen 5:29 our work and the toil of our **h**,
19:10 But the men reached out their **h**
19:16 and the **h** of his two daughters,
20: 5 my heart and innocence of my **h**
27:16 the kids of the goats on his **h**
27:22 but the **h** are the hands of
27:22 but the hands are the **h** of
27:23 because his **h** were hairy like
27:23 hairy like his brother Esau's **h**;
31:42 and the labor of my **h**,
35: 4 gods which were in their **h**,
37:21 he delivered him out of their **h**,
37:22 deliver him out of their **h**,
42:37 back to you; put him in my **h**,
43:22 down other money in our **h** to
48:14 guiding his **h** knowingly, for
49:24 And the arms of his **h** were
49:24 were made strong By the **h** of
Ex 9:29 I will spread out my **h** to the
9:33 Pharaoh and spread out his **h**
15:17 which Your **h** have established.
17:12 But Moses' **h** became heavy;
17:12 Aaron and Hur supported his **h**,
17:12 and his **h** were steady until the
29:10 and his sons shall put their **h**
29:15 and his sons shall put their **h**
29:19 and his sons shall put their **h**
29:24 shall put all these in the **h**
29:24 hands of Aaron and in the **h** of
29:25 receive them back from their **h**
30:19 and his sons shall wash their **h**
30:21 So they shall wash their **h** and
32:19 cast the tablets out of his **h**
35:25 artisans spun yarn with their **h**,
40:31 and his sons would wash their **h**
Lev 4:15 congregation shall lay their **h**
7:30 His own **h** shall bring the
8:14 and his sons laid their **h** on
8:18 and his sons laid their **h** on
8:22 and his sons laid their **h** on
8:24 on the thumbs of their right **h**,
8:27 he put all these in Aaron's **h**
8:27 hands and in his sons' **h**,
8:28 Moses took them from their **h**
15:11 and has not rinsed his **h** in
16:12 with his **h** full of sweet
16:21 Aaron shall lay both his **h** on
24:14 all who heard him lay their **h**
Num 5:18 for remembering in her **h**,
6:19 and put them upon the **h** of the
8:10 of Israel shall lay their **h** on
8:12 the Levites shall lay their **h**
24:10 and he struck his **h** together;
27:23 And he laid his **h** on him and
36: 7 of Israel shall not change **h**
36: 9 no inheritance shall change **h**
Deut 1:25 fruit of the land in their **h**
3: 3 God also delivered into our **h**
4:28 serve gods, the work of men's **h**,
9:15 the covenant were in my two **h**.
9:17 and threw them out of my two **h**
12:18 in all to which you put your **h**.
16:15 and in all the work of your **h**,
17: 7 The **h** of the witnesses shall be
17: 7 and afterward the **h** of all the
20:13 God delivers it into your **h**,
21: 6 slain man shall wash their **h**
21: 7 Our **h** have not shed this blood,
24:19 you in all the work of your **h**.
27:15 the work of the **h** of the
31:29 through the work of your **h**.
33: 7 Let his **h** be sufficient for
33:11 And accept the work of his **h**;
34: 9 for Moses had laid his **h** on
Josh 2:24 all the land into our **h**,
9:25 now, here we are, in your **h**;
Judg 2:14 So He delivered them into the **h**
2:14 and He sold them into the **h** of
6:13 us and delivered us into the **h**
7: 2 the Midianites into their **h**,
7: 8 and their trumpets in their **h**.
7:11 and afterward your **h** shall be
7:19 pitchers that were in their **h**.

7:20 the torches in their left **h**
7:20 the trumpets in their right **h**
8: 3 God has delivered into your **h**
8: 6 Are the **h** of Zebah and Zalmunna
8:15 Are the **h** of Zebah and Zalmunna
8:34 had delivered them from the **h**
10: 7 and He sold them into the **h** of
10: 7 the Philistines and into the **h**
11:30 the people of Ammon into my **h**,
11:32 LORD delivered them into his **h**.
12: 2 not deliver me out of their **h**.
12: 3 I took my life in my **h** and
13:23 and a grain offering from our **h**,
14: 9 He took some of it in his **h** and
15:14 bonds broke loose from his **h**.
16:23 god has delivered into our **h**
16:24 god has delivered into our **h**
18:10 God has given it into your **h**,
19:27 door of the house with her **h**
1 Sam 5: 4 and both the palms of its **h**
7:14 its territory from the **h** of
10: 4 you shall receive from their **h**.
11: 7 territory of Israel by the **h**
14:13 Jonathan climbed up on his **h**
14:48 delivered Israel from the **h** of
17:47 and He will give you into our **h**.
19: 5 For he took his life in his **h**
21:13 feigned madness in their **h**,
22:17 king would not lift their **h** to
28:21 and I have put my life in my **h**
30:15 me nor deliver me into the **h**
2 Sam 2: 7 let your **h** be strengthened, and
3:34 Your **h** were not bound Nor your
4:12 cut off their **h** and feet, and
16:21 Then the **h** of all who are with
21: 9 he delivered them into the **h**
22:21 to the cleanness of my **h** He
22:35 He teaches my **h** to make war,
23: 6 they cannot be taken with **h**.
1 Ki 8:22 and spread out his **h** toward
8:38 and spreads out his **h** toward
8:54 on his knees with his **h** spread
14:27 and committed them to the **h** of
16: 7 to anger with the work of his **h**,
20: 6 they will put it in their **h**
2 Ki 3:11 who poured water on the **h** of
4:34 and his **h** on his hands; and he
4:34 eyes, and his hands on his **h**;
5:20 while not receiving from his **h**
9:35 feet and the palms of her **h**.
10:24 whom I have brought into your **h**
11:12 and they clapped their **h** and
12:11 into the **h** of those who did the
13:16 and Elisha put his **h** on the
13:16 put his hands on the king's **h**.
19:18 gods, but the work of men's **h**—
22:17 with all the works of their **h**.
1 Chr 12:17 there is no wrong in my **h**,
29: 5 of work to be done by the **h**
2 Chr 6: 4 who has fulfilled with His **h**
6:12 and spread out his **h**
6:13 and spread out his **h** toward
6:29 and spreads out his **h** to this
12:10 and committed them to the **h** of
15: 7 be strong and do not let your **h**
29:23 and they laid their **h** on them.
32:19 the earth—the work of men's **h**.
34:25 with all the works of their **h**.
35:11 the blood with their **h**,
Ezra 5: 8 and prospers in their **h**.
6:22 to strengthen their **h** in the
9: 5 on my knees and spread out my **h**
Neh 2:18 Then they set their **h** to
6: 9 Their **h** will be weakened in the
6: 9 O God, strengthen my **h**.
8: 6 while lifting up their **h**.
9:24 And gave them into their **h**,
13:21 I will lay **h** on you!" From
Esth 2:21 furious and sought to lay **h** on
3: 6 But he disdained to lay **h** on
3: 9 talents of silver into the **h**
6: 2 who had sought to lay **h** on
9: 2 of King Ahasuerus to lay **h** on
Job 1:10 have blessed the work of his **h**,
4: 3 you have strengthened weak **h**.
5:12 So that their **h** cannot carry
5:18 but His **h** make whole.
9:30 And cleanse my **h** with soap,
10: 3 despise the work of Your **h**,
10: 8 Your **h** have made me and
11:13 And stretch out your **h** toward
13:14 teeth, And put my life in my **h**?
14:15 shall desire the work of Your **h**.
16:11 And turned me over to the **h** of
16:17 no violence is in my **h**,
17: 3 Who is he who will shake **h**
17: 9 And he who has clean **h** will be
20:10 And his **h** will restore his
22:30 by the purity of your **h**.
27:23 Men shall clap their **h** at him,
30: 2 is the strength of their **h** to
31: 7 Or if any spot adheres to my **h**,
34:19 they are all the work of His **h**.
34:37 He claps his **h** among us,
36:32 He covers His **h** with
Ps 7: 3 If there is iniquity in my **h**,
8: 6 over the works of Your **h**;
9:16 snared in the work of his own **h**.
18:20 to the cleanness of my **h** He
18:24 to the cleanness of my **h** in
18:34 He teaches my **h** to make war,
22:16 They pierced My **h** and My feet;

24: 4 He who has clean **h** and a pure
26: 6 I will wash my **h** in innocence;
26:10 In whose **h** is a sinister
28: 2 When I lift up my **h** toward
28: 4 to the work of their **h**;
28: 5 Nor the operation of His **h**,
44:20 Or stretched out our **h** to a
47: 1 Oh, clap your **h**, all you
55:20 He has put forth his **h** against
58: 2 out the violence of your **h** in
63: 4 I will lift up my **h** in Your
68:31 will quickly stretch out her **h**
73:13 And washed my **h** in innocence.
76: 5 have found the use of their **h**.
78:72 by the skillfulness of his **h**.
81: 6 His **h** were freed from the
88: 9 I have stretched out my **h** to
90:17 establish the work of our **h**
90:17 establish the work of our **h**.
91:12 In their **h** they shall bear you
92: 4 triumph in the works of Your **h**.
95: 5 And His **h** formed the dry
98: 8 Let the rivers clap their **h**;
102:25 heavens are the work of Your **h**.
111: 7 The works of His **h** are verity
115: 4 and gold, The work of men's **h**.
115: 7 They have **h**, but they do
119:48 My **h** also I will lift up to
119:73 Your **h** have made me and
125: 3 righteous reach out their **h** to
128: 2 you eat the labor of your **h**,
134: 2 Lift up your **h** in the
135:15 and gold, The work of men's **h**.
138: 8 not forsake the works of Your **h**.
140: 4 from the **h** of the wicked;
141: 2 The lifting up of my **h** as the
143: 5 I muse on the work of Your **h**.
143: 6 I spread out my **h** to You;
144: 1 Who trains my **h** for war, And
Prov 6: 1 If you have shaken **h** in
6:10 A little folding of the **h** to
6:17 ***H*** that shed innocent blood,
12:14 the recompense of a man's **h**
14: 1 pulls it down with her **h**.
17:18 of understanding shakes **h** in a
21:25 For his **h** refuse to labor.
22:26 be one of those who shakes **h**
24:33 A little folding of the **h** to
30:28 skillfully grasps with its **h**,
31:13 And willingly works with her **h**.
31:19 She stretches out her **h** to the
31:20 she reaches out her **h** to the
31:31 Give her of the fruit of her **h**,
Eccl 2:11 on all the works that my **h** had
4: 5 The fool folds his **h** And
4: 6 with quietness Than both **h**
5: 6 and destroy the work of your **h**?
7:26 Whose **h** are fetters. He who
10:18 And through idleness of **h** the
Song 5: 5 And my **h** dripped with myrrh,
5:14 His **h** are rods of gold Set
7: 1 The work of the **h** of a
Isa 1:15 When you spread out your **h**,
1:15 Your **h** are full of blood.
2: 8 worship the work of their own **h**,
3:11 For the reward of his **h** shall
5:12 consider the operation of His **h**.
13: 7 Therefore all **h** will be limp,
17: 8 the altars, The work of his **h**;
19:25 and Assyria the work of My **h**,
25:11 And He will spread out His **h** in
25:11 with the trickery of their **h**.
29:23 his children, The work of My **h**,
31: 7 which your own **h** have made for
33:15 Who gestures with his **h**,
35: 3 Strengthen the weak **h**,
37:19 gods, but the work of men's **h**—
45: 9 handiwork say, 'He has no **h**'?
45:11 concerning the work of My **h**,
45:12 I—My **h**— stretched out the
49:16 you on the palms of My **h**;
55:12 the field shall clap their **h**.
59: 3 For your **h** are defiled with
59: 6 act of violence is in their **h**.
60:21 My planting, The work of My **h**,
65: 2 I have stretched out My **h** all
65:22 long enjoy the work of their **h**.
Jer 1:16 the works of their own **h**.
2:37 go forth from him With your **h**
4:31 She spreads her **h**,
6:24 Our **h** grow feeble.
10: 3 The work of the **h** of the
10: 9 of the craftsman And of the **h**
19: 7 their enemies and by the **h** of
21: 4 of war that are in your **h**,
23:14 They also strengthen the **h** of
25: 6 anger with the works of your **h**;
25: 7 anger with the works of your **h**
25:14 to the works of their own **h**.
30: 6 do I see every man with his **h**
32:30 anger with the work of their **h**,
33:13 shall again pass under the **h**
38: 4 for thus he weakens the **h** of
38: 4 and the **h** of all the people, by
44: 8 wrath with the works of your **h**,
44:25 and fulfilled with your **h**,
48:37 On all the **h** shall be cuts,
50:43 And his **h** grow feeble;
Lam 1:14 were woven together by His **h**,
1:14 Lord delivered me into the **h**
1:17 Zion spreads out her **h**,
2:15 All who pass by clap their **h**
2:19 Lift your **h** toward Him For
3:41 Let us lift our hearts and **h**
3:64 to the work of their **h**.
4: 2 The work of the **h** of the
4:10 The **h** of the compassionate
5:12 were hung up by their **h**,
Ezek 1: 8 The **h** of a man were under their
7:21 give it as plunder Into the **h**
7:27 And the **h** of the common people
10: 2 fill your **h** with coals of fire
10: 7 of it and put it into the **h**
10:12 body, with their back, their **h**,
10:21 and the likeness of the **h** of a
11: 9 and deliver you into the **h** of
13:22 you have strengthened the **h** of
21: 7 all **h** will be feeble, every
21:14 And strike your **h** together.
21:31 And deliver you into the **h** of
22:14 or can your **h** remain strong, in
23:37 and blood is on their **h**.
23:45 and blood is on their **h**.
25: 6 "Because you clapped your **h**,
Dan 2:34 a stone was cut out without **h**,
2:45 out of the mountain without **h**,
3:15 who will deliver you from my **h**?
10:10 knees and on the palms of my **h**.
Hos 14: 3 anymore to the work of our **h**,
Ob 13 Nor laid **h** on their substance
Jon 3: 8 the violence that is in his **h**.
Mic 5:13 more worship the work of your **h**;
7: 3 do evil with both **h**—
Nah 3:19 news of you Will clap their **h**
Hab 3:10 And lifted its **h** on high.
Zeph 3:16 let not your **h** be weak.
Hag 1:11 and on all the labor of your **h**.
2:14 so is every work of their **h**;
2:17 in all the labors of your **h**;
Zech 4: 9 The **h** of Zerubbabel Have laid
4: 9 His **h** shall also finish it.
8: 9 Let your **h** be strong, You who
8:13 Let your **h** be strong.'
Mal 1: 9 this is being done by your **h**,
1:10 accept an offering from your **h**.
2:13 it with goodwill from your **h**.
Mt 4: 6 In their **h** they shall bear
15: 2 For they do not wash their **h**
15:20 but to eat with unwashed **h** does
17:12 also about to suffer at their **h**.
17:22 to be betrayed into the **h** of
18: 8 rather than having two **h** or two
18:28 and he laid **h** on him and took
19:13 to Him that He might put His **h**
19:15 And He laid His **h** on them and
21:46 But when they sought to lay **h** on
26:45 is being betrayed into the **h**
26:50 Then they came and laid **h** on
26:67 Him with the palms of their **h**,
27:24 he took water and washed his **h**
Mk 5:23 Come and lay Your **h** on her,
6: 2 works are performed by His **h**!
6: 5 except that He laid His **h** on a
7: 2 that is, with unwashed **h**,
7: 3 eat unless they wash their **h**
7: 5 but eat bread with unwashed **h**?
8:23 spit on his eyes and put His **h**
8:25 Then He put His **h** on his eyes
9:31 is being betrayed into the **h**
9:43 rather than having two **h**,
10:16 put His **h** on them, and blessed
12:12 And they sought to lay **h** on Him,
14:41 is being betrayed into the **h**
14:46 Then they laid their **h** on Him
14:58 destroy this temple made with **h**,
14:58 build another made without **h**.
14:65 Him with the palms of their **h**.
16:18 they will lay **h** on the sick,
Lk 4:11 In their **h** they shall bear
4:40 and He laid His **h** on every one
6: 1 rubbing them in their **h**.
9:44 to be betrayed into the **h** of
13:13 And He laid His **h** on her, and
20:19 that very hour sought to lay **h**
21:12 they will lay their **h** on you
23:46 into Your **h** I commit My
24: 7 must be delivered into the **h**
24:39 Behold My **h** and My feet, that it
24:40 He showed them His **h** and His
24:50 and He lifted up His **h** and
Jn 7:44 but no one laid **h** on Him.
8:20 and no one laid **h** on Him, for
13: 3 had given all things into His **h**,
13: 9 but also my **h** and my head!"
19: 3 they struck Him with their **h**.
20:20 He showed them His **h** and His
20:25 Unless I see in His **h** the print
20:27 finger here, and look at My **h**;
21:18 you will stretch out your **h**,
Acts 2:23 you have taken by lawless **h**,
4: 3 And they laid **h** on them, and put
5:12 And through the **h** of the
5:18 and laid their **h** on the apostles
6: 6 they laid **h** on them.
7:41 in the works of their own **h**.
7:48 dwell in temples made with **h**,
8:17 Then they laid **h** on them, and
8:18 laying on of the apostles' **h**
8:19 that anyone on whom I lay **h** may
9:17 and laying his **h** on him he
11:30 sent it to the elders by the **h**
12: 7 And his chains fell off his **h**.
13: 3 and laid **h** on them, they sent
14: 3 wonders to be done by their **h**.
17:24 dwell in temples made with **h**.
17:25 is He worshiped with men's **h**,
19: 6 And when Paul had laid **h** on
19:11 unusual miracles by the **h** of
19:26 not gods which are made with **h**.
20:34 yourselves know that these **h**
21:11 bound his own **h** and feet, and
21:11 and deliver him into the **h** of
21:27 up the whole crowd and laid **h**
24: 7 violence took him out of our **h**,
27:19 tackle overboard with our own **h**.
28: 8 and he laid his **h** on him and
28:17 from Jerusalem into the **h** of
Rom 10:21 I have stretched out My **h**
1 Cor 4:12 labor, working with our own **h**.
2 Cor 5: 1 God, a house not made with **h**,
11:33 wall, and escaped from his **h**.
Eph 2:11 made in the flesh by **h**—
4:28 working with his **h** what is
Col 2:11 the circumcision made without **h**,
1 Th 4:11 and to work with your own **h**,
1 Tim 2: 8 everywhere, lifting up holy **h**,
4:14 with the laying on of the **h** of
5:22 Do not lay **h** on anyone hastily,
2 Tim 1: 6 through the laying on of my **h**.
Heb 1:10 are the work of Your **h**.
2: 7 over the works of Your **h**.
6: 2 of baptisms, of laying on of **h**,
9:11 tabernacle not made with **h**,
9:24 the holy places made with **h**,
10:31 thing to fall into the **h** of
12:12 Therefore strengthen the **h**
Jas 4: 8 near to you. Cleanse your **h**,
1 Jn 1: 1 and our **h** have handled,
Rev 7: 9 with palm branches in their **h**,
9:20 repent of the works of their **h**,
20: 4 their foreheads or on their **h**.

HANDSOME (5/4)

Gen 39: 6 Now Joseph was **h** in form and
1 Sam 9: 2 And he had a choice and **h** son
9: 2 There was not a more **h** person
16:18 and a **h** person; and the LORD
Song 1:16 Behold, you are **h**,

HANDSTAVES (KJV) See JAVELINS

HANDWRITING (1/1)

Col 2:14 having wiped out the **h** of

HANDYWORK (KJV) See HANDIWORK

HANES (1/1)

Isa 30: 4 And his ambassadors came to ***H***.

HANG (19/19) HANGED, HANGING, HANGS, HUNG

Gen 40:19 your head from you and **h** you
Ex 26:12 shall **h** over the back of the
26:13 shall **h** over the sides of the
26:32 You shall **h** it upon the four
26:33 And you shall **h** the veil from
40: 8 and **h** up the screen at the
Num 25: 4 people and **h** the offenders
Deut 21:22 and you **h** him on a tree,
28:66 Your life shall **h** in doubt
2 Sam 21: 6 and we will **h** them before the
Esth 6: 4 to suggest that the king **h**
7: 9 king said, "***H*** him on it!"
Job 28: 4 forgotten by feet They **h** far
Prov 26: 7 legs of the lame that **h** limp
Song 4: 4 On which **h** a thousand
Isa 22:24 They will **h** on him all the glory
Ezek 15: 3 men make a peg from it to **h**
Mt 22:40 On these two commandments **h** all
Heb 12:12 the hands which **h** down,

HANGED (19/19) HANG

Gen 40:22 But he **h** the chief baker, as
41:13 my office, and he **h** him."
Deut 21:23 for he who is **h** is accursed of
Josh 8:29 And the king of Ai he **h** on a
10:26 and **h** them on five trees;
2 Sam 4:12 and **h** them by the pool in
17:23 and **h** himself, and died; and he
21: 9 and they **h** them on the hill
21:13 bones of those who had been **h**.
Ezra 6:11 and let him be **h** on it; and let
Esth 2:23 and both were **h** on a gallows;
5:14 to the king that Mordecai be **h**
7:10 So they **h** Haman on the gallows
8: 7 and they have **h** him on the
9:13 and let Haman's ten sons be **h**
9:14 and they **h** Haman's ten sons.
9:25 he and his sons should be **h** on
Mt 27: 5 and went and **h** himself.
Lk 23:39 one of the criminals who were **h**

HANGING (6/6) HANG, HANGINGS

Josh 10:26 and they were **h** on the trees
2 Sam 18: 9 so he was left **h** between heaven
18:10 I just saw Absalom **h** in a
Acts 5:30 up Jesus whom you murdered by **h**
10:39 whom they killed by **h** on a
28: 4 the natives saw the creature **h**

HANGINGS (18/18) HANGING

Ex 27: 9 south side there shall be ***h***
27:11 north side there shall be ***h***
27:12 on the west side shall be ***h***
27:14 The ***h*** on one side of the
27:15 on the other side shall be ***h***
35:17 the ***h*** of the court, its pillars,
38: 9 the ***h*** of the court were of
38:11 On the north side the ***h*** were
38:12 were ***h*** of fifty cubits,
38:13 For the east side the ***h*** were
38:14 The ***h*** of one side of the gate
38:15 were ***h*** of fifteen cubits,
38:16 All the ***h*** of the court all
38:18 corresponding to the ***h*** of the
39:40 the ***h*** of the court, its pillars
Num 3:26 the ***h*** of the court which are
4:26 the ***h*** of the court which are
2 Ki 23: 7 where the women wove ***h*** for the

HANGS (2/2) HANG

Job 26: 7 He ***h*** the earth on nothing.
Gal 3:13 Cursed is everyone who ***h*** on

HANIEL (1/1)

1 Chr 7:39 The sons of Ulla were Arah, ***H***,

HANNAH (13/11)

1 Sam 1: 2 wives: the name of one was ***H***,
1: 2 but ***H*** had no children.
1: 5 But to ***H*** he would give a double
1: 5 double portion, for he loved ***H***,
1: 8 her husband said to her, "***H***,
1: 9 So ***H*** arose after they had
1:13 Now ***H*** spoke in her heart;
1:15 And ***H*** answered and said, "No,
1:19 And Elkanah knew ***H*** his wife,
1:20 in the process of time that ***H***
1:22 But ***H*** did not go up, for she
2: 1 And ***H*** prayed and said: "My
2:21 And the LORD visited ***H***,

HANNATHON (1/1)

Josh 19:14 it on the north side of ***H***,

HANNIEL (1/1)

Num 34:23 ***H*** the son of Ephod,

HANOCH (6/6)

Gen 25: 4 of Midian were Ephah, Epher, ***H***,
46: 9 The sons of Reuben were ***H***,
Ex 6:14 firstborn of Israel, were ***H***,
Num 26: 5 children of Reuben were: of ***H***,
1 Chr 1:33 of Midian were Ephah, Epher, ***H***,
5: 3 the firstborn of Israel were ***H***,

HANOCHITES (1/1)

Num 26: 5 of Hanoch, the family of the ***H***;

HANUN (11/10)

2 Sam 10: 1 and ***H*** his son reigned in his
10: 2 I will show kindness to ***H*** the
10: 3 the people of Ammon said to ***H***
10: 4 Therefore ***H*** took David's
1 Chr 19: 2 I will show kindness to ***H*** the
19: 2 And David's servants came to ***H***
19: 3 the people of Ammon said to ***H***,
19: 4 Therefore ***H*** took David's
19: 6 ***H*** and the people of Ammon sent
Neh 3:13 ***H*** and the inhabitants of Zanoah
3:30 the son of Shelemiah, and ***H***,

HAP (KJV) See HAPPENED

HAPHRAIM (1/1)

Josh 19:19 ***H***, Shion, Anaharath,

HAPLY (KJV) See (IN THE) HOPE, PERHAPS

HAPPEN (31/31)

Gen 4:14 and it will ***h*** that anyone who
12:12 "Therefore it will ***h***,
44:31 'it will ***h***, when he sees
Ex 1:10 lest they multiply, and it ***h***,
Num 11:23 see whether what I say will ***h***
Deut 18:22 if the thing does not ***h*** or come
29:19 "and so it may not ***h***,
Judg 20: 3 us, how did this wicked deed ***h***?
1 Sam 10: 5 garrison is. And it will ***h***,
1 Ki 1:21 "Otherwise it will ***h***,
Eccl 3:22 bring him to see what will ***h***
6:12 Who can tell a man what will ***h***
8: 7 he does not know what will ***h***;
9:11 But time and chance ***h*** to them
Isa 7:23 It shall ***h*** in that day, That
8:21 and hungry; and it shall ***h***,
23:15 end of seventy years it will ***h***
41:22 forth and show us what will ***h***;
Ezek 16:16 them. Such things should not ***h***,
Dan 8:19 known to you what shall ***h*** in
10:14 you understand what will ***h*** to
Zech 12: 3 And it shall ***h*** in that day that
14: 7 But at evening time it shall ***h***
Mt 16:22 this shall not ***h*** to You!"
26:54 that it must ***h*** thus?"
Mk 10:32 them the things that would ***h***
13: 7 for such things must ***h***,
Lk 21:28 when these things begin to ***h***,
22:49 Him saw what was going to ***h***,
Acts 20:22 knowing the things that will ***h***
Jas 4:14 you do not know what will ***h***

HAPPENED (221/221)

Gen 19:34 It ***h*** on the next day that the
24:15 And it ***h***, before he had
27:30 Now it ***h***, as soon as Isaac
31:10 'And it ***h***, at the time when
35:22 And it ***h***, when Israel dwelt
38:29 Then it ***h***, as he drew back
39:11 But it ***h*** about this time, when
39:15 'And it ***h***, when he heard
39:18 'so it ***h***, as I lifted my
41:13 he interpreted for us, so it ***h***.
42:29 and told him all that had ***h*** to
42:35 Then it ***h*** as they emptied their
43:21 'but it ***h***, when we came to
Ex 2:23 Now it ***h*** in the process of time
16:27 Now it ***h*** that some of the
Num 11:25 the seventy elders; and it ***h***,
16:42 Now it ***h***, when the
Deut 4:32 great thing like this has ***h***,
Josh 2: 5 And it ***h*** as the gate was being
6:16 And the seventh time it ***h***,
6:20 And it ***h*** when the people heard
8:14 Now it ***h***, when the king
9:16 And it ***h*** at the end of three
10:11 And it ***h***, as they fled
10:20 Then it ***h***, while Joshua and
17:13 And it ***h***, when the children
Judg 1:14 Now it ***h***, when she came
3:27 And it ***h***, when he arrived,
6:13 why then has all this ***h*** to us?
7: 9 It ***h*** on the same night that the
13:20 it ***h*** as the flame went up toward
14:11 And it ***h***, when they saw him,
14:17 And it ***h*** on the seventh day
15: 1 it ***h*** that Samson visited his
16: 4 Afterward it ***h*** that he loved a
16:25 So it ***h***, when their hearts
Ruth 1:19 came to Bethlehem. And it ***h***,
2: 3 And she ***h*** to come to the part
3: 8 Now it ***h*** at midnight that the
1 Sam 1:12 And it ***h***, as she continued
4: 7 For such a thing has never ***h***
4:16 And he said, "What ***h***,
4:18 Then it ***h***, when he made
6: 9 it ***h*** to us by chance."
10:11 And it ***h***, when all who knew
11:11 And it ***h*** that those who
13:10 Now it ***h***, as soon as he had
14: 1 Now it ***h*** one day that Jonathan
14:19 Now it ***h***, while Saul talked
18: 6 Now it had ***h*** as they were coming
18:10 And it ***h*** on the next day that
18:19 But it ***h*** at the time when Merab,
20:26 Something has ***h*** to him; he is
20:27 And it ***h*** the next day, the
23: 6 Now it ***h***, when Abiathar
24: 1 Now it ***h***, when Saul had
24: 5 Now it ***h*** afterward that David's
28: 1 Now it ***h*** in those days that the
30: 1 Now it ***h***, when David and
31: 8 So it ***h*** the next day, when the
2 Sam 1: 2 it ***h*** that a man came from
1: 6 As I ***h*** by chance to be on
2: 1 It ***h*** after this that David
4: 4 took him up and fled. And it ***h***,
7: 4 But it ***h*** that night that the
10: 1 It ***h*** after this that the king of
11: 1 It ***h*** in the spring of the year,
11: 2 Then it ***h*** one evening that
11:14 In the morning it ***h*** that David
15: 1 After this it ***h*** that Absalom
15:32 Now it ***h*** when David had come to
17:27 Now it ***h***, when David had
20: 1 And there ***h*** to be there a rebel,
21:18 Now it ***h*** afterward that there
1 Ki 2:39 Now it ***h*** at the end of three
3:18 'Then it ***h***, the third day
9:10 Now it ***h*** at the end of twenty
11:15 For it ***h***, when David was in
11:29 Now it ***h*** at that time, when
12: 2 So it ***h***, when Jeroboam the
13:20 Now it ***h***, as they sat at
14:25 It ***h*** in the fifth year of King
15:21 Now it ***h***, when Baasha heard
16:18 And it ***h***, when Zimri saw
17: 7 And it ***h*** after a while that the
17:17 Now it ***h*** after these things
18:17 Then it ***h***, when Ahab saw
18:45 Now it ***h*** in the meantime that
20:12 And it ***h*** when Ben-Hadad heard
22:33 And it ***h***, when the captains
2 Ki 2:11 Then it ***h***, as they continued
3: 5 But it ***h***, when Ahab died,
3:15 me a musician." Then it ***h***,
3:20 Now it ***h*** in the morning, when
4: 8 Now it ***h*** one day that Elisha
4:11 And it ***h*** one day that he came
4:18 Now it ***h*** one day that he went
4:40 it to the men to eat. Now it ***h***,
5: 7 And it ***h***, when the king of
6:24 And it ***h*** after this that
6:30 Now it ***h***, when the king
7:18 So it ***h*** just as the man of God
7:20 And so it ***h*** to him, for the
8: 5 Now it ***h***, as he was telling
8:15 But it ***h*** on the next day that he
9:22 Now it ***h***, when Joram saw
10:25 Now it ***h***, as soon as he
14: 5 Now it ***h***, as soon as the
20: 4 And it ***h***, before Isaiah had
22:11 Now it ***h***, when the king
24:20 the anger of the LORD this ***h***
25:25 But it ***h*** in the seventh month
1 Chr 10: 8 So it ***h*** the next day, when the
15:29 And it ***h***, as the ark of the
17: 3 But it ***h*** that night that the
19: 1 It ***h*** after this that Nahash the
20: 1 It ***h*** in the spring of the year,
20: 4 Now it ***h*** afterward that war
29:30 and the events that ***h*** to him,
2 Chr 10: 2 So it ***h***, when Jeroboam
12: 2 And it ***h*** in the fifth year of
13:15 it ***h*** that God struck Jeroboam
16: 5 Now it ***h***, when Baasha heard
20: 1 It ***h*** after this that the people
21:19 Then it ***h*** in the course of time,
22: 8 And it ***h***, when Jehu was
24: 4 Now it ***h*** after this that Joash
24:23 So it ***h*** in the spring of the
25: 3 Now it ***h***, as soon as the
34:19 Thus it ***h***, when the king
Neh 4: 1 But it so ***h***, when Sanballat
4: 7 Now it ***h***, when Sanballat,
4:15 And it ***h***, when our enemies
6: 1 Now it ***h*** when Sanballat, Tobiah,
6:16 And it ***h***, when all our
Esth 3: 4 Now it ***h***, when they spoke
4: 1 Mordecai learned all that had ***h***,
4: 7 told him all that had ***h*** to him,
5: 1 Now it ***h*** on the third day that
6:13 friends everything that had ***h***
9:26 and what had ***h*** to them,
Job 3:25 And what I dreaded has ***h*** to
Jer 20: 3 And it ***h*** on the next day that
26: 8 Now it ***h***, when Jeremiah had
28: 1 And it ***h*** in the same year, at
29: 2 (This ***h*** after Jeconiah the king,
32:24 What You have spoken has ***h***;
36:16 Now it ***h***, when they had
36:23 And it ***h***, when Jehudi had
37:11 And it ***h***, when the army
41: 4 And it ***h***, on the second day
41: 6 and it ***h*** as he met them that he
42: 7 And it ***h*** after ten days that
43: 1 Now it ***h***, when Jeremiah
44:23 therefore this calamity has ***h***
48:19 who escapes; Say, 'What has ***h***?
52: 3 the anger of the LORD this ***h***
Ezek 10: 6 Then it ***h***, when He
11:13 Now it ***h***, while I was
Dan 8: 2 and it so ***h*** while I was
8:15 Then it ***h***, when I, Daniel,
Joel 1: 2 Has anything like this ***h*** in
Jon 4: 8 And it ***h***, when the sun
Zech 7:13 'Therefore it ***h***, that just
Mt 8:33 including what had ***h*** to the
9:10 Now it ***h***, as Jesus sat at
27:54 and the things that had ***h***,
28:11 all the things that had ***h***.
Mk 2:15 Now it ***h***, as He was dining
2:23 Now it ***h*** that He went through
4: 4 'And it ***h***, as he sowed,
5:14 to see what it was that had ***h***.
5:16 who saw it told them how it ***h***
5:33 knowing what had ***h*** to her, came
Lk 1:41 And it ***h***, when Elizabeth
5:12 And it ***h*** when He was in a
5:17 Now it ***h*** on a certain day, as
6: 1 Now it ***h*** on the second Sabbath
6: 6 Now it ***h*** on another Sabbath,
7:11 Now it ***h***, the day after,
8:22 Now it ***h***, on a certain day,
8:34 who fed them saw what had ***h***,
8:35 they went out to see what had ***h***,
8:56 them to tell no one what had ***h***.
9:18 And it ***h***, as He was alone
9:33 Then it ***h***, as they were
9:37 Now it ***h*** on the next day, when
9:57 Now it ***h*** as they journeyed on
10:38 Now it ***h*** as they went that He
11:27 And it ***h***, as He spoke these
14: 1 Now it ***h***, as He went into
17:11 Now it ***h*** as He went to
18:35 Then it ***h***, as He was
20: 1 Now it ***h*** on one of those days,
23:47 the centurion saw what had ***h***,
24: 4 And it ***h***, as they were
24:12 to himself at what had ***h***.
24:14 of all these things which had ***h***.
24:18 not known the things which ***h***
24:21 third day since these things ***h***.
24:35 about the things that had ***h***
Jn 15:25 But this ***h*** that the word might
Acts 3:10 and amazement at what had ***h*** to
5: 7 came in, not knowing what had ***h***.
9:37 But it ***h*** in those days that she
11:28 which also ***h*** in the days of
14: 1 Now it ***h*** in Iconium that they
16:16 Now it ***h***, as we went to
17:17 daily with those who ***h*** to be

19: 1 And it *h*, while Apollos was
20:19 many tears and trials which *h*
22: 6 'Now it *h*, as I journeyed
22:17 'Now it *h*, when I
28: 8 And it *h* that the father of
Rom 11:25 that blindness in part has *h* to
1 Cor 10:11 Now all these things *h* to them
Phil 1:12 that the things which *h* to me
1 Th 3: 4 tribulation, just as it *h*,
2 Tim 3:11 which *h* to me at Antioch, at
1 Pe 4:12 as though some strange thing *h*
2 Pe 2:22 But it has *h* to them according

HAPPENING (5/5)

Esth 2:11 welfare and what was *h* to her.
Mk 9:21 How long has this been *h* to
13:29 when you see these things *h*,
Lk 21:31 when you see these things *h*,
Col 4: 9 to you all things which are *h*

HAPPENS (15/12)

Deut 15:16 And if it *h* that he says to you,
22: 6 If a bird's nest *h* to be before
24: 1 and it *h* that she finds no
2 Sam 11:20 if it *h* that the king's wrath
18:22 again to Joab, "But whatever *h*,
18:23 'But whatever *h*," he said,
Eccl 2:14 That the same event *h* to them
2:15 As it *h* to the fool, It also
2:15 It also *h* to me, And why was
3:19 For what *h* to the sons of men
3:19 to the sons of men also *h* to
8:14 are just men to whom it *h*
8:14 are wicked men to whom it *h*
9: 2 One event *h* to the righteous
9: 3 that one thing *h* to all.

HAPPIER (1/1) HAPPY

1 Cor 7:40 But she is *h* if she remains as

HAPPINESS (1/1) HAPPY

Deut 24: 5 and bring *h* to his wife whom he

HAPPIZZEZ (1/1)

1 Chr 24:15 to Hezir, the eighteenth to *H*,

HAPPY (24/21) BLESSED, HAPPIER, HAPPINESS

Gen 30:13 Then Leah said, "I am *h*,
Deut 33:29 *H* are you, O Israel! Who is
1 Ki 10: 8 *H* are your men and happy are
10: 8 Happy are your men and *h* are
2 Chr 9: 7 *H* are your men and happy are
9: 7 Happy are your men and *h* are
Job 5:17 *h* is the man whom God
Ps 127: 5 *H* is the man who has his
128: 2 your hands, You shall be *h*,
137: 8 *H* the one who repays you as
137: 9 *H* the one who takes and dashes
144:15 *H* are the people who are in
144:15 *H* are the people whose God
146: 5 *H* is he who has the God of
Prov 3:13 *H* is the man who finds
3:18 And *h* are all who retain
14:21 on the poor, *h* is he.
16:20 in the LORD, *h* is he.
28:14 *H* is the man who is always
29:18 But *h* is he who keeps the
Isa 32:13 on all the *h* homes in the
Jer 12: 1 Why are those *h* who deal so
Acts 26: 2 "I think myself *h*,
Rom 14:22 *H* is he who does not condemn

HARA (1/1)

1 Chr 5:26 He took them to Halah, Habor, *H*,

HARADAH (2/2)

Num 33:24 Mount Shepher and camped at *H*.
33:25 They moved from *H* and camped at

HARAN (22/19) BETH HARAN

Gen 11:26 and begot Abram, Nahor, and *H*.
11:27 Terah begot Abram, Nahor, and *H*.
11:27 and Haran. *H* begot Lot.
11:28 And *H* died before his father
11:29 the daughter of *H* the father of
11:31 his grandson Lot, the son of *H*,
11:31 and they came to *H* and dwelt
11:32 five years, and Terah died in *H*.
12: 4 old when he departed from *H*.
12: 5 whom they had acquired in *H*,
27:43 flee to my brother Laban in *H*.
28:10 Beersheba and went toward *H*.
29: 4 And they said, "We are from *H*.
2 Ki 19:12 Gozan and *H* and Rezeph, and the
1 Chr 2:46 Caleb's concubine, bore *H*,
2:46 and Gazez; and *H* begot Gazez.
23: 9 Shelomith, Haziel, and *H*—
Isa 37:12 Gozan and *H* and Rezeph, and the
Ezek 27:23 '*H*, Canneh, Eden, the
Acts 7: 2 before he dwelt in *H*,
7: 4 of the Chaldeans and dwelt in *H*.

HARARITE (5/4)

2 Sam 23:11 Shammah the son of Agee the *H*.
23:33 Shammah the *H*, Ahiam the
23:33 Ahiam the son of Sharar the *H*,
1 Chr 11:34 the son of Shageh the *H*,
11:35 Ahiam the son of Sacar the *H*,

HARASS (6/6) HARASSED

Num 25:17 *H* the Midianites, and attack
33:55 and they shall *h* you in the
Deut 2: 9 Do not *h* Moab, nor contend with
2:19 do not *h* them or meddle with
Isa 11:13 And Judah shall not *h* Ephraim.
Acts 12: 1 stretched out his hand to *h*

HARASSED (4/4) HARASS

Num 25:18 for they *h* you with their
Judg 2:18 those who oppressed them and *h*
10: 8 From that year they *h* and
1 Sam 14:47 he turned, he *h* them.

HARBONA (1/1)

Esth 1:10 he commanded Mehuman, Biztha, *H*,

HARBONAH (1/1)

Esth 7: 9 Now *H*, one of the eunuchs,

HARBOR (3/2) HARBORED

Isa 23: 1 that there is no house, no *h*;
Acts 27:12 And because the *h* was not
27:12 a *h* of Crete opening toward the

HARBORED (1/1) HARBOR

Acts 17: 7 Jason has *h* them, and these are

HARD (54/53) HARDEN, HARDER, HARDNESS, HARDSHIP

Gen 18:14 Is anything too *h* for the LORD?
19: 9 So they pressed *h* against the
33:13 if the men should drive them *h*
35:16 and she had *h* labor.
35:17 when she was in *h* labor, that
Ex 1:14 lives bitter with *h* bondage—in
7:13 And Pharaoh's heart grew *h*,
7:14 Moses: "Pharaoh's heart is *h*;
7:22 and Pharaoh's heart grew *h*,
8:19 But Pharaoh's heart grew *h*,
9: 7 the heart of Pharaoh became *h*,
9:35 So the heart of Pharaoh was *h*;
18:26 the *h* cases they brought to
Deut 1:17 The case that is too *h* for you,
15:18 It shall not seem *h* to you when
17: 8 a matter arises which is too *h*
26: 6 and laid *h* bondage on us.
1 Sam 14:22 they also followed *h* after them
31: 2 Philistines followed *h* after
2 Sam 1: 6 and horsemen followed *h* after
1 Ki 10: 1 test him with *h* questions.
2 Ki 2:10 You have asked a *h* thing.
1 Chr 10: 2 Philistines followed *h* after
2 Chr 9: 1 to test Solomon with *h* questions,
Job 7: 1 Is there not a time of *h*
14:14 All the days of my *h* service I
41:24 His heart is as *h* as stone,
41:24 Even as *h* as the lower
Ps 60: 3 shown Your people *h* things;
Prov 13:15 the way of the unfaithful is *h*.
Isa 8:21 pass through it *h* pressed
14: 3 your fear and the *h* bondage
Jer 32:17 There is nothing too *h* for You.
32:27 Is there anything too *h* for Me?
Lam 1: 3 affliction and *h* servitude;
Ezek 3: 5 speech and of *h* language,
3: 6 speech and of *h* language,
Jon 1:13 Nevertheless the men rowed *h* to
Mt 13:15 Their ears are *h* of
19:23 I say to you that it is *h* for a
23: 4 *h* to bear, and lay them on
25:24 I knew you to be a *h* man,
Mk 10:23 How *h* it is for those who have
10:24 how *h* it is for those who trust
Lk 11:46 you load men with burdens *h* to
18:24 How *h* it is for those who have
Jn 6:60 This is a *h* saying; who can
Acts 9: 5 It is *h* for you to kick
26:14 It is *h* for you to kick
28:27 Their ears are *h* of
2 Cor 4: 8 We are *h* pressed on every
Phil 1:23 For I am *h* pressed between the
Heb 5:11 and *h* to explain, since you
2 Pe 3:16 in which are some things *h* to

HARD-HEARTED (1/1)

Ezek 3: 7 of Israel are impudent and *h*.

HARD-WORKING (1/1)

2 Tim 2: 6 The *h* farmer must be first to

HARDEN (12/12) HARD, HARDENED, HARDENS

Ex 4:21 But I will *h* his heart, so that
7: 3 And I will *h* Pharaoh's heart,
14: 4 Then I will *h* Pharaoh's heart,
14:17 And I indeed will *h* the hearts
Deut 15: 7 you shall not *h* your heart nor
Josh 11:20 For it was of the LORD to *h*
1 Sam 6: 6 Why then do you *h* your hearts as
Job 38:30 The waters *h* like stone, And
Ps 95: 8 Do not *h* your hearts, as in the
Heb 3: 8 Do not *h* your hearts as
3:15 Do not *h* your hearts as
4: 7 Do not *h* your hearts."

HARDENED (22/22) BLINDED, HARDEN

Ex 8:15 he *h* his heart and did not heed
8:32 But Pharaoh *h* his heart at this
9:12 But the LORD *h* the heart of
9:34 and he *h* his heart, he and his
10: 1 for I have *h* his heart and the
10:20 But the LORD *h* Pharaoh's heart,
10:27 But the LORD *h* Pharaoh's
11:10 and the LORD *h* Pharaoh's
14: 8 And the LORD *h* the heart of
Deut 2:30 for the LORD your God *h* his
1 Sam 6: 6 as the Egyptians and Pharaoh *h*
2 Chr 36:13 but he stiffened his neck and *h*
Neh 9:16 *H* their necks, And did not
9:17 But they *h* their necks, And
Job 9: 4 Who has *h* himself against Him
Isa 63:17 And *h* our heart from Your
Dan 5:20 and his spirit was *h* in pride,
Mk 6:52 because their heart was *h*.
8:17 Is your heart still *h*?
Jn 12:40 eyes and *h* their hearts,
Acts 19: 9 But when some were *h* and did not
Heb 3:13 lest any of you be *h* through

HARDENS (5/5) HARDEN

Job 38:38 When the dust *h* in clumps, And
Prov 21:29 A wicked man *h* his face, But
28:14 But he who *h* his heart will
29: 1 and *h* his neck, Will
Rom 9:18 wills, and whom He wills He *h*.

HARDER (3/3) HARD

Prov 18:19 A brother offended is *h* to
Jer 5: 3 They have made their faces *h*
Ezek 3: 9 *h* than flint, I have made your

HARDNESS (5/5) HARD

Mt 19: 8 because of the *h* of your
Mk 3: 5 being grieved by the *h* of their
10: 5 Because of the *h* of your heart
16:14 He rebuked their unbelief and *h*
Rom 2: 5 But in accordance with your *h*

HARDSHIP (3/3) HARD

Ex 18: 8 all the *h* that had come upon
Num 20:14 You know all the *h* that has
2 Tim 2: 3 You therefore must endure *h* as a

HARE (2/2)

Lev 11: 6 'the *h*, because it chews
Deut 14: 7 as these: the camel, the *h*,

HAREPH (1/1)

1 Chr 2:51 and *H* the father of Beth

HARETH (KJV) See HERETH

HARHAIAH (1/1)

Neh 3: 8 Next to him Uzziel the son of *H*,

HARHAS (1/1)

2 Ki 22:14 the son of Tikvah, the son of *H*,

HARHUR (2/2)

Ezra 2:51 sons of Hakupha, the sons of *H*,
Neh 7:53 sons of Hakupha, the sons of *H*,

HARIM (11/11)

1 Chr 24: 8 the third to *H*, the fourth to
Ezra 2:32 the people of *H*, three
2:39 the sons of *H*, one thousand
10:21 of the sons of *H*: Maaseiah,
10:31 of the sons of *H*: Eliezer,
Neh 3:11 Malchijah the son of *H* and
7:35 the sons of *H*, three hundred
7:42 the sons of *H*, one thousand
10: 5 *H*, Meremoth, Obadiah,
10:27 Malluch, *H*, and Baanah.
12:15 of *H*, Adna; of Meraioth,

HARIPH (2/2)

Neh 7:24 the sons of *H*, one hundred
10:19 *H*, Anathoth, Nebai,

HARLOT (76/71) HARLOTRY, HARLOTS

Gen 34:31 he treat our sister like a **h**?
38:15 her, he thought she was a **h**,
38:21 Where is the **h** who was openly
38:21 There was no **h** in this place."
38:22 the place said there was no **h**
38:24 has played the **h**;
Ex 34:15 and they play the **h** with their
34:16 and his daughters play the **h**
34:16 and make your sons play the **h**
Lev 17: 7 whom they have played the **h**.
19:29 to cause her to be a **h**,
21: 7 not take a wife who is a **h**
21: 9 herself by playing the **h**,
21:14 or a defiled woman or a **h**—
Deut 22:21 to play the **h** in her father's
23:17 There shall be no ritual **h** of
23:18 not bring the wages of a **h** or
31:16 will rise and play the **h** with
Josh 2: 1 and came to the house of a **h**
6:17 Only Rahab the **h** shall live,
6:25 And Joshua spared Rahab the **h**,
Judg 2:17 but they played the **h** with
8:27 And all Israel played the **h**
8:33 of Israel again played the **h**
11: 1 but he was the son of a **h**;
16: 1 went to Gaza and saw a **h** there,
19: 2 But his concubine played the **h**
1 Chr 5:25 and played the **h** after the gods
2 Chr 21:13 of Jerusalem to play the **h**
Ps 106:39 And played the **h** by their own
Prov 6:26 For by means of a **h** A man
7:10 him, With the attire of a **h**,
23:27 For a **h** is a deep pit, And a
Isa 1:21 faithful city has become a **h**!
23:15 Tyre as in the song of the **h**:
23:16 the city, You forgotten **h**;
57: 3 of the adulterer and the **h**!
Jer 2:20 You lay down, playing the **h**.
3: 1 But you have played the **h** with
3: 6 tree, and there played the **h**.
3: 8 but went and played the **h** also.
Ezek 6: 9 by their eyes which play the **h**
16:15 played the **h** because of your
16:16 and played the **h** on them.
16:17 male images and played the **h**
16:28 You also played the **h** with the
16:28 indeed you played the **h** with
16:30 the deeds of a brazen **h**.
16:31 Yet you were not like a **h**,
16:34 no one solicited you to be a **h**.
16:35 Now then, O **h**, hear the
16:41 make you cease playing the **h**,
23: 5 Oholah played the **h** even though
23:19 When she had played the **h** in
23:30 because you have gone as a **h**
23:44 in to a woman who plays the **h**;
Hos 2: 5 their mother has played the **h**;
3: 3 days; you shall not play the **h**,
4:12 And they have played the **h**
4:14 sacrifices with a ritual **h**.
4:15 you, Israel, play the **h**,
9: 1 For you have played the **h**
Joel 3: 3 a boy as payment for a **h**,
Am 7:17 Your wife shall be a **h** in the
Mic 1: 7 And all her pay as a **h** shall
1: 7 it from the pay of a **h**,
1: 7 shall return to the pay of a **h**.
Nah 3: 4 harlotries of the seductive **h**,
1 Cor 6:15 and make them members of a **h**?
6:16 that he who is joined to a **h**
Heb 11:31 By faith the **h** Rahab did not
Jas 2:25 was not Rahab the **h** also
Rev 17: 1 you the judgment of the great **h**
17:15 where the **h** sits, are peoples,
17:16 beast, these will hate the **h**,
19: 2 He has judged the great **h** who

HARLOT'S (2/2)

Josh 6:22 Go into the **h** house, and from
Jer 3: 3 You have had a **h** forehead;

HARLOTRIES (5/4) HARLOTRY

2 Ki 9:22 as long as the **h** of your mother
Jer 3: 2 polluted the land With your **h**
Hos 2: 2 Let her put away her **h** from
Nah 3: 4 Because of the multitude of **h**
3: 4 sells nations through her **h**,

HARLOTRY (50/44) HARLOT, HARLOTRIES

Gen 38:24 she is with child by **h**.
Lev 19:29 lest the land fall into **h**,
20: 5 with him to commit **h** with
Num 15:39 that you may not follow the **h**
25: 1 the people began to commit **h**
2 Chr 21:11 of Jerusalem to commit **h**,
21:13 to play the harlot like the **h**
Ps 73:27 all those who desert You for **h**.
Jer 3: 9 to pass, through her casual **h**,
13:27 The lewdness of your **h**,
Ezek 16:15 and poured out your **h** on
16:20 Were your acts of **h** a small
16:22 abominations and acts of **h** you
16:25 and multiplied your acts of **h**.
16:26 You also committed **h** with the
16:26 and increased your acts of **h** to
16:29 you multiplied your acts of **h**
16:33 you from all around for your **h**.
16:34 of other women in your **h**,
16:36 nakedness uncovered in your **h**
20:30 and committing **h** according to
23: 3 They committed **h** in Egypt,
23: 3 They committed **h** in their
23: 7 Thus she committed her **h** with
23: 8 She has never given up her **h**
23:11 and in her **h** more corrupt than
23:11 corrupt than her sister's **h**.
23:14 But she increased her **h**;
23:18 She revealed her **h** and
23:19 Yet she multiplied her **h** In
23:27 cease your lewdness and your **h**
23:29 The nakedness of your **h** shall
23:29 both your lewdness and your **h**.
23:35 Of your lewdness and your **h**.
23:43 Will they commit **h** with her now,
43: 7 by their **h** or with the
43: 9 Now let them put their **h** and the
Hos 1: 2 take yourself a wife of **h** And
1: 2 of harlotry And children of **h**,
1: 2 the land has committed great **h**
2: 4 they are the children of **h**.
4:10 They shall commit **h**,
4:11 **H**, wine, and new wine
4:12 For the spirit of **h** has caused
4:13 your daughters commit **h**,
4:14 daughters when they commit **h**,
4:18 They commit **h** continually.
5: 3 now, O Ephraim, you commit **h**;
5: 4 For the spirit of **h** is in
6:10 There is the **h** of Ephraim;

HARLOTS (9/9) HARLOT

1 Ki 3:16 Now two women who were **h** came
22:38 licked up his blood while the **h**
Prov 29: 3 But a companion of **h** wastes
Ezek 16:33 "Men make payment to all **h**,
Hos 4:14 men themselves go apart with **h**,
Mt 21:31 you that tax collectors and **h**
21:32 but tax collectors and **h**
Lk 15:30 devoured your livelihood with **h**,
Rev 17: 5 THE MOTHER OF **H** AND OF THE

HARLOTS' (1/1)

Jer 5: 7 by troops in the **h** houses.

HARM (48/46) HARMFUL, HARMLESS

Gen 26:29 'that you will do us no **h**,
31:29 "It is in my power to do you **h**,
31:52 and this pillar to me, for **h**.
Ex 21:22 yet no **h** follows, he shall
21:23 But if any **h** follows, then you
32:12 He brought them out to **h** them,
32:12 and relent from this **h** to Your
32:14 the LORD relented from the **h**
Lev 5:16 make restitution for the **h**
Num 35:23 not his enemy or seeking his **h**,
Josh 24:20 then He will turn and do you **h**
Judg 15: 3 the Philistines if I **h** them!"
1 Sam 20:21 is safety for you and no **h**.
24: 9 'Indeed David seeks your **h**'?
25:17 for **h** is determined against our
25:26 enemies and those who seek **h**
26:21 For I will **h** you no more,
2 Sam 12:18 He may do some **h**!"
18:32 who rise against you to do **h**,
20: 6 son of Bichri will do us more **h**
1 Chr 16:22 ones, And do My prophets no **h**.
Neh 6: 2 But they thought to do me **h**.
Esth 9: 2 on those who sought their **h**.
Ps 37: 8 Do not fret—it only causes **h**.
105:15 ones, And do My prophets no **h**.
Prov 3:30 cause, If he has done you no **h**.
Jer 24: 9 of the earth, for their **h**,
25: 6 and I will not **h** you.'
38: 4 of this people, but their **h**.
39:12 look after him, and do him no **h**;
Joel 2:13 And He relents from doing **h**.
Am 9: 4 will set My eyes on them for **h**
Jon 4: 2 One who relents from doing **h**.
Mic 3:11 No **h** can come upon us."
Acts 9:13 how much **h** he has done to Your
16:28 saying, "Do yourself no **h**,
28: 5 into the fire and suffered no **h**.
28: 6 for a long time and saw no **h**
Rom 13:10 Love does no **h** to a neighbor;
2 Tim 4:14 the coppersmith did me much **h**.
1 Pe 3:13 And who is he who will **h** you
Rev 6: 6 and do not **h** the oil and the
7: 2 to whom it was granted to **h**
7: 3 Do not **h** the earth, the sea, or
9: 4 They were commanded not to **h** the
9:19 and with them they do **h**.
11: 5 And if anyone wants to **h** them,
11: 5 And if anyone wants to **h** them,

HARMFUL (5/5) HARM

Josh 23:15 LORD will bring upon you all **h**
2 Ki 4:41 And there was nothing **h** in
Ezra 4:15 **h** to kings and provinces, and
Eccl 8: 5 will experience nothing **h**;
1 Tim 6: 9 and into many foolish and **h**

HARMLESS (3/3) HARM

Mt 10:16 be wise as serpents and **h** as
Phil 2:15 you may become blameless and **h**,
Heb 7:26 for us, who is holy, **h**,

HARMON (1/1)

Am 4: 3 And you will be cast into **H**,

HARMONIOUS (1/1)

Ps 92: 3 on the harp, With **h** sound.

HARMS (1/1)

Prov 9: 7 rebukes a wicked man only **h**

HARNEPHER (1/1)

1 Chr 7:36 sons of Zophah were Suah, **H**,

HARNESS (2/2)

Jer 46: 4 **H** the horses, And mount up,
Mic 1:13 **H** the chariot to the swift

HARNESSED (2/2)

Ps 32: 9 Which must be **h** with bit and
Hos 10:11 But I **h** her fair neck, I will

HAROD (1/1)

Judg 7: 1 encamped beside the well of **H**,

HARODITE (2/1)

2 Sam 23:25 Shammah the **H**, Elika the
23:25 the Harodite, Elika the **H**,

HAROEH (1/1)

1 Chr 2:52 Jearim had descendants: **H**,

HARORITE (1/1)

1 Chr 11:27 Shammoth the **H**, Helez the

HAROSHETH HAGOYIM (3/3)

Judg 4: 2 was Sisera, who dwelt in **H**.
4:13 from **H** to the River Kishon.
4:16 and the army as far as **H**,

HARP (34/33) HARPS

Gen 4:21 of all those who play the **h**
31:27 and songs, with timbrel and **h**?
1 Sam 10: 5 and a **h** before them; and they
16:16 is a skillful player on the **h**;
16:23 that David would take a **h** and
1 Chr 25: 3 who prophesied with a **h** to give
Job 21:12 sing to the tambourine and **h**,
30:31 My **h** is turned to mourning,
Ps 6: On an eight-stringed **h**.
12: On an eight-stringed **h**.
33: 2 Praise the LORD with the **h**;
43: 4 And on the **h** I will praise
49: 4 my dark saying on the **h**.
57: 8 lute and **h**! I will awaken the
71:22 To You I will sing with the **h**,
81: 2 The pleasant **h** with the lute.
92: 3 On the lute, And on the **h**,
98: 5 Sing to the LORD with the **h**,
98: 5 With the **h** and the sound of a
108: 2 lute and **h**! I will awaken the
144: 9 On a **h** of ten strings I will
147: 7 Sing praises on the **h** to our
149: 3 to Him with the timbrel and **h**.
150: 3 Him with the lute and **h**!
Isa 5:12 The **h** and the strings, The
16:11 my heart shall resound like a **h**
23:16 'Take a **h**, go about the
24: 8 The joy of the **h** ceases.
Dan 3: 5 the sound of the horn, flute, **h**,
3: 7 the sound of the horn, flute, **h**,
3:10 the sound of the horn, flute, **h**,
3:15 the sound of the horn, flute, **h**,
1 Cor 14: 7 life, whether flute or **h**,
Rev 5: 8 the Lamb, each having a **h**,

HARPISTS (2/2)

Rev 14: 2 And I heard the sound of **h**
18:22 'The sound of **h**, musicians,

HARPOONS (1/1)

Job 41: 7 Can you fill his skin with **h**,

HARPS (19/19) HARP

2 Sam 6: 5 instruments of fir wood, on **h**,
1 Ki 10:12 also **h** and stringed instruments
1 Chr 13: 8 might, with singing, on **h**,
15:16 music, stringed instruments, **h**,
15:21 to direct with **h** on the
15:28 with stringed instruments and **h**.

16: 5 with stringed instruments and **h**,
25: 1 who should prophesy with **h**,
25: 6 stringed instruments, and **h**,
2 Chr 5:12 stringed instruments and **h**,
9:11 also **h** and stringed instruments
20:28 stringed instruments and **h** and
29:25 instruments, and with **h**,
Neh 12:27 and stringed instruments and **h**.
Ps 137: 2 We hung our **h** Upon the willows
Isa 30:32 will be with tambourines and **h**;
Ezek 26:13 and the sound of your **h** shall
Rev 14: 2 of harpists playing their **h**.
15: 2 of glass, having **h** of God.

HARROW (KJV) See PLOW

HARSH (8/8) HARSHLY

1 Sam 5: 7 for His hand is **h** toward us and
25: 3 but the man was **h** and evil in
2 Sam 3:39 are too **h** for me. The LORD
Prov 15: 1 But a **h** word stirs up anger.
15:10 **H** discipline is for him who
Mal 3:13 Your words have been **h** against
1 Pe 2:18 and gentle, but also to the **h**.
Jude 15 and of all the **h** things which

HARSHA (4/4)

Ezra 2:52 sons of Mehida, the sons of **H**,
Neh 7:54 sons of Mehida, the sons of **H**,

HARSHLY (3/3) HARSH

Gen 16: 6 And when Sarai dealt **h** with
Judg 4: 3 and for twenty years he **h**
Job 39:16 She treats her young **h**,

HART (KJV) See DEER

HARUM (1/1)

1 Chr 4: 8 of Aharhel the son of **H**.

HARUMAPH (1/1)

Neh 3:10 to them Jedaiah the son of **H**

HARUPHITE (1/1)

1 Chr 12: 5 Shemariah, and Shephatiah the **H**;

HARUZ (1/1)

2 Ki 21:19 Meshullemeth the daughter of **H**

HARVEST (68/58)

Gen 8:22 earth remains, Seedtime and **h**,
30:14 went in the days of wheat **h**
47:24 it shall come to pass in the **h**
Ex 23:16 "and the Feast of **H**,
34:21 in plowing time and in **h** you
34:22 of the firstfruits of wheat **h**,
Lev 19: 9 When you reap the **h** of your
19: 9 gather the gleanings of your **h**.
23:10 I give to you, and reap its **h**,
23:10 of the firstfruits of your **h**
23:22 When you reap the **h** of your
23:22 gather any gleaning from your **h**.
25: 5 of its own accord of your **h**
25:22 you shall eat of the old **h**.
26:10 You shall eat the old **h**,
Deut 24:19 When you reap your **h** in your
Josh 3:15 during the whole time of **h**),
Judg 15: 1 a while, in the time of wheat **h**,
Ruth 1:22 at the beginning of barley **h**.
2:21 they have finished all my **h**.
2:23 until the end of barley **h** and
2:23 of barley harvest and wheat **h**;
1 Sam 6:13 were reaping their wheat **h** in
8:12 plow his ground and reap his **h**,
12:17 "Is today not the wheat **h**?
2 Sam 9:10 and you shall bring in the **h**,
21: 9 put to death in the days of **h**,
21: 9 in the beginning of barley **h**.
21:10 from the beginning of **h** until
23:13 chief men went down at **h** time
2 Chr 32:28 storehouses for the **h** of grain,
Job 5: 5 the hungry eat up his **h**,
31: 8 let my **h** be rooted out.
Ps 107:37 they may yield a fruitful **h**.
Prov 6: 8 And gathers her food in the **h**.
10: 5 He who sleeps in **h** is a son
20: 4 He will beg during **h** and have
25:13 the cold of snow in time of **h**
26: 1 snow in summer and rain in **h**,
Isa 9: 3 You According to the joy of **h**,
16: 9 your summer fruits and your **h**.
17:11 But the **h** will be a heap of
18: 4 a cloud of dew in the heat of **h**.
18: 5 For before the **h**, when the
23: 3 The **h** of the River, is her
Jer 5:17 And they shall eat up your **h**
5:24 us the appointed weeks of the **h**.
8:20 The **h** is past, The summer is
12:13 But be ashamed of your **h**
50:16 him who handles the sickle at **h**
51:33 while And the time of her **h**
Hos 6:11 a **h** is appointed for you, When
Joel 1:11 Because the **h** of the field has
3:13 for the **h** is ripe. Come, go
Am 4: 7 still three months to the **h**.
Mt 9:37 The **h** truly is plentiful, but
9:38 pray the Lord of the **h** to send
9:38 to send out laborers into His **h**.
13:30 both grow together until the **h**,
13:30 and at the time of **h** I will say
13:39 the **h** is the end of the age,
Mk 4:29 because the **h** has come."
Lk 10: 2 The **h** truly is great, but the
10: 2 pray the Lord of the **h** to send
10: 2 to send out laborers into His **h**.
Jn 4:35 months and then comes the **h**'?
4:35 they are already white for **h**!
Rev 14:15 for the **h** of the earth is

HARVESTER (2/2)

Isa 17: 5 It shall be as when the **h**
Jer 9:22 Like cuttings after the **h**,

HARVESTING (1/1)

Gen 45: 6 will be neither plowing nor **h**.

HAS (292/268) See APPENDIX

Gen 23: 9 cave of Mechpelah which he **h**
24:36 him he has given all that he **h**.
39: 8 he has committed all that he **h**
Ex 3:14 I AM **h** sent me to you."
24:14 If any man **h** a difficulty, let
32:24 whoever **h** any gold, let them
Lev 11: 9 whatever in the water **h** fins
11:42 or whatever **h** many feet among
13: 2 When a man **h** on the skin of his
13:29 If a man or woman **h** a sore on
13:38 If a man or a woman **h** bright
13:41 He whose hair **h** fallen from his
13:46 All the days he **h** the sore he
15: 2 When any man **h** a discharge from
15:16 If any man **h** an emission of
15:19 If a woman **h** a discharge,
15:25 If a woman **h** a discharge of
15:32 This is the law for one who **h**
15:33 and for one who **h** a discharge,
20:27 or who **h** familiar spirits,
21:17 who **h** any defect, may approach
21:18 For any man who **h** a defect shall
21:18 who **h** a marred face or any
21:19 a man who **h** a broken foot or
21:21 who **h** a defect, shall come near
21:21 He **h** a defect; he shall not
21:23 because he **h** a defect, lest he
22: 3 while he **h** uncleanness upon
22: 4 is a leper or **h** a discharge
22:20 Whatever **h** a defect, you shall
22:23 bull or a lamb that **h** any limb
25:26 Or if the man **h** no one to redeem
27:28 to the LORD of all that he **h**,
Num 5: 2 everyone who **h** a discharge,
5: 8 But if the man **h** no relative to
14:24 because he **h** a different spirit
27: 8 If a man dies and **h** no son, then
27: 9 If he **h** no daughter, then you
27:10 If he **h** no brothers, then you
27:11 And if his father **h** no brothers,
Deut 4: 7 nation is there that **h** God,
4: 8 is there that **h** such statutes
10: 9 Therefore Levi **h** no portion not
12:12 since he **h** no portion nor
14:27 for he **h** no part no
14:29 because he **h** no portion nor
15:21 it is lame or blind or **h**
17: 1 or sheep which **h** any blemish
21:15 If a man **h** two wives, one loved
21:17 double portion of all that he **h**,
21:18 If a man **h** a stubborn and
25: 5 one of them dies and **h** no son
Josh 6:22 the woman and all that she **h**,
7:15 with fire, he and all that he **h**,
Judg 6:25 of Baal that your father **h**,
1 Sam 2: 5 And she who **h** many children
25:21 all that this fellow **h** in the
2 Sam 3:29 or Joab one who **h** a discharge
13:24 your servant **h** sheepshearers;
14:30 and he **h** barley there; go and
2 Ki 4: 2 Your maidservant **h** nothing in
4:14 she **h** no son, and her husband
2 Chr 2: 7 who **h** skill to engrave with the
25: 8 for God **h** power to help and to
Esth 4:11 he **h** but one law: put all to
6: 8 which **h** a royal crest placed on
Job 1:10 and around all that he **h** on
1:11 hand and touch all that he **h**,
1:12 all that he **h** is in your
2: 4 all that a man **h** he will give
12:13 He **h** counsel and
17: 9 And he who **h** clean hands will
18:17 And he **h** no name among the
18:19 HE **h** neither son nor posterity
26: 2 the arm that **h** no strength?
26: 3 one who **h** no wisdom?
26: 6 And Destruction **h** no covering.
32:19 is like wine that **h** no rent;
38:28 **H** the rain a father
Ps 24: 4 He who **h** clean hands and a pure
35:27 Who **h** pleasure in the
37:16 little that a righteous man **h**
69:31 Which **h** horns and hooves.
72:12 and him who **h** no helper.
88: 4 like a man who **h** no strength,
101: 5 The one who **h** a haughty look
104:17 The stork **h** her home in the
109:11 creditor seize all that he **h**,
123: 2 Until He **h** mercy on us.
127: 5 is the man who **h** his quiver
146: 5 Happy is he who **h** the God of
150: 6 Let everything that **h** breath
Prov 10: 4 He who **h** a slack hand becomes
10:18 hides hatred **h** lying lips,
10:23 man of understanding **h** wisdom.
10:25 But the righteous **h** an
12: 9 is slighted but **h** a servant,
13: 4 and **h** nothing; But the soul
13: 7 yet **h** nothing; And one who
13: 7 yet **h** great riches.
14:20 But the rich **h** many friends.
14:21 But he who **h** mercy on the
14:29 He who is slow to wrath **h**
14:31 But he who honors Him **h** mercy
14:32 But the righteous **h** a refuge
14:33 of him who **h** understanding,
15:14 heart of him who **h** understanding
15:15 he who is of a merry heart **h**
15:23 A man **h** joy by the answer of
16:22 of life to him who **h** it.
17:16 Since he **h** no heart for
17:20 He who **h** a deceitful heart
17:20 And he who **h** a perverse tongue
17:21 the father of a fool **h** no joy.
17:24 of him who **h** understanding,
17:27 He who **h** knowledge spares his
18: 2 A fool **h** no delight in
18:24 A man who **h** friends must
19:17 He who **h** pity on the poor lends
19:23 And he who **h** it will abide
19:25 one who **h** understanding;
22: 9 He who **h** a generous eye will be
22:11 purity of heart And **h** grace
23:29 Who **h** woe? Who has sorrow?
23:29 Who **h** sorrow? Who has
23:29 Who **h** contentions? Who has
23:29 Who **h** complaints? Who has
23:29 Who **h** wounds without cause?
23:29 Who **h** redness of eyes?
28:11 the poor who **h** understanding
30:15 The leech **h** two daughters-Give
Eccl 1: 3 What profit **h** a man from all
2:22 For what **h** man for all his
3: 9 What profit **h** the worker from
3:19 man **h** no advantage over
4: 8 He **h** neither son nor brother.
4:10 For he **h** no one to help him
5: 4 For He **h** no pleasure in
5:16 And what profit **h** he who has
5:17 And he **h** much sorrow and
6: 3 or indeed he **h** no burial, I say
6: 5 this **h** more rest than that man,
6: 8 For what more **h** the wise man
8: 8 No one **h** power over the spirit
8: 8 And no one **h** power in the day
8:15 because a man **h** nothing better
Song 3: 8 Every man **h** his sword on his
8: 8 And she **h** no breasts.
Isa 1:30 as a garden that **h** no water.
5: 1 My well-beloved **h** a vineyard
28: 2 the Lord **h** a mighty and strong
29:16 He **h** no understanding'?
34: 6 For the LORD **h** a sacrifice in
45: 9 He **h** no hands'?
49:10 For He who **h** mercy on them
50:10 in darkness And **h** no light?
53: 2 He **h** no form or comeliness,
54:10 who **h** mercy on you.
57:15 With him who **h** a contrite and
Jer 5:23 But this people **h** a defiant and
11:15 What **h** My beloved to do in My
23:28 The prophet who **h** a dream, let
23:28 And he who **h** My word, let him
25:31 For the LORD **h** a controversy
49: 1 **h** Israel no sons? Has he no
49: 1 **h** he no heir? Why then does
49:31 Which **h** neither gates nor bars,
Lam 1: 2 Among all her lovers She **h**
Ezek 12: 2 which **h** eyes to see but does
19:14 that she **h** no strong branch—
33:32 of one who **h** a pleasant voice
Hos 8: 7 The stalk **h** no bud; It shall
12:11 Though Gilead **h** idols—Surely
Joel 1: 6 And he **h** the fangs of a fierce
Am 3: 4 when he **h** no prey? Will a
Mic 6: 2 For the LORD **h** a complaint
Nah 3:19 Your injury **h** no healing,
Mal 1:14 cursed be the deceiver Who **h**
Mt 11:18 and they say, 'He **h** a demon.'
12:11 among you who **h** one sheep,
13:12 "For whoever **h**, to him more
13:21 yet he **h** no root in himself,
13:43 He who **h** ears to hear, let him
13:44 he goes and sells all that he **h**
18:12 If a man **h** a hundred sheep,
25:28 it to him who **h** ten talents.
25:29 'For to everyone who **h**,
Mk 3:22 He **h** Beelzebub," and, "By the
3:26 he cannot stand, but **h** an end.
3:29 Holy Spirit never **h** forgiveness,
3:30 He **h** an unclean spirit."
4: 9 He who **h** ears to hear, let him
4:23 If anyone **h** ears to hear, let
4:25 "For whoever **h**, to him more
7:16 If anyone **h** ears to hear, let
9:17 who **h** a mute spirit.

Lk 3:11 He who **h** two tunics, let him
3:11 let him give to him who **h** none:
3:11 and he who **h** food, let him do
7:33 and you say, 'He **h** a demon.'
8:18 how you hear. For whoever **h**,
9:58 but the Son of Man **h** nowhere to
12: 5 **h** power to cast into hell;
12:44 him ruler over all that he **h**.
14: 5 having a donkey or an ox that **h**
14:28 whether he **h** enough to finish
14:35 He who **h** ears to hear, let him
19:24 it to him who **h** ten minas.
19:25 'Master, he **h** ten minas.')
22:36 he who **h** a money bag, let him
22:36 and he who **h** no sword, let him
Jn 3:29 He who **h** the bride is the
5:26 For as the Father **h** life in
6: 9 There is a lad here who **h** five
6:47 in Me **h** everlasting life.
8:37 because My word **h** no place in
10:20 He **h** a demon and is mad. Why do
10:21 words of one who **h** a demon.
14:30 and he **h** nothing in Me.
15:13 Greater love **h** no one than this,
16:15 All things that the Father **h** are
16:21 **h** sorrow because her hour has
Acts 9:14 And here he **h** authority from the
15:21 For Moses **h** had throughout many
23:17 for he **h** something to tell
23:18 He **h** something to say to you."
25:16 and **h** opportunity to answer for
Rom 3: 1 What advantage the **h** the Jew,
4: 2 he **h** something to boast about,
6: 9 Death no longer **h** dominion over
7: 1 that the law **h** dominion over a
7: 2 For the woman who **h** a husband is
9:18 Therefore He **h** mercy on whom He
1 Cor 5: 1 that a man **h** his father's wife
7: 7 But each one **h** his own gift
7:12 If any brother **h** a wife who
7:13 And a woman who **h** a husband who
7:37 but **h** power over his own will,
11:15 But if a woman **h** long hair,
12:12 is one and **h** many members
14:26 each of you **h** a psalm, has a
14:26 **h** a teaching, has a tongue, has
14:26 **h** a tongue, has a revelation,
14:26 **h** a revelation, has an
14:26 **h** an interpretation. Let all
16:12 he will come when he **h** a
2 Cor 6:14 what fellowship **h** righteousness
6:14 And what communion **h** light with
6:15 And what accord **h** Christ with
6:15 Or what part **h** a believer with
6:16 And what agreement **h** the temple
8:12 according to what one **h**,
Gal 4:27 For the desolate **h** many
4:27 she who **h** a husband.'
Eph 5: 5 **h** any inheritance in the
1 Tim 5: 4 But if any widow **h** children or
6:16 who alone **h** immortality,
Heb 7:24 **h** an unchangeable priesthood.
9:17 since it **h** no power at all
10:35 which **h** great reward.
10:38 My soul **h** no pleasure in
1 Jn 2:23 the Son **h** the Father also.
3:17 But whoever **h** this world's
4:16 the love that God **h** for us.
4:18 But he who fears **h** not been
5:12 He who **h** the Son has life;
5:12 He who has the Son **h** life;
2 Jn 1: 9 the doctrine of Christ **h** both
3 Jn 1:12 Demetrius **h** a good testimony
Rev 2: 7 He who **h** an ear, let him hear
2:11 He who **h** an ear, let him hear
2:12 These things says He who **h** the
2:17 He who **h** an ear, let him hear
2:18 who **h** eyes like a flame of
2:29 He who **h** an ear, let him hear
3: 1 These things says He who **h** the
3: 6 He who **h** an ear, let him hear
3: 7 He who **h** the key of David
3:13 He who **h** an ear, let him hear
3:22 He who **h** an ear, let him hear
9:11 but in Greek he **h** the name
12: 6 where she **h** a place prepared by
12:12 knows that he **h** a short time.'
13: 9 If anyone **h** an ear, let him
13:18 Let him who **h** understanding
16: 9 the name of God who **h** power
17: 7 which **h** the seven heads and the
17: 9 is the mind which **h** wisdom:
19:16 And He **h** on His robe and on His
20: 6 and holy is he who **h** part
20: 6 the second death **h** no power,

HASADIAH (1/1)

1 Chr 3:20 Hashubah, Ohel, Berechiah, **H**,

HASHABIAH (15/15)

1 Chr 6:45 the son of **H**, the son of
9:14 son of Azrikam, the son of **H**,
25: 3 Zeri, Jeshaiah, Shimei, **H**,
25:19 the twelfth for **H**, his sons
26:30 **H** and his brethren, one
27:17 **H** the son of Kemuel; over the
2 Chr 35: 9 and **H** and Jeiel and Jozabad,
Ezra 8:19 and **H**, and with him Jeshaiah
8:24 of the priests—Sherebiah, **H**,
Neh 3:17 made repairs. Next to him **H**,
10:11 Micha, Rehob, **H**,
11:15 son of Azrikam, the son of **H**,
11:22 the son of Bani, the son of **H**,
12:21 of Hilkiah, **H**; and of
12:24 heads of the Levites were **H**,

HASHABNAH (1/1)

Neh 10:25 Rehum, **H**, Maaseiah,

HASHABNIAH (2/2)

Neh 3:10 to him Hattush the son of **H**
9: 5 Jeshua, Kadmiel, Bani, **H**,

HASHBADANA (1/1)

Neh 8: 4 Mishael, Malchijah, Hashum, **H**,

HASHEM (1/1)

1 Chr 11:34 the sons of **H** the Gizonite,

HASHMONAH (2/2)

Num 33:29 from Mithkah and camped at **H**.
33:30 They departed from **H** and camped

HASHUB (1/1)

Neh 3:11 the son of Harim and **H** the son

HASHUBAH (1/1)

1 Chr 3:20 and **H**, Ohel, Berechiah,

HASHUM (5/5)

Ezra 2:19 the people of **H**, two hundred
10:33 of the sons of **H**: Mattenai,
Neh 7:22 the sons of **H**, three hundred
8: 4 Pedaiah, Mishael, Malchijah, **H**,
10:18 Hodijah, **H**, Bezai,

HASHUPHA (KJV) See HASUPHA

HASRAH (1/1)

2 Chr 34:22 son of Tokhath, the son of **H**,

HASSENAAH (1/1)

Neh 3: 3 Also the sons of **H** built the

HASSENUAH (1/1)

1 Chr 9: 7 son of Hodaviah, the son of **H**;

HASSHUB (4/4)

1 Chr 9:14 Levites: Shemaiah the son of **H**,
Neh 3:23 After him Benjamin and **H** made
10:23 Hoshea, Hananiah, **H**,
11:15 Levites: Shemaiah the son of **H**,

HASTE (47/46) HASTEN, HASTILY, HASTY

Gen 24:46 And she made **h** and let her
43:30 so Joseph made **h** and sought
Ex 10:16 called for Moses and Aaron in **h**,
12:11 So you shall eat it in **h**.
12:33 send them out of the land in **h**.
34: 8 So Moses made **h** and bowed his
Deut 16: 3 out of the land of Egypt in **h**),
Judg 9:48 make **h** and do as I have
13:10 Then the woman ran in **h** and told
1 Sam 20:38 out after the lad, "Make **h**,
21: 8 the king's business required **h**.
23:26 So David made **h** to get away
25:18 Then Abigail made **h** and took
25:42 So Abigail rose in **h** and rode on
2 Sam 4: 4 as she made **h** to flee, that he
15:14 Make **h** to depart, lest he
1 Ki 12:18 mounted his chariot in **h** to
2 Ki 7:15 had thrown away in their **h**.
2 Chr 10:18 mounted his chariot in **h** to
35:21 for God commanded me to make **h**.
Ezra 4:23 they went up in **h** to Jerusalem
Ps 31:22 For I said in my **h**,
38:22 Make **h** to help me, O Lord, my
40:13 make **h** to help me!
70: 1 Make **h**, O God, to deliver
70: 1 to deliver me! Make **h** to help
70: 5 Make **h** to me, O God! You are
71:12 O my God, make **h** to help me!
116:11 I said in my **h**, "All men
119:60 I made **h**, and did not delay
141: 1 Make **h** to me! Give ear to my
Prov 1:16 And they make **h** to shed blood.
Song 8:14 Make **h**, my beloved, And be
Isa 49:17 Your sons shall make **h**;
52:12 you shall not go out with **h**,
59: 7 And they make **h** to shed
Jer 9:18 Let them make **h** And take up a
Dan 3:24 and he rose in **h** and spoke,
6:19 in the morning and went in **h**
Nah 2: 5 They make **h** to her walls, And
Mk 6:25 Immediately she came in with **h**
Lk 1:39 into the hill country with **h**,
2:16 And they came with **h** and found
19: 5 make **h** and come down, for today
19: 6 So he made **h** and came down, and
Acts 22:18 Make **h** and get out of Jerusalem
Titus 3:13 Apollos on their journey with **h**,

HASTEN (9/9) HASTE, HASTENED, HASTENING, HASTENS, HURRY

Deut 32:35 And the things to come **h** upon
Josh 10:13 and did not **h** to go down for
1 Sam 23:27 **H** and come, for the Philistines
Ps 16: 4 shall be multiplied who **h**
22:19 My Strength, **h** to help Me!
55: 8 I would **h** my escape From the
Eccl 7: 9 Do not **h** in your spirit to be
Isa 5:19 Let Him make speed and **h** His
60:22 will **h** it in its time."

HASTENED (14/14) HASTEN, HURRIED, QUICKLY

Gen 18: 7 and he **h** to prepare it.
1 Sam 17:48 that David **h** and ran toward the
25:23 she **h** to dismount from the
25:34 unless you had **h** and come to
28:24 and she **h** to kill it. And she
2 Sam 19:16 **h** and came down with the men of
1 Ki 20:41 And he **h** to take the bandage
2 Ki 9:13 Then each man **h** to take his
Esth 3:15 **h** by the king's command;
6:14 and **h** to bring Haman to the
8:14 **h** and pressed on by the king's
Job 31: 5 Or if my foot has **h** to deceit,
Ps 48: 5 were troubled, they **h** away.
104: 7 voice of Your thunder they **h**

HASTENING (2/2) HASTEN

Isa 16: 5 and **h** righteousness."
2 Pe 3:12 looking for and **h** the coming of

HASTENS (8/8) HASTEN

Prov 7:23 As a bird **h** to the snare, He
19: 2 And he sins who **h** with his
28:20 But he who **h** to be rich will
28:22 A man with an evil eye **h** after
Eccl 1: 5 And **h** to the place where it
Isa 51:14 The captive exile **h**,
Hab 1: 8 They fly as the eagle that **h**
Zeph 1:14 It is near and **h** quickly.

HASTILY (5/5) HASTE, QUICKLY

Prov 20:21 An inheritance gained **h** at the
25: 8 Do not go **h** to court; For what
Eccl 5: 2 not your heart utter anything **h**
Isa 28:16 believes will not act **h**.
1 Tim 5:22 Do not lay hands on anyone **h**,

HASTY (4/4) HASTE

Prov 21: 5 those of everyone who is **h**,
29:20 Do you see a man **h** in his
Eccl 8: 3 Do not be **h** to go from his
Hab 1: 6 A bitter and **h** nation Which

HASUPHA (2/2)

Ezra 2:43 the sons of Ziha, the sons of **H**,
Neh 7:46 the sons of Ziha, the sons of **H**,

HATACH (KJV) See HATHACH

HATCH (3/3)

Isa 34:15 her nest and lay eggs And **h**,
59: 5 They **h** vipers' eggs and weave
Jer 17:11 that broods but does not **h**,

HATE (86/83) HATED, HATEFUL, HATERS, HATES, HATING, HATRED

Gen 24:60 The gates of those who **h** them.
26:27 since you **h** me and have sent me
50:15 Perhaps Joseph will **h** us, and
Ex 20: 5 generations of those who **h** Me,
Lev 19:17 You shall not **h** your brother in
26:17 Those who **h** you shall reign
Num 10:35 And let those who **h** You flee
Deut 5: 9 generations of those who **h** Me,
7:10 and He repays those who **h** Him to
7:15 on all those who **h** you.
30: 7 enemies and on those who **h** you,
32:41 And repay those who **h** Me.
33:11 And of those who **h** him, that
Josh 20: 5 but did not **h** him beforehand.
Judg 11: 7 Did you not **h** me, and expel me
14:16 You only **h** me! You do not love
2 Sam 19: 6 enemies and **h** your friends.
1 Ki 22: 8 but I **h** him, because he does
2 Chr 18: 7 but I **h** him, because he never
19: 2 love those who **h** the LORD?
Job 8:22 Those who **h** you will be clothed
Ps 5: 5 You **h** all workers of iniquity.
9:13 my trouble from those who **h** me,
21: 8 hand will find those who **h** You.
25:19 And they **h** me with cruel
34:21 And those who **h** the righteous
35:19 wink with the eye who **h** me
38:19 And those who **h** me wrongfully
41: 7 All who **h** me whisper together
44:10 And those who **h** us have taken
45: 7 and **h** wickedness;

50:17 Seeing you ***h*** instruction And
55: 3 And in wrath they ***h*** me.
68: 1 Let those also who ***h*** Him flee
69: 4 Those who ***h*** me without a cause
69:14 from those who ***h*** me,
83: 2 And those who ***h*** You have
86:17 That those who ***h*** me may see
89:23 And plague those who ***h*** him.
97:10 ***h*** evil! He preserves the souls
101: 3 I ***h*** the work of those who fall
105:25 He turned their heart to ***h*** His
118: 7 my desire on those who ***h*** me.
119:104 Therefore I ***h*** every false way.
119:113 I ***h*** the double-minded, But I
119:128 I ***h*** every false way.
119:163 I ***h*** and abhor lying, But I
129: 5 Let all those who ***h*** Zion Be
139:21 Do I not ***h*** them, O LORD, who
139:21 who ***h*** You? And do I not loathe
139:22 I ***h*** them with perfect hatred;
Prov 1:22 And fools ***h*** knowledge.
8:13 the LORD is to ***h*** evil;
8:13 way And the perverse mouth I ***h***.
8:36 All those who ***h*** me love
9: 8 lest he ***h*** you; Rebuke a wise
19: 7 the brothers of the poor ***h*** him;
25:17 weary of you and ***h*** you.
29:10 The bloodthirsty ***h*** the
Eccl 3: 8 time to love, And a time to ***h***;
Isa 61: 8 I ***h*** robbery for burnt
Jer 44: 4 this abominable thing that I ***h***!
Ezek 16:27 the will of those who ***h*** you,
23:28 into the hand of those you ***h***,
Dan 4:19 the dream concern those who ***h***
Am 5:10 They ***h*** the one who rebukes in
5:15 ***H*** evil, love good
5:21 I ***h***, I despise your
6: 8 of Jacob, And ***h*** his palaces;
Mic 3: 2 You who ***h*** good and love evil;
Zech 8:17 all these are things that I ***h***,
Mt 5:43 neighbor and ***h*** your enemy.'
5:44 do good to those who ***h*** you, and
6:24 for either he will ***h*** the one
24:10 and will ***h*** one another.
Lk 1:71 from the hand of all who ***h*** us,
6:22 Blessed are you when men ***h*** you,
6:27 do good to those who ***h*** you,
14:26 comes to Me and does not ***h*** his
16:13 for either he will ***h*** the one
Jn 7: 7 The world cannot ***h*** you, but it
Rom 7:15 I do not practice; but what I ***h***,
Rev 2: 6 that you ***h*** the deeds of the
2: 6 the Nicolaitans, which I also ***h***.
2:15 Nicolaitans, which thing I ***h***.
17:16 these will ***h*** the harlot, make

HATED (53/51) HATE

Gen 27:41 So Esau ***h*** Jacob because of the
37: 4 they ***h*** him and could not speak
37: 5 and they ***h*** him even more.
37: 8 So they ***h*** him even more for
49:23 Shot at him and ***h*** him.
Deut 4:42 without having ***h*** him in time
9:28 and because He ***h*** them, He has
19: 4 not having ***h*** him in time past—
19: 6 since he had not ***h*** the victim
Judg 15: 2 that you thoroughly ***h*** her;
2 Sam 5: 8 who are ***h*** by David's soul),
13:15 Then Amnon ***h*** her exceedingly,
13:15 the hatred with which he ***h*** her
13:22 For Absalom ***h*** Amnon, because he
22:18 From those who ***h*** me; For they
22:41 I destroyed those who ***h*** me.
Esth 9: 1 overpowered those who ***h*** them.
9: 5 with those who ***h*** them.
Job 31:29 at the destruction of him who ***h***
Ps 18:17 From those who ***h*** me, For they
18:40 I destroyed those who ***h*** me.
26: 5 I have ***h*** the assembly of
31: 6 I have ***h*** those who regard
44: 7 put to shame those who ***h*** us.
106:10 the hand of him who ***h*** them,
106:41 And those who ***h*** them ruled
Prov 1:29 Because they ***h*** knowledge And
5:12 How I have ***h*** instruction, And
14:17 a man of wicked intentions is ***h***.
14:20 The poor man is ***h*** even by his
Eccl 2:17 Therefore I ***h*** life because the
2:18 Then I ***h*** all my labor in which
Isa 60:15 you have been forsaken and ***h***,
66: 5 Your brethren who ***h*** you, Who
Jer 12: 8 Therefore I have ***h*** it.
Ezek 16:37 you loved, and all those you ***h***;
35: 6 since you have not ***h*** blood,
Hos 9:15 For there I ***h*** them.
Mal 1: 3 But Esau I have ***h***,
Mt 10:22 And you will be ***h*** by all for My
24: 9 and you will be ***h*** by all
Mk 13:13 And you will be ***h*** by all for My
Lk 19:14 But his citizens ***h*** him, and sent
21:17 And you will be ***h*** by all for My
Jn 15:18 you know that it ***h*** Me before
15:18 it hated Me before it ***h*** you.
15:24 have seen and also ***h*** both Me
15:25 They ***h*** Me without a cause.'
17:14 and the world has ***h*** them
Rom 9:13 loved, but Esau I have ***h***.
Eph 5:29 For no one ever ***h*** his own flesh,
Heb 1: 9 and ***h*** lawlessness;
Rev 18: 2 every unclean and ***h*** bird!

HATEFUL (2/2) HATE

Prov 30:23 A ***h*** woman when she is married,
Titus 3: 3 ***h*** and hating one another.

HATEFULLY (1/1)

Ezek 23:29 They will deal ***h*** with you, take

HATERS (2/2) HATE

Ps 81:15 The ***h*** of the LORD would
Rom 1:30 ***h*** of God, violent, proud,

HATES (37/36) HATE

Ex 23: 5 the donkey of one who ***h*** you
Deut 1:27 Because the LORD ***h*** us, He has
7:10 not be slack with him who ***h***
12:31 to the LORD which He ***h*** they
16:22 which the LORD your God ***h***.
19:11 But if anyone ***h*** his neighbor,
Job 16: 9 and ***h*** me; He gnashes at me
34:17 Should one who ***h*** justice
Ps 11: 5 who loves violence His soul ***h***.
36: 2 out his iniquity and when he ***h***.
55:12 Nor is it one who ***h*** me who
120: 6 dwelt too long With one who ***h***
Prov 6:16 These six things the LORD ***h***,
11:15 But one who ***h*** being surety is
12: 1 But he who ***h*** correction is
13: 5 A righteous man ***h*** lying, But
13:24 He who spares his rod ***h*** his
15:10 And he who ***h*** correction will
15:27 But he who ***h*** bribes will live.
26:24 He who ***h***, disguises it with
26:28 A lying tongue ***h*** those who
28:16 But he who ***h*** covetousness
29:24 with a thief ***h*** his own life;
Isa 1:14 appointed feasts My soul ***h***;
Mal 2:16 God of Israel says That He ***h***
Jn 3:20 everyone practicing evil ***h***
7: 7 but it ***h*** Me because I testify
12:25 and he who ***h*** his life in this
15:18 If the world ***h*** you, you know
15:19 therefore the world ***h*** you.
15:23 He who ***h*** Me hates My Father
15:23 He who hates Me ***h*** My Father
1 Jn 2: 9 and ***h*** his brother, is in
2:11 But he who ***h*** his brother is in
3:13 brethren, if the world ***h*** you.
3:15 Whoever ***h*** his brother is a
4:20 and ***h*** his brother, he is a

HATHACH (4/4)

Esth 4: 5 Then Esther called ***H***,
4: 6 So ***H*** went out to Mordecai in the
4: 9 So ***H*** returned and told Esther
4:10 Then Esther spoke to ***H***,

HATHATH (1/1)

1 Chr 4:13 The sons of Othniel were ***H***,

HATING (3/3) HATE

Ex 18:21 ***h*** covetousness; and place such
Titus 3: 3 hateful and ***h*** one another.
Jude 23 ***h*** even the garment defiled by

HATIPHA (2/2)

Ezra 2:54 of Neziah, and the sons of ***H***.
Neh 7:56 of Neziah, and the sons of ***H***.

HATITA (2/2)

Ezra 2:42 sons of Akkub, the sons of ***H***,
Neh 7:45 sons of Akkub, the sons of ***H***,

HATRED (16/16) HATE

Num 35:20 If he pushes him out of ***h*** or,
2 Sam 13:15 so that the ***h*** with which he
Ps 25:19 And they hate me with cruel ***h***.
109: 3 surrounded me with words of ***h***,
109: 5 good, And ***h*** for my love.
139:22 I hate them with perfect ***h***;
Prov 10:12 ***H*** stirs up strife, But love
10:18 Whoever hides ***h*** has lying
15:17 is, Than a fatted calf with ***h***.
26:26 Though his ***h*** is covered by
Eccl 9: 1 People know neither love nor ***h***
9: 6 Also their love, their ***h***,
Ezek 25:15 to destroy because of the old ***h***,
35: 5 you have had an ancient ***h***,
35:11 envy which you showed in your ***h***
Gal 5:20 idolatry, sorcery, ***h***,

HATS (4/4)

Ex 28:40 And you shall make ***h*** for them,
29: 9 and put the ***h*** on them.
39:28 exquisite ***h*** of fine linen,
Lev 8:13 and put ***h*** on them, as the LORD

HATTIL (2/2)

Ezra 2:57 of Shephatiah, the sons of ***H***,
Neh 7:59 of Shephatiah, the sons of ***H***,

HATTUSH (5/5)

1 Chr 3:22 The sons of Shemaiah were ***H***,
Ezra 8: 2 Daniel; of the sons of David, ***H***;
Neh 3:10 And next to him ***H*** the son of
10: 4 ***H***, Shebaniah, Malluch,
12: 2 Amariah, Malluch, ***H***,

HAUGHTILY (1/1)

Mic 2: 3 Nor shall you walk ***h***, For

HAUGHTINESS (6/6) HAUGHTY

Job 20: 6 Though his ***h*** mounts up to the
Isa 2:11 The ***h*** of men shall be bowed
2:17 And the ***h*** of men shall be
13:11 And will lay low the ***h*** of the
16: 6 Of his ***h*** and his pride and his
Jer 48:29 And of the ***h*** of his heart."

HAUGHTY (18/18) HAUGHTINESS

2 Sam 22:28 But Your eyes are on the ***h***,
Ps 18:27 But will bring down ***h*** looks.
101: 5 The one who has a ***h*** look and a
131: 1 LORD, my heart is not ***h***,
Prov 16:18 And a ***h*** spirit before a fall.
18:12 the heart of a man is ***h***,
21: 4 A ***h*** look, a proud heart, And
21:24 A proud and ***h*** man—Scoffer"
Isa 3:16 the daughters of Zion are ***h***,
10:12 and the glory of his ***h*** looks."
10:33 And the ***h*** will be humbled.
24: 4 The ***h*** people of the earth
Jer 50:31 O most ***h*** one!" says the Lord
Ezek 16:50 And they were ***h*** and committed
Zeph 3:11 And you shall no longer be ***h***
Rom 11:20 you stand by faith. Do not be ***h***,
1 Tim 6:17 in this present age not to be ***h***,
2 Tim 3: 4 traitors, headstrong, ***h***,

HAUNTS (1/1)

Ps 74:20 full of the ***h*** of cruelty.

HAURAN (2/2)

Ezek 47:16 (which is on the border of ***H***).
47:18 between ***H*** and Damascus,

HAVE (4940/3825) See APPENDIX

HAVE (593/538)

Gen 1:26 let them ***h*** dominion over the
1:26 ***h*** dominion over the fish of the
1:29 I ***h*** given you every herb that
11: 6 people are one and they all ***h***
18:10 Sarah your wife shall ***h*** a
18:12 shall I ***h*** pleasure, my lord
18:14 and Sarah shall ***h*** a son."
19: 8 I ***h*** two daughters who have not
19:12 ***H*** you anyone else here?
19:12 and whomever you ***h*** in the
27:38 ***H*** you only one blessing,
31:32 identify what I ***h*** of yours and
32: 5 I ***h*** oxen, donkeys, flocks, and
33: 9 I ***h*** enough, my brother;
33: 9 keep what you ***h*** for yourself."
33:11 and because I ***h*** enough." So he
35:17 you will ***h*** this son also."
37: 8 Or shall you indeed ***h*** dominion
43: 7 ***H*** you another brother?' And we
44:19 ***H*** you a father or a brother?'
44:20 We ***h*** a father, an old man, and a
45:10 your herds, and all that you ***h***.
45:11 household, and all that you ***h***.
46:32 and they ***h*** brought their
47:26 Pharaoh should ***h*** one-fifth,
Ex 9:19 livestock and all that you ***h***
17:16 the LORD will ***h*** war with
18:16 when they ***h*** a difficulty, they
20: 3 You shall ***h*** no other gods
21: 8 He shall ***h*** no right to sell her
27:16 It shall ***h*** four pillars and
28: 3 Whom I ***h*** filled with the spirit
28: 7 It shall ***h*** two shoulder straps
28:32 it shall ***h*** a woven binding all
Lev 7: 7 atonement with it shall ***h*** it.
11: 4 chew the cud or those that***h***
11: 4 it chews the cud but does not ***h***
11: 5 it chews the cud but does not ***h***
11: 6 it chews the cud but does not ***h***
11:10 or in the rivers that do not ***h***
11:12 in the water does not ***h*** fins
11:21 those which ***h*** jointed legs
11:23 other flying insects which ***h***
19:36 You shall ***h*** honest scales,
24:22 You shall ***h*** the same law for the
25:31 the houses of villages which ***h***
25:44 female slaves whom you may ***h***
26:37 and you shall ***h*** no power to
Num 9:14 you shall ***h*** one ordinance,
15:29 You shall ***h*** one law for him who
15:39 And you shall ***h*** the tassel,
18:20 You shall ***h*** no inheritance in
18:20 nor shall you ***h*** any portion
18:23 of Israel they shall ***h*** no
22:38 I ***h*** come to you! Now have I
28:26 you shall ***h*** a holy convocation.
29: 1 you shall ***h*** a holy convocation.

H

29: 7 this seventh month you shall ***h***
29:12 the seventh month you shall ***h***
29:35 'On the eighth day you shall ***h*** 32.
32: 4 and your servants ***h***
32:30 they shall ***h*** possessions among
34: 6 you shall ***h*** the Great Sea for a
Deut 3:19 livestock (I know that you ***h***
5: 7 You shall ***h*** no other gods
8:13 and all that you ***h*** is
14: 7 of those that chew the cud or ***h***
14:10 And whatever does not ***h*** fins and
18: 1 shall ***h*** no part nor inheritance
18: 2 Therefore they shall ***h*** no
18: 8 They shall ***h*** equal portions to
23:12 Also you shall ***h*** a place outside
23:13 and you shall ***h*** an implement
25:13 You shall not ***h*** in your bag
25:14 You shall not ***h*** in your house
25:15 You shall ***h*** a perfect and just
28:40 You shall ***h*** olive trees
32:36 will judge His people And ***h***
Josh 17:17 You are a great people and ***h***
17:17 you shall not ***h*** only one lot,
17:18 though they ***h*** iron chariots
18: 7 But the Levites ***h*** no part among
22:24 what ***h*** you to do with the LORD
22:25 You ***h*** no part in the LORD."
22:27 You ***h*** no part inn the LORD."'
Judg 3:19 I ***h*** a secret message for you,
3:20 I ***h*** a message from God for
18:24 gone away. Now what more do I ***h***?
19:19 although we ***h*** both straw and
21:22 it is not as though you ***h***
Ruth 1:12 for I am too old to ***h*** a husband.
1:12 if I should ***h*** a husband
2:12 under whose wings you ***h*** come
1 Sam 8:19 but we will ***h*** a king over us,
9: 7 to the man of God. What do we ***h***?
9: 8 I ***h*** here at hand one fourth of
11: 9 you shall ***h*** help." Then the
15: 3 utterly destroy all that they ***h***,
18: 8 Now what more can he ***h*** but the
21: 3 what ***h*** you on hand? Give one
21: 4 if the young men ***h*** at least
25: 7 Now I have heard that you ***h***
25:31 either that you ***h*** shed blood
28:22 that you may ***h*** strength when
2 Sam 9:10 that your master's son may ***h***
16:10 What ***h*** I to do with you,
18:18 I ***h*** no son to keep my name in
18:22 since you ***h*** no news ready?"
19:22 What ***h*** I to do with you
19:28 Therefore what right ***h*** I still
19:34 How long ***h*** I to live, that I
19:43 We ***h*** ten shares in the king;
19:43 therefore we also ***h*** more right
20: 1 We ***h*** no share in David, Nor do
20: 1 Nor do we ***h*** inheritance in the
1 Ki 2:14 I ***h*** something to say to you.'
8:50 that they may ***h*** compassion on
11:36 My servant David may always ***h***
12:16 What share ***h*** we in David?
12:16 We ***h*** no inheritance in the
17:12 I do not ***h*** bread, only a
17:18 What ***h*** I to do with you, O man
20: 4 I and all that I ***h*** are
21: 2 that I may ***h*** it for a vegetable
22:17 as sheep that ***h*** no shepherd.
22:17 These ***h*** no master. Let each
2 Ki 3:13 What ***h*** I to do with you? Go to
4: 2 what do you ***h*** in the house?'
4:13 you ***h*** been concerned for us
4:43 that I ***h*** sent Naaman my servant
7:17 on whose hand he leaned to ***h***
9: 5 I ***h*** a message for you,
9:18 What ***h*** you to do with peace?
9:19 What ***h*** you to do with peace?
10: 2 and you ***h*** chariots and horses,
10:19 for I ***h*** a great sacrifice for
22: 4 which the doorkeepers ***h***
1 Chr 4:27 but his brothers did not ***h*** many
29: 3 over and above all that I ***h***
2 Chr 1:12 nor shall any after you ***h*** the
10:16 What share ***h*** we in David?
10:16 we ***h*** no inheritance in the
13:10 and we ***h*** not forsaken Him;
18:16 as sheep that ***h*** no shepherd.
18:16 These ***h*** no master. Let each
31:10 we have had enough to eat and ***h***
35:21 What ***h*** I to do with you, king of
Ezra 4:16 result will be that you will ***h***
Neh 2:20 but you ***h*** no heritage or right
9:37 increase to the kings You ***h***
Esth 8: 5 and if I ***h*** found favor in his
Job 3: 9 but ***h*** none, And not see the
3:26 I ***h*** no rest, for trouble
5:16 So the poor ***h*** hope,
6: 8 that I might ***h*** my request,
10: 4 Do You ***h*** eyes of flesh? Or do
12: 3 But I ***h*** understanding as well
24: 7 And ***h*** no covering in the cold.
33:32 If you ***h*** anything to say,
34:16 If you ***h*** understanding, hear
35: 3 to You? What profit shall I ***h***,
38: 4 if you ***h*** understanding.
40: 9 ***H*** you an arm like God
Ps 14: 4 ***H*** all the workers of iniquity
16: 6 I ***h*** a good inheritance.
17:14 From men of the world who ***h***
19:13 Let them not ***h*** dominion over
35:25 so we would ***h*** it!" Let them
50:16 What right ***h*** you to declare My
51: 1 ***H*** mercy upon me, O God,
53: 4 ***H*** the workers of iniquity no
72: 8 He shall ***h*** dominion also from
73:25 whom ***h*** I in heaven but You?
74:20 ***H*** respect to the covenant
89:13 You ***h*** a mighty arm; Strong is
90:13 And ***h*** compassion on Your
102:27 And Your years will ***h*** no end.
111:10 A good understanding ***h*** all
115: 5 They ***h*** mouths, but they do not
115: 5 they do not speak; Eyes they ***h***,
115: 6 They ***h*** ears, but they do not
115: 6 they do not hear; Noses they ***h***,
115: 7 They ***h*** hands, but they do not
115: 7 do not handle; Feet they ***h***,
119:42 So shall I ***h*** an answer for him
119:99 I ***h*** more understanding than all
119:165 Great peace ***h*** those who love
123: 3 ***H*** mercy on us, O LORD,
123: 3 ***h*** mercy on us! For we are
135:14 And He will ***h*** compassion on
135:16 They ***h*** mouths, but they do not
135:16 they do not speak; Eyes they ***h***,
135:17 They ***h*** ears, but they do not
Prov 1:14 Let us all ***h*** one purse"
1:25 And would ***h*** none of my rebuke,
1:30 They would ***h*** none of my counsel
3:28 When you ***h*** it with you.
8:14 understanding, I ***h*** strength.
12:20 But counselors of peace ***h*** joy.
14:26 And His children will ***h*** a
19:19 you will ***h*** to do it again.
22: 2 The rich and the poor ***h*** this in
22:27 If you ***h*** nothing with which
24:25 who rebuke the wicked will ***h***
28:19 He who tills his land will ***h***
28:19 he who follows frivolity will ***h***
29:13 poor man and the oppressor ***h***
30: 2 And do not ***h*** the understanding
30: 3 neither learned wisdom Nor ***h***
30:27 The locusts ***h*** no king,
31:11 So he will ***h*** no lack of gain.
Eccl 2:25 or who can ***h*** enjoyment,
3:19 they all ***h*** one breath; man has
4: 9 Because they ***h*** a good reward
6: 8 What does the poor man ***h***,
9: 5 And they ***h*** no more reward,
9: 6 Nevermore will they ***h*** a share
12: 1 I ***h*** no pleasure in them":
Song 8: 8 We ***h*** a little sister, And she
8:12 may ***h*** a thousand, And those
Isa 3: 6 You ***h*** clothing; You be our
9:17 Therefore the LORD will ***h*** no
10:13 the strength of my hand I ***h***
13:18 And they will ***h*** no pity on the
14: 1 For the LORD will ***h*** mercy on
17: 8 not respect what his fingers ***h***
22:11 Nor did you ***h*** respect for Him
22:16 What ***h*** you here, and whom have
22:16 and whom ***h*** you here, That you
23:12 There also you will ***h*** no
26: 1 We ***h*** a strong city; God will
30:29 You shall ***h*** a song As in the
43: 8 but the blind people who ***h***
43: 8 And the deaf who ***h*** ears.
45:20 They ***h*** no knowledge,
45:21 ***H*** not I, the LORD?
49:13 And will ***h*** mercy on His
50: 2 Or ***h*** I no power to deliver?
50:11 This you shall ***h*** from My hand:
55: 1 And you who ***h*** no money, Come,
55: 7 And He will ***h*** mercy on him;
56:11 greedy dogs which never ***h***
Jer 2:28 are your gods that you ***h*** made
3: 3 Therefore the showers ***h*** been
4:22 And they ***h*** no understanding.
4:22 But to do good they ***h*** no
5:21 Who ***h*** eyes and see not,
5:21 And who ***h*** ears and hear not:
5:31 And My people love to ***h*** it
6:23 They are cruel and ***h*** no
12:15 that I will return and ***h***
13:14 will not pity nor spare not ***h***
14:13 nor shall you ***h*** famine, but I
15: 5 For who will ***h*** pity on you,
16: 2 nor shall you ***h*** sons or
21: 7 or ***h*** pity or mercy."'
29:32 he shall not ***h*** anyone to dwell
30:10 ***h*** rest and be quiet, And no
30:18 And ***h*** mercy on his dwelling
31:20 I will surely ***h*** mercy on him,
33:21 so that he shall not ***h*** a son to
33:26 and will ***h*** mercy on them.'"
35: 9 nor do we ***h*** vineyard, field, or
36:30 He shall ***h*** no one to sit on the
39:18 because you ***h*** put your trust in
41: 8 for we ***h*** treasures of wheat,
42:12 that he may ***h*** mercy on you and
44:17 as we ***h*** come, we and our
46:27 ***h*** rest and be at ease; No one
46:28 all the nations To which I ***h***
49:12 was not to drink of the cup ***h***
Lam 3:21 Therefore I ***h*** hope.
Ezek 5:11 nor will I ***h*** any pity.
7: 4 Nor will I ***h*** pity; But I will
7: 9 Nor will I ***h*** pity; I will
8:18 eye will not spare nor will I ***h***
9:10 nor will I ***h*** pity, but I will
10: 8 The cherubim appeared to ***h*** the
18:32 For I ***h*** no pleasure in the death
33:11 I ***h*** no pleasure in the death of
37:24 and they shall all ***h*** one
39:25 and ***h*** mercy on the whole house
44:18 They shall ***h*** linen turbans on
45:10 You shall ***h*** honest scales,
47:13 Joseph shall ***h*** two portions.
48:13 the Levites shall ***h*** an area
Dan 3:16 we ***h*** no need to answer you in
5: 7 be clothed with purple and ***h***
5:16 be clothed with purple and ***h***
Hos 1: 6 For I will no longer ***h*** mercy
1: 7 Yet I will ***h*** mercy on the house
2: 4 I will not ***h*** mercy on her
2:23 And I will ***h*** mercy on her
10: 3 We ***h*** no king, Because we did
14: 8 What ***h*** I to do anymore with
Mic 2: 5 Therefore you will ***h*** no one to
5:12 And you shall ***h*** no
7:19 He will again ***h*** compassion on
Hab 1:14 Like creeping things that ***h***
Hag 1: 6 You ***h*** sown much, and bring in
1: 6 but do not ***h*** enough;
Mal 1:10 I ***h*** no pleasure in you,'
2:10 ***H*** we not all one Father?
Mt 3: 9 We ***h*** Abraham as our father.'
5:46 what reward ***h*** you? Do not even
6: 2 that they may ***h*** glory from men.
6: 2 they ***h*** their reward.
6: 5 they ***h*** their reward.
6:16 they ***h*** their reward.
8:20 Foxes ***h*** holes and birds of the
8:20 holes and birds of the air ***h***
8:29 What ***h*** we to do with You, Jesus,
9:12 Those who are well ***h*** no need of
9:27 ***h*** mercy on us!'
11: 5 are raised up and the poor ***h***
13: 5 Where they did not ***h*** much
13:12 and he will ***h*** abundance;
13:12 but whoever does not ***h***,
14: 4 It is not lawful for you to ***h***
14:17 We ***h*** here only five loaves and
15:22 ***H*** mercy on me, O Lord, Son of
15:32 I ***h*** compassion on the multitude,
15:34 "How many loaves do you ***h***?
17:15 ***h*** mercy on my son, for he is an
17:20 if you ***h*** faith as a mustard
18:26 ***H*** patience with me, and I will
18:29 ***H*** patience with me, and I will
18:33 Should you not also ***h*** had
19:16 thing shall I do that I may ***h***
19:21 sell what you ***h*** and give to the
19:21 and you will ***h*** treasure in
19:27 we ***h*** left all and followed You.
19:27 Therefore what shall we ***h***?
20:30 ***H*** mercy on us, O Lord, Son of
20:31 ***H*** mercy on us, O Lord, Son of
21:21 if you ***h*** faith and do not
25:29 and he will ***h*** abundance;
25:29 but from him who does not ***h***,
26:11 For you ***h*** the poor with you
26:11 but Me you do not ***h*** always.
27:19 ***H*** nothing to do with that just
27:65 You ***h*** a guard; go your way, make
Mk 1:24 Let us alone! What ***h*** we to do
2:17 Those who are well ***h*** no need of
2:19 As long as they ***h*** the
3:15 and to ***h*** power to heal
4: 5 where it did not ***h*** much earth;
4:17 and they ***h*** no root in
4:25 but whoever does not ***h***,
4:40 How is it that you ***h*** no
5: 7 What ***h*** I to do with You, Jesus,
6:18 It is not lawful for you to ***h***
6:38 "How many loaves do you ***h***?
8: 2 I ***h*** compassion on the multitude
8: 5 "How many loaves do you ***h***
8:16 It is because we ***h*** no bread."
9:22 ***h*** compassion on us and help
9:50 ***H*** salt in yourselves, and have
9:50 and ***h*** peace with one another."
10:21 sell whatever you ***h*** and give to
10:21 and you will ***h*** treasure in
10:23 hard it is for those who ***h***
10:47 ***H*** mercy on me!"
10:48 ***H*** mercy on me!"
11:22 ***H*** faith in God.
11:25 if you ***h*** anything against
14: 7 For you ***h*** the poor with you
14: 7 but Me you do not ***h*** always.
Lk 1:14 And you will ***h*** joy and gladness,
3: 8 We ***h*** Abraham as your father.'
5:31 Those who are well ***h*** no need of
7:22 the poor ***h*** the gospel preached
7:40 I ***h*** something to say to you."
8:13 and these ***h*** no root, who
8:18 and whoever does not ***h***
8:18 even what he seems to ***h*** will be
8:28 What ***h*** I to do with You, Jesus,
9:18 We ***h*** no more than five loaves
9:58 Foxes ***h*** holes and birds of the
9:58 holes and birds of the air ***h***
11: 6 and I ***h*** nothing to set before
12:17 since I ***h*** no room to store my
12:19 you ***h*** many goods laid up for
12:24 which ***h*** neither storehouse nor
12:50 But I ***h*** a baptism to be baptized
16:24 ***h*** mercy on me, and send Lazarus
16:28 For I ***h*** five brothers, that he
16:29 They ***h*** Moses and the prophets;
17:13 ***h*** mercy on us!'
18:22 Sell all that you ***h*** and
18:22 and you will ***h*** treasure in
18:24 hard it is for those who ***h***
18:38 ***h*** mercy on me!'

18:39 ***h*** mercy on me!'
19:26 and from him who does not ***h***,
24:39 for a spirit does not ***h*** flesh
24:39 flesh and bones as you and I ***h***.
24:41 ***H*** you any food here?'
Jn 2: 3 They ***h*** no wine.'
3:15 in Him should not perish but ***h***
3:16 in Him should not perish but ***h***
4:11 You ***h*** nothing to draw with,
4:17 I ***h*** no husband.' Jesus said to
4:17 I ***h*** no husband,'
4:18 for you ***h*** had five husbands,
4:18 and the one whom you now ***h*** is
4:32 I ***h*** food to eat of which you do
5: 7 I ***h*** no man to put me into the
5:36 But I ***h*** a greater witness than
5:38 But you do not ***h*** His word
5:39 for in them you think you ***h***
5:40 to come to Me that you may ***h***
5:42 that you do not ***h*** the love of
6:40 Son and believes in Him may ***h***
6:53 you ***h*** no life in you.
6:68 You ***h*** the words of eternal
7:20 You ***h*** a demon. Who is seeking to
8: 6 that they might ***h*** something of
8:12 but ***h*** the light of life.'
8:26 I ***h*** many things to say and to
8:41 we ***h*** one Father—God.'
8:48 that You are a Samaritan and ***h***
8:49 I do not ***h*** a demon; but I honor
8:52 Now we know that You ***h*** a demon!
9:41 you would ***h*** no sin, but now you
10:10 I have come that they may ***h***
10:10 and that they may ***h*** it more
10:16 And other sheep I ***h*** which are
10:18 I ***h*** power to lay it down, and I
10:18 and I ***h*** power to take it again.
12: 8 For the poor you ***h*** with you
12: 8 but Me you do not ***h*** always.'
12:35 Walk while you ***h*** the light,
12:36 While you ***h*** the light, believe
13: 8 you ***h*** no part with Me.'
15:22 they would ***h*** no sin, but now
15:22 but now they ***h*** no excuse for
15:24 they would ***h*** no sin; but now
16:12 I still ***h*** many things to say to
16:22 Therefore you now ***h*** sorrow;
16:30 and ***h*** have no need that anyone
16:33 that in Me you may ***h*** peace.
17:13 that they may ***h*** My joy
18:39 But you ***h*** a custom that I
19: 7 We ***h*** a law, and according to our
19:10 Do You not know that I ***h*** power
19:11 You could ***h*** no power at all
19:15 We ***h*** no king but Caesar!'
20:31 and that believing you may ***h***
21: 5 ***h*** you any food?' They answered
21:10 some of the fish which you ***h***
Acts 3: 6 "Silver and gold I do not ***h***,
3: 6 but what I do ***h*** I give you:
8:21 You ***h*** neither part nor portion
13:15 if you ***h*** any word of
17:28 in Him we live and move and ***h***
19:38 and his fellow craftsmen ***h*** a
21:23 We ***h*** four men who have taken a
24:15 I ***h*** hope in God, which they
24:16 I myself always strive to ***h*** a
24:19 They ought to ***h*** been here before
24:23 to keep Paul and to let him ***h***
24:25 when I ***h*** a convenient time I
25: 5 let those who ***h*** authority among
25:26 I ***h*** nothing certain to write to
Rom 5: 1 we ***h*** peace with God through our
6:14 For sin shall not ***h*** dominion
8: 9 Now if anyone does not ***h*** the
8:23 but we also who ***h*** the
9: 2 that I ***h*** great sorrow and
9:15 I will ***h*** mercy on whomever
9:15 on whomever I will ***h***
9:15 and I will ***h*** compassion
9:15 on whomever I will ***h***
10: 2 I bear them witness that they ***h***
12: 4 For as we ***h*** many members in one
12: 4 but all the members do not ***h***
13: 3 and you will ***h*** praise from the
14:22 Do you ***h*** faith? Have it to
14:22 ***h*** it to yourself before God.
15: 4 of the Scriptures might ***h*** hope.
15:17 Therefore I ***h*** reason to glory in
1 Cor 2:16 But we ***h*** the mind of Christ.
4: 7 And what do you ***h*** that you did
4: 8 You are already rich! You ***h***
4:15 For though you might ***h*** ten
4:15 yet you do not ***h*** many
5:12 For what ***h*** I to do with
6: 4 If then you ***h*** judgments
6:19 whom you ***h*** from God, and you
7: 2 let each man ***h*** his own wife,
7: 2 and let each woman ***h*** her own
7: 4 The wife does not ***h*** authority
7: 4 likewise the husband does not ***h***
7:25 I ***h*** no commandment from the
7:29 from now on even those who ***h***
7:40 and I think I also ***h*** the Spirit
9: 4 Do we ***h*** no right to eat and
9: 5 Do we ***h*** no right to take along a
9: 6 it only Barnabas and I who ***h***
9:17 I ***h*** a reward; but if against my
11:10 reason the woman ought to ***h*** a
11:16 we ***h*** no such custom, nor do
11:22 What! Do you not ***h*** houses to eat
11:22 of God and shame those who ***h***
12:21 I ***h*** no need of you'; nor again
12:21 I ***h*** no need of you.'
12:25 but that the members should ***h***
13: 1 but ***h*** not love, I have become
13: 2 And though I ***h*** the gift of
13: 2 and though I ***h*** all faith,
13: 2 but ***h*** not love, I am nothing.
13: 3 but ***h*** not love, it profits me
15:34 for some do not ***h*** the knowledge
2 Cor 1:15 that you might ***h*** a second
2: 4 might know the love which I ***h***
3:12 since we ***h*** such hope, we use
4: 7 But we ***h*** this treasure in
4:13 And since we ***h*** the same spirit
5: 1 we ***h*** a building from God,
7:16 Therefore I rejoice that I ***h***
8:11 a completion out of what you ***h***.
8:12 according to what he does not ***h***.
Gal 6:10 as we ***h*** opportunity, let us do
Eph 1: 7 In Him we ***h*** redemption through
3:12 in whom we ***h*** boldness and access
4:28 that he may ***h*** something to give
Phil 2:20 For I ***h*** no one like-minded, who
2:27 lest I should ***h*** sorrow upon
3: 3 and ***h*** no confidence in the
3: 4 though I also might ***h*** confidence
3: 4 If anyone else thinks he may ***h***
3:16 to the degree that we ***h***
4:11 for I ***h*** learned in whatever
4:12 and in all things I ***h*** learned
4:18 Indeed I ***h*** all and abound. I am
Col 1:14 in whom we ***h*** redemption through
2:23 These things indeed ***h*** an
1 Th 5: 1 you ***h*** no need that I should
2 Th 3: 2 for not all ***h*** faith.
3: 4 And we ***h*** confidence in the Lord
1 Tim 6: 2 And those who ***h*** believing
Phm 1:20 let me ***h*** joy from you in the
Heb 4:14 Seeing then that we ***h*** a great
4:15 For we do not ***h*** a High Priest
5:11 of whom we ***h*** much to say,
6:19 This hope we ***h*** as an anchor of
8: 1 We ***h*** such a High Priest, who is
12: 8 of which all ***h*** become
13: 5 with such things as you ***h***.
13:10 We ***h*** an altar from which those
13:14 For here we ***h*** no continuing
13:18 for we are confident that we ***h***
Jas 1: 4 But let patience ***h*** its perfect
2:14 he has faith but does not ***h***
2:18 You ***h*** faith, and I have works.'
2:18 and I ***h*** works." Show me your
3:14 But if you ***h*** bitter envy and
4: 2 You lust and do not ***h***.
4: 2 Yet you do not ***h*** because you do
2 Pe 1:19 And so we ***h*** the prophetic word
2:14 They ***h*** a heart trained in
1 Jn 1: 6 If we say that w ***h*** fellowship
1: 7 we ***h*** fellowship with one
1: 8 If we say that we ***h*** no sin, we
1:10 If we say that we ***h*** not sinned,
2: 1 we ***h*** an Advocate with the
2:20 But you ***h*** an anointing, from the
3:21 we ***h*** confidence toward God.
4:17 that we may ***h*** boldness in the
5:12 he who does not ***h*** the Son of
5:12 have the Son of God does not ***h***
5:13 that you may know that you ***h***
5:14 is the confidence that we ***h*** in
2 Jn 1: 9 doctrine of Christ does not ***h***
3 Jn 1: 4 I ***h*** no greater joy than to hear
Jude 1:22 And on some ***h*** compassion, making
Rev 1:18 And I ***h*** the keys of Hades and
2: 4 Nevertheless I ***h*** this against
2: 6 "But this you ***h***, that you hate
2:14 But I ***h*** a few things against
2:14 because you ***h*** there those who
2:15 Thus you also ***h*** those who hold
2:20 Nevertheless I ***h*** a few things
3: 1 that you ***h*** a name that you are
3: 4 You ***h*** a few names even in Sardis
3: 8 for you ***h*** a little strength,
3:11 Hold fast what you ***h***,
11: 6 These ***h*** power to shut heaven,
11: 6 and they ***h*** power over waters to
14:11 and they ***h*** no rest day or
15: 2 and those who ***h*** the victory
19:10 brethren who ***h*** the testimony
21: 8 all liars shall ***h*** their part
22:14 that they may ***h*** the right to

HAVEN (3/2) HAVENS

Gen 49:13 Zebulun shall dwell by the ***h*** of
49:13 He shall become a ***h*** for
Ps 107:30 guides them to their desired ***h***.

HAVENS (1/1) HAVEN

Acts 27: 8 came to a place called Fair ***H***,

HAVILAH (7/7)

Gen 2:11 skirts the whole land of ***H***,
10: 7 The sons of Cush were Seba, ***H***,
10:29 Ophir, ***H***, and Jobab.
25:18 (They dwelt from ***H*** as far as
1 Sam 15: 7 from ***H*** all the way to Shur,
1 Chr 1: 9 The sons of Cush were Seba, ***H***,
1:23 Ophir, ***H***, and Jobab.

HAVING (234/226)

Ex 12:34 ***h*** their kneading bowls bound up
Lev 11: 3 ***h*** cloven hooves and chewing
11: 7 ***h*** cloven hooves, yet does not
Deut 4:42 without ***h*** hated him in time
10: 3 ***h*** the two tablets in my hand.
14: 6 ***h*** the hoof split into two
19: 4 not ***h*** hated him in time past—
Josh 10: 9 ***h*** marched all night from
Judg 19: 3 ***h*** his servant and a couple of
Ruth 1:13 yourselves from ***h*** husbands?
1 Sam 26: 2 ***h*** three thousand chosen men of
1 Ki 22:10 ***h*** put on their robes, sat each
2 Ki 8:16 Jehoshaphat ***h*** been king of
18:20 You speak of ***h*** plans and power
1 Chr 4:42 ***h*** as their captains Pelatiah,
21:16 ***h*** in his hand a drawn sword
26:12 ***h*** duties just like their
27: 1 each division ***h*** twenty-four
2 Chr 5:12 ***h*** cymbals, stringed instruments
9: 1 ***h*** a very great retinue, camels
11:12 ***h*** Judah and Benjamin on his
Ezra 9: 5 and ***h*** torn my garment and my
Neh 13: 4 ***h*** authority over the storerooms
Job 21:25 Never ***h*** eaten with pleasure.
Ps 13: 2 ***H*** sorrow in my heart daily?
Prov 6: 7 ***h*** no captain, Overseer or
Isa 6: 6 ***h*** in his hand a live coal
36: 5 I say you speak of ***h*** plans and
Jer 11:15 ***H*** done lewd deeds with many?
41: 5 ***h*** cut themselves, with
Ezek 10: 1 ***h*** the appearance of the
38:11 and ***h*** neither bars nor gates'—
Dan 8:15 ***h*** the appearance of a man.
8:20 ***h*** the two horns—they are the
8:23 ***H*** fierce features, Who
10:16 one ***h*** the likeness of the sons
10:18 the one ***h*** the likeness of a
Zech 9: 9 He is just and ***h*** salvation,
Mal 2:15 ***H*** a remnant of the Spirit?
Mt 7:29 them as one ***h*** authority,
8: 9 ***h*** soldiers under me. And I say
9:36 like sheep ***h*** no shepherd.
14: 8 ***h*** been prompted by her mother,
15:30 ***h*** with them the lame, blind,
18: 8 rather than ***h*** two hands or two
18: 9 rather than ***h*** two eyes, to be
22:24 ***h*** no children, his brother
22:25 and ***h*** no offspring, left his
26: 7 to Him ***h*** an alabaster flask
Mk 1:22 them as one ***h*** authority,
1:35 ***h*** risen a long while before
6:34 they were like sheep not ***h*** a
7: 1 ***h*** come from Jerusalem.
8: 1 being very great and ***h*** nothing
8: 7 and ***h*** blessed them, He said to
8:18 '***H*** eyes, do you not see?
8:18 And ***h*** ears, do you not hear?
9:43 rather than ***h*** two hands, to go
9:45 rather than ***h*** two feet, to be
9:47 rather than ***h*** two eyes, to be
11:13 afar a fig tree ***h*** leaves,
12: 6 Therefore still ***h*** one son, his
12:28 and ***h*** heard them reasoning
14: 3 a woman came ***h*** an alabaster
14:51 ***h*** a linen cloth thrown around
Lk 1: 3 ***h*** had perfect understanding of
1:28 And ***h*** come in, the angel said to
5:39 ***h*** drunk old wine, immediately
7: 8 ***h*** soldiers under me. And I say
7:29 ***h*** been baptized with the
7:30 not ***h*** been baptized by him.
8:15 ***h*** heard the word with a noble
8:43 ***h*** a flow of blood for twelve
9:62 ***h*** put his hand to the plow, and
11:36 ***h*** no part dark, the whole
14: 5 ***h*** a donkey or an ox that has
15: 4 ***h*** a hundred sheep, if he loses
15: 8 ***h*** ten silver coins, if she
17: 7 ***h*** a servant plowing or tending
19:15 ***h*** received the kingdom, he then
20:28 ***h*** a wife, and he dies without
22:54 ***H*** arrested Him, they led Him
22:64 And ***h*** blindfolded Him, they
23:14 ***h*** examined Him in your
23:46 ***H*** said this, He breathed
Jn 4:45 ***h*** seen all the things He did in
5: 2 Bethesda, ***h*** five porches.
7:15 letters, ***h*** never studied?"
13: 1 ***h*** loved His own who were in the
13: 2 the devil ***h*** already put it into
13:26 And ***h*** dipped the bread, He
13:30 ***H*** received the piece of bread,
18: 3 ***h*** received a detachment of
18:10 ***h*** a sword, drew it and struck
Acts 2:24 ***h*** loosed the pains of death,
2:33 and ***h*** received from the Father
2:47 praising God and ***h*** favor with
3:26 ***h*** raised up His Servant Jesus,
4:37 ***h*** land, sold it, and brought
7:45 ***h*** received it in turn, also
11:11 ***h*** been sent to me from
12:20 and ***h*** made Blastus the king's
13: 3 ***h*** fasted and prayed, and laid
14:19 and ***h*** persuaded the multitudes,
16:24 ***H*** received such a charge, he put
16:34 ***h*** believed in God with all his
19: 1 ***h*** passed through the upper
19:29 ***h*** seized Gaius and Aristarchus,
21:26 ***h*** been purified with them,
22:12 ***h*** a good testimony with all the

23:27 **h** learned that he was a Roman.
24:22 **h** more accurate knowledge of
26:10 **h** received authority from the
26:22 **h** obtained help from God, to
Rom 2:14 although not **h** the law, are a
2:20 **h** the form of knowledge and
5: 1 **h** been justified by faith, we
5: 9 **h** now been justified by His
5:10 **h** been reconciled, we shall be
6: 9 **h** been raised from the dead,
6:18 And **h** been set free from sin,
6:22 But now **h** been set free from
6:22 and **h** become slaves of God, you
7: 6 **h** died to what we were held by,
9:11 nor **h** done any good or evil,
12: 6 **H** then gifts differing according
15:23 But now no longer **h** a place in
15:23 and **h** a great desire these many
1 Cor 6: 1 **h** a matter against another, go
7:37 **h** no necessity, but has power
11: 4 **h** his head covered, dishonors
12:24 **h** given greater honor to that
2 Cor 2: 3 **h** confidence in you all that my
4:15 **h** spread through the many, may
5: 3 **h** been clothed, we shall not be
6:10 as **h** nothing, and yet
7: 1 **h** these promises, beloved, let
9: 8 always **h** all sufficiency in all
10:15 but **h** hope, that as your faith
Gal 3: 3 **H** begun in the Spirit, are you
3:13 **h** become a curse for us (for it
Eph 1: 5 **h** predestined us to adoption as
1: 9 **h** made known to us the mystery
1:13 **h** believed, you were sealed
2:12 **h** no hope and without God in
2:15 **h** abolished in His flesh the
2:20 **h** been built on the foundation
4:18 **h** their understanding darkened,
5:27 not **h** spot or wrinkle or any
6:13 and **h** done all, to stand.
6:14 **h** girded your waist with truth,
6:14 **h** put on the breastplate of
6:15 and **h** shod your feet with the
Phil 1:14 **h** become confident by my
1:23 **h** a desire to depart and be
1:30 **h** the same conflict which you
2: 2 **h** the same love, being of one
3: 9 not **h** my own righteousness,
4:18 **h** received from Epaphroditus
Col 1:20 **h** made peace through the blood
2:13 **h** forgiven you all trespasses,
2:14 **h** wiped out the handwriting of
2:14 **h** nailed it to the cross.
2:15 **H** disarmed principalities and
1 Th 1: 6 **h** received the word in much
2:17 **h** been taken away from you for
1 Tim 1: 6 **h** strayed, have turned aside to
1:19 **h** faith and a good conscience,
1:19 which some **h** rejected,
3: 4 **h** his children in submission
4: 2 **h** their own conscience seared
4: 8 **h** promise of the life that now
5:12 **h** condemnation because they have
6: 8 And **h** food and clothing, with
2 Tim 2:19 **h** this seal: "The Lord knows
2:26 **h** been taken captive by him to
3: 5 **h** a form of godliness but
4:10 **h** loved this present world, and
Titus 1: 6 **h** faithful children not accused
2: 8 **h** nothing evil to say of you.
3: 7 that **h** been justified by His
Phm 1:21 **H** confidence in your obedience,
Heb 1: 4 **h** become so much better than the
3:16 **h** heard, rebelled? Indeed, was
5: 9 And **h** been perfected, He became
6:20 **h** become High Priest forever
7: 3 **h** neither beginning of days nor
9:12 **h** obtained eternal redemption.
10: 1 **h** a shadow of the good things
10:19 **h** boldness to enter the Holiest
10:21 and **h** a High Priest over the
10:22 **h** our hearts sprinkled from an
11:13 not **h** received the promises,
11:13 but **h** seen them afar off were
11:39 **h** obtained a good testimony
11:40 God **h** provided something better
1 Pe 1: 8 whom **h** not seen you love.
1:23 **h** been born again, not of
2:12 **h** your conduct honorable among
2:24 **h** died to sins, might live for
3: 8 **h** compassion for one another;
3:16 **h** a good conscience, that when
3:22 and authorities and powers **h**
2 Pe 1: 4 **h** escaped the corruption that
2:14 **h** eyes full of adultery and that
2:21 than **h** known it, to turn from
2:22 **h** washed, to her wallowing in
2 Jn 12 **H** many things to write to you,
Jude 5 **h** saved the people out of the
7 **h** given themselves over to
19 divisions, not **h** the Spirit.
Rev 1:12 And **h** turned I saw seven golden
4: 8 each **h** six wings, were full of
5: 6 **h** seven horns and seven eyes,
5: 8 each **h** a harp, and golden bowls
7: 2 **h** the seal of the living God.
8: 3 **h** a golden censer, came and
9:19 **h** heads; and with them they do
12: 3 fiery red dragon **h** seven heads
12:12 **h** great wrath, because he knows
13: 1 **h** seven heads and ten horns,
14: 1 **h** His Father's name written on
14: 6 **h** the everlasting gospel to
14:14 **h** on His head a golden crown,
14:17 he also **h** a sharp sickle.
15: 1 seven angels **h** the seven last
15: 2 of glass, **h** harps of God.
15: 6 seven angels **h** the seven
15: 6 and **h** their chests girded with
17: 3 **h** seven heads and ten horns.
17: 4 **h** in her hand a golden cup full
18: 1 **h** great authority, and the
20: 1 **h** the key to the bottomless pit
21:11 **h** the glory of God. Her light

HAVOC (1/1)

Acts 8: 3 he made **h** of the church,

HAVOCK (KJV) See HAVOC

HAVOTH (3/3)

Num 32:41 and called them **H** Jair.
Deut 3:14 **H** Jair, to this day.)
Judg 10: 4 **H** Jair" to this day, which are

HAWK (3/3)

Lev 11:16 and the **h** after its kind;
Deut 14:15 and the **h** after their kinds;
Job 39:26 Does the **h** fly by your wisdom,

HAWKS (1/1)

Isa 34:15 There also shall the **h** be

HAY (2/2)

Prov 27:25 When the **h** is removed, and the
1 Cor 3:12 precious stones, wood, **h**,

HAZAEL (23/21)

1 Ki 19:15 anoint **H** as king over Syria.
19:17 whoever escapes the sword of **H**,
2 Ki 8: 8 And the king said to **H**,
8: 9 So **H** went to meet him and took a
8:12 And **H** said, "Why is my lord
8:13 So **H** said, "But what is your
8:15 and **H** reigned in his place.
8:28 son of Ahab to war against **H**
8:29 when he fought against **H** king
9:14 against **H** king of Syria.
9:15 on him when he fought with **H**
10:32 and **H** conquered them in all the
12:17 **H** king of Syria went up and
12:17 then **H** set his face to go up to
12:18 and sent them to **H** king of
13: 3 them into the hand of **H** king
13: 3 hand of Ben-Hadad the son of **H**,
13:22 And **H** king of Syria oppressed
13:24 Now **H** king of Syria died.
13:25 hand of Ben-Hadad, the son of **H**,
2 Chr 22: 5 king of Israel to war against **H**
22: 6 when he fought against **H** king
Am 1: 4 send a fire into the house of **H**,

HAZAIAH (1/1)

Neh 11: 5 son of Col-Hozeh, the son of **H**,

HAZAR ADDAR (1/1)

Num 34: 4 then it shall go on to **H**,

HAZAR ENAN (4/4)

Num 34: 9 Ziphron, and it shall end at **H**.
34:10 out your eastern border from **H**
Ezek 47:17 shall be from the Sea to **H**,
48: 1 at the entrance of Hamath, to **H**,

HAZAR GADDAH (1/1)

Josh 15:27 **H**, Heshmon, Beth Pelet,

HAZAR HATTICON (1/1)

Ezek 47:16 to **H** (which is on the border of

HAZAR SHUAL (4/4)

Josh 15:28 **H**, Beersheba, Bizjothjah,
19: 3 **H**, Balah, Ezem,
1 Chr 4:28 dwelt at Beersheba, Moladah, **H**,
Neh 11:27 **H**, and Beersheba and its

HAZAR SUSAH (1/1)

Josh 19: 5 Ziklag, Beth Marcaboth, **H**,

HAZAR SUSIM (1/1)

1 Chr 4:31 Beth Marcaboth, **H**,

HAZARDED (KJV) See RISKED

HAZARHATTICON (KJV) See HAZAR HATTICON

HAZARMAVETH (2/2)

Gen 10:26 begot Almodad, Sheleph, **H**,
1 Chr 1:20 begot Almodad, Sheleph, **H**,

HAZAZON TAMAR (1/1)

2 Chr 20: 2 and they are in **H**" (which is

HAZEL (KJV) See ALMOND

HAZELELPONI (1/1)

1 Chr 4: 3 the name of their sister was **H**;

HAZERIM (KJV) See VILLAGES

HAZEROTH (6/5)

Num 11:35 Hattaavah the people moved to **H**,
11:35 to Hazeroth, and camped at **H**.
12:16 the people moved from **H** and
33:17 Hattaavah and camped at **H**.
33:18 They departed from **H** and camped
Deut 1: 1 between Paran, Tophel, Laban, **H**,

HAZEZON TAMAR (1/1)

Gen 14: 7 the Amorites who dwelt in **H**.

HAZIEL (1/1)

1 Chr 23: 9 sons of Shimei: Shelomith, **H**,

HAZO (1/1)

Gen 22:22 'Chesed, **H**, Pildash,

HAZOR (21/19)

Josh 11: 1 when Jabin king of **H** heard
11:10 back at that time and took **H**,
11:10 for **H** was formerly the head of
11:11 Then he burned **H** with fire.
11:13 except **H** only, which Joshua
12:19 of Madon, one; the king of **H**,
15:23 Kedesh, **H**, Ithnan,
15:25 **H**, Hadattah, Kerioth, Hezron
15:25 Kerioth, Hezron (which is **H**),
19:36 Adamah, Ramah, **H**,
Judg 4: 2 of Canaan, who reigned in **H**.
4:17 peace between Jabin king of **H**
1 Sam 12: 9 commander of the army of **H**,
1 Ki 9:15 Millo, the wall of Jerusalem, **H**,
2 Ki 15:29 Beth Maachah, Janoah, Kedesh, **H**,
Neh 11:33 in **H**, Ramah, Gittaim;
Jer 49:28 and against the kingdoms of **H**,
49:30 O inhabitants of **H**!" says the
49:33 **H** shall be a dwelling for

HE (10435/7554) See APPENDIX

HEAD (361/331) HEADED, HEADS

Gen 3:15 He shall bruise your **h**,
24:26 Then the man bowed down his **h**
24:48 And I bowed my **h** and worshiped
28:11 that place and put it at his **h**,
28:18 stone that he had put at his **h**,
40:13 Pharaoh will lift up your **h**
40:16 three white baskets on my **h**.
40:17 them out of the basket on my **h**.
40:19 Pharaoh will lift off your **h**
40:20 and he lifted up the **h** of the
47:31 Israel bowed himself on the **h**
48:14 and laid it on Ephraim's **h**,
48:14 his left hand on Manasseh's **h**,
48:17 laid his right hand on the **h**
48:17 to remove it from Ephraim's **h**
48:17 Ephraim's head to Manasseh's **h**.
48:18 put your right hand on his **h**.
49:26 They shall be on the **h** of
49:26 And on the crown of the **h** of
Ex 9:31 for the barley was in the **h**
12: 9 its **h** with its legs and its
28:32 shall be an opening for his **h**
29: 6 shall put the turban on his **h**,
29: 7 oil, pour it on his **h**,
29:10 shall put their hands on the **h**
29:15 shall put their hands on the **h**
29:17 with its pieces and with its **h**.
29:19 shall put their hands on the **h**
34: 8 made haste and bowed his **h**
Lev 1: 4 he shall put his hand on the **h**
1: 8 shall lay the parts, the **h**,
1:12 with its **h** and its fat; and the
1:15 to the altar, wring off its **h**,
3: 2 he shall lay his hand on the **h**
3: 8 he shall lay his hand on the **h**
3:13 'He shall lay his hand on its **h**
4: 4 lay his hand on the bull's **h**,
4:11 with its **h** and legs, its
4:15 shall lay their hands on the **h**
4:24 he shall lay his hand on the **h**
4:29 he shall lay his hand on the **h**
4:33 he shall lay his hand on the **h**
5: 8 and wring off its **h** from its
8: 9 And he put the turban on his **h**.
8:12 the anointing oil on Aaron's **h**
8:14 sons laid their hands on the **h**
8:18 sons laid their hands on the **h**
8:20 and Moses burned the **h**,
8:22 sons laid their hands on the **h**
9:13 to him, with its pieces and **h**,
13:12 from his **h** to his foot,
13:29 or woman has a sore on the **h**
13:30 It is a scaly leprosy of the **h**

13:40 hair has fallen from his ***h***,
13:42 And if there is on the bald ***h*** or
13:42 breaking out on his bald ***h*** or
13:43 reddish-white on his bald ***h*** or
13:44 unclean; his sore is on his ***h***.
13:45 shall be torn and his ***h*** bare;
14: 9 shave all the hair off his ***h***
14:18 hand he shall put on the ***h*** of
14:29 hand he shall put on the ***h*** of
16:21 lay both his hands on the ***h*** of
16:21 putting them on the ***h*** of the
19:27 around the sides of your ***h***,
21:10 on whose ***h*** the anointing oil
21:10 shall not uncover his ***h*** nor
24:14 him lay their hands on his ***h***,
Num 1: 4 each one the ***h*** of his father's
5:18 LORD, uncover the woman's ***h***,
6: 5 no razor shall come upon his ***h***;
6: 5 the locks of the hair of his ***h***
6: 7 separation to God is on his ***h***.
6: 9 he defiles his consecrated ***h***,
6: 9 then he shall shave his ***h*** on
6:11 and he shall sanctify his ***h***
6:18 shall shave his consecrated ***h***
6:18 the hair from his consecrated ***h***
17: 3 shall be one rod for the ***h*** of
22:31 and he bowed his ***h*** and fell
25:15 he was ***h*** of the people of a
Deut 14: 1 nor shave the front of your ***h***
19: 5 and the ***h*** slips from the handle
21:12 and she shall shave her ***h*** and
28:13 the LORD will make you the ***h***
28:23 heavens which are over your ***h***
28:35 your foot to the top of your ***h***.
28:44 lend to him; he shall be the ***h***,
33:16 on the ***h*** of Joseph, And on the
33:16 And on the crown of the ***h*** of
33:20 the arm and the crown of his ***h***.
Josh 2:19 blood shall be on his own ***h***,
2:19 his blood shall be on our ***h***
11:10 for Hazor was formerly the ***h*** of
22:14 and each one was the ***h*** of the
Judg 5:26 Sisera, she pierced his ***h***,
9:53 millstone on Abimelech's ***h*** and
10:18 He shall be ***h*** over all the
11: 8 and be our ***h*** over all the
11: 9 them to me, shall I be your ***h***?
11:11 and the people made him ***h*** and
13: 5 no razor shall come upon his ***h***,
16:13 weave the seven locks of my ***h***
16:17 razor has ever come upon my ***h***,
16:19 off the seven locks of his ***h***.
16:22 the hair of his ***h*** began to grow
1 Sam 1:11 no razor shall come upon his ***h***.
4:12 clothes torn and dirt on his ***h***.
5: 4 The ***h*** of Dagon and both the
10: 1 of oil and poured it on his ***h***,
14:45 not one hair of his ***h*** shall
15:17 were you not ***h*** of the tribes
17: 5 had a bronze helmet on his ***h***,
17:38 he put a bronze helmet on his ***h***;
17:46 will strike you and take your ***h***
17:51 and cut off his ***h*** with it.
17:54 And David took the ***h*** of the
17:57 with the ***h*** of the Philistine
19:13 cover of goats' hair for his ***h***,
19:16 cover of goats' hair for his ***h***.
25:39 of Nabal on his own ***h***.
26: 7 stuck in the ground by his ***h***.
26:11 jug of water that are by his ***h***,
26:12 the jug of water by Saul's ***h***,
26:16 jug of water that was by his ***h***.
31: 9 And they cut off his ***h*** and
2 Sam 1: 2 clothes torn and dust on his ***h***.
1:10 the crown that was on his ***h***
1:16 "Your blood is on your own ***h***,
2:16 grasped his opponent by the ***h***
3: 8 Am I a dog's ***h*** that belongs to
3:29 Let it rest on the ***h*** of Joab and
4: 7 beheaded him and took his ***h***,
4: 8 And they brought the ***h*** of
4: 8 Here is the ***h*** of Ishbosheth, the
4:12 But they took the ***h*** of
12:30 their king's crown from his ***h***.
12:30 And it was set on David's ***h***.
13:19 Then Tamar put ashes on her ***h***,
13:19 and laid her hand on her ***h*** and
14:25 his foot to the crown of his ***h***
14:26 when he cut the hair of his ***h***—
14:26 he weighed the hair of his ***h*** at
15:30 and he had his ***h*** covered and
15:32 his robe torn and dust on his ***h***.
16: 9 me go over and take off his ***h***!
18: 9 and his ***h*** caught in the
20:21 his ***h*** will be thrown to you
20:22 And they cut off the ***h*** of Sheba
22:44 as the ***h*** of the nations.
1 Ki 2:32 will return his blood on his ***h***,
2:33 return upon the ***h*** of Joab
2:33 the ***h*** of his descendants
2:37 blood shall be on your own ***h***.
2:44 your wickedness on your own ***h***.
8:32 bringing his way on his ***h***,
19: 6 and there by his ***h*** was a cake
2 Ki 4:19 he said to his father, "My ***h***,
4:19 my ***h***!" So he said to a
6: 5 the iron ax ***h*** fell into the
6:25 besieged it until a donkey's ***h***
6:31 if the ***h*** of Elisha the son of
6:32 sent someone to take away my ***h***?
9: 3 of oil, and pour it on his ***h***,
9: 6 And he poured the oil on his ***h***,
9:30 on her eyes and adorned her ***h***,
19:21 of Jerusalem Has shaken her ***h***
1 Chr 10: 9 stripped him and took his ***h***
10:10 and fastened his ***h*** in the
20: 2 their king's crown from his ***h***,
20: 2 And it was set on David's ***h***.
26:31 Jerijah was ***h*** of the
29:11 You are exalted as ***h*** over all.
2 Chr 6:23 bringing his way on his own ***h***,
13:12 Himself is with us as our ***h***,
20:18 And Jehoshaphat bowed his ***h*** with
Ezra 9: 3 out some of the hair of my ***h***
Esth 2:17 set the royal crown upon her ***h***
6: 8 a royal crest placed on its ***h***.
6:12 mourning and with his ***h***
9:25 Jews should return on his own ***h***,
Job 1:20 tore his robe, and shaved his ***h***;
2: 7 his foot to the crown of his ***h***.
2:12 and sprinkled dust on his ***h***
10:15 I cannot lift up my ***h***.
10:16 If my ***h*** is exalted, You hunt
16: 4 And shake my ***h*** at you;
16:15 And laid my ***h*** in the dust.
19: 9 And taken the crown from my ***h***.
20: 6 And his ***h*** reaches to the
29: 3 When His lamp shone upon my ***h***,
41: 7 Or his ***h*** with fishing spears?
Ps 3: 3 and the One who lifts up my ***h***.
7:16 shall return upon his own ***h***,
18:43 You have made me the ***h*** of the
21: 3 a crown of pure gold upon his ***h***.
22: 7 out the lip, they shake the ***h***,
23: 5 You anoint my ***h*** with oil;
27: 6 And now my ***h*** shall be lifted up
38: 4 iniquities have gone over my ***h***;
40:12 are more than the hairs of my ***h***;
44:14 A shaking of the ***h*** among the
60: 7 also is the helmet for My ***h***;
68:21 But God will wound the ***h*** of His
69: 4 more than the hairs of my ***h***;
83: 2 hate You have lifted up their ***h***.
108: 8 also is the helmet for My ***h***;
110: 7 He shall lift up the ***h***.
133: 2 the precious oil upon the ***h***,
140: 7 You have covered my ***h*** in the
140: 9 As for the ***h*** of those who
141: 5 Let my ***h*** not refuse it.
Prov 1: 9 a graceful ornament on your ***h***,
4: 9 She will place on your ***h*** an
10: 6 Blessings are on the ***h*** of the
11:26 blessing will be on the ***h*** of
16:31 The silver-haired ***h*** is a crown
20:29 of old men is their gray ***h***.
25:22 heap coals of fire on his ***h***,
Eccl 2:14 wise man's eyes are in his ***h***,
9: 8 And let your ***h*** lack no oil.
Song 2: 6 His left hand is under my ***h***,
5: 2 For my ***h*** is covered with dew,
5:11 His ***h*** is like the finest
7: 5 Your ***h*** crowns you like Mount
7: 5 And the hair of your ***h*** is
8: 3 His left hand is under my ***h***,
Isa 1: 5 The whole ***h*** is sick, And the
1: 6 sole of the foot even to the ***h***,
3:17 a scab The crown of the ***h*** of
7: 8 For the ***h*** of Syria is
7: 8 And the ***h*** of Damascus is
7: 9 The ***h*** of Ephraim is Samaria,
7: 9 And the ***h*** of Samaria is
7:20 The ***h*** and the hair of the
9:14 the LORD will cut off ***h*** and
9:15 and honorable, he is the ***h***;
19:15 Which the ***h*** or tail, Palm
28: 1 flower Which is at the ***h*** of
28: 4 flower Which is at the ***h*** of
37:22 of Jerusalem Has shaken her ***h***
51:20 They lie at the ***h*** of all the
58: 5 Is it to bow down his ***h*** like
59:17 a helmet of salvation on His ***h***;
Jer 2:16 broken the crown of your ***h***.
2:37 him With your hands on your ***h***;
9: 1 that my ***h*** were waters, And my
13:21 to be ***h*** over you. Will not
18:16 be astonished And shake his ***h***.
22: 6 The ***h*** of Lebanon; Yet I
23:19 will fall violently on the ***h***
30:23 will fall violently on the ***h***
48:27 You shake your ***h*** in scorn.
48:37 For every ***h*** shall be bald, and
48:45 The crown of the ***h*** of the sons
52:31 lifted up the ***h*** of Jehoiachin
Lam 2:19 at the ***h*** of every street."
3:54 The waters flowed over my ***h***;
4: 1 are scattered At the ***h*** of
5:16 crown has fallen from our ***h***.
Ezek 5: 1 and pass it over your ***h*** and
9:10 their deeds on their own ***h***.
10: 1 firmament that was above the ***h***
10:11 in the direction the ***h*** was
16:12 and a beautiful crown on your ***h***.
16:25 your high places at the ***h*** of
16:31 erected your shrine at the ***h***
16:43 your deeds on your own ***h***,
17:19 I will recompense on his own ***h***.
21:19 put it at the ***h*** of the road to
24:17 bind your turban on your ***h***,
29:18 every ***h*** was made bald, and
33: 4 blood shall be on his own ***h***.
Dan 1:10 Then you would endanger my ***h***
2:28 and the visions of your ***h*** upon
2:32 This image's ***h*** was of fine
2:38 you are this ***h*** of gold.
3:27 the hair of their ***h*** was not
4: 5 my bed and the visions of my ***h***
4:10 were the visions of my ***h***
4:13 I saw in the visions of my ***h***
7: 1 a dream and visions of his ***h***
7: 9 And the hair of His ***h*** was
7:15 and the visions of my ***h***
7:20 ten horns that were on its ***h***,
Hos 1:11 appoint for themselves one ***h***;
Joel 3: 4 retaliation upon your own ***h***;
3: 7 retaliation upon your own ***h***.
Am 2: 7 the earth which is on the ***h***
8:10 waist, And baldness on every ***h***;
Ob 15 shall return upon your own ***h***.
Jon 2: 5 Weeds were wrapped around my ***h***.
4: 6 shade for his ***h*** to deliver
4: 8 and the sun beat on Jonah's ***h***,
Mic 2:13 With the LORD at their ***h***.
Nah 3:10 At the ***h*** of every street;
Hab 3:13 You struck the ***h*** from the
3:14 The ***h*** of his villages.
Zech 1:21 that no one could lift up his ***h***;
3: 5 put a clean turban on his ***h***.
3: 5 put a clean turban on his ***h***,
6:11 and set it on the ***h*** of Joshua
Mt 5:36 "Nor shall you swear by your ***h***,
6:17 anoint your ***h*** and wash your
8:20 Man has nowhere to lay His ***h***.
10:30 But the very hairs of your ***h*** are
14: 8 Give me John the Baptist's ***h***
14:11 And his ***h*** was brought on a
26: 7 and she poured it on His ***h*** as
27:29 thorns, they put it on His ***h***,
27:30 reed and struck Him on the ***h***.
27:37 up over His ***h*** the accusation
Mk 4:28 first the blade, then the ***h***,
4:28 that the full grain in the ***h***.
6:24 The ***h*** of John the Baptist!"
6:25 you to give me at once the ***h***
6:27 and commanded his ***h*** to be
6:28 brought his ***h*** on a platter, and
12: 4 stones, wounded him in the ***h***,
14: 3 flask and poured it on His ***h***.
15:17 of thorns, put it on His ***h***,
15:19 Then they struck Him on the ***h***
Lk 7:38 them with the hair of her ***h***;
7:44 them with the hair of her ***h***.
7:46 You did not anoint My ***h*** with
9:58 Man has nowhere to lay His ***h***.
12: 7 But the very hairs of your ***h*** are
21:18 But not a hair of your ***h*** shall
Jn 13: 9 but also my hands and my ***h***!"
19: 2 of thorns and put it on His ***h***,
19:30 is finished!" And bowing His ***h***,
20: 7 that had been around His ***h***,
20:12 one at the ***h*** and the other at
Acts 27:14 a tempestuous ***h*** wind arose,
27:15 and could not ***h*** into the wind,
27:34 from the ***h*** of any of you."
Rom 12:20 coals of fire on his ***h***.
1 Cor 11: 3 I want you to know that the ***h***
11: 3 the ***h*** of woman is man, and the
11: 3 and the ***h*** of Christ is God.
11: 4 having his ***h*** covered,
11: 4 head covered, dishonors his ***h***.
11: 5 prays or prophesies with her ***h***
11: 5 head uncovered dishonors her ***h***,
11: 5 is one and the same as if her ***h***
11: 7 ought not to cover his ***h***,
11:10 symbol of authority on her ***h***,
11:13 woman to pray to God with her ***h***
12:21 nor again the ***h*** to the feet,
Eph 1:22 and gave Him to be ***h*** over all
4:15 things into Him who is the ***h***—
5:23 husband is ***h*** of the wife,
5:23 Christ is ***h*** of the church;
Col 1:18 And He is the ***h*** of the body, the
2:10 who is the ***h*** of all
2:19 and not holding fast to the ***H***,
Rev 1:14 His ***h*** and hair were white like
10: 1 And a rainbow was on his ***h***,
12: 1 and on her ***h*** a garland of
14:14 having on His ***h*** a golden crown,
19:12 and on His ***h*** were many crowns.

HEADBANDS (1/1)

Isa 3:20 the leg ornaments, and the ***h***;

HEADDRESSES (1/1)

Isa 3:20 The ***h***, the leg ornaments,

HEADED (3/3) HEAD

Gen 31:21 and ***h*** toward the mountains of
Lev 19:32 before the gray ***h*** and honor
1 Sam 6:12 Then the cows ***h*** straight for the

HEADLONG (2/2)

Jer 49: 5 shall be driven out, everyone ***h***,
Acts 1:18 of iniquity; and falling ***h***,

HEADS (172/158) HEAD

Gen 41: 5 and suddenly seven ***h*** of grain
41: 6 Then behold, seven thin ***h***,
41: 7 And the seven thin ***h*** devoured
41: 7 the seven plump and full ***h***.
41:22 and suddenly seven ***h*** came up on
41:23 "Then behold, seven ***h***,
41:24 And the thin ***h*** devoured the

H

41:24 heads devoured the seven good **h**.
41:26 and the seven good **h** are seven
41:27 and the seven empty **h** blighted
43:28 And they bowed their **h** down
Ex 4:31 then they bowed their **h** and
6:14 These are the **h** of their
6:25 These are the **h** of the
12:27 ' So the people bowed their **h**
18:25 and made them **h** over the
Lev 2:14 firstfruits green **h** of grain
2:14 fire, grain beaten from full **h**.
10: 6 Do not uncover your **h** nor tear
21: 5 make any bald place on their **h**,
Num 1:16 **h** of the divisions in Israel.
7: 2 the **h** of their fathers' houses,
8:12 shall lay their hands on the **h**
10: 4 the **h** of the divisions of
13: 3 who were **h** of the children
30: 1 spoke to the **h** of the tribes
Deut 1:13 will make them **h** over you.'
1:15 So I took the **h** of your tribes,
1:15 and made them **h** over you,
5:23 all the **h** of your tribes and
23:25 you may pluck the **h** with your
32:42 From the **h** of the leaders of
33:21 with the **h** of the people;
Josh 7: 6 and they put dust on their **h**.
14: 1 and the **h** of the fathers of the
19:51 and the **h** of the fathers of the
21: 1 Then the **h** of the fathers'
21: 1 and to the **h** of the fathers'
22:21 answered and said to the **h** of
22:30 the **h** of the divisions of
23: 2 for their elders, for their **h**,
24: 1 elders of Israel, for their **h**,
Judg 7:25 and brought the **h** of Oreb
8:28 so that they lifted their **h** no
9:57 God returned on their own **h**,
Ruth 2: 2 and glean **h** of grain after him
1 Sam 29: 4 if not with the **h** of these men?
2 Sam 15:30 were with him covered their **h**
1 Ki 8: 1 elders of Israel and all the **h**
20:31 waists and ropes around our **h**,
20:32 and put ropes around their **h**,
2 Ki 10: 6 take the **h** of the men, your
10: 7 put their **h** in baskets and sent
10: 8 They have brought the **h** of the
1 Chr 5:24 These were the **h** of their
5:24 and **h** of their fathers'
7: 2 **h** of their father's house.
7: 7 They were **h** of their fathers'
7: 9 **h** of their fathers' houses,
7:11 these sons of Jediael were **h**
7:40 **h** of their fathers' houses,
8: 6 who were the **h** of the fathers'
8:10 **h** of their fathers' houses.
8:13 who were **h** of their fathers'
8:28 These were **h** of the fathers'
9: 9 were **h** of a father's house
9:13 **h** of their fathers' houses—one
9:33 **h** of the fathers' houses of
9:34 These **h** of the fathers' houses
9:34 houses of the Levites were **h**
11:10 Now these were the **h** of the
12:19 Saul and endanger our **h**.
15:12 You are the **h** of the fathers'
23: 9 These were the **h** of the
23:24 the **h** of the fathers' houses as
24: 4 of Eleazar were sixteen **h** of
24: 4 and eight **h** of their fathers'
24: 6 and the **h** of the fathers'
24:31 and the **h** of the fathers'
26:21 **h** of their fathers' houses, of
26:26 which King David and the **h** of
26:32 **h** of fathers' houses, whom
27: 1 the **h** of fathers' houses, the
29:20 and bowed their **h** and
2 Chr 1: 2 the **h** of the fathers' houses.
5: 2 elders of Israel and all the **h**
28:12 Then some of the **h** of the
29:30 and they bowed their **h** and
Ezra 1: 5 Then the **h** of the fathers'
2:68 Some of the **h** of the fathers'
3:12 the priests and Levites and **h**
4: 2 came to Zerubbabel and the **h**
4: 3 Jeshua and the rest of the **h**
8: 1 These are the **h** of their
8:29 priests and the Levites and **h**
9: 6 have risen higher than our **h**,
10:16 with certain **h** of the fathers'
Neh 4: 4 their reproach on their own **h**,
7:70 And some of the **h** of the
7:71 Some of the **h** of the fathers'
8: 6 And they bowed their **h** and
8:13 the **h** of the fathers' houses
9: 1 and with dust on their **h**.
11: 3 are the **h** of the province
11:13 **h** of the fathers' houses,
11:16 of the **h** of the Levites, had
12: 7 were the **h** of the priests
12:12 the **h** of the fathers' houses
12:22 and priests who had been **h**
12:23 the **h** of the fathers' houses
12:24 And the **h** of the Levites were
Job 24:24 out like the **h** of grain.
Ps 24: 7 Lift up your **h**, O you gates!
24: 9 Lift up your **h**, O you gates!
66:12 caused men to ride over our **h**;
74:13 You broke the **h** of the sea
74:14 You broke the **h** of Leviathan in
109:25 look at me, they shake their **h**.
110: 6 He shall execute the **h** of many
Isa 15: 2 On all their **h** will be
17: 5 And reaps the **h** with his arm;
17: 5 shall be as he who gathers **h**
29:10 And He has covered your **h**,
35:10 everlasting joy on their **h**.
51:11 everlasting joy on their **h**.
Jer 14: 3 confounded And covered their **h**.
14: 4 They covered their **h**.
Lam 2:10 They throw dust on their **h**
2:10 of Jerusalem Bow their **h** to
2:15 They hiss and shake their **h**
Ezek 1:22 of the firmament above the **h**
1:22 stretched out over their **h**.
1:25 that was over their **h**;
1:26 the firmament over their **h**
7:18 face, Baldness on all their **h**.
11:21 their deeds on their own **h**,
13:18 veils for the **h** of people
22:31 their deeds on their own **h**,
23:15 Flowing turbans on their **h**,
23:42 and beautiful crowns on their **h**.
24:23 turbans shall be on your **h** and
27:30 and cast dust on their **h**;
32:27 laid their swords under their **h**,
44:18 have linen turbans on their **h**
44:20 shall neither shave their **h**
Dan 7: 6 The beast also had four **h**,
Am 9: 1 them on the **h** of them all.
Mic 3: 1 O **h** of Jacob, And you rulers
3: 9 You **h** of the house of Jacob
3:11 Her **h** judge for a bribe, Her
Mt 12: 1 and began to pluck **h** of grain
27:39 Him, wagging their **h**
Mk 2:23 disciples began to pluck the **h**
15:29 wagging their **h** and saying,
Lk 6: 1 plucked the **h** of grain
21:28 look up and lift up your **h**,
Acts 18: 6 blood be upon your own **h**;
21:24 so that they may shave their **h**,
Rev 4: 4 had crowns of gold on their **h**.
9: 7 On their **h** were crowns of
9:17 and the **h** of the horses were
9:17 of the horses were like the **h**
9:19 are like serpents, having **h**;
12: 3 red dragon having seven **h** and
12: 3 and seven diadems on his **h**.
13: 1 having seven **h** and ten horns,
13: 1 and on his **h** a blasphemous
13: 3 And I saw one of his **h** as if
17: 3 having seven **h** and ten horns.
17: 7 which has the seven **h** and the
17: 9 The seven **h** are seven mountains
18:19 They threw dust on their **h** and

HEADSTONE (KJV) See CAPSTONE

HEADSTRONG (1/1)

2 Tim 3: 4 traitors, **h**, haughty, lovers

HEADY (KJV) See HEADSTRONG

HEAL (46/45) HEALED, HEALING, HEALS

Num 12:13 Please **h** her, O God, I pray!"
Deut 32:39 I make alive; I wound and I **h**;
2 Ki 5: 3 is in Samaria! For he would **h**
5: 6 that you may **h** him of his
5: 7 man sends a man to me to **h** him
5:11 place, and **h** the leprosy.'
20: 5 surely I will **h** you. On the
20: 8 the sign that the LORD will **h**
2 Chr 7:14 their sin and **h** their land.
Ps 6: 2 **h** me, for my bones are
41: 4 **H** my soul, for I have sinned
60: 2 **H** its breaches, for it is
Eccl 3: 3 time to kill, And a time to **h**;
Isa 19:22 He will strike and **h** it;
19:22 will be entreated by them and **h**
57:18 and will **h** him; I will also
57:19 LORD, "And I will **h** him."
61: 1 He has sent Me to **h** the
Jer 3:22 And I will **h** your
17:14 **H** me, O LORD, and I shall be
30:17 health to you And **h** you
33: 6 I will **h** them and reveal to
Lam 2:13 as the sea; Who can **h** you?
Hos 5:13 Nor **h** you of your wound.
6: 1 but He will **h** us; He has
14: 4 I will **h** their backsliding, I
Zech 11:16 nor **h** those that are broken,
Mt 8: 7 I will come and **h** him."
10: 1 and to **h** all kinds of sickness
10: 8 **H** the sick, cleanse the lepers,
12:10 Is it lawful to **h** on the
13:15 that I should **h** them.'
Mk 3: 2 whether He would **h** him on the
3:15 have power to **h** sicknesses
Lk 4:18 to **h** the brokenhearted,
4:23 **h** yourself! Whatever we have
5:17 of the Lord was present to **h**
6: 7 whether He would **h** on the
7: 3 with Him to come and **h** his
9: 2 the kingdom of God and to **h**
10: 9 And **h** the sick there, and say to
14: 3 Is it lawful to **h** on the
Jn 4:47 Him to come down and **h** his son,
12:40 So that I should **h**
Acts 4:30 stretching out Your hand to **h**,
28:27 I should **h** them."

HEALED (78/76) HEAL

Gen 20:17 and God **h** Abimelech, his wife,
Ex 21:19 for him to be thoroughly **h**.
Lev 13:18 a boil in the skin, and it is **h**,
13:37 grown up in it, the scale has **h**.
14: 3 if the leprosy is **h** in the
14:48 clean, because the plague is **h**.
Deut 28:27 from which you cannot be **h**.
28:35 severe boils which cannot be **h**,
Josh 5: 8 in the camp till they were **h**.
1 Sam 6: 3 Then you will be **h**,
2 Ki 2:21 I have **h** this water; from it
2:22 So the water remains **h** to this
2 Chr 30:20 listened to Hezekiah and **h** the
Ps 30: 2 out to You, And You **h** me.
107:20 He sent His word and **h** them,
Isa 6:10 heart, And return and be **h**.
53: 5 And by His stripes we are **h**.
Jer 6:14 They have also **h** the hurt of My
8:11 For they have **h** the hurt of the
15:18 Which refuses to be **h**?
17:14 me, O LORD, and I shall be **h**;
51: 8 her pain; Perhaps she may be **h**.
51: 9 We would have **h** Babylon, But
51: 9 Babylon, But she is not **h**.
Ezek 34: 4 nor have you **h** those who were
47: 8 the sea, its waters are **h**.
47: 9 go there; for they will be **h**,
47:11 and marshes will not be **h**;
Hos 7: 1 When I would have **h** Israel,
11: 3 But they did not know that I **h**
Mt 4:24 paralytics; and He **h** them.
8: 8 word, and my servant will be **h**.
8:13 And his servant was **h** that
8:16 and **h** all who were sick,
12:15 Him, and He **h** them all.
12:22 and He **h** him, so that the blind
14:14 for them, and **h** their sick.
15:28 And her daughter was **h** from
15:30 Jesus' feet, and He **h** them.
19: 2 and He **h** them there.
21:14 the temple, and He **h** them.
Mk 1:34 Then He **h** many who were sick
3:10 For He **h** many, so that as many
5:23 hands on her, that she may be **h**,
5:29 in her body that she was **h** of
5:34 and be **h** of your affliction."
6: 5 on a few sick people and **h**
6:13 were sick, and **h** them.
Lk 4:40 on every one of them and **h**
5:15 and to be **h** by Him of their
6:17 who came to hear Him and be **h**
6:18 And they were **h**.
6:19 out from Him and **h** them all.
7: 7 word, and my servant will be **h**.
8: 2 certain women who had been **h**
8:36 had been demon-possessed was **h**.
8:43 physicians and could not be **h**
8:47 touched Him and how she was **h**
9:11 and **h** those who had need of
9:42 **h** the child, and gave him back
13:14 because Jesus had **h** on the
13:14 come and be **h** on them,
14: 4 And He took him and **h** him, and
17:15 them, when he saw that he was **h**,
22:51 And He touched his ear and **h**
Jn 5:13 But the one who was **h** did not
Acts 3:11 Now as the lame man who was **h**
4:14 seeing the man who had been **h**
5:16 spirits, and they were all **h**.
8: 7 were paralyzed and lame were **h**.
14: 9 that he had faith to be **h**,
28: 8 he laid his hands on him and **h**
28: 9 diseases also came and were **h**.
Heb 12:13 be dislocated, but rather be **h**.
Jas 5:16 one another, that you may be **h**.
1 Pe 2:24 whose stripes you were **h**.
Rev 13: 3 and his deadly wound was **h**.
13:12 beast, whose deadly wound was **h**.

HEALING (15/14) HEAL, HEALINGS

Isa 58: 8 Your **h** shall spring forth
Jer 14:19 us so that there is no **h** for
14:19 no good; And for the time of **h**,
30:13 You have no **h** medicines.
33: 6 I will bring it health and **h**;
Ezek 30:21 it has not been bandaged for **h**,
Nah 3:19 Your injury has no **h**,
Mal 4: 2 shall arise With **h** in His
Mt 4:23 and **h** all kinds of sickness and
9:35 and **h** every sickness and every
Lk 9: 6 the gospel and **h** everywhere.
9:11 healed those who had need of **h**.
Acts 4:22 old on whom this miracle of **h**
10:38 went about doing good and **h** all
Rev 22: 2 for the **h** of the nations.

HEALINGS (3/3) HEALING

1 Cor 12: 9 to another gifts of **h** by the
12:28 that miracles, then gifts of **h**,
12:30 Do all have gifts of **h**?

HEALS (5/5) HEAL

Ex 15:26 For I am the LORD who **h**
Ps 103: 3 Who **h** all your diseases,
147: 3 He **h** the brokenhearted And
Isa 30:26 the bruise of His people And **h**

Acts 9:34 Jesus the Christ ***h*** you.

HEALTH (13/13) HEALTHY

Gen 43:28 our father is in good ***h***;
2 Sam 20: 9 said to Amasa, "Are you in ***h***,
Ps 38: 3 Nor any ***h*** in my bones
Prov 3: 8 It will be ***h*** to your flesh,
4:22 And ***h*** to all their flesh.
12:18 tongue of the wise promotes ***h***.
13:17 a faithful ambassador brings ***h***.
16:24 Sweetness to the soul and ***h*** to
Jer 8:15 And for a time of ***h***,
8:22 is there no recovery For the ***h***
30:17 For I will restore ***h*** to you
33: 6 I will bring it ***h*** and healing;
3 Jn 2 in all things and be in ***h***,

HEALTHY (2/2) HEALTH

Job 39: 4 Their young ones are ***h***,
Prov 15:30 a good report makes the bones ***h***.

HEAP (47/43) HEAPED, HEAPS

Gen 31:46 they took stones and made a ***h***,
31:46 and they ate there on the ***h***.
31:48 This ***h*** is a witness between you
31:51 Here is this ***h*** and here is this
31:52 This ***h*** is a witness, and this
31:52 I will not pass beyond this ***h***
31:52 you will not pass beyond this ***h***
Ex 15: 8 floods stood upright like a ***h***;
Deut 13:16 It shall be a ***h*** forever;
32:23 I will ***h*** disasters on them;
Josh 3:13 and they shall stand as a ***h***.
3:16 and rose in a ***h*** very far away
7:26 they raised over him a great ***h***
8:28 burned Ai and made it a ***h***
8:29 and raise over it a great ***h*** of
Ruth 3: 7 to lie down at the end of the ***h***
1 Sam 2: 8 lifts the beggar from the ash ***h***,
2 Sam 18:17 and laid a very large ***h*** of
Ezra 6:11 his house be made a refuse ***h***
Job 8:17 roots wrap around the rock ***h***,
16: 4 I could ***h*** up words against
30:24 out His hand against a ***h*** of
Ps 33: 7 of the sea together as a ***h***;
78:13 the waters stand up like a ***h***.
113: 7 the needy out of the ash ***h***,
Prov 25:22 For so you will ***h*** coals of
Song 7: 2 Your waist is a ***h*** of wheat
Isa 17: 1 And it will be a ruinous ***h***.
17:11 the harvest will be a ***h*** of
25:10 trampled down for the refuse ***h***.
57:14 '***H*** it up! Heap it up!
57:14 'Heap it up! ***H*** it up!
Jer 9:11 I will make Jerusalem a ***h*** of
51:37 Babylon shall become a ***h***,
Ezek 4: 2 and ***h*** up a mound against it;
17:17 when they ***h*** up a siege mound
21:22 to ***h*** up a siege mound, and to
24:10 ***H*** on the wood, Kindle the fire
26: 8 he will ***h*** up a siege mound
Dan 2: 5 houses shall be made an ash ***h***.
3:29 houses shall be made an ash ***h***;
Mic 1: 6 I will make Samaria a ***h*** of
Hab 1:10 For they ***h*** up earthen mounds
3:15 Through the ***h*** of great waters.
Hag 2:16 when one came to a ***h*** of twenty
Rom 12:20 in so doing you will ***h***
2 Tim 4: 3 they will ***h*** up for themselves

HEAPED (2/2) HEAP

Zech 9: 3 ***H*** up silver like the dust,
Jas 5: 3 You have ***h*** up treasure in the

HEAPS (20/19) HEAP

Ex 8:14 gathered them together in ***h***,
Judg 15:16 ***H*** upon heaps, With the
15:16 of a donkey, Heaps upon ***h***,
2 Ki 10: 8 Lay them in two ***h*** at the
19:25 fortified cities into ***h*** of
2 Chr 31: 6 LORD their God they laid in ***h***.
31: 7 they began laying them in ***h***,
31: 8 the leaders came and saw the ***h***,
31: 9 the Levites concerning the ***h***.
Neh 4: 2 revive the stones from the ***h***
Job 27:16 Though he ***h*** up silver like
Ps 39: 6 He ***h*** up riches, And does not
79: 1 They have laid Jerusalem in ***h***.
Isa 37:26 fortified cities into ***h*** of
Jer 26:18 Jerusalem shall become ***h*** of
50:26 Cast her up as ***h*** of ruins,
Lam 4: 5 up in scarlet Embrace ash ***h***.
Hos 12:11 their altars shall be ***h*** in
Mic 3:12 Jerusalem shall become ***h*** of
Hab 2: 5 to himself all nations And ***h***

HEAR (537/504) HEARD, HEARER, HEARING, HEARS, UNHEARD

Gen 4:23 ***h*** my voice; Wives of Lamech,
21: 6 and all who ***h*** will laugh with
23: 6 ***H*** us, my lord: You are a mighty
23: 8 ***h*** me, and meet with Ephron the
23:11 ***h*** me: I give you the field and
23:13 please ***h*** me. I will give you
37: 6 Please ***h*** this dream which I have
42:21 with us, and we would not ***h***;
49: 2 "Gather together and ***h***,
Ex 7:16 until now you would not ***h***!
15:14 The people will ***h*** and be
19: 9 that the people may ***h*** when I
20:19 speak with us, and we will ***h***;
22:23 I will surely ***h*** their cry;
22:27 when he cries to Me, I will ***h***,
32:18 But the sound of singing I ***h***.
Num 9: 8 that I may ***h*** what the LORD
12: 6 ***H*** now My words: If there is a
14:13 Then the Egyptians will ***h*** it,
16: 8 ***H*** now, you sons of Levi:
20:10 ***H*** now, you rebels! Must we bring
23:18 'Rise up, Balak, and ***h***!
Deut 1:16 ***H*** the cases between your
1:17 you shall ***h*** the small as well
1:17 to me, and I will ***h*** it.'
2:25 who shall ***h*** the report of you,
4: 6 of the peoples who will ***h*** all
4:10 and I will let them ***h*** My words,
4:28 which neither see nor ***h*** nor eat
4:33 Did any people ever ***h*** the
4:36 Out of heaven He let you ***h*** His
5: 1 said to them: "***H***, O Israel,
5:25 if we ***h*** the voice of the LORD
5:27 You go near and ***h*** all that the
5:27 and we will ***h*** and do it.'
6: 3 'Therefore ***h***, O Israel, and
6: 4 ***H***, O Israel: The LORD our
9: 1 '***H***, O Israel: You are to
13:11 So all Israel shall ***h*** and fear,
13:12 If you ***h*** someone in one of your
17: 4 and you ***h*** of it, then you
17:13 And all the people shall ***h*** and
18:15 your brethren. Him you shall ***h***,
18:16 Let me not ***h*** again the voice of
18:19 be that whoever will not ***h*** My
19:20 And those who remain shall ***h*** and
20: 3 say to them, '***H***, O Israel:
21:21 and all Israel shall ***h*** and
29: 4 and eyes to see and ears to ***h***,
30:12 that we may ***h*** it and do it?'
30:13 that we may ***h*** it and do it?'
30:17 turns away so that you do not ***h***,
31:12 that they may ***h*** and that they
31:13 may ***h*** and learn to fear the
32: 1 will speak; And ***h***, O earth,
33: 7 Judah: "***H***, LORD, the voice
Josh 3: 9 and ***h*** the words of the LORD
6: 5 and when you ***h*** the sound of
7: 9 inhabitants of the land will ***h***
Judg 5: 3 '***H***, O kings! Give ear,
5:16 To ***h*** the pipings for the
7:11 and you shall ***h*** what they say;
14:13 riddle, that we may ***h*** it."
1 Sam 2:23 For I ***h*** of your evil dealings
2:24 is not a good report that I ***h***.
8:18 and the LORD will not ***h*** you in
13: 3 Let the Hebrews ***h***!"
15:14 lowing of the oxen which I ***h***?
22: 7 ***H*** now, you Benjamites! Will the
22:12 ***H*** now, son of Ahitub!" And he
25:24 and ***h*** the words of your
26:19 let my lord the king ***h*** the
2 Sam 5:24 when you ***h*** the sound of
14:16 For the king will ***h*** and deliver
15: 3 is no deputy of the king to ***h***
15:10 As soon as you ***h*** the sound of
15:35 it will be that whatever you ***h***
15:36 shall send me everything you ***h***.
16:21 and all Israel will ***h*** that you
17: 5 and let us ***h*** what he says
19:35 Can I ***h*** any longer the voice of
20:16 out from the city, "***H***, Hear!
20:16 'Hear, ***H***! Please say to
20:17 ***H*** the words of your
22:45 to me; As soon as they ***h***,
1 Ki 4:34 came to ***h*** the wisdom of
8:29 that You may ***h*** the prayer
8:30 And may You ***h*** the supplication
8:30 ***H*** in heaven Your dwelling
8:30 dwelling place; and when You ***h***,
8:32 then ***h*** in heaven, and act, and
8:34 then ***h*** in heaven, and forgive
8:36 then ***h*** in heaven, and forgive
8:39 then ***h*** in heaven Your dwelling
8:42 (for they will ***h*** of Your great
8:43 ***h*** in heaven Your dwelling place,
8:45 then ***h*** in heaven their prayer
8:49 then ***h*** in heaven Your dwelling
10: 8 continually before you and ***h***
10:24 the presence of Solomon to ***h***
18:26 ***h*** us!" But there was no
18:37 ***H*** me, O LORD, hear me, that
18:37 ***h*** me, that this people may know
22:19 Therefore ***h*** the word of the
2 Ki 7: 1 '***H*** the word of the LORD.
7: 6 the army of the Syrians to ***h***
17:14 Nevertheless they would not ***h***,
18:12 and they would neither ***h*** nor do
18:28 ***H*** the word of the great king,
19: 4 that the LORD your God will ***h***
19: 7 and he shall ***h*** a rumor and
19:16 Your ear, O LORD, and ***h***;
19:16 and ***h*** the words of Sennacherib,
19:25 Did you not ***h*** long ago How I
20:16 ***H*** the word of the LORD:
1 Chr 14:15 when you ***h*** a sound of marching
28: 2 ***H*** me, my brethren and my people:
2 Chr 6:20 that You may ***h*** the prayer which
6:21 And may You ***h*** the supplications
6:21 ***H*** from heaven Your dwelling
6:21 dwelling place, and when You ***h***,
6:23 then ***h*** from heaven, and act, and
6:25 then ***h*** from heaven and forgive
6:27 then ***h*** in heaven, and forgive
6:30 then ***h*** from heaven Your dwelling
6:33 then ***h*** from heaven Your dwelling
6:35 then ***h*** from heaven their prayer
6:39 then ***h*** from heaven Your dwelling
7:14 then I will ***h*** from heaven, and
9: 7 continually before you and ***h***
9:23 the presence of Solomon to ***h***
13: 4 ***H*** me, Jeroboam and all Israel:
15: 2 ***H*** me, Asa, and all Judah and
18:18 Therefore ***h*** the word of the
20: 9 and You will ***h*** and save.'
20:20 ***H*** me, O Judah and you
28:11 Now ***h*** me, therefore, and return
29: 5 ***H*** me, Levites! Now sanctify
Neh 1: 6 that You may ***h*** the prayer of
4: 4 ***H***, O our God, for we are
4:20 Wherever you ***h*** the sound of the
8: 2 and women and all who could ***h***
9:29 their necks, And would not ***h***.
13:27 Should we then ***h*** of your doing
Job 3:18 They do not ***h*** the voice of the
5:27 ***H*** it, and know for
13: 6 Now ***h*** my reasoning, And heed
15:17 ***h*** me; What I have seen I will
22:27 He will ***h*** you, And you will
26:14 And how small a whisper we ***h***
27: 9 Will God ***h*** his cry When
31:35 that I had one to ***h*** me!
33: 1 ***h*** my speech, And listen to all
34: 2 '***H*** my words, you wise men;
34:16 ***h*** this; listen to the sound of
37: 2 ***H*** attentively the thunder of
Ps 4: 1 ***H*** me when I call, O God of my
4: 1 on me, and ***h*** my prayer.
4: 3 The LORD will ***h*** when I call
5: 3 My voice You shall ***h*** in the
10:17 You will cause Your ear to ***h***,
13: 3 Consider and ***h*** me, O LORD my
17: 1 ***H*** a just cause, O LORD,
17: 6 for You will ***h*** me, O God;
17: 6 to me, and ***h*** my speech.
18:44 As soon as they ***h*** of me they
22: 2 the daytime, but You do not ***h***;
27: 7 ***H***, O LORD, when I cry with
28: 2 ***H*** the voice of my supplications
30:10 ***H***, O LORD, and have mercy
31:13 For I ***h*** the slander of many;
34: 2 The humble shall ***h*** of it and
38:13 I, like a deaf man, do not ***h***;
38:14 I am like a man who does not ***h***,
38:15 O LORD, I hope; You will ***h***,
38:16 ***H*** me, lest they rejoice over
39:12 ***H*** my prayer, O LORD, And give
49: 1 ***H*** this, all peoples
50: 7 '***H***, O My people, and I
51: 8 Make me ***h*** joy and gladness,
54: 2 ***H*** my prayer, O God; Give ear
55: 2 and ***h*** me; I am restless in my
55:17 And He shall ***h*** my voice.
55:19 God will ***h***, and afflict
60: 5 Your right hand, and ***h*** me.
61: 1 ***H*** my cry, O God; Attend to
64: 1 ***H*** my voice, O God, in my
65: 2 O You who ***h*** prayer, To You all
66:16 Come and ***h***, all you who
66:18 my heart, The Lord will not ***h***.
69:13 ***H*** me in the truth of Your
69:16 ***H*** me, O LORD, for Your
69:17 in trouble; ***H*** me speedily.
81: 8 '***H***, O My people, and I
84: 8 ***h*** my prayer; Give ear, O God
85: 8 I will ***h*** what God the LORD
86: 1 ***h*** me; For I am poor and
92:11 My ears ***h*** my desire on the
94: 9 planted the ear, shall He not ***h***?
95: 7 if you will ***h*** His voice:
102: 1 ***H*** my prayer, O LORD, And let
102:20 To ***h*** the groaning of the
108: 6 Your right hand, and ***h*** me.
115: 6 have ears, but they do not ***h***;
119:145 ***H*** me, O LORD! I will keep
119:149 ***H*** my voice according to Your
130: 2 ***h*** my voice! Let Your ears be
135:17 have ears, but they do not ***h***;
138: 4 When they ***h*** the words of Your
140: 6 ***H*** the voice of my
141: 6 And they ***h*** my words, for they
143: 1 ***H*** my prayer, O LORD, Give ear
143: 8 Cause me to ***h*** Your
145:19 He also will ***h*** their cry and
Prov 1: 5 A wise man will ***h*** and increase
1: 8 ***h*** the instruction of your
4: 1 ***H***, my children, the
4:10 ***H***, my son, and receive my
5: 7 Therefore ***h*** me now, my
8:33 ***H*** instruction and be wise, And
13: 8 But the poor does not ***h***
22:17 Incline your ear and ***h*** the
23:19 ***H***, my son, and be wise;
Eccl 5: 1 and draw near to ***h*** rather than
7: 5 It is better to ***h*** the rebuke
7: 5 the wise Than for a man to ***h***
7:21 Lest you ***h*** your servant
12:13 Let us ***h*** the conclusion of the
Song 2:14 Let me ***h*** your voice; For your
8:13 Let me ***h*** it! THE SHULAMITE
Isa 1: 2 ***H***, O heavens, and give
1:10 ***H*** the word of the LORD, You
1:15 many prayers, I will not ***h***.

6:10 And ***h*** with their ears, And
7:13 ***H*** now, O house of David! Is it
18: 3 blows a trumpet, you ***h*** it.
28:12 Yet they would not ***h***.
28:14 Therefore ***h*** the word of the
28:23 Give ear and ***h*** my voice,
28:23 Listen and ***h*** my speech.
29:18 In that day the deaf shall ***h***
30: 9 Children who will not ***h*** the
30:21 Your ears shall ***h*** a word behind
32: 3 And the ears of those who ***h***
32: 9 ***H*** my voice; You complacent
33:13 ***H***, you who are afar off,
34: 1 Come near, you nations, to ***h***;
34: 1 you people! Let the earth ***h***,
36:13 ***H*** the words of the great king,
37: 4 that the LORD your God will ***h***
37: 7 and he shall ***h*** a rumor and
37:17 Your ear, O LORD, and ***h***;
37:17 and ***h*** all the words of
37:26 Did you not ***h*** long ago How I
39: 5 ***H*** the word of the LORD of
41:17 will ***h*** them; I, the God of
42:18 ***H***, you deaf; And look,
42:20 the ears, but he does not ***h***.
42:23 Who will listen and ***h*** for the
43: 9 Or let them ***h*** and say, "It
44: 1 Yet ***h*** now, O Jacob My servant,
47: 8 Therefore ***h*** this now, you who
48: 1 ***H*** this, O house of Jacob, Who
48: 3 and I caused them to ***h*** it.
48: 6 I have made you ***h*** new things
48: 8 Surely you did not ***h***,
48:14 assemble yourselves, and ***h***!
48:16 ***h*** this: I have not spoken in
50: 4 He awakens My ear To ***h*** as the
51:21 Therefore please ***h*** this, you
55: 3 ***H***, and your soul shall live;
59: 1 ear heavy, That it cannot ***h***.
59: 2 you, So that He will not ***h***.
65:12 When I spoke, you did not ***h***,
65:24 are still speaking, I will ***h***.
66: 4 When I spoke they did not ***h***;
66: 5 ***H*** the word of the LORD, You
Jer 2: 4 ***H*** the word of the LORD,
4:21 And ***h*** the sound of the
5:21 ***H*** this now, O foolish people,
5:21 And who have ears and ***h*** not:
6:10 give warning, That they may ***h***?
6:18 Therefore ***h***, you nations,
6:19 ***H***, O earth! Behold, I will
7: 2 ***H*** the word of the LORD, all
7:13 and speaking, but you did not ***h***,
7:16 for I will not ***h*** you.
9:10 Nor can men ***h*** the voice of
9:20 Yet ***h*** the word of the LORD, O
10: 1 ***H*** the word which the LORD
11: 2 ***H*** the words of this covenant,
11: 6 ***H*** the words of this covenant and
11:10 forefathers who refused to ***h***
11:14 for I will not ***h*** them in the
13:10 who refuse to ***h*** My words, who
13:11 for glory; but they would not ***h***.
13:15 ***H*** and give ear: Do not be
13:17 But if you will not ***h*** it, My
14:12 I will not ***h*** their cry;
17:20 ***H*** the word of the LORD, you
17:23 that they might not ***h*** nor
18: 2 there I will cause you to ***h*** My
19: 3 ***H*** the word of the LORD, O kings
19:15 necks that they might not ***h*** My
20:16 Let him ***h*** the cry in the
21:11 ***H*** the word of the LORD,
22: 2 ***H*** the word of the LORD, O king
22: 5 But if you will not ***h*** these
22:21 But you said, 'I will not ***h***.
22:29 ***H*** the word of the LORD!
23:22 And had caused My people to ***h***
25: 4 nor inclined your ear to ***h***.
28: 7 Nevertheless ***h*** now this word
28:15 ***H*** now, Hananiah, the LORD has
29:20 Therefore ***h*** the word of the
31:10 ***H*** the word of the LORD,
33: 9 who shall ***h*** all the good that I
34: 4 'Yet ***h*** the word of the LORD,
36: 3 that the house of Judah will ***h***
37:20 Therefore please ***h*** now, O my
38:25 But if the princes ***h*** that I have
42:14 nor ***h*** the sound of the trumpet,
42:15 Then ***h*** now the word of the
44:24 ***H*** the word of the LORD, all
44:26 Therefore ***h*** the word of the
49:20 Therefore ***h*** the counsel of the
50:45 Therefore ***h*** the counsel of the
Lam 1:18 ***H*** now, all peoples, And
Ezek 2: 5 whether they ***h*** or whether they
2: 7 whether they ***h*** or whether they
2: 8 ***h*** what I say to you. Do not be
3:10 you, and ***h*** with your ears.
3:11 the Lord GOD,' whether they ***h***,
3:17 therefore ***h*** a word from My
3:27 He who hears, let him ***h***;
6: 3 ***h*** the word of the Lord GOD!'
8:18 voice, I will not ***h*** them."
12: 2 and ears to ***h*** but does not
12: 2 and ears to hear but does not ***h***;
13: 2 ***H*** the word of the LORD!'"
16:35 ***h*** the word of the LORD!
18:25 ***H*** now, O house of Israel, is
20:47 '***H*** the word of the LORD!
24:26 will come to you to let you ***h***
25: 3 ***H*** the word of the Lord GOD!
33: 7 therefore you shall ***h*** a word
33:30 Please come and ***h*** what the word
33:31 and they ***h*** your words, but they
33:32 for they ***h*** your words, but they
34: 7 ***h*** the word of the LORD:
34: 9 ***h*** the word of the LORD!
36: 1 ***h*** the word of the LORD!
36: 4 ***h*** the word of the Lord GOD!
36:15 Nor will I let you ***h*** the taunts
37: 4 ***h*** the word of the LORD!
40: 4 look with your eyes and ***h*** with
44: 5 see with your eyes and ***h*** with
Dan 3: 5 that at the time you ***h*** the
3:15 you are ready at the time you ***h***
5:23 which do not see or ***h*** or know;
9:17 ***h*** the prayer of Your servant,
9:18 my God, incline Your ear and ***h***;
9:19 'O Lord, ***h***! O Lord, forgive!
Hos 5: 1 '***H*** this, O priests! Take heed,
Joel 1: 2 ***H*** this, you elders, And give
Am 3: 1 ***H*** this word that the LORD has
3:13 ***H*** and testify against the house
4: 1 ***H*** this word, you cows of
5: 1 ***H*** this word which I take up
5:23 For I will not ***h*** the melody of
7:16 ***h*** the word of the LORD: You
8: 4 ***H*** this, you who swallow up the
Mic 1: 2 ***H***, all you peoples!
3: 1 '***H*** now, O heads of Jacob,
3: 4 But He will not ***h*** them;
3: 9 Now ***h*** this, You heads of the
6: 1 ***H*** now what the LORD says:
6: 1 And let the hills ***h*** your
6: 2 ***H***, O you mountains, the
6: 9 ***H*** the Rod! Who has appointed
7: 7 My God will ***h*** me.
Nah 3:19 All who ***h*** news of you Will
Hab 1: 2 I cry, And You will not ***h***?
Zech 1: 4 ' But they did not ***h*** nor heed
3: 8 '***H***, O Joshua, the high
7:11 ears so that they could not ***h***.
7:12 refusing to ***h*** the law and the
7:13 proclaimed and they would not ***h***,
10: 6 their God, And I will ***h*** them.
Mal 2: 2 If you will not ***h***, And if
Mt 10:14 will not receive you nor ***h***
10:27 and what you ***h*** in the ear,
11: 4 John the things which you ***h***
11: 5 are cleansed and the deaf ***h***;
11:15 "He who has ears to ***h***,
11:15 ears to hear, let him ***h***!
12:19 Nor will anyone ***h*** His
12:42 the ends of the earth to ***h*** the
13: 9 "He who has ears to ***h***,
13: 9 ears to hear, let him ***h***!"
13:13 see, and hearing they do not ***h***,
13:14 Hearing you will ***h*** and
13:15 see with their eyes and ***h***
13:16 see, and your ears for they ***h***;
13:17 and to ***h*** what you hear, and did
13:17 see it, and to hear what you ***h***,
13:17 you hear, and did not ***h*** it.
13:18 Therefore ***h*** the parable of the
13:43 ears to ***h***, let him hear!
13:43 ears to hear, let him ***h***!
15:10 to them, "***H*** and understand:
17: 5 I am well pleased. ***H*** Him!"
18:16 "But if he will not ***h***,
18:17 And if he refuses to ***h*** them,
18:17 But if he refuses even to ***h*** the
21:16 Do You ***h*** what these are
21:33 ***H*** another parable: There was a
24: 6 And you will ***h*** of wars and
27:13 Do You not ***h*** how many things
Mk 4: 9 ears to ***h***, let him hear!"
4: 9 ears to hear, let him ***h***!"
4:12 And hearing they may ***h***
4:15 the word is sown. When they ***h***,
4:16 when they ***h*** the word,
4:18 they are the ones who ***h*** the
4:20 those who ***h*** the word, accept
4:23 "If anyone has ears to ***h***,
4:23 has ears to hear, let him ***h***.
4:24 to them, "Take heed what you ***h***.
4:24 to you; and to you who ***h***,
4:33 to them as they were able to ***h***
6:11 will not receive you nor ***h*** you,
7:14 ***H*** Me, everyone, and understand:
7:16 'If anyone has ears to ***h***,
7:16 has ears to hear, let him ***h***!"
7:37 He makes both the deaf to ***h*** and
8:18 And having ears, do you not ***h***?
9: 7 My beloved Son. ***H*** Him!"
12:29 all the commandments is: '***H***,
13: 7 But when you ***h*** of wars and
Lk 5: 1 pressed about Him to ***h*** the
5:15 multitudes came together to ***h***,
6:17 who came to ***h*** Him and be healed
6:27 "But I say to you who ***h***:
7:22 are cleansed, the deaf ***h***,
8: 8 ears to ***h***, let him hear!"
8: 8 ears to hear, let him ***h***!"
8:12 the wayside are the ones who ***h***;
8:13 are those who, when they ***h***,
8:18 "Therefore take heed how you ***h***.
8:21 and My brothers are these who ***h***
9: 9 but who is this of whom I ***h***
9:35 My beloved Son. ***H*** Him!"
10:24 and to ***h*** what you hear, and
10:24 it, and to hear what you ***h***,
11:28 blessed are those who ***h*** the
11:31 the ends of the earth to ***h*** the
14:35 it out. He who has ears to ***h***,
14:35 ears to hear, let him ***h***!"
15: 1 sinners drew near to Him to ***h***
16: 2 'What is this I ***h*** about you?
16:29 let them ***h*** them.'
16:31 If they do not ***h*** Moses and the
18: 6 ***H*** what the unjust judge said.
19:48 were very attentive to ***h*** Him.
21: 9 But when you ***h*** of wars and
21:38 came to Him in the temple to ***h***
Jn 3: 8 and you ***h*** the sound of it, but
5:25 when the dead will ***h*** the voice
5:25 and those who ***h*** will live.
5:28 who are in the graves will ***h***
5:30 of Myself do nothing. As I ***h***,
8: 6 finger, as though He did not ***h***.
8:47 words; therefore you do not ***h***,
9:27 Why do you want to ***h*** it again?
9:31 we know that God does not ***h***
10: 3 and the sheep ***h*** his voice;
10: 8 but the sheep did not ***h*** them.
10:16 and they will ***h*** My voice;
10:27 My sheep ***h*** My voice, and I know
11:42 And I know that You always ***h*** Me,
14:24 and the word which you ***h*** is not
Acts 2: 8 "And how is it that we ***h***,
2:11 we ***h*** them speaking in our own
2:22 ***h*** these words: Jesus of
2:33 this which you now see and ***h***.
3:22 Him you shall ***h*** in all
3:23 soul who will not ***h*** that
7:37 Him you shall ***h***.'
10:22 and to ***h*** words from you."
10:33 to ***h*** all the things commanded
13: 7 and Saul and sought to ***h*** the
13:44 whole city came together to ***h***
15: 7 my mouth the Gentiles should ***h***
17:21 else but either to tell or to ***h***
17:32 We will ***h*** you again on this
19:26 Moreover you see and ***h*** that not
21:22 for they will ***h*** that you have
22: 1 ***h*** my defense before you now."
22: 9 but they did not ***h*** the voice of
22:14 and ***h*** the voice of His mouth.
23:35 I will ***h*** you when your accusers
24: 4 you any further, I beg you to ***h***,
25:22 I also would like to ***h*** the man
25:22 he said, "you shall ***h*** him."
26: 3 Therefore I beg you to ***h*** me
26:29 but also all who ***h*** me today,
28:22 But we desire to ***h*** from you what
28:26 'Hearing you will ***h***,
28:27 see with their eyes and ***h***
28:28 and they will ***h*** it!"
Rom 10:14 And how shall they ***h*** without a
11: 8 that they should not ***h***,
1 Cor 11:18 I ***h*** that there are divisions
14:21 they will not ***h*** Me,"
Gal 4:21 do you not ***h*** the law?
Phil 1:27 I may ***h*** of your affairs, that
1:30 which you saw in me and now ***h***
2 Th 3:11 For we ***h*** that there are some who
1 Tim 4:16 both yourself and those who ***h***
2 Tim 4:17 that all the Gentiles might ***h***.
Heb 3: 7 if you will ***h*** His voice,
3:15 if you will ***h*** His voice,
4: 7 if you will ***h*** His voice,
Jas 1:19 let every man be swift to ***h***,
1 Jn 4: 6 he who is not of God does not ***h***
3 Jn 4 I have no greater joy than to ***h***
Rev 1: 3 he who reads and those who ***h***
2: 7 let him ***h*** what the Spirit says
2:11 let him ***h*** what the Spirit says
2:17 let him ***h*** what the Spirit says
2:29 let him ***h*** what the Spirit says
3: 6 let him ***h*** what the Spirit says
3:13 let him ***h*** what the Spirit says
3:22 let him ***h*** what the Spirit says
9:20 which can neither see nor ***h*** nor
13: 9 If anyone has an ear, let him ***h***.

HEARD (632/611) HEAR

Gen 3: 8 And they ***h*** the sound of the
3:10 I ***h*** Your voice in the garden,
14:14 Now when Abram ***h*** that his
16:11 Because the LORD has ***h*** your
17:20 I have ***h*** you. Behold, I have
21:17 And God ***h*** the voice of the lad.
21:17 for God has ***h*** the voice of the
21:26 nor had I ***h*** of it until
24:30 and when he ***h*** the words of his
24:52 when Abraham's servant ***h*** their
27: 6 Indeed I ***h*** your father speak to
27:34 When Esau ***h*** the words of his
29:13 when Laban ***h*** the report about
29:33 Because the LORD has ***h*** that I
30: 6 and He has also ***h*** my voice and
31: 1 Now Jacob ***h*** the words of
34: 5 And Jacob ***h*** that he had defiled
34: 7 in from the field when they ***h***
35:22 and Israel ***h*** about it.
37:17 for I ***h*** them say, 'Let us go to
37:21 But Reuben ***h*** it, and he
39:15 when he ***h*** that I lifted my
39:19 when his master ***h*** the words
41:15 But I have ***h*** it said of you
42: 2 Indeed I have ***h*** that there is
43:25 for they ***h*** that they would eat
45: 2 and the house of Pharaoh ***h*** it.
45:16 Now the report of it was ***h*** in

Ex 2:15 When Pharaoh ***h*** of this matter,
2:24 So God ***h*** their groaning, and God
3: 7 and have ***h*** their cry because of
4:31 and when they ***h*** that the LORD
6: 5 And I have also ***h*** the groaning
16: 9 for He has ***h*** your complaints.'
16:12 I have ***h*** the complaints of the
18: 1 ***h*** of all that God had done for
23:13 nor let it be ***h*** from your
28:35 and its sound will be ***h*** when he
32:17 And when Joshua ***h*** the noise of
33: 4 And when the people ***h*** this bad
Lev 10:20 So when Moses ***h*** that, he was
24:14 then let all who ***h*** him lay
Num 7:89 he ***h*** the voice of One speaking
11: 1 for the LORD ***h*** it, and His
11:10 Then Moses ***h*** the people weeping
12: 2 And the LORD ***h*** it.
14:14 They have ***h*** that You, LORD,
14:15 then the nations which have ***h***
14:27 I have ***h*** the complaints which
16: 4 So when Moses ***h*** it, he fell on
20:16 He ***h*** our voice and sent the
21: 1 ***h*** that Israel was coming on the
22:36 Now when Balak ***h*** that Balaam
30:11 and her husband ***h*** it, and made
30:12 made them void on the day he ***h***
30:14 to her on the day that he ***h***
30:15 make them void after he has ***h***
33:40 ***h*** of the coming of the children
Deut 1:34 And the LORD ***h*** the sound of
4:12 You ***h*** the sound of the words,
4:12 you only ***h*** a voice.
4:32 or anything like it has been ***h***.
4:33 of the fire, as you have ***h***,
4:36 and you ***h*** His words out of the
5:23 when you ***h*** the voice from the
5:24 and we have ***h*** His voice from
5:26 there of all flesh who has ***h***
5:28 Then the LORD ***h*** the voice of
5:28 I have ***h*** the voice of the words
9: 2 and of whom you ***h*** it said,
10:10 the LORD also ***h*** me at that
26: 7 and the LORD ***h*** our voice and
Josh 2:10 For we have ***h*** how the LORD
2:11 And as soon as we ***h*** these
5: 1 ***h*** that the LORD had dried up
6:20 it happened when the people ***h***
9: 1 the Jebusite—***h*** about it,
9: 3 the inhabitants of Gibeon ***h***
9: 9 for we have ***h*** of His fame, and
9:16 that they ***h*** that they were
10: 1 king of Jerusalem ***h*** how Joshua
11: 1 when Jabin king of Hazor ***h***
14:12 for you ***h*** in that day how the
22:11 Now the children of Israel ***h***
22:12 when the children of Israel ***h***
22:30 ***h*** the words that the children
24:27 for it has ***h*** all the words of
Judg 7:15 when Gideon ***h*** the telling of
9:30 ***h*** the words of Gaal the son of
9:46 of the tower of Shechem had ***h***
18:25 Do not let your voice be ***h*** among
20: 3 (Now the children of Benjamin ***h***
Ruth 1: 6 for she had ***h*** in the country of
1 Sam 1:13 moved, but her voice was not ***h***.
2:22 and he ***h*** everything his sons
4: 6 Now when the Philistines ***h*** the
4:14 When Eli ***h*** the noise of the
4:19 and when she ***h*** the news that
7: 7 Now when the Philistines ***h*** that
7: 7 when the children of Israel ***h***
8:21 And Samuel ***h*** all the words of
11: 6 of God came upon Saul when he ***h***
13: 3 and the Philistines ***h*** of it.
13: 4 Now all Israel ***h*** it said that
14:22 when they ***h*** that the
14:27 But Jonathan had not ***h*** his
17:11 When Saul and all Israel ***h*** these
17:23 same words. So David ***h*** them.
17:28 Now Eliab his oldest brother ***h***
17:31 words which David spoke were ***h***,
22: 1 and all his father's house ***h***
22: 6 When Saul ***h*** that David and the
23:10 Your servant has certainly ***h***
23:11 down, as Your servant has ***h***?
23:25 And when Saul ***h*** that, he
25: 4 When David ***h*** in the wilderness
25: 7 Now I have ***h*** that you have
25:39 So when David ***h*** that Nabal was
31:11 inhabitants of Jabesh Gilead ***h***
2 Sam 3:28 when David ***h*** it, he said, "My
4: 1 When Saul's son ***h*** that Abner had
5:17 Now when the Philistines ***h*** that
5:17 And David ***h*** of it and went
7:22 to all that we have ***h*** with our
8: 9 When Toi king of Hamath ***h*** that
10: 7 Now when David ***h*** of it, he
11:26 When the wife of Uriah ***h*** that
13:21 But when King David ***h*** of all
18: 5 And all the people ***h*** when the
19: 2 For the people ***h*** it said that
22: 7 He ***h*** my voice from His temple,
1 Ki 1:11 Have you not ***h*** that Adonijah the
1:41 the guests who were with him ***h***
1:41 And when Joab ***h*** the sound of
1:45 is the noise that you have ***h***.
2:42 The word I have ***h*** is good.'
3:28 And all Israel ***h*** of the judgment
4:34 kings of the earth who had ***h***
5: 1 because he ***h*** that they had
5: 7 when Hiram ***h*** the words of
6: 7 chisel or any iron tool was ***h***
9: 3 I have ***h*** your prayer and your
10: 1 Now when the queen of Sheba ***h*** of
10: 6 was a true report which I ***h***
10: 7 exceed the fame of which I ***h***.
11:21 So when Hadad ***h*** in Egypt that
12: 2 Jeroboam the son of Nebat ***h***
12:20 came to pass when all Israel ***h***
13: 4 to pass when King Jeroboam ***h***
13:26 him back from the way ***h*** it,
14: 6 when Ahijah ***h*** the sound of her
15:21 when Baasha ***h*** it, that he
16:16 people who were encamped ***h***
17:22 Then the LORD ***h*** the voice of
19:13 when Elijah ***h*** it, that he
20:12 it happened when Ben-Hadad ***h***
20:31 we have ***h*** that the kings of the
21:15 when Jezebel ***h*** that Naboth had
21:16 when Ahab ***h*** that Naboth was
21:27 when Ahab ***h*** those words, that
2 Ki 3:21 And when all the Moabites ***h*** that
5: 8 when Elisha the man of God ***h***
6:30 when the king ***h*** the words of
9:30 Jezebel ***h*** of it; and she put
11:13 Now when Athaliah ***h*** the noise
19: 1 when King Hezekiah ***h*** it, that
19: 4 which the LORD your God has ***h***.
19: 6 of the words which you have ***h***,
19: 8 for he ***h*** that he had departed
19: 9 And the king ***h*** concerning
19:11 Look! You have ***h*** what the kings
19:20 king of Assyria, I have ***h***.
20: 5 I have ***h*** your prayer, I have
20:12 for he ***h*** that Hezekiah had been
22:11 when the king ***h*** the words of
22:18 the words which you have ***h***—
22:19 before the LORD when you ***h***
22:19 I also have ***h*** you," says the
25:23 ***h*** that the king of Babylon had
1 Chr 10:11 And when all Jabesh Gilead ***h***
14: 8 Now when the Philistines ***h*** that
14: 8 And David ***h*** of it and went
17:20 to all that we have ***h*** with our
18: 9 Now when Tou king of Hamath ***h***
19: 8 Now when David ***h*** of it, he
2 Chr 5:13 to make one sound to be ***h*** in
7:12 I have ***h*** your prayer, and have
9: 1 Now when the queen of Sheba ***h***
9: 5 was a true report which I ***h***
9: 6 exceed the fame of which I ***h***.
10: 2 Jeroboam the son of Nebat ***h***
15: 8 And when Asa ***h*** these words and
16: 5 when Baasha ***h*** it, that he
20:29 of those countries when they ***h***
23:12 Now when Athaliah ***h*** the noise
30:27 people, and their voice was ***h***;
33:13 ***h*** his supplication, and brought
34:19 when the king ***h*** the words of
34:26 the words which you have ***h***—
34:27 yourself before God when you ***h***
34:27 I also have ***h*** you," says the
Ezra 3:13 and the sound was ***h*** afar off.
4: 1 of Judah and Benjamin ***h*** that
9: 3 So when I ***h*** this thing, I tore
Neh 1: 4 when I ***h*** these words, that I
2:10 Tobiah the Ammonite official ***h***
2:19 and Geshem the Arab ***h*** of it,
4: 1 when Sanballat ***h*** that we were
4: 7 and the Ashdodites ***h*** that the
4:15 when our enemies ***h*** that it was
5: 6 I became very angry when I ***h***
6: 1 and the rest of our enemies ***h***
6:16 when all our enemies ***h*** of it,
8: 9 when they ***h*** the words of the
9: 9 And ***h*** their cry by the Red
9:27 to You, You ***h*** from heaven;
9:28 You ***h*** from heaven; And many
12:43 that the joy of Jerusalem was ***h***
13: 3 when they had ***h*** the Law, that
Esth 1:18 officials that they have ***h*** of
2: 8 command and decree were ***h***,
Job 2:11 when Job's three friends ***h*** of
4:16 Then I ***h*** a voice saying:
13: 1 My ear has ***h*** and understood
15: 8 Have you ***h*** the counsel of God?
16: 2 I have ***h*** many such things;
19: 7 concerning wrong, I am not ***h***.
20: 3 I have ***h*** the rebuke that
28:22 We have ***h*** a report about it with
29:11 When the ear ***h***, then it
33: 8 And I have ***h*** the sound of
37: 4 them when His voice is ***h***.
42: 5 I have ***h*** of You by the hearing
Ps 3: 4 And He ***h*** me from His holy
6: 8 For the LORD has ***h*** the voice
6: 9 The LORD has ***h*** my
10:17 You have ***h*** the desire of the
18: 6 He ***h*** my voice from His temple,
19: 3 Where their voice is not ***h***.
22:24 But when He cried to Him, He ***h***.
28: 6 Because He has ***h*** the voice of
31:22 Nevertheless You ***h*** the voice
34: 4 and He ***h*** me, And delivered me
34: 6 and the LORD ***h*** him, And
40: 1 to me, And ***h*** my cry.
44: 1 We have ***h*** with our ears, O God,
48: 8 As we have ***h***, So we have
61: 5 have ***h*** my vows; You have given
62:11 Twice I have ***h*** this:
66: 8 the voice of His praise to be ***h***,
66:19 But certainly God has ***h*** me;
76: 8 You caused judgment to be ***h***
78: 3 Which we have ***h*** and known, And
78:21 Therefore the LORD ***h*** this and
78:59 When God ***h*** this, He was
81: 5 Where I ***h*** a language I did
106:44 When He ***h*** their cry;
116: 1 because He has ***h*** My voice and
120: 1 to the LORD, And He ***h*** me.
132: 6 we ***h*** of it in Ephrathah; We
Prov 21:13 also cry himself and not be ***h***.
Eccl 9:16 And his words are not ***h***.
9:17 should be ***h*** Rather than the
Song 2:12 voice of the turtledove Is ***h***
Isa 6: 8 Also I ***h*** the voice of the Lord,
10:30 of Gallim! Cause it to be ***h***
15: 4 Their voice shall be ***h*** as far
16: 6 We have ***h*** of the pride of
21: 3 I was distressed when I ***h***
21:10 my floor! That which I have ***h***
24:16 the ends of the earth we have ***h***
28:22 For I have ***h*** from the Lord
30:30 His glorious voice to be ***h***,
37: 1 when King Hezekiah ***h*** it, that
37: 4 which the LORD your God has ***h***.
37: 6 of the words which you have ***h***,
37: 8 for he ***h*** that he had departed
37: 9 And the king ***h*** concerning
37: 9 So when he ***h*** it, he sent
37:11 You have ***h*** what the kings
38: 5 I have ***h*** your prayer, I have
39: 1 for he ***h*** that he had been sick
40:21 you not known? Have you not ***h***?
40:28 you not known? Have you not ***h***?
42: 2 Nor cause His voice to be ***h*** in
48: 6 'You have ***h***; See all this.
48: 7 before this day you have not ***h***
49: 8 an acceptable time I have ***h***
52:15 And what they had not ***h*** they
58: 4 To make your voice ***h*** on high.
60:18 Violence shall no longer be ***h***
64: 4 of the world Men have not ***h***
65:19 of weeping shall no longer be ***h***
66: 8 Who has ***h*** such a thing?
66:19 afar off who have not ***h*** My
Jer 3:21 A voice was ***h*** on the desolate
4:19 my peace, Because you have ***h***,
4:31 For I have ***h*** a voice as of a
6: 7 Violence and plundering are ***h***
6:24 We have ***h*** the report of it;
8: 6 I listened and ***h***, But they
8:16 snorting of His horses was ***h***
9:19 For a voice of wailing is ***h***
18:13 Who has ***h*** such things?
18:22 Let a cry be ***h*** from their
20: 1 ***h*** that Jeremiah prophesied
20:10 For I ***h*** many mocking: "Fear
23:18 And has perceived and ***h*** His
23:18 Who has marked His word and ***h***
23:25 I have ***h*** what the prophets have
25: 8 Because you have not ***h*** My words,
25:36 to the flock will be ***h***.
26: 7 prophets and all the people ***h***
26:10 When the princes of Judah ***h***
26:11 as you have ***h*** with your ears."
26:12 all the words that you have ***h***.
26:21 ***h*** his words, the king sought to
26:21 but when Urijah ***h*** it, he was
30: 5 We have ***h*** a voice of trembling,
31:15 A voice was ***h*** in Ramah,
31:18 I have surely ***h*** Ephraim
33:10 Again there shall be ***h*** in this
34:10 ***h*** that everyone should set free
35:17 to them but they have not ***h***,
36:11 ***h*** all the words of the LORD
36:13 all the words that he had ***h***
36:16 when they had ***h*** all the words,
36:24 nor any of his servants who ***h***
37: 5 who were besieging Jerusalem ***h***
38: 1 Pashhur the son of Malchiah ***h***
38: 7 ***h*** that they had put Jeremiah in
38:27 the conversation had not been ***h***.
40: 7 ***h*** that the king of Babylon had
40:11 ***h*** that the king of Babylon had
41:11 forces that were with him ***h***
42: 4 said to them, "I have ***h***.
46:12 The nations have ***h*** of your
48: 4 ones have caused a cry to be ***h***;
48: 5 of Horonaim the enemies have ***h***
48:29 'We have ***h*** the pride of Moab
49: 2 That I will cause to be ***h*** an
49:14 I have ***h*** a message from the
49:21 At the cry its noise is ***h*** at
49:23 For they have ***h*** bad news.
50:43 The king of Babylon has ***h*** the
50:46 And the cry is ***h*** among the
51:46 for the rumor that will be ***h***
51:51 are ashamed because we have ***h***
Lam 1:21 They have ***h*** that I sigh, But
1:21 All my enemies have ***h*** of my
3:56 You have ***h*** my voice: "Do not
3:61 You have ***h*** their reproach,
Ezek 1:24 I ***h*** the noise of their wings,
1:28 and I ***h*** a voice of One
2: 2 and I ***h*** Him who spoke to me.
3:12 and I ***h*** behind me a great
3:13 I also ***h*** the noise of the
10: 5 the wings of the cherubim was ***h***
19: 4 The nations also ***h*** of him;
19: 9 voice should no longer be ***h*** on
26:13 sound of your harps shall be ***h***
27:30 They will make their voice ***h***
33: 5 He ***h*** the sound of the trumpet,
35:12 I have ***h*** all your blasphemies

35:13 I have ***h*** them."
43: 6 Then I ***h*** Him speaking to me
Dan 3: 7 when all the people ***h*** the sound
5:14 I have ***h*** of you, that the Spirit
5:16 And I have ***h*** of you, that you
6:14 when he ***h*** these words, was
8:13 Then I ***h*** a holy one speaking;
8:16 And I ***h*** a man's voice between
10: 9 Yet I ***h*** the sound of his words;
10: 9 and while I ***h*** the sound of his
10:12 your God, your words were ***h***;
12: 7 Then I ***h*** the man clothed in
12: 8 Although I ***h***, I did not
Hos 7:12 what their congregation has ***h***.
14: 8 I have ***h*** and observed him.
Ob 1 concerning Edom (We have ***h*** a
Jon 2: 2 And You ***h*** my voice.
Mic 5:15 On the nations that have not ***h***.
Nah 2:13 of your messengers shall be ***h***
Hab 3: 2 I have ***h*** your speech and was
3:16 When I ***h***, my body trembled;
Zeph 2: 8 I have ***h*** the reproach of Moab,
Zech 8:23 for we have ***h*** that God is
Mal 3:16 And the LORD listened and ***h***
Mt 2: 3 When Herod the king ***h*** this, he
2: 9 When they ***h*** the king, they
2:18 A voice was ***h*** in Ramah,
2:22 But when he ***h*** that Archelaus was
4:12 Now when Jesus ***h*** that John had
5:21 You have ***h*** that it was said to
5:27 You have ***h*** that it was said to
5:33 Again you have ***h*** that it was
5:38 You have ***h*** that it was said,
5:43 You have ***h*** that it was said,
6: 7 they think that they will be ***h***
8:10 When Jesus ***h*** it, He marveled,
9:12 When Jesus ***h*** that, He said to
11: 2 And when John had ***h*** in prison
12:24 Now when the Pharisees ***h*** it
14: 1 that time Herod the tetrarch ***h***
14:13 When Jesus ***h*** it, He departed
14:13 But when the multitudes ***h*** it,
15:12 were offended when they ***h*** this
17: 6 And when the disciples ***h*** it,
19:22 But when the young man ***h*** that
19:25 When His disciples ***h*** it, they
20:24 And when the ten ***h*** it, they
20:30 when they ***h*** that Jesus was
21:45 chief priests and Pharisees ***h***
22: 7 But when the king ***h*** about it,
22:22 When they had ***h*** these words,
22:33 And when the multitudes ***h*** this,
22:34 But when the Pharisees ***h*** that
25: 6 "And at midnight a cry was ***h***:
26:65 now you have ***h*** His blasphemy!
27:47 when they ***h*** that, said, "This
Mk 2: 1 and it was ***h*** that He was in the
2:17 When Jesus ***h*** it, He said to
3: 8 when they ***h*** how many things He
3:21 But when His own people ***h*** about
5:27 When she ***h*** about Jesus, she came
5:36 As soon as Jesus ***h*** the word that
6:14 Now King Herod ***h*** of Him, for
6:16 But when Herod ***h***, he said,
6:20 And when he ***h*** him, he did many
6:20 many things, and ***h*** him gladly.
6:29 When his disciples ***h*** of it,
6:55 were sick to wherever they ***h***
7:25 had an unclean spirit ***h*** about
10:41 And when the ten ***h*** it, they
10:47 And when he ***h*** that it was Jesus
11:14 And His disciples ***h*** it.
11:18 scribes and chief priests ***h*** it
12:28 and having ***h*** them reasoning
12:37 And the common people ***h*** Him
14:11 And when they ***h*** it, they were
14:58 We ***h*** Him say, 'I will destroy
14:64 'You have ***h*** the blasphemy!
15:35 when they ***h*** that, said,
16:11 And when they ***h*** that He was
Lk 1:13 Zacharias, for your prayer is ***h***;
1:41 when Elizabeth ***h*** the greeting
1:58 her neighbors and relatives ***h***
1:66 And all those who ***h*** them kept
2:18 And all those who ***h*** it marveled
2:20 all the things that they had ***h***
2:47 And all who ***h*** Him were
4:23 Whatever we have ***h*** done
4:28 when they ***h*** these things, were
6:49 But he who ***h*** and did nothing is
7: 3 So when he ***h*** about Jesus, he
7: 9 When Jesus ***h*** these things, He
7:22 the things you have seen and ***h***:
7:29 And when all the people ***h*** Him,
8:14 are those who, when they have ***h***,
8:15 having ***h*** the word with a noble
8:50 But when Jesus ***h*** it, He
9: 7 Now Herod the tetrarch ***h*** of all
10:24 and have not ***h*** it."
10:39 also sat at Jesus' feet and ***h***
12: 3 spoken in the dark will be ***h***
14:15 who sat at the table with Him ***h***
15:25 he ***h*** music and dancing.
16:14 also ***h*** all these things, and
18:22 So when Jesus ***h*** these things, He
18:23 But when he ***h*** this, he became
18:26 And those who ***h*** it said, "Who
19:11 Now as they ***h*** these things, He
20:16 And when they ***h*** it they
22:71 For we have ***h*** it ourselves from
23: 6 When Pilate ***h*** of Galilee, he
23: 8 because he had ***h*** many things
Jn 1:37 The two disciples ***h*** him speak,
1:40 One of the two who ***h*** John
3:32 "And what He has seen and ***h***,
4: 1 knew that the Pharisees had ***h***
4:42 for we ourselves have ***h*** Him
4:47 When he ***h*** that Jesus had come
5:37 You have neither ***h*** His voice at
6:45 Therefore everyone who has ***h***
6:60 when they ***h*** this, said, "This
7:32 The Pharisees ***h*** the crowd
7:40 when they ***h*** this saying, said,
8: 9 Then those who ***h*** it, being
8:26 world those things which I ***h***
8:40 told you the truth which I ***h***
9:35 Jesus ***h*** that they had cast him
9:40 Pharisees who were with Him ***h***
11: 4 When Jesus ***h*** that, He said,
11: 6 when He ***h*** that he was sick, He
11:20 as soon as she ***h*** that Jesus was
11:29 As soon as she ***h*** that, she
11:41 I thank You that You have ***h*** Me.
12:12 when they ***h*** that Jesus was
12:18 because they ***h*** that He had done
12:29 the people who stood by and ***h***
12:34 We have ***h*** from the law that the
14:28 You have ***h*** Me say to you, 'I am
15:15 for all things that I ***h*** from My
18:21 Ask those who have ***h*** Me what I
19: 8 when Pilate ***h*** that saying, he
19:13 When Pilate therefore ***h*** that
21: 7 Lord!" Now when Simon Peter ***h***
Acts 1: 4 you have ***h*** from Me;
2: 6 because everyone ***h*** them speak
2:37 Now when they ***h*** this, they were
4: 4 many of those who ***h*** the word
4:20 things which we have seen and ***h***.
4:24 So when they ***h*** that, they raised
5: 5 fear came upon all those who ***h***
5:11 the church and upon all who ***h***
5:21 And when they ***h*** that, they
5:24 and the chief priests ***h*** these
5:33 When they ***h*** this, they were
6:11 We have ***h*** him speak blasphemous
6:14 for we have ***h*** him say that this
7:12 But when Jacob ***h*** that there was
7:34 I have ***h*** their groaning
7:54 When they ***h*** these things they
8:14 who were at Jerusalem ***h*** that
8:30 and ***h*** him reading the prophet
9: 4 and ***h*** a voice saying to him,
9:13 I have ***h*** from many about this
9:21 Then all who ***h*** were amazed, and
9:38 and the disciples had ***h*** that
10:31 your prayer has been ***h***,
10:44 fell upon all those who ***h*** the
10:46 For they ***h*** them speak with
11: 1 brethren who were in Judea ***h***
11: 7 And I ***h*** a voice saying to me,
11:18 When they ***h*** these things they
13:48 Now when the Gentiles ***h*** this,
14: 9 This man ***h*** Paul speaking.
14:14 apostles Barnabas and Paul ***h***
15:24 Since we have ***h*** that some who
16:14 a certain woman named Lydia ***h***
16:38 they were afraid when they ***h***
17: 8 rulers of the city when they ***h***
17:32 And when they ***h*** of the
18:26 When Aquila and Priscilla ***h***
19: 2 We have not so much as ***h*** whether
19: 5 When they ***h*** this, they were
19:10 so that all who dwelt in Asia ***h***
19:28 Now when they ***h*** this, they were
21:12 Now when we ***h*** these things, both
21:20 And when they ***h*** it, they
22: 2 And when they ***h*** that he spoke to
22: 7 I fell to the ground and ***h***
22:15 men of what you have seen and ***h***.
22:26 When the centurion ***h*** that, he
23:16 So when Paul's sister's son ***h*** of
24:22 But when Felix ***h*** these things,
24:24 he sent for Paul and ***h*** him
26:14 I ***h*** a voice speaking to me and
28:15 when the brethren ***h*** about us,
Rom 10:14 in Him of whom they have not ***h***?
10:18 But I say, have they not ***h***?
15:21 And those who have not ***h***
1 Cor 2: 9 has not seen, nor ear ***h***,
2 Cor 6: 2 acceptable time I have ***h***
12: 4 caught up into Paradise and ***h***
Gal 1:13 For you have ***h*** of my former
Eph 1:13 after you ***h*** the word of truth,
1:15 after I ***h*** of your faith in the
3: 2 if indeed you have ***h*** of the
4:21 if indeed you have ***h*** Him and
Phil 2:26 distressed because you had ***h***
4: 9 you learned and received and ***h***
Col 1: 4 since we ***h*** of your faith in
1: 5 of which you ***h*** before in the
1: 6 among you since the day you ***h***
1: 9 since the day we ***h*** it, do not
1:23 hope of the gospel which you ***h***,
1 Th 2:13 the word of God which you ***h***
2 Tim 1:13 of sound words which you have ***h***
2: 2 And the things that you have ***h***
Heb 2: 1 heed to the things we have ***h***,
2: 3 confirmed to us by those who ***h***
3:16 For who, having ***h***,
4: 2 but the word which they ***h*** did
4: 2 with faith in those who ***h*** it.
5: 7 and was ***h*** because of His godly
12:19 so that those who ***h*** it begged
Jas 5:11 You have ***h*** of the perseverance
2 Pe 1:18 And we ***h*** this voice which came
1 Jn 1: 1 the beginning, which we have ***h***,
1: 3 that which we have seen and ***h*** we
1: 5 is the message which we have ***h***
2: 7 is the word which you ***h*** from
2:18 and as you have ***h*** that the
2:24 that abide in you which you ***h***
2:24 If what you ***h*** from the
3:11 this is the message that you ***h***
4: 3 which you have ***h*** was coming,
2 Jn 6 that as you have ***h*** from the
Rev 1:10 and I ***h*** behind me a loud voice,
3: 3 how you have received and ***h***;
4: 1 And the first voice which I ***h***
5:11 and I ***h*** the voice of many
5:13 I ***h*** saying: "Blessing and
6: 1 and I ***h*** one of the four living
6: 3 I ***h*** the second living creature
6: 5 I ***h*** the third living creature
6: 6 And I ***h*** a voice in the midst of
6: 7 I ***h*** the voice of the fourth
7: 4 And I ***h*** the number of those who
8:13 and I ***h*** an angel flying through
9:13 And I ***h*** a voice from the four
9:16 I ***h*** the number of them.
10: 4 but I ***h*** a voice from heaven
10: 8 Then the voice which I ***h*** from
11:12 And they ***h*** a loud voice from
12:10 Then I ***h*** a loud voice saying in
14: 2 And I ***h*** a voice from heaven,
14: 2 And I ***h*** the sound of harpists
14:13 Then I ***h*** a voice from heaven
16: 1 Then I ***h*** a loud voice from the
16: 5 And I ***h*** the angel of the waters
16: 7 And I ***h*** another from the altar
18: 4 And I ***h*** another voice from
18:22 and trumpeters shall not be ***h***
18:22 of a millstone shall not be ***h***
18:23 and bride shall not be ***h*** in
19: 1 After these things I ***h*** a loud
19: 6 And I ***h***, as it were,
21: 3 And I ***h*** a loud voice from heaven
22: 8 saw and ***h*** these things.
22: 8 And when I ***h*** and saw, I fell

HEARER (2/2) HEAR, HEARERS

Jas 1:23 For if anyone is a ***h*** of the word
1:25 and is not a forgetful ***h*** but a

HEARERS (4/4) HEARER

Rom 2:13 (for not the ***h*** of the law are
Eph 4:29 it may impart grace to the ***h***.
2 Tim 2:14 no profit, to the ruin of the ***h***.
Jas 1:22 and not ***h*** only, deceiving

HEARING (91/84) HEAR

Gen 20: 8 all these things in their ***h***;
23:13 he spoke to Ephron in the ***h*** of
23:16 which he had named in the ***h*** of
44:18 speak a word in my lord's ***h***,
50: 4 please speak in the ***h*** of
Ex 10: 2 that you may tell in the ***h***
11: 2 Speak now in the ***h*** of the
17:14 book and recount it in the ***h***
24: 7 the Covenant and read in the ***h***
Lev 5: 1 If a person sins in ***h*** the
Num 11:18 for you have wept in the ***h*** of
14:28 as you have spoken in My ***h***,
Deut 5: 1 which I speak in your ***h*** today,
31:11 before all Israel in their ***h***.
31:28 speak these words in their ***h***
31:30 Then Moses spoke in the ***h*** of
32:44 words of this song in the ***h*** of
Josh 20: 4 and declares his case in the ***h***
Judg 7: 3 proclaim in the ***h*** of the
9: 2 Please speak in the ***h*** of all the
9: 3 words concerning him in the ***h***
1 Sam 8:21 and he repeated them in the ***h***
11: 4 and told the news in the ***h*** of
18:23 spoke those words in the ***h*** of
2 Sam 3:19 And Abner also spoke in the ***h*** of
3:19 also went to speak in the ***h*** of
18:12 For in our ***h*** the king commanded
2 Ki 4:31 there was neither voice nor ***h***.
18:26 speak to us in Hebrew in the ***h***
23: 2 And he read in their ***h*** all the
1 Chr 28: 8 and in the ***h*** of our God, be
2 Chr 34:30 And he read in their ***h*** all the
Neh 13: 1 the Book of Moses in the ***h*** of
Job 33: 8 you have spoken in my ***h***,
42: 5 I have heard of You by the ***h*** of
Prov 20:12 The ***h*** ear and the seeing eye,
23: 9 Do not speak in the ***h*** of a
28: 9 who turns away his ear from ***h***
Eccl 1: 8 Nor the ear filled with ***h***.
Isa 5: 9 In my ***h*** the LORD of hosts
6: 9 tell this people: 'Keep on ***h***,
11: 3 Nor decide by the ***h*** of His
22:14 Then it was revealed in my ***h*** by
33:15 Who stops his ears from ***h*** of
36:11 speak to us in Hebrew in the ***h***
Jer 2: 2 Go and cry in the ***h*** of
26:15 speak all these words in your ***h***.
28: 7 word that I speak in your ***h***
28: 7 in your hearing and in the ***h***
29:29 read this letter in the ***h*** of
36: 6 in the ***h*** of the people in the
36: 6 shall also read them in the ***h***
36:10 in the ***h*** of all the people.

36:13 Baruch read the book in the **h**
36:14 which you have read in the **h**
36:15 down now, and read it in our **h**.
36:15 So Baruch read it in their **h**.
36:20 told all the words in the **h** of
36:21 And Jehudi read it in the **h** of
36:21 of the king and in the **h** of
Ezek 9: 1 Then He called out in my **h** with
9: 5 To the others He said in my **h**,
10:13 they were called in my **h**,
Am 8:11 But of **h** the words of the
Zech 8: 9 You who have been **h** in these
Mt 13:13 and **h** they do not hear, nor do
13:14 ***H*** you will hear and shall
13:15 Their ears are hard of **h**,
Mk 4:12 And **h** they may hear and
6: 2 And many **h** Him were
Lk 4:21 is fulfilled in your **h**.
7: 1 all His sayings in the **h** of
8:10 And **h** they may not
18:36 And **h** a multitude passing by, he
20:45 in the **h** of all the people, He
Acts 5: 5 **h** these words, fell down and
8: 6 **h** and seeing the miracles which
9: 7 **h** a voice but seeing no one.
18: 8 And many of the Corinthians, **h**,
28:26 ***H*** you will hear, and shall
28:27 Their ears are hard of **h**,
Rom 10:17 So then faith comes by **h**,
10:17 and **h** by the word of God.
1 Cor 12:17 an eye, where would be the **h**?
12:17 If the whole were **h**,
Gal 1:23 But they were **h** only, "He who
3: 2 or by the **h** of faith?
3: 5 or by the **h** of faith?—
Phm 1: 5 **h** of your love and faith which
Heb 5:11 since you have become dull of **h**.
2 Pe 2: 8 from day to day by seeing and **h**

HEARKEN, HEARKENED, HEARKENETH, HEARKENING (KJV)

See ANSWER, HEED, LISTEN, LISTENING

HEARS (58/56) HEAR

Ex 16: 7 for He **h** your complaints
16: 8 for the LORD **h** your complaints
Num 24: 4 The utterance of him who **h** the
24:16 The utterance of him who **h** the
30: 4 and her father **h** her vow and the
30: 5 her on the day that he **h**,
30: 7 and her husband **h** it, and makes
30: 7 to her on the day that he **h**,
30: 8 her on the day that he **h** it,
Deut 29:19 when he **h** the words of this
1 Sam 3: 9 LORD, for Your servant **h**.
3:10 "Speak, for Your servant **h**.
3:11 both ears of everyone who **h** it
16: 2 If Saul **h** it, he will kill
2 Sam 17: 9 that whoever **h** it will say,
2 Ki 21:12 that whoever **h** of it, both his
Job 34:28 For He **h** the cry of the
Ps 34:17 cry out, and the LORD **h**,
59: 7 For they say, "Who **h**?"
69:33 For the LORD **h** the poor,
97: 8 Zion **h** and is glad, And the
Prov 15:29 But He **h** the prayer of the
15:31 The ear that **h** the rebukes of
18:13 answers a matter before he **h**
21:28 But the man who **h** him will
25:10 Lest he who **h** it expose your
Isa 30:19 When He **h** it, He will answer
41:26 there is no one who **h** your
Jer 19: 3 that whoever **h** of it, his ears
Ezek 3:27 says the Lord GOD.' He who **h**,
33: 4 then whoever **h** the sound of the
Dan 3:10 a decree that everyone who **h**
Mt 7:24 Therefore whoever **h** these
7:26 But everyone who **h** these sayings
13:19 When anyone **h** the word of the
13:20 this is he who **h** the word and
13:22 among the thorns is he who **h**
13:23 on the good ground is he who **h**
18:15 If he **h** you, you have gained
Lk 6:47 and **h** My sayings and does them,
10:16 He who **h** you hears Me, he who
10:16 He who hears you **h** Me, he who
Jn 3:29 who stands and **h** him, rejoices
5:24 he who **h** My word and believes
7:51 our law judge a man before it **h**
8:47 He who is of God **h** God's words;
9:31 does His will, He **h** him.
12:47 And if anyone **h** My words and
16:13 but whatever He **h** He will
18:37 Everyone who is of the truth **h**
2 Cor 12: 6 what he sees me to be or **h**
1 Jn 4: 5 and the world **h** them.
4: 6 He who knows God **h** us; he who
5:14 to His will, He **h** us.
5:15 And if we know that He **h** us,
Rev 3:20 If anyone **h** My voice and opens
22:17 And let him who **h** say,
22:18 I testify to everyone who **h**

HEART (833/772) BROKENHEARTED, HEART'S, HEARTS, WHOLE-HEARTED

Gen 6: 5 of the thoughts of his **h** was
6: 6 and He was grieved in His **h**.
8:21 Then the LORD said in His **h**,
8:21 the imagination of man's **h** is
17:17 and laughed, and said in his **h**,
20: 5 In the integrity of my **h** and
20: 6 this in the integrity of your **h**.
24:45 I had finished speaking in my **h**,
27:41 him, and Esau said in his **h**,
43:30 Now his **h** yearned for his
45:26 And Jacob's **h** stood still,
Ex 4:14 you, he will be glad in his **h**.
4:21 But I will harden his **h**,
7: 3 "And I will harden Pharaoh's **h**,
7:13 And Pharaoh's **h** grew hard, and
7:14 Pharaoh's **h** is hard; he refuses
7:22 and Pharaoh's **h** grew hard, and
7:23 Neither was his **h** moved by
8:15 he hardened his **h** and did not
8:19 But Pharaoh's **h** grew hard,
8:32 But Pharaoh hardened his **h** at
9: 7 But the **h** of Pharaoh became
9:12 But the LORD hardened the **h** of
9:14 all My plagues to your very **h**,
9:34 yet more; and he hardened his **h**,
9:35 So the **h** of Pharaoh was hard;
10: 1 for I have hardened his **h** and
10:20 the LORD hardened Pharaoh's **h**,
10:27 the LORD hardened Pharaoh's **h**,
11:10 the LORD hardened Pharaoh's **h**,
14: 4 I will harden Pharaoh's **h**,
14: 5 and the **h** of Pharaoh and his
14: 8 And the LORD hardened the **h** of
15: 8 The depths congealed in the **h**
23: 9 for you know the **h** of a
25: 2 gives it willingly with his **h**
28:29 of judgment over his **h**,
28:30 they shall be over Aaron's **h**
28:30 children of Israel over his **h**
35: 5 Whoever is of a willing **h**,
35:21 Then everyone came whose **h** was
35:22 as many as had a willing **h**,
35:26 And all the women whose **h**
35:34 And He has put in his **h** the
36: 2 gifted artisan in whose **h** the
36: 2 everyone whose **h** was stirred,
Lev 19:17 not hate your brother in your **h**.
26:16 the eyes and cause sorrow of **h**.
Num 15:39 harlotry to which your own **h**
32: 7 why will you discourage the **h**
32: 9 they discouraged the **h** of the
Deut 2:30 his spirit and made his **h**
4: 9 lest they depart from your **h**
4:29 if you seek Him with all your **h**
4:39 day, and consider it in your **h**,
5:29 that they had such a **h** in them
6: 5 LORD your God with all your **h**,
6: 6 you today shall be in your **h**.
7:17 "If you should say in your **h**,
8: 2 to know what was in your **h**,
8: 5 You should know in your **h** that
8:14 when your **h** is lifted up, and
8:17 "then you say in your **h**,
9: 4 "Do not think in your **h**,
9: 5 or the uprightness of your **h**
10:12 LORD your God with all your **h**
10:16 the foreskin of your **h**,
11:13 and serve Him with all your **h**
11:16 lest your **h** be deceived, and
11:18 these words of mine in your **h**
12:15 whatever your **h** desires,
12:20 may eat as much meat as your **h**
12:21 your gates as much as your **h**
13: 3 LORD your God with all your **h**
14:26 that money for whatever your **h**
14:26 for whatever your **h** desires;
15: 7 you shall not harden your **h** nor
15: 9 be a wicked thought in your **h**,
15:10 and your **h** should not be
17:17 lest his **h** turn away; nor shall
17:20 that his **h** may not be lifted
18:21 "And if you say in your **h**,
20: 3 Do not let your **h** faint, do not
20: 8 lest the **h** of his brethren
20: 8 his brethren faint like his **h**.
24:15 he is poor and has set his **h**
26:16 to observe them with all your **h**
28:28 blindness and confusion of **h**.
28:47 God with joy and gladness of **h**,
28:65 will give you a trembling **h**,
28:67 the fear which terrifies your **h**,
29: 4 LORD has not given you a **h** to
29:18 whose **h** turns away today from
29:19 he blesses himself in his **h**,
29:19 I follow the dictates of my **h**'—
30: 2 with all your **h** and with all
30: 6 God will circumcise your **h** and
30: 6 your heart and the **h** of your
30: 6 LORD your God with all your **h**
30:10 LORD your God with all your **h**
30:14 in your mouth and in your **h**,
30:17 But if your **h** turns away so that
Josh 5: 1 that their **h** melted; and there
14: 7 word to him as it was in my **h**.
14: 8 who went up with me made the **h**
22: 5 to serve Him with all your **h**
24:23 and incline your **h** to the LORD
Judg 5: 9 My **h** is with the rulers of
5:15 were great resolves of **h**.
5:16 have great searchings of **h**.
9: 3 and their **h** was inclined to
16:15 when your **h** is not with me?
16:17 that he told her all his **h**,
16:18 that he had told her all his **h**,
16:18 for he has told me all his **h**.
18:20 So the priest's **h** was glad;
19: 5 Refresh your **h** with a morsel of
19: 6 and let your **h** be merry."
19: 8 said, "Please refresh your **h**.
19: 9 that your **h** may be merry.
Ruth 3: 7 and his **h** was cheerful, he went
1 Sam 1: 8 And why is your **h** grieved?
1:13 Now Hannah spoke in her **h**;
2: 1 'My **h** rejoices in the LORD;
2:16 may take as much as your **h**
2:33 your eyes and grieve your **h**.
2:35 according to what is in My **h**
4:13 for his **h** trembled for the ark
9:19 tell you all that is in your **h**.
10: 9 that God gave him another **h**;
12:20 serve the LORD with all your **h**.
12:24 Him in truth with all your **h**;
13:14 Himself a man after His own **h**,
14: 7 him, "Do all that is in your **h**.
14: 7 with you, according to your **h**.
16: 7 but the LORD looks at the **h**.
17:28 and the insolence of your **h**,
17:32 Let no man's **h** fail because of
21:12 Now David took these words to **h**,
24: 5 afterward that David's **h**
25:31 nor offense of **h** to my lord,
25:36 And Nabal's **h** was merry within
25:37 that his **h** died within him, and
27: 1 And David said in his **h**,
28: 5 and his **h** trembled greatly.
2 Sam 3:21 may reign over all that your **h**
4: 1 had died in Hebron, he lost **h**,
6:16 and she despised him in her **h**.
7: 3 "Go, do all that is in your **h**,
7:21 and according to Your own **h**,
7:27 servant has found it in his **h**
13:20 do not take this thing to **h**.
13:28 when Amnon's **h** is merry with
13:33 king take the thing to his **h**,
14: 1 perceived that the king's **h**
17:10 whose **h** is like the heart of a
17:10 whose heart is like the **h** of a
18:14 thrust them through Absalom's **h**,
19:14 just as the **h** of one man, so
19:19 the king should take it to **h**.
24:10 And David's **h** condemned him
1 Ki 2: 4 Me in truth with all their **h**
2:44 as your **h** acknowledges, all the
3: 6 and in uprightness of **h** with
3: 9 servant an understanding **h** to
3:12 you a wise and understanding **h**,
4:29 and largeness of **h** like the
8:17 Now it was in the **h** of my father
8:18 Whereas it was in your **h** to
8:18 did well that it was in your **h**.
8:38 knows the plague of his own **h**,
8:39 whose **h** You know (for You alone
8:48 return to You with all their **h**
8:61 Let your **h** therefore be loyal to
8:66 tents joyful and glad of **h** for
9: 3 and My eyes and My **h** will be
9: 4 in integrity of **h** and in
10: 2 him about all that was in her **h**.
10:24 which God had put in his **h**.
11: 3 and his wives turned away his **h**.
11: 4 that his wives turned his **h**
11: 4 and his **h** was not loyal to the
11: 4 as was the **h** of his father
11: 9 because his **h** had turned from
11:37 you shall reign over all your **h**
12:26 And Jeroboam said in his **h**,
12:27 then the **h** of this people will
12:33 he had devised in his own **h**.
14: 8 who followed Me with all his **h**,
15: 3 his **h** was not loyal to the
15: 3 as was the **h** of his father
15:14 Nevertheless Asa's **h** was loyal
21: 7 and let your **h** be cheerful;
2 Ki 5:26 Did not my **h** go with you when
6:11 Therefore the **h** of the king of
9:24 and the arrow came out at his **h**,
10:15 Is your **h** right, as my heart is
10:15 as my **h** is toward your
10:15 as my heart is toward your **h**?
10:30 of Ahab all that was in My **h**,
10:31 God of Israel with all his **h**;
12: 4 that a man purposes in his **h**
14:10 and your **h** has lifted you up.
20: 3 You in truth and with a loyal **h**,
22:19 because your **h** was tender, and
23: 3 with all his **h** and all his
23:25 to the LORD with all his **h**,
1 Chr 12:17 my **h** will be united with you;
12:38 came to Hebron with a loyal **h**,
15:29 and she despised him in her **h**.
17: 2 "Do all that is in your **h**,
17:19 and according to Your own **h**,
17:25 has found it in his **h** to
22:19 Now set your **h** and your soul to
28: 2 I had it in my **h** to build a
28: 9 and serve Him with a loyal **h**
29: 9 because with a loyal **h** they had
29:17 that You test the **h** and have
29:17 in the uprightness of my **h** I
29:18 of the thoughts of the **h** of
29:18 and fix their **h** toward You.
29:19 give my son Solomon a loyal **h**
2 Chr 1:11 "Because this was in your **h**,
6: 7 Now it was in the **h** of my father
6: 8 Whereas it was in your **h** to

6: 8 well in that it was in your ***h***.
6:30 whose ***h*** You know (for You alone
6:38 return to You with all their ***h***
7:10 joyful and glad of ***h*** for the
7:11 all that came into his ***h*** to
7:16 and My eyes and My ***h*** will be
9: 1 him about all that was in her ***h***.
9:23 which God had put in his ***h***.
11:16 such as set their ***h*** to seek the
12:14 he did not prepare his ***h*** to
15:12 their fathers with all their ***h***
15:15 had sworn with all their ***h*** and
15:17 Nevertheless the ***h*** of Asa was
16: 9 on behalf of those whose ***h***
17: 6 And his ***h*** took delight in the
19: 3 and have prepared your ***h*** to
19: 9 faithfully and with a loyal ***h***:
22: 9 sought the LORD with all his ***h***.
24: 4 this that Joash set his ***h*** on
25: 2 LORD, but not with a loyal ***h***.
25:19 and your ***h*** is lifted up to
26:16 But when he was strong his ***h***
29:10 Now it is in my ***h*** to make a
29:31 as many as were of a willing ***h***
30:12 to give them singleness of ***h***
30:19 who prepares his ***h*** to seek God,
31:21 God, he did it with all his ***h***.
32:25 for his ***h*** was lifted up;
32:26 himself for the pride of his ***h***,
32:31 know all that was in his ***h***.
34:27 because your ***h*** was tender, and
34:31 and His statutes with all his ***h***
36:13 his neck and hardened his ***h***
Ezra 6:22 and turned the ***h*** of the king of
7:10 For Ezra had prepared his ***h*** to
7:27 thing as this in the king's ***h***,
Neh 2: 2 is nothing but sorrow of ***h***.
2:12 what my God had put in my ***h*** to
6: 8 you invent them in your own ***h***.
7: 5 Then my God put it into my ***h*** to
9: 8 You found his ***h*** faithful before
Esth 1:10 when the ***h*** of the king was
4:13 Do not think in your ***h*** that you
5: 9 day joyful and with a glad ***h***;
6: 6 Now Haman thought in his ***h***,
7: 5 would dare presume in his ***h*** to
Job 7:17 That You should set Your ***h*** on
8:10 And utter words from their ***h***?
9: 4 God is wise in ***h*** and mighty in
10:13 You have hidden in Your ***h***;
11:13 "If you would prepare your ***h***,
15:12 Why does your ***h*** carry you away,
16:13 He pierces my ***h*** and does not
17: 4 For You have hidden their ***h***
17:11 Even the thoughts of my ***h***.
19:27 How my ***h*** yearns within me!
20:20 he knows no quietness in his ***h***,
22:22 And lay up His words in your ***h***.
23:16 For God made my ***h*** weak, And
27: 6 My ***h*** shall not reproach me as
29:13 And I caused the widow's ***h*** to
30:27 My ***h*** is in turmoil and cannot
31: 7 Or my ***h*** walked after my eyes,
31: 9 If my ***h*** has been enticed by a
31:20 If his ***h*** has not blessed me,
31:27 So that my ***h*** has been secretly
33: 3 words come from my upright ***h***;
34:14 If He should set His ***h*** on it,
36:13 But the hypocrites in ***h*** store
37: 1 At this also my ***h*** trembles, And
37:24 to any who are wise of ***h***.
38:36 given understanding to the ***h***?
41:24 His ***h*** is as hard as stone,
Ps 4: 4 Meditate within your ***h*** on your
4: 7 You have put gladness in my ***h***,
7:10 Who saves the upright in ***h***.
9: 1 You, O LORD, with my whole ***h***;
10: 6 He has said in his ***h***,
10:11 He has said in his ***h***,
10:13 God? He has said in his ***h***,
10:17 You will prepare their ***h***;
11: 2 secretly at the upright in ***h***.
12: 2 lips and a double ***h*** they
13: 2 Having sorrow in my ***h*** daily?
13: 5 My ***h*** shall rejoice in Your
14: 1 The fool has said in his ***h***,
15: 2 And speaks the truth in his ***h***;
16: 7 My ***h*** also instructs me in the
16: 9 Therefore my ***h*** is glad, and my
17: 3 You have tested my ***h***;
19: 8 are right, rejoicing the ***h***;
19:14 and the meditation of my ***h*** Be
22:14 My ***h*** is like wax; It has
22:26 Let your ***h*** live forever!
24: 4 has clean hands and a pure ***h***,
25:17 The troubles of my ***h*** have
26: 2 prove me; Try my mind and my ***h***.
27: 3 My ***h*** shall not fear;
27: 8 My ***h*** said to You, "Your
27:13 I would have lost ***h***,
27:14 And He shall strengthen your ***h***;
28: 7 My ***h*** trusted in Him, and I am
28: 7 Therefore my ***h*** greatly
31:24 And He shall strengthen your ***h***,
32:11 all you upright in ***h***!
33:11 The plans of His ***h*** to all
33:21 For our ***h*** shall rejoice in Him,
34:18 to those who have a broken ***h***,
35:13 prayer would return to my own ***h***.
36: 1 An oracle within my ***h***
36:10 to the upright in ***h***.
37: 4 give you the desires of your ***h***.
37:15 sword shall enter their own ***h***,
37:31 law of his God is in his ***h***;
38: 8 because of the turmoil of my ***h***.
38:10 My ***h*** pants, my strength fails
39: 3 My ***h*** was hot within me;
40: 8 And Your law is within my ***h***.
40:10 Your righteousness within my ***h***;
40:12 Therefore my ***h*** fails me.
41: 6 His ***h*** gathers iniquity to
44:18 Our ***h*** has not turned back,
44:21 He knows the secrets of the ***h***.
45: 1 My ***h*** is overflowing with a good
45: 5 arrows are sharp in the ***h*** of
49: 3 And the meditation of my ***h***
51:10 Create in me a clean ***h***,
51:17 A broken and a contrite ***h***—
53: 1 The fool has said in his ***h***,
55: 4 My ***h*** is severely pained within
55:21 butter, But war was in his ***h***;
57: 7 My ***h*** is steadfast, O God, my
57: 7 my ***h*** is steadfast; I will sing
58: 2 in ***h*** you work wickedness;
61: 2 When my ***h*** is overwhelmed;
62: 8 Pour out your ***h*** before Him;
62:10 Do not set your ***h*** on them.
64: 6 the inward thought and the ***h***
64:10 And all the upright in ***h*** shall
66:18 If I regard iniquity in my ***h***,
69:20 Reproach has broken my ***h***,
73: 1 To such as are pure in ***h***.
73: 7 They have more than ***h*** could
73:13 Surely I have cleansed my ***h*** in
73:21 Thus my ***h*** was grieved, And I
73:26 My flesh and my ***h*** fail;
73:26 God is the strength of my ***h***
77: 6 I meditate within my ***h***,
78: 8 that did not set its ***h*** aright,
78:18 they tested God in their ***h*** By
78:37 For their ***h*** was not steadfast
78:72 to the integrity of his ***h***,
81:12 over to their own stubborn ***h***,
84: 2 My ***h*** and my flesh cry out for
84: 5 Whose ***h*** is set on pilgrimage.
86:11 Unite my ***h*** to fear Your name.
86:12 O Lord my God, with all my ***h***,
90:12 That we may gain a ***h*** of
94:15 And all the upright in ***h*** will
97:11 gladness for the upright in ***h***.
101: 2 my house with a perfect ***h***.
101: 4 A perverse ***h*** shall depart from
101: 5 a haughty look and a proud ***h***,
102: 4 My ***h*** is stricken and withered
104:15 wine that makes glad the ***h*** of
104:15 which strengthens man's ***h***.
105:25 He turned their ***h*** to hate His
107:12 He brought down their ***h*** with
108: 1 my ***h*** is steadfast; I will sing
109:16 might even slay the broken in ***h***.
109:22 And my ***h*** is wounded within me.
111: 1 the LORD with my whole ***h***,
112: 7 His ***h*** is steadfast, trusting
112: 8 His ***h*** is established; He will
119: 2 Who seek Him with the whole ***h***!
119: 7 You with uprightness of ***h***,
119:10 With my whole ***h*** I have sought
119:11 word I have hidden in my ***h***,
119:32 For You shall enlarge my ***h***.
119:34 observe it with my whole ***h***.
119:36 Incline my ***h*** to Your
119:58 Your favor with my whole ***h***;
119:69 Your precepts with my whole ***h***.
119:70 Their ***h*** is as fat as grease,
119:80 Let my ***h*** be blameless regarding
119:111 they are the rejoicing of my ***h***.
119:112 I have inclined my ***h*** to perform
119:145 I cry out with my whole ***h***;
119:161 But my ***h*** stands in awe of Your
128: 3 a fruitful vine In the very ***h***
131: 1 my ***h*** is not haughty, Nor my
138: 1 will praise You with my whole ***h***;
139:23 me, O God, and know my ***h***;
141: 4 Do not incline my ***h*** to any evil
143: 4 My ***h*** within me is distressed.
Prov 2: 2 And apply your ***h*** to
2:10 When wisdom enters your ***h***,
3: 1 But let your ***h*** keep my
3: 3 them on the tablet of your ***h***,
3: 5 in the LORD with all your ***h***,
4: 4 Let your ***h*** retain my words;
4:21 them in the midst of your ***h***;
4:23 Keep your ***h*** with all diligence,
5:12 And my ***h*** despised correction!
6:14 Perversity is in his ***h***,
6:18 A ***h*** that devises wicked plans,
6:21 them continually upon your ***h***;
6:25 lust after her beauty in your ***h***,
7: 3 them on the tablet of your ***h***.
7:10 of a harlot, and a crafty ***h***.
7:25 Do not let your ***h*** turn aside to
8: 5 fools, be of an understanding ***h***.
10: 8 The wise in ***h*** will receive
10:20 The ***h*** of the wicked is worth
11:20 Those who are of a perverse ***h***
11:29 be servant to the wise of ***h***.
12: 8 But he who is of a perverse ***h***
12:20 Deceit is in the ***h*** of those who
12:23 But the ***h*** of fools proclaims
12:25 Anxiety in the ***h*** of man causes
13:12 Hope deferred makes the ***h*** sick,
14:10 The ***h*** knows its own bitterness,
14:13 Even in laughter the ***h*** may
14:14 The backslider in ***h*** will be
14:30 A sound ***h*** is life to the body,
14:33 Wisdom rests in the ***h*** of him
14:33 But what is in the ***h*** of
15: 7 But the ***h*** of the fool does
15:13 A merry ***h*** makes a cheerful
15:13 But by sorrow of the ***h*** the
15:14 The ***h*** of him who has
15:15 But he who is of a merry ***h***
15:28 The ***h*** of the righteous studies
15:30 of the eyes rejoices the ***h***,
16: 1 The preparations of the ***h***
16: 5 Everyone proud in ***h*** is an
16: 9 A man's ***h*** plans his way, But
16:21 The wise in ***h*** will be called
16:23 The ***h*** of the wise teaches his
17:16 Since he has no ***h*** for it?
17:20 He who has a deceitful ***h*** finds
17:22 A merry ***h*** does good, like
18: 2 But in expressing his own ***h***.
18:12 Before destruction the ***h*** of a
18:15 The ***h*** of the prudent acquires
19: 3 And his ***h*** frets against the
19:18 And do not set your ***h*** on his
19:21 are many plans in a man's ***h***,
20: 5 Counsel in the ***h*** of man is
20: 9 I have made my ***h*** clean, I am
20:27 all the inner depths of his ***h***.
20:30 the inner depths of the ***h***.
21: 1 The king's ***h*** is in the hand of
21: 4 A haughty look, a proud ***h***,
22:11 He who loves purity of ***h*** And
22:15 is bound up in the ***h*** of a
22:17 And apply your ***h*** to my
23: 7 For as he thinks in his ***h***,
23: 7 But his ***h*** is not with you.
23:12 Apply your ***h*** to instruction,
23:15 if your ***h*** is wise, My heart
23:15 My ***h*** will rejoice—indeed, I
23:17 Do not let your ***h*** envy sinners,
23:19 And guide your ***h*** in the way.
23:26 My son, give me your ***h***,
23:33 And your ***h*** will utter perverse
24: 2 For their ***h*** devises violence,
24:17 And do not let your ***h*** be glad
25: 3 So the ***h*** of kings is
25:20 who sings songs to a heavy ***h***.
26:23 Fervent lips with a wicked ***h***
26:25 seven abominations in his ***h***;
27: 9 and perfume delight the ***h***,
27:11 and make my ***h*** glad, That I may
27:19 So a man's ***h*** reveals the man.
28:14 But he who hardens his ***h*** will
28:25 He who is of a proud ***h*** stirs up
28:26 He who trusts in his own ***h*** is a
31: 6 to those who are bitter of ***h***.
31:11 The ***h*** of her husband safely
Eccl 1:13 And I set my ***h*** to seek and
1:16 I communed with my ***h***,
1:16 My ***h*** has understood great
1:17 And I set my ***h*** to know wisdom
2: 1 I said in my ***h***,
2: 3 I searched in my ***h*** how to
2: 3 while guiding my ***h*** with wisdom,
2:10 I did not withhold my ***h*** from
2:10 For my ***h*** rejoiced in all my
2:15 So I said in my ***h***,
2:15 Then I said in my ***h***,
2:20 Therefore I turned my ***h*** and
2:22 and for the striving of his ***h***
2:23 even in the night his ***h*** takes
3:17 I said in my ***h***,
3:18 I said in my ***h***,
5: 2 And let not your ***h*** utter
5:20 him busy with the joy of his ***h***.
7: 2 the living will take it to ***h***.
7: 3 by a sad countenance the ***h*** is
7: 4 The ***h*** of the wise is in the
7: 4 But the ***h*** of fools is in the
7: 7 And a bribe debases the ***h***.
7:21 Also do not take to ***h***
7:22 your own ***h*** has known That even
7:25 I applied my ***h*** to know, To
7:26 than death The woman whose ***h***
8: 5 And a wise man's ***h*** discerns
8: 9 and applied my ***h*** to every work
8:11 therefore the ***h*** of the sons of
8:16 When I applied my ***h*** to know
9: 1 I considered all this in my ***h***,
9: 7 drink your wine with a merry ***h***;
10: 2 A wise man's ***h*** is at his right
10: 2 But a fool's ***h*** at his left.
11: 9 And let your ***h*** cheer you in
11: 9 Walk in the ways of your ***h***,
11:10 remove sorrow from your ***h***,
Song 3:11 day of the gladness of his ***h***.
4: 9 You have ravished my ***h***,
4: 9 You have ravished my ***h*** With
5: 2 but my ***h*** is awake; It is the
5: 4 And my ***h*** yearned for him.
5: 6 My ***h*** leaped up when he spoke.
8: 6 Set me as a seal upon your ***h***,
Isa 1: 5 And the whole ***h*** faints.
6:10 Make the ***h*** of this people dull,
6:10 And understand with their ***h***,
7: 2 So his ***h*** and the heart of his
7: 2 So his heart and the ***h*** of his
9: 9 say in pride and arrogance of ***h***:
10: 7 Nor does his ***h*** think so;
10: 7 But it is in his ***h*** to
10:12 the fruit of the arrogant ***h*** of
13: 7 Every man's ***h*** will melt,
14:13 For you have said in your ***h***:

15: 5 'My **h** will cry out for Moab;
16:11 Therefore my **h** shall resound
19: 1 And the **h** of Egypt will melt
21: 4 My **h** wavered, fearfulness
30:29 And gladness of **h** as when one
32: 4 Also the **h** of the rash will
32: 6 And his **h** will work iniquity:
33:18 Your **h** will meditate on terror:
38: 3 You in truth and with a loyal **h**,
42:25 Yet he did not take it to **h**.
44:19 And no one considers in his **h**,
44:20 A deceived **h** has turned him
47: 7 did not take these things to **h**,
47: 8 securely, Who say in your **h**,
47:10 And you have said in your **h**,
49:21 Then you will say in your **h**,
51: 7 You people in whose **h** is My
57: 1 And no man takes it to **h**;
57:11 Me, Nor taken it to your **h**?
57:15 And to revive the **h** of the
57:17 backsliding in the way of his **h**.
59:13 and uttering from the **h** words
60: 5 And your **h** shall swell with
63: 4 day of vengeance is in My **h**,
63:15 The yearning of Your **h** and
63:17 And hardened our **h** from Your
65:14 shall sing for joy of **h**,
65:14 you shall cry for sorrow of **h**,
66:14 your **h** shall rejoice, And your
Jer 3:10 turned to Me with her whole **h**,
3:15 you shepherds according to My **h**,
4: 9 That the **h** of the king shall
4: 9 And the **h** of the princes;
4:10 the sword reaches to the **h**.
4:14 wash your **h** from wickedness,
4:18 Because it reaches to your **h**.
4:19 I am pained in my very **h**!
4:19 pained in my very heart! My **h**
5:23 has a defiant and rebellious **h**;
5:24 They do not say in their **h**,
7:31 nor did it come into My **h**.
8:18 My **h** is faint in me.
9: 8 But in his **h** he lies in wait.
9:26 are uncircumcised in the **h**.
11: 8 the dictates of his evil **h**;
11:20 Testing the mind and the **h**,
12: 3 And You have tested my **h**
12:11 Because no one takes it to **h**.
13:22 And if you say in your **h**,
14:14 and the deceit of their **h**.
15:16 the joy and rejoicing of my **h**;
16:12 the dictates of his own evil **h**,
17: 1 On the tablet of their **h**,
17: 5 Whose **h** departs from the
17: 9 The **h** is deceitful above all
17:10 I, the LORD, search the **h**,
18:12 obey the dictates of his evil **h**.
20: 9 But His word was in my **h**
20:12 And see the mind and **h**,
22:17 Yet your eyes and your **h** are
23: 9 My **h** within me is broken
23:16 speak a vision of their own **h**,
23:17 to the dictates of his own **h**,
23:20 performed the thoughts of His **h**.
23:26 long will this be in the **h** of
23:26 of the deceit of their own **h**,
24: 7 Then I will give them a **h** to
24: 7 return to Me with their whole **h**.
29:13 search for Me with all your **h**.
30:21 who is this who pledged his **h**
30:24 performed the intents of His **h**.
31:20 Therefore My **h** yearns for him;
31:21 Set your **h** toward the highway,
32:39 then I will give them one **h** and
32:41 with all My **h** and with all My
48:29 of the haughtiness of his **h**.
48:36 Therefore My **h** shall wail like
48:36 And like flutes My **h** shall
48:41 that day shall be Like the **h**
49:16 you, The pride of your **h**,
49:22 The **h** of the mighty men of
49:22 that day shall be Like the **h**
51:46 And lest your **h** faint, And you
Lam 1:20 My **h** is overturned within me,
1:22 And my **h** is faint."
2:11 My **h** is troubled; My bile is
2:18 Their **h** cried out to the Lord,
2:19 Pour out your **h** like water
3:65 Give them a veiled **h**;
5:15 The joy of our **h** has ceased;
5:17 Because of this our **h** is faint;
Ezek 3:10 receive into your **h** all My
6: 9 crushed by their adulterous **h**
11:19 "Then I will give them one **h**,
11:19 and take the stony **h** out of
11:19 and give them a **h** of flesh,
13: 2 who prophesy out of their own **h**,
13:17 who prophesy out of their own **h**;
13:22 with lies you have made the **h**
14: 4 who sets up his idols in his **h**,
14: 5 the house of Israel by their **h**,
14: 7 and sets up his idols in his **h**
16:30 'How degenerate is your **h**!"
18:31 and get yourselves a new **h** and
20:16 for their **h** went after their
21: 6 son of man, with a breaking **h**,
21: 7 every **h** will melt, all hands
21:15 That the **h** may melt and many
22:14 Can your **h** endure, or can your
25: 6 and rejoiced in **h** with all your
25:15 vengeance with a spiteful **h**,
27:31 for you With bitterness of **h**

28: 2 Because your **h** is lifted up,
28: 2 Though you set your **h** as the
28: 2 you set your heart as the **h** of
28: 5 And your **h** is lifted up
28: 6 Because you have set your **h** as
28: 6 have set your heart as the **h**
28:17 Your **h** was lifted up because of
31:10 and its **h** was lifted up in its
36:26 I will give you a new **h** and put
36:26 I will take the **h** of stone out
36:26 of your flesh and give you a **h**
44: 7 uncircumcised in **h** and
44: 9 uncircumcised in **h** or
Dan 1: 8 But Daniel purposed in his **h**
2:30 may know the thoughts of your **h**.
4:16 Let his **h** be changed from that
4:16 Let him be given the **h** of a
5:20 But when his **h** was lifted up,
5:21 his **h** was made like the beasts,
5:22 have not humbled your **h**,
6:14 and set his **h** on Daniel to
7: 4 and a man's **h** was given to it.
7:28 but I kept the matter in my **h**.
8:25 shall exalt himself in his **h**.
10:12 first day that you set your **h**
11:12 his **h** will be lifted up; and he
11:28 his **h** shall be moved against
Hos 4: 8 They set their **h** on their
4:11 and new wine enslave the **h**.
7: 6 They prepare their **h** like an
7:14 not cry out to Me with their **h**
10: 2 Their **h** is divided; Now they
11: 8 My **h** churns within Me;
13: 6 They were filled and their **h**
Joel 2:12 "Turn to Me with all your **h**,
2:13 So rend your **h**, and not your
Ob 3 The pride of your **h** has
3 high; You who say in your **h**,
Jon 2: 3 Into the **h** of the seas, And
Nah 2:10 and waste! The **h** melts, and
Zeph 1:12 Who say in their **h**,
2:15 securely, That said in her **h**,
3:14 and rejoice with all your **h**,
Zech 7:10 none of you plan evil in his **h**
8:17 of you think evil in your **h**
10: 7 And their **h** shall rejoice as
10: 7 Their **h** shall rejoice in the
12: 5 of Judah shall say in their **h**,
Mal 2: 2 if you will not take it to **h**,
2: 2 you do not take it to **h**.
Mt 5: 8 Blessed are the pure in **h**,
5:28 adultery with her in his **h**.
6:21 there your **h** will be also.
11:29 for I am gentle and lowly in **h**,
12:34 out of the abundance of the **h**
12:35 of the good treasure of his **h**
12:40 days and three nights in the **h**
13:19 away what was sown in his **h**.
15: 8 But their **h** is far from
15:18 of the mouth come from the **h**,
15:19 For out of the **h** proceed evil
18:35 you if each of you, from his **h**,
22:37 your God with all your **h**,
24:48 that evil servant says in his **h**,
Mk 6:52 because their **h** was hardened.
7: 6 But their **h** is far from
7:19 it does not enter his **h** but
7:21 out of the **h** of men, proceed
8:17 Is your **h** still hardened?
10: 5 of the hardness of your **h** he
11:23 and does not doubt in his **h**,
12:30 your God with all your **h**,
12:33 to love Him with all the **h**,
16:14 unbelief and hardness of **h**,
Lk 2:19 and pondered them in her **h**.
2:51 kept all these things in her **h**.
6:45 of the good treasure of his **h**
6:45 of the evil treasure of his **h**
6:45 out of the abundance of the **h**
8:15 word with a noble and good **h**,
9:47 the thought of their **h**,
10:27 your God with all your **h**,
12:34 there your **h** will be also.
12:45 if that servant says in his **h**,
18: 1 ought to pray and not lose **h**,
24:25 and slow of **h** to believe in all
24:32 Did not our **h** burn within us
Jn 7:38 out of his **h** will flow rivers
13: 2 already put it into the **h** of
14: 1 Let not your **h** be troubled; you
14:27 Let not your **h** be troubled,
16: 6 you, sorrow has filled your **h**.
16:22 I will see you again and your **h**
Acts 2:26 Therefore my **h** rejoiced,
2:37 this, they were cut to the **h**,
2:46 gladness and simplicity of **h**,
4:32 who believed were of one **h** and
5: 3 why has Satan filled your **h** to
5: 4 conceived this thing in your **h**?
7:23 it came into his **h** to visit his
7:51 and uncircumcised in **h** and
7:54 things they were cut to the **h**,
8:21 for your **h** is not right in the
8:22 perhaps the thought of your **h**
8:37 you believe with all your **h**,
11:23 them all that with purpose of **h**
13:22 a man after My own **h**,
15: 8 "So God, who knows the **h**,
16:14 The Lord opened her **h** to heed
21:13 by weeping and breaking my **h**?
27:22 "And now I urge you to take **h**,
27:25 "Therefore take **h**,

Rom 2: 5 hardness and your impenitent **h**
2:29 circumcision is that of the **h**,
6:17 yet you obeyed from the **h** that
9: 2 and continual grief in my **h**.
10: 6 "Do not say in your **h**,
10: 8 your mouth and in your **h**'
10: 9 Jesus and believe in your **h**
10:10 For with the **h** one believes unto
1 Cor 2: 9 have entered into the **h**
7:37 who stands steadfast in his **h**,
7:37 and has so determined in his **h**
14:25 And thus the secrets of his **h**
2 Cor 2: 4 affliction and anguish of **h** I
3: 3 of flesh, that is, of the **h**.
3:15 is read, a veil lies on their **h**.
4: 1 mercy, we do not lose **h**.
4:16 Therefore we do not lose **h**.
5:12 in appearance and not in **h**.
6:11 our **h** is wide open.
8:16 care for you into the **h** of
9: 7 give as he purposes in his **h**,
Gal 6: 9 shall reap if we do not lose **h**.
Eph 3:13 I ask that you do not lose **h**
4:18 of the blindness of their **h**;
5:19 and making melody in your **h** to
6: 5 trembling, in sincerity of **h**,
6: 6 the will of God from the **h**,
Phil 1: 7 all, because I have you in my **h**,
Col 3:22 but in sincerity of **h**,
1 Th 2:17 time in presence, not in **h**,
1 Tim 1: 5 is love from a pure **h**,
2 Tim 2:22 on the Lord out of a pure **h**.
Phm 1:12 receive him, that is, my own **h**,
1:20 refresh my **h** in the Lord.
Heb 3:10 go astray in their **h**,
3:12 be in any of you an evil **h** of
4:12 thoughts and intents of the **h**.
10:22 let us draw near with a true **h**
13: 9 For it is good that the **h** be
Jas 1:26 tongue but deceives his own **h**,
1 Pe 1:22 another fervently with a pure **h**,
3: 4 be the hidden person of the **h**,
2 Pe 2:14 They have a **h** trained in
1 Jn 3:17 and shuts up his **h** from him,
3:20 For if our **h** condemns us, God is
3:20 us, God is greater than our **h**,
3:21 if our **h** does not condemn us,
Rev 18: 7 sorrow; for she says in her **h**,

HEART'S (4/4) HEART

Ps 10: 3 wicked boasts of his **h** desire;
20: 4 grant you according to your **h**
21: 2 given him his **h** desire,
Rom 10: 1 my **h** desire and prayer to God

HEARTH (9/7)

Lev 6: 9 offering shall be on the **h**
Ps 102: 3 my bones are burned like a **h**.
Isa 30:14 shard to take fire from the **h**,
Jer 36:22 with a fire burning on the **h**
36:23 the fire that was on the **h**,
36:23 in the fire that was on the **h**.
Ezek 43:15 The altar **h** is four cubits
43:15 extending upward from the **h**.
43:16 The altar **h** is twelve cubits

HEARTHS (1/1)

Ezek 46:23 and cooking **h** were made under

HEARTILY (2/2)

1 Cor 16:19 and Priscilla greet you **h** in
Col 3:23 And whatever you do, do it **h**,

HEARTS (142/135) HEART

Gen 18: 5 that you may refresh your **h**.
42:28 in my sack!" Then their **h**
Ex 10: 1 hardened his heart and the **h**
14:17 I indeed will harden the **h**
31: 6 and I have put wisdom in the **h**
35:29 all the men and women whose **h**
Lev 26:36 send faintness into their **h** in
26:41 if their uncircumcised **h** are
Deut 1:28 brethren have discouraged our **h**,
32:46 Set your **h** on all the words
Josh 2:11 our **h** melted; neither did there
7: 5 therefore the **h** of the people
11:20 of the LORD to harden their **h**,
23:14 And you know in all your **h** and
Judg 16:25 when their **h** were merry, that
1 Sam 6: 6 Why then do you harden your **h** as
6: 6 and Pharaoh hardened their **h**?
7: 3 to the LORD with all your **h**,
7: 3 and prepare your **h** for the
10:26 whose **h** God had touched.
2 Sam 15: 6 So Absalom stole the **h** of the
15:13 The **h** of the men of Israel are
19:14 So he swayed the **h** of all the
1 Ki 8:23 before You with all their **h**.
8:39 (for You alone know the **h** of
8:58 that He may incline our **h** to
11: 2 they will turn away your **h**
18:37 that You have turned their **h**
1 Chr 16:10 Let the **h** of those rejoice who
28: 9 for the LORD searches all **h**
2 Chr 6:14 before You with all their **h**.
6:30 (for You alone know the **h** of
20:33 had not directed their **h** to
Job 1: 5 and cursed God in their **h**.

Ps 7: 9 the righteous God tests the *h*
17:10 have closed up their fat *h*;
28: 3 But evil is in their *h*.
33:15 He fashions their *h*
35:25 Let them not say in their *h*,
69:32 your *h* shall live.
74: 8 They said in their *h*,
95: 8 "Do not harden your *h*,
95:10 people who go astray in their *h*,
105: 3 Let the *h* of those rejoice who
125: 4 who are upright in their *h*.
140: 2 plan evil things in their *h*;
Prov 15:11 So how much more the *h* of the
17: 3 But the LORD tests the *h*.
21: 2 But the LORD weighs the *h*.
24:12 Does not He who weighs the *h*
Eccl 3:11 He has put eternity in their *h*,
9: 3 Truly the *h* of the sons of men
9: 3 madness is in their *h* while
Isa 29:13 But have removed their *h* far
44:18 they cannot see, And their *h*,
Jer 3:17 the dictates of their evil *h*.
4: 4 away the foreskins of your *h*,
7:24 the dictates of their evil *h*,
9:14 to the dictates of their own *h*
13:10 follow the dictates of their *h*,
31:33 minds, and write it on their *h*;
32:40 I will put My fear in their *h*
42:20 you were hypocrites in your *h*
48:41 The mighty men's *h* in Moab on
Lam 3:41 Let us lift our *h* and hands To
Ezek 11:21 But as for those whose *h*
14: 3 set up their idols in their *h*,
32: 9 I will also trouble the *h* of
33:31 but their *h* pursue their own
Dan 11:27 Both these kings' *h* shall be
Hos 7: 2 do not consider in their *h*
Zech 7:12 they made their *h* like flint,
Mal 4: 6 And he will turn The *h* of the
4: 6 And the *h* of the children to
Mt 9: 4 do you think evil in your *h*?
13:15 For the *h* of this people
13:15 understand with their *h*
19: 8 of the hardness of your *h*,
Mk 2: 6 there and reasoning in their *h*,
2: 8 about these things in your *h*?
3: 5 by the hardness of their *h*,
4:15 word that was sown in their *h*.
Lk 1:17 to turn the *h* of the
1:51 in the imagination of their *h*.
1:66 them kept them in their *h*,
2:35 that the thoughts of many *h* may
3:15 and all reasoned in their *h*
5:22 are you reasoning in your *h*?
8:12 away the word out of their *h*,
16:15 men, but God knows your *h*.
21:14 settle it in your *h*
21:26 men's *h* failing them from fear
21:34 lest your *h* be weighed down
24:38 why do doubts arise in your *h*?
Jn 12:40 eyes and hardened their *h*,
12:40 understand with their *h*
Acts 1:24 who know the *h* of all, show
7:39 And in their *h* they turned back
14:17 filling our *h* with food and
15: 9 purifying their *h* by faith.
28:27 For the *h* of this people
28:27 understand with their *h*
Rom 1:21 and their foolish *h* were
1:24 in the lusts of their *h*,
2:15 of the law written in their *h*,
5: 5 has been poured out in our *h*
8:27 Now He who searches the *h* knows
16:18 speech deceive the *h* of the
1 Cor 4: 5 reveal the counsels of the *h*.
2 Cor 1:22 given us the Spirit in our *h*
3: 2 our epistle written in our *h*,
4: 6 who has shone in our *h* to give
7: 2 Open your *h* to us. We have
7: 3 before that you are in our *h*,
Gal 4: 6 Spirit of His Son into your *h*,
Eph 3:17 that Christ may dwell in your *h*
6:22 and that he may comfort your *h*.
Phil 4: 7 will guard your *h* and minds
Col 2: 2 that their *h* may be encouraged,
3:15 the peace of God rule in your *h*,
3:16 singing with grace in your *h* to
4: 8 and comfort your *h*,
1 Th 2: 4 men, but God who tests our *h*.
3:13 so that He may establish your *h*
2 Th 2:17 comfort your *h* and establish you
3: 5 Now may the Lord direct your *h*
Phm 1: 7 because the *h* of the saints
Heb 3: 8 Do not harden your *h* as
3:15 Do not harden your *h* as
4: 7 Do not harden your *h*.
8:10 and write them on their *h*;
10:16 put My laws into their *h*,
10:22 having our *h* sprinkled from an
Jas 3:14 envy and self-seeking in your *h*,
4: 8 and purify your *h*,
5: 5 you have fattened your *h* as in
5: 8 be patient. Establish your *h*,
1 Pe 3:15 sanctify the Lord God in your *h*,
2 Pe 1:19 morning star rises in your *h*;
1 Jn 3:19 and shall assure our *h* before
Rev 2:23 He who searches the minds and *h*.
17:17 God has put it into their *h* to

HEARTY (1/1)

Prov 27: 9 delight by *h* counsel.

HEAT (25/23) HEATED

Gen 8:22 and harvest, Cold and *h*,
18: 1 in the tent door in the *h* of
Deut 29:24 What does the *h* of this great
1 Sam 11:11 killed Ammonites until the *h*
2 Sam 4: 5 out and came at about the *h* of
Job 24:19 As drought and *h* consume the
Ps 19: 6 is nothing hidden from its *h*.
Isa 4: 6 shade in the daytime from the *h*,
18: 4 My dwelling place Like clear *h*
18: 4 Like a cloud of dew in the *h*
25: 4 the storm, A shade from the *h*;
25: 5 As *h* in a dry place; As heat
25: 5 As *h* in the shadow of a
49:10 Neither *h* nor sun shall strike
Jer 17: 8 And will not fear when *h*
36:30 shall be cast out to the *h* of
Ezek 3:14 in the *h* of my spirit; but the
Dan 3:19 and commanded that they *h* the
Mt 20:12 borne the burden and the *h* of
Acts 28: 3 viper came out because of the *h*,
Jas 1:11 the sun risen with a burning *h*
2 Pe 3:10 will melt with fervent *h*;
3:12 will melt with fervent *h*?
Rev 7:16 not strike them, nor any *h*;
16: 9 men were scorched with great *h*,

HEATED (2/2) HEAT

Dan 3:19 more than it was usually *h*.
Hos 7: 4 Like an oven *h* by a baker—He

HEATH (KJV) See SHRUB

HEATHEN (2/2)

Mt 6: 7 use vain repetitions as the *h*
18:17 let him be to you like a *h* and

HEAVE (30/26)

Ex 29:27 and the thigh of the *h* offering
29:28 For it is a *h* offering;
29:28 it shall be a *h* offering from
29:28 their *h* offering to the LORD.
Lev 7:14 cake from each offering as a *h*
7:32 give to the priest as a *h*
7:34 offering and the thigh of the *h*
10:14 offering and the thigh of the *h*
10:15 The thigh of the *h* offering and
Num 6:20 offering and the thigh of the *h*
15:19 that you shall offer up a *h*
15:20 of your ground meal as a *h*
15:20 as a *h* offering of the
15:21 you shall give to the LORD a *h*
18: 8 also given you charge of My *h*
18:11 the *h* offering of their gift,
18:19 All the *h* offerings of the holy
18:24 which they offer up as a *h*
18:26 then you shall offer up a *h*
18:27 And your *h* offering shall be
18:28 Thus you shall also offer a *h*
18:28 you shall give the LORD's *h*
18:29 you shall offer up every *h*
31:29 to Eleazar the priest as a *h*
31:41 which was the LORD's *h*
Deut 12: 6 the *h* offerings of your hand,
12:11 the *h* offerings of your hand,
12:17 or of the *h* offering of your
Am 8: 8 *H* and subside Like the River
Zech 12: 3 all who would *h* it away will

HEAVEN (532/502) HEAVEN'S, HEAVENLY, HEAVENS

Gen 1: 8 And God called the firmament *H*.
6:17 to destroy from under *h* all
7:11 and the windows of *h* were
7:19 high hills under the whole *h*
8: 2 the deep and the windows of *h*
8: 2 and the rain from *h* was
14:19 Possessor of *h* and earth;
14:22 the Possessor of *h* and earth,
15: 5 and said, "Look now toward *h*,
21:17 of God called to Hagar out of *h*,
22:11 the LORD called to him from *h*
22:15 Abraham a second time out of *h*,
22:17 as the stars of the *h* and as
24: 3 the God of *h* and the God of the
24: 7 "The LORD God of *h*,
26: 4 multiply as the stars of *h*;
27:28 God give you Of the dew of *h*,
27:39 And of the dew of *h* from
28:12 earth, and its top reached to *h*;
28:17 and this is the gate of *h*!"
49:25 bless you With blessings of *h*
Ex 9:10 Moses scattered them toward *h*.
9:22 out your hand toward *h*,
9:23 stretched out his rod toward *h*;
10:21 out your hand toward *h*,
10:22 stretched out his hand toward *h*,
16: 4 I will rain bread from *h* for
17:14 of Amalek from under *h*.
20: 4 of anything that is in *h*
20:22 I have talked with you from *h*.
32:13 descendants as the stars of *h*;
Deut 1:10 as the stars of *h* in multitude.
1:28 great and fortified up to *h*;
2:25 the nations under the whole *h*,
3:24 for what god is there in *h* or
4:11 with fire to the midst of *h*,
4:19 lest you lift your eyes to *h*,
4:19 the stars, all the host of *h*,
4:19 the peoples under the whole *h*
4:26 I call *h* and earth to witness
4:32 and ask from one end of *h* to
4:36 Out of *h* He let you hear His
4:39 the LORD Himself is God in *h*
5: 8 of anything that is in *h*
7:24 destroy their name from under *h*;
9: 1 great and fortified up to *h*,
9:14 out their name from under *h*;
10:14 Indeed *h* and the highest heavens
10:22 has made you as the stars of *h*
11:11 drinks water from the rain of *h*,
17: 3 or moon or any of the host of *h*,
25:19 of Amalek from under *h*.
26:15 Your holy habitation, from *h*,
28:24 from the *h* it shall come down
28:62 you were as the stars of *h* in
29:20 blot out his name from under *h*.
30: 4 to the farthest parts under *h*,
30:12 "It is not in *h*, that you should
30:12 Who will ascend into *h* for us
30:19 I call *h* and earth as witnesses
31:28 in their hearing and call *h*
32:40 For I raise My hand to *h*,
33:13 With the precious things of *h*,
Josh 2:11 He is God in *h* above and on
8:20 smoke of the city ascended to *h*.
10:11 down large hailstones from *h*
10:13 stood still in the midst of *h*,
Judg 13:20 as the flame went up toward *h*
20:40 city going up in smoke to *h*.
1 Sam 2:10 From *h* He will thunder against
5:12 cry of the city went up to *h*.
2 Sam 18: 9 he was left hanging between *h*
21:10 rains poured on them from *h*.
22: 8 The foundations of *h* quaked
22:14 "The LORD thundered from *h*,
1 Ki 8:22 spread out his hands toward *h*;
8:23 there is no God in *h* above or
8:27 *h* and the heaven of heavens
8:27 heaven and the *h* of heavens
8:30 Hear in *h* Your dwelling place;
8:32 "then hear in *h*, and act,
8:34 "then hear in *h*, and forgive
8:36 "then hear in *h*, and forgive
8:39 then hear in *h* Your dwelling
8:43 hear in *h* Your dwelling place,
8:45 then hear in *h* their prayer and
8:49 then hear in *h* Your dwelling
8:54 with his hands spread up to *h*.
22:19 and all the host of *h* standing
2 Ki 1:10 then let fire come down from *h*
1:10 And fire came down from *h* and
1:12 let fire come down from *h* and
1:12 fire of God came down from *h*
1:14 fire has come down from *h* and
2: 1 about to take up Elijah into *h*
2:11 went up by a whirlwind into *h*.
7: 2 LORD would make windows in *h*,
7:19 LORD would make windows in *h*,
14:27 the name of Israel from under *h*;
17:16 and worshiped all the host of *h*,
19:15 You have made *h* and earth.
21: 3 he worshiped all the host of *h*
21: 5 altars for all the host of *h*
23: 4 and for all the host of *h*;
23: 5 and to all the host of *h*.
1 Chr 21:16 standing between earth and *h*,
21:26 and He answered him from *h* by
29:11 For all that is in *h* and in
2 Chr 2: 6 since *h* and the heaven of
2: 6 since heaven and the *h* of
2:12 who made *h* and earth, for He
6:13 spread out his hands toward *h*);
6:14 there is no God in *h* or on
6:18 *h* and the heaven of heavens
6:18 heaven and the *h* of heavens
6:21 Hear from *h* Your dwelling
6:23 "then hear from *h*,
6:25 then hear from *h* and forgive the
6:27 "then hear in *h*, and forgive
6:30 then hear from *h* Your dwelling
6:33 then hear from *h* Your dwelling
6:35 then hear from *h* their prayer
6:39 then hear from *h* Your dwelling
7: 1 fire came down from *h* and
7:13 When I shut up *h* and there is no
7:14 ways, then I will hear from *h*,
18:18 and all the host of *h* standing
20: 6 fathers, are You not God in *h*,
28: 9 in a rage that reaches up to *h*.
30:27 His holy dwelling place, to *h*.
32:20 Amoz, prayed and cried out to *h*.
33: 3 he worshiped all the host of *h*
33: 5 altars for all the host of *h*
36:23 of the earth the LORD God of *h*
Ezra 1: 2 of the earth the LORD God of *h*
5:11 the servants of the God of *h*
5:12 fathers provoked the God of *h*
6: 9 burnt offerings of the God of *h*,
6:10 of sweet aroma to the God of *h*,
7:12 of the Law of the God of *h*:
7:21 of the Law of the God of *h*,
7:23 is commanded by the God of *h*,
7:23 for the house of the God of *h*.
Neh 1: 4 and praying before the God of *h*.
1: 5 said: "I pray, LORD God of *h*,
2: 4 So I prayed to the God of *h*.
2:20 The God of *h* Himself will
9: 6 the LORD; You have made *h*,

9: 6 The **h** of heavens, with all
9: 6 The host of **h** worships You.
9:13 And spoke with them from **h**,
9:15 You gave them bread from **h** for
9:23 children as the stars of **h**,
9:27 cried to You, You heard from **h**;
9:28 out to You, You heard from **h**;
Job 1:16 The fire of God fell from **h** and
2:12 dust on his head toward **h**.
11: 8 They are higher than **h**—
16:19 even now my witness is in **h**,
22:12 not God in the height of **h**?
22:14 He walks above the circle of **h**.
26:11 The pillars of **h** tremble, And
35:11 us wiser than the birds of **h**?
37: 3 it forth under the whole **h**,
38:29 the ice? And the frost of **h**,
38:37 can pour out the bottles of **h**,
41:11 Everything under **h** is Mine.
Ps 11: 4 The LORD's throne is in **h**;
14: 2 The LORD looks down from **h**
18:13 The LORD thundered from **h**,
19: 6 rising is from one end of **h**,
20: 6 will answer him from His holy **h**
33:13 The LORD looks from **h**;
53: 2 God looks down from **h** upon the
57: 3 He shall send from **h** and save
68:33 To Him who rides on the **h** of
69:34 Let **h** and earth praise Him,
73:25 Whom have I in **h** but You?
76: 8 judgment to be heard from **h**;
78:23 And opened the doors of **h**,
78:24 given them of the bread of **h**.
80:14 Look down from **h** and see, And
85:11 shall look down from **h**.
89:29 his throne as the days of **h**.
102:19 From **h** the LORD viewed the
103:19 has established His throne in **h**,
105:40 them with the bread of **h**.
115: 3 But our God is in **h**;
115:15 Who made **h** and earth.
115:16 The **h**, even the heavens,
119:89 Your word is settled in **h**.
121: 2 Who made **h** and earth.
124: 8 Who made **h** and earth.
134: 3 The LORD who made **h** and earth
135: 6 In **h** and in earth, In the
136:26 give thanks to the God of **h**!
139: 8 If I ascend into **h**,
146: 6 Who made **h** and earth, The sea,
148:13 glory is above the earth and **h**.
Prov 23: 5 away like an eagle toward **h**.
30: 4 Who has ascended into **h**,
Eccl 1:13 all that is done under **h**;
2: 3 the sons of men to do under **h**
3: 1 time for every purpose under **h**:
5: 2 before God. For God is in **h**,
Isa 13: 5 far country, From the end of **h**—
13:10 For the stars of **h** and their
14:12 "How you are fallen from **h**,
14:13 heart: 'I will ascend into **h**,
34: 4 All the host of **h** shall be
34: 5 My sword shall be bathed in **h**;
37:16 You have made **h** and earth.
40:12 Measured **h** with a span And
55:10 comes down, and the snow from **h**,
63:15 Look down from **h**,
66: 1 ***H*** is My throne, And earth is
Jer 7:18 make cakes for the queen of **h**;
7:33 be food for the birds of the **h**
8: 2 the moon and all the host of **h**,
10: 2 be dismayed at the signs of **h**,
16: 4 be meat for the birds of **h** and
19: 7 as meat for the birds of the **h**
19:13 incense to all the host of **h**,
23:24 Do I not fill **h** and earth?"
31:37 If **h** above can be measured, And
33:22 As the host of **h** cannot be
33:25 appointed the ordinances of **h**
34:20 for meat for the birds of the **h**
44:17 burn incense to the queen of **h**
44:18 incense to the queen of **h**
44:19 incense to the queen of **h** and
44:25 burn incense to the queen of **h**
49:36 From the four quarters of **h**,
51: 9 For her judgment reaches to **h**
51:15 And stretched out the **h** by His
51:53 Babylon were to mount up to **h**,
Lam 2: 1 He cast down from **h** to
3:41 hearts and hands To God in **h**.
3:50 Till the LORD from **h** Looks
Ezek 8: 3 me up between earth and **h**,
Dan 2:18 seek mercies from the God of **h**
2:19 So Daniel blessed the God of **h**.
2:28 But there is a God in **h** who
2:37 For the God of **h** has given you
2:38 field and the birds of the **h**,
2:44 of these kings the God of **h**
4:13 a holy one, coming down from **h**.
4:15 it be wet with the dew of **h**,
4:21 branches the birds of the **h**
4:23 coming down from **h** and saying,
4:23 let it be wet with the dew of **h**,
4:25 shall wet you with the dew of **h**,
4:26 after you come to know that ***H***
4:31 mouth, a voice fell from **h**:
4:33 body was wet with the dew of **h**
4:34 lifted my eyes to **h**,
4:35 to His will in the army of **h**
4:37 extol and honor the King of **h**,
5:21 body was wet with the dew of **h**,
5:23 up against the Lord of **h**.

6:27 works signs and wonders In **h**
7: 2 the four winds of **h** were
7:13 Coming with the clouds of **h**!
7:27 the kingdoms under the whole **h**,
8: 8 up toward the four winds of **h**.
8:10 And it grew up to the host of **h**;
9:12 for under the whole **h** such has
11: 4 toward the four winds of **h**,
12: 7 hand and his left hand to **h**,
Am 9: 2 Though they climb up to **h**,
Jon 1: 9 I fear the LORD, the God of **h**,
Nah 3:16 more than the stars of **h**.
Zeph 1: 5 who worship the host of **h** on
Hag 2: 6 a little while) I will shake **h**
2:21 I will shake **h** and earth.
Zech 2: 6 abroad like the four winds of **h**,
5: 9 the basket between earth and **h**.
6: 5 "These are four spirits of **h**,
Mal 3:10 open for you the windows of **h**
Mt 3: 2 for the kingdom of **h** is at
3:17 suddenly a voice came from **h**,
4:17 for the kingdom of **h** is at
5: 3 For theirs is the kingdom of **h**.
5:10 For theirs is the kingdom of **h**.
5:12 for great is your reward in **h**,
5:16 and glorify your Father in **h**.
5:18 till **h** and earth pass away, one
5:19 least in the kingdom of **h**;
5:19 great in the kingdom of **h**.
5:20 no means enter the kingdom of **h**.
5:34 not swear at all: neither by **h**,
5:45 may be sons of your Father in **h**;
5:48 just as your Father in **h** is
6: 1 no reward from your Father in **h**.
6: 9 pray: Our Father in **h**,
6:10 done On earth as it is in **h**.
6:20 for yourselves treasures in **h**,
7:11 will your Father who is in **h**
7:21 shall enter the kingdom of **h**,
7:21 does the will of My Father in **h**.
8:11 and Jacob in the kingdom of **h**.
10: 7 The kingdom of **h** is at hand.'
10:32 before My Father who is in **h**.
10:33 before My Father who is in **h**.
11:11 is least in the kingdom of **h**
11:12 until now the kingdom of **h**
11:23 Capernaum, who are exalted to **h**,
11:25 Lord of **h** and earth, that You
12:50 the will of My Father in **h** is
13:11 mysteries of the kingdom of **h**,
13:24 The kingdom of **h** is like a man
13:31 The kingdom of **h** is like a
13:33 The kingdom of **h** is like leaven,
13:44 the kingdom of **h** is like
13:45 the kingdom of **h** is like a
13:47 the kingdom of **h** is like a
13:52 concerning the kingdom of **h** is
14:19 two fish, and looking up to **h**,
16: 1 would show them a sign from **h**.
16:17 you, but My Father who is in **h**.
16:19 the keys of the kingdom of **h**,
16:19 on earth will be bound in **h**,
16:19 on earth will be loosed in **h**.
18: 1 is greatest in the kingdom of **h**?
18: 3 no means enter the kingdom of **h**.
18: 4 greatest in the kingdom of **h**.
18:10 for I say to you that in **h**
18:10 face of My Father who is in **h**.
18:14 will of your Father who is in **h**
18:18 on earth will be bound in **h**,
18:18 on earth will be loosed in **h**.
18:19 done for them by My Father in **h**.
18:23 Therefore the kingdom of **h** is
19:14 for of such is the kingdom of **h**.
19:21 and you will have treasure in **h**;
19:23 man to enter the kingdom of **h**.
20: 1 For the kingdom of **h** is like a
21:25 From **h** or from men?" And they
21:25 saying, "If we say, 'From **h**,
22: 2 The kingdom of **h** is like a
22:30 but are like angels of God in **h**.
23: 9 is your Father, He who is in **h**.
23:13 you shut up the kingdom of **h**
23:22 "And he who swears by **h**,
24:29 the stars will fall from **h**,
24:30 the Son of Man will appear in **h**,
24:30 Man coming on the clouds of **h**
24:31 from one end of **h** to the other.
24:35 ***H*** and earth will pass away, but
24:36 knows, not even the angels of **h**,
25: 1 Then the kingdom of **h** shall be
25:14 For the kingdom of **h** is
26:64 and coming on the clouds of **h**.
28: 2 of the Lord descended from **h**,
28:18 has been given to Me in **h** and
Mk 1:11 Then a voice came from **h**,
6:41 the two fish, He looked up to **h**,
7:34 Then, looking up to **h**,
8:11 seeking from Him a sign from **h**,
10:21 and you will have treasure in **h**;
11:25 that your Father in **h** may also
11:26 neither will your Father in **h**
11:30 was it from **h** or from men?
11:31 saying, "If we say, 'From **h**,
12:25 but are like angels in **h**.
13:25 the stars of **h** will fall, and
13:27 earth to the farthest part of **h**.
13:31 ***H*** and earth will pass away, but
13:32 knows, not even the angels in **h**,
14:62 and coming with the clouds of **h**.
16:19 them, He was received up into **h**,
Lk 2:15 had gone away from them into **h**,

3:21 the **h** was opened.
3:22 and a voice came from **h** which
4:25 when the **h** was shut up three
6:23 your reward is great in **h**,
9:16 two fish, and looking up to **h**,
9:54 fire to come down from **h** and
10:15 Capernaum, who are exalted to **h**,
10:18 fall like lightning from **h**.
10:20 your names are written in **h**.
10:21 Lord of **h** and earth, that You
11: 2 pray, say: Our Father in **h**,
11: 2 done On earth as it is in **h**.
11:16 sought from Him a sign from **h**.
15: 7 there will be more joy in **h**
15:18 I have sinned against **h** and
15:21 I have sinned against **h** and in
16:17 And it is easier for **h** and earth
17:24 out of one part under **h**
17:24 to the other part under **h**,
17:29 fire and brimstone from **h** and
18:13 so much as raise his eyes to **h**,
18:22 and you will have treasure in **h**;
19:38 Peace in **h** and glory in the
20: 4 was it from **h** or from men?"
20: 5 saying, "If we say, 'From **h**,
21:11 sights and great signs from **h**.
21:26 for the powers of **h** will be
21:33 ***H*** and earth will pass away, but
22:43 an angel appeared to Him from **h**,
24:51 from them and carried up into **h**.
Jn 1:32 the Spirit descending from **h**
1:51 hereafter you shall see **h** open,
3:13 No one has ascended to **h** but He
3:13 but He who came down from **h**,
3:13 is, the Son of Man who is in **h**.
3:27 it has been given to him from **h**.
3:31 He who comes from **h** is above
6:31 gave them bread from **h**
6:32 not give you the bread from **h**,
6:32 gives you the true bread from **h**.
6:33 God is He who comes down from **h**
6:38 "For I have come down from **h**,
6:41 bread which came down from **h**.
6:42 says, 'I have come down from **h**'?
6:50 bread which comes down from **h**,
6:51 bread which came down from **h**.
6:58 bread which came down from **h**—
12:28 Then a voice came from **h**,
17: 1 words, lifted up His eyes to **h**,
Acts 1:10 looked steadfastly toward **h** as
1:11 do you stand gazing up into **h**?
1:11 was taken up from you into **h**,
1:11 manner as you saw Him go into **h**.
2: 2 there came a sound from **h**,
2: 5 men, from every nation under **h**.
2:19 I will show wonders in **h**
3:21 whom **h** must receive until the
4:12 there is no other name under **h**
4:24 who made **h** and earth and the
7:42 up to worship the host of **h**,
7:49 ***H*** is My throne, And earth
7:55 gazed into **h** and saw the glory
9: 3 a light shone around him from **h**.
10:11 and saw **h** opened and an object
10:16 the object was taken up into **h**
11: 5 let down from **h** by four
11: 9 voice answered me again from **h**,
11:10 all were drawn up again into **h**.
14:15 the living God, who made the **h**,
14:17 gave us rain from **h** and
17:24 since He is Lord of **h** and
22: 6 suddenly a great light from **h**
26:13 the road I saw a light from **h**,
Rom 1:18 wrath of God is revealed from **h**
10: 6 'Who will ascend into **h**?
1 Cor 8: 5 whether in **h** or on earth
15:47 second Man is the Lord from **h**.
2 Cor 5: 2 our habitation which is from **h**,
12: 2 was caught up to the third **h**.
Gal 1: 8 even if we, or an angel from **h**,
Eph 1:10 both which are in **h** and which
3:15 whom the whole family in **h** and
6: 9 your own Master also is in **h**,
Phil 2:10 knee should bow, of those in **h**,
3:20 For our citizenship is in **h**,
Col 1: 5 which is laid up for you in **h**,
1:16 were created that are in **h** and
1:20 things on earth or things in **h**,
1:23 to every creature under **h**,
4: 1 you also have a Master in **h**.
1 Th 1:10 and to wait for His Son from **h**,
4:16 Himself will descend from **h**
2 Th 1: 7 Lord Jesus is revealed from **h**
Heb 9:24 but into **h** itself, now to
10:34 possession for yourselves in **h**.
12:23 who are registered in **h**,
12:25 from Him who speaks from **h**,
12:26 the earth, but also **h**.
Jas 5:12 either by **h** or by earth or with
5:18 and the **h** gave rain, and the
1 Pe 1: 4 reserved in **h** for you,
1:12 by the Holy Spirit sent from **h**—
3:22 who has gone into **h** and is at
2 Pe 1:18 this voice which came from **h**
1 Jn 5: 7 three that bear witness in **h**:
Rev 3:12 which comes down out of **h** from
4: 1 a door standing open in **h**.
4: 2 and behold, a throne set in **h**,
5: 3 And no one in **h** or on the earth
5:13 every creature which is in **h**
6:13 And the stars of **h** fell to the
8: 1 there was silence in **h** for

8:10 And a great star fell from ***h***,
8:13 flying through the midst of ***h***,
9: 1 And I saw a star fallen from ***h***
10: 1 mighty angel coming down from ***h***,
10: 4 but I heard a voice from ***h***
10: 5 land raised up his hand to ***h***
10: 6 who created ***h*** and the things
10: 8 the voice which I heard from ***h***
11: 6 These have power to shut ***h***,
11:12 they heard a loud voice from ***h***
11:12 And they ascended to ***h*** in a
11:13 and gave glory to the God of ***h***.
11:15 And there were loud voices in ***h***,
11:19 temple of God was opened in ***h***,
12: 1 Now a great sign appeared in ***h***:
12: 3 And another sign appeared in ***h***:
12: 4 drew a third of the stars of ***h***
12: 7 And war broke out in ***h***:
12: 8 was a place found for them in ***h***
12:10 heard a loud voice saying in ***h***,
13: 6 and those who dwell in ***h***.
13:13 makes fire come down from ***h*** on
14: 2 And I heard a voice from ***h***,
14: 6 angel flying in the midst of ***h***,
14: 7 and worship Him who made ***h*** and
14:13 Then I heard a voice from ***h***
14:17 out of the temple which is in ***h***,
15: 1 Then I saw another sign in ***h***,
15: 5 of the testimony in ***h*** was
16:11 They blasphemed the God of ***h***
16:17 came out of the temple of ***h***,
16:21 And great hail from ***h*** fell upon
18: 1 angel coming down from ***h***,
18: 4 I heard another voice from ***h***
18: 5 her sins have reached to ***h***,
18:20 "Rejoice over her, O ***h***,
19: 1 voice of a great multitude in ***h***,
19:11 Now I saw ***h*** opened, and behold,
19:14 And the armies in ***h***,
19:17 that fly in the midst of ***h***,
20: 1 saw an angel coming down from ***h***,
20: 9 came down from God out of ***h***
20:11 whose face the earth and the ***h***
21: 1 Now I saw a new ***h*** and a new
21: 1 for the first ***h*** and the first
21: 2 coming down out of ***h*** from God,
21: 3 And I heard a loud voice from ***h***
21:10 descending out of ***h*** from God,

HEAVEN'S (1/1) HEAVEN

Mt 19:12 for the kingdom of ***h*** sake.

HEAVENLY (24/23) HEAVEN

Mt 6:14 your ***h*** Father will also forgive
6:26 yet your ***h*** Father feeds them.
6:32 For your ***h*** Father knows that
15:13 Every plant which My ***h*** Father
18:35 So My ***h*** Father also will do to
Lk 2:13 a multitude of the ***h*** host
11:13 more will your ***h*** Father
Jn 3:12 if I tell you ***h*** things?
Acts 26:19 disobedient to the ***h*** vision,
1 Cor 15:48 and as is the ***h*** Man, so also
15:48 so also are those who are ***h***.
15:49 the image of the ***h*** Man.
Eph 1: 3 blessing in the ***h*** places
1:20 His right hand in the ***h*** places,
2: 6 sit together in the ***h*** places
3:10 and powers in the ***h*** places,
6:12 wickedness in the ***h*** places.
2 Tim 4:18 preserve me for His ***h*** kingdom.
Heb 3: 1 partakers of the ***h*** calling,
6: 4 and have tasted the ***h*** gift, and
8: 5 and shadow of the ***h*** things,
9:23 but the ***h*** things themselves
11:16 a ***h*** country. Therefore God is
12:22 the ***h*** Jerusalem, to an

HEAVENS (171/166) HEAVEN

Gen 1: 1 the beginning God created the ***h***
1: 9 Let the waters under the ***h*** be
1:14 in the firmament of the ***h*** to
1:15 in the firmament of the ***h*** to
1:17 them in the firmament of the ***h***
1:20 face of the firmament of the ***h***.
2: 1 Thus the ***h*** and the earth, and
2: 4 This is the history of the ***h***
2: 4 God made the earth and the ***h***,
11: 4 a tower whose top is in the ***h***;
19:24 from the LORD out of the ***h***.
Ex 9: 8 Moses scatter it toward the ***h***
20:11 six days the LORD made the ***h***
24:10 and it was like the very ***h*** in
31:17 six days the LORD made the ***h***
Lev 26:19 I will make your ***h*** like iron
Deut 10:14 heaven and the highest ***h***
11:17 and He shut up the ***h*** so that
11:21 like the days of the ***h*** above
28:12 to you His good treasure, the ***h***,
28:23 And your ***h*** which are over your
32: 1 "Give ear, O ***h***, and I will
33:26 Who rides the ***h*** to help you,
33:28 His ***h*** shall also drop dew.
Judg 5: 4 The earth trembled and the ***h***
5:20 They fought from the ***h***;
2 Sam 22:10 He bowed the ***h*** also, and came
1 Ki 8:27 heaven and the heaven of ***h***
8:35 When the ***h*** are shut up and
1 Chr 16:26 But the LORD made the ***h***.
16:31 Let the ***h*** rejoice, and let the
27:23 Israel like the stars of the ***h***.
2 Chr 2: 6 heaven and the heaven of ***h***
6:18 heaven and the heaven of ***h***
6:26 When the ***h*** are shut up and
Ezra 9: 6 our guilt has grown up to the ***h***.
Neh 1: 9 to the farthest part of the ***h***,
9: 6 made heaven, The heaven of ***h***,
Job 9: 8 He alone spreads out the ***h***,
14:12 Till the ***h*** are no more, They
15:15 And the ***h*** are not pure in His
20: 6 haughtiness mounts up to the ***h***,
20:27 The ***h*** will reveal his iniquity,
26:13 By His Spirit He adorned the ***h***;
28:24 And sees under the whole ***h***,
35: 5 Look to the ***h*** and see;
38:33 know the ordinances of the ***h***?
Ps 2: 4 He who sits in the ***h*** shall
8: 1 set Your glory above the ***h***!
8: 3 When I consider Your ***h***,
18: 9 He bowed the ***h*** also, and came
19: 1 The ***h*** declare the glory of God;
33: 6 By the word of the LORD the ***h***
36: 5 mercy, O LORD, is in the ***h***;
50: 4 He shall call to the ***h*** from
50: 6 Let the ***h*** declare His
57: 5 Be exalted, O God, above the ***h***;
57:10 Your mercy reaches unto the ***h***,
57:11 Be exalted, O God, above the ***h***;
68: 8 The ***h*** also dropped rain at
68:33 who rides on the heaven of ***h***,
73: 9 set their mouth against the ***h***,
78:26 an east wind to blow in the ***h***;
79: 2 as food for the birds of the ***h***,
89: 2 shall establish in the very ***h***.
89: 5 And the ***h*** will praise Your
89: 6 For who in the ***h*** can be
89:11 The ***h*** are Yours, the earth
96: 5 But the LORD made the ***h***.
96:11 Let the ***h*** rejoice, and let the
97: 6 The ***h*** declare His
102:25 And the ***h*** are the work of
103:11 For as the ***h*** are high above the
104: 2 Who stretch out the ***h*** like a
104:12 By them the birds of the ***h*** have
107:26 They mount up to the ***h***,
108: 4 mercy is great above the ***h***,
108: 5 Be exalted, O God, above the ***h***,
113: 4 nations, His glory above the ***h***.
113: 6 things that are in the ***h***
115:16 The heaven, even the ***h***,
123: 1 eyes, O You who dwell in the ***h***.
136: 5 Him who by wisdom made the ***h***,
144: 5 Bow down Your ***h***,
147: 8 Who covers the ***h*** with clouds,
148: 1 Praise the LORD from the ***h***;
148: 4 you ***h*** of heavens, And you
148: 4 Praise Him, you heavens of ***h***,
148: 4 And you waters above the ***h***!
Prov 3:19 He established the ***h***;
8:27 When He prepared the ***h***,
25: 3 As the ***h*** for height and the
Isa 1: 2 Hear, O ***h***, and give ear,
13:13 Therefore I will shake the ***h***,
34: 4 And the ***h*** shall be rolled up
40:22 Who stretches out the ***h*** like a
42: 5 Who created the ***h*** and
44:23 Sing, O ***h***, for the LORD has
44:24 Who stretches out the ***h*** all
45: 8 "Rain down, you ***h***,
45:12 hands— stretched out the ***h***,
45:18 the LORD, Who created the ***h***,
48:13 hand has stretched out the ***h***;
49:13 O ***h***! Be joyful, O earth!
50: 3 I clothe the ***h*** with blackness,
51: 6 Lift up your eyes to the ***h***,
51: 6 For the ***h*** will vanish away
51:13 Who stretched out the ***h*** And
51:16 hand, That I may plant the ***h***,
55: 9 For as the ***h*** are higher than
64: 1 that You would rend the ***h***!
65:17 I create new ***h*** and a new earth;
66:22 For as the new ***h*** and the new
Jer 2:12 Be astonished, O ***h***,
4:23 form, and void; And the ***h***,
4:25 And all the birds of the ***h*** had
4:28 And the ***h*** above be black,
8: 7 Even the stork in the ***h*** Knows
9:10 Both the birds of the ***h*** and
10:11 gods that have not made the ***h***
10:11 earth and from under these ***h***.
10:12 And has stretched out the ***h*** at
10:13 a multitude of waters in the ***h***:
14:22 Or can the ***h*** give showers?
15: 3 the birds of the ***h*** and the
32:17 You have made the ***h*** and the
51:16 a multitude of waters in the ***h***:
51:48 Then the ***h*** and the earth and
Lam 3:66 destroy them From under the ***h***
4:19 Than the eagles of the ***h***.
Ezek 1: 1 that the ***h*** were opened and I
29: 5 And to the birds of the ***h***.
31: 6 All the birds of the ***h*** made
31:13 remain all the birds of the ***h***,
32: 4 on you all the birds of the ***h***.
32: 7 your light, I will cover the ***h***,
32: 8 the bright lights of the ***h*** I
38:20 of the sea, the birds of the ***h***,
Dan 4:11 Its height reached to the ***h***,
4:12 The birds of the ***h*** dwelt in
4:20 whose height reached to the ***h***
4:22 has grown and reaches to the ***h***,
Hos 2:21 'I will answer the ***h***,
Joel 2:10 The ***h*** tremble; The sun and
2:30 I will show wonders in the ***h***
3:16 The ***h*** and earth will shake;
Hab 3: 3 Selah His glory covered the ***h***,
Zeph 1: 3 will consume the birds of the ***h***,
Hag 1:10 Therefore the ***h*** above you
Zech 8:12 And the ***h*** shall give their
12: 1 LORD, who stretches out the ***h***,
Mt 3:16 the ***h*** were opened to Him, and
24:29 and the powers of the ***h*** will be
Mk 1:10 He saw the ***h*** parting and the
13:25 and the powers in the ***h*** will be
Lk 12:33 a treasure in the ***h*** that does
Acts 2:34 David did not ascend into the ***h***,
7:56 I see the ***h*** opened and the
2 Cor 5: 1 with hands, eternal in the ***h***.
Eph 4:10 ascended far above all the ***h***,
Heb 1:10 And the ***h*** are the work
4:14 who has passed through the ***h***,
7:26 has become higher than the ***h***;
8: 1 throne of the Majesty in the ***h***,
9:23 copies of the things in the ***h***
2 Pe 3: 5 that by the word of God the ***h***
3: 7 But the ***h*** and the earth which
3:10 in which the ***h*** will pass away
3:12 because of which the ***h*** will be
3:13 look for new ***h*** and a new earth
Rev 12:12 "Therefore rejoice, O ***h***,

HEAVES (1/1)

Nah 1: 5 And the earth ***h*** at His

HEAVIER (2/2)

Job 6: 3 it would be ***h*** than the sand
Prov 27: 3 But a fool's wrath is ***h*** than

HEAVILY (4/4)

Ps 35:14 or brother; I bowed down ***h***,
Isa 9: 1 And afterward more ***h*** oppressed
46: 1 Your carriages were ***h*** loaded,
47: 6 you laid your yoke very ***h***.

HEAVINESS (4/4) HEAVY

Ps 69:20 my heart, And I am full of ***h***;
119:28 My soul melts from ***h***;
Isa 29: 2 There shall be ***h*** and sorrow,
61: 3 of praise for the spirit of ***h***;

HEAVY (46/43) HEAVINESS

Ex 9:18 this time I will cause very ***h***
9:24 so very ***h*** that there was none
17:12 But Moses' hands became ***h***;
Num 11:14 because the burden is too ***h***
Deut 25:13 weights, a ***h*** and a light.
1 Sam 4:18 died, for the man was old and ***h***.
5: 6 the hand of the LORD was ***h*** on
5:11 the hand of God was very ***h***
2 Sam 14:26 he cut it because it was ***h*** on
1 Ki 12: 4 "Your father made our yoke ***h***;
12: 4 and his ***h*** yoke which he put on
12:10 'Your father made our yoke ***h***,
12:11 whereas my father put a ***h*** yoke
12:14 "My father made your yoke ***h***,
18:45 and there was a ***h*** rain. So Ahab
2 Chr 10: 4 "Your father made our yoke ***h***;
10: 4 of your father and his ***h*** yoke
10:10 'Your father made our yoke ***h***,
10:11 whereas my father put a ***h*** yoke
10:14 "My father made your yoke ***h***,
Ezra 5: 8 which is being built with ***h***
6: 4 with three rows of ***h*** stones and
10: 9 this matter and because of ***h***
10:13 it is the season for ***h*** rain,
Neh 5:18 because the bondage was ***h*** on
Job 15:27 And made his waist ***h*** with
33: 7 Nor will my hand be ***h*** on you.
37: 6 to the gentle rain and the ***h***
Ps 32: 4 day and night Your hand was ***h***
38: 4 Like a ***h*** burden they are too
38: 4 a heavy burden they are too ***h***
88: 7 Your wrath lies ***h*** upon me, And
Prov 25:20 Is one who sings songs to a ***h***
27: 3 A stone is ***h*** and sand is
Isa 6:10 people dull, And their ears ***h***,
24:20 Its transgression shall be ***h***
30:27 anger, And His burden is ***h***;
58: 6 To undo the ***h*** burdens, To let
59: 1 it cannot save; Nor His ear ***h***,
Lam 3: 7 He has made my chain ***h***.
Zech 12: 3 I will make Jerusalem a very ***h***
Mt 11:28 all you who labor and are ***h***
23: 4 For they bind ***h*** burdens, hard to
26:43 again, for their eyes were ***h***.
Mk 14:40 again, for their eyes were ***h***;
Lk 9:32 and those with him were ***h*** with

HEBER (10/9) HEBER'S

Gen 46:17 And the sons of Beriah were ***H***
Num 26:45 Of the sons of Beriah: of ***H***,
Judg 4:11 Now ***H*** the Kenite, of the
4:17 the wife of ***H*** the Kenite;
4:17 of Hazor and the house of ***H***
5:24 The wife of ***H*** the Kenite,
1 Chr 4:18 ***H*** the father of Sochoh, and
7:31 The sons of Beriah were ***H*** and
7:32 And ***H*** begot Japhlet, Shomer,

8:17 Zebadiah, Meshullam, Hizki, ***H***,

HEBER'S (1/1) HEBER

Judg 4:21 ***H*** wife, took a tent peg and

HEBERITES (1/1)

Num 26:45 of Heber, the family of the ***H***;

HEBREW (32/31) HEBREWS

Gen 14:13 came and told Abram the ***H***,
39:14 he has brought in to us a ***H*** to
39:17 The ***H*** servant whom you brought
41:12 Now there was a young ***H*** man
Ex 1:15 king of Egypt spoke to the ***H***
1:16 duties of a midwife for the ***H***
1:19 Because the ***H*** women are not
2: 7 call a nurse for you from the ***H***
2:11 he saw an Egyptian beating a ***H***,
2:13 two ***H*** men were fighting, and he
21: 2 If you buy a ***H*** servant, he shall
Deut 15:12 a ***H*** man, or a Hebrew woman, is
15:12 or a ***H*** woman, is sold to you
2 Ki 18:26 and do not speak to us in ***H*** in
18:28 out with a loud voice in ***H***,
2 Chr 32:18 out with a loud voice in ***H*** to
Isa 36:11 and do not speak to us in ***H*** in
36:13 out with a loud voice in ***H***,
Jer 34: 9 a ***H*** man or woman—that no one
34:14 let every man set free his ***H***
Jon 1: 9 So he said to them, "I am a ***H***;
Lk 23:38 letters of Greek, Latin, and ***H***:
Jn 5: 2 a pool, which is called in ***H***,
19:13 called The Pavement, but in ***H***,
19:17 a Skull, which is called in ***H***,
19:20 and it was written in ***H***,
Acts 21:40 he spoke to them in the ***H***
22: 2 that he spoke to them in the ***H***
26:14 to me and saying in the ***H***
Phil 3: 5 a ***H*** of the Hebrews; concerning
Rev 9:11 whose name in ***H*** is Abaddon,
16:16 to the place called in ***H***,

HEBREWS (19/19) HEBREW, HEBREWS'

Gen 40:15 away from the land of the ***H***;
43:32 could not eat food with the ***H***,
Ex 3:18 The LORD God of the ***H*** has met
5: 3 The God of the ***H*** has met with
7:16 The LORD God of the ***H*** has sent
9: 1 says the LORD God of the ***H***:
9:13 says the LORD God of the ***H***:
10: 3 says the LORD God of the ***H***:
1 Sam 4: 6 shout in the camp of the ***H***
4: 9 do not become servants of the ***H***,
13: 3 saying, "Let the ***H*** hear!"
13: 7 And some of the ***H*** crossed over
13:19 Lest the ***H*** make swords or
14:11 the ***H*** are coming out of the
14:21 Moreover the ***H*** who were with
29: 3 What are these ***H*** doing
Acts 6: 1 a complaint against the ***H*** by
2 Cor 11:22 Are they ***H***? So am I.
Phil 3: 5 of Benjamin, a Hebrew of the ***H***;

HEBREWS' (1/1)

Ex 2: 6 This is one of the ***H*** children."

HEBRON (72/67) KIRJATH ARBA

Gen 13:18 trees of Mamre, which are in ***H***,
23: 2 ***H***) in the land of Canaan, and
23:19 ***H***) in the land of Canaan.
35:27 or Kirjath Arba (that is, ***H***),
37:14 sent him out of the Valley of ***H***,
Ex 6:18 of Kohath were Amram, Izhar, ***H***,
Num 3:19 families: Amram, Izehar, ***H***,
13:22 through the South and came to ***H***;
13:22 (Now ***H*** was built seven years
Josh 10: 3 sent to Hoham king of ***H***,
10: 5 of Jerusalem, the king of ***H***,
10:23 of Jerusalem, the king of ***H***,
10:36 and all Israel with him, to ***H***;
10:39 remaining; as he had done to ***H***,
11:21 from the mountains: from ***H***,
12:10 Jerusalem, one; the king of ***H***,
14:13 and gave ***H*** to Caleb the son of
14:14 ***H*** therefore became the
14:15 And the name of ***H*** formerly was
15:13 which is ***H*** (Arba was the
15:54 Kirjath Arba (which is ***H***),
20: 7 and Kirjath Arba (which is ***H***)
21:11 father of Anak), which is ***H***,
21:13 of Aaron the priest they gave ***H***
Judg 1:10 the Canaanites who dwelt in ***H***.
1:10 (Now the name of ***H*** was
1:20 And they gave ***H*** to Caleb, as
16: 3 top of the hill that faces ***H***.
1 Sam 30:31 those who were in ***H***,
2 Sam 2: 1 I go up?" And He said, "To ***H***.
2: 3 they dwelt in the cities of ***H***.
2:11 time that David was king in ***H***
2:32 and they came to ***H*** at daybreak.
3: 2 Sons were born to David in ***H***:
3: 5 These were born to David in ***H***.
3:19 in the hearing of David in ***H***
3:20 men with him came to David at ***H***.
3:22 Abner was not with David in ***H***,
3:27 when Abner had returned to ***H***,
3:32 So they buried Abner in ***H***;
4: 1 heard that Abner had died in ***H***,
4: 8 of Ishbosheth to David at ***H***,
4:12 hanged them by the pool in ***H***.
4:12 it in the tomb of Abner in ***H***.
5: 1 of Israel came to David at ***H***
5: 3 of Israel came to the king at ***H***,
5: 3 made a covenant with them at ***H***
5: 5 In ***H*** he reigned over Judah seven
5:13 after he had come from ***H***.
15: 7 let me go to ***H*** and pay the vow
15: 9 So he arose and went to ***H***.
15:10 Absalom reigns in ***H***!'"
1 Ki 2:11 seven years he reigned in ***H***,
1 Chr 2:42 of Mareshah the father of ***H***.
2:43 The sons of ***H*** were Korah,
3: 1 David who were born to him in ***H***:
3: 4 six were born to him in ***H***.
6: 2 of Kohath were Amram, Izhar, ***H***,
6:18 of Kohath were Amram, Izhar, ***H***,
6:55 They gave them ***H*** in the land of
6:57 of the cities of refuge, ***H***;
11: 1 came together to David at ***H***,
11: 3 of Israel came to the king at ***H***,
11: 3 made a covenant with them at ***H***
12:23 and came to David at ***H*** to turn
12:38 came to ***H*** with a loyal heart,
15: 9 of the sons of ***H***,
23:12 sons of Kohath: Amram, Izhar, ***H***,
23:19 Of the sons of ***H***,
24:23 Of the sons of ***H***,
29:27 seven years he reigned in ***H***,
2 Chr 11:10 Zorah, Aijalon, and ***H***,

HEBRONITES (6/5)

Num 3:27 Izharites, the family of the ***H***,
26:58 Libnites, the family of the ***H***,
1 Chr 26:23 Amramites, the Izharites, the ***H***,
26:30 Of the ***H***, Hashabiah and his
26:31 Among the ***H***, Jerijah was
26:31 Jerijah was head of the ***H***

HEDGE (7/7) HEDGED, HEDGES

Job 1:10 Have You not made a ***h*** around
Prov 15:19 of the lazy man is like a ***h***
Isa 5: 5 I will take away its ***h***,
Hos 2: 6 I will ***h*** up your way with
Mic 7: 4 is sharper than a thorn ***h***;
Mt 21:33 planted a vineyard and set a ***h***
Mk 12: 1 planted a vineyard and set a ***h***

HEDGED (3/3) HEDGE

Job 3:23 And whom God has ***h*** in?
Ps 139: 5 You have ***h*** me behind and
Lam 3: 7 He has ***h*** me in so that I cannot

HEDGES (4/4) HEDGE

Ps 80:12 Why have You broken down her ***h***,
89:40 You have broken down all his ***h***;
Nah 3:17 Which camp in the ***h*** on a cold
Lk 14:23 'Go out into the highways and ***h***,

HEED (121/121) HEEDED, HEEDING, HEEDS

Gen 34:17 But if you will not ***h*** us and be
39:10 that he did not ***h*** her, to lie
Ex 3:18 'Then they will ***h*** your voice;
4: 8 nor ***h*** the message of the first
6: 9 but they did not ***h*** Moses,
6:12 How then shall Pharaoh ***h*** me,
6:30 and how shall Pharaoh ***h*** me?"
7: 4 But Pharaoh will not ***h*** you, so
7:13 and he did not ***h*** them, as the
7:22 and he did not ***h*** them, as the
8:15 his heart and did not ***h*** them,
8:19 and he did not ***h*** them, just as
9:12 and he did not ***h*** them, just as
10:28 Get away from me! Take ***h*** to
11: 9 Pharaoh will not ***h*** you, so that
15:26 If you diligently ***h*** the voice of
16:20 Notwithstanding they did not ***h***
19:12 Take ***h*** to yourselves that you
34:12 Take ***h*** to yourself, lest you
Num 23:12 Must I not take ***h*** to speak what
Deut 4: 9 Only take ***h*** to yourself, and
4:15 Take careful ***h*** to yourselves,
4:19 'And take ***h***, lest you lift
4:23 Take ***h*** to yourselves, lest you
11:16 Take ***h*** to yourselves, lest your
12:13 Take ***h*** to yourself that you do
12:19 Take ***h*** to yourself that you do
12:30 take ***h*** to yourself that you are
17:12 presumptuously and will not ***h***
21:18 him, will not ***h*** them,
24: 8 Take ***h*** in an outbreak of
27: 9 Take ***h*** and listen, O Israel:
28:13 if you ***h*** the commandments of
Josh 1:17 so we will ***h*** you. Only the
1:18 your command and does not ***h***
22: 5 But take careful ***h*** to do the
23:11 Therefore take careful ***h*** to
Judg 11:17 the king of Edom would not ***h***.
11:28 the people of Ammon did not ***h***
19:25 But the men would not ***h*** him.
1 Sam 2:25 Nevertheless they did not ***h***
8: 7 ***H*** the voice of the people in all
8: 9 ***h*** their voice. However, you
8:22 ***H*** their voice, and make them a
15: 1 ***h*** the voice of the words of the
15:22 And to ***h*** than the fat of
28:22 ***h*** also the voice of your
30:24 For who will ***h*** you in this
2 Sam 12:18 and he would not ***h*** our voice.
13:14 he would not ***h*** her voice;
1 Ki 2: 4 If your sons take ***h*** to their
8:25 only if your sons take ***h*** to
11:38 if you ***h*** all that I command
22:28 by me." And he said, "Take ***h***,
2 Ki 10:31 But Jehu took no ***h*** to walk in
14:11 But Amaziah would not ***h***.
2 Chr 6:16 only if your sons take ***h*** to
18:27 by me." And he said, "Take ***h***,
19: 6 Take ***h*** to what you are doing,
25:20 But Amaziah would not ***h***,
35:22 and did not ***h*** the words of
Ezra 4:22 Take ***h*** now that you do not fail
Neh 9:16 And did not ***h*** Your
9:29 And did not ***h*** Your
Job 13: 6 And ***h*** the pleadings of my
36:21 Take ***h***, do not turn to
39: 7 He does not ***h*** the shouts of
Ps 5: 2 Give ***h*** to the voice of my cry,
58: 5 Which will not ***h*** the voice of
81:11 But My people would not ***h*** My
106:25 And did not ***h*** the voice of
119: 9 By taking ***h*** according to Your
Prov 17: 4 An evildoer gives ***h*** to false
Isa 7: 4 "and say to him: 'Take ***h***,
34: 1 you nations, to hear; And ***h***,
49: 1 coastlands, to Me, And take ***h***,
Jer 6:10 And they cannot give ***h***.
9: 4 Everyone take ***h*** to his neighbor,
17:21 Take ***h*** to yourselves, and bear
17:24 if you ***h*** Me carefully," says
17:27 But if you will not ***h*** Me to
18:18 and let us not give ***h*** to any of
18:19 Give ***h*** to me, O LORD, And
26: 5 to ***h*** the words of My servants
29:19 them; neither would you ***h***.
36:31 them; but they did not ***h***.
37: 2 the people of the land gave ***h***
Hos 5: 1 this, O priests! Take ***h***,
Zech 1: 4 But they did not hear nor ***h***
7:11 "But they refused to ***h***,
Mal 2:15 Therefore take ***h*** to your
2:16 Therefore take ***h*** to your spirit,
Mt 6: 1 Take ***h*** that you do not do your
16: 6 Take ***h*** and beware of the leaven
18:10 Take ***h*** that you do not despise
24: 4 Take ***h*** that no one deceives you.
Mk 4:24 Take ***h*** what you hear. With the
8:15 charged them, saying, "Take ***h***,
13: 5 Take ***h*** that no one deceives you.
13:23 'But take ***h***; see, I have
13:33 'Take ***h***, watch and pray;
Lk 8:18 Therefore take ***h*** how you hear.
11:35 Therefore take ***h*** that the light
12:15 Take ***h*** and beware of
17: 3 Take ***h*** to yourselves. If your
21: 8 Take ***h*** that you not be deceived.
21:34 But take ***h*** to yourselves, lest
Acts 2:14 known to you, and ***h*** my words.
5:35 take ***h*** to yourselves what you
8:10 to whom they all gave ***h***,
16:14 The Lord opened her heart to ***h***
20:28 Therefore take ***h*** to yourselves
1 Cor 3:10 But let each one take ***h*** how he
10:12 him who thinks he stands take ***h***
Col 4:17 Take ***h*** to the ministry which you
1 Tim 1: 4 nor give ***h*** to fables and endless
4: 1 giving ***h*** to deceiving spirits
4:16 Take ***h*** to yourself and to the
Titus 1:14 not giving ***h*** to Jewish fables
Heb 2: 1 we must give the more earnest ***h***
2 Pe 1:19 which you do well to ***h*** as a

HEEDED (30/30) HEED

Gen 3:17 Because you have ***h*** the voice of
16: 2 And Abram ***h*** the voice of
34:24 the gate of his city ***h*** Hamor
Ex 6:12 Israel have not ***h*** me.
18:24 So Moses ***h*** the voice of his
Num 14:22 and have not ***h*** My voice,
Deut 34: 9 children of Israel ***h*** him,
Josh 1:17 Just as we ***h*** Moses in all
10:14 that the LORD ***h*** the voice of a
Judg 2:20 and has not ***h*** My voice,
1 Sam 12: 1 Indeed I have ***h*** your voice in
19: 6 So Saul ***h*** the voice of Jonathan,
25:35 I have ***h*** your voice and
28:21 in my hands and ***h*** the words
28:23 and he ***h*** their voice. Then he
2 Sam 21:14 And after that God ***h*** the prayer
24:25 So the LORD ***h*** the prayers for
1 Ki 15:20 So Ben-Hadad ***h*** King Asa, and
2 Ki 16: 9 So the king of Assyria ***h*** him;
1 Chr 5:20 He ***h*** their prayer, because they
2 Chr 16: 4 So Ben-Hadad ***h*** King Asa, and
25:16 and have not ***h*** my advice."
Neh 9:34 Nor ***h*** Your commandments and
Isa 48:18 that you had ***h*** My commandments!
Jer 6:19 Because they have not ***h*** My
26: 5 them (but you have not ***h***),
29:19 because they have not ***h*** My
Dan 9: 6 Neither have we ***h*** Your servants
Acts 8: 6 one accord ***h*** the things
8:11 And they ***h*** him because he had

H

HEEDING (1/1) HEED
Ps 103:20 **H** the voice of His word.

HEEDS (4/4) HEED
Prov 12:15 But he who **h** counsel is wise.
13: 1 A wise son **h** his father's
15:32 But he who **h** rebuke gets
16:20 He who **h** the word wisely will

HEEL (6/6) HEELS
Gen 3:15 And you shall bruise His **h**.
25:26 his hand took hold of Esau's **h**;
Job 18: 9 The net takes him by the **h**,
Ps 41: 9 Has lifted up his **h** against
Hos 12: 3 He took his brother by the **h** in
Jn 13:18 Me has lifted up his **h**

HEELS (6/6) HEEL
Gen 49:17 That bites the horse's **h** So
1 Sam 25:12 young men turned on their **h**
Ps 49: 5 When the iniquity at my **h**
Jer 13:22 Your **h** made bare.
Lam 5: 5 They pursue at our **h**;
Dan 11:43 shall follow at his **h**.

HEGAI (4/3)
Esth 2: 3 under the custody of **H** the
2: 8 under the custody of **H**,
2: 8 into the care of **H** the
2:15 requested nothing but what **H**

HEIFER (18/18) HEIFER'S
Gen 15: 9 "Bring Me a three-year-old **h**,
Num 19: 2 that they bring you a red **h**
19: 5 Then the **h** shall be burned in
19: 6 midst of the fire burning the **h**.
19: 9 gather up the ashes of the **h**,
19:10 who gathers the ashes of the **h**
19:17 take some of the ashes of the **h**
Deut 21: 3 to the slain man will take a **h**
21: 4 of that city shall bring the **h**
21: 6 wash their hands over the **h**
Judg 14:18 you had not plowed with my **h**,
1 Sam 16: 2 Take a **h** with you, and say, 'I
Isa 15: 5 Zoar, Like a three-year-old **h**.
Jer 46:20 "Egypt is a very pretty **h**,
48:34 Like a three-year-old **h**;
50:11 you have grown fat like a **h**
Hos 10:11 Ephraim is a trained **h** That
Heb 9:13 and goats and the ashes of a **h**,

HEIFER'S (1/1) HEIFER
Deut 21: 4 and they shall break the **h** neck

HEIGHT (65/60) HEIGHTS
Gen 6:15 and its **h** thirty cubits.
Ex 25:10 and a cubit and a half its **h**.
25:23 and a cubit and a half its **h**.
27: 1 and its **h** shall be three
27:18 and the **h** five cubits, made
30: 2 two cubits shall be its **h**.
37: 1 and a cubit and a half its **h**.
37:10 and a cubit and a half its **h**.
37:25 two cubits was its **h**.
38: 1 and its **h** was three cubits.
38:18 and the **h** along its width was
Num 23: 3 So he went to a desolate **h**.
1 Sam 16: 7 at his appearance or at the **h**
17: 4 whose **h** was six cubits and a
1 Ki 6: 2 and its **h** thirty cubits.
6:26 The **h** of one cherub was ten
7: 2 and its **h** thirty cubits, with
7:16 The **h** of one capital was five
7:16 and the **h** of the other capital
7:23 Its **h** was five cubits, and a
7:27 width, and three cubits its **h**.
7:32 The **h** of a wheel was one and a
7:35 at the **h** of half a cubit, it
2 Ki 19:23 I have come up to the **h** of
25:17 The **h** of one pillar was
25:17 The **h** of the capital was three
1 Chr 11:23 an Egyptian, a man of GREAT **h**,
2 Chr 3: 4 and the **h** was one hundred and
4: 1 its width, and ten cubits its **h**.
4: 2 Its **h** was five cubits, and a
33:14 he raised it to a very great **h**.
Ezra 6: 3 its **h** sixty cubits and its
Neh 4: 6 together up to half its **h**,
Job 22:12 Is not God in the **h** of heaven?
Ps 102:19 For He looked down from the **h**
Prov 25: 3 As the heavens for **h** and the
Eccl 12: 5 Also they are afraid of **h**,
Isa 7:11 in the depth or in the **h** above.
37:24 I have come up to the **h** of
37:24 I will enter its farthest **h**,
Jer 31:12 shall come and sing in the **h**
49:16 Who hold the **h** of the hill!
51:53 she were to fortify the **h** of
52:21 the **h** of one pillar was
52:22 and the **h** of one capital was
Ezek 13:18 the heads of people of every **h**
17:23 On the mountain **h** of Israel I
19:11 And was seen in her **h** amid the
20:40 on the mountain **h** of Israel,"
31: 4 Underground waters gave it **h**,
31: 5 Therefore its **h** was exalted
31:10 you have increased in **h**,
31:10 heart was lifted up in its **h**,
31:14 exalt themselves for their **h**,
40: 5 structure, one rod; and the **h**,
43:13 This is the **h** of the altar:
Dan 3: 1 whose **h** was sixty cubits and
4:10 And its **h** was great.
4:11 Its **h** reached to the heavens,
4:20 whose **h** reached to the heavens
Am 2: 9 Whose **h** was like the height
2: 9 Whose height was like the **h**
Rom 8:39 nor **h** nor depth, nor any other
Eph 3:18 and length and depth and **h**—
Rev 21:16 breadth, and **h** are equal.

HEIGHTS (19/19) HEIGHT
Num 21:28 The lords of the **h** of the
Deut 32:13 He made him ride in the **h** of the
Josh 11: 2 and in the **h** of Dor on the
12:23 the king of Dor in the **h** of Dor,
Judg 5:18 on the **h** of the battlefield.
Ps 42: 6 And from the **h** of Hermon,
78:69 built His sanctuary like the **h**,
95: 4 The **h** of the hills are His
148: 1 Praise Him in the **h**!
Isa 14:14 I will ascend above the **h** of
41:18 will open rivers in desolate **h**,
49: 9 shall be on all desolate **h**.
Jer 3: 2 up your eyes to the desolate **h**
3:21 was heard on the desolate **h**,
4:11 A dry wind of the desolate **h**
7:29 a lamentation on the desolate **h**;
12:12 come On all the desolate **h** in
14: 6 donkeys stood in the desolate **h**;
Ezek 36: 2 Aha! The ancient **h** have become

HEINOUS (KJV) See WICKEDNESS

HEIR (21/19) HEIRS
Gen 15: 2 and the **h** of my house is
15: 3 one born in my house is my **h**!
15: 4 "This one shall not be your **h**,
15: 4 your own body shall be your **h**.
21:10 this bondwoman shall not be **h**
38: 8 and raise up an **h** to your
38: 9 But Onan knew that the **h** would
38: 9 lest he should give an **h** to his
2 Sam 14: 7 and we will destroy the **h**
Isa 65: 9 And from Judah an **h** of My
Jer 49: 1 Israel no sons? Has he no **h**?
Mic 1:15 I will yet bring an **h** to you, O
Mt 21:38 themselves, 'This is the **h**.
Mk 12: 7 themselves, 'This is the **h**.
Lk 20:14 saying, 'This is the **h**.
Rom 4:13 promise that he would be the **h**
Gal 4: 1 Now I say that the **h**,
4: 7 then an **h** of God through
4:30 bondwoman shall not be **h**
Heb 1: 2 whom He has appointed **h** of all
11: 7 the world and became **h** of the

HEIRS (13/11) HEIR
2 Ki 11: 1 and destroyed all the royal **h**.
2 Chr 22:10 and destroyed all the royal **h**
Rom 4:14 those who are of the law are **h**,
8:17 and if children, then **h**—
8:17 **h** of God and joint heirs with
8:17 heirs of God and joint **h** with
Gal 3:29 and **h** according to the promise.
Eph 3: 6 the Gentiles should be fellow **h**,
Titus 3: 7 by His grace we should become **h**
Heb 6:17 show more abundantly to the **h**
11: 9 the **h** with him of the same
Jas 2: 5 to be rich in faith and **h** of
1 Pe 3: 7 and as being **h** together of the

HELAH (2/2)
1 Chr 4: 5 two wives, **H** and Naarah.
4: 7 The sons of **H** were Zereth,

HELAM (2/2)
2 Sam 10:16 the River, and they came to **H**.
10:17 over the Jordan, and came to **H**.

HELBAH (1/1)
Judg 1:31 Sidon, or of Ahlab, Achzib, **H**,

HELBON (1/1)
Ezek 27:18 with the wine of **H** and with

HELD (50/50) HOLD
Gen 34: 5 so Jacob **h** his peace until they
Ex 17:11 when Moses **h** up his hand, that
36:12 the loops **h** one curtain to
Lev 10: 3 So Aaron **h** his peace.
Deut 4: 4 But you who **h** fast to the LORD
Judg 7:20 they **h** the torches in their left
16:26 Samson said to the lad who **h**
Ruth 3:15 And when she **h** it, he
1 Sam 10:27 But he **h** his peace.
25:26 since the LORD has **h** you back
2 Sam 6:22 by them I will be **h** in honor."
18:16 For Joab **h** back the people.
1 Ki 8:65 At that time Solomon **h** a feast,
2 Ki 18: 6 For he **h** fast to the LORD;
18:36 But the people **h** their peace
23:22 surely had never been **h** since
23:23 King Josiah this Passover was **h**
2 Chr 7: 9 And on the eighth day they **h** a
Neh 4:16 while the other half **h** the
4:17 and with the other **h** a weapon.
4:21 and half of the men **h** the
Esth 5: 2 and the king **h** out to Esther
7: 4 I would have **h** my tongue,
8: 4 And the king **h** out the golden
Job 23:11 My foot has **h** fast to His
36: 8 **H** in the cords of affliction,
Ps 18:35 Your right hand has **h** me up,
39: 2 I **h** my peace even from good;
89: 7 And to be **h** in reverence by
Song 3: 4 I **h** him and would not let him
7: 5 A king is **h** captive by your
Isa 36:21 But they **h** their peace and
42:14 I have **h** My peace a long time,
45: 1 whose right hand I have **h**—
57:11 Is it not because I have **h** My
Jer 50:33 who took them captive have **h**
Ezek 23:32 be laughed to scorn And **h** in
31:15 and the great waters were **h**
Dan 12: 7 when he **h** up his right hand and
Hos 10: 2 Now they are **h** guilty.
13:16 Samaria is **h** guilty, For she
Mt 28: 9 So they came and **h** Him
Mk 6:19 Therefore Herodias **h** it against
15: 1 the chief priests **h** a
Lk 22:63 Now the men who **h** Jesus mocked
Acts 2:24 possible that He should be **h**
3:11 the lame man who was healed **h**
5:34 a teacher of the law **h** in
Rom 7: 6 having died to what we were **h**
Rev 6: 9 for the testimony which they **h**.

HELDAI (2/2)
1 Chr 27:15 for the twelfth month was **H**
Zech 6:10 gift from the captives—from **H**,

HELEB (1/1)
2 Sam 23:29 **H** the son of Baanah

HELED (1/1)
1 Chr 11:30 **H** the son of Baanah the

HELEK (2/2)
Num 26:30 family of the Jeezerites; of **H**,
Josh 17: 2 of Abiezer, the children of **H**,

HELEKITES (1/1)
Num 26:30 of Helek, the family of the **H**;

HELEM (2/2)
1 Chr 7:35 And the sons of his brother **H**
Zech 6:14 the temple of the LORD for **H**,

HELEPH (2/2)
Josh 19:33 And their border began at **H**,
19:34 From **H** the border extended

HELEZ (5/4)
2 Sam 23:26 **H** the Paltite, Ira the son of
1 Chr 2:39 Azariah begot **H**,
2:39 and **H** begot Eleasah;
11:27 Harorite, **H** the Pelonite,
27:10 for the seventh month was **H**

HELI (1/1)
Lk 3:23 son of Joseph, the son of **H**,

HELKAI (1/1)
Neh 12:15 of Harim, Adna; of Meraioth, **H**;

HELKATH (2/2)
Josh 19:25 And their territory included **H**,
21:31 **H** with its common-land, and

HELL (32/32)
Deut 32:22 And shall burn to the lowest **h**;
Ps 9:17 wicked shall be turned into **h**,
55:15 Let them go down alive into **h**,
139: 8 If I make my bed in **h**,
Prov 5: 5 death, Her steps lay hold of **h**.
7:27 Her house is the way to **h**,
9:18 guests are in the depths of **h**.
15:11 **H** and Destruction are before
15:24 That he may turn away from **h**
23:14 And deliver his soul from **h**.
27:20 **H** and Destruction are never
Isa 14: 9 **H** from beneath is excited about
Ezek 31:15 the day when it went down to **h**,
31:16 when I cast it down to **h**
31:17 They also went down to **h** with
32:21 to him out of the midst of **h**
32:27 Who have gone down to **h** with
Am 9: 2 "Though they dig into **h**,
Hab 2: 5 he enlarges his desire as **h**,
Mt 5:22 shall be in danger of **h** fire.
5:29 whole body to be cast into **h**.

5:30 whole body to be cast into ***h***.
10:28 destroy both soul and body in ***h***.
18: 9 to be cast into ***h*** fire.
23:15 him twice as much a son of ***h***
23:33 escape the condemnation of ***h***?
Mk 9:43 having two hands, to go to ***h***,
9:45 two feet, to be cast into ***h***,
9:47 to be cast into ***h*** fire—
Lk 12: 5 has power to cast into ***h***;
Jas 3: 6 and it is set on fire by ***h***.
2 Pe 2: 4 but cast them down to ***h*** and

HELLENISTS (3/3)

Acts 6: 1 against the Hebrews by the ***H***,
9:29 and disputed against the ***H***,
11:20 come to Antioch, spoke to the ***H***,

HELM (KJV) See RUDDER

HELMET (10/10)

1 Sam 17: 5 He had a bronze ***h*** on his head,
17:38 and he put a bronze ***h*** on his
Ps 60: 7 Ephraim also is the ***h*** for My
108: 8 Ephraim also is the ***h*** for My
Isa 59:17 And a ***h*** of salvation on His
Ezek 23:24 shield, and ***h*** all around.
27:10 They hung shield and ***h*** in you;
38: 5 all of them with shield and ***h***;
Eph 6:17 And take the ***h*** of salvation, and
1 Th 5: 8 and as a ***h*** the hope of

HELMETS (2/2)

2 Chr 26:14 entire army, shields, spears, ***h***,
Jer 46: 4 Stand forth with your ***h***,

HELMSMAN (1/1)

Acts 27:11 was more persuaded by the ***h***

HELON (5/5)

Num 1: 9 Zebulun, Eliab the son of ***H***;
2: 7 and Eliab the son of ***H*** shall
7:24 third day Eliab the son of ***H***,
7:29 offering of Eliab the son of ***H***.
10:16 Zebulun was Eliab the son of ***H***.

HELP (137/129) HELPED, HELPER, HELPFUL, HELPING, HELPLESS, HELPS

Gen 49:25 God of your father who will ***h***
Ex 18: 4 God of my father was my ***h***,
23: 5 you shall surely ***h*** him with it.
Lev 25:35 then you shall ***h*** him, like a
Deut 22: 4 you shall surely ***h*** him lift
32:38 Let them rise and ***h*** you, And
33: 7 And may You be a ***h*** against his
33:26 Who rides the heavens to ***h***
33:29 The shield of your ***h*** And the
Josh 1:14 men of valor, and ***h*** them,
10: 4 Come up to me and ***h*** me, that we
10: 6 save us and ***h*** us, for all the
10:33 king of Gezer came up to ***h***
Judg 5:23 they did not come to the ***h*** of
5:23 To the ***h*** of the LORD against
1 Sam 11: 9 sun is hot, you shall have ***h***.
2 Sam 8: 5 Syrians of Damascus came to ***h***
10:11 then you shall ***h*** me; but if the
10:11 then I will come and ***h*** you.
10:19 So the Syrians were afraid to ***h***
14: 4 herself, and said, "***H***,
18: 3 For you are now more ***h*** to us in
2 Ki 6:26 cried out to him, saying, "***H***,
6:27 If the LORD does not ***h*** you,
6:27 where can I find ***h*** for you?
1 Chr 12:17 have come peaceably to me to ***h***
12:19 but they did not ***h*** them, for
12:22 came to David day by day to ***h***
18: 5 Syrians of Damascus came to ***h***
19:12 then you shall ***h*** me; but if the
19:12 then I will ***h*** you.
19:19 Syrians were not willing to ***h***
22:17 all the leaders of Israel to ***h***
23:28 because their duty was to ***h*** the
2 Chr 14:11 it is nothing for You to ***h***,
14:11 ***h*** us, O LORD our God, for we
19: 2 Should you ***h*** the wicked and love
20: 4 gathered together to ask ***h***
25: 8 for God has power to ***h*** and to
26:13 to ***h*** the king against the
28:16 to the kings of Assyria to ***h***
28:21 but he did not ***h*** him.
28:23 gods of the kings of Syria ***h***
28:23 to them that they may ***h*** me.
32: 8 to ***h*** us and to fight our
Ezra 1: 4 let the men of his place ***h*** him
8:22 of soldiers and horsemen to ***h***
Job 6:13 Is my ***h*** not within me? And is
30:28 the assembly and cry out for ***h***.
31:21 When I saw I had ***h*** in the
35: 9 They cry out for ***h*** because of
36:13 They do not cry for ***h*** when He
36:18 a large ransom would not ***h*** you
Ps 3: 2 There is no ***h*** for him in
12: 1 ***H***, LORD, for the godly man
20: 2 May He send you ***h*** from the
22:11 For there is none to ***h***.
22:19 hasten to ***h*** Me!
27: 9 in anger; You have been my ***h***;
33:20 He is our ***h*** and our shield.
35: 2 buckler, And stand up for my ***h***.
37:40 And the LORD shall ***h*** them and
38:22 Make haste to ***h*** me, O Lord, my
40:13 make haste to ***h*** me!
40:17 You are my ***h*** and my
42: 5 yet praise Him For the ***h*** of
42:11 The ***h*** of my countenance and my
43: 5 The ***h*** of my countenance and my
44:26 Arise for our ***h***, And redeem
46: 1 A very present ***h*** in trouble.
46: 5 God shall ***h*** her, just at the
59: 4 Awake to ***h*** me, and behold!
60:11 Give us ***h*** from trouble, For
60:11 For the ***h*** of man is useless.
63: 7 Because You have been my ***h***,
70: 1 to deliver me! Make haste to ***h***
70: 5 O God! You are my ***h*** and my
71:12 make haste to ***h*** me!
79: 9 ***H*** us, O God of our salvation,
89:19 I have given ***h*** to one who is
94:17 the LORD had been my ***h***,
107:12 down, and there was none to ***h***.
108:12 Give us ***h*** from trouble, For
108:12 For the ***h*** of man is useless.
109:26 ***H*** me, O LORD my God! Oh, save
115: 9 He is their ***h*** and their
115:10 He is their ***h*** and their
115:11 He is their ***h*** and their
118: 7 is for me among those who ***h*** me;
119:86 me wrongfully; ***H*** me!
119:147 of the morning, And cry for ***h***;
119:173 Let Your hand become my ***h***,
119:175 And let Your judgments ***h*** me.
121: 1 hills—From whence comes my ***h***?
121: 2 My ***h*** comes from the LORD,
124: 8 Our ***h*** is in the name of the
146: 3 of man, in whom there is no ***h***.
146: 5 has the God of Jacob for his ***h***,
Prov 28:17 Let no one ***h*** him.
Eccl 4:10 For he has no one to ***h*** him
Isa 5: 7 but behold, a cry for ***h***.
10: 3 To whom will you flee for ***h***?
20: 6 wherever we flee for ***h*** to be
30: 5 Or be ***h*** or benefit, But a
30: 7 For the Egyptians shall ***h*** in
31: 1 who go down to Egypt for ***h***,
31: 2 And against the ***h*** of those who
41:10 I will ***h*** you, I will uphold
41:13 'Fear not, I will ***h*** you.'
41:14 You men of Israel! I will ***h***
44: 2 who will ***h*** you: 'Fear not,
50: 7 For the Lord GOD will ***h*** Me;
50: 9 Surely the Lord GOD will ***h*** Me;
63: 5 but there was no one to ***h***,
Jer 37: 7 army which has come up to ***h***
Lam 1: 7 With no one to ***h*** her, The
3:56 my sighing, from my cry for ***h***.
4: 6 With no hand to ***h*** her!
4:17 us, Watching vainly for our ***h***;
Ezek 12:14 all who are around him to ***h***
32:21 of hell With those who ***h*** him:
39:14 with the ***h*** of a search party,
Dan 10:13 came to ***h*** me, for I had been
11:34 shall be aided with a little ***h***;
11:45 and no one will ***h*** him.
Hos 12: 6 by the ***h*** of your God,
13: 9 But your ***h*** is from Me.
Mt 15:25 saying, "Lord, ***h*** me!"
Mk 9:22 have compassion on us and ***h***
9:24 I believe; ***h*** my unbelief!"
Lk 5: 7 in the other boat to come and ***h***
10:40 Therefore tell her to ***h*** me."
Acts 16: 9 Come over to Macedonia and ***h***
21:28 'Men of Israel, ***h***! This is
26:22 having obtained ***h*** from God, to
Phil 4: 3 ***h*** these women who labored with
Heb 4:16 mercy and find grace to ***h*** in

HELPED (30/30) HELP

Ex 2:17 but Moses stood up and ***h*** them,
1 Sam 7:12 Thus far the LORD has ***h*** us."
1 Ki 1: 7 and they followed and ***h***
1 Chr 5:20 And they were ***h*** against them,
12:21 And they ***h*** David against the
15:26 when God ***h*** the Levites who bore
2 Chr 18:31 and the LORD ***h*** him, and God
20:23 they ***h*** to destroy one another.
26: 7 God ***h*** him against the
26:15 for he was marvelously ***h*** till
29:34 their brethren the Levites ***h***
32: 3 the city; and they ***h*** him.
Neh 8: 7 ***h*** the people to understand the
8: 8 and ***h*** them to understand the
Esth 9: 3 ***h*** the Jews, because the fear of
Job 26: 2 How have you ***h*** him who is
Ps 28: 7 trusted in Him, and I am ***h***;
83: 8 They have ***h*** the children of
86:17 have ***h*** me and comforted me.
118:13 But the LORD ***h*** me.
Isa 31: 3 And he who is ***h*** will fall
41: 6 Everyone ***h*** his neighbor, And
49: 8 the day of salvation I have ***h***
Zech 1:15 was a little angry, And they ***h***—
Lk 1:54 He has ***h*** His servant Israel,
Acts 18:27 he greatly ***h*** those who had
Rom 15:24 and to be ***h*** on my way there by
2 Cor 1:16 and be ***h*** by you on my way to
6: 2 day of salvation I have ***h***
Rev 12:16 But the earth ***h*** the woman, and

HELPER (16/16) HELP

Gen 2:18 I will make him a ***h*** comparable
2:20 Adam there was not found a ***h***
2 Ki 14:26 there was no ***h*** for Israel.
Job 29:12 and the one who had no ***h***.
30:13 my calamity; They have no ***h***.
Ps 10:14 You are the ***h*** of the
30:10 on me; LORD, be my ***h***!"
54: 4 Behold, God is my ***h***;
72:12 also, and him who has no ***h***.
Jer 47: 4 off from Tyre and Sidon every ***h***
Jn 14:16 and He will give you another ***H***,
14:26 'But the ***H***, the Holy Spirit,
15:26 But when the ***H*** comes, whom I
16: 7 the ***H*** will not come to you;
Rom 16: 2 for indeed she has been a ***h*** of
Heb 13: 6 say: "The LORD is my ***h***;

HELPERS (4/4)

1 Chr 12: 1 mighty men, ***h*** in the war,
12:18 And peace to your ***h***! For your
Ezek 30: 8 a fire in Egypt And all her ***h***
Nah 3: 9 Put and Lubim were your ***h***.

HELPFUL (3/3) HELP

Acts 20:20 I kept back nothing that was ***h***,
1 Cor 6:12 me, but all things are not ***h***.
10:23 me, but not all things are ***h***;

HELPING (5/5) HELP

Ex 23: 5 and you would refrain from ***h***
1 Ki 20:16 and the thirty-two kings ***h*** him
Ezra 5: 2 were with them, ***h*** them.
Ps 22: 1 Why are You so far from ***h***
2 Cor 1:11 you also ***h*** together in prayer

HELPLESS (4/4) HELP

Ps 10: 8 are secretly fixed on the ***h***.
10:10 That the ***h*** may fall by his
10:14 The ***h*** commits himself to You;
Acts 4: 9 for a good deed done to a ***h***

HELPS (4/4) HELP

1 Chr 12:18 your helpers! For your God ***h***
Isa 31: 3 Both he who ***h*** will fall, And
Rom 8:26 Likewise the Spirit also ***h*** in
1 Cor 12:28 then gifts of healings, ***h***,

HEM (9/8)

Ex 28:33 And upon its ***h*** you shall make
28:33 and scarlet, all around its ***h***,
28:34 upon the ***h*** of the robe all
39:24 They made on the ***h*** of the robe
39:25 the pomegranates on the ***h*** of
39:26 all around the ***h*** of the robe to
Mt 9:20 from behind and touched the ***h***
14:36 they might only touch the ***h*** of
Mk 6:56 they might just touch the ***h*** of

HEMAM (1/1)

Gen 36:22 sons of Lotan were Hori and ***H***.

HEMAN (17/15)

1 Ki 4:31 Ethan the Ezrahite, and ***H***,
1 Chr 2: 6 of Zerah were Zimri, Ethan, ***H***,
6:33 sons of the Kohathites were ***H***
15:17 So the Levites appointed ***H*** the
15:19 the singers, ***H***, Asaph,
16:41 and with them ***H*** and Jeduthun and
16:42 and with them ***H*** and Jeduthun, to
25: 1 of the sons of Asaph, of ***H***,
25: 4 Of ***H***, the sons of Heman:
25: 4 Of Heman, the sons of ***H***:
25: 5 All these were the sons of ***H***
25: 5 For God gave ***H*** fourteen sons
25: 6 and ***H*** were under the authority
2 Chr 5:12 all those of Asaph and ***H*** and
29:14 of the sons of ***H***,
35:15 the command of David, Asaph, ***H***,
Ps 88: A Contemplation of ***H*** the

HEMATH (KJV) See HAMATH

HEMDAN (1/1)

Gen 36:26 were the sons of Dishon: ***H***,

HEMLOCK (1/1)

Hos 10: 4 judgment springs up like ***h*** in

HEN (3/3)

Zech 6:14 and ***H*** the son of Zephaniah.
Mt 23:37 as a ***h*** gathers her chicks under
Lk 13:34 as a ***h*** gathers her brood under

HENA (3/3)

2 Ki 18:34 the gods of Sepharvaim and ***H***
19:13 of the city of Sepharvaim, ***H***,
Isa 37:13 of the city of Sepharvaim, ***H***,

HENADAD (4/4)
Ezra 3: 9 the sons of ***H*** with their sons
Neh 3:18 under Bavai the son of ***H***,
3:24 After him Binnui the son of ***H***
10: 9 Binnui of the sons of ***H***,

HENCE (KJV) See AWAY, (FROM) HERE

HENCEFORTH (1/1)
Lk 1:48 ***h*** all generations will call me

HENNA (2/2)
Song 1:14 is to me a cluster of ***h***
4:13 Fragrant ***h*** with spikenard,

HENOCH (KJV) See ENOCH

HEPHER (11/11)
Num 26:32 of the Shemidaites; of ***H***,
26:33 Now Zelophehad the son of ***H*** had
27: 1 of Zelophehad the son of ***H***,
Josh 12:17 of Tappuah, one; the king of ***H***,
17: 2 of Shechem, the children of ***H***,
17: 3 But Zelophehad the son of ***H***,
1 Ki 4:10 Sochoh and all the land of ***H***;
1 Chr 4: 6 Naarah bore him Ahuzzam, ***H***,
11:36 ***H*** the Mecherathite, Ahijah the

HEPHERITES (1/1)
Num 26:32 of Hepher, the family of the ***H***.

HEPHZIBAH (2/2)
2 Ki 21: 1 His mother's name was ***H***.
Isa 62: 4 But you shall be called ***H***,

HER (1791/1088) See APPENDIX

HERALD (1/1)
Dan 3: 4 Then a ***h*** cried aloud: "To you

HERB (14/14) HERBS
Gen 1:11 the ***h*** that yields seed, and
1:12 the ***h*** that yields seed
1:29 I have given you every ***h*** that
1:30 I have given every green ***h***
2: 5 in the earth and before any ***h***
3:18 And you shall eat the ***h*** of the
Ex 9:22 and on every ***h*** of the field,
9:25 and the hail struck every ***h*** of
10:12 and eat every ***h*** of the land—all
10:15 and they ate every ***h*** of the
Deut 32: 2 As raindrops on the tender ***h***,
2 Ki 19:26 of the field And the green ***h***,
Ps 37: 2 And wither as the green ***h***.
Isa 37:27 of the field And the green ***h***,

HERBS (13/13) HERB
Gen 9: 3 all things, even as the green ***h***.
Ex 12: 8 bread and with bitter ***h*** they
Num 9:11 unleavened bread and bitter ***h***.
2 Ki 4:39 out into the field to gather ***h***,
Prov 15:17 Better is a dinner of ***h*** where
27:25 And the ***h*** of the mountains are
Song 5:13 of spices, Banks of scented ***h***.
Isa 26:19 your dew is like the dew of ***h***,
Jer 12: 4 And the ***h*** of every field
Mt 13:32 grown it is greater than the ***h***
Mk 4:32 and becomes greater than all ***h***,
Lk 11:42 and rue and all manner of ***h***,
Heb 6: 7 and bears ***h*** useful for those by

HERD (26/24) HERDS
Gen 18: 7 And Abraham ran to the ***h***,
Lev 1: 2 of the ***h*** and of the flock.
1: 3 is a burnt sacrifice of the ***h***,
3: 1 if he offers it of the ***h***,
27:32 concerning the tithe of the ***h***
Num 15: 3 from the ***h*** or the flock,
Deut 12:17 of the firstborn of your ***h*** or
12:21 you may slaughter from your ***h***
15:19 males that come from your ***h***
15:19 with the firstborn of your ***h***,
16: 2 God, from the flock and the ***h***,
1 Sam 11: 5 coming behind the ***h*** from the
2 Sam 12: 4 own flock and from his own ***h***
17:29 sheep and cheese of the ***h***,
Ps 68:30 The ***h*** of bulls with the calves
Jer 31:12 young of the flock and the ***h***;
Jon 3: 7 ***h*** nor flock, taste anything;
Hab 3:17 And there be no ***h*** in the
Mt 8:30 off from them there was a ***h*** of
8:31 us to go away into the ***h*** of
8:32 they went into the ***h*** of swine.
8:32 And suddenly the whole ***h*** of
Mk 5:11 Now a large ***h*** of swine was
5:13 and the ***h*** ran violently down
Lk 8:32 Now a ***h*** of many swine was
8:33 and the ***h*** ran violently down

HERDS (36/35) HERD
Gen 13: 5 had flocks and ***h*** and tents.
24:35 He has given him flocks and ***h***,
26:14 of flocks and possessions of ***h***
32: 7 and the flocks and ***h*** and
33:13 and the flocks and ***h*** which are
45:10 your flocks and your ***h***,
46:32 brought their flocks, their ***h***,
47: 1 their flocks and their ***h*** and
47:17 the flocks, the cattle of the ***h***,
47:18 my lord also has our ***h*** of
50: 8 and their ***h*** they left in the
Ex 10: 9 with our flocks and our ***h*** we
10:24 let your flocks and your ***h*** be
12:32 take your flocks and your ***h***,
12:38 them also, and flocks and ***h***—
34: 3 let neither flocks nor ***h*** feed
Num 11:22 Shall flocks and ***h*** be
35: 3 for their cattle, for their ***h***,
Deut 8:13 and when your ***h*** and your flocks
12: 6 and the firstborn of your ***h*** and
14:23 of the firstborn of your ***h*** and
28: 4 and the increase of your ***h***,
1 Sam 30:20 took all the flocks and ***h*** they
2 Sam 12: 2 exceedingly many flocks and ***h***.
1 Chr 27:29 the Sharonite was over the ***h***
27:29 the son of Adlai was over the ***h***
2 Chr 32:29 possessions of flocks and ***h*** in
Neh 10:36 and the firstborn of our ***h*** and
Prov 27:23 flocks, And attend to your ***h***;
Eccl 2: 7 I had greater possessions of ***h***
Isa 65:10 Valley of Achor a place for ***h***
Jer 3:24 youth—Their flocks and their ***h***,
5:17 eat up your flocks and your ***h***;
Hos 5: 6 With their flocks and ***h*** They
Joel 1:18 How the animals groan! The ***h***
Zeph 2:14 The ***h*** shall lie down in her

HERDSMEN (8/5) SHEEPBREEDERS
Gen 13: 7 there was strife between the ***h***
13: 7 of Abram's livestock and the ***h***
13: 8 and between my ***h*** and your
13: 8 between my herdsmen and your ***h***;
26:20 But the ***h*** of Gerar quarreled
26:20 Gerar quarreled with Isaac's ***h***,
47: 6 then make them chief ***h*** over my
1 Sam 21: 7 the chief of the ***h*** who

HERE (303/284)
Gen 12:19 ***h*** is your wife; take her and
15:16 generation they shall return ***h***,
16:13 Have I also ***h*** seen Him who sees
18: 9 your wife?" So he said, "***H***,
19: 2 ***H*** now, my lords, please turn in
19: 9 "This one came in to stay ***h***,
19:12 Lot, "Have you anyone else ***h***?
19:15 your two daughters who are ***h***,
22: 1 And he said, "***H*** I am."
22: 5 Stay ***h*** with the donkey; the lad
22: 7 ***H*** I am, my son." Then he said,
22:11 So he said, "***H*** I am."
24:13 ***h*** I stand by the well of
24:51 ***H*** is Rebekah before you; take
27: 1 he answered him, "***H*** I am."
27:18 ***H*** I am. Who are you, my son?"
30: 3 ***H*** is my maid Bilhah; go in to
31:11 And I said, '***H*** I am.'
31:37 Set it ***h*** before my brethren
31:51 ***H*** is this heap and here is this
31:51 Here is this heap and ***h*** is this
37:13 he said to him, "***H*** I am."
37:17 "They have departed from ***h***,
40:15 and also I have done nothing ***h***
42:15 your youngest brother comes ***h***.
42:33 Leave one of your brothers ***h***
44:16 ***h*** we are, my lord's slaves,
45: 5 because you sold me ***h***;
45: 8 it was not you who sent me ***h***,
45:13 and bring my father down ***h***.
46: 2 And he said, "***H*** I am."
47:23 ***h*** is seed for you, and you
50:25 shall carry up my bones from ***h***.
Ex 3: 4 And he said, "***H*** I am."
11: 1 he will let you go from ***h***.
11: 1 will surely drive you out of ***h***
13:19 shall carry up my bones from ***h***
24:14 Wait ***h*** for us until we come back
33: 1 "Depart and go up from ***h***,
33:15 us, do not bring us up from ***h***.
33:21 ***H*** is a place by Me, and you
Num 11:15 please kill me ***h*** and now—if I
14:40 ***H*** we are, and we will go up to
18: 8 '***H***, I Myself have also
20: 4 we and our animals should die ***h***?
20:16 now ***h*** we are in Kadesh, a city
22: 8 Lodge ***h*** tonight, and I will
22:19 you also stay ***h*** tonight, that I
23: 1 "Build seven altars for me ***h***,
23: 1 and prepare for me ***h*** seven
23:15 Stand ***h*** by your burnt offering
23:29 Build for me ***h*** seven altars, and
23:29 and prepare for me ***h*** seven
32: 6 go to war while you sit ***h***?
32:16 We will build sheepfolds ***h*** for
Deut 1:10 and ***h*** you are today, as the
5: 3 those who are ***h*** today, all of
5:31 stand ***h*** by Me, and I will speak
9:12 'Arise, go down quickly from ***h***,
12: 8 not at all do as we are doing ***h***
29:15 but with him who stands ***h*** with
29:15 well as with him who is not ***h***
Josh 2: 2 men have come ***h*** tonight from
3: 9 children of Israel, "Come ***h***,
4: 3 yourselves twelve stones from ***h***,
9:25 ***h*** we are, in your hands;
14:10 ***h*** I am this day, eighty-five
18: 6 parts and bring the survey ***h***
18: 6 that I may cast lots for you ***h***
18: 8 that I may cast lots for you ***h***
22:28 ***H*** is the replica of the altar of
Judg 4:20 and says, 'Is there any man ***h***?
6:18 "Do not depart from ***h***,
8:15 ***H*** are Zebah and Zalmunna, about
9:31 and ***h*** they are, fortifying the
16: 2 'Samson has come ***h***!"
17: 2 ***h*** is the silver with me; I took
18: 3 to him, "Who brought you ***h***?
18: 3 this place? What do you have ***h***?
19: 9 is coming to an end; lodge ***h***,
19:12 We will not turn aside ***h*** into a
19:24 ***h*** is my virgin daughter and
20: 7 give your advice and counsel ***h***
Ruth 2: 8 in another field, nor go from ***h***,
2:14 to her at mealtime, "Come ***h***,
4: 1 aside, friend, sit down ***h***.
4: 2 city, and said, "Sit down ***h***.
1 Sam 1:26 the woman who stood by you ***h***,
3: 4 he answered, "***H*** I am!"
3: 5 '***H*** I am, for you called me."
3: 6 '***H*** I am, for you called me."
3: 8 ***H*** I am, for you did call me."
3:16 he answered, "***H*** I am."
9: 8 I have ***h*** at hand one fourth of
9:11 said to them, "Is the seer ***h***?
9:24 '***H*** it is, what was kept back.
9:27 But you stand ***h*** awhile, that I
10:22 'Has the man come ***h*** yet?"
12: 2 And now ***h*** is the king, walking
12: 3 ***H*** I am. Witness against me
12:13 ***h*** is the king whom you have
13: 9 offering and peace offerings ***h***
14: 7 ***h*** I am with you, according to
14:16 and they went ***h*** and there.
14:18 'Bring the ark of God ***h***"
14:34 Bring me ***h*** every man's ox and
14:34 man's sheep, slaughter them ***h***,
14:36 "Let us draw near to God ***h***.
14:38 And Saul said, "Come over ***h***,
15:32 Agag king of the Amalekites ***h***
16:11 "Are all the young men ***h***?
16:11 not sit down till he comes ***h***.
17:28 said, "Why did you come down ***h***?
18:17 '***H*** is my older daughter Merab;
21: 8 Is there not ***h*** on hand a spear
21: 9 is no other except that one ***h***.
22: 3 let my father and mother come ***h***
22:12 ***H*** I am, my lord."
23: 3 we are afraid ***h*** in Judah.
23: 9 the priest, "Bring the ephod ***h***.
25:41 ***H*** is your maidservant, a servant
26:22 ***H*** is the king's spear. Let one
29: 3 are these Hebrews doing ***h***?
30: 7 Please bring the ephod ***h*** to
30:26 ***H*** is a present for you from the
2 Sam 1: 7 And I answered, '***H*** I am.'
1:10 and have brought them ***h*** to my
4: 8 ***H*** is the head of Ishbosheth, the
5: 6 "You shall not come in ***h***;
5: 6 "David cannot come in ***h***.
9: 6 ***H*** is your servant!"
11:12 Wait ***h*** today also, and tomorrow
13:17 ***H***! Put this woman out, away
14:32 I sent to you, saying, 'Come ***h***,
15:26 ***h*** I am, let Him do to me as
16: 4 So the king said to Ziba, "***H***,
18:30 said, "Turn aside and stand ***h***.
19:20 Therefore ***h*** I am, the first to
19:37 But ***h*** is your servant Chimham;
20: 4 and be present ***h*** yourself."
24:22 ***h*** are oxen for burnt
1 Ki 1:23 '***H*** is Nathan the prophet."
2:30 he said, "No, but I will die ***h***.
12:28 ***H*** are your gods, O Israel,
14: 5 ***H*** is the wife of Jeroboam,
17: 3 Get away from ***h*** and turn
18: 8 your master, 'Elijah is ***h***.
18:10 when they said, 'He is not ***h***,
18:11 Elijah is ***h***" '!
18:14 your master, "Elijah is ***h***.
19: 9 to him, "What are you doing ***h***,
19:13 said, "What are you doing ***h***,
20:40 While your servant was busy ***h***
22: 7 still a prophet of the LORD ***h***,
2 Ki 2: 2 Elijah said to Elisha, "Stay ***h***,
2: 4 said to him, "Elisha, stay ***h***,
2: 6 Elijah said to him, "Stay ***h***,
3:11 no prophet of the LORD ***h***,
3:11 the son of Shaphat is ***h***,
7: 3 Why are we sitting ***h*** until we
7: 4 die there. And if we sit ***h***,
8: 7 "The man of God has come ***h***.
9:37 ***H*** lies Jezebel." ' "
10:23 no servants of the LORD are ***h***
1 Chr 11: 5 You shall not come in ***h***!"
28:21 ***H*** are the divisions of the
29:17 who are present ***h*** to offer
2 Chr 18: 6 still a prophet of the LORD ***h***,
20:10 ***h*** are the people of Ammon,
20:11 ***h*** they are, rewarding us by
28:13 shall not bring the captives ***h***,
Ezra 4: 2 of Assyria, who brought us ***h***.
9:15 ***H*** we are before You, in our
Neh 9:36 ***H*** we are, servants today! And

9:36 ***H*** we are, servants in it!
Job 31:35 to hear me! ***H*** is my mark.
38:11 And ***h*** your proud waves must
38:35 say to you, '***H*** we are!'?
Ps 52:7 ***H*** is the man who did not make
73:10 Therefore his people return ***h***,
132:14 ***H*** I will dwell, for I have
Prov 9:4 let him turn in ***h***!" As for
9:16 let him turn in ***h***"; And as
25:7 he say to you, "Come up ***h***,
Eccl 5:18 ***H*** is what I have seen
7:27 ***H*** is what I have found," says
Isa 6:8 ***H*** am I! Send me."
8:18 ***H*** am I and the children whom
21:9 ***h*** comes a chariot of men with
22:16 'What have you ***h***,
22:16 you here, and whom have you ***h***,
22:16 you have hewn a sepulcher ***h***,
28:10 ***H*** a little, there a little."
28:13 ***H*** a little, there a little,"
52:5 Now therefore, what have I ***h***,
56:3 ***H*** I am, a dry tree."
57:3 But come ***h***, You sons of
58:9 ***H*** I am.' "If you take away
65:1 ***H*** I am, here I am,' To a nation
65:1 ***h*** I am,' To a nation that was
Jer 22:11 He shall not return ***h*** anymore,
26:14 ***h*** I am, in your hand; do with
36:29 man and beast to cease from ***h***?
38:10 Take from ***h*** thirty men with you,
40:4 with me to Babylon, remain ***h***.
Lam 4:15 shall no longer dwell ***h***.
Ezek 8:6 the house of Israel commits ***h***,
8:17 which they commit ***h***?
40:4 for you were brought ***h*** so that
Dan 3:26 High God, come out, and come ***h***.
Hos 7:9 gray hairs are ***h*** and there on
Zech 3:7 walk Among these who stand ***h***.
5:7 ***H*** is a lead disc lifted up, and
Mt 8:29 Have You come ***h*** to torment us
12:41 a greater than Jonah is ***h***.
12:42 a greater than Solomon is ***h***.
12:49 ***H*** are My mother and My brothers!
14:8 me John the Baptist's head ***h***
14:17 We have ***h*** only five loaves and
14:18 Bring them ***h*** to Me."
16:28 there are some standing ***h*** who
17:4 it is good for us to be ***h***;
17:4 let us make ***h*** three
17:17 Bring him ***h*** to Me."
17:20 Move from ***h*** to there,' and it
20:6 Why have you been standing ***h***
22:12 how did you come in ***h*** without a
24:2 not one stone shall be left ***h***
24:23 ***h*** is the Christ!' or 'There!'
26:36 Sit ***h*** while I go and pray over
26:38 Stay ***h*** and watch with Me."
28:6 'He is not ***h***; for He is
Mk 3:34 ***H*** are My mother and My brothers!
6:3 And are not His sisters ***h*** with
8:4 these people with bread ***h*** in
9:1 that there are some standing ***h***
9:5 it is good for us to be ***h***;
11:3 immediately he will send it ***h***.
13:1 and what buildings are ***h***!"
13:21 ***h*** is the Christ!' or, 'Look,
14:32 Sit ***h*** while I pray."
14:34 Stay ***h*** and watch."
16:6 He is risen! He is not ***h***.
Lk 4:9 God, throw Yourself down from ***h***.
4:23 do also ***h*** in Your country.'"
6:8 hand, "Arise and stand ***h***.
9:12 we are in a deserted place ***h***.
9:27 there are some standing ***h*** who
9:33 it is good for us to be ***h***;
9:41 bear with you? Bring your son ***h***.
11:31 a greater than Solomon is ***h***.
11:32 a greater than Jonah is ***h***.
13:31 "Get out and depart from ***h***,
14:21 and bring in ***h*** the poor and
15:23 And bring the fatted calf ***h*** and
16:26 those who want to pass from ***h***
17:21 'See ***h***!' or 'See there!'
17:23 Look ***h***!' or 'Look there!' Do not
19:20 ***h*** is your mina, which I have
19:27 But bring ***h*** those enemies of
19:30 Loose it and bring it ***h***.
22:38 look, ***h*** are two swords."
24:6 'He is not ***h***, but is risen!
24:41 to them, "Have you any food ***h***?
Jn 4:15 nor come ***h*** to draw."
4:16 call your husband, and come ***h***.
6:9 There is a lad ***h*** who has five
6:25 "Rabbi, when did You come ***h***?
7:3 Depart from ***h*** and go into Judea,
11:21 "Lord, if You had been ***h***,
11:32 Him, "Lord, if You had been ***h***,
14:31 I do. Arise, let us go from ***h***.
18:36 now My kingdom is not from ***h***.
20:27 Thomas, "Reach your finger ***h***,
20:27 and reach your hand ***h***,
Acts 4:10 by Him this man stands ***h*** before
8:36 ***h*** is water. What hinders me
9:10 he said, "***H*** I am, Lord."
9:14 And ***h*** he has authority from the
9:21 and has come ***h*** for that
10:32 to Joppa and call Simon ***h***,
16:28 no harm, for we are all ***h***.
17:6 world upside down have come ***h***
19:37 you have brought these men ***h***
22:21 for I will send you far from ***h***
24:19 They ought to have been ***h*** before
24:20 Or else let those who are ***h***
25:24 and all the men who are ***h***
25:24 me, both at Jerusalem and ***h***,
Col 4:9 things which are happening ***h***.
Heb 2:13 ***H*** am I and the children
7:8 ***H*** mortal men receive tithes, but
13:14 For ***h*** we have no continuing
Jas 2:3 You sit ***h*** in a good place," and
2:3 Sit ***h*** at my footstool,"
1 Pe 1:17 the time of your stay ***h*** in
Rev 4:1 with me, saying, "Come up ***h***,
11:12 saying to them, "Come up ***h***.
13:10 ***H*** is the patience and the faith
13:18 ***H*** is wisdom. Let him who has
14:12 ***H*** is the patience of the saints;
14:12 ***h*** are those who keep the
17:9 ***H*** is the mind which has wisdom:

HEREAFTER (8/8)

Num 18:22 ***H*** the children of Israel shall
Deut 19:20 and ***h*** they shall not again
Prov 23:18 For surely there is a ***h***,
Isa 41:23 the things that are to come ***h***,
Ezek 20:39 one of you his idols—and ***h***—
Mt 26:64 ***h*** you will see the Son of Man
Lk 22:69 ***H*** the Son of Man will sit on the
Jn 1:51 ***h*** you shall see heaven open,

HEREIN (KJV) See (BY) THIS, (IN) THIS

HERES (5/6)

Judg 1:35 determined to dwell in Mount ***H***,
8:13 battle, from the Ascent of ***H***.
Isa 16:11 And my inner being for Kir ***H***.
Jer 48:31 will mourn for the men of Kir ***H***.
48:36 wail For the men of Kir ***H***.

HERESH (1/1)

1 Chr 9:15 Bakbakkar, ***H***, Galal,

HERESIES (2/2)

Gal 5:20 ambitions, dissensions, ***h***,
2 Pe 2:1 secretly bring in destructive ***h***,

HERETH (1/1)

1 Sam 22:5 and went into the forest of ***H***.

HERETICK (KJV) See DIVISIVE

HERETOFORE (KJV) See BEFORE

HERITAGE (36/35)

Ex 6:8 I will give it to you as a ***h***:
Deut 4:19 under the whole heaven as a ***h***.
33:4 A ***h*** of the congregation of
Neh 2:20 but you have no ***h*** or right or
Job 20:29 The ***h*** appointed to him by
27:13 And the ***h*** of oppressors,
Ps 61:5 You have given me the ***h*** of
94:5 O LORD, And afflict Your ***h***.
111:6 In giving them the ***h*** of the
119:111 I have taken as a ***h*** forever,
127:3 children are a ***h*** from the
135:12 And gave their land as a ***h***,
135:12 A ***h*** to Israel His people.
136:21 And gave their land as a ***h***,
136:22 A ***h*** to Israel His servant, For
Eccl 2:21 yet he must leave his ***h*** to a
3:22 own works, for that is his ***h***.
5:18 God gives him; for it is his ***h***.
5:19 to receive his ***h*** and rejoice in
Isa 54:17 This is the ***h*** of the servants
58:14 And feed you with the ***h*** of
Jer 2:7 defiled My land And made My ***h***
3:19 A beautiful ***h*** of the hosts of
12:7 My house, I have left My ***h***;
12:8 My ***h*** is to Me like a lion in
12:9 My ***h*** is to Me like a speckled
12:15 everyone to his ***h*** and everyone
17:4 Shall let go of your ***h*** which I
50:11 You destroyers of My ***h***,
Hos 5:7 shall devour them and their ***h***.
Joel 2:17 And do not give Your ***h*** to
3:2 My ***h*** Israel, Whom they have
Mic 2:4 He has changed the ***h*** of my
7:14 staff, The flock of Your ***h***,
7:18 of the remnant of His ***h***?
Mal 1:3 waste his mountains and his ***h***

HERITAGES (1/1)

Isa 49:8 them to inherit the desolate ***h***;

HERMAS (1/1)

Rom 16:14 Greet Asyncritus, Phlegon, ***H***,

HERMES (2/2)

Acts 14:12 they called Zeus, and Paul, ***H***,
Rom 16:14 Phlegon, Hermas, Patrobas, ***H***,

HERMOGENES (1/1)

2 Tim 1:15 among whom are Phygellus and ***H***.

HERMON (16/15) SENIR, SIRION

Deut 3:8 the River Arnon to Mount ***H***
3:9 (the Sidonians call ***H*** Sirion,
4:48 even to Mount Sion (that is, ***H***),
Josh 11:3 and the Hivite below ***H*** in the
11:17 Valley of Lebanon below Mount ***H***.
12:1 from the River Arnon to Mount ***H***,
12:5 and reigned over Mount ***H***,
13:5 from Baal Gad below Mount ***H*** as
13:11 and Maachathites, all Mount ***H***,
1 Chr 5:23 that is, to Senir, or Mount ***H***.
Ps 42:6 And from the heights of ***H***,
89:12 Tabor and ***H*** rejoice in Your
133:3 It is like the dew of ***H***,
Song 4:8 From the top of Senir and ***H***,

HEROD (40/39) HEROD'S, HERODIANS

Mt 2:1 of Judea in the days of ***H*** the
2:3 When ***H*** the king heard this, he
2:7 Then ***H***, when he had secretly
2:12 they should not return to ***H***,
2:13 for ***H*** will seek the young Child
2:15 was there until the death of ***H***,
2:16 Then ***H***, when he saw that
2:19 But when ***H*** was dead, behold, an
2:22 Judea instead of his father ***H***,
14:1 At that time ***H*** the tetrarch
14:3 For ***H*** had laid hold of John and
14:6 before them and pleased ***H***.
Mk 6:14 Now King ***H*** heard of Him, for
6:16 But when ***H*** heard, he said,
6:17 For ***H*** himself had sent and laid
6:18 For John had said to ***H***,
6:20 for ***H*** feared John, knowing that
6:21 an opportune day came when ***H***
6:22 and pleased ***H*** and those who sat
8:15 Pharisees and the leaven of ***H***.
Lk 1:5 There was in the days of ***H***,
3:1 ***H*** being tetrarch of Galilee,
3:19 But ***H*** the tetrarch, being
3:19 and for all the evils which ***H***
9:7 Now ***H*** the tetrarch heard of all
9:9 ***H*** said, "John I have beheaded,
13:31 for ***H*** wants to kill You."
23:7 jurisdiction, he sent Him to ***H***,
23:8 Now when ***H*** saw Jesus, he was
23:11 Then ***H***, with his men of war,
23:12 That very day Pilate and ***H***
23:15 "no, neither did ***H***,
Acts 4:27 both ***H*** and Pontius Pilate, with
12:1 Now about that time ***H*** the king
12:6 And when ***H*** was about to bring
12:11 me from the hand of ***H*** and
12:19 But when ***H*** had searched for him
12:20 Now ***H*** had been very angry with
12:21 So on a set day ***H***,
13:1 who had been brought up with ***H***

HEROD'S (4/4) HEROD

Mt 14:6 But when ***H*** birthday was
Lk 8:3 ***H*** steward, and Susanna, and
23:7 he knew that He belonged to ***H***
Acts 23:35 commanded him to be kept in ***H***

HERODIANS (3/3) HEROD

Mt 22:16 Him their disciples with the ***H***,
Mk 3:6 immediately plotted with the ***H***
12:13 some of the Pharisees and the ***H***,

HERODIAS (5/5)

Mt 14:3 in prison for the sake of ***H***,
14:6 the daughter of ***H*** danced before
Mk 6:17 him in prison for the sake of ***H***,
6:19 Therefore ***H*** held it against him
Lk 3:19 rebuked by him concerning ***H***,

HERODIAS' (1/1)

Mk 6:22 And when ***H*** daughter herself came

HERODION (1/1)

Rom 16:11 Greet ***H***, my countryman.

HEROES (2/2)

2 Sam 23:20 He had killed two lion-like ***h***
1 Chr 11:22 He had killed two lion-like ***h***

HERON (2/2)

Lev 11:19 the ***h*** after its kind, the
Deut 14:18 the ***h*** after its kind, and the

HESED (KJV) See BEN-HESED

HERS See APPENDIX

HERSELF (54/50) See APPENDIX

HESHBON (38/37)

Num 21:25 in ***H*** and in all its villages.
21:26 For ***H*** was the city of Sihon
21:27 in proverbs say: "Come to ***H***,
21:28 "For fire went out from ***H***,
21:30 ***H*** has perished as far as

21:34 of the Amorites, who dwelt at ***H***.
32: 3 Dibon, Jazer, Nimrah, ***H***,
32:37 the children of Reuben built ***H***
Deut 1: 4 of the Amorites, who dwelt in ***H***,
2:24 Sihon the Amorite, king of ***H***,
2:26 of Kedemoth to Sihon king of ***H***,
2:30 But Sihon king of ***H*** would not
3: 2 of the Amorites, who dwelt at ***H***.
3: 6 as we did to Sihon king of ***H***,
4:46 of the Amorites, who dwelt at ***H***,
29: 7 Sihon king of ***H*** and Og king of
Josh 9:10 the Jordan—to Sihon king of ***H***,
12: 2 who dwelt in ***H*** and ruled half
12: 5 the border of Sihon king of ***H***.
13:10 the Amorites, who reigned in ***H***,
13:17 ***H*** and all its cities that are
13:21 the Amorites, who reigned in ***H***,
13:26 and from ***H*** to Ramath Mizpah and
13:27 the kingdom of Sihon king of ***H***,
21:39 ***H*** with its common-land, and
Judg 11:19 king of the Amorites, king of ***H***;
11:26 While Israel dwelt in ***H*** and its
1 Chr 6:81 ***H*** with its common-lands, and
Neh 9:22 The land of the king of ***H***,
Song 7: 4 eyes like the pools in ***H*** By
Isa 15: 4 ***H*** and Elealeh will cry out,
16: 8 For the fields of ***H*** languish,
16: 9 O ***H*** and Elealeh; For battle
Jer 48: 2 In ***H*** they have devised evil
48:34 From the cry of ***H*** to Elealeh
48:45 stood under the shadow of ***H***
48:45 But a fire shall come out of ***H***,
49: 3 'Wail, O ***H***, for Ai is

HESHMON (1/1)

Josh 15:27 Hazar Gaddah, ***H***,

HESITATE (3/3)

Judg 18: 9 Do not ***h*** to go, and enter to
1 Ki 22: 3 but we ***h*** to take it out of the
Job 30:10 They do not ***h*** to spit in my

HETH (14/12)

Gen 10:15 Sidon his firstborn, and ***H***;
23: 3 and spoke to the sons of ***H***,
23: 5 And the sons of ***H*** answered
23: 7 of the land, the sons of ***H***.
23:10 dwelt among the sons of ***H***;
23:10 the presence of the sons of ***H***,
23:16 in the hearing of the sons of ***H***,
23:18 the presence of the sons of ***H***,
23:20 to Abraham by the sons of ***H*** as
25:10 purchased from the sons of ***H***.
27:46 because of the daughters of ***H***;
27:46 a wife of the daughters of ***H***,
49:32 purchased from the sons of ***H***.
1 Chr 1:13 Sidon, his firstborn, and ***H***;

HETHLON (2/2)

Ezek 47:15 Great Sea, by the road to ***H***,
48: 1 border along the road to ***H*** at

HEW (1/1) HEWED, HEWN, HEWS

Deut 10: 1 ***H*** for yourself two tablets of

HEWED (1/1) HEW

Deut 10: 3 ***h*** two tablets of stone like the

HEWER (KJV) See (ONE WHO) CUTS

HEWN (22/22) HEW

Ex 20:25 build it of ***h*** stone;
1 Ki 5:17 and ***h*** stones, to lay the
6:36 with three rows of ***h*** stone
7:11 ***h*** to size, and cedar wood.
7:12 with three rows of ***h*** stones
2 Ki 12:12 buying timber and ***h*** stone,
22: 6 and to buy timber and ***h*** stone to
1 Chr 22: 2 masons to cut ***h*** stones
2 Chr 34:11 and builders to buy ***h*** stone
Prov 9: 1 She has ***h*** out her seven
Isa 9:10 will rebuild with ***h*** stones;
10:33 stature will be ***h*** down,
22:16 That you have ***h*** a sepulcher
51: 1 rock from which you were ***h***,
Jer 2:13 ***h*** themselves cisterns—broken
Lam 3: 9 blocked my ways with ***h*** stone;
Ezek 40:42 four tables of ***h*** stone
Hos 6: 5 Therefore I have ***h*** them by the
Am 5:11 built houses of ***h*** stone,
Mt 27:60 in his new tomb which he had ***h***
Mk 15:46 Him in a tomb which had been ***h***
Lk 23:53 laid it in a tomb that was ***h***

HEWN-OUT (1/1)

Deut 6:11 ***h*** wells which you did not dig,

HEWS (1/1) HEW

Isa 22:16 As he who ***h*** himself a

HEZEKI (KJV) See HIZKI

HEZEKIAH (132/121)

2 Ki 16:20 Then ***H*** his son reigned in his
18: 1 that ***H*** the son of Ahaz, king
18: 9 in the fourth year of King ***H***,
18:10 took it. In the sixth year of ***H***,
18:13 the fourteenth year of King ***H***,
18:14 Then ***H*** king of Judah sent to the
18:14 the king of Assyria assessed ***H***
18:15 So ***H*** gave him all the silver
18:16 At that time ***H*** stripped the
18:16 and from the pillars which ***H***
18:17 against Jerusalem, to King ***H***.
18:19 said to them, "Say now to ***H***,
18:22 high places and whose altars ***H***
18:29 Do not let ***H*** deceive you, for he
18:30 nor let ***H*** make you trust in the
18:31 "Do not listen to ***H***;
18:32 not die. But do not listen to ***H***,
18:37 came to ***H*** with their clothes
19: 1 when King ***H*** heard it, that he
19: 3 they said to him, "Thus says ***H***:
19: 5 So the servants of King ***H*** came
19: 9 he again sent messengers to ***H***,
19:10 Thus you shall speak to ***H*** king
19:14 And ***H*** received the letter from
19:14 and ***H*** went up to the house of
19:15 Then ***H*** prayed before the LORD,
19:20 the son of Amoz sent to ***H***,
20: 1 In those days ***H*** was sick and
20: 3 And ***H*** wept bitterly.
20: 5 Return and tell ***H*** the leader of
20: 8 And ***H*** said to Isaiah, "What
20:10 And ***H*** answered, "It is an easy
20:12 sent letters and a present to ***H***,
20:12 for he heard that ***H*** had been
20:13 And ***H*** was attentive to them, and
20:13 or in all his dominion that ***H***
20:14 the prophet went to King ***H***,
20:14 So ***H*** said, "They came from a
20:15 So ***H*** answered, "They have
20:16 Then Isaiah said to ***H***,
20:19 So ***H*** said to Isaiah, "The word
20:20 Now the rest of the acts of ***H***—
20:21 So ***H*** rested with his fathers.
21: 3 the high places which ***H*** his
1 Chr 3:13 ***H*** his son, Manasseh his son,
3:23 of Neariah were Elioenai, ***H***,
4:41 by name came in the days of ***H***
2 Chr 28:27 Then ***H*** his son reigned in his
29: 1 ***H*** became king when he was
29:18 Then they went in to King ***H*** and
29:20 Then King ***H*** rose early,
29:27 Then ***H*** commanded them to offer
29:30 Moreover King ***H*** and the leaders
29:31 Then ***H*** answered and said, "Now
29:36 Then ***H*** and all the people
30: 1 And ***H*** sent to all Israel and
30:18 But ***H*** prayed for them, saying,
30:20 And the LORD listened to ***H*** and
30:22 And ***H*** gave encouragement to all
30:24 For ***H*** king of Judah gave to the
31: 2 And ***H*** appointed the divisions
31: 8 And when ***H*** and the leaders came
31: 9 Then ***H*** questioned the priests
31:11 Now ***H*** commanded them to
31:13 at the commandment of ***H*** the
31:20 Thus ***H*** did throughout all
32: 2 And when ***H*** saw that Sennacherib
32: 8 strengthened by the words of ***H***
32: 9 to ***H*** king of Judah, and to all
32:11 Does not ***H*** persuade you to give
32:12 Has not the same ***H*** taken away
32:15 do not let ***H*** deceive you or
32:16 God and against His servant ***H***.
32:17 so the God of ***H*** will not
32:20 Now because of this King ***H*** and
32:22 Thus the LORD saved ***H*** and the
32:23 and presents to ***H*** king of
32:24 In those days ***H*** was sick and
32:25 But ***H*** did not repay according to
32:26 Then ***H*** humbled himself for the
32:26 come upon them in the days of ***H***.
32:27 ***H*** had very great riches and
32:30 This same ***H*** also stopped the
32:30 ***H*** prospered in all his works.
32:32 Now the rest of the acts of ***H***,
32:33 So ***H*** rested with his fathers,
33: 3 the high places which ***H*** his
Ezra 2:16 the people of Ater of ***H***,
Neh 7:21 the sons of Ater of ***H***,
10:17 Ater, ***H***, Azzur,
Prov 25: 1 of Solomon which the men of ***H***
Isa 1: 1 of Uzziah, Jotham, Ahaz, and ***H***,
36: 1 the fourteenth year of King ***H***
36: 2 army from Lachish to King ***H*** at
36: 4 said to them, "Say now to ***H***,
36: 7 high places and whose altars ***H***
36:14 Do not let ***H*** deceive you, for he
36:15 nor let ***H*** make you trust in the
36:16 "Do not listen to ***H***;
36:18 Beware lest ***H*** persuade you,
36:22 came to ***H*** with their clothes
37: 1 when King ***H*** heard it, that he
37: 3 they said to him, "Thus says ***H***:
37: 5 So the servants of King ***H*** came
37: 9 it, he sent messengers to ***H***,
37:10 Thus you shall speak to ***H*** king
37:14 And ***H*** received the letter from
37:14 and ***H*** went up to the house of
37:15 Then ***H*** prayed to the LORD,
37:21 the son of Amoz sent to ***H***,
38: 1 In those days ***H*** was sick and
38: 2 Then ***H*** turned his face toward
38: 3 And ***H*** wept bitterly.
38: 5 'Go and tell ***H***, 'Thus says
38: 9 This is the writing of ***H*** king
38:22 And ***H*** had said, "What is the
39: 1 sent letters and a present to ***H***,
39: 2 And ***H*** was pleased with them, and
39: 2 or in all his dominion that ***H***
39: 3 the prophet went to King ***H***,
39: 3 So ***H*** said, "They came to me
39: 4 So ***H*** answered, "They have
39: 5 Then Isaiah said to ***H***,
39: 8 So ***H*** said to Isaiah, "The word
Jer 15: 4 of Manasseh the son of ***H***,
26:18 prophesied in the days of ***H***
26:19 Did ***H*** king of Judah and all
Hos 1: 1 of Uzziah, Jotham, Ahaz, and ***H***,
Mic 1: 1 days of Jotham, Ahaz, and ***H***,
Zeph 1: 1 son of Amariah, the son of ***H***,
Mt 1: 9 begot Ahaz, and Ahaz begot ***H***.
1:10 ***H*** begot Manasseh, Manasseh begot

HEZION (1/1)

1 Ki 15:18 son of Tabrimmon, the son of ***H***,

HEZIR (2/2)

1 Chr 24:15 the seventeenth to ***H***,
Neh 10:20 Magpiash, Meshullam, ***H***,

HEZRAI (1/1)

2 Sam 23:35 ***H*** the Carmelite, Paarai the

HEZRO (1/1)

1 Chr 11:37 ***H*** the Carmelite, Naarai the son

HEZRON (20/19)

Gen 46: 9 Reuben were Hanoch, Pallu, ***H***,
46:12 The sons of Perez were ***H*** and
Ex 6:14 Israel, were Hanoch, Pallu, ***H***,
Num 26: 6 of ***H***, the family of the
26:21 the sons of Perez were: of ***H***,
Josh 15: 3 Barnea, passed along to ***H***,
15:25 ***H*** (which is Hazor),
Ruth 4:18 of Perez: Perez begot ***H***;
4:19 ***H*** begot Ram, and Ram begot
1 Chr 2: 5 The sons of Perez were ***H*** and
2: 9 Also the sons of ***H*** who were
2:18 Caleb the son of ***H*** had children
2:21 Now afterward ***H*** went in to the
2:24 After ***H*** died in Caleb Ephrathah,
2:25 Jerahmeel, the firstborn of ***H***,
4: 1 sons of Judah were Perez, ***H***,
5: 3 of Israel were Hanoch, Pallu, ***H***,
Mt 1: 3 Zerah by Tamar, Perez begot ***H***,
1: 3 begot Hezron, and ***H*** begot Ram.
Lk 3:33 son of Ram, the son of ***H***,

HEZRON'S (1/1)

1 Chr 2:24 ***H*** wife Abijah bore him Ashhur

HEZRONITES (2/2)

Num 26: 6 of Hezron, the family of the ***H***;
26:21 of Hezron, the family of the ***H***;

HID (37/36) HIDE

Gen 3: 8 and Adam and his wife ***h***
3:10 was naked; and I ***h*** myself."
35: 4 and Jacob ***h*** them under the
Ex 2: 2 she ***h*** him three months.
2:12 he killed the Egyptian and ***h***
3: 6 And Moses ***h*** his face, for he
Josh 2: 4 woman took the two men and ***h***
6:17 because she ***h*** the messengers
6:25 because she ***h*** the messengers
Judg 9: 5 because he ***h*** himself.
1 Sam 3:18 and ***h*** nothing from him. And he
13: 6 then the people ***h*** in caves, in
20:19 come to the place where you ***h***
20:24 Then David ***h*** in the field.
1 Ki 18:13 how I ***h*** one hundred men of the
2 Ki 7: 8 and went and ***h*** them; then they
7: 8 and went and ***h*** it.
11: 2 and they ***h*** him and his nurse in
1 Chr 21:20 four sons who were with him ***h***
2 Chr 22:11 ***h*** him from Athaliah so that she
Job 29: 8 The young men saw me and ***h***,
Ps 9:15 In the net which they ***h***,
30: 7 You ***h*** Your face, and I was
Isa 53: 3 with grief. And we ***h***,
54: 8 With a little wrath I ***h*** My face
57:17 I ***h*** and was angry, And he
Jer 13: 5 So I went and ***h*** it by the
36:26 but the LORD ***h*** them.
Ezek 39:23 therefore I ***h*** My face from
Mt 13:33 which a woman took and ***h*** in
13:44 field, which a man found and ***h***;
25:18 and ***h*** his lord's money.
25:25 and went and ***h*** your talent in
Lk 1:24 and she ***h*** herself five months,
13:21 which a woman took and ***h*** in
Jn 8:59 but Jesus ***h*** Himself and went

Rev 6:15 **h** themselves in the caves and

HIDDAI (1/1)

2 Sam 23:30 **H** from the brooks of Gaash,

HIDDEKEL (1/1)

Gen 2:14 name of the third river is **H**;

HIDDEN (98/96) HIDE

Gen 4:14 I shall be **h** from Your face;
Lev 4:13 and the thing is **h** from the
Num 5:13 and it is **h** from the eyes of
Deut 33:19 the seas And of treasures **h**
Josh 2: 6 them up to the roof and **h** them
7:21 **h** in the earth in the midst of
7:22 **h** in his tent, with the silver
10:16 these five kings had fled and **h**
10:17 five kings have been found **h**
10:27 the cave where they had been **h**,
1 Sam 10:22 **h** among the equipment."
14:11 of the holes where they have **h**.
14:22 the men of Israel who had **h** in
2 Sam 17: 9 Surely by now he is **h** in some
18:13 For there is nothing **h** from the
1 Ki 18: 4 one hundred prophets and **h**
2 Ki 4:27 and the LORD has **h** it from
6:29 but she has **h** her son."
11: 3 So he was **h** with her in the
2 Chr 22:12 And he was **h** with them in the
Job 3:16 Or why was I not **h** like a
3:21 And search for it more than **h**
3:23 given to a man whose way is **h**,
5:21 You shall be **h** from the scourge
10:13 And these things You have **h** in
15:20 And the number of years is **h**
17: 4 For You have **h** their heart from
18:10 A noose is **h** for him on the
24: 1 Since times are not **h** from the
28:11 What is **h** he brings forth to
28:21 It is **h** from the eyes of all
40:13 Bind their faces in **h**
Ps 17:14 belly You fill with Your **h**
19: 6 And there is nothing **h** from
22:24 Nor has He **h** His face from
32: 5 And my iniquity I have not **h**.
35: 7 For without cause they have **h**
35: 8 And let his net that he has **h**
38: 9 And my sighing is not **h** from
40:10 I have not **h** Your righteousness
51: 6 And in the **h** part You will
69: 5 And my sins are not **h** from
119:11 Your word I have **h** in my heart,
139:15 My frame was not **h** from You,
140: 5 The proud have **h** a snare for
Prov 2: 4 And search for her as for **h**
Isa 28:15 And under falsehood we have **h**
29:14 their prudent men shall be **h**.
40:27 My way is **h** from the LORD, And
42:22 And they are **h** in prison
45: 3 treasures of darkness And **h**
48: 6 Even **h** things, and you did not
49: 2 shadow of His hand He has **h** Me,
49: 2 In His quiver He has **h** Me."
59: 2 And your sins have **h** His face
64: 7 For You have **h** Your face from
65:16 And because they are **h** from My
Jer 13: 7 from the place where I had **h**
16:17 they are not **h** from My face,
16:17 nor is their iniquity **h** from My
18:22 And **h** snares for my feet.
33: 5 for whose wickedness I have **h**
43:10 these stones that I have **h**.
Ezek 22:26 and they have **h** their eyes from
28: 3 is no secret that can be **h**
39:24 and **h** My face from them." '
Hos 5: 3 And Israel is not **h** from Me;
13:14 be your destruction! Pity is **h**
Ob 6 be searched out! How his **h**
Nah 3:11 will be drunk; You will be **h**;
Hab 3: 4 And there His power was **h**.
Zeph 2: 3 It may be that you will be **h**
Mt 5:14 is set on a hill cannot be **h**.
10:26 and **h** that will not be known.
11:25 that You have **h** these things
13:44 of heaven is like treasure **h**
Mk 4:22 For there is nothing **h** which
7:24 know it, but He could not be **h**.
Lk 8:17 nor anything **h** that will not
8:47 woman saw that she was not **h**,
9:45 and it was **h** from them so that
10:21 that You have **h** these things
12: 2 nor **h** that will not be known.
18:34 this saying was **h** from them,
19:42 your peace! But now they are **h**
Jn 12:36 and was **h** from them.
1 Cor 2: 7 the **h** wisdom which God
4: 5 will both bring to light the **h**
2 Cor 4: 2 But we have renounced the **h**
Eph 3: 9 of the ages has been **h** in God
Col 1:26 the mystery which has been **h**
2: 3 in whom are **h** all the treasures
3: 3 and your life is **h** with Christ
1 Tim 5:25 that are otherwise cannot be **h**.
Heb 4:13 And there is no creature **h** from
11:23 was **h** three months by his
1 Pe 3: 4 rather let it be the **h** person
Rev 2:17 I will give some of the **h**

HIDE (85/82) HID, HIDDEN, HIDEOUT, HIDES, HIDING

Gen 18:17 Shall I **h** from Abraham what I am
47:18 We will not **h** from my lord that
Ex 2: 3 But when she could no longer **h**
Lev 4:11 But the bull's **h** and all its
8:17 But the bull, its **h**,
9:11 The flesh and the **h** he burned
20: 4 of the land should in any way **h**
Num 19: 5 be burned in his sight: its **h**,
Deut 7:20 who **h** themselves from you, are
22: 1 and **h** yourself from them;
22: 3 you must not **h** yourself.
22: 4 and **h** yourself from them; you
31:17 and I will **h** My face from them,
31:18 And I will surely **h** My face in
32:20 I will **h** My face from them, I
Josh 2:16 **H** there three days, until the
7:19 do not **h** it from me."
Judg 6:11 in order to **h** it from the
1 Sam 3:17 Please do not **h** it from me.
3:17 if you **h** anything from me of
19: 2 stay in a secret place and **h**.
20: 2 And why should my father **h** this
20: 5 that I may **h** in the field until
2 Sam 14:18 Please do not **h** from me anything
1 Ki 17: 3 and **h** by the Brook Cherith,
22:25 go into an inner chamber to **h**!
2 Ki 7:12 have gone out of the camp to **h**
2 Chr 18:24 go into an inner chamber to **h**!
Job 3:10 Nor **h** sorrow from my eyes.
13:20 Then I will not **h** myself from
13:24 Why do You **h** Your face, And
14:13 that You would **h** me in the
23:17 And He did not **h** deep
24: 4 of the land are forced to **h**.
34:22 the workers of iniquity may **h**
40:13 **H** them in the dust together,
Ps 10: 1 Why do You **h** in times of
13: 1 How long will You **h** Your face
17: 8 **H** me under the shadow of Your
27: 5 time of trouble He shall **h** me
27: 5 of His tabernacle He shall **h**
27: 9 Do not **h** Your face from me;
31:20 You shall **h** them in the secret
44:24 Why do You **h** Your face, And
51: 9 **H** Your face from my sins, And
55: 1 And do not **h** Yourself from my
55:12 Then I could **h** from him.
56: 6 They gather together, They **h**,
64: 2 **H** me from the secret plots of
69:17 And do not **h** Your face from
78: 4 We will not **h** them from their
88:14 Why do You **h** Your face from
89:46 Will You **h** Yourself forever?
102: 2 Do not **h** Your face from me in
104:29 You **h** Your face, they are
119:19 Do not **h** Your commandments
139:12 the darkness shall not **h** from
143: 7 My spirit fails! Do not **h**
Prov 28:12 arise, men **h** themselves.
28:28 men **h** themselves; But when
Isa 1:15 I will **h** My eyes from you;
2:10 and **h** in the dust, From the
3: 9 They do not **h** it. Woe to
16: 3 **H** the outcasts, Do not betray
26:20 **H** yourself, as it were, for a
29:15 to those who seek deep to **h**
45:15 who **h** Yourself, O God of
50: 6 I did not **h** My face from shame
58: 7 And not **h** yourself from your
Jer 13: 4 and **h** it there in a hole in the
13: 6 sash which I commanded you to **h**
23:24 Can anyone **h** himself in secret
36:19 said to Baruch, "Go and **h**,
38:14 **H** nothing from me."
38:25 do not **h** it from us, and we
43: 9 and **h** them in the sight of the
49:10 And he shall not be able to **h**
Lam 3:56 Do not **h** Your ear From my
Ezek 31: 8 the garden of God could not **h**
39:29 And I will not **h** My face from
Dan 10: 7 so that they fled to **h**
Am 9: 3 And though they **h** themselves on
9: 3 Though they **h** from My sight at
Mic 3: 4 He will even **h** His face from
Rev 6:16 Fall on us and **h** us from the

HIDEOUT (1/1) HIDE

1 Sam 23:22 and see the place where his **h**

HIDEOUTS (2/2)

2 Sam 22:46 come frightened from their **h**.
Ps 18:45 come frightened from their **h**.

HIDES (10/10) HIDE

1 Sam 23:23 the lurking places where he **h**;
Job 20:12 And he **h** it under his tongue,
34:29 And when He **h** His face, who
42: 3 Who is this who **h** counsel
Ps 10:11 He **h** His face; He will never
Prov 10:18 Whoever **h** hatred has lying
22: 3 man foresees evil and **h**
27:12 man foresees evil and **h**
28:27 But he who **h** his eyes will
Isa 8:17 Who **h** His face from the house

HIDING (10/10) HIDE

1 Sam 23:19 Is David not **h** with us in
26: 1 Is David not **h** in the hill of
2 Chr 22: 9 and they caught him (he was **h**
Job 15:18 Not **h** anything received from
31:33 By **h** my iniquity in my bosom,
Ps 32: 7 You are my **h** place; You shall
54: Is David not **h** with us?"
119:114 You are my **h** place and my
Isa 28:17 the waters will overflow the **h**
32: 2 A man will be as a **h** place from

HIEL (1/1)

1 Ki 16:34 In his days **H** of Bethel built

HIERAPOLIS (1/1)

Col 4:13 are in Laodicea, and those in **H**.

HIGH (376/357) HIGHER, HIGHEST, HIGHLY, LOUD

Gen 7:17 and it rose **h** above the earth.
7:19 and all the **h** hills under the
14:18 was the priest of God Most **H**.
14:19 be Abram of God Most **H**,
14:20 And blessed be God Most **H**,
14:22 hand to the LORD, God Most **H**,
29: 7 it is still **h** day; it is
Lev 21:10 He who is the **h** priest among
26:30 I will destroy your **h** places,
Num 22:41 and brought him up to the **h**
24:16 has the knowledge of the Most **H**,
33:52 and demolish all their **h**
35:25 there until the death of the **h**
35:28 refuge until the death of the **h**
35:28 But after the death of the **h**
Deut 3: 5 cities were fortified with **h**
12: 2 on the **h** mountains and on the
26:19 and that He will set you **h** above
28: 1 LORD your God will set you **h**
28:52 at all your gates until your **h**
32: 8 When the Most **H** divided their
32:27 should say, "Our hand is **h**;
33:29 you shall tread down their **h**
Josh 20: 6 the death of the one who is **h**
1 Sam 9:12 of the people today on the **h**
9:13 him before he goes up to the **h**
9:14 them on his way up to the **h**
9:19 Go up before me to the **h** place,
9:25 they had come down from the **h**
10: 5 coming down from the **h** place
10:13 he went to the **h** place.
2 Sam 1:19 of Israel is slain on your **h**
1:25 Jonathan was slain in your **h**
22:14 And the Most **H** uttered His
22:34 And sets me on my **h** places.
23: 1 says the man raised up on **h**,
1 Ki 3: 2 the people sacrificed at the **h**
3: 3 and burned incense at the **h**
3: 4 for that was the great **h**
6:10 temple, each five cubits **h**;
6:20 wide, and twenty cubits **h**.
6:23 olive wood, each ten cubits **h**.
7:15 each one eighteen cubits **h**,
11: 7 Then Solomon built a **h** place for
12:31 He made shrines on the **h** places,
12:32 installed the priests of the **h**
13: 2 sacrifice the priests of the **h**
13:32 all the shrines on the **h**
13:33 every class of people for the **h**
13:33 one of the priests of the **h**
14:23 also built for themselves **h**
14:23 and wooden images on every **h**
15:14 But the **h** places were not
21: 9 and seat Naboth with **h** honor
21:12 and seated Naboth with **h** honor
22:43 Nevertheless the **h** places were
22:43 and burned incense on the **h**
2 Ki 12: 3 But the **h** places were not taken
12: 3 and burned incense on the **h**
12:10 the king's scribe and the **h**
14: 4 However the **h** places were not
14: 4 and burned incense on the **h**
15: 4 except that the **h** places were
15: 4 and burned incense on the **h**
15:35 However the **h** places were not
15:35 and burned incense on the **h**
16: 4 and burned incense on the **h**
17: 9 and they built for themselves **h**
17:10 and wooden images on every **h**
17:11 burned incense on all the **h**
17:29 them in the shrines on the **h**
17:32 for themselves priests of the **h**
17:32 them in the shrines of the **h**
18: 4 He removed the **h** places and
18:22 is it not He whose **h** places
19:22 And lifted up your eyes on **h**?
21: 3 For he rebuilt the **h** places
22: 4 Go up to Hilkiah the **h** priest,
22: 8 Then Hilkiah the **h** priest said
23: 4 king commanded Hilkiah the **h**
23: 5 to burn incense on the **h**
23: 8 and defiled the **h** places where
23: 8 also he broke down the **h** places
23: 9 the priests of the **h** places
23:13 Then the king defiled the **h**
23:15 and the **h** place which Jeroboam
23:15 both that altar and the **h** place
23:15 and he burned the **h** place and

23:19 away all the shrines of the **h**
23:20 all the priests of the **h**
1 Chr 16:39 of the LORD at the **h** place
17:17 to the rank of a man of **h**
21:29 were at that time at the **h**
2 Chr 1: 3 went to the **h** place that was
1:13 came to Jerusalem from the **h**
3:15 pillars thirty-five cubits **h**,
6:13 cubits wide, and three cubits **h**,
11:15 for himself priests for the **h**
14: 3 of the foreign gods and the **h**
14: 5 He also removed the **h** places and
15:17 But the **h** places were not
17: 6 moreover he removed the **h**
20:19 Israel with voices loud and **h**.
20:33 Nevertheless the **h** places were
21:11 Moreover he made **h** places in the
24:11 the king's scribe and the **h**
28: 4 and burned incense on the **h**
28:25 single city of Judah he made **h**
31: 1 and threw down the **h** places and
32:12 same Hezekiah taken away His **h**
33: 3 For he rebuilt the **h** places
33:17 still sacrificed on the **h**
33:19 and the sites where he built **h**
34: 3 Judah and Jerusalem of the **h**
34: 9 When they came to Hilkiah the **h**
Neh 3: 1 Then Eliashib the **h** priest rose
3:20 of the house of Eliashib the **h**
13:28 the son of Eliashib the **h**
Esth 5:14 gallows be made, fifty cubits **h**,
7: 9 The gallows, fifty cubits **h**,
Job 5:11 He sets on **h** those who are
16:19 And my evidence is on **h**.
21:22 Since He judges those on **h**?
25: 2 He makes peace in His **h**
31: 2 of the Almighty from on **h**?
39:18 When she lifts herself on **h**,
39:27 And make its nest on **h**?
41:34 He beholds every **h** thing;
Ps 7: 7 sakes, therefore, return on **h**.
7:17 to the name of the LORD Most **H**.
9: 2 praise to Your name, O Most **H**.
18:13 And the Most **H** uttered His
18:33 And sets me on my **h** places.
21: 7 the mercy of the Most **H** he
27: 5 He shall set me **h** upon a rock.
46: 4 of the tabernacle of the Most **H**.
47: 2 For the LORD Most **H** is
49: 2 Both low and **h**, Rich and
50:14 pay your vows to the Most **H**.
56: 2 who fight against me, O Most **H**.
57: 2 I will cry out to God Most **H**,
62: 4 to cast him down from his **h**
62: 9 Men of **h** degree are a lie;
68:18 You have ascended on **h**,
69:29 O God, set me up on **h**.
71:19 O God, is very **h**,
73:11 there knowledge in the Most **H**?
75: 5 Do not lift up your horn on **h**;
77:10 of the right hand of the Most **H**.
78:17 rebelling against the Most **H**
78:35 And the Most **H** God their
78:56 tested and provoked the Most **H**
78:58 Him to anger with their **h**
82: 6 you are children of the Most **H**.
83:18 Are the Most **H** over all the
87: 5 And the Most **H** Himself shall
89:13 and **h** is Your right hand.
91: 1 the secret place of the Most **H**
91: 9 my refuge, Even the Most **H**,
91:14 I will set him on **h**,
92: 1 praises to Your name, O Most **H**;
92: 8 are on **h** forevermore.
93: 4 The LORD on **h** is mightier
97: 9 are most **h** above all the
99: 2 And He is **h** above all the
103:11 For as the heavens are **h** above
104:18 The **h** hills are for the wild
107:11 the counsel of the Most **H**,
107:41 Yet He sets the poor on **h**,
113: 4 The LORD is **h** above all
113: 5 LORD our God, Who dwells on **h**,
138: 6 Though the LORD is on **h**,
139: 6 too wonderful for me; It is **h**,
144: 2 My **h** tower and my deliverer,
149: 6 Let the **h** praises of God be
Prov 3: 4 And so find favor and **h** esteem
8: 2 her stand on the top of the **h**
18:11 And like a **h** wall in his own
Eccl 5: 8 for **h** official watches over
5: 8 high official watches over **h**
Isa 2:13 cedars of Lebanon that are **h**
2:14 Upon all the **h** mountains, And
2:15 Upon every **h** tower, And upon
6: 1 **h** and lifted up, and the train
10:33 Those of **h** stature will be
13: 2 Lift up a banner on the **h**
14:14 I will be like the Most **H**.
15: 2 To the **h** places to weep.
16:12 that Moab is weary on the **h**
22:16 hews himself a sepulcher on **h**,
24:18 For the windows from on **h** are
24:21 the LORD will punish on **h** the
25:12 The fortress of the **h** fort of
26: 5 down those who dwell on **h**,
30:13 A bulge in a **h** wall, Whose
30:25 There will be on every **h**
30:25 high mountain And on every **h**
32:15 is poured upon us from on **h**,
33: 5 is exalted, for He dwells on **h**;
33:16 He will dwell on **h**;
36: 7 is it not He whose **h** places
37:23 And lifted up your eyes on **h**?
40: 9 Get up into the **h** mountain;
40:26 Lift up your eyes on **h**,
52:13 and extolled and be very **h**.
57: 7 On a lofty and **h** mountain You
57:15 For thus says the **H** and Lofty
57:15 I dwell in the **h** and holy
58: 4 To make your voice heard on **h**.
58:14 will cause you to ride on the **h**
Jer 2:20 When on every **h** hill and
3: 6 She has gone up on every **h**
7:31 And they have built the **h** places
17: 2 By the green trees on the **h**
17: 3 And your **h** places of sin
17:12 A glorious **h** throne from the
19: 5 (they have also built the **h**
20: 2 the stocks that were in the **h**
25:30 LORD will roar from on **h**,
32:35 And they built the **h** places of
48: 1 The **h** stronghold is shamed and
48:35 who offers sacrifices in the **h**
49:16 you make your nest as **h** as the
51:58 And her **h** gates shall be
Lam 3:35 Before the face of the Most **H**,
3:38 from the mouth of the Most **H**
Ezek 1:18 they were so **h** they were
1:26 with the appearance of a man **h**
6: 3 and I will destroy your **h**
6: 6 and the **h** places shall be
6:13 on every **h** hill, on all the
11:22 of the God of Israel was **h**
16:16 and adorned multicolored **h**
16:24 and made a **h** place for yourself
16:25 You built your **h** places at the
16:31 and built your **h** place in every
16:39 shrines and break down your **h**
17:22 the highest branches of the **h**
17:22 and will plant it on a **h** and
17:24 have brought down the **h** tree
20:28 and they saw all the **h** hills
20:29 What is this **h** place to which
31: 3 And of **h** stature; And its top
31:14 drinks water may ever be **h**
34: 6 and on every **h** hill; yes, My
34:14 their fold shall be on the **h**
40: 2 Israel and set me on a very **h**
40:14 the gateposts, sixty cubits **h**,
40:42 a half wide, and one cubit **h**;
41: 3 and the entrance, six cubits **h**;
41: 8 rod, that is, six cubits **h**.
41:22 was of wood, three cubits **h**,
43: 7 of their kings on their **h**
43:13 the base one cubit **h** and one
43:15 altar hearth is four cubits **h**,
Dan 3:26 servants of the Most **H** God,
4: 2 and wonders that the Most **H**
4:17 may know That the Most **H**
4:24 is the decree of the Most **H**,
4:25 till you know that the Most **H**
4:32 until you know that the Most **H**
4:34 and I blessed the Most **H** and
5:18 the Most **H** God gave
5:21 till he knew that the Most **H**
7:18 But the saints of the Most **H**
7:22 of the saints of the Most **H**,
7:25 words against the Most **H**,
7:25 the saints of the Most **H**,
7:27 the saints of the Most **H**.
8: 3 and the two horns were **h**;
8:11 He even exalted himself as **h** as
Hos 7:16 return, but not to the Most **H**;
10: 8 Also the **h** places of Aven, the
11: 7 Though they call to the Most **H**,
Am 4:13 Who treads the **h** places of the
7: 9 The **h** places of Isaac shall be
Ob 3 rock, Whose habitation is **h**;
4 Though you ascend as **h** as the
Mic 1: 3 come down And tread on the **h**
1: 5 And what are the **h** places of
6: 6 And bow myself before the **H**
Hab 2: 9 That he may set his nest on **h**,
3:10 And lifted its hands on **h**.
3:19 He will make me walk on my **h**
Zeph 1:16 cities And against the **h**
Hag 1: 1 the **h** priest, saying,
1:12 the **h** priest, with all the
1:14 the **h** priest, and the spirit of
2: 2 the **h** priest, and to the
2: 4 the **h** priest; and be strong,
Zech 3: 1 Then he showed me Joshua the **h**
3: 8 the **h** priest, You and your
6:11 Jehozadak, the **h** priest.
Mt 4: 8 took Him up on an exceedingly **h**
17: 1 led them up on a **h** mountain by
26: 3 at the palace of the **h** priest,
26:51 struck the servant of the **h**
26:57 led Him away to Caiaphas the **h**
26:58 Him at a distance to the **h**
26:62 And the **h** priest arose and said
26:63 And the **h** priest answered and
26:65 Then the **h** priest tore his
Mk 2:26 the days of Abiathar the **h**
5: 7 Son of the Most **H** God?
6:21 the **h** officers, and the chief
9: 2 and led them up on a **h** mountain
14:47 and struck the servant of the **h**
14:53 they led Jesus away to the **h**
14:54 into the courtyard of the **h**
14:60 And the **h** priest stood up in the
14:61 Again the **h** priest asked Him,
14:63 Then the **h** priest tore his
14:66 of the servant girls of the **h**
Lk 1:78 which the Dayspring from on **h**
3: 2 while Annas and Caiaphas were **h**
4: 5 taking Him up on a **h** mountain,
4:38 mother was sick with a **h** fever,
6:35 you will be sons of the Most **H**.
8:28 Son of the Most **H** God? I beg
22:50 struck the servant of the **h**
22:54 Him and brought Him into the **h**
24:49 are endued with power from on **h**.
Jn 11:49 being **h** priest that year, said
11:51 but being **h** priest that year he
18:10 drew it and struck the **h**
18:13 of Caiaphas who was **h** priest
18:15 disciple was known to the **h**
18:15 into the courtyard of the **h**
18:16 who was known to the **h** priest,
18:19 The **h** priest then asked Jesus
18:22 Do You answer the **h** priest like
18:24 Him bound to Caiaphas the **h**
18:26 One of the servants of the **h**
19:31 (for that Sabbath was a **h** day),
Acts 4: 6 as well as Annas the **h** priest,
4: 6 as were of the family of the **h**
5:17 Then the **h** priest rose up, and
5:21 But the **h** priest and those with
5:24 Now when the **h** priest, the
5:27 And the **h** priest asked them,
7: 1 Then the **h** priest said, "Are
7:48 the Most **H** does not dwell in
9: 1 went to the **h** priest
16:17 are the servants of the Most **H**
22: 5 as also the **h** priest bears me
23: 2 And the **h** priest Ananias
23: 4 Do you revile God's **h** priest?"
23: 5 that he was the **h** priest; for
24: 1 after five days Ananias the **h**
25: 2 Then the **h** priest and the chief
Rom 12:16 Do not set your mind on **h**
13:11 that now it is **h** time to
2 Cor 10: 5 down arguments and every **h**
Eph 4: 8 "When He ascended on **h**,
Heb 1: 3 right hand of the Majesty on **h**,
2:17 be a merciful and faithful **H**
3: 1 consider the Apostle and **H**
4:14 then that we have a great **H**
4:15 For we do not have a **H** Priest
5: 1 For every **h** priest taken from
5: 5 not glorify Himself to become **H**
5:10 called by God as **H** Priest
6:20 having become **H** Priest forever
7: 1 priest of the Most **H** God, who
7:26 For such a **H** Priest was fitting
7:27 as those **h** priests, to offer up
7:28 For the law appoints as **h**
8: 1 We have such a **H** Priest, who is
8: 3 For every **h** priest is appointed
9: 7 But into the second part the **h**
9:11 But Christ came as **H** Priest of
9:25 as the **h** priest enters the Most
10:21 and having a **H** Priest over the
13:11 into the sanctuary by the **h**
Rev 21:10 in the Spirit to a great and **h**
21:12 Also she had a great and **h** wall

HIGHER (14/11) HIGH

Num 24: 7 His king shall be **h** than Agag,
Deut 28:43 who is among you shall rise **h**
28:43 you shall rise higher and **h**
Ezra 9: 6 for our iniquities have risen **h**
Job 11: 8 They are **h** than heaven—what
35: 5 They are **h** than you.
Ps 61: 2 Lead me to the rock that is **h**
Eccl 5: 8 and **h** officials are over them.
Isa 55: 9 For as the heavens are **h** than
55: 9 So are My ways **h** than your
Dan 8: 3 but one was **h** than the other,
8: 3 and the **h** one came up last.
Lk 14:10 say to you, 'Friend, go up **h**.
Heb 7:26 and has become **h** than the

HIGHEST (17/17) HIGH

Deut 10:14 Indeed heaven and the **h** heavens
Esth 1:14 and who ranked **h** in the
Job 22:12 And see the **h** stars, how lofty
Ps 89:27 The **h** of the kings of the
Prov 9: 3 She cries out from the **h**
9:14 On a seat by the **h** places of
Jer 2:21 a seed of **h** quality. How then
Ezek 17: 3 And took from the cedar the **h**
17:22 will take also one of the **h**
41: 7 the lowest story to the **h** by
Mt 21: 9 Hosanna in the **h**!"
Mk 11:10 of the Lord! Hosanna in the **h**!
Lk 1:32 will be called the Son of the **H**;
1:35 and the power of the **H** will
1:76 be called the prophet of the **H**;
2:14 "Glory to God in the **h**,
19:38 in heaven and glory in the **h**!

HIGHLY (8/8) HIGH

1 Sam 18:30 so that his name became **h**
1 Chr 14: 2 for his kingdom was **h** exalted
Lk 1:28 **h** favored one, the Lord is
16:15 For what is **h** esteemed among
Acts 5:13 but the people esteemed them **h**.
Rom 12: 3 to think of himself more **h**
Phil 2: 9 Therefore God also has **h** exalted

1 Th 5:13 and to esteem them very **h** in

HIGHMINDED (KJV) See HAUGHTY

HIGHWAY (23/21) HIGHWAYS

Num 20:17 we will go along the King's **H**;
20:19 to him, "We will go by the **H**,
21:22 We will go by the King's **H**
Judg 21:19 on the east side of the **h** that
1 Sam 6:12 Shemesh, and went along the **h**,
2 Sam 20:12 blood in the middle of the **h**.
20:12 he moved Amasa from the **h** to
20:13 When he was removed from the **h**,
2 Ki 18:17 which was on the **h** to the
1 Chr 26:16 Gate on the ascending **h**—
26:18 there were four on the **h** and
Prov 15:19 the way of the upright is a **h**.
16:17 The **h** of the upright is to
Isa 7:3 on the **h** to the Fuller's Field,
11:16 There will be a **h** for the
19:23 In that day there will be a **h**
35:8 A **h** shall be there, and a
35:8 And it shall be called the **H**
36:2 on the **h** to the Fuller's Field.
40:3 straight in the desert A **h**
62:10 Build up the **h**! Take out the
Jer 18:15 walk in pathways and not on a **h**,
31:21 Set your heart toward the **h**,

HIGHWAYS (11/11) HIGHWAY

Lev 26:22 and your **h** shall be desolate.
Judg 5:6 The **h** were deserted, And the
20:31 in the **h** (one of which goes up
20:32 away from the city to the **h**.
20:45 five thousand of them on the **h**.
Isa 33:8 The **h** lie waste, The traveling
49:11 And My **h** shall be elevated.
Am 5:16 they shall say in all the **h**,
Mt 22:9 'Therefore go into the **h**,
22:10 servants went out into the **h**
Lk 14:23 Go out into the **h** and hedges,

HILEN (1/1)

1 Chr 6:58 **H** with its common-lands, Debir

HILKIAH (34/31)

2 Ki 18:18 the king, Eliakim the son of **H**,
18:26 Then Eliakim the son of **H**,
18:37 Then Eliakim the son of **H**,
22:4 Go up to **H** the high priest, that
22:8 Then **H** the high priest said to
22:8 And **H** gave the book to
22:10 **H** the priest has given me a
22:12 Then the king commanded **H** the
22:14 So **H** the priest, Ahikam,
23:4 And the king commanded **H** the
23:24 written in the book that **H** the
1 Chr 6:13 Shallum begot **H**, and Hilkiah
6:13 and **H** begot Azariah;
6:45 son of Amaziah, the son of **H**,
9:11 Azariah the son of **H**,
26:11 **H** the second, Tebaliah the
2 Chr 34:9 When they came to **H** the high
34:14 **H** the priest found the Book of
34:15 Then **H** answered and said to
34:15 And **H** gave the book to
34:18 **H** the priest has given me a
34:20 Then the king commanded **H**,
34:22 So **H** and those the king had
35:8 priests, and to the Levites. **H**,
Ezra 7:1 son of Azariah, the son of **H**,
Neh 8:4 Shema, Anaiah, Urijah, **H**,
11:11 Seraiah the son of **H**,
12:7 Sallu, Amok, **H**, and Jedaiah.
12:21 of **H**, Hashabiah; and of
Isa 22:20 My servant Eliakim the son of **H**;
36:3 And Eliakim the son of **H**,
36:22 Then Eliakim the son of **H**,
Jer 1:1 words of Jeremiah the son of **H**,
29:3 and Gemariah the son of **H**,

HILL (60/58) HILLS, HILLSIDE

Ex 17:9 will stand on the top of the **h**
17:10 Hur went up to the top of the **h**.
Josh 5:3 the sons of Israel at the **h** of
15:9 around from the top of the **h**
18:13 near the **h** that lies on the
18:14 from the **h** that lies before
24:33 They buried him in a **h**
Judg 7:1 north side of them by the **h** of
16:3 them to the top of the **h** that
1 Sam 7:1 the house of Abinadab on the **h**,
9:11 As they went up the **h** to the
10:5 that you shall come to the **h**
10:10 When they came there to the **h**,
23:19 in the **h** of Hachilah, which is
25:20 went down under cover of the **h**;
26:1 Is David not hiding in the **h** of
26:3 And Saul encamped in the **h** of
26:13 and stood on the top of a **h**
2 Sam 2:24 down when they came to the **h**
2:25 took their stand on top of a **h**.
6:3 Abinadab, which was on the **h**;
6:4 Abinadab, which was on the **h**,
21:9 and they hanged them on the **h**
1 Ki 11:7 on the **h** that is east of
14:23 wooden images on every high **h**
16:24 And he bought the **h** of Samaria
16:24 then he built on the **h**,
16:24 name of Shemer, owner of the **h**.
2 Ki 1:9 was, sitting on the top of a **h**.
4:27 came to the man of God at the **h**,
17:10 wooden images on every high **h**
Ps 2:6 have set My King On My holy **h**
3:4 He heard me from His holy **h**.
15:1 Who may dwell in Your holy **h**?
24:3 Who may ascend into the **h** of
42:6 From the **H** Mizar.
43:3 them bring me to Your holy **h**
99:9 God, And worship at His holy **h**;
Prov 8:2 stand on the top of the high **h**,
Song 4:6 of myrrh And to the **h** of
Isa 5:1 vineyard On a very fruitful **h**.
7:25 And to any **h** which could be dug
10:32 The **h** of Jerusalem.
30:17 And as a banner on a **h**.
30:25 mountain And on every high **h**
31:4 for Mount Zion and for its **h**.
40:4 And every mountain and **h**
Jer 2:20 When on every high **h** and
16:16 from every mountain and every **h**,
31:39 straight forward over the **h**
49:16 Who hold the height of the **h**!
50:6 have gone from mountain to **h**;
Ezek 6:13 their altars, on every high **h**,
34:6 mountains, and on every high **h**;
34:26 and the places all around My **h**
Mt 5:14 A city that is set on a **h**
Lk 1:39 those days and went into the **h**
1:65 discussed throughout all the **h**
3:5 And every mountain and **h**
4:29 led Him to the brow of the **h**

HILLEL (2/2)

Judg 12:13 Abdon the son of **H** the
12:15 Then Abdon the son of **H** the

HILLS (63/63) HILL

Gen 7:19 and all the high **h** under the
49:26 bound of the everlasting **h**.
Num 23:9 And from the **h** I behold him;
Deut 8:7 that flow out of valleys and **h**;
8:9 are iron and out of whose **h**
11:11 to possess is a land of **h** and
12:2 the high mountains and on the **h**
33:15 things of the everlasting **h**,
Josh 9:1 in the **h** and in the lowland and
1 Ki 20:23 "Their gods are gods of the **h**.
20:28 "The LORD is God of the **h**,
2 Ki 16:4 on the high places, on the **h**,
2 Chr 28:4 on the high places, on the **h**,
Job 15:7 Or were you made before the **h**?
Ps 18:7 The foundations of the **h** also
50:10 the cattle on a thousand **h**.
65:12 And the little **h** rejoice on
72:3 the people, And the little **h**,
80:10 The **h** were covered with its
95:4 The heights of the **h** are His
98:8 Let the **h** be joyful together
104:10 valleys, They flow among the **h**.
104:13 He waters the **h** from His upper
104:18 The high **h** are for the wild
104:32 it trembles; He touches the **h**,
114:4 The little **h** like lambs.
114:6 skipped like rams? O little **h**,
121:1 will lift up my eyes to the **h**—
148:9 Mountains and all **h**;
Prov 8:25 were settled, Before the **h**,
Song 2:8 mountains, Skipping upon the **h**.
Isa 2:2 shall be exalted above the **h**;
2:14 And upon all the **h** that are
5:25 And the **h** trembled.
40:12 mountains in scales And the **h**
41:15 And make the **h** like chaff.
42:15 lay waste the mountains and **h**,
54:10 shall depart And the **h** be
55:12 The mountains and the **h** Shall
58:14 you to ride on the high **h** of
65:7 And blasphemed Me on the **h**;
Jer 3:23 hoped for from the **h**,
4:24 And all the **h** moved back and
13:27 Your abominations on the **h** in
17:2 the green trees on the high **h**.
26:18 of the temple Like the bare **h**
Ezek 6:3 GOD to the mountains, to the **h**,
20:28 and they saw all the high **h** and
35:8 on your **h** and in your valleys
36:4 GOD to the mountains, the **h**,
36:6 and say to the mountains, the **h**,
Hos 4:13 And burn incense on the **h**,
10:8 "Cover us!" And to the **h**,
Joel 3:18 The **h** shall flow with milk,
Am 9:13 And all the **h** shall flow with
Mic 3:12 of the temple Like the bare **h**
4:1 shall be exalted above the **h**;
6:1 And let the **h** hear your voice.
Nah 1:5 The **h** melt, And the earth
Hab 3:6 The perpetual **h** bowed.
3:19 will make me walk on my high **h**.
Zeph 1:10 And a loud crashing from the **h**.
Lk 23:30 on us!" and to the **h**,

HILLSIDE (2/2) HILL

2 Sam 13:34 coming from the road on the **h**
16:13 Shimei went along the **h**

HILLY (1/1)

Josh 17:11 its towns—three **h** regions.

HILT (1/1)

Judg 3:22 Even the **h** went in after the

HIM (6281/4723) See APPENDIX

HIMSELF (545/507) See APPENDIX

HIN (22/19)

Ex 29:40 mixed with one-fourth of a **h**
29:40 and one-fourth of a **h** of wine
30:24 and a **h** of olive oil.
Lev 19:36 honest ephah, and an honest **h**:
23:13 be of wine, one-fourth of a **h**.
Num 15:4 mixed with one-fourth of a **h**
15:5 and one-fourth of a **h** of wine
15:6 mixed with one-third of a **h**
15:7 shall offer one-third of a **h**
15:9 flour mixed with half a **h** of
15:10 as the drink offering half a **h**
28:5 mixed with one-fourth of a **h**
28:7 shall be one-fourth of a **h**
28:14 offering shall be half a **h** of
28:14 one-third of a **h** for a ram, and
28:14 and one-fourth of a **h** for a
Ezek 4:11 by measure, one-sixth of a **h**;
45:24 together with a **h** of oil for
46:5 as well as a **h** of oil with
46:7 and a **h** of oil with every
46:11 and a **h** of oil with every
46:14 and a third of a **h** of oil to

HIND (KJV) See DEER

HINDER (5/5) HINDERED, HINDERS

Gen 24:56 Do not **h** me, since the LORD has
Num 22:16 Please let nothing **h** you from
Job 9:12 who can **h** Him? Who can say to
11:10 Then who can **h** Him?
1 Cor 9:12 but endure all things lest we **h**

HINDERED (8/8) HINDER

Ezra 6:8 men, so that they are not **h**.
Prov 4:12 walk, your steps will not be **h**,
Lk 11:52 who were entering in you **h**.
Rom 1:13 to come to you (but was **h**
15:22 reason I also have been much **h**
Gal 5:7 Who **h** you from obeying the
1 Th 2:18 and again—but Satan **h** us.
1 Pe 3:7 that your prayers may not be **h**.

HINDERMOST (KJV) See LAST, LEAST

HINDERS (2/2) HINDER

Isa 14:6 Is persecuted and no one **h**.
Acts 8:36 What **h** me from being

HINDMOST (KJV) See LAST, REAR

HINGES (2/2)

1 Ki 7:50 and the **h** of gold, both for
Prov 26:14 As a door turns on its **h**,

HINNOM (13/11)

Josh 15:8 by the Valley of the Son of **H**
15:8 lies before the Valley of **H**
18:16 the Valley of the Son of **H**,
18:16 descended to the Valley of **H**,
2 Ki 23:10 in the Valley of the Son of **H**,
2 Chr 28:3 in the Valley of the Son of **H**,
33:6 in the Valley of the Son of **H**;
Neh 11:30 Beersheba to the Valley of **H**.
Jer 7:31 in the Valley of the Son of **H**,
7:32 or the Valley of the Son of **H**,
19:2 to the Valley of the Son of **H**,
19:6 or the Valley of the Son of **H**,
32:35 in the Valley of the Son of **H**,

HIP (6/4) HIPS

Gen 32:25 He touched the socket of his **h**;
32:25 and the socket of Jacob's **h** was
32:31 on him, and he limped on his **h**.
32:32 which is on the **h** socket,
32:32 the socket of Jacob's **h** in the
Judg 15:8 So he attacked them **h** and thigh

HIPS (3/3) HIP

2 Sam 20:8 fastened in its sheath at his **h**;
Job 40:16 now, his strength is in his **h**,
Dan 5:6 so that the joints of his **h**

HIRAH (2/2)

Gen 38:1 Adullamite whose name was **H**.
38:12 he and his friend **H** the

HIRAM (25/22) HURAM

2 Sam 5:11 Then **H** king of Tyre sent
1 Ki 5:1 Now **H** king of Tyre sent his

5: 1 for **H** had always loved David.
5: 2 Then Solomon sent to **H**,
5: 7 when **H** heard the words of
5: 8 Then **H** sent to Solomon, saying:
5:10 Then **H** gave Solomon cedar and
5:11 And Solomon gave **H** twenty
5:11 Thus Solomon gave to **H** year by
5:12 and there was peace between **H**
9:11 (**H** the king of Tyre had supplied
9:11 that King Solomon then gave **H**
9:12 Then **H** went from Tyre to see the
9:14 Then **H** sent the king one hundred
9:27 Then **H** sent his servants with
10:11 Also, the ships of **H**,
10:22 at sea with the fleet of **H**.
1 Chr 14: 1 Now **H** king of Tyre sent
2 Chr 2: 3 Then Solomon sent to **H** king of
2:11 Then **H** king of Tyre answered in
2:12 **H** also said: Blessed be the
8: 2 that the cities which **H** had
8:18 And **H** sent him ships by the hand
9:10 the servants of **H** and the
9:21 Tarshish with the servants of **H**.

HIRAM'S (1/1)

1 Ki 5:18 **H** builders, and the Gebalites

HIRE (9/9) HIRED, HIRELING

Ex 22:15 was hired, it came for its **h**.
1 Chr 19: 6 talents of silver to **h** for
Prov 26:10 Gives the fool his **h** and the
Isa 23:17 She will return to her **h**,
46: 6 They **h** a goldsmith, and he
Ezek 16:41 and you shall no longer **h**
Hos 9: 1 You have made love for **h** on
Zech 8:10 no wages for man nor any **h** for
Mt 20: 1 out early in the morning to **h**

HIRED (38/38) HIRE

Gen 30:16 for I have surely **h** you with my
Ex 12:45 A sojourner and a **h** servant
22:15 not make it good; if it was **h**,
Lev 19:13 The wages of him who is **h** shall
22:10 or a **h** servant, shall not eat
25: 6 your **h** man, and the stranger
25:40 As a **h** servant and a sojourner
25:50 to the time of a **h** servant
25:53 with him as a yearly **h** servant,
Deut 15:18 worth a double **h** servant
23: 4 and because they **h** against you
24:14 not oppress a **h** servant
Judg 9: 4 with which Abimelech **h**
18: 4 He has **h** me, and I have become
1 Sam 2: 5 were full have **h** themselves
2 Sam 10: 6 the people of Ammon sent and **h**
2 Ki 7: 6 has **h** against us the kings
1 Chr 19: 7 So they **h** for themselves
2 Chr 24:12 and they **h** masons and
25: 6 He also **h** one hundred thousand
Ezra 4: 5 and **h** counselors against them to
Neh 6:12 Tobiah and Sanballat had **h** him.
6:13 For this reason he was **h**,
13: 2 but **h** Balaam against them to
Job 7: 1 like the days of a **h** man?
7: 2 And like a **h** man who eagerly
14: 6 Till like a **h** man he finishes
Isa 7:20 will shave with a **h** razor,
16:14 as the years of a **h** man, the
21:16 to the year of a **h** man,
Ezek 16:33 and **h** them to come to you from
Hos 8: 9 Ephraim has **h** lovers.
8:10 though they have **h** among the
Mt 20: 7 Because no one **h** us.' He said to
20: 9 when those came who were **h**
Mk 1:20 the boat with the **h** servants,
Lk 15:17 of my father's **h** servants
15:19 one of your **h** servants."

HIRELING (3/2) HIRE

Jn 10:12 'But a **h**, he who is
10:13 The **h** flees because he is a
10:13 flees because he is a **h** and

HIS (7947/5676) See APPENDIX

HISS (9/9) HISSING

1 Ki 9: 8 will be astonished and will **h**,
Job 27:23 And shall **h** him out of his
Jer 19: 8 by it will be astonished and **h**
49:17 will be astonished And will **h**
50:13 shall be horrified And **h** at
Lam 2:15 They **h** and shake their heads
2:16 They **h** and gnash their teeth.
Ezek 27:36 among the peoples will **h** at
Zeph 2:15 who passes by her Shall **h** and

HISSING (7/7) HISS

Jer 18:16 desolate and a perpetual **h**;
19: 8 make this city desolate and a **h**;
25: 9 make them an astonishment, a **h**,
25:18 an astonishment, a **h**,
29:18 a curse, an astonishment, a **h**,
51:37 An astonishment and a **h**,
Mic 6:16 And your inhabitants a **h**.

HISTORY (2/2)

Gen 2: 4 This is the **h** of the heavens
37: 2 This is the **h** of Jacob.

HIT (2/2)

1 Sam 31: 3 The archers **h** him, and he was
1 Chr 10: 3 The archers **h** him, and he was

HITCH (1/1) HITCHED

1 Sam 6: 7 and **h** the cows to the cart;

HITCHED (1/1) HITCH

1 Sam 6:10 they took two milk cows and **h**

HITHER (KJV) See HERE

HITHERTO (KJV) See ONWARD, PREVIOUSLY, THIS (FAR)

HITTITE (27/26) HITTITES

Gen 23:10 and Ephron the **H** answered
25: 9 Ephron the son of Zohar the **H**,
26:34 the daughter of Beeri the **H**,
26:34 the daughter of Elon the **H**.
36: 2 Adah the daughter of Elon the **H**;
49:29 in the field of Ephron the **H**,
49:30 with the field of Ephron the **H**
50:13 the field from Ephron the **H** as
Ex 23:28 and the **H** from before you.
33: 2 and the Amorite and the **H** and
34:11 and the Canaanite and the **H**
Deut 20:17 the **H** and the Amorite and the
Josh 9: 1 Great Sea toward Lebanon—the **H**,
11: 3 in the west, the Amorite, the **H**,
1 Sam 26: 6 and said to Ahimelech the **H** and
2 Sam 11: 3 Eliam, the wife of Uriah the **H**?
11: 6 saying, "Send me Uriah the **H**.
11:17 and Uriah the **H** died also.
11:21 Your servant Uriah the **H** is dead
11:24 and your servant Uriah the **H** is
12: 9 You have killed Uriah the **H**
12:10 taken the wife of Uriah the **H**
23:39 and Uriah the **H**:
1 Ki 15: 5 in the matter of Uriah the **H**.
1 Chr 11:41 Uriah the **H**, Zabad the son
Ezek 16: 3 an Amorite and your mother a **H**.
16:45 your mother was a **H** and your

HITTITES (21/21) HITTITE

Gen 15:20 'the **H**, the Perizzites,
Ex 3: 8 of the Canaanites and the **H**
3:17 of the Canaanites and the **H**
13: 5 of the Canaanites and the **H**
23:23 in to the Amorites and the **H**
Num 13:29 in the land of the South; the **H**,
Deut 7: 1 the **H** and the Girgashites and
Josh 1: 4 all the land of the **H**,
3:10 you the Canaanites and the **H**
12: 8 and in the South—the **H**,
24:11 the Canaanites, the **H**,
Judg 1:26 man went to the land of the **H**,
3: 5 among the Canaanites, the **H**,
1 Ki 9:20 were left of the Amorites, **H**,
10:29 to all the kings of the **H** and
11: 1 Edomites, Sidonians, and **H**—
2 Ki 7: 6 against us the kings of the **H**
2 Chr 1:17 them to all the kings of the **H**
8: 7 people who were left of the **H**,
Ezra 9: 1 of the Canaanites, the **H**,
Neh 9: 8 land of the Canaanites, The **H**,

HIVITE (10/10) HIVITES

Gen 10:17 the **H**, the Arkite,
34: 2 Shechem the son of Hamor the **H**,
36: 2 the daughter of Zibeon the **H**;
Ex 23:28 which shall drive out the **H**,
33: 2 and the Perizzite and the **H**
34:11 and the Perizzite and the **H**
Deut 20:17 and the Perizzite and the **H**
Josh 9: 1 Canaanite, the Perizzite, the **H**,
11: 3 and the **H** below Hermon in the
1 Chr 1:15 the **H**, the Arkite,

HIVITES (15/15) HIVITE

Ex 3: 8 and the Perizzites and the **H**
3:17 and the Perizzites and the **H**
13: 5 and the Amorites and the **H** and
23:23 and the Canaanites and the **H**
Deut 7: 1 and the Perizzites and the **H**
Josh 3:10 and the Hittites and the **H** and
9: 7 the men of Israel said to the **H**,
11:19 of Israel, except the **H**,
12: 8 the Perizzites, the **H**,
24:11 the Girgashites, the **H**,
Judg 3: 3 and the **H** who dwelt in Mount
3: 5 Amorites, the Perizzites, the **H**,
2 Sam 24: 7 and to all the cities of the **H**
1 Ki 9:20 Hittites, Perizzites, **H**,
2 Chr 8: 7 Amorites, Perizzites, **H**,

HIZKI (1/1)

1 Chr 8:17 Zebadiah, Meshullam, **H**,

HO (1/1)

Isa 55: 1 **H**! Everyone who thirsts, Come

HOAR (KJV) See GRAY (HAIR)

HOARY (KJV) See GRAY (HEAD)

HOBAB (2/2) JETHRO

Num 10:29 Now Moses said to **H** the son of
Judg 4:11 of the children of **H** the

HOBAH (1/1)

Gen 14:15 and pursued them as far as **H**,

HOD (1/1)

1 Chr 7:37 Bezer, **H**, Shamma, Shilshah,

HODAIAH (KJV) See HODAVIAH

HODAVIAH (4/4)

1 Chr 3:24 The sons of Elioenai were **H**,
5:24 Eliel, Azriel, Jeremiah, **H**,
9: 7 son of Meshullam, the son of **H**,
Ezra 2:40 and Kadmiel, of the sons of **H**,

HODESH (1/1)

1 Chr 8: 9 By **H** his wife he begot Jobab,

HODEVAH (1/1)

Neh 7:43 Kadmiel, and of the sons of **H**,

HODIAH'S (1/1)

1 Chr 4:19 The sons of **H** wife, the sister

HODIJAH (5/5)

Neh 8: 7 Jamin, Akkub, Shabbethai, **H**,
9: 5 Bani, Hashabniah, Sherebiah, **H**,
10:10 Their brethren: Shebaniah, **H**,
10:13 **H**, Bani, and Beninu.
10:18 **H**, Hashum, Bezai,

HOE (1/1)

Isa 7:25 which could be dug with the **h**,

HOGLAH (7/7)

Num 26:33 were Mahlah, Noah, **H**,
27: 1 his daughters: Mahlah, Noah, **H**,
36:11 for Mahlah, Tirzah, **H**,
Josh 17: 3 his daughters: Mahlah, Noah, **H**,

HOHAM (1/1)

Josh 10: 3 king of Jerusalem sent to **H**

HOISED (KJV) See HOISTED

HOISTED (1/1)

Acts 27:40 and they **h** the mainsail to the

HOLD (135/134) HELD, HOLDERS, HOLDING, HOLDS

Gen 19:16 the men took **h** of his hand, his
21:18 lift up the lad and **h** him with
25:26 and his hand took **h** of Esau's
48:17 so he took **h** of his father's
Ex 5: 1 that they may **h** a feast to Me
9: 2 and still **h** them,
10: 9 for we must **h** a feast to the
14:14 and you shall **h** your peace."
15:14 Sorrow will take **h** of the
15:15 Trembling will take **h** of them;
20: 7 for the LORD will not **h** him
Deut 5:11 for the LORD will not **h** him
10:20 and to Him you shall **h** fast,
11:22 and to **h** fast to Him—
13: 4 and you shall serve Him and **h**
21:19 and his mother shall take **h** of
32:41 And My hand takes **h** on
Josh 22: 5 to **h** fast to Him, and to serve
23: 8 but you shall **h** fast to the
Judg 16: 3 took **h** of the doors of the gate
16:29 And Samson took **h** of the two
19:29 laid **h** of his concubine, and
20: 6 So I took **h** of my concubine, cut
Ruth 3:15 shawl that is on you and **h** it.
1 Sam 11: 3 **H** off for seven days, that we
2 Sam 1:11 Therefore David took **h** of his
2:21 and lay **h** on one of the young
3: 6 was strengthening his **h** on
6: 6 to the ark of God and took **h**
13:11 he took **h** of her and said to
13:20 But now **h** your peace, my
1 Ki 1:50 and went and took **h** of the
1:51 he has taken **h** of the horns of
2: 9 do not **h** him guiltless, for you
2:28 and took **h** of the horns of the
11:30 Then Ahijah took **h** of the new
18:32 the altar large enough to **h**
2 Ki 2:12 And he took **h** of his own
6:32 and **h** him fast at the door.

1 Chr 13: 9 Uzza put out his hand to ***h*** the
Job 2: 9 Do you still ***h*** fast to your
6:24 and I will ***h*** my tongue;
9:28 I know that You will not ***h*** me
11: 3 your empty talk make men ***h***
13:13 ***H*** your peace with me, and let
13:19 If now I ***h*** my tongue, I
17: 9 Yet the righteous will ***h*** to his
18: 9 And a snare lays ***h*** of him.
21: 6 And trembling takes ***h*** of my
27: 6 My righteousness I ***h*** fast, and
30:16 The days of affliction take ***h***
33:31 ***H*** your peace, and I will
33:33 ***H*** your peace, and I will teach
36:17 Judgment and justice take ***h***
38:13 That it might take ***h*** of the
Ps 2: 4 The LORD shall ***h*** them in
35: 2 Take ***h*** of shield and buckler,
48: 6 Fear took ***h*** of them there,
69:24 let Your wrathful anger take ***h***
73:23 You ***h*** me by my right hand.
77: 4 You ***h*** my eyelids open; I am
83: 1 O God! Do not ***h*** Your peace,
94:18 mercy, O LORD, will ***h*** me up.
116: 3 And the pangs of Sheol laid ***h***
119:53 Indignation has taken ***h*** of me
119:117 ***H*** me up, and I shall be safe,
139:10 And Your right hand shall ***h***
Prov 3:18 of life to those who take ***h*** of
4:13 Take firm ***h*** of instruction, do
5: 5 Her steps lay ***h*** of hell.
20:16 And ***h*** it as a pledge when it
24:11 And ***h*** back those stumbling to
27:13 And ***h*** it in pledge when he is
Eccl 2: 3 and how to lay ***h*** on folly, till
Song 3: 8 They all ***h*** swords, Being
7: 8 I will take ***h*** of its
Isa 3: 6 When a man takes ***h*** of his
4: 1 day seven women shall take ***h***
5:29 they will roar And lay ***h*** of
13: 8 Pangs and sorrows will take ***h***
21: 3 Pangs have taken ***h*** of me, like
27: 5 Or let him take ***h*** of My
41:13 will ***h*** your right hand, Saying
42: 6 And will ***h*** Your hand; I will
56: 2 the son of man who lays ***h*** on
56: 4 And ***h*** fast My covenant,
62: 1 For Zion's sake I will not ***h*** My
62: 6 They shall never ***h*** their peace
64: 7 stirs himself up to take ***h*** of
64:12 Will You ***h*** Your peace, and
Jer 2:13 broken cisterns that can ***h*** no
4:19 I cannot ***h*** my peace, Because
6:23 They will lay ***h*** on bow and
6:24 Anguish has taken ***h*** of us,
8: 5 They ***h*** fast to deceit, They
8:21 Astonishment has taken ***h*** of
49:16 Who ***h*** the height of the hill!
50:42 They shall ***h*** the bow and the
50:43 Anguish has taken ***h*** of him,
Ezek 24:14 I will not ***h*** back, Nor will I
29: 7 When they took ***h*** of you with
30:21 to make it strong enough to ***h***
Am 6:10 ***H*** your tongue! For we dare not
Hab 1:13 And ***h*** Your tongue when the
Mt 12:11 will not lay ***h*** of it and lift
14: 3 For Herod had laid ***h*** of John and
26:57 And those who had laid ***h*** of
Mk 3:21 they went out to lay ***h*** of Him,
6:17 himself had sent and laid ***h*** of
7: 4 which they have received and ***h***,
7: 8 you ***h*** the tradition of men—the
14:51 And the young men laid ***h*** of
Lk 23:26 they laid ***h*** of a certain man,
1 Cor 15: 2 if you ***h*** fast that word which I
Phil 2:29 and ***h*** such men in esteem;
3:12 that I may lay ***h*** of that for
3:12 Christ Jesus has also laid ***h***
1 Th 5:21 ***H*** fast what is good.
2 Th 2:15 stand fast and ***h*** the traditions
1 Tim 6:12 lay ***h*** on eternal life, to which
6:19 that they may lay ***h*** on eternal
2 Tim 1:13 ***H*** fast the pattern of sound
Heb 3: 6 whose house we are if we ***h*** fast
3:14 partakers of Christ if we ***h***
4:14 let us ***h*** fast our confession.
6:18 have fled for refuge to lay ***h***
10:23 Let us ***h*** fast the confession of
Jas 2: 1 do not ***h*** the faith of our Lord
Rev 2:13 And you ***h*** fast to My name, and
2:14 you have there those who ***h*** the
2:15 you also have those who ***h***
2:25 But ***h*** fast what you have till I
3: 3 ***h*** fast and repent. Therefore if
3:11 I am coming quickly! ***H*** fast
20: 2 He laid ***h*** of the dragon, that

HOLDERS (7/7) HOLD

Ex 25:27 as ***h*** for the poles to bear the
26:29 make their rings of gold as ***h***
30: 4 and they will be ***h*** for the
36:34 their rings of gold to be ***h***
37:14 as ***h*** for the poles to bear the
37:27 as ***h*** for the poles with which
38: 5 as ***h*** for the poles.

HOLDING (9/9) HOLD

1 Sam 25:36 ***h*** a feast in his house, like
Jer 6:11 I am weary of ***h*** it in.
20: 9 I was weary of ***h*** it back,
Mk 7: 3 ***h*** the tradition of the elders.
Phil 2:16 ***h*** fast the word of life, so that
Col 2:19 and not ***h*** fast to the Head, from
1 Tim 3: 9 ***h*** the mystery of the faith with
Titus 1: 9 ***h*** fast the faithful word as he
Rev 7: 1 ***h*** the four winds of the earth,

HOLDS (13/13) HOLD

Num 30: 4 and her father ***h*** his peace,
Esth 4:11 the one to whom the king ***h*** out
Job 2: 3 And still he ***h*** fast to his
8:15 He ***h*** it fast, but it does not
Prov 11:12 But a man of understanding ***h***
17:28 fool is counted wise when he ***h***
29:11 But a wise man ***h*** them back.
31:19 And her hand ***h*** the spindle.
Isa 56: 6 And ***h*** fast My covenant—
Dan 5:23 and the God who ***h*** your breath
Am 1: 5 And the one who ***h*** the scepter
1: 8 And the one who ***h*** the scepter
Rev 2: 1 These things says He who ***h*** the

HOLE (5/5) HOLES

2 Ki 12: 9 bored a ***h*** in its lid, and set
Isa 11: 8 shall play by the cobra's ***h***,
51: 1 And to the ***h*** of the pit from
Jer 13: 4 and hide it there in a ***h*** in the
Ezek 8: 7 there was a ***h*** in the wall.

HOLES (9/9) HOLE

1 Sam 13: 6 in thickets, in rocks, in ***h***,
14:11 are coming out of the ***h*** where
Isa 2:19 They shall go into the ***h*** of the
42:22 All of them are snared in ***h***,
Jer 16:16 and out of the ***h*** of the rocks.
Mic 7:17 They shall crawl from their ***h***
Hag 1: 6 to put into a bag with ***h***.
Mt 8:20 Foxes have ***h*** and birds of the
Lk 9:58 Foxes have ***h*** and birds of the

HOLIDAY (4/4)

Esth 2:18 and he proclaimed a ***h*** in the
8:17 and gladness, a feast and a ***h***.
9:19 gladness and feasting, as a ***h***,
9:22 them, and from mourning to a ***h***;

HOLIER (1/1) HOLY

Isa 65: 5 For I am ***h*** than you!'

HOLIEST (3/3) HOLY

Heb 9: 3 which is called the ***H*** of All,
9: 8 that the way into the ***H*** of All
10:19 having boldness to enter the ***H***

HOLILY (KJV) See DEVOUTLY

HOLINESS (32/32) HOLY

Ex 15:11 is like You, glorious in ***h***,
28:36 of a signet: ***H*** TO THE LORD.
39:30 of a signet: ***H*** TO THE LORD.
1 Chr 16:29 the LORD in the beauty of ***h***!
2 Chr 20:21 should praise the beauty of ***h***,
31:18 they sanctified themselves in ***h***.
Ps 29: 2 the LORD in the beauty of ***h***.
60: 6 God has spoken in His ***h***:
89:35 Once I have sworn by My ***h***;
93: 5 ***H*** adorns Your house, O LORD,
96: 9 the LORD in the beauty of ***h***!
108: 7 God has spoken in His ***h***:
110: 3 In the beauties of ***h***,
Eccl 8:10 and gone from the place of ***h***,
Isa 35: 8 be called the Highway of ***H***.
Jer 2: 3 Israel was ***h*** to the LORD,
31:23 and mountain of ***h***!'
Am 4: 2 Lord GOD has sworn by His ***h***:
Ob 17 And there shall be ***h***;
Zech 14:20 ***H*** TO THE LORD" shall be
14:21 Jerusalem and Judah shall be ***h***
Lk 1:75 In ***h*** and righteousness before
Rom 1: 4 according to the Spirit of ***h***,
6:19 slaves of righteousness for ***h***.
6:22 God, you have your fruit to ***h***,
2 Cor 7: 1 perfecting ***h*** in the fear of
Eph 4:24 in true righteousness and ***h***.
1 Th 3:13 your hearts blameless in ***h***
4: 7 us to uncleanness, but in ***h***.
1 Tim 2:15 continue in faith, love, and ***h***,
Heb 12:10 we may be partakers of His ***h***.
12:14 peace with all people, and ***h***,

HOLLOW (6/6)

Ex 27: 8 You shall make it ***h*** with boards;
38: 7 He made the altar ***h*** with
Judg 15:19 So God split the ***h*** place that
Isa 40:12 measured the waters in the ***h***
Jer 52:21 was four fingers; it was ***h***.
Zech 1: 8 among the myrtle trees in the ***h***;

HOLON (3/3)

Josh 15:51 Goshen, ***H***, and Giloh:
21:15 ***H*** with its common-land, Debir
Jer 48:21 On ***H*** and Jahzah and Mephaath,

HOLPEN (KJV) See HELPED

HOLY (637/567) HOLIER, HOLIEST, HOLINESS, SPIRIT, UNHOLY

Ex 3: 5 the place where you stand is ***h***
12:16 first day there shall be a ***h***
12:16 seventh day there shall be a ***h***
15:13 in Your strength To Your ***h***
16:23 a ***h*** Sabbath to the LORD.
19: 6 Me a kingdom of priests and a ***h***
20: 8 the Sabbath day, to keep it ***h***.
22:31 And you shall be ***h*** men to Me:
26:33 a divider for you between the ***h***
26:33 the holy place and the Most ***H***.
26:34 of the Testimony in the Most ***H***.
28: 2 And you shall make ***h*** garments
28: 4 So they shall make ***h*** garments
28:29 when he goes into the ***h*** place,
28:35 heard when he goes into the ***h***
28:38 may bear the iniquity of the ***h***
28:38 of Israel hallow in all their ***h***
28:43 the altar to minister in the ***h***
29: 6 and put the ***h*** crown on the
29:29 And the ***h*** garments of Aaron
29:30 of meeting to minister in the ***h***
29:31 and boil its flesh in the ***h***
29:33 eat them, because they are ***h***.
29:34 not be eaten, because it is ***h***.
29:37 And the altar shall be most ***h***.
29:37 touches the altar must be ***h***.
30:10 It is most ***h*** to the LORD."
30:25 you shall make from these a ***h***
30:25 It shall be a ***h*** anointing oil.
30:29 them, that they may be most ***h***;
30:29 whatever touches them must be ***h***.
30:31 This shall be a ***h*** anointing oil
30:32 to its composition. It is ***h***,
30:32 and it shall be ***h*** to you.
30:35 perfumer, salted, pure, and ***h***.
30:36 It shall be most ***h*** to you.
30:37 It shall be to you ***h*** for the
31:10 the ***h*** garments for Aaron the
31:11 oil and sweet incense for the ***h***
31:14 for it is ***h*** to you. Everyone
31:15 ***h*** to the LORD. Whoever does
35: 2 the seventh day shall be a ***h***
35:19 for ministering in the ***h***
35:19 the ***h*** garments for Aaron the
35:21 and for the ***h*** garments.
37:29 He also made the ***h*** anointing
38:24 used in all the work of the ***h***
39: 1 for ministering in the ***h***
39: 1 and made the ***h*** garments for
39:30 they made the plate of the ***h***
39:41 to minister in the ***h*** place:
39:41 the ***h*** garments for Aaron the
40: 9 its utensils, and it shall be ***h***.
40:10 The altar shall be most ***h***.
40:13 You shall put the ***h*** garments on
Lev 2: 3 It is most ***h*** of the offerings
2:10 It is most ***h*** of the offerings
5:15 in regard to the ***h*** things of
5:16 he has done in regard to the ***h***
6:16 bread it shall be eaten in a ***h***
6:17 made by fire; it is most ***h***,
6:18 who touches them must be ***h***.
6:25 before the LORD. It is most ***h***.
6:26 In a ***h*** place it shall be eaten,
6:27 who touches its flesh must be ***h***.
6:27 was sprinkled, in a ***h*** place.
6:29 may eat it. It is most ***h***.
6:30 to make atonement in the ***h***
7: 1 offering (it is most ***h***):
7: 6 It shall be eaten in a ***h*** place.
7: 6 in a holy place. It is most ***h***.
8: 9 the ***h*** crown, as the LORD had
10: 3 Me I must be regarded as ***h***;
10:10 you may distinguish between ***h***
10:12 the altar; for it is most ***h***.
10:13 You shall eat it in a ***h*** place,
10:17 eaten the sin offering in a ***h***
10:17 holy place, since it is most ***h***,
10:18 was not brought inside the ***h***
10:18 you should have eaten it in a ***h***
11:44 yourselves, and you shall be ***h***;
11:44 you shall be holy; for I am ***h***.
11:45 You shall therefore be ***h***,
11:45 therefore be holy, for I am ***h***.
14:13 in a ***h*** place; for as the sin
14:13 offering. It is most ***h***.
16: 2 at just any time into the ***H***
16: 3 Aaron shall come into the ***H***
16: 4 He shall put the ***h*** linen tunic
16: 4 These are ***h*** garments.
16:16 shall make atonement for the ***H***
16:17 in to make atonement in the ***H***
16:20 an end of atoning for the ***H***
16:23 put on when he went into the ***H***
16:24 wash his body with water in a ***h***
16:27 in to make atonement in the ***H***
16:32 clothes, the ***h*** garments;
16:33 shall make atonement for the ***H***
19: 2 say to them: 'You shall be ***h***,
19: 2 for I the LORD your God am ***h***.
19:24 year all its fruit shall be ***h***,
20: 3 My sanctuary and profane My ***h***
20: 7 yourselves therefore, and be ***h***,
20:26 And you shall be ***h*** to Me, for I
20:26 to Me, for I the LORD am ***h***,
21: 6 They shall be ***h*** to their God and
21: 6 therefore they shall be ***h***.
21: 7 for the priest is ***h*** to his

H

21: 8 He shall be ***h*** to you, for I the
21: 8 LORD, who sanctify you, am ***h***.
21:22 both the most ***h*** and the holy;
21:22 both the most holy and the ***h***;
22: 2 separate themselves from the ***h***
22: 2 that they do not profane My ***h***
22: 3 who goes near the ***h*** things
22: 4 shall not eat the ***h*** offerings
22: 6 and shall not eat the ***h***
22: 7 and afterward he may eat the ***h***
22:10 No outsider shall eat the ***h***
22:10 shall not eat the ***h*** thing.
22:12 she may not eat of the ***h***
22:14 And if a man eats the ***h***
22:14 then he shall restore a ***h***
22:15 They shall not profane the ***h***
22:16 trespass when they eat their ***h***
22:32 You shall not profane My ***h*** name,
23: 2 you shall proclaim to be ***h***
23: 3 a ***h*** convocation. You shall do
23: 4 ***h*** convocations which you shall
23: 7 first day you shall have a ***h***
23: 8 The seventh day shall be a ***h***
23:20 They shall be ***h*** to the LORD
23:21 on the same day that it is a ***h***
23:24 trumpets, a ***h*** convocation.
23:27 It shall be a ***h*** convocation for
23:35 first day there shall be a ***h***
23:36 eighth day you shall have a ***h***
23:37 you shall proclaim to be ***h***
24: 9 and they shall eat it in a ***h***
24: 9 for it is most ***h*** to him from
25:12 it shall be ***h*** to you; you shall
27: 9 gives to the LORD shall be ***h***.
27:10 one exchanged for it shall be ***h***.
27:14 dedicates his house to be ***h***
27:21 shall be ***h*** to the LORD, as a
27:23 valuation on that day as a ***h***
27:28 devoted offering is most ***h***
27:30 It is ***h*** to the LORD.
27:32 the tenth one shall be ***h*** to the
27:33 one exchanged for it shall be ***h***;
Num 4: 4 relating to the most ***h***
4:15 but they shall not touch any ***h***
4:19 when they approach the most ***h***
4:20 not go in to watch while the ***h***
5: 9 Every offering of all the ***h***
5:10 And every man's ***h*** things shall
5:17 The priest shall take ***h*** water in
6: 5 to the LORD, he shall be ***h***.
6: 8 of his separation he shall be ***h***
6:20 they are ***h*** for the priest,
7: 9 was the service of the ***h***
10:21 carrying the ***h*** things.
15:40 and be ***h*** for your God.
16: 3 for all the congregation is ***h***,
16: 5 show who is His and who is ***h***,
16: 7 the LORD chooses is the ***h***
16:37 of the blaze, for they are ***h***,
16:38 the LORD, therefore they are ***h***;
18: 8 all the ***h*** gifts of the children
18: 9 shall be yours of the most ***h***
18: 9 shall be most ***h*** for you and
18:10 In a most ***h*** place you shall eat
18:10 It shall be ***h*** to you.
18:17 shall not redeem; they are ***h***.
18:19 the heave offerings of the ***h***
18:32 But you shall not profane the ***h***
28: 7 in a ***h*** place you shall pour
28:18 first day you shall have a ***h***
28:25 seventh day you shall have a ***h***
28:26 you shall have a ***h*** convocation.
29: 1 you shall have a ***h*** convocation.
29: 7 month you shall have a ***h***
29:12 month you shall have a ***h***
31: 6 with the ***h*** articles and the
35:25 who was anointed with the ***h***
Deut 5:12 the Sabbath day, to keep it ***h***,
7: 6 For you are a ***h*** people to the
12:26 Only the ***h*** things which you
14: 2 For you are a ***h*** people to the
14:21 for you are a ***h*** people to the
23:14 therefore your camp shall be ***h***,
26:13 I have removed the ***h*** tithe from
26:15 Look down from Your ***h***
26:19 and that you may be a ***h*** people
28: 9 LORD will establish you as a ***h***
33: 8 and Your Urim be with Your ***h***
Josh 5:15 the place where you stand is ***h***.
24:19 for He is a ***h*** God. He is a
1 Sam 2: 2 No one is ***h*** like the LORD, For
6:20 is able to stand before this ***h***
21: 4 but there is ***h*** bread, if the
21: 5 vessels of the young men are ***h***,
21: 6 So the priest gave him ***h*** bread;
1 Ki 6:16 as the Most ***H*** Place.
7:50 of the inner room (the Most ***H***
8: 4 and all the ***h*** furnishings that
8: 6 to the Most ***H*** Place, under the
8: 8 poles could be seen from the ***h***
8:10 the priests came out of the ***h***
2 Ki 4: 9 I know that this is a ***h*** man of
19:22 Against the ***H*** One of Israel.
1 Chr 6:49 for all the work of the Most ***H***
16:10 Glory in His ***h*** name; Let the
16:35 To give thanks to Your ***h*** name,
22:19 covenant of the LORD and the ***h***
23:13 he should sanctify the most ***h***
23:28 in the purifying of all ***h***
23:32 the needs of the ***h*** place, and
29: 3 that I have prepared for the ***h***
29:16 to build You a house for Your ***h***
2 Chr 3: 8 And he made the Most ***H*** Place.
3:10 In the Most ***H*** Place he made two
4:22 its inner doors to the Most ***H***
5: 5 and all the ***h*** furnishings that
5: 7 to the Most ***H*** Place, under the
5: 9 ark could be seen from the ***h***
5:11 came out of the Most ***H*** Place
8:11 ark of the LORD has come are ***h***.
23: 6 They may go in, for they are ***h***;
29: 5 out the rubbish from the ***h***
29: 7 burnt offerings in the ***h***
30:27 their prayer came up to His ***h***
31: 6 also the tithe of ***h*** things
31:14 of the LORD and the most ***h***
35: 3 who were ***h*** to the LORD: "Put
35: 3 Put the ***h*** ark in the house which
35: 5 And stand in the ***h*** place
35:13 but the other ***h*** offerings
Ezra 2:63 should not eat of the most ***h***
8:28 'You are ***h*** to the LORD;
8:28 the articles are ***h*** also;
9: 2 so that the ***h*** seed is mixed
9: 8 and to give us a peg in His ***h***
Neh 7:65 should not eat of the most ***h***
8: 9 This day is ***h*** to the LORD your
8:10 for this day is ***h*** to our
8:11 "Be still, for the day is ***h***;
9:14 You made known to them Your ***h***
10:31 or on a ***h*** day; and we would
10:33 for the ***h*** things, for the sin
11: 1 the ***h*** city, and nine-tenths
11:18 All the Levites in the ***h*** city
12:47 They also consecrated ***h***
Job 5: 1 And to which of the ***h*** ones
6:10 concealed the words of the ***H***
Ps 2: 6 I have set My King On My ***h***
3: 4 And He heard me from His ***h***
5: 7 I will worship toward Your ***h***
11: 4 The LORD is in His ***h*** temple,
15: 1 Who may dwell in Your ***h*** hill?
16:10 Nor will You allow Your ***H*** One
20: 6 He will answer him from His ***h***
22: 3 But You are ***h***, Enthroned
24: 3 Or who may stand in His ***h***
28: 2 lift up my hands toward Your ***h***
30: 4 at the remembrance of His ***h***
33:21 we have trusted in His ***h*** name.
43: 3 Let them bring me to Your ***h***
46: 4 The ***h*** place of the tabernacle
47: 8 God sits on His ***h*** throne.
48: 1 In His ***h*** mountain.
51:11 And do not take Your ***H*** Spirit
65: 4 house, Of Your ***h*** temple.
68: 5 Is God in His ***h*** habitation.
68:17 in Sinai, in the ***H*** Place.
68:35 are more awesome than Your ***h***
71:22 O ***H*** One of Israel.
78:41 And limited the ***H*** One of
78:54 And He brought them to His ***h***
79: 1 Your ***h*** temple they have
86: 2 Preserve my life, for I am ***h***;
87: 1 His foundation is in the ***h***
89:18 And our king to the ***H*** One of
89:19 You spoke in a vision to Your ***h***
89:20 With My ***h*** oil I have anointed
97:12 at the remembrance of His ***h***
98: 1 His right hand and His ***h*** arm
99: 3 and awesome name—He is ***h***.
99: 5 at His footstool— He is ***h***.
99: 9 And worship at His ***h*** hill;
99: 9 For the LORD our God is ***h***.
103: 1 bless His ***h*** name!
105: 3 Glory in His ***h*** name; Let the
105:42 For He remembered His ***h***
106:47 To give thanks to Your ***h*** name,
111: 9 ***H*** and awesome is His name.
138: 2 I will worship toward Your ***h***
145:21 all flesh shall bless His ***h***
Prov 9:10 And the knowledge of the ***H*** One
20:25 devote rashly something as ***h***,
30: 3 Nor have knowledge of the ***H***
Isa 1: 4 have provoked to anger The ***H***
4: 3 in Jerusalem will be called ***h***—
5:16 And God who is ***h*** shall be
5:19 And let the counsel of the ***H***
5:24 despised the word of the ***H*** One
6: 3 to another and said: "***H***,
6: 3 another and said: "Holy, ***h***,
6: 3 ***h*** is the LORD of hosts; The
6:13 So the ***h*** seed shall be its
10:17 And his ***H*** One for a flame; It
10:20 the ***H*** One of Israel, in truth.
11: 9 hurt nor destroy in all My ***h***
12: 6 For great is the ***H*** One of
17: 7 will have respect for the ***H***
27:13 worship the LORD in the ***h***
29:19 men shall rejoice In the ***H***
29:23 And hallow the ***H*** One of Jacob,
30:11 Cause the ***H*** One of Israel To
30:12 Therefore thus says the ***H*** One
30:15 the ***H*** One of Israel: "In
30:29 song As in the night when a ***h***
31: 1 But who do not look to the ***H***
37:23 Against the ***H*** One of Israel.
40:25 be equal?" says the ***H*** One.
41:14 the ***H*** One of Israel.
41:16 And glory in the ***H*** One of
41:20 And the ***H*** One of Israel has
43: 3 The ***H*** One of Israel, your
43:14 The ***H*** One of Israel: "For
43:15 your ***H*** One, The Creator of
45:11 The ***H*** One of Israel, and his
47: 4 The ***H*** One of Israel.
48: 2 call themselves after the ***h***
48:17 The ***H*** One of Israel: "I am
49: 7 their ***H*** One, To Him whom man
49: 7 The ***H*** One of Israel; And He
52: 1 the ***h*** city! For the
52:10 The LORD has made bare His ***h***
54: 5 And your Redeemer is the ***H***
55: 5 And the ***H*** One of Israel;
56: 7 Even them I will bring to My ***h***
57:13 And shall inherit My ***h***
57:15 eternity, whose name is ***H***:
57:15 I dwell in the high and ***h***
58:13 doing your pleasure on My ***h***
58:13 The ***h*** day of the LORD
60: 9 And to the ***H*** One of Israel,
60:14 Zion of the ***H*** One of Israel.
62: 9 shall drink it in My ***h*** courts.
62:12 And they shall call them The ***H***
63:10 they rebelled and grieved His ***H***
63:11 Where is He who put His ***H***
63:15 habitation, ***h*** and glorious.
63:18 Your ***h*** people have possessed
64:10 Your ***h*** cities are a wilderness,
64:11 Our ***h*** and beautiful temple,
65:11 Who forget My ***h*** mountain, Who
65:25 hurt nor destroy in all My ***h***
66:20 to My ***h*** mountain Jerusalem,"
Jer 11:15 And the ***h*** flesh has passed
23: 9 And because of His ***h*** words.
25:30 And utter His voice from His ***h***
31:40 shall be ***h*** to the LORD.
50:29 Against the ***H*** One of Israel.
51: 5 filled with sin against the ***H***
Ezek 7:24 And their ***h*** places shall be
20:39 but profane My ***h*** name no more
20:40 For on My ***h*** mountain, on the
20:40 together with all your ***h***
21: 2 preach against the ***h*** places,
22: 8 You have despised My ***h*** things
22:26 My law and profaned My ***h***
22:26 not distinguished between the ***h***
28:14 You were on the ***h*** mountain of
36:20 they profaned My ***h*** name—when
36:21 But I had concern for My ***h*** name,
36:22 but for My ***h*** name's sake, which
36:38 Like a flock offered as ***h***
39: 7 So I will make My ***h*** name known
39: 7 not let them profane My ***h***
39: 7 the ***H*** One in Israel.
39:25 and I will be jealous for My ***h***
41: 4 This is the Most ***H*** Place."
42:13 are the ***h*** chambers where the
42:13 the LORD shall eat the most ***h***
42:13 There they shall lay the most ***h***
42:13 offering—for the place is ***h***.
42:14 they shall not go out of the ***h***
42:14 they minister, for they are ***h***.
42:20 to separate the ***h*** areas from
43: 7 the house of Israel defile My ***h***
43: 8 they defiled My ***h*** name by the
43:12 the mountaintop is most ***h***.
44: 8 have not kept charge of My ***h***
44:13 nor come near any of My ***h***
44:13 nor into the Most ***H*** Place;
44:19 leave them in the ***h*** chambers,
44:19 and in their ***h*** garments they
44:23 the difference between the ***h***
45: 1 a ***h*** section of the land; its
45: 1 It shall be ***h*** throughout its
45: 3 the Most ***H*** Place.
45: 4 It shall be a ***h*** section of the
45: 4 place for their houses and a ***h***
45: 6 to the district of the ***h***
45: 7 one side and the other of the ***h***
45: 7 and bordering on the ***h*** district
46:19 into the ***h*** chambers of the
48:10 —the ***h*** district shall belong:
48:12 be to them a thing most ***h*** by
48:14 for it is ***h*** to the LORD.
48:18 the district of the ***h*** section,
48:18 to the district of the ***h***
48:20 You shall set apart the ***h***
48:21 side and on the other of the ***h***
48:21 thousand cubits of the ***h***
48:21 It shall be the ***h*** district, and
Dan 4: 8 in him is the Spirit of the ***H***
4: 9 I know that the Spirit of the ***H***
4:13 a ***h*** one, coming down from
4:17 sentence by the word of the ***h***
4:18 for the Spirit of the ***H*** God is
4:23 a ***h*** one, coming down from
5:11 in whom is the Spirit of the ***H***
8:13 Then I heard a ***h*** one speaking;
8:13 and another ***h*** one said to that
8:24 and also the ***h*** people.
9:16 Your ***h*** mountain; because for
9:20 the LORD my God for the ***h***
9:24 For your people and for your ***h***
9:24 And to anoint the Most ***H***.
11:28 shall be moved against the ***h***
11:30 return in rage against the ***h***
11:30 for those who forsake the ***h***
11:45 the seas and the glorious ***h***
12: 7 and when the power of the ***h***
Hos 11: 9 The ***H*** One in your midst;
11:12 Even with the ***H*** One who is
Joel 2: 1 And sound an alarm in My ***h***
3:17 Dwelling in Zion My ***h***
3:17 Then Jerusalem shall be ***h***,
Am 2: 7 To defile My ***h*** name.
Ob 16 For as you drank on my ***h***

Jon 2: 4 I will look again toward Your ***h***
2: 7 Into Your ***h*** temple.
Mic 1: 2 The Lord from His ***h*** temple.
Hab 1:12 my ***H*** One? We shall not die.
2:20 But the LORD is in His ***h***
3: 3 The ***H*** One from Mount Paran.
Zeph 3:11 no longer be haughty In My ***h***
Hag 2:12 If one carries ***h*** meat in the
2:12 or any food, will it become ***h***?
Zech 2:12 as His inheritance in the ***H***
2:13 for He is aroused from His ***h***
8: 3 The ***H*** Mountain.'
Mal 2:11 has profaned The LORD's ***h***
Mt 1:18 was found with child of the ***H***
1:20 is conceived in her is of the ***H***
3:11 He will baptize you with the ***H***
4: 5 devil took Him up into the ***h***
7: 6 Do not give what is ***h*** to the
12:32 whoever speaks against the ***H***
24:15 standing in the ***h*** place"
25:31 and all the ***h*** angels with Him,
27:53 they went into the ***h*** city and
28:19 and of the Son and of the ***H***
Mk 1: 8 He will baptize you with the ***H***
1:24 the ***H*** One of God!"
3:29 he who blasphemes against the ***H***
6:20 that he was a just and ***h*** man,
8:38 glory of His Father with the ***h***
12:36 David himself said by the ***H***
13:11 but the ***H*** Spirit.
Lk 1:15 will also be filled with the ***H***
1:35 The ***H*** Spirit will come upon
1:35 that ***H*** One who is to be born
1:41 was filled with the ***H*** Spirit.
1:49 And ***h*** is His name.
1:67 was filled with the ***H*** Spirit,
1:70 He spoke by the mouth of His ***h***
1:72 fathers And to remember His ***h***
2:23 womb shall be called ***h***
2:25 and the ***H*** Spirit was upon him.
2:26 been revealed to him by the ***H***
3:16 He will baptize you with the ***H***
3:22 And the ***H*** Spirit descended in
4: 1 being filled with the ***H*** Spirit,
4:34 the ***H*** One of God!"
9:26 and of the ***h*** angels.
11:13 heavenly Father give the ***H***
12:10 who blasphemes against the ***H***
12:12 For the ***H*** Spirit will teach you
Jn 1:33 is He who baptizes with the ***H***
7:39 for the ***H*** Spirit was not yet
14:26 the ***H*** Spirit, whom the Father
17:11 ***H*** Father, keep through Your
20:22 Receive the ***H*** Spirit.
Acts 1: 2 after He through the ***H*** Spirit
1: 5 shall be baptized with the ***H***
1: 8 shall receive power when the ***H***
1:16 which the ***H*** Spirit spoke before
2: 4 they were all filled with the ***H***
2:27 will You allow Your ***H***
2:33 the Father the promise of the ***H***
2:38 shall receive the gift of the ***H***
3:14 But you denied the ***H*** One and the
3:21 by the mouth of all His ***h***
4: 8 filled with the ***H*** Spirit, said
4:27 For truly against Your ***h*** Servant
4:30 done through the name of Your ***h***
4:31 they were all filled with the ***H***
5: 3 your heart to lie to the ***H***
5:32 and so also is the ***H*** Spirit
6: 3 full of the ***H*** Spirit and
6: 5 a man full of faith and the ***H***
6:13 words against this ***h*** place and
7:33 where you stand is ***h***
7:51 You always resist the ***H*** Spirit;
7:55 being full of the ***H*** Spirit,
8:15 that they might receive the ***H***
8:17 and they received the ***H*** Spirit.
8:18 on of the apostles' hands the ***H***
8:19 I lay hands may receive the ***H***
9:17 sight and be filled with the ***H***
9:31 and in the comfort of the ***H***
10:22 was divinely instructed by a ***h***
10:38 Jesus of Nazareth with the ***H***
10:44 the ***H*** Spirit fell upon all
10:45 because the gift of the ***H***
10:47 who have received the ***H*** Spirit
11:15 the ***H*** Spirit fell upon them, as
11:16 shall be baptized with the ***H***
11:24 full of the ***H*** Spirit and of
13: 2 the ***H*** Spirit said, "Now
13: 4 being sent out by the ***H*** Spirit,
13: 9 filled with the ***H*** Spirit,
13:35 will not allow Your ***H***
13:52 filled with joy and with the ***H***
15: 8 them by giving them the ***H***
15:28 For it seemed good to the ***H***
16: 6 they were forbidden by the ***H***
19: 2 Did you receive the ***H*** Spirit
19: 2 as heard whether there is a ***H***
19: 6 the ***H*** Spirit came upon them,
20:23 except that the ***H*** Spirit
20:28 among which the ***H*** Spirit has
21:11 Thus says the ***H*** Spirit, 'So
21:28 temple and has defiled this ***h***
28:25 The ***H*** Spirit spoke rightly
Rom 1: 2 through His prophets in the ***H***
5: 5 out in our hearts by the ***H***
7:12 Therefore the law is ***h***,
7:12 and the commandment ***h*** and just
9: 1 bearing me witness in the ***H***
11:16 For if the firstfruit is ***h***,
11:16 is holy, the lump is also ***h***;
11:16 and if the root is ***h***,
12: 1 bodies a living sacrifice, ***h***,
14:17 and peace and joy in the ***H***
15:13 in hope by the power of the ***H***
15:16 sanctified by the ***H*** Spirit.
16:16 Greet one another with a ***h*** kiss.
1 Cor 2:13 wisdom teaches but which the ***H***
3:17 For the temple of God is ***h***,
6:19 body is the temple of the ***H***
7:14 be unclean, but now they are ***h***.
7:34 that she may be ***h*** both in body
9:13 that those who minister the ***h***
12: 3 Jesus is Lord except by the ***H***
16:20 Greet one another with a ***h***
2 Cor 6: 6 by the ***H*** Spirit, by sincere
13:12 Greet one another with a ***h*** kiss.
13:14 and the communion of the ***H***
Eph 1: 4 that we should be ***h*** and without
1:13 you were sealed with the ***H***
2:21 grows into a ***h*** temple in the
3: 5 revealed by the Spirit to His ***h***
4:30 And do not grieve the ***H*** Spirit
5:27 but that she should be ***h*** and
Col 1:22 through death, to present you ***h***,
3:12 ***h*** and beloved, put on tender
1 Th 1: 5 and in the ***H*** Spirit and in much
1: 6 with joy of the ***H*** Spirit,
4: 8 who has also given us His ***H***
5:26 all the brethren with a ***h*** kiss.
5:27 epistle be read to all the ***h***
1 Tim 2: 8 lifting up ***h*** hands, without
2 Tim 1: 9 us and called us with a ***h***
1:14 keep by the ***H*** Spirit who dwells
3:15 childhood you have known the ***H***
Titus 1: 8 is good, sober-minded, just, ***h***,
3: 5 and renewing of the ***H*** Spirit,
Heb 2: 4 and gifts of the ***H*** Spirit,
3: 1 ***h*** brethren, partakers of the
3: 7 as the ***H*** Spirit says:
6: 4 have become partakers of the ***H***
7:26 was fitting for us, who is ***h***,
9: 8 the ***H*** Spirit indicating this,
9:12 own blood He entered the Most ***H***
9:24 Christ has not entered the ***h***
9:25 high priest enters the Most ***H***
10:15 But the ***H*** Spirit also witnesses
1 Pe 1:12 the gospel to you by the ***H***
1:15 but as He who called you is ***h***,
1:15 you also be ***h*** in all your
1:16 it is written, "Be ***h***,
1:16 "Be holy, for I am ***h***.
2: 5 a ***h*** priesthood, to offer up
2: 9 a ***h*** nation, His own special
3: 5 the ***h*** women who trusted in God
2 Pe 1:18 when we were with Him on the ***h***
1:21 but ***h*** men of God spoke as
1:21 as they were moved by the ***H***
2:21 to turn from the ***h*** commandment
3: 2 were spoken before by the ***h***
3:11 persons ought you to be in ***h***
1 Jn 2:20 have an anointing from the ***H***
5: 7 and the ***H*** Spirit; and these
Jude 20 yourselves up on your most ***h***
20 praying in the ***H*** Spirit,
Rev 3: 7 "These things says He who is ***h***,
4: 8 day or night, saying: "***H***,
4: 8 or night, saying: "Holy, ***h***,
4: 8 saying: "Holy, holy, ***h***,
6:10 ***h*** and true, until You judge and
11: 2 And they will tread the ***h*** city
14:10 in the presence of the ***h***
15: 4 For You alone are ***h***.
18:20 and you ***h*** apostles and
20: 6 Blessed and ***h*** is he who has
21: 2 saw the ***h*** city, New Jerusalem,
21:10 the ***h*** Jerusalem, descending out
22: 6 And the Lord God of the ***h***
22:11 be righteous still; he who is ***h***,
22:11 let him be ***h*** still."
22:19 from the ***h*** city, and from the

HOLYDAY (KJV) See (PILGRIM) FEAST, FESTIVAL

HOMAGE (5/4)

1 Ki 1:16 And Bathsheba bowed and did ***h*** to
1:31 and paid ***h*** to the king, and
Esth 3: 2 king's gate bowed and paid ***h***
3: 2 Mordecai would not bow or pay ***h***.
3: 5 did not bow or pay him ***h***,

HOMAM (1/1)

1 Chr 1:39 sons of Lotan were Hori and ***H***;

HOME (67/66) HOMELAND, HOMELESS, HOMEMAKERS, HOMES

Gen 39:16 her until his master came ***h***.
43:16 "Take these men to my ***h***,
43:26 And when Joseph came ***h***,
Ex 9:19 the field and is not brought ***h***;
Lev 18: 9 whether born at ***h*** or
Deut 21:12 then you shall bring her ***h*** to
24: 5 he shall be free at ***h*** one year,
Josh 2:18 household to your own ***h***.
Judg 11: 9 If you take me back ***h*** to fight
19: 9 early, so that you may get ***h***.
Ruth 1:21 and the LORD has brought me ***h***
1 Sam 2:20 they would go to their own ***h***.
6: 7 cart; and take their calves ***h***.
6:10 and shut up their calves at ***h***.
7:17 for his ***h*** was there. There he
10:26 And Saul also went ***h*** to Gibeah;
18: 2 and would not let him go ***h*** to
18: 6 happened as they were coming ***h***,
24:22 swore to Saul. And Saul went ***h***,
25: 1 and buried him at his ***h*** in
2 Sam 13: 7 And David sent ***h*** to Tamar,
14:13 not bring his banished one ***h***
17:23 and arose and went ***h*** to his
1 Ki 5:14 in Lebanon and two months at ***h***;
13: 7 Come ***h*** with me and refresh
13:15 Come ***h*** with me and eat bread."
2 Ki 14:10 Glory in that, and stay at ***h***;
19:36 and went away, returned ***h***,
2 Chr 25:10 him from Ephraim, to go back ***h***.
25:10 and they returned ***h*** in great
25:19 Stay at ***h*** now; why should you
Esth 5:10 restrained himself and went ***h***,
Job 38:20 may know the paths to its ***h***?
39: 6 Whose ***h*** I have made the
39:12 Will you trust him to bring ***h***
Ps 68:12 And she who remains at ***h***
84: 3 Even the sparrow has found a ***h***,
104:12 of the heavens have their ***h***;
104:17 The stork has her ***h*** in the fir
113: 9 He grants the barren woman a ***h***,
Prov 3:33 But He blesses the ***h*** of the
7:11 Her feet would not stay at ***h***.
7:19 For my husband is not at ***h***;
7:20 And will come ***h*** on the
Eccl 12: 5 For man goes to his eternal ***h***,
Isa 33:20 will see Jerusalem, a quiet ***h***,
37:37 and went away, returned ***h***,
Jer 31:23 O ***h*** of justice, and mountain
39:14 that he should take him ***h***.
50:19 will bring back Israel to his ***h***,
Lam 1:20 At ***h*** it is like death.
Ezek 31: 6 all great nations made their ***h***.
Dan 4:21 birds of the heaven had their ***h***—
6:10 writing was signed, he went ***h***.
Hab 2: 5 man, And he does not stay at ***h***.
Hag 1: 9 and when you brought it ***h***,
Mt 8: 6 my servant is lying at ***h***
Mk 5:19 Go ***h*** to your friends, and tell
Lk 15: 6 "And when he comes ***h***,
16: 9 you into an everlasting ***h***.
Jn 14:23 will come to him and make Our ***h***
19:27 disciple took her to his own ***h***.
Acts 21: 6 the ship, and they returned ***h***.
1 Cor 11:34 is hungry, let him eat at ***h***,
14:35 ask their own husbands at ***h***;
2 Cor 5: 6 knowing that while we are at ***h***
1 Tim 5: 4 first learn to show piety at ***h***

HOMEBORN (1/1)

Jer 2:14 Is he a ***h*** slave? Why is he

HOMELAND (1/1) HOME

Heb 11:14 plainly that they seek a ***h***.

HOMELESS (1/1) HOME

1 Cor 4:11 clothed, and beaten, and ***h***.

HOMEMAKERS (1/1) HOME

Titus 2: 5 to be discreet, chaste, ***h***,

HOMER (9/5)

Lev 27:16 A ***h*** of barley seed shall be
Isa 5:10 And a ***h*** of seed shall yield
Ezek 45:11 bath contains one-tenth of a ***h***,
45:11 and the ephah one-tenth of a ***h***;
45:11 shall be according to the ***h***.
45:13 one-sixth of an ephah from a ***h***
45:13 one-sixth of an ephah from a ***h***
45:14 A kor is a ***h*** or ten baths, for
45:14 baths, for ten baths are a ***h***.

HOMERS (2/2)

Num 11:32 gathered least gathered ten ***h***);
Hos 3: 2 and one and one-half ***h*** of

HOMES (4/4) HOME

Num 32:18 We will not return to our ***h***
Prov 30:26 Yet they make their ***h*** in the
Isa 32:13 on all the happy ***h*** in the
Jn 20:10 went away again to their own ***h***.

HOMOSEXUALS (1/1)

1 Cor 6: 9 nor adulterers, nor ***h***,

HONEST (14/9)

Gen 42:11 we are ***h*** men; your servants
42:19 If you are ***h*** men, let one of
42:31 We are ***h*** men; we are not
42:33 I will know that you are ***h***
42:34 but that you are ***h*** men.
Lev 19:36 You shall have ***h*** scales, honest
19:36 ***h*** weights, an honest ephah, and
19:36 an ***h*** ephah, and an honest hin:
19:36 and an ***h*** hin: I am the LORD
Job 31: 6 Let me be weighed on ***h*** scales,
Prov 16:11 ***H*** weights and scales are the

Ezek 45:10 You shall have ***h*** scales, an
45:10 an ***h*** ephah, and an honest bath.
45:10 ephah, and an ***h*** bath.

HONEY (57/57) HONEYCOMB

Gen 43:11 little balm and a little ***h***,
Ex 3: 8 a land flowing with milk and ***h***,
3:17 a land flowing with milk and ***h***.
13: 5 a land flowing with milk and ***h***,
16:31 was like wafers made with ***h***.
33: 3 a land flowing with milk and ***h***;
Lev 2:11 shall burn no leaven nor any ***h***
20:24 a land flowing with milk and ***h***.
Num 13:27 It truly flows with milk and ***h***,
14: 8 which flows with milk and ***h***.
16:13 a land flowing with milk and ***h***,
16:14 a land flowing with milk and ***h***,
Deut 6: 3 land flowing with milk and ***h***.
8: 8 a land of olive oil and ***h***;
11: 9 'a land flowing with milk and ***h***.
26: 9 land flowing with milk and ***h***'
26:15 land flowing with milk and ***h***.
27: 3 'a land flowing with milk and ***h***,
31:20 land flowing with milk and ***h***,
32:13 He made him draw ***h*** from the
Josh 5: 6 land flowing with milk and ***h***.
Judg 14: 8 a swarm of bees and ***h*** were in
14: 9 them that he had taken the ***h***
14:18 "What is sweeter than ***h***?
1 Sam 14:25 and there was ***h*** on the ground.
14:26 into the woods, there was the ***h***,
14:29 I tasted a little of this ***h***.
14:43 I only tasted a little ***h*** with
2 Sam 17:29 ***h*** and curds, sheep and cheese of
1 Ki 14: 3 some cakes, and a jar of ***h***,
2 Ki 18:32 a land of olive groves and ***h***,
2 Chr 31: 5 of grain and wine, oil and ***h***,
Job 20:17 The rivers flowing with ***h*** and
Ps 19:10 Sweeter also than ***h*** and the
81:16 And with ***h*** from the rock I
119:103 Sweeter than ***h*** to my mouth!
Prov 5: 3 lips of an immoral woman drip ***h***,
24:13 eat ***h*** because it is good,
25:16 Have you found ***h***?
25:27 It is not good to eat much ***h***;
Song 4:11 ***H*** and milk are under your
5: 1 eaten my honeycomb with my ***h***;
Isa 7:15 Curds and ***h*** He shall eat, that
7:22 For curds and ***h*** everyone will
Jer 11: 5 'a land flowing with milk and ***h***,
32:22 land flowing with milk and ***h***.
41: 8 and ***h*** in the field." So he
Ezek 3: 3 and it was in my mouth like ***h***
16:13 ate pastry of fine flour, ***h***,
16:19 and ***h*** which I fed you—you set
20: 6 them, 'flowing with milk and ***h***,
20:15 them, 'flowing with milk and ***h***,
27:17 wheat of Minnith, millet, ***h***,
Mt 3: 4 his food was locusts and wild ***h***.
Mk 1: 6 and he ate locusts and wild ***h***.
Rev 10: 9 but it will be as sweet as ***h*** in
10:10 and it was as sweet as ***h*** in my

HONEYCOMB (8/8) HONEY

1 Sam 14:27 his hand and dipped it in a ***h***,
Ps 19:10 also than honey and the ***h***.
Prov 16:24 Pleasant words are like a ***h***,
24:13 And the ***h*** which is sweet to
27: 7 A satisfied soul loathes the ***h***,
Song 4:11 O my spouse, Drip as the ***h***;
5: 1 I have eaten my ***h*** with my
Lk 24:42 of a broiled fish and some ***h***.

HONOR (144/132) HONORABLE, HONORED, HONORS

Gen 49: 6 Let not my ***h*** be united to
Ex 8: 9 Accept the ***h*** of saying when I
14: 4 and I will gain ***h*** over Pharaoh
14:17 So I will gain ***h*** over Pharaoh
14:18 when I have gained ***h*** for Myself
20:12 ***H*** your father and your mother,
Lev 19:15 nor ***h*** the person of the mighty.
19:32 before the gray headed and ***h***
Num 22:17 for I will certainly ***h*** you
22:37 Am I not able to ***h*** you?"
24:11 I said I would greatly ***h*** you,
24:11 LORD has kept you back from ***h***.
Deut 5:16 ***H*** your father and your mother,
26:19 in praise, in name, and in ***h***,
Judg 9: 9 With which they ***h*** God and men,
13:17 words come to pass we may ***h***
1 Sam 2:29 and ***h*** your sons more than Me,
2:30 for those who ***h*** Me I will
2:30 for those who honor Me I will ***h***,
9:22 had them sit in the place of ***h***
15:30 yet ***h*** me now, please, before
2 Sam 6:22 by them I will be held in ***h***.
1 Ki 3:13 not asked: both riches and ***h***,
21: 9 and seat Naboth with high ***h***
21:12 and seated Naboth with high ***h***
1 Chr 16:27 ***H*** and majesty are before Him
17:18 David say to You for the ***h*** of
29:12 Both riches and ***h*** come from
29:28 full of days and riches and ***h***;
2 Chr 1:11 asked riches or wealth or ***h*** or
1:12 you riches and wealth and ***h***,
17: 5 and he had riches and ***h*** in
18: 1 Jehoshaphat had riches and ***h*** in
26:18 You shall have no ***h*** from the
32:27 had very great riches and ***h***.
Esth 1:20 all wives will ***h*** their
6: 3 What ***h*** or dignity has been
6: 6 man whom the king delights to ***h***?
6: 6 would the king delight to ***h***
6: 7 man whom the king delights to ***h***,
6: 9 man whom the king delights to ***h***.
6: 9 whom the king delights to ***h***!'
6:11 whom the king delights to ***h***!"
8:16 light and gladness, joy and ***h***.
Job 14:21 His sons come to ***h***,
30:15 They pursue my ***h*** as the wind,
Ps 7: 5 And lay my ***h*** in the dust.
8: 5 crowned him with glory and ***h***.
21: 5 ***H*** and majesty You have placed
49:12 Nevertheless man, though in ***h***,
49:20 A man who is in ***h***,
66: 2 Sing out the ***h*** of His name;
91:15 I will deliver him and ***h*** him.
96: 6 ***H*** and majesty are before Him
104: 1 You are clothed with ***h*** and
112: 9 horn will be exalted with ***h***.
149: 9 This ***h*** have all His saints.
Prov 3: 9 ***H*** the LORD with your
3:16 In her left hand riches and ***h***.
4: 8 She will bring you ***h***,
5: 9 Lest you give your ***h*** to others,
8:18 Riches and ***h*** are with me,
11:16 A gracious woman retains ***h***,
14:28 of people is a king's ***h***,
15:33 And before ***h*** is humility.
18:12 And before ***h*** is humility.
21:21 life, righteousness and ***h***.
22: 4 of the LORD Are riches and ***h***
26: 1 So ***h*** is not fitting for a
26: 8 in a sling Is he who gives ***h***
29:23 humble in spirit will retain ***h***.
31:25 Strength and ***h*** are her
Eccl 6: 2 given riches and wealth and ***h***,
10: 1 one respected for wisdom and ***h***.
Isa 29:13 near with their mouths And ***h***
43:20 The beast of the field will ***h***
58:13 And shall ***h*** Him, not doing
61: 7 you shall have double ***h***,
Jer 33: 9 and an ***h*** before all nations of
Dan 2: 6 me gifts, rewards, and great ***h***.
4:30 my mighty power and for the ***h***
4:36 my ***h*** and splendor returned to
4:37 praise and extol and ***h*** the King
5:18 and majesty, glory and ***h***.
11:21 whom they will not give the ***h***
11:38 But in their place he shall ***h*** a
11:38 did not know he shall ***h*** with
Mal 1: 6 am the Father, Where is My ***h***?
Mt 13:57 A prophet is not without ***h***
15: 4 ***H*** your father and your
15: 6 then he need not ***h*** his father or
15: 8 And ***h*** Me with their
19:19 ***H*** your father and your
Mk 6: 4 A prophet is not without ***h***
7:10 ***H*** your father and your
10:19 ***H*** your father and your
Lk 18:20 ***H*** your father and your
Jn 4:44 that a prophet has no ***h*** in his
5:23 that all should ***h*** the Son just
5:23 honor the Son just as they ***h***
5:23 He who does not ***h*** the Son does
5:23 not honor the Son does not ***h***
5:41 I do not receive ***h*** from men.
5:44 who receive ***h*** from one another,
5:44 and do not seek the ***h*** that
8:49 but I ***h*** My Father, and you
8:54 If I ***h*** Myself, My honor is
8:54 My ***h*** is nothing. It is My
12:26 Me, him My Father will ***h***.
Rom 2: 7 in doing good seek for glory, ***h***,
2:10 but glory, ***h***, and peace
9:21 lump to make one vessel for ***h***
12:10 in ***h*** giving preference to one
13: 7 ***h*** to whom honor.
13: 7 to whom fear, honor to whom ***h***.
1 Cor 12:23 on these we bestow greater ***h***;
12:24 having given greater ***h*** to that
2 Cor 6: 8 by ***h*** and dishonor, by evil
Eph 6: 2 ***H*** your father and mother,"
1 Th 4: 4 vessel in sanctification and ***h***,
1 Tim 1:17 be ***h*** and glory forever and
5: 3 ***H*** widows who are really widows
5:17 be counted worthy of double ***h***,
6: 1 own masters worthy of all ***h***,
6:16 to whom be ***h*** and everlasting
2 Tim 2:20 some for ***h*** and some for
2:21 he will be a vessel for ***h***,
Heb 2: 7 him with glory and ***h***,
2: 9 death crowned with glory and ***h***,
3: 3 who built the house has more ***h***
5: 4 And no man takes this ***h*** to
1 Pe 1: 7 fire, may be found to praise, ***h***,
2:17 ***H*** all people. Love the
2:17 Fear God. ***H*** the king.
3: 7 giving ***h*** to the wife, as to the
2 Pe 1:17 received from God the Father ***h***
Rev 4: 9 creatures give glory and ***h*** and
4:11 To receive glory and ***h*** and
5:12 And strength and ***h*** and glory
5:13 Blessing and ***h*** and glory and
7:12 Thanksgiving and ***h*** and power
19: 1 Salvation and glory and ***h*** and
21:24 earth bring their glory and ***h***
21:26 bring the glory and the ***h*** of

HONORABLE (25/25) HONOR, HONORABLY

Gen 34:19 He was more ***h*** than all the
Num 22:15 more numerous and more ***h*** than
1 Sam 9: 6 and he is an ***h*** man; all that
22:14 and is ***h*** in your house?
2 Ki 5: 1 was a great and ***h*** man in the
1 Chr 4: 9 Now Jabez was more ***h*** than his
Job 22: 8 And the ***h*** man dwelt in it.
Ps 45: 9 daughters are among Your ***h***
111: 3 His work is ***h*** and glorious,
Prov 20: 3 It is ***h*** for a man to stop
Isa 3: 3 captain of fifty and the ***h*** man,
3: 5 And the base toward the ***h***.
5:13 Their ***h*** men are famished,
9:15 The elder and ***h***, he is the
23: 8 Whose traders are the ***h*** of
23: 9 bring into contempt all the ***h***
42:21 exalt the law and make it ***h***.
58:13 The holy day of the LORD ***h***,
Nah 3:10 They cast lots for her ***h*** men,
Lk 14: 8 lest one more ***h*** than you be
1 Cor 12:23 which we think to be less ***h***,
2 Cor 8:21 providing ***h*** things, not only in
13: 7 that you should do what is ***h***,
Heb 13: 4 Marriage is ***h*** among all, and
1 Pe 2:12 having your conduct ***h*** among the

HONORABLY (1/1) HONORABLE

Heb 13:18 all things desiring to live ***h***.

HONORED (13/13) HONOR

2 Sam 23:19 Was he not the most ***h*** of three?
23:23 He was more ***h*** than the thirty,
1 Chr 11:21 Of the three he was more ***h*** than
11:25 Indeed he was more ***h*** than the
2 Chr 32:33 the inhabitants of Jerusalem ***h***
Prov 13:18 who regards a rebuke will be ***h***.
27:18 waits on his master will be ***h***.
Isa 43: 4 in My sight, You have been ***h***,
43:23 Nor have you ***h*** Me with your
Lam 1: 8 All who ***h*** her despise her
Dan 4:34 the Most High and praised and ***h***
Acts 28:10 They also ***h*** us in many ways; and
1 Cor 12:26 with it; or if one member is ***h***,

HONORS (8/8) HONOR

2 Sam 10: 3 you think that David really ***h***
1 Chr 19: 3 you think that David really ***h***
Ps 15: 4 But he ***h*** those who fear the
Prov 12: 9 Than he who ***h*** himself but
14:31 But he who ***h*** Him has mercy on
Mal 1: 6 A son ***h*** his father, And a
Mk 7: 6 This people ***h*** Me with their
Jn 8:54 It is My Father who ***h*** Me, of

HOOF (4/4) HOOVES

Ex 10:26 not a ***h*** shall be left behind.
Lev 11: 3 animals, whatever divides the ***h***,
11: 7 swine, though it divides the ***h***,
Deut 14: 6 having the ***h*** split into two

HOOK (6/6) HOOKS

2 Ki 19:28 Therefore I will put My ***h*** in
Job 41: 1 you draw out Leviathan with a ***h***,
41: 2 Or pierce his jaw with a ***h***?
Isa 37:29 Therefore I will put My ***h*** in
Hab 1:15 take up all of them with a ***h***,
Mt 17:27 go to the sea, cast in a ***h***,

HOOKS (22/22) HOOK

Ex 26:32 Their ***h*** shall be gold, upon
26:37 their ***h*** shall be of gold,
27:10 The ***h*** of the pillars and their
27:11 and the ***h*** of the pillars and
27:17 their ***h*** shall be of silver
36:36 with their ***h*** of gold; and he
36:38 its five pillars with their ***h***.
38:10 The ***h*** of the pillars and their
38:11 The ***h*** of the pillars and their
38:12 The ***h*** of the pillars and their
38:17 the ***h*** of the pillars and their
38:19 their ***h*** were silver, and the
38:28 shekels he made ***h*** for the
2 Chr 33:11 who took Manasseh with ***h***,
Isa 2: 4 their spears into pruning ***h***;
18: 5 off the sprigs with pruning ***h***
19: 8 those will lament who cast ***h***
Ezek 29: 4 But I will put ***h*** in your jaws,
38: 4 put ***h*** into your jaws, and lead
40:43 Inside were ***h***, a handbreadth
Joel 3:10 into swords And your pruning ***h***
Mic 4: 3 their spears into pruning ***h***;

HOOPOE (2/2)

Lev 11:19 the heron after its kind, the ***h***,
Deut 14:18 and the ***h*** and the bat.

HOOVES (18/16) HOOF

Lev 11: 3 having cloven ***h*** and chewing
11: 4 cud or those that have cloven ***h***:
11: 4 cud but does not have cloven ***h***,
11: 5 cud but does not have cloven ***h***,
11: 6 cud but does not have cloven ***h***,

11: 7 the hoof, having cloven ***h***,
Deut 14: 6 eat every animal with cloven ***h***,
14: 7 chew the cud or have cloven ***h***,
14: 7 cud but do not have cloven ***h***;
14: 8 you, because it has cloven ***h***,
Judg 5:22 Then the horses' ***h*** pounded,
Ps 69:31 bull, Which has horns and ***h***.
Isa 5:28 Their horses' ***h*** will seem like
Jer 47: 3 the noise of the stamping ***h*** of
Ezek 26:11 With the ***h*** of his horses he will
32:13 Nor shall the ***h*** of animals
Mic 4:13 And I will make your ***h*** bronze;
Zech 11:16 of the fat and tear their ***h*** in

HOPE (142/134) HOPED, HOPES, HOPING

Ruth 1:12 If I should say I have ***h***,
1 Chr 29:15 as a shadow, And without ***h***.
Ezra 10: 2 yet now there is ***h*** in Israel in
Job 4: 6 integrity of your ways your ***h***?
5:16 So the poor have ***h***,
6:11 do I have, that I should ***h***?
6:19 The travelers of Sheba ***h*** for
7: 6 And are spent without ***h***.
8:13 And the ***h*** of the hypocrite
11:18 be secure, because there is ***h***;
11:20 shall not escape, And their ***h***—
14: 7 For there is ***h*** for a tree, If
14:19 So You destroy the ***h*** of man.
17:15 Where then is my ***h***?
17:15 then is my hope? As for my ***h***,
19:10 My ***h*** He has uprooted like a
27: 8 For what is the ***h*** of the
31:24 "If I have made gold my ***h***,
41: 9 any ***h*** of overcoming him is
Ps 16: 9 My flesh also will rest in ***h***.
31:24 All you who ***h*** in the LORD.
33:17 A horse is a vain ***h*** for
33:18 On those who ***h*** in His mercy,
33:22 Just as we ***h*** in You.
38:15 For in You, O LORD, I ***h***;
39: 7 My ***h*** is in You.
42: 5 ***H*** in God, for I shall yet
42:11 ***H*** in God; For I shall yet
43: 5 ***H*** in God; For I shall yet
62:10 Nor vainly ***h*** in robbery;
71: 5 For You are my ***h***,
71:14 But I will ***h*** continually, And
78: 7 That they may set their ***h*** in
119:49 which You have caused me to ***h***.
119:81 But I ***h*** in Your word.
119:114 I ***h*** in Your word.
119:116 not let me be ashamed of my ***h***.
119:147 I ***h*** in Your word.
119:166 I ***h*** for Your salvation, And I
130: 5 waits, And in His word I do ***h***.
130: 7 ***h*** in the LORD; For with the
131: 3 ***h*** in the LORD From this time
146: 5 Whose ***h*** is in the LORD his
147:11 In those who ***h*** in His mercy.
Prov 10:28 The ***h*** of the righteous will
11: 7 And the ***h*** of the unjust
13:12 ***H*** deferred makes the heart
19:18 your son while there is ***h***,
23:18 And your ***h*** will not be cut
24:14 And your ***h*** will not be cut
26:12 There is more ***h*** for a fool
29:20 There is more ***h*** for a fool
Eccl 9: 4 to all the living there is ***h***,
Isa 8:17 And I will ***h*** in Him.
38:18 who go down to the pit cannot ***h***
57:10 you did not say, 'There is no ***h***.
Jer 2:25 But you said, 'There is no ***h***.
14: 8 O the ***H*** of Israel, his Savior
17: 7 And whose ***h*** is the LORD.
17:13 the ***h*** of Israel, All who
17:17 You are my ***h*** in the day of
29:11 to give you a future and a ***h***.
31:17 There is ***h*** in your future, says
50: 7 the ***h*** of their fathers.'
Lam 3:18 My strength and my ***h*** Have
3:21 to my mind, Therefore I have ***h***.
3:24 Therefore I ***h*** in Him!"
3:26 is good that one should ***h***
3:29 in the dust—There may yet be ***h***.
Ezek 13: 6 yet they ***h*** that the word may be
19: 5 that her ***h*** was lost, She took
37:11 our ***h*** is lost, and we ourselves
Hos 2:15 Valley of Achor as a door of ***h***;
Zech 9:12 stronghold, You prisoners of ***h***.
Lk 6:34 to those from whom you ***h*** to
Acts 2:26 flesh also will rest in ***h***.
16:19 her masters saw that their ***h***
17:27 in the ***h*** that they might grope
23: 6 concerning the ***h*** and
24:15 I have ***h*** in God, which they
26: 6 I stand and am judged for the ***h***
26: 7 ***h*** to attain. For this hope's
27:20 all ***h*** that we would be saved
28:20 because for the ***h*** of Israel I
Rom 4:18 who, contrary to ***h***,
4:18 in ***h*** believed, so that he
5: 2 and rejoice in ***h*** of the glory
5: 4 character; and character, ***h***.
5: 5 Now ***h*** does not disappoint,
8:20 of Him who subjected it in ***h***;
8:24 For we were saved in this ***h***,
8:24 but ***h*** that is seen is not hope;
8:24 but hope that is seen is not ***h***;
8:24 for why does one still ***h*** for
8:25 But if we ***h*** for what we do not
12:12 rejoicing in ***h***, patient in
15: 4 of the Scriptures might have ***h***.
15:12 Him the Gentiles shall ***h***.
15:13 Now may the God of ***h*** fill you
15:13 that you may abound in ***h*** by the
15:24 For I ***h*** to see you on my
1 Cor 9:10 he who plows should plow in ***h***,
9:10 and he who threshes in ***h*** should
9:10 should be partaker of his ***h***.
13:13 And now abide faith, ***h***,
15:19 If in this life only we have ***h***
16: 7 but I ***h*** to stay a while with
2 Cor 1: 7 And our ***h*** for you is steadfast,
3:12 Therefore, since we have such ***h***,
10:15 men's labors, but having ***h***,
Gal 5: 5 Spirit eagerly wait for the ***h***
Eph 1:18 you may know what is the ***h*** of
2:12 having no ***h*** and without God in
4: 4 as you were called in one ***h*** of
Phil 1:20 to my earnest expectation and ***h***
2:23 Therefore I ***h*** to send him at
Col 1: 5 because of the ***h*** which is laid
1:23 are not moved away from the ***h***
1:27 in you, the ***h*** of glory.
1 Th 1: 3 and patience of ***h*** in our Lord
2:19 For what is our ***h***,
4:13 sorrow as others who have no ***h***.
5: 8 and as a helmet the ***h*** of
2 Th 2:16 consolation and good ***h*** by
1 Tim 1: 1 the Lord Jesus Christ, our ***h***,
3:14 though I ***h*** to come to you
Titus 1: 2 in ***h*** of eternal life which God,
2:13 looking for the blessed ***h*** and
3: 7 heirs according to the ***h*** of
Heb 3: 6 and the rejoicing of the ***h***
6:11 to the full assurance of ***h***
6:18 for refuge to lay hold of the ***h***
6:19 This ***h*** we have as an anchor of
7:19 the bringing in of a better ***h***,
10:23 fast the confession of our ***h***
1 Pe 1: 3 us again to a living ***h*** through
1:13 and rest your ***h*** fully upon the
1:21 so that your faith and ***h*** are in
3:15 who asks you a reason for the ***h***
1 Jn 3: 3 And everyone who has this ***h*** in
2 Jn 12 but I ***h*** to come to you and
3 Jn 14 but I ***h*** to see you shortly, and

HOPE'S (1/1)

Acts 26: 7 For this ***h*** sake, King Agrippa,

HOPED (8/8) HOPE

Esth 9: 1 the enemies of the Jews had ***h***
Ps 119:43 For I have ***h*** in Your
119:74 Because I have ***h*** in Your word.
Jer 3:23 in vain is salvation ***h*** for
Lk 23: 8 and he ***h*** to see some miracle
Acts 24:26 Meanwhile he also ***h*** that money
2 Cor 8: 5 And not only as we had ***h***,
Heb 11: 1 is the substance of things ***h***

HOPELESS (1/1)

Jer 18:12 That is ***h***! So we will walk

HOPES (1/1) HOPE

1 Cor 13: 7 ***h*** all things, endures all

HOPHNI (5/5)

1 Sam 1: 3 ***H*** and Phinehas, the priests of
2:34 on ***H*** and Phinehas: in one day
4: 4 ***H*** and Phinehas, were there
4:11 ***H*** and Phinehas, died.
4:17 ***H*** and Phinehas, are dead; and

HOPHRA (1/1) PHARAOH

Jer 44:30 I will give Pharaoh ***H*** king of

HOPING (2/2) HOPE

Lk 6:35 ***h*** for nothing in return;
24:21 But we were ***h*** that it was He who

HOR (14/14)

Num 20:22 from Kadesh and came to Mount ***H***.
20:23 to Moses and Aaron in Mount ***H***
20:25 and bring them up to Mount ***H***;
20:27 and they went up to Mount ***H*** in
21: 4 they journeyed from Mount ***H*** by
33:37 Kadesh and camped at Mount ***H***,
33:38 the priest went up to Mount ***H***
33:39 old when he died on Mount ***H***.
33:41 So they departed from Mount ***H***
34: 7 your border line to Mount ***H***;
34: 8 from Mount ***H*** you shall mark out
Deut 32:50 your brother died on Mount ***H***

HOR HAGIDGAD (2/2)

Num 33:32 Bene Jaakan and camped at ***H***.
33:33 They went from ***H*** and camped at

HORAM (1/1)

Josh 10:33 Then ***H*** king of Gezer came up to

HORDE (1/1)

Ezek 23:24 With a ***h*** of people.

HOREB (17/17) SINAI

Ex 3: 1 of the desert, and came to ***H***.
17: 6 you there on the rock in ***H***;
33: 6 of their ornaments by Mount ***H***.
Deut 1: 2 eleven days' journey from ***H***
1: 6 LORD our God spoke to us in ***H***,
1:19 "So we departed from ***H***,
4:10 before the LORD your God in ***H***,
4:15 the LORD spoke to you at ***H***
5: 2 made a covenant with us in ***H***.
9: 8 Also in ***H*** you provoked the LORD
18:16 of the LORD your God in ***H*** in
29: 1 which He made with them in ***H***.
1 Ki 8: 9 which Moses put there at ***H***,
19: 8 and forty nights as far as ***H***,
2 Chr 5:10 which Moses put there at ***H***,
Ps 106:19 They made a calf in ***H***,
Mal 4: 4 Which I commanded him in ***H*** for

HOREM (1/1)

Josh 19:38 Iron, Migdal El, ***H***,

HORI (3/3)

Gen 36:22 And the sons of Lotan were ***H*** and
Num 13: 5 of Simeon, Shaphat the son of ***H***;
1 Chr 1:39 And the sons of Lotan were ***H***

HORIMS (KJV) See HORITES

HORITE (1/1)

Gen 36:20 were the sons of Seir the ***H***

HORITES (6/6)

Gen 14: 6 and the ***H*** in their mountain of
36:21 These were the chiefs of the ***H***,
36:29 were the chiefs of the ***H***:
36:30 These were the chiefs of the ***H***,
Deut 2:12 The ***H*** formerly dwelt in Seir,
2:22 when He destroyed the ***H*** from

HORIZON (1/1)

Job 26:10 He drew a circular ***h*** on the

HORMAH (9/9)

Num 14:45 and drove them back as far as ***H***.
21: 3 name of that place was called ***H***.
Deut 1:44 drove you back from Seir to ***H***.
Josh 12:14 the king of ***H***, one; the king
15:30 Eltolad, Chesil, ***H***,
19: 4 Eltolad, Bethul, ***H***,
Judg 1:17 name of the city was called ***H***.
1 Sam 30:30 those who were in ***H***,
1 Chr 4:30 Bethuel, ***H***, Ziklag,

HORN (47/44) HORNS

Ex 21:29 ox tended to thrust with its ***h***
Josh 6: 5 a long blast with the ram's ***h***,
1 Sam 2: 1 My ***h*** is exalted in the LORD.
2:10 And exalt the ***h*** of His
16: 1 Fill your ***h*** with oil, and go;
16:13 Then Samuel took the ***h*** of oil
2 Sam 22: 3 My shield and the ***h*** of my
1 Ki 1:34 over Israel; and blow the ***h***,
1:39 Then Zadok the priest took a ***h***
1:39 Solomon. And they blew the ***h***,
1:41 Joab heard the sound of the ***h***,
1 Chr 15:28 and with the sound of the ***h***,
25: 5 words of God, to exalt his ***h***.
Ps 18: 2 My shield and the ***h*** of my
75: 4 wicked, 'Do not lift up the ***h***.
75: 5 Do not lift up your ***h*** on high;
89:17 And in Your favor our ***h*** is
89:24 And in My name his ***h*** shall be
92:10 But my ***h*** You have exalted like
98: 6 trumpets and the sound of a ***h***;
112: 9 His ***h*** will be exalted with
132:17 There I will make the ***h*** of
148:14 And He has exalted the ***h*** of His
Jer 48:25 The ***h*** of Moab is cut off, And
Lam 2: 3 off in fierce anger Every ***h***
2:17 He has exalted the ***h*** of your
Ezek 29:21 that day I will cause the ***h*** of
Dan 3: 5 you hear the sound of the ***h***,
3: 7 people heard the sound of the ***h***,
3:10 who hears the sound of the ***h***,
3:15 you hear the sound of the ***h***,
7: 8 horns, and there was another ***h***,
7: 8 the roots. And there, in this ***h***,
7:11 the pompous words which the ***h***
7:20 and the other ***h*** which came up,
7:20 that ***h*** which had eyes and a
7:21 and the same ***h*** was making war
8: 5 and the goat had a notable ***h***
8: 8 the large ***h*** was broken, and in
8: 9 of one of them came a little ***h***
8:12 was given over to the ***h*** to
8:21 The large ***h*** that is between
8:22 As for the broken ***h*** and the
Hos 5: 8 Blow the ram's ***h*** in Gibeah,
Mic 4:13 For I will make your ***h*** iron,
Zech 1:21 nations that lifted up their ***h***
Lk 1:69 And has raised up a ***h*** of

H

HORNET (2/2) HORNETS

Deut 7:20 LORD your God will send the **h**
Josh 24:12 I sent the **h** before you which

HORNETS (1/1) HORNET

Ex 23:28 And I will send **h** before you,

HORNS (65/57) HORN

Gen 22:13 caught in a thicket by its **h**.
Ex 27: 2 You shall make its **h** on its four
27: 2 its **h** shall be of one piece
29:12 the bull and put it on the **h**
30: 2 Its **h** shall be of one piece
30: 3 and its **h** with pure gold;
30:10 make atonement upon its **h** once
37:25 Its **h** were of one piece with
37:26 its sides all around, and its **h**.
38: 2 He made its **h** on its four
38: 2 the **h** were of one piece with
Lev 4: 7 put some of the blood on the **h**
4:18 some of the blood on the **h** of
4:25 put it on the **h** of the altar
4:30 put it on the **h** of the altar
4:34 put it on the **h** of the altar
8:15 and put some on the **h** of the
9: 9 put it on the **h** of the altar,
16:18 and put it on the **h** of the
Deut 33:17 And his **h** like the horns of
33:17 And his horns like the **h** of
Josh 6: 4 bear seven trumpets of rams' **h**
6: 6 bear seven trumpets of rams' **h**
6: 8 the seven trumpets of rams' **h**
6:13 seven trumpets of rams' **h**
1 Ki 1:50 went and took hold of the **h** of
1:51 he has taken hold of the **h** of
2:28 and took hold of the **h** of the
22:11 son of Chenaanah had made **h** of
2 Chr 15:14 and trumpets and rams' **h**.
18:10 son of Chenaanah had made **h** of
Ps 22:21 lion's mouth And from the **h**
69:31 Which has **h** and hooves.
75:10 All the **h** of the wicked I will
75:10 But the **h** of the righteous
118:27 sacrifice with cords to the **h**
Jer 17: 1 And on the **h** of your altars,
Ezek 34:21 all the weak ones with your **h**,
43:15 with four **h** extending upward
43:20 and put it on the four **h** of
Dan 7: 7 before it, and it had ten **h**.
7: 8 "I was considering the **h**,
7: 8 whom three of the first **h** were
7:20 and the ten **h** that were on its
7:24 The ten **h** are ten kings Who
8: 3 was a ram which had two **h**,
8: 3 and the two **h** were high;
8: 6 came to the ram that had two **h**,
8: 7 the ram, and broke his two **h**.
8:20 which you saw, having the two **h**—
Am 3:14 And the **h** of the altar shall
Zech 1:18 looked, and there were four **h**.
1:19 These are the **h** that have
1:21 These are the **h** that scattered
1:21 to cast out the **h** of the
Rev 5: 6 having seven **h** and seven eyes,
9:13 I heard a voice from the four **h**
12: 3 having seven heads and ten **h**,
13: 1 having seven heads and ten **h**,
13: 1 and on his **h** ten crowns, and on
13:11 and he had two **h** like a lamb
17: 3 having seven heads and ten **h**.
17: 7 the seven heads and the ten **h**.
17:12 The ten **h** which you saw are ten
17:16 And the ten **h** which you saw on

HORONAIM (4/4)

Isa 15: 5 For in the way of **H** They will
Jer 48: 3 of crying shall be from **H**:
48: 5 For in the descent of **H** the
48:34 their voice, From Zoar to **H**,

HORONITE (3/3)

Neh 2:10 When Sanballat the **H** and Tobiah
2:19 But when Sanballat the **H**,
13:28 a son-in-law of Sanballat the **H**;

HORRIBLE (5/5) HORROR

Ps 40: 2 also brought me up out of a **h**
Jer 5:30 An astonishing and **h** thing Has
18:13 of Israel has done a very **h**
23:14 Also I have seen a **h** thing in
Hos 6:10 I have seen a **h** thing in the

HORRIBLY (2/2)

Jer 2:12 And be **h** afraid; Be very
Ezek 32:10 and their kings shall be **h**

HORRIFIED (1/1)

Jer 50:13 who goes by Babylon shall be **h**

HORROR (6/6) HORRIBLE

Gen 15:12 **h** and great darkness fell upon
Ps 55: 5 And **h** has overwhelmed me.
Ezek 7:18 **H** will cover them;
23:33 The cup of **h** and desolation,
27:36 at you; You will become a **h**,
28:19 at you; You have become a **h**,

HORSE (40/38) HORSEBACK, HORSEMEN, HORSES, WAR-HORSES

Ex 15: 1 The **h** and its rider He
15:21 The **h** and its rider He
1 Ki 10:29 and a **h** one hundred and fifty;
20:20 king of Syria escaped on a **h**
20:25 **h** for horse and chariot for
20:25 horse for **h** and chariot for
2 Chr 1:17 and a **h** for one hundred and
23:15 of the entrance of the **H** Gate
Neh 3:28 Beyond the **H** Gate the priests
Esth 6: 8 and a **h** on which the king has
6: 9 Then let this robe and **h** be
6:10 take the robe and the **h**,
6:11 Haman took the robe and the **h**,
Job 39:18 She scorns the **h** and its
39:19 Have you given the **h** strength?
Ps 32: 9 Do not be like the **h** or like
33:17 A **h** is a vain hope for safety;
76: 6 Both the chariot and **h** were
147:10 in the strength of the **h**;
Prov 21:31 The **h** is prepared for the day
26: 3 A whip for the **h**,
Isa 43:17 brings forth the chariot and **h**,
63:13 As a **h** in the wilderness,
Jer 8: 6 As the **h** rushes into the
31:40 to the corner of the **H** Gate
51:21 I will break in pieces the **h**
Am 2:15 Nor shall he who rides a **h**
Zech 1: 8 behold, a man riding on a red **h**,
9:10 from Ephraim And the **h** from
10: 3 will make them as His royal **h**
12: 4 I will strike every **h** with
12: 4 and will strike every **h** of the
14:15 shall be the plague On the **h**
Rev 6: 2 I looked, and behold, a white **h**.
6: 4 Another **h**, fiery red, went
6: 5 I looked, and behold, a black **h**,
6: 8 I looked, and behold, a pale **h**.
19:11 opened, and behold, a white **h**.
19:19 against Him who sat on the **h**
19:21 mouth of Him who sat on the **h**.

HORSE'S (1/1)

Gen 49:17 That bites the **h** heels So

HORSEBACK (3/3) HORSE

Esth 6: 9 Then parade him on **h** through
6:11 Mordecai and led him on **h**
8:10 sent letters by couriers on **h**,

HORSELEACH (KJV) See LEECH

HORSEMAN (3/3)

2 Ki 9:17 Get a **h** and send him to meet
9:18 So the **h** went to meet him, and
9:19 Then he sent out a second **h** who

HORSEMEN (51/49)

Gen 50: 9 up with him both chariots and **h**.
Ex 14: 9 his **h** and his army, and
14:17 army, his chariots, and his **h**.
14:18 his chariots, and his **h**.
14:23 horses, his chariots, and his **h**.
14:26 their chariots, and on their **h**.
14:28 and covered the chariots, the **h**,
15:19 with his chariots and his **h**
Josh 24: 6 fathers with chariots and **h** to
1 Sam 8:11 own chariots and to be his **h**,
13: 5 chariots and six thousand **h**,
2 Sam 1: 6 and indeed the chariots and **h**
8: 4 chariots, seven hundred **h**,
10:18 and forty thousand **h** of the
1 Ki 1: 5 for himself chariots and **h**,
4:26 chariots, and twelve thousand **h**.
10:26 Solomon gathered chariots and **h**;
10:26 chariots and twelve thousand **h**,
2 Ki 2:12 chariot of Israel and its **h**!"
13: 7 army of Jehoahaz only fifty **h**,
13:14 chariots of Israel and their **h**!
18:24 in Egypt for chariots and **h**?
1 Chr 18: 4 chariots, seven thousand **h**,
19: 6 for themselves chariots and **h**
2 Chr 1:14 Solomon gathered chariots and **h**;
1:14 chariots and twelve thousand **h**,
9:25 and twelve thousand **h** whom he
12: 3 chariots, sixty thousand **h**,
16: 8 with very many chariots and **h**?
Ezra 8:22 an escort of soldiers and **h** to
Neh 2: 9 sent captains of the army and **h**
Isa 21: 7 saw a chariot with a pair of **h**,
21: 9 of men with a pair of **h**!"
22: 6 With chariots of men and **h**,
22: 7 And the **h** shall set themselves
28:28 Or crush it with his **h**.
31: 1 And in **h** because they are very
36: 9 in Egypt for chariots and **h**?
Jer 4:29 flee from the noise of the **h**
46: 4 And mount up, you **h**!
Ezek 23: 6 **H** riding on horses.
23:12 **H** riding on horses, All of
26: 7 with chariots, and with **h**,
26:10 shake at the noise of the **h**,
38: 4 all your army, horses, and **h**,
Dan 11:40 a whirlwind, with chariots, **h**,
Hos 1: 7 or battle, By horses or **h**.
Nah 3: 3 **H** charge with bright sword and
Acts 23:23 two hundred soldiers, seventy **h**,
23:32 The next day they left the **h** to
Rev 9:16 the number of the army of the **h**

HORSES (109/102) HORSE, HORSES'

Gen 47:17 bread in exchange for the **h**,
Ex 9: 3 cattle in the field, on the **h**,
14: 9 all the **h** and chariots of
14:23 of the sea, all Pharaoh's **h**,
15:19 For the **h** of Pharaoh went with
Deut 11: 4 to their **h** and their chariots:
17:16 But he shall not multiply **h** for
17:16 return to Egypt to multiply **h**,
20: 1 and see **h** and chariots and
Josh 11: 4 with very many **h** and chariots.
11: 6 You shall hamstring their **h** and
11: 9 he hamstrung their **h** and burned
2 Sam 8: 4 hamstrung all the chariot **h**,
15: 1 himself with chariots and **h**,
1 Ki 4:26 had forty thousand stalls of **h**
4:28 for the **h** and steeds, each man
10:25 garments, armor, spices, **h**,
10:28 Also Solomon had **h** imported
18: 5 we may find grass to keep the **h**
20: 1 with **h** and chariots. And he
20:21 went out and attacked the **h**
22: 4 my **h** as your horses."
22: 4 people, my horses as your **h**.
2 Ki 2:11 of fire appeared with **h** of
3: 7 my **h** as your horses."
3: 7 people, my horses as your **h**.
5: 9 Then Naaman went with his **h** and
6:14 Therefore he sent **h** and chariots
6:15 surrounding the city with **h** and
6:17 the mountain was full of **h** and
7: 6 of chariots and the noise of **h**—
7: 7 intact—their tents, their **h**,
7:10 only **h** and donkeys tied, and the
7:13 take five of the remaining **h**
7:14 they took two chariots with **h**;
9:33 on the wall and on the **h**;
10: 2 and you have chariots and **h**,
14:20 Then they brought him on **h**,
18:23 I will give you two thousand **h**—
23:11 Then he removed the **h** that the
1 Chr 18: 4 hamstrung all the chariot **h**,
2 Chr 1:16 And Solomon had **h** imported from
9:24 garments, armor, spices, **h**,
9:25 had four thousand stalls for **h**
9:28 And they brought **h** to Solomon
25:28 Then they brought him on **h** and
Ezra 2:66 Their **h** were seven hundred and
Neh 7:68 Their **h** were seven hundred and
Esth 8:10 riding on royal **h** bred from
8:14 couriers who rode on royal **h**
Ps 20: 7 in chariots, and some in **h**;
Eccl 10: 7 I have seen servants on **h**,
Isa 2: 7 Their land is also full of **h**,
30:16 will flee on **h**"—Therefore
30:16 ride on swift **h**"—THEREFORE
31: 1 Egypt for help, And rely on **h**,
31: 3 And their **h** are flesh, and not
36: 8 I will give you two thousand **h**—
66:20 on **h** and in chariots and in
Jer 4:13 His **h** are swifter than eagles.
6:23 the sea; And they ride on **h**,
8:16 The snorting of His **h** was heard
12: 5 how can you contend with **h**?
17:25 riding in chariots and on **h**,
22: 4 riding on **h** and in chariots,
46: 4 Harness the **h**, And mount
46: 9 Come up, O **h**, and rage,
47: 3 stamping hooves of his strong **h**,
50:37 A sword is against their **h**,
50:42 the sea; They shall ride on **h**,
51:27 Cause the **h** to come up like
Ezek 17:15 that they might give him **h** and
23: 6 men, Horsemen riding on **h**.
23:12 Horsemen riding on **h**,
23:20 issue is like the issue of **h**.
23:23 All of them riding on **h**.
26: 7 Babylon, king of kings, with **h**,
26:10 of the abundance of his **h**,
26:11 With the hooves of his **h** he will
27:14 traded for your wares with **h**,
38: 4 you out, with all your army, **h**,
38:15 you, all of them riding on **h**,
39:20 be filled at My table With **h**
Hos 1: 7 By **h** or horsemen."
14: 3 save us, We will not ride on **h**,
Joel 2: 4 is like the appearance of **h**;
Am 4:10 Along with your captive **h**;
6:12 Do **h** run on rocks? Does one
Mic 5:10 That I will cut off your **h** from
Nah 3: 2 wheels, Of galloping **h**,
Hab 1: 8 Their **h** also are swifter than
3: 8 sea, That You rode on Your **h**,
3:15 through the sea with Your **h**,
Hag 2:22 The **h** and their riders shall
Zech 1: 8 hollow; and behind him were **h**:
6: 2 the first chariot were red **h**,
6: 2 with the second chariot black **h**,
6: 3 with the third chariot white **h**,
6: 3 the fourth chariot dappled **h**—
6: 6 The one with the black **h** is
10: 5 And the riders on **h** shall be
14:20 engraved on the bells of the **h**.
Rev 9: 7 shape of the locusts was like **h**

9: 9 sound of chariots with many **h**
9:17 And thus I saw the **h** in the
9:17 and the heads of the **h** were
18:13 **h** and chariots, and bodies and
19:14 clean, followed Him on white **h**.
19:18 the flesh of **h** and of those who

HORSES' (5/5)

Judg 5:22 Then the **h** hooves pounded, The
2 Ki 11:16 and she went by way of the **h**
Isa 5:28 Their **h** hooves will seem like
Jas 3: 3 we put bits in **h** mouths that
Rev 14:20 up to the **h** bridles, for one

HOSAH (5/5)

Josh 19:29 then the border turned to **H**,
1 Chr 16:38 the son of Jeduthun, and **H**,
26:10 Also **H**, of the children of
26:11 all the sons and brethren of **H**
26:16 To Shuppim and **H** the lot came

HOSANNA (6/5)

Mt 21: 9 '**H** to the Son of David!
21: 9 **H** in the highest!"
21:15 '**H** to the Son of David!"
Mk 11: 9 **H**! 'Blessed is He who
11:10 in the name of the Lord! **H** in
Jn 12:13 **H**! 'Blessed is He who

HOSEA (4/3) HOSHEA, JOSHUA

Hos 1: 1 of the LORD that came to **H**
1: 2 the LORD began to speak by **H**,
1: 2 by Hosea, the LORD said to **H**:
Rom 9:25 As He says also in **H**:

HOSEN (KJV) See TROUSERS

HOSHAIAH (3/3)

Neh 12:32 After them went **H** and half of
Jer 42: 1 Kareah, Jezaniah the son of **H**,
43: 2 that Azariah the son of **H**,

HOSHAMA (1/1)

1 Chr 3:18 Pedaiah, Shenazzar, Jecamiah, **H**,

HOSHEA (12/12) HOSEA, JOSHUA

Num 13: 8 **H** the son of Nun;
13:16 And Moses called **H** the son of
2 Ki 15:30 Then **H** the son of Elah led a
17: 1 **H** the son of Elah became king
17: 3 and **H** became his vassal, and
17: 4 uncovered a conspiracy by **H**;
17: 6 In the ninth year of **H**,
18: 1 to pass in the third year of **H**
18: 9 was the seventh year of **H** the
18:10 the ninth year of **H** king of
1 Chr 27:20 **H** the son of Azaziah; over the
Neh 10:23 **H**, Hananiah, Hasshub,

HOSPITABLE (3/3) HOSPITALITY

1 Tim 3: 2 of good behavior, **h**,
Titus 1: 8 but **h**, a lover of what is
1 Pe 4: 9 Be **h** to one another without

HOSPITALITY (1/1) HOSPITABLE

Rom 12:13 needs of the saints, given to **h**.

HOST (33/29) HOSTS

Gen 2: 1 and all the **h** of them, were
Deut 4:19 all the **h** of heaven, you feel
17: 3 sun or moon or any of the **h** of
1 Ki 22:19 and all the **h** of heaven
2 Ki 17:16 image and worshiped all the **h**
21: 3 and he worshiped all the **h** of
21: 5 he built altars for all the **h**
23: 4 and for all the **h** of heaven;
23: 5 and to all the **h** of heaven.
2 Chr 18:18 and all the **h** of heaven
33: 3 and he worshiped all the **h** of
33: 5 he built altars for all the **h**
Neh 9: 6 of heavens, with all their **h**,
9: 6 The **h** of heaven worships You.
Ps 33: 6 And all the **h** of them by the
Isa 24:21 will punish on high the **h** of
34: 4 All the **h** of heaven shall be
34: 4 All their **h** shall fall down
40:26 Who brings out their **h** by
45:12 And all their **h** I have
Jer 8: 2 sun and the moon and all the **h**
19:13 burned incense to all the **h** of
33:22 As the **h** of heaven cannot be
Dan 8:10 And it grew up to the **h** of
8:10 and it cast down some of the **h**
8:11 as high as the Prince of the **h**;
8:13 of both the sanctuary and the **h**
Ob 20 And the captives of this **h** of
Zeph 1: 5 Those who worship the **h** of
Lk 2:13 a multitude of the heavenly **h**
Acts 7:42 gave them up to worship the **h**
Rom 16:23 my **h** and the host of the
16:23 my host and the **h** of the

HOSTAGES (2/2)

2 Ki 14:14 of the king's house, and **h**,
2 Chr 25:24 of the king's house, and **h**,

HOSTILE (1/1)

Deut 28:54 man among you will be **h** toward

HOSTILITY (1/1)

Heb 12: 3 Him who endured such **h** from

HOSTS (289/277) HOST

1 Sam 1: 3 sacrifice to the LORD of **h** in
1:11 a vow and said, "O LORD of **h**,
4: 4 the covenant of the LORD of **h**,
15: 2 "Thus says the LORD of **h**:
17:45 in the name of the LORD of **h**,
2 Sam 5:10 and the LORD God of **h** was
6: 2 by the Name, the LORD of **H**,
6:18 in the name of the LORD of **h**.
7: 8 'Thus says the LORD of **h**:
7:26 The LORD of **h** is the God over
7:27 "For You, O LORD of **h**,
1 Ki 18:15 As the LORD of **h** lives, before
19:10 zealous for the LORD God of **h**;
19:14 zealous for the LORD God of **h**;
2 Ki 3:14 As the LORD of **h** lives, before
19:31 The zeal of the LORD of **h**
1 Chr 11: 9 and the LORD of **h** was with
17: 7 'Thus says the LORD of **h**:
17:24 saying, 'The LORD of **h**,
Ps 24:10 King of glory? The LORD of **h**,
46: 7 The LORD of **h** is with us;
46:11 The LORD of **h** is with us;
48: 8 In the city of the LORD of **h**,
59: 5 therefore, O LORD God of **h**,
69: 6 wait for You, O Lord GOD of **h**,
80: 4 O LORD God of **h**, How long
80: 7 Restore us, O God of **h**;
80:14 we beseech You, O God of **h**;
80:19 Restore us, O LORD God of **h**;
84: 1 tabernacle, O LORD of **h**!
84: 3 Your altars, O LORD of **h**,
84: 8 O LORD God of **h**,
84:12 O LORD of **h**, Blessed is the
89: 8 O LORD God of **h**, Who is
103:21 the LORD, all you His **h**,
148: 2 Praise Him, all His **h**!
Isa 1: 9 Unless the LORD of **h** Had left
1:24 the Lord says, The LORD of **h**,
2:12 For the day of the LORD of **h**
3: 1 the Lord, the LORD of **h**,
3:15 Says the Lord GOD of **h**.
5: 7 the vineyard of the LORD of **h**
5: 9 In my hearing the LORD of **h**
5:16 But the LORD of **h** shall be
5:24 the law of the LORD of **h**,
6: 3 holy, holy is the LORD of **h**;
6: 5 seen the King, The LORD of **h**.
8:13 The LORD of **h**, Him you
8:18 in Israel From the LORD of **h**,
9: 7 The zeal of the LORD of **h**
9:13 do they seek the LORD of **h**.
9:19 the wrath of the LORD of **h**
10:16 the Lord, the Lord of **h**,
10:23 For the Lord GOD of **h** Will
10:24 thus says the Lord GOD of **h**:
10:26 And the LORD of **h** will stir up
10:33 the Lord, The LORD of **h**,
13: 4 The LORD of **h** musters
13:13 In the wrath of the LORD of **h**
14:22 them," says the LORD of **h**,
14:23 says the LORD of **h**.
14:24 The LORD of **h** has sworn,
14:27 For the LORD of **h** has
17: 3 Israel," Says the LORD of **h**.
18: 7 be brought to the LORD of **h**
18: 7 of the name of the LORD of **h**,
19: 4 Says the Lord, the LORD of **h**.
19:12 them know what the LORD of **h**
19:16 of the hand of the LORD of **h**,
19:17 the counsel of the LORD of **h**
19:18 and swear by the LORD of **h**;
19:20 a witness to the LORD of **h** in
19:25 whom the LORD of **h** shall bless,
21:10 have heard from the LORD of **h**,
22: 5 By the Lord GOD of **h** In the
22:12 in that day the Lord GOD of **h**
22:14 in my hearing by the LORD of **h**,
22:14 says the Lord GOD of **h**.
22:15 Thus says the Lord GOD of **h**:
22:25 that day,' says the LORD of **h**,
23: 9 The LORD of **h** has purposed it,
24:23 For the LORD of **h** will reign
25: 6 this mountain The LORD of **h**
28: 5 In that day the LORD of **h**
28:22 heard from the Lord GOD of **h**,
28:29 also comes from the LORD of **h**,
29: 6 be punished by the LORD of **h**
31: 4 So the LORD of **h** will come
31: 5 So will the LORD of **h** defend
37:16 'O LORD of **h**, God of Israel,
37:32 The zeal of the LORD of **h**
39: 5 the word of the LORD of **h**:
44: 6 his Redeemer, the LORD of **h**:
45:13 reward," Says the LORD of **h**.
47: 4 the LORD of **h** is His name,
48: 2 The LORD of **h** is His name:
51:15 The LORD of **h** is His name.
54: 5 The LORD of **h** is His name;
Jer 2:19 you," Says the Lord GOD of **h**.
3:19 A beautiful heritage of the **h**
5:14 thus says the LORD God of **h**:
6: 6 For thus has the LORD of **h**
6: 9 Thus says the LORD of **h**:
7: 3 Thus says the LORD of **h**,
7:21 Thus says the LORD of **h**,
8: 3 them," says the LORD of **h**.
9: 7 thus says the LORD of **h**:
9:15 thus says the LORD of **h**,
9:17 Thus says the LORD of **h**:
10:16 The LORD of **h** is His name.
11:17 "For the LORD of **h**,
11:20 But, O LORD of **h**,
11:22 thus says the LORD of **h**:
15:16 by Your name, O LORD God of **h**.
16: 9 For thus says the LORD of **h**,
19: 3 Thus says the LORD of **h**,
19:11 them, 'Thus says the LORD of **h**:
19:15 "Thus says the LORD of **h**,
20:12 But, O LORD of **h**,
23:15 thus says the LORD of **h**
23:16 Thus says the LORD of **h**:
23:36 the living God, the LORD of **h**,
25: 8 thus says the LORD of **h**:
25:27 them, 'Thus says the LORD of **h**,
25:28 them, 'Thus says the LORD of **h**:
25:29 earth," says the LORD of **h**.
25:32 Thus says the LORD of **h**:
26:18 'Thus says the LORD of **h**:
27: 4 "Thus says the LORD of **h**,
27:18 intercession to the LORD of **h**,
27:19 For thus says the LORD of **h**
27:21 "yes, thus says the LORD of **h**,
28: 2 "Thus speaks the LORD of **h**,
28:14 'For thus says the LORD of **h**,
29: 4 Thus says the LORD of **h**,
29: 8 For thus says the LORD of **h**,
29:17 thus says the LORD of **h**,
29:21 Thus says the LORD of **h**,
29:25 Thus speaks the LORD of **h**,
30: 8 that day,' Says the LORD of **h**,
31:23 Thus says the LORD of **h**,
31:35 its waves roar (The LORD of **h**
32:14 'Thus says the LORD of **h**,
32:15 'For thus says the LORD of **h**,
32:18 whose name is the LORD of **h**.
33:11 say: "Praise the LORD of **h**,
33:12 "Thus says the LORD of **h**:
35:13 "Thus says the LORD of **h**,
35:17 thus says the LORD God of **h**,
35:18 "Thus says the LORD of **h**,
35:19 thus says the LORD of **h**,
38:17 says the LORD, the God of **h**,
39:16 'Thus says the LORD of **h**,
42:15 Thus says the LORD of **h**,
42:18 "For thus says the LORD of **h**,
43:10 them, 'Thus says the LORD of **h**,
44: 2 "Thus says the LORD of **h**,
44: 7 says the LORD, the God of **h**,
44:11 thus says the LORD of **h**,
44:25 "Thus says the LORD of **h**,
46:10 the day of the Lord GOD of **h**,
46:10 For the Lord GOD of **h** has a
46:18 Whose name is the LORD of **h**,
46:25 The LORD of **h**, the God of
48: 1 Thus says the LORD of **h**,
48:15 Whose name is the LORD of **h**.
49: 5 you," Says the Lord GOD of **h**,
49: 7 Thus says the LORD of **h**:
49:26 that day," says the LORD of **h**.
49:35 "Thus says the LORD of **h**:
50:18 thus says the LORD of **h**,
50:25 the work of the Lord GOD of **h**
50:31 one!" says the Lord GOD of **h**;
50:33 Thus says the LORD of **h**:
50:34 The LORD of **h** is His name.
51: 5 By his God, the LORD of **h**,
51:14 The LORD of **h** has sworn by
51:19 The LORD of **h** is His name.
51:33 For thus says the LORD of **h**,
51:57 Whose name is the LORD of **h**.
51:58 Thus says the LORD of **h**:
Hos 12: 5 That is, the LORD God of **h**.
Am 3:13 the Lord GOD, the God of **h**,
4:13 The LORD God of **h** is His
5:14 So the LORD God of **h** will be
5:15 may be that the LORD God of **h**
5:16 Therefore the LORD God of **h**,
5:27 whose name is the God of **h**.
6: 8 The LORD God of **h** says: "I
6:14 Says the LORD God of **h**;
9: 5 The Lord GOD of **h**,
Mic 4: 4 the mouth of the LORD of **h**
Nah 2:13 you," says the LORD of **h**,
3: 5 you," says the LORD of **h**;
Hab 2:13 is it not of the LORD of **h**
Zeph 2: 9 I live," Says the LORD of **h**,
2:10 the people of the LORD of **h**.
Hag 1: 2 "Thus speaks the LORD of **h**,
1: 5 thus says the LORD of **h**:
1: 7 Thus says the LORD of **h**:
1: 9 Why?" says the LORD of **h**.
1:14 on the house of the LORD of **h**,
2: 4 with you,' says the LORD of **h**.
2: 6 "For thus says the LORD of **h**:
2: 7 glory,' says the LORD of **h**.
2: 8 is Mine,' says the LORD of **h**.
2: 9 former,' says the LORD of **h**.
2: 9 peace,' says the LORD of **h**.
2:11 "Thus says the LORD of **h**:

2:23 that day,' says the LORD of ***h***,
2:23 you,' says the LORD of ***h***.
Zech 1: 3 them, 'Thus says the LORD of ***h***:
1: 3 to Me," says the LORD of ***h***,
1: 3 to you," says the LORD of ***h***.
1: 4 'Thus says the LORD of ***h***:
1: 6 Just as the LORD of ***h***
1:12 and said, "O LORD of ***h***,
1:14 'Thus says the LORD of ***h***:
1:16 in it," says the LORD of ***h***,
1:17 'Thus says the LORD of ***h***:
2: 8 For thus says the LORD of ***h***:
2: 9 will know that the LORD of ***h***
2:11 will know that the LORD of ***h***
3: 7 "Thus says the LORD of ***h***:
3: 9 Says the LORD of ***h***,
3:10 that day,' says the LORD of ***h***,
4: 6 Spirit,' Says the LORD of ***h***.
4: 9 will know That the LORD of ***h***
5: 4 curse," says the LORD of ***h***;
6:12 'Thus says the LORD of ***h***,
6:15 shall know that the LORD of ***h***
7: 3 in the house of the LORD of ***h***,
7: 4 the word of the LORD of ***h***
7: 9 "Thus says the LORD of ***h***:
7:12 the words which the LORD of ***h***
7:12 wrath came from the LORD of ***h***.
7:13 listen," says the LORD of ***h***.
8: 1 the word of the LORD of ***h***
8: 2 "Thus says the LORD of ***h***:
8: 3 The Mountain of the LORD of ***h***,
8: 4 "Thus says the LORD of ***h***:
8: 6 "Thus says the LORD of ***h***:
8: 6 My eyes?' Says the LORD of ***h***.
8: 7 "Thus says the LORD of ***h***:
8: 9 "Thus says the LORD of ***h***:
8: 9 the house of the LORD of ***h***,
8:11 days,' says the LORD of ***h***.
8:14 "For thus says the LORD of ***h***:
8:14 to wrath,' Says the LORD of ***h***,
8:18 the word of the LORD of ***h***
8:19 "Thus says the LORD of ***h***:
8:20 "Thus says the LORD of ***h***:
8:21 LORD, And seek the LORD of ***h***.
8:22 come to seek the LORD of ***h*** in
8:23 "Thus says the LORD of ***h***:
9:15 The LORD of ***h*** will defend
10: 3 For the LORD of ***h*** will visit
12: 5 my strength in the LORD of ***h***,
13: 2 that day," says the LORD of ***h***,
13: 7 Says the LORD of ***h***.
14:16 the King, the LORD of ***h***,
14:17 the King, the LORD of ***h***,
14:21 be holiness to the LORD of ***h***.
14:21 in the house of the LORD of ***h***.
Mal 1: 4 Thus says the LORD of ***h***:
1: 6 Says the LORD of ***h*** To you
1: 8 Says the LORD of ***h***.
1: 9 Says the LORD of ***h***.
1:10 in you," Says the LORD of ***h***,
1:11 nations," Says the LORD of ***h***.
1:13 at it," Says the LORD of ***h***.
1:14 King," Says the LORD of ***h***,
2: 2 My name," Says the LORD of ***h***,
2: 4 Says the LORD of ***h***.
2: 7 the messenger of the LORD of ***h***.
2: 8 of Levi," Says the LORD of ***h***.
2:12 an offering to the LORD of ***h***!
2:16 Says the LORD of ***h***.
3: 1 coming," Says the LORD of ***h***.
3: 5 fear Me," Says the LORD of ***h***.
3: 7 to you," Says the LORD of ***h***.
3:10 in this," Says the LORD of ***h***,
3:11 field," Says the LORD of ***h***;
3:12 land," Says the LORD of ***h***.
3:14 mourners Before the LORD of ***h***?
3:17 be Mine," says the LORD of ***h***,
4: 1 them up," Says the LORD of ***h***,
4: 3 this," Says the LORD of ***h***.
Eph 6:12 spiritual ***h*** of wickedness

HOT (31/30) HOTTEST

Ex 16:21 And when the sun became ***h***,
22:24 "and My wrath will become ***h***,
32:10 that My wrath may burn ***h***
32:11 why does Your wrath burn ***h***
32:19 So Moses' anger became ***h***,
32:22 the anger of my lord become ***h***.
Deut 9:19 I was afraid of the anger and ***h***
19: 6 of blood, while his anger is ***h***,
Josh 9:12 we took ***h*** for our provision
Judg 2:14 the anger of the LORD was ***h***
2:20 the anger of the LORD was ***h***
3: 8 the anger of the LORD was ***h***
10: 7 So the anger of the LORD was ***h***
1 Sam 11: 9 by the time the sun is ***h***,
21: 6 in order to put ***h*** bread in
Neh 7: 3 be opened until the sun is ***h***;
Job 6:17 cease to flow; When it is ***h***,
37:17 Why are your garments ***h***,
Ps 6: 1 Nor chasten me in Your ***h***
38: 1 Nor chasten me in Your ***h***
39: 3 My heart was ***h*** within me;
Prov 6:28 Can one walk on ***h*** coals, And
Lam 5:10 Our skin is ***h*** as an oven,
Ezek 24:11 That it may become ***h*** and its
Dan 3:22 and the furnace exceedingly ***h***,
Hos 7: 7 are all ***h***, like an oven,
Lk 12:55 'There will be ***h*** weather';
1 Tim 4: 2 own conscience seared with a ***h***
Rev 3:15 that you are neither cold nor ***h***.
3:15 I could wish you were cold or ***h***.
3:16 and neither cold nor ***h***,

HOTHAM (2/2)

1 Chr 7:32 Heber begot Japhlet, Shomer, ***H***,
11:44 Shama and Jeiel the sons of ***H***

HOTHIR (2/2)

1 Chr 25: 4 Joshbekashah, Mallothi, ***H***,
25:28 the twenty-first for ***H***,

HOTLY (1/1)

Gen 31:36 that you have so ***h*** pursued me?

HOTTEST (1/1) HOT

2 Sam 11:15 the forefront of the ***h*** battle,

HOUGH (KJV) See HAMSTRING

HOUND (1/1)

Ps 56: 2 My enemies would ***h*** me all day,

HOUR (97/89) HOURS

Dan 4:33 That very ***h*** the word was
5: 5 In the same ***h*** the fingers of a
Mt 8:13 servant was healed that same ***h***.
9:22 woman was made well from that ***h***.
10:19 will be given to you in that ***h***
14:15 and the ***h*** is already late.
15:28 was healed from that very ***h***.
17:18 was cured from that very ***h***.
20: 3 he went out about the third ***h***
20: 5 about the sixth and the ninth ***h***,
20: 6 And about the eleventh ***h*** he went
20: 9 hired about the eleventh ***h***,
20:12 men have worked only one ***h***,
24:36 But of that day and ***h*** no one
24:42 for you do not know what ***h*** your
24:43 of the house had known what ***h***
24:44 Son of Man is coming at an ***h***
24:50 looking for him and at an ***h***
25:13 know neither the day nor the ***h***
26:40 you not watch with Me one ***h***?
26:45 the ***h*** is at hand, and the Son
26:55 In that ***h*** Jesus said to the
27:45 Now from the sixth ***h*** until the
27:45 sixth hour until the ninth ***h***
27:46 And about the ninth ***h*** Jesus
Mk 6:35 and already the ***h*** is late.
11:11 as the ***h*** was already late, He
13:11 whatever is given you in that ***h***,
13:32 But of that day and ***h*** no one
14:35 the ***h*** might pass from Him.
14:37 Could you not watch one ***h***?
14:41 It is enough! The ***h*** has come;
15:25 Now it was the third ***h***,
15:33 Now when the sixth ***h*** had come,
15:33 whole land until the ninth ***h***.
15:34 And at the ninth ***h*** Jesus cried
Lk 1:10 was praying outside at the ***h***
7:21 And that very ***h*** He cured many of
10:21 In that ***h*** Jesus rejoiced in the
12:12 will teach you in that very ***h***
12:39 of the house had known what ***h***
12:40 Son of Man is coming at an ***h***
12:46 and at an ***h*** when he is not
20:19 and the scribes that very ***h***
22:14 When the ***h*** had come, He sat
22:53 to seize Me. But this is your ***h***,
22:59 Then after about an ***h*** had
23:44 Now it was about the sixth ***h***,
23:44 all the earth until the ninth ***h***.
24:33 So they rose up that very ***h*** and
Jn 1:39 (now it was about the tenth ***h***).
2: 4 My ***h*** has not yet come."
4: 6 It was about the sixth ***h***.
4:21 the ***h*** is coming when you will
4:23 But the ***h*** is coming, and now is,
4:52 Then he inquired of them the ***h***
4:52 Yesterday at the seventh ***h*** the
4:53 that it was at the same ***h*** in
5:25 the ***h*** is coming, and now is,
5:28 for the ***h*** is coming in which
7:30 because His ***h*** had not yet come.
8:20 for His ***h*** had not yet come.
12:23 The ***h*** has come that the Son of
12:27 'Father, save Me from this ***h***'?
12:27 this purpose I came to this ***h***.
13: 1 when Jesus knew that His ***h*** had
16:21 has sorrow because her ***h*** has
16:32 Indeed the ***h*** is coming, yes, has
17: 1 the ***h*** has come. Glorify Your
19:14 Passover, and about the sixth ***h***.
19:27 your mother!" And from that ***h***
Acts 2:15 since it is only the third ***h***
3: 1 to the temple at the ***h*** of
3: 1 hour of prayer, the ninth ***h***.
10: 3 About the ninth ***h*** of the day he
10: 9 to pray, about the sixth ***h***.
10:30 ago I was fasting until this ***h***;
10:30 and at the ninth ***h*** I prayed in
16:18 And he came out that very ***h***.
16:33 And he took them the same ***h*** of
22:13 And at that same ***h*** I looked up
23:23 go to Caesarea at the third ***h***
1 Cor 4:11 To the present ***h*** we both hunger
15:30 do we stand in jeopardy every ***h***?
Gal 2: 5 yield submission even for an ***h***,
1 Jn 2:18 children, it is the last ***h***;
2:18 we know that it is the last ***h***.
Rev 3: 3 and you will not know what ***h*** I
3:10 I also will keep you from the ***h***
8: 1 in heaven for about half an ***h***.
9:15 who had been prepared for the ***h***
11:13 In the same ***h*** there was a great
14: 7 for the ***h*** of His judgment has
17:12 receive authority for one ***h*** as
18:10 that mighty city! For in one ***h***
18:17 For in one ***h*** such great riches
18:19 by her wealth! For in one ***h***

HOURS (3/3) HOUR

Jn 11: 9 Are there not twelve ***h*** in the
Acts 5: 7 Now it was about three ***h*** later
19:34 voice cried out for about two ***h***,

HOUSE (1739/1490) HOUSEHOLD, HOUSES, HOUSETOP

Gen 12: 1 And from your father's ***h***,
12:15 woman was taken to Pharaoh's ***h***.
12:17 plagued Pharaoh and his ***h*** with
14:14 who were born in his own ***h***,
15: 2 and the heir of my ***h*** is
15: 3 indeed one born in my ***h*** is my
17:12 he who is born in your ***h*** or
17:13 He who is born in your ***h*** and he
17:23 all who were born in his ***h*** and
17:23 among the men of Abraham's ***h***,
17:27 and all the men of his ***h***,
17:27 born in the ***h*** or bought with
19: 2 turn in to your servant's ***h***
19: 3 in to him and entered his ***h***.
19: 4 every quarter, surrounded the ***h***.
19:10 and pulled Lot into the ***h*** with
19:11 were at the doorway of the ***h***
20:13 me to wander from my father's ***h***,
20:18 wombs of the ***h*** of Abimelech
24: 2 to the oldest servant of his ***h***,
24: 7 who took me from my father's ***h***
24:23 there room in your father's ***h***
24:27 ***h*** of my master's brethren."
24:31 For I have prepared the ***h***,
24:32 Then the man came to the ***h***.
24:38 you shall go to my father's ***h***
24:40 family and from my father's ***h***.
27:15 which were with her in the ***h***,
28: 2 to the ***h*** of Bethuel your
28:17 This is none other than the ***h***
28:21 I come back to my father's ***h***
28:22 as a pillar shall be God's ***h***,
29:13 him, and brought him to his ***h***.
30:30 I also provide for my own ***h***?
31:14 for us in our father's ***h***?
31:30 long for your father's ***h***,
31:41 Thus I have been in your ***h***
33:17 to Succoth, built himself a ***h***,
34:26 and took Dinah from Shechem's ***h***,
38:11 a widow in your father's ***h***
38:11 and dwelt in her father's ***h***.
39: 2 was in the ***h*** of his master
39: 4 he made him overseer of his ***h***,
39: 5 had made him overseer of his ***h***
39: 5 LORD blessed the Egyptian's ***h***
39: 5 was on all that he had in the ***h***
39: 8 know what is with me in the ***h***,
39: 9 is no one greater in this ***h***
39:11 when Joseph went into the ***h*** to
39:11 and none of the men of the ***h***
39:14 she called to the men of her ***h***
40: 3 he put them in custody in the ***h***
40: 7 in the custody of his lord's ***h***,
40:14 and get me out of this ***h***.
41:10 and put me in custody in the ***h***
41:40 "You shall be over my ***h***,
41:51 my toil and all my father's ***h***.
42:19 be confined to your prison ***h***;
43:16 he said to the steward of his ***h***,
43:17 brought the men into Joseph's ***h***.
43:18 were brought into Joseph's ***h***;
43:19 to the steward of Joseph's ***h***,
43:19 with him at the door of the ***h***,
43:24 the men into Joseph's ***h*** and
43:26 was in their hand into the ***h***,
44: 1 commanded the steward of his ***h***,
44: 8 or gold from your lord's ***h***?
44:14 his brothers came to Joseph's ***h***,
45: 2 and the ***h*** of Pharaoh heard
45: 8 Pharaoh, and lord of all his ***h***,
45:16 of it was heard in Pharaoh's ***h***,
46:27 persons of the ***h*** of Jacob
46:31 and those of my father's ***h***,
47:14 the money into Pharaoh's ***h***.
50: 7 of Pharaoh, the elders of his ***h***,
50: 8 as well as all the ***h*** of Joseph,
50: 8 brothers, and his father's ***h***.
Ex 2: 1 And a man of the ***h*** of Levi went
3:22 of her who dwells near her ***h***,
7:23 turned and went into his ***h***.
8: 3 go up and come into your ***h***,
8:24 came into the ***h*** of Pharaoh,
12: 3 according to the ***h*** of his
12: 4 and his neighbor next to his ***h***
12:22 go out of the door of his ***h***
12:30 for there was not a ***h*** where
12:46 'In one ***h*** it shall be eaten;
12:46 any of the flesh outside the ***h***,

13: 3 out of the ***h*** of bondage; for by
13:14 out of the ***h*** of bondage.
16:31 And the ***h*** of Israel called its
19: 3 shall say to the ***h*** of Jacob,
20: 2 out of the ***h*** of bondage.
20:17 not covet your neighbor's ***h***;
22: 7 it is stolen out of the man's ***h***,
22: 8 then the master of the ***h*** shall
23:19 bring into the ***h*** of the LORD
34:26 land you shall bring to the ***h***
40:38 of all the ***h*** of Israel,
Lev 10: 6 the whole ***h*** of Israel, bewail
14:34 I put the leprous plague in a ***h***
14:35 and he who owns the ***h*** comes and
14:35 there is some plague in the ***h***,
14:36 command that they empty the ***h***,
14:36 that all that is in the ***h*** may
14:36 shall go in to examine the ***h***.
14:37 is on the walls of the ***h*** with
14:38 priest shall go out of the ***h***,
14:38 the house, to the door of the ***h***,
14:38 and shut up the ***h*** seven days.
14:39 spread on the walls of the ***h***,
14:41 And he shall cause the ***h*** to be
14:42 other mortar and plaster the ***h***.
14:43 back and breaks out in the ***h***,
14:43 after he has scraped the ***h***,
14:44 the plague has spread in the ***h***,
14:44 is an active leprosy in the ***h***.
14:45 "And he shall break down the ***h***,
14:45 and all the plaster of the ***h***,
14:46 he who goes into the ***h*** at all
14:47 And he who lies down in the ***h***
14:47 and he who eats in the ***h*** shall
14:48 plague has not spread in the ***h***
14:48 in the house after the ***h*** was
14:48 priest shall pronounce the ***h***
14:49 he shall take, to cleanse the ***h***,
14:51 and sprinkle the ***h*** seven times.
14:52 And he shall cleanse the ***h*** with
14:53 and make atonement for the ***h***,
14:55 leprosy of a garment and of a ***h***,
16: 6 for himself and for his ***h***.
16:11 for himself and for his ***h***,
17: 3 Whatever man of the ***h*** of Israel
17: 8 Whatever man of the ***h*** of Israel,
17:10 man of the ***h*** of Israel,
22:11 and one who is born in his ***h***
22:13 has returned to her father's ***h***
22:18 Whatever man of the ***h*** of Israel,
25:29 If a man sells a ***h*** in a walled
25:30 then the ***h*** in the walled city
25:33 And if a man purchases a ***h*** from
25:33 then the ***h*** that was sold in the
27:14 when a man dedicates his ***h*** to
27:15 it wants to redeem his ***h***,
Num 1: 4 one the head of his father's ***h***.
1:20 families, by their fathers' ***h***,
1:22 families, by their fathers' ***h***,
1:24 families, by their fathers' ***h***,
1:26 families, by their fathers' ***h***,
1:28 families, by their fathers' ***h***,
1:30 families, by their fathers' ***h***,
1:32 families, by their fathers' ***h***,
1:34 families, by their fathers' ***h***,
1:36 families, by their fathers' ***h***,
1:38 families, by their fathers' ***h***,
1:40 families, by their fathers' ***h***,
1:42 families, by their fathers' ***h***,
1:44 one representing his father's ***h***.
2: 2 the emblems of his father's ***h***;
3:24 the leader of the fathers' ***h***
3:30 the leader of the fathers' ***h***
3:35 ***h*** of the families of Merari
4: 2 families, by their fathers' ***h***,
4:22 of Gershon, by their fathers' ***h***,
4:29 and by their fathers' ***h***.
4:34 and by their fathers' ***h***,
4:38 and by their fathers' ***h***,
4:40 families, by their fathers' ***h***,
4:42 families, by their fathers' ***h***,
12: 7 He is faithful in all My ***h***.
17: 2 them a rod from each father's ***h***,
17: 3 the head of each father's ***h***.
17: 8 of the ***h*** of Levi, had sprouted
18: 1 your sons and your father's ***h***
18:11 who is clean in your ***h*** may eat
18:13 who is clean in your ***h*** may eat
20:29 all the ***h*** of Israel mourned for
22:18 Balak were to give me his ***h***
24:13 'If Balak were to give me his ***h***
25:14 a leader of a father's ***h*** among
25:15 of the people of a father's ***h***
30: 3 while in her father's ***h*** in her
30:10 she vowed in her husband's ***h***,
30:16 in her youth in her father's ***h***.
34:14 to the ***h*** of their fathers,
34:14 of Gad according to the ***h*** of
Deut 5: 6 out of the ***h*** of bondage.
5:21 not desire your neighbor's ***h***,
6: 7 of them when you sit in your ***h***,
6: 9 on the doorposts of your ***h*** and
6:12 from the ***h*** of bondage.
7: 8 you from the ***h*** of bondage,
7:26 an abomination into your ***h***,
8:14 from the ***h*** of bondage;
11:19 of them when you sit in your ***h***,
11:20 on the doorposts of your ***h*** and
13: 5 you from the ***h*** of bondage,
13:10 from the ***h*** of bondage.
15:16 because he loves you and your ***h***,
20: 5 there who has built a new ***h***
20: 5 Let him go and return to his ***h***,
20: 6 Let him go and return to his ***h***,
20: 7 Let him go and return to his ***h***,
20: 8 Let him go and return to his ***h***,
21:12 shall bring her home to your ***h***,
21:13 her captivity, remain in your ***h***,
22: 2 shall bring it to your own ***h***,
22: 8 "When you build a new ***h***,
22:21 to the door of her father's ***h***,
22:21 the harlot in her father's ***h***.
23:18 or the price of a dog to the ***h***
24: 1 and sends her out of his ***h***,
24: 2 she has departed from his ***h***,
24: 3 and sends her out of his ***h***,
24:10 you shall not go into his ***h*** to
25: 9 not build up his brother's ***h***.
25:10 The ***h*** of him who had his sandal
25:14 You shall not have in your ***h***
26:11 God has given to you and your ***h***,
26:13 the holy tithe from my ***h***,
28:30 with her; you shall build a ***h***,
Josh 2: 1 and came to the ***h*** of a harlot
2: 3 to you, who have entered your ***h***,
2:12 show kindness to my father's ***h***,
2:15 for her ***h*** was on the city
2:19 outside the doors of your ***h***
2:19 whoever is with you in the ***h***,
6:17 all who are with her in the ***h***,
6:22 "Go into the harlot's ***h***,
6:24 put into the treasury of the ***h***
9:23 and water carriers for the ***h***
17:17 to the ***h*** of Joseph—to
18: 5 and the ***h*** of Joseph shall
20: 6 to his own city and his own ***h***,
21:45 the LORD had spoken to the ***h***
22:14 the chief ***h*** of every tribe
22:14 head of the ***h*** of his father
24:15 But as for me and my ***h***,
24:17 from the ***h*** of bondage, who did
Judg 1:22 And the ***h*** of Joseph also went
1:23 So the ***h*** of Joseph sent men to
1:35 yet when the strength of the ***h***
4:17 Jabin king of Hazor and the ***h***
6: 8 and brought you out of the ***h***
6:15 am the least in my father's ***h***.
8:27 a snare to Gideon and to his ***h***.
8:29 went and dwelt in his own ***h***.
8:35 to the ***h*** of Jerubbaal
9: 1 with all the family of the ***h***
9: 5 Then he went to his father's ***h***
9:16 well with Jerubbaal and his ***h***,
9:18 risen up against my father's ***h***
9:19 with Jerubbaal and with his ***h***
9:27 into the ***h*** of their god,
10: 9 and against the ***h*** of Ephraim,
11: 2 inheritance in our father's ***h***,
11: 7 and expel me from my father's ***h***?
11:31 comes out of the doors of my ***h***
11:34 When Jephthah came to his ***h*** at
12: 1 We will burn your ***h*** down on you
14:15 burn you and your father's ***h***
14:19 went back up to his father's ***h***.
17: 4 were in the ***h*** of Micah.
17: 8 to the ***h*** of Micah, as he
17:12 and lived in the ***h*** of Micah.
18: 2 to the ***h*** of Micah, and lodged
18: 3 were at the ***h*** of Micah,
18:13 and came to the ***h*** of Micah.
18:15 and came to the ***h*** of the young
18:15 to the ***h*** of Micah—and greeted
18:18 When these went into Micah's ***h***
18:22 way from the ***h*** of Micah,
18:22 in the houses near Micah's ***h***
18:26 turned and went back to his ***h***.
18:31 all the time that the ***h*** of God
19: 2 from him to her father's ***h*** at
19: 3 brought him into her father's ***h***;
19:15 would take them into his ***h*** to
19:18 going to the ***h*** of the LORD.
19:18 one who will take me into his ***h***,
19:21 So he brought him into his ***h***,
19:22 surrounded the ***h*** and beat on
19:22 spoke to the master of the ***h***,
19:22 out the man who came to your ***h***,
19:23 the man, the master of the ***h***,
19:23 this man has come into my ***h***,
19:26 down at the door of the man's ***h***
19:27 and opened the doors of the ***h***
19:27 fallen at the door of the ***h***
19:29 When he entered his ***h*** he took a
20: 5 and surrounded the ***h*** at night
20: 8 nor will any turn back to his ***h***;
20:18 and went up to the ***h*** of God
20:26 up and came to the ***h*** of God
21: 2 people came to the ***h*** of God,
Ruth 1: 8 return each to her mother's ***h***.
1: 9 each in the ***h*** of her husband."
2: 7 she rested a little in the ***h***.
4:11 woman who is coming to your ***h***
4:11 who built the ***h*** of Israel;
4:12 ***h*** be like the house of Perez,
4:12 house be like the ***h*** of Perez,
1 Sam 1: 7 went up to the ***h*** of the LORD,
1:19 returned and came to their ***h***
1:21 the man Elkanah and all his ***h***
1:24 and brought him to the ***h*** of the
2:11 Then Elkanah went to his ***h*** at
2:27 clearly reveal Myself to the ***h***
2:27 were in Egypt in Pharaoh's ***h***?
2:28 give to the ***h*** of your father
2:30 I said indeed that your ***h*** and
2:30 and the ***h*** of your father
2:31 and the arm of your father's ***h***,
2:31 not be an old man in your ***h***.
2:32 not be an old man in your ***h***
2:33 all the descendants of your ***h***
2:35 I will build him a sure ***h***,
2:36 everyone who is left in your ***h***
3:12 I have spoken concerning his ***h***,
3:13 him that I will judge his ***h***
3:14 I have sworn to the ***h*** of Eli
3:14 that the iniquity of Eli's ***h***
3:15 and opened the doors of the ***h***
5: 5 nor any who come into Dagon's ***h***
7: 1 it into the ***h*** of Abinadab
7: 2 And all the ***h*** of Israel
7: 3 Then Samuel spoke to all the ***h***
9:18 tell me, where is the seer's ***h***?
9:20 you and on all your father's ***h***?
9:25 with Saul on the top of the ***h***.
9:26 to Saul on the top of the ***h***,
10:25 people away, every man to his ***h***.
15:34 and Saul went up to his ***h*** at
17:25 and give his father's ***h***
18: 2 him go home to his father's ***h***
18:10 and he prophesied inside the ***h***.
19: 9 upon Saul as he sat in his ***h***
19:11 sent messengers to David's ***h***
20:15 cut off your kindness from my ***h***
20:16 made a covenant with the ***h***
21:15 this fellow come into my ***h***?
22: 1 and all his father's ***h*** heard
22:11 Ahitub, and all his father's ***h***,
22:14 and is honorable in your ***h***?
22:15 or to any in the ***h*** of my
22:16 you and all your father's ***h***!"
22:22 the persons of your father's ***h***.
23:18 and Jonathan went to his own ***h***.
24:21 my name from my father's ***h***.
25: 3 was of the ***h*** of Caleb.
25: 6 be to you, peace to your ***h***,
25:28 make for my lord an enduring ***h***,
25:35 her, "Go up in peace to your ***h***.
25:36 was, holding a feast in his ***h***,
28:24 had a fatted calf in the ***h***,
2 Sam 1:12 and for the ***h*** of Israel,
2: 4 anointed David king over the ***h***
2: 7 and also the ***h*** of Judah has
2:10 Only the ***h*** of Judah followed
2:11 was king in Hebron over the ***h***
3: 1 was a long war between the ***h***
3: 1 of Saul and the ***h*** of David.
3: 1 and the ***h*** of Saul grew weaker
3: 6 war between the ***h*** of Saul
3: 6 of Saul and the ***h*** of David,
3: 6 his hold on the ***h*** of Saul.
3: 8 Today I show loyalty to the ***h***
3:10 the kingdom from the ***h*** of Saul,
3:19 good to Israel and the whole ***h***
3:29 Joab and on all his father's ***h***;
3:29 fail to be in the ***h*** of Joab
4: 5 the heat of the day to the ***h***
4: 6 there, all the way into the ***h***,
4: 7 For when they came into the ***h***,
4:11 a righteous person in his own ***h***
5: 8 lame shall not come into the ***h***.
5:11 And they built David a ***h***.
6: 3 it out of the ***h*** of Abinadab,
6: 4 they brought it out of the ***h***
6: 5 and all the ***h*** of Israel
6:10 David took it aside into the ***h***
6:11 of the LORD remained in the ***h***
6:12 blessed the ***h*** of Obed-Edom
6:12 up the ark of God from the ***h***
6:15 So David and all the ***h*** of Israel
6:19 departed, everyone to his ***h***.
6:21 of your father and all his ***h***,
7: 1 the king was dwelling in his ***h***,
7: 2 I dwell in a ***h*** of cedar, but
7: 5 Would you build a ***h*** for Me to
7: 6 For I have not dwelt in a ***h***
7: 7 built Me a ***h*** of cedar?'
7:11 you that He will make you a ***h***.
7:13 He shall build a ***h*** for My name,
7:16 And your ***h*** and your kingdom
7:18 O Lord GOD? And what is my ***h***,
7:19 spoken of Your servant's ***h*** for
7:25 servant and concerning his ***h***,
7:26 And let the ***h*** of Your servant
7:27 saying, 'I will build you a ***h***.
7:29 it please You to bless the ***h***
7:29 with Your blessing let the ***h***
9: 1 left of the ***h*** of Saul,
9: 2 there was a servant of the ***h***
9: 3 someone of the ***h*** of Saul,
9: 4 Indeed he is in the ***h*** of Machir
9: 5 and brought him out of the ***h***
9: 9 to Saul and to all his ***h***.
9:12 who dwelt in the ***h*** of Ziba
11: 2 on the roof of the king's ***h***.
11: 4 and she returned to her ***h***.
11: 8 Go down to your ***h*** and wash your
11: 8 departed from the king's ***h***,
11: 9 at the door of the king's ***h***
11: 9 and did not go down to his ***h***.
11:10 did not go down to his ***h***,
11:10 did you not go down to your ***h***?
11:11 Shall I then go to my ***h*** to eat
11:13 but he did not go down to his ***h***.
11:27 sent and brought her to his ***h***,
12: 8 I gave you your master's ***h*** and
12: 8 and gave you the ***h*** of Israel
12:10 shall never depart from your ***h***,
12:11 against you from your own ***h***;

12:15 Then Nathan departed to his *h*.
12:17 So the elders of his *h* arose
12:20 into the *h* of the LORD
12:20 Then he went to his own *h*;
13: 7 go to your brother Amnon's *h*,
13: 8 went to her brother Amnon's *h*;
13:20 in her brother Absalom's *h*.
14: 8 to the woman, "Go to your *h*,
14: 9 be on me and on my father's *h*,
14:24 "Let him return to his own *h*,
14:24 Absalom returned to his own *h*,
14:31 arose and came to Absalom's *h*,
15:16 concubines, to keep the *h*.
15:35 you hear from the king's *h*,
16: 3 Today the *h* of Israel will
16: 5 a man from the family of the *h*
16: 8 the blood of the *h* of Saul,
16:21 whom he has left to keep the *h*;
16:22 for Absalom on the top of the *h*,
17:18 quickly and came to a man's *h*
17:20 came to the woman at the *h*,
17:23 arose and went home to his *h*,
19: 5 came into the *h* to the king,
19:11 to bring the king back to his *h*,
19:11 to the king, to his very *h*?
19:17 and Ziba the servant of the *h*
19:20 today of all the *h* of Joseph
19:28 For all my father's *h* were but
19:30 come back in peace to his own *h*.
20: 3 Now David came to his *h* at
20: 3 whom he had left to keep the *h*,
21: 1 of Saul and his bloodthirsty *h*,
21: 4 or gold from Saul or from his *h*,
23: 5 Although my *h* is not so with
24:17 me and against my father's *h*.
1 Ki 1:53 said to him, "Go to your *h*.
2:24 and who has established a *h* for
2:27 concerning the *h* of Eli
2:31 and from the *h* of my father
2:33 upon his *h* and his throne,
2:34 and he was buried in his own *h*
2:36 Build yourself a *h* in Jerusalem
3: 1 had finished building his own *h*,
3: 1 and the *h* of the LORD, and the
3: 2 because there was no *h* built
3:17 woman and I dwell in the same *h*;
3:17 birth while she was in the *h*.
3:18 no one was with us in the *h*,
3:18 except the two of us in the *h*.
5: 3 David could not build a *h* for
5: 5 I propose to build a *h* for the
5: 5 he shall build the *h* for My
6: 1 to build the *h* of the LORD.
6: 2 Now the *h* which King Solomon
6: 3 of the sanctuary of the *h* was
6: 3 long across the width of the *h*,
6: 3 cubits from the front of the *h*.
6: 4 And he made for the *h* windows
6:37 year the foundation of the *h*
6:38 the *h* was finished in all its
7: 1 years to build his own *h*;
7: 1 so he finished all his *h*.
7: 2 *H* of the Forest of Lebanon;
7: 8 And the *h* where he dwelt had
7: 8 Solomon also made a *h* like this
7:12 were the inner court of the *h*
7:39 on the right side of the *h*,
7:39 five on the left side of the *h*.
7:39 Sea on the right side of the *h*,
7:40 do for King Solomon for the *h*
7:45 for the *h* of the LORD
7:48 the furnishings made for the *h*
7:51 done for the *h* of the LORD
7:51 of the *h* of the LORD.
8:10 filled the *h* of the LORD,
8:11 filled the *h* of the LORD.
8:13 surely built You an exalted *h*,
8:16 Israel in which to build a *h*,
8:63 dedicated the *h* of the LORD.
8:64 front of the *h* of the LORD;
9: 1 building the *h* of the LORD
9: 1 of the LORD and the king's *h*,
9: 3 I have consecrated this *h* which
9: 7 and this *h* which I have
9: 8 "And as for this *h*,
9: 8 thus to this land and to this *h*?
9:10 the *h* of the LORD and the
9:10 of the LORD and the king's *h*
9:15 to build the *h* of the LORD,
9:15 house of the LORD, his own *h*,
9:24 from the City of David to her *h*
10: 4 the *h* that he had built,
10: 5 by which he went up to the *h*
10:12 wood for the *h* of the LORD
10:12 the LORD and for the king's *h*,
10:17 *H* of the Forest of Lebanon.
10:21 *H* of the Forest of Lebanon
11:18 king of Egypt, who gave him a *h*,
11:20 Tahpenes weaned in Pharaoh's *h*.
11:28 all the labor force of the *h*
11:38 and build for you an enduring *h*,
12:16 Now, see to your own *h*,
12:19 against the *h* of David
12:20 who followed the *h* of David,
12:21 he assembled all the *h* of Judah
12:21 against the *h* of Israel,
12:23 to all the *h* of Judah and
12:24 Let every man return to his *h*,
12:26 may return to the *h* of David:
12:27 up to offer sacrifices in the *h*
13: 2 born to the *h* of David;
13: 8 you were to give me half your *h*,
13:18 him back with you to your *h*,
13:19 him, and ate bread in his *h*,
13:34 the sin of the *h* of Jeroboam,
14: 4 and came to the *h* of Ahijah.
14: 8 away from the *h* of David,
14:10 I will bring disaster on the *h*
14:10 take away the remnant of the *h*
14:12 therefore, go to your own *h*.
14:13 LORD God of Israel in the *h*
14:14 Israel who shall cut off the *h*
14:17 came to the threshold of the *h*,
14:26 of the *h* of the LORD
14:26 the treasures of the king's *h*;
14:27 the doorway of the king's *h*.
14:28 entered the *h* of the LORD,
15:15 into the *h* of the LORD
15:18 of the *h* of the LORD
15:18 the treasuries of the king's *h*,
15:27 of the *h* of Issachar, conspired
15:29 all the *h* of Jeroboam.
16: 3 and the posterity of his *h*,
16: 3 and I will make your *h* like the
16: 3 like the *h* of Jeroboam
16: 7 Hanani against Baasha and his *h*,
16: 7 like the *h* of Jeroboam,
16: 9 himself drunk in the *h* of Arza,
16: 9 steward of his *h* in Tirzah.
16:18 the citadel of the king's *h*
16:18 house and burned the king's *h*
17:17 of the woman who owned the *h*
17:23 from the upper room into the *h*,
18: 3 who was in charge of his *h*.
18:18 but you and your father's *h*
20: 6 and they shall search your *h*
20:31 heard that the kings of the *h*
20:43 king of Israel went to his *h*
21: 2 it is near, next to my *h*;
21: 4 So Ahab went into his *h* sullen
21:22 *h* like the house of Jeroboam
21:22 make your house like the *h* of
21:22 and like the *h* of Baasha the
21:29 bring the calamity on his *h*.
22:17 Let each return to his *h* in
22:39 the ivory *h* which he built and
2 Ki 4: 2 me, what do you have in the *h*?
4: 2 has nothing in the *h* but a jar
4:32 When Elisha came into the *h*,
4:35 walked back and forth in the *h*,
5: 9 stood at the door of Elisha's *h*.
5:24 and stored them away in the *h*;
6:32 But Elisha was sitting in his *h*,
8: 3 an appeal to the king for her *h*
8: 5 to the king for her *h* and for
8:18 just as the *h* of Ahab had done,
8:27 he walked in the way of the *h*
8:27 like the *h* of Ahab, for he was
8:27 he was the son-in-law of the *h*
9: 6 he arose and went into the *h*.
9: 7 strike down the *h* of Ahab
9: 8 For the whole *h* of Ahab shall
9: 9 So I will make the *h* of Ahab
9: 9 the house of Ahab like the *h*
9: 9 and like the *h* of Baasha the
10: 3 and fight for your master's *h*.
10: 5 he who was in charge of the *h*,
10:10 LORD spoke concerning the *h*
10:11 remained of the *h* of Ahab
10:30 and have done to the *h* of Ahab
11: 3 he was hidden with her in the *h*
11: 4 them into the *h* of the LORD
11: 4 them in the *h* of the LORD,
11: 5 keeping watch over the king's *h*,
11: 6 shall keep the watch of the *h*,
11: 7 shall keep the watch of the *h*
11:11 temple, by the altar and the *h*.
11:15 not let her be killed in the *h*
11:16 entrance into the king's *h*,
11:18 appointed officers over the *h*
11:19 down from the *h* of the LORD,
11:19 of the escorts to the king's *h*.
11:20 with the sword in the king's *h*.
12: 4 into the *h* of the LORD—EACH
12: 4 his heart to bring into the *h*
12: 9 side as one comes into the *h*
12: 9 the money brought into the *h*
12:10 money that was found in the *h*
12:11 who had the oversight of the *h*
12:11 builders who worked on the *h*
12:12 to repair the damage of the *h*
12:13 there were not made for the *h*
12:13 the money brought into the *h*
12:14 and they repaired the *h* of the
12:16 was not brought into the *h* of
12:18 in the treasuries of the *h* of
12:18 the LORD and in the king's *h*,
12:20 and killed Joash in the *h* of
13: 6 depart from the sins of the *h*
14:14 that were found in the *h* of
14:14 the treasuries of the king's *h*,
15: 5 so he dwelt in an isolated *h*.
15: 5 son was over the royal *h*,
15:25 in the citadel of the king's *h*,
15:35 built the Upper Gate of the *h*
16: 8 gold that was found in the *h*
16: 8 the treasuries of the king's *h*,
16:14 the new altar and the *h* of
16:18 outer entrance from the *h* of
17:21 For He tore Israel from the *h* of
18:15 silver that was found in the *h*
18:15 the treasuries of the king's *h*.
19: 1 went into the *h* of the LORD.
19:14 and Hezekiah went up to the *h*
19:30 escaped of the *h* of Judah
20: 1 Set your *h* in order, for you
20: 5 day you shall go up to the *h*
20: 8 go up to the *h* of the LORD
20:13 all the *h* of his treasures—the
20:13 There was nothing in his *h* or
20:15 "What have they seen in your *h*?
20:15 have seen all that is in my *h*;
20:17 when all that is in your *h*,
21: 4 altars in the *h* of the LORD,
21: 5 courts of the *h* of the LORD.
21: 7 in the *h* of which the LORD had
21: 7 In this *h* and in Jerusalem,
21:13 plummet of the *h* of Ahab;
21:18 in the garden of his own *h*,
21:23 killed the king in his own *h*.
22: 3 to the *h* of the LORD, saying:
22: 4 has been brought into the *h* of
22: 5 who are the overseers in the *h*
22: 5 it to those who are in the *h*
22: 5 to repair the damages of the *h*—
22: 6 and hewn stone to repair the *h*.
22: 8 the Book of the Law in the *h*
22: 9 money that was found in the *h*,
22: 9 who oversee the *h* of the
23: 2 The king went up to the *h* of
23: 2 which had been found in the *h*
23: 6 the wooden image from the *h* of
23: 7 persons that were in the *h* of
23:11 at the entrance to the *h* of
23:12 in the two courts of the *h* of
23:24 the priest found in the *h* of
23:27 and the *h* of which I said, 'My
24:13 all the treasures of the *h* of
24:13 the treasures of the king's *h*,
25: 9 He burned the *h* of the LORD and
25: 9 of the LORD and the king's *h*;
25:13 pillars that were in the *h* of
25:13 bronze Sea that were in the *h*
25:16 Solomon had made for the *h* of
1 Chr 2:55 the father of the *h* of Rechab.
4:21 and the families of the *h* of
4:21 of the linen workers of the *h*
4:38 and their father's *h* increased
5:13 brethren of their father's *h*:
5:15 was chief of their father's *h*.
6:31 the service of song in the *h*
6:32 until Solomon had built the *h*
6:48 of the tabernacle of the *h* of
7: 2 heads of their father's *h*.
7:23 tragedy had come upon his *h*.
9: 9 were heads of a father's *h*
9:11 the officer over the *h* of God;
9:13 work of the service of the *h*
9:19 brethren, from his father's *h*,
9:23 in charge of the gates of the *h*
9:23 the *h* of the tabernacle, by
9:26 and treasuries of the *h* of God.
9:27 they lodged all around the *h*
10: 6 and all his *h* died together.
12:28 and from his father's *h*
12:29 had remained loyal to the *h* of
12:30 men throughout their father's *h*;
13: 7 of God on a new cart from the *h*
13:13 but took it aside into the *h* of
13:14 family of Obed-Edom in his *h*
13:14 And the LORD blessed the *h* of
14: 1 carpenters, to build him a *h*.
15:25 of the LORD from the *h* of
16:43 departed, every man to his *h*;
16:43 David returned to bless his *h*.
17: 1 David was dwelling in his *h*,
17: 1 I dwell in a *h* of cedar, but
17: 4 You shall not build Me a *h* to
17: 5 For I have not dwelt in a *h*
17: 6 'Why have you not built Me a *h* of
17:10 the LORD will build you a *h*.
17:12 "He shall build Me a *h*,
17:14 I will establish him in My *h*
17:16 O LORD God? And what is my *h*,
17:17 spoken of Your servant's *h* for
17:23 servant and concerning his *h*,
17:24 And let the *h* of Your servant
17:25 that You will build him a *h*.
17:27 been pleased to bless the *h* of
21:17 be against me and my father's *h*,
22: 1 This is the *h* of the LORD God,
22: 2 cut hewn stones to build the *h*
22: 5 and the *h* to be built for the
22: 6 and charged him to build a *h*
22: 7 it was in my mind to build a *h*
22: 8 you shall not build a *h* for My
22:10 He shall build a *h* for My name,
22:11 and build the *h* of the LORD
22:14 trouble to prepare for the *h*
22:19 holy articles of God into the *h*
23: 4 to look after the work of the *h*
23:11 were assigned as one father's *h*.
23:24 work for the service of the *h*
23:28 Aaron in the service of the *h*
23:28 work of the service of the *h*
23:32 brethren in the work of the *h*
24: 5 and officials of the *h* of
24: 6 one father's *h* taken for
24:19 service for coming into the *h*
25: 6 father for the music in the *h*
25: 6 for the service of the *h* of
26:12 to serve in the *h* of the LORD.
26:13 according to their father's *h*.
26:20 over the treasuries of the *h*
26:22 over the treasuries of the *h*
26:27 dedicated to maintain the *h* of

28: 2 it in my heart to build a ***h*** of
28: 3 You shall not build a ***h*** for My
28: 4 chose me above all the ***h*** of my
28: 4 and of the ***h*** of Judah, the
28: 4 the ***h*** of my father, and among
28: 6 Solomon who shall build My ***h***
28:10 has chosen you to build a ***h***
28:12 of the courts of the ***h*** of the
28:12 of the treasuries of the ***h*** of
28:13 work of the service of the ***h***
28:13 articles of service in the ***h***
28:20 work for the service of the ***h***
28:21 for all the service of the ***h***
29: 2 Now for the ***h*** of my God I have
29: 3 have set my affection on the ***h***
29: 3 I have given to the ***h*** of my
29: 3 I have prepared for the holy ***h***,
29: 7 gave for the work of the ***h*** of
29: 8 them to the treasury of the ***h***
29:16 have prepared to build You a ***h***
2 Chr 2: 1 and a royal ***h*** for himself.
2: 3 cedars to build himself a ***h*** to
2:12 for the LORD and a royal ***h***
3: 1 Solomon began to build the ***h***
3: 3 laid for building the ***h*** of God:
3: 4 long across the width of the ***h***,
3: 6 And he decorated the ***h*** with
3: 7 He also overlaid the ***h***—
3: 8 according to the width of the ***h***,
4:11 do for King Solomon for the ***h***
4:16 for King Solomon for the ***h*** of
4:19 the furnishings made for the ***h***
5: 1 Solomon had done for the ***h*** of
5: 1 in the treasuries of the ***h*** of
5:13 endures forever," that the ***h***,
5:13 the ***h*** of the LORD, was filled
5:14 of the LORD filled the ***h*** of
6: 2 surely built You an exalted ***h***,
6: 5 Israel in which to build a ***h***,
7: 2 priests could not enter the ***h***
7: 2 LORD had filled the LORD's ***h***.
7: 5 all the people dedicated the ***h***
7: 7 that was in front of the ***h*** of
7:11 Thus Solomon finished the ***h*** of
7:11 of the LORD and the king's ***h***;
7:11 his heart to make in the ***h*** of
7:11 of the LORD and in his own ***h***.
7:12 this place for Myself as a ***h***
7:16 chosen and sanctified this ***h***,
7:20 and this ***h*** which I have
7:21 "And as for this ***h***,
7:21 thus to this land and this ***h***?
8: 1 which Solomon had built the ***h***
8: 1 of the LORD and his own ***h***,
8:11 the City of David to the ***h*** he
8:11 wife shall not dwell in the ***h***
8:16 day of the foundation of the ***h***
8:16 So the ***h*** of the LORD was
9: 3 the ***h*** that he had built,
9: 4 by which he went up to the ***h***
9:11 of the algum wood for the ***h***
9:11 the LORD and for the king's ***h***,
9:16 The king put them in the ***H*** of
9:20 and all the vessels of the ***H*** of
10:16 Now see to your own ***h***,
10:19 in rebellion against the ***h*** of
11: 1 he assembled from the ***h*** of
11: 4 Let every man return to his ***h***,
12: 9 away the treasures of the ***h*** of
12: 9 the treasures of the king's ***h***;
12:10 the doorway of the king's ***h***.
12:11 the king entered the ***h*** of
15:18 He also brought into the ***h*** of
16: 2 from the treasuries of the ***h***
16: 2 the LORD and of the king's ***h***,
18:16 Let each return to his ***h*** in
19: 1 Judah returned safely to his ***h***
19:11 the ruler of the ***h*** of Judah,
20: 5 in the ***h*** of the LORD, before
20:28 to the ***h*** of the LORD.
21: 6 just as the ***h*** of Ahab had done,
21: 7 LORD would not destroy the ***h***
21:13 like the harlotry of the ***h*** of
21:17 that were found in the king's ***h***,
22: 3 walked in the ways of the ***h*** of
22: 4 like the ***h*** of Ahab; for they
22: 7 had anointed to cut off the ***h***
22: 8 executing judgment on the ***h*** of
22: 9 So the ***h*** of Ahaziah had no
22:10 all the royal heirs of the ***h***
22:12 was hidden with them in the ***h***
23: 3 with the king in the ***h*** of God.
23: 5 be at the king's ***h***;
23: 5 be in the courts of the ***h*** of
23: 6 let no one come into the ***h***
23: 7 and whoever comes into the ***h***,
23:14 Do not kill her in the ***h*** of the
23:15 Horse Gate into the king's ***h***,
23:18 the oversight of the ***h*** of the
23:18 David had assigned in the ***h*** of
23:19 at the gates of the ***h*** of the
23:20 the king down from the ***h*** of
23:20 the Upper Gate to the king's ***h***,
24: 4 his heart on repairing the ***h***
24: 5 Israel money to repair the ***h***
24: 7 had broken into the ***h*** of God,
24: 7 the dedicated things of the ***h***
24: 8 it outside at the gate of the ***h***
24:12 work of the service of the ***h*** of
24:12 and carpenters to repair the ***h*** of
24:12 and bronze to restore the ***h*** of
24:13 they restored the ***h*** of God to
24:14 from it articles for the ***h*** of
24:14 burnt offerings in the ***h*** of
24:16 both toward God and His ***h***.
24:18 Therefore they left the ***h*** of
24:21 stones in the court of the ***h***
24:27 and the repairing of the ***h*** of
25:24 that were found in the ***h*** of
25:24 the treasures of the king's ***h***,
26:19 before the priests in the ***h*** of
26:21 He dwelt in an isolated ***h***,
26:21 for he was cut off from the ***h***
26:21 his son was over the king's ***h***,
27: 3 built the Upper Gate of the ***h***
28: 7 Azrikam the officer over the ***h***,
28:21 of the treasures from the ***h***
28:21 from the ***h*** of the king, and
28:24 gathered the articles of the ***h***
28:24 in pieces the articles of the ***h***
28:24 shut up the doors of the ***h*** of
29: 3 he opened the doors of the ***h*** of
29: 5 sanctify the ***h*** of the LORD God
29:15 to cleanse the ***h*** of the LORD.
29:16 into the inner part of the ***h***
29:16 LORD to the court of the ***h*** of
29:17 Then they sanctified the ***h*** of
29:18 'We have cleansed all the ***h*** of
29:20 and went up to the ***h*** of the
29:25 stationed the Levites in the ***h***
29:31 and thank offerings into the ***h***
29:35 So the service of the ***h*** of the
30: 1 that they should come to the ***h***
30:15 the burnt offerings to the ***h***
31:10 from the ***h*** of Zadok, answered
31:10 bring the offerings into the ***h***
31:11 to prepare rooms in the ***h*** of
31:13 and Azariah the ruler of the ***h***
31:16 to everyone who entered the ***h***
31:17 according to their father's ***h***,
31:21 began in the service of the ***h***
33: 4 He also built altars in the ***h*** of
33: 5 in the two courts of the ***h*** of
33: 7 in the ***h*** of God, of which God
33: 7 In this ***h*** and in Jerusalem,
33:15 gods and the idol from the ***h***
33:15 built in the mount of the ***h*** of
33:20 they buried him in his own ***h***.
33:24 and killed him in his own ***h***.
34: 8 to repair the ***h*** of the LORD
34: 9 that was brought into the ***h*** of
34:10 who had the oversight of the ***h***
34:10 workmen who worked in the ***h*** of
34:10 to repair and restore the ***h***.
34:14 that was brought into the ***h*** of
34:15 the Book of the Law in the ***h***
34:17 money that was found in the ***h***
34:30 The king went up to the ***h*** of
34:30 which had been found in the ***h***
35: 2 them for the service of the ***h***
35: 3 Put the holy ark in the ***h*** which
35: 5 the division of the father's ***h***
35: 8 rulers of the ***h*** of God, gave to
35:21 but against the ***h*** with which I
36: 7 of the articles from the ***h*** of
36:10 the costly articles from the ***h***
36:14 and defiled the ***h*** of the LORD
36:17 men with the sword in the ***h*** of
36:18 all the articles from the ***h*** of
36:18 the treasures of the ***h*** of
36:19 Then they burned the ***h*** of God,
36:23 commanded me to build Him a ***h***
Ezra 1: 2 commanded me to build Him a ***h***
1: 3 and build the ***h*** of the LORD
1: 4 freewill offerings for the ***h***
1: 5 arose to go up and build the ***h***
1: 7 out the articles of the ***h*** of
2:36 of the ***h*** of Jeshua, nine
2:59 not identify their father's ***h***
2:68 when they came to the ***h*** of
2:68 offered freely for the ***h*** of
3: 8 year of their coming to the ***h***
3: 8 to oversee the work of the ***h***
3: 9 oversee those working on the ***h***
3:11 the foundation of the ***h*** of
4: 3 do nothing with us to build a ***h***
4:24 Thus the work of the ***h*** of God
5: 2 up and began to build the ***h*** of
5:13 a decree to build this ***h*** of
5:14 and silver articles of the ***h***
5:15 and let the ***h*** of God be rebuilt
5:16 laid the foundation of the ***h***
5:17 made in the king's treasure ***h***,
5:17 by King Cyrus to build this ***h***
6: 3 a decree concerning the ***h*** of
6: 3 Let the ***h*** be rebuilt, the place
6: 5 and silver articles of the ***h*** of
6: 5 and deposit them in the ***h*** of
6: 7 Let the work of this ***h*** of God
6: 7 of the Jews build this ***h*** of
6: 8 for the building of this ***h*** of
6:11 a timber be pulled from his ***h***
6:11 and let his ***h*** be made a refuse
6:12 or to destroy this ***h*** of God
6:16 the dedication of this ***h*** of
6:17 at the dedication of this ***h*** of
6:22 hands in the work of the ***h*** of
7:16 be freely offered for the ***h***
7:17 them on the altar of the ***h*** of
7:19 to you for the service of the ***h***
7:20 more may be needed for the ***h***
7:23 it diligently be done for the ***h***
7:24 or servants of this ***h*** of God.
7:27 to beautify the ***h*** of the LORD
8:17 bring us servants for the ***h*** of
8:25 the offering for the ***h*** of our
8:29 in the chambers of the ***h*** of
8:30 them to Jerusalem to the ***h*** of
8:33 articles were weighed in the ***h***
8:36 to the people and the ***h*** of God.
9: 9 to repair the ***h*** of our God, to
10: 1 and bowing down before the ***h*** of
10: 6 Ezra rose up from before the ***h***
10: 9 in the open square of the ***h*** of
Neh 1: 6 Both my father's ***h*** and I have
2: 8 and for the ***h*** that I will
3:10 made repairs in front of his ***h***.
3:16 and as far as the ***H*** of
3:20 buttress to the door of the ***h***
3:21 from the door of the ***h*** of
3:21 of Eliashib to the end of the ***h***
3:23 made repairs opposite their ***h***.
3:23 Ananiah, made repairs by his ***h***.
3:24 from the ***h*** of Azariah to the
3:25 from the king's upper ***h*** that
3:28 each in front of his own ***h***.
3:29 repairs in front of his own ***h***.
3:31 made repairs as far as the ***h*** of
4:16 leaders were behind all the ***h***
5:13 shake out each man from his ***h***,
6:10 Afterward I came to the ***h*** of
6:10 'Let us meet together in the ***h*** of
7: 3 another in front of his own ***h***.
7:39 of the ***h*** of Jeshua, nine
7:61 not identify their father's ***h***
8:16 each one on the roof of his ***h***,
8:16 or the courts of the ***h*** of God,
10:32 for the service of the ***h*** of
10:33 and all the work of the ***h*** of
10:34 the wood offering into the ***h***
10:35 to the ***h*** of the LORD;
10:36 to the ***h*** of our God, to the
10:36 priests who minister in the ***h***
10:37 to the storerooms of the ***h*** of
10:38 a tenth of the tithes to the ***h***
10:39 and we will not neglect the ***h***
11:11 was the leader of the ***h*** of
11:12 who did the work of the ***h***
11:16 the business outside of the ***h***
11:22 charge of the service of the ***h***
12:29 from the ***h*** of Gilgal, and from
12:37 beyond the ***h*** of David, as far
12:40 choirs stood in the ***h*** of God,
13: 4 over the storerooms of the ***h***
13: 7 for him in the courts of the ***h***
13: 9 them the articles of the ***h*** of
13:11 Why is the ***h*** of God forsaken?"
13:14 that I have done for the ***h*** of
Esth 1:22 should be master in his own ***h***,
2: 9 to the best place in the ***h*** of
2:14 she returned to the second ***h***
4:14 but you and your father's ***h***
5: 1 across from the king's ***h***,
5: 1 his royal throne in the royal ***h***,
5: 1 facing the entrance of the ***h***.
6:12 But Haman hurried to his ***h***,
7: 8 the queen while I am in the ***h***?
7: 9 is standing at the ***h*** of
8: 1 gave Queen Esther the ***h*** of
8: 2 appointed Mordecai over the ***h***
8: 7 I have given Esther the ***h*** of
Job 1:13 in their oldest brother's ***h***;
1:18 in their oldest brother's ***h***,
1:19 the four corners of the ***h***,
7:10 He shall never return to his ***h***,
8:15 He leans on his ***h***,
17:13 I wait for the grave as my ***h***,
19:15 Those who dwell in my ***h***,
20:19 He has violently seized a ***h***
20:28 The increase of his ***h*** will
21:28 Where is the ***h*** of the prince?
27:18 He builds his ***h*** like a moth,
30:23 And to the ***h*** appointed for
42:11 and ate food with him in his ***h***;
Ps 5: 7 I will come into Your ***h*** in the
23: 6 And I will dwell in the ***h*** of
26: 8 loved the habitation of Your ***h***,
27: 4 That I may dwell in the ***h*** of
30: at the dedication of the ***h*** of
36: 8 with the fullness of Your ***h***,
42: 4 I went with them to the ***h*** of
45:10 also, and your father's ***h***;
49:16 When the glory of his ***h*** is
50: 9 not take a bull from your ***h***,
52: David has gone to the ***h*** of
52: 8 a green olive tree in the ***h*** of
55:14 And walked to the ***h*** of God in
59: and they watched the the ***h*** in
65: 4 with the goodness of Your ***h***,
66:13 I will go into Your ***h*** with
69: 9 Because zeal for Your ***h*** has
84: 4 are those who dwell in Your ***h***;
84:10 be a doorkeeper in the ***h*** of
92:13 who are planted in the ***h*** of
93: 5 sure; Holiness adorns Your ***h***,
98: 3 and His faithfulness to the ***h***
101: 2 I will walk within my ***h*** with a
101: 7 shall not dwell within my ***h***;
105:21 He made him lord of his ***h***,
112: 3 and riches will be in his ***h***,
114: 1 The ***h*** of Jacob from a people
115:10 O ***h*** of Aaron, trust in the
115:12 He will bless the ***h*** of Israel;
115:12 He will bless the ***h*** of Aaron.
116:19 In the courts of the LORD's ***h***,
118: 3 Let the ***h*** of Aaron now say,

118:26 have blessed you from the **h** of
119:54 have been my songs In the **h**
122: 1 Let us go into the **h** of the
122: 5 The thrones of the **h** of David.
122: 9 Because of the **h** of the LORD
127: 1 Unless the LORD builds the **h**,
128: 3 In the very heart of your **h**,
132: 3 not go into the chamber of my **h**,
134: 1 Who by night stand in the **h** of
135: 2 You who stand in the **h** of
135: 2 In the courts of the **h** of
135:19 O **h** of Israel! Bless the
135:19 Bless the LORD, O **h** of Aaron!
135:20 O **h** of Levi! You who fear the
Prov 2:18 For her **h** leads down to death,
3:33 of the LORD is on the **h** of
5: 8 not go near the door of her **h**,
5:10 And your labors go to the **h**
6:31 up all the substance of his **h**.
7: 6 For at the window of my **h** I
7: 8 And he took the path to her **h**
7:27 Her **h** is the way to hell,
9: 1 Wisdom has built her **h**,
9:14 she sits at the door of her **h**,
11:29 He who troubles his own **h** will
12: 7 But the **h** of the righteous
14: 1 The wise woman builds her **h**,
14:11 The **h** of the wicked will be
15: 6 In the **h** of the righteous
15:25 The LORD will destroy the **h** of
15:27 for gain troubles his own **h**,
17: 1 Than a **h** full of feasting
17:13 will not depart from his **h**.
21: 9 Than in a **h** shared with a
21:12 God wisely considers the **h** of
24: 3 Through wisdom a **h** is built,
24:27 And afterward build your **h**.
25:17 set foot in your neighbor's **h**,
25:24 Than in a **h** shared with a
27:10 Nor go to your brother's **h** in
Eccl 2: 7 and had servants born in my **h**.
5: 1 prudently when you go to the **h**
7: 2 Better to go to the **h** of
7: 2 mourning Than to go to the **h**
7: 4 heart of the wise is in the **h**
7: 4 heart of fools is in the **h** of
10:18 idleness of hands the **h** leaks.
12: 3 day when the keepers of the **h**
Song 2: 4 brought me to the banqueting **h**,
3: 4 I had brought him to the **h** of
8: 2 you and bring you Into the **h**
8: 7 love All the wealth of his **h**,
Isa 2: 2 the mountain of the LORD's **h**
2: 3 To the **h** of the God of Jacob;
2: 5 O **h** of Jacob, come and let us
2: 6 the **h** of Jacob, Because they
3: 6 hold of his brother In the **h**
3: 7 For in my **h** is neither food
5: 7 of the LORD of hosts is the **h**
5: 8 Woe to those who join **h** to
5: 8 to those who join house to **h**;
6: 4 and the **h** was filled with
7: 2 And it was told to the **h** of
7:13 O **h** of David! Is it a small
7:17 your people and your father's **h**—
8:17 Who hides His face from the **h**
10:20 such as have escaped of the **h**
14: 1 and they will cling to the **h** of
14: 2 and the **h** of Israel will
14:17 Who did not open the **h** of his
14:18 glory, Everyone in his own **h**;
22: 8 that day to the armor of the **H**
22:15 To Shebna, who is over the **h**,
22:18 the shame of your master's **h**.
22:21 of Jerusalem And to the **h** of
22:22 The key of the **h** of David I
22:23 throne to his father's **h**.
22:24 all the glory of his father's **h**,
23: 1 waste, So that there is no **h**,
24:10 Every **h** is shut up, so that
29:22 concerning the **h** of Jacob:
31: 2 But will arise against the **h**
37: 1 and went into the **h** of
37:14 and Hezekiah went up to the **h**
37:31 who have escaped of the **h** of
37:38 as he was worshiping in the **h**
38: 1 Set your **h** in order, for you
38:20 in the **h** of the LORD."
38:22 that I shall go up to the **h** of
39: 2 and showed them the **h** of his
39: 2 There was nothing in his **h** or
39: 4 "What have they seen in your **h**?
39: 4 have seen all that is in my **h**;
39: 6 when all that is in your **h**,
42: 7 in darkness from the prison **h**.
44:13 that it may remain in the **h**.
46: 3 O **h** of Jacob, And all the
46: 3 And all the remnant of the **h**
48: 1 O **h** of Jacob, Who are called
56: 5 to them I will give in My **h**
56: 7 And make them joyful in My **h**
56: 7 For My **h** shall be called a
56: 7 My house shall be called a **h**
58: 1 And the **h** of Jacob their sins.
58: 7 And that you bring to your **h**
60: 7 And I will glorify the **h** of My
63: 7 great goodness toward the **h** of
66: 1 Where is the **h** that you will
66:20 in a clean vessel into the **h**
Jer 2: 4 O **h** of Jacob and all the
2: 4 and all the families of the **h**
2:26 So is the **h** of Israel ashamed;
3:18 In those days the **h** of Judah
3:18 of Judah shall walk with the **h**
3:20 O **h** of Israel," says the
5:11 For the **h** of Israel and the
5:11 the house of Israel and the **h**
5:15 O **h** of Israel," says the
5:20 Declare this in the **h** of Jacob
7: 2 in the gate of the LORD's **h**,
7:10 and stand before Me in this **h**
7:11 'Has this **h**, which is called
7:14 therefore I will do to the **h**
7:30 set their abominations in the **h**
9:26 and all the **h** of Israel are
10: 1 to you, O **h** of Israel.
11:10 the **h** of Israel and the house
11:10 the house of Israel and the **h**
11:15 has My beloved to do in My **h**,
11:17 you for the evil of the **h** of
11:17 house of Israel and of the **h**
12: 6 the **h** of your father, Even
12: 7 "I have forsaken My **h**,
12:14 their land and pluck out the **h**
13:11 so I have caused the whole **h** of
13:11 of Israel and the whole **h** of
16: 5 Do not enter the **h** of mourning,
16: 8 you shall not go into the **h** of
17:26 sacrifices of praise to the **h**
18: 2 and go down to the potter's **h**,
18: 3 I went down to the potter's **h**,
18: 6 O **h** of Israel, can I not do with
18: 6 My hand, O **h** of Israel!
19:14 in the court of the Lord's **h**
20: 1 also chief governor in the **h**
20: 2 which was by the **h** of
20: 6 and all who dwell in your **h**,
21:11 And concerning the **h** of the
21:12 O **h** of David! Thus says the
22: 1 'Go down to the **h** of the king
22: 4 shall enter the gates of this **h**,
22: 5 that this **h** shall become a
22: 6 thus says the LORD to the **h**
22:13 Woe to him who builds his **h** by
22:14 I will build myself a wide **h**
23: 8 led the descendants of the **h**
23:11 in My **h** I have found their
23:34 even punish that man and his **h**.
26: 2 in the court of the LORD's **h**,
26: 2 to worship in the LORD's **h**,
26: 6 then I will make this **h** like
26: 7 speaking these words in the **h**
26: 9 This **h** shall be like Shiloh, and
26: 9 against Jeremiah in the **h** of
26:10 they came up from the king's **h**
26:10 from the king's house to the **h**
26:10 the New Gate of the LORD's **h**.
26:12 me to prophesy against this **h**
27:16 the vessels of the LORD's **h**
27:18 which are left in the **h** of
27:18 in the **h** of the king of Judah,
27:21 vessels that remain in the **h**
27:21 and in the **h** of the king
28: 1 spoke to me in the **h** of
28: 3 the vessels of the LORD's **h**,
28: 5 the people who stood in the **h**
28: 6 the vessels of the LORD's **h**
29:26 should be officers in the **h**
31:27 that I will sow the **h** of Israel
31:27 the house of Israel and the **h**
31:31 make a new covenant with the **h**
31:31 house of Israel and with the **h**
31:33 that I will make with the **h** of
32: 2 was in the king of Judah's **h**.
32:34 set their abominations in the **h**
33:11 sacrifice of praise into the **h**
33:14 which I have promised to the **h**
33:14 house of Israel and to the **h**
33:17 to sit on the throne of the **h**
34:13 out of the **h** of bondage,
34:15 a covenant before Me in the **h**
35: 2 Go to the **h** of the Rechabites,
35: 2 and bring them into the **h** of
35: 3 and the whole **h** of the
35: 4 and I brought them into the **h** of
35: 5 I set before the sons of the **h**
35: 7 'You shall not build a **h**,
35:18 And Jeremiah said to the **h** of
36: 3 It may be that the **h** of Judah
36: 5 I cannot go into the **h** of the
36: 6 of the people in the LORD's **h**
36: 8 of the LORD in the LORD's **h**.
36:10 the words of Jeremiah in the **h**
36:10 the New Gate of the LORD's **h**,
36:12 then went down to the king's **h**,
36:22 was sitting in the winter **h** in
37:15 and put him in prison in the **h**
37:17 asked him secretly in his **h**,
37:20 do not make me return to the **h**
38: 7 who was in the king's **h**,
38: 8 went out of the king's **h** and
38:11 with him and went into the **h**
38:14 at the third entrance of the **h**
38:17 and you and your **h** shall live.
38:22 left in the king of Judah's **h**
38:26 make me return to Jonathan's **h**
39: 8 Chaldeans burned the king's **h**
41: 5 to bring them to the **h** of the
43: 9 at the entrance to Pharaoh's **h**
48:13 As the **h** of Israel was ashamed
51:51 sanctuaries of the LORD's **h**.
52:13 He burned the **h** of the LORD and
52:13 of the LORD and the king's **h**;
52:17 pillars that were in the **h** of
52:17 bronze Sea that were in the **h**
52:20 Solomon had made for the **h** of
Lam 2: 7 have made a noise in the **h** of
Ezek 2: 5 they are a rebellious **h**—
2: 6 though they are a rebellious **h**.
2: 8 like that rebellious **h**;
3: 1 speak to the **h** of Israel."
3: 4 go to the **h** of Israel and speak
3: 5 but to the **h** of Israel,
3: 7 But the **h** of Israel will not
3: 7 for all the **h** of Israel are
3: 9 though they are a rebellious **h**.
3:17 made you a watchman for the **h**
3:24 shut yourself inside your **h**.
3:26 for they are a rebellious **h**.
3:27 for they are a rebellious **h**.
4: 3 This will be a sign to the **h**
4: 4 and lay the iniquity of the **h**
4: 5 bear the iniquity of the **h** of
4: 6 bear the iniquity of the **h** of
5: 4 will go out into all the **h** of
6:11 the evil abominations of the **h**
8: 1 as I sat in my **h** with the
8: 6 great abominations that the **h**
8:10 and all the idols of the **h** of
8:11 men of the elders of the **h** of
8:12 seen what the elders of the **h**
8:14 the north gate of the LORD's **h**;
8:16 inner court of the LORD's **h**;
8:17 Is it a trivial thing to the **h**
9: 9 The iniquity of the **h** of Israel
10: 4 and the **h** was filled with the
10:19 the east gate of the LORD's **h**,
11: 1 the East Gate of the LORD's **h**,
11: 5 O **h** of Israel; for I know the
11:15 and all the **h** of Israel in its
12: 2 in the midst of a rebellious **h**,
12: 2 for they are a rebellious **h**.
12: 3 though they are a rebellious **h**.
12: 6 I have made you a sign to the **h**
12: 9 has not the **h** of Israel, the
12: 9 of Israel, the rebellious **h**,
12:10 in Jerusalem and all the **h** of
12:24 divination within the **h** of
12:25 in your days, O rebellious **h**,
12:27 the **h** of Israel is saying, 'The
13: 5 gaps to build a wall for the **h**
13: 9 written in the record of the **h**
14: 4 Everyone of the **h** of Israel who
14: 5 that I may seize the **h** of Israel
14: 6 Therefore say to the **h** of
14: 7 For anyone of the **h** of Israel,
14:11 that the **h** of Israel may no
17: 2 and speak a parable to the **h** of
17:12 "Say now to the rebellious **h**:
18: 6 his eyes to the idols of the **h**
18:15 his eyes to the idols of the **h**
18:25 O **h** of Israel, is it not My way
18:29 Yet the **h** of Israel says, 'The
18:29 O **h** of Israel, is it not My
18:30 O **h** of Israel, every one
18:31 you die, O **h** of Israel?
20: 5 to the descendants of the **h** of
20:13 Yet the **h** of Israel rebelled
20:27 speak to the **h** of Israel, and
20:30 Therefore say to the **h** of
20:31 O **h** of Israel? As I live,"
20:39 O **h** of Israel," thus says the
20:40 there all the **h** of Israel, all
20:44 O **h** of Israel," says the Lord
22:18 the **h** of Israel has become
23:39 have done in the midst of My **h**.
24: 3 a parable to the rebellious **h**,
24:21 Speak to the **h** of Israel, "Thus
25: 3 and against the **h** of Judah when
25: 8 Look! The **h** of Judah is like
25:12 of what Edom did against the **h**
27:14 Those from the **h** of Togarmah
28:24 or a painful thorn for the **h**
28:25 'When I have gathered the **h** of
29: 6 been a staff of reed to the **h**
29:16 it be the confidence of the **h**
29:21 I will cause the horn of the **h**
33: 7 made you a watchman for the **h**
33:10 say to the **h** of Israel: 'Thus
33:11 you die, O **h** of Israel?'
33:20 O **h** of Israel, I will judge
34:30 the **h** of Israel, are My
35:15 the inheritance of the **h** of
36:10 all the **h** of Israel, all of it;
36:17 when the **h** of Israel dwelt in
36:21 which the **h** of Israel had
36:22 Therefore say to the **h** of
36:22 O **h** of Israel, but for My holy
36:32 own ways, O **h** of Israel!"
36:37 I will also let the **h** of Israel
37:11 these bones are the whole **h** of
37:16 and for all the **h** of Israel,
38: 6 the **h** of Togarmah from the far
39:12 For seven months the **h** of Israel
39:22 So the **h** of Israel shall know
39:23 Gentiles shall know that the **h**
39:25 and have mercy on the whole **h**
39:29 poured out My Spirit on the **h**
40: 4 Declare to the **h** of Israel
43: 7 No more shall the **h** of Israel
43:10 describe the temple to the **h** of
44: 4 of the LORD filled the **h** of
44: 5 all the ordinances of the **h** of
44: 5 Mark well who may enter the **h**
44: 6 to the **h** of Israel, 'Thus says
44: 6 O **h** of Israel, let us have no

44: 7 My sanctuary to defile it—My **h**—
44:11 as gatekeepers of the **h** and
44:11 house and ministers of the **h**;
44:12 their idols and caused the **h**
44:17 the inner court or within the **h**.
44:22 of the descendants of the **h** of
44:30 a blessing to rest on your **h**.
45: 6 it shall belong to the whole **h**
45: 8 rest of the land to the **h** of
45:17 the appointed seasons of the **h**
45:17 to make atonement for the **h** of
Dan 1: 2 some of the articles of the **h**
1: 2 the land of Shinar to the **h** of
1: 2 articles into the treasure **h**
2:17 Then Daniel went to his **h**,
4: 4 was at rest in my **h**,
5: 3 taken from the temple of the **h**
5:23 brought the vessels of His **h**
Hos 1: 4 bloodshed of Jezreel on the **h**
1: 4 an end to the kingdom of the **h**
1: 6 no longer have mercy on the **h** of
1: 7 I will have mercy on the **h** of
5: 1 O **h** of Israel! Give ear, O
5: 1 O **h** of the king! For yours is
5:12 And to the **h** of Judah like
5:14 like a young lion to the **h** of
6:10 seen a horrible thing in the **h**
8: 1 like an eagle against the **h** of
9: 4 It shall not come into the **h**
9: 8 Enmity in the **h** of his God.
9:15 I will drive them from My **h**;
11:12 And the **h** of Israel with
Joel 1: 9 Have been cut off from the **h**
1:13 Are withheld from the **h** of
1:14 of the land Into the **h** of
1:16 Joy and gladness from the **h** of
3:18 fountain shall flow from the **h**
Am 1: 4 I will send a fire into the **h**
2: 8 of the condemned in the **h** of
3:13 and testify against the **h** of
3:15 I will destroy the winter **h**
3:15 house along with the summer **h**;
5: 1 lamentation, O **h** of Israel:
5: 3 Shall have ten left to the **h**
5: 4 thus says the LORD to the **h**
5: 6 break out like fire in the **h**
5:19 as though he went into the **h**,
5:25 forty years, O **h** of Israel?
6: 1 To whom the **h** of Israel comes!
6: 9 that if ten men remain in one **h**,
6:10 to take them out of the **h**,
6:10 he will say to one inside the **h**,
6:11 He will break the great **h** into
6:11 And the little **h** into pieces.
6:14 O **h** of Israel," Says the
7: 9 with the sword against the **h**
7:10 you in the midst of the **h** of
7:16 do not spout against the **h** of
9: 8 will not utterly destroy the **h**
9: 9 And will sift the **h** of Israel
Ob 17 The **h** of Jacob shall possess
18 The **h** of Jacob shall be a fire,
18 And the **h** of Joseph a flame;
18 But the **h** of Esau shall be
18 shall remain of the **h** of Esau,
Mic 1: 5 And for the sins of the **h** of
2: 2 they oppress a man and his **h**,
2: 7 You who are named the **h** of
3: 1 And you rulers of the **h** of
3: 9 You heads of the **h** of Jacob
3: 9 of Jacob And rulers of the **h** of
4: 1 the mountain of the LORD's **h**
4: 2 To the **h** of the God of Jacob;
6: 4 I redeemed you from the **h** of
6:10 of wickedness In the **h** of
6:16 All the works of Ahab's **h** are
Nah 1:14 Out of the **h** of your gods I
Hab 2: 9 who covets evil gain for his **h**,
2:10 give shameful counsel to your **h**,
3:13 struck the head from the **h** of
Zeph 2: 7 be for the remnant of the **h** of
Hag 1: 2 the time that the LORD's **h**
1: 9 Because of My **h** that is in
1: 9 one of you runs to his own **h**.
1:14 they came and worked on the **h**
Zech 1:16 My **h** shall be built in it,"
3: 7 Then you shall also judge My **h**,
5: 4 'It shall enter the **h** of
5: 4 house of the thief And the **h**
5: 4 remain in the midst of his **h**
5:11 To build a **h** for it in the land
6:10 go the same day and enter the **h**
7: 2 to the **h** of God, to pray
7: 3 the priests who were in the **h**
8: 9 foundation was laid For the **h**
8:13 O **h** of Judah and house
8:13 O house of Judah and **h** of
8:15 To Jerusalem and to the **h** of
8:19 and cheerful feasts For the **h**
9: 8 I will camp around My **h**
10: 3 The **h** of Judah, And will make
10: 6 'I will strengthen the **h** of
10: 6 And I will save the **h** of
11:13 and threw them into the **h** of
12: 4 I will open My eyes on the **h** of
12: 7 so that the glory of the **h** of
12: 8 and the **h** of David shall be
12:10 And I will pour on the **h** of
12:12 the family of the **h** of David by
12:12 the family of the **h** of Nathan
12:13 the family of the **h** of Levi by
13: 1 shall be opened for the **h** of
13: 6 which I was wounded in the **h**
14:20 The pots in the LORD's **h** shall
14:21 longer be a Canaanite in the **h**
Mal 3:10 That there may be food in My **h**,
Mt 2:11 when they had come into the **h**,
5:15 light to all who are in the **h**.
7:24 to a wise man who built his **h**
7:25 winds blew and beat on that **h**;
7:26 a foolish man who built his **h**
7:27 winds blew and beat on that **h**;
8:14 Jesus had come into Peter's **h**,
9: 6 up your bed, and go to your **h**.
9: 7 he arose and departed to his **h**.
9:10 Jesus sat at the table in the **h**,
9:23 Jesus came into the ruler's **h**,
9:28 And when He had come into the **h**,
10: 6 to the lost sheep of the **h** of
10:14 when you depart from that **h** or
10:25 have called the master of the **h**
12: 4 how he entered the **h** of God and
12:25 and every city or **h** divided
12:29 can one enter a strong man's **h**
12:29 And then he will plunder his **h**.
12:44 I will return to my **h** from which
13: 1 day Jesus went out of the **h**
13:36 away and went into the **h**.
13:57 own country and in his own **h**.
15:24 to the lost sheep of the **h** of
17:25 And when he had come into the **h**,
21:13 My **h** shall be called a
21:13 shall be called a **h** of
23:38 See! Your **h** is left to you
24:17 to take anything out of his **h**.
24:43 that if the master of the **h** had
24:43 watched and not allowed his **h**
26: 6 Jesus was in Bethany at the **h**
26:18 keep the Passover at your **h**
Mk 1:29 they entered the **h** of Simon and
2: 1 was heard that He was in the **h**.
2:11 up your bed, and go to your **h**.
2:15 as He was dining in Levi's **h**,
2:26 how he went into the **h** of God
3:19 And they went into a **h**.
3:25 And if a **h** is divided against
3:25 that **h** cannot stand.
3:27 one can enter a strong man's **h**
3:27 And then he will plunder his **h**.
5:35 the ruler of the synagogue's **h**
5:38 Then He came to the **h** of
6: 4 own relatives, and in his own **h**.
6:10 whatever place you enter a **h**,
7:17 When He had entered a **h** away
7:24 And He entered a **h** and wanted
7:30 And when she had come to her **h**,
8:26 Then He sent him away to his **h**,
9:28 And when He had come into the **h**,
9:33 And when He was in the **h** He
10:10 In the **h** His disciples also
10:29 there is no one who has left **h**
11:17 My **h** shall be called a
11:17 shall be called a **h** of
13:15 housetop not go down into the **h**,
13:15 to take anything out of his **h**.
13:34 who left his **h** and gave
13:35 know when the master of the **h**
14: 3 And being in Bethany at the **h**
14:14 in, say to the master of the **h**,
Lk 1:23 that he departed to his own **h**.
1:27 of the **h** of David. The virgin's
1:33 'And He will reign over the **h** of
1:40 and entered the **h** of Zacharias
1:56 months, and returned to her **h**.
1:69 of salvation for us In the **h**
2: 4 because he was of the **h** and
4:38 synagogue and entered Simon's **h**.
5:24 up your bed, and go to your **h**.
5:25 on, and departed to his own **h**,
5:29 Him a great feast in his own **h**.
6: 4 how he went into the **h** of God,
6:48 "He is like a man building a **h**,
6:48 beat vehemently against that **h**,
6:49 is like a man who built a **h** on
6:49 And the ruin of that **h** was
7: 6 was already not far from the **h**,
7:10 were sent, returning to the **h**,
7:36 And He went to the Pharisee's **h**,
7:37 the table in the Pharisee's **h**,
7:44 this woman? I entered your **h**;
8:27 nor did he live in a **h** but in
8:39 "Return to your own **h**,
8:41 and begged Him to come to his **h**,
8:49 the ruler of the synagogue's **h**,
8:51 When He came into the **h**,
9: 4 Whatever **h** you enter, stay
9:61 them farewell who are at my **h**.
10: 5 But whatever **h** you enter, first
10: 5 first say, 'Peace to this **h**.
10: 7 "And remain in the same **h**,
10: 7 Do not go from **h** to house.
10: 7 Do not go from house to **h**.
10:38 Martha welcomed Him into her **h**.
11:17 and a **h** divided against a
11:17 a house divided against a **h**
11:24 I will return to my **h** from which
12:39 that if the master of the **h** had
12:39 watched and not allowed his **h**
12:52 For from now on five in one **h**
13:25 When once the Master of the **h**
13:35 See! Your **h** is left to you
14: 1 as He went into the **h** of one
14:21 Then the master of the **h**,
14:23 that my **h** may be filled.
15: 8 not light a lamp, sweep the **h**,
15:25 he came and drew near to the **h**,
16:27 would send him to my father's **h**,
17:31 and his goods are in the **h**,
18:14 this man went down to his **h**
18:29 there is no one who has left **h**
19: 5 for today I must stay at your **h**.
19: 9 salvation has come to this **h**,
19:46 'My **h** is a house
19:46 'My house is a **h** of
22:10 follow him into the **h** which he
22:11 say to the master of the **h**,
22:54 Him into the high priest's **h**.
Jn 2:16 Do not make My Father's **h** a
2:16 not make My Father's house a **h**
2:17 Zeal for Your **h** has eaten
7:53 everyone went to his own **h**.
8:35 a slave does not abide in the **h**
11:20 but Mary was sitting in the **h**.
11:31 Jews who were with her in the **h**,
12: 3 And the **h** was filled with the
14: 2 In My Father's **h** are many
Acts 2: 2 and it filled the whole **h** where
2:36 'Therefore let all the **h** of
2:46 and breaking bread from **h** to
2:46 breaking bread from house to **h**,
5:42 in the temple, and in every **h**,
7:10 over Egypt and all his **h**.
7:20 brought up in his father's **h**
7:42 O **h** of Israel?
7:47 "But Solomon built Him a **h**.
7:49 What **h** will you build
8: 3 of the church, entering every **h**,
9:11 and inquire at the **h** of Judas
9:17 went his way and entered the **h**;
10: 6 whose **h** is by the sea. He will
10:17 had made inquiry for Simon's **h**,
10:22 angel to summon you to his **h**,
10:30 the ninth hour I prayed in my **h**,
10:32 He is lodging in the **h** of
11:11 three men stood before the **h**
11:12 me, and we entered the man's **h**.
11:13 seen an angel standing in his **h**,
12:12 he came to the **h** of Mary, the
16:15 come to my **h** and stay." So she
16:32 and to all who were in his **h**.
16:34 he had brought them into his **h**,
16:40 the prison and entered the **h**
17: 5 in an uproar and attacked the **h**
18: 7 from there and entered the **h**
18: 7 whose **h** was next door to the
19:16 so that they fled out of that **h**
20:20 taught you publicly and from **h**
20:20 publicly and from house to **h**,
21: 8 and entered the **h** of Philip the
28:30 whole years in his own rented **h**,
Rom 16: 5 the church that is in their **h**.
1 Cor 16:19 the church that is in their **h**.
2 Cor 5: 1 we know that if our earthly **h**,
5: 1 a **h** not made with hands,
Col 4:15 the church that is in his **h**.
1 Tim 3: 4 one who rules his own **h** well,
3: 5 not know how to rule his own **h**,
3:15 to conduct yourself in the **h**
5:13 wandering about from **h** to
5:13 wandering about from house to **h**,
5:14 bear children, manage the **h**,
2 Tim 2:20 But in a great **h** there are not
Phm 1: 2 and to the church in your **h**:
Heb 3: 2 was faithful in all His **h**.
3: 3 inasmuch as He who built the **h**
3: 3 house has more honor than the **h**.
3: 4 For every **h** is built by someone,
3: 5 was faithful in all His **h** as
3: 6 Christ as a Son over His own **h**,
3: 6 whose **h** we are if we hold fast
8: 8 a new covenant with the **h**
8: 8 of Israel and with the **h**
8:10 I will make with the **h**
10:21 a High Priest over the **h** of
1 Pe 2: 5 being built up a spiritual **h**,
4:17 for judgment to begin at the **h**
2 Jn 10 do not receive him into your **h**

HOUSEHOLD (104/103) HOUSE, HOUSEHOLDER, HOUSEHOLDS

Gen 7: 1 the ark, you and all your **h**,
18:19 command his children and his **h**
24:28 ran and told her mother's **h**
31:19 and Rachel had stolen the **h**
31:34 Now Rachel had taken the **h**
31:35 but did not find the **h** idols.
31:37 what part of your **h** things have
34:19 more honorable than all the **h**
34:30 be destroyed, my **h** and I."
35: 2 And Jacob said to his **h** and to
36: 6 and all the persons of his **h**,
45:11 for you, lest you and your **h**,
46:31 brothers and to his father's **h**,
47:12 and all his father's **h** with
50: 4 Joseph spoke to the **h** of
50:22 in Egypt, he and his father's **h**.
Ex 1: 1 each man and his **h** came with
12: 3 of his father, a lamb for a **h**.
12: 4 And if the **h** is too small for
Lev 16:17 for himself, for his **h**,
Deut 6:22 Egypt, Pharaoh, and all his **h**.
14:26 shall rejoice, you and your **h**.
15:20 You and your **h** shall eat it
22: 8 guilt of bloodshed on your **h**

H

Josh 2:18 and all your father's **h** to your
6:25 the harlot, her father's **h**,
7:14 and the **h** which the LORD takes
7:18 Then he brought his **h** man by
Judg 6:27 he feared his father's **h** and
16:31 and all his father's **h** came
17: 5 and made an ephod and **h** idols;
18:14 **h** idols, a carved image, and a
18:17 the **h** idols, and the molded
18:18 the **h** idols, and the molded
18:19 you to be a priest to the **h** of
18:20 the **h** idols, and the carved
18:25 with the lives of your **h**!"
1 Sam 25:17 master and against all his **h**.
27: 3 his men, each man with his **h**,
2 Sam 2: 3 with him, every man with his **h**.
6:11 blessed Obed-Edom and all his **h**.
6:20 David returned to bless his **h**.
15:16 king went out with all his **h**
16: 2 donkeys are for the king's **h**
17:23 Then he put his **h** in order, and
19:18 to carry over the king's **h**,
19:41 and brought the king, his **h**,
1 Ki 4: 6 Ahishar, over the **h**;
4: 7 food for the king and his **h**;
5: 9 desire by giving food for my **h**.
5:11 of wheat as food for his **h**,
11:20 And Genubath was in Pharaoh's **h**
16:11 that he killed all the **h** of
16:12 Thus Zimri destroyed all the **h**
17:15 and she and he and her **h** ate
2 Ki 7: 9 let us go and tell the king's **h**.
7:11 they told it to the king's **h**
8: 1 "Arise and go, you and your **h**,
8: 2 and she went with her **h** and
18:18 of Hilkiah, who was over the **h**,
18:37 of Hilkiah, who was over the **h**,
19: 2 Eliakim, who was over the **h**,
23:24 the **h** gods and idols, all the
2 Chr 21:13 those of your father's **h**,
Neh 13: 8 therefore I threw all the **h**
Esth 1: 8 all the officers of his **h**,
Job 1: 3 donkeys, and a very large **h**,
1:10 hedge around him, around his **h**,
21:21 what does he care about his **h**
Prov 27:27 food, For the food of your **h**,
31:15 And provides food for her **h**,
31:21 is not afraid of snow for her **h**,
31:21 For all her **h** is clothed with
31:27 watches over the ways of her **h**,
Isa 36: 3 of Hilkiah, who was over the **h**,
36:22 of Hilkiah, who was over the **h**,
37: 2 Eliakim, who was over the **h**,
Mic 7: 6 are the men of his own **h**.
Mt 10:12 "And when you go into a **h**,
10:13 If the **h** is worthy, let your
10:25 they call those of his **h**!
10:36 be those of his own **h**.
24:45 master made ruler over his **h**,
Lk 12:42 will make ruler over his **h**,
Jn 4:53 believed, and his whole **h**.
Acts 10: 2 who feared God with all his **h**,
10: 7 Cornelius called two of his **h**
11:14 by which you and all your **h**
16:15 And when she and her **h** were
16:31 will be saved, you and your **h**.
16:34 believed in God with all his **h**.
18: 8 on the Lord with all his **h**.
Rom 16:10 Greet those who are of the **h**
16:11 Greet those who are of the **h**
1 Cor 1:11 by those of Chloe's **h**,
1:16 I also baptized the **h** of
16:15 you know the **h** of Stephanas,
Gal 6:10 to those who are of the **h** of
Eph 2:19 saints and members of the **h** of
Phil 4:22 those who are of Caesar's **h**.
1 Tim 5: 8 especially for those of his **h**,
2 Tim 1:16 The Lord grant mercy to the **h** of
4:19 and the **h** of Onesiphorus.
Heb 11: 7 an ark for the saving of his **h**,

HOUSEHOLDER (1/1) HOUSEHOLD

Mt 13:52 kingdom of heaven is like a **h**

HOUSEHOLDS (14/13) HOUSEHOLD

Gen 42:33 food for the famine of your **h**,
45:18 Bring your father and your **h** and
47:24 for those of your **h** and as food
Ex 1:21 that He provided **h** for them.
12:27 Egyptians and delivered our **h**.
Num 16:32 with their **h** and all the men
18:31 it in any place, you and your **h**,
Deut 11: 6 and swallowed them up, their **h**,
12: 7 put your hand, you and your **h**,
Josh 7:14 the LORD takes shall come by **h**;
Ezra 10:16 heads of the fathers' **h**,
10:16 set apart by the fathers' **h**,
2 Tim 3: 6 are those who creep into **h** and
Titus 1:11 be stopped, who subvert whole **h**,

HOUSES (187/172) HOUSE

Gen 34:29 even all that was in the **h**.
42:19 grain for the famine of your **h**.
Ex 6:14 the heads of their fathers' **h**:
6:25 the heads of the fathers' **h** of
8: 3 into the **h** of your servants, on
8: 9 the frogs from you and your **h**,
8:11 depart from you, from your **h**,
8:13 And the frogs died out of the **h**,
8:21 on your people and into your **h**.
8:21 The **h** of the Egyptians shall be
8:24 Pharaoh, into his servants' **h**,
9:20 and his livestock flee to the **h**.
10: 6 'They shall fill your **h**,
10: 6 the **h** of all your servants, and
10: 6 and the **h** of all the
12: 7 and on the lintel of the **h**
12:13 be a sign for you on the **h**
12:15 shall remove leaven from your **h**.
12:19 leaven shall be found in your **h**,
12:23 destroyer to come into your **h**
12:27 who passed over the **h** of the
Lev 25:31 However the **h** of villages which
25:32 and the **h** in the cities of
25:33 for the **h** in the cities
Num 1: 2 families, by their fathers' **h**,
1:18 families, by their fathers' **h**,
1:45 of Israel, by their fathers' **h**,
2:32 of Israel by their fathers' **h**.
2:34 according to their fathers' **h**.
3:15 of Levi by their fathers' **h**,
3:20 the Levites by their fathers' **h**.
4:46 and by their fathers' **h**,
7: 2 the heads of their fathers' **h**,
17: 2 according to their fathers' **h**—
17: 6 according to their fathers' **h**,
26: 2 and above, by their fathers' **h**,
Deut 6:11 **h** full of all good things, which
8:12 and have built beautiful **h** and
19: 1 in their cities and in their **h**,
Josh 9:12 for our provision from our **h**
21: 1 the heads of the fathers' **h**
21: 1 to the heads of the fathers' **h**
Judg 18:14 know that there are in these **h**
18:22 the men who were in the **h** near
1 Ki 9:10 Solomon had built the two **h**,
20: 6 search your house and the **h** of
2 Ki 25: 9 all the **h** of Jerusalem, that
25: 9 all the **h** of the great, he
1 Chr 5:24 the heads of their fathers' **h**:
5:24 and heads of their fathers' **h**.
7: 4 according to their fathers' **h**,
7: 7 heads of their fathers' **h**,
7: 9 heads of their fathers' **h**,
7:11 were heads of their fathers' **h**;
7:40 heads of their fathers' **h**,
8: 6 the heads of the fathers' **h**
8:10 heads of their fathers' **h**.
8:13 heads of their fathers' **h** of
8:28 were heads of the fathers' **h**
9: 9 house in their fathers' **h**.
9:13 heads of their fathers' **h**—
9:33 heads of the fathers' **h** of
9:34 These heads of the fathers' **h**
15: 1 David built **h** for himself in
15:12 the heads of the fathers' **h**
23: 9 the heads of the fathers' **h**
23:24 of Levi by their fathers' **h**—
23:24 the heads of the fathers' **h** as
24: 4 heads of their fathers' **h**,
24: 4 eight heads of their fathers' **h**
24: 6 the heads of the fathers' **h**
24:30 according to their fathers' **h**.
24:31 the heads of the fathers' **h**
26: 6 who governed their fathers' **h**,
26:21 heads of their fathers' **h**,
26:26 and the heads of fathers' **h**,
26:32 able men, heads of fathers' **h**,
27: 1 the heads of fathers' **h**,
28:11 plans for the vestibule, its **h**,
29: 4 to overlay the walls of the **h**;
29: 6 the leaders of the fathers' **h**,
2 Chr 1: 2 the heads of the fathers' **h**.
17:14 according to their fathers' **h**.
25: 5 according to their fathers' **h**,
34:11 and to floor the **h** which the
35: 4 according to your fathers' **h**,
35: 5 divisions of the fathers' **h** of
35:12 divisions of the fathers' **h** of
Ezra 1: 5 the heads of the fathers' **h**
2:68 of the heads of the fathers' **h**,
3:12 and heads of the fathers' **h**,
4: 2 the heads of the fathers' **h**,
4: 3 of the heads of the fathers' **h**
8: 1 the heads of their fathers' **h**,
8:29 and heads of the fathers' **h**
Neh 4:14 your wives, and your **h**.
5: 3 our lands and vineyards and **h**,
5:11 their olive groves, and their **h**,
7: 4 and the **h** were not rebuilt.
7:70 of the heads of the fathers' **h**
7:71 of the heads of the fathers' **h**
8:13 the heads of the fathers' **h**
9:25 And possessed **h** full of all
10:34 according to our fathers' **h**,
11:13 heads of the fathers' **h**,
12:12 the heads of the fathers' **h**
12:22 heads of their fathers' **h** in
12:23 the heads of the fathers' **h**
Job 1: 4 would go and feast in their **h**,
3:15 Who filled their **h** with
4:19 much more those who dwell in **h**
15:28 In **h** which no one inhabits,
21: 9 Their **h** are safe from fear,
22:18 Yet He filled their **h** with good
24:16 In the dark they break into **h**
Ps 49:11 inner thought is that their **h**
Prov 1:13 We shall fill our **h** with
19:14 **H** and riches are an
Eccl 2: 4 works great, I built myself **h**,
Song 1:17 The beams of our **h** are cedar,
Isa 3:14 of the poor is in your **h**.
5: 9 many **h** shall be desolate,
6:11 The **h** are without a man, The
8:14 rock of offense To both the **h**
13:16 Their **h** will be plundered And
13:21 And their **h** will be full of
15: 3 On the tops of their **h** And in
22:10 You numbered the **h** of
22:10 And the **h** you broke down To
42:22 they are hidden in prison **h**;
65:21 They shall build **h** and inhabit
Jer 5: 7 by troops in the harlots' **h**.
5:27 So their **h** are full of
6:12 And their **h** shall be turned
17:22 carry a burden out of your **h**
18:22 a cry be heard from their **h**,
19:13 And the **h** of Jerusalem and the
19:13 houses of Jerusalem and the **h**
19:13 because of all the **h** on whose
29: 5 Build **h** and dwell in them;
29:28 build **h** and dwell in them,
32:15 **H** and fields and vineyards shall
32:29 with the **h** on whose roofs they
33: 4 concerning the **h** of this city
33: 4 houses of this city and the **h**
35: 9 nor to build ourselves **h** to
39: 8 the king's house and the **h** of
43:12 'I will kindle a fire in the **h** of
43:13 and the **h** of the gods of the
52:13 all the **h** of Jerusalem, that
52:13 all the **h** of the great, he
Lam 5: 2 And our **h** to foreigners.
Ezek 7:24 And they will possess their **h**;
11: 3 time is not near to build **h**;
16:41 They shall burn your **h** with
23:47 and burn their **h** with fire.
26:12 and destroy your pleasant **h**;
28:26 dwell safely there, build **h**,
33:30 walls and in the doors of the **h**;
45: 4 it shall be a place for their **h**
Dan 2: 5 and your **h** shall be made an ash
3:29 and their **h** shall be made an
Hos 11:11 will let them dwell in their **h**,
Joel 2: 9 They climb into the **h**,
Am 3:15 The **h** of ivory shall perish,
3:15 And the great **h** shall have an
5:11 Though you have built **h** of
Mic 1:14 The **h** of Achzib shall be a
2: 2 take them by violence, Also **h**,
2: 9 cast out From their pleasant **h**;
Zeph 1: 9 Who fill their masters' **h** with
1:13 And their **h** a desolation;
1:13 desolation; They shall build **h**,
2: 7 In the **h** of Ashkelon they
Hag 1: 4 to dwell in your paneled **h**,
Zech 14: 2 The **h** rifled, And the women
Mt 11: 8 soft clothing are in kings' **h**.
19:29 And everyone who has left **h** or
23:14 For you devour widows' **h**,
Mk 8: 3 them away hungry to their own **h**,
10:30 **h** and brothers and sisters and
12:40 "who devour widows' **h**,
Lk 16: 4 may receive me into their **h**.
20:47 "who devour widows' **h**,
Acts 4:34 were possessors of lands or **h**
1 Cor 11:22 What! Do you not have **h** to eat
1 Tim 3:12 children and their own **h** well.

HOUSETOP (8/8) HOUSE, HOUSETOPS

Ps 102: 7 like a sparrow alone on the **h**.
Prov 21: 9 to dwell in a corner of a **h**,
25:24 to dwell in a corner of a **h**,
Mt 24:17 Let him who is on the **h** not go
Mk 13:15 Let him who is on the **h** not go
Lk 5:19 they went up on the **h** and let
17:31 that day, he who is on the **h**,
Acts 10: 9 Peter went up on the **h** to pray,

HOUSETOPS (8/8) HOUSETOP

2 Ki 19:26 As the grass on the **h** And
Ps 129: 6 them be as the grass on the **h**,
Isa 22: 1 you have all gone up to the **h**,
37:27 As the grass on the **h** And
Jer 48:38 lamentation On all the **h** of
Zeph 1: 5 the host of heaven on the **h**;
Mt 10:27 in the ear, preach on the **h**.
Lk 12: 3 will be proclaimed on the **h**.

HOVERING (1/1) HOVERS

Gen 1: 2 And the Spirit of God was **h**

HOVERS (1/1) HOVERING

Deut 32:11 **H** over its young, Spreading

HOW (522/472)

Gen 6:15 And this is **h** you shall make it:
15: 8 **h** shall I know that I will
20: 9 **H** have I offended you, that you
26: 9 so **h** could you say, 'She is my
27:20 **H** is it that you have found
28:17 '**H** awesome is this place!
30:29 You know **h** I have served you and
30:29 how I have served you and **h**
38:29 '**H** did you break through?
39: 9 **H** then can I do this great
44: 8 **H** then could we steal silver or
44:16 Or **h** shall we clear ourselves?

44:34 For ***h*** shall I go up to my father
47: 8 to Jacob, "***H*** old are you?"
Ex 2:18 ***H*** is it that you have come so
6:12 ***H*** then shall Pharaoh heed me,
6:30 and ***h*** shall Pharaoh heed me?"
10: 3 ***H*** long will you refuse to humble
10: 7 ***H*** long shall this man be a snare
16:28 ***H*** long do you refuse to keep My
18: 8 and ***h*** the LORD had delivered
19: 4 and ***h*** I bore you on eagles'
33:16 For ***h*** then will it be known that
36: 1 to know ***h*** to do all manner of
Num 10:31 inasmuch as you know ***h*** we are
14:11 ***H*** long will these people reject
14:11 And ***h*** long will they not
14:27 ***H*** long shall I bear with
20:15 ***h*** our fathers went down to
23: 8 ***H*** shall I curse whom God has not
23: 8 And ***h*** shall I denounce whom
24: 5 '***H*** lovely are your tents,
24:22 ***H*** long until Asshur carries
Deut 1:12 ***H*** can I alone bear your problems
1:31 the wilderness where you saw ***h***
7:17 ***h*** can I dispossess them?'—
9: 7 Do not forget ***h*** you provoked
11: 4 ***h*** He made the waters of the Red
11: 4 and ***h*** the LORD has destroyed
11: 6 ***h*** the earth opened its mouth
12:30 ***H*** did these nations serve their
18:21 ***H*** shall we know the word which
25:18 ***h*** he met you on the way and
31:27 then ***h*** much more after my
32:30 ***H*** could one chase a thousand,
Josh 2:10 For we have heard ***h*** the LORD
9: 7 so ***h*** can we make a covenant
10: 1 king of Jerusalem heard ***h***
10: 1 and ***h*** the inhabitants of Gibeon
14:12 for you heard in that day ***h*** the
18: 3 ***H*** long will you neglect to go
Judg 6:15 ***h*** can I save Israel? Indeed my
16:15 ***H*** can you say, 'I love you,'
18: 7 ***h*** they dwelt safely, in the
18:24 ***H*** can you say to me, 'What ails
20: 3 ***h*** did this wicked deed
Ruth 2:11 and ***h*** you have left your
3:18 until you know ***h*** the matter
1 Sam 1:14 '***H*** long will you be drunk?
2:22 and ***h*** they lay with the women
5: 7 when the men of Ashdod saw ***h***
6: 2 Tell us ***h*** we should send it to
10:27 '***H*** can this man save us?"
14:29 ***h*** my countenance has brightened
14:30 ***H*** much better if the people had
15: 2 ***h*** he ambushed him on the way
16: 1 ***H*** long will you mourn for Saul,
16: 2 ***H*** can I go? If Saul hears it,
17:18 and see ***h*** your brothers fare,
23: 3 ***H*** much more then if we go to
24:18 And you have shown this day ***h***
28: 9 ***h*** he has cut off the mediums
2 Sam 1: 4 ***H*** did the matter go? Please tell
1: 5 ***H*** do you know that Saul and
1:14 ***H*** was it you were not afraid to
1:19 ***H*** the mighty have fallen!
1:25 ***H*** the mighty have fallen in the
1:27 ***H*** the mighty have fallen, And
2:22 ***H*** then could I face your
2:26 ***H*** long will it be then until
4:11 ***H*** much more, when wicked men
6: 9 ***H*** can the ark of the LORD come
6:20 ***H*** glorious was the king of
11: 7 David asked ***h*** Joab was doing,
11: 7 and ***h*** the people were doing,
11: 7 and ***h*** the war prospered.
12:18 ***H*** can we tell him that the
16:11 See ***h*** my son who came from my
16:11 ***H*** much more now may this
18:19 ***h*** the LORD has avenged him of
19:34 ***H*** long have I to live, that I
1 Ki 3: 7 I do not know ***h*** to go out or
5: 3 You know ***h*** my father David could
8:27 ***H*** much less this temple which I
12: 6 ***H*** do you advise me to answer
12: 9 ***H*** should we answer this people
14:19 ***h*** he made war and how he
14:19 how he made war and ***h*** he
18: 9 ***H*** have I sinned, that you are
18:13 ***h*** I hid one hundred men of the
18:21 ***H*** long will you falter between
19: 1 also ***h*** he had executed all the
20: 7 and see ***h*** this man seeks
21:29 See ***h*** Ahab has humbled himself
22:16 ***H*** many times shall I make you
22:45 and ***h*** he made war, are they
2 Ki 5: 7 and see ***h*** he seeks a quarrel
5:13 ***H*** much more then, when he says
6:32 Do you see ***h*** this son of a
8: 5 as he was telling the king ***h*** he
10: 4 ***h*** then can we stand?"
14:15 and ***h*** he fought with Amaziah
14:28 ***h*** he made war, and how he
14:28 and ***h*** he recaptured for Israel,
17:28 and taught them ***h*** they should
18:24 ***H*** then will you repel one
19:25 you not hear long ago ***H***
20: 3 ***h*** I have walked before You in
20:20 and ***h*** he made a pool and a
1 Chr 13:12 ***H*** can I bring the ark of God to
2 Chr 6:18 ***H*** much less this temple which I
7: 3 the children of Israel saw ***h***
10: 6 ***H*** do you advise me to answer
10: 9 ***H*** should we answer this people
18:15 ***H*** many times shall I make you
32:15 ***H*** much less will your God
33:19 Also his prayer and ***h*** God
Neh 2: 6 '***H*** long will your journey be?
2:17 ***h*** Jerusalem lies waste, and
Esth 5:11 and ***h*** he had advanced him above
8: 1 for Esther had told ***h*** he was
8: 6 For ***h*** can I endure to see the
8: 6 Or ***h*** can I endure to see the
Job 4:19 ***H*** much more those who dwell in
6:25 ***H*** forceful are right words!
7:19 ***H*** long? Will You not look
8: 2 ***H*** long will you speak these
9: 2 But ***h*** can a man be righteous
9:14 ***H*** then can I answer Him, And
13:23 ***H*** many are my iniquities and
15:16 ***H*** much less man, who is
16: 6 ***h*** am I eased?
18: 2 ***H*** long till you put an end to
19: 2 ***H*** long will you torment my soul,
19:27 ***H*** my heart yearns within me!
19:28 ***H*** shall we persecute him?'—
21:17 ***H*** often is the lamp of the
21:17 ***H*** often does their
21:34 ***H*** then can you comfort me with
22:12 ***h*** lofty they are!
25: 4 ***H*** then can man be righteous
25: 4 Or ***h*** can he be pure who is
25: 6 ***H*** much less man, who is a
26: 2 ***H*** have you helped him who is
26: 2 ***H*** have you saved the arm
26: 3 ***H*** have you counseled one who
26: 3 And ***h*** have you declared sound
26:14 And ***h*** small a whisper we hear
31:14 ***h*** shall I answer Him?
32:22 For I do not know ***h*** to flatter,
37:16 Do you know ***h*** the clouds are
Ps 3: 1 ***h*** they have increased who
4: 2 ***H*** long, O you sons of men,
4: 2 ***H*** long will you love
6: 3 But You, O LORD—***h*** long?
8: 1 ***H*** excellent is Your name in
8: 9 ***H*** excellent is Your name in
11: 1 ***H*** can you say to my soul,
13: 1 ***H*** long, O LORD? Will You
13: 1 ***H*** long will You hide Your face
13: 2 ***H*** long shall I take counsel in
13: 2 ***H*** long will my enemy be
21: 1 And in Your salvation ***h***
31:19 ***h*** great is Your goodness,
35:17 ***h*** long will You look on?
36: 7 ***H*** precious is Your
39: 4 That I may know ***h*** frail I
62: 3 ***H*** long will you attack a man
66: 3 ***H*** awesome are Your works!
73:11 ***H*** does God know? And is there
73:16 When I thought ***h*** to understand
73:19 ***h*** they are brought to
74: 9 any among us who knows ***h*** long.
74:10 ***h*** long will the adversary
74:22 Remember ***h*** the foolish man
78:40 ***H*** often they provoked Him in
79: 5 ***H*** long, LORD? Will You be
80: 4 ***H*** long will You be angry
82: 2 ***H*** long will you judge unjustly,
84: 1 ***H*** lovely is Your tabernacle,
89:46 ***H*** long, LORD? Will You
89:47 Remember ***h*** short my time is;
89:50 ***H*** I bear in my bosom the
90:13 O LORD! ***H*** long? And have
92: 5 ***h*** great are Your works!
94: 3 ***h*** long will the wicked, How
94: 3 ***H*** long will the wicked
104:24 ***h*** manifold are Your works!
119: 9 ***H*** can a young man cleanse his
119:84 ***H*** many are the days of Your
119:97 ***h*** I love Your law! It is my
119:103 ***H*** sweet are Your words to my
119:159 Consider ***h*** I love Your
132: 2 ***H*** he swore to the LORD, And
133: 1 ***h*** good and how pleasant it is
133: 1 how good and ***h*** pleasant it is
137: 4 ***H*** shall we sing the LORD's
139:17 ***H*** precious also are Your
139:17 O God! ***H*** great is the sum of
Prov 1:22 ***H*** long, you simple ones, will
5:12 ***H*** I have hated instruction, And
6: 9 ***H*** long will you slumber,
11:31 ***H*** much more the ungodly and
15:11 So ***h*** much more the hearts of
15:23 due season, ***h*** good it is!
15:28 of the righteous studies ***h*** to
16:16 ***H*** much better to get wisdom
19: 7 ***H*** much more do his friends go
20:24 ***H*** then can a man understand
21:27 ***H*** much more when he brings it
30:13 ***h*** lofty are their eyes!
Eccl 2: 3 I searched in my heart ***h*** to
2: 3 and ***h*** to lay hold on folly,
2:16 And ***h*** does a wise man die?
4:11 But ***h*** can one be warm alone?
6: 8 Who knows ***h*** to walk before
6:11 ***H*** is man the better?
10:15 know ***h*** to go to the city!
11: 5 Or ***h*** the bones grow in the
Song 4:10 ***H*** fair is your love, My
4:10 my spouse! ***H*** much better than
5: 3 ***H*** can I put it on again?
5: 3 ***H*** can I defile them?
7: 1 ***H*** beautiful are your feet in
7: 6 ***H*** fair and how pleasant you
7: 6 How fair and ***h*** pleasant you
Isa 1:21 ***H*** the faithful city has become
6:11 I said, "Lord, ***h*** long?"
14: 4 ***H*** the oppressor has ceased, The
14:12 ***H*** you are fallen from heaven,
14:12 ***H*** you are cut down to the
19:11 ***H*** do you say to Pharaoh, "I
20: 6 and ***h*** shall we escape?'"
36: 9 ***H*** then will you repel one
37:26 hear long ago ***H*** I made it,
38: 3 ***h*** I have walked before You in
48:11 For ***h*** should My name be
50: 4 That I should know ***h*** to speak
52: 7 ***H*** beautiful upon the mountains
Jer 2:21 ***H*** then have you turned before
2:23 ***H*** can you say, 'I am not
3:19 ***H*** can I put you among the
4:14 ***H*** long shall your evil
4:21 ***H*** long will I see the standard,
5: 7 ***H*** shall I pardon you for this?
6:15 Nor did they know ***h*** to blush.
8: 8 ***H*** can you say, 'We are wise,
8:12 Nor did they know ***h*** to blush.
9: 7 For ***h*** shall I deal with the
9:19 ***H*** we are plundered! We are
12: 4 ***H*** long will the land mourn,
12: 5 Then ***h*** can you contend with
12: 5 Then ***h*** will you do in the
15: 5 to ask ***h*** you are doing?
22:23 ***H*** gracious will you be when
23:26 ***H*** long will this be in the
31:22 ***H*** long will you gad about,
36:17 ***h*** did you write all these
46:13 ***h*** Nebuchadnezzar king of
47: 5 ***H*** long will you cut yourself?
47: 6 ***H*** long until you are quiet?
47: 7 ***H*** can it be quiet, Seeing the
48:14 ***H*** can you say, 'We are mighty
48:17 ***H*** the strong staff is broken,
48:39 ***H*** she is broken down! How Moab
48:39 How she is broken down! ***H*** Moab
50:23 ***H*** the hammer of the whole earth
50:23 ***H*** Babylon has become a
51:41 ***h*** Sheshach is taken! Oh, how
51:41 ***h*** the praise of the whole earth
51:41 the whole earth is seized! ***H***
Lam 1: 1 ***H*** lonely sits the city That
1: 1 was full of people! ***H*** like
2: 1 ***H*** the Lord has covered the
2:13 ***H*** shall I console you
3:59 You have seen ***h*** I am wronged;
4: 1 ***H*** the gold has become dim!
4: 1 ***H*** changed the fine gold!
4: 2 ***H*** they are regarded as clay
Ezek 14:21 ***H*** much more it shall be when I
15: 2 ***h*** is the wood of the vine
15: 5 ***H*** much less will it be useful
16:30 ***H*** degenerate is your heart!"
26:17 ***H*** you have perished, O one
33:10 ***h*** can we then live?"'
Dan 4: 3 ***H*** great are His signs, And
4: 3 And ***h*** mighty His wonders!
8:13 ***H*** long will the vision be,
10:17 For ***h*** can this servant of my
12: 6 ***H*** long shall the fulfillment of
Hos 8: 5 ***H*** long until they attain to
11: 8 ***H*** can I give you up, Ephraim?
11: 8 ***H*** can I hand you over,
11: 8 ***H*** can I make you like Admah?
11: 8 ***H*** can I set you like Zeboiim?
Joel 1:18 ***H*** the animals groan! The herds
Ob 5 ***h*** you will be cut off!—Would
6 ***h*** Esau shall be searched out!
6 ***H*** his hidden treasures
Mic 2: 4 ***H*** He has removed it from me!
6: 3 And ***h*** have I wearied you?
Hab 1: 2 ***h*** long shall I cry, And You
2: 6 ***h*** long? And to him who loads
Zeph 2:15 ***H*** has she become a
Hag 2: 3 And ***h*** do you see it now?
Zech 1:12 ***h*** long will You not have mercy
9:17 For ***h*** great is its goodness
9:17 goodness And ***h*** great its
Mt 5:13 ***h*** shall it be seasoned? It is
6:23 ***h*** great is that darkness!
6:28 ***h*** they grow: they neither toil
7: 4 Or ***h*** can you say to your
7:11 know ***h*** to give good gifts to
7:11 ***h*** much more will your Father
10:19 do not worry about ***h*** or what
10:25 ***h*** much more will they call
12: 4 ***h*** he entered the house of God
12:12 Of ***h*** much more value then is a
12:14 ***h*** they might destroy Him.
12:26 ***H*** then will his kingdom stand?
12:29 Or ***h*** can one enter a strong
12:34 Brood of vipers! ***H*** can you,
13:27 ***H*** then does it have tares?'
15:34 '***H*** many loaves do you have?"
16: 3 You know ***h*** to discern the
16: 9 ***h*** many baskets you took up?
16:10 and ***h*** many large baskets
16:11 ***H*** is it you do not understand
17:17 ***h*** long shall I be with you?
17:17 ***H*** long shall I bear with you?
18:21 ***h*** often shall my brother sin
21:20 ***H*** did the fig tree wither away
22:12 ***h*** did you come in here without
22:15 ***h*** they might entangle Him
22:43 ***H*** then does David in the Spirit
22:45 ***h*** is He his Son?"
23:33 ***H*** can you escape the
23:37 ***H*** often I wanted to gather

26:54 ***H*** then could the Scriptures be
27:13 Do You not hear ***h*** many things
27:63 ***h*** that deceiver said, 'After
27:65 it as secure as you know ***h***.
Mk 2:16 ***H*** is it that He eats and
2:26 ***h*** he went into the house of God
3: 6 ***h*** they might destroy Him.
3: 8 when they heard ***h*** many things
3:23 ***H*** can Satan cast out Satan?
4:13 ***H*** then will you understand all
4:27 he himself does not know ***h***.
4:40 ***H*** is it that you have no
5:16 those who saw it told them ***h***
5:19 and ***h*** He has had compassion on
6:38 ***H*** many loaves do you have? Go
8: 4 ***H*** can one satisfy these people
8: 5 '***H*** many loaves do you have?"
8:19 ***h*** many baskets full of
8:20 ***h*** many large baskets full of
8:21 ***H*** is it you do not
9:12 And ***h*** is it written concerning
9:19 ***h*** long shall I be with you?
9:19 ***H*** long shall I bear with you?
9:21 ***H*** long has this been happening
9:50 ***h*** will you season it? Have salt
10:23 ***H*** hard it is for those who have
10:24 ***h*** hard it is for those who
11:18 ***h*** they might destroy Him;
12:26 ***h*** God spoke to him, saying, 'I
12:35 ***H*** is it that the scribes say
12:37 ***h*** is He then his Son?"
12:41 the treasury and saw ***h*** the
14: 1 and the scribes sought ***h*** they
14:11 So he sought ***h*** he might
15: 4 See ***h*** many things they testify
Lk 1:18 ***H*** shall I know this? For I am an
1:34 ***H*** can this be, since I do not
1:58 and relatives heard ***h*** the Lord
5:19 ***h*** they might bring him in,
6: 4 ***h*** he went into the house of God,
6:42 Or ***h*** can you say to your
8:18 Therefore take heed ***h*** you hear.
8:47 Him and ***h*** she was healed
9:41 ***h*** long shall I be with you and
11:13 know ***h*** to give good gifts to
11:13 ***h*** much more will your heavenly
11:18 ***h*** will his kingdom stand?
12:11 do not worry about ***h*** or what
12:24 Of ***h*** much more value are you
12:27 ***h*** they grow: they neither toil
12:28 ***h*** much more will He clothe
12:49 and ***h*** I wish it were already
12:50 and ***h*** distressed I am till it
12:56 but ***h*** is it you do not
13:34 ***H*** often I wanted to gather
14: 7 when He noted ***h*** they chose the
14:34 ***h*** shall it be seasoned?
15:17 ***H*** many of my father's hired
16: 5 ***H*** much do you owe my master?'
16: 7 And ***h*** much do you owe?' So he
18:24 ***H*** hard it is for those who have
19:15 that he might know ***h*** much every
20:41 ***H*** can they say that the Christ
20:44 ***h*** is He then his Son?"
21: 5 ***h*** it was adorned with beautiful
22: 2 sought ***h*** they might kill Him,
22: 4 ***h*** he might betray Him to them.
22:61 ***h*** He had said to him, "Before
23:55 and ***h*** His body was laid.
24: 6 Remember ***h*** He spoke to you
24:20 and ***h*** the chief priests and our
24:35 and ***h*** He was known to them in
Jn 1:48 ***H*** do You know me?" Jesus
3: 4 ***H*** can a man be born when he is
3: 9 ***H*** can these things be?"
3:12 ***h*** will you believe if I tell
4: 9 ***H*** is it that You, being a Jew,
5:44 ***H*** can you believe, who receive
5:47 ***h*** will you believe My words?"
6:42 ***H*** is it then that He says, 'I
6:52 ***H*** can this Man give us His
7:15 ***H*** does this Man know letters,
8:33 ***H*** can you say, 'You will be
9:10 ***H*** were your eyes opened?"
9:15 also asked him again ***h*** he had
9:16 ***H*** can a man who is a sinner do
9:19 ***H*** then does he now see?"
9:26 ***H*** did He open your eyes?"
10:24 ***H*** long do You keep us in doubt?
11:36 See ***h*** He loved him!"
12:34 and ***h*** can You say, 'The Son of
14: 5 and ***h*** can we know the way?"
14: 9 so ***h*** can you say, 'Show us the
14:22 ***h*** is it that You will manifest
Acts 2: 8 And ***h*** is it that we hear,
5: 9 ***H*** is it that you have agreed
8:31 ***H*** can I, unless someone guides
9:13 ***h*** much harm he has done to Your
9:16 For I will show him ***h*** many
9:27 And he declared to them ***h*** he
9:27 and ***h*** he had preached boldly at
10:28 You know ***h*** unlawful it is for a
10:38 ***h*** God anointed Jesus of Nazareth
11:13 And he told us ***h*** he had seen an
11:16 ***h*** He said, 'John indeed
12:17 he declared to them ***h*** the Lord
15:12 declaring ***h*** many miracles
15:14 Simon has declared ***h*** God at the
15:36 and see ***h*** they are doing."
20:20 ***h*** I kept back nothing that was
21:20 ***h*** many myriads of Jews there
Rom 3: 6 Certainly not! For then ***h*** will
4:10 ***H*** then was it accounted? While
6: 2 Certainly not! ***H*** shall we who
7:18 but ***h*** to perform what is good
8:32 ***h*** shall He not with Him also
10:14 ***H*** then shall they call on Him
10:14 And ***h*** shall they believe in Him
10:14 And ***h*** shall they hear without a
10:15 And ***h*** shall they preach unless
10:15 ***H*** beautiful are the feet of
11: 2 ***h*** he pleads with God against
11:12 ***h*** much more their fullness!
11:24 ***h*** much more will these, who
11:33 ***H*** unsearchable are His
1 Cor 3:10 take heed ***h*** he builds on it.
6: 3 ***H*** much more, things that
7:16 For ***h*** do you know, O wife,
7:16 Or ***h*** do you know, O husband,
7:32 ***h*** he may please the Lord.
7:33 ***h*** he may please his wife.
7:34 ***h*** she may please her husband.
14: 7 ***h*** will it be known what is
14: 9 ***h*** will it be known what is
14:16 ***h*** will he who occupies the
14:26 ***H*** is it then, brethren
15:12 ***h*** do some among you say that
15:35 '***H*** are the dead raised up?
2 Cor 3: 8 ***h*** will the ministry of the
7:15 ***h*** with fear and trembling you
12: 4 ***h*** he was caught up into Paradise
Gal 1:13 ***h*** I persecuted the church of
4: 9 ***h*** is it that you turn again
Eph 3: 3 ***h*** that by revelation He made
6:21 affairs and ***h*** I am doing,
Phil 1: 8 ***h*** greatly I long for you all
2:23 as soon as I see ***h*** it goes with
4:12 I know ***h*** to be abased, and I
4:12 and I know ***h*** to abound.
Col 4: 6 that you may know ***h*** you ought
1 Th 1: 9 and ***h*** you turned to God from
2:10 ***h*** devoutly and justly and
2:11 as you know ***h*** we exhorted, and
4: 1 from us ***h*** you ought to walk
4: 4 you should know ***h*** to possess
2 Th 3: 7 ***h*** you ought to follow us,
3: 9 of ***h*** you should follow us.
1 Tim 3: 5 know ***h*** to rule his own house,
3: 5 ***h*** will he take care of the
3:15 know ***h*** you ought to conduct
2 Tim 1:18 and you know very well ***h*** many
Phm 1:16 especially to me but ***h*** much
Heb 2: 3 ***h*** shall we escape if we neglect
7: 4 Now consider ***h*** great this man
9:14 ***h*** much more shall the blood of
10:29 Of ***h*** much worse punishment, do
Jas 3: 5 See ***h*** great a forest a little
5: 7 See ***h*** the farmer waits for the
2 Pe 2: 9 then the Lord knows ***h*** to
1 Jn 3:17 ***h*** does the love of God abide in
4:20 ***h*** can he love God whom he has
Jude 18 ***h*** they told you that there would
Rev 3: 3 Remember therefore ***h*** you have
6:10 ***H*** long, O Lord, holy and true,

HOWBEIT (KJV) See HOWEVER

HOWEVER (71/71) See APPENDIX

HOWL (4/4) HOWLING

Ps 59:15 And ***h*** if they are not
Isa 13:22 The hyenas will ***h*** in their
Mic 1: 8 Therefore I will wail and ***h***,
Jas 5: 1 weep and ***h*** for your miseries

HOWLING (1/1) HOWL

Deut 32:10 a ***h*** wilderness; He encircled

HOWSOEVER (KJV) See DESPITE, HOWEVER

HOZAI (1/1)

2 Chr 33:19 written among the sayings of ***H***.

HUBS (1/1)

1 Ki 7:33 and their ***h*** were all of cast

HUDDLE (1/1)

Job 24: 8 And ***h*** around the rock for want

HUGE (2/2)

2 Chr 16: 8 and the Lubim not a ***h*** army
Dan 7: 7 It had ***h*** iron teeth; it was

HUKKOK (1/1)

Josh 19:34 went out from there toward ***H***;

HUKOK (1/1)

1 Chr 6:75 ***H*** with its common-lands, and

HUL (2/2)

Gen 10:23 The sons of Aram were Uz, ***H***,
1 Chr 1:17 Arphaxad, Lud, Aram, Uz, ***H***,

HULDAH (2/2)

2 Ki 22:14 and Asaiah went to ***H*** the
2 Chr 34:22 king had appointed went to ***H***

HUMAN (15/15)

Lev 5: 3 Or if he touches ***h*** uncleanness—
7:21 such as ***h*** uncleanness, an
Num 9: 6 men who were defiled by a ***h***
9: 7 We became defiled by a ***h***
2 Ki 7:10 not a ***h*** sound—only horses and
Ezek 4:12 and bake it using fuel of ***h***
4:15 you cow dung instead of ***h***
27:13 They bartered ***h*** lives and
Dan 8:25 he shall be broken without ***h***
Hos 5:11 he willingly walked by ***h***
Jn 16:21 for joy that a ***h*** being has been
Rom 6:19 I speak in ***h*** terms because of
1 Cor 2: 4 not with persuasive words of ***h***
4: 3 be judged by you or by a ***h***
Heb 12: 9 we have had ***h*** fathers who

HUMBLE (43/40) HUMBLED, HUMBLES, HUMBLY

Ex 10: 3 How long will you refuse to ***h***
Num 12: 3 (Now the man Moses was very ***h***,
Deut 8: 2 to ***h*** you and test you, to know
8:16 that He might ***h*** you and that He
Judg 19:24 ***H*** them, and do with them as you
2 Sam 6:22 and will be ***h*** in my own sight.
22:28 You will save the ***h*** people;
2 Chr 7:14 are called by My name will ***h***
33:23 And he did not ***h*** himself before
36:12 and did not ***h*** himself before
Ezra 8:21 that we might ***h*** ourselves
Job 22:29 Then He will save the ***h***
40:11 who is proud, and ***h*** him.
Ps 9:12 not forget the cry of the ***h***.
10:12 Your hand! Do not forget the ***h***.
10:17 have heard the desire of the ***h***;
18:27 For You will save the ***h*** people,
25: 9 The ***h*** He guides in justice,
25: 9 And the ***h*** He teaches His way.
34: 2 The ***h*** shall hear of it and
69:32 The ***h*** shall see this and be
147: 6 The LORD lifts up the ***h***;
149: 4 He will beautify the ***h*** with
Prov 3:34 But gives grace to the ***h***.
6: 3 Go and ***h*** yourself; Plead with
11: 2 But with the ***h*** is wisdom.
16:19 Better to be of a ***h*** spirit
29:23 But the ***h*** in spirit will
Isa 29:19 The ***h*** also shall increase
57:15 him who has a contrite and ***h***
57:15 To revive the spirit of the ***h***,
Jer 13:18 ***H*** yourselves; Sit down, For
Ezek 21:26 remain the same. Exalt the ***h***,
21:26 and ***h*** the exalted.
Dan 10:12 and to ***h*** yourself before your
Am 2: 7 And pervert the way of the ***h***.
Zeph 3:12 in your midst A meek and ***h***
Rom 12:16 but associate with the ***h***.
2 Cor 12:21 my God will ***h*** me among you, and
Jas 4: 6 But gives grace to the ***h***.
4:10 ***H*** yourselves in the sight of the
1 Pe 5: 5 But gives grace to the ***h***.
5: 6 Therefore ***h*** yourselves under the

HUMBLED (30/26) HUMBLE

Lev 26:41 uncircumcised hearts are ***h***,
Deut 8: 3 So He ***h*** you, allowed you to
21:14 because you have ***h*** her.
22:24 and the man because he ***h*** his
22:29 be his wife because he has ***h***
1 Ki 21:29 See how Ahab has ***h*** himself
21:29 Because he has ***h*** himself before
2 Ki 22:19 and you ***h*** yourself before the
2 Chr 12: 6 of Israel and the king ***h***
12: 7 when the LORD saw that they ***h***
12: 7 They have ***h*** themselves;
12:12 When he ***h*** himself, the wrath of
30:11 and Zebulun ***h*** themselves and
32:26 Then Hezekiah ***h*** himself for the
33:12 and ***h*** himself greatly before
33:19 carved images, before he was ***h***,
33:23 as his father Manasseh had ***h***
34:27 and you ***h*** yourself before God
34:27 and you ***h*** yourself before Me,
Ps 35:13 I ***h*** myself with fasting;
Isa 2:11 lofty looks of man shall be ***h***,
5:15 down, Each man shall be ***h***,
5:15 eyes of the lofty shall be ***h***.
10:33 And the haughty will be ***h***.
Jer 44:10 'They have not been ***h***,
Dan 5:22 have not ***h*** your heart, although
Mt 23:12 exalts himself will be ***h***,
Lk 14:11 exalts himself will be ***h***,
18:14 who exalts himself will be ***h***,
Phil 2: 8 He ***h*** Himself and became

HUMBLES (6/6) HUMBLE

Ps 113: 6 Who ***h*** Himself to behold The
Isa 2: 9 And each man ***h*** himself;
Mt 18: 4 Therefore whoever ***h*** himself as
23:12 and he who ***h*** himself will be
Lk 14:11 and he who ***h*** himself will be
18:14 and he who ***h*** himself will be

HUMBLING (1/1)

2 Cor 11: 7 Did I commit sin in ***h*** myself

HUMBLY (2/2) HUMBLE

2 Sam 16: 4 I ***h*** bow before you, that I may
Mic 6: 8 And to walk ***h*** with your God?

HUMILIATED (5/5) HUMILIATION, HUMILITY

Deut 25: 3 and your brother be ***h*** in your
Ezra 9: 6 I am too ashamed and ***h*** to lift
Jer 22:22 then you will be ashamed and ***h***
31:19 I was ashamed, yes, even ***h***,
50: 2 in pieces; Her idols are ***h***,

HUMILIATION (5/5) HUMILIATED

Ezra 9: 7 captivity, to plunder, and to ***h***,
Isa 30: 3 of Egypt Shall be your ***h***.
32:19 the city is brought low in ***h***.
Acts 8:33 In His ***h*** His justice was
Jas 1:10 but the rich in his ***h***,

HUMILITY (12/12) HUMILIATED

Ps 45: 4 because of truth, ***h***,
Prov 15:33 wisdom, And before honor is ***h***.
18:12 And before honor is ***h***.
22: 4 By ***h*** and the fear of the LORD
Zeph 2: 3 Seek righteousness, seek ***h***.
Acts 20:19 "serving the Lord with all ***h***,
Col 2:18 taking delight in false ***h*** and
2:23 self-imposed religion, false ***h***,
3:12 on tender mercies, kindness, ***h***,
2 Tim 2:25 in ***h*** correcting those who are in
Titus 3: 2 showing all ***h*** to all men.
1 Pe 5: 5 another, and be clothed with ***h***,

HUMPS (1/1)

Isa 30: 6 And their treasures on the ***h***

HUMTAH (1/1)

Josh 15:54 ***H***, Kirjath Arba (which is

HUNCHBACK (1/1)

Lev 21:20 or is a ***h*** or a dwarf, or a man

HUNDRED (595/522) HUNDREDFOLD, HUNDREDS, HUNDREDTH

Gen 5: 3 And Adam lived one ***h*** and thirty
5: 4 the days of Adam were eight ***h***
5: 5 that Adam lived were nine ***h***
5: 6 Seth lived one ***h*** and five
5: 7 Seth lived eight ***h*** and seven
5: 8 the days of Seth were nine ***h***
5:10 Enosh lived eight ***h*** and fifteen
5:11 the days of Enosh were nine ***h***
5:13 Cainan lived eight ***h*** and forty
5:14 the days of Cainan were nine ***h***
5:16 Mahalalel lived eight ***h*** and
5:17 days of Mahalalel were eight ***h***
5:18 Jared lived one ***h*** and sixty-two
5:19 Jared lived eight ***h*** years, and
5:20 the days of Jared were nine ***h***
5:22 Enoch walked with God three ***h***
5:23 the days of Enoch were three ***h***
5:25 Methuselah lived one ***h*** and
5:26 Methuselah lived seven ***h*** and
5:27 days of Methuselah were nine ***h***
5:28 Lamech lived one ***h*** and
5:30 Lamech lived five ***h*** and
5:31 the days of Lamech were seven ***h***
5:32 And Noah was five ***h*** years old,
6: 3 yet his days shall be one ***h*** and
6:15 of the ark shall be three ***h***
7: 6 Noah was six ***h*** years old when
7:24 prevailed on the earth one ***h***
8: 3 At the end of the ***h*** and fifty
8:13 it came to pass in the six ***h***
9:28 lived after the flood three ***h***
9:29 the days of Noah were nine ***h***
11:10 Shem was one ***h*** years old, and
11:11 Shem lived five ***h*** years, and
11:13 Arphaxad lived four ***h*** and three
11:15 Salah lived four ***h*** and three
11:17 Eber lived four ***h*** and thirty
11:19 Peleg lived two ***h*** and nine
11:21 Reu lived two ***h*** and seven
11:23 Serug lived two ***h*** years, and
11:25 Nahor lived one ***h*** and nineteen
11:32 So the days of Terah were two ***h***
14:14 he armed his three ***h*** and
15:13 they will afflict them four ***h***
17:17 be born to a man who is one ***h***
21: 5 Now Abraham was one ***h*** years old
23: 1 Sarah lived one ***h*** and
23:15 the land is worth four ***h***
23:16 four ***h*** shekels of silver,
25: 7 one ***h*** and seventy-five years.
25:17 one ***h*** and thirty-seven years;
32: 6 and four ***h*** men are with him."
32:14 two ***h*** female goats and twenty
32:14 two ***h*** ewes and twenty rams,
33: 1 and with him were four ***h*** men.
33:19 for one ***h*** pieces of money.
35:28 the days of Isaac were one ***h***
45:22 but to Benjamin he gave three ***h***
47: 9 of my pilgrimage are one ***h***
47:28 of Jacob's life was one ***h*** and
50:22 And Joseph lived one ***h*** and ten
50:26 being one ***h*** and ten years old;
Ex 6:16 of the life of Levi were one ***h***
6:18 the life of Kohath were one ***h***
6:20 the life of Amram were one ***h***
12:37 about six ***h*** thousand men on
12:40 who lived in Egypt was four ***h***
12:41 pass at the end of the four ***h***
14: 7 he took six ***h*** choice chariots,
27: 9 one ***h*** cubits long for one side.
27:11 shall be hangings one ***h***
27:18 of the court shall be one ***h***
30:23 five ***h*** shekels of liquid myrrh,
30:23 (two ***h*** and fifty shekels),
30:23 two ***h*** and fifty shekels of
30:24 five ***h*** shekels of cassia,
38: 9 one ***h*** cubits long.
38:11 side the hangings were one ***h***
38:24 talents and seven ***h*** and thirty
38:25 of the congregation was one ***h***
38:25 and one thousand seven ***h*** and
38:26 for six ***h*** and three thousand,
38:26 five ***h*** and fifty men.
38:27 And from the ***h*** talents of silver
38:27 one ***h*** sockets from the hundred
38:27 one hundred sockets from the ***h***
38:28 from the one thousand seven ***h***
38:29 talents and two thousand four ***h***
Lev 26: 8 Five of you shall chase a ***h***,
26: 8 and a ***h*** of you shall put ten
Num 1:21 were forty-six thousand five ***h***.
1:23 fifty-nine thousand three ***h***.
1:25 forty-five thousand six ***h*** and
1:27 seventy-four thousand six ***h***.
1:29 fifty-four thousand four ***h***.
1:31 fifty-seven thousand four ***h***.
1:33 were forty thousand five ***h***.
1:35 were thirty-two thousand two ***h***.
1:37 thirty-five thousand four ***h***.
1:39 sixty-two thousand seven ***h***.
1:41 were forty-one thousand five ***h***.
1:43 fifty-three thousand four ***h***.
1:46 who were numbered were six ***h***
1:46 and three thousand five ***h*** and
2: 4 at seventy-four thousand six ***h***.
2: 6 at fifty-four thousand four ***h***.
2: 8 at fifty-seven thousand four ***h***.
2: 9 one ***h*** and eighty-six thousand
2: 9 and eighty-six thousand four ***h***—
2:11 at forty-six thousand five ***h***.
2:13 at fifty-nine thousand three ***h***.
2:15 at forty-five thousand six ***h***
2:16 one ***h*** and fifty-one thousand
2:16 and fifty-one thousand four ***h***
2:19 at forty thousand five ***h***.
2:21 at thirty-two thousand two ***h***.
2:23 at thirty-five thousand four ***h***.
2:24 one ***h*** and eight thousand one
2:24 and eight thousand one ***h***—
2:26 at sixty-two thousand seven ***h***.
2:28 at forty-one thousand five ***h***.
2:30 at fifty-three thousand four ***h***.
2:31 one ***h*** and fifty-seven thousand
2:31 and fifty-seven thousand six ***h***—
2:32 of the forces were six ***h*** and
2:32 and three thousand five ***h*** and
3:22 were seven thousand five ***h***.
3:28 were eight thousand six ***h***
3:34 above, were six thousand two ***h***.
3:43 were twenty-two thousand two ***h***
3:46 for the redemption of the two ***h***
3:50 one thousand three ***h*** and
4:36 were two thousand seven ***h*** and
4:40 were two thousand six ***h*** and
4:44 were three thousand two ***h***.
4:48 were eight thousand five ***h*** and
7:13 the weight of which was one ***h***
7:19 the weight of which was one ***h***
7:25 the weight of which was one ***h***
7:31 the weight of which was one ***h***
7:37 the weight of which was one ***h***
7:43 the weight of which was one ***h***
7:49 the weight of which was one ***h***
7:55 the weight of which was one ***h***
7:61 the weight of which was one ***h***
7:67 the weight of which was one ***h***
7:73 the weight of which was one ***h***
7:79 the weight of which was one ***h***
7:85 silver platter weighed one ***h***
7:85 weighed two thousand four ***h***
7:86 of the pans weighed one ***h*** and
11:21 whom I am among are six ***h***
16: 2 two ***h*** and fifty leaders of the
16:17 two ***h*** and fifty censers;
16:35 LORD and consumed the two ***h***
16:49 were fourteen thousand seven ***h***,
26: 7 forty-three thousand seven ***h***
26:10 when the fire devoured two ***h***
26:14 twenty-two thousand two ***h***.
26:18 of them: forty thousand five ***h***.
26:22 seventy-six thousand five ***h***.
26:25 sixty-four thousand three ***h***.
26:27 of them: sixty thousand five ***h***.
26:34 fifty-two thousand seven ***h***.
26:37 thirty-two thousand five ***h***.
26:41 were forty-five thousand six ***h***.
26:43 sixty-four thousand four ***h***.
26:47 fifty-three thousand four ***h***.
26:50 forty-five thousand four ***h***.
26:51 six ***h*** and one thousand seven
26:51 and one thousand seven ***h*** and
31:28 one of every five ***h*** of the
31:32 was six ***h*** and seventy-five
31:36 was in number three ***h*** and
31:36 thirty-seven thousand five ***h***
31:37 tribute of the sheep was six ***h***
31:39 were thirty thousand five ***h***,
31:43 to the congregation was three ***h***
31:43 thirty-seven thousand five ***h***
31:45 thirty thousand five ***h*** donkeys,
31:52 was sixteen thousand seven ***h***
33:39 Aaron was one ***h*** and
Deut 22:19 and they shall fine him one ***h***
31: 2 I am one ***h*** and twenty years old
34: 7 Moses was one ***h*** and twenty
Josh 7:21 two ***h*** shekels of silver, and a
24:29 being one ***h*** and ten years old.
24:32 the father of Shechem for one ***h***
Judg 2: 8 died when he was one ***h*** and
3:31 who killed six ***h*** men of the
4: 3 for Jabin had nine ***h*** chariots
4:13 nine ***h*** chariots of iron, and
7: 6 was three ***h*** men; but all the
7: 7 By the three ***h*** men who lapped I
7: 8 and retained those three ***h*** men.
7:16 Then he divided the three ***h*** men
7:19 So Gideon and the ***h*** men who
7:22 When the three ***h*** blew the
8: 4 he and the three ***h*** men who
8:10 for one ***h*** and twenty thousand
8:26 was one thousand seven ***h***
11:26 for three ***h*** years, why did you
15: 4 Samson went and caught three ***h***
16: 5 of us will give you eleven ***h***
17: 2 The eleven ***h*** shekels of silver
17: 3 he had returned the eleven ***h***
17: 4 Then his mother took two ***h***
18:11 And six ***h*** men of the family of
18:16 The six ***h*** men armed with their
18:17 of the gate with the six ***h*** men
20: 2 four ***h*** thousand foot soldiers
20:10 take ten men out of every ***h***
20:10 a ***h*** out of every thousand, and
20:15 who numbered seven ***h*** select
20:16 all this people were seven ***h***
20:17 men of Israel numbered four ***h***
20:35 day twenty-five thousand one ***h***
20:47 But six ***h*** men turned and fled
21:12 of Jabesh Gilead four ***h*** young
1 Sam 11: 8 children of Israel were three ***h***
13:15 about six ***h*** men.
14: 2 with him were about six ***h*** men.
15: 4 two ***h*** thousand foot soldiers
17: 7 iron spearhead weighed six ***h***
18:25 not desire any dowry but one ***h***
18:27 and killed two ***h*** men of the
22: 2 And there were about four ***h*** men
23:13 David and his men, about six ***h***,
25:13 And about four ***h*** men went with
25:13 and two ***h*** stayed with the
25:18 made haste and took two ***h***
25:18 one ***h*** clusters of raisins, and
25:18 and two ***h*** cakes of figs, and
27: 2 and went over with the six ***h***
30: 9 he and the six ***h*** men who were
30:10 he and four ***h*** men; for two
30:10 for two ***h*** stayed behind, who
30:17 except four ***h*** young men who
30:21 Now David came to the two ***h*** men
2 Sam 2:31 three ***h*** and sixty men who died.
3:14 I betrothed to myself for a ***h***
8: 4 seven ***h*** horsemen, and twenty
8: 4 enough of them for one ***h***
10:18 and David killed seven ***h***
14:26 the hair of his head at two ***h***
15:11 And with Absalom went two ***h*** men
15:18 six ***h*** men who had followed him
16: 1 and on them two ***h*** loaves of
16: 1 one ***h*** clusters of raisins, one
16: 1 one ***h*** summer fruits, and a skin
21:16 whose bronze spear was three ***h***
23: 8 because he had killed eight ***h***
23:18 his spear against three ***h*** men,
24: 3 your God add to the people a ***h***
24: 9 there were in Israel eight ***h***
24: 9 the men of Judah were five ***h***
1 Ki 4:23 and one ***h*** sheep, besides deer,
5:16 besides three thousand three ***h***
6: 1 it came to pass in the four ***h***
7: 2 its length was one ***h*** cubits,
7:20 and there were two ***h*** such
7:42 four ***h*** pomegranates for the two
8:63 thousand bulls and one ***h*** and
9:14 Then Hiram sent the king one ***h***
9:23 five ***h*** and fifty, who ruled
9:28 and acquired four ***h*** and twenty
10:10 Then she gave the king one ***h*** and
10:14 to Solomon yearly was six ***h***
10:16 And King Solomon made two ***h***
10:16 six ***h*** shekels of gold went
10:17 He also made three ***h*** shields
10:26 he had one thousand four ***h***
10:29 imported from Egypt cost six ***h***
10:29 and a horse one ***h*** and fifty;
11: 3 And he had seven ***h*** wives,
11: 3 and three ***h*** concubines; and his
12:21 one ***h*** and eighty thousand
18: 4 that Obadiah had taken one ***h***
18:13 how I hid one ***h*** men of the
18:19 the four ***h*** and fifty prophets
18:19 and the four ***h*** prophets of

H

18:22 but Baal's prophets are four ***h***
20:15 and there were two ***h*** and
20:29 children of Israel killed one ***h***
22: 6 about four ***h*** men, and said to
2 Ki 3: 4 paid the king of Israel one ***h***
3: 4 lambs and the wool of one ***h***
3:26 he took with him seven ***h*** men
4:43 Shall I set this before one ***h***
14:13 Corner Gate—four ***h*** cubits.
18:14 Hezekiah king of Judah three ***h***
19:35 the camp of the Assyrians one ***h***
23:33 on the land a tribute of one ***h***
1 Chr 4:42 five ***h*** men of the sons of
5:18 forty-four thousand seven ***h***
5:21 two ***h*** and fifty thousand of
5:21 also one ***h*** thousand of their
7: 2 was twenty-two thousand six ***h***.
7: 9 twenty thousand two ***h*** mighty
7:11 were seventeen thousand two ***h***
8:40 one ***h*** and fifty in all.
9: 6 six ***h*** and ninety.
9: 9 nine ***h*** and fifty-six. All these
9:13 one thousand seven ***h*** and sixty.
9:22 as gatekeepers were two ***h*** and
11:11 up his spear against three ***h***,
11:20 up his spear against three ***h***
12:14 the least was over a ***h***,
12:24 six thousand eight ***h*** armed for
12:25 for war, seven thousand one ***h***;
12:26 of Levi four thousand six ***h***;
12:27 with him three thousand seven ***h***;
12:30 Ephraim twenty thousand eight ***h***,
12:32 to do, their chiefs were two ***h***;
12:35 twenty-eight thousand six ***h***;
12:37 one ***h*** and twenty thousand armed
15: 5 and one ***h*** and twenty of his
15: 6 and two ***h*** and twenty of his
15: 7 and one ***h*** and thirty of his
15: 8 and two ***h*** of his brethren;
15:10 and one ***h*** and twelve of his
18: 4 spared enough of them for one ***h***
21: 3 the LORD make His people a ***h***
21: 5 Israel had one million one ***h***
21: 5 and Judah had four ***h*** and
21:25 So David gave Ornan six ***h***
22:14 the house of the LORD one ***h***
25: 7 was two ***h*** and eighty-eight.
26:30 one thousand seven ***h*** able men,
26:32 were two thousand seven ***h***
29: 7 and one ***h*** thousand talents of
2 Chr 1:14 he had one thousand four ***h***
1:17 from Egypt a chariot for six ***h***
1:17 and a horse for one ***h*** and
2: 2 and three thousand six ***h*** to
2:17 there were found to be one ***h***
2:17 and fifty-three thousand six ***h***.
2:18 and three thousand six ***h***
3: 4 and the height was one ***h*** and
3: 8 He overlaid it with six ***h***
3:16 and he made one ***h*** pomegranates,
4: 8 And he made one ***h*** bowls of
4:13 four ***h*** pomegranates for the two
5:12 and with them one ***h*** and twenty
7: 5 thousand bulls and one ***h*** and
8:10 two ***h*** and fifty, who ruled over
8:18 and acquired four ***h*** and fifty
9: 9 And she gave the king one ***h*** and
9:13 to Solomon yearly was six ***h***
9:15 And King Solomon made two ***h***
9:15 six ***h*** shekels of hammered gold
9:16 He also made three ***h*** shields
9:16 three ***h*** shekels of gold went
11: 1 of Judah and Benjamin one ***h***
12: 3 with twelve ***h*** chariots, sixty
13: 3 four ***h*** thousand choice men.
13: 3 against him with eight ***h***
13:17 so five ***h*** thousand choice men
14: 8 And Asa had an army of three ***h***
14: 8 and from Benjamin two ***h*** and
14: 9 of a million men and three ***h***
15:11 the LORD at that time seven ***h***
17:11 seven thousand seven ***h*** rams and
17:11 rams and seven thousand seven ***h***
17:14 and with him three ***h*** thousand
17:15 and with him two ***h*** and eighty
17:16 and with him two ***h*** thousand
17:17 and with him two ***h*** thousand men
17:18 and with him one ***h*** and eighty
18: 5 four ***h*** men, and said to them,
24:15 he was one ***h*** and thirty years
25: 5 and found them to be three ***h***
25: 6 He also hired one ***h*** thousand
25: 6 of valor from Israel for one ***h***
25: 9 what shall we do about the ***h***
25:23 Corner Gate—four ***h*** cubits.
26:12 valor was two thousand six ***h***.
26:13 was an army of three ***h*** and
26:13 and seven thousand five ***h***,
27: 5 gave him in that year one ***h***
28: 6 son of Remaliah killed one ***h***
28: 8 captive of their brethren two ***h***
29:32 one ***h*** rams, and two hundred
29:32 and two ***h*** lambs; all these
29:33 consecrated things were six ***h***
35: 8 offerings two thousand six ***h***
35: 8 and three ***h*** cattle.
35: 9 from the flock and five ***h***
36: 3 on the land a tribute of one ***h***
Ezra 1:10 four ***h*** and ten silver basins of
1:11 were five thousand four ***h***.
2: 3 two thousand one ***h*** and
2: 4 three ***h*** and seventy-two;

2: 5 seven ***h*** and seventy-five;
2: 6 two thousand eight ***h*** and
2: 7 one thousand two ***h*** and
2: 8 nine ***h*** and forty-five;
2: 9 seven ***h*** and sixty;
2:10 six ***h*** and forty-two;
2:11 six ***h*** and twenty-three;
2:12 one thousand two ***h*** and
2:13 six ***h*** and sixty-six;
2:15 four ***h*** and fifty-four;
2:17 three ***h*** and twenty-three;
2:18 Jorah, one ***h*** and twelve;
2:19 two ***h*** and twenty-three;
2:21 one ***h*** and twenty-three;
2:23 one ***h*** and twenty-eight;
2:25 seven ***h*** and forty-three;
2:26 six ***h*** and twenty-one;
2:27 one ***h*** and twenty-two;
2:28 two ***h*** and twenty-three;
2:30 one ***h*** and fifty-six;
2:31 one thousand two ***h*** and
2:32 three ***h*** and twenty;
2:33 seven ***h*** and twenty-five;
2:34 three ***h*** and forty-five;
2:35 three thousand six ***h*** and
2:36 nine ***h*** and seventy-three;
2:38 one thousand two ***h*** and
2:41 one ***h*** and twenty-eight.
2:42 one ***h*** and thirty-nine in all.
2:58 servants were three ***h*** and
2:60 six ***h*** and fifty-two;
2:64 was forty-two thousand three ***h***
2:65 were seven thousand three ***h***
2:65 and they had two ***h*** men and
2:66 Their horses were seven ***h*** and
2:66 their mules two ***h*** and
2:67 their camels four ***h*** and
2:67 donkeys six thousand seven ***h***
2:69 and one ***h*** priestly garments.
6:17 one ***h*** bulls, two hundred rams,
6:17 two ***h*** rams, four hundred lambs,
6:17 four ***h*** lambs, and as a sin
7:22 up to one ***h*** talents of silver,
7:22 one ***h*** kors of wheat, one
7:22 one ***h*** baths of wine, one
7:22 one ***h*** baths of oil, and salt
8: 3 with him were one ***h*** and fifty
8: 4 and with him two ***h*** males;
8: 5 and with him three ***h*** males;
8: 9 and with him two ***h*** and eighteen
8:10 and with him one ***h*** and sixty
8:12 and with him one ***h*** and ten
8:20 two ***h*** and twenty Nethinim.
8:26 I weighed into their hand six ***h***
8:26 silver articles weighing one ***h***
8:26 one ***h*** talents of gold,
Neh 3: 1 as far as the Tower of the ***H***,
5:17 And at my table were one ***h*** and
7: 8 two thousand one ***h*** and
7: 9 three ***h*** and seventy-two;
7:10 six ***h*** and fifty-two;
7:11 two thousand eight ***h*** and
7:12 one thousand two ***h*** and
7:13 eight ***h*** and forty-five;
7:14 seven ***h*** and sixty;
7:15 six ***h*** and forty-eight;
7:16 six ***h*** and twenty-eight;
7:17 two thousand three ***h*** and
7:18 six ***h*** and sixty-seven;
7:20 six ***h*** and fifty-five;
7:22 three ***h*** and twenty-eight;
7:23 three ***h*** and twenty-four;
7:24 one ***h*** and twelve;
7:26 one ***h*** and eighty-eight;
7:27 one ***h*** and twenty-eight;
7:29 seven ***h*** and forty-three;
7:30 six ***h*** and twenty-one;
7:31 one ***h*** and twenty-two;
7:32 one ***h*** and twenty-three;
7:34 one thousand two ***h*** and
7:35 three ***h*** and twenty;
7:36 three ***h*** and forty-five;
7:37 seven ***h*** and twenty-one;
7:38 three thousand nine ***h*** and
7:39 nine ***h*** and seventy-three;
7:41 one thousand two ***h*** and
7:44 one ***h*** and forty-eight.
7:45 one ***h*** and thirty-eight.
7:60 were three ***h*** and ninety-two.
7:62 six ***h*** and forty-two;
7:66 forty-two thousand three ***h*** and
7:67 were seven thousand three ***h***
7:67 and they had two ***h*** and
7:68 Their horses were seven ***h*** and
7:68 their mules two ***h*** and
7:69 their camels four ***h*** and
7:69 donkeys six thousand seven ***h***
7:70 and five ***h*** and thirty priestly
7:71 and two thousand two ***h*** silver
11: 6 at Jerusalem were four ***h*** and
11: 8 nine ***h*** and twenty-eight.
11:12 of the house were eight ***h*** and
11:13 were two ***h*** and forty-two;
11:14 were one ***h*** and twenty-eight.
11:18 in the holy city were two ***h***
11:19 were one ***h*** and seventy-two.
12:39 of Hananel, the Tower of the ***H***,
Esth 1: 1 who reigned over one ***h*** and
1: 4 one ***h*** and eighty days in all.
8: 9 one ***h*** and twenty-seven
9: 6 killed and destroyed five ***h***
9:12 killed and destroyed five ***h***

9:15 of Adar and killed three ***h*** men
9:30 to the one ***h*** and twenty-seven
Job 1: 3 five ***h*** yoke of oxen, five
1: 3 five ***h*** female donkeys, and a
42:16 After this Job lived one ***h*** and
Prov 17:10 for a wise man Than a ***h***
Eccl 6: 3 If a man begets a ***h*** children
8:12 Though a sinner does evil a ***h***
Song 8:12 those who tend its fruit two ***h***.
Isa 37:36 the camp of the Assyrians one ***h***
65:20 For the child shall die one ***h***
65:20 But the sinner being one ***h***
Jer 52:23 on the network, were one ***h***.
52:29 captive from Jerusalem eight ***h***
52:30 captive of the Jews seven ***h***
52:30 were four thousand six ***h***.
Ezek 4: 5 three ***h*** and ninety days; so you
4: 9 three ***h*** and ninety days, you
40:19 one ***h*** cubits toward the east
40:23 to gateway, one ***h*** cubits.
40:27 the south, one ***h*** cubits.
40:47 one ***h*** cubits long and one
40:47 hundred cubits long and one ***h***
41:13 one ***h*** cubits long; and the
41:13 and its walls was one ***h***
41:14 was one ***h*** cubits.
41:15 one ***h*** cubits, as well as the
42: 2 which was one ***h*** cubits
42: 8 facing the temple was one ***h***
42:16 five ***h*** rods by the measuring
42:17 five ***h*** rods by the measuring
42:18 five ***h*** rods by the measuring
42:19 west side and measured five ***h***
42:20 five ***h*** cubits long and five
42:20 cubits long and five ***h*** wide,
45: 2 five ***h*** by five hundred rods,
45: 2 five hundred by five ***h*** rods,
45:15 be given from a flock of two ***h***,
48:16 north side four thousand five ***h***
48:16 south side four thousand five ***h***,
48:16 east side four thousand five ***h***,
48:16 west side four thousand five ***h***.
48:17 to the north two ***h*** and fifty
48:17 to the south two ***h*** and fifty,
48:17 to the east two ***h*** and fifty,
48:17 and to the west two ***h*** and
48:30 measuring four thousand five ***h***
48:32 four thousand five ***h*** cubits,
48:33 measuring four thousand five ***h***
48:34 four thousand five ***h*** cubits
Dan 6: 1 to set over the kingdom one ***h***
8:14 For two thousand three ***h*** days;
12:11 shall be one thousand two ***h***
12:12 to the one thousand three ***h***
Am 5: 3 by a thousand Shall have a ***h***
5: 3 And that which goes out by a ***h***
Jon 4:11 in which are more than one ***h***
Mt 18:12 If a man has a ***h*** sheep, and one
18:28 servants who owed him a ***h***
Mk 4: 8 some sixty, and some a ***h***.
4:20 some sixty, and some a ***h***.
6:37 Shall we go and buy two ***h***
14: 5 been sold for more than three ***h***
Lk 7:41 One owed five ***h*** denarii, and
15: 4 having a ***h*** sheep, if he loses
16: 6 A ***h*** measures of oil.' So he said
16: 7 A ***h*** measures of wheat.' And he
Jn 6: 7 Two ***h*** denarii worth of bread is
12: 5 oil not sold for three ***h***
19:39 about a ***h*** pounds.
21: 8 but about two ***h*** cubits),
21:11 one ***h*** and fifty-three;
Acts 1:15 number of names was about a ***h***
5:36 A number of men, about four ***h***,
7: 6 and oppress them four ***h*** years.
13:20 them judges for about four ***h***
23:23 Prepare two ***h*** soldiers, seventy
23:23 and two ***h*** spearmen to go to
27:37 And in all we were two ***h*** and
Rom 4:19 (since he was about a ***h*** years
1 Cor 15: 6 that He was seen by over five ***h***
Gal 3:17 which was four ***h*** and thirty
Rev 7: 4 One ***h*** and forty-four thousand
9:16 army of the horsemen was two ***h***
11: 3 prophesy one thousand two ***h***
12: 6 her there one thousand two ***h***
14: 1 and with Him one ***h*** and
14: 3 learn that song except the ***h***
14:20 for one thousand six ***h***
21:17 one ***h*** and forty-four cubits,

HUNDREDFOLD (6/6) HUNDRED

Gen 26:12 and reaped in the same year a ***h***;
Mt 13: 8 and yielded a crop: some a ***h***,
13:23 fruit and produces: some a ***h***,
19:29 name's sake, shall receive a ***h***,
Mk 10:30 who shall not receive a ***h*** now in
Lk 8: 8 up, and yielded a crop a ***h***.

HUNDREDS (28/28) HUNDRED

Ex 18:21 of thousands, rulers of ***h***,
18:25 of thousands, rulers of ***h***,
Num 31:14 thousands and captains over ***h***,
31:48 of thousands and captains of ***h***,
31:52 of thousands and captains of ***h***,
31:54 captains of thousands and of ***h***,
Deut 1:15 of thousands, leaders of ***h***,
1 Sam 22: 7 of thousands and captains of ***h***?
29: 2 passed in review by ***h*** and by
2 Sam 18: 1 of thousands and captains of ***h***

18: 4 all the people went out by ***h***
2 Ki 11: 4 and brought the captains of ***h***—
11: 9 So the captains of the ***h*** did
11:10 priest gave the captains of ***h***
11:15 commanded the captains of the ***h***,
11:19 Then he took the captains of ***h***,
1 Chr 13: 1 the captains of thousands and ***h***,
26:26 captains over thousands and ***h***,
27: 1 the captains of thousands and ***h***
28: 1 thousands and captains over ***h***,
29: 6 captains of thousands and of ***h***,
2 Chr 1: 2 captains of thousands and of ***h***,
23: 1 covenant with the captains of ***h***:
23: 9 gave to the captains of ***h*** the
23:14 brought out the captains of ***h***
23:20 Then he took the captains of ***h***,
25: 5 of thousands and captains of ***h***,
Mk 6:40 in ***h*** and in fifties.

HUNDREDTH (2/2) HUNDRED

Gen 7:11 In the six ***h*** year of Noah's
Neh 5:11 also a ***h*** of the money and the

HUNG (19/19) HANG

Ex 40:21 ***h*** up the veil of the covering,
40:28 He ***h*** up the screen at the door
40:33 and ***h*** up the screen of the
2 Sam 21:12 where the Philistines had ***h***
Neh 3: 1 they consecrated it and ***h*** its
3: 3 they laid its beams and ***h*** its
3: 6 they laid its beams and ***h*** its
3:13 ***h*** its doors with its bolts and
3:14 he built it and ***h*** its doors
3:15 ***h*** its doors with its bolts and
6: 1 at that time I had not ***h*** the
7: 1 the wall was built and I had ***h***
Ps 137: 2 We ***h*** our harps Upon the
Lam 5:12 Princes were ***h*** up by their
Ezek 27:10 They ***h*** shield and helmet in
27:11 They ***h*** their shields on your
Mt 18: 6 for him if a millstone were ***h***
Mk 9:42 for him if a millstone were ***h***
Lk 17: 2 for him if a millstone were ***h***

HUNGER (23/23) HUNGRY

Ex 16: 3 kill this whole assembly with ***h***.
Deut 8: 3 humbled you, allowed you to ***h***,
28:48 will send against you, in ***h***,
32:24 They shall be wasted with ***h***,
1 Sam 2: 5 the hungry have ceased to ***h***.
Neh 9:15 bread from heaven for their ***h***,
Ps 34:10 young lions lack and suffer ***h***;
Prov 19:15 an idle person will suffer ***h***.
Isa 49:10 They shall neither ***h*** nor
Jer 38: 9 and he is likely to die from ***h***
Lam 2:19 Who faint from ***h*** at the head
4: 9 off Than those who die of ***h***;
Ezek 34:29 no longer be consumed with ***h***
Mic 6:14 ***H*** shall be in your midst.
Mt 5: 6 Blessed are those who ***h*** and
Lk 6:21 Blessed are you who ***h*** now,
6:25 who are full, For you shall ***h***.
15:17 and I perish with ***h***!
Jn 6:35 who comes to Me shall never ***h***,
1 Cor 4:11 To the present hour we both ***h***
2 Cor 11:27 in ***h*** and thirst, in fastings
Rev 6: 8 to kill with sword, with ***h***,
7:16 They shall neither ***h*** anymore nor

HUNGRY (46/45) HUNGER

1 Sam 2: 5 And the ***h*** have ceased to
2 Sam 17:29 The people are ***h*** and weary and
2 Ki 7:12 to us. They know that we are ***h***;
Job 5: 5 Because the ***h*** eat up his
22: 7 have withheld bread from the ***h***.
24:10 away the sheaves from the ***h***.
Ps 50:12 'If I were ***h***, I would not
107: 5 ***H*** and thirsty, Their soul
107: 9 And fills the ***h*** soul with
107:36 There He makes the ***h*** dwell,
146: 7 Who gives food to the ***h***.
Prov 16:26 For his ***h*** mouth drives him
25:21 If your enemy is ***h***,
27: 7 But to a ***h*** soul every bitter
Isa 8:21 through it hard pressed and ***h***;
8:21 shall happen, when they are ***h***,
9:20 on the right hand And be ***h***;
29: 8 It shall even be as when a ***h***
32: 6 To keep the ***h*** unsatisfied,
44:12 of his arms. Even so, he is ***h***,
58: 7 to share your bread with the ***h***,
58:10 you extend your soul to the ***h***
65:13 shall eat, But you shall be ***h***;
Jer 42:14 nor be ***h*** for bread, and there
Ezek 18: 7 has given his bread to the ***h***
18:16 has given his bread to the ***h***
Mt 4: 2 nights, afterward He was ***h***.
12: 1 And His disciples were ***h***,
12: 3 what David did when he was ***h***,
15:32 do not want to send them away ***h***,
21:18 returned to the city, He was ***h***.
25:35 for I was ***h*** and you gave Me
25:37 when did we see You ***h*** and feed
25:42 for I was ***h*** and you gave Me no
25:44 when did we see You ***h*** or
Mk 2:25 did when he was in need and ***h***,
8: 3 And if I send them away ***h*** to
11:12 come out from Bethany, He was ***h***.
Lk 1:53 He has filled the ***h*** with good
4: 2 when they had ended, He was ***h***.
6: 3 what David did when he was ***h***,
Acts 10:10 Then he became very ***h*** and wanted
Rom 12:20 "If your enemy is ***h***,
1 Cor 11:21 and one is ***h*** and another is
11:34 But if anyone is ***h***,
Phil 4:12 both to be full and to be ***h***,

HUNT (12/10) HUNTED, HUNTER, HUNTING

Gen 27: 3 and go out to the field and ***h***
27: 5 And Esau went to the field to ***h***
1 Sam 24:11 Yet you ***h*** my life to take it.
1 Ki 18:10 has not sent someone to ***h*** for
Job 10:16 You ***h*** me like a fierce lion,
38:39 Can you ***h*** the prey for the
Ps 140:11 Let evil ***h*** the violent man to
Jer 16:16 and they shall ***h*** them from
Ezek 13:18 of people of every height to ***h***
13:18 to hunt souls! Will you ***h*** the
13:20 magic charms by which you ***h***
13:20 the souls you ***h*** like birds.

HUNTED (3/3) HUNT

Gen 27:33 Where is the one who ***h*** game
Isa 13:14 It shall be as the ***h*** gazelle,
Lam 3:52 My enemies without cause ***H*** me

HUNTER (4/3) HUNT

Gen 10: 9 He was a mighty ***h*** before the
10: 9 Like Nimrod the mighty ***h*** before
25:27 And Esau was a skillful ***h***,
Prov 6: 5 from the hand of the ***h***,

HUNTERS (1/1)

Jer 16:16 I will send for many ***h***,

HUNTING (2/2) HUNT

Gen 27:30 his brother came in from his ***h***.
Prov 12:27 not roast what he took in ***h***,

HUNTS (3/3)

Lev 17:13 who ***h*** and catches any animal or
1 Sam 26:20 as when one ***h*** a partridge in
Mic 7: 2 Every man ***h*** his brother with a

HUPHAM (1/1)

Num 26:39 family of the Shuphamites; of ***H***,

HUPHAMITES (1/1)

Num 26:39 of Hupham, the family of the ***H***.

HUPPAH (1/1)

1 Chr 24:13 the thirteenth to ***H***,

HUPPIM (3/3)

Gen 46:21 Naaman, Ehi, Rosh, Muppim, ***H***,
1 Chr 7:12 Shuppim and ***H*** were the sons of
7:15 as his wife the sister of ***H***

HUR (15/15)

Ex 17:10 and ***H*** went up to the top of the
17:12 And Aaron and ***H*** supported his
24:14 Indeed Aaron and ***H*** are with
31: 2 the son of Uri, the son of ***H***,
35:30 the son of Uri, the son of ***H***,
38:22 the son of Uri, the son of ***H***,
Num 31: 8 were killed—Evi, Rekem, Zur, ***H***,
Josh 13:21 of Midian: Evi, Rekem, Zur, ***H***,
1 Chr 2:19 as his wife, who bore him ***H***.
2:20 And ***H*** begot Uri, and Uri begot
2:50 of Caleb: The sons of ***H***,
4: 1 were Perez, Hezron, Carmi, ***H***,
4: 4 These were the sons of ***H***,
2 Chr 1: 5 the son of Uri, the son of ***H***,
Neh 3: 9 to them Rephaiah the son of ***H***,

HURAI (1/1)

1 Chr 11:32 ***H*** of the brooks of Gaash, Abiel

HURAM (9/7) HIRAM

1 Ki 7:13 King Solomon sent and brought ***H***
7:40 ***H*** made the lavers and the
7:40 So ***H*** finished doing all the
7:45 All these articles which ***H*** made
1 Chr 8: 5 Gera, Shephuphan, and ***H***.
2 Chr 2:13 ***H*** my master craftsman
4:11 Then ***H*** made the pots and the
4:11 So ***H*** finished doing the work
4:16 and all their articles ***H*** his

HURI (1/1)

1 Chr 5:14 of Abihail the son of ***H***,

HURLING (1/1)

1 Chr 12: 2 right hand and the left in ***h***

HURLS (2/2)

Num 35:20 ***h*** something at him so that he
Job 27:22 It ***h*** against him and does not

HURRIED (7/7)

Gen 18: 6 So Abraham ***h*** into the tent to
Josh 4:10 and the people ***h*** and crossed
8:14 that the men of the city ***h*** and
8:19 and ***h*** to set the city on fire.
2 Chr 26:20 Indeed he also ***h*** to get out,
Esth 6:12 But Haman ***h*** to his house,
Jer 17:16 I have not ***h*** away from being a

HURRY (8/8)

Gen 19:15 the angels urged Lot to ***h***,
19:22 '***H***, escape there.
45: 9 ***H*** and go up to my father, and
45:13 and you shall ***h*** and bring my
Ex 5:13 taskmasters forced them to ***h***,
1 Sam 9:12 ***H*** now; for today he came to
20:38 after the lad, "Make haste, ***h***,
Esth 6:10 the king said to Haman, "***H***,

HURRYING (1/1)

Acts 20:16 for he was ***h*** to be at

HURT (39/38) HURTING, HURTS

Gen 31: 7 but God did not allow him to ***h***
Ex 21:22 and ***h*** a woman with child, so
22:10 to keep, and it dies, is ***h***,
Num 16:15 nor have I ***h*** one of them."
1 Sam 25: 7 and we did not ***h*** them, nor was
25:15 good to us, and we were not ***h***,
Ezra 4:22 damage increase to the ***h*** of
Ps 15: 4 He who swears to his own ***h***
35: 4 to confusion Who plot my ***h***.
35:26 confusion Who rejoice at my ***h***;
38:12 Those who seek my ***h*** speak of
41: 7 Against me they devise my ***h***.
70: 2 and confused Who desire my ***h***.
71:13 and dishonor Who seek my ***h***.
71:24 brought to shame Who seek my ***h***.
105:18 They ***h*** his feet with fetters,
Prov 20:30 Blows that ***h*** cleanse away evil,
23:35 struck me, but I was not ***h***;
Eccl 5:13 kept for their owner to his ***h***.
8: 9 rules over another to his own ***h***.
10: 9 who quarries stones may be ***h***
Isa 11: 9 They shall not ***h*** nor destroy in
27: 3 Lest any ***h*** it, I keep it
65:25 They shall not ***h*** nor destroy
Jer 6:14 They have also healed the ***h*** of
7: 6 walk after other gods to your ***h***,
8:11 For they have healed the ***h*** of
8:21 For the ***h*** of the daughter of my
8:21 daughter of my people I am ***h***.
10:19 Woe is me for my ***h***! My wound
25: 7 of your hands to your own ***h***.
Dan 3:25 of the fire; and they are not ***h***,
6:22 so that they have not ***h*** me,
Mk 16:18 it will by no means ***h*** them;
Lk 4:35 came out of him and did not ***h***
10:19 nothing shall by any means ***h***
Acts 18:10 and no one will attack you to ***h***
Rev 2:11 He who overcomes shall not be ***h***
9:10 Their power was to ***h*** men five

HURTING (2/2) HURT

Gen 4:23 Even a young man for ***h*** me.
1 Sam 25:34 kept me back from ***h*** you,

HURTS (1/1) HURT

Ex 21:35 If one man's ox ***h*** another's, so

HUSBAND (119/103) HUSBAND'S, HUSBANDS

Gen 3: 6 She also gave to her ***h*** with
3:16 desire shall be for your ***h***,
16: 3 and gave her to her ***h*** Abram to
29:32 my ***h*** will love me."
29:34 Now this time my ***h*** will become
30:15 that you have taken away my ***h***?
30:18 I have given my maid to my ***h***.
30:20 now my ***h*** will dwell with me,
Ex 4:25 Surely you are a ***h*** of blood to
4:26 You are a ***h*** of
21:22 accordingly as the woman's ***h***
Lev 21: 3 near to him, who has had no ***h***,
21: 7 a woman divorced from her ***h***;
Num 5:13 hidden from the eyes of her ***h***,
5:20 and some man other than your ***h***
5:27 unfaithfully toward her ***h***,
30: 6 "If indeed she takes a ***h***,
30: 7 and her ***h*** hears it, and makes
30: 8 But if her ***h*** overrules her on
30:11 and her ***h*** heard it, and made no
30:12 But if her ***h*** truly made them
30:12 her ***h*** has made them void, and
30:13 her ***h*** may confirm it, or her
30:13 or her ***h*** may make it void.
30:14 Now if her ***h*** makes no response
Deut 21:13 may go in to her and be her ***h***,
22:22 with a woman married to a ***h***,
22:23 a virgin is betrothed to a ***h***,
24: 3 if the latter ***h*** detests her and

24: 3 or if the latter *h* dies who
24: 4 then her former *h* who divorced
25:11 one draws near to rescue her *h*
28:56 will refuse to the *h* of her
Judg 13: 6 the woman came and told her *h*,
13: 9 but Manoah her *h* was not with
13:10 ran in haste and told her *h*,
14:15 Samson's wife, "Entice your *h*,
19: 3 Then her *h* arose and went after
20: 4 the *h* of the woman who was
Ruth 1: 3 Then Elimelech, Naomi's *h*,
1: 5 survived her two sons and her *h*.
1: 9 each in the house of her *h*.
1:12 go—for I am too old to have a *h*.
1:12 if I should have a *h* tonight
2: 1 was a relative of Naomi's *h*,
2:11 since the death of your *h*,
1 Sam 1: 8 Then Elkanah her *h* said to her,
1:22 go up, for she said to her *h*,
1:23 And Elkanah her *h* said to her,
2:19 when she came up with her *h* to
4:19 her father-in-law and her *h*
4:21 of her father-in-law and her *h*.
25:19 But she did not tell her *h*
2 Sam 3:15 sent and took her from her *h*,
3:16 Then her *h* went along with her
11:26 of Uriah heard that Uriah her *h*
11:26 was dead, she mourned for her *h*.
14: 5 am a widow, my *h* is dead.
14: 7 and leave to my *h* neither name
2 Ki 4: 1 Your servant my *h* is dead, and
4: 9 And she said to her *h*,
4:14 and her *h* is old."
4:22 Then she called to her *h*,
4:26 Is it well with your *h*?
Prov 7:19 For my *h* is not at home;
12: 4 wife is the crown of her *h*,
31:11 The heart of her *h* safely
31:23 Her *h* is known in the gates,
31:28 Her *h* also, and he praises
Isa 54: 5 For your Maker is your *h*,
Jer 3:20 departs from her *h*,
6:11 For even the *h* shall be taken
31:32 though I was a *h* to them, says
Ezek 16:32 strangers instead of her *h*.
16:45 loathing *h* and children;
Hos 2: 2 nor am I her *H*! Let her put
2: 7 go and return to my first *h*,
2:16 "That you will call Me 'My *H*,
Joel 1: 8 with sackcloth For the *h* of
Mt 1:16 And Jacob begot Joseph the *h* of
1:19 Then Joseph her *h*,
Mk 10:12 And if a woman divorces her *h*
Lk 2:36 and had lived with a *h* seven
16:18 her who is divorced from her *h*
Jn 4:16 said to her, "Go, call your *h*,
4:17 and said, "I have no *h*."
4:17 have well said, 'I have no *h*,
4:18 whom you now have is not your *h*;
Acts 5: 9 of those who have buried your *h*
5:10 her out, buried her by her *h*.
Rom 7: 2 For the woman who has a *h* is
7: 2 is bound by the law to her *h*
7: 2 But if the *h* dies, she is
7: 2 released from the law of her *h*.
7: 3 while her *h* lives, she marries
7: 3 but if her *h* dies, she is free
1 Cor 7: 2 let each woman have her own *h*.
7: 3 Let the *h* render to his wife the
7: 3 likewise also the wife to her *h*.
7: 4 but the *h* does. And likewise
7: 4 And likewise the *h* does not
7:10 is not to depart from her *h*.
7:11 or be reconciled to her *h*.
7:11 And a *h* is not to divorce his
7:13 And a woman who has a *h* who does
7:14 For the unbelieving *h* is
7:14 wife is sanctified by the *h*;
7:16 whether you will save your *h*?
7:16 Or how do you know, O *h*,
7:34 world—how she may please her *h*.
7:39 bound by law as long as her *h*
7:39 but if her *h* dies, she is at
2 Cor 11: 2 I have betrothed you to one *h*,
Gal 4:27 Than she who has a *h*.
Eph 5:23 For the *h* is head of the wife,
5:33 see that she respects her *h*.
1 Tim 3: 2 the *h* of one wife, temperate,
Titus 1: 6 the *h* of one wife, having
Rev 21: 2 as a bride adorned for her *h*.

HUSBAND'S (9/7) HUSBAND

Num 5:19 while under your *h* authority,
5:20 while under your *h* authority,
5:29 while under her *h* authority,
30:10 If she vowed in her *h* house, or
Deut 25: 5 her *h* brother shall go in to
25: 5 duty of a *h* brother to her.
25: 7 My *h* brother refuses to raise up
25: 7 the duty of my *h* brother.'
Prov 6:34 For jealousy is a *h* fury;

HUSBANDMAN (KJV) See FARMER

HUSBANDS (21/21) HUSBAND

Ruth 1:11 womb, that they may be your *h*?
1:13 yourselves from having *h*?
Esth 1:17 that they will despise their *h*
1:20 all wives will honor their *h*,
Jer 29: 6 and give your daughters to *h*,
Ezek 16:45 who loathed their *h* and
Am 4: 1 the needy, Who say to your *h*,
Jn 4:18 "for you have had five *h*,
1 Cor 14:35 let them ask their own *h* at
Eph 5:22 Wives, submit to your own *h*,
5:24 the wives be to their own *h*
5:25 *H*, love your wives, just as
5:28 So *h* ought to love their own
Col 3:18 Wives, submit to your own *h*,
3:19 *H*, love your wives and do
1 Tim 3:12 Let deacons be the *h* of one
Titus 2: 4 the young women to love their *h*,
2: 5 good, obedient to their own *h*,
1 Pe 3: 1 be submissive to your own *h*,
3: 5 being submissive to their own *h*,
3: 7 *H*, likewise, dwell with

HUSBANDS' (1/1)

Jer 44:19 without our *h* permission?"

HUSHAH (1/1)

1 Chr 4: 4 and Ezer was the father of *H*.

HUSHAI (14/13)

2 Sam 15:32 there was *H* the Archite coming
15:37 So *H*, David's friend,
16:16 when *H* the Archite, David's
16:16 that *H* said to Absalom, "Long
16:17 So Absalom said to *H*,
16:18 And *H* said to Absalom, "No, but
17: 5 Now call *H* the Archite also, and
17: 6 And when *H* came to Absalom,
17: 7 So *H* said to Absalom: "The
17: 8 'For,' said *H*, "you know
17:14 The advice of *H* the Archite is
17:15 Then *H* said to Zadok and
1 Ki 4:16 Baanah the son of *H*,
1 Chr 27:33 and *H* the Archite was the

HUSHAM (4/4)

Gen 36:34 *H* of the land of the Temanites
36:35 And when *H* died, Hadad the son
1 Chr 1:45 *H* of the land of the Temanites
1:46 And when *H* died, Hadad the son

HUSHATHITE (5/5)

2 Sam 21:18 Then Sibbechai the *H* killed
23:27 the Anathothite, Mebunnai the *H*,
1 Chr 11:29 Sibbechai the *H*, Ilai the
20: 4 at which time Sibbechai the *H*
27:11 month was Sibbechai the *H*,

HUSHED (1/1)

Job 29:10 The voice of nobles was *h*,

HUSHIM (4/4)

Gen 46:23 The son of Dan was *H*.
1 Chr 7:12 and *H* was the son of Aher.
8: 8 after he had sent away *H* and
8:11 And by *H* he begot Abitub and

HUSK (KJV) See KNAPSACK, SKIN

HUT (2/2)

Isa 1: 8 As a *h* in a garden of
24:20 And shall totter like a *h*;

HUZ (1/1)

Gen 22:21 *H* his firstborn, Buz his

HYACINTH (1/1)

Rev 9:17 *h* blue, and sulfur yellow;

HYENAS (1/1)

Isa 13:22 The *h* will howl in their

HYMENAEUS (2/2)

1 Tim 1:20 of whom are *H* and Alexander,
2 Tim 2:17 *H* and Philetus are of this

HYMN (2/2) HYMNS

Mt 26:30 And when they had sung a *h*,
Mk 14:26 And when they had sung a *h*,

HYMNS (3/3) HYMN

Acts 16:25 were praying and singing *h* to
Eph 5:19 to one another in psalms and *h*
Col 3:16 one another in psalms and *h*

HYPOCRISY (8/8) HYPOCRITE

Mt 23:28 but inside you are full of *h*
Mk 12:15 But He, knowing their *h*,
Lk 12: 1 of the Pharisees, which is *h*.
Rom 12: 9 Let love be without *h*.
Gal 2:13 was carried away with their *h*.
1 Tim 4: 2 speaking lies in *h*,
Jas 3:17 partiality and without *h*.
1 Pe 2: 1 aside all malice, all deceit, *h*,

HYPOCRITE (12/12) HYPOCRISY, HYPOCRITES

Job 8:13 And the hope of the *h* shall
13:16 For a *h* could not come before
17: 8 stirs himself up against the *h*.
20: 5 And the joy of the *h* is but
27: 8 For what is the hope of the *h*,
34:30 That the *h* should not reign,
Prov 11: 9 The *h* with his mouth destroys
Isa 9:17 For everyone is a *h* and an
Mt 7: 5 *H*! First remove the plank from
Lk 6:42 *H*! First remove the plank from
13:15 *H*! Does not each one of you on
Gal 2:13 of the Jews also played the *h*

HYPOCRITES (22/22) HYPOCRITE

Job 15:34 For the company of *h* will be
36:13 But the *h* in heart store up
Ps 26: 4 Nor will I go in with *h*.
Isa 33:14 Fearfulness has seized the *h*:
Jer 42:20 For you were *h* in your hearts
Mt 6: 2 a trumpet before you as the *h*
6: 5 you shall not be like the *h*.
6:16 you fast, do not be like the *h*,
15: 7 *H*! Well did Isaiah prophesy
16: 3 *H*! You know how to discern the
22:18 "Why do you test Me, you *h*?
23:13 Pharisees, *h*! For you shut up
23:14 Pharisees, *h*! For you devour
23:15 Pharisees, *h*! For you travel
23:23 Pharisees, *h*! For you pay
23:25 Pharisees, *h*! For you cleanse
23:27 Pharisees, *h*! For you are
23:29 Pharisees, *h*! Because you
24:51 him his portion with the *h*.
Mk 7: 6 did Isaiah prophesy of you *h*,
Lk 11:44 Pharisees, *h*! For you are
12:56 *H*! You can discern the face of

HYRAX (2/2)

Lev 11: 5 'the rock *h*, because it chews
Deut 14: 7 camel, the hare, and the rock *h*;

HYSSOP (12/12)

Ex 12:22 you shall take a bunch of *h*,
Lev 14: 4 cedar wood, scarlet, and *h*.
14: 6 wood and the scarlet and the *h*,
14:49 cedar wood, scarlet, and *h*.
14:51 take the cedar wood, the *h*,
14:52 with the cedar wood, the *h*,
Num 19: 6 shall take cedar wood and *h*
19:18 A clean person shall take *h* and
1 Ki 4:33 tree of Lebanon even to the *h*
Ps 51: 7 Purge me with *h*, and I
Jn 19:29 with sour wine, put it on *h*,
Heb 9:19 with water, scarlet wool, and *h*,

I

I (8690/5913) See APPENDIX

I AM (816/758)

Gen 6: 7 for *I* sorry that I have made
15: 1 *I* your shield, your exceedingly
15: 7 *I* the LORD, who brought you out
16: 8 *I* fleeing from the presence of
17: 1 *I* Almighty God; walk before Me
18:13 bear a child, since *I* old?'
18:17 I hide from Abraham what *I*
22: 1 And he said, "Here *I*."
22: 7 And he said, "Here *I*,
22:11 So he said, "Here *I*."
23: 4 *I* a foreigner and a visitor
24:24 *I* the daughter of Bethuel,
24:34 *I* Abraham's servant.
25:30 for *I* weary." Therefore his
25:32 *I* about to die; so what is
26:24 *I* the God of your father
26:24 for *I* with you. I will bless
27: 1 And he answered him, "Here *I*."
27: 2 *I* old. I do not know the day of
27:11 and *I* a smooth-skinned man.
27:18 And he said, "Here *I*.
27:19 *I* Esau your firstborn; I have
27:24 my son Esau?" He said, "*I*."
27:32 *I* your son, your firstborn,
27:46 *I* weary of my life because of
28:13 *I* the LORD God of Abraham your
28:15 *I* with you and will keep you
28:20 and keep me in this way that *I*
29:33 the LORD has heard that *I*
30:13 *I* happy, for the daughters will
31:11 'Jacob.' And I said, 'Here *I*.'
31:13 *I* the God of Bethel, where you
32:10 *I* not worthy of the least of all
34:30 and since *I* few in number, they
35:11 *I* God Almighty. Be fruitful and
37:13 So he said to him, "Here *I*."
37:16 '*I* seeking my brothers.
38:25 *I* with child." And she said,

41:44 *I* Pharaoh, and without your
43:14 If *I* bereaved, I am bereaved!"
43:14 am bereaved, *I* bereaved!"
45: 3 *I* Joseph; does my father still
45: 4 *I* Joseph your brother, whom you
46: 2 Jacob!" And he said, "Here *I*.
46: 3 *I* God, the God of your father;
48:21 *I* dying, but God will be with
49:29 *I* to be gathered to my people;
50: 5 *I* dying; in my grave which I
50:24 *I* dying; but God will surely
Ex 3: 4 Moses!" And he said, "Here *I*.
3: 6 *I* the God of your father—the God
3:14 *I* WHO I AM." And He said,
3:14 God said to Moses, "I AM WHO *I*.
3:14 *I* has sent me to you.'"
3:19 But *I* sure that the king of
4:10 *I* not eloquent, neither before
4:10 but *I* slow of speech and slow
6: 2 to him: "*I* the LORD.
6: 6 *I* the LORD; I will bring you
6: 7 Then you shall know that *I* the
6: 8 heritage: *I* the LORD.'
6:12 for *I* of uncircumcised lips?"
6:29 *I* the LORD. Speak to Pharaoh
6:30 *I* of uncircumcised lips, and
7: 5 the Egyptians shall know that *I*
7:17 By this you shall know that *I*
8:22 order that you may know that *I*
8:29 Indeed *I* going out from you, and
10: 2 that you may know that *I* the
12:12 judgment: *I* the LORD.
14: 4 the Egyptians may know that *I*
14:18 the Egyptians shall know that *I*
15:26 For *I* the LORD who heals
16:12 And you shall know that *I* the
20: 2 *I* the LORD your God, who
22:27 I will hear, for *I* gracious.
29:46 And they shall know that *I* the
29:46 *I* the LORD their God.
31:13 that you may know that *I* the
34:11 *I* driving out from before you
Lev 11:44 For *I* the LORD your God. You
11:44 for *I* holy. Neither shall you
11:45 For *I* the LORD who brings you
11:45 be holy, for *I* holy.
18: 2 *I* the LORD your God.
18: 3 where *I* bringing you, you shall
18: 4 *I* the LORD your God.
18: 5 by them: *I* the LORD.
18: 6 nakedness: *I* the LORD.
18:21 your God: *I* the LORD.
18:24 which *I* casting out before you.
18:30 *I* the LORD your God.'"
19: 3 *I* the LORD your God.
19: 4 *I* the LORD your God.
19:10 *I* the LORD your God.
19:12 your God: *I* the LORD.
19:14 your God: *I* the LORD.
19:16 neighbor: *I* the LORD.
19:18 as yourself: *I* the LORD.
19:25 *I* the LORD your God.
19:28 marks on you: *I* the LORD.
19:30 sanctuary: *I* the LORD.
19:31 *I* the LORD your God.
19:32 your God: *I* the LORD.
19:34 *I* the LORD your God.
19:36 *I* the LORD your God, who
19:37 them: *I* the LORD.'
20: 7 for *I* the LORD your God.
20: 8 *I* the LORD who sanctifies you.
20:22 that the land where *I* bringing
20:23 statutes of the nation which *I*
20:24 *I* the LORD your God, who has
21:12 upon him: *I* the LORD.
22: 2 to Me: *I* the LORD.
22: 3 My presence: *I* the LORD.
22: 8 with it: *I* the LORD.
22:30 morning: *I* the LORD.
22:31 perform them: *I* the LORD.
22:32 *I* the LORD who sanctifies you,
22:33 your God: *I* the LORD."
23:22 *I* the LORD your God.'"
23:43 *I* the LORD your God.'"
24:22 for *I* the LORD your God.'"
25:17 for *I* the LORD your God.
25:38 *I* the LORD your God, who
25:55 *I* the LORD your God.
26: 1 for *I* the LORD your God.
26: 2 My sanctuary: *I* the LORD.
26:13 *I* the LORD your God, who
26:44 for *I* the LORD their God.
26:45 their God: *I* the LORD.'
Num 3:13 be Mine: *I* the LORD."
3:41 *I* the LORD—INSTEAD of all the
3:45 be Mine: *I* the LORD.
10:10 *I* the LORD your God."
11:14 *I* not able to bear all these
11:21 The people whom *I* among are six
13: 2 which *I* giving to the children
15: 2 which *I* giving to you,
15:41 *I* the LORD your God, who
15:41 *I* the LORD your God."
18:20 *I* your portion and your
24:14 *I* going to my people. Come, I
Deut 1:36 and to him and his children *I*
1:42 for *I* not among you; lest you
5: 6 *I* the LORD your God who
5:31 them in the land which *I*
29: 6 that you may know that *I* the
31: 2 *I* one hundred and twenty years
31:27 while *I* yet alive with you, you
32:39 *I*, even I, ***am*** He, And there is no
32:52 into the land which *I* giving to
Josh 1: 2 to the land which *I* giving to
14:10 here *I* this day, eighty-five
14:11 As yet *I* as strong this day as
23: 2 *I* old, advanced in age.
23:14 this day *I* going the way of all
Judg 4:19 for *I* thirsty." So she opened
6:10 *I* the LORD your God; do not
6:15 and *I* the least in my father's
8: 5 and *I* pursuing Zebah and
9: 2 Remember that *I* your own flesh
13:11 this woman?" And He said, "*I*.
16:17 If *I* shaven, then my strength
17: 9 *I* a Levite from Bethlehem in
17: 9 and *I* on my way to find a
19:18 *I* from there. I went to
19:18 now *I* going to the house of
Ruth 1:12 for *I* too old to have a husband.
2:10 since *I* a foreigner?"
2:13 though *I* not like one of your
3: 9 '*I* Ruth, your maidservant.
3:12 Now it is true that *I* a close
4: 4 and *I* next after you.'" And
1 Sam 1:15 *I* a woman of sorrowful spirit.
1:26 *I* the woman who stood by you
3: 4 he answered, "Here *I*!"
3: 5 ran to Eli and said, "Here *I*,
3: 6 went to Eli, and said, "Here *I*,
3: 8 went to Eli, and said, "Here *I*,
3:16 And he answered, "Here *I*.
4:16 *I* he who came from the battle.
9:19 *I* the seer. Go up before me to
12: 2 and *I* old and grayheaded, and
12: 3 'Here *I*. Witness against me
14: 7 here *I* with you, according to
16: 1 *I* sending you to Jesse the
17:58 *I* the son of your servant Jesse
18:23 seeing *I* a poor and lightly
22:12 And he answered, "Here *I*,
23:22 For *I* told he is very crafty.
25:19 *I* coming after you." But she
28:15 *I* deeply distressed; for the
30:13 *I* a young man from Egypt,
2 Sam 1: 7 to me. And I answered, 'Here *I*.
1: 8 him, '*I* an Amalekite.'
1:13 *I* the son of an alien, an
1:26 *I* distressed for you, my
2:20 you Asahel?" He answered, "*I*.
3:39 And *I* weak today, though
11: 5 and said, "*I* with child."
14: 5 Indeed *I* a widow, my husband is
15:26 have no delight in you,' here *I*,
19:20 I have sinned. Therefore here *I*,
19:22 today *I* king over Israel?"
19:35 '*I* today eighty years old.
20:17 you Joab?" He answered, "*I*."
20:17 answered, "*I* listening."
20:19 *I* among the peaceable and
24:14 *I* in great distress. Please let
1 Ki 3: 7 but *I* a little child; I do not
13:14 from Judah?" And he said, "*I*.
13:31 When *I* dead, then bury me in the
17:12 *I* gathering a couple of sticks
18:12 as soon as *I* gone from you,
18:36 You are God in Israel and *I*
19: 4 for *I* no better than my
20:13 and you shall know that *I* the
20:28 and you shall know that *I* the
22: 4 *I* as you are, my people as your
22:34 the battle, for *I* wounded."
2 Ki 1:10 If *I* a man of God, then let fire
1:12 If *I* a man of God, let fire come
2: 9 before *I* taken away from you?"
2:10 if you see me when *I* taken
3: 7 *I* as you are, my people as
16: 7 *I* your servant and your son.
21:12 *I* bringing such calamity upon
1 Chr 21:13 *I* in great distress. Please let
21:17 *I* the one who has sinned and
2 Chr 2: 4 *I* building a temple for the
2: 9 for the temple which *I* about to
18: 3 *I* as you are, and my people as
18:33 the battle, for *I* wounded."
35:23 for *I* severely wounded."
Ezra 9: 6 *I* too ashamed and humiliated to
Neh 6: 3 *I* doing a great work, so that I
Esth 5:12 and tomorrow *I* again invited by
7: 8 while *I* in the house?"
8: 5 and *I* pleasing in his eyes,
Job 3:26 *I* not at ease, nor am I quiet
7:20 So that *I* a burden to myself?
9:21 *I* blameless, yet I do not know
9:28 *I* afraid of all my sufferings
9:29 If *I* condemned, Why then do I
9:32 "For He is not a man, as *I*,
10: 7 Although You know that *I* not
10:15 If *I* wicked, woe to me;
10:15 Even if *I* righteous, I cannot
10:15 *I* full of disgrace; See my
11: 4 And *I* clean in your eyes.'
12: 3 *I* not inferior to you.
12: 4 *I* one mocked by his friends,
13: 2 *I* not inferior to you.
19: 7 *I* not heard. If I cry aloud,
19:10 And *I* gone; My hope He has
19:15 *I* an alien in their sight.
19:17 And *I* repulsive to the
21: 6 Even when I remember *I*
23:15 Therefore *I* terrified at His
23:15 this, *I* afraid of Him.
30: 9 'And now *I* their taunting song;
30: 9 Yes, *I* their byword.
30:29 *I* a brother of jackals, And a
32: 6 *I* young in years, and you are
32:18 For *I* full of words;
33: 6 Truly *I* as your spokesman
33: 9 *I* pure, without transgression;
33: 9 *I* innocent, and there is no
34: 5 *I* righteous, But God has taken
34: 6 though *I* without
40: 4 *I* vile; What shall I answer
Ps 6: 2 for *I* weak; O LORD, heal me,
6: 6 *I* weary with my groaning
13: 4 who trouble me rejoice when *I*
22: 6 But *I* a worm, and no man;
22:14 *I* poured out like water, And
25:16 For *I* desolate and afflicted.
28: 7 and *I* helped; Therefore my
31: 9 for *I* in trouble; My eye
31:11 *I* a reproach among all my
31:12 *I* forgotten like a dead man,
31:12 *I* like a broken vessel.
31:22 *I* cut off from before Your
35: 3 my soul, "*I* your salvation."
38: 6 *I* troubled, I am bowed down
38: 6 *I* bowed down greatly; I go
38: 8 *I* feeble and severely broken
38:13 And *I* like a mute who does
38:14 Thus *I* like a man who does not
38:17 For *I* ready to fall, And my
39: 4 That I may know how frail *I*.
39:10 *I* consumed by the blow of Your
39:12 For *I* a stranger with You, A
40:12 so that *I* not able to look up;
40:17 But *I* poor and needy; Yet the
46:10 and know that *I* God; I will be
50: 7 *I* God, your God!
52: 8 But *I* like a green olive tree
55: 2 *I* restless in my complaint,
56: 3 Whenever *I* afraid, I will
69: 3 *I* weary with my crying
69:12 And *I* the song of the
69:17 For *I* in trouble; Hear me
69:20 And *I* full of heaviness;
69:29 But *I* poor and sorrowful;
70: 5 But *I* poor and needy;
71:18 Now also when *I* old and
73:23 Nevertheless *I* continually with
77: 4 *I* so troubled that I cannot
81:10 *I* the LORD your God, Who
86: 1 For *I* poor and needy.
86: 2 for *I* holy; You are my God;
88: 4 *I* counted with those who go
88: 4 *I* like a man who has no
88: 8 *I* shut up, and I cannot get
88:15 Your terrors; *I* distraught.
102: 6 *I* like a pelican of the
102: 6 *I* like an owl of the desert.
109:22 For *I* poor and needy, And my
109:23 *I* gone like a shadow when it
109:23 *I* shaken off like a locust.
116:10 *I* greatly afflicted."
116:16 truly *I* Your servant; I am
116:16 *I* Your servant, the son of
119:19 *I* a stranger in the earth
119:63 *I* a companion of all who fear
119:94 *I* Yours, save me
119:107 *I* afflicted very much
119:120 And *I* afraid of Your
119:125 *I* Your servant; Give me
119:141 *I* small and despised, Yet I
120: 7 *I* for peace; But when
139:14 for *I* fearfully and
139:18 awake, *I* still with You.
142: 6 For *I* brought very low;
143:12 For *I* Your servant.
Prov 8:14 *I* understanding, I have
20: 9 *I* pure from my sin"?
30: 2 Surely *I* more stupid than any
Song 1: 5 *I* dark, but lovely,
1: 6 because *I* dark, Because the
2: 1 *I* the rose of Sharon, And the
2: 5 apples, For *I* lovesick.
2:16 and *I* his. He feeds his
5: 8 That you tell him *I* lovesick!
6: 3 *I* my beloved's, And my beloved
7:10 *I* my beloved's, And his desire
8:10 *I* a wall, And my breasts like
Isa 1:14 *I* weary of bearing them.
6: 5 for *I* undone! Because I am a
6: 5 for I am undone! Because *I* a
10:13 for *I* prudent; Also I have
19:11 *I* the son of the wise, The son
24:16 *I* ruined, ruined! Woe to me!
29:12 says, "*I* not literate."
33:24 *I* sick"; The people who dwell
38:10 *I* deprived of the remainder of
38:14 *I* oppressed; Undertake for me!
41: 4 And with the last *I* He.'"
41:10 for *I* with you; Be not
41:10 for *I* your God. I will
42: 8 *I* the LORD, that is My name
43: 3 For *I* the LORD your God, The
43: 5 for *I* with you; I will bring
43:10 And understand that *I* He.
43:11 *I*, even I, ***am*** the LORD, And
43:12 LORD, "that *I* God.
43:13 *I* He; And there is no one
43:15 *I* the LORD, your Holy One,
43:25 *I*, even I, ***am*** He who blots out
44: 5 *I* the LORD's'; Another will
44: 6 *I* the First and I am the Last;
44: 6 I am the First and *I* the Last;

44:16 Ah! *I* warm, I have seen the
44:24 *I* the LORD, who makes all
45: 5 *I* the LORD, and there is no
45: 6 *I* the LORD, and there is no
45:18 *I* the LORD, and there is no
45:22 For *I* God, and there is no
46: 4 *I* He, And even to gray hairs
46: 9 For *I* God, and there is no
46: 9 *I* God, and there is none
47: 8 '*I*, and there is no one
47:10 '*I*, and there is no one
48:12 *I* He, I am the First, I am
48:12 *I* the First, I am also the
48:12 *I* also the Last.
48:17 *I* the LORD your God, Who
49:23 Then you will know that *I* the
51:12 am He who comforts you. Who are
51:15 But *I* the LORD your God, Who
52: 6 know in that day That *I* He
56: 3 let the eunuch say, "Here *I*,
58: 9 cry, and He will say, 'Here *I*.
65: 1 not seek Me. I said, 'Here *I*,
65: 1 Me. I said, 'Here I am, here *I*,
65: 5 For *I* holier than you!'
Jer 1: 6 speak, for *I* a youth."
1: 7 *I* a youth,' For you shall go to
1: 8 For *I* with you to deliver
1:12 for *I* ready to perform My
1:15 *I* calling All the families of
1:19 For *I* with you," says the
2:23 *I* not polluted, I have not gone
2:35 Because *I* innocent, Surely His
3:12 For *I* merciful,' says the
3:14 for *I* married to you. I will
4:19 my soul! *I* pained in my very
6:11 Therefore *I* full of the fury of
6:11 *I* weary of holding it in.
8:21 daughter of my people *I* hurt.
8:21 *I* mourning; Astonishment has
9:24 That *I* the LORD, exercising
15: 6 *I* weary of relenting!
15:16 For *I* called by Your name,
15:20 For *I* with you to save you
18:11 *I* fashioning a disaster and
20: 7 *I* in derision daily;
21:13 *I* against you, O inhabitant of
23: 9 *I* like a drunken man, And
23:30 *I* against the prophets," says
23:31 *I* against the prophets," says
23:32 *I* against those who prophesy
24: 7 that *I* the LORD; and they
26:14 "As for me, here *I*,
30:11 For *I* with you,' says the
31: 9 For *I* a Father to Israel, And
32:27 *I* the LORD, the God of all
36: 5 *I* confined, I cannot go into the
37:14 *I* not defecting to the
38:19 *I* afraid of the Jews who have
42:11 for *I* with you, to save you and
46:28 For *I* with you; For I will make
50:31 *I* against you, O most haughty
51:25 *I* against you, O destroying
Lam 1:11 consider, For *I* scorned."
1:14 the hands of those whom *I*
1:20 that *I* in distress; My soul is
3: 1 *I* the man who has seen
3:54 I said, "*I* cut off!"
3:59 You have seen how *I* wronged;
3:63 *I* their taunting song.
Ezek 2: 3 *I* sending you to the children
2: 4 *I* sending you to them, and you
4:15 *I* giving you cow dung instead
5: 8 *I*, even I, ***am*** against you and will
6: 7 and you shall know that *I* the
6:10 And they shall know that *I* the
6:13 Then you shall know that *I* the
6:14 Then they shall know that *I* the
7: 4 Then you shall know that *I* the
7: 9 Then you shall know that *I* the
7:27 Then they shall know that *I*
11:10 Then you shall know that *I* the
11:12 And you shall know that *I* the
12:11 *I* a sign to you. As I have done,
12:15 Then they shall know that *I* the
12:16 Then they shall know that *I* the
12:20 and you shall know that *I* the
12:25 For *I* the LORD. I speak, and
13: 8 therefore *I* indeed against
13: 9 Then you shall know that *I* the
13:14 Then you shall know that *I* the
13:20 *I* against your magic charms by
13:21 Then you shall know that *I* the
13:23 and you shall know that *I* the
14: 8 Then you shall know that *I* the
15: 7 Then you shall know that *I* the
16:62 Then you shall know that *I* the
20: 5 *I* the LORD your God.'
20: 7 *I* the LORD your God.'
20:12 that they might know that *I* the
20:19 *I* the LORD your God
20:20 that you may know that *I* the
20:26 know that *I* the LORD."
20:38 Then you will know that *I* the
20:42 Then you shall know that *I* the
20:44 Then you shall know that *I* the
21: 3 *I* against you, and I will draw
22:16 then you shall know that *I* the
22:26 so that *I* profaned among them.
23:49 Then you shall know that *I* the
24:24 you shall know that *I* the Lord
24:27 and they shall know that *I* the
25: 5 Then you shall know that *I* the
25: 7 and you shall know that *I* the
25:11 and they shall know that *I* the
25:17 and they shall know that *I* the
26: 3 *I* against you, O Tyre, and will
26: 6 Then they shall know that *I* the
27: 3 *I* perfect in beauty.'
28: 2 *I* a god, I sit in the seat of
28: 9 *I* a god'? But you shall be a
28:22 *I* against you, O Sidon; I will
28:22 And they shall know that *I* the
28:23 shall know that *I* the LORD.
28:24 Then they shall know that *I* the
28:26 Then they shall know that *I* the
29: 3 *I* against you, O Pharaoh king
29: 6 Shall know that *I* the LORD,
29: 9 then they will know that *I* the
29:10 *I* against you and against your
29:16 Then they shall know that *I* the
29:21 Then they shall know that *I* the
30: 8 Then they will know that *I* the
30:19 know that *I* the LORD."
30:22 Surely *I* against Pharaoh king of
30:25 they shall know that *I* the
30:26 Then they shall know that *I* the
32:15 shall know that *I* the LORD.
33:29 Then they shall know that *I* the
34:10 *I* against the shepherds, and I
34:27 and they shall know that *I* the
34:31 and *I* your God," says the
35: 3 *I* against you; I will stretch
35: 4 Then you shall know that *I* the
35: 9 then you shall know that *I* the
35:12 Then you shall know that *I* the
35:15 know that *I* the LORD."
36: 9 For indeed *I* for you, and I will
36:11 Then you shall know that *I* the
36:23 know that *I* the LORD,"
36:23 when *I* hallowed in you before
36:38 Then they shall know that *I* the
37: 6 Then you shall know that *I* the
37:13 Then you shall know that *I* the
38: 3 *I* against you, O Gog, the
38:16 when *I* hallowed in you, O Gog,
38:23 Then they shall know that *I* the
39: 1 *I* against you, O Gog, the
39: 6 Then they shall know that *I* the
39: 7 shall know that *I* the LORD,
39:13 the day that *I* glorified,"
39:17 Which *I* sacrificing for you,
39:19 Which *I* sacrificing for you.
39:22 shall know that *I* the LORD
39:27 and *I* hallowed in them in the
39:28 then they shall know that *I* the
44:28 that *I* their inheritance.
44:28 for *I* their possession.
Dan 8:19 *I* making known to you what
Hos 11: 9 For *I* God, and not man, The
12: 9 But *I* the LORD your God, Ever
13: 4 Yet *I* the LORD your God Ever
14: 8 *I* like a green cypress tree;
Joel 2:27 Then you shall know that *I* in
2:27 *I* the LORD your God And
3:10 the weak say, '*I* strong.'
3:17 So you shall know that *I* the
Am 2:13 *I* weighed down by you, As a
7: 8 *I* setting a plumb line In the
Jon 1: 9 *I* a Hebrew; and I fear the
Mic 2: 3 against this family *I* devising
3: 8 But truly *I* full of power by
7: 1 Woe is me! For *I* like those
Nah 2:13 *I* against you," says the LORD
3: 5 *I* against you," says the LORD
Hab 1: 6 For indeed *I* raising up the
2: 1 will answer when *I* corrected.
Zeph 2:15 *I* it, and there is none
Hag 1:13 *I* with you, says the LORD."
2: 4 for *I* with you,' says the LORD
Zech 1:14 *I* zealous for Jerusalem And for
1:15 *I* exceedingly angry with the
1:16 *I* returning to Jerusalem with
2:10 *I* coming and I will dwell in
3: 8 *I* bringing forth My Servant the
4: 2 *I* looking, and there is a
8: 2 *I* zealous for Zion with great
8: 2 With great fervor *I* zealous
8:15 *I* determined to do good
10: 6 For *I* the LORD their God,
11: 5 for *I* rich'; and their
13: 5 *I* no prophet, I am a farmer;
13: 5 *I* a farmer; for a man taught me
Mal 1: 6 If then *I* the Father, Where
1: 6 And if *I* a Master, Where is
1:14 For *I* a great King," Says the
3: 6 For *I* the LORD, I do not
Mt 3:11 whose sandals *I* not worthy to
3:17 in whom *I* well pleased."
8: 3 *I* willing; be cleansed."
8: 8 *I* not worthy that You should
9:28 Do you believe that *I* able to do
11:29 for *I* gentle and lowly in
16:15 "But who do you say that *I*?
17: 5 in whom *I* well pleased.
18:20 *I* there in the midst of them."
20:13 *I* doing you no wrong. Did you
20:15 eye evil because *I* good?'
20:22 cup that *I* about to drink,
20:22 that *I* baptized with?"
20:23 baptism that *I* baptized with;
22:32 *I* the God of Abraham, the
24: 5 *I* the Christ,' and will deceive
26:61 *I* able to destroy the temple of
27:24 *I* innocent of the blood of this
27:43 said, '*I* the Son of God.'
28:20 *I* with you always, even to the
Mk 1: 7 whose sandal strap *I* not worthy
1:11 in whom *I* well pleased."
1:41 *I* willing; be cleansed."
8:27 them, "Who do men say that *I*?
8:29 "But who do you say that *I*?
10:38 with the baptism that *I*
10:39 and with the baptism *I* baptized
12:26 *I* the God of Abraham, the
13: 6 *I* He,' and will deceive many.
14:62 Jesus said, "*I*. And you
Lk 1:18 For *I* an old man, and my wife
1:19 *I* Gabriel, who stands in the
3:16 whose sandal strap *I* not worthy
3:22 in You *I* well pleased."
5: 8 for *I* a sinful man, O Lord!"
5:13 *I* willing; be cleansed."
7: 6 for *I* not worthy that You
9:18 "Who do the crowds say that *I*?
9:20 "But who do you say that *I*?
12:50 and how distressed *I* till it is
14:19 and *I* going to test them. I ask
15:19 and *I* no longer worthy to be
16: 3 *I* ashamed to beg.
16: 4 that when *I* put out of the
16:24 for *I* tormented in this flame.'
18:11 I thank You that *I* not like
21: 8 *I* He,' and, 'The time has drawn
22:27 Yet *I* among you as the One who
22:33 *I* ready to go with You, both to
22:58 Peter said, "Man, *I* not!"
22:70 them, "You rightly say that *I*.
Jn 1:20 *I* not the Christ."
1:21 *I* not." "Are you the
1:23 He said: "*I* 'The voice
1:27 whose sandal strap *I* not worthy
3:28 *I* not the Christ,' but, 'I have
5: 7 but while *I* coming, another
6:35 *I* the bread of life. He who
6:41 *I* the bread which came down from
6:48 *I* the bread of life.
6:51 *I* the living bread which came
7: 8 *I* not yet going up to this
7:28 and you know where *I* from; and
7:29 for *I* from Him, and He sent
7:34 and where *I* you cannot come."
7:36 and where *I* you cannot come'?"
8:12 *I* the light of the world. He who
8:14 came from and where *I* going;
8:14 come from and where *I* going.
8:16 for *I* not alone, but I am with
8:16 but *I* with the Father who sent
8:18 *I* One who bears witness of
8:21 *I* going away, and you will seek
8:23 *I* from above. You are of this
8:23 *I* not of this world.
8:24 do not believe that *I* He,
8:28 then you will know that *I* He,
8:58 to you, before Abraham was, *I*.
9: 5 As long as *I* in the world, I am
9: 5 *I* the light of the world."
9: 9 He said, "*I* he."
10: 7 *I* the door of the sheep.
10: 9 *I* the door. If anyone enters by
10:11 *I* the good shepherd. The good
10:14 *I* the good shepherd; and I know
10:36 *I* the Son of God'?
11:15 And *I* glad for your sakes that I
11:25 *I* the resurrection and the life.
12:26 let him follow Me; and where *I*,
12:32 if *I* lifted up from the earth,
13: 7 What *I* doing you do not
13:13 and you say well, for so *I*.
13:19 you may believe that *I* He.
13:33 Where *I* going, you cannot come,'
13:36 Where *I* going you cannot follow
14: 3 you to Myself; that where *I*,
14: 6 *I* the way, the truth, and the
14:10 Do you not believe that *I* in the
14:11 Believe Me that *I* in the Father
14:20 know that *I* in My Father,
14:28 *I* going away and coming back to
14:28 *I* going to the Father,' for My
15: 1 *I* the true vine, and My Father
15: 5 *I* the vine, you are the
16:32 And yet *I* not alone, because
17:10 and *I* glorified in them.
17:11 Now *I* no longer in the world,
17:14 just as *I* not of the world.
17:16 just as *I* not of the world.
17:24 gave Me may be with Me where *I*,
18: 5 *I* He." And Judas, who betrayed
18: 6 *I* He," they drew back and fell
18: 8 I have told you that *I* He.
18:17 He said, "*I* not."
18:25 it and said, "*I* not!"
18:37 You say rightly that *I* a king.
19: 4 *I* bringing Him out to you, that
19:21 *I* the King of the Jews." '"
20:17 *I* ascending to My Father and
21: 3 *I* going fishing." They said to
Acts 7:32 *I* the God of your
9: 5 *I* Jesus, whom you are
9:10 And he said, "Here *I*,
10:21 *I* he whom you seek. For what
13:25 he said, 'Who do you think *I*?
13:25 *I* not He. But behold, there
13:25 the sandals of whose feet *I* not
18: 6 *I* clean. From now on I will go
18:10 for *I* with you, and no one will
20:26 you this day that *I* innocent

21:13 For I ready not only to be
21:39 I a Jew from Tarsus, in Cilicia,
22: 3 I indeed a Jew, born in Tarsus
22: 8 I Jesus of Nazareth, whom you
23: 6 I a Pharisee, the son of a
23: 6 of the dead I being judged!"
24:21 of the dead I being judged
25:11 For if I an offender, or have
26: 2 things of which I accused
26: 7 I accused by the Jews.
26:15 I Jesus, whom you are
26:25 I not mad, most noble Festus,
26:26 for I convinced that none of
26:29 almost and altogether such as I,
28:20 for the hope of Israel I bound
Rom 1:14 I a debtor both to Greeks and to
1:15 I ready to preach the gospel
1:16 For I not ashamed of the gospel
7:14 but I carnal, sold under sin.
7:15 For what I doing, I do not
7:24 O wretched man that I! Who will
8:38 For I persuaded that neither
9: 1 I not lying, my conscience also
11:13 inasmuch as I an apostle to the
15:25 But now I going to Jerusalem to
16:19 Therefore I glad on your
1 Cor 1:12 'I of Paul," or "I am of
1:12 'I of Apollos," or "I am of
1:12 'I of Cephas," or "I am of
1:12 Cephas," or "I of Christ."
3: 4 I of Paul," and another, "I
3: 4 I of Apollos," are you not
4: 4 yet I not justified by this;
7: 8 them if they remain even as I;
9: 2 If I not an apostle to others,
9: 2 yet doubtless I to you. For you
9:19 For though I free from all
12:15 Because I not a hand, I am not
12:15 I not of the body," is it
12:16 Because I not an eye, I am not
12:16 I not of the body," is it
13: 2 have not love, I nothing.
15: 9 For I the least of the apostles,
15:10 But by the grace of God I what I
15:10 by the grace of God I am what I,
16: 5 (for I passing through
16:11 for I waiting for him with the
16:17 I glad about the coming of
2 Cor 7: 4 I filled with comfort.
7: 4 I exceedingly joyful in all our
7:14 I not ashamed. But as we spoke
8: 8 but I testing the sincerity of
10: 2 But I beg you that when I
11: 2 For I jealous for you with godly
11: 5 For I consider that I not at
11: 6 Even though I untrained in
11: 6 yet I not in knowledge. But we
11:21 foolishly—I bold also.
11:23 I more: in labors more abundant,
11:29 and I not weak? Who is made to
11:31 knows that I not lying.
12:10 For when I weak, then I am
12:10 weak, then I strong.
12:11 though I nothing.
12:14 Now for the third time I ready
12:15 the less I loved.
13: 1 will be the third time I
Gal 4:11 I afraid for you, lest I have
4:18 and not only when I present
Eph 6:20 for which I an ambassador in
6:21 may know my affairs and how I
Phil 1:17 knowing that I appointed for
1:23 For I hard pressed between the
2:17 and if I being poured out as
2:17 I glad and rejoice with you
4:11 learned in whatever state I,
4:18 I full, having received from
Col 2: 5 For though I absent in the
2: 5 yet I with you in spirit,
4: 3 for which I also in chains,
4: 8 I sending him to you for this
1 Tim 1:15 sinners, of whom I chief.
2: 7 I speaking the truth in Christ
3:15 but if I delayed, I write so
2 Tim 1: 5 and I persuaded is in you also.
1:12 nevertheless I not ashamed, for
4: 6 For I already being poured out
Phm 1:12 I sending him back. You
Heb 12:21 I exceedingly afraid and
Jas 1:13 I tempted by God"; for God
1 Pe 1:16 "Be holy, for I holy."
2 Pe 1:13 as long as I in this tent, to
1:17 in whom I well pleased."
Rev 1: 8 I the Alpha and the Omega, the
1:11 I the Alpha and the Omega, the
1:17 I the First and the Last.
1:18 I He who lives, and was dead,
1:18 I alive forevermore. Amen. And
2:23 the churches shall know that I
3:11 I coming quickly! Hold fast
3:17 I rich, have become wealthy, and
16:15 I coming as a thief. Blessed
19:10 you do not do that! I your
21: 6 It is done! I the Alpha and the
22: 7 I coming quickly! Blessed is
22: 9 For I your fellow servant, and
22:12 I coming quickly, and My reward
22:13 I the Alpha and the Omega, the
22:16 I the Root and the Offspring of
22:20 Surely I coming quickly." Amen.

IBHAR (3/3)

2 Sam 5:15 I, Elishua, Nepheg, Japhia,
1 Chr 3: 6 Also there were I,
14: 5 I, Elishua, Elpelet,

IBLEAM (3/3)

Josh 17:11 I and its towns, the
Judg 1:27 or the inhabitants of I and its
2 Ki 9:27 Ascent of Gur, which is by I.

IBNEIAH (1/1)

1 Chr 9: 8 I the son of Jeroham; Elah the

IBNIJAH (1/1)

1 Chr 9: 8 the son of Reuel, the son of I;

IBRI (1/1)

1 Chr 24:27 Beno, Shoham, Zaccur, and I.

IBZAN (2/2)

Judg 12: 8 I of Bethlehem judged Israel.
12:10 Then I died and was buried at

ICE (3/3)

Job 6:16 are dark because of the i,
37:10 By the breath of God i is
38:29 From whose womb comes the i?

ICHABOD (1/1)

1 Sam 4:21 Then she named the child I,

ICHABOD'S (1/1)

1 Sam 14: 3 I brother, the son of Phinehas,

ICONIUM (6/6)

Acts 13:51 against them, and came to I.
14: 1 Now it happened in I that they
14:19 Then Jews from Antioch and I
14:21 they returned to Lystra, I,
16: 2 who were at Lystra and I.
2 Tim 3:11 happened to me at Antioch, at I,

IDALAH (1/1)

Josh 19:15 Kattath, Nahallal, Shimron, I,

IDBASH (1/1)

1 Chr 4: 3 of Etam: Jezreel, Ishma, and I;

IDDO (14/13)

1 Ki 4:14 Ahinadab the son of I,
1 Chr 6:21 I his son, Zerah his son, and
27:21 I the son of Zechariah;
2 Chr 9:29 and in the visions of I the
12:15 and of I the seer concerning
13:22 in the annals of the prophet I.
Ezra 5: 1 and Zechariah the son of I,
6:14 and Zechariah the son of I.
8:17 And I gave them a command for I
8:17 them what they should say to I
Neh 12: 4 I, Ginnethoi, Abijah,
12:16 of I, Zechariah; of
Zech 1: 1 the son of I the prophet,
1: 7 the son of I the prophet:

IDENTIFY (3/3)

Gen 31:32 i what I have of yours and take
Ezra 2:59 but they could not i their
Neh 7:61 but they could not i their

IDLE (17/14) IDLENESS

Ex 5: 8 not reduce it. For they are i;
5:17 You are i! Idle! Therefore you
5:17 You are idle! I! Therefore you
Prov 14:23 But i chatter leads only to
19:15 And an i person will suffer
Mt 12:36 I say to you that for every i
20: 3 hour and saw others standing i
20: 6 out and found others standing i,
20: 6 have you been standing here i
Lk 24:11 words seemed to them like i
1 Tim 1: 6 have turned aside to i talk,
5:13 besides they learn to be i,
5:13 and not only i but also gossips
6:20 avoiding the profane and i
2 Tim 2:16 But shun profane and i
Titus 1:10 both i talkers and deceivers,
2 Pe 2: 3 their judgment has not been i,

IDLENESS (3/3) IDLE

Prov 31:27 does not eat the bread of i.
Eccl 10:18 And through i of hands the
Ezek 16:49 of food, and abundance of i;

IDLY (2/2)

Ps 12: 2 They speak i everyone with his
Am 6: 5 Who sing i to the sound of

IDOL (14/13) IDOL'S, IDOLATER, IDOLATRY, IDOLS

2 Chr 33: 7 the i which he had made, in the
33:15 away the foreign gods and the i
Ps 24: 4 not lifted up his soul to an i,
Isa 48: 5 My i has done them, And my
66: 3 as if he blesses an i.
66:17 to the gardens After an i in
Jer 10: 8 A wooden i is a worthless
22:28 man Coniah a despised, broken i—
Hos 10: 6 The i also shall be carried
Acts 7:41 offered sacrifices to the i,
1 Cor 8: 4 we know that an i is nothing
8: 7 with consciousness of the i,
8: 7 it as a thing offered to an i;
10:19 That an i is anything, or what

IDOL'S (1/1) IDOL

1 Cor 8:10 have knowledge eating in an i

IDOLATER (2/2) IDOL, IDOLATERS

1 Cor 5:11 immoral, or covetous, or an i,
Eph 5: 5 nor covetous man, who is an i,

IDOLATERS (7/7) IDOLATER

2 Ki 17:15 they followed idols, became i,
Jer 2: 5 idols, And have become i?
1 Cor 5:10 covetous, or extortioners, or i,
6: 9 Neither fornicators, nor i,
10: 7 And do not become i as were
Rev 21: 8 sexually immoral, sorcerers, i,
22:15 immoral and murderers and i,

IDOLATRIES (1/1) IDOLATRY

1 Pe 4: 3 parties, and abominable i.

IDOLATROUS (4/4) IDOLATRY

2 Ki 23: 5 Then he removed the i priests
Ps 26: 4 I have not sat with i mortals,
Ezek 23:49 and you shall pay for your i
Zeph 1: 4 The names of the i priests

IDOLATRY (4/4) IDOL, IDOLATRIES, IDOLATROUS

1 Sam 15:23 is as iniquity and i.
1 Cor 10:14 my beloved, flee from i.
Gal 5:20 i, sorcery, hatred,
Col 3: 5 and covetousness, which is i.

IDOLS (124/118) IDOL

Gen 31:19 had stolen the household i
31:34 had taken the household i,
31:35 did not find the household i.
Lev 19: 4 'Do not turn to i,
26: 1 You shall not make i for
26:30 on the lifeless forms of your i;
Deut 29:17 their abominations and their i
32:21 Me to anger by their foolish i.
Judg 17: 5 made an ephod and household i;
18:14 houses an ephod, household i,
18:17 the ephod, the household i,
18:18 the ephod, the household i,
18:20 took the ephod, the household i,
1 Sam 31: 9 it in the temple of their i
1 Ki 15:12 and removed all the i that his
16:13 of Israel to anger with their i.
16:26 of Israel to anger with their i.
21:26 very abominably in following i,
2 Ki 17:12 for they served i,
17:15 against them; they followed i,
21:11 also made Judah sin with his i)
21:21 and he served the i that his
23:24 the household gods and i,
1 Chr 10: 9 in the temple of their i
16:26 the gods of the peoples are i,
2 Chr 11:15 and the calf i which he had
15: 8 and removed the abominable i
24:18 and served wooden images and i;
Ps 31: 6 those who regard useless i;
96: 5 the gods of the peoples are i,
97: 7 carved images, Who boast of i.
106:36 They served their i,
106:38 Whom they sacrificed to the i
115: 4 Their i are silver and gold,
135:15 The i of the nations are
Isa 2: 8 Their land is also full of i;
2:18 But the i He shall utterly
2:20 day a man will cast away his i
2:20 his idols of silver And his i
10:10 has found the kingdoms of the i,
10:11 have done to Samaria and her i,
10:11 do also to Jerusalem and her i?
19: 1 The i of Egypt will totter at
19: 3 And they will consult the i
31: 7 man shall throw away his i of
31: 7 his idols of silver and his i
45:16 Who are makers of i.
46: 1 Their i were on the beasts and
57:13 Let your collection of i
Jer 2: 5 far from Me, Have followed i,
8:19 carved images—With foreign i?
14:22 Are there any among the i of
16:18 detestable and abominable i
18:15 burned incense to worthless i.
50: 2 Her i are humiliated, Her

50:38 they are insane with their *i*.
Ezek 6: 4 your slain men before your *i*.
6: 5 of Israel before their *i*,
6: 6 your *i* may be broken and made
6: 9 play the harlot after their *i*;
6:13 their slain are among their *i*
6:13 sweet incense to all their *i*.
8:10 and all the *i* of the house of
8:12 every man in the room of his *i*?
14: 3 these men have set up their *i*
14: 4 of Israel who sets up his *i* in
14: 4 to the multitude of his *i*,
14: 5 estranged from Me by their *i*.
14: 6 "Repent, turn away from your *i*,
14: 7 from Me and sets up his *i* in
16:36 and with all your abominable *i*,
18: 6 lifted up his eyes to the *i* of
18:12 Lifted his eyes to the *i*,
18:15 Nor lifted his eyes to the *i*
20: 7 defile yourselves with the *i*
20: 8 nor did they forsake the *i* of
20:16 their heart went after their *i*.
20:18 defile yourselves with their *i*.
20:24 were fixed on their fathers' *i*.
20:31 yourselves with all your *i*,
20:39 serve every one of you his *i*—
20:39 more with your gifts and your *i*.
22: 3 and she makes *i* within herself
22: 4 defiled yourself with the *i*
23: 7 she lusted, With all their *i*,
23:30 have become defiled by their *i*.
23:37 committed adultery with their *i*,
23:39 their children for their *i*,
30:13 "I will also destroy the *i*,
33:25 lift up your eyes toward your *i*,
36:18 and for their *i* with which
36:25 filthiness and from all your *i*.
37:23 themselves anymore with their *i*,
44:10 away from Me after their *i*,
44:12 to them before their *i* and
Hos 4:12 counsel from their wooden *i*,
4:17 "Ephraim is joined to *i*,
8: 4 silver and gold They made *i*
12:11 Though Gilead has *i*—
13: 2 *I* of their silver, according
14: 8 have I to do anymore with *i*?
Am 5:26 your king And Chiun, your *i*,
Jon 2: 8 Those who regard worthless *i*
Mic 1: 7 All her *i* I will lay desolate,
Hab 2:18 trust in it, To make mute *i*?
Zech 10: 2 For the *i* speak delusion;
13: 2 will cut off the names of the *i*
Acts 15:20 from things polluted by *i*,
15:29 from things offered to *i*,
17:16 the city was given over to *i*.
21:25 from things offered to *i*,
Rom 2:22 You who abhor *i*, do you
1 Cor 8: 1 concerning things offered to *i*:
8: 4 eating of things offered to *i*,
8:10 eat those things offered to *i*?
10:19 or what is offered to *i* is
10:28 to you, "This was offered to *i*,
12: 2 carried away to these dumb *i*,
2 Cor 6:16 has the temple of God with *i*?
1 Th 1: 9 how you turned to God from *i*
1 Jn 5:21 keep yourselves from *i*.
Rev 2:14 to eat things sacrificed to *i*,
2:20 and eat things sacrificed to *i*.
9:20 and *i* of gold, silver, brass,

IDUMEA (1/1) EDOM
Mk 3: 8 and Jerusalem and *I* and beyond

IF (1637/1455) See APPENDIX

IGAL (3/3)
Num 13: 7 *I* the son of Joseph;
2 Sam 23:36 *I* the son of Nathan of Zobah,
1 Chr 3:22 of Shemaiah were Hattush, *I*,

IGDALIAH (1/1)
Jer 35: 4 the sons of Hanan the son of *I*,

IGEAL (KJV) See IGAL

IGNOMINY (KJV) See DISHONOR

IGNORANCE (8/8) IGNORANT
Lev 5:18 for him regarding his *i* in
Ezek 45:20 sinned unintentionally or in *i*.
Acts 3:17 I know that you did it in *i*,
17:30 these times of *i* God
Eph 4:18 because of the *i* that is in
Heb 9: 7 people's sins committed in *i*;
1 Pe 1:14 the former lusts, as in your *i*;
2:15 you may put to silence the *i*

IGNORANT (13/12) IGNORANCE, IGNORANTLY
Ps 73:22 I was so foolish and *i*;
Isa 56:10 are blind, They are all *i*;
63:16 Though Abraham was *i* of us,
Rom 10: 3 For they being *i* of God's
11:25 that you should be *i* of this
1 Cor 12: 1 I do not want you to be *i*:
14:38 But if anyone is *i*,
14:38 is ignorant, let him be *i*.
2 Cor 1: 8 For we do not want you to be *i*,
2:11 for we are not *i* of his
1 Th 4:13 But I do not want you to be *i*,
2 Tim 2:23 But avoid foolish and *i*
Heb 5: 2 compassion on those who are *i*

IGNORANTLY (1/1) IGNORANT
1 Tim 1:13 mercy because I did it *i* in

IJE ABARIM (2/2)
Num 21:11 from Oboth and camped at *I*,
33:44 from Oboth and camped at *I*,

IJE-ABARIM (KJV) See IJE ABARIM

IJIM (2/2)
Num 33:45 They departed from *I* and camped
Josh 15:29 Baalah, *I*, Ezem,

IJON (3/3)
1 Ki 15:20 cities of Israel. He attacked *I*,
2 Ki 15:29 king of Assyria came and took *I*,
2 Chr 16: 4 of Israel. They attacked *I*,

IKKESH (3/3)
2 Sam 23:26 Ira the son of *I* the Tekoite,
1 Chr 11:28 Ira the son of *I* the Tekoite,
27: 9 month was Ira the son of *I*

ILAI (1/1)
1 Chr 11:29 Hushathite, *I* the Ahohite,

ILL (7/7) ILLNESS, ILLS
Judg 9:23 God sent a spirit of *i* will
2 Sam 12:15 bore to David, and it became *i*.
13: 5 on your bed and pretend to be *i*.
13: 6 lay down and pretended to be *i*;
Job 20:26 It shall go *i* with who is
Ps 106:32 So that it went *i* with Moses
Isa 3:11 to the wicked! It shall be *i*

ILLEGITIMATE (2/2)
Deut 23: 2 One of *i* birth shall not enter
Heb 12: 8 then you are *i* and not sons.

ILLITERATE (1/1)
Isa 29:12 is delivered to one who is *i*,

ILLNESS (2/2) ILL
2 Ki 13:14 had become sick with the *i* of
Ps 41: 3 strengthen him on his bed of *i*;

ILLS (1/1) ILL
Isa 3: 7 "I cannot cure your *i*,

ILLUMINATED (3/3)
Heb 10:32 days in which, after you were *i*,
Rev 18: 1 and the earth was *i* with his
21:23 for the glory of God *i* it.

ILLUSTRATION (1/1)
Jn 10: 6 Jesus used this *i*, but they

ILLYRICUM (1/1)
Rom 15:19 Jerusalem and round about to *I*

IMAGE (110/91) IMAGE'S, IMAGES
Gen 1:26 "Let Us make man in Our *i*,
1:27 God created man in His own *i*;
1:27 in the *i* of God He created him;
5: 3 his own likeness, after his *i*,
9: 6 For in the *i* of God He made
Ex 20: 4 make for yourself a carved *i*,
Lev 26: 1 neither a carved *i* nor a
Deut 4:16 make for yourselves a carved *i*
4:23 make for yourselves a carved *i*
4:25 corruptly and make a carved *i*
5: 8 make for yourself a carved *i*—
9:12 have made themselves a molded *i*.
16:21 any tree, as a wooden *i*,
27:15 who makes a carved or molded *i*,
Judg 6:25 and cut down the wooden *i* that
6:26 with the wood of the *i* which
6:28 and the wooden *i* that was
6:30 he has cut down the wooden *i*
17: 3 to make a carved *i* and a molded
17: 3 a carved image and a molded *i*;
17: 4 and he made it into a carved *i*
17: 4 a carved image and a molded *i*;
18:14 household idols, a carved *i*,
18:14 a carved image, and a molded *i*?
18:17 there, they took the carved *i*,
18:17 idols, and the molded *i*.
18:18 house and took the carved *i*,
18:18 idols, and the molded *i*,
18:20 idols, and the carved *i*,
18:30 up for themselves the carved *i*;
18:31 for themselves Micah's carved *i*
1 Sam 19:13 And Michal took an *i* and laid
19:16 there was the *i* in the bed,
1 Ki 15:13 she had made an obscene *i* of
15:13 And Asa cut down her obscene *i*
16:33 And Ahab made a wooden *i*.
2 Ki 13: 6 and the wooden *i* also remained
17:16 made for themselves a molded *i*
17:16 made a wooden *i* and worshiped
18: 4 cut down the wooden *i* and broke
21: 3 for Baal, and made a wooden *i*,
21: 7 He even set a carved *i* of
23: 6 And he brought out the wooden *i*
23: 7 wove hangings for the wooden *i*.
23:15 powder, and burned the wooden *i*.
2 Chr 15:16 she had made an obscene *i* of
15:16 and Asa cut down her obscene *i*,
33: 7 He even set a carved *i*,
Ps 73:20 You shall despise their *i*.
106:19 And worshiped the molded *i*.
106:20 their glory Into the *i* of an
Isa 40:19 The workman molds an *i*,
40:20 workman To prepare a carved *i*
44: 9 Those who make an *i*,
44:10 would form a god or mold an *i*
44:15 He makes it a carved *i*,
44:17 makes into a god, His carved *i*.
45:20 the wood of their carved *i*,
48: 5 And my carved *i* and my molded
48: 5 my carved image and my molded *i*
Jer 10:14 is put to shame by an *i*;
10:14 For his molded *i* is
51:17 is put to shame by the carved *i*;
51:17 For his molded *i* is
Ezek 8: 3 where the seat of the *i* of
8: 5 was this *i* of jealousy in the
Dan 2:31 and behold, a great *i*!
2:31 a great image! This great *i*,
2:34 which struck the *i* on its feet
2:35 And the stone that struck the *i*
3: 1 the king made an *i* of gold,
3: 2 come to the dedication of the *i*
3: 3 for the dedication of the *i*
3: 3 and they stood before the *i*
3: 5 down and worship the gold *i*
3: 7 down and worshiped the gold *i*
3:10 down and worship the gold *i*;
3:12 your gods or worship the gold *i*
3:14 my gods or worship the gold *i*
3:15 you fall down and worship the *i*
3:18 nor will we worship the gold *i*
Nah 1:14 I will cut off the carved *i*
1:14 carved image and the molded *i*.
Hab 2:18 "What profit is the *i*,
2:18 should carve it, The molded *i*,
Mt 22:20 Whose *i* and inscription is
Mk 12:16 Whose *i* and inscription is
Lk 20:24 Whose *i* and inscription does it
Acts 19:35 and of the *i* which fell down
Rom 1:23 the incorruptible God into an *i*
8:29 to be conformed to the *i* of
1 Cor 11: 7 since he is the *i* and glory of
15:49 And as we have borne the *i* of
15:49 we shall also bear the *i* of the
2 Cor 3:18 transformed into the same *i*
4: 4 who is the *i* of God, should
Col 1:15 He is the *i* of the invisible
3:10 in knowledge according to the *i*
Heb 1: 3 of His glory and the express *i*
10: 1 and not the very *i* of the
Rev 13:14 on the earth to make an *i* to
13:15 power to give breath to the *i*
13:15 that the *i* of the beast should
13:15 as would not worship the *i* of
14: 9 worships the beast and his *i*,
14:11 who worship the beast and his *i*,
15: 2 over his *i* and over his mark
16: 2 and those who worshiped his *i*.
19:20 and those who worshiped his *i*.
20: 4 worshiped the beast or his *i*,

IMAGE'S (1/1) IMAGE
Dan 2:32 This *i* head was of fine gold,

IMAGES (68/57) IMAGE
Ex 34:13 and cut down their wooden *i*
Num 33:52 destroy all their molded *i*,
Deut 7: 5 and cut down their wooden *i*,
7: 5 and burn their carved *i* with
7:25 You shall burn the carved *i* of
12: 3 and burn their wooden *i* with
12: 3 shall cut down the carved *i* of
Judg 3:19 turned back from the stone *i*
3:26 and passed beyond the stone *i*
1 Sam 6: 5 Therefore you shall make *i* of
6: 5 images of your tumors and *i* of
6:11 with the gold rats and the *i*
2 Sam 5:21 And they left their *i* there, and
1 Ki 14: 9 other gods and molded *i* to
14:15 they have made their wooden *i*,
14:23 and wooden *i* on every high hill
2 Ki 11:18 in pieces its altars and *i*,
17:10 sacred pillars and wooden *i*
17:41 yet served their carved *i*;
23:14 and cut down the wooden *i*,
2 Chr 14: 3 and cut down the wooden *i*.
17: 6 the high places and wooden *i*
19: 3 you have removed the wooden *i*
23:17 in pieces its altars and *i*,
24:18 and served wooden *i* and idols;
28: 2 and made molded *i* for the

31: 1 pieces, cut down the wooden *i*,
33: 3 the Baals, and made wooden *i*;
33:19 places and set up wooden *i* and
33:19 up wooden images and carved *i*,
33:22 sacrificed to all the carved *i*
34: 3 the high places, the wooden *i*,
34: 3 the wooden images, the carved *i*,
34: 3 carved images, and the molded *i*.
34: 4 he cut down; and the wooden *i*,
34: 4 the wooden images, the carved *i*,
34: 4 and the molded *i* he broke in
34: 7 the altars and the wooden *i*,
34: 7 had beaten the carved *i* into
Ps 78:58 to jealousy with their carved *i*.
97: 7 put to shame who serve carved *i*,
Isa 10:10 Whose carved *i* excelled those
17: 8 Nor the wooden *i* nor the
21: 9 And all the carved *i* of her
27: 9 Wooden *i* and incense altars
30:22 the covering of your graven *i*
30:22 the ornament of your molded *i*
41:29 Their molded *i* are wind and
42: 8 Nor My praise to carved *i*.
42:17 ashamed, Who trust in carved *i*,
42:17 Who say to the molded *i*,
Jer 8:19 to anger With their carved *i*—
17: 2 altars and their wooden *i* By
50: 2 Her *i* are broken in pieces.'
50:38 it is the land of carved *i*,
51:47 bring judgment on the carved *i*
51:52 bring judgment on her carved *i*,
Ezek 7:20 made from it The *i* of their
16:17 and made for yourself male *i*
21:21 the arrows, he consults the *i*,
23:14 *I* of Chaldeans portrayed in
30:13 And cause the *i* to cease from
Hos 11: 2 And burned incense to carved *i*.
13: 2 made for themselves molded *i*,
Mic 1: 7 All her carved *i* shall be
5:13 Your carved *i* I will also cut
5:14 I will pluck your wooden *i* from
Acts 7:43 *I* which you made to

IMAGINATION (2/2)

Gen 8:21 although the *i* of man's heart
Lk 1:51 scattered the proud in the *i*

IMITATE (5/4) IMITATORS

1 Cor 4:16 Therefore I urge you, *i* me.
11: 1 *I* me, just as I also imitate
11: 1 just as I also *i* Christ.
Heb 6:12 but *i* those who through faith
3 Jn 11 do not *i* what is evil, but what

IMITATORS (2/2) IMITATE

Eph 5: 1 Therefore be *i* of God as dear
1 Th 2:14 became *i* of the churches of God

IMLA (2/2)

2 Chr 18: 7 He is Micaiah the son of *I*.
18: 8 Bring Micaiah the son of *I*

IMLAH (2/2)

1 Ki 22: 8 one man, Micaiah the son of *I*,
22: 9 Bring Micaiah the son of *I*

IMMANUEL (3/3)

Isa 7:14 Son, and shall call His name *I*.
8: 8 the breadth of Your land, O *I*.
Mt 1:23 shall call His name *I*,

IMMEASURABLE (1/1)

Gen 41:49 counting, for it was *i*.

IMMEDIATELY (108/108)

Judg 2:23 without driving them out *i*;
1 Sam 28:20 Then *i* Saul fell full length on
1 Ki 1:13 Go *i* to King David and say to
Ezra 6: 8 this is to be given *i* to these
Prov 7:22 *I* he went after her, as an ox
Dan 3: 6 and worship shall be cast *i*
3:15 you shall be cast *i* into the
Mt 3:16 Jesus came up *i* from the water;
4:20 They *i* left their nets and
4:22 and *i* they left the boat and
8: 3 *I* his leprosy was cleansed.
13: 5 and they *i* sprang up because
13:20 is he who hears the word and *i*
13:21 the word, *i* he stumbles.
14:22 *I* Jesus made His disciples get
14:27 But *i* Jesus spoke to them,
14:31 And *i* Jesus stretched out His
20:34 And *i* their eyes received
21: 2 and *i* you will find a donkey
21: 3 and *i* he will send them."
21:19 *I* the fig tree withered away.
24:29 *I* after the tribulation of
25:15 and *i* he went on a journey.
26:49 *I* he went up to Jesus and said,
26:74 the Man!" *I* a rooster crowed.
27:48 *I* one of them ran and took a
Mk 1:10 And *i*, coming up from the
1:12 *I* the Spirit drove Him into the
1:18 They *i* left their nets and
1:20 And *i* He called them, and they
1:21 and *i* on the Sabbath He entered
1:28 And *i* His fame spread throughout
1:31 and *i* the fever left her.
1:42 *i* the leprosy left him, and he
2: 2 *I* many gathered together, so
2: 8 But *i*, when Jesus perceived
2:12 *I* he arose, took up the bed, and
3: 6 the Pharisees went out and *i*
4: 5 and *i* it sprang up because it
4:15 Satan comes *i* and takes away
4:16 *i* receive it with gladness;
4:17 word's sake, *i* they stumble.
4:29 *i* he puts in the sickle,
5: 2 *i* there met Him out of the
5:29 *I* the fountain of her blood was
5:30 *i* knowing in Himself that power
5:42 *I* the girl arose and walked, for
6:25 *I* she came in with haste to the
6:27 *I* the king sent an executioner
6:45 *I* He made His disciples get
6:50 But *i* He talked with them and
6:54 *i* the people recognized Him,
7:35 *I* his ears were opened, and the
8:10 *i* got into the boat with His
9:15 *I*, when they saw Him, all
9:20 *i* the spirit convulsed him, and
9:24 *I* the father of the child cried
10:52 And *i* he received his sight
11: 3 and *i* he will send it here."
14:43 And *i*, while He was still
14:45 *i* he went up to Him and said to
15: 1 *I*, in the morning, the chief
Lk 1:64 *I* his mouth was opened and his
4:39 And *i* she arose and served
5:13 *I* the leprosy left him.
5:25 *I* he rose up before them, took
5:39 *i* desires new; for he says,
6:49 and *i* it fell. And the ruin of
8:44 And *i* her flow of blood
8:47 Him and how she was healed *i*.
8:55 returned, and she arose *i*.
12:36 knocks they may open to him *i*.
12:54 *i* you say, 'A shower is
13:13 and *i* she was made straight,
14: 5 will not *i* pull him out on the
18:43 And *i* he received his sight, and
19:11 kingdom of God would appear *i*.
19:40 the stones would *i* cry out."
21: 9 but the end will not come *i*.
22:60 *I*, while he was still speaking,
Jn 5: 9 And *i* the man was made well,
6:21 and *i* the boat was at the land
13:30 of bread, he then went out *i*.
13:32 in Himself, and glorify Him *i*.
18:27 and *i* a rooster crowed.
19:34 and *i* blood and water came out.
21: 3 They went out and *i* got into
Acts 3: 7 and *i* his feet and ankle bones
5:10 Then *i* she fell down at his feet
9:18 *I* there fell from his eyes
9:20 *I* he preached the Christ in the
9:34 your bed." Then he arose *i*.
10:33 "So I sent to you *i*,
12:10 and *i* the angel departed from
12:23 Then *i* an angel of the Lord
13:11 And *i* a dark mist fell on
16:10 *i* we sought to go to Macedonia,
16:26 and *i* all the doors were opened
16:33 And *i* he and all his family
17:10 Then the brethren *i* sent Paul
17:14 Then *i* the brethren sent Paul
21:30 and *i* the doors were shut.
21:32 He *i* took soldiers and
22:29 Then *i* those who were about to
23:30 I sent him *i* to you, and also
Gal 1:16 I did not *i* confer with flesh
Jas 1:24 and *i* forgets what kind of man
Rev 4: 2 *I* I was in the Spirit;

IMMER (10/10)

1 Chr 9:12 of Meshillemith, the son of *I*;
24:14 to Bilgah, the sixteenth to *I*,
Ezra 2:37 the sons of *I*, one thousand
2:59 Harsha, Cherub, Addan, and *I*;
10:20 Also of the sons of *I*:
Neh 3:29 After them Zadok the son of *I*
7:40 the sons of *I*, one thousand
7:61 Harsha, Cherub, Addon, and *I*,
11:13 of Meshillemoth, the son of *I*,
Jer 20: 1 Now Pashhur the son of *I*,

IMMORAL (10/10) IMMORALITY

Prov 2:16 To deliver you from the *i*
5: 3 For the lips of an *i* woman drip
5:20 be enraptured by an *i* woman,
7: 5 they may keep you from the *i*
22:14 The mouth of an *i* woman is a
1 Cor 5: 9 to keep company with sexually *i*
5:10 not mean with the sexually *i*
5:11 a brother, who is sexually *i*,
Rev 21: 8 murderers, sexually *i*,
22:15 and sorcerers and sexually *i*

IMMORALITY (21/19) IMMORAL

Ezek 23: 8 And poured out their *i* upon
23:17 they defiled her with their *i*;
Mt 5:32 for any reason except sexual *i*
19: 9 his wife, except for sexual *i*,
Acts 15:20 by idols, from sexual *i*,
15:29 strangled, and from sexual *i*.
21:25 strangled, and from sexual *i*.
Rom 1:29 all unrighteousness, sexual *i*,
1 Cor 5: 1 that there is sexual *i*
5: 1 and such sexual *i* as is not
6:13 the body is not for sexual *i*
6:18 Flee sexual *i*. Every sin that
6:18 but he who commits sexual *i*
7: 2 because of sexual *i*,
10: 8 Nor let us commit sexual *i*,
1 Th 4: 3 should abstain from sexual *i*;
Jude 7 themselves over to sexual *i*
Rev 2:14 idols, and to commit sexual *i*.
2:20 My servants to commit sexual *i*
2:21 time to repent of her sexual *i*,
9:21 sorceries or their sexual *i* or

IMMORTAL (1/1) IMMORTALITY

1 Tim 1:17 Now to the King eternal, *i*,

IMMORTALITY (5/5) IMMORTAL

Rom 2: 7 seek for glory, honor, and *i*;
1 Cor 15:53 and this mortal must put on *i*.
15:54 and this mortal has put on *i*,
1 Tim 6:16 who alone has *i*, dwelling in
2 Tim 1:10 death and brought life and *i*

IMMOVABLE (2/2)

Acts 27:41 prow stuck fast and remained *i*,
1 Cor 15:58 brethren, be steadfast, *i*,

IMMUTABILITY (1/1) IMMUTABLE

Heb 6:17 to the heirs of promise the *i*

IMMUTABLE (1/1) IMMUTABILITY

Heb 6:18 that by two *i* things, in which

IMNA (1/1)

1 Chr 7:35 brother Helem were Zophah, *I*,

IMNAH (2/2)

1 Chr 7:30 The sons of Asher were *I*,
2 Chr 31:14 Kore the son of *I* the Levite,

IMPART (3/3)

Rom 1:11 that I may *i* to you some
Eph 4:29 that it may *i* grace to the
1 Th 2: 8 we were well pleased to *i* to

IMPATIENT (1/1)

Job 21: 4 were, why should I not be *i*?

IMPEDIMENT (2/2)

Mk 7:32 one who was deaf and had an *i*
7:35 and the *i* of his tongue was

IMPENITENT (1/1)

Rom 2: 5 hardness and your *i* heart

IMPERISHABLE (1/1)

1 Cor 9:25 but we for an *i* crown.

IMPLACABLE (KJV) See UNFORGIVING

IMPLANTED (1/1)

Jas 1:21 *i* word, which is able to save

IMPLEAD (KJV) See BRING (CHARGES)

IMPLEMENT (2/2)

Num 35:16 he strikes him with an iron *i*,
Deut 23:13 and you shall have an *i* among

IMPLEMENTS (6/6)

Num 4:14 shall put on it all its *i*
2 Sam 24:22 and threshing *i* and the yokes
1 Chr 9:29 furnishings and over all the *i*
21:23 the threshing *i* for wood, and
Am 1: 3 have threshed Gilead with *i* of
Zech 11:15 take for yourself the *i* of a

IMPLORE (7/6) IMPLORED, IMPLORING

Ps 116: 4 I *i* You, deliver my soul!"
Mk 5: 7 I *i* You by God that You do not
Lk 9:38 I *i* You, look on my son, for he
Acts 21:39 and I *i* you, permit me to speak
2 Cor 5:20 we *i* you on Christ's behalf,
Phil 4: 2 I *i* Euodia and I implore
4: 2 I implore Euodia and I *i*

IMPLORED (7/7) IMPLORE

2 Chr 33:12 he *i* the LORD his God, and
Esth 8: 3 and *i* him with tears to
Jer 36:25 and Gemariah *i* the king not to
Lk 5:12 and he fell on his face and *i*
9:40 So I *i* Your disciples to cast it

I

Jn 4:47 he went to Him and *i* Him to
Acts 27:33 Paul *i* them all to take food,

IMPLORING (3/3) IMPLORE

Mk 1:40 *i* Him, kneeling down to Him and
Acts 9:38 *i* him not to delay in coming
2 Cor 8: 4 *i* us with much urgency that we

IMPORTED (4/4)

1 Ki 10:28 Also Solomon had horses *i* from
10:29 Now a chariot that was *i* from
2 Chr 1:16 And Solomon had horses *i* from
1:17 They also acquired and *i* from

IMPORTUNITY (KJV) See PERSISTENCE

IMPOSE (2/2)

2 Ki 18:14 whatever you *i* on me I will
Ezra 7:24 it shall not be lawful to *i*

IMPOSED (8/7)

Ex 21:30 If there is *i* on him a sum of
21:30 whatever is *i* on him.
2 Ki 23:33 and he *i* on the land a tribute
2 Chr 24: 9 the servant of God had *i* on
36: 3 and he *i* on the land a tribute
Esth 9:27 the Jews established and *i* it
10: 1 And King Ahasuerus *i* tribute on
Heb 9:10 and fleshly ordinances *i* until

IMPOSES (2/2)

Ex 21:22 as the woman's husband *i* on
Dan 11:20 arise in his place one who *i*

IMPOSSIBLE (9/9)

Mt 17:20 and nothing will be *i* for you.
19:26 to them, "With men this is *i*,
Mk 10:27 and said, "With men it is *i*,
Lk 1:37 with God nothing will be *i*.
17: 1 It is *i* that no offenses should
18:27 The things which are *i* with men
Heb 6: 4 For it is *i* for those who were
6:18 in which it is *i* for God to
11: 6 But without faith it is *i* to

IMPOSTORS (1/1)

2 Tim 3:13 But evil men and *i* will grow

IMPOTENT (KJV) See HELPLESS, SICK

IMPOVERISHED (3/3)

Judg 6: 6 So Israel was greatly *i* because
Isa 40:20 Whoever is too *i* for such a
Mal 1: 4 has said, "We have been *i*,

IMPRESSIVE (1/1)

Josh 22:10 —a great, *i* altar.

IMPRISONED (1/1) IMPRISONMENT

Acts 22:19 that in every synagogue I *i*

IMPRISONMENT (2/2) IMPRISONED, IMPRISONMENTS

Ezra 7:26 or confiscation of goods, or *i*.
Heb 11:36 yes, and of chains and *i*.

IMPRISONMENTS (1/1) IMPRISONMENT

2 Cor 6: 5 in stripes, in *i*, in tumults,

IMPRISONS (2/2)

Job 11:10 "If He passes by, *i*,
12:14 If He *i* a man, there can be

IMPROPER (1/1) IMPROPERLY

2 Sam 13: 2 And it was *i* for Amnon to do

IMPROPERLY (1/1) IMPROPER

1 Cor 7:36 any man thinks he is behaving *i*

IMPUDENT (3/3)

Prov 7:13 With an *i* face she said to
Ezek 2: 4 For they are *i* and stubborn
3: 7 all the house of Israel are *i*

IMPULSIVE (1/1)

Prov 14:29 But he who is *i* exalts

IMPURITY (16/13)

Lev 12: 2 in the days of her customary *i*
12: 5 weeks, as in her customary *i*,
15:20 that she lies on during her *i*
15:24 so that her *i* is on him, he
15:25 at the time of her customary *i*,
15:25 beyond her usual time of *i*,
15:25 as the days of her customary *i*.
15:26 be to her as the bed of her *i*;
15:26 as the uncleanness of her *i*.
15:33 because of her customary *i*,
18:19 as she is in her customary *i*.
2 Sam 11: 4 for she was cleansed from her *i*;
Ezra 9:11 one end to another with their *i*.
Ezek 18: 6 approached a woman during her *i*;
22:10 are set apart during their *i*.
36:17 of a woman in her customary *i*.

IMPUTE (4/4) IMPUTED, IMPUTES, IMPUTING

1 Sam 22:15 it from me! Let not the king *i*
2 Sam 19:19 Do not let my lord *i* iniquity to
Ps 32: 2 to whom the LORD does not *i*
Rom 4: 8 the LORD shall not *i*

IMPUTED (6/6) IMPUTE

Lev 7:18 nor shall it be *i* to him;
17: 4 guilt of bloodshed shall be *i*
Rom 4:11 that righteousness might be *i*
4:23 his sake alone that it was *i*
4:24 It shall be *i* to us who believe
5:13 but sin is not *i* when there is

IMPUTES (1/1) IMPUTE

Rom 4: 6 of the man to whom God *i*

IMPUTETH (KJV) See IMPUTE

IMPUTING (1/1) IMPUTE

2 Cor 5:19 not *i* their trespasses to them,

IMRAH (1/1)

1 Chr 7:36 Suah, Harnepher, Shual, Beri, *I*,

IMRI (2/2)

1 Chr 9: 4 the son of Omri, the son of *I*,
Neh 3: 2 to them Zaccur the son of *I*

IN (12234/9398) See APPENDIX

IN MY NAME (28/28)

Deut 18:19 My words, which He speaks *i*,
18:20 who presumes to speak a word *i*,
1 Sam 25: 5 go to Nabal, and greet him *i*.
Ps 89:24 And *i* his horn shall be
Jer 14:14 "The prophets prophesy lies *i*.
14:15 the prophets who prophesy *i*,
23:25 have said who prophesy lies *i*,
27:15 "yet they prophesy a lie *i*,
29: 9 they prophesy falsely to you *i*;
29:21 who prophesy a lie to you *i*:
29:23 and have spoken lying words *i*,
Mt 18: 5 one little child like this *i*
18:20 three are gathered together *i*,
24: 5 "For many will come *i*,
Mk 9:37 one of these little children *i*
9:39 no one who works a miracle *i*
9:41 you a cup of water to drink *i*,
13: 6 "For many will come *i*,
16:17 *I* they will cast out demons;
Lk 9:48 receives this little child *i*
21: 8 For many will come *i*, saying,
Jn 14:13 "And whatever you ask *i*,
14:14 "If you ask anything *i*,
14:26 whom the Father will send *i*,
15:16 whatever you ask the Father *i*
16:23 whatever you ask the Father *i*
16:24 now you have asked nothing *i*.
16:26 "In that day you will ask *i*,

INASMUCH (25/25)

Gen 18: 5 *i* as you have come to your
33:10 *i* as I have seen your face as
41:39 *I* as God has shown you all this,
Num 10:31 *i* as you know how we are to
Josh 17:14 *i* as the LORD has blessed us
2 Sam 19:30 *i* as my lord the king has come
1 Ki 16: 2 *I* as I lifted you out of the
Isa 8: 6 *I* as these people refused The
29:13 *I* as these people draw near with
Jer 10: 6 *I* as there is none like You,
Dan 2:40 *i* as iron breaks in pieces and
2:45 *I* as you saw that the stone was
4:23 And *i* as the king saw a watcher,
4:26 And *i* as they gave the command
5:12 *I* as an excellent spirit,
Mt 25:40 *i* as you did it to one of the
25:45 *i* as you did not do it to one
Lk 1: 1 *I* as many have taken in hand to
Acts 24:10 *I* as I know that you have been
Rom 11:13 *i* as I am an apostle to the
Phil 1: 7 *i* as both in my chains and in
Heb 2:14 *I* then as the children have
3: 3 *i* as He who built the house has
7:20 And *i* as He was not made
8: 6 *i* as He is also Mediator of a

INAUGURATE (2/2)

Num 27:19 and *i* him in their sight.
Deut 31:14 that I may *i* him." So Moses

INAUGURATED (2/2)

Num 27:23 he laid his hands on him and *i*
Deut 31:23 Then He *i* Joshua the son of Nun,

INCENSE (144/136)

Ex 25: 6 oil and for the sweet *i*;
30: 1 shall make an altar to burn *i*
30: 7 shall burn on it sweet *i*
30: 7 he shall burn *i* on it.
30: 8 he shall burn *i* on it, a
30: 8 a perpetual *i* before the LORD
30: 9 You shall not offer strange *i* on
30:27 utensils, and the altar of *i*;
30:35 "You shall make of these an *i*,
30:37 But as for the *i* which you
31: 8 its utensils, the altar of *i*,
31:11 the anointing oil and sweet *i*
35: 8 oil and for the sweet *i*;
35:15 the *i* altar, its poles, the
35:15 the anointing oil, the sweet *i*,
35:28 oil, and for the sweet *i*.
37:25 He made the *i* altar of acacia
37:29 anointing oil and the pure *i*
39:38 anointing oil, and the sweet *i*;
40: 5 set the altar of gold for the *i*
40:27 and he burned sweet *i* on it, as
Lev 4: 7 horns of the altar of sweet *i*
10: 1 put *i* on it, and offered
16:12 with his hands full of sweet *i*
16:13 And he shall put the *i* on the
16:13 that the cloud of *i* may cover
26:30 cut down your *i* altars, and
Num 4:16 oil for the light, the sweet *i*,
7:14 pan of ten shekels, full of *i*;
7:20 pan of ten shekels, full of *i*;
7:26 pan of ten shekels, full of *i*;
7:32 pan of ten shekels, full of *i*;
7:38 pan of ten shekels, full of *i*;
7:44 pan of ten shekels, full of *i*;
7:50 pan of ten shekels, full of *i*;
7:56 pan of ten shekels, full of *i*;
7:62 pan of ten shekels, full of *i*;
7:68 pan of ten shekels, full of *i*;
7:74 pan of ten shekels, full of *i*;
7:80 pan of ten shekels, full of *i*;
7:86 The twelve gold pans full of *i*
16: 7 put fire in them and put *i* in
16:17 each take his censer and put *i*
16:18 laid *i* on it, and stood at the
16:35 fifty men who were offering *i*.
16:40 should come near to offer *i*
16:46 put *i* on it, and take it
16:47 So he put in the *i* and made
Deut 33:10 They shall put *i* before You,
1 Sam 2:28 offer upon My altar, to burn *i*,
1 Ki 3: 3 he sacrificed and burned *i* at
9:25 and he burned *i* with them on
11: 8 who burned *i* and sacrificed to
12:33 on the altar and burned *i*.
13: 1 stood by the altar to burn *i*.
13: 2 of the high places who burn *i*
22:43 sacrifices and burned *i* on the
2 Ki 12: 3 still sacrificed and burned *i*
14: 4 still sacrificed and burned *i*
15: 4 still sacrificed and burned *i*
15:35 still sacrificed and burned *i*
16: 4 And he sacrificed and burned *i*
17:11 There they burned *i* on all the
18: 4 children of Israel burned *i* to
22:17 have forsaken Me and burned *i*
23: 5 of Judah had ordained to burn *i*
23: 5 and those who burned *i* to Baal,
23: 8 where the priests had burned *i*,
1 Chr 6:49 offering and on the altar of *i*,
9:29 the wine and the oil and the *i*
23:13 to burn *i* before the LORD, to
28:18 by weight for the altar of *i*,
2 Chr 2: 4 Him, to burn before Him sweet *i*,
13:11 burnt sacrifices and sweet *i*;
14: 5 the high places and the *i*
25:14 down before them and burned *i*
26:16 temple of the LORD to burn *i*
26:16 burn incense on the altar of *i*.
26:18 to burn *i* to the LORD, but for
26:18 who are consecrated to burn *i*.
26:19 a censer in his hand to burn *i*.
26:19 beside the *i* altar.
28: 3 He burned *i* in the Valley of the
28: 4 And he sacrificed and burned *i*
28:25 he made high places to burn *i*
29: 7 and have not burned *i* or
29:11 minister to Him and burn *i*.
30:14 and they took away all the *i*
32:12 before one altar and burn *i* on
34: 4 and the *i* altars which were
34: 7 and cut down all the *i* altars
34:25 have forsaken Me and burned *i*
Ps 141: 2 prayer be set before You as *i*,
Isa 1:13 *I* is an abomination to Me.
17: 8 the wooden images nor the *i*
27: 9 Wooden images and *i* altars
43:23 Nor wearied you with *i*.
60: 6 They shall bring gold and *i*,
65: 3 And burn *i* on altars of brick;
65: 7 Who have burned *i* on the
66: 3 swine's blood; He who burns *i*,
Jer 1:16 Burned *i* to other gods, And
7: 9 burn *i* to Baal, and walk after
11:12 the gods to whom they offer *i*,
11:13 altars to burn *i* to Baal.

11:17 Me to anger in offering *i* to
17:26 grain offerings and *i*,
18:15 They have burned *i* to
19: 4 because they have burned *i* in
19:13 whose roofs they have burned *i*
32:29 roofs they have offered *i* to
34: 5 so they shall burn *i* for you
41: 5 with offerings and *i* in their
44: 3 in that they went to burn *i*
44: 5 to burn no *i* to other gods.
44: 8 burning *i* to other gods in the
44:15 that their wives had burned *i*
44:17 to burn *i* to the queen of
44:18 since we stopped burning *i*
44:19 And when we burned *i* to the
44:21 The *i* that you burned in the
44:23 Because you have burned *i* and
44:25 to burn *i* to the queen of
48:35 in the high places And burns *i*
Ezek 6: 4 your *i* altars shall be broken,
6: 6 your *i* altars may be cut down,
6:13 wherever they offered sweet *i*
8:11 and a thick cloud of *i* went up.
16:18 and you set My oil and My *i*
16:19 set it before them as sweet *i*;
23:41 on which you had set My *i* and
Dan 2:46 present an offering and *i* to
Hos 2:13 the Baals to which she burned *i*.
4:13 And burn *i* on the hills,
11: 2 And burned *i* to carved images.
Hab 1:16 And burn *i* to their dragnet;
Mal 1:11 In every place *i* shall be
Lk 1: 9 his lot fell to burn *i* when he
1:10 outside at the hour of *i*.
1:11 right side of the altar of *i*.
Rev 5: 8 and golden bowls full of *i*,
8: 3 the altar. He was given much *i*,
8: 4 And the smoke of the *i*,
18:13 "and cinnamon and *i*,

INCENSED (2/2)

Isa 41:11 all those who were *i* against
45:24 all shall be ashamed Who are *i*

INCIDENT (2/2)

Num 16:49 those who died in the Korah *i*.
31:16 against the LORD in the *i* of

INCITED (2/2) INCITING

Ezra 4:15 and that they have *i* sedition
Job 2: 3 although you *i* Me against him,

INCITING (1/1) INCITED

Acts 24:12 disputing with anyone nor *i*

INCLINATION (1/1) INCLINE

Deut 31:21 for I know the *i* of their

INCLINE (24/24) INCLINATION, INCLINED

Josh 24:23 and *i* your heart to the LORD
1 Ki 8:58 that He may *i* our hearts to
2 Ki 19:16 *I* your ear, O LORD, and hear;
Ps 17: 6 *I* Your ear to me, and hear my
45:10 Consider and *i* your ear;
49: 4 I will *i* my ear to a proverb;
71: 2 *I* Your ear to me, and save me.
78: 1 *I* your ears to the words of my
88: 2 *I* Your ear to my cry.
102: 2 *I* Your ear to me; In the day
119:36 *I* my heart to Your testimonies,
141: 4 Do not *i* my heart to any evil
Prov 2: 2 So that you *i* your ear to
4:20 *I* your ear to my sayings.
22:17 *I* your ear and hear the words
Isa 37:17 *I* Your ear, O LORD, and hear;
55: 3 *I* your ear, and come to Me
Jer 7:24 Yet they did not obey or *i* their
7:26 Yet they did not obey Me or *i*
11: 8 Yet they did not obey or *i* their
17:23 But they did not obey nor *i*
34:14 fathers did not obey Me nor *i*
44: 5 But they did not listen or *i*
Dan 9:18 *i* Your ear and hear; open Your

INCLINED (8/8) INCLINE

Num 15:39 heart and your own eyes are *i*,
Judg 9: 3 and their heart was *i* to follow
Ps 40: 1 And He *i* to me, And heard my
116: 2 Because He has *i* His ear to me,
119:112 I have *i* my heart to perform
Prov 5:13 Nor *i* my ear to those who
Jer 25: 4 but you have not listened nor *i*
35:15 But you have not *i* your ear,

INCLOSE (KJV) See ENCLOSE

INCLUDED (11/11) INCLUDING

Ex 30:14 Everyone *i* among those who are
38:26 for everyone *i* in the numbering
Num 3:25 in the tabernacle of meeting *i*
3:31 Their duty *i* the ark, the
3:36 of the children of Merari *i*
Deut 29:19 though the drunkard could be *i*
Josh 19: 9 the children of Simeon was *i*
19:15 *I* were Kattath, Nahallal,
19:18 and *i* Chesulloth, Shunem,
19:25 And their territory *i* Helkath,
19:30 Aphek, and Rehob were *i*:

INCLUDES (1/1)

2 Cor 10:13 a sphere which especially *i* you.

INCLUDING (11/11) INCLUDED

Josh 19:28 *i* Ebron, Rehob, Hammon, and
24: 2 *i* Terah, the father of Abraham
24:18 *i* the Amorites who dwelt in the
Judg 21:10 *i* the women and children.
2 Ki 10:33 *i* Gilead and Bashan.
1 Chr 16:38 *i* Obed-Edom the son of
Eccl 12:14 *I* every secret thing, Whether
Ezek 21:12 Terrors *i* the sword will be
41:14 *i* the separating courtyard,
44: 9 *i* any foreigner who is among
Mt 8:33 *i* what had happened to the

INCOME (1/1)

1 Ki 10:15 from the *i* of traders, from all

INCONTINENCY (KJV) See LACK (OF SELF-CONTROL)

INCORRUPTIBILITY (1/1) INCORRUPTIBLE

Titus 2: 7 integrity, reverence, *i*,

INCORRUPTIBLE (5/5) INCORRUPTIBILITY, INCORRUPTION

Rom 1:23 and changed the glory of the *i*
1 Cor 15:52 and the dead will be raised *i*,
1 Pe 1: 4 to an inheritance *i* and
1:23 not of corruptible seed but *i*,
3: 4 with the *i* beauty of a gentle

INCORRUPTION (4/4) INCORRUPTIBLE

1 Cor 15:42 corruption, it is raised in *i*.
15:50 nor does corruption inherit *i*.
15:53 this corruptible must put on *i*,
15:54 this corruptible has put on *i*,

INCREASE (67/64) INCREASED, INCREASES, INCREASING

Lev 19:25 that it may yield to you its *i*:
25:16 multitude of years you shall *i*
Num 32:14 to *i* still more the fierce
Deut 7:13 the *i* of your cattle and the
14:22 shall truly tithe all the *i* of
26:12 aside all the tithe of your *i*
28: 4 of your ground and the *i* of
28: 4 the *i* of your cattle and the
28:11 in the *i* of your livestock, and
28:18 the *i* of your cattle and the
28:51 And they shall eat the *i* of your
28:51 or the *i* of your cattle or the
30: 9 in the *i* of your livestock, and
32:22 consume the earth with her *i*,
Judg 9:29 *I* your army and come out!"
1 Sam 14:19 the Philistines continued to *i*;
2 Sam 23: 5 Will He not make it *i*?
Ezra 4:22 Why should damage *i* to the hurt
Neh 9:37 And it yields much *i* to the
Job 8: 7 Yet your latter end would *i*
10:17 And *i* Your indignation toward
20:28 The *i* of his house will depart,
31:12 And would root out all my *i*.
Ps 62:10 hope in robbery; If riches *i*,
67: 6 the earth shall yield her *i*;
71:21 You shall *i* my greatness, And
73:12 They *i* in riches.
85:12 And our land will yield its *i*.
115:14 May the LORD give you *i* more
Prov 1: 5 A wise man will hear and *i*
3: 9 the firstfruits of all your *i*;
9: 9 and he will *i* in learning.
13:11 he who gathers by labor will *i*.
14: 4 But much *i* comes by the
22:16 He who oppresses the poor to *i*
28:28 they perish, the righteous *i*.
Eccl 5:10 he who loves abundance, with *i*.
5:11 When goods *i*, They increase
5:11 They *i* who eat them; So what
6:11 there are many things that *i*
Isa 9: 7 Of the *i* of His government and
29:19 The humble also shall *i* their
30:23 And bread of the *i* of the
Jer 2: 3 The firstfruits of His *i*.
23: 3 they shall be fruitful and *i*.
Ezek 5:16 I will *i* the famine upon you
18: 8 exacted usury Nor taken any *i*,
18:13 has exacted usury Or taken *i*—
18:17 And not received usury or *i*,
22:12 you take usury and *i*;
34:27 and the earth shall yield her *i*.
36:11 and they shall *i* and bear
36:30 fruit of your trees and the *i*
36:37 I will *i* their men like a
Dan 12: 4 and fro, and knowledge shall *i*.
Hos 4:10 commit harlotry, but not *i*;
Zech 8:12 The ground shall give her *i*,
10: 8 And they shall *i* as they once
Lk 17: 5 to the Lord, "*I* our faith."
Jn 3:30 'He must *i*, but I must
1 Cor 3: 6 watered, but God gave the *i*.
3: 7 waters, but God who gives the *i*.
2 Cor 9:10 the seed you have sown and *i*
Col 2:19 grows with the *i* that is from
1 Th 3:12 And may the Lord make you *i* and
4:10 that you *i* more and more;
2 Tim 2:16 for they will *i* to more

INCREASED (43/42) INCREASE

Gen 7:17 The waters *i* and lifted up the
7:18 waters prevailed and greatly *i*
19:19 and you have *i* your mercy which
30:30 and it has *i* to a great amount;
Ex 1: 7 of Israel were fruitful and *i*
23:30 before you, until you have *i*,
2 Sam 15:12 with Absalom continually *i* in
1 Ki 22:35 The battle *i* that day; and the
1 Chr 4:38 and their father's house *i*
5:23 Their numbers *i* from Bashan to
2 Chr 18:34 The battle *i* that day, and the
Job 1:10 and his possessions have *i* in
Ps 3: 1 how they have *i* who trouble me!
4: 7 that their grain and wine *i*.
49:16 the glory of his house is *i*;
105:24 He *i* His people greatly, And
Isa 9: 3 multiplied the nation And *i*
26:15 You have *i* the nation, O LORD,
26:15 You have *i* the nation;
51: 2 And blessed him and *i* him."
57: 9 And *i* your perfumes; You sent
Jer 3:16 when you are multiplied and *i*
5: 6 Their backslidings have *i*.
15: 8 Their widows will be *i* to Me
29: 6 that you may be *i* there, and not
30:14 Because your sins have *i*.
30:15 Because your sins have *i*,
Lam 2: 5 And has *i* mourning and
Ezek 16:26 and *i* your acts of harlotry to
23:14 But she *i* her harlotry;
28: 5 wisdom in trade you have *i*
31:10 Because you have *i* in height,
41: 7 the width of the structure *i*
Hos 4: 7 "The more they *i*,
10: 1 of his fruit He has *i* the
Am 4: 9 When your gardens *i*, Your
Zech 10: 8 shall increase as they once *i*.
Mk 4: 8 *i* and produced: some
Lk 2:52 And Jesus *i* in wisdom and
Acts 9:22 But Saul *i* all the more in
16: 5 and *i* in number daily.
Rom 3: 7 For if the truth of God has *i*
2 Cor 10:15 hope, that as your faith is *i*,

INCREASES (13/12) INCREASE

Ps 74:23 those who rise up against You *i*
Prov 11:24 yet *i* more; And there is one
16:21 And sweetness of the lips *i*
23:28 And *i* the unfaithful among
24: 5 a man of knowledge *i* strength;
28: 8 One who *i* his possessions by
29:16 are multiplied, transgression *i*;
Eccl 1:18 And he who *i* knowledge
1:18 he who increases knowledge *i*
8: 6 Though the misery of man *i*
Isa 40:29 those who have no might He *i*
Hos 12: 1 He daily *i* lies and
Hab 2: 6 Woe to him who *i* What is not

INCREASING (1/1) INCREASE, INCREASINGLY

Col 1:10 in every good work and *i* in

INCREASINGLY (4/4) INCREASING

2 Chr 17:12 So Jehoshaphat became *i*
28:22 his distress King Ahaz became *i*
Esth 9: 4 for this man Mordecai became *i*
Acts 5:14 And believers were *i* added to

INCREDIBLE (1/1)

Acts 26: 8 Why should it be thought *i* by

INCUR (1/1)

Ex 28:43 that they do not *i* iniquity and

INCURABLE (6/6)

2 Chr 21:18 him in his intestines with an *i*
Job 34: 6 my right? My wound is *i*,
Jer 15:18 pain perpetual And my wound *i*,
30:12 LORD: 'Your affliction is *i*,
30:15 Your sorrow is *i*. Because of
Mic 1: 9 For her wounds are *i*.

INCURRED (1/1)

Acts 27:21 have sailed from Crete and *i*

INDEBTED (1/1)

Lk 11: 4 also forgive everyone who is *i*

INDEED (423/420)

Gen 1:31 and *i* it was very good.
3: 1 Has God *i* said, 'You shall not
6: 3 for he is *i* flesh; yet his
6:12 and *i* it was corrupt; for all
8:13 and *i* the surface of the ground
11: 6 *I* the people are one and they
12:11 *I* I know that you are a woman
15: 3 *i* one born in my house is my
16: 6 '*I* your maid is in your hand;
18:27 *I* now, I who am but dust and
18:31 *I* now, I have taken it upon
19:19 *I* now, your servant has found
19:34 *I* I lay with my father last
20: 3 *I* you are a dead man because of
20:12 But *i* she is truly my sister.
20:16 *i* this vindicates you before
22:20 *I* Milcah also has borne children
25:24 *i* there were twins in her
27: 6 *I* I heard your father speak to
27:33 and *i* he shall be blessed."
27:37 *I* I have made him your master,
30: 8 and *i* I have prevailed."
31: 2 and *i* it was not favorable
34:21 For *i* the land is large enough
37: 7 and *i* your sheaves stood all
37: 8 'Shall you *i* reign over us?
37: 8 Or shall you *i* have dominion
37:10 and I and your brothers *i* come
37:29 and *i* Joseph was not in the
40:15 For *i* I was stolen away from the
41: 7 So Pharaoh awoke, and *i*,
41:29 *I* seven years of great plenty
42: 2 *I* I have heard that there is
43:20 we *i* came down the first time
44: 5 and with which he *i* practices
47: 1 and *i* they are in the land of
47:23 *I* I have bought you and your
48: 1 *I* your father is sick"; and he
Ex 3:13 Then Moses said to God, "*I*,
4:23 *i* I will kill your son, your
5:16 Make brick!' And *i* your servants
7:16 Me in the wilderness"; but *i*,
8:29 *I* I am going out from you, and I
9: 7 Then Pharaoh sent, and *i*,
9:16 But *i* for this purpose I have
14:17 And I *i* will harden the hearts
19: 5 if you will *i* obey My voice and
23:22 But if you *i* obey His voice and
24:14 *I* Aaron and Hur are with you.
31: 6 *i* I, have appointed with him
32: 9 and *i* it is a stiff-necked
36: 7 to be done—*i* too much.
39:43 and *i* they had done it; as the
Lev 10:18 *i* you should have eaten it in a
13: 5 and *i* if the sore appears to
13: 6 and *i* if the sore has faded,
13: 8 priest sees that the scab has *i*
13:10 and *i* if the swelling on the
13:13 and *i* if the leprosy has
13:17 and *i* if the sore has turned
13:20 it *i* appears deeper than the
13:21 and *i* there are no white
13:25 and *i* if the hair of the
13:26 and *i* there are no white
13:30 and *i* if it appears deeper than
13:31 and *i* it does not appear deeper
13:32 and *i* if the scale has not
13:34 and *i* if the scale has not
13:36 and *i* if the scale has spread
13:39 and *i* if the bright spots on
13:43 and *i* if the swelling of the
13:53 and *i* the plague has not spread
13:55 and *i* if the plague has not
13:56 and *i* the plague has faded
14: 3 shall examine him; and *i*,
14:37 and *i* if the plague is on the
14:39 and *i* if the plague has spread
14:44 and *i* if the plague has spread
14:48 and *i* the plague has not spread
Num 10:32 *i* it shall be—that whatever good
12: 2 Has the LORD *i* spoken only
21: 2 If You will *i* deliver this
24:14 'And now, *i*, I am going to
25: 6 And *i*, one of the children
30: 6 If *i* she takes a husband, while
32: 1 that *i* the region was a place
Deut 2:15 For *i* the hand of the LORD was
3:11 *I* his bedstead was an iron
9:13 and *i* they are a stiff-necked
10:14 *I* heaven and the highest heavens
13:14 And if it is *i* true and
17: 4 And if it is *i* true and
19:18 make careful inquiry, and *i*,
Josh 2:24 for *i* all the inhabitants of
7:20 *I* I have sinned against the
22: 7 And *i*, when Joshua sent them
23:12 if *i* you do go back, and cling
Judg 1: 2 *I* I have delivered the land
6:15 *I* my clan is the weakest in
9:38 Where *i* is your mouth now, with
11:30 If You will *i* deliver the people
13: 3 *I* now, you are barren and have
18: 9 and *i* it is very good. Would
21: 9 when the people were counted, *i*,
1 Sam 1:11 if You will *i* look on the
2:30 I said *i* that your house and
10:11 knew him formerly saw that he *i*
12: 1 *I* I have heeded your voice in
14:20 and *i* every man's sword was
15:12 "Saul went to Carmel, and *i*,
19:22 *I* they are at Naioth in
20: 2 *I*, my father will do nothing
20: 5 *I* tomorrow is the New Moon, and
20:12 and *i* there is good toward
20:23 *i* the LORD be between you and
24: 9 *I* David seeks your harm'?
24:20 And now I know *i* that you shall
25:34 'For *i*, as the LORD God
26: 4 and understood that Saul had *i*
26:21 *I* I have played the fool and
26:24 'And *i*, as your life was
2 Sam 1: 6 and *i* the chariots and horsemen
1:18 *i* it is written in the Book
3:12 and *i* my hand shall be with
5: 1 *I* we are your bone and your
9: 4 *I* he is in the house of Machir
12:18 '*I*, while the child was
13:16 she said to him, "No, *i*!
13:36 that the king's sons *i* came,
14: 5 *I* I am a widow, my husband is
15: 8 If the LORD *i* brings me back to
15:36 *I* they have there with them
16: 3 *I* he is staying in Jerusalem,
1 Ki 1:51 *I* Adonijah is afraid of King
3:15 and *i* it had been a dream.
3:21 examined him in the morning, *i*,
8:27 But will God *i* dwell on the
10: 7 and *i* the half was not told me.
14: 2 *I*, Ahijah the prophet is
14:19 *i* they are written in the book
17:10 *i* a widow was there gathering
20: 5 *I* I have sent to you, saying,
22:25 And Micaiah said, "*I*,
2 Ki 5:11 said, "*I*, I said to myself,
5:15 said, "*I*, now I know that
5:22 '*I*, just now two young men
6:25 and *i* they besieged it until a
7:13 in it; or *i*, I say, they
7:15 and *i* all the road was full of
10: 9 *I* I conspired against my master
14:10 You have *i* defeated Edom, and
15:11 *i* they are written in the book
15:15 *i* they are written in the book
15:26 *i* they are written in the book
15:31 *i* they are written in the book
16: 3 *i* he made his son pass through
17:26 sent lions among them, and *i*,
18:34 *I*, have they delivered
1 Chr 4:10 "Oh, that You would bless me *i*,
5: 1 he was *i* the firstborn, but
9: 1 recorded by genealogies, and *i*,
11: 1 *I* we are your bone and your
11:25 *I* he was more honored than the
16:19 *I* very few, and strangers in
21:17 who has sinned and done evil *i*;
22:14 *I* I have taken much trouble to
29:29 *i* they are written in the book
2 Chr 2: 8 and *i* my servants will be
2:10 And *i* I will give to your
5:13 *i* it came to pass, when the
6:18 But will God *i* dwell with men
9: 6 and *i* the half of the greatness
16:11 are *i* written in the book of
18:24 *I* you shall see on that day when
20:34 *i* they are written in the book
24:27 *i* they are written in the
25:19 *I* you say that you have defeated
25:26 *i* are they not written in the
26:20 *I* he also hurried to get out,
27: 7 *i* they are written in the book
28:26 *i* they are written in the book
29: 9 'For *i*, because of this our
32:32 *i* they are written in the
33:18 *i* they are written in the
33:19 *i* they are written among the
35:25 and *i* they are written in the
35:27 *i* they are written in the book
36: 8 *i* they are written in the book
Ezra 9: 2 *I*, the hand of the leaders
Neh 5: 5 and *i* we are forcing our sons
5: 8 Now *i*, will you even sell
5:16 *I*, I also continued the work
6:10 *i*, at night they will come
Esth 8: 7 '*I*, I have given Esther
Job 1:15 *i* they have killed the servants
2:10 Shall we *i* accept good from
9:19 *i* He is strong; And if of
12: 3 *I*, who does not know such
14:10 *I* he breathes his last And
18: 5 The light of the wicked *i* goes
19: 4 And if *i* I have erred, My
19: 5 If *i* you exalt yourselves
21:16 *I* their prosperity is not in
24: 5 *I*, like wild donkeys in the
26:14 *I* these are the mere edges of
28:27 declared it; He prepared it, *i*,
30: 2 *I*, what profit is the
31:30 (*I* I have not allowed my mouth
32:11 *I* I waited for your words, I
32:19 *I* my belly is like wine that
36:16 *I* He would have brought you out
36:29 *I*, can anyone understand
40: 8 Would you *i* annul My judgment?
40:23 *I* the river may rage, Yet he
41: 9 *I*, any hope of overcoming
42:10 *I* the LORD gave Job twice as
Ps 25: 3 *I*, let no one who waits on
37:10 wicked shall be no more; *I*,
37:36 *I* I sought him, but he could
39: 5 *I*, You have made my days
40: 9 In the great assembly; *I*,
55: 7 *I*, I would wander far off,
58: 1 Do you *i* speak righteousness,
59: 7 *I*, they belch with their
68:33 *I*, He sends out His voice,
73:27 For *i*, those who are far
105:12 *I* very few, and strangers in
119:34 *I*, I shall observe it with
139:12 *I*, the darkness shall not
Prov 23:15 wise, My heart will rejoice—*i*,
Eccl 1:14 are done under the sun; and *i*,
2:11 And *i* all was vanity and
6: 3 or *i* he has no burial, I say
Isa 14: 8 *I* the cypress trees rejoice
22:17 *I*, the LORD will throw you
24:16 *I*, the treacherous dealers
29: 8 and *i* he is faint, And his
34: 5 *I* it shall come down on Edom,
36:19 *I*, have they delivered
38:17 *I* it was for my own peace
41:24 *I* you are nothing, And your
41:29 *I* they are all worthless
43:13 *I* before the day was, I am He
44: 8 *I* there is no other Rock;
44:15 *I* he makes a god and worships
46:11 *I* I have spoken it; I will
48:13 *I* My hand has laid the
49: 6 *I* He says, 'It is too small a
50: 2 *I* with My rebuke I dry up the
50: 9 *I* they will all grow old like
54:15 *I* they shall surely assemble,
55: 4 *I* I have given him as a
58: 4 *I* you fast for strife and
62:11 *I* the LORD has proclaimed To
64: 5 You are *i* angry, for we have
64: 9 *I*, please look—we all are
Jer 2:37 *I* you will go forth from him
3:22 *I* we do come to You, For You
4:23 and *i* it was without form,
4:24 and *i* they trembled, And all
4:25 and *i* there was no man, And
4:26 and *i* the fruitful land was a
6:10 *I* their ear is uncircumcised,
17:15 *I* they say to me, "Where is
22: 4 For if you *i* do this thing, then
23:26 *I* they are prophets of the
29:23 *I* I know, and am a witness,
40:10 I will *i* dwell at Mizpah and
42: 4 *I*, I will pray to the LORD
49:15 For *i*, I will make you
50:24 You have *i* been trapped, O
Ezek 4:14 Lord GOD! *I* I have never
5: 8 *I* I, even I, am against you and
6: 3 *I* I, even I, will bring a sword
8:17 *I* they put the branch to their
13: 8 therefore I am *i* against
13:10 'Because, *i*, because they
15: 5 '*I*, when it was whole,
16: 8 *i* your time was the time of
16:28 *i* you played the harlot with
16:44 *I* everyone who quotes proverbs
17:12 *I* the king of Babylon went to
23:39 and *i* thus they have done in
25: 4 '*i*, therefore, I will deliver
25: 7 '*i*, therefore, I will stretch
29:10 '*I*, therefore, I am against
30: 9 For *i* it is coming!"
31: 3 *I* Assyria was a cedar in
33:32 *I* you are to them as a very
34:11 *I* I Myself will search for My
36: 9 For *i* I am for you, and I will
37: 2 and *i* they were very dry.
37: 8 *I*, as I looked, the sinews
37:11 They *i* say, 'Our bones are dry,
37:27 *i* I will be their God, and they
39:13 *I* all the people of the land
Dan 10:20 *i* the prince of Greece will
Hos 9: 6 For *i* they are gone because of
12:11 *I* their altars shall be
Joel 3: 4 *I*, what have you to do
Am 7: 1 *i* it was the late crop after
Ob 13 *I*, you should not have gazed
Mic 3: 7 *I* they shall all cover their
Hab 1: 6 For *i* I am raising up the
2: 5 *I*, because he
Zeph 2:11 *I* all the shores of the
Hag 1: 9 but *i* it came to little;
Zech 11: 6 But *i* I will give everyone into
11:16 For *i* I will raise up a shepherd
Mt 3:11 I *i* baptize you with water unto
11: 8 *I*, those who wear soft
12:41 and *i* a greater than Jonah is
12:42 and *i* a greater than Solomon
13:23 who *i* bears fruit and produces:
13:32 which *i* is the least of all the
17:11 '*I*, Elijah is coming first
20:23 You will *i* drink My cup, and be
23:27 like whitewashed tombs which *i*
23:34 'Therefore, *i*, I send you
26:24 The Son of Man *i* goes just as it
26:41 The spirit *i* is willing, but
28: 7 and *i* He is going before you
Mk 1: 8 I *i* baptized you with water, but
9:12 '*I*, Elijah is coming first
10:39 You will *i* drink the cup that I
11:32 John to have been a prophet *i*.
14:21 The Son of Man *i* goes just as it
14:38 The spirit *i* is willing, but
Lk 1:36 'Now *i*, Elizabeth your
1:44 'For *i*, as soon as the
3:16 'I *i* baptize you with water;
6:23 For *i* your reward is great
7:25 *I* those who are gorgeously
11:31 and *i* a greater than Solomon

11:32 and *i* a greater than Jonah is
11:41 then *i* all things are clean to
11:48 for they *i* killed them, and you
13:30 And *i* there are last who will be
17:21 here!' or 'See there!' For *i*,
22:31 Lord said, "Simon, Simon! *I*,
23:14 And *i*, having examined Him
23:15 and *i* nothing deserving of
23:29 For *i* the days are coming in
23:41 And we *i* justly, for we receive
24:21 *I*, besides all this, today
24:34 saying, "The Lord is risen *i*,
Jn 1:47 him, "Behold, an Israelite *i*,
4:42 and we know that this is *i* the
6:55 "For My flesh is food *i*,
6:55 indeed, and My blood is drink *i*.
7:26 Do the rulers know *i* that this
8:31 My word, you are My disciples *i*.
8:36 you free, you shall be free *i*.
16:32 *I* the hour is coming, yes, has
18:21 *I* they know what I said."
Acts 4:16 For, *i*, that a notable
5:23 *I* we found the prison shut
11:16 John *i* baptized with water, but
13:11 'And now, *i*, the hand of
16:37 No *i*! Let them come themselves
19: 4 John *i* baptized with a baptism
20:25 'And *i*, now I know that you
22: 3 I am *i* a Jew, born in Tarsus of
22: 9 And those who were with me *i* saw
26: 9 '*I*, I myself thought I must
27:24 and *i* God has granted you all
Rom 2:17 *I* you are called a Jew, and
2:25 For circumcision is *i*
3: 4 Certainly not! *I*, let God be
6:11 reckon yourselves to be dead *i*
8: 7 law of God, nor *i* can be.
8: 9 if *i* the Spirit of God dwells
8:17 if *i* we suffer with Him, that
9:20 But *i*, O man, who are you to
10:18 *i*: "Their sound has gone
14: 4 *I*, he will be made to stand,
14:20 All things *i* are pure, but it
15:27 It pleased them *i*,
16: 2 for *i* she has been a helper of
1 Cor 4: 7 Now if you did *i* receive it,
4: 8 and *i* I could wish you did
5: 3 For I *i*, as absent in body
5: 7 For *i* Christ, our Passover, was
11: 7 For a man *i* ought not to cover
12:20 But now *i* there are many
14: 5 unless *i* he interprets, that
14:17 For you *i* give thanks well, but
2 Cor 2:10 For if *i* I have forgiven
5: 3 if *i*, having been clothed,
7: 5 For *i*, when we came to
11: 1 and *i* you do bear with me.
13: 5 unless *i* you are disqualified.
Gal 1:20 things which I write to you, *i*,
3: 4 if *i* it was in vain?
4: 8 But then, *i*, when you did
5: 2 *I* I, Paul, say to you that if
Eph 3: 2 if *i* you have heard of the
4:21 if *i* you have heard Him and have
Phil 1:15 Some *i* preach Christ even from
2:27 For *i* he was sick almost unto
3: 8 Yet *i* I also count all things
4:18 *I* I have all and abound. I am
Col 1:23 if *i* you continue in the faith,
2:23 These things *i* have an
1 Th 4:10 and *i* you do so toward all the
Heb 2:16 For *i* He does not give aid to
3: 5 And Moses *i* was faithful in all
3:16 *I*, was it not all who came
4: 2 For *i* the gospel was preached to
6:16 For men *i* swear by the greater,
7: 5 And *i* those who are of the sons
9: 1 Then *i*, even the first
12:10 For they *i* for a few days
Jas 3: 3 *I*, we put bits in horses'
5: 4 *I* the wages of the laborers who
5:11 *I* we count them blessed who
1 Pe 1:20 He *i* was foreordained before the
2: 3 if *i* you have tasted that the
2: 4 rejected *i* by men, but chosen
Rev 2:10 *I*, the devil is about to
2:22 *I* I will cast her into a
3: 9 *I* I will make those of the
3: 9 *i* I will make them come and

INDEPENDENT (2/1)

1 Cor 11:11 neither is man *i* of woman, nor
11:11 nor woman *i* of man, in the

INDESCRIBABLE (1/1)

2 Cor 9:15 Thanks be to God for His *i*

INDIA (2/2)

Esth 1: 1 from *I* to Ethiopia),
8: 9 of the provinces from *I* to

INDICATE (1/1)

1 Ki 5: 9 by sea to the place you *i* to

INDICATED (1/1)

Lk 24:28 and He *i* that He would have

INDICATES (1/1) INDICATING

Heb 12:27 *i* the removal of those things

INDICATING (2/2) INDICATES

Heb 9: 8 the Holy Spirit *i* this, that the
1 Pe 1:11 of Christ who was in them was *i*

INDIGNANT (4/4) INDIGNATION

Neh 4: 1 that he was furious and very *i*,
Mt 21:15 Son of David!" they were *i*
26: 8 disciples saw it, they were *i*,
Mk 14: 4 But there were some who were *i*

INDIGNATION (36/36) INDIGNANT

Deut 29:28 anger, in wrath, and in great *i*,
2 Ki 3:27 and there was great *i* against
Esth 5: 9 he was filled with *i* against
Job 10:17 And increase Your *i* toward me;
Ps 69:24 Pour out Your *i* upon them, And
78:49 of His anger, Wrath, *i*,
102:10 Because of Your *i* and Your
119:53 *I* has taken hold of me Because
Isa 10: 5 the staff in whose hand is My *i*.
10:25 a very little while and the *i*
13: 5 LORD and His weapons of *i*,
26:20 Until the *i* is past.
30:27 His lips are full of *i*,
30:30 With the *i* of His anger And
34: 2 For the *i* of the LORD is
66:14 And His *i* to His enemies.
Jer 10:10 not be able to endure His *i*.
15:17 For You have filled me with *i*.
50:25 out the weapons of His *i*;
Lam 2: 6 In His burning *i* He has
Ezek 21:31 I will pour out My *i* on you;
22:24 or rained on in the day of *i*.
22:31 I have poured out My *i* on them;
Dan 8:19 in the latter time of the *i*;
Mic 7: 9 I will bear the *i* of the LORD,
Nah 1: 6 Who can stand before His *i*?
Hab 3:12 marched through the land in *i*;
Zeph 3: 8 kingdoms, To pour on them My *i*,
Mal 1: 4 whom the LORD will have *i*
Lk 13:14 the synagogue answered with *i*,
Acts 5:17 and they were filled with *i*,
Rom 2: 8 unrighteousness—*i* and wrath,
2 Cor 7:11 of yourselves, what *i*,
11:29 and I do not burn with *i*?
Heb 10:27 and fiery *i* which will devour
Rev 14:10 strength into the cup of His *i*.

INDISPOSED (1/1)

Lev 15:33 and for her who is *i* because of

INDIVIDUAL (2/2)

1 Chr 23: 3 and the number of *i* males was
Rev 21:21 each *i* gate was of one pearl.

INDIVIDUALLY (10/10)

Num 1: 2 number of names, every male *i*,
1:18 years old and above, each one *i*.
1:20 number of names, every male *i*,
1:22 number of names, every male *i*,
3:47 five shekels for each one *i*;
1 Chr 23:24 houses as they were counted *i*
Ps 33:15 He fashions their hearts *i*;
Rom 12: 5 and *i* members of one another.
1 Cor 12:11 distributing to each one *i* as
12:27 body of Christ, and members *i*.

INDUCED (5/4)

Jer 20: 7 You *i* me, and I was persuaded;
20:10 saying, "Perhaps he can be *i*;
Ezek 14: 9 And if the prophet is *i* to speak
14: 9 I the LORD have *i* that
Acts 6:11 Then they secretly *i* men to say,

INDULGENCE (1/1)

Col 2:23 are of no value against the *i*

INDUSTRIOUS (1/1)

1 Ki 11:28 seeing that the young man was *i*,

INEXCUSABLE (1/1)

Rom 2: 1 Therefore you are *i*,

INEXPERIENCED (3/3)

1 Chr 22: 5 my son is young and *i*,
29: 1 God has chosen, is young and *i*;
2 Chr 13: 7 when Rehoboam was young and *i*

INEXPRESSIBLE (2/2)

2 Cor 12: 4 up into Paradise and heard *i*
1 Pe 1: 8 you rejoice with joy *i* and full

INFALLIBLE (1/1)

Acts 1: 3 after His suffering by many *i*

INFAMOUS (1/1)

Ezek 22: 5 far from you will mock you as *i*

INFANT (4/4) INFANTS

1 Sam 15: 3 *i* and nursing child, ox and
Isa 65:20 No more shall an *i* from there
Jer 44: 7 you man and woman, child and *i*,
Lam 4: 4 The tongue of the *i* clings To

INFANTS (7/7) INFANT

1 Sam 22:19 women, children and nursing *i*,
Job 3:16 Like *i* who never saw light?
Ps 8: 2 mouth of babes and nursing *i*
Lam 2:11 the children and the *i* Faint
Hos 13:16 Their *i* shall be dashed in
Mt 21:16 of babes and nursing *i*
Lk 18:15 Then they also brought *i* to Him

INFERIOR (6/6)

Job 12: 3 I am not *i* to you. Indeed,
13: 2 I am not *i* to you.
Dan 2:39 shall arise another kingdom *i*
Jn 2:10 have well drunk, then the *i*.
2 Cor 11: 5 that I am not at all *i* to the
12:13 what is it in which you were *i*

INFIDEL (KJV) See UNBELIEVER

INFIDELITY (1/1)

Num 14:33 and bear the brunt of your *i*,

INFINITE (1/1)

Ps 147: 5 power; His understanding is *i*.

INFIRMITIES (8/8) INFIRMITY

Mt 8:17 He Himself took our *i* And
Lk 5:15 to be healed by Him of their *i*.
7:21 very hour He cured many of *i*,
8: 2 healed of evil spirits and *i*—
2 Cor 12: 5 will not boast, except in my *i*.
12: 9 I will rather boast in my *i*,
12:10 Therefore I take pleasure in *i*,
1 Tim 5:23 sake and your frequent *i*.

INFIRMITY (6/6) INFIRMITIES

Jer 10:19 I say, "Truly this is an *i*,
Lk 13:11 a woman who had a spirit of *i*
13:12 you are loosed from your *i*.
Jn 5: 5 man was there who had an *i*
2 Cor 11:30 the things which concern my *i*.
Gal 4:13 that because of physical *i* I

INFLAMED (1/1)

Hos 7: 5 *i* with wine; He stretched out

INFLAMES (1/1)

Isa 5:11 night, till wine *i* them!

INFLAMING (1/1)

Isa 57: 5 *I* yourselves with gods under

INFLAMMATION (2/2)

Deut 28:22 consumption, with fever, with *i*,
Ps 38: 7 For my loins are full of *i*,

INFLICT (1/1)

Deut 7:23 and will *i* defeat upon them

INFLICTED (4/4)

2 Ki 8:29 wounds which the Syrians had *i*
9:15 wounds which the Syrians had *i*
Lam 1:12 Which the LORD has *i* In the
2 Cor 2: 6 This punishment which was *i* by

INFLICTING (1/1)

1 Ki 20:37 man struck him, *i* a wound.

INFLICTS (1/1)

Rom 3: 5 Is God unjust who *i* wrath?

INFORM (6/6) INFORMED

Ruth 4: 4 And I thought to *i* you, saying,
1 Sam 27:11 Lest they should *i* on us,
2 Sam 15:28 until word comes from you to *i*
Ezra 4:16 We *i* the king that if this city
5:10 asked them their names to *i*
7:24 Also we *i* you that it shall not

INFORMED (7/7) INFORM

Ezra 4:14 therefore we have sent and *i*
Esth 2:22 and Esther *i* the king in
Dan 9:22 And he *i* me, and talked with
Acts 21:21 but they have been *i* about you
21:24 things of which they were *i*
25: 2 and the chief men of the Jews *i*
25:15 and the elders of the Jews *i*

INFORMER (1/1)
Neh 6:10 Mehetabel, who was a secret *i*;

INFORMS (1/1)
Hos 4:12 And their staff *i* them.

INGATHERING (2/2)
Ex 23:16 and the Feast of *I* at the end
34:22 and the Feast of *I* at the

INGRAINED (1/1)
Lev 14:37 the walls of the house with *i*

INGREDIENTS (1/1)
2 Chr 16:14 with spices and various *i*

INHABIT (10/10) ENTHRONED, INHABITANT, INHABITED, INHABITING, INHABITS, UNINHABITED
Num 13:19 whether the cities they *i* are
15: 2 come into the land you are to *i*,
35:34 not defile the land which you *i*,
Prov 10:30 But the wicked will not *i* the
Isa 65:21 They shall build houses and *i*
65:22 shall not build and another *i*;
Jer 17: 6 But shall *i* the parched places
Ezek 33:24 they who *i* those ruins in the
Am 9:14 build the waste cities and *i*
Zeph 1:13 but not *i* them; They shall

INHABITANT (32/31) INHABIT, INHABITANTS
Isa 5: 9 and beautiful ones, without *i*.
6:11 are laid waste and without *i*,
9: 9 Ephraim and the *i* of
12: 6 O *i* of Zion, For great is the
20: 6 And the *i* of this territory will
24:17 you, O *i* of the earth.
33:24 And the *i* will not say, "I am
Jer 2:15 cities are burned, without *i*.
4: 7 will be laid waste, Without *i*.
9:11 of Judah desolate, without an *i*.
10:17 O *i* of the fortress!
21:13 O *i* of the valley, And rock
22:23 O *i* of Lebanon, Making your
26: 9 be desolate, without an *i*'?
33:10 without man and without *i* and
34:22 of Judah a desolation without *i*.
44:22 a curse, and without an *i*,
46:19 waste and desolate, without *i*.
48:19 O *i* of Aroer, Stand by the way
48:43 O *i* of Moab," says the LORD.
51:29 Babylon a desolation without *i*.
51:35 The *i* of Zion will say;
51:37 and a hissing, Without an *i*.
Am 1: 5 And cut off the *i* from the
1: 8 I will cut off the *i* from
Mic 1:11 shame, you *i* of Shaphir;
1:11 The *i* of Zaanan does not go
1:12 For the *i* of Maroth pined for
1:13 O *i* of Lachish, Harness the
1:15 O *i* of Mareshah; The glory of
Zeph 2: 5 So there shall be no *i*."
3: 6 There is no one, no *i*.

INHABITANTS (200/184) INHABITANT
Gen 19:25 all the *i* of the cities, and
34:30 me obnoxious among the *i* of
50:11 And when the *i* of the land, the
Ex 15:14 will take hold of the *i* of
15:15 All the *i* of Canaan will melt
23:31 For I will deliver the *i* of the
34:12 you make a covenant with the *i*
34:15 you make a covenant with the *i*
Lev 18:25 and the land vomits out its *i*.
25:10 all the land to all its *i*.
Num 13:32 is a land that devours its *i*,
14:14 they will tell it to the *i* of
32:17 cities because of the *i* of the
33:52 you shall drive out all the *i*
33:53 you shall dispossess the *i* of
33:55 if you do not drive out the *i*
Deut 13:13 among you and enticed the *i* of
13:15 you shall surely strike the *i* of
Josh 2: 9 and that all the *i* of the land
2:24 for indeed all the *i* of the
7: 9 the Canaanites and all the *i*
8:24 an end of slaying all the *i* of
8:26 utterly destroyed all the *i* of
9: 3 But when the *i* of Gibeon heard
9:11 our elders and all the *i* of
9:24 and to destroy all the *i* of the
10: 1 and how the *i* of Gibeon had made
11:19 the *i* of Gibeon. All the
13: 6 all the *i* of the mountains from
15:15 he went up from there to the *i*
15:63 the *i* of Jerusalem, the
17: 7 went along south to the *i* of
17:11 the *i* of Dor and its towns, the
17:11 the *i* of En Dor and its towns,
17:11 the *i* of Taanach and its towns,
17:11 and the *i* of Megiddo and its
17:12 could not drive out the *i*
Judg 1:11 there they went against the *i*
1:19 they could not drive out the *i*
1:27 did not drive out the *i* of
1:27 or the *i* of Dor and its
1:27 or the *i* of Ibleam and its
1:27 or the *i* of Megiddo and its
1:30 did Zebulun drive out the *i* of
1:30 inhabitants of Kitron or the *i*
1:31 Nor did Asher drive out the *i*
1:31 inhabitants of Acco or the *i*
1:32 the *i* of the land; for they did
1:33 did Naphtali drive out the *i* of
1:33 of Beth Shemesh or the *i* of
1:33 the *i* of the land. Nevertheless
1:33 the *i* of Beth Shemesh
2: 2 make no covenant with the *i* of
5:23 Curse its *i* bitterly, Because
10:18 He shall be head over all the *i*
11: 8 and be our head over all the *i*
20:15 besides the *i* of Gibeah, who
21: 9 not one of the *i* of Jabesh
21:10 Go and strike the *i* of Jabesh
21:12 So they found among the *i* of
Ruth 4: 4 back in the presence of the *i*
1 Sam 6:21 they sent messengers to the *i*
23: 5 So David saved the *i* of Keilah.
27: 8 For those nations were the *i* of
31:11 Now when the *i* of Jabesh Gilead
2 Sam 5: 6 the *i* of the land, who spoke to
1 Ki 17: 1 of the *i* of Gilead, said to
21:11 elders and nobles who were *i*
2 Ki 19:26 Therefore their *i* had little
22:16 on this place and on its *i*—
22:19 this place and against its *i*,
23: 2 and with him all the *i* of
1 Chr 8: 6 the fathers' houses of the *i*
8:13 fathers' houses of the *i* of
8:13 who drove out the *i* of Gath.
9: 2 And the first *i* who dwelt in
11: 4 the *i* of the land.
11: 5 Then the *i* of Jebus said to
22:18 For He has given the *i* of the
2 Chr 15: 5 turmoil was on all the *i* of
20: 7 who drove out the *i* of this
20:15 all you of Judah and you *i* of
20:18 and all Judah and the *i* of
20:20 O Judah and you *i* of Jerusalem:
20:23 Moab stood up against the *i* of
20:23 they had made an end of the *i*
21:11 and caused the *i* of Jerusalem
21:13 and have made Judah and the *i*
22: 1 Then the *i* of Jerusalem made
32:22 LORD saved Hezekiah and the *i*
32:26 he and the *i* of Jerusalem, so
32:33 and all Judah and the *i* of
33: 9 seduced Judah and the *i* of
34:24 on this place and on its *i*,
34:27 this place and against its *i*,
34:28 bring on this place and its *i*.
34:30 all the men of Judah and the *i*
34:32 So the *i* of Jerusalem did
35:18 and the *i* of Jerusalem.
Ezra 4: 6 an accusation against the *i* of
Neh 3:13 Hanun and the *i* of Zanoah
7: 3 guards from among the *i* of
9:24 You subdued before them the *i*
Ps 33: 8 Let all the *i* of the world
33:14 He looks On all the *i* of the
49: 1 all *i* of the world,
75: 3 The earth and all its *i* are
83: 7 Philistia with the *i* of Tyre;
Isa 5: 3 O *i* of Jerusalem and men of
8:14 a trap and a snare to the *i* of
10:13 So I have put down the *i* like
10:31 The *i* of Gebim seek refuge.
18: 3 All *i* of the world and dwellers
21:14 O *i* of the land of Tema, Bring
22:21 He shall be a father to the *i*
23: 2 you *i* of the coastland, You
23: 6 you *i* of the coastland!
24: 1 And scatters abroad its *i*.
24: 5 is also defiled under its *i*,
24: 6 Therefore the *i* of the earth
26: 9 The *i* of the world will learn
26:18 Nor have the *i* of the world
26:21 of His place To punish the *i*
37:27 Therefore their *i* had little
38:11 man no more among the *i* of the
40:22 And its *i* are like
42:10 You coastlands and you *i* of
42:11 Let the *i* of Sela sing, Let
49:19 even now be too small for the *i*;
Jer 1:14 break forth On all the *i* of
4: 4 You men of Judah and *i* of
6:12 out My hand Against the *i* of
8: 1 and the bones of the *i* of
10:18 throw out at this time The *i*
11: 2 the men of Judah and to the *i*
11: 9 men of Judah and among the *i*
11:12 the cities of Judah and the *i*
13:13 I will fill all the *i* of this
13:13 and all the *i* of Jerusalem—with
17:20 and all the *i* of Jerusalem, who
17:25 by the men of Judah and the *i*
18:11 the men of Judah and to the *i*
19: 3 O kings of Judah and *i* of
19:12 says the LORD, "and to its *i*,
21: 6 I will strike the *i* of this
23:14 And her *i* like Gomorrah.
25: 2 of Judah and to all the *i* of
25: 9 this land, against its *i*,
25:29 call for a sword on all the *i*
25:30 Against all the *i* of the
26:15 on this city, and on its *i*;
32:32 and the *i* of Jerusalem.
35:13 the men of Judah and the *i* of
35:17 on Judah and on all the *i* of
36:31 on the *i* of Jerusalem, and on
42:18 have been poured out on the *i*
46: 8 will destroy the city and its *i*.
47: 2 And all the *i* of the land
49: 8 O *i* of Dedan! For I will bring
49:20 He has proposed against the *i*
49:30 O *i* of Hazor!" says the
50:21 And against the *i* of Pekod.
50:34 And disquiet the *i* of Babylon.
50:35 Against the *i* of Babylon, And
51:12 What He spoke against the *i*
51:24 repay Babylon And all the *i*
51:35 And my blood be upon the *i* of
Lam 4:12 And all *i* of the world, Would
Ezek 11:15 are those about whom the *i* of
12:19 says the Lord GOD to the *i* of
15: 6 so I will give up the *i* of
26:17 strong at sea, She and her *i*,
26:17 terror to be on all her *i*!
27: 8 *I* of Sidon and Arvad were your
27:35 All the *i* of the isles will be
29: 6 Then all the *i* of Egypt Shall
Dan 4:35 All the *i* of the earth are
4:35 of heaven And among the *i* of
9: 7 to the *i* of Jerusalem and all
Hos 4: 1 brings a charge against the *i*
10: 5 The *i* of Samaria fear Because
Joel 1: 2 all you *i* of the land! Has
1:14 the elders And all the *i* of
2: 1 holy mountain! Let all the *i*
Mic 6:12 Her *i* have spoken lies, And
6:16 And your *i* a hissing.
Zeph 1: 4 And against all the *i* of
1:11 you *i* of Maktesh! For all the
2: 5 Woe to the *i* of the seacoast,
Zech 8:20 come, *I* of many cities;
8:21 The *i* of one city shall go to
11: 6 I will no longer pity the *i* of
12: 5 The *i* of Jerusalem are my
12: 7 of David and the glory of the *i*
12: 8 the LORD will defend the *i* of
12:10 house of David and on the *i* of
13: 1 house of David and for the *i*
Rev 8:13 woe to the *i* of the earth,
12:12 dwell in them! Woe to the *i* of
17: 2 and the *i* of the earth were

INHABITED (32/31) INHABIT
Gen 36:20 sons of Seir the Horite who *i*
Ex 16:35 until they came to an *i* land;
Judg 1:17 attacked the Canaanites who *i*
1:21 drive out the Jebusites who *i*
11:21 Amorites, who *i* that country.
Prov 8:31 Rejoicing in His *i* world, And
Isa 13:20 It will never be *i*,
44:26 to Jerusalem, 'You shall be *i*,
45:18 in vain, Who formed it to be *i*:
54: 3 And make the desolate cities *i*.
Jer 6: 8 you desolate, A land not *i*.
17: 6 a salt land which is not *i*.
22: 6 Cities which are not *i*.
46:26 Afterward it shall be *i* as in
50:13 the LORD She shall not be *i*,
50:39 It shall be *i* no more forever,
Ezek 12:20 Then the cities that are *i* shall
26:17 O one *i* by seafaring men,
26:19 like cities that are not *i*,
26:20 Pit, so that you may never be *i*;
34:13 in the valleys and in all the *i*
36:10 and the cities shall be *i* and
36:11 I will make you *i* as in former
36:35 are now fortified and *i*.
38:12 places that are again *i*,
Zech 2: 4 Jerusalem shall be *i* as towns
7: 7 and the cities around it were *i*
7: 7 South and the Lowland were *i*?
9: 5 And Ashkelon shall not be *i*.
12: 6 but Jerusalem shall be *i* again
14:10 shall be raised up and *i* in
14:11 Jerusalem shall be safely *i*.

INHABITING (3/3) INHABIT
Job 26: 5 under the waters and those *i*
Ps 74:14 him as food to the people *i*
Jer 48:18 O daughter *i* Dibon, Come down

INHABITS (3/3) INHABIT
Job 15:28 In houses which no one *i*,
Isa 42:11 The villages that Kedar *i*.
57:15 the High and Lofty One Who *i*

INHERIT (62/61) INHERITANCE, INHERITED
Gen 15: 7 to give you this land to *i*
15: 8 how shall I know that I will *i*
28: 4 That you may *i* the land In
Ex 23:30 and you *i* the land.
32:13 and they shall *i* it forever.'
Lev 20:24 You shall *i* their land, and I
25:46 to *i* them as a possession;
Num 14:24 and his descendants shall *i* it.
26:55 they shall *i* according to the
32:19 For we will not *i* with them on
33:54 You shall *i* according to the

34:13 is the land which you shall *i*
Deut 1:38 for he shall cause Israel to *i*
2:31 that you may *i* his land.'
3:28 and he shall cause them to *i*
12:10 your God is giving you to *i*,
16:20 that you may live and *i* the
19: 3 your God is giving you to *i*,
19:14 inheritance which you will *i*
31: 7 and you shall cause them to *i*
Josh 17:14 one lot and one share to *i*,
1 Sam 2: 8 among princes And make them *i*
2 Chr 20:11 which You have given us to *i*.
Job 13:26 And make me *i* the iniquities
Ps 25:13 And his descendants shall *i*
37: 9 They shall *i* the earth.
37:11 But the meek shall *i* the earth,
37:22 those blessed by Him shall *i*
37:29 The righteous shall *i* the land,
37:34 And He shall exalt you to *i*
69:36 of His servants shall *i* it,
82: 8 For You shall *i* all nations.
Prov 3:35 The wise shall *i* glory, But
8:21 cause those who love me to *i*
11:29 troubles his own house will *i*
14:18 The simple *i* folly, But the
28:10 But the blameless will *i* good.
Isa 49: 8 To cause them to *i* the
54: 3 And your descendants will *i*
57:13 And shall *i* My holy
60:21 They shall *i* the land forever,
65: 9 My elect shall *i* it, And My
Jer 8:10 fields to those who will *i*
12:14 caused My people Israel to *i*—
49: 1 Why then does Milcom *i* Gad,
Ezek 47:14 You shall *i* it equally with one
Mt 5: 5 For they shall *i* the earth.
19:29 and *i* eternal life.
25:34 *i* the kingdom prepared for you
Mk 10:17 what shall I do that I may *i*
Lk 10:25 what shall I do to *i* eternal
18:18 what shall I do to *i* eternal
1 Cor 6: 9 the unrighteous will not *i* the
6:10 nor extortioners will *i* the
15:50 that flesh and blood cannot *i*
15:50 nor does corruption *i*
Gal 5:21 such things will not *i* the
Heb 1:14 minister for those who will *i*
6:12 through faith and patience *i*
12:17 when he wanted to *i* the
1 Pe 3: 9 that you may *i* a blessing.
Rev 21: 7 He who overcomes shall *i* all

INHERITANCE (246/210) INHERIT, INHERITANCES

Gen 31:14 there still any portion or *i*
48: 6 of their brothers in their *i*.
Ex 15:17 them In the mountain of Your *i*,
34: 9 our sin, and take us as Your *i*.
Lev 25:46 And you may take them as an *i*
Num 16:14 nor given us *i* of fields and
18:20 You shall have no *i* in their
18:20 I am your portion and your *i*
18:21 the tithes in Israel as an *i*
18:23 of Israel they shall have no *i*.
18:24 given to the Levites as an *i*;
18:24 of Israel they shall have no *i*.
18:26 given you from them as your *i*,
26:53 land shall be divided as an *i*,
26:54 you shall give a larger *i*,
26:54 you shall give a smaller *i*.
26:54 Each shall be given its *i*
26:56 According to the lot their *i*
26:62 because there was no *i* given to
27: 7 give them a possession of *i*
27: 7 and cause the *i* of their father
27: 8 then you shall cause his *i* to
27: 9 then you shall give his *i* to
27:10 then you shall give his *i* to
27:11 then you shall give his *i* to
32:18 of Israel has received his *i*.
32:19 because our *i* has fallen to us
32:32 but the possession of our *i*
33:54 divide the land by lot as an *i*
33:54 you shall give a larger *i*,
33:54 you shall give a smaller *i*;
33:54 there everyone's *i* shall be
34: 2 that shall fall to you as an *i*—
34:14 have received their *i*;
34:14 of Manasseh has received its *i*.
34:15 have received their *i* on this
34:17 the land among you as an *i*:
34:18 to divide the land for the *i*.
34:29 LORD commanded to divide the *i*
35: 2 cities to dwell in from the *i*
35: 8 in proportion to the *i* that
36: 2 to give the land as an *i* by
36: 2 by the LORD to give the *i* of
36: 3 then their *i* will be taken from
36: 3 will be taken from the *i* of
36: 3 and it will be added to the *i*
36: 3 be taken from the lot of our *i*.
36: 4 then their *i* will be added to
36: 4 will be added to the *i* of the
36: 4 so their *i* will be taken away
36: 4 will be taken away from the *i*
36: 7 So the *i* of the children of
36: 7 of Israel shall keep the *i* of
36: 8 daughter who possesses an *i* in
36: 8 Israel each may possess the *i*
36: 9 Thus no *i* shall change hands
36: 9 of Israel shall keep its own *i*.
36:12 and their *i* remained in the
Deut 4:20 Egypt, to be His people, an *i*,
4:21 your God is giving you as an *i*.
4:38 to give you their land as an *i*,
9:26 destroy Your people and Your *i*
9:29 are Your people and Your *i*,
10: 9 Levi has no portion nor *i* with
10: 9 the LORD is his *i*, just as
12: 9 not come to the rest and the *i*
12:12 since he has no portion nor *i*
14:27 for he has no part nor *i* with
14:29 he has no portion nor *i* with
15: 4 giving you to possess as an *i*—
18: 1 shall have no part nor *i* with
18: 2 they shall have no *i*
18: 2 the LORD is their *i*, as He
18: 8 comes from the sale of his *i*.
19:10 your God is giving you as an *i*,
19:14 in your *i* which you will
20:16 your God gives you as an *i*,
21:23 your God is giving you as an *i*;
24: 4 your God is giving you as an *i*.
25:19 giving you to possess as an *i*,
26: 1 your God is giving you as an *i*,
29: 8 their land and gave it as an *i*
32: 8 the Most High divided their *i*
32: 9 Jacob is the place of His *i*.
Josh 1: 6 you shall divide as an *i* the
11:23 and Joshua gave it as an *i* to
13: 6 it by lot to Israel as an *i*,
13: 7 divide this land as an *i* to the
13: 8 the Gadites received their *i*,
13:14 tribe of Levi he had given no *i*;
13:14 made by fire are their *i*,
13:15 the children of Reuben an *i*
13:23 This was the *i* of the children
13:24 Moses also had given an *i* to
13:28 This is the *i* of the children
13:29 Moses also had given an *i* to
13:32 Moses had distributed as an *i*
13:33 of Levi Moses had given no *i*;
13:33 God of Israel was their *i*,
14: 1 of Israel distributed as an *i*
14: 2 Their *i* was by lot, as the
14: 3 For Moses had given the *i* of the
14: 3 the Levites he had given no *i*
14: 9 has trodden shall be your *i*
14:13 the son of Jephunneh as an *i*.
14:14 Hebron therefore became the *i* of
15:20 This was the *i* of the tribe of
16: 4 and Ephraim, took their *i*.
16: 5 The border of their *i* on the
16: 8 This was the *i* of the tribe of
16: 9 of Ephraim were among the *i*
17: 4 Moses to give us an *i* among
17: 4 he gave them an *i* among their
17: 6 of Manasseh received an *i*
18: 2 had not yet received their *i*.
18: 4 survey it according to their *i*,
18: 7 of the LORD is their *i*.
18: 7 Manasseh have received their *i*
18:20 This was the *i* of the children
18:28 This was the *i* of the children
19: 1 And their *i* was within the
19: 1 inheritance was within the *i*
19: 2 They had in their *i* Beersheba
19: 8 This was the *i* of the tribe of
19: 9 The *i* of the children of Simeon
19: 9 of Simeon had their *i* within
19: 9 inheritance within the *i* of
19:10 and the border of their *i* was
19:16 This was the *i* of the children
19:23 This was the *i* of the tribe of
19:31 This was the *i* of the tribe of
19:39 This was the *i* of the tribe of
19:41 And the territory of their *i* was
19:48 This is the *i* of the tribe of
19:49 of dividing the land as an *i*
19:49 children of Israel gave an *i*
19:51 of Israel divided as an *i* by
21: 3 to the Levites from their *i*,
23: 4 to be an *i* for your tribes,
24:28 depart, each to his own *i*.
24:30 him within the border of his *i*
24:32 and which had become an *i* of
Judg 2: 6 Israel went each to his own *i*
2: 9 him within the border of his *i*
11: 2 You shall have no *i* in our
18: 1 of the Danites was seeking an *i*
18: 1 for until that day their *i*
20: 6 all the territory of the *i* of
21:17 There must be an *i* for the
21:23 went and returned to their *i*,
21:24 from there, every man to his *i*.
Ruth 4: 5 name of the dead through his *i*.
4: 6 myself, lest I ruin my own *i*.
4:10 name of the dead through his *i*,
1 Sam 10: 1 you commander over His *i*?
26:19 this day from sharing in the *i*
2 Sam 14:16 and my son together from the *i*
20: 1 Nor do we have *i* in the son of
20:19 Why would you swallow up the *i*
21: 3 that you may bless the *i* of the
1 Ki 8:36 given to Your people as an *i*.
8:51 are Your people and Your *i*,
8:53 of the earth to be Your *i*,
12:16 We have no *i* in the son of
21: 3 that I should give the *i* of my
21: 4 I will not give you the *i* of my
2 Ki 21:14 forsake the remnant of My *i*
1 Chr 16:18 As the allotment of your *i*,
28: 8 and leave it as an *i* for your
2 Chr 6:27 given to Your people as an *i*.
10:16 We have no *i* in the son of
Ezra 9:12 and leave it as an *i* to your
Neh 11:20 of Judah, everyone in his *i*.
Job 31: 2 And the *i* of the Almighty from
42:15 and their father gave them an *i*
Ps 2: 8 You The nations for Your *i*,
16: 5 You are the portion of my *i*
16: 6 Yes, I have a good *i*.
28: 9 Your people, And bless Your *i*;
33:12 He has chosen as His own *i*.
37:18 And their *i* shall be forever.
47: 4 He will choose our *i* for us,
68: 9 Whereby You confirmed Your *i*,
74: 2 of old, The tribe of Your *i*,
78:55 Allotted them an *i* by survey,
78:62 And was furious with His *i*.
78:71 His people, And Israel His *i*.
79: 1 nations have come into Your *i*;
94:14 Nor will He forsake His *i*.
105:11 As the allotment of your *i*,
106: 5 That I may glory with Your *i*.
106:40 So that He abhorred His own *i*.
Prov 13:22 A good man leaves an *i* to his
17: 2 And will share an *i* among the
19:14 Houses and riches are an *i*
20:21 An *i* gained hastily at the
Eccl 7:11 Wisdom is good with an *i*,
Isa 19:25 of My hands, and Israel My *i*.
47: 6 I have profaned My *i*,
63:17 sake, The tribes of Your *i*.
Jer 3:18 land that I have given as an *i*
10:16 Israel is the tribe of His *i*;
12:14 evil neighbors who touch the *i*
16:18 they have filled My *i* with the
32: 8 for the right of *i* is yours,
49: 2 shall take possession of his *i*,
51:19 Israel is the tribe of His *i*.
Lam 5: 2 Our *i* has been turned over to
Ezek 35:15 As you rejoiced because the *i* of
36:12 you, and you shall be their *i*;
44:28 shall be, in regard to their *i*,
44:28 that I am their *i*.
45: 1 divide the land by lot into *i*,
46:16 a gift of some of his *i* to
46:16 it is their possession by *i*.
46:17 gives a gift of some of his *i*
46:17 But his *i* shall belong to his
46:18 not take any of the people's *i*
46:18 he shall provide an *i* for his
47:13 shall divide the land as an *i*
47:14 shall fall to you as your *i*.
47:22 will divide it by lot as an *i*
47:22 they shall have an *i* with you
47:23 there you shall give him his *i*,
48:29 you shall divide by lot as an *i*
Dan 12:13 and will arise to your *i* at the
Mic 2: 2 and his house, A man and his *i*.
Zech 2:12 possession of Judah as His *i*
Mt 21:38 let us kill him and seize his *i*.
Mk 12: 7 and the *i* will be ours.'
Lk 12:13 tell my brother to divide the *i*
20:14 that the *i* may be ours.'
Acts 7: 5 And God gave him no *i* in it,
20:32 build you up and give you an *i*
26:18 forgiveness of sins and an *i*
Gal 3:18 For if the *i* is of the law, it
Eph 1:11 Him also we have obtained an *i*,
1:14 who is the guarantee of our *i*
1:18 riches of the glory of His *i*
5: 5 has any *i* in the kingdom of
Col 1:12 us to be partakers of the *i* of
3:24 receive the reward of the *i*;
Heb 1: 4 as He has by *i* obtained a more
9:15 the promise of the eternal *i*.
11: 8 which he would receive as an *i*.
1 Pe 1: 4 to an *i* incorruptible and

INHERITANCES (1/1)

Josh 19:51 These were the *i* which Eleazar

INHERITED (4/4) INHERIT

Josh 14: 1 which the children of Israel *i*
Ps 105:44 And they *i* the labor of the
Jer 16:19 Surely our fathers have *i* lies,
Ezek 33:24 and he *i* the land. But we are

INIQUITIES (53/52) INIQUITY

Lev 16:21 confess over it all the *i* of
16:22 bear on itself all their *i* to
26:39 also in their fathers' *i*,
Ezra 9: 6 for our *i* have risen higher
9: 7 and for our *i* we, our kings,
9:13 punished us less than our *i*
Neh 9: 2 confessed their sins and the *i*
Job 13:23 How many are my *i* and sins?
13:26 And make me inherit the *i* of
Ps 38: 4 For my *i* have gone over my
40:12 My *i* have overtaken me, so
51: 9 my sins, And blot out all my *i*.
64: 6 They devise *i*: "We have
65: 3 *I* prevail against me
79: 8 do not remember former *i*
90: 8 You have set our *i* before You,
103: 3 Who forgives all your *i*,
103:10 punished us according to our *i*.
107:17 And because of their *i*,
130: 3 If You, LORD, should mark *i*,
130: 8 redeem Israel From all his *i*.

I

Prov 5:22 His own *i* entrap the wicked
Isa 43:24 have wearied Me with your *i*.
50: 1 For your *i* you have sold
53: 5 He was bruised for our *i*;
53:11 For He shall bear their *i*.
59: 2 But your *i* have separated you
59:12 with us, And as for our *i*,
64: 6 all fade as a leaf, And our *i*,
64: 7 consumed us because of our *i*.
65: 7 Your *i* and the iniquities of
65: 7 Your iniquities and the *i* of
Jer 5:25 Your *i* have turned these
11:10 have turned back to the *i*
14: 7 though our *i* testify against
30:14 For the multitude of your *i*,
30:15 of the multitude of your *i*,
33: 8 and I will pardon all their *i*
Lam 4:13 of her prophets And the *i* of
5: 7 no more, But we bear their *i*.
Ezek 24:23 you shall pine away in your *i*
28:18 By the multitude of your *i*,
32:27 But their *i* will be on their
36:31 for your *i* and your
36:33 I cleanse you from all your *i*,
43:10 they may be ashamed of their *i*;
Dan 4:27 and your *i* by showing mercy to
9:13 that we might turn from our *i*
9:16 and for the *i* of our fathers,
Am 3: 2 will punish you for all your *i*.
Mic 7:19 on us, And will subdue our *i*.
Acts 3:26 every one of you from your *i*.
Rev 18: 5 and God has remembered her *i*.

INIQUITY (241/229) INIQUITIES

Gen 15:16 for the *i* of the Amorites is
44:16 God has found out the *i* of your
Ex 20: 5 visiting the *i* of the fathers
28:38 that Aaron may bear the *i* of
28:43 that they do not incur *i* and
34: 7 forgiving *i* and transgression
34: 7 visiting the *i* of the fathers
34: 9 and pardon our *i* and our sin,
Lev 5:17 is guilty and shall bear his *i*.
18:25 I visit the punishment of its *i*
19: 8 who eats it shall bear his *i*,
26:39 shall waste away in their *i* in
26:40 But if they confess their *i*
26:40 their iniquity and the *i* of
Num 5:15 for bringing *i* to remembrance.
5:31 the man shall be free from *i*,
14:18 forgiving *i* and transgression;
14:18 visiting the *i* of the fathers
14:19 Pardon the *i* of this people, I
18: 1 house with you shall bear the *i*
18: 1 sons with you shall bear the *i*
18:23 and they shall bear their *i*;
23:21 He has not observed *i* in Jacob,
Deut 5: 9 visiting the *i* of the fathers
19:15 against a man concerning any *i*
Josh 22:17 Is the *i* of Peor not enough for
22:20 did not perish alone in his *i*.
1 Sam 3:13 his house forever for the *i*
3:14 to the house of Eli that the *i*
15:23 And stubbornness is as *i* and
20: 1 have I done? What is my *i*,
20: 8 if there is *i* in me, kill me
25:24 on me let this *i* be!
2 Sam 7:14 be My son. If he commits *i*,
14: 9 let the *i* be on me and on my
14:32 but if there is *i* in me, let
19:19 Do not let my lord impute *i* to
22:24 And I kept myself from my *i*.
24:10 take away the *i* of Your
1 Chr 21: 8 take away the *i* of Your
2 Chr 19: 7 for there is no *i* with the
Neh 4: 5 Do not cover their *i*,
Job 4: 8 Those who plow *i* And sow
7:21 And take away my *i*?
10: 6 That You should seek for my *i*
10:14 And will not acquit me of my *i*.
11: 6 from you Less than your *i*
11:14 If *i* were in your hand, and
14:17 in a bag, And You cover my *i*.
15: 5 For your *i* teaches your mouth,
15:16 Who drinks *i* like water!
20:27 The heavens will reveal his *i*,
21:19 God lays up one's *i* for his
22: 5 And your *i* without end?
22:23 You will remove *i* far from
31: 3 disaster for the workers of *i*?
31:11 it would be *i* deserving of
31:28 This also would be an *i*
31:33 By hiding my *i* in my bosom,
33: 9 and there is no *i* in me.
34: 8 company with the workers of *i*,
34:10 from the Almighty to commit *i*.
34:22 death Where the workers of *i*
34:32 I do not see; If I have done *i*,
36:10 commands that they turn from *i*.
36:21 Take heed, do not turn to *i*,
Ps 5: 5 You hate all workers of *i*.
6: 8 from me, all you workers of *i*;
7: 3 If there is *i* in my hands,
7:14 the wicked brings forth *i*;
10: 7 his tongue is trouble and *i*.
14: 4 Have all the workers of *i* no
18:23 And I kept myself from my *i*.
25:11 sake, O LORD, Pardon my *i*,
28: 3 And with the workers of *i*,
31:10 strength fails because of my *i*,
32: 2 the LORD does not impute *i*,
32: 5 And my *i* I have not hidden. I
32: 5 And You forgave the *i* of my
36: 2 When he finds out his *i* and
36:12 There the workers of *i* have
37: 1 be envious of the workers of *i*.
38:18 For I will declare my *i*;
39:11 rebukes You correct man for *i*,
41: 6 His heart gathers *i* to itself;
49: 5 When the *i* at my heels
51: 2 Wash me thoroughly from my *i*,
51: 5 I was brought forth in *i*,
53: 1 and have done abominable *i*;
53: 4 Have the workers of *i* no
55:10 *I* and trouble are also in the
56: 7 Shall they escape by *i*?
59: 2 me from the workers of *i*,
64: 2 rebellion of the workers of *i*,
66:18 If I regard *i* in my heart, The
69:27 Add *i* to their iniquity, And
69:27 Add iniquity to their *i*,
78:38 of compassion, forgave their *i*,
85: 2 You have forgiven the *i* of Your
89:32 And their *i* with stripes.
92: 7 And when all the workers of *i*
92: 9 All the workers of *i* shall be
94: 4 All the workers of *i* boast in
94:16 for me against the workers of *i*?
94:20 Shall the throne of *i*,
94:23 has brought on them their own *i*,
106: 6 fathers, We have committed *i*,
106:43 were brought low for their *i*.
107:42 And all *i* stops its mouth.
109:14 Let the *i* of his fathers be
119: 3 They also do no *i*;
119:133 And let no *i* have dominion
125: 3 reach out their hands to *i*.
125: 5 away With the workers of *i*.
141: 4 works With men who work *i*;
141: 9 the traps of the workers of *i*.
Prov 10:29 will come to the workers of *i*.
16: 6 Atonement is provided for *i*;
19:28 mouth of the wicked devours *i*.
21:15 will come to the workers of *i*.
22: 8 He who sows *i* will reap sorrow,
Eccl 3:16 *I* was there.
Isa 1: 4 nation, A people laden with *i*,
1:13 I cannot endure *i* and the
5:18 Woe to those who draw *i* with
6: 7 Your *i* is taken away, And
13:11 And the wicked for their *i*;
14:21 his children Because of the *i*
22:14 Surely for this *i* there will be
26:21 of the earth for their *i*;
27: 9 Therefore by this the *i* of
29:20 And all who watch for *i* are
30:13 Therefore this *i* shall be to
31: 2 the help of those who work *i*.
32: 6 And his heart will work *i*:
33:24 it will be forgiven their *i*.
40: 2 That her *i* is pardoned;
53: 6 LORD has laid on Him the *i* of
57:17 For the *i* of his covetousness
59: 3 blood, And your fingers with *i*;
59: 4 conceive evil and bring forth *i*.
59: 6 Their works are works of *i*,
59: 7 thoughts are thoughts of *i*;
64: 9 Nor remember *i* forever;
Jer 2:22 Yet your *i* is marked before
3:13 Only acknowledge your *i*,
9: 5 weary themselves to commit *i*.
13:22 For the greatness of your *i*
14:10 He will remember their *i* now,
14:20 our wickedness And the *i* of
16:10 against us? Or what is our *i*?
16:17 nor is their *i* hidden from My
16:18 I will repay double for their *i*
18:23 no atonement for their *i*,
25:12 of the Chaldeans, for their *i*,
31:30 one shall die for his own *i*;
31:34 For I will forgive their *i*,
32:18 and repay the *i* of the fathers
33: 8 cleanse them from all their *i*
36: 3 that I may forgive their *i* and
36:31 and his servants for their *i*;
50:20 The *i* of Israel shall be sought,
51: 6 Do not be cut off in her *i*,
Lam 2:14 They have not uncovered your *i*,
4: 6 The punishment of the *i* of the
4:22 The punishment of your *i* is
4:22 He will punish your *i*,
Ezek 3:18 wicked man shall die in his *i*;
3:19 way, he shall die in his *i*;
3:20 his righteousness and commits *i*,
4: 4 and lay the *i* of the house of
4: 4 on it, you shall bear their *i*.
4: 5 on you the years of their *i*,
4: 5 so you shall bear the *i* of the
4: 6 then you shall bear the *i* of
4:17 waste away because of their *i*.
7:13 himself Who lives in *i*.
7:16 them mourning, Each for his *i*.
7:19 their stumbling block of *i*.
9: 9 The *i* of the house of Israel and
11: 2 are the men who devise *i* and
14: 3 causes them to stumble into *i*.
14: 4 causes him to stumble into *i*,
14: 7 causes him to stumble into *i*,
14:10 "And they shall bear their *i*;
16:49 this was the *i* of your sister
18: 8 has withdrawn his hand from *i*
18:17 He shall not die for the *i* of
18:18 Behold, he shall die for his *i*.
18:24 his righteousness and commits *i*,
18:26 his righteousness, commits *i*,
18:26 it is because of the *i* which he
18:30 so that *i* will not be your
21:23 but he will bring their *i* to
21:24 Because you have made your *i* to
21:25 whose *i* shall end,
21:29 Whose *i* shall end.
28:15 Till *i* was found in you.
28:18 By the *i* of your trading;
29:16 will remind them of their *i*
33: 6 them, he is taken away in his *i*;
33: 8 wicked man shall die in his *i*;
33: 9 his way, he shall die in his *i*;
33:13 own righteousness and commits *i*,
33:13 but because of the *i* that he
33:15 of life without committing *i*,
33:18 his righteousness and commits *i*,
35: 5 when their *i* came to an
39:23 went into captivity for their *i*;
44:10 idols, they shall bear their *i*.
44:12 house of Israel to fall into *i*,
44:12 "that they shall bear their *i*.
Dan 9: 5 have sinned and committed *i*,
9:24 To make reconciliation for *i*,
Hos 4: 8 set their heart on their *i*.
5: 5 and Ephraim stumble in their *i*;
7: 1 Then the *i* of Ephraim was
8:13 Now He will remember their *i*
9: 7 of the greatness of your *i* and
9: 9 He will remember their *i*;
10: 9 against the children of *i* Did
10:13 wickedness; You have reaped *i*.
12: 8 They shall find in me no *i*
13:12 The *i* of Ephraim is bound up;
14: 1 have stumbled because of your *i*;
14: 2 Say to Him, "Take away all *i*;
Mic 2: 1 Woe to those who devise *i*,
3:10 bloodshed And Jerusalem with *i*:
7:18 Pardoning *i* And passing over
Hab 1: 3 Why do You show me *i*,
2:12 Who establishes a city by *i*!
Zech 3: 4 I have removed your *i* from you,
3: 9 And I will remove the *i* of that
Mal 2: 6 And turned many away from *i*.
Lk 13:27 from Me, all you workers of *i*.
Acts 1:18 a field with the wages of *i*;
8:23 by bitterness and bound by *i*.
1 Cor 13: 6 does not rejoice in *i*,
2 Tim 2:19 name of Christ depart from *i*.
Jas 3: 6 tongue is a fire, a world of *i*.
2 Pe 2:16 but he was rebuked for his *i*:

INJURED (3/3) INJURY

Ex 22:14 and it becomes *i* or dies, the
2 Ki 1: 2 room in Samaria, and was *i*;
Gal 4:12 You have not *i* me at all.

INJURY (3/3) INJURED

2 Ki 1: 2 I shall recover from this *i*.
Dan 6:23 and no *i* whatever was found on
Nah 3:19 Your *i* has no healing, Your

INJUSTICE (9/9)

Lev 19:15 You shall do no *i* in judgment.
19:35 You shall do no *i* in judgment,
Deut 32: 4 A God of truth and without *i*;
Job 5:16 And *i* shuts her mouth.
6:29 let there be no *i*!
6:30 Is there *i* on my tongue?
Jer 2: 5 What *i* have your fathers found
22:13 And his chambers by *i*,
Mal 2: 6 And *i* was not found on his

INK (4/4)

Jer 36:18 and I wrote them with *i* in the
2 Cor 3: 3 written not with *i* but by the
2 Jn 12 to do so with paper and *i*;
3 Jn 13 to write to you with pen and *i*;

INKHORN (3/3)

Ezek 9: 2 linen and had a writer's *i* at
9: 3 who had the writer's *i* at his
9:11 who had the *i* at his side,

INLAID (2/2)

Song 5:14 His body is carved ivory *I*
Ezek 27: 6 company of Ashurites have *i*

INLETS (1/1)

Judg 5:17 seashore, And stayed by his *i*.

INMOST (3/3)

Prov 18: 8 they go down into the *i* body.
23:16 my *i* being will rejoice When
26:22 And they go down into the *i*

INN (2/2) INNKEEPER

Lk 2: 7 was no room for them in the *i*.
10:34 own animal, brought him to an *i*,

INNER (62/60)

Ex 28:26 which is on the *i* side of the
1 Ki 6: 5 sanctuary and the *i* sanctuary.

6:16 inside as the *i* sanctuary,
6:19 And he prepared the *i* sanctuary
6:20 The *i* sanctuary was twenty
6:21 front of the *i* sanctuary,
6:22 that was by the *i* sanctuary.
6:23 Inside the *i* sanctuary he made
6:27 cherubim inside the *i* room;
6:29 both the *i* and outer
6:30 both the *i* and outer
6:31 entrance of the *i* sanctuary
6:36 And he built the *i* court with
7:12 So were the *i* court of the
7:49 in front of the *i* sanctuary,
7:50 for the doors of the *i* room
8: 6 into the *i* sanctuary of the
8: 8 in front of the *i* sanctuary;
20:30 the city, into an *i* chamber.
22:25 when you go into an *i* chamber
2 Ki 9: 2 and take him to an *i* room.
10:25 and went into the *i* room of the
1 Chr 28:11 its *i* chambers, and the place
2 Chr 3:16 as in the *i* sanctuary, and put
4:20 in front of the *i* sanctuary,
4:22 its *i* doors to the Most Holy
5: 7 into the *i* sanctuary of the
5: 9 in front of the *i* sanctuary;
18:24 when you go into an *i* chamber
29:16 went into the *i* part
Esth 4:11 who goes into the *i* court
5: 1 and stood in the *i* court
Ps 49:11 Their *i* thought is that their
Prov 20:27 Searching all the *i* depths of
20:30 As do stripes the *i* depths of
Isa 16:11 And my *i* being for Kir Heres.
Ezek 8: 3 the north gate of the *i* court,
8:16 brought me into the *i* court
10: 3 cloud filled the *i* court.
40:15 of the vestibule of the *i* gate
40:19 to the front of the *i* court
40:23 A gate of the *i* court was
40:27 a gateway on the *i* court,
40:28 he brought me to the *i* court
40:32 brought me into the *i* court
40:44 Outside the *i* gate were the
40:44 for the singers in the *i* court,
41:15 as well as the *i* temple and the
41:17 even to the *i* room, as well as
42: 3 Opposite the *i* court of twenty
42:15 measuring the *i* temple,
43: 5 brought me into the *i* court;
44:17 the gates of the *i* court,
44:17 the gates of the *i* court
44:21 when he enters the *i* court.
44:27 sin offering in the *i* court,"
45:19 of the gate of the *i* court.
46: 1 The gateway of the *i* court that
Mt 24:26 He is in the *i* rooms!' do not
Lk 12: 3 spoken in the ear in *i* rooms
Acts 16:24 he put them into the *i* prison
Eph 3:16 His Spirit in the *i* man,

INNKEEPER (1/1) INN

Lk 10:35 denarii, gave them to the *i*,

INNOCENCE (4/4) INNOCENT

Gen 20: 5 integrity of my heart and *i* of
Ps 26: 6 I will wash my hands in *i*;
73:13 vain, And washed my hands in *i*.
Hos 8: 5 long until they attain to *i*?

INNOCENT (39/38) INNOCENCE, INNOCENTS

Ex 23: 7 do not kill the *i* and
Deut 19:10 lest *i* blood be shed in the
19:13 put away the guilt of *i*
21: 8 and do not lay *i* blood to the
21: 9 shall put away the guilt of *i*
27:25 who takes a bribe to slay an *i*
1 Sam 19: 5 Why then will you sin against *i*
1 Ki 2:31 the house of my father the *i*
2 Ki 21:16 Manasseh shed very much *i*
24: 4 and also because of the *i* blood
24: 4 he had filled Jerusalem with *i*
Job 4: 7 now, who ever perished being *i*?
9:23 laughs at the plight of the *i*.
9:28 that You will not hold me *i*.
17: 8 And the *i* stirs himself up
22:19 And the *i* laugh at them:
22:30 even deliver one who is not *i*;
27:17 And the *i* will divide the
33: 9 without transgression; I am *i*,
Ps 10: 8 secret places he murders the *i*;
15: 5 he take a bribe against the *i*.
19:13 And I shall be *i* of great
94:21 And condemn *i* blood.
106:38 And shed *i* blood, The blood of
Prov 1:11 Let us lurk secretly for the *i*
6:17 Hands that shed *i* blood,
6:29 touches her shall not be *i*.
Isa 59: 7 And they make haste to shed *i*
Jer 2:35 Yet you say, 'Because I am *i*,
7: 6 and do not shed *i* blood in this
22: 3 nor shed *i* blood in this place.
22:17 For shedding *i* blood, And
26:15 you will surely bring *i* blood
Dan 6:22 because I was found *i* before
Joel 3:19 For they have shed *i* blood in
Jon 1:14 and do not charge us with *i*
Mt 27: 4 I have sinned by betraying *i*
27:24 I am *i* of the blood of this just
Acts 20:26 to you this day that I am *i*

INNOCENTLY (1/1)

2 Sam 15:11 and they went along *i* and did

INNOCENTS (2/2) INNOCENT

Jer 2:34 of the lives of the poor *i*.
19: 4 place with the blood of the *i*

INNS (1/1)

Acts 28:15 far as Appii Forum and Three *I*.

INNUMERABLE (6/6)

Ps 40:12 For *i* evils have surrounded me;
104:25 In which are *i* teeming
Jer 46:23 searched, Because they are *i*,
Lk 12: 1 when an *i* multitude of people
Heb 11:12 *i* as the sand which is by the
12:22 to an *i* company of angels,

INORDINATE (KJV) See LUST, PASSION

INQUIRE (50/48) INQUIRED, INQUIRY

Gen 25:22 So she went to *i* of the
Ex 18:15 the people come to me to *i* of
Lev 27:33 He shall not *i* whether it is
Num 27:21 who shall *i* before the LORD
Deut 12:30 and that you do not *i* after
13:14 "then you shall *i*,
17: 4 then you shall *i* diligently.
17: 9 and *i* of them; they shall
Judg 18: 5 Please *i* of God, that we may
20:18 up to the house of God to *i* of
1 Sam 9: 9 when a man went to *i* of God, he
17:56 *I* whose son this young man
22:15 Did I then begin to *i* of God for
28: 7 that I may go to her and *i* of
1 Ki 22: 5 Please *i* for the word of the
22: 7 that we may *i* of Him?"
22: 8 by whom we may *i* of the LORD;
2 Ki 1: 2 *i* of Baal-Zebub, the god of
1: 3 that you are going to *i* of
1: 6 that you are sending to *i* of
1:16 you have sent messengers to *i*
1:16 is no God in Israel to *i* of
3:11 that we may *i* of the LORD by
8: 8 and *i* of the LORD by him,
16:15 altar shall be for me to *i* by.
22:13 *i* of the LORD for me, for the
22:18 who sent you to *i* of the LORD,
1 Chr 10:14 But he did not *i* of the LORD;
21:30 could not go before it to *i* of
2 Chr 18: 4 Please *i* for the word of the
18: 6 that we may *i* of Him?"
18: 7 still one man by whom we may *i*
32:31 whom they sent to him to *i*
34:21 *i* of the LORD for me, and for
34:26 who sent you to *i* of the LORD,
Ezra 7:14 and his seven counselors to *i*
Job 8: 8 'For *i*, please, of the
Ps 27: 4 And to *i* in His temple.
Eccl 7:10 For you do not *i* wisely
Isa 21:12 also the night. If you will *i*,
21:12 If you will inquire, *i*;
Jer 21: 2 Please *i* of the LORD for us,
37: 7 who sent you to Me to *i* of Me:
Ezek 14: 7 then comes to a prophet to *i* of
20: 1 the elders of Israel came to *i*
20: 3 Have you come to *i* of Me? As I
36:37 also let the house of Israel *i*
Mt 10:11 *i* who in it is worthy, and stay
Acts 9:11 and *i* at the house of Judas for
23:20 as though they were going to *i*

INQUIRED (28/27) INQUIRE

Judg 6:29 And when they had *i* and
20:27 So the children of Israel *i* of
1 Sam 10:22 Therefore they *i* of the LORD
22:10 And he *i* of the LORD for him,
22:13 and have *i* of God for him, that
23: 2 Therefore David *i* of the LORD,
23: 4 Then David *i* of the LORD once
28: 6 And when Saul *i* of the LORD,
30: 8 So David *i* of the LORD, saying,
2 Sam 2: 1 after this that David *i* of the
5:19 So David *i* of the LORD, saying,
5:23 Therefore David *i* of the LORD,
11: 3 So David sent and *i* about the
16:23 was as if one had *i* at the
21: 1 and David *i* of the LORD.
1 Chr 13: 3 for we have not *i* at it since
14:10 And David *i* of God, saying,
14:14 Therefore David *i* again of God,
Ezek 14: 3 Should I let Myself be *i* of at
14:10 the punishment of the one who *i*,
20: 3 I will not be *i* of by you." '
20:31 So shall I be *i* of by you,
20:31 I will not be *i* of by you.
Zeph 1: 6 the LORD, nor *i* of Him."
Mt 2: 4 he *i* of them where the Christ
Jn 4:52 Then he *i* of them the hour when
2 Cor 8:23 Or if our brethren are *i*
1 Pe 1:10 salvation the prophets have *i*

INQUIRES (2/2)

Judg 4:20 and if any man comes and *i* of
2 Cor 8:23 If anyone *i* about Titus, he

INQUIRIES (1/1)

Acts 23:15 were going to make further *i*

INQUIRING (1/1)

Jn 16:19 Are you *i* among yourselves about

INQUIRY (6/6) INQUIRE

Lev 10:16 Then Moses made careful *i* about
Deut 19:18 the judges shall make careful *i*,
Esth 2:23 And when an *i* was made into the
Job 34:24 in pieces mighty men without *i*,
Acts 10:17 sent from Cornelius had made *i*
19:39 But if you have any other *i* to

INQUISITION (KJV) See AVENGES, INQUIRY

INSANE (3/3)

1 Sam 21:14 "Look, you see the man is *i*.
Jer 50:38 And they are *i* with their
Hos 9: 7 fool, The spiritual man is *i*,

INSATIABLE (1/1)

Ezek 16:28 Assyrians, because you were *i*;

INSCRIBED (3/3) INSCRIPTION

1 Chr 9: 1 they were *i* in the book of the
Job 19:23 that they were *i* in a book!
Isa 49:16 I have *i* you on the palms of

INSCRIPTION (9/9) INSCRIBED

Ex 39:30 and wrote on it an *i* like the
Dan 5:25 And this is the *i* that was
Zech 3: 9 Behold, I will engrave its *i*,
Mt 22:20 Whose image and *i* is this?"
Mk 12:16 Whose image and *i* is this?"
15:26 And the *i* of His accusation was
Lk 20:24 Whose image and *i* does it
23:38 And an *i* also was written over
Acts 17:23 even found an altar with this *i*:

INSECT (1/1)

Lev 11:21 you may eat of every flying *i*

INSECTS (2/2)

Lev 11:20 All flying *i* that creep on all
11:23 But all other flying *i* which

INSERT (4/4)

Num 4: 6 and they shall *i* its poles.
4: 8 and they shall *i* its poles.
4:11 and they shall *i* its poles.
4:14 skins, and *i* its poles.

INSERTED (1/1)

Ex 40:20 *i* the poles through the rings

INSIDE (51/49)

Gen 6:14 and cover it *i* and outside with
39:11 of the men of the house was *i*,
Ex 25:11 *i* and out you shall overlay it,
37: 2 He overlaid it with pure gold *i*
Lev 10:18 Its blood was not brought *i*
13:55 the damage is outside or *i*.
14:41 cause the house to be scraped *i*,
16: 2 any time into the Holy Place *i*
16:12 and bring it *i* the veil.
16:15 bring its blood *i* the veil, do
Deut 23:10 he shall not come *i* the camp.
Judg 7:16 and torches *i* the pitchers.
1 Sam 18:10 and he prophesied *i* the house.
2 Sam 7: 2 but the ark of God dwells *i*
1 Ki 6:15 And he built the *i* walls of the
6:15 to the ceiling he paneled the *i*
6:16 he built it *i* as the inner
6:18 The *i* of the temple was cedar,
6:19 prepared the inner sanctuary *i*
6:21 So Solomon overlaid the *i* of the
6:23 *I* the inner sanctuary he made
6:27 Then he set the cherubim *i* the
7: 8 he dwelt had another court *i*
7: 9 *i* and out, from the foundation
7:31 Its opening *i* the crown at the
2 Ki 6:20 there they were, *i* Samaria!
7:11 it to the king's household *i*.
2 Chr 3: 4 He overlaid the *i* with pure
Ezek 2:10 there was writing on the *i*
3:24 shut yourself *i* your house.
40: 7 by the vestibule of the *i* gate
40: 8 the vestibule of the *i* gate,
40: 9 of the gate was on the *i*.
40:16 intervening archways on the *i*
40:16 windows all around on the *i*.
40:43 *I* were hooks, a handbreadth
41: 3 Also he went *i* and measured the
41:17 *i* and outside, by measure.
42: 4 of the chambers, toward the *i*,

I

Am 6:10 he will say to one *i* the house,
Zech 5: 7 and this is a woman sitting *i*
Mt 23:25 but *i* they are full of
23:26 first cleanse the *i* of the cup
23:27 but *i* are full of dead men's
23:28 but *i* you are full of hypocrisy
Lk 11:40 who made the outside make the *i*
Jn 20:26 days His disciples were again *i*,
Acts 5:23 we found no one *i*!"
1 Cor 5:12 you not judge those who are *i*?
2 Cor 7: 5 were conflicts, *i* were fears.
Rev 5: 1 the throne a scroll written *i*

INSISTED (2/2)

Gen 19: 3 But he *i* strongly; so they
Acts 15:38 But Paul *i* that they should not

INSISTENT (1/1)

Lk 23:23 But they were *i*,

INSISTING (1/1)

Acts 12:15 Yet she kept *i* that it was so.

INSOLENCE (1/1)

1 Sam 17:28 I know your pride and the *i* of

INSOLENT (5/5)

Ps 31:18 Which speak *i* things proudly
94: 4 and speak *i* things; All the
Isa 3: 5 The child will be *i* toward the
Zeph 3: 4 Her prophets are *i*,
1 Tim 1:13 and an *i* man; but I obtained

INSOMUCH (KJV) See SO

INSPIRATION (1/1) INSPIRED

2 Tim 3:16 All Scripture is given by *i* of

INSPIRED (1/1) INSPIRATION

Isa 41: 7 who smooths with the hammer *i*

INSTALLED (1/1)

1 Ki 12:32 And at Bethel he *i* the priests

INSTANT (5/5)

Isa 29: 5 Yes, it shall be in an *i*,
30:13 comes suddenly, in an *i*.
Jer 18: 7 The *i* I speak concerning a
18: 9 And the *i* I speak concerning a
Lk 2:38 And coming in that *i* she gave

INSTEAD (53/41)

Gen 4:25 another seed for me *i* of Abel,
22:13 it up for a burnt offering *i*
44:33 let your servant remain *i* of
Ex 5:12 of Egypt to gather stubble *i*
Num 3:12 among the children of Israel *i*
3:41 *i* of all the firstborn among the
3:41 the livestock of the Levites *i*
3:45 Take the Levites *i* of all the
3:45 the livestock of the Levites *i*
8:16 I have taken them for Myself *i*
8:18 I have taken the Levites *i* of
Judg 15: 2 than she? Please, take her *i*.
20: 5 but *i* they ravished my
20:14 *I*, the children of Benjamin
2 Sam 6:21 who chose me *i* of your father
17:25 Amasa captain of the army *i* of
1 Ki 3: 7 have made Your servant king *i*
2 Ki 14:21 and made him king *i* of his
17:24 in the cities of Samaria *i* of
1 Chr 29:23 throne of the LORD as king *i*
2 Chr 26: 1 and made him king *i* of his
Esth 2: 4 pleases the king be queen *i* of
2:17 her head and made her queen *i*
3: 6 of the people of Mordecai. *I*,
Job 31:40 Then let thistles grow *i* of
31:40 And weeds *i* of barley."
Ps 45:16 *I* of Your fathers shall be Your
Prov 11: 8 And it comes to the wicked *i*.
Isa 3:24 *Id* of a sweet smell there will
3:24 *I* of a sash, a rope; Instead
3:24 *I* of well-set hair, baldness;
3:24 *I* of a rich robe, a girding of
3:24 And branding *i* of beauty.
22:13 But *i*, joy and gladness,
55:13 *I* of the thorn shall come up
55:13 And *i* of the brier shall come
60:17 *I* of bronze I will bring gold,
60:17 *I* of iron I will bring silver,
60:17 *I* of wood, bronze, And
60:17 And *i* of stones, iron. I will
61: 7 *I* of your shame you shall
61: 7 And *i* of confusion they
Jer 22:11 who reigned *i* of Josiah his
29:26 LORD has made you priest *i* of
37: 1 the son of Josiah reigned *i* of
Ezek 4:15 I am giving you cow dung *i* of
15: 4 '*I*, it is thrown into the
16:32 who takes strangers *i* of her
36:34 land shall be tilled *i* of
Hab 2:16 You are filled with shame *i* of
Mt 2:22 was reigning over Judea *i* of
Lk 11:11 will he give him a serpent *i* of
Jas 4:15 *I* you ought to say, "If the

INSTITUTION (1/1)

Mal 2:11 profaned The LORD's holy *i*

INSTRUCT (9/9) INSTRUCTED, INSTRUCTION, INSTRUCTOR, INSTRUCTS

Deut 4:36 that He might *i* you; on earth
17:11 of the law in which they *i* you,
Neh 9:20 also gave Your good Spirit to *i*
Ps 32: 8 I will *i* you and teach you in
94:12 Blessed is the man whom You *i*,
Song 8: 2 She who used to *i* me.
Dan 11:33 people who understand shall *i*
1 Cor 2:16 the LORD that he may *i*
1 Tim 4: 6 If you *i* the brethren in these

INSTRUCTED (22/22) INSTRUCT

Deut 32:10 He *i* him, He kept him as the
Judg 21:20 Therefore they *i* the children of
Ruth 3: 6 to all that her mother-in-law *i*
2 Ki 12: 2 in which Jehoiada the priest *i*
1 Chr 25: 7 with their brethren who were *i*
Job 4: 3 Surely you have *i* many, And
Ps 2:10 be wise, O kings; Be *i*,
Prov 5:13 inclined my ear to those who *i*
21:11 wise; But when the wise is *i*,
22:19 I have *i* you today, even you.
Isa 8:11 and *i* me that I should not walk
40:14 and who *i* Him, And taught Him
Jer 6: 8 Be *i*, O Jerusalem, Lest My
31:19 I repented; And after I was *i*,
Dan 1: 3 Then the king *i* Ashpenaz, the
Mt 13:52 Therefore every scribe *i*
28:15 money and did as they were *i*;
Lk 1: 4 things in which you were *i*.
Acts 10:22 was divinely *i* by a holy angel
18:25 This man had been *i* in the way
Rom 2:18 being *i* out of the law,
Heb 8: 5 as Moses was divinely *i* when he

INSTRUCTING (1/1)

Acts 7:44 *i* Moses to make it according to

INSTRUCTION (40/39) INSTRUCT, INSTRUCTIONS

2 Chr 35: 4 following the written *i* of
35: 4 of Israel and the written *i* of
Job 22:22 *i* from His mouth, And lay up
33:16 ears of men, And seals their *i*.
36:10 He also opens their ear to *i*,
Ps 50:17 Seeing you hate *i* And cast My
Prov 1: 2 To know wisdom and *i*,
1: 3 To receive the *i* of wisdom,
1: 7 fools despise wisdom and *i*.
1: 8 hear the *i* of your father, And
4: 1 the *i* of a father, And give
4:13 Take firm hold of *i*,
5:12 And say: "How I have hated *i*,
5:23 He shall die for lack of *i*,
6:23 Reproofs of *i* are the way of
8:10 Receive my *i*, and not silver,
8:33 Hear *i* and be wise, And do not
9: 9 Give *i* to a wise man, and he
10:17 He who keeps *i* is in the way
12: 1 Whoever loves *i* loves
13: 1 wise son heeds his father's *i*,
15: 5 A fool despises his father's *i*,
15:32 He who disdains *i* despises his
15:33 fear of the LORD is the *i* of
19:20 to counsel and receive *i*,
19:27 Cease listening to *i*,
23:12 Apply your heart to *i*,
23:23 Also wisdom and *i* and
24:32 looked on it and received *i*:
Jer 17:23 might not hear nor receive *i*.
32:33 have not listened to receive *i*.
35:13 Will you not receive *i* to obey
36: 4 at the *i* of Jeremiah, all the
36: 6 which you have written at my *i*,
36:17 write all these words—at his *i*?
36:27 Baruch had written at the *i* of
36:32 who wrote on it at the *i* of
45: 1 these words in a book at the *i*
Zeph 3: 7 fear Me, You will receive *i*'—
2 Tim 3:16 for *i* in righteousness,

INSTRUCTIONS (5/5) INSTRUCTION

Ezra 10: 8 according to the *i* of the
Esth 9:27 according to the written *i* and
1 Cor 11:17 Now in giving these *i* I do not
Col 4:10 (about whom you received *i*:
Heb 11:22 and gave *i* concerning his

INSTRUCTOR (3/3) INSTRUCT

Gen 4:22 an *i* of every craftsman in
1 Chr 15:22 was *i* in charge of the
Rom 2:20 an *i* of the foolish, a teacher

INSTRUCTORS (1/1)

1 Cor 4:15 you might have ten thousand *i*

INSTRUCTS (3/3) INSTRUCT

Ps 16: 7 My heart also *i* me in the
94:10 He who *i* the nations, shall He
Isa 28:26 For He *i* him in right judgment,

INSTRUMENT (9/9) INSTRUMENTS

1 Sam 10: 5 high place with a stringed *i*,
Ps 8: On the *i* of Gath. A Psalm of
33: 2 Make melody to Him with an *i*
61: Chief Musician. On a stringed *i*.
81: On an *i* of Gath. A Psalm of
84: On an *i* of Gath. A Psalm of the
92: 3 On an *i* of ten strings, On the
Isa 54:16 Who brings forth an *i* for his
Ezek 33:32 voice and can play well on an *i*;

INSTRUMENTS (47/43) INSTRUMENT

Gen 49: 5 *I* of cruelty are in their
1 Sam 18: 6 with joy, and with musical *i*.
2 Sam 6: 5 the LORD on all kinds of *i*
6: 5 wood, on harps, on stringed *i*,
1 Ki 10:12 also harps and stringed *i* for
1 Chr 13: 8 on harps, on stringed *i*,
15:16 the singers accompanied by *i*
15:16 of music, stringed *i*,
15:28 making music with stringed *i*
16: 5 Jeiel with stringed *i* and
16:42 and cymbals and the musical *i*
23: 5 the LORD with musical *i*,
25: 1 prophesy with harps, stringed *i*,
25: 6 LORD, with cymbals, stringed *i*,
2 Chr 5:12 stringed *i* and harps, and with
5:13 the trumpets and cymbals and *i*
7: 6 the Levites also with *i* of the
9:11 also harps and stringed *i* for
20:28 with stringed *i* and harps and
23:13 also the singers with musical *i*,
29:25 with cymbals, with stringed *i*,
29:26 The Levites stood with the *i* of
29:27 the trumpets and with the *i* of
30:21 LORD, accompanied by loud *i*.
34:12 of whom were skillful with *i*
Neh 12:27 with cymbals and stringed *i*
12:36 with the musical *i* of David the
Ps 4: Chief Musician. With stringed *i*.
6: Chief Musician. With stringed *i*.
7:13 also prepares for Himself *i* of
54: Chief Musician. With stringed *i*.
55: Chief Musician. With stringed *i*.
67: Chief Musician. On stringed *i*.
68:25 the players on *i* followed
76: Chief Musician. On stringed *i*.
87: 7 singers and the players on *i*
150: 4 Praise Him with stringed *i* and
Eccl 2: 8 and musical *i* of all kinds.
Isa 14:11 the sound of your stringed *i*;
38:20 sing my songs with stringed *i*
Ezek 40:42 on these they laid the *i* with
Am 5:23 the melody of your stringed *i*.
6: 5 idly to the sound of stringed *i*,
6: 5 for yourselves musical *i* like
Hab 3:19 With my stringed *i*.
Rom 6:13 not present your members as *i*
6:13 and your members as *i* of

INSUBORDINATE (2/2)

1 Tim 1: 9 but for the lawless and *i*,
Titus 1:10 For there are many *i*,

INSUBORDINATION (1/1)

Titus 1: 6 not accused of dissipation or *i*.

INSULT (2/1)

Mic 2: 6 They shall not return *i* for
2: 6 shall not return insult for *i*.

INSULTED (2/2)

Lk 18:32 and will be mocked and *i* and
Heb 10:29 and *i* the Spirit of grace?

INSULTS (2/2)

Isa 51: 7 men, Nor be afraid of their *i*.
Zeph 2: 8 And the *i* of the people of

INTACT (3/3)

2 Ki 3:25 the stones of Kir Haraseth *i*.
7: 7 twilight, and left the camp *i*—
7:10 donkeys tied, and the tents *i*.

INTEGRITY (20/20)

Gen 20: 5 In the *i* of my heart and
20: 6 that you did this in the *i* of
1 Ki 9: 4 in *i* of heart and in
Job 2: 3 still he holds fast to his *i*,
2: 9 you still hold fast to your *i*?
4: 6 And the *i* of your ways your
27: 5 I die I will not put away my *i*
31: 6 scales, That God may know my *i*.
Ps 7: 8 And according to my *i* within
25:21 Let *i* and uprightness preserve
26: 1 For I have walked in my *i*.
26:11 as for me, I will walk in my *i*;
41:12 for me, You uphold me in my *i*,

78:72 them according to the *i* of his
Prov 10: 9 He who walks with *i* walks
11: 3 The *i* of the upright will guide
19: 1 is the poor who walks in his *i*
20: 7 righteous man walks in his *i*;
28: 6 is the poor who walks in his *i*
Titus 2: 7 works; in doctrine showing *i*,

INTELLIGENT (1/1)
Acts 13: 7 an *i* man. This man called for

INTEND (9/8) INTENDED, INTENDING, UNINTENDED
Ex 2:14 Do you *i* to kill me as you
2 Chr 28:13 You *i* to add to our sins and to
Job 6:26 Do you *i* to rebuke my words,
Dan 7:25 And shall *i* to change times
Jn 7:35 Where does He *i* to go that we
7:35 Does He *i* to go to the
Acts 5:28 and *i* to bring this Man's blood
5:35 heed to yourselves what you *i*
2 Cor 10: 2 that confidence by which I *i*

INTENDED (7/7) INTEND
Gen 31:20 he did not tell him that he *i*
Judg 20: 5 They *i* to kill me, but instead
2 Chr 11:22 for he *i* to make him king.
Ps 21:11 For they *i* evil against You;
44:11 have given us up like sheep *i*
2 Cor 1:15 And in this confidence I *i* to
Jas 5:11 of Job and seen the end *i* by

INTENDING (6/5) INTEND
Gen 27:42 himself concerning you by *i*
Lk 14:28 *i* to build a tower, does not
Acts 12: 4 *i* to bring him before the
14:13 *i* to sacrifice with the
20:13 there *i* to take Paul on board;
20:13 *i* himself to go on foot.

INTENSE (1/1) FIERCE
Num 11: 4 among them yielded to *i* craving;

INTENT (10/10) INTENTLY, INTENTS
Gen 6: 5 and that every *i* of the
2 Sam 3:37 it had not been the king's *i*
17:14 to the *i* that the LORD might
2 Ki 10:19 with the *i* of destroying the
1 Chr 28: 9 and understands all the *i* of
29:18 keep this forever in the *i* of
Prov 21:27 he brings it with wicked *i*!
Zech 1:15 they helped—but with evil *i*.
1 Cor 10: 6 to the *i* that we should not
Eph 3:10 to the *i* that now the manifold

INTENTIONS (2/2)
Prov 12: 2 But a man of wicked *i* He will
14:17 And a man of wicked *i* is

INTENTLY (5/5) INTENT
Lk 22:56 looked *i* at him and said,
Acts 3:12 Or why look so *i* at us, as
11: 6 When I observed it *i* and
13: 9 Holy Spirit, looked *i* at him
14: 9 observing him *i* and seeing that

INTENTS (2/2) INTENT
Jer 30:24 until He has performed the *i*
Heb 4:12 of the thoughts and *i* of the

INTERCEDE (4/4) INTERCESSION
Ex 8: 9 honor of saying when I shall *i*
8:28 very far away. *I* for me."
1 Sam 2:25 who will *i* for him?"
Jer 15:11 I will cause the enemy to *i*

INTERCESSION (7/7) INTERCEDE, INTERCESSIONS
Isa 53:12 And made *i* for the
Jer 7:16 nor make *i* to Me; for I will
27:18 let them now make *i* to the
Rom 8:26 but the Spirit Himself makes *i*
8:27 because He makes *i* for the
8:34 who also makes *i* for us.
Heb 7:25 He always lives to make *i* for

INTERCESSIONS (1/1) INTERCESSION
1 Tim 2: 1 that supplications, prayers, *i*,

INTERCESSOR (1/1)
Isa 59:16 wondered that there was no *i*;

INTEREST (11/7) INTERESTS
Ex 22:25 you shall not charge him *i*.
Lev 25:36 Take no usury or *i* from him; but
Deut 23:19 You shall not charge *i* to your
23:19 *i* on money or food or anything
23:19 anything that is lent out at *i*.
23:20 a foreigner you may charge *i*,
23:20 brother you shall not charge *i*,
Jer 15:10 I have neither lent for *i*,
15:10 Nor have men lent to me for *i*.
Mt 25:27 received back my own with *i*.
Lk 19:23 might have collected it with *i*?

INTERESTS (2/1) INTEREST
Phil 2: 4 look out not only for his own *i*,
2: 4 but also for the *i* of others.

INTERIOR (1/1)
Song 3:10 Its *i* paved with love By the

INTERMARRY (1/1)
1 Ki 11: 2 You shall not *i* with them, nor

INTERMEDDLE (KJV) See SHARE

INTERPRET (6/5) INTERPRETATION, INTERPRETED, INTERPRETER, INTERPRETING, INTERPRETS
Gen 41: 8 there was no one who could *i*
41:15 there is no one who can *i* it.
41:15 a dream, to *i* it."
1 Cor 12:30 speak with tongues? Do all *i*?
14:13 in a tongue pray that he may *i*.
14:27 each in turn, and let one *i*.

INTERPRETATION (40/36) INTERPRET, INTERPRETATIONS
Gen 40: 5 man's dream with its own *i*.
40:12 This is the *i* of it: The three
40:16 the chief baker saw that the *i*
40:18 This is the *i* of it: The three
41:11 us dreamed according to the *i*
Judg 7:15 telling of the dream and its *i*,
Eccl 8: 1 And who knows the *i* of a
Dan 2: 4 dream, and we will give the *i*.
2: 5 the dream to me, and its *i*,
2: 6 if you tell the dream and its *i*,
2: 6 tell me the dream and its *i*.
2: 7 dream, and we will give its *i*.
2: 9 know that you can give me its *i*.
2:16 he might tell the king the *i*.
2:24 and I will tell the king the *i*.
2:25 make known to the king the *i*.
2:26 which I have seen, and its *i*?
2:30 sakes who make known the *i* to
2:36 Now we will tell the *i* of it
2:45 and its *i* is sure."
4: 6 might make known to me the *i*
4: 7 did not make known to me its *i*.
4: 9 that I have seen, and its *i*.
4:18 Belteshazzar, declare its *i*,
4:18 able to make known to me the *i*;
4:19 do not let the dream or its *i*
4:19 and its *i* concern your enemies!
4:24 this is the *i*, O king,
5: 7 writing, and tells me its *i*,
5: 8 or make known to the king its *i*.
5:12 called, and he will give the *i*.
5:15 and make known to me its *i*,
5:15 but they could not give the *i*
5:16 and make known to me its *i*,
5:17 and make known to him the *i*.
5:26 This is the *i* of each word.
7:16 me and made known to me the *i*
1 Cor 12:10 to another the *i* of tongues.
14:26 has a revelation, has an *i*.
2 Pe 1:20 Scripture is of any private *i*,

INTERPRETATIONS (2/2) INTERPRETATION
Gen 40: 8 'Do not *i* belong to God?
Dan 5:16 that you can give *i* and explain

INTERPRETED (4/3) INTERPRET
Gen 40:22 as Joseph had *i* to them.
41:12 and he *i* our dreams for us; to
41:12 to each man he *i* according to
41:13 just as he *i* for us, so it

INTERPRETER (3/3) INTERPRET
Gen 40: 8 and there is no *i* of it."
42:23 he spoke to them through an *i*.
1 Cor 14:28 But if there is no *i*,

INTERPRETING (1/1) INTERPRET
Dan 5:12 *i* dreams, solving riddles, and

INTERPRETS (2/2) INTERPRET
Deut 18:10 or one who *i* omens, or a
1 Cor 14: 5 tongues, unless indeed he *i*,

INTERROGATED (1/1)
Judg 8:14 man of the men of Succoth and *i*

INTERRUPTION (1/1)
Lam 3:49 and do not cease, Without *i*,

INTERVENE (1/1)
Zeph 2: 7 the LORD their God will *i* for

INTERVENED (1/1)
Ps 106:30 Then Phinehas stood up and *i*,

INTERVENING (1/1)
Ezek 40:16 and in their *i* archways in the

INTERVIEWED (1/1)
Dan 1:19 Then the king *i* them, and among

INTESTINES (4/3)
2 Chr 21:15 sick with a disease of your *i*,
21:15 until your *i* come out by reason
21:18 the LORD struck him in his *i*
21:19 that his *i* came out because of

INTIMATELY (5/5)
Num 31:17 woman who has known a man *i*.
31:18 who have not known a man *i*.
31:35 women who had not known a man *i*.
Judg 21:11 woman who has known a man *i*.
21:12 who had not known a man *i*;

INTIMIDATE (1/1)
Lk 3:14 Do not *i* anyone or accuse

INTO (1457/1339) See APPENDIX

I

INTOXICATING (10/8)
Lev 10: 9 Do not drink wine or *i* drink,
1 Sam 1:15 drunk neither wine nor *i* drink,
Prov 31: 4 Nor for princes *i* drink;
Isa 5:11 That they may follow *i* drink;
5:22 valiant for mixing *i* drink,
28: 7 And through *i* drink are out of
28: 7 have erred through *i* drink,
28: 7 of the way through *i* drink;
29: 9 but not with *i* drink.
56:12 fill ourselves with *i* drink;

INTREAT, INTREATED, INTREATIES, INTREATY (KJV) See BEGGED, ENTREAT, MEET, PLEADED, (WILLING TO) YIELD

INTRICATE (1/1)
Job 10: 8 An *i* unity; Yet You would

INTRICATELY (8/8)
Ex 28: 8 And the *i* woven band of the
28:27 seam above the *i* woven band
28:28 it is above the *i* woven band
29: 5 him with the *i* woven band
39: 5 And the *i* woven band of his
39:20 seam above the *i* woven band
39:21 would be above the *i* woven band
Lev 8: 7 him with the *i* woven band

INTRIGUE (2/2)
Dan 11:21 and seize the kingdom by *i*.
11:34 many shall join with them by *i*.

INTRUDING (1/1)
Col 2:18 *i* into those things which he

INVADE (2/2)
2 Chr 20:10 You would not let Israel *i*
Hab 3:16 He will *i* them with his

INVADED (5/5)
1 Sam 23:27 for the Philistines have *i* the
30: 1 that the Amalekites had *i* the
2 Ki 13:20 the raiding bands from Moab *i*
2 Chr 21:17 they came up into Judah and *i*
28:18 The Philistines also had *i* the

INVASION (1/1)
1 Sam 30:14 We made an *i* of the southern

INVENT (2/2) INVENTORS
Neh 6: 8 but you *i* them in your own
Am 6: 5 And *i* for yourselves musical

INVENTED (1/1)
2 Chr 26:15 *i* by skillful men, to be on the

INVENTORS (1/1) INVENT
Rom 1:30 *i* of evil things, disobedient

INVENTORY (1/1)
Ex 38:21 This is the *i* of the

INVISIBLE (5/5)
Rom 1:20 the creation of the world His *i*
Col 1:15 He is the image of the *i* God,
1:16 are on earth, visible and *i*,
1 Tim 1:17 the King eternal, immortal, *i*,
Heb 11:27 endured as seeing Him who is *i*.

INVITE (7/7) INVITED, INVITES
1 Sam 16: 3 Then *i* Jesse to the sacrifice,
1 Ki 1:10 But he did not *i* Nathan the
Job 1: 4 and would send and *i* their
Zech 3:10 Everyone will *i* his neighbor
Mt 22: 9 you find, *i* to the wedding.'
Lk 14:12 lest they also *i* you back, and
14:13 *i* the poor, the maimed, the

INVITED (34/30) INVITE
Num 25: 2 They *i* the people to the
Judg 14:15 Have you *i* us in order to take
1 Sam 9:13 afterward those who are *i* will
9:22 of honor among those who were *i*;
9:24 since I said I *i* the people."
16: 5 and *i* them to the sacrifice.
2 Sam 13:23 so Absalom *i* all the king's
15:11 Absalom went two hundred men *i*
1 Ki 1: 9 he also *i* all his brothers, the
1:19 and has *i* all the sons of the
1:19 your servant he has not *i*.
1:25 and has *i* all the king's sons,
1:26 But he has not *i* me—me your
Esth 5:12 Queen Esther *i* no one but me to
5:12 and tomorrow I am again *i* by
Lam 2:22 You have *i* as to a feast day
Zeph 1: 7 He has *i* His guests.
Mt 22: 3 to call those who were *i* to
22: 4 saying, 'Tell those who are *i*,
22: 8 but those who were *i* were not
Lk 7:39 Now when the Pharisee who had *i*
14: 7 a parable to those who were *i*,
14: 8 When you are *i* by anyone to a
14: 8 more honorable than you be *i*
14: 9 and he who *i* you and him come
14:10 "But when you are *i*,
14:10 so that when he who *i* you comes
14:12 Then He also said to him who *i*
14:16 man gave a great supper and *i*
14:17 time to say to those who were *i*,
14:24 none of those men who were *i*
Jn 2: 2 Jesus and His disciples were *i*
Acts 10:23 Then he *i* them in and lodged
28:14 and were *i* to stay with them

INVITES (2/2) INVITE
Ex 34:15 and one of them *i* you and
1 Cor 10:27 of those who do not believe *i*

INVOLVED (1/1)
Hos 5: 2 The revolters are deeply *i* in

INVOLVES (1/1)
1 Jn 4:18 because fear *i* torment. But he

INWARD (12/12) INWARDLY
Ex 39:19 which was on the *i* side of the
2 Sam 5: 9 all around from the Millo and *i*.
1 Ki 7:25 all their back parts pointed *i*.
2 Chr 3:13 on their feet, and they faced *i*.
4: 4 all their back parts pointed *i*.
Ps 5: 9 Their *i* part is destruction;
51: 6 You desire truth in the *i*
64: 6 Both the *i* thought and the
139:13 For You formed my *i* parts;
Lk 11:39 but your *i* part is full of
Rom 7:22 law of God according to the *i*
2 Cor 4:16 yet the *i* man is being renewed

INWARDLY (3/3) INWARD
Ps 62: 4 their mouth, But they curse *i*.
Mt 7:15 but *i* they are ravenous wolves.
Rom 2:29 he is a Jew who is one *i*;

INWARDS (KJV) See ENTRAILS

IPHDEIAH (1/1)
1 Chr 8:25 *I*, and Penuel were the sons

IR (1/1)
1 Chr 7:12 and Huppim were the sons of *I*,

IR SHEMESH (1/1)
Josh 19:41 was Zorah, Eshtaol, *I*,

IR-NAHASH (1/1)
1 Chr 4:12 and Tehinnah the father of *I*.

IRA (6/6)
2 Sam 20:26 and *I* the Jairite was a chief
23:26 *I* the son of Ikkesh the
23:38 *I* the Ithrite, Gareb the
1 Chr 11:28 *I* the son of Ikkesh the Tekoite,
11:40 *I* the Ithrite, Gareb the
27: 9 for the sixth month was *I* the

IRAD (2/1)
Gen 4:18 To Enoch was born *I*;
4:18 and *I* begot Mehujael, and

IRAM (2/2)
Gen 36:43 Chief Magdiel, and Chief *I*.
1 Chr 1:54 Chief Magdiel, and Chief *I*.

IRI (1/1)
1 Chr 7: 7 Uzzi, Uzziel, Jerimoth, and *I*—

IRIJAH (2/2)
Jer 37:13 was there whose name was *I*
37:14 So *I* seized Jeremiah and

IRON (99/87) IRONS
Gen 4:22 every craftsman in bronze and *i*.
Lev 26:19 I will make your heavens like *i*
Num 31:22 the silver, the bronze, the *i*,
35:16 if he strikes him with an *i*
Deut 3:11 Indeed his bedstead was an *i*
4:20 and brought you out of the *i*
8: 9 a land whose stones are *i* and
27: 5 you shall not use an *i* tool on
28:23 which is under you shall be *i*.
28:48 and He will put a yoke of *i* on
33:25 Your sandals shall be *i* and
Josh 6:19 and vessels of bronze and *i*,
6:24 and the vessels of bronze and *i*,
8:31 which no man has wielded an *i*
17:16 the valley have chariots of *i*,
17:18 though they have *i* chariots
19:38 *I*, Migdal El, Horem,
22: 8 with gold, with bronze, with *i*,
Judg 1:19 because they had chariots of *i*.
4: 3 had nine hundred chariots of *i*,
4:13 nine hundred chariots of *i*,
1 Sam 17: 7 and his *i* spearhead weighed
2 Sam 12:31 them to work with saws and *i*
12:31 with saws and iron picks and *i*
23: 7 them Must be armed with *i* and
1 Ki 6: 7 no hammer or chisel or any *i*
8:51 out of the *i* furnace),
22:11 Chenaanah had made horns of *i*
2 Ki 6: 5 the *i* ax head fell into the
6: 6 and he made the *i* float.
1 Chr 20: 3 with *i* picks, and with axes.
22: 3 And David prepared *i* in
22:14 and bronze and *i* beyond
22:16 and silver and bronze and *i*
29: 2 *i* for things of iron, wood
29: 2 bronze, iron for things of *i*,
29: 7 hundred thousand talents of *i*.
2 Chr 2: 7 and silver, in bronze and *i*,
2:14 gold and silver, bronze and *i*,
18:10 Chenaanah had made horns of *i*
24:12 and also those who worked in *i*
Job 19:24 engraved on a rock With an *i*
20:24 He will flee from the *i* weapon;
28: 2 *I* is taken from the earth, And
40:18 His ribs like bars of *i*.
41:27 He regards *i* as straw, And
Ps 2: 9 break them with a rod of *i*;
107:16 And cut the bars of *i* in two.
149: 8 their nobles with fetters of *i*;
Prov 27:17 As *i* sharpens iron, So a man
27:17 As iron sharpens *i*,
Isa 10:34 thickets of the forest with *i*,
45: 2 bronze And cut the bars of *i*.
48: 4 And your neck was an *i* sinew,
60:17 Instead of *i* I will bring
60:17 And instead of stones, *i*.
Jer 1:18 day A fortified city and an *i*
6:28 They are bronze and *i*,
11: 4 from the *i* furnace, saying,
15:12 Can anyone break *i*,
15:12 The northern *i* and the bronze?
17: 1 is written with a pen of *i*;
28:13 made in their place yokes of *i*.
28:14 I have put a yoke of *i* on the
Ezek 4: 3 take for yourself an *i* plate,
4: 3 and set it as an *i* wall
22:18 they are all bronze, tin, *i*,
22:20 men gather silver, bronze, *i*,
27:12 They gave you silver, *i*,
27:19 back and forth. Wrought *i*,
Dan 2:33 'its legs of *i*, its feet
2:33 its feet partly of *i* and partly
2:34 the image on its feet of *i* and
2:35 'Then the *i*, the clay, the
2:40 kingdom shall be as strong as *i*,
2:40 inasmuch as *i* breaks in pieces
2:40 and like *i* that crushes, that
2:41 potter's clay and partly of *i*,
2:41 yet the strength of the *i* shall
2:41 just as you saw the *i* mixed
2:42 of the feet were partly of *i*
2:43 As you saw *i* mixed with ceramic
2:43 just as *i* does not mix with
2:45 that it broke in pieces the *i*,
4:15 Bound with a band of *i* and
4:23 bound with a band of *i* and
5: 4 gold and silver, bronze and *i*,
5:23 silver and gold, bronze and *i*,
7: 7 It had huge *i* teeth; it was
7:19 with its teeth of *i* and its
Am 1: 3 Gilead with implements of *i*.
Mic 4:13 For I will make your horn *i*,
Acts 12:10 they came to the *i* gate that
1 Tim 4: 2 conscience seared with a hot *i*,
Rev 2:27 them with a rod of *i*;
9: 9 like breastplates of *i*,
12: 5 all nations with a rod of *i*.
18:12 most precious wood, bronze, *i*,
19:15 will rule them with a rod of *i*.

IRONS (2/2)
Ps 105:18 with fetters, He was laid in *i*.
107:10 Bound in affliction and *i*—

IRPEEL (1/1)
Josh 18:27 Rekem, *I*, Taralah,

IRREVOCABLE (1/1)
Rom 11:29 and the calling of God are *i*.

IRRITANTS (1/1)
Num 33:55 you let remain shall be *i* in

IRU (1/1)
1 Chr 4:15 the son of Jephunneh were *I*,

IS (6944/5487) See APPENDIX

ISAAC (128/119) ISAAC'S
Gen 17:19 and you shall call his name *I*;
17:21 I will establish with *I*,
21: 3 to him—whom Sarah bore to him—*I*.
21: 4 Abraham circumcised his son *I*
21: 5 years old when his son *I* was
21: 8 feast on the same day that *I*
21:10 with my son, namely with *I*.
21:12 for in *I* your seed shall be
22: 2 now your son, your only son *I*,
22: 3 and *I* his son; and he split the
22: 6 offering and laid it on *I* his
22: 7 But *I* spoke to Abraham his
22: 9 and he bound *I* his son and laid
24: 4 and take a wife for my son *I*.
24:14 appointed for Your servant *I*.
24:62 Now *I* came from the way of Beer
24:63 And *I* went out to meditate in
24:64 and when she saw *I* she
24:66 And the servant told *I* all the
24:67 Then *I* brought her into his
24:67 So *I* was comforted after his
25: 5 gave all that he had to *I*.
25: 6 away from *I* his son, to the
25: 9 And his sons *I* and Ishmael
25:11 that God blessed his son *I*.
25:11 And *I* dwelt at Beer Lahai Roi.
25:19 This is the genealogy of *I*,
25:19 Abraham's son. Abraham begot *I*.
25:20 *I* was forty years old when he
25:21 Now *I* pleaded with the LORD for
25:26 *I* was sixty years old when she
25:28 And *I* loved Esau because he ate
26: 1 And *I* went to Abimelech king of
26: 6 So *I* dwelt in Gerar.
26: 8 and saw, and there was *I*,
26: 9 Then Abimelech called *I* and
26: 9 And *I* said to him, "Because
26:12 Then *I* sowed in that land, and
26:16 And Abimelech said to *I*,
26:17 Then *I* departed from there and
26:18 And *I* dug again the wells of
26:27 And *I* said to them, "Why have
26:31 and *I* sent them away, and they
26:35 they were a grief of mind to *I*
27: 1 when *I* was old and his eyes
27: 5 Rebekah was listening when *I*
27:20 But *I* said to his son, "How is
27:21 Then *I* said to Jacob, "Please
27:22 So Jacob went near to *I* his
27:26 Then his father *I* said to him,
27:30 as soon as *I* had finished
27:30 out from the presence of *I* his
27:32 And his father *I* said to him,
27:33 Then *I* trembled exceedingly, and
27:37 Then *I* answered and said to
27:39 Then *I* his father answered and
27:46 And Rebekah said to *I*,
28: 1 Then *I* called Jacob and blessed
28: 5 So *I* sent Jacob away, and he
28: 6 Esau saw that *I* had blessed
28: 8 did not please his father *I*.
28:13 your father and the God of *I*;
31:18 to go to his father *I* in the
31:42 of Abraham and the Fear of *I*,
31:53 by the Fear of his father *I*.
32: 9 Abraham and God of my father *I*,
35:12 which I gave Abraham and *I* I
35:27 Jacob came to his father *I* at
35:27 where Abraham and *I* had dwelt.
35:28 Now the days of *I* were one

35:29 So *I* breathed his last and died,
46: 1 to the God of his father *I*.
48:15 whom my fathers Abraham and *I*
48:16 of my fathers Abraham and *I*;
49:31 there they buried *I* and Rebekah
50:24 which He swore to Abraham, to *I*,
Ex 2:24 covenant with Abraham, with *I*,
3: 6 God of Abraham, the God of *I*,
3:15 God of Abraham, the God of *I*,
3:16 the God of Abraham, of *I*,
4: 5 God of Abraham, the God of *I*,
6: 3 "I appeared to Abraham, to *I*,
6: 8 I swore to give to Abraham, *I*,
32:13 "Remember Abraham, *I*,
33: 1 of which I swore to Abraham, *I*,
Lev 26:42 and My covenant with *I* and My
Num 32:11 of which I swore to Abraham, *I*,
Deut 1: 8 to your fathers—to Abraham, *I*,
6:10 to your fathers, to Abraham, *I*,
9: 5 to your fathers, to Abraham, *I*,
9:27 Your servants, Abraham, *I*,
29:13 to your fathers, to Abraham, *I*,
30:20 to your fathers, to Abraham, *I*,
34: 4 I swore to give Abraham, *I*,
Josh 24: 3 his descendants and gave him *I*.
24: 4 'To *I* I gave Jacob and Esau.
1 Ki 18:36 said, "LORD God of Abraham, *I*,
2 Ki 13:23 of His covenant with Abraham, *I*,
1 Chr 1:28 The sons of Abraham were *I* and
1:34 And Abraham begot *I*.
1:34 The sons of *I* were Esau and
16:16 Abraham, And His oath to *I*,
29:18 "O LORD God of Abraham, *I*,
2 Chr 30: 6 to the LORD God of Abraham, *I*,
Ps 105: 9 Abraham, And His oath to *I*,
Jer 33:26 the descendants of Abraham, *I*,
Am 7: 9 The high places of *I* shall be
7:16 spout against the house of *I*.
Mt 1: 2 Abraham begot *I*, Isaac begot
1: 2 *I* begot Jacob, and Jacob begot
8:11 and sit down with Abraham, *I*,
22:32 of Abraham, the God of *I*,
Mk 12:26 of Abraham, the God of *I*,
Lk 3:34 son of Jacob, the son of *I*,
13:28 when you see Abraham and *I* and
20:37 of Abraham, the God of *I*,
Acts 3:13 "The God of Abraham, *I*,
7: 8 and so Abraham begot *I* and
7: 8 and *I* begot Jacob, and Jacob
7:32 of Abraham, the God of *I*,
Rom 9: 7 In *I* your seed shall be
9:10 even by our father *I*
Gal 4:28 as *I* was, are children of
Heb 11: 9 dwelling in tents with *I* and
11:17 he was tested, offered up *I*,
11:18 In *I* your seed shall be
11:20 By faith *I* blessed Jacob and
Jas 2:21 by works when he offered *I* his

ISAAC'S (4/4) ISAAC

Gen 26:19 Also *I* servants dug in the
26:20 quarreled with *I* herdsmen,
26:25 and there *I* servants dug a
26:32 the same day that *I* servants

ISAIAH (53/53)

2 Ki 19: 2 to *I* the prophet, the son of
19: 5 of King Hezekiah came to *I*.
19: 6 And *I* said to them, "Thus you
19:20 Then *I* the son of Amoz sent to
20: 1 And *I* the prophet, the son of
20: 4 before *I* had gone out into the
20: 7 Then *I* said, "Take a lump of
20: 8 And Hezekiah said to *I*,
20: 9 Then *I* said, "This is the sign
20:11 So *I* the prophet cried out to
20:14 Then *I* the prophet went to King
20:16 Then *I* said to Hezekiah, "Hear
20:19 So Hezekiah said to *I*,
2 Chr 26:22 the prophet *I* the son of Amoz
32:20 King Hezekiah and the prophet *I*,
32:32 written in the vision of *I* the
Isa 1: 1 The vision of *I* the son of
2: 1 The word that *I* the son of Amoz
7: 3 Then the LORD said to *I*,
13: 1 burden against Babylon which *I*
20: 2 same time the LORD spoke by *I*
20: 3 Just as My servant *I* has walked
37: 2 to *I* the prophet, the son of
37: 5 of King Hezekiah came to *I*.
37: 6 And *I* said to them, "Thus shall
37:21 Then *I* the son of Amoz sent to
38: 1 And *I* the prophet, the son of
38: 4 the word of the LORD came to *I*,
38:21 Now *I* had said, "Let them take
39: 3 Then *I* the prophet went to King
39: 5 Then *I* said to Hezekiah, "Hear
39: 8 So Hezekiah said to *I*,
Mt 3: 3 was spoken of by the prophet *I*,
4:14 which was spoken by *I* the
8:17 which was spoken by *I* the
12:17 which was spoken by *I* the
13:14 And in them the prophecy of *I* is
15: 7 Hypocrites! Well did *I* prophesy
Mk 7: 6 Well did *I* prophesy of you
Lk 3: 4 in the book of the words of *I*
4:17 the book of the prophet *I*.
Jn 1:23 as the prophet *I* said."
12:38 that the word of *I* the prophet
12:39 because *I* said again:
12:41 These things *I* said when he saw
Acts 8:28 he was reading *I* the prophet.
8:30 heard him reading the prophet *I*,
28:25 Spirit spoke rightly through *I*
Rom 9:27 *I* also cries out concerning
9:29 And as *I* said before:
10:16 For *I* says, "Lord, who has
10:20 But *I* is very bold and says:
15:12 *I* says: "There shall be

ISCAH (1/1)

Gen 11:29 of Milcah and the father of *I*.

ISCARIOT (11/11) JUDAS

Mt 10: 4 the Canaanite, and Judas *I*,
26:14 of the twelve, called Judas *I*,
Mk 3:19 and Judas *I*, who also betrayed
14:10 Then Judas *I*, one of the
Lk 6:16 and Judas *I* who also became a
22: 3 Satan entered Judas, surnamed *I*,
Jn 6:71 He spoke of Judas *I*,
12: 4 one of His disciples, Judas *I*,
13: 2 it into the heart of Judas *I*,
13:26 bread, He gave it to Judas *I*,
14:22 Judas (not *I*) said to Him,

ISH-TOB (2/2)

2 Sam 10: 6 and from *I* twelve thousand men.
10: 8 Syrians of Zoba, Beth Rehob, *I*,

ISHBAH (1/1)

1 Chr 4:17 and *I* the father of Eshtemoa.

ISHBAK (2/2)

Gen 25: 2 Jokshan, Medan, Midian, *I*,
1 Chr 1:32 Jokshan, Medan, Midian, *I*,

ISHBI-BENOB (1/1)

2 Sam 21:16 Then *I*, who was one of the

ISHBOSHETH (12/11) ESH-BAAL

2 Sam 2: 8 took *I* the son of Saul and
2:10 *I*, Saul's son, was forty
2:12 and the servants of *I* the son
2:15 followers of *I* the son of
3: 7 So *I* said to Abner, "Why have
3: 8 very angry at the words of *I*,
3:14 So David sent messengers to *I*,
3:15 And *I* sent and took her from
4: 5 of the day to the house of *I*,
4: 8 And they brought the head of *I*
4: 8 king, "Here is the head of *I*,
4:12 But they took the head of *I* and

ISHHOD (1/1)

1 Chr 7:18 His sister Hammoleketh bore *I*,

ISHI (5/4)

1 Chr 2:31 The son of Appaim was *I*,
2:31 the son of *I* was Sheshan, and
4:20 And the sons of *I* were Zoheth
4:42 and Uzziel, the sons of *I*.
5:24 their fathers' houses: Epher, *I*,

ISHIAH (1/1)

1 Chr 7: 3 Michael, Obadiah, Joel, and *I*.

ISHIJAH (1/1)

Ezra 10:31 the sons of Harim: Eliezer, *I*,

ISHMA (1/1)

1 Chr 4: 3 father of Etam: Jezreel, *I*,

ISHMAEL (47/43) ISHMAELITES

Gen 16:11 You shall call his name *I*,
16:15 his son, whom Hagar bore, *I*.
16:16 years old when Hagar bore *I* to
17:18 that *I* might live before You!"
17:20 'And as for *I*, I have heard
17:23 So Abraham took *I* his son, all
17:25 And *I* his son was thirteen
17:26 was circumcised, and his son *I*;
25: 9 And his sons Isaac and *I* buried
25:12 this is the genealogy of *I*,
25:13 the names of the sons of *I*,
25:13 generations: The firstborn of *I*,
25:16 These were the sons of *I* and
25:17 the years of the life of *I*:
28: 9 So Esau went to *I* and took
28: 9 took Mahalath the daughter of *I*,
2 Ki 25:23 *I* the son of Nethaniah, Johanan
25:25 in the seventh month that *I*
1 Chr 1:28 of Abraham were Isaac and *I*.
1:29 The firstborn of *I* was
1:31 These were the sons of *I*.
8:38 these: Azrikam, Bocheru, *I*,
9:44 these: Azrikam, Bocheru, *I*,
2 Chr 19:11 and Zebadiah the son of *I*,
23: 1 *I* the son of Jehohanan, Azariah
Ezra 10:22 Pashhur: Elioenai, Maaseiah, *I*,
Jer 40: 8 *I* the son of Nethaniah, Johanan
40:14 of the Ammonites has sent *I*
40:15 and I will kill *I* the son of
40:16 you speak falsely concerning *I*.
41: 1 in the seventh month that *I*
41: 2 Then *I* the son of Nethaniah, and
41: 3 *I* also struck down all the Jews
41: 6 Now *I* the son of Nethaniah went
41: 7 that *I* the son of Nethaniah
41: 8 found among them who said to *I*,
41: 9 Now the pit into which *I* had
41: 9 *I* the son of Nethaniah filled
41:10 Then *I* carried away captive all
41:10 And *I* the son of Nethaniah
41:11 heard of all the evil that *I*
41:12 men and went to fight with *I*
41:13 all the people who were with *I*
41:14 Then all the people whom *I* had
41:15 But *I* the son of Nethaniah
41:16 whom he had recovered from *I*
41:18 because *I* the son of Nethaniah

ISHMAEL'S (1/1)

Gen 36: 3 *I* daughter, sister of Nebajoth.

ISHMAELITE (2/2)

1 Chr 2:17 of Amasa was Jether the *I*.
27:30 Obil the *I* was over the camels,

ISHMAELITES (6/6) ISHMAEL

Gen 37:25 and there was a company of *I*,
37:27 and let us sell him to the *I*,
37:28 and sold him to the *I* for
39: 1 bought him from the *I* who had
Judg 8:24 earrings, because they were *I*.
Ps 83: 6 The tents of Edom and the *I*;

ISHMAIAH (2/2)

1 Chr 12: 4 *I* the Gibeonite, a mighty man
27:19 *I* the son of Obadiah;

ISHMEELETE, ISHMEELITES (KJV) See ISHMAELITE, ISHMAELITES

ISHMERAI (1/1)

1 Chr 8:18 *I*, Jizliah, and Jobab were

ISHOD (KJV) See ISHHOD

ISHPAN (1/1)

1 Chr 8:22 *I*, Eber, Eliel,

ISHUAH (1/1)

Gen 46:17 sons of Asher were Jimnah, *I*,

ISHUAI (KJV) See ISHVI

ISHUI (KJV) See JISHUI

ISHVAH (1/1)

1 Chr 7:30 sons of Asher were Imnah, *I*,

ISHVI (1/1)

1 Chr 7:30 of Asher were Imnah, Ishvah, *I*,

ISLAND (10/10) ISLANDS

Acts 13: 6 they had gone through the ***i*** to
27:16 under the shelter of an ***i***
27:26 must run aground on a certain ***i***.
28: 1 they then found out that the ***i***
28: 7 of the leading citizen of the ***i***,
28: 9 the rest of those on the ***i*** who
28:11 which had wintered at the ***i***.
Rev 1: 9 was on the ***i*** that is called
6:14 and every mountain and ***i*** was
16:20 Then every ***i*** fled away, and the

ISLANDS (2/2) ISLAND

Esth 10: 1 on the land and on the ***i*** of
Isa 11:11 From Hamath and the ***i*** of the

ISLES (6/6)

Ps 72:10 kings of Tarshish and of the ***i***
97: 1 Let the multitude of ***i*** be
Isa 40:15 He lifts up the ***i*** as a very
Jer 31:10 And declare it in the ***i*** afar
Ezek 27:15 many ***i*** were the market of your
27:35 All the inhabitants of the ***i***

ISMACHIAH (1/1)

2 Chr 31:13 Jerimoth, Jozabad, Eliel, *I*,

ISMAIAH (KJV) See ISHMAIAH

ISOLATE (9/9) ISOLATED

Lev 13: 4 then the priest shall ***i*** the
13: 5 then the priest shall ***i*** him
13:11 and shall not ***i*** him, for he is
13:21 then the priest shall ***i*** him

13:26 then the priest shall *i* him
13:31 then the priest shall *i* the
13:33 And the priest shall *i* the
13:50 shall examine the plague and *i*
13:54 and he shall *i* it another seven

ISOLATED (2/2) ISOLATE

2 Ki 15: 5 so he dwelt in an *i* house.
2 Chr 26:21 He dwelt in an *i* house, because

ISOLATES (1/1)

Prov 18: 1 A man who *i* himself seeks his

ISPAH (1/1)

1 Chr 8:16 Michael, *I*, and Joha were

ISRAEL (2567/2294) ISRAEL'S, ISRAELITE, JACOB

Gen 32:28 longer be called Jacob, but *I*;
32:32 to this day the children of *I*
34: 7 done a disgraceful thing in *I*
35:10 but *I* shall be your name."
35:10 So He called his name *I*.
35:21 Then *I* journeyed and pitched
35:22 when *I* dwelt in that land, that
35:22 and *I* heard about it.
36:31 reigned over the children of *I*:
37: 3 Now *I* loved Joseph more than all
37:13 And *I* said to Joseph, "Are not
42: 5 And the sons of *I* went to buy
43: 6 And *I* said, "Why did you deal
43: 8 Then Judah said to *I* his
43:11 And their father *I* said to them,
45:21 Then the sons of *I* did so;
45:28 Then *I* said, "It is enough.
46: 1 So *I* took his journey with all
46: 2 Then God spoke to *I* in the
46: 5 and the sons of *I* carried their
46: 8 the names of the children of *I*,
46:29 to Goshen to meet his father *I*;
46:30 And *I* said to Joseph, "Now let
47:27 So *I* dwelt in the land of
47:29 When the time drew near that *I*
47:31 So *I* bowed himself on the head
48: 2 and *I* strengthened himself and
48: 8 Then *I* saw Joseph's sons, and
48:10 Now the eyes of *I* were dim with
48:11 And *I* said to Joseph, "I had
48:14 Then *I* stretched out his right
48:20 By you *I* will bless, saying,
48:21 Then *I* said to Joseph, "Behold,
49: 2 And listen to *I* your father.
49: 7 in Jacob And scatter them in *I*.
49:16 As one of the tribes of *I*.
49:24 the Shepherd, the Stone of *I*),
49:28 are the twelve tribes of *I*,
50: 2 So the physicians embalmed *I*.
50:25 an oath from the children of *I*,
Ex 1: 1 the names of the children of *I*
1: 7 But the children of *I* were
1: 9 the people of the children of *I*
1:12 in dread of the children of *I*.
1:13 made the children of *I* serve
2:23 Then the children of *I* groaned
2:25 looked upon the children of *I*,
3: 9 the cry of the children of *I*
3:10 My people, the children of *I*,
3:11 should bring the children of *I*
3:13 I come to the children of *I*
3:14 shall say to the children of *I*,
3:15 shall say to the children of *I*:
3:16 Go and gather the elders of *I*
3:18 come, you and the elders of *I*,
4:22 *I* is My son, My firstborn.
4:29 the elders of the children of *I*.
4:31 had visited the children of *I*
5: 1 "Thus says the LORD God of *I*:
5: 2 should obey His voice to let *I*
5: 2 nor will I let *I* go."
5:14 officers of the children of *I*,
5:15 officers of the children of *I*
5:19 officers of the children of *I*
6: 5 groaning of the children of *I*
6: 6 say to the children of *I*:
6: 9 spoke thus to the children of *I*;
6:11 Egypt to let the children of *I*
6:12 The children of *I* have not
6:13 a command for the children of *I*
6:13 to bring the children of *I* out
6:14 of Reuben, the firstborn of *I*,
6:26 Bring out the children of *I* from
6:27 to bring out the children of *I*
7: 2 to send the children of *I* out
7: 4 My people, the children of *I*,
7: 5 and bring out the children of *I*
9: 4 between the livestock of *I* and
9: 4 belongs to the children of *I*.
9: 6 livestock of the children of *I*,
9:26 where the children of *I* were,
9:35 would he let the children of *I*
10:20 did not let the children of *I*
10:23 But all the children of *I* had
11: 7 none of the children of *I*
11: 7 between the Egyptians and *I*.
11:10 did not let the children of *I*
12: 3 to all the congregation of *I*,
12: 6 of the congregation of *I* shall
12:15 person shall be cut off from *I*.
12:19 off from the congregation of *I*,
12:21 called for all the elders of *I*
12:27 houses of the children of *I* in
12:28 Then the children of *I* went away
12:31 both you and the children of *I*.
12:35 Now the children of *I* had done
12:37 Then the children of *I*
12:40 sojourn of the children of *I*
12:42 for all the children of *I*
12:47 All the congregation of *I* shall
12:50 Thus all the children of *I* did;
12:51 brought the children of *I* out
13: 2 womb among the children of *I*,
13:18 And the children of *I* went up
13:19 he had placed the children of *I*
14: 2 "Speak to the children of *I*,
14: 3 will say of the children of *I*,
14: 5 that we have let *I* go from
14: 8 he pursued the children of *I*;
14: 8 and the children of *I* went out
14:10 the children of *I* lifted their
14:10 and the children of *I* cried out
14:15 Tell the children of *I* to go
14:16 And the children of *I* shall go
14:19 who went before the camp of *I*,
14:20 the Egyptians and the camp of *I*.
14:22 So the children of *I* went into
14:25 us flee from the face of *I*,
14:29 But the children of *I* had walked
14:30 So the LORD saved *I* that day
14:30 and *I* saw the Egyptians dead on
14:31 Thus *I* saw the great work which
15: 1 Moses and the children of *I*
15:19 But the children of *I* went on
15:22 So Moses brought *I* from the Red
16: 1 of the children of *I* came to
16: 2 of the children of *I*
16: 3 And the children of *I* said to
16: 6 said to all the children of *I*,
16: 9 of the children of *I*,
16:10 of the children of *I*,
16:12 complaints of the children of *I*.
16:15 So when the children of *I* saw
16:17 Then the children of *I* did so
16:31 And the house of *I* called its
16:35 And the children of *I* ate manna
17: 1 of the children of *I* set out
17: 5 you some of the elders of *I*.
17: 6 in the sight of the elders of *I*.
17: 7 contention of the children of *I*,
17: 8 Amalek came and fought with *I*
17:11 that *I* prevailed; and when he
18: 1 had done for Moses and for *I*
18: 1 that the LORD had brought *I* out
18: 9 which the LORD had done for *I*,
18:12 came with all the elders of *I*
18:25 chose able men out of all *I*,
19: 1 month after the children of *I*
19: 2 So *I* camped there before the
19: 3 and tell the children of *I*:
19: 6 speak to the children of *I*.
20:22 shall say to the children of *I*:
24: 1 and seventy of the elders of *I*,
24: 4 to the twelve tribes of *I*.
24: 5 young men of the children of *I*,
24: 9 and seventy of the elders of *I*,
24:10 and they saw the God of *I*.
24:11 nobles of the children of *I* He
24:17 the eyes of the children of *I*.
25: 2 "Speak to the children of *I*,
25:22 to the children of *I*.
27:20 command the children of *I* that
27:21 on behalf of the children of *I*.
28: 1 from among the children of *I*,
28: 9 them the names of the sons of *I*:
28:11 with the names of the sons of *I*.
28:12 stones for the sons of *I*.
28:21 have the names of the sons of *I*,
28:29 the names of the sons of *I* on
28:30 judgment of the children of *I*
28:38 things which the children of *I*
29:28 be from the children of *I* for
29:28 from the children of *I* from
29:43 meet with the children of *I*,
29:45 dwell among the children of *I*
30:12 the census of the children of *I*
30:16 money of the children of *I*,
30:16 memorial for the children of *I*
30:31 speak to the children of *I*,
31:13 also to the children of *I*,
31:16 Therefore the children of *I*
31:17 Me and the children of *I*
32: 4 said, "This is your god, O *I*,
32: 8 said, 'This is your god, O *I*,
32:13 Abraham, Isaac, and *I*,
32:20 and made the children of *I*
32:27 "Thus says the LORD God of *I*:
33: 5 "Say to the children of *I*,
33: 6 So the children of *I* stripped
34:23 the Lord, the LORD God of *I*.
34:27 a covenant with you and with *I*.
34:30 and all the children of *I* saw
34:32 all the children of *I* came
34:34 and speak to the children of *I*
34:35 And whenever the children of *I*
35: 1 of the children of *I* together,
35: 4 of the children of *I*,
35:20 of the children of *I* departed
35:29 The children of *I* brought a
35:30 Moses said to the children of *I*,
36: 3 which the children of *I* had
39: 6 with the names of the sons of *I*.
39: 7 stones for the sons of *I*,
39:14 to the names of the sons of *I*:
39:32 And the children of *I* did
39:42 so the children of *I* did all
40:36 the children of *I* would go
40:38 the sight of all the house of *I*,
Lev 1: 2 "Speak to the children of *I*,
4: 2 "Speak to the children of *I*,
4:13 if the whole congregation of *I*
7:23 "Speak to the children of *I*,
7:29 "Speak to the children of *I*,
7:34 taken from the children of *I*,
7:34 sons from the children of *I* by
7:36 to them by the children of *I*,
7:38 He commanded the children of *I*
9: 1 his sons and the elders of *I*.
9: 3 And to the children of *I* you
10: 6 brethren, the whole house of *I*,
10:11 you may teach the children of *I*
10:14 offerings of the children of *I*.
11: 2 "Speak to the children of *I*,
12: 2 "Speak to the children of *I*,
15: 2 "Speak to the children of *I*,
15:31 separate the children of *I*
16: 5 of the children of *I* two kids
16:16 of the children of *I*,
16:17 and for all the assembly of *I*.
16:19 of the children of *I*.
16:21 iniquities of the children of *I*,
16:34 atonement for the children of *I*,
17: 2 and to all the children of *I*,
17: 3 man of the house of *I*
17: 5 the end that the children of *I*
17: 8 'Whatever man of the house of *I*,
17:10 whatever man of the house of *I*,
17:12 I said to the children of *I*,
17:13 man of the children of *I*,
17:14 I said to the children of *I*,
18: 2 "Speak to the children of *I*,
19: 2 of the children of *I*,
20: 2 shall say to the children of *I*:
20: 2 'Whoever of the children of *I*,
20: 2 of the strangers who dwell in *I*,
21:24 and to all the children of *I*.
22: 2 things of the children of *I*,
22: 3 things which the children of *I*
22:15 offerings of the children of *I*,
22:18 and to all the children of *I*,
22:18 'Whatever man of the house of *I*,
22:18 or of the strangers in *I*,
22:32 among the children of *I*.
23: 2 "Speak to the children of *I*,
23:10 "Speak to the children of *I*,
23:24 "Speak to the children of *I*,
23:34 "Speak to the children of *I*,
23:43 that I made the children of *I*
23:44 declared to the children of *I*
24: 2 Command the children of *I* that
24: 8 taken from the children of *I*
24:10 out among the children of *I*;
24:10 woman's son and a man of *I*
24:15 speak to the children of *I*,
24:23 spoke to the children of *I*;
24:23 So the children of *I* did as the
25: 2 "Speak to the children of *I*,
25:33 among the children of *I*.
25:46 brethren, the children of *I*,
25:55 For the children of *I* are
26:46 Himself and the children of *I*
27: 2 "Speak to the children of *I*,
27:34 Moses for the children of *I* on
Num 1: 2 of the children of *I*,
1: 3 are able to go to war in *I*.
1:16 heads of the divisions in *I*.
1:44 numbered, with the leaders of *I*,
1:45 numbered of the children of *I*,
1:45 were able to go to war in *I*—
1:49 of them among the children of *I*;
1:52 The children of *I* shall pitch
1:53 of the children of *I*;
1:54 Thus the children of *I* did;
2: 2 Everyone of the children of *I*
2:32 numbered of the children of *I*
2:33 among the children of *I*,
2:34 Thus the children of *I* did
3: 8 the needs of the children of *I*,
3: 9 from among the children of *I*.
3:12 from among the children of *I*
3:12 womb among the children of *I*.
3:13 Myself all the firstborn in *I*,
3:38 the needs of the children of *I*;
3:40 males of the children of *I*
3:41 among the children of *I*,
3:41 livestock of the children of *I*.
3:42 among the children of *I*,
3:45 among the children of *I*,
3:46 firstborn of the children of *I*,
3:50 firstborn of the children of *I*
4:46 and the leaders of *I* numbered,
5: 2 Command the children of *I* that
5: 4 And the children of *I* did so,
5: 4 so the children of *I* did.
5: 6 "Speak to the children of *I*:
5: 9 things of the children of *I*,
5:12 "Speak to the children of *I*,
6: 2 "Speak to the children of *I*,
6:23 shall bless the children of *I*.
6:27 My name on the children of *I*,
7: 2 Then the leaders of *I*,
7:84 the altar from the leaders of *I*,
8: 6 from among the children of *I*
8: 9 of the children of *I*.

8:10 and the children of *I* shall lay
8:11 offering from the children of *I*,
8:14 from among the children of *I*,
8:16 Me from among the children of *I*;
8:16 of all the children of *I*.
8:17 among the children of *I* are
8:18 firstborn of the children of *I*.
8:19 from among the children of *I*,
8:19 the work for the children of *I*
8:19 atonement for the children of *I*,
8:19 plague among the children of *I*
8:19 Israel when the children of *I*
8:20 of the children of *I* did to
8:20 so the children of *I* did to
9: 2 Let the children of *I* keep the
9: 4 So Moses told the children of *I*
9: 5 so the children of *I* did.
9: 7 time among the children of *I*?
9:10 "Speak to the children of *I*,
9:17 after that the children of *I*
9:17 there the children of *I* would
9:18 of the LORD the children of *I*
9:19 the children of *I* kept the
9:22 the children of *I* would remain
10: 4 the heads of the divisions of *I*,
10:12 And the children of *I* set out
10:28 of march of the children of *I*,
10:29 has promised good things to *I*.
10:36 To the many thousands of *I*.
11: 4 so the children of *I* also wept
11:16 seventy men of the elders of *I*,
11:30 both he and the elders of *I*.
13: 2 am giving to the children of *I*;
13: 3 heads of the children of *I*.
13:24 the cluster which the men of *I*
13:26 of the children of *I* in the
13:32 they gave the children of *I* a
14: 2 And all the children of *I*
14: 5 of the children of *I*.
14: 7 of the children of *I*,
14:10 before all the children of *I*.
14:27 which the children of *I* make
14:39 words to all the children of *I*,
15: 2 "Speak to the children of *I*,
15:18 "Speak to the children of *I*,
15:25 of the children of *I*,
15:26 of the children of *I* and the
15:29 among the children of *I* and
15:32 Now while the children of *I*
15:38 "Speak to the children of *I*:
16: 2 with some of the children of *I*,
16: 9 thing to you that the God of *I*
16: 9 you from the congregation of *I*,
16:25 and the elders of *I* followed
16:34 Then all *I* who were around them
16:38 be a sign to the children of *I*.
16:40 a memorial to the children of *I*
16:41 of the children of *I* murmured
17: 2 "Speak to the children of *I*,
17: 5 complaints of the children of *I*,
17: 6 spoke to the children of *I*,
17: 9 LORD to all the children of *I*;
17:12 So the children of *I* spoke to
18: 5 more wrath on the children of *I*.
18: 6 from among the children of *I*;
18: 8 holy gifts of the children of *I*;
18:11 offerings of the children of *I*;
18:14 Every devoted thing in *I* shall
18:19 which the children of *I* offer
18:20 among the children of *I*.
18:21 of Levi all the tithes in *I* as
18:22 Hereafter the children of *I*
18:23 that among the children of *I*
18:24 the tithes of the children of *I*,
18:24 Among the children of *I* they
18:26 you take from the children of *I*
18:28 receive from the children of *I*,
18:32 holy gifts of the children of *I*,
19: 2 'Speak to the children of *I*,
19: 9 of the children of *I* for the
19:10 forever to the children of *I*
19:13 person shall be cut off from *I*.
20: 1 Then the children of *I*,
20:12 the eyes of the children of *I*,
20:13 because the children of *I*
20:14 "Thus says your brother *I*:
20:19 So the children of *I* said to
20:21 Thus Edom refused to give *I*
20:21 so *I* turned away from him.
20:22 Then the children of *I*,
20:24 have given to the children of *I*,
20:29 all the house of *I* mourned for
21: 1 heard that *I* was coming on the
21: 1 then he fought against *I* and
21: 2 So *I* made a vow to the LORD,
21: 3 listened to the voice of *I* and
21: 6 and many of the people of *I*
21:10 Now the children of *I* moved on
21:17 Then *I* sang this song:
21:21 Then *I* sent messengers to Sihon
21:23 But Sihon would not allow *I* to
21:23 and went out against *I* in the
21:23 to Jahaz and fought against *I*.
21:24 Then *I* defeated him with the
21:25 So *I* took all these cities, and
21:25 and *I* dwelt in all the cities
21:31 Thus *I* dwelt in the land of the
22: 1 Then the children of *I* moved,
22: 2 son of Zippor saw all that *I*
22: 3 because of the children of *I*.
23: 7 And come, denounce *I*!'
23:10 Or number one-fourth of *I*?
23:21 has He seen wickedness in *I*.
23:23 Nor any divination against *I*.
23:23 must be said of Jacob And of *I*,
24: 1 it pleased the LORD to bless *I*,
24: 2 and saw *I* encamped according to
24: 5 Your dwellings, O *I*!
24:17 A Scepter shall rise out of *I*,
24:18 While *I* does valiantly.
25: 1 Now *I* remained in Acacia Grove,
25: 3 So *I* was joined to Baal of Peor,
25: 3 the LORD was aroused against *I*.
25: 4 the LORD may turn away from *I*.
25: 5 Moses said to the judges of *I*,
25: 6 one of the children of *I* came
25: 6 of the children of *I*,
25: 8 and he went after the man of *I*
25: 8 of them through, the man of *I*,
25: 8 stopped among the children of *I*.
25:11 My wrath from the children of *I*,
25:11 not consume the children of *I*
25:13 atonement for the children of *I*.
26: 2 of the children of *I* from
26: 2 who are able to go to war in *I*.
26: 4 Moses and the children of *I*
26: 5 Reuben was the firstborn of *I*.
26:51 numbered of the children of *I*:
26:62 among the other children of *I*,
26:62 to them among the children of *I*.
26:63 who numbered the children of *I*
26:64 numbered the children of *I* in
27: 8 speak to the children of *I*,
27:11 shall be to the children of *I*
27:12 have given to the children of *I*.
27:20 of the children of *I* may be
27:21 he and all the children of *I*
28: 2 "Command the children of *I*,
29:40 Moses told the children of *I*
30: 1 concerning the children of *I*,
31: 2 for the children of *I*.
31: 4 tribe of all the tribes of *I*
31: 5 from the divisions of *I* one
31: 9 And the children of *I* took the
31:12 of the children of *I*,
31:16 women caused the children of *I*,
31:54 memorial for the children of *I*
32: 4 before the congregation of *I*,
32: 7 the heart of the children of *I*
32: 9 the heart of the children of *I*,
32:13 anger was aroused against *I*,
32:14 anger of the LORD against *I*.
32:17 go before the children of *I*
32:18 every one of the children of *I*
32:22 before the LORD and before *I*;
32:28 the tribes of the children of *I*.
33: 1 journeys of the children of *I*,
33: 3 the Passover the children of *I*
33: 5 Then the children of *I* moved
33:38 year after the children of *I*
33:40 the coming of the children of *I*.
33:51 "Speak to the children of *I*,
34: 2 "Command the children of *I*,
34:13 commanded the children of *I*,
34:29 among the children of *I* in the
35: 2 Command the children of *I* that
35: 8 possession of the children of *I*;
35:10 "Speak to the children of *I*,
35:15 refuge for the children of *I*,
35:34 dwell among the children of *I*.
36: 1 fathers of the children of *I*.
36: 2 by lot to the children of *I*,
36: 3 tribes of the children of *I*,
36: 4 Jubilee of the children of *I*
36: 5 commanded the children of *I*
36: 7 of the children of *I* shall not
36: 7 every one of the children of *I*
36: 8 any tribe of the children of *I*
36: 8 so that the children of *I* each
36: 9 tribe of the children of *I*
36:13 commanded the children of *I* by
Deut 1: 1 which Moses spoke to all *I* on
1: 3 spoke to the children of *I*
1:38 for he shall cause *I* to inherit
2:12 just as *I* did to the land of
3:18 brethren, the children of *I*.
4: 1 'Now, O *I*, listen to the
4:44 set before the children of *I*.
4:45 spoke to the children of *I*
4:46 Moses and the children of *I*
5: 1 And Moses called all *I*,
5: 1 and said to them: "Hear, O *I*,
6: 3 "Therefore hear, O *I*,
6: 4 Hear, O *I*: The LORD our
9: 1 'Hear, O *I*: You are to
10: 6 (Now the children of *I*
10:12 And now, *I*, what does the
11: 6 in the midst of all *I*—
13:11 So all *I* shall hear and fear,
17: 4 has been committed in *I*,
17:12 shall put away the evil from *I*.
17:20 his children in the midst of *I*.
18: 1 no part nor inheritance with *I*;
18: 6 where he dwells among all *I*,
19:13 of innocent blood from *I*,
20: 3 shall say to them, 'Hear, O *I*:
21: 8 O LORD, for Your people *I*,
21: 8 to the charge of Your people *I*.
21:21 and all *I* shall hear and fear.
22:19 a bad name on a virgin of *I*.
22:21 done a disgraceful thing in *I*,
22:22 shall put away the evil from *I*.
23:17 harlot of the daughters of *I*,
23:17 perverted one of the sons of *I*.
24: 7 brethren of the children of *I*,
25: 6 may not be blotted out of *I*.
25: 7 up a name to his brother in *I*;
25:10 his name shall be called in *I*,
26:15 and bless Your people *I* and the
27: 1 Now Moses, with the elders of *I*,
27: 9 the Levites, spoke to all *I*,
27: 9 "Take heed and listen, O *I*:
27:14 and say to all the men of *I*:
29: 1 to make with the children of *I*
29: 2 Now Moses called all *I* and said
29:10 your officers, all the men of *I*,
29:21 him from all the tribes of *I*
31: 1 and spoke these words to all *I*.
31: 7 to him in the sight of all *I*,
31: 9 and to all the elders of *I*.
31:11 when all *I* comes to appear
31:11 read this law before all *I* in
31:19 teach it to the children of *I*;
31:19 Me against the children of *I*.
31:22 taught it to the children of *I*.
31:23 shall bring the children of *I*
31:30 of all the assembly of *I* the
32: 8 the number of the children of *I*.
32:45 all these words to all *I*,
32:49 I give to the children of *I* as
32:51 Me among the children of *I* at
32:51 the midst of the children of *I*.
32:52 am giving to the children of *I*.
33: 1 God blessed the children of *I*
33: 5 All the tribes of *I* together.
33:10 And *I* Your law. They shall
33:21 And His judgments with *I*.
33:28 Then *I* shall dwell in safety,
33:29 O *I*! Who is like you, a
34: 8 And the children of *I* wept for
34: 9 so the children of *I* heeded
34:10 then there has not arisen in *I*
34:12 performed in the sight of all *I*.
Josh 1: 2 to them—the children of *I*.
2: 2 tonight from the children of *I*
3: 1 he and all the children of *I*,
3: 7 exalt you in the sight of all *I*,
3: 9 said to the children of *I*,
3:12 twelve men from the tribes of *I*,
3:17 and all *I* crossed over on dry
4: 4 from the children of *I*,
4: 5 the tribes of the children of *I*,
4: 7 a memorial to the children of *I*
4: 8 And the children of *I* did so,
4: 8 the tribes of the children of *I*,
4:12 armed before the children of *I*,
4:14 Joshua in the sight of all *I*;
4:21 he spoke to the children of *I*,
4:22 *I* crossed over this Jordan on
5: 1 from before the children of *I*
5: 1 because of the children of *I*.
5: 2 and circumcise the sons of *I*
5: 3 and circumcised the sons of *I*
5: 6 For the children of *I* walked
5:10 Now the children of *I* camped in
5:12 and the children of *I* no longer
6: 1 up because of the children of *I*;
6:18 and make the camp of *I* a curse,
6:23 left them outside the camp of *I*.
6:25 So she dwells in *I* to this day,
7: 1 But the children of *I* committed
7: 1 against the children of *I*.
7: 6 evening, he and the elders of *I*;
7: 8 what shall I say when *I* turns
7:11 *I* has sinned, and they have also
7:12 Therefore the children of *I*
7:13 thus says the LORD God of *I*:
7:13 thing in your midst, O *I*;
7:15 done a disgraceful thing in *I*.
7:16 in the morning and brought *I*
7:19 glory to the LORD God of *I*,
7:20 against the LORD God of *I*,
7:23 and to all the children of *I*,
7:24 and all *I* with him, took Achan
7:25 So all *I* stoned him with
8:10 went up, he and the elders of *I*,
8:14 early and went out against *I*
8:15 And Joshua and all *I* made as if
8:17 who did not go out after *I*.
8:17 the city open and pursued *I*.
8:21 Now when Joshua and all *I* saw
8:22 were caught in the midst of *I*,
8:24 And it came to pass when *I* had
8:27 and the spoil of that city *I*
8:30 an altar to the LORD God of *I*
8:31 had commanded the children of *I*,
8:32 presence of the children of *I*,
8:33 Then all *I*, with their
8:33 should bless the people of *I*.
8:35 before all the assembly of *I*,
9: 2 to fight with Joshua and *I*
9: 6 said to him and to the men of *I*,
9: 7 Then the men of *I* said to the
9:14 Then the men of *I* took some of
9:17 Then the children of *I* journeyed
9:18 But the children of *I* did not
9:18 to them by the LORD God of *I*.
9:19 to them by the LORD God of *I*;
9:26 the hand of the children of *I*,
10: 1 of Gibeon had made peace with *I*
10: 4 and with the children of *I*.
10:10 the LORD routed them before *I*,
10:11 as they fled before *I* and were
10:11 than the children of *I* killed
10:12 before the children of *I*,
10:12 and he said in the sight of *I*:

10:14 for the LORD fought for *I*.
10:15 and all *I* with him, to the camp
10:20 Joshua and the children of *I*
10:21 any of the children of *I*.
10:24 called for all the men of *I*,
10:29 and all *I* with him, to Libnah;
10:30 and its king into the hand of *I*;
10:31 and all *I* with him, to Lachish;
10:32 Lachish into the hand of *I*,
10:34 and all *I* with him; and they
10:36 and all *I* with him, to Hebron;
10:38 and all *I* with him, to Debir;
10:40 as the LORD God of *I* had
10:42 because the LORD God of *I*
10:42 God of Israel fought for *I*.
10:43 and all *I* with him, to the camp
11: 5 of Merom to fight against *I*.
11: 6 all of them slain before *I*.
11: 8 them into the hand of *I*,
11:13 *I* burned none of them, except
11:14 the children of *I* took as booty
11:16 the mountains of *I* and its
11:19 peace with the children of *I*,
11:20 they should come against *I* in
11:21 and from all the mountains of *I*;
11:22 the land of the children of *I*;
11:23 gave it as an inheritance to *I*
12: 1 the land whom the children of *I*
12: 6 the LORD and the children of *I*
12: 7 Joshua and the children of *I*
12: 7 Joshua gave to the tribes of *I*
13: 6 from before the children of *I*;
13: 6 only divide it by lot to *I* as
13:13 Nevertheless the children of *I*
13:14 of the LORD God of *I* made by
13:22 The children of *I* also killed
13:33 the LORD God of *I* was their
14: 1 areas which the children of *I*
14: 1 the tribes of the children of *I*
14: 5 so the children of *I* did;
14:10 this word to Moses while *I*
14:14 followed the LORD God of *I*.
17:13 when the children of *I* grew
18: 1 of the children of *I* assembled
18: 2 among the children of *I* seven
18: 3 said to the children of *I*:
18:10 the land to the children of *I*
19:49 the children of *I* gave an
19:51 the tribes of the children of *I*
20: 2 "Speak to the children of *I*,
20: 9 for all the children of *I* and
21: 1 the tribes of the children of *I*.
21: 3 So the children of *I* gave to the
21: 8 And the children of *I* gave these
21:41 of the children of *I* were
21:43 So the LORD gave to *I* all the
21:45 had spoken to the house of *I*.
22: 9 from the children of *I* at
22:11 Now the children of *I* heard
22:12 And when the children of *I* heard
22:12 of the children of *I* gathered
22:13 Then the children of *I* sent
22:14 chief house of every tribe of *I*;
22:14 father among the divisions of *I*.
22:16 committed against the God of *I*,
22:18 the whole congregation of *I*.
22:20 on all the congregation of *I*?
22:21 the heads of the divisions of *I*:
22:22 and let *I* itself know—if it
22:24 to do with the LORD God of *I*?
22:30 the heads of the divisions of *I*
22:31 delivered the children of *I*
22:32 of Canaan, to the children of *I*,
22:33 thing pleased the children of *I*,
22:33 and the children of *I* blessed
23: 1 the LORD had given rest to *I*
23: 2 And Joshua called for all *I*,
24: 1 gathered all the tribes of *I*
24: 1 and called for the elders of *I*,
24: 2 "Thus says the LORD God of *I*:
24: 9 arose to make war against *I*,
24:23 heart to the LORD God of *I*.
24:31 *I* served the LORD all the days
24:31 LORD which He had done for *I*.
24:32 which the children of *I* had
Judg 1: 1 to pass that the children of *I*
1:28 when *I* was strong, that they
2: 4 words to all the children of *I*,
2: 6 the children of *I* went each to
2: 7 LORD which He had done for *I*.
2:10 work which He had done for *I*.
2:11 Then the children of *I* did evil
2:14 of the LORD was hot against *I*.
2:20 of the LORD was hot against *I*;
2:22 that through them I may test *I*,
3: 1 that He might test *I* by them,
3: 2 of the children of *I* might be
3: 4 that He might test *I* by
3: 5 Thus the children of *I* dwelt
3: 7 So the children of *I* did evil
3: 8 of the LORD was hot against *I*,
3: 8 and the children of *I* served
3: 9 When the children of *I* cried out
3: 9 deliverer for the children of *I*,
3:10 came upon him, and he judged *I*.
3:12 And the children of *I* again did
3:12 Eglon king of Moab against *I*,
3:13 and Amalek, went and defeated *I*,
3:14 So the children of *I* served
3:15 But when the children of *I*
3:15 By him the children of *I* sent
3:27 and the children of *I* went down
3:30 that day under the hand of *I*.
3:31 and he also delivered *I*.
4: 1 the children of *I* again did
4: 3 And the children of *I* cried out
4: 3 oppressed the children of *I*.
4: 4 was judging *I* at that time.
4: 5 And the children of *I* came up
4: 6 Has not the LORD God of *I*
4:23 presence of the children of *I*.
4:24 the hand of the children of *I*
5: 2 "When leaders lead in *I*,
5: 3 praise to the LORD God of *I*.
5: 5 before the LORD God of *I*.
5: 7 life ceased, it ceased in *I*,
5: 7 arose, Arose a mother in *I*.
5: 8 seen among forty thousand in *I*.
5: 9 heart is with the rulers of *I*
5:11 acts for His villagers in *I*;
6: 1 Then the children of *I* did evil
6: 2 of Midian prevailed against *I*.
6: 2 the children of *I* made for
6: 3 whenever *I* had sown, Midianites
6: 4 and leave no sustenance for *I*,
6: 6 So *I* was greatly impoverished
6: 6 and the children of *I* cried out
6: 7 when the children of *I* cried
6: 8 a prophet to the children of *I*,
6: 8 "Thus says the LORD God of *I*:
6:14 and you shall save *I* from the
6:15 "O my Lord, how can I save *I*?
6:36 If You will save *I* by my hand as
6:37 know that You will save *I* by
7: 2 lest *I* claim glory for itself
7: 8 sent away all the rest of *I*,
7:14 a man of *I*! Into his hand God
7:15 He returned to the camp of *I*,
7:23 And the men of *I* gathered
8:22 Then the men of *I* said to
8:27 And all *I* played the harlot
8:28 before the children of *I*,
8:33 that the children of *I* again
8:34 Thus the children of *I* did not
8:35 with the good he had done for *I*.
9:22 Abimelech had reigned over *I*
9:55 And when the men of *I* saw that
10: 1 there arose to save *I* Tola the
10: 2 He judged *I* twenty-three years;
10: 3 and he judged *I* twenty-two
10: 6 Then the children of *I* again
10: 7 of the LORD was hot against *I*;
10: 8 and oppressed the children of *I*
10: 8 all the children of *I* who were
10: 9 so that *I* was severely
10:10 And the children of *I* cried out
10:11 LORD said to the children of *I*,
10:15 And the children of *I* said to
10:16 longer endure the misery of *I*.
10:17 And the children of *I* assembled
11: 4 of Ammon made war against *I*.
11: 5 of Ammon made war against *I*,
11:13 Because *I* took away my land when
11:15 *I* did not take away the land of
11:16 for when *I* came up from Egypt,
11:17 Then *I* sent messengers to the
11:17 So *I* remained in Kadesh.
11:19 Then *I* sent messengers to Sihon
11:19 and *I* said to him, "Please let
11:20 But Sihon did not trust *I* to
11:20 in Jahaz, and fought against *I*.
11:21 And the LORD God of *I* delivered
11:21 his people into the hand of *I*,
11:21 Thus *I* gained possession of all
11:23 And now the LORD God of *I* has
11:23 from before His people *I*;
11:25 Did he ever strive against *I*?
11:26 While *I* dwelt in Heshbon and its
11:27 day between the children of *I*
11:33 before the children of *I*.
11:39 And it became a custom in *I*
11:40 that the daughters of *I* went
12: 7 And Jephthah judged *I* six years.
12: 8 Ibzan of Bethlehem judged *I*.
12: 9 He judged *I* seven years.
12:11 Elon the Zebulunite judged *I*.
12:11 He judged *I* ten years.
12:13 Hillel the Pirathonite judged *I*.
12:14 He judged *I* eight years.
13: 1 Again the children of *I* did evil
13: 5 and he shall begin to deliver *I*
14: 4 Philistines had dominion over *I*.
15:20 And he judged *I* twenty years in
16:31 He had judged *I* twenty years.
17: 6 days there was no king in *I*;
18: 1 days there was no king in *I*.
18: 1 among the tribes of *I* had not
18:19 to a tribe and a family in *I*?
18:29 their father, who was born to *I*.
19: 1 when there was no king in *I*,
19:12 are not of the children of *I*;
19:29 all the territory of *I*.
19:30 the day that the children of *I*
20: 1 So all the children of *I* came
20: 2 the people, all the tribes of *I*,
20: 3 heard that the children of *I*
20: 3) Then the children of *I* said,
20: 6 of the inheritance of *I*,
20: 6 lewdness and outrage in *I*.
20: 7 All of you are children of *I*;
20:10 throughout all the tribes of *I*,
20:10 that they have done in *I*.
20:11 So all the men of *I* were
20:12 Then the tribes of *I* sent men
20:13 and remove the evil from *I*!"
20:13 brethren, the children of *I*.
20:14 against the children of *I*.
20:17 the men of *I* numbered four
20:18 Then the children of *I* arose
20:19 So the children of *I* rose in the
20:20 And the men of *I* went out to
20:20 and the men of *I* put themselves
20:22 people, that is, the men of *I*,
20:23 Then the children of *I* went up
20:24 So the children of *I* approached
20:25 more of the children of *I*;
20:26 Then all the children of *I*,
20:27 So the children of *I* inquired of
20:29 Then *I* set men in ambush all
20:30 And the children of *I* went up
20:31 field, about thirty men of *I*.
20:32 But the children of *I* said,
20:33 So all the men of *I* rose from
20:34 thousand select men from all *I*
20:35 defeated Benjamin before *I*.
20:35 And the children of *I* destroyed
20:36 The men of *I* had given ground
20:38 signal between the men of *I*
20:39 whereupon the men of *I* would
20:39 about thirty of the men of *I*.
20:41 And when the men of *I* turned
20:42 backs before the men of *I* in
20:48 And the men of *I* turned back
21: 1 Now the men of *I* had sworn an
21: 3 and said, "O LORD God of *I*,
21: 3 why has this come to pass in *I*,
21: 3 be one tribe missing in *I*?
21: 5 The children of *I* said, "Who
21: 5 among all the tribes of *I* who
21: 6 And the children of *I* grieved
21: 6 One tribe is cut off from *I*
21: 8 is there from the tribes of *I*
21:15 made a void in the tribes of *I*.
21:17 may not be destroyed from *I*.
21:18 for the children of *I* have
21:24 So the children of *I* departed
21:25 days there was no king in *I*;
Ruth 2:12 given you by the LORD God of *I*,
4: 7 custom in former times in *I*
4: 7 this was a confirmation in *I*.
4:11 two who built the house of *I*;
4:14 may his name be famous in *I*!
1 Sam 1:17 and the God of *I* grant your
2:22 his sons did to all *I*,
2:28 him out of all the tribes of *I*
2:28 offerings of the children of *I*
2:29 best of all the offerings of *I*
2:30 Therefore the LORD God of *I*
2:32 the good which God does for *I*.
3:11 I will do something in *I* at
3:20 And all *I* from Dan to Beersheba
4: 1 word of Samuel came to all *I*.
4: 1 Now *I* went out to battle
4: 2 in battle array against *I*.
4: 2 *I* was defeated by the
4: 3 the elders of *I* said, "Why has
4: 5 all *I* shouted so loudly that
4:10 and *I* was defeated, and every
4:10 and there fell of *I* thirty
4:17 *I* has fled before the
4:18 And he had judged *I* forty
4:21 The glory has departed from *I*!"
4:22 "The glory has departed from *I*,
5: 7 The ark of the God of *I* must not
5: 8 do with the ark of the God of *I*?
5: 8 Let the ark of the God of *I* be
5: 8 the ark of the God of *I* away.
5:10 the ark of the God of *I* to us,
5:11 away the ark of the God of *I*,
6: 3 away the ark of the God of *I*,
6: 5 give glory to the God of *I*;
7: 2 And all the house of *I* lamented
7: 3 spoke to all the house of *I*,
7: 4 So the children of *I* put away
7: 5 Gather all *I* to Mizpah, and I
7: 6 judged the children of *I* at
7: 7 heard that the children of *I*
7: 7 Philistines went up against *I*.
7: 7 And when the children of *I*
7: 8 So the children of *I* said to
7: 9 cried out to the LORD for *I*,
7:10 drew near to battle against *I*.
7:10 they were overcome before *I*.
7:11 And the men of *I* went out of
7:13 anymore into the territory of *I*.
7:14 Philistines had taken from *I*
7:14 from Israel were restored to *I*,
7:14 and *I* recovered its territory
7:14 Also there was peace between *I*
7:15 And Samuel judged *I* all the
7:16 and judged *I* in all those
7:17 was there. There he judged *I*,
8: 1 he made his sons judges over *I*.
8: 4 Then all the elders of *I*
8:22 And Samuel said to the men of *I*,
9: 2 than he among the children of *I*.
9: 9 (Formerly in *I*, when a man
9:16 him commander over My people *I*,
9:20 on whom is all the desire of *I*?
9:21 the smallest of the tribes of *I*,
10:18 and said to the children of *I*,
10:18 "Thus says the LORD God of *I*:
10:18 I brought up *I* out of Egypt, and
10:20 had caused all the tribes of *I*
11: 2 and bring reproach on all *I*.
11: 3 to all the territory of *I*.

11: 7 all the territory of *I* by the
11: 8 the children of *I* were three
11:13 has accomplished salvation in *I*.
11:15 there Saul and all the men of *I*
12: 1 Now Samuel said to all *I*:
13: 1 he had reigned two years over *I*,
13: 2 three thousand men of *I*.
13: 4 Now all *I* heard it said that
13: 4 and that *I* had also become an
13: 5 together to fight with *I*,
13: 6 When the men of *I* saw that they
13:13 your kingdom over *I* forever.
13:19 throughout all the land of *I*,
14:12 them into the hand of *I*.
14:18 God was with the children of *I*)
14:22 Likewise all the men of *I* who
14:23 So the LORD saved *I* that day,
14:24 And the men of *I* were
14:37 deliver them into the hand of *I*?
14:39 the LORD lives, who saves *I*,
14:40 Then he said to all *I*,
14:41 Saul said to the LORD God of *I*,
14:45 this great deliverance in *I*?
14:47 his sovereignty over *I*,
14:48 and delivered *I* from the hands
15: 1 king over His people, over *I*.
15: 2 Amalek for what he did to *I*,
15: 6 to all the children of *I* when
15:17 you not head of the tribes of *I*?
15:17 LORD anoint you king over *I*?
15:26 you from being king over *I*.
15:28 has torn the kingdom of *I* from
15:29 And also the Strength of *I* will
15:30 of my people and before *I*,
15:35 He had made Saul king over *I*.
16: 1 him from reigning over *I*?
17: 2 And Saul and the men of *I* were
17: 3 and *I* stood on a mountain on
17: 8 cried out to the armies of *I*,
17:10 I defy the armies of *I* this day;
17:11 When Saul and all *I* heard these
17:19 and they and all the men of *I*
17:21 For *I* and the Philistines had
17:24 And all the men of *I*,
17:25 So the men of *I* said, "Have you
17:25 Surely he has come up to defy *I*;
17:25 exemption from taxes in *I*.
17:26 takes away the reproach from *I*?
17:45 the God of the armies of *I*,
17:46 know that there is a God in *I*.
17:52 Now the men of *I* and Judah arose
17:53 Then the children of *I* returned
18: 6 come out of all the cities of *I*,
18:16 But all *I* and Judah loved David,
18:18 or my father's family in *I*,
19: 5 a great deliverance for all *I*.
20:12 The LORD God of *I* is witness!
23:10 David said, "O LORD God of *I*,
23:11 has heard? O LORD God of *I*,
23:17 You shall be king over *I*,
24: 2 thousand chosen men from all *I*,
24:14 After whom has the king of *I*
24:20 and that the kingdom of *I* shall
25:30 has appointed you ruler over *I*,
25:32 is the LORD God of *I*,
25:34 as the LORD God of *I* lives,
26: 2 three thousand chosen men of *I*
26:15 And who is like you in *I*?
26:20 For the king of *I* has come out
27: 1 me anymore in any part of *I*.
27:12 He has made his people *I* utterly
28: 1 for war, to fight with *I*.
28: 3 and all *I* had lamented for him
28: 4 So Saul gathered all *I*
28:19 the LORD will also deliver *I*
28:19 will also deliver the army of *I*
29: 3 the servant of Saul king of *I*,
30:25 statute and an ordinance for *I*
31: 1 Philistines fought against *I*;
31: 1 and the men of *I* fled from
31: 7 And when the men of *I* who were
31: 7 saw that the men of *I* had fled
2 Sam 1: 3 have escaped from the camp of *I*.
1:12 LORD and for the house of *I*,
1:19 The beauty of *I* is slain on your
1:24 "O daughters of *I*,
2: 9 over Benjamin, and over all *I*.
2:10 when he began to reign over *I*,
2:17 and Abner and the men of *I* were
2:28 still and did not pursue *I*
3:10 up the throne of David over *I*
3:12 be with you to bring all *I* to
3:17 with the elders of *I*,
3:18 I will save My people *I* from
3:19 all that seemed good to *I* and
3:21 and gather all *I* to my lord the
3:37 For all the people and all *I*
3:38 man has fallen this day in *I*?
4: 1 and all *I* was troubled.
5: 1 Then all the tribes of *I* came to
5: 2 you were the one who led *I* out
5: 2 'You shall shepherd My people *I*,
5: 2 Israel, and be ruler over *I*.'
5: 3 Therefore all the elders of *I*
5: 3 they anointed David king over *I*.
5: 5 thirty-three years over all *I*
5:12 established him as king over *I*,
5:12 for the sake of His people *I*.
5:17 had anointed David king over *I*,
6: 1 all the choice men of *I*,
6: 5 David and all the house of *I*
6:15 So David and all the house of *I*
6:19 among the whole multitude of *I*,
6:20 glorious was the king of *I*
6:21 the people of the LORD, over *I*.
7: 6 I brought the children of *I* up
7: 7 with all the children of *I*,
7: 7 to anyone from the tribes of *I*,
7: 7 to shepherd My people *I*,
7: 8 be ruler over My people, over *I*.
7:10 appoint a place for My people *I*,
7:11 judges to be over My people *I*,
7:23 is like Your people, like *I*,
7:24 You have made Your people *I*
7:26 of hosts is the God over *I*.'
7:27 You, O LORD of hosts, God of *I*,
8:15 So David reigned over all *I*;
10:15 they had been defeated by *I*,
10:17 told David, he gathered all *I*,
10:18 Then the Syrians fled before *I*;
10:19 that they were defeated by *I*,
10:19 they made peace with *I* and
11: 1 servants with him, and all *I*;
11:11 The ark and *I* and Judah are
12: 7 Thus says the LORD God of *I*:
12: 7 'I anointed you king over *I*,
12: 8 and gave you the house of *I* and
12:12 will do this thing before all *I*,
13:12 such thing should be done in *I*.
13:13 be like one of the fools in *I*.
14:25 Now in all *I* there was no one
15: 2 from such and such a tribe of *I*.
15: 6 Absalom acted toward all *I* who
15: 6 the hearts of the men of *I*.
15:10 throughout all the tribes of *I*,
15:13 The hearts of the men of *I* are
16: 3 Today the house of *I* will
16:15 all the people, the men of *I*,
16:18 people and all the men of *I*
16:21 and all *I* will hear that you
16:22 in the sight of all *I*.
17: 4 Absalom and all the elders of *I*.
17:10 For all *I* knows that your
17:11 Therefore I advise that all *I* be
17:13 then all *I* shall bring ropes to
17:14 So Absalom and all the men of *I*
17:15 Absalom and the elders of *I*,
17:24 he and all the men of *I* with
17:26 So *I* and Absalom encamped in the
18: 6 the field of battle against *I*.
18: 7 The people of *I* were overthrown
18:16 people returned from pursuing *I*.
18:17 Then all *I* fled, everyone to
19: 8 For everyone of *I* had fled to
19: 9 throughout all the tribes of *I*,
19:11 since the words of all *I* have
19:22 man be put to death today in *I*?
19:22 that today I am king over *I*?
19:40 and also half the people of *I*.
19:41 Just then all the men of *I* came
19:42 of Judah answered the men of *I*,
19:43 And the men of *I* answered the
19:43 than the words of the men of *I*.
20: 1 to his tents, O *I*!"
20: 2 So every man of *I* deserted
20:14 through all the tribes of *I* to
20:19 peaceable and faithful in *I*.
20:19 a city and a mother in *I*.
20:23 was over all the army of *I*;
21: 2 were not of the children of *I*,
21: 2 the children of *I* had sworn
21: 2 his zeal for the children of *I*
21: 4 nor shall you kill any man in *I*
21: 5 in any of the territories of *I*,
21:15 were at war again with *I*,
21:17 lest you quench the lamp of *I*.
21:21 So when he defied *I*,
23: 1 And the sweet psalmist of *I*:
23: 3 The God of *I* said, The Rock of
23: 3 The Rock of *I* spoke to me:
23: 9 and the men of *I* had retreated.
24: 1 the LORD was aroused against *I*,
24: 1 number *I* and Judah."
24: 2 throughout all the tribes of *I*,
24: 4 king to count the people of *I*.
24: 9 And there were in *I* eight
24:15 the LORD sent a plague upon *I*
24:25 the plague was withdrawn from *I*.
1 Ki 1: 3 all the territory of *I*,
1:20 the eyes of all *I* are on you,
1:30 to you by the LORD God of *I*,
1:34 prophet anoint him king over *I*;
1:35 him to be ruler over *I* and
1:48 'Blessed be the LORD God of *I*,
2: 4 lack a man on the throne of *I*.'
2: 5 commanders of the armies of *I*,
2:11 that David reigned over *I* was
2:15 and all *I* had set their
2:32 the commander of the army of *I*,
3:28 And all *I* heard of the judgment
4: 1 Solomon was king over all *I*.
4: 7 had twelve governors over all *I*,
4:20 Judah and *I* were as numerous
4:25 And Judah and *I* dwelt safely,
5:13 up a labor force out of all *I*;
6: 1 year after the children of *I*
6: 1 year of Solomon's reign over *I*,
6:13 dwell among the children of *I*,
6:13 will not forsake My people *I*.
8: 1 assembled the elders of *I* and
8: 1 fathers of the children of *I*,
8: 2 Therefore all the men of *I*
8: 3 So all the elders of *I* came, and
8: 5 and all the congregation of *I*
8: 9 with the children of *I*,
8:14 blessed the whole assembly of *I*,
8:14 while all the assembly of *I* was
8:15 be the LORD God of *I*,
8:16 day that I brought My people *I*
8:16 no city from any tribe of *I*
8:16 David to be over My people *I*.
8:17 the name of the LORD God of *I*.
8:20 and sit on the throne of *I*,
8:20 the name of the LORD God of *I*.
8:22 of all the assembly of *I*,
8:23 and he said: "LORD God of *I*,
8:25 "Therefore, LORD God of *I*,
8:25 before Me on the throne of *I*,
8:26 "And now I pray, O God of *I*,
8:30 servant and of Your people *I*,
8:33 When Your people *I* are defeated
8:34 the sin of Your people *I*,
8:36 of Your servants, Your people *I*,
8:38 or by all Your people *I*,
8:41 who is not of Your people *I*,
8:43 fear You, as do Your people *I*,
8:52 supplication of Your people *I*,
8:55 blessed all the assembly of *I*
8:56 has given rest to His people *I*,
8:59 and the cause of His people *I*,
8:62 Then the king and all *I* with
8:63 king and all the children of *I*
8:65 and all *I* with him, a great
8:66 and for *I* His people.
9: 5 throne of your kingdom over *I*
9: 5 have a man on the throne of *I*.'
9: 7 then I will cut off *I* from the
9: 7 *I* will be a proverb and a
9:20 were not of the children of *I*—
9:21 whom the children of *I* had not
9:22 But of the children of *I* Solomon
10: 9 setting you on the throne of *I*!
10: 9 Because the LORD has loved *I*
11: 2 had said to the children of *I*,
11: 9 turned from the LORD God of *I*,
11:16 Joab remained there with all *I*,
11:25 He was an adversary of *I* all the
11:25 caused); and he abhorred *I*,
11:31 says the LORD, the God of *I*:
11:32 out of all the tribes of *I*),
11:37 and you shall be king over *I*.
11:38 and will give *I* to you.
11:42 in Jerusalem over all *I* was
12: 1 for all *I* had gone to Shechem
12: 3 and the whole assembly of *I*
12:16 Now when all *I* saw that the
12:16 O *I*! Now, see to your own
12:16 So *I* departed to their tents.
12:17 reigned over the children of *I*
12:18 but all *I* stoned him with
12:19 So *I* has been in rebellion
12:20 Now it came to pass when all *I*
12:20 and made him king over all *I*.
12:21 to fight against the house of *I*,
12:24 your brethren the children of *I*.
12:28 Here are your gods, O *I*,
12:33 a feast for the children of *I*,
14: 7 'Thus says the LORD God of *I*:
14: 7 made you ruler over My people *I*,
14:10 from Jeroboam every male in *I*,
14:13 And all *I* shall mourn for him
14:13 good toward the LORD God of *I*
14:14 up for Himself a king over *I*
14:15 "For the LORD will strike *I*,
14:15 He will uproot *I* from this good
14:16 And He will give *I* up because of
14:16 who sinned and who made *I*
14:18 and all *I* mourned for him,
14:19 chronicles of the kings of *I*.
14:21 out of all the tribes of *I*,
14:24 out before the children of *I*.
15: 9 year of Jeroboam king of *I*,
15:16 Asa and Baasha king of *I* all
15:17 And Baasha king of *I* came up
15:19 treaty with Baasha king of *I*,
15:20 armies against the cities of *I*.
15:25 of Jeroboam became king over *I*
15:25 and he reigned over *I* two
15:26 his sin by which he had made *I*
15:27 while Nadab and all *I* laid
15:30 and by which he had made *I* sin,
15:30 provoked the LORD God of *I* to
15:31 chronicles of the kings of *I*?
15:32 Asa and Baasha king of *I* all
15:33 Ahijah became king over all *I*
15:34 his sin by which he had made *I*
16: 2 made you ruler over My people *I*,
16: 2 and have made My people *I* sin,
16: 5 chronicles of the kings of *I*?
16: 8 of Baasha became king over *I*,
16:13 and by which they had made *I*
16:13 in provoking the LORD God of *I*
16:14 chronicles of the kings of *I*?
16:16 So all *I* made Omri, the
16:16 king over *I* that day in the
16:17 Then Omri and all *I* with him
16:19 he had committed to make *I* sin.
16:20 chronicles of the kings of *I*?
16:21 Then the people of *I* were
16:23 Judah, Omri became king over *I*,
16:26 his sin by which he had made *I*
16:26 provoking the LORD God of *I* to
16:27 chronicles of the kings of *I*?
16:29 son of Omri became king over *I*;
16:29 the son of Omri reigned over *I*
16:33 to provoke the LORD God of *I*

16:33 anger than all the kings of *I*
17: 1 As the LORD God of *I* lives,
17:14 thus says the LORD God of *I*:
18:17 that you, O troubler of *I*?
18:18 "I have not troubled *I*,
18:19 send and gather all *I* to me on
18:20 sent for all the children of *I*,
18:31 *I* shall be your name."
18:36 God of Abraham, Isaac, and *I*,
18:36 day that You are God in *I* and
19:10 for the children of *I* have
19:14 because the children of *I* have
19:16 son of Nimshi as king over *I*.
19:18 reserved seven thousand in *I*,
20: 2 into the city to Ahab king of *I*,
20: 4 And the king of *I* answered and
20: 7 So the king of *I* called all the
20:11 So the king of *I* answered and
20:13 approached Ahab king of *I*,
20:15 people, all the children of *I*—
20:20 and *I* pursued them; and
20:21 Then the king of *I* went out and
20:22 prophet came to the king of *I*
20:26 up to Aphek to fight against *I*.
20:27 And the children of *I* were
20:27 Now the children of *I* encamped
20:28 came and spoke to the king of *I*,
20:29 and the children of *I* killed
20:31 the kings of the house of *I*
20:31 and go out to the king of *I*;
20:32 and came to the king of *I* and
20:40 Then the king of *I* said to
20:41 and the king of *I* recognized
20:43 So the king of *I* went to his
21: 7 now exercise authority over *I*!
21:18 go down to meet Ahab king of *I*,
21:21 off from Ahab every male in *I*,
21:22 Me to anger, and made *I* sin.'
21:26 out before the children of *I*.
22: 1 without war between Syria and *I*.
22: 2 down to visit the king of *I*.
22: 3 And the king of *I* said to his
22: 4 said to the king of *I*,
22: 5 said to the king of *I*,
22: 6 Then the king of *I* gathered the
22: 8 So the king of *I* said to
22: 9 Then the king of *I* called an
22:10 The king of *I* and Jehoshaphat
22:17 I saw all *I* scattered on the
22:18 And the king of *I* said to
22:26 So the king of *I* said, "Take
22:29 So the king of *I* and
22:30 And the king of *I* said to
22:30 So the king of *I* disguised
22:31 but only with the king of *I*.
22:32 Surely it is the king of *I*!"
22:33 that it was not the king of *I*,
22:34 and struck the king of *I*
22:39 chronicles of the kings of *I*?
22:41 fourth year of Ahab king of *I*.
22:44 made peace with the king of *I*.
22:51 son of Ahab became king over *I*
22:51 and reigned two years over *I*.
22:52 who had made *I* sin;
22:53 provoked the LORD God of *I* to
2 Ki 1: 1 Moab rebelled against *I* after
1: 3 because there is no God in *I*
1: 6 because there is no God in *I*
1:16 because there is no God in *I*
1:18 chronicles of the kings of *I*?
2:12 the chariot of *I* and its
3: 1 son of Ahab became king over *I*
3: 3 who had made *I* sin; he did not
3: 4 he regularly paid the king of *I*
3: 5 rebelled against the king of *I*.
3: 6 at that time and mustered all *I*.
3: 9 So the king of *I* went with the
3:10 And the king of *I* said, "Alas!
3:11 the servants of the king of *I*
3:12 So the king of *I* and
3:13 Elisha said to the king of *I*,
3:13 But the king of *I* said to
3:24 when they came to the camp of *I*,
3:24 *I* rose up and attacked the
3:27 was great indignation against *I*.
5: 2 a young girl from the land of *I*.
5: 4 girl who is from the land of *I*.
5: 5 send a letter to the king of *I*.
5: 6 the letter to the king of *I*,
5: 7 when the king of *I* read the
5: 8 of God heard that the king of *I*
5: 8 that there is a prophet in *I*.
5:12 better than all the waters of *I*?
5:15 in all the earth, except in *I*;
6: 8 Syria was making war against *I*;
6: 9 of God sent to the king of *I*,
6:10 Then the king of *I* sent someone
6:11 of us is for the king of *I*?
6:12 the prophet who is in *I*,
6:12 tells the king of *I* the words
6:21 Now when the king of *I* saw them,
6:23 came no more into the land of *I*.
6:26 as the king of *I* was passing by
7: 6 the king of *I* has hired against
7:13 like all the multitude of *I*
7:13 like all the multitude of *I*
8:12 will do to the children of *I*:
8:16 the son of Ahab, king of *I*,
8:18 in the way of the kings of *I*,
8:25 the son of Ahab, king of *I*,
8:26 of Omri, king of *I*.
9: 3 have anointed you king over *I*.
9: 6 "Thus says the LORD God of *I*:
9: 6 the people of the LORD, over *I*.
9: 8 from Ahab all the males in *I*,
9:12 have anointed you king over *I*.
9:14 Ramoth Gilead, he and all *I*,
9:21 Then Joram king of *I* and
10:21 Then Jehu sent throughout all *I*;
10:28 Thus Jehu destroyed Baal from *I*.
10:29 who had made *I* sin, that is,
10:30 shall sit on the throne of *I*
10:31 the law of the LORD God of *I*
10:31 who had made *I* sin.
10:32 began to cut off parts of *I*;
10:32 them in all the territory of *I*
10:34 chronicles of the kings of *I*?
10:36 that Jehu reigned over *I* in
13: 1 son of Jehu became king over *I*
13: 2 who had made *I* sin. He did not
13: 3 the LORD was aroused against *I*,
13: 4 for He saw the oppression of *I*,
13: 5 Then the LORD gave *I* a
13: 5 and the children of *I* dwelt in
13: 6 who had made *I* sin, but walked
13: 8 chronicles of the kings of *I*?
13:10 of Jehoahaz became king over *I*
13:11 who made *I* sin, but walked in
13:12 chronicles of the kings of *I*?
13:13 in Samaria with the kings of *I*.
13:14 Then Joash the king of *I* came
13:14 the chariots of *I* and their
13:16 Then he said to the king of *I*,
13:18 And he said to the king of *I*,
13:22 king of Syria oppressed *I* all
13:25 and recaptured the cities of *I*.
14: 1 the son of Jehoahaz, king of *I*,
14: 8 the son of Jehu, king of *I*,
14: 9 And Jehoash king of *I* sent to
14:11 Therefore Jehoash king of *I*
14:12 And Judah was defeated by *I*,
14:13 Then Jehoash king of *I* captured
14:15 chronicles of the kings of *I*?
14:16 in Samaria with the kings of *I*.
14:17 the son of Jehoahaz, king of *I*.
14:23 the son of Joash, king of *I*,
14:24 who had made *I* sin.
14:25 He restored the territory of *I*
14:25 the word of the LORD God of *I*,
14:26 saw that the affliction of *I*
14:26 free, there was no helper for *I*.
14:27 He would blot out the name of *I*
14:28 and how he recaptured for *I*,
14:28 chronicles of the kings of *I*?
14:29 his fathers, the kings of *I*.
15: 1 year of Jeroboam king of *I*,
15: 8 son of Jeroboam reigned over *I*
15: 9 Nebat, who had made *I* sin.
15:11 chronicles of the kings of *I*.
15:12 shall sit on the throne of *I*
15:15 chronicles of the kings of *I*.
15:17 son of Gadi became king over *I*,
15:18 Nebat, who had made *I* sin.
15:20 exacted the money from *I*,
15:21 chronicles of the kings of *I*?
15:23 of Menahem became king over *I*
15:24 Nebat, who had made *I* sin.
15:26 chronicles of the kings of *I*.
15:27 of Remaliah became king over *I*
15:28 Nebat, who had made *I* sin.
15:29 In the days of Pekah king of *I*,
15:31 chronicles of the kings of *I*.
15:32 the son of Remaliah, king of *I*,
16: 3 in the way of the kings of *I*;
16: 3 from before the children of *I*.
16: 5 the son of Remaliah, king of *I*,
16: 7 from the hand of the king of *I*,
17: 1 son of Elah became king of *I*
17: 2 but not as the kings of *I* who
17: 6 took Samaria and carried *I*
17: 7 it was that the children of *I*
17: 8 from before the children of *I*,
17: 8 Israel, and of the kings of *I*,
17: 9 Also the children of *I* secretly
17:13 the LORD testified against *I*
17:18 the LORD was very angry with *I*,
17:19 but walked in the statutes of *I*
17:20 all the descendants of *I*,
17:21 For He tore *I* from the house of
17:21 Then Jeroboam drove *I* from
17:22 For the children of *I* walked in
17:23 until the LORD removed *I* out of
17:23 So *I* was carried away from
17:24 instead of the children of *I*;
17:34 of Jacob, whom He named *I*,
18: 1 the son of Elah, king of *I*,
18: 4 those days the children of *I*
18: 5 trusted in the LORD God of *I*,
18: 9 the son of Elah, king of *I*,
18:10 ninth year of Hoshea king of *I*,
18:11 the king of Assyria carried *I*
19:15 and said: "O LORD God of *I*,
19:20 "Thus says the LORD God of *I*:
19:22 Against the Holy One of *I*.
21: 2 out before the children of *I*.
21: 3 as Ahab king of *I* had done; and
21: 7 out of all the tribes of *I*,
21: 8 I will not make the feet of *I*
21: 9 before the children of *I*.
21:12 thus says the LORD God of *I*:
22:15 "Thus says the LORD God of *I*,
22:18 'Thus says the LORD God of *I*:
23:13 which Solomon king of *I* had
23:15 who made *I* sin, had made, both
23:19 which the kings of *I* had made
23:22 days of the judges who judged *I*,
23:22 all the days of the kings of *I*
23:27 My sight, as I have removed *I*,
24:13 of gold which Solomon king of *I*
1 Chr 1:34 sons of Isaac were Esau and *I*.
1:43 reigned over the children of *I*:
2: 1 These were the sons of *I*:
2: 7 was Achar, the troubler of *I*,
4:10 Jabez called on the God of *I*
5: 1 of Reuben the firstborn of *I*—
5: 1 sons of Joseph, the son of *I*,
5: 3 of Reuben the firstborn of *I*
5:17 the days of Jeroboam king of *I*.
5:26 So the God of *I* stirred up the
6:38 the son of Levi, the son of *I*.
6:49 and to make atonement for *I*,
6:64 So the children of *I* gave these
7:29 of Joseph, the son of *I*.
9: 1 So all *I* was recorded by
9: 1 in the book of the kings of *I*.
10: 1 Philistines fought against *I*;
10: 1 and the men of *I* fled from
10: 7 And when all the men of *I* who
11: 1 Then all *I* came together to
11: 2 you were the one who led *I* out
11: 2 'You shall shepherd My people *I*,
11: 2 and be ruler over My people *I*.
11: 3 Therefore all the elders of *I*
11: 3 they anointed David king over *I*,
11: 4 And David and all *I* went to
11:10 him in his kingdom, with all *I*,
11:10 word of the LORD concerning *I*.
12:32 to know what *I* ought to do,
12:38 to make David king over all *I*;
12:38 and all the rest of *I* were of
12:40 for there was joy in *I*.
13: 2 said to all the assembly of *I*,
13: 2 are left in all the land of *I*,
13: 5 So David gathered all *I*
13: 6 And David and all *I* went up to
13: 8 Then David and all *I* played
14: 2 established him as king over *I*,
14: 2 for the sake of His people *I*.
14: 8 been anointed king over all *I*,
15: 3 And David gathered all *I*
15:12 the ark of the LORD God of *I*
15:14 the ark of the LORD God of *I*.
15:25 So David, the elders of *I*,
15:28 Thus all *I* brought up the ark of
16: 3 he distributed to everyone of *I*,
16: 4 to praise the LORD God of *I*:
16:13 O seed of *I* His servant, You
16:17 To *I* for an everlasting
16:36 be the LORD God of *I* From
16:40 the LORD which He commanded *I*;
17: 5 the time that I brought up *I*,
17: 6 I have moved about with all *I*,
17: 6 word to any of the judges of *I*,
17: 7 to be ruler over My people *I*.
17: 9 appoint a place for My people *I*,
17:10 judges to be over My people *I*.
17:21 who is like Your people *I*,
17:22 You have made Your people *I*
17:24 LORD of hosts, the God of *I*,
18:14 So David reigned over all *I*,
19:16 they had been defeated by *I*,
19:17 told David, he gathered all *I*,
19:18 Then the Syrians fled before *I*;
19:19 that they were defeated by *I*,
20: 7 So when he defied *I*,
21: 1 Now Satan stood up against *I*,
21: 1 and moved David to number *I*.
21: 2 number *I* from Beersheba to Dan,
21: 3 he be a cause of guilt in *I*?
21: 4 and went throughout all *I* and
21: 5 All *I* had one million one
21: 7 therefore He struck *I*.
21:12 all the territory of *I*.
21:14 the LORD sent a plague upon *I*,
21:14 and seventy thousand men of *I*
22: 1 altar of burnt offering for *I*.
22: 2 who were in the land of *I*;
22: 6 a house for the LORD God of *I*.
22: 9 give peace and quietness to *I*
22:10 throne of his kingdom over *I*
22:12 give you charge concerning *I*,
22:13 charged Moses concerning *I*.
22:17 commanded all the leaders of *I*
23: 1 his son Solomon king over *I*.
23: 2 together all the leaders of *I*,
23:25 The LORD God of *I* has given
24:19 as the LORD God of *I* had
26:29 as officials and judges over *I*
26:30 had the oversight of *I* on the
27: 1 And the children of *I*,
27:16 over the tribes of *I*:
27:22 the leaders of the tribes of *I*.
27:23 had said He would multiply *I*
27:24 for wrath came upon *I* because
28: 1 Jerusalem all the leaders of *I*:
28: 4 However the LORD God of *I* chose
28: 4 of my father to be king over *I*
28: 4 me to make me king over all *I*.
28: 5 the kingdom of the LORD over *I*.
28: 8 in the sight of all *I*,
29: 6 leaders of the tribes of *I*,
29:10 are You, LORD God of *I*,
29:18 God of Abraham, Isaac, and *I*,
29:21 in abundance for all *I*.
29:23 and all *I* obeyed him.
29:25 in the sight of all *I*,

29:25 on any king before him in *I*.
29:26 son of Jesse reigned over all *I*.
29:27 period that he reigned over *I*
29:30 that happened to him, to *I*,
2 Chr 1: 2 And Solomon spoke to all *I*,
1: 2 and to every leader in all *I*,
1:13 of meeting, and reigned over *I*.
2: 4 is an ordinance forever to *I*.
2:12 Blessed be the LORD God of *I*,
2:17 who were in the land of *I*,
5: 2 assembled the elders of *I* and
5: 2 fathers of the children of *I*,
5: 3 Therefore all the men of *I*
5: 4 So all the elders of *I* came, and
5: 6 and all the congregation of *I*
5:10 with the children of *I*,
6: 3 blessed the whole assembly of *I*,
6: 3 while all the assembly of *I* was
6: 4 be the LORD God of *I*,
6: 5 no city from any tribe of *I*
6: 5 to be a ruler over My people *I*.
6: 6 David to be over My people *I*.
6: 7 the name of the LORD God of *I*.
6:10 and sit on the throne of *I*,
6:10 the name of the LORD God of *I*.
6:11 He made with the children of *I*.
6:12 of all the assembly of *I*,
6:13 before all the assembly of *I*,
6:14 and he said: "LORD God of *I*,
6:16 "Therefore, LORD God of *I*,
6:16 before Me on the throne of *I*,
6:17 "And now, O LORD God of *I*,
6:21 servant and of Your people *I*,
6:24 Or if Your people *I* are
6:25 the sin of Your people *I*,
6:27 of Your servants, Your people *I*,
6:29 anyone, or by all Your people *I*,
6:32 who is not of Your people *I*,
6:33 fear You, as do Your people *I*,
7: 3 When all the children of *I* saw
7: 6 them, while all *I* stood.
7: 8 and all *I* with him, a very
7:10 Solomon, and for His people *I*.
7:18 to have a man as ruler in *I*.
8: 2 he settled the children of *I*
8: 7 Jebusites, who were not of *I*—
8: 8 whom the children of *I* did not
8: 9 did not make the children of *I*
8:11 in the house of David king of *I*,
9: 8 Because your God has loved *I*,
9:30 in Jerusalem over all *I* forty
10: 1 for all *I* had gone to Shechem
10: 3 And Jeroboam and all *I* came and
10:16 Now when all *I* saw that the
10:16 O *I*! Now see to your own
10:16 So all *I* departed to their
10:17 reigned over the children of *I*
10:18 but the children of *I* stoned
10:19 So *I* has been in rebellion
11: 1 warriors, to fight against *I*,
11: 3 and to all *I* in Judah and
11:13 the Levites who were in all *I*
11:16 those from all the tribes of *I*,
11:16 to seek the LORD God of *I*,
12: 1 and all *I* along with him.
12: 6 So the leaders of *I* and the king
12:13 out of all the tribes of *I*,
13: 4 "Hear me, Jeroboam and all *I*:
13: 5 know that the LORD God of *I*
13: 5 gave the dominion over *I* to
13:12 against you. O children of *I*,
13:15 God struck Jeroboam and all *I*
13:16 And the children of *I* fled
13:17 thousand choice men of *I* fell
13:18 Thus the children of *I* were
15: 3 For a long time *I* has been
15: 4 turned to the LORD God of *I*,
15: 9 to him in great numbers from *I*
15:13 not seek the LORD God of *I*
15:17 places were not removed from *I*.
16: 1 Baasha king of *I* came up
16: 3 treaty with Baasha king of *I*,
16: 4 armies against the cities of *I*.
16:11 of the kings of Judah and *I*.
17: 1 strengthened himself against *I*.
17: 4 not according to the acts of *I*.
18: 3 So Ahab king of *I* said to
18: 4 said to the king of *I*,
18: 5 Then the king of *I* gathered the
18: 7 So the king of *I* said to
18: 8 Then the king of *I* called one
18: 9 The king of *I* and Jehoshaphat
18:16 I saw all *I* scattered on the
18:17 And the king of *I* said to
18:19 will persuade Ahab king of *I*
18:25 Then the king of *I* said, "Take
18:28 So the king of *I* and
18:29 And the king of *I* said to
18:29 So the king of *I* disguised
18:30 but only with the king of *I*.
18:31 It is the king of *I*!"
18:32 that it was not the king of *I*,
18:33 and struck the king of *I*
18:34 and the king of *I* propped
19: 8 some of the chief fathers of *I*,
20: 7 this land before Your people *I*,
20:10 whom You would not let *I* invade
20:19 up to praise the LORD God of *I*
20:29 fought against the enemies of *I*.
20:34 in the book of the kings of *I*.
20:35 himself with Ahaziah king of *I*,
21: 2 sons of Jehoshaphat king of *I*.
21: 4 others of the princes of *I*.
21: 6 in the way of the kings of *I*,
21:13 in the way of the kings of *I*,
22: 5 the son of Ahab king of *I* to
23: 2 and the chief fathers of *I*,
24: 5 and gather from all *I* money to
24: 6 LORD and of the assembly of *I*,
24: 9 of God had imposed on *I* in
24:16 because he had done good in *I*,
25: 6 mighty men of valor from *I* for
25: 7 do not let the army of *I* go
25: 7 for the LORD is not with *I*—
25: 9 I have given to the troops of *I*?
25:17 the son of Jehu, king of *I*,
25:18 And Joash king of *I* sent to
25:21 So Joash king of *I* went out;
25:22 And Judah was defeated by *I*,
25:23 Then Joash the king of *I*
25:25 the son of Jehoahaz, king of *I*.
25:26 of the kings of Judah and *I*?
27: 7 in the book of the kings of *I*
28: 2 in the ways of the kings of *I*,
28: 3 out before the children of *I*.
28: 5 into the hand of the king of *I*,
28: 8 And the children of *I* carried
28:13 is fierce wrath against *I*.
28:19 low because of Ahaz king of *I*,
28:23 the ruin of him and of all *I*.
28:26 of the kings of Judah and *I*.
28:27 the tombs of the kings of *I*.
29: 7 the holy place to the God of *I*.
29:10 with the LORD God of *I*,
29:24 to make an atonement for all *I*,
29:24 offering be made for all *I*.
29:27 instruments of David king of *I*.
30: 1 And Hezekiah sent to all *I* and
30: 1 Passover to the LORD God of *I*.
30: 5 a proclamation throughout all *I*,
30: 5 Passover to the LORD God of *I*
30: 6 runners went throughout all *I*
30: 6 of the king: "Children of *I*,
30: 6 God of Abraham, Isaac, and *I*;
30:21 So the children of *I* who were
30:25 the assembly that came from *I*,
30:25 who came from the land of *I*,
30:26 the son of David, king of *I*,
31: 1 all *I* who were present went out
31: 1 Then all the children of *I*
31: 5 the children of *I* brought in
31: 6 And the children of *I* and Judah,
31: 8 the LORD and His people *I*.
32:17 to revile the LORD God of *I*,
32:32 of the kings of Judah and *I*.
33: 2 out before the children of *I*.
33: 7 out of all the tribes of *I*,
33: 8 not again remove the foot of *I*
33: 9 before the children of *I*.
33:16 to serve the LORD God of *I*.
33:18 the name of the LORD God of *I*,
33:18 in the book of the kings of *I*.
34: 7 throughout all the land of *I*,
34: 9 from all the remnant of *I*,
34:21 and for those who are left in *I*
34:23 "Thus says the LORD God of *I*,
34:26 'Thus says the LORD God of *I*:
34:33 belonged to the children of *I*,
34:33 made all who were present in *I*
35: 3 to the Levites who taught all *I*,
35: 3 the son of David, king of *I*,
35: 3 LORD your God and His people *I*.
35: 4 instruction of David king of *I*
35:17 And the children of *I* who were
35:18 had been no Passover kept in *I*
35:18 and none of the kings of *I* had
35:18 all Judah and *I* who were
35:25 They made it a custom in *I*;
35:27 in the book of the kings of *I*
36: 8 in the book of the kings of *I*
36:13 turning to the LORD God of *I*.
Ezra 1: 3 the house of the LORD God of *I*
2: 2 of the men of the people of *I*:
2:59 whether they were of *I*:
2:70 and all *I* in their cities.
3: 1 and the children of *I* were in
3: 2 built the altar of the God of *I*,
3:10 ordinance of David king of *I*.
3:11 mercy endures forever toward *I*.
4: 1 temple of the LORD God of *I*,
4: 3 of the fathers' houses of *I*
4: 3 build to the LORD God of *I*,
5: 1 in the name of the God of *I*,
5:11 which a great king of *I* built
6:14 the commandment of the God of *I*,
6:16 Then the children of *I*,
6:17 and as a sin offering for all *I*
6:17 the number of the tribes of *I*.
6:21 Then the children of *I* who had
6:21 to seek the LORD God of *I*.
6:22 the house of God, the God of *I*.
7: 6 which the LORD God of *I* had
7: 7 Some of the children of *I*,
7:10 statutes and ordinances in *I*.
7:11 LORD, and of His statutes to *I*:
7:13 all those of the people of *I*
7:15 freely offered to the God of *I*,
7:28 I gathered leading men of *I* to
8:18 the son of Levi, the son of *I*,
8:25 and all *I* who were present,
8:29 of the fathers' houses of *I*
8:35 burnt offerings to the God of *I*:
8:35 Israel: twelve bulls for all *I*,
9: 1 The people of *I* and the priests
9: 4 at the words of the God of *I*
9:15 "O LORD God of *I*,
10: 1 children gathered to him from *I*;
10: 2 yet now there is hope in *I* in
10: 5 and all *I* swear an oath that
10:10 wives, adding to the guilt of *I*.
10:25 And others of *I*: of the sons
Neh 1: 6 for the children of *I* Your
1: 6 the sins of the children of *I*
2:10 well-being of the children of *I*.
7: 7 of the men of the people of *I*:
7:61 whether they were of *I*:
7:73 and all *I* dwelt in their
7:73 the children of *I* were in
8: 1 which the LORD had commanded *I*.
8:14 that the children of *I* should
8:17 that day the children of *I* had
9: 1 of this month the children of *I*
10:33 to make atonement for *I*,
10:39 For the children of *I* and the
11:20 And the rest of *I*, of the
12:47 in the days of Nehemiah all *I*
13: 2 had not met the children of *I*
13: 3 all the mixed multitude from *I*.
13:18 Yet you bring added wrath on *I*
13:26 Did not Solomon king of *I* sin by
13:26 God made him king over all *I*.
Ps 14: 7 that the salvation of *I* would
14: 7 Let Jacob rejoice and *I* be
22: 3 Enthroned in the praises of *I*.
22:23 all you offspring of *I*!
25:22 Redeem *I*, O God,
41:13 be the LORD God of *I* From
50: 7 people, and I will speak, O *I*,
53: 6 that the salvation of *I* would
53: 6 Let Jacob rejoice and *I* be
59: 5 God of hosts, the God of *I*,
68: 8 presence of God, the God of *I*.
68:26 Lord, from the fountain of *I*.
68:34 His excellence is over *I*,
68:35 The God of *I* is He who gives
69: 6 because of me, O God of *I*.
71:22 with the harp, O Holy One of *I*.
72:18 be the LORD God, the God of *I*,
73: 1 Truly God is good to *I*,
76: 1 His name is great in *I*.
78: 5 And appointed a law in *I*,
78:21 anger also came up against *I*,
78:31 down the choice men of *I*.
78:41 And limited the Holy One of *I*.
78:55 And made the tribes of *I* dwell
78:59 And greatly abhorred *I*,
78:71 And *I* His inheritance.
80: 1 Give ear, O Shepherd of *I*,
81: 4 For this is a statute for *I*,
81: 8 and I will admonish you! O *I*,
81:11 And *I* would have none of Me.
81:13 That *I* would walk in My ways!
83: 4 That the name of *I* may be
89:18 our king to the Holy One of *I*.
98: 3 faithfulness to the house of *I*;
103: 7 His acts to the children of *I*.
105:10 To *I* as an everlasting
105:23 *I* also came into Egypt, And
106:48 be the LORD God of *I* From
114: 1 When *I* went out of Egypt, The
114: 2 And *I* His dominion.
115: 9 O *I*, trust in the LORD;
115:12 He will bless the house of *I*;
118: 2 Let *I* now say, "His mercy
121: 4 He who keeps *I* Shall neither
122: 4 LORD, To the Testimony of *I*,
124: 1 on our side," Let *I* now say—
125: 5 Peace be upon *I*!
128: 6 Peace be upon *I*!
129: 1 my youth," Let *I* now say—
130: 7 O *I*, hope in the LORD;
130: 8 And He shall redeem *I* From all
131: 3 O *I*, hope in the LORD
135: 4 *I* for His special treasure.
135:12 A heritage to *I* His people.
135:19 O house of *I*! Bless the LORD,
136:11 And brought out *I* from among
136:14 And made *I* pass through the
136:22 A heritage to *I* His servant,
147: 2 together the outcasts of *I*.
147:19 statutes and His judgments to *I*.
148:14 saints—Of the children of *I*,
149: 2 Let *I* rejoice in their Maker;
Prov 1: 1 the son of David, king of *I*:
Eccl 1:12 was king over *I* in Jerusalem.
Song 3: 7 around it, Of the valiant of *I*.
Isa 1: 3 But *I* does not know, My
1: 4 to anger The Holy One of *I*,
1:24 of hosts, the Mighty One of *I*,
4: 2 and appealing For those of *I*
5: 7 of hosts is the house of *I*,
5:19 counsel of the Holy One of *I*
5:24 the word of the Holy One of *I*.
7: 1 the son of Remaliah, king of *I*,
8:14 To both the houses of *I*,
8:18 are for signs and wonders in *I*
9: 8 Jacob, And it has fallen on *I*.
9:12 And they shall devour *I* with
9:14 cut off head and tail from *I*,
10:17 So the Light of *I* will be for a
10:20 day That the remnant of *I*,
10:20 on the LORD, the Holy One of *I*,
10:22 For though your people, O *I*,
11:12 will assemble the outcasts of *I*,
11:16 As it was for *I* In the day
12: 6 great is the Holy One of *I* in

I

14: 1 Jacob, and will still choose *I*,
14: 2 and the house of *I* will possess
17: 3 the glory of the children of *I*,
17: 6 Says the LORD God of *I*.
17: 7 respect for the Holy One of *I*.
17: 9 because of the children of *I*;
19:24 In that day *I* will be one of
19:25 and *I* My inheritance."
21:10 LORD of hosts, The God of *I*,
21:17 for the LORD God of *I* has
24:15 name of the LORD God of *I* in
27: 6 *I* shall blossom and bud, And
27: 7 Has He struck *I* as He struck
27:12 by one, O you children of *I*.
29:19 rejoice In the Holy One of *I*.
29:23 Jacob, And fear the God of *I*.
30:11 Cause the Holy One of *I* To
30:12 thus says the Holy One of *I*:
30:15 Lord GOD, the Holy One of *I*:
30:29 LORD, To the Mighty One of *I*.
31: 1 not look to the Holy One of *I*,
31: 6 against whom the children of *I*
37:16 "O LORD of hosts, God of *I*,
37:21 "Thus says the LORD God of *I*,
37:23 Against the Holy One of *I*.
40:27 say, O Jacob, And speak, O *I*:
41: 8 But you, *I*, are My
41:14 You men of *I*! I will help
41:14 Redeemer, the Holy One of *I*.
41:16 glory in the Holy One of *I*.
41:17 hear them; I, the God of *I*,
41:20 And the Holy One of *I* has
42:24 and *I* to the robbers? Was it
43: 1 And He who formed you, O *I*:
43: 3 your God, The Holy One of *I*,
43:14 Redeemer, The Holy One of *I*:
43:15 Holy One, The Creator of *I*,
43:22 you have been weary of Me, O *I*.
43:28 And *I* to reproaches.
44: 1 And *I* whom I have chosen.
44: 5 name himself by the name of *I*.
44: 6 says the LORD, the King of *I*,
44:21 these, O Jacob, And *I*,
44:21 you, you are My servant; O *I*,
44:23 And glorified Himself in *I*.
45: 3 by your name, Am the God of *I*.
45: 4 And *I* My elect, I have even
45:11 the LORD, The Holy One of *I*,
45:15 who hide Yourself, O God of *I*,
45:17 But *I* shall be saved by the
45:25 LORD all the descendants of *I*
46: 3 the remnant of the house of *I*,
46:13 in Zion, For *I* My glory.
47: 4 His name, The Holy One of *I*.
48: 1 are called by the name of *I*,
48: 1 make mention of the God of *I*,
48: 2 city, And lean on the God of *I*;
48:12 to Me, O Jacob, And *I*,
48:17 Redeemer, The Holy One of *I*:
49: 3 me, 'You are My servant, O *I*,
49: 5 So that *I* is gathered to Him
49: 6 restore the preserved ones of *I*;
49: 7 the LORD, The Redeemer of *I*,
49: 7 is faithful, The Holy One of *I*;
52:12 And the God of *I* will be
54: 5 Redeemer is the Holy One of *I*;
55: 5 God, And the Holy One of *I*;
56: 8 who gathers the outcasts of *I*,
60: 9 God, And to the Holy One of *I*,
60:14 Zion of the Holy One of *I*.
63: 7 goodness toward the house of *I*,
63:16 And *I* does not acknowledge us.
66:20 as the children of *I* bring an
Jer 2: 3 *I* was holiness to the LORD,
2: 4 the families of the house of *I*.
2:14 Is *I* a servant? Is he a
2:26 So is the house of *I* ashamed;
2:31 Have I been a wilderness to *I*,
3: 6 you seen what backsliding *I*
3: 8 causes for which backsliding *I*
3:11 Backsliding *I* has shown herself
3:12 say: 'Return, backsliding *I*,
3:18 shall walk with the house of *I*,
3:20 with Me, O house of *I*,
3:21 of the children of *I*.
3:23 our God Is the salvation of *I*.
4: 1 "If you will return, O *I*,
5:11 For the house of *I* and the
5:15 you from afar, O house of *I*,
6: 9 as a vine the remnant of *I*;
7: 3 LORD of hosts, the God of *I*:
7:12 the wickedness of My people *I*.
7:21 LORD of hosts, the God of *I*:
9:15 LORD of hosts, the God of *I*:
9:26 and all the house of *I* are
10: 1 speaks to you, O house of *I*.
10:16 And *I* is the tribe of His
11: 3 'Thus says the LORD God of *I*:
11:10 the house of *I* and the house of
11:17 for the evil of the house of *I*
12:14 I have caused My people *I* to
13:11 caused the whole house of *I*
13:12 'Thus says the LORD God of *I*:
14: 8 O the Hope of *I*, his Savior
16: 9 LORD of hosts, the God of *I*:
16:14 brought up the children of *I*
16:15 brought up the children of *I*
17:13 O LORD, the hope of *I*,
18: 6 'O house of *I*, can I not do
18: 6 in My hand, O house of *I*!
18:13 The virgin of *I* has done a
19: 3 LORD of hosts, the God of *I*:

19:15 LORD of hosts, the God of *I*:
21: 4 'Thus says the LORD God of *I*:
23: 2 thus says the LORD God of *I*
23: 6 And *I* will dwell safely; Now
23: 7 brought up the children of *I*
23: 8 descendants of the house of *I*
23:13 by Baal And caused My people *I*
24: 5 says the LORD, the God of *I*:
25:15 thus says the LORD God of *I*
25:27 LORD of hosts, the God of *I*:
27: 4 LORD of hosts, the God of *I*—
27:21 LORD of hosts, the God of *I*,
28: 2 LORD of hosts, the God of *I*,
28:14 LORD of hosts, the God of *I*:
29: 4 LORD of hosts, the God of *I*,
29: 8 LORD of hosts, the God of *I*:
29:21 LORD of hosts, the God of *I*,
29:23 done disgraceful things in *I*,
29:25 LORD of hosts, the God of *I*,
30: 2 speaks the LORD God of *I*,
30: 3 from captivity My people *I* and
30: 4 the LORD spoke concerning *I*
30:10 LORD, 'Nor be dismayed, O *I*;
31: 1 God of all the families of *I*,
31: 2 grace in the wilderness—*I*,
31: 4 O virgin of *I*! You shall
31: 7 The remnant of *I*!'
31: 9 For I am a Father to *I*,
31:10 He who scattered *I* will gather
31:21 Turn back, O virgin of *I*,
31:23 LORD of hosts, the God of *I*:
31:27 that I will sow the house of *I*
31:31 covenant with the house of *I*
31:33 I will make with the house of *I*
31:36 Then the seed of *I* shall also
31:37 also cast off all the seed of *I*
32:14 LORD of hosts, the God of *I*:
32:15 LORD of hosts, the God of *I*:
32:20 and in *I* and among other men;
32:21 'You have brought Your people *I*
32:30 because the children of *I* and
32:30 For the children of *I* have
32:32 the evil of the children of *I*
32:36 says the LORD, the God of *I*,
33: 4 says the LORD, the God of *I*,
33: 7 of Judah and the captives of *I*
33:14 promised to the house of *I* and
33:17 on the throne of the house of *I*;
34: 2 says the LORD, the God of *I*:
34:13 says the LORD, the God of *I*:
35:13 LORD of hosts, the God of *I*:
35:17 God of hosts, the God of *I*:
35:18 LORD of hosts, the God of *I*:
35:19 LORD of hosts, the God of *I*:
36: 2 I have spoken to you against *I*,
37: 7 says the LORD, the God of *I*,
38:17 the God of hosts, the God of *I*:
39:16 LORD of hosts, the God of *I*:
41: 9 for fear of Baasha king of *I*.
42: 9 says the LORD, the God of *I*,
42:15 LORD of hosts, the God of *I*:
42:18 LORD of hosts, the God of *I*:
43:10 LORD of hosts, the God of *I*:
44: 2 LORD of hosts, the God of *I*:
44: 7 the God of hosts, the God of *I*:
44:11 LORD of hosts, the God of *I*:
44:25 LORD of hosts, the God of *I*,
45: 2 says the LORD, the God of *I*,
46:25 LORD of hosts, the God of *I*,
46:27 O *I*! For behold, I will save
48: 1 LORD of hosts, the God of *I*:
48:13 As the house of *I* was ashamed
48:27 For was not *I* a derision to
49: 1 Has *I* no sons? Has he no heir?
49: 2 Then *I* shall take possession
50: 4 The children of *I* shall come,
50:17 *I* is like scattered sheep;
50:18 LORD of hosts, the God of *I*:
50:19 But I will bring back *I* to his
50:20 The iniquity of *I* shall be
50:29 Against the Holy One of *I*.
50:33 The children of *I* were
51: 5 For *I* is not forsaken, nor
51: 5 sin against the Holy One of *I*.
51:19 And *I* is the tribe of His
51:33 LORD of hosts, the God of *I*:
51:49 has caused the slain of *I* to
Lam 2: 1 to the earth The beauty of *I*,
2: 3 fierce anger Every horn of *I*;
2: 5 He has swallowed up *I*,
Ezek 2: 3 you to the children of *I*,
3: 1 and go, speak to the house of *I*.
3: 4 go to the house of *I* and speak
3: 5 but to the house of *I*,
3: 7 But the house of *I* will not
3: 7 for all the house of *I* are
3:17 a watchman for the house of *I*;
4: 3 be a sign to the house of *I*.
4: 4 the iniquity of the house of *I*
4: 5 the iniquity of the house of *I*.
4:13 So shall the children of *I* eat
5: 4 go out into all the house of *I*.
6: 2 face toward the mountains of *I*,
6: 3 "and say, 'O mountains of *I*,
6: 5 corpses of the children of *I*
6:11 abominations of the house of *I*!
7: 2 the Lord GOD to the land of *I*:
8: 4 the glory of the God of *I* was
8: 6 that the house of *I* commits
8:10 all the idols of the house of *I*,
8:11 of the elders of the house of *I*,
8:12 the elders of the house of *I*

9: 3 Now the glory of the God of *I*
9: 8 destroy all the remnant of *I*
9: 9 iniquity of the house of *I*
10:19 and the glory of the God of *I*
10:20 I saw under the God of *I* by
11: 5 you have said, O house of *I*;
11:10 judge you at the border of *I*.
11:11 judge you at the border of *I*.
11:13 end of the remnant of *I*?
11:15 and all the house of *I* in its
11:17 I will give you the land of *I*.
11:22 and the glory of the God of *I*
12: 6 you a sign to the house of *I*.
12: 9 of man, has not the house of *I*,
12:10 and all the house of *I* who are
12:19 Jerusalem and to the land of *I*:
12:22 have about the land of *I*,
12:23 more use it as a proverb in *I*.
12:24 within the house of *I*.
12:27 the house of *I* is saying, 'The
13: 2 against the prophets of *I* who
13: 4 'O *I*, your prophets are like
13: 5 a wall for the house of *I* to
13: 9 in the record of the house of *I*,
13: 9 they enter into the land of *I*.
13:16 the prophets of *I* who prophesy
14: 1 Now some of the elders of *I* came
14: 4 Everyone of the house of *I* who
14: 5 I may seize the house of *I* by
14: 6 say to the house of *I*,
14: 7 "For anyone of the house of *I*,
14: 7 of the strangers who dwell in *I*,
14: 9 him from among My people *I*.
14:11 that the house of *I* may no
17: 2 a parable to the house of *I*,
17:23 On the mountain height of *I* I
18: 2 concerning the land of *I*,
18: 3 no longer use this proverb in *I*.
18: 6 to the idols of the house of *I*,
18:15 to the idols of the house of *I*,
18:25 Hear now, O house of *I*,
18:29 Yet the house of *I* says, 'The
18:29 Lord is not fair.' O house of *I*,
18:30 I will judge you, O house of *I*,
18:31 should you die, O house of *I*?
19: 1 for the princes of *I*,
19: 9 be heard on the mountains of *I*.
20: 1 certain of the elders of *I*
20: 3 man, speak to the elders of *I*,
20: 5 On the day when I chose *I* and
20:13 Yet the house of *I* rebelled
20:27 of man, speak to the house of *I*,
20:30 say to the house of *I*,
20:31 of by you, O house of *I*?
20:38 shall not enter the land of *I*.
20:39 "As for you, O house of *I*,
20:40 on the mountain height of *I*,
20:40 "there all the house of *I*,
20:42 I bring you into the land of *I*,
20:44 corrupt doings, O house of *I*,
21: 2 prophesy against the land of *I*;
21: 3 "and say to the land of *I*,
21:12 Against all the princes of *I*.
21:25 O profane, wicked prince of *I*,
22: 6 "Look, the princes of *I*:
22:18 the house of *I* has become dross
24:21 'Speak to the house of *I*,
25: 3 and against the land of *I* when
25: 6 your disdain for the land of *I*,
25:14 Edom by the hand of My people *I*,
27:17 Judah and the land of *I* were
28:24 thorn for the house of *I* from
28:25 I have gathered the house of *I*
29: 6 staff of reed to the house of *I*.
29:16 confidence of the house of *I*,
29:21 the horn of the house of *I* to
33: 7 a watchman for the house of *I*;
33:10 of man, say to the house of *I*:
33:11 should you die, O house of *I*?
33:20 is not fair.' O house of *I*,
33:24 those ruins in the land of *I*
33:28 and the mountains of *I* shall be
34: 2 against the shepherds of *I*,
34: 2 Woe to the shepherds of *I* who
34:13 feed them on the mountains of *I*,
34:14 be on the high mountains of *I*.
34:14 pasture on the mountains of *I*.
34:30 them, and they, the house of *I*,
35: 5 blood of the children of *I*
35:12 against the mountains of *I*,
35:15 inheritance of the house of *I*
36: 1 prophesy to the mountains of *I*,
36: 1 and say, 'O mountains of *I*,
36: 4 'therefore, O mountains of *I*,
36: 6 concerning the land of *I*,
36: 8 "But you, O mountains of *I*,
36: 8 yield your fruit to My people *I*,
36:10 upon you, all the house of *I*,
36:12 men to walk on you, My people *I*;
36:17 when the house of *I* dwelt in
36:21 which the house of *I* had
36:22 say to the house of *I*,
36:22 for your sake, O house of *I*,
36:32 own ways, O house of *I*!"
36:37 will also let the house of *I*
37:11 bones are the whole house of *I*.
37:12 bring you into the land of *I*.
37:16 Judah and for the children of *I*,
37:16 and for all the house of *I*,
37:19 of Ephraim, and the tribes of *I*,
37:21 I will take the children of *I*
37:22 the land, on the mountains of *I*;

37:28 that I, the LORD, sanctify *I*,
38: 8 people on the mountains of *I*,
38:14 On that day when My people *I*
38:16 come up against My people *I*
38:17 My servants the prophets of *I*,
38:18 Gog comes against the land of *I*,
38:19 earthquake in the land of *I*,
39: 2 you against the mountains of *I*.
39: 4 fall upon the mountains of *I*,
39: 7 in the midst of My people *I*,
39: 7 the LORD, the Holy One in *I*.
39: 9 who dwell in the cities of *I*
39:11 Gog a burial place there in *I*,
39:12 seven months the house of *I*
39:17 meal on the mountains of *I*,
39:22 So the house of *I* shall know
39:23 shall know that the house of *I*
39:25 mercy on the whole house of *I*;
39:29 out My Spirit on the house of *I*,
40: 2 He took me into the land of *I*
40: 4 Declare to the house of *I*
43: 2 the glory of the God of *I* came
43: 7 the midst of the children of *I*
43: 7 No more shall the house of *I*
43:10 the temple to the house of *I*,
44: 2 because the LORD God of *I* has
44: 6 rebellious, to the house of *I*,
44: 6 the Lord GOD: "O house of *I*,
44: 9 who is among the children of *I*.
44:10 when *I* went astray, who strayed
44:12 and caused the house of *I* to
44:15 when the children of *I* went
44:22 descendants of the house of *I*,
44:28 give them no possession in *I*,
44:29 every dedicated thing in *I*
45: 6 belong to the whole house of *I*.
45: 8 shall be his possession in *I*;
45: 8 of the land to the house of *I*,
45: 9 O princes of *I*! Remove violence
45:15 from the rich pastures of *I*.
45:16 offering for the prince in *I*.
45:17 seasons of the house of *I*.
45:17 atonement for the house of *I*.
47:13 among the twelve tribes of *I*.
47:18 Gilead and the land of *I*,
47:21 according to the tribes of *I*.
47:22 among the children of *I*;
47:22 with you among the tribes of *I*.
48:11 astray when the children of *I*
48:19 city, from all the tribes of *I*,
48:29 among the tribes of *I*,
48:31 named after the tribes of *I*),
Dan 1: 3 some of the children of *I* and
9: 7 of Jerusalem and all *I*,
9:11 all *I* has transgressed Your
9:20 sin and the sin of my people *I*,
Hos 1: 1 the son of Joash, king of *I*.
1: 4 the kingdom of the house of *I*.
1: 5 I will break the bow of *I* in
1: 6 have mercy on the house of *I*,
1:10 the number of the children of *I*
1:11 of Judah and the children of *I*
3: 1 the LORD for the children of *I*,
3: 4 For the children of *I* shall
3: 5 Afterward the children of *I*
4: 1 the LORD, You children of *I*,
4:15 Though you, *I*, play the
4:16 For *I* is stubborn Like a
5: 1 O house of *I*! Give ear, O
5: 3 And *I* is not hidden from Me;
5: 3 harlotry; *I* is defiled.
5: 5 The pride of *I* testifies to his
5: 5 Therefore *I* and Ephraim
5: 9 Among the tribes of *I* I make
6:10 thing in the house of *I*:
6:10 Ephraim; *I* is defiled.
7: 1 "When I would have healed *I*,
7:10 And the pride of *I* testifies to
8: 2 *I* will cry to Me, 'My God, we
8: 3 *I* has rejected the good
8: 6 For from *I* is even this:
8: 8 *I* is swallowed up; Now they
8:14 For *I* has forgotten his Maker,
9: 1 Do not rejoice, O *I*,
9: 7 *I* knows! The prophet is a
9:10 I found *I* Like grapes in the
10: 1 *I* empties his vine
10: 6 And *I* shall be ashamed of his
10: 8 places of Aven, the sin of *I*,
10: 9 O *I*, you have sinned from
10:15 At dawn the king of *I* Shall
11: 1 When *I* was a child, I loved
11: 8 How can I hand you over, *I*?
11:12 And the house of *I* with
12:12 *I* served for a spouse, And
12:13 a prophet the LORD brought *I*
13: 1 He exalted himself in *I*;
13: 9 O *I*, you are destroyed,
14: 1 O *I*, return to the LORD
14: 5 I will be like the dew to *I*;
Joel 2:27 that I am in the midst of *I*:
3: 2 of My people, My heritage *I*,
3:16 strength of the children of *I*.
Am 1: 1 which he saw concerning *I* in
1: 1 the son of Joash, king of *I*,
2: 6 three transgressions of *I*,
2:11 it not so, O you children of *I*?
3: 1 against you, O children of *I*,
3:12 So shall the children of *I* be
3:14 That in the day I punish *I* for
4: 5 You children of *I*!" Says
4:12 thus will I do to you, O *I*;
4:12 meet your God, O *I*!"
5: 1 a lamentation, O house of *I*:
5: 2 The virgin of *I* has fallen;
5: 3 have ten left to the house of *I*.
5: 4 the LORD to the house of *I*:
5:25 forty years, O house of *I*?
6: 1 To whom the house of *I* comes!
6:14 against you, O house of *I*,
7: 8 In the midst of My people *I*;
7: 9 And the sanctuaries of *I* shall
7:10 sent to Jeroboam king of *I*,
7:10 in the midst of the house of *I*.
7:11 And *I* shall surely be led away
7:15 'Go, prophesy to My people *I*.
7:16 say, 'Do not prophesy against *I*,
7:17 And *I* shall surely be led away
8: 2 end has come upon My people *I*;
9: 7 to Me, O children of *I*?
9: 7 Did I not bring up *I* from the
9: 9 And will sift the house of *I*
9:14 the captives of My people *I*;
Ob 20 this host of the children of *I*
Mic 1: 5 for the sins of the house of *I*.
1:13 For the transgressions of *I*
1:14 be a lie to the kings of *I*.
1:15 The glory of *I* shall come to
2:12 surely gather the remnant of *I*;
3: 1 you rulers of the house of *I*:
3: 8 his transgression And to *I*
3: 9 And rulers of the house of *I*,
5: 1 will strike the judge of *I*
5: 2 to Me The One to be Ruler in *I*,
5: 3 return to the children of *I*.
6: 2 And He will contend with *I*.
Nah 2: 2 Jacob Like the excellence of *I*,
Zeph 2: 9 LORD of hosts, the God of *I*,
3:13 The remnant of *I* shall do no
3:14 O *I*! Be glad and rejoice with
3:15 out your enemy. The King of *I*,
Zech 1:19 that have scattered Judah, *I*,
8:13 house of Judah and house of *I*,
9: 1 of men And all the tribes of *I*
11:14 brotherhood between Judah and *I*.
12: 1 the word of the LORD against *I*.
Mal 1: 1 of the word of the LORD to *I*
1: 5 beyond the border of *I*.
2:11 has been committed in *I* and in
2:16 For the LORD God of *I* says
4: 4 him in Horeb for all *I*,
Mt 2: 6 will shepherd My people *I*.
2:20 mother, and go to the land of *I*,
2:21 and came into the land of *I*.
8:10 great faith, not even in *I*!
9:33 was never seen like this in *I*!
10: 6 lost sheep of the house of *I*.
10:23 gone through the cities of *I*
15:24 lost sheep of the house of *I*.
15:31 and they glorified the God of *I*.
19:28 judging the twelve tribes of *I*.
27: 9 whom they of the children of *I*
27:42 If He is the King of *I*,
Mk 12:29 commandments is: 'Hear, O *I*,
15:32 "Let the Christ, the King of *I*,
Lk 1:16 turn many of the children of *I*
1:54 He has helped His servant *I*,
1:68 is the Lord God of *I*,
1:80 day of his manifestation to *I*.
2:25 for the Consolation of *I*,
2:32 And the glory of Your people *I*.
2:34 fall and rising of many in *I*,
4:25 many widows were in *I* in the
4:27 And many lepers were in *I* in the
7: 9 great faith, not even in *I*!"
22:30 judging the twelve tribes of *I*.
24:21 He who was going to redeem *I*.
Jn 1:31 that He should be revealed to *I*,
1:49 of God! You are the King of *I*!
3:10 him, "Are you the teacher of *I*,
12:13 the LORD!' The King of *I*!
Acts 1: 6 time restore the kingdom to *I*?
2:22 Men of *I*, hear these
2:36 let all the house of *I* know
3:12 to the people: "Men of *I*,
4: 8 of the people and elders of *I*:
4:10 all, and to all the people of *I*,
4:27 Gentiles and the people of *I*,
5:21 the elders of the children of *I*,
5:31 to give repentance to *I* and
5:35 And he said to them: "Men of *I*,
7:23 his brethren, the children of *I*.
7:37 who said to the children of *I*,
7:42 wilderness, O house of *I*?
9:15 kings, and the children of *I*.
10:36 God sent to the children of *I*,
13:16 with his hand said, "Men of *I*,
13:17 The God of this people *I* chose
13:23 God raised up for *I* a
13:24 to all the people of *I*.
21:28 crying out, "Men of *I*,
28:20 because for the hope of *I* I am
Rom 9: 6 For they are not all *I* who
9: 6 not all Israel who are of *I*,
9:27 also cries out concerning *I*:
9:27 of the children of *I* be
9:31 but *I*, pursuing the law
10: 1 desire and prayer to God for *I*
10:19 did *I* not know? First Moses
10:21 But to *I* he says: "All day
11: 2 he pleads with God against *I*,
11: 7 *I* has not obtained what it
11:25 in part has happened to *I*
11:26 And so all *I* will be saved, as
1 Cor 10:18 Observe *I* after the flesh: Are
2 Cor 3: 7 so that the children of *I* could
3:13 face so that the children of *I*
Gal 6:16 and upon the *I* of God.
Eph 2:12 from the commonwealth of *I* and
Phil 3: 5 eighth day, of the stock of *I*,
Heb 8: 8 with the house of *I* and
8:10 make with the house of *I*
11:22 departure of the children of *I*,
Rev 2:14 block before the children of *I*,
7: 4 the tribes of the children of *I*
21:12 tribes of the children of *I*:

ISRAEL'S (12/11) ISRAEL

Gen 48:13 hand toward *I* left hand,
48:13 left hand toward *I* right hand,
Ex 18: 8 the Egyptians for *I* sake,
Num 1:20 *I* oldest son, their genealogies
31:30 And from the children of *I* half
31:42 the children of *I* half,
31:47 and from the children of *I* half
Josh 22:11 on the children of *I* side."
Judg 20:33 Then *I* men in ambush burst
2 Sam 10: 9 he chose some of *I* best and put
1 Chr 17:24 is *I* God.' And let the house
19:10 he chose some of *I* best and put

ISRAELITE (8/7) ISRAEL, ISRAELITES

Lev 24:10 Now the son of an *I* woman,
24:10 and this *I* woman's son and a
24:11 And the *I* woman's son blasphemed
Num 25:14 Now the name of the *I* who was
2 Sam 17:25 whose name was Jithra, an *I*,
Neh 9: 2 Then those of *I* lineage
Jn 1:47 an *I* indeed, in whom is no
Rom 11: 1 For I also am an *I*,

ISRAELITES (14/14) ISRAELITE

Ex 9: 7 one of the livestock of the *I*
Lev 23:42 All who are native *I* shall
Josh 8:24 that all the *I* returned to Ai
13:13 Maachathites dwell among the *I*
Judg 20:21 thousand men of the *I*.
1 Sam 2:14 did in Shiloh to all the *I* who
13:20 But all the *I* would go down to
14:21 they also joined the *I* who
25: 1 and the *I* gathered together and
29: 1 and the *I* encamped by a
1 Chr 9: 2 in their cities were *I*,
Neh 11: 3 possession in their cities—*I*,
Rom 9: 4 who are *I*, to whom pertain
2 Cor 11:22 So am I. Are they *I*? So am

ISSACHAR (44/41)

Gen 30:18 So she called his name *I*.
35:23 and Simeon, Levi, Judah, *I*,
46:13 The sons of *I* were Tola, Puvah,
49:14 *I* is a strong donkey, Lying
Ex 1: 3 *I*, Zebulun, and Benjamin;
Num 1: 8 'from *I*, Nethanel the son
1:28 From the children of *I*,
1:29 were numbered of the tribe of *I*
2: 5 him shall be the tribe of *I*,
2: 5 the leader of the children of *I*.
7:18 the son of Zuar, leader of *I*,
10:15 the tribe of the children of *I*
13: 7 from the tribe of *I*,
26:23 The sons of *I* according to
26:25 These are the families of *I*
34:26 the tribe of the children of *I*,
Deut 27:12 Jordan: Simeon, Levi, Judah, *I*,
33:18 And *I* in your tents!
Josh 17:10 Asher on the north and *I* on
17:11 And in *I* and in Asher, Manasseh
19:17 The fourth lot came out to *I*,
19:17 for the children of *I* according
19:23 the tribe of the children of *I*
21: 6 the families of the tribe of *I*,
21:28 and from the tribe of *I*,
Judg 5:15 And the princes of *I* were with
5:15 were with Deborah; As *I*,
10: 1 the son of Dodo, a man of *I*;
1 Ki 4:17 the son of Paruah, in *I*;
15:27 of Ahijah, of the house of *I*,
1 Chr 2: 1 Reuben, Simeon, Levi, Judah, *I*,
6:62 cities from the tribe of *I*,
6:72 And from the tribe of *I*:
7: 1 The sons of *I* were Tola, Puah,
7: 5 among all the families of *I*
12:32 of the sons of *I* who had
12:40 from as far away as *I* and
26: 5 *I* the seventh, Peulthai the
27:18 of David's brothers; over *I*,
2 Chr 30:18 many from Ephraim, Manasseh, *I*,
Ezek 48:25 *I* shall have one section;
48:26 "by the border of *I*,
48:33 gate for Simeon, one gate for *I*,
Rev 7: 7 of the tribe of *I* twelve

ISSHIAH (3/2)

1 Chr 24:21 of Rehabiah, the first was *I*.
24:25 The brother of Michah, *I*;
24:25 Isshiah; of the sons of *I*,

ISSUE (7/6) ISSUED, ISSUES, POSTERITY

Ezra 6: 8 Moreover I *i* a decree as to
6:11 Also I *i* a decree that whoever

6:12 I Darius *i* a decree; let it be
7:13 I *i* a decree that all those of
7:21 *i* a decree to all the
Ezek 23:20 And whose *i* is like the
23:20 whose issue is like the *i* of

ISSUED (13/13) ISSUE

Ezra 5:13 King Cyrus *i* a decree to build
5:17 it is so that a decree was *i*
6: 1 Then King Darius *i* a decree, and
6: 3 King Cyrus *i* a decree
10: 7 And they *i* a proclamation
Esth 3:14 of the document was to be *i* as
8:13 of the document was to be *i* as
8:14 And the decree was *i* in Shushan
9:14 the decree was *i* in Shushan,
Job 38: 8 When it burst forth and *i*
Dan 4: 6 Therefore I *i* a decree to bring
7:10 A fiery stream *i* And came
Zeph 2: 2 Before the decree is *i*,

ISSUES (1/1) ISSUE

Prov 4:23 For out of it spring the *i* of

ISUAH (KJV) See ISHVAH

ISUI (1/1)

Gen 46:17 Asher were Jimnah, Ishuah, *I*,

IT (6202/4735) See APPENDIX

IT IS WRITTEN (78/78)

Josh 8:31 as *i* in the Book of the Law of
2 Sam 1:18 indeed *i* in the Book of
1 Ki 2: 3 as *i* in the Law of Moses, that
2 Ki 23:21 as *i* in this Book of the
2 Chr 23:18 as *i* in the Law of Moses, with
25: 4 but did as *i* in the Law in
31: 3 as *i* in the Law of the LORD.
35:12 as *i* in the Book of Moses. And
Ezra 3: 2 as *i* in the Law of Moses the
3: 4 the Feast of Tabernacles, as *i*,
6:18 as *i* in the Book of Moses.
Neh 8:15 trees, to make booths, as *i*.
10:34 of the LORD our God as *i* in
10:36 as *i* in the Law, and the
Ps 40: 7 In the scroll of the book *i*
Isa 65: 6 *i* before Me: I will not keep
Dan 9:13 As *i* in the Law of Moses, all
Mt 2: 5 for thus *i* by the prophet:
4: 4 But He answered and said, "*I*,
4: 6 God, throw Yourself down. For *i*:
4: 7 *I* again, 'You shall not
4:10 "Away with you, Satan! For *i*,
11:10 "For this is he of whom *i*:
21:13 And He said to them, "*I*,
26:24 of Man indeed goes just as *i*
26:31 because of Me this night, for *i*:
Mk 1: 2 As *i* in the Prophets:
7: 6 of you hypocrites, as *i*:
9:13 they wished, as *i* of him."
14:21 of Man indeed goes just as *i*
14:27 because of Me this night, for *i*:
Lk 2:23 (as *i* in the law of the Lord,
3: 4 as *i* in the book of the words of
4: 4 Jesus answered him, saying, "*I*,
4: 8 "Get behind Me, Satan! For *i*,
4:10 'For *i*: 'He shall give His
7:27 "This is he of whom *i*:
19:46 saying to them, "*I*,
24:46 Then He said to them, "Thus *i*,
Jn 6:31 the manna in the desert; as *i*,
6:45 *I* in the prophets, 'And they
12:14 a young donkey, sat on it; as *i*:
Acts 1:20 For *i* in the book of Psalms:
7:42 as *i* in the book of the
15:15 the prophets agree, just as *i*:
23: 5 he was the high priest; for *i*,
Rom 1:17 from faith to faith; as *i*,
2:24 because of you," as *i*.
3: 4 true but every man a liar. As *i*:
3:10 As *i*: "There is none
4:17 (as *i*, "I have made you
8:36 As *i*: "For Your sake we
9:13 As *i*, "Jacob I have loved,
9:33 *i*: "Behold, I lay in Zion
10:15 unless they are sent? As *i*:
11: 8 Just as *i*: "God has given
11:26 all Israel will be saved, as *i*:
12:19 give place to wrath; for *i*,
14:11 For *i*: "As I live, says
15: 3 not please Himself; but as *i*,
15: 9 God for His mercy, as *i*:
15:21 but as *i*: "To whom He was
1 Cor 1:19 For *i*: "I will destroy
1:31 that, as *i*, "He who glories,
2: 9 *i*: "Eye has not seen,
3:19 is foolishness with God. For *i*,
9: 9 For *i* in the law of Moses,
10: 7 as were some of them. As *i*,
14:21 In the law *i*: "With men of
15:45 And so *i*, "The first man
2 Cor 8:15 As *i*, "He who gathered much
9: 9 As *i*: "He has dispersed
Gal 3:10 law are under the curse; for *i*,
3:13 become a curse for us (for *i*,
4:22 For *i* that Abraham had two sons:
4:27 For *i*: "Rejoice, O barren,
Heb 10: 7 the volume of the book *i*
1 Pe 1:16 because *i*, "Be holy, for I

ITALIAN (1/1) ITALY

Acts 10: 1 what was called the *I* Regiment,

ITALY (4/4) ITALIAN

Acts 18: 2 who had recently come from *I*
27: 1 that we should sail to *I*,
27: 6 Alexandrian ship sailing to *I*,
Heb 13:24 Those from *I* greet you.

ITCH (1/1)

Deut 28:27 with the scab, and with the *i*,

ITCHING (1/1)

2 Tim 4: 3 because they have *i* ears, they

ITEM (2/1)

Lev 11:32 whether it is any *i* of wood
11:32 whatever *i* it is, in which

ITEMS (4/4)

Num 4:32 to each man by name the *i*
2 Chr 32:27 for all kinds of desirable *i*;
Ezek 27:18 because of your many luxury *i*,
27:24 your merchants in choice *i*—

ITHAI (1/1)

1 Chr 11:31 *I* the son of Ribai of Gibeah, of

ITHAMAR (21/20)

Ex 6:23 Nadab, Abihu, Eleazar, and *I*.
28: 1 Nadab, Abihu, Eleazar, and *I*.
38:21 the Levites, by the hand of *I*,
Lev 10: 6 to Aaron, and to Eleazar and *I*,
10:12 to Aaron, and to Eleazar and *I*,
10:16 he was angry with Eleazar and *I*,
Num 3: 2 and Abihu, Eleazar, and *I*.
3: 4 So Eleazar and *I* ministered as
4:28 be under the authority of *I*
4:33 under the authority of *I* the
7: 8 under the authority of *I* the
26:60 Nadab and Abihu, Eleazar and *I*.
1 Chr 6: 3 Nadab, Abihu, Eleazar, and *I*.
24: 1 Nadab, Abihu, Eleazar, and *I*.
24: 2 therefore Eleazar and *I*
24: 3 and Ahimelech of the sons of *I*,
24: 4 Eleazar than of the sons of *I*,
24: 4 houses among the sons of *I*.
24: 5 Eleazar and from the sons of *I*.
24: 6 for Eleazar and one for *I*.
Ezra 8: 2 Gershom; of the sons of *I*,

ITHIEL (3/2)

Neh 11: 7 son of Maaseiah, the son of *I*,
Prov 30: 1 to *I*—to Ithiel and Ucal:
30: 1 to *I* and Ucal:

ITHMAH (1/1)

1 Chr 11:46 of Elnaam, *I* the Moabite,

ITHNAN (1/1)

Josh 15:23 Kedesh, Hazor, *I*,

ITHRAN (2/2)

Gen 36:26 of Dishon: Hemdan, Eshban, *I*,
1 Chr 1:41 Dishon were Hamran, Eshban, *I*,

ITHREAM (2/2)

2 Sam 3: 5 and the sixth, *I*,
1 Chr 3: 3 by Abital; the sixth, *I*,

ITHRITE (4/2)

2 Sam 23:38 Ira the *I*, Gareb the
23:38 Ira the Ithrite, Gareb the *I*,
1 Chr 11:40 Ira the *I*, Gareb the
11:40 Ira the Ithrite, Gareb the *I*,

ITHRITES (1/1)

1 Chr 2:53 of Kirjath Jearim were the *I*,

ITINERANT (1/1)

Acts 19:13 Then some of the *i* Jewish

ITS (1350/917) See APPENDIX

ITSELF (58/52) See APPENDIX

ITTAI (8/7)

2 Sam 15:19 Then the king said to *I* the
15:21 And *I* answered the king and
15:22 So David said to *I*,
15:22 Then *I* the Gittite and all
18: 2 one third under the hand of *I*
18: 5 commanded Joab, Abishai, and *I*,
18:12 commanded you and Abishai and *I*,
23:29 *I* the son of Ribai from Gibeah

ITTAH-KAZIN (KJV) See ETH KAZIN

ITUREA (1/1)

Lk 3: 1 brother Philip tetrarch of *I*

IVAH (3/3)

2 Ki 18:34 of Sepharvaim and Hena and *I*?
19:13 city of Sepharvaim, Hena, and *I*?
Isa 37:13 city of Sepharvaim, Hena, and *I*?

IVORY (13/13)

1 Ki 10:18 king made a great throne of *i*,
10:22 came bringing gold, silver, *i*,
22:39 the *i* house which he built and
2 Chr 9:17 king made a great throne of *i*,
9:21 came, bringing gold, silver, *i*,
Ps 45: 8 Out of the *i* palaces, by which
Song 5:14 His body is carved *i* Inlaid
7: 4 Your neck is like an *i* tower,
Ezek 27: 6 inlaid your planks With *i*
27:15 They brought you *i* tusks and
Am 3:15 The houses of *i* shall perish,
6: 4 Who lie on beds of *i*,
Rev 18:12 wood, every kind of object of *i*,

IZEHAR (1/1)

Num 3:19 by their families: Amram, *I*,

IZEHARITES (KJV) See IZHARITES

IZHAR (8/8)

Ex 6:18 sons of Kohath were Amram, *I*,
6:21 The sons of *I* were Korah,
Num 16: 1 Now Korah the son of *I*,
1 Chr 6: 2 sons of Kohath were Amram, *I*,
6:18 sons of Kohath were Amram, *I*,
6:38 the son of *I*, the son of
23:12 The sons of Kohath: Amram, *I*,
23:18 Of the sons of *I*,

IZHARITES (4/4)

Num 3:27 Amramites, the family of the *I*,
1 Chr 24:22 Of the *I*, Shelomoth;
26:23 Of the Amramites, the *I*,
26:29 Of the *I*, Chenaniah

IZRAHIAH (2/1)

1 Chr 7: 3 The son of Uzzi was *I*,
7: 3 and the sons of *I* were

IZRAHITE (1/1)

1 Chr 27: 8 fifth month was Shamhuth the *I*;

J

JAAKAN (4/4)

Num 33:31 Moseroth and camped at Bene *J*.
33:32 They moved from Bene *J* and
Deut 10: 6 from the wells of Bene *J* to
1 Chr 1:42 were Bilhan, Zaavan, and *J*.

JAAKOBAH (1/1)

1 Chr 4:36 Elioenai, *J*, Jeshohaiah,

JAALA (2/2)

Ezra 2:56 the sons of *J*, the sons of
Neh 7:58 the sons of *J*, the sons of

JAALAM (4/4)

Gen 36: 5 And Aholibamah bore Jeush, *J*,
36:14 And she bore to Esau: Jeush, *J*,
36:18 wife: Chief Jeush, Chief *J*,
1 Chr 1:35 were Eliphaz, Reuel, Jeush, *J*,

JAAN (1/1)

2 Sam 24: 6 they came to Dan *J* and around

JAANAI (1/1)

1 Chr 5:12 then *J* and Shaphat in Bashan,

JAARE-OREGIM (1/1)

2 Sam 21:19 where Elhanan the son of *J* the

JAARESHIAH (1/1)

1 Chr 8:27 *J*, Elijah, and Zichri were

JAASAI (1/1)

Ezra 10:37 Mattaniah, Mattenai, *J*,

JAASAU (KJV) See JAASAI

JAASIEL (2/2)
1 Chr 11:47 and *J* the Mezobaite.
27:21 *J* the son of Abner;

JAAZANIAH (4/4)
2 Ki 25:23 and *J* the son of a Maachathite,
Jer 35: 3 Then I took *J* the son of
Ezek 8:11 and in their midst stood *J* the
11: 1 among whom I saw *J* the son of

JAAZER (KJV) See JAZER

JAAZIAH (2/2)
1 Chr 24:26 Mahli and Mushi; the son of *J*,
24:27 The sons of Merari by *J* were

JAAZIEL (1/1)
1 Chr 15:18 second rank: Zechariah, Ben, *J*,

JABAL (1/1)
Gen 4:20 And Adah bore *J*. He was the

JABBOK (7/7)
Gen 32:22 and crossed over the ford of *J*.
Num 21:24 land from the Arnon to the *J*,
Deut 2:37 along the River *J*,
3:16 border, as far as the River *J*,
Josh 12: 2 even as far as the River *J*,
Judg 11:13 from the Arnon as far as the *J*,
11:22 from the Arnon to the *J* and

JABESH (12/11) JABESH GILEAD
1 Sam 11: 1 and all the men of *J* said to
11: 3 Then the elders of *J* said to
11: 5 him the words of the men of *J*.
11: 9 reported it to the men of *J*,
11:10 Therefore the men of *J* said,
31:12 and they came to *J* and burned
31:13 under the tamarisk tree at *J*,
2 Ki 15:10 Then Shallum the son of *J*
15:13 Shallum the son of *J* became
15:14 struck Shallum the son of *J* in
1 Chr 10:12 and they brought them to *J*,
10:12 under the tamarisk tree at *J*,

JABESH GILEAD (12/12) GILEAD, JABESH
Judg 21: 8 had come to the camp from *J* to
21: 9 not one of the inhabitants of *J*
21:10 and strike the inhabitants of *J*
21:12 among the inhabitants of *J*
21:14 saved alive of the women of *J*;
1 Sam 11: 1 came up and encamped against *J*;
11: 9 you shall say to the men of *J*:
31:11 Now when the inhabitants of *J*
2 Sam 2: 4 The men of *J* were the ones
2: 5 messengers to the men of *J*,
21:12 from the men of *J* who had
1 Chr 10:11 And when all *J* heard all that

JABEZ (4/3)
1 Chr 2:55 of the scribes who dwelt at *J*
4: 9 Now *J* was more honorable than
4: 9 his mother called his name *J*,
4:10 And *J* called on the God of

JABIN (8/7) JABIN'S
Josh 11: 1 when *J* king of Hazor heard
Judg 4: 2 sold them into the hand of *J*
4: 3 for *J* had nine hundred chariots
4:17 for there was peace between *J*
4:23 So on that day God subdued *J*
4:24 and stronger against *J* king of
4:24 until they had destroyed *J* king
Ps 83: 9 As with *J* at the Brook

JABIN'S (1/1) JABIN
Judg 4: 7 the commander of *J* army, with

JABNEEL (2/2)
Josh 15:11 Mount Baalah, and extended to *J*;
19:33 Zaanannim, Adami Nekeb, and *J*,

JABNEH (1/1)
2 Chr 26: 6 the wall of Gath, the wall of *J*,

JACHAN (1/1)
1 Chr 5:13 Meshullam, Sheba, Jorai, *J*,

JACHIN (8/8)
Gen 46:10 were Jemuel, Jamin, Ohad, *J*,
Ex 6:15 were Jemuel, Jamin, Ohad, *J*,
Num 26:12 family of the Jaminites; of *J*,
1 Ki 7:21 the right and called its name *J*,
1 Chr 9:10 Jedaiah, Jehoiarib, and *J*;
24:17 the twenty-first to *J*,
2 Chr 3:17 of the one on the right hand *J*,
Neh 11:10 the son of Joiarib, and *J*;

JACHINITES (1/1)
Num 26:12 of Jachin, the family of the *J*;

JACINTH (3/3)
Ex 28:19 "the third row, a *j*,
39:12 the third row, a *j*,
Rev 21:20 chrysoprase, the eleventh *j*,

JACKALS (17/17)
Job 30:29 I am a brother of *j*,
Ps 44:19 broken us in the place of *j*,
63:10 They shall be a portion for *j*.
Isa 13:22 And *j* in their pleasant
34:13 It shall be a habitation of *j*,
34:14 shall also meet with the *j*,
35: 7 water; In the habitation of *j*,
43:20 The *j* and the ostriches,
Jer 9:11 a heap of ruins, a den of *j*.
10:22 of Judah desolate, a den of *j*.
14: 6 sniffed at the wind like *j*;
49:33 shall be a dwelling for *j*,
50:39 shall dwell there with the *j*,
51:37 a heap, A dwelling place for *j*,
Lam 4: 3 Even the *j* present their
Mic 1: 8 will make a wailing like the *j*
Mal 1: 3 and his heritage For the *j* of

JACKDAW (2/2)
Lev 11:18 'the white owl, the *j*,
Deut 14:17 'the *j*, the carrion vulture,

JACOB (363/336) ISRAEL, JACOB'S, JAMES
Gen 25:26 heel; so his name was called *J*.
25:27 but *J* was a mild man, dwelling
25:28 his game, but Rebekah loved *J*.
25:29 Now *J* cooked a stew; and Esau
25:30 And Esau said to *J*,
25:31 But *J* said, "Sell me your
25:33 Then *J* said, "Swear to me as of
25:33 and sold his birthright to *J*.
25:34 And *J* gave Esau bread and stew
27: 6 So Rebekah spoke to *J* her son,
27:11 And *J* said to Rebekah his
27:15 and put them on *J* her younger
27:17 into the hand of her son *J*.
27:19 *J* said to his father, "I am
27:21 Then Isaac said to *J*,
27:22 So *J* went near to Isaac his
27:30 Isaac had finished blessing *J*,
27:30 and *J* had scarcely gone out
27:36 "Is he not rightly named *J*?
27:41 So Esau hated *J* because of the
27:41 then I will kill my brother *J*.
27:42 So she sent and called *J* her
27:46 if *J* takes a wife of the
28: 1 Then Isaac called *J* and blessed
28: 5 So Isaac sent *J* away, and he
28: 5 the mother of *J* and Esau.
28: 6 saw that Isaac had blessed *J*
28: 7 and that *J* had obeyed his father
28:10 Now *J* went out from Beersheba
28:16 Then *J* awoke from his sleep and
28:18 Then *J* rose early in the
28:20 Then *J* made a vow, saying, "If
29: 1 So *J* went on his journey and
29: 4 And *J* said to them, "My
29:10 when *J* saw Rachel the daughter
29:10 that *J* went near and rolled the
29:11 Then *J* kissed Rachel, and lifted
29:12 And *J* told Rachel that he was
29:13 Laban heard the report about *J*
29:15 Then Laban said to *J*,
29:18 Now *J* loved Rachel; so he said,
29:20 So *J* served seven years for
29:21 Then *J* said to Laban, "Give
29:23 daughter and brought her to *J*;
29:28 Then *J* did so and fulfilled her
29:30 Then *J* also went in to Rachel,
30: 1 Rachel saw that she bore *J* no
30: 1 her sister, and said to *J*,
30: 4 and *J* went in to her.
30: 5 Bilhah conceived and bore *J* a
30: 7 conceived again and bore *J* a
30: 9 her maid and gave her to *J* as
30:10 And Leah's maid Zilpah bore *J* a
30:12 And Leah's maid Zilpah bore *J* a
30:16 When *J* came out of the field in
30:17 and she conceived and bore *J* a
30:19 conceived again and bore *J* a
30:25 that *J* said to Laban, "Send me
30:29 So *J* said to him, "You know
30:31 And *J* said, "You shall not
30:36 journey between himself and *J*,
30:36 and *J* fed the rest of Laban's
30:37 Now *J* took for himself rods of
30:40 Then *J* separated the lambs, and
30:41 that *J* placed the rods before
31: 1 Now *J* heard the words of
31: 1 *J* has taken away all that was
31: 2 And *J* saw the countenance of
31: 3 Then the LORD said to *J*,
31: 4 So *J* sent and called Rachel and
31:11 to me in a dream, saying, '*J*.
31:17 Then *J* rose and set his sons
31:20 And *J* stole away, unknown to
31:22 told on the third day that *J*
31:24 careful that you speak to *J*
31:25 So Laban overtook *J*.
31:25 Now *J* had pitched his tent in
31:26 And Laban said to *J*:
31:29 'Be careful that you speak to *J*
31:31 Then *J* answered and said to
31:32 For *J* did not know that
31:36 Then *J* was angry and rebuked
31:36 and *J* answered and said to
31:43 Laban answered and said to *J*,
31:45 So *J* took a stone and set it up
31:46 Then *J* said to his brethren,
31:47 but *J* called it Galeed.
31:51 Then Laban said to *J*,
31:53 And *J* swore by the Fear of
31:54 Then *J* offered a sacrifice on
32: 1 So *J* went on his way, and the
32: 2 When *J* saw them, he said, "This
32: 3 Then *J* sent messengers before
32: 4 Thus your servant *J* says: "I
32: 6 the messengers returned to *J*,
32: 7 So *J* was greatly afraid and
32: 9 Then *J* said, "O God of my
32:20 your servant *J* is behind us.'
32:24 Then *J* was left alone; and a Man
32:27 is your name?" He said, "*J*.
32:28 shall no longer be called *J*,
32:29 Then *J* asked, saying, "Tell me
32:30 And *J* called the name of the
33: 1 Now *J* lifted his eyes and
33:10 And *J* said, "No, please, if I
33:13 But *J* said to him, "My lord
33:17 And *J* journeyed to Succoth,
33:18 Then *J* came safely to the city
34: 1 Leah, whom she had borne to *J*,
34: 3 to Dinah the daughter of *J*,
34: 5 And *J* heard that he had defiled
34: 5 so *J* held his peace until they
34: 6 of Shechem went out to *J* to
34: 7 And the sons of *J* came in from
34:13 But the sons of *J* answered
34:25 pain, that two of the sons of *J*,
34:27 The sons of *J* came upon the
34:30 Then *J* said to Simeon and Levi,
35: 1 Then God said to *J*, "Arise,
35: 2 And *J* said to his household and
35: 4 So they gave *J* all the foreign
35: 4 and *J* hid them under the
35: 5 did not pursue the sons of *J*.
35: 6 So *J* came to Luz (that is,
35: 9 Then God appeared to *J* again,
35:10 said to him, "Your name is *J*;
35:10 your name shall not be called *J*
35:14 So *J* set up a pillar in the
35:15 And *J* called the name of the
35:20 And *J* set a pillar on her grave,
35:22 Now the sons of *J* were twelve:
35:26 These were the sons of *J* who
35:27 Then *J* came to his father Isaac
35:29 And his sons Esau and *J* buried
36: 6 the presence of his brother *J*.
37: 1 Now *J* dwelt in the land where
37: 2 This is the history of *J*.
37:34 Then *J* tore his clothes, put
42: 1 When *J* saw that there was grain
42: 1 *J* said to his sons, "Why do
42: 4 But *J* did not send Joseph's
42:29 Then they went to *J* their
42:36 And *J* their father said to them,
45:25 came to the land of Canaan to *J*
45:27 the spirit of *J* their father
46: 2 of the night, and said, "*J*,
46: 2 'Jacob, *J*!" And he said,
46: 5 Then *J* arose from Beersheba; and
46: 5 Israel carried their father *J*,
46: 6 *J* and all his descendants with
46: 8 *J* and his sons, who went to
46:15 whom she bore to *J* in Padan
46:18 and these she bore to *J*:
46:22 of Rachel, who were born to *J*:
46:25 and she bore these to *J*:
46:26 the persons who went with *J* to
46:27 the persons of the house of *J*
47: 7 Joseph brought in his father *J*
47: 7 and *J* blessed Pharaoh.
47: 8 Pharaoh said to *J*, "How
47: 9 And *J* said to Pharaoh, "The
47:10 So *J* blessed Pharaoh, and went
47:28 And *J* lived in the land of Egypt
48: 2 And *J* was told, "Look, your son
48: 3 Then *J* said to Joseph: "God
49: 1 And *J* called his sons and said,
49: 2 and hear, you sons of *J*,
49: 7 I will divide them in *J* And
49:24 hands of the Mighty God of *J*
49:33 And when *J* had finished
50:24 to Abraham, to Isaac, and to *J*.
Ex 1: 1 and his household came with *J*:
1: 5 who were descendants of *J* were
2:24 Abraham, with Isaac, and with *J*.
3: 6 God of Isaac, and the God of *J*.
3:15 God of Isaac, and the God of *J*,
3:16 of Abraham, of Isaac, and of *J*,
4: 5 God of Isaac, and the God of *J*,
6: 3 to Abraham, to Isaac, and to *J*,
6: 8 give to Abraham, Isaac, and *J*;
19: 3 you shall say to the house of *J*,
33: 1 swore to Abraham, Isaac, and *J*,
Lev 26:42 remember My covenant with *J*,
Num 23: 7 curse *J* for me, And come,
23:10 "Who can count the dust of *J*,
23:21 has not observed iniquity in *J*,
23:23 there is no sorcery against *J*,

23:23 It now must be said of J And
24: 5 O J! Your dwellings, O Israel!
24:17 A Star shall come out of J;
24:19 Out of J One shall have
32:11 swore to Abraham, Isaac, and J,
Deut 1: 8 Abraham, Isaac, and J—
6:10 to Abraham, Isaac, and J,
9: 5 to Abraham, Isaac, and J.
9:27 servants, Abraham, Isaac, and J;
29:13 to Abraham, Isaac, and J.
30:20 to Abraham, Isaac, and J,
32: 9 J is the place of His
33: 4 of the congregation of J.
33:10 They shall teach J Your
33:28 The fountain of J alone, In a
34: 4 to give Abraham, Isaac, and J,
Josh 24: 4 'To Isaac I gave J and Esau.
24: 4 but J and his children went
24:32 in the plot of ground which J
1 Sam 12: 8 When J had gone into Egypt, and
2 Sam 23: 1 The anointed of the God of J,
1 Ki 18:31 of the tribes of the sons of J,
2 Ki 13:23 with Abraham, Isaac, and J,
17:34 had commanded the children of J,
1 Chr 16:13 His servant, You children of J,
16:17 And confirmed it to J for a
Ps 14: 7 Let J rejoice and Israel be
20: 1 May the name of the God of J
22:23 All you descendants of J,
24: 6 This is J, the generation
44: 4 O God; Command victories for J.
46: 7 The God of J is our refuge.
46:11 The God of J is our refuge.
47: 4 The excellence of J whom He
53: 6 Let J rejoice and Israel be
59:13 them know that God rules in J
75: 9 sing praises to the God of J.
76: 6 At Your rebuke, O God of J,
77:15 The sons of J and Joseph.
78: 5 He established a testimony in J,
78:21 a fire was kindled against J,
78:71 To shepherd J His people, And
79: 7 For they have devoured J,
81: 1 a joyful shout to the God of J.
81: 4 Israel, A law of the God of J.
84: 8 O God of J! Selah
85: 1 brought back the captivity of J.
87: 2 than all the dwellings of J.
94: 7 Nor does the God of J
99: 4 justice and righteousness in J.
105: 6 His servant, You children of J,
105:10 And confirmed it to J for a
105:23 And J dwelt in the land of
114: 1 The house of J from a people
114: 7 the presence of the God of J,
132: 2 vowed to the Mighty One of J:
132: 5 place for the Mighty One of J.
135: 4 For the LORD has chosen J for
146: 5 is he who has the God of J
147:19 He declares His word to J,
Isa 2: 3 To the house of the God of J;
2: 5 O house of J, come and let
2: 6 Your people, the house of J,
8:17 His face from the house of J;
9: 8 LORD sent a word against J,
10:20 have escaped of the house of J,
10:21 will return, the remnant of J,
14: 1 the LORD will have mercy on J,
14: 1 will cling to the house of J.
17: 4 to pass That the glory of J
27: 6 shall cause to take root in J;
27: 9 by this the iniquity of J will
29:22 concerning the house of J:
29:22 J shall not now be ashamed, Nor
29:23 And hallow the Holy One of J,
40:27 Why do you say, O J,
41: 8 J whom I have chosen, The
41:14 "Fear not, you worm J,
41:21 reasons," says the King of J.
42:24 Who gave J for plunder, and
43: 1 the LORD, who created you, O J,
43:22 have not called upon Me, O J;
43:28 I will give J to the curse,
44: 1 O J My servant, And Israel
44: 2 O J My servant; And you,
44: 5 call himself by the name of J;
44:21 "Remember these, O J,
44:23 For the LORD has redeemed J,
45: 4 For J My servant's sake, And
45:19 I did not say to the seed of J,
46: 3 "Listen to Me, O house of J,
48: 1 "Hear this, O house of J,
48:12 "Listen to Me, O J,
48:20 has redeemed His servant J!"
49: 5 To bring J back to Him, So
49: 6 To raise up the tribes of J,
49:26 Redeemer, the Mighty One of J.
58: 1 And the house of J their sins.
58:14 feed you with the heritage of J
59:20 turn from transgression in J,
60:16 Redeemer, the Mighty One of J.
65: 9 bring forth descendants from J,
Jer 2: 4 O house of J and all the
5:20 this in the house of J And
10:16 The Portion of J is not like
10:25 name; For they have eaten up J,
30:10 do not fear, O My servant J,
30:10 J shall return, have rest and
31: 7 "Sing with gladness for J,
31:11 For the LORD has redeemed J,
33:26 cast away the descendants of J
33:26 of Abraham, Isaac, and J.
46:27 do not fear, O My servant J,
46:27 J shall return, have rest and
46:28 O J My servant," says the
51:19 The Portion of J is not like
Lam 1:17 has commanded concerning J
2: 2 All the dwelling places of J.
2: 3 He has blazed against J like a
Ezek 20: 5 descendants of the house of J,
28:25 which I gave to My servant J.
37:25 land that I have given to J My
39:25 bring back the captives of J,
Hos 10:11 J shall break his clods."
12: 2 And will punish J according to
12:12 J fled to the country of Syria
Am 3:13 testify against the house of J,
6: 8 says: "I abhor the pride of J,
7: 2 that J may stand, For he is
7: 5 that J may stand, For he is
8: 7 has sworn by the pride of J:
9: 8 utterly destroy the house of J,
Ob 10 violence against your brother J,
17 The house of J shall possess
18 The house of J shall be a fire,
Mic 1: 5 is for the transgression of J
1: 5 is the transgression of J?
2: 7 who are named the house of J:
2:12 surely assemble all of you, O J,
3: 1 "Hear now, O heads of J,
3: 8 To declare to J his
3: 9 You heads of the house of J
4: 2 To the house of the God of J;
5: 7 Then the remnant of J Shall
5: 8 And the remnant of J Shall be
7:20 You will give truth to J And
Nah 2: 2 restore the excellence of J
Mal 1: 2 Yet J I have loved;
2:12 cut off from the tents of J
3: 6 are not consumed, O sons of J.
Mt 1: 2 begot Isaac, Isaac begot J,
1: 2 and J begot Judah and his
1:15 Matthan, and Matthan begot J.
1:16 And J begot Joseph the husband
8:11 and J in the kingdom of heaven.
22:32 Isaac, and the God of J'?
Mk 12:26 Isaac, and the God of J'?
Lk 1:33 will reign over the house of J
3:34 the son of J, the son of
13:28 you see Abraham and Isaac and J
20:37 Isaac, and the God of J.
Jn 4: 5 near the plot of ground that J
4:12 You greater than our father J,
Acts 3:13 God of Abraham, Isaac, and J,
7: 8 eighth day; and Isaac begot J,
7: 8 and J begot the twelve
7:12 But when J heard that there was
7:14 sent and called his father J
7:15 So J went down to Egypt; and he
7:32 Isaac, and the God of J.
7:46 a dwelling for the God of J.
Rom 9:13 J I have loved, but Esau I
11:26 away ungodliness from J;
Heb 11: 9 in tents with Isaac and J,
11:20 By faith Isaac blessed J and
11:21 By faith J, when he was

JACOB'S (19/19) JACOB

Gen 27:22 The voice is J voice, but the
30: 2 And J anger was aroused against
30:42 were Laban's and the stronger J.
31:33 And Laban went into J tent,
32:18 say, 'They are your servant J.
32:25 and the socket of J hip was out
32:32 He touched the socket of J hip
34: 7 thing in Israel by lying with J
34:19 because he delighted in J
35:23 J firstborn, and Simeon, Levi,
45:26 And J heart stood still,
46: 8 Reuben was J firstborn.
46:19 J wife, were Joseph and
46:26 besides J sons' wives, were
47:28 So the length of J life was one
Jer 30: 7 And it is the time of J
30:18 bring back the captivity of J
Mal 1: 2 Was not Esau J brother?"
Jn 4: 6 Now J well was there.

JADA (2/2)

1 Chr 2:28 sons of Onam were Shammai and J.
2:32 The sons of J, the brother

JADAU (KJV) See JADDAI

JADDAI (1/1)

Ezra 10:43 Mattithiah, Zabad, Zebina, J,

JADDUA (3/3)

Neh 10:21 Meshezabel, Zadok, J,
12:11 Jonathan, and Jonathan begot J.
12:22 Joiada, Johanan, and J.

JADON (1/1)

Neh 3: 7 J the Meronothite, the men of

JAEL (6/6)

Judg 4:17 away on foot to the tent of J,
4:18 And J went out to meet Sisera,
4:21 Then J, Heber's wife, took
4:22 J came out to meet him, and
5: 6 son of Anath, In the days of J,
5:24 blessed among women is J,

JAGUR (1/1)

Josh 15:21 South, were Kabzeel, Eder, J,

JAH (KJV) See YAH

JAHATH (8/7)

1 Chr 4: 2 the son of Shobal begot J,
4: 2 and J begot Ahumai and Lahad.
6:20 J his son, Zimmah his son,
6:43 the son of J, the son of
23:10 And the sons of Shimei: J,
23:11 J was the first and Zizah the
24:22 of the sons of Shelomoth, J.
2 Chr 34:12 Their overseers were J and

JAHAZ (6/6)

Num 21:23 and he came to J and fought
Deut 2:32 out against us to fight at J.
Josh 21:36 J with its common-land,
Judg 11:20 people together, encamped in J,
Isa 15: 4 shall be heard as far as J;
Jer 48:34 of Heshbon to Elealeh and to J

JAHAZA (1/1)

Josh 13:18 J, Kedemoth, Mephaath,

JAHAZAH (KJV) See JAHAZ

JAHAZIAH (1/1)

Ezra 10:15 the son of Asahel and J the

JAHAZIEL (5/5)

1 Chr 12: 4 over the thirty; Jeremiah, J,
16: 6 Benaiah and J the priests
23:19 J the third, and Jekameam the
24:23 J the third, and Jekameam the
2 Chr 20:14 of the LORD came upon J the

JAHDAI (1/1)

1 Chr 2:47 And the sons of J were Regem,

JAHDIEL (1/1)

1 Chr 5:24 Jeremiah, Hodaviah, and J.

JAHDO (1/1)

1 Chr 5:14 son of Jeshishai, the son of J,

JAHLEEL (2/2)

Gen 46:14 were Sered, Elon, and J.
Num 26:26 family of the Elonites; of J,

JAHLEELITES (1/1)

Num 26:26 of Jahleel, the family of the J.

JAHMAI (1/1)

1 Chr 7: 2 were Uzzi, Rephaiah, Jeriel, J,

JAHZAH (2/2)

1 Chr 6:78 J with its common-lands,
Jer 48:21 On Holon and J and Mephaath,

JAHZEEL (2/2)

Gen 46:24 The sons of Naphtali were J,
Num 26:48 to their families were: of J,

JAHZEELITES (1/1)

Num 26:48 of Jahzeel, the family of the J;

JAHZERAH (1/1)

1 Chr 9:12 the son of Adiel, the son of J,

JAHZIEL (1/1)

1 Chr 7:13 The sons of Naphtali were J,

JAILER (1/1)

Acts 16:23 commanding the j to keep them

JAIR (13/11)

Num 32:41 Also J the son of Manasseh went
32:41 towns, and called them Havoth J.
Deut 3:14 J the son of Manasseh took all
3:14 after his own name, Havoth J,
Josh 13:30 and all the towns of J which
Judg 10: 3 After him arose J,
10: 4 Havoth J" to this day, which
10: 5 And J died and was buried in
1 Ki 4:13 to him belonged the towns of J
1 Chr 2:22 Segub begot J, who had
2:23 took from them the towns of J,
20: 5 and Elhanan the son of J killed
Esth 2: 5 name was Mordecai the son of J,

JAIRITE (1/1)
2 Sam 20:26 and Ira the *J* was a chief

JAIRUS (2/2)
Mk 5:22 *J* by name. And when he saw Him,
Lk 8:41 there came a man named *J*,

JAKAN (KJV) See JAAKAN

JAKEH (1/1)
Prov 30: 1 The words of Agur the son of *J*,

JAKIM (2/2)
1 Chr 8:19 *J*, Zichri, Zabdi,
24:12 to Eliashib, the twelfth to *J*,

JALON (1/1)
1 Chr 4:17 Jether, Mered, Epher, and *J*.

JAMBRES (1/1)
2 Tim 3: 8 Now as Jannes and *J* resisted

JAMES (42/38) JACOB
Mt 4:21 *J* the son of Zebedee, and
10: 2 *J* the son of Zebedee, and John
10: 3 *J* the son of Alphaeus, and
13:55 called Mary? And His brothers *J*,
17: 1 six days Jesus took Peter, *J*,
27:56 Mary the mother of *J* and Joses,
Mk 1:19 He saw *J* the son of Zebedee,
1:29 Andrew, with *J* and John.
3:17 *J* the son of Zebedee and John
3:17 and John the brother of *J*,
3:18 *J* the son of Alphaeus,
5:37 to follow Him except Peter, *J*,
5:37 and John the brother of *J*.
6: 3 Son of Mary, and brother of *J*,
9: 2 six days Jesus took Peter, *J*,
10:35 Then *J* and John, the sons of
10:41 to be greatly displeased with *J*
13: 3 opposite the temple, Peter, *J*,
14:33 And He took Peter, *J*,
15:40 Mary the mother of *J* the Less
16: 1 Mary the mother of *J*,
Lk 5:10 and so also were *J* and John,
6:14 *J* and John; Philip and
6:15 *J* the son of Alphaeus, and
6:16 Judas the son of *J*,
8:51 no one to go in except Peter, *J*,
9:28 and *J* and went up on the
9:54 And when His disciples *J* and
24:10 Joanna, Mary the mother of *J*,
Acts 1:13 they were staying: Peter, *J*,
1:13 *J* the son of Alphaeus and
1:13 and Judas the son of *J*.
12: 2 Then he killed *J* the brother of
12:17 tell these things to *J* and to
15:13 *J* answered, saying, "Men and
21:18 day Paul went in with us to *J*,
1 Cor 15: 7 After that He was seen by *J*,
Gal 1:19 of the other apostles except *J*,
2: 9 and when *J*, Cephas, and John,
2:12 before certain men came from *J*,
Jas 1: 1 *J*, a bondservant of God
Jude 1 Jesus Christ, and brother of *J*,

JAMIN (6/6)
Gen 46:10 sons of Simeon were Jemuel, *J*,
Ex 6:15 sons of Simeon were Jemuel, *J*,
Num 26:12 family of the Nemuelites; of *J*,
1 Chr 2:27 of Jerahmeel, were Maaz, *J*,
4:24 sons of Simeon were Nemuel, *J*,
Neh 8: 7 Also Jeshua, Bani, Sherebiah, *J*,

JAMINITES (1/1)
Num 26:12 of Jamin, the family of the *J*;

JAMLECH (1/1)
1 Chr 4:34 Meshobab, *J*, and Joshah the

JANGLING (KJV) See TALK

JANNA (1/1)
Lk 3:24 son of Melchi, the son of *J*,

JANNES (1/1)
2 Tim 3: 8 Now as *J* and Jambres resisted

JANOAH (1/1)
2 Ki 15:29 took Ijon, Abel Beth Maachah, *J*,

JANOHAH (2/2)
Josh 16: 6 passed by it on the east of *J*.
16: 7 Then it went down from *J* to

JANUM (1/1)
Josh 15:53 *J*, Beth Tappuah, Aphekah,

JAPHETH (11/11)
Gen 5:32 and Noah begot Shem, Ham, and *J*.
6:10 three sons: Shem, Ham, and *J*.
7:13 Noah's sons, Shem, Ham, and *J*,
9:18 the ark were Shem, Ham, and *J*.
9:23 But Shem and *J* took a garment,
9:27 May God enlarge *J*,
10: 1 sons of Noah: Shem, Ham, and *J*.
10: 2 The sons of *J* were Gomer,
10:21 the brother of *J* the elder.
1 Chr 1: 4 Noah, Shem, Ham, and *J*.
1: 5 The sons of *J* were Gomer,

JAPHIA (5/5)
Josh 10: 3 *J* king of Lachish, and Debir
19:12 toward Daberath, bypassing *J*.
2 Sam 5:15 Ibhar, Elishua, Nepheg, *J*,
1 Chr 3: 7 Nogah, Nepheg, *J*,
14: 6 Nogah, Nepheg, *J*,

JAPHLET (3/2)
1 Chr 7:32 And Heber begot *J*,
7:33 The sons of *J* were Pasach,
7:33 These were the children of *J*.

JAPHLETITES (1/1)
Josh 16: 3 to the boundary of the *J*,

JAPHO (KJV) See JOPPA

JAR (6/6)
1 Ki 14: 3 and a *j* of honey, and go to
17:12 a bin, and a little oil in a *j*;
17:14 nor shall the *j* of oil run dry,
17:16 nor did the *j* of oil run dry,
19: 6 and a *j* of water. So he ate and
2 Ki 4: 2 nothing in the house but a *j*

JARAH (2/1)
1 Chr 9:42 And Ahaz begot *J*;
9:42 *J* begot Alemeth, Azmaveth, and

JAREB (2/2)
Hos 5:13 to Assyria And sent to King *J*;
10: 6 As a present for King *J*.

JARED (7/7)
Gen 5:15 sixty-five years, and begot *J*.
5:16 After he begot *J*, Mahalalel
5:18 *J* lived one hundred and
5:19 *J* lived eight hundred years,
5:20 So all the days of *J* were nine
1 Chr 1: 2 Cainan, Mahalalel, *J*,
Lk 3:37 son of Enoch, the son of *J*,

JARESIAH (KJV) See JAARESHIAH

JARHA (2/2)
1 Chr 2:34 servant whose name was *J*.
2:35 Sheshan gave his daughter to *J*

JARIB (3/3)
1 Chr 4:24 Simeon were Nemuel, Jamin, *J*,
Ezra 8:16 Ariel, Shemaiah, Elnathan, *J*,
10:18 brothers: Maaseiah, Eliezer, *J*,

JARKON (1/1)
Josh 19:46 Me *J*, and Rakkon, with

JARMUTH (7/7) RAMOTH
Josh 10: 3 king of Hebron, Piram king of *J*,
10: 5 king of Hebron, the king of *J*,
10:23 king of Hebron, the king of *J*,
12:11 the king of *J*, one; the king
15:35 *J*, Adullam, Socoh, Azekah,
21:29 *J* with its common-land, and En
Neh 11:29 in En Rimmon, Zorah, *J*,

JAROAH (1/1)
1 Chr 5:14 the son of Huri, the son of *J*,

JASHEN (1/1)
2 Sam 23:32 Shaalbonite (of the sons of *J*),

JASHER (2/2)
Josh 10:13 not written in the Book of *J*?
2 Sam 1:18 is written in the Book of *J*:

JASHOBEAM (3/3)
1 Chr 11:11 *J* the son of a Hachmonite,
12: 6 Jisshiah, Azarel, Joezer, and *J*,
27: 2 for the first month was *J* the

JASHUB (3/3)
Num 26:24 of *J*, the family of the
1 Chr 7: 1 of Issachar were Tola, Puah, *J*,
Ezra 10:29 Meshullam, Malluch, Adaiah, *J*,

JASHUBI-LEHEM (1/1)
1 Chr 4:22 who ruled in Moab, and *J*.

JASHUBITES (1/1)
Num 26:24 of Jashub, the family of the *J*;

JASIEL (KJV) See JAASIEL

JASON (5/5)
Acts 17: 5 and attacked the house of *J*,
17: 6 they dragged *J* and some
17: 7 *J* has harbored them, and these
17: 9 they had taken security from *J*
Rom 16:21 my fellow worker, and Lucius, *J*,

JASPER (7/7)
Ex 28:20 row, a beryl, an onyx, and a *j*.
39:13 row, a beryl, an onyx, and a *j*.
Ezek 28:13 diamond, Beryl, onyx, and *j*,
Rev 4: 3 He who sat there was like a *j*
21:11 like a *j* stone, clear as
21:18 of its wall was of *j*;
21:19 the first foundation was *j*,

JATHNIEL (1/1)
1 Chr 26: 2 the third, *J* the fourth,

JATTIR (4/4)
Josh 15:48 the mountain country: Shamir, *J*,
21:14 *J* with its common-land, Eshtemoa
1 Sam 30:27 South, those who were in *J*,
1 Chr 6:57 Libnah with its common-lands, *J*,

JAVAN (7/7)
Gen 10: 2 were Gomer, Magog, Madai, *J*,
10: 4 The sons of *J* were Elishah,
1 Chr 1: 5 were Gomer, Magog, Madai, *J*,
1: 7 The sons of *J* were Elishah,
Isa 66:19 draw the bow, and Tubal and *J*,
Ezek 27:13 '*J*, Tubal, and Meshech
27:19 Dan and *J* paid for your wares,

JAVELIN (5/5)
Num 25: 7 the congregation and took a *j*
1 Sam 17: 6 on his legs and a bronze *j*
17:45 with a spear, and with a *j*.
Job 39:23 The glittering spear and *j*.
41:26 Nor does spear, dart, or *j*.

JAVELINS (2/2)
Job 41:29 He laughs at the threat of *j*.
Ezek 39: 9 the *j* and spears; and they will

JAW (1/1) JAWBONE, JAWS
Job 41: 2 Or pierce his *j* with a hook?

JAWBONE (4/3) JAW
Judg 15:15 He found a fresh *j* of a donkey,
15:16 With the *j* of a donkey, Heaps
15:16 With the *j* of a donkey I have
15:17 that he threw the *j* from his

JAWS (4/4) JAW
Ps 22:15 And My tongue clings to My *j*;
Isa 30:28 shall be a bridle in the *j*
Ezek 29: 4 But I will put hooks in your *j*,
38: 4 around, put hooks into your *j*,

JAZER (13/12)
Num 21:32 Then Moses sent to spy out *J*;
32: 1 and when they saw the land of *J*
32: 3 "Ataroth, Dibon, *J*,
32:35 Atroth and Shophan and *J* and
Josh 13:25 Their territory was *J*,
21:39 and *J* with its common-land:
2 Sam 24: 5 the ravine of Gad, and toward *J*.
1 Chr 6:81 and *J* with its common-lands.
26:31 among them capable men at *J* of
Isa 16: 8 Which have reached to *J* And
16: 9 Sibmah, With the weeping of *J*;
Jer 48:32 for you with the weeping of *J*.
48:32 They reach to the sea of *J*.

JAZIZ (1/1)
1 Chr 27:31 and *J* the Hagrite was over the

JEALOUS (13/11) JEALOUSY
Ex 20: 5 am a *j* God, visiting the
34:14 for the LORD, whose name is *J*,
34:14 is Jealous, is a *j* God),
Num 5:14 upon him and he becomes *j* of
5:14 upon him and he becomes *j* of
5:30 and he becomes *j* of his wife;
Deut 4:24 a consuming fire, a *j* God.
5: 9 am a *j* God, visiting the
6:15 the LORD your God is a *j* God
Josh 24:19 He is a *j* God; He will not
Ezek 39:25 and I will be *j* for My holy
Nah 1: 2 God is *j*, and the LORD

2 Cor 11: 2 For I am *j* for you with godly

JEALOUSIES (2/2) JEALOUSY

2 Cor 12:20 lest there be contentions, *j*,
Gal 5:20 sorcery, hatred, contentions, *j*,

JEALOUSLY (1/1)

Jas 4: 5 who dwells in us yearns *j*"?

JEALOUSY (33/30) JEALOUS, JEALOUSIES

Num 5:14 if the spirit of *j* comes upon
5:14 or if the spirit of *j* comes
5:15 it is a grain offering of *j*,
5:18 is the grain offering of *j*.
5:25 take the grain offering of *j*
5:29 'This is the law of *j*,
5:30 or when the spirit of *j* comes
Deut 29:20 anger of the LORD and His *j*
32:16 They provoked Him to *j* with
32:21 They have provoked Me to *j* by
32:21 But I will provoke them to *j*
1 Ki 14:22 and they provoked Him to *j* with
Ps 78:58 And moved Him to *j* with their
79: 5 Will Your *j* burn like fire?
Prov 6:34 For *j* is a husband's fury;
27: 4 who is able to stand before *j*?
Song 8: 6 *J* as cruel as the grave; Its
Ezek 8: 3 the seat of the image of *j*
8: 3 was, which provokes to *j*.
8: 5 was this image of *j* in the
16:38 blood upon you in fury and *j*.
16:42 and My *j* shall depart from you.
23:25 I will set My *j* against you,
36: 5 I have spoken in My burning *j*
36: 6 I have spoken in My *j* and My
38:19 For in My *j* and in the fire of
Zeph 1:18 devoured By the fire of His *j*,
3: 8 devoured With the fire of My *j*.
Rom 10:19 I will provoke you to *j* by
11:11 fall, to provoke them to *j*,
11:14 by any means I may provoke to *j*
1 Cor 10:22 Or do we provoke the Lord to *j*?
2 Cor 11: 2 am jealous for you with godly *j*.

JEARIM (1/1) KIRJATH JEARIM

Josh 15:10 along to the side of Mount *J*

JEATHERAI (1/1)

1 Chr 6:21 his son, and *J* his son.

JEBERECHIAH (1/1)

Isa 8: 2 and Zechariah the son of *J*.

JEBUS (5/5) JEBUSITE, JERUSALEM

Josh 18:28 *J* (which is Jerusalem),
Judg 19:10 and came to opposite *J*
19:11 They were near *J*,
1 Chr 11: 4 went to Jerusalem, which is *J*,
11: 5 Then the inhabitants of *J* said

JEBUSI (KJV) See JEBUSITE

JEBUSITE (16/16) JEBUS, JEBUSITES

Gen 10:16 the *J*, the Amorite, and the
Ex 33: 2 and the Hivite and the *J*.
34:11 and the Hivite and the *J*.
Deut 20:17 and the Hivite and the *J*,
Josh 9: 1 the Hivite, and the *J*—
11: 3 the *J* in the mountains, and the
15: 8 to the southern slope of the *J*
18:16 to the side of the *J* city on
2 Sam 24:16 floor of Araunah the *J*.
24:18 floor of Araunah the *J*.
1 Chr 1:14 the *J*, the Amorite, and the
21:15 threshing floor of Ornan the *J*.
21:18 threshing floor of Ornan the *J*.
21:28 threshing floor of Ornan the *J*,
2 Chr 3: 1 threshing floor of Ornan the *J*.
Zech 9: 7 in Judah, And Ekron like a *J*.

JEBUSITES (24/22) JEBUSITE

Gen 15:21 the Girgashites, and the *J*.
Ex 3: 8 and the Hivites and the *J*.
3:17 and the Hivites and the *J*,
13: 5 and the Hivites and the *J*,
23:23 and the Hivites and the *J*;
Num 13:29 the South; the Hittites, the *J*,
Deut 7: 1 and the Hivites and the *J*,
Josh 3:10 and the Amorites and the *J*:
12: 8 the Hivites, and the *J*:
15:63 As for the *J*, the inhabitants
15:63 but the *J* dwell with the
24:11 the Hivites, and the *J*.
Judg 1:21 did not drive out the *J* who
1:21 so the *J* dwell with the
3: 5 the Hivites, and the *J*.
19:11 aside into this city of the *J*
2 Sam 5: 6 went to Jerusalem against the *J*,
5: 8 water shaft and defeats the *J*
1 Ki 9:20 Perizzites, Hivites, and *J*,
1 Chr 11: 4 where the *J* were, the
11: 6 Whoever attacks the *J* first
2 Chr 8: 7 Perizzites, Hivites, and *J*,
Ezra 9: 1 Hittites, the Perizzites, the *J*,
Neh 9: 8 the Perizzites, the *J*,

JECAMIAH (1/1)

1 Chr 3:18 Pedaiah, Shenazzar, *J*,

JECHOLIAH (2/2)

2 Ki 15: 2 His mother's name was *J* of
2 Chr 26: 3 His mother's name was *J* of

JECHONIAS (KJV) See JECONIAH

JECONIAH (9/9) JEHOIACHIN

1 Chr 3:16 The sons of Jehoiakim were *J*
3:17 And the sons of *J* were Assir,
Esth 2: 6 who had been captured with *J*
Jer 24: 1 had carried away captive *J* the
27:20 when he carried away captive *J*
28: 4 bring back to this place *J* the
29: 2 (This happened after *J* the king,
Mt 1:11 Josiah begot *J* and his brothers
1:12 *J* begot Shealtiel, and

JEDAIAH (13/13)

1 Chr 4:37 the son of Allon, the son of *J*,
9:10 Of the priests: *J*,
24: 7 to Jehoiarib, the second to *J*,
Ezra 2:36 The priests: the sons of *J*,
Neh 3:10 Next to them *J* the son of
7:39 The priests: the sons of *J*,
11:10 *J* the son of Joiarib, and
12: 6 Shemaiah, Joiarib, *J*,
12: 7 Sallu, Amok, Hilkiah, and *J*.
12:19 of Joiarib, Mattenai; of *J*,
12:21 Hilkiah, Hashabiah; and of *J*,
Zech 6:10 Heldai, Tobijah, and *J*,
6:14 the LORD for Helem, Tobijah, *J*,

JEDIAEL (6/6)

1 Chr 7: 6 were Bela, Becher, and *J*—
7:10 The son of *J* was Bilhan, and
7:11 All these sons of *J* were heads
11:45 *J* the son of Shimri, and Joha
12:20 to him were Adnah, Jozabad, *J*,
26: 2 *J* the second, Zebadiah the

JEDIDAH (1/1)

2 Ki 22: 1 His mother's name was *J* the

JEDIDIAH (1/1) SOLOMON

2 Sam 12:25 So he called his name *J*,

JEDUTHUN (17/14)

1 Chr 9:16 the son of Galal, the son of *J*;
16:38 Obed-Edom the son of *J*,
16:41 and with them Heman and *J* and
16:42 and with them Heman and *J*,
16:42 Now the sons of *J* were
25: 1 of Asaph, of Heman, and of *J*,
25: 3 Of *J*, the sons of Jeduthun:
25: 3 Of Jeduthun, the sons of *J*:
25: 3 the direction of their father *J*,
25: 6 of the house of God. Asaph, *J*,
2 Chr 5:12 those of Asaph and Heman and *J*,
29:14 Shimei; and of the sons of *J*,
35:15 and *J* the king's seer. Also the
Neh 11:17 the son of Galal, the son of *J*.
Ps 39: To the Chief Musician. To *J*.
62: To the Chief Musician. To *J*.
77: To the Chief Musician. To *J*.

JEERING (1/1)

2 Chr 29: 8 to desolation, and to *j*,

JEEZER (1/1)

Num 26:30 are the sons of Gilead: of *J*,

JEEZERITES (1/1)

Num 26:30 of Jeezer, the family of the *J*;

JEGAR SAHADUTHA (1/1)

Gen 31:47 Laban called it *J*,

JEHALLELEL (2/2)

1 Chr 4:16 The sons of *J* were Ziph,
2 Chr 29:12 Abdi and Azariah the son of *J*;

JEHDEIAH (2/2)

1 Chr 24:20 of the sons of Shubael, *J*.
27:30 *J* the Meronothite was over the

JEHEZEKEL (1/1)

1 Chr 24:16 Pethahiah, the twentieth to *J*,

JEHIAH (1/1)

1 Chr 15:24 ark of God; and Obed-Edom and *J*,

JEHIEL (14/14)

1 Chr 15:18 Ben, Jaaziel, Shemiramoth, *J*,
15:20 Aziel, Shemiramoth, *J*,
16: 5 then Jeiel, Shemiramoth, *J*,
23: 8 The sons of Laadan: the first *J*,
27:32 and *J* the son of Hachmoni was
29: 8 into the hand of *J* the
2 Chr 21: 2 sons of Jehoshaphat: Azariah, *J*,
29:14 *J* and Shimei; and of the sons
31:13 *J*, Azaziah, Nahath, Asahel,
35: 8 Hilkiah, Zechariah, and *J*,
Ezra 8: 9 of Joab, Obadiah the son of *J*,
10: 2 And Shechaniah the son of *J*,
10:21 Maaseiah, Elijah, Shemaiah, *J*,
10:26 Elam: Mattaniah, Zechariah, *J*,

JEHIELI (2/2)

1 Chr 26:21 of Laadan the Gershonite: *J*.
26:22 The sons of *J*, Zetham and

JEHIZKIAH (1/1)

2 Chr 28:12 *J* the son of Shallum, and Amasa

JEHOADDAH (2/1)

1 Chr 8:36 And Ahaz begot *J*;
8:36 *J* begot Alemeth, Azmaveth, and

JEHOADDAN (2/2)

2 Ki 14: 2 His mother's name was *J* of
2 Chr 25: 1 His mother's name was *J* of

JEHOAHAZ (23/22) AHAZIAH, SHALLUM

2 Ki 10:35 Then *J* his son reigned in his
13: 1 *J* the son of Jehu became king
13: 4 So *J* pleaded with the LORD, and
13: 7 For He left of the army of *J*
13: 8 Now the rest of the acts of *J*,
13: 9 So *J* rested with his fathers,
13:10 Jehoash the son of *J* became
13:22 Israel all the days of *J*.
13:25 And Jehoash the son of *J*
13:25 had taken out of the hand of *J*
14: 1 year of Joash the son of *J*,
14: 8 to Jehoash the son of *J*,
14:17 death of Jehoash the son of *J*,
23:30 the people of the land took *J*
23:31 *J* was twenty-three years old
23:34 And Pharaoh took *J* and went to
2 Chr 21:17 not a son left to him except *J*,
25:17 and sent to Joash the son of *J*,
25:23 the son of Joash, the son of *J*,
25:25 the death of Joash the son of *J*,
36: 1 the people of the land took *J*
36: 2 *J* was twenty-three years old
36: 4 And Necho took *J* his brother

JEHOAHAZ'S (1/1)

2 Chr 36: 4 king of Egypt made *J* brother

JEHOASH (17/16) JOASH

2 Ki 11:21 *J* was seven years old when he
12: 1 *J* became king, and he reigned
12: 2 *J* did what was right in the
12: 4 And *J* said to the priests,
12: 6 the twenty-third year of King *J*,
12: 7 So King *J* called Jehoiada the
12:18 And *J* king of Judah took all the
13:10 *J* the son of Jehoahaz became
13:25 And *J* the son of Jehoahaz
14: 8 Amaziah sent messengers to *J*
14: 9 And *J* king of Israel sent to
14:11 Therefore *J* king of Israel went
14:13 Then *J* king of Israel captured
14:13 king of Judah, the son of *J*,
14:15 Now the rest of the acts of *J*
14:16 So *J* rested with his fathers,
14:17 years after the death of *J* the

JEHOHANAN (8/8)

1 Chr 26: 3 *J* the sixth, Eliehoenai the
2 Chr 17:15 and next to him was *J* the
23: 1 Jeroham, Ishmael the son of *J*,
Ezra 10: 6 and went into the chamber of *J*
10:28 of the sons of Bebai: *J*,
Neh 6:18 and his son *J* had married the
12:13 Ezra, Meshullam; of Amariah, *J*;
12:42 Shemaiah, Eleazar, Uzzi, *J*,

JEHOIACHIN (12/10) JECONIAH, JEHOIACHIN'S

2 Ki 24: 6 Then *J* his son reigned in his
24: 8 *J* was eighteen years old when
24:12 Then *J* king of Judah, his
24:15 And he carried *J* captive to
25:27 year of the captivity of *J*
25:27 released *J* king of Judah from
25:29 So *J* changed from his prison
2 Chr 36: 8 Then *J* his son reigned in his
36: 9 *J* was eight years old when he
Jer 52:31 year of the captivity of *J*
52:31 lifted up the head of *J* king of
52:33 So *J* changed from his prison

JEHOIACHIN'S (2/2) JEHOIACHIN

2 Ki 24:17 *J* uncle, king in his place,
Ezek 1: 2 in the fifth year of King *J*

JEHOIADA (52/49)

2 Sam 8:18 Benaiah the son of *J* was over
20:23 Benaiah the son of *J* was over
23:20 Benaiah was the son of *J*,
23:22 things Benaiah the son of *J*
1 Ki 1: 8 priest, Benaiah the son of *J*,
1:26 nor Benaiah the son of *J*,
1:32 and Benaiah the son of *J*.
1:36 Benaiah the son of *J* answered
1:38 prophet, Benaiah the son of *J*,
1:44 prophet, Benaiah the son of *J*,
2:25 hand of Benaiah the son of *J*;
2:29 sent Benaiah the son of *J*,
2:34 So Benaiah the son of *J* went up
2:35 king put Benaiah the son of *J*
2:46 commanded Benaiah the son of *J*;
4: 4 Benaiah the son of *J*,
2 Ki 11: 4 In the seventh year *J* sent and
11: 9 did according to all that *J*
11: 9 and came to *J* the priest.
11:15 And *J* the priest commanded the
11:17 Then *J* made a covenant between
12: 2 LORD all the days in which *J*
12: 7 So King Jehoash called *J* the
12: 9 Then *J* the priest took a chest,
1 Chr 11:22 Benaiah was the son of *J*,
11:24 things Benaiah the son of *J*
12:27 *J*, the leader of the
18:17 Benaiah the son of *J* was over
27: 5 the son of *J* the priest, who
27:34 After Ahithophel was *J* the son
2 Chr 22:11 the wife of *J* the priest
23: 1 In the seventh year *J*
23: 8 did according to all that *J*
23: 8 for *J* the priest had not
23: 9 And *J* the priest gave to the
23:11 Then *J* and his sons anointed
23:14 And *J* the priest brought out
23:16 Then *J* made a covenant between
23:18 Also *J* appointed the oversight
24: 2 of the LORD all the days of *J*
24: 3 And *J* took two wives for him,
24: 6 So the king called *J* the chief
24:12 The king and *J* gave it to those
24:14 the money before the king and *J*;
24:14 continually all the days of *J*.
24:15 But *J* grew old and was full of
24:17 Now after the death of *J* the
24:20 upon Zechariah the son of *J*
24:22 remember the kindness which *J*
24:25 of the blood of the sons of *J*
Neh 3: 6 Moreover *J* the son of Paseah
Jer 29:26 made you priest instead of *J*

JEHOIAKIM (37/37) ELIAKIM, JEHOIAKIM'S

2 Ki 23:34 and changed his name to *J*.
23:35 So *J* gave the silver and gold
23:36 *J* was twenty-five years old
24: 1 and *J* became his vassal for
24: 5 Now the rest of the acts of *J*,
24: 6 So *J* rested with his fathers.
24:19 according to all that *J* had
1 Chr 3:15 the firstborn, the second *J*,
3:16 The sons of *J* were Jeconiah his
2 Chr 36: 4 and changed his name to *J*.
36: 5 *J* was twenty-five years old
36: 8 Now the rest of the acts of *J*,
Jer 1: 3 It came also in the days of *J*
22:18 says the LORD concerning *J*
22:24 "though Coniah the son of *J*,
24: 1 captive Jeconiah the son of *J*,
25: 1 in the fourth year of *J* the son
26: 1 the beginning of the reign of *J*
26:21 And when *J* the king, with all
26:22 Then *J* the king sent men to
26:23 Egypt and brought him to *J* the
27: 1 the beginning of the reign of *J*
27:20 captive Jeconiah the son of *J*,
28: 4 place Jeconiah the son of *J*,
35: 1 the LORD in the days of *J* the
36: 1 to pass in the fourth year of *J*
36: 9 to pass in the fifth year of *J*
36:28 in the first scroll which *J*
36:29 And you shall say to *J* king of
36:30 says the LORD concerning *J*
36:32 the words of the book which *J*
37: 1 instead of Coniah the son of *J*,
45: 1 in the fourth year of *J* the son
46: 2 in the fourth year of *J* the
52: 2 according to all that *J* had
Dan 1: 1 third year of the reign of *J*
1: 2 And the Lord gave *J* king of

JEHOIAKIM'S (1/1) JEHOIAKIM

2 Chr 36:10 *J* brother, king over Judah and

JEHOIARIB (2/2)

1 Chr 9:10 Of the priests: Jedaiah, *J*,
24: 7 Now the first lot fell to *J*,

JEHONADAB (3/2) JONADAB

2 Ki 10:15 he met *J* the son of Rechab,
10:15 And *J* answered, "It is."
10:23 Then Jehu and *J* the son of

JEHONATHAN (4/4)

1 Chr 27:25 and *J* the son of Uzziah was
27:32 Also *J*, David's uncle, was a
2 Chr 17: 8 Asahel, Shemiramoth, *J*,
Neh 12:18 Bilgah, Shammua; of Shemaiah, *J*;

JEHORAM (23/21) JORAM

1 Ki 22:50 Then *J* his son reigned in his
2 Ki 1:17 *J* became king in his place, in
1:17 in the second year of *J* the son
3: 1 Now *J* the son of Ahab became
3: 6 So King *J* went out of Samaria
8:16 *J* the son of Jehoshaphat began
8:25 of Israel, Ahaziah the son of *J*,
8:29 And Ahaziah the son of *J*,
9:24 with full strength and shot *J*
12:18 Jehoshaphat and *J* and Ahaziah,
2 Chr 17: 8 and with them Elishama and *J*,
21: 1 Then *J* his son reigned in his
21: 3 but he gave the kingdom to *J*,
21: 4 Now when *J* was established over
21: 5 *J* was thirty-two years old when
21: 9 So *J* went out with his officers,
21:16 the LORD stirred up against *J*
22: 1 So Ahaziah the son of *J*,
22: 5 and went with *J* the son of Ahab
22: 6 And Azariah the son of *J*,
22: 6 went down to see *J* the son of
22: 7 he went out with *J* against Jehu
22:11 the daughter of King *J*,

JEHOSHABEATH (2/1)

2 Chr 22:11 But *J*, the daughter of the
22:11 So *J*, the daughter of

JEHOSHAPHAT (86/76)

2 Sam 8:16 *J* the son of Ahilud was
20:24 *J* the son of Ahilud was
1 Ki 4: 3 *J* the son of Ahilud, the
4:17 *J* the son of Paruah, in
15:24 Then *J* his son reigned in his
22: 2 that *J* the king of Judah went
22: 4 So he said to *J*, "Will you
22: 4 *J* said to the king of Israel,
22: 5 Also *J* said to the king of
22: 7 And *J* said, "Is there not
22: 8 So the king of Israel said to *J*,
22: 8 And *J* said, "Let not the
22:10 The king of Israel and *J* the
22:18 the king of Israel said to *J*,
22:29 So the king of Israel and *J* the
22:30 the king of Israel said to *J*,
22:32 captains of the chariots saw *J*,
22:32 him, and *J* cried out.
22:41 *J* the son of Asa had become
22:42 *J* was thirty-five years old
22:44 Also *J* made peace with the king
22:45 Now the rest of the acts of *J*,
22:48 *J* made merchant ships to go to
22:49 the son of Ahab said to *J*,
22:49 But *J* would not.
22:50 And *J* rested with his fathers,
22:51 in the seventeenth year of *J*
2 Ki 1:17 year of Jehoram the son of *J*,
3: 1 in the eighteenth year of *J*
3: 7 Then he went and sent to *J* king
3:11 But *J* said, "Is there no
3:12 And *J* said, "The word of the
3:12 So the king of Israel and *J*
3:14 that I regard the presence of *J*
8:16 *J* having been king of Judah,
8:16 Jehoram the son of *J* began to
9: 2 there for Jehu the son of *J*,
9:14 So Jehu the son of *J*,
12:18 *J* and Jehoram and Ahaziah,
1 Chr 3:10 Asa his son, *J* his son,
18:15 *J* the son of Ahilud was
2 Chr 17: 1 Then *J* his son reigned in his
17: 3 Now the LORD was with *J*,
17: 5 all Judah gave presents to *J*,
17:10 they did not make war against *J*.
17:11 of the Philistines brought *J*
17:12 So *J* became increasingly
18: 1 *J* had riches and honor in
18: 3 Ahab king of Israel said to *J*
18: 4 And *J* said to the king of
18: 6 But *J* said, "Is there not
18: 7 So the king of Israel said to *J*,
18: 7 And *J* said, "Let not the
18: 9 The king of Israel and *J* king of
18:17 the king of Israel said to *J*,
18:28 So the king of Israel and *J* the
18:29 the king of Israel said to *J*,
18:31 captains of the chariots saw *J*,
18:31 but *J* cried out, and the LORD
19: 1 Then *J* the king of Judah
19: 2 to meet him, and said to King *J*,
19: 4 So *J* dwelt at Jerusalem; and he
19: 8 *J* appointed some of the Levites
20: 1 came to battle against *J*.
20: 2 Then some came and told *J*,
20: 3 And *J* feared, and set himself to
20: 5 Then *J* stood in the assembly of
20:15 King *J*! Thus says the LORD to
20:18 And *J* bowed his head with his
20:20 *J* stood and said, "Hear me,
20:25 When *J* and his people came to
20:27 with *J* in front of them, to go
20:30 Then the realm of *J* was quiet,
20:31 So *J* was king over Judah.
20:34 Now the rest of the acts of *J*,
20:35 After this *J* king of Judah
20:37 Mareshah prophesied against *J*,
21: 1 And *J* rested with his fathers,
21: 2 He had brothers, the sons of *J*:
21: 2 all these were the sons of *J*
21:12 not walked in the ways of *J*
22: 9 they said, "he is the son of *J*,
Joel 3: 2 them down to the Valley of *J*;
3:12 and come up to the Valley of *J*;
Mt 1: 8 Asa begot *J*, Jehoshaphat begot
1: 8 *J* begot Joram, and Joram begot

JEHOSHEBA (1/1)

2 Ki 11: 2 But *J*, the daughter of King

JEHOSHUA, JEHOSHUAH (KJV) See JOSHUA

JEHOVAH (KJV) See LORD, YAH

JEHOVAH-JIREH (KJV) See THE-LORD-WILL-PROVIDE

JEHOVAH-NISSI (KJV) See THE-LORD-IS-MY-BANNER

JEHOVAH-SHALOM (KJV) See THE-LORD-IS-PEACE

J

JEHOZABAD (4/4)

2 Ki 12:21 the son of Shimeath and *J* the
1 Chr 26: 4 *J* the second, Joah the third,
2 Chr 17:18 and next to him was *J*,
24:26 and *J* the son of Shimrith the

JEHOZADAK (8/8) JOZADAK

1 Chr 6:14 Seraiah, and Seraiah begot *J*.
6:15 *J* went into captivity when the
Hag 1: 1 and to Joshua the son of *J*,
1:12 and Joshua the son of *J*,
1:14 spirit of Joshua the son of *J*,
2: 2 and to Joshua the son of *J*,
2: 4 be strong, Joshua, son of *J*,
Zech 6:11 the head of Joshua the son of *J*,

JEHU (60/56)

1 Ki 16: 1 the word of the LORD came to *J*
16: 7 the LORD came by the prophet *J*
16:12 He spoke against Baasha by *J*
19:16 Also you shall anoint *J* the son
19:17 *J* will kill; and whoever
19:17 whoever escapes the sword of *J*,
2 Ki 9: 2 look there for *J* the son of
9: 5 *J* said, "For which one of
9:11 Then *J* came out to the servants
9:13 saying, "*J* is king!"
9:14 So *J* the son of Jehoshaphat,
9:15 And *J* said, "If you are so
9:16 So *J* rode in a chariot and went
9:17 and he saw the company of *J* as
9:18 And *J* said, "What have you
9:19 And *J* answered, "What have
9:20 is like the driving of *J* the
9:21 and they went out to meet *J*,
9:22 it happened, when Joram saw *J*,
9:22 he said, "Is it peace, *J*?
9:24 Now *J* drew his bow with full
9:25 Then *J* said to Bidkar his
9:27 So *J* pursued him, and said,
9:30 Now when *J* had come to Jezreel,
9:31 as *J* entered at the gate, she
10: 1 And *J* wrote and sent letters to
10: 5 reared the sons, sent to *J*,
10:11 So *J* killed all who remained of
10:13 *J* met with the brothers of
10:15 *J* said, "If it is, give
10:18 Then *J* gathered all the people
10:18 *J* will serve him much.
10:19 But *J* acted deceptively, with
10:20 And *J* said, "Proclaim a solemn
10:21 Then *J* sent throughout all
10:23 Then *J* and Jehonadab the son of
10:24 Now *J* had appointed for himself
10:25 that *J* said to the guard and to
10:28 Thus *J* destroyed Baal from
10:29 However *J* did not turn away
10:30 And the LORD said to *J*,
10:31 But *J* took no heed to walk in
10:34 Now the rest of the acts of *J*,
10:35 So *J* rested with his fathers,
10:36 And the period that *J* reigned
12: 1 In the seventh year of *J*,
13: 1 Jehoahaz the son of *J* became
14: 8 son of Jehoahaz, the son of *J*,
15:12 the LORD which He spoke to *J*,
1 Chr 2:38 Obed begot *J*, and Jehu begot
2:38 and *J* begot Azariah;

4:35 and *J* the son of Joshibiah, the
12: 3 and *J* the Anathothite;
2 Chr 19: 2 And *J* the son of Hanani the seer
20:34 are written in the book of *J*
22: 7 out with Jehoram against *J* the
22: 8 when *J* was executing judgment
22: 9 and brought him to *J*.
25:17 son of Jehoahaz, the son of *J*,
Hos 1: 4 of Jezreel on the house of *J*,

JEHUBBAH (1/1)
1 Chr 7:34 of Shemer were Ahi, Rohgah, *J*,

JEHUCAL (1/1)
Jer 37: 3 And Zedekiah the king sent *J*

JEHUD (1/1)
Josh 19:45 *J*, Bene Berak, Gath Rimmon,

JEHUDI (4/3)
Jer 36:14 all the princes sent *J* the son
36:21 So the king sent *J* to bring the
36:21 And *J* read it in the hearing of
36:23 when *J* had read three or four

JEHUDIJAH (1/1)
1 Chr 4:18 (His wife *J* bore Jered the

JEHUSH (KJV) See JEUSH

JEIEL (13/12)
1 Chr 5: 7 was registered: the chief, *J*,
9:35 *J* the father of Gibeon, whose
11:44 Shama and *J* the sons of Hotham
15:18 Mikneiah, Obed-Edom, and *J*,
15:21 Mikneiah, Obed-Edom, *J*,
16: 5 next to him Zechariah, then *J*,
16: 5 *J* with stringed instruments and
2 Chr 20:14 son of Benaiah, the son of *J*,
26:11 on their roll as prepared by *J*
29:13 sons of Elizaphan, Shimri and *J*;
35: 9 and Hashabiah and *J* and
Ezra 8:13 names are these—Eliphelet, *J*,
10:43 of the sons of Nebo: *J*,

JEKABZEEL (1/1)
Neh 11:25 *J* and its villages;

JEKAMEAM (2/2)
1 Chr 23:19 the third, and *J* the fourth.
24:23 the third, and *J* the fourth.

JEKAMIAH (2/1)
1 Chr 2:41 Shallum begot *J*, and Jekamiah
2:41 and *J* begot Elishama.

JEKUTHIEL (1/1)
1 Chr 4:18 and *J* the father of Zanoah.)

JEMIMAH (1/1)
Job 42:14 called the name of the first *J*,

JEMUEL (2/2)
Gen 46:10 The sons of Simeon were *J*,
Ex 6:15 And the sons of Simeon were *J*,

JEOPARDED (KJV) See JEOPARDIZED

JEOPARDIZED (1/1)
Judg 5:18 Zebulun is a people who *j*

JEOPARDY (4/4)
2 Sam 23:17 of the men who went in *j* of
1 Chr 11:19 have put their lives in *j*?
Lk 8:23 with water, and were in *j*.
1 Cor 15:30 And why do we stand in *j* every

JEPHTHAE (KJV) See JEPHTHAH

JEPHTHAH (30/26) JIPHTHAH EL
Judg 11: 1 Now *J* the Gileadite was a mighty
11: 1 of a harlot; and Gilead begot *J*.
11: 2 they drove *J* out, and said to
11: 3 Then *J* fled from his brothers
11: 3 men banded together with *J* and
11: 5 elders of Gilead went to get *J*
11: 6 Then they said to *J*,
11: 7 So *J* said to the elders of
11: 8 the elders of Gilead said to *J*,
11: 9 So *J* said to the elders of
11:10 the elders of Gilead said to *J*,
11:11 Then *J* went with the elders of
11:11 and *J* spoke all his words
11:12 Now *J* sent messengers to the
11:13 answered the messengers of *J*,
11:14 So *J* again sent messengers to
11:15 and said to him, "Thus says *J*:
11:28 did not heed the words which *J*
11:29 Spirit of the LORD came upon *J*,
11:30 And *J* made a vow to the LORD,
11:32 So *J* advanced toward the people
11:34 When *J* came to his house at
11:40 to lament the daughter of *J*
12: 1 toward Zaphon, and said to *J*,
12: 2 And *J* said to them, "My people
12: 4 Now *J* gathered together all the
12: 7 And *J* judged Israel six years.
12: 7 Then *J* the Gileadite died and
1 Sam 12:11 LORD sent Jerubbaal, Bedan, *J*,
Heb 11:32 and Barak and Samson and *J*,

JEPHUNNEH (16/16)
Num 13: 6 of Judah, Caleb the son of *J*;
14: 6 of Nun and Caleb the son of *J*,
14:30 Except for Caleb the son of *J*
14:38 of Nun and Caleb the son of *J*
26:65 except Caleb the son of *J* and
32:12 'except Caleb the son of *J*,
34:19 of Judah, Caleb the son of *J*;
Deut 1:36 'except Caleb the son of *J*;
Josh 14: 6 And Caleb the son of *J* the
14:13 Hebron to Caleb the son of *J*
14:14 of Caleb the son of *J* the
15:13 Now to Caleb the son of *J* he
21:12 gave to Caleb the son of *J* as
1 Chr 4:15 The sons of Caleb the son of *J*
6:56 they gave to Caleb the son of *J*.
7:38 The sons of Jether were *J*,

JERAH (2/2)
Gen 10:26 Sheleph, Hazarmaveth, *J*,
1 Chr 1:20 Sheleph, Hazarmaveth, *J*,

JERAHMEEL (8/8)
1 Chr 2: 9 who were born to him were *J*,
2:25 The sons of *J*, the firstborn
2:26 *J* had another wife, whose name
2:27 sons of Ram, the firstborn of *J*,
2:33 These were the sons of *J*.
2:42 of Caleb the brother of *J*
24:29 Of Kish: the son of Kish, *J*.
Jer 36:26 And the king commanded *J* the

JERAHMEELITES (2/2)
1 Sam 27:10 the southern area of the *J*,
30:29 were in the cities of the *J*,

JERED (1/1)
1 Chr 4:18 (His wife Jehudijah bore *J* the

JEREMAI (1/1)
Ezra 10:33 Mattattah, Zabad, Eliphelet, *J*,

JEREMIAH (150/136) JEREMIAH'S
2 Ki 23:31 was Hamutal the daughter of *J*
24:18 was Hamutal the daughter of *J*
1 Chr 5:24 Epher, Ishi, Eliel, Azriel, *J*,
12: 4 thirty, and over the thirty; *J*,
12:10 the fourth, *J* the fifth,
12:13 *J* the tenth, and Machbanai the
2 Chr 35:25 *J* also lamented for Josiah.
36:12 did not humble himself before *J*
36:21 of the LORD by the mouth of *J*,
36:22 of the LORD by the mouth of *J*
Ezra 1: 1 of the LORD by the mouth of *J*
Neh 10: 2 Seraiah, Azariah, *J*,
12: 1 and Jeshua: Seraiah, *J*,
12:12 of Seraiah, Meraiah; of *J*,
12:34 Judah, Benjamin, Shemaiah, *J*,
Jer 1: 1 The words of *J* the son of
1:11 LORD came to me, saying, "*J*,
7: 1 The word that came to *J* from the
11: 1 The word that came to *J* from the
14: 1 of the LORD that came to *J*
18: 1 The word which came to *J* from
18:18 let us devise plans against *J*;
19:14 Then *J* came from Tophet, where
20: 1 heard that *J* prophesied these
20: 2 Then Pashhur struck *J* the
20: 3 day that Pashhur brought *J* out
20: 3 Then *J* said to him, "The LORD
21: 1 The word which came to *J* from
21: 3 Then *J* said to them, "Thus you
24: 3 to me, "What do you see, *J*?
25: 1 The word that came to *J*
25: 2 which *J* the prophet spoke to all
25:13 which *J* has prophesied
26: 7 and all the people heard *J*
26: 8 when *J* had made an end of
26: 9 people were gathered against *J*
26:12 Then *J* spoke to all the princes
26:20 according to all the words of *J*.
26:24 the son of Shaphan was with *J*,
27: 1 this word came to *J* from the
28: 5 Then the prophet *J* spoke to the
28: 6 and the prophet *J* said, "Amen!
28:11 " And the prophet *J* went his
28:12 the word of the LORD came to *J*,
28:12 from the neck of the prophet *J*,
28:15 Then the prophet *J* said to
29: 1 the words of the letter that *J*
29:27 why have you not reproved *J* of
29:29 letter in the hearing of *J* the
29:30 the word of the LORD came to *J*,
30: 1 The word that came to *J* from the
32: 1 The word that came to *J* from the
32: 2 and *J* the prophet was shut up
32: 6 And *J* said, "The word of the
32:26 the word of the LORD came to *J*,
33: 1 word of the LORD came to *J* a
33:19 the word of the LORD came to *J*,
33:23 the word of the LORD came to *J*,
34: 1 The word which came to *J* from
34: 6 Then *J* the prophet spoke all
34: 8 is the word that came to *J*
34:12 the word of the LORD came to *J*
35: 1 The word which came to *J* from
35: 3 I took Jaazaniah the son of *J*,
35:12 came the word of the LORD to *J*,
35:18 And *J* said to the house of the
36: 1 that this word came to *J* from
36: 4 Then *J* called Baruch the son of
36: 4 a book, at the instruction of *J*,
36: 5 And *J* commanded Baruch, saying,
36: 8 did according to all that *J*
36:10 from the book the words of *J*
36:19 "Go and hide, you and *J*;
36:26 seize Baruch the scribe and *J*
36:27 written at the instruction of *J*,
36:27 the word of the LORD came to *J*,
36:32 Then *J* took another scroll and
36:32 on it at the instruction of *J*
37: 2 which He spoke by the prophet *J*.
37: 3 the priest, to the prophet *J*,
37: 4 Now *J* was coming and going among
37: 6 the LORD came to the prophet *J*,
37:12 that *J* went out of Jerusalem to
37:13 and he seized *J* the prophet,
37:14 Then *J* said, "False! I am not
37:14 So Irijah seized *J* and brought
37:15 the princes were angry with *J*,
37:16 When *J* entered the dungeon and
37:16 and *J* had remained there many
37:17 And *J* said, "There is."
37:18 Moreover *J* said to King
37:21 that they should commit *J* to
37:21 Thus *J* remained in the court of
38: 1 heard the words that *J* had
38: 6 So they took *J* and cast him into
38: 6 and they let *J* down with ropes.
38: 6 So *J* sank in the mire.
38: 7 heard that they had put *J* in
38: 9 in all that they have done to *J*
38:10 and lift *J* the prophet out of
38:11 by ropes into the dungeon to *J*.
38:12 the Ethiopian said to *J*,
38:12 the ropes." And *J* did so.
38:13 So they pulled *J* up with ropes
38:13 And *J* remained in the court of
38:14 the king sent and had *J* the
38:14 LORD. And the king said to *J*,
38:15 *J* said to Zedekiah, "If I
38:16 the king swore secretly to *J*,
38:17 Then *J* said to Zedekiah, "Thus
38:19 And Zedekiah the king said to *J*,
38:20 But *J* said, "They shall not
38:24 Then Zedekiah said to *J*,
38:27 Then all the princes came to *J*
38:28 Now *J* remained in the court of
39:11 gave charge concerning *J* to
39:14 they sent someone to take *J*
39:15 word of the LORD had come to *J*
40: 1 The word that came to *J* from the
40: 2 the captain of the guard took *J*
40: 5 Now while *J* had not yet gone
40: 6 Then *J* went to Gedaliah the son
42: 2 and said to *J* the prophet,
42: 4 Then *J* the prophet said to them,
42: 5 So they said to *J*,
42: 7 the word of the LORD came to *J*.
43: 1 when *J* had stopped speaking to
43: 2 proud men spoke, saying to *J*,
43: 6 and *J* the prophet and Baruch
43: 8 word of the LORD came to *J* in
44: 1 The word that came to *J*
44:15 Egypt, in Pathros, answered *J*,
44:20 Then *J* spoke to all the
44:24 Moreover *J* said to all the
45: 1 The word that *J* the prophet
45: 1 a book at the instruction of *J*,
46: 1 of the LORD which came to *J*
46:13 word that the LORD spoke to *J*
47: 1 of the LORD that came to *J*
49:34 of the LORD that came to *J*
50: 1 the land of the Chaldeans by *J*
51:59 The word which *J* the prophet
51:60 So *J* wrote in a book all the
51:61 And *J* said to Seraiah, "When
51:64 Thus far are the words of *J*.
52: 1 was Hamutal the daughter of *J*
Dan 9: 2 the word of the LORD through *J*
Mt 2:17 fulfilled what was spoken by *J*
16:14 and others *J* or one of the
27: 9 fulfilled what was spoken by *J*

JEREMIAH'S (1/1) JEREMIAH
Jer 28:10 the yoke off the prophet *J* neck

JEREMIAS, JEREMY (KJV) See JEREMIAH

JEREMOTH (5/5)
1 Chr 8:14 Ahio, Shashak, *J*,
23:23 Mushi were Mahli, Eder, and *J*—
25:22 the fifteenth for *J*,

Ezra 10:26 Zechariah, Jehiel, Abdi, J,
10:27 Eliashib, Mattaniah, J,

JERIAH (2/2)

1 Chr 23:19 J was the first, Amariah the
24:23 J was the first, Amariah the

JERIBAI (1/1)

1 Chr 11:46 J and Joshaviah the sons of

JERICHO (64/59)

Num 22: 1 of the Jordan across from J.
26: 3 by the Jordan, across from J,
26:63 by the Jordan, across from J.
31:12 by the Jordan, across from J.
33:48 by the Jordan, across from J.
33:50 by the Jordan, across from J,
34:15 across from J eastward,
35: 1 by the Jordan across from J,
36:13 by the Jordan, across from J.
Deut 32:49 the land of Moab, across from J;
34: 1 Pisgah, which is across from J.
34: 3 the plain of the Valley of J,
Josh 2: 1 view the land, especially J.
2: 2 And it was told the king of J,
2: 3 So the king of J sent to Rahab,
3:16 people crossed over opposite J.
4:13 for battle, to the plains of J.
4:19 Gilgal on the east border of J.
5:10 at twilight on the plains of J.
5:13 to pass, when Joshua was by J,
6: 1 Now J was securely shut up
6: 2 See! I have given J into your
6:25 whom Joshua sent to spy out J.
6:26 rises up and builds this city J;
7: 2 Now Joshua sent men from J to
8: 2 Ai and its king as you did to J
9: 3 what Joshua had done to J and
10: 1 as he had done to J and its
10:28 as he had done to the king of J.
10:30 as he had done to the king of J.
12: 9 the king of J, one; the king
13:32 the Jordan, by J eastward.
16: 1 of Joseph from the Jordan, by J,
16: 1 to the waters of J on the east,
16: 1 wilderness that goes up from J
16: 7 and Naarah, reached to J,
18:12 went up to the side of J on
18:21 to their families, were J,
20: 8 by J eastward, they assigned
24:11 over the Jordan and came to J.
24:11 And the men of J fought against
2 Sam 10: 5 Wait at J until your beards have
1 Ki 16:34 his days Hiel of Bethel built J.
2 Ki 2: 4 the LORD has sent me on to J.
2: 4 leave you!" So they came to J.
2: 5 of the prophets who were at J
2:15 the prophets who were from J
2:18 to him, for he had stayed in J,
25: 5 overtook him in the plains of J.
1 Chr 6:78 of the Jordan, across from J,
19: 5 Wait at J until your beards have
2 Chr 28:15 them to their brethren at J,
Ezra 2:34 the people of J, three
Neh 3: 2 Next to Eliashib the men of J
7:36 the sons of J, three
Jer 39: 5 Zedekiah in the plains of J.
52: 8 Zedekiah in the plains of J.
Mt 20:29 Now as they went out of J,
Mk 10:46 Now they came to J.
10:46 As He went out of J with His
Lk 10:30 went down from Jerusalem to J,
18:35 as He was coming near J,
19: 1 entered and passed through J.
Heb 11:30 By faith the walls of J fell

JERIEL (1/1)

1 Chr 7: 2 of Tola were Uzzi, Rephaiah, J,

JERIJAH (1/1)

1 Chr 26:31 J was head of the Hebronites

JERIMOTH (8/8)

1 Chr 7: 7 were Ezbon, Uzzi, Uzziel, J,
7: 8 Eliezer, Elioenai, Omri, J,
12: 5 Eluzai, J, Bealiah,
24:30 Mushi were Mahli, Eder, and J.
25: 4 Mattaniah, Uzziel, Shebuel, J,
27:19 J the son of Azriel;
2 Chr 11:18 Mahalath the daughter of J the
31:13 Azaziah, Nahath, Asahel, J,

JERIOTH (1/1)

1 Chr 2:18 by Azubah, his wife, and by J.

JEROBOAM (101/93)

1 Ki 11:26 J the son of Nebat, an
11:28 The man J was a mighty man of
11:29 when J went out of Jerusalem,
11:31 And he said to J, "Take for
11:40 therefore sought to kill J.
11:40 But J arose and fled to Egypt,
12: 2 when J the son of Nebat heard
12: 3 Then J and the whole assembly
12:12 So J and all the people came to
12:15 by Ahijah the Shilonite to J
12:20 when all Israel heard that J
12:25 Then J built Shechem in the
12:26 And J said in his heart, "Now
12:32 J ordained a feast on the
13: 1 and J stood by the altar to
13: 4 So it came to pass when King J
13:33 After this event J did not turn
13:34 was the sin of the house of J,
14: 1 that time Abijah the son of J
14: 2 And J said to his wife, "Please
14: 2 recognize you as the wife of J,
14: 5 Ahijah, "Here is the wife of J,
14: 6 he said, "Come in, wife of J.
14: 7 'Go, tell J, 'Thus says the
14:10 disaster on the house of J,
14:10 and will cut off from J every
14:10 the remnant of the house of J,
14:11 shall eat whoever belongs to J
14:13 for he is the only one of J who
14:13 God of Israel in the house of J.
14:14 shall cut off the house of J;
14:16 up because of the sins of J,
14:19 Now the rest of the acts of J,
14:20 The period that J reigned was
14:30 was war between Rehoboam and J
15: 1 the eighteenth year of King J
15: 6 was war between Rehoboam and J
15: 7 was war between Abijam and J.
15: 9 In the twentieth year of J king
15:25 Now Nadab the son of J became
15:29 he killed all the house of J.
15:29 He did not leave to J anyone
15:30 because of the sins of J,
15:34 and walked in the way of J,
16: 2 you have walked in the way of J,
16: 3 your house like the house of J
16: 7 in being like the house of J,
16:19 in walking in the way of J,
16:26 he walked in all the ways of J
16:31 him to walk in the sins of J
21:22 your house like the house of J
22:52 his mother and in the way of J
2 Ki 3: 3 he persisted in the sins of J
9: 9 of Ahab like the house of J
10:29 turn away from the sins of J
10:31 not depart from the sins of J,
13: 2 and followed the sins of J the
13: 6 from the sins of the house of J,
13:11 depart from all the sins of J
13:13 Then J sat on his throne.
14:16 Then J his son reigned in his
14:23 J the son of Joash, king of
14:24 depart from all the sins of J
14:27 He saved them by the hand of J
14:28 Now the rest of the acts of J,
14:29 So J rested with his fathers,
15: 1 In the twenty-seventh year of J
15: 8 Zechariah the son of J reigned
15: 9 not depart from the sins of J
15:18 all his days from the sins of J
15:24 not depart from the sins of J
15:28 not depart from the sins of J
17:21 and they made J the son of
17:21 Then J drove Israel from
17:22 walked in all the sins of J
23:15 and the high place which J the
1 Chr 5:17 and in the days of J king of
2 Chr 9:29 of Iddo the seer concerning J
10: 2 when J the son of Nebat heard
10: 2 that J returned from Egypt.
10: 3 And J and all Israel came and
10:12 So J and all the people came to
10:15 of Ahijah the Shilonite to J
11: 4 turned back from attacking J.
11:14 for J and his sons had rejected
12:15 wars between Rehoboam and J
13: 1 the eighteenth year of King J,
13: 2 was war between Abijah and J.
13: 3 J also drew up in battle
13: 4 'Hear me, J and all Israel:
13: 6 Yet J the son of Nebat, the
13: 8 you are the gold calves which J
13:13 But J caused an ambush to go
13:15 it happened that God struck J
13:19 And Abijah pursued J and took
13:20 So J did not recover strength
Hos 1: 1 and in the days of J the son of
Am 1: 1 and in the days of J the son of
7: 9 sword against the house of J.
7:10 the priest of Bethel sent to J
7:11 J shall die by the sword, And

JEROBOAM'S (2/2)

1 Ki 14: 4 And J wife did so; she arose and
14:17 Then J wife arose and departed,

JEROHAM (10/10)

1 Sam 1: 1 name was Elkanah the son of J,
1 Chr 6:27 J his son, and Elkanah his
6:34 son of Elkanah, the son of J,
8:27 and Zichri were the sons of J.
9: 8 Ibneiah the son of J;
9:12 Adaiah the son of J,
12: 7 and Zebadiah the sons of J of
27:22 over Dan, Azarel the son of J.
2 Chr 23: 1 hundreds: Azariah the son of J,
Neh 11:12 and Adaiah the son of J,

JERUBBAAL (14/13) GIDEON, JERUBBESHETH

Judg 6:32 on that day he called him J,
7: 1 Then J (that is, Gideon) and
8:29 Then J the son of Joash went
8:35 show kindness to the house of J
9: 1 Then Abimelech the son of J went
9: 2 all seventy of the sons of J
9: 5 brothers, the seventy sons of J,
9: 5 Jotham the youngest son of J
9:16 if you have dealt well with J
9:19 in truth and sincerity with J
9:24 done to the seventy sons of J
9:28 Is he not the son of J,
9:57 curse of Jotham the son of J.
1 Sam 12:11 "And the LORD sent J,

JERUBBESHETH (1/1) JERUBBAAL

2 Sam 11:21 struck Abimelech the son of J?

JERUEL (1/1)

2 Chr 20:16 before the Wilderness of J.

JERUSALEM (814/764) ARIEL, JEBUS, SALEM

Josh 10: 1 pass when Adoni-Zedek king of J
10: 3 Adoni-Zedek king of J sent to
10: 5 of the Amorites, the king of J,
10:23 from the cave: the king of J,
12:10 the king of J, one; the king
15: 8 Jebusite city (which is J).
15:63 Jebusites, the inhabitants of J,
15:63 the children of Judah at J to
18:28 Eleph, Jebus (which is J),
Judg 1: 7 Then they brought him to J,
1: 8 of Judah fought against J and
1:21 the Jebusites who inhabited J;
1:21 the children of Benjamin in J
19:10 to opposite Jebus (that is, J).
1 Sam 17:54 Philistine and brought it to J,
2 Sam 5: 5 months, and in J he reigned
5: 6 the king and his men went to J
5:13 concubines and wives from J,
5:14 those who were born to him in J:
8: 7 and brought them to J.
9:13 So Mephibosheth dwelt in J,
10:14 people of Ammon and went to J.
11: 1 But David remained at J.
11:12 So Uriah remained in J that
12:31 all the people returned to J.
14:23 and brought Absalom to J.
14:28 dwelt two full years in J,
15: 8 indeed brings me back to J,
15:11 two hundred men invited from J,
15:14 who were with him at J,
15:29 the ark of God back to J.
15:37 And Absalom came into J.
16: 3 "Indeed he is staying in J,
16:15 the men of Israel, came to J;
17:20 find them, they returned to J.
19:19 that my lord the king left J,
19:25 when he had come to J to meet
19:33 you while you are with me in J.
19:34 should go up with the king to J?
20: 2 from the Jordan as far as J,
20: 3 David came to his house at J.
20: 7 And they went out of J to
20:22 Joab returned to the king at J.
24: 8 they came to J at the end of
24:16 stretched out His hand over J
1 Ki 2:11 Hebron, and in J he reigned
2:36 Build yourself a house in J and
2:38 So Shimei dwelt in J many
2:41 that Shimei had gone from J to
3: 1 and the wall all around J.
3:15 And he came to J and stood
8: 1 of Israel, to King Solomon in J,
9:15 house, the Millo, the wall of J,
9:19 Solomon desired to build in J,
10: 2 She came to J with a very great
10:26 cities and with the king in J.
10:27 made silver as common in J
11: 7 on the hill that is east of J,
11:13 and for the sake of J which I
11:29 when Jeroboam went out of J,
11:32 David, and for the sake of J,
11:36 have a lamp before Me in J,
11:42 that Solomon reigned in J over
12:18 chariot in haste to flee to J.
12:21 And when Rehoboam came to J,
12:27 in the house of the LORD at J,
12:28 too much for you to go up to J.
14:21 He reigned seventeen years in J,
14:25 king of Egypt came up against J.
15: 2 He reigned three years in J.
15: 4 his God gave him a lamp in J,
15: 4 after him and by establishing J;
15:10 he reigned forty-one years in J.
22:42 reigned twenty-five years in J.
2 Ki 8:17 and he reigned eight years in J.
8:26 and he reigned one year in J.
9:28 carried him in the chariot to J,
12: 1 and he reigned forty years in J.
12:17 set his face to go up to J.
12:18 Then he went away from J.
14: 2 reigned twenty-nine years in J.
14: 2 name was Jehoaddan of J.
14:13 Beth Shemesh; and he went to J,

J

14:13 and broke down the wall of *J*
14:19 a conspiracy against him in *J*,
14:20 and he was buried at *J* with his
15: 2 he reigned fifty-two years in *J*.
15: 2 name was Jecholiah of *J*.
15:33 he reigned sixteen years in *J*.
16: 2 he reigned sixteen years in *J*;
16: 5 came up to *J* to make war;
18: 2 reigned twenty-nine years in *J*.
18:17 with a great army against *J*,
18:17 And they went up and came to *J*.
18:22 away, and said to Judah and *J*,
18:22 worship before this altar in *J*'
18:35 that the LORD should deliver *J*
19:10 *J* shall not be given into the
19:21 The daughter of *J* Has shaken
19:31 For out of *J* shall go a
21: 1 reigned fifty-five years in *J*.
21: 4 In *J* I will put My name."
21: 7 son, "In this house and in *J*,
21:12 bringing such calamity upon *J*
21:13 And I will stretch over *J* the
21:13 I will wipe *J* as one wipes a
21:16 till he had filled *J* from one
21:19 and he reigned two years in *J*.
22: 1 reigned thirty-one years in *J*.
22:14 (She dwelt in *J* in the Second
23: 1 all the elders of Judah and *J*
23: 2 him all the inhabitants of *J*—
23: 4 and he burned them outside *J* in
23: 5 and in the places all around *J*,
23: 6 to the Brook Kidron outside *J*,
23: 9 to the altar of the LORD in *J*,
23:13 places that were east of *J*,
23:20 on them; and he returned to *J*.
23:23 was held before the LORD in *J*.
23:24 in the land of Judah and in *J*,
23:27 and will cast off this city *J*
23:30 from Megiddo, brought him to *J*,
23:31 he reigned three months in *J*.
23:33 that he might not reign in *J*;
23:36 he reigned eleven years in *J*.
24: 4 for he had filled *J* with
24: 8 and he reigned in *J* three
24: 8 the daughter of Elnathan of *J*.
24:10 of Babylon came up against *J*,
24:14 he carried into captivity all *J*:
24:15 carried into captivity from *J*
24:18 he reigned eleven years in *J*.
24:20 the LORD this happened in *J*
25: 1 and all his army came against *J*
25: 8 the king of Babylon, came to *J*.
25: 9 house; all the houses of *J*,
25:10 broke down the walls of *J* all
1 Chr 3: 4 and in *J* he reigned
3: 5 And these were born to him in *J*:
6:10 temple that Solomon built in *J*)
6:15 the LORD carried Judah and *J*
6:32 the house of the LORD in *J*,
8:28 chief men. These dwelt in *J*.
8:32 alongside their relatives in *J*,
9: 3 Now in *J* the children of Judah
9:34 They dwelt at *J*.
9:38 alongside their relatives in *J*,
11: 4 David and all Israel went to *J*,
14: 3 David took more wives in *J*,
14: 4 his children whom he had in *J*:
15: 3 all Israel together at *J*,
18: 7 and brought them to *J*.
19:15 the city. So Joab went to *J*.
20: 1 But David stayed at *J*.
20: 3 all the people returned to *J*.
21: 4 all Israel and came to *J*.
21:15 And God sent an angel to *J* to
21:16 sword stretched out over *J*.
23:25 that they may dwell in *J*
26:29 judges over Israel outside *J*.
28: 1 Now David assembled at *J* all the
29:27 years he reigned in *J*.
2 Chr 1: 4 had pitched a tent for it at *J*.
1:13 So Solomon came to *J* from the
1:14 cities and with the king in *J*.
1:15 silver and gold as common in *J*
2: 7 who are with me in Judah and *J*,
2:16 and you will carry it up to *J*.
3: 1 the house of the LORD at *J* on
5: 2 of the children of Israel, in *J*,
6: 6 'Yet I have chosen *J*,
8: 6 Solomon desired to build in *J*,
9: 1 she came to *J* to test Solomon
9:25 cities and with the king at *J*.
9:27 made silver as common in *J*
9:30 Solomon reigned in *J* over all
10:18 chariot in haste to flee to *J*.
11: 1 Now when Rehoboam came to *J*,
11: 5 So Rehoboam dwelt in *J*,
11:14 and came to Judah and *J*,
11:16 came to *J* to sacrifice to the
12: 2 king of Egypt came up against *J*,
12: 4 cities of Judah and came to *J*.
12: 5 who were gathered together in *J*
12: 7 shall not be poured out on *J*
12: 9 king of Egypt came up against *J*,
12:13 strengthened himself in *J* and
12:13 he reigned seventeen years in *J*,
13: 2 He reigned three years in *J*.
14:15 in abundance, and returned to *J*.
15:10 they gathered together at *J* in
17:13 mighty men of valor, were in *J*.
19: 1 safely to his house in *J*.
19: 4 So Jehoshaphat dwelt at *J*;
19: 8 Moreover in *J*, for the
19: 8 Israel, when they returned to *J*.
20: 5 in the assembly of Judah and *J*,
20:15 Judah and you inhabitants of *J*,
20:17 O Judah and *J*!' Do not fear or
20:18 Judah and the inhabitants of *J*
20:20 Judah and you inhabitants of *J*:
20:27 every man of Judah and *J*,
20:27 to go back to *J* with joy, for
20:28 So they came to *J*,
20:31 reigned twenty-five years in *J*.
21: 5 and he reigned eight years in *J*.
21:11 caused the inhabitants of *J* to
21:13 Judah and the inhabitants of *J*
21:20 He reigned in *J* eight years
22: 1 Then the inhabitants of *J* made
22: 2 and he reigned one year in *J*.
23: 2 of Israel, and they came to *J*.
24: 1 and he reigned forty years in *J*.
24: 6 bring in from Judah and from *J*
24: 9 throughout Judah and *J* to
24:18 and wrath came upon Judah and *J*
24:23 and they came to Judah and *J*,
25: 1 reigned twenty-nine years in *J*.
25: 1 name was Jehoaddan of *J*.
25:23 and he brought him to *J*,
25:23 and broke down the wall of *J*
25:27 a conspiracy against him in *J*,
26: 3 he reigned fifty-two years in *J*.
26: 3 name was Jecholiah of *J*.
26: 9 And Uzziah built towers in *J* at
26:15 And he made devices in *J*,
27: 1 he reigned sixteen years in *J*.
27: 8 he reigned sixteen years in *J*.
28: 1 he reigned sixteen years in *J*;
28:10 the children of Judah and *J* to
28:24 altars in every corner of *J*.
28:27 buried him in the city, in *J*;
29: 1 reigned twenty-nine years in *J*.
29: 8 the LORD fell upon Judah and *J*,
30: 1 to the house of the LORD at *J*,
30: 2 and all the assembly in *J* had
30: 3 people gathered together at *J*.
30: 5 to the LORD God of Israel at *J*,
30:11 themselves and came to *J*.
30:13 gathered at *J* to keep the Feast
30:14 away the altars that were in *J*,
30:21 of Israel who were present at *J*
30:26 So there was great joy in *J*,
30:26 been nothing like this in *J*.
31: 4 the people who dwelt in *J* to
32: 2 was to make war against *J*,
32: 9 Assyria sent his servants to *J*
32: 9 and to all Judah who were in *J*,
32:10 you remain under siege in *J*?
32:12 and commanded Judah and *J*,
32:18 in Hebrew to the people of *J*
32:19 they spoke against the God of *J*,
32:22 and the inhabitants of *J* from
32:23 brought gifts to the LORD at *J*,
32:25 over him and over Judah and *J*.
32:26 he and the inhabitants of *J*,
32:33 Judah and the inhabitants of *J*
33: 1 reigned fifty-five years in *J*.
33: 4 In *J* shall My name be forever."
33: 7 son, "In this house and in *J*,
33: 9 Judah and the inhabitants of *J*
33:13 and brought him back to *J* into
33:15 the house of the LORD and in *J*;
33:21 and he reigned two years in *J*.
34: 1 reigned thirty-one years in *J*.
34: 3 he began to purge Judah and *J*
34: 5 and cleansed Judah and *J*.
34: 7 of Israel, he returned to *J*.
34: 9 they had brought back to *J*.
34:22 (She dwelt in *J* in the Second
34:29 all the elders of Judah and *J*.
34:30 Judah and the inhabitants of *J*—
34:32 made all who were present in *J*
34:32 So the inhabitants of *J* did
35: 1 a Passover to the LORD in *J*,
35:18 and the inhabitants of *J*.
35:24 had, and they brought him to *J*.
35:24 And all Judah and *J* mourned for
36: 1 king in his father's place in *J*.
36: 2 he reigned three months in *J*.
36: 3 king of Egypt deposed him at *J*;
36: 4 Eliakim king over Judah and *J*,
36: 5 he reigned eleven years in *J*.
36: 9 and he reigned in *J* three
36:10 brother, king over Judah and *J*.
36:11 he reigned eleven years in *J*.
36:14 which He had consecrated in *J*.
36:19 God, broke down the wall of *J*,
36:23 me to build Him a house at *J*
Ezra 1: 2 me to build Him a house at *J*
1: 3 and let him go up to *J* which
1: 3 (He is God), which is in *J*.
1: 4 the house of God which is in *J*.
1: 5 of the LORD which is in *J*.
1: 7 had taken from *J* and put in
1:11 were brought from Babylon to *J*.
2: 1 and who returned to *J* and
2:68 of the LORD which is in *J*,
3: 1 together as one man to *J*.
3: 8 coming to the house of God at *J*,
3: 8 come out of the captivity to *J*,
4: 6 the inhabitants of Judah and *J*.
4: 8 wrote a letter against *J* to
4:12 from you have come to us at *J*,
4:20 also been mighty kings over *J*,
4:23 they went up in haste to *J*
4:24 the house of God which is at *J*
5: 1 Jews who were in Judah and *J*,
5: 2 the house of God which is in *J*;
5:14 from the temple that was in *J*
5:15 the temple site that is in *J*,
5:16 the house of God which is in *J*;
5:17 to build this house of God at *J*,
6: 3 the house of God at *J*:
6: 5 from the temple which is in *J*
6: 5 to the temple which is in *J*,
6: 9 of the priests who are in *J*—
6:12 this house of God which is in *J*.
6:18 over the service of God in *J*,
7: 7 and the Nethinim came up to *J*
7: 8 And Ezra came to *J* in the fifth
7: 9 of the fifth month he came to *J*,
7:13 who volunteer to go up to *J*,
7:14 inquire concerning Judah and *J*,
7:15 Israel, whose dwelling is in *J*;
7:16 for the house of their God in *J*—
7:17 of the house of your God in *J*.
7:19 in full before the God of *J*.
7:27 of the LORD which is in *J*,
8:29 fathers' houses of Israel in *J*,
8:30 to bring them to *J* to the
8:31 of the first month, to go to *J*.
8:32 So we came to *J*, and stayed
9: 9 give us a wall in Judah and *J*.
10: 7 throughout Judah and *J* to all
10: 7 that they must gather at *J*,
10: 9 and Benjamin gathered at *J*
Neh 1: 2 the captivity, and concerning *J*.
1: 3 The wall of *J* is also broken
2:11 So I came to *J* and was there
2:12 had put in my heart to do at *J*;
2:13 and viewed the walls of *J* which
2:17 how *J* lies waste, and its
2:17 and let us build the wall of *J*,
2:20 or right or memorial in *J*.
3: 8 and they fortified *J* as far as
3: 9 of half the district of *J*,
3:12 of half the district of *J*;
4: 7 heard that the walls of *J* were
4: 8 together to come and attack *J*
4:22 his servant stay at night in *J*,
6: 7 to proclaim concerning you at *J*,
7: 2 that I gave the charge of *J* to
7: 3 Do not let the gates of *J* be
7: 3 from among the inhabitants of *J*,
7: 6 and who returned to *J* and
8:15 in all their cities and in *J*,
11: 1 of the people dwelt at *J*;
11: 1 one out of ten to dwell in *J*,
11: 2 themselves to dwell at *J*.
11: 3 of the province who dwelt in *J*.
11: 4 Also in *J* dwelt some of the
11: 6 sons of Perez who dwelt at *J*
11:22 overseer of the Levites at *J*
12:27 the dedication of the wall of *J*
12:27 to bring them to *J* to celebrate
12:28 from the countryside around *J*,
12:29 villages all around *J*.
12:43 so that the joy of *J* was heard
13: 6 during all this I was not in *J*,
13: 7 and I came to *J* and discovered
13:15 which they brought into *J* on
13:16 the children of Judah, and in *J*.
13:19 So it was, at the gates of *J*,
13:20 of wares lodged outside *J* once
Esth 2: 6 had been carried away from *J*
Ps 51:18 to Zion; Build the walls of *J*.
68:29 Because of Your temple at *J*,
79: 1 They have laid *J* in heaps.
79: 3 shed like water all around *J*,
102:21 in Zion, And His praise in *J*,
116:19 In the midst of you, O *J*.
122: 2 Within your gates, O *J*!
122: 3 *J* is built As a city that is
122: 6 Pray for the peace of *J*:
125: 2 As the mountains surround *J*,
128: 5 And may you see the good of *J*
135:21 Who dwells in *J*! Praise the
137: 5 If I forget you, O *J*,
137: 6 If I do not exalt *J* Above my
137: 7 the sons of Edom The day of *J*,
147: 2 The LORD builds up *J*;
147:12 O *J*! Praise your God, O Zion!
Eccl 1: 1 the son of David, king in *J*.
1:12 was king over Israel in *J*.
1:16 all who were before me in *J*.
2: 7 flocks than all who were in *J*
2: 9 all who were before me in *J*.
Song 1: 5 but lovely, O daughters of *J*,
2: 7 I charge you, O daughters of *J*,
3: 5 I charge you, O daughters of *J*,
3:10 love By the daughters of *J*.
5: 8 I charge you, O daughters of *J*,
5:16 O daughters of *J*!
6: 4 as Tirzah, Lovely as *J*,
8: 4 I charge you, O daughters of *J*,
Isa 1: 1 he saw concerning Judah and *J*
2: 1 Amoz saw concerning Judah and *J*.
2: 3 the word of the LORD from *J*.
3: 1 Takes away from *J* and from
3: 8 For *J* stumbled, And Judah is
4: 3 left in Zion and remains in *J*
4: 3 recorded among the living in *J*.
4: 4 and purged the blood of *J* from
5: 3 O inhabitants of *J* and men of
7: 1 went up to *J* to make war
8:14 a snare to the inhabitants of *J*.
10:10 images excelled those of *J* and

10:11 Shall I not do also to *J* and
10:12 His work on Mount Zion and on *J*,
10:32 of Zion, The hill of *J*.
22:10 You numbered the houses of *J*,
22:21 father to the inhabitants of *J*
24:23 reign On Mount Zion and in *J*
27:13 LORD in the holy mount at *J*.
28:14 rule this people who are in *J*,
30:19 people shall dwell in Zion at *J*;
31: 5 the LORD of hosts defend *J*.
31: 9 And whose furnace is in *J*.
33:20 Your eyes will see *J*,
36: 2 Lachish to King Hezekiah at *J*.
36: 7 away, and said to Judah and *J*,
36:20 that the LORD should deliver *J*
37:10 *J* shall not be given into the
37:22 The daughter of *J* Has shaken
37:32 For out of *J* shall go a
40: 2 "Speak comfort to *J*,
40: 9 up into the high mountain; O *J*,
41:27 And I will give to *J* one
44:26 His messengers; Who says to *J*,
44:28 all My pleasure, Saying to *J*,
51:17 Awake, awake! Stand up, O *J*,
52: 1 your beautiful garments, O *J*,
52: 2 O *J*! Loose yourself from the
52: 9 You waste places of *J*!
52: 9 His people, He has redeemed *J*.
62: 6 set watchmen on your walls, O *J*;
62: 7 And till He makes *J* a praise
64:10 wilderness, *J* a desolation.
65:18 I create *J* as a rejoicing,
65:19 I will rejoice in *J*,
66:10 "Rejoice with *J*,
66:13 you shall be comforted in *J*.
66:20 camels, to My holy mountain *J*,
Jer 1: 3 until the carrying away of *J*
1:15 the entrance of the gates of *J*,
2: 2 and cry in the hearing of *J*,
3:17 At that time *J* shall be called
3:17 to the name of the LORD, to *J*.
4: 3 LORD to the men of Judah and *J*:
4: 4 of Judah and inhabitants of *J*,
4: 5 in Judah and proclaim in *J*,
4:10 deceived this people and *J*,
4:11 said To this people and to *J*,
4:14 O *J*, wash your heart from
4:16 Yes, proclaim against *J*,
5: 1 fro through the streets of *J*;
6: 1 to flee from the midst of *J*!
6: 6 And build a mound against *J*.
6: 8 Be instructed, O *J*,
7:17 Judah and in the streets of *J*?
7:34 and from the streets of *J* the
8: 1 bones of the inhabitants of *J*,
8: 5 this people slidden back, *J*,
9:11 I will make *J* a heap of ruins, a
11: 2 and to the inhabitants of *J*;
11: 6 Judah and in the streets of *J*,
11: 9 and among the inhabitants of *J*.
11:12 Judah and the inhabitants of *J*
11:13 the number of the streets of *J*
13: 9 Judah and the great pride of *J*.
13:13 and all the inhabitants of *J*—
13:27 O *J*! Will you still not be
14: 2 And the cry of *J* has gone up.
14:16 be cast out in the streets of *J*
15: 4 of Judah, for what he did in *J*.
15: 5 who will have pity on you, O *J*?
17:19 out, and in all the gates of *J*;
17:20 and all the inhabitants of *J*,
17:21 bring it in by the gates of *J*;
17:25 Judah and the inhabitants of *J*;
17:26 and from the places around *J*,
17:27 when entering the gates of *J*
17:27 shall devour the palaces of *J*,
18:11 and to the inhabitants of *J*,
19: 3 of Judah and inhabitants of *J*.
19: 7 the counsel of Judah and *J* in
19:13 And the houses of *J* and the
22:19 cast out beyond the gates of *J*.
23:14 thing in the prophets of *J*:
23:15 For from the prophets of *J*
24: 1 craftsmen and smiths, from *J*,
24: 8 the residue of *J* who remain in
25: 2 and to all the inhabitants of *J*,
25:18 *J* and the cities of Judah, its
26:18 *J* shall become heaps of ruins,
27: 3 of the messengers who come to *J*
27:18 of the king of Judah, and at *J*,
27:20 from *J* to Babylon, and all the
27:20 all the nobles of Judah and *J*—
27:21 of the king of Judah and of *J*:
29: 1 the prophet sent from *J* to the
29: 1 carried away captive from *J* to
29: 2 the princes of Judah and *J*,
29: 2 the smiths had departed from *J*.
29: 4 to be carried away from *J* to
29:20 whom I have sent from *J* to
29:25 to all the people who are at *J*,
32: 2 of Babylon's army besieged *J*,
32:32 Judah, and the inhabitants of *J*.
32:44 in the places around *J*,
33:10 in the streets of *J* that are
33:13 in the places around *J*,
33:16 And *J* will dwell safely.
34: 1 fought against *J* and all its
34: 6 to Zedekiah king of Judah in *J*,
34: 7 army fought against *J* and all
34: 8 all the people who were at *J*
34:19 of Judah, the princes of *J*,
35:11 let us go to *J* for fear of the
35:11 the Syrians.' So we dwell at *J*.
35:13 Judah and the inhabitants of *J*,
35:17 and on all the inhabitants of *J*
36: 9 LORD to all the people in *J*,
36: 9 from the cities of Judah to *J*.
36:31 them, on the inhabitants of *J*,
37: 5 Chaldeans who were besieging *J*
37: 5 of them, they departed from *J*.
37:11 left the siege of *J* for fear
37:12 that Jeremiah went out of *J* to
38:28 the prison until the day that *J*
38:28 And he was there when *J* was
39: 1 and all his army came against *J*,
39: 8 and broke down the walls of *J*.
40: 1 carried away captive from *J*
42:18 out on the inhabitants of *J*,
44: 2 that I have brought on *J* and
44: 6 Judah and in the streets of *J*;
44: 9 Judah and in the streets of *J*?
44:13 of Egypt, as I have punished *J*,
44:17 Judah and in the streets of *J*.
44:21 Judah and in the streets of *J*,
51:35 of Chaldea!" *J* will say.
51:50 And let *J* come to your mind.
52: 1 he reigned eleven years in *J*.
52: 3 the LORD this happened in *J*
52: 4 and all his army came against *J*
52:12 the king of Babylon, came to *J*.
52:13 all the houses of *J*,
52:14 broke down all the walls of *J*
52:29 he carried away captive from *J*
Lam 1: 7 *J* remembers all her pleasant
1: 8 *J* has sinned gravely,
1:17 *J* has become an unclean thing
2:10 The virgins of *J* Bow their
2:13 I liken you, O daughter of *J*?
2:15 heads At the daughter of *J*:
4:12 Could enter the gates of *J*—
Ezek 4: 1 and portray on it a city, *J*.
4: 7 your face toward the siege of *J*;
4:16 off the supply of bread in *J*;
5: 5 says the Lord GOD: 'This is *J*;
8: 3 me in visions of God to *J*,
9: 4 city, through the midst of *J*,
9: 8 in pouring out Your fury on *J*?
11:15 whom the inhabitants of *J* have
12:10 concerns the prince in *J* and
12:19 GOD to the inhabitants of *J*
13:16 who prophesy concerning *J*,
14:21 My four severe judgments on *J*—
14:22 that I have brought upon *J*,
15: 6 give up the inhabitants of *J*;
16: 2 cause *J* to know her
16: 3 'Thus says the Lord GOD to *J*:
17:12 the king of Babylon went to *J*
21: 2 of man, set your face toward *J*,
21:20 and to Judah, into fortified *J*.
21:22 hand is the divination for *J*:
22:19 gather you into the midst of *J*.
23: 4 and *J* is Oholibah.
24: 2 started his siege against *J*
26: 2 because Tyre has said against *J*,
33:21 one who had escaped from *J*
36:38 like the flock at *J* on its
Dan 1: 1 king of Babylon came to *J* and
5: 2 temple which had been in *J*,
5: 3 of God which had been in *J*;
6:10 with his windows open toward *J*,
9: 2 years in the desolations of *J*.
9: 7 to the inhabitants of *J* and all
9:12 done as what has been done to *J*.
9:16 be turned away from Your city *J*,
9:16 *J* and Your people are a
9:25 To restore and build *J* Until
Joel 2:32 For in Mount Zion and in *J*
3: 1 the captives of Judah and *J*,
3: 6 of Judah and the people of *J*
3:16 And utter His voice from *J*;
3:17 Then *J* shall be holy, And no
3:20 And *J* from generation to
Am 1: 2 And utters His voice from *J*;
2: 5 shall devour the palaces of *J*.
Ob 11 his gates And cast lots for *J*—
20 The captives of *J* who are in
Mic 1: 1 he saw concerning Samaria and *J*.
1: 5 of Judah? Are they not *J*?
1: 9 to the gate of My people—To *J*.
1:12 the LORD To the gate of *J*.
3:10 up Zion with bloodshed And *J*
3:12 *J* shall become heaps of ruins,
4: 2 the word of the LORD from *J*.
4: 8 kingdom of the daughter of *J*.
Zeph 1: 4 all the inhabitants of *J*.
1:12 time That I will search *J*
3:14 heart, O daughter of *J*!
3:16 that day it shall be said to *J*:
Zech 1:12 will You not have mercy on *J*
1:14 I am zealous for *J* And for Zion
1:16 I am returning to *J* with mercy;
1:16 shall be stretched out over *J*.
1:17 Zion, And will again choose *J*.
1:19 scattered Judah, Israel, and *J*.
2: 2 he said to me, "To measure *J*,
2: 4 *J* shall be inhabited as towns
2:12 Land, and will again choose *J*.
3: 2 The LORD who has chosen *J*
7: 7 the former prophets when *J* and
8: 3 And dwell in the midst of *J*.
8: 3 *J* shall be called the City of
8: 4 again sit In the streets of *J*,
8: 8 shall dwell in the midst of *J*.
8:15 am determined to do good To *J*
8:22 to seek the LORD of hosts in *J*,
9: 9 O daughter of *J*! Behold, your
9:10 Ephraim And the horse from *J*;
12: 2 I will make *J* a cup of
12: 2 lay siege against Judah and *J*.
12: 3 in that day that I will make *J*
12: 5 The inhabitants of *J* are my
12: 6 but *J* shall be inhabited again
12: 6 again in her own place—*J*.
12: 7 glory of the inhabitants of *J*
12: 8 defend the inhabitants of *J*;
12: 9 the nations that come against *J*.
12:10 and on the inhabitants of *J*
12:11 shall be a great mourning in *J*,
13: 1 and for the inhabitants of *J*,
14: 2 the nations to battle against *J*;
14: 4 Which faces *J* on the east.
14: 8 living waters shall flow from *J*,
14:10 from Geba to Rimmon south of *J*.
14:10 *J* shall be raised up and
14:11 But *J* shall be safely
14:12 the people who fought against *J*:
14:14 Judah also will fight at *J*.
14:16 nations which came against *J*
14:17 the earth do not come up to *J*
14:21 every pot in *J* and Judah shall
Mal 2:11 committed in Israel and in *J*,
3: 4 the offering of Judah and *J*
Mt 2: 1 men from the East came to *J*,
2: 3 and all *J* with him.
3: 5 Then *J*, all Judea, and all
4:25 Galilee, and from Decapolis, *J*,
5:35 it is His footstool; nor by *J*,
15: 1 and Pharisees who were from *J*
16:21 disciples that He must go to *J*,
20:17 Now Jesus, going up to *J*,
20:18 "Behold, we are going up to *J*,
21: 1 Now when they drew near *J*,
21:10 And when He had come into *J*,
23:37 O *J*, Jerusalem, the one
23:37 O Jerusalem, *J*, the one
Mk 1: 5 land of Judea, and those from *J*,
3: 8 and *J* and Idumea and beyond the
3:22 scribes who came down from *J*
7: 1 to Him, having come from *J*.
10:32 were on the road, going up to *J*,
10:33 "Behold, we are going up to *J*,
11: 1 Now when they drew near *J*,
11:11 And Jesus went into *J* and into
11:15 So they came to *J*.
11:27 Then they came again to *J*.
15:41 women who came up with Him to *J*.
Lk 2:22 they brought Him to *J* to
2:25 there was a man in *J* whose name
2:38 who looked for redemption in *J*.
2:41 His parents went to *J* every
2:42 they went up to *J* according to
2:43 Boy Jesus lingered behind in *J*.
2:45 find Him, they returned to *J*,
4: 9 Then he brought Him to *J*,
5:17 town of Galilee, Judea, and *J*.
6:17 of people from all Judea and *J*,
9:31 He was about to accomplish at *J*.
9:51 set His face to go to *J*,
9:53 was set for the journey to *J*.
10:30 certain man went down from *J*
13: 4 all other men who dwelt in *J*?
13:22 and journeying toward *J*.
13:33 should perish outside of *J*.
13:34 O *J*, Jerusalem, the one
13:34 O Jerusalem, *J*, the one
17:11 it happened as He went to *J*
18:31 "Behold, we are going up to *J*,
19:11 because He was near *J* and
19:28 He went on ahead, going up to *J*.
21:20 But when you see *J* surrounded
21:24 And *J* will be trampled by
23: 7 who was also in *J* at that time.
23:28 to them, said, "Daughters of *J*,
24:13 which was seven miles from *J*.
24:18 You the only stranger in *J*,
24:33 very hour and returned to *J*,
24:47 to all nations, beginning at *J*.
24:49 but tarry in the city of *J*
24:52 and returned to *J* with great
Jn 1:19 priests and Levites from *J* to
2:13 at hand, and Jesus went up to *J*.
2:23 Now when He was in *J* at the
4:20 and you Jews say that in *J* is
4:21 on this mountain, nor in *J*,
4:45 all the things He did in *J* at
5: 1 Jews, and Jesus went up to *J*.
5: 2 Now there is in *J* by the Sheep
7:25 Now some of them from *J* said,
10:22 the Feast of Dedication in *J*,
11:18 Now Bethany was near *J*,
11:55 went from the country up to *J*
12:12 that Jesus was coming to *J*,
Acts 1: 4 them not to depart from *J*,
1: 8 shall be witnesses to Me in *J*,
1:12 Then they returned to *J* from
1:12 called Olivet, which is near *J*,
1:19 to all those dwelling in *J*;
2: 5 And there were dwelling in *J*
2:14 of Judea and all who dwell in *J*,
4: 6 were gathered together at *J*.
4:16 evident to all who dwell in *J*,
5:16 the surrounding cities to *J*,
5:28 you have filled *J* with your

6: 7 multiplied greatly in *J*,
8: 1 the church which was at *J*;
8:14 when the apostles who were at *J*
8:25 of the Lord, they returned to *J*,
8:26 road which goes down from *J* to
8:27 and had come to *J* to worship,
9: 2 he might bring them bound to *J*.
9:13 he has done to Your saints in *J*.
9:21 who called on this name in *J*,
9:26 And when Saul had come to *J*,
9:28 So he was with them at *J*,
10:39 the land of the Jews and in *J*,
11: 2 And when Peter came up to *J*,
11:22 to the ears of the church in *J*,
11:27 days prophets came from *J* to
12:25 and Saul returned from *J* when
13:13 from them, returned to *J*.
13:27 "For those who dwell in *J*,
13:31 up with Him from Galilee to *J*,
15: 2 of them should go up to *J*,
15: 4 And when they had come to *J*,
16: 4 by the apostles and elders at *J*.
18:21 keep this coming feast in *J*;
19:21 and Achaia, to go to *J*,
20:16 for he was hurrying to be at *J*,
20:22 I go bound in the spirit to *J*,
21: 4 the Spirit not to go up to *J*.
21:11 So shall the Jews at *J* bind the
21:12 with him not to go up to *J*.
21:13 but also to die at *J* for the
21:15 days we packed and went up to *J*.
21:17 And when we had come to *J*,
21:31 of the garrison that all *J* was
22: 5 even those who were there to *J*
22:17 when I returned to *J* and was
22:18 Make haste and get out of *J*
23:11 you have testified for Me in *J*,
24:11 days since I went up to *J* to
25: 1 he went up from Caesarea to *J*.
25: 3 that he would summon him to *J*—
25: 7 Jews who had come down from *J*
25: 9 Are you willing to go up to *J*
25:15 informed me, when I was in *J*,
25:20 he was willing to go to *J* and
25:24 both at *J* and here, crying out
26: 4 among my own nation at *J*,
26:10 "This I also did in *J*,
26:20 to those in Damascus and in *J*,
28:17 delivered as a prisoner from *J*
Rom 15:19 so that from *J* and round about
15:25 But now I am going to *J* to
15:26 among the saints who are in *J*.
15:31 and that my service for *J* may
1 Cor 16: 3 send to bear your gift to *J*.
Gal 1:17 nor did I go up to *J* to those
1:18 three years I went up to *J* to
2: 1 years I went up again to *J*
4:25 and corresponds to *J* which now
4:26 but the *J* above is free, which
Heb 12:22 the living God, the heavenly *J*,
Rev 3:12 the city of My God, the New *J*,
21: 2 John, saw the holy city, New *J*,
21:10 me the great city, the holy *J*,

JERUSALEM'S (1/1)
Isa 62: 1 And for *J* sake I will not

JERUSHA (1/1)
2 Ki 15:33 His mother's name was *J* the

JERUSHAH (1/1)
2 Chr 27: 1 His mother's name was *J* the

JESAIAH (KJV) See JESHAIAH

JESHAIAH (7/7)
1 Chr 3:21 Hananiah were Pelatiah and *J*,
25: 3 of Jeduthun: Gedaliah, Zeri, *J*,
25:15 the eighth for *J*, his sons
26:25 *J* his son, Joram his son,
Ezra 8: 7 *J* the son of Athaliah, and with
8:19 and with him *J* of the sons of
Neh 11: 7 the son of Ithiel, the son of *J*;

JESHANAH (1/1)
2 Chr 13:19 *J* with its villages, and

JESHARELAH (1/1)
1 Chr 25:14 the seventh for *J*, his sons

JESHEBEAB (1/1)
1 Chr 24:13 to Huppah, the fourteenth to *J*,

JESHER (1/1)
1 Chr 2:18 Now these were her sons: *J*,

JESHIMON (4/4)
1 Sam 23:19 which is on the south of *J*?
23:24 in the plain on the south of *J*.
26: 1 hill of Hachilah, opposite *J*?
26: 3 Hachilah, which is opposite *J*,

JESHISHAI (1/1)
1 Chr 5:14 son of Michael, the son of *J*,

JESHOHAIAH (1/1)
1 Chr 4:36 Elioenai, Jaakobah, *J*,

JESHUA (29/29) JOSHUA
1 Chr 24:11 the ninth to *J*, the tenth to
2 Chr 31:15 him were Eden, Miniamin, *J*,
Ezra 2: 2 came with Zerubbabel were *J*,
2: 6 of the people of *J* and Joab,
2:36 of Jedaiah, of the house of *J*,
2:40 the sons of *J* and Kadmiel, of
3: 2 Then *J* the son of Jozadak and
3: 8 *J* the son of Jozadak, and the
3: 9 Then *J* with his sons and
4: 3 But Zerubbabel and *J* and the
5: 2 the son of Shealtiel and *J* the
8:33 Jozabad the son of *J* and
10:18 were found of the sons of *J*
Neh 3:19 next to him Ezer the son of *J*,
7: 7 came with Zerubbabel were *J*,
7:11 of the sons of *J* and Joab, two
7:39 of Jedaiah, of the house of *J*,
7:43 The Levites: the sons of *J*,
8: 7 Also *J*, Bani, Sherebiah,
9: 4 Then *J*, Bani, Kadmiel,
9: 5 And the Levites, *J*,
10: 9 *J* the son of Azaniah, Binnui of
11:26 in *J*, Moladah, Beth Pelet,
12: 1 the son of Shealtiel, and *J*:
12: 7 their brethren in the days of *J*.
12: 8 Moreover the Levites were *J*,
12:10 *J* begot Joiakim, Joiakim begot
12:24 and *J* the son of Kadmiel, with
12:26 days of Joiakim the son of *J*,

JESHURUN (4/4)
Deut 32:15 But *J* grew fat and kicked;
33: 5 And He was King in *J*,
33:26 is no one like the God of *J*,
Isa 44: 2 O Jacob My servant; And you, *J*,

JESIAH (KJV) See JESSHIAH, JISSHIAH

JESIMIEL (1/1)
1 Chr 4:36 Jeshohaiah, Asaiah, Adiel, *J*,

JESSE (47/44)
Ruth 4:17 He is the father of *J*,
4:22 Obed begot *J*, and Jesse
4:22 and *J* begot David.
1 Sam 16: 1 I am sending you to *J* the
16: 3 Then invite *J* to the sacrifice,
16: 5 Then he consecrated *J* and his
16: 8 So *J* called Abinadab, and made
16: 9 Then *J* made Shammah pass by.
16:10 Thus *J* made seven of his sons
16:10 And Samuel said to *J*,
16:11 And Samuel said to *J*,
16:11 And Samuel said to *J*,
16:18 I have seen a son of *J* the
16:19 Saul sent messengers to *J*,
16:20 And *J* took a donkey loaded
16:22 Then Saul sent to *J*,
17:12 Judah, whose name was *J*,
17:13 The three oldest sons of *J* had
17:17 Then *J* said to his son David,
17:20 the things and went as *J* had
17:58 am the son of your servant *J*
20:27 Why has the son of *J* not come to
20:30 you have chosen the son of *J*
20:31 For as long as the son of *J*
22: 7 Will the son of *J* give every
22: 8 a covenant with the son of *J*;
22: 9 I saw the son of *J* going to Nob,
22:13 me, you and the son of *J*,
25:10 David, and who is the son of *J*?
2 Sam 20: 1 inheritance in the son of *J*;
23: 1 says David the son of *J*;
1 Ki 12:16 no inheritance in the son of *J*.
1 Chr 2:12 begot Obed, and Obed begot *J*;
2:13 *J* begot Eliab his firstborn,
10:14 over to David the son of *J*.
12:18 O son of *J*! Peace, peace to
29:26 Thus David the son of *J* reigned
2 Chr 10:16 no inheritance in the son of *J*.
11:18 daughter of Eliah the son of *J*.
Ps 72:20 prayers of David the son of *J*
Isa 11: 1 forth a Rod from the stem of *J*,
11:10 day there shall be a Root of *J*,
Mt 1: 5 Obed by Ruth, Obed begot *J*,
1: 6 and *J* begot David the king.
Lk 3:32 the son of *J*, the son of
Acts 13:22 found David the son of *J*,
Rom 15:12 shall be a root of *J*;

JESSHIAH (1/1)
1 Chr 23:20 Michah was the first and *J* the

JESTING (1/1)
Eph 5: 4 foolish talking, nor coarse *j*,

JESUI (1/1)
Num 26:44 family of the Jimnites; of *J*,

JESUITES (1/1)
Num 26:44 of Jesui, the family of the *J*;

JESURUN (KJV) See JESHURUN

JESUS (971/934) CHRIST, JESUS', JUSTUS
Mt 1: 1 The book of the genealogy of *J*
1:16 of whom was born *J* who is
1:18 Now the birth of *J* Christ was
1:21 and you shall call His name *J*,
1:25 Son. And he called His name *J*.
2: 1 Now after *J* was born in
3:13 Then *J* came from Galilee to
3:15 But *J* answered and said to him,
3:16 *J* came up immediately from the
4: 1 Then *J* was led up by the Spirit
4: 7 *J* said to him, "It is written
4:10 Then *J* said to him, "Away with
4:12 Now when *J* heard that John had
4:17 From that time *J* began to preach
4:18 And *J*, walking by the Sea
4:23 And *J* went about all Galilee,
7:28 when *J* had ended these sayings,
8: 3 Then *J* put out His hand and
8: 4 And *J* said to him, "See that
8: 5 Now when *J* had entered
8: 7 And *J* said to him, "I will come
8:10 When *J* heard it, He marveled,
8:13 Then *J* said to the centurion,
8:14 Now when *J* had come into
8:18 And when *J* saw great multitudes
8:20 And *J* said to him, "Foxes have
8:22 But *J* said to him, "Follow Me,
8:29 have we to do with You, *J*,
8:34 whole city came out to meet *J*.
9: 2 When *J* saw their faith, He said
9: 4 But *J*, knowing their
9: 9 As *J* passed on from there, He
9:10 as *J* sat at the table in the
9:12 When *J* heard that, He said to
9:15 And *J* said to them, "Can the
9:19 So *J* arose and followed him, and
9:22 But *J* turned around, and when He
9:23 When *J* came into the ruler's
9:27 When *J* departed from there, two
9:28 And *J* said to them, "Do you
9:30 And *J* sternly warned them,
9:35 Then *J* went about all the
10: 5 These twelve *J* sent out and
11: 1 when *J* finished commanding His
11: 4 *J* answered and said to them,
11: 7 *J* began to say to the
11:25 At that time *J* answered and
12: 1 At that time *J* went through the
12:15 But when *J* knew it, He
12:25 But *J* knew their thoughts, and
13: 1 On the same day *J* went out of
13:34 All these things *J* spoke to the
13:36 Then *J* sent the multitude away
13:51 *J* said to them, "Have you
13:53 when *J* had finished these
13:57 But *J* said to them, "A prophet
14: 1 heard the report about *J*
14:12 buried it, and went and told *J*.
14:13 When *J* heard it, He departed
14:14 And when *J* went out He saw a
14:16 But *J* said to them, "They do
14:22 Immediately *J* made His
14:25 the fourth watch of the night *J*
14:27 But immediately *J* spoke to them,
14:29 walked on the water to go to *J*.
14:31 And immediately *J* stretched out
15: 1 were from Jerusalem came to *J*,
15:16 So *J* said, "Are you also still
15:21 Then *J* went out from there and
15:28 Then *J* answered and said to her,
15:29 *J* departed from there, skirted
15:32 Now *J* called His disciples to
15:34 *J* said to them, "How many
16: 6 Then *J* said to them, "Take heed
16: 8 But *J*, being aware of it,
16:13 When *J* came into the region of
16:17 *J* answered and said to him,
16:20 tell no one that He was *J* the
16:21 From that time *J* began to show
16:24 Then *J* said to His disciples,
17: 1 Now after six days *J* took Peter,
17: 4 Peter answered and said to *J*,
17: 7 But *J* came and touched them and
17: 8 they saw no one but *J* only.
17: 9 *J* commanded them, saying,
17:11 *J* answered and said to them,
17:17 Then *J* answered and said,
17:18 And *J* rebuked the demon, and it
17:19 Then the disciples came to *J*
17:20 So *J* said to them, "Because of
17:22 *J* said to them, "The Son of
17:25 *J* anticipated him, saying,
17:26 *J* said to him, "Then the
18: 1 time the disciples came to *J*,
18: 2 Then *J* called a little child to
18:22 *J* said to him, "I do not say to
19: 1 when *J* had finished these
19:14 But *J* said, "Let the little
19:18 *J* said, " 'You shall not
19:21 *J* said to him, "If you want to

19:23 Then *J* said to His disciples,
19:26 But *J* looked at them and said
19:28 So *J* said to them, "Assuredly I
20:17 Now *J*, going up to
20:22 But *J* answered and said, "You
20:25 But *J* called them to Himself
20:30 when they heard that *J* was
20:32 So *J* stood still and called
20:34 So *J* had compassion and touched
21: 1 then *J* sent two disciples,
21: 6 the disciples went and did as *J*
21:11 multitudes said, "This is *J*,
21:12 Then *J* went into the temple of
21:16 And *J* said to them, "Yes.
21:21 So *J* answered and said to them,
21:24 But *J* answered and said to them,
21:27 So they answered *J* and said,
21:31 *J* said to them, "Assuredly,
21:42 *J* said to them, "Have you never
22: 1 And *J* answered and spoke to them
22:18 But *J* perceived their
22:29 *J* answered and said to them,
22:37 *J* said to him, " 'You shall
22:41 together, *J* asked them,
23: 1 Then *J* spoke to the multitudes
24: 1 Then *J* went out and departed
24: 2 And *J* said to them, "Do you not
24: 4 And *J* answered and said to them:
26: 1 when *J* had finished all these
26: 4 and plotted to take *J* by
26: 6 And when *J* was in Bethany at
26:10 But when *J* was aware of it, He
26:17 Bread the disciples came to *J*,
26:19 So the disciples did as *J* had
26:26 *J* took bread, blessed and broke
26:31 Then *J* said to them, "All of
26:34 *J* said to him, "Assuredly, I
26:36 Then *J* came with them to a
26:49 Immediately he went up to *J* and
26:50 But *J* said to him, "Friend, why
26:50 they came and laid hands on *J*
26:51 one of those who were with *J*
26:52 But *J* said to him, "Put your
26:55 In that hour *J* said to the
26:57 those who had laid hold of *J*
26:59 false testimony against *J* to
26:63 But *J* kept silent. And the high
26:64 *J* said to him, "It is as you
26:69 You also were with *J* of
26:71 This fellow also was with *J* of
26:75 Peter remembered the word of *J*
27: 1 of the people plotted against *J*
27:11 Now *J* stood before the
27:11 So *J* said to him, "It is
27:17 or *J* who is called Christ?"
27:20 ask for Barabbas and destroy *J*.
27:22 What then shall I do with *J* who
27:26 and when he had scourged *J*,
27:27 of the governor took *J* into
27:37 IS *J* THE KING OF THE JEWS.
27:46 And about the ninth hour *J* cried
27:50 And *J* cried out again with a
27:54 with him, who were guarding *J*,
27:55 And many women who followed *J*
27:57 had also become a disciple of *J*.
27:58 and asked for the body of *J*.
28: 5 for I know that you seek *J* who
28: 9 *J* met them, saying,
28:10 Then *J* said to them, "Do not be
28:16 to the mountain which *J* had
28:18 And *J* came and spoke to them,
Mk 1: 1 beginning of the gospel of *J*
1: 9 to pass in those days that *J*
1:14 *J* came to Galilee, preaching
1:17 Then *J* said to them, "Follow
1:24 do with You, *J* of Nazareth?
1:25 But *J* rebuked him, saying, "Be
1:41 Then *J*, moved with
1:45 so that *J* could no longer
2: 5 When *J* saw their faith, He said
2: 8 when *J* perceived in His spirit
2:15 also sat together with *J* and
2:17 When *J* heard it, He said to
2:19 And *J* said to them, "Can the
3: 7 But *J* withdrew with His
5: 6 When he saw *J* from afar, he ran
5: 7 "What have I to do with You, *J*,
5:13 And at once *J* gave them
5:15 Then they came to *J*,
5:19 *J* did not permit him, but said
5:20 in Decapolis all that *J* had
5:21 Now when *J* had crossed over
5:24 So *J* went with him, and a great
5:27 When she heard about *J*,
5:30 And *J*, immediately knowing
5:36 As soon as *J* heard the word that
6: 4 But *J* said to them, "A prophet
6:30 the apostles gathered to *J* and
6:34 And *J*, when He came out,
7:27 But *J* said to her, "Let the
8: 1 *J* called His disciples to Him
8:17 But *J*, being aware of it,
8:27 Now *J* and His disciples went
9: 2 Now after six days *J* took
9: 4 and they were talking with *J*.
9: 5 Peter answered and said to *J*,
9: 8 but only *J* with themselves.
9:23 *J* said to him, "If you can
9:25 When *J* saw that the people came
9:27 But *J* took him by the hand and
9:39 But *J* said, "Do not forbid him,
10: 5 And *J* answered and said to them,
10:14 But when *J* saw it, He was
10:18 So *J* said to him, "Why do you
10:21 Then *J*, looking at him,
10:23 Then *J* looked around and said
10:24 But *J* answered again and said
10:27 But *J* looked at them and said,
10:29 So *J* answered and said,
10:32 and *J* was going before them;
10:38 But *J* said to them, "You do not
10:39 So *J* said to them, "You will
10:42 But *J* called them to Himself
10:47 when he heard that it was *J* of
10:47 began to cry out and say, "*J*,
10:49 So *J* stood still and commanded
10:50 garment, he rose and came to *J*.
10:51 So *J* answered and said to him,
10:52 Then *J* said to him, "Go your
10:52 his sight and followed *J* on
11: 6 they spoke to them just as *J*
11: 7 they brought the colt to *J* and
11:11 And *J* went into Jerusalem and
11:14 In response *J* said to it, "Let
11:15 Then *J* went into the temple and
11:22 So *J* answered and said to them,
11:29 But *J* answered and said to them,
11:33 So they answered and said to *J*,
11:33 And *J* answered and said to
12:17 And *J* answered and said to them,
12:24 *J* answered and said to them,
12:29 *J* answered him, "The first of
12:34 Now when *J* saw that he answered
12:35 Then *J* answered and said, while
12:41 Now *J* sat opposite the treasury
13: 2 And *J* answered and said to him,
13: 5 And *J*, answering them, began
14: 6 But *J* said, "Let her alone. Why
14:18 *J* said, "Assuredly, I say to
14:22 *J* took bread, blessed and broke
14:27 Then *J* said to them, "All of
14:30 *J* said to him, "Assuredly, I
14:48 Then *J* answered and said to
14:53 And they led *J* away to the high
14:55 sought testimony against *J* to
14:60 up in the midst and asked *J*,
14:62 *J* said, "I am. And you will see
14:67 You also were with *J* of
14:72 called to mind the word that *J*
15: 1 whole council; and they bound *J*,
15: 5 But *J* still answered nothing, so
15:15 to them; and he delivered *J*,
15:34 And at the ninth hour *J* cried
15:37 And *J* cried out with a loud
15:43 and asked for the body of *J*.
16: 6 You seek *J* of Nazareth, who was
Lk 1:31 Son, and shall call His name *J*.
2:21 Child, His name was called *J*,
2:27 parents brought in the Child *J*,
2:43 the Boy *J* lingered behind in
2:52 And *J* increased in wisdom and
3:21 it came to pass that *J* also was
3:23 Now *J* Himself began His
4: 1 Then *J*, being filled with
4: 4 But *J* answered him, saying, "It
4: 8 And *J* answered and said to him,
4:12 And *J* answered and said to him,
4:14 Then *J* returned in the power of
4:34 *J* of Nazareth? Did You come to
4:35 But *J* rebuked him, saying, "Be
5:10 And *J* said to Simon, "Do not
5:12 who was full of leprosy saw *J*;
5:19 tiling into the midst before *J*.
5:22 But when *J* perceived their
5:31 *J* answered and said to them,
6: 3 But *J* answering them said,
6: 9 Then *J* said to them, "I will
6:11 another what they might do to *J*.
7: 3 So when he heard about *J*,
7: 4 And when they came to *J*,
7: 6 Then *J* went with them. And when
7: 9 When *J* heard these things, He
7:19 to him, sent them to *J*,
7:22 *J* answered and said to them,
7:37 when she knew that *J* sat at
7:40 And *J* answered and said to him,
8:28 When he saw *J*, he cried out,
8:28 "What have I to do with You, *J*,
8:30 *J* asked him, saying, "What is
8:35 had happened, and came to *J*,
8:35 sitting at the feet of *J*,
8:38 But *J* sent him away, saying,
8:39 whole city what great things *J*
8:40 when *J* returned, that the
8:45 And *J* said, "Who touched Me?"
8:46 But *J* said, "Somebody touched
8:50 But when *J* heard it, He
9:33 from Him, that Peter said to *J*,
9:36 *J* was found alone. But they
9:41 Then *J* answered and said,
9:42 Then *J* rebuked the unclean
9:43 at all the things which *J* did,
9:47 And *J*, perceiving the thought
9:50 But *J* said to him, "Do not
9:58 And *J* said to him, "Foxes have
9:60 *J* said to him, "Let the dead
9:62 But *J* said to him, "No one,
10:21 In that hour *J* rejoiced in the
10:29 to justify himself, said to *J*,
10:30 Then *J* answered and said: "A
10:37 Then *J* said to him, "Go and
10:41 And *J* answered and said to her,
13: 2 And *J* answered and said to them,
13:12 But when *J* saw her, He called
13:14 because *J* had healed on the
14: 3 And *J*, answering, spoke to
17:13 up their voices and said, "*J*,
17:17 So *J* answered and said, "Were
18:16 But *J* called them to Him and
18:19 So *J* said to him, "Why do you
18:22 So when *J* heard these things, He
18:24 And when *J* saw that he became
18:37 So they told him that *J* of
18:38 And he cried out, saying, "*J*,
18:40 So *J* stood still and commanded
18:42 Then *J* said to him, "Receive
19: 1 Then *J* entered and passed
19: 3 And he sought to see who *J* was,
19: 5 And when *J* came to the place, He
19: 9 And *J* said to him, "Today
19:35 Then they brought him to *J*.
19:35 and they set *J* on him.
20: 8 And *J* said to them, "Neither
20:34 And *J* answered and said to them,
22:47 before them and drew near to *J*
22:48 But *J* said to him, "Judas, are
22:51 But *J* answered and said,
22:52 Then *J* said to the chief
22:63 Now the men who held *J* mocked
23: 8 Now when Herod saw *J*,
23:20 therefore, wishing to release *J*,
23:25 but he delivered *J* to their
23:26 that he might bear it after *J*.
23:28 But *J*, turning to them,
23:34 Then *J* said, "Father, forgive
23:42 Then he said to *J*,
23:43 And *J* said to him, "Assuredly,
23:46 And when *J* had cried out with a
23:52 and asked for the body of *J*.
24: 3 not find the body of the Lord *J*.
24:15 that *J* Himself drew near and
24:19 The things concerning *J* of
24:36 *J* Himself stood in the midst of
Jn 1:17 grace and truth came through *J*
1:29 The next day John saw *J* coming
1:36 And looking at *J* as He walked,
1:37 him speak, and they followed *J*.
1:38 Then *J* turned, and seeing them
1:42 And he brought him to *J*.
1:42 Now when *J* looked at him, He
1:43 The following day *J* wanted to
1:45 *J* of Nazareth, the son of
1:47 *J* saw Nathanael coming toward
1:48 *J* answered and said to him,
1:50 *J* answered and said to him,
2: 1 and the mother of *J* was there.
2: 2 Now both *J* and His disciples
2: 3 the mother of *J* said to Him,
2: 4 *J* said to her, "Woman, what
2: 7 *J* said to them, "Fill the
2:11 This beginning of signs *J* did in
2:13 and *J* went up to Jerusalem.
2:19 *J* answered and said to them,
2:22 Scripture and the word which *J*
2:24 But *J* did not commit Himself to
3: 2 This man came to *J* by night and
3: 3 *J* answered and said to him,
3: 5 *J* answered, "Most assuredly, I
3:10 *J* answered and said to him,
3:22 After these things *J* and His
4: 1 the Pharisees had heard that *J*
4: 2 (though *J* Himself did not
4: 6 *J* therefore, being wearied from
4: 7 *J* said to her, "Give Me a
4:10 *J* answered and said to her, "If
4:13 *J* answered and said to her,
4:16 *J* said to her, "Go, call your
4:17 *J* said to her, "You have
4:21 *J* said to her, "Woman, believe
4:26 *J* said to her, "I who speak to
4:34 *J* said to them, "My food is to
4:44 For *J* Himself testified that a
4:46 So *J* came again to Cana of
4:47 When he heard that *J* had come
4:48 Then *J* said to him, "Unless you
4:50 *J* said to him, "Go your way;
4:50 man believed the word that *J*
4:53 at the same hour in which *J*
4:54 again is the second sign *J*
5: 1 and *J* went up to Jerusalem.
5: 6 When *J* saw him lying there, and
5: 8 *J* said to him, "Rise, take up
5:13 for *J* had withdrawn, a
5:14 Afterward *J* found him in the
5:15 and told the Jews that it was *J*
5:16 reason the Jews persecuted *J*,
5:17 But *J* answered them, "My Father
5:19 Then *J* answered and said to
6: 1 After these things *J* went over
6: 3 And *J* went up on the mountain,
6: 5 Then *J* lifted up His eyes, and
6:10 Then *J* said, "Make the people
6:11 And *J* took the loaves, and when
6:14 they had seen the sign that *J*
6:15 Therefore when *J* perceived that
6:17 and *J* had not come to them.
6:19 they saw *J* walking on the sea
6:22 and that *J* had not entered the
6:24 the people therefore saw that *J*
6:24 came to Capernaum, seeking *J*.
6:26 *J* answered them and said, "Most
6:29 *J* answered and said to them,
6:32 Then *J* said to them, "Most
6:35 And *J* said to them, "I am the
6:42 And they said, "Is not this *J*,

6:43 *J* therefore answered and said to
6:53 Then *J* said to them, "Most
6:61 When *J* knew in Himself that His
6:64 For *J* knew from the beginning
6:67 Then *J* said to the twelve, "Do
6:70 *J* answered them, "Did I not
7: 1 After these things *J* walked in
7: 6 Then *J* said to them, "My time
7:14 the middle of the feast *J* went
7:16 *J* answered them and said, "My
7:21 *J* answered and said to them, "I
7:28 Then *J* cried out, as He taught
7:33 Then *J* said to them, "I shall
7:37 *J* stood and cried out, saying,
7:39 because *J* was not yet
7:50 (he who came to *J* by night,
8: 1 But *J* went to the Mount of
8: 6 But *J* stooped down and wrote on
8: 9 And *J* was left alone, and the
8:10 When *J* had raised Himself up and
8:11 And *J* said to her, "Neither
8:12 Then *J* spoke to them again,
8:14 *J* answered and said to them,
8:19 *J* answered, "You know
8:20 These words *J* spoke in the
8:21 Then *J* said to them again, "I
8:25 And *J* said to them, "Just
8:28 Then *J* said to them, "When you
8:31 Then *J* said to those Jews who
8:34 *J* answered them, "Most
8:39 *J* said to them, "If you were
8:42 *J* said to them, "If God were
8:49 *J* answered, "I do not have a
8:54 *J* answered, "If I honor Myself,
8:58 *J* said to them, "Most
8:59 but *J* hid Himself and went out
9: 1 Now as *J* passed by, He saw a
9: 3 *J* answered, "Neither this man
9:11 A Man called *J* made clay and
9:14 Now it was a Sabbath when *J* made
9:35 *J* heard that they had cast him
9:37 And *J* said to him, "You have
9:39 And *J* said, "For judgment I
9:41 *J* said to them, "If you were
10: 6 *J* used this illustration, but
10: 7 Then *J* said to them again,
10:23 And *J* walked in the temple, in
10:25 *J* answered them, "I told you,
10:32 *J* answered them, "Many good
10:34 *J* answered them, "Is it not
11: 4 When *J* heard that, He said,
11: 5 Now *J* loved Martha and her
11: 9 *J* answered, "Are there not
11:13 *J* spoke of his death, but they
11:14 Then *J* said to them plainly,
11:17 So when *J* came, He found that
11:20 as soon as she heard that *J* was
11:21 Then Martha said to *J*,
11:23 *J* said to her, "Your brother
11:25 *J* said to her, "I am the
11:30 Now *J* had not yet come into the
11:32 when Mary came where *J* was, and
11:33 when *J* saw her weeping, and the
11:35 *J* wept.
11:38 Then *J*, again groaning in
11:39 *J* said, "Take away the stone."
11:40 *J* said to her, "Did I not say
11:41 And *J* lifted up His eyes and
11:44 *J* said to them, "Loose him,
11:45 and had seen the things *J* did,
11:46 and told them the things *J* did.
11:51 that year he prophesied that *J*
11:54 Therefore *J* no longer walked
11:56 Then they sought *J*,
12: 1 *J* came to Bethany, where
12: 3 anointed the feet of *J*,
12: 7 But *J* said, "Let her alone;
12:11 went away and believed in *J*.
12:12 when they heard that *J* was
12:14 Then *J*, when He had found
12:16 but when *J* was glorified, then
12:21 saying, "Sir, we wish to see *J*.
12:22 turn Andrew and Philip told *J*.
12:23 But *J* answered them, saying,
12:30 *J* answered and said, "This
12:35 Then *J* said to them, "A little
12:36 These things *J* spoke, and
12:44 Then *J* cried out and said, "He
13: 1 when *J* knew that His hour had
13: 3 *J*, knowing that the Father
13: 7 *J* answered and said to him,
13: 8 my feet!" *J* answered him,
13:10 *J* said to him, "He who is
13:21 When *J* had said these things, He
13:23 His disciples, whom *J* loved.
13:26 *J* answered, "It is he to whom I
13:27 Then *J* said to him, "What you
13:29 that *J* had said to him, "Buy
13:31 *J* said, "Now the Son of Man is
13:36 *J* answered him, "Where I am
13:38 *J* answered him, "Will you lay
14: 6 *J* said to him, "I am the way,
14: 9 *J* said to him, "Have I been
14:23 *J* answered and said to him, "If
16:19 Now *J* knew that they desired to
16:31 *J* answered them, "Do you now
17: 1 *J* spoke these words, lifted up
17: 3 and *J* Christ whom You have
18: 1 When *J* had spoken these words,
18: 2 for *J* often met there with His
18: 4 *J* therefore, knowing all things
18: 5 *J* of Nazareth." Jesus said to
18: 5 *J* said to them, "I am He."
18: 7 they said, "*J* of Nazareth."
18: 8 *J* answered, "I have told you
18:11 So *J* said to Peter, "Put your
18:12 of the Jews arrested *J* and
18:15 And Simon Peter followed *J*,
18:15 and went with *J* into the
18:19 The high priest then asked *J*
18:20 *J* answered him, "I spoke openly
18:22 officers who stood by struck *J*
18:23 *J* answered him, "If I have
18:28 Then they led *J* from Caiaphas
18:32 that the saying of *J* might be
18:33 the Praetorium again, called *J*,
18:34 *J* answered him, "Are you
18:36 *J* answered, "My kingdom is not
18:37 *J* answered, "You say
19: 1 So then Pilate took *J* and
19: 5 Then *J* came out, wearing the
19: 9 the Praetorium, and said to *J*,
19: 9 But *J* gave him no answer.
19:11 *J* answered, "You could have no
19:13 he brought *J* out and sat down
19:16 So they took *J* and led Him
19:18 and *J* in the center.
19:19 *J* OF NAZARETH, THE KING OF
19:20 for the place where *J* was
19:23 when they had crucified *J*,
19:25 there stood by the cross of *J*
19:26 When *J* therefore saw His mother,
19:28 After this, *J*, knowing that
19:30 So when *J* had received the sour
19:33 But when they came to *J* and saw
19:38 being a disciple of *J*,
19:38 might take away the body of *J*;
19:38 he came and took the body of *J*.
19:39 who at first came to *J* by
19:40 Then they took the body of *J*,
19:42 So there they laid *J*,
20: 2 whom *J* loved, and said to them,
20:12 where the body of *J* had lain.
20:14 she turned around and saw *J*
20:14 and did not know that it was *J*.
20:15 *J* said to her, "Woman, why are
20:16 *J* said to her, "Mary!"
20:17 *J* said to her, "Do not cling to
20:19 *J* came and stood in the midst,
20:21 So *J* said to them again, "Peace
20:24 was not with them when *J* came.
20:26 *J* came, the doors being shut,
20:29 *J* said to him, "Thomas, because
20:30 And truly *J* did many other
20:31 that you may believe that *J* is
21: 1 After these things *J* showed
21: 4 *J* stood on the shore; yet the
21: 4 did not know that it was *J*.
21: 5 Then *J* said to them, "Children,
21: 7 Therefore that disciple whom *J*
21:10 *J* said to them, "Bring some of
21:12 *J* said to them, "Come and eat
21:13 *J* then came and took the bread
21:14 This is now the third time *J*
21:15 *J* said to Simon Peter, "Simon,
21:17 *J* said to him, "Feed My
21:20 saw the disciple whom *J* loved
21:21 Peter, seeing him, said to *J*,
21:22 *J* said to him, "If I will that
21:23 Yet *J* did not say to him that
21:25 also many other things that *J*

Acts
1: 1 of all that *J* began both to do
1:11 up into heaven? This same *J*,
1:14 women and Mary the mother of *J*,
1:16 a guide to those who arrested *J*;
1:21 us all the time that the Lord *J*
2:22 *J* of Nazareth, a Man attested
2:32 This *J* God has raised up, of
2:36 that God has made this *J*,
2:38 be baptized in the name of *J*
3: 6 In the name of *J* Christ of
3:13 glorified His Servant *J*,
3:20 and that He may send *J* Christ,
3:26 having raised up His Servant *J*,
4: 2 the people and preached in *J*
4:10 that by the name of *J* Christ of
4:13 that they had been with *J*.
4:18 all nor teach in the name of *J*.
4:27 against Your holy Servant *J*,
4:30 the name of Your holy Servant *J*.
4:33 the resurrection of the Lord *J*.
5:30 God of our fathers raised up *J*
5:40 not speak in the name of *J*,
5:42 cease teaching and preaching *J*
6:14 have heard him say that this *J*
7:55 and *J* standing at the right
7:59 on God and saying, "Lord *J*,
8:12 of God and the name of *J*
8:16 in the name of the Lord *J*.
8:35 Scripture, preached *J* to him.
8:37 I believe that *J* Christ is the
9: 5 Then the Lord said, "I am *J*,
9:17 "Brother Saul, the Lord *J*,
9:22 proving that this *J* is the
9:27 at Damascus in the name of *J*.
9:29 in the name of the Lord *J* and
9:34 *J* the Christ heals you.
10:36 preaching peace through *J*
10:38 how God anointed *J* of Nazareth
11:17 when we believed on the Lord *J*
11:20 preaching the Lord *J*.
13:23 raised up for Israel a Savior—*J*—
13:33 in that He has raised up *J*.
15:11 the grace of the Lord *J* Christ
15:26 for the name of our Lord *J*
16:18 command you in the name of *J*
16:31 Believe on the Lord *J* Christ,
17: 3 This *J* whom I preach to you is
17: 7 saying there is another king—*J*.
17:18 because he preached to them *J*
18: 5 testified to the Jews that *J*
18:28 from the Scriptures that *J* is
19: 4 after him, that is, on Christ *J*.
19: 5 in the name of the Lord *J*.
19:10 heard the word of the Lord *J*,
19:13 to call the name of the Lord *J*
19:13 We exorcise you by the *J* whom
19:15 '*J* I know, and Paul I know;
19:17 and the name of the Lord *J* was
20:21 God and faith toward our Lord *J*
20:24 I received from the Lord *J*,
20:35 the words of the Lord *J*,
21:13 for the name of the Lord *J*.
22: 8 I am *J* of Nazareth, whom you are
25:19 religion and about a certain *J*,
26: 9 contrary to the name of *J* of
26:15 And He said, 'I am *J*,
28:23 persuading them concerning *J*
28:31 things which concern the Lord *J*

Rom
1: 1 a bondservant of *J* Christ,
1: 3 concerning His Son *J* Christ our
1: 6 you also are the called of *J*
1: 7 God our Father and the Lord *J*
1: 8 I thank my God through *J* Christ
2:16 judge the secrets of men by *J*
3:22 through faith in *J* Christ, to
3:24 redemption that is in Christ *J*,
3:26 of the one who has faith in *J*.
4:24 believe in Him who raised up *J*
5: 1 with God through our Lord *J*
5:11 in God through our Lord *J*
5:15 *J* Christ, abounded to many.
5:17 through the One, *J* Christ.)
5:21 to eternal life through *J*
6: 3 as were baptized into Christ *J*
6:11 but alive to God in Christ *J*
6:23 is eternal life in Christ *J*
7:25 —through *J* Christ our Lord!
8: 1 to those who are in Christ *J*,
8: 2 the Spirit of life in Christ *J*
8:11 the Spirit of Him who raised *J*
8:39 of God which is in Christ *J*
10: 9 with your mouth the Lord *J* and
13:14 But put on the Lord *J* Christ,
14:14 and am convinced by the Lord *J*
15: 5 another, according to Christ *J*,
15: 6 God and Father of our Lord *J*
15: 8 Now I say that *J* Christ has
15:16 that I might be a minister of *J*
15:17 reason to glory in Christ *J* in
15:30 through the Lord *J* Christ, and
16: 3 my fellow workers in Christ *J*,
16:18 such do not serve our Lord *J*
16:20 The grace of our Lord *J* Christ
16:24 The grace of our Lord *J* Christ
16:25 gospel and the preaching of *J*
16:27 be glory through *J* Christ

1 Cor
1: 1 called to be an apostle of *J*
1: 2 who are sanctified in Christ *J*,
1: 2 place call on the name of *J*
1: 3 God our Father and the Lord *J*
1: 4 was given to you by Christ *J*,
1: 7 the revelation of our Lord *J*
1: 8 in the day of our Lord *J*
1: 9 His Son, *J* Christ our Lord.
1:10 by the name of our Lord *J*
1:30 But of Him you are in Christ *J*,
2: 2 anything among you except *J*
3:11 is laid, which is *J* Christ.
4:15 for in Christ *J* I have begotten
5: 4 In the name of our Lord *J*
5: 4 with the power of our Lord *J*
5: 5 saved in the day of the Lord *J*.
6:11 in the name of the Lord *J* and
8: 6 and one Lord *J* Christ, through
9: 1 Have I not seen *J* Christ our
11:23 that the Lord *J* on the same
12: 3 by the Spirit of God calls *J*
12: 3 and no one can say that *J* is
15:31 in you which I have in Christ *J*
15:57 the victory through our Lord *J*
16:22 anyone does not love the Lord *J*
16:23 The grace of our Lord *J* Christ
16:24 be with you all in Christ *J*.

2 Cor
1: 1 an apostle of *J* Christ by the
1: 2 God our Father and the Lord *J*
1: 3 God and Father of our Lord *J*
1:14 ours, in the day of the Lord *J*.
1:19 *J* Christ, who was preached
4: 5 but Christ *J* the Lord, and
4: 6 glory of God in the face of *J*
4:10 body the dying of the Lord *J*,
4:10 that the life of *J* also may be
4:11 that the life of *J* also may be
4:14 He who raised up the Lord *J*
4:14 will also raise us up with *J*,
5:18 us to Himself through *J* Christ,
8: 9 know the grace of our Lord *J*
11: 4 he who comes preaches another *J*
11:31 God and Father of our Lord *J*
13: 5 that *J* Christ is in you?—unless
13:14 The grace of the Lord *J* Christ,

Gal
1: 1 but through *J* Christ and God
1: 3 God the Father and our Lord *J*
1:12 through the revelation of *J*

2: 4 which we have in Christ *J*,
2:16 of the law but by faith in *J*
2:16 we have believed in Christ *J*,
3: 1 before whose eyes *J* Christ was
3:14 upon the Gentiles in Christ *J*,
3:22 that the promise by faith in *J*
3:26 God through faith in Christ *J*.
3:28 for you are all one in Christ *J*.
4:14 angel of God, even as Christ *J*.
5: 6 For in Christ *J* neither
6:14 in the cross of our Lord *J*
6:15 For in Christ *J* neither
6:17 my body the marks of the Lord *J*.
6:18 the grace of our Lord *J* Christ
Eph 1: 1 an apostle of *J* Christ by the
1: 1 and faithful in Christ *J*:
1: 2 God our Father and the Lord *J*
1: 3 God and Father of our Lord *J*
1: 5 us to adoption as sons by *J*
1:15 of your faith in the Lord *J*
1:17 that the God of our Lord *J*
2: 6 heavenly places in Christ *J*,
2: 7 kindness toward us in Christ *J*.
2:10 created in Christ *J* for good
2:13 But now in Christ *J* you who once
2:20 *J* Christ Himself being the
3: 1 the prisoner of Christ *J* for
3: 9 created all things through *J*
3:11 He accomplished in Christ *J*
3:14 to the Father of our Lord *J*
3:21 in the church by Christ *J* to
4:21 by Him, as the truth is in *J*:
5:20 in the name of our Lord *J*
6:23 God the Father and the Lord *J*
6:24 all those who love our Lord *J*
Phil 1: 1 bondservants of *J* Christ, To
1: 1 To all the saints in Christ *J*
1: 2 God our Father and the Lord *J*
1: 6 it until the day of *J* Christ;
1: 8 you all with the affection of *J*
1:11 righteousness which are by *J*
1:19 the supply of the Spirit of *J*
1:26 me may be more abundant in *J*
2: 5 you which was also in Christ *J*,
2:10 that at the name of *J* every knee
2:11 tongue should confess that *J*
2:19 But I trust in the Lord *J* to
2:21 things which are of Christ *J*.
3: 3 the Spirit, rejoice in Christ *J*,
3: 8 of the knowledge of Christ *J*
3:12 of that for which Christ *J* has
3:14 upward call of God in Christ *J*.
3:20 Savior, the Lord *J* Christ,
4: 7 and minds through Christ *J*.
4:19 His riches in glory by Christ *J*.
4:21 Greet every saint in Christ *J*.
4:23 The grace of our Lord *J* Christ
Col 1: 1 an apostle of *J* Christ by the
1: 2 God our Father and the Lord *J*
1: 3 God and Father of our Lord *J*
1: 4 of your faith in Christ *J* and
1:28 every man perfect in Christ *J*.
2: 6 therefore received Christ *J*
3:17 all in the name of the Lord *J*,
4:11 and *J* who is called Justus.
1 Th 1: 1 God the Father and the Lord *J*
1: 1 God our Father and the Lord *J*
1: 3 patience of hope in our Lord *J*
1:10 even *J* who delivers us from
2:14 which are in Judea in Christ *J*.
2:15 who killed both the Lord *J* and
2:19 in the presence of our Lord *J*
3:11 and our Lord *J* Christ, direct
3:13 at the coming of our Lord *J*
4: 1 urge and exhort in the Lord *J*
4: 2 we gave you through the Lord *J*.
4:14 For if we believe that *J* died
4:14 with Him those who sleep in *J*.
5: 9 salvation through our Lord *J*
5:18 is the will of God in Christ *J*
5:23 at the coming of our Lord *J*
5:28 The grace of our Lord *J* Christ
2 Th 1: 1 God our Father and the Lord *J*
1: 2 God our Father and the Lord *J*
1: 7 rest with us when the Lord *J*
1: 8 obey the gospel of our Lord *J*
1:12 that the name of our Lord *J*
1:12 grace of our God and the Lord *J*
2: 1 the coming of our Lord *J*
2:14 of the glory of our Lord *J*
2:16 Now may our Lord *J* Christ
3: 6 in the name of our Lord *J*
3:12 and exhort through our Lord *J*
3:18 The grace of our Lord *J* Christ
1 Tim 1: 1 an apostle of *J* Christ, by the
1: 1 God our Savior and the Lord *J*
1: 2 peace from God our Father and *J*
1:12 And I thank Christ *J* our Lord
1:14 and love which are in Christ *J*.
1:15 that Christ *J* came into the
1:16 that in me first *J* Christ might
2: 5 God and men, the Man Christ *J*,
3:13 the faith which is in Christ *J*.
4: 6 will be a good minister of *J*
5:21 you before God and the Lord *J*
6: 3 even the words of our Lord *J*
6:13 and before Christ *J* who
6:14 blameless until our Lord *J*
2 Tim 1: 1 an apostle of *J* Christ by the
1: 1 of life which is in Christ *J*,
1: 2 God the Father and Christ *J*
1: 9 was given to us in Christ *J*
1:10 the appearing of our Savior *J*
1:13 and love which are in Christ *J*.
2: 1 the grace that is in Christ *J*.
2: 3 as a good soldier of *J* Christ.
2: 8 Remember that *J* Christ, of the
2:10 salvation which is in Christ *J*
3:12 to live godly in Christ *J* will
3:15 faith which is in Christ *J*.
4: 1 before God and the Lord *J*
4:22 The Lord *J* Christ be with your
Titus 1: 1 of God and an apostle of *J*
1: 4 God the Father and the Lord *J*
2:13 of our great God and Savior *J*
3: 6 out on us abundantly through *J*
Phm 1: 1 Paul, a prisoner of Christ *J*,
1: 3 God our Father and the Lord *J*
1: 5 you have toward the Lord *J* and
1: 6 which is in you in Christ *J*.
1: 9 and now also a prisoner of *J*
1:23 my fellow prisoner in Christ *J*,
1:25 The grace of our Lord *J* Christ
Heb 2: 9 But we see *J*, who was made
3: 1 of our confession, Christ *J*,
4:14 *J* the Son of God, let us hold
6:20 has entered for us, even *J*,
7:22 by so much more *J* has become a
10:10 the offering of the body of *J*
10:19 the Holiest by the blood of *J*,
12: 2 looking unto *J*, the author
12:24 to *J* the Mediator of the new
13: 8 *J* Christ is the same yesterday,
13:12 Therefore *J* also, that He might
13:20 who brought up our Lord *J* from
13:21 through *J* Christ, to whom be
Jas 1: 1 of God and of the Lord *J*
2: 1 hold the faith of our Lord *J*
1 Pe 1: 1 an apostle of *J* Christ, To the
1: 2 sprinkling of the blood of *J*
1: 3 God and Father of our Lord *J*
1: 3 through the resurrection of *J*
1: 7 glory at the revelation of *J*
1:13 to you at the revelation of *J*
2: 5 acceptable to God through *J*
3:21 through the resurrection of *J*
4:11 God may be glorified through *J*
5:10 His eternal glory by Christ *J*,
5:14 to you all who are in Christ *J*.
2 Pe 1: 1 a bondservant and apostle of *J*
1: 1 of our God and Savior *J* Christ:
1: 2 the knowledge of God and of *J*
1: 8 in the knowledge of our Lord *J*
1:11 of our Lord and Savior *J*
1:14 just as our Lord *J* Christ
1:16 power and coming of our Lord *J*
2:20 of the Lord and Savior *J*
3:18 of our Lord and Savior *J*
1 Jn 1: 3 the Father and with His Son *J*
1: 7 and the blood of *J* Christ His
2: 1 *J* Christ the righteous.
2:22 a liar but he who denies that *J*
3:23 on the name of His Son *J*
4: 2 spirit that confesses that *J*
4: 3 that does not confess that *J*
4:15 Whoever confesses that *J* is the
5: 1 Whoever believes that *J* is the
5: 5 but he who believes that *J* is
5: 6 *J* Christ; not only by water, but
5:20 in His Son *J* Christ. This is
2 Jn 3 the Father and from the Lord *J*
7 the world who do not confess *J*
Jude 1 a bondservant of *J* Christ, and
1 and preserved in *J* Christ:
4 only Lord God and our Lord *J*
17 by the apostles of our Lord *J*
21 for the mercy of our Lord *J*
Rev 1: 1 The Revelation of *J* Christ,
1: 2 and to the testimony of *J*
1: 5 and from *J* Christ, the faithful
1: 9 and kingdom and patience of *J*
1: 9 God and for the testimony of *J*
12:17 God and have the testimony of *J*
14:12 of God and the faith of *J*.
17: 6 the blood of the martyrs of *J*.
19:10 who have the testimony of *J*.
19:10 God! For the testimony of *J* is
20: 4 for their witness to *J* and for
22:16 'I, *J*, have sent My angel
22:20 Even so, come, Lord *J*!
22:21 The grace of our Lord *J* Christ

JESUS' (9/9) JESUS

Mt 15:30 laid them down at *J* feet,
Lk 5: 8 he fell down at *J* knees,
8:41 And he fell down at *J* feet and
10:39 who also sat at *J* feet and
Jn 12: 9 not for *J* sake only, but that
13:23 Now there was leaning on *J* bosom
13:25 leaning back on *J* breast, he
2 Cor 4: 5 your bondservants for *J* sake.
4:11 delivered to death for *J* sake,

JETHER (8/7) JETHRO

Judg 8:20 And he said to *J* his firstborn,
1 Ki 2: 5 of Ner and Amasa the son of *J*,
2:32 Israel, and Amasa the son of *J*,
1 Chr 2:17 and the father of Amasa was *J*
2:32 were *J* and Jonathan;
2:32 *J* died without children.
4:17 The sons of Ezrah were *J*,
7:38 The sons of *J* were Jephunneh,

JETHETH (2/2)

Gen 36:40 Timnah, Chief Alvah, Chief *J*,
1 Chr 1:51 Timnah, Chief Aliah, Chief *J*,

JETHLAH (1/1)

Josh 19:42 Shaalabbin, Aijalon, *J*,

JETHRO (10/9) HOBAB, JETHER, REUEL

Ex 3: 1 was tending the flock of *J* his
4:18 Moses went and returned to *J*
4:18 And *J* said to Moses, "Go in
18: 1 And *J*, the priest of Midian,
18: 2 Then *J*, Moses' father-in-law,
18: 5 and *J*, Moses' father-in-law,
18: 6 "I, your father-in-law *J*,
18: 9 Then *J* rejoiced for all the good
18:10 And *J* said, "Blessed be the
18:12 Then *J*, Moses' father-in-law,

JETUR (3/3)

Gen 25:15 Hadar, Tema, *J*,
1 Chr 1:31 *J*, Naphish, and Kedemah.
5:19 made war with the Hagrites, *J*,

JEUEL (1/1)

1 Chr 9: 6 Of the sons of Zerah: *J*,

JEUSH (9/9)

Gen 36: 5 And Aholibamah bore *J*,
36:14 And she bore to Esau: *J*,
36:18 Esau's wife: Chief *J*,
1 Chr 1:35 of Esau were Eliphaz, Reuel, *J*,
7:10 and the sons of Bilhan were *J*,
8:39 *J* the second, and Eliphelet the
23:10 sons of Shimei: Jahath, Zina, *J*,
23:11 But *J* and Beriah did not have
2 Chr 11:19 And she bore him children: *J*,

J

JEUZ (1/1)

1 Chr 8:10 *J*, Sachiah, and Mirmah.

JEW (28/28) JEWISH, JEWS, JUDAISM

Esth 2: 5 citadel there was a certain *J*
3: 4 had told them that he was a *J*.
5:13 so long as I see Mordecai the *J*
6:10 and do so for Mordecai the *J*
8: 7 Queen Esther and Mordecai the *J*,
9:29 of Abihail, with Mordecai the *J*,
9:31 as Mordecai the *J* and Queen
10: 3 For Mordecai the *J* was second
Jn 4: 9 "How is it that You, being a *J*,
18:35 Pilate answered, "Am I a *J*?
Acts 13: 6 a *J* whose name was Bar-Jesus,
18: 2 And he found a certain *J* named
18:24 Now a certain *J* named Apollos,
19:34 they found out that he was a *J*,
21:39 I am a *J* from Tarsus, in
22: 3 'I am indeed a *J*, born in
Rom 1:16 for the *J* first and also for
2: 9 of the *J* first and also of the
2:10 to the *J* first and also to the
2:17 Indeed you are called a *J*,
2:28 For he is not a *J* who is one
2:29 but he is a *J* who is one
3: 1 What advantage then has the *J*,
10:12 is no distinction between *J*
1 Cor 9:20 and to the Jews I became as a *J*,
Gal 2:14 them all, "If you, being a *J*,
3:28 There is neither *J* nor Greek,
Col 3:11 there is neither Greek nor *J*,

JEWEL (2/2) JEWELRY, JEWELS

Prov 20:15 of knowledge are a precious *j*.
Ezek 16:12 And I put a *j* in your nose,

JEWELRY (10/9) JEWEL

Gen 24:53 Then the servant brought out *j*
24:53 *j* of gold, and clothing, and
Ex 35:22 all *j* of gold, that is, every
2 Chr 20:25 the dead bodies, and precious *j*,
Job 28:17 Nor can it be exchanged for *j*
Prov 25: 4 go to the silversmith for *j*.
Ezek 16:17 also taken your beautiful *j*
16:39 clothes, take your beautiful *j*,
23:26 And take away your beautiful *j*.
Hos 2:13 herself with her earrings and *j*,

JEWELS (7/7) JEWEL

Ex 31: 5 in cutting *j* for setting, in
35:33 in cutting *j* for setting, in
Song 7: 1 of your thighs are like *j*,
Isa 3:21 and the rings; The nose *j*,
61:10 adorns herself with her *j*.
Zech 9:16 they shall be like the *j* of
Mal 3:17 the day that I make them My *j*.

JEWISH (14/14) JEW

Neh 5: 1 wives against their *J* brethren.
5: 8 have redeemed our *J* brethren
Esth 6:13 is of *J* descent, you will not
Jer 34: 9 no one should keep a *J* brother
Zech 8:23 grasp the sleeve of a *J* man

Acts 10:28 how unlawful it is for a *J* man
12:11 all the expectation of the *J*
16: 1 the son of a certain *J* woman
19:13 of the itinerant *J* exorcists
19:14 a *J* chief priest, who did so.
24:24 his wife Drusilla, who was *J*,
26:17 deliver you from the *J* people,
26:23 would proclaim light to the *J*
Titus 1:14 not giving heed to *J* fables and

JEWRY (KJV) See JUDAH, JUDEA

JEWS (241/228) JEW, JEWS'

2 Ki 25:25 and killed Gedaliah, the *J*,
Ezra 4:12 be known to the king that the *J*
4:23 to Jerusalem against the *J*,
5: 1 prophesied to the *J* who were
5: 5 was upon the elders of the *J*,
6: 7 let the governor of the *J* and
6: 7 Jews and the elders of the *J*
6: 8 do for the elders of these *J*
6:14 So the elders of the *J* built,
Neh 1: 2 I asked them concerning the *J*
2:16 I had not yet told the *J*,
4: 1 indignant, and mocked the *J*.
4: 2 What are these feeble *J* doing?
4:12 when the *J* who dwelt near them
5:17 were one hundred and fifty *J*
6: 6 that you and the *J* plan to
13:23 In those days I also saw *J* who
Esth 3: 6 sought to destroy all the *J*
3:10 the Agagite, the enemy of the *J*.
3:13 and to annihilate all the *J*,
4: 3 was great mourning among the *J*,
4: 7 treasuries to destroy the *J*.
4:13 any more than all the other *J*.
4:14 will arise for the *J* from
4:16 gather all the *J* who are
8: 1 of Haman, the enemy of the *J*.
8: 3 he had devised against the *J*.
8: 5 he wrote to annihilate the *J*
8: 7 to lay his hand on the *J*.
8: 8 a decree concerning the *J*,
8: 9 Mordecai commanded, to the *J*,
8: 9 and to the *J* in their own
8:11 the king permitted the *J* who
8:13 so that the *J* would be ready on
8:16 The *J* had light and gladness,
8:17 the *J* had joy and gladness, a
8:17 the people of the land became *J*,
8:17 because fear of the *J* fell upon
9: 1 day that the enemies of the *J*
9: 1 in that the *J* themselves
9: 2 The *J* gathered together in their
9: 3 the king's work, helped the *J*,
9: 5 Thus the *J* defeated all their
9: 6 in Shushan the citadel the *J*
9:10 Hammedatha, the enemy of the *J*—
9:12 The *J* have killed and destroyed
9:13 let it be granted to the *J* who
9:15 And the *J* who were in Shushan
9:16 The remainder of the *J* in the
9:18 But the *J* who were at Shushan
9:19 Therefore the *J* of the villages
9:20 and sent letters to all the *J*,
9:22 as the days on which the *J* had
9:23 So the *J* accepted the custom
9:24 Agagite, the enemy of all the *J*,
9:24 had plotted against the *J* to
9:25 had devised against the *J*
9:27 the *J* established and imposed it
9:28 to be observed among the *J*,
9:30 sent letters to all the *J*,
10: 3 and was great among the *J* and
Jer 32:12 before all the *J* who sat in the
38:19 I am afraid of the *J* who have
40:11 when all the *J* who were in
40:12 then all the *J* returned out of
40:15 so that all the *J* who are
41: 3 also struck down all the *J* who
44: 1 Jeremiah concerning all the *J*
52:28 thousand and twenty-three *J*;
52:30 carried away captive of the *J*
Dan 3: 8 came forward and accused the *J*.
3:12 There are certain *J* whom you
Mt 2: 2 who has been born King of the *J*?
27:11 "Are You the King of the *J*?
27:29 'Hail, King of the *J*!"
27:37 JESUS THE KING OF THE *J*.
28:15 commonly reported among the *J*
Mk 7: 3 the Pharisees and all the *J* do
15: 2 "Are You the King of the *J*?
15: 9 to you the King of the *J*?
15:12 whom you call the King of the *J*?
15:18 'Hail, King of the *J*!"
15:26 above: THE KING OF THE *J*.
Lk 7: 3 he sent elders of the *J* to Him,
23: 3 "Are You the King of the *J*?
23:37 "If You are the King of the *J*,
23:38 THIS IS THE KING OF THE *J*.
23:51 from Arimathea, a city of the *J*,
Jn 1:19 when the *J* sent priests and
2: 6 manner of purification of the *J*,
2:13 Now the Passover of the *J* was
2:18 So the *J* answered and said to
2:20 Then the *J* said, "It has taken
3: 1 Nicodemus, a ruler of the *J*.
3:25 of John's disciples and the *J*
4: 9 For *J* have no dealings with
4:20 and you *J* say that in
4:22 for salvation is of the *J*.
5: 1 this there was a feast of the *J*,
5:10 The *J* therefore said to him who
5:15 The man departed and told the *J*
5:16 For this reason the *J*
5:18 Therefore the *J* sought all the
6: 4 the Passover, a feast of the *J*,
6:41 The *J* then complained about
6:52 The *J* therefore quarreled among
7: 1 because the *J* sought to kill
7:11 Then the *J* sought Him at the
7:13 openly of Him for fear of the *J*.
7:15 And the *J* marveled, saying,
7:35 Then the *J* said among
8:22 So the *J* said, "Will He kill
8:31 Then Jesus said to those *J* who
8:48 Then the *J* answered and said to
8:52 Then the *J* said to Him, "Now we
8:57 Then the *J* said to Him, "You
9:18 But the *J* did not believe
9:22 because they feared the *J*,
9:22 for the *J* had agreed already
10:19 a division again among the *J*
10:24 Then the *J* surrounded Him and
10:31 Then the *J* took up stones again
10:33 The *J* answered Him, saying,
11: 8 lately the *J* sought to stone
11:19 And many of the *J* had joined the
11:31 Then the *J* who were with her in
11:33 and the *J* who came with her
11:36 Then the *J* said, "See how He
11:45 Then many of the *J* who had come
11:54 walked openly among the *J*,
11:55 And the Passover of the *J* was
12: 9 Now a great many of the *J* knew
12:11 on account of him many of the *J*
13:33 seek Me; and as I said to the *J*,
18:12 and the officers of the *J*
18:14 was Caiaphas who advised the *J*
18:20 where the *J* always meet, and in
18:31 Therefore the *J* said to him,
18:33 "Are You the King of the *J*?
18:36 not be delivered to the *J*;
18:38 he went out again to the *J*,
18:39 to you the King of the *J*?
19: 3 King of the *J*!" And they
19: 7 The *J* answered him, "We have a
19:12 but the *J* cried out, saying,
19:14 hour. And he said to the *J*,
19:19 THE KING OF THE *J*.
19:20 Then many of the *J* read this
19:21 the chief priests of the *J*
19:21 not write, 'The King of the *J*,'
19:21 said, "I am the King of the *J*."
19:31 the *J* asked Pilate that their
19:38 but secretly, for fear of the *J*,
19:40 as the custom of the *J* is to
20:19 assembled, for fear of the *J*,
Acts 2: 5 were dwelling in Jerusalem *J*,
2:10 both *J* and proselytes,
9:22 and confounded the *J* who dwelt
9:23 the *J* plotted to kill him.
10:22 among all the nation of the *J*,
10:39 did both in the land of the *J*
11:19 the word to no one but the *J*
12: 3 he saw that it pleased the *J*,
13: 5 God in the synagogues of the *J*.
13:42 So when the *J* went out of the
13:43 many of the *J* and devout
13:45 But when the *J* saw the
13:50 But the *J* stirred up the devout
14: 1 to the synagogue of the *J*,
14: 1 a great multitude both of the *J*
14: 2 But the unbelieving *J* stirred up
14: 4 divided: part sided with the *J*,
14: 5 made by both the Gentiles and *J*,
14:19 Then *J* from Antioch and Iconium
16: 3 him because of the *J* who were
16:20 and said, "These men, being *J*,
17: 1 there was a synagogue of the *J*.
17: 5 But the *J* who were not
17:10 into the synagogue of the *J*.
17:13 But when the *J* from Thessalonica
17:17 in the synagogue with the *J*
18: 2 had commanded all the *J* to
18: 4 and persuaded both *J* and
18: 5 and testified to the *J* that
18:12 the *J* with one accord rose up
18:14 mouth, Gallio said to the *J*,
18:14 or wicked crimes, O *J*,
18:19 and reasoned with the *J*.
18:28 for he vigorously refuted the *J*
19:10 both *J* and Greeks.
19:17 became known both to all *J* and
19:33 the *J* putting him forward.
20: 3 And when the *J* plotted against
20:19 to me by the plotting of the *J*;
20:21 'testifying to *J*, and also
21:11 So shall the *J* at Jerusalem bind
21:20 how many myriads of *J* there are
21:21 you that you teach all the *J*
21:27 the *J* from Asia, seeing him in
22:12 a good testimony with all the *J*
22:30 why he was accused by the *J*,
23:12 some of the *J* banded together
23:20 The *J* have agreed to ask that
23:27 This man was seized by the *J* and
23:30 when it was told me that the *J*
24: 5 of dissension among all the *J*
24: 9 And the *J* also assented,
24:18 in the midst of which some *J*
24:27 wanting to do the *J* a favor,
25: 2 and the chief men of the *J*
25: 7 the *J* who had come down from
25: 8 against the law of the *J*,
25: 9 wanting to do the *J* a favor,
25:10 To the *J* I have done no wrong,
25:15 priests and the elders of the *J*
25:24 the whole assembly of the *J*
26: 2 of which I am accused by the *J*,
26: 3 which have to do with the *J*.
26: 4 Jerusalem, all the *J* know.
26: 7 Agrippa, I am accused by the *J*.
26:21 For these reasons the *J* seized
28:17 called the leaders of the *J*
28:19 But when the *J* spoke against
28:29 the *J* departed and had a great
Rom 3: 9 have previously charged both *J*
3:29 Or is He the God of the *J*
9:24 not of the *J* only, but also of
1 Cor 1:22 For *J* request a sign, and Greeks
1:23 to the *J* a stumbling block and
1:24 both *J* and Greeks, Christ the
9:20 and to the *J* I became as a Jew,
9:20 as a Jew, that I might win *J*;
10:32 either to the *J* or to the
12:13 whether *J* or Greeks, whether
2 Cor 11:24 From the *J* five times I received
Gal 2:13 And the rest of the *J* also
2:14 of Gentiles and not as the *J*,
2:14 compel Gentiles to live as *J*?
2:15 We who are *J* by nature, and
Rev 2: 9 of those who say they are *J*
3: 9 who say they are *J* and are not,

JEWS' (2/2) JEWS

Jn 7: 2 Now the *J* Feast of Tabernacles
19:42 because of the *J* Preparation

JEZANIAH (2/2)

Jer 40: 8 and *J* the son of a Maachathite,
42: 1 *J* the son of Hoshaiah, and all

JEZEBEL (22/19) JEZEBEL'S

1 Ki 16:31 that he took as wife *J* the
18: 4 while *J* massacred the prophets
18:13 to my lord what I did when *J*
19: 1 And Ahab told *J* all that Elijah
19: 2 Then *J* sent a messenger to
21: 5 But *J* his wife came to him, and
21: 7 Then *J* his wife said to him,
21:11 did as *J* had sent to them, as
21:14 Then they sent to *J*, saying,
21:15 when *J* heard that Naboth had
21:15 that *J* said to Ahab, "Arise,
21:23 And concerning *J* the LORD also
21:23 The dogs shall eat *J* by the wall
21:25 because *J* his wife stirred him
2 Ki 9: 7 of the LORD, at the hand of *J*.
9:10 The dogs shall eat *J* on the plot
9:22 the harlotries of your mother *J*
9:30 *J* heard of it; and she put
9:36 dogs shall eat the flesh of *J*;
9:37 and the corpse of *J* shall be as
9:37 shall not say, "Here lies *J*."
Rev 2:20 because you allow that woman *J*,

JEZEBEL'S (1/1) JEZEBEL

1 Ki 18:19 who eat at *J* table."

JEZER (3/3)

Gen 46:24 Naphtali were Jahzeel, Guni, *J*,
Num 26:49 of *J*, the family of the
1 Chr 7:13 Naphtali were Jahziel, Guni, *J*,

JEZERITES (1/1)

Num 26:49 of Jezer, the family of the *J*;

JEZIAH (1/1)

Ezra 10:25 the sons of Parosh: Ramiah, *J*,

JEZIEL (1/1)

1 Chr 12: 3 *J* and Pelet the sons of

JEZLIAH (KJV) See JIZLIAH

JEZOAR (KJV) See ZOHAR

JEZRAHIAH (1/1)

Neh 12:42 The singers sang loudly with *J*

JEZREEL (36/32) JEZREELITE

Josh 15:56 *J*, Jokdeam, Zanoah,
17:16 who are of the Valley of *J*.
19:18 And their territory went to *J*,
Judg 6:33 and encamped in the Valley of *J*.
1 Sam 25:43 David also took Ahinoam of *J*,
29: 1 by a fountain which is in *J*.
29:11 the Philistines went up to *J*.
2 Sam 2: 9 over the Ashurites, over *J*,
4: 4 Saul and Jonathan came from *J*;
1 Ki 4:12 is beside Zaretan below *J*,
18:45 So Ahab rode away and went to *J*.

18:46 of Ahab to the entrance of *J*.
21: 1 had a vineyard which was in *J*,
21:23 eat Jezebel by the wall of *J*.
2 Ki 8:29 Then King Joram went back to *J*
8:29 see Joram the son of Ahab in *J*,
9:10 on the plot of ground at *J*,
9:15 King Joram had returned to *J*
9:15 city to go and tell it in *J*.
9:16 rode in a chariot and went to *J*,
9:17 stood on the tower in *J*,
9:30 Now when Jehu had come to *J*,
9:36 On the plot of ground at *J*
9:37 of the field, in the plot at *J*,
10: 1 to Samaria, to the rulers of *J*,
10: 6 and come to me at *J* by this
10: 7 and sent them to him at *J*.
10:11 of the house of Ahab in *J*,
1 Chr 4: 3 of the father of Etam: *J*,
2 Chr 22: 6 Then he returned to *J* to recover
22: 6 Jehoram the son of Ahab in *J*,
Hos 1: 4 to him: "Call his name *J*,
1: 4 will avenge the bloodshed of *J*
1: 5 of Israel in the Valley of *J*.
1:11 great will be the day of *J*!
2:22 with oil; They shall answer *J*.

JEZREELITE (8/8) JEZREEL

1 Ki 21: 1 things that Naboth the *J* had
21: 4 of the word which Naboth the *J*
21: 6 I spoke to Naboth the *J*,
21: 7 the vineyard of Naboth the *J*.
21:15 of the vineyard of Naboth the *J*,
21:16 of the vineyard of Naboth the *J*.
2 Ki 9:21 on the property of Naboth the *J*.
9:25 of the field of Naboth the *J*;

JEZREELITESS (5/5)

1 Sam 27: 3 his two wives, Ahinoam the *J*,
30: 5 two wives, Ahinoam the *J*,
2 Sam 2: 2 two wives also, Ahinoam the *J*,
3: 2 was Amnon by Ahinoam the *J*;
1 Chr 3: 1 was Amnon, by Ahinoam the *J*;

JIBSAM (1/1)

1 Chr 7: 2 Rephaiah, Jeriel, Jahmai, *J*,

JIDLAPH (1/1)

Gen 22:22 "Chesed, Hazo, Pildash, *J*,

JIMNA (1/1)

Num 26:44 to their families were: of *J*,

JIMNAH (1/1)

Gen 46:17 The sons of Asher were *J*,

JIMNITES (1/1)

Num 26:44 of Jimna, the family of the *J*;

JINGLING (2/2)

Isa 3:16 Making a *j* with their feet,
3:18 The *j* anklets, the scarves,

JIPHTAH (1/1)

Josh 15:43 *J*, Ashnah, Nezib,

JIPHTHAH EL (2/2)

Josh 19:14 and it ended in the Valley of *J*.
19:27 Zebulun and to the Valley of *J*,

JIPHTHAH-EL (KJV) See JIPHTHAH EL

JISHUI (1/1)

1 Sam 14:49 *J* and Malchishua. And the names

JISSHIAH (1/1)

1 Chr 12: 6 Elkanah, *J*, Azarel,

JITHRA (1/1)

2 Sam 17:25 son of a man whose name was *J*,

JITHRAN (1/1)

1 Chr 7:37 Bezer, Hod, Shamma, Shilshah, *J*,

JIZLIAH (1/1)

1 Chr 8:18 Ishmerai, *J*, and Jobab were

JIZRI (1/1)

1 Chr 25:11 the fourth for *J*, his sons

JOAB (139/122) JOAB'S

1 Sam 26: 6 son of Zeruiah, brother of *J*,
2 Sam 2:13 And *J* the son of Zeruiah, and
2:14 Then Abner said to *J*,
2:14 And *J* said, "Let them
2:18 *J* and Abishai and Asahel.
2:22 could I face your brother *J*?
2:24 *J* and Abishai also pursued
2:26 Then Abner called to *J* and said,
2:27 And *J* said, "As God lives,
2:28 So *J* blew a trumpet; and all the
2:30 So *J* returned from pursuing
2:32 And *J* and his men went all
3:22 the servants of David and *J*
3:23 When *J* and all the troops that
3:23 with him had come, they told *J*,
3:24 Then *J* came to the king and
3:26 And when *J* had gone from David's
3:27 *J* took him aside in the gate to
3:29 Let it rest on the head of *J* and
3:29 fail to be in the house of *J*
3:30 So *J* and Abishai his brother
3:31 Then David said to *J* and to all
8:16 *J* the son of Zeruiah was over
10: 7 he sent *J* and all the army of
10: 9 When *J* saw that the battle line
10:13 So *J* and the people who were
10:14 So *J* returned from the people
11: 1 that David sent *J* and his
11: 6 Then David sent to *J*,
11: 6 And *J* sent Uriah to David.
11: 7 David asked how *J* was doing,
11:11 and my lord *J* and the servants
11:14 that David wrote a letter to *J*
11:16 while *J* besieged the city, that
11:17 city came out and fought with *J*.
11:18 Then *J* sent and told David all
11:22 came and told David all that *J*
11:25 "Thus you shall say to *J*:
12:26 Now *J* fought against Rabbah of
12:27 And *J* sent messengers to David,
14: 1 So *J* the son of Zeruiah
14: 2 And *J* sent to Tekoa and brought
14: 3 So *J* put the words in her
14:19 Is the hand of *J* with you in
14:19 For your servant *J* commanded
14:20 of affairs your servant *J* has
14:21 And the king said to *J*,
14:22 Then *J* fell to the ground on his
14:22 And *J* said, "Today your
14:23 So *J* arose and went to Geshur,
14:29 Therefore Absalom sent for *J*,
14:31 Then *J* arose and came to
14:32 And Absalom answered *J*,
14:33 So *J* went to the king and told
17:25 of the army instead of *J*.
18: 2 the people under the hand of *J*,
18: 5 Now the king had commanded *J*,
18:10 certain man saw it and told *J*,
18:11 So *J* said to the man who told
18:12 But the man said to *J*,
18:14 Then *J* said, "I cannot linger
18:16 So *J* blew the trumpet, and the
18:16 For *J* held back the people.
18:20 And *J* said to him, "You shall
18:21 Then *J* said to the Cushite,
18:21 the Cushite bowed himself to *J*
18:22 son of Zadok said again to *J*,
18:22 So *J* said, "Why will you
18:29 When *J* sent the king's servant
19: 1 And *J* was told, "Behold, the
19: 5 Then *J* came into the house to
19:13 me continually in place of *J*.
20: 8 Now *J* was dressed in battle
20: 9 Then *J* said to Amasa, "Are you
20: 9 And *J* took Amasa by the beard
20:10 Then *J* and Abishai his brother
20:11 Whoever favors *J* and whoever is
20:11 for David—follow *J*!"
20:13 all the people went on after *J*
20:15 all the people who were with *J*
20:16 "Hear, Hear! Please say to *J*,
20:17 the woman said, "Are you *J*?
20:20 And *J* answered and said, "Far
20:21 So the woman said to *J*,
20:22 Bichri, and threw it out to *J*.
20:22 So *J* returned to the king at
20:23 And *J* was over all the army of
23:18 Now Abishai the brother of *J*,
23:24 Asahel the brother of *J* was
23:37 Beerothite (armorbearer of *J*
24: 2 So the king said to *J* the
24: 3 And *J* said to the king, "Now
24: 4 word prevailed against *J* and
24: 4 Therefore *J* and the captains of
24: 9 Then *J* gave the sum of the
1 Ki 1: 7 Then he conferred with *J* the son
1:19 and *J* the commander of the
1:41 And when *J* heard the sound of
2: 5 Moreover you know also what *J*
2:22 and for *J* the son of Zeruiah."
2:28 Then news came to *J*,
2:28 for *J* had defected to Adonijah,
2:28 So *J* fled to the tabernacle of
2:29 *J* has fled to the tabernacle of
2:30 the king, saying, "Thus said *J*,
2:31 the innocent blood which *J*
2:33 return upon the head of *J* and
11:15 and *J* the commander of the army
11:16 (because for six months *J*
11:21 and that *J* the commander of the
1 Chr 2:16 of Zeruiah were Abishai, *J*,
4:14 Seraiah begot *J* the father of
11: 6 And *J* the son of Zeruiah went
11: 8 *J* repaired the rest of the
11:20 Abishai the brother of *J* was
11:26 were Asahel the brother of *J*,
11:39 (the armorbearer of *J* the son
18:15 *J* the son of Zeruiah was over
19: 8 he sent *J* and all the army of
19:10 When *J* saw that the battle line
19:14 So *J* and the people who were
19:15 So *J* went to Jerusalem.
20: 1 that *J* led out the armed forces
20: 1 And *J* defeated Rabbah and
21: 2 So David said to *J* and to the
21: 3 And *J* answered, "May the LORD
21: 4 king's word prevailed against *J*.
21: 4 Therefore *J* departed and went
21: 5 Then *J* gave the sum of the
21: 6 king's word was abominable to *J*.
26:28 and *J* the son of Zeruiah had
27: 7 was Asahel the brother of *J*,
27:24 *J* the son of Zeruiah began a
27:34 of the king's army was *J*.
Ezra 2: 6 of the people of Jeshua and *J*,
8: 9 of the sons of *J*,
Neh 7:11 of the sons of Jeshua and *J*,
Ps 60: and *J* returned and killed

JOAB'S (7/7) JOAB

2 Sam 14:30 *J* field is near mine, and he
17:25 sister of Zeruiah, *J* mother.
18: 2 *J* brother, and one third under
18:15 young men who bore *J* armor
20: 7 So *J* men, with the Cherethites,
20:10 the sword that was in *J* hand.
20:11 Meanwhile one of *J* men stood

JOAH (11/10)

2 Ki 18:18 and *J* the son of Asaph, the
18:26 and *J* said to the Rabshakeh,
18:37 and *J* the son of Asaph, the
1 Chr 6:21 *J* his son, Iddo his son, Zerah
26: 4 *J* the third, Sacar the fourth,
2 Chr 29:12 *J* the son of Zimmah and Eden
29:12 of Zimmah and Eden the son of *J*;
34: 8 and *J* the son of Joahaz the
Isa 36: 3 and *J* the son of Asaph, the
36:11 and *J* said to the Rabshakeh,
36:22 and *J* the son of Asaph, the

JOAHAZ (1/1)

2 Chr 34: 8 and Joah the son of *J* the

JOANNA (2/2)

Lk 8: 3 and *J* the wife of Chuza, Herod's
24:10 It was Mary Magdalene, *J*,

JOANNAS (1/1)

Lk 3:27 the son of *J*, the son of

JOASH (49/43) JEHOASH

Judg 6:11 which belonged to *J* the
6:29 Gideon the son of *J* has done
6:30 the men of the city said to *J*,
6:31 But *J* said to all who stood
7:14 sword of Gideon the son of *J*,
8:13 Then Gideon the son of *J*
8:29 Then Jerubbaal the son of *J*
8:32 Now Gideon the son of *J* died at
8:32 and was buried in the tomb of *J*
1 Ki 22:26 governor of the city and to *J*
2 Ki 11: 2 took *J* the son of Ahaziah, and
12:19 Now the rest of the acts of *J*,
12:20 and killed *J* in the house of
13: 1 In the twenty-third year of *J*
13: 9 Then *J* his son reigned in his
13:10 the thirty-seventh year of *J*
13:12 Now the rest of the acts of *J*,
13:13 So *J* rested with his fathers.
13:13 And *J* was buried in Samaria
13:14 Then *J* the king of Israel came
13:25 Three times *J* defeated him and
14: 1 In the second year of *J* the son
14: 1 of Israel, Amaziah the son of *J*,
14: 3 did everything as his father *J*
14:17 Amaziah the son of *J*,
14:23 year of Amaziah the son of *J*,
14:23 of Judah, Jeroboam the son of *J*,
14:27 hand of Jeroboam the son of *J*.
1 Chr 3:11 Ahaziah his son, *J* his son,
4:22 the men of Chozeba, and *J*;
7: 8 sons of Becher were Zemirah, *J*,
12: 3 The chief was Ahiezer, then *J*,
27:28 and *J* was over the store of
2 Chr 18:25 governor of the city and to *J*
22:11 took *J* the son of Ahaziah, and
24: 1 *J* was seven years old when he
24: 2 *J* did what was right in the
24: 4 it happened after this that *J*
24:22 Thus *J* the king did not remember
24:24 executed judgment against *J*.
25:17 asked advice and sent to *J* the
25:18 And *J* king of Israel sent to
25:21 So *J* king of Israel went out;
25:23 Then *J* the king of Israel
25:23 king of Judah, the son of *J*,
25:25 Amaziah the son of *J*,
25:25 years after the death of *J* the
Hos 1: 1 days of Jeroboam the son of *J*,
Am 1: 1 days of Jeroboam the son of *J*,

JOATHAM (KJV) See JOTHAM

JOB (58/53) JASHUB, JOB'S

Gen 46:13 Issachar were Tola, Puvah, *J*,

J

Job 1: 1 land of Uz, whose name was *J*;
1: 5 that *J* would send and sanctify
1: 5 For *J* said, "It may be that my
1: 5 Thus *J* did regularly.
1: 8 you considered My servant *J*,
1: 9 Does *J* fear God for nothing?
1:14 and a messenger came to *J* and
1:20 Then *J* arose, tore his robe,
1:22 In all this *J* did not sin nor
2: 3 you considered My servant *J*,
2: 7 and struck *J* with painful boils
2:10 In all this *J* did not sin
3: 1 After this *J* opened his mouth
3: 2 And *J* spoke, and said:
6: 1 Then *J* answered and said:
9: 1 Then *J* answered and said:
12: 1 Then *J* answered and said:
16: 1 Then *J* answered and said:
19: 1 Then *J* answered and said:
21: 1 Then *J* answered and said:
23: 1 Then *J* answered and said:
26: 1 But *J* answered and said:
27: 1 Moreover *J* continued his
29: 1 *J* further continued his
31:40 The words of *J* are ended.
32: 1 three men ceased answering *J*,
32: 2 of Ram, was aroused against *J*;
32: 3 and yet had condemned *J*.
32: 4 Elihu had waited to speak to *J*.
32:12 not one of you convinced *J*,
33: 1 'But please, *J*, hear my
33:31 'Give ear, *J*, listen to
34: 5 For *J* has said, 'I am righteous,
34: 7 What man is like *J*,
34:35 *J* speaks without knowledge, His
34:36 that *J* were tried to the
35:16 Therefore *J* opens his mouth in
37:14 "Listen to this, O *J*;
38: 1 Then the LORD answered *J* out of
40: 1 Moreover the LORD answered *J*,
40: 3 Then *J* answered the LORD and
40: 6 Then the LORD answered *J* out
42: 1 Then *J* answered the LORD and
42: 7 had spoken these words to *J*,
42: 7 as My servant *J* has.
42: 8 seven rams, go to My servant *J*,
42: 8 and My servant *J* shall pray for
42: 8 as My servant *J* has."
42: 9 for the LORD had accepted *J*.
42:10 Indeed the LORD gave *J* twice
42:12 blessed the latter days of *J*
42:15 beautiful as the daughters of *J*;
42:16 After this *J* lived one hundred
42:17 So *J* died, old and full of days.
Ezek 14:14 three men, Noah, Daniel, and *J*,
14:20 and *J* were in it, as I
Jas 5:11 heard of the perseverance of *J*

JOB'S (2/2) JOB

Job 2:11 Now when *J* three friends heard
42:10 And the LORD restored *J* losses

JOBAB (9/9)

Gen 10:29 Ophir, Havilah, and *J*.
36:33 *J* the son of Zerah of Bozrah
36:34 When *J* died, Husham of the land
Josh 11: 1 that he sent to *J* king of
1 Chr 1:23 Ophir, Havilah, and *J*.
1:44 *J* the son of Zerah of Bozrah
1:45 When *J* died, Husham of the land
8: 9 By Hodesh his wife he begot *J*,
8:18 and *J* were the sons of Elpaal.

JOCHEBED (2/2)

Ex 6:20 Now Amram took for himself *J*,
Num 26:59 The name of Amram's wife was *J*

JOED (1/1)

Neh 11: 7 son of Meshullam, the son of *J*,

JOEL (21/21)

1 Sam 8: 2 The name of his firstborn was *J*,
1 Chr 4:35 *J*, and Jehu the son of
5: 4 The sons of *J* were Shemaiah his
5: 8 the son of Shema, the son of *J*,
5:12 *J* was the chief, Shapham the
6:28 The sons of Samuel were *J* the
6:33 Heman the singer, the son of *J*,
6:36 son of Elkanah, the son of *J*,
7: 3 were Michael, Obadiah, *J*,
11:38 *J* the brother of Nathan, Mibhar
15: 7 *J* the chief, and one hundred
15:11 Levites: for Uriel, Asaiah, *J*,
15:17 appointed Heman the son of *J*;
23: 8 first Jehiel, then Zetham and *J*—
26:22 Zetham and *J* his brother, were
27:20 *J* the son of Pedaiah;
2 Chr 29:12 Mahath the son of Amasai and *J*
Ezra 10:43 Zabad, Zebina, Jaddai, *J*,
Neh 11: 9 *J* the son of Zichri was their
Joel 1: 1 of the LORD that came to *J*
Acts 2:16 was spoken by the prophet *J*:

JOELAH (1/1)

1 Chr 12: 7 and *J* and Zebadiah the sons of

JOEZER (1/1)

1 Chr 12: 6 Elkanah, Jisshiah, Azarel, *J*,

JOGBEHAH (2/2)

Num 32:35 and Shophan and Jazer and *J*,
Judg 8:11 on the east of Nobah and *J*;

JOGLI (1/1)

Num 34:22 of Dan, Bukki the son of *J*;

JOHA (2/2)

1 Chr 8:16 and *J* were the sons of Beriah.
11:45 and *J* his brother, the Tizite,

JOHANAN (25/25)

2 Ki 25:23 *J* the son of Careah, Seraiah
1 Chr 3:15 The sons of Josiah were *J* the
3:24 Eliashib, Pelaiah, Akkub, *J*,
6: 9 Azariah, and Azariah begot *J*;
6:10 *J* begot Azariah (it was he who
12: 4 Jeremiah, Jahaziel, *J*,
12:12 *J* the eighth, Elzabad the ninth,
2 Chr 28:12 Ephraim, Azariah the son of *J*,
Ezra 8:12 *J* the son of Hakkatan, and with
Neh 12:22 the days of Eliashib, Joiada, *J*,
12:23 houses until the days of *J*
Jer 40: 8 *J* and Jonathan the sons of
40:13 Moreover *J* the son of Kareah
40:15 Then *J* the son of Kareah spoke
40:16 the son of Ahikam said to *J*
41:11 But when *J* the son of Kareah
41:13 who were with Ishmael saw *J*
41:14 and went to *J* the son of
41:15 son of Nethaniah escaped from *J*
41:16 Then *J* the son of Kareah, and
42: 1 *J* the son of Kareah, Jezaniah
42: 8 Then he called *J* the son of
43: 2 *J* the son of Kareah, and all
43: 4 So *J* the son of Kareah, all the
43: 5 But *J* the son of Kareah and all

JOHN (130/127) BAPTIST, JOHN'S, MARK

Mt 3: 1 In those days *J* the Baptist came
3: 4 And *J* himself was clothed in
3:13 Jesus came from Galilee to *J*
3:14 And *J* tried to prevent Him,
4:12 Now when Jesus heard that *J* had
4:21 and *J* his brother, in the boat
9:14 Then the disciples of *J* came to
10: 2 Zebedee, and *J* his brother;
11: 2 And when *J* had heard in prison
11: 4 Go and tell *J* the things which
11: 7 to the multitudes concerning *J*:
11:11 not risen one greater than *J*
11:12 And from the days of *J* the
11:13 and the law prophesied until *J*.
11:18 For *J* came neither eating nor
14: 2 This is *J* the Baptist; he is
14: 3 For Herod had laid hold of *J* and
14: 4 Because *J* had said to him, "It
14: 8 Give me *J* the Baptist's head
14:10 So he sent and had *J* beheaded in
16:14 Some say *J* the Baptist, some
17: 1 and *J* his brother, led them up
17:13 that He spoke to them of *J* the
21:25 "The baptism of *J*—
21:26 for all count *J* as a prophet."
21:32 For *J* came to you in the way of
Mk 1: 4 *J* came baptizing in the
1: 6 Now *J* was clothed with camel's
1: 9 and was baptized by *J* in the
1:14 Now after *J* was put in prison,
1:19 and *J* his brother, who also
1:29 and Andrew, with James and *J*.
2:18 The disciples of *J* and of the
2:18 Why do the disciples of *J* and of
3:17 the son of Zebedee and *J* the
5:37 and *J* the brother of James.
6:14 *J* the Baptist is risen from the
6:16 heard, he said, "This is *J*,
6:17 had sent and laid hold of *J*,
6:18 For *J* had said to Herod, "It is
6:20 for Herod feared *J*, knowing
6:24 The head of *J* the Baptist!"
6:25 give me at once the head of *J*
8:28 *J* the Baptist; but some say,
9: 2 Jesus took Peter, James, and *J*,
9:38 Now *J* answered Him, saying,
10:35 Then James and *J*, the sons
10:41 displeased with James and *J*.
11:30 'The baptism of *J*—was it
11:32 for all counted *J* to have been
13: 3 the temple, Peter, James, *J*,
14:33 and *J* with Him, and He began to
Lk 1:13 and you shall call his name *J*.
1:60 "No; he shall be called *J*.
1:63 wrote, saying, "His name is *J*.
3: 2 the word of God came to *J* the
3:15 in their hearts about *J*
3:16 *J* answered, saying to all, "I
3:20 that he shut *J* up in prison.
5:10 and so also were James and *J*,
5:33 Why do the disciples of *J* fast
6:14 Andrew his brother; James and *J*;
7:18 Then the disciples of *J*
7:19 And *J*, calling two of his
7:20 *J* the Baptist has sent us to
7:22 Go and tell *J* the things you
7:24 When the messengers of *J* had
7:24 to the multitudes concerning *J*:
7:28 is not a greater prophet than *J*
7:29 baptized with the baptism of *J*.
7:33 For *J* the Baptist came neither
8:51 in except Peter, James, and *J*,
9: 7 it was said by some that *J* had
9: 9 *J* I have beheaded, but who is
9:19 *J* the Baptist, but some say
9:28 sayings, that He took Peter, *J*,
9:49 Now *J* answered and said,
9:54 when His disciples James and *J*
11: 1 as *J* also taught his
16:16 and the prophets were until *J*.
20: 4 'The baptism of *J*—was it
20: 6 for they are persuaded that *J*
22: 8 And He sent Peter and *J*,
Jn 1: 6 from God, whose name was *J*.
1:15 *J* bore witness of Him and cried
1:19 Now this is the testimony of *J*,
1:26 *J* answered them, saying, "I
1:28 where *J* was baptizing.
1:29 The next day *J* saw Jesus coming
1:32 And *J* bore witness, saying, "I
1:35 *J* stood with two of his
1:40 One of the two who heard *J*
3:23 Now *J* also was baptizing in
3:24 For *J* had not yet been thrown
3:26 And they came to *J* and said to
3:27 *J* answered and said, "A man can
4: 1 baptized more disciples than *J*
5:33 "You have sent to *J*,
10:40 the Jordan to the place where *J*
10:41 *J* performed no sign, but all the
10:41 but all the things that *J* spoke
Acts 1: 5 for *J* truly baptized with water,
1:13 were staying: Peter, James, *J*,
1:22 from the baptism of *J* to that
3: 1 Now Peter and *J* went up together
3: 3 seeing Peter and *J* about to go
3: 4 fixing his eyes on him, with *J*,
3:11 healed held on to Peter and *J*,
4: 6 the high priest, Caiaphas, *J*,
4:13 saw the boldness of Peter and *J*,
4:19 But Peter and *J* answered and
8:14 they sent Peter and *J* to them,
10:37 after the baptism which *J*
11:16 *J* indeed baptized with water,
12: 2 killed James the brother of *J*
12:12 the mother of *J* whose surname
12:25 and they also took with them *J*
13: 5 They also had *J* as their
13:13 and *J*, departing from them,
13:24 after *J* had first preached,
13:25 And as *J* was finishing his
15:37 determined to take with them *J*
18:25 he knew only the baptism of *J*.
19: 4 *J* indeed baptized with a baptism
Gal 2: 9 and when James, Cephas, and *J*,
Rev 1: 1 by His angel to His servant *J*,
1: 4 *J*, to the seven churches
1: 9 I, *J*, both your brother
21: 2 Then I, *J*, saw the holy city,
22: 8 Now I, *J*, saw and heard

JOHN'S (3/3) JOHN

Jn 3:25 between some of *J* disciples
5:36 I have a greater witness than *J*;
Acts 19: 3 they said, "Into *J* baptism."

JOIADA (4/4)

Neh 12:10 Eliashib, Eliashib begot *J*,
12:11 *J* begot Jonathan, and Jonathan
12:22 in the days of Eliashib, *J*,
13:28 And one of the sons of *J*,

JOIAKIM (4/3)

Neh 12:10 Jeshua begot *J*, Joiakim
12:10 Joiakim, *J* begot Eliashib,
12:12 Now in the days of *J*,
12:26 These lived in the days of *J*

JOIARIB (5/5)

Ezra 8:16 also for *J* and Elnathan, men of
Neh 11: 5 the son of Adaiah, the son of *J*,
11:10 priests: Jedaiah the son of *J*,
12: 6 Shemaiah, *J*, Jedaiah,
12:19 of *J*, Mattenai; of Jedaiah,

JOIN (15/15) JOINED

Ex 1:10 that they also *j* our enemies
Ezra 9:14 and *j* in marriage with the
Esth 9:27 and all who would *j* them,
Prov 11:21 Though they *j* forces, the
16: 5 Though they *j* forces, none
Isa 5: 8 Woe to those who *j* house to
56: 6 sons of the foreigner Who *j*
Jer 50: 5 Come and let us *j* ourselves to
Ezek 37:17 Then *j* them one to another for
37:19 and I will *j* them with it, with
Dan 11: 6 end of some years they shall *j*
11:34 but many shall *j* with them by
Acts 5:13 Yet none of the rest dared *j*
9:26 he tried to *j* the disciples;
Phil 3:17 *j* in following my example, and

JOINED (43/42) JOIN

Gen 2:24 his father and mother and be *j*
14: 3 All these *j* together in the
14: 8 went out and *j* together
Ex 28: 7 have two shoulder straps *j* at
28: 7 and so it shall be *j* together.
Num 18: 2 that they may be *j* with you and
18: 4 They shall be *j* with you and
25: 3 So Israel was *j* to Baal of Peor,
25: 5 of you kill his men who were *j*
1 Sam 4: 2 And when they *j* battle, Israel
14:21 they also *j* the Israelites who
1 Ki 7:32 axles of the wheels were *j*
20:29 seventh day the battle was *j*;
1 Chr 12: 8 Some Gadites *j* David at the
Neh 4: 6 and the entire wall was *j*
10:29 these *j* with their brethren,
Job 41:17 They are *j* one to another,
41:23 The folds of his flesh are *j*
Ps 83: 8 Assyria also has *j* with them;
106:28 They *j* themselves also to Baal
Eccl 9: 4 But for him who is *j* to all the
Isa 14: 1 The strangers will be *j* with
14:20 You will not be *j* with them in
56: 3 son of the foreigner Who has *j*
Hos 4:17 Ephraim is *j* to idols, Let him
Zech 2:11 Many nations shall be *j* to the
Mt 19: 5 and mother and be *j* to
19: 6 Therefore what God has *j*
Mk 10: 7 and mother and be *j* to
10: 9 Therefore what God has *j*
Lk 9:18 that His disciples *j* Him, and
15:15 Then he went and *j* himself to a
Jn 11:19 And many of the Jews had *j* the
Acts 5:36 about four hundred, *j* him.
17: 4 women, *j* Paul and Silas.
17:34 some men *j* him and believed,
20: 6 and in five days *j* them at
1 Cor 1:10 but that you be perfectly *j*
6:16 you not know that he who is *j*
6:17 But he who is *j* to the Lord is
Eph 2:21 being *j* together, grows into a
4:16 *j* and knit together by what
5:31 and be *j* to his wife,

JOINT (5/5) JOINTS

Gen 32:25 of Jacob's hip was out of *j* as
Ps 22:14 And all My bones are out of *j*;
Prov 25:19 a bad tooth and a foot out of *j*.
Rom 8:17 heirs of God and *j* heirs with
Eph 4:16 knit together by what every *j*

JOINTED (1/1)

Lev 11:21 those which have *j* legs above

JOINTS (6/6) JOINT

1 Ki 22:34 king of Israel between the *j*
1 Chr 22: 3 of the gates and for the *j*,
2 Chr 18:33 king of Israel between the *j*
Dan 5: 6 so that the *j* of his hips were
Col 2:19 and knit together by *j* and
Heb 4:12 and of *j* and marrow, and is a

JOKDEAM (1/1)

Josh 15:56 Jezreel, *J*, Zanoah,

JOKIM (1/1)

1 Chr 4:22 also *J*, the men of Chozeba,

JOKING (2/2)

Gen 19:14 sons-in-law he seemed to be *j*.
Prov 26:19 And says, "I was only *j*!"

JOKMEAM (1/1)

1 Chr 6:68 *J* with its common-lands,

JOKNEAM (4/4)

Josh 12:22 the king of *J* in Carmel, one;
19:11 the brook that is east of *J*.
21:34 *J* with its common-land, Kartah
1 Ki 4:12 as far as the other side of *J*;

JOKSHAN (4/3)

Gen 25: 2 And she bore him Zimran, *J*,
25: 3 *J* begot Sheba and Dedan. And the
1 Chr 1:32 concubine, were Zimran, *J*,
1:32 The sons of *J* were Sheba and

JOKTAN (6/6)

Gen 10:25 and his brother's name was *J*.
10:26 *J* begot Almodad, Sheleph,
10:29 All these were the sons of *J*.
1 Chr 1:19 and his brother's name was *J*.
1:20 *J* begot Almodad, Sheleph,
1:23 All these were the sons of *J*.

JOKTHEEL (2/2)

Josh 15:38 Dilean, Mizpah, *J*,
2 Ki 14: 7 and called its name *J* to this

JONA (KJV) See JONAH

JONADAB (12/11) JEHONADAB

2 Sam 13: 3 had a friend whose name was *J*
13: 3 Now *J* was a very crafty man.
13: 5 So *J* said to him, "Lie down on
13:32 Then *J* the son of Shimeah,
13:35 And *J* said to the king, "Look,
Jer 35: 6 for *J* the son of Rechab, our
35: 8 we have obeyed the voice of *J*
35:10 done according to all that *J*
35:14 The words of *J* the son of
35:16 Surely the sons of *J* the son of
35:18 obeyed the commandment of *J*
35:19 *J* the son of Rechab shall not

JONAH (31/27) JONAH'S

2 Ki 14:25 spoken through His servant *J*
Jon 1: 1 the word of the LORD came to *J*
1: 3 But *J* arose to flee to Tarshish
1: 5 But *J* had gone down into the
1: 7 lots, and the lot fell on *J*.
1:15 So they picked up *J* and threw
1:17 a great fish to swallow *J*.
1:17 And *J* was in the belly of the
2: 1 Then *J* prayed to the LORD his
2:10 and it vomited *J* onto dry
3: 1 the word of the LORD came to *J*
3: 3 So *J* arose and went to Nineveh,
3: 4 And *J* began to enter the city on
4: 1 But it displeased *J* exceedingly,
4: 5 So *J* went out of the city and
4: 6 and made it come up over *J*,
4: 6 So *J* was very grateful for the
4: 9 Then God said to *J*,
Mt 12:39 the sign of the prophet *J*.
12:40 For as *J* was three days and
12:41 repented at the preaching of *J*;
12:41 and indeed a greater than *J* is
16: 4 the sign of the prophet *J*.
Lk 11:29 to it except the sign of *J* the
11:30 For as *J* became a sign to the
11:32 repented at the preaching of *J*;
11:32 and indeed a greater than *J* is
Jn 1:42 "You are Simon the son of *J*.
21:15 Simon Peter, "Simon, son of *J*,
21:16 second time, "Simon, son of *J*,
21:17 third time, "Simon, son of *J*,

JONAH'S (1/1) JONAH

Jon 4: 8 and the sun beat on *J* head, so

JONAN (1/1)

Lk 3:30 son of Joseph, the son of *J*,

JONAS (KJV) See JONAH

JONATHAN (118/103) JONATHAN'S

Judg 18:30 and *J* the son of Gershom, the
1 Sam 13: 2 and a thousand were with *J* in
13: 3 And *J* attacked the garrison of
13:16 *J* his son, and the people
13:22 who were with Saul and *J*.
13:22 were found with Saul and *J* his
14: 1 Now it happened one day that *J*
14: 3 the people did not know that *J*
14: 4 by which *J* sought to go over to
14: 6 Then *J* said to the young man
14: 8 Then *J* said, "Very well, let us
14:12 men of the garrison called to *J*
14:12 *J* said to his armorbearer,
14:13 And *J* climbed up on his hands
14:13 and they fell before *J*.
14:14 That first slaughter which *J* and
14:17 *J* and his armorbearer were not
14:21 who were with Saul and *J*.
14:27 But *J* had not heard his father
14:29 But *J* said, "My father has
14:39 though it be in *J* my son, he
14:40 and my son *J* and I will be on
14:41 So Saul and *J* were taken, but
14:42 Cast lots between my son *J* and
14:42 and me." So *J* was taken.
14:43 Then Saul said to *J*,
14:43 And *J* told him, and said, "I
14:44 for you shall surely die, *J*.
14:45 Shall *J* die, who has
14:45 So the people rescued *J*,
14:49 The sons of Saul were *J*,
18: 1 the soul of *J* was knit to the
18: 1 and *J* loved him as his own
18: 3 Then *J* and David made a
18: 4 And *J* took off the robe that
19: 1 Now Saul spoke to *J* his son and
19: 1 they should kill David; but *J*,
19: 2 So *J* told David, saying, "My
19: 4 Thus *J* spoke well of David to
19: 6 So Saul heeded the voice of *J*,
19: 7 Then *J* called David, and
19: 7 and *J* told him all these
19: 7 So *J* brought David to Saul, and
20: 1 Ramah, and went and said to *J*,
20: 2 So *J* said to him, "By no means!
20: 3 Do not let *J* know this, lest he
20: 4 So *J* said to David, "Whatever
20: 5 And David said to *J*,
20: 9 But *J* said, "Far be it from
20:10 Then David said to *J*,
20:11 And *J* said to David, "Come, and
20:12 Then *J* said to David: "The
20:13 LORD do so and much more to *J*.
20:16 So *J* made a covenant with the
20:17 Now *J* again caused David to
20:18 Then *J* said to David, "Tomorrow
20:25 And *J* arose, and Abner sat by
20:27 And Saul said to *J* his son,
20:28 So *J* answered Saul, "David
20:30 anger was aroused against *J*,
20:32 And *J* answered Saul his father,
20:33 by which *J* knew that it was
20:34 So *J* arose from the table in
20:35 that *J* went out into the field
20:37 where the arrow was which *J*
20:37 *J* cried out after the lad and
20:38 And *J* cried out after the lad,
20:39 Only *J* and David knew of the
20:40 Then *J* gave his weapons to his
20:42 Then *J* said to David, "Go in
20:42 and *J* went into the city.
23:16 Then *J*, Saul's son, arose
23:18 and *J* went to his own house.
31: 2 And the Philistines killed *J*,
2 Sam 1: 4 and Saul and *J* his son are dead
1: 5 do you know that Saul and *J*
1:12 evening for Saul and for *J* his
1:17 over Saul and over *J* his son,
1:22 The bow of *J* did not turn
1:23 Saul and *J* were beloved and
1:25 in the midst of the battle! *J*
1:26 for you, my brother *J*;
4: 4 *J*, Saul's son, had a son
4: 4 when the news about Saul and *J*
9: 3 There is still a son of *J* who
9: 6 when Mephibosheth the son of *J*,
9: 7 surely show you kindness for *J*
15:27 and *J* the son of Abiathar.
15:36 Ahimaaz, Zadok's son, and *J*,
17:17 Now *J* and Ahimaaz stayed at En
17:20 "Where are Ahimaaz and *J*?
21: 7 Mephibosheth the son of *J*,
21: 7 between David and *J* the son of
21:12 and the bones of *J* his son,
21:13 of Saul and the bones of *J* his
21:14 buried the bones of Saul and *J*
21:21 *J* the son of Shimea, David's
23:32 (of the sons of Jashen), *J*,
1 Ki 1:42 still speaking, there came *J*,
1:43 Then *J* answered and said to
1 Chr 2:32 of Shammai, were Jether and *J*;
2:33 The sons of *J* were Peleth and
8:33 begot Saul, and Saul begot *J*,
8:34 The son of *J* was Merib-Baal,
9:39 begot Saul, and Saul begot *J*,
9:40 The son of *J* was Merib-Baal,
10: 2 And the Philistines killed *J*,
11:34 *J* the son of Shageh the
20: 7 *J* the son of Shimea, David's
Ezra 8: 6 sons of Adin, Ebed the son of *J*,
10:15 Only *J* the son of Asahel and
Neh 12:11 Joiada begot *J*,
12:11 and *J* begot Jaddua.
12:14 of Melichu, *J*; of Shebaniah,
12:35 trumpets—Zechariah the son of *J*,
Jer 37:15 him in prison in the house of *J*
37:20 me return to the house of *J*
40: 8 Johanan and *J* the sons of

JONATHAN'S (3/3) JONATHAN

1 Sam 20:38 do not delay!" So *J* lad
2 Sam 9: 1 him kindness for *J* sake?"
Jer 38:26 make me return to *J* house

JOPPA (14/14)

Josh 19:46 Rakkon, with the region near *J*.
2 Chr 2:16 it to you in rafts by sea to *J*,
Ezra 3: 7 from Lebanon to the sea, to *J*,
Jon 1: 3 of the LORD. He went down to *J*,
Acts 9:36 At *J* there was a certain
9:38 And since Lydda was near *J*,
9:42 became known throughout all *J*,
9:43 that he stayed many days in *J*
10: 5 "Now send men to *J*,
10: 8 to them, he sent them to *J*.
10:23 and some brethren from *J*
10:32 Send therefore to *J* and call
11: 5 I was in the city of *J* praying;
11:13 who said to him, 'Send men to *J*,

JORAH (1/1)

Ezra 2:18 the people of *J*, one hundred

JORAI (1/1)

1 Chr 5:13 Michael, Meshullam, Sheba, *J*,

JORAM (29/22) JEHORAM

2 Sam 8:10 then Toi sent *J* his son to King
8:10 and *J* brought with him
2 Ki 8:16 Now in the fifth year of *J* the
8:21 So *J* went to Zair, and all his
8:23 Now the rest of the acts of *J*,
8:24 So *J* rested with his fathers,
8:25 In the twelfth year of *J* the
8:28 Now he went with *J* the son of
8:28 and the Syrians wounded *J*.
8:29 Then King *J* went back to Jezreel
8:29 went down to see *J* the son of
9:14 of Nimshi, conspired against *J*.

J

9:14 (Now *J* had been defending
9:15 But King *J* had returned to
9:16 for *J* was laid up there; and
9:16 of Judah had come down to see *J*.
9:17 And *J* said, "Get a horseman
9:21 Then *J* said, "Make ready."
9:21 Then *J* king of Israel and
9:22 when *J* saw Jehu, that he said,
9:23 Then *J* turned around and fled,
9:29 In the eleventh year of *J* the
11: 2 the daughter of King *J*,
1 Chr 3:11 *J* his son, Ahaziah his son,
26:25 *J* his son, Zichri his son, and
2 Chr 22: 5 and the Syrians wounded *J*.
22: 7 His going to *J* was God's
Mt 1: 8 Jehoshaphat begot *J*,
1: 8 and *J* begot Uzziah.

JORDAN (201/182)

Gen 13:10 eyes and saw all the plain of *J*,
13:11 for himself all the plain of *J*,
32:10 for I crossed over this *J* with
50:10 of Atad, which is beyond the *J*,
50:11 Mizraim, which is beyond the *J*.
Num 13:29 and along the banks of the *J*.
22: 1 of Moab on the side of the *J*
26: 3 in the plains of Moab by the *J*,
26:63 in the plains of Moab by the *J*,
31:12 in the plains of Moab by the *J*,
32: 5 Do not take us over the *J*.
32:19 on the other side of the *J* and
32:19 on this eastern side of the *J*.
32:21 your armed men cross over the *J*
32:29 of Reuben cross over the *J*
32:32 with us on this side of the *J*.
33:48 in the plains of Moab by the *J*,
33:49 They camped by the *J*,
33:50 in the plains of Moab by the *J*,
33:51 When you have crossed the *J* into
34:12 shall go down along the *J*,
34:15 on this side of the *J*,
35: 1 in the plains of Moab by the *J*
35:10 When you cross the *J* into the
35:14 cities on this side of the *J*,
36:13 in the plains of Moab by the *J*,
Deut 1: 1 Israel on this side of the *J*
1: 5 On this side of the *J* in the
2:29 until I cross the *J* to the land
3: 8 who were on this side of the *J*,
3:17 with the *J* as the border, from
3:20 God is giving them beyond the *J*.
3:25 see the good land beyond the *J*,
3:27 you shall not cross over this *J*.
4:21 I would not cross over the *J*,
4:22 I must not cross over the *J*;
4:26 which you cross over the *J* to
4:41 cities on this side of the *J*,
4:46 on this side of the *J*,
4:47 who were on this side of the *J*,
4:49 on the east side of the *J* as
9: 1 You are to cross over the *J*
11:30 not on the other side of the *J*,
11:31 For you will cross over the *J*
12:10 when you cross over the *J*
27: 2 day when you cross over the *J*
27: 4 you have crossed over the *J*,
27:12 you have crossed over the *J*:
30:18 which you cross over the *J* to
31: 2 shall not cross over this *J*.
31:13 the land which you cross the *J*
32:47 which you cross over the *J* to
Josh 1: 2 arise, go over this *J*,
1:11 days you will cross over this *J*,
1:14 gave you on this side of the *J*.
1:15 gave you on this side of the *J*
2: 7 them by the road to the *J*,
2:10 on the other side of the *J*,
3: 1 Acacia Grove and came to the *J*,
3: 8 the edge of the water of the *J*,
3: 8 you shall stand in the *J*.
3:11 over before you into the *J*.
3:13 rest in the waters of the *J*,
3:13 that the waters of the *J* shall
3:14 their camp to cross over the *J*,
3:15 who bore the ark came to the *J*,
3:15 edge of the water (for the *J*
3:17 ground in the midst of the *J*;
3:17 crossed completely over the *J*.
4: 1 completely crossed over the *J*,
4: 3 here, out of the midst of the *J*,
4: 5 God into the midst of the *J*,
4: 7 them that the waters of the *J*
4: 7 when it crossed over the *J*,
4: 7 the waters of the *J* were cut
4: 8 stones from the midst of the *J*,
4: 9 stones in the midst of the *J*,
4:10 ark stood in the midst of the *J*
4:16 Testimony to come up from the *J*.
4:17 saying, "Come up from the *J*.
4:18 come from the midst of the *J*,
4:18 that the waters of the *J*
4:19 the people came up from the *J*
4:20 which they took out of the *J*,
4:22 Israel crossed over this *J* on
4:23 dried up the waters of the *J*
5: 1 were on the west side of the *J*,
5: 1 dried up the waters of the *J*
7: 7 brought this people over the *J*
7: 7 on the other side of the *J*!
9: 1 who were on this side of the *J*,
9:10 Amorites who were beyond the *J*—
11:16 and the *J* plain—the mountains
12: 1 on the other side of the *J*
12: 1 and all the eastern *J* plain:
12: 3 and the eastern *J* plain from the
12: 7 conquered on this side of the *J*,
12: 8 in the *J* plain, in the slopes,
13: 8 beyond the *J* eastward, as Moses
13:23 of Reuben was the bank of the *J*.
13:27 with the *J* as its border, as
13:27 on the other side of the *J*
13:32 Moab on the other side of the *J*,
14: 3 on the other side of the *J*;
15: 5 as far as the mouth of the *J*.
15: 5 the sea at the mouth of the *J*.
16: 1 children of Joseph from the *J*,
16: 7 Jericho, and came out at the *J*.
17: 5 on the other side of the *J*,
18: 7 their inheritance beyond the *J*
18:12 the north side began at the *J*,
18:19 Sea, at the south end of the *J*.
18:20 The *J* was its border on the east
19:22 their border ended at the *J*:
19:33 as Lakkum; it ended at the *J*.
19:34 and ended at Judah by the *J*
20: 8 And on the other side of the *J*,
22: 4 you on the other side of the *J*.
22: 7 brethren on this side of the *J*,
22:10 came to the region of the *J*
22:10 built an altar there by the *J*—
22:11 Canaan, in the region of the *J*—
22:25 For the LORD has made the *J* a
23: 4 for your tribes, from the *J*,
24: 8 on the other side of the *J*,
24:11 Then you went over the *J* and
Judg 3:28 seized the fords of the *J*
5:17 Gilead stayed beyond the *J*,
7:24 as far as Beth Barah and the *J*.
7:24 as far as Beth Barah and the *J*.
7:25 on the other side of the *J*.
8: 4 When Gideon came to the *J*,
10: 8 on the other side of the *J* in
10: 9 of Ammon crossed over the *J* to
11:13 far as the Jabbok, and to the *J*.
11:22 from the wilderness to the *J*.
12: 5 seized the fords of the *J*
12: 6 kill him at the fords of the *J*.
1 Sam 13: 7 the Hebrews crossed over the *J*
31: 7 on the other side of the *J*,
2 Sam 2:29 the plain, crossed over the *J*,
10:17 all Israel, crossed over the *J*,
17:22 arose and crossed over the *J*.
17:22 who had not gone over the *J*.
17:24 And Absalom crossed over the *J*,
19:15 king returned and came to the *J*.
19:15 to escort the king across the *J*.
19:17 and they went over the *J* before
19:18 king when he had crossed the *J*.
19:31 Rogelim and went across the *J*
19:31 to escort him across the *J*.
19:36 go a little way across the *J*
19:39 all the people went over the *J*.
19:41 men with him across the *J*?
20: 2 from the *J* as far as Jerusalem,
24: 5 And they crossed over the *J* and
1 Ki 2: 8 came down to meet me at the *J*,
7:46 In the plain of *J* the king had
17: 3 Cherith, which flows into the *J*.
17: 5 Cherith, which flows into the *J*.
2 Ki 2: 6 LORD has sent me on to the *J*.
2: 7 the two of them stood by the *J*.
2:13 and stood by the bank of the *J*.
5:10 Go and wash in the *J* seven
5:14 and dipped seven times in the *J*,
6: 2 "Please, let us go to the *J*,
6: 4 And when they came to the *J*,
7:15 they went after them to the *J*;
10:33 from the *J* eastward: all the
1 Chr 6:78 And on the other side of the *J*,
6:78 on the east side of the *J*,
12:15 the ones who crossed the *J* in
12:37 from the other side of the *J*,
19:17 crossed over the *J* and came
26:30 on the west side of the *J* for
2 Chr 4:17 In the plain of *J* the king had
Job 40:23 though the *J* gushes into his
Ps 42: 6 You from the land of the *J*,
114: 3 it and fled; *J* turned back.
114: 5 O *J*, that you turned
Isa 9: 1 way of the sea, beyond the *J*,
Jer 12: 5 do in the floodplain of the *J*?
49:19 from the floodplain of the *J*
50:44 from the floodplain of the *J*
Ezek 47:18 the land of Israel, along the *J*,
Zech 11: 3 lions! For the pride of the *J*
Mt 3: 5 and all the region around the *J*
3: 6 were baptized by him in the *J*,
3:13 from Galilee to John at the *J*
4:15 of the sea, beyond the *J*,
4:25 Judea, and beyond the *J*.
19: 1 region of Judea beyond the *J*.
Mk 1: 5 all baptized by him in the *J*
1: 9 was baptized by John in the *J*.
3: 8 and Idumea and beyond the *J*;
10: 1 by the other side of the *J*.
Lk 3: 3 all the region around the *J*,
4: 1 returned from the *J* and was led
Jn 1:28 done in Bethabara beyond the *J*,
3:26 who was with you beyond the *J*,
10:40 He went away again beyond the *J*

JORIM (1/1)

Lk 3:29 son of Eliezer, the son of *J*,

JORKOAM (1/1)

1 Chr 2:44 begot Raham the father of *J*,

JOSABAD (KJV) See JOZABAD

JOSAPHAT (KJV) See JEHOSHAPHAT

JOSE (1/1)

Lk 3:29 the son of *J*, the son of

JOSEDECH (KJV) See JEHOZADAK

JOSEPH (227/214) BARSABAS, JOSEPH'S

Gen 30:24 So she called his name *J*,
30:25 pass, when Rachel had borne *J*,
33: 2 and Rachel and *J* last.
33: 7 Afterward *J* and Rachel came
35:24 the sons of Rachel were *J* and
37: 2 is the history of Jacob. *J*,
37: 2 and *J* brought a bad report of
37: 3 Now Israel loved *J* more than all
37: 5 Now *J* had a dream, and he told
37:13 And Israel said to *J*,
37:17 " So *J* went after his
37:23 when *J* had come to his
37:23 that they stripped *J* of his
37:28 so the brothers pulled *J* up
37:28 And they took *J* to Egypt.
37:29 and indeed *J* was not in the
37:33 Without doubt *J* is torn to
39: 1 Now *J* had been taken down to
39: 2 The LORD was with *J*,
39: 4 So *J* found favor in his sight,
39: 6 Now *J* was handsome in form and
39: 7 wife cast longing eyes on *J*,
39:10 as she spoke to *J* day by day,
39:11 when *J* went into the house to
39:21 But the LORD was with *J* and
40: 3 the place where *J* was
40: 4 captain of the guard charged *J*
40: 6 And *J* came in to them in the
40: 8 So *J* said to them, "Do not
40: 9 butler told his dream to *J*,
40:12 And *J* said to him, "This is
40:16 was good, he said to *J*,
40:18 So *J* answered and said, "This
40:22 as *J* had interpreted to them.
40:23 chief butler did not remember *J*,
41:14 Then Pharaoh sent and called *J*,
41:15 And Pharaoh said to *J*,
41:16 So *J* answered Pharaoh, saying,
41:17 Then Pharaoh said to *J*:
41:25 Then *J* said to Pharaoh, "The
41:39 Then Pharaoh said to *J*,
41:41 And Pharaoh said to *J*,
41:44 Pharaoh also said to *J*,
41:45 So *J* went out over all the
41:46 *J* was thirty years old when he
41:46 And *J* went out from the
41:49 *J* gathered very much grain, as
41:50 And to *J* were born two sons
41:51 *J* called the name of the
41:54 as *J* had said. The famine was
41:55 to all the Egyptians, "Go to *J*;
41:56 and *J* opened all the
41:57 So all countries came to *J* in
42: 6 Now *J* was governor over the
42: 7 *J* saw his brothers and
42: 8 So *J* recognized his brothers,
42: 9 Then *J* remembered the dreams
42:14 But *J* said to them, "It is as
42:18 Then *J* said to them the third
42:23 But they did not know that *J*
42:25 Then *J* gave a command to fill
42:36 *J* is no more, Simeon is no
43:15 and they stood before *J*.
43:16 When *J* saw Benjamin with them,
43:17 Then the man did as *J* ordered,
43:26 And when *J* came home, they
43:30 so *J* made haste and sought
44: 2 according to the word that *J*
44: 4 *J* said to his steward, "Get
44:15 And *J* said to them, "What deed
45: 1 Then *J* could not restrain
45: 1 no one stood with him while *J*
45: 3 Then *J* said to his brothers, "I
45: 3 said to his brothers, "I am *J*;
45: 4 And *J* said to his brothers,
45: 4 I am *J* your brother, whom you
45: 9 to him, 'Thus says your son *J*:
45:17 And Pharaoh said to *J*,
45:21 and *J* gave them carts,
45:26 *J* is still alive, and he is
45:27 told him all the words which *J*
45:27 when he saw the carts which *J*
45:28 *J* my son is still alive.
46: 4 and *J* will put his hand on your
46:19 were *J* and Benjamin.
46:20 And to *J* in the land of Egypt
46:27 And the sons of *J* who were born
46:28 he sent Judah before him to *J*,
46:29 So *J* made ready his chariot and
46:30 And Israel said to *J*,
46:31 Then *J* said to his brothers and

47: 1 Then *J* went and told Pharaoh,
47: 5 Then Pharaoh spoke to *J*,
47: 7 Then *J* brought in his father
47:11 And *J* situated his father and
47:12 Then *J* provided his father, his
47:14 And *J* gathered up all the money
47:14 and *J* brought the money into
47:15 all the Egyptians came to *J* and
47:16 Then *J* said, "Give your
47:17 brought their livestock to *J*,
47:17 and *J* gave them bread in
47:20 Then *J* bought all the land of
47:23 Then *J* said to the people,
47:26 And *J* made it a law over the
47:29 he called his son *J* and said to
48: 1 pass after these things that *J*
48: 2 your son *J* is coming to you";
48: 3 Then Jacob said to *J*:
48: 9 And *J* said to his father, "They
48:10 Then *J* brought them near him,
48:11 And Israel said to *J*,
48:12 So *J* brought them from beside
48:13 And *J* took them both, Ephraim
48:15 And he blessed *J*, and said:
48:17 Now when *J* saw that his father
48:18 And *J* said to his father, "Not
48:21 Then Israel said to *J*,
49:22 *J* is a fruitful bough, A
49:26 They shall be on the head of *J*,
50: 1 Then *J* fell on his father's
50: 2 And *J* commanded his servants the
50: 4 *J* spoke to the household of
50: 7 So *J* went up to bury his
50: 8 as well as all the house of *J*,
50:14 *J* returned to Egypt, he and his
50:15 Perhaps *J* will hate us, and may
50:16 So they sent messengers to *J*,
50:17 'Thus you shall say to *J*:
50:17 And *J* wept when they spoke to
50:19 *J* said to them, "Do not be
50:22 So *J* dwelt in Egypt, he and his
50:22 And *J* lived one hundred and ten
50:23 *J* saw Ephraim's children to the
50:24 And *J* said to his brethren, "I
50:25 Then *J* took an oath from the
50:26 So *J* died, being one hundred
Ex 1: 5 were seventy persons (for *J*
1: 6 And *J* died, all his brothers,
1: 8 over Egypt, who did not know *J*.
13:19 And Moses took the bones of *J*
Num 1:10 "from the sons of *J*:
1:32 From the sons of *J*,
13: 7 of Issachar, Igal the son of *J*;
13:11 from the tribe of *J*,
26:28 The sons of *J* according to
26:37 These are the sons of *J*
27: 1 of Manasseh the son of *J*;
32:33 tribe of Manasseh the son of *J*,
34:23 "from the sons of *J*:
36: 1 the families of the sons of *J*,
36: 5 the tribe of the sons of *J*
36:12 of Manasseh the son of *J*,
Deut 27:12 Levi, Judah, Issachar, *J*,
33:13 And of *J* he said: "Blessed
33:16 come 'on the head of *J*,
Josh 14: 4 For the children of *J* were two
16: 1 lot fell to the children of *J*
16: 4 So the children of *J*,
17: 1 for he was the firstborn of *J*:
17: 2 of Manasseh the son of *J*
17:14 Then the children of *J* spoke to
17:16 But the children of *J* said,
17:17 Joshua spoke to the house of *J*—
18: 5 and the house of *J* shall remain
18:11 of Judah and the children of *J*.
24:32 The bones of *J*, which the
24:32 of the children of *J*.
Judg 1:22 And the house of *J* also went up
1:23 So the house of *J* sent men to
1:35 the strength of the house of *J*
2 Sam 19:20 today of all the house of *J* to
1 Ki 11:28 labor force of the house of *J*.
1 Chr 2: 2 Dan, *J*, Benjamin, Naphtali,
5: 1 was given to the sons of *J*,
7:29 these dwelt the children of *J*,
25: 2 Of the sons of Asaph: Zaccur, *J*,
25: 9 lot for Asaph came out for *J*;
Ezra 10:42 Shallum, Amariah, and *J*;
Neh 12:14 Jonathan; of Shebaniah, *J*;
Ps 77:15 The sons of Jacob and *J*.
78:67 He rejected the tent of *J*,
80: 1 You who lead *J* like a flock;
81: 5 This He established in *J* as a
105:17 He sent a man before them—*J*—
Ezek 37:16 stick and write on it, 'For *J*,
37:19 I will take the stick of *J*,
47:13 *J* shall have two portions.
48:32 three gates: one gate for *J*,
Am 5: 6 like fire in the house of *J*,
5:15 be gracious to the remnant of *J*.
6: 6 grieved for the affliction of *J*.
Ob 18 And the house of *J* a flame;
Zech 10: 6 And I will save the house of *J*.
Mt 1:16 And Jacob begot *J* the husband of
1:18 mother Mary was betrothed to *J*,
1:19 Then *J* her husband, being a just
1:20 to him in a dream, saying, "*J*,
1:24 Then *J*, being aroused from
2:13 of the Lord appeared to *J* in a
2:19 Lord appeared in a dream to *J*
27:57 man from Arimathea, named *J*,
27:59 When *J* had taken the body, he
Mk 15:43 *J* of Arimathea, a prominent
15:45 he granted the body to *J*.
Lk 1:27 to a man whose name was *J*,
2: 4 *J* also went up from Galilee, out
2:16 with haste and found Mary and *J*,
2:33 And *J* and His mother marveled at
2:43 And *J* and His mother did not
3:23 (as was supposed) the son of *J*,
3:24 son of Janna, the son of *J*,
3:26 son of Semei, the son of *J*,
3:30 son of Judah, the son of *J*,
23:50 there was a man named *J*,
Jn 1:45 of Nazareth, the son of *J*.
4: 5 that Jacob gave to his son *J*.
6:42 not this Jesus, the son of *J*,
19:38 *J* of Arimathea, being a
Acts 1:23 *J* called Barsabas, who was
7: 9 sold *J* into Egypt. But God was
7:13 And the second time *J* was made
7:14 Then *J* sent and called his
7:18 king arose who did not know *J*.
Heb 11:21 blessed each of the sons of *J*,
11:22 By faith *J*, when he was
Rev 7: 8 of the tribe of *J* twelve

JOSEPH'S (24/24) JOSEPH

Gen 37:31 So they took *J* tunic, killed a
39: 5 Egyptian's house for *J* sake;
39: 6 all that he had in *J* hand,
39:20 Then *J* master took him and put
39:22 prison committed to *J* hand
39:23 was under *J* authority,
41:42 hand and put it on *J* hand;
41:45 And Pharaoh called *J* name
42: 3 So *J* ten brothers went down to
42: 4 But Jacob did not send *J* brother
42: 6 And *J* brothers came and bowed
43:17 brought the men into *J* house.
43:18 they were brought into *J* house;
43:19 to the steward of *J* house,
43:24 brought the men into *J* house
43:25 present ready for *J* coming
44:14 brothers came to *J* house,
45:16 *J* brothers have come." So it
48: 8 Then Israel saw *J* sons, and
50:15 When *J* brothers saw that their
50:23 also brought up on *J* knees.
1 Chr 5: 2 although the birthright was *J*—
Lk 4:22 Is this not *J* son?"
Acts 7:13 and *J* family became known to

JOSES (6/6) BARNABAS

Mt 13:55 Mary? And His brothers James, *J*,
27:56 Mary the mother of James and *J*,
Mk 6: 3 Mary, and brother of James, *J*,
15:40 of James the Less and of *J*,
15:47 and Mary the mother of *J*
Acts 4:36 And *J*, who was also named

JOSHAH (1/1)

1 Chr 4:34 and *J* the son of Amaziah;

JOSHAPHAT (2/2)

1 Chr 11:43 Maachah, *J* the Mithnite,
15:24 Shebaniah, *J*, Nethanel,

JOSHAVIAH (1/1)

1 Chr 11:46 Jeribai and *J* the sons of

JOSHBEKASHAH (2/2)

1 Chr 25: 4 Giddalti, Romamti-Ezer, *J*,
25:24 the seventeenth for *J*,

JOSHEB-BASSHEBETH (1/1)

2 Sam 23: 8 *J* the Tachmonite, chief among

JOSHIBIAH (1/1)

1 Chr 4:35 Joel, and Jehu the son of *J*,

JOSHUA (222/203) HOSEA, HOSHEA, JESHUA

Ex 17: 9 And Moses said to *J*,
17:10 So *J* did as Moses said to him,
17:13 So *J* defeated Amalek and his
17:14 recount it in the hearing of *J*,
24:13 arose with his assistant *J*,
32:17 And when *J* heard the noise of
33:11 but his servant *J* the son of
Num 11:28 So *J* the son of Nun, Moses'
13:16 called Hoshea the son of Nun, *J*.
14: 6 But *J* the son of Nun and Caleb
14:30 the son of Jephunneh and *J* the
14:38 But *J* the son of Nun and Caleb
26:65 the son of Jephunneh and *J* the
27:18 Take *J* the son of Nun with you,
27:22 He took *J* and set him before
32:12 and *J* the son of Nun, for they
32:28 to *J* the son of Nun, and to the
34:17 Eleazar the priest and *J* the
Deut 1:38 *J* the son of Nun, who stands
3:21 And I commanded *J* at that time,
3:28 'But command *J*, and encourage
31: 3 *J* himself crosses over before
31: 7 Then Moses called *J* and said to
31:14 when you must die; call *J*,
31:14 So Moses and *J* went and
31:23 Then He inaugurated *J* the son of
32:44 So Moses came with *J* the son of
34: 9 Now *J* the son of Nun was full
Josh 1: 1 pass that the LORD spoke to *J*
1:10 Then *J* commanded the officers
1:12 half the tribe of Manasseh *J*
1:16 So they answered *J*,
2: 1 Now *J* the son of Nun sent out
2:23 and they came to *J* the son of
2:24 And they said to *J*, "Truly
3: 1 Then *J* rose early in the
3: 5 And *J* said to the people,
3: 6 Then *J* spoke to the priests,
3: 7 And the LORD said to *J*,
3: 9 So *J* said to the children of
3:10 And *J* said, "By this you shall
4: 1 that the LORD spoke to *J*,
4: 4 Then *J* called the twelve men
4: 5 and *J* said to them: "Cross over
4: 8 just as *J* commanded, and took
4: 8 as the LORD had spoken to *J*,
4: 9 Then *J* set up twelve stones in
4:10 that the LORD had commanded *J*
4:10 all that Moses had commanded *J*;
4:14 On that day the LORD exalted *J*
4:15 Then the LORD spoke to *J*,
4:17 *J* therefore commanded the
4:20 *J* set up in Gilgal.
5: 2 that time the LORD said to *J*,
5: 3 So *J* made flint knives for
5: 4 And this is the reason why *J*
5: 7 Then *J* circumcised their sons
5: 9 Then the LORD said to *J*,
5:13 when *J* was by Jericho, that he
5:13 And *J* went to Him and said to
5:14 And *J* fell on his face to the
5:15 of the LORD's army said to *J*,
5:15 stand is holy." And *J* did so.
6: 2 And the LORD said to *J*:
6: 6 Then *J* the son of Nun called
6: 8 when *J* had spoken to the
6:10 Now *J* had commanded the people,
6:12 And *J* rose early in the
6:16 that *J* said to the people:
6:22 But *J* had said to the two men
6:25 And *J* spared Rahab the harlot,
6:25 she hid the messengers whom *J*
6:26 Then *J* charged them at that
6:27 So the LORD was with *J*,
7: 2 Now *J* sent men from Jericho to
7: 3 And they returned to *J* and said
7: 6 Then *J* tore his clothes, and
7: 7 And *J* said, "Alas, Lord GOD,
7:10 So the LORD said to *J*:
7:16 So *J* rose early in the morning
7:19 Now *J* said to Achan, "My son, I
7:20 And Achan answered *J* and said,
7:22 So *J* sent messengers, and they
7:23 brought them to *J* and to all
7:24 Then *J*, and all Israel with
7:25 And *J* said, "Why have you
8: 1 Now the LORD said to *J*:
8: 3 So *J* arose, and all the people
8: 3 and *J* chose thirty thousand
8: 9 *J* therefore sent them out
8: 9 but *J* lodged that night among
8:10 Then *J* rose up early in the
8:13 *J* went that night into the
8:15 And *J* and all Israel made as if
8:16 And they pursued *J* and were
8:18 Then the LORD said to *J*,
8:18 And *J* stretched out the spear
8:21 Now when *J* and all Israel saw
8:23 alive, and brought him to *J*.
8:26 For *J* did not draw back his
8:27 LORD which He had commanded *J*.
8:28 So *J* burned Ai and made it a
8:29 *J* commanded that they should
8:30 Now *J* built an altar to the
8:35 Moses had commanded which *J*
9: 2 together to fight with *J* and
9: 3 of Gibeon heard what *J* had
9: 6 And they went to *J*,
9: 8 But they said to *J*,
9: 8 And *J* said to them, "Who
9:15 So *J* made peace with them, and
9:22 Then *J* called for them, and he
9:24 So they answered *J* and said,
9:27 And that day *J* made them
10: 1 king of Jerusalem heard how *J*
10: 4 for it has made peace with *J*
10: 6 the men of Gibeon sent to *J* at
10: 7 So *J* ascended from Gilgal, he
10: 8 And the LORD said to *J*,
10: 9 *J* therefore came upon them
10:12 Then *J* spoke to the LORD in
10:15 Then *J* returned, and all Israel
10:17 And it was told *J*, saying,
10:18 So *J* said, "Roll large stones
10:20 while *J* and the children of
10:21 to *J* at Makkedah, in peace.
10:22 Then *J* said, "Open the mouth
10:24 brought out those kings to *J*,
10:24 that *J* called for all the men
10:25 Then *J* said to them, "Do not be
10:26 And afterward *J* struck them and
10:27 going down of the sun that *J*
10:28 On that day *J* took Makkedah,
10:29 Then *J* passed from Makkedah,
10:31 Then *J* passed from Libnah, and

J

10:33 and *J* struck him and his
10:34 From Lachish *J* passed to Eglon,
10:36 So *J* went up from Eglon, and
10:38 Then *J* returned, and all Israel
10:40 So *J* conquered all the land:
10:41 And *J* conquered them from Kadesh
10:42 these kings and their land *J*
10:43 Then *J* returned, and all Israel
11: 6 But the LORD said to *J*,
11: 7 So *J* and all the people of war
11: 9 So *J* did to them as the LORD
11:10 *J* turned back at that time and
11:12 *J* took and struck with the edge
11:13 Hazor only, which *J* burned.
11:15 servant, so Moses commanded *J*,
11:15 and so *J* did. He left nothing
11:16 Thus *J* took all this land: the
11:18 *J* made war a long time with all
11:21 And at that time *J* came and cut
11:21 *J* utterly destroyed them with
11:23 So *J* took the whole land,
11:23 and *J* gave it as an inheritance
12: 7 kings of the country which *J*
12: 7 which *J* gave to the tribes of
13: 1 Now *J* was old, advanced in
14: 1 *J* the son of Nun, and the heads
14: 6 children of Judah came to *J* in
14:13 And *J* blessed him, and gave
15:13 commandment of the LORD to *J*,
17: 4 before *J* the son of Nun, and
17:14 children of Joseph spoke to *J*,
17:15 So *J* answered them, "If you
17:17 And *J* spoke to the house of
18: 3 Then *J* said to the children of
18: 8 and *J* charged those who went to
18: 9 and they came to *J* at the camp
18:10 Then *J* cast lots for them in
18:10 and there *J* divided the land to
19:49 an inheritance among them to *J*
19:51 *J* the son of Nun, and the heads
20: 1 The LORD also spoke to *J*,
21: 1 to *J* the son of Nun, and to the
22: 1 Then *J* called the Reubenites,
22: 6 So *J* blessed them and sent them
22: 7 but to the other half of it *J*
22: 7 when *J* sent them away to their
23: 1 that *J* was old, advanced in
23: 2 And *J* called for all Israel, for
24: 1 Then *J* gathered all the tribes
24: 2 And *J* said to all the people,
24:19 But *J* said to the people, "You
24:21 And the people said to *J*,
24:22 So *J* said to the people, "You
24:24 And the people said to *J*,
24:25 So *J* made a covenant with the
24:26 Then *J* wrote these words in the
24:27 And *J* said to all the people,
24:28 So *J* let the people depart, each
24:29 pass after these things that *J*
24:31 the LORD all the days of *J*,
24:31 of the elders who outlived *J*,
Judg 1: 1 Now after the death of *J* it
2: 6 And when *J* had dismissed the
2: 7 the LORD all the days of *J*,
2: 7 of the elders who outlived *J*,
2: 8 Now *J* the son of Nun, the
2:21 them any of the nations which *J*
2:23 deliver them into the hand of *J*.
1 Sam 6:14 cart came into the field of *J*
6:18 to this day in the field of *J*
1 Ki 16:34 which He had spoken through *J*
2 Ki 23: 8 the entrance of the Gate of *J*
1 Chr 7:27 Nun his son, and *J* his son.
Neh 8:17 for since the days of *J* the son
Hag 1: 1 and to *J* the son of Jehozadak,
1:12 and *J* the son of Jehozadak, the
1:14 and the spirit of *J* the son of
2: 2 and to *J* the son of Jehozadak,
2: 4 the LORD; 'and be strong, *J*,
Zech 3: 1 Then he showed me *J* the high
3: 3 Now *J* was clothed with filthy
3: 6 Angel of the LORD admonished *J*,
3: 8 'Hear, O *J*, the high priest,
3: 9 That I have laid before *J*:
6:11 and set it on the head of *J*
Acts 7:45 also brought with *J* into the
Heb 4: 8 For if *J* had given them rest,

JOSIAH (55/50)

1 Ki 13: 2 *J* by name, shall be born to the
2 Ki 21:24 of the land made his son *J*
21:26 Then *J* his son reigned in his
22: 1 *J* was eight years old when he
22: 3 the eighteenth year of King *J*,
23:16 As *J* turned, he saw the tombs
23:19 Now *J* also took away all the
23:23 the eighteenth year of King *J*
23:24 Moreover *J* put away those who
23:28 Now the rest of the acts of *J*,
23:29 and King *J* went against him.
23:30 land took Jehoahaz the son of *J*,
23:34 made Eliakim the son of *J* king
23:34 king in place of his father *J*,
1 Chr 3:14 his son, and *J* his son.
3:15 The sons of *J* were Johanan the
2 Chr 33:25 of the land made his son *J*
34: 1 *J* was eight years old when he
34:33 Thus *J* removed all the
35: 1 Now *J* kept a Passover to the
35: 7 Then *J* gave the lay people
35:16 to the command of King *J*.
35:18 had kept such a Passover as *J*
35:19 year of the reign of *J* this
35:20 when *J* had prepared the temple,
35:20 and *J* went out against him.
35:22 Nevertheless *J* would not turn
35:23 And the archers shot King *J*;
35:24 and Jerusalem mourned for *J*.
35:25 Jeremiah also lamented for *J*.
35:25 the singing women speak of *J*
35:26 Now the rest of the acts of *J*
36: 1 land took Jehoahaz the son of *J*,
Jer 1: 2 the LORD came in the days of *J*
1: 3 days of Jehoiakim the son of *J*,
1: 3 year of Zedekiah the son of *J*,
3: 6 also to me in the days of *J*
22:11 concerning Shallum the son of *J*,
22:11 who reigned instead of *J* his
22:18 Jehoiakim the son of *J*,
25: 1 year of Jehoiakim the son of *J*,
25: 3 From the thirteenth year of *J*
26: 1 reign of Jehoiakim the son of *J*,
27: 1 reign of Jehoiakim the son of *J*,
35: 1 days of Jehoiakim the son of *J*,
36: 1 year of Jehoiakim the son of *J*,
36: 2 from the days of *J* even to this
36: 9 year of Jehoiakim the son of *J*,
37: 1 Now King Zedekiah the son of *J*
45: 1 year of Jehoiakim the son of *J*,
46: 2 year of Jehoiakim the son of *J*,
Zeph 1: 1 in the days of *J* the son of
Zech 6:10 day and enter the house of *J*
Mt 1:10 begot Amon, and Amon begot *J*.
1:11 *J* begot Jeconiah and his

JOSIAS (KJV) See JOSIAH

JOSIBIAH (KJV) See JOSHIBIAH

JOSTLE (1/1)

Nah 2: 4 They *j* one another in the

JOT (1/1)

Mt 5:18 one *j* or one tittle will by no

JOTBAH (1/1)

2 Ki 21:19 the daughter of Haruz of *J*.

JOTBATHAH (3/3)

Num 33:33 Hor Hagidgad and camped at *J*.
33:34 They moved from *J* and camped at
Deut 10: 7 and from Gudgodah to *J*,

JOTHAM (26/25)

Judg 9: 5 But *J* the youngest son of
9: 7 Now when they told *J*,
9:21 And *J* ran away and fled; and he
9:57 and on them came the curse of *J*
2 Ki 15: 5 And *J* the king's son was over
15: 7 Then *J* his son reigned in his
15:30 in the twentieth year of *J* the
15:32 *J* the son of Uzziah, king of
15:36 Now the rest of the acts of *J*,
15:38 So *J* rested with his fathers,
16: 1 of Remaliah, Ahaz the son of *J*,
1 Chr 2:47 sons of Jahdai were Regem, *J*,
3:12 Azariah his son, *J* his son,
5:17 by genealogies in the days of *J*
2 Chr 26:21 Then *J* his son was over the
26:23 Then *J* his son reigned in his
27: 1 *J* was twenty-five years old
27: 6 So *J* became mighty, because he
27: 7 Now the rest of the acts of *J*,
27: 9 So *J* rested with his fathers,
Isa 1: 1 in the days of Uzziah, *J*,
7: 1 the days of Ahaz the son of *J*,
Hos 1: 1 Beeri, in the days of Uzziah, *J*,
Mic 1: 1 of Moresheth in the days of *J*,
Mt 1: 9 Uzziah begot *J*, Jotham begot
1: 9 *J* begot Ahaz, and Ahaz begot

JOURNEY (71/66) JOURNEYED, JOURNEYING, JOURNEYS

Gen 13: 3 And he went on his *j* from the
24:21 the LORD had made his *j*
29: 1 So Jacob went on his *j* and came
30:36 Then he put three days' *j*
31:23 pursued him for seven days' *j*,
33:12 Esau said, "Let us take our *j*;
42:25 give them provisions for the *j*.
45:21 gave them provisions for the *j*.
45:23 food for his father for the *j*.
46: 1 So Israel took his *j* with all
Ex 3:18 let us go three days' *j* into
5: 3 let us go three days' *j* into
8:27 We will go three days' *j* into
13:20 So they took their *j* from
17: 1 of Israel set out on their *j*
40:37 then they did not *j* till the
Num 4: 5 "When the camp prepares to *j*,
9:10 corpse, or is far away on a *j*,
9:13 who is clean and is not on a *j*,
9:17 the children of Israel would *j*;
9:18 the children of Israel would *j*,
9:19 of the LORD and did not *j*.
9:20 of the LORD they would *j*.
9:21 the morning, then they would *j*;
9:21 was taken up, they would *j*.
9:22 would remain encamped and not *j*;
9:22 it was taken up, they would *j*.
10: 5 side shall then begin their *j*.
10: 6 south side shall begin their *j*;
10:28 armies, when they began their *j*.
10:33 mountain of the LORD on a *j*
10:33 them for the three days' *j*,
11:31 about a day's *j* on this side
11:31 this side and about a day's *j*
12:15 and the people did not *j* till
33: 8 went three days' *j* in the
Deut 1: 2 It is eleven days' *j* from
1: 7 'Turn and take your *j*,
1:40 turn and take your *j* into the
2:24 "'Rise, take your *j*,
10:11 begin your *j* before the
14:24 But if the *j* is too long for
Josh 9:11 provisions with you for the *j*,
9:13 old because of the very long *j*.
Judg 4: 9 be no glory for you in the *j*
18: 5 that we may know whether the *j*
2 Sam 11:10 "Did you not come from a *j*?
1 Ki 18:27 or he is busy, or he is on a *j*,
19: 4 But he himself went a day's *j*
19: 7 because the *j* is too great for
Ezra 7: 9 the first month he began his *j*
Neh 2: 6 'How long will your *j* be?
Prov 7:19 He has gone on a long *j*;
Jon 3: 3 a three-day *j* in extent.
Mt 10:10 "nor bag for your *j*,
25:15 and immediately he went on a *j*.
Mk 6: 8 them to take nothing for the *j*
Lk 2:44 company, they went a day's *j*,
9: 3 them, "Take nothing for the *j*,
9:53 His face was set for the *j* to
11: 6 of mine has come to me on his *j*,
13:33 Nevertheless I must *j* today,
Jn 4: 6 being wearied from His *j*,
Acts 1:12 Jerusalem, a Sabbath day's *j*.
10: 9 as they went on their *j* and
Rom 15:24 whenever I *j* to Spain, I shall
15:24 For I hope to see you on my *j*,
1 Cor 16: 6 that you may send me on my *j*,
16:11 But send him on his *j* in peace,
Titus 3:13 lawyer and Apollos on their *j*
3 Jn 6 send them forward on their *j*

JOURNEYED (30/30) JOURNEY

Gen 11: 2 as they *j* from the east, that
12: 9 So Abram *j*, going on still
13:11 and Lot *j* east. And they
20: 1 And Abraham *j* from there to the
33:17 And Jacob *j* to Succoth, built
35: 5 And they *j*, and the terror
35:16 Then they *j* from Bethel. And
35:21 Then Israel *j* and pitched his
42: 5 to buy grain among those who *j*,
Ex 12:37 Then the children of Israel *j*
16: 1 And they *j* from Elim, and all
Num 9:23 the command of the LORD they *j*;
20:22 *j* from Kadesh and came to Mount
21: 4 Then they *j* from Mount Hor by
21:11 And they *j* from Oboth and camped
33:12 They *j* from the Wilderness of
33:22 They *j* from Rissah and camped at
Deut 2: 1 Then we turned and *j* into the
10: 6 (Now the children of Israel *j*
10: 7 From there they *j* to Gudgodah,
Josh 9:17 Then the children of Israel *j*
Judg 17: 8 to the house of Micah, as he *j*.
Lk 9:57 Now it happened as they *j* on
10:33 a certain Samaritan, as he *j*,
15:13 *j* to a far country, and there
Acts 9: 3 As he *j* he came near Damascus,
9: 7 And the men who *j* with him stood
22: 6 as I *j* and came near Damascus
26:12 as I *j* to Damascus with
26:13 around me and those who *j* with

JOURNEYING (1/1) JOURNEY

Lk 13:22 and *j* toward Jerusalem.

JOURNEYS (8/7) JOURNEY

Ex 40:36 would go onward in all their *j*.
40:38 Israel, throughout all their *j*.
Num 10: 6 call for them to begin their *j*.
10:12 Wilderness of Sinai on their *j*;
33: 1 These are the *j* of the children
33: 2 the starting points of their *j*
33: 2 And these are their *j*
2 Cor 11:26 in *j* often, in perils of

JOY (158/150) JOYFUL

Gen 31:27 have sent you away with *j* and
Deut 28:47 the LORD your God with *j* and
1 Sam 18: 6 Saul, with tambourines, with *j*,
1 Ki 1:40 and rejoiced with great *j*,
1 Chr 12:40 for there was *j* in Israel.
15:16 the voice with resounding *j*.
15:25 the house of Obed-Edom with *j*.
29:17 and now with *j* I have seen Your
2 Chr 20:27 to go back to Jerusalem with *j*,
30:26 So there was great *j* in
Ezra 3:12 Yet many shouted aloud for *j*,
3:13 the noise of the shout of *j*
6:16 of this house of God with *j*.
6:22 Bread seven days with *j*;

Neh 8:10 for the *j* of the LORD is your
12:43 made them rejoice with great *j*;
12:43 so that the *j* of Jerusalem was
Esth 8:16 gladness, *j* and honor.
8:17 the Jews had *j* and gladness, a
9:22 was turned from sorrow to *j*
9:22 them days of feasting and *j*,
Job 8:19 this is the *j* of His way, And
20: 5 And the *j* of the hypocrite is
29:13 the widow's heart to sing for *j*.
33:26 He shall see His face with *j*,
38: 7 the sons of God shouted for *j*?
Ps 5:11 Let them ever shout for *j*,
16:11 Your presence is fullness of *j*;
21: 1 The king shall have *j* in Your
27: 6 I will offer sacrifices of *j*
30: 5 But *j* comes in the morning.
32:11 you righteous; And shout for *j*,
33: 3 skillfully with a shout of *j*.
35:27 Let them shout for *j* and be
42: 4 With the voice of *j* and
43: 4 of God, To God my exceeding *j*;
48: 2 The *j* of the whole earth, Is
51: 8 Make me hear *j* and gladness,
51:12 Restore to me the *j* of Your
65:13 with grain; They shout for *j*,
67: 4 nations be glad and sing for *j*!
105:43 brought out His people with *j*,
126: 5 sow in tears Shall reap in *j*.
132: 9 let Your saints shout for *j*.
132:16 saints shall shout aloud for *j*.
137: 6 Jerusalem Above my chief *j*.
Prov 12:20 But counselors of peace have *j*.
14:10 a stranger does not share its *j*.
15:21 Folly is *j* to him who is
15:23 A man has *j* by the answer of
17:21 the father of a fool has no *j*.
21:15 It is a *j* for the just to do
Eccl 2:26 wisdom and knowledge and *j* to
5:20 God keeps him busy with the *j*
9: 7 Go, eat your bread with *j*,
Isa 9: 3 nation And increased its *j*;
9: 3 before You According to the *j*
9:17 the LORD will have no *j* in
12: 3 Therefore with *j* you will draw
16:10 And *j* from the plentiful
22:13 *j* and gladness, Slaying oxen
24: 8 The *j* of the harp ceases.
24:11 All *j* is darkened, The mirth
29:19 also shall increase their *j*
32:14 A *j* of wild donkeys, a pasture
35: 2 Even with *j* and singing.
35:10 With everlasting *j* on their
35:10 They shall obtain *j* and
51: 3 *J* and gladness will be found
51:11 With everlasting *j* on their
51:11 They shall obtain *j* and
52: 9 Break forth into *j*,
55:12 "For you shall go out with *j*,
60: 5 your heart shall swell with *j*;
60:15 A *j* of many generations.
61: 3 The oil of *j* for mourning,
61: 7 Everlasting *j* shall be theirs.
65:14 My servants shall sing for *j* of
65:18 rejoicing, And her people a *j*.
65:19 And *j* in My people; The voice
66: 5 That we may see your *j*.
66:10 Rejoice for *j* with her, all
Jer 15:16 And Your word was to me the *j*
31:13 I will turn their mourning to *j*,
33: 9 it shall be to Me a name of *j*,
33:11 the voice of *j* and the voice of
48:33 *J* and gladness are taken From
49:25 not deserted, the city of My *j*?
Lam 2:15 The *j* of the whole earth'?"
5:15 The *j* of our heart has ceased;
Ezek 24:25 their *j* and their glory, the
36: 5 with whole-hearted *j* and
Hos 9: 1 with *j* like other peoples,
Joel 1:12 Surely *j* has withered away
1:16 *J* and gladness from the house
Hab 3:18 I will *j* in the God of my
Zech 8:19 Shall be *j* and gladness and
Mt 2:10 with exceedingly great *j*.
13:20 immediately receives it with *j*;
13:44 and for *j* over it he goes and
25:21 Enter into the *j* of your lord.'
25:23 Enter into the *j* of your lord.'
28: 8 the tomb with fear and great *j*,
Lk 1:14 And you will have *j* and
1:44 babe leaped in my womb for *j*.
2:10 you good tidings of great *j*
6:23 in that day and leap for *j*!
8:13 hear, receive the word with *j*;
10:17 the seventy returned with *j*,
15: 7 likewise there will be more *j*
15:10 there is *j* in the presence of
24:41 still did not believe for *j*,
24:52 to Jerusalem with great *j*,
Jn 3:29 Therefore this *j* of mine is
15:11 that My *j* may remain in you,
15:11 and that your *j* may be full.
16:20 sorrow will be turned into *j*.
16:21 for *j* that a human being has
16:22 and your *j* no one will take
16:24 that your *j* may be full.
17:13 that they may have My *j*
Acts 2:28 will make me full of *j*
8: 8 And there was great *j* in that
13:52 disciples were filled with *j*
15: 3 and they caused great *j* to all
20:24 I may finish my race with *j*,

Rom 14:17 righteousness and peace and *j*
15:13 God of hope fill you with all *j*
15:32 that I may come to you with *j* by
2 Cor 1:24 are fellow workers for your *j*;
2: 3 from whom I ought to have *j*,
2: 3 in you all that my *j* is the
2: 3 you all that my joy is the *j*
7:13 exceedingly more for the *j* of
8: 2 the abundance of their *j* and
Gal 5:22 fruit of the Spirit is love, *j*,
Phil 1: 4 request for you all with *j*,
1:25 all for your progress and *j* of
2: 2 fulfill my *j* by being
4: 1 my *j* and crown, so stand fast
Col 1:11 and longsuffering with *j*;
1 Th 1: 6 with *j* of the Holy Spirit,
2:19 For what is our hope, or *j*,
2:20 For you are our glory and *j*.
3: 9 for all the *j* with which we
2 Tim 1: 4 that I may be filled with *j*,
Phm 1: 7 For we have great *j* and
1:20 let me have *j* from you in the
Heb 12: 2 who for the *j* that was set
13:17 Let them do so with *j* and not
Jas 1: 2 count it all *j* when you fall
4: 9 turned to mourning and your *j*
1 Pe 1: 8 you rejoice with *j* inexpressible
4:13 also be glad with exceeding *j*.
1 Jn 1: 4 we write to you that your *j*
2 Jn 12 that our *j* may be full.
3 Jn 4 I have no greater *j* than to hear
Jude 24 of His glory with exceeding *j*,

JOYFUL (23/23) JOY, JOYFULLY

1 Ki 8:66 and went to their tents *j* and
2 Chr 7:10 *j* and glad of heart for the
Ezra 6:22 joy; for the LORD made them *j*,
Esth 5: 9 So Haman went out that day *j*
Job 3: 7 May no *j* shout come into it!
Ps 5:11 also who love Your name Be *j*
35: 9 And my soul shall be *j* in the
63: 5 mouth shall praise You with *j*
66: 1 Make a *j* shout to God, all the
81: 1 Make a *j* shout to the God of
89:15 are the people who know the *j*
96:12 Let the field be *j*,
98: 8 Let the hills be *j* together
100: 1 Make a *j* shout to the LORD,
113: 9 Like a *j* mother of children.
149: 2 Let the children of Zion be *j*
149: 5 Let the saints be *j* in glory;
Eccl 7:14 In the day of prosperity be *j*,
Isa 49:13 Sing, O heavens! Be *j*,
56: 7 And make them *j* in My house of
61:10 My soul shall be *j* in my God;
2 Cor 7: 4 I am exceedingly *j* in all our
Heb 12:11 Now no chastening seems to be *j*

JOYFULLY (7/7) JOYFUL

Ps 95: 1 to the LORD! Let us shout *j*
95: 2 Let us shout *j* to Him with
98: 4 Shout *j* to the LORD, all the
98: 6 Shout *j* before the LORD, the
Eccl 9: 9 Live *j* with the wife whom you
Lk 19: 6 came down, and received Him *j*.
Heb 10:34 and *j* accepted the plundering

JOYOUS (5/4)

Isa 22: 2 a *j* city? Your slain men are
23: 7 Is this your *j* city, Whose
32:13 happy homes in the *j* city;
Jer 48:33 will tread with *j* shouting—Not
48:33 shouting—Not *j* shouting!

JOYOUSLY (1/1)

Jer 51:48 that is in them Shall sing *j*

JOZABAD (10/9)

1 Chr 12: 4 and *J* the Gederathite;
12:20 defected to him were Adnah, *J*,
12:20 Jozabad, Jediael, Michael, *J*,
2 Chr 31:13 Nahath, Asahel, Jerimoth, *J*,
35: 9 and Hashabiah and Jeiel and *J*,
Ezra 8:33 *J* the son of Jeshua and Noadiah
10:22 Maaseiah, Ishmael, Nethanel, *J*,
10:23 Also of the Levites: *J*,
Neh 8: 7 Maaseiah, Kelita, Azariah, *J*,
11:16 Shabbethai and *J*, of the

JOZACHAR (1/1)

2 Ki 12:21 For *J* the son of Shimeath and

JOZADAK (5/5) JEHOZADAK

Ezra 3: 2 Then Jeshua the son of *J* and his
3: 8 Shealtiel, Jeshua the son of *J*,
5: 2 and Jeshua the son of *J* rose
10:18 the sons of Jeshua the son of *J*,
Neh 12:26 the son of Jeshua, the son of *J*,

JUBAL (1/1)

Gen 4:21 His brother's name was *J*.

JUBILANT (2/2)

Isa 5:14 their pomp, And he who is *j*,
24: 8 The noise of the *j* ends, The

JUBILATION (1/1)

Prov 11:10 the wicked perish, there is *j*.

JUBILEE (22/20)

Lev 25: 9 cause the trumpet of the *J* to
25:10 It shall be a *J* for you; and
25:11 fiftieth year shall be a *J* to
25:12 'For it is the *J*; it shall
25:13 'In this Year of *J*,
25:15 the number of years after the *J*
25:28 bought it until the Year of *J*;
25:28 and in the *J* it shall be
25:30 shall not be released in the *J*.
25:31 they shall be released in the *J*.
25:33 shall be released in the *J*;
25:40 serve you until the Year of *J*.
25:50 sold to him until the Year of *J*;
25:52 a few years until the Year of *J*,
25:54 be released in the Year of *J*—
27:17 his field from the Year of *J*,
27:18 dedicates his field after the *J*,
27:18 that remain till the Year of *J*,
27:21 when it is released in the *J*,
27:23 valuation, up to the Year of *J*,
27:24 In the Year of *J* the field shall
Num 36: 4 And when the *J* of the children

JUCAL (1/1)

Jer 38: 1 *J* the son of Shelemiah, and

JUDAH (832/767) JUDAH'S, JUDEA

Gen 29:35 Therefore she called his name *J*.
35:23 firstborn, and Simeon, Levi, *J*,
37:26 So *J* said to his brothers,
38: 1 to pass at that time that *J*
38: 2 And *J* saw there a daughter of a
38: 6 Then *J* took a wife for Er his
38: 8 And *J* said to Onan, "Go in to
38:11 Then *J* said to Tamar his
38:12 and *J* was comforted, and went
38:15 When *J* saw her, he thought she
38:20 And *J* sent the young goat by the
38:22 So he returned to *J* and said,
38:23 Then *J* said, "Let her take
38:24 that *J* was told, saying,
38:24 So *J* said, "Bring her out
38:26 So *J* acknowledged them and
43: 3 But *J* spoke to him, saying,
43: 8 Then *J* said to Israel his
44:14 So *J* and his brothers came to
44:16 Then *J* said, "What shall we say
44:18 Then *J* came near to him and
46:12 The sons of *J* were Er, Onan,
46:28 Then he sent *J* before him to
49: 8 '*J*, you are he whom your
49: 9 *J* is a lion's whelp
49:10 scepter shall not depart from *J*,
Ex 1: 2 Reuben, Simeon, Levi, and *J*;
31: 2 son of Hur, of the tribe of *J*.
35:30 son of Hur, of the tribe of *J*;
38:22 son of Hur, of the tribe of *J*,
Num 1: 7 'from *J*, Nahshon the son of
1:26 From the children of *J*,
1:27 were numbered of the tribe of *J*
2: 3 standard of the forces with *J*
2: 3 the leader of the children of *J*.
2: 9 armies of the forces with *J*,
7:12 Amminadab, from the tribe of *J*.
10:14 the camp of the children of *J*
13: 6 from the tribe of *J*,
26:19 The sons of *J* were Er and
26:20 And the sons of *J* according to
26:22 These are the families of *J*
34:19 of the men: from the tribe of *J*,
Deut 27:12 the Jordan: Simeon, Levi, *J*,
33: 7 And this he said of *J*:
33: 7 "Hear, LORD, the voice of *J*,
34: 2 all the land of *J* as far as the
Josh 7: 1 son of Zerah, of the tribe of *J*,
7:16 and the tribe of *J* was taken.
7:17 He brought the clan of *J*,
7:18 son of Zerah, of the tribe of *J*,
11:21 from all the mountains of *J*,
14: 6 Then the children of *J* came to
15: 1 the tribe of the children of *J*
15:12 boundary of the children of *J*
15:13 a share among the children of *J*,
15:20 the tribe of the children of *J*
15:21 the tribe of the children of *J*,
15:63 the children of *J* could not
15:63 dwell with the children of *J*
18: 5 *J* shall remain in their
18:11 out between the children of *J*
18:14 a city of the children of *J*.
19: 1 of the children of *J*.
19: 9 the share of the children of *J*,
19: 9 the share of the children of *J*,
19:34 and ended at *J* by the Jordan
20: 7 Hebron) in the mountains of *J*.
21: 4 by lot from the tribe of *J*,
21: 9 the tribe of the children of *J*
21:11 Hebron, in the mountains of *J*,
Judg 1: 2 *J* shall go up. Indeed I have

J

1: 3 So *J* said to Simeon his brother,
1: 4 Then *J* went up, and the LORD
1: 8 Now the children of *J* fought
1: 9 And afterward the children of *J*
1:10 Then *J* went against the
1:16 of Palms with the children of *J*
1:16 Judah into the Wilderness of *J*,
1:17 And *J* went with his brother
1:18 Also *J* took Gaza with its
1:19 So the LORD was with *J*.
10: 9 the Jordan to fight against *J*
15: 9 went up, encamped in *J*,
15:10 And the men of *J* said, "Why
15:11 Then three thousand men of *J*
17: 7 a young man from Bethlehem in *J*,
17: 7 in Judah, of the family of *J*;
17: 8 the city of Bethlehem in *J* to
17: 9 a Levite from Bethlehem in *J*,
18:12 encamped in Kirjath Jearim in *J*.
19: 1 a concubine from Bethlehem in *J*.
19: 2 house at Bethlehem in *J*,
19:18 passing from Bethlehem in *J*
19:18 there. I went to Bethlehem in *J*;
20:18 The LORD said, "*J* first!"
Ruth 1: 1 a certain man of Bethlehem, *J*,
1: 2 —Ephrathites of Bethlehem, *J*.
1: 7 way to return to the land of *J*.
4:12 of Perez, whom Tamar bore to *J*,
1 Sam 11: 8 and the men of *J* thirty
15: 4 and ten thousand men of *J*.
17: 1 at Sochoh, which belongs to *J*;
17:12 that Ephrathite of Bethlehem *J*,
17:52 Now the men of Israel and *J*
18:16 But all Israel and *J* loved
22: 5 depart, and go to the land of *J*.
23: 3 "Look, we are afraid here in *J*.
23:23 throughout all the clans of *J*.
27: 6 has belonged to the kings of *J*
27:10 the southern area of *J*,
30:14 territory which belongs to *J*,
30:16 and from the land of *J*.
30:26 of the spoil to the elders of *J*,
2 Sam 1:18 to teach the children of *J*
2: 1 go up to any of the cities of *J*?
2: 4 Then the men of *J* came, and
2: 4 David king over the house of *J*.
2: 7 and also the house of *J* has
2:10 Only the house of *J* followed
2:11 in Hebron over the house of *J*
3: 8 a dog's head that belongs to *J*?
3:10 of David over Israel and over *J*,
5: 5 In Hebron he reigned over *J*
5: 5 years over all Israel and *J*.
11:11 The ark and Israel and *J* are
12: 8 you the house of Israel and *J*.
19:11 "Speak to the elders of *J*,
19:14 the hearts of all the men of *J*,
19:15 And *J* came to Gilgal, to go to
19:16 came down with the men of *J* to
19:40 And all the people of *J*
19:41 have our brethren, the men of *J*,
19:42 So all the men of *J* answered the
19:43 of Israel answered the men of *J*,
19:43 Yet the words of the men of *J*
20: 2 son of Bichri. But the men of *J*,
20: 4 Assemble the men of *J* for me
20: 5 to assemble the men of *J*.
21: 2 the children of Israel and *J*.
24: 1 say, "Go, number Israel and *J*.
24: 7 Then they went out to South *J*
24: 9 and the men of *J* were five
1 Ki 1: 9 sons, and all the men of *J*,
1:35 to be ruler over Israel and *J*.
2:32 the commander of the army of *J*—
4:20 *J* and Israel were as numerous
4:25 And *J* and Israel dwelt safely,
9:18 wilderness, in the land of *J*,
12:17 who dwelt in the cities of *J*.
12:20 but the tribe of *J* only.
12:21 he assembled all the house of *J*
12:23 the son of Solomon, king of *J*,
12:23 to all the house of *J* and
12:27 their lord, Rehoboam king of *J*,
12:27 go back to Rehoboam king of *J*.
12:32 like the feast that was in *J*,
13: 1 a man of God went from *J* to
13:12 man of God went who came from *J*.
13:14 the man of God who came from *J*?
13:21 the man of God who came from *J*,
14:21 the son of Solomon reigned in *J*.
14:22 Now *J* did evil in the sight of
14:29 chronicles of the kings of *J*?
15: 1 Abijam became king over *J*.
15: 7 chronicles of the kings of *J*?
15: 9 Israel, Asa became king over *J*.
15:17 of Israel came up against *J*,
15:17 out or come in to Asa king of *J*.
15:22 a proclamation throughout all *J*;
15:23 chronicles of the kings of *J*?
15:25 second year of Asa king of *J*,
15:28 the third year of Asa king of *J*,
15:33 the third year of Asa king of *J*,
16: 8 year of Asa king of *J*,
16:10 year of Asa king of *J*,
16:15 year of Asa king of *J*,
16:23 year of Asa king of *J*,
16:29 year of Asa king of *J*,
19: 3 Beersheba, which belongs to *J*,
22: 2 that Jehoshaphat the king of *J*
22:10 and Jehoshaphat the king of *J*,
22:29 and Jehoshaphat the king of *J*
22:41 of Asa had become king over *J*
22:45 chronicles of the kings of *J*?
22:51 year of Jehoshaphat king of *J*,
2 Ki 1:17 son of Jehoshaphat, king of *J*.
3: 1 year of Jehoshaphat king of *J*,
3: 7 sent to Jehoshaphat king of *J*,
3: 9 Israel went with the king of *J*
3:14 of Jehoshaphat king of *J*,
8:16 having been king of *J*,
8:16 began to reign as king of *J*.
8:19 the LORD would not destroy *J*,
8:23 chronicles of the kings of *J*?
8:25 the son of Jehoram, king of *J*,
8:29 the son of Jehoram, king of *J*,
9:16 and Ahaziah king of *J* had come
9:21 of Israel and Ahaziah king of *J*
9:27 But when Ahaziah king of *J* saw
9:29 Ahaziah had become king over *J*.
10:13 brothers of Ahaziah king of *J*,
12:18 And Jehoash king of *J* took all
12:18 Jehoram and Ahaziah, kings of *J*,
12:19 chronicles of the kings of *J*?
13: 1 the son of Ahaziah, king of *J*,
13:10 year of Joash king of *J*,
13:12 against Amaziah king of *J*,
14: 1 the son of Joash, king of *J*,
14: 9 sent to Amaziah king of *J*,
14:10 you and *J* with you?"
14:11 so he and Amaziah king of *J*
14:11 Shemesh, which belongs to *J*.
14:12 And *J* was defeated by Israel,
14:13 captured Amaziah king of *J*,
14:15 fought with Amaziah king of *J*—
14:17 the son of Joash, king of *J*,
14:18 chronicles of the kings of *J*?
14:21 And all the people of *J* took
14:22 Elath and restored it to *J*,
14:23 the son of Joash, king of *J*,
14:28 what had belonged to *J*—
15: 1 the son of Amaziah, king of *J*,
15: 6 chronicles of the kings of *J*?
15: 8 year of Azariah king of *J*,
15:13 year of Uzziah king of *J*;
15:17 year of Azariah king of *J*,
15:23 year of Azariah king of *J*,
15:27 year of Azariah king of *J*,
15:32 the son of Uzziah, king of *J*,
15:36 chronicles of the kings of *J*?
15:37 the son of Remaliah against *J*.
16: 1 the son of Jotham, king of *J*,
16: 6 and drove the men of *J* from
16:19 chronicles of the kings of *J*?
17: 1 twelfth year of Ahaz king of *J*,
17:13 against Israel and against *J*,
17:18 none left but the tribe of *J*
17:19 Also *J* did not keep the
18: 1 the son of Ahaz, king of *J*,
18: 5 him among all the kings of *J*,
18:13 all the fortified cities of *J*
18:14 Then Hezekiah king of *J* sent to
18:14 assessed Hezekiah king of *J*
18:16 which Hezekiah king of *J* had
18:22 and said to *J* and Jerusalem,
19:10 speak to Hezekiah king of *J*,
19:30 have escaped of the house of *J*
20:20 chronicles of the kings of *J*?
21:11 Because Manasseh king of *J* has
21:11 and has also made *J* sin with
21:12 calamity upon Jerusalem and *J*,
21:16 his sin by which he made *J* sin,
21:17 chronicles of the kings of *J*?
21:25 chronicles of the kings of *J*?
22:13 for the people and for all *J*,
22:16 of the book which the king of *J*
22:18 "But as for the king of *J*,
23: 1 to gather all the elders of *J*
23: 2 the LORD with all the men of *J*,
23: 5 priests whom the kings of *J*
23: 5 high places in the cities of *J*
23: 8 priests from the cities of *J*,
23:11 the horses that the kings of *J*
23:12 which the kings of *J* had made,
23:17 the man of God who came from *J*
23:22 of Israel and the kings of *J*.
23:24 were seen in the land of *J* and
23:26 His anger was aroused against *J*,
23:27 I will also remove *J* from My
23:28 chronicles of the kings of *J*?
24: 2 He sent them against *J* to
24: 3 of the LORD this came upon *J*,
24: 5 chronicles of the kings of *J*?
24:12 Then Jehoiachin king of *J*,
24:20 happened in Jerusalem and *J*,
25:21 Thus *J* was carried away captive
25:22 who remained in the land of *J*,
25:27 of Jehoiachin king of *J*,
25:27 released Jehoiachin king of *J*
1 Chr 2: 1 Israel: Reuben, Simeon, Levi, *J*,
2: 3 The sons of *J* were Er, Onan,
2: 3 Er, the firstborn of *J*,
2: 4 All the sons of *J* were five.
2:10 leader of the children of *J*;
4: 1 The sons of *J* were Perez,
4:21 The sons of Shelah the son of *J*
4:27 as much as the children of *J*.
4:41 the days of Hezekiah king of *J*;
5: 2 yet *J* prevailed over his
5:17 in the days of Jotham king of *J*,
6:15 when the LORD carried *J* and
6:55 them Hebron in the land of *J*,
6:65 the tribe of the children of *J*,
9: 1 But *J* was carried away captive
9: 3 in Jerusalem the children of *J*
9: 4 of Perez, the son of *J*.
12:16 of the sons of Benjamin and *J*
12:24 of the sons of *J* bearing shield
13: 6 Jearim, which belonged to *J*,
21: 5 and *J* had four hundred and
27:18 over *J*, Elihu, one of
28: 4 for He has chosen *J* to be the
28: 4 and of the house of *J*,
2 Chr 2: 7 men who are with me in *J* and
9:11 seen before in the land of *J*.
10:17 who dwelt in the cities of *J*.
11: 1 assembled from the house of *J*
11: 3 the son of Solomon, king of *J*,
11: 3 and to all Israel in *J* and
11: 5 built cities for defense in *J*.
11:10 which are in *J* and Benjamin,
11:12 having *J* and Benjamin on his
11:14 possessions and came to *J* and
11:17 strengthened the kingdom of *J*,
11:23 all the territories of *J* and
12: 4 took the fortified cities of *J*
12: 5 Rehoboam and the leaders of *J*,
12:12 and things also went well in *J*.
13: 1 Abijah became king over *J*.
13:13 so they were in front of *J*,
13:14 And when *J* looked around, to
13:15 Then the men of *J* gave a shout;
13:15 and as the men of *J* shouted, it
13:15 all Israel before Abijah and *J*.
13:16 of Israel fled before *J*,
13:18 and the children of *J*
14: 4 He commanded *J* to seek the LORD
14: 5 altars from all the cities of *J*,
14: 6 he built fortified cities in *J*,
14: 7 Therefore he said to *J*,
14: 8 three hundred thousand from *J*
14:12 the Ethiopians before Asa and *J*,
15: 2 and all *J* and Benjamin.
15: 8 idols from all the land of *J*
15: 9 Then he gathered all *J* and
15:15 And all *J* rejoiced at the oath,
16: 1 of Israel came up against *J*
16: 1 out or come in to Asa king of *J*.
16: 6 Then King Asa took all *J*,
16: 7 the seer came to Asa king of *J*,
16:11 in the book of the kings of *J*
17: 2 all the fortified cities of *J*,
17: 2 set garrisons in the land of *J*
17: 5 and all *J* gave presents to
17: 6 places and wooden images from *J*.
17: 7 to teach in the cities of *J*.
17: 9 So they taught in *J*,
17: 9 throughout all the cities of *J*
17:10 the lands that were around *J*,
17:12 and storage cities in *J*.
17:13 property in the cities of *J*;
17:14 Of *J*, the captains of
17:19 cities throughout all *J*.
18: 3 said to Jehoshaphat king of *J*,
18: 9 and Jehoshaphat king of *J*,
18:28 and Jehoshaphat the king of *J*
19: 1 Then Jehoshaphat the king of *J*
19: 5 all the fortified cities of *J*,
19:11 the ruler of the house of *J*,
20: 3 a fast throughout all *J*.
20: 4 So *J* gathered together to ask
20: 4 and from all the cities of *J*
20: 5 stood in the assembly of *J* and
20:13 Now all *J*, with their little
20:15 all you of *J* and you
20:17 O *J* and Jerusalem!' Do not fear
20:18 and all *J* and the inhabitants
20:20 O *J* and you inhabitants of
20:22 Seir, who had come against *J*;
20:24 So when *J* came to a place
20:27 every man of *J* and Jerusalem,
20:31 So Jehoshaphat was king over *J*.
20:35 this Jehoshaphat king of *J*
21: 3 with fortified cities in *J*;
21:11 places in the mountains of *J*,
21:11 harlotry, and led *J* astray.
21:12 or in the ways of Asa king of *J*,
21:13 and have made *J* and the
21:17 And they came up into *J* and
22: 1 the son of Jehoram, king of *J*,
22: 6 the son of Jehoram, king of *J*,
22: 8 and found the princes of *J* and
22:10 royal heirs of the house of *J*.
23: 2 And they went throughout *J* and
23: 2 from all the cities of *J*,
23: 8 So the Levites and all *J* did
24: 5 "Go out to the cities of *J*,
24: 6 the Levites to bring in from *J*
24: 9 a proclamation throughout *J*
24:17 of Jehoiada the leaders of *J*
24:18 and wrath came upon *J* and
24:23 and they came to *J* and
25: 5 Moreover Amaziah gathered *J*
25: 5 throughout all *J* and Benjamin;
25:10 was greatly aroused against *J*,
25:12 Also the children of *J* took
25:13 they raided the cities of *J*
25:17 Now Amaziah king of *J* asked
25:18 sent to Amaziah king of *J*,
25:19 you and *J* with you?"
25:21 and he and Amaziah king of *J*
25:21 Shemesh, which belongs to *J*.
25:22 And *J* was defeated by Israel,
25:23 captured Amaziah king of *J*,
25:25 the son of Joash, king of *J*,
25:26 in the book of the kings of *J*
25:28 his fathers in the City of *J*.

26: 1 Now all the people of *J* took
26: 2 Elath and restored it to *J*,
27: 4 cities in the mountains of *J*,
27: 7 of the kings of Israel and *J*.
28: 6 and twenty thousand in *J* in
28: 9 your fathers was angry with *J*,
28:10 to force the children of *J* and
28:17 Edomites had come, attacked *J*,
28:18 lowland and of the South of *J*,
28:19 For the LORD brought *J* low
28:19 encouraged moral decline in *J*
28:25 And in every single city of *J* he
28:26 in the book of the kings of *J*
29: 8 wrath of the LORD fell upon *J*
29:21 for the sanctuary, and for *J*.
30: 1 sent to all Israel and *J*,
30: 6 throughout all Israel and *J*
30:12 Also the hand of God was on *J* to
30:24 For Hezekiah king of *J* gave to
30:25 The whole assembly of *J*
30:25 and those who dwelt in *J*.
31: 1 went out to the cities of *J*
31: 1 and the altars—from all *J*,
31: 6 the children of Israel and *J*,
31: 6 who dwelt in the cities of *J*,
31:20 Hezekiah did throughout all *J*,
32: 1 of Assyria came and entered *J*;
32: 8 the words of Hezekiah king of *J*.
32: 9 to Hezekiah king of *J*,
32: 9 and to all *J* who were in
32:12 and commanded *J* and Jerusalem,
32:23 presents to Hezekiah king of *J*,
32:25 was looming over him and over *J*
32:32 in the book of the kings of *J*
32:33 and all *J* and the inhabitants
33: 9 So Manasseh seduced *J* and the
33:14 all the fortified cities of *J*.
33:16 and commanded *J* to serve the
34: 3 year he began to purge *J* and
34: 5 and cleansed *J* and Jerusalem.
34: 9 from all *J* and Benjamin, and
34:11 the houses which the kings of *J*
34:21 who are left in Israel and *J*,
34:24 have read before the king of *J*,
34:26 "But as for the king of *J*,
34:29 gathered all the elders of *J*
34:30 with all the men of *J* and the
35:18 all *J* and Israel who were
35:21 I to do with you, king of *J*?
35:24 And all *J* and Jerusalem mourned
35:27 of the kings of Israel and *J*.
36: 4 brother Eliakim king over *J*
36: 8 of the kings of Israel and *J*.
36:10 king over *J* and Jerusalem.
36:23 at Jerusalem which is in *J*.
Ezra 1: 2 at Jerusalem which is in *J*.
1: 3 up to Jerusalem which is in *J*,
1: 5 of the fathers' houses of *J*
1: 8 to Sheshbazzar the prince of *J*.
2: 1 who returned to Jerusalem and *J*,
3: 9 his sons, and the sons of *J*,
4: 1 Now when the adversaries of *J*
4: 4 to discourage the people of *J*.
4: 6 against the inhabitants of *J*
5: 1 to the Jews who were in *J* and
7:14 to inquire concerning *J* and
9: 9 and to give us a wall in *J* and
10: 7 a proclamation throughout *J*
10: 9 So all the men of *J* and
10:23 same is Kelita), Pethahiah, *J*,
Neh 1: 2 brethren came with men from *J*;
2: 5 I ask that you send me to *J*,
2: 7 pass through till I come to *J*,
4:10 Then *J* said, "The strength of
4:16 were behind all the house of *J*.
5:14 their governor in the land of *J*,
6: 7 There is a king in *J*!'
6:17 in those days the nobles of *J*
6:18 For many in *J* were pledged to
7: 6 who returned to Jerusalem and *J*,
11: 3 (But in the cities of *J*
11: 4 some of the children of *J* and
11: 4 of Benjamin. The children of *J*:
11: 9 and *J* the son of Senuah was
11:20 were in all the cities of *J*,
11:24 children of Zerah the son of *J*,
11:25 some of the children of *J*
12: 8 Binnui, Kadmiel, Sherebiah, *J*,
12:31 So I brought the leaders of *J*
12:32 and half of the leaders of *J*,
12:34 *J*, Benjamin, Shemaiah,
12:36 Gilalai, Maai, Nethanel, *J*,
12:44 for *J* rejoiced over the priests
13:12 Then all *J* brought the tithe of
13:15 those days I saw people in *J*
13:16 Sabbath to the children of *J*,
13:17 contended with the nobles of *J*,
13:24 not speak the language of *J*,
Esth 2: 6 with Jeconiah king of *J*,
Ps 48:11 Let the daughters of *J* be
60: 7 *J* is My lawgiver.
63: he was in the wilderness of *J*.
68:27 The princes of *J* and their
69:35 Zion And build the cities of *J*,
76: 1 In *J* God is known; His name
78:68 But chose the tribe of *J*,
97: 8 And the daughters of *J* rejoice
108: 8 *J* is My lawgiver.
114: 2 *J* became His sanctuary, And
Prov 25: 1 the men of Hezekiah king of *J*
Isa 1: 1 which he saw concerning *J* and
1: 1 Ahaz, and Hezekiah, kings of *J*.

2: 1 son of Amoz saw concerning *J*
3: 1 away from Jerusalem and from *J*
3: 8 And *J* is fallen, Because
5: 3 of Jerusalem and men of *J*,
5: 7 And the men of *J* are His
7: 1 the son of Uzziah, king of *J*,
7: 6 Let us go up against *J* and
7:17 that Ephraim departed from *J*.
8: 8 He will pass through *J*,
9:21 they shall be against *J*.
11:12 together the dispersed of *J*
11:13 And the adversaries of *J* shall
11:13 off; Ephraim shall not envy *J*,
11:13 And *J* shall not harass
19:17 And the land of *J* will be a
22: 8 removed the protection of *J*.
22:21 And to the house of *J*.
26: 1 will be sung in the land of *J*:
36: 1 all the fortified cities of *J*
36: 7 and said to *J* and Jerusalem,
37:10 speak to Hezekiah king of *J*,
37:31 have escaped of the house of *J*
38: 9 writing of Hezekiah king of *J*,
40: 9 Say to the cities of *J*,
44:26 inhabited,' To the cities of *J*,
48: 1 forth from the wellsprings of *J*;
65: 9 And from *J* an heir of My
Jer 1: 2 the son of Amon, king of *J*,
1: 3 the son of Josiah, king of *J*,
1: 3 the son of Josiah, king of *J*,
1:15 against all the cities of *J*.
1:18 land—Against the kings of *J*,
2:28 your cities Are your gods, O *J*.
3: 7 And her treacherous sister *J*
3: 8 yet her treacherous sister *J*
3:10 this her treacherous sister *J*
3:11 righteous than treacherous *J*.
3:18 In those days the house of *J*
4: 3 says the LORD to the men of *J*
4: 4 You men of *J* and inhabitants
4: 5 Declare in *J* and proclaim in
4:16 voice against the cities of *J*.
5:11 of Israel and the house of *J*
5:20 of Jacob And proclaim it in *J*,
7: 2 all you of *J* who enter in at
7:17 they do in the cities of *J* and
7:30 For the children of *J* have done
7:34 to cease from the cities of *J*
8: 1 out the bones of the kings of *J*,
9:11 I will make the cities of *J*
9:26 'Egypt, *J*, Edom, the people
10:22 To make the cities of *J*
11: 2 and speak to the men of *J* and
11: 6 these words in the cities of *J*
11: 9 been found among the men of *J*
11:10 of Israel and the house of *J*
11:12 Then the cities of *J* and the
11:13 your cities were your gods, O *J*;
11:17 of Israel and of the house of *J*,
12:14 and pluck out the house of *J*
13: 9 I will ruin the pride of *J* and
13:11 and the whole house of *J* to
13:19 *J* shall be carried away
14: 2 *J* mourns, And her gates
14:19 Have You utterly rejected *J*?
15: 4 the son of Hezekiah, king of *J*,
17: 1 The sin of *J* is written with a
17:19 by which the kings of *J* come in
17:20 of the LORD, you kings of *J*,
17:20 you kings of Judah, and all *J*,
17:25 accompanied by the men of *J* and
17:26 come from the cities of *J* and
18:11 speak to the men of *J* and to
19: 3 O kings of *J* and inhabitants of
19: 4 nor the kings of *J* have known,
19: 7 make void the counsel of *J* and
19:13 the houses of the kings of *J*
20: 4 I will give all *J* into the hand
20: 5 treasures of the kings of *J* I
21: 7 will deliver Zedekiah king of *J*,
21:11 the house of the king of *J*,
22: 1 to the house of the king of *J*,
22: 2 word of the LORD, O king of *J*,
22: 6 to the house of the king of *J*:
22:11 the son of Josiah, king of *J*,
22:18 the son of Josiah, king of *J*:
22:24 the son of Jehoiakim, king of *J*,
22:30 David, And ruling anymore in *J*.
23: 6 In His days *J* will be saved,
24: 1 the son of Jehoiakim, king of *J*,
24: 1 and the princes of *J* with the
24: 5 are carried away captive from *J*,
24: 8 give up Zedekiah the king of *J*,
25: 1 concerning all the people of *J*,
25: 1 king of *J* (which was the first
25: 2 spoke to all the people of *J*
25: 3 the son of Amon, king of *J*,
25:18 Jerusalem and the cities of *J*,
26: 1 the son of Josiah, king of *J*,
26: 2 speak to all the cities of *J*,
26:10 When the princes of *J* heard
26:18 the days of Hezekiah king of *J*,
26:18 spoke to all the people of *J*,
26:19 Did Hezekiah king of *J* and all
26:19 king of Judah and all *J* ever
27: 1 the son of Josiah, king of *J*,
27: 3 Jerusalem to Zedekiah king of *J*.
27:12 spoke to Zedekiah king of *J*
27:18 in the house of the king of *J*,
27:20 the son of Jehoiakim, king of *J*,
27:20 and all the nobles of *J* and
27:21 in the house of the king of *J*

28: 1 the reign of Zedekiah king of *J*,
28: 4 the son of Jehoiakim, king of *J*,
28: 4 with all the captives of *J* who
29: 2 the princes of *J* and Jerusalem,
29: 3 whom Zedekiah king of *J* sent to
29:22 up by all the captivity of *J*
30: 3 My people Israel and *J*,
30: 4 spoke concerning Israel and *J*.
31:23 this speech in the land of *J*
31:24 And there shall dwell in *J*
31:27 of Israel and the house of *J*
31:31 Israel and with the house of *J*—
32: 1 year of Zedekiah king of *J*,
32: 3 For Zedekiah king of *J* had shut
32: 4 and Zedekiah king of *J* shall not
32:30 of Israel and the children of *J*
32:32 of Israel and the children of *J*,
32:32 their prophets, the men of *J*,
32:35 to cause *J* to sin.'
32:44 Jerusalem, in the cities of *J*,
33: 4 the houses of the kings of *J*,
33: 7 I will cause the captives of *J*
33:10 beast"—in the cities of *J*,
33:13 and in the cities of *J*,
33:14 of Israel and to the house of *J*:
33:16 In those days *J* will be saved,
34: 2 and speak to Zedekiah king of *J*
34: 4 O Zedekiah king of *J*! Thus says
34: 6 words to Zedekiah king of *J* in
34: 7 and all the cities of *J* that
34: 7 remained of the cities of *J*.
34:19 'the princes of *J*,
34:21 I will give Zedekiah king of *J*
34:22 I will make the cities of *J* a
35: 1 the son of Josiah, king of *J*,
35:13 Go and tell the men of *J* and the
35:17 I will bring on *J* and on all
36: 1 the son of Josiah, king of *J*,
36: 2 you against Israel, against *J*,
36: 3 It may be that the house of *J*
36: 6 them in the hearing of all *J*
36: 9 the son of Josiah, king of *J*,
36: 9 who came from the cities of *J*
36:28 which Jehoiakim the king of *J*
36:29 say to Jehoiakim king of *J*,
36:30 concerning Jehoiakim king of *J*:
36:31 and on the men of *J* all the
36:32 book which Jehoiakim king of *J*
37: 1 made king in the land of *J*.
37: 7 you shall say to the king of *J*,
39: 1 year of Zedekiah king of *J*,
39: 4 when Zedekiah the king of *J* and
39: 6 also killed all the nobles of *J*.
39:10 the guard left in the land of *J*
40: 1 captive from Jerusalem and *J*,
40: 5 governor over the cities of *J*,
40:11 Babylon had left a remnant of *J*,
40:12 and came to the land of *J*,
40:15 and the remnant in *J* perish?"
42:15 O remnant of *J*! Thus says the
42:19 concerning you, O remnant of *J*,
43: 4 to remain in the land of *J*.
43: 5 took all the remnant of *J* who
43: 5 to dwell in the land of *J*,
43: 9 in the sight of the men of *J*,
44: 2 and on all the cities of *J*;
44: 6 and kindled in the cities of *J*
44: 7 child and infant, out of *J*,
44: 9 wickedness of the kings of *J*,
44: 9 committed in the land of *J* and
44:11 and for cutting off all *J*.
44:12 I will take the remnant of *J*
44:14 that none of the remnant of *J*
44:14 they return to the land of *J*,
44:17 in the cities of *J* and in the
44:21 you burned in the cities of *J*
44:24 all *J* who are in the land of
44:26 all *J* who dwell in the land of
44:26 in the mouth of any man of *J*
44:27 And all the men of *J* who are
44:28 land of Egypt to the land of *J*;
44:28 and all the remnant of *J*,
44:30 as I gave Zedekiah king of *J*
45: 1 the son of Josiah, king of *J*
46: 2 the son of Josiah, king of *J*:
49:34 the reign of Zedekiah king of *J*,
50: 4 They and the children of *J*
50:20 be none; And the sins of *J*,
50:33 Along with the children of *J*;
51: 5 Israel is not forsaken, nor *J*,
51:59 with Zedekiah the king of *J* to
52: 3 happened in Jerusalem and *J*,
52:10 he killed all the princes of *J*
52:27 Thus *J* was carried away captive
52:31 of Jehoiachin king of *J*,
52:31 head of Jehoiachin king of *J*
Lam 1: 3 *J* has gone into captivity,
1:15 The virgin daughter of *J*.
2: 2 of the daughter of *J*;
2: 5 In the daughter of *J*.
5:11 The maidens in the cities of *J*.
Ezek 4: 6 the iniquity of the house of *J*
8: 1 my house with the elders of *J*
8:17 thing to the house of *J* to
9: 9 of the house of Israel and *J*
21:20 of the Ammonites, and to *J*,
25: 3 and against the house of *J* when
25: 8 Look! The house of *J* is like
25:12 did against the house of *J* by
27:17 *J* and the land of Israel were
37:16 For *J* and for the children of
37:19 with it, with the stick of *J*,

48: 7 the west, one section for *J*;
48: 8 "by the border of *J*,
48:22 area between the border of *J*
48:31 gate for Reuben, one gate for *J*,
Dan 1: 1 reign of Jehoiakim king of *J*,
1: 2 Lord gave Jehoiakim king of *J*
1: 6 among those of the sons of *J*
2:25 a man of the captives of *J*,
5:13 is one of the captives from *J*,
5:13 father the king brought from *J*?
6:13 is one of the captives from *J*,
9: 7 is this day—to the men of *J*,
Hos 1: 1 Ahaz, and Hezekiah, kings of *J*,
1: 7 have mercy on the house of *J*,
1:11 Then the children of *J* and the
4:15 Let not *J* offend. Do not come
5: 5 *J* also stumbles with them.
5:10 The princes of *J* are like those
5:12 And to the house of *J* like
5:13 And *J* saw his wound, Then
5:14 a young lion to the house of *J*.
6: 4 what shall I do to you? O *J*,
6:11 Also, O *J*, a harvest is
8:14 *J* also has multiplied
10:11 *J* shall plow; Jacob shall
11:12 But *J* still walks with God,
12: 2 also brings a charge against *J*,
Joel 3: 1 I bring back the captives of *J*
3: 6 Also the people of *J* and the
3: 8 the hand of the people of *J*,
3:18 And all the brooks of *J* shall
3:19 against the people of *J*,
3:20 But *J* shall abide forever, And
Am 1: 1 in the days of Uzziah king of *J*,
2: 4 three transgressions of *J*,
2: 5 But I will send a fire upon *J*,
7:12 Flee to the land of *J*.
Ob 12 over the children of *J* In the
Mic 1: 1 Ahaz, and Hezekiah, kings of *J*,
1: 5 what are the high places of *J*?
1: 9 For it has come to *J*;
5: 2 little among the thousands of *J*,
Nah 1:15 Who proclaims peace! O *J*,
Zeph 1: 1 the son of Amon, king of *J*.
1: 4 stretch out My hand against *J*,
2: 7 the remnant of the house of *J*;
Hag 1: 1 son of Shealtiel, governor of *J*,
1:14 son of Shealtiel, governor of *J*,
2: 2 son of Shealtiel, governor of *J*,
2:21 to Zerubbabel, governor of *J*,
Zech 1:12 and on the cities of *J*,
1:19 the horns that have scattered *J*,
1:21 are the horns that scattered *J*,
1:21 horn against the land of *J* to
2:12 will take possession of *J* as
8:13 O house of *J* and house of
8:15 Jerusalem and to the house of *J*.
8:19 feasts For the house of *J*.
9: 7 shall be like a leader in *J*,
9:13 For I have bent *J*,
10: 3 His flock, The house of *J*,
10: 6 will strengthen the house of *J*,
11:14 the brotherhood between *J* and
12: 2 when they lay siege against *J*
12: 4 open My eyes on the house of *J*,
12: 5 And the governors of *J* shall say
12: 6 I will make the governors of *J*
12: 7 LORD will save the tents of *J*
12: 7 become greater than that of *J*.
14: 5 the days of Uzziah king of *J*.
14:14 *J* also will fight at Jerusalem
14:21 every pot in Jerusalem and *J*
Mal 2:11 *J* has dealt treacherously, And
2:11 For *J* has profaned The
3: 4 Then the offering of *J* and
Mt 1: 2 and Jacob begot *J* and his
1: 3 *J* begot Perez and Zerah by
2: 6 in the land of *J*,
2: 6 among the rulers of *J*;
Lk 1:39 with haste, to a city of *J*,
3:26 son of Joseph, the son of *J*,
3:30 son of Simeon, the son of *J*,
3:33 son of Perez, the son of *J*,
Heb 7:14 that our Lord arose from *J*,
8: 8 and with the house of *J*—
Rev 5: 5 the Lion of the tribe of *J*,
7: 5 of the tribe of *J* twelve

JUDAH'S (8/8) JUDAH

Gen 38: 7 *J* firstborn, was wicked in the
38:12 *J* wife, died; and Judah was
2 Ki 8:20 revolted against *J* authority,
8:22 revolt against *J* authority
2 Chr 21: 8 revolted against *J* authority,
21:10 revolt against *J* authority
Jer 32: 2 in the king of *J* house.
38:22 left in the king of *J* house

JUDAISM (2/2) JEW

Gal 1:13 heard of my former conduct in *J*,
1:14 And I advanced in *J* beyond many

JUDAS (32/31) BARSABAS, ISCARIOT, JUDE, THADDAEUS

Mt 10: 4 and *J* Iscariot, who also
13:55 James, Joses, Simon, and *J*?
26:14 called *J* Iscariot, went to the
26:25 Then *J*, who was betraying
26:47 was still speaking, behold, *J*,
27: 3 Then *J*, His betrayer,
Mk 3:19 and *J* Iscariot, who also
6: 3 and brother of James, Joses, *J*,
14:10 Then *J* Iscariot, one of the
14:43 while He was still speaking, *J*,
Lk 6:16 *J* the son of James, and Judas
6:16 and *J* Iscariot who also became
22: 3 Then Satan entered *J*,
22:47 and he who was called *J*,
22:48 But Jesus said to him, "*J*,
Jn 6:71 He spoke of *J* Iscariot, the
12: 4 *J* Iscariot, Simon's son, who
13: 2 put it into the heart of *J*
13:26 He gave it to *J* Iscariot, the
13:29 because *J* had the money box,
14:22 *J* (not Iscariot) said to Him,
18: 2 And *J*, who betrayed Him,
18: 3 Then *J*, having received a
18: 5 to them, "I am He." And *J*,
Acts 1:13 and *J* the son of James.
1:16 the mouth of David concerning *J*,
1:25 and apostleship from which *J*
5:37 *J* of Galilee rose up in the
9:11 and inquire at the house of *J*
15:22 *J* who was also named Barsabas,
15:27 We have therefore sent *J* and
15:32 Now *J* and Silas, themselves

JUDE (1/1) JUDAS

Jude 1 *J*, a bondservant of Jesus

JUDEA (46/46) JUDAH

Ezra 5: 8 we went into the province of *J*,
Mt 2: 1 was born in Bethlehem of *J* in
2: 5 to him, "In Bethlehem of *J*,
2:22 Archelaus was reigning over *J*
3: 1 in the wilderness of *J*,
3: 5 Then Jerusalem, all *J*,
4:25 from Decapolis, Jerusalem, *J*,
19: 1 and came to the region of *J*
24:16 then let those who are in *J* flee
Mk 1: 5 Then all the land of *J*,
3: 7 followed Him, and from *J*
10: 1 and came to the region of *J* by
13:14 then let those who are in *J* flee
Lk 1: 5 days of Herod, the king of *J*,
1:65 all the hill country of *J*.
2: 4 of the city of Nazareth, into *J*,
3: 1 Pilate being governor of *J*,
5:17 out of every town of Galilee, *J*,
6:17 multitude of people from all *J*
7:17 Him went throughout all *J* and
21:21 Then let those who are in *J* flee
23: 5 teaching throughout all *J*,
Jn 3:22 came into the land of *J*,
4: 3 He left *J* and departed again to
4:47 that Jesus had come out of *J*
4:54 did when He had come out of *J*
7: 1 He did not want to walk in *J*,
7: 3 from here and go into *J*,
11: 7 Let us go to *J* again."
Acts 1: 8 and in all *J* and Samaria, and
2: 9 *J* and Cappadocia, Pontus and
2:14 Men of *J* and all who dwell in
8: 1 throughout the regions of *J*
9:31 the churches throughout all *J*,
10:37 was proclaimed throughout all *J*,
11: 1 and brethren who were in *J*
11:29 to the brethren dwelling in *J*.
12:19 And he went down from *J* to
15: 1 certain men came down from *J*
21:10 named Agabus came down from *J*.
26:20 throughout all the region of *J*,
28:21 neither received letters from *J*
Rom 15:31 be delivered from those in *J*
2 Cor 1:16 be helped by you on my way to *J*.
Gal 1:22 by face to the churches of *J*
1 Th 2:14 churches of God which are in *J*

JUDEAN (1/1)

Neh 11:36 Some of the *J* divisions of

JUDEANS (1/1)

1 Th 2:14 just as they did from the *J*,

JUDGE (188/170) JUDGED, JUDGES, JUDGING, JUDGMENT

Gen 15:14 nation whom they serve I will *j*;
16: 5 The LORD *j* between you and
18:25 be it from You! Shall not the *J*
19: 9 and he keeps acting as a *j*;
31:37 that they may *j* between us
31:53 and the God of their father *j*
49:16 Dan shall *j* his people As one
Ex 2:14 Who made you a prince and a *j*
5:21 the LORD look on you and *j*,
18:13 that Moses sat to *j* the people;
18:16 and I *j* between one and
18:22 And let them *j* the people at all
18:22 matter they themselves shall *j*.
Lev 19:15 In righteousness you shall *j*
Num 35:24 then the congregation shall *j*
Deut 1:16 and *j* righteously between a man
16:18 and they shall *j* the people
17: 8 which is too hard for you to *j*,
17: 9 and to the *j* there in those
17:12 the LORD your God, or the *j*,
25: 1 that the judges may *j* them,
25: 2 that the *j* will cause him to
32:36 For the LORD will *j* His people
Judg 2:18 the LORD was with the *j* and
2:18 enemies all the days of the *j*;
2:19 when the *j* was dead, that they
11:27 me. May the LORD, the *J*,
1 Sam 2:10 The LORD will *j* the ends of
2:25 God will *j* him. But if a man
3:13 I have told him that I will *j*
8: 5 Now make us a king to *j* us like
8: 6 Give us a king to *j* us." So
8:20 and that our king may *j* us and
24:12 Let the LORD *j* between you and
24:15 "Therefore let the LORD be *j*,
24:15 and *j* between you and me, and
2 Sam 15: 4 that I were made *j* in the land,
1 Ki 3: 9 an understanding heart to *j*
3: 9 For who is able to *j* this great
7: 7 of Judgment, where he might *j*;
8:32 and *j* Your servants, condemning
1 Chr 16:33 For He is coming to *j* the
2 Chr 1:10 for who can *j* this great people
1:11 that you may *j* My people over
6:23 and *j* Your servants, bringing
19: 6 for you do not *j* for man but
20:12 will You not *j* them? For we
Ezra 7:25 and judges who may *j* all the
Job 9:15 Him; I would beg mercy of my *J*.
22:13 Can He *j* through the deep
23: 7 be delivered forever from my *J*.
Ps 7: 8 The LORD shall *j* the peoples;
7: 8 *J* me, O LORD, according to my
7:11 God is a just *j*,
9: 8 He shall *j* the world in
50: 4 that He may *j* His people:
50: 6 For God Himself is *J*.
51: 4 And blameless when You *j*.
58: 1 Do you *j* uprightly, you sons
67: 4 sing for joy! For You shall *j*
72: 2 He will *j* Your people with
75: 2 I will *j* uprightly.
75: 7 But God is the *J*:
82: 2 How long will you *j* unjustly,
82: 8 *j* the earth; For You shall
94: 2 O *J* of the earth; Render
96:10 He shall *j* the peoples
96:13 for He is coming to *j* the
96:13 He shall *j* the world with
98: 9 For He is coming to *j* the
98: 9 With righteousness He shall *j*
110: 6 He shall *j* among the nations,
135:14 For the LORD will *j* His
Prov 31: 9 *j* righteously, And plead the
Eccl 3:17 God shall *j* the righteous and
Isa 2: 4 He shall *j* between the nations,
3: 2 The *j* and the prophet, And
3:13 And stands to *j* the people.
5: 3 Jerusalem and men of Judah, *J*,
11: 3 And He shall not *j* by the
11: 4 with righteousness He shall *j*
33:22 (For the LORD is our *J*,
51: 5 And My arms will *j* the
66:16 by His sword The LORD will *j*
Jer 11:20 You who *j* righteously,
Lam 3:59 I am wronged; *J* my case.
Ezek 7: 3 I will *j* you according to your
7: 8 I will *j* you according to your
7:27 to what they deserve I will *j*
11:10 I will *j* you at the border of
11:11 I will *j* you at the border of
16:38 And I will *j* you as women who
18:30 Therefore I will *j* you, O house
20: 4 Will you *j* them, son of man,
20: 4 will you *j* them? Then make
21:30 I will *j* you In the place
22: 2 "Now, son of man, will you *j*,
22: 2 will you *j* the bloody city?
23:24 And they shall *j* you according
23:36 will you *j* Oholah and Oholibah?
23:45 But righteous men will *j* them
24:14 to your deeds They will *j* you,
33:20 I will *j* every one of you
34:17 I shall *j* between sheep and
34:20 I Myself will *j* between the fat
34:22 and I will *j* between sheep and
35:11 known among them when I *j* you.
44:24 and *j* it according to My
Joel 3:12 For there I will sit to *j* all
Am 2: 3 And I will cut off the *j* from
Ob 21 shall come to Mount Zion To *j*
Mic 3:11 Her heads *j* for a bribe, Her
4: 3 He shall *j* between many
5: 1 They will strike the *j* of
7: 3 The *j* seeks a bribe, And the
Zech 3: 7 Then you shall also *j* My
Mt 5:25 adversary deliver you to the *j*,
5:25 the *j* hand you over to the
7: 1 *J* not, that you be not judged.
7: 2 "For with what judgment you *j*,
Lk 6:37 *J* not, and you shall not be
12:14 who made Me a *j* or an
12:57 do you not *j* what is right?
12:58 him, lest he drag you to the *j*,
12:58 the *j* deliver you to the
18: 2 was in a certain city a *j* who
18: 6 Hear what the unjust *j* said.
19:22 'Out of your own mouth I will *j*
Jn 5:30 do nothing. As I hear, I *j*;
7:24 Do not *j* according to
7:24 but *j* with righteous
7:51 Does our law *j* a man before it

8:15 You *j* according to the flesh; I
8:15 the flesh; I *j* no one.
8:16 "And yet if I do *j*,
8:26 many things to say and to *j*
12:47 I do not *j* him; for I did not
12:47 for I did not come to *j* the
12:48 word that I have spoken will *j*
18:31 You take Him and *j* Him according
Acts 4:19 to you more than to God, you *j*.
7: 7 be in bondage I will *j*,
7:27 made you a ruler and a *j*
7:35 made you a ruler and a *j*?
10:42 was ordained by God to be *J*
13:46 and *j* yourselves unworthy of
15:19 Therefore I *j* that we should not
17:31 a day on which He will *j* the
18:15 for I do not want to be a *j* of
23: 3 wall! For you sit to *j* me
24: 6 and wanted to *j* him according
24:10 have been for many years a *j*
Rom 2: 1 O man, whoever you are who *j*,
2: 1 for in whatever you *j* another
2: 1 for you who *j* practice the same
2: 3 you who *j* those practicing such
2:16 in the day when God will *j* the
2:27 *j* you who, even with your
3: 6 not! For then how will God *j*
14: 3 let not him who does not eat *j*
14: 4 Who are you to *j* another's
14:10 But why do you *j* your brother?
14:13 Therefore let us not *j* one
1 Cor 4: 3 I do not even *j* myself.
4: 5 Therefore *j* nothing before the
5:12 Do you not *j* those who are
6: 2 not know that the saints will *j*
6: 2 are you unworthy to *j* the
6: 3 Do you not know that we shall *j*
6: 4 esteemed by the church to *j*?
6: 5 who will be able to *j* between
10:15 *j* for yourselves what I say.
11:13 *J* among yourselves. Is it proper
11:31 For if we would *j* ourselves, we
14:29 speak, and let the others *j*.
2 Cor 5:14 because we *j* thus: that if One
Col 2:16 So let no one *j* you in food or
2 Tim 4: 1 who will *j* the living and the
4: 8 which the Lord, the righteous *J*,
Heb 10:30 The LORD will *j* His
12:23 to God the *J* of all, to the
13: 4 and adulterers God will *j*.
Jas 4:11 But if you *j* the law, you are
4:11 not a doer of the law but a *j*.
4:12 Who are you to *j* another?
5: 9 the *J* is standing at the door!
1 Pe 4: 5 to Him who is ready to *j* the
Rev 6:10 until You *j* and avenge our

JUDGED (61/59) JUDGE

Gen 30: 6 God has *j* my case; and He has
Ex 18:26 So they *j* the people at all
18:26 but they *j* every small case
Judg 3:10 and he *j* Israel. He went out to
10: 2 He *j* Israel twenty-three years;
10: 3 and he *j* Israel twenty-two
12: 7 And Jephthah *j* Israel six years.
12: 8 Ibzan of Bethlehem *j* Israel.
12: 9 He *j* Israel seven years.
12:11 Elon the Zebulunite *j* Israel.
12:11 He *j* Israel ten years.
12:13 son of Hillel the Pirathonite *j*
12:14 He *j* Israel eight years.
15:20 And he *j* Israel twenty years in
16:31 He had *j* Israel twenty years.
1 Sam 4:18 And he had *j* Israel forty
7: 6 And Samuel *j* the children of
7:15 And Samuel *j* Israel all the
7:16 and *j* Israel in all those
7:17 There he *j* Israel, and there he
2 Ki 23:22 the days of the judges who *j*
Ps 9:19 Let the nations be *j* in Your
37:33 Nor condemn him when he is *j*.
109: 7 When he is *j*, let him be
Jer 22:16 He *j* the cause of the poor and
Ezek 16:38 wedlock or shed blood are *j*;
16:52 You who *j* your sisters, bear
28:23 The wounded shall be *j* in her
36:19 I *j* them according to their
Dan 9:12 us and against our judges who *j*
Mt 7: 1 "Judge not, that you be not *j*.
7: 2 you judge, you will be *j*;
Lk 6:37 not, and you shall not be *j*.
7:43 to him, "You have rightly *j*.
Jn 16:11 the ruler of this world is *j*.
Acts 4: 9 If we this day are *j* for a good
16:15 If you have *j* me to be faithful
23: 6 of the dead I am being *j*!"
24:21 of the dead I am being *j* by
25: 9 up to Jerusalem and there be *j*
25:10 seat, where I ought to be *j*.
25:20 go to Jerusalem and there be *j*
26: 6 And now I stand and am *j* for the
Rom 2:12 sinned in the law will be *j* by
3: 4 overcome when You are *j*.
3: 7 why am I also still *j* as a
1 Cor 2:15 yet he himself is rightly *j* by
4: 3 small thing that I should be *j*
5: 3 have already *j* (as though I
6: 2 And if the world will be *j* by
10:29 For why is my liberty *j* by
11:31 ourselves, we would not be *j*.
11:32 But when we are *j*,
Heb 11:11 because she *j* Him faithful who
Jas 2:12 so do as those who will be *j*
1 Pe 4: 6 that they might be *j* according
Rev 11:18 the dead, that they should be *j*,
16: 5 Because You have *j* these
19: 2 because He has *j* the great
20:12 And the dead were *j* according
20:13 were in them. And they were *j*,

JUDGES (69/67) JUDGE

Ex 21: 6 master shall bring him to the *j*.
21:22 and he shall pay as the *j*
22: 8 shall be brought to the *j* to
22: 9 parties shall come before the *j*;
22: 9 and whomever the *j* condemn
Num 25: 5 So Moses said to the *j* of
Deut 1:16 Then I commanded your *j* at that
16:18 You shall appoint *j* and
19:17 before the priests and the *j*
19:18 And the *j* shall make careful
21: 2 then your elders and your *j*
25: 1 that the *j* may judge them,
32:31 our enemies themselves being *j*.
Josh 8:33 their elders and officers and *j*,
23: 2 for their heads, for their *j*,
24: 1 for their heads, for their *j*,
Judg 2:16 the LORD raised up *j* who
2:17 would not listen to their *j*,
2:18 And when the LORD raised up *j*
Ruth 1: 1 in the days when the *j* ruled,
1 Sam 8: 1 was old that he made his sons *j*
8: 2 they were *j* in Beersheba.
2 Sam 7:11 the time that I commanded *j*
2 Ki 23:22 held since the days of the *j*
1 Chr 17: 6 spoken a word to any of the *j*
17:10 the time that I commanded *j*
23: 4 thousand were officers and *j*,
26:29 duties as officials and *j* over
2 Chr 1: 2 and of hundreds, to the *j*,
19: 5 Then he set *j* in the land
19: 6 and said to the *j*, "Take
Ezra 7:25 set magistrates and *j* who may
10:14 together with the elders and *j*
Job 9:24 He covers the faces of its *j*.
12:17 And makes fools of the *j*.
21:22 Since He *j* those on high?
36:31 For by these He *j* the peoples;
Ps 2:10 you *j* of the earth.
58:11 Surely He is God who *j* in the
82: 1 He *j* among the gods.
141: 6 Their *j* are overthrown by the
148:11 Princes and all *j* of the
Prov 8:16 All the *j* of the earth.
29:14 The king who *j* the poor with
Isa 1:26 I will restore your *j* as at the
40:23 He makes the *j* of the earth
Ezek 44:24 they shall stand as *j*,
Dan 3: 2 the treasurers, the *j*,
3: 3 the treasurers, the *j*,
9:12 against us and against our *j*
Hos 7: 7 And have devoured their *j*;
13:10 And your *j* to whom you said,
Zeph 3: 3 Her *j* are evening wolves
Mt 12:27 Therefore they shall be your *j*.
Lk 11:19 Therefore they will be your *j*.
Jn 5:22 For the Father *j* no one, but has
8:50 there is One who seeks and *j*.
12:48 has that which *j* him—the word
Acts 13:20 After that He gave them *j* for
1 Cor 2:15 But he who is spiritual *j* all
4: 4 but He who *j* me is the Lord.
5:13 But those who are outside God *j*.
Jas 2: 4 and become *j* with evil
4:11 speaks evil of a brother and *j*
4:11 speaks evil of the law and *j*
1 Pe 1:17 who without partiality *j*
2:23 committed Himself to Him who *j*
Rev 18: 8 strong is the Lord God who *j*
19:11 and in righteousness He *j* and

JUDGES' (1/1)

Judg 5:10 Who sit in *j* attire, And who

JUDGING (8/8) JUDGE

Judg 4: 4 was *j* Israel at that time.
2 Ki 15: 5 *j* the people of the land.
2 Chr 26:21 *j* the people of the land.
Ps 9: 4 You sat on the throne *j* in
Isa 16: 5 *J* and seeking justice and
Mt 19:28 *j* the twelve tribes of Israel.
Lk 22:30 and sit on thrones *j* the twelve
1 Cor 5:12 For what have I to do with *j*

JUDGMENT (190/186) JUDGE, JUDGMENTS

Ex 12:12 gods of Egypt I will execute *j*:
21:31 according to this *j* it shall be
23: 6 You shall not pervert the *j* of
28:15 shall make the breastplate of *j*
28:29 Israel on the breastplate of *j*
28:30 put in the breastplate of *j*
28:30 So Aaron shall bear the *j* of
Lev 19:15 shall do no injustice in *j*.
19:35 shall do no injustice in *j*,
Num 27:11 of Israel a statute of *j*,
27:21 the LORD for him by the *j* of
35:12 before the congregation in *j*.
35:29 shall be a statute of *j* to you
Deut 1:17 shall not show partiality in *j*;
1:17 for the *j* is God's. The case
16:18 judge the people with just *j*.
17: 8 between one *j* or another, or
17: 9 upon you the sentence of *j*.
17:11 according to the *j* which they
32:41 And My hand takes hold on *j*,
Josh 20: 6 before the congregation for *j*,
Judg 4: 5 of Israel came up to her for *j*.
11:27 render *j* this day between the
2 Sam 8:15 and David administered *j* and
15: 6 who came to the king for *j*.
1 Ki 3:28 And all Israel heard of the *j*
7: 7 for the throne, the Hall of *J*,
20:40 'So shall your *j* be;
2 Ki 25: 6 and they pronounced *j* on him.
1 Chr 12:17 of our fathers look and bring *j*.
18:14 and administered *j* and justice
2 Chr 19: 6 who is with you in the *j*.
19: 8 for the *j* of the LORD and for
20: 9 disaster comes upon us—sword, *j*,
22: 8 when Jehu was executing *j* on
24:24 So they executed *j* against
Ezra 7:26 let *j* be executed speedily on
Job 8: 3 Does God subvert *j*?
11:10 imprisons, and gathers to *j*,
14: 3 And bring me to *j* with
19:29 you may know there is a *j*.
22: 4 And enters into *j* with you?
31:11 be iniquity deserving of *j*.
31:28 an iniquity deserving of *j*,
34:23 he should go before God in *j*.
36:17 But you are filled with the *j*
36:17 *J* and justice take hold of
37:23 In *j* and abundant justice;
40: 8 "Would you indeed annul My *j*?
Ps 1: 5 shall not stand in the *j*,
7: 6 Rise up for me to the *j* You
9: 7 has prepared His throne for *j*.
9: 8 And He shall administer *j* for
9:16 The LORD is known by the *j* He
76: 8 You caused *j* to be heard from
76: 9 When God arose to *j*,
94:15 But *j* will return to
119:66 Teach me good *j* and knowledge,
119:84 When will You execute *j* on
122: 5 thrones are set there for *j*,
143: 2 Do not enter into *j* with Your
149: 9 execute on them the written *j*—
Prov 1: 3 of wisdom, Justice, *j*,
16:10 mouth must not transgress in *j*.
18: 1 He rages against all wise *j*.
18: 5 to overthrow the righteous in *j*.
20: 8 who sits on the throne of *j*
24:23 good to show partiality in *j*.
Eccl 3:16 the sun: In the place of *j*,
8: 5 heart discerns both time and *j*,
8: 6 matter there is a time and *j*,
11: 9 God will bring you into *j*.
12:14 will bring every work into *j*,
Isa 3:14 The LORD will enter into *j*
4: 4 by the spirit of *j* and by the
5:16 of hosts shall be exalted in *j*,
9: 7 it and establish it with *j* and
16: 3 "Take counsel, execute *j*;
28: 6 of justice to him who sits in *j*,
28: 7 in vision, they stumble in *j*.
28:26 He instructs him in right *j*,
34: 5 the people of My curse, for *j*.
41: 1 us come near together for *j*.
53: 8 taken from prison and from *j*,
54:17 which rises against you in *j*
Jer 4: 2 LORD lives,' In truth, in *j*,
4:12 Now I will also speak *j*
5: 1 there is anyone who executes *j*,
5: 4 The *j* of their God.
5: 5 The *j* of their God."
7: 5 if you thoroughly execute *j*
8: 7 My people do not know the *j* of
9:24 exercising lovingkindness, *j*,
21:12 'Execute *j* in the morning;
22: 3 Execute *j* and righteousness, and
23: 5 And execute *j* and
33:15 He shall execute *j* and
39: 5 where he pronounced *j* on him.
48:21 And *j* has come on the plain
48:47 Thus far is the *j* of Moab.
49:12 those whose *j* was not to drink
51: 9 For her *j* reaches to heaven
51:47 coming That I will bring *j* on
51:52 That I will bring *j* on her
52: 9 and he pronounced *j* on him.
Ezek 18: 8 iniquity And executed true *j*
23:10 For they had executed *j* on
23:24 I will delegate *j* to them, And
34:16 the strong, and feed them in *j*.
38:22 And I will bring him to *j* with
39:21 all the nations shall see My *j*
Dan 7:22 and a *j* was made in favor of
Hos 5: 1 the king! For yours is the *j*,
5:11 is oppressed and broken in *j*,
10: 4 Thus *j* springs up like hemlock
Joel 3: 2 And I will enter into *j* with
Hab 1: 4 Therefore perverse *j* proceeds.
1: 7 Their *j* and their dignity
1:12 You have appointed them for *j*;
Zech 8:16 Give *j* in your gates for
Mal 3: 5 And I will come near you for *j*;
Mt 5:21 will be in danger of the *j*.
5:22 shall be in danger of the *j*.
7: 2 For with what *j* you judge, you
10:15 and Gomorrah in the day of *j*

11:22 Tyre and Sidon in the day of *j*
11:24 land of Sodom in the day of *j*
12:36 account of it in the day of *j*.
12:41 Nineveh will rise up in the *j*
12:42 the South will rise up in the *j*
27:19 While he was sitting on the *j*
Mk 6:11 and Gomorrah in the day of *j*
Lk 10:14 for Tyre and Sidon at the *j*
11:31 the South will rise up in the *j*
11:32 Nineveh will rise up in the *j*
Jn 5:22 but has committed all *j* to the
5:24 life, and shall not come into *j*,
5:27 Him authority to execute *j*
5:30 and My *j* is righteous, because
7:24 but judge with righteous *j*.
8:16 My *j* is true; for I am not
9:39 For *j* I have come into this
12:31 'Now is the *j* of this world;
16: 8 and of righteousness, and of *j*:
16:11 'of *j*, because the ruler of
19:13 out and sat down in the *j* seat
Acts 18:12 Paul and brought him to the *j*
18:16 And he drove them from the *j*
18:17 and beat him before the *j*
24:25 and the *j* to come, Felix was
25: 6 sitting on the *j* seat, he
25:10 I stand at Caesar's *j* seat,
25:15 asking for a *j* against him.
25:17 the next day I sat on the *j*
Rom 1:32 knowing the righteous *j* of God,
2: 2 But we know that the *j* of God is
2: 3 that you will escape the *j* of
2: 5 revelation of the righteous *j*
5:16 For the *j* which came from one
5:18 as through one man's offense *j*
13: 2 those who resist will bring *j*
14:10 we shall all stand before the *j*
1 Cor 1:10 the same mind and in the same *j*.
7:25 yet I give *j* as one whom the
7:40 as she is, according to my *j*—
11:29 manner eats and drinks *j* to
11:34 lest you come together for *j*.
2 Cor 5:10 we must all appear before the *j*
Gal 5:10 troubles you shall bear his *j*,
2 Th 1: 5 evidence of the righteous *j* of
1 Tim 5:24 evident, preceding them to *j*,
Heb 6: 2 of the dead, and of eternal *j*.
9:27 die once, but after this the *j*,
10:27 fearful expectation of *j*,
Jas 2:13 For *j* is without mercy to the
2:13 no mercy. Mercy triumphs over *j*.
3: 1 we shall receive a stricter *j*.
5:12 "No," lest you fall into *j*.
1 Pe 4:17 For the time has come for *j* to
2 Pe 2: 3 for a long time their *j* has not
2: 4 darkness, to be reserved for *j*;
2: 9 punishment for the day of *j*,
3: 7 for fire until the day of *j*
1 Jn 4:17 have boldness in the day of *j*;
Jude 6 under darkness for the *j* of
15 to execute *j* on all, to convict
Rev 14: 7 for the hour of His *j* has come;
17: 1 I will show you the *j* of the
18:10 For in one hour your *j* has
20: 4 and *j* was committed to them.

JUDGMENTS (122/120) JUDGMENT

Ex 6: 6 arm and with great *j*.
7: 4 of the land of Egypt by great *j*.
21: 1 Now these are the *j* which you
24: 3 of the LORD and all the *j*.
Lev 18: 4 You shall observe My *j* and keep
18: 5 keep My statutes and My *j*,
18:26 keep My statutes and My *j*,
19:37 all My statutes and all My *j*,
20:22 all My statutes and all My *j*,
25:18 My statutes and keep My *j*,
26:15 or if your soul abhors My *j*,
26:43 because they despised My *j* and
26:46 These are the statutes and *j*
Num 33: 4 gods the LORD had executed *j*.
35:24 of blood according to these *j*.
36:13 are the commandments and the *j*
Deut 4: 1 to the statutes and the *j*
4: 5 have taught you statutes and *j*,
4: 8 such statutes and righteous *j*
4:14 to teach you statutes and *j*,
4:45 and the *j* which Moses spoke to
5: 1 the statutes and *j* which I
5:31 and the *j* which you shall teach
6: 1 these are the statutes and *j*
6:20 and the *j* which the LORD our
7:11 and the *j* which I command you
7:12 because you listen to these *j*,
8:11 keeping His commandments, His *j*,
11: 1 His charge, His statutes, His *j*,
11:32 observe all the statutes and *j*
12: 1 These are the statutes and *j*
26:16 to observe these statutes and *j*;
26:17 His commandments, and His *j*,
30:16 His statutes, and His *j*,
33:10 They shall teach Jacob Your *j*,
33:21 And His *j* with Israel."
2 Sam 22:23 For all His *j* were before me;
1 Ki 2: 3 His commandments, His *j*,
6:12 in My statutes, execute My *j*,
8:58 and His statutes and His *j*,
9: 4 you keep My statutes and My *j*,
11:33 and keep My statutes and My *j*,
1 Chr 16:12 and the *j* of His mouth,
16:14 His *j* are in all the earth.
22:13 to fulfill the statutes and *j*
28: 7 My commandments and My *j*,
2 Chr 7:17 you keep My statutes and My *j*,
Neh 9:29 But sinned against Your *j*,
Ps 10: 5 Your *j* are far above, out of
18:22 For all His *j* were before me,
19: 9 The *j* of the LORD are true
36: 6 Your *j* are a great deep;
48:11 be glad, Because of Your *j*.
72: 1 Give the king Your *j*,
89:30 My law And do not walk in My *j*,
97: 8 rejoice Because of Your *j*,
105: 5 and the *j* of His mouth,
105: 7 His *j* are in all the earth.
119: 7 When I learn Your righteous *j*.
119:13 I have declared All the *j* of
119:20 with longing For Your *j* at
119:30 Your *j* I have laid before
119:39 For Your *j* are good.
119:52 I remembered Your *j* of old,
119:62 Because of Your righteous *j*.
119:75 that Your *j* are right, And
119:102 have not departed from Your *j*,
119:106 I will keep Your righteous *j*.
119:108 O LORD, And teach me Your *j*.
119:120 You, And I am afraid of Your *j*.
119:137 LORD, And upright are Your *j*.
119:156 Revive me according to Your *j*.
119:160 every one of Your righteous *j*
119:164 Because of Your righteous *j*.
119:175 And let Your *j* help me.
147:19 His statutes and His *j* to
147:20 nation; And as for His *j*,
Prov 19:29 *J* are prepared for scoffers,
Isa 26: 8 Yes, in the way of Your *j*,
26: 9 For when Your *j* are in the
Jer 1:16 I will utter My *j* Against them
12: 1 me talk with You about Your *j*.
Ezek 5: 6 She has rebelled against My *j* by
5: 6 for they have refused My *j*,
5: 7 in My statutes nor kept My *j*,
5: 7 even done according to the *j*
5: 8 against you and will execute *j*
5:10 and I will execute *j* among you,
5:15 when I execute *j* among you in
11: 9 and execute *j* on you.
11:12 My statutes nor executed My *j*,
11:20 in My statutes and keep My *j*
14:21 be when I send My four severe *j*
16:41 and execute *j* on you in the
18: 9 in My statutes And kept My *j*
18:17 But has executed My *j* And
20:11 statutes and showed them My *j*,
20:13 My statutes; they despised My *j*,
20:16 because they despised My *j* and
20:18 fathers, nor observe their *j*,
20:19 Walk in My statutes, keep My *j*,
20:21 not careful to observe My *j*,
20:24 they had not executed My *j*,
20:25 and *j* by which they could not
23:24 judge you according to their *j*.
25:11 And I will execute *j* upon Moab,
28:22 When I execute *j* in her and am
28:26 when I execute *j* on all those
30:14 And execute *j* in No.
30:19 Thus I will execute *j* on Egypt,
36:27 and you will keep My *j* and do
37:24 they shall also walk in My *j*
44:24 and judge it according to My *j*.
Dan 9: 5 from Your precepts and Your *j*.
Hos 6: 5 And your *j* are like light
Zeph 3:15 LORD has taken away your *j*,
Mal 4: 4 With the statutes and *j*.
Rom 11:33 How unsearchable are His *j*
1 Cor 6: 4 If then you have *j* concerning
Rev 15: 4 For Your *j* have been
16: 7 true and righteous are Your *j*.
19: 2 true and righteous are His *j*,

JUDITH (1/1)

Gen 26:34 he took as wives *J* the daughter

JUG (4/4)

Judg 4:19 So she opened a *j* of milk,
1 Sam 26:11 take now the spear and the *j* of
26:12 David took the spear and the *j*
26:16 and the *j* of water that was by

JUICE (2/2)

Num 6: 3 shall he drink any grape *j*,
Song 8: 2 Of the *j* of my pomegranate.

JUICES (1/1)

Ex 22:29 of your ripe produce and your *j*.

JULIA (1/1)

Rom 16:15 Greet Philologus and *J*,

JULIUS (2/2)

Acts 27: 1 other prisoners to one named *J*,
27: 3 And *J* treated Paul kindly and

JUMP (1/1)

Acts 27:43 those who could swim should *j*

JUNIA (1/1)

Rom 16: 7 Greet Andronicus and *J*,

JUNIPER (1/1)

Jer 48: 6 your lives! And be like the *j*

JUPITER (KJV) See ZEUS

JURISDICTION (1/1)

Lk 23: 7 that He belonged to Herod's *j*,

JUSHAB-HESED (1/1)

1 Chr 3:20 Berechiah, Hasadiah, and *J*—

JUST (262/256) HONEST, JUSTICE, JUSTIFY, JUSTLY, UNJUST

Gen 6: 9 Noah was a *j* man, perfect in
27:19 I have done *j* as you told me;
32:31 *J* as he crossed over Penuel the
41:13 *j* as he interpreted for us, so
41:21 for they were *j* as ugly as at
50:12 So his sons did for him *j* as he
Ex 7: 6 *j* as the LORD commanded them,
7:10 *j* as the LORD commanded.
7:20 *j* as the LORD commanded.
8:19 *j* as the LORD had said.
9:12 *j* as the LORD had spoken to
12:25 *j* as He promised, that you
12:28 *j* as the LORD had commanded
25: 9 *j* so you shall make it.
39:43 *j* so they had done it.
Lev 16: 2 your brother not to come at *j*
Num 2:33 *j* as the LORD commanded Moses.
14:17 *j* as You have spoken, saying,
14:19 *j* as You have forgiven this
14:28 *j* as you have spoken in My
15:14 *j* as you do, so shall he do.
16:40 *j* as the LORD had said to him
17:11 *j* as the LORD had commanded
18:18 *j* as the wave breast and the
20:27 So Moses did *j* as the LORD
23: 2 And Balak did *j* as Balaam had
26: 4 *j* as the LORD commanded Moses
27:11 *j* as the LORD commanded Moses.
27:23 *j* as the LORD commanded by the
29:40 *j* as the LORD commanded Moses.
31: 7 *j* as the LORD commanded Moses,
32:27 *j* as my lord says."
36:10 *J* as the LORD commanded Moses,
Deut 1:41 *j* as the LORD our God
2:12 *j* as Israel did to the land of
2:14 *j* as the LORD had sworn to
2:22 *j* as He had done for the
2:29 *j* as the descendants of Esau who
4: 5 *j* as the LORD my God commanded
10: 5 *j* as the LORD commanded me."
10: 9 *j* as the LORD your God
11:25 *j* as He has said to you.
12:21 *j* as I have commanded you, and
12:22 *J* as the gazelle and the deer
13:17 *j* as He swore to your fathers,
15: 6 your God will bless you *j* as
16:18 shall judge the people with *j*
16:20 follow what is altogether *j*,
20:17 *j* as the LORD your God has
22:26 for *j* as when a man rises
24: 8 *j* as I commanded them, so you
25:15 shall have a perfect and *j*
25:15 a perfect and *j* measure, that
26:15 *j* as You swore to our fathers,
26:18 *j* as He promised you, that you
26:19 *j* as He has spoken."
27: 3 *j* as the LORD God of your
28: 9 *j* as He has sworn to you, if
28:63 that *j* as the LORD rejoiced
29:13 *j* as He has spoken to you, and
29:13 and *j* as He has sworn to your
31: 3 *j* as the LORD has said.
32:50 *j* as Aaron your brother died on
Josh 1:17 *J* as we heeded Moses in all
4: 8 *j* as Joshua commanded, and took
14:11 *j* as my strength was then, so
Judg 6:39 but let me speak *j* once more:
6:39 *j* once more with the fleece;
7:19 *j* as they had posted the watch;
13:10 to me the other day has *j* now
16:28 *j* this once, O God, that I may
19:16 *J* then an old man came in from
21:21 and *j* when the daughters of
1 Sam 9:12 *j* ahead of you. Hurry now; for
2 Sam 18:10 I *j* saw Absalom hanging in a
18:11 You *j* saw him! And why did you
18:31 *J* then the Cushite came, and the
19:14 *j* as the heart of one man,
19:41 *J* then all the men of Israel
23: 3 who rules over men must be *j*,
1 Ki 1:22 And *j* then, while she was still
1:30 *j* as I swore to you by the LORD
20: 4 *j* as you say, I and all that I
2 Ki 4: 3 do not gather *j* a few.
5:22 *j* now two young men of the sons
6:10 not *j* once or twice.
7:17 *j* as the man of God had said,
7:18 So it happened *j* as the man of
8:18 *j* as the house of Ahab had
1 Chr 24:31 These also cast lots *j* as their
24:31 The chief fathers did *j* as

26:12 having duties *j* like their
2 Chr 21: 6 *j* as the house of Ahab had
Neh 9:13 And gave them *j* ordinances and
9:33 However You are *j* in all that
Esth 2:20 *j* as Mordecai had charged her,
6: 4 Now Haman had *j* entered the
Job 12: 4 The *j* and blameless who is
27:17 but the *j* will wear it, And
29: 4 *J* as I was in the days of my
34:17 condemn Him who is most *j*?
34:33 *J* because you disavow it?
Ps 7: 9 to an end, But establish the *j*;
7:11 God is a *j* judge, And God is
17: 1 Hear a *j* cause, O LORD,
33:22 *J* as we hope in You.
37:12 The wicked plots against the *j*,
46: 5 *j* at the break of dawn.
51: 4 That You may be found *j* when
Prov 3:12 *J* as a father the son in
3:33 He blesses the home of the *j*.
4:18 But the path of the *j* is like
9: 9 Teach a *j* man, and he will
11: 1 But a *j* weight is His
17:15 and he who condemns the *j*,
21:15 It is a joy for the *j* to do
24:29 I will do to him *j* as he has
Eccl 5:16 *J* exactly as he came, so shall
7:15 There is a *j* man who perishes
7:20 For there is not a *j* man on
8:14 that there are *j* men to whom
Isa 20: 3 *J* as My servant Isaiah has
26: 7 The way of the *j* is
26: 7 You weigh the path of the *j*.
28: 9 Those *j* weaned from milk?
28: 9 Those *j* drawn from the
28:19 It will be a terror *j* to
29:21 And turn aside the *j* by empty
40:27 And my *j* claim is passed over
45:21 A *j* God and a Savior;
49: 4 Yet surely my *j* reward is
52:14 *J* as many were astonished at
66: 3 *J* as they have chosen their
Jer 5:19 *J* as you have forsaken Me and
13:10 shall be *j* like this sash which
32:42 *J* as I have brought all this
39:12 but do to him *j* as he says to
40: 3 and has done *j* as He said.
Lam 4:13 her midst The blood of the *j*.
Ezek 9:11 *J* then, the man clothed with
18: 5 But if a man is *j* And does
18: 9 judgments faithfully—He is *j*;
20:36 *J* as I pleaded My case with your
40:23 *j* as the eastern gateway;
41:25 on the doors of the temple *j*
Dan 2:41 *j* as you saw the iron mixed
2:43 *j* as iron does not mix with
Hos 3: 1 *j* like the love of the LORD
9:13 *J* as I saw Ephraim like Tyre,
Am 5:12 Afflicting the *j* and taking
Hab 2: 4 But the *j* shall live by his
Zech 1: 6 *J* as the LORD of hosts
7:13 that *j* as He proclaimed and
8:13 it shall come to pass That *j*
8:14 *J* as I determined to punish you
9: 9 He is *j* and having salvation,
Mt 1:19 being a *j* man, and not wanting
5:45 and sends rain on the *j* and on
5:48 *j* as your Father in heaven is
9:18 My daughter has *j* died, but come
13:49 the wicked from among the *j*,
18:33 *j* as I had pity on you?'
19: 3 man to divorce his wife for *j*
20:28 *j* as the Son of Man did not come
26:24 The Son of Man indeed goes *j* as
27:19 nothing to do with that *j*
27:24 of the blood of this *j* Person.
Mk 6:20 knowing that he was a *j* and
6:56 begged Him that they might *j*
11: 6 And they spoke to them *j* as
14:16 and found it *j* as He had said
14:21 The Son of Man indeed goes *j* as
15: 8 began to ask him to do *j* as
Lk 1: 2 *j* as those who from the
1:17 to the wisdom of the *j*,
2:25 and this man was *j* and devout,
5:14 *j* as Moses commanded."
6:31 And *j* as you want men to do to
6:36 *j* as your Father also is
9:54 them, *j* as Elijah did?"
14:14 at the resurrection of the *j*.
15: 7 repents than over ninety-nine *j*
19:32 went their way and found it *j*
22:13 So they went and found it *j* as
22:29 *j* as My Father bestowed one
23:50 member, a good and *j* man.
24:24 to the tomb and found it *j* as
Jn 5:23 all should honor the Son *j* as
8:25 *J* what I have been saying to you
12:50 *j* as the Father has told Me, so
15:10 *j* as I have kept My Father's
17:14 *j* as I am not of the world.
17:16 *j* as I am not of the world.
17:22 that they may be one *j* as We
21:10 of the fish which you have *j*
Acts 3:14 denied the Holy One and the *J*,
7:52 foretold the coming of the *J*
10:22 a *j* man, one who fears God and
10:47 received the Holy Spirit *j* as
15: 8 *j* as He did to us,
15:15 agree, *j* as it is written:
22:14 and see the *J* One, and hear the
24:15 both of the *j* and the unjust.
27:25 I believe God that it will be *j*
Rom 1:13 *j* as among the other Gentiles.
1:17 The *j* shall live by
2:13 the hearers of the law are *j*
3: 8 we say. Their condemnation is *j*.
3:26 that He might be *j* and the
4: 6 *j* as David also describes the
5:12 *j* as through one man sin
6: 4 that *j* as Christ was raised
6:19 For *j* as you presented your
7:12 and the commandment holy and *j*
11: 8 *J* as it is written: "God
15: 7 *j* as Christ also received us,
1 Cor 10:33 *j* as I also please all men in
11: 1 *j* as I also imitate Christ.
11: 2 and keep the traditions *j* as I
12:18 in the body *j* as He pleased.
13:12 but then I shall know *j* as I
2 Cor 3:18 *j* as by the Spirit of the Lord.
10: 7 that *j* as he is Christ's, even
11:12 to be regarded *j* as we are
Gal 3: 6 *j* as Abraham "believed God,
3:11 the *j* shall live by
5:21 *j* as I also told you in time
Eph 1: 4 *j* as He chose us in Him before
2: 3 wrath, *j* as the others.
4: 4 *j* as you were called in one
4:32 *j* as God in Christ forgave you.
5:24 *j* as the church is subject to
5:25 *j* as Christ also loved the
5:29 *j* as the Lord does the church.
Phil 1: 7 *j* as it is right for me to think
4: 8 noble, whatever things are *j*,
Col 4: 1 your bondservants what is *j*
1 Th 2: 7 *j* as a nursing mother
2:14 *j* as they did from the
3: 4 *j* as it happened, and you know.
3:12 *j* as we do to you,
4: 1 *j* as you received from us how
5:11 *j* as you also are doing.
2 Th 3: 1 *j* as it is with you,
Titus 1: 8 what is good, sober-minded, *j*,
Heb 2: 2 and disobedience received a *j*
5: 4 by God, *j* as Aaron was.
10:38 Now the *j* shall live by
12:23 to the spirits of *j* men made
Jas 5: 6 you have murdered the *j*;
1 Pe 3:18 the *j* for the unjust, that He
2 Pe 1:14 *j* as our Lord Jesus Christ
1 Jn 1: 9 He is faithful and *j* to forgive
2: 6 ought himself also to walk *j*
2:27 and *j* as it has taught you, you
3: 3 himself, *j* as He is pure.
3: 7 *j* as He is righteous.
3 Jn 2 *j* as your soul prospers.
3 *j* as you walk in the truth.
Rev 15: 3 *J* and true are Your ways,
16: 6 For it is their *j* due."
18: 6 Render to her *j* as she rendered

JUSTICE (130/129) JUST

Gen 18:19 to do righteousness and *j*,
Ex 23: 2 aside after many to pervert *j*.
Deut 10:18 He administers *j* for the
16:19 "You shall not pervert *j*;
24:17 You shall not pervert *j* due the
27:19 is the one who perverts the *j*
32: 4 For all His ways are *j*,
33:21 He administered the *j* of the
1 Sam 8: 3 took bribes, and perverted *j*.
2 Sam 8:15 administered judgment and *j* to
15: 4 to me; then I would give him *j*.
1 Ki 3:11 understanding to discern *j*,
3:28 God was in him to administer *j*.
10: 9 to do *j* and righteousness."
1 Chr 18:14 administered judgment and *j* to
2 Chr 9: 8 to do *j* and righteousness."
Esth 1:13 toward all who knew law and *j*,
Job 8: 3 Or does the Almighty pervert *j*?
9:19 He is strong; And if of *j*,
19: 7 I cry aloud, there is no *j*.
27: 2 lives, who has taken away my *j*,
29:14 My *j* was like a robe and a
32: 9 the aged always understand *j*.
34: 4 Let us choose *j* for ourselves;
34: 5 But God has taken away my *j*;
34:12 will the Almighty pervert *j*.
34:17 Should one who hates *j* govern?
35:14 Yet *j* is before Him, and you
36: 6 But gives *j* to the oppressed.
36:17 Judgment and *j* take hold of
37:23 In judgment and abundant *j*;
Ps 10:18 To do *j* to the fatherless and
25: 9 The humble He guides in *j*,
33: 5 He loves righteousness and *j*;
37: 6 And your *j* as the noonday.
37:28 For the LORD loves *j*,
37:30 And his tongue talks of *j*.
72: 2 And Your poor with *j*.
72: 4 He will bring *j* to the poor of
82: 3 Do *j* to the afflicted and
89:14 Righteousness and *j* are the
97: 2 Righteousness and *j* are the
99: 4 King's strength also loves *j*;
99: 4 You have executed *j* and
101: 1 I will sing of mercy and *j*;
103: 6 executes righteousness And *j*
106: 3 Blessed are those who keep *j*,
111: 7 of His hands are verity and *j*;
119:121 I have done *j* and
119:149 revive me according to Your *j*.
140:12 And *j* for the poor.
146: 7 Who executes *j* for the
Prov 1: 3 the instruction of wisdom, *J*,
2: 8 He guards the paths of *j*,
2: 9 understand righteousness and *j*,
8:15 reign, And rulers decree *j*.
8:20 In the midst of the paths of *j*,
13:23 And for lack of *j* there is
16: 8 Than vast revenues without *j*.
17:23 back To pervert the ways of *j*.
19:28 disreputable witness scorns *j*,
21: 3 To do righteousness and *j* Is
21: 7 Because they refuse to do *j*.
21:15 is a joy for the just to do *j*,
28: 5 Evil men do not understand *j*,
29: 4 king establishes the land by *j*,
29:26 But *j* for man comes from the
31: 5 And pervert the *j* of all the
Eccl 5: 8 and the violent perversion of *j*
Isa 1:17 Learn to do good; Seek *j*,
1:21 a harlot! It was full of *j*;
1:27 Zion shall be redeemed with *j*,
5: 7 He looked for *j*, but behold,
5:23 And take away *j* from the
9: 7 it with judgment and *j* From
10: 2 To rob the needy of *j*,
16: 5 Judging and seeking *j* and
28: 6 For a spirit of *j* to him who
28:17 Also I will make *j* the
30:18 For the LORD is a God of *j*;
32: 1 And princes will rule with *j*.
32: 7 Even when the needy speaks *j*.
32:16 Then *j* will dwell in the
33: 5 He has filled Zion with *j* and
40:14 taught Him in the path of *j*?
42: 1 He will bring forth *j* to the
42: 3 He will bring forth *j* for
42: 4 Till He has established *j* in
51: 4 And I will make My *j* rest
56: 1 Thus says the LORD: "Keep *j*,
58: 2 ask of Me the ordinances of *j*;
59: 4 No one calls for *j*,
59: 8 And there is no *j* in their
59: 9 Therefore *j* is far from us,
59:11 like doves; We look for *j*,
59:14 *J* is turned back, And
59:15 Him That there was no *j*.
61: 8 "For I, the LORD, love *j*;
Jer 10:24 LORD, correct me, but with *j*;
22:15 And do *j* and righteousness?
30:11 But I will correct you in *j*,
31:23 LORD bless you, O home of *j*,
50: 7 the LORD, the habitation of *j*,
Lam 3:35 To turn aside the *j* due a man
Ezek 45: 9 execute *j* and righteousness,
Dan 4:37 are truth, and His ways *j*.
Hos 2:19 to Me In righteousness and *j*,
12: 6 Observe mercy and *j*,
Am 5: 7 You who turn *j* to wormwood,
5:12 Diverting the poor from *j* at
5:15 Establish *j* in the gate.
5:24 But let *j* run down like water,
6:12 Yet you have turned *j* into
Mic 3: 1 Is it not for you to know *j*?
3: 8 And of *j* and might, To
3: 9 Who abhor *j* And pervert all
7: 9 pleads my case And executes *j*
Hab 1: 4 And *j* never goes forth.
Zeph 2: 3 earth, Who have upheld His *j*.
3: 5 Every morning He brings His *j*
Zech 7: 9 of hosts: 'Execute true *j*,
8:16 in your gates for truth, *j*,
Mal 2:17 Or, "Where is the God of *j*?
Mt 12:18 And He will declare *j* to
12:20 Till He sends forth *j* to
23:23 *j* and mercy and faith.
Lk 11:42 and pass by *j* and the love of
18: 3 Get *j* for me from my adversary.'
Acts 8:33 In His humiliation His *j*
28: 4 yet *j* does not allow to live."

JUSTIFICATION (3/3) JUSTIFY

Rom 4:25 and was raised because of our *j*.
5:16 many offenses resulted in *j*.
5:18 resulting in *j* of life.

JUSTIFIED (37/33) JUSTIFY

Job 32: 2 wrath was aroused because he *j*
40: 8 condemn Me that you may be *j*?
Isa 43: 9 witnesses, that they may be *j*;
45:25 of Israel Shall be *j*,
Ezek 16:51 and have *j* your sisters by all
16:52 because you *j* your sisters.
Mt 11:19 and sinners!' But wisdom is *j*
12:37 by your words you will be *j*,
Lk 7:29 even the tax collectors *j* God,
7:35 But wisdom is *j* by all her
18:14 man went down to his house *j*
Acts 13:39 Him everyone who believes is *j*
13:39 from which you could not be *j*
Rom 2:13 the doers of the law will be *j*;
3: 4 That You may be *j* in Your
3:20 of the law no flesh will be *j*
3:24 being *j* freely by His grace
3:28 we conclude that a man is *j* by
4: 2 For if Abraham was *j* by works,
5: 1 having been *j* by faith, we have
5: 9 having now been *j* by His blood,
8:30 whom He called, these He also *j*;
8:30 also justified; and whom He *j*,

J

1 Cor 4: 4 yet I am not *j* by this; but He
6:11 but you were *j* in the name of
Gal 2:16 knowing that a man is not *j* by
2:16 that we might be *j* by faith in
2:16 of the law no flesh shall be *j*.
2:17 while we seek to be *j* by
3:11 But that no one is *j* by the law
3:24 that we might be *j* by faith.
5: 4 you who attempt to be *j* by
1 Tim 3:16 *J* in the Spirit, Seen by
Titus 3: 7 that having been *j* by His grace
Jas 2:21 Was not Abraham our father *j* by
2:24 You see then that a man is *j* by
2:25 not Rahab the harlot also *j* by

JUSTIFIER (1/1) JUSTIFY

Rom 3:26 He might be just and the *j* of

JUSTIFIES (4/4) JUSTIFY

Prov 17:15 He who *j* the wicked, and he who
Isa 50: 8 He is near who *j* Me;
Rom 4: 5 work but believes on Him who *j*
8:33 God's elect? It is God who *j*.

JUSTIFY (9/9) JUST, JUSTIFICATION, JUSTIFIED, JUSTIFIER, JUSTIFIES

Ex 23: 7 For I will not *j* the wicked.
Deut 25: 1 and they *j* the righteous and
Job 33:32 for I desire to *j* you.
Isa 5:23 Who *j* the wicked for a bribe,
53:11 My righteous Servant shall *j*
Lk 10:29 wanting to *j* himself, said to
16:15 You are those who *j* yourselves
Rom 3:30 there is one God who will *j*
Gal 3: 8 foreseeing that God would *j* the

JUSTIFYING (2/2)

1 Ki 8:32 and *j* the righteous by giving
2 Chr 6:23 and *j* the righteous by giving

JUSTLE (KJV) See JOSTLE

JUSTLY (3/3) JUST

Mic 6: 8 require of you But to do *j*,
Lk 23:41 'And we indeed *j*, for we
1 Th 2:10 how devoutly and *j* and

JUSTUS (3/3) BARSABAS, JESUS

Acts 1:23 Barsabas, who was surnamed *J*,
18: 7 house of a certain man named *J*,
Col 4:11 and Jesus who is called *J*.

JUTTAH (2/2)

Josh 15:55 Maon, Carmel, Ziph, *J*,
21:16 *J* with its common-land, and

K

KAB (1/1)

2 Ki 6:25 and one-fourth of a *k* of dove

KABZEEL (3/3)

Josh 15:21 of Edom in the South, were *K*,
2 Sam 23:20 the son of a valiant man from *K*,
1 Chr 11:22 the son of a valiant man from *K*,

KADESH (18/18) KADESH BARNEA, KEDESH

Gen 14: 7 to En Mishpat (that is, *K*),
16:14 it is between *K* and Bered.
20: 1 and dwelt between *K* and Shur,
Num 13:26 the Wilderness of Paran, at *K*;
20: 1 and the people stayed in *K*;
20:14 Moses sent messengers from *K*
20:16 of Egypt; now here we are in *K*,
20:22 journeyed from *K* and came to
27:14 at *K* in the Wilderness of Zin.)
33:36 Wilderness of Zin, which is *K*.
33:37 They moved from *K* and camped at
Deut 1:46 So you remained in *K* many days,
32:51 at the waters of Meribah *K*,
Judg 11:16 as the Red Sea and came to *K*.
11:17 So Israel remained in *K*.
Ps 29: 8 shakes the Wilderness of *K*.
Ezek 47:19 to the waters of Meribah by *K*,
48:28 to the waters of Meribah by *K*,

KADESH BARNEA (10/10) KADESH

Num 32: 8 when I sent them away from *K*
34: 4 Zin, and be on the south of *K*;
Deut 1: 2 Horeb by way of Mount Seir to *K*.
1:19 commanded us. Then we came to *K*.
2:14 the time we took to come from *K*
9:23 when the LORD sent you from *K*,
Josh 10:41 Joshua conquered them from *K*
14: 6 God concerning you and me in *K*.
14: 7 of the LORD sent me from *K* to
15: 3 ascended on the south side of *K*,

KADMIEL (8/8)

Ezra 2:40 the sons of Jeshua and *K*,
3: 9 *K* with his sons, and the sons
Neh 7:43 the sons of Jeshua, of *K*,
9: 4 Then Jeshua, Bani, *K*,
9: 5 And the Levites, Jeshua, *K*,
10: 9 of the sons of Henadad, and *K*.
12: 8 Levites were Jeshua, Binnui, *K*,
12:24 and Jeshua the son of *K*,

KADMONITES (1/1)

Gen 15:19 Kenites, the Kenezzites, the *K*,

KAIN (2/2)

Num 24:22 Nevertheless *K* shall be burned.
Josh 15:57 *K*, Gibeah, and Timnah:

KALLAI (1/1)

Neh 12:20 of Sallai, *K*; of Amok, Eber;

KAMAI (1/1)

Jer 51: 1 those who dwell in Leb *K*,

KANAH (3/3)

Josh 16: 8 Tappuah westward to the Brook *K*,
17: 9 border descended to the Brook *K*,
19:28 Ebron, Rehob, Hammon, and *K*,

KAREAH (13/13)

Jer 40: 8 and Jonathan the sons of *K*,
40:13 Moreover Johanan the son of *K*
40:15 Then Johanan the son of *K* spoke
40:16 said to Johanan the son of *K*,
41:11 But when Johanan the son of *K*
41:13 saw Johanan the son of *K*,
41:14 went to Johanan the son of *K*.
41:16 Then Johanan the son of *K*,
42: 1 forces, Johanan the son of *K*,
42: 8 he called Johanan the son of *K*,
43: 2 Hoshaiah, Johanan the son of *K*,
43: 4 So Johanan the son of *K*,
43: 5 But Johanan the son of *K* and all

KARKAA (1/1)

Josh 15: 3 to Adar, and went around to *K*.

KARKOR (1/1)

Judg 8:10 Zebah and Zalmunna were at *K*,

KARNAIM (2/2) ASHTEROTH

Gen 14: 5 the Rephaim in Ashteroth *K*,
Am 6:13 Have we not taken *K* for

KARTAH (1/1)

Josh 21:34 *K* with its common-land,

KARTAN (1/1)

Josh 21:32 and *K* with its common-land:

KATTATH (1/1)

Josh 19:15 Included were *K*, Nahallal,

KEDAR (12/11)

Gen 25:13 of Ishmael, Nebajoth; then *K*,
1 Chr 1:29 Ishmael was Nebajoth; then *K*,
Ps 120: 5 I dwell among the tents of *K*!
Song 1: 5 Jerusalem, Like the tents of *K*,
Isa 21:16 all the glory of *K* will fail;
21:17 mighty men of the people of *K*,
42:11 The villages that *K* inhabits.
60: 7 All the flocks of *K* shall be
Jer 2:10 Send to *K* and consider
49:28 Against *K* and against the
49:28 LORD: "Arise, go up to *K*,
Ezek 27:21 and all the princes of *K* were

KEDEMAH (2/2)

Gen 25:15 Tema, Jetur, Naphish, and *K*.
1 Chr 1:31 Jetur, Naphish, and *K*.

KEDEMOTH (4/4)

Deut 2:26 from the Wilderness of *K* to
Josh 13:18 Jahaza, *K*, Mephaath,
21:37 *K* with its common-land, and
1 Chr 6:79 *K* with its common-lands, and

KEDESH (12/12) KADESH, KISHION

Josh 12:22 the king of *K*, one; the king
15:23 *K*, Hazor, Ithnan,
19:37 *K*, Edrei, En Hazor,
20: 7 So they appointed *K* in Galilee,
21:32 *K* in Galilee with its
Judg 4: 6 the son of Abinoam from *K* in
4: 9 arose and went with Barak to *K*.
4:10 Zebulun and Naphtali to *K*;
4:11 at Zaanaim, which is beside *K*.
2 Ki 15:29 Abel Beth Maachah, Janoah, *K*,
1 Chr 6:72 *K* with its common-lands,
6:76 *K* in Galilee with its

KEEP (371/362) KEEPER, KEEPING, KEEPS, KEPT

Gen 2:15 garden of Eden to tend and *k*
6:19 to *k* them alive with you; they
6:20 kind will come to you to *k*
7: 3 to *k* the species alive on the
17: 9 you shall *k* My covenant, you
17:10 My covenant which you shall *k*,
18:19 that they *k* the way of the
28:15 I am with you and will *k* you
28:20 and *k* me in this way that I am
30:31 I will again feed and *k* your
33: 9 *k* what you have for yourself."
41:35 and let them *k* food in the
Ex 6: 5 of Israel whom the Egyptians *k*
12: 6 Now you shall *k* it until the
12:14 and you shall *k* it as a feast
12:14 You shall *k* it as a feast by an
12:25 that you shall *k* this service.
12:47 congregation of Israel shall *k*
12:48 with you and wants to *k* the
12:48 then let him come near and *k*
13: 5 that you shall *k* this service
13:10 You shall therefore *k* this
15:26 ear to His commandments and *k*
16:28 How long do you refuse to *k* My
19: 5 indeed obey My voice and *k* My
20: 6 to those who love Me and *k* My
20: 8 Sabbath day, to *k* it holy.
22: 7 neighbor money or articles to *k*,
22:10 ox, a sheep, or any animal to *k*,
23: 7 *K* yourself far from a false
23:14 Three times you shall *k* a feast
23:15 You shall *k* the Feast of
23:20 I send an Angel before you to *k*
31:13 'Surely My Sabbaths you shall *k*,
31:14 You shall *k* the Sabbath,
31:16 the children of Israel shall *k*
34:18 of Unleavened Bread you shall *k*.
Lev 8:35 and *k* the charge of the LORD,
18: 4 observe My judgments and *k* My
18: 5 You shall therefore *k* My
18:26 You shall therefore *k* My
18:30 Therefore you shall *k* My
19: 3 and *k* My Sabbaths: I am the
19:19 You shall *k* My statutes. You
19:30 You shall *k* My Sabbaths and
20: 8 And you shall *k* My statutes,
20:22 You shall therefore *k* all My
22: 9 They shall therefore *k* My
22:31 Therefore you shall *k* My
23:39 you shall *k* the feast of the
23:41 You shall *k* it as a feast to the
25: 2 then the land shall *k* a sabbath
25:18 observe My statutes and *k* My
26: 2 You shall *k* My Sabbaths and
26: 3 you walk in My statutes and *k*
Num 1:53 and the Levites shall *k* charge
6:24 The LORD bless you and *k* you;
9: 2 Let the children of Israel *k* the
9: 3 you shall *k* it at its appointed
9: 3 and ceremonies you shall *k* it.
9: 4 of Israel that they should *k*
9: 6 so that they could not *k* the
9:10 he may still *k* the LORD's
9:11 they may *k* it. They shall eat
9:12 of the Passover they shall *k*
9:13 and ceases to *k* the Passover,
9:14 and would *k* the LORD's
16:13 that you should *k* acting like a
29:12 and you shall *k* a feast to the
31:18 But *k* alive for yourselves all
31:30 give them to the Levites who *k*
36: 7 the children of Israel shall *k*
36: 9 the children of Israel shall *k*
Deut 2:27 I will *k* strictly to the road,
4: 2 that you may *k* the commandments
4: 9 and diligently *k* yourself, lest
4:40 You shall therefore *k* His
5:10 to those who love Me and *k* My
5:12 to *k* it holy, as the LORD your
5:15 your God commanded you to *k*
5:29 would fear Me and always *k* all
6: 2 to *k* all His statutes and His
6:17 You shall diligently *k* the
7: 8 and because He would *k* the oath
7: 9 with those who love Him and *k*
7:11 Therefore you shall *k* the
7:12 and *k* and do them, that the
7:12 that the LORD your God will *k*
8: 2 whether you would *k* His
8: 6 Therefore you shall *k* the
10:13 and to *k* the commandments of
11: 1 and *k* His charge, His statutes,
11: 8 Therefore you shall *k* every
11:22 For if you carefully *k* all
13: 4 and *k* His commandments and obey
13:18 to *k* all His commandments which
16: 1 and *k* the Passover to the LORD
16:10 Then you shall *k* the Feast of
16:15 Seven days you shall *k* a sacred
19: 9 and if you *k* all these
23: 9 then *k* yourself from every
23:23 from your lips you shall *k* and
24:12 you shall not *k* his pledge
26:17 you will walk in His ways and *k*
26:18 that you should *k* all His
27: 1 *K* all the commandments which I
28: 9 if you *k* the commandments of

28:45 to ***k*** His commandments and His
29: 9 Therefore ***k*** the words of this
30:10 to ***k*** His commandments and His
30:16 and to ***k*** His commandments, His
Josh 22: 5 to ***k*** His commandments, to hold
23: 6 be very courageous to ***k*** and to
Judg 2:22 whether they will ***k*** the ways of
3:19 ***K*** silence!" And all who
1 Sam 7: 1 Eleazar his son to ***k*** the ark
17:34 Your servant used to ***k*** his
2 Sam 15:16 concubines, to ***k*** the house.
16:21 whom he has left to ***k*** the
18:18 I have no son to ***k*** my name in
20: 3 whom he had left to ***k*** the
1 Ki 2: 3 And ***k*** the charge of the LORD
2: 3 to ***k*** His statutes, His
3:14 to ***k*** My statutes and My
6:12 ***k*** all My commandments, and walk
8:23 who ***k*** Your covenant and mercy
8:25 now ***k*** what You promised Your
8:58 and to ***k*** His commandments and
8:61 to walk in His statutes and ***k***
9: 4 and if you ***k*** My statutes and
9: 6 and do not ***k*** My commandments
11:10 but he did not ***k*** what the LORD
11:33 is right in My eyes and ***k*** My
11:38 to ***k*** My statutes and My
18: 5 perhaps we may find grass to ***k***
2 Ki 2: 3 'Yes, I know; ***k*** silent!"
2: 5 'Yes, I know; ***k*** silent!"
7: 4 If they ***k*** us alive, we shall
11: 6 You shall ***k*** the watch of the
11: 7 off duty on the Sabbath shall ***k***
17:13 and ***k*** My commandments and My
17:19 Also Judah did not ***k*** the
23: 3 to follow the LORD and to ***k***
23:21 ***K*** the Passover to the LORD your
1 Chr 4:10 and that You would ***k*** me from
10:13 because he did not ***k*** the word
12:33 stouthearted men who could ***k***
12:35 of the Danites who could ***k***
12:36 able to ***k*** battle formation,
12:38 who could ***k*** ranks, came to
22:12 that you may ***k*** the law of the
29:18 ***k*** this forever in the intent of
29:19 son Solomon a loyal heart to ***k***
2 Chr 6:14 who ***k*** Your covenant and mercy
6:16 now ***k*** what You promised Your
7:17 and if you ***k*** My statutes and My
13:11 for we ***k*** the command of the
23: 6 but all the people shall ***k*** the
30: 1 to ***k*** the Passover to the LORD
30: 2 in Jerusalem had agreed to ***k***
30: 3 For they could not ***k*** it at the
30: 5 that they should come to ***k*** the
30:13 gathered at Jerusalem to ***k*** the
30:23 the whole assembly agreed to ***k***
34:31 and to ***k*** His commandments and
35:16 to ***k*** the Passover and to offer
Ezra 6: 6 ***k*** yourselves far from there.
8:29 Watch and ***k*** them until you
Neh 1: 5 You who ***k*** Your covenant and
1: 9 and ***k*** My commandments and do
Esth 3: 8 and they do not ***k*** the king's
Job 21: 3 I have spoken, ***k*** mocking.
22:15 Will you ***k*** to the old way
30:10 they ***k*** far from me; They do
36:19 ***K*** you from distress?
Ps 12: 7 You shall ***k*** them, O LORD, You
17: 8 ***K*** me as the apple of Your eye
19:13 ***K*** back Your servant also from
22:29 Even he who cannot ***k*** himself
25:10 To such as ***k*** His covenant and
25:20 ***K*** my soul, and deliver me
31:20 You shall ***k*** them secretly in a
33:19 And to ***k*** them alive in famine.
34:13 ***K*** your tongue from evil, And
35:22 Do not ***k*** silence. O Lord, do
37:34 And ***k*** His way, And He shall
41: 2 LORD will preserve him and ***k***
50: 3 and shall not ***k*** silent; A fire
78: 7 But ***k*** His commandments;
78:10 They did not ***k*** the covenant of
78:56 And did not ***k*** His testimonies,
83: 1 Do not ***k*** silent, O God! Do not
89:28 My mercy I will ***k*** for him
89:31 My statutes And do not ***k*** My
91:11 To ***k*** you in all your ways.
103: 9 Nor will He ***k*** His anger
103:18 To such as ***k*** His covenant, And
105:45 observe His statutes And ***k***
106: 3 Blessed are those who ***k***
109: 1 Do not ***k*** silent, O God of my
119: 2 Blessed are those who ***k*** His
119: 4 You have commanded us To ***k***
119: 5 my ways were directed To ***k***
119: 8 I will ***k*** Your statutes; Oh, do
119:17 That I may live and ***k*** Your
119:33 And I shall ***k*** it to the end.
119:34 and I shall ***k*** Your law;
119:44 So shall I ***k*** Your law
119:55 And I ***k*** Your law.
119:57 I have said that I would ***k***
119:60 and did not delay To ***k*** Your
119:63 And of those who ***k*** Your
119:67 But now I ***k*** Your word.
119:69 But I will ***k*** Your precepts
119:88 So that I may ***k*** the testimony
119:100 Because I ***k*** Your precepts.
119:101 That I may ***k*** Your word.
119:106 and confirmed That I will ***k***
119:115 For I will ***k*** the commandments
119:134 That I may ***k*** Your precepts.
119:136 Because men do not ***k*** Your
119:145 O LORD! I will ***k*** Your
119:146 and I will ***k*** Your testimonies.
119:158 Because they do not ***k*** Your
119:168 I ***k*** Your precepts and Your
132:12 If your sons will ***k*** My covenant
140: 4 ***K*** me, O LORD, from the hands
141: 3 ***K*** watch over the door of my
141: 9 ***K*** me from the snares they have
Prov 1:15 ***K*** your foot from their path;
2:11 Understanding will ***k*** you,
2:20 And ***k*** to the paths of
3: 1 But let your heart ***k*** my
3:21 ***K*** sound wisdom and discretion;
3:26 And will ***k*** your foot from
4: 4 ***K*** my commands, and live.
4: 6 and she will ***k*** you.
4:13 ***K*** her, for she is your life.
4:21 ***K*** them in the midst of your
4:23 ***K*** your heart with all
5: 2 And your lips may ***k*** knowledge.
6:20 ***k*** your father's command, And
6:22 they will ***k*** you; And when you
6:24 To ***k*** you from the evil woman,
7: 1 ***k*** my words, And treasure my
7: 2 ***K*** my commands and live, And my
7: 5 That they may ***k*** you from the
8:32 blessed are those who ***k*** my
22:18 is a pleasant thing if you ***k***
28: 4 But such as ***k*** the law contend
Eccl 2:10 my eyes desired I did not ***k***
3: 6 a time to lose; A time to ***k***,
3: 7 A time to ***k*** silence, And a
4:11 they will ***k*** warm; But how can
8: 2 ***K*** the king's commandment for the
12:13 Fear God and ***k*** His
Isa 6: 9 ***K*** on hearing, but do not
6: 9 ***K*** on seeing, but do not
7:21 in that day That a man will ***k***
26: 3 You will ***k*** him in perfect
27: 3 ***k*** it, I water it every moment;
27: 3 I ***k*** it night and day.
28:24 Does the plowman ***k*** plowing all
28:24 Does he ***k*** turning his soil and
32: 6 To ***k*** the hungry unsatisfied,
41: 1 ***K*** silence before Me, O
42: 6 I will ***k*** You and give You as a
43: 6 Do not ***k*** them back!' Bring My
56: 1 ***K*** justice, and do righteousness,
56: 4 To the eunuchs who ***k*** My
62: 6 of the LORD, do not ***k*** silent,
65: 5 ***K*** to yourself, Do not come near
65: 6 I will not ***k*** silence, but will
Jer 3: 5 Will He ***k*** it to the end?'
31:10 And ***k*** him as a shepherd does
34: 9 that no one should ***k*** a Jewish
34:10 that no one should ***k*** them in
42: 4 I will ***k*** nothing back from
44:25 We will surely ***k*** our vows that
44:25 You will surely ***k*** your vows
Lam 2:10 Zion Sit on the ground and ***k***
3:28 Let him sit alone and ***k*** silent,
Ezek 11:20 may walk in My statutes and ***k***
13:18 and ***k*** yourselves alive?
20:19 ***k*** My judgments, and do them;
36:27 and you will ***k*** My judgments and
43:11 so that they may ***k*** its whole
44: 8 but you have set others to ***k***
44:14 I will make them ***k*** charge of
44:16 and they shall ***k*** My charge.
44:20 but they shall ***k*** their hair
44:24 They shall ***k*** My laws and My
Dan 9: 4 and with those who ***k*** His
Am 5:13 Therefore the prudent ***k*** silent
Nah 1:15 ***k*** your appointed feasts,
Hab 2:20 Let all the earth ***k*** silence
Zech 3: 7 And if you will ***k*** My command,
13: 5 for a man taught me to ***k*** cattle
14:16 and to ***k*** the Feast of
14:18 who do not come up to ***k*** the
14:19 that do not come up to ***k*** the
Mal 2: 7 the lips of a priest should ***k***
Mt 19:17 ***k*** the commandments."
26:18 I will ***k*** the Passover at your
Mk 7: 9 that you may ***k*** your tradition.
Lk 4:10 charge over you, To ***k*** you,'
4:42 and tried to ***k*** Him from leaving
8:15 ***k*** it and bear fruit with
11:28 who hear the word of God and ***k***
19:40 tell you that if these should ***k***
Jn 8:55 but I do know Him and ***k*** His
9:16 because He does not ***k*** the
10:24 How long do You ***k*** us in doubt?
12:25 his life in this world will ***k***
14:15 love Me, ***k*** My commandments.
14:23 he will ***k*** My word; and My
14:24 does not love Me does not ***k*** My
15:10 If you ***k*** My commandments, you
15:20 they will ***k*** yours also.
17:11 ***k*** through Your name those whom
17:15 but that You should ***k*** them from
Acts 5: 3 to lie to the Holy Spirit and ***k***
5:38 ***k*** away from these men and let
10:28 it is for a Jewish man to ***k***
12: 4 to four squads of soldiers to ***k***
12:17 to them with his hand to ***k***
15: 5 and to command them to ***k*** the
15:24 must be circumcised and ***k*** the
15:29 If you ***k*** yourselves from these,
16: 4 to them the decrees to ***k***,
16:23 commanding the jailer to ***k*** them
18: 9 and do not ***k*** silent;
18:21 I must by all means ***k*** this
21:24 also walk orderly and ***k*** the
21:25 except that they should ***k***
24:23 he commanded the centurion to ***k***
Rom 2:25 is indeed profitable if you ***k***
1 Cor 5: 8 Therefore let us ***k*** the feast,
5: 9 to you in my epistle not to ***k***
5:11 I have written to you not to ***k***
7:37 in his heart that he will ***k***
11: 2 me in all things and ***k*** the
14:28 let him ***k*** silent in church, and
14:30 let the first ***k*** silent.
14:34 Let your women ***k*** silent in the
2 Cor 11: 9 and so I will ***k*** myself.
Gal 5: 3 that he is a debtor to ***k*** the
6:13 those who are circumcised ***k***
Eph 4: 3 endeavoring to ***k*** the unity of
2 Th 3:14 note that person and do not ***k***
1 Tim 5:22 sins; ***k*** yourself pure.
6:14 that you ***k*** this commandment
2 Tim 1:12 persuaded that He is able to ***k***
1:14 ***k*** by the Holy Spirit who dwells
Phm 1:13 whom I wished to ***k*** with me, that
Jas 1:27 and to ***k*** oneself unspotted
2:10 For whoever shall ***k*** the whole
1 Jn 2: 3 if we ***k*** His commandments.
2: 4 and does not ***k*** His
3:22 because we ***k*** His commandments
5: 2 when we love God and ***k*** His
5: 3 that we ***k*** His commandments. And
5:21 ***k*** yourselves from idols. Amen.
Jude 6 And the angels who did not ***k***
21 ***k*** yourselves in the love of God,
24 Now to Him who is able to ***k*** you
Rev 1: 3 and ***k*** those things which are
3:10 I also will ***k*** you from the hour
12:17 who ***k*** the commandments of God
14:12 here are those who ***k*** the
22: 9 and of those who ***k*** the words of

KEEPER (19/19) KEEP, KEEPERS

Gen 4: 2 Now Abel was a ***k*** of sheep, but
4: 9 not know. Am I my brother's ***k***?
39:21 favor in the sight of the ***k*** of
39:22 And the ***k*** of the prison
39:23 The ***k*** of the prison did not look
1 Sam 17:20 left the sheep with a ***k***,
17:22 in the hand of the supply ***k***,
2 Ki 22:14 ***k*** of the wardrobe. (She dwelt
1 Chr 9:21 the son of Meshelemiah was ***k***
2 Chr 31:14 the ***k*** of the East Gate, was
34:22 ***k*** of the wardrobe. (She dwelt
Neh 2: 8 and a letter to Asaph the ***k*** of
3:29 the ***k*** of the East Gate, made
Ps 121: 5 The LORD is your ***k***;
Song 1: 6 They made me the ***k*** of the
Jer 35: 4 Shallum, the ***k*** of the door.
Lk 13: 7 Then he said to the ***k*** of his
Acts 16:27 And the ***k*** of the prison, awaking
16:36 So the ***k*** of the prison reported

KEEPERS (5/5) KEEPER

1 Chr 9:19 Their fathers had been ***k*** of the
Eccl 12: 3 In the day when the ***k*** of the
Song 5: 7 The ***k*** of the walls Took my
8:11 He leased the vineyard to ***k***;
Jer 4:17 Like ***k*** of a field they are

KEEPING (19/19) KEEP

Ex 34: 7 ***k*** mercy for thousands, forgiving
Num 3:28 eight thousand six hundred ***k***
3:38 ***k*** charge of the sanctuary, to
Deut 8:11 the LORD your God by not ***k***
1 Sam 16:11 ***k*** the sheep." And Samuel said
25:16 the time we were with them ***k***
2 Sam 12: 8 your master's wives into your ***k***,
13:34 And the young man who was ***k***
2 Ki 11: 5 duty on the Sabbath shall be ***k***
2 Chr 5:11 without ***k*** to their divisions),
23: 4 shall be ***k*** watch over the
Neh 12:25 and Akkub were gatekeepers ***k***
Ps 19:11 And in ***k*** them there is
Prov 15: 3 ***K*** watch on the evil and the
Ezek 13:19 and ***k*** people alive who should
17:14 but that by ***k*** his covenant it
Lk 2: 8 ***k*** watch over their flock by
Acts 12: 6 guards before the door were ***k***
1 Cor 7:19 but ***k*** the commandments of God

KEEPS (42/40) KEEP

Gen 19: 9 and he ***k*** acting as a judge; now
Deut 7: 9 the faithful God who ***k*** covenant
Neh 9:32 Who ***k*** covenant and mercy: Do
Job 20:13 But still ***k*** it in his mouth,
33:18 He ***k*** back his soul from the
Ps 66: 9 Who ***k*** our soul among the
119:129 Therefore my soul ***k*** them.
119:167 My soul ***k*** Your testimonies,
121: 3 He who ***k*** you will not slumber.
121: 4 He who ***k*** Israel Shall neither
146: 6 Who ***k*** truth forever,
Prov 10:17 He who ***k*** instruction is in
16:17 He who ***k*** his way preserves his
18:18 And ***k*** the mighty apart.
19: 8 He who ***k*** understanding will
19:16 He who ***k*** the commandment keeps
19:16 He who keeps the commandment ***k***

21:23 guards his mouth and tongue **K**
24:12 He who **k** your soul, does He
27:18 Whoever **k** the fig tree will eat
28: 7 Whoever **k** the law is a
29:18 But happy is he who **k** the
Eccl 5:20 because God **k** him busy with
8: 5 He who **k** his command will
Isa 26: 2 the righteous nation which **k**
56: 2 Who **k** from defiling the
56: 2 And **k** his hand from doing any
56: 6 Everyone who **k** from defiling
Jer 48:10 And cursed is he who **k** back
Ezek 18:21 **k** all My statutes, and does
Dan 9: 4 who **k** His covenant and mercy
Jn 7:19 yet none of you **k** the law? Why
8:51 if anyone **k** My word he shall
8:52 If anyone **k** My word he shall
14:21 who has My commandments and **k**
Rom 2:26 if an uncircumcised man **k** the
1 Jn 2: 5 But whoever **k** His word, truly
3:24 Now he who **k** His commandments
5:18 he who has been born of God **k**
Rev 2:26 and **k** My works until the end,
16:15 and **k** his garments, lest he
22: 7 quickly! Blessed is he who **k**

KEHELATHAH (2/2)

Num 33:22 from Rissah and camped at **K**.
33:23 They went from **K** and camped at

KEILAH (18/16)

Josh 15:44 **K**, Achzib, and Mareshah:
1 Sam 23: 1 are fighting against **K**,
23: 2 the Philistines, and save **K**.
23: 3 much more then if we go to **K**
23: 4 and said, "Arise, go down to **K**.
23: 5 And David and his men went to **K**
23: 5 saved the inhabitants of **K**.
23: 6 of Ahimelech fled to David at **K**,
23: 7 told that David had gone to **K**.
23: 8 to go down to **K** to besiege
23:10 that Saul seeks to come to **K**
23:11 Will the men of **K** deliver me
23:12 Will the men of **K** deliver me and
23:13 arose and departed from **K** and
23:13 that David had escaped from **K**;
1 Chr 4:19 were the fathers of **K** the
Neh 3:17 of half the district of **K**,
3:18 half of the district of **K**,

KELAIAH (1/1)

Ezra 10:23 **K** (the same is Kelita),

KELITA (3/3)

Ezra 10:23 Kelaiah (the same is **K**),
Neh 8: 7 Hodijah, Maaseiah, **K**,
10:10 brethren: Shebaniah, Hodijah, **K**,

KEMUEL (3/3)

Gen 22:21 **K** the father of Aram,
Num 34:24 **K** the son of Shiphtan;
1 Chr 27:17 Levites, Hashabiah the son of **K**;

KENATH (2/2)

Num 32:42 Then Nobah went and took **K** and
1 Chr 2:23 with **K** and its towns—sixty

KENAZ (11/11)

Gen 36:11 Omar, Zepho, Gatam, and **K**.
36:15 Omar, Chief Zepho, Chief **K**,
36:42 Chief **K**, Chief Teman, Chief
Josh 15:17 So Othniel the son of **K**,
Judg 1:13 And Othniel the son of **K**,
3: 9 them: Othniel the son of **K**,
3:11 Then Othniel the son of **K** died.
1 Chr 1:36 Omar, Zephi, Gatam, and **K**;
1:53 Chief **K**, Chief Teman, Chief
4:13 The sons of **K** were Othniel and
4:15 Naam. The son of Elah was **K**.

KENEZITE (KJV) See KENIZZITE

KENEZZITES (1/1)

Gen 15:19 "the Kenites, the **K**,

KENITE (5/4) KENITES

Judg 1:16 Now the children of the **K**,
4:11 Now Heber the **K**, of the
4:17 Jael, the wife of Heber the **K**;
4:17 and the house of Heber the **K**.
5:24 Jael, The wife of Heber the **K**;

KENITES (8/7) KENITE, MIDIANITES

Gen 15:19 'the **K**, the Kenezzites,
Num 24:21 Then he looked on the **K**,
Judg 4:11 separated himself from the **K**
1 Sam 15: 6 Then Saul said to the **K**,
15: 6 So the **K** departed from among
27:10 the southern area of the **K**.
30:29 were in the cities of the **K**,
1 Chr 2:55 These were the **K** who came from

KENIZZITE (3/3)

Num 32:12 the son of Jephunneh, the **K**,
Josh 14: 6 the son of Jephunneh the **K**
14:14 the son of Jephunneh the **K** to

KEPT (170/165) KEEP, TENDING

Gen 8: 7 which **k** going to and fro until
26: 5 Abraham obeyed My voice and **k**
37:11 but his father **k** the matter in
39: 9 nor has he **k** back anything from
39:16 So she **k** his garment with her
42:16 and you shall be **k** in prison,
Ex 10:24 your flocks and your herds be **k**
16:23 to be **k** until morning.'"
16:32 to be **k** for your generations,
16:33 to be **k** for your generations."
16:34 before the Testimony, to be **k**.
21:29 and he has not **k** it confined,
21:36 and its owner has not **k** it
Lev 6: 9 fire of the altar shall be **k**
6:12 fire on the altar shall be **k**
Num 3:32 with oversight of those who **k**
9: 5 And they **k** the Passover on the
9: 7 Why are we **k** from presenting
9:19 the children of Israel **k** the
9:23 they **k** the charge of the LORD,
17:10 to be **k** as a sign against the
19: 9 and they shall be **k** for the
24:11 the LORD has **k** you back from
31:15 Have you **k** all the women alive?
31:47 who **k** charge of the tabernacle
Deut 9:25 forty days and forty nights I **k**
32:10 He **k** him as the apple of His
33: 9 have observed Your word And **k**
Josh 5:10 and **k** the Passover on the
14:10 the LORD has **k** me alive, as He
22: 2 You have **k** all that Moses the
22: 3 but have **k** the charge of the
Judg 2:22 walk in them as their fathers **k**
Ruth 2:14 satisfied, and **k** some back.
2:18 and gave to her what she had **k**
1 Sam 9:24 what was **k** back. It was set
9:24 until this time it has been **k**
13:13 You have not **k** the commandment
13:14 because you have not **k** what the
21: 4 the young men have at least **k**
21: 5 women have been **k** from us
25:33 because you have **k** me this day
25:34 who has **k** me back from hurting
25:39 and has **k** His servant from
2 Sam 8: 2 one full line those to be **k**
22:22 For I have **k** the ways of the
22:24 And I **k** myself from my
22:44 You have **k** me as the head of
1 Ki 2:43 Why then have you not **k** the oath
8:24 You have **k** what You promised
11:11 and have not **k** My covenant and
11:34 whom I chose because he **k** My
13:21 and have not **k** the commandment
14: 8 who **k** My commandments and who
2 Ki 12: 9 and the priests who **k** the door
18: 6 but **k** His commandments, which
2 Chr 6:15 You have **k** what You promised
7: 8 At that time Solomon **k** the
30:21 who were present at Jerusalem **k**
30:23 and they **k** it another seven
34: 9 which the Levites who **k** the
34:21 because our fathers have not **k**
35: 1 Now Josiah **k** a Passover to the
35:17 of Israel who were present **k**
35:18 There had been no Passover **k** in
35:18 of the kings of Israel had **k**
35:18 such a Passover as Josiah **k**,
35:19 of Josiah this Passover was **k**.
36:21 long as she lay desolate she **k**
Ezra 3: 4 They also **k** the Feast of
6:19 descendants of the captivity **k**
6:22 And they **k** the Feast of
Neh 1: 7 and have not **k** the
8:18 And they **k** the feast seven
9:34 Have **k** Your law, Nor heeded
11:19 and their brethren who **k** the
12:22 a record was also **k** of the
12:45 singers and the gatekeepers **k**
Esth 2:14 the king's eunuch who **k** the
9:28 should be remembered and **k**
Job 21:32 And a vigil **k** over the tomb.
23:11 I have **k** His way and not
29:21 And **k** silence for my counsel.
31:16 If I have **k** the poor from their
31:34 So that I **k** silence And did
Ps 17: 4 I have **k** away from the paths
18:21 For I have **k** the ways of the
18:23 And I **k** myself from my
30: 3 You have **k** me alive, that I
32: 3 When I **k** silent, my bones grew
42: 4 With a multitude that **k** a
50:21 and I **k** silent; You thought
56:13 Have You not **k** my feet from
99: 7 They **k** His testimonies and the
119:22 For I have **k** Your testimonies.
119:56 Because I **k** Your precepts.
Eccl 5:13 Riches **k** for their owner to
Song 1: 6 my own vineyard I have not **k**.
Isa 30:29 when a holy festival is **k**,
Jer 16:11 and have forsaken Me and not **k**
35:18 and **k** all his precepts and done
Ezek 5: 7 walked in My statutes nor **k** My
18: 9 walked in My statutes And **k**
18:19 and has **k** all My statutes and
44: 8 And you have not **k** charge of My
44:15 who **k** charge of My sanctuary
48:11 who have **k** My charge, who did
Dan 5:19 he **k** alive; whomever he wished,
7:28 but I **k** the matter in my
9:14 Therefore the LORD has **k** the
Am 1:11 And he **k** his wrath forever.
2: 4 And have not **k** His
Mic 6:16 For the statutes of Omri are **k**;
Mal 2: 9 Because you have not **k** My ways
3: 7 My ordinances And have not **k**
3:14 profit is it that we have **k**
Mt 8:33 Then those who **k** them fled; and
13:35 I will utter things **k**
19:20 All these things I have **k** from
26:63 But Jesus **k** silent. And the high
27:36 they **k** watch over Him there.
Mk 3: 4 But they **k** silent.
3: 9 that a small boat should be **k**
4:22 nor has anything been **k** secret
7:26 and she **k** asking Him to cast
9:10 So they **k** this word to
9:34 But they **k** silent, for on the
10:20 all these things I have **k** from
14:61 But He **k** silent and answered
Lk 1:66 And all those who heard them **k**
2:19 But Mary **k** all these things and
2:51 but His mother **k** all these
8:29 and he was **k** under guard, bound
9:36 But they **k** quiet, and told no
14: 4 But they **k** silent. And He took
18:21 All these things I have **k** from
19:20 which I have **k** put away in a
20:26 marveled at His answer and **k**
Jn 2:10 You have **k** the good wine until
11:37 also have **k** this man from
12: 7 she has **k** this for the day of
15:10 just as I have **k** My Father's
15:20 If they **k** My word, they will
17: 6 and they have **k** Your word.
17:12 I **k** them in Your name. Those
17:12 Those whom You gave Me I have **k**;
18:16 out and spoke to her who **k** the
18:17 Then the servant girl who **k** the
Acts 5: 2 And he **k** back part of the
7:53 of angels and have not **k** it.
12: 5 Peter was therefore **k** in
12:15 beside yourself!" Yet she **k**
12:22 And the people **k** shouting, "The
15:12 Then all the multitude **k** silent
20:20 how I **k** back nothing that was
22: 2 they **k** all the more silent.
23:35 And he commanded him to be **k**
25: 4 answered that Paul should be **k**
25:21 I commanded him to be **k** till I
27:43 **k** them from their purpose, and
Rom 16:25 the revelation of the mystery **k**
2 Cor 11: 9 And in everything I **k** myself
Gal 3:23 we were **k** under guard by the
3:23 **k** for the faith which would
2 Tim 4: 7 I have **k** the faith.
Heb 11:28 By faith he **k** the Passover and
Jas 5: 4 which you **k** back by fraud, cry
1 Pe 1: 5 who are **k** by the power of God
Rev 3: 8 have **k** My word, and have not
3:10 Because you have **k** My command to

KERCHIEFS (KJV) See VEILS

KEREN-HAPPUCH (1/1)

Job 42:14 and the name of the third **K**.

KERIOTH (4/4)

Josh 15:25 Hazor, Hadattah, **K**,
Jer 48:24 On **K** and Bozrah, On all the
48:41 **K** is taken, And the
Am 2: 2 shall devour the palaces of **K**;

KEROS (2/2)

Ezra 2:44 the sons of **K**, the sons of
Neh 7:47 the sons of **K**, the sons of

KETTLE (1/1)

1 Sam 2:14 thrust it into the pan, or **k**,

KETURAH (4/4)

Gen 25: 1 a wife, and her name was **K**.
25: 4 these were the children of **K**.
1 Chr 1:32 Now the sons born to **K**,
1:33 these were the children of **K**.

KEVEH (4/2)

1 Ki 10:28 imported from Egypt and **K**;
10:28 merchants bought them in **K** at
2 Chr 1:16 imported from Egypt and **K**;
1:16 merchants bought them in **K** at

KEY (6/6) KEYS

Judg 3:25 Therefore they took the **k** and
Isa 22:22 The **k** of the house of David I
Lk 11:52 For you have taken away the **k**
Rev 3: 7 He who has the **k** of David,
9: 1 To him was given the **k** to the
20: 1 having the **k** to the bottomless

KEYS (2/2) KEY

Mt 16:19 And I will give you the **k** of the
Rev 1:18 And I have the **k** of Hades and

KEZIAH (1/1)

Job 42:14 the name of the second **K**,

KIBROTH HATTAAVAH (5/5)

Num 11:34 called the name of that place **K**,
11:35 From **K** the people moved to
33:16 of Sinai and camped at **K**.
33:17 They departed from **K** and camped
Deut 9:22 at Taberah and Massah and **K**

KIBZAIM (1/1)

Josh 21:22 **K** with its common-land, and Beth

KICK (3/3) KICKED

1 Sam 2:29 Why do you **k** at My sacrifice and
Acts 9: 5 It is hard for you to **k**
26:14 It is hard for you to **k**

KICKED (2/2) KICK

Deut 32:15 "But Jeshurun grew fat and **k**;
2 Sam 16:13 threw stones at him and **k** up

KID (28/28) KIDS

Gen 37:31 killed a **k** of the goats, and
Lev 4:23 bring as his offering a **k** of
4:28 bring as his offering a **k** of
5: 6 a lamb or a **k** of the goats as a
9: 3 Take a **k** of the goats as a sin
23:19 'Then you shall sacrifice one **k**
Num 7:16 one **k** of the goats as a sin
7:22 one **k** of the goats as a sin
7:28 one **k** of the goats as a sin
7:34 one **k** of the goats as a sin
7:40 one **k** of the goats as a sin
7:46 one **k** of the goats as a sin
7:52 one **k** of the goats as a sin
7:58 one **k** of the goats as a sin
7:64 one **k** of the goats as a sin
7:70 one **k** of the goats as a sin
7:76 one **k** of the goats as a sin
7:82 one **k** of the goats as a sin
15:24 and one **k** of the goats as a sin
28:15 Also one **k** of the goats as a sin
28:30 also one **k** of the goats, to
29: 5 also one **k** of the goats as a
29:11 also one **k** of the goats as a
29:16 also one **k** of the goats as a
29:19 also one **k** of the goats as a
29:25 also one **k** of the goats as a
Ezek 43:22 second day you shall offer a **k**
45:23 and a **k** of the goats daily for

KIDNAPPER (1/1)

Deut 24: 7 then that **k** shall die; and you

KIDNAPPERS (1/1)

1 Tim 1:10 for sodomites, for **k**,

KIDNAPPING (1/1)

Deut 24: 7 If a man is found **k** any of his

KIDNAPS (1/1)

Ex 21:16 He who **k** a man and sells him,

KIDNEYS (17/12)

Ex 29:13 and the two **k** and the fat that
29:22 the two **k** and the fat on them,
Lev 3: 4 the two **k** and the fat that is
3: 4 to the liver above the **k**,
3:10 the two **k** and the fat that is
3:10 to the liver above the **k**,
3:15 the two **k** and the fat that is
3:15 to the liver above the **k**,
4: 9 the two **k** and the fat that is
4: 9 to the liver above the **k**,
7: 4 the two **k** and the fat that is
7: 4 to the liver above the **k**,
8:16 and the two **k** with their fat,
8:25 the two **k** and their fat, and
9:10 But the fat, the **k**, and the
9:19 covers the entrails and the **k**,
Isa 34: 6 With the fat of the **k** of rams.

KIDRON (12/11)

2 Sam 15:23 also crossed over the Brook **K**,
1 Ki 2:37 go out and cross the Brook **K**,
15:13 and burned it by the Brook **K**.
2 Ki 23: 4 Jerusalem in the fields of **K**,
23: 6 to the Brook **K** outside
23: 6 burned it at the Brook **K** and
23:12 their dust into the Brook **K**.
2 Chr 15:16 and burned it by the Brook **K**.
29:16 and carried it to the Brook **K**.
30:14 and cast them into the Brook **K**.
Jer 31:40 fields as far as the Brook **K**,
Jn 18: 1 His disciples over the Brook **K**,

KIDS (4/4) KID

Gen 27: 9 me from there two choice **k** of
27:16 And she put the skins of the **k**
Lev 16: 5 of the children of Israel two **k**
Num 7:87 and the **k** of the goats as a sin

KILL (196/184) KILLED, KILLING, KILLS

Gen 4:14 anyone who finds me will **k** me.
4:15 anyone finding him should **k**
12:12 and they will **k** me, but they
20:11 and they will **k** me on account
26: 7 lest the men of the place **k** me
27:41 then I will **k** my brother
27:42 you by intending to **k** you.
34:30 together against me and **k** me.
37:18 conspired against him to **k** him.
37:20 let us now **k** him and cast him
37:21 Let us not **k** him."
37:26 profit is there if we **k**
42:37 **K** my two sons if I do not bring
Ex 1:16 then you shall **k** him; but if it
2:14 Do you intend to **k** me as you
2:15 he sought to **k** Moses. But Moses
4:23 indeed I will **k** your son, your
4:24 LORD met him and sought to **k**
5:21 put a sword in their hand to **k**
12: 6 congregation of Israel shall **k**
12:21 and **k** the Passover lamb.
16: 3 out into this wilderness to **k**
17: 3 to **k** us and our children and
21:14 to **k** him by treachery, you
22:24 and I will **k** you with the
23: 7 do not **k** the innocent and
29:11 Then you shall **k** the bull before
29:16 and you shall **k** the ram, and you
29:20 Then you shall **k** the ram, and
32:12 to **k** them in the mountains, and
32:27 and let every man **k** his
Lev 1: 5 He shall **k** the bull before the
1:11 He shall **k** it on the north side
3: 2 and **k** it at the door of the
3: 8 and **k** it before the tabernacle
3:13 lay his hand on its head and **k**
4: 4 and **k** the bull before the
4:24 and **k** it at the place where
4:24 it at the place where they **k**
4:29 and **k** the sin offering at the
4:33 and **k** it as a sin offering at
4:33 at the place where they **k** the
7: 2 In the place where they **k** the
7: 2 the burnt offering they shall **k**
14:13 Then he shall **k** the lamb in the
14:19 Afterward he shall **k** the burnt
14:25 Then he shall **k** the lamb of the
14:50 Then he shall **k** one of the birds
16:11 and shall **k** the bull as the sin
16:15 Then he shall **k** the goat of the
20: 4 and they do not **k** him,
20:15 and you shall **k** the animal.
20:16 you shall **k** the woman and the
22:28 do not **k** both her and her young
Num 11:15 please **k** me here and now—if I
14:15 Now if You **k** these people as
16:13 to **k** us in the wilderness, that
22:29 for now I would **k** you!"
25: 5 Every one of you **k** his men who
31:17 **k** every male among the little
31:17 and **k** every woman who has known
Deut 9:28 He has brought them out to **k**
13: 9 but you shall surely **k** him; your
19: 6 and **k** him, though he was not
32:39 I **k** and I make alive; I wound
Josh 9:26 so that they did not **k** them.
Judg 8:19 I would not **k** you."
8:20 **k** them!" But the youth would
8:21 and **k** us; for as a man is, so
9:54 Draw your sword and **k** me, lest
12: 6 Then they would take him and **k**
13:23 If the LORD had desired to **k**
15:12 to me that you will not **k** me
15:13 but we will surely not **k** you."
16: 2 daylight, we will **k** him."
20: 5 They intended to **k** me, but
20:31 began to strike down and **k**
20:39 had begun to strike and **k**
1 Sam 2:25 because the LORD desired to **k**
5:10 to **k** us and our people!"
5:11 so that it does not **k** us and
15: 3 But **k** both man and woman,
16: 2 he will **k** me." And the LORD
17: 9 is able to fight with me and **k**
17: 9 if I prevail against him and **k**
19: 1 that they should **k** David; but
19: 2 My father Saul seeks to **k** you.
19: 5 to **k** David without a cause?"
19:11 house to watch him and to **k**
19:15 the bed, that I may **k** him."
19:17 Let me go! Why should I **k** you?'
20: 8 **k** me yourself, for why should
20:33 Saul cast a spear at him to **k**
20:33 determined by his father to **k**
22:17 Turn and **k** the priests of the
22:18 You turn and **k** the priests!" So
24:10 and someone urged me to **k**
24:11 and did not **k** you, know and see
24:18 your hand, you did not **k** me.
28:24 and she hastened to **k** it. And
30: 2 they did not **k** anyone, but
30:15 by God that you will neither **k**
2 Sam 1: 9 Please stand over me and **k** me,
3:37 been the king's intent to **k**
13:28 Strike Amnon!' then **k** him. Do
21: 2 but Saul had sought to **k** them
21: 4 nor shall you **k** any man in
21:16 thought he could **k** David.
1 Ki 3:26 and by no means **k** him!" But
3:27 and by no means **k** him; she is
11:40 Solomon therefore sought to **k**
12:27 and they will **k** me and go back
17:18 and to **k** my son?"
18: 5 so that we will not have to **k**
18: 9 hand of Ahab, to **k** me?
18:12 he will **k** me. But I your
18:14 He will **k** me!"
19:17 sword of Hazael, Jehu will **k**;
19:17 sword of Jehu, Elisha will **k**.
20:36 a lion shall **k** you." And as
2 Ki 5: 7 to **k** and make alive, that this
6:21 shall I **k** them? Shall I kill
6:21 Shall I **k** them?"
6:22 You shall not **k** them. Would you
6:22 Would you **k** those whom you have
7: 4 and if they **k** us, we shall only
8:12 and their young men you will **k**
10:25 Go in and **k** them; let no one
2 Chr 20:23 of Mount Seir to utterly **k** and
22:11 Athaliah so that she did not **k**
23:14 Do not **k** her in the house of the
Neh 4:11 we come into their midst and **k**
6:10 for they are coming to **k** you;
6:10 at night they will come to **k**
Esth 3:13 provinces, to destroy, to **k**,
8:11 their lives—to destroy, **k**,
Ps 59: the the house in order to **k**
Eccl 3: 3 A time to **k**, And a time to
Isa 14:30 I will **k** your roots with
Jer 9:21 To **k** off the children—no
20:17 Because he did not **k** me from
40:15 and I will **k** Ishmael the son of
41: 8 Do not **k** us, for we have
41: 8 So he desisted and did not **k**
Ezek 9: 5 him through the city and **k**;
Dan 2:13 companions, to **k** them.
2:14 who had gone out to **k** the wise
Hos 9:16 I would **k** the darlings of
Mt 10:28 And do not fear those who **k** the
10:28 who kill the body but cannot **k**
17:23 and they will **k** Him, and the
21:38 let us **k** him and seize his
23:34 some of them you will **k** and
24: 9 you up to tribulation and **k**
26: 4 to take Jesus by trickery and **k**
Mk 3: 4 do evil, to save life or to **k**?
6:19 it against him and wanted to **k**
9:31 and they will **k** Him. And after
10:34 and **k** Him. And the third day He
12: 7 let us **k** him, and the
Lk 11:49 and some of them they will **k**
12: 4 do not be afraid of those who **k**
13:31 for Herod wants to **k** You."
15:23 the fatted calf here and **k** it,
18:33 They will scourge Him and **k**
20:14 let us **k** him, that the
22: 2 sought how they might **k** Him,
Jn 5:16 and sought to **k** Him, because He
5:18 Jews sought all the more to **k**
7: 1 because the Jews sought to **k**
7:19 Why do you seek to **k** Me?"
7:20 Who is seeking to **k** You?"
7:25 this not He whom they seek to **k**?
8:22 Will He **k** Himself, because He
8:37 but you seek to **k** Me, because
8:40 But now you seek to **k** Me, a Man
10:10 come except to steal, and to **k**,
Acts 5:33 were furious and plotted to **k**
7:28 Do you want to **k** me as
9:23 the Jews plotted to **k** him.
9:24 day and night, to **k** him.
9:29 but they attempted to **k** him.
10:13 'Rise, Peter; **k** and eat.'
11: 7 'Rise, Peter; **k** and eat.'
16:27 his sword and was about to **k**
21:31 Now as they were seeking to **k**
23:15 but we are ready to **k** him
25: 3 in ambush along the road to **k**
26:21 me in the temple and tried to **k**
27:42 And the soldiers' plan was to **k**
Rev 2:23 I will **k** her children with
6: 4 and that people should **k** one
6: 8 to **k** with sword, with hunger,
9: 5 were not given authority to **k**
9:15 were released to **k** a third of
11: 7 overcome them, and **k** them.

KILLED (266/246) KILL

Gen 4: 8 against Abel his brother and **k**
4:23 to my speech! For I have **k** a
4:25 me instead of Abel, whom Cain **k**.
34:25 boldly upon the city and **k** all
34:26 And they **k** Hamor and Shechem his
37:31 **k** a kid of the goats, and
38: 7 and the LORD **k** him.
38:10 therefore He **k** him also.
Ex 2:12 he **k** the Egyptian and hid him
2:14 you intend to kill me as you **k**
13:15 that the LORD **k** all the
21:29 so that it has **k** a man or a
Lev 4:15 Then the bull shall be **k** before
6:25 where the burnt offering is **k**,
6:25 the sin offering shall be **k**
8:15 and Moses **k** it. Then he took

8:19 and Moses **k** it. Then he
8:23 and Moses **k** it. Also he took
9: 8 went to the altar and **k** the
9:12 And he **k** the burnt offering;
9:15 and **k** it and offered it for
9:18 He also **k** the bull and the ram
14: 5 that one of the birds be **k** in
14: 6 blood of the bird that was **k**
Num 14:16 therefore He **k** them in the
16:41 You have **k** the people of the
22:33 surely I would also have **k** you
25:14 name of the Israelite who was **k**,
25:14 who was **k** with the Midianite
25:15 the Midianite woman who was **k**
25:18 who was **k** in the day of the
31: 7 and they **k** all the males.
31: 8 They **k** the kings of Midian with
31: 8 the rest of those who were **k**—
31: 8 the son of Beor they also **k**
31:19 whoever has **k** any person, and
33: 4 whom the LORD had **k** among
Deut 1: 4 after he had **k** Sihon king of the
21: 1 and it is not known who **k** him,
Josh 10:10 **k** them with a great slaughter
10:11 than the children of Israel **k**
10:26 Joshua struck them and **k** them,
11:17 and struck them down and **k**
13:22 The children of Israel also **k**
13:22 among those who were **k** by them.
20: 9 that whoever **k** a person
Judg 1: 4 and they **k** ten thousand men at
1:10) And they **k** Sheshai, Ahiman,
3:29 And at that time they **k** about
3:31 who **k** six hundred men of the
7:25 They **k** Oreb at the rock of
7:25 and Zeeb they **k** at the
8:17 down the tower of Penuel and **k**
8:18 of men were they whom you **k**
8:21 So Gideon arose and **k** Zebah
9: 5 father's house at Ophrah and **k**
9:18 and **k** his seventy sons on one
9:24 who **k** them, and on the men of
9:44 who were in the fields and **k**
9:45 he took the city and **k** the
9:54 A woman **k** him.'" So his young
14:19 he went down to Ashkelon and **k**
15:15 and **k** a thousand men with it.
16:30 So the dead that he **k** at his
16:30 death were more than he had **k**
20:45 and **k** two thousand of them.
1 Sam 4: 2 who **k** about four thousand men
11:11 and **k** Ammonites until the heat
14:13 his armorbearer **k** them.
17:35 and struck and **k** it.
17:36 Your servant has **k** both lion and
17:50 and struck the Philistine and **k**
17:51 it out of its sheath and **k** him,
18:27 and **k** two hundred men of the
19: 5 his life in his hands and **k**
19: 6 LORD lives, he shall not be **k**.
19:11 tonight, tomorrow you will be **k**.
20:32 to him, "Why should he be **k**?
21: 9 whom you **k** in the Valley of
22:18 and **k** on that day eighty-five
22:21 told David that Saul had **k** the
25:11 and my meat that I have **k** for
31: 2 And the Philistines **k** Jonathan,
2 Sam 1:10 So I stood over him and **k** him,
1:16 I have **k** the LORD's anointed.'
3:30 Joab and Abishai his brother **k**
3:30 because he had **k** their brother
4: 7 then they struck him and **k** him,
4:11 when wicked men have **k** a
8: 5 David **k** twenty-two thousand of
10:18 and David **k** seven hundred
12: 9 You have **k** Uriah the Hittite
12: 9 and have **k** him with the sword
13:30 Absalom has **k** all the king's
13:32 not my lord suppose they have **k**
14: 6 the one struck the other and **k**
14: 7 life of his brother whom he **k**;
18:15 and struck and **k** him.
21: 1 because he **k** the Gibeonites."
21:17 and struck the Philistine and **k**
21:18 Then Sibbechai the Hushathite **k**
21:19 the Bethlehemite **k** the
21:21 David's brother, **k** him.
23: 8 because he had **k** eight hundred
23:12 and **k** the Philistines. And the
23:18 **k** them, and won a name among
23:20 He had **k** two lion-like heroes
23:20 He also had gone down and **k** a
23:21 And he **k** an Egyptian, a
23:21 and **k** him with his own spear.
1 Ki 2: 5 the son of Jether, whom he **k**.
2:32 and **k** them with the sword—Abner
2:34 went up and struck and **k** him;
9:16 had **k** the Canaanites who dwelt
11:15 after he had **k** every male in
11:24 when David **k** those of Zobah.
13:24 lion met him on the road and **k**
13:26 which has torn him and **k** him,
15:27 And Baasha **k** him at Gibbethon,
15:28 Baasha **k** him in the third year
15:29 that he **k** all the house of
16: 7 and because he **k** them.
16:10 went in and struck him and **k**
16:11 that he **k** all the household of
16:16 has conspired and also has **k**
18:13 lord what I did when Jezebel **k**
19:10 and **k** Your prophets with the
19:14 and **k** Your prophets with the

20:20 And each one **k** his man; so the
20:21 and **k** the Syrians with a great
20:29 and the children of Israel **k**
20:36 a lion found him and **k** him.
2 Ki 3:23 struck swords and have **k** one
10: 9 against my master and **k** him;
10: 9 but who **k** all these?
10:11 So Jehu **k** all who remained of
10:14 and **k** them at the well of Beth
10:17 he **k** all who remained to Ahab
10:25 no one come out!" And they **k**
11: 2 Athaliah, so that he was not **k**.
11:15 Do not let her be **k** in the house
11:16 house, and there she was **k**.
11:18 and **k** Mattan the priest of Baal
12:20 and **k** Joash in the house of the
14: 7 He **k** ten thousand Edomites in
14:19 after him to Lachish and **k** him
15:10 and struck and **k** him in front
15:14 son of Jabesh in Samaria and **k**
15:25 conspired against him and **k** him
15:25 He **k** him and reigned in his
15:30 and struck and **k** him; so he
16: 9 captive to Kir, and **k** Rezin.
17:25 which **k** some of them.
19:35 and **k** in the camp of the
21:23 and **k** the king in his own
23:29 And Pharaoh Necho **k** him at
25: 7 Then they **k** the sons of Zedekiah
25:25 with ten men and struck and **k**
1 Chr 2: 3 of the LORD; so He **k** him.
7:21 who were born in that land **k**
10: 2 And the Philistines **k** Jonathan,
10:14 therefore He **k** him, and turned
11:11 **k** by him at one time.
11:14 and **k** the Philistines. So the
11:20 **k** them, and won a name among
11:22 He had **k** two lion-like heroes
11:22 He also had gone down and **k** a
11:23 And he **k** an Egyptian, a man of
11:23 and **k** him with his own spear.
18: 5 David **k** twenty-two thousand of
18:12 Abishai the son of Zeruiah **k**
19:18 and David **k** seven thousand
19:18 and **k** Shophach the commander of
20: 4 time Sibbechai the Hushathite **k**
20: 5 and Elhanan the son of Jair **k**
20: 7 David's brother, **k** him.
2 Chr 18: 2 and Ahab **k** sheep and oxen in
21: 4 he strengthened himself and **k**
21:13 and also have **k** your brothers,
22: 1 Arabians into the camp had **k**
22: 8 Ahaziah, that he **k** them.
22: 9 When they had **k** him, they
23:15 and they **k** her there.
23:17 and **k** Mattan the priest of Baal
24:22 but **k** his son; and as he died,
24:25 and **k** him on his bed. So he
25:11 to the Valley of Salt and **k**
25:13 **k** three thousand in them, and
25:16 Cease! Why should you be **k**?
25:27 after him to Lachish and **k** him
28: 6 For Pekah the son of Remaliah **k**
28: 7 **k** Maaseiah the king's son,
28: 9 but you have **k** them in a rage
29:22 So they **k** the bulls, and the
29:22 Likewise they **k** the rams and
29:22 They also **k** the lambs and
29:24 And the priests **k** them; and they
33:24 and **k** him in his own house.
36:17 who **k** their young men with the
Neh 9:26 law behind their backs And **k**
Esth 7: 4 and I, to be destroyed, to be **k**,
9: 6 Shushan the citadel the Jews **k**
9:10 the enemy of the Jews—they **k**;
9:11 the number of those who were **k**
9:12 The Jews have **k** and destroyed
9:15 day of the month of Adar and **k**
9:16 and **k** seventy-five thousand of
Job 1:15 indeed they have **k** the servants
1:17 and **k** the servants with the
Ps 44:22 Yet for Your sake we are **k** all
60: and Joab returned and **k** twelve
105:29 And **k** their fish.
Isa 37:36 and **k** in the camp of the
Jer 26:23 who **k** him with the sword and
39: 6 Then the king of Babylon **k** the
39: 6 the king of Babylon also **k** all
41: 2 and **k** him whom the king of
41: 4 the second day after he had **k**
41: 7 Ishmael the son of Nethaniah **k**
52:10 Then the king of Babylon **k** the
52:10 And he **k** all the princes of
Ezek 9: 7 out!" And they went out and **k**
Dan 3:22 the flame of the fire **k** those
Am 4:10 Your young men I **k** with a
Nah 2:12 *K* for his lionesses, Filled
Mt 16:21 priests and scribes, and be **k**,
21:35 **k** one, and stoned another.
21:39 him out of the vineyard and **k**
22: 4 oxen and fatted cattle are **k**,
22: 6 them spitefully, and **k** them.
Mk 8:31 priests and scribes, and be **k**,
9:31 kill Him. And after He is **k**,
12: 5 he sent another, and him they **k**;
12: 8 So they took him and **k** him and
14:12 when they **k** the Passover lamb,
Lk 9:22 priests and scribes, and be **k**,
11:47 and your fathers **k** them.
11:48 for they indeed **k** them, and you
12: 5 Fear Him who, after He has **k**,
13: 4 the tower in Siloam fell and **k**

15:27 your father has **k** the fatted
15:30 you **k** the fatted calf for him.'
20:15 him out of the vineyard and **k**
22: 7 when the Passover must be **k**.
Acts 3:15 and **k** the Prince of life, whom
7:52 And they **k** those who foretold
10:39 whom they **k** by hanging on a
12: 2 Then he **k** James the brother of
23:12 eat nor drink till they had **k**
23:14 eat nothing until we have **k**
23:21 eat nor drink till they have **k**
23:27 the Jews and was about to be **k**
Rom 7:11 deceived me, and by it **k** me.
8:36 For Your sake we are **k** all
11: 3 they have **k** Your prophets
2 Cor 6: 9 as chastened, and yet not **k**;
1 Th 2:15 who **k** both the Lord Jesus and
Rev 2:13 who was **k** among you, where
6:11 who would be **k** as they were,
9:18 a third of mankind was **k**—
9:20 who were not **k** by these
11: 5 he must be **k** in this manner.
11:13 seven thousand people were **k**,
13:10 kills with the sword must be **k**
13:15 the image of the beast to be **k**.
19:21 And the rest were **k** with the

KILLING (13/13) KILL

Judg 9:24 who aided him in the **k** of his
9:56 he had done to his father by **k**
2 Sam 8:13 a name when he returned from **k**
1 Ki 17:20 whom I lodge, by **k** her son?"
2 Ki 3:24 their land, **k** the Moabites.
17:26 they are **k** them because they do
Isa 22:13 Slaying oxen and **k** sheep,
Ezek 9: 8 that while they were **k** them, I
13:19 **k** people who should not die,
Dan 2:13 and they began **k** the wise men;
Hos 4: 2 *K* and stealing and committing
Mk 12: 5 beating some and **k** some.
Acts 22:20 the clothes of those who were **k**

KILLS (29/27) KILL

Gen 4:15 whoever **k** Cain, vengeance shall
Lev 14:13 lamb in the place where he **k**
17: 3 of the house of Israel who **k**
17: 3 or who **k** it outside the camp,
24:17 Whoever **k** any man shall surely
24:18 Whoever **k** an animal shall make
24:21 And whoever **k** an animal shall
24:21 but whoever **k** a man shall be
Num 35:11 that the manslayer who **k** any
35:15 that anyone who **k** a person
35:27 and the avenger of blood **k** the
35:30 Whoever **k** a person, the murderer
Deut 4:42 flee there, who **k** his neighbor
19: 4 Whoever **k** his neighbor
22:26 against his neighbor and **k** him,
Josh 20: 3 that the slayer who **k** a person
1 Sam 2: 6 The LORD **k** and makes alive; He
17:25 it shall be that the man who **k**
17:26 be done for the man who **k** this
17:27 it be done for the man who **k**
Job 5: 2 For wrath **k** a foolish man, And
24:14 He **k** the poor and needy; And
Prov 21:25 The desire of the lazy man **k**
Isa 66: 3 He who **k** a bull is as if he
Mt 23:37 the one who **k** the prophets and
Lk 13:34 the one who **k** the prophets and
Jn 16: 2 time is coming that whoever **k**
2 Cor 3: 6 of the Spirit; for the letter **k**,
Rev 13:10 he who **k** with the sword must be

KILN (1/1)

Nah 3:14 Make strong the brick **k**!

KIN (7/7) KINDRED

Lev 18: 6 anyone who is near of **k** to him,
18:12 she is near of **k** to your
18:13 for she is near of **k** to your
18:17 They are near of **k** to her. It
20:19 would uncover his near of **k**.
25:49 or anyone who is near of **k** to
Prov 7: 4 understanding your nearest **k**,

KINAH (1/1)

Josh 15:22 *K*, Dimonah, Adadah,

KIND (65/46) KINDLY, KINDNESS, KINDS

Gen 1:11 yields fruit according to its **k**,
1:12 yields seed according to its **k**,
1:12 in itself according to its **k**.
1:21 abounded, according to their **k**,
1:21 winged bird according to its **k**.
1:24 creature according to its **k**:
1:24 each according to its **k**"; and
1:25 of the earth according to its **k**,
1:25 kind, cattle according to its **k**,
1:25 on the earth according to its **k**.
6:20 "Of the birds after their **k**,
6:20 kind, of animals after their **k**,
6:20 thing of the earth after its **k**,
6:20 two of every **k** will come to
7:14 and every beast after its **k**,
7:14 kind, all cattle after their **k**,
7:14 creeps on the earth after its **k**,
7:14 and every bird after its **k**,

Ex 22: 9 For any *k* of trespass, whether
22: 9 or for any *k* of lost thing
Lev 11:14 and the falcon after its *k*;
11:15 'every raven after its *k*,
11:16 gull, and the hawk after its *k*;
11:19 stork, the heron after its *k*,
11:22 may eat: the locust after its *k*,
11:22 destroying locust after its *k*,
11:22 kind, the cricket after its *k*,
11:22 and the grasshopper after its *k*.
11:29 the large lizard after its *k*;
19:19 livestock breed with another *k*.
20:25 or by any *k* of living thing
Deut 14:14 "every raven after its *k*;
14:18 stork, the heron after its *k*,
27:21 the one who lies with any *k* of
Judg 8:18 What *k* of men were they whom
21:22 Be *k* to them for our sakes,
1 Ki 9:13 What *k* of cities are these
2 Ki 1: 7 What *k* of man was it who came
1 Chr 6:48 were appointed to every *k* of
12:37 armed for battle with every *k*
22:15 of skillful men for every *k* of
28:14 all articles used in every *k*
28:14 all articles used in every *k*
28:21 for every *k* of service; also
2 Chr 10: 7 If you are *k* to these people,
34:13 of all who did work in any *k*
Ezra 1:10 silver basins of a similar *k*,
Ezek 44:30 of all firstfruits of any *k*,
44:30 and every sacrifice of any *k*
Mt 13:47 and gathered some of every *k*,
17:21 this *k* does not go out except
Mk 9:29 This *k* can come out by nothing
Lk 1:66 What *k* of child will this be?"
6:35 For He is *k* to the unthankful
24:17 What *k* of conversation is this
1 Cor 13: 4 Love suffers long and is *k*;
15:39 but there is one *k* of flesh
Eph 4:32 And be *k* to one another,
1 Th 1: 5 as you know what *k* of men we
Jas 1:18 that we might be a *k* of
1:24 and immediately forgets what *k*
3: 7 For every *k* of beast and bird,
Rev 18:12 every *k* of citron wood, every
18:12 every *k* of object of ivory,
18:12 every *k* of object of most

KINDLE (17/17) KINDLED, KINDLES

Ex 35: 3 You shall *k* no fire throughout
Prov 26:21 So is a contentious man to *k*
Isa 9:18 And *k* in the thickets of the
10:16 under his glory He will *k* a
50:11 all you who *k* a fire, Who
Jer 7:18 the fathers *k* the fire, and the
17:27 then I will *k* a fire in its
21:14 I will *k* a fire in its forest,
33:18 to *k* grain offerings, and to
43:12 I will *k* a fire in the houses of
49:27 I will *k* a fire in the wall of
50:32 I will *k* a fire in his cities,
Ezek 20:47 I will *k* a fire in you, and it
24:10 *K* the fire; Cook the meat
Am 1:14 But I will *k* a fire in the wall
Ob 18 They shall *k* them and devour
Mal 1:10 So that you would not *k* fire

KINDLED (24/24) KINDLE

Ex 4:14 So the anger of the LORD was *k*
22: 6 he who *k* the fire shall surely
Lev 10: 6 burning which the LORD has *k*.
Deut 32:22 For a fire is *k* by my anger,
2 Sam 22: 9 Coals were *k* by it.
22:13 Him Coals of fire were *k*.
Job 19:11 He has also *k* His wrath against
Ps 2:12 When His wrath is *k* but a
18: 8 Coals were *k* by it.
78:21 So a fire was *k* against Jacob,
106:18 A fire was *k* in their company;
106:40 the wrath of the LORD was *k*
124: 3 When their wrath was *k* against
Isa 50:11 and in the sparks you have *k*—
Jer 11:16 of a great tumult He has *k*
15:14 For a fire is *k* in My anger,
17: 4 For you have *k* a fire in My
44: 6 My anger were poured out and *k*
Lam 4:11 He *k* a fire in Zion, And it
Ezek 20:48 have *k* it; it shall not be
Zech 10: 3 My anger is *k* against the
Lk 12:49 how I wish it were already *k*!
22:55 Now when they had *k* a fire in
Acts 28: 2 for they *k* a fire and made us

KINDLES (4/4) KINDLE

Job 41:21 His breath *k* coals, And a
Isa 30:33 stream of brimstone, *K* it.
44:15 he *k* it and bakes bread;
Jas 3: 5 great a forest a little fire *k*!

KINDLY (16/16) KIND

Gen 24:49 Now if you will deal *k* and truly
34: 3 the young woman and spoke *k* to
47:29 and deal *k* and truly with me.
50:21 he comforted them and spoke *k*
Josh 2:14 that we will deal *k* and truly
Judg 19: 3 to speak *k* to her and bring
Ruth 1: 8 The LORD deal *k* with you, as
2:13 and have spoken *k* to your
1 Sam 20: 8 Therefore you shall deal *k* with
2 Sam 13:24 *K* note, your servant has
2 Ki 25:28 He spoke *k* to him, and gave him
Job 39:13 wings and pinions like the *k*
Prov 26:25 When he speaks *k*,
Jer 52:32 And he spoke *k* to him and gave
Acts 27: 3 And Julius treated Paul *k* and
Rom 12:10 Be *k* affectionate to one

KINDNESS (46/41) KIND

Gen 20:13 This is your *k* that you should
21:23 but that according to the *k*
24:12 and show *k* to my master
24:14 know that You have shown *k* to
40:14 and please show *k* to me; make
Josh 2:12 LORD, since I have shown you *k*,
2:12 that you also will show *k* to my
Judg 8:35 nor did they show *k* to the house
Ruth 2:20 who has not forsaken His *k* to
3:10 For you have shown more *k* at
1 Sam 15: 6 For you showed *k* to all the
20:14 shall not only show me the *k*
20:15 you shall not cut off your *k*
2 Sam 2: 5 for you have shown this *k* to
2: 6 And now may the LORD show *k* and
2: 6 I also will repay you this *k*,
9: 1 that I may show him *k* for
9: 3 to whom I may show the *k* of
9: 7 for I will surely show you *k*
10: 2 I will show *k* to Hanun the son
10: 2 as his father showed *k* to me."
1 Ki 2: 7 But show *k* to the sons of
3: 6 You have continued this great *k*
1 Chr 19: 2 I will show *k* to Hanun the son
19: 2 because his father showed *k* to
2 Chr 24:22 the king did not remember the *k*
Neh 9:17 Slow to anger, Abundant in *k*,
Job 6:14 *k* should be shown by his
Ps 31:21 He has shown me His marvelous *k*
117: 2 For His merciful *k* is great
119:76 Your merciful *k* be for my
141: 5 strike me; It shall be a *k*.
Prov 19:22 What is desired in a man is *k*,
31:26 on her tongue is the law of *k*.
Isa 54: 8 But with everlasting *k* I will
54:10 But My *k* shall not depart from
Jer 2: 2 The *k* of your youth, The love
Joel 2:13 Slow to anger, and of great *k*;
Acts 28: 2 the natives showed us unusual *k*;
2 Cor 6: 6 by longsuffering, by *k*,
Gal 5:22 joy, peace, longsuffering, *k*,
Eph 2: 7 riches of His grace in His *k*
Col 3:12 put on tender mercies, *k*,
Titus 3: 4 But when the *k* and the love of
2 Pe 1: 7 to godliness brotherly *k*,
1: 7 and to brotherly *k* love.

KINDRED, KINDREDS (KJV) See FAMILIES, FAMILY, RELATIVES, TRIBES

KINDS (41/39) KIND

Gen 40:17 uppermost basket were all *k*
Ex 35:29 to bring material for all *k*
Lev 11:27 among all *k* of animals that go
19:23 and have planted all *k* of trees
Deut 14:13 and the kite after their *k*;
14:15 and the hawk after their *k*;
22: 9 your vineyard with different *k*
2 Sam 6: 5 before the LORD on all *k* of
1 Ki 7:14 skill in working with all *k* of
1 Chr 18:10 brought with him all *k* of
23:29 what is mixed and with all *k*
29: 2 all *k* of precious stones, and
29: 5 and for all *k* of work to be
2 Chr 32:27 and for all *k* of desirable
32:28 and stalls for all *k* of
Neh 5:18 ten days an abundance of all *k*
10:37 the fruit from all *k* of trees,
13:15 and all *k* of burdens, which
13:16 who brought in fish and all *k*
13:20 merchants and sellers of all *k*
Ps 144:13 Supplying all *k* of produce;
Prov 1:13 We shall find all *k* of
Eccl 2: 5 and I planted all *k* of fruit
2: 8 musical instruments of all *k*.
Ezek 27:22 all *k* of precious stones, and
47:10 fish will be of the same *k* as
47:12 will grow all *k* of trees used
Dan 3: 5 in symphony with all *k* of
3: 7 in symphony with all *k* of
3:10 in symphony with all *k* of
3:15 in symphony with all *k* of
Mt 4:23 and healing all *k* of sickness
4:23 kinds of sickness and all *k* of
5:11 and say all *k* of evil against
10: 1 and to heal all *k* of sickness
10: 1 kinds of sickness and all *k* of
Acts 10:12 In it were all *k* of four-footed
1 Cor 12:10 to another different *k* of
14:10 so many *k* of languages in the
1 Tim 6:10 of money is a root of all *k*
Rev 21:19 city were adorned with all *k*

KINE (KJV) See CATTLE, COWS, HERD

KING (2337/1801) KING'S, KINGLY, KINGS

Gen 14: 1 pass in the days of Amraphel *k*
14: 1 Arioch *k* of Ellasar,
14: 1 Chedorlaomer *k* of Elam, and
14: 1 and Tidal *k* of nations,
14: 2 they made war with Bera *k* of
14: 2 Birsha *k* of Gomorrah, Shinab
14: 2 Shinab *k* of Admah, Shemeber
14: 2 Shemeber *k* of Zeboiim, and the
14: 2 and the *k* of Bela (that is,
14: 8 And the *k* of Sodom, the king of
14: 8 the *k* of Gomorrah, the king of
14: 8 the *k* of Admah, the king of
14: 8 the *k* of Zeboiim, and the king
14: 8 and the *k* of Bela (that is,
14: 9 against Chedorlaomer *k* of Elam,
14: 9 Tidal *k* of nations, Amraphel
14: 9 Amraphel *k* of Shinar, and
14: 9 and Arioch *k* of Ellasar—four
14:17 And the *k* of Sodom went out to
14:18 Then Melchizedek *k* of Salem
14:21 Now the *k* of Sodom said to
14:22 But Abram said to the *k* of
20: 2 And Abimelech *k* of Gerar sent
26: 1 And Isaac went to Abimelech *k*
26: 8 that Abimelech *k* of the
36:31 the land of Edom before any *k*
40: 1 butler and the baker of the *k*
40: 1 their lord, the *k* of Egypt.
40: 5 butler and the baker of the *k*
41:46 when he stood before Pharaoh *k*
Ex 1: 8 Now there arose a new *k* over
1:15 Then the *k* of Egypt spoke to
1:17 and did not do as the *k* of
1:18 So the *k* of Egypt called for the
2:23 the process of time that the *k*
3:18 to the *k* of Egypt; and you
3:19 But I am sure that the *k* of
5: 4 Then the *k* of Egypt said to
6:11 tell Pharaoh *k* of Egypt to let
6:13 of Israel and for Pharaoh *k* of
6:27 ones who spoke to Pharaoh *k* of
6:29 Speak to Pharaoh *k* of Egypt all
14: 5 Now it was told the *k* of Egypt
14: 8 the heart of Pharaoh *k* of
Num 20:14 from Kadesh to the *k* of Edom.
21: 1 The *k* of Arad, the Canaanite,
21:21 sent messengers to Sihon *k* of
21:26 was the city of Sihon *k* of
21:26 fought against the former *k* of
21:29 To Sihon *k* of the Amorites.
21:33 So Og *k* of Bashan went out
21:34 do to him as you did to Sihon *k*
22: 4 Balak the son of Zippor was *k*
22:10 *k* of Moab, has sent to me,
23: 7 Balak the *k* of Moab has brought
23:21 And the shout of a *K* is among
24: 7 His *k* shall be higher than Agag,
32:33 the kingdom of Sihon *k* of the
32:33 and the kingdom of Og *k* of
33:40 Now the *k* of Arad, the
Deut 1: 4 after he had killed Sihon *k* of
1: 4 and Og *k* of Bashan, who dwelt
2:24 *k* of Heshbon, and his land.
2:26 of Kedemoth to Sihon *k* of
2:30 But Sihon *k* of Heshbon would not
3: 1 and Og *k* of Bashan came out
3: 2 do to him as you did to Sihon *k*
3: 3 delivered into our hands Og *k*
3: 6 as we did to Sihon *k* of
3:11 For only Og *k* of Bashan remained
4:46 in the land of Sihon *k* of the
4:47 his land and the land of Og *k*
7: 8 from the hand of Pharaoh *k* of
11: 3 to Pharaoh *k* of Egypt, and to
17:14 I will set a *k* over me like all
17:15 you shall surely set a *k* over
17:15 brethren you shall set as *k*
28:36 LORD will bring you and the *k*
29: 7 Sihon *k* of Heshbon and Og king
29: 7 Sihon king of Heshbon and Og *k*
33: 5 And He was *K* in Jeshurun, When
Josh 2: 2 And it was told the *k* of
2: 3 So the *k* of Jericho sent to
6: 2 Jericho into your hand, its *k*,
8: 1 given into your hand the *k* of
8: 2 you shall do to Ai and its *k*
8: 2 as you did to Jericho and its *k*.
8:14 when the *k* of Ai saw it, that
8:23 But the *k* of Ai they took alive,
8:29 And the *k* of Ai he hanged on a
9:10 to Sihon *k* of Heshbon, and Og
9:10 and Og *k* of Bashan, who was at
10: 1 to pass when Adoni-Zedek *k* of
10: 1 had done to Jericho and its *k*,
10: 1 so he had done to Ai and its *k*—
10: 3 Therefore Adoni-Zedek *k* of
10: 3 of Jerusalem sent to Hoham *k*
10: 3 Piram *k* of Jarmuth, Japhia king
10: 3 Japhia *k* of Lachish, and Debir
10: 3 and Debir *k* of Eglon, saying,
10: 5 the *k* of Jerusalem, the king of
10: 5 the *k* of Hebron, the king of
10: 5 the *k* of Jarmuth, the king of
10: 5 the *k* of Lachish, and the king
10: 5 and the *k* of Eglon, gathered
10:23 the *k* of Jerusalem, the king of
10:23 the *k* of Hebron, the king of
10:23 the *k* of Jarmuth, the king of
10:23 the *k* of Lachish, and the king
10:23 and the *k* of Eglon.
10:28 and struck it and its *k* with
10:28 He also did to the *k* of
10:28 as he had done to the *k* of

10:30 also delivered it and its ***k***
10:30 but did to its ***k*** as he had done
10:30 king as he had done to the ***k***
10:33 Then Horam ***k*** of Gezer came up to
10:37 the edge of the sword—its ***k***,
10:39 And he took it and its ***k*** and all
10:39 so he did to Debir and its ***k***,
10:39 done also to Libnah and its ***k***.
11: 1 when Jabin ***k*** of Hazor heard
11: 1 that he sent to Jobab ***k*** of
11: 1 to the ***k*** of Shimron, to the
11: 1 to the ***k*** of Achshaph,
11:10 and struck its ***k*** with the
12: 2 One ***k*** was Sihon king of the
12: 2 One king was Sihon ***k*** of the
12: 4 The other ***k*** was Og king of
12: 4 The other king was Og ***k*** of
12: 5 to the border of Sihon ***k*** of
12: 9 the ***k*** of Jericho, one; the king
12: 9 the ***k*** of Ai, which is beside
12:10 the ***k*** of Jerusalem, one; the
12:10 the ***k*** of Hebron, one;
12:11 the ***k*** of Jarmuth, one; the king
12:11 the ***k*** of Lachish, one;
12:12 the ***k*** of Eglon, one; the king of
12:12 the ***k*** of Gezer, one;
12:13 the ***k*** of Debir, one; the king of
12:13 the ***k*** of Geder, one;
12:14 the ***k*** of Hormah, one; the king
12:14 the ***k*** of Arad, one;
12:15 the ***k*** of Libnah, one; the king
12:15 the ***k*** of Adullam, one;
12:16 the ***k*** of Makkedah, one; the king
12:16 the ***k*** of Bethel, one;
12:17 the ***k*** of Tappuah, one; the king
12:17 the ***k*** of Hepher, one;
12:18 the ***k*** of Aphek, one; the king of
12:18 the ***k*** of Lasharon, one;
12:19 the ***k*** of Madon, one; the king of
12:19 the ***k*** of Hazor, one;
12:20 the ***k*** of Shimron Meron, one; the
12:20 the ***k*** of Achshaph, one;
12:21 the ***k*** of Taanach, one; the king
12:21 the ***k*** of Megiddo, one;
12:22 the ***k*** of Kedesh, one; the king
12:22 the ***k*** of Jokneam in Carmel,
12:23 the ***k*** of Dor in the heights of
12:23 the ***k*** of the people of Gilgal,
12:24 the ***k*** of Tirzah, one—all the
13:10 all the cities of Sihon ***k*** of the
13:21 and all the kingdom of Sihon ***k***
13:27 rest of the kingdom of Sihon ***k***
13:30 all the kingdom of Og ***k*** of
24: 9 ***k*** of Moab, arose to make war
Judg 3: 8 hand of Cushan-Rishathaim ***k*** of
3:10 delivered Cushan-Rishathaim ***k***
3:12 the LORD strengthened Eglon ***k***
3:14 of Israel served Eglon ***k*** of
3:15 Israel sent tribute to Eglon ***k***
3:17 brought the tribute to Eglon ***k***
3:19 a secret message for you, O ***k***.
4: 2 them into the hand of Jabin ***k***
4:17 was peace between Jabin ***k*** of
4:23 on that day God subdued Jabin ***k***
4:24 and stronger against Jabin ***k***
4:24 they had destroyed Jabin ***k*** of
8:18 one resembled the son of a ***k***.
9: 6 they went and made Abimelech ***k***
9: 8 once went forth to anoint a ***k***
9:15 in truth you anoint me as ***k***
9:16 sincerity in making Abimelech ***k***,
9:18 ***k*** over the men of Shechem,
11:12 sent messengers to the ***k*** of
11:13 And the ***k*** of the people of Ammon
11:14 again sent messengers to the ***k***
11:17 sent messengers to the ***k*** of
11:17 But the ***k*** of Edom would not
11:17 like manner they sent to the ***k***
11:19 sent messengers to Sihon ***k*** of
11:19 ***k*** of Heshbon; and Israel said
11:25 ***k*** of Moab? Did he ever strive
11:28 the ***k*** of the people of Ammon
17: 6 In those days there was no ***k***
18: 1 In those days there was no ***k***
19: 1 when there was no ***k*** in
21:25 those days there was no ***k*** in
1 Sam 2:10 will give strength to His ***k***,
8: 5 Now make us a ***k*** to judge us
8: 6 Give us a ***k*** to judge us." So
8: 9 them the behavior of the ***k*** who
8:10 people who asked him for a ***k***.
8:11 will be the behavior of the ***k***
8:18 in that day because of your ***k***
8:19 but we will have a ***k*** over us,
8:20 and that our ***k*** may judge us and
8:22 their voice, and make them a ***k***.
10:19 set a ***k*** over us!' Now
10:24 Long live the ***k***!"
11:15 and there they made Saul ***k***
12: 1 and have made a ***k*** over you.
12: 2 "And now here is the ***k***,
12: 9 and into the hand of the ***k*** of
12:12 when you saw that Nahash ***k***
12:12 but a ***k*** shall reign over us,'
12:12 the LORD your God was your ***k***.
12:13 here is the ***k*** whom you have
12:13 the LORD has set a ***k*** over you.
12:14 then both you and the ***k*** who
12:17 in asking a ***k*** for yourselves."
12:19 our sins the evil of asking a ***k***
12:25 swept away, both you and your ***k***.
15: 1 LORD sent me to anoint you ***k***
15: 8 He also took Agag ***k*** of the
15:11 that I have set up Saul as ***k***,
15:17 did not the LORD anoint you ***k***
15:20 and brought back Agag ***k*** of
15:23 has rejected you from being ***k***.
15:26 has rejected you from being ***k***
15:32 Bring Agag ***k*** of the Amalekites
15:35 that He had made Saul ***k*** over
16: 1 For I have provided Myself a ***k***
17:25 the man who kills him the ***k***
17:55 said, "As your soul lives, O ***k***,
17:56 So the ***k*** said, "Inquire whose
18: 6 to meet ***K*** Saul, with
18:18 I should be son-in-law to the ***k***?
18:22 the ***k*** has delight in you, and
18:25 The ***k*** does not desire any dowry
18:27 them in full count to the ***k***,
19: 4 Let not the ***k*** sin against his
20: 5 not fail to sit with the ***k*** to
20:24 the ***k*** sat down to eat the
20:25 Now the ***k*** sat on his seat, as at
21: 2 The ***k*** has ordered me on some
21:10 and went to Achish the ***k*** of
21:11 Is this not David the ***k*** of the
21:12 much afraid of Achish the ***k*** of
22: 3 and he said to the ***k*** of Moab,
22: 4 So he brought them before the ***k***
22:11 So the ***k*** sent to call Ahimelech
22:11 Nob. And they all came to the ***k***.
22:14 So Ahimelech answered the ***k*** and
22:15 be it from me! Let not the ***k***
22:16 And the ***k*** said, "You shall
22:17 Then the ***k*** said to the guards
22:17 But the servants of the ***k***
22:18 And the ***k*** said to Doeg, "You
23:17 You shall be ***k*** over Israel, and
23:20 "Now therefore, O ***k***,
24: 8 My lord the ***k***!" And when Saul
24:14 After whom has the ***k*** of Israel
24:20 that you shall surely be ***k***,
25:36 house, like the feast of a ***k***.
26:14 are you, calling out to the ***k***?
26:15 you not guarded your lord the ***k***?
26:15 in to destroy your lord the ***k***.
26:17 is my voice, my lord, O ***k***.
26:19 let my lord the ***k*** hear the
26:20 For the ***k*** of Israel has come
27: 2 son of Maoch, ***k*** of Gath.
28:13 And the ***k*** said to her, "Do not
29: 3 the servant of Saul ***k*** of
29: 8 the enemies of my lord the ***k***?
2 Sam 2: 4 and there they anointed David ***k***
2: 7 of Judah has anointed me ***k***
2: 9 and he made him ***k*** over Gilead,
2:11 And the time that David was ***k*** in
3: 3 of Talmai, ***k*** of Geshur;
3:17 seeking for David to be ***k***
3:21 all Israel to my lord the ***k***,
3:23 the son of Ner came to the ***k***,
3:24 Then Joab came to the ***k*** and
3:31 And ***K*** David followed the
3:32 and the ***k*** lifted up his voice
3:33 And the ***k*** sang a lament over
3:36 since whatever the ***k*** did
3:38 Then the ***k*** said to his servants,
3:39 weak today, though anointed ***k***;
4: 8 at Hebron, and said to the ***k***,
4: 8 has avenged my lord the ***k*** this
5: 2 when Saul was ***k*** over us, you
5: 3 elders of Israel came to the ***k***
5: 3 and ***K*** David made a covenant
5: 3 And they anointed David ***k*** over
5: 6 And the ***k*** and his men went to
5:11 Then Hiram ***k*** of Tyre sent
5:12 LORD had established him as ***k***
5:17 that they had anointed David ***k***
6:12 Now it was told ***K*** David,
6:16 through a window and saw ***K***
6:20 How glorious was the ***k*** of Israel
7: 1 Now it came to pass when the ***k***
7: 2 that the ***k*** said to Nathan the
7: 3 Then Nathan said to the ***k***,
7:18 Then ***K*** David went in and sat
8: 3 ***k*** of Zobah, as he went to
8: 5 came to help Hadadezer ***k*** of
8: 8 ***K*** David took a large amount of
8: 9 When Toi ***k*** of Hamath heard that
8:10 Toi sent Joram his son to ***K***
8:11 ***K*** David also dedicated these to
8:12 son of Rehob, ***k*** of Zobah.
9: 2 the ***k*** said to him, "Are you
9: 3 Then the ***k*** said, "Is there not
9: 3 And Ziba said to the ***k***,
9: 4 So the ***k*** said to him, "Where
9: 4 And Ziba said to the ***k***,
9: 5 Then ***K*** David sent and brought
9: 9 And the ***k*** called to Ziba,
9:11 Then Ziba said to the ***k***,
9:11 to all that my lord the ***k*** has
9:11 Mephibosheth," said the ***k***,
10: 1 happened after this that the ***k***
10: 5 And the ***k*** said, "Wait at
10: 6 and from the ***k*** of Maacah one
11: 8 and a gift of food from the ***k***
11:19 the matters of the war to the ***k***,
12: 7 I anointed you ***k*** over Israel,
13: 6 and when the ***k*** came to see him,
13: 6 to see him, Amnon said to the ***k***,
13:13 please speak to the ***k***;
13:21 But when ***K*** David heard of all
13:24 Then Absalom came to the ***k*** and
13:24 let the ***k*** and his servants go
13:25 But the ***k*** said to Absalom, "No,
13:26 And the ***k*** said to him, "Why
13:31 So the ***k*** arose and tore his
13:33 let not my lord the ***k*** take the
13:35 And Jonadab said to the ***k***,
13:36 Also the ***k*** and all his servants
13:37 ***k*** of Geshur. And David mourned
13:39 And ***K*** David longed to go to
14: 3 Go to the ***k*** and speak to him in
14: 4 woman of Tekoa spoke to the ***k***,
14: 4 and said, "Help, O ***k***!"
14: 5 Then the ***k*** said to her, "What
14: 8 Then the ***k*** said to the woman,
14: 9 woman of Tekoa said to the ***k***,
14: 9 to the king, "My lord, O ***k***,
14: 9 and the ***k*** and his throne be
14:10 So the ***k*** said, "Whoever says
14:11 Please let the ***k*** remember the
14:12 another word to my lord the ***k***.
14:13 For the ***k*** speaks this thing as
14:13 in that the ***k*** does not bring
14:15 of this thing to my lord the ***k***
14:15 'I will now speak to the ***k***;
14:15 it may be that the ***k*** will
14:16 For the ***k*** will hear and deliver
14:17 The word of my lord the ***k*** will
14:17 so is my lord the ***k*** in
14:18 Then the ***k*** answered and said to
14:18 let my lord the ***k*** speak."
14:19 So the ***k*** said, "Is the hand of
14:19 "As you live, my lord the ***k***,
14:19 anything that my lord the ***k***
14:21 And the ***k*** said to Joab, "All
14:22 himself, and thanked the ***k***.
14:22 in your sight, my lord, O ***k***,
14:22 in that the ***k*** has fulfilled the
14:24 And the ***k*** said, "Let him return
14:29 for Joab, to send him to the ***k***,
14:32 so that I may send you to the ***k***,
14:33 So Joab went to the ***k*** and told
14:33 he came to the ***k*** and bowed
14:33 face to the ground before the ***k***.
14:33 Then the ***k*** kissed Absalom.
15: 2 who had a lawsuit came to the ***k***
15: 3 there is no deputy of the ***k***
15: 6 all Israel who came to the ***k***
15: 7 that Absalom said to the ***k***,
15: 9 And the ***k*** said to him, "Go in
15:15 king's servants said to the ***k***,
15:15 to do whatever my lord the ***k***
15:16 Then the ***k*** went out with all his
15:16 But the ***k*** left ten women,
15:17 And the ***k*** went out with all the
15:18 from Gath, passed before the ***k***.
15:19 Then the ***k*** said to Ittai the
15:19 Return and remain with the ***k***.
15:21 And Ittai answered the ***k*** and
15:21 and as my lord the ***k*** lives,
15:21 in whatever place my lord the ***k***
15:23 The ***k*** himself also crossed over
15:25 Then the ***k*** said to Zadok,
15:27 The ***k*** also said to Zadok the
15:34 'I will be your servant, O ***k***;
16: 2 And the ***k*** said to Ziba, "What
16: 3 Then the ***k*** said, "And where is
16: 3 son?" And Ziba said to the ***k***,
16: 4 So the ***k*** said to Ziba, "Here,
16: 4 sight, my lord, O ***k***!"
16: 5 Now when ***K*** David came to
16: 6 and at all the servants of ***K***
16: 9 son of Zeruiah said to the ***k***,
16: 9 dead dog curse my lord the ***k***?
16:10 But the ***k*** said, "What have I to
16:14 Now the ***k*** and all the people who
16:16 Long live the ***k***! Long live the
16:16 the king! Long live the ***k***!"
17: 2 and I will strike only the ***k***.
17:16 lest the ***k*** and all the people
17:17 and they would go and tell ***K***
17:21 of the well and went and told ***K***
18: 2 And the ***k*** said to the people,
18: 4 Then the ***k*** said to them,
18: 4 So the ***k*** stood beside the
18: 5 Now the ***k*** had commanded Joab,
18: 5 all the people heard when the ***k***
18:12 For in our hearing the ***k***
18:13 is nothing hidden from the ***k***,
18:19 now and take the news to the ***k***,
18:21 tell the ***k*** what you have
18:25 cried out and told the ***k***.
18:25 And the ***k*** said, "If he is
18:26 running alone!" And the ***k***
18:27 And the ***k*** said, "He is a
18:28 called out and said to the ***k***,
18:28 face to the earth before the ***k***,
18:28 hand against my lord the ***k***!"
18:29 The ***k*** said, "Is the young man
18:30 And the ***k*** said, "Turn aside
18:31 my lord the ***k***! For the LORD
18:32 And the ***k*** said to the Cushite,
18:32 the enemies of my lord the ***k***,
18:33 Then the ***k*** was deeply moved,
19: 1 the ***k*** is weeping and mourning
19: 2 The ***k*** is grieved for his son."
19: 4 But the ***k*** covered his face, and
19: 4 and the ***k*** cried out with a loud
19: 5 came into the house to the ***k***,
19: 8 Then the ***k*** arose and sat in the
19: 8 saying, "There is the ***k***,
19: 8 the people came before the ***k***.
19: 9 The ***k*** saved us from the hand of
19:10 about bringing back the ***k***?

19:11 So *K* David sent to Zadok and
19:11 are you the last to bring the ***k***
19:11 all Israel have come to the ***k***,
19:12 the last to bring back the ***k***?
19:14 they sent this word to the ***k***:
19:15 Then the ***k*** returned and came to
19:15 to Gilgal, to go to meet the ***k***,
19:15 to escort the ***k*** across the
19:16 with the men of Judah to meet *K*
19:17 over the Jordan before the ***k***.
19:18 of Gera fell down before the ***k***
19:19 Then he said to the ***k***,
19:19 on the day that my lord the ***k***
19:19 that the ***k*** should take it to
19:20 go down to meet my lord the ***k***.
19:22 I not know that today I am ***k***
19:23 Therefore the ***k*** said to Shimei,
19:23 And the ***k*** swore to him.
19:24 of Saul came down to meet the ***k***.
19:24 from the day the ***k*** departed
19:25 come to Jerusalem to meet the ***k***,
19:25 that the ***k*** said to him, "Why
19:26 And he answered, "My lord, O ***k***,
19:26 may ride on it and go to the ***k***,
19:27 your servant to my lord the ***k***,
19:27 but my lord the ***k*** is like the
19:28 dead men before my lord the ***k***.
19:28 to cry out anymore to the ***k***?
19:29 So the ***k*** said to him, "Why do
19:30 Then Mephibosheth said to the ***k***,
19:30 inasmuch as my lord the ***k*** has
19:31 across the Jordan with the ***k***,
19:32 And he had provided the ***k*** with
19:33 And the ***k*** said to Barzillai,
19:34 But Barzillai said to the ***k***,
19:34 that I should go up with the ***k***
19:35 further burden to my lord the ***k***?
19:36 across the Jordan with the ***k***.
19:36 And why should the ***k*** repay me
19:37 cross over with my lord the ***k***,
19:38 And the ***k*** answered, "Chimham
19:39 And when the ***k*** had crossed
19:39 the ***k*** kissed Barzillai and
19:40 Now the ***k*** went on to Gilgal,
19:40 people of Judah escorted the ***k***,
19:41 the men of Israel came to the ***k***,
19:41 to the king, and said to the ***k***,
19:41 you away and brought the ***k***,
19:42 Because the ***k*** is a close
19:43 "We have ten shares in the ***k***;
19:43 to advise bringing back our ***k***?
20: 2 remained loyal to their ***k***.
20: 3 And the ***k*** took the ten women,
20: 4 And the ***k*** said to Amasa,
20:21 raised his hand against the ***k***,
20:22 So Joab returned to the ***k*** at
21: 2 So the ***k*** called the Gibeonites
21: 5 Then they answered the ***k***,
21: 6 And the ***k*** said, "I will give
21: 7 But the ***k*** spared Mephibosheth
21: 8 So the ***k*** took Armoni and
21:14 they performed all that the ***k***
22:51 the tower of salvation to His ***k***,
24: 2 So the ***k*** said to Joab the
24: 3 And Joab said to the ***k***,
24: 3 may the eyes of my lord the ***k***
24: 3 But why does my lord the ***k***
24: 4 out from the presence of the ***k***
24: 9 number of the people to the ***k***.
24:20 and saw the ***k*** and his servants
24:20 went out and bowed before the ***k***
24:21 Why has my lord the ***k*** come to
24:22 Let my lord the ***k*** take and offer
24:23 'All these, O ***k***, Araunah has
24:23 Araunah has given to the ***k***.
24:23 And Araunah said to the ***k***,
24:24 Then the ***k*** said to Araunah,
1 Ki 1: 1 Now *K* David was old, advanced
1: 2 be sought for our lord the ***k***,
1: 2 and let her stand before the ***k***,
1: 2 that our lord the ***k*** may be
1: 3 and brought her to the ***k***.
1: 4 lovely; and she cared for the ***k***,
1: 4 but the ***k*** did not know her.
1: 5 I will be ***k***"; and he prepared
1:11 the son of Haggith has become ***k***,
1:13 Go immediately to *K* David and
1:13 him, 'Did you not, my lord, O ***k***,
1:13 Why then has Adonijah become ***k***?
1:14 still talking there with the ***k***,
1:15 went into the chamber to the ***k***.
1:15 (Now the ***k*** was very old, and
1:15 Shunammite was serving the ***k***.
1:16 bowed and did homage to the ***k***.
1:16 Then the ***k*** said, "What is your
1:18 look! Adonijah has become ***k***;
1:18 king; and now, my lord the ***k***,
1:19 invited all the sons of the ***k***,
1:20 "And as for you, my lord, O ***k***,
1:20 on the throne of my lord the ***k***
1:21 when my lord the ***k*** rests with
1:22 was still talking with the ***k***,
1:23 So they told the ***k***,
1:23 when he came in before the ***k***,
1:23 he bowed down before the ***k*** with
1:24 And Nathan said, "My lord, O ***k***,
1:25 Long live *K* Adonijah!'
1:27 been done by my lord the ***k***,
1:27 on the throne of my lord the ***k***
1:28 Then *K* David answered and said,
1:28 presence and stood before the ***k***.
1:29 And the ***k*** took an oath and said,
1:30 Solomon your son shall be ***k***
1:31 earth, and paid homage to the ***k***,
1:31 Let my lord *K* David live
1:32 And *K* David said, "Call to me
1:32 So they came before the ***k***.
1:33 The ***k*** also said to them, "Take
1:34 the prophet anoint him ***k*** over
1:34 Long live *K* Solomon!'
1:35 and he shall be ***k*** in my place.
1:36 son of Jehoiada answered the ***k***
1:36 the LORD God of my lord the ***k***
1:37 has been with my lord the ***k***,
1:37 than the throne of my lord *K*
1:38 down and had Solomon ride on *K*
1:39 Long live *K* Solomon!"
1:43 No! Our lord *K* David has made
1:43 King David has made Solomon ***k***.
1:44 The ***k*** has sent with him Zadok
1:45 prophet have anointed him ***k*** at
1:47 have gone to bless our lord *K*
1:47 Then the ***k*** bowed himself on
1:48 Also the ***k*** said thus, 'Blessed
1:51 Adonijah is afraid of *K*
1:51 Let *K* Solomon swear to me today
1:53 So *K* Solomon sent them to bring
1:53 he came and fell down before *K*
2:17 Please speak to *K* Solomon, for
2:18 I will speak for you to the ***k***.
2:19 Bathsheba therefore went to *K*
2:19 And the ***k*** rose up to meet her
2:20 And the ***k*** said to her, "Ask
2:22 And *K* Solomon answered and said
2:23 Then *K* Solomon swore by the
2:25 So *K* Solomon sent by the hand of
2:26 to Abiathar the priest the ***k***
2:29 And *K* Solomon was told, "Joab
2:30 said to him, "Thus says the ***k***,
2:30 brought back word to the ***k***,
2:31 Then the ***k*** said to him, "Do as
2:35 The ***k*** put Benaiah the son of
2:35 and the ***k*** put Zadok the priest
2:36 Then the ***k*** sent and called for
2:38 And Shimei said to the ***k***,
2:38 As my lord the ***k*** has said, so
2:39 ***k*** of Gath. And they told
2:42 Then the ***k*** sent and called for
2:44 The ***k*** said moreover to Shimei,
2:45 But *K* Solomon shall be
2:46 So the ***k*** commanded Benaiah the
3: 1 made a treaty with Pharaoh ***k***
3: 4 Now the ***k*** went to Gibeon to
3: 7 You have made Your servant ***k***
3:16 were harlots came to the ***k***,
3:22 Thus they spoke before the ***k***.
3:23 And the ***k*** said, "The one says,
3:24 Then the ***k*** said, "Bring me a
3:24 brought a sword before the ***k***.
3:25 And the ***k*** said, "Divide the
3:26 son was living spoke to the ***k***,
3:27 So the ***k*** answered and said,
3:28 of the judgment which the ***k***
3:28 rendered; and they feared the ***k***,
4: 1 So *K* Solomon was king over all
4: 1 So King Solomon was ***k*** over all
4: 7 who provided food for the ***k*** and
4:19 in the country of Sihon ***k*** of
4:19 and of Og ***k*** of Bashan. He was
4:27 provided food for *K* Solomon and
4:27 and for all who came to *K*
5: 1 Now Hiram ***k*** of Tyre sent his
5: 1 that they had anointed him ***k***
5:13 Then *K* Solomon raised up a
5:17 And the ***k*** commanded them to
6: 2 Now the house which *K* Solomon
7:13 Now *K* Solomon sent and brought
7:14 So he came to *K* Solomon and did
7:40 work that he was to do for *K*
7:45 which Huram made for *K* Solomon
7:46 In the plain of Jordan the ***k*** had
7:51 So all the work that *K* Solomon
8: 1 to *K* Solomon in Jerusalem, that
8: 2 men of Israel assembled with *K*
8: 5 Also *K* Solomon, and all the
8:14 Then the ***k*** turned around and
8:62 Then the ***k*** and all Israel with
8:63 So the ***k*** and all the children
8:64 On the same day the ***k***
8:66 away; and they blessed the ***k***,
9:11 (Hiram the ***k*** of Tyre had
9:11 that *K* Solomon then gave Hiram
9:14 Then Hiram sent the ***k*** one
9:15 for the labor force which *K*
9:16 (Pharaoh ***k*** of Egypt had gone up
9:26 *K* Solomon also built a fleet of
9:28 and brought it to *K* Solomon.
10: 3 nothing so difficult for the ***k***
10: 6 Then she said to the ***k***:
10: 9 therefore He made you ***k***,
10:10 Then she gave the ***k*** one hundred
10:10 as the queen of Sheba gave to *K*
10:12 And the ***k*** made steps of the
10:13 Now *K* Solomon gave the queen of
10:16 And *K* Solomon made two hundred
10:17 The ***k*** put them in the House of
10:18 Moreover the ***k*** made a great
10:21 All *K* Solomon's drinking
10:22 For the ***k*** had merchant ships at
10:23 So *K* Solomon surpassed all the
10:26 chariot cities and with the ***k***
10:27 The ***k*** made silver as common in
11: 1 But *K* Solomon loved many foreign
11:14 he was a descendant of the ***k***
11:18 to Pharaoh ***k*** of Egypt, who gave
11:23 Hadadezer ***k*** of Zobah.
11:26 also rebelled against the ***k***.
11:27 him to rebel against the ***k***:
11:37 and you shall be ***k*** over Israel.
11:40 to Shishak ***k*** of Egypt, and was
12: 1 gone to Shechem to make him ***k***.
12: 2 had fled from the presence of *K*
12: 6 Then *K* Rehoboam consulted the
12:12 as the ***k*** had directed, saying,
12:13 Then the ***k*** answered the people
12:15 So the ***k*** did not listen to the
12:16 when all Israel saw that the ***k***
12:16 them, the people answered the ***k***,
12:18 Then *K* Rehoboam sent Adoram,
12:18 Therefore *K* Rehoboam mounted
12:20 and made him ***k*** over all Israel.
12:23 ***k*** of Judah, to all the house of
12:27 Rehoboam ***k*** of Judah, and they
12:27 me and go back to Rehoboam ***k***
12:28 Therefore the ***k*** asked advice,
13: 4 So it came to pass when *K*
13: 6 Then the ***k*** answered and said to
13: 7 Then the ***k*** said to the man of
13: 8 the man of God said to the ***k***,
13:11 which he had spoken to the ***k***.
14: 2 told me that I would be ***k***
14:14 will raise up for Himself a ***k***
14:21 years old when he became ***k***.
14:25 happened in the fifth year of *K*
14:25 King Rehoboam that Shishak ***k***
14:27 Then *K* Rehoboam made bronze
14:28 And whenever the ***k*** entered the
15: 1 In the eighteenth year of *K*
15: 1 Abijam became ***k*** over Judah.
15: 9 twentieth year of Jeroboam ***k***
15: 9 Asa became ***k*** over Judah.
15:16 war between Asa and Baasha ***k***
15:17 And Baasha ***k*** of Israel came up
15:17 go out or come in to Asa ***k*** of
15:18 And *K* Asa sent them to
15:18 ***k*** of Syria, who dwelt in
15:19 your treaty with Baasha ***k*** of
15:20 So Ben-Hadad heeded *K* Asa, and
15:22 Then *K* Asa made a proclamation
15:22 and with them *K* Asa built Geba
15:25 the son of Jeroboam became ***k***
15:25 in the second year of Asa ***k*** of
15:28 him in the third year of Asa ***k***
15:29 And it was so, when he became ***k***,
15:32 war between Asa and Baasha ***k***
15:33 In the third year of Asa ***k*** of
15:33 the son of Ahijah became ***k***
16: 8 the twenty-sixth year of Asa ***k***
16: 8 Elah the son of Baasha became ***k***
16:10 twenty-seventh year of Asa ***k***
16:15 twenty-seventh year of Asa ***k***
16:16 and also has killed the ***k***.
16:16 ***k*** over Israel that day in the
16:21 son of Ginath, to make him ***k***,
16:23 the thirty-first year of Asa ***k***
16:23 Omri became ***k*** over Israel, and
16:29 thirty-eighth year of Asa ***k*** of
16:29 Ahab the son of Omri became ***k***
16:31 ***k*** of the Sidonians; and he went
19:15 anoint Hazael as ***k*** over Syria.
19:16 Jehu the son of Nimshi as ***k***
20: 1 Now Ben-Hadad the ***k*** of Syria
20: 2 into the city to Ahab ***k*** of
20: 4 And the ***k*** of Israel answered and
20: 4 and said, "My lord, O ***k***,
20: 7 So the ***k*** of Israel called all
20: 9 Ben-Hadad, "Tell my lord the ***k***,
20:11 So the ***k*** of Israel answered and
20:13 a prophet approached Ahab ***k*** of
20:20 and Ben-Hadad the ***k*** of Syria
20:21 Then the ***k*** of Israel went out
20:22 And the prophet came to the ***k*** of
20:22 in the spring of the year the ***k***
20:23 Then the servants of the ***k*** of
20:28 of God came and spoke to the ***k***
20:31 and go out to the ***k*** of Israel;
20:32 and came to the ***k*** of Israel and
20:38 departed and waited for the ***k***
20:39 Now as the ***k*** passed by, he cried
20:39 he cried out to the ***k*** and said,
20:40 Then the ***k*** of Israel said to
20:41 and the ***k*** of Israel recognized
20:43 So the ***k*** of Israel went to his
21: 1 next to the palace of Ahab ***k*** of
21:10 have blasphemed God and the ***k***.
21:13 has blasphemed God and the ***k***!
21:18 go down to meet Ahab ***k*** of
22: 2 that Jehoshaphat the ***k*** of Judah
22: 2 went down to visit the ***k*** of
22: 3 And the ***k*** of Israel said to his
22: 3 it out of the hand of the ***k*** of
22: 4 Jehoshaphat said to the ***k*** of
22: 5 Jehoshaphat said to the ***k*** of
22: 6 Then the ***k*** of Israel gathered
22: 6 it into the hand of the ***k***.
22: 8 So the ***k*** of Israel said to
22: 8 Let not the ***k*** say such things!"
22: 9 Then the ***k*** of Israel called an
22:10 The ***k*** of Israel and Jehoshaphat
22:10 of Israel and Jehoshaphat the ***k***
22:13 with one accord encourage the ***k***.
22:15 Then he came to the ***k***;
22:15 and the ***k*** said to him,
22:15 it into the hand of the ***k***!"
22:16 So the ***k*** said to him, "How many

22:18 And the ***k*** of Israel said to
22:26 So the ***k*** of Israel said, "Take
22:27 "and say, 'Thus says the ***k***:
22:29 So the ***k*** of Israel and
22:29 of Israel and Jehoshaphat the ***k***
22:30 And the ***k*** of Israel said to
22:30 So the ***k*** of Israel disguised
22:31 Now the ***k*** of Syria had commanded
22:31 but only with the ***k*** of
22:32 Surely it is the ***k*** of Israel!"
22:33 saw that it was not the ***k*** of
22:34 and struck the ***k*** of Israel
22:35 and the ***k*** was propped up in his
22:37 So the ***k*** died, and was brought
22:37 And they buried the ***k*** in
22:41 the son of Asa had become ***k***
22:41 in the fourth year of Ahab ***k***
22:42 years old when he became ***k***,
22:44 made peace with the ***k*** of
22:47 There was then no ***k*** in Edom,
22:47 in Edom, only a deputy of the ***k***.
22:51 the son of Ahab became ***k*** over
22:51 year of Jehoshaphat ***k*** of Judah,
2 Ki 1: 3 to meet the messengers of the ***k***
1: 6 return to the ***k*** who sent you,
1: 9 Then the ***k*** sent to him a
1: 9 the ***k*** has said, 'Come down!'"
1:11 thus has the ***k*** said, 'Come down
1:15 and went down with him to the ***k***.
1:17 Jehoram became ***k*** in his place,
1:17 Jehoshaphat, ***k*** of Judah.
3: 1 the son of Ahab became ***k*** over
3: 1 year of Jehoshaphat ***k*** of Judah,
3: 4 Now Mesha ***k*** of Moab was a
3: 4 and he regularly paid the ***k*** of
3: 5 that the ***k*** of Moab rebelled
3: 5 of Moab rebelled against the ***k***
3: 6 So ***K*** Jehoram went out of
3: 7 went and sent to Jehoshaphat ***k***
3: 7 The ***k*** of Moab has rebelled
3: 9 So the ***k*** of Israel went with the
3: 9 king of Israel went with the ***k***
3: 9 the king of Judah and the ***k*** of
3:10 And the ***k*** of Israel said,
3:11 So one of the servants of the ***k***
3:12 So the ***k*** of Israel and
3:12 and Jehoshaphat and the ***k*** of
3:13 Then Elisha said to the ***k*** of
3:13 But the ***k*** of Israel said to
3:14 the presence of Jehoshaphat ***k***
3:26 And when the ***k*** of Moab saw that
3:26 to break through to the ***k*** of
4:13 speak on your behalf to the ***k***
5: 1 commander of the army of the ***k***
5: 5 Then the ***k*** of Syria said, "Go
5: 5 I will send a letter to the ***k***
5: 6 he brought the letter to the ***k***
5: 7 when the ***k*** of Israel read the
5: 8 man of God heard that the ***k*** of
5: 8 clothes, that he sent to the ***k***,
6: 8 Now the ***k*** of Syria was making
6: 9 the man of God sent to the ***k***
6:10 Then the ***k*** of Israel sent
6:11 Therefore the heart of the ***k*** of
6:11 me which of us is for the ***k***
6:12 said, "None, my lord, O ***k***;
6:12 tells the ***k*** of Israel the words
6:21 Now when the ***k*** of Israel saw
6:24 after this that Ben-Hadad ***k*** of
6:26 as the ***k*** of Israel was passing
6:26 'Help, my lord, O ***k***!"
6:28 Then the ***k*** said to her, "What
6:30 when the ***k*** heard the words of
6:32 And the ***k*** sent a man ahead of
6:33 and then the ***k*** said, "Surely
7: 2 an officer on whose hand the ***k***
7: 6 the ***k*** of Israel has hired
7:12 So the ***k*** arose in the night and
7:14 and the ***k*** sent them in the
7:15 returned and told the ***k***.
7:17 Now the ***k*** had appointed the
7:17 who spoke when the ***k*** came down
7:18 man of God had spoken to the ***k***,
8: 3 to make an appeal to the ***k*** for
8: 4 Then the ***k*** talked with Gehazi,
8: 5 as he was telling the ***k*** how he
8: 5 appealing to the ***k*** for her
8: 5 And Gehazi said, "My lord, O ***k***,
8: 6 And when the ***k*** asked the woman,
8: 6 So the ***k*** appointed a certain
8: 7 and Ben-Hadad ***k*** of Syria was
8: 8 And the ***k*** said to Hazael, "Take
8: 9 Your son Ben-Hadad ***k*** of Syria
8:13 me that you will become ***k***
8:16 ***k*** of Israel, Jehoshaphat
8:16 Jehoshaphat having been ***k*** of
8:16 began to reign as ***k*** of Judah.
8:17 years old when he became ***k***,
8:20 and made a ***k*** over themselves.
8:25 ***k*** of Israel, Ahaziah the son of
8:25 ***k*** of Judah, began to reign.
8:26 years old when he became ***k***,
8:26 of Omri, ***k*** of Israel.
8:28 of Ahab to war against Hazael ***k***
8:29 Then ***K*** Joram went back to
8:29 he fought against Hazael ***k*** of
8:29 ***k*** of Judah, went down to see
9: 3 I have anointed you ***k*** over
9: 6 I have anointed you ***k*** over the
9:12 I have anointed you ***k*** over
9:13 saying, "Jehu is ***k***!"
9:14 against Hazael ***k*** of Syria.
9:15 But ***K*** Joram had returned to
9:15 when he fought with Hazael ***k***
9:16 and Ahaziah ***k*** of Judah had come
9:18 and said, "Thus says the ***k***:
9:19 and said, "Thus says the ***k***:
9:21 Then Joram ***k*** of Israel and
9:21 king of Israel and Ahaziah ***k***
9:27 But when Ahaziah ***k*** of Judah saw
9:29 Ahaziah had become ***k*** over
10: 5 but we will not make anyone ***k***.
10:13 with the brothers of Ahaziah ***k***
10:13 to greet the sons of the ***k*** and
11: 2 the daughter of ***K*** Joram, sister
11: 7 house of the LORD for the ***k***.
11: 8 But you shall surround the ***k*** on
11: 8 You are to be with the ***k*** as he
11:10 which had belonged to ***K***
11:11 in his hand, all around the ***k***,
11:12 they made him ***k*** and anointed
11:12 Long live the ***k***!"
11:14 there was the ***k*** standing by a
11:14 the trumpeters were by the ***k***.
11:17 between the LORD, the ***k***,
11:17 and also between the ***k*** and the
11:19 and they brought the ***k*** down
11:21 years old when he became ***k***.
12: 1 year of Jehu, Jehoash became ***k***,
12: 6 by the twenty-third year of ***K***
12: 7 So ***K*** Jehoash called Jehoiada the
12:17 Hazael ***k*** of Syria went up and
12:18 And Jehoash ***k*** of Judah took all
12:18 and sent them to Hazael ***k*** of
13: 1 ***k*** of Judah, Jehoahaz the son of
13: 1 the son of Jehu became ***k*** over
13: 3 them into the hand of Hazael ***k***
13: 4 because the ***k*** of Syria
13: 7 for the ***k*** of Syria had
13:10 thirty-seventh year of Joash ***k***
13:10 the son of Jehoahaz became ***k***
13:12 he fought against Amaziah ***k*** of
13:14 Then Joash the ***k*** of Israel came
13:16 Then he said to the ***k*** of Israel,
13:18 And he said to the ***k*** of Israel,
13:22 And Hazael ***k*** of Syria oppressed
13:24 Now Hazael ***k*** of Syria died.
14: 1 ***k*** of Israel, Amaziah the son of
14: 1 ***k*** of Judah, became king.
14: 1 Joash, king of Judah, became ***k***.
14: 2 years old when he became ***k***,
14: 5 had murdered his father the ***k***.
14: 8 ***k*** of Israel, saying, "Come,
14: 9 And Jehoash ***k*** of Israel sent to
14: 9 of Israel sent to Amaziah ***k*** of
14:11 Therefore Jehoash ***k*** of Israel
14:11 so he and Amaziah ***k*** of Judah
14:13 Then Jehoash ***k*** of Israel
14:13 of Israel captured Amaziah ***k***
14:15 how he fought with Amaziah ***k***
14:17 ***k*** of Judah, lived fifteen years
14:17 son of Jehoahaz, ***k*** of Israel.
14:21 and made him ***k*** instead of his
14:22 after the ***k*** rested with his
14:23 ***k*** of Judah, Jeroboam the son of
14:23 ***k*** of Israel, became king in
14:23 became ***k*** in Samaria, and
15: 1 year of Jeroboam ***k*** of Israel,
15: 1 ***k*** of Judah, became king.
15: 1 king of Judah, became ***k***.
15: 2 years old when he became ***k***,
15: 5 Then the LORD struck the ***k***,
15: 8 year of Azariah ***k*** of Judah,
15:13 the son of Jabesh became ***k*** in
15:13 thirty-ninth year of Uzziah ***k***
15:17 thirty-ninth year of Azariah ***k***
15:17 the son of Gadi became ***k*** over
15:19 Pul ***k*** of Assyria came against
15:20 to give to the ***k*** of Assyria. So
15:20 So the ***k*** of Assyria turned
15:23 the fiftieth year of Azariah ***k***
15:23 the son of Menahem became ***k***
15:27 fifty-second year of Azariah ***k***
15:27 the son of Remaliah became ***k***
15:29 In the days of Pekah ***k*** of
15:29 Tiglath-Pileser ***k*** of Assyria
15:32 ***k*** of Israel, Jotham the son of
15:32 ***k*** of Judah, began to reign.
15:33 years old when he became ***k***,
15:37 LORD began to send Rezin ***k*** of
16: 1 ***k*** of Judah, began to reign.
16: 2 years old when he became ***k***,
16: 5 Then Rezin ***k*** of Syria and Pekah
16: 5 ***k*** of Israel, came up to
16: 6 At that time Rezin ***k*** of Syria
16: 7 to Tiglath-Pileser ***k*** of
16: 7 save me from the hand of the ***k***
16: 7 and from the hand of the ***k*** of
16: 8 it as a present to the ***k*** of
16: 9 So the ***k*** of Assyria heeded him;
16: 9 for the ***k*** of Assyria went up
16:10 Now ***K*** Ahaz went to Damascus to
16:10 to meet Tiglath-Pileser ***k*** of
16:10 and ***K*** Ahaz sent to Urijah the
16:11 altar according to all that ***K***
16:11 the priest made it before ***K***
16:12 And when the ***k*** came back from
16:12 the ***k*** saw the altar; and the
16:12 and the ***k*** approached the altar
16:15 Then ***K*** Ahaz commanded Urijah the
16:16 according to all that ***K*** Ahaz
16:17 And ***K*** Ahaz cut off the panels
16:18 on account of the ***k*** of Assyria.
17: 1 In the twelfth year of Ahaz ***k*** of
17: 1 the son of Elah became ***k*** of
17: 3 Shalmaneser ***k*** of Assyria came up
17: 4 And the ***k*** of Assyria uncovered a
17: 4 ***k*** of Egypt, and brought no
17: 4 brought no tribute to the ***k*** of
17: 4 Therefore the ***k*** of Assyria shut
17: 5 Now the ***k*** of Assyria went
17: 6 the ***k*** of Assyria took Samaria
17: 7 under the hand of Pharaoh ***k*** of
17:21 Jeroboam the son of Nebat ***k***.
17:24 Then the ***k*** of Assyria brought
17:26 So they spoke to the ***k*** of
17:27 Then the ***k*** of Assyria commanded,
18: 1 ***k*** of Israel, that Hezekiah the
18: 1 ***k*** of Judah, began to reign.
18: 2 years old when he became ***k***,
18: 7 And he rebelled against the ***k***
18: 9 to pass in the fourth year of ***K***
18: 9 ***k*** of Israel, that Shalmaneser
18: 9 that Shalmaneser ***k*** of Assyria
18:10 the ninth year of Hoshea ***k*** of
18:11 Then the ***k*** of Assyria carried
18:13 in the fourteenth year of ***K***
18:13 Sennacherib ***k*** of Assyria came
18:14 Then Hezekiah ***k*** of Judah sent to
18:14 king of Judah sent to the ***k*** of
18:14 And the ***k*** of Assyria assessed
18:14 of Assyria assessed Hezekiah ***k***
18:16 the pillars which Hezekiah ***k***
18:16 and gave it to the ***k*** of
18:17 Then the ***k*** of Assyria sent the
18:17 to ***K*** Hezekiah. And they went up
18:18 when they had called to the ***k***,
18:19 'Thus says the great ***k***,
18:19 the ***k*** of Assyria: "What
18:21 So is Pharaoh ***k*** of Egypt to
18:23 a pledge to my master the ***k*** of
18:28 "Hear the word of the great ***k***,
18:28 great king, the ***k*** of Assyria!
18:29 'Thus says the ***k***: 'Do not let
18:30 be given into the hand of the ***k***
18:31 for thus says the ***k*** of Assyria:
18:33 land from the hand of the ***k*** of
19: 1 when ***K*** Hezekiah heard it, that
19: 4 whom his master the ***k*** of
19: 5 So the servants of ***K*** Hezekiah
19: 6 which the servants of the ***k*** of
19: 8 returned and found the ***k*** of
19: 9 And the ***k*** heard concerning
19: 9 heard concerning Tirhakah ***k*** of
19:10 you shall speak to Hezekiah ***k***
19:10 be given into the hand of the ***k***
19:13 Where is the ***k*** of Hamath, the
19:13 the ***k*** of Arpad, and the king of
19:13 and the ***k*** of the city of
19:20 to Me against Sennacherib ***k*** of
19:32 the LORD concerning the ***k*** of
19:36 So Sennacherib ***k*** of Assyria
20: 6 city from the hand of the ***k*** of
20:12 ***k*** of Babylon, sent letters and
20:14 Isaiah the prophet went to ***K***
20:18 eunuchs in the palace of the ***k***
21: 1 years old when he became ***k***,
21: 3 as Ahab ***k*** of Israel had done;
21:11 Because Manasseh ***k*** of Judah has
21:19 years old when he became ***k***,
21:23 and killed the ***k*** in his own
21:24 who had conspired against ***K***
21:24 the land made his son Josiah ***k***
22: 1 years old when he became ***k***,
22: 3 in the eighteenth year of ***K***
22: 3 that the ***k*** sent Shaphan the
22: 9 the scribe went to the ***k***,
22: 9 bringing the ***k*** word, saying,
22:10 Shaphan the scribe showed the ***k***,
22:10 Shaphan read it before the ***k***.
22:11 when the ***k*** heard the words of
22:12 Then the ***k*** commanded Hilkiah the
22:12 and Asaiah a servant of the ***k***,
22:16 words of the book which the ***k***
22:18 But as for the ***k*** of Judah, who
22:20 they brought back word to the ***k***.
23: 1 Now the ***k*** sent them to gather
23: 2 The ***k*** went up to the house of
23: 3 Then the ***k*** stood by a pillar
23: 4 And the ***k*** commanded Hilkiah the
23:12 the ***k*** broke down and pulverized
23:13 Then the ***k*** defiled the high
23:13 which Solomon ***k*** of Israel had
23:21 Then the ***k*** commanded all the
23:23 But in the eighteenth year of ***K***
23:25 Now before him there was no ***k***
23:29 In his days Pharaoh Necho ***k*** of
23:29 Egypt went to the aid of the ***k***
23:29 and ***K*** Josiah went against him.
23:30 and made him ***k*** in his father's
23:31 years old when he became ***k***,
23:34 Eliakim the son of Josiah ***k*** in
23:36 years old when he became ***k***,
24: 1 In his days Nebuchadnezzar ***k*** of
24: 7 And the ***k*** of Egypt did not come
24: 7 for the ***k*** of Babylon had taken
24: 7 all that belonged to the ***k*** of
24: 8 years old when he became ***k***,
24:10 servants of Nebuchadnezzar ***k***
24:11 And Nebuchadnezzar ***k*** of Babylon
24:12 Then Jehoiachin ***k*** of Judah, his
24:12 his officers went out to the ***k***
24:12 and the ***k*** of Babylon, in the
24:13 of gold which Solomon ***k*** of
24:16 these the ***k*** of Babylon brought
24:17 Then the ***k*** of Babylon made

24:17 ***k*** in his place, and changed his
24:18 years old when he became ***k***,
24:20 rebelled against the ***k*** of
25: 1 that Nebuchadnezzar ***k*** of
25: 2 until the eleventh year of ***K***
25: 4 And the ***k*** went by way of the
25: 5 of the Chaldeans pursued the ***k***,
25: 6 So they took the ***k*** and brought
25: 6 and brought him up to the ***k*** of
25: 8 was the nineteenth year of ***K***
25: 8 year of King Nebuchadnezzar ***k***
25: 8 a servant of the ***k*** of Babylon,
25:11 who had deserted to the ***k*** of
25:20 and brought them to the ***k*** of
25:21 Then the ***k*** of Babylon struck
25:22 whom Nebuchadnezzar ***k*** of
25:23 heard that the ***k*** of Babylon had
25:24 in the land and serve the ***k*** of
25:27 the captivity of Jehoiachin ***k***
25:27 that Evil-Merodach ***k*** of
25:27 released Jehoiachin ***k*** of Judah
25:29 bread regularly before the ***k***
25:30 ration given him by the ***k***,
1 Chr 1:43 in the land of Edom before a ***k***
3: 2 ***k*** of Geshur; the fourth,
4:23 there they dwelt with the ***k*** for
4:41 came in the days of Hezekiah ***k***
5: 6 whom Tiglath-Pileser ***k*** of
5:17 in the days of Jotham ***k*** of
5:17 and in the days of Jeroboam ***k***
5:26 stirred up the spirit of Pul ***k***
5:26 Tiglath-Pileser ***k*** of Assyria.
11: 2 time past, even when Saul was ***k***,
11: 3 elders of Israel came to the ***k***
11: 3 Then they anointed David ***k*** over
11:10 with all Israel, to make him ***k***,
12:31 name to come and make David ***k***;
12:38 to make David ***k*** over all
12:38 of one mind to make David ***k***.
14: 1 Now Hiram ***k*** of Tyre sent
14: 2 LORD had established him as ***k***
14: 8 that David had been anointed ***k***
15:29 through a window and saw ***K***
17:16 Then ***K*** David went in and sat
18: 3 David defeated Hadadezer ***k*** of
18: 5 came to help Hadadezer ***k*** of
18: 9 Now when Tou ***k*** of Hamath heard
18: 9 all the army of Hadadezer ***k*** of
18:10 he sent Hadoram his son to ***K***
18:11 ***K*** David also dedicated these to
19: 1 after this that Nahash the ***k***
19: 5 And the ***k*** said, "Wait at
19: 7 with the ***k*** of Maachah and his
21: 3 they are. But, my lord the ***k***,
21:23 and let my lord the ***k*** do what
21:24 Then ***K*** David said to Ornan,
23: 1 he made his son Solomon ***k*** over
24: 6 wrote them down before the ***k***,
24:31 in the presence of ***K*** David,
25: 2 according to the order of the ***k***.
25: 6 under the authority of the ***k***.
26:26 of the dedicated things which ***K***
26:30 and in the service of the ***k***.
26:32 whom ***K*** David made officials
26:32 to God and the affairs of the ***k***.
27: 1 served the ***k*** in every matter of
27:24 account of the chronicles of ***K***
27:31 were the officials over ***K***
28: 1 the divisions who served the ***k***,
28: 1 and possessions of the ***k*** and
28: 2 Then ***K*** David rose to his feet
28: 4 the house of my father to be ***k***
28: 4 pleased with me to make me ***k***
29: 1 Furthermore ***K*** David said to all
29: 9 and ***K*** David also rejoiced
29:20 before the LORD and the ***k***.
29:22 Solomon the son of David ***k*** the
29:23 on the throne of the LORD as ***k***
29:24 and also all the sons of ***K***
29:24 submitted themselves to ***K***
29:25 as had not been on any ***k***
29:29 Now the acts of ***K*** David, first
2 Chr 1: 8 and have made me ***k*** in his
1: 9 for You have made me ***k*** over a
1:11 over whom I have made you ***k***—
1:14 chariot cities and with the ***k***
1:15 Also the ***k*** made silver and gold
2: 3 Then Solomon sent to Hiram ***k*** of
2:11 Then Hiram ***k*** of Tyre answered
2:11 He has made you ***k*** over them.
2:12 for He has given ***K*** David a wise
4:11 work that he was to do for ***K***
4:16 made of burnished bronze for ***K***
4:17 In the plain of Jordan the ***k*** had
5: 3 of Israel assembled with the ***k***
5: 6 Also ***K*** Solomon, and all the
6: 3 Then the ***k*** turned around and
7: 4 Then the ***k*** and all the people
7: 5 ***K*** Solomon offered a sacrifice of
7: 5 So the ***k*** and all the people
7: 6 which ***K*** David had made to
8:10 chiefs of the officials of ***K***
8:11 dwell in the house of David ***k***
8:15 from the command of the ***k*** to
8:18 and brought it to ***K*** Solomon.
9: 5 Then she said to the ***k***:
9: 8 you on His throne to be ***k***
9: 8 therefore He made you ***k*** over
9: 9 And she gave the ***k*** one hundred
9: 9 the queen of Sheba gave to ***K***
9:11 And the ***k*** made walkways of the
9:12 Now ***K*** Solomon gave to the queen
9:12 than she had brought to the ***k***.
9:15 And ***K*** Solomon made two hundred
9:16 The ***k*** put them in the House of
9:17 Moreover the ***k*** made a great
9:20 All ***K*** Solomon's drinking vessels
9:22 So ***K*** Solomon surpassed all the
9:25 chariot cities and with the ***k***
9:27 The ***k*** made silver as common in
10: 1 gone to Shechem to make him ***k***.
10: 2 had fled from the presence of ***K***
10: 6 Then ***K*** Rehoboam consulted the
10:12 as the ***k*** had directed, saying,
10:13 Then the ***k*** answered them
10:13 ***K*** Rehoboam rejected the advice
10:15 So the ***k*** did not listen to the
10:16 all Israel saw that the ***k*** did
10:16 them, the people answered the ***k***,
10:18 Then ***K*** Rehoboam sent Hadoram,
10:18 Therefore ***K*** Rehoboam mounted
11: 3 ***k*** of Judah, and to all Israel
11:22 for he intended to make him ***k***.
12: 2 happened in the fifth year of ***K***
12: 2 that Shishak ***k*** of Egypt came
12: 6 the leaders of Israel and the ***k***
12: 9 So Shishak ***k*** of Egypt came up
12:10 Then ***K*** Rehoboam made bronze
12:11 And whenever the ***k*** entered the
12:13 years old when he became ***k***;
13: 1 In the eighteenth year of ***K***
13: 1 Abijah became ***k*** over Judah.
15:16 the mother of Asa the ***k***,
16: 1 Baasha ***k*** of Israel came up
16: 1 go out or come in to Asa ***k*** of
16: 2 and sent to Ben-Hadad ***k*** of
16: 3 your treaty with Baasha ***k*** of
16: 4 So Ben-Hadad heeded ***K*** Asa, and
16: 6 Then ***K*** Asa took all Judah, and
16: 7 Hanani the seer came to Asa ***k***
16: 7 you have relied on the ***k*** of
16: 7 therefore the army of the ***k*** of
17:19 These served the ***k***,
17:19 besides those the ***k*** put in the
18: 3 So Ahab ***k*** of Israel said to
18: 3 of Israel said to Jehoshaphat ***k***
18: 4 And Jehoshaphat said to the ***k***
18: 5 Then the ***k*** of Israel gathered
18: 7 So the ***k*** of Israel said to
18: 7 Let not the ***k*** say such things!"
18: 8 Then the ***k*** of Israel called one
18: 9 The ***k*** of Israel and Jehoshaphat
18: 9 of Israel and Jehoshaphat ***k*** of
18:12 with one accord encourage the ***k***.
18:14 Then he came to the ***k***;
18:14 and the ***k*** said to him,
18:15 So the ***k*** said to him, "How many
18:17 And the ***k*** of Israel said to
18:19 Who will persuade Ahab ***k*** of
18:25 Then the ***k*** of Israel said,
18:26 "and say, 'Thus says the ***k***:
18:28 So the ***k*** of Israel and
18:28 of Israel and Jehoshaphat the ***k***
18:29 And the ***k*** of Israel said to
18:29 So the ***k*** of Israel disguised
18:30 Now the ***k*** of Syria had commanded
18:30 but only with the ***k*** of
18:31 It is the ***k*** of Israel!"
18:32 saw that it was not the ***k*** of
18:33 and struck the ***k*** of Israel
18:34 and the ***k*** of Israel propped
19: 1 Then Jehoshaphat the ***k*** of Judah
19: 2 and said to ***K*** Jehoshaphat,
20:15 ***K*** Jehoshaphat! Thus says the
20:31 So Jehoshaphat was ***k*** over
20:31 years old when he became ***k***,
20:35 After this Jehoshaphat ***k*** of
20:35 allied himself with Ahaziah ***k***
21: 2 the sons of Jehoshaphat ***k*** of
21: 5 years old when he became ***k***,
21: 8 and made a ***k*** over themselves.
21:12 or in the ways of Asa ***k*** of
21:20 years old when he became ***k***.
22: 1 Ahaziah his youngest son ***k*** in
22: 1 ***k*** of Judah, reigned.
22: 2 years old when he became ***k***,
22: 5 with Jehoram the son of Ahab ***k***
22: 5 Israel to war against Hazael ***k***
22: 6 he fought against Hazael ***k*** of
22: 6 ***k*** of Judah, went down to see
22:11 the daughter of the ***k***,
22:11 the daughter of ***K*** Jehoram, the
23: 3 made a covenant with the ***k*** in
23: 7 Levites shall surround the ***k***
23: 7 You are to be with the ***k*** when
23: 9 which had belonged to ***K***
23:10 by the temple, all around the ***k***.
23:11 the Testimony, and made him ***k***.
23:11 Long live the ***k***!"
23:12 running and praising the ***k***,
23:13 there was the ***k*** standing by his
23:13 the trumpeters were by the ***k***.
23:16 himself, the people, and the ***k***,
23:20 and brought the ***k*** down from the
23:20 and set the ***k*** on the throne of
24: 1 years old when he became ***k***,
24: 6 So the ***k*** called Jehoiada the
24:12 The ***k*** and Jehoiada gave it to
24:14 rest of the money before the ***k***
24:17 came and bowed down to the ***k***.
24:17 And the ***k*** listened to them.
24:21 and at the command of the ***k***
24:22 Thus Joash the ***k*** did not
24:23 sent all their spoil to the ***k***
25: 1 years old when he became ***k***,
25: 3 had murdered his father the ***k***.
25: 7 God came to him, saying, "O ***k***,
25:16 that the ***k*** said to him,
25:17 Now Amaziah ***k*** of Judah asked
25:17 ***k*** of Israel, saying, "Come,
25:18 And Joash ***k*** of Israel sent to
25:18 of Israel sent to Amaziah ***k*** of
25:21 So Joash ***k*** of Israel went out;
25:21 and he and Amaziah ***k*** of Judah
25:23 Then Joash the ***k*** of Israel
25:23 of Israel captured Amaziah ***k***
25:25 ***k*** of Judah, lived fifteen years
25:25 of Jehoahaz, ***k*** of Israel.
26: 1 and made him ***k*** instead of his
26: 2 after the ***k*** rested with his
26: 3 years old when he became ***k***,
26:13 to help the ***k*** against the
26:18 And they withstood ***K*** Uzziah, and
26:21 ***K*** Uzziah was a leper until the
27: 1 years old when he became ***k***,
27: 5 He also fought with the ***k*** of the
27: 8 years old when he became ***k***,
28: 1 years old when he became ***k***,
28: 5 him into the hand of the ***k*** of
28: 5 into the hand of the ***k*** of
28: 7 who was second to the ***k***.
28:16 At the same time ***K*** Ahaz sent to
28:19 Judah low because of Ahaz ***k*** of
28:20 Also Tiglath-Pileser ***k*** of
28:21 LORD, from the house of the ***k***,
28:21 and he gave it to the ***k*** of
28:22 in the time of his distress ***K***
28:22 This is that ***K*** Ahaz.
29: 1 Hezekiah became ***k*** when he was
29:15 to the commandment of the ***k***,
29:18 Then they went in to ***K*** Hezekiah
29:19 all the articles which ***K*** Ahaz
29:20 Then ***K*** Hezekiah rose early,
29:23 the sin offering before the ***k***
29:24 for the ***k*** commanded that the
29:27 the instruments of David ***k*** of
29:29 the ***k*** and all who were present
29:30 Moreover ***K*** Hezekiah and the
30: 2 For the ***k*** and his leaders and
30: 4 And the matter pleased the ***k*** and
30: 6 with the letters from the ***k***
30: 6 to the command of the ***k***:
30:12 to obey the command of the ***k***
30:24 For Hezekiah ***k*** of Judah gave to
30:26 ***k*** of Israel, there had been
31: 3 The ***k*** also appointed a portion
31:13 commandment of Hezekiah the ***k***
32: 1 Sennacherib ***k*** of Assyria came
32: 7 nor dismayed before the ***k*** of
32: 8 by the words of Hezekiah ***k*** of
32: 9 After this Sennacherib ***k*** of
32: 9 to Hezekiah ***k*** of Judah, and to
32:10 Thus says Sennacherib ***k*** of
32:11 us from the hand of the ***k*** of
32:20 Now because of this ***K*** Hezekiah
32:21 captain in the camp of the ***k***
32:22 the hand of Sennacherib the ***k***
32:23 and presents to Hezekiah ***k*** of
33: 1 years old when he became ***k***,
33:11 captains of the army of the ***k***
33:21 years old when he became ***k***,
33:25 who had conspired against ***K***
33:25 the land made his son Josiah ***k***
34: 1 years old when he became ***k***,
34:16 carried the book to the ***k***,
34:16 bringing the ***k*** word, saying,
34:18 Shaphan the scribe told the ***k***,
34:18 Shaphan read it before the ***k***.
34:19 when the ***k*** heard the words of
34:20 Then the ***k*** commanded Hilkiah,
34:20 and Asaiah a servant of the ***k***,
34:22 So Hilkiah and those the ***k*** had
34:24 they have read before the ***k*** of
34:26 But as for the ***k*** of Judah, who
34:28 they brought back word to the ***k***.
34:29 Then the ***k*** sent and gathered
34:30 The ***k*** went up to the house of
34:31 Then the ***k*** stood in his place
35: 3 ***k*** of Israel, built. It shall
35: 4 written instruction of David ***k***
35:16 according to the command of ***K***
35:20 Necho ***k*** of Egypt came up to
35:21 ***k*** of Judah? I have not come
35:23 And the archers shot ***K*** Josiah;
35:23 and the ***k*** said to his servants,
36: 1 and made him ***k*** in his father's
36: 2 years old when he became ***k***,
36: 3 Now the ***k*** of Egypt deposed him
36: 4 Then the ***k*** of Egypt made
36: 4 Jehoahaz's brother Eliakim ***k***
36: 5 years old when he became ***k***,
36: 6 Nebuchadnezzar ***k*** of Babylon came
36: 9 years old when he became ***k***,
36:10 At the turn of the year ***K***
36:10 ***k*** over Judah and Jerusalem.
36:11 years old when he became ***k***,
36:13 And he also rebelled against ***K***
36:17 He brought against them the ***k***
36:18 and the treasures of the ***k*** and
36:22 in the first year of Cyrus ***k***
36:22 up the spirit of Cyrus ***k*** of
36:23 Thus says Cyrus ***k*** of Persia: All
Ezra 1: 1 in the first year of Cyrus ***k***
1: 1 up the spirit of Cyrus ***k*** of
1: 2 Thus says Cyrus ***k*** of Persia: All
1: 7 ***K*** Cyrus also brought out the

K

	1: 8	and Cyrus ***k*** of Persia brought
	2: 1	whom Nebuchadnezzar the ***k*** of
	3: 7	which they had from Cyrus ***k*** of
	3:10	to the ordinance of David ***k*** of
	4: 2	since the days of Esarhaddon ***k***
	4: 3	as ***K*** Cyrus the king of Persia
	4: 3	as King Cyrus the ***k*** of Persia
	4: 5	all the days of Cyrus ***k*** of
	4: 5	until the reign of Darius ***k*** of
	4: 7	wrote to Artaxerxes ***k*** of
	4: 8	a letter against Jerusalem to ***K***
	4:11	letter that they sent him) To ***K***
	4:12	Let it be known to the ***k*** that
	4:13	Let it now be known to the ***k***
	4:14	we have sent and informed the ***k***,
	4:16	We inform the ***k*** that if this
	4:17	The ***k*** sent an answer: To Rehum
	4:23	Now when the copy of ***K***
	4:24	year of the reign of Darius ***k***
	5: 6	the River, to Darius the ***k***.
	5: 7	written thus—To Darius the ***k***:
	5: 8	Let it be known to the ***k*** that we
	5:11	which a great ***k*** of Israel built
	5:12	the hand of Nebuchadnezzar ***k***
	5:13	in the first year of Cyrus ***k*** of
	5:13	***K*** Cyrus issued a decree to
	5:14	those ***K*** Cyrus took from the
	5:17	if it seems good to the ***k***,
	5:17	that a decree was issued by ***K***
	5:17	and let the ***k*** send us his
	6: 1	Then ***K*** Darius issued a decree,
	6: 3	In the first year of ***K*** Cyrus,
	6: 3	***K*** Cyrus issued a decree
	6:10	and pray for the life of the ***k***
	6:12	to dwell there destroy any ***k***
	6:13	did according to what ***K*** Darius
	6:14	and Artaxerxes ***k*** of Persia.
	6:15	sixth year of the reign of ***K***
	6:22	and turned the heart of the ***k***
	7: 1	in the reign of Artaxerxes ***k*** of
	7: 6	The ***k*** granted him all his
	7: 7	in the seventh year of ***K***
	7: 8	in the seventh year of the ***k***.
	7:11	is a copy of the letter that ***K***
	7:12	***k*** of kings, To Ezra the priest,
	7:14	you are being sent by the ***k***
	7:15	the silver and gold which the ***k***
	7:21	I, even I, Artaxerxes the ***k***,
	7:23	against the realm of the ***k*** and
	7:26	your God and the law of the ***k***,
	7:28	mercy to me before the ***k*** and
	8: 1	in the reign of ***K*** Artaxerxes:
	8:22	ashamed to request of the ***k*** an
	8:22	because we had spoken to the ***k***,
	8:25	house of our God which the ***k***
Neh	2: 1	in the twentieth year of ***K***
	2: 1	the wine and gave it to the ***k***.
	2: 2	Therefore the ***k*** said to me,
	2: 3	and said to the ***k***, "May the
	2: 3	May the ***k*** live forever! Why
	2: 4	Then the ***k*** said to me, "What do
	2: 5	And I said to the ***k***,
	2: 5	the king, "If it pleases the ***k***,
	2: 6	Then the ***k*** said to me (the queen
	2: 6	So it pleased the ***k*** to send
	2: 7	Furthermore I said to the ***k***,
	2: 7	the king, "If it pleases the ***k***,
	2: 8	And the ***k*** granted them to me
	2: 9	Now the ***k*** had sent captains of
	2:19	Will you rebel against the ***k***?
	5:14	the thirty-second year of ***K***
	6: 6	wall, that you may be their ***k***.
	6: 7	There is a ***k*** in Judah!' Now
	6: 7	will be reported to the ***k***.
	7: 6	whom Nebuchadnezzar the ***k*** of
	9:22	The land of the ***k*** of Heshbon,
	9:22	And the land of Og ***k*** of
	13: 6	year of Artaxerxes ***k*** of
	13: 6	Babylon I had returned to the ***k***.
	13: 6	I obtained leave from the ***k***,
	13:26	Did not Solomon ***k*** of Israel sin
	13:26	many nations there was no ***k***
	13:26	and God made him ***k*** over all
Esth	1: 2	in those days when ***K*** Ahasuerus
	1: 5	the ***k*** made a feast lasting
	1: 7	to the generosity of the ***k***.
	1: 8	for so the ***k*** had ordered all
	1: 9	palace which belonged to ***K***
	1:10	when the heart of the ***k*** was
	1:10	who served in the presence of ***K***
	1:11	bring Queen Vashti before the ***k***,
	1:12	therefore the ***k*** was furious,
	1:13	Then the ***k*** said to the wise men
	1:15	did not obey the command of ***K***
	1:16	Memucan answered before the ***k***
	1:16	has not only wronged the ***k***,
	1:16	are in all the provinces of ***K***
	1:17	***K*** Ahasuerus commanded Queen
	1:19	"If it pleases the ***k***,
	1:19	shall come no more before ***K***
	1:19	and let the ***k*** give her royal
	1:21	And the reply pleased the ***k*** and
	1:21	and the ***k*** did according to the
	2: 1	when the wrath of ***K*** Ahasuerus
	2: 2	virgins be sought for the ***k***;
	2: 3	and let the ***k*** appoint officers
	2: 4	young woman who pleases the ***k***
	2: 4	This thing pleased the ***k***,
	2: 6	been captured with Jeconiah ***k***
	2: 6	whom Nebuchadnezzar the ***k*** of
	2:12	woman's turn came to go in to ***K***
	2:13	each young woman went to the ***k***,
	2:14	She would not go in to the ***k***
	2:14	to the king again unless the ***k***
	2:15	his daughter, to go in to the ***k***,
	2:16	So Esther was taken to ***K***
	2:17	The ***k*** loved Esther more than all
	2:18	Then the ***k*** made a great feast,
	2:18	to the generosity of a ***k***.
	2:21	and sought to lay hands on ***K***
	2:22	and Esther informed the ***k*** in
	2:23	in the presence of the ***k***.
	3: 1	After these things ***K*** Ahasuerus
	3: 2	for so the ***k*** had commanded
	3: 7	in the twelfth year of ***K***
	3: 8	Then Haman said to ***K*** Ahasuerus,
	3: 8	it is not fitting for the ***k***
	3: 9	"If it pleases the ***k***,
	3:10	So the ***k*** took his signet ring
	3:11	And the ***k*** said to Haman, "The
	3:12	In the name of ***K*** Ahasuerus it
	3:15	So the ***k*** and Haman sat down to
	4: 8	command her to go in to the ***k***
	4:11	into the inner court to the ***k***,
	4:11	except the one to whom the ***k***
	4:11	been called to go in to the ***k***
	4:16	And so I will go to the ***k***,
	5: 1	while the ***k*** sat on his royal
	5: 2	when the ***k*** saw Queen Esther
	5: 2	and the ***k*** held out to Esther
	5: 3	And the ***k*** said to her, "What do
	5: 4	answered, "If it pleases the ***k***,
	5: 4	let the ***k*** and Haman come today
	5: 5	Then the ***k*** said, "Bring Haman
	5: 5	So the ***k*** and Haman went to
	5: 6	At the banquet of wine the ***k***
	5: 8	favor in the sight of the ***k***,
	5: 8	and if it pleases the ***k*** to
	5: 8	then let the ***k*** and Haman come
	5: 8	and tomorrow I will do as the ***k***
	5:11	everything in which the ***k*** had
	5:11	officials and servants of the ***k***.
	5:12	but me to come in with the ***k***
	5:12	by her, along with the ***k***.
	5:14	in the morning suggest to the ***k***
	5:14	then go merrily with the ***k*** to
	6: 1	That night the ***k*** could not
	6: 1	and they were read before the ***k***.
	6: 2	had sought to lay hands on ***K***
	6: 3	Then the ***k*** said, "What honor or
	6: 4	So the ***k*** said, "Who is in the
	6: 4	palace to suggest that the ***k***
	6: 5	And the ***k*** said, "Let him
	6: 6	and the ***k*** asked him, "What
	6: 6	be done for the man whom the ***k***
	6: 6	Whom would the ***k*** delight to
	6: 7	And Haman answered the ***k***,
	6: 7	For the man whom the ***k*** delights
	6: 8	robe be brought which the ***k***
	6: 8	and a horse on which the ***k*** has
	6: 9	he may array the man whom the ***k***
	6: 9	be done to the man whom the ***k***
	6:10	Then the ***k*** said to Haman,
	6:11	be done to the man whom the ***k***
	7: 1	So the ***k*** and Haman went to dine
	7: 2	the ***k*** again said to Esther,
	7: 3	found favor in your sight, O ***k***,
	7: 3	O king, and if it pleases the ***k***,
	7: 5	So ***K*** Ahasuerus answered and
	7: 6	was terrified before the ***k*** and
	7: 7	Then the ***k*** arose in his wrath
	7: 7	determined against him by the ***k***.
	7: 8	When the ***k*** returned from the
	7: 8	Then the ***k*** said, "Will he also
	7: 9	of the eunuchs, said to the ***k***,
	7: 9	Then the ***k*** said, "Hang him
	8: 1	On that day ***K*** Ahasuerus gave
	8: 1	And Mordecai came before the ***k***,
	8: 2	So the ***k*** took off his signet
	8: 3	Esther spoke again to the ***k***,
	8: 4	And the ***k*** held out the golden
	8: 4	arose and stood before the ***k***,
	8: 5	and said, "If it pleases the ***k***,
	8: 5	the thing seems right to the ***k***
	8: 7	Then ***K*** Ahasuerus said to Queen
	8:10	And he wrote in the name of ***K***
	8:11	By these letters the ***k*** permitted
	8:12	day in all the provinces of ***K***
	8:15	out from the presence of the ***k***
	9: 2	all the provinces of ***K***
	9:11	citadel was brought to the ***k***.
	9:12	And the ***k*** said to Queen Esther,
	9:13	said, "If it pleases the ***k***,
	9:14	So the ***k*** commanded this to be
	9:20	were in all the provinces of ***K***
	9:25	when Esther came before the ***k***,
	10: 1	And ***K*** Ahasuerus imposed tribute
	10: 2	to which the ***k*** advanced him,
	10: 3	the Jew was second to ***K***
Job	15:24	like a ***k*** ready for battle.
	18:14	they parade him before the ***k***
	29:25	So I dwell as a ***k*** in the army,
	34:18	Is it fitting to say to a ***k***,
	41:34	He is ***k*** over all the children
Ps	2: 6	Yet I have set My ***K*** On My holy
	5: 2	My ***K*** and my God, For to You I
	10:16	The LORD is ***K*** forever and
	18:50	deliverance He gives to His ***k***,
	20: 9	LORD! May the ***K*** answer us
	21: 1	The ***k*** shall have joy in Your
	21: 7	For the ***k*** trusts in the LORD,
	24: 7	everlasting doors! And the ***K***
	24: 8	Who is this ***K*** of glory? The
	24: 9	everlasting doors! And the ***K***
	24:10	Who is this ***K*** of glory? The
	24:10	He is the ***K*** of glory. Selah
	29:10	And the LORD sits as ***K***
	33:16	No ***k*** is saved by the multitude
	44: 4	You are my ***K***,
	45: 1	my composition concerning the ***K***;
	45:11	So the ***K*** will greatly desire
	45:14	She shall be brought to the ***K***
	47: 2	He is a great ***K*** over all the
	47: 6	praises! Sing praises to our ***K***,
	47: 7	For God is the ***K*** of all the
	48: 2	north, The city of the great ***K***.
	63:11	But the ***k*** shall rejoice in God;
	68:24	The procession of my God, my ***K***,
	72: 1	Give the ***k*** Your judgments, O
	74:12	For God is my ***K*** from of old,
	84: 3	My ***K*** and my God.
	89:18	And our ***k*** to the Holy One of
	95: 3	And the great ***K*** above all
	98: 6	before the LORD, the ***K***.
	105:20	The ***k*** sent and released him,
	135:11	Sihon ***k*** of the Amorites, Og
	135:11	Og ***k*** of Bashan, And all the
	136:19	Sihon ***k*** of the Amorites, For
	136:20	And Og ***k*** of Bashan, For His
	145: 1	I will extol You, my God, O ***K***;
	149: 2	of Zion be joyful in their ***K***.
Prov	1: 1	of David, ***k*** of Israel:
	16:10	is on the lips of the ***k***;
	20: 2	The wrath of a ***k*** is like the
	20: 8	A ***k*** who sits on the throne of
	20:26	A wise ***k*** sifts out the wicked,
	20:28	Mercy and truth preserve the ***k***,
	22:11	The ***k*** will be his friend.
	24:21	son, fear the LORD and the ***k***;
	25: 1	which the men of Hezekiah ***k*** of
	25: 5	the wicked from before the ***k***,
	25: 6	in the presence of the ***k***,
	29: 4	The ***k*** establishes the land by
	29:14	The ***k*** who judges the poor with
	30:27	The locusts have no ***k***,
	30:31	And a ***k*** whose troops are
	31: 1	The words of ***K*** Lemuel, the
Eccl	1: 1	of David, ***k*** in Jerusalem.
	1:12	was ***k*** over Israel in Jerusalem.
	2:12	the man do who succeeds the ***k***?
	4:13	Than an old and foolish ***k*** who
	4:14	he comes out of prison to be ***k***,
	4:16	people over whom he was made ***k***;
	5: 9	even the ***k*** is served from the
	8: 4	Where the word of a ***k*** is,
	9:14	and a great ***k*** came against it,
	10:16	when your ***k*** is a child, And
	10:17	when your ***k*** is the son of
	10:20	Do not curse the ***k***,
Song	1: 4	The ***k*** has brought me into his
	1:12	While the ***k*** is at his table,
	3: 9	wood of Lebanon Solomon the ***K***
	3:11	And see ***K*** Solomon with the
	7: 5	A ***k*** is held captive by your
Isa	6: 1	In the year that ***K*** Uzziah died,
	6: 5	For my eyes have seen the ***K***,
	7: 1	***k*** of Judah, that Rezin king of
	7: 1	that Rezin ***k*** of Syria and
	7: 1	***k*** of Israel, went up to
	7: 6	and set a ***k*** over them, the son
	7:17	The LORD will bring the ***k*** of
	7:20	with the ***k*** of Assyria, The
	8: 4	be taken away before the ***k*** of
	8: 7	The ***k*** of Assyria and all his
	8:21	be enraged and curse their ***k***
	10:12	of the arrogant heart of the ***k***
	14: 4	up this proverb against the ***k***
	14:28	which came in the year that ***K***
	19: 4	And a fierce ***k*** will rule over
	20: 1	when Sargon the ***k*** of Assyria
	20: 4	so shall the ***k*** of Assyria lead
	20: 6	to be delivered from the ***k*** of
	23:15	according to the days of one ***k***.
	30:33	for the ***k*** it is prepared. He
	32: 1	Behold, a ***k*** will reign in
	33:17	Your eyes will see the ***K*** in
	33:22	Lawgiver, The LORD is our ***K***;
	36: 1	in the fourteenth year of ***K***
	36: 1	Hezekiah that Sennacherib ***k***
	36: 2	Then the ***k*** of Assyria sent the
	36: 2	a great army from Lachish to ***K***
	36: 4	'Thus says the great ***k***,
	36: 4	the ***k*** of Assyria: "What
	36: 6	So is Pharaoh ***k*** of Egypt to
	36: 8	a pledge to my master the ***k*** of
	36:13	"Hear the words of the great ***k***,
	36:13	great king, the ***k*** of Assyria!
	36:14	'Thus says the ***k***: 'Do not
	36:15	be given into the hand of the ***k***
	36:16	for thus says the ***k*** of Assyria:
	36:18	land from the hand of the ***k*** of
	37: 1	when ***K*** Hezekiah heard it, that
	37: 4	whom his master the ***k*** of
	37: 5	So the servants of ***K*** Hezekiah
	37: 6	which the servants of the ***k*** of
	37: 8	and found the ***k*** of Assyria
	37: 9	And the ***k*** heard concerning
	37: 9	heard concerning Tirhakah ***k*** of
	37:10	you shall speak to Hezekiah ***k***
	37:10	be given into the hand of the ***k***
	37:13	Where is the ***k*** of Hamath, the
	37:13	the ***k*** of Arpad, and the king of
	37:13	and the ***k*** of the city of
	37:21	to Me against Sennacherib ***k*** of
	37:33	the LORD concerning the ***k*** of
	37:37	So Sennacherib ***k*** of Assyria

38: 6 city from the hand of the **k** of
38: 9 is the writing of Hezekiah **k**
39: 1 **k** of Babylon, sent letters and
39: 3 Isaiah the prophet went to **K**
39: 7 eunuchs in the palace of the **k**
41:21 says the **K** of Jacob.
43:15 The Creator of Israel, your **K**.
44: 6 the **K** of Israel, And his
57: 9 You went to the **k** with
Jer 1: 2 **k** of Judah, in the thirteenth
1: 3 **k** of Judah, until the end of
1: 3 **k** of Judah, until the carrying
3: 6 me in the days of Josiah the **k**:
4: 9 That the heart of the **k** shall
8:19 Is not her **K** in her?" "Why
10: 7 O **K** of the nations? For this
10:10 God and the everlasting **K**.
13:18 Say to the **k** and to the queen
15: 4 **k** of Judah, for what he did in
20: 4 Judah into the hand of the **k**
21: 1 Jeremiah from the LORD when **K**
21: 2 for Nebuchadnezzar **k** of Babylon
21: 2 that the **k** may go away from
21: 4 which you fight against the **k**
21: 7 I will deliver Zedekiah **k** of
21: 7 the hand of Nebuchadnezzar **k**
21:10 be given into the hand of the **k**
21:11 concerning the house of the **k**
22: 1 Go down to the house of the **k** of
22: 2 O **k** of Judah, you who sit on
22: 6 LORD to the house of the **k** of
22:11 **k** of Judah, who reigned instead
22:18 **k** of Judah: "They shall not
22:24 **k** of Judah, were the signet on
22:25 the hand of Nebuchadnezzar **k** of
23: 5 A **K** shall reign and prosper,
24: 1 after Nebuchadnezzar **k** of
24: 1 **k** of Judah, and the princes of
24: 8 will I give up Zedekiah the **k**
25: 1 **k** of Judah (which was the
25: 1 first year of Nebuchadnezzar **k**
25: 3 **k** of Judah, even to this day,
25: 9 and Nebuchadnezzar the **k** of
25:11 nations shall serve the **k** of
25:12 that I will punish the **k** of
25:19 Pharaoh **k** of Egypt, his
25:26 Also the **k** of Sheshach shall
26: 1 **k** of Judah, this word came from
26:18 in the days of Hezekiah **k** of
26:19 Did Hezekiah **k** of Judah and all
26:21 And when Jehoiakim the **k**,
26:21 the **k** sought to put him to
26:22 Then Jehoiakim the **k** sent men to
26:23 brought him to Jehoiakim the **k**,
27: 1 **k** of Judah, this word came to
27: 3 and send them to the **k** of Edom,
27: 3 the **k** of Moab, the king of the
27: 3 the **k** of the Ammonites, the
27: 3 the **k** of Tyre, and the king of
27: 3 and the **k** of Sidon, by the hand
27: 3 to Jerusalem to Zedekiah **k** of
27: 6 hand of Nebuchadnezzar the **k**
27: 8 not serve Nebuchadnezzar the **k**
27: 8 neck under the yoke of the **k**
27: 9 You shall not serve the **k** of
27:11 necks under the yoke of the **k**
27:12 I also spoke to Zedekiah **k** of
27:12 necks under the yoke of the **k**
27:13 that will not serve the **k** of
27:14 You shall not serve the **k** of
27:17 serve the **k** of Babylon, and
27:18 in the house of the **k** of
27:20 which Nebuchadnezzar **k** of
27:20 **k** of Judah, from Jerusalem to
27:21 and in the house of the **k** of
28: 1 of the reign of Zedekiah **k** of
28: 2 have broken the yoke of the **k**
28: 3 that Nebuchadnezzar **k** of
28: 4 **k** of Judah, with all the
28: 4 I will break the yoke of the **k**
28:11 the yoke of Nebuchadnezzar **k**
28:14 may serve Nebuchadnezzar **k** of
29: 2 happened after Jeconiah the **k**,
29: 3 whom Zedekiah **k** of Judah sent
29: 3 to Nebuchadnezzar **k** of Babylon,
29:16 the LORD concerning the **k** who
29:21 the hand of Nebuchadnezzar **k**
29:22 whom the **k** of Babylon roasted
30: 9 their God, And David their **k**,
32: 1 in the tenth year of Zedekiah **k**
32: 2 For then the **k** of Babylon's army
32: 2 which was in the **k** of Judah's
32: 3 For Zedekiah **k** of Judah had shut
32: 3 city into the hand of the **k** of
32: 4 and Zedekiah **k** of Judah shall
32: 4 into the hand of the **k** of
32:28 the hand of Nebuchadnezzar **k**
32:36 into the hand of the **k** of
34: 1 when Nebuchadnezzar **k** of
34: 2 Go and speak to Zedekiah **k** of
34: 2 city into the hand of the **k** of
34: 3 shall see the eyes of the **k** of
34: 4 O Zedekiah **k** of Judah! Thus
34: 6 all these words to Zedekiah **k**
34: 7 when the **k** of Babylon's army
34: 8 after **K** Zedekiah had made a
34:21 And I will give Zedekiah **k** of
34:21 and into the hand of the **k** of
35: 1 **k** of Judah, saying,
35:11 when Nebuchadnezzar **k** of
36: 1 **k** of Judah, that this word
36: 9 **k** of Judah, in the ninth month,
36:16 We will surely tell the **k** of all
36:20 And they went to the **k**,
36:20 words in the hearing of the **k**.
36:21 So the **k** sent Jehudi to bring
36:21 it in the hearing of the **k** and
36:21 princes who stood beside the **k**.
36:22 Now the **k** was sitting in the
36:23 that the **k** cut it with the
36:24 the **k** nor any of his servants
36:25 and Gemariah implored the **k** not
36:26 And the **k** commanded Jerahmeel
36:27 Now after the **k** had burned the
36:28 scroll which Jehoiakim the **k**
36:29 you shall say to Jehoiakim **k**
36:29 you written in it that the **k**
36:30 LORD concerning Jehoiakim **k**
36:32 of the book which Jehoiakim **k**
37: 1 Now **K** Zedekiah the son of Josiah
37: 1 whom Nebuchadnezzar **k** of
37: 1 king of Babylon made **k** in the
37: 3 And Zedekiah the **k** sent Jehucal
37: 7 Thus you shall say to the **k** of
37:17 then Zedekiah the **k** sent and
37:17 The **k** asked him secretly in his
37:17 into the hand of the **k** of
37:18 Moreover Jeremiah said to **K**
37:19 The **k** of Babylon will not come
37:20 hear now, O my lord the **k**.
37:21 Then Zedekiah the **k** commanded
38: 3 be given into the hand of the **k**
38: 4 the princes said to the **k**,
38: 5 Then Zedekiah the **k** said,
38: 5 For the **k** can do nothing
38: 7 When the **k** was sitting at the
38: 8 king's house and spoke to the **k**,
38: 9 "My lord the **k**,
38:10 Then the **k** commanded
38:11 went into the house of the **k**
38:14 Then Zedekiah the **k** sent and
38:14 And the **k** said to Jeremiah, "I
38:16 So Zedekiah the **k** swore secretly
38:17 you surely surrender to the **k**
38:18 you do not surrender to the **k**
38:19 And Zedekiah the **k** said to
38:22 women who are left in the **k** of
38:22 be surrendered to the **k** of
38:23 be taken by the hand of the **k**
38:25 now what you have said to the **k**,
38:25 and also what the **k** said to
38:26 my request before the **k**,
38:27 to all these words that the **k**
39: 1 the ninth year of Zedekiah **k**
39: 1 Nebuchadnezzar **k** of Babylon and
39: 3 Then all the princes of the **k** of
39: 3 rest of the princes of the **k**
39: 4 when Zedekiah the **k** of Judah
39: 5 him up to Nebuchadnezzar **k** of
39: 6 Then the **k** of Babylon killed the
39: 6 the **k** of Babylon also killed
39:11 Now Nebuchadnezzar **k** of Babylon
39:13 and all the **k** of Babylon's
40: 5 whom the **k** of Babylon has made
40: 7 heard that the **k** of Babylon had
40: 9 in the land and serve the **k** of
40:11 heard that the **k** of Babylon had
40:14 know that Baalis the **k** of the
41: 1 and of the officers of the **k**,
41: 2 and killed him whom the **k** of
41: 9 was the same one Asa the **k** had
41: 9 had made for fear of Baasha **k**
41:18 whom the **k** of Babylon had made
42:11 Do not be afraid of the **k** of
43:10 and bring Nebuchadnezzar the **k**
44:30 I will give Pharaoh Hophra **k** of
44:30 as I gave Zedekiah **k** of Judah
44:30 the hand of Nebuchadnezzar **k**
45: 1 Josiah, **k** of Judah, saying,
46: 2 **k** of Egypt, which was by the
46: 2 and which Nebuchadnezzar **k** of
46: 2 son of Josiah, **k** of Judah:
46:13 how Nebuchadnezzar **k** of Babylon
46:17 **k** of Egypt, is but a noise.
46:18 "As I live," says the **K**,
46:26 the hand of Nebuchadnezzar **k**
48:15 to the slaughter," says the **K**,
49:28 which Nebuchadnezzar **k** of
49:30 For Nebuchadnezzar **k** of Babylon
49:34 of the reign of Zedekiah **k** of
49:38 will destroy from there the **k**
50:17 First the **k** of Assyria
50:17 at last this Nebuchadnezzar **k**
50:18 I will punish the **k** of Babylon
50:18 As I have punished the **k** of
50:43 The **k** of Babylon has heard the
51:31 To show the **k** of Babylon that
51:34 Nebuchadnezzar the **k** of Babylon
51:57 And not awake," says the **K**,
51:59 he went with Zedekiah the **k** of
52: 1 years old when he became **k**,
52: 3 rebelled against the **k** of
52: 4 that Nebuchadnezzar **k** of
52: 5 until the eleventh year of **K**
52: 8 of the Chaldeans pursued the **k**,
52: 9 So they took the **k** and brought
52: 9 and brought him up to the **k** of
52:10 Then the **k** of Babylon killed the
52:11 and the **k** of Babylon bound him
52:12 was the nineteenth year of **K**
52:12 year of King Nebuchadnezzar **k**
52:12 who served the **k** of Babylon,
52:15 who had deserted to the **k** of
52:20 which **K** Solomon had made for
52:26 and brought them to the **k** of
52:27 Then the **k** of Babylon struck
52:31 the captivity of Jehoiachin **k**
52:31 that Evil-Merodach **k** of
52:31 up the head of Jehoiachin **k** of
52:33 bread regularly before the **k**
52:34 ration given him by the **k** of
Lam 2: 6 He has spurned the **k** and the
2: 9 Her **k** and her princes are
Ezek 1: 2 was in the fifth year of **K**
7:27 The **k** will mourn, The prince
17:12 Indeed the **k** of Babylon went to
17:12 to Jerusalem and took its **k**
17:16 in the place where the **k**
17:16 the king dwells who made him **k**,
19: 9 And brought him to the **k** of
21:19 ways for the sword of the **k** of
21:21 For the **k** of Babylon stands at
24: 2 the **k** of Babylon started his
26: 7 the north Nebuchadnezzar **k** of
26: 7 **k** of kings, with horses, with
28:12 up a lamentation for the **k** of
29: 2 your face against Pharaoh **k** of
29: 3 O Pharaoh **k** of Egypt, O great
29:18 Nebuchadnezzar **k** of Babylon
29:19 of Egypt to Nebuchadnezzar **k**
30:10 the hand of Nebuchadnezzar **k**
30:21 broken the arm of Pharaoh **k** of
30:22 'Surely I am against Pharaoh **k**
30:24 strengthen the arms of the **k**
30:25 strengthen the arms of the **k**
30:25 My sword into the hand of the **k**
31: 2 say to Pharaoh **k** of Egypt and
32: 2 up a lamentation for Pharaoh **k**
32:11 The sword of the **k** of Babylon
37:22 and one **k** shall be king over
37:22 and one king shall be **k** over
37:24 My servant shall be **k**
Dan 1: 1 of the reign of Jehoiakim **k** of
1: 1 Nebuchadnezzar **k** of Babylon
1: 2 And the Lord gave Jehoiakim **k** of
1: 3 Then the **k** instructed Ashpenaz,
1: 5 And the **k** appointed for them a
1: 5 they might serve before the **k**.
1:10 Daniel, "I fear my lord the **k**,
1:10 endanger my head before the **k**.
1:18 when the **k** had said that they
1:19 Then the **k** interviewed them, and
1:19 they served before the **k**.
1:20 about which the **k** examined
1:21 until the first year of **K**
2: 2 Then the **k** gave the command to
2: 2 and the Chaldeans to tell the **k**
2: 2 came and stood before the **k**.
2: 3 And the **k** said to them, "I have
2: 4 the Chaldeans spoke to the **k**
2: 4 to the king in Aramaic, "O **k**,
2: 5 The **k** answered and said to the
2: 7 Let the **k** tell his servants the
2: 8 The **k** answered and said, "I
2:10 The Chaldeans answered the **k**,
2:10 king's matter; therefore no **k**,
2:11 a difficult thing that the **k**
2:11 other who can tell it to the **k**
2:12 For this reason the **k** was angry
2:15 Why is the decree from the **k** so
2:16 Daniel went in and asked the **k**
2:16 that he might tell the **k** the
2:24 whom the **k** had appointed to
2:24 Babylon; take me before the **k**,
2:24 and I will tell the **k** the
2:25 brought Daniel before the **k**,
2:25 who will make known to the **k**
2:26 The **k** answered and said to
2:27 in the presence of the **k**,
2:27 The secret which the **k** has
2:27 cannot declare to the **k**.
2:28 and He has made known to **K**
2:29 "As for you, O **k**,
2:30 the interpretation to the **k**,
2:31 You, O **k**, were watching;
2:36 of it before the **k**.
2:37 'You, O **k**, are a king of
2:37 are a **k** of kings. For the God
2:45 God has made known to the **k**
2:46 Then **K** Nebuchadnezzar fell on
2:47 The **k** answered Daniel, and said,
2:48 Then the **k** promoted Daniel and
2:49 Also Daniel petitioned the **k**,
2:49 sat in the gate of the **k**.
3: 1 Nebuchadnezzar the **k** made an
3: 2 And **K** Nebuchadnezzar sent word
3: 2 dedication of the image which **K**
3: 3 dedication of the image that **K**
3: 5 worship the gold image that **K**
3: 7 the gold image which **K**
3: 9 They spoke and said to **K**
3: 9 to King Nebuchadnezzar, "O **k**,
3:10 'You, O **k**, have made a
3:12 and Abed-Nego; these men, O **k**,
3:13 brought these men before the **k**.
3:16 answered and said to the **k**,
3:17 deliver us from your hand, O **k**.
3:18 let it be known to you, O **k**,
3:24 Then **K** Nebuchadnezzar was
3:24 They answered and said to the **k**,
3:24 said to the king, "True, O **k**.
3:30 Then the **k** promoted Shadrach,
4: 1 Nebuchadnezzar the **k**,
4:18 **K** Nebuchadnezzar, have seen.
4:19 So the **k** spoke, and said,

4:22 it is you, O ***k***, who have
4:23 And inasmuch as the ***k*** saw a
4:24 this is the interpretation, O ***k***,
4:24 has come upon my lord the ***k***:
4:27 Therefore, O ***k***, let my advice
4:28 All this came upon *K*
4:30 The ***k*** spoke, saying, "Is not
4:31 *K* Nebuchadnezzar, to you it is
4:37 and extol and honor the *K* of
5: 1 Belshazzar the ***k*** made a great
5: 2 that the ***k*** and his lords, his
5: 3 and the ***k*** and his lords, his
5: 5 and the ***k*** saw the part of the
5: 7 The ***k*** cried aloud to bring in
5: 7 The ***k*** spoke, saying to the wise
5: 8 or make known to the ***k*** its
5: 9 Then *K* Belshazzar was greatly
5:10 because of the words of the ***k***
5:10 The queen spoke, saying, "O ***k***,
5:11 and *K* Nebuchadnezzar your
5:11 your father—your father the ***k***—
5:12 whom the ***k*** named Belteshazzar,
5:13 was brought in before the ***k***.
5:13 The ***k*** spoke, and said to
5:13 whom my father the ***k*** brought
5:17 answered, and said before the ***k***,
5:17 will read the writing to the ***k***,
5:18 'O ***k***, the Most High God gave
5:30 ***k*** of the Chaldeans, was slain.
6: 2 so that the ***k*** would suffer no
6: 3 and the ***k*** gave thought to
6: 6 satraps thronged before the ***k***,
6: 6 *K* Darius, live forever!
6: 7 thirty days, except you, O ***k***,
6: 8 'Now, O ***k***, establish the
6: 9 Therefore *K* Darius signed the
6:12 And they went before the ***k***,
6:12 thirty days, except you, O ***k***,
6:12 The ***k*** answered and said,
6:13 answered and said before the ***k***,
6:13 show due regard for you, O ***k***,
6:14 And the ***k***, when he heard
6:15 Then these men approached the ***k***,
6:15 the king, and said to the ***k***,
6:15 said to the king, "Know, O ***k***,
6:15 decree or statute which the ***k***
6:16 So the ***k*** gave the command, and
6:16 But the ***k*** spoke, saying to
6:17 and the ***k*** sealed it with his
6:18 Now the ***k*** went to his palace
6:19 Then the ***k*** arose very early in
6:20 The ***k*** spoke, saying to Daniel,
6:21 Then Daniel said to the ***k***,
6:21 Daniel said to the king, "O ***k***,
6:22 before Him; and also, O ***k***,
6:23 Then the ***k*** was exceedingly glad
6:24 And the ***k*** gave the command, and
6:25 Then *K* Darius wrote: To all
7: 1 the first year of Belshazzar ***k***
8: 1 third year of the reign of *K*
8:21 its eyes is the first ***k***.
8:23 A ***k*** shall arise, Having
9: 1 who was made ***k*** over the realm
10: 1 In the third year of Cyrus ***k*** of
11: 3 Then a mighty ***k*** shall arise, who
11: 5 Also the ***k*** of the South shall
11: 6 for the daughter of the ***k*** of
11: 6 of the South shall go to the ***k***
11: 7 enter the fortress of the ***k*** of
11: 8 more years than the ***k*** of the
11: 9 Also the ***k*** of the North
11: 9 come to the kingdom of the ***k***
11:11 And the ***k*** of the South shall be
11:11 with the ***k*** of the North, who
11:13 For the ***k*** of the North will
11:14 shall rise up against the ***k*** of
11:15 So the ***k*** of the North shall come
11:25 and his courage against the ***k***
11:25 And the ***k*** of the South shall be
11:36 Then the ***k*** shall do according
11:40 At the time of the end the ***k*** of
11:40 and the ***k*** of the North shall
Hos 1: 1 son of Joash, ***k*** of Israel.
3: 4 abide many days without ***k*** or
3: 5 their God and David their ***k***.
5: 1 O house of the ***k***! For yours
5:13 went to Assyria And sent to *K*
7: 3 They make a ***k*** glad with their
7: 5 In the day of our ***k*** Princes
8:10 of the burden of the ***k*** of
10: 3 now they say, "We have no ***k***,
10: 3 fear the LORD. And as for a ***k***,
10: 6 to Assyria As a present for *K*
10: 7 her ***k*** is cut off Like a twig
10:15 At dawn the ***k*** of Israel Shall
11: 5 the Assyrian shall be his ***k***,
13:10 I will be your *K*;
13:10 Give me a ***k*** and princes'?
13:11 I gave you a ***k*** in My anger,
Am 1: 1 Israel in the days of Uzziah ***k***
1: 1 ***k*** of Israel, two years before
1:15 Their ***k*** shall go into
2: 1 he burned the bones of the ***k***
5:26 also carried Sikkuth your ***k***
7:10 of Bethel sent to Jeroboam ***k***
Jon 3: 6 Then word came to the ***k*** of
3: 7 Nineveh by the decree of the ***k***
Mic 2:13 Their ***k*** will pass before them,
4: 9 Is there no ***k*** in your midst?
6: 5 remember now What Balak ***k*** of
Nah 3:18 O ***k*** of Assyria; Your nobles
Zeph 1: 1 son of Amon, ***k*** of Judah.
3:15 The *K* of Israel, the LORD,
Hag 1: 1 In the second year of *K* Darius,
1:15 in the second year of *K* Darius.
Zech 7: 1 Now in the fourth year of *K*
9: 5 The ***k*** shall perish from Gaza,
9: 9 your *K* is coming to you; He
11: 6 hand and into the hand of his ***k***.
14: 5 In the days of Uzziah ***k*** of
14: 9 And the LORD shall be *K* over
14:16 year to year to worship the *K*,
14:17 to Jerusalem to worship the *K*,
Mal 1:14 blemished—For I am a great *K*,
Mt 1: 6 and Jesse begot David the ***k***.
1: 6 David the ***k*** begot Solomon by
2: 1 in the days of Herod the ***k***,
2: 2 is He who has been born *K* of
2: 3 When Herod the ***k*** heard this, he
2: 9 When they heard the ***k***,
5:35 it is the city of the great *K*.
14: 9 And the ***k*** was sorry;
18:23 of heaven is like a certain ***k***
21: 5 your *K* is coming to you,
22: 2 of heaven is like a certain ***k***
22: 7 But when the ***k*** heard about it,
22:11 But when the ***k*** came in to see
22:13 Then the ***k*** said to the servants,
25:34 Then the *K* will say to those on
25:40 And the *K* will answer and say to
27:11 Are You the *K* of the Jews?" So
27:29 'Hail, *K* of the Jews!"
27:37 THIS IS JESUS THE *K* OF THE
27:42 If He is the *K* of Israel, let
Mk 6:14 Now *K* Herod heard of Him, for
6:22 the ***k*** said to the girl, "Ask
6:25 she came in with haste to the ***k***
6:26 And the ***k*** was exceedingly sorry;
6:27 Immediately the ***k*** sent an
15: 2 Are You the *K* of the Jews?" He
15: 9 me to release to you the *K* of
15:12 with Him whom you call the *K*
15:18 Him, "Hail, *K* of the Jews!"
15:26 THE *K* OF THE JEWS.
15:32 the *K* of Israel, descend now
Lk 1: 5 the ***k*** of Judea, a certain
14:31 'Or what ***k***, going to make war
14:31 to make war against another ***k***,
19:38 Blessed is the *K* who comes
23: 2 that He Himself is Christ, a *K*.
23: 3 Are You the *K* of the Jews?" He
23:37 If You are the *K* of the Jews,
23:38 THIS IS THE *K* OF THE JEWS.
Jn 1:49 the Son of God! You are the *K*
6:15 take Him by force to make Him ***k***,
12:13 name of the LORD!' The *K*
12:15 your *K* is coming, Sitting
18:33 Are You the *K* of the Jews?"
18:37 Are You a ***k*** then?" Jesus
18:37 say rightly that I am a ***k***.
18:39 me to release to you the *K* of
19: 3 *K* of the Jews!" And they
19:12 Whoever makes himself a ***k***
19:14 to the Jews, "Behold your *K*!"
19:15 them, "Shall I crucify your *K*?
19:15 We have no ***k*** but Caesar!"
19:19 THE *K* OF THE JEWS.
19:21 The *K* of the Jews,' but, 'He
19:21 I am the *K* of the Jews." '"
Acts 7:10 ***k*** of Egypt; and he made him
7:18 till another ***k*** arose who did not
12: 1 Now about that time Herod the ***k***
13:21 afterward they asked for a ***k***;
13:22 raised up for them David as ***k***,
17: 7 saying there is another ***k***—
25:13 And after some days *K* Agrippa
25:14 laid Paul's case before the ***k***,
25:24 *K* Agrippa and all the men who
25:26 *K* Agrippa, so that after the
26: 2 *K* Agrippa, because today I
26: 7 *K* Agrippa, I am accused by the
26:13 'at midday, O ***k***, along the
26:19 *K* Agrippa, I was not
26:26 'For the ***k***, before whom I
26:27 *K* Agrippa, do you believe the
26:30 the ***k*** stood up, as well as the
2 Cor 11:32 governor, under Aretas the ***k***,
1 Tim 1:17 Now to the *K* eternal, immortal,
6:15 the *K* of kings and Lord of
Heb 7: 1 ***k*** of Salem, priest of the Most
7: 2 ***k*** of righteousness," and then
7: 2 and then also ***k*** of Salem,
7: 2 meaning "***k*** of peace,"
11:27 not fearing the wrath of the ***k***;
1 Pe 2:13 whether to the ***k*** as supreme,
2:17 Fear God. Honor the ***k***.
Rev 9:11 And they had as ***k*** over them the
15: 3 O *K* of the saints!
17:14 for He is Lord of lords and *K*
19:16 *K* OF KINGS AND LORD OF

KING'S (283/263) KING

Gen 14:17 the *K* Valley), after his return
39:20 a place where the ***k*** prisoners
Num 20:17 we will go along the *K* Highway;
21:22 We will go by the *K* Highway
1 Sam 18:22 become the ***k*** son-in-law.'"
18:23 you a light thing to be a ***k***
18:25 vengeance on the ***k*** enemies.
18:26 David well to become the ***k***
18:27 he might become the ***k*** son-in-law.
20:29 he has not come to the ***k*** table.
21: 8 because the ***k*** business required
22:14 who is the ***k*** son-in-law, who
23:20 deliver him into the ***k*** hand.
26:16 And now see where the ***k*** spear
26:22 Here is the ***k*** spear. Let one of
2 Sam 3:37 it had not been the ***k*** intent
9:11 table like one of the ***k*** sons.
9:13 ate continually at the ***k*** table.
11: 2 on the roof of the ***k*** house.
11: 8 So Uriah departed from the ***k***
11: 9 at the door of the ***k*** house,
11:20 if it happens that the ***k*** wrath
11:24 and some of the ***k*** servants are
12:30 Then he took their ***k*** crown from
13: 4 the ***k*** son, becoming thinner day
13:18 for the ***k*** virgin daughters wore
13:23 Absalom invited all the ***k*** sons.
13:27 so he let Amnon and all the ***k***
13:29 Then all the ***k*** sons arose, and
13:30 has killed all the ***k*** sons,
13:32 the ***k*** sons, for only Amnon is
13:33 to think that all the ***k*** sons
13:35 the ***k*** sons are coming; as your
13:36 that the ***k*** sons indeed came,
14: 1 perceived that the ***k*** heart
14:24 but did not see the ***k*** face.
14:26 according to the ***k*** standard.
14:28 but did not see the ***k*** face.
14:32 let me see the ***k*** face; but if
15:15 And the ***k*** servants said to the
15:35 you hear from the ***k*** house,
16: 2 The donkeys are for the ***k***
18:12 raise my hand against the ***k*** son.
18:18 which is in the *K* Valley. For
18:20 because the ***k*** son is dead."
18:29 When Joab sent the ***k*** servant and
19:18 to carry over the ***k*** household,
19:42 Have we ever eaten at the ***k***
24: 4 Nevertheless the ***k*** word
1 Ki 1: 9 the ***k*** sons, and all the men of
1: 9 men of Judah, the ***k*** servants.
1:25 and has invited all the ***k*** sons,
1:28 she came into the ***k*** presence
1:44 made him ride on the ***k*** mule.
1:47 And moreover the ***k*** servants have
2:19 a throne set for the ***k*** mother;
4: 5 a priest and the ***k*** friend;
9: 1 of the LORD and the ***k*** house,
9:10 house of the LORD and the ***k***
10:12 of the LORD and for the ***k*** house,
10:28 the ***k*** merchants bought them in
13: 6 and the ***k*** hand was restored to
14:26 treasures of the ***k*** house;
14:27 guarded the doorway of the ***k***
15:18 treasuries of the ***k*** house,
16:18 into the citadel of the ***k*** house
16:18 king's house and burned the ***k***
22:12 will deliver it into the ***k*** hand.
22:26 city and to Joash the ***k*** son;
2 Ki 7: 9 us go and tell the ***k*** household.
7:11 and they told it to the ***k***
9:34 for she was a ***k*** daughter."
10: 6 Now the ***k*** sons, seventy
10: 7 that they took the ***k*** sons and
10: 8 brought the heads of the ***k*** sons.
11: 2 him away from among the ***k*** sons
11: 4 and showed them the ***k*** son.
11: 5 keeping watch over the ***k*** house,
11:12 And he brought out the ***k*** son,
11:16 entrance into the ***k*** house,
11:19 gate of the escorts to the ***k***
11:20 with the sword in the ***k*** house.
12:10 that the ***k*** scribe and the high
12:18 of the LORD and in the ***k*** house,
13:16 Elisha put his hands on the ***k***
14:14 the treasuries of the ***k*** house,
15: 5 And Jotham the ***k*** son was over
15:25 in the citadel of the ***k*** house,
16: 8 the treasuries of the ***k*** house,
16:15 the ***k*** burnt sacrifice, and his
16:18 removed the ***k*** outer entrance
18:15 and in the treasuries of the ***k***
18:36 for the ***k*** commandment was, "Do
24:13 treasures of the ***k*** house,
24:15 The ***k*** mother, the king's wives,
24:15 the ***k*** wives, his officers, and
25: 4 which was by the ***k*** garden, even
25: 9 house of the LORD and the ***k***
25:19 men of the ***k*** close associates
1 Chr 9:18 the children of Levi at the *K*
18:17 chief ministers at the ***k*** side.
20: 2 Then David took their ***k*** crown
21: 4 Nevertheless the ***k*** word
21: 6 for the ***k*** word was abominable
25: 5 the sons of Heman the ***k*** seer
27:25 Adiel was over the ***k*** treasuries;
27:32 Hachmoni was with the ***k*** sons.
27:33 Ahithophel was the ***k*** counselor,
27:33 the Archite was the ***k*** companion.
27:34 And the general of the ***k*** army
29: 6 the officers over the ***k*** work,
2 Chr 1:16 the ***k*** merchants bought them in
7:11 of the LORD and the ***k*** house;
9:11 of the LORD and for the ***k*** house,
9:21 For the ***k*** ships went to Tarshish
12: 9 treasures of the ***k*** house;
12:10 guarded the doorway of the ***k***
16: 2 of the LORD and of the ***k*** house,
18: 5 will deliver it into the ***k*** hand.
18:11 will deliver it into the ***k*** hand.
18:25 of the city and to Joash the ***k***
19:11 for all the ***k*** matters; also the
21:17 that were found in the ***k*** house,

22:11 him away from among the **k** sons
23: 3 the **k** son shall reign, as the
23: 5 one-third shall be at the **k**
23:11 And they brought out the **k** son,
23:15 Horse Gate into the **k** house,
23:20 the Upper Gate to the **k** house,
24: 8 Then at the **k** command they made
24:11 was brought to the **k** official
24:11 that the **k** scribe and the high
25:16 we made you the **k** counselor?
25:24 the treasures of the **k** house,
26:11 one of the **k** captains.
26:21 his son was over the **k** house,
28: 7 killed Maaseiah the **k** son,
29:25 of Gad the **k** seer, and of
35: 7 were from the **k** possessions.
35:10 according to the **k** command.
35:15 and Jeduthun the **k** seer. Also
Ezra 4:13 and the **k** treasury will be
4:14 for us to see the **k** dishonor;
5:17 be made in the **k** treasure house,
6: 4 the expenses be paid from the **k**
6: 8 cost be paid at the **k** expense
7:20 pay for it from the **k** treasury.
7:27 a thing as this in the **k** heart,
7:28 and before all the **k** mighty
8:36 And they delivered the **k** orders
8:36 king's orders to the **k** satraps
Neh 1:11 For I was the **k** cupbearer.
2: 8 the keeper of the **k** forest,
2: 9 and gave them the **k** letters.
2:14 Fountain Gate and to the **K** Pool,
2:18 and also of the **k** words that he
3:15 Pool of Shelah by the **K** Garden,
3:25 projects from the **k** upper house
5: 4 borrowed money for the **k** tax
11:23 For it was the **k** command
11:24 was the **k** deputy in all
Esth 1: 5 of the garden of the **k** palace.
1:12 refused to come at the **k** command
1:13 (for this was the **k** manner
1:14 had access to the **k** presence
1:18 will say to all the **k** officials
1:20 When the **k** decree which he will
1:22 letters to all the **k** provinces,
2: 2 Then the **k** servants who attended
2: 3 custody of Hegai the **k** eunuch
2: 8 when the **k** command and decree
2: 8 Esther also was taken to the **k**
2: 9 for her from the **k** palace,
2:13 the women's quarters to the **k**
2:14 the **k** eunuch who kept the
2:15 but what Hegai the **k** eunuch,
2:19 Mordecai sat within the **k** gate.
2:21 Mordecai sat within the **k** gate,
2:21 two of the **k** eunuchs, Bigthan
3: 2 And all the **k** servants who were
3: 2 who were within the **k** gate
3: 3 Then the **k** servants who were
3: 3 who were within the **k** gate
3: 3 do you transgress the **k** command?
3: 8 they do not keep the **k** laws.
3: 9 bring it into the **k** treasuries.
3:12 Then the **k** scribes were called
3:12 to the **k** satraps, to the
3:12 and sealed with the **k** signet
3:13 into all the **k** provinces,
3:15 hastened by the **k** command; and
4: 2 far as the front of the **k** gate,
4: 2 one might enter the **k** gate
4: 3 province where the **k** command
4: 5 one of the **k** eunuchs whom he
4: 6 that was in front of the **k** gate.
4: 7 had promised to pay into the **k**
4:11 All the **k** servants and the
4:11 the people of the **k** provinces
4:13 will escape in the **k** palace
5: 1 in the inner court of the **k**
5: 1 across from the **k** house, while
5: 9 Haman saw Mordecai in the **k**
5:13 the Jew sitting at the **k** gate.
6: 2 two of the **k** eunuchs, the
6: 3 And the **k** servants who
6: 4 the outer court of the **k** palace
6: 5 The **k** servants said to him,
6: 9 one of the **k** most noble princes,
6:10 Jew who sits within the **k** gate!
6:12 Mordecai went back to the **k**
6:14 the **k** eunuchs came, and
7: 4 compensate for the **k** loss.
7: 8 As the word left the **k** mouth,
7: 9 who spoke good on the **k** behalf,
7:10 Then the **k** wrath subsided.
8: 5 who are in all the **k** provinces.
8: 8 in the **k** name, and seal it
8: 8 and seal it with the **k** signet
8: 8 is written in the **k** name,
8: 8 sealed with the **k** signet ring
8: 9 So the **k** scribes were called at
8:10 sealed it with the **k** signet
8:14 and pressed on by the **k**
8:17 wherever the **k** command and
9: 1 the time came for the **k**
9: 3 and all those doing the **k** work,
9: 4 Mordecai was great in the **k**
9:12 in the rest of the **k** provinces?
9:16 of the Jews in the **k** provinces
Ps 45: 5 in the heart of the **K** enemies;
45:15 They shall enter the **K** palace.
61: 6 You will prolong the **k** life,
72: 1 righteousness to the **k** Son.
99: 4 The **K** strength also loves
Prov 14:28 of people is a **k** honor,
14:35 The **k** favor is toward a wise
16:14 of death is the **k** wrath,
16:15 In the light of the **k** face is
19:12 The **k** wrath is like the
21: 1 The **k** heart is in the hand of
Eccl 8: 2 Keep the **k** commandment for the
Isa 36:21 for the **k** commandment was, "Do
Jer 26:10 they came up from the **k** house
36:12 went down to the **k** house,
36:26 commanded Jerahmeel the **k** son,
38: 6 dungeon of Malchiah the **k** son,
38: 7 who was in the **k** house, heard
38: 8 Ebed-Melech went out of the **k**
39: 4 by way of the **k** garden, by the
39: 8 Chaldeans burned the **k** house
41:10 the **k** daughters and all the
43: 6 the **k** daughters, and every
52: 7 which was by the **k** garden,
52:13 house of the LORD and the **k**
52:25 men of the **k** close associates,
Ezek 17:13 And he took the **k** offspring,
Dan 1: 3 and some of the **k** descendants
1: 4 to serve in the **k** palace,
1: 5 them a daily provision of the **k**
1: 8 the portion of the **k** delicacies,
1:13 who eat the portion of the **k**
1:15 the portion of the **k** delicacies.
2:10 earth who can tell the **k** matter;
2:14 the captain of the **k** guard, who
2:15 to Arioch the **k** captain,
2:23 You have made known to us the **k**
3:22 because the **k** command was
3:27 and the **k** counselors gathered
3:28 they have frustrated the **k** word,
4:31 word was still in the **k** mouth,
5: 5 plaster of the wall of the **k**
5: 6 Then the **k** countenance changed,
5: 8 Now all the **k** wise men came,
6:12 spoke concerning the **k** decree:
8:27 and went about the **k** business.
Am 7: 1 late crop after the **k** mowings.
7:13 For it is the **k** sanctuary,
Zeph 1: 8 the princes and the **k** children,
Zech 14:10 the Tower of Hananeel to the **k**
Acts 12:20 made Blastus the **k** personal aide
12:20 with food by the **k** country.
Heb 11:23 were not afraid of the **k** command.

KINGDOM (333/308) KINGDOMS

Gen 10:10 And the beginning of his **k** was
20: 9 have brought on me and on my **k**
Ex 19: 6 And you shall be to Me a **k** of
Num 24: 7 And his **k** shall be exalted.
32:33 the **k** of Sihon king of the
32:33 king of the Amorites and the **k**
Deut 3: 4 the **k** of Og in Bashan.
3:10 cities of the **k** of Og in
3:13 the **k** of Og, I gave to half the
17:18 he sits on the throne of his **k**,
17:20 may prolong his days in his **k**,
Josh 13:12 all the **k** of Og in Bashan, who
13:21 of the plain and all the **k** of
13:27 the rest of the **k** of Sihon king
13:30 all the **k** of Og king of Bashan,
13:31 cities of the **k** of Og in
1 Sam 10:16 But about the matter of the **k**,
11:14 us go to Gilgal and renew the **k**
13:13 would have established your **k**
13:14 But now your **k** shall not
15:28 The LORD has torn the **k** of
18: 8 more can he have but the **k**?
20:31 not be established, nor your **k**.
24:20 and that the **k** of Israel shall
28:17 For the LORD has torn the **k**
2 Sam 3:10 to transfer the **k** from the house
3:28 My **k** and I are guiltless before
5:12 and that He had exalted His **k**
7:12 and I will establish his **k**.
7:13 establish the throne of his **k**
7:16 And your house and your **k** shall
16: 3 of Israel will restore the **k**
16: 8 the LORD has delivered the **k**
1 Ki 1:46 sits on the throne of the **k**.
2:12 and his **k** was firmly
2:15 You know that the **k** was mine,
2:15 the **k** has been turned over, and
2:22 Ask for him the **k** also—for he
2:46 Thus the **k** was established in
9: 5 establish the throne of your **k**
10:20 had been made for any other **k**.
11:11 I will surely tear the **k** away
11:13 will not tear away the whole **k**;
11:31 I will tear the **k** out of the
11:34 I will not take the whole **k**
11:35 But I will take the **k** out of his
12:21 that he might restore the **k** to
12:26 Now the **k** may return to the
14: 8 and tore the **k** away from the
18:10 there is no nation or **k** where
18:10 he took an oath from the **k** or
2 Ki 14: 5 as soon as the **k** was
15:19 be with him to strengthen the **k**
1 Chr 10:14 and turned the **k** over to David
11:10 themselves with him in his **k**,
12:23 at Hebron to turn over the **k**
14: 2 for his **k** was highly exalted
16:20 And from one **k** to another
17:11 and I will establish his **k**.
17:14 him in My house and in My **k**
22:10 establish the throne of his **k**
28: 5 to sit on the throne of the **k**
28: 7 I will establish his **k** forever,
29:11 is Yours; Yours is the **k**,
2 Chr 1: 1 David was strengthened in his **k**,
7:18 establish the throne of your **k**,
9:19 had been made for any other **k**.
11: 1 that he might restore the **k** to
11:17 So they strengthened the **k** of
12: 1 Rehoboam had established the **k**
13: 8 you think to withstand the **k**
14: 5 and the **k** was quiet under him.
17: 5 the LORD established the **k** in
21: 3 but he gave the **k** to Jehoram,
21: 4 was established over the **k** of
22: 9 one to assume power over the **k**.
23:20 the king on the throne of the **k**.
25: 3 as soon as the **k** was
29:21 for a sin offering for the **k**,
32:15 for no god of any nation or **k**
33:13 back to Jerusalem into his **k**.
36:20 sons until the rule of the **k**
36:22 throughout all his **k**,
Ezra 1: 1 throughout all his **k**,
Neh 9:35 have not served You in their **k**,
Esth 1: 2 sat on the throne of his **k**,
1: 4 the riches of his glorious **k**
1:14 who ranked highest in the **k**):
2: 3 in all the provinces of his **k**,
3: 6 were throughout the whole **k**
3: 8 in all the provinces of your **k**;
4:14 whether you have come to the **k**
5: 3 to you—up to half the **k**!"
5: 6 your request, up to half the **k**?
7: 2 your request, up to half the **k**?
9:30 provinces of the **k** of
Ps 22:28 For the **k** is the LORD's, And
45: 6 is the scepter of Your **k**.
103:19 And His **k** rules over all.
105:13 From one **k** to another people,
145:11 speak of the glory of Your **k**,
145:12 the glorious majesty of His **k**.
145:13 Your **k** is an everlasting
145:13 kingdom is an everlasting **k**,
Eccl 4:14 he was born poor in his **k**.
Isa 9: 7 throne of David and over His **k**,
17: 3 The **k** from Damascus, And the
19: 2 city, **k** against kingdom.
19: 2 against city, kingdom against **k**.
34:12 shall call its nobles to the **k**,
60:12 For the nation and **k** which will
Jer 18: 7 a nation and concerning a **k**,
18: 9 a nation and concerning a **k**,
27: 8 that the nation and **k** which
Lam 2: 2 He has profaned the **k** and its
Ezek 17:14 that the **k** might be brought low
29:14 there they shall be a lowly **k**.
Dan 2:37 God of heaven has given you a **k**,
2:39 after you shall arise another **k**
2:39 a third **k** of bronze, which
2:40 And the fourth **k** shall be as
2:40 that **k** will break in pieces
2:41 the **k** shall be divided; yet the
2:42 so the **k** shall be partly
2:44 God of heaven will set up a **k**
2:44 and the **k** shall not be left to
4: 3 how mighty His wonders! His **k**
4: 3 kingdom is an everlasting **k**,
4:17 the Most High rules in the **k**
4:18 all the wise men of my **k** are
4:25 the Most High rules in the **k**
4:26 your **k** shall be assured to you,
4:31 the **k** has departed from you!
4:32 the Most High rules in the **k**
4:34 And His **k** is from generation
4:36 me, and for the glory of my **k**,
4:36 to me, I was restored to my **k**,
5: 7 be the third ruler in the **k**.
5:11 There is a man in your **k** in whom
5:16 be the third ruler in the **k**.
5:18 Nebuchadnezzar your father a **k**
5:21 Most High God rules in the **k**
5:26 MENE: God has numbered your **k**,
5:28 Your **k** has been divided, and
5:29 be the third ruler in the **k**.
5:31 Darius the Mede received the **k**,
6: 1 Darius to set over the **k** one
6: 1 satraps, to be over the whole **k**;
6: 4 against Daniel concerning the **k**;
6: 7 "All the governors of the **k**,
6:26 that in every dominion of my **k**
6:26 His **k** is the one which
7:14 dominion and glory and a **k**,
7:14 And His **k** the one Which
7:18 Most High shall receive the **k**,
7:18 and possess the **k** forever, even
7:22 for the saints to possess the **k**.
7:23 beast shall be A fourth **k** on
7:24 Who shall arise from this **k**.
7:27 Then the **k** and dominion, And
7:27 His **k** is an everlasting
7:27 kingdom is an everlasting **k**,
8:21 And the male goat is the **k** of
8:23 in the latter time of their **k**,
10:13 But the prince of the **k** of
11: 4 his **k** shall be broken up and
11: 4 for his **k** shall be uprooted,
11: 9 North shall come to the **k** of
11:17 the strength of his whole **k**,
11:20 taxes on the glorious **k**;
11:21 and seize the **k** by intrigue.
Hos 1: 4 And bring an end to the **k** of

Am 9: 8 Lord GOD are on the sinful ***k***,
Ob 21 And the ***k*** shall be the
Mic 4: 8 The ***k*** of the daughter of
Mt 3: 2 for the ***k*** of heaven is at
4:17 for the ***k*** of heaven is at
4:23 preaching the gospel of the ***k***,
5: 3 For theirs is the ***k*** of heaven.
5:10 For theirs is the ***k*** of heaven.
5:19 shall be called least in the ***k***
5:19 shall be called great in the ***k***
5:20 will by no means enter the ***k***
6:10 Your ***k*** come. Your will be done
6:13 For Yours is the ***k*** and the
6:33 But seek first the ***k*** of God and
7:21 shall enter the ***k*** of heaven,
8:11 and Jacob in the ***k*** of heaven.
8:12 But the sons of the ***k*** will be
9:35 preaching the gospel of the ***k***,
10: 7 The ***k*** of heaven is at hand.'
11:11 but he who is least in the ***k*** of
11:12 the Baptist until now the ***k*** of
12:25 Every ***k*** divided against itself
12:26 How then will his ***k*** stand?
12:28 surely the ***k*** of God has come
13:11 to know the mysteries of the ***k***
13:19 anyone hears the word of the ***k***,
13:24 The ***k*** of heaven is like a man
13:31 The ***k*** of heaven is like a
13:33 The ***k*** of heaven is like leaven,
13:38 seeds are the sons of the ***k***,
13:41 they will gather out of His ***k***
13:43 forth as the sun in the ***k*** of
13:44 the ***k*** of heaven is like
13:45 the ***k*** of heaven is like a
13:47 the ***k*** of heaven is like a
13:52 instructed concerning the ***k*** of
16:19 give you the keys of the ***k*** of
16:28 the Son of Man coming in His ***k***.
18: 1 Who then is greatest in the ***k*** of
18: 3 will by no means enter the ***k***
18: 4 child is the greatest in the ***k***
18:23 Therefore the ***k*** of heaven is
19:12 themselves eunuchs for the ***k***
19:14 for of such is the ***k*** of
19:23 for a rich man to enter the ***k***
19:24 for a rich man to enter the ***k***
20: 1 For the ***k*** of heaven is like a
20:21 other on the left, in Your ***k***.
21:31 and harlots enter the ***k*** of God
21:43 the ***k*** of God will be taken from
22: 2 The ***k*** of heaven is like a
23:13 For you shut up the ***k*** of
24: 7 and ***k*** against kingdom. And
24: 7 nation, and kingdom against ***k***.
24:14 And this gospel of the ***k*** will be
25: 1 Then the ***k*** of heaven shall be
25:14 For the ***k*** of heaven is
25:34 inherit the ***k*** prepared for you
26:29 new with you in My Father's ***k***.
Mk 1:14 preaching the gospel of the ***k***
1:15 and the ***k*** of God is at hand.
3:24 If a ***k*** is divided against
3:24 that ***k*** cannot stand.
4:11 to know the mystery of the ***k***
4:26 The ***k*** of God is as if a man
4:30 To what shall we liken the ***k*** of
6:23 give you, up to half of my ***k***.
9: 1 death till they see the ***k*** of
9:47 better for you to enter the ***k***
10:14 for of such is the ***k*** of God.
10:15 whoever does not receive the ***k***
10:23 who have riches to enter the ***k***
10:24 trust in riches to enter the ***k***
10:25 for a rich man to enter the ***k***
11:10 Blessed is the ***k*** of our father
12:34 You are not far from the ***k*** of
13: 8 and ***k*** against kingdom. And
13: 8 nation, and kingdom against ***k***.
14:25 when I drink it new in the ***k***
15:43 was himself waiting for the ***k***
Lk 1:33 and of His ***k*** there will be no
4:43 I must preach the ***k*** of God to
6:20 For yours is the ***k*** of God.
7:28 but he who is least in the ***k*** of
8: 1 the glad tidings of the ***k*** of
8:10 to know the mysteries of the ***k***
9: 2 He sent them to preach the ***k*** of
9:11 and spoke to them about the ***k***
9:27 death till they see the ***k*** of
9:60 but you go and preach the ***k*** of
9:62 is fit for the ***k*** of God."
10: 9 The ***k*** of God has come near to
10:11 that the ***k*** of God has come near
11: 2 Your ***k*** come. Your will be
11:17 Every ***k*** divided against itself
11:18 how will his ***k*** stand? Because
11:20 surely the ***k*** of God has come
12:31 But seek the ***k*** of God, and all
12:32 good pleasure to give you the ***k***.
13:18 What is the ***k*** of God like? And
13:20 To what shall I liken the ***k*** of
13:28 and all the prophets in the ***k***
13:29 and sit down in the ***k*** of God.
14:15 he who shall eat bread in the ***k***
16:16 Since that time the ***k*** of God
17:20 by the Pharisees when the ***k*** of
17:20 The ***k*** of God does not come with
17:21 the ***k*** of God is within you."
18:16 for of such is the ***k*** of God.
18:17 whoever does not receive the ***k***
18:24 who have riches to enter the ***k***
18:25 for a rich man to enter the ***k***
18:29 for the sake of the ***k*** of God,
19:11 and because they thought the ***k***
19:12 to receive for himself a ***k*** and
19:15 returned, having received the ***k***,
21:10 and ***k*** against kingdom.
21:10 nation, and kingdom against ***k***.
21:31 know that the ***k*** of God is near.
22:16 until it is fulfilled in the ***k***
22:18 fruit of the vine until the ***k***
22:29 "And I bestow upon you a ***k***,
22:30 and drink at My table in My ***k***,
23:42 me when You come into Your ***k***.
23:51 was also waiting for the ***k*** of
Jn 3: 3 he cannot see the ***k*** of God."
3: 5 he cannot enter the ***k*** of God.
18:36 My ***k*** is not of this world. If My
18:36 If My ***k*** were of this world, My
18:36 but now My ***k*** is not from
Acts 1: 3 the things pertaining to the ***k***
1: 6 You at this time restore the ***k***
8:12 the things concerning the ***k*** of
14:22 many tribulations enter the ***k***
19: 8 concerning the things of the ***k***
20:25 I have gone preaching the ***k*** of
28:23 solemnly testified of the ***k*** of
28:31 preaching the ***k*** of God and
Rom 14:17 for the ***k*** of God is not eating
1 Cor 4:20 For the ***k*** of God is not in word
6: 9 will not inherit the ***k*** of God?
6:10 will inherit the ***k*** of God.
15:24 when He delivers the ***k*** to God
15:50 and blood cannot inherit the ***k***
Gal 5:21 things will not inherit the ***k***
Eph 5: 5 has any inheritance in the ***k*** of
Col 1:13 and conveyed us into the ***k*** of
4:11 only fellow workers for the ***k***
1 Th 2:12 who calls you into His own ***k***
2 Th 1: 5 may be counted worthy of the ***k***
2 Tim 4: 1 dead at His appearing and His ***k***:
4:18 preserve me for His heavenly ***k***.
Heb 1: 8 is the scepter of Your ***K***.
12:28 since we are receiving a ***k***
Jas 2: 5 in faith and heirs of the ***k***
2 Pe 1:11 into the everlasting ***k*** of our
Rev 1: 9 in the tribulation and ***k*** and
12:10 and the ***k*** of our God, and the
16:10 and his ***k*** became full of
17:12 kings who have received no ***k***
17:17 and to give their ***k*** to the

KINGDOM OF GOD (70/69)

Mt 6:33 But seek first the ***k*** and His
12:28 surely the ***k*** has come upon you.
19:24 for a rich man to enter the ***k***.
21:31 and harlots enter the ***k*** before
21:43 the ***k*** will be taken from you
Mk 1:14 preaching the gospel of the ***k***,
1:15 and the ***k*** is at hand.
4:11 to know the mystery of the ***k***;
4:26 The ***k*** is as if a man should
4:30 "To what shall we liken the ***k***?
9: 1 taste death till they see the ***k***
9:47 better for you to enter the ***k***
10:14 for of such is the ***k***.
10:15 whoever does not receive the ***k***
10:23 who have riches to enter the ***k***!
10:24 trust in riches to enter the ***k***!
10:25 for a rich man to enter the ***k***.
12:34 "You are not far from the ***k***.
14:25 when I drink it new in the ***k***.
15:43 was himself waiting for the ***k***,
Lk 4:43 'I must preach the ***k*** to the
6:20 you poor, For yours is the ***k***.
7:28 but he who is least in the ***k*** is
8: 1 the glad tidings of the ***k***.
8:10 to know the mysteries of the ***k***,
9: 2 He sent them to preach the ***k*** and
9:11 and spoke to them about the ***k***,
9:27 death till they see the ***k***."
9:60 but you go and preach the ***k***.
9:62 looking back, is fit for the ***k***.
10: 9 The ***k*** has come near to you.'
10:11 that the ***k*** has come near you.'
11:20 surely the ***k*** has come upon you.
12:31 'But seek the ***k***, and all
13:18 What is the ***k*** like? And to what
13:20 "To what shall I liken the ***k***?
13:28 and all the prophets in the ***k***,
13:29 south, and sit down in the ***k***.
14:15 who shall eat bread in the ***k***!"
16:16 Since that time the ***k*** has been
17:20 by the Pharisees when the ***k***
17:20 The ***k*** does not come with
17:21 the ***k*** is within you."
18:16 them; for of such is the ***k***.
18:17 whoever does not receive the ***k***
18:24 who have riches to enter the ***k***!
18:25 for a rich man to enter the ***k***.
18:29 children, for the sake of the ***k***,
19:11 and because they thought the ***k***
21:31 know that the ***k*** is near.
22:16 until it is fulfilled in the ***k***.
22:18 fruit of the vine until the ***k***
23:51 was also waiting for the ***k***.
Jn 3: 3 born again, he cannot see the ***k***.
3: 5 Spirit, he cannot enter the ***k***.
Acts 1: 3 the things pertaining to the ***k***.
8:12 the things concerning the ***k***
14:22 many tribulations enter the ***k***.
19: 8 concerning the things of the ***k***.
20:25 I have gone preaching the ***k***,
28:23 and solemnly testified of the ***k***,
28:31 preaching the ***k*** and teaching the
Rom 14:17 for the ***k*** is not eating and
1 Cor 4:20 For the ***k*** is not in word but in
6: 9 will not inherit the ***k***?
6:10 extortioners will inherit the ***k***.
15:50 and blood cannot inherit the ***k***;
Gal 5:21 things will not inherit the ***k***.
Col 4:11 only fellow workers for the ***k***
2 Th 1: 5 may be counted worthy of the ***k***,

KINGDOMS (58/56) KINGDOM

Deut 3:21 will the LORD do to all the ***k***
28:25 troublesome to all the ***k*** of
Josh 11:10 the head of all those ***k***.
1 Sam 10:18 and from the hand of all ***k***
1 Ki 4:21 So Solomon reigned over all ***k***
2 Ki 19:15 of all the ***k*** of the earth. You
19:19 that all the ***k*** of the earth may
1 Chr 29:30 and to all the ***k*** of the lands.
2 Chr 12: 8 from the service of the ***k*** of
17:10 of the LORD fell on all the ***k***
20: 6 do You not rule over all the ***k***
20:29 fear of God was on all the ***k***
36:23 All the ***k*** of the earth the
Ezra 1: 2 All the ***k*** of the earth the
Neh 9:22 Moreover You gave them ***k*** and
Ps 46: 6 the ***k*** were moved; He uttered
68:32 you ***k*** of the earth; Oh, sing
79: 6 And on the ***k*** that do not call
102:22 gathered together, And the ***k***,
135:11 And all the ***k*** of Canaan—
Isa 10:10 As my hand has found the ***k*** of
13: 4 A tumultuous noise of the ***k***
13:19 And Babylon, the glory of ***k***,
14:16 the earth tremble, Who shook ***k***,
23:11 over the sea, He shook the ***k***;
23:17 fornication with all the ***k*** of
37:16 of all the ***k*** of the earth. You
37:20 that all the ***k*** of the earth may
47: 5 longer be called The Lady of ***K***.
Jer 1:10 over the nations and over the ***k***,
1:15 All the families of the ***k*** of
10: 7 nations, And in all their ***k***,
15: 4 to all ***k*** of the earth, because
24: 9 them to trouble into all the ***k***
25:26 and all the ***k*** of the world
28: 8 many countries and great ***k***—
29:18 to trouble among all the ***k*** of
34: 1 all the ***k*** of the earth under
34:17 you to trouble among all the ***k***
49:28 Kedar and against the ***k*** of
51:20 With you I will destroy ***k***;
51:27 Call the ***k*** together against
Ezek 29:15 "It shall be the lowliest of ***k***;
37:22 they ever be divided into two ***k***
Dan 2:44 pieces and consume all these ***k***,
7:23 be different from all other ***k***,
7:27 And the greatness of the ***k***
8:22 four ***k*** shall arise out of that
Am 6: 2 Are you better than these ***k***?
Nah 3: 5 And the ***k*** your shame.
Zeph 3: 8 nations To My assembly of ***k***,
Hag 2:22 will overthrow the throne of ***k***;
2:22 the strength of the Gentile ***k***.
Mt 4: 8 and showed Him all the ***k*** of the
Lk 4: 5 showed Him all the ***k*** of the
Heb 11:33 who through faith subdued ***k***,
Rev 11:15 The ***k*** of this world have become
11:15 this world have become the ***k***

KINGLY (1/1) KING

Dan 5:20 deposed from his ***k*** throne,

KINGS (326/302) KING, KINGS'

Gen 14: 5 year Chedorlaomer and the ***k***
14: 9 four ***k*** against five.
14:10 and the ***k*** of Sodom and Gomorrah
14:17 of Chedorlaomer and the ***k*** who
17: 6 and ***k*** shall come from you.
17:16 ***k*** of peoples shall be from
35:11 and ***k*** shall come from your
36:31 Now these were the ***k*** who
Num 31: 8 They killed the ***k*** of Midian with
31: 8 the five ***k*** of Midian. Balaam
Deut 3: 8 from the hand of the two ***k*** of
3:21 God has done to these two ***k***;
4:47 two ***k*** of the Amorites, who
7:24 And He will deliver their ***k*** into
31: 4 the ***k*** of the Amorites and their
Josh 2:10 and what you did to the two ***k***
5: 1 when all the ***k*** of the Amorites
5: 1 and all the ***k*** of the Canaanites
9: 1 it came to pass when all the ***k***
9:10 all that He did to the two ***k***
10: 5 Therefore the five ***k*** of the
10: 6 for all the ***k*** of the Amorites
10:16 But these five ***k*** had fled and
10:17 The five ***k*** have been found
10:22 and bring out those five ***k*** to
10:23 and brought out those five ***k*** to
10:24 when they brought out those ***k***
10:24 feet on the necks of these ***k***.
10:40 slopes, and all their ***k***;
10:42 All these ***k*** and their land
11: 2 and to the ***k*** who were from the
11: 5 And when all these ***k*** had met
11:12 So all the cities of those ***k***,
11:12 of those kings, and all their ***k***,

11:17 Hermon. He captured all their ***k***,
11:18 a long time with all those ***k***.
12: 1 These are the ***k*** of the land
12: 7 And these are the ***k*** of the
12:24 king of Tirzah, one—all the ***k***,
24:12 also the two ***k*** of the
Judg 1: 7 Seventy ***k*** with their thumbs and
5: 3 O ***k***! Give ear, O princes! I,
5:19 The ***k*** came and fought, Then
5:19 Then the ***k*** of Canaan fought
8: 5 Zalmunna, ***k*** of Midian."
8:12 and he took the two ***k*** of
8:26 robes which were on the ***k*** of
1 Sam 14:47 against the ***k*** of Zobah, and
27: 6 Ziklag has belonged to the ***k***
2 Sam 10:19 And when all the ***k*** who were
11: 1 at the time when ***k*** go out to
1 Ki 3:13 be anyone like you among the ***k***
4:24 namely over all the ***k*** on this
4:34 from all the ***k*** of the earth who
10:15 from all the ***k*** of Arabia, and
10:23 Solomon surpassed all the ***k*** of
10:29 exported them to all the ***k*** of
10:29 of the Hittites and the ***k*** of
14:19 of the chronicles of the ***k*** of
14:29 of the chronicles of the ***k*** of
15: 7 of the chronicles of the ***k*** of
15:23 of the chronicles of the ***k*** of
15:31 of the chronicles of the ***k*** of
16: 5 of the chronicles of the ***k*** of
16:14 of the chronicles of the ***k*** of
16:20 of the chronicles of the ***k*** of
16:27 of the chronicles of the ***k*** of
16:33 Israel to anger than all the ***k***
20: 1 thirty-two ***k*** were with him,
20:12 as he and the ***k*** were drinking
20:16 Ben-Hadad and the thirty-two ***k***
20:24 do this thing: Dismiss the ***k***,
20:31 we have heard that the ***k*** of the
20:31 house of Israel are merciful ***k***.
22:39 of the chronicles of the ***k*** of
22:45 of the chronicles of the ***k*** of
2 Ki 1:18 of the chronicles of the ***k*** of
3:10 LORD has called these three ***k***
3:13 LORD has called these three ***k***
3:21 the Moabites heard that the ***k***
3:23 the ***k*** have surely struck swords
7: 6 has hired against us the ***k*** of
7: 6 of the Hittites and the ***k*** of
8:18 he walked in the way of the ***k***
8:23 of the chronicles of the ***k*** of
10: 4 two ***k*** could not stand up to
10:34 of the chronicles of the ***k*** of
11:19 he sat on the throne of the ***k***.
12:18 ***k*** of Judah, had dedicated, and
12:19 of the chronicles of the ***k*** of
13: 8 of the chronicles of the ***k*** of
13:12 of the chronicles of the ***k*** of
13:13 buried in Samaria with the ***k***
14:15 of the chronicles of the ***k*** of
14:16 buried in Samaria with the ***k***
14:18 of the chronicles of the ***k*** of
14:28 of the chronicles of the ***k*** of
14:29 the ***k*** of Israel. Then Zechariah
15: 6 of the chronicles of the ***k*** of
15:11 of the chronicles of the ***k*** of
15:15 of the chronicles of the ***k*** of
15:21 of the chronicles of the ***k*** of
15:26 of the chronicles of the ***k*** of
15:31 of the chronicles of the ***k*** of
15:36 of the chronicles of the ***k*** of
16: 3 he walked in the way of the ***k***
16:19 of the chronicles of the ***k*** of
17: 2 but not as the ***k*** of Israel who
17: 8 and of the ***k*** of Israel, which
18: 5 none like him among all the ***k***
19:11 You have heard what the ***k*** of
19:17 the ***k*** of Assyria have laid
20:20 of the chronicles of the ***k*** of
21:17 of the chronicles of the ***k*** of
21:25 of the chronicles of the ***k*** of
23: 5 idolatrous priests whom the ***k***
23:11 removed the horses that the ***k***
23:12 which the ***k*** of Judah had made,
23:19 which the ***k*** of Israel had made
23:22 nor in all the days of the ***k*** of
23:22 the kings of Israel and the ***k***
23:28 of the chronicles of the ***k*** of
24: 5 of the chronicles of the ***k*** of
25:28 seat than those of the ***k*** who
1 Chr 1:43 Now these were the ***k*** who
9: 1 inscribed in the book of the ***k***
16:21 He rebuked ***k*** for their sakes,
19: 9 and the ***k*** who had come were by
20: 1 at the time ***k*** go out to
2 Chr 1:12 such as none of the ***k*** have had
1:17 exported them to all the ***k*** of
1:17 of the Hittites and the ***k*** of
9:14 And all the ***k*** of Arabia and
9:22 Solomon surpassed all the ***k*** of
9:23 And all the ***k*** of the earth
9:26 So he reigned over all the ***k***
16:11 written in the book of the ***k***
20:34 mentioned in the book of the ***k***
21: 6 he walked in the way of the ***k***
21:13 walked in the way of the ***k*** of
21:20 but not in the tombs of the ***k***.
24:16 the City of David among the ***k***,
24:25 bury him in the tombs of the ***k***.
24:27 the annals of the book of the ***k***.
25:26 written in the book of the ***k***
26:23 burial which belonged to the ***k***,
27: 7 written in the book of the ***k***
28: 2 he walked in the ways of the ***k***
28:16 time King Ahaz sent to the ***k***
28:23 Because the gods of the ***k*** of
28:26 written in the book of the ***k***
28:27 him into the tombs of the ***k*** of
30: 6 escaped from the hand of the ***k***
32: 4 Why should the ***k*** of Assyria come
32:32 and in the book of the ***k*** of
33:18 written in the book of the ***k***
34:11 to floor the houses which the ***k***
35:18 and none of the ***k*** of Israel had
35:27 written in the book of the ***k***
36: 8 written in the book of the ***k***
Ezra 4:15 harmful to ***k*** and provinces, and
4:19 times has revolted against ***k***,
4:20 There have also been mighty ***k***
4:22 increase to the hurt of the ***k***?
7:12 Artaxerxes, king of ***k***,
9: 7 for our iniquities we, our ***k***,
9: 7 into the hand of the ***k*** of the
9: 9 to us in the sight of the ***k*** of
Neh 9:24 With their ***k*** And the people
9:32 Our ***k*** and our princes, Our
9:32 from the days of the ***k*** of
9:34 Neither our ***k*** nor our princes,
9:37 yields much increase to the ***k***
Esth 10: 2 of the chronicles of the ***k*** of
Job 3:14 With ***k*** and counselors of the
12:18 He loosens the bonds of ***k***,
36: 7 they are on the throne with ***k***,
Ps 2: 2 The ***k*** of the earth set
2:10 Now therefore, be wise, O ***k***;
48: 4 the ***k*** assembled, They passed
68:12 ***K*** of armies flee, they flee,
68:14 When the Almighty scattered ***k***
68:29 ***K*** will bring presents to You.
72:10 The ***k*** of Tarshish and of the
72:10 The ***k*** of Sheba and Seba Will
72:11 all ***k*** shall fall down before
76:12 He is awesome to the ***k*** of
89:27 The highest of the ***k*** of the
102:15 And all the ***k*** of the earth
105:14 He rebuked ***k*** for their sakes,
105:30 in the chambers of their ***k***.
110: 5 He shall execute ***k*** in the day
119:46 Your testimonies also before ***k***,
135:10 many nations And slew mighty ***k***—
136:17 To Him who struck down great ***k***,
136:18 slew famous ***k***, For His mercy
138: 4 All the ***k*** of the earth shall
144:10 One who gives salvation to ***k***,
148:11 ***K*** of the earth and all peoples
149: 8 To bind their ***k*** with chains,
Prov 8:15 By me ***k*** reign, And rulers
16:12 It is an abomination for ***k*** to
16:13 lips are the delight of ***k***,
22:29 work? He will stand before ***k***;
25: 2 But the glory of ***k*** is to
25: 3 So the heart of ***k*** is
31: 3 ways to that which destroys ***k***.
31: 4 It is not for ***k***,
31: 4 It is not for ***k*** to drink
Eccl 2: 8 and the special treasures of ***k***
Isa 1: 1 and Hezekiah, ***k*** of Judah.
7:16 will be forsaken by both her ***k***.
10: 8 not my princes altogether ***k***?
14: 9 from their thrones All the ***k***
14:18 All the ***k*** of the nations, All
19:11 the wise, The son of ancient ***k***?
24:21 And on the earth the ***k*** of the
37:11 You have heard what the ***k*** of
37:18 the ***k*** of Assyria have laid
41: 2 him, And made him rule over ***k***?
45: 1 him And loose the armor of ***k***,
49: 7 ***K*** shall see and arise, Princes
49:23 ***K*** shall be your foster fathers,
52:15 ***K*** shall shut their mouths at
60: 3 And ***k*** to the brightness of
60:10 And their ***k*** shall minister to
60:11 And their ***k*** in procession.
60:16 And milk the breast of ***k***;
62: 2 And all ***k*** your glory. You
Jer 1:18 Against the ***k*** of Judah,
2:26 They and their ***k*** and their
8: 1 bring out the bones of the ***k***
13:13 even the ***k*** who sit on David's
17:19 by which the ***k*** of Judah come in
17:20 you ***k*** of Judah, and all Judah,
17:25 enter the gates of this city ***k***
19: 3 O ***k*** of Judah and inhabitants of
19: 4 nor the ***k*** of Judah have known,
19:13 and the houses of the ***k*** of
20: 5 all the treasures of the ***k*** of
22: 4 ***k*** who sit on the throne of
25:14 (For many nations and great ***k***
25:18 its ***k*** and its princes, to make
25:20 all the ***k*** of the land of Uz,
25:20 all the ***k*** of the land of the
25:22 all the ***k*** of Tyre, all the kings
25:22 all the ***k*** of Sidon, and all the
25:22 and the ***k*** of the coastlands
25:24 all the ***k*** of Arabia and all the
25:24 kings of Arabia and all the ***k***
25:25 all the ***k*** of Zimri, all the
25:25 all the ***k*** of Elam, and all the
25:25 and all the ***k*** of the Medes;
25:26 all the ***k*** of the north, far and
27: 7 then many nations and great ***k***
32:32 Me to anger—they, their ***k***,
33: 4 city and the houses of the ***k***
34: 5 the former ***k*** who were before
44: 9 the wickedness of the ***k*** of
44:17 our ***k*** and our princes, in the
44:21 your ***k*** and your princes, and
46:25 with their gods and their ***k***—
50:41 And a great nation and many ***k***
51:11 raised up the spirit of the ***k***
51:28 With the ***k*** of the Medes, Its
52:32 seat than those of the ***k*** who
Lam 4:12 The ***k*** of the earth, And all
Ezek 26: 7 king of Babylon, king of ***k***,
27:33 You enriched the ***k*** of the
27:35 Their ***k*** will be greatly
28:17 ground, I laid you before ***k***,
32:10 and their ***k*** shall be horribly
32:29 Her ***k*** and all her princes,
43: 7 My holy name, they nor their ***k***,
43: 7 with the carcasses of their ***k***
43: 9 and the carcasses of their ***k***
Dan 2:21 He removes ***k*** and raises up
2:21 removes kings and raises up ***k***;
2:37 "You, O king, are a king of ***k***.
2:44 And in the days of these ***k*** the
2:47 the God of gods, the Lord of ***k***,
7:17 are four ***k*** which arise out of
7:24 The ten horns are ten ***k*** Who
7:24 And shall subdue three ***k***.
8:20 they are the ***k*** of Media and
9: 6 who spoke in Your name to our ***k***
9: 8 shame of face, to our ***k***,
10:13 left alone there with the ***k*** of
11: 2 three more ***k*** will arise in
Hos 1: 1 ***k*** of Judah, and in the days of
7: 7 All their ***k*** have fallen. None
8: 4 'They set up ***k***, but not by
Mic 1: 1 ***k*** of Judah, which he saw
1:14 shall be a lie to the ***k*** of
Hab 1:10 They scoff at ***k***, And princes
Mt 10:18 brought before governors and ***k***
17:25 From whom do the ***k*** of the earth
Mk 13: 9 be brought before rulers and ***k***
Lk 10:24 you that many prophets and ***k***
21:12 You will be brought before ***k***
22:25 The ***k*** of the Gentiles exercise
Acts 4:26 The ***k*** of the earth took
9:15 bear My name before Gentiles, ***k***,
1 Cor 4: 8 rich! You have reigned as ***k***
1 Tim 2: 2 for ***k*** and all who are in
6:15 the King of ***k*** and Lord of
Heb 7: 1 from the slaughter of the ***k***
Rev 1: 5 and the ruler over the ***k*** of the
1: 6 and has made us ***k*** and priests to
5:10 And have made us ***k*** and priests
6:15 And the ***k*** of the earth, the
10:11 nations, tongues, and ***k***.
16:12 so that the way of the ***k*** from
16:14 which go out to the ***k*** of the
17: 2 with whom the ***k*** of the earth
17:10 "There are also seven ***k***.
17:12 horns which you saw are ten ***k***
17:12 authority for one hour as ***k***
17:14 is Lord of lords and King of ***k***;
17:18 city which reigns over the ***k***
18: 3 the ***k*** of the earth have
18: 9 The ***k*** of the earth who
19:16 KING OF ***K*** AND LORD OF LORDS.
19:18 you may eat the flesh of ***k***,
19:19 the ***k*** of the earth, and their
21:24 and the ***k*** of the earth bring

KINGS' (5/5) KINGS

Ps 45: 9 ***K*** daughters are among Your
Prov 30:28 And it is in ***k*** palaces.
Dan 11:27 Both these ***k*** hearts shall be
Mt 11: 8 wear soft clothing are in ***k***
Lk 7:25 and live in luxury are in ***k***

KIR (8/8)

2 Ki 16: 9 its people captive to ***K***,
Isa 15: 1 Because in the night ***K*** of Moab
16:11 And my inner being for ***K***
22: 6 And ***K*** uncovered the shield.
Jer 48:31 I will mourn for the men of ***K***
48:36 shall wail For the men of ***K***
Am 1: 5 of Syria shall go captive to ***K***,
9: 7 And the Syrians from ***K***?

KIR HARASETH (1/1)

2 Ki 3:25 But they left the stones of ***K***

KIR HARESETH (1/1)

Isa 16: 7 For the foundations of ***K*** you

KIR-HARASETH, KIR-HARESH, KIR-HERES (KJV) See KIR HARASETH, (KIR) HERES

KIRIOTH (KJV) See KERIOTH

KIRJATH (1/1)

Josh 18:28 is Jerusalem), Gibeath, and ***K***:

KIRJATH ARBA (9/9) HEBRON

Gen 23: 2 So Sarah died in ***K*** (that is,
35:27 or ***K*** (that is, Hebron), where
Josh 14:15 name of Hebron formerly was ***K***
15:13 the LORD to Joshua, namely, ***K***,

15:54 *K* (which is Hebron), and Zior:
20: 7 and *K* (which is Hebron) in the
21:11 And they gave them *K* (Arba was
Judg 1:10 name of Hebron was formerly *K*.
Neh 11:25 children of Judah dwelt in *K*

KIRJATH ARIM (1/1)

Ezra 2:25 the people of *K*, Chephirah,

KIRJATH BAAL (2/2)

Josh 15:60 *K* (which is Kirjath Jearim)
18:14 and it ended at *K* (which is

KIRJATH HUZOTH (1/1)

Num 22:39 with Balak, and they came to *K*.

KIRJATH JEARIM (18/17)

Josh 9:17 Chephirah, Beeroth, and *K*.
15: 9 around to Baalah (which is *K*).
15:60 Kirjath Baal (which is *K*) and
18:14 at Kirjath Baal (which is *K*),
18:15 side began at the end of *K*,
Judg 18:12 they went up and encamped in *K*
18:12 There it is, west of *K*.)
1 Sam 6:21 to the inhabitants of *K*,
7: 1 Then the men of *K* came and took
7: 2 was that the ark remained in *K*
1 Chr 2:50 were Shobal the father of *K*,
2:52 And Shobal the father of *K* had
2:53 The families of *K* were the
13: 5 to bring the ark of God from *K*.
13: 6 Israel went up to Baalah, to *K*,
2 Chr 1: 4 up the ark of God from *K* to
Neh 7:29 the men of *K*, Chephirah,
Jer 26:20 Urijah the son of Shemaiah of *K*,

KIRJATH SANNAH (1/1)

Josh 15:49 *K* (which is Debir),

KIRJATH SEPHER (4/4)

Josh 15:15 the name of Debir was *K*).
15:16 He who attacks *K* and takes it,
Judg 1:11 name of Debir was formerly *K*.
1:12 Whoever attacks *K* and takes it,

KIRJATHAIM (6/6)

Num 32:37 built Heshbon and Elealeh and *K*,
Josh 13:19 *K*, Sibmah, Zereth Shahar on
1 Chr 6:76 and *K* with its common-lands.
Jer 48: 1 *K* is shamed and taken; The
48:23 On *K* and Beth Gamul and Beth
Ezek 25: 9 Jeshimoth, Baal Meon, and *K*.

KIRJATH-ARBA (KJV) See ARBA, KIRJATH ARBA

KIRJATH-ARIM (KJV) See KIRJATH ARIM

KIRJATH-BAAL (KJV) See KIRJATH BAAL

KIRJATH-HUZOTH (KJV) See KIRJATH HUZOTH

KIRJATH-JEARIM (KJV) See KIRJATH JEARIM

KIRJATH-SANNAH (KJV) See KIRJATH SANNAH

KIRJATH-SEPHER (KJV) See KIRJATH SEPHER

KISH (23/19)

1 Sam 9: 1 of Benjamin whose name was *K*
9: 3 Now the donkeys of *K*,
9: 3 And *K* said to his son Saul,
10:11 has come upon the son of *K*?
10:21 And Saul the son of *K* was
14:51 *K* was the father of Saul, and
2 Sam 21:14 in the tomb of *K* his father. So
1 Chr 8:30 son was Abdon, then Zur, *K*,
8:33 Ner begot *K*, Kish begot Saul,
8:33 *K* begot Saul, and Saul begot
9:36 son was Abdon, then Zur, *K*,
9:39 Ner begot *K*, Kish begot Saul,
9:39 *K* begot Saul, and Saul begot
12: 1 fugitive from Saul the son of *K*;
23:21 of Mahli were Eleazar and *K*.
23:22 their brethren, the sons of *K*,
24:29 Of *K*: the son of Kish,
24:29 Of Kish: the son of *K*,
26:28 the seer, Saul the son of *K*,
2 Chr 29:12 *K* the son of Abdi and Azariah
Esth 2: 5 the son of Shimei, the son of *K*,
2: 6 *K* had been carried away from
Acts 13:21 God gave them Saul the son of *K*,

KISHI (1/1)

1 Chr 6:44 hand, were Ethan the son of *K*,

KISHION (2/2)

Josh 19:20 Rabbith, *K*, Abez,
21:28 *K* with its common-land,

KISHON (6/5)

Judg 4: 7 his multitude at the River *K*;
4:13 Hagoyim to the River *K*.
5:21 The torrent of *K* swept them
5:21 torrent, the torrent of *K*.
1 Ki 18:40 them down to the Brook *K* and
Ps 83: 9 As with Jabin at the Brook *K*,

KISON (KJV) See KISHON

KISS (20/19) KISSED, KISSES

Gen 27:26 Come near now and *k* me, my
31:28 And you did not allow me to *k* my
2 Sam 15: 5 out his hand and take him and *k*
20: 9 beard with his right hand to *k*
1 Ki 19:20 Please let me *k* my father and my
Ps 2:12 *K* the Son, lest He be angry,
Song 1: 2 Let him *k* me with the kisses of
8: 1 I would *k* you; I would not be
Hos 13: 2 Let the men who sacrifice *k* the
Mt 26:48 a sign, saying, "Whomever I *k*,
Mk 14:44 signal, saying, "Whomever I *k*,
Lk 7:45 "You gave Me no *k*,
7:45 this woman has not ceased to *k*
22:47 and drew near to Jesus to *k*
22:48 the Son of Man with a *k*?
Rom 16:16 Greet one another with a holy *k*.
1 Cor 16:20 Greet one another with a holy *k*.
2 Cor 13:12 Greet one another with a holy *k*.
1 Th 5:26 all the brethren with a holy *k*.
1 Pe 5:14 Greet one another with a *k* of

KISSED (25/25) KISS

Gen 27:27 And he came near and *k* him; and
29:11 Then Jacob *k* Rachel, and lifted
29:13 and embraced him and *k* him, and
31:55 and *k* his sons and daughters
33: 4 and fell on his neck and *k* him,
45:15 Moreover he *k* all his brothers
48:10 and he *k* them and embraced
50: 1 wept over him, and *k* him.
Ex 4:27 of God, and *k* him.
18: 7 and *k* him. And they asked each
Ruth 1: 9 Then she *k* them, and they
1:14 and Orpah *k* her mother-in-law,
1 Sam 10: 1 and *k* him and said: "Is it
20:41 And they *k* one another; and
2 Sam 14:33 Then the king *k* Absalom.
19:39 the king *k* Barzillai and
1 Ki 19:18 and every mouth that has not *k*
Job 31:27 And my mouth has *k* my hand;
Ps 85:10 Righteousness and peace have *k*.
Prov 7:13 So she caught him and *k* him;
Mt 26:49 'Greetings, Rabbi!" and *k* Him.
Mk 14:45 'Rabbi, Rabbi!" and *k* Him.
Lk 7:38 and she *k* His feet and anointed
15:20 ran and fell on his neck and *k*
Acts 20:37 and fell on Paul's neck and *k*

KISSES (3/3) KISS

Prov 24:26 He who gives a right answer *k*
27: 6 But the *k* of an enemy are
Song 1: 2 Let him kiss me with the *k* of

KITCHENS (1/1)

Ezek 46:24 These are the *k* where the

KITE (3/2)

Lev 11:14 'the *k*, and the falcon after
Deut 14:13 'the red *k*, the falcon,
14:13 and the *k* after their kinds;

KITHLISH (1/1)

Josh 15:40 Cabbon, Lahmas, *K*,

KITRON (1/1)

Judg 1:30 drive out the inhabitants of *K*

KITTIM (2/2)

Gen 10: 4 were Elishah, Tarshish, *K*,
1 Chr 1: 7 were Elishah, Tarshishah, *K*,

KNAPSACK (4/4)

2 Ki 4:42 newly ripened grain in his *k*.
Lk 10: 4 "Carry neither money bag, *k*,
22:35 I sent you without money bag, *k*,
22:36 him take it, and likewise a *k*;

KNEAD (2/2) KNEADED, KNEADING

Gen 18: 6 *k* it and make cakes."
Jer 7:18 and the women *k* dough, to make

KNEADED (2/2) KNEAD

1 Sam 28:24 And she took flour and *k* it,
2 Sam 13: 8 Then she took flour and *k* it,

KNEADING (5/5) KNEAD

Ex 8: 3 and into your *k* bowls.
12:34 having their *k* bowls bound up
Deut 28: 5 be your basket and your *k*
28:17 be your basket and your *k*
Hos 7: 4 stirring the fire after *k*

KNEE (8/8) KNEES

Gen 41:43 Bow the *k*!" So he set him over
Isa 45:23 That to Me every *k* shall bow,
Ezek 7:17 And every *k* will be as weak
Mt 27:29 And they bowed the *k* before Him
Mk 15:19 spat on Him; and bowing the *k*,
Rom 11: 4 who have not bowed the *k*
14:11 Every *k* shall bow to Me,
Phil 2:10 at the name of Jesus every *k*

KNEEL (2/2) KNEELING, KNELT

Gen 24:11 And he made his camels *k* down
Ps 95: 6 Let us *k* before the LORD our

KNEELING (4/4) KNEEL

1 Ki 8:54 from *k* on his knees with his
Mt 17:14 *k* down to Him and saying,
20:20 *k* down and asking something
Mk 1:40 *k* down to Him and saying to

KNEES (29/29) KNEE

Gen 30: 3 she will bear a child on my *k*,
48:12 brought them from beside his *k*,
50:23 also brought up on Joseph's *k*.
Deut 28:35 LORD will strike you in the *k*
Judg 7: 5 who gets down on his *k* to
7: 6 the people got down on their *k*
16:19 lulled him to sleep on her *k*,
1 Sam 14:13 climbed up on his hands and *k*
1 Ki 8:54 from kneeling on his *k* with his
18:42 and put his face between his *k*,
19:18 all whose *k* have not bowed to
2 Ki 1:13 and came and fell on his *k*
4:20 he sat on her *k* till noon, and
2 Chr 6:13 knelt down on his *k* before all
Ezra 9: 5 I fell on my *k* and spread out
Job 3:12 Why did the *k* receive me? Or
4: 4 have strengthened the feeble *k*;
Ps 109:24 My *k* are weak through fasting,
Isa 35: 3 And make firm the feeble *k*.
66:12 And be dandled on her *k*.
Ezek 21: 7 and all *k* will be weak as
47: 4 the water came up to my *k*.
Dan 5: 6 hips were loosened and his *k*
6:10 he knelt down on his *k* three
10:10 which made me tremble on my *k*
Nah 2:10 and the *k* shake; Much pain is
Lk 5: 8 it, he fell down at Jesus' *k*,
Eph 3:14 For this reason I bow my *k* to
Heb 12:12 hang down, and the feeble *k*,

KNELT (8/8) KNEEL

2 Chr 6:13 *k* down on his knees before all
Dan 6:10 he *k* down on his knees three
Mk 10:17 *k* before Him, and asked Him,
Lk 22:41 and He *k* down and prayed,
Acts 7:60 Then he *k* down and cried out
9:40 and *k* down and prayed. And
20:36 he *k* down and prayed with them
21: 5 And we *k* down on the shore and

KNEW (98/98) KNOW

Gen 3: 7 and they *k* that they were
4: 1 Now Adam *k* Eve his wife, and she
4:17 And Cain *k* his wife, and she
4:25 And Adam *k* his wife again, and
8:11 and Noah *k* that the waters had
9:24 and *k* what his younger son had
38: 9 But Onan *k* that the heir would
38:26 And he never *k* her again.
Deut 9:24 the LORD from the day that I *k*
34:10 whom the LORD *k* face to face,
Judg 11:39 She *k* no man. And it became a
13:21 then Manoah *k* that He was the
19:25 And they *k* her and abused her
1 Sam 1:19 And Elkanah *k* Hannah his wife,
3:20 Israel from Dan to Beersheba *k*
10:11 when all who *k* him formerly saw
18:28 Thus Saul saw and *k* that the
20: 9 be it from you! For if I *k*
20:33 by which Jonathan *k* that it was
20:39 Only Jonathan and David *k* of
22:15 For your servant *k* nothing of
22:17 and because they *k* when he fled
22:22 I *k* that day, when Doeg the
23: 9 When David *k* that Saul plotted
26:12 and no man saw it or *k* it or
26:17 Then Saul *k* David's voice, and
2 Sam 5:12 So David *k* that the LORD had
11:16 Uriah to a place where he *k*
1 Ki 9:27 seamen who *k* the sea, to work
1 Chr 14: 2 So David *k* that the LORD had
2 Chr 8:18 and servants who *k* the sea.
33:13 Then Manasseh *k* that the LORD
Neh 9:10 For You *k* that they acted
Esth 1:13 king's manner toward all who *k*
Job 23: 3 that I *k* where I might find
Ps 142: 3 Then You *k* my path. In the
Isa 48: 4 Because I *k* that you were

48: 7 Of course I ***k*** them.'
48: 8 For I ***k*** that you would deal
Jer 1: 5 I formed you in the womb I ***k***
32: 8 Then I ***k*** that this was the
41: 4 when as yet no one ***k*** it,
44:15 Then all the men who ***k*** that
Ezek 10:20 and I ***k*** they were cherubim.
19: 7 He ***k*** their desolate places,
28:19 All who ***k*** you among the peoples
Dan 5:21 till he ***k*** that the Most High
5:22 although you ***k*** all this.
6:10 Now when Daniel ***k*** that the
Hos 13: 5 I ***k*** you in the wilderness, In
Jon 1:10 For the men ***k*** that he fled
Zech 11:11 ***k*** that it was the word of the
Mt 7:23 I never ***k*** you; depart from Me,
12:15 But when Jesus ***k*** it, He
12:25 But Jesus ***k*** their thoughts, and
25:24 I ***k*** you to be a hard man,
25:26 you ***k*** that I reap where I have
27:18 For he ***k*** that they had handed
Mk 1:34 because they ***k*** Him.
6:33 and many ***k*** Him and ran there on
12:12 for they ***k*** He had spoken the
15:10 For he ***k*** that the chief priests
Lk 4:41 for they ***k*** that He was the
6: 8 But He ***k*** their thoughts, and
7:37 when she ***k*** that Jesus sat at
9:11 But when the multitudes ***k*** it,
12:47 And that servant who ***k*** his
19:22 You ***k*** that I was an austere
20:19 for they ***k*** He had spoken this
23: 7 And as soon as he ***k*** that He
24:31 eyes were opened and they ***k***
Jn 2: 9 who had drawn the water ***k***),
2:24 because He ***k*** all men,
2:25 for He ***k*** what was in man.
4: 1 when the Lord ***k*** that the
4:10 If you ***k*** the gift of God, and
4:53 So the father ***k*** that it was at
5: 6 and ***k*** that he already had been
6: 6 for He Himself ***k*** what He would
6:61 When Jesus ***k*** in Himself that His
6:64 For Jesus ***k*** from the
11:57 that if anyone ***k*** where He was,
12: 9 Now a great many of the Jews ***k***
13: 1 when Jesus ***k*** that His hour had
13:11 For He ***k*** who would betray Him;
13:28 But no one at the table ***k*** for
16:19 Now Jesus ***k*** that they desired to
18: 2 also ***k*** the place; for Jesus
Acts 3:10 Then they ***k*** that it was he who
16: 3 for they all ***k*** that his father
18:25 though he ***k*** only the baptism of
26: 5 They ***k*** me from the first, if
Rom 1:21 although they ***k*** God, they did
1 Cor 2: 8 of the rulers of this age ***k***;
2 Cor 5:21 For He made Him who ***k*** no sin to
Col 1: 6 since the day you heard and ***k***
Jude 5 though you once ***k*** this, that
Rev 19:12 a name written that no one ***k***

KNIFE (5/5) KNIVES

Gen 22: 6 the fire in his hand, and a ***k***,
22:10 out his hand and took the ***k*** to
Judg 19:29 entered his house he took a ***k***,
Prov 23: 2 And put a ***k*** to your throat If
Jer 36:23 cut it with the scribe's ***k*** and

KNIT (6/6)

1 Sam 18: 1 the soul of Jonathan was ***k*** to
Job 10:11 And ***k*** me together with bones
40:17 of his thighs are tightly ***k***.
Eph 4:16 joined and ***k*** together by what
Col 2: 2 being ***k*** together in love, and
2:19 nourished and ***k*** together by

KNIVES (5/5) KNIFE

Josh 5: 2 Make flint ***k*** for yourself, and
5: 3 So Joshua made flint ***k*** for
1 Ki 18:28 with ***k*** and lances, until the
Ezra 1: 9 silver platters, twenty-nine ***k***,
Prov 30:14 And whose fangs are like ***k***,

KNOB (12/6)

Ex 25:33 with an ornamental ***k*** and a
25:33 with an ornamental ***k*** and a
25:34 each with its ornamental ***k***
25:35 And there shall be a ***k*** under
25:35 a ***k*** under the second two
25:35 and a ***k*** under the third two
37:19 with an ornamental ***k*** and a
37:19 with an ornamental ***k*** and a
37:20 each with its ornamental ***k***
37:21 There was a ***k*** under the first
37:21 a ***k*** under the second two
37:21 and a ***k*** under the third two

KNOBS (4/4)

Ex 25:31 its bowls, its ornamental ***k***,
25:36 Their ***k*** and their branches
37:17 its bowls, its ornamental ***k***,
37:22 Their ***k*** and their branches were

KNOCK (5/5) KNOCKED, KNOCKING, KNOCKS

Ezek 39: 3 Then I will ***k*** the bow out of
Mt 7: 7 you; seek, and you will find; ***k***,
Lk 11: 9 you; seek, and you will find; ***k***,
13:25 begin to stand outside and ***k***
Rev 3:20 I stand at the door and ***k***.

KNOCKED (2/2) KNOCK

Dan 5: 6 were loosened and his knees ***k***
Acts 12:13 And as Peter ***k*** at the door of

KNOCKING (1/1) KNOCK

Acts 12:16 Now Peter continued ***k***;

KNOCKS (5/5) KNOCK

Ex 21:27 And if he ***k*** out the tooth of his
Song 5: 2 the voice of my beloved! He ***k***,
Mt 7: 8 and to him who ***k*** it will be
Lk 11:10 and to him who ***k*** it will be
12:36 that when he comes and ***k*** they

KNOP, KNOPS (KJV) See KNOB, KNOBS

KNOW (964/904) KNEW, KNOWING, KNOWLEDGE, KNOWN, KNOWS, UNKNOWN

Gen 3:22 to ***k*** good and evil. And now,
4: 9 He said, "I do not ***k***.
12:11 Indeed I ***k*** that you are a woman
15: 8 how shall I ***k*** that I will
15:13 ***K*** certainly that your
18:21 to Me; and if not, I will ***k***.
19: 5 them out to us that we may ***k***
19:33 and he did not ***k*** when she lay
19:35 and he did not ***k*** when she lay
20: 6 I ***k*** that you did this in the
20: 7 ***k*** that you shall surely die,
21:26 I do not ***k*** who has done this
22:12 for now I ***k*** that you fear God,
24:14 And by this I will ***k*** that You
24:21 remained silent so as to ***k***
27: 2 I do not ***k*** the day of my death.
28:16 and I did not ***k*** it."
29: 5 Do you ***k*** Laban the son of
29: 5 they said, "We ***k*** him."
30:26 for you ***k*** my service which I
30:29 You ***k*** how I have served you and
31: 6 And you ***k*** that with all my might
31:32 For Jacob did not ***k*** that
37:32 Do you ***k*** whether it is your
38:16 for he did not ***k*** that she was
39: 6 and he did not ***k*** what he had
39: 8 my master does not ***k*** what is
42:23 But they did not ***k*** that Joseph
42:33 By this I will ***k*** that you are
42:34 so I shall ***k*** that you are not
43:22 We do not ***k*** who put our money
44:15 Did you not ***k*** that such a man
44:27 You ***k*** that my wife bore me two
47: 6 And if you ***k*** any competent men
48:19 father refused and said, "I ***k***,
48:19 and said, "I know, my son, I ***k***.
Ex 1: 8 who did not ***k*** Joseph.
2: 4 to ***k*** what would be done to him.
3: 7 for I ***k*** their sorrows.
4:14 I ***k*** that he can speak well. And
5: 2 I do not ***k*** the LORD, nor will
6: 7 Then you shall ***k*** that I am the
7: 5 And the Egyptians shall ***k*** that I
7:17 By this you shall ***k*** that I am
8:10 that you may ***k*** that there is
8:22 in order that you may ***k*** that I
9:14 that you may ***k*** that there is
9:29 that you may ***k*** that the earth
9:30 I ***k*** that you will not yet fear
10: 2 that you may ***k*** that I am the
10: 7 Do you not yet ***k*** that Egypt is
10:26 and even we do not ***k*** with what
11: 7 that you may ***k*** that the LORD
14: 4 that the Egyptians may ***k*** that I
14:18 Then the Egyptians shall ***k*** that
16: 6 At evening you shall ***k*** that the
16:12 And you shall ***k*** that I am the
16:15 For they did not ***k*** what it
18:11 Now I ***k*** that the LORD is
23: 9 for you ***k*** the heart of a
29:46 And they shall ***k*** that I am the
31:13 that you may ***k*** that I am the
32: 1 we do not ***k*** what has become of
32:22 You ***k*** the people, that they
32:23 we do not ***k*** what has become of
33: 5 that I may ***k*** what to do to
33:12 But You have not let me ***k*** whom
33:12 I ***k*** you by name, and you have
33:13 that I may ***k*** You and that I may
33:17 and I ***k*** you by name."
34:29 that Moses did not ***k*** that the
36: 1 to ***k*** how to do all manner of
Lev 5:17 though he does not ***k*** it, yet
5:18 in which he erred and did not ***k***
23:43 that your generations may ***k*** that
Num 10:31 inasmuch as you ***k*** how we are to
11:16 whom you ***k*** to be the elders of
14:31 and they shall ***k*** the land which
14:34 and you shall ***k*** My rejection.
16:28 By this you shall ***k*** that the
20:14 You ***k*** all the hardship that has
22: 6 for I ***k*** that he whom you bless
22:19 that I may ***k*** what more the
22:34 for I did not ***k*** You stood in
Deut 3:19 and your livestock (I ***k*** that
4:35 that you might ***k*** that the LORD
4:39 Therefore ***k*** this day, and
7: 9 Therefore ***k*** that the LORD your
8: 2 to ***k*** what was in your heart,
8: 3 with manna which you did not ***k***
8: 3 not know nor did your fathers ***k***,
8: 3 that He might make you ***k*** that
8: 5 You should ***k*** in your heart that
8:16 which your fathers did not ***k***,
9: 2 of the Anakim, whom you ***k***,
11: 2 ***K*** today that I do not speak
13: 3 your God is testing you to ***k***
18:21 How shall we ***k*** the word which
20:20 Only the trees which you ***k*** are
22: 2 or if you do not ***k*** him, then
29: 6 that you may ***k*** that I am the
29:16 (for you ***k*** that we dwelt in the
29:26 gods that they did not ***k*** and
31:21 for I ***k*** the inclination of
31:27 for I ***k*** your rebellion and your
31:29 For I ***k*** that after my death you
32:17 God, To gods they did not ***k***,
33: 9 Or ***k*** his own children; For
Josh 2: 4 but I did not ***k*** where they
2: 5 Where the men went I do not ***k***;
2: 9 I ***k*** that the LORD has given you
3: 4 that you may ***k*** the way by which
3: 7 that they may ***k*** that, as I was
3:10 By this you shall ***k*** that the
4:22 you shall let your children ***k***,
4:24 the peoples of the earth may ***k***
8:14 But he did not ***k*** that there
14: 6 You ***k*** the word which the LORD
22:22 knows, and let Israel itself ***k***—
23:13 ***k*** for certain that the LORD
23:14 And you ***k*** in all your hearts
Judg 2:10 arose after them who did not ***k***
3: 2 of Israel might be taught to ***k***
3: 4 to ***k*** whether they would obey
6:37 then I shall ***k*** that You will
13:16 (For Manoah did not ***k*** He was
14: 4 his father and mother did not ***k***
15:11 Do you not ***k*** that the
16:20 free!" But he did not ***k*** that
17:13 Now I ***k*** that the LORD will be
18: 5 that we may ***k*** whether the
18:14 Do you ***k*** that there are in these
19:22 that we may ***k*** him carnally!"
20:34 But the Benjamites did not ***k***
Ruth 2:11 to a people whom you did not ***k***
3:11 for all the people of my town ***k***
3:18 until you ***k*** how the matter will
4: 4 then tell me, that I may ***k***;
1 Sam 2:12 they did not ***k*** the LORD.
3: 7 (Now Samuel did not yet ***k*** the
6: 9 then we shall ***k*** that it is
14: 3 But the people did not ***k*** that
14:38 and ***k*** and see what this sin was
17:28 I ***k*** your pride and the
17:46 that all the earth may ***k*** that
17:47 all this assembly shall ***k***
17:55 soul lives, O king, I do not ***k***.
20: 3 Do not let Jonathan ***k*** this, lest
20:30 rebellious woman! Do I not ***k***
20:39 But the lad did not ***k*** anything.
21: 2 Do not let anyone ***k*** anything
22: 3 till I ***k*** what God will do for
24:11 ***k*** and see that there is
24:20 And now I ***k*** indeed that you
25:11 give it to men when I do not ***k***
25:17 ***k*** and consider what you will
28: 1 You assuredly ***k*** that you will go
28: 2 Surely you ***k*** what your servant
28: 9 you ***k*** what Saul has done, how
29: 9 I ***k*** that you are as good in my
2 Sam 1: 5 How do you ***k*** that Saul and
2:26 Do you not ***k*** that it will be
3:25 to ***k*** your going out and your
3:25 and to ***k*** all that you are
3:26 But David did not ***k*** it.
3:38 Do you not ***k*** that a prince and a
7:20 Lord GOD, ***k*** Your servant.
7:21 to make Your servant ***k*** them.
11:20 Did you not ***k*** that they would
14:20 to ***k*** everything that is in the
15:11 along innocently and did not ***k***
15:20 since I go I ***k*** not where?
17: 8 you ***k*** your father and his men,
18:29 but I did not ***k*** what it was
19:20 ***k*** that I have sinned. Therefore
19:22 For do I not ***k*** that today I am
24: 2 that I may ***k*** the number of the
1 Ki 1: 4 but the king did not ***k*** her.
1:11 and David our lord does not ***k***
1:18 you do not ***k*** about it.
2: 5 Moreover you ***k*** also what Joab
2: 9 for you are a wise man and ***k***
2:15 You ***k*** that the kingdom was mine,
2:32 my father David did not ***k*** it.
2:37 ***k*** for certain you shall surely
2:42 ***K*** for certain that on the day
2:44 moreover to Shimei, "You ***k***,
3: 7 I do not ***k*** how to go out or
5: 3 You ***k*** how my father David could
5: 6 For you ***k*** there is none among
8:39 whose heart You ***k*** (for You
8:39 You know (for You alone ***k*** the
8:43 all peoples of the earth may ***k***
8:43 and that they may ***k*** that this

K

8:60 the peoples of the earth may ***k***
17:24 Now by this I ***k*** that you are a
18:12 carry you to a place I do not ***k***;
18:37 that this people may ***k*** that You
20:13 and you shall ***k*** that I am the
20:28 and you shall ***k*** that I am the
22: 3 Do you ***k*** that Ramoth in Gilead
2 Ki 2: 3 Do you ***k*** that the LORD will
2: 3 And he said, "Yes, I ***k***;
2: 5 Do you ***k*** that the LORD will
2: 5 So he answered, "Yes, I ***k***;
4: 1 and you ***k*** that your servant
4: 9 I ***k*** that this is a holy man of
4:39 though they did not ***k*** what
5: 8 and he shall ***k*** that there is a
5:15 now I ***k*** that there is no God
7:12 They ***k*** that we are hungry;
8:12 Because I ***k*** the evil that you
9:11 You ***k*** the man and his babble."
10:10 ***K*** now that nothing shall fall to
17:26 the cities of Samaria do not ***k***
17:26 them because they do not ***k*** the
19:19 the kingdoms of the earth may ***k***
19:27 But I ***k*** your dwelling place,
1 Chr 12:32 to ***k*** what Israel ought to do,
17:18 For You ***k*** Your servant.
21: 2 of them to me that I may ***k*** it.
28: 9 ***k*** the God of your father, and
29:17 I ***k*** also, my God, that You test
2 Chr 2: 8 for I ***k*** that your servants have
6:30 whose heart You ***k*** (for You
6:30 You know (for You alone ***k*** the
6:33 all peoples of the earth may ***k***
6:33 and that they may ***k*** that this
13: 5 Should you not ***k*** that the LORD
20:12 nor do we ***k*** what to do, but our
25:16 I ***k*** that God has determined to
32:13 Do you not ***k*** what I and my
32:31 that He might ***k*** all that was
Ezra 4:15 the book of the records and ***k***
7:25 all such as ***k*** the laws of your
7:25 and teach those who do not ***k***
Neh 2:16 And the officials did not ***k***
4:11 They will neither ***k*** nor see
Esth 4:11 of the king's provinces ***k*** that
Job 5:24 You shall ***k*** that your tent is
5:25 You shall also ***k*** that your
5:27 Hear it, and ***k*** for yourself."
7:10 Nor shall his place ***k*** him
8: 9 and ***k*** nothing, Because our
9: 2 Truly I ***k*** it is so, But how
9: 5 and they do not ***k*** When He
9:21 yet I do not ***k*** myself; I
9:28 I ***k*** that You will not hold me
10: 7 Although You ***k*** that I am not
10:13 I ***k*** that this was with You:
11: 6 ***K*** therefore that God exacts
11: 8 than Sheol—what can you ***k***?
12: 3 who does not ***k*** such things as
12: 9 Who among all these does not ***k***
13: 2 What you ***k***, I also know;
13: 2 What you know, I also ***k***;
13:18 I ***k*** that I shall be
13:23 Make me ***k*** my transgression and
14:21 and he does not ***k*** it; They
15: 9 What do you ***k*** that we do not
15: 9 do you know that we do not ***k***?
18:21 place of him who does not ***k***
19: 6 ***K*** then that God has wronged me,
19:25 For I ***k*** that my Redeemer
19:26 skin is destroyed, this I ***k***,
19:29 That you may ***k*** there is a
20: 4 Do you not ***k*** this of old,
21:19 him, that he may ***k*** it.
21:27 I ***k*** your thoughts, And the
21:29 And do you not ***k*** their signs?
22:13 And you say, 'What does God ***k***?
23: 5 I would ***k*** the words which He
24: 1 Why do those who ***k*** Him see not
24:13 They do not ***k*** its ways Nor
24:16 They do not ***k*** the light.
28:13 Man does not ***k*** its value, Nor
29:16 out the case that I did not ***k***.
30:23 For I ***k*** that You will bring me
31: 6 That God may ***k*** my integrity.
32:22 For I do not ***k*** how to flatter,
34: 4 Let us ***k*** among ourselves what
34:33 I; Therefore speak what you ***k***.
36:26 and we do not ***k*** Him; Nor can
37: 7 That all men may ***k*** His work.
37:15 Do you ***k*** when God dispatches
37:16 Do you ***k*** how the clouds are
38: 5 Surely you ***k***! Or who
38:12 And caused the dawn to ***k*** its
38:18 Tell Me, if you ***k*** all this.
38:20 That you may ***k*** the paths to
38:21 Do you ***k*** it, because you were
38:33 Do you ***k*** the ordinances of the
39: 1 Do you ***k*** the time when the wild
39: 2 Or do you ***k*** the time when they
42: 2 I ***k*** that You can do everything,
42: 3 for me, which I did not ***k***.
Ps 4: 3 But ***k*** that the LORD has set
9:10 And those who ***k*** Your name will
9:20 That the nations may ***k***
20: 6 Now I ***k*** that the LORD saves
35:11 ask me things that I do not ***k***.
35:15 And I did not ***k*** it; They
36:10 lovingkindness to those who ***k***
39: 4 make me to ***k*** my end, And what
39: 4 That I may ***k*** how frail I am.
39: 6 And does not ***k*** who will gather
40: 9 lips, O LORD, You Yourself ***k***.
41:11 By this I ***k*** that You are well
46:10 and ***k*** that I am God; I will
50:11 I ***k*** all the birds of the
51: 6 part You will make me to ***k***
56: 9 will turn back; This I ***k***,
59:13 And let them ***k*** that God rules
69: 5 You ***k*** my foolishness; And my
69:19 You ***k*** my reproach, my shame,
71:15 For I do not ***k*** their limits.
73:11 And they say, "How does God ***k***?
78: 6 the generation to come might ***k***
79: 6 on the nations that do not ***k***
82: 5 They do not ***k***, nor do they
83:18 That they may ***k*** that You, whose
87: 4 and Babylon to those who ***k*** Me;
89:15 Blessed are the people who ***k***
92: 6 A senseless man does not ***k***,
95:10 And they do not ***k*** My ways.'
100: 3 ***K*** that the LORD, He is God
101: 4 I will not ***k*** wickedness.
109:27 That they may ***k*** that this is
119:75 I ***k***, O LORD, that Your
119:79 Those who ***k*** Your testimonies.
119:125 That I may ***k*** Your testimonies.
135: 5 For I ***k*** that the LORD is
139: 2 You ***k*** my sitting down and my
139: 4 You ***k*** it altogether.
139:23 and ***k*** my heart; Try me, and
139:23 Try me, and ***k*** my anxieties;
140:12 I ***k*** that the LORD will
143: 8 Cause me to ***k*** the way in which
Prov 1: 2 To ***k*** wisdom and instruction,
4: 1 And give attention to ***k***
4:19 They do not ***k*** what makes them
5: 6 You do not ***k*** them.
7:23 He did not ***k*** it would cost
9:18 But he does not ***k*** that the dead
10:32 The lips of the righteous ***k***
22:21 That I may make you ***k*** the
24:12 Surely we did not ***k*** this,"
24:12 does He not ***k*** it? And will
27: 1 For you do not ***k*** what a day
27:23 Be diligent to ***k*** the state of
30: 4 is His Son's name, If you ***k***?
Eccl 1:17 And I set my heart to ***k*** wisdom
1:17 heart to know wisdom and to ***k***
3:12 I ***k*** that nothing is better for
3:14 I ***k*** that whatever God does, It
5: 1 for they do not ***k*** that they do
7:25 I applied my heart to ***k***,
7:25 To ***k*** the wickedness of folly,
8: 7 For he does not ***k*** what will
8:12 yet I surely ***k*** that it will be
8:16 When I applied my heart to ***k***
8:17 a wise man attempts to ***k*** it,
9: 1 People ***k*** neither love nor
9: 5 For the living ***k*** that they will
9: 5 But the dead ***k*** nothing, And
9:12 For man also does not ***k*** his
10:15 For they do not even ***k*** how to
11: 2 For you do not ***k*** what evil
11: 5 As you do not ***k*** what is the
11: 5 So you do not ***k*** the works of
11: 6 For you do not ***k*** which will
11: 9 But ***k*** that for all these God
Song 1: 8 If you do not ***k***, O fairest
Isa 1: 3 crib; But Israel does not ***k***,
5:19 That we may ***k*** it."
7:15 that He may ***k*** to refuse the
7:16 For before the Child shall ***k*** to
9: 9 All the people will ***k***—
19:12 And let them ***k*** what the LORD
19:21 and the Egyptians will ***k*** the
37:20 the kingdoms of the earth may ***k***
37:28 But I ***k*** your dwelling place,
41:20 That they may see and ***k***,
41:22 And ***k*** the latter end of them;
41:23 That we may ***k*** that you are
41:26 the beginning, that we may ***k***?
42:16 blind by a way they did not ***k***;
42:25 all around, Yet he did not ***k***;
43:10 That you may ***k*** and believe Me,
43:19 Shall you not ***k*** it? I will
44: 8 other Rock; I ***k*** not one.'
44: 9 They neither see nor ***k***,
44:18 They do not ***k*** nor understand;
45: 3 That you may ***k*** that I, the
45: 6 That they may ***k*** from the rising
47: 8 Nor shall I ***k*** the loss of
47:11 You shall not ***k*** from where it
47:11 Which you shall not ***k***.
48: 6 and you did not ***k*** them.
48: 8 not hear, Surely you did not ***k***;
49:23 Then you will ***k*** that I am the
49:26 All flesh shall ***k*** That I, the
50: 4 That I should ***k*** how to speak
50: 7 And I ***k*** that I will not be
51: 7 you who ***k*** righteousness, You
52: 6 Therefore My people shall ***k*** My
52: 6 Therefore they shall ***k*** in
55: 5 call a nation you do not ***k***,
55: 5 And nations who do not ***k*** you
58: 2 And delight to ***k*** My ways, As
59: 8 takes that way shall not ***k***
59:12 our iniquities, we ***k*** them:
60:16 You shall ***k*** that I, the LORD,
66:18 For I ***k*** their works and their
Jer 2: 8 who handle the law did not ***k***
2:19 ***K*** therefore and see that it
2:23 ***K*** what you have done: You
5: 1 of Jerusalem; See now and ***k***;
5: 4 For they do not ***k*** the way of
5:15 whose language you do not ***k***,
6:15 Nor did they ***k*** how to blush.
6:18 hear, you nations, And ***k***,
6:27 That you may ***k*** and test their
7: 9 other gods whom you do not ***k***,
8: 7 But My people do not ***k*** the
8:12 Nor did they ***k*** how to blush.
9: 3 And they do not ***k*** Me," says
9: 6 deceit they refuse to ***k*** Me,
10:23 I ***k*** the way of man is not in
10:25 who do not ***k*** You, And on the
11:18 and I ***k*** it; for You showed me
11:19 and I did not ***k*** that they had
12: 3 ***k*** me; You have seen me, And
13:12 Do we not certainly ***k*** that every
14:18 about in a land they do not ***k***.
15:14 a land which you do not ***k***;
15:15 O LORD, You ***k***; Remember
15:15 ***K*** that for Your sake I have
16:13 into a land that you do not ***k***,
16:21 will this once cause them to ***k***,
16:21 I will cause them to ***k*** My
16:21 And they shall ***k*** that My name
17: 4 In the land which you do not ***k***;
17: 9 wicked; Who can ***k*** it?
17:16 You ***k*** what came out of my
18:23 You ***k*** all their counsel Which
22:28 into a land which they do not ***k***?
24: 7 I will give them a heart to ***k***
26:15 But ***k*** for certain that if you
29:11 For I ***k*** the thoughts that I
29:23 not commanded them. Indeed I ***k***,
31:34 ***K*** the LORD,' for they all shall
31:34 for they all shall ***k*** Me, from
33: 3 things, which you do not ***k***.
36:19 and let no one ***k*** where you
38:24 Let no one ***k*** of these words, and
40:14 Do you certainly ***k*** that Baalis
40:15 and no one will ***k*** it. Why
42:19 Do not go to Egypt!' ***K*** certainly
42:22 ***k*** certainly that you shall die
44: 3 other gods whom they did not ***k***,
44:28 shall ***k*** whose words will stand,
44:29 that you may ***k*** that My words
48:17 And all you who ***k*** his name,
48:30 I ***k*** his wrath," says the LORD,
Ezek 2: 5 yet they will ***k*** that a prophet
5:13 and they shall ***k*** that I, the
6: 7 and you shall ***k*** that I am the
6:10 And they shall ***k*** that I am the
6:13 Then you shall ***k*** that I am the
6:14 Then they shall ***k*** that I am
7: 4 Then you shall ***k*** that I am
7: 9 Then you shall ***k*** that I am
7:27 Then they shall ***k*** that I am
11: 5 for I ***k*** the things that come
11:10 Then you shall ***k*** that I am the
11:12 And you shall ***k*** that I am the
12:15 Then they shall ***k*** that I am the
12:16 Then they shall ***k*** that I am
12:20 and you shall ***k*** that I am the
13: 9 Then you shall ***k*** that I am the
13:14 Then you shall ***k*** that I am the
13:21 Then you shall ***k*** that I am the
13:23 and you shall ***k*** that I am the
14: 8 Then you shall ***k*** that I am the
14:23 and you shall ***k*** that I have
15: 7 Then you shall ***k*** that I am the
16: 2 cause Jerusalem to ***k*** her
16:62 Then you shall ***k*** that I am the
17:12 Do you not ***k*** what these things
17:21 and you shall ***k*** that I, the
17:24 the trees of the field shall ***k***
20:12 that they might ***k*** that I am
20:20 that you may ***k*** that I am the
20:26 desolate and that they might ***k***
20:38 Then you will ***k*** that I am the
20:42 Then you shall ***k*** that I am the
20:44 Then you shall ***k*** that I am the
21: 5 that all flesh may ***k*** that I, the
22:16 then you shall ***k*** that I am the
22:22 then you shall ***k*** that I, the
23:49 Then you shall ***k*** that I am the
24:24 you shall ***k*** that I am the Lord
24:27 and they shall ***k*** that I am the
25: 5 Then you shall ***k*** that I am the
25: 7 and you shall ***k*** that I am the
25:11 and they shall ***k*** that I am the
25:14 and they shall ***k*** My
25:17 and they shall ***k*** that I am the
26: 6 Then they shall ***k*** that I am
28:22 And they shall ***k*** that I am
28:23 Then they shall ***k*** that I am
28:24 Then they shall ***k*** that I am
28:26 Then they shall ***k*** that I am
29: 6 inhabitants of Egypt Shall ***k***
29: 9 then they will ***k*** that I am the
29:16 Then they shall ***k*** that I am
29:21 Then they shall ***k*** that I am
30: 8 Then they will ***k*** that I am the
30:19 Then they shall ***k*** that I am
30:25 they shall ***k*** that I am the
30:26 Then they shall ***k*** that I am
32:15 Then they shall ***k*** that I am
33:29 Then they shall ***k*** that I am the
33:33 then they will ***k*** that a prophet
34:27 and they shall ***k*** that I am the
34:30 Thus they shall ***k*** that I, the
35: 4 Then you shall ***k*** that I am
35: 9 then you shall ***k*** that I am the
35:12 Then you shall ***k*** that I am the

35:15 all of it! Then they shall ***k***
36:11 Then you shall ***k*** that I am the
36:23 and the nations shall ***k*** that I
36:36 are left all around you shall ***k***
36:38 Then they shall ***k*** that I am
37: 3 answered, "O Lord GOD, You ***k***.
37: 6 Then you shall ***k*** that I am the
37:13 Then you shall ***k*** that I am the
37:14 Then you shall ***k*** that I, the
37:28 The nations also will ***k*** that I,
38:14 will you not ***k*** it?
38:16 so that the nations may ***k*** Me,
38:23 Then they shall ***k*** that I am
39: 6 Then they shall ***k*** that I am
39: 7 Then the nations shall ***k*** that
39:22 the house of Israel shall ***k***
39:23 The Gentiles shall ***k*** that the
39:28 then they shall ***k*** that I am the
Dan 2: 3 and my spirit is anxious to ***k***
2: 8 I ***k*** for certain that you would
2: 9 and I shall ***k*** that you can give
2:30 and that you may ***k*** the thoughts
4: 9 because I ***k*** that the Spirit of
4:17 In order that the living may ***k***
4:25 till you ***k*** that the Most High
4:26 after you come to ***k*** that Heaven
4:32 until you ***k*** that the Most High
5:23 which do not see or hear or ***k***;
6:15 king, and said to the king, "***K***,
7:19 Then I wished to ***k*** the truth
9:25 ***K*** therefore and understand,
10:20 Do you ***k*** why I have come to you?
11:32 but the people who ***k*** their God
11:38 which his fathers did not ***k*** he
Hos 2: 8 For she did not ***k*** That I gave
2:20 And you shall ***k*** the LORD.
5: 3 I ***k*** Ephraim, And Israel is not
5: 4 And they do not ***k*** the LORD.
6: 3 Let us ***k***, Let us pursue
7: 9 But he does not ***k*** it; Yes,
7: 9 Yet he does not ***k*** it.
8: 2 'My God, we ***k*** You!'
11: 3 But they did not ***k*** that I
13: 4 And you shall ***k*** no God but Me;
14: 9 Let him ***k*** them. For the ways
Joel 2:27 Then you shall ***k*** that I am in
3:17 So you shall ***k*** that I am the
Am 3:10 For they do not ***k*** to do right,'
5:12 For I ***k*** your manifold
Jon 1: 7 that we may ***k*** for whose cause
1:12 For I ***k*** that this great tempest
4: 2 for I ***k*** that You are a
Mic 3: 1 Is it not for you to ***k***
4:12 But they do not ***k*** the thoughts
6: 5 That you may ***k*** the
Zech 2: 9 Then you will ***k*** that the LORD
2:11 Then you will ***k*** that the LORD
4: 5 Do you not ***k*** what these are?"
4: 9 Then you will ***k*** That the
4:13 Do you not ***k*** what these are?"
6:15 Then you shall ***k*** that the LORD
Mal 2: 4 Then you shall ***k*** that I have
Mt 1:25 and did not ***k*** her till she had
6: 3 do not let your left hand ***k***
7:11 ***k*** how to give good gifts to
7:16 You will ***k*** them by their fruits.
7:20 by their fruits you will ***k***
9: 6 But that you may ***k*** that the Son
11:27 Nor does anyone ***k*** the Father
13:11 it has been given to you to ***k***
15:12 Do You ***k*** that the Pharisees were
16: 3 Hypocrites! You ***k*** how to
17:12 and they did not ***k*** him but did
20:22 You do not ***k*** what you ask. Are
20:25 You ***k*** that the rulers of the
21:27 Jesus and said, "We do not ***k***.
22:16 we ***k*** that You are true, and
24:32 you ***k*** that summer is near.
24:33 ***k*** that it is near—at the doors!
24:39 and did not ***k*** until the flood
24:42 for you do not ***k*** what hour your
24:43 But ***k*** this, that if the master
25:12 I do not ***k*** you.'
25:13 for you ***k*** neither the day nor
26: 2 You ***k*** that after two days is the
26:70 I do not ***k*** what you are
26:72 I do not ***k*** the Man!"
26:74 I do not ***k*** the Man!"
27:65 make it as secure as you ***k***
28: 5 for I ***k*** that you seek Jesus who
Mk 1:24 I ***k*** who You are—the Holy One of
2:10 But that you may ***k*** that the Son
4:11 To you it has been given to ***k***
4:27 he himself does not ***k*** how.
5:43 strictly that no one should ***k***
7:24 a house and wanted no one to ***k***
9: 6 because he did not ***k*** what to
9:30 and He did not want anyone to ***k***
10:19 You ***k*** the commandments: 'Do
10:38 You do not ***k*** what you ask. Are
10:42 You ***k*** that those who are
11:33 said to Jesus, "We do not ***k***.
12:14 we ***k*** that You are true, and
12:24 because you do not ***k*** the
13:28 you ***k*** that summer is near.
13:29 ***k*** that it is near—at the doors!
13:33 for you do not ***k*** when the time
13:35 for you do not ***k*** when the
14:40 and they did not ***k*** what to
14:68 I neither ***k*** nor understand what
14:71 I do not ***k*** this Man of whom you
Lk 1: 4 that you may ***k*** the certainty of
1:18 How shall I ***k*** this? For I am an
1:34 since I do not ***k*** a man?"
2:43 and His mother did not ***k*** it;
2:49 Did you not ***k*** that I must be
4:34 I ***k*** who You are—the Holy One of
5:24 But that you may ***k*** that the Son
7:39 would ***k*** who and what manner of
8:10 To you it has been given to ***k***
9:55 You do not ***k*** what manner of
10:11 Nevertheless ***k*** this, that the
11:13 ***k*** how to give good gifts to
12:39 But ***k*** this, that if the master
12:48 "But he who did not ***k***,
13:25 I do not ***k*** you, where you are
13:27 I tell you I do not ***k*** you, where
18:20 You ***k*** the commandments: 'Do
18:34 and they did not ***k*** the things
19:15 that he might ***k*** how much every
19:44 because you did not ***k*** the time
20: 7 answered that they did not ***k***
20:21 we ***k*** that You say and teach
21:20 then ***k*** that its desolation is
21:30 you see and ***k*** for yourselves
21:31 ***k*** that the kingdom of God is
22:34 deny three times that you ***k*** Me.
22:57 'Woman, I do not ***k*** Him."
22:60 I do not ***k*** what you are
23:34 for they do not ***k*** what they
24:16 so that they did not ***k*** Him.
Jn 1:10 and the world did not ***k*** Him.
1:26 One among you whom you do not ***k***.
1:31 I did not ***k*** Him; but that He
1:33 I did not ***k*** Him, but He who sent
1:48 How do You ***k*** me?" Jesus
2: 9 and did not ***k*** where it came
3: 2 we ***k*** that You are a teacher
3:10 and do not ***k*** these things?
3:11 We speak what We ***k*** and testify
4:22 "You worship what you do not ***k***;
4:22 we ***k*** what we worship, for
4:25 I ***k*** that Messiah is coming"
4:32 to eat of which you do not ***k***.
4:42 have heard Him and we ***k*** that
5:13 one who was healed did not ***k***
5:32 and I ***k*** that the witness which
5:42 But I ***k*** you, that you do not
6:42 whose father and mother we ***k***?
6:69 we have come to believe and ***k***
7:15 How does this Man ***k*** letters,
7:17 he shall ***k*** concerning the
7:26 Do the rulers ***k*** indeed that
7:27 we ***k*** where this Man is from;
7:28 You both ***k*** Me, and you know
7:28 and you ***k*** where I am from; and
7:28 Me is true, whom you do not ***k***.
7:29 But I ***k*** Him, for I am from Him,
7:49 this crowd that does not ***k***
8:14 for I ***k*** where I came from and
8:14 but you do not ***k*** where I come
8:19 You ***k*** neither Me nor My Father.
8:28 then you will ***k*** that I am He,
8:32 And you shall ***k*** the truth, and
8:37 I ***k*** that you are Abraham's
8:52 Now we ***k*** that You have a demon!
8:55 but I ***k*** Him. And if I say, 'I
8:55 I do not ***k*** Him,' I shall be a
8:55 but I do ***k*** Him and keep His
9:12 is He?" He said, "I do not ***k***.
9:20 We ***k*** that this is our son, and
9:21 means he now sees we do not ***k***,
9:21 who opened his eyes we do not ***k***.
9:24 Give God the glory! We ***k*** that
9:25 is a sinner or not I do not ***k***.
9:25 I do not know. One thing I ***k***:
9:29 We ***k*** that God spoke to Moses;
9:29 we do not ***k*** where He is from."
9:30 that you do not ***k*** where He is
9:31 Now we ***k*** that God does not hear
10: 4 for they ***k*** his voice.
10: 5 for they do not ***k*** the voice of
10:14 and I ***k*** My sheep, and am known
10:15 even so I ***k*** the Father; and I
10:27 and I ***k*** them, and they follow
10:38 that you may ***k*** and believe that
11:22 But even now I ***k*** that whatever
11:24 I ***k*** that he will rise again in
11:42 And I ***k*** that You always hear Me,
11:49 You ***k*** nothing at all,
12:35 walks in darkness does not ***k***
12:50 And I ***k*** that His command is
13: 7 but you will ***k*** after this."
13:12 Do you ***k*** what I have done to
13:17 If you ***k*** these things, blessed
13:18 I ***k*** whom I have chosen; but
13:35 By this all will ***k*** that you are
14: 4 "And where I go you ***k***,
14: 4 go you know, and the way you ***k***.
14: 5 we do not ***k*** where You are
14: 5 and how can we ***k*** the way?"
14: 7 and from now on you ***k*** Him and
14:17 but you ***k*** Him, for He dwells
14:20 At that day you will ***k*** that I
14:31 But that the world may ***k*** that I
15:15 for a servant does not ***k*** what
15:18 you ***k*** that it hated Me before
15:21 because they do not ***k*** Him who
16:18 We do not ***k*** what He is
16:30 Now we are sure that You ***k*** all
17: 3 that they may ***k*** You, the only
17:23 and that the world may ***k*** that
18:21 Indeed they ***k*** what I said."
19: 4 that you may ***k*** that I find no
19:10 Do You not ***k*** that I have power
20: 2 and we do not ***k*** where they have
20: 9 For as yet they did not ***k*** the
20:13 and I do not ***k*** where they have
20:14 and did not ***k*** that it was
21: 4 yet the disciples did not ***k***
21:15 You ***k*** that I love You." He
21:16 You ***k*** that I love You." He
21:17 You ***k*** all things; You know that
21:17 You ***k*** that I love You." Jesus
21:24 and we ***k*** that his testimony is
Acts 1: 7 It is not for you to ***k*** times or
1:24 who ***k*** the hearts of all, show
2:22 midst, as you yourselves also ***k***—
2:36 let all the house of Israel ***k***
3:16 man strong, whom you see and ***k***.
3:17 I ***k*** that you did it in
7:18 king arose who did not ***k***
7:40 we do not ***k*** what has
10:28 You ***k*** how unlawful it is for a
10:37 'that word you ***k***, which was
12: 9 and did not ***k*** that what was
12:11 Now I ***k*** for certain that the
13:27 because they did not ***k*** Him, nor
15: 7 you ***k*** that a good while ago God
17:19 May we ***k*** what this new doctrine
17:20 Therefore we want to ***k*** what
19:15 answered and said, "Jesus I ***k***,
19:15 "Jesus I know, and Paul I ***k***;
19:25 you ***k*** that we have our
19:32 and most of them did not ***k*** why
19:35 man is there who does not ***k***
20:18 him, he said to them: "You ***k***,
20:25 now I ***k*** that you all, among
20:29 For I ***k*** this, that after my
20:34 you yourselves ***k*** that these
21:24 and that all may ***k*** that those
22:14 chosen you that you should ***k***
22:19 they ***k*** that in every synagogue
22:24 so that he might ***k*** why they
22:30 because he wanted to ***k*** for
23: 5 Then Paul said, "I did not ***k***,
23:28 And when I wanted to ***k*** the
24:10 Inasmuch as I ***k*** that you have
25:10 no wrong, as you very well ***k***.
26: 4 at Jerusalem, all the Jews ***k***.
26:27 I ***k*** that you do believe."
28:22 we ***k*** that it is spoken against
Rom 2: 2 But we ***k*** that the judgment of
2:18 and ***k*** His will, and approve the
3:19 Now we ***k*** that whatever the law
6: 3 Or do you not ***k*** that as many of
6:16 Do you not ***k*** that to whom you
7: 1 Or do you not ***k***, brethren
7: 1 (for I speak to those who ***k***
7:14 For we ***k*** that the law is
7:18 For I ***k*** that in me (that is, in
8:22 For we ***k*** that the whole creation
8:26 For we do not ***k*** what we should
8:28 And we ***k*** that all things work
10:19 But I say, did Israel not ***k***?
11: 2 Or do you not ***k*** what the
14:14 I ***k*** and am convinced by the
15:29 But I ***k*** that when I come to you,
1 Cor 1:16 I do not ***k*** whether I baptized
1:21 world through wisdom did not ***k***
2: 2 For I determined not to ***k***
2:12 that we might ***k*** the things that
2:14 nor can he ***k*** them, because
3:16 Do you not ***k*** that you are the
4: 4 For I ***k*** nothing against myself,
4:19 if the Lord wills, and I will ***k***,
5: 6 Do you not ***k*** that a little
6: 2 Do you not ***k*** that the saints
6: 3 Do you not ***k*** that we shall judge
6: 9 Do you not ***k*** that the
6:15 Do you not ***k*** that your bodies
6:16 Or do you not ***k*** that he who is
6:19 Or do you not ***k*** that your body
7:16 For how do you ***k***, O wife,
7:16 your husband? Or how do you ***k***,
8: 1 We ***k*** that we all have
8: 2 nothing yet as he ought to ***k***.
8: 4 we ***k*** that an idol is nothing
9:13 Do you not ***k*** that those who
9:24 Do you not ***k*** that those who run
11: 3 But I want you to ***k*** that the
12: 2 You ***k*** that you were Gentiles,
13: 9 For we ***k*** in part and we prophesy
13:12 Now I ***k*** in part, but then I
13:12 but then I shall ***k*** just as I
14:11 if I do not ***k*** the meaning of
16:15 you ***k*** the household of
2 Cor 1: 7 because we ***k*** that as you are
2: 4 but that you might ***k*** the love
5: 1 For we ***k*** that if our earthly
5:16 yet now we ***k*** Him thus no
8: 9 For you ***k*** the grace of our Lord
9: 2 for I ***k*** your willingness, about
12: 2 I ***k*** a man in Christ who fourteen
12: 2 in the body I do not ***k***,
12: 2 out of the body I do not ***k***,
12: 3 And I ***k*** such a man—whether in
12: 3 or out of the body I do not ***k***,
13: 5 Do you not ***k*** yourselves, that
13: 6 But I trust that you will ***k*** that
Gal 3: 7 Therefore ***k*** that only those who
4: 8 when you did not ***k*** God, you
4:13 You ***k*** that because of physical
Eph 1:18 that you may ***k*** what is the hope
3:19 to ***k*** the love of Christ which
5: 5 For this you ***k***,

K

6:21 But that you also may **k** my
6:22 that you may **k** our affairs, and
Phil 1:12 But I want you to **k**,
1:19 For I **k** that this will turn out
1:25 I **k** that I shall remain and
2:19 also may be encouraged when I **k**
2:22 But you **k** his proven character,
3:10 that I may **k** Him and the power
4:12 I **k** how to be abased, and I know
4:12 and I **k** how to abound.
4:15 Now you Philippians **k** also that
Col 2: 1 For I want you to **k** what a great
4: 6 that you may **k** how you ought to
4: 8 purpose, that he may **k** your
1 Th 1: 5 as you **k** what kind of men we
2: 1 For you yourselves **k**,
2: 2 treated at Philippi, as you **k**,
2: 5 use flattering words, as you **k**,
2:11 as you **k** how we exhorted, and
3: 3 for you yourselves **k** that we
3: 4 just as it happened, and you **k**.
3: 5 I sent to **k** your faith, lest by
4: 2 for you **k** what commandments we
4: 4 that each of you should **k** how to
4: 5 like the Gentiles who do not **k**
5: 2 For you yourselves **k** perfectly
2 Th 1: 8 on those who do not **k** God,
2: 6 And now you **k** what is
3: 7 For you yourselves **k** how you
1 Tim 1: 8 But we **k** that the law is good
3: 5 (for if a man does not **k** how to
3:15 I write so that you may **k** how
4: 3 by those who believe and **k** the
2 Tim 1:12 for I **k** whom I have believed
1:15 This you **k**, that all those in
1:18 and you **k** very well how many
2:25 so that they may **k** the truth,
3: 1 But **k** this, that in the last
Titus 1:16 They profess to **k** God, but in
Heb 8:11 **K** the LORD,' for all shall
8:11 for all shall **k** Me, from
10:30 For we **k** Him who said,
12:17 For you **k** that afterward, when
13:23 **K** that our brother Timothy has
Jas 2:20 But do you want to **k**,
4: 4 and adulteresses! Do you not **k**
4:14 whereas you do not **k** what will
5:20 let him **k** that he who turns a
2 Pe 1:12 though you **k** and are
3:17 since you **k** this beforehand,
1 Jn 2: 3 Now by this we **k** that we know
2: 3 Now by this we know that we **k**
2: 4 I **k** Him," and does not keep His
2: 5 By this we **k** that we are in
2:11 and does not **k** where he is
2:18 by which we **k** that it is the
2:20 and you **k** all things.
2:21 to you because you do not **k**
2:21 but because you **k** it, and that
2:29 If you **k** that He is righteous,
2:29 you **k** that everyone who
3: 1 Therefore the world does not **k**
3: 1 because it did not **k** Him.
3: 2 but we **k** that when He is
3: 5 And you **k** that He was manifested
3:14 We **k** that we have passed from
3:15 and you **k** that no murderer has
3:16 By this we **k** love, because He
3:19 And by this we **k** that we are of
3:24 And by this we **k** that He abides
4: 2 By this you **k** the Spirit of God:
4: 6 By this we **k** the spirit of
4: 8 He who does not love does not **k**
4:13 By this we **k** that we abide in
5: 2 By this we **k** that we love the
5:13 that you may **k** that you have
5:15 And if we **k** that He hears us,
5:15 we **k** that we have the petitions
5:18 We **k** that whoever is born of
5:19 We **k** that we are of God, and the
5:20 And we **k** that the Son of God has
5:20 that we may **k** Him who is true;
3 Jn 12 and you **k** that our testimony is
Jude 10 evil of whatever they do not **k**;
10 and whatever they **k** naturally,
Rev 2: 2 I **k** your works, your labor, your
2: 9 I **k** your works, tribulation, and
2: 9 and I **k** the blasphemy of
2:13 I **k** your works, and where you
2:19 I **k** your works, love, service,
2:23 and all the churches shall **k**
3: 1 I **k** your works, that you have a
3: 3 and you will not **k** what hour I
3: 8 I **k** your works. See, I have set
3: 9 and to **k** that I have loved you.
3:15 I **k** your works, that you are
3:17 and do not **k** that you are
7:14 And I said to him, "Sir, you **k**.

KNOWING (52/52) KNOW

Gen 3: 5 **k** good and evil."
Jer 22:16 Was not this **k** Me?" says the
Mt 9: 4 **k** their thoughts, said, "Why
22:29 not **k** the Scriptures nor the
Mk 5:30 immediately **k** in Himself that
5:33 **k** what had happened to her,
6:20 **k** that he was a just and holy
12:15 **k** their hypocrisy, said to
Lk 8:53 **k** that she was dead.
9:33 not **k** what he said.
11:17 **k** their thoughts, said to them:
Jn 13: 3 **k** that the Father had given all
18: 4 **k** all things that would come
19:28 **k** that all things were now
21:12 **k** that it was the Lord.
Acts 2:30 and **k** that God had sworn with
5: 7 not **k** what had happened.
17:23 One whom you worship without **k**,
20:22 not **k** the things that will
Rom 1:32 **k** the righteous judgment of
2: 4 not **k** that the goodness of God
5: 3 **k** that tribulation produces
6: 6 **k** this, that our old man was
6: 9 **k** that Christ, having been
13:11 **k** the time, that now it is
1 Cor 15:58 **k** that your labor is not in
2 Cor 4:14 **k** that He who raised up the Lord
5: 6 **k** that while we are at home in
5:11 **K**, therefore, the terror of
Gal 2:16 **k** that a man is not justified by
Eph 6: 8 **k** that whatever good anyone
6: 9 **k** that your own Master also is
Phil 1:17 **k** that I am appointed for the
Col 3:24 **k** that from the Lord you will
4: 1 **k** that you also have a Master
1 Th 1: 4 **k**, beloved brethren, your
1 Tim 1: 9 **k** this: that the law is not made
6: 4 **k** nothing, but is obsessed with
2 Tim 2:23 **k** that they generate strife.
3:14 **k** from whom you have learned
Titus 3:11 **k** that such a person is warped
Phm 1:21 **k** that you will do even more
Heb 10:34 **k** that you have a better and an
11: 8 not **k** where he was going.
Jas 1: 3 **k** that the testing of your faith
3: 1 **k** that we shall receive a
1 Pe 1:18 **k** that you were not redeemed
3: 9 **k** that you were called to this,
5: 9 **k** that the same sufferings are
2 Pe 1:14 **k** that shortly I must put off
1:20 **k** this first, that no prophecy
3: 3 **k** this first: that scoffers will

KNOWINGLY (1/1)

Gen 48:14 head, guiding his hands **k**,

KNOWLEDGE (164/161) KNOW

Gen 2: 9 and the tree of the **k** of good
2:17 but of the tree of the **k** of good
Ex 31: 3 wisdom, in understanding, in **k**,
35:31 in **k** and all manner of
Lev 4:23 he has committed comes to his **k**,
4:28 he has committed comes to his **k**,
Num 15:24 without the **k** of the
24:16 And has the **k** of the Most
Deut 1:39 who today have no **k** of good and
1 Sam 2: 3 For the LORD is the God of **k**;
23:23 and take **k** of all the lurking
2 Chr 1:10 "Now give me wisdom and **k**,
1:11 but have asked wisdom and **k** for
1:12 wisdom and **k** are granted to
30:22 Levites who taught the good **k**
Neh 10:28 everyone who had **k** and
Job 15: 2 a wise man answer with empty **k**,
21:14 For we do not desire the **k** of
21:22 "Can anyone teach God **k**,
33: 3 heart; My lips utter pure **k**.
34: 2 Give ear to me, you who have **k**.
34:35 'Job speaks without **k**,
35:16 He multiplies words without **k**.
36: 3 I will fetch my **k** from afar; I
36: 4 One who is perfect in **k** is
36:12 And they shall die without **k**.
37:16 of Him who is perfect in **k**?
38: 2 counsel By words without **k**?
42: 3 who hides counsel without **k**?
Ps 14: 4 the workers of iniquity no **k**,
19: 2 And night unto night reveals **k**.
53: 4 the workers of iniquity no **k**,
73:11 And is there **k** in the Most
94:10 correct, He who teaches man **k**?
119:66 Teach me good judgment and **k**,
139: 6 Such **k** is too wonderful for
144: 3 that You take **k** of him? Or
Prov 1: 4 To the young man **k** and
1: 7 LORD is the beginning of **k**,
1:22 scorning, And fools hate **k**.
1:29 Because they hated **k** And did
2: 5 And find the **k** of God.
2: 6 From His mouth come **k** and
2:10 And **k** is pleasant to your
3:20 By His **k** the depths were broken
5: 2 And your lips may keep **k**.
8: 9 And right to those who find **k**.
8:10 And **k** rather than choice gold;
8:12 And find out **k** and
9:10 And the **k** of the Holy One is
10:14 Wise people store up **k**,
11: 9 But through **k** the righteous
12: 1 loves instruction loves **k**,
12:23 A prudent man conceals **k**,
13:16 Every prudent man acts with **k**,
14: 6 But **k** is easy to him who
14: 7 perceive in him the lips of **k**.
14:18 the prudent are crowned with **k**.
15: 2 The tongue of the wise uses **k**
15: 7 lips of the wise disperse **k**,
15:14 who has understanding seeks **k**,
17:27 He who has **k** spares his words,
18:15 heart of the prudent acquires **k**,
18:15 the ear of the wise seeks **k**.
19: 2 for a soul to be without **k**,
19:25 and he will discern **k**.
19:27 will stray from the words of **k**.
20:15 But the lips of **k** are a
21:11 is instructed, he receives **k**.
22:12 eyes of the LORD preserve **k**,
22:17 And apply your heart to my **k**;
22:20 things Of counsels and **k**,
23:12 And your ears to words of **k**.
24: 4 By **k** the rooms are filled With
24: 5 a man of **k** increases strength;
24:14 So shall the **k** of wisdom be
28: 2 a man of understanding and **k**
29: 7 does not understand such **k**.
30: 3 learned wisdom Nor have **k** of
Eccl 1:16 understood great wisdom and **k**.
1:18 And he who increases **k**
2:21 whose labor is with wisdom, **k**,
2:26 For God gives wisdom and **k** and
7:12 But the excellence of **k** is
9:10 is no work or device or **k** or
12: 9 he still taught the people **k**;
Isa 5:13 Because they have no **k**;
8: 4 before the child shall have **k**
11: 2 The Spirit of **k** and of the
11: 9 earth shall be full of the **k**
28: 9 "Whom will he teach **k**?
32: 4 of the rash will understand **k**,
33: 6 Wisdom and **k** will be the
40:14 of justice? Who taught Him **k**,
44:19 Nor is there **k** nor
44:25 And makes their **k** foolishness;
45:20 the nations. They have no **k**,
47:10 Your wisdom and your **k** have
53:11 By His **k** My righteous Servant
Jer 3:15 who will feed you with **k** and
4:22 But to do good they have no **k**.
10:14 is dull-hearted, without **k**;
11:18 Now the LORD gave me **k** of
51:17 is dull-hearted, without **k**;
Dan 1: 4 possessing **k** and quick to
1:17 God gave them **k** and skill in
2:21 wisdom to the wise And **k** to
5:12 as an excellent spirit, **k**,
12: 4 and **k** shall increase."
Hos 4: 1 is no truth or mercy Or **k** of
4: 6 are destroyed for lack of **k**.
4: 6 Because you have rejected **k**,
6: 3 Let us pursue the **k** of the
6: 6 And the **k** of God more than
Hab 2:14 will be filled With the **k** of
Mal 2: 7 lips of a priest should keep **k**,
Lk 1:77 To give **k** of salvation to His
11:52 have taken away the key of **k**.
Acts 24:22 having more accurate **k** of the
Rom 1:28 like to retain God in their **k**,
2:20 having the form of **k** and truth
3:20 for by the law is the **k** of
10: 2 for God, but not according to **k**.
11:33 both of the wisdom and **k** of
15:14 of goodness, filled with all **k**,
1 Cor 1: 5 Him in all utterance and all **k**,
8: 1 We know that we all have **k**.
8: 1 **K** puffs up, but love edifies.
8: 7 is not in everyone that **k**;
8:10 if anyone sees you who have **k**
8:11 And because of your **k** shall the
12: 8 to another the word of **k**
13: 2 all mysteries and all **k**,
13: 8 cease; whether there is **k**,
14: 6 you either by revelation, by **k**,
15:34 for some do not have the **k** of
2 Cor 2:14 the fragrance of His **k** in
4: 6 to give the light of the **k** of
6: 6 by purity, by **k**, by
8: 7 faith, in speech, in **k**,
10: 5 exalts itself against the **k** of
11: 6 in speech, yet I am not in **k**.
Eph 1:17 wisdom and revelation in the **k**
3: 4 you may understand my **k** in the
3:19 love of Christ which passes **k**;
4:13 of the faith and of the **k** of
Phil 1: 9 still more and more in **k** and
3: 8 for the excellence of the **k** of
Col 1: 9 you may be filled with the **k**
1:10 work and increasing in the **k**
2: 2 to the **k** of the mystery of God,
2: 3 the treasures of wisdom and **k**.
3:10 new man who is renewed in **k**
1 Tim 2: 4 be saved and to come to the **k**
6:20 of what is falsely called **k**—
2 Tim 3: 7 never able to come to the **k** of
Heb 10:26 after we have received the **k**
2 Pe 1: 2 be multiplied to you in the **k**
1: 3 through the **k** of Him who called
1: 5 your faith virtue, to virtue **k**,
1: 6 to **k** self-control, to
1: 8 barren nor unfruitful in the **k**
2:20 of the world through the **k** of
3:18 but grow in the grace and **k** of

KNOWLEDGEABLE (2/2)

Deut 1:13 and **k** men from among your
1:15 wise and **k** men, and made them

KNOWN (229/218) KNOW

Gen 18:19 For I have **k** him, in order that
19: 8 two daughters who have not **k** a
24:16 no man had **k** her. And she went
41:21 no one would have **k** that they

41:31 So the plenty will not be **k** in
43: 7 Could we possibly have **k** that
45: 1 while Joseph made himself **k** to
Ex 2:14 Surely this thing is **k**!"
6: 3 by My name LORD I was not **k**
18:16 and I make **k** the statutes of
21:29 and it has been made **k** to his
21:36 Or if it was **k** that the ox
33:16 For how then will it be **k** that
Lev 4:14 they have committed becomes **k**,
5: 1 whether he has seen or **k** of
Num 12: 6 make Myself **k** to him in a
31:17 and kill every woman who has **k**
31:18 the young girls who have not **k**
31:35 of women who had not **k** a man
Deut 7:15 of Egypt which you have **k**,
11: 2 who have not **k** and who have not
11:28 other gods which you have not **k**.
13: 2 gods'—which you have not **k**—
13: 6 gods,' which you have not **k**,
13:13 gods" '—which you have not **k**—
21: 1 and it is not **k** who killed
28:33 A nation whom you have not **k**
28:36 you nor your fathers have **k**,
28:64 you nor your fathers have **k**—
31:13 who have not **k** it, may hear and
Josh 24:31 who had **k** all the works of the
Judg 3: 1 all who had not **k** any of the
3: 2 those who had not formerly **k**
16: 9 of his strength was not **k**.
21:11 and every woman who has **k** a man
21:12 young virgins who had not **k** a
Ruth 3: 3 but do not make yourself **k** to
3:14 Do not let it be **k** that the
1 Sam 6: 3 and it will be **k** to you why His
2 Sam 17:19 on it; and the thing was not **k**.
22:44 A people I have not **k** shall
1 Ki 18:36 let it be **k** this day that You
1 Chr 16: 8 Make **k** His deeds among the
17:19 in making **k** all these great
Ezra 4:12 Let it be **k** to the king that the
4:13 Let it now be **k** to the king
5: 8 Let it be **k** to the king that we
Neh 4:15 enemies heard that it was **k** to
9:14 You made **k** to them Your holy
Esth 1:17 queen's behavior will become **k**
2:22 So the matter became **k** to
Ps 9:16 The LORD is **k** by the judgment
18:43 A people I have not **k** shall
31: 7 You have **k** my soul in
48: 3 He is **k** as her refuge.
67: 2 That Your way may be **k** on
76: 1 In Judah God is **k**;
77:19 And Your footsteps were not **k**.
78: 3 Which we have heard and **k**,
78: 5 That they should make them **k**
79:10 Let there be **k** among the
88:12 Shall Your wonders be **k** in the
89: 1 With my mouth will I make **k**
91:14 because he has **k** My name.
98: 2 The LORD has made **k** His
103: 7 He made **k** His ways to Moses,
105: 1 Make **k** His deeds among the
106: 8 might make His mighty power **k**.
119:152 I have **k** of old that You have
139: 1 You have searched me and **k** me.
145:12 To make **k** to the sons of men
147:20 they have not **k** them. Praise
Prov 1:23 I will make my words **k** to you.
10: 9 perverts his ways will become **k**.
12:16 A fool's wrath is **k** at once,
14:33 in the heart of fools is made **k**.
20:11 Even a child is **k** by his deeds,
31:23 Her husband is **k** in the gates,
Eccl 5: 3 And a fool's voice is **k** by
6: 5 it has not seen the sun or **k**
6:10 For it is **k** that he is man;
7:22 your own heart has **k** That even
Isa 12: 5 This is **k** in all the earth.
19:21 Then the LORD will be **k** to
38:19 The father shall make **k** Your
40:21 Have you not **k**? Have you not
40:28 Have you not **k**? Have you not
42:16 them in paths they have not **k**.
45: 4 though you have not **k** Me.
45: 5 though you have not **k** Me,
59: 8 way of peace they have not **k**,
61: 9 Their descendants shall be **k**
64: 2 To make Your name **k** to Your
66:14 hand of the LORD shall be **k**
Jer 4:22 They have not **k** Me. They are
5: 5 For they have **k** the way of the
9:16 they nor their fathers have **k**.
19: 4 nor the kings of Judah have **k**,
28: 9 the prophet will be **k** as one
Ezek 20: 4 Then make **k** to them the
20: 5 and made Myself **k** to them in
20: 9 sight I had made Myself **k** to
22:26 nor have they made **k** the
32: 9 countries which you have not **k**.
35:11 and I will make Myself **k** among
36:32 let it be **k** to you. Be ashamed
38:23 and I will be **k** in the eyes of
39: 7 So I will make My holy name **k** in
43:11 make **k** to them the design of
Dan 2: 5 if you do not make **k** the dream
2: 9 if you do not make **k** the dream
2:15 Arioch made the decision **k** to
2:17 and made the decision **k** to
2:23 And have now made **k** to me what
2:23 For You have made **k** to us the
2:25 who will make **k** to the king the
2:26 Are you able to make **k** to me the
2:28 and He has made **k** to King
2:29 who reveals secrets has made **k**
2:30 but for our sakes who make **k**
2:45 the great God has made **k** to the
3:18 let it be **k** to you, O king,
4: 6 that they might make **k** to me
4: 7 but they did not make **k** to me
4:18 kingdom are not able to make **k**
5: 8 or make **k** to the king its
5:15 read this writing and make **k**
5:16 read the writing and make **k** to
5:17 and make **k** to him the
7:16 So he told me and made **k** to me
8:19 I am making **k** to you what shall
Hos 5: 9 the tribes of Israel I make **k**
Am 3: 2 You only have I **k** of all the
Nah 3:17 place where they are is not **k**.
Hab 3: 2 midst of the years make it **k**;
Zech 7:14 nations which they had not **k**.
14: 7 shall be one day Which is **k**
Mt 10:26 and hidden that will not be **k**.
12: 7 But if you had **k** what this
12:16 warned them not to make Him **k**,
12:33 for a tree is **k** by its fruit.
24:43 the master of the house had **k**
Mk 3:12 that they should not make Him **k**.
6:14 for His name had become well **k**.
Lk 2:15 which the Lord has made **k** to
2:17 they made widely **k** the saying
6:44 For every tree is **k** by its own
8:17 hidden that will not be **k** and
12: 2 nor hidden that will not be **k**.
12:39 the master of the house had **k**
19:42 saying, "If you had **k**,
24:18 and have You not **k** the things
24:35 and how He was **k** to them in the
Jn 7: 4 while he himself seeks to be **k**
8:19 If you had **k** Me, you would have
8:19 you would have **k** My Father
8:55 Yet you have not **k** Him, but I
10:14 sheep, and am **k** by My own.
14: 7 If you had **k** Me, you would have
14: 7 you would have **k** My Father
14: 9 and yet you have not **k** Me,
15:15 from My Father I have made **k**
16: 3 to you because they have not **k**
17: 7 Now they have **k** that all things
17: 8 and have **k** surely that I came
17:25 Father! The world has not **k**
17:25 but I have **k** You; and these
17:25 and these have **k** that You sent
18:15 Now that disciple was **k** to the
18:16 who was **k** to the high priest,
Acts 1:19 And it became **k** to all those
2:14 let this be **k** to you, and heed
2:28 You have made **k** to me
4:10 let it be **k** to you all, and to
7:13 second time Joseph was made **k**
7:13 and Joseph's family became **k** to
9:24 But their plot became **k** to Saul.
9:42 And it became **k** throughout all
13:38 Therefore let it be **k** to you,
15:18 **K** to God from eternity are all
19:17 This became **k** both to all Jews
28:28 Therefore let it be **k** to you
Rom 1:19 because what may be **k** of God is
3:17 of peace they have not **k**.
7: 7 I would not have **k** sin except
7: 7 For I would not have **k**
9:22 wrath and to make His power **k**,
9:23 and that He might make **k** the
11:34 For who has **k** the mind of the
16:19 your obedience has become **k** to
16:26 Scriptures has been made **k** to
1 Cor 2: 8 this age knew; for had they **k**,
2:16 who has **k** the mind of the
8: 3 this one is **k** by Him.
12: 3 Therefore I make **k** to you that
13:12 shall know just as I also am **k**.
14: 7 how will it be **k** what is piped
14: 9 how will it be **k** what is
2 Cor 3: 2 **k** and read by all men;
5:16 Even though we have **k** Christ
8: 1 we make **k** to you the grace of
Gal 1:11 But I make **k** to you, brethren,
4: 9 But now after you have **k** God, or
4: 9 or rather are **k** by God, how is
Eph 1: 9 having made **k** to us the mystery
3: 3 that by revelation He made **k**
3: 5 in other ages was not made **k**
3:10 wisdom of God might be made **k**
6:19 open my mouth boldly to make **k**
6:21 will make all things **k** to you;
Phil 4: 5 Let your gentleness be **k** to all
4: 6 let your requests be made **k** to
Col 1:27 To them God willed to make **k**
4: 9 They will make **k** to you all
2 Tim 3:15 that from childhood you have **k**
Heb 3:10 And they have not **k** My
2 Pe 1:16 devised fables when we made **k**
2:21 better for them not to have **k**
2:21 than having **k** it, to turn from
1 Jn 2:13 Because you have **k** Him who
2:13 Because you have **k** the Father.
2:14 Because you have **k** Him who
3: 6 has neither seen Him nor **k** Him.
4:16 And we have **k** and believed the
2 Jn 1 but also all those who have **k**
Rev 2:24 who have not **k** the depths of

KNOWS (82/80) KNOW, KNOWLEDGE

Gen 3: 5 For God **k** that in the day you
33:13 My lord **k** that the children are
Deut 2: 7 He **k** your trudging through this
34: 6 but no one **k** his grave to this
Josh 22:22 the LORD God of gods, He **k**,
1 Sam 3:13 for the iniquity which he **k**,
20: 3 Your father certainly **k** that I
23:17 Even my father Saul **k** that."
2 Sam 14:22 Today your servant **k** that I have
17:10 For all Israel **k** that your
1 Ki 8:38 when each one **k** the plague of
2 Chr 6:29 when each one **k** his own burden
Esth 4:14 Yet who **k** whether you have come
Job 11:11 For He **k** deceitful men; He
15:23 He **k** that a day of darkness
20:20 Because he **k** no quietness in his
23:10 But He **k** the way that I take;
28: 7 That path no bird **k**,
28:23 And He **k** its place.
34:25 Therefore he **k** their works; He
Ps 1: 6 For the LORD **k** the way of the
37:18 The LORD **k** the days of the
44:21 For He **k** the secrets of the
74: 9 is there any among us who **k**
90:11 Who **k** the power of Your anger?
94:11 The LORD **k** the thoughts of
103:14 For He **k** our frame; He
104:19 The sun **k** its going down.
138: 6 But the proud He **k** from afar.
139:14 And that my soul **k** very well.
Prov 9:13 She is simple, and **k** nothing.
14:10 The heart **k** its own bitterness,
24:22 And who **k** the ruin those two
Eccl 2:19 And who **k** whether he will be
3:21 Who **k** the spirit of the sons of
6: 8 Who **k** how to walk before the
6:12 For who **k** what is good for man
8: 1 And who **k** the interpretation
10:14 No man **k** what is to be; Who
Isa 1: 3 The ox **k** its owner And the
29:15 sees us?" and, "Who **k** us?"
Jer 8: 7 the stork in the heavens **K**
9:24 That he understands and **k** Me,
Dan 2:22 He **k** what is in the darkness,
Hos 9: 7 Israel **k**! The prophet is a
Joel 2:14 Who **k** if He will turn and
Nah 1: 7 And He **k** those who trust in
Zeph 3: 5 But the unjust **k** no shame.
Mt 6: 8 For your Father **k** the things
6:32 For your heavenly Father **k** that
9:30 See that no one **k** it."
11:27 and no one **k** the Son except the
24:36 of that day and hour no one **k**,
Mk 13:32 of that day and hour no one **k**,
Lk 10:22 and no one **k** who the Son is
12:30 and your Father **k** that you need
16:15 but God **k** your hearts. For what
Jn 7:27 no one **k** where He is from."
7:51 a man before it hears him and **k**
10:15 As the Father **k** Me, even so I
14:17 it neither sees Him nor **k** Him;
19:35 and he **k** that he is telling the
Acts 15: 8 who **k** the heart, acknowledged
26:26 **k** these things; for I am
Rom 8:27 He who searches the hearts **k**
1 Cor 2:11 For what man **k** the things of a
2:11 Even so no one **k** the things of
3:20 The LORD **k** the thoughts of
8: 2 And if anyone thinks that he **k**
8: 2 he **k** nothing yet as he ought to
2 Cor 11:11 do not love you? God **k**!
11:31 **k** that I am not lying.
12: 2 the body I do not know, God **k**—
12: 3 the body I do not know, God **k**—
2 Tim 2:19 The Lord **k** those who are His,"
Jas 4:17 to him who **k** to do good and
2 Pe 2: 9 then the Lord **k** how to deliver
1 Jn 3:20 our heart, and **k** all things.
4: 6 He who **k** God hears us; he who
4: 7 who loves is born of God and **k**
Rev 2:17 new name written which no one **k**
12:12 because he **k** that he has a

KOA (1/1)

Ezek 23:23 the Chaldeans, Pekod, Shoa, **K**,

KOHATH (31/28) KOHATHITES

Gen 46:11 sons of Levi were Gershon, **K**,
Ex 6:16 their generations: Gershon, **K**,
6:18 And the sons of **K** were Amram,
6:18 And the years of the life of **K**
Num 3:17 Levi by their names: Gershon, **K**,
3:19 And the sons of **K** by their
3:27 From **K** came the family of the
3:29 families of the children of **K**
4: 2 a census of the sons of **K**
4: 4 the service of the sons of **K**
4:15 then the sons of **K** shall come
4:15 of meeting which the sons of **K**
7: 9 But to the sons of **K** he gave
16: 1 the son of Izhar, the son of **K**,
26:57 family of the Gershonites; of **K**,
26:58 And **K** begot Amram.
Josh 21: 5 The rest of the children of **K**
21:20 families of the children of **K**,
21:20 the rest of the children of **K**,
21:26 families of the children of **K**.
1 Chr 6: 1 sons of Levi were Gershon, **K**,

6: 2 The sons of *K* were Amram,
6:16 sons of Levi were Gershon, *K*,
6:18 The sons of *K* were Amram,
6:22 The sons of *K* were Amminadab
6:38 the son of Izhar, the son of *K*,
6:66 the families of the sons of *K*
6:70 of the family of the sons of *K*.
15: 5 of the sons of *K*, Uriel the
23: 6 the sons of Levi: Gershon, *K*,
23:12 The sons of *K*: Amram, Izhar,

KOHATHITES (16/16) KOHATH

Num 3:27 were the families of the *K*.
3:30 house of the families of the *K*
4:18 tribe of the families of the *K*
4:34 numbered the sons of the *K* by
4:37 of the families of the *K*,
10:21 Then the *K* set out, carrying the
26:57 of Kohath, the family of the *K*;
Josh 21: 4 out for the families of the *K*.
21:10 one of the families of the *K*,
1 Chr 6:33 Of the sons of the *K* were
6:54 Aaron, of the family of the *K*:
6:61 family of the tribe of the *K*
9:32 brethren of the sons of the *K*
2 Chr 20:19 of the children of the *K* and
29:12 Azariah, of the sons of the *K*;
34:12 Meshullam, of the sons of the *K*,

KOLAIAH (2/2)

Neh 11: 7 son of Pedaiah, the son of *K*,
Jer 29:21 concerning Ahab the son of *K*,

KOR (2/1)

Ezek 45:14 one-tenth of a bath from a *k*.
45:14 A *k* is a homer or ten baths,

KORAH (39/39)

Gen 36: 5 bore Jeush, Jaalam, and *K*.
36:14 to Esau: Jeush, Jaalam, and *K*.
36:16 Chief *K*, Chief Gatam, and
36:18 Chief Jaalam, and Chief *K*.
Ex 6:21 The sons of Izhar were *K*,
6:24 And the sons of *K* were Assir,
Num 16: 1 Now *K* the son of Izhar, the son
16: 5 and he spoke to *K* and all his
16: 6 *K* and all your company;
16: 8 Then Moses said to *K*,
16:16 And Moses said to *K*,
16:19 And *K* gathered all the
16:24 'Get away from the tents of *K*,
16:27 away from around the tents of *K*,
16:32 and all the men with *K*,
16:40 he might not become like *K* and
16:49 besides those who died in the *K*
26: 9 and Aaron in the company of *K*,
26:10 them up together with *K* when
26:11 Nevertheless the children of *K*
27: 3 the LORD, in company with *K*,
1 Chr 1:35 Reuel, Jeush, Jaalam, and *K*.
2:43 The sons of Hebron were *K*,
6:22 *K* his son, Assir his son,
6:37 son of Ebiasaph, the son of *K*,
9:19 son of Ebiasaph, the son of *K*,
26:19 among the sons of *K* and among
Ps 42: Contemplation of the sons of *K*.
44: Contemplation of the sons of *K*.
45: Contemplation of the sons of *K*.
46: A Psalm of the sons of *K*.
47: A Psalm of the sons of *K*.
48: Song. A Psalm of the sons of *K*.
49: A Psalm of the sons of *K*.
84: Gath. A Psalm of the sons of *K*.
85: A Psalm of the sons of *K*.
87: A Psalm of the sons of *K*.
88: Song. A Psalm of the sons of *K*.
Jude 11 perished in the rebellion of *K*.

KORAHITE (1/1)

1 Chr 9:31 the firstborn of Shallum the *K*,

KORAHITES (5/5)

Ex 6:24 These are the families of the *K*.
1 Chr 9:19 from his father's house, the *K*,
12: 6 Joezer, and Jashobeam, the *K*;
26: 1 of the gatekeepers: of the *K*,
2 Chr 20:19 and of the children of the *K*

KORATHITES (1/1)

Num 26:58 and the family of the *K*.

KORATHITS, KORHITES (KJV) See KORAHITES

KORE (3/3)

1 Chr 9:19 Shallum the son of *K*,
26: 1 Meshelemiah the son of *K*,
2 Chr 31:14 *K* the son of Imnah the Levite,

KORS (8/5)

1 Ki 4:22 for one day was thirty *k* of
4:22 fine flour, sixty *k* of meal,
5:11 gave Hiram twenty thousand *k*
5:11 and twenty *k* of pressed oil.
2 Chr 2:10 twenty thousand *k* of ground
2:10 twenty thousand *k* of barley,
27: 5 ten thousand *k* of wheat, and
Ezra 7:22 one hundred *k* of wheat, one

KOZ (5/5)

1 Chr 4: 8 and *K* begot Anub, Zobebah, and
Ezra 2:61 sons of Habaiah, the sons of *K*,
Neh 3: 4 the son of Urijah, the son of *K*,
3:21 the son of Urijah, the son of *K*,
7:63 sons of Habaiah, the sons of *K*,

KUSHAIAH (1/1)

1 Chr 15:17 of Merari, Ethan the son of *K*;

L

LAADAH (1/1)

1 Chr 4:21 *L* the father of Mareshah, and

LAADAN (7/5)

1 Chr 7:26 *L* his son, Ammihud his son,
23: 7 Gershonites: *L* and Shimei.
23: 8 The sons of *L*: the first
23: 9 of the fathers' houses of *L*.
26:21 The sons of *L*, the descendants
26:21 of the Gershonites of *L*,
26:21 of *L* the Gershonite: Jehieli.

LABAN (52/45) LABAN'S

Gen 24:29 had a brother whose name was *L*,
24:29 and *L* ran out to the man by the
24:50 Then *L* and Bethuel answered and
25:20 the sister of *L* the Syrian.
27:43 flee to my brother *L* in Haran.
28: 2 there of the daughters of *L*
28: 5 to *L* the son of Bethuel the
29: 5 Do you know *L* the son of
29:10 saw Rachel the daughter of *L*
29:10 and the sheep of *L* his mother's
29:10 and watered the flock of *L* his
29:13 when *L* heard the report about
29:13 So he told *L* all these things.
29:14 And *L* said to him, "Surely you
29:15 Then *L* said to Jacob, "Because
29:16 Now *L* had two daughters:
29:19 And *L* said, "It is better
29:21 Then Jacob said to *L*,
29:22 And *L* gathered together all the
29:24 And *L* gave his maid Zilpah to
29:25 it was Leah. And he said to *L*,
29:26 And *L* said, "It must not be
29:29 And *L* gave his maid Bilhah to
29:30 And he served with *L* still
30:25 Joseph, that Jacob said to *L*,
30:27 And *L* said to him, "Please
30:34 And *L* said, "Oh, that it were
30:40 all the brown in the flock of *L*;
31: 2 Jacob saw the countenance of *L*,
31:12 for I have seen all that *L* is
31:19 Now *L* had gone to shear his
31:20 unknown to *L* the Syrian, in
31:22 And *L* was told on the third day
31:24 But God had come to *L* the Syrian
31:25 So *L* overtook Jacob. Now Jacob
31:25 and *L* with his brethren pitched
31:26 And *L* said to Jacob: "What have
31:31 Jacob answered and said to *L*,
31:33 And *L* went into Jacob's tent,
31:34 And *L* searched all about the
31:36 Jacob was angry and rebuked *L*,
31:36 Jacob answered and said to *L*:
31:43 And *L* answered and said to
31:47 *L* called it Jegar Sahadutha, but
31:48 And *L* said, "This heap is a
31:51 Then *L* said to Jacob, "Here is
31:55 And early in the morning *L*
31:55 Then *L* departed and returned to
32: 4 I have dwelt with *L* and stayed
46:18 whom *L* gave to Leah his
46:25 whom *L* gave to Rachel his
Deut 1: 1 Suph, between Paran, Tophel, *L*,

LABAN'S (4/4) LABAN

Gen 30:36 Jacob fed the rest of *L* flocks.
30:40 did not put them with *L* flock.
30:42 so the feebler were *L* and the
31: 1 Jacob heard the words of *L* sons,

LABOR (109/105) LABORED, LABORER, LABORING, LABORS

Gen 31:42 seen my affliction and the *l*
35:16 childbirth, and she had hard *l*.
35:17 to pass, when she was in hard *l*,
Ex 5: 4 their work? Get back to your *l*.
5: 5 make them rest from their *l*!"
5: 9 that they may *l* in it, and let
20: 9 Six days you shall *l* and do all
Deut 5:13 Six days you shall *l* and do all
26: 7 on our affliction and our *l*
28:33 land and the produce of your *l*,
Josh 17:13 put the Canaanites to forced *l*,
24:13 a land for which you did not *l*,
1 Sam 4:19 for her *l* pains came upon her.
1 Ki 4: 6 son of Abda, over the *l* force.
5:13 King Solomon raised up a *l*
5:13 and the *l* force was thirty
5:14 was in charge of the *l* force.
9:15 this is the reason for the *l*
9:21 these Solomon raised forced *l*,
11:28 him the officer over all the *l*
2 Chr 8: 8 these Solomon raised forced *l*,
Job 9:29 Why then do I *l* in vain?
39:11 Or will you leave your *l* to
39:16 Her *l* is in vain, without
Ps 78:46 And their *l* to the locust.
90:10 Yet their boast is only *l* and
104:23 out to his work And to his *l*
105:44 And they inherited the *l* of
107:12 brought down their heart with *l*;
109:11 let strangers plunder his *l*.
127: 1 They *l* in vain who build it;
128: 2 When you eat the *l* of your
Prov 10:16 The *l* of the righteous leads
12:24 man will be put to forced *l*.
13:11 But he who gathers by *l* will
14:23 In all *l* there is profit,
21:25 For his hands refuse to *l*.
Eccl 1: 3 has a man from all his *l* In
1: 8 All things are full of *l*;
2:10 my heart rejoiced in all my *l*;
2:10 was my reward from all my *l*.
2:11 my hands had done And on the *l*
2:18 Then I hated all my *l* in which
2:19 Yet he will rule over all my *l*
2:20 and despaired of all the *l* in
2:21 For there is a man whose *l* is
2:22 For what has man for all his *l*,
2:24 soul should enjoy good in his *l*.
3:13 and enjoy the good of all his *l*—
4: 9 have a good reward for their *l*.
5:15 shall take nothing from his *l*
5:18 to enjoy the good of all his *l*
5:19 heritage and rejoice in his *l*—
6: 7 All the *l* of man is for his
8:15 will remain with him in his *l*
9: 9 and in the *l* which you perform
10:15 The *l* of fools wearies them,
Isa 21: 3 like the pangs of a woman in *l*.
22: 4 Do not *l* to comfort me
23: 4 the sea, saying, "I do not *l*,
31: 8 young men shall become forced *l*.
42:14 I will cry like a woman in *l*,
45:14 The *l* of Egypt and merchandise
53:11 He shall see the *l* of His soul,
65:23 They shall not *l* in vain,
66: 7 "Before she was in *l*,
66: 8 For as soon as Zion was in *l*,
Jer 3:24 For shame has devoured The *l*
4:31 a voice as of a woman in *l*,
6:24 of us, Pain as of a woman in *l*.
13:21 seize you, Like a woman in *l*?
20:18 forth from the womb to see *l*
22:23 Like the pain of a woman in *l*?
30: 6 Whether a man is ever in *l*
30: 6 on his loins Like a woman in *l*,
49:24 taken her like a woman in *l*.
51:58 The people will *l* in vain,
Lam 5: 5 We *l* and have no rest.
Ezek 29:18 of Babylon caused his army to *l*
29:18 for the *l* which they expended
29:20 the land of Egypt for his *l*,
Mic 4: 9 seized you like a woman in *l*.
4:10 and *l* to bring forth,
5: 3 the time that she who is in *l*
Hab 2:13 of hosts That the peoples *l*
3:17 Though the *l* of the olive may
Hag 1:11 and on all the *l* of your
Mt 11:28 all you who *l* and are heavy
Jn 6:27 Do not *l* for the food which
16:21 "A woman, when she is in *l*,
1 Cor 3: 8 reward according to his own *l*.
4:12 And we *l*, working with our
15:58 knowing that your *l* is not in
Gal 4:19 for whom I *l* in birth again
4:27 You who are not in *l*!
Eph 4:28 no longer, but rather let him *l*,
Phil 1:22 will mean fruit from my *l*;
Col 1:29 To this end I also *l*,
1 Th 1: 3 *l* of love, and patience of hope
2: 9 our *l* and toil; for laboring
3: 5 and our *l* might be in vain.
5: 3 as *l* pains upon a pregnant
5:12 to recognize those who *l* among
2 Th 3: 8 but worked with *l* and toil
1 Tim 4:10 For to this end we both *l* and
5:17 especially those who *l* in the
Heb 6:10 to forget your work and *l* of
Rev 2: 2 "I know your works, your *l*,
12: 2 she cried out in *l* and in pain

LABORED (24/22) LABOR

Gen 35:16 Rachel *l* in childbirth, and
1 Ki 5:16 supervised the people who *l* in
2 Chr 24:13 So the workmen *l*, and the work
Neh 4:21 So we *l* in the work, and half
Job 20:18 restore that for which he *l*,
Eccl 2:21 to a man who has not *l* for it.
5:16 what profit has he who has *l*
Isa 47:12 In which you have *l* from your
47:15 be to you With whom you have *l*,
49: 4 I have *l* in vain, I have spent
54: 1 You who have not *l* with
62: 8 new wine, For which you have *l*.

Dan 6:14 and he *l* till the going down of
Jon 4:10 plant for which you have not *l*,
Jn 4:38 that for which you have not *l*;
4:38 have not labored; others have *l*,
Rom 16: 6 Greet Mary, who *l* much for us.
16:12 who have *l* in the Lord.
16:12 who *l* much in the Lord.
1 Cor 15:10 but I *l* more abundantly than
Gal 4:11 lest I have *l* for you in vain.
Phil 2:16 I have not run in vain or *l* in
4: 3 help these women who *l* with me
Rev 2: 3 and have *l* for My name's sake

LABORER (4/4) LABOR, LABORERS

Lk 10: 7 for the *l* is worthy of his
1 Th 3: 2 and our fellow *l* in the gospel
1 Tim 5:18 The *l* is worthy of his wages."
Phm 1: 1 beloved friend and fellow *l*,

LABORERS (13/12) LABORER

Josh 16:10 day and have become forced *l*.
1 Ki 9:22 Israel Solomon made no forced *l*,
Neh 4:10 The strength of the *l* is
Isa 58: 3 And exploit all your *l*.
Mt 9:37 but the *l* are few.
9:38 of the harvest to send out *l*
20: 1 early in the morning to hire *l*
20: 2 when he had agreed with the *l*
20: 8 Call the *l* and give them their
Lk 10: 2 but the *l* are few; therefore
10: 2 of the harvest to send out *l*
Phm 1:24 Demas, Luke, my fellow *l*.
Jas 5: 4 Indeed the wages of the *l* who

LABORING (4/4) LABOR

Eccl 5:12 The sleep of a *l* man is sweet,
Acts 20:35 by *l* like this, that you must
Col 4:12 always *l* fervently for you in
1 Th 2: 9 for *l* night and day, that we

LABORS (18/16) LABOR

Ex 23:16 the firstfruits of your *l* which
23:16 in the fruit of your *l* from
Prov 5:10 And your *l* go to the house of
16:26 The person who *l*, labors for
16:26 *l* for himself, For his hungry
Eccl 3: 9 worker from that in which he *l*?
4: 8 there is no end to all his *l*,
8:17 For though a man *l* to discover
Jer 31: 8 with child And the one who *l*
Hos 12: 8 In all my *l* They shall find
Hag 2:17 mildew and hail in all the *l*
Jn 4:38 you have entered into their *l*.
Rom 8:22 the whole creation groans and *l*
1 Cor 16:16 and to everyone who works and *l*
2 Cor 6: 5 imprisonments, in tumults, in *l*,
10:15 that is, in other men's *l*,
11:23 in *l* more abundant, in stripes
Rev 14:13 they may rest from their *l*,

LACE (KJV) See CORD

LACHISH (24/22)

Josh 10: 3 of Jarmuth, Japhia king of *L*,
10: 5 king of Jarmuth, the king of *L*,
10:23 king of Jarmuth, the king of *L*,
10:31 and all Israel with him, to *L*;
10:32 And the LORD delivered *L* into
10:33 king of Gezer came up to help *L*;
10:34 From *L* Joshua passed to Eglon,
10:35 to all that he had done to *L*.
12:11 of Jarmuth, one; the king of *L*,
15:39 *L*, Bozkath, Eglon,
2 Ki 14:19 in Jerusalem, and he fled to *L*;
14:19 but they sent after him to *L*
18:14 to the king of Assyria at *L*,
18:17 and the Rabshakeh from *L*,
19: 8 that he had departed from *L*.
2 Chr 11: 9 Adoraim, *L*, Azekah,
25:27 in Jerusalem, and he fled to *L*;
25:27 but they sent after him to *L*
32: 9 him laid siege against *L*),
Neh 11:30 in *L* and its fields; in Azekah
Isa 36: 2 with a great army from *L* to
37: 8 that he had departed from *L*.
Jer 34: 7 against *L* and Azekah; for only
Mic 1:13 O inhabitant of *L*, Harness

LACK (39/37) LACKED, LACKING, LACKS

Gen 18:28 destroy all of the city for *l*
Ex 16:18 he who gathered little had no *l*.
Deut 8: 9 in which you will *l* nothing;
28:57 will eat them secretly for *l*
Judg 18:10 a place where there is no *l*
19:19 there is no *l* of anything."
1 Ki 2: 4 you shall not *l* a man on the
4:27 There was no *l* in their supply.
Job 4:11 The old lion perishes for *l* of
31:19 I have seen anyone perish for *l*
38:41 And wander about for *l* of
Ps 34:10 The young lions *l* and suffer
34:10 who seek the LORD shall not *l*
109:24 And my flesh is feeble from *l*
Prov 5:23 He shall die for *l* of
10:21 But fools die for *l* of wisdom.
13:23 And for *l* of justice there is
14:28 But in the *l* of people is the
28:27 gives to the poor will not *l*,
31:11 So he will have no *l* of gain.
Eccl 9: 8 And let your head *l* no oil.
Isa 34:16 Not one shall *l* her mate.
Jer 33:17 David shall never *l* a man to sit
33:18 *l* a man to offer burnt
35:19 the son of Rechab shall not *l*
Lam 4: 9 Stricken for *l* of the fruits
Ezek 4:17 that they may *l* bread and water,
Hos 4: 6 My people are destroyed for *l*
Am 4: 6 And *l* of bread in all your
Mt 19:20 my youth. What do I still *l*?
Mk 10:21 said to him, "One thing you *l*:
Lk 18:22 You still *l* one thing. Sell all
22:35 did you *l* anything?" So they
1 Cor 7: 5 tempt you because of your *l* of
2 Cor 8:14 abundance may supply their *l*,
8:14 also may supply your *l*—
8:15 gathered little had no *l*.
1 Th 4:12 and that you may *l* nothing.
Titus 3:13 that they may *l* nothing.

LACKED (8/8) LACK

Deut 2: 7 you have *l* nothing." '
1 Ki 11:22 But what have you *l* with me,
Neh 9:21 They *l* nothing; Their clothes
Jer 44:18 we have *l* everything and have
Lk 8: 6 it withered away because it *l*
Acts 4:34 there anyone among them who *l*;
2 Cor 11: 9 for what I *l* the brethren who
Phil 4:10 but you *l* opportunity.

LACKING (12/12) LACK

Lev 2:13 covenant of your God to be *l*
1 Sam 30:19 And nothing of theirs was *l*,
Prov 10:19 multitude of words sin is not *l*,
Eccl 1:15 And what is *l* cannot be
Jer 23: 4 dismayed, nor shall they be *l*,
47: 3 their children, *L* courage,
1 Cor 16:17 for what was *l* on your part
Phil 2:30 to supply what was *l* in your
Col 1:24 fill up in my flesh what is *l*
1 Th 3:10 face and perfect what is *l* in
Titus 1: 5 in order the things that are *l*,
Jas 1: 4 complete, *l* nothing.

LACKS (13/13) LACK

2 Sam 3:29 the sword, or who *l* bread."
Prov 6:32 commits adultery with a woman *l*
9: 4 in here!" As for him who *l*
9:16 And as for him who *l*
11:22 So is a lovely woman who *l*
12: 9 he who honors himself but *l*
28:16 A ruler who *l* understanding is
Eccl 6: 2 so that he *l* nothing for
10: 3 He *l* wisdom, And he shows
Song 7: 2 It *l* no blended beverage.
1 Cor 12:24 honor to that part which *l* it,
Jas 1: 5 If any of you *l* wisdom, let him
2 Pe 1: 9 For he who *l* these things is

LAD (32/27) LAD'S, LADS

Gen 21:12 in your sight because of the *l*
21:17 God heard the voice of the *l*.
21:17 has heard the voice of the *l*
21:18 lift up the *l* and hold him with
21:19 and gave the *l* a drink.
21:20 So God was with the *l*;
22: 5 the *l* and I will go yonder and
22:12 "Do not lay your hand on the *l*,
37: 2 And the *l* was with the sons of
37:30 The *l* is no more; and I, where
43: 8 Send the *l* with me, and we will
44:22 The *l* cannot leave his father,
44:30 and the *l* is not with us,
44:31 when he sees that the *l* is not
44:32 became surety for the *l* to my
44:33 remain instead of the *l* as a
44:33 and let the *l* go up with his
44:34 I go up to my father if the *l*
Judg 16:26 Then Samson said to the *l* who
1 Sam 20:21 "and there I will send a *l*,
20:35 and a little *l* was with him.
20:36 Then he said to his *l*,
20:36 As the *l* ran, he shot an
20:37 When the *l* had come to the place
20:37 Jonathan cried out after the *l*
20:38 Jonathan cried out after the *l*,
20:38 do not delay!" So Jonathan's *l*
20:39 But the *l* did not know anything.
20:40 gave his weapons to his *l*,
20:41 As soon as the *l* had gone,
2 Sam 17:18 Nevertheless a *l* saw them, and
Jn 6: 9 There is a *l* here who has five

LAD'S (1/1) LAD

Gen 44:30 life is bound up in the *l* life,

LADDER (1/1)

Gen 28:12 a *l* was set up on the earth,

LADE, LADED, LADING (KJV) See CARGO, LOAD, LOADED, LOADING, PROVIDED, PUT

LADEN (2/2)

Isa 1: 4 A people *l* with iniquity,
Mt 11:28 you who labor and are heavy *l*,

LADIES (2/2) LADY

Judg 5:29 Her wisest *l* answered her,
Esth 1:18 This very day the noble *l* of

LADLES (2/2)

1 Ki 7:50 the trimmers, the bowls, the *l*,
2 Chr 4:22 the trimmers, the bowls, the *l*,

LADS (2/2) LAD

Gen 48:16 me from all evil, Bless the *l*;
Jer 14: 3 nobles have sent their *l* for

LADY (4/4) LADIES

Isa 47: 5 no longer be called The *L* of
47: 7 'I shall be a *l* forever,'
2 Jn 1 To the elect *l* and her
5 And now I plead with you, *l*,

LAEL (1/1)

Num 3:24 was Eliasaph the son of *L*.

LAGGING (1/1)

Rom 12:11 not *l* in diligence, fervent in

LAHAD (1/1)

1 Chr 4: 2 and Jahath begot Ahumai and *L*.

LAHAI ROI BEER LAHAI ROI

LAHAI-ROI (KJV) See LAHAI (ROI)

LAHMAS (1/1)

Josh 15:40 Cabbon, *L*, Kithlish,

LAHMI (1/1)

1 Chr 20: 5 the son of Jair killed *L* the

LAID (211/206) LAY

Gen 9:23 *l* it on both their shoulders,
22: 6 of the burnt offering and *l*
22: 9 he bound Isaac his son and *l*
38:19 and *l* aside her veil and put on
41:48 and *l* up the food in the
41:48 he *l* up in every city the food
48:14 out his right hand and *l* it
48:17 Joseph saw that his father *l*
Ex 2: 3 and *l* it in the reeds by the
5: 9 Let more work be *l* on the men,
16:24 So they *l* it up till morning, as
16:34 so Aaron *l* it up before the
19: 7 and *l* before them all these
Lev 8:14 Then Aaron and his sons *l* their
8:18 And Aaron and his sons *l* their
8:22 Then Aaron and his sons *l* their
Num 11:11 that You have *l* the burden of
16:18 *l* incense on it, and stood at
21:30 Then we *l* waste as far as
27:23 And he *l* his hands on him and
Deut 26: 6 and *l* hard bondage on us.
29:22 which the LORD has *l* on it:
32:34 Is this not *l* up in store with
34: 9 for Moses had *l* his hands on
Josh 2: 6 which she had *l* in order on the
2:19 be on our head if a hand is *l*
4: 8 and *l* them down there.
7:23 and *l* them out before the
10:27 and *l* large stones against the
Judg 9:24 be settled and their blood be *l*
9:48 and took it and *l* it on his
19:29 *l* hold of his concubine, and
Ruth 3:15 and *l* it on her. Then she went
4:16 Naomi took the child and *l* him
1 Sam 10:25 and wrote it in a book and *l*
19:13 And Michal took an image and *l*
2 Sam 13:19 and *l* her hand on her head and
18:17 and *l* a very large heap of
1 Ki 3:20 and *l* him in her bosom, and
3:20 and *l* her dead child in my
6:37 of the house of the LORD was *l*,
13:29 *l* it on the donkey, and brought
13:30 Then he *l* the corpse in his own
15:27 while Nadab and all Israel *l*
16:34 He *l* its foundation with Abiram
17:19 and *l* him on his own bed.
18:33 and *l* it on the wood, and
2 Ki 4:21 And she went up and *l* him on the
4:31 and *l* the staff on the face of
9:16 for Joram was *l* up there;
9:25 that the LORD *l* this burden
19:17 the kings of Assyria have *l*
20: 7 So they took and *l* it on the
2 Chr 3: 3 the foundation which Solomon *l*
16:14 and they *l* him in the bed which
29:23 and they *l* their hands on them.
31: 6 to the LORD their God they *l*
32: 9 and all the forces with him *l*
Ezra 3: 6 of the LORD had not been *l*.
3:10 When the builders *l* the

L

3:11 of the house of the LORD was *l*.
3:12 of this temple was *l* before
5: 8 and timber is being *l* in the
5:16 same Sheshbazzar came and *l*
6: 3 foundations of it be firmly *l*,
Neh 3: 3 they *l* its beams and hung its
3: 6 they *l* its beams and hung its
5:15 who were before me *l* burdens
Job 6: 2 And my calamity *l* with it on
14:10 But man dies and is *l* away;
16:15 And *l* my head in the dust.
38: 4 Where were you when I *l* the
38: 6 Or who *l* its cornerstone,
Ps 31: 4 net which they have secretly *l*
31:19 Which You have *l* up for those
49:14 Like sheep they are *l* in the
66:11 You *l* affliction on our backs.
79: 1 They have *l* Jerusalem in
79: 7 And *l* waste his dwelling
88: 6 You have *l* me in the lowest
102:25 Of old You *l* the foundation of
104: 5 You who *l* the foundations of
105:18 He was *l* in irons.
116: 3 And the pangs of Sheol *l* hold
119:30 Your judgments I have *l*
119:110 The wicked have *l* a snare for
136: 6 To Him who *l* out the earth
139: 5 And *l* Your hand upon me.
141: 9 me from the snares they have *l*
Song 7:13 Which I have *l* up for you, my
Isa 6:11 Until the cities are *l* waste and
15: 1 in the night Ar of Moab is *l*
15: 1 in the night Kir of Moab is *l*
15: 7 And what they have *l* up,
23: 1 ships of Tarshish! For it is *l*
23:14 For your strength is *l* waste.
23:18 it will not be treasured nor *l*
37:18 the kings of Assyria have *l*
44:28 "Your foundation shall be *l*.
47: 6 On the elderly you *l* your yoke
48:13 Indeed My hand has *l* the
49:17 destroyers and those who *l* you
51:13 out the heavens And *l* the
51:23 And you have *l* your body like
53: 6 And the LORD has *l* on Him the
64:11 all our pleasant things are *l*
Jer 4: 7 Your cities will be *l* waste,
27:17 live! Why should this city be *l*
50:23 among the nations! I have *l* a
Lam 3:28 Because God has *l* it on him;
Ezek 4: 5 For I have *l* on you the years of
4: 6 I have *l* on you a day for each
6: 6 places the cities shall be *l*
6: 6 so that your altars may be *l*
11: 7 Your slain whom you have *l* in
12:20 that are inhabited shall be *l*
19: 7 And *l* waste their cities;
26: 2 be filled; she is *l* waste.'
28:17 I *l* you before kings,
29:12 among the cities that are *l*
30: 7 of the cities that are *l*
32:27 They have *l* their swords under
32:29 Who despite their might Are *l*
39:21 and My hand which I have *l* on
40:42 on these they *l* the instruments
Dan 6:17 Then a stone was brought and *l*
Joel 1: 7 He has *l* waste My vine,
Am 7: 9 of Israel shall be *l* waste.
Ob 13 Nor *l* hands on their
Jon 3: 6 he arose from his throne and *l*
Mic 5: 1 He has *l* siege against us;
Nah 3: 7 Nineveh is *l* waste! Who will
Hag 2:15 from before stone was *l* upon
2:18 of the LORD's temple was *l*—
Zech 3: 9 the stone That I have *l* before
4: 9 hands of Zerubbabel Have *l*
8: 9 in the day the foundation was *l*
Mal 1: 3 And *l* waste his mountains and
Mt 3:10 And even now the ax is *l* to the
14: 3 For Herod had *l* hold of John and
15:30 and they *l* them down at Jesus'
18:28 and he *l* hands on him and took
19:15 And He *l* His hands on them and
21: 7 *l* their clothes on them,
26:50 Then they came and *l* hands on
26:57 And those who had *l* hold of
27:60 and *l* it in his new tomb which
Mk 6: 5 except that He *l* His hands on a
6:17 Herod himself had sent and *l*
6:29 and took away his corpse and *l*
6:56 they *l* the sick in the
14:46 Then they *l* their hands on Him
14:51 And the young men *l* hold of
15:46 And he *l* Him in a tomb which
15:47 Joses observed where He was *l*.
16: 6 See the place where they *l* Him.
Lk 2: 7 and *l* Him in a manger, because
3: 9 And even now the ax is *l* to the
4:40 and He *l* His hands on every one
6:48 who dug deep and *l* the
12:19 you have many goods *l* up for
13:13 And He *l* His hands on her,
14:29 after he has *l* the foundation,
16:20 who was *l* at his gate,
23:26 they *l* hold of a certain man,
23:26 and on him they *l* the cross
23:53 and *l* it in a tomb that was
23:55 the tomb and how His body was *l*.
Jn 7:30 but no one *l* a hand on Him,
7:44 but no one *l* hands on Him.
8:20 and no one *l* hands on Him,
11:34 'Where have you *l* him?"
13: 4 rose from supper and *l* aside His
19:41 in which no one had yet been *l*.
19:42 So there they *l* Jesus, because
20: 2 do not know where they have *l*
20:13 I do not know where they have *l*
20:15 tell me where You have *l* Him,
21: 9 and fish *l* on it, and bread.
Acts 3: 2 whom they *l* daily at the gate
4: 3 And they *l* hands on them,
4:35 and *l* them at the apostles'
4:37 and brought the money and *l* it
5: 2 brought a certain part and *l*
5:15 sick out into the streets and *l*
5:18 and *l* their hands on the
6: 6 they *l* hands on them.
7:16 carried back to Shechem and *l*
7:58 And the witnesses *l* down their
8:17 Then they *l* hands on them,
9:37 they *l* her in an upper room.
13: 3 and *l* hands on them, they sent
13:29 Him down from the tree and *l*
16:23 And when they had *l* many stripes
19: 6 And when Paul had *l* hands on
21:27 up the whole crowd and *l* hands
25: 7 Jerusalem stood about and *l*
25:14 Festus *l* Paul's case before the
28: 3 a bundle of sticks and *l* them
28: 8 and he *l* his hands on him and
1 Cor 3:10 a wise master builder I have *l*
3:11 anyone lay than that which is *l*,
9:16 for necessity is *l* upon me;
Phil 3:12 which Christ Jesus has also *l*
Col 1: 5 because of the hope which is *l*
2 Tim 4: 8 there is *l* up for me the crown
Heb 1:10 in the beginning *l* the
1 Jn 3:16 because He *l* down His life for
Rev 1:17 But He *l* His right hand on me,
20: 2 He *l* hold of the dragon, that
21:16 The city is *l* out as a square;

LAIN (9/9) LIE

Gen 26:10 of the people might soon have *l*
Num 5:19 If no man has *l* with you, and if
5:20 other than your husband has *l*
Job 3:13 For now I would have *l* still
Jer 3: 2 Where have you not *l* with
Ezek 23: 8 For in her youth they had *l*
Jon 1: 5 had *l* down, and was fast
Lk 23:53 where no one had ever *l* before.
Jn 20:12 where the body of Jesus had *l*.

LAIR (1/1)

Jer 25:38 He has left His *l* like the

LAIRS (3/3)

Job 37: 8 And remain in their *l*.
38:40 Or lurk in their *l* to lie in
Isa 32:14 forts and towers will become *l*

LAISH (7/7) DAN, LESHEM

Judg 18: 7 five men departed and went to *L*.
18:14 to spy out the country of *L*
18:27 belonged to him, and went to *L*,
18:29 of the city formerly was *L*.
1 Sam 25:44 wife, to Palti the son of *L*,
2 Sam 3:15 from Paltiel the son of *L*.
Isa 10:30 it to be heard as far as *L*—

LAKE (10/10)

Lk 5: 1 that He stood by the *L* of
5: 2 saw two boats standing by the *l*;
8:22 over to the other side of the *l*.
8:23 a windstorm came down on the *l*,
8:33 the steep place into the *l* and
Rev 19:20 two were cast alive into the *l*
20:10 was cast into the *l* of fire and
20:14 and Hades were cast into the *l*
20:15 of Life was cast into the *l* of
21: 8 shall have their part in the *l*

LAKKUM (1/1)

Josh 19:33 Nekeb, and Jabneel, as far as *L*;

LAMA (2/2)

Mt 27:46 *l* sabachthani?" that is, "My
Mk 15:34 *l* sabachthani?" which is

LAMB (102/95) LAMB'S, LAMBS

Gen 22: 7 but where is the *l* for a burnt
22: 8 will provide for Himself the *l*
Ex 12: 3 man shall take for himself a *l*,
12: 3 father, a *l* for a household.
12: 4 is too small for the *l*,
12: 4 shall make your count for the *l*.
12: 5 Your *l* shall be without blemish,
12:21 and kill the Passover *l*.
13:13 you shall redeem with a *l*;
29:39 One *l* you shall offer in the
29:39 and the other *l* you shall offer
29:40 With the one *l* shall be
29:41 And the other *l* you shall offer
34:20 you shall redeem with a *l*.
Lev 3: 7 If he offers a *l* as his
4:32 If he brings a *l* as his sin
4:35 as the fat of the *l* is removed
5: 6 a *l* or a kid of the goats as a
5: 7 he is not able to bring a *l*,
9: 3 offering, and a calf and a *l*,
12: 6 shall bring to the priest a *l*
12: 8 if she is not able to bring a *l*,
14:10 one ewe *l* of the first year
14:12 priest shall take one male *l*
14:13 Then he shall kill the *l* in the
14:21 then he shall take one male *l*
14:24 the priest shall take the *l* of
14:25 Then he shall kill the *l* of the
17: 3 of Israel who kills an ox or *l*
22:23 Either a bull or a *l* that has
23:12 a male *l* of the first year,
Num 6:12 and bring a male *l* in its first
6:14 one male *l* in its first year
6:14 one ewe *l* in its first year
7:15 and one male *l* in its first
7:21 and one male *l* in its first
7:27 and one male *l* in its first
7:33 and one male *l* in its first
7:39 and one male *l* in its first
7:45 and one male *l* in its first
7:51 and one male *l* in its first
7:57 and one male *l* in its first
7:63 and one male *l* in its first
7:69 and one male *l* in its first
7:75 and one male *l* in its first
7:81 and one male *l* in its first
15: 5 or the sacrifice, for each *l*.
15:11 or for each *l* or young goat.
28: 4 The one *l* you shall offer in the
28: 4 the other *l* you shall offer in
28: 7 one-fourth of a hin for each *l*;
28: 8 The other *l* you shall offer in
28:13 as a grain offering for each *l*,
28:14 and one-fourth of a hin for a *l*;
1 Sam 7: 9 And Samuel took a suckling *l*
17:34 or a bear came and took a *l*
17:35 and delivered the *l* from its
2 Sam 12: 3 except one little ewe *l* which
12: 4 but he took the poor man's *l*
12: 6 restore fourfold for the *l*,
Isa 11: 6 also shall dwell with the *l*,
16: 1 Send the *l* to the ruler of the
53: 7 He was led as a *l* to the
65:25 The wolf and the *l* shall feed
66: 3 a man; He who sacrifices a *l*,
Jer 11:19 But I was like a docile *l*
Ezek 45:15 And one *l* shall be given from a
46:13 offering to the LORD of a *l*
46:15 "Thus they shall prepare the *l*,
Hos 4:16 will let them forage Like a *l*
Mk 14:12 they killed the Passover *l*,
Jn 1:29 Behold! The *L* of God who takes
1:36 Behold the *L* of God!"
Acts 8:32 And as a *l* before its
1 Pe 1:19 as of a *l* without blemish and
Rev 5: 6 stood a *L* as though it had been
5: 8 elders fell down before the *L*,
5:12 Worthy is the *L* who was slain
5:13 on the throne, And to the *L*,
6: 1 Now I saw when the *L* opened one
6:16 and from the wrath of the *L*!
7: 9 the throne and before the *L*,
7:10 the throne, and to the *L*!"
7:14 white in the blood of the *L*.
7:17 for the *L* who is in the midst of
12:11 him by the blood of the *L* and
13: 8 in the Book of Life of the *L*
13:11 and he had two horns like a *l*
14: 1 a *L* standing on Mount Zion,
14: 4 are the ones who follow the *L*
14: 4 firstfruits to God and to the *L*.
14:10 and in the presence of the *L*.
15: 3 of God, and the song of the *L*,
17:14 will make war with the *L*,
17:14 and the *L* will overcome them,
19: 7 for the marriage of the *L* has
19: 9 the marriage supper of the *L*!'
21:14 of the twelve apostles of the *L*.
21:22 the Lord God Almighty and the *L*
21:23 The *L* is its light.
22: 1 the throne of God and of the *L*.
22: 3 the throne of God and of the *L*

LAMB'S (2/2) LAMB

Rev 21: 9 the bride, the *L* wife."
21:27 written in the *L* Book of Life.

LAMBS (88/88) LAMB

Gen 21:28 And Abraham set seven ewe *l* of
21:29 meaning of these seven ewe *l*
21:30 will take these seven ewe *l*
30:32 all the brown ones among the *l*,
30:33 goats, and brown among the *l*,
30:35 all the brown ones among the *l*,
30:40 Then Jacob separated the *l*,
Ex 12:21 Pick out and take *l* for
29:38 two *l* of the first year, day by
Lev 14:10 day he shall take two male *l*
23:18 offer with the bread seven *l*
23:19 and two male *l* of the first
23:20 the LORD, with the two *l*.
Num 7:17 and five male *l* in their first
7:23 and five male *l* in their first
7:29 and five male *l* in their first
7:35 and five male *l* in their first
7:41 and five male *l* in their first
7:47 and five male *l* in their first

7:53 and five male l in their first
7:59 and five male l in their first
7:65 and five male l in their first
7:71 and five male l in their first
7:77 and five male l in their first
7:83 and five male l in their first
7:87 the male l in their first year
7:88 and the l in their first year
28: 3 two male l in their first year
28: 9 And on the Sabbath day two l in
28:11 and seven l in their first
28:19 and seven l in their first
28:21 ephah for each of the seven l;
28:27 and seven l in their first
28:29 for each of the seven l;
29: 2 and seven l in their first
29: 4 for each of the seven l;
29: 8 and seven l in their first
29:10 for each of the seven l;
29:13 and fourteen l in their first
29:15 for each of the fourteen l;
29:17 fourteen l in their first year
29:18 for the rams, and for the l,
29:20 fourteen l in their first year
29:21 for the rams, and for the l,
29:23 and fourteen l in their first
29:24 for the rams, and for the l,
29:26 and fourteen l in their first
29:27 for the rams, and for the l,
29:29 and fourteen l in their first
29:30 for the rams, and for the l,
29:32 and fourteen l in their first
29:33 for the rams, and for the l,
29:36 seven l in their first year
29:37 for the ram, and for the l,
Deut 32:14 of the flock, With fat of l;
1 Sam 15: 9 the oxen, the fatlings, the l,
2 Ki 3: 4 Israel one hundred thousand l
1 Chr 29:21 a thousand rams, a thousand l,
2 Chr 29:21 bulls, seven rams, seven l,
29:22 They also killed the l and
29:32 rams, and two hundred l;
30:15 slaughtered the Passover l on
30:17 slaughter of the Passover l
35: 1 slaughtered the Passover l on
35: 7 Josiah gave the lay people l
Ezra 6: 9 and l for the burnt offerings
6:17 hundred rams, four hundred l,
6:20 slaughtered the Passover l
7:17 this money bulls, rams, and l,
8:35 rams, seventy-seven l,
Ps 114: 4 rams, The little hills like l.
114: 6 rams? O little hills, like l?
Prov 27:26 The l will provide your
Isa 1:11 of bulls, Or of l or goats.
5:17 Then the l shall feed in their
34: 6 With the blood of l and goats,
40:11 He will gather the l with His
Jer 51:40 will bring them down Like l
Ezek 27:21 They traded with you in l,
39:18 of the earth, Of rams and l,
46: 4 Sabbath day shall be six l
46: 5 the grain offering for the l,
46: 6 bull without blemish, six l,
46: 7 as he wants to give for the l,
46:11 as he wants to give for the l,
Am 6: 4 Eat l from the flock And
Lk 10: 3 I send you out as l among
Jn 21:15 He said to him, "Feed My l.

LAME (34/32)

Lev 21:18 not approach: a man blind or l,
Deut 15:21 if it is l or blind or has
2 Sam 4: 4 had a son who was l in his
4: 4 flee, that he fell and became l.
5: 6 but the blind and the l will
5: 8 defeats the Jebusites (the l
5: 8 The blind and the l shall not
9: 3 a son of Jonathan who is l
9:13 And he was l in both his feet.
19:26 because your servant is l.
Job 29:15 And I was feet to the l.
Prov 26: 7 Like the legs of the l that
Isa 33:23 The l take the prey.
35: 6 Then the l shall leap like a
Jer 31: 8 them the blind and the l,
Mic 4: 6 LORD, "I will assemble the l,
4: 7 I will make the l a remnant,
Zeph 3:19 afflict you; I will save the l,
Mal 1: 8 And when you offer the l and
1:13 you bring the stolen, the l,
Mt 11: 5 The blind see and the l walk;
15:30 to Him, having with them the l,
15:31 the l walking, and the blind
18: 8 for you to enter into life l
21:14 Then the blind and the l came
Mk 9:45 better for you to enter life l,
Lk 7:22 the l walk, the lepers are
14:13 the poor, the maimed, the l,
14:21 and the maimed and the l and
Jn 5: 3 of sick people, blind, l,
Acts 3: 2 And a certain man l from his
3:11 Now as the l man who was healed
8: 7 many who were paralyzed and l
Heb 12:13 so that what is l may not be

LAMECH (12/11)

Gen 4:18 and Methushael begot L.
4:19 Then L took for himself two
4:23 Then L said to his wives:
4:23 hear my voice; Wives of L,
4:24 Then L seventy-sevenfold."
5:25 eighty-seven years, and begot L.
5:26 After he begot L, Methuselah
5:28 L lived one hundred and
5:30 L lived five hundred and
5:31 So all the days of L were seven
1 Chr 1: 3 Enoch, Methuselah, L,
Lk 3:36 son of Noah, the son of L,

LAMENT (23/20) LAMENTATION, LAMENTED, LAMENTING, LAMENTS

Judg 11:40 went four days each year to l
2 Sam 3:33 And the king sang a l over
Isa 3:26 Her gates shall l and mourn,
19: 8 All those will l who cast
Jer 4: 8 L and wail. For the fierce
16: 5 nor go to l or bemoan them; for
16: 6 neither shall men l for them,
22:18 They shall not l for him,
22:18 my sister!' They shall not l
34: 5 burn incense for you and l for
49: 3 yourselves with sackcloth! L
Lam 2: 8 the rampart and wall to l;
Ezek 27:32 And l for you: 'What city
32:16 With which they shall l her;
32:16 of the nations shall l her;
32:16 They shall l for her, for
Joel 1: 8 L like a virgin girded with
1:13 Gird yourselves and l,
Mic 2: 4 And l with a bitter
Mt 11:17 to you, And you did not l.
Jn 16:20 to you that you will weep and l,
Jas 4: 9 L and mourn and weep! Let your
Rev 18: 9 with her will weep and l for

LAMENTATION (24/23) LAMENT, LAMENTATIONS

Gen 50:10 with a great and very solemn l.
2 Sam 1:17 David lamented with this l
Ps 78:64 And their widows made no l.
Jer 6:26 for an only son, most bitter l;
7:29 and take up a l on the desolate
9:10 places of the wilderness a l,
9:20 And everyone her neighbor a l.
31:15 L and bitter weeping, Rachel
48:38 A general l On all the
Lam 2: 5 has increased mourning and l
Ezek 19: 1 Moreover take up a l for the
19:14 for ruling.'" This is a l,
19:14 lamentation, and has become a l.
26:17 And they will take up a l for
27: 2 take up a l for Tyre,
27:32 for you They will take up a l,
28:12 take up a l for the king of
32: 2 take up a l for Pharaoh king of
32:16 This is the l With which they
Am 5: 1 I take up against you, a l,
8:10 And all your songs into l;
Mic 2: 4 And lament with a bitter l,
Mt 2:18 was heard in Ramah, L,
Acts 8: 2 and made great l over him.

LAMENTATIONS (2/2) LAMENTATION

2 Chr 35:25 speak of Josiah in their l.
Ezek 2:10 and written on it were l and

LAMENTED (9/9) LAMENT

1 Sam 6:19 and the people l because the
7: 2 And all the house of Israel l
25: 1 gathered together and l for
28: 3 and all Israel had l for him
2 Sam 1:17 Then David l with this
2 Chr 35:25 Jeremiah also l for Josiah. And
Jer 16: 4 they shall not be l nor shall
25:33 the earth. They shall not be l,
Lk 23:27 women who also mourned and l

LAMENTERS (1/1)

Am 5:16 And skillful l to wailing.

LAMENTING (2/2) LAMENT

Esth 9:31 matters of their fasting and l.
Dan 6:20 he cried out with a l voice to

LAMENTS (1/1) LAMENT

2 Chr 35:25 they are written in the L.

LAMP (34/34) LAMPS, LAMPSTAND

Ex 27:20 to cause the l to burn
1 Sam 3: 3 and before the l of God went out
2 Sam 21:17 lest you quench the l of
22:29 'For You are my l, O LORD;
1 Ki 11:36 David may always have a l
15: 4 the LORD his God gave him a l
2 Ki 8:19 as He promised him to give a l
2 Chr 21: 7 He had promised to give a l to
Job 12: 5 A l is despised in the thought
18: 6 And his l beside him is put
21:17 How often is the l of the
29: 3 When His l shone upon my head,
Ps 18:28 For You will light my l;
119:105 Your word is a l to my feet
132:17 I will prepare a l for My
Prov 6:23 For the commandment is a l,
13: 9 But the l of the wicked will
20:20 His l will be put out in deep
20:27 The spirit of a man is the l
24:20 The l of the wicked will be
31:18 And her l does not go out by
Isa 62: 1 And her salvation as a l that
Jer 25:10 and the light of the l.
Mt 5:15 Nor do they light a l and put it
6:22 The l of the body is the eye.
Mk 4:21 Is a l brought to be put under a
Lk 8:16 "No one, when he has lit a l,
11:33 "No one, when he has lit a l,
11:34 The l of the body is the eye.
11:36 when the bright shining of a l
15: 8 one coin, does not light a l,
Jn 5:35 was the burning and shining l,
Rev 18:23 The light of a l shall not shine
22: 5 They need no l nor light of the

LAMPS (35/29) LAMP

Ex 25:37 You shall make seven l for it,
25:37 and they shall arrange its l so
30: 7 morning; when he tends the l,
30: 8 And when Aaron lights the l at
35:14 the light, its utensils, its l,
37:23 And he made its seven l,
39:37 pure gold lampstand with its l
39:37 with its lamps (the l set in
40: 4 the lampstand and light its l.
40:25 and he lit the l before the
Lev 24: 2 to make the l burn continually.
24: 4 shall be in charge of the l
Num 4: 9 of the light, with its l,
8: 2 to him, 'When you arrange the l,
8: 2 the seven l shall give light in
8: 3 he arranged the l to face
1 Ki 7:49 with the flowers and the l and
1 Chr 28:15 and their l of gold, by weight
28:15 for each lampstand and its l;
28:15 for the lampstand and its l,
2 Chr 4:20 the lampstands with their l of
4:21 with the flowers and the l and
13:11 lampstand of gold with its l
29: 7 of the vestibule, put out the l,
Zeph 1:12 I will search Jerusalem with l,
Zech 4: 2 and on the stand seven l with
4: 2 with seven pipes to the seven l.
Mt 25: 1 to ten virgins who took their l
25: 3 who were foolish took their l
25: 4 in their vessels with their l.
25: 7 arose and trimmed their l.
25: 8 for our l are going out.'
Lk 12:35 waist be girded and your l
Acts 20: 8 There were many l in the upper
Rev 4: 5 Seven l of fire were burning

LAMPSTAND (41/34) LAMP, LAMPSTANDS

Ex 25:31 You shall also make a l of pure
25:31 the l shall be of hammered
25:32 three branches of the l out of
25:32 and three branches of the l out
25:33 branches that come out of the l.
25:34 On the l itself four bowls
25:35 branches that extend from the l.
26:35 and the l across from the table
30:27 the l and its utensils, and the
31: 8 the pure gold l with all its
35:14 also the l for the light, its
37:17 He also made the l of pure
37:17 of hammered work he made the l.
37:18 three branches of the l out of
37:18 and three branches of the l out
37:19 branches coming out of the l.
37:20 And on the l itself were four
39:37 the pure gold l with its lamps
40: 4 and you shall bring in the l
40:24 He put the l in the tabernacle
Lev 24: 4 the lamps on the pure gold l
Num 3:31 the ark, the table, the l,
4: 9 a blue cloth and cover the l
8: 2 give light in front of the l.
8: 3 face toward the front of the l,
8: 4 Now this workmanship of the l
8: 4 shown Moses, so he made the l.
2 Ki 4:10 and a table and a chair and a l;
1 Chr 28:15 by weight for each l and its
28:15 for the l and its lamps,
28:15 according to the use of each l.
2 Chr 13:11 and the l of gold with its
Dan 5: 5 and wrote opposite the l on
Zech 4: 2 and there is a l of solid gold
4:11 at the right of the l and at its
Mt 5:15 it under a basket, but on a l,
Mk 4:21 bed? Is it not to be set on a l?
Lk 8:16 a bed, but sets it on a l,
11:33 or under a basket, but on a l,
Heb 9: 2 part, in which was the l,
Rev 2: 5 you quickly and remove your l

LAMPSTANDS (12/10) LAMPSTAND

1 Ki 7:49 the l of pure gold, five on the
1 Chr 28:15 the weight for the l of gold,
28:15 for the l of silver by weight,
2 Chr 4: 7 And he made ten l of gold
4:20 the l with their lamps of pure
Jer 52:19 the bowls, the pots, the l,
Rev 1:12 turned I saw seven golden l,

1:13 and in the midst of the seven *l*
1:20 hand, and the seven golden *l*:
1:20 and the seven *l* which you saw
2: 1 the midst of the seven golden *l*:
11: 4 two olive trees and the two *l*

LANCE (1/1)

Jer 50:42 shall hold the bow and the *l*;

LANCES (1/1)

1 Ki 18:28 their custom, with knives and *l*,

LANCETS (KJV) See LANCES

LAND (1745/1511) LANDMARK, LANDOWNER, LANDS

Gen 1: 9 and let the dry *l* appear";
1:10 And God called the dry *l* Earth,
2:11 one which skirts the whole *l*
2:12 And the gold of that *l* is good.
2:13 which goes around the whole *l*
4:16 of the LORD and dwelt in the *l*
7:22 all that was on the dry *l*,
10:10 Calneh, in the *l* of Shinar.
10:11 From that *l* he went to Assyria
11: 2 they found a plain in the *l* of
11:28 father Terah in his native *l*,
11:31 of the Chaldeans to go to the *l*
12: 1 To a *l* that I will show you.
12: 5 they departed to go to the *l*
12: 5 So they came to the *l* of
12: 6 Abram passed through the *l* to
12: 6 Canaanites were then in the *l*.
12: 7 descendants I will give this *l*.
12:10 there was a famine in the *l*,
12:10 the famine was severe in the *l*.
13: 6 Now the *l* was not able to
13: 7 Perizzites then dwelt in the *l*.
13: 9 Is not the whole *l* before you?
13:10 like the *l* of Egypt as you go
13:12 Abram dwelt in the *l* of Canaan,
13:15 for all the *l* which you see I
13:17 walk in the *l* through its
15: 7 to give you this *l* to inherit
15:13 will be strangers in a *l* that
15:18 descendants I have given this *l*,
16: 3 had dwelt ten years in the *l*
17: 8 descendants after you the *l* in
17: 8 all the *l* of Canaan, as an
19:28 and toward all the *l* of the
19:28 the smoke of the *l* which went
20:15 my *l* is before you; dwell
21:21 took a wife for him from the *l*
21:23 you will do to me and to the *l*
21:32 and they returned to the *l* of
21:34 And Abraham stayed in the *l* of
22: 2 and go to the *l* of Moriah, and
23: 2 Hebron) in the *l* of Canaan, and
23: 7 himself to the people of the *l*,
23:12 down before the people of the *l*;
23:13 hearing of the people of the *l*,
23:15 the *l* is worth four hundred
23:19 Hebron) in the *l* of Canaan.
24: 5 willing to follow me to this *l*.
24: 5 I take your son back to the *l*
24: 7 father's house and from the *l*
24: 7 your descendants I give this *l*,
24:37 in whose *l* I dwell;
26: 1 There was a famine in the *l*,
26: 2 live in the *l* of which I shall
26: 3 'Dwell in this *l*, and I will
26:12 Then Isaac sowed in that *l*,
26:22 we shall be fruitful in the *l*.
27:46 are the daughters of the *l*,
28: 4 That you may inherit the *l* In
28:13 the *l* on which you lie I will
28:15 will bring you back to this *l*;
29: 1 his journey and came to the *l*
31: 3 Return to the *l* of your fathers
31:13 Now arise, get out of this *l*,
31:13 and return to the *l* of your
31:18 go to his father Isaac in the *l*
32: 3 to Esau his brother in the *l*
33:18 which is in the *l* of Canaan,
33:19 And he bought the parcel of *l*,
34: 1 to see the daughters of the *l*.
34:10 and the *l* shall be before you.
34:21 let them dwell in the *l* and
34:21 For indeed the *l* is large
34:30 among the inhabitants of the *l*,
35: 6 which is in the *l* of Canaan,
35:12 The *l* which I gave Abraham and
35:12 after you I give this *l*.
35:22 when Israel dwelt in that *l*,
36: 5 who were born to him in the *l*
36: 6 which he had gained in the *l*
36: 7 and the *l* where they were
36:16 the chiefs of Eliphaz in the *l*
36:17 the chiefs of Reuel in the *l*
36:20 the Horite who inhabited the *l*:
36:21 of Seir, in the *l* of Edom.
36:30 to their chiefs in the *l* of
36:31 the kings who reigned in the *l*
36:34 Husham of the *l* of the
36:43 their dwelling places in the *l*
37: 1 Now Jacob dwelt in the *l* where
37: 1 stranger, in the *l* of Canaan.
40:15 I was stolen away from the *l*
41:19 I have never seen in all the *l*
41:29 will come throughout all the *l*
41:30 will be forgotten in the *l* of
41:30 the famine will deplete the *l*.
41:31 will not be known in the *l*
41:33 and set him over the *l* of
41:34 him appoint officers over the *l*,
41:34 of the produce of the *l* of
41:36 be as a reserve for the *l* for
41:36 famine which shall be in the *l*
41:36 that the *l* may not perish
41:41 I have set you over all the *l*
41:43 So he set him over all the *l*
41:44 his hand or foot in all the *l*
41:45 went out over all the *l* of
41:46 and went throughout all the *l*
41:48 years which were in the *l* of
41:52 me to be fruitful in the *l* of
41:53 of plenty which were in the *l*
41:54 but in all the *l* of Egypt there
41:55 So when all the *l* of Egypt was
41:56 famine became severe in the *l*
42: 5 for the famine was in the *l* of
42: 6 Joseph was governor over the *l*;
42: 6 sold to all the people of the *l*.
42: 7 From the *l* of Canaan to buy
42: 9 to see the nakedness of the *l*!
42:12 to see the nakedness of the *l*.
42:13 the sons of one man in the *l* of
42:29 to Jacob their father in the *l*
42:30 man who is lord of the *l*
42:32 our father this day in the *l*
42:34 you, and you may trade in the *l*.
43: 1 the famine was severe in the *l*.
43:11 of the best fruits of the *l* in
44: 8 brought back to you from the *l*
45: 6 the famine has been in the *l*,
45: 8 a ruler throughout all the *l*
45:10 You shall dwell in the *l* of
45:17 go to the *l* of Canaan.
45:18 give you the best of the *l* of
45:18 you will eat the fat of the *l*.
45:19 Take carts out of the *l* of
45:20 for the best of all the *l* of
45:25 and came to the *l* of Canaan to
45:26 he is governor over all the *l*
46: 6 they had acquired in the *l* of
46:12 (but Er and Onan died in the *l*
46:20 And to Joseph in the *l* of Egypt
46:28 And they came to the *l* of
46:31 who were in the *l* of Canaan,
46:34 that you may dwell in the *l* of
47: 1 have come from the *l* of Canaan;
47: 1 and indeed they are in the *l*
47: 4 have come to dwell in the *l*,
47: 4 the famine is severe in the *l*
47: 4 your servants dwell in the *l*
47: 6 The *l* of Egypt is before you.
47: 6 dwell in the best of the *l*;
47: 6 let them dwell in the *l*
47:11 them a possession in the *l* of
47:11 of Egypt, in the best of the *l*,
47:11 in the *l* of Rameses, as Pharaoh
47:13 was no bread in all the *l*;
47:13 so that the *l* of Egypt and the
47:13 the land of Egypt and the *l* of
47:14 money that was found in the *l*
47:14 the land of Egypt and in the *l*
47:15 when the money failed in the *l*
47:15 the land of Egypt and in the *l*
47:19 your eyes, both we and our *l*?
47:19 Buy us and our *l* for bread, and
47:19 and we and our *l* will be
47:19 that the *l* may not be
47:20 Then Joseph bought all the *l* of
47:20 So the *l* became Pharaoh's.
47:22 Only the *l* of the priests he did
47:23 I have bought you and your *l*
47:23 you, and you shall sow the *l*.
47:26 made it a law over the *l* of
47:26 except for the *l* of the priests
47:27 So Israel dwelt in the *l* of
47:28 And Jacob lived in the *l* of
48: 3 appeared to me at Luz in the *l*
48: 4 and give this *l* to your
48: 5 who were born to you in the *l*
48: 7 Rachel died beside me in the *l*
48:21 and bring you back to the *l* of
49:15 And that the *l* was pleasant;
49:30 is before Mamre in the *l* of
50: 5 I dug for myself in the *l* of
50: 7 and all the elders of the *l* of
50: 8 their herds they left in the *l*
50:11 when the inhabitants of the *l*,
50:13 his sons carried him to the *l*
50:24 and bring you out of this *l* to
50:24 you out of this land to the *l*

Ex 1: 7 and the *l* was filled with them.
1:10 us, and so go up out of the *l*.
2:15 of Pharaoh and dwelt in the *l*
2:22 been a stranger in a foreign *l*.
3: 8 to bring them up from that *l*
3: 8 that land to a good and large *l*,
3: 8 to a *l* flowing with milk and
3:17 affliction of Egypt to the *l*
3:17 to a *l* flowing with milk and
4: 9 and pour it on the dry *l*.
4: 9 will become blood on the dry *l*.
4:20 and he returned to the *l* of
5: 5 the people of the *l* are many
5:12 abroad throughout all the *l* of
6: 1 he will drive them out of his *l*.
6: 4 to give them the *l* of Canaan,
6: 4 the *l* of their pilgrimage, in
6: 8 I will bring you into the *l*
6:11 of Israel go out of his *l*.
6:13 of Israel out of the *l* of
6:26 children of Israel from the *l*
6:28 LORD spoke to Moses in the *l*
7: 2 children of Israel out of his *l*.
7: 3 signs and My wonders in the *l*
7: 4 out of the *l* of Egypt by great
7:19 be blood throughout all the *l*
7:21 was blood throughout all the *l*
8: 5 frogs to come up on the *l* of
8: 6 came up and covered the *l* of
8: 7 and brought up frogs on the *l*
8:14 in heaps, and the *l* stank.
8:16 and strike the dust of the *l*,
8:16 lice throughout all the *l* of
8:17 All the dust of the *l* became
8:17 lice throughout all the *l* of
8:22 day I will set apart the *l* of
8:22 the LORD in the midst of the *l*.
8:24 and into all the *l* of Egypt.
8:24 The *l* was corrupted because of
8:25 sacrifice to your God in the *l*.
9: 5 will do this thing in the *l*.
9: 9 become fine dust in all the *l*
9: 9 and beast throughout all the *l*
9:22 there may be hail in all the *l*
9:22 throughout the *l* of Egypt."
9:23 the LORD rained hail on the *l*
9:24 was none like it in all the *l*
9:25 struck throughout the whole *l*
9:26 Only in the *l* of Goshen, where
10:12 out your hand over the *l* of
10:12 that they may come upon the *l*
10:12 and eat every herb of the *l*—
10:13 out his rod over the *l* of
10:13 brought an east wind on the *l*
10:14 locusts went up over all the *l*
10:15 so that the *l* was darkened; and
10:15 they ate every herb of the *l*
10:15 the field throughout all the *l*
10:21 may be darkness over the *l* of
10:22 thick darkness in all the *l* of
11: 3 Moses was very great in the *l*
11: 5 'and all the firstborn in the *l*
11: 6 great cry throughout all the *l*
11: 9 may be multiplied in the *l* of
11:10 of Israel go out of his *l*.
12: 1 to Moses and Aaron in the *l* of
12:12 For I will pass through the *l* of
12:12 all the firstborn in the *l* of
12:13 you when I strike the *l* of
12:17 your armies out of the *l* of
12:19 a stranger or a native of the *l*.
12:25 to pass when you come to the *l*
12:29 all the firstborn in the *l* of
12:33 might send them out of the *l*
12:41 the LORD went out from the *l*
12:42 for bringing them out of the *l*
12:48 shall be as a native of the *l*.
12:51 of Israel out of the *l* of
13: 5 LORD brings you into the *l* of
13: 5 a *l* flowing with milk and
13:11 LORD brings you into the *l* of
13:15 all the firstborn in the *l* of
13:17 not lead them by way of the *l*
13:18 in orderly ranks out of the *l*
14: 3 'They are bewildered by the *l*;
14:21 and made the sea into dry *l*,
14:29 of Israel had walked on dry *l*
15:19 of Israel went on dry *l* in
16: 1 after they departed from the *l*
16: 3 the hand of the LORD in the *l*
16: 6 has brought you out of the *l*
16:32 I brought you out of the *l* of
16:35 they came to an inhabited *l*;
16:35 came to the border of the *l* of
18: 3 been a stranger in a foreign *l*'
18:27 he went his way to his own *l*.
19: 1 of Israel had gone out of the *l*
20: 2 who brought you out of the *l* of
20:12 days may be long upon the *l*
22:21 you were strangers in the *l* of
23: 9 you were strangers in the *l* of
23:10 years you shall sow your *l* and
23:19 of the firstfruits of your *l*
23:26 or be barren in your *l*;
23:29 lest the *l* become desolate and
23:30 and you inherit the *l*.
23:31 the inhabitants of the *l* into
23:33 shall not dwell in your *l*,
29:46 brought them up out of the *l*
32: 1 who brought us up out of the *l*
32: 4 that brought you out of the *l*
32: 7 whom you brought out of the *l*
32: 8 that brought you out of the *l*
32:11 You have brought out of the *l*
32:13 and all this *l* that I have
32:23 who brought us out of the *l* of
33: 1 you have brought out of the *l*
33: 1 to the *l* of which I swore to
33: 3 Go up to a *l* flowing with milk
34:12 with the inhabitants of the *l*
34:15 with the inhabitants of the *l*,
34:24 will any man covet your *l* when
34:26 of the firstfruits of your *l*

Lev 11:45 who brings you up out of the *l*
14:34 When you have come into the *l* of
14:34 plague in a house in the *l* of
16:22 iniquities to an uninhabited *l*;
18: 3 to the doings of the *l* of

18: 3 to the doings of the *l* of
18:25 For the *l* is defiled; therefore
18:25 and the *l* vomits out its
18:27 abominations the men of the *l*
18:27 and thus the *l* is defiled),
18:28 lest the *l* vomit you out also
19: 9 you reap the harvest of your *l*,
19:23 'When you come into the *l*,
19:29 lest the *l* fall into harlotry,
19:29 and the *l* become full of
19:33 dwells with you in your *l*,
19:34 you were strangers in the *l* of
19:36 who brought you out of the *l* of
20: 2 The people of the *l* shall stone
20: 4 And if the people of the *l*
20:22 that the *l* where I am bringing
20:24 "You shall inherit their *l*,
20:24 a *l* flowing with milk and
22:24 offering of them in your *l*.
22:33 who brought you out of the *l* of
23:10 When you come into the *l* which I
23:22 you reap the harvest of your *l*,
23:39 gathered in the fruit of the *l*,
23:43 I brought them out of the *l* of
24:16 as him who is born in the *l*.
25: 2 When you come into the *l* which I
25: 2 then the *l* shall keep a sabbath
25: 4 of solemn rest for the *l*,
25: 5 it is a year of rest for the *l*.
25: 6 the sabbath produce of the *l*
25: 7 the beasts that are in your *l*—
25: 9 to sound throughout all your *l*.
25:10 liberty throughout all the *l*
25:18 and you will dwell in the *l* in
25:19 Then the *l* will yield its fruit,
25:23 The *l* shall not be sold
25:23 for the *l* is Mine; for you
25:24 And in all the *l* of your
25:24 shall grant redemption of the *l*.
25:38 who brought you out of the *l* of
25:38 to give you the *l* of Canaan
25:42 whom I brought out of the *l* of
25:45 you, which they beget in your *l*;
25:55 whom I brought out of the *l* of
26: 1 up an engraved stone in your *l*,
26: 4 the *l* shall yield its produce,
26: 5 and dwell in your *l* safely.
26: 6 I will give peace in the *l*,
26: 6 I will rid the *l* of evil
26: 6 will not go through your *l*.
26:13 who brought you out of the *l* of
26:20 for your *l* shall not yield its
26:20 nor shall the trees of the *l*
26:32 I will bring the *l* to
26:33 your *l* shall be desolate and
26:34 Then the *l* shall enjoy its
26:34 and you are in your enemies' *l*;
26:34 then the *l* shall rest and enjoy
26:38 and the *l* of your enemies shall
26:41 have brought them into the *l*
26:42 remember; I will remember the *l*.
26:43 The *l* also shall be left empty
26:44 when they are in the *l* of their
26:45 whom I brought out of the *l* of
27:24 to the one who owned the *l* as
27:30 'And all the tithe of the *l*,
27:30 whether of the seed of the *l*
Num 1: 1 they had come out of the *l* of
3:13 all the firstborn in the *l* of
8:17 all the firstborn in the *l* of
9: 1 they had come out of the *l* of
9:14 and the native of the *l*.
10: 9 When you go to war in your *l*
10:30 but I will depart to my own *l*
11:12 to the *l* which You swore to
13: 2 Send men to spy out the *l* of
13:16 Moses sent to spy out the *l*.
13:17 sent them to spy out the *l* of
13:18 and see what the *l* is like:
13:19 whether the *l* they dwell in is
13:20 whether the *l* is rich or poor;
13:20 some of the fruit of the *l*.
13:21 went up and spied out the *l*
13:25 returned from spying out the *l*
13:26 showed them the fruit of the *l*.
13:27 We went to the *l* where you sent
13:28 the people who dwell in the *l*
13:29 The Amalekites dwell in the *l* of
13:32 of Israel a bad report of the *l*
13:32 The *l* through which we have gone
13:32 we have gone as spies is a *l*
14: 2 If only we had died in the *l* of
14: 3 the LORD brought us to this *l*
14: 6 those who had spied out the *l*,
14: 7 The *l* we passed through to spy
14: 7 out is an exceedingly good *l*.
14: 8 He will bring us into this *l*
14: 8 a *l* which flows with milk and
14: 9 nor fear the people of the *l*,
14:14 to the inhabitants of this *l*.
14:16 to bring this people to the *l*
14:23 certainly shall not see the *l*
14:24 I will bring into the *l* where
14:30 shall by no means enter the *l*
14:31 and they shall know the *l* which
14:34 in which you spied out the *l*,
14:36 Moses sent to spy out the *l*,
14:36 bringing a bad report of the *l*,
14:37 the evil report about the *l*,
14:38 men who went to spy out the *l*.
15: 2 When you have come into the *l*
15:18 When you come into the *l* to
15:19 you eat of the bread of the *l*,
15:41 who brought you out of the *l* of
16:13 have brought us up out of a *l*
16:14 have not brought us into a *l*
18:13 first ripe fruit is in their *l*,
18:20 have no inheritance in their *l*,
20:12 bring this assembly into the *l*
20:18 shall not pass through my *l*,
20:23 Hor by the border of the *l* of
20:24 for he shall not enter the *l*
21: 4 to go around the *l* of Edom; and
21:22 "Let me pass through your *l*.
21:24 and took possession of his *l*
21:26 and had taken all his *l* from
21:31 Thus Israel dwelt in the *l* of
21:34 with all his people and his *l*;
21:35 they took possession of his *l*.
22: 5 is near the River in the *l* of
22: 6 and drive them out of the *l*,
22:13 of Balak, "Go back to your *l*,
26: 4 of Israel who came out of the *l*
26:19 and Er and Onan died in the *l*
26:53 To these the *l* shall be divided
26:55 But the *l* shall be divided by
27:12 and see the *l* which I have
32: 1 and when they saw the *l* of
32: 1 the land of Jazer and the *l* of
32: 4 is a *l* for livestock, and your
32: 5 let this *l* be given to your
32: 7 from going over into the *l*
32: 8 from Kadesh Barnea to see the *l*.
32: 9 Valley of Eshcol and saw the *l*,
32: 9 that they did not go into the *l*
32:11 shall see the *l* of which I
32:17 of the inhabitants of the *l*.
32:22 and the *l* is subdued before the
32:22 and this *l* shall be your
32:29 and the *l* is subdued before
32:29 then you shall give them the *l*
32:30 possessions among you in the *l*
32:32 before the LORD into the *l* of
32:33 the *l* with its cities within
33: 1 who went out of the *l* of Egypt
33:37 on the boundary of the *l* of
33:38 of Israel had come out of the *l*
33:40 dwelt in the South in the *l* of
33:51 crossed the Jordan into the *l*
33:52 all the inhabitants of the *l*
33:53 the inhabitants of the *l*
33:53 for I have given you the *l* to
33:54 And you shall divide the *l* by
33:55 out the inhabitants of the *l*
33:55 they shall harass you in the *l*
34: 2 When you come into the *l* of
34: 2 this is the *l* that shall fall
34: 2 the *l* of Canaan to its
34:12 This shall be your *l* with its
34:13 This is the *l* which you shall
34:17 the men who shall divide the *l*
34:18 of every tribe to divide the *l*
34:29 children of Israel in the *l* of
35:10 cross the Jordan into the *l* of
35:14 you shall appoint in the *l* of
35:28 manslayer may return to the *l*
35:32 he may return to dwell in the *l*
35:33 'So you shall not pollute the *l*
35:33 are; for blood defiles the *l*,
35:33 atonement can be made for the *l*,
35:34 Therefore do not defile the *l*
36: 2 my lord Moses to give the *l*
Deut 1: 5 side of the Jordan in the *l* of
1: 7 to the *l* of the Canaanites and
1: 8 I have set the *l* before you; go
1: 8 go in and possess the *l* which
1:21 LORD your God has set the *l*
1:22 and let them search out the *l*
1:25 some of the fruit of the *l* in
1:25 It is a good *l* which the LORD
1:27 He has brought us out of the *l*
1:35 shall see that good *l* of which
1:36 his children I am giving the *l*
2: 5 not give you any of their *l*,
2: 9 not give you any of their *l*
2:12 just as Israel did to the *l* of
2:19 not give you any of the *l* of
2:20 (That was also regarded as a *l*
2:24 king of Heshbon, and his *l*.
2:27 'Let me pass through your *l*;
2:29 I cross the Jordan to the *l*
2:31 begun to give Sihon and his *l*
2:31 it, that you may inherit his *l*.
2:37 you did not go near the *l* of
3: 2 and all his people and his *l*
3: 8 at that time we took the *l*
3:12 And this *l*, which we
3:13 was called the *l* of the giants.
3:18 your God has given you this *l*
3:20 and they also possess the *l*
3:25 cross over and see the good *l*
3:28 cause them to inherit the *l*
4: 1 and go in and possess the *l*
4: 5 according to them in the *l*
4:14 you might observe them in the *l*
4:21 I would not enter the good *l*
4:22 "But I must die in this *l*,
4:22 over and possess that good *l*.
4:25 and have grown old in the *l*,
4:26 soon utterly perish from the *l*
4:38 to give you their *l* as an
4:40 may prolong your days in the *l*
4:46 in the *l* of Sihon king of the
4:47 they took possession of his *l*
4:47 of his land and the *l* of Og
5: 6 who brought you out of the *l*
5:15 that you were a slave in the *l*
5:16 may be well with you in the *l*
5:31 they may observe them in the *l*
5:33 may prolong your days in the *l*
6: 1 you may observe them in the *l*
6: 3 a *l* flowing with milk and
6:10 your God brings you into the *l*
6:12 who brought you out of the *l*
6:18 go in and possess the good *l*
6:23 to give us the *l* of which He
7: 1 your God brings you into the *l*
7:13 womb and the fruit of your *l*,
7:13 in the *l* of which He swore to
8: 1 and go in and possess the *l* of
8: 7 is bringing you into a good *l*,
8: 7 a *l* of brooks of water, of
8: 8 a *l* of wheat and barley, of
8: 8 a *l* of olive oil and honey;
8: 9 a *l* in which you will eat bread
8: 9 a *l* whose stones are iron and
8:10 LORD your God for the good *l*
8:14 who brought you out of the *l*
8:15 and scorpions and thirsty *l*
9: 4 me in to possess this *l*';
9: 5 you go in to possess their *l*,
9: 6 is not giving you this good *l*
9: 7 that you departed from the *l*
9:23 Go up and possess the *l* which I
9:28 lest the *l* from which You
9:28 not able to bring them to the *l*
10: 7 a *l* of rivers of water.
10:11 may go in and possess the *l*
10:19 you were strangers in the *l* of
11: 3 king of Egypt, and to all his *l*;
11: 8 and go in and possess the *l*
11: 9 may prolong your days in the *l*
11: 9 a *l* flowing with milk and
11:10 For the *l* which you go to
11:10 to possess is not like the *l*
11:11 but the *l* which you cross over
11:11 cross over to possess is a *l*
11:12 a *l* for which the LORD your God
11:14 give you the rain for your *l*
11:17 and the *l* yield no produce, and
11:17 perish quickly from the good *l*
11:21 may be multiplied in the *l* of
11:25 the fear of you upon all the *l*
11:29 God has brought you into the *l*
11:30 in the *l* of the Canaanites who
11:31 and go in to possess the *l*
12: 1 be careful to observe in the *l*
12:10 the Jordan and dwell in the *l*
12:19 as long as you live in your *l*.
12:29 them and dwell in their *l*,
13: 5 who brought you out of the *l* of
13:10 who brought you out of the *l* of
15: 4 will greatly bless you in the *l*
15: 7 any of the gates in your *l*
15:11 will never cease from the *l*;
15:11 poor and your needy, in your *l*.
15:15 that you were a slave in the *l*
16: 3 (for you came out of the *l* of
16: 3 in which you came out of the *l*
16:20 you may live and inherit the *l*
17:14 When you come to the *l* which
18: 9 When you come into the *l* which
19: 1 has cut off the nations whose *l*
19: 2 in the midst of your *l* which
19: 3 parts the territory of your *l*
19: 8 and gives you the *l* which He
19:10 be shed in the midst of your *l*
19:14 you will inherit in the *l* that
20: 1 who brought you up from the *l*
21: 1 lying in the field in the *l*
21:23 so that you do not defile the *l*
23: 7 you were an alien in his *l*.
23:20 you set your hand in the *l*
24: 4 shall not bring sin on the *l*
24:14 of the aliens who is in your *l*
24:22 that you were a slave in the *l*
25:15 days may be lengthened in the *l*
25:19 in the *l* which the LORD your
26: 1 when you come into the *l* which
26: 2 you shall bring from your *l*
26: 9 place and has given us this *l*,
26: 9 a *l* flowing with milk and
26:10 the firstfruits of the *l* which
26:15 Your people Israel and the *l*
26:15 a *l* flowing with milk and
27: 2 cross over the Jordan to the *l*
27: 3 that you may enter the *l* which
27: 3 a *l* flowing with milk and
28: 8 and He will bless you in the *l*
28:11 in the *l* of which the LORD
28:12 to give the rain to your *l* in
28:18 body and the produce of your *l*,
28:21 He has consumed you from the *l*
28:24 will change the rain of your *l*
28:33 shall eat the fruit of your *l*
28:42 trees and the produce of your *l*.
28:51 and the produce of your *l*,
28:52 come down throughout all your *l*;
28:52 gates throughout all your *l*
28:63 shall be plucked from off the *l*
29: 1 children of Israel in the *l* of
29: 2 did before your eyes in the *l*
29: 2 his servants and to all his *l*—
29: 8 We took their *l* and gave it as
29:16 know that we dwell in the *l* of
29:22 who comes from a far *l*,

L

29:22 they see the plagues of that *l*
29:23 The whole *l* is brimstone, salt,
29:24 has the LORD done so to this *l*?
29:25 He brought them out of the *l*
29:27 was aroused against this *l*,
29:28 uprooted them from their *l* in
29:28 and cast them into another *l*,
30: 5 God will bring you to the *l*
30: 9 and in the produce of your *l*
30:16 God will bless you in the *l*
30:18 not prolong your days in the *l*
30:20 and that you may dwell in the *l*
31: 4 of the Amorites and their *l*,
31: 7 go with this people to the *l*
31:13 as long as you live in the *l*
31:16 gods of the foreigners of the *l*,
31:20 I have brought them to the *l*
31:21 I have brought them to the *l*
31:23 children of Israel into the *l*
32:10 He found him in a desert *l* And
32:43 provide atonement for His *l*
32:47 prolong your days in the *l*
32:49 which is in the *l* of Moab,
32:49 view the *l* of Canaan, which I
32:52 Yet you shall see the *l* before
32:52 into the *l* which I am giving to
33:13 of the LORD is his *l*,
33:28 In a *l* of grain and new wine;
34: 1 the LORD showed him all the *l*
34: 2 all Naphtali and the *l* of
34: 2 all the *l* of Judah as far as
34: 4 This is the *l* of which I swore
34: 5 the LORD died there in the *l*
34: 6 him in a valley in the *l* of
34:11 LORD sent him to do in the *l*
34:11 his servants, and in all his *l*,
Josh 1: 2 to the *l* which I am giving to
1: 4 all the *l* of the Hittites, and
1: 6 divide as an inheritance the *l*
1:11 to go in to possess the *l* which
1:13 rest and is giving you this *l*.
1:14 shall remain in the *l* which
1:15 have taken possession of the *l*
1:15 Then you shall return to the *l*
2: 1 saying, "Go, view the *l*,
2: 9 the LORD has given you the *l*,
2: 9 all the inhabitants of the *l*
2:14 the LORD has given us the *l*,
2:18 when we come into the *l*,
2:24 LORD has delivered all the *l*
4:18 priests' feet touched the dry *l*,
4:22 over this Jordan on dry *l*';
5: 6 He would not show them the *l*
5: 6 a *l* flowing with milk and
5:11 ate of the produce of the *l* on
5:12 had eaten the produce of the *l*;
5:12 but they ate the food of the *l*
7: 9 all the inhabitants of the *l*
8: 1 his people, his city, and his *l*.
9:24 Moses to give you all the *l*,
9:24 all the inhabitants of the *l*
10:40 So Joshua conquered all the *l*:
10:42 All these kings and their *l*
11: 3 Hivite below Hermon in the *l*
11:16 Thus Joshua took all this *l*:
11:16 all the *l* of Goshen, the
11:22 the Anakim were left in the *l*
11:23 So Joshua took the whole *l*,
11:23 Then the *l* rested from war.
12: 1 These are the kings of the *l*
12: 1 and whose *l* they possessed on
13: 1 and there remains very much *l*
13: 2 This is the *l* that yet remains:
13: 4 all the *l* of the Canaanites,
13: 5 the *l* of the Gebalites, and all
13: 7 divide this *l* as an inheritance
13:25 and half the *l* of the Ammonites
14: 1 of Israel inherited in the *l*
14: 4 no part to the Levites in the *l*,
14: 5 did; and they divided the *l*.
14: 7 Kadesh Barnea to spy out the *l*,
14: 9 Surely the *l* where your foot has
14:15 Then the *l* had rest from war.
15:19 since you have given me *l* in
17: 5 besides the *l* of Gilead and
17: 6 of Manasseh's sons had the *l*
17: 8 Manasseh had the *l* of Tappuah,
17:12 determined to dwell in that *l*.
17:15 for yourself there in the *l* of
17:16 Canaanites who dwell in the *l*
18: 1 And the *l* was subdued before
18: 3 to go and possess the *l* which
18: 4 shall rise and go through the *l*,
18: 6 shall therefore survey the *l*
18: 8 those who went to survey the *l*,
18: 8 "Go, walk through the *l*,
18: 9 men went, passed through the *l*,
18:10 and there Joshua divided the *l*
19:49 made an end of dividing the *l*
21: 2 to them at Shiloh in the *l* of
21:43 LORD gave to Israel all the *l*
22: 4 go to your tents and to the *l*
22: 9 which is in the *l* of Canaan,
22: 9 to the *l* of their possession,
22:10 the Jordan which is in the *l*
22:11 altar on the frontier of the *l*
22:13 into the *l* of Gilead,
22:15 to the *l* of Gilead, and they
22:19 if the *l* of your possession is
22:19 then cross over to the *l* of
22:32 from the *l* of Gilead to the
22:32 the land of Gilead to the *l* of
22:33 to destroy the *l* where the
23: 5 So you shall possess their *l*,
23:13 you perish from this good *l*
23:15 destroyed you from this good *l*
23:16 perish quickly from the good *l*
24: 3 led him throughout all the *l* of
24: 8 And I brought you into the *l* of
24: 8 that you might possess their *l*,
24:13 I have given you a *l* for which
24:15 in whose *l* you dwell. But as
24:17 our fathers up out of the *l* of
24:18 the Amorites who dwelt in the *l*.
Judg 1: 2 Indeed I have delivered the *l*
1:15 since you have given me *l* in
1:26 And the man went to the *l* of the
1:27 determined to dwell in that *l*.
1:32 the inhabitants of the *l*;
1:33 the inhabitants of the *l*.
2: 1 Egypt and brought you to the *l*
2: 2 with the inhabitants of this *l*;
2: 6 inheritance to possess the *l*.
2:12 had brought them out of the *l*
3:11 So the *l* had rest for forty
3:30 And the *l* had rest for eighty
5:31 So the *l* had rest for forty
6: 5 and they would enter the *l* to
6: 9 before you and gave you their *l*.
6:10 in whose *l* you dwell." But you
9:37 down from the center of the *l*,
10: 4 which are in the *l* of Gilead.
10: 8 side of the Jordan in the *l* of
11: 3 brothers and dwelt in the *l* of
11: 5 to get Jephthah from the *l* of
11:12 to fight against me in my *l*?
11:13 Because Israel took away my *l*
11:15 'Israel did not take away the *l*
11:15 nor the *l* of the people of
11:17 let me pass through your *l*.
11:18 wilderness and bypassed the *l*
11:18 the land of Edom and the *l* of
11:18 came to the east side of the *l*
11:19 let us pass through your *l*
11:21 gained possession of all the *l*
12:15 buried in Pirathon in the *l* of
16:24 enemy, The destroyer of our *l*,
18: 2 to spy out the *l* and search it.
18: 2 to them, "Go, search the *l*.
18: 7 were no rulers in the *l* who
18: 9 them. For we have seen the *l*,
18: 9 go, and enter to possess the *l*.
18:10 a secure people and a large *l*.
18:17 who had gone to spy out the *l*
18:30 day of the captivity of the *l*.
19:30 of Israel came up from the *l*
20: 1 as well as from the *l* of
21:12 which is in the *l* of Canaan.
21:21 then go to the *l* of Benjamin.
Ruth 1: 1 there was a famine in the *l*.
1: 7 on the way to return to the *l*
2:11 and your mother and the *l* of
4: 3 sold the piece of *l* which
1 Sam 6: 5 of your rats that ravage the *l*,
6: 5 from your gods, and from your *l*.
9: 4 of Ephraim and through the *l*
9: 4 Then they passed through the *l*
9: 4 Then he passed through the *l* of
9: 5 When they had come to the *l* of
9:16 will send you a man from the *l*
12: 6 your fathers up from the *l* of
13: 3 trumpet throughout all the *l*,
13: 7 over the Jordan to the *l* of
13:17 Ophrah, to the *l* of Shual,
13:19 be found throughout all the *l*
14:14 within about half an acre of *l*.
14:25 Now all the people of the *l*
14:29 "My father has troubled the *l*.
21:11 not David the king of the *l*?
22: 5 and go to the *l* of Judah." So
23:23 it shall be, if he is in the *l*,
23:27 Philistines have invaded the *l*!
27: 1 speedily escape to the *l* of
27: 8 were the inhabitants of the *l*
27: 8 even as far as the *l* of Egypt.
27: 9 Whenever David attacked the *l*,
28: 3 and the spiritists out of the *l*.
28: 9 and the spiritists from the *l*.
29:11 to return to the *l* of the
30:16 were, spread out over all the *l*,
30:16 they had taken from the *l* of
30:16 the Philistines and from the *l*
31: 9 sent word throughout the *l* of
2 Sam 3:12 saying, "Whose is the *l*?
5: 6 the inhabitants of the *l*,
7:23 and awesome deeds for Your *l*—
9: 7 will restore to you all the *l*
9:10 shall work the *l* for him, and
10: 2 servants came into the *l* of
15: 4 that I were made judge in the *l*,
17:26 and Absalom encamped in the *l*
19: 9 and now he has fled from the *l*
19:29 'You and Ziba divide the *l*.
21:14 God heeded the prayer for the *l*.
24: 6 came to Gilead and to the *l* of
24: 8 they had gone through all the *l*,
24:13 of famine come to you in your *l*?
24:13 be three days' plague in your *l*?
24:25 heeded the prayers for the *l*,
1 Ki 4:10 belonged Sochoh and all the *l*
4:19 in the *l* of Gilead, in the
4:19 only governor who was in the *l*.
4:21 from the River to the *l* of
6: 1 of Israel had come out of the *l*
8: 9 when they came out of the *l* of
8:21 He brought them out of the *l*
8:34 and bring them back to the *l*
8:36 and send rain on Your *l* which
8:37 there is famine in the *l*,
8:37 enemy besieges them in the *l*
8:40 days that they live in the *l*
8:46 take them captive to the *l* of
8:47 come to themselves in the *l*
8:47 supplication to You in the *l*
8:48 with all their soul in the *l*
8:48 and pray to You toward their *l*
9: 7 will cut off Israel from the *l*
9: 8 the LORD done thus to this *l*
9: 9 their fathers out of the *l* of
9:11 Hiram twenty cities in the *l*
9:13 And he called them the *l* of
9:18 in the *l* of Judah,
9:19 and in all the *l* of his
9:21 who were left in the *l* after
9:26 Red Sea, in the *l* of Edom.
10: 6 which I heard in my own *l*
11:18 food for him, and gave him *l*.
12:28 brought you up from the *l* of
14:15 uproot Israel from this good *l*
14:24 also perverted persons in the *l*.
15:12 perverted persons from the *l*,
15:20 with all the *l* of Naphtali.
17: 7 there had been no rain in the *l*.
18: 5 Go into the *l* to all the springs
18: 6 So they divided the *l* between
20: 7 called all the elders of the *l*,
22:46 Asa, he banished from the *l*.
2 Ki 3:19 and ruin every good piece of *l*
3:20 and the *l* was filled with
3:24 them; and they entered their *l*,
3:25 stone on every good piece of *l*
3:27 and returned to their own *l*.
4:38 there was a famine in the *l*.
5: 2 a young girl from the *l* of
5: 4 the girl who is from the *l* of
6:23 came no more into the *l* of
8: 1 it will come upon the *l* for
8: 2 household and dwelt in the *l*
8: 3 the woman returned from the *l*
8: 3 for her house and for her *l*.
8: 5 for her house and for her *l*.
8: 6 the day that she left the *l*
10:33 all the *l* of Gilead—Gad,
11: 3 Athaliah reigned over the *l*.
11:14 All the people of the *l* were
11:18 And all the people of the *l* went
11:19 and all the people of the *l*;
11:20 So all the people of the *l*
13:20 bands from Moab invaded the *l*
15: 5 judging the people of the *l*.
15:19 of Assyria came against the *l*;
15:20 and did not stay there in the *l*.
15:29 all the *l* of Naphtali; and he
16:15 of all the people of the *l*,
17: 5 went throughout all the *l*,
17: 7 brought them up out of the *l*
17:23 carried away from their own *l*
17:26 the rituals of the God of the *l*;
17:26 the rituals of the God of the *l*.
17:27 the rituals of the God of the *l*.
17:36 who brought you up from the *l*
18:25 to me, 'Go up against this *l*,
18:32 I come and take you away to a *l*
18:32 away to a land like your own *l*,
18:32 a *l* of grain and new wine, a
18:32 a *l* of bread and vineyards, a
18:32 a *l* of olive groves and honey,
18:33 nations at all delivered its *l*
19: 7 a rumor and return to his own *l*;
19: 7 fall by the sword in his own *l*.
19:37 and they escaped into the *l* of
21: 8 wander anymore from the *l*
21:24 But the people of the *l* executed
21:24 Then the people of the *l* made
23:24 that were seen in the *l* of
23:30 And the people of the *l* took
23:33 in prison at Riblah in the *l*
23:33 and he imposed on the *l* a
23:35 but he taxed the *l* to give
23:35 gold from the people of the *l*,
24: 7 Egypt did not come out of his *l*
24:14 the poorest people of the *l*.
24:15 and the mighty of the *l* he
25: 3 no food for the people of the *l*.
25:12 some of the poor of the *l* as
25:19 mustered the people of the *l*,
25:19 men of the people of the *l*
25:21 to death at Riblah in the *l* of
25:21 away captive from its own *l*.
25:22 people who remained in the *l*
25:24 Dwell in the *l* and serve the
1 Chr 1:43 the kings who reigned in the *l*
1:45 Husham of the *l* of the
2:22 twenty-three cities in the *l*
4:40 and the *l* was broad, quiet,
5: 9 cattle had multiplied in the *l*
5:11 dwelt next to them in the *l* of
5:23 of Manasseh dwelt in the *l*.
5:25 gods of the peoples of the *l*,
6:55 They gave them Hebron in the *l*
7:21 Gath who were born in that *l*
10: 9 sent word throughout the *l* of
11: 4 were, the inhabitants of the *l*.
13: 2 who are left in all the *l* of
16:18 To you I will give the *l* of
19: 2 came to Hanun in the *l* of the

19: 3 overthrow and to spy out the *l*?
21:12 the LORD—THE plague in the *l*,
22: 2 the aliens who were in the *l*
22:18 given the inhabitants of the *l*
22:18 and the *l* is subdued before the
28: 8 you may possess this good *l*,
2 Chr 2:17 the aliens who were in the *l*
6: 5 brought My people out of the *l*
6:25 and bring them back to the *l*
6:27 and send rain on Your *l* which
6:28 there is famine in the *l*,
6:28 enemies besiege them in the *l*
6:31 as long as they live in the *l*
6:36 they take them captive to a *l*
6:37 come to themselves in the *l*
6:37 supplication to You in the *l*
6:38 with all their soul in the *l*
6:38 and pray toward their *l* which
7:13 the locusts to devour the *l*,
7:14 their sin and heal their *l*.
7:20 I will uproot them from My *l*
7:21 the LORD done thus to this *l*
7:22 who brought them out of the *l*
8: 6 and in all the *l* of his
8: 8 who were left in the *l* after
8:17 seacoast, in the *l* of Edom.
9: 5 which I heard in my own *l*
9:11 these seen before in the *l* of
9:26 kings from the River to the *l*
14: 1 In his days the *l* was quiet for
14: 6 for the *l* had rest; he had no
14: 7 while the *l* is yet before us,
15: 8 idols from all the *l* of Judah
17: 2 and set garrisons in the *l* of
19: 3 the wooden images from the *l*,
19: 5 Then he set judges in the *l*
20: 7 out the inhabitants of this *l*
20:10 when they came out of the *l* of
22:12 Athaliah reigned over the *l*.
23:13 All the people of the *l* were
23:20 and all the people of the *l*,
23:21 So all the people of the *l*
26:21 judging the people of the *l*.
30: 9 they may come back to this *l*;
30:25 sojourners who came from the *l*
32: 4 brook that ran through the *l*,
32:21 shamefaced to his own *l*.
32:31 wonder that was done in the *l*,
33: 8 the foot of Israel from the *l*
33:25 But the people of the *l* executed
33:25 Then the people of the *l* made
34: 7 altars throughout all the *l* of
34: 8 when he had purged the *l* and
36: 1 Then the people of the *l* took
36: 3 and he imposed on the *l* a
36:21 until the *l* had enjoyed her
Ezra 4: 4 Then the people of the *l* tried
6:21 filth of the nations of the *l*
9:11 The *l* which you are entering to
9:11 to possess is an unclean *l*,
9:12 and eat the good of the *l*,
10: 2 wives from the peoples of the *l*;
10:11 from the peoples of the *l*,
Neh 4: 4 give them as plunder to a *l* of
5:14 to be their governor in the *l*
5:16 wall, and we did not buy any *l*.
9: 8 with him To give the *l* of the
9:10 against all the people of his *l*.
9:11 midst of the sea on the dry *l*;
9:15 them to go in to possess the *l*
9:22 they took possession of the *l*
9:22 The *l* of the king of Heshbon,
9:22 And the *l* of Og king of
9:23 And brought them into the *l*
9:24 went in And possessed the *l*;
9:24 them the inhabitants of the *l*,
9:24 kings And the people of the *l*,
9:25 took strong cities and a rich *l*,
9:35 Or in the large and rich *l*
9:36 servants today! And the *l* that
10:30 wives to the peoples of the *l*,
10:31 if the peoples of the *l* brought
10:37 to bring the tithes of our *l*
Esth 8:17 many of the people of the *l*
10: 1 imposed tribute on the *l* and
Job 1: 1 There was a man in the *l* of Uz,
1:10 have increased in the *l*.
10:21 To the *l* of darkness and the
10:22 A *l* as dark as darkness
15:19 To whom alone the *l* was given,
22: 8 the mighty man possessed the *l*,
24: 4 All the poor of the *l* are
28:13 Nor is it found in the *l* of
30: 8 They were scourged from the *l*.
31:38 If my *l* cries out against me,
37:13 for correction, Or for His *l*,
38:26 To cause it to rain on a *l*
39: 6 And the barren *l* his dwelling?
42:15 In all the *l* were found no women
Ps 10:16 have perished out of His *l*.
27:13 of the LORD In the *l* of the
35:20 the quiet ones in the *l*.
37: 3 and do good; Dwell in the *l*,
37:29 righteous shall inherit the *l*,
37:34 exalt you to inherit the *l*;
42: 6 I will remember You from the *l*
44: 3 not gain possession of the *l*
52: 5 And uproot you from the *l* of
63: 1 for You In a dry and thirsty *l*
66: 6 He turned the sea into dry *l*;
68: 6 rebellious dwell in a dry *l*.
74: 8 meeting places of God in the *l*.
78:12 In the *l* of Egypt, in the
80: 9 deep root, And it filled the *l*.
81: 5 When He went throughout the *l*
81:10 Who brought you out of the *l*
85: 1 have been favorable to Your *l*;
85: 9 That glory may dwell in our *l*.
85:12 And our *l* will yield its
88:12 Your righteousness in the *l* of
95: 5 His hands formed the dry *l*.
101: 6 be on the faithful of the *l*,
101: 8 destroy all the wicked of the *l*,
105:11 To you I will give the *l* of
105:16 He called for a famine in the *l*;
105:23 And Jacob dwelt in the *l* of
105:27 And wonders in the *l* of Ham.
105:30 Their *l* abounded with frogs,
105:32 And flaming fire in their *l*.
105:35 all the vegetation in their *l*,
105:36 all the firstborn in their *l*,
106:22 Wondrous works in the *l* of Ham,
106:24 they despised the pleasant *l*;
106:38 And the *l* was polluted with
107:34 A fruitful *l* into barrenness,
107:35 And dry *l* into watersprings.
116: 9 before the LORD In the *l* of
125: 3 shall not rest On the *l*
135:12 And gave their *l* as a
136:21 And gave their *l* as a heritage,
137: 4 LORD's song In a foreign *l*?
142: 5 My portion in the *l* of the
143: 6 longs for You like a thirsty *l*.
143:10 Lead me in the *l* of
Prov 2:21 the upright will dwell in the *l*,
12:11 He who tills his *l* will be
28: 2 of the transgression of a *l*,
28:19 He who tills his *l* will have
29: 4 The king establishes the *l* by
31:23 sits among the elders of the *l*.
Eccl 5: 9 Moreover the profit of the *l* is
10:16 Woe to you, O *l*,
10:17 Blessed are you, O *l*,
Song 2:12 turtledove Is heard in our *l*.
Isa 1: 7 Strangers devour your *l* in
1:19 shall eat the good of the *l*;
2: 7 Their *l* is also full of silver
2: 7 Their *l* is also full of
2: 8 Their *l* is also full of idols;
5: 8 alone in the midst of the *l*!
5:30 And if one looks to the *l*,
6:11 The *l* is utterly desolate,
6:12 are many in the midst of the *l*.
7:16 the *l* that you dread will be
7:18 for the bee that is in the *l*
7:22 will eat who is left in the *l*
7:24 Because all the *l* will become
8: 8 fill the breadth of Your *l*,
9: 1 He lightly esteemed The *l* of
9: 1 The land of Zebulun and the *l*
9: 2 Those who dwelt in the *l* of
9:19 of the LORD of hosts The *l*
10:23 end In the midst of all the *l*.
11:16 day that he came up from the *l*
13: 5 To destroy the whole *l*.
13: 9 To lay the *l* desolate; And He
13:14 everyone will flee to his own *l*.
14: 1 and settle them in their own *l*.
14: 2 servants and maids in the *l* of
14:20 you have destroyed your *l*
14:21 they rise up and possess the *l*,
14:25 will break the Assyrian in My *l*,
15: 9 And on the remnant of the *l*.
16: 1 the lamb to the ruler of the *l*,
16: 4 are consumed out of the *l*.
18: 1 Woe to the *l* shadowed with
18: 2 Whose *l* the rivers divide."
18: 7 Whose *l* the rivers divide—To
19:17 And the *l* of Judah will be a
19:18 that day five cities in the *l*
19:19 LORD in the midst of the *l* of
19:20 to the LORD of hosts in the *l*
19:24 blessing in the midst of the *l*,
21: 1 the desert, from a terrible *l*.
21:14 O inhabitants of the *l* of Tema,
23: 1 From the *l* of Cyprus it is
23:10 Overflow through your *l* like
23:13 the *l* of the Chaldeans, This
24: 3 The *l* shall be entirely emptied
24:11 The mirth of the *l* is gone.
24:13 be thus in the midst of the *l*
26: 1 song will be sung in the *l* of
26:10 In the *l* of uprightness he
26:15 all the borders of the *l*.
27:13 are about to perish in the *l*
27:13 they who are outcasts in the *l*
30: 6 Through a *l* of trouble and
32: 2 of a great rock in a weary *l*.
32:13 On the *l* of my people will come
33:17 They will see the *l* that is
34: 6 a great slaughter in the *l* of
34: 7 Their *l* shall be soaked with
34: 9 Its *l* shall become burning
35: 7 And the thirsty *l* springs of
36:10 the LORD against this *l* to
36:10 to me, 'Go up against this *l*,
36:17 I come and take you away to a *l*
36:17 away to a land like your own *l*,
36:17 a *l* of grain and new wine, a
36:17 a *l* of bread and vineyards.
36:18 of the nations delivered its *l*
37: 7 a rumor and return to his own *l*;
37: 7 fall by the sword in his own *l*.
37:38 and they escaped into the *l* of
38:11 The LORD in the *l* of the
41:18 And the dry *l* springs of
49:12 And these from the *l* of
49:19 And the *l* of your destruction,
53: 8 For He was cut off from the *l*
57:13 trust in Me shall possess the *l*,
60: 6 of camels shall cover your *l*,
60:18 no longer be heard in your *l*,
60:21 They shall inherit the *l*
61: 7 Therefore in their *l* they
62: 4 Nor shall your *l* any more be
62: 4 and your *l* Beulah; For the
62: 4 And your *l* shall be married.
Jer 1: 1 who were in Anathoth in the *l*
1:14 all the inhabitants of the *l*.
1:18 walls against the whole *l*—
1:18 against the people of the *l*.
2: 2 In a *l* not sown.
2: 6 brought us up out of the *l* of
2: 6 Through a *l* of deserts and
2: 6 Through a *l* of drought and the
2: 6 Through a *l* that no one
2: 7 you defiled My *l* And made My
2:15 They made his *l* waste; His
2:31 Or a *l* of darkness? Why do My
3: 1 Would not that *l* be greatly
3: 2 And you have polluted the *l*
3: 9 that she defiled the *l* and
3:16 and increased in the *l* in
3:18 come together out of the *l* of
3:18 the land of the north to the *l*
3:19 And give you a pleasant *l*,
4: 5 "Blow the trumpet in the *l*;
4: 7 from his place To make your *l*
4:20 For the whole *l* is plundered.
4:26 and indeed the fruitful *l* was
4:27 The whole *l* shall be desolate;
5:19 served foreign gods in your *l*,
5:19 you shall serve aliens in a *l*
5:30 Has been committed in the *l*:
6: 8 A *l* not inhabited."
6:12 the inhabitants of the *l*,
7: 7 in the *l* that I gave to your
7:22 I brought them out of the *l* of
7:25 your fathers came out of the *l*
7:34 For the *l* shall be desolate.
8:16 The whole *l* trembled at the
8:16 have come and devoured the *l*
9:12 Why does the *l* perish and burn
9:19 Because we have forsaken the *l*,
10:17 up your wares from the *l*,
10:18 time The inhabitants of the *l*,
11: 4 I brought them out of the *l* of
11: 5 a *l* flowing with milk and
11: 7 I brought them up out of the *l*
11:19 let us cut him off from the *l*
12: 4 How long will the *l* mourn, And
12: 5 And if in the *l* of peace,
12:11 The whole *l* is made desolate,
12:12 devour From one end of the *l*
12:12 land to the other end of the *l*;
12:14 will pluck them out of their *l*
12:15 heritage and everyone to his *l*.
13:13 all the inhabitants of this *l*—
14: 2 languish; They mourn for the *l*,
14: 4 For there was no rain in the *l*,
14: 8 You be like a stranger in the *l*,
14:15 famine shall not be in this *l*'—
14:18 and priest go about in a *l*
15: 7 fan in the gates of the *l*;
15:14 with your enemies Into a *l*
16: 3 who begot them in this *l*:
16: 6 the small shall die in this *l*.
16:13 I will cast you out of this *l*
16:13 you out of this land into a *l*
16:14 children of Israel from the *l*
16:15 children of Israel from the *l*
16:15 bring them back into their *l*
16:18 because they have defiled My *l*;
17: 4 to serve your enemies In the *l*
17: 6 In a salt *l* which is not
17:26 from the *l* of Benjamin and from
18:16 To make their *l* desolate and a
22:12 and shall see this *l* no more.
22:27 But to the *l* to which they
22:28 And cast into a *l* which they
23: 7 children of Israel from the *l*
23: 8 they shall dwell in their own *l*.
23:10 For the *l* is full of
23:10 For because of a curse the *l*
23:15 has gone out into all the *l*.
24: 5 into the *l* of the Chaldeans.
24: 6 will bring them back to this *l*;
24: 8 Jerusalem who remain in this *l*,
24: 8 and those who dwell in the *l* of
24:10 they are consumed from the *l*
25: 5 and dwell in the *l* that the
25: 9 will bring them against this *l*,
25:11 And this whole *l* shall be a
25:12 the *l* of the Chaldeans, for
25:13 So I will bring on that *l* all My
25:20 all the kings of the *l* of Uz,
25:20 all the kings of the *l* of the
25:38 For their *l* is desolate
26:17 certain of the elders of the *l*
26:20 this city and against this *l*
27: 7 until the time of his *l* comes;
27:10 to remove you far from your *l*;
27:11 let them remain in their own *l*,
30: 3 cause them to return to the *l*
30:10 And your seed from the *l* of
31:16 shall come back from the *l* of

31:23 again use this speech in the l
31:32 hand to lead them out of the l
32:15 be possessed again in this l.
32:20 set signs and wonders in the l
32:21 people Israel out of the l of
32:22 'You have given them this l,
32:22 a l flowing with milk and
32:41 assuredly plant them in this l,
32:43 will be bought in this l of
32:44 in the l of Benjamin, in the
33:11 cause the captives of the l to
33:13 in the l of Benjamin, in the
34:13 I brought them out of the l of
34:19 and all the people of the l who
35: 7 you may live many days in the l
35:11 of Babylon came up into the l,
35:15 then you will dwell in the l
36:29 come and destroy this l,
37: 1 of Babylon made king in the l
37: 2 nor the people of the l gave
37: 7 return to Egypt, to their own l.
37:12 of Jerusalem to go into the l
37:19 against you or against this l'?
39: 5 to Riblah in the l of Hamath,
39:10 of the guard left in the l of
40: 4 all the l is before you;
40: 6 people who were left in the l.
40: 7 son of Ahikam governor in the l,
40: 7 and the poorest of the l who
40: 9 Dwell in the l and serve the
40:12 and came to the l of Judah, to
41: 2 had made governor over the l.
41:18 had made governor in the l.
42:10 you will still remain in this l,
42:12 you to return to your own l.
42:13 'We will not dwell in this l,
42:14 but we will go to the l of
42:16 overtake you there in the l of
43: 4 to remain in the l of Judah.
43: 5 had returned to dwell in the l
43: 7 So they went to the l of Egypt,
43:11 he shall strike the l of Egypt
43:12 shall array himself with the l
43:13 Shemesh that are in the l of
44: 1 the Jews who dwell in the l of
44: 8 incense to other gods in the l
44: 9 which they committed in the l
44:12 their faces to go into the l
44:12 be consumed and fall in the l
44:13 those who dwell in the l of
44:14 Judah who have gone into the l
44:14 lest they return to the l of
44:15 the people who dwelt in the l
44:21 and the people of the l,
44:22 Therefore your l is a
44:24 all Judah who are in the l of
44:26 all Judah who dwell in the l of
44:26 any man of Judah in all the l
44:27 men of Judah who are in the l
44:28 sword shall return from the l
44:28 the land of Egypt to the l of
44:28 who have gone to the l of Egypt
45: 4 pluck up, that is, this whole l.
46:12 And your cry has filled the l;
46:13 would come and strike the l
46:16 to our own people And to the l
46:27 And your offspring from the l
47: 2 They shall overflow the l and
47: 2 all the inhabitants of the l
48:24 On all the cities of the l of
48:33 field And from the l of Moab;
50: 1 Babylon and against the l of
50: 3 Which shall make her l
50: 8 Go out of the l of the
50:12 A dry l and a desert.
50:16 shall flee to his own l.
50:18 the king of Babylon and his l,
50:21 Go up against the l of
50:22 A sound of battle is in the l,
50:25 Lord God of hosts In the l of
50:28 who flee and escape from the l
50:34 That He may give rest to the l,
50:38 For it is the l of carved
50:45 He has proposed against the l
51: 2 winnow her and empty her l.
51: 4 the slain shall fall in the l
51: 5 Though their l was filled with
51:27 Set up a banner in the l,
51:28 All the l of his dominion.
51:29 And the l will tremble and
51:29 To make the l of Babylon a
51:43 A dry l and a wilderness,
51:43 A l where no one dwells,
51:46 that will be heard in the l
51:46 come, And violence in the l,
51:47 Her whole l shall be ashamed,
51:52 And throughout all her l the
51:54 great destruction from the l
52: 6 no food for the people of the l.
52: 9 of Babylon at Riblah in the l
52:16 some of the poor of the l as
52:25 mustered the people of the l,
52:25 men of the people of the l who
52:27 to death at Riblah in the l of
52:27 away captive from its own l.
Lam 4:21 You who dwell in the l of Uz!
Ezek 1: 3 in the l of the Chaldeans by
6:14 against them and make the l
7: 2 says the Lord GOD to the l of
7: 2 upon the four corners of the l.
7: 7 to you, you who dwell in the l;
7:23 For the l is filled with
8:12 the LORD has forsaken the l.
8:17 For they have filled the l with
9: 9 and the l is full of bloodshed,
9: 9 'The LORD has forsaken the l,
11:15 this l has been given to us as
11:17 and I will give you the l of
12:13 to the l of the Chaldeans; yet
12:19 say to the people of the l,
12:19 of Jerusalem and to the l of
12:19 so that her l may be emptied of
12:20 and the l shall become
12:22 you people have about the l
13: 9 shall they enter into the l of
14:13 when a l sins against Me by
14:15 beasts to pass through the l,
14:16 and the l would be desolate.
14:17 if I bring a sword on that l,
14:17 say, 'Sword, go through the l,
14:19 I send a pestilence into that l
15: 8 Thus I will make the l desolate,
16: 3 your nativity are from the l
16:29 of harlotry as far as the l of
17: 4 twig And carried it to a l of
17: 5 took some of the seed of the l
17:13 took away the mighty of the l,
18: 2 this proverb concerning the l
19: 4 him with chains to the l of
19: 7 The l with its fullness was
19:13 In a dry and thirsty l.
20: 5 Myself known to them in the l
20: 6 to bring them out of the l of
20: 6 of the land of Egypt into a l
20: 8 them in the midst of the l of
20: 9 to bring them out of the l of
20:10 I made them go out of the l of
20:15 would not bring them into the l
20:28 I brought them into the l
20:36 in the wilderness of the l of
20:38 but they shall not enter the l
20:40 of Israel, all of them in the l,
20:42 when I bring you into the l of
20:46 prophesy against the forest l,
21: 2 and prophesy against the l of
21: 3 and say to the l of Israel,
21:19 them shall go from the same l.
21:30 In the l of your nativity.
21:32 shall be in the midst of the l.
22:24 You are a l that is not
22:29 The people of the l have used
22:30 before Me on behalf of the l,
23:15 The l of their nativity.
23:19 had played the harlot in the l
23:27 harlotry Brought from the l
23:48 lewdness to cease from the l,
25: 3 and against the l of Israel
25: 6 all your disdain for the l of
26:20 shall establish glory in the l
27:17 Judah and the l of Israel were
28:25 they will dwell in their own l
29: 9 And the l of Egypt shall become
29:10 and I will make the l of Egypt
29:12 I will make the l of Egypt
29:14 cause them to return to the l
29:14 to the l of their origin, and
29:19 Surely I will give the l of
29:20 I have given him the l of Egypt
30:11 be brought to destroy the l;
30:11 And fill the l with the slain.
30:12 And sell the l into the hand
30:12 I will make the l waste, and
30:13 no longer be princes from the l
30:13 I will put fear in the l of
30:25 stretches it out against the l
31:12 by all the rivers of the l;
32: 4 Then I will leave you on the l;
32: 6 I will also water the l with the
32: 8 And bring darkness upon your l,
32:15 When I make the l of Egypt
32:23 Who caused terror in the l of
32:24 caused their terror in the l
32:25 terror was caused In the l of
32:26 caused their terror in the l
32:27 terror of the mighty in the l
32:32 have caused My terror in the l
33: 2 I bring the sword upon a l,
33: 2 and the people of the l take a
33: 3 the sword coming upon the l,
33:24 inhabit those ruins in the l
33:24 one, and he inherited the l.
33:24 the l has been given to us as a
33:25 Should you then possess the l?
33:26 Should you then possess the l?
33:28 For I will make the l most
33:29 when I have made the l most
34:13 will bring them to their own l;
34:25 wild beasts to cease from the l;
34:27 They shall be safe in their l;
34:28 nor shall beasts of the l
34:29 consumed with hunger in the l,
36: 5 who gave My l to themselves as
36: 6 prophesy concerning the l of
36:17 of Israel dwelt in their own l,
36:18 blood they had shed on the l,
36:20 yet they have gone out of His l.
36:24 and bring you into your own l.
36:28 Then you shall dwell in the l
36:34 The desolate l shall be tilled
36:35 This l that was desolate has
37:12 and bring you into the l of
37:14 I will place you in your own l.
37:21 and bring them into their own l;
37:22 make them one nation in the l,
37:25 they shall dwell in the l
38: 2 of the l of Magog, the prince
38: 8 years you will come into the l
38: 9 covering the l like a cloud,
38:11 I will go up against a l of
38:12 who dwell in the midst of the l.
38:16 like a cloud, to cover the l.
38:16 I will bring you against My l,
38:18 when Gog comes against the l of
38:19 be a great earthquake in the l
39:12 them, in order to cleanse the l.
39:13 all the people of the l
39:14 to pass through the l and bury
39:15 party will pass through the l;
39:16 Thus they shall cleanse the l.
39:26 dwelt safely in their own l
39:28 brought them back to their l,
40: 2 of God He took me into the l
45: 1 when you divide the l by lot
45: 1 LORD, a holy section of the l;
45: 4 be a holy section of the l,
45: 8 The l shall be his possession in
45: 8 give the rest of the l to
45:16 All the people of the l shall
45:22 for all the people of the l a
46: 3 Likewise the people of the l
46: 9 But when the people of the l
47:13 by which you shall divide the l
47:14 and this l shall fall to you as
47:15 shall be the border of the l
47:18 and between Gilead and the l of
47:21 Thus you shall divide this l
48:12 And this district of l that is
48:14 this best part of the l,
48:29 This is the l which you shall
Dan 1: 2 which he carried into the l of
8: 9 and toward the Glorious L.
9: 6 and all the people of the l.
9:15 Your people out of the l of
11: 9 but shall return to his own l.
11:16 shall stand in the Glorious L
11:19 the fortress of his own l;
11:28 While returning to his l with
11:28 damage and return to his own l.
11:39 and divide the l for gain.
11:41 shall also enter the Glorious L,
11:42 and the l of Egypt shall not
Hos 1: 2 For the l has committed great
1:11 they shall come up out of the l,
2: 3 And set her like a dry l,
2:15 when she came up from the l of
4: 1 the inhabitants of the l:
4: 1 Or knowledge of God in the l.
4: 3 Therefore the l will mourn;
7:16 be their derision in the l of
9: 3 not dwell in the LORD's l,
10: 1 to the bounty of his l They
11: 5 He shall not return to the l of
11:11 Like a dove from the l of
12: 9 Ever since the l of Egypt;
13: 4 your God Ever since the l of
13: 5 In the l of great drought.
Joel 1: 2 all you inhabitants of the l!
1: 6 nation has come up against My l,
1:10 The l mourns; For the grain
1:14 all the inhabitants of the l
2: 1 all the inhabitants of the l
2: 3 The l is like the Garden of
2:18 LORD will be zealous for His l,
2:20 into a barren and desolate l,
2:21 Fear not, O l; Be glad
3: 2 They have also divided up My l.
3:19 shed innocent blood in their l.
Am 2:10 who brought you up from the l
2:10 To possess the l of the
3: 1 which I brought up from the l
3: 9 And in the palaces in the l of
3:11 shall be all around the l;
5: 2 She lies forsaken on her l;
7: 2 eating the grass of the l,
7:10 The l is not able to bear all
7:11 away captive From their own l.
7:12 you seer! Flee to the l of
7:17 Your l shall be divided by
7:17 You shall die in a defiled l;
7:17 away captive From his own l.
8: 4 And make the poor of the l
8: 8 Shall the l not tremble for
8:11 I will send a famine on the l,
9: 7 not bring up Israel from the l
9:15 I will plant them in their l,
9:15 they be pulled up From the l
Ob 20 Shall possess the l of
Jon 1: 9 who made the sea and the dry l.
1:13 men rowed hard to return to l,
2:10 it vomited Jonah onto dry l.
Mic 5: 5 the Assyrian comes into our l,
5: 6 waste with the sword the l of
5: 6 And the l of Nimrod at its
5: 6 When he comes into our l And
5:11 cut off the cities of your l
6: 4 I brought you up from the l of
7:13 Yet the l shall be desolate
7:15 when you came out of the l of
Nah 3:13 women! The gates of your l
Hab 2: 8 And the violence of the l
2:17 And the violence of the l
3: 7 The curtains of the l of
3:12 You marched through the l in
Zeph 1: 2 From the face of the l,
1: 3 off man from the face of the l,
1:18 But the whole l shall be

1:18 all those who dwell in the *l*.
2: 5 *l* of the Philistines: "I will
3:19 for praise and fame In every *l*
Hag 1:11 I called for a drought on the *l*
2: 4 strong, all you people of the *l*,
2: 6 and earth, the sea and dry *l*;
Zech 1:21 up their horn against the *l*
2: 6 up! Flee from the *l* of the
2:12 His inheritance in the Holy *L*,
3: 9 remove the iniquity of that *l*
5:11 build a house for it in the *l*
7: 5 to all the people of the *l*,
7:14 Thus the *l* became desolate
7:14 for they made the pleasant *l*
8: 7 will save My people from the *l*
8: 7 of the east And from the *l* of
9: 1 of the LORD Against the *l* of
9:16 like a banner over His *l*—
10:10 bring them back from the *l* of
10:10 I will bring them into the *l*
11: 6 pity the inhabitants of the *l*,
11: 6 king. They shall attack the *l*,
11:16 raise up a shepherd in the *l*
12:12 And the *l* shall mourn, every
13: 2 names of the idols from the *l*,
13: 2 spirit to depart from the *l*.
13: 8 shall come to pass in all the *l*,
14:10 All the *l* shall be turned into a
Mal 3:12 For you will be a delightful *l*,
Mt 2: 6 in the *l* of Judah, Are
2:20 and go to the *l* of Israel, for
2:21 and came into the *l* of Israel.
4:15 The *l* of Zebulun and the
4:15 of Zebulun and the *l* of
9:26 this went out into all that *l*.
10:15 be more tolerable for the *l* of
11:24 be more tolerable for the *l* of
14:34 they came to the *l* of
23:15 hypocrites! For you travel *l*
27:45 was darkness over all the *l*.
Mk 1: 5 Then all the *l* of Judea, and
4: 1 whole multitude was on the *l*
6:47 sea; and He was alone on the *l*.
6:53 they came to the *l* of
15:33 was darkness over the whole *l*
Lk 4:25 famine throughout all the *l*;
5: 3 to put out a little from the *l*.
5:11 had brought their boats to *l*,
8:27 when He stepped out on the *l*,
14:35 It is neither fit for the *l* nor
15:14 arose a severe famine in that *l*,
21:23 be great distress in the *l* and
Jn 3:22 His disciples came into the *l*
6:21 the boat was at the *l* where
21: 8 (for they were not far from *l*,
21: 9 as soon as they had come to *l*,
21:11 up and dragged the net to *l*,
Acts 4:37 having *l*, sold it, and brought
5: 3 part of the price of the *l*
5: 8 me whether you sold the *l*
7: 3 and come to a *l* that I
7: 4 Then he came out of the *l* of the
7: 4 He moved him to this *l* in which
7: 6 would dwell in a foreign *l*,
7:11 trouble came over all the *l* of
7:29 and became a dweller in the *l*
7:36 wonders and signs in the *l* of
7:40 brought us out of the *l*
7:45 brought with Joshua into the *l*
10:39 which He did both in the *l* of
13:17 dwelt as strangers in the *l* of
13:19 seven nations in the *l* of
13:19 He distributed their *l* to them
27:27 they were drawing near some *l*.
27:39 they did not recognize the *l*;
27:43 overboard first and get to *l*,
27:44 they all escaped safely to *l*.
Heb 8: 9 lead them out of the *l*
11: 9 By faith he dwelt in the *l* of
11:29 the Red Sea as by dry *l*,
Jas 5:17 and it did not rain on the *l*
Jude 5 saved the people out of the *l*
Rev 10: 2 and his left foot on the *l*,
10: 5 on the sea and on the *l* raised

LANDED (3/3)

Acts 18:22 And when he had *l* at Caesarea,
21: 3 and *l* at Tyre; for there the
27: 3 And the next day we *l* at Sidon.

LANDING (1/1)

Acts 28:12 And *l* at Syracuse, we stayed

LANDMARK (5/5) LAND, LANDMARKS

Deut 19:14 not remove your neighbor's *l*,
27:17 one who moves his neighbor's *l*.
Prov 22:28 Do not remove the ancient *l*
23:10 Do not remove the ancient *l*,
Hos 5:10 are like those who remove a *l*;

LANDMARKS (2/2) LANDMARK

Job 24: 2 Some remove *l*; They seize
Jer 31:21 "Set up signposts, Make *l*;

LANDOWNER (3/3) LAND

Mt 20: 1 kingdom of heaven is like a *l*
20:11 they complained against the *l*,
21:33 There was a certain *l* who

LANDS (54/52) LAND

Gen 10: 5 were separated into their *l*,
10:20 in their *l* and in their
10:31 to their languages, in their *l*,
26: 3 descendants I give all these *l*,
26: 4 to your descendants all these *l*;
41:54 said. The famine was in all *l*,
41:57 the famine was severe in all *l*.
47:18 lord but our bodies and our *l*.
47:22 they did not sell their *l*.
Lev 26:36 into their hearts in the *l* of
26:39 iniquity in your enemies' *l*;
Judg 11:13 restore those *l* peaceably."
2 Ki 18:35 among all the gods of the *l*
19:11 of Assyria have done to all *l*
19:17 waste the nations and their *l*,
1 Chr 14:17 of David went out into all *l*,
29:30 to all the kingdoms of the *l*.
2 Chr 9:28 from Egypt and from all *l*.
13: 9 like the peoples of other *l*,
15: 5 on all the inhabitants of the *l*.
17:10 on all the kingdoms of the *l*
32:13 to all the peoples of other *l*?
32:13 gods of the nations of those *l*
32:13 any way able to deliver their *l*
32:17 gods of the nations of other *l*
Ezra 9: 1 from the peoples of the *l*,
9: 2 with the peoples of those *l*.
9: 7 the hand of the kings of the *l*,
9:11 of the peoples of the *l*,
Neh 5: 3 We have mortgaged our *l* and
5: 4 for the king's tax on our *l*
5: 5 for other men have our *l* and
5:11 to them, even this day, their *l*,
9:30 hand of the peoples of the *l*.
10:28 from the peoples of the *l* to
Ps 49:11 They call their *l* after their
56: "The Silent Dove in Distant *L*.
100: 1 shout to the LORD, all you *l*!
105:44 He gave them the *l* of the
106:27 And to scatter them in the *l*.
107: 3 And gathered out of the *l*,
Isa 36:20 among all the gods of these *l*
37:11 of Assyria have done to all *l*
37:18 all the nations and their *l*,
Jer 16:15 of the north and from all the *l*
27: 6 now I have given all these *l*
Ezek 20: 6 and honey,' the glory of all *l*.
20:15 and honey,' the glory of all *l*,
30: 5 and the men of the *l* who are
39:27 them out of their enemies' *l*,
Mt 19:29 mother or wife or children or *l*,
Mk 10:29 mother or wife or children or *l*,
10:30 and mothers and children and *l*,
Acts 4:34 all who were possessors of *l*

LANES (1/1)

Lk 14:21 quickly into the streets and *l*

LANGUAGE (38/33) LANGUAGES

Gen 10: 5 everyone according to his *l*,
11: 1 Now the whole earth had one *l*
11: 6 one and they all have one *l*,
11: 7 down and there confuse their *l*,
11: 9 there the LORD confused the *l*
Deut 28:49 a nation whose *l* you will not
Ezra 4: 7 translated into the Aramaic *l*.
Neh 13:24 of their children spoke the *l*
13:24 and could not speak the *l* of
13:24 but spoke according to the *l* of
Esth 1:22 to every people in their own *l*,
1:22 and speak in the *l* of his own
3:12 and to every people in their *l*.
8: 9 to every people in their own *l*,
8: 9 Jews in their own script and *l*.
Ps 19: 3 There is no speech nor *l*
81: 5 Where I heard a *l* I did not
114: 1 from a people of strange *l*,
Isa 19:18 land of Egypt will speak the *l*
36:11 your servants in the Aramaic *l*,
Jer 5:15 A nation whose *l* you do not
Ezek 3: 5 unfamiliar speech and of hard *l*,
3: 6 unfamiliar speech and of hard *l*,
Dan 1: 4 and whom they might teach the *l*
3:29 or *l* which speaks anything
Zeph 3: 9 restore to the peoples a pure *l*,
Zech 8:23 days ten men from every *l* of
Jn 16:25 spoken to you in figurative *l*;
16:25 speak to you in figurative *l*,
Acts 1:19 field is called in their own *l*,
2: 6 heard them speak in his own *l*.
2: 8 each in our own *l* in which we
14:11 saying in the Lycaonian *l*,
21:40 spoke to them in the Hebrew *l*,
22: 2 spoke to them in the Hebrew *l*,
26:14 me and saying in the Hebrew *l*,
1 Cor 14:11 not know the meaning of the *l*,
Col 3: 8 filthy *l* out of your mouth.

LANGUAGES (9/9) LANGUAGE

Gen 10:20 families, according to their *l*,
10:31 families, according to their *l*,
Dan 3: 4 O peoples, nations, and *l*,
3: 7 and *l* fell down and worshiped
4: 1 and *l* that dwell in all the
5:19 and *l* trembled and feared
6:25 and *l* that dwell in all the
7:14 and *l* should serve Him. His
1 Cor 14:10 so many kinds of *l* in the

LANGUISH (4/4) LANGUISHED, LANGUISHES

Isa 16: 8 For the fields of Heshbon *l*,
19: 8 And they will *l* who spread
24: 4 haughty people of the earth *l*.
Jer 14: 2 mourns, And her gates *l*;

LANGUISHED (2/2) LANGUISH

Gen 47:13 Egypt and the land of Canaan *l*
Lam 2: 8 They *l* together.

LANGUISHES (4/4) LANGUISH

Isa 24: 4 The world *l* and fades away;
24: 7 new wine fails, the vine *l*,
33: 9 The earth mourns and *l*,
Jer 15: 9 She *l* who has borne seven; She

LANTERNS (1/1)

Jn 18: 3 Pharisees, came there with *l*,

LAODICEA (5/5) LAODICEANS

Col 2: 1 I have for you and those in *L*,
4:13 for you, and those who are in *L*,
4:15 Greet the brethren who are in *L*,
4:16 read the epistle from *L*.
Rev 1:11 to Philadelphia, and to *L*.

LAODICEANS (2/2) LAODICEA

Col 4:16 also in the church of the *L*,
Rev 3:14 angel of the church of the *L*

LAP (1/1) LAPPED, LAPS

Prov 16:33 The lot is cast into the *l*,

LAPFUL (1/1)

2 Ki 4:39 and gathered from it a *l* of

LAPIDOTH (1/1)

Judg 4: 4 a prophetess, the wife of *L*,

LAPPED (2/2) LAP

Judg 7: 6 And the number of those who *l*,
7: 7 the three hundred men who *l*

LAPS (2/1) LAP

Judg 7: 5 Everyone who *l* from the water
7: 5 with his tongue, as a dog *l*,

LAPWING (KJV) See HOOPOE

LARGE (70/69)

Gen 29: 2 A *l* stone was on the well's
30:43 and had *l* flocks, female and
34:21 For indeed the land is *l*
Ex 3: 8 from that land to a good and *l*
Lev 11:29 and the *l* lizard after its
Num 13:28 are fortified and very *l*;
26:54 To a *l* tribe you shall give a
Deut 6:10 to give you *l* and beautiful
25:14 measures, a *l* and a small.
27: 2 set up for yourselves *l* stones,
Josh 10:11 LORD cast down *l* hailstones
10:18 Roll *l* stones against the mouth
10:27 and laid *l* stones against the
24:26 And he took a *l* stone, and set
Judg 18:10 to a secure people and a *l* land.
1 Sam 6:14 a *l* stone was there. So they
6:15 and put them on the *l* stone.
6:18 even as far as the *l* stone of
14:33 roll a *l* stone to me this
2 Sam 8: 8 King David took a *l* amount of
18:17 and cast him into a *l* pit
18:17 and laid a very *l* heap of
20: 8 When they were at the *l* stone
1 Ki 4:13 sixty *l* cities with walls and
5:17 king commanded them to quarry *l*
7:10 *l* stones, some ten cubits and
10:16 made two hundred *l* shields
18:32 a trench around the altar *l*
2 Ki 4:38 Put on the *l* pot, and boil stew
1 Chr 18: 8 David brought a *l* amount of
2 Chr 9:15 made two hundred *l* shields
23: 9 and the *l* and small shields
26:15 to shoot arrows and *l* stones.
Ezra 10: 1 a very *l* assembly of men,
Neh 7: 4 Now the city was *l* and
9:35 Or in the *l* and rich land
12:31 two *l* thanksgiving choirs.
13: 5 And he had prepared for him a *l*
Job 1: 3 and a very *l* household, so that
36:18 For a *l* ransom would not help
Isa 8: 1 Take a *l* scroll, and write on it
22:18 you like a ball Into a *l* country;
30:23 cattle will feed In *l* pastures.
30:33 He has made it deep and *l*;
Jer 43: 9 Take *l* stones in your hand, and
Ezek 17: 3 A great eagle with *l* wings and
17: 7 was another great eagle with *l*
Dan 8: 8 the *l* horn was broken, and in
8:21 The *l* horn that is between its

L

Am 8: 5 ephah small and the shekel *l*,
Zech 14: 4 Making a very *l* valley; Half
Mt 15:37 they took up seven *l* baskets
16:10 four thousand and how many *l*
27:60 and he rolled a *l* stone against
28:12 they gave a *l* sum of money to
Mk 4:32 and shoots out *l* branches, so
5:11 Now a *l* herd of swine was
8: 8 they took up seven *l* baskets
8:20 how many *l* baskets full of
14:15 Then he will show you a *l* upper
16: 4 rolled away—for it was very *l*.
Lk 7:11 went with Him, and a *l* crowd.
7:12 And a *l* crowd from the city was
13:19 it grew and became a *l* tree,
22:12 "Then he will show you a *l*,
Jn 21:11 full of *l* fish, one hundred and
Acts 9:25 through the wall in a *l* basket.
22:28 With a *l* sum I obtained this
Gal 6:11 See with what *l* letters I have
Jas 3: 4 although they are so *l* and are

LARGENESS (1/1)

1 Ki 4:29 and *l* of heart like the sand on

LARGER (7/6)

Num 26:54 large tribe you shall give a *l*
26:56 shall be divided between the *l*
33:54 to the *l* you shall give a
33:54 the larger you shall give a *l*
35: 8 from the *l* tribe you shall
2 Chr 3: 5 The *l* room he paneled with
Ezek 43:14 from the smaller ledge to the *l*

LASCIVIOUSNESS (KJV) See LEWDNESS

LASEA (1/1)

Acts 27: 8 Havens, near the city of *L*.

LASHA (1/1)

Gen 10:19 Admah, and Zeboiim, as far as *L*.

LASHARON (1/1)

Josh 12:18 of Aphek, one; the king of *L*,

LAST (107/101)

Gen 19:34 I lay with my father *l* night;
25: 8 Then Abraham breathed his *l* and
25:17 and he breathed his *l* and died,
31:29 your father spoke to me *l* night,
31:42 and rebuked you *l* night."
33: 2 behind, and Rachel and Joseph *l*.
35:29 So Isaac breathed his *l* and
49: 1 shall befall you in the *l* days:
49:19 him, But he shall triumph at *l*.
49:33 into the bed and breathed his *l*,
Lev 26: 5 Your threshing shall *l* till the
26: 5 and the vintage shall *l* till
Num 2:31 hundred—they shall break camp *l*,
24:20 But shall be *l* until he
1 Sam 15:16 the LORD said to me *l* night.
2 Sam 19:11 Why are you the *l* to bring the
19:12 Why then are you the *l* to bring
23: 1 Now these are the *l* words of
1 Chr 23:27 For by the *l* words of David the
29:29 acts of King David, first and *l*,
2 Chr 9:29 acts of Solomon, first and *l*,
12:15 acts of Rehoboam, first and *l*,
16:11 the acts of Asa, first and *l*,
20:34 of Jehoshaphat, first and *l*,
25:26 of Amaziah, from first to *l*,
26:22 acts of Uzziah, from first to *l*,
28:26 all his ways, from first to *l*,
35:27 and his deeds from first to *l*,
Ezra 8:13 of the *l* sons of Adonikam, whose
Neh 8:18 from the first day until the *l*
Job 14:10 Indeed he breathes his *l* And
19:25 And He shall stand at *l* on the
20:21 his well-being will not *l*.
Ps 49:11 is that their houses will *l*
Prov 5:11 And you mourn at *l*,
23:32 At the *l* it bites like a
Isa 41: 4 And with the *l* I am He.'"
44: 6 am the First and I am the *L*;
48:12 the First, I am also the *L*.
Jer 15: 9 seven; She has breathed her *l*;
32:14 that they may *l* many days."
50:17 Now at *l* this Nebuchadnezzar
Lam 1:19 my elders Breathed their *l* in
Dan 4: 8 But at *l* Daniel came before me
8: 3 and the higher one came up *l*.
Hos 9:12 will bereave them to the *l* man.
Am 9: 1 I will slay the *l* of them with
Mt 5:26 till you have paid the *l* penny.
12:45 and the *l* state of that man is
19:30 be *l*, and the last first.
19:30 and the *l* first.
20: 8 beginning with the *l* to the
20:12 These *l* men have worked only
20:14 I wish to give to this *l* man
20:16 So the *l* will be first, and the
20:16 will be first, and the first *l*.
21:37 Then *l* of all he sent his son to
22:27 *L* of all the woman died also.
26:60 But at *l* two false witnesses
27:64 So the *l* deception will be
Mk 9:35 he shall be *l* of all and
10:31 be *l*, and the last first."
10:31 and the *l* first."
12: 6 he also sent him to them *l*,
12:22 *L* of all the woman died also.
15:37 loud voice, and breathed His *l*.
15:39 like this and breathed His *l*,
Lk 11:26 and the *l* state of that man is
12:59 you have paid the very *l* mite.
13:30 And indeed there are *l* who will
13:30 there are first who will be *l*.
20:32 *L* of all the woman died also.
23:46 said this, He breathed His *l*.
Jn 6:39 should raise it up at the *l* day.
6:40 I will raise him up at the *l* day.
6:44 I will raise him up at the *l* day.
6:54 I will raise him up at the *l* day.
7:37 On the *l* day, that great day
8: 9 with the oldest even to the *l*.
11:24 resurrection at the *l* day.
12:48 spoken will judge him in the *l*
Acts 2:17 come to pass in the *l* days,
5: 5 fell down and breathed his *l*.
5:10 at his feet and breathed her *l*.
Rom 1:10 now at *l* I may find a way in
1 Cor 4: 9 the apostles, *l*, as men
15: 8 Then *l* of all He was seen by me
15:26 The *l* enemy that will be
15:45 The *l* Adam became a
15:52 at the *l* trumpet. For the
Phil 4:10 the Lord greatly that now at *l*
2 Tim 3: 1 that in the *l* days perilous
Heb 1: 2 has in these *l* days spoken to us
Jas 5: 3 heaped up treasure in the *l* days.
1 Pe 1: 5 to be revealed in the *l* times.
1:20 was manifest in these *l* times
2 Pe 3: 3 scoffers will come in the *l*
1 Jn 2:18 it is the *l* hour; and as you
2:18 we know that it is the *l* hour.
Jude 18 would be mockers in the *l* time
Rev 1:11 the Omega, the First and the *L*,
1:17 I am the First and the *L*.
2: 8 things says the First and the *L*,
2:19 the *l* are more than the first.
15: 1 having the seven *l* plagues,
21: 9 bowls filled with the seven *l*
22:13 the End, the First and the *L*.

LASTED (1/1)

Judg 14:17 seven days while their feast *l*.

LASTING (1/1)

Esth 1: 5 the king made a feast *l* seven

LATCH (1/1)

Song 5: 4 beloved put his hand By the *l*

LATCHET (KJV) See STRAP

LATE (11/10) LATER

Ex 9:32 for they are *l* crops.
2 Sam 21:10 of harvest until the *l* rains
Job 30: 3 Fleeing *l* to the wilderness,
Ps 127: 2 to rise up early, To sit up *l*,
Am 7: 1 at the beginning of the *l* crop;
7: 1 indeed it was the *l* crop
Mt 14:15 and the hour is already *l*.
Mk 6:35 and already the hour is *l*.
11:11 as the hour was already *l*,
Jude 12 *l* autumn trees without fruit,
Rev 6:13 as a fig tree drops its *l* figs

LATELY (2/2)

Mic 2: 8 *L* My people have risen up as an
Jn 11: 8 *l* the Jews sought to stone You,

LATER (6/6) LATE

Mt 26:73 And a little *l* those who stood
Mk 14:70 And a little *l* those who stood
16:14 *L* He appeared to the eleven as
Acts 5: 7 Now it was about three hours *l*
Gal 3:17 four hundred and thirty years *l*,
1 Tim 5:24 but those of some men follow *l*.

LATIN (2/2)

Lk 23:38 over Him in letters of Greek, *L*,
Jn 19:20 in Hebrew, Greek, and *L*.

LATTER (40/39)

Ex 4: 8 the message of the *l* sign.
Num 24:14 do to your people in the *l* days.
Deut 4:30 things come upon you in the *l*
11:14 the early rain and the *l* rain,
24: 3 if the *l* husband detests her
24: 3 or if the *l* husband dies who
31:29 will befall you in the *l* days,
32:29 would consider their *l* end!
2 Sam 2:26 it will be bitter in the *l* end?
Job 8: 7 Yet your *l* end would increase
42:12 the LORD blessed the *l* days
Prov 16:15 is like a cloud of the *l* rain.
19:20 you may be wise in your *l* days.
Isa 2: 2 it shall come to pass in the *l*
41:22 And know the *l* end of them;
47: 7 Nor remember the *l* end of
Jer 3: 3 And there has been no *l* rain.
5:24 rain, both the former and the *l*,
23:20 In the *l* days you will
30:24 In the *l* days you will
48:47 captives of Moab In the *l* days,
49:39 it shall come to pass in the *l*
Ezek 38: 8 In the *l* years you will come
38:16 It will be in the *l* days that I
Dan 2:28 what will be in the *l* days.
8:19 what shall happen in the *l* time
8:23 And in the *l* time of their
10:14 happen to your people in the *l*
11:29 not be like the former or the *l*.
Hos 3: 5 and His goodness in the *l* days.
6: 3 Like the *l* and former rain to
Joel 2:23 And the *l* rain in the first
Mic 4: 1 it shall come to pass in the *l*
Hag 2: 9 The glory of this *l* temple shall
Zech 10: 1 for rain In the time of the *l*
Phil 1:17 but the *l* out of love, knowing
1 Tim 4: 1 expressly says that in *l* times
2 Tim 2:21 cleanses himself from the *l*,
Jas 5: 7 receives the early and *l* rain.
2 Pe 2:20 the *l* end is worse for them

LATTICE (5/5)

Judg 5:28 And cried out through the *l*,
1 Ki 7:17 He made a *l* network, with
2 Ki 1: 2 Now Ahaziah fell through the *l*
Prov 7: 6 my house I looked through my *l*,
Song 2: 9 windows, Gazing through the *l*.

LAUD (2/2)

Ps 117: 1 all you Gentiles! *L* Him, all
Rom 15:11 all you Gentiles! *L* Him,

LAUGH (15/13) LAUGHED, LAUGHS, LAUGHTER, RIDICULE

Gen 18:13 to Abraham, "Why did Sarah *l*,
18:15 it, saying, "I did not *l*,
18:15 'No, but you did *l*!"
21: 6 Sarah said, "God has made me *l*,
21: 6 and all who hear will *l* with
Job 5:22 You shall *l* at destruction and
22:19 And the innocent *l* at them:
Ps 2: 4 who sits in the heavens shall *l*;
52: 6 And shall *l* at him, saying,
59: 8 shall *l* at them; You shall
80: 6 And our enemies *l* among
Prov 1:26 I also will *l* at your calamity;
Eccl 3: 4 time to weep, And a time to *l*;
Lk 6:21 who weep now, For you shall *l*.
6:25 Woe to you who *l* now, For you

LAUGHED (7/7) LAUGH, RIDICULED

Gen 17:17 Abraham fell on his face and *l*,
18:12 Therefore Sarah *l* within
2 Ki 19:21 *l* you to scorn; The daughter
2 Chr 30:10 but they *l* at them and mocked
Neh 2:19 they *l* at us and despised us,
Isa 37:22 *l* you to scorn; The daughter
Ezek 23:32 You shall be *l* to scorn

LAUGHING (1/1)

Job 8:21 will yet fill your mouth with *l*,

LAUGHS (4/4) LAUGH

Job 9:23 He *l* at the plight of the
41:29 He *l* at the threat of
Ps 37:13 The Lord *l* at him, For He sees
Prov 29: 9 Whether the fool rages or *l*,

LAUGHTER (7/7) LAUGH

Ps 126: 2 our mouth was filled with *l*,
Prov 14:13 Even in *l* the heart may sorrow,
Eccl 2: 2 I said of *l*—"Madness!";
7: 3 Sorrow is better than *l*,
7: 6 So is the *l* of the fool.
10:19 A feast is made for *l*,
Jas 4: 9 and mourn and weep! Let your *l*

LAUNCH (1/1) LAUNCHED

Lk 5: 4 *L* out into the deep and let down

LAUNCHED (1/1) LAUNCH

Lk 8:22 And they *l* out.

LAUNDERER (1/1)

Mk 9: 3 such as no *l* on earth can

LAUNDERER'S (1/1)

Mal 3: 2 a refiner's fire And like *l*

LAVER (14/12) LAVERS

Ex 30:18 You shall also make a *l* of
30:28 and the *l* and its base.
31: 9 and the *l* and its base—
35:16 and the *l* and its base;
38: 8 He made the *l* of bronze and its
39:39 the *l* with its base;
40: 7 And you shall set the *l* between

40:11 And you shall anoint the *l* and
40:30 He set the *l* between the
Lev 8:11 and the *l* and its base, to
1 Ki 7:30 Under the *l* were supports of
7:38 each *l* contained forty baths,
7:38 and each *l* was four cubits.
7:38 each of the ten carts was a *l*.

LAVERS (6/6) LAVER

1 Ki 7:38 Then he made ten *l* of bronze;
7:40 Huram made the *l* and the
7:43 and ten *l* on the carts;
2 Ki 16:17 and removed the *l* from them;
2 Chr 4: 6 He also made ten *l*,
4:14 he also made carts and the *l* on

LAVISH (2/2)

Isa 46: 6 They *l* gold out of the bag,
2 Cor 8:20 should blame us in this *l* gift

LAW (441/388) LAWFUL, LAWGIVER, LAWLESS, LAWS, LAWYER

Gen 47:26 And Joseph made it a *l* over the
Ex 12:49 One *l* shall be for the
13: 9 that the LORD's *l* may be in
16: 4 whether they will walk in My *l*
24:12 and the *l* and commandments
Lev 6: 9 This is the *l* of the burnt
6:14 This is the *l* of the grain
6:25 This is the *l* of the sin
7: 1 Likewise this is the *l* of the
7: 7 there is one *l* for them both:
7:11 This is the *l* of the sacrifice
7:37 This is the *l* of the burnt
11:46 This is the *l* of the animals
12: 7 This is the *l* for her who has
13:59 This is the *l* of the leprous
14: 2 This shall be the *l* of the leper
14:32 This is the *l* for one who had
14:54 This is the *l* for any leprous
14:57 This is the *l* of leprosy."
15:32 This is the *l* for one who has a
24:22 You shall have the same *l* for
Num 5:29 This is the *l* of jealousy,
5:30 shall execute all this *l* upon
6:13 Now this is the *l* of the
6:21 This is the *l* of the Nazirite
6:21 he must do according to the *l*
15:16 One *l* and one custom shall be
15:29 You shall have one *l* for him who
19: 2 is the ordinance of the *l*
19:14 This is the *l* when a man dies
31:21 is the ordinance of the *l*
Deut 1: 5 Moses began to explain this *l*,
4: 8 judgments as are in all this *l*
4:44 Now this is the *l* which Moses
17:11 to the sentence of the *l* in
17:18 for himself a copy of this *l*
17:19 all the words of this *l* and
27: 3 on them all the words of this *l*,
27: 8 stones all the words of this *l*.
27:26 all the words of this *l*.
28:58 all the words of this *l* that
28:61 written in this Book of the *L*,
29:21 written in this Book of the *L*,
29:29 may do all the words of this *l*.
30:10 written in this Book of the *L*,
31: 9 So Moses wrote this *l* and
31:11 you shall read this *l* before
31:12 observe all the words of this *l*,
31:24 writing the words of this *l* in
31:26 "Take this Book of the *L*,
32:46 observe—all the words of this *l*.
33: 2 His right hand Came a fiery *l*
33: 4 Moses commanded a *l* for us, A
33:10 judgments, And Israel Your *l*.
Josh 1: 7 to do according to all the *l*
1: 8 This Book of the *L* shall not
8:31 is written in the Book of the *L*
8:32 on the stones a copy of the *l*
8:34 he read all the words of the *l*,
8:34 is written in the Book of the *L*.
22: 5 to do the commandment and the *l*
23: 6 is written in the Book of the *L*
24:26 words in the Book of the *L* of
1 Ki 2: 3 as it is written in the *L* of
2 Ki 10:31 took no heed to walk in the *l*
14: 6 is written in the Book of the *L*
17:13 according to all the *l* which I
17:34 or the *l* and commandment which
17:37 statutes, the ordinances, the *l*,
21: 8 and according to all the *l* that
22: 8 have found the Book of the *L*
22:11 the words of the Book of the *L*,
23:24 perform the words of the *l*
23:25 according to all the *L* of
1 Chr 16:40 to all that is written in the *L*
22:12 that you may keep the *l* of the
2 Chr 6:16 that they walk in My *l* as you
12: 1 that he forsook the *l* of the
14: 4 and to observe the *l* and the
15: 3 teaching priest, and without *l*;
17: 9 and had the Book of the *L* of
19:10 or offenses against *l* or
23:18 as it is written in the *L* of
25: 4 as it is written in the *L* in
30:16 according to the *L* of Moses the
31: 3 as it is written in the *L* of
31: 4 devote themselves to the *L* of
31:21 in the *l* and in the
33: 8 according to the whole *l* and
34:14 priest found the Book of the *L*
34:15 have found the Book of the *L*
34:19 king heard the words of the *L*,
35:26 to what was written in the *L*
Ezra 3: 2 as it is written in the *L* of
7: 6 was a skilled scribe in the *L*
7:10 his heart to seek the *L* of the
7:12 a scribe of the *L* of the God of
7:14 with regard to the *L* of your
7:21 the scribe of the *L* of the God
7:26 Whoever will not observe the *l*
7:26 the law of your God and the *l*
10: 3 it be done according to the *l*.
Neh 8: 1 to bring the Book of the *L* of
8: 2 Ezra the priest brought the *L*
8: 3 attentive to the Book of the *L*.
8: 7 the people to understand the *L*;
8: 8 in the *L* of God; and they gave
8: 9 they heard the words of the *L*.
8:13 understand the words of the *L*.
8:14 And they found written in the *L*,
8:18 he read from the Book of the *L*
9: 3 read from the Book of the *L* of
9:26 Cast Your *l* behind their backs
9:29 might bring them back to Your *l*.
9:34 our fathers, Have kept Your *l*,
10:28 peoples of the lands to the *L*
10:29 and an oath to walk in God's *L*,
10:34 God as it is written in the *L*.
10:36 as it is written in the *L*,
12:44 the portions specified by the *L*
13: 3 was, when they had heard the *L*,
Esth 1: 8 In accordance with the *l*,
1:13 manner toward all who knew *l*
1:15 to Queen Vashti, according to *l*,
3:14 document was to be issued as *l*
4:11 been called, he has but one *l*:
4:16 king, which is against the *l*;
Job 28:26 When He made a *l* for the rain,
Ps 1: 2 But his delight is in the *l* of
1: 2 And in His *l* he meditates day
19: 7 The *l* of the LORD is perfect,
37:31 The *l* of his God is in his
40: 8 And Your *l* is within my
78: 1 ear, O my people, to my *l*;
78: 5 And appointed a *l* in Israel,
78:10 They refused to walk in His *l*,
81: 4 A *l* of the God of Jacob.
89:30 If his sons forsake My *l* And do
94:12 LORD, And teach out of Your *l*,
94:20 which devises evil by *l*,
119: 1 Who walk in the *l* of the
119:18 Wondrous things from Your *l*.
119:29 And grant me Your *l*
119:34 and I shall keep Your *l*;
119:44 So shall I keep Your *l*
119:51 I do not turn aside from Your *l*.
119:53 the wicked, who forsake Your *l*.
119:55 O LORD, And I keep Your *l*.
119:61 I have not forgotten Your *l*.
119:70 But I delight in Your *l*.
119:72 The *l* of Your mouth is better
119:77 For Your *l* is my delight.
119:85 is not according to Your *l*.
119:92 Unless Your *l* had been my
119:97 how I love Your *l*! It is my
119:109 Yet I do not forget Your *l*.
119:113 But I love Your *l*.
119:126 they have regarded Your *l* as
119:136 men do not keep Your *l*.
119:142 And Your *l* is truth.
119:150 They are far from Your *l*.
119:153 For I do not forget Your *l*.
119:163 lying, But I love Your *l*.
119:165 have those who love Your *l*,
119:174 And Your *l* is my delight.
Prov 1: 8 And do not forsake the *l* of
3: 1 My son, do not forget my *l*,
4: 2 Do not forsake my *l*.
6:20 And do not forsake the *l* of
6:23 And the *l* a light; Reproofs
7: 2 And my *l* as the apple of your
13:14 The *l* of the wise is a
28: 4 Those who forsake the *l* praise
28: 4 But such as keep the *l* contend
28: 7 Whoever keeps the *l* is a
28: 9 away his ear from hearing the *l*,
29:18 happy is he who keeps the *l*.
31: 5 they drink and forget the *l*,
31:26 And on her tongue is the *l* of
Isa 1:10 Give ear to the *l* of our God,
2: 3 of Zion shall go forth the *l*,
5:24 they have rejected the *l* of
8:16 Seal the *l* among my disciples.
8:20 To the *l* and to the testimony!
30: 9 who will not hear the *l* of
42: 4 coastlands shall wait for His *l*.
42:21 He will exalt the *l* and make
42:24 were they obedient to His *l*.
51: 4 For *l* will proceed from Me,
51: 7 people in whose heart is My *l*:
Jer 2: 8 And those who handle the *l*
6:19 not heeded My words, Nor My *l*,
8: 8 And the *l* of the LORD is
9:13 they have forsaken My *l* which
16:11 forsaken Me and not kept My *l*.
18:18 for the *l* shall not perish from
26: 4 to walk in My *l* which I have
31:33 I will put My *l* in their minds,
32:11 was sealed according to the *l*
32:23 Your voice or walked in Your *l*.
44:10 they have not walked in My *l* or
44:23 of the LORD or walked in His *l*,
Lam 2: 9 The *L* is no more, And her
Ezek 7:26 But the *l* will perish from the
22:26 priests have violated My *l*
43:12 This is the *l* of the temple:
43:12 this is the *l* of the temple.
Dan 6: 5 against him concerning the *l*
6: 8 according to the *l* of the Medes
6:12 according to the *l* of the Medes
6:15 that it is the *l* of the Medes
7:25 intend to change times and *l*.
9:11 Israel has transgressed Your *l*,
9:11 and the oath written in the *L*
9:13 As it is written in the *L* of
Hos 4: 6 you have forgotten the *l* of
8: 1 And rebelled against My *l*.
8:12 him the great things of My *l*,
Am 2: 4 they have despised the *l* of
Mic 4: 2 For out of Zion the *l* shall
Hab 1: 4 Therefore the *l* is powerless,
Zeph 3: 4 have done violence to the *l*.
Hag 2:11 the priests concerning the *l*,
Zech 7:12 refusing to hear the *l* and the
Mal 2: 6 The *l* of truth was in his
2: 7 And people should seek the *l*
2: 8 caused many to stumble at the *l*.
2: 9 have shown partiality in the *l*.
4: 4 Remember the *L* of Moses, My
Mt 5:17 that I came to destroy the *L*
5:18 by no means pass from the *l*
7:12 for this is the *L* and the
11:13 all the prophets and the *l*
12: 5 Or have you not read in the *l*
22:36 the great commandment in the *l*?
22:40 two commandments hang all the *L*
23:23 the weightier matters of the *l*:
Lk 2:22 according to the *l* of Moses
2:23 (as it is written in the *l* of
2:24 to what is said in the *l* of
2:27 to the custom of the *l*,
2:39 all things according to the *l*
5:17 and teachers of the *l* sitting
10:26 him, "What is written in the *l*?
16:16 The *l* and the prophets were
16:17 than for one tittle of the *l*
24:44 which were written in the *L* of
Jn 1:17 For the *l* was given through
1:45 Him of whom Moses in the *l*,
7:19 "Did not Moses give you the *l*,
7:19 yet none of you keeps the *l*?
7:23 so that the *l* of Moses should
7:49 crowd that does not know the *l*
7:51 Does our *l* judge a man before it
8: 5 "Now Moses, in the *l*,
8:17 It is also written in your *l*
10:34 "Is it not written in your *l*,
12:34 We have heard from the *l* that
15:25 which is written in their *l*,
18:31 judge Him according to your *l*.
19: 7 answered him, "We have a *l*,
19: 7 and according to our *l* He ought
Acts 5:34 a teacher of the *l* held in
6:13 this holy place and the *l*;
7:53 who have received the *l* by the
13:15 And after the reading of the *L*
13:39 not be justified by the *l* of
15: 5 to command them to keep the *l*
15:24 be circumcised and keep the *l*'
18:13 worship God contrary to the *l*.
18:15 words and names and your own *l*,
21:20 they are all zealous for the *l*;
21:24 walk orderly and keep the *l*.
21:28 against the people, the *l*,
22: 3 strictness of our fathers' *l*,
22:12 a devout man according to the *l*,
23: 3 to judge me according to the *l*,
23: 3 to be struck contrary to the *l*?
23:29 concerning questions of their *l*,
24: 6 to judge him according to our *l*.
24:14 which are written in the *L* and
25: 8 Neither against the *l* of the
28:23 Jesus from both the *L* of Moses
Rom 2:12 many as have sinned without *l*
2:12 law will also perish without *l*,
2:12 as many as have sinned in the *l*
2:12 law will be judged by the *l*
2:13 (for not the hearers of the *l*
2:13 but the doers of the *l* will be
2:14 Gentiles, who do not have the *l*,
2:14 nature do the things in the *l*,
2:14 although not having the *l*,
2:14 are a *l* to themselves,
2:15 who show the work of the *l*
2:17 called a Jew, and rest on the *l*,
2:18 being instructed out of the *l*,
2:20 of knowledge and truth in the *l*.
2:23 who make your boast in the *l*,
2:23 God through breaking the *l*?
2:25 profitable if you keep the *l*;
2:25 if you are a breaker of the *l*,
2:26 righteous requirements of the *l*,
2:27 if he fulfills the *l*,
2:27 are a transgressor of the *l*?
3:19 Now we know that whatever the *l*
3:19 to those who are under the *l*,
3:20 by the deeds of the *l* no flesh
3:20 for by the *l* is the knowledge
3:21 of God apart from the *l* is
3:21 being witnessed by the *L* and
3:27 It is excluded. By what *l*?

L

3:27 but by the *l* of faith.
3:28 apart from the deeds of the *l*.
3:31 Do we then make void the *l*
3:31 contrary, we establish the *l*.
4:13 or to his seed through the *l*,
4:14 For if those who are of the *l*
4:15 because the *l* brings about
4:15 for where there is no *l* there
4:16 only to those who are of the *l*,
5:13 (For until the *l* sin was in the
5:13 not imputed when there is no *l*.
5:20 Moreover the *l* entered that the
6:14 for you are not under *l* but
6:15 sin because we are not under *l*
7: 1 speak to those who know the *l*),
7: 1 that the *l* has dominion over a
7: 2 a husband is bound by the *l* to
7: 2 she is released from the *l* of
7: 3 dies, she is free from that *l*,
7: 4 also have become dead to the *l*
7: 5 which were aroused by the *l*
7: 6 have been delivered from the *l*,
7: 7 Is the *l* sin? Certainly not!
7: 7 known sin except through the *l*.
7: 7 covetousness unless the *l* had
7: 8 For apart from the *l* sin was
7: 9 I was alive once without the *l*,
7:12 Therefore the *l* is holy, and
7:14 For we know that the *l* is
7:16 I agree with the *l* that it is
7:21 I find then a *l*, that evil is
7:22 For I delight in the *l* of God
7:23 But I see another *l* in my
7:23 warring against the *l* of my
7:23 me into captivity to the *l* of
7:25 the mind I myself serve the *l*
7:25 but with the flesh the *l* of
8: 2 For the *l* of the Spirit of life
8: 2 has made me free from the *l* of
8: 3 For what the *l* could not do in
8: 4 righteous requirement of the *l*
8: 7 for it is not subject to the *l*
9: 4 covenants, the giving of the *l*,
9:31 but Israel, pursuing the *l* of
9:31 has not attained to the *l* of
9:32 it were, by the works of the *l*.
10: 4 For Christ is the end of the *l*
10: 5 righteousness which is of the *l*,
13: 8 another has fulfilled the *l*.
13:10 is the fulfillment of the *l*.
1 Cor 6: 1 go to *l* before the unrighteous,
6: 6 But brother goes to *l* against
6: 7 for you that you go to *l*
7:39 A wife is bound by *l* as long as
9: 8 Or does not the *l* say the same
9: 9 For it is written in the *l* of
9:20 to those who are under the *l*,
9:20 under the law, as under the *l*,
9:20 win those who are under the *l*;
9:21 to those who are without *l*,
9:21 as without *l* (not being without
9:21 law (not being without *l*
9:21 but under *l* toward Christ),
9:21 win those who are without *l*;
14:21 In the *l* it is written:
14:34 as the *l* also says.
15:56 the strength of sin is the *l*.
Gal 2:16 by the works of the *l* but by
2:16 and not by the works of the *l*;
2:16 for by the works of the *l* no
2:19 For I through the *l* died to the
2:19 I through the law died to the *l*
2:21 comes through the *l*,
3: 2 Spirit by the works of the *l*,
3: 5 do it by the works of the *l*,
3:10 as are of the works of the *l*
3:10 in the book of the *l*,
3:11 no one is justified by the *l*
3:12 Yet the *l* is not of faith, but
3:13 us from the curse of the *l*,
3:17 And this I say, that the *l*,
3:18 if the inheritance is of the *l*,
3:19 What purpose then does the *l*
3:21 Is the *l* then against the
3:21 not! For if there had been a *l*
3:21 would have been by the *l*.
3:23 were kept under guard by the *l*,
3:24 Therefore the *l* was our tutor
4: 4 of a woman, born under the *l*,
4: 5 those who were under the *l*,
4:21 who desire to be under the *l*,
4:21 the law, do you not hear the *l*?
5: 3 is a debtor to keep the whole *l*.
5: 4 attempt to be justified by *l*;
5:14 For all the *l* is fulfilled in
5:18 Spirit, you are not under the *l*.
5:23 Against such there is no *l*.
6: 2 and so fulfill the *l* of Christ.
6:13 who are circumcised keep the *l*,
Eph 2:15 the *l* of commandments
Phil 3: 5 the Hebrews; concerning the *l*,
3: 6 righteousness which is in the *l*,
3: 9 which is from the *l*,
1 Tim 1: 7 to be teachers of the *l*,
1: 8 But we know that the *l* is good
1: 9 that the *l* is not made for a
Titus 3: 9 and strivings about the *l*;
Heb 7: 5 the people according to the *l*,
7:11 it the people received the *l*),
7:12 there is also a change of the *l*.
7:16 not according to the *l* of a
7:19 for the *l* made nothing perfect;
7:28 For the *l* appoints as high
7:28 oath, which came after the *l*,
8: 4 the gifts according to the *l*;
9:19 the people according to the *l*,
9:22 And according to the *l* almost
10: 1 For the *l*, having a shadow
10: 8 are offered according to the *l*)
10:28 who has rejected Moses' *l* dies
Jas 1:25 he who looks into the perfect *l*
2: 8 you really fulfill the royal *l*
2: 9 and are convicted by the *l* as
2:10 whoever shall keep the whole *l*,
2:11 become a transgressor of the *l*.
2:12 who will be judged by the *l* of
4:11 speaks evil of the *l* and judges
4:11 of the law and judges the *l*.
4:11 the law. But if you judge the *l*,
4:11 you are not a doer of the *l* but

LAW OF MOSES (21/21)

Josh 8:31 is written in the Book of the *L*:
8:32 on the stones a copy of the *L*,
23: 6 is written in the Book of the *L*,
1 Ki 2: 3 as it is written in the *L*,
2 Ki 14: 6 is written in the Book of the *L*,
23:25 might, according to all the *L*;
2 Chr 23:18 as it is written in the *L*,
30:16 according to the *L* the man of
Ezra 3: 2 as it is written in the *L* the
7: 6 was a skilled scribe in the *L*,
Neh 8: 1 to bring the Book of the *L*,
Dan 9:11 and the oath written in the *L*
9:13 "As it is written in the *L*,
Mal 4: 4 'Remember the *L*, My servant,
Lk 2:22 according to the *L* were
24:44 which were written in the *L*
Jn 7:23 so that the *l* should not be
Acts 13:39 could not be justified by the *l*.
15: 5 to command them to keep the *l*.
28:23 Jesus from both the *L* and the
1 Cor 9: 9 For it is written in the *l*,

LAWFUL (38/36) LAW, LAWFULLY, UNLAWFUL

Ezra 7:24 you that it shall not be *l* to
Ezek 18: 5 man is just And does what is *l*
18:19 the son has done what is *l* and
18:21 and does what is *l* and right,
18:27 and does what is *l* and right,
33:14 his sin and does what is *l* and
33:16 he has done what is *l* and
33:19 wickedness and does what is *l*
Mt 12: 2 are doing what is not *l* to do
12: 4 the showbread which was not *l*
12:10 Is it *l* to heal on the
12:12 Therefore it is *l* to do good on
14: 4 It is not *l* for you to have
19: 3 Is it *l* for a man to divorce his
20:15 Is it not *l* for me to do what I
22:17 Is it *l* to pay taxes to Caesar,
27: 6 It is not *l* to put them into the
Mk 2:24 why do they do what is not *l* on
2:26 which is not *l* to eat, except
3: 4 Is it *l* on the Sabbath to do
6:18 It is not *l* for you to have your
10: 2 Is it *l* for a man to divorce
12:14 Is it *l* to pay taxes to Caesar,
Lk 6: 2 are you doing what is not *l* to
6: 4 which is not *l* for any but the
6: 9 Is it *l* on the Sabbath to do
14: 3 Is it *l* to heal on the
20:22 Is it *l* for us to pay taxes to
Jn 5:10 it is not *l* for you to carry
18:31 It is not *l* for us to put anyone
Acts 16:21 teach customs which are not *l*
19:39 it shall be determined in the *l*
22:25 Is it *l* for you to scourge a man
1 Cor 6:12 All things are *l* for me, but
6:12 All things are *l* for me, but I
10:23 All things are *l* for me, but
10:23 all things are *l* for me, but
2 Cor 12: 4 which it is not *l* for a man to

LAWFULLY (1/1) LAWFUL

1 Tim 1: 8 law is good if one uses it *l*,

LAWGIVER (6/6) LAW

Gen 49:10 Nor a *l* from between his feet,
Num 21:18 the nation's nobles, By the *l*,
Ps 60: 7 for My head; Judah is My *l*.
108: 8 for My head; Judah is My *l*.
Isa 33:22 our Judge, The LORD is our *L*,
Jas 4:12 There is one *L*, who is able

LAWGIVER'S (1/1)

Deut 33:21 Because a *l* portion was

LAWLESS (9/9) LAW, LAWLESSNESS

Acts 2:23 you have taken by *l* hands, have
Rom 4: 7 Blessed are those whose *l* deeds
2 Th 2: 8 And then the *l* one will be
2: 9 The coming of the *l* one is
1 Tim 1: 9 person, but for the *l* and
Titus 2:14 redeem us from every *l* deed
Heb 8:12 their sins and their *l* deeds
10:17 Their sins and their *l* deeds
2 Pe 2: 8 by seeing and hearing their *l*

LAWLESSNESS (11/9) LAWLESS

Mt 7:23 from Me, you who practice *l*!'
13:41 and those who practice *l*,
23:28 you are full of hypocrisy and *l*.
24:12 And because *l* will abound, the
Rom 6:19 and of *l* leading to more
6:19 lawlessness leading to more *l*,
2 Cor 6:14 has righteousness with *l*?
2 Th 2: 7 For the mystery of *l* is already
Heb 1: 9 righteousness and hated *l*;
1 Jn 3: 4 commits sin also commits *l*,
3: 4 lawlessness, and sin is *l*.

LAWS (19/18) LAW

Gen 26: 5 My statutes, and My *l*.
Ex 16:28 keep My commandments and My *l*?
18:16 the statutes of God and His *l*.
18:20 them the statutes and the *l*,
Lev 26:46 statutes and judgments and *l*
Ezra 7:25 all such as know the *l* of your
Neh 9:13 them just ordinances and true *l*,
9:14 them precepts, statutes and *l*,
Esth 1:19 let it be recorded in the *l* of
3: 8 their *l* are different from all
3: 8 they do not keep the king's *l*.
Ps 105:45 His statutes And keep His *l*.
Isa 24: 5 they have transgressed the *l*,
Ezek 43:11 all its forms and all its *l*.
44: 5 of the LORD and all its *l*.
44:24 They shall keep My *l* and My
Dan 9:10 LORD our God, to walk in His *l*,
Heb 8:10 I will put My *l* in their
10:16 I will put My *l* into

LAWSUIT (1/1)

2 Sam 15: 2 whenever anyone who had a *l*

LAWYER (3/3) LAW, LAWYERS

Mt 22:35 Then one of them, a *l*,
Lk 10:25 a certain *l* stood up and tested
Titus 3:13 Send Zenas the *l* and Apollos on

LAWYERS (5/5) LAWYER

Lk 7:30 But the Pharisees and *l* rejected
11:45 Then one of the *l* answered and
11:46 *l*! For you load men with
11:52 Woe to you *l*! For you have taken
14: 3 spoke to the *l* and Pharisees,

LAY (203/196) LAID, LAYING, LAYS, LIE

Gen 19: 4 Now before they *l* down, the men
19:33 And the firstborn went in and *l*
19:33 and he did not know when she *l*
19:34 Indeed I *l* with my father last
19:35 And the younger arose and *l*
19:35 and he did not know when she *l*
22:12 Do not *l* your hand on the lad,
28:11 and he *l* down in that place to
30:16 And he *l* with her that night.
34: 2 he took her and *l* with her, and
35:22 that Reuben went and *l* with
37:22 and do not *l* a hand on
Ex 5: 8 And you shall *l* on them the
7: 4 so that I may *l* My hand on
16:13 and in the morning the dew *l*
16:23 and *l* up for yourselves all
16:33 and *l* it up before the LORD,
24:11 of Israel He did not *l* His
Lev 1: 7 and *l* the wood in order on the
1: 8 shall *l* the parts, the head,
1:12 and the priest shall *l* them in
2:15 and *l* frankincense on it. It
3: 2 And he shall *l* his hand on the
3: 8 And he shall *l* his hand on the
3:13 He shall *l* his hand on its head
4: 4 *l* his hand on the bull's head,
4:15 of the congregation shall *l*
4:24 And he shall *l* his hand on the
4:29 And he shall *l* his hand on the
4:33 Then he shall *l* his hand on the
6:12 and *l* the burnt offering in
16:21 Aaron shall *l* both his hands on
24:14 then let all who heard him *l*
26:31 I will *l* your cities waste and
Num 8:10 the children of Israel shall *l*
8:12 Then the Levites shall *l* their
12:11 my lord! Please do not *l* this
22:27 she *l* down under Balaam;
27:18 and *l* your hand on him;
Deut 7:15 but will *l* them on all those
11:18 Therefore you shall *l* up these
21: 8 and do not *l* innocent blood to
22:22 the man that *l* with the woman,
22:25 then only the man who *l* with
22:29 then the man who *l* with her
Josh 2: 8 Now before they *l* down, she
6:26 he shall *l* its foundation with
8: 2 *L* an ambush for the city behind
8:11 Now a valley *l* between them
15:46 all that *l* near Ashdod, with
Judg 4:22 there *l* Sisera, dead with the
5:27 he *l* still; At her feet he
6:20 and the unleavened bread and *l*
9:34 and *l* in wait against Shechem
9:43 and *l* in wait in the field.
16: 2 surrounded the place and *l*
16: 3 And Samson *l* low till midnight;

Ruth 3: 7 his feet, and *l* down.
3:14 So she *l* at his feet until
1 Sam 2:22 and how they *l* with the women
3: 5 And he went and *l* down.
3: 9 " So Samuel went and *l* down
3:15 So Samuel *l* down until morning,
15: 5 and *l* in wait in the valley.
19:24 and *l* down naked all that day
26: 5 saw the place where Saul *l*,
26: 5 Now Saul *l* within the camp,
26: 7 and there Saul *l* sleeping
26: 7 And Abner and the people *l* all
28: 9 Why then do you *l* a snare for
2 Sam 2:21 and *l* hold on one of the young
11: 4 and he *l* with her, for she was
12: 3 drank from his own cup and *l*
12:16 David fasted and went in and *l*
12:24 and went in to her and *l* with
13: 6 Then Amnon *l* down and pretended
13:14 he forced her and *l* with her.
13:31 and tore his garments and *l* on
1 Ki 3:19 because she *l* on him.
5:17 to *l* the foundation of the
13:31 *l* my bones beside his bones.
18:23 and *l* it on the wood, but put
18:23 and *l* it on the wood, but put
19: 5 Then as he *l* and slept under a
19: 6 drank, and *l* down again.
21: 4 And he *l* down on his bed, and
21:27 and fasted and *l* in sackcloth,
2 Ki 4:11 in to the upper room and *l*
4:29 but *l* my staff on the face of
4:34 And he went up and *l* on the
10: 8 *L* them in two heaps at the
2 Chr 35: 5 houses of your brethren the *l*
35: 7 Then Josiah gave the *l* people
35:12 the fathers' houses of the *l*
35:13 them quickly among all the *l*
36:21 As long as she *l* desolate she
Neh 13:21 I will *l* hands on you!"
Esth 2:21 became furious and sought to *l*
3: 6 But he disdained to *l* hands on
4: 3 and many *l* in sackcloth and
6: 2 who had sought to *l* hands on
8: 7 because he tried to *l* his
9: 2 of King Ahasuerus to *l* hands
9:10 but they did not *l* a hand on
9:15 but they did not *l* a hand on
9:16 but they did not *l* a hand on
Job 1:12 only do not *l* a hand on his
9:33 Who may *l* his hand on us
22:22 And *l* up His words in your
22:24 Then you will *l* your gold in
40: 4 I *l* my hand over my mouth.
41: 8 *L* your hand on him
Ps 3: 5 I *l* down and slept; I awoke,
7: 5 And *l* my honor in the dust.
38:12 Those also who seek my life *l*
84: 3 Where she may *l* her
Prov 5: 5 Her steps *l* hold of hell.
Eccl 2: 3 and how to *l* hold on folly,
Isa 5: 6 I will *l* it waste; It shall
5:29 they will roar And *l* hold of
11:14 They shall *l* their hand on
13: 9 To *l* the land desolate;
13:11 And will *l* low the haughtiness
22:22 of the house of David I will *l*
25:12 *l* low, And bring to the
28:16 I *l* in Zion a stone for a
29: 3 I will *l* siege against you
29:21 And *l* a snare for him who
34:15 snake shall make her nest and *l*
35: 7 of jackals, where each *l*,
42:15 I will *l* waste the mountains
51:16 *L* the foundations of the
54:11 I will *l* your stones with
54:11 And *l* your foundations with
Jer 2:20 under every green tree You *l*
6:21 I will *l* stumbling blocks
6:23 They will *l* hold on bow and
Lam 4:19 us on the mountains And *l* in
Ezek 3:20 and I *l* a stumbling block
4: 1 take a clay tablet and *l* it
4: 2 *L* siege against it, build a
4: 3 and you shall *l* siege against
4: 4 and *l* the iniquity of the house
6: 5 And I will *l* the corpses of the
12:23 I will *l* this proverb to rest,
16:42 So I will *l* to rest My fury
19: 2 She *l* down among the lions;
25:14 I will *l* My vengeance on Edom by
25:17 when I *l* My vengeance upon
26:12 they will *l* your stones, your
26:16 *l* aside their robes, and take
32: 5 I will *l* your flesh on the
35: 4 I shall *l* your cities waste,
42:13 There they shall *l* the most
Am 5: 7 And *l* righteousness to rest in
Ob 7 who eat your bread shall *l* a
Mic 1: 7 All her idols I will *l*
Zeph 2:14 For He will *l* bare the cedar
Zech 12: 2 when they *l* siege against Judah
Mt 6:19 Do not *l* up for yourselves
6:20 but *l* up for yourselves
8:20 the Son of Man has nowhere to *l*
9:18 but come and *l* Your hand on her
12:11 will not *l* hold of it and lift
21:46 But when they sought to *l* hands
23: 4 and *l* them on men's shoulders;
28: 6 see the place where the Lord *l*.
Mk 1:30 But Simon's wife's mother *l* sick
3:21 they went out to *l* hold of Him,
5:23 Come and *l* Your hands on her,
12:12 And they sought to *l* hands on
16:18 they will *l* hands on the sick,
Lk 5:18 they sought to bring in and *l*
9:58 the Son of Man has nowhere to *l*
20:19 that very hour sought to *l*
21:12 they will *l* their hands on you
Jn 5: 3 In these *l* a great multitude of
10:15 and I *l* down My life for the
10:17 because I *l* down My life that I
10:18 but I *l* it down of Myself.
10:18 I have power to *l* it down,
11:38 and a stone *l* against it.
13:37 I will *l* down my life for Your
13:38 Will you *l* down your life for My
15:13 than to *l* down one's life for
Acts 8:19 that anyone on whom I *l* hands
15:28 to *l* upon you no greater burden
23:30 it was told me that the Jews *l*
25: 3 while they *l* in ambush along
28: 8 that the father of Publius *l*
Rom 9:33 I *l* in Zion a stumbling
1 Cor 3:11 other foundation can anyone *l*
16: 2 the week let each one of you *l*
2 Cor 12:14 the children ought not to *l* up
Phil 3:12 that I may *l* hold of that for
1 Tim 5:22 Do not *l* hands on anyone
6:12 *l* hold on eternal life, to
6:19 that they may *l* hold on eternal
Heb 6:18 who have fled for refuge to *l*
12: 1 let us *l* aside every weight,
Jas 1:21 Therefore *l* aside all
1 Pe 2: 6 I *l* in Zion A chief
1 Jn 3:16 And we also ought to *l* down

LAYER (1/1)

Ex 16:14 And when the *l* of dew lifted,

LAYERS (1/1)

Am 9: 6 He who builds His *l* in the sky,

LAYING (12/12) LAY

Deut 26:12 When you have finished *l* aside
2 Chr 31: 7 the third month they began *l*
Ps 64: 5 They talk of *l* snares
Hab 3:13 By *l* bare from foundation to
Mk 7: 8 For *l* aside the commandment of
Acts 8:18 Simon saw that through the *l*
9:17 and *l* his hands on him he said,
1 Tim 4:14 to you by prophecy with the *l*
2 Tim 1: 6 which is in you through the *l*
Heb 6: 1 not *l* again the foundation of
6: 2 baptisms, of *l* on of hands,
1 Pe 2: 1 *l* aside all malice, all deceit,

LAYS (14/13) LAY

Job 18: 9 And a snare *l* hold of him.
21:19 God *l* up one's iniquity for his
Ps 33: 7 He *l* up the deep in
91: 6 of the destruction that *l*
104: 3 He *l* the beams of His upper
Prov 13:16 But a fool *l* open his folly.
26:24 And *l* up deceit within
Isa 26: 5 He *l* it low, He lays it low
26: 5 He *l* it low to the ground,
30:32 Which the LORD *l* on him,
56: 2 And the son of man who *l* hold
Zech 12: 1 *l* the foundation of the earth,
Lk 12:21 So is he who *l* up treasure for
15: 5 he *l* it on his shoulders,

LAZARUS (15/15)

Lk 16:20 was a certain beggar named *L*,
16:23 and *L* in his bosom.
16:24 and send *L* that he may dip the
16:25 and likewise *L* evil things;
Jn 11: 1 *L* of Bethany, the town of Mary
11: 2 whose brother *L* was sick.
11: 5 Martha and her sister and *L*.
11:11 Our friend *L* sleeps, but I go
11:14 them plainly, "*L* is dead.
11:43 He cried with a loud voice, "*L*,
12: 1 where *L* was who had been dead,
12: 2 but *L* was one of those who sat
12: 9 but that they might also see *L*,
12:10 chief priests plotted to put *L*
12:17 were with Him when He called *L*

LAZINESS (2/2)

Prov 19:15 *L* casts one into a deep sleep,
Eccl 10:18 Because of *l* the building

LAZY (16/16)

Prov 10:26 So is the *l* man to those who
12:24 But the *l* man will be put to
12:27 The *l* man does not roast what
13: 4 The soul of a *l* man desires,
15:19 The way of the *l* man is like
19:24 A *l* man buries his hand in the
20: 4 The *l* man will not plow
21:25 The desire of the *l* man kills
22:13 The *l* man says, "There is a
24:30 I went by the field of the *l*
26:13 The *l* man says, "There is
26:14 So does the *l* man on his
26:15 The *l* man buries his hand in
26:16 The *l* man is wiser in his own
Mt 25:26 You wicked and *l* servant, you
Titus 1:12 evil beasts, *l* gluttons."

LEAD (62/62) LEADER, LEADING, LEADS, LED

Gen 33:14 I will *l* on slowly at a pace
Ex 13:17 that God did not *l* them by way
13:21 day in a pillar of cloud to *l*
15:10 They sank like *l* in the mighty
32:34 *l* the people to the place of
Num 27:17 who may *l* them out and bring
31:22 the iron, the tin, and the *l*,
Deut 20: 9 captains of the armies to *l*
Judg 5: 2 'When leaders *l* in Israel,
5:12 and *l* your captives away, O
1 Sam 30:22 that they may *l* them away and
2 Chr 30: 9 with compassion by those who *l*
Neh 9:19 To *l* them on the road;
Job 19:24 a rock With an iron pen and *l*,
Ps 5: 8 *L* me, O LORD, in Your
25: 5 *L* me in Your truth and teach
27:11 And *l* me in a smooth path,
31: 3 *L* me and guide me.
43: 3 and Your truth! Let them *l* me;
60: 9 Who will *l* me to Edom?
61: 2 *L* me to the rock that is
80: 1 You who *l* Joseph like a flock;
108:10 Who will *l* me to Edom?
125: 5 The LORD shall *l* them away
139:10 Even there Your hand shall *l*
139:24 And *l* me in the way
143:10 *L* me in the land of
Prov 6:22 they will *l* you; When you
21: 5 The plans of the diligent *l*
Song 8: 2 I would *l* you and bring you
Isa 3:12 O My people! Those who *l* you
11: 6 And a little child shall *l*
20: 4 shall the king of Assyria *l*
40:11 And gently *l* those who are
42:16 I will *l* them in paths they
49:10 He who has mercy on them will *l*
57:18 I will also *l* him,
63:14 So You *l* Your people, To make
Jer 6:29 The *l* is consumed by the fire;
31: 9 with supplications I will *l*
31:32 I took them by the hand to *l*
32: 5 then he shall *l* Zedekiah to
Ezek 22:18 all bronze, tin, iron, and *l*,
22:20 gather silver, bronze, iron, *l*,
27:12 and *l* for your goods.
38: 4 and *l* you out, with all your
39: 2 I will turn you around and *l*
Am 2: 4 Their lies *l* them astray,
Nah 2: 7 And her maidservants shall *l*
Zech 5: 7 Here is a *l* disc lifted up, and
5: 8 and threw the *l* cover over its
Mt 6:13 And do not *l* us into
Mk 14:44 seize Him and *l* Him away
Lk 6:39 'Can the blind *l* the blind?
11: 4 And do not *l* us into
13:15 and *l* it away to water it?
Acts 13:11 around seeking someone to *l*
1 Th 4:11 that you also aspire to *l* a
1 Tim 2: 2 that we may *l* a quiet and
Heb 8: 9 them by the hand to *l*
1 Jn 5:16 a sin which does not *l* to
Rev 7:17 will shepherd them and *l* them

LEADER (67/67) LEAD, LEADERS

Num 2: 3 of Amminadab shall be the *l*
2: 5 son of Zuar shall be the *l*
2: 7 son of Helon shall be the *l*
2:10 and the *l* of the children of
2:12 and the *l* of the children of
2:14 and the *l* of the children of
2:18 and the *l* of the children of
2:20 and the *l* of the children of
2:22 and the *l* of the children of
2:25 and the *l* of the children of
2:27 and the *l* of the children of
2:29 and the *l* of the children of
3:24 And the *l* of the fathers' house
3:30 And the *l* of the fathers' house
3:35 The *l* of the fathers' house of
7:11 one *l* each day, for the
7:18 *l* of Issachar, presented an
7:24 *l* of the children of Zebulun,
7:30 *l* of the children of Reuben,
7:36 *l* of the children of Simeon,
7:42 *l* of the children of Gad,
7:48 *l* of the children of Ephraim,
7:54 *l* of the children of Manasseh,
7:60 *l* of the children of Benjamin,
7:66 *l* of the children of Dan,
7:72 *l* of the children of Asher,
7:78 *l* of the children of Naphtali,
13: 2 every one a *l* among them."
14: 4 Let us select a *l* and return to
17: 6 for each *l* according to their
25:14 a *l* of a father's house among
25:18 the daughter of a *l* of Midian,
34:18 And you shall take one *l* of
34:22 a *l* from the tribe of the
34:23 a *l* from the tribe of the
34:24 and a *l* from the tribe of the
34:25 a *l* from the tribe of the
34:26 a *l* from the tribe of the
34:27 a *l* from the tribe of the
34:28 and a *l* from the tribe of the

L

1 Sam 19:20 and Samuel standing as *l* over
2 Ki 20: 5 and tell Hezekiah the *l*
1 Chr 2:10 *l* of the children of Judah;
5: 6 He was *l* of the Reubenites.
12:27 the *l* of the Aaronites, and
13: 1 and hundreds, and with every *l*.
15:22 *l* of the Levites, was
27: 4 Mikloth also was the *l*;
29:22 before the LORD to be the *l*,
2 Chr 1: 2 and to every *l* in all Israel,
11:22 to be *l* among his brothers;
32:21 every mighty man of valor, *l*,
Neh 3: 9 *l* of half the district of
3:12 *l* of half the district of
3:14 *l* of the district of Beth
3:15 *l* of the district of Mizpah,
3:16 *l* of half the district of Beth
3:17 *l* of half the district of
3:18 *l* of the other half of the
3:19 the *l* of Mizpah, repaired
7: 2 and Hananiah the *l* of the
9:17 They appointed a *l* To
11:11 was the *l* of the house of God.
11:17 the *l* who began the
Ps 68:27 is little Benjamin, their *l*,
Isa 55: 4 A *l* and commander for the
Zech 9: 7 And shall be like a *l* in

LEADERS (94/88) LEADER

Num 1:16 *l* of their fathers' tribes,
1:44 with the *l* of Israel, twelve
3:32 was to be chief over the *l*
4:34 and the *l* of the congregation
4:46 and the *l* of Israel numbered,
7: 2 Then the *l* of Israel, the heads
7: 2 who were the *l* of the tribes
7: 3 a cart for every two of the *l*,
7:10 Now the *l* offered the
7:10 so the *l* offered their offering
7:84 for the altar from the *l* of
10: 4 they blow only one, then the *l*,
16: 2 two hundred and fifty *l* of the
17: 2 all their *l* according to their
17: 6 and each of their *l* gave him a
21:18 The well the *l* sank, Dug by
25: 4 Take all the *l* of the people and
27: 2 and before the *l* and all the
31:13 and all the *l* of the
32: 2 and to the *l* of the
36: 1 before Moses and before the *l*,
Deut 1:15 *l* of thousands, leaders of
1:15 *l* of hundreds, leaders of
1:15 *l* of fifties, leaders of tens,
1:15 *l* of tens, and officers for
29:10 your *l* and your tribes and your
32:42 From the heads of the *l* of the
33: 5 When the *l* of the people were
Judg 5: 2 When *l* lead in Israel, When the
8: 6 And the *l* of Succoth said,
8:14 he wrote down for him the *l* of
10:18 the *l* of Gilead, said to one
20: 2 And the *l* of all the people, all
1 Ki 20:14 By the young *l* of the
20:15 Then he mustered the young *l* of
20:17 The young *l* of the provinces
20:19 Then these young *l* of the
2 Ki 11:14 and the *l* and the trumpeters
1 Chr 4:38 mentioned by name were *l* in
7:40 mighty men of valor, chief *l*.
15:16 Then David spoke to the *l* of
21: 2 said to Joab and to the *l* of
22:17 also commanded all the *l* of
23: 2 he gathered together all the *l*
24: 4 There were more *l* found of the
24: 6 down before the king, the *l*,
27:22 These were the *l* of the tribes
28: 1 at Jerusalem all the *l* of
28:21 also the *l* and all the people
29: 6 Then the *l* of the fathers'
29: 6 *l* of the tribes of Israel, the
29:24 All the *l* and the mighty men,
2 Chr 12: 5 came to Rehoboam and the *l* of
12: 6 So the *l* of Israel and the king
17: 7 year of his reign he sent his *l*,
23:13 and the *l* and the trumpeters
24:10 Then all the *l* and all the
24:17 the death of Jehoiada the *l* of
24:23 and destroyed all the *l* of the
28:14 and the spoil before the *l* and
28:21 of the king, and from the *l*,
29:30 King Hezekiah and the *l*
30: 2 For the king and his *l* and all
30: 6 letters from the king and his *l*,
30:12 command of the king and the *l*,
30:24 and the *l* gave to the assembly
31: 8 And when Hezekiah and the *l* came
32: 3 he consulted with his *l* and
35: 8 And his *l* gave willingly to the
36:14 Moreover all the *l* of the
36:18 of the king and of his *l*,
Ezra 8:16 Zechariah, and Meshullam, *l*;
8:20 whom David and the *l* had
8:24 I separated twelve of the *l* of
8:29 you weigh them before the *l*
9: 1 the *l* came to me, saying, "The
9: 2 the hand of the *l* and rulers
10: 5 and made the *l* of the priests,
10: 8 to the instructions of the *l*
10:14 let the *l* of our entire
Neh 4:14 said to the nobles, to the *l*,
4:16 and the *l* were behind all the
9:38 covenant, and write it; our *l*,
10:14 The *l* of the people: Parosh,
11: 1 Now the *l* of the people dwelt at
12:31 So I brought the *l* of Judah up
12:32 Hoshaiah and half of the *l* of
Isa 9:16 For the *l* of this people cause
Jer 25:34 You *l* of the flock! For the
25:35 Nor the *l* of the flock to
25:36 And a wailing of the *l* to the
Mt 15:14 They are blind *l* of the blind.
Lk 19:47 and the *l* of the people sought
Acts 28:17 days that Paul called the *l* of

LEADING (17/14) LEAD

Judg 3:28 the fords of the Jordan *l* to
9:39 *l* the men of Shechem, and
2 Chr 25:11 and *l* his people, he went to
Ezra 7:28 and I gathered *l* men of Israel
Acts 15:22 *l* men among the brethren.
17: 4 and not a few of the *l* women,
28: 7 there was an estate of the *l*
Rom 6:16 whether of sin *l* to death, or
6:16 or of obedience *l* to
6:19 and of lawlessness *l* to more
15: 2 his good, *l* to edification.
2 Cor 2:16 we are the aroma of death *l*
2:16 the other the aroma of life *l*
7:10 sorrow produces repentance *l*
1 Jn 5:16 those who commit sin not *l* to
5:16 There is sin *l* to death. I do
5:17 and there is sin not *l* to

LEADS (22/22) LEAD

Job 12:17 He *l* counselors away plundered,
12:19 He *l* princes away plundered,
Ps 23: 2 He *l* me beside the still
23: 3 He *l* me in the paths of
Prov 2:18 For her house *l* down to death,
10:16 The labor of the righteous *l*
11:19 As righteousness *l* to life,
11:24 But it *l* to poverty.
12:26 For the way of the wicked *l*
14:23 But idle chatter *l* only to
16:29 And *l* him in a way that is
19:23 The fear of the LORD *l* to
Isa 48:17 Who *l* you by the way you
Mt 7:13 and broad is the way that *l*
7:14 difficult is the way which *l*
15:14 And if the blind *l* the blind,
Jn 10: 3 his own sheep by name and *l*
Acts 12:10 came to the iron gate that *l*
Rom 2: 4 that the goodness of God *l* you
12: 8 with liberality; he who *l*,
2 Cor 2:14 thanks be to God who always *l*
Rev 13:10 He who *l* into captivity shall go

LEAF (9/9) LEAVES

Gen 8:11 a freshly plucked olive *l* was
Lev 26:36 the sound of a shaken *l* shall
Job 13:25 Will You frighten a *l* driven to
Ps 1: 3 Whose *l* also shall not wither;
Isa 1:30 shall be as a terebinth whose *l*
34: 4 host shall fall down As the *l*
64: 6 We all fade as a *l*,
Jer 8:13 And the *l* shall fade;
17: 8 But its *l* will be green, And

LEAFY (3/3)

Lev 23:40 the boughs of *l* trees, and
Neh 8:15 and branches of *l* trees, to
Mk 11: 8 and others cut down *l* branches

LEAGUE (1/1)

Dan 11:23 And after the *l* is made with

LEAH (28/27) LEAH'S

Gen 29:16 the name of the elder was *L*,
29:23 that he took *L* his daughter and
29:24 maid Zilpah to his daughter *L*
29:25 morning, that behold, it was *L*.
29:30 also loved Rachel more than *L*.
29:31 When the LORD saw that *L* was
29:32 So *L* conceived and bore a son,
30: 9 When *L* saw that she had stopped
30:11 Then *L* said, "A troop comes!"
30:13 Then *L* said, "I am happy, for
30:14 brought them to his mother *L*.
30:14 Then Rachel said to *L*,
30:16 *L* went out to meet him and
30:17 And God listened to *L*,
30:18 *L* said, "God has given me my
30:19 Then *L* conceived again and bore
30:20 And *L* said, "God has endowed me
31: 4 sent and called Rachel and *L*
31:14 Then Rachel and *L* answered and
33: 1 he divided the children among *L*,
33: 2 *L* and her children behind, and
33: 7 And *L* also came near with her
34: 1 Now Dinah the daughter of *L*,
35:23 the sons of *L* were Reuben,
46:15 These were the sons of *L*,
46:18 whom Laban gave to *L* his
49:31 his wife, and there I buried *L*.
Ruth 4:11 to your house like Rachel and *L*,

LEAH'S (6/5) LEAH

Gen 29:17 *L* eyes were delicate, but
30:10 And *L* maid Zilpah bore Jacob a
30:12 And *L* maid Zilpah bore Jacob a
31:33 into *L* tent, and into the two
31:33 Then he went out of *L* tent and
35:26 *L* maidservant, were Gad and

LEAKS (1/1)

Eccl 10:18 idleness of hands the house *l*.

LEAN (6/6) LEANED, LEANING, LEANNESS, LEANS

Judg 16:26 so that I can *l* on them."
Prov 3: 5 And *l* not on your own
Isa 17: 4 the fatness of his flesh grow *l*.
48: 2 And *l* on the God of Israel;
Ezek 34:20 judge between the fat and the *l*
Mic 3:11 Yet they *l* on the LORD, and

LEANED (5/5) LEAN

2 Ki 7: 2 on whose hand the king *l*
7:17 the officer on whose hand he *l*
Ezek 29: 7 When they *l* on you, You broke
Am 5:19 *L* his hand on the wall, And a
Jn 21:20 who also had *l* on His breast at

LEANFLESHED (KJV) See GAUNT

LEANING (6/6) LEAN

2 Sam 1: 6 *l* on his spear; and indeed the
Ps 62: 3 Like a *l* wall and a tottering
Song 8: 5 *L* upon her beloved?
Jn 13:23 Now there was *l* on Jesus' bosom
13:25 *l* back on Jesus' breast, he
Heb 11:21 *l* on the top of his staff.

LEANNESS (3/3) LEAN

Job 16: 8 My *l* rises up against me And
Ps 106:15 But sent *l* into their soul.
Isa 10:16 Will send *l* among his fat

LEANNOTH (1/1)

Ps 88: Set to "Mahalath *L*."

LEANS (5/5) LEAN

2 Sam 3:29 who *l* on a staff or falls by
2 Ki 5:18 and he *l* on my hand, and I bow
18:21 Egypt, on which if a man *l*,
Job 8:15 He *l* on his house, but it does
Isa 36: 6 Egypt, on which if a man *l*,

LEAP (9/9) LEAPED, LEAPING

Gen 31:12 all the rams which *l* on the
Lev 11:21 their feet with which to *l* on
Deut 33:22 He shall *l* from Bashan."
2 Sam 22:30 By my God I can *l* over a wall.
Ps 18:29 By my God I can *l* over a wall.
Isa 35: 6 Then the lame shall *l* like a
Joel 2: 5 Over mountaintops they *l*,
Zeph 1: 9 I will punish All those who *l*
Lk 6:23 Rejoice in that day and *l* for

LEAPED (7/7) LEAP

Gen 31:10 the rams which *l* upon the
1 Ki 18:26 Then they *l* about the altar
Song 5: 6 My heart *l* up when he spoke.
Lk 1:41 that the babe *l* in her womb;
1:44 the babe *l* in my womb for joy.
Acts 14:10 on your feet!" And he *l* and
19:16 in whom the evil spirit was *l*

LEAPING (4/3) LEAP

2 Sam 6:16 a window and saw King David *l*
Song 2: 8 he comes *L* upon the mountains,
Acts 3: 8 *l* up, stood and walked and
3: 8 the temple with them—walking, *l*,

LEAPS (1/1)

Job 37: 1 And *l* from its place.

LEARN (35/35) LEARNED, LEARNING

Deut 4:10 that they may *l* to fear Me all
5: 1 that you may *l* them and be
14:23 that you may *l* to fear the
17:19 that he may *l* to fear the LORD
18: 9 you shall not *l* to follow the
31:12 may hear and that they may *l*
31:13 may hear and *l* to fear the
Esth 2:11 to *l* of Esther's welfare and
4: 5 to *l* what and why this was.
Ps 119: 7 When I *l* Your righteous
119:71 That I may *l* Your statutes.
119:73 that I may *l* Your commandments.
Prov 22:25 Lest you *l* his ways And set a
Isa 1:17 *L* to do good; Seek justice,
2: 4 Neither shall they *l* war
26: 9 inhabitants of the world will *l*
26:10 Yet he will not *l*
29:24 those who complained will *l*
Jer 10: 2 Do not *l* the way of the

12:16 if they will l carefully the
Mic 4: 3 Neither shall they l war any
Mt 9:13 But go and l what this means:
11:29 Take My yoke upon you and l from
24:32 Now l this parable from the fig
Mk 13:28 Now l this parable from the fig
1 Cor 4: 6 that you may l in us not to
14:31 that all may l and all may be
14:35 And if they want to l something,
Gal 3: 2 This only I want to l from you:
1 Tim 1:20 to Satan that they may l not
2:11 Let a woman l in silence with
5: 4 let them first l to show piety
5:13 And besides they l to be idle,
Titus 3:14 And let our people also l to
Rev 14: 3 and no one could l that song

LEARNED (21/19) LEARN

Gen 30:27 for I have l by experience
Esth 4: 1 When Mordecai l all that had
Ps 106:35 with the Gentiles And l their
Prov 30: 3 I neither l wisdom Nor have
Isa 50: 4 given Me The tongue of the l,
50: 4 My ear To hear as the l.
Ezek 19: 3 He l to catch prey, And he
19: 6 He l to catch prey;
Jn 6:45 everyone who has heard and l
Acts 7:22 And Moses was l in all the
17:13 the Jews from Thessalonica l
23:27 having l that he was a Roman.
Rom 16:17 to the doctrine which you l,
Eph 4:20 But you have not so l Christ,
Phil 4: 9 The things which you l and
4:11 for I have l in whatever state
4:12 and in all things I have l
Col 1: 7 as you also l from Epaphras, our
2 Tim 3:14 in the things which you have l
3:14 knowing from whom you have l
Heb 5: 8 yet He l obedience by the

LEARNING (7/7) LEARN

Prov 1: 5 man will hear and increase l,
9: 9 man, and he will increase in l.
16:21 of the lips increases l.
16:23 And adds l to his lips.
Acts 26:24 are beside yourself! Much l is
Rom 15: 4 before were written for our l,
2 Tim 3: 7 always l and never able to come

LEASE (1/1) LEASED

Mt 21:41 and l his vineyard to other

LEASED (4/4) LEASE

Song 8:11 He l the vineyard to keepers;
Mt 21:33 And he l it to vinedressers and
Mk 12: 1 And he l it to vinedressers and
Lk 20: 9 l it to vinedressers, and went

LEASH (2/2)

Job 41: 5 Or will you l him for your
1 Cor 7:35 not that I may put a l on you,

LEASING (KJV) See FALSEHOOD

LEAST (42/40)

Gen 24:55 at l ten; after that she may
32:10 I am not worthy of the l of all
Num 11:32 the quail (he who gathered l
Deut 7: 7 for you were the l of all
Judg 3: 2 at l those who had not formerly
6:15 and I am the l in my father's
1 Sam 9:21 and my family the l of all the
21: 4 if the young men have at l kept
2 Ki 18:24 you repel one captain of the l
20:19 not be peace and truth at l in
1 Chr 12:14 the l was over a hundred, and
Isa 36: 9 you repel one captain of the l
39: 8 At l there will be peace and
Jer 6:13 Because from the l of them even
8:10 Because from the l even to the
31:34 from the l of them to the
42: 1 from the l to the greatest,
42: 8 and all the people from the l
44:12 from the l to the greatest, by
49:20 Surely the l of the flock
50:12 the l of the nations shall be
50:45 Surely the l of the flock
Jon 3: 5 from the greatest to the l of
Mt 2: 6 Are not the l among the
5:19 therefore breaks one of the l
5:19 shall be called l in the
11:11 but he who is l in the kingdom
13:32 which indeed is the l of all the
25:40 as you did it to one of the l
25:45 did not do it to one of the l
Lk 7:28 but he who is l in the kingdom
9:48 For he who is l among you all
12:26 then are not able to do the l,
16:10 is faithful in what is l is
16:10 he who is unjust in what is l
Acts 5:15 that at l the shadow of Peter
8:10 from the l to the greatest,
1 Cor 6: 4 do you appoint those who are l
15: 9 For I am the l of the apostles,
2 Cor 11:16 at l receive me as a fool, that
Eph 3: 8 who am less than the l of all

Heb 8:11 from the l of them to

LEATHER (17/14)

Lev 13:48 whether in l or in anything
13:48 or in anything made of l,
13:49 in the garment or in the l,
13:49 woof, or in anything made of l,
13:51 in the l or in anything made
13:51 or in anything made of l,
13:52 or in linen, or anything of l,
13:53 woof, or in anything made of l,
13:56 of the woof, or out of the l.
13:57 woof, or in anything made of l,
13:58 woof, or whatever is made of l,
13:59 woof, or in anything made of l,
15:17 And any garment and any l on
Num 31:20 garment, everything made of l,
2 Ki 1: 8 A hairy man wearing a l belt
Mt 3: 4 with a l belt around his waist;
Mk 1: 6 with camel's hair and with a l

LEATHERN (KJV) See LEATHER

LEAVE (107/106)

Gen 2:24 Therefore a man shall l his
28:15 for I will not l you until I
33:15 Now let me l with you some of
42:15 you shall not l this place
42:33 L one of your brothers here
44:22 The lad cannot l his father, for
44:22 for if he should l his father,
Ex 16:19 Let no one l any of it till
23:11 people may eat; and what they l,
Lev 7:15 He shall not l any of it until
16:23 and shall l them there.
19:10 you shall l them for the poor
22:30 you shall l none of it until
23:22 You shall l them for the poor
Num 9:12 They shall l none of it until
10:31 Moses said, "Please do not l,
32:15 He will once again l them in
Deut 28:51 they shall not l you grain or
31: 6 He will not l you nor forsake
31: 8 He will not l you nor forsake
Josh 1: 5 I will not l you nor forsake
4: 3 carry them over with you and l
Judg 6: 4 and l no sustenance for Israel,
16:17 then my strength will l me, and
Ruth 1:16 'Entreat me not to l you,
2:16 l it that she may glean, and
1 Sam 14:36 and let us not l a man of
25:22 if I l one male of all who
2 Sam 14: 7 and l to my husband neither
1 Ki 8:57 May He not l us nor forsake us,
15:29 He did not l to Jeroboam anyone
16:11 he did not l him one male,
2 Ki 2: 2 I will not l you!" So they
2: 4 I will not l you!" So they
2: 6 I will not l you!" So the two
4:30 I will not l you." So he arose
9:15 let no one l or escape from
1 Chr 28: 8 and l it as an inheritance for
28:20 He will not l you nor forsake
2 Chr 35:15 they did not have to l their
Ezra 9: 8 to l us a remnant to escape,
9:12 and l it as an inheritance to
Neh 6: 3 the work cease while I l it
13: 6 certain days I obtained l from
Esth 6:10 sits within the king's gate! L
Job 10:20 Cease! L me alone, that I may
39:11 Or will you l your labor to
Ps 16:10 For You will not l my soul in
17:14 And l the rest of their
27: 9 Do not l me nor forsake me,
37:33 The LORD will not l him in his
49:10 And l their wealth to others.
119:121 Do not l me to my oppressors.
141: 8 Do not l my soul destitute.
Prov 2:13 From those who l the paths of
22:10 scoffer, and contention will l;
Eccl 2:18 because I must l it to the man
2:21 yet he must l his heritage to a
10: 4 Do not l your post; For
Isa 10: 3 And where will you l your
65:15 You shall l your name as a
Jer 9: 2 That I might l my people,
14: 9 Do not l us!
17:11 It will l him in the midst of
18:14 Will a man l the snow water
46:28 For I will not l you wholly
48:28 L the cities and dwell in the
49: 9 Would they not l some
49:11 L your fatherless children,
Ezek 6: 8 Yet I will l a remnant, so that
16:39 and l you naked and bare.
17: 9 And l it to wither? All of
22:20 and I will l you there and
23:29 and l you naked and bare.
29: 5 I will l you in the wilderness,
32: 4 Then I will l you on the land;
42:14 but there they shall l their
44:19 l them in the holy chambers,
Dan 4:15 Nevertheless l the stump and
4:23 but l its stump and roots in
4:26 as they gave the command to l
Hos 12:14 Therefore his Lord will l the
Joel 2:14 And l a blessing behind Him—A
Zeph 3: 3 are evening wolves That l
3:12 I will l in your midst A meek
Mal 4: 1 That will l them neither root

Mt 5:24 l your gift there before the
18:12 does he not l the ninety-nine
19: 5 reason a man shall l his
Mk 10: 7 reason a man shall l his
12:21 nor did he l any offspring. And
Lk 15: 4 does not l the ninety-nine in
19:44 and they will not l in you one
Jn 14:18 I will not l you orphans; I will
14:27 Peace I l with you, My peace I
16:28 I l the world and go to the
16:32 and will l Me alone. And yet I
Acts 2:27 For You will not l my
6: 2 not desirable that we should l
14:17 Nevertheless He did not l
18:18 Then he took l of the brethren
18:21 but took l of them, saying, "I
21: 6 When we had taken our l of one
2 Cor 2:13 but taking my l of them, I
Eph 5:31 reason a man shall l his
Heb 13: 5 I will never l you nor
Rev 11: 2 But l out the court which is

LEAVED (KJV) See DOUBLE

LEAVEN (24/21) LEAVENED, LEAVENS, UNLEAVENED

Ex 12:15 first day you shall remove l
12:19 For seven days no l shall be
13: 7 nor shall l be seen among you
34:25 blood of My sacrifice with l,
Lev 2:11 the LORD shall be made with l,
2:11 for you shall burn no l nor any
6:17 'It shall not be baked with l.
10:12 and eat it without l beside the
23:17 they shall be baked with l.
Deut 16: 4 And no l shall be seen among you
Am 4: 5 of thanksgiving with l,
Mt 13:33 kingdom of heaven is like l,
16: 6 Take heed and beware of the l of
16:11 but to beware of the l of the
16:12 tell them to beware of the l
Mk 8:15 beware of the l of the
8:15 of the Pharisees and the l of
Lk 12: 1 Beware of the l of the
13:21 'It is like l, which a woman
1 Cor 5: 6 Do you not know that a little l
5: 7 Therefore purge out the old l,
5: 8 keep the feast, not with old l,
5: 8 nor with the l of malice and
Gal 5: 9 A little l leavens the whole

LEAVENED (13/13) LEAVEN

Ex 12:15 For whoever eats l bread from
12:19 since whoever eats what is l,
12:20 'You shall eat nothing l;
12:34 their dough before it was l,
12:39 out of Egypt; for it was not l,
13: 3 No l bread shall be eaten.
13: 7 And no l bread shall be seen
23:18 blood of My sacrifice with l
Lev 7:13 his offering he shall offer l
Deut 16: 3 You shall eat no l bread with
Hos 7: 4 the dough, Until it is l.
Mt 13:33 of meal till it was all l.
Lk 13:21 of meal till it was all l.

LEAVENS (2/2) LEAVEN

1 Cor 5: 6 not know that a little leaven l
Gal 5: 9 A little leaven l the whole

LEAVES (23/20)

Gen 3: 7 and they sewed fig l together
Deut 28:54 rest of his children whom he l
Job 39:14 For she l her eggs on the
41:32 He l a shining wake behind him;
Prov 13:22 A good man l an inheritance to
28: 3 like a driving rain which l
Ezek 17: 9 All of its spring l will
35: 7 cut off from it the one who l
47:12 their l will not wither, and
47:12 and their l for medicine."
Dan 4:12 Its l were lovely, Its fruit
4:14 Strip off its l and scatter
4:21 whose l were lovely and its
Zech 11:17 Who l the flock! A sword
Mt 21:19 and found nothing on it but l,
24:32 become tender and puts forth l,
Mk 11:13 from afar a fig tree having l,
11:13 to it, He found nothing but l,
12:19 and l his wife behind, and
12:19 and l no children, his brother
13:28 become tender, and puts forth l,
Jn 10:12 sees the wolf coming and l the
Rev 22: 2 The l of the tree were for the

LEAVING (9/9)

Jer 44: 7 Judah, l none to remain,
Mt 4:13 And l Nazareth, He came and
23:23 without l the others undone.
Lk 4:42 and tried to keep Him from l
10:30 departed, l him half dead.
11:42 without l the others undone.
Rom 1:27 l the natural use of the woman,
Heb 6: 1 l the discussion of the
1 Pe 2:21 l us an example, that you

L

LEB (1/1)
Jer 51: 1 Against those who dwell in *L*

LEBANA (1/1)
Neh 7:48 the sons of *L*, the sons of

LEBANAH (1/1)
Ezra 2:45 the sons of *L*, the sons of

LEBANON (71/64)
Deut 1: 7 land of the Canaanites and to *L*,
3:25 those pleasant mountains, and *L*.
11:24 from the wilderness and *L*,
Josh 1: 4 the wilderness and this *L*
9: 1 of the Great Sea toward *L*—
11:17 as Baal Gad in the Valley of *L*
12: 7 Baal Gad in the Valley of *L* as
13: 5 of the Gebalites, and all *L*,
13: 6 of the mountains from *L* as far
Judg 3: 3 Hivites who dwelt in Mount *L*,
9:15 And devour the cedars of *L*!'
1 Ki 4:33 from the cedar tree of *L* even
5: 6 cut down cedars for me from *L*;
5: 9 shall bring them down from *L*
5:14 And he sent them to *L*,
5:14 they were one month in *L* and
7: 2 the House of the Forest of *L*;
9:19 to build in Jerusalem, in *L*,
10:17 in the House of the Forest of *L*.
10:21 of the House of the Forest of *L*
2 Ki 14: 9 The thistle that was in *L* sent
14: 9 to the cedar that was in *L*,
14: 9 and a wild beast that was in *L*
19:23 mountains, To the limits of *L*;
2 Chr 2: 8 cypress and algum logs from *L*,
2: 8 have skill to cut timber in *L*;
2:16 And we will cut wood from *L*,
8: 6 to build in Jerusalem, in *L*,
9:16 in the House of the Forest of *L*.
9:20 of the House of the Forest of *L*
25:18 The thistle that was in *L* sent
25:18 sent to the cedar that was in *L*,
25:18 and a wild beast that was in *L*
Ezra 3: 7 to bring cedar logs from *L* to
Ps 29: 5 LORD splinters the cedars of *L*.
29: 6 *L* and Sirion like a young wild
72:16 Its fruit shall wave like *L*;
92:12 shall grow like a cedar in *L*.
104:16 The cedars of *L* which He
Song 3: 9 Of the wood of *L* Solomon the
4: 8 Come with me from *L*,
4: 8 my spouse, With me from *L*.
4:11 Is like the fragrance of *L*.
4:15 waters, And streams from *L*.
5:15 His countenance is like *L*,
7: 4 nose is like the tower of *L*
Isa 2:13 Upon all the cedars of *L* that
10:34 And *L* will fall by the Mighty
14: 8 over you, And the cedars of *L*,
29:17 yet a very little while Till *L*
33: 9 *L* is shamed and shriveled;
35: 2 The glory of *L* shall be given
37:24 mountains, To the limits of *L*;
40:16 And *L* is not sufficient to
60:13 The glory of *L* shall come to
Jer 18:14 man leave the snow water of *L*,
22: 6 Gilead to Me, The head of *L*;
22:20 Go up to *L*, and cry out,
22:23 O inhabitant of *L*,
Ezek 17: 3 Came to *L* And took from the
27: 5 They took a cedar from *L* to
31: 3 Assyria was a cedar in *L*,
31:15 I caused *L* to mourn for it, and
31:16 Eden, the choice and best of *L*,
Hos 14: 5 And lengthen his roots like *L*.
14: 6 And his fragrance like *L*.
14: 7 shall be like the wine of *L*.
Nah 1: 4 And the flower of *L* wilts.
Hab 2:17 For the violence done to *L*
Zech 10:10 into the land of Gilead and *L*,
11: 1 Open your doors, O *L*,

LEBAOTH (2/2)
Josh 15:32 *L*, Shilhim, Ain, and Rimmon:

LEBBAEUS (1/1)
Mt 10: 3 the son of Alphaeus, and *L*,

LEBONAH (1/1)
Judg 21:19 to Shechem, and south of *L*.

LECAH (1/1)
1 Chr 4:21 Judah were Er the father of *L*,

LED (89/89) LEAD
Gen 24:27 the LORD *l* me to the house of
24:48 who had *l* me in the way of
Ex 3: 1 And he *l* the flock to the back
13:18 So God *l* the people around by
15:13 You in Your mercy have *l* forth
Deut 8: 2 that the LORD your God *l* you
8:15 who *l* you through that great and
29: 5 And I have *l* you forty years in
32:12 So the LORD alone *l* him,
Josh 24: 3 *l* him throughout all the land
Judg 2: 1 I *l* you up from Egypt and
3:27 mountains; and he *l* them.
2 Sam 5: 2 you were the one who *l* Israel
1 Ki 8:48 the land of their enemies who *l*
2 Ki 6:19 But he *l* them to Samaria.
15:15 and the conspiracy which he *l*,
15:30 Then Hoshea the son of Elah *l* a
1 Chr 11: 2 you were the one who *l* Israel
20: 1 that Joab *l* out the armed
2 Chr 21:11 and *l* Judah astray.
23:13 and those who *l* in praise.
Neh 9:12 Moreover You *l* them by day with
12: 8 and Mattaniah who *l* the
Esth 6:11 arrayed Mordecai and *l* him on
Ps 68:18 You have *l* captivity captive;
77:20 You *l* Your people like a flock
78:14 In the daytime also He *l* them
78:53 And He *l* them on safely, so
106: 9 So He *l* them through the
107: 7 And He *l* them forth by the
136:16 To Him who *l* His people through
Prov 4:11 I have *l* you in right paths.
20: 1 And whoever is *l* astray by it
Isa 9:16 And those who are *l* by them
48:21 they did not thirst When He *l*
53: 7 He was *l* as a lamb to the
55:12 And be *l* out with peace;
63:12 Who *l* them by the right hand
63:13 Who *l* them through the deep,
Jer 2: 6 Who *l* us through the
2:17 the LORD your God When He *l*
22:12 in the place where they have *l*
23: 8 lives who brought up and *l* the
50: 6 Their shepherds have *l* them
Lam 3: 2 He has *l* me and made me walk
Ezek 17:12 and *l* them with him to Babylon.
40:26 Seven steps *l* up to it, and its
40:49 and by the steps which *l* up to
47: 2 and *l* me around on the outside
Am 2:10 And *l* you forty years through
7:11 And Israel shall surely be *l*
7:17 And Israel shall surely be *l*
Nah 2: 7 She shall be *l* away captive,
Mt 4: 1 Then Jesus was *l* up by the
17: 1 *l* them up on a high mountain by
26:57 who had laid hold of Jesus *l*
27: 2 they *l* Him away and delivered
27:31 and *l* Him away to be crucified.
Mk 8:23 the blind man by the hand and *l*
9: 2 and *l* them up on a high
14:53 And they *l* Jesus away to the
15: 1 *l* Him away, and delivered Him
15:16 Then the soldiers *l* Him away
15:20 and *l* Him out to crucify Him.
Lk 4: 1 from the Jordan and was *l* by
4:29 and they *l* Him to the brow of
21:24 and be *l* away captive into all
22:54 they *l* Him and brought Him
22:66 came together and *l* Him into
23: 1 multitude of them arose and *l*
23:26 Now as they *l* Him away, they
23:32 *l* with Him to be put to death.
24:50 And He *l* them out as far as
Jn 18:13 And they *l* Him away to Annas
18:28 Then they *l* Jesus from Caiaphas
19:16 So they took Jesus and *l* Him
Acts 8:32 He was *l* as a sheep to
9: 8 But they *l* him by the hand and
21:37 as Paul was about to be *l* into
21:38 stirred up a rebellion and *l*
22:11 being *l* by the hand of those
Rom 8:14 For as many as are *l* by the
1 Cor 12: 2 dumb idols, however you were *l*.
2 Cor 7: 9 but that your sorrow *l* to
Gal 5:18 But if you are *l* by the Spirit,
Eph 4: 8 He *l* captivity captive,
2 Tim 3: 6 *l* away by various lusts,
Heb 3:16 out of Egypt, *l* by Moses?
2 Pe 3:17 being *l* away with the error of

LEDGE (8/4)
Ezek 43:14 on the ground to the lower *l*,
43:14 two cubits; the width of the *l*,
43:14 from the smaller *l* to the
43:14 smaller ledge to the larger *l*,
43:14 cubits; and the width of the *l*,
43:17 'the *l*, fourteen cubits long
43:20 on the four corners of the *l*,
45:19 on the four corners of the *l* of

LEDGES (3/3)
1 Ki 6: 6 for he made narrow *l* around the
Ezek 41: 6 they rested on *l* which were
41: 7 because their supporting *l* in

LEECH (1/1)
Prov 30:15 The *l* has two daughters—Give

LEEKS (1/1)
Num 11: 5 cucumbers, the melons, the *l*,

LEES (2/1)
Isa 25: 6 A feast of wines on the *l*,
25: 6 Of well-refined wines on the *l*.

LEFT (335/324)
Gen 13: 9 from me. If you take the *l*,
13: 9 right, then I will go to the *l*.
24:49 to the right hand or to the *l*.
32: 8 the other company which is *l*
32:24 Then Jacob was *l* alone; and a
39: 6 Thus he *l* all that he had in
39:12 But he *l* his garment in her
39:13 when she saw that he had *l* his
39:15 that he *l* his garment with me,
39:18 that he *l* his garment with me
42:38 and he is *l* alone. If any
44:12 He began with the oldest and *l*
44:20 and he alone is *l* of his
47:18 There is nothing *l* in the sight
48:13 right hand toward Israel's *l*
48:13 and Manasseh with his *l* hand
48:14 and his *l* hand on Manasseh's
50: 8 and their herds they *l* in the
Ex 2:20 Why is it that you have *l* the
9:21 regard the word of the LORD *l*
10: 5 eat the residue of what is *l*,
10:12 land—all that the hail has *l*.
10:15 the trees which the hail had *l*.
10:26 not a hoof shall be *l* behind.
14:22 their right hand and on their *l*.
14:29 their right hand and on their *l*.
16:18 who gathered much had nothing *l*
16:20 But some of them *l* part of it
34:25 the Feast of the Passover be *l*
Lev 2:10 And what is *l* of the grain
10:12 Ithamar, his sons who were *l*:
10:16 the sons of Aaron who were *l*,
14:15 it into the palm of his own *l*
14:16 in the oil that is in his *l*
14:26 oil into the palm of his own *l*
14:27 of the oil that is in his *l*
26:36 as for those of you who are *l*,
26:39 And those of you who are *l* shall
26:43 The land also shall be *l* empty
Num 11:31 quail from the sea and *l* them
20:17 to the right hand or to the *l*
21:35 until there was no survivor *l*
22:26 to the right hand or to the *l*.
26:65 So there was not *l* a man of
Deut 2:27 to the right nor to the *l*.
2:34 we *l* none remaining.
4:27 and you will be *l* few in number
5:32 to the right hand or to the *l*.
7:20 them until those who are *l*,
17:11 to the right hand or to the *l*
17:20 to the right hand or to the *l*,
28:14 day, to the right or the *l*,
28:55 because he has nothing *l* in the
28:62 You shall be *l* few in number,
Josh 1: 7 to the right hand or to the *l*,
6:23 out all her relatives and *l*
8:17 There was not a man *l* in Ai or
8:17 So they *l* the city open and
10:33 until he *l* him none remaining.
10:37 he *l* none remaining, according
10:39 He *l* none remaining; as he had
10:40 he *l* none remaining, but
11: 8 they attacked them until they *l*
11:11 There was none *l* breathing.
11:14 and they *l* none breathing.
11:15 He *l* nothing undone of all that
11:22 None of the Anakim were *l* in the
19:27 Cabul which was on the *l*,
22: 3 You have not *l* your brethren
23: 6 to the right hand or to the *l*,
Judg 2:21 of the nations which Joshua *l*
2:23 Therefore the LORD *l* those
3: 1 the nations which the LORD *l*,
3: 4 And they were *l*, that He
3:21 Then Ehud reached with his *l*
4:16 of the sword; not a man was *l*.
7:20 held the torches in their *l*
8:10 all who were *l* of all the army
9: 5 youngest son of Jerubbaal was *l*,
16:19 and his strength *l* him.
16:29 right and the other on his *l*.
Ruth 1: 3 husband, died; and she was *l*,
2: 3 Then she *l*, and went
2:11 and how you have *l* your father
4:14 who has not *l* you this day
1 Sam 2:36 to pass that everyone who is *l*
5: 4 only Dagon's torso was *l* of it.
6:12 to the right hand or the *l*.
11:11 so that no two of them were *l*
17:20 *l* the sheep with a keeper, and
17:22 And David *l* his supplies in the
17:28 And with whom have you *l* those
25:34 no males would have been *l* to
27: 9 he *l* neither man nor woman
30: 9 where those stayed who were *l*
30:13 and my master *l* me behind,
2 Sam 2:19 to the right hand or to the *l*
2:21 to your right hand or to your *l*,
5:21 And they *l* their images there,
9: 1 there still anyone who is *l*
13:30 and not one of them is *l*!"
14: 7 extinguish my ember that is *l*,
14:19 to the right hand or to the *l*
15:16 But the king *l* ten women,
16: 6 on his right hand and on his *l*.
16:21 whom he has *l* to keep the
17:12 with him there shall not be *l*
17:22 light not one of them was *l*
18: 9 so he was *l* hanging between
19:19 the day that my lord the king *l*

20: 3 his concubines whom he had *l* to
1 Ki 7:21 he set up the pillar on the *l*
7:39 and five on the *l* side of the
7:49 right side and five on the *l*
9:20 All the people who were *l* of
9:21 their descendants who were *l* in
15:18 silver and gold that was *l*
17:17 that there was no breath *l* in
18:22 I alone am *l* a prophet of the
19: 3 and *l* his servant there.
19:10 with the sword. I alone am *l*;
19:14 with the sword. I alone am *l*;
19:20 And he *l* the oxen and ran after
20:10 if enough dust is *l* of Samaria
20:30 of the men who were *l*.
20:36 And as soon as he *l* him, a
22:19 on His right hand and on His *l*.
2 Ki 3:25 But they *l* the stones of Kir
4:43 shall eat and have some *l*
4:44 and they ate and had some *l*
7: 7 and *l* the camp intact—their
7:13 remaining horses which are *l*
7:13 multitude of Israel that are *l*
7:13 all the multitude of Israel *l*
8: 6 field from the day that she *l*
10:11 until he *l* him none remaining.
10:14 and he *l* none of them.
10:21 so that there was not a man *l*
11:11 side of the temple to the *l*
13: 7 For He *l* of the army of Jehoahaz
17:16 So they *l* all the commandments
17:18 there was none *l* but the tribe
19: 4 for the remnant that is *l*.
20:17 to Babylon; nothing shall be *l*,
22: 2 to the right hand or to the *l*.
23: 8 which were to the *l* of the
25:12 But the captain of the guard *l*
25:22 king of Babylon had *l*.
1 Chr 6:44 on the *l* hand, were Ethan the
12: 2 both the right hand and the *l*
13: 2 everywhere who are *l* in all
14:12 And when they *l* their gods
16:37 So he *l* Asaph and his brothers
2 Chr 3:17 hand and the other on the *l*;
3:17 the name of the one on the *l*
4: 6 right side and five on the *l*,
4: 7 right side and five on the *l*.
4: 8 right side and five on the *l*.
8: 7 All the people who were *l* of
8: 8 their descendants who were *l* in
11:14 For the Levites *l* their
11:16 And after the Levites *l*,
12: 5 and therefore I also have *l* you
18:18 on His right hand and His *l*.
21:17 so that there was not a son *l*
23:10 side of the temple to the *l*
24:18 Therefore they *l* the house of
24:25 withdrawn from him (for they *l*
28:14 So the armed men *l* the captives
31:10 enough to eat and have plenty *l*,
31:10 and what is *l* is this great
34: 2 to the right hand or to the *l*.
34:21 and for those who are *l* in
Ezra 1: 4 And whoever is *l* in any place
9:15 for we are *l* as a remnant, as
Neh 1: 3 The survivors who are *l* from the
6: 1 that there were no breaks *l*
8: 4 and at his *l* hand Pedaiah,
9:28 Therefore You *l* them in the
Esth 7: 8 As the word *l* the king's
Job 20:21 Nothing is *l* for him to eat;
20:26 shall go ill with him who is *l*
23: 9 When He works on the *l* hand, I
Ps 106:11 There was not one of them *l*.
Prov 3:16 In her *l* hand riches and
4:27 not turn to the right or the *l*;
29:15 But a child *l* to himself
Eccl 10: 2 But a fool's heart at his *l*.
Song 2: 6 His *l* hand is under my head,
8: 3 His *l* hand is under my head,
Isa 1: 8 So the daughter of Zion is *l* as
1: 9 the LORD of hosts Had *l* to
4: 3 to pass that he who is *l* in
7:22 everyone will eat who is *l* in
9:20 He shall devour on the *l* hand
10:14 one gathers eggs that are *l*,
11:11 remnant of His people who are *l*,
11:16 of His people Who will be *l*
17: 6 Yet gleaning grapes will be *l*
17: 9 Which they *l* because of the
18: 6 They will be *l* together for
24: 6 are burned, And few men are *l*.
24:12 In the city desolation is *l*,
27:10 The habitation forsaken and *l*
30:17 Till you are *l* as a pole on
30:21 Or whenever you turn to the *l*.
37: 4 for the remnant that is *l*.
39: 6 to Babylon; nothing shall be *l*,
49:21 *l* alone; But these, where
54: 3 to the right and to the *l*,
Jer 12: 7 I have *l* My heritage; I have
14: 5 But *l* because there was no
21: 7 and such as are *l* in this city
25:38 He has *l* His lair like the
27:18 that the vessels which are *l* in
34: 7 the cities of Judah that were *l*,
37:11 the army of the Chaldeans *l*
38:22 all the women who are *l* in the
39:10 the captain of the guard *l* in
40: 6 among the people who were *l* in
40:11 that the king of Babylon had *l*
42: 2 this remnant (since we are *l*
43: 6 the captain of the guard had *l*
50:26 Let nothing of her be *l*.
52:16 the captain of the guard *l*
Ezek 1:10 had the face of an ox on the *l*
4: 4 Lie also on your *l* side, and
9: 8 I was *l* alone; and I fell on
14:22 there shall be *l* in it a
21:16 Set your blade! Thrust *l*—
24:21 sons and daughters whom you *l*
31:12 have cut it down and *l* it; its
31:12 from under its shadow and *l* it.
36:36 Then the nations which are *l* all
39: 3 knock the bow out of your *l*
39:28 and *l* none of them captive any
Dan 2: 1 so troubled that his sleep *l*
2:44 and the kingdom shall not be *l*
10: 8 Therefore I was *l* alone when I
10:13 for I had been *l* alone there
10:17 nor is any breath *l* in me."
12: 7 up his right hand and his *l*
Joel 1: 4 What the chewing locust *l*,
1: 4 What the swarming locust *l*,
1: 4 And what the crawling locust *l*,
Am 5: 3 Shall have a hundred *l*,
5: 3 by a hundred Shall have ten *l*
Ob 5 Would they not have *l* some
Jon 4:11 their right hand and their *l*—
Hag 2: 3 Who is *l* among you who saw this
Zech 4: 3 the bowl and the other at its *l*.
4:11 of the lampstand and at its *l*?
11: 9 Let those that are *l* eat each
12: 6 on the right hand and on the *l*,
13: 8 But one- third shall be *l* in
14:16 to pass that everyone who is *l*
Mt 4:11 Then the devil *l* Him, and
4:20 They immediately *l* their nets
4:22 and immediately they *l* the boat
6: 3 do not let your *l* hand know
8:15 and the fever *l* her. And she
15:37 of the fragments that were *l*.
16: 4 And He *l* them and departed.
19:27 we have *l* all and followed You.
19:29 And everyone who has *l* houses or
20:21 hand and the other on the *l*,
20:23 on My right hand and on My *l*
21:17 Then He *l* them and went out of
22:22 and *l* Him and went their way.
22:25 *l* his wife to his brother.
23:38 See! Your house is *l* to you
24: 2 not one stone shall be *l* here
24:40 will be taken and the other *l*.
24:41 will be taken and the other *l*.
25:33 hand, but the goats on the *l*.
25:41 will also say to those on the *l*
26:44 So He *l* them, went away again,
27:38 the right and another on the *l*.
Mk 1:18 They immediately *l* their nets
1:20 and they *l* their father Zebedee
1:31 and immediately the fever *l*
1:42 immediately the leprosy *l* him,
4:36 Now when they had *l* the
8:13 And He *l* them, and getting into
10:28 we have *l* all and followed
10:29 there is no one who has *l* house
10:37 hand and the other on Your *l*,
10:40 on My right hand and on My *l*
12:12 So they *l* Him and went away.
12:20 and dying, he *l* no offspring.
12:22 So the seven had her and *l* no
13: 2 Not one stone shall be *l* upon
13:34 who *l* his house and gave
14:52 and he *l* the linen cloth and
15:27 right and the other on His *l*.
Lk 4:39 and it *l* her. And immediately
5:13 Immediately the leprosy *l*
5:28 So he *l* all, rose up, and
10:40 not care that my sister has *l*
13:35 See! Your house is *l* to you
17:34 taken and the other will be *l*.
17:35 will be taken and the other *l*.
17:36 will be taken and the other *l*.
18:28 we have *l* all and followed
18:29 there is no one who has *l* house
20:31 and they *l* no children, and
21: 6 not one stone shall be *l* upon
23:33 hand and the other on the *l*.
Jn 4: 3 He *l* Judea and departed again to
4:28 The woman then *l* her waterpot,
4:52 at the seventh hour the fever *l*
6:13 five barley loaves which were *l*
8: 9 And Jesus was *l* alone, and the
8:29 The Father has not *l* Me alone,
Acts 2:31 that His soul was not *l* in
18:19 and *l* them there; but he
19:12 and the diseases *l* them and the
21: 3 Cyprus, we passed it on the *l*,
23:32 The next day they *l* the horsemen
24:27 Jews a favor, *l* Paul bound.
25:14 There is a certain man *l* a
27:40 they let go the anchors and *l*
Rom 9:29 LORD of Sabaoth had *l*
11: 3 altars, and I alone am *l*,
2 Cor 6: 7 on the right hand and on the *l*,
8:15 much had nothing *l* over,
1 Th 3: 1 we thought it good to be *l* in
1 Tim 5: 5 and *l* alone, trusts in God and
2 Tim 4:13 Bring the cloak that I *l* with
4:20 but Trophimus I have *l* in
Titus 1: 5 For this reason I *l* you in
Heb 2: 8 He *l* nothing that is not put
Jude 6 but *l* their own abode, He has
Rev 2: 4 that you have *l* your first
10: 2 foot on the sea and his *l*

LEFT-HANDED (2/2) LEFT

Judg 3:15 a *l* man. By him the children of
20:16 hundred select men who were *l*;

LEFTOVER (2/2)

Mk 8: 8 up seven large baskets of *l*
Lk 9:17 and twelve baskets of the *l*

LEG (1/1)

Isa 3:20 the *l* ornaments, and the

LEGACY (1/1)

Prov 3:35 But shame shall be the *l* of

LEGION (3/3) LEGIONS

Mk 5: 9 saying, "My name is *L*;
5:15 demon-possessed and had the *l*,
Lk 8:30 your name?" And he said, "*L*,

LEGIONS (1/1) LEGION

Mt 26:53 Me with more than twelve *l* of

LEGS (22/22)

Ex 12: 9 its head with its *l* and its
25:26 corners that are at its four *l*.
29:17 wash its entrails and its *l*,
37:13 that were at its four *l*.
Lev 1: 9 wash its entrails and its *l*
1:13 wash the entrails and the *l*
4:11 its flesh, with its head and *l*,
8:21 washed the entrails and the *l*
9:14 washed the entrails and the *l*,
11:21 those which have jointed *l*
Deut 28:35 you in the knees and on the *l*
1 Sam 17: 6 he had bronze armor on his *l*
Ps 147:10 He takes no pleasure in the *l*
Prov 26: 7 Like the *l* of the lame that
Song 5:15 His *l* are pillars of marble
Isa 7:20 The head and the hair of the *l*,
Ezek 1: 7 Their *l* were straight, and the
Dan 2:33 its *l* of iron, its feet partly
Am 3:12 the mouth of a lion Two *l* or
Jn 19:31 Jews asked Pilate that their *l*
19:32 soldiers came and broke the *l*
19:33 dead, they did not break His *l*.

LEHABIM (2/2)

Gen 10:13 Mizraim begot Ludim, Anamim, *L*,
1 Chr 1:11 Mizraim begot Ludim, Anamim, *L*,

LEHI (4/3)

Judg 15: 9 deployed themselves against *L*.
15:14 When he came to *L*,
15:19 the hollow place that is in *L*,
15:19 which is in *L* to this day.

LEISURE (KJV) See TIME

LEMUEL (2/2)

Prov 31: 1 The words of King *L*,
31: 4 It is not for kings, O *L*,

LEND (15/12) LENDER, LENDS, LENT

Ex 22:25 If you *l* money to any of My
Lev 25:37 You shall not *l* him your money
25:37 nor *l* him your food at a
Deut 15: 6 you shall *l* to many nations,
15: 8 wide to him and willingly *l*
24:10 When you *l* your brother
24:11 and the man to whom you *l* shall
28:12 You shall *l* to many nations,
28:44 He shall *l* to you, but you shall
28:44 but you shall not *l* to him;
Prov 5: 1 wisdom; *L* your ear to my
Lk 6:34 And if you *l* to those from
6:34 For even sinners *l* to sinners
6:35 your enemies, do good, and *l*,
11: 5 'Friend, *l* me three loaves;

LENDER (2/2) LEND

Prov 22: 7 borrower is servant to the *l*.
Isa 24: 2 with the seller; As with the *l*,

LENDING (1/1)

Neh 5:10 am *l* them money and grain.

LENDS (3/3) LEND

Ps 37:26 He is ever merciful, and *l*;
112: 5 good man deals graciously and *l*;
Prov 19:17 He who has pity on the poor *l*

LENGTH (73/69) LENGTHEN

Gen 6:15 The *l* of the ark shall be
13:17 walk in the land through its *l*
47:28 So the *l* of Jacob's life was
Ex 25:10 a half cubits shall be its *l*,
25:17 a half cubits shall be its *l*

L

25:23 two cubits shall be its *l*,
26: 2 The *l* of each curtain shall be
26: 8 The *l* of each curtain shall be
26:13 of what remains of the *l* of the
26:16 Ten cubits shall be the *l* of a
27:11 Likewise along the *l* of the
27:18 The *l* of the court shall be
28:16 square: a span shall be its *l*,
30: 2 A cubit shall be its *l* and a
36: 9 The *l* of each curtain was
36:15 The *l* of each curtain was
36:21 The *l* of each board was ten
37: 1 and a half cubits was its *l*,
37: 6 and a half cubits was its *l*
37:10 wood; two cubits was its *l*,
37:25 Its *l* was a cubit and its
38: 1 five cubits was its *l* and five
38:18 The *l* was twenty cubits, and
39: 9 a span was its *l* and a span
Lev 19:35 judgment, in measurement of *l*,
Deut 3:11 Nine cubits is its *l* and four
30:20 for He is your life and the *l*
Judg 3:16 double-edged and a cubit in *l*)
1 Sam 28:20 immediately Saul fell full *l*
1 Ki 6: 2 its *l* was sixty cubits, its
7: 2 its *l* was one hundred cubits,
7: 6 its *l* was fifty cubits, and
7:27 four cubits was the *l* of each
2 Chr 3: 3 The *l* was sixty cubits (by
3: 8 Its *l* was according to the
3:11 twenty cubits in overall *l*:
4: 1 altar: twenty cubits was its *l*,
Job 12:12 And with *l* of days,
Ps 21: 4 *L* of days forever and ever.
Prov 3: 2 For *l* of days and long life
3:16 *L* of days is in her right
Isa 57:10 You are wearied in the *l* of
Ezek 31: 7 in greatness and in the *l* of
40:11 and the *l* of the gate,
40:18 corresponding to the *l* of the
40:20 and he measured its *l* and its
40:21 its *l* was fifty cubits and its
40:25 its *l* was fifty cubits and its
40:36 its *l* was fifty cubits and its
40:49 The *l* of the vestibule was
41: 2 side; and he measured its *l*,
41: 4 He measured the *l*, twenty
41:12 and its *l* ninety cubits.
41:15 He measured the *l* of the
41:22 and its *l* two cubits. Its
41:22 two cubits. Its corners, its *l*,
42: 2 Facing the *l*, which was one
42: 7 its *l* was fifty cubits.
42: 8 The *l* of the chambers toward the
45: 1 its *l* shall be twenty-five
45: 7 the *l* shall be side by side
48: 8 and in *l* the same as one of
48: 9 thousand cubits in *l* and ten
48:10 thousand cubits in *l*,
48:10 south twenty-five thousand in *l*.
48:13 thousand cubits in *l* and ten
48:13 its entire *l* shall be
48:18 'The rest of the *l*, alongside
Zech 2: 2 its width and what is its *l*.
5: 2 Its *l* is twenty cubits and its
Eph 3:18 what is the width and *l* and
Rev 21:16 its *l* is as great as its
21:16 twelve thousand furlongs. Its *l*,

LENGTHEN (3/3) LENGTH, LENGTHENED, LENGTHENING, LENGTHENS
1 Ki 3:14 then I will *l* your days."
Isa 54: 2 *L* your cords, And strengthen
Hos 14: 5 And *l* his roots like Lebanon.

LENGTHENED (1/1) LENGTHEN
Deut 25:15 that your days may be *l* in the

LENGTHENING (2/2) LENGTHEN
Jer 6: 4 shadows of the evening are *l*.
Dan 4:27 Perhaps there may be a *l* of

LENGTHENS (2/2) LENGTHEN
Ps 102:11 days are like a shadow that *l*,
109:23 am gone like a shadow when it *l*;

LENT (6/4) LEND
Deut 15: 2 Every creditor who has *l*
23:19 or food or anything that is *l*
1 Sam 1:28 Therefore I also have *l* him to
1:28 long as he lives he shall be *l*
Jer 15:10 whole earth! I have neither *l*
15:10 Nor have men *l* to me for

LENTILS (4/4)
Gen 25:34 gave Esau bread and stew of *l*;
2 Sam 17:28 beans, *l* and parched seeds,
23:11 was a piece of ground full of *l*.
Ezek 4: 9 wheat, barley, beans, *l*,

LEOPARD (6/6) LEOPARDS
Isa 11: 6 The *l* shall lie down with the
Jer 5: 6 A *l* will watch over their
13:23 change his skin or the *l* its
Dan 7: 6 and there was another, like a *l*,
Hos 13: 7 Like a *l* by the road I will
Rev 13: 2 beast which I saw was like a *l*,

LEOPARDS (2/2) LEOPARD
Song 4: 8 From the mountains of the *l*.
Hab 1: 8 horses also are swifter than *l*,

LEPER (16/15) LEPERS, LEPROSY
Lev 13:45 Now the *l* on whom the sore is,
14: 2 shall be the law of the *l*
14: 3 the leprosy is healed in the *l*,
22: 4 who is a *l* or has a discharge,
Num 5: 2 put out of the camp every *l*,
12:10 Miriam, and there she was, a *l*.
2 Sam 3:29 who has a discharge or is a *l*,
2 Ki 5: 1 a mighty man of valor, but a *l*.
15: 5 so that he was a *l* until the
2 Chr 26:21 King Uzziah was a *l* until the
26:21 house, because he was a *l*;
26:23 for they said, "He is a *l*.
Mt 8: 2 a *l* came and worshiped Him,
26: 6 at the house of Simon the *l*,
Mk 1:40 Now a *l* came to Him, imploring
14: 3 at the house of Simon the *l*,

LEPERS (6/6) LEPER
2 Ki 7: 8 And when these *l* came to the
Mt 10: 8 "Heal the sick, cleanse the *l*,
11: 5 the *l* are cleansed and the
Lk 4:27 And many *l* were in Israel in the
7:22 the *l* are cleansed, the deaf
17:12 met Him ten men who were *l*,

LEPROSY (28/27) LEPER, LEPROUS
Lev 13: 8 pronounce him unclean. It is *l*.
13:11 it is an old *l* on the skin of
13:12 And if *l* breaks out all over
13:12 and the *l* covers all the skin
13:13 and indeed if the *l* has
13:15 raw flesh is unclean. It is *l*.
13:25 it is *l* broken out in the
13:30 It is a scaly *l* of the head or
13:42 it is *l* breaking out on his
13:43 as the appearance of *l* on the
13:51 the plague is an active *l*.
13:52 leather, for it is an active *l*;
14: 3 if the *l* is healed in the
14: 7 is to be cleansed from the *l*,
14:44 it is an active *l* in the
14:55 for the *l* of a garment and of a
14:57 This is the law of *l*."
Deut 24: 8 heed in an outbreak of *l*,
2 Ki 5: 3 For he would heal him of his *l*.
5: 6 that you may heal him of his *l*.
5: 7 man to me to heal him of his *l*?
5:11 over the place, and heal the *l*.
5:27 Therefore the *l* of Naaman shall
2 Chr 26:19 *l* broke out on his forehead,
Mt 8: 3 Immediately his *l* was cleansed.
Mk 1:42 immediately the *l* left him, and
Lk 5:12 a man who was full of *l* saw
5:13 Immediately the *l* left him.

LEPROUS (19/19) LEPROSY
Ex 4: 6 it out, behold, his hand was *l*,
Lev 13: 2 the skin of his body like a *l*
13: 3 it is a *l* sore. Then the
13: 9 When the *l* sore is on a person,
13:20 It is a *l* sore which has
13:22 It is a *l* sore.
13:25 It is a *l* sore.
13:27 It is a *l* sore.
13:44 he is a *l* man. He is unclean.
13:47 if a garment has a *l* plague in
13:49 it is a *l* plague and shall be
13:59 This is the law of the *l*
14:32 the law for one who had a *l*
14:34 and I put the *l* plague in a
14:54 This is the law for any *l* sore
Num 12:10 suddenly Miriam became *l*,
2 Ki 5:27 he went out from his presence *l*,
7: 3 Now there were four *l* men at
2 Chr 26:20 on his forehead, he was *l*;

LESHEM (2/1) LAISH
Josh 19:47 Dan went up to fight against *L*
19:47 and dwelt in it. They called *L*,

LESS (20/20)
Gen 18:28 Suppose there were five *l* than
Ex 16:17 and gathered, some more, some *l*.
30:15 and the poor shall not give *l*
Num 22:18 my God, to do *l* or more.
1 Ki 8:27 How much *l* this temple which I
2 Chr 6:18 How much *l* this temple which I
32:15 How much *l* will your God
Ezra 9:13 You our God have punished us *l*
Job 11: 6 that God exacts from you *L*
15:16 How much *l* man, who is
25: 6 How much *l* man, who is a
Prov 17: 7 Much *l* lying lips to a prince.
19:10 Much *l* for a servant to rule
Isa 40:17 And they are counted by Him *l*
Ezek 15: 5 How much *l* will it be useful
Mk 15:40 Mary the mother of James the *L*
1 Cor 12:23 the body which we think to be *l*
2 Cor 12:15 I love you, the *l* I am loved.
Eph 3: 8 who am *l* than the least of all
Phil 2:28 and I may be *l* sorrowful.

LESSER (2/2)
Gen 1:16 and the *l* light to rule the
Heb 7: 7 beyond all contradiction the *l*

LESSON (1/1)
Ezek 5:15 be a reproach, a taunt, a *l*,

LEST (272/257)
Gen 3: 3 touch it, *l* you die.'
3:22 *l* he put out his hand and take
4:15 *l* anyone finding him should
11: 4 *l* we be scattered abroad over
14:23 *l* you should say, 'I have made
19:15 *l* you be consumed in the
19:17 *l* you be destroyed."
19:19 *l* some evil overtake me and I
26: 7 *l* the men of the place kill me
26: 9 *L* I die on account of her.'"
32:11 *l* he come and attack me and
38: 9 *l* he should give an heir to his
38:11 *L* he also die like his
38:23 *l* we be shamed; for I sent this
42: 4 *L* some calamity befall him."
44:34 *l* perhaps I see the evil that
45:11 *l* you and your household, and
Ex 1:10 *l* they multiply, and it happen,
5: 3 *l* He fall upon us with
13:17 *L* perhaps the people change
19:21 *l* they break through to gaze at
19:22 *l* the LORD break out against
19:24 *l* He break out against them."
20:19 speak with us, *l* we die."
23:29 *l* the land become desolate and
23:33 *l* they make you sin against Me.
30:20 wash with water, *l* they die.
30:21 *l* they die. And it shall be a
33: 3 *l* I consume you on the way, for
34:12 *l* you make a covenant with the
34:12 *l* it be a snare in your midst.
34:15 *l* you make a covenant with the
Lev 10: 6 *l* you die, and wrath come upon
10: 7 *l* you die, for the anointing
10: 9 *l* you die. It shall be a
11:43 *l* you be defiled by them.
15:31 *l* they die in their uncleanness
16: 2 *l* he die; for I will appear in
16:13 on the Testimony, *l* he die.
18:28 *l* the land vomit you out also
19:29 *l* the land fall into harlotry,
21:23 *l* he profane My sanctuaries;
22: 9 *l* they bear sin for it and die
Num 4:15 *l* they die. These are the
4:20 being covered, *l* they die."
14:42 *l* you be defeated by your
16:26 *l* you be consumed in all their
16:34 *L* the earth swallow us up
17:10 away from Me, *l* they die."
18: 3 *l* they die—they and you also.
18:22 *l* they bear sin and die.
18:32 of Israel, *l* you die.'
20:18 *l* I come out against you with
Deut 1:42 *l* you be defeated before your
4: 9 *l* you forget the things your
4: 9 and *l* they depart from your
4:16 *l* you act corruptly and make for
4:19 *l* you lift your eyes to heaven,
4:23 *l* you forget the covenant of
6:12 *l* you forget the LORD who
6:15 *l* the anger of the LORD your
7:22 *l* the beasts of the field
7:25 *l* you be snared by it; for it
7:26 *l* you be doomed to destruction
8:12 '*l*—when you have eaten
9:28 *l* the land from which You
11:16 *l* your heart be deceived, and
11:17 *l* the LORD's anger be aroused
15: 9 Beware *l* there be a wicked
17:17 *l* his heart turn away; nor
18:16 great fire anymore, *l* I die.'
19: 6 *l* the avenger of blood, while
19:10 *l* innocent blood be shed in the
20: 5 *l* he die in the battle and
20: 6 *l* he die in the battle and
20: 7 *l* he die in the battle and
20: 8 *l* the heart of his brethren
20:18 *l* they teach you to do according
22: 9 *l* the yield of the seed which
24:15 *l* he cry out against you to the
25: 3 *l* he should exceed this and
32:27 *L* their adversaries should
32:27 *L* they should say, "Our hand
Josh 2:16 *l* the pursuers meet you.
6:18 *l* you become accursed when you
9:20 *l* wrath be upon us because of
23: 6 *l* you turn aside from it to the
23: 7 and *l* you go among these
24:27 *l* you deny your God."
Judg 7: 2 *l* Israel claim glory for itself
9:54 *l* men say of me, 'A woman
18:25 *l* angry men fall upon you, and
Ruth 4: 6 *l* I ruin my own inheritance.
1 Sam 9: 5 *l* my father cease caring about
13:19 *L* the Hebrews make swords or
15: 6 *l* I destroy you with them.
20: 3 *l* he be grieved.' But truly,

27:11 *L* they should inform on us,
29: 4 *l* in the battle he become our
31: 4 *l* these uncircumcised men come
2 Sam 1:20 *L* the daughters of the
1:20 *L* the daughters of the
12:28 *l* I take the city and it be
13:25 *l* we be a burden to you."
14:11 *l* they destroy my son." And he
15:14 *l* he overtake us suddenly and
17:16 *l* the king and all the people
18:12 Beware *l* anyone touch the young
20: 6 *l* he find for himself fortified
21:17 *l* you quench the lamp of
2 Ki 2:16 *l* perhaps the Spirit of the
11: 6 *l* it be broken down.
18:32 *l* he persuade you, saying,
1 Chr 10: 4 *l* these uncircumcised men come
2 Chr 19:10 *l* they trespass against the
35:21 with me, *l* He destroy you."
Job 32:13 *L* you say, 'We have found
34:30 *L* the people be ensnared.
36:18 beware *l* He take you away with
42: 8 *l* I deal with you according
Ps 2:12 *l* He be angry, And you perish
7: 2 *L* they tear me like a lion,
13: 3 *L* I sleep the sleep of
13: 4 *L* my enemy say, "I have
13: 4 *L* those who trouble me
28: 1 Do not be silent to me, *L*,
38:16 *l* they rejoice over me, Lest,
38:16 lest they rejoice over me, *L*,
39: 1 *L* I sin with my tongue;
50:22 *L* I tear you in pieces,
59:11 *l* my people forget; Scatter
91:12 *L* you dash your foot against a
106:23 *l* He destroy them.
125: 3 *L* the righteous reach out
140: 8 *L* they be exalted. Selah
143: 7 *L* I be like those who go down
Prov 5: 6 *L* you ponder her path of life
5: 9 *L* you give your honor to
5:10 *L* aliens be filled with your
9: 8 *l* he hate you; Rebuke a wise
20:13 *l* you come to poverty;
22:25 *L* you learn his ways And set a
24:18 *L* the LORD see it, and it
25:10 *L* he who hears it expose your
25:16 *L* you be filled with it and
25:17 *L* he become weary of you and
26: 4 *L* you also be like him.
26: 5 *L* he be wise in his own eyes.
30: 6 *L* He rebuke you, and you be
30: 9 *L* I be full and deny You,
30: 9 Or *l* I be poor and steal,
30:10 *L* he curse you, and you be
31: 5 *L* they drink and forget the
Eccl 7:21 *L* you hear your servant
Isa 6:10 *L* they see with their eyes,
14:21 *L* they rise up and possess the
27: 3 *L* any hurt it, I keep it
28:22 *L* your bonds be made strong;
36:18 Beware *l* Hezekiah persuade you,
48: 5 *L* you should say, 'My idol has
48: 7 *L* you should say, 'Of course I
Jer 1:17 *L* I dismay you before them.
4: 4 *L* My fury come forth like
6: 8 *L* My soul depart from you;
6: 8 *L* I make you desolate, A land
10:24 *l* You bring me to nothing.
11:21 *l* you die by our hand'—
21:12 *L* My fury go forth like fire
37:20 the scribe, *l* I die there."
38:19 *l* they deliver me into their
44:14 *l* they return to the land of
51:46 And *l* your heart faint,
Hos 2: 3 *L* I strip her naked And expose
Am 5: 6 *L* He break out like fire in
Mal 4: 6 *L* I come and strike the earth
Mt 4: 6 *L* you dash your foot
5:25 *l* your adversary deliver you to
7: 6 *l* they trample them under their
13:15 *L* they should see with
13:15 *L* they should understand
13:29 *l* while you gather up the tares
15:32 *l* they faint on the way."
17:27 *l* we offend them, go to the
25: 9 *l* there should not be enough
26: 5 *l* there be an uproar among the
26:41 *l* you enter into temptation.
27:64 *l* His disciples come by night
Mk 3: 9 *l* they should crush Him.
4:12 *L* they should turn, And
13:36 '*l*, coming suddenly, he find
14: 2 *l* there be an uproar of the
14:38 *l* you enter into temptation.
Lk 4:11 *L* you dash your foot
8:12 *l* they should believe and be
12:58 *l* he drag you to the judge, the
14: 8 *l* one more honorable than you
14:12 *l* they also invite you back,
14:29 '*l*, after he has laid
16:28 *l* they also come to this place
18: 5 *l* by her continual coming she
21:34 *l* your hearts be weighed down
22:46 *l* you enter into temptation."
Jn 3:20 *l* his deeds should be exposed.
5:14 *l* a worse thing come upon
12:35 *l* darkness overtake you; he who
12:40 *L* they should see with
12:40 *L* they should understand
12:42 *l* they should be put out of the
18:28 *l* they should be defiled, but
Acts 5:26 *l* they should be stoned.
5:39 *l* you even be found to fight
13:40 *l* what has been spoken in the
23:10 fearing *l* Paul might be pulled
27:17 and fearing *l* they should run
27:29 fearing *l* we should run aground
27:42 *l* any of them should swim away
28:27 *L* they should see with
28:27 *L* they should understand
Rom 11:25 *l* you should be wise in your
15:20 *l* I should build on another
1 Cor 1:15 *l* anyone should say that I had
1:17 *l* the cross of Christ should be
8: 9 But beware *l* somehow this
8:13 *l* I make my brother stumble.
9:12 but endure all things *l* we
9:27 bring it into subjection, *l*,
10:12 thinks he stands take heed *l*
11:34 *l* you come together for
2 Cor 2: 3 wrote this very thing to you, *l*,
2: 7 *l* perhaps such a one be
2:11 *l* Satan should take advantage of
4: 4 *l* the light of the gospel of
9: 3 *l* our boasting of you should be
9: 4 *l* if some Macedonians come with
10: 9 *l* I seem to terrify you by
11: 3 *l* somehow, as the serpent
12: 6 *l* anyone should think of me
12: 7 And *l* I should be exalted above
12: 7 *l* I be exalted above measure.
12:20 For I fear *l*, when I come,
12:20 *l* there be contentions,
12:21 *l*, when I come again,
13:10 *l* being present I should use
Gal 2: 2 *l* by any means I might run, or
4:11 *l* I have labored for you in
5:15 beware *l* you be consumed by one
6: 1 considering yourself *l* you also
Eph 2: 9 *l* anyone should boast.
Phil 2:27 *l* I should have sorrow upon
Col 2: 4 Now this I say *l* anyone should
2: 8 Beware *l* anyone cheat you
3:21 *l* they become discouraged.
1 Th 3: 5 *l* by some means the tempter had
4:13 *l* you sorrow as others who have
1 Tim 3: 6 *l* being puffed up with pride he
3: 7 *l* he fall into reproach and the
Heb 2: 1 heard, *l* we drift away.
3:12 *l* there be in any of you an
3:13 *l* any of you be hardened
4: 1 let us fear *l* any of you seem
4:11 *l* anyone fall according to the
11:28 *l* he who destroyed the
12: 3 *l* you become weary and
12:15 looking carefully *l* anyone fall
12:15 *l* any root of bitterness
12:16 *l* there be any fornicator or
Jas 5: 9 *l* you be condemned. Behold, the
5:12 *l* you fall into judgment.
2 Pe 3:17 beware *l* you also fall from
Rev 16:15 *l* he walk naked and they see
18: 4 *l* you share in her sins, and
18: 4 and *l* you receive of her

LET (1557/1272)

Gen 1: 3 *L* there be light"; and there
1: 6 *L* there be a firmament in the
1: 6 and *l* it divide the waters from
1: 9 *L* the waters under the heavens
1: 9 and *l* the dry land appear";
1:11 *L* the earth bring forth grass,
1:14 *L* there be lights in the
1:14 and *l* them be for signs and
1:15 and *l* them be for lights in the
1:20 *L* the waters abound with an
1:20 and *l* birds fly above the earth
1:22 and *l* birds multiply on the
1:24 *L* the earth bring forth the
1:26 *L* Us make man in Our image,
1:26 *l* them have dominion over the
11: 3 *l* us make bricks and bake them
11: 4 *l* us build ourselves a city,
11: 4 *l* us make a name for ourselves,
11: 7 *l* Us go down and there confuse
12:12 but they will *l* you live.
13: 8 Please *l* there be no strife
14:24 *l* them take their portion."
18: 4 Please *l* a little water be
18:30 *L* not the Lord be angry, and I
18:32 *L* not the Lord be angry, and I
19: 8 *l* me bring them out to you, and
19:20 please *l* me escape there (is
19:32 *l* us make our father drink
19:34 *l* us make him drink wine
20: 6 therefore I did not *l* you touch
21:12 Do not *l* it be displeasing in
21:16 *L* me not see the death of the
23: 9 *L* him give it to me at the full
24:14 Now *l* it be that the young woman
24:14 Please *l* down your pitcher that
24:14 *l* her be the one You have
24:17 Please *l* me drink a little water
24:18 Then she quickly *l* her
24:44 *l* her be the woman whom the
24:45 Please *l* me drink.'
24:46 And she made haste and *l* her
24:51 and *l* her be your master's
24:55 *L* the young woman stay with us
26:28 *L* there now be an oath between
26:28 and *l* us make a covenant with
27:13 *L* your curse be on me, my son;
27:29 *L* peoples serve you,
27:29 And *l* your mother's sons bow
27:31 *L* my father arise and eat of his
30:26 and *l* me go; for you know my
30:32 *L* me pass through all your flock
31:32 do not *l* him live. In the
31:35 *L* it not displease my lord that
31:44 *l* us make a covenant, you and
31:44 and *l* it be a witness between
32:26 *L* Me go, for the day breaks."
32:26 I will not *l* You go unless You
33:12 *L* us take our journey; let us
33:12 *l* us go, and I will go before
33:14 Please *l* my lord go on ahead
33:15 Now *l* me leave with you some of
33:15 *L* me find favor in the sight of
34:11 *L* me find favor in your eyes,
34:21 Therefore *l* them dwell in the
34:21 *L* us take their daughters to us
34:21 and *l* us give them our
34:23 Only *l* us consent to them, and
35: 3 Then *l* us arise and go up to
37:17 *L* us go to Dothan.'" So Joseph
37:20 *l* us now kill him and cast him
37:21 *L* us not kill him."
37:27 Come and *l* us sell him to the
37:27 and *l* not our hand be upon him,
38:16 Please *l* me come in to you";
38:23 *L* her take them for herself,
38:24 Bring her out and *l* her be
41:33 *l* Pharaoh select a discerning
41:34 *L* Pharaoh do this, and let him
41:34 and *l* him appoint officers over
41:35 And *l* them gather all the food
41:35 and *l* them keep food in the
42:16 and *l* him bring your brother;
42:19 *l* one of your brothers be
43: 9 then *l* me bear the blame
44: 9 *l* him die, and we also will be
44:10 Now also *l* it be according to
44:11 Then each man speedily *l* down
44:18 please *l* your servant speak a
44:18 and do not *l* your anger burn
44:33 please *l* your servant remain
44:33 and *l* the lad go up with his
46:30 Now *l* me die, since I have seen
47: 4 please *l* your servants dwell in
47: 6 *l* them dwell in the land of
47:25 *l* us find favor in the sight of
47:30 but *l* me lie with my fathers;
48:16 *L* my name be named upon them,
48:16 And *l* them grow into a
49: 6 *L* not my soul enter their
49: 6 *L* not my honor be united to
49:21 'Naphtali is a deer *l* loose;
50: 5 please *l* me go up and bury my
Ex 1:10 *l* us deal shrewdly with them,
3:18 *l* us go three days' journey
3:19 the king of Egypt will not *l*
3:20 and after that he will *l* you
4:18 Please *l* me go and return to my
4:21 so that he will not *l* the
4:23 *l* My son go that he may serve
4:23 But if you refuse to *l* him go,
4:26 So He *l* him go. Then she said,
5: 1 *L* My people go, that they may
5: 2 I should obey His voice to *l*
5: 2 nor will I *l* Israel go."
5: 3 *l* us go three days' journey
5: 7 *L* them go and gather straw for
5: 8 *L* us go and sacrifice to our
5: 9 *L* more work be laid on the men,
5: 9 and *l* them not regard false
5:17 *L* us go and sacrifice to the
5:21 *L* the LORD look on you and
6: 1 with a strong hand he will *l*
6:11 Pharaoh king of Egypt to *l* the
7: 9 and *l* it become a serpent.'"
7:14 he refuses to *l* the people go.
7:16 *L* My people go, that they may
8: 1 *L* My people go, that they may
8: 2 But if you refuse to *l* them go,
8: 8 and I will *l* the people go,
8:10 *L* it be according to your
8:20 *L* My people go, that they may
8:21 if you will not *l* My people go,
8:28 I will *l* you go, that you may
8:29 But *l* Pharaoh not deal
8:32 neither would he *l* the people
9: 1 *L* My people go, that they may
9: 2 For if you refuse to *l* them go,
9: 7 and he did not *l* the people go.
9: 8 and *l* Moses scatter it toward
9:13 *L* My people go, that they may
9:17 people in that you will not *l*
9:28 I will *l* you go, and you shall
9:35 neither would he *l* the children
10: 3 *L* My people go, that they may
10: 4 if you refuse to *l* My people
10: 7 *L* the men go, that they may
10:10 had better be with you when I *l*
10:20 and he did not *l* the children
10:24 only *l* your flocks and your
10:24 *L* your little ones also go with
10:27 and he would not *l* them go.
11: 1 Afterward he will *l* you go from
11: 2 and *l* every man ask from his
11:10 and he did not *l* the children
12: 4 *l* him and his neighbor next to
12:10 You shall *l* none of it remain
12:48 *l* all his males be circumcised,
12:48 and then *l* him come near and

L

13:17 when Pharaoh had l the people
14: 5 that we have l Israel go from
14:12 L us alone that we may serve the
14:25 L us flee from the face of
16:16 L every man gather it according
16:16 l every man take for those who
16:19 L no one leave any of it till
16:29 L every man remain in his
16:29 l no man go out of his place on
17:11 and when he l down his hand,
18:22 And l them judge the people at
18:27 Then Moses l his father-in-law
19:10 and l them wash their clothes.
19:11 And l them be ready for the
19:22 Also l the priests who come near
19:24 But do not l the priests and
20:19 but l not God speak with us,
21: 8 then he shall l her be
21:26 he shall l him go free for the
21:27 he shall l him go free for the
23:11 the seventh year you shall l
23:13 nor l it be heard from your
24:14 difficulty, l him go to them."
25: 8 And l them make Me a sanctuary,
32:10 l Me alone, that My wrath may
32:22 Do not l the anger of my lord
32:24 l them break it off.' So they
32:27 L every man put his sword on his
32:27 and l every man kill his
33:12 But You have not l me know
34: 3 and l no man be seen throughout
34: 3 l neither flocks nor herds feed
34: 9 l my Lord, I pray, go among us,
35: 5 l him bring it as an offering
36: 6 L neither man nor woman do any
Lev 1: 3 l him offer a male without
4: 3 then l him offer to the LORD
10: 6 But l your brethren, the whole
14: 7 and shall l the living bird
14:53 Then he shall l the living bird
16:10 and to l it go as the
18:21 And you shall not l any of your
19:19 You shall not l your livestock
24:14 then l all who heard him lay
24:14 and l all the congregation
25:27 then l him count the years since
Num 6: 5 Then he shall l the locks of
8: 7 and l them shave all their
8: 7 and l them wash their clothes,
8: 8 Then l them take a young bull
9: 2 L the children of Israel keep
10:35 O LORD! L Your enemies be
10:35 And l those who hate You flee
11:15 and do not l me see my
12:12 Please do not l her be as one
12:14 L her be shut out of the camp
13:30 L us go up at once and take
14: 4 L us select a leader and return
14:17 l the power of my LORD be
16:17 L each take his censer and put
16:38 l them be made into hammered
20:17 Please l us pass through your
20:19 l me only pass through on foot,
21:22 'L me pass through your land.
21:27 l it be built; Let the city of
21:27 L the city of Sihon be
22:16 Please l nothing hinder you from
22:33 you by now, and l her live."
23:10 L me die the death of the
23:10 And l my end be like his!"
27:16 L the LORD, the God of the
31: 3 and l them go against the
32: 5 l this land be given to your
33:55 shall be that those whom you l
36: 6 L them marry whom they think
Deut 1:22 L us send men before us, and let
1:22 and l them search out the land
2:27 L me pass through your land
2:28 only l me pass through on foot,
2:30 king of Heshbon would not l us
3:25 l me cross over and see the
4:10 and I will l them hear My
4:36 Out of heaven He l you hear His
9:14 L Me alone, that I may destroy
12:20 L me eat meat,' because you long
13: 2 L us go after other gods'—which
13: 2 and l us serve them,'
13: 6 L us go and serve other gods,'
13:13 L us go and serve other gods"
15:12 in the seventh year you shall l
15:13 you shall not l him go away
18:16 L me not hear again the voice of
18:16 nor l me see this great fire
20: 3 Do not l your heart faint, do
20: 5 L him go and return to his
20: 6 L him go and return to his
20: 7 L him go and return to his
20: 8 L him go and return to his
20:16 you shall l nothing that
22: 7 you shall surely l the mother
24:15 and not l the sun go down on
25: 7 then l his brother's wife go up
32: 2 L my teaching drop as the rain,
32:38 L them rise and help you,
33: 6 L Reuben live, and not die,
33: 6 Nor l his men be few."
33: 7 L his hands be sufficient for
33: 8 L Your Thummim and Your Urim
33:16 L the blessing come 'on the
33:24 L him be favored by his
33:24 And l him dip his foot in oil.
Josh 2:15 Then she l them down by a rope
2:18 the window through which you l
4:22 then you shall l your children
6: 6 and l seven priests bear seven
6: 7 and l him who is armed advance
7: 3 Do not l all the people go up,
7: 3 but l about two or three
8:22 so that they l none of them
9:15 made a covenant with them to l
9:20 We will l them live, lest wrath
9:21 L them live, but let them be
9:21 but l them be woodcutters and
10:28 He l none remain. He also did
10:30 He l none remain in it, but did
22:22 and l Israel itself know—if it
22:23 l the LORD Himself require an
22:26 L us now prepare to build
24:28 So Joshua l the people depart,
Judg 1:25 but they l the man and all his
5:31 Thus l all Your enemies perish,
5:31 O LORD! But l those who love
6:31 L the one who would plead for
6:31 l him plead for himself,
6:32 L Baal plead against him,
6:39 but l me speak just once more:
6:39 L me test, I pray, just once
6:39 l it now be dry only on the
6:39 but on all the ground l there
7: 3 l him turn and depart at once
7: 7 L all the other people go,
8:19 if you had l them live, I would
9:15 l fire come out of the bramble
9:19 and l him also rejoice in you.
9:20 l fire come from Abimelech and
9:20 and l fire come from the men of
10:14 l them deliver you in your time
11:17 Please l me pass through your
11:19 Please l us pass through your
11:37 L this thing be done for me:
11:37 l me alone for two months, that
12: 5 L me cross over," the men of
13: 8 please l the Man of God whom
13:12 Now l Your words come to pass!
13:13 all that I said to the woman l
13:14 All that I commanded her l her
13:15 Please l us detain You, and we
14:12 'L me pose a riddle to you.
15: 1 L me go in to my wife, into her
15: 5 he l the foxes go into the
16:26 L me feel the pillars which
16:30 L me die with the Philistines!"
18: 9 l us go up against them. For we
18:25 Do not l your voice be heard
19: 6 and l your heart be merry."
19:11 and l us turn aside into this
19:13 l us draw near to one of these
19:20 l all your needs be my
19:24 l me bring them out now.
19:25 to break, they l her go.
19:28 Get up and l us be going." But
20:32 L us flee and draw them away
Ruth 2: 2 Please l me go to the field, and
2: 7 Please l me glean and gather
2: 9 L your eyes be on the field
2:13 L me find favor in your sight,
2:15 L her glean even among the
2:16 Also l grain from the bundles
3:13 l him do it. But if he does not
3:14 Do not l it be known that the
1 Sam 1:18 L your maidservant find favor in
1:23 Only l the LORD establish His
2: 3 L no arrogance come from your
3:18 L Him do what seems good to
3:19 the LORD was with him and l
4: 3 L us bring the ark of the
5: 8 L the ark of the God of Israel
5:11 and l it go back to its own
6: 6 did they not l the people go,
6: 8 send it away, and l it go.
9: 5 l us return, lest my father
9: 6 So l us go there; perhaps he
9: 9 l us go to the seer"; for he
9:10 l us go." So they went to the
9:19 and tomorrow I will l you go
10: 7 And l it be, when these signs
11:14 l us go to Gilgal and renew the
13: 3 L the Hebrews hear!"
14: 1 l us go over to the
14: 6 l us go over to the garrison of
14: 8 l us cross over to these men,
14:36 L us go down after the
14:36 and l us not leave a man of
14:36 L us draw near to God here."
16:16 L our master now command your
16:22 Please l David stand before me,
17: 8 and l him come down to me.
17:32 L no man's heart fail because of
18: 2 and would not l him go home to
18:17 L my hand not be against him,
18:17 but l the hand of the
19: 4 L not the king sin against his
19:12 So Michal l David down through a
19:17 L me go! Why should I kill you?'
20: 3 Do not l Jonathan know this,
20: 5 But l me go, that I may hide in
20:11 and l us go out into the
20:16 L the LORD require it at the
20:29 Please l me go, for our family
20:29 please l me get away and see my
21: 2 Do not l anyone know anything
21:13 and l his saliva fall down on
22: 3 Please l my father and mother
22:15 Far be it from me! L not the
24:12 L the LORD judge between you
24:12 and l the LORD avenge me on
24:15 Therefore l the LORD be judge,
24:19 will he l him get away safely?
25: 8 Therefore l my young men find
25:24 on me l this iniquity be!
25:24 this iniquity be! And please l
25:25 l not my lord regard this
25:26 l your enemies and those who
25:27 l it be given to the young men
26: 8 l me strike him at once with
26:11 by his head, and l us go."
26:19 l my lord the king hear the
26:19 l Him accept an offering. But
26:20 do not l my blood fall to the
26:22 L one of the young men come
26:24 so l my life be valued much in
26:24 and l Him deliver me out of all
27: 5 l them give me a place in some
28:22 and l me set a piece of bread
29: 4 and do not l him go down with
30:11 and they l him drink water.
2 Sam 1:21 L there be no dew nor rain
2: 7 l your hands be strengthened,
2:14 L the young men now arise and
2:14 Joab said, "L them arise."
3:29 L it rest on the head of Joab
3:29 and l there never fail to be in
7:26 So l Your name be magnified
7:26 And l the house of Your
7:29 l it please You to bless the
7:29 and with Your blessing l the
10:12 and l us be strong for our
11:12 and tomorrow I will l you
11:25 Do not l this thing displease
13: 5 Please l my sister Tamar come
13: 6 Please l Tamar my sister come
13:24 l the king and his servants go
13:25 l us not all go now, lest we be
13:26 please l my brother Amnon go
13:27 so he l Amnon and all the
13:32 L not my lord suppose they have
13:33 l not my lord the king take the
14: 9 l the iniquity be on me and
14:11 Please l the king remember the
14:12 l your maidservant speak
14:18 l my lord the king speak."
14:24 L him return to his own house,
14:24 but do not l him see my face."
14:32 l me see the king's face; but
14:32 l him execute me."
15: 7 l me go to Hebron and pay the
15:14 and l us flee; or we shall not
15:26 l Him do to me as seems good to
16: 9 l me go over and take off his
16:10 So l him curse, because the
16:11 L him alone, and let him curse;
16:11 and l him curse; for so the
17: 1 Now l me choose twelve thousand
17: 5 and l us hear what he says
18:19 L me run now and take the news
18:22 please l me also run after the
18:23 l me run." So he said to him,
19:19 Do not l my lord impute iniquity
19:30 l him take it all, inasmuch as
19:37 Please l your servant turn back
19:37 l him cross over with my lord
21: 6 l seven men of his descendants
22:47 Blessed be my Rock! L God
24:14 Please l us fall into the hand
24:14 but do not l me fall into the
24:17 L Your hand, I pray, be against
24:22 L my lord the king take and
1 Ki 1: 2 L a young woman, a virgin, be
1: 2 and l her stand before the
1: 2 and l her care for him; and let
1: 2 and l her lie in your bosom,
1:12 l me now give you advice, that
1:31 L my lord King David live
1:34 There l Zadok the priest and
1:51 L King Solomon swear to me today
2: 6 and do not l his gray hair go
2: 7 and l them be among those who
2:21 L Abishag the Shunammite be
3:26 L him be neither mine nor yours,
8:26 l Your word come true, which
8:61 L your heart therefore be loyal
11:21 L me depart, that I may go to my
11:22 but do l me go anyway."
12:24 L every man return to his
15:17 that he might l none go out or
15:19 L there be a treaty between
17:21 l this child's soul come back
18:23 Therefore l them give us two
18:23 and l them choose one bull for
18:36 l it be known this day that You
18:40 the prophets of Baal! Do not l
19: 2 So l the gods do to me, and
19:20 Please l me kiss my father and
20:11 L not the one who puts on his
20:31 l us put sackcloth around our
20:32 Please l me live.'" And he
20:42 Because you have l slip out of
21: 7 and l your heart be cheerful;
22: 8 L not the king say such
22:13 l your word be like the word of
22:17 L each return to his house in
22:49 L my servants go with your
2 Ki 1:10 then l fire come down from
1:12 l fire come down from heaven
1:13 please l my life and the life
1:14 But l my life now be precious

2: 9 Please *l* a double portion of
2:16 Please *l* them go and search for
4:10 *l* us make a small upper room on
4:10 and *l* us put a bed for him
4:27 *L* her alone; for her soul is in
5: 8 Please *l* him come to me, and he
5:17 please *l* your servant be given
5:24 then he *l* the men go, and they
6: 2 *l* us go to the Jordan, and let
6: 2 and *l* every man take a beam
6: 2 and *l* us make there a place
7: 4 *l* us surrender to the army of
7: 9 *l* us go and tell the king's
7:12 *L* me now tell you what the
7:13 *l* several men take five of the
7:13 so *l* us send them and see."
9:15 *l* no one leave or escape from
9:17 and *l* him say, 'Is it peace?'
10:19 *L* no one be missing, for I have
10:25 *l* no one come out!" And they
11: 8 *l* him be put to death. You are
11:15 Do not *l* her be killed in the
12: 5 *l* the priests take it
12: 5 and *l* them repair the damages
13:21 and when the man was *l* down and
14: 8 *l* us face one another in
17:27 *l* him go and dwell there, and
17:27 and *l* him teach them the
18:29 Do not *l* Hezekiah deceive you,
18:30 nor *l* Hezekiah make you trust in
19:10 Do not *l* your God in whom you
20:10 but *l* the shadow go backward
22: 5 And *l* them deliver it into the
22: 5 *l* them give it to those who
23:18 *L* him alone; let no one move his
23:18 *l* no one move his bones."
23:18 So they *l* his bones alone,
1 Chr 13: 2 *l* us send out to our brethren
13: 3 and *l* us bring the ark of our
16:10 *L* the hearts of those rejoice
16:31 *L* the heavens rejoice, and let
16:31 and *l* the earth be glad;
16:31 And *l* them say among the
16:32 *L* the sea roar, and all its
16:32 *L* the field rejoice, and all
17:23 *l* it be established forever,
17:24 So *l* it be established, that
17:24 And *l* the house of Your
19:13 and *l* us be strong for our
21:13 Please *l* me fall into the hand
21:13 but do not *l* me fall into the
21:17 *L* Your hand, I pray, O LORD my
21:23 and *l* my lord the king do what
2 Chr 1: 9 *l* Your promise to David my
2:15 *l* him send to his servants.
6:17 *l* Your word come true, which
6:40 *l* Your eyes be open and let
6:40 let Your eyes be open and *l*
6:41 *L* Your priests, O LORD God,
6:41 And *l* Your saints rejoice in
11: 4 fight against your brethren! *L*
14: 7 *L* us build these cities and make
14:11 do not *l* man prevail against
15: 7 be strong and do not *l* your
16: 1 that he might *l* none go out or
16: 3 *L* there be a treaty between
18: 7 *L* not the king say such
18:12 Therefore please *l* your word be
18:16 *L* each return to his house in
19: 7 *l* the fear of the LORD be upon
20:10 whom You would not *l* Israel
23: 6 But *l* no one come into the house
23: 7 *l* him be put to death. You are
25: 7 do not *l* the army of Israel go
25:17 *l* us face one another in
28:15 and they *l* all the feeble ones
32:15 do not *l* Hezekiah deceive you
36:23 be with him, and *l* him go up!
Ezra 1: 3 and *l* him go up to Jerusalem
1: 4 *l* the men of his place help him
4: 2 *L* us build with you, for we seek
4:12 *L* it be known to the king that
4:13 *L* it now be known to the king
5: 8 *L* it be known to the king that
5:15 and *l* the house of God be
5:17 *l* a search be made in the
5:17 and *l* the king send us his
6: 3 *L* the house be rebuilt, the
6: 3 and *l* the foundations of it be
6: 4 *L* the expenses be paid from the
6: 5 Also *l* the gold and silver
6: 7 *L* the work of this house of God
6: 7 *l* the governor of the Jews and
6: 8 *L* the cost be paid at the
6: 9 *l* it be given them day by day
6:11 *l* a timber be pulled from his
6:11 and *l* him be hanged on it;
6:11 and *l* his house be made a
6:12 *l* it be done diligently.
7:21 *l* it be done diligently,
7:23 *l* it diligently be done for the
7:26 *l* judgment be executed speedily
10: 3 *l* us make a covenant with our
10: 3 and *l* it be done according to
10:14 *l* the leaders of our entire
10:14 and *l* all those in our cities
Neh 1: 6 please *l* Your ear be attentive
1:11 please *l* Your ear be attentive
1:11 and *l* Your servant prosper this
2: 7 *l* letters be given to me for
2:17 Come and *l* us build the wall of
2:18 '*L* us rise up and build."

4: 5 and do not *l* their sin be
4:22 *L* each man and his servant stay
5: 2 therefore *l* us get grain, that
5:10 *l* us stop this usury!
6: 2 *l* us meet together among the
6: 7 and *l* us consult together.
6:10 *L* us meet together in the house
6:10 and *l* us close the doors of the
7: 3 Do not *l* the gates of Jerusalem
7: 3 *l* them shut and bar the doors;
9:32 Do not *l* all the trouble seem
Esth 1:19 *l* a royal decree go out from
1:19 and *l* it be recorded in the
1:19 and *l* the king give her royal
2: 2 *L* beautiful young virgins be
2: 3 and *l* the king appoint officers
2: 3 And *l* beauty preparations be
2: 4 Then *l* the young woman who
3: 8 not fitting for the king to *l*
3: 9 *l* a decree be written that
5: 4 *l* the king and Haman come today
5: 8 then *l* the king and Haman come
5:14 *L* a gallows be made, fifty
6: 5 king said, "*L* him come in."
6: 8 *l* a royal robe be brought which
6: 9 Then *l* this robe and horse be
7: 3 *l* my life be given me at my
8: 5 *l* it be written to revoke the
9:13 *l* it be granted to the Jews who
9:13 and *l* Haman's ten sons be
Job 6:29 *l* there be no injustice!
7:16 *L* me alone, For my days are
7:19 And *l* me alone till I swallow
9:34 *L* Him take His rod away from
9:34 And do not *l* dread of Him
11:14 And would not *l* wickedness
13:13 and *l* me speak, Then let come
13:13 Then *l* come on me what may!
13:21 And *l* not the dread of You
13:22 Or *l* me speak, then You
15:13 And *l* such words go out of
15:31 *L* him not trust in futile
16:18 And *l* my cry have no resting
21: 2 And *l* this be your
21:19 *L* Him recompense him, that he
21:20 *L* his eyes see his destruction,
21:20 And *l* him drink of the wrath
27: 6 and will not *l* it go; My heart
31: 6 *L* me be weighed on honest
31: 8 Then *l* me sow, and another
31: 8 *l* my harvest be rooted out.
31:10 Then *l* my wife grind for
31:10 And *l* others bow down over
31:22 Then *l* my arm fall from my
31:22 *L* my arm be torn from the
31:40 Then *l* thistles grow instead
32:21 *L* me not, I pray, show
32:21 Nor *l* me flatter any man.
34: 4 *L* us choose justice for
34: 4 *L* us know among ourselves what
40: 2 *l* him answer it."
42: 4 and *l* me speak; You said, 'I
Ps 2: 3 *L* us break Their bonds in pieces
5:10 O God! *L* them fall by their
5:11 But *l* all those rejoice who put
5:11 *L* them ever shout for joy,
5:11 *L* those also who love Your
6:10 *L* all my enemies be ashamed and
6:10 *L* them turn back and be
7: 5 *L* the enemy pursue me and
7: 5 *l* him trample my life to the
7: 9 *l* the wickedness of the wicked
9:19 Do not *l* man prevail; Let the
9:19 *L* the nations be judged in
10: 2 *L* them be caught in the plots
14: 7 *L* Jacob rejoice and Israel be
17: 2 *L* my vindication come from Your
17: 2 *L* Your eyes look on the things
18:46 Blessed be my Rock! *L* the
19:13 *L* them not have dominion over
19:14 *L* the words of my mouth and the
22: 8 *l* Him rescue Him; Let Him
22: 8 *L* Him deliver Him, since He
22:26 *L* your heart live forever!
25: 2 *L* me not be ashamed; Let not
25: 2 *L* not my enemies triumph over
25: 3 *l* no one who waits on You be
25: 3 *L* those be ashamed who deal
25:20 *L* me not be ashamed, for I put
25:21 *L* integrity and uprightness
30: 1 And have not *l* my foes rejoice
31: 1 *L* me never be ashamed;
31:17 Do not *l* me be ashamed,
31:17 *L* the wicked be ashamed;
31:17 *L* them be silent in the grave.
31:18 *L* the lying lips be put to
33: 8 *L* all the earth fear the LORD
33: 8 *L* all the inhabitants of the
33:22 *L* Your mercy, O LORD, be upon
34: 3 And *l* us exalt His name
35: 4 *L* those be put to shame and
35: 4 *L* those be turned back and
35: 5 *L* them be like chaff before the
35: 5 And *l* the angel of the LORD
35: 6 *L* their way be dark and
35: 6 And *l* the angel of the LORD
35: 8 *L* destruction come upon him
35: 8 And *l* his net that he has
35: 8 Into that very destruction *l*
35:19 *L* them not rejoice over me who
35:19 Nor *l* them wink with the eye
35:24 And *l* them not rejoice over

35:25 *L* them not say in their hearts,
35:25 so we would have it!" *L* them
35:26 *L* them be ashamed and brought
35:26 *L* them be clothed with shame
35:27 *L* them shout for joy and be
35:27 And *l* them say continually,
35:27 '*L* the LORD be magnified,
36:11 *L* not the foot of pride come
36:11 And *l* not the hand of the
40:11 *L* Your lovingkindness and Your
40:14 *L* them be ashamed and brought
40:14 *L* them be driven backward and
40:15 *L* them be confounded because of
40:16 *L* all those who seek You
40:16 *L* such as love Your salvation
43: 3 Your light and Your truth! *L*
43: 3 *L* them bring me to Your holy
48:11 *L* Mount Zion rejoice, Let the
48:11 *L* the daughters of Judah be
50: 6 *L* the heavens declare His
53: 6 *L* Jacob rejoice and Israel be
55:15 *L* death seize them
55:15 *L* them go down alive into
57: 5 *L* Your glory be above all
57:11 *L* Your glory be above all
58: 7 *L* them flow away as waters
58: 7 *L* his arrows be as if cut in
58: 8 *L* them be like a snail which
59:10 God shall *l* me see my desire
59:12 *L* them even be taken in their
59:13 And *l* them know that God rules
66: 7 Do not *l* the rebellious exalt
67: 3 *L* the peoples praise You, O God
67: 3 *L* all the peoples praise You.
67: 4 *l* the nations be glad and sing
67: 5 *L* the peoples praise You, O God
67: 5 *L* all the peoples praise You.
68: 1 *L* God arise, Let His enemies
68: 1 *L* His enemies be scattered;
68: 1 *L* those also who hate Him flee
68: 2 So *l* the wicked perish at the
68: 3 But *l* the righteous be glad;
68: 3 *L* them rejoice before God;
68: 3 *l* them rejoice exceedingly.
69: 6 *L* not those who wait for You,
69: 6 *L* not those who seek You be
69:14 And *l* me not sink; Let me be
69:14 *L* me be delivered from those
69:15 *L* not the floodwater overflow
69:15 Nor *l* the deep swallow me up;
69:15 And *l* not the pit shut its
69:22 *L* their table become a snare
69:23 *L* their eyes be darkened, so
69:24 And *l* Your wrathful anger take
69:25 *L* their dwelling place be
69:25 *L* no one live in their tents.
69:27 And *l* them not come into Your
69:28 *L* them be blotted out of the
69:29 *L* Your salvation, O God, set
69:34 *L* heaven and earth praise Him,
70: 2 *L* them be ashamed and
70: 2 *L* them be turned back and
70: 3 *L* them be turned back because
70: 4 *L* all those who seek You
70: 4 And *l* those who love Your
70: 4 *L* God be magnified!"
71: 1 *L* me never be put to shame.
71: 8 *L* my mouth be filled with Your
71:13 *L* them be confounded and
71:13 *L* them be covered with
72:19 glorious name forever! And *l*
74: 8 *L* us destroy them altogether."
74:21 do not *l* the oppressed return
74:21 oppressed return ashamed! *L*
76:11 *L* all who are around Him bring
78:28 And He *l* them fall in the
79: 8 iniquities against us! *L* Your
79:10 *L* there be known among the
79:11 *L* the groaning of the prisoner
80:17 *L* Your hand be upon the man of
83: 4 and *l* us cut them off from
83:12 *L* us take for ourselves The
83:17 *L* them be confounded and
83:17 *l* them be put to shame and
85: 8 But *l* them not turn back to
88: 2 *L* my prayer come before You
90:16 *L* Your work appear to Your
90:17 And *l* the beauty of the LORD
95: 1 *l* us sing to the LORD! Let us
95: 1 let us sing to the LORD! *L* us
95: 2 *L* us come before His presence
95: 2 *L* us shout joyfully to Him
95: 6 *l* us worship and bow down;
95: 6 *L* us kneel before the LORD
96:11 *L* the heavens rejoice, and let
96:11 and *l* the earth be glad;
96:11 *L* the sea roar, and all its
96:12 *L* the field be joyful, and all
97: 1 *L* the earth rejoice; Let the
97: 1 *L* the multitude of isles be
97: 7 *L* all be put to shame who serve
98: 7 *L* the sea roar, and all its
98: 8 *L* the rivers clap their hands
98: 8 *L* the hills be joyful together
99: 1 *L* the peoples tremble!
99: 1 *L* the earth be moved!
99: 3 *L* them praise Your great and
102: 1 And *l* my cry come to You.
105: 3 *L* the hearts of those rejoice
105:20 The ruler of the people *l* him
106:48 to everlasting! And *l* all the
107: 2 *L* the redeemed of the LORD say

L

107:22 *L* them sacrifice the sacrifices
107:32 *L* them exalt Him also in the
107:38 And He does not *l* their cattle
109: 6 And *l* an accuser stand at his
109: 7 *l* him be found guilty, And let
109: 7 And *l* his prayer become sin.
109: 8 *L* his days be few, And let
109: 8 And *l* another take his
109: 9 *L* his children be fatherless,
109:10 *L* his children continually be
109:10 *L* them seek their bread also
109:11 *L* the creditor seize all that
109:11 And *l* strangers plunder his
109:12 *L* there be none to extend mercy
109:12 Nor *l* there be any to favor
109:13 *L* his posterity be cut off,
109:13 in the generation following *l*
109:14 *L* the iniquity of his fathers
109:14 And *l* not the sin of his
109:15 *L* them be continually before
109:17 so *l* it come to him; As he did
109:17 so *l* it be far from him.
109:18 So *l* it enter his body like
109:19 *L* it be to him like the garment
109:20 *L* this be the LORD's reward
109:28 *L* them curse, but You bless
109:28 *l* them be ashamed, But let
109:28 But *l* Your servant rejoice.
109:29 *L* my accusers be clothed with
109:29 And *l* them cover themselves
118: 2 *L* Israel now say, "His mercy
118: 3 *L* the house of Aaron now say,
118: 4 *L* those who fear the LORD now
119:10 *l* me not wander from Your
119:41 *L* Your mercies come also to
119:76 *L*, I pray, Your merciful
119:77 *L* Your tender mercies come to
119:78 *L* the proud be ashamed,
119:79 *L* those who fear You turn to
119:80 *L* my heart be blameless
119:116 And do not *l* me be ashamed of
119:122 Do not *l* the proud oppress me.
119:133 And *l* no iniquity have
119:169 *L* my cry come before You,
119:170 *L* my supplication come before
119:173 *L* Your hand become my help,
119:175 *L* my soul live, and it shall
119:175 And *l* Your judgments help me.
122: 1 *L* us go into the house of the
124: 1 *L* Israel now say—
129: 1 *L* Israel now say—
129: 5 *L* all those who hate Zion Be
129: 6 *L* them be as the grass on the
129: 8 Neither *l* those who pass by
130: 2 hear my voice! *L* Your ears be
132: 7 *L* us go into His tabernacle
132: 7 *L* us worship at His footstool.
132: 9 *L* Your priests be clothed with
132: 9 And *l* Your saints shout for
137: 5 *L* my right hand forget its
137: 6 *L* my tongue cling to the roof
140: 9 *L* the evil of their lips cover
140:10 *L* burning coals fall upon them
140:10 *L* them be cast into the fire,
140:11 *L* not a slanderer be
140:11 *L* evil hunt the violent man to
141: 2 *L* my prayer be set before You
141: 4 And do not *l* me eat of their
141: 5 *L* the righteous strike me
141: 5 And *l* him rebuke me;
141: 5 *L* my head not refuse it.
141:10 *L* the wicked fall into their
148: 5 *L* them praise the name of the
148:13 *L* them praise the name of the
149: 2 *L* Israel rejoice in their Maker
149: 2 *L* the children of Zion be
149: 3 *L* them praise His name with the
149: 3 *L* them sing praises to Him
149: 5 *L* the saints be joyful in glory
149: 5 *L* them sing aloud on their
149: 6 *L* the high praises of God be
150: 6 *L* everything that has breath
Prov 1:11 *L* us lie in wait to shed
1:11 *L* us lurk secretly for the
1:12 *L* us swallow them alive like
1:14 *L* us all have one purse"—
3: 1 But *l* your heart keep my
3: 3 *L* not mercy and truth forsake
3:21 *l* them not depart from your
4: 4 *L* your heart retain my words;
4:13 do not *l* go; Keep her, for she
4:21 Do not *l* them depart from your
4:25 *L* your eyes look straight
4:26 And *l* all your ways be
5:17 *L* them be only your own,
5:18 *L* your fountain be blessed,
5:19 *L* her breasts satisfy you at
6:25 Nor *l* her allure you with her
7:18 *l* us take our fill of love
7:18 *L* us delight ourselves with
7:25 Do not *l* your heart turn aside
9: 4 *l* him turn in here!" As for
9:16 *l* him turn in here"; And as
17:12 *L* a man meet a bear robbed of
22:18 *L* them all be fixed upon your
23:17 Do not *l* your heart envy
23:25 *L* your father and your mother
23:25 And *l* her who bore you
23:26 And *l* your eyes observe my
24:17 And do not *l* your heart be
27: 2 *L* another man praise you, and
28:17 *L* no one help him.
31: 7 *L* him drink and forget his
31:31 And *l* her own works praise her
Eccl 5: 2 And *l* not your heart utter
5: 2 Therefore *l* your words be few.
5: 6 Do not *l* your mouth cause your
9: 8 *L* your garments always be
9: 8 And *l* your head lack no oil.
11: 8 Yet *l* him remember the days of
11: 9 And *l* your heart cheer you in
12:13 *L* us hear the conclusion of the
Song 1: 2 *L* him kiss me with the kisses
2:14 *L* me see your face, Let me
2:14 *L* me hear your voice;
3: 4 I held him and would not *l* him
4:16 *L* my beloved come to his
7: 8 *L* now your breasts be like
7:11 *L* us go forth to the field;
7:11 *L* us lodge in the villages.
7:12 *L* us get up early to the
7:12 *L* us see if the vine has
8:13 *L* me hear it! THE SHULAMITE
Isa 1:18 and *l* us reason together,"
2: 3 and *l* us go up to the mountain
2: 5 come and *l* us walk In the
3: 6 And *l* these ruins be under
4: 1 Only *l* us be called by your
5: 1 Now *l* me sing to my
5: 5 please *l* Me tell you what I
5:19 *L* Him make speed and hasten His
5:19 And *l* the counsel of the Holy
7: 6 *L* us go up against Judah and
7: 6 and *l* us make a gap in its wall
8:13 *L* Him be your fear,
8:13 And *l* Him be your dread.
16: 4 *L* My outcasts dwell with you,
19:12 *L* them tell you now, And let
19:12 And *l* them know what the LORD
21: 6 *L* him declare what he sees."
22:13 *L* us eat and drink, for tomorrow
26:10 *L* grace be shown to the wicked,
27: 5 Or *l* him take hold of My
29: 1 *L* feasts come around.
34: 1 you people! *L* the earth hear,
36:14 Do not *l* Hezekiah deceive you,
36:15 nor *l* Hezekiah make you trust in
37:10 Do not *l* your God in whom you
38:21 *L* them take a lump of figs, and
41: 1 And *l* the people renew their
41: 1 renew their strength! *L* them
41: 1 then *l* them speak; Let us come
41: 1 *L* us come near together for
41:22 *L* them bring forth and show us
41:22 *L* them show the former things,
42:11 *L* the wilderness and its cities
42:11 *L* the inhabitants of Sela
42:11 *L* them shout from the top of
42:12 *L* them give glory to the LORD,
43: 9 *L* all the nations be gathered
43: 9 And *l* the people be assembled.
43: 9 *L* them bring out their
43: 9 Or *l* them hear and say, "It
43:26 *L* us contend together;
44: 7 Then *l* him declare it and set
44: 7 *L* them show these to them.
44:11 *L* them all be gathered
44:11 *L* them stand up; Yet they
45: 8 And *l* the skies pour down
45: 8 *L* the earth open, let them
45: 8 *l* them bring forth salvation,
45: 8 And *l* righteousness spring up
45: 9 *L* the potsherd strive with
45:13 And *l* My exiles go free,
45:21 *l* them take counsel together.
47:13 *L* now the astrologers, the
50: 8 *L* us stand together. Who is
50: 8 *L* him come near Me.
50:10 *L* him trust in the name of the
54: 2 And *l* them stretch out the
55: 2 And *l* your soul delight itself
55: 7 *L* the wicked forsake his way,
55: 7 *L* him return to the LORD,
56: 3 Do not *l* the son of the
56: 3 Nor *l* the eunuch say, "Here
57:13 *L* your collection of idols
58: 6 To *l* the oppressed go free,
66: 5 *L* the LORD be glorified, That
Jer 2:28 *L* them arise, If they can
4: 5 And *l* us go into the fortified
5:24 *L* us now fear the LORD our God,
6: 4 and *l* us go up at noon. Woe to
6: 5 and *l* us go by night, And let
6: 5 And *l* us destroy her
8:14 And *l* us enter the fortified
8:14 And *l* us be silent there.
9:18 *L* them make haste And take up
9:20 And *l* your ear receive the
9:23 *L* not the wise man glory in his
9:23 *L* not the mighty man glory in
9:23 Nor *l* the rich man glory in
9:24 But *l* him who glories glory in
11:19 *L* us destroy the tree with its
11:19 and *l* us cut him off from the
11:20 *L* me see Your vengeance on
12: 1 Yet *l* me talk with You about
14:17 *L* my eyes flow with tears night
14:17 And *l* them not cease; For the
15: 1 and *l* them go forth.
15:19 *L* them return to you, But you
17: 4 Shall *l* go of your heritage
17:15 *L* it come now!"
17:18 *L* them be ashamed who persecute
17:18 But do not *l* me be put to
17:18 *L* them be dismayed, But do
17:18 But do not *l* me be dismayed.
18:18 Come and *l* us devise plans
18:18 Come and *l* us attack him with
18:18 and *l* us not give heed to any
18:21 *L* their wives become widows
18:21 *L* their men be put to death,
18:22 *L* a cry be heard from their
18:23 But *l* them be overthrown
20:12 *L* me see Your vengeance on
20:14 the day in which I was born! *L*
20:15 *L* the man be cursed Who
20:16 And *l* that man be like the
20:16 *L* him hear the cry in the
23:28 *l* him tell a dream; And he who
23:28 *l* him speak My word faithfully.
27:11 I will *l* them remain in their
27:18 *l* them now make intercession to
29: 8 Do not *l* your prophets and your
30:11 And will not *l* you go
31: 6 and *l* us go up to Zion,
34:10 they obeyed and *l* them go.
34:14 At the end of seven years *l*
34:14 you shall *l* him go free from
35:11 *l* us go to Jerusalem for fear
36:19 and *l* no one know where you
37:20 *l* my petition be accepted
38: 4 *l* this man be put to death, for
38: 6 and they *l* Jeremiah down with
38:11 and *l* them down by ropes into
38:24 *L* no one know of these words,
40: 1 the captain of the guard had *l*
40: 5 him rations and a gift and *l*
40:15 *L* me go, please, and I will kill
42: 2 *l* our petition be acceptable to
42: 5 *L* the LORD be a true and
46: 6 Do not *l* the swift flee away,
46: 9 O chariots! And *l* the mighty
46:16 Arise! *L* us go back to our own
48: 2 and *l* us cut her off as a
49:11 And *l* your widows trust in
50: 5 Come and *l* us join ourselves to
50:26 *L* nothing of her be left.
50:27 *L* them go down to the
50:29 *L* none of them escape.
50:33 They have refused to *l* them
51: 3 Against her *l* the archer bend
51: 9 and *l* us go everyone to his own
51:10 Come and *l* us declare in Zion
51:35 *L* the violence done to me and
51:45 out of the midst of her! And *l*
51:50 And *l* Jerusalem come to your
Lam 1:22 *L* all their wickedness come
2:18 *L* tears run down like a river
3:28 *L* him sit alone and keep
3:29 *L* him put his mouth in the dust
3:30 *L* him give his cheek to the
3:40 *L* us search out and examine our
3:41 *L* us lift our hearts and hands
Ezek 1:24 they *l* down their wings.
1:25 they *l* down their wings.
3:27 *l* him hear; and he who refuses,
3:27 *l* him refuse; for they are a
7:12 '*L* not the buyer rejoice,
9: 1 *L* those who have charge over the
9: 5 do not *l* your eye spare, nor
13:20 and *l* the souls go, the souls
14: 3 Should I *l* Myself be inquired
21:14 The third time *l* the sword do
24: 5 And *l* the cuts simmer in
24:10 And *l* the cuts be burned up.
24:12 *L* her scum be in the fire!
24:26 escapes will come to you to *l*
36:15 Nor will I *l* you hear the taunts
36:32 *l* it be known to you. Be ashamed
36:37 I will also *l* the house of
39: 7 and I will not *l* them profane
43: 9 Now *l* them put their harlotry
43:10 and *l* them measure the pattern.
44: 6 *l* us have no more of all your
44:20 shave their heads nor *l* their
Dan 1:12 and *l* them give us vegetables
1:13 Then *l* our appearance be
2: 7 *L* the king tell his servants the
3:18 *l* it be known to you, O king,
4:14 *L* the beasts get out from
4:15 *L* it be wet with the dew of
4:15 And *l* him graze with the
4:16 *L* his heart be changed from
4:16 *L* him be given the heart of a
4:16 And *l* seven times pass over
4:19 do not *l* the dream or its
4:23 *l* it be wet with the dew of
4:23 and *l* him graze with the beasts
4:27 *l* my advice be acceptable to
5:10 live forever! Do not *l* your
5:10 nor *l* your countenance change.
5:12 now *l* Daniel be called, and he
5:17 *L* your gifts be for yourself,
9:16 *l* Your anger and Your fury be
10:19 *L* my lord speak, for you have
Hos 2: 2 nor am I her Husband! *L* her
4: 4 Now *l* no man contend, or rebuke
4:15 *L* not Judah offend. Do not
4:16 Now the LORD will *l* them
4:17 joined to idols, *L* him alone.
6: 1 and *l* us return to the LORD;
6: 3 *L* us know, Let us pursue the
6: 3 *L* us pursue the knowledge of
11:11 And I will *l* them dwell in
13: 2 *L* the men who sacrifice kiss the
14: 9 *L* him understand these things.

14: 9 *L* him know them. For the ways
Joel 1: 3 *L* your children tell their
2: 1 alarm in My holy mountain! *L*
2:16 *L* the bridegroom go out from
2:17 *L* the priests, who minister to
2:17 *L* them say, "Spare Your
3: 9 *L* all the men of war draw
3: 9 *L* them come up.
3:10 *L* the weak say, 'I am
3:12 *L* the nations be wakened, and
Am 4: 1 'Bring wine, *l* us drink!"
5:24 But *l* justice run down like
Ob 1 and *l* us rise up against her
Jon 1: 7 *l* us cast lots, that we may
1:14 please do not *l* us perish for
3: 7 *L* neither man nor beast, herd
3: 7 do not *l* them eat, or drink
3: 8 But *l* man and beast be covered
3: 8 *l* every one turn from his evil
Mic 1: 2 and all that is in it! *L* the
4: 2 and *l* us go up to the mountain
4:11 *L* her be defiled, And let our
4:11 And *l* our eye look upon
6: 1 And *l* the hills hear your
7:14 *L* them feed in Bashan and
Hab 2:20 *L* all the earth keep silence
Zeph 3:16 *l* not your hands be weak.
Zech 3: 5 *L* them put a clean turban on his
7:10 *L* none of you plan evil in his
8: 9 *L* your hands be strong, You who
8:13 *L* your hands be strong.'
8:17 *L* none of you think evil in
8:21 *L* us continue to go and pray
8:23 *L* us go with you, for we have
11: 9 *L* what is dying die, and what
11: 9 *L* those that are left eat each
Mal 2:15 And *l* none deal treacherously
Mt 5:16 *L* your light so shine before
5:31 *l* him give her a certificate of
5:37 But *l* your 'Yes' be 'Yes,' and
5:40 *l* him have your cloak also.
6: 3 do not *l* your left hand know
7: 4 *L* me remove the speck from your
8:13 so *l* it be done for you."
8:21 *l* me first go and bury my
8:22 and *l* the dead bury their own
9:29 According to your faith *l* it be
10:13 *l* your peace come upon it.
10:13 *l* your peace return to you.
11:15 ears to hear, *l* him hear!
13: 9 ears to hear, *l* him hear!"
13:30 *L* both grow together until the
13:43 ears to hear, *l* him hear!
15: 4 *l* him be put to death.'
15:14 *L* them alone. They are blind
15:28 great is your faith! *L* it be
16:24 *l* him deny himself, and take up
17: 4 *l* us make here three
18:17 *l* him be to you like a heathen
19: 6 *l* not man separate."
19:12 *l* him accept it."
19:14 *L* the little children come to
20:26 *l* him be your servant.
20:27 *l* him be your slave—
21:19 *L* no fruit grow on you ever
21:38 *l* us kill him and seize his
24:15 reads, *l* him understand),
24:16 then *l* those who are in Judea
24:17 *L* him who is on the housetop not
24:18 And *l* him who is in the field
26:39 *l* this cup pass from Me;
26:46 *l* us be going. See, My betrayer
27:22 *L* Him be crucified!"
27:23 *L* Him be crucified!"
27:42 *l* Him now come down from the
27:43 *l* Him deliver Him now if He
27:49 *L* Him alone; let us see if
27:49 *l* us see if Elijah will come to
Mk 1:24 *L* us alone! What have we to do
1:38 *L* us go into the next towns,
2: 4 they *l* down the bed on which
4: 9 ears to hear, *l* him hear!"
4:23 ears to hear, *l* him hear."
4:35 *L* us cross over to the other
7:10 *l* him be put to death.'
7:12 then you no longer *l* him do
7:16 ears to hear, *l* him hear!"
7:27 *L* the children be filled first,
8:34 *l* him deny himself, and take up
9: 5 and *l* us make three
10: 9 *l* not man separate."
10:14 *L* the little children come to
11: 6 So they *l* them go.
11:14 *L* no one eat fruit from you ever
12: 7 *l* us kill him, and the
13:14 where it ought not" (*l* the
13:14 then *l* those who are in Judea
13:15 *L* him who is on the housetop not
13:16 And *l* him who is in the field
14: 6 *L* her alone. Why do you trouble
14:42 *l* us be going. See, My betrayer
15:32 *L* the Christ, the King of
15:36 *L* Him alone; let us see if
15:36 *l* us see if Elijah will come to
Lk 1:38 the maidservant of the Lord! *L*
2:15 *L* us now go to Bethlehem and see
3:11 *l* him give to him who has none;
3:11 *l* him do likewise."
4:34 *L* us alone! What have we to do
5: 4 out into the deep and *l*
5: 5 at Your word I will *l* down the
5:19 went up on the housetop and *l*
6:42 *l* me remove the speck that is
8: 8 ears to hear, *l* him hear!"
8:22 *L* us cross over to the other
9:23 *l* him deny himself, and take up
9:33 and *l* us make three
9:44 *L* these words sink down into
9:59 *l* me first go and bury my
9:60 *L* the dead bury their own dead,
9:61 but *l* me first go and bid them
12:35 *L* your waist be girded and
13: 8 *l* it alone this year also,
14: 4 healed him, and *l* him go.
14:35 ears to hear, *l* him hear!"
15:23 and *l* us eat and be merry;
16:29 *l* them hear them.'
17:31 *l* him not come down to take
17:31 *l* him not turn back.
18:16 *L* the little children come to
20:14 *l* us kill him, that the
21:21 Then *l* those who are in Judea
21:21 *l* those who are in the midst of
21:21 and *l* not those who are in the
22:26 *l* him be as the younger, and he
22:36 *l* him take it, and likewise a
22:36 *l* him sell his garment and buy
22:68 by no means answer Me or *l* Me
23:22 therefore chastise Him and *l*
23:35 *l* Him save Himself if He is the
Jn 7:37 *l* him come to Me and drink.
8: 7 *l* him throw a stone at her
11: 7 *L* us go to Judea again."
11:15 Nevertheless *l* us go to him."
11:16 *L* us also go, that we may die
11:44 'Loose him, and *l* him go."
11:48 If we *l* Him alone like this,
12: 7 *L* her alone; she has kept this
12:26 *l* him follow Me; and where I
14: 1 *L* not your heart be troubled;
14:27 *L* not your heart be troubled,
14:27 neither *l* it be afraid.
14:31 *l* us go from here.
18: 8 *l* these go their way,"
19:12 If you *l* this Man go, you are
19:24 *L* us not tear it, but cast lots
Acts 1:20 *L* his dwelling place be
1:20 And *l* no one live in
1:20 *L* another take his office.'
2:14 *l* this be known to you, and
2:29 *l* me speak freely to you of
2:36 Therefore *l* all the house of
2:38 and *l* every one of you be
3:13 when he was determined to *l*
4:10 *l* it be known to you all, and to
4:17 *l* us severely threaten them,
4:21 they *l* them go, finding no way
4:23 And being *l* go, they went to
5:38 keep away from these men and *l*
5:40 name of Jesus, and *l* them go.
9:25 took him by night and *l* him
10:11 descending to him and *l* down to
11: 5 *l* down from heaven by four
13:38 Therefore *l* it be known to you,
15:36 *L* us now go back and visit our
16:35 *L* those men go."
16:36 magistrates have sent to *l*
16:37 No indeed! *L* them come
17: 9 the rest, they *l* them go.
19:38 *L* them bring charges against
23: 9 *l* us not fight against God."
23:22 So the commander *l* the young man
24:20 Or else *l* those who are here
24:23 to keep Paul and to *l* him
25: 5 *l* those who have authority among
27:15 the wind, we *l* her drive.
27:30 when they had *l* down the skiff
27:32 the ropes of the skiff and *l*
27:40 And they *l* go the anchors and
28:18 wanted to *l* me go, because
28:28 Therefore *l* it be known to you
Rom 3: 4 *l* God be true but every man a
3: 8 *L* us do evil that good may
6:12 Therefore do not *l* sin reign in
11: 9 *L* their table become a
11:10 *L* their eyes be darkened,
12: 6 *l* us use them: if prophecy,
12: 6 *l* us prophesy in proportion
12: 7 *l* us use it in our
12: 9 *L* love be without hypocrisy.
13: 1 *L* every soul be subject to the
13:12 Therefore *l* us cast off the
13:12 and *l* us put on the armor of
13:13 *L* us walk properly, as in the
14: 3 *L* not him who eats despise him
14: 3 and *l* not him who does not eat
14: 5 *L* each be fully convinced in
14:13 Therefore *l* us not judge one
14:16 Therefore do not *l* your good be
14:19 Therefore *l* us pursue the things
15: 2 *L* each of us please his
1 Cor 1:31 *l* him glory in the
3:10 But *l* each one take heed how he
3:18 *L* no one deceive himself
3:18 *l* him become a fool that he may
3:21 Therefore *l* no one boast in men.
4: 1 *L* a man so consider us, as
5: 8 Therefore *l* us keep the feast,
6: 7 Why do you not rather *l*
7: 2 *l* each man have his own wife,
7: 2 and *l* each woman have her own
7: 3 *L* the husband render to his wife
7: 9 *l* them marry. For it is better
7:11 *l* her remain unmarried or be
7:12 *l* him not divorce her.
7:13 *l* her not divorce him.
7:15 *l* him depart; a brother or a
7:17 so *l* him walk. And so I ordain
7:18 *L* him not become uncircumcised.
7:18 *L* him not be circumcised.
7:20 *L* each one remain in the same
7:24 *l* each one remain with God in
7:36 *l* him do what he wishes.
7:36 does not sin; *l* them marry.
10: 8 Nor *l* us commit sexual
10: 9 nor *l* us tempt Christ, as some
10:12 Therefore *l* him who thinks he
10:24 *L* no one seek his own, but each
11: 6 *l* her also be shorn. But if it
11: 6 shaved, *l* her be covered.
11:28 But *l* a man examine himself, and
11:28 and so *l* him eat of the bread
11:34 *l* him eat at home, lest you
14:12 *l* it be for the edification
14:13 Therefore *l* him who speaks in a
14:26 *L* all things be done for
14:27 *l* there be two or at the
14:27 and *l* one interpret.
14:28 *l* him keep silent in church,
14:28 and *l* him speak to himself and
14:29 *L* two or three prophets speak,
14:29 and *l* the others judge.
14:30 *l* the first keep silent.
14:34 *L* your women keep silent in the
14:35 *l* them ask their own husbands
14:37 *l* him acknowledge that the
14:38 ignorant, *l* him be ignorant.
14:40 *L* all things be done decently
15:32 *L* us eat and drink, for
16: 2 On the first day of the week *l*
16:11 Therefore *l* no one despise him.
16:14 *L* all that you do be done with
16:22 *l* him be accursed. O Lord,
2 Cor 7: 1 *l* us cleanse ourselves from all
9: 7 So *l* each one give as he
10: 7 *l* him again consider this in
10:11 *L* such a person consider this,
10:17 *l* him glory in the
11:16 *l* no one think me a fool. If
11:33 but I was *l* down in a basket
Gal 1: 8 to you, *l* him be accursed.
1: 9 received, *l* him be accursed.
5:25 *l* us also walk in the Spirit.
5:26 *L* us not become conceited,
6: 4 But *l* each one examine his own
6: 6 *L* him who is taught the word
6: 9 And *l* us not grow weary while
6:10 *l* us do good to all, especially
6:17 From now on *l* no one trouble me,
Eph 4:25 *L* each one of you speak
4:26 do not *l* the sun go down on
4:28 *L* him who stole steal no longer,
4:28 but rather *l* him labor, working
4:29 *L* no corrupt word proceed out of
4:31 *L* all bitterness, wrath, anger,
5: 3 *l* it not even be named among
5: 6 *L* no one deceive you with empty
5:24 so *l* the wives be to their
5:33 Nevertheless *l* each one of you
5:33 and *l* the wife see that she
Phil 1:27 Only *l* your conduct be worthy
2: 3 *L* nothing be done through
2: 3 but in lowliness of mind *l* each
2: 4 *L* each of you look out not only
2: 5 *L* this mind be in you which was
3:15 Therefore *l* us, as many as are
3:16 *l* us walk by the same rule, let
3:16 *l* us be of the same mind.
4: 5 *L* your gentleness be known to
4: 6 *l* your requests be made known
Col 2:16 So *l* no one judge you in food or
2:18 *L* no one cheat you of your
3:15 And *l* the peace of God rule in
3:16 *L* the word of Christ dwell in
4: 6 *L* your speech always be with
1 Th 5: 6 Therefore *l* us not sleep, as
5: 6 but *l* us watch and be sober.
5: 8 But *l* us who are of the day be
2 Th 2: 3 *L* no one deceive you by any
1 Tim 2:11 *L* a woman learn in silence with
3:10 But *l* these also first be
3:10 then *l* them serve as deacons,
3:12 *L* deacons be the husbands of one
4:12 *L* no one despise your youth,
5: 4 *l* them first learn to show
5: 9 Do not *l* a widow under sixty
5:16 *l* them relieve them, and do not
5:16 and do not *l* the church be
5:17 *L* the elders who rule well be
6: 1 *L* as many bondservants as are
6: 2 *l* them not despise them
6:18 *L* them do good, that they be
2 Tim 2:19 *L* everyone who names the name of
Titus 2:15 *L* no one despise you.
3:14 And *l* our people also learn to
Phm 1:20 *l* me have joy from you in the
Heb 1: 6 *L* all the angels of God
4: 1 *l* us fear lest any of you seem
4:11 *L* us therefore be diligent to
4:14 *l* us hold fast our confession.
4:16 *L* us therefore come boldly to
6: 1 *l* us go on to perfection, not
10:22 *l* us draw near with a true heart
10:23 *L* us hold fast the confession of
10:24 And *l* us consider one another in
12: 1 *l* us lay aside every weight,

12: 1 and l us run with endurance the
12:28 l us have grace, by which we
13: 1 L brotherly love continue.
13: 5 L your conduct be without
13:13 Therefore l us go forth to Him,
13:15 Therefore by Him l us
13:17 L them do so with joy and not
Jas 1: 4 But l patience have its perfect
1: 5 l him ask of God, who gives to
1: 6 But l him ask in faith, with no
1: 7 For l not that man suppose that
1: 9 L the lowly brother glory in
1:13 L no one say when he is tempted,
1:19 l every man be swift to hear,
3: 1 l not many of you become
3:13 L him show by good conduct
4: 9 Lament and mourn and weep! L
5:12 But l your "Yes," be "Yes,"
5:13 L him pray. Is anyone cheerful?
5:13 L him sing psalms.
5:14 L him call for the elders of
5:14 and l them pray over him,
5:20 l him know that he who turns a
1 Pe 3: 3 Do not l your adornment be
3: 4 rather l it be the hidden
3:10 L him refrain his tongue
3:11 L him turn away from evil
3:11 L him seek peace and
4:11 l him speak as the oracles
4:11 l him do it as with the
4:15 But l none of you suffer as a
4:16 l him not be ashamed, but let
4:16 but l him glorify God in this
4:19 Therefore l those who suffer
1 Jn 2:24 Therefore l that abide in you
3: 7 l no one deceive you. He who
3:18 l us not love in word or in
4: 7 l us love one another, for love
Rev 2: 7 l him hear what the Spirit says
2:11 l him hear what the Spirit says
2:17 l him hear what the Spirit says
2:29 l him hear what the Spirit says
3: 6 l him hear what the Spirit says
3:13 l him hear what the Spirit says
3:22 l him hear what the Spirit says
13: 9 has an ear, l him hear.
13:18 L him who has understanding
19: 7 L us be glad and rejoice and
22:11 l him be unjust still; he who
22:11 l him be filthy still; he who
22:11 l him be righteous still;
22:11 l him be holy still."
22:17 Come!" And l him who hears say,
22:17 Come!" And l him who thirsts
22:17 l him take the water of life

LETS (3/3)

Ex 11: 1 When he l you go, he will
22: 5 and l loose his animal, and it
2 Ki 10:24 whoever l him escape, it

LETTER (38/36) LETTERS

2 Sam 11:14 happened that David wrote a l
11:15 And he wrote in the l,
2 Ki 5: 5 and I will send a l to the king
5: 6 Then he brought the l to the
5: 6 when this l comes to you, that
5: 7 the king of Israel read the l,
10: 2 Now as soon as this l comes to
10: 6 Then he wrote a second l to
10: 7 when the l came to them, that
19:14 And Hezekiah received the l
2 Chr 21:12 And a l came to him from Elijah
Ezra 4: 7 and the l was written in
4: 8 Shimshai the scribe wrote a l
4:11 (This is a copy of the l that
4:18 The l which you sent to us has
4:23 the copy of King Artaxerxes' l
5: 6 This is a copy of the l that
5: 7 They sent a l to him, in which
7:11 This is a copy of the l that
Neh 2: 8 and a l to Asaph the keeper of
6: 5 with an open l in his hand.
Esth 9:25 he commanded by l that this
9:26 of all the words of this l,
9:29 to confirm this second l about
Isa 37:14 And Hezekiah received the l
Jer 29: 1 these are the words of the l
29: 3 The l was sent by the hand
29:29 the priest read this l in the
Acts 15:23 They wrote this l by them:
15:30 together, they delivered the l.
23:25 He wrote a l in the following
23:33 and had delivered the l to the
Rom 2:29 in the Spirit, not in the l;
7: 6 not in the oldness of the l.
2 Cor 3: 6 not of the l but of the Spirit;
3: 6 for the l kills, but the Spirit
7: 8 if I made you sorry with my l,
2 Th 2: 2 by spirit or by word or by l,

LETTERS (34/32) LETTER

1 Ki 21: 8 And she wrote l in Ahab's name,
21: 8 and sent the l to the elders
21: 9 She wrote in the l,
21:11 as it was written in the l
2 Ki 10: 1 And Jehu wrote and sent l to
20:12 sent l and a present to
2 Chr 30: 1 and also wrote l to Ephraim and
30: 6 all Israel and Judah with the l
32:17 He also wrote l to revile the
Neh 2: 7 let l be given to me for the
2: 9 and gave them the king's l.
6:17 nobles of Judah sent many l to
6:17 and the l of Tobiah came to
6:19 Tobiah sent l to frighten me.
Esth 1:22 Then he sent l to all the king's
3:13 And the l were sent by couriers
8: 5 it be written to revoke the l
8:10 and sent l by couriers on
8:11 By these l the king permitted
9:20 wrote these things and sent l
9:30 And Mordecai sent l to all the
Isa 39: 1 sent l and a present to
Jer 29:25 You have sent l in your name to
Lk 23:38 also was written over Him in l
Jn 7:15 "How does this Man know l,
Acts 9: 2 and asked l from him to the
22: 5 from whom I also received l to
28:21 We neither received l from Judea
1 Cor 16: 3 you approve by your l I will
2 Cor 3: 1 of commendation to you or l
10: 9 lest I seem to terrify you by l.
10:10 'For his l,' they say,
10:11 that what we are in word by l
Gal 6:11 See with what large l I have

LETTING (3/3)

Ex 8:29 deceitfully anymore in not l
13:15 Pharaoh was stubborn about l
Lk 2:29 now You are l Your servant

LETUSHIM (1/1)

Gen 25: 3 sons of Dedan were Asshurim, L,

LEUMMIM (1/1)

Gen 25: 3 were Asshurim, Letushim, and L.

LEVEL (3/3)

Ezek 42: 6 therefore the upper l was
Lk 6:17 down with them and stood on a l
19:44 and l you, and your children

LEVELED (1/1)

Isa 28:25 When he has l its surface,

LEVELS (1/1)

Ezek 42: 6 than the lower and middle l

LEVI (72/69) LEVI'S, LEVITE, MATTHEW

Gen 29:34 Therefore his name was called L.
34:25 the sons of Jacob, Simeon and L,
34:30 Then Jacob said to Simeon and L,
35:23 firstborn, and Simeon, L,
46:11 The sons of L were Gershon,
49: 5 Simeon and L are brothers;
Ex 1: 2 Reuben, Simeon, L, and Judah;
2: 1 And a man of the house of L went
2: 1 took as wife a daughter of L.
6:16 are the names of the sons of L
6:16 And the years of the life of L
6:19 These are the families of L
32:26 And all the sons of L
32:28 So the sons of L did according
Num 1:49 Only the tribe of L you shall
3: 6 Bring the tribe of L near, and
3:15 Number the children of L by
3:17 These were the sons of L by
4: 2 from among the children of L,
16: 1 the son of Kohath, the son of L,
16: 7 you sons of L!"
16: 8 "Hear now, you sons of L:
16:10 your brethren, the sons of L,
17: 3 Aaron's name on the rod of L.
17: 8 rod of Aaron, of the house of L,
18: 2 your brethren of the tribe of L,
18:21 I have given the children of L
26:59 was Jochebed the daughter of L,
26:59 who was born to L in Egypt;
Deut 10: 8 LORD separated the tribe of L
10: 9 Therefore L has no portion nor
18: 1 the Levites—all the tribe of L—
21: 5 the priests, the sons of L,
27:12 over the Jordan: Simeon, L,
31: 9 to the priests, the sons of L,
33: 8 And of L he said: "Let Your
Josh 13:14 Only to the tribe of L he had
13:33 But to the tribe of L Moses had
21:10 who were of the children of L;
1 Ki 12:31 who were not of the sons of L.
1 Chr 2: 1 of Israel: Reuben, Simeon, L,
6: 1 The sons of L were Gershon,
6:16 The sons of L were Gershon,
6:38 the son of Kohath, the son of L,
6:43 son of Gershon, the son of L.
6:47 the son of Merari, the son of L.
9:18 the camps of the children of L
12:26 of the sons of L four thousand
21: 6 But he did not count L and
23: 6 divisions among the sons of L:
23:14 were reckoned to the tribe of L.
23:24 These were the sons of L by
24:20 And the rest of the sons of L:
Ezra 8:15 and found none of the sons of L
8:18 the sons of Mahli the son of L,
Neh 10:39 of Israel and the children of L
12:23 The sons of L, the heads of
Ps 135:20 O house of L! You who fear the
Ezek 40:46 of Zadok, from the sons of L,
48:31 for Judah, and one gate for L;
Zech 12:13 the family of the house of L by
Mal 2: 4 That My covenant with L may
2: 8 corrupted the covenant of L,
3: 3 He will purify the sons of L,
Mk 2:14 He saw L the son of Alphaeus
Lk 3:24 son of Matthat, the son of L,
3:29 son of Matthat, the son of L,
5:27 and saw a tax collector named L,
5:29 Then L gave Him a great feast in
Heb 7: 5 those who are of the sons of L,
7: 9 Even L, who receives tithes,
Rev 7: 7 of the tribe of L twelve

LEVI'S (1/1) LEVI

Mk 2:15 as He was dining in L house,

LEVIATHAN (6/5)

Job 3: 8 who are ready to arouse L.
41: 1 Can you draw out L with a hook,
Ps 74:14 You broke the heads of L in
104:26 There is that L Which You
Isa 27: 1 Will punish L the fleeing
27: 1 L that twisted serpent;

LEVITE (28/28) LEVI, LEVITES, LEVITICAL

Ex 4:14 Is not Aaron the L your brother?
Deut 12:12 and the L who is within your
12:18 and the L who is within your
12:19 that you do not forsake the L
14:27 You shall not forsake the L who
14:29 'And the L, because he has
16:11 the L who is within your
16:14 your female servant and the L,
18: 6 So if a L comes from any of
26:11 you and the L and the stranger
26:12 have given it to the L,
26:13 also have given them to the L,
Judg 17: 7 family of Judah; he was a L,
17: 9 I am a L from Bethlehem in
17:10 So the L went in.
17:11 Then the L was content to dwell
17:12 So Micah consecrated the L,
17:13 since I have a L as priest!"
18: 3 the voice of the young L.
18:15 to the house of the young L
19: 1 that there was a certain L
20: 4 So the L, the husband of
2 Chr 20:14 a L of the sons of Asaph, in
31:12 Cononiah the L had charge of
31:14 Kore the son of Imnah the L,
Ezra 10:15 Meshullam and Shabbethai the L
Lk 10:32 'Likewise a L, when he arrived
Acts 4:36 a L of the country of Cyprus,

LEVITES (266/238) LEVITE

Ex 6:25 of the fathers' houses of the L
38:21 Moses, for the service of the L,
Lev 25:32 the cities of the L,
25:32 the L may redeem at any time.
25:33 purchases a house from the L,
25:33 houses in the cities of the L
Num 1:47 But the L were not numbered
1:50 but you shall appoint the L over
1:51 the L shall take it down;
1:51 the L shall set it up.
1:53 but the L shall camp around the
1:53 and the L shall keep charge of
2:17 out with the camp of the L in
2:33 But the L were not numbered
3: 9 And you shall give the L to
3:12 I Myself have taken the L from
3:12 Therefore the L shall be Mine,
3:20 are the families of the L by
3:32 chief over the leaders of the L,
3:39 All who were numbered of the L,
3:41 And you shall take the L for
3:41 and the livestock of the L
3:45 Take the L instead of all the
3:45 and the livestock of the L
3:45 The L shall be Mine: I am the
3:46 more than the number of the L,
3:49 who were redeemed by the L.
4:18 the Kohathites from among the L;
4:46 All who were numbered of the L,
7: 5 you shall give them to the L,
7: 6 oxen, and gave them to the L.
8: 6 Take the L from among the
8: 9 And you shall bring the L before
8:10 So you shall bring the L before
8:10 shall lay their hands on the L;
8:11 and Aaron shall offer the L
8:12 Then the L shall lay their hands
8:12 to make atonement for the L.
8:13 And you shall stand the L before
8:14 Thus you shall separate the L
8:14 and the L shall be Mine.
8:15 After that the L shall go in to
8:18 I have taken the L instead of
8:19 And I have given the L as a gift
8:20 children of Israel did to the L;
8:20 Moses concerning the L,
8:21 And the L purified themselves

8:22 After that the L went in to do
8:22 Moses concerning the L,
8:24 is what pertains to the L:
8:26 Thus you shall do to the L
18: 6 have taken your brethren the L
18:23 But the L shall perform the work
18:24 I have given to the L as an
18:26 "Speak thus to the L,
18:30 shall be accounted to the L as
26:57 who were numbered of the L
26:58 are the families of the L:
31:30 and give them to the L who keep
31:47 beast, and gave them to the L,
35: 2 of Israel that they give the L
35: 2 and you shall also give the L
35: 4 which you shall give the L
35: 6 which you will give to the L
35: 7 cities you will give to the L
35: 8 some of its cities to the L,
Deut 17: 9 come to the priests, the L,
17:18 one before the priests, the L.
18: 1 "The priests, the L—
18: 7 God as all his brethren the L
24: 8 to all that the priests, the L,
27: 9 Moses and the priests, the L,
27:14 And the L shall speak with a
31:25 that Moses commanded the L,
Josh 3: 3 God, and the priests, the L,
8:33 ark before the priests, the L,
14: 3 but to the L he had given no
14: 4 And they gave no part to the L
18: 7 But the L have no part among
21: 1 the fathers' houses of the L
21: 3 of Israel gave to the L from
21: 4 the priest, who were of the L,
21: 8 common-lands by lot to the L,
21:20 the children of Kohath, the L,
21:27 of the families of the L,
21:34 of Merari, the rest of the L,
21:40 rest of the families of the L,
21:41 All the cities of the L within
1 Sam 6:15 The L took down the ark of the
2 Sam 15:24 and all the L with him, bearing
1 Ki 8: 4 The priests and the L brought
1 Chr 6:19 are the families of the L
6:48 And their brethren, the L,
6:64 their common-lands to the L.
9: 2 were Israelites, priests, L,
9:14 Of the L: Shemaiah the son
9:26 chief gatekeepers; they were L.
9:31 Mattithiah of the L,
9:33 the fathers' houses of the L,
9:34 the fathers' houses of the L
13: 2 with them to the priests and L
15: 2 carry the ark of God but the L,
15: 4 the children of Aaron and the L:
15:11 the priests, and for the L:
15:12 the fathers' houses of the L;
15:14 So the priests and the L
15:15 And the children of the L bore
15:16 spoke to the leaders of the L
15:17 So the L appointed Heman the son
15:22 Chenaniah, leader of the L,
15:26 when God helped the L who bore
15:27 as were all the L who bore the
16: 4 he appointed some of the L to
23: 2 with the priests and the L.
23: 3 Now the L were numbered from the
23:26 and also to the L,
23:27 the last words of David the L
24: 6 son of Nethanel, one of the L,
24: 6 houses of the priests and L,
24:30 These were the sons of the L
24:31 houses of the priests and L.
26:17 On the east were six L,
26:20 Of the L, Ahijah was over
27:17 over the L, Hashabiah the
28:13 of the priests and the L,
28:21 of the priests and the L for
2 Chr 5: 4 and the L took up the ark.
5: 5 The priests and the L brought
5:12 and the L who were the
7: 6 the L also with instruments of
8:14 the L for their duties (to
8:15 the king to the priests and L
11:13 the priests and the L who
11:14 For the L left their
11:16 And after the L left, those
13: 9 the sons of Aaron, and the L,
13:10 and the L attend to their
17: 8 And with them he sent L:
17: 8 Tobijah, and Tobadonijah—the L;
19: 8 appointed some of the L and
19:11 also the L will be officials
20:19 Then the L of the children of
23: 2 Judah and gathered the L from
23: 4 of the priests and the L,
23: 6 the priests and those of the L
23: 7 And the L shall surround the
23: 8 So the L and all Judah did
23:18 the hand of the priests, the L,
24: 5 gathered the priests and the L,
24: 5 However the L did not do it
24: 6 have you not required the L to
24:11 official by the hand of the L,
29: 4 in the priests and the L,
29: 5 L! Now sanctify yourselves,
29:12 Then these L arose: Mahath the
29:16 And the L took it out and
29:25 And he stationed the L in the
29:26 The L stood with the instruments
29:30 the leaders commanded the L to
29:34 therefore their brethren the L
29:34 for the L were more diligent in
30:15 The priests and the L were
30:16 from the hand of the L.
30:17 therefore the L had charge of
30:21 and the L and the priests
30:22 encouragement to all the L who
30:25 also the priests and L,
30:27 Then the priests, the L,
31: 2 of the priests and the L
31: 2 the priests and L for burnt
31: 4 for the priests and the L,
31: 9 the priests and the L
31:17 and to the L from twenty years
31:19 by genealogies among the L.
34: 9 which the L who kept the doors
34:12 were Jahath and Obadiah the L,
34:12 to supervise. Others of the L,
34:13 And some of the L were
34:30 Jerusalem—the priests and the L,
35: 3 Then he said to the L who taught
35: 5 of the father's house of the L.
35: 8 to the priests, and to the L.
35: 9 and Jozabad, chief of the L,
35: 9 gave to the L for Passover
35:10 and the L in their divisions,
35:11 while the L skinned the
35:14 therefore the L prepared
35:15 because their brethren the L
35:18 with the priests and the L,
Ezra 1: 5 and the priests and the L,
2:40 The L: the sons of Jeshua
2:70 So the priests and the L,
3: 8 brethren the priests and the L,
3: 8 work and appointed the L from
3: 9 sons and their brethren the L.
3:10 with trumpets, and the L,
3:12 But many of the priests and L
6:16 the priests and the L and the
6:18 to their divisions and the L
6:20 For the priests and the L had
7: 7 of Israel, the priests, the L,
7:13 of Israel and the priests and L
7:24 on any of the priests, L,
8:20 for the service of the L,
8:29 of the priests and the L and
8:30 So the priests and the L
8:33 Phinehas; with them were the L,
9: 1 and the priests and the L have
10: 5 leaders of the priests, the L,
10:23 Also of the L: Jozabad, Shimei,
Neh 3:17 After him the L, under Rehum
7: 1 and the L had been appointed,
7:43 The L: the sons of Jeshua,
7:73 So the priests, the L,
8: 7 Hanan, Pelaiah, and the L,
8: 9 and the L who taught the people
8:11 So the L quieted all the people,
8:13 people, with the priests and L,
9: 4 stood on the stairs of the L
9: 5 And the L, Jeshua, Kadmiel,
9:38 write it; our leaders, our L,
10: 9 The L: Jeshua the son of
10:28 the people—the priests, the L,
10:34 lots among the priests, the L,
10:37 the tithes of our land to the L,
10:37 for the L should receive the
10:38 shall be with the L when the
10:38 be with the Levites when the L
10:38 and the L shall bring up a
11: 3 cities—Israelites, priests, L,
11:15 Also of the L: Shemaiah the
11:16 Jozabad, of the heads of the L,
11:18 All the L in the holy city were
11:20 Israel, of the priests and L,
11:22 Also the overseer of the L at
11:36 of the Judean divisions of L
12: 1 are the priests and the L who
12: 8 Moreover the L were Jeshua,
12:22 was also kept of the L and
12:24 And the heads of the L were
12:27 they sought out the L in all
12:30 Then the priests and the L purified
12:44 the Law for the priests and L;
12:44 over the priests and L who
12:47 holy things for the L,
12:47 and the L consecrated them for
13: 5 to be given to the L and
13:10 that the portions for the L
13:10 for each of the L and the
13:13 Zadok the scribe, and of the L,
13:22 And I commanded the L that they
13:29 of the priesthood and the L.
13:30 duties to the priests and the L,
Isa 66:21 some of them for priests and L,
Jer 33:18 'nor shall the priests, the L,
33:21 on his throne, and with the L,
33:22 of David My servant and the L
Ezek 43:19 offering to the priests, the L,
44:10 And the L who went far from Me,
44:15 "But the priests, the L,
45: 5 wide shall belong to the L,
48:11 as the L went astray.
48:12 holy by the border of the L.
48:13 the L shall have an area
48:22 from the possession of the L
Jn 1:19 the Jews sent priests and L

LEVITICAL (1/1) LEVITE

Heb 7:11 perfection were through the L

LEVY (1/1)

Num 31:28 And l a tribute for the LORD on

LEWD (3/3) LEWDNESS

Jer 11:15 Having done l deeds with many?
Ezek 16:27 who were ashamed of your l
23:44 and Oholibah, the l women.

LEWDLY (1/1)

Ezek 22:11 another l defiles his

LEWDNESS (23/22) LEWD

Judg 20: 6 because they committed l and
Jer 13:27 The l of your harlotry,
Ezek 16:43 And you shall not commit l in
16:58 You have paid for your l and
22: 9 in your midst they commit l.
23:21 called to remembrance the l of
23:27 I will make you cease your l
23:29 both your l and your harlotry.
23:35 bear the penalty Of your l
23:48 Thus I will cause l to cease
23:48 taught not to practice your l.
23:49 shall repay you for your l,
24:13 In your filthiness is l.
Hos 2:10 Now I will uncover her l in the
6: 9 Surely they commit l.
Mk 7:22 wickedness, deceit, l,
Rom 13:13 not in l and lust, not in
2 Cor 12:21 and l which they have
Gal 5:19 fornication, uncleanness, l,
Eph 4:19 have given themselves over to l,
1 Pe 4: 3 Gentiles—when we walked in l,
2 Pe 2:18 lusts of the flesh, through l,
Jude 4 the grace of our God into l

LIAR (12/12) LIARS, LIE

Job 24:25 not so, who will prove me a l,
Prov 17: 4 A l listens eagerly to a
19:22 a poor man is better than a l.
30: 6 you, and you be found a l.
Jn 8:44 for he is a l and the father of
8:55 I shall be a l like you; but I
Rom 3: 4 God be true but every man a l.
1 Jn 1:10 not sinned, we make Him a l,
2: 4 keep His commandments, is a l,
2:22 Who is a l but he who denies
4:20 hates his brother, he is a l;
5:10 believe God has made Him a l,

LIARS (5/5) LIAR

Ps 116:11 in my haste, "All men are l.
1 Tim 1:10 for kidnappers, for l,
Titus 1:12 said, "Cretans are always l,
Rev 2: 2 are not, and have found them l;
21: 8 and all l shall have their part

LIBERAL (1/1)

2 Cor 9:13 and for your l sharing with

LIBERALITY (3/3) LIBERALLY

Rom 12: 8 he who gives, with l;
2 Cor 8: 2 in the riches of their l.
9:11 in everything for all l,

LIBERALLY (2/2) LIBERALITY

Deut 15:14 you shall supply him l from your
Jas 1: 5 who gives to all l and without

LIBERTINES (KJV) See FREEDMEN

LIBERTY (26/23)

Lev 25:10 and proclaim l throughout all
Ps 119:45 And I will walk at l,
Isa 61: 1 To proclaim l to the captives,
Jer 34: 8 at Jerusalem to proclaim l to
34:15 every man proclaiming l to his
34:16 slaves, whom he had set at l,
34:17 not obeyed Me in proclaiming l,
34:17 I proclaim l to you,' says the
Ezek 46:17 be his until the year of l,
Lk 4:18 To proclaim l to the
4:18 To set at l those who
Acts 24:23 Paul and to let him have l,
27: 3 Paul kindly and gave him l to
Rom 8:21 corruption into the glorious l
1 Cor 7:39 she is at l to be married to
8: 9 But beware lest somehow this l
10:29 For why is my l judged by
2 Cor 3:17 of the Lord is, there is l.
Gal 2: 4 in by stealth to spy out our l
5: 1 Stand fast therefore in the l by
5:13 brethren, have been called to l;
5:13 only do not use l as an
Jas 1:25 into the perfect law of l and
2:12 will be judged by the law of l.
1 Pe 2:16 yet not using l as a cloak for
2 Pe 2:19 While they promise them l,

LIBNAH (18/17)

Num 33:20 Rimmon Perez and camped at L.
33:21 They moved from L and camped at

L

Josh 10:29 and all Israel with him, to *L*;
10:29 and they fought against *L*.
10:31 Then Joshua passed from *L*,
10:32 to all that he had done to *L*.
10:39 as he had done also to *L* and
12:15 the king of *L*, one;
15:42 *L*, Ether, Ashan,
21:13 *L* with its common-land,
2 Ki 8:22 And *L* revolted at that time.
19: 8 of Assyria warring against *L*,
23:31 the daughter of Jeremiah of *L*.
24:18 the daughter of Jeremiah of *L*.
1 Chr 6:57 also *L* with its common-lands,
2 Chr 21:10 At that time *L* revolted against
Isa 37: 8 of Assyria warring against *L*,
Jer 52: 1 the daughter of Jeremiah of *L*.

LIBNI (5/5)

Ex 6:17 The sons of Gershon were *L* and
Num 3:18 their families: *L* and Shimei.
1 Chr 6:17 sons of Gershon: *L* and Shimei.
6:20 Of Gershon were *L* his son,
6:29 *L* his son, Shimei his son,

LIBNITES (2/2)

Num 3:21 came the family of the *L* and
26:58 Levites: the family of the *L*,

LIBYA (4/4)

Ezek 27:10 and *L* Were in your army as men
30: 5 'Ethiopia, *L*, Lydia, all the
38: 5 and *L* are with them, all of
Acts 2:10 Egypt and the parts of *L*

LIBYANS (2/2)

Jer 46: 9 The Ethiopians and the *L* who
Dan 11:43 also the *L* and Ethiopians

LICE (6/4)

Ex 8:16 so that it may become *l*
8:17 and it became *l* on man and
8:17 the dust of the land became *l*
8:18 enchantments to bring forth *l*,
8:18 So there were *l* on man and
Ps 105:31 And *l* in all their territory.

LICK (5/5) LICKED

Num 22: 4 Now this company will *l* up
1 Ki 21:19 dogs shall *l* your blood, even
Ps 72: 9 And His enemies will *l* the
Isa 49:23 And *l* up the dust of your
Mic 7:17 They shall *l* the dust like a

LICKED (4/4) LICK

1 Ki 18:38 and it *l* up the water that was
21:19 In the place where dogs *l* the
22:38 and the dogs *l* up his blood
Lk 16:21 Moreover the dogs came and *l*

LICKS (1/1)

Num 22: 4 as an ox *l* up the grass of the

LID (1/1)

2 Ki 12: 9 a chest, bored a hole in its *l*,

LIE (151/149) LAIN, LAY, LIAR, LIED, LIES, LYING

Gen 19:32 and we will *l* with him, that we
19:34 and you go in and *l* with him,
28:13 the land on which you *l* I will
30:15 Therefore he will *l* with you
39: 7 she said, "*L* with me."
39:10 to *l* with her or to be with
39:12 *L* with me." But he left his
39:14 He came in to me to *l* with me,
47:30 but let me *l* with my fathers;
Ex 21:13 if he did not *l* in wait, but
23:11 you shall let it rest and *l*
Lev 18:20 Moreover you shall not *l*
18:22 You shall not *l* with a male as
19:11 nor *l* to one another.
26: 6 and you shall *l* down, and none
Num 10: 5 the camps that *l* on the east
10: 6 then the camps that *l* on the
23:19 is not a man, that He should *l*,
23:24 It shall not *l* down until it
Deut 6: 7 when you *l* down, and when you
11:19 when you *l* down, and when you
25: 2 the judge will cause him to *l*
28:30 but another man shall *l* with
Josh 7:10 Get up! Why do you *l* thus on
8: 4 you shall *l* in ambush against
8: 9 and they went to *l* in ambush,
Judg 9:32 and *l* in wait in the field.
21:20 *l* in wait in the vineyards,
Ruth 3: 4 and *l* down; and he will tell
3: 7 he went to *l* down at the end of
3:13 as the LORD lives! *L* down
1 Sam 3: 5 *l* down again." And he went and
3: 6 my son; *l* down again."
3: 9 *l* down; and it shall be, if He
15:29 Strength of Israel will not *l*
22: 8 to *l* in wait, as it is this
22:13 to *l* in wait, as it is this
2 Sam 11:11 and to *l* with my wife? As you
11:13 at evening he went out to *l* on
12:11 and he shall *l* with your wives
13: 5 *L* down on your bed and pretend
13:11 *l* with me, my sister."
1 Ki 1: 2 and let her *l* in your bosom,
2 Ki 4:16 do not *l* to your maidservant!"
9:12 A *l*! Tell us now." So he said,
Job 6:28 For I would never *l* to your
7: 4 When I *l* down, I say, 'When
7:21 For now I will *l* down in the
9:13 The allies of the proud *l*
11:19 You would also *l* down, and no
20:11 But it will *l* down with him in
21:26 They *l* down alike in the dust,
27:19 The rich man will *l* down,
34: 6 Should I *l* concerning my right?
38:40 Or lurk in their lairs to *l*
Ps 4: 8 I will both *l* down in peace,
23: 2 He makes me to *l* down in green
56: 6 When they *l* in wait for my
57: 4 I *l* among the sons of men
59: 3 they *l* in wait for my life;
62: 9 Men of high degree are a *l*;
68:13 Though you *l* down among the
71:10 And those who *l* in wait for my
88: 5 Like the slain who *l* in the
89:35 I will not *l* to David:
102: 7 I *l* awake, And am like a
104:22 they gather together And *l*
119:69 The proud have forged a *l*
Prov 1:11 Let us *l* in wait to shed
1:18 But they *l* in wait for their
3:24 When you *l* down, you will not
3:24 you will *l* down and your sleep
12: 6 *L* in wait for blood," But the
14: 5 A faithful witness does not *l*,
24:15 Do not *l* in wait, O wicked
Eccl 4:11 if two *l* down together, they
11: 3 tree falls, there it shall *l*.
Isa 11: 6 The leopard shall *l* down with
11: 7 Their young ones shall *l* down
13:21 beasts of the desert will *l*
14:30 And the needy will *l* down in
17: 2 will be for flocks Which *l*
27:10 and there it will *l* down And
33: 8 The highways *l* waste,
34:10 to generation it shall *l* waste;
43:17 and the power (They shall *l*
44:20 Is there not a *l* in my right
50:11 You shall *l* down in torment.
51:20 They *l* at the head of all the
51:23 *L* down, that we may walk over
63: 8 Children who will not *l*.
65:10 of Achor a place for herds to *l*
Jer 3:25 We *l* down in our shame, And
5:26 They *l* in wait as one who sets
27:10 For they prophesy a *l* to you, to
27:14 for they prophesy a *l* to you;
27:15 yet they prophesy a *l* in My
27:16 for they prophesy a *l* to you.
28:15 make this people trust in a *l*.
29:21 who prophesy a *l* to you in My
29:31 has caused you to trust in a *l*—
33:12 causing their flocks to *l*
Lam 2:21 Young and old *l* On the ground
Ezek 4: 4 *L* also on your left side, and
4: 4 number of the days that you *l*
4: 6 *l* again on your right side;
4: 9 the number of days that you *l*
21:29 While they divine a *l* to you,
31:12 its boughs *l* broken by all the
31:18 you shall *l* in the midst of the
32:21 They *l* with the uncircumcised,
32:27 They do not *l* with the mighty
32:28 And *l* with those slain by the
32:29 They shall *l* with the
32:30 They *l* uncircumcised with
33:10 transgressions and our sins *l*
34:14 There they shall *l* down in a
34:15 and I will make them *l* down,"
Hos 2:18 To make them *l* down safely.
6: 9 As bands of robbers *l* in wait
7: 6 While they *l* in wait;
Joel 1:13 *l* all night in sackcloth,
Am 2: 8 They *l* down by every altar on
6: 4 Who *l* on beds of ivory,
Mic 1:14 of Achzib shall be a *l* to
2:11 a false spirit And speak a *l*,
7: 2 They all *l* in wait for blood;
Hab 2: 3 will speak, and it will not *l*.
Zeph 2: 7 of Ashkelon they shall *l* down
2:14 The herds shall *l* down in her
2:15 A place for beasts to *l* down!
3:13 shall feed their flocks and *l*
Hag 1: 4 and this temple to *l* in
Jn 8:44 in him. When he speaks a *l*,
Acts 5: 3 Satan filled your heart to *l*
23:21 for more than forty of them *l*
Rom 1:25 the truth of God for the *l*,
3: 7 God has increased through my *l*
Gal 1:20 indeed, before God, I do not *l*.
Col 3: 9 Do not *l* to one another, since
2 Th 2:11 that they should believe the *l*,
Titus 1: 2 life which God, who cannot *l*,
Heb 6:18 it is impossible for God to *l*,
Jas 3:14 do not boast and *l* against the
1 Jn 1: 6 we *l* and do not practice the
2:21 and that no *l* is of the truth.
2:27 and is true, and is not a *l*,
Rev 3: 9 are Jews and are not, but *l*—
11: 8 And their dead bodies will *l*
21:27 or causes an abomination or a *l*,
22:15 whoever loves and practices a *l*.

LIED (4/4) LIE

Ps 78:36 And they *l* to Him with their
Isa 57:11 That you have *l* And not
Jer 5:12 They have *l* about the LORD,
Acts 5: 4 You have not *l* to men but to

LIEN (KJV) See LAIN

LIES (121/115) LIE

Gen 4: 7 sin *l* at the door. And its
49: 9 he *l* down as a lion; And as a
49:25 Blessings of the deep that *l*
Ex 22:16 and *l* with her, he shall surely
22:19 Whoever *l* with an animal shall
Lev 6: 3 has found what was lost and *l*
14:47 And he who *l* down in the house
15: 4 he who has the discharge *l*,
15:18 when a woman *l* with a man, and
15:20 Everything that she *l* on during
15:24 And if any man *l* with her at
15:24 and every bed on which he *l*
15:26 Every bed on which she *l* all the
15:33 and for him who *l* with her who
19:20 Whoever *l* carnally with a woman
20:11 The man who *l* with his father's
20:12 If a man *l* with his
20:13 If a man *l* with a male as he
20:13 a man lies with a male as he *l*
20:18 If a man *l* with a woman during
20:20 If a man *l* with his uncle's
26:34 its sabbaths as long as it *l*
26:35 As long as it *l* desolate it
26:43 enjoy its sabbaths while it *l*
Num 5:13 and a man *l* with her carnally,
21:15 And *l* on the border of
24: 9 he *l* down as a lion; And as a
Deut 19:11 *l* in wait for him, rises
22:23 man finds her in the city and *l*
22:25 and the man forces her and *l*
22:28 and he seizes her and *l* with
27:20 Cursed is the one who *l* with
27:21 Cursed is the one who *l* with
27:22 Cursed is the one who *l* with
27:23 Cursed is the one who *l* with
Josh 15: 8 the top of the mountain that *l*
17: 7 that *l* east of Shechem;
18:13 near the hill that *l* on the
18:14 from the hill that *l* before
18:16 the end of the mountain that *l*
Judg 1:16 which *l* in the South near
16: 5 out where his great strength *l*,
16: 6 me where your great strength *l*,
16:10 have mocked me and told me *l*.
16:13 have mocked me and told me *l*.
16:15 me where your great strength *l*.
Ruth 3: 4 when he *l* down, that you shall
3: 4 notice the place where he *l*;
2 Ki 9:37 not say, "Here *l* Jezebel."
Neh 2: 3 *l* waste, and its gates are
2:17 how Jerusalem *l* waste, and its
Job 13: 4 But you forgers of *l*,
14:12 So man *l* down and does not
29:19 And the dew *l* all night on my
40:21 He *l* under the lotus trees,
Ps 10: 9 He *l* in wait secretly, as a
10: 9 He *l* in wait to catch the
10:10 he *l* low, That the helpless
40: 4 nor such as turn aside to *l*.
41: 6 comes to see me, he speaks *l*;
41: 8 And now that he *l* down, he
58: 3 as they are born, speaking *l*.
62: 4 They delight in *l*;
63:11 the mouth of those who speak *l*
88: 7 Your wrath *l* heavy upon me,
101: 7 He who tells *l* shall not
Prov 6:19 A false witness who speaks *l*,
14: 5 a false witness will utter *l*.
14:25 a deceitful witness speaks *l*.
19: 5 And he who speaks *l* will not
19: 9 And he who speaks *l* shall
23:28 She also *l* in wait as for a
23:34 you will be like one who *l* down
23:34 Or like one who *l* at the top
29:12 If a ruler pays attention to *l*,
30: 8 Remove falsehood and *l* far from
Song 1:13 That *l* all night between my
Isa 9:15 The prophet who teaches *l*,
16: 6 But his *l* shall not be so.
28:15 For we have made *l* our refuge,
28:17 will sweep away the refuge of *l*,
59: 3 Your lips have spoken *l*,
59: 4 in empty words and speak *l*;
Jer 9: 3 have bent their tongues for *l*.
9: 5 taught their tongue to speak *l*;
9: 8 But in his heart he *l* in wait.
14:14 The prophets prophesy *l* in My
16:19 our fathers have inherited *l*,
20: 6 to whom you have prophesied *l*.
23:14 commit adultery and walk in *l*;
23:25 have said who prophesy *l* in My
23:26 of the prophets who prophesy *l*?
23:32 My people to err by their *l*
48:30 His *l* have made nothing right.
Ezek 13: 8 nonsense and envisioned *l*,
13: 9 futility and who divine *l*;
13:19 to My people who listen to *l*?

13:22 Because with *l* you have made the
22:28 and divining *l* for them,
24:12 She has grown weary with *l*,
29: 3 O great monster who *l* in the
Dan 11:27 and they shall speak *l* at the
Hos 7: 3 And princes with their *l*.
7:13 Yet they have spoken *l* against
10:13 You have eaten the fruit of *l*,
11:12 has encircled Me with *l*,
12: 1 He daily increases *l* and
Am 2: 4 Their *l* lead them astray,
2: 4 *L* which their fathers
5: 2 She *l* forsaken on her land;
Mic 6:12 Her inhabitants have spoken *l*,
7: 5 of your mouth From her who *l*
Nah 3: 1 city! It is all full of *l*
Hab 2:18 molded image, a teacher of *l*,
Zeph 3:13 unrighteousness And speak no *l*,
Zech 10: 2 The diviners envision *l*,
13: 3 because you have spoken *l* in
Mk 5:23 My little daughter *l* at the
2 Cor 3:15 a veil *l* on their heart.
1 Tim 4: 2 speaking *l* in hypocrisy, having
1 Jn 5:19 and the whole world *l* under

LIEUTENANTS (KJV) See SATRAPS

LIFE (495/449) LIFE-GIVING, LIFEBLOOD, LIFELESS, LIFETIME, LIVE

Gen 1:30 earth, in which there is *l*,
2: 7 his nostrils the breath of *l*;
2: 9 The tree of *l* was also in the
3:14 All the days of your *l*.
3:17 of it All the days of your *l*.
3:22 and take also of the tree of *l*,
3:24 guard the way to the tree of *l*.
6:17 in which is the breath of *l*;
7:11 six hundredth year of Noah's *l*,
7:15 in which is the breath of *l*.
7:22 the breath of the spirit of *l*,
9: 4 shall not eat flesh with its *l*,
9: 5 brother I will require the *l*
18:10 you according to the time of *l*,
18:14 you, according to the time of *l*,
19:17 Escape for your *l*! Do not look
19:19 have shown me by saving my *l*;
23: 1 were the years of the *l* of
25: 7 sum of the years of Abraham's *l*
25:17 These were the years of the *l*
27:46 I am weary of my *l* because of
27:46 what good will my *l* be to me?"
32:30 and my *l* is preserved."
42:15 By the *l* of Pharaoh, you shall
42:16 by the *l* of Pharaoh, surely you
44:30 since his *l* is bound up in the
44:30 life is bound up in the lad's *l*,
45: 5 me before you to preserve *l*.
47: 9 the days of the years of my *l*,
47: 9 the days of the years of the *l*
47:28 So the length of Jacob's *l* was
48:15 God who has fed me all my *l*
Ex 4:19 all the men who sought your *l*
6:16 And the years of the *l* of Levi
6:18 And the years of the *l* of
6:20 And the years of the *l* of Amram
21:23 then you shall give *l* for life,
21:23 then you shall give life for *l*,
21:30 he shall pay to redeem his *l*,
Lev 17:11 For the *l* of the flesh is in
17:14 for it is the *l* of all flesh.
17:14 flesh. Its blood sustains its *l*.
17:14 for the *l* of all flesh is its
19:16 you take a stand against the *l*
Num 35:31 shall take no ransom for the *l*
Deut 4: 9 heart all the days of your *l*.
6: 2 all the days of your *l*,
12:23 blood, for the blood is the *l*;
12:23 you may not eat the *l* with the
16: 3 of Egypt all the days of your *l*.
17:19 read it all the days of his *l*,
19:21 *l* shall be for life, eye for
19:21 not pity: life shall be for *l*,
28:66 Your *l* shall hang in doubt
28:66 and have no assurance of *l*.
30:15 I have set before you today *l*
30:19 that I have set before you *l*
30:19 and cursing; therefore choose *l*,
30:20 for He is your *l* and the
32:47 for you, because it is your *l*,
Josh 1: 5 you all the days of your *l*;
4:14 Moses, all the days of his *l*.
Judg 5: 7 Village *l* ceased, it ceased in
9:17 fought for you, risked his *l*,
12: 3 I took my *l* in my hands and
13:12 will be the boy's rule of *l*,
16:30 than he had killed in his *l*.
18:25 upon you, and you lose your *l*,
Ruth 4:15 he be to you a restorer of *l*
1 Sam 1:11 the LORD all the days of his *l*,
7:15 Israel all the days of his *l*.
18:18 and what is my *l* or my
19: 5 For he took his *l* in his hands
19:11 If you do not save your *l*
20: 1 your father, that he seeks my *l*?
22:23 For he who seeks my *l* seeks
22:23 who seeks my life seeks your *l*,
23:15 Saul had come out to seek his *l*.
24:11 Yet you hunt my *l* to take it.
25:29 to pursue you and seek your *l*,
25:29 but the *l* of my lord shall be
26:21 because my *l* was precious in
26:24 as your *l* was valued much this
26:24 so let my *l* be valued much in
28: 9 do you lay a snare for my *l*,
28:21 and I have put my *l* in my hands
2 Sam 1: 9 but my *l* still remains in me.'
4: 8 your enemy, who sought your *l*;
4: 9 who has redeemed my *l* from all
14: 7 we may execute him for the *l*
14:14 Yet God does not take away a *l*;
15:21 shall be, whether in death or *l*,
16:11 from my own body seeks my *l*.
18:13 dealt falsely against my own *l*.
19: 5 who today have saved your *l*,
1 Ki 1:12 that you may save your own *l*
1:12 save your own life and the *l*
1:29 who has redeemed my *l* from
2:23 this word against his own *l*!
3:11 and have not asked long *l* for
3:11 nor have asked the *l* of your
4:21 Solomon all the days of his *l*.
11:34 him ruler all the days of his *l*
15: 5 him all the days of his *l*,
15: 6 Jeroboam all the days of his *l*.
19: 2 if I do not make your *l* as the
19: 2 do not make your life as the *l*
19: 3 he arose and ran for his *l*,
19: 4 enough! Now, LORD, take my *l*,
19:10 and they seek to take my *l*.
19:14 and they seek to take my *l*.
20:31 perhaps he will spare your *l*.
20:39 your *l* shall be for his life,
20:39 your life shall be for his *l*,
20:42 therefore your *l* shall go for
20:42 your life shall go for his *l*.
2 Ki 1:13 please let my *l* and the life of
1:13 please let my life and the *l* of
1:14 But let my *l* now be precious in
8: 1 whose son he had restored to *l*,
8: 5 he had restored the dead to *l*,
8: 5 whose son he had restored to *l*,
8: 5 son whom Elisha restored to *l*.
10:24 it shall be his *l* for the
10:24 shall be his life for the *l*
25:29 the king all the days of his *l*.
25:30 each day, all the days of his *l*.
2 Chr 1:11 or wealth or honor or the *l* of
1:11 nor have you asked long *l*—
Ezra 6:10 and pray for the *l* of the king
Neh 6:11 into the temple to save his *l*?
Esth 7: 3 let my *l* be given me at my
7: 7 Esther, pleading for his *l*,
Job 2: 4 man has he will give for his *l*.
2: 6 in your hand, but spare his *l*.
3:20 And *l* to the bitter of soul,
6:11 end, that I should prolong my *l*?
7: 7 remember that my *l* is a
7:16 I loathe my *l*; I would not
9:21 know myself; I despise my *l*.
10: 1 "My soul loathes my *l*;
10:12 You have granted me *l* and
11:17 And your *l* would be brighter
11:20 their hope—loss of *l*!"
12:10 In whose hand is the *l* of
13:14 And put my *l* in my hands?
24:22 up, but no man is sure of *l*.
27: 8 much, If God takes away his *l*?
33: 4 of the Almighty gives me *l*.
33:18 And his *l* from perishing by
33:20 So that his *l* abhors bread,
33:22 And his *l* to the executioners.
33:28 And his *l* shall see the light.
33:30 enlightened with the light of *l*.
36: 6 He does not preserve the *l* of
36:14 And their *l* ends among the
Ps 7: 5 let him trample my *l* to the
16:11 You will show me the path of *l*;
17:13 Deliver my *l* from the wicked
17:14 have their portion in this *l*,
21: 4 He asked *l* from You, and You
22:20 My precious *l* from the power
23: 6 follow me All the days of my *l*;
26: 9 Nor my *l* with bloodthirsty
27: 1 LORD is the strength of my *l*;
27: 4 the LORD All the days of my *l*,
30: 5 a moment, His favor is for *l*;
31:10 For my *l* is spent with grief,
31:13 They scheme to take away my *l*.
34:12 Who is the man who desires *l*,
35: 4 dishonor Who seek after my *l*;
35: 7 have dug without cause for my *l*.
35:17 My precious *l* from the lions.
36: 9 with You is the fountain of *l*;
38:12 Those also who seek my *l* lay
40:14 Who seek to destroy my *l*;
42: 8 me—A prayer to the God of my *l*.
54: 3 have sought after my *l*;
54: 4 is with those who uphold my *l*.
56: 6 When they lie in wait for my *l*.
59: 3 look, they lie in wait for my *l*;
61: 6 You will prolong the king's *l*,
63: 3 is better than *l*,
63: 9 But those who seek my *l*,
64: 1 Preserve my *l* from fear of the
70: 2 and confounded Who seek my *l*;
71:10 those who lie in wait for my *l*
71:13 Who are adversaries of my *l*;
72:14 He will redeem their *l* from
74:19 do not deliver the *l* of Your
74:19 not forget the *l* of Your poor
78:50 But gave their *l* over to the
86: 2 Preserve my *l*, for I am holy;
86:14 violent men have sought my *l*,
88: 3 And my *l* draws near to the
89:48 Can he deliver his *l* from the
91:16 With long *l* I will satisfy him,
94:21 gather together against the *l*
103: 4 Who redeems your *l* from
119:50 For Your word has given me *l*.
119:93 by them You have given me *l*.
119:109 My *l* is continually in my
128: 5 All the days of your *l*.
133: 3 the blessing—*L* forevermore.
143: 3 He has crushed my *l* to the
Prov 1:19 It takes away the *l* of its
2:19 do they regain the paths of *l*—
3: 2 For length of days and long *l*
3:18 She is a tree of *l* to those
3:22 So they will be *l* to your soul
4:10 And the years of your *l* will
4:13 Keep her, for she is your *l*.
4:22 For they are *l* to those who
4:23 of it spring the issues of *l*.
5: 6 Lest you ponder her path of *l*—
6:23 instruction are the way of *l*,
6:26 will prey upon his precious *l*.
7:23 not know it would cost his *l*.
8:35 For whoever finds me finds *l*,
9:11 And years of *l* will be added
10:11 the righteous is a well of *l*,
10:16 of the righteous leads to *l*,
10:17 is in the way of *l*,
11:19 As righteousness leads to *l*,
11:30 the righteous is a tree of *l*,
12:10 A righteous man regards the *l*
12:28 the way of righteousness is *l*,
13: 3 his mouth preserves his *l*,
13: 8 The ransom of a man's *l* is his
13:12 comes, it is a tree of *l*.
13:14 of the wise is a fountain of *l*,
14:27 the LORD is a fountain of *l*,
14:30 A sound heart is *l* to the
15: 4 tongue is a tree of *l*,
15:24 The way of *l* winds upward for
15:31 ear that hears the rebukes of *l*
16:15 light of the king's face is *l*,
16:22 is a wellspring of *l* to him
18:21 Death and *l* are in the power
19:23 fear of the LORD leads to *l*,
20: 2 anger sins against his own *l*.
21:21 and mercy Finds *l*,
22: 4 Are riches and honor and *l*.
29:24 with a thief hates his own *l*;
31:12 not evil All the days of her *l*.
Eccl 2:17 Therefore I hated *l* because the
5:18 the sun all the days of his *l*
5:20 unduly on the days of his *l*,
6:12 what is good for man in *l*,
6:12 all the days of his vain *l*
7:12 is that wisdom gives *l* to
7:15 a wicked man who prolongs *l*
8:15 labor all the days of his *l*
9: 9 all the days of your vain *l*
9: 9 for that is your portion in *l*,
Isa 15: 4 His *l* will be burdensome to
38:10 In the prime of my *l* I shall go
38:12 My *l* span is gone, Taken from
38:12 I have cut off my *l* like a
38:16 in all these things is the *l*
38:20 All the days of our *l*,
43: 4 for you, And people for your *l*.
57:10 You have found the *l* of your
Jer 4:30 They will seek your *l*.
8: 3 shall be chosen rather than *l*
11:21 men of Anathoth who seek your *l*,
18:20 they have dug a pit for my *l*.
20:13 For He has delivered the *l* of
21: 7 hand of those who seek their *l*;
21: 8 I set before you the way of *l*
21: 9 and his *l* shall be as a prize
22:25 hand of those who seek your *l*,
23:10 Their course of *l* is evil,
34:20 hand of those who seek their *l*.
34:21 hand of those who seek their *l*,
38: 2 his *l* shall be as a prize to
38:16 of these men who seek your *l*.
39:18 but your *l* shall be as a prize
44:30 hand of those who seek his *l*,
44:30 his enemy who sought his *l*.
45: 5 But I will give your *l* to you as
49:37 before those who seek their *l*.
51: 6 And every one save his *l*!
52:33 the king all the days of his *l*.
52:34 death, all the days of his *l*.
Lam 1:11 valuables for food to restore *l*.
1:16 who should restore my *l*,
1:19 sought food To restore their *l*.
2:12 As their *l* is poured out
2:19 hands toward Him For the *l* of
3:53 They silenced my *l* in the pit
3:58 You have redeemed my *l*.
Ezek 3:18 his wicked way, to save his *l*,
13:22 his wicked way to save his *l*.
32:10 moment, every man for his own *l*,
33: 5 takes warning will save his *l*.
33:15 and walks in the statutes of *l*
Dan 12: 2 awake, Some to everlasting *l*,
Hos 9: 4 shall be for their own *l*;
Jon 1:14 let us perish for this man's *l*,
2: 6 Yet You have brought up my *l*
4: 3 please take my *l* from me, for
Mal 2: 5 one of *l* and peace, And I
Mt 2:20 who sought the young Child's *l*
6:25 you, do not worry about your *l*,

6:25 Is not *l* more than food and the
7:14 is the way which leads to *l*,
10:39 He who finds his *l* will lose it,
10:39 and he who loses his *l* for My
16:25 whoever desires to save his *l*
16:25 but whoever loses his *l* for My
18: 8 better for you to enter into *l*
18: 9 better for you to enter into *l*
19:16 I do that I may have eternal *l*?
19:17 But if you want to enter into *l*,
19:29 and inherit eternal *l*.
20:28 and to give His *l* a ransom for
25:46 the righteous into eternal *l*.
Mk 3: 4 to save *l* or to kill?"
8:35 whoever desires to save his *l*
8:35 but whoever loses his *l* for My
9:43 better for you to enter into *l*
9:45 It is better for you to enter *l*
10:17 do that I may inherit eternal *l*?
10:30 in the age to come, eternal *l*.
10:45 and to give His *l* a ransom for
Lk 1:75 Him all the days of our *l*.
6: 9 to save *l* or to destroy?"
8:14 riches, and pleasures of *l*,
9:24 whoever desires to save his *l*
9:24 but whoever loses his *l* for My
10:25 shall I do to inherit eternal *l*?
12:15 for one's *l* does not consist in
12:22 you, do not worry about your *l*,
12:23 *L* is more than food, and the
14:26 and his own *l* also, he cannot
17:33 Whoever seeks to save his *l* will
17:33 and whoever loses his *l* will
18:18 shall I do to inherit eternal *l*?
18:30 in the age to come eternal *l*.
21:34 and cares of this *l*,
Jn 1: 4 In Him was *l*, and the life
1: 4 and the *l* was the light of men.
3:15 not perish but have eternal *l*.
3:16 perish but have everlasting *l*.
3:36 in the Son has everlasting *l*;
3:36 believe the Son shall not see *l*,
4:14 springing up into everlasting *l*.
4:36 and gathers fruit for eternal *l*,
5:21 raises the dead and gives *l* to
5:21 even so the Son gives *l* to whom
5:24 who sent Me has everlasting *l*,
5:24 has passed from death into *l*.
5:26 For as the Father has *l* in
5:26 has granted the Son to have *l*
5:29 good, to the resurrection of *l*,
5:39 you think you have eternal *l*;
5:40 come to Me that you may have *l*.
6:27 which endures to everlasting *l*,
6:33 down from heaven and gives *l*
6:35 to them, "I am the bread of *l*.
6:40 in Him may have everlasting *l*;
6:47 in Me has everlasting *l*.
6:48 "I am the bread of *l*.
6:51 which I shall give for the *l* of
6:53 you have no *l* in you.
6:54 drinks My blood has eternal *l*,
6:63 "It is the Spirit who gives *l*;
6:63 you are spirit, and they are *l*.
6:68 You have the words of eternal *l*.
8:12 but have the light of *l*.
10:10 have come that they may have *l*,
10:11 The good shepherd gives His *l*
10:15 and I lay down My *l* for the
10:17 because I lay down My *l* that I
10:28 "And I give them eternal *l*,
11:25 am the resurrection and the *l*.
12:25 He who loves his *l* will lose it,
12:25 and he who hates his *l* in this
12:25 will keep it for eternal *l*.
12:50 His command is everlasting *l*.
13:37 I will lay down my *l* for Your
13:38 Will you lay down your *l* for My
14: 6 the way, the truth, and the *l*.
15:13 than to lay down one's *l* for
17: 2 that He should give eternal *l*
17: 3 "And this is eternal *l*,
20:31 that believing you may have *l*
Acts 2:28 to me the ways of *l*;
3:15 "and killed the Prince of *l*,
5:20 people all the words of this *l*.
8:33 For His *l* is taken from
11:18 to the Gentiles repentance to *l*.
13:46 unworthy of everlasting *l*,
13:48 had been appointed to eternal *l*
17:25 since He gives to all *l*,
20:10 for his *l* is in him."
20:24 nor do I count my *l* dear to
26: 4 My manner of *l* from my youth,
27:22 for there will be no loss of *l*
Rom 2: 7 eternal *l* to those who by
4:17 who gives *l* to the dead and
5:10 we shall be saved by His *l*.
5:17 righteousness will reign in *l*
5:18 resulting in justification of *l*.
5:21 righteousness to eternal *l*
6: 4 should walk in newness of *l*.
6:10 but the *l* that He lives, He
6:22 and the end, everlasting *l*.
6:23 the gift of God is eternal *l*
7:10 which was to bring *l*,
8: 2 For the law of the Spirit of *l*
8: 6 to be spiritually minded is *l*
8:10 but the Spirit is *l* because of
8:11 from the dead will also give *l*
8:38 that neither death nor *l*,
11: 3 and they seek my *l*"?
11:15 their acceptance be but *l*
16: 4 risked their own necks for my *l*,
1 Cor 3:22 or the world or *l* or death, or
6: 3 things that pertain to this *l*?
6: 4 things pertaining to this *l*,
14: 7 Even things without *l*,
15:19 If in this *l* only we have hope
2 Cor 1: 8 so that we despaired even of *l*.
2:16 and to the other the aroma of *l*
2:16 the aroma of life leading to *l*.
3: 6 kills, but the Spirit gives *l*.
4:10 that the *l* of Jesus also may be
4:11 that the *l* of Jesus also may be
4:12 working in us, but *l* in you.
5: 4 may be swallowed up by *l*.
Gal 2:20 and the *l* which I now live in
3:21 given which could have given *l*,
6: 8 the Spirit reap everlasting *l*.
Eph 4:18 being alienated from the *l* of
Phil 1:20 whether by *l* or by death.
2:16 holding fast the word of *l*,
2:30 to death, not regarding his *l*,
4: 3 names are in the Book of *L*.
Col 3: 3 and your *l* is hidden with
3: 4 When Christ who is our *l*
1 Th 4:11 also aspire to lead a quiet *l*,
1 Tim 1:16 on Him for everlasting *l*.
2: 2 lead a quiet and peaceable *l*
4: 8 having promise of the *l* that
6:12 of faith, lay hold on eternal *l*,
6:13 in the sight of God who gives *l*
6:19 they may lay hold on eternal *l*.
2 Tim 1: 1 according to the promise of *l*
1:10 abolished death and brought *l*
2: 4 with the affairs of this *l*,
3:10 my doctrine, manner of *l*,
Titus 1: 2 in hope of eternal *l* which God,
3: 7 to the hope of eternal *l*.
Heb 7: 3 beginning of days nor end of *l*,
7:16 to the power of an endless *l*.
11:35 their dead raised to *l* again.
Jas 1:12 he will receive the crown of *l*
4:14 For what is your *l*?
1 Pe 3: 7 together of the grace of *l*,
3:10 He who would love *l* And
2 Pe 1: 3 all things that pertain to *l*
1 Jn 1: 1 concerning the Word of *l*—
1: 2 the *l* was manifested, and we
1: 2 declare to you that eternal *l*
2:16 of the eyes, and the pride of *l*—
2:25 He has promised us—eternal *l*.
3:14 we have passed from death to *l*,
3:15 that no murderer has eternal *l*
3:16 because He laid down His *l* for
5:11 that God has given us eternal *l*,
5:11 and this *l* is in His Son.
5:12 He who has the Son has *l*;
5:12 the Son of God does not have *l*.
5:13 know that you have eternal *l*,
5:16 and He will give him *l* for
5:20 is the true God and eternal *l*.
Jude 21 Jesus Christ unto eternal *l*.
Rev 2: 7 give to eat from the tree of *l*,
2: 8 who was dead, and came to *l*:
2:10 I will give you the crown of *l*.
3: 5 out his name from the Book of *L*;
11:11 days the breath of *l* from God
13: 8 been written in the Book of *L*
17: 8 not written in the Book of *L*
20:12 which is the Book of *L*.
20:15 found written in the Book of *L*
21: 6 the fountain of the water of *l*
21:27 written in the Lamb's Book of *L*.
22: 1 me a pure river of water of *l*,
22: 2 the river, was the tree of *l*,
22:14 have the right to the tree of *l*,
22:17 let him take the water of *l*
22:19 his part from the Book of *L*,

LIFE-GIVING (1/1) LIFE

1 Cor 15:45 last Adam became a *l* spirit.

LIFEBLOOD (1/1) BLOOD, LIFE

Gen 9: 5 Surely for your *l* I will demand

LIFELESS (1/1) LIFE

Lev 26:30 cast your carcasses on the *l*

LIFETIME (4/4) LIFE

2 Sam 18:18 Now Absalom in his *l* had taken
Lk 16:25 remember that in your *l* you
Heb 2:15 fear of death were all their *l*
1 Pe 4: 3 spent enough of our past *l* in

LIFT (94/91) LIFTED, LIFTING, LIFTS, RAISE, UNLIFTED, UPLIFTED

Gen 13:14 *L* your eyes now and look from
21:18 *l* up the lad and hold him with
31:12 *L* your eyes now and see, all the
40:13 three days Pharaoh will *l* up
40:19 three days Pharaoh will *l* off
41:44 your consent no man may *l* his
Ex 14:16 But *l* up your rod, and stretch
Num 6:26 The LORD *l* up His countenance
Deut 3:27 and *l* your eyes toward the
4:19 lest you *l* your eyes to heaven,
22: 4 you shall surely help him *l*
1 Sam 22:17 of the king would not *l* their
2 Sam 22:49 You also *l* me up above those
2 Ki 19: 4 Therefore *l* up your prayer for
Ezra 9: 6 ashamed and humiliated to *l* up
Job 10:15 I cannot *l* up my head. I am
11:15 Then surely you could *l* up your
22:26 And *l* up your face to God.
30:22 You *l* me up to the wind and
38:34 Can you *l* up your voice to the
Ps 4: 6 *l* up the light of Your
7: 6 *L* Yourself up because of the
9:13 You who *l* me up from the gates
10:12 *l* up Your hand! Do not forget
18:48 You also *l* me up above those
24: 7 *L* up your heads, O you gates!
24: 9 *L* up your heads, O you gates!
24: 9 O you gates! *L* up, you
25: 1 O LORD, I *l* up my soul.
28: 2 When I *l* up my hands toward
63: 4 I will *l* up my hands in Your
74: 3 *L* up Your feet to the perpetual
74: 5 They seem like men who *l* up
75: 4 Do not *l* up the horn.
75: 5 Do not *l* up your horn on high;
86: 4 O Lord, I *l* up my soul.
93: 3 The floods *l* up their waves.
110: 7 Therefore He shall *l* up the
119:48 My hands also I will *l* up to
121: 1 I will *l* up my eyes to the
123: 1 Unto You I *l* up my eyes, O You
134: 2 *L* up your hands in the
143: 8 For I *l* up my soul to You.
Prov 2: 3 And *l* up your voice for
8: 1 And understanding *l* up her
Eccl 4:10 one will *l* up his companion.
Isa 2: 4 Nation shall not *l* up sword
5:26 He will *l* up a banner to the
10:15 itself against those who *l* it
10:15 Or as if a staff could *l* up,
10:24 strike you with a rod and *l* up
10:26 so will He *l* it up in the
10:30 *L* up your voice, O daughter of
13: 2 *L* up a banner on the high
24:14 They shall *l* up their voice,
33: 3 When You *l* Yourself up, the
33:10 Now I will *l* Myself up.
37: 4 Therefore *l* up your prayer for
40: 9 *L* up your voice with strength,
40: 9 *L* it up, be not afraid;
40:26 *L* up your eyes on high,
42:11 wilderness and its cities *l* up
49:18 *L* up your eyes, look around and
49:22 I will *l* My hand in an oath to
51: 6 *L* up your eyes to the heavens,
52: 8 Your watchmen shall *l* up their
58: 1 *L* up your voice like a
59:19 Spirit of the LORD will *l* up
60: 4 *L* up your eyes all around, and
62:10 *L* up a banner for the peoples!
Jer 3: 2 *L* up your eyes to the desolate
7:16 nor *l* up a cry or prayer for
11:14 or *l* up a cry or prayer for
13:20 *L* up your eyes and see
22:20 And *l* up your voice in Bashan;
38:10 and *l* Jeremiah the prophet out
51: 3 And *l* himself up against her
51:14 And they shall *l* up a shout
Lam 2:19 *L* your hands toward Him
3:41 Let us *l* our hearts and hands
Ezek 8: 5 *l* your eyes now toward the
17:14 might be brought low and not *l*
21:22 to *l* the voice with shouting,
23:27 So that you will not *l* your
33:25 you *l* up your eyes toward your
Mic 4: 3 Nation shall not *l* up sword
Nah 3: 5 I will *l* your skirts over your
Zech 1:21 so that no one could *l* up his
5: 5 *L* your eyes now, and see what
Mt 12:11 will not lay hold of it and *l*
Lk 21:28 look up and *l* up your heads,
Jn 4:35 *l* up your eyes and look at the
8:28 When you *l* up the Son of Man,
Jas 4:10 and He will *l* you up.

LIFTED (133/128) LIFT, RAISED

Gen 7:17 The waters increased and *l* up
13:10 And Lot *l* his eyes and saw all
18: 2 So he *l* his eyes and looked, and
21:16 and *l* her voice and wept.
22: 4 on the third day Abraham *l* his
22:13 Then Abraham *l* his eyes and
24:63 and he *l* his eyes and looked,
24:64 Then Rebekah *l* her eyes, and
27:38 O my father!" And Esau *l* up
29:11 and *l* up his voice and wept.
31:10 that I *l* my eyes and saw in a
33: 1 Now Jacob *l* his eyes and looked,
33: 5 And he *l* his eyes and saw the
37:25 Then they *l* their eyes and
37:28 pulled Joseph up and *l* him out
39:15 when he heard that I *l* my voice
39:18 as I *l* my voice and cried out,
40:20 and he *l* up the head of the
43:29 Then he *l* his eyes and saw his
Ex 7:20 So he *l* up the rod and struck
14:10 the children of Israel *l* their
16:14 And when the layer of dew *l*,
Lev 9:22 Then Aaron *l* his hand toward
Num 14: 1 So all the congregation *l* up
18:30 When you have *l* up the best of
18:32 when you have *l* up the best of

20:11 Then Moses *l* his hand and struck
Deut 8:14 when your heart is *l* up, and you
17:20 that his heart may not be *l*
Josh 5:13 that he *l* his eyes and looked,
Judg 2: 4 that the people *l* up their
8:28 so that they *l* their heads no
9: 7 and *l* his voice and cried out.
19:28 So the man *l* her onto the
21: 2 They *l* up their voices and wept
Ruth 1: 9 and they *l* up their voices and
1:14 Then they *l* up their voices and
1 Sam 6:13 and they *l* their eyes and saw
11: 4 And all the people *l* up their
24:16 And Saul *l* up his voice and
30: 4 people who were with him *l* up
2 Sam 3:32 and the king *l* up his voice and
13:34 man who was keeping watch *l*
13:36 and they *l* up their voice and
18:24 *l* his eyes and looked, and
23:18 He *l* his spear against three
1 Ki 16: 2 Inasmuch as I *l* you out of the
2 Ki 14:10 and your heart has *l* you up.
19:22 And *l* up your eyes on high?
1 Chr 11:11 he had *l* up his spear against
11:20 He had *l* up his spear against
21:16 Then David *l* his eyes and saw
2 Chr 5:13 and when they *l* up their voice
25:19 and your heart is *l* up to
26:16 he was strong his heart was *l*
32:25 for his heart was *l* up;
Job 2:12 they *l* their voices and wept;
5:11 And those who mourn are *l* to
31:29 Or *l* myself up when evil found
Ps 24: 4 Who has not *l* up his soul to
24: 7 O you gates! And be *l* up, you
27: 6 And now my head shall be *l* up
30: 1 for You have *l* me up, And have
41: 9 Has *l* up his heel against me.
83: 2 And those who hate You have *l*
93: 3 The floods have *l* up, O LORD,
93: 3 The floods have *l* up their
102:10 For You have *l* me up and cast
Prov 30:13 And their eyelids are *l* up.
Isa 2:12 Upon everything *l* up—And it
2:13 Lebanon that are high and *l*
2:14 all the hills that are *l* up;
6: 1 high and *l* up, and the train of
26:11 when Your hand is *l* up, they
37:23 And *l* up your eyes on high?
Jer 38:13 Jeremiah up with ropes and *l*
51: 9 reaches to heaven and is *l* up
52:31 *l* up the head of Jehoiachin
Ezek 1:19 the living creatures were *l* up
1:19 the wheels were *l* up.
1:20 and the wheels were *l* together
1:21 and when those were *l* up from
1:21 the wheels were *l* up together
3:12 Then the Spirit *l* me up, and I
3:14 So the Spirit *l* me up and took
8: 3 and the Spirit *l* me up between
8: 5 So I *l* my eyes toward the
10:15 And the cherubim were *l* up.
10:16 and when the cherubim *l* their
10:17 and when one was *l* up, the
10:17 the other *l* itself up, for
10:19 And the cherubim *l* their wings
11: 1 Then the Spirit *l* me up and
11:22 So the cherubim *l* up their
18: 6 Nor *l* up his eyes to the idols
18:12 *L* his eyes to the idols,
18:15 Nor *l* his eyes to the idols of
28: 2 Because your heart is *l* up,
28: 5 And your heart is *l* up because
28:17 Your heart was *l* up because of
31:10 and its heart was *l* up in its
43: 5 The Spirit *l* me up and brought
Dan 4:34 *l* my eyes to heaven, and my
5:20 But when his heart was *l* up, and
5:23 And you have *l* yourself up
7: 4 and it was *l* up from the earth
8: 3 Then I *l* my eyes and saw, and
10: 5 I *l* my eyes and looked, and
11:12 his heart will be *l* up; and he
Mic 5: 9 Your hand shall be *l* against
Hab 3:10 And *l* its hands on high.
Zech 1:21 horns of the nations that *l* up
5: 7 Here is a lead disc *l* up, and
5: 9 and they *l* up the basket
9:16 *L* like a banner over His land—
Mt 17: 8 When they had *l* up their eyes,
Mk 1:31 and took her by the hand and *l*
9:27 took him by the hand and *l* him
Lk 6:20 Then He *l* up His eyes toward
16:23 he *l* up his eyes and saw
17:13 And they *l* up their voices and
24:50 and He *l* up His hands and
Jn 3:14 And as Moses *l* up the serpent in
3:14 so must the Son of Man be *l* up,
6: 5 Then Jesus *l* up His eyes, and
11:41 And Jesus *l* up His eyes and
12:32 if I am *l* up from the earth,
12:34 The Son of Man must be *l* up'?
13:18 eats bread with Me has *l*
17: 1 *l* up His eyes to heaven, and
Acts 3: 7 him by the right hand and *l*
9:41 he gave her his hand and *l*
10:26 But Peter *l* him up, saying,

LIFTING (3/3) LIFT

Neh 8: 6 Amen!" while *l* up their hands.
Ps 141: 2 The *l* up of my hands as the
1 Tim 2: 8 *l* up holy hands, without wrath

LIFTS (10/10) LIFT

Num 23:24 And *l* itself up like a lion;
1 Sam 2: 7 He brings low and *l* up.
2: 8 the poor from the dust And *l*
Job 39:18 When she *l* herself on high,
Ps 3: 3 My glory and the One who *l* up
107:25 Which *l* up the waves of the
113: 7 And *l* the needy out of the
147: 6 The LORD *l* up the humble;
Isa 18: 3 When he *l* up a banner on the
40:15 He *l* up the isles as a very

LIGAMENTS (1/1)

Col 2:19 knit together by joints and *l*,

LIGHT (253/221) LIGHTEN, LIGHTER, LIGHTLY, LIGHTS, LIT

Gen 1: 3 Let there be *l*"; and there was
1: 3 be light"; and there was *l*.
1: 4 And God saw the *l*, that it
1: 4 and God divided the *l* from the
1: 5 God called the *l* Day, and the
1:15 of the heavens to give *l* on
1:16 the greater *l* to rule the day,
1:16 and the lesser *l* to rule the
1:17 of the heavens to give *l* on
1:18 and to divide the *l* from the
Ex 10:23 the children of Israel had *l*
13:21 a pillar of fire to give them *l*,
14:20 and it gave *l* by night to the
25: 6 'oil for the *l*, and spices for
25:37 its lamps so that they give *l*
27:20 oil of pressed olives for the *l*,
35: 8 'oil for the *l*, and spices for
35:14 'also the lampstand for the *l*,
35:14 lamps, and the oil for the *l*;
35:28 and spices and oil for the *l*,
39:37 its utensils, and the oil for *l*;
40: 4 bring in the lampstand and *l*
Lev 24: 2 oil of pressed olives for the *l*,
Num 4: 9 cover the lampstand of the *l*,
4:16 priest is the oil for the *l*,
8: 2 the seven lamps shall give *l* in
Deut 25:13 weights, a heavy and a *l*.
Judg 19:26 her master was, till it was *l*.
1 Sam 14:36 them until the morning *l*;
18:23 Does it seem to you a *l* thing
25:22 who belong to him by morning *l*.
25:34 surely by morning *l* no males
25:36 little or much, until morning *l*.
29:10 early in the morning and have *l*,
2 Sam 17:22 By morning *l* not one of them
23: 4 And he shall be like the *l*
2 Ki 7: 9 If we wait until morning *l*,
Neh 9:12 To give them *l* on the road
9:19 fire by night, To show them *l*,
Esth 8:16 The Jews had *l* and gladness, joy
Job 3: 4 Nor the *l* shine upon it.
3: 9 be dark; May it look for *l*,
3:16 Like infants who never saw *l*?
3:20 Why is *l* given to him who is in
3:23 Why is *l* given to a man
10:22 Where even the *l* is like
12:22 brings the shadow of death to *l*.
12:25 grope in the dark without *l*,
17:12 The *l* is near,' they say, in
18: 5 The *l* of the wicked indeed goes
18: 6 The *l* is dark in his tent,
18:18 He is driven from *l* into
22:28 So *l* will shine on your ways.
24:13 those who rebel against the *l*;
24:14 The murderer rises with the *l*;
24:16 They do not know the *l*.
25: 3 Upon whom does His *l* not rise?
26:10 At the boundary of *l* and
28:11 is hidden he brings forth to *l*.
29: 3 And when by His *l* I walked
29:24 And the *l* of my countenance
30:26 And when I waited for *l*,
33:28 And his life shall see the *l*.
33:30 may be enlightened with the *l*
36:30 He scatters his *l* upon it,
37:15 And causes the *l* of His cloud
37:21 now men cannot look at the *l*
38:15 From the wicked their *l* is
38:19 the way to the dwelling of *l*?
38:24 By what way is *l* diffused,
41:18 His sneezings flash forth *l*,
Ps 4: 6 lift up the *l* of Your
18:28 For You will *l* my lamp;
27: 1 The LORD is my *l* and my
36: 9 In Your *l* we see light.
36: 9 In Your light we see *l*.
37: 6 your righteousness as the *l*,
38:10 As for the *l* of my eyes, it
43: 3 send out Your *l* and Your truth!
44: 3 and the *l* of Your countenance,
49:19 They shall never see *l*.
56:13 I may walk before God In the *l*
74:16 You have prepared the *l* and
78:14 And all the night with a *l* of
89:15 in the *l* of Your countenance.
90: 8 Our secret sins in the *l* of
97: 4 His lightnings *l* the world;
97:11 *L* is sown for the righteous,
104: 2 Who cover Yourself with *l* as
105:39 And fire to give *l* in the
112: 4 the upright there arises *l* in
118:27 And He has given us *l*;
119:105 is a lamp to my feet And a *l*
119:130 entrance of Your words gives *l*;
139:11 Even the night shall be *l*
139:12 The darkness and the *l* are
148: 3 all you stars of *l*!
Prov 6:23 is a lamp, And the law a *l*;
13: 9 The *l* of the righteous
15:30 The *l* of the eyes rejoices the
16:15 In the *l* of the king's face is
29:13 The LORD gives *l* to the eyes
Eccl 2:13 that wisdom excels folly As *l*
11: 7 Truly the *l* is sweet, And it
12: 2 While the sun and the *l*,
Isa 2: 5 come and let us walk In the *l*
5:20 Who put darkness for *l*,
5:20 and *l* for darkness; Who put
5:30 And the *l* is darkened by the
8:20 is because there is no *l* in
9: 2 darkness Have seen a great *l*;
9: 2 Upon them a *l* has shined.
10:17 So the *L* of Israel will be for
13:10 Will not give their *l*;
13:10 the moon will not cause its *l*
24:15 the LORD in the dawning *l*,
30:26 Moreover the *l* of the moon will
30:26 of the moon will be as the *l*
30:26 And the *l* of the sun will be
30:26 As the *l* of seven days,
42: 6 As a *l* to the Gentiles,
42:16 I will make darkness *l* before
45: 7 I form the *l* and create
49: 6 I will also give You as a *l* to
50:10 walks in darkness And has no *l*?
50:11 Walk in the *l* of your fire and
51: 4 make My justice rest As a *l*
58: 8 Then your *l* shall break forth
58:10 Then your *l* shall dawn in the
59: 9 overtake us; We look for *l*,
60: 1 For your *l* has come! And the
60: 3 Gentiles shall come to your *l*,
60:19 sun shall no longer be your *l*
60:19 shall the moon give *l* to you;
60:19 will be to you an everlasting *l*,
60:20 will be your everlasting *l*,
Jer 4:23 the heavens, they had no *l*.
13:16 while you are looking for *l*,
25:10 of the millstones and the *l* of
31:35 Who gives the sun for a *l* by
31:35 the moon and the stars for a *l*
Lam 3: 2 In darkness and not in *l*.
Ezek 22: 7 In you they have made *l* of
32: 7 When I put out your *l*,
32: 7 the moon shall not give her *l*.
Dan 2:22 And *l* dwells with Him.
5:11 *l* and understanding and wisdom,
5:14 and that *l* and understanding
Hos 6: 5 your judgments are like *l*
Am 5:18 will be darkness, and not *l*.
5:20 the LORD darkness, and not *l*?
Mic 2: 1 on their beds! At morning *l*
7: 8 The LORD will be a *l* to me.
7: 9 will bring me forth to the *l*;
Hab 3: 4 His brightness was like the *l*;
3:11 At the *l* of Your arrows they
Zeph 3: 5 He brings His justice to *l*;
Zech 14: 6 That there will be no *l*;
14: 7 happen That it will be *l*.
Mt 4:16 have seen a great *l*,
4:16 and shadow of death *L*
5:14 'You are the *l* of the world.
5:15 Nor do they *l* a lamp and put it
5:15 and it gives *l* to all who are
5:16 Let your *l* so shine before men,
6:22 whole body will be full of *l*.
6:23 If therefore the *l* that is in
10:27 you in the dark, speak in the *l*;
11:30 is easy and My burden is *l*.
17: 2 became as white as the *l*.
22: 5 But they made *l* of it and went
24:29 the moon will not give its *l*;
Mk 4:22 but that it should come to *l*.
13:24 the moon will not give its *l*;
Lk 1:79 To give *l* to those who sit in
2:32 A *l* to bring revelation to the
8:16 those who enter may see the *l*.
8:17 will not be known and come to *l*.
11:33 those who come in may see the *l*.
11:34 whole body also is full of *l*.
11:35 take heed that the *l*
11:36 your whole body is full of *l*,
11:36 whole body will be full of *l*,
11:36 shining of a lamp gives you *l*.
12: 3 the dark will be heard in the *l*,
15: 8 does not *l* a lamp, sweep the
16: 8 generation than the sons of *l*.
Jn 1: 4 and the life was the *l* of men.
1: 5 And the *l* shines in the
1: 7 to bear witness of the *L*,
1: 8 He was not that *L*,
1: 8 sent to bear witness of that *L*.
1: 9 That was the true *L* which gives
1: 9 the true Light which gives *l*
3:19 that the *l* has come into the
3:19 loved darkness rather than *l*,
3:20 practicing evil hates the *l*
3:20 and does not come to the *l*,
3:21 does the truth comes to the *l*,
5:35 for a time to rejoice in his *l*.
8:12 I am the *l* of the world. He who
8:12 but have the *l* of life."

9: 5 I am the l of the world."
11: 9 because he sees the l of this
11:10 because the l is not in him."
12:35 A little while longer the l is
12:35 Walk while you have the l,
12:36 "While you have the l,
12:36 the light, believe in the l,
12:36 that you may become sons of l.
12:46 I have come as a l into the
Acts 9: 3 and suddenly a l shone around
12: 7 and a l shone in the prison;
13:47 I have set you as a l to
16:29 Then he called for a l,
22: 6 suddenly a great l from heaven
22: 9 were with me indeed saw the l
22:11 not see for the glory of that l,
26:13 along the road I saw a l from
26:18 turn them from darkness to l,
26:23 and would proclaim l to the
Rom 2:19 a l to those who are in
13:12 let us put on the armor of l.
1 Cor 4: 5 who will both bring to l the
2 Cor 4: 4 lest the l of the gospel of the
4: 6 it is the God who commanded l
4: 6 in our hearts to give the l
4:17 For our l affliction, which is
6:14 And what communion has l with
11:14 himself into an angel of l.
Eph 5: 8 but now you are l in the
5: 8 Walk as children of l
5:13 are made manifest by the l,
5:13 whatever makes manifest is l.
5:14 And Christ will give you l.
Col 1:12 of the saints in the l.
1 Th 5: 5 You are all sons of l and sons
1 Tim 6:16 dwelling in unapproachable l,
2 Tim 1:10 life and immortality to l
1 Pe 2: 9 darkness into His marvelous l;
2 Pe 1:19 you do well to heed as a l
1 Jn 1: 5 that God is l and in Him is no
1: 7 But if we walk in the l as He is
1: 7 in the light as He is in the l,
2: 8 and the true l is already
2: 9 He who says he is in the l,
2:10 his brother abides in the l,
Rev 18:23 The l of a lamp shall not shine
21:11 Her l was like a most precious
21:23 The Lamb is its l.
21:24 are saved shall walk in its l,
22: 5 They need no lamp nor l of the
22: 5 for the Lord God gives them l.

LIGHTEN (6/6) LIGHT, LIGHTENED

1 Sam 6: 5 perhaps He will l His hand from
1 Ki 12: 4 l the burdensome service of
12: 9 L the yoke which your father put
2 Chr 10: 4 l the burdensome service of
10: 9 L the yoke which your father put
Jon 1: 5 to l the load. But Jonah had

LIGHTENED (2/2) LIGHTEN

Acts 27:18 the next day they l the ship.
27:38 they l the ship and threw out

LIGHTER (3/3) LIGHT

1 Ki 12:10 but you make it l on us'—thus
2 Chr 10:10 but you make it l on us'—thus
Ps 62: 9 They are altogether l than

LIGHTLY (4/4) LIGHT

1 Sam 2:30 those who despise Me shall be l
18:23 seeing I am a poor and l
Isa 9: 1 As when at first He l esteemed
2 Cor 1:17 planning this, did I do it l?

LIGHTNING (18/18) LIGHTNINGS

Ex 20:18 the l flashes, the sound of the
2 Sam 22:15 L bolts, and He vanquished
Job 36:32 He covers His hands with l,
37: 3 His l to the ends of the
Ps 78:48 And their flocks to fiery l.
135: 7 He makes l for the rain;
144: 6 Flash forth l and scatter them;
Jer 10:13 He makes l for the rain,
Ezek 1:13 and out of the fire went l.
1:14 in appearance like a flash of l.
21:10 Polished to flash like l!
Dan 10: 6 face like the appearance of l,
Nah 2: 4 like torches, They run like l.
Zech 9:14 His arrow will go forth like l.
Mt 24:27 For as the l comes from the east
28: 3 His countenance was like l,
Lk 10:18 I saw Satan fall like l from
17:24 For as the l that flashes out of

LIGHTNINGS (10/10) LIGHTNING

Ex 19:16 there were thunderings and l,
Job 38:35 Can you send out l,
Ps 18:14 L in abundance, and He
77:18 The l lit up the world;
97: 4 His l light the world;
Jer 51:16 He makes l for the rain;
Rev 4: 5 And from the throne proceeded l,
8: 5 were noises, thunderings, l,
11:19 in His temple. And there were l,
16:18 noises and thunderings and l;

LIGHTS (10/10) LIGHT

Gen 1:14 Let there be l in the firmament
1:15 and let them be for l in the
1:16 Then God made two great l:
Ex 30: 8 And when Aaron l the lamps at
Job 41:19 Out of his mouth go burning l;
Ps 136: 7 To Him who made great l,
Ezek 32: 8 All the bright l of the heavens
Zech 14: 6 The l will diminish.
Phil 2:15 among whom you shine as l in
Jas 1:17 comes down from the Father of l,

LIGURE (KJV) See JACINTH

LIKE (1278/1013) See APPENDIX

LIKE-MINDED (3/3)

Rom 15: 5 and comfort grant you to be l
Phil 2: 2 fulfill my joy by being l,
2:20 For I have no one l,

LIKELY (1/1)

Jer 38: 9 and he is l to die from hunger

LIKEN (9/9) LIKENED, LIKENESS

Isa 40:18 To whom then will you l God?
40:25 To whom then will you l Me,
46: 5 To whom will you l Me, and make
Lam 2:13 To what shall I l you,
Mt 7:24 I will l him to a wise man who
11:16 But to what shall I l this
Mk 4:30 To what shall we l the kingdom
Lk 7:31 To what then shall I l the men
13:20 To what shall I l the kingdom of

LIKENED (4/4) LIKEN

Ps 89: 6 sons of the mighty can be l to
Jer 6: 2 I have l the daughter of Zion
Ezek 31:18 in Eden will you then be l in
Mt 25: 1 kingdom of heaven shall be l

LIKENESS (36/30) LIKEN

Gen 1:26 Our image, according to Our l;
5: 1 He made him in the l of God.
5: 3 and begot a son in his own l,
Ex 20: 4 or any l of anything that is
Deut 4:16 the l of male or female,
4:17 the l of any animal that is on
4:17 that is on the earth or the l
4:18 the l of anything that creeps on
4:18 creeps on the ground or the l
5: 8 any l of anything that is in
2 Chr 4: 3 And under it was the l of oxen
Ps 17:15 when I awake in Your l.
Isa 40:18 Or what l will you compare to
Ezek 1: 5 from within it came the l of
1: 5 they had the l of a man.
1:10 As for the l of their faces,
1:13 As for the l of the living
1:16 and all four had the same l.
1:22 The l of the firmament above
1:26 over their heads was the l of
1:26 on the l of the throne was a
1:26 of the throne was a l with
1:28 was the appearance of the l
8: 2 I looked, and there was a l,
10: 1 having the appearance of the l
10:21 and the l of the hands of a man
10:22 And the l of their faces was
Dan 10:16 one having the l of the sons
10:18 the one having the l of a man
Acts 14:11 have come down to us in the l
Rom 5:14 not sinned according to the l
6: 5 been united together in the l
6: 5 we also shall be in the l
8: 3 by sending His own Son in the l
Phil 2: 7 and coming in the l of men.
Heb 7:15 in the l of Melchizedek, there

LIKEWISE (87/87)

Ex 22:30 L you shall do with your oxen
26: 4 and l you shall do on the outer
27:11 L along the length of the north
36:11 l he did on the outer edge of
Lev 7: 1 L this is the law of the
Deut 9:23 'L, when the LORD sent you
12:30 their gods? I also will do l.
15:17 female servant you shall do l.
22: 3 you have found, you shall do l;
Judg 1: 3 and I will l go with you to
7: 5 l everyone who gets down on his
7:17 to them, "Look at me and do l;
9:49 So each of the people l cut down
1 Sam 14:22 L all the men of Israel who had
19:21 and they prophesied l.
1 Ki 11: 8 And he did l for all his foreign
1 Chr 23:30 the LORD, and l at evening;
2 Chr 29:22 L they killed the rams and
Neh 12:40 l I and the half of the rulers
Esth 4:16 day. My maids and I will fast l.
Job 37: 6 L to the gentle rain and the
Ps 49:10 L the fool and the senseless
52: 5 God shall l destroy you
Isa 30:24 L the oxen and the young
Jer 40:11 L, when all the Jews who were
Ezek 13:17 L, son of man, set your face
18:14 considers but does not do l;
40:16 and l in the vestibules.
45:25 he shall do l for seven days,
46: 3 L the people of the land shall
Nah 1:12 and l many, Yet in this manner
Zech 3: 7 And l have charge of My
Mt 17:12 L the Son of Man is also about
20: 5 and the ninth hour, and did l.
20:10 and they l received each a
21:24 I l will tell you by what
21:30 came to the second and said l.
21:36 and they did l to them.
22:26 L the second also, and the
25:17 And l he who had received two
27:41 L the chief priests also,
Mk 4:16 These l are the ones sown on
12:21 any offspring. And the third l.
14:31 deny You!" And they all said l.
15:31 L the chief priests also,
Lk 3:11 he who has food, let him do l.
3:14 L the soldiers asked him,
5:33 and l those of the Pharisees,
6:31 to you, you also do to them l.
10:32 L a Levite, when he arrived at
10:37 said to him, "Go and do l.
13: 3 you repent you will all l
13: 5 you repent you will all l
14:33 'So l, whoever of you does
15: 7 I say to you that l there will
15:10 'L, I say to you, there is
16:25 and l Lazarus evil things;
17:10 So l you, when you have done all
17:28 L as it was also in the days of
17:31 And l the one who is in the
19:19 L he said to him, 'You also be
22:20 L He also took the cup after
22:36 and l a knapsack; and he who
Jn 6:11 and l of the fish, as much as
21:13 it to them, and l the fish.
Rom 1:27 L also the men, leaving the
6:11 L you also, reckon yourselves to
8:26 L the Spirit also helps in our
16: 5 L greet the church that is in
1 Cor 7: 3 and l also the wife to her
7: 4 And l the husband does not have
7:22 L he who is called while free
14: 9 So l you, unless you utter by
Col 4:16 and that you l read the epistle
1 Tim 3: 8 L deacons must be reverent,
3:11 L their wives must be
5:25 L, the good works of some
Titus 2: 3 the older women l, that they
2: 6 L exhort the young men to be
Heb 2:14 He Himself l shared in the
9:21 Then l he sprinkled with blood
Jas 2:25 L, was not Rahab the harlot
1 Pe 3: 1 Wives, l, be submissive to
3: 7 Husbands, l, dwell with
5: 5 L you younger people, submit
Jude 8 L also these dreamers defile the
Rev 8:12 not shine, and l the night.

LIKHI (1/1)

1 Chr 7:19 Shemida were Ahian, Shechem, L,

LILIES (13/13) LILY

1 Ki 7:19 hall were in the shape of l,
7:22 pillars were in the shape of l.
Ps 45: Chief Musician. Set to "The L.
69: Chief Musician. Set to "The L.
80: Chief Musician. Set to "The L.
Song 2:16 feeds his flock among the l.
4: 5 Which feed among the l.
5:13 scented herbs. His lips are l,
6: 2 the gardens, And to gather l.
6: 3 feeds his flock among the l.
7: 2 heap of wheat Set about with l.
Mt 6:28 Consider the l of the field,
Lk 12:27 'Consider the l, how they

LILY (6/6) LILIES

1 Ki 7:26 like a l blossom. It contained
2 Chr 4: 5 like a l blossom. It contained
Ps 60: L of the Testimony." A Michtam
Song 2: 1 And the l of the valleys.
2: 2 Like a l among thorns, So is
Hos 14: 5 He shall grow like the l,

LIMB (4/3)

Lev 21:18 has a marred face or any l
22:23 a bull or a lamb that has any l
Judg 19:29 l by limb, and sent her
19:29 into twelve pieces, limb by l,

LIMBS (2/2)

Job 18:13 of death devours his l.
41:12 "I will not conceal his l,

LIME (4/4)

Deut 27: 2 and whitewash them with l.
27: 4 you shall whitewash them with l.
Isa 33:12 be like the burnings of l;
Am 2: 1 bones of the king of Edom to l.

LIMIT (6/6) LIMITS

1 Chr 22:16 bronze and iron there is no *l*.
Ezra 7:22 and salt without prescribed *l*.
Job 13:27 You set a *l* for the soles of
15: 8 Do you *l* wisdom to yourself?
38:10 When I fixed My *l* for it,
Prov 8:29 He assigned to the sea its *l*,

LIMITED (1/1)

Ps 78:41 And *l* the Holy One of Israel.

LIMITS (9/9) LIMIT

Num 35:26 at any time goes outside the *l*
35:27 blood finds him outside the *l*
Josh 15:21 The cities at the *l* of the tribe
2 Ki 19:23 To the *l* of Lebanon; I will
Job 11: 7 Can you find out the *l* of the
14: 5 You have appointed his *l*,
Ps 71:15 For I do not know their *l*.
Isa 37:24 To the *l* of Lebanon; I will
2 Cor 10:13 but within the *l* of the sphere

LIMP (2/2) LIMPED

Prov 26: 7 legs of the lame that hang *l*
Isa 13: 7 Therefore all hands will be *l*,

LIMPED (1/1) LIMP

Gen 32:31 and he *l* on his hip.

LINE (42/33) LINEAGE, LINES

Num 34: 7 shall mark out your border *l*
Josh 2:18 you bind this *l* of scarlet cord
Judg 20:22 and again formed the battle *l*
1 Sam 4:12 Benjamin ran from the battle *l*
4:16 I fled today from the battle *l*.
17: 8 Why have you come out to *l* up
2 Sam 8: 2 he measured them off with a *l*.
8: 2 and with one full *l* those to be
10: 9 Joab saw that the battle *l* was
1 Ki 7:15 and a *l* of twelve cubits
7:23 and a *l* of thirty cubits
2 Ki 21:13 over Jerusalem the measuring *l*
1 Chr 19:10 Joab saw that the battle *l* was
2 Chr 4: 2 and a *l* of thirty cubits
13:14 to their surprise the battle *l*
Job 38: 5 Or who stretched the *l* upon
41: 1 Or snare his tongue with a *l*
Ps 19: 4 Their *l* has gone out through
Isa 28:10 *L* upon line, line upon line,
28:10 upon precept, Line upon *l*,
28:10 *l* upon line, Here a little,
28:10 Line upon line, line upon *l*,
28:13 *L* upon line, line upon line,
28:13 upon precept, Line upon *l*,
28:13 *l* upon line, Here a little,
28:13 Line upon line, line upon *l*,
28:17 make justice the measuring *l*,
34:11 stretch out over it The *l* of
34:17 among them with a measuring *l*.
Jer 31:39 The surveyor's *l* shall again
52:21 a measuring *l* of twelve cubits
Lam 2: 8 He has stretched out a *l*;
Ezek 40: 3 He had a *l* of flax and a
47: 3 out to the east with the *l* in
Am 7: 7 on a wall made with a plumb *l*,
7: 7 with a plumb *l* in His hand.
7: 8 And I said, "A plumb *l*."
7: 8 I am setting a plumb *l* In the
7:17 shall be divided by survey *l*;
Zech 1:16 And a surveyor's *l* shall be
2: 1 a man with a measuring *l* in his
4:10 rejoice to see The plumb *l* in

LINEAGE (6/6) LINE

Gen 19:32 that we may preserve the *l* of
19:34 that we may preserve the *l* of
Neh 7:61 father's house nor their *l*,
9: 2 Then those of Israelite *l*
Dan 9: 1 of the *l* of the Medes, who was
Lk 2: 4 he was of the house and *l* of

LINEN (105/93)

Gen 41:42 him in garments of fine *l* and
Ex 25: 4 and scarlet thread, fine *l*,
26: 1 ten curtains of fine woven *l*
26:31 thread, and fine woven *l*.
26:36 thread, and fine woven *l*,
27: 9 court made of fine woven *l*,
27:16 thread, and fine woven *l*,
27:18 cubits, made of fine woven *l*,
28: 5 and scarlet thread, and fine *l*,
28: 6 thread, and fine woven *l*,
28: 8 thread, and fine woven *l*.
28:15 thread, and fine woven *l*,
28:39 weave the tunic of fine *l*
28:39 shall make the turban of fine *l*,
28:42 And you shall make for them *l*
35: 6 and scarlet thread, fine *l*,
35:23 and scarlet thread, fine *l*,
35:25 and scarlet, and fine *l*.
35:35 and scarlet thread, and fine *l*,
36: 8 ten curtains woven of fine *l*,
36:35 thread, and fine woven *l*;
36:37 thread, and fine woven *l*,
38: 9 court were of fine woven *l*,
38:16 around were of fine woven *l*.
38:18 thread, and of fine woven *l*.
38:23 scarlet thread, and of fine *l*.
39: 2 thread, and of fine woven *l*.
39: 3 scarlet thread and the fine *l*,
39: 5 thread, and of fine woven *l*,
39: 8 thread, and of fine woven *l*.
39:24 scarlet, and of fine woven *l*.
39:27 artistically woven of fine *l*,
39:28 a turban of fine *l*,
39:28 linen, exquisite hats of fine *l*,
39:28 short trousers of fine woven *l*,
39:29 and a sash of fine woven *l* with
Lev 6:10 the priest shall put on his *l*
6:10 and his *l* trousers he shall put
13:47 it is a woolen garment or a *l*
13:48 is in the warp or woof of *l*
13:52 warp or woof, in wool or in *l*,
13:59 in a garment of wool or *l*,
16: 4 He shall put the holy *l* tunic
16: 4 the holy linen tunic and the *l*
16: 4 he shall be girded with a *l*
16: 4 and with the *l* turban he shall
16:23 shall take off the *l* garments
16:32 and put on the *l* clothes, the
19:19 Nor shall a garment of mixed *l*
Deut 22:11 such as wool and *l* mixed
Judg 14:12 then I will give you thirty *l*
14:13 then you shall give me thirty *l*
1 Sam 2:18 wearing a *l* ephod.
22:18 eighty-five men who wore a *l*
2 Sam 6:14 and David was wearing a *l*
1 Chr 4:21 families of the house of the *l*
15:27 clothed with a robe of fine *l*,
15:27 David also wore a *l* ephod.
2 Chr 2:14 fine *l* and crimson, and to make
3:14 purple, crimson, and fine *l*,
5:12 the altar, clothed in white *l*,
Esth 1: 6 There were white and blue *l*
1: 6 fastened with cords of fine *l*
8:15 of gold and a garment of fine *l*
Prov 7:16 coverings of Egyptian *l*.
31:22 Her clothing is fine *l* and
31:24 She makes *l* garments and sells
Isa 3:23 and the mirrors; The fine *l*,
Jer 13: 1 Go and get yourself a *l* sash,
Ezek 9: 2 among them was clothed with *l*
9: 3 to the man clothed with *l*,
9:11 then, the man clothed with *l*,
10: 2 spoke to the man clothed with *l*,
10: 6 commanded the man clothed in *l*,
10: 7 of the man clothed with *l*,
16:10 I clothed you with fine *l* and
16:13 your clothing was of fine *l*,
27: 7 Fine embroidered *l* from Egypt
27:16 purple, embroidery, fine *l*,
44:17 that they shall put on *l*
44:18 They shall have *l* turbans on
44:18 turbans on their heads and *l*
Dan 10: 5 a certain man clothed in *l*,
12: 6 said to the man clothed in *l*,
12: 7 I heard the man clothed in *l*,
Hos 2: 5 and my water, My wool and my *l*,
2: 9 will take back My wool and My *l*,
Mt 27:59 he wrapped it in a clean *l*
Mk 14:51 having a *l* cloth thrown around
14:52 and he left the *l* cloth and fled
15:46 Then he bought fine *l*,
15:46 down, and wrapped Him in the *l*.
Lk 16:19 clothed in purple and fine *l*
23:53 took it down, wrapped it in *l*,
24:12 he saw the *l* cloths lying by
Jn 19:40 and bound it in strips of *l*
20: 5 saw the *l* cloths lying there;
20: 6 and he saw the *l* cloths lying
20: 7 not lying with the *l* cloths,
Rev 15: 6 clothed in pure bright *l*,
18:12 fine *l* and purple, silk and
18:16 city that was clothed in fine *l*,
19: 8 granted to be arrayed in fine *l*,
19: 8 for the fine *l* is the righteous
19:14 in heaven, clothed in fine *l*,

LINES (2/2) LINE

2 Sam 8: 2 With two *l* he measured off
Ps 16: 6 The *l* have fallen to me in

LINGER (3/3) LINGERED

2 Sam 18:14 I cannot *l* with you." And he
Prov 23:30 Those who *l* long at the wine,
Isa 46:13 My salvation shall not *l*.

LINGERED (4/4) LINGER

Gen 19:16 And while he *l*, the men
43:10 "For if we had not *l*,
Lk 1:21 and marveled that he *l* so long
2:43 the Boy Jesus *l* behind in

LINK (1/1)

Song 4: 9 With one *l* of your necklace.

LINTEL (4/4)

Ex 12: 7 the two doorposts and on the *l*
12:22 and strike the *l* and the two
12:23 He sees the blood on the *l* and
1 Ki 6:31 the *l* and doorposts were

LINUS (1/1)

2 Tim 4:21 you, as well as Pudens, *L*,

LION (97/82) LION'S, LIONESS, LIONS

Gen 49: 9 bows down, he lies down as a *l*;
49: 9 down as a lion; And as a *l*,
Num 23:24 And lifts itself up like a *l*;
24: 9 bows down, he lies down as a *l*;
24: 9 down as a lion; And as a *l*,
Deut 33:20 enlarges Gad; He dwells as a *l*,
Judg 14: 5 a young *l* came roaring against
14: 6 and he tore the *l* apart as one
14: 8 to see the carcass of the *l*.
14: 8 were in the carcass of the *l*.
14: 9 out of the carcass of the *l*.
14:18 And what is stronger than a *l*?
1 Sam 17:34 and when a *l* or a bear came and
17:36 servant has killed both *l*
17:37 me from the paw of the *l* and
2 Sam 17:10 heart is like the heart of a *l*,
23:20 had gone down and killed a *l*
1 Ki 13:24 a *l* met him on the road and
13:24 The *l* also stood by the corpse.
13:25 and the *l* standing by the
13:26 has delivered him to the *l*,
13:28 and the donkey and the *l*
13:28 The *l* had not eaten the corpse
20:36 a *l* shall kill you." And as
20:36 a *l* found him and killed him.
1 Chr 11:22 had gone down and killed a *l*
Job 4:10 The roaring of the *l*,
4:10 The voice of the fierce *l*,
4:11 The old *l* perishes for lack of
10:16 You hunt me like a fierce *l*,
28: 8 Nor has the fierce *l* passed
38:39 you hunt the prey for the *l*,
Ps 7: 2 Lest they tear me like a *l*,
10: 9 as a *l* in his den; He lies in
17:12 As a *l* is eager to tear his
17:12 And like a young *l* lurking in
22:13 Like a raging and roaring *l*.
91:13 You shall tread upon the *l* and
91:13 The young *l* and the serpent
Prov 19:12 is like the roaring of a *l*,
20: 2 is like the roaring of a *l*;
22:13 There is a *l* outside! I shall
26:13 There is a *l* in the road!
26:13 a lion in the road! A fierce *l*
28: 1 the righteous are bold as a *l*.
28:15 Like a roaring *l* and a
30:30 A *l*, which is mighty among
Eccl 9: 4 dog is better than a dead *l*.
Isa 5:29 roaring will be like a *l*,
11: 6 The calf and the young *l* and
11: 7 And the *l* shall eat straw like
21: 8 Then he cried, "A *l*,
30: 6 which came the lioness and *l*,
31: 4 As a *l* roars, And a young lion
31: 4 And a young *l* over his prey
35: 9 No *l* shall be there, Nor shall
38:13 until morning—Like a *l*,
65:25 The *l* shall eat straw like the
Jer 2:30 Like a destroying *l*.
4: 7 The *l* has come up from his
5: 6 Therefore a *l* from the forest
12: 8 My heritage is to Me like a *l*
25:38 has left His lair like the *l*;
49:19 he shall come up like a *l* from
50:44 he shall come up like a *l* from
Lam 3:10 Like a *l* in ambush.
Ezek 1:10 of the four had the face of a *l*
10:14 man, the third the face of a *l*,
19: 3 And he became a young *l*;
19: 5 cubs and made him a young *l*.
19: 6 And became a young *l*;
22:25 her midst is like a roaring *l*
32: 2 You are like a young *l* among the
41:19 and the face of a young *l*
Dan 7: 4 "The first was like a *l*,
Hos 5:14 For I will be like a *l* to
5:14 And like a young *l* to the
11:10 He will roar like a *l*.
13: 7 I will be to them like a *l*;
13: 8 I will devour them like a *l*.
Joel 1: 6 teeth are the teeth of a *l*,
1: 6 he has the fangs of a fierce *l*.
Am 3: 4 Will a *l* roar in the forest,
3: 4 Will a young *l* cry out of his
3: 8 A *l* has roared! Who will not
3:12 takes from the mouth of a *l*
5:19 as though a man fled from a *l*,
Mic 5: 8 Like a *l* among the beasts of
5: 8 Like a young *l* among flocks of
Nah 2:11 Where the *l* walked, the
2:12 The *l* tore in pieces enough for
2 Tim 4:17 out of the mouth of the *l*.
1 Pe 5: 8 walks about like a roaring *l*,
Rev 4: 7 living creature was like a *l*,
5: 5 the *L* of the tribe of Judah,
10: 3 as when a *l* roars. When he
13: 2 his mouth like the mouth of a *l*.

LION-LIKE (2/2)

2 Sam 23:20 He had killed two *l* heroes of
1 Chr 11:22 He had killed two *l* heroes of

LION'S (4/4) LION

Gen 49: 9 Judah is a *l* whelp; From the

Deut 33:22 Dan is a *l* whelp; He shall
Ps 22:21 Save Me from the *l* mouth And
Nah 2:11 the lioness and *l* cub, And no

LIONESS (5/5) LION

Num 23:24 Look, a people rises like a *l*,
Job 4:11 And the cubs of the *l* are
Isa 30: 6 From which came the *l* and
Ezek 19: 2 'What is your mother? A *l*:
Nah 2:11 the *l* and lion's cub, And no

LIONESSES (1/1)

Nah 2:12 for his cubs, Killed for his *l*,

LIONS (43/39) LION, LIONS'

2 Sam 1:23 They were stronger than *l*.
1 Ki 7:29 between the frames were *l*,
7:29 Below the *l* and oxen were
7:36 panels he engraved cherubim, *l*,
10:19 and two *l* stood beside the
10:20 Twelve *l* stood there, one on
2 Ki 17:25 therefore the LORD sent *l*
17:26 therefore He has sent *l* among
1 Chr 12: 8 were like the faces of *l*,
2 Chr 9:18 and two *l* stood beside the
9:19 Twelve *l* stood there, one on
Job 4:10 And the teeth of the young *l*
28: 8 The proud *l* have not trodden
38:39 the appetite of the young *l*,
Ps 34:10 The young *l* lack and suffer
35:17 My precious life from the *l*.
57: 4 My soul is among *l*;
58: 6 out the fangs of the young *l*,
104:21 The young *l* roar after their
Isa 5:29 They will roar like young *l*;
15: 9 *L* upon him who escapes from
Jer 2:15 The young *l* roared at him, and
50:17 The *l* have driven him away.
51:38 shall roar together like *l*,
Ezek 19: 2 She lay down among the *l*;
19: 2 Among the young *l* she
19: 6 He roved among the *l*,
38:13 and all their young *l* will say
Dan 6: 7 shall be cast into the den of *l*.
6:12 shall be cast into the den of *l*?
6:16 and cast him into the den of *l*.
6:19 went in haste to the den of *l*.
6:20 able to deliver you from the *l*?
6:24 cast them into the den of *l*—
6:24 and the *l* overpowered them, and
6:27 Daniel from the power of the *l*.
Nah 2:11 is the dwelling of the *l*,
2:11 feeding place of the young *l*,
2:13 sword shall devour your young *l*;
Zeph 3: 3 in her midst are roaring *l*;
Zech 11: 3 is the sound of roaring *l*!
Heb 11:33 stopped the mouths of *l*,
Rev 9:17 were like the heads of *l*;

LIONS' (4/4) LIONS

Song 4: 8 From the *l* dens, From the
Jer 51:38 shall growl like *l* whelps.
Dan 6:22 angel and shut the *l* mouths,
Rev 9: 8 their teeth were like *l* teeth.

LIP (2/2) LIPS

Ps 22: 7 They shoot out the *l*,
Prov 12:19 The truthful *l* shall be

LIPS (118/117) LIP

Ex 6:12 for I am of uncircumcised *l*?
6:30 I am of uncircumcised *l*,
Lev 5: 4 thoughtlessly with his *l* to
Num 30: 6 by a rash utterance from her *l*
30: 8 and what she uttered with her *l*,
30:12 whatever proceeded from her *l*
Deut 23:23 which has gone from your *l* you
1 Sam 1:13 only her *l* moved, but her voice
2 Ki 19:28 And My bridle in your *l*,
Job 2:10 this Job did not sin with his *l*.
8:21 And your *l* with rejoicing.
11: 5 And open His *l* against you,
13: 6 And heed the pleadings of my *l*.
15: 6 your own *l* testify against you.
16: 5 And the comfort of my *l* would
23:12 from the commandment of His *l*;
27: 4 My *l* will not speak wickedness,
32:20 I must open my *l* and answer.
33: 3 My *l* utter pure knowledge.
Ps 12: 2 With flattering *l* and a
12: 3 LORD cut off all flattering *l*,
12: 4 Our *l* are our own; Who is
16: 4 take up their names on my *l*.
17: 1 which is not from deceitful *l*.
17: 4 of men, By the word of Your *l*,
21: 2 withheld the request of his *l*.
31:18 Let the lying *l* be put to
34:13 And your *l* from speaking
40: 9 Indeed, I do not restrain my *l*,
45: 2 Grace is poured upon Your *l*;
51:15 O Lord, open my *l*,
59: 7 Swords are in their *l*;
59:12 mouth and the words of their *l*,
63: 3 My *l* shall praise You.
63: 5 shall praise You with joyful *l*.
66:14 Which my *l* have uttered And my
71:23 My *l* shall greatly rejoice when
89:34 word that has gone out of My *l*.
106:33 that he spoke rashly with his *l*.
119:13 With my *l* I have declared All
119:171 My *l* shall utter praise,
120: 2 from lying *l* And from a
140: 3 of asps is under their *l*.
140: 9 Let the evil of their *l* cover
141: 3 watch over the door of my *l*.
Prov 4:24 And put perverse *l* far from
5: 2 And your *l* may keep knowledge.
5: 3 For the *l* of an immoral woman
7:21 With her flattering *l* she
8: 6 And from the opening of my *l*
8: 7 is an abomination to my *l*.
10:13 Wisdom is found on the *l* of him
10:18 hides hatred has lying *l*,
10:19 But he who restrains his *l* is
10:21 The *l* of the righteous feed
10:32 The *l* of the righteous know
12:13 by the transgression of his *l*,
12:22 Lying *l* are an abomination to
13: 3 But he who opens wide his *l*
14: 3 But the *l* of the wise will
14: 7 do not perceive in him the *l*
15: 7 The *l* of the wise disperse
16:10 Divination is on the *l* of the
16:13 Righteous *l* are the delight of
16:21 And sweetness of the *l*
16:23 And adds learning to his *l*.
16:27 And it is on his *l* like a
16:30 He purses his *l* and brings
17: 4 evildoer gives heed to false *l*;
17: 7 Much less lying *l* to a prince.
17:28 When he shuts his *l*,
18: 6 A fool's *l* enter into
18: 7 And his *l* are the snare of
18:20 From the produce of his *l* he
19: 1 one who is perverse in his *l*,
20:15 But the *l* of knowledge are a
20:19 one who flatters with his *l*.
22:11 heart And has grace on his *l*,
22:18 them all be fixed upon your *l*,
23:16 being will rejoice When your *l*
24: 2 And their *l* talk of
24:26 a right answer kisses the *l*.
24:28 would you deceive with your *l*?
26:23 Fervent *l* with a wicked heart
26:24 hates, disguises it with his *l*,
27: 2 A stranger, and not your own *l*.
Eccl 10:12 But the *l* of a fool shall
Song 4: 3 Your *l* are like a strand of
4:11 Your *l*, O my spouse,
5:13 His *l* are lilies, Dripping
7: 9 Moving gently the *l* of
Isa 6: 5 I am a man of unclean *l*,
6: 5 midst of a people of unclean *l*;
6: 7 this has touched your *l*;
11: 4 And with the breath of His *l*
28:11 For with stammering *l* and
29:13 And honor Me with their *l*,
30:27 His *l* are full of indignation,
37:29 And My bridle in your *l*,
57:19 "I create the fruit of the *l*:
59: 3 Your *l* have spoken lies,
Jer 17:16 You know what came out of my *l*;
Lam 3:62 The *l* of my enemies And their
Ezek 24:17 your feet; do not cover your *l*,
24:22 you shall not cover your *l* nor
36: 3 and you are taken up by the *l*
Dan 10:16 of the sons of men touched my *l*;
Hos 14: 2 offer the sacrifices of our *l*.
Mic 3: 7 they shall all cover their *l*;
Hab 3:16 My *l* quivered at the voice;
Mal 2: 6 was not found on his *l*.
2: 7 For the *l* of a priest should
Mt 15: 8 honor Me with their *l*,
Mk 7: 6 honors Me with their *l*,
Rom 3:13 of asps is under their *l*'
1 Cor 14:21 other tongues and other *l*
Heb 13:15 that is, the fruit of our *l*,
1 Pe 3:10 And his *l* from speaking

LIQUID (3/3)

Ex 30:23 five hundred shekels of *l*
Song 5: 5 My fingers with *l* myrrh, On
5:13 Dripping *l* myrrh.

LIQUOR (KJV) See JUICES

LISTED (5/5)

Num 11:26 Now they were among those *l*,
1 Chr 5: 1 so that the genealogy is not *l*
7: 5 *l* by their genealogies,
7: 7 and they were *l* by their
2 Chr 31:19 priests and to all who were *l*

LISTEN (112/109) LISTENED, LISTENING, LISTENS

Gen 4:23 *l* to my speech! For I have
21:12 *l* to her voice; for in Isaac
23:15 *l* to me; the land is worth
42:22 the boy'; and you would not *l*?
49: 2 And *l* to Israel your father.
Ex 4: 1 they will not believe me or *l*
4: 9 or *l* to your voice, that you
18:19 *L* now to my voice; I will give
Num 23:18 and hear! *L* to me, son of
Deut 1:43 to you; yet you would not *l*,
1:45 but the LORD would not *l* to
3:26 and would not *l* to me. So the
4: 1 *l* to the statutes and the
7:12 because you *l* to these
13: 3 you shall not *l* to the words of
13: 8 shall not consent to him or *l*
23: 5 the LORD your God would not *l*
27: 9 saying, "Take heed and *l*,
Josh 24:10 But I would not *l* to Balaam;
Judg 2:17 Yet they would not *l* to their
9: 7 *L* to me, you men of Shechem,
9: 7 That God may *l* to you!
20:13 of Benjamin would not *l* to the
Ruth 2: 8 Boaz said to Ruth, "You will *l*,
1 Sam 24: 9 Why do you *l* to the words of men
2 Sam 13:16 But he would not *l* to her.
1 Ki 8:28 and *l* to the cry and the prayer
8:52 to *l* to them whenever they call
12:15 So the king did not *l* to the
12:16 saw that the king did not *l* to
20: 8 Do not *l* or consent."
22:13 spoke to him, saying, "Now *l*,
2 Ki 18:31 Do not *l* to Hezekiah; for thus
18:32 But do not *l* to Hezekiah, lest
2 Chr 6:19 and *l* to the cry and the prayer
10:15 So the king did not *l* to the
10:16 saw that the king did not *l*
18:12 spoke to him, saying, "Now *l*,
20:15 And he said, "*L*, all you of
24:19 them, but they would not *l*.
33:10 people, but they would not *l*.
Neh 9:30 Yet they would not *l*;
Esth 3: 4 to him daily and he would not *l*
Job 13:17 *L* carefully to my speech,
21: 2 *L* carefully to my speech, And
32:10 *L* to me, I also will declare my
33: 1 And *l* to all my words.
33:31 *l* to me; Hold your peace, and
33:33 *l* to me; Hold your peace, and
34:10 Therefore *l* to me, you men of
34:16 *l* to the sound of my words:
34:34 Wise men who *l* to me:
35:13 Surely God will not *l* to empty
37:14 *L* to this, O Job; Stand still
42: 4 *L*, please, and let me speak;
Ps 34:11 *l* to me; I will teach you the
45:10 *L*, O daughter, Consider and
81: 8 if you will *l* to Me!
81:13 that My people would *l* to Me,
Prov 7:24 *l* to me, my children;
8: 6 *L*, for I will speak of
8:32 *l* to me, my children,
13: 1 But a scoffer does not *l* to
19:20 *L* to counsel and receive
23:22 *L* to your father who begot you,
Song 8:13 The companions *l* for your
Isa 28:23 *L* and hear my speech.
32: 3 ears of those who hear will *l*.
36:16 Do not *l* to Hezekiah; for thus
42:23 Who will *l* and hear for the
46: 3 *L* to Me, O house of Jacob,
46:12 *L* to Me, you stubborn-hearted,
48:12 *L* to Me, O Jacob, And Israel,
49: 1 '*L*, O coastlands, to Me,
51: 1 *L* to Me, you who follow after
51: 4 *L* to Me, My people; And give
51: 7 *L* to Me, you who know
55: 2 *L* carefully to Me, and eat
Jer 6:17 *L* to the sound of the trumpet!'
6:17 But they said, 'We will not *l*.
8:19 *L*! The voice, The cry of the
11:11 I will not *l* to them.
18:19 And *l* to the voice of those
23:16 Do not *l* to the words of the
26: 3 Perhaps everyone will *l* and turn
26: 4 If you will not *l* to Me, to walk
27: 9 Therefore do not *l* to your
27:14 Therefore do not *l* to the words
27:16 Do not *l* to the words of your
27:17 Do not *l* to them; serve the king
29: 8 nor *l* to your dreams which you
29:12 and I will *l* to you.
36:25 but he would not *l* to them.
37:14 But he did not *l* to him.
38:15 you will not *l* to me."
44: 5 But they did not *l* or incline
44:16 we will not *l* to you!
Ezek 3: 7 the house of Israel will not *l*
3: 7 because they will not *l* to Me;
13:19 your lying to My people who *l*
Dan 9:19 *l* and act! Do not delay for
Mic 1: 2 Hear, all you peoples! *L*,
Zech 7:13 called out and I would not *l*,
Mk 4: 3 *L*! Behold, a sower went out to
Jn 8:43 Because you are not able to *l*
9:27 you already, and you did not *l*.
10:20 Why do you *l* to Him?"
Acts 4:19 right in the sight of God to *l*
7: 2 said, "Brethren and fathers, *l*:
13:16 Israel, and you who fear God, *l*:
15:13 'Men and brethren, *l* to me:
Jas 2: 5 *L*, my beloved brethren:

LISTENED (26/26) LISTEN

Gen 23:16 And Abraham *l* to Ephron;
30:17 And God *l* to Leah, and she
30:22 and God *l* to her and opened her
37:27 our flesh." And his brothers *l*.
Num 21: 3 And the LORD *l* to the voice of
Deut 9:19 But the LORD *l* to me at that
13:18 because you have *l* to the voice
18:14 which you will dispossess *l* to

Judg 13: 9 And God *l* to the voice of
1 Ki 20:25 And he *l* to their voice and
2 Ki 13: 4 and the LORD *l* to him; for He
2 Chr 24:17 And the king *l* to them.
30:20 And the LORD *l* to Hezekiah and
Job 29:21 Men *l* to me and waited,
32:11 I *l* to your reasonings, while
Isa 21: 7 And he *l* earnestly with great
Jer 8: 6 I *l* and heard, But they do
25: 3 speaking, but you have not *l*.
25: 4 but you have not *l* nor inclined
25: 7 Yet you have not *l* to Me," says
32:33 yet they have not *l* to receive
Ezek 3: 6 they would have *l* to you.
Mal 3:16 And the LORD *l* and heard
Acts 15:12 multitude kept silent and *l* to
22:22 And they *l* to him until this
27:21 you should have *l* to me, and

LISTENING (7/7) LISTEN

Gen 18:10 (Sarah was *l* in the tent door
27: 5 Now Rebekah was *l* when Isaac
2 Sam 20:17 And he answered, "I am *l*.
Job 9:16 not believe that He was *l* to
Prov 19:27 Cease *l* to instruction, my son,
Lk 2:46 both *l* to them and asking them
Acts 16:25 and the prisoners were *l* to

LISTENS (4/4) LISTEN

Prov 1:33 But whoever *l* to me will dwell
8:34 Blessed is the man who *l* to me,
17: 4 A liar *l* eagerly to a spiteful
Jer 16:12 so that no one *l* to Me.

LISTETH (KJV) See WISHES

LISTING (2/2)

Ezra 2:62 These sought their *l* among
Neh 7:64 These sought their *l* among

LISTLESS (1/1)

Job 23: 2 My hand is *l* because of my

LIT (4/4) LIGHT

Ex 40:25 and he *l* the lamps before the
Ps 77:18 The lightnings *l* up the world;
Lk 8:16 when he has *l* a lamp, covers it
11:33 when he has *l* a lamp, puts it

LITERATE (2/2)

Isa 29:11 men deliver to one who is *l*,
29:12 And he says, "I am not *l*.

LITERATURE (2/2)

Dan 1: 4 might teach the language and *l*
1:17 knowledge and skill in all *l*

LITTERS (1/1)

Isa 66:20 horses and in chariots and in *l*,

LITTLE (231/215)

Gen 18: 4 Please let a *l* water be brought,
19:20 and it is a *l* one; please let
19:20 me escape there (is it not a *l*
24:17 Please let me drink a *l* water
24:43 Please give me a *l* water from
30:30 you had before I came was *l*,
34:29 All their *l* ones and their
35:16 And when there was but a *l*
43: 2 'Go back, buy us a *l* food."
43: 8 both we and you and also our *l*
43:11 a *l* balm and a little honey,
43:11 a little balm and a *l* honey,
44:25 Go back and buy us a *l* food.'
45:19 of the land of Egypt for your *l*
46: 5 their *l* ones, and their wives,
47:24 and as food for your *l* ones.
48: 7 when there was but a *l*
50: 8 Only their *l* ones, their
50:21 will provide for you and your *l*
Ex 10:10 you when I let you and your *l*
10:24 Let your *l* ones also go with
16:18 and he who gathered *l* had no
23:30 *L* by little I will drive them
23:30 Little by *l* I will drive them
Lev 11:17 the *l* owl, the fisher owl, and
Num 14:31 But your *l* ones, whom you said
16:27 and their *l* children.
31: 9 with their *l* ones, and took as
31:17 kill every male among the *l*
32:16 and cities for our *l* ones,
32:17 and our *l* ones will dwell in
32:24 Build cities for your *l* ones and
32:26 Our *l* ones, our wives, our
Deut 1:39 Moreover your *l* ones and your
2:34 and *l* ones of every city;
3:19 your *l* ones, and your livestock
7:22 out those nations before you *l*
7:22 nations before you little by *l*;
14:16 the *l* owl, the screech owl, the
20:14 the *l* ones, the livestock, and
28:38 out to the field but gather *l*
29:11 your *l* ones and your wives—also
31:12 men and women and *l* ones, and
Josh 1:14 your *l* ones, and your livestock
8:35 the *l* ones, and the strangers
Judg 4:19 Please give me a *l* water to
18:21 and put the *l* ones, the
Ruth 2: 7 though she rested a *l* in the
1 Sam 2:19 his mother used to make him a *l*
14:29 because I tasted a *l* of this
14:43 I only tasted a *l* honey with the
15:17 When you were *l* in your own
20:35 and a *l* lad was with him.
22:15 of all this, *l* or much."
25:36 *l* or much, until morning light.
2 Sam 12: 3 except one *l* ewe lamb which he
12: 8 And if that had been too *l*,
15:22 and all his men and all the *l*
16: 1 When David was a *l* past the top
19:36 Your servant will go a *l* way
1 Ki 3: 7 but I am a *l* child; I do not
11:17 Hadad was still a *l* child.
12:10 My *l* finger shall be thicker
17:10 Please bring me a *l* water in a
17:12 and a *l* oil in a jar; and see,
20:27 before them like two *l* flocks
2 Ki 5:14 restored like the flesh of a *l*
10:18 to them, "Ahab served Baal a *l*,
19:26 their inhabitants had *l* power;
2 Chr 10:10 My *l* finger shall be thicker
20:13 with their *l* ones, their wives,
31:18 their *l* ones and their wives,
Ezra 8:21 the right way for us and our *l*
9: 8 And now for a *l* while grace has
Esth 3:13 *l* children and women, in one
8:11 both *l* children and women, and
Job 10:20 that I may take a *l* comfort,
21:11 They send forth their *l* ones
24:24 They are exalted for a *l* while,
36: 2 "Bear with me a *l*,
Ps 2:12 His wrath is kindled but a *l*.
8: 5 For You have made him a *l* lower
37:10 For yet a *l* while and the
37:16 A *l* that a righteous man has
65:12 And the *l* hills rejoice on
68:27 There is *l* Benjamin, their
72: 3 And the *l* hills, by
114: 4 The *l* hills like lambs.
114: 6 O *l* hills, like lambs?
137: 9 who takes and dashes Your *l*
Prov 6:10 A *l* sleep, a little slumber,
6:10 a *l* slumber, A little folding
6:10 A *l* folding of the hands to
10:20 of the wicked is worth *l*.
15:16 Better is a *l* with the fear of
16: 8 Better is a *l* with
24:33 A *l* sleep, a little slumber,
24:33 a *l* slumber, A little folding
24:33 A *l* folding of the hands to
30:24 are four things which are *l*
Eccl 5:12 Whether he eats *l* or much;
9:14 There was a *l* city with few
10: 1 So does a *l* folly to one
Song 1: 8 And feed your *l* goats
2:15 The *l* foxes that spoil the
8: 8 We have a *l* sister, And she
Isa 10:25 For yet a very *l* while and the
11: 6 And a *l* child shall lead them.
26:20 for a *l* moment, Until the
28:10 line, line upon line, Here a *l*,
28:10 Here a little, there a *l*."
28:13 line, line upon line, Here a *l*,
28:13 Here a little, there a *l*,"
29:17 Is it not yet a very *l* while
37:27 their inhabitants had *l* power;
40:15 lifts up the isles as a very *l*
54: 8 With a *l* wrath I hid My face
60:22 A *l* one shall become a
63:18 have possessed it but a *l*
Jer 48: 4 Her *l* ones have caused a cry
51:33 Yet a *l* while And the time of
Ezek 9: 6 maidens and *l* children and
11:16 yet I shall be a *l* sanctuary
16:47 but, as if that were too *l*,
34:18 Is it too *l* for you to have
Dan 7: 8 a *l* one, coming up among them,
8: 9 out of one of them came a *l*
11:34 they shall be aided with a *l*
Hos 1: 4 For in a *l* while I will
8:10 And they shall sorrow a *l*,
Am 6:11 And the *l* house into pieces.
Mic 5: 2 Though you are *l* among the
Hag 1: 6 have sown much, and bring in *l*;
1: 9 but indeed it came to *l*;
2: 6 Once more (it is a *l* while) I
Zech 1:15 For I was a *l* angry, And they
13: 7 will turn My hand against the *l*
Mt 6:30 O you of *l* faith?
8:26 O you of *l* faith?" Then He
10:42 whoever gives one of these *l*
14:31 O you of *l* faith, why did you
15:26 bread and throw it to the *l*
15:27 yet even the *l* dogs eat the
15:34 'Seven, and a few *l* fish."
16: 8 O you of *l* faith, why do you
18: 2 Then Jesus called a *l* child to
18: 3 are converted and become as *l*
18: 4 humbles himself as this *l*
18: 5 Whoever receives one *l* child
18: 6 whoever causes one of these *l*
18:10 do not despise one of these *l*
18:14 in heaven that one of these *l*
19:13 Then *l* children were brought to
19:14 Let the *l* children come to Me,
26:39 He went a *l* farther and fell on
26:73 And a *l* later those who stood by
Mk 1:19 When He had gone a *l* farther
4:36 And other *l* boats were also
5:23 My *l* daughter lies at the point
5:41 *L* girl, I say to you, arise."
7:27 bread and throw it to the *l*
7:28 yet even the *l* dogs under the
9:36 Then He took a *l* child and set
9:37 receives one of these *l*
9:42 whoever causes one of these *l*
10:13 Then they brought *l* children to
10:14 Let the *l* children come to Me,
10:15 the kingdom of God as a *l*
14:35 He went a *l* farther, and fell on
14:70 And a *l* later those who stood
Lk 5: 3 and asked him to put out a *l*
7:47 But to whom *l* is forgiven, the
7:47 is forgiven, the same loves *l*.
8:54 saying, "*L* girl, arise."
9:47 took a *l* child and set him by
9:48 Whoever receives this *l* child in
12:28 O you of *l* faith?
12:32 *l* flock, for it is your
17: 2 he should offend one of these *l*
18:16 Let the *l* children come to Me,
18:17 the kingdom of God as a *l*
19:17 you were faithful in a very *l*,
22:58 And after a *l* while another saw
Jn 6: 7 every one of them may have a *l*.
7:33 I shall be with you a *l* while
12:35 A *l* while longer the light is
13:33 *L* children, I shall be with you
13:33 I shall be with you a *l* while
14:19 A *l* while longer and the world
16:16 A *l* while, and you will not see
16:16 and again a *l* while, and you
16:17 A *l* while, and you will not see
16:17 and again a *l* while, and you
16:18 A *l* while'? We do not know what
16:19 A *l* while, and you will not see
16:19 and again a *l* while, and you
21: 8 other disciples came in the *l*
Acts 5:34 the apostles outside for a *l*
20:12 and they were not a *l*
27:28 and when they had gone a *l*
1 Cor 5: 6 Do you not know that a *l* leaven
2 Cor 8:15 and he who gathered *l* had
11: 1 you would bear with me in a *l*
11:16 fool, that I also may boast a *l*.
Gal 4:19 My *l* children, for whom I labor
5: 9 A *l* leaven leavens the whole
1 Tim 4: 8 For bodily exercise profits a *l*,
5:23 but use a *l* wine for your
Heb 2: 7 You have made him a *l*
2: 9 who was made a *l* lower than the
10:37 For yet a *l* while, And He
Jas 3: 5 Even so the tongue is a *l* member
3: 5 See how great a forest a *l* fire
4:14 a vapor that appears for a *l*
1 Pe 1: 6 though now for a *l* while, if
1 Jn 2: 1 My *l* children, these things I
2:12 *l* children, Because your sins
2:13 *l* children, Because you have
2:18 *L* children, it is the last hour
2:28 *l* children, abide in Him, that
3: 7 *L* children, let no one deceive
3:18 My *l* children, let us not love
4: 4 *l* children, and have overcome
5:21 *L* children, keep yourselves from
Rev 3: 8 for you have a *l* strength, have
6:11 them that they should rest a *l*
10: 2 He had a *l* book open in his
10: 8 take the *l* book which is open
10: 9 Give me the *l* book." And he
10:10 Then I took the *l* book out of
20: 3 he must be released for a *l*

LIVE (272/254) LIFE, LIVED, LIVES, LIVING

Gen 3:22 and eat, and *l* forever"—
12:12 me, but they will let you *l*.
12:13 and that I may *l* because of
17:18 that Ishmael might *l* before
19:20 one?) and my soul shall *l*."
20: 7 pray for you and you shall *l*.
26: 2 *l* in the land of which I shall
27:40 By your sword you shall *l*,
31:32 your gods, do not let him *l*.
42: 2 that we may *l* and not die."
42:18 the third day, "Do this and *l*,
43: 8 that we may *l* and not die, both
45: 3 Joseph; does my father still *l*?
47:19 that we may *l* and not die, that
Ex 1:16 a daughter, then she shall *l*.
2:21 Then Moses was content to *l* with
19:13 man or beast, he shall not *l*.
21:35 then they shall sell the *l* ox
22:18 not permit a sorceress to *l*.
33:20 for no man shall see Me, and *l*.
Lev 16:20 he shall bring the *l* goat.
16:21 his hands on the head of the *l*
18: 5 he shall *l* by them: I am the
25:35 that he may *l* with you.
25:36 that your brother may *l* with
Num 4:19 that they may *l* and not die
14:21 'but truly, as I *l*, all the
14:28 "Say to them, 'As I *l*,
21: 8 when he looks at it, shall *l*.
22:33 you by now, and let her *l*.
24:23 Alas! Who shall *l* when God does
Deut 2: 4 who *l* in Seir; and they will be
4: 1 you to observe, that you may *l*,

L

4:10 to fear Me all the days they *l*
4:33 fire, as you have heard, and *l*?
4:42 one of these cities he might *l*:
5:33 that you may *l* and that it
8: 1 that you may *l* and multiply,
8: 3 you know that man shall not *l*
12: 1 all the days that you *l* on the
12:19 the Levite as long as you *l* in
16:20 that you may *l* and inherit the
19: 4 who flees there, that he may *l*:
19: 5 to one of these cities and *l*;
30: 6 all your soul, that you may *l*.
30:16 that you may *l* and multiply;
30:19 you and your descendants may *l*;
31:13 your God as long as you *l* in
32:40 And say, "As I *l* forever,
33: 6 Let Reuben *l*, and not die,
Josh 6:17 Only Rahab the harlot shall *l*,
9:15 with them to let them *l*;
9:20 do to them: We will let them *l*,
9:21 said to them, "Let them *l*,
Judg 8:19 lives, if you had let them *l*,
1 Sam 10:24 and said, "Long *l* the king!"
20:14 of the LORD while I still *l*,
2 Sam 1:10 I was sure that he could not *l*
11:11 to lie with my wife? As you *l*,
12:22 to me, that the child may *l*?
14:19 answered and said, "As you *l*,
16:16 Long *l* the king! Long live the
16:16 Long live the king! Long *l* the
19:34 king, "How long have I to *l*,
1 Ki 1:25 Long *l* King Adonijah!'
1:31 Let my lord King David *l*
1:34 Long *l* King Solomon!'
1:39 Long *l* King Solomon!"
8:40 You all the days that they *l*
20:32 says, 'Please let me *l*.'
2 Ki 4: 7 and you and your sons *l* on the
7: 4 they keep us alive, we shall *l*;
10:19 Whoever is missing shall not *l*.
11:12 and said, "Long *l* the king!"
18:32 that you may *l* and not die. But
20: 1 for you shall die, and not *l*.
2 Chr 6:31 in Your ways as long as they *l*
23:11 and said, "Long *l* the king!"
Neh 2: 3 May the king *l* forever! Why
5: 2 grain, that we may eat and *l*.
9:29 he shall *l* by them.' And they
Esth 4:11 golden scepter, that he may *l*.
Job 7:16 I would not *l* forever. Let me
14:14 shall he *l* again? All the
21: 7 Why do the wicked *l* and become
27: 6 not reproach me as long as I *l*.
30: 6 They had to *l* in the clefts
Ps 22:26 Let your heart *l* forever!
49: 9 That he should continue to *l*
55:23 and deceitful men shall not *l*
63: 4 I will bless You while I *l*;
69:25 Let no one *l* in their tents.
69:32 seek God, your hearts shall *l*.
72:15 And He shall *l*; And the
89:48 What man can *l* and not see
104:33 to the LORD as long as I *l*;
116: 2 call upon Him as long as I *l*.
118:17 I shall not die, but *l*,
119:17 That I may *l* and keep Your
119:77 come to me, that I may *l*;
119:116 to Your word, that I may *l*;
119:144 me understanding, and I shall *l*.
119:175 Let my soul *l*, and it shall
146: 2 While I *l* I will praise the
Prov 4: 4 Keep my commands, and *l*.
7: 2 Keep my commands and *l*,
9: 6 Forsake foolishness and *l*,
15:27 But he who hates bribes will *l*.
Eccl 9: 3 in their hearts while they *l*,
9: 9 *L* joyfully with the wife whom
Isa 6: 6 having in his hand a *l* coal
26:14 are dead, they will not *l*;
26:19 Your dead shall *l*;
38: 1 for you shall die and not *l*.
38:16 LORD, by these things men *l*;
38:16 will restore me and make me *l*.
49:18 and come to you. As I *l*,
55: 3 Hear, and your soul shall *l*;
65:20 shall an infant from there *l*
Jer 21: 9 who besiege you, he shall *l*,
22:24 "As I *l*, says the LORD,
27:12 him and his people, and *l*!
27:17 and *l*! Why should this city be
35: 7 that you may *l* many days in the
38: 2 over to the Chaldeans shall *l*;
38: 2 a prize to him, and he shall *l*.'
38:17 princes, then your soul shall *l*;
38:17 and you and your house shall *l*.
38:20 with you, and your soul shall *l*.
46:18 As I *l*," says the King,
Lam 4:20 Under his shadow We shall *l*
Ezek 3:21 he shall surely *l* because he
5:11 'Therefore, as I *l*,' says the
13:19 people alive who should not *l*,
14:16 three men were in it, as I *l*,
14:18 three men were in it, as I *l*,
14:20 and Job were in it, as I *l*,
16: 6 *L*!' Yes, I said to you in your
16: 6 you in your blood, '*L*!'
16:48 As I *l*," says the Lord GOD,
17:16 As I *l*,' says the Lord GOD,
17:19 says the Lord GOD: "As I *l*,
18: 3 As I *l*," says the Lord GOD,
18: 9 He shall surely *l*!" Says the
18:13 taken increase—Shall he then *l*?
18:13 He shall not *l*! If he has
18:17 He shall surely *l*!
18:19 them, he shall surely *l*.
18:21 and right, he shall surely *l*;
18:22 which he has done, he shall *l*.
18:23 should turn from his ways and *l*?
18:24 wicked man does, shall he *l*?
18:28 he committed, he shall surely *l*;
18:32 Therefore turn and *l*!"
20: 3 come to inquire of Me? As I *l*,
20:11 he shall *l* by them.'
20:13 he shall *l* by them'; and they
20:21 he shall *l* by them'; but they
20:25 by which they could not *l*;
20:31 you, O house of Israel? As I *l*,
20:33 As I *l*," says the Lord GOD,
33:10 away in them, how can we then *l*?
33:11 "Say to them: 'As I *l*,
33:11 wicked turn from his way and *l*.
33:12 the righteous be able to *l*
33:13 that he shall surely *l*,
33:15 iniquity, he shall surely *l*;
33:16 and right; he shall surely *l*.
33:19 he shall *l* because of it.
33:27 says the Lord GOD: "As I *l*,
34: 8 As I *l*," says the Lord GOD,
35: 6 "therefore, as I *l*,
35:11 "therefore, as I *l*,
37: 3 "Son of man, can these bones *l*?
37: 5 enter into you, and you shall *l*.
37: 6 breath in you; and you shall *l*.
37: 9 on these slain, that they may *l*.
37:14 Spirit in you, and you shall *l*,
39: 6 on Magog and on those who *l* in
47: 9 wherever the rivers go, will *l*.
47: 9 and everything will *l* wherever
Dan 2: 4 *l* forever! Tell your servants
3: 9 'O king, *l* forever!
5:10 *l* forever! Do not let your
6: 6 'King Darius, *l* forever!
6:21 'O king, *l* forever!
Hos 6: 2 That we may *l* in His sight.
Am 5: 4 of Israel: "Seek Me and *l*;
5: 6 Seek the LORD and *l*,
5:14 and not evil, That you may *l*;
Jon 4: 3 better for me to die than to *l*!
4: 8 better for me to die than to *l*.
Hab 2: 4 But the just shall *l* by his
Zeph 2: 9 Therefore, as I *l*,
Zech 1: 5 prophets, do they *l* forever?
10: 9 in far countries; They shall *l*,
13: 3 say to him, 'You shall not *l*,
Mt 4: 4 Man shall not *l* by bread
9:18 Your hand on her and she will *l*.
Mk 5:23 may be healed, and she will *l*.
Lk 4: 4 Man shall not *l* by bread
7:25 are gorgeously appareled and *l*
8:27 nor did he *l* in a house but in
10:28 rightly; do this and you will *l*.
20:38 the living, for all *l* to Him."
Jn 5:25 God; and those who hear will *l*.
6:51 he will *l* forever; and the
6:57 and I *l* because of the Father,
6:57 so he who feeds on Me will *l*
6:58 He who eats this bread will *l*
11:25 though he may die, he shall *l*.
14:19 you will see Me. Because I *l*,
14:19 I live, you will *l* also.
Acts 1:20 And let no one *l* in
7:19 so that they might not *l*.
17:28 for in Him we *l* and move and
22:22 for he is not fit to *l*!"
25:24 out that he was not fit to *l*
28: 4 yet justice does not allow to *l*.
Rom 1:17 The just shall *l* by
6: 2 How shall we who died to sin *l*
6: 8 we believe that we shall also *l*
8: 5 For those who *l* according to the
8: 5 but those who *l* according to
8:12 to *l* according to the flesh.
8:13 For if you *l* according to the
8:13 deeds of the body, you will *l*.
10: 5 does those things shall *l*
12:18 *l* peaceably with all men.
14: 8 For if we *l*, we live to the
14: 8 we *l* to the Lord; and if we
14: 8 whether we *l* or die, we are the
14:11 it is written: As I *l*,
1 Cor 7:12 and she is willing to *l* with
7:13 if he is willing to *l* with her,
8: 6 things, and through whom we *l*.
9:14 who preach the gospel should *l*
2 Cor 4:11 For we who *l* are always
5:15 that those who *l* should live no
5:15 that those who live should *l* no
6: 9 as dying, and behold we *l*;
7: 3 to die together and to *l*
13: 4 but we shall *l* with Him by the
13:11 *l* in peace; and the God of love
Gal 2:14 *l* in the manner of Gentiles and
2:14 do you compel Gentiles to *l* as
2:19 died to the law that I might *l*
2:20 it is no longer I who *l*,
2:20 and the life which I now *l* in
2:20 I now live in the flesh I *l* by
3:11 the just shall *l* by
3:12 who does them shall *l* by
5:25 If we *l* in the Spirit, let us
Eph 6: 3 with you and you may *l*
Phil 1:21 to *l* is Christ, and to die is
1:22 But if I *l* on in the flesh,
1 Th 3: 8 For now we *l*, if you stand
5:10 we should *l* together with Him.
2 Tim 2:11 We shall also *l* with Him.
3:12 and all who desire to *l* godly
Titus 2:12 we should *l* soberly,
Heb 10:38 Now the just shall *l* by
12: 9 to the Father of spirits and *l*?
13:18 in all things desiring to *l*
Jas 4:15 we shall *l* and do this or
1 Pe 2:24 might *l* for righteousness—by
4: 2 that he no longer should *l* the
4: 6 but *l* according to God in the
2 Pe 2: 6 to those who afterward would *l*
2:18 escaped from those who *l* in
1 Jn 4: 9 that we might *l* through Him.
Rev 20: 5 the rest of the dead did not *l*

LIVED (65/65) LIVE

Gen 5: 3 And Adam *l* one hundred and
5: 5 So all the days that Adam *l* were
5: 6 Seth *l* one hundred and five
5: 7 Seth *l* eight hundred and seven
5: 9 Enosh *l* ninety years, and begot
5:10 Enosh *l* eight hundred and
5:12 Cainan *l* seventy years, and
5:13 Cainan *l* eight hundred and
5:15 Mahalalel *l* sixty-five years,
5:16 Mahalalel *l* eight hundred and
5:18 Jared *l* one hundred and
5:19 Jared *l* eight hundred years,
5:21 Enoch *l* sixty-five years, and
5:25 Methuselah *l* one hundred and
5:26 Methuselah *l* seven hundred and
5:28 Lamech *l* one hundred and
5:30 Lamech *l* five hundred and
9:28 And Noah *l* after the flood
11:11 Shem *l* five hundred years, and
11:12 Arphaxad *l* thirty-five years,
11:13 Arphaxad *l* four hundred and
11:14 Salah *l* thirty years, and begot
11:15 Salah *l* four hundred and three
11:16 Eber *l* thirty-four years, and
11:17 Eber *l* four hundred and thirty
11:18 Peleg *l* thirty years, and begot
11:19 Peleg *l* two hundred and nine
11:20 Reu *l* thirty-two years, and
11:21 Reu *l* two hundred and seven
11:22 Serug *l* thirty years, and begot
11:23 Serug *l* two hundred years, and
11:24 Nahor *l* twenty-nine years, and
11:25 Nahor *l* one hundred and
11:26 Now Terah *l* seventy years, and
23: 1 Sarah *l* one hundred and
25: 7 of Abraham's life which he *l*:
47:28 And Jacob *l* in the land of Egypt
50:22 And Joseph *l* one hundred and
Ex 12:40 of the children of Israel who *l*
Num 21: 9 at the bronze serpent, he *l*.
Deut 5:26 of the fire, as we have, and *l*?
Judg 17:12 and *l* in the house of Micah.
2 Sam 19: 6 perceive that if Absalom had *l*
1 Ki 12: 6 father Solomon while he still *l*,
2 Ki 14:17 *l* fifteen years after the death
1 Chr 4:40 for some Hamites formerly *l*
9:16 who *l* in the villages of the
2 Chr 10: 6 father Solomon while he still *l*,
25:25 *l* fifteen years after the death
26: 7 against the Arabians who *l* in
Neh 12:26 These *l* in the days of Joiakim
Job 42:16 After this Job *l* one hundred and
Ezek 37:10 came into them, and they *l*,
Mt 23:30 If we had *l* in the days of our
Lk 2:36 and had *l* with a husband seven
Acts 20:18 in what manner I always *l* among
23: 1 I have *l* in all good conscience
26: 5 sect of our religion I *l* a
Rom 14: 9 end Christ died and rose and *l*
Col 3: 7 once walked when you *l* in them.
Jas 5: 5 You have *l* on the earth in
Rev 13:14 was wounded by the sword and *l*.
18: 7 she glorified herself and *l*
18: 9 who committed fornication and *l*
20: 4 And they *l* and reigned with

LIVELIHOOD (5/5)

Mk 12:44 all that she had, her whole *l*.
Lk 8:43 who had spent all her *l* on
15:12 So he divided to them his *l*.
15:30 who has devoured your *l* with
21: 4 of her poverty put in all the *l*

LIVELY (1/1)

Ex 1:19 for they are *l* and give birth

LIVER (13/13)

Ex 29:13 fatty lobe attached to the *l*,
29:22 fatty lobe attached to the *l*,
Lev 3: 4 fatty lobe attached to the *l*
3:10 fatty lobe attached to the *l*
3:15 fatty lobe attached to the *l*
4: 9 fatty lobe attached to the *l*
7: 4 fatty lobe attached to the *l*
8:16 fatty lobe attached to the *l*,
8:25 fatty lobe attached to the *l*,
9:10 and the fatty lobe from the *l*

9:19 fatty lobe attached to the *l*;
Prov 7:23 Till an arrow struck his *l*.
Ezek 21:21 the images, he looks at the *l*.

LIVES (138/125) LIVE

Gen 9: 3 Every moving thing that *l* shall
45: 7 and to save your *l* by a great
47:25 said, "You have saved our *l*;
Ex 1:14 And they made their *l* bitter
Deut 5:24 with man; yet he still *l*.
8: 3 but man *l* by every word that
Josh 2:13 and deliver our *l* from death."
2:14 Our *l* for yours, if none of you
9:24 were very much afraid for our *l*
Judg 5:18 who jeopardized their *l* to
8:19 of my mother. As the LORD *l*,
18:25 with the *l* of your household!"
Ruth 3:13 as the LORD *l*! Lie down until
1 Sam 1:26 "O my lord! As your soul *l*,
1:28 as long as he *l* he shall be
14:39 "For as the LORD *l*,
14:45 Certainly not! As the LORD *l*,
17:55 Abner said, "As your soul *l*,
19: 6 Saul swore, "As the LORD *l*,
20: 3 as the LORD *l* and as your
20: 3 LORD lives and as your soul *l*,
20:21 and come'—then, as the LORD *l*,
20:31 as long as the son of Jesse *l*
25: 6 you shall say to him who *l* in
25:26 as the LORD *l* and as your
25:26 LORD lives and as your soul *l*,
25:29 and the *l* of your enemies He
25:34 as the LORD God of Israel *l*,
26:10 furthermore, "As the LORD *l*,
26:16 is not good. As the LORD *l*,
28:10 saying, "As the LORD *l*,
29: 6 him, "Surely, as the LORD *l*,
2 Sam 1:23 beloved and pleasant in their *l*,
2:27 And Joab said, "As God *l*,
4: 9 said to them, "As the LORD *l*,
11:11 you live, and as your soul *l*,
12: 5 to Nathan, "As the LORD *l*,
14:11 And he said, "As the LORD *l*,
15:21 and said, "As the LORD *l*,
15:21 and as my lord the king *l*,
19: 5 the *l* of your sons and
19: 5 the *l* of your wives and the
19: 5 lives of your wives and the *l*
22:47 The LORD *l*! Blessed be my
23:17 went in jeopardy of their *l*?
1 Ki 1:29 and said, "As the LORD *l*,
2:24 therefore, as the LORD *l*,
3:23 says, 'This is my son, who *l*,
17: 1 "As the LORD God of Israel *l*,
17:12 said, "As the LORD your God *l*,
17:23 said, "See, your son *l*!"
18:10 "As the LORD your God *l*,
18:15 "As the LORD of hosts *l*,
21:18 who *l* in Samaria. There he
22:14 Micaiah said, "As the LORD *l*,
2 Ki 2: 2 Elisha said, "As the LORD *l*,
2: 2 lives, and as your soul *l*,
2: 4 But he said, "As the LORD *l*,
2: 4 lives, and as your soul *l*,
2: 6 But he said, "As the LORD *l*,
2: 6 lives, and as your soul *l*,
3:14 "As the LORD of hosts *l*,
4:30 child said, "As the LORD *l*,
4:30 lives, and as your soul *l*,
5:16 But he said, "As the LORD *l*,
5:20 he brought; but as the LORD *l*,
7: 7 they fled for their *l*.
1 Chr 11:19 men who have put their *l*
11:19 For at the risk of their *l* they
2 Chr 18:13 Micaiah said, "As the LORD *l*,
Esth 8:11 together and protect their *l*—
9:16 together and protected their *l*,
Job 19:25 For I know that my Redeemer *l*,
27: 2 As God *l*, who has taken away
31:39 its owners to lose their *l*;
Ps 18:46 The LORD *l*! Blessed be my
49:18 Though while he *l* he blesses
90:10 The days of our *l* are seventy
Prov 1:18 lurk secretly for their own *l*.
Eccl 2: 3 heaven all the days of their *l*.
3:12 and to do good in their *l*,
6: 3 a hundred children and *l* many
6: 6 even if he *l* a thousand years
11: 8 But if a man *l* many years And
Jer 2:34 is found The blood of the *l*
4: 2 you shall swear, 'The LORD *l*,
5: 2 they say, 'As the LORD *l*,
12:16 by My name, 'As the LORD *l*,
16:14 The LORD *l* who brought up the
16:15 The LORD *l* who brought up the
19: 7 hands of those who seek their *l*;
19: 9 and those who seek their *l*
23: 7 As the LORD *l* who brought up
23: 8 As the LORD *l* who brought up
38:16 saying, "As the LORD *l*,
44:26 saying, "The Lord GOD *l*.
46:26 hand of those who seek their *l*,
48: 6 save your *l*! And be like the
Lam 5: 9 bread at the risk of our *l*
Ezek 7:13 will strengthen himself Who *l*
27:13 They bartered human *l* and
Dan 4:34 praised and honored Him who *l*
7:12 yet their *l* were prolonged for
12: 7 and swore by Him who *l* forever,
Hos 4:15 oath, saying, 'As the LORD *l*'—
Am 8:14 Who say, 'As your god *l*,
8:14 As the way of Beersheba *l*!'
Lk 9:56 did not come to destroy men's *l*
Jn 4:50 him, "Go your way; your son *l*.
4:51 saying, "Your son *l*!"
4:53 Jesus said to him, "Your son *l*.
11:26 And whoever *l* and believes in Me
Acts 15:26 men who have risked their *l* for
27:10 cargo and ship, but also our *l*.
Rom 6:10 but the life that He *l*,
6:10 He lives, He *l* to God.
7: 1 over a man as long as he *l*?
7: 2 to her husband as long as he *l*.
7: 3 then if, while her husband *l*,
14: 7 For none of us *l* to himself, and
1 Cor 7:39 by law as long as her husband *l*;
2 Cor 13: 4 yet He *l* by the power of God.
Gal 2:20 but Christ *l* in me; and the
1 Th 2: 8 of God, but also our own *l*,
1 Tim 5: 6 But she who *l* in pleasure is
5: 6 in pleasure is dead while she *l*.
Heb 7: 8 whom it is witnessed that he *l*.
7:25 since He always *l* to make
9:17 at all while the testator *l*.
1 Pe 1:23 the word of God which *l* and
1 Jn 3:16 also ought to lay down our *l*
Rev 1:18 "I am He who *l*,
4: 9 who *l* forever and ever,
4:10 throne and worship Him who *l*
5:14 down and worshiped Him who *l*
10: 6 and swore by Him who *l* forever
12:11 and they did not love their *l*
15: 7 full of the wrath of God who *l*

LIVESTOCK (88/76)

Gen 4:20 who dwell in tents and have *l*.
13: 2 Abram was very rich in *l*,
13: 7 the herdsmen of Abram's *l* and
13: 7 and the herdsmen of Lot's *l*.
30:29 have served you and how your *l*
30:41 whenever the stronger *l*
30:41 rods before the eyes of the *l*
31: 9 So God has taken away the *l* of
31:18 And he carried away all his *l*
31:18 his acquired *l* which he had
33:14 on slowly at a pace which the *l*
33:17 and made booths for his *l*.
34: 5 Now his sons were with his *l* in
34:23 "Will not their *l*,
36: 7 support them because of their *l*.
46: 6 So they took their *l* and their
46:32 occupation has been to feed *l*;
46:34 occupation has been with *l*
47: 6 them chief herdsmen over my *l*.
47:16 Then Joseph said, "Give your *l*,
47:16 will give you bread for your *l*,
47:17 So they brought their *l* to
47:17 in exchange for all their *l*
47:18 my lord also has our herds of *l*.
Ex 9: 4 a difference between the *l* of
9: 4 livestock of Israel and the *l*
9: 6 and all the *l* of Egypt died;
9: 6 but of the *l* of the children of
9: 7 not even one of the *l* of the
9:19 send now and gather your *l*
9:20 made his servants and his *l*
9:21 left his servants and his *l* in
10:26 'Our *l* also shall go with us;
12:29 and all the firstborn of *l*.
12:38 and herds—a great deal of *l*.
17: 3 us and our children and our *l*
34:19 male firstborn among your *l*,
Lev 1: 2 bring your offering of the *l*—
5: 2 or the carcass of unclean *l*,
19:19 You shall not let your *l* breed
25: 7 for your *l* and the beasts that
26:22 your children, destroy your *l*,
Num 3:41 and the *l* of the Levites
3:41 all the firstborn among the *l*
3:45 and the *l* of the Levites
3:45 the Levites instead of their *l*.
20:19 and if I or my *l* drink any of
31:30 and the sheep, from all the *l*,
32: 1 had a very great multitude of *l*;
32: 1 the region was a place for *l*,
32: 4 of Israel, is a land for *l*,
32: 4 and your servants have *l*.
32:16 build sheepfolds here for our *l*,
32:26 and all our *l* will be there in
Deut 2:35 We took only the *l* as plunder
3: 7 But all the *l* and the spoil of
3:19 and your *l* (I know that you
3:19 (I know that you have much *l*)
7:14 among you or among your *l*.
11:15 grass in your fields for your *l*,
13:15 it, all that is in it and its *l*,
20:14 women, the little ones, the *l*,
28:11 body, in the increase of your *l*,
28:51 eat the increase of your *l* and
30: 9 body, in the increase of your *l*,
Josh 1:14 and your *l* shall remain in the
8:27 Only the *l* and the spoil of that
11:14 spoil of these cities and the *l*,
14: 4 their common-lands for their *l*
21: 2 their common-lands for our *l*.
22: 8 to your tents, with very much *l*,
Judg 6: 5 would come up with their *l* and
18:21 and put the little ones, the *l*,
1 Sam 23: 5 blow, and took away their *l*.
30:20 driven before those other *l*,
1 Ki 18: 5 we will not have to kill any *l*.
1 Chr 5:21 Then they took away their *l*—
2 Chr 14:15 They also attacked the *l*
26:10 many wells, for he had much *l*,
32:28 and stalls for all kinds of *l*,
Ezra 1: 4 and gold, with goods and *l*,
1: 6 and gold, with goods and *l*,
Ezek 38:12 who have acquired *l* and goods,
38:13 to take away *l* and goods, to
Jon 4:11 hand and their left—and much *l*?
Hag 1:11 brings forth, on men and *l*,
Zech 2: 4 of the multitude of men and *l*
Jn 4:12 as well as his sons and his *l*?

LIVING (179/168) LIVE

Gen 1:20 an abundance of *l* creatures,
1:21 great sea creatures and every *l*
1:24 earth bring forth the *l* creature
1:28 and over every *l* thing that
2: 7 and man became a *l* being.
2:19 Adam called each *l* creature,
3:20 she was the mother of all *l*.
6:19 And of every *l* thing of all
7: 4 face of the earth all *l* things
7:23 So He destroyed all *l* things
8: 1 and every *l* thing, and all the
8:17 Bring out with you every *l* thing
8:21 will I again destroy every *l*
9:10 and with every *l* creature that
9:12 and every *l* creature that is
9:15 between Me and you and every *l*
9:16 God and every *l* creature
25: 6 and while he was still *l* he
Lev 11:10 move in the water or any *l* thing
11:46 and the birds and every *l*
14: 4 cleansed two *l* and clean birds,
14: 6 As for the *l* bird, he shall take
14: 6 and dip them and the *l* bird in
14: 7 and shall let the *l* bird loose
14:51 and the *l* bird, and dip them in
14:52 the running water and the *l* bird
14:53 Then he shall let the *l* bird
20:25 or by any kind of *l* thing that
Num 16:48 between the dead and the *l*;
Deut 5:26 has heard the voice of the *l* God
24: 6 for he takes one's *l* in
Josh 3:10 you shall know that the *l* God
8:35 and the strangers who were *l*
Ruth 2:20 forsaken His kindness to the *l*
1 Sam 17:26 defy the armies of the *l* God?
17:36 defied the armies of the *l* God
25:29 be bound in the bundle of the *l*
2 Sam 20: 3 their death, *l* in widowhood.
1 Ki 3:22 No! But the *l* one is my son,
3:22 and the *l* one is my son."
3:23 and my son is the *l* one.'"
3:25 Divide the *l* child in two, and
3:26 Then the woman whose son was *l*
3:26 give her the *l* child, and by no
3:27 Give the first woman the *l* child
2 Ki 19: 4 has sent to reproach the *l* God,
19:16 has sent to reproach the *l* God.
Job 12:10 hand is the life of every *l*
28:13 it found in the land of the *l*.
28:21 hidden from the eyes of all *l*,
30:23 the house appointed for all *l*.
Ps 27:13 the LORD In the land of the *l*.
42: 2 for the *l* God. When shall I
52: 5 you from the land of the *l*.
56:13 God In the light of the *l*?
58: 9 As in His *l* and burning wrath.
66: 9 Who keeps our soul among the *l*,
69:28 out of the book of the *l*,
84: 2 and my flesh cry out for the *l*
104:25 *L* things both small and great.
116: 9 the LORD In the land of the *l*.
142: 5 portion in the land of the *l*.
143: 2 For in Your sight no one *l* is
145:16 the desire of every *l* thing.
Eccl 4: 2 More than the *l* who are still
4:15 I saw all the *l* who walk under
6: 8 knows how to walk before the *l*?
7: 2 And the *l* will take it to
9: 4 him who is joined to all the *l*
9: 4 for a *l* dog is better than a
9: 5 For the *l* know that they will
Song 4:15 A well of *l* waters, And
Isa 4: 3 who is recorded among the *l* in
8:19 the dead on behalf of the *l*?
37: 4 has sent to reproach the *l* God,
37:17 he has sent to reproach the *l*
38:11 The LORD in the land of the *l*;
38:19 The *l*, the living man,
38:19 the *l* man, he shall praise You,
53: 8 cut off from the land of the *l*;
Jer 2:13 the fountain of *l* waters, And
10:10 He is the *l* God and the
11:19 him off from the land of the *l*,
17:13 The fountain of *l* waters."
23:36 perverted the words of the *l*
Lam 3:39 Why should a *l* man complain,
Ezek 1: 5 likeness of four *l* creatures.
1:13 As for the likeness of the *l*
1:13 and forth among the *l* creatures.
1:14 And the *l* creatures ran back and
1:15 Now as I looked at the *l*
1:15 the earth beside each *l* creature
1:19 When the *l* creatures went, the
1:19 and when the *l* creatures were
1:20 the spirit of the *l* creatures

L

1:21 the spirit of the *l* creatures
1:22 the heads of the *l* creatures
3:13 the noise of the wings of the *l*
10:15 This was the *l* creature I saw
10:17 the spirit of the *l* creature
10:20 This is the *l* creature I saw
26:20 glory in the land of the *l*.
32:23 terror in the land of the *l*.
32:24 terror in the land of the *l*;
32:25 caused In the land of the *l*,
32:26 terror in the land of the *l*.
32:27 the mighty in the land of the *l*.
32:32 My terror in the land of the *l*;
47: 9 it shall be that every *l* thing
Dan 2:30 have more wisdom than anyone *l*,
4:17 In order that the *l* may know
6:20 servant of the *l* God, has your
6:26 For He is the *l* God, And
Hos 1:10 You are sons of the *l* God.'
Zech 14: 8 day it shall be That *l* waters
Mt 16:16 the Son of the *l* God."
22:32 God of the dead, but of the *l*.
26:63 I put You under oath by the *l*
Mk 12:27 the dead, but the God of the *l*.
Lk 2: 8 in the same country shepherds *l*
15:13 his possessions with prodigal *l*.
20:38 God of the dead but of the *l*,
24: 5 Why do you seek the *l* among the
Jn 4:10 He would have given you *l* water
4:11 Where then do You get that *l*
6:51 I am the *l* bread which came down
6:57 As the *l* Father sent Me, and I
6:69 the Son of the *l* God."
7:38 will flow rivers of *l* water.
Acts 7:38 one who received the *l* oracles
10:42 by God to be Judge of the *l*
14:15 useless things to the *l* God
Rom 9:26 be called sons of the *l* God.
12: 1 your bodies a *l* sacrifice,
14: 9 Lord of both the dead and the *l*.
1 Cor 15:45 first man Adam became a *l* being.
2 Cor 3: 3 but by the Spirit of the *l* God,
6:16 For you are the temple of the *l*
Col 2:20 as though *l* in the world, do
1 Th 1: 9 God from idols to serve the *l*
1 Tim 3:15 is the church of the *l* God,
4:10 because we trust in the *l* God,
6:17 uncertain riches but in the *l*
2 Tim 4: 1 who will judge the *l* and the
Titus 3: 3 *l* in malice and envy, hateful
Heb 3:12 in departing from the *l* God;
4:12 For the word of God is *l* and
9:14 dead works to serve the *l* God?
10:20 by a new and *l* way which He
10:31 to fall into the hands of the *l*
12:22 Zion and to the city of the *l*
1 Pe 1: 3 begotten us again to a *l* hope
2: 4 Coming to Him as to a *l* stone,
2: 5 as *l* stones, are being built up
4: 5 Him who is ready to judge the *l*
Rev 4: 6 were four *l* creatures full of
4: 7 The first *l* creature was like a
4: 7 the second *l* creature like a
4: 7 the third *l* creature had a face
4: 7 and the fourth *l* creature was
4: 8 The four *l* creatures, each
4: 9 Whenever the *l* creatures give
5: 6 of the throne and of the four *l*
5: 8 the four *l* creatures and the
5:11 the *l* creatures, and the
5:14 Then the four *l* creatures said,
6: 1 and I heard one of the four *l*
6: 3 I heard the second *l* creature
6: 5 I heard the third *l* creature
6: 6 in the midst of the four *l*
6: 7 heard the voice of the fourth *l*
7: 2 having the seal of the *l* God.
7:11 and the elders and the four *l*
7:17 and lead them to *l* fountains
8: 9 And a third of the *l* creatures
14: 3 before the four *l* creatures,
15: 7 Then one of the four *l* creatures
16: 3 and every *l* creature in the sea
19: 4 elders and the four *l* creatures

LIZARD (3/2)

Lev 11:29 and the large *l* after its kind;
11:30 'the gecko, the monitor *l*,
11:30 the sand reptile, the sand *l*,

LO (3/3)

Mt 28:20 I have commanded you; and *l*,
Lk 15:29 and said to his father, '*L*,

LO DEBAR (3/3)

2 Sam 9: 4 the son of Ammiel, in *L*."
9: 5 the son of Ammiel, in *L*."
17:27 the son of Ammiel from *L*,
Am 6:13 You who rejoice over *L*, Who say

LO-AMMI (1/1)

Hos 1: 9 God said: "Call his name *L*,

LO-RUHAMAH (2/2)

Hos 1: 6 to him: "Call her name *L*,
1: 8 Now when she had weaned *L*,

LOAD (4/4) LOADED, LOADS, UNLOAD

Gen 45:17 *L* your animals and depart;
Jon 1: 5 into the sea, to lighten the *l*.
Lk 11:46 For you *l* men with burdens
Gal 6: 5 each one shall bear his own *l*.

LOADED (9/8) LOAD

Gen 42:26 So they *l* their donkeys with the
44:13 and each man *l* his donkey and
45:23 ten donkeys *l* with the good
45:23 and ten female donkeys *l* with
1 Sam 16:20 And Jesse took a donkey *l* with
25:18 and *l* them on donkeys.
Neh 4:17 *l* themselves so that with one
Isa 46: 1 Your carriages were heavily *l*,
2 Tim 3: 6 captives of gullible women *l*

LOADING (1/1)

Neh 13:15 and *l* donkeys with wine,

LOADS (3/3) LOAD

Ps 68:19 Who daily *l* us with
Lam 5:13 Boys staggered under *l* of
Hab 2: 6 And to him who *l* himself with

LOAF (5/5) LOAVES

Ex 29:23 one *l* of bread, one cake made
Judg 7:13 a *l* of barley bread tumbled
2 Sam 6:19 to everyone a *l* of bread, a
1 Chr 16: 3 to everyone a *l* of bread, a
Mk 8:14 did not have more than one *l*

LOAN (1/1)

1 Sam 2:20 from this woman for the *l* that

LOATHE (6/6) LOATHED, LOATHES, LOATHSOME

Ex 7:18 and the Egyptians will *l* to
Job 7:16 I *l* my life; I would not
Ps 139:21 And do I not *l* those who rise
Ezek 6: 9 they will *l* themselves for the
20:43 and you shall *l* yourselves in
36:31 and you will *l* yourselves in

LOATHED (4/4) LOATHE

Jer 14:19 Has Your soul *l* Zion?
Ezek 16: 5 when you yourself were *l* on the
16:45 who *l* their husbands and
Zech 11: 8 My soul *l* them, and their soul

LOATHES (3/3) LOATHE

Num 21: 5 and our soul *l* this worthless
Job 10: 1 My soul *l* my life; I will give
Prov 27: 7 A satisfied soul *l* the

LOATHING (1/1)

Ezek 16:45 *l* husband and children; and you

LOATHSOME (4/4) LOATHE

Num 11:20 of your nostrils and becomes *l*
Job 6: 7 They are as *l* food to me.
Prov 13: 5 But a wicked man is *l* and
Rev 16: 2 and a foul and *l* sore came upon

LOAVES (32/30) LOAF

Lev 23:17 your dwellings two wave *l* of
Judg 8: 5 Please give *l* of bread to the
1 Sam 10: 3 another carrying three *l* of
10: 4 greet you and give you two *l*
17:17 dried grain and these ten *l*,
21: 3 Give me five *l* of bread in
25:18 haste and took two hundred *l*
2 Sam 16: 1 and on them two hundred *l* of
1 Ki 14: 3 "Also take with you ten *l*,
2 Ki 4:42 twenty *l* of barley bread, and
Mt 14:17 We have here only five *l* and two
14:19 And He took the five *l* and the
14:19 and broke and gave the *l* to
15:34 'How many *l* do you have?"
15:36 And He took the seven *l* and the
16: 9 or remember the five *l* of the
16:10 Nor the seven *l* of the four
Mk 6:38 How many *l* do you have? Go and
6:41 when He had taken the five *l*
6:41 heaven, blessed and broke the *l*,
6:44 Now those who had eaten the *l*
6:52 had not understood about the *l*,
8: 5 'How many *l* do you have?"
8: 6 And He took the seven *l* and
8:19 When I broke the five *l* for the
Lk 9:13 We have no more than five *l* and
9:16 Then He took the five *l* and the
11: 5 him, 'Friend, lend me three *l*;
Jn 6: 9 lad here who has five barley *l*
6:11 And Jesus took the *l*,
6:13 fragments of the five barley *l*
6:26 but because you ate of the *l*

LOBE (11/11)

Ex 29:13 the fatty *l* attached to the
29:22 the fatty *l* attached to the
Lev 3: 4 and the fatty *l* attached to
3:10 and the fatty *l* attached to
3:15 and the fatty *l* attached to
4: 9 and the fatty *l* attached to
7: 4 and the fatty *l* attached to
8:16 the fatty *l* attached to the
8:25 the fatty *l* attached to the
9:10 and the fatty *l* from the liver
9:19 and the fatty *l* attached to

LOCK (2/2) LOCKED, LOCKS

Song 5: 5 myrrh, On the handles of the *l*.
Ezek 8: 3 and took me by a *l* of my hair;

LOCKED (2/2) LOCK

Judg 3:23 the upper room behind him and *l*
3:24 doors of the upper room were *l*.

LOCKS (5/5) LOCK

Num 6: 5 Then he shall let the *l* of the
Judg 16:13 If you weave the seven *l* of my
16:19 had him shave off the seven *l*
Song 5: 2 My *l* with the drops of the
5:11 His *l* are wavy, And black

LOCUST (22/12) LOCUSTS

Ex 10:19 There remained not one *l* in all
Lev 11:22 the *l* after its kind, the
11:22 the destroying *l* after its
Deut 28:38 for the *l* shall consume it.
Job 39:20 Can you frighten him like a *l*?
Ps 78:46 And their labor to the *l*.
109:23 I am shaken off like a *l*.
Joel 1: 4 What the chewing *l* left, the
1: 4 the swarming *l* has eaten;
1: 4 What the swarming *l* left, the
1: 4 the crawling *l* has eaten;
1: 4 And what the crawling *l* left,
1: 4 the consuming *l* has eaten.
2:25 the years that the swarming *l*
2:25 has eaten, The crawling *l*,
2:25 locust, The consuming *l*,
2:25 locust, And the chewing *l*,
Am 4: 9 The *l* devoured them; Yet you
7: 1 He formed *l* swarms at the
Nah 3:15 It will eat you up like a *l*.
3:15 like the *l*! Make yourself
3:16 The *l* plunders and flies away.

LOCUSTS (24/22) LOCUST

Ex 10: 4 tomorrow I will bring *l* into
10:12 the land of Egypt for the *l*,
10:13 the east wind brought the *l*.
10:14 And the *l* went up over all the
10:14 there had been no such *l* as
10:19 which took the *l* away and blew
Deut 28:42 *L* shall consume all your trees
Judg 6: 5 coming in as numerous as *l*;
7:12 in the valley as numerous as *l*;
1 Ki 8:37 *l* or grasshoppers; when their
2 Chr 6:28 *l* or grasshoppers; when their
7:13 or command the *l* to devour the
Ps 105:34 and *l* came, Young locusts
105:34 Young *l* without number,
Prov 30:27 The *l* have no king, Yet they
Isa 33: 4 As the running to and fro of *l*,
Jer 51:14 fill you with men, as with *l*,
51:27 to come up like the bristling *l*.
Nah 3:15 like the swarming *l*!
3:17 are like swarming *l*,
Mt 3: 4 and his food was *l* and wild
Mk 1: 6 and he ate *l* and wild honey.
Rev 9: 3 Then out of the smoke *l* came
9: 7 The shape of the *l* was like

LOD (4/4)

1 Chr 8:12 who built Ono and *L* with its
Ezra 2:33 the people of *L*, Hadid, and
Neh 7:37 the sons of *L*, Hadid, and Ono,
11:35 in *L*, Ono, and the Valley

LODGE (17/16) LODGED, LODGING

Gen 24:23 your father's house for us to *l*?
24:25 and feed enough, and room to *l*.
Num 22: 8 *L* here tonight, and I will bring
Josh 4: 3 the lodging place where you *l*
Judg 19: 9 *l* here, that your heart may be
19:11 city of the Jebusites and *l* in
19:15 aside there to go in to *l* in
Ruth 1:16 I will go; And wherever you *l*,
1:16 wherever you lodge, I will *l*;
1 Ki 17:20 on the widow with whom I *l*,
Job 31:32 (But no sojourner had to *l* in
Song 7:11 Let us *l* in the villages.
Isa 21:13 the forest in Arabia you will *l*,
Jer 4:14 long shall your evil thoughts *l*
Zeph 2:14 and the bittern Shall *l* on
Lk 9:12 and *l* and get provisions;
Acts 21:16 with whom we were to *l*.

LODGED (17/17) LODGE

Gen 32:13 So he *l* there that same night,
32:21 but he himself *l* that night in
Josh 2: 1 named Rahab, and *l* there.
3: 1 and *l* there before they crossed

4: 8 them to the place where they l,
6:11 they came into the camp and l
8: 9 but Joshua l that night among
Judg 18: 2 house of Micah, and l there.
19: 4 So they ate and drank and l
19: 7 so he l there again.
1 Chr 9:27 And they l all around the house
9:33 who l in the chambers, and
Neh 13:20 sellers of all kinds of wares l
Isa 1:21 Righteousness l in it, But
Mt 21:17 to Bethany, and He l there.
Acts 10:23 Then he invited them in and l
1 Tim 5:10 if she has l strangers, if she

LODGING (7/7) LODGE

Josh 4: 3 you and leave them in the l
Isa 10:29 They have taken up l at Geba.
Jer 9: 2 I had in the wilderness A l
Acts 10: 6 He is l with Simon, a tanner,
10:18 was Peter, was l there.
10:32 He is l in the house of Simon,
28:23 day, many came to him at his l,

LOFT (KJV) See (UPPER) ROOM

LOFTILY (1/1)

Ps 73: 8 oppression; They speak l.

LOFTINESS (2/2)

Isa 2:17 The l of man shall be bowed
Jer 48:29 Of his l and arrogance and

LOFTY (10/10) LOFTINESS

Job 22:12 highest stars, how l they are!
Ps 131: 1 is not haughty, Nor my eyes l.
Prov 24: 7 Wisdom is too l for a fool;
30:13 how l are their eyes!
Isa 2:11 The l looks of man shall be
2:12 upon everything proud and l,
5:15 And the eyes of the l shall be
26: 5 The l city; He lays it low,
57: 7 'On a l and high mountain
57:15 For thus says the High and L

LOG (5/5)

Lev 14:10 and one l of oil.
14:12 and the l of oil, and wave them
14:15 shall take some of the l of
14:21 grain offering, a l of oil,
14:24 trespass offering and the l of

LOGS (4/4)

1 Ki 5: 8 the cedar and cypress l.
5:10 Solomon cedar and cypress l
2 Chr 2: 8 cedar and cypress and algum l
Ezra 3: 7 and Tyre to bring cedar l from

LOINS (13/13)

Deut 33:11 Strike the l of those who rise
1 Ki 18:46 and he girded up his l and ran
Ps 38: 7 For my l are full of
69:23 And make their l shake
Isa 5:27 Nor will the belt on their l
11: 5 shall be the belt of His l,
21: 3 Therefore my l are filled with
Jer 30: 6 man with his hands on his l
48:37 and on the l sackcloth—
Lam 3:13 of His quiver To pierce my l.
Heb 7: 5 they have come from the l of
7:10 for he was still in the l of his
1 Pe 1:13 Therefore gird up the l of your

LOIS (1/1)

2 Tim 1: 5 first in your grandmother L

LONELY (1/1)

Lam 1: 1 How l sits the city

LONG (236/227) LONGED, LONGED-FOR, LONGER, LONGING, LONGS

Gen 26: 8 when he had been there a l
31:30 gone because you greatly l for
48:15 who has fed me all my life l
Ex 10: 3 How l will you refuse to humble
10: 7 How l shall this man be a snare
16:28 How l do you refuse to keep My
19:13 When the trumpet sounds l,
19:19 blast of the trumpet sounded l
20:12 that your days may be l upon
27: 1 five cubits l and five cubits
27: 9 one hundred cubits l for one
27:11 hangings one hundred cubits l,
27:16 be a screen twenty cubits l,
38: 9 linen, one hundred cubits l.
38:11 were one hundred cubits l,
38:14 gate were fifteen cubits l,
Lev 18:19 to uncover her nakedness as l
21:18 marred face or any limb too l,
22:23 a lamb that has any limb too l
26:34 shall enjoy its sabbaths as l
26:35 As l as it lies desolate it
Num 9:18 as l as the cloud stayed above
9:19 Even when the cloud continued l,
14:11 How l will these people reject
14:11 And how l will they not believe
14:27 How l shall I bear with this
20:15 and we dwelt in Egypt a l time,
24:22 How l until Asshur carries you
Deut 1: 6 You have dwelt l enough at this
2: 3 have skirted this mountain l
5:16 you, that your days may be l,
12:19 do not forsake the Levite as l
12:20 because you l to eat meat, you
14:24 But if the journey is too l for
19: 6 him, because the way is l,
20:19 you besiege a city for a l
28:32 longing for them all day l;
31:13 to fear the LORD your God as l
33:12 shelters him all the day l;
Josh 6: 5 when they make a l blast with
9:13 old because of the very l
11:18 Joshua made war a l time with
18: 3 How l will you neglect to go and
23: 1 a l time after the LORD had
24: 7 you dwelt in the wilderness a l
Judg 5:28 Why is his chariot so l in
1 Sam 1:14 'How l will you be drunk?
1:28 as l as he lives he shall be
7: 2 remained in Kirjath Jearim a l
10:24 L live the king!"
16: 1 How l will you mourn for Saul,
20:31 For as l as the son of Jesse
25:15 nor did we miss anything as l
29: 8 you found in your servant as l
2 Sam 2:26 How l will it be then until you
3: 1 Now there was a l war between
14: 2 who has been mourning a l time
16:16 L live the king! Long live the
16:16 Long live the king! L live the
19:34 How l have I to live, that I
1 Ki 1:25 L live King Adonijah!'
1:34 L live King Solomon!'
1:39 L live King Solomon!"
3:11 and have not asked l life for
6: 3 the house was twenty cubits l
6:17 sanctuary was forty cubits l.
6:20 sanctuary was twenty cubits l,
18:21 How l will you falter between
2 Ki 9:22 as l as the harlotries of your
11:12 L live the king!"
19:25 Did you not hear l ago How I
2 Chr 1:11 nor have you asked l life—but
3: 4 sanctuary was twenty cubits l
6:13 a bronze platform five cubits l,
6:31 to walk in Your ways as l as
15: 3 For a l time Israel has been
23:11 L live the king!"
26: 5 and as l as he sought the
30: 5 they had not done it for a l
36:21 As l as she lay desolate she
Neh 2: 6 'How l will your journey be?
Esth 5:13 so l as I see Mordecai the Jew
Job 3:21 Who l for death, but it does
6: 8 grant me the thing that I l
7:19 How l? Will You not look
8: 2 How l will you speak these
18: 2 How l till you put an end to
19: 2 How l will you torment my soul,
27: 3 As l as my breath is in me,
27: 6 shall not reproach me as l as
Ps 4: 2 How l, O you sons of men,
4: 2 How l will you love
6: 3 But You, O LORD—HOW l?
13: 1 How l, O LORD?
13: 1 How l will You hide Your face
13: 2 How l shall I take counsel in
13: 2 How l will my enemy be exalted
32: 3 my groaning all the day l.
35:17 how l will You look on?
35:28 of Your praise all the day l.
38: 6 I go mourning all the day l.
38:12 plan deception all the day l.
42:10 While they say to me all day l,
44: 8 In God we boast all day l,
44:22 sake we are killed all day l;
62: 3 How l will you attack a man?
71:24 righteousness all the day l;
72: 5 They shall fear You As l as
72:17 His name shall continue as l
73:14 For all day l I have been
74: 9 any among us who knows how l.
74:10 how l will the adversary
79: 5 How l, LORD?
80: 4 How l will You be angry
82: 2 How l will you judge unjustly,
86: 3 For I cry to You all day l.
88:17 They came around me all day l
89:16 name they rejoice all day l,
89:46 How l, LORD?
90:13 Return, O LORD! How l?
91:16 With l life I will satisfy him,
94: 3 how l will the wicked,
94: 3 How l will the wicked triumph?
102: 8 enemies reproach me all day l,
104:33 I will sing to the LORD as l
116: 2 I will call upon Him as l as
119:40 I l for Your precepts;
119:174 I l for Your salvation,
120: 6 My soul has dwelt too l With
129: 3 They made their furrows l.
143: 3 Like those who have l been
Prov 1:22 'How l, you simple ones,
3: 2 For length of days and l life
6: 9 How l will you slumber,
7:19 He has gone on a l journey;
21:26 He covets greedily all day l,
23:30 Those who linger l at the wine,
25:15 By l forbearance a ruler is
Isa 6:11 Then I said, "Lord, how l?
22:11 for Him who fashioned it l ago.
37:26 Did you not hear l ago How I
42:14 I have held My peace a l time,
48: 8 Surely from l ago your ear was
65: 2 out My hands all day l to a
65:22 And My elect shall l enjoy the
Jer 4:14 How l shall your evil thoughts
4:21 How l will I see the standard,
12: 4 How l will the land mourn,
23:26 How l will this be in the heart
29:28 saying, 'This captivity is l;
31:22 How l will you gad about,
47: 5 How l will you cut yourself?
47: 6 How l until you are quiet?
Lam 3: 6 places Like the dead of l ago.
5:20 And forsake us for so l a
Ezek 17: 3 eagle with large wings and l
31: 5 And its branches became l
38: 8 which had l been desolate;
40: 5 a measuring rod six cubits l,
40: 7 gate chamber was one rod l
40:29 it was fifty cubits l and
40:30 twenty-five cubits l and five
40:33 it was fifty cubits l and
40:42 one cubit and a half l,
40:47 one hundred cubits l and one
41:13 temple, one hundred cubits l;
41:13 walls was one hundred cubits l;
42:11 they were as l and as wide as
42:20 five hundred cubits l and five
43:16 hearth is twelve cubits l,
43:17 fourteen cubits l and fourteen
44:20 heads nor let their hair grow l;
45: 3 twenty-five thousand cubits l
45: 5 twenty-five thousand cubits l
45: 6 wide and twenty-five thousand l,
46:22 forty cubits l and thirty
Dan 8:13 How l will the vision be,
10: 1 but the appointed time was l;
12: 6 How l shall the fulfillment of
Hos 8: 5 How l until they attain to
13:13 For he should not stay l where
Hab 1: 2 how l shall I cry, And You
2: 6 What is not his—how l?
Zech 1:12 how l will You not have mercy
Mt 9:15 of the bridegroom mourn as l
11:21 they would have repented l ago
17:17 how l shall I be with you?
17:17 How l shall I bear with you?
23:14 and for a pretense make l
25:19 After a l time the lord of those
Mk 1:35 having risen a l while before
2:19 As l as they have the
9:19 how l shall I be with you?
9:19 How l shall I bear with you?
9:21 How l has this been happening to
12:38 who desire to go around in l
12:40 and for a pretense make l
16: 5 saw a young man clothed in a l
Lk 1:21 marveled that he lingered so l
8:27 the city who had demons for a l
9:41 how l shall I be with you and
10:13 they would have repented l ago,
18: 7 though He bears l with them?
20: 9 went into a far country for a l
20:46 who desire to go around in l
20:47 and for a pretense make l
23: 8 for he had desired for a l
Jn 5: 6 been in that condition a l
9: 5 As l as I am in the world, I am
10:24 How l do You keep us in doubt?
14: 9 "Have I been with you so l,
Acts 8:11 them with his sorceries for a l
14: 3 they stayed there a l time,
14:28 So they stayed there a l time
20:11 and talked a l while, even till
27:14 But not l after, a tempestuous
27:21 But after l abstinence from
28: 6 after they had looked for a l
Rom 1:11 For I l to see you, that I may
7: 1 has dominion over a man as l
7: 2 by the law to her husband as l
8:36 we are killed all day l;
10:21 All day l I have stretched
1 Cor 7:39 A wife is bound by law as l as
11:14 teach you that if a man has l
11:15 But if a woman has l hair, it is
13: 4 Love suffers l and is kind;
2 Cor 9:14 who l for you because of the
Gal 4: 1 as l as he is a child, does not
Eph 6: 3 you and you may live l
Phil 1: 8 how greatly I l for you all
Heb 4: 7 after such a l time, as it
2 Pe 1:13 as l as I am in this tent, to
2: 3 for a l time their judgment has
Jude 4 who l ago were marked out for
Rev 6:10 a loud voice, saying, "How l,

LONGED (4/4) LONG

2 Sam 13:39 And King David l to go to
Ps 119:131 For I l for Your commandments.
Isa 21: 4 The night for which I l He
Rev 18:14 The fruit that your soul l for

LONGED-FOR (1/1) LONG

Phil 4: 1 my beloved and l brethren, my

L

LONGER (126/122) LONG

Gen 4:12 it shall no *l* yield its
17: 5 No *l* shall your name be called
32:28 Your name shall no *l* be called
Ex 2: 3 But when she could no *l* hide
5: 7 You shall no *l* give the people
9:28 you go, and you shall stay no *l*.
Deut 10:16 heart, and be stiff-necked no *l*.
17:13 and no *l* act presumptuously.
31: 2 I can no *l* go out and come in.
Josh 5: 1 was no spirit in them any *l*
5:12 and the children of Israel no *l*
23:13 the LORD your God will no *l*
Judg 2:14 so that they could no *l* stand
2:21 I also will no *l* drive out
10:16 And His soul could no *l* endure
1 Sam 1:18 and her face was no *l* sad.
2 Sam 19:35 Can I hear any *l* the voice of
20: 5 But he delayed *l* than the set
2 Ki 5:17 for your servant will no *l*
6:33 I wait for the LORD any *l*?
1 Chr 23:26 They shall no *l* carry the
2 Chr 35: 3 It shall no *l* be a burden on
Neh 2:17 that we may no *l* be a
Job 7: 8 I shall no *l* be.
7:21 But I will no *l* be."
11: 9 Their measure is *l* than the
Ps 74: 9 There is no *l* any prophet;
Isa 32: 5 The foolish person will no *l* be
47: 5 For you shall no *l* be called
51:22 You shall no *l* drink it.
52: 1 and the unclean Shall no *l*
54: 9 the waters of Noah would no *l*
60:18 Violence shall no *l* be heard in
60:19 The sun shall no *l* be your
60:20 Your sun shall no *l* go down,
62: 4 You shall no *l* be termed
62: 8 Surely I will no *l* give your
65:19 voice of weeping shall no *l* be
Jer 9:21 no *l* to be outside!
9:21 no *l* on the streets!
23: 7 that they shall no *l* say, 'As
44:22 So the LORD could no *l* bear
Lam 4:15 They shall no *l* dwell here."
4:16 He no *l* regards them.
4:22 He will no *l* send you into
Ezek 13:21 and they shall no *l* be as prey
13:23 Therefore you shall no *l*
14:11 the house of Israel may no *l*
16:41 and you shall no *l* hire lovers.
18: 3 you shall no *l* use this proverb
19: 9 That his voice should no *l* be
21:27 It shall be no *l*,
24:27 you shall speak and no *l* be
28:24 And there shall no *l* be a
29:16 No *l* shall it be the confidence
30:13 There shall no *l* be princes
33:22 and I was no *l* mute.
34:10 that they may no *l* be food for
34:22 and they shall no *l* be a prey;
34:28 And they shall no *l* be a prey
34:29 and they shall no *l* be consumed
37:22 they shall no *l* be two nations,
39:28 left none of them captive any *l*.
Hos 1: 6 For I will no *l* have mercy on
2:16 And no *l* call Me 'My Master,'
Joel 2:19 I will no *l* make you a
Am 9:15 And no *l* shall they be pulled
Nah 1:14 name shall be perpetuated no *l*.
Zeph 3:11 And you shall no *l* be haughty
Zech 11: 6 For I will no *l* pity the
13: 2 and they shall no *l* be
14:11 And no *l* shall there be utter
14:21 In that day there shall no *l* be
Mt 19: 6 they are no *l* two but one
Mk 1:45 so that Jesus could no *l* openly
2: 2 so that there was no *l* room to
7:12 then you no *l* let him do
10: 8 so then they are no *l* two, but
14:25 I will no *l* drink of the fruit
Lk 15:19 and I am no *l* worthy to be
15:21 and am no *l* worthy to be called
16: 2 for you can no *l* be steward.'
22:16 I will no *l* eat of it until it
Jn 7:33 be with you a little while *l*,
11:54 Therefore Jesus no *l* walked
12:35 A little while *l* the light is
13:33 be with you a little while *l*.
14:19 A little while *l* and the world
14:30 I will no *l* talk much with you,
15:15 No *l* do I call you servants, for
16:21 she no *l* remembers the anguish,
16:25 time is coming when I will no *l*
17:11 Now I am no *l* in the world, but
Acts 18:20 they asked him to stay a *l*
25:24 he was not fit to live any *l*.
Rom 6: 2 we who died to sin live any *l*
6: 6 that we should no *l* be slaves
6: 9 Death no *l* has dominion over
7:17 it is no *l* I who do it, but
7:20 it is no *l* I who do it, but sin
11: 6 then it is no *l* of works;
11: 6 otherwise grace is no *l* grace.
11: 6 it is no *l* grace; otherwise
11: 6 otherwise work is no *l* work.
14:15 you are no *l* walking in love.
15:23 But now no *l* having a place in
2 Cor 5:15 who live should live no *l* for
5:16 yet now we know Him thus no *l*.
Gal 2:20 it is no *l* I who live, but
3:18 it is no *l* of promise;
3:25 we are no *l* under a tutor.
4: 7 Therefore you are no *l* a slave
Eph 2:19 you are no *l* strangers and
4:14 that we should no *l* be children,
4:17 that you should no *l* walk as
4:28 Let him who stole steal no *l*,
1 Th 3: 1 when we could no *l* endure it,
3: 5 when I could no *l* endure it, I
1 Tim 5:23 No *l* drink only water, but use a
Phm 1:16 no *l* as a slave but more than a
Heb 10:18 there is no *l* an offering for
10:26 there no *l* remains a sacrifice
1 Pe 4: 2 that he no *l* should live the
Rev 6:11 should rest a little while *l*,
10: 6 that there should be delay no *l*,
12: 8 found for them in heaven any *l*.

LONGING (8/8) LONG

Gen 39: 7 that his master's wife cast *l*
Deut 28:32 shall look and fail with *l*
2 Sam 23:15 And David said with *l*,
1 Chr 11:17 And David said with *l*,
Ps 107: 9 For He satisfies the *l* soul,
119:20 My soul breaks with *l* For Your
Phil 2:26 since he was *l* for you all, and
1 Th 2: 8 affectionately *l* for you, we

LONGS (4/4) LONG

Gen 34: 8 The soul of my son Shechem *l* for
Ps 63: 1 My flesh *l* for You In a dry
84: 2 My soul *l*, yes, even faints
143: 6 My soul *l* for You like a

LONGSUFFERING (16/16)

Ex 34: 6 God, merciful and gracious, *l*,
Num 14:18 The LORD is *l* and abundant in
Ps 86:15 *L* and abundant in mercy and
Rom 2: 4 goodness, forbearance, and *l*,
9:22 endured with much *l* the vessels
2 Cor 6: 6 by purity, by knowledge, by *l*,
Gal 5:22 Spirit is love, joy, peace, *l*,
Eph 4: 2 and gentleness, with *l*,
Col 1:11 for all patience and *l* with
3:12 kindness, humility, meekness, *l*;
1 Tim 1:16 Jesus Christ might show all *l*,
2 Tim 3:10 of life, purpose, faith, *l*,
4: 2 with all *l* and teaching.
1 Pe 3:20 when once the Divine *l* waited
2 Pe 3: 9 but is *l* toward us, not willing
3:15 and consider that the *l* of our

LOOK (295/287) EXAMINE, LOOKED, LOOKING, LOOKS

Gen 9:16 and I will *l* on it to remember
13:14 Lift your eyes now and *l* from
15: 3 Then Abram said, "*L*,
15: 5 *L* now toward heaven, and count
19:17 for your life! Do not *l*
22: 7 am, my son." Then he said, "*L*,
25:32 And Esau said, "*L*, I am about
27:11 said to Rebekah his mother, "*L*,
27:36 away my birthright, and now *l*,
29: 6 said, "He is well. And *l*,
29: 7 Then he said, "*L*, it is still
37: 9 to his brothers, and said, "*L*,
37:19 they said to one another, "*L*,
38:13 it was told Tamar, saying, "*L*,
39: 8 said to his master's wife, "*L*,
39:23 keeper of the prison did not *l*
40: 7 Why do you *l* so sad today?"
42: 1 Why do you *l* at one another?"
44: 8 '*L*, we brought back to you
47:23 land this day for Pharaoh. *L*,
48: 2 And Jacob was told, "*L*,
Ex 1: 9 And he said to his people, "*L*,
3: 4 saw that he turned aside to *l*,
3: 6 for he was afraid to *l* upon
4:14 that he can speak well. And *l*,
5: 5 And Pharaoh said, "*L*,
5:21 Let the LORD *l* on you and
Lev 10:19 And Aaron said to Moses, "*L*,
13:39 "then the priest shall *l*;
14:39 again on the seventh day and *l*;
14:44 the priest shall come and *l*;
26: 9 For I will *l* on you favorably
Num 15:39 that you may *l* upon it and
22: 5 to call him, saying: "*L*,
22:11 '*L*, a people has come out of
22:38 And Balaam said to Balak, "*L*,
23:11 you to curse my enemies, and *l*,
23:24 *L*, a people rises like a
24:10 you to curse my enemies, and *l*,
31:16 '*L*, these women caused
32:14 And *l*! You have risen in your
Deut 1:21 '*L*, the LORD your God has set
2:24 River Arnon. *L*, I have given
9:27 do not *l* on the stubbornness of
26:15 *L* down from Your holy
28:32 and your eyes shall *l* and fail
Josh 9:12 to come to you. But now *l*,
Judg 3:24 out, Eglon's servants came to *l*,
6:37 '*l*, I shall put a fleece
7:17 *L* at me and do likewise; watch,
9:36 people, he said to Zebul, "*L*,
13:10 husband, and said to him, "*L*,
14:16 And he said to her, "*L*,
16:10 Delilah said to Samson, "*L*,
19: 9 father, said to him, "*L*,
19:24 '*L*, here is my virgin
20: 7 *L*! All of you are children of
Ruth 1:15 And she said, "*L*,
1 Sam 1:11 if You will indeed *l* on the
8: 5 and said to him, "*L*,
9: 3 go and *l* for the donkeys."
9: 6 *L* now, there is in this city a
9: 7 said to his servant, "But *l*,
9: 8 Saul again and said, "*L*,
10: 2 donkeys which you went to *l*
10:14 To *l* for the donkeys. When we
12: 2 I am old and grayheaded, and *l*,
14:11 And the Philistines said, "*L*,
14:29 *L* now, how my countenance has
14:33 they told Saul, saying, "*L*,
16: 7 Do not *l* at his appearance or at
16:18 servants answered and said, "*L*,
18:22 David secretly, and say, '*L*,
20:21 If I expressly say to him, '*L*,
20:22 I say thus to the young man, '*L*,
21:14 said to his servants, "*L*,
23: 1 they told David, saying, "*L*,
23: 3 David's men said to him, "*L*,
24:10 '*L*, this day your eyes have
25:14 Nabal's wife, saying, "*L*,
28: 9 Then the woman said to him, "*L*,
28:21 troubled, and said to him, "*L*,
2 Sam 3:24 said, "What have you done? *L*,
4:10 someone told me, saying, '*L*,
9: 8 that you should *l* upon such a
13:35 Jonadab said to the king, "*L*,
14:32 And Absalom answered Joab, "*L*,
15: 3 Absalom would say to him, "*L*,
16:12 may be that the LORD will *l*
24:22 whatever seems good to him. *L*,
1 Ki 1:18 *l*! Adonijah has become king;
1:25 and *l*! They are eating and
1:51 afraid of King Solomon; for *l*,
2:39 they told Shimei, saying, "*L*,
18:43 *l* toward the sea." So he went
20:31 *L* now, we have heard that the
22:23 Therefore *l*! The LORD has put a
2 Ki 1:14 '*L*, fire has come down
2:16 *L* now, there are fifty strong
3:14 I would not *l* at you, nor see
4: 9 *L* now, I know that this is a
4:13 to him, "Say now to her, '*L*,
4:25 said to his servant Gehazi, "*L*,
5:20 the man of God, said, "*L*,
6:32 someone to take away my head? *L*,
7: 2 the man of God and said, "*L*,
7: 6 they said to one another, "*L*,
7:13 which are left in the city. *L*,
7:19 man of God, and said, "Now *l*,
9: 2 *l* there for Jehu the son of
10: 4 afraid, and said, "*L*,
18:21 Now *l*! You are trusting in the
19: 9 Tirhakah king of Ethiopia, "*L*,
19:11 *L*! You have heard what the kings
1 Chr 12:17 may the God of our fathers *l*
21:23 what is good in his eyes. *L*,
23: 4 thousand were to *l* after the
2 Chr 13:12 'Now *l*, God Himself is with
18:22 Therefore *l*! The LORD has put a
24:22 The LORD *l* on it, and repay!"
28: 9 Samaria, and said to them: "*L*,
Esth 7: 9 *L*! The gallows, fifty cubits
Job 3: 9 May it *l* for light, but have
6:19 The caravans of Tema *l*,
6:28 be pleased to *l* at me; For I
7:19 Will You not *l* away from me,
8:17 And *l* for a place in the
14: 6 *L* away from him that he may
21: 5 *L* at me and be astonished
21:27 '*L*, I know your thoughts,
23: 8 '*L*, I go forward, but He
31: 1 Why then should I *l* upon a
33:12 *L*, in this you are not
35: 5 *L* to the heavens and see
36:30 *L*, He scatters his light
37:21 Even now men cannot *l* at the
40:11 *L* on everyone who is proud,
40:12 *L* on everyone who is proud,
40:15 *L* now at the behemoth, which I
Ps 5: 3 And I will *l* up.
11: 2 For *l*! The wicked bend their
17: 2 Let Your eyes *l* on the things
22:17 They *l* and stare at Me.
25:18 *L* on my affliction and my pain,
35:17 how long will You *l* on?
37:10 you will *l* carefully for his
40:12 so that I am not able to *l* up;
59: 3 For *l*, they lie in wait
80:14 *L* down from heaven and see,
84: 9 And *l* upon the face of Your
85:11 And righteousness shall *l* down
91: 8 with your eyes shall you *l*,
101: 5 The one who has a haughty *l*
109:25 When they *l* at me, they shake
119: 6 When I *l* into all Your
119:132 *L* upon me and be merciful to
123: 2 as the eyes of servants *l* to
123: 2 So our eyes *l* to the LORD
142: 4 *L* on my right hand and see,
145:15 The eyes of all *l* expectantly
Prov 4:25 Let your eyes *l* straight ahead,
4:25 And your eyelids *l* right
6:17 A proud *l*, A lying tongue,
21: 4 A haughty *l*, a proud heart,
23:31 Do not *l* on the wine when it is
Eccl 1:16 with my heart, saying, "*L*,
4: 1 And *l*! The tears of the

12: 3 And those that *l* through the
Song 1: 6 Do not *l* upon me, because I am
4: 8 *L* from the top of Amana,
4: 9 ravished my heart With one *l*
6:13 that we may *l* upon you!
Isa 3: 9 The *l* on their countenance
8:21 their God, and *l* upward.
8:22 Then they will *l* to the earth,
17: 7 In that day a man will *l* to
17: 8 He will not *l* to the altars,
18: 4 And I will *l* from My dwelling
21: 9 And *l*, here comes a chariot
22: 4 *L* away from me, I will weep
22:11 But you did not *l* to its
29: 8 a hungry man dreams, And *l*—
29: 8 a thirsty man dreams, And *l*—
31: 1 But who do not *l* to the Holy
33:20 *L* upon Zion, the city of our
36: 6 *L*! You are trusting in the staff
37:11 *L*! You have heard what the kings
40:15 small dust on the scales; *L*,
41:27 time I said to Zion, '*L*,
42:18 "Hear, you deaf; And *l*,
45:22 *L* to Me, and be saved, All you
49:12 *L*! Those from the north and
49:18 *l* around and see; All these
50:11 *L*, all you who kindle a fire,
51: 1 *L* to the rock from which you
51: 2 *L* to Abraham your father,
51: 6 And *l* on the earth beneath.
56:11 They all *l* to their own way,
59: 9 We *l* for light, but there is
59:11 We *l* for justice, but there
63:15 *L* down from heaven, And see
64: 3 things for which we did not *l*,
64: 9 forever; Indeed, please *l*—
66: 2 "But on this one will I *l*:
66:24 And they shall go forth and *l*
Jer 8: 8 of the LORD is with us'? *L*,
18: 6 says the LORD. "*L*,
32:24 '*L*, the siege mounds!
38: 5 Zedekiah the king said, "*L*,
39:12 Take him and *l* after him, and do
40: 4 'And now *l*, I free you this
40: 4 and I will *l* after you. But if
46: 5 And did not *l* back, For fear
47: 3 The fathers will not *l* back
Lam 3:63 *L* at their sitting down and
5: 1 what has come upon us; *L*,
Ezek 12:27 'Son of man, *l*, the house of
16:49 '*L*, this was the iniquity
22: 6 *L*, the princes of Israel:
25: 8 *L*! The house of Judah is like
40: 4 *l* with your eyes and hear with
Dan 3:25 *L*!" he answered, "I see four
8:19 And he said, "*L*, I am making
Hos 3: 1 who *l* to other gods and love
5: 8 *L* behind you, O Benjamin!'
Jon 2: 4 Yet I will *l* again toward Your
Mic 4:11 And let our eye *l* upon Zion."
7: 7 Therefore I will *l* to the
Nah 3: 7 come to pass that all who *l*
Hab 1: 5 *L* among the nations and
1:13 And cannot *l* on wickedness.
1:13 Why do You *l* on those who deal
2:15 That you may *l* on his
Zech 12:10 then they will *l* on Me whom
Mt 6:26 *L* at the birds of the air, for
7: 3 And why do you *l* at the speck in
7: 4 the speck from your eye'; and *l*,
11: 3 or do we *l* for another?"
11:19 and drinking, and they say, '*L*,
12: 2 saw it, they said to Him, "*L*,
12:47 Then one said to Him, "*L*,
24:23 if anyone says to you, '*L*,
24:26 if they say to you, '*L*,
24:26 do not go out; or '*L*,
25:20 delivered to me five talents; *l*,
25:22 delivered to me two talents; *l*,
25:25 your talent in the ground. *L*,
26:65 need do we have of witnesses? *L*,
Mk 2:24 the Pharisees said to Him, "*L*,
3:32 and they said to Him, "*L*,
8:25 his eyes again and made him *l*
11:21 *l*! The fig tree which You
13:21 if anyone says to you, '*L*,
13:21 here is the Christ!' or, '*L*,
15:35 they heard that, said, "*L*,
Lk 2:48 why have You done this to us? *L*,
6:41 And why do you *l* at the speck in
7:19 or do we *l* for another?"
7:20 or do we *l* for another?'"
7:34 and drinking, and you say, '*L*,
9:38 *l* on my son, for he is my only
13: 7 the keeper of his vineyard, '*L*,
17:23 *L* here!' or 'Look there!' Do not
17:23 *L* there!' Do not go after them
19: 8 stood and said to the Lord, "*L*,
21:28 *l* up and lift up your heads,
21:29 *L* at the fig tree, and all the
22:38 So they said, "Lord, *l*,
Jn 4:35 lift up your eyes and *l* at the
7:26 But *l*! He speaks boldly, and
7:52 also from Galilee? Search and *l*,
12:19 are accomplishing nothing. *L*,
19:37 They shall *l* on Him whom
20:27 and *l* at My hands; and reach
Acts 2: 7 saying to one another, "*L*,
3: 4 Peter said, "*L* at us."
3:12 Or why *l* so intently at us, as
4:29 *l* on their threats, and grant
5: 9 *L*, the feet of those who have
5:25 came and told them, saying, "*L*,
5:28 to teach in this name? And *l*,
7:32 Moses trembled and dared not *l*.
7:56 *L*! I see the heavens opened and
18:15 *l* to it yourselves; for I do
2 Cor 3: 7 children of Israel could not *l*
3:13 children of Israel could not *l*
4:18 while we do not *l* at the things
10: 7 Do you *l* at things according to
Phil 2: 4 Let each of you *l* out not only
Jas 3: 4 *L* also at ships: although they
1 Pe 1:12 which angels desire to *l* into.
2 Pe 3:13 *l* for new heavens and a new
2 Jn 8 *L* to yourselves, that we do not
Rev 5: 3 open the scroll, or to *l* at it.
5: 4 read the scroll, or to *l* at it.

LOOKED (146/144) LOOK

Gen 6:12 So God *l* upon the earth, and
8:13 the covering of the ark and *l*,
18: 2 So he lifted his eyes and *l*,
18:16 the men rose from there and *l*
19:26 But his wife *l* back behind him,
19:28 Then he *l* toward Sodom and
22:13 Abraham lifted his eyes and *l*,
24:63 and he lifted his eyes and *l*,
26: 8 king of the Philistines *l*
29: 2 And he *l*, and saw a well
29:32 The LORD has surely *l* on my
33: 1 Now Jacob lifted his eyes and *l*,
37:25 they lifted their eyes and *l*,
40: 6 in to them in the morning and *l*
43:33 and the men *l* in astonishment
Ex 2:11 went out to his brethren and *l*
2:12 So he *l* this way and that way,
2:25 And God *l* upon the children of
3: 2 the midst of a bush. So he *l*,
4:31 of Israel and that He had *l* on
14:24 that the LORD *l* down upon the
16:10 that they *l* toward the
39:43 Then Moses *l* over all the work,
Num 17: 9 children of Israel; and they *l*,
21: 9 when he *l* at the bronze
24:20 Then he *l* on Amalek, and he
24:21 Then he *l* on the Kenites, and
Deut 9:16 'And I *l*, and behold, you
26: 7 LORD heard our voice and *l* on
Josh 5:13 that he lifted his eyes and *l*,
8:20 And when the men of Ai *l* behind
Judg 5:28 The mother of Sisera *l* through
9:43 in wait in the field. And he *l*,
13:19 while Manoah and his wife *l* on—
20:40 the Benjamites *l* behind them,
1 Sam 6:19 because they had *l* into the ark
9:16 for I have *l* upon My people,
14:16 of Saul in Gibeah of Benjamin *l*,
16: 6 that he *l* at Eliab and said,
17:42 And when the Philistine *l* about
24: 8 the king!" And when Saul *l*
2 Sam 1: 7 Now when he *l* behind him, he saw
2:20 Then Abner *l* behind him and
6:16 *l* through a window and saw King
13:34 watch lifted his eyes and *l*,
18:24 the wall, lifted his eyes and *l*,
22:42 They *l*, but there was none
24:20 Now Araunah *l*, and saw the
1 Ki 18:43 the sea." So he went up and *l*,
19: 6 Then he *l*, and there by his
2 Ki 2:24 So he turned around and *l* at
6:30 by on the wall, the people *l*,
9:30 and *l* through a window.
9:32 And he *l* up at the window, and
9:32 So two or three eunuchs *l*
11:14 When she *l*, there was the king
1 Chr 15:29 *l* through a window and saw King
21:15 the LORD *l* and relented of the
21:21 and Ornan *l* and saw David.
2 Chr 13:14 And when Judah *l* around, to
20:24 they *l* toward the multitude;
23:13 When she *l*, there was the king
26:20 priest and all the priests *l*
Ezra 8:15 And I *l* among the people and
Neh 4:14 And I *l*, and arose and said to
Job 30:26 But when I *l* for good, evil
Ps 34: 5 They *l* to Him and were radiant,
63: 2 So I have *l* for You in the
69:20 I *l* for someone to take
102:19 For He *l* down from the height
Prov 7: 6 at the window of my house I *l*
24:32 I *l* on it and received
Eccl 2:11 Then I *l* on all the works that
Isa 5: 7 He *l* for justice, but behold,
22: 8 You *l* in that day to the armor
41:28 I *l*, and there was no man;
41:28 I *l* among them, but there
63: 5 I *l*, but there was no one to
Jer 8:15 We *l* for peace, but no good
14:19 We *l* for peace, but there
31:26 After this I awoke and *l* around,
36:16 that they *l* in fear from one to
Ezek 1: 4 I *l*, and behold, a whirlwind
1:15 Now as I *l* at the living
2: 9 Now when I *l*, there was a hand
8: 2 Then I *l*, and there was a
8: 7 door of the court; and when I *l*,
10: 1 And I *l*, and there in the
10: 9 And when I *l*, there were four
10:10 all four *l* alike—as it were, a
16: 8 I passed by you again and *l*
23:14 She *l* at men portrayed on the
37: 8 Indeed, as I *l*, the sinews and
44: 4 the front of the temple; so I *l*,
Dan 7: 6 'After this I *l*, and there was
10: 5 I lifted my eyes and *l*,
12: 5 Then I, Daniel, *l*;
Hab 3: 6 He *l* and startled the nations.
Hag 1: 9 You *l* for much, but indeed it
Zech 1:18 Then I raised my eyes and *l*,
2: 1 Then I raised my eyes and *l*,
5: 9 Then I raised my eyes and *l*,
6: 1 turned and raised my eyes and *l*,
Mt 19:26 But Jesus *l* at them and said to
Mk 3: 5 And when He had *l* around at them
3:34 And He *l* around in a circle at
5:32 And He *l* around to see her who
6:41 He *l* up to heaven, blessed and
8:24 And he *l* up and said, "I see
8:33 He had turned around and *l* at
9: 8 when they had *l* around, they
10:23 Then Jesus *l* around and said to
10:27 But Jesus *l* at them and said,
11:11 So when He had *l* around at all
14:67 she *l* at him and said, "You
16: 4 But when they *l* up, they saw
Lk 1:25 in the days when He *l* on me,
2:38 of Him to all those who *l* for
6:10 And when He had *l* around at them
10:32 at the place, came and *l*,
19: 5 He *l* up and saw him, and said
20:17 Then He *l* at them and said,
21: 1 And He *l* up and saw the rich
22:56 *l* intently at him and said,
22:61 And the Lord turned and *l* at
Jn 1:42 Now when Jesus *l* at him, He
13:22 Then the disciples *l* at one
20:11 wept she stooped down and *l*
Acts 1:10 And while they *l* steadfastly
13: 9 *l* intently at him
22:13 And at that same hour I *l* up
28: 6 But after they had *l* for a long
Heb 11:26 for he *l* to the reward.
1 Jn 1: 1 which we have *l* upon, and our
Rev 4: 1 After these things I *l*,
5: 6 And I *l*, and behold, in the
5:11 Then I *l*, and I heard the
6: 2 And I *l*, and behold, a white
6: 5 say, "Come and see." So I *l*,
6: 8 So I *l*, and behold, a pale
6:12 I *l* when He opened the sixth
7: 9 After these things I *l*,
8:13 And I *l*, and I heard an
14: 1 Then I *l*, and behold, a
14:14 Then I *l*, and behold, a
15: 5 After these things I *l*,

LOOKING (41/35) LOOK

Gen 41: 2 fine *l* and fat; and they fed in
41: 4 cows ate up the seven fine *l*
41:18 fine *l* and fat; and they fed in
1 Ki 7:25 three *l* toward the north, three
7:25 three *l* toward the west, three
7:25 three *l* toward the south, and
7:25 and three *l* toward the east;
2 Chr 4: 4 three *l* toward the north, three
4: 4 three *l* toward the west, three
4: 4 three *l* toward the south, and
4: 4 and three *l* toward the east;
Ps 119:37 Turn away my eyes from *l* at
Song 2: 9 He is *l* through the windows,
Isa 38:14 My eyes fail from *l* upward.
Jer 13:16 And while you are *l* for light,
Ezek 23:15 All of them *l* like captains,
Dan 1:10 why should he see your faces *l*
4:10 while on my bed: "I was *l*,
8: 2 it so happened while I was *l*,
Zech 4: 2 you see?" So I said, "I am *l*,
Mt 14:19 and *l* up to heaven, He blessed
24:50 come on a day when he is not *l*
27:55 were there *l* on from afar,
Mk 1:37 Everyone is *l* for You."
7:34 *l* up to heaven, He sighed, and
10:21 *l* at him, loved him, and said
15:40 There were also women *l* on from
Lk 9:16 and *l* up to heaven, He blessed
9:62 and *l* back, is fit for the
12:46 come on a day when he is not *l*
23:35 And the people stood *l* on.
Jn 1:36 And *l* at Jesus as He walked, he
20: 5 stooping down and *l* in, saw the
Acts 6:15 *l* steadfastly at him, saw his
23: 1 *l* earnestly at the council,
Titus 2:13 *l* for the blessed hope and
Heb 12: 2 *l* unto Jesus, the author and
12:15 *l* carefully lest anyone fall
2 Pe 3:12 *l* for and hastening the coming
3:14 *l* forward to these things, be
Jude 21 *l* for the mercy of our Lord

LOOKINGGLASSES (KJV) See MIRRORS

LOOKS (27/26) LOOK

Lev 13:12 his foot, wherever the priest *l*,
Num 21: 8 when he *l* at it, shall live."
21:20 to the top of Pisgah which *l*
1 Sam 16: 7 for man *l* at the outward
16: 7 but the LORD *l* at the heart."
2 Sam 14:25 much as Absalom for his good *l*.
Job 7: 2 like a hired man who eagerly *l*
28:24 For He *l* to the ends of the
33:27 Then he *l* at men and says, 'I

36:25 Man l on it from afar.
Ps 14: 2 The LORD l down from heaven
18:27 But will bring down haughty l.
33:13 The LORD l from heaven;
33:14 the place of His dwelling He l
53: 2 God l down from heaven upon the
104:32 He l on the earth, and it
Song 6:10 Who is she who l forth as the
7: 4 the tower of Lebanon Which l
Isa 2:11 The lofty l of man shall be
5:30 And if one l to the land,
10:12 and the glory of his haughty l.
Lam 3:50 Till the LORD from heaven L
Ezek 2: 6 words or dismayed by their l,
3: 9 nor be dismayed at their l,
21:21 he l at the liver.
Mt 5:28 I say to you that whoever l at
Jas 1:25 But he who l into the perfect

LOOM (4/3)

Judg 16:13 my head into the web of the l"
16:14 with the batten of the l,
16:14 batten and the web from the l.
Isa 38:12 He cuts me off from the l;

LOOMING (1/1)

2 Chr 32:25 therefore wrath was l over him

LOOPS (13/7)

Ex 26: 4 And you shall make l of blue
26: 5 Fifty l you shall make in the
26: 5 and fifty l you shall make on
26: 5 that the l may be clasped to
26:10 You shall make fifty l on the
26:10 and fifty l on the edge of the
26:11 put the clasps into the l,
36:11 He made l of blue yarn on the
36:12 Fifty l he made on one curtain,
36:12 and fifty l he made on the edge
36:12 the l held one curtain to
36:17 And he made fifty l on the edge
36:17 and fifty l he made on the edge

LOOSE (27/27) LOOSED, LOOSING, RELEASE

Gen 49:21 "Naphtali is a deer let l;
Ex 22: 5 and lets l his animal, and it
28:28 the breastplate does not come l
39:21 breastplate would not come l
Lev 14: 7 shall let the living bird l in
14:53 he shall let the living bird l
Judg 15:14 and his bonds broke l from his
Job 6: 9 That He would l His hand and
38:31 Or l the belt of Orion?
Isa 45: 1 nations before him And l the
52: 2 O Jerusalem! L yourself from
58: 6 To l the bonds of wickedness,
Jer 2:23 a swift dromedary breaking l
Dan 3:25 he answered, "I see four men l,
Mt 16:19 and whatever you l on earth
18:18 and whatever you l on earth
21: 2 L them and bring them to Me.
Mk 1: 7 not worthy to stoop down and l.
11: 2 L it and bring it.
Lk 3:16 strap I am not worthy to l.
13:15 one of you on the Sabbath l
19:30 L it and bring it here.
Jn 1:27 strap I am not worthy to l.
11:44 L him, and let him go."
Acts 13:25 whose feet I am not worthy to l.
Rev 5: 2 to open the scroll and to l
5: 5 to open the scroll and to l

LOOSED (18/17) LOOSE

Job 30:11 Because He has l my bowstring
39: 5 Who l the bonds of the onager,
Ps 116:16 You have l my bonds.
Eccl 12: 6 before the silver cord is l,
Isa 5:27 the belt on their loins be l,
33:23 Your tackle is l,
51:14 exile hastens, that he may be l,
Mt 16:19 you loose on earth will be l
18:18 you loose on earth will be l
Mk 7:35 impediment of his tongue was l,
11: 4 the street, and they l it.
Lk 1:64 was opened and his tongue l,
13:12 you are l from your
13:16 be l from this bond on the
Acts 2:24 having l the pains of death,
16:26 and everyone's chains were l.
1 Cor 7:27 to a wife? Do not seek to be l.
7:27 Are you l from a wife? Do not

LOOSENED (1/1)

Dan 5: 6 the joints of his hips were l

LOOSENS (1/1)

Job 12:18 He l the bonds of kings,

LOOSING (5/4) LOOSE

Mk 11: 5 you doing, l the colt?"
Lk 19:31 Why are you l it?' thus you
19:33 But as they were l the colt, the
19:33 Why are you l the colt?"
Acts 27:40 meanwhile l the rudder ropes;

LOOTER (1/1)

Judg 5:30 for the neck of the l?

LOP (1/1)

Isa 10:33 Will l off the bough with

LORD (7773/6614) LORD'S, LORDLY, LORDS, LORDSHIP, THE-LORD-IS-MY-BANNER, THE-LORD-IS-MY-PEACE, THE-LORD-WILL-PROVIDE

Gen 2: 4 in the day that the L God made
2: 5 For the L God had not caused
2: 7 And the L God formed man of
2: 8 The L God planted a garden
2: 9 And out of the ground the L God
2:15 Then the L God took the man
2:16 And the L God commanded the
2:18 And the L God said, "It is
2:19 Out of the ground the L God
2:21 And the L God caused a deep
2:22 Then the rib which the L God
3: 1 of the field which the L God
3: 8 they heard the sound of the L
3: 8 from the presence of the L
3: 9 Then the L God called to Adam
3:13 And the L God said to the
3:14 So the L God said to the
3:21 for Adam and his wife the L
3:22 Then the L God said, "Behold,
3:23 therefore the L God sent him
4: 1 have acquired a man from the L.
4: 3 fruit of the ground to the L.
4: 4 And the L respected Abel and
4: 6 So the L said to Cain, "Why
4: 9 Then the L said to Cain,
4:13 And Cain said to the L,
4:15 And the L said to him,
4:15 And the L set a mark on
4:16 out from the presence of the L
4:26 to call on the name of the L.
5:29 of the ground which the L has
6: 3 And the L said, "My Spirit
6: 5 Then the L saw that the
6: 6 And the L was sorry that He had
6: 7 So the L said, "I will destroy
6: 8 grace in the eyes of the L.
7: 1 Then the L said to Noah, "Come
7: 5 according to all that the L
7:16 and the L shut him in.
8:20 Noah built an altar to the L,
8:21 And the L smelled a soothing
8:21 Then the L said in His heart,
9:26 he said: "Blessed be the L,
10: 9 a mighty hunter before the L;
10: 9 the mighty hunter before the L."
11: 5 But the L came down to see the
11: 6 And the L said, "Indeed the
11: 8 So the L scattered them abroad
11: 9 because there the L confused
11: 9 and from there the L scattered
12: 1 Now the L had said to Abram:
12: 4 So Abram departed as the L had
12: 7 Then the L appeared to Abram
12: 7 he built an altar to the L,
12: 8 he built an altar to the L
12: 8 called on the name of the L.
12:17 But the L plagued Pharaoh and
13: 4 called on the name of the L.
13:10 everywhere (before the L
13:10 like the garden of the L,
13:13 and sinful against the L.
13:14 And the L said to Abram, after
13:18 built an altar there to the L.
14:22 have raised my hand to the L,
15: 1 things the word of the L came
15: 2 L GOD, what will You give me,
15: 4 the word of the L came to
15: 6 And he believed in the L,
15: 7 He said to him, "I am the L,
15: 8 L GOD, how shall I know that I
15:18 On the same day the L made a
16: 2 the L has restrained me from
16: 5 The L judge between you and
16: 7 Now the Angel of the L found
16: 9 The Angel of the L said to her,
16:10 Then the Angel of the L said to
16:11 And the Angel of the L said to
16:11 Because the L has heard your
16:13 she called the name of the L
17: 1 the L appeared to Abram and
18: 1 Then the L appeared to him by
18: 3 and said, "My L, if I have
18:12 my l being old also?"
18:13 And the L said to Abraham,
18:14 anything too hard for the L?
18:17 And the L said, "Shall I hide
18:19 they keep the way of the L,
18:19 that the L may bring to
18:20 And the L said, "Because the
18:22 still stood before the L.
18:26 So the L said, "If I find in
18:27 upon myself to speak to the L:
18:30 Let not the L be angry, and I
18:31 upon myself to speak to the L:
18:32 Let not the L be angry, and I
18:33 So the L went His way as soon
19:13 great before the face of the L,
19:13 and the L has sent us to
19:14 for the L will destroy this
19:16 the L being merciful to him,
19:24 Then the L rained brimstone and
19:24 from the L out of the heavens.
19:27 he had stood before the L.
20: 4 come near her; and he said, "L,
20:18 for the L had closed up all the
21: 1 And the L visited Sarah as He
21: 1 and the L did for Sarah as He
21:33 called on the name of the L,
22:11 But the Angel of the L called
22:14 In the Mount of The L it shall
22:15 Then the Angel of the L called
22:16 I have sworn, says the L,
23: 6 'Hear us, my l: You are a
23:11 'No, my l, hear me:
23:15 'My l, listen to me;
24: 1 and the L had blessed Abraham
24: 3 I will make you swear by the L,
24: 7 The L God of heaven, who took
24:12 O L God of my master Abraham,
24:18 So she said, "Drink, my l.
24:21 so as to know whether the L
24:26 his head and worshiped the L.
24:27 Blessed be the L God of my
24:27 the L led me to the house of
24:31 O blessed of the L! Why do you
24:35 The L has blessed my master
24:40 "But he said to me, 'The L,
24:42 O L God of my master Abraham,
24:44 her be the woman whom the L
24:48 my head and worshiped the L,
24:48 and blessed the L God of my
24:50 "The thing comes from the L;
24:51 as the L has spoken."
24:52 words, that he worshiped the L,
24:56 since the L has prospered my
25:21 Now Isaac pleaded with the L
25:21 and the L granted his plea,
25:22 she went to inquire of the L.
25:23 And the L said to her: "Two
26: 2 Then the L appeared to him and
26:12 and the L blessed him.
26:22 For now the L has made room for
26:24 And the L appeared to him the
26:25 called on the name of the L,
26:28 certainly seen that the L is
26:29 are now the blessed of the L.
27: 7 you in the presence of the L
27:20 Because the L your God brought
27:27 smell of a field Which the L
28:13 the L stood above it and said:
28:13 I am the L God of Abraham your
28:16 Surely the L is in this place,
28:21 then the L shall be my God.
29:31 When the L saw that Leah was
29:32 The L has surely looked on my
29:33 Because the L has heard that I
29:35 "Now I will praise the L.
30:24 The L shall add to me another
30:27 by experience that the L has
30:30 the L has blessed you since my
31: 3 Then the L said to Jacob,
31:35 Let it not displease my l that I
31:49 May the L watch between you and
32: 4 Speak thus to my l Esau, 'Thus
32: 5 and I have sent to tell my l,
32: 9 the L who said to me, 'Return
32:18 It is a present sent to my l
33: 8 find favor in the sight of my l.
33:13 My l knows that the children
33:14 Please let my l go on ahead
33:14 until I come to my l in Seir."
33:15 find favor in the sight of my l.
38: 7 wicked in the sight of the L,
38: 7 and the L killed him.
38:10 which he did displeased the L;
39: 2 The L was with Joseph, and he
39: 3 And his master saw that the L
39: 3 was with him and that the L
39: 5 that the L blessed the
39: 5 and the blessing of the L was
39:21 But the L was with Joseph and
39:23 because the L was with him;
39:23 the L made it prosper.
40: 1 king of Egypt offended their l,
42:10 they said to him, "No, my l,
42:30 The man who is l of the land
42:33 the l of the country, said to
44: 5 this the one from which my l
44: 7 Why does my l say these words?
44:16 "What shall we say to my l?
44:18 near to him and said: "O my l,
44:19 My l asked his servants, saying,
44:20 "And we said to my l,
44:22 "And we said to my l,
44:24 we told him the words of my l.
44:33 of the lad as a slave to my l,
45: 8 and l of all his house, and a
45: 9 God has made me l of all Egypt;
47:18 We will not hide from my l that
47:18 my l also has our herds of
47:18 left in the sight of my l but
47:25 find favor in the sight of my l,
49:18 for your salvation, O L!
Ex 3: 2 And the Angel of the L appeared
3: 4 So when the L saw that he
3: 7 And the L said: "I have
3:15 The L God of your fathers, the
3:16 The L God of your fathers, the
3:18 The L God of the Hebrews has
3:18 we may sacrifice to the L our

4: 1 The *L* has not appeared to you.'
4: 2 So the *L* said to him, "What
4: 4 Then the *L* said to Moses,
4: 5 they may believe that the *L*
4: 6 Furthermore the *L* said to him,
4:10 Then Moses said to the *L*,
4:10 said to the LORD, "O my *L*,
4:11 So the *L* said to him, "Who has
4:11 the blind? Have not I, the *L*?
4:13 But he said, "O my *L*,
4:14 So the anger of the *L* was
4:19 And the *L* said to Moses in
4:21 And the *L* said to Moses, "When
4:22 to Pharaoh, 'Thus says the *L*:
4:24 that the *L* met him and sought
4:27 And the *L* said to Aaron, "Go
4:28 Aaron all the words of the *L*
4:30 all the words which the *L* had
4:31 and when they heard that the *L*
5: 1 Thus says the *L* God of Israel:
5: 2 Pharaoh said, "Who is the *L*,
5: 2 Israel go? I do not know the *L*,
5: 3 desert and sacrifice to the *L*
5:17 us go and sacrifice to the *L*.
5:21 Let the *L* look on you and
5:22 So Moses returned to the *L* and
5:22 to the LORD and said, "*L*,
6: 1 Then the *L* said to Moses, "Now
6: 2 and said to him: "I am the *L*.
6: 3 but by My name *L* I was not
6: 6 of Israel: 'I am the *L*;
6: 7 shall know that I am the *L*
6: 8 as a heritage: I am the *L*.
6:10 And the *L* spoke to Moses,
6:12 And Moses spoke before the *L*,
6:13 Then the *L* spoke to Moses and
6:26 Aaron and Moses to whom the *L*
6:28 on the day the *L* spoke to
6:29 that the *L* spoke to Moses,
6:29 Moses, saying, "I am the *L*.
6:30 But Moses said before the *L*,
7: 1 So the *L* said to Moses: "See,
7: 5 shall know that I am the *L*,
7: 6 just as the *L* commanded them,
7: 8 Then the *L* spoke to Moses and
7:10 so, just as the *L* commanded.
7:13 as the *L* had said.
7:14 So the *L* said to Moses:
7:16 The *L* God of the Hebrews has
7:17 'Thus says the *L*: "By this
7:17 shall know that I am the *L*.
7:19 Then the *L* spoke to Moses,
7:20 just as the *L* commanded. So he
7:22 heed them, as the *L* had said.
7:25 seven days passed after the *L*
8: 1 And the *L* spoke to Moses, "Go
8: 1 say to him, 'Thus says the *L*:
8: 5 Then the *L* spoke to Moses,
8: 8 Entreat the *L* that He may take
8: 8 they may sacrifice to the *L*.
8:10 there is no one like the *L*
8:12 And Moses cried out to the *L*
8:13 So the *L* did according to the
8:15 heed them, as the *L* had said.
8:16 So the *L* said to Moses, "Say
8:19 just as the *L* had said.
8:20 And the *L* said to Moses,
8:20 say to him, 'Thus says the *L*:
8:22 you may know that I am the *L*
8:24 And the *L* did so. Thick swarms
8:26 of the Egyptians to the *L* our
8:27 and sacrifice to the *L* our
8:28 you may sacrifice to the *L*
8:29 you, and I will entreat the *L*,
8:29 go to sacrifice to the *L*.
8:30 Pharaoh and entreated the *L*.
8:31 And the *L* did according to the
9: 1 Then the *L* said to Moses, "Go
9: 1 Thus says the *L* God of the
9: 3 the hand of the *L* will be on
9: 4 And the *L* will make a
9: 5 Then the *L* appointed a set
9: 5 Tomorrow the *L* will do this
9: 6 So the *L* did this thing on the
9: 8 So the *L* said to Moses and
9:12 But the *L* hardened the heart of
9:12 just as the *L* had spoken to
9:13 Then the *L* said to Moses,
9:13 Thus says the *L* God of the
9:20 who feared the word of the *L*
9:21 not regard the word of the *L*
9:22 Then the *L* said to Moses,
9:23 and the *L* sent thunder and
9:23 And the *L* rained hail on the
9:27 The *L* is righteous, and my
9:28 'Entreat the *L*, that there
9:29 spread out my hands to the *L*;
9:30 you will not yet fear the *L*
9:33 spread out his hands to the *L*;
9:35 as the *L* had spoken by Moses.
10: 1 Now the *L* said to Moses, "Go
10: 2 you may know that I am the *L*.
10: 3 Thus says the *L* God of the
10: 7 that they may serve the *L*
10: 8 serve the *L* your God. Who are
10: 9 we must hold a feast to the *L*.
10:10 The *L* had better be with you
10:11 who are men, and serve the *L*,
10:12 Then the *L* said to Moses,
10:13 and the *L* brought an east wind
10:16 I have sinned against the *L*
10:17 and entreat the *L* your God,
10:18 Pharaoh and entreated the *L*.
10:19 And the *L* turned a very strong
10:20 But the *L* hardened Pharaoh's
10:21 Then the *L* said to Moses,
10:24 and said, "Go, serve the *L*;
10:25 we may sacrifice to the *L* our
10:26 some of them to serve the *L*
10:26 with what we must serve the *L*
10:27 But the *L* hardened Pharaoh's
11: 1 And the *L* said to Moses, "I
11: 3 And the *L* gave the people favor
11: 4 Moses said, "Thus says the *L*:
11: 7 that you may know that the *L*
11: 9 But the *L* said to Moses,
11:10 and the *L* hardened Pharaoh's
12: 1 Now the *L* spoke to Moses and
12:12 execute judgment: I am the *L*.
12:14 keep it as a feast to the *L*
12:23 For the *L* will pass through to
12:23 the *L* will pass over the door
12:25 come to the land which the *L*
12:27 Passover sacrifice of the *L*,
12:28 just as the *L* had commanded
12:29 to pass at midnight that the *L*
12:31 serve the *L* as you have said.
12:36 And the *L* had given the people
12:41 that all the armies of the *L*
12:42 of solemn observance to the *L*
12:42 This is that night of the *L*,
12:43 And the *L* said to Moses and
12:48 to keep the Passover to the *L*,
12:50 as the *L* commanded Moses and
12:51 that the *L* brought the
13: 1 Then the *L* spoke to Moses,
13: 3 for by strength of hand the *L*
13: 5 when the *L* brings you into the
13: 6 shall be a feast to the *L*.
13: 8 done because of what the *L*
13: 9 for with a strong hand the *L*
13:11 when the *L* brings you into the
13:12 you shall set apart to the *L*
13:14 By strength of hand the *L*
13:15 that the *L* killed all the
13:15 I sacrifice to the *L* all
13:16 for by strength of hand the *L*
13:21 And the *L* went before them by
14: 1 Now the *L* spoke to Moses,
14: 4 may know that I am the *L*.
14: 8 And the *L* hardened the heart of
14:10 of Israel cried out to the *L*.
14:13 and see the salvation of the *L*,
14:14 The *L* will fight for you, and
14:15 And the *L* said to Moses, "Why
14:18 shall know that I am the *L*,
14:21 and the *L* caused the sea to go
14:24 that the *L* looked down upon
14:25 for the *L* fights for them
14:26 Then the *L* said to Moses,
14:27 So the *L* overthrew the
14:30 So the *L* saved Israel that day
14:31 saw the great work which the *L*
14:31 so the people feared the *L*,
14:31 and believed the *L* and His
15: 1 Israel sang this song to the *L*,
15: 1 "I will sing to the *L*,
15: 2 The *L* is my strength and
15: 3 The *L* is a man of war;
15: 3 The *L* is His name.
15: 6 "Your right hand, O *L*,
15: 6 Your right hand, O *L*,
15:11 "Who is like You, O *L*,
15:16 Your people pass over, O *L*,
15:17 In the place, O *L*,
15:17 dwelling, The sanctuary, O *L*,
15:18 The *L* shall reign forever and
15:19 and the *L* brought back the
15:21 them: "Sing to the *L*,
15:25 So he cried out to the *L*,
15:25 and the *L* showed him a tree.
15:26 heed the voice of the *L* your
15:26 For I am the *L* who heals
16: 3 had died by the hand of the *L*
16: 4 Then the *L* said to Moses,
16: 6 you shall know that the *L* has
16: 7 shall see the glory of the *L*;
16: 7 your complaints against the *L*.
16: 8 shall be seen when the *L*
16: 8 for the *L* hears your
16: 8 against us but against the *L*.
16: 9 'Come near before the *L*,
16:10 the glory of the *L* appeared in
16:11 And the *L* spoke to Moses,
16:12 shall know that I am the *L*
16:15 is the bread which the *L* has
16:16 is the thing which the *L*
16:23 This is what the *L* has said:
16:23 rest, a holy Sabbath to the *L*.
16:25 today is a Sabbath to the *L*;
16:28 And the *L* said to Moses, "How
16:29 See! For the *L* has given you
16:32 is the thing which the *L* has
16:33 it, and lay it up before the *L*,
16:34 As the *L* commanded Moses, so
17: 1 to the commandment of the *L*,
17: 2 Why do you tempt the *L*?"
17: 4 So Moses cried out to the *L*,
17: 5 And the *L* said to Moses, "Go
17: 7 and because they tempted the *L*,
17: 7 Is the *L* among us or not?"
17:14 Then the *L* said to Moses,
17:16 'Because the *L* has sworn:
17:16 the *L* will have war with
18: 1 that the *L* had brought Israel
18: 8 father-in-law all that the *L*
18: 8 and how the *L* had delivered
18: 9 for all the good which the *L*
18:10 said, "Blessed be the *L*,
18:11 Now I know that the *L* is
19: 3 and the *L* called to him from
19: 7 all these words which the *L*
19: 8 All that the *L* has spoken we
19: 8 words of the people to the *L*.
19: 9 And the *L* said to Moses,
19: 9 words of the people to the *L*.
19:10 Then the *L* said to Moses, "Go
19:11 For on the third day the *L*
19:18 because the *L* descended upon
19:20 Then the *L* came down upon Mount
19:20 And the *L* called Moses to the
19:21 And the *L* said to Moses, "Go
19:21 break through to gaze at the *L*,
19:22 priests who come near the *L*
19:22 lest the *L* break out against
19:23 But Moses said to the *L*,
19:24 Then the *L* said to him, "Away!
19:24 through to come up to the *L*,
20: 2 I am the *L* your God, who
20: 5 the *L* your God, am a jealous
20: 7 not take the name of the *L*
20: 7 for the *L* will not hold him
20:10 day is the Sabbath of the *L*
20:11 For in six days the *L* made the
20:11 Therefore the *L* blessed the
20:12 long upon the land which the *L*
20:22 Then the *L* said to Moses,
22:11 then an oath of the *L* shall be
22:20 except to the *L* only, he shall
23:17 shall appear before the *L* GOD.
23:19 bring into the house of the *L*
23:25 So you shall serve the *L* your
24: 1 to Moses, "Come up to the *L*,
24: 2 alone shall come near the *L*,
24: 3 people all the words of the *L*
24: 3 All the words which the *L* has
24: 4 wrote all the words of the *L*.
24: 5 offerings of oxen to the *L*.
24: 7 All that the *L* has said we will
24: 8 of the covenant which the *L*
24:12 Then the *L* said to Moses,
24:16 Now the glory of the *L* rested
24:17 sight of the glory of the *L*
25: 1 Then the *L* spoke to Moses,
27:21 until morning before the *L*.
28:12 bear their names before the *L*
28:29 as a memorial before the *L*
28:30 when he goes in before the *L*.
28:30 over his heart before the *L*
28:35 the holy place before the *L*
28:36 of a signet: HOLINESS TO THE *L*.
28:38 may be accepted before the *L*.
29:11 kill the bull before the *L*,
29:18 is a burnt offering to the *L*;
29:18 offering made by fire to the *L*.
29:23 bread that is before the *L*;
29:24 a wave offering before the *L*.
29:25 as a sweet aroma before the *L*.
29:25 offering made by fire to the *L*.
29:26 a wave offering before the *L*;
29:28 their heave offering to the *L*.
29:41 offering made by fire to the *L*.
29:42 of meeting before the *L*,
29:46 shall know that I am the *L*
29:46 I am the *L* their God.
30: 8 perpetual incense before the *L*
30:10 It is most holy to the *L*.
30:11 Then the *L* spoke to Moses,
30:12 a ransom for himself to the *L*,
30:13 be an offering to the *L*.
30:14 give an offering to the *L*.
30:15 you give an offering to the *L*,
30:16 of Israel before the *L*,
30:17 Then the *L* spoke to Moses,
30:20 offering made by fire to the *L*,
30:22 Moreover the *L* spoke to Moses,
30:34 And the *L* said to Moses:
30:37 shall be to you holy for the *L*.
31: 1 Then the *L* spoke to Moses,
31:12 And the *L* spoke to Moses,
31:13 may know that I am the *L* who
31:15 Sabbath of rest, holy to the *L*.
31:17 for in six days the *L* made
32: 5 is a feast to the *L*.
32: 7 And the *L* said to Moses, "Go,
32: 9 And the *L* said to Moses, "I
32:11 Moses pleaded with the *L* his
32:11 LORD his God, and said: "*L*,
32:14 So the *L* relented from the harm
32:22 Do not let the anger of my *l*
32:27 Thus says the *L* God of Israel:
32:29 yourselves today to the *L*,
32:30 So now I will go up to the *L*;
32:31 Then Moses returned to the *L*
32:33 And the *L* said to Moses,
32:35 So the *L* plagued the people
33: 1 Then the *L* said to Moses,
33: 5 For the *L* had said to Moses,
33: 7 everyone who sought the *L*
33: 9 and the *L* talked with Moses.
33:11 So the *L* spoke to Moses face to
33:12 Then Moses said to the *L*,
33:17 So the *L* said to Moses, "I
33:19 proclaim the name of the *L*
33:21 And the *L* said, "Here is a
34: 1 And the *L* said to Moses, "Cut

34: 4 as the *L* had commanded him;
34: 5 Now the *L* descended in the
34: 5 proclaimed the name of the *L*.
34: 6 And the *L* passed before him and
34: 6 him and proclaimed, "The *L*,
34: 6 the *L* God, merciful and
34: 9 found grace in Your sight, O *L*,
34: 9 in Your sight, O Lord, let my *L*,
34:10 shall see the work of the *L*.
34:14 no other god, for the *L*,
34:23 men shall appear before the *L*,
34:23 the *L* God of Israel.
34:24 go up to appear before the *L*
34:26 bring to the house of the *L*
34:27 Then the *L* said to Moses,
34:28 So he was there with the *L*
34:32 as commandments all that the *L*
34:34 Moses went in before the *L* to
35: 1 are the words which the *L*
35: 2 a Sabbath of rest to the *L*.
35: 4 is the thing which the *L*
35: 5 among you an offering to the *L*.
35: 5 it as an offering to the *L*:
35:10 come and make all that the *L*
35:22 an offering of gold to the *L*.
35:29 a freewill offering to the *L*,
35:29 all kinds of work which the *L*,
35:30 the *L* has called by name
36: 1 gifted artisan in whom the *L*
36: 1 do according to all that the *L*
36: 2 artisan in whose heart the *L*
36: 5 of the work which the *L*
38:22 made all that the *L* had
39: 1 as the *L* had commanded Moses.
39: 5 as the *L* had commanded Moses.
39: 7 as the *L* had commanded Moses.
39:21 as the *L* had commanded Moses.
39:26 as the *L* had commanded Moses.
39:29 as the *L* had commanded Moses.
39:30 of a signet: HOLINESS TO THE *L*.
39:31 as the *L* had commanded Moses.
39:32 according to all that the *L*
39:42 According to all that the *L*
39:43 as the *L* had commanded, just
40: 1 Then the *L* spoke to Moses,
40:16 according to all that the *L*
40:19 as the *L* had commanded Moses.
40:21 as the *L* had commanded Moses.
40:23 in order upon it before the *L*,
40:23 as the *L* had commanded Moses.
40:25 he lit the lamps before the *L*,
40:25 as the *L* had commanded Moses.
40:27 as the *L* had commanded Moses.
40:29 as the *L* had commanded Moses.
40:32 as the *L* had commanded Moses.
40:34 and the glory of the *L* filled
40:35 and the glory of the *L* filled
40:38 For the cloud of the *L* was
Lev 1: 1 Now the *L* called to Moses, and
1: 2 brings an offering to the *L*,
1: 3 of meeting before the *L*.
1: 5 kill the bull before the *L*;
1: 9 fire, a sweet aroma to the *L*.
1:11 side of the altar before the *L*;
1:13 fire, a sweet aroma to the *L*.
1:14 of his offering to the *L* is
1:17 fire, a sweet aroma to the *L*.
2: 1 a grain offering to the *L*,
2: 2 fire, a sweet aroma to the *L*.
2: 3 holy of the offerings to the *L*
2: 8 made of these things to the *L*.
2: 9 fire, a sweet aroma to the *L*.
2:10 holy of the offerings to the *L*
2:11 which you bring to the *L*
2:11 in any offering to the *L* made
2:12 you shall offer them to the *L*,
2:14 of your firstfruits to the *L*,
2:16 offering made by fire to the *L*.
3: 1 without blemish before the *L*.
3: 3 offering made by fire to the *L*.
3: 5 fire, a sweet aroma to the *L*.
3: 6 of a peace offering to the *L*
3: 7 he shall offer it before the *L*.
3: 9 offering made by fire to the *L*,
3:11 offering made by fire to the *L*.
3:12 he shall offer it before the *L*.
3:14 offering made by fire to the *L*.
4: 1 Now the *L* spoke to Moses,
4: 2 of the commandments of the *L*
4: 3 then let him offer to the *L*
4: 4 of meeting before the *L*,
4: 4 and kill the bull before the *L*.
4: 6 blood seven times before the *L*,
4: 7 of sweet incense before the *L*,
4:13 of the commandments of the *L*
4:15 head of the bull before the *L*.
4:15 shall be killed before the *L*.
4:17 it seven times before the *L*,
4:18 altar which is before the *L*,
4:22 of the commandments of the *L*
4:24 burnt offering before the *L*.
4:27 of the commandments of the *L*
4:31 for a sweet aroma to the *L*.
4:35 made by fire to the *L*.
5: 6 his trespass offering to the *L*
5: 7 then he shall bring to the *L*,
5:12 made by fire to the *L*.
5:14 Then the *L* spoke to Moses,
5:15 to the holy things of the *L*,
5:15 then he shall bring to the *L*
5:17 by the commandments of the *L*,
5:19 trespassed against the *L*.
6: 1 And the *L* spoke to Moses,
6: 2 a trespass against the *L* by
6: 6 his trespass offering to the *L*,
6: 7 atonement for him before the *L*,
6: 8 Then the *L* spoke to Moses,
6:14 it on the altar before the *L*.
6:15 aroma, as a memorial to the *L*.
6:18 made by fire to the *L*.
6:19 And the *L* spoke to Moses,
6:20 they shall offer to the *L*,
6:21 for a sweet aroma to the *L*.
6:22 is a statute forever to the *L*.
6:24 And the *L* spoke to Moses,
6:25 shall be killed before the *L*.
7: 5 offering made by fire to the *L*.
7:11 which he shall offer to the *L*:
7:14 as a heave offering to the *L*.
7:20 that belongs to the *L*,
7:21 that belongs to the *L*,
7:22 And the *L* spoke to Moses,
7:25 offering made by fire to the *L*,
7:28 Then the *L* spoke to Moses,
7:29 of his peace offering to the *L*
7:29 bring his offering to the *L*
7:30 made by fire to the *L*.
7:30 a wave offering before the *L*.
7:35 made by fire to the *L*,
7:35 them to minister to the *L* as
7:36 The *L* commanded this to be
7:38 which the *L* commanded Moses on
7:38 their offerings to the *L* in
8: 1 And the *L* spoke to Moses,
8: 4 So Moses did as the *L* commanded
8: 5 This is what the *L* commanded
8: 9 as the *L* had commanded Moses.
8:13 as the *L* had commanded Moses.
8:17 as the *L* had commanded Moses.
8:21 offering made by fire to the *L*,
8:21 as the *L* had commanded Moses.
8:26 bread that was before the *L*
8:27 a wave offering before the *L*.
8:28 offering made by fire to the *L*.
8:29 a wave offering before the *L*.
8:29 as the *L* had commanded Moses.
8:34 so the *L* has commanded to do,
8:35 and keep the charge of the *L*,
8:36 did all the things that the *L*
9: 2 and offer them before the *L*.
9: 4 to sacrifice before the *L*,
9: 4 for today the *L* will appear to
9: 5 near and stood before the *L*.
9: 6 is the thing which the *L*
9: 6 and the glory of the *L* will
9: 7 as the *L* commanded."
9:10 as the *L* had commanded Moses.
9:21 a wave offering before the *L*,
9:23 Then the glory of the *L*
9:24 came out from before the *L*
10: 1 profane fire before the *L*,
10: 2 So fire went out from the *L* and
10: 2 and they died before the *L*.
10: 3 This is what the *L* spoke,
10: 6 the burning which the *L* has
10: 7 for the anointing oil of the *L*
10: 8 Then the *L* spoke to Aaron,
10:11 all the statutes which the *L*
10:12 made by fire to the *L*,
10:13 made by fire to the *L*;
10:15 a wave offering before the *L*.
10:15 as the *L* has commanded."
10:17 for them before the *L*?
10:19 burnt offering before the *L*,
10:19 accepted in the sight of the *L*?
11: 1 Now the *L* spoke to Moses and
11:44 For I am the *L* your God. You
11:45 For I am the *L* who brings you
12: 1 Then the *L* spoke to Moses,
12: 7 he shall offer it before the *L*,
13: 1 And the *L* spoke to Moses and
14: 1 Then the *L* spoke to Moses,
14:11 and those things, before the *L*,
14:12 a wave offering before the *L*.
14:16 seven times before the *L*.
14:18 atonement for him before the *L*.
14:23 of meeting, before the *L*.
14:24 a wave offering before the *L*.
14:27 hand seven times before the *L*.
14:29 atonement for him before the *L*.
14:31 is to be cleansed before the *L*.
14:33 And the *L* spoke to Moses and
15: 1 And the *L* spoke to Moses and
15:14 pigeons, and come before the *L*,
15:15 for him before the *L* because
15:30 for her before the *L* for the
16: 1 Now the *L* spoke to Moses after
16: 1 profane fire before the *L*,
16: 2 and the *L* said to Moses: "Tell
16: 7 and present them before the *L*
16: 8 one lot for the *L* and the
16:10 presented alive before the *L*,
16:12 from the altar before the *L*,
16:13 on the fire before the *L*,
16:18 altar that is before the *L*,
16:30 all your sins before the *L*.
16:34 And he did as the *L*
17: 1 And the *L* spoke to Moses,
17: 2 is the thing which the *L* has
17: 4 to offer an offering to the *L*
17: 4 before the tabernacle of the *L*,
17: 5 they may bring them to the *L*
17: 5 as peace offerings to the *L*.
17: 6 blood on the altar of the *L*
17: 6 fat for a sweet aroma to the *L*.
17: 9 meeting, to offer it to the *L*,
18: 1 Then the *L* spoke to Moses,
18: 2 I am the *L* your God.
18: 4 I am the *L* your God.
18: 5 live by them: I am the *L*.
18: 6 his nakedness: I am the *L*.
18:21 name of your God: I am the *L*.
18:30 I am the *L* your God.'"
19: 1 And the *L* spoke to Moses,
19: 2 for I the *L* your God am holy.
19: 3 I am the *L* your God.
19: 4 I am the *L* your God.
19: 5 of a peace offering to the *L*,
19: 8 hallowed offering of the *L*;
19:10 I am the *L* your God.
19:12 name of your God: I am the *L*.
19:14 fear your God: I am the *L*.
19:16 of your neighbor: I am the *L*.
19:18 as yourself: I am the *L*.
19:21 his trespass offering to the *L*,
19:22 offering before the *L* for his
19:24 be holy, a praise to the *L*.
19:25 I am the *L* your God.
19:28 any marks on you: I am the *L*.
19:30 My sanctuary: I am the *L*.
19:31 I am the *L* your God.
19:32 and fear your God: I am the *L*.
19:34 I am the *L* your God.
19:36 I am the *L* your God, who
19:37 and perform them: I am the *L*.
20: 1 Then the *L* spoke to Moses,
20: 7 for I am the *L* your God.
20: 8 I am the *L* who sanctifies
20:24 I am the *L* your God, who
20:26 for I the *L* am holy, and have
21: 1 And the *L* said to Moses,
21: 6 offer the offerings of the *L*
21: 8 be holy to you, for I the *L*,
21:12 God is upon him: I am the *L*.
21:15 for I the *L* sanctify him.'"
21:16 And the *L* spoke to Moses,
21:21 made by fire to the *L*.
21:23 for I the *L* sanctify them.'"
22: 1 Then the *L* spoke to Moses,
22: 2 dedicate to Me: I am the *L*.
22: 3 of Israel dedicate to the *L*,
22: 3 from My presence: I am the *L*.
22: 8 himself with it: I am the *L*.
22: 9 I the *L* sanctify them.
22:15 which they offer to the *L*,
22:16 for I the *L* sanctify them.'"
22:17 And the *L* spoke to Moses,
22:18 which they offer to the *L* as a
22:21 of a peace offering to the *L*,
22:22 you shall not offer to the *L*,
22:22 of them on the altar to the *L*.
22:24 You shall not offer to the *L*
22:26 And the *L* spoke to Moses,
22:27 offering made by fire to the *L*.
22:29 of thanksgiving to the *L*,
22:30 it until morning: I am the *L*.
22:31 and perform them: I am the *L*.
22:32 I am the *L* who sanctifies
22:33 to be your God: I am the *L*.
23: 1 And the *L* spoke to Moses,
23: 2 to them: 'The feasts of the *L*,
23: 3 it is the Sabbath of the *L* in
23: 4 are the feasts of the *L*,
23: 6 of Unleavened Bread to the *L*;
23: 8 made by fire to the *L* for
23: 9 And the *L* spoke to Moses,
23:11 wave the sheaf before the *L*,
23:12 as a burnt offering to the *L*,
23:13 offering made by fire to the *L*,
23:16 a new grain offering to the *L*.
23:17 are the firstfruits to the *L*.
23:18 as a burnt offering to the *L*,
23:18 for a sweet aroma to the *L*.
23:20 a wave offering before the *L*,
23:20 They shall be holy to the *L*
23:22 I am the *L* your God.'"
23:23 Then the *L* spoke to Moses,
23:25 offering made by fire to the *L*.
23:26 And the *L* spoke to Moses,
23:27 offering made by fire to the *L*.
23:28 for you before the *L* your God.
23:33 Then the *L* spoke to Moses,
23:34 for seven days to the *L*.
23:36 offering made by fire to the *L*.
23:36 offering made by fire to the *L*.
23:37 are the feasts of the *L*
23:37 offering made by fire to the *L*,
23:38 'besides the Sabbaths of the *L*,
23:38 which you give to the *L*.
23:39 shall keep the feast of the *L*
23:40 you shall rejoice before the *L*
23:41 keep it as a feast to the *L*
23:43 I am the *L* your God.'"
23:44 of Israel the feasts of the *L*.
24: 1 Then the *L* spoke to Moses,
24: 3 until morning before the *L*
24: 4 gold lampstand before the *L*
24: 6 pure gold table before the *L*.
24: 7 offering made by fire to the *L*.
24: 8 set it in order before the *L*
24: 9 from the offerings of the *L*
24:11 the name of the *L* and
24:12 that the mind of the *L* might
24:13 And the *L* spoke to Moses,
24:16 blasphemes the name of the *L*
24:16 the name of the *L*,

24:22 for I am the *L* your God.'"
24:23 of Israel did as the *L*
25: 1 And the *L* spoke to Moses on
25: 2 shall keep a sabbath to the *L*.
25: 4 the land, a sabbath to the *L*.
25:17 for I am the *L* your God.
25:38 I am the *L* your God, who
25:55 I am the *L* your God.
26: 1 for I am the *L* your God.
26: 2 My sanctuary: I am the *L*.
26:13 I am the *L* your God, who
26:44 for I am the *L* their God.
26:45 be their God: I am the *L*.
26:46 and laws which the *L* made
27: 1 Now the *L* spoke to Moses,
27: 2 a vow certain persons to the *L*,
27: 9 bring as an offering to the *L*,
27: 9 that anyone gives to the *L*
27:11 offer as a sacrifice to the *L*,
27:14 house to be holy to the *L*,
27:16 If a man dedicates to the *L*
27:21 shall be holy to the *L*,
27:22 if a man dedicates to the *L* a
27:23 as a holy offering to the *L*.
27:28 a man may devote to the *L* of
27:28 is most holy to the *L*.
27:30 It is holy to the *L*.
27:32 one shall be holy to the *L*.
27:34 the commandments which the *L*
Num 1: 1 Now the *L* spoke to Moses in
1:19 As the *L* commanded Moses, so he
1:48 for the *L* had spoken to Moses,
1:54 according to all that the *L*
2: 1 And the *L* spoke to Moses and
2:33 just as the *L* commanded Moses.
2:34 according to all that the *L*
3: 1 of Aaron and Moses when the *L*
3: 4 Abihu had died before the *L*
3: 4 profane fire before the *L* in
3: 5 And the *L* spoke to Moses,
3:11 Then the *L* spoke to Moses,
3:13 shall be Mine: I am the *L*.
3:14 Then the *L* spoke to Moses in
3:16 according to the word of the *L*,
3:39 at the commandment of the *L*,
3:40 Then the *L* said to Moses:
3:41 the Levites for Me—I am the *L*—
3:42 as the *L* commanded him.
3:44 Then the *L* spoke to Moses,
3:45 shall be Mine: I am the *L*.
3:51 according to the word of the *L*,
3:51 as the *L* commanded Moses.
4: 1 Then the *L* spoke to Moses and
4:17 Then the *L* spoke to Moses and
4:21 Then the *L* spoke to Moses,
4:37 to the commandment of the *L*
4:41 to the commandment of the *L*.
4:45 to the word of the *L* by the
4:49 to the commandment of the *L*
4:49 as the *L* commanded Moses.
5: 1 And the *L* spoke to Moses,
5: 4 as the *L* spoke to Moses, so
5: 5 Then the *L* spoke to Moses,
5: 6 unfaithfulness against the *L*,
5: 8 the wrong must go to the *L*
5:11 And the *L* spoke to Moses,
5:16 near, and set her before the *L*.
5:18 stand the woman before the *L*,
5:21 the *L* make you a curse and an
5:21 when the *L* makes your thigh
5:25 wave the offering before the *L*,
5:30 stand the woman before the *L*,
6: 1 Then the *L* spoke to Moses,
6: 2 to separate himself to the *L*,
6: 5 he separated himself to the *L*,
6: 6 he separates himself to the *L*
6: 8 he shall be holy to the *L*.
6:12 He shall consecrate to the *L*
6:14 present his offering to the *L*:
6:16 bring them before the *L* and
6:17 of peace offering to the *L*,
6:20 a wave offering before the *L*;
6:21 the Nazirite who vows to the *L*
6:22 And the *L* spoke to Moses,
6:24 The *L* bless you and keep you;
6:25 The *L* make His face shine upon
6:26 The *L* lift up His countenance
7: 3 their offering before the *L*,
7: 4 Then the *L* spoke to Moses,
7:11 For the *L* said to Moses, "They
8: 1 And the *L* spoke to Moses,
8: 3 as the *L* commanded Moses.
8: 4 to the pattern which the *L*
8: 5 Then the *L* spoke to Moses,
8:10 bring the Levites before the *L*,
8:11 offer the Levites before the *L*,
8:11 may perform the work of the *L*.
8:12 as a burnt offering to the *L*,
8:13 like a wave offering to the *L*.
8:20 according to all that the *L*
8:21 a wave offering before the *L*,
8:22 as the *L* commanded Moses
8:23 Then the *L* spoke to Moses,
9: 1 Now the *L* spoke to Moses in the
9: 5 according to all that the *L*
9: 7 the offering of the *L* at its
9: 8 that I may hear what the *L*
9: 9 Then the *L* spoke to Moses,
9:13 bring the offering of the *L*
9:18 At the command of the *L* the
9:18 and at the command of the *L*
9:19 kept the charge of the *L* and

9:20 to the command of the *L* they
9:20 to the command of the *L* they
9:23 At the command of the *L* they
9:23 and at the command of the *L*
9:23 they kept the charge of the *L*,
9:23 at the command of the *L* by the
10: 1 And the *L* spoke to Moses,
10: 9 be remembered before the *L*
10:10 I am the *L* your God."
10:13 to the command of the *L* by
10:29 for the place of which the *L*
10:29 for the *L* has promised good
10:32 that whatever good the *L* will
10:33 from the mountain of the *L* on
10:33 ark of the covenant of the *L*
10:34 And the cloud of the *L* was
10:35 O *L*! Let Your enemies be
10:36 he said: "Return, O *L*,
11: 1 it displeased the *L*;
11: 1 for the *L* heard it, and His
11: 1 So the fire of the *L* burned
11: 2 and when Moses prayed to the *L*,
11: 3 because the fire of the *L* had
11:10 and the anger of the *L* was
11:11 So Moses said to the *L*,
11:16 So the *L* said to Moses:
11:18 wept in the hearing of the *L*,
11:18 Therefore the *L* will give
11:20 you have despised the *L* who
11:23 And the *L* said to Moses, "Has
11:24 the people the words of the *L*,
11:25 Then the *L* came down in the
11:28 answered and said, "Moses my *l*,
11:29 were prophets and that the *L*
11:31 a wind went out from the *L*,
11:33 the wrath of the *L* was aroused
11:33 and the *L* struck the people
12: 2 Has the *L* indeed spoken only
12: 2 And the *L* heard it.
12: 4 Suddenly the *L* said to Moses,
12: 5 Then the *L* came down in the
12: 6 prophet among you, I, the *L*,
12: 8 And he sees the form of the *L*.
12: 9 So the anger of the *L* was
12:11 my *l*! Please do not lay this
12:13 So Moses cried out to the *L*,
12:14 Then the *L* said to Moses, "If
13: 1 And the *L* spoke to Moses,
13: 3 to the command of the *L*,
14: 3 Why has the *L* brought us to
14: 8 If the *L* delights in us, then
14: 9 do not rebel against the *L*,
14: 9 and the *L* is with us. Do not
14:10 Now the glory of the *L*
14:11 Then the *L* said to Moses:
14:13 And Moses said to the *L*:
14:14 They have heard that You, *L*,
14:14 these people; that You, *L*,
14:16 Because the *L* was not able to
14:17 let the power of my *L* be
14:18 The *L* is longsuffering and
14:20 Then the *L* said: "I have
14:21 filled with the glory of the *L*—
14:26 And the *L* spoke to Moses and
14:28 them, 'As I live,' says the *L*,
14:35 'I the *L* have spoken this;
14:37 by the plague before the *L*.
14:40 go up to the place which the *L*
14:41 the command of the *L*?
14:42 for the *L* is not among you.
14:43 have turned away from the *L*,
14:43 the *L* will not be with you."
14:44 ark of the covenant of the *L*
15: 1 And the *L* spoke to Moses,
15: 3 an offering by fire to the *L*,
15: 3 to make a sweet aroma to the *L*,
15: 4 his offering to the *L* shall
15: 7 wine as a sweet aroma to the *L*.
15: 8 as a peace offering to the *L*,
15:10 fire, a sweet aroma to the *L*.
15:13 fire, a sweet aroma to the *L*.
15:14 fire, a sweet aroma to the *L*,
15:15 the stranger be before the *L*.
15:17 Again the *L* spoke to Moses,
15:19 up a heave offering to the *L*.
15:21 meal you shall give to the *L*
15:22 commandments which the *L* has
15:23 all that the *L* has commanded
15:23 from the day the *L* gave
15:24 as a sweet aroma to the *L*,
15:25 offering made by fire to the *L*,
15:25 sin offering before the *L*,
15:28 unintentionally before the *L*,
15:30 one brings reproach on the *L*,
15:31 has despised the word of the *L*,
15:35 Then the *L* said to Moses, "The
15:36 as the *L* commanded Moses, all
15:37 Again the *L* spoke to Moses,
15:39 all the commandments of the *L*
15:41 I am the *L* your God, who
15:41 I am the *L* your God."
16: 3 and the *L* is among them.
16: 3 above the assembly of the *L*?
16: 5 Tomorrow morning the *L* will
16: 7 incense in them before the *L*
16: 7 be that the man whom the *L*
16: 9 of the tabernacle of the *L*,
16:11 together against the *L*.
16:15 very angry, and said to the *L*,
16:16 be present before the *L*—
16:17 bring his censer before the *L*,
16:19 Then the glory of the *L*

16:20 And the *L* spoke to Moses and
16:23 So the *L* spoke to Moses,
16:28 you shall know that the *L* has
16:29 then the *L* has not sent me.
16:30 But if the *L* creates a new
16:30 these men have rejected the *L*.
16:35 And a fire came out from the *L*
16:36 Then the *L* spoke to Moses,
16:38 presented them before the *L*,
16:40 to offer incense before the *L*,
16:40 just as the *L* had said to him
16:41 killed the people of the *L*.
16:42 and the glory of the *L*
16:44 And the *L* spoke to Moses,
16:46 wrath has gone out from the *L*.
17: 1 And the *L* spoke to Moses,
17: 7 placed the rods before the *L*
17: 9 the rods from before the *L* to
17:10 And the *L* said to Moses,
17:11 just as the *L* had commanded
17:13 near the tabernacle of the *L*
18: 1 Then the *L* said to Aaron: "You
18: 6 a gift to you, given by the *L*,
18: 8 And the *L* spoke to Aaron:
18:12 which they offer to the *L*,
18:13 which they bring to the *L*,
18:15 which they bring to the *L*,
18:17 for a sweet aroma to the *L*.
18:19 of Israel offer to the *L*,
18:19 of salt forever before the *L*
18:20 Then the *L* said to Aaron: "You
18:24 as a heave offering to the *L*,
18:25 Then the *L* spoke to Moses,
18:26 heave offering of it to the *L*,
18:28 a heave offering to the *L*
18:29 heave offering due to the *L*,
19: 1 Now the *L* spoke to Moses and
19: 2 of the law which the *L* has
19:13 the tabernacle of the *L*.
19:20 defiled the sanctuary of the *L*.
20: 3 brethren died before the *L*!
20: 4 up the assembly of the *L* into
20: 6 And the glory of the *L*
20: 7 Then the *L* spoke to Moses,
20: 9 the rod from before the *L* as
20:12 Then the *L* spoke to Moses and
20:13 of Israel contended with the *L*,
20:16 'When we cried out to the *L*,
20:23 And the *L* spoke to Moses and
20:27 So Moses did just as the *L*
21: 2 So Israel made a vow to the *L*,
21: 3 And the *L* listened to the voice
21: 6 So the *L* sent fiery serpents
21: 7 we have spoken against the *L*
21: 7 pray to the *L* that He take
21: 8 Then the *L* said to Moses,
21:14 the Book of the Wars of the *L*:
21:16 is the well where the *L* said
21:34 Then the *L* said to Moses, "Do
22: 8 as the *L* speaks to me."
22:13 for the *L* has refused to give
22:18 go beyond the word of the *L*
22:19 I may know what more the *L*
22:22 and the Angel of the *L* took
22:23 donkey saw the Angel of the *L*
22:24 Then the Angel of the *L* stood
22:25 donkey saw the Angel of the *L*,
22:26 Then the Angel of the *L* went
22:27 donkey saw the Angel of the *L*,
22:28 Then the *L* opened the mouth of
22:31 Then the *L* opened Balaam's
22:31 and he saw the Angel of the *L*
22:32 And the Angel of the *L* said to
22:34 said to the Angel of the *L*,
22:35 Then the Angel of the *L* said to
23: 3 perhaps the *L* will come to
23: 5 Then the *L* put a word in
23: 8 shall I denounce whom the *L*
23:12 take heed to speak what the *L*
23:15 offering while I meet the *L*
23:16 Then the *L* met Balaam, and put
23:17 What has the *L* spoken?"
23:21 The *L* his God is with him,
23:26 All that the *L* speaks, that I
24: 1 saw that it pleased the *L* to
24: 6 Like aloes planted by the *L*,
24:11 the *L* has kept you back from
24:13 go beyond the word of the *L*,
24:13 What the *L* says, that I must
25: 3 and the anger of the *L* was
25: 4 Then the *L* said to Moses,
25: 4 the offenders before the *L*,
25: 4 the fierce anger of the *L* may
25:10 Then the *L* spoke to Moses,
25:16 Then the *L* spoke to Moses,
26: 1 that the *L* spoke to Moses and
26: 4 just as the *L* commanded Moses
26: 9 they contended against the *L*;
26:52 Then the *L* spoke to Moses,
26:61 profane fire before the *L*.
26:65 For the *L* had said of them,
27: 3 together against the *L*,
27: 5 their case before the *L*.
27: 6 And the *L* spoke to Moses,
27:11 just as the *L* commanded Moses.
27:12 Now the *L* said to Moses: "Go
27:15 Then Moses spoke to the *L*,
27:16 'Let the *L*, the God of
27:17 the congregation of the *L* may
27:18 And the *L* said to Moses:
27:21 who shall inquire before the *L*
27:22 So Moses did as the *L* commanded

27:23 just as the *L* commanded by the
28: 1 Now the *L* spoke to Moses,
28: 3 which you shall offer to the *L*:
28: 6 offering made by fire to the *L*.
28: 7 pour out the drink to the *L*
28: 8 fire, a sweet aroma to the *L*.
28:11 a burnt offering to the *L*:
28:13 offering made by fire to the *L*.
28:15 as a sin offering to the *L*
28:16 is the Passover of the *L*.
28:19 as a burnt offering to the *L*:
28:24 as a sweet aroma to the *L*;
28:26 a new grain offering to the *L*
28:27 as a sweet aroma to the *L*:
29: 2 as a sweet aroma to the *L*:
29: 6 offering made by fire to the *L*.
29: 8 a burnt offering to the *L* as
29:12 shall keep a feast to the *L*
29:13 fire as a sweet aroma to the *L*:
29:36 fire as a sweet aroma to the *L*:
29:39 you shall present to the *L* at
29:40 just as the *L* commanded Moses.
30: 1 is the thing which the *L* has
30: 2 a man makes a vow to the *L*,
30: 3 a woman makes a vow to the *L*,
30: 5 and the *L* will release her,
30: 8 and the *L* will release her.
30:12 and the *L* will release her.
30:16 are the statutes which the *L*
31: 1 And the *L* spoke to Moses,
31: 3 to take vengeance for the *L*
31: 7 just as the *L* commanded Moses,
31:16 to trespass against the *L* in
31:16 the congregation of the *L*.
31:21 of the law which the *L*
31:25 Now the *L* spoke to Moses,
31:28 And levy a tribute for the *L* on
31:29 as a heave offering to the *L*.
31:30 of the tabernacle of the *L*.
31:31 the priest did as the *L*
31:41 as the *L* commanded Moses.
31:47 of the tabernacle of the *L*,
31:47 as the *L* commanded Moses.
31:50 brought an offering for the *L*,
31:50 for ourselves before the *L*.
31:52 that they offered to the *L*,
31:54 of Israel before the *L*.
32: 4 the country which the *L*
32: 7 into the land which the *L* has
32: 9 go into the land which the *L*
32:12 have wholly followed the *L*.
32:13 evil in the sight of the *L*
32:14 more the fierce anger of the *L*
32:20 arm yourselves before the *L*
32:21 over the Jordan before the *L*
32:22 land is subdued before the *L*,
32:22 and be blameless before the *L*
32:22 your possession before the *L*.
32:23 you have sinned against the *L*;
32:25 Your servants will do as my *l*
32:27 before the *L* to battle, just
32:27 just as my *l* says."
32:29 armed for battle before the *L*,
32:31 As the *L* has said to your
32:32 cross over armed before the *L*
33: 2 at the command of the *L*.
33: 4 whom the *L* had killed among
33: 4 Also on their gods the *L* had
33:38 Hor at the command of the *L*,
33:50 Now the *L* spoke to Moses in
34: 1 Then the *L* spoke to Moses,
34:13 which the *L* has commanded to
34:16 And the *L* spoke to Moses,
34:29 These are the ones the *L*
35: 1 And the *L* spoke to Moses in the
35: 9 Then the *L* spoke to Moses,
35:34 for I the *L* dwell among the
36: 2 The *L* commanded my lord Moses
36: 2 The LORD commanded my *l* Moses
36: 2 and my *l* was commanded by the
36: 2 my lord was commanded by the *L*
36: 5 according to the word of the *L*,
36: 6 This is what the *L* commands
36:10 Just as the *L* commanded Moses,
36:13 and the judgments which the *L*
Deut 1: 3 according to all that the *L*
1: 6 The *L* our God spoke to us in
1: 8 possess the land which the *L*
1:10 The *L* your God has multiplied
1:11 May the *L* God of your fathers
1:19 as the *L* our God had commanded
1:20 which the *L* our God is giving
1:21 the *L* your God has set the
1:21 as the *L* God of your fathers
1:25 is a good land which the *L*
1:26 against the command of the *L*
1:27 Because the *L* hates us, He has
1:30 The *L* your God, who goes before
1:31 where you saw how the *L* your
1:32 you did not believe the *L* your
1:34 And the *L* heard the sound of
1:36 he wholly followed the *L*.
1:37 The *L* was also angry with me
1:41 'We have sinned against the *L*;
1:41 just as the *L* our God
1:42 And the *L* said to me, 'Tell
1:43 against the command of the *L*,
1:45 returned and wept before the *L*,
1:45 but the *L* would not listen to
2: 1 as the *L* spoke to me, and we
2: 2 And the *L* spoke to me, saying:
2: 7 For the *L* your God has blessed
2: 7 These forty years the *L* your
2: 9 Then the *L* said to me, 'Do not
2:12 their possession which the *L*
2:14 just as the *L* had sworn to
2:15 For indeed the hand of the *L*
2:17 that the *L* spoke to me, saying:
2:21 But the *L* destroyed them
2:29 to the land which the *L* our
2:30 for the *L* your God hardened
2:31 And the *L* said to me, 'See, I
2:33 And the *L* our God delivered him
2:36 the *L* our God delivered all to
2:37 or wherever the *L* our God had
3: 2 And the *L* said to me, 'Do not
3: 3 So the *L* our God also delivered
3:18 The *L* your God has given you
3:20 until the *L* has given rest to
3:20 possess the land which the *L*
3:21 eyes have seen all that the *L*
3:21 so will the *L* do to all the
3:22 for the *L* your God Himself
3:23 Then I pleaded with the *L* at
3:24 O *L* GOD, You have begun to show
3:26 But the *L* was angry with me on
3:26 So the *L* said to me: 'Enough
4: 1 possess the land which the *L*
4: 2 keep the commandments of the *L*
4: 3 eyes have seen what the *L* did
4: 3 for the *L* your God has
4: 4 you who held fast to the *L*
4: 5 just as the *L* my God commanded
4: 7 as the *L* our God is to us,
4:10 the day you stood before the *L*
4:10 when the *L* said to me, 'Gather
4:12 And the *L* spoke to you out of
4:14 And the *L* commanded me at that
4:15 for you saw no form when the *L*
4:19 which the *L* your God has given
4:20 But the *L* has taken you and
4:21 Furthermore the *L* was angry
4:21 the good land which the *L*
4:23 forget the covenant of the *L*
4:23 form of anything which the *L*
4:24 For the *L* your God is a
4:25 do evil in the sight of the *L*
4:27 And the *L* will scatter you
4:27 among the nations where the *L*
4:29 from there you will seek the *L*
4:30 when you turn to the *L* your
4:31 (for the *L* your God is a
4:34 according to all that the *L*
4:35 that you might know that the *L*
4:39 that the *L* Himself is God in
4:40 days in the land which the *L*
5: 2 The *L* our God made a covenant
5: 3 The *L* did not make this
5: 4 The *L* talked with you face to
5: 5 I stood between the *L* and you
5: 5 to you the word of the *L*;
5: 6 I am the *L* your God who
5: 9 the *L* your God, am a jealous
5:11 not take the name of the *L*
5:11 for the *L* will not hold him
5:12 as the *L* your God commanded
5:14 day is the Sabbath of the *L*
5:15 and the *L* your God brought you
5:15 therefore the *L* your God
5:16 as the *L* your God has
5:16 you in the land which the *L*
5:22 These words the *L* spoke to all
5:24 Surely the *L* our God has shown
5:25 if we hear the voice of the *L*
5:27 near and hear all that the *L*
5:27 and tell us all that the *L* our
5:28 Then the *L* heard the voice of
5:28 and the *L* said to me: 'I have
5:32 be careful to do as the *L*
5:33 in all the ways which the *L*
6: 1 and judgments which the *L*
6: 2 that you may fear the *L* your
6: 3 may multiply greatly as the *L*
6: 4 The *L* our God, the LORD is
6: 4 LORD our God, the *L* is one!
6: 5 You shall love the *L* your God
6:10 when the *L* your God brings you
6:12 lest you forget the *L* who
6:13 You shall fear the *L* your God
6:15 (for the *L* your God is a
6:15 lest the anger of the *L* your
6:16 You shall not tempt the *L* your
6:17 keep the commandments of the *L*
6:18 and good in the sight of the *L*,
6:18 the good land of which the *L*
6:19 as the *L* has spoken.
6:20 and the judgments which the *L*
6:21 and the *L* brought us out of
6:22 and the *L* showed signs and
6:24 And the *L* commanded us to
6:24 to fear the *L* our God, for our
6:25 commandments before the *L* our
7: 1 When the *L* your God brings you
7: 2 and when the *L* your God
7: 4 so the anger of the *L* will be
7: 6 are a holy people to the *L*
7: 6 the *L* your God has chosen you
7: 7 The *L* did not set His love on
7: 8 but because the *L* loves you,
7: 8 the *L* has brought you out with
7: 9 Therefore know that the *L* your
7:12 that the *L* your God will keep
7:15 And the *L* will take away from
7:16 all the peoples whom the *L*
7:18 remember well what the *L* your
7:19 by which the *L* your God
7:19 So shall the *L* your God do to
7:20 Moreover the *L* your God will
7:21 for the *L* your God, the great
7:22 And the *L* your God will drive
7:23 But the *L* your God will deliver
7:25 it is an abomination to the *L*
8: 1 the land of which the *L* swore
8: 2 you shall remember that the *L*
8: 3 from the mouth of the *L*.
8: 5 so the *L* your God chastens
8: 6 keep the commandments of the *L*
8: 7 For the *L* your God is bringing
8:10 then you shall bless the *L*
8:11 that you do not forget the *L*
8:14 and you forget the *L* your God
8:18 And you shall remember the *L*
8:19 you by any means forget the *L*
8:20 As the nations which the *L*
8:20 to the voice of the *L* your
9: 3 understand today that the *L*
9: 3 as the *L* has said to you.
9: 4 after the *L* your God has cast
9: 4 of my righteousness the *L* has
9: 4 of these nations that the *L*
9: 5 of these nations that the *L*
9: 5 fulfill the word which the *L*
9: 6 understand that the *L* your
9: 7 forget how you provoked the *L*
9: 7 been rebellious against the *L*.
9: 8 in Horeb you provoked the *L*
9: 8 so that the *L* was angry
9: 9 of the covenant which the *L*
9:10 Then the *L* delivered to me two
9:10 all the words which the *L* had
9:11 that the *L* gave me the two
9:12 Then the *L* said to me, 'Arise,
9:13 Furthermore the *L* spoke to me,
9:16 you had sinned against the *L*
9:16 from the way which the *L* had
9:18 "And I fell down before the *L*,
9:18 wickedly in the sight of the *L*,
9:19 displeasure with which the *L*
9:19 But the *L* listened to me at
9:20 And the *L* was very angry with
9:22 Hattaavah you provoked the *L*
9:23 when the *L* sent you from
9:23 the commandment of the *L* your
9:24 been rebellious against the *L*
9:25 prostrated myself before the *L*;
9:25 because the *L* had said He
9:26 "Therefore I prayed to the *L*,
9:26 O *L* GOD, do not destroy Your
9:28 Because the *L* was not able to
10: 1 At that time the *L* said to me,
10: 4 which the *L* had spoken to you
10: 4 and the *L* gave them to me.
10: 5 just as the *L* commanded me."
10: 8 At that time the *L* separated
10: 8 ark of the covenant of the *L*,
10: 8 to stand before the *L* to
10: 9 the *L* is his inheritance,
10: 9 just as the *L* your God
10:10 the *L* also heard me at that
10:10 and the *L* chose not to
10:11 Then the *L* said to me, 'Arise,
10:12 what does the *L* your God
10:12 but to fear the *L* your God, to
10:12 to serve the *L* your God with
10:13 the commandments of the *L* and
10:14 heavens belong to the *L* your
10:15 The *L* delighted only in your
10:17 For the *L* your God is God of
10:17 your God is God of gods and *L*
10:20 You shall fear the *L* your God;
10:22 and now the *L* your God has
11: 1 you shall love the *L* your God,
11: 2 seen the chastening of the *L*
11: 4 and how the *L* has destroyed
11: 7 seen every great act of the *L*
11: 9 days in the land which the *L*
11:12 a land for which the *L* your God
11:12 the eyes of the *L* your God
11:13 to love the *L* your God and
11:17 the good land which the *L* is
11:21 in the land of which the *L*
11:22 to love the *L* your God, to walk
11:23 then the *L* will drive out all
11:25 the *L* your God will put the
11:27 obey the commandments of the *L*
11:28 obey the commandments of the *L*
11:29 when the *L* your God has
11:31 possess the land which the *L*
12: 1 in the land which the *L* God
12: 4 You shall not worship the *L*
12: 5 seek the place where the *L*
12: 7 you shall eat before the *L*
12: 7 in which the *L* your God has
12: 9 the inheritance which the *L*
12:10 dwell in the land which the *L*
12:11 will be the place where the *L*
12:11 which you vow to the *L*.
12:12 you shall rejoice before the *L*
12:14 but in the place which the *L*
12:15 to the blessing of the *L* your
12:18 you must eat them before the *L*
12:18 God in the place which the *L*
12:18 you shall rejoice before the *L*
12:20 When the *L* your God enlarges
12:21 If the place where the *L* your
12:21 from your flock which the *L*

12:25 right in the sight of the *L*.
12:26 go to the place which the *L*
12:27 on the altar of the *L* your
12:27 out on the altar of the *L*
12:28 right in the sight of the *L*
12:29 When the *L* your God cuts off
12:31 You shall not worship the *L*
12:31 for every abomination to the *L*
13: 3 for the *L* your God is testing
13: 3 to know whether you love the *L*
13: 4 You shall walk after the *L* your
13: 5 to turn you away from the *L*
13: 5 from the way in which the *L*
13:10 to entice you away from the *L*
13:12 which the *L* your God gives you
13:16 for the *L* your God. It shall
13:17 that the *L* may turn from the
13:18 to the voice of the *L* your
13:18 is right in the eyes of the *L*
14: 1 are the children of the *L*
14: 2 are a holy people to the *L*
14: 2 and the *L* has chosen you to be
14:21 are a holy people to the *L*
14:23 you shall eat before the *L*
14:23 you may learn to fear the *L*
14:24 or if the place where the *L*
14:24 when the *L* your God has
14:25 go to the place which the *L*
14:26 shall eat there before the *L*
14:29 that the *L* your God may bless
15: 4 for the *L* will greatly bless
15: 4 you in the land which the *L*
15: 5 obey the voice of the *L* your
15: 6 For the *L* your God will bless
15: 7 in your land which the *L* your
15: 9 and he cry out to the *L*
15:10 because for this thing the *L*
15:14 From what the *L* has blessed
15:15 and the *L* your God redeemed
15:18 Then the *L* your God will bless
15:19 you shall sanctify to the *L*
15:20 shall eat it before the *L*
15:20 year in the place which the *L*
15:21 not sacrifice it to the *L*
16: 1 and keep the Passover to the *L*
16: 1 for in the month of Abib the *L*
16: 2 the Passover to the *L* your
16: 2 in the place where the *L*
16: 5 any of your gates which the *L*
16: 6 but at the place where the *L*
16: 7 it in the place which the *L*
16: 8 be a sacred assembly to the *L*
16:10 the Feast of Weeks to the *L*
16:10 which you shall give as the *L*
16:11 shall rejoice before the *L*
16:11 at the place where the *L* your
16:15 keep a sacred feast to the *L*
16:15 God in the place which the *L*
16:15 because the *L* your God will
16:16 shall appear before the *L*
16:16 shall not appear before the *L*
16:17 to the blessing of the *L* your
16:18 which the *L* your God gives
16:20 inherit the land which the *L*
16:21 build for yourself to the *L*
16:22 which the *L* your God hates.
17: 1 shall not sacrifice to the *L*
17: 1 is an abomination to the *L*
17: 2 any of your gates which the *L*
17: 2 wicked in the sight of the *L*
17: 8 go up to the place which the *L*
17:10 you in that place which the *L*
17:12 to minister there before the *L*
17:14 come to the land which the *L*
17:15 set a king over you whom the *L*
17:16 for the *L* has said to you,
17:19 he may learn to fear the *L*
18: 1 eat the offerings of the *L*
18: 2 the *L* is their inheritance, as
18: 5 For the *L* your God has chosen
18: 5 minister in the name of the *L*,
18: 6 mind to the place which the *L*
18: 7 may serve in the name of the *L*
18: 7 who stand there before the *L*.
18: 9 come into the land which the *L*
18:12 are an abomination to the *L*,
18:12 of these abominations the *L*
18:13 be blameless before the *L*
18:14 the *L* your God has not
18:15 The *L* your God will raise up
18:16 to all you desired of the *L*
18:16 hear again the voice of the *L*
18:17 And the *L* said to me: 'What
18:21 we know the word which the *L*
18:22 speaks in the name of the *L*,
18:22 is the thing which the *L* has
19: 1 When the *L* your God has cut off
19: 1 the nations whose land the *L*
19: 2 of your land which the *L* your
19: 3 of your land which the *L* your
19: 8 Now if the *L* your God enlarges
19: 9 to love the *L* your God and to
19:10 of your land which the *L* your
19:14 in the land that the *L* your
19:17 shall stand before the *L*,
20: 1 for the *L* your God is with
20: 4 for the *L* your God is He who
20:13 And when the *L* your God
20:14 enemies' plunder which the *L*
20:16 of these peoples which the *L*
20:17 just as the *L* your God has
20:18 and you sin against the *L* your

21: 1 field in the land which the *L*
21: 5 for the *L* your God has chosen
21: 5 to bless in the name of the *L*;
21: 8 'Provide atonement, O *L*,
21: 9 right in the sight of the *L*.
21:10 and the *L* your God delivers
21:23 defile the land which the *L*
22: 5 are an abomination to the *L*
23: 1 enter the assembly of the *L*.
23: 2 enter the assembly of the *L*;
23: 2 enter the assembly of the *L*.
23: 3 enter the assembly of the *L*;
23: 3 enter the assembly of the *L*
23: 5 Nevertheless the *L* your God
23: 5 but the *L* your God turned the
23: 5 because the *L* your God loves
23: 8 enter the assembly of the *L*.
23:14 For the *L* your God walks in the
23:18 of a dog to the house of the *L*
23:18 are an abomination to the *L*
23:20 that the *L* your God may bless
23:21 you make a vow to the *L*
23:21 for the *L* your God will surely
23:23 you voluntarily vowed to the *L*
24: 4 an abomination before the *L*,
24: 4 sin on the land which the *L*
24: 9 Remember what the *L* your God
24:13 to you before the *L* your God.
24:15 cry out against you to the *L*,
24:18 and the *L* your God redeemed
24:19 that the *L* your God may bless
25:15 in the land which the *L* your
25:16 are an abomination to the *L*
25:19 when the *L* your God has given
25:19 in the land which the *L* your
26: 1 come into the land which the *L*
26: 2 from your land that the *L*
26: 2 go to the place where the *L*
26: 3 I declare today to the *L* your
26: 3 to the country which the *L*
26: 4 down before the altar of the *L*
26: 5 answer and say before the *L*
26: 7 Then we cried out to the *L* God
26: 7 and the *L* heard our voice and
26: 8 So the *L* brought us out of
26:10 of the land which you, O *L*,
26:10 you shall set it before the *L*
26:10 and worship before the *L* your
26:11 every good thing which the *L*
26:13 you shall say before the *L*
26:14 obeyed the voice of the *L* my
26:16 This day the *L* your God
26:17 you have proclaimed the *L* to
26:18 Also today the *L* has proclaimed
26:19 may be a holy people to the *L*
27: 2 to the land which the *L* your
27: 3 may enter the land which the *L*
27: 3 just as the *L* God of your
27: 5 shall build an altar to the *L*
27: 6 stones the altar of the *L*
27: 6 offerings on it to the *L* your
27: 7 and rejoice before the *L* your
27: 9 become the people of the *L*
27:10 shall obey the voice of the *L*
27:15 image, an abomination to the *L*,
28: 1 obey the voice of the *L* your
28: 1 that the *L* your God will set
28: 2 you obey the voice of the *L*
28: 7 The *L* will cause your enemies
28: 8 The *L* will command the blessing
28: 8 you in the land which the *L*
28: 9 The *L* will establish you as a
28: 9 keep the commandments of the *L*
28:10 called by the name of the *L*,
28:11 And the *L* will grant you plenty
28:11 in the land of which the *L*
28:12 The *L* will open to you His good
28:13 And the *L* will make you the
28:13 heed the commandments of the *L*
28:15 do not obey the voice of the *L*
28:20 The *L* will send on you
28:21 The *L* will make the plague
28:22 The *L* will strike you with
28:24 The *L* will change the rain of
28:25 The *L* will cause you to be
28:27 The *L* will strike you with the
28:28 The *L* will strike you with
28:35 The *L* will strike you in the
28:36 The *L* will bring you and the
28:37 among all nations where the *L*
28:45 not obey the voice of the *L*
28:47 you did not serve the *L* your
28:48 whom the *L* will send against
28:49 The *L* will bring a nation
28:52 all your land which the *L*
28:53 and your daughters whom the *L*
28:58 THE *L* YOUR GOD,
28:59 then the *L* will bring upon you
28:61 will the *L* bring upon you
28:62 not obey the voice of the *L*
28:63 that just as the *L* rejoiced
28:63 so the *L* will rejoice over you
28:64 Then the *L* will scatter you
28:65 but there the *L* will give you
28:68 And the *L* will take you back to
29: 1 of the covenant which the *L*
29: 2 You have seen all that the *L*
29: 4 Yet the *L* has not given you a
29: 6 you may know that I am the *L*
29:10 you stand today before the *L*
29:12 into covenant with the *L* your
29:12 which the *L* your God makes

29:15 with us today before the *L*
29:18 turns away today from the *L*
29:20 'The *L* would not spare him;
29:20 for then the anger of the *L*
29:20 and the *L* would blot out his
29:21 And the *L* would separate him
29:22 and the sicknesses which the *L*
29:23 which the *L* overthrew in His
29:24 Why has the *L* done so to this
29:25 the covenant of the *L* God of
29:27 Then the anger of the *L* was
29:28 And the *L* uprooted them from
29:29 things belong to the *L* our
30: 1 all the nations where the *L*
30: 2 and you return to the *L* your
30: 3 that the *L* your God will bring
30: 3 all the nations where the *L*
30: 4 from there the *L* your God will
30: 5 Then the *L* your God will bring
30: 6 And the *L* your God will
30: 6 to love the *L* your God with
30: 7 Also the *L* your God will put
30: 8 again obey the voice of the *L*
30: 9 The *L* your God will make you
30: 9 For the *L* will again rejoice
30:10 you obey the voice of the *L*
30:10 and if you turn to the *L* your
30:16 you today to love the *L* your
30:16 and the *L* your God will bless
30:20 that you may love the *L* your
30:20 dwell in the land which the *L*
31: 2 Also the *L* has said to me,
31: 3 The *L* your God Himself crosses
31: 3 just as the *L* has said.
31: 4 And the *L* will do to them as He
31: 5 The *L* will give them over to
31: 6 for the *L* your God, He is the
31: 7 to the land which the *L* has
31: 8 'And the *L*, He is the one
31: 9 ark of the covenant of the *L*,
31:11 comes to appear before the *L*
31:12 they may learn to fear the *L*
31:13 hear and learn to fear the *L*
31:14 Then the *L* said to Moses,
31:15 Now the *L* appeared at the
31:16 And the *L* said to Moses:
31:25 ark of the covenant of the *L*,
31:26 ark of the covenant of the *L*
31:27 been rebellious against the *L*,
31:29 do evil in the sight of the *L*,
32: 3 I proclaim the name of the *L*:
32: 6 Do you thus deal with the *L*,
32:12 So the *L* alone led him,
32:19 And when the *L* saw it, He
32:27 And it is not the *L* who has
32:30 And the *L* had surrendered
32:36 For the *L* will judge His people
32:48 Then the *L* spoke to Moses that
33: 2 The *L* came from Sinai, And
33: 7 he said of Judah: "Hear, *L*,
33:11 Bless his substance, *L*,
33:12 The beloved of the *L* shall
33:13 Blessed of the *L* is his land,
33:21 the justice of the *L*,
33:23 full of the blessing of the *L*,
33:29 you, a people saved by the *L*,
34: 1 And the *L* showed him all the
34: 4 Then the *L* said to him, "This
34: 5 So Moses the servant of the *L*
34: 5 according to the word of the *L*.
34: 9 and did as the *L* had commanded
34:10 whom the *L* knew face to face,
34:11 signs and wonders which the *L*
Josh 1: 1 of Moses the servant of the *L*,
1: 1 it came to pass that the *L*
1: 9 for the *L* your God is with
1:11 possess the land which the *L*
1:13 Moses the servant of the *L*
1:13 The *L* your God is giving you
1:15 until the *L* has given your
1:15 of the land which the *L* your
1:17 Only the *L* your God be with
2: 9 I know that the *L* has given you
2:10 For we have heard how the *L*
2:11 for the *L* your God, He is God
2:12 beg you, swear to me by the *L*,
2:14 when the *L* has given us the
2:24 Truly the *L* has delivered all
3: 3 ark of the covenant of the *L*
3: 5 for tomorrow the *L* will do
3: 7 And the *L* said to Joshua,
3: 9 and hear the words of the *L*
3:11 ark of the covenant of the *L*
3:13 who bear the ark of the *L*,
3:13 the *L* of all the earth, shall
3:17 ark of the covenant of the *L*
4: 1 that the *L* spoke to Joshua,
4: 5 over before the ark of the *L*
4: 7 ark of the covenant of the *L*;
4: 8 as the *L* had spoken to Joshua,
4:10 was finished that the *L* had
4:11 that the ark of the *L* and the
4:13 war crossed over before the *L*
4:14 On that day the *L* exalted
4:15 Then the *L* spoke to Joshua,
4:18 ark of the covenant of the *L*
4:23 for the *L* your God dried up the
4:23 as the *L* your God did to the
4:24 may know the hand of the *L*,
4:24 that you may fear the *L* your
5: 1 heard that the *L* had dried up
5: 2 At that time the *L* said to

5: 6 not obey the voice of the *L*—
5: 6 to whom the *L* swore that He
5: 6 them the land which the *L* had
5: 9 Then the *L* said to Joshua,
5:14 of the army of the *L* I have
5:14 What does my *L* say to His
6: 2 And the *L* said to Joshua:
6: 6 horns before the ark of the *L*.
6: 7 before the ark of the *L*.
6: 8 of rams' horns before the *L*
6: 8 ark of the covenant of the *L*
6:11 So he had the ark of the *L*
6:12 took up the ark of the *L*.
6:13 horns before the ark of the *L*
6:13 came after the ark of the *L*,
6:16 for the *L* has given you the
6:17 city shall be doomed by the *L*
6:19 are consecrated to the *L*;
6:19 into the treasury of the *L*.
6:24 treasury of the house of the *L*.
6:26 be the man before the *L* who
6:27 So the *L* was with Joshua, and
7: 1 so the anger of the *L* burned
7: 6 face before the ark of the *L*
7: 7 *L* GOD, why have You brought
7: 8 'O *L*, what shall I say when
7:10 So the *L* said to Joshua: "Get
7:13 because thus says the *L* God of
7:14 be that the tribe which the *L*
7:14 and the family which the *L*
7:14 and the household which the *L*
7:15 the covenant of the *L*,
7:19 give glory to the *L* God of
7:20 I have sinned against the *L*
7:23 and laid them out before the *L*.
7:25 The *L* will trouble you this
7:26 So the *L* turned from the
8: 1 Now the *L* said to Joshua: "Do
8: 7 for the *L* your God will
8: 8 to the commandment of the *L*
8:18 Then the *L* said to Joshua,
8:27 to the word of the *L* which He
8:30 built an altar to the *L* God
8:31 as Moses the servant of the *L*
8:31 on it burnt offerings to the *L*,
8:33 ark of the covenant of the *L*,
8:33 as Moses the servant of the *L*
9: 9 because of the name of the *L*
9:14 did not ask counsel of the *L*.
9:18 had sworn to them by the *L*
9:19 have sworn to them by the *L*
9:24 were clearly told that the *L*
9:27 and for the altar of the *L*,
10: 8 And the *L* said to Joshua, "Do
10:10 So the *L* routed them before
10:11 that the *L* cast down large
10:12 Then Joshua spoke to the *L* in
10:12 LORD in the day when the *L*
10:14 that the *L* heeded the voice of
10:14 for the *L* fought for Israel.
10:19 for the *L* your God has
10:25 for thus the *L* will do to all
10:30 And the *L* also delivered it and
10:32 And the *L* delivered Lachish
10:40 as the *L* God of Israel had
10:42 because the *L* God of Israel
11: 6 But the *L* said to Joshua, "Do
11: 8 And the *L* delivered them into
11: 9 So Joshua did to them as the *L*
11:12 as Moses the servant of the *L*
11:15 As the *L* had commanded Moses
11:15 undone of all that the *L* had
11:20 For it was of the *L* to harden
11:20 as the *L* had commanded Moses.
11:23 according to all that the *L*
12: 6 Moses the servant of the *L*
12: 6 and Moses the servant of the *L*
13: 1 And the *L* said to him: "You
13: 8 as Moses the servant of the *L*
13:14 the sacrifices of the *L* God of
13:33 the *L* God of Israel was their
14: 2 as the *L* had commanded by the
14: 5 As the *L* had commanded Moses,
14: 6 know the word which the *L*
14: 7 Moses the servant of the *L*
14: 8 but I wholly followed the *L* my
14: 9 have wholly followed the *L* my
14:10 the *L* has kept me alive, as He
14:10 ever since the *L* spoke this
14:12 this mountain of which the *L*
14:12 It may be that the *L* will be
14:12 to drive them out as the *L*
14:14 he wholly followed the *L* God
15:13 to the commandment of the *L*
17: 4 The *L* commanded Moses to give
17: 4 to the commandment of the *L*,
17:14 inasmuch as the *L* has blessed
18: 3 possess the land which the *L*
18: 6 for you here before the *L* our
18: 7 for the priesthood of the *L*
18: 7 Moses the servant of the *L*
18: 8 for you here before the *L* in
18:10 them in Shiloh before the *L*,
19:50 to the word of the *L* they
19:51 by lot in Shiloh before the *L*,
20: 1 The *L* also spoke to Joshua,
21: 2 The *L* commanded through Moses
21: 3 at the commandment of the *L*,
21: 8 as the *L* had commanded by the
21:43 So the *L* gave to Israel all
21:44 The *L* gave them rest all
21:44 the *L* delivered all their
21:45 of any good thing which the *L*
22: 2 Moses the servant of the *L*
22: 3 of the commandment of the *L*
22: 4 And now the *L* your God has
22: 4 Moses the servant of the *L*
22: 5 Moses the servant of the *L*
22: 5 to love the *L* your God, to
22: 9 to the word of the *L* by the
22:16 whole congregation of the *L*:
22:16 this day from following the *L*,
22:16 rebel this day against the *L*?
22:17 in the congregation of the *L*,
22:18 this day from following the *L*?
22:18 you rebel today against the *L*,
22:19 of the possession of the *L*,
22:19 but do not rebel against the *L*,
22:19 besides the altar of the *L*
22:22 The *L* God of gods, the LORD
22:22 the *L* God of gods, He knows,
22:22 if in treachery against the *L*,
22:23 to turn from following the *L*,
22:23 let the *L* Himself require an
22:24 have you to do with the *L* God
22:25 For the *L* has made the Jordan a
22:25 You have no part in the *L*."
22:25 cease fearing the *L*.
22:27 perform the service of the *L*
22:27 "You have no part in the *L*.
22:28 replica of the altar of the *L*
22:29 we should rebel against the *L*,
22:29 and turn from following the *L*
22:29 besides the altar of the *L* our
22:31 day we perceive that the *L*
22:31 this treachery against the *L*.
22:31 out of the hand of the *L*.
22:34 witness between us that the *L*
23: 1 a long time after the *L* had
23: 3 You have seen all that the *L*
23: 3 for the *L* your God is He who
23: 5 And the *L* your God will expel
23: 5 as the *L* your God promised
23: 8 you shall hold fast to the *L*
23: 9 For the *L* has driven out from
23:10 for the *L* your God is He who
23:11 that you love the *L* your God.
23:13 know for certain that the *L*
23:13 this good land which the *L*
23:14 the good things which the *L*
23:15 have come upon you which the *L*
23:15 so the *L* will bring upon you
23:15 this good land which the *L*
23:16 the covenant of the *L* your
23:16 then the anger of the *L* will
24: 2 Thus says the *L* God of Israel:
24: 7 'So they cried out to the *L*;
24:14 "Now therefore, fear the *L*,
24:14 and in Egypt. Serve the *L*!
24:15 evil to you to serve the *L*,
24:15 my house, we will serve the *L*.
24:16 that we should forsake the *L*
24:17 for the *L* our God is He who
24:18 And the *L* drove out from before
24:18 We also will serve the *L*,
24:19 "You cannot serve the *L*,
24:20 If you forsake the *L* and serve
24:21 but we will serve the *L*!"
24:22 that you have chosen the *L*
24:23 incline your heart to the *L*
24:24 The *L* our God we will serve,
24:26 was by the sanctuary of the *L*.
24:27 heard all the words of the *L*
24:29 of Nun, the servant of the *L*,
24:31 Israel served the *L* all the
24:31 known all the works of the *L*
Judg 1: 1 children of Israel asked the *L*,
1: 2 And the *L* said, "Judah shall
1: 4 and the *L* delivered the
1:19 So the *L* was with Judah.
1:22 and the *L* was with them.
2: 1 Then the Angel of the *L* came up
2: 4 when the Angel of the *L* spoke
2: 5 they sacrificed there to the *L*.
2: 7 So the people served the *L* all
2: 7 all the great works of the *L*
2: 8 of Nun, the servant of the *L*,
2:10 them who did not know the *L*
2:11 did evil in the sight of the *L*,
2:12 and they forsook the *L* God of
2:12 and they provoked the *L* to
2:13 They forsook the *L* and served
2:14 And the anger of the *L* was hot
2:15 the hand of the *L* was against
2:15 as the *L* had said, and as the
2:15 and as the *L* had sworn to
2:16 the *L* raised up judges who
2:17 the commandments of the *L*;
2:18 And when the *L* raised up judges
2:18 the *L* was with the judge and
2:18 for the *L* was moved to pity by
2:20 Then the anger of the *L* was
2:22 will keep the ways of the *L*,
2:23 Therefore the *L* left those
3: 1 are the nations which the *L*
3: 4 obey the commandments of the *L*,
3: 7 did evil in the sight of the *L*.
3: 7 They forgot the *L* their God,
3: 8 Therefore the anger of the *L*
3: 9 of Israel cried out to the *L*,
3: 9 the *L* raised up a deliverer
3:10 The Spirit of the *L* came upon
3:10 and the *L* delivered
3:12 did evil in the sight of the *L*.
3:12 So the *L* strengthened Eglon
3:12 evil in the sight of the *L*.
3:15 of Israel cried out to the *L*,
3:15 the *L* raised up a deliverer
3:28 for the *L* has delivered your
4: 1 did evil in the sight of the *L*.
4: 2 So the *L* sold them into the
4: 3 of Israel cried out to the *L*;
4: 6 Has not the *L* God of Israel
4: 9 for the *L* will sell Sisera
4:14 is the day in which the *L*
4:14 Has not the *L* gone out before
4:15 And the *L* routed Sisera and all
4:18 said to him, "Turn aside, my *l*,
5: 2 themselves, Bless the *L*!
5: 3 even I, will sing to the *L*;
5: 3 I will sing praise to the *L*
5: 4 *L*, when You went out from
5: 5 mountains gushed before the *L*,
5: 5 before the *L* God of Israel.
5: 9 with the people. Bless the *L*!
5:11 the righteous acts of the *L*,
5:11 Then the people of the *L*
5:13 The *L* came down for me
5:23 said the angel of the *L*,
5:23 not come to the help of the *L*,
5:23 To the help of the *L* against
5:31 O *L*! But let those who love
6: 1 did evil in the sight of the *L*.
6: 1 So the *L* delivered them into
6: 6 of Israel cried out to the *L*.
6: 7 of Israel cried out to the *L*
6: 8 that the *L* sent a prophet to
6: 8 Thus says the *L* God of Israel:
6:10 I am the *L* your God; do not
6:11 Now the Angel of the *L* came
6:12 And the Angel of the *L* appeared
6:12 The *L* is with you, you mighty
6:13 Gideon said to Him, "O my *l*,
6:13 if the *L* is with us, why then
6:13 Did not the *L* bring us up from
6:13 But now the *L* has forsaken us
6:14 Then the *L* turned to him and
6:15 So he said to Him, "O my *L*,
6:16 And the *L* said to him, "Surely
6:21 Then the Angel of the *L* put
6:21 And the Angel of the *L*
6:22 He was the Angel of the *L*.
6:22 O *L* GOD! For I have seen the
6:22 I have seen the Angel of the *L*
6:23 Then the *L* said to him, "Peace
6:24 built an altar there to the *L*,
6:25 pass the same night that the *L*
6:26 and build an altar to the *L*
6:27 his servants and did as the *L*
6:34 But the Spirit of the *L* came
7: 2 And the *L* said to Gideon,
7: 4 But the *L* said to Gideon,
7: 5 And the *L* said to Gideon,
7: 7 Then the *L* said to Gideon, "By
7: 9 on the same night that the *L*
7:15 for the *L* has delivered the
7:18 The sword of the *L* and of
7:20 The sword of the *L* and of
7:22 the *L* set every man's sword
8: 7 when the *L* has delivered Zebah
8:19 As the *L* lives, if you had
8:23 the *L* shall rule over you."
8:34 Israel did not remember the *L*
10: 6 did evil in the sight of the *L*,
10: 6 and they forsook the *L* and did
10: 7 So the anger of the *L* was hot
10:10 of Israel cried out to the *L*,
10:11 So the *L* said to the children
10:15 of Israel said to the *L*,
10:16 among them and served the *L*.
11: 9 and the *L* delivers them to me,
11:10 The *L* will be a witness between
11:11 all his words before the *L* in
11:21 And the *L* God of Israel
11:23 And now the *L* God of Israel has
11:24 So whatever the *L* our God
11:27 fighting against me. May the *L*,
11:29 Then the Spirit of the *L* came
11:30 Jephthah made a vow to the *L*,
11:32 and the *L* delivered them into
11:35 I have given my word to the *L*,
11:36 have given your word to the *L*,
11:36 because the *L* has avenged you
12: 3 and the *L* delivered them into
13: 1 did evil in the sight of the *L*,
13: 1 and the *L* delivered them into
13: 3 And the Angel of the *L* appeared
13: 8 Then Manoah prayed to the *L*,
13: 8 the LORD, and said, "O my *L*,
13:13 So the Angel of the *L* said to
13:15 said to the Angel of the *L*,
13:16 And the Angel of the *L* said to
13:16 you must offer it to the *L*.
13:16 He was the Angel of the *L*.
13:17 said to the Angel of the *L*,
13:18 And the Angel of the *L* said to
13:19 it upon the rock to the *L*.
13:20 the Angel of the *L* ascended in
13:21 When the Angel of the *L*
13:21 He was the Angel of the *L*.
13:23 If the *L* had desired to kill
13:24 and the *L* blessed him.
13:25 And the Spirit of the *L* began
14: 4 not know that it was of the *L*—
14: 6 And the Spirit of the *L* came
14:19 Then the Spirit of the *L* came

15:14 Then the Spirit of the *L* came
15:18 so he cried out to the *L* and
16:20 But he did not know that the *L*
16:28 Then Samson called to the *L*,
16:28 O *L* GOD, remember me, I pray!
17: 2 you be blessed by the *L*,
17: 3 silver from my hand to the *L*
17:13 Now I know that the *L* will be
18: 6 The presence of the *L* be with
19:18 am going to the house of the *L*.
20: 1 as one man before the *L* at
20:18 The *L* said, "Judah first!"
20:23 went up and wept before the *L*
20:23 and asked counsel of the *L*,
20:23 And the *L* said, "Go up
20:26 They sat there before the *L*
20:26 peace offerings before the *L*.
20:27 of Israel inquired of the *L*
20:28 And the *L* said, "Go up, for
20:35 The *L* defeated Benjamin before
21: 3 O *L* God of Israel, why has this
21: 5 up with the assembly to the *L*?
21: 5 who had not come up to the *L*
21: 7 seeing we have sworn by the *L*
21: 8 not come up to Mizpah to the *L*?
21:15 because the *L* had made a void
21:19 is a yearly feast of the *L*
Ruth 1: 6 the country of Moab that the *L*
1: 8 The *L* deal kindly with you, as
1: 9 The *L* grant that you may find
1:13 sakes that the hand of the *L*
1:17 The *L* do so to me, and more
1:21 and the *L* has brought me home
1:21 since the *L* has testified
2: 4 The *L* be with you!" And they
2: 4 The *L* bless you!"
2:12 The *L* repay your work, and a
2:12 reward be given you by the *L*
2:13 find favor in your sight, my *l*;
2:20 "Blessed be he of the *L*,
3:10 "Blessed are you of the *L*,
3:13 as the *L* lives! Lie down
4:11 The *L* make the woman who is
4:12 of the offspring which the *L*
4:13 the *L* gave her conception, and
4:14 to Naomi, "Blessed be the *L*,
1 Sam 1: 3 and sacrifice to the *L* of
1: 3 Phinehas, the priests of the *L*,
1: 5 although the *L* had closed her
1: 6 because the *L* had closed her
1: 7 went up to the house of the *L*,
1: 9 of the tabernacle of the *L*.
1:10 and prayed to the *L* and wept
1:11 O *L* of hosts, if You will
1:11 then I will give him to the *L*
1:12 continued praying before the *L*,
1:15 answered and said, "No, my *l*,
1:15 out my soul before the *L*.
1:19 and worshiped before the *L*,
1:19 and the *L* remembered her.
1:20 have asked for him from the *L*.
1:21 went up to offer to the *L* the
1:22 he may appear before the *L*
1:23 Only let the *L* establish His
1:24 him to the house of the *L* in
1:26 O my *l*! As your soul lives, my
1:26 lord! As your soul lives, my *l*,
1:26 by you here, praying to the *L*.
1:27 and the *L* has granted me my
1:28 I also have lent him to the *L*;
1:28 he shall be lent to the *L*.
1:28 So they worshiped the *L*
2: 1 "My heart rejoices in the *L*;
2: 1 My horn is exalted in the *L*.
2: 2 "No one is holy like the *L*,
2: 3 For the *L* is the God of
2: 6 The *L* kills and makes alive;
2: 7 The *L* makes poor and makes
2:10 The adversaries of the *L* shall
2:10 The *L* will judge the ends of
2:11 the child ministered to the *L*
2:12 they did not know the *L*.
2:17 was very great before the *L*,
2:17 abhorred the offering of the *L*.
2:18 Samuel ministered before the *L*,
2:20 The *L* give you descendants from
2:20 loan that was given to the *L*.
2:21 And the *L* visited Hannah, so
2:21 child Samuel grew before the *L*.
2:25 if a man sins against the *L*,
2:25 because the *L* desired to kill
2:26 and in favor both with the *L*
2:27 said to him, "Thus says the *L*:
2:30 Therefore the *L* God of Israel
2:30 But now the *L* says: 'Far be
3: 1 boy Samuel ministered to the *L*
3: 1 And the word of the *L* was rare
3: 3 out in the tabernacle of the *L*
3: 4 that the *L* called Samuel.
3: 6 Then the *L* called yet again,
3: 7 Samuel did not yet know the *L*,
3: 7 nor was the word of the *L* yet
3: 8 And the *L* called Samuel again
3: 8 Then Eli perceived that the *L*
3: 9 that you must say, 'Speak, *L*,
3:10 Now the *L* came and stood and
3:11 Then the *L* said to Samuel:
3:15 doors of the house of the *L*.
3:17 is the word that the *L*
3:18 And he said, "It is the *L*.
3:19 and the *L* was with him and let
3:20 as a prophet of the *L*.
3:21 Then the *L* appeared again in
3:21 For the *L* revealed Himself to
3:21 in Shiloh by the word of the *L*.
4: 3 Why has the *L* defeated us today
4: 3 ark of the covenant of the *L*
4: 4 ark of the covenant of the *L*
4: 5 ark of the covenant of the *L*
4: 6 that the ark of the *L* had
5: 3 earth before the ark of the *L*.
5: 4 ground before the ark of the *L*.
5: 6 But the hand of the *L* was
5: 9 that the hand of the *L* was
6: 1 Now the ark of the *L* was in the
6: 2 we do with the ark of the *L*?
6: 8 Then take the ark of the *L* and
6:11 And they set the ark of the *L*
6:14 as a burnt offering to the *L*.
6:15 took down the ark of the *L*
6:15 the same day to the *L*.
6:17 a trespass offering to the *L*:
6:18 they set the ark of the *L*,
6:19 looked into the ark of the *L*.
6:19 people lamented because the *L*
6:20 to stand before this holy *L*
6:21 brought back the ark of the *L*;
7: 1 came and took the ark of the *L*,
7: 1 son to keep the ark of the *L*.
7: 2 of Israel lamented after the *L*.
7: 3 If you return to the *L* with all
7: 3 prepare your hearts for the *L*,
7: 4 and served the *L* only.
7: 5 and I will pray to the *L* for
7: 6 poured it out before the *L*.
7: 6 "We have sinned against the *L*.
7: 8 not cease to cry out to the *L*
7: 9 whole burnt offering to the *L*.
7: 9 Samuel cried out to the *L* for
7: 9 and the *L* answered him.
7:10 But the *L* thundered with a
7:12 Thus far the *L* has helped us."
7:13 And the hand of the *L* was
7:17 he built an altar to the *L*.
8: 6 So Samuel prayed to the *L*.
8: 7 And the *L* said to Samuel,
8:10 told all the words of the *L*
8:18 and the *L* will not hear you in
8:21 them in the hearing of the *L*.
8:22 So the *L* said to Samuel, "Heed
9:15 Now the *L* had told Samuel in
9:17 the *L* said to him, "There he
10: 1 Is it not because the *L* has
10: 6 Then the Spirit of the *L* will
10:17 the people together to the *L*
10:18 Thus says the *L* God of Israel:
10:19 yourselves before the *L* by
10:22 they inquired of the *L*
10:22 And the *L* answered, "There
10:24 Do you see him whom the *L* has
10:25 and laid it up before the *L*.
11: 7 And the fear of the *L* fell
11:13 for today the *L* has
11:15 made Saul king before the *L*
11:15 peace offerings before the *L*,
12: 3 against me before the *L* and
12: 5 The *L* is witness against you,
12: 6 It is the *L* who raised up
12: 7 reason with you before the *L*
12: 7 the righteous acts of the *L*
12: 8 fathers cried out to the *L*,
12: 8 then the *L* sent Moses and
12: 9 And when they forgot the *L*
12:10 "Then they cried out to the *L*,
12:10 we have forsaken the *L* and
12:11 And the *L* sent Jerubbaal,
12:12 when the *L* your God was your
12:13 the *L* has set a king over you.
12:14 If you fear the *L* and serve Him
12:14 the commandment of the *L*,
12:14 will continue following the *L*
12:15 do not obey the voice of the *L*,
12:15 the commandment of the *L*,
12:15 then the hand of the *L* will be
12:16 this great thing which the *L*
12:17 I will call to the *L*,
12:17 done in the sight of the *L*,
12:18 So Samuel called to the *L*,
12:18 and the *L* sent thunder and
12:18 people greatly feared the *L*
12:19 for your servants to the *L*
12:20 aside from following the *L*,
12:20 but serve the *L* with all your
12:22 For the *L* will not forsake His
12:22 because it has pleased the *L*
12:23 I should sin against the *L* in
12:24 'Only fear the *L*, and serve
13:12 not made supplication to the *L*.
13:13 kept the commandment of the *L*
13:13 For now the *L* would have
13:14 The *L* has sought for Himself a
13:14 and the *L* has commanded him
13:14 you have not kept what the *L*
14: 6 it may be that the *L* will work
14: 6 For nothing restrains the *L*
14:10 For the *L* has delivered them
14:12 for the *L* has delivered them
14:23 So the *L* saved Israel that day,
14:33 are sinning against the *L* by
14:34 and do not sin against the *L*
14:35 Saul built an altar to the *L*.
14:35 altar that he built to the *L*.
14:39 For as the *L* lives, who saves
14:41 Therefore Saul said to the *L*
14:45 Certainly not! As the *L*
15: 1 The *L* sent me to anoint you
15: 1 voice of the words of the *L*.
15: 2 Thus says the *L* of hosts: 'I
15:10 Now the word of the *L* came to
15:11 and he cried out to the *L* all
15:13 'Blessed are you of the *L*!
15:13 the commandment of the *L*.
15:15 to sacrifice to the *L* your
15:16 And I will tell you what the *L*
15:17 And did not the *L* anoint you
15:18 Now the *L* sent you on a
15:19 not obey the voice of the *L*?
15:19 do evil in the sight of the *L*?
15:20 have obeyed the voice of the *L*,
15:20 on the mission on which the *L*
15:21 to sacrifice to the *L* your God
15:22 Has the *L* as great delight in
15:22 in obeying the voice of the *L*?
15:23 rejected the word of the *L*,
15:24 the commandment of the *L* and
15:25 me, that I may worship the *L*.
15:26 rejected the word of the *L*,
15:26 and the *L* has rejected you
15:28 The *L* has torn the kingdom of
15:30 that I may worship the *L* your
15:31 Saul, and Saul worshiped the *L*.
15:33 Agag in pieces before the *L*
15:35 and the *L* regretted that He
16: 1 Now the *L* said to Samuel, "How
16: 2 And the *L* said, "Take a
16: 2 come to sacrifice to the *L*.
16: 4 So Samuel did what the *L* said,
16: 5 come to sacrifice to the *L*.
16: 7 But the *L* said to Samuel, "Do
16: 7 For the *L* does not see as
16: 7 but the *L* looks at the
16: 8 Neither has the *L* chosen this
16: 9 Neither has the *L* chosen this
16:10 The *L* has not chosen these."
16:12 And the *L* said, "Arise,
16:13 and the Spirit of the *L* came
16:14 But the Spirit of the *L*
16:14 distressing spirit from the *L*
16:18 and the *L* is with him."
17:37 Moreover David said, "The *L*,
17:37 and the *L* be with you!"
17:45 to you in the name of the *L*
17:46 This day the *L* will deliver you
17:47 shall know that the *L* does
18:12 because the *L* was with him,
18:14 and the *L* was with him.
18:28 Saul saw and knew that the *L*
19: 5 and the *L* brought about a
19: 6 As the *L* lives, he shall not
19: 9 distressing spirit from the *L*
20: 3 as the *L* lives and as your
20: 8 into a covenant of the *L* with
20:12 The *L* God of Israel is
20:13 may the *L* do so and much more
20:13 And the *L* be with you as He
20:14 show me the kindness of the *L*
20:15 not when the *L* has cut off
20:16 Let the *L* require it at the
20:21 as the *L* lives, there is
20:22 for the *L* has sent you away.
20:23 indeed the *L* be between you
20:42 sworn in the name of the *L*,
20:42 May the *L* be between you and
21: 6 been taken from before the *L*,
21: 7 day, detained before the *L*.
22:10 And he inquired of the *L* for
22:12 he answered, "Here I am, my *l*.
22:17 and kill the priests of the *L*,
22:17 to strike the priests of the *L*.
23: 2 David inquired of the *L*,
23: 2 And the *L* said to David,
23: 4 Then David inquired of the *L*
23: 4 And the *L* answered him and
23:10 O *L* God of Israel, Your servant
23:11 O *L* God of Israel, I pray,
23:11 And the *L* said, "He will
23:12 And the *L* said, "They will
23:18 made a covenant before the *L*.
23:21 "Blessed are you of the *L*,
24: 4 is the day of which the *L*
24: 6 The *L* forbid that I should do
24: 6 he is the anointed of the *L*.
24: 8 My *l* the king!" And when Saul
24:10 your eyes have seen that the *L*
24:10 out my hand against my *l*,
24:12 Let the *L* judge between you and
24:12 and let the *L* avenge me on
24:15 Therefore let the *L* be judge,
24:18 for when the *L* delivered me
24:19 Therefore may the *L* reward you
24:21 swear now to me by the *L* that
25:24 feet and said: "On me, my *l*,
25:25 let not my *l* regard this
25:25 not see the young men of my *l*
25:26 'Now therefore, my *l*, as the
25:26 as the *L* lives and as your
25:26 since the *L* has held you back
25:26 those who seek harm for my *l*
25:27 maidservant has brought to my *l*,
25:27 the young men who follow my *l*.
25:28 For the *L* will certainly make
25:28 will certainly make for my *l*
25:28 because my *l* fights the battles
25:28 fights the battles of the *L*,
25:29 but the life of my *l* shall be
25:29 of the living with the *L* your

25:30 when the *L* has done for my
25:30 the LORD has done for my *l*
25:31 nor offense of heart to my *l*,
25:31 or that my *l* has avenged
25:31 But when the *L* has dealt well
25:31 LORD has dealt well with my *l*,
25:32 Blessed is the *L* God of
25:34 as the *L* God of Israel lives,
25:38 that the *L* struck Nabal, and
25:39 he said, "Blessed be the *L*,
25:39 servant from evil! For the *L*
25:41 feet of the servants of my *l*.
26:10 As the *L* lives, the LORD
26:10 the *L* shall strike him, or his
26:11 The *L* forbid that I should
26:12 a deep sleep from the *L* had
26:15 have you not guarded your *l*
26:15 came in to destroy your *l* the
26:16 As the *L* lives, you deserve
26:17 said, "It is my voice, my *l*,
26:18 Why does my *l* thus pursue his
26:19 let my *l* the king hear the
26:19 If the *L* has stirred you up
26:19 they be cursed before the *L*,
26:19 in the inheritance of the *L*,
26:20 earth before the face of the *L*.
26:23 May the *L* repay every man for
26:23 for the *L* delivered you into
26:24 much in the eyes of the *L*,
28: 6 when Saul inquired of the *L*,
28: 6 the *L* did not answer him,
28:10 And Saul swore to her by the *L*,
28:10 As the *L* lives, no punishment
28:16 seeing the *L* has departed from
28:17 And the *L* has done for Himself
28:17 For the *L* has torn the kingdom
28:18 not obey the voice of the *L*,
28:18 therefore the *L* has done this
28:19 Moreover the *L* will also
28:19 The *L* will also deliver the
29: 6 as the *L* lives, you have been
29: 8 against the enemies of my *l*
30: 6 strengthened himself in the *L*
30: 8 So David inquired of the *L*,
30:23 not do so with what the *L* has
30:26 spoil of the enemies of the *L*
2 Sam 1:10 have brought them here to my *l*.
1:12 for the people of the *L* and
2: 1 that David inquired of the *L*,
2: 1 And the *L* said to him, "Go
2: 5 "You are blessed of the *L*,
2: 5 shown this kindness to your *l*,
2: 6 And now may the *L* show kindness
3: 9 I do not do for David as the *L*
3:18 do it! For the *L* has spoken
3:21 and gather all Israel to my *l*
3:28 I are guiltless before the *L*
3:39 The *L* shall repay the evildoer
4: 8 and the *L* has avenged my lord
4: 8 and the LORD has avenged my *l*
4: 9 As the *L* lives, who has
5: 2 and the *L* said to you, 'You
5: 3 them at Hebron before the *L*.
5:10 and the *L* God of hosts was
5:12 So David knew that the *L* had
5:19 So David inquired of the *L*,
5:19 And the *L* said to David,
5:20 The *L* has broken through my
5:23 David inquired of the *L*,
5:24 For then the *L* will go out
5:25 as the *L* commanded him; and he
6: 2 the *L* of Hosts, who dwells
6: 5 played music before the *L* on
6: 7 Then the anger of the *L* was
6: 9 David was afraid of the *L* that
6: 9 How can the ark of the *L* come
6:10 not move the ark of the *L*
6:11 The ark of the *L* remained in
6:11 And the *L* blessed Obed-Edom
6:12 The *L* has blessed the house of
6:13 bearing the ark of the *L* had
6:14 Then David danced before the *L*
6:15 brought up the ark of the *L*
6:16 Now as the ark of the *L* came
6:16 and whirling before the *L*;
6:17 they brought the ark of the *L*,
6:17 peace offerings before the *L*.
6:18 people in the name of the *L*
6:21 "It was before the *L*,
6:21 ruler over the people of the *L*,
6:21 will play music before the *L*.
7: 1 and the *L* had given him rest
7: 3 for the *L* is with you."
7: 4 night that the word of the *L*
7: 5 David, 'Thus says the *L*:
7: 8 Thus says the *L* of hosts: "I
7:11 Also the *L* tells you that He
7:18 went in and sat before the *L*;
7:18 O *L* GOD? And what is my house,
7:19 O *L* GOD; and You have also
7:19 manner of man, O *L* GOD?
7:20 *L* GOD, know Your servant.
7:22 O *L* GOD. For there is none
7:24 own people forever; and You, *L*,
7:25 O *L* God, the word which You
7:26 The *L* of hosts is the God over
7:27 O *L* of hosts, God of Israel,
7:28 O *L* GOD, You are God, and Your
7:29 O *L* GOD, have spoken it, and
8: 6 The *L* preserved David wherever
8:11 also dedicated these to the *L*,
8:14 And the *L* preserved David
9:11 According to all that my *l* the
10: 3 of Ammon said to Hanun their *l*,
10:12 And may the *L* do what is
11: 9 with all the servants of his *l*,
11:11 and my *l* Joab and the servants
11:11 Joab and the servants of my *l*
11:13 bed with the servants of his *l*,
11:27 had done displeased the *L*.
12: 1 Then the *L* sent Nathan to
12: 5 As the *L* lives, the man who
12: 7 are the man! Thus says the *L*
12: 9 the commandment of the *L*,
12:11 'Thus says the *L*: 'Behold, I
12:13 "I have sinned against the *L*.
12:13 The *L* also has put away your
12:14 to the enemies of the *L* to
12:15 And the *L* struck the child
12:20 went into the house of the *L*
12:22 Who can tell whether the *L*
12:24 Now the *L* loved him,
12:25 Jedidiah, because of the *L*.
13:32 Let not my *l* suppose they have
13:33 let not my *l* the king take the
14: 9 Tekoa said to the king, "My *l*,
14:11 let the king remember the *L*
14:11 As the *L* lives, not one hair
14:12 speak another word to my *l*
14:15 to speak of this thing to my *l*
14:17 The word of my *l* the king will
14:17 so is my *l* the king in
14:17 And may the *L* your God be with
14:18 let my *l* the king speak."
14:19 my *l* the king, no one can turn
14:19 left from anything that my *l*
14:20 but my *l* is wise, according to
14:22 found favor in your sight, my *l*,
15: 7 the vow which I made to the *L*.
15: 8 If the *L* indeed brings me back
15: 8 then I will serve the *L*.
15:15 ready to do whatever my *l*
15:21 As the *L* lives, and as my
15:21 and as my *l* the king lives,
15:21 surely in whatever place my *l*
15:25 favor in the eyes of the *L*,
15:31 And David said, "O *L*,
16: 4 find favor in your sight, my *l*,
16: 8 The *L* has brought upon you all
16: 8 and the *L* has delivered the
16: 9 this dead dog curse my *l* the
16:10 because the *L* has said to him,
16:11 for so the *L* has ordered him.
16:12 It may be that the *L* will look
16:12 and that the *L* will repay me
16:18 but whom the *L* and this people
17:14 For the *L* had purposed to
17:14 to the intent that the *L* might
18:19 how the *L* has avenged him of
18:28 Blessed be the *L* your God, who
18:28 raised their hand against my *l*
18:31 my *l* the king! For the LORD
18:31 my lord the king! For the *L*
18:32 May the enemies of my *l* the
19: 7 For I swear by the *L*,
19:19 Do not let my *l* impute iniquity
19:19 did on the day that my *l* the
19:20 Joseph to go down to meet my *l*
19:26 And he answered, "My *l*,
19:27 slandered your servant to my *l*
19:27 but my *l* the king is like the
19:28 were but dead men before my *l*
19:30 inasmuch as my *l* the king has
19:35 be a further burden to my *l*
19:37 let him cross over with my *l*
20:19 up the inheritance of the *L*?
21: 1 and David inquired of the *L*.
21: 1 And the *L* answered, "It is
21: 3 bless the inheritance of the *L*?
21: 6 we will hang them before the *L*
21: 6 whom the *L* chose." And the
21: 9 them on the hill before the *L*.
22: 1 Then David spoke to the *L* the
22: 1 on the day when the *L* had
22: 2 The *L* is my rock and my
22: 4 I will call upon the *L*,
22: 7 distress I called upon the *L*,
22:14 The *L* thundered from heaven,
22:16 At the rebuke of the *L*,
22:19 But the *L* was my support.
22:21 The *L* rewarded me according to
22:22 I have kept the ways of the *L*,
22:25 Therefore the *L* has
22:29 "For You are my lamp, O *L*;
22:29 The *L* shall enlighten my
22:31 The word of the *L* is proven;
22:32 who is God, except the *L*?
22:42 none to save; Even to the *L*,
22:47 The *L* lives! Blessed be my
22:50 I will give thanks to You, O *L*,
23: 2 The Spirit of the *L* spoke by
23:10 The *L* brought about a great
23:12 And the *L* brought about a
23:16 it, but poured it out to the *L*.
23:17 said, "Far be it from me, O *L*,
24: 1 Again the anger of the *L* was
24: 3 Now may the *L* your God add to
24: 3 and may the eyes of my *l* the
24: 3 But why does my *l* the king
24:10 So David said to the *L*,
24:10 but now, I pray, O *L*,
24:11 the word of the *L* came to the
24:12 tell David, 'Thus says the *L*:
24:14 us fall into the hand of the *L*,
24:15 So the *L* sent a plague upon
24:16 the *L* relented from the
24:16 And the angel of the *L* was
24:17 Then David spoke to the *L* when
24:18 erect an altar to the *L* on the
24:19 went up as the *L* commanded.
24:21 Why has my *l* the king come to
24:21 to build an altar to the *L*,
24:22 Let my *l* the king take and offer
24:23 May the *L* your God accept
24:24 burnt offerings to the *L* my
24:25 built there an altar to the *L*,
24:25 So the *L* heeded the prayers
1 Ki 1: 2 be sought for our *l* the king,
1: 2 that our *l* the king may be
1:11 and David our *l* does not know
1:13 say to him, 'Did you not, my *l*,
1:17 Then she said to him, "My *l*,
1:17 you swore by the *L* your God to
1:18 my *l* the king, you do not know
1:20 "And as for you, my *l*,
1:20 will sit on the throne of my *l*
1:21 when my *l* the king rests with
1:24 And Nathan said, "My *l*,
1:27 this thing been done by my *l*
1:27 sit on the throne of my *l* the
1:29 As the *L* lives, who has
1:30 as I swore to you by the *L*
1:31 Let my *l* King David live
1:33 with you the servants of your *l*,
1:36 Amen! May the *L* God of my lord
1:36 May the LORD God of my *l* the
1:37 As the *L* has been with my lord
1:37 the LORD has been with my *l*
1:37 than the throne of my *l* King
1:43 No! Our *l* King David has made
1:47 have gone to bless our *l* King
1:48 Blessed be the *L* God of
2: 3 And keep the charge of the *L*
2: 4 that the *L* may fulfill His word
2: 8 and I swore to him by the *L*,
2:15 for it was his from the *L*.
2:23 King Solomon swore by the *L*,
2:24 as the *L* lives, who has
2:26 you carried the ark of the *L*
2:27 from being priest to the *L*,
2:27 fulfill the word of the *L*
2:28 to the tabernacle of the *L*,
2:29 to the tabernacle of the *L*;
2:30 to the tabernacle of the *L*,
2:32 So the *L* will return his blood
2:33 be peace forever from the *L*.
2:38 As my *l* the king has said, so
2:42 I not make you swear by the *L*,
2:43 you not kept the oath of the *L*
2:44 therefore the *L* will return
2:45 be established before the *L*
3: 1 house, and the house of the *L*,
3: 2 built for the name of the *L*
3: 3 And Solomon loved the *L*,
3: 5 At Gibeon the *L* appeared to
3: 7 O *L* my God, You have made Your
3:10 The speech pleased the *L*,
3:15 ark of the covenant of the *L*,
3:17 And one woman said, "O my *l*,
3:26 her son; and she said, "O my *l*,
5: 3 a house for the name of the *L*
5: 3 until the *L* put his foes
5: 4 But now the *L* my God has given
5: 5 a house for the name of the *L*
5: 5 as the *L* spoke to my father
5: 7 Blessed be the *L* this day,
5:12 So the *L* gave Solomon wisdom,
6: 1 to build the house of the *L*.
6: 2 King Solomon built for the *L*,
6:11 Then the word of the *L* came to
6:19 ark of the covenant of the *L*
6:37 of the house of the *L* was
7:12 court of the house of the *L*
7:40 for the house of the *L*:
7:45 for the house of the *L* were
7:48 made for the house of the *L*:
7:51 done for the house of the *L*
7:51 of the house of the *L*.
8: 1 ark of the covenant of the *L*
8: 4 brought up the ark of the *L*,
8: 6 ark of the covenant of the *L*
8: 9 when the *L* made a covenant
8:10 filled the house of the *L*,
8:11 for the glory of the *L* filled
8:11 filled the house of the *L*.
8:12 The *L* said He would dwell in
8:15 Blessed be the *L* God of
8:17 a temple for the name of the *L*
8:18 But the *L* said to my father
8:20 So the *L* has fulfilled His word
8:20 as the *L* promised; and I have
8:20 a temple for the name of the *L*
8:21 is the covenant of the *L*
8:22 before the altar of the *L* in
8:23 *L* God of Israel, there is no
8:25 *L* God of Israel, now keep what
8:28 O *L* my God, and listen to the
8:44 and when they pray to the *L*
8:53 out of Egypt, O *L* GOD.'
8:54 and supplication to the *L*,
8:54 from before the altar of the *L*,
8:56 'Blessed be the *L*, who has
8:57 May the *L* our God be with us,
8:59 made supplication before the *L*,
8:59 be near the *L* our God day and
8:60 the earth may know that the *L*

8:61 therefore be loyal to the L
8:62 sacrifices before the L.
8:63 which he offered to the L,
8:63 dedicated the house of the L.
8:64 in front of the house of the L;
8:64 altar that was before the L
8:65 before the L our God, seven
8:66 for all the good that the L
9: 1 building the house of the L
9: 2 that the L appeared to Solomon
9: 3 And the L said to him: "I have
9: 8 Why has the L done thus to this
9: 9 Because they forsook the L
9: 9 therefore the L has brought
9:10 the house of the L and the
9:15 to build the house of the L,
9:25 which he had built for the L,
9:25 altar that was before the L.
10: 1 concerning the name of the L,
10: 5 went up to the house of the L,
10: 9 Blessed be the L your God, who
10: 9 of Israel! Because the L has
10:12 wood for the house of the L
11: 2 the nations of whom the L had
11: 4 heart was not loyal to the L
11: 6 did evil in the sight of the L,
11: 6 and did not fully follow the L,
11: 9 So the L became angry with
11: 9 heart had turned from the L
11:10 but he did not keep what the L
11:11 Therefore the L said to
11:14 Now the L raised up an
11:23 who had fled from his l,
11:31 pieces, for thus says the L,
12:15 of events was from the L,
12:15 which the L had spoken by
12:24 'Thus says the L: "You shall
12:24 they obeyed the word of the L,
12:24 according to the word of the L.
12:27 in the house of the L at
12:27 will turn back to their l,
13: 1 to Bethel by the word of the L,
13: 2 the altar by the word of the L,
13: 2 altar, altar! Thus says the L:
13: 3 is the sign which the L
13: 5 had given by the word of the L.
13: 6 entreat the favor of the L
13: 6 the man of God entreated the L,
13: 9 me by the word of the L,
13:17 been told by the word of the L,
13:18 to me by the word of the L,
13:20 that the word of the L came to
13:21 saying, "Thus says the L:
13:21 disobeyed the word of the L,
13:21 the commandment which the L
13:22 in the place of which the L
13:26 to the word of the L.
13:26 Therefore the L has delivered
13:26 to the word of the L which He
13:32 cried out by the word of the L
14: 5 Now the L had said to Ahijah,
14: 7 Thus says the L God of Israel:
14:11 for the L has spoken!" '
14:13 something good toward the L
14:14 Moreover the L will raise up
14:15 For the L will strike Israel,
14:15 provoking the L to anger.
14:18 to the word of the L which He
14:21 the city which the L had
14:22 did evil in the sight of the L,
14:24 of the nations which the L
14:26 of the house of the L and the
14:28 entered the house of the L,
15: 3 heart was not loyal to the L
15: 4 for David's sake the L his
15: 5 right in the eyes of the L,
15:11 right in the eyes of the L,
15:14 heart was loyal to the L all
15:15 into the house of the L the
15:18 of the house of the L and the
15:26 did evil in the sight of the L,
15:29 to the word of the L which He
15:30 which he had provoked the L
15:34 did evil in the sight of the L,
16: 1 Then the word of the L came to
16: 7 And also the word of the L came
16: 7 he did in the sight of the L
16:12 according to the word of the L,
16:13 in provoking the L God of
16:19 evil in the sight of the L,
16:25 did evil in the eyes of the L,
16:26 provoking the L God of Israel
16:30 did evil in the sight of the L,
16:33 did more to provoke the L God
16:34 according to the word of the L,
17: 1 As the L God of Israel lives,
17: 2 Then the word of the L came to
17: 5 according to the word of the L,
17: 8 Then the word of the L came to
17:12 As the L your God lives, I do
17:14 For thus says the L God of
17:14 until the day the L sends rain
17:16 to the word of the L which He
17:20 Then he cried out to the L and
17:20 O L my God, have You also
17:21 and cried out to the L and
17:21 O L my God, I pray, let this
17:22 Then the L heard the voice of
17:24 and that the word of the L in
18: 1 days that the word of the L
18: 3 (Now Obadiah feared the L
18: 4 the prophets of the L,
18: 7 Is that you, my l Elijah?"
18:10 As the L your God lives, there
18:12 that the Spirit of the L will
18:12 your servant have feared the L
18:13 Was it not reported to my l what
18:13 killed the prophets of the L,
18:15 As the L of hosts lives,
18:18 the commandments of the L and
18:21 If the L is God, follow Him;
18:22 am left a prophet of the L;
18:24 will call on the name of the L;
18:30 he repaired the altar of the L
18:31 to whom the word of the L had
18:32 an altar in the name of the L;
18:36 L God of Abraham, Isaac, and
18:37 'Hear me, O L, hear me,
18:37 may know that You are the L
18:38 Then the fire of the L fell and
18:39 and they said, "The L,
18:39 "The LORD, He is God! The L,
18:46 Then the hand of the L came
19: 4 said, "It is enough! Now, L,
19: 7 And the angel of the L came
19: 9 the word of the L came to
19:10 been very zealous for the L
19:11 on the mountain before the L.
19:11 the L passed by, and a great
19:11 rocks in pieces before the L,
19:11 but the L was not in the
19:11 but the L was not in the
19:12 but the L was not in the
19:14 been very zealous for the L
19:15 Then the L said to him: "Go,
20: 4 answered and said, "My l,
20: 9 Tell my l the king, 'All that
20:13 saying, "Thus says the L:
20:13 shall know that I am the L.
20:14 And he said, "Thus says the L:
20:28 and said, "Thus says the L:
20:28 The L is God of the hills, but
20:28 shall know that I am the L."
20:35 neighbor by the word of the L,
20:36 not obeyed the voice of the L,
20:42 said to him, "Thus says the L:
21: 3 The L forbid that I should give
21:17 Then the word of the L came to
21:19 him, saying, 'Thus says the L:
21:19 him, saying, 'Thus says the L:
21:20 do evil in the sight of the L:
21:23 And concerning Jezebel the L
21:25 in the sight of the L,
21:26 whom the L had cast out before
21:28 And the word of the L came to
22: 5 inquire for the word of the L
22: 6 for the L will deliver it into
22: 7 not still a prophet of the L
22: 8 whom we may inquire of the L;
22:11 and he said, "Thus says the L:
22:12 for the L will deliver it
22:14 As the L lives, whatever the
22:14 whatever the L says to me,
22:15 for the L will deliver it
22:16 the truth in the name of the L?
22:17 And the L said, 'These have no
22:19 hear the word of the L:
22:19 I saw the L sitting on His
22:20 And the L said, 'Who will
22:21 forward and stood before the L,
22:22 The L said to him, 'In what
22:22 And the L said, 'You shall
22:23 Therefore look! The L has put a
22:23 and the L has declared
22:24 way did the spirit from the L
22:28 the L has not spoken by me."
22:38 to the word of the L which He
22:43 right in the eyes of the L.
22:52 did evil in the sight of the L,
22:53 and provoked the L God of
2 Ki 1: 3 But the angel of the L said to
1: 4 therefore, thus says the L:
1: 6 say to him, "Thus says the L:
1:15 And the angel of the L said to
1:16 said to him, "Thus says the L:
1:17 to the word of the L which
2: 1 when the L was about to take
2: 2 for the L has sent me on to
2: 2 As the L lives, and as your
2: 3 Do you know that the L will
2: 4 for the L has sent me on to
2: 4 As the L lives, and as your
2: 5 Do you know that the L will
2: 6 for the L has sent me on to
2: 6 As the L lives, and as your
2:14 Where is the L God of
2:16 perhaps the Spirit of the L
2:19 as my l sees; but the water is
2:21 and said, "Thus says the L:
2:24 on them in the name of the L.
3: 2 did evil in the sight of the L,
3:10 Alas! For the L has called
3:11 there no prophet of the L
3:11 that we may inquire of the L
3:12 The word of the L is with
3:13 for the L has called these
3:14 As the L of hosts lives,
3:15 that the hand of the L came
3:16 And he said, "Thus says the L:
3:17 "For thus says the L:
3:18 matter in the sight of the L;
4: 1 that your servant feared the L.
4:16 son." And she said, "No, my l.
4:27 and the L has hidden it from
4:28 said, "Did I ask a son of my l?
4:30 As the L lives, and as your
4:33 of them, and prayed to the L.
4:43 may eat; for thus says the L:
4:44 according to the word of the L.
5: 1 because by him the L had given
5:11 and call on the name of the L
5:16 As the L lives, before whom I
5:17 to other gods, but to the L.
5:18 Yet in this thing may the L
5:18 may the L please pardon your
5:20 but as the L lives, I will
6:12 his servants said, "None, my l,
6:17 Elisha prayed, and said, "L,
6:17 Then the L opened the eyes
6:18 to him, Elisha prayed to the L,
6:20 Samaria, that Elisha said, "L,
6:20 And the L opened their eyes,
6:26 to him, saying, "Help, my l,
6:27 If the L does not help you,
6:33 this calamity is from the L;
6:33 why should I wait for the L
7: 1 said, "Hear the word of the L.
7: 1 of the LORD. Thus says the L:
7: 2 if the L would make windows
7: 6 For the L had caused the army
7:16 according to the word of the L.
7:19 if the L would make windows
8: 1 for the L has called for a
8: 5 And Gehazi said, "My l,
8: 8 and inquire of the L by him,
8:10 However the L has shown me
8:12 'Why is my l weeping?"
8:13 The L has shown me that you
8:18 did evil in the sight of the L.
8:19 Yet the L would not destroy
8:27 did evil in the sight of the L,
9: 3 and say, 'Thus says the L:
9: 6 Thus says the L God of Israel:
9: 6 king over the people of the L,
9: 7 of all the servants of the L,
9:12 me, saying, 'Thus says the L:
9:25 that the L laid this burden
9:26 blood of his sons,' says the L,
9:26 you in this plot,' says the L.
9:26 according to the word of the L.
9:36 "This is the word of the L,
10:10 the earth of the word of the L
10:10 word of the LORD which the L
10:10 for the L has done what He
10:16 me, and see my zeal for the L.
10:17 to the word of the L which He
10:23 see that no servants of the L
10:30 And the L said to Jehu,
10:31 to walk in the law of the L
10:32 In those days the L began to
11: 3 her in the house of the L for
11: 4 them into the house of the L
11: 4 them in the house of the L,
11: 7 watch of the house of the L
11:10 were in the temple of the L.
11:13 people in the temple of the L.
11:15 killed in the house of the L.
11:17 made a covenant between the L,
11:18 over the house of the L.
11:19 down from the house of the L,
12: 2 right in the sight of the L
12: 4 into the house of the L—
12: 4 bring into the house of the L,
12: 9 comes into the house of the L;
12: 9 into the house of the L.
12:10 found in the house of the L.
12:11 of the house of the L;
12:11 worked on the house of the L,
12:12 damage of the house of the L,
12:13 made for the house of the L
12:13 into the house of the L.
12:14 repaired the house of the L
12:16 into the house of the L.
12:18 of the house of the L and in
13: 2 did evil in the sight of the L,
13: 3 Then the anger of the L was
13: 4 So Jehoahaz pleaded with the L,
13: 4 and the L listened to him;
13: 5 Then the L gave Israel a
13:11 did evil in the sight of the L,
13:23 But the L was gracious to them,
14: 3 right in the sight of the L,
14: 6 in which the L commanded,
14:14 found in the house of the L
14:24 did evil in the sight of the L;
14:25 to the word of the L God of
14:26 For the L saw that the
14:27 And the L did not say that He
15: 3 right in the sight of the L,
15: 5 Then the L struck the king, so
15: 9 did evil in the sight of the L,
15:12 This was the word of the L
15:18 did evil in the sight of the L;
15:24 did evil in the sight of the L;
15:28 did evil in the sight of the L;
15:34 right in the sight of the L;
15:35 Gate of the house of the L.
15:37 In those days the L began to
16: 2 right in the sight of the L
16: 3 of the nations whom the L had
16: 8 found in the house of the L,
16:14 altar which was before the L,
16:14 altar and the house of the L—
16:18 from the house of the L,
17: 2 did evil in the sight of the L,
17: 7 had sinned against the L

L

17: 8 of the nations whom the *L* had
17: 9 secretly did against the *L*
17:11 like the nations whom the *L*
17:11 things to provoke the *L* to
17:12 of which the *L* had said to
17:13 Yet the *L* testified against
17:14 who did not believe in the *L*
17:15 concerning whom the *L* had
17:16 all the commandments of the *L*
17:17 do evil in the sight of the *L*,
17:18 Therefore the *L* was very angry
17:19 keep the commandments of the *L*
17:20 And the *L* rejected all the
17:21 Israel from following the *L*,
17:23 until the *L* removed Israel out
17:25 that they did not fear the *L*;
17:25 therefore the *L* sent lions
17:28 how they should fear the *L*.
17:32 So they feared the *L*,
17:33 They feared the *L*,
17:34 they do not fear the *L*,
17:34 and commandment which the *L*
17:35 with whom the *L* had made a
17:36 'but the *L*, who brought you
17:39 But the *L* your God you shall
17:41 So these nations feared the *L*,
18: 3 right in the sight of the *L*,
18: 5 He trusted in the *L* God of
18: 6 For he held fast to the *L*;
18: 6 which the *L* had commanded
18: 7 The *L* was with him;
18:12 not obey the voice of the *L*
18:12 Moses the servant of the *L*
18:15 found in the house of the *L*
18:16 doors of the temple of the *L*,
18:22 We trust in the *L* our God,' is
18:25 I now come up without the *L*
18:25 The *L* said to me, 'Go up
18:30 make you trust in the *L*,
18:30 The *L* will surely deliver us;
18:32 The *L* will deliver us."
18:35 that the *L* should deliver
19: 1 went into the house of the *L*.
19: 4 It may be that the *L* your God
19: 4 rebuke the words which the *L*
19: 6 your master, 'Thus says the *L*:
19:14 went up to the house of the *L*,
19:14 and spread it before the *L*.
19:15 Hezekiah prayed before the *L*,
19:15 O *L* God of Israel, the One
19:16 "Incline Your ear, O *L*,
19:16 and hear; open Your eyes, O *L*,
19:17 'Truly, *L*, the kings of
19:19 O *L* our God, I pray, save us
19:19 may know that You are the *L*
19:20 Thus says the *L* God of Israel:
19:21 is the word which the *L*
19:23 you have reproached the *L*,
19:31 The zeal of the *L* of hosts
19:32 Therefore thus says the *L*
19:33 into this city,' Says the *L*.
19:35 night that the angel of the *L*
20: 1 said to him, "Thus says the *L*:
20: 2 the wall, and prayed to the *L*,
20: 3 'Remember now, O *L*, I pray,
20: 4 that the word of the *L* came to
20: 5 of My people, 'Thus says the *L*,
20: 5 go up to the house of the *L*.
20: 8 What is the sign that the *L*
20: 8 go up to the house of the *L*
20: 9 is the sign to you from the *L*,
20: 9 that the *L* will do the thing
20:11 the prophet cried out to the *L*,
20:16 "Hear the word of the *L*:
20:17 shall be left,' says the *L*.
20:19 The word of the *L* which you
21: 2 did evil in the sight of the *L*,
21: 2 of the nations whom the *L* had
21: 4 altars in the house of the *L*,
21: 4 of which the *L* had said, "In
21: 5 courts of the house of the *L*.
21: 6 evil in the sight of the *L*,
21: 7 in the house of which the *L*
21: 9 than the nations whom the *L*
21:10 And the *L* spoke by His
21:12 therefore thus says the *L* God
21:16 evil in the sight of the *L*.
21:20 did evil in the sight of the *L*,
21:22 He forsook the *L* God of his
21:22 not walk in the way of the *L*.
22: 2 right in the sight of the *L*,
22: 3 to the house of the *L*,
22: 4 into the house of the *L*,
22: 5 in the house of the *L*;
22: 5 who are in the house of the *L*
22: 8 the Law in the house of the *L*.
22: 9 who oversee the house of the *L*.
22:13 inquire of the *L* for me, for
22:13 great is the wrath of the *L*
22:15 Thus says the *L* God of Israel,
22:16 'Thus says the *L*: 'Behold, I
22:18 sent you to inquire of the *L*,
22:18 Thus says the *L* God of Israel:
22:19 humbled yourself before the *L*
22:19 have heard you," says the *L*.
23: 2 went up to the house of the *L*
23: 2 found in the house of the *L*.
23: 3 made a covenant before the *L*,
23: 3 to follow the *L* and to keep
23: 4 out of the temple of the *L*
23: 6 image from the house of the *L*,
23: 7 were in the house of the *L*,
23: 9 come up to the altar of the *L*
23:11 entrance to the house of the *L*,
23:12 courts of the house of the *L*,
23:16 to the word of the *L* which
23:19 had made to provoke the *L* to
23:21 Keep the Passover to the *L* your
23:23 was held before the *L* in
23:24 found in the house of the *L*.
23:25 who turned to the *L* with all
23:26 Nevertheless the *L* did not
23:27 And the *L* said, "I will also
23:32 did evil in the sight of the *L*,
23:37 did evil in the sight of the *L*,
24: 2 And the *L* sent against him
24: 2 to the word of the *L* which He
24: 3 at the commandment of the *L*
24: 4 which the *L* would not pardon.
24: 9 did evil in the sight of the *L*,
24:13 of the house of the *L* and the
24:13 made in the temple of the *L*,
24:13 as the *L* had said.
24:19 did evil in the sight of the *L*,
24:20 because of the anger of the *L*
25: 9 He burned the house of the *L*
25:13 were in the house of the *L*,
25:13 were in the house of the *L*,
25:16 made for the house of the *L*,
1 Chr 2: 3 wicked in the sight of the *L*;
6:15 into captivity when the *L*
6:31 of song in the house of the *L*,
6:32 had built the house of the *L*
9:19 entrance to the camp of the *L*.
9:20 the *L* was with him.
9:23 gates of the house of the *L*,
10:13 he had committed against the *L*,
10:13 did not keep the word of the *L*,
10:14 he did not inquire of the *L*;
11: 2 and the *L* your God said to
11: 3 them at Hebron before the *L*.
11: 3 to the word of the *L* by
11: 9 and the *L* of hosts was with
11:10 according to the word of the *L*
11:14 So the *L* brought about a great
11:18 it, but poured it out to the *L*.
12:23 according to the word of the *L*:
13: 2 and if it is of the *L* our God,
13: 6 there the ark of God the *L*,
13:10 Then the anger of the *L* was
13:14 And the *L* blessed the house of
14: 2 So David knew that the *L* had
14:10 And the *L* said to him, "Go
14:17 and the *L* brought the fear of
15: 2 for the *L* has chosen them to
15: 3 to bring up the ark of the *L*
15:12 may bring up the ark of the *L*
15:13 the *L* our God broke out
15:14 to bring up the ark of the *L*
15:15 according to the word of the *L*.
15:25 ark of the covenant of the *L*
15:26 ark of the covenant of the *L*,
15:28 ark of the covenant of the *L*
15:29 ark of the covenant of the *L*
16: 2 people in the name of the *L*.
16: 4 before the ark of the *L*,
16: 4 and to praise the *L* God of
16: 7 his brethren, to thank the *L*:
16: 8 give thanks to the *L*!
16:10 those rejoice who seek the *L*!
16:11 Seek the *L* and His strength;
16:14 He is the *L* our God;
16:23 Sing to the *L*, all the earth;
16:25 For the *L* is great and
16:26 But the *L* made the heavens.
16:28 Give to the *L*, O families
16:28 Give to the *L* glory and
16:29 Give to the *L* the glory due
16:29 worship the *L* in the beauty of
16:31 the nations, "The *L* reigns."
16:33 shall rejoice before the *L*,
16:34 Oh, give thanks to the *L*,
16:36 Blessed be the *L* God of
16:36 "Amen!" and praised the *L*.
16:37 ark of the covenant of the *L*
16:39 the tabernacle of the *L* at
16:40 burnt offerings to the *L* on
16:40 is written in the Law of the *L*
16:41 name, to give thanks to the *L*,
17: 1 ark of the covenant of the *L*
17: 4 David, 'Thus says the *L*:
17: 7 Thus says the *L* of hosts: "I
17:10 I tell you that the *L* will
17:16 went in and sat before the *L*;
17:16 O *L* God? And what is my house,
17:17 man of high degree, O *L* God.
17:19 'O *L*, for Your servant's sake,
17:20 'O *L*, there is none like
17:22 own people forever; and You, *L*,
17:23 And now, O *L*, the word
17:24 The *L* of hosts, the God of
17:26 'And now, *L*, You are God,
17:27 for You have blessed it, O *L*,
18: 6 So the *L* preserved David
18:11 also dedicated these to the *L*,
18:13 And the *L* preserved David
19:13 And may the *L* do what is
21: 3 May the *L* make His people a
21: 3 my *l* the king, are they not
21: 3 Why then does my *l* require this
21: 9 And the *L* spoke to Gad,
21:10 saying, 'Thus says the *L*:
21:11 said to him, "Thus says the *L*:
21:12 three days the sword of the *L*—
21:12 with the angel of the *L*
21:13 me fall into the hand of the *L*,
21:14 So the *L* sent a plague upon
21:15 the *L* looked and relented of
21:15 And the angel of the *L* stood
21:16 and saw the angel of the *L*
21:17 O *L* my God, be against me and
21:18 the angel of the *L* commanded
21:18 go and erect an altar to the *L*
21:19 spoken in the name of the *L*.
21:22 build an altar on it to the *L*.
21:23 and let my *l* the king do what
21:24 take what is yours for the *L*,
21:26 built there an altar to the *L*,
21:26 offerings, and called on the *L*;
21:27 So the *L* commanded the angel,
21:28 when David saw that the *L* had
21:29 For the tabernacle of the *L* and
21:30 sword of the angel of the *L*.
22: 1 This is the house of the *L*
22: 5 house to be built for the *L*
22: 6 him to build a house for the *L*
22: 7 a house to the name of the *L*
22: 8 but the word of the *L* came to
22:11 may the *L* be with you; and may
22:11 and build the house of the *L*
22:12 Only may the *L* give you wisdom
22:12 you may keep the law of the *L*
22:13 and judgments with which the *L*
22:14 for the house of the *L* one
22:16 and the *L* be with you."
22:18 Is not the *L* your God with
22:18 land is subdued before the *L*
22:19 and your soul to seek the *L*
22:19 build the sanctuary of the *L*
22:19 ark of the covenant of the *L*
22:19 be built for the name of the *L*.
23: 4 the work of the house of the *L*,
23: 5 four thousand praised the *L*
23:13 to burn incense before the *L*,
23:24 service of the house of the *L*,
23:25 The *L* God of Israel has given
23:28 service of the house of the *L*,
23:30 to thank and praise the *L*,
23:31 of a burnt offering to the *L*
23:31 them, regularly before the *L*;
23:32 the work of the house of the *L*.
24:19 coming into the house of the *L*
24:19 as the *L* God of Israel had
25: 3 thanks and to praise the *L*.
25: 6 music in the house of the *L*,
25: 7 in the songs of the *L*,
26:12 to serve in the house of the *L*.
26:22 of the house of the *L*.
26:27 to maintain the house of the *L*.
26:30 for all the business of the *L*,
27:23 because the *L* had said He
28: 2 ark of the covenant of the *L*,
28: 4 However the *L* God of Israel
28: 5 of all my sons (for the *L*
28: 5 of the kingdom of the *L* over
28: 8 Israel, the assembly of the *L*,
28: 8 all the commandments of the *L*
28: 9 for the *L* searches all hearts
28:10 for the *L* has chosen you to
28:12 courts of the house of the *L*,
28:13 service of the house of the *L*,
28:13 service in the house of the *L*.
28:18 ark of the covenant of the *L*.
28:19 the *L* made me understand in
28:20 for the *L* God—my God—will be
28:20 service of the house of the *L*.
29: 1 is not for man but for the *L*
29: 5 himself this day to the *L*?
29: 8 treasury of the house of the *L*,
29: 9 had offered willingly to the *L*;
29:10 David blessed the *L* before
29:10 *L* God of Israel, our Father,
29:11 Yours, O *L*, is the
29:11 Yours is the kingdom, O *L*,
29:16 O *L* our God, all this
29:18 O *L* God of Abraham, Isaac, and
29:20 'Now bless the *L* your God."
29:20 all the assembly blessed the *L*
29:20 themselves before the *L* and
29:21 they made sacrifices to the *L*
29:21 burnt offerings to the *L* on
29:22 ate and drank before the *L*
29:22 and anointed him before the *L*
29:23 sat on the throne of the *L* as
29:25 So the *L* exalted Solomon
2 Chr 1: 1 and the *L* his God was with
1: 3 Moses the servant of the *L*
1: 5 before the tabernacle of the *L*;
1: 6 the bronze altar before the *L*,
1: 9 O *L* God, let Your promise to
2: 1 a temple for the name of the *L*,
2: 4 a temple for the name of the *L*
2: 4 and on the set feasts of the *L*
2:11 Because the *L* loves His
2:12 Blessed be the *L* God of
2:12 will build a temple for the *L*
2:14 with the skillful men of my *l*
2:15 and the wine which my *l* has
3: 1 to build the house of the *L*
3: 1 where the *L* had appeared to
4:16 Solomon for the house of the *L*.
5: 1 done for the house of the *L*
5: 2 ark of the covenant of the *L*
5: 7 ark of the covenant of the *L*
5:10 when the *L* made a covenant
5:13 in praising and thanking the *L*,

5:13 of music, and praised the *L*,
5:13 the house, the house of the *L*,
5:14 for the glory of the *L* filled
6: 1 The *L* said He would dwell in
6: 4 Blessed be the *L* God of
6: 7 a temple for the name of the *L*
6: 8 But the *L* said to my father
6:10 So the *L* has fulfilled His word
6:10 as the *L* promised; and I have
6:10 temple for the name of the *L*
6:11 is the covenant of the *L*
6:12 before the altar of the *L* in
6:14 *L* God of Israel, there is no
6:16 *L* God of Israel, now keep what
6:17 O *L* God of Israel, let Your
6:19 O *L* my God, and listen to the
6:41 O *L* God, to Your resting
6:41 O *L* God, be clothed with
6:42 O *L* God, do not turn away the
7: 1 and the glory of the *L* filled
7: 2 not enter the house of the *L*,
7: 2 because the glory of the *L* had
7: 3 and the glory of the *L* on the
7: 3 worshiped and praised the *L*,
7: 4 sacrifices before the *L*.
7: 6 of the music of the *L*,
7: 6 David had made to praise the *L*,
7: 7 in front of the house of the *L*;
7:10 heart for the good that the *L*
7:11 finished the house of the *L*
7:11 to make in the house of the *L*
7:12 Then the *L* appeared to Solomon
7:21 Why has the *L* done thus to this
7:22 Because they forsook the *L* God
8: 1 had built the house of the *L*
8:11 to which the ark of the *L* has
8:12 burnt offerings to the *L* on
8:12 LORD on the altar of the *L*
8:16 of the house of the *L* until
8:16 So the house of the *L* was
9: 4 went up to the house of the *L*,
9: 8 Blessed be the *L* your God, who
9: 8 throne to be king for the *L*
9:11 wood for the house of the *L*
10:15 that the *L* might fulfill His
11: 2 But the word of the *L* came to
11: 4 'Thus says the *L*: "You shall
11: 4 they obeyed the words of the *L*,
11:14 serving as priests to the *L*.
11:16 set their heart to seek the *L*
11:16 to sacrifice to the *L* God of
12: 1 he forsook the law of the *L*,
12: 2 had transgressed against the *L*,
12: 5 to them, "Thus says the *L*:
12: 6 The *L* is righteous."
12: 7 Now when the *L* saw that they
12: 7 the word of the *L* came to
12: 9 of the house of the *L* and the
12:11 entered the house of the *L*,
12:12 the wrath of the *L* turned from
12:13 the city which the *L* had
12:14 his heart to seek the *L*.
13: 5 you not know that the *L* God
13: 6 up and rebelled against his *l*.
13: 8 withstand the kingdom of the *L*,
13: 9 cast out the priests of the *L*,
13:10 the *L* is our God, and we have
13:10 priests who minister to the *L*
13:11 And they burn to the *L* every
13:11 we keep the command of the *L*
13:12 do not fight against the *L* God
13:14 and they cried out to the *L*,
13:18 because they relied on the *L*
13:20 and the *L* struck him, and he
14: 2 and right in the eyes of the *L*
14: 4 commanded Judah to seek the *L*
14: 6 because the *L* had given him
14: 7 because we have sought the *L*
14:11 And Asa cried out to the *L* his
14:11 LORD his God, and said, "*L*,
14:11 O *L* our God, for we rest on
14:11 go against this multitude. O *L*,
14:12 So the *L* struck the Ethiopians
14:13 they were broken before the *L*
14:14 for the fear of the *L* came
15: 2 The *L* is with you while you
15: 4 trouble they turned to the *L*
15: 8 he restored the altar of the *L*
15: 8 before the vestibule of the *L*.
15: 9 when they saw that the *L* his
15:11 And they offered to the *L* at
15:12 into a covenant to seek the *L*
15:13 whoever would not seek the *L*
15:14 they took an oath before the *L*
15:15 and the *L* gave them rest all
16: 2 of the house of the *L* and of
16: 7 and have not relied on the *L*
16: 8 because you relied on the *L*,
16: 9 For the eyes of the *L* run to
16:12 disease he did not seek the *L*,
17: 3 Now the *L* was with Jehoshaphat,
17: 5 Therefore the *L* established the
17: 6 delight in the ways of the *L*;
17: 9 the Book of the Law of the *L*
17:10 And the fear of the *L* fell on
17:16 offered himself to the *L*,
18: 4 inquire for the word of the *L*
18: 6 not still a prophet of the *L*
18: 7 whom we may inquire of the *L*;
18:10 and he said, "Thus says the *L*:
18:11 for the *L* will deliver it
18:13 As the *L* lives, whatever my
18:15 the truth in the name of the *L*?
18:16 And the *L* said, 'These have no
18:18 hear the word of the *L*:
18:18 I saw the *L* sitting on His
18:19 And the *L* said, 'Who will
18:20 forward and stood before the *L*,
18:20 The *L* said to him, 'In what
18:21 And the *L* said, 'You shall
18:22 Therefore look! The *L* has put a
18:22 and the *L* has declared
18:23 way did the spirit from the *L*
18:27 the *L* has not spoken by me."
18:31 and the *L* helped him, and God
19: 2 and love those who hate the *L*?
19: 2 Therefore the wrath of the *L*
19: 4 and brought them back to the *L*
19: 6 judge for man but for the *L*,
19: 7 let the fear of the *L* be upon
19: 7 is no iniquity with the *L*
19: 8 for the judgment of the *L* and
19: 9 shall act in the fear of the *L*,
19:10 they trespass against the *L*
19:11 you in all matters of the *L*;
19:11 and the *L* will be with the
20: 3 and set himself to seek the *L*,
20: 4 to ask help from the *L*;
20: 4 Judah they came to seek the *L*.
20: 5 in the house of the *L*,
20: 6 O *L* God of our fathers, are
20:13 children, stood before the *L*.
20:14 Then the Spirit of the *L* came
20:15 Jehoshaphat! Thus says the *L*
20:17 and see the salvation of the *L*,
20:17 for the *L* is with you."
20:18 Jerusalem bowed before the *L*,
20:18 the LORD, worshiping the *L*.
20:19 stood up to praise the *L* God
20:20 Believe in the *L* your God, and
20:21 those who should sing to the *L*,
20:21 were saying: "Praise the *L*,
20:22 the *L* set ambushes against the
20:26 for there they blessed the *L*;
20:27 for the *L* had made them
20:28 to the house of the *L*.
20:29 when they heard that the *L*
20:32 right in the sight of the *L*.
20:37 the *L* has destroyed your
21: 6 did evil in the sight of the *L*.
21: 7 Yet the *L* would not destroy the
21:10 because he had forsaken the *L*
21:12 Thus says the *L* God of your
21:14 the *L* will strike your people
21:16 Moreover the *L* stirred up
21:18 After all this the *L* struck
22: 4 did evil in the sight of the *L*,
22: 7 whom the *L* had anointed to cut
22: 9 who sought the *L* with all his
23: 3 as the *L* has said of the sons
23: 5 courts of the house of the *L*.
23: 6 come into the house of the *L*
23: 6 shall keep the watch of the *L*.
23:12 people in the temple of the *L*.
23:14 kill her in the house of the *L*.
23:18 of the house of the *L* to the
23:18 assigned in the house of the *L*,
23:18 the burnt offerings of the *L*,
23:19 gates of the house of the *L*,
23:20 down from the house of the *L*;
24: 2 right in the sight of the *L*
24: 4 repairing the house of the *L*.
24: 6 of Moses the servant of the *L*
24: 7 things of the house of the *L*
24: 8 the gate of the house of the *L*.
24: 9 Jerusalem to bring to the *L*
24:12 service of the house of the *L*;
24:12 to repair the house of the *L*,
24:12 to restore the house of the *L*.
24:14 for the house of the *L*,
24:14 in the house of the *L*
24:18 they left the house of the *L*
24:19 to bring them back to the *L*;
24:20 the commandments of the *L*,
24:20 you have forsaken the *L*,
24:21 court of the house of the *L*.
24:22 The *L* look on it, and repay!"
24:24 but the *L* delivered a very
24:24 they had forsaken the *L* God
25: 2 right in the sight of the *L*,
25: 4 where the *L* commanded, saying,
25: 7 for the *L* is not with
25: 9 The *L* is able to give you much
25:15 Therefore the anger of the *L*
25:27 away from following the *L*,
26: 4 right in the sight of the *L*,
26: 5 and as long as he sought the *L*,
26:16 he transgressed against the *L*
26:16 entering the temple of the *L*
26:17 were eighty priests of the *L*—
26:18 to burn incense to the *L*,
26:18 have no honor from the *L* God.
26:19 priests in the house of the *L*,
26:20 because the *L* had struck him.
26:21 off from the house of the *L*.
27: 2 right in the sight of the *L*,
27: 2 not enter the temple of the *L*)
27: 3 Gate of the house of the *L*,
27: 6 his ways before the *L* his God.
28: 1 right in the sight of the *L*,
28: 3 of the nations whom the *L* had
28: 5 Therefore the *L* his God
28: 6 they had forsaken the *L* God
28: 9 But a prophet of the *L* was
28: 9 because the *L* God of your
28:10 not also guilty before the *L*
28:11 for the fierce wrath of the *L*
28:13 already have offended the *L*.
28:19 For the *L* brought Judah low
28:19 unfaithful to the *L*.
28:21 from the house of the *L*,
28:22 unfaithful to the *L*.
28:24 doors of the house of the *L*,
28:25 and provoked to anger the *L*
29: 2 right in the sight of the *L*,
29: 3 doors of the house of the *L*
29: 5 sanctify the house of the *L*
29: 6 evil in the eyes of the *L* our
29: 6 the dwelling place of the *L*,
29: 8 Therefore the wrath of the *L*
29:10 to make a covenant with the *L*
29:11 for the *L* has chosen you to
29:15 king, at the words of the *L*,
29:15 to cleanse the house of the *L*.
29:16 part of the house of the *L* to
29:16 found in the temple of the *L*
29:16 court of the house of the *L*.
29:17 came to the vestibule of the *L*.
29:17 sanctified the house of the *L*
29:18 all the house of the *L*,
29:19 before the altar of the *L*.
29:20 went up to the house of the *L*.
29:21 them on the altar of the *L*.
29:25 Levites in the house of the *L*
29:25 was the commandment of the *L*
29:27 the song of the *L* also began,
29:30 to sing praise to the *L* with
29:31 yourselves to the *L*,
29:31 into the house of the *L*.
29:32 for a burnt offering to the *L*.
29:35 service of the house of the *L*
30: 1 come to the house of the *L* at
30: 1 to keep the Passover to the *L*
30: 5 to keep the Passover to the *L*
30: 6 return to the *L* God of
30: 7 who trespassed against the *L*
30: 8 but yield yourselves to the *L*;
30: 8 and serve the *L* your God, that
30: 9 "For if you return to the *L*,
30: 9 for the *L* your God is
30:12 leaders, at the word of the *L*.
30:15 to the house of the *L*.
30:17 to sanctify them to the *L*.
30:18 May the good *L* provide
30:19 the *L* God of his fathers,
30:20 And the *L* listened to Hezekiah
30:21 and the priests praised the *L*
30:21 day by day, singing to the *L*,
30:22 the good knowledge of the *L*;
30:22 and making confession to the *L*
31: 2 the gates of the camp of the *L*.
31: 3 written in the Law of the *L*.
31: 4 themselves to the Law of the *L*.
31: 6 were consecrated to the *L*
31: 8 they blessed the *L* and His
31:10 into the house of the *L*,
31:10 for the *L* has blessed His
31:11 rooms in the house of the *L*,
31:14 the offerings of the *L* and
31:16 who entered the house of the *L*
31:20 right and true before the *L*
32: 8 but with us is the *L* our God,
32:11 The *L* our God will deliver us
32:16 servants spoke against the *L*
32:17 wrote letters to revile the *L*
32:21 Then the *L* sent an angel who
32:22 Thus the *L* saved Hezekiah and
32:23 many brought gifts to the *L*
32:24 death, and he prayed to the *L*;
32:26 so that the wrath of the *L* did
33: 2 did evil in the sight of the *L*,
33: 2 of the nations whom the *L* had
33: 4 altars in the house of the *L*,
33: 4 of which the *L* had said, "In
33: 5 courts of the house of the *L*.
33: 6 evil in the sight of the *L*,
33: 9 than the nations whom the *L*
33:10 And the *L* spoke to Manasseh
33:11 Therefore the *L* brought upon
33:12 he implored the *L* his God, and
33:13 Then Manasseh knew that the *L*
33:15 idol from the house of the *L*,
33:15 mount of the house of the *L*
33:16 repaired the altar of the *L*,
33:16 Judah to serve the *L* God of
33:17 but only to the *L* their God.
33:18 to him in the name of the *L*
33:22 did evil in the sight of the *L*,
33:23 humble himself before the *L*,
34: 2 right in the sight of the *L*,
34: 8 to repair the house of the *L*
34:10 of the house of the *L*;
34:10 worked in the house of the *L*,
34:14 into the house of the *L*,
34:14 the Book of the Law of the *L*
34:15 the Law in the house of the *L*.
34:17 found in the house of the *L*,
34:21 inquire of the *L* for me, and
34:21 great is the wrath of the *L*
34:21 not kept the word of the *L*,
34:23 Thus says the *L* God of Israel,
34:24 'Thus says the *L*: 'Behold, I
34:26 sent you to inquire of the *L*,
34:26 Thus says the *L* God of Israel:
34:27 have heard you," says the *L*.
34:30 went up to the house of the *L*,

34:30 found in the house of the *L*.
34:31 made a covenant before the *L*,
34:31 the LORD, to follow the *L*,
34:33 Israel diligently serve the *L*
34:33 depart from following the *L*
35: 1 kept a Passover to the *L* in
35: 2 service of the house of the *L*.
35: 3 Israel, who were holy to the *L*:
35: 3 Now serve the *L* your God and
35: 6 to the word of the *L* by the
35:12 lay people, to offer to the *L*,
35:16 So all the service of the *L* was
35:16 on the altar of the *L*,
35:26 written in the Law of the *L*,
36: 5 did evil in the sight of the *L*
36: 7 from the house of the *L* to
36: 9 did evil in the sight of the *L*.
36:10 from the house of the *L*,
36:12 did evil in the sight of the *L*
36:12 spoke from the mouth of the *L*.
36:13 against turning to the *L* God
36:14 and defiled the house of the *L*
36:15 And the *L* God of their fathers
36:16 until the wrath of the *L* arose
36:18 of the house of the *L*,
36:21 to fulfill the word of the *L* by
36:22 that the word of the *L* by the
36:22 the *L* stirred up the spirit of
36:23 kingdoms of the earth the *L*
36:23 May the *L* his God be with
Ezra 1: 1 that the word of the *L* by the
1: 1 the *L* stirred up the spirit of
1: 2 kingdoms of the earth the *L*
1: 3 and build the house of the *L*
1: 5 and build the house of the *L*
1: 7 articles of the house of the *L*,
2:68 came to the house of the *L*
3: 3 burnt offerings on it to the *L*,
3: 5 the appointed feasts of the *L*
3: 5 a freewill offering to the *L*.
3: 6 offer burnt offerings to the *L*,
3: 6 of the temple of the *L* had
3: 8 the work of the house of the *L*.
3:10 of the temple of the *L*,
3:10 with cymbals, to praise the *L*,
3:11 and giving thanks to the *L*:
3:11 shout, when they praised the *L*,
3:11 of the house of the *L* was
4: 1 building the temple of the *L*
4: 3 we alone will build to the *L*
6:21 land in order to seek the *L*
6:22 for the *L* made them joyful,
7: 6 which the *L* God of Israel had
7: 6 to the hand of the *L* his God
7:10 heart to seek the Law of the *L*,
7:11 of the commandments of the *L*,
7:27 Blessed be the *L* God of our
7:27 to beautify the house of the *L*
7:28 as the hand of the *L* my God
8:28 them, "You are holy to the *L*;
8:28 a freewill offering to the *L*
8:29 chambers of the house of the *L*.
8:35 was a burnt offering to the *L*.
9: 5 spread out my hands to the *L*
9: 8 has been shown from the *L*
9:15 O *L* God of Israel, You are
10:11 make confession to the *L* God
Neh 1: 5 *L* God of heaven, O great and
1:11 'O *L*, I pray, please let
3: 5 to the work of their *L*.
4:14 afraid of them. Remember the *L*,
5:13 "Amen!" and praised the *L*.
8: 1 which the *L* had commanded
8: 6 And Ezra blessed the *L*,
8: 6 heads and worshiped the *L*
8: 9 This day is holy to the *L* your
8:10 this day is holy to our *L*.
8:10 for the joy of the *L* is your
8:14 which the *L* had commanded by
9: 3 the Book of the Law of the *L*
9: 3 confessed and worshiped the *L*
9: 4 out with a loud voice to the *L*
9: 5 Stand up and bless the *L* your
9: 6 You alone are the *L*;
9: 7 You are the *L* God, Who chose
10:29 all the commandments of the *L*
10:29 commandments of the LORD our *L*,
10:34 to burn on the altar of the *L*
10:35 by year, to the house of the *L*;
Job 1: 6 themselves before the *L*,
1: 7 And the *L* said to Satan, "From
1: 7 So Satan answered the *L* and
1: 8 Then the *L* said to Satan,
1: 9 So Satan answered the *L* and
1:12 And the *L* said to Satan,
1:12 out from the presence of the *L*.
1:21 The *L* gave, and the LORD has
1:21 and the *L* has taken away;
1:21 Blessed be the name of the *L*.
2: 1 themselves before the *L*,
2: 1 present himself before the *L*.
2: 2 And the *L* said to Satan, "From
2: 2 So Satan answered the *L* and
2: 3 Then the *L* said to Satan,
2: 4 So Satan answered the *L* and
2: 6 And the *L* said to Satan,
2: 7 out from the presence of the *L*,
12: 9 That the hand of the *L* has
28:28 'Behold, the fear of the *L*,
38: 1 Then the *L* answered Job out of
40: 1 Moreover the *L* answered Job,
40: 3 Then Job answered the *L* and
40: 6 Then the *L* answered Job out of
42: 1 Then Job answered the *L* and
42: 7 after the *L* had spoken these
42: 7 that the *L* said to Eliphaz the
42: 9 went and did as the *L*
42: 9 for the *L* had accepted Job.
42:10 And the *L* restored Job's losses
42:10 Indeed the *L* gave Job twice as
42:11 all the adversity that the *L*
42:12 Now the *L* blessed the latter
Ps 1: 2 is in the law of the *L*,
1: 6 For the *L* knows the way of the
2: 2 Against the *L* and against His
2: 4 The *L* shall hold them in
2: 7 The *L* has said to Me, 'You
2:11 Serve the *L* with fear,
3: 1 *L*, how they have increased
3: 3 But You, O *L*, are a shield
3: 4 I cried to the *L* with my
3: 5 for the *L* sustained me.
3: 7 Arise, O *L*; Save me, O my
3: 8 Salvation belongs to the *L*.
4: 3 But know that the *L* has set
4: 3 The *L* will hear when I call
4: 5 And put your trust in the *L*.
4: 6 will show us any good?" *L*,
4: 8 and sleep; For You alone, O *L*,
5: 1 Give ear to my words, O *L*,
5: 3 shall hear in the morning, O *L*;
5: 6 The *L* abhors the bloodthirsty
5: 8 Lead me, O *L*, in Your
5:12 For You, O *L*, will bless the
6: 1 O *L*, do not rebuke me in
6: 2 Have mercy on me, O *L*,
6: 2 O LORD, for I am weak; O *L*,
6: 3 troubled; But You, O *L*—
6: 4 Return, O *L*, deliver me!
6: 8 For the *L* has heard the voice
6: 9 The *L* has heard my
6: 9 The *L* will receive my prayer.
7: which he sang to the *L*
7: 1 O *L* my God, in You I put my
7: 3 O *L* my God, if I have done
7: 6 Arise, O *L*, in Your anger;
7: 8 The *L* shall judge the peoples;
7: 8 the peoples; Judge me, O *L*,
7:17 I will praise the *L* according
7:17 praise to the name of the *L*
8: 1 O *L*, our Lord, How excellent
8: 1 O LORD, our *L*, How excellent
8: 9 O *L*, our Lord, How excellent
8: 9 O LORD, our *L*, How excellent
9: 1 I will praise You, O *L*,
9: 7 But the *L* shall endure
9: 9 The *L* also will be a refuge
9:10 trust in You; For You, *L*,
9:11 Sing praises to the *L*,
9:13 O *L*! Consider my trouble from
9:16 The *L* is known by the
9:19 Arise, O *L*, Do not let man
9:20 Put them in fear, O *L*,
10: 1 do You stand afar off, O *L*?
10: 3 greedy and renounces the *L*.
10:12 O *L*! O God, lift up Your
10:16 The *L* is King forever and
10:17 *L*, You have heard the
11: 1 In the *L* I put my trust;
11: 4 The *L* is in His holy temple,
11: 5 The *L* tests the righteous,
11: 7 For the *L* is righteous,
12: 1 Help, *L*, for the godly
12: 3 May the *L* cut off all
12: 4 Who is *l* over us?"
12: 5 I will arise," says the *L*;
12: 6 The words of the *L* are pure
12: 7 You shall keep them, O *L*,
13: 1 How long, O *L*? Will You
13: 3 O *L* my God; Enlighten my
13: 6 I will sing to the *L*,
14: 2 The *L* looks down from heaven
14: 4 And do not call on the *L*?
14: 6 But the *L* is his refuge.
14: 7 come out of Zion! When the *L*
15: 1 *L*, who may abide in Your
15: 4 he honors those who fear the *L*;
16: 2 soul, you have said to the *L*,
16: 2 to the LORD, "You are my *L*,
16: 5 O *L*,YOU are the portion
16: 7 I will bless the *L* who has
16: 8 I have set the *L* always before
17: 1 Hear a just cause, O *L*,
17:13 Arise, O *L*, Confront him,
17:14 With Your hand from men, O *L*,
18: of David the servant of the *L*,
18: who spoke to the *L* the words
18: song on the day that the *L*
18: 1 I will love You, O *L*,
18: 2 The *L* is my rock and my
18: 3 I will call upon the *L*,
18: 6 distress I called upon the *L*,
18:13 The *L* thundered from heaven,
18:15 At Your rebuke, O *L*,
18:18 But the *L* was my support.
18:20 The *L* rewarded me according to
18:21 I have kept the ways of the *L*,
18:24 Therefore the *L* has
18:28 The *L* my God will enlighten
18:30 The word of the *L* is proven;
18:31 For who is God, except the *L*?
18:41 none to save; Even to the *L*,
18:46 The *L* lives! Blessed be my
18:49 I will give thanks to You, O *L*,
19: 7 The law of the *L* is perfect,
19: 7 The testimony of the *L* is
19: 8 The statutes of the *L* are
19: 8 The commandment of the *L* is
19: 9 The fear of the *L* is clean,
19: 9 The judgments of the *L* are
19:14 acceptable in Your sight, O *L*,
20: 1 May the *L* answer you in the
20: 5 up our banners! May the *L*
20: 6 Now I know that the *L* saves
20: 7 remember the name of the *L*
20: 9 *L*! May the King answer us
21: 1 have joy in Your strength, O *L*;
21: 7 For the king trusts in the *L*,
21: 9 The *L* shall swallow them up
21:13 Be exalted, O *L*, in Your own
22: 8 "He trusted in the *L*,
22:19 But You, O *L*, do not be far
22:23 You who fear the *L*,
22:26 who seek Him will praise the *L*.
22:27 remember and turn to the *L*,
22:30 It will be recounted of the *L*
23: 1 The *L* is my shepherd;
23: 6 dwell in the house of the *L*
24: 3 ascend into the hill of the *L*?
24: 5 receive blessing from the *L*,
24: 8 The *L* strong and mighty,
24: 8 The *L* mighty in battle.
24:10 The *L* of hosts, He is the
25: 1 To You, O *L*, I lift up my
25: 4 Show me Your ways, O *L*;
25: 6 Remember, O *L*, Your tender
25: 7 For Your goodness' sake, O *L*.
25: 8 Good and upright is the *L*;
25:10 All the paths of the *L* are
25:11 For Your name's sake, O *L*,
25:12 is the man that fears the *L*?
25:14 The secret of the *L* is with
25:15 eyes are ever toward the *L*,
26: 1 Vindicate me, O *L*, For I
26: 1 I have also trusted in the *L*;
26: 2 Examine me, O *L*, and prove me;
26: 6 will go about Your altar, O *L*,
26: 8 *L*, I have loved the
26:12 I will bless the *L*.
27: 1 The *L* is my light and my
27: 1 The *L* is the strength of my
27: 4 thing I have desired of the *L*,
27: 4 dwell in the house of the *L*
27: 4 To behold the beauty of the *L*,
27: 6 I will sing praises to the *L*.
27: 7 Hear, O *L*, when I cry with
27: 8 said to You, "Your face, *L*,
27:10 Then the *L* will take care of
27:11 Teach me Your way, O *L*,
27:13 see the goodness of the *L* In
27:14 Wait on the *L*; Be of good
27:14 Wait, I say, on the *L*!
28: 1 O *L* my Rock: Do not be silent
28: 5 not regard the works of the *L*,
28: 6 Blessed be the *L*, Because He
28: 7 The *L* is my strength and my
28: 8 The *L* is their strength,
29: 1 Give unto the *L*, O you
29: 1 Give unto the *L* glory and
29: 2 Give unto the *L* the glory due
29: 2 Worship the *L* in the beauty
29: 3 The voice of the *L* is over
29: 3 The *L* is over many waters.
29: 4 The voice of the *L* is
29: 4 The voice of the *L* is full
29: 5 The voice of the *L* breaks the
29: 5 the *L* splinters the cedars of
29: 7 The voice of the *L* divides the
29: 8 The voice of the *L* shakes the
29: 8 The *L* shakes the Wilderness
29: 9 The voice of the *L* makes the
29:10 The *L* sat enthroned at the
29:10 And the *L* sits as King
29:11 The *L* will give strength to
29:11 The *L* will bless His people
30: 1 I will extol You, O *L*,
30: 2 O *L* my God, I cried out to
30: 3 O *L*, You brought my soul
30: 4 Sing praise to the *L*,
30: 7 *L*, by Your favor You have
30: 8 I cried out to You, O *L*;
30: 8 And to the *L* I made
30:10 Hear, O *L*, and have mercy
30:10 and have mercy on me; *L*,
30:12 O *L* my God, I will give
31: 1 In You, O *L*, I put my trust;
31: 5 O *L* God of truth.
31: 6 But I trust in the *L*.
31: 9 Have mercy on me, O *L*,
31:14 as for me, I trust in You, O *L*;
31:17 Do not let me be ashamed, O *L*,
31:21 Blessed be the *L*, For He has
31:23 Oh, love the *L*, all you His
31:23 you His saints! For the *L*
31:24 All you who hope in the *L*.
32: 2 is the man to whom the *L*
32: 5 my transgressions to the *L*,
32:10 But he who trusts in the *L*,
32:11 Be glad in the *L* and rejoice,
33: 1 Rejoice in the *L*, O you
33: 2 Praise the *L* with the harp;
33: 4 For the word of the *L* is
33: 5 full of the goodness of the *L*.
33: 6 By the word of the *L* the
33: 8 Let all the earth fear the *L*;
33:10 The *L* brings the counsel of

33:11 The counsel of the *L* stands
33:12 the nation whose God is the *L*,
33:13 The *L* looks from heaven;
33:18 the eye of the *L* is on those
33:20 Our soul waits for the *L*;
33:22 Let Your mercy, O *L*,
34: 1 I will bless the *L* at all
34: 2 shall make its boast in the *L*;
34: 3 magnify the *L* with me, And
34: 4 I sought the *L*, and He heard
34: 6 and the *L* heard him, And
34: 7 The angel of the *L* encamps all
34: 8 taste and see that the *L* is
34: 9 Oh, fear the *L*, you His
34:10 But those who seek the *L*
34:11 teach you the fear of the *L*.
34:15 The eyes of the *L* are on the
34:16 The face of the *L* is against
34:17 and the *L* hears, And delivers
34:18 The *L* is near to those who
34:19 But the *L* delivers him out of
34:22 The *L* redeems the soul of His
35: 1 Plead my cause, O *L*,
35: 5 And let the angel of the *L*
35: 6 And let the angel of the *L*
35: 9 soul shall be joyful in the *L*;
35:10 All my bones shall say, "*L*,
35:17 *L*, how long will You look on?
35:22 This You have seen, O *L*;
35:22 Do not keep silence. O *L*,
35:23 To my cause, my God and my *L*.
35:24 O *L* my God, according to Your
35:27 'Let the *L* be magnified,
36: of David the servant of the *L*.
36: 5 Your mercy, O *L*, is in the
36: 6 are a great deep; O *L*,
37: 3 Trust in the *L*, and do
37: 4 yourself also in the *L*,
37: 5 Commit your way to the *L*,
37: 7 Rest in the *L*, and wait
37: 9 But those who wait on the *L*,
37:13 The *L* laughs at him, For He
37:17 But the *L* upholds the
37:18 The *L* knows the days of the
37:20 And the enemies of the *L*,
37:23 good man are ordered by the *L*,
37:24 For the *L* upholds him with
37:28 For the *L* loves justice,
37:33 The *L* will not leave him in
37:34 Wait on the *L*, And keep His
37:39 the righteous is from the *L*;
37:40 And the *L* shall help them and
38: 1 O *L*, do not rebuke me in
38: 9 *L*, all my desire is before
38:15 For in You, O *L*, I hope;
38:15 You will hear, O *L* my God.
38:21 Do not forsake me, O *L*;
38:22 Make haste to help me, O *L*,
39: 4 *L*, make me to know my
39: 7 'And now, *L*, what do I wait
39:12 "Hear my prayer, O *L*,
40: 1 I waited patiently for the *L*;
40: 3 And will trust in the *L*.
40: 4 is that man who makes the *L*
40: 5 O *L* my God, are Your
40: 9 do not restrain my lips, O *L*,
40:11 tender mercies from me, O *L*;
40:13 Be pleased, O *L*,
40:13 O LORD, to deliver me; O *L*,
40:16 The *L* be magnified!"
40:17 Yet the *L* thinks upon me.
41: 1 The *L* will deliver him in
41: 2 The *L* will preserve him and
41: 3 The *L* will strengthen him on
41: 4 I said, "*L*, be merciful to
41:10 But You, O *L*, be merciful to
41:13 Blessed be the *L* God of
42: 8 The *L* will command His
44:23 Awake! Why do You sleep, O *L*?
45:11 Because He is your *L*,
46: 7 The *L* of hosts is with us;
46: 8 behold the works of the *L*,
46:11 The *L* of hosts is with us;
47: 2 For the *L* Most High is
47: 5 The *L* with the sound of a
48: 1 Great is the *L*,
48: 8 In the city of the *L* of
50: 1 The Mighty One, God the *L*,
51:15 O *L*, open my lips, And my
54: 4 The *L* is with those who
54: 6 I will praise Your name, O *L*,
55: 9 Destroy, O *L*, and divide
55:16 And the *L* shall save me.
55:22 Cast your burden on the *L*,
56:10 In the *L* (I will praise His
57: 9 I will praise You, O *L*,
58: 6 of the young lions, O *L*!
59: 3 nor for my sin, O *L*.
59: 5 O *L* God of hosts, the God of
59: 8 But You, O *L*,
59:11 them down, O *L* our shield.
62:12 Also to You, O *L*, belongs
64:10 shall be glad in the *L*,
66:18 The *L* will not hear.
68:11 The *L* gave the word;
68:16 the *L* will dwell in it
68:17 The *L* is among them as in
68:18 That the *L* God might dwell
68:19 Blessed be the *L*, Who daily
68:20 And to GOD the *L* belong
68:22 The *L* said, "I will bring back
68:26 in the congregations, The *L*,
68:32 Oh, sing praises to the *L*,
69: 6 O *L* GOD of hosts, be ashamed
69:13 me, my prayer is to You, O *L*,
69:16 Hear me, O *L*, for Your
69:31 This also shall please the *L*
69:33 For the *L* hears the poor,
70: 1 Make haste to help me, O *L*!
70: 5 my help and my deliverer; O *L*,
71: 1 In You, O *L*, I put my trust;
71: 5 O *L* GOD; You are my trust
71:16 go in the strength of the *L*
72:18 Blessed be the *L* God, the God
73:20 dream when one awakes, So, *L*,
73:28 I have put my trust in the *L*
74:18 the enemy has reproached, O *L*,
75: 8 For in the hand of the *L*
76:11 Make vows to the *L* your God,
77: 2 of my trouble I sought the *L*;
77: 7 Will the *L* cast off forever?
77:11 remember the works of the *L*;
78: 4 to come the praises of the *L*,
78:21 Therefore the *L* heard this
78:65 Then the *L* awoke as from
79: 5 How long, *L*? Will You be
79:12 they have reproached You, O *L*.
80: 4 O *L* God of hosts, How long
80:19 O *L* God of hosts; Cause Your
81:10 I am the *L* your God,
81:15 The haters of the *L* would
83:16 they may seek Your name, O *L*.
83:18 whose name alone is the *L*,
84: 1 O *L* of hosts!
84: 2 For the courts of the *L*;
84: 3 O *L* of hosts, My King and my
84: 8 O *L* God of hosts, hear my
84:11 For the *L* God is a sun and
84:11 The *L* will give grace and
84:12 O *L* of hosts, Blessed is the
85: 1 *L*, You have been favorable
85: 7 Show us Your mercy, *L*,
85: 8 I will hear what God the *L*
85:12 the *L* will give what is
86: 1 Bow down Your ear, O *L*,
86: 3 Be merciful to me, O *L*,
86: 4 Your servant, For to You, O *L*,
86: 5 For You, *L*, are good,
86: 6 Give ear, O *L*, to my prayer;
86: 8 there is none like You, O *L*;
86: 9 and worship before You, O *L*,
86:11 Teach me Your way, O *L*;
86:12 O *L* my God, with all my heart,
86:15 But You, O *L*, are a God full
86:17 be ashamed, Because You, *L*,
87: 2 The *L* loves the gates of Zion
87: 6 The *L* will record, When He
88: 1 O *L*, God of my salvation,
88: 9 away because of affliction. *L*,
88:13 to You I have cried out, O *L*,
88:14 *L*, why do You cast off my
89: 1 sing of the mercies of the *L*
89: 5 will praise Your wonders, O *L*;
89: 6 can be compared to the *L*?
89: 6 mighty can be likened to the *L*?
89: 8 O *L* God of hosts, Who is
89: 8 Who is mighty like You, O *L*?
89:15 joyful sound! They walk, O *L*,
89:18 our shield belongs to the *L*,
89:46 How long, *L*? Will You hide
89:49 *L*, where are Your former
89:50 Remember, *L*, the reproach
89:51 enemies have reproached, O *L*,
89:52 Blessed be the *L* forevermore!
90: 1 *L*, You have been our
90:13 O *L*! How long? And have
90:17 And let the beauty of the *L*
91: 2 I will say of the *L*,
91: 9 Because you have made the *L*,
92: 1 good to give thanks to the *L*,
92: 4 For You, *L*, have made me
92: 5 O *L*, how great are Your
92: 8 But You, *L*, are on high
92: 9 For behold, Your enemies, O *L*,
92:13 planted in the house of the *L*
92:15 To declare that the *L* is
93: 1 The *L* reigns, He is clothed
93: 1 The *L* is clothed, He has
93: 3 floods have lifted up, O *L*,
93: 4 The *L* on high is mightier
93: 5 adorns Your house, O *L*,
94: 1 O *L* God, to whom vengeance
94: 3 *L*, how long will the wicked,
94: 5 in pieces Your people, O *L*,
94: 7 The *L* does not see, Nor does
94:11 The *L* knows the thoughts of
94:12 the man whom You instruct, O *L*,
94:14 For the *L* will not cast off
94:17 Unless the *L* had been my
94:18 foot slips," Your mercy, O *L*,
94:22 But the *L* has been my defense,
94:23 The *L* our God shall cut them
95: 1 let us sing to the *L*! Let us
95: 3 For the *L* is the great God,
95: 6 Let us kneel before the *L* our
96: 1 sing to the *L* a new song!
96: 1 a new song! Sing to the *L*,
96: 2 Sing to the *L*, bless His
96: 4 For the *L* is great and
96: 5 But the *L* made the heavens.
96: 7 Give to the *L*, O families of
96: 7 Give to the *L* glory and
96: 8 Give to the *L* the glory due
96: 9 worship the *L* in the beauty of
96:10 The *L* reigns; The world also
96:12 will rejoice before the *L*.
97: 1 The *L* reigns; Let the earth
97: 5 wax at the presence of the *L*,
97: 5 At the presence of the *L* of
97: 8 of Your judgments, O *L*.
97: 9 For You, *L*, are most high
97:10 You who love the *L*,
97:12 Rejoice in the *L*,
98: 1 sing to the *L* a new song!
98: 2 The *L* has made known His
98: 4 Shout joyfully to the *L*,
98: 5 Sing to the *L* with the harp,
98: 6 Shout joyfully before the *L*,
98: 8 joyful together before the *L*,
99: 1 The *L* reigns; Let the peoples
99: 2 The *L* is great in Zion,
99: 5 Exalt the *L* our God,
99: 6 They called upon the *L*,
99: 8 O *L* our God; You were to them
99: 9 Exalt the *L* our God,
99: 9 For the *L* our God is holy.
100: 1 Make a joyful shout to the *L*,
100: 2 Serve the *L* with gladness;
100: 3 Know that the *L*,
100: 5 For the *L* is good; His mercy
101: 1 and justice; To You, O *L*,
101: 8 from the city of the *L*.
102: out his complaint before the *L*.
102: 1 Hear my prayer, O *L*,
102:12 But You, O *L*, shall endure
102:15 shall fear the name of the *L*,
102:16 For the *L* shall build up Zion;
102:18 to be created may praise the *L*.
102:19 From heaven the *L* viewed the
102:21 To declare the name of the *L*
102:22 the kingdoms, to serve the *L*.
103: 1 Bless the *L*, O my soul;
103: 2 Bless the *L*, O my soul,
103: 6 The *L* executes righteousness
103: 8 The *L* is merciful and
103:13 So the *L* pities those who
103:17 But the mercy of the *L* is
103:19 The *L* has established His
103:20 Bless the *L*, you His angels,
103:21 Bless the *L*, all you His
103:22 Bless the *L*, all His works,
103:22 of His dominion. Bless the *L*,
104: 1 Bless the *L*, O my soul!
104: 1 O my soul! O *L* my God, You
104:16 The trees of the *L* are full
104:24 O *L*, how manifold are Your
104:31 May the glory of the *L* endure
104:31 May the *L* rejoice in His
104:33 I will sing to the *L* as long
104:34 I will be glad in the *L*.
104:35 be no more. Bless the *L*,
104:35 O my soul! Praise the *L*!
105: 1 give thanks to the *L*!
105: 3 those rejoice who seek the *L*!
105: 4 Seek the *L* and His strength;
105: 7 He is the *L* our God;
105:19 The word of the *L* tested him.
105:21 He made him *l* of his house,
105:45 Praise the *L*!
106: 1 Praise the *L*! Oh, give thanks
106: 1 Oh, give thanks to the *L*,
106: 2 utter the mighty acts of the *L*?
106: 4 Remember me, O *L*,
106:16 And Aaron the saint of the *L*,
106:25 not heed the voice of the *L*.
106:34 Concerning whom the *L* had
106:40 Therefore the wrath of the *L*
106:47 O *L* our God, And gather us
106:48 Blessed be the *L* God of
106:48 Amen!" Praise the *L*!
107: 1 Oh, give thanks to the *L*,
107: 2 Let the redeemed of the *L* say
107: 6 Then they cried out to the *L*
107: 8 would give thanks to the *L*
107:13 Then they cried out to the *L*
107:15 would give thanks to the *L*
107:19 Then they cried out to the *L*
107:21 would give thanks to the *L*
107:24 They see the works of the *L*,
107:28 Then they cry out to the *L* in
107:31 would give thanks to the *L*
107:43 the lovingkindness of the *L*.
108: 3 I will praise You, O *L*,
109:14 be remembered before the *L*,
109:15 be continually before the *L*,
109:21 But You, O GOD the *L*,
109:26 O *L* my God! Oh, save me
109:27 is Your hand—That You, *L*,
109:30 I will greatly praise the *L*
110: 1 The *L* said to my Lord, "Sit
110: 1 The LORD said to my *L*,
110: 2 The *L* shall send the rod of
110: 4 The *L* has sworn And will not
110: 5 The *L* is at Your right hand;
111: 1 Praise the *L*! I will praise
111: 1 I will praise the *L* with
111: 2 The works of the *L* are great,
111: 4 The *L* is gracious and full
111:10 The fear of the *L* is the
112: 1 Praise the *L*! Blessed is the
112: 1 is the man who fears the *L*,
112: 7 steadfast, trusting in the *L*.
113: 1 Praise the *L*! Praise,
113: 1 Praise, O servants of the *L*,
113: 1 Praise the name of the *L*!
113: 2 Blessed be the name of the *L*

113: 4 The *L* is high above all
113: 5 Who is like the *L* our God,
113: 9 Praise the *L*!
114: 7 earth, at the presence of the *L*,
115: 1 Not unto us, O *L*,
115: 9 O Israel, trust in the *L*;
115:10 house of Aaron, trust in the *L*;
115:11 You who fear the *L*,
115:11 fear the LORD, trust in the *L*;
115:12 The *L* has been mindful of us;
115:13 bless those who fear the *L*,
115:14 May the *L* give you increase
115:15 May you be blessed by the *L*,
115:17 The dead do not praise the *L*,
115:18 But we will bless the *L* From
115:18 Praise the *L*!
116: 1 I love the *L*, because He
116: 4 called upon the name of the *L*:
116: 4 the name of the LORD: "O *L*,
116: 5 Gracious is the *L*,
116: 6 The *L* preserves the simple;
116: 7 For the *L* has dealt
116: 9 I will walk before the *L* In
116:12 What shall I render to the *L*
116:13 call upon the name of the *L*.
116:14 I will pay my vows to the *L*
116:15 in the sight of the *L* Is
116:16 O *L*, truly I am Your
116:17 call upon the name of the *L*.
116:18 I will pay my vows to the *L*
116:19 Praise the *L*!
117: 1 Praise the *L*, all you
117: 2 And the truth of the *L*
117: 2 Praise the *L*!
118: 1 Oh, give thanks to the *L*,
118: 4 Let those who fear the *L* now
118: 5 I called on the *L* in distress;
118: 5 The *L* answered me and set
118: 6 The *L* is on my side; I will
118: 7 The *L* is for me among those
118: 8 is better to trust in the *L*
118: 9 is better to trust in the *L*
118:10 But in the name of the *L* I
118:11 But in the name of the *L* I
118:12 For in the name of the *L* I
118:13 But the *L* helped me.
118:14 The *L* is my strength and
118:15 The right hand of the *L* does
118:16 The right hand of the *L* is
118:16 The right hand of the *L* does
118:17 declare the works of the *L*.
118:18 The *L* has chastened me
118:19 And I will praise the *L*.
118:20 This is the gate of the *L*,
118:24 This is the day the *L* has
118:25 Save now, I pray, O *L*;
118:25 now, I pray, O LORD; O *L*,
118:26 comes in the name of the *L*!
118:26 you from the house of the *L*.
118:27 God is the *L*, And He has
118:29 Oh, give thanks to the *L*,
119: 1 Who walk in the law of the *L*!
119:12 O *L*! Teach me Your statutes!
119:31 to Your testimonies; O *L*,
119:33 Teach me, O *L*, the way of
119:41 mercies come also to me, O *L*—
119:52 Your judgments of old, O *L*,
119:55 Your name in the night, O *L*,
119:57 You are my portion, O *L*;
119:64 The earth, O *L*, is full of
119:65 well with Your servant, O *L*,
119:75 I know, O *L*, that Your
119:89 Forever, O *L*, Your word
119:107 very much; Revive me, O *L*,
119:108 offerings of my mouth, O *L*,
119:126 is time for You to act, O *L*,
119:137 Righteous are You, O *L*,
119:145 O *L*! I will keep Your
119:149 to Your lovingkindness; O *L*,
119:151 You are near, O *L*,
119:156 are Your tender mercies, O *L*;
119:159 Your precepts; Revive me, O *L*,
119:166 *L*, I hope for Your
119:169 my cry come before You, O *L*;
119:174 long for Your salvation, O *L*,
120: 1 my distress I cried to the *L*,
120: 2 Deliver my soul, O *L*,
121: 2 My help comes from the *L*,
121: 5 The *L* is your keeper;
121: 5 The *L* is your shade at your
121: 7 The *L* shall preserve you from
121: 8 The *L* shall preserve your
122: 1 us go into the house of the *L*.
122: 4 go up, The tribes of the *L*,
122: 4 thanks to the name of the *L*.
122: 9 of the house of the *L* our God
123: 2 So our eyes look to the *L*
123: 3 Have mercy on us, O *L*,
124: 1 If it had not been the *L* who
124: 2 If it had not been the *L* who
124: 6 Blessed be the *L*,
124: 8 help is in the name of the *L*,
125: 1 Those who trust in the *L* Are
125: 2 So the *L* surrounds His people
125: 4 Do good, O *L*, to those who
125: 5 The *L* shall lead them away
126: 1 When the *L* brought back the
126: 2 The *L* has done great things for
126: 3 The *L* has done great things
126: 4 Bring back our captivity, O *L*,
127: 1 Unless the *L* builds the house,
127: 1 Unless the *L* guards the city,
127: 3 are a heritage from the *L*,
128: 1 is every one who fears the *L*,
128: 4 be blessed Who fears the *L*.
128: 5 The *L* bless you out of Zion,
129: 4 The *L* is righteous; He has
129: 8 The blessing of the *L* be upon
129: 8 you in the name of the *L*!"
130: 1 I have cried to You, O *L*;
130: 2 *L*, hear my voice!
130: 3 If You, *L*, should mark
130: 3 should mark iniquities, O *L*,
130: 5 I wait for the *L*,
130: 6 My soul waits for the *L* More
130: 7 O Israel, hope in the *L*;
130: 7 For with the *L* there is
131: 1 *L*, my heart is not haughty,
131: 3 hope in the *L* From this time
132: 1 *L*, remember David And all
132: 2 How he swore to the *L*,
132: 5 I find a place for the *L*,
132: 8 Arise, O *L*, to Your resting
132:11 The *L* has sworn in truth to
132:13 For the *L* has chosen Zion;
133: 3 For there the *L* commanded the
134: 1 Behold, bless the *L*,
134: 1 All you servants of the *L*,
134: 1 stand in the house of the *L*!
134: 2 sanctuary, And bless the *L*.
134: 3 The *L* who made heaven and
135: 1 Praise the *L*! Praise the name
135: 1 Praise the name of the *L*;
135: 1 O you servants of the *L*!
135: 2 stand in the house of the *L*,
135: 3 Praise the *L*,
135: 3 for the *L* is good;
135: 4 For the *L* has chosen Jacob for
135: 5 For I know that the *L* is
135: 5 And our *L* is above all gods.
135: 6 Whatever the *L* pleases He
135:13 Your name, O *L*, endures
135:13 forever, Your fame, O *L*,
135:14 For the *L* will judge His
135:19 Bless the *L*, O house of
135:19 house of Israel! Bless the *L*,
135:20 Bless the *L*, O house of
135:20 of Levi! You who fear the *L*,
135:20 fear the LORD, bless the *L*!
135:21 Blessed be the *L* out of Zion,
135:21 in Jerusalem! Praise the *L*!
136: 1 Oh, give thanks to the *L*,
136: 3 give thanks to the *L* of lords!
137: 7 Remember, O *L*, against
138: 4 earth shall praise You, O *L*,
138: 5 sing of the ways of the *L*,
138: 5 great is the glory of the *L*.
138: 6 Though the *L* is on high,
138: 8 The *L* will perfect that
138: 8 concerns me; Your mercy, O *L*,
139: 1 O *L*, You have searched me
139: 4 my tongue, But behold, O *L*,
139:21 Do I not hate them, O *L*,
140: 1 Deliver me, O *L*, from evil
140: 4 Keep me, O *L*, from the
140: 6 I said to the *L*: "You are my
140: 6 voice of my supplications, O *L*.
140: 7 O GOD the *L*, the strength
140: 8 Do not grant, O *L*,
140:12 I know that the *L* will
141: 1 *L*, I cry out to You;
141: 3 Set a guard, O *L*,
141: 8 are upon You, O GOD the *L*;
142: 1 I cry out to the *L* with my
142: 1 With my voice to the *L* I make
142: 5 I cried out to You, O *L*:
143: 1 Hear my prayer, O *L*,
143: 7 Answer me speedily, O *L*;
143: 9 Deliver me, O *L*, from my
143:11 Revive me, O *L*, for Your
144: 1 Blessed be the *L* my Rock,
144: 3 *L*, what is man, that You take
144: 5 Bow down Your heavens, O *L*,
144:15 people whose God is the *L*!
145: 3 Great is the *L*,
145: 8 The *L* is gracious and full of
145: 9 The *L* is good to all, And
145:10 works shall praise You, O *L*,
145:14 The *L* upholds all who fall,
145:17 The *L* is righteous in all His
145:18 The *L* is near to all who call
145:20 The *L* preserves all who love
145:21 speak the praise of the *L*,
146: 1 Praise the *L*! Praise the
146: 1 the LORD! Praise the *L*,
146: 2 I live I will praise the *L*;
146: 5 Whose hope is in the *L* his
146: 7 The *L* gives freedom to the
146: 8 The *L* opens the eyes of the
146: 8 The *L* raises those who are
146: 8 The *L* loves the righteous.
146: 9 The *L* watches over the
146:10 The *L* shall reign
146:10 Praise the *L*!
147: 1 Praise the *L*! For it is
147: 2 The *L* builds up Jerusalem;
147: 5 Great is our *L*, and mighty
147: 6 The *L* lifts up the humble; He
147: 7 Sing to the *L* with
147:11 The *L* takes pleasure in those
147:12 Praise the *L*, O Jerusalem!
147:20 Praise the *L*!
148: 1 Praise the *L*! Praise the
148: 1 the LORD! Praise the *L* from
148: 5 them praise the name of the *L*,
148: 7 Praise the *L* from the earth,
148:13 them praise the name of the *L*,
148:14 Praise the *L*!
149: 1 Praise the *L*! Sing to the
149: 1 the LORD! Sing to the *L* a
149: 4 For the *L* takes pleasure in
149: 9 Praise the *L*!
150: 1 Praise the *L*! Praise God in
150: 6 that has breath praise the *L*.
150: 6 Praise the *L*!
Prov 1: 7 The fear of the *L* is the
1:29 not choose the fear of the *L*,
2: 5 understand the fear of the *L*,
2: 6 For the *L* gives wisdom;
3: 5 Trust in the *L* with all your
3: 7 Fear the *L* and depart from
3: 9 Honor the *L* with your
3:11 the chastening of the *L*,
3:12 For whom the *L* loves He
3:19 The *L* by wisdom founded the
3:26 For the *L* will be your
3:32 is an abomination to the *L*,
3:33 The curse of the *L* is on the
5:21 are before the eyes of the *L*,
6:16 These six things the *L*
8:13 The fear of the *L* is to hate
8:22 The *L* possessed me at the
8:35 And obtains favor from the *L*;
9:10 The fear of the *L* is the
10: 3 The *L* will not allow the
10:22 The blessing of the *L* makes
10:27 The fear of the *L* prolongs
10:29 The way of the *L* is strength
11: 1 are an abomination to the *L*,
11:20 are an abomination to the *L*,
12: 2 man obtains favor from the *L*,
12:22 are an abomination to the *L*,
14: 2 in his uprightness fears the *L*,
14:26 In the fear of the *L* there
14:27 The fear of the *L* is a
15: 3 The eyes of the *L* are in
15: 8 is an abomination to the *L*,
15: 9 is an abomination to the *L*,
15:11 Destruction are before the *L*;
15:16 little with the fear of the *L*,
15:25 The *L* will destroy the house
15:26 are an abomination to the *L*,
15:29 The *L* is far from the wicked,
15:33 The fear of the *L* is the
16: 1 of the tongue is from the *L*.
16: 2 But the *L* weighs the spirits.
16: 3 Commit your works to the *L*,
16: 4 The *L* has made all for
16: 5 is an abomination to the *L*;
16: 6 And by the fear of the *L* one
16: 7 a man's ways please the *L*,
16: 9 But the *L* directs his steps.
16:20 And whoever trusts in the *L*,
16:33 every decision is from the *L*.
17: 3 But the *L* tests the hearts.
17:15 are an abomination to the *L*.
18:10 The name of the *L* is a strong
18:22 And obtains favor from the *L*.
19: 3 his heart frets against the *L*.
19:14 a prudent wife is from the *L*.
19:17 on the poor lends to the *L*,
19:23 The fear of the *L* leads to
20:10 alike, an abomination to the *L*.
20:12 The *L* has made them both.
20:22 Wait for the *L*,
20:23 are an abomination to the *L*,
20:24 A man's steps are of the *L*;
20:27 of a man is the lamp of the *L*,
21: 1 heart is in the hand of the *L*,
21: 2 But the *L* weighs the hearts.
21: 3 Is more acceptable to the *L*
21:30 Or counsel against the *L*.
21:31 But deliverance is of the *L*.
22: 2 The *L* is the maker of them
22: 4 and the fear of the *L* Are
22:12 The eyes of the *L* preserve
22:14 He who is abhorred by the *L*
22:19 your trust may be in the *L*;
22:23 For the *L* will plead their
23:17 for the fear of the *L* all the
24:18 Lest the *L* see it, and it
24:21 fear the *L* and the king;
25:22 And the *L* will reward you.
28: 5 But those who seek the *L*
28:25 But he who trusts in the *L*
29:13 The *L* gives light to the eyes
29:25 But whoever trusts in the *L*
29:26 for man comes from the *L*.
30: 9 And say, "Who is the *L*?
31:30 But a woman who fears the *L*,
Isa 1: 2 O earth! For the *L* has
1: 4 They have forsaken the *L*,
1: 9 Unless the *L* of hosts Had
1:10 Hear the word of the *L*,
1:11 to Me?" Says the *L*.
1:18 reason together," Says the *L*,
1:20 For the mouth of the *L* has
1:24 Therefore the *L* says,
1:24 The *L* of hosts, the Mighty
1:28 And those who forsake the *L*
2: 3 go up to the mountain of the *L*,
2: 3 And the word of the *L* from
2: 5 us walk In the light of the *L*.
2:10 From the terror of the *L* And
2:11 And the *L* alone shall be
2:12 For the day of the *L* of hosts

2:17 The *L* alone will be exalted
2:19 From the terror of the *L* And
2:21 From the terror of the *L* And
3: 1 For behold, the *L*,
3: 1 the *L* of hosts, Takes away
3: 8 doings Are against the *L*,
3:13 The *L* stands up to plead,
3:14 The *L* will enter into judgment
3:15 Says the *L* GOD of hosts.
3:16 Moreover the *L* says:
3:17 Therefore the *L* will strike
3:17 And the *L* will uncover their
3:18 In that day the *L* will take
4: 2 that day the Branch of the *L*
4: 4 When the *L* has washed away the
4: 5 then the *L* will create above
5: 7 For the vineyard of the *L* of
5: 9 In my hearing the *L* of hosts
5:12 not regard the work of the *L*,
5:16 But the *L* of hosts shall be
5:24 rejected the law of the *L* of
5:25 Therefore the anger of the *L*
6: 1 I saw the *L* sitting on a
6: 3 holy is the *L* of hosts;
6: 5 The *L* of hosts."
6: 8 I heard the voice of the *L*,
6:11 Then I said, "*L*, how long?"
6:12 The *L* has removed men far
7: 3 Then the *L* said to Isaiah,
7: 7 thus says the *L* GOD: "It
7:10 Moreover the *L* spoke again to
7:11 a sign for yourself from the *L*
7:12 nor will I test the *L*!"
7:14 Therefore the *L* Himself will
7:17 The *L* will bring the king of
7:18 pass in that day That the *L*
7:20 In the same day the *L* will
8: 1 Moreover the *L* said to me,
8: 3 Then the *L* said to me, "Call
8: 5 The *L* also spoke to me again,
8: 7 the *L* brings up over them The
8:11 For the *L* spoke thus to me
8:13 The *L* of hosts, Him you shall
8:17 And I will wait on the *L*,
8:18 I and the children whom the *L*
8:18 wonders in Israel From the *L*
9: 7 The zeal of the *L* of hosts
9: 8 The *L* sent a word against
9:11 Therefore the *L* shall set up
9:13 Nor do they seek the *L* of
9:14 Therefore the *L* will cut off
9:17 Therefore the *L* will have no
9:19 Through the wrath of the *L* of
10:12 when the *L* has performed all
10:16 Therefore the *L*, the Lord
10:16 the *L* of hosts, Will send
10:20 But will depend on the *L*,
10:23 For the *L* GOD of hosts Will
10:24 Therefore thus says the *L* GOD
10:26 And the *L* of hosts will stir up
10:33 Behold, the *L*, The LORD of
10:33 The *L* of hosts, Will lop off
11: 2 The Spirit of the *L* shall rest
11: 2 and of the fear of the *L*.
11: 3 is in the fear of the *L*,
11: 9 of the knowledge of the *L* As
11:11 pass in that day That the *L*
11:15 The *L* will utterly destroy the
12: 1 that day you will say: "O *L*,
12: 2 be afraid; 'For YAH, the *L*,
12: 4 you will say: "Praise the *L*,
12: 5 Sing to the *L*, For He has
13: 4 gathered together! The *L* of
13: 5 The *L* and His weapons of
13: 6 for the day of the *L* is at
13: 9 the day of the *L* comes,
13:13 In the wrath of the *L* of
14: 1 For the *L* will have mercy on
14: 2 and maids in the land of the *L*;
14: 3 come to pass in the day the *L*
14: 5 The *L* has broken the staff of
14:22 says the *L* of hosts, "And
14:22 and posterity," says the *L*.
14:23 says the *L* of hosts.
14:24 The *L* of hosts has sworn,
14:27 For the *L* of hosts has
14:32 That the *L* has founded Zion,
16:13 is the word which the *L* has
16:14 But now the *L* has spoken,
17: 3 Says the *L* of hosts.
17: 6 Says the *L* God of Israel.
18: 4 For so the *L* said to me, "I
18: 7 will be brought to the *L* of
18: 7 place of the name of the *L* of
19: 1 the *L* rides on a swift cloud,
19: 4 rule over them," Says the *L*,
19: 4 Says the Lord, the *L* of hosts.
19:12 And let them know what the *L*
19:14 The *L* has mingled a perverse
19:16 waving of the hand of the *L*
19:17 of the counsel of the *L* of
19:18 of Canaan and swear by the *L*
19:19 will be an altar to the *L* in
19:19 and a pillar to the *L* at its
19:20 and for a witness to the *L* of
19:20 for they will cry to the *L*
19:21 Then the *L* will be known to
19:21 the Egyptians will know the *L*
19:21 they will make a vow to the *L*
19:22 And the *L* will strike Egypt, He
19:22 they will return to the *L*,
19:25 whom the *L* of hosts shall
20: 2 at the same time the *L* spoke by
20: 3 Then the *L* said, "Just as My
21: 6 For thus has the *L* said to me:
21: 8 my *L*! I stand continually on
21:10 which I have heard from the *L*
21:16 For thus the *L* has said to me:
21:17 for the *L* God of Israel has
22: 5 down and perplexity By the *L*
22:12 And in that day the *L* GOD of
22:14 in my hearing by the *L* of
22:14 says the *L* GOD of hosts.
22:15 Thus says the *L* GOD of hosts:
22:17 the *L* will throw you away
22:25 says the *L* of hosts, 'the peg
22:25 for the *L* has spoken.'"
23: 9 The *L* of hosts has purposed
23:11 The *L* has given a commandment
23:17 that the *L* will visit Tyre.
23:18 will be set apart for the *L*;
23:18 those who dwell before the *L*,
24: 1 the *L* makes the earth empty
24: 3 For the *L* has spoken this
24:14 For the majesty of the *L*
24:15 Therefore glorify the *L* in the
24:15 The name of the *L* God of
24:21 pass in that day That the *L*
24:23 For the *L* of hosts will reign
25: 1 O *L*, You are my God.
25: 6 And in this mountain The *L*
25: 8 And the *L* GOD will wipe away
25: 8 For the *L* has spoken.
25: 9 will save us. This is the *L*;
25:10 mountain the hand of the *L*
26: 4 Trust in the *L* forever,
26: 4 forever, For in YAH, the *L*,
26: 8 way of Your judgments, O *L*,
26:10 behold the majesty of the *L*.
26:11 *L*, when Your hand is lifted
26:12 *L*, You will establish
26:13 O *L* our God, masters besides
26:15 have increased the nation, O *L*,
26:16 *L*, in trouble they have
26:17 we been in Your sight, O *L*.
26:21 the *L* comes out of His place
27: 1 In that day the *L* with His
27: 3 I, the *L*, keep it,
27:12 pass in that day That the *L*
27:13 And shall worship the *L* in
28: 2 the *L* has a mighty and strong
28: 5 In that day the *L* of hosts
28:13 But the word of the *L* was to
28:14 hear the word of the *L*,
28:16 Therefore thus says the *L* GOD:
28:21 For the *L* will rise up as at
28:22 For I have heard from the *L*
28:29 This also comes from the *L* of
29: 6 will be punished by the *L* of
29:10 For the *L* has poured out on
29:13 Therefore the *L* said:
29:15 their counsel far from the *L*,
29:19 increase their joy in the *L*,
29:22 Therefore thus says the *L*,
30: 1 children," says the *L*,
30: 9 will not hear the law of the *L*;
30:15 For thus says the *L* GOD, the
30:18 Therefore the *L* will wait,
30:18 For the *L* is a God of
30:20 And though the *L* gives you
30:26 In the day that the *L* binds
30:27 the name of the *L* comes from
30:29 into the mountain of the *L*,
30:30 The *L* will cause His glorious
30:31 through the voice of the *L*
30:32 Which the *L* lays on him,
30:33 The breath of the *L*,
31: 1 Nor seek the *L*!
31: 3 When the *L* stretches out His
31: 4 For thus the *L* has spoken to
31: 4 So the *L* of hosts will come
31: 5 So will the *L* of hosts defend
31: 9 of the banner," Says the *L*,
32: 6 To utter error against the *L*,
33: 2 O *L*, be gracious to us;
33: 5 The *L* is exalted, for He
33: 6 The fear of the *L* is His
33:10 I will rise," says the *L*;
33:21 But there the majestic *L* will
33:22 (For the *L* is our Judge,
33:22 The *L* is our Lawgiver,
33:22 The *L* is our King; He will
34: 2 For the indignation of the *L*
34: 6 The sword of the *L* is filled
34: 6 For the *L* has a sacrifice in
34:16 from the book of the *L*,
35: 2 shall see the glory of the *L*,
35:10 And the ransomed of the *L*
36: 7 We trust in the *L* our God,' is
36:10 I now come up without the *L*
36:10 The *L* said to me, 'Go up
36:15 make you trust in the *L*,
36:15 The *L* will surely deliver us;
36:18 'The *L* will deliver us."
36:20 that the *L* should deliver
37: 1 went into the house of the *L*.
37: 4 It may be that the *L* your God
37: 4 rebuke the words which the *L*
37: 6 your master, 'Thus says the *L*:
37:14 went up to the house of the *L*,
37:14 and spread it before the *L*.
37:15 Then Hezekiah prayed to the *L*,
37:16 O *L* of hosts, God of Israel,
37:17 "Incline Your ear, O *L*,
37:17 and hear; open Your eyes, O *L*,
37:18 'Truly, *L*, the kings of
37:20 O *L* our God, save us from his
37:20 may know that You are the *L*,
37:21 Thus says the *L* God of Israel,
37:22 'this is the word which the *L*
37:24 you have reproached the *L*,
37:32 The zeal of the *L* of hosts
37:33 Therefore thus says the *L*
37:34 into this city,' Says the *L*.
37:36 Then the angel of the *L* went
38: 1 said to him, "Thus says the *L*:
38: 2 the wall, and prayed to the *L*,
38: 3 and said, "Remember now, O *L*,
38: 4 And the word of the *L* came to
38: 5 Hezekiah, 'Thus says the *L*,
38: 7 is the sign to you from the *L*,
38: 7 that the *L* will do this thing
38:11 The *L* in the land of the
38:14 from looking upward. O *L*,
38:16 O *L*, by these things men
38:20 The *L* was ready to save me;
38:20 life, in the house of the *L*.
38:22 go up to the house of the *L*?
39: 5 Hear the word of the *L* of
39: 6 shall be left,' says the *L*.
39: 8 The word of the *L* which you
40: 3 "Prepare the way of the *L*;
40: 5 The glory of the *L* shall be
40: 5 For the mouth of the *L* has
40: 7 Because the breath of the *L*
40:10 the *L* GOD shall come with a
40:13 directed the Spirit of the *L*,
40:27 "My way is hidden from the *L*,
40:28 The everlasting God, the *L*,
40:31 But those who wait on the *L*
41: 4 from the beginning? 'I, the *L*,
41:13 the *L* your God, will hold your
41:14 says the *L* And your
41:16 You shall rejoice in the *L*,
41:17 fail for thirst. I, the *L*,
41:20 That the hand of the *L* has
41:21 your case," says the *L*.
42: 5 Thus says God the *L*,
42: 6 'I, the *L*, have called You
42: 8 I am the *L*, that is My
42:10 Sing to the *L* a new song,
42:12 Let them give glory to the *L*,
42:13 The *L* shall go forth like a
42:21 The *L* is well pleased for His
42:24 the robbers? Was it not the *L*,
43: 1 But now, thus says the *L*,
43: 3 For I am the *L* your God,
43:10 My witnesses," says the *L*,
43:11 I, even I, am the *L*,
43:12 My witnesses," Says the *L*,
43:14 says the *L*, your Redeemer,
43:15 I am the *L*, your Holy One,
43:16 Thus says the *L*,
44: 2 Thus says the *L* who made you
44: 6 "Thus says the *L*,
44: 6 the *L* of hosts: 'I am the
44:23 for the *L* has done it!
44:23 every tree in it! For the *L*
44:24 Thus says the *L*,
44:24 from the womb: "I am the *L*,
45: 1 Thus says the *L* to His
45: 3 you may know that I, the *L*,
45: 5 I am the *L*, and there is
45: 6 none besides Me. I am the *L*,
45: 7 and create calamity; I, the *L*,
45: 8 spring up together. I, the *L*,
45:11 Thus says the *L*, The Holy
45:13 Says the *L* of hosts.
45:14 Thus says the *L*: "The labor
45:17 shall be saved by the *L* With
45:18 For thus says the *L*,
45:18 be inhabited: "I am the *L*,
45:19 'Seek Me in vain'; I, the *L*,
45:21 that time? Have not I, the *L*?
45:24 Surely in the *L* I have
45:25 In the *L* all the descendants
47: 4 the *L* of hosts is His name,
48: 1 swear by the name of the *L*,
48: 2 The *L* of hosts is His name:
48:14 The *L* loves him; He shall do
48:16 And now the *L* GOD and His
48:17 Thus says the *L*,
48:17 I am the *L* your God, Who
48:20 The *L* has redeemed His servant
48:22 is no peace," says the *L*,
49: 1 you peoples from afar! The *L*
49: 4 my just reward is with the *L*,
49: 5 And now the *L* says, Who
49: 5 glorious in the eyes of the *L*,
49: 7 Thus says the *L*,
49: 7 Because of the *L* who is
49: 8 Thus says the *L*:
49:13 O mountains! For the *L* has
49:14 The *L* has forsaken me, And my
49:14 And my *L* has forgotten me."
49:18 As I live," says the *L*,
49:22 Thus says the *L* GOD:
49:23 you will know that I am the *L*,
49:25 But thus says the *L*:
49:26 shall know That I, the *L*,
50: 1 Thus says the *L*:
50: 4 The *L* GOD has given Me The
50: 5 The *L* GOD has opened My ear;
50: 7 For the *L* GOD will help Me;
50: 9 Surely the *L* GOD will help Me;
50:10 "Who among you fears the *L*?

50:10 him trust in the name of the *L*
51: 1 You who seek the *L*:
51: 3 For the *L* will comfort Zion,
51: 3 like the garden of the *L*;
51: 9 O arm of the *L*! Awake as in
51:11 So the ransomed of the *L* shall
51:13 And you forget the *L* your
51:15 But I am the *L* your God,
51:15 The *L* of hosts is His name.
51:17 drunk at the hand of the *L*
51:20 are full of the fury of the *L*,
51:22 Thus says your *L*,
51:22 The *L* and your God, Who
52: 3 For thus says the *L*:
52: 4 For thus says the *L* GOD: "My
52: 5 what have I here," says the *L*,
52: 5 Make them wail," says the *L*,
52: 8 see eye to eye When the *L*
52: 9 of Jerusalem! For the *L* has
52:10 The *L* has made bare His holy
52:11 who bear the vessels of the *L*.
52:12 For the *L* will go before you,
53: 1 to whom has the arm of the *L*
53: 6 And the *L* has laid on Him the
53:10 Yet it pleased the *L* to
53:10 And the pleasure of the *L*
54: 1 married woman," says the *L*.
54: 5 The *L* of hosts is His name;
54: 6 For the *L* has called you Like
54: 8 mercy on you," Says the *L*,
54:10 be removed," Says the *L*,
54:13 shall be taught by the *L*,
54:17 of the servants of the *L*,
54:17 is from Me," Says the *L*.
55: 5 Because of the *L* your God,
55: 6 Seek the *L* while He may be
55: 7 Let him return to the *L*,
55: 8 ways My ways," says the *L*.
55:13 And it shall be to the *L* for
56: 1 Thus says the *L*:
56: 3 has joined himself to the *L*
56: 3 The *L* has utterly separated me
56: 4 For thus says the *L*:
56: 6 Who join themselves to the *L*,
56: 6 And to love the name of the *L*,
56: 8 The *L* GOD, who gathers the
57:19 who is near," Says the *L*,
58: 5 an acceptable day to the *L*?
58: 8 The glory of the *L* shall be
58: 9 and the *L* will answer;
58:11 The *L* will guide you
58:13 The holy day of the *L*
58:14 delight yourself in the *L*;
58:14 The mouth of the *L* has
59:13 and lying against the *L*,
59:15 Then the *L* saw it, and it
59:19 they fear The name of the *L*
59:19 The Spirit of the *L* will lift
59:20 in Jacob," Says the *L*.
59:21 "As for Me," says the *L*,
59:21 descendants," says the *L*,
60: 1 And the glory of the *L* is
60: 2 But the *L* will arise over
60: 6 proclaim the praises of the *L*.
60: 9 To the name of the *L* your
60:14 call you The City of the *L*,
60:16 You shall know that I, the *L*,
60:19 But the *L* will be to you an
60:20 For the *L* will be your
60:22 one a strong nation. I, the *L*,
61: 1 The Spirit of the *L* GOD is
61: 1 Because the *L* has anointed Me
61: 2 the acceptable year of the *L*,
61: 3 The planting of the *L*,
61: 6 be named the priests of the *L*,
61: 8 'For I, the *L*, love justice;
61: 9 the posterity whom the *L* has
61:10 will greatly rejoice in the *L*,
61:11 So the *L* GOD will cause
62: 2 Which the mouth of the *L* will
62: 3 of glory In the hand of the *L*,
62: 4 For the *L* delights in you,
62: 6 You who make mention of the *L*,
62: 8 The *L* has sworn by His right
62: 9 eat it, And praise the *L*;
62:11 Indeed the *L* has proclaimed
62:12 People, The Redeemed of the *L*;
63: 7 the lovingkindnesses of the *L*
63: 7 And the praises of the *L*,
63: 7 According to all that the *L*
63:14 And the Spirit of the *L*
63:16 not acknowledge us. You, O *L*,
63:17 O *L*, why have You made us
64: 8 But now, O *L*, You are our
64: 9 Do not be furious, O *L*,
64:12 because of these things, O *L*?
65: 7 together," Says the *L*,
65: 8 says the *L*: "As the new
65:11 are those who forsake the *L*,
65:13 Therefore thus says the *L* GOD:
65:15 For the *L* GOD will slay you,
65:23 of the blessed of the *L*,
65:25 holy mountain," Says the *L*.
66: 1 Thus says the *L*: "Heaven is
66: 2 things exist," Says the *L*.
66: 5 Hear the word of the *L*,
66: 5 'Let the *L* be glorified,
66: 6 The voice of the *L*,
66: 9 cause delivery?" says the *L*.
66:12 For thus says the *L*:
66:14 The hand of the *L* shall be
66:15 the *L* will come with fire
66:16 fire and by His sword The *L*
66:16 And the slain of the *L* shall
66:17 together," says the *L*.
66:20 for an offering to the *L* out
66:20 Jerusalem," says the *L*,
66:20 vessel into the house of the *L*.
66:21 and Levites," says the *L*.
66:22 remain before Me," says the *L*,
66:23 before Me," says the *L*.
Jer 1: 2 to whom the word of the *L* came
1: 4 Then the word of the *L* came to
1: 6 *L* GOD! Behold, I cannot
1: 7 But the *L* said to me: "Do
1: 8 to deliver you," says the *L*.
1: 9 Then the *L* put forth His hand
1: 9 and the *L* said to me:
1:11 Moreover the word of the *L*
1:12 Then the *L* said to me, "You
1:13 And the word of the *L* came to
1:14 Then the *L* said to me: "Out
1:15 of the north," says the *L*;
1:19 I am with you," says the *L*,
2: 1 Moreover the word of the *L* came
2: 2 saying, 'Thus says the *L*:
2: 3 Israel was holiness to the *L*,
2: 3 come upon them," says the *L*.
2: 4 Hear the word of the *L*,
2: 5 Thus says the *L*:
2: 6 did they say, 'Where is the *L*,
2: 8 did not say, 'Where is the *L*?
2: 9 against you," says the *L*,
2:12 very desolate," says the *L*.
2:17 that you have forsaken the *L*
2:19 That you have forsaken the *L*
2:19 Says the *L* GOD of hosts.
2:22 before Me," says the *L* GOD.
2:29 against Me," says the *L*.
2:31 see the word of the *L*! Have I
2:37 For the *L* has rejected your
3: 1 return to Me," says the *L*.
3: 6 The *L* said also to me in the
3:10 but in pretense," says the *L*.
3:11 Then the *L* said to me,
3:12 Israel,' says the *L*;
3:12 I am merciful,' says the *L*;
3:13 transgressed against the *L*
3:13 obeyed My voice,' says the *L*.
3:14 children," says the *L*;
3:16 in those days," says the *L*,
3:16 ark of the covenant of the *L*.
3:17 be called The Throne of the *L*,
3:17 to it, to the name of the *L*,
3:20 house of Israel," says the *L*.
3:21 They have forgotten the *L*
3:22 For You are the *L* our God.
3:23 in the *L* our God Is the
3:25 we have sinned against the *L*
3:25 not obeyed the voice of the *L*
4: 1 return, O Israel," says the *L*,
4: 2 The *L* lives,' In truth, in
4: 3 For thus says the *L* to the men
4: 4 yourselves to the *L*,
4: 8 For the fierce anger of the *L*
4: 9 pass in that day," says the *L*,
4:10 *L* GOD! Surely You have
4:17 against Me," says the *L*.
4:26 At the presence of the *L*,
4:27 For thus says the *L*:
5: 2 As the *L* lives,' Surely they
5: 3 O *L*, are not Your eyes on the
5: 4 do not know the way of the *L*,
5: 5 have known the way of the *L*,
5: 9 these things?" says the *L*.
5:11 with Me," says the *L*.
5:12 They have lied about the *L*,
5:14 Therefore thus says the *L* God
5:15 house of Israel," says the *L*.
5:18 in those days," says the *L*,
5:19 Why does the *L* our God do all
5:22 you not fear Me?' says the *L*.
5:24 Let us now fear the *L* our God,
5:29 for these things?' says the *L*.
6: 6 For thus has the *L* of hosts
6: 9 Thus says the *L* of hosts:
6:10 the word of the *L* is a
6:11 I am full of the fury of the *L*.
6:12 of the land," says the *L*.
6:15 be cast down," says the *L*.
6:16 Thus says the *L*:
6:21 Therefore thus says the *L*:
6:22 Thus says the *L*:
6:30 Because the *L* has rejected
7: 1 came to Jeremiah from the *L*,
7: 2 say, 'Hear the word of the *L*,
7: 2 these gates to worship the *L*!
7: 3 Thus says the *L* of hosts, the
7: 4 saying, 'The temple of the *L*,
7: 4 the LORD, the temple of the *L*,
7: 4 the temple of the *L* are
7:11 I, have seen it," says the *L*.
7:13 all these works," says the *L*,
7:19 Me to anger?" says the *L*.
7:20 Therefore thus says the *L* GOD:
7:21 Thus says the *L* of hosts, the
7:28 not obey the voice of the *L*
7:29 for the *L* has rejected and
7:30 evil in My sight," says the *L*.
7:32 days are coming," says the *L*,
8: 1 "At that time," says the *L*,
8: 3 says the *L* of hosts.
8: 4 say to them, 'Thus says the *L*:
8: 7 not know the judgment of the *L*.
8: 8 And the law of the *L* is with
8: 9 rejected the word of the *L*;
8:12 be cast down," says the *L*.
8:13 consume them," says the *L*.
8:14 For the *L* our God has put us
8:14 we have sinned against the *L*.
8:17 shall bite you," says the *L*.
8:19 Is not the *L* in Zion? Is not
9: 3 do not know Me," says the *L*.
9: 6 to know Me," says the *L*.
9: 7 Therefore thus says the *L* of
9: 9 these things?" says the *L*.
9:12 he to whom the mouth of the *L*
9:13 And the *L* said, "Because they
9:15 therefore thus says the *L* of
9:17 Thus says the *L* of hosts:
9:20 Yet hear the word of the *L*,
9:22 Speak, "Thus says the *L*:
9:23 Thus says the *L*: "Let not
9:24 knows Me, That I am the *L*,
9:24 these I delight," says the *L*.
9:25 days are coming," says the *L*,
10: 1 Hear the word which the *L*
10: 2 Thus says the *L*: "Do not
10: 6 O *L* (You are great, and Your
10:10 But the *L* is the true God;
10:16 The *L* of hosts is His name.
10:18 For thus says the *L*:
10:21 And have not sought the *L*;
10:23 O *L*, I know the way of man
10:24 O *L*, correct me, but with
11: 1 came to Jeremiah from the *L*,
11: 3 Thus says the *L* God of Israel:
11: 5 and said, "So be it, *L*.
11: 6 Then the *L* said to me,
11: 9 And the *L* said to me, "A
11:11 Therefore thus says the *L*.
11:16 The *L* called your name,
11:17 For the *L* of hosts, who planted
11:18 Now the *L* gave me knowledge
11:20 O *L* of hosts, You who judge
11:21 Therefore thus says the *L*
11:21 prophesy in the name of the *L*,
11:22 therefore thus says the *L* of
12: 1 Righteous are You, O *L*,
12: 3 But You, O *L*, know me;
12:12 For the sword of the *L* shall
12:13 of the fierce anger of the *L*.
12:14 Thus says the *L*:
12:16 As the *L* lives,' as they taught
12:17 that nation," says the *L*.
13: 1 Thus the *L* said to me: "Go and
13: 2 according to the word of the *L*,
13: 3 And the word of the *L* came to
13: 5 as the *L* commanded me.
13: 6 after many days that the *L*
13: 8 Then the word of the *L* came to
13: 9 'Thus says the *L*: 'In this
13:11 to cling to Me,' says the *L*,
13:12 Thus says the *L* God of Israel:
13:13 say to them, 'Thus says the *L*:
13:14 sons together," says the *L*.
13:15 For the *L* has spoken.
13:16 Give glory to the *L* your God
13:25 measures from Me," says the *L*,
14: 1 The word of the *L* that came to
14: 7 O *L*, though our iniquities
14: 9 cannot save? Yet You, O *L*,
14:10 Thus says the *L* to this
14:10 Therefore the *L* does not
14:11 Then the *L* said to me, "Do
14:13 *L* GOD! Behold, the prophets
14:14 And the *L* said to me, "The
14:15 Therefore thus says the *L*
14:20 We acknowledge, O *L*,
14:22 O *L* our God? Therefore we
15: 1 Then the *L* said to me, "Even
15: 2 tell them, 'Thus says the *L*:
15: 3 of destruction," says the *L*:
15: 6 have forsaken Me," says the *L*,
15: 9 their enemies," says the *L*.
15:11 The *L* said: "Surely it will
15:15 O *L*, You know; Remember me
15:16 O *L* God of hosts.
15:19 Therefore thus says the *L*:
15:20 And deliver you," says the *L*.
16: 1 The word of the *L* also came to
16: 3 For thus says the *L* concerning
16: 5 For thus says the *L*:
16: 5 from this people," says the *L*,
16: 9 For thus says the *L* of hosts,
16:10 Why has the *L* pronounced all
16:10 have committed against the *L*
16:11 have forsaken Me,' says the *L*;
16:14 days are coming," says the *L*,
16:14 The *L* lives who brought up the
16:15 The *L* lives who brought up the
16:16 many fishermen," says the *L*,
16:19 O *L*, my strength and my
16:21 know that My name is the *L*.
17: 5 says the *L*: "Cursed is
17: 5 heart departs from the *L*.
17: 7 the man who trusts in the *L*,
17: 7 And whose hope is the *L*.
17:10 I, the *L*, search the heart,
17:13 O *L*, the hope of Israel,
17:13 they have forsaken the *L*,
17:14 Heal me, O *L*, and I shall
17:15 "Where is the word of the *L*?
17:19 Thus the *L* said to me: "Go
17:20 them, 'Hear the word of the *L*,
17:21 'Thus says the *L*: "Take heed

17:24 Me carefully," says the *L*,
17:26 praise to the house of the *L*.
18: 1 came to Jeremiah from the *L*,
18: 5 Then the word of the *L* came to
18: 6 as this potter?" says the *L*.
18:11 saying, 'Thus says the *L*:
18:13 Therefore thus says the *L*:
18:19 Give heed to me, O *L*,
18:23 Yet, *L*, You know all their
19: 1 Thus says the *L*: "Go and
19: 3 say, 'Hear the word of the *L*,
19: 3 Thus says the *L* of hosts, the
19: 6 days are coming," says the *L*,
19:11 Thus says the *L* of hosts:
19:12 do to this place," says the *L*,
19:14 where the *L* had sent him to
19:15 Thus says the *L* of hosts, the
20: 1 governor in the house of the *L*,
20: 2 was by the house of the *L*.
20: 3 The *L* has not called your name
20: 4 "For thus says the *L*:
20: 7 O *L*, You induced me, and I
20: 8 Because the word of the *L*
20:11 But the *L* is with me as a
20:12 O *L* of hosts, You who test
20:13 Sing to the *L*! Praise the
20:13 to the LORD! Praise the *L*!
20:16 like the cities Which the *L*
21: 1 came to Jeremiah from the *L*
21: 2 Please inquire of the *L* for us,
21: 2 Perhaps the *L* will deal with
21: 4 Thus says the *L* God of Israel:
21: 7 "And afterward," says the *L*,
21: 8 this people, 'Thus says the *L*:
21:10 and not for good," says the *L*.
21:11 say, 'Hear the word of the *L*,
21:12 of David! Thus says the *L*:
21:13 of the plain," says the *L*,
21:14 of your doings," says the *L*;
22: 1 Thus says the *L*: "Go down
22: 2 say, 'Hear the word of the *L*,
22: 3 'Thus says the *L*: "Execute
22: 5 swear by Myself," says the *L*,
22: 6 For thus says the *L* to the
22: 8 Why has the *L* done so to this
22: 9 the covenant of the *L* their
22:11 For thus says the *L* concerning
22:16 this knowing Me?" says the *L*.
22:18 Therefore thus says the *L*
22:24 "As I live," says the *L*,
22:29 Hear the word of the *L*!
22:30 Thus says the *L*: 'Write this
23: 1 of My pasture!" says the *L*.
23: 2 Therefore thus says the *L* God
23: 2 of your doings," says the *L*.
23: 4 they be lacking," says the *L*.
23: 5 days are coming," says the *L*,
23: 6 THE *L* OUR RIGHTEOUSNESS.
23: 7 days are coming," says the *L*,
23: 7 As the *L* lives who brought up
23: 8 As the *L* lives who brought up
23: 9 overcome, Because of the *L*,
23:11 their wickedness," says the *L*.
23:12 their punishment," says the *L*.
23:15 Therefore thus says the *L* of
23:16 Thus says the *L* of hosts:
23:16 Not from the mouth of the *L*.
23:17 The *L* has said, "You shall
23:18 stood in the counsel of the *L*,
23:19 a whirlwind of the *L* has gone
23:20 The anger of the *L* will not
23:23 God near at hand," says the *L*,
23:24 not see him?" says the *L*;
23:24 heaven and earth?" says the *L*.
23:28 to the wheat?" says the *L*.
23:29 word like a fire?" says the *L*,
23:30 the prophets," says the *L*,
23:31 the prophets," says the *L*,
23:32 false dreams," says the *L*,
23:32 people at all," says the *L*.
23:33 'What is the oracle of the *L*?
23:33 even forsake you," says the *L*.
23:34 The oracle of the *L*!' I will
23:35 What has the *L* answered?' and,
23:35 What has the *L* spoken?'
23:36 And the oracle of the *L* you
23:36 the *L* of hosts, our God.
23:37 What has the *L* answered you?'
23:37 What has the *L* spoken?'
23:38 The oracle of the *L*!' therefore
23:38 therefore thus says the *L*:
23:38 The oracle of the *L*!" and I
23:38 The oracle of the *L*!'"
24: 1 The *L* showed me, and there were
24: 1 set before the temple of the *L*,
24: 3 Then the *L* said to me, "What
24: 4 Again the word of the *L* came
24: 5 'Thus says the *L*, the God of
24: 7 to know Me, that I am the *L*;
24: 8 so bad'—surely thus says the *L*—
25: 3 in which the word of the *L*
25: 4 And the *L* has sent to you all
25: 5 dwell in the land that the *L*
25: 7 listened to Me," says the *L*,
25: 8 Therefore thus says the *L* of
25: 9 of the north,' says the *L*,
25:12 their iniquity,' says the *L*;
25:15 For thus says the *L* God of
25:17 to whom the *L* had sent me:
25:27 Thus says the *L* of hosts, the
25:28 Thus says the *L* of hosts: "You
25:29 says the *L* of hosts.'
25:30 The *L* will roar from on high,
25:31 For the *L* has a controversy
25:31 to the sword,' says the *L*.
25:32 Thus says the *L* of hosts:
25:33 at that day the slain of the *L*
25:36 For the *L* has plundered their
25:37 of the fierce anger of the *L*.
26: 1 this word came from the *L*,
26: 2 'Thus says the *L*: 'Stand in
26: 4 say to them, 'Thus says the *L*:
26: 7 words in the house of the *L*.
26: 8 end of speaking all that the *L*
26: 9 in the name of the *L*,
26: 9 Jeremiah in the house of the *L*.
26:10 house to the house of the *L*
26:12 The *L* sent me to prophesy
26:13 and obey the voice of the *L*
26:13 then the *L* will relent
26:15 for truly the *L* has sent me to
26:16 to us in the name of the *L*
26:18 Thus says the *L* of hosts:
26:19 Did he not fear the *L* and seek
26:19 And the *L* relented concerning
26:20 in the name of the *L*,
27: 1 came to Jeremiah from the *L*,
27: 2 Thus says the *L* to me: 'Make
27: 4 Thus says the *L* of hosts, the
27: 8 I will punish,' says the *L*,
27:11 in their own land,' says the *L*,
27:13 as the *L* has spoken against
27:15 not sent them," says the *L*,
27:16 saying, "Thus says the *L*:
27:18 and if the word of the *L* is
27:18 make intercession to the *L* of
27:18 are left in the house of the *L*,
27:19 For thus says the *L* of hosts
27:21 thus says the *L* of hosts, the
27:21 remain in the house of the *L*,
27:22 that I visit them,' says the *L*.
28: 1 to me in the house of the *L*
28: 2 Thus speaks the *L* of hosts, the
28: 4 went to Babylon,' says the *L*,
28: 5 stood in the house of the *L*,
28: 6 Amen! The *L* do so; the LORD
28: 6 the *L* perform your words which
28: 9 be known as one whom the *L*
28:11 saying, "Thus says the *L*:
28:12 Now the word of the *L* came to
28:13 saying, 'Thus says the *L*:
28:14 For thus says the *L* of hosts,
28:15 the *L* has not sent you, but
28:16 "Therefore thus says the *L*:
28:16 taught rebellion against the *L*.
29: 4 Thus says the *L* of hosts, the
29: 7 and pray to the *L* for it; for
29: 8 For thus says the *L* of hosts,
29: 9 have not sent them, says the *L*.
29:10 For thus says the *L*:
29:11 I think toward you, says the *L*,
29:14 be found by you, says the *L*,
29:14 I have driven you, says the *L*,
29:15 The *L* has raised up prophets
29:16 therefore thus says the *L*
29:17 thus says the *L* of hosts:
29:19 heeded My words, says the *L*,
29:19 would you heed, says the *L*.
29:20 hear the word of the *L*,
29:21 Thus says the *L* of hosts, the
29:22 The *L* make you like Zedekiah
29:23 and am a witness, says the *L*.
29:25 Thus speaks the *L* of hosts, the
29:26 The *L* has made you priest
29:26 in the house of the *L* over
29:30 Then the word of the *L* came to
29:31 Thus says the *L* concerning
29:32 therefore thus says the *L*:
29:32 do for My people, says the *L*,
29:32 taught rebellion against the *L*.
30: 1 came to Jeremiah from the *L*,
30: 2 Thus speaks the *L* God of
30: 3 days are coming,' says the *L*,
30: 3 Israel and Judah,' says the *L*.
30: 4 are the words that the *L*
30: 5 "For thus says the *L*:
30: 8 Says the *L* of hosts, 'That
30: 9 But they shall serve the *L*
30:10 My servant Jacob,' says the *L*,
30:11 I am with you,' says the *L*,
30:12 "For thus says the *L*:
30:17 of your wounds,' says the *L*,
30:18 Thus says the *L*: 'Behold, I
30:21 to approach Me?' says the *L*.
30:23 the whirlwind of the *L* Goes
30:24 The fierce anger of the *L* will
31: 1 the same time," says the *L*,
31: 2 says the *L*: "The people
31: 3 The *L* has appeared of old to
31: 6 To the *L* our God.'"
31: 7 For thus says the *L*:
31: 7 give praise, and say, 'O *L*,
31:10 "Hear the word of the *L*,
31:11 For the *L* has redeemed Jacob,
31:12 to the goodness of the *L*—
31:14 with My goodness, says the *L*.
31:15 Thus says the *L*: "A voice
31:16 Thus says the *L*: "Refrain
31:16 shall be rewarded, says the *L*,
31:17 in your future, says the *L*,
31:18 For You are the *L* my God.
31:20 have mercy on him, says the *L*.
31:22 For the *L* has created a new
31:23 Thus says the *L* of hosts, the
31:23 The *L* bless you, O home of
31:27 days are coming, says the *L*,
31:28 build and to plant, says the *L*.
31:31 days are coming, says the *L*,
31:32 a husband to them, says the *L*.
31:33 after those days, says the *L*:
31:34 brother, saying, 'Know the *L*,
31:34 greatest of them, says the *L*.
31:35 Thus says the *L*, Who gives
31:35 And its waves roar (The *L* of
31:36 From before Me, says the *L*,
31:37 Thus says the *L*: "If heaven
31:37 they have done, says the *L*.
31:38 days are coming, says the *L*,
31:38 city shall be built for the *L*
31:40 east, shall be holy to the *L*.
32: 1 came to Jeremiah from the *L*
32: 3 and say, 'Thus says the *L*:
32: 5 I visit him," says the *L*;
32: 6 The word of the *L* came to me,
32: 8 according to the word of the *L*,
32: 8 this was the word of the *L*.
32:14 Thus says the *L* of hosts, the
32:15 For thus says the *L* of hosts,
32:16 of Neriah, I prayed to the *L*,
32:17 *L* GOD! Behold, You have made
32:18 whose name is the *L* of hosts.
32:25 O *L* GOD, "Buy the field for
32:26 Then the word of the *L* came to
32:27 "Behold, I am the *L*,
32:28 "Therefore thus says the *L*:
32:30 of their hands," says the *L*.
32:36 therefore, thus says the *L*,
32:42 "For thus says the *L*:
32:44 to return,' says the *L*.
33: 1 Moreover the word of the *L* came
33: 2 Thus says the *L* who made it,
33: 2 the *L* who formed it to
33: 2 it to establish it (the *L* is
33: 4 "For thus says the *L*,
33:10 Thus says the *L*: 'Again there
33:11 Praise the *L* of hosts, For the
33:11 For the *L* is good, For His
33:11 praise into the house of the *L*.
33:11 as at the first,' says the *L*.
33:12 Thus says the *L* of hosts: 'In
33:13 who counts them,' says the *L*.
33:14 days are coming,' says the *L*,
33:16 THE *L* OUR RIGHTEOUSNESS.'
33:17 "For thus says the *L*:
33:19 And the word of the *L* came to
33:20 'Thus says the *L*: 'If you
33:23 Moreover the word of the *L*
33:24 The two families which the *L*
33:25 Thus says the *L*: 'If My
34: 1 came to Jeremiah from the *L*,
34: 2 'Thus says the *L*, the God
34: 2 tell him, "Thus says the *L*:
34: 4 "Yet hear the word of the *L*,
34: 4 king of Judah! Thus says the *L*
34: 5 *l*!" For I have pronounced the
34: 5 the word, says the *L*.
34: 8 came to Jeremiah from the *L*,
34:12 Therefore the word of the *L*
34:12 came to Jeremiah from the *L*,
34:13 'Thus says the *L*, the God
34:17 "Therefore thus says the *L*:
34:17 liberty to you,' says the *L*—
34:22 I will command,' says the *L*,
35: 1 came to Jeremiah from the *L*
35: 2 them into the house of the *L*,
35: 4 them into the house of the *L*,
35:12 Then came the word of the *L* to
35:13 Thus says the *L* of hosts, the
35:13 to obey My words?" says the *L*.
35:17 Therefore thus says the *L* God
35:18 Thus says the *L* of hosts, the
35:19 therefore thus says the *L* of
36: 1 came to Jeremiah from the *L*,
36: 4 all the words of the *L* which
36: 5 go into the house of the *L*.
36: 6 the words of the *L*,
36: 7 supplication before the *L*,
36: 7 anger and the fury that the *L*
36: 8 the book the words of the *L*
36: 9 a fast before the *L* to all
36:10 Jeremiah in the house of the *L*,
36:11 heard all the words of the *L*
36:26 but the *L* hid them.
36:27 the word of the *L* came to
36:29 of Judah, 'Thus says the *L*:
36:30 Therefore thus says the *L*
37: 2 heed to the words of the *L*
37: 3 Pray now to the *L* our God for
37: 6 Then the word of the *L* came to
37: 7 'Thus says the *L*, the God
37: 9 'Thus says the *L*: 'Do not
37:17 there any word from the *L*?
37:20 O my *l* the king. Please, let my
38: 2 'Thus says the *L*: 'He who
38: 3 'Thus says the *L*: 'This city
38: 9 My *l* the king, these men have
38:14 entrance of the house of the *L*.
38:16 As the *L* lives, who made our
38:17 to Zedekiah, "Thus says the *L*,
38:20 obey the voice of the *L* which
38:21 this is the word that the *L*
39:15 Meanwhile the word of the *L*
39:16 Thus says the *L* of hosts, the
39:17 you in that day," says the *L*,
39:18 your trust in Me," says the *L*.
40: 1 came to Jeremiah from the *L*

40: 2 The *L* your God has pronounced
40: 3 Now the *L* has brought it, and
40: 3 have sinned against the *L*,
41: 5 them to the house of the *L*.
42: 2 and pray for us to the *L* your
42: 3 that the *L* your God may show us
42: 4 I will pray to the *L* your God
42: 4 that whatever the *L* answers
42: 5 Let the *L* be a true and
42: 5 to everything which the *L*
42: 6 will obey the voice of the *L*
42: 6 we obey the voice of the *L*
42: 7 days that the word of the *L*
42: 9 to them, "Thus says the *L*,
42:11 be afraid of him,' says the *L*,
42:13 disobeying the voice of the *L*
42:15 hear now the word of the *L*,
42:15 of Judah! Thus says the *L* of
42:18 For thus says the *L* of hosts,
42:19 The *L* has said concerning you,
42:20 when you sent me to the *L*
42:20 Pray for us to the *L* our God,
42:20 according to all that the *L*
42:21 not obeyed the voice of the *L*
43: 1 people all the words of the *L*
43: 1 for which the *L* their God had
43: 2 You speak falsely! The *L* our
43: 4 not obey the voice of the *L*,
43: 7 not obey the voice of the *L*.
43: 8 Then the word of the *L* came to
43:10 Thus says the *L* of hosts, the
44: 2 Thus says the *L* of hosts, the
44: 7 therefore, thus says the *L*,
44:11 Therefore thus says the *L* of
44:16 to us in the name of the *L*,
44:21 did not the *L* remember them,
44:22 So the *L* could no longer bear
44:23 you have sinned against the *L*,
44:23 not obeyed the voice of the *L*
44:24 "Hear the word of the *L*,
44:25 Thus says the *L* of hosts, the
44:26 hear the word of the *L*,
44:26 by My great name,' says the *L*,
44:26 saying, "The *L* GOD lives."
44:29 be a sign to you,' says the *L*,
44:30 'Thus says the *L*: 'Behold, I
45: 2 'Thus says the *L*, the God
45: 3 Woe is me now! For the *L* has
45: 4 say to him, 'Thus says the *L*:
45: 5 on all flesh," says the *L*.
46: 1 The word of the *L* which came to
46: 5 was all around," says the *L*.
46:10 For this is the day of the *L*
46:10 For the *L* GOD of hosts has a
46:13 The word that the *L* spoke to
46:15 did not stand Because the *L*
46:18 Whose name is the *L* of
46:23 down her forest," says the *L*,
46:25 The *L* of hosts, the God of
46:26 the days of old," says the *L*.
46:28 Jacob My servant," says the *L*,
47: 1 The word of the *L* that came to
47: 2 Thus says the *L*: "Behold,
47: 4 For the *L* shall plunder the
47: 6 "O you sword of the *L*,
47: 7 Seeing the *L* has given it a
48: 1 Thus says the *L* of hosts, the
48: 8 As the *L* has spoken.
48:10 he who does the work of the *L*
48:12 days are coming," says the *L*,
48:15 Whose name is the *L* of
48:25 arm is broken," says the *L*.
48:26 exalted himself against the *L*.
48:30 know his wrath," says the *L*,
48:35 "Moreover," says the *L*,
48:38 is no pleasure," says the *L*.
48:40 For thus says the *L*:
48:42 exalted himself against the *L*.
48:43 of Moab," says the *L*.
48:44 their punishment," says the *L*.
48:47 the latter days," says the *L*.
49: 1 the Ammonites. Thus says the *L*:
49: 2 days are coming," says the *L*,
49: 2 his inheritance," says the *L*.
49: 5 Says the *L* GOD of hosts,
49: 6 people of Ammon," says the *L*.
49: 7 Thus says the *L* of hosts:
49:12 For thus says the *L*:
49:13 sworn by Myself," says the *L*,
49:14 heard a message from the *L*,
49:16 down from there," says the *L*.
49:18 their neighbors," says the *L*,
49:20 hear the counsel of the *L*
49:26 says the *L* of hosts.
49:28 shall strike. Thus says the *L*:
49:30 of Hazor!" says the *L*.
49:31 dwells securely," says the *L*,
49:32 all its sides," says the *L*.
49:34 The word of the *L* that came to
49:35 Thus says the *L* of hosts:
49:37 My fierce anger,' says the *L*;
49:38 and the princes,' says the *L*.
49:39 captives of Elam,' says the *L*.
50: 1 The word that the *L* spoke
50: 4 and in that time," says the *L*,
50: 4 And seek the *L* their God.
50: 5 let us join ourselves to the *L*
50: 7 they have sinned against the *L*,
50: 7 habitation of justice, The *L*,
50:10 be satisfied," says the *L*.
50:13 of the wrath of the *L*
50:14 she has sinned against the *L*.
50:15 it is the vengeance of the *L*.
50:18 Therefore thus says the *L* of
50:20 and in that time," says the *L*,
50:21 destroy them," says the *L*,
50:24 have contended against the *L*.
50:25 The *L* has opened His armory,
50:25 this is the work of the *L* God
50:28 in Zion the vengeance of the *L*
50:29 has been proud against the *L*,
50:30 off in that day," says the *L*.
50:31 most haughty one!" says the *L*
50:33 Thus says the *L* of hosts:
50:34 The *L* of hosts is His name.
50:35 the Chaldeans," says the *L*,
50:40 their neighbors," says the *L*,
50:45 hear the counsel of the *L*
51: 1 Thus says the *L*: "Behold, I
51: 5 the *L* of hosts, Though their
51:10 The *L* has revealed our
51:10 in Zion the work of the *L* our
51:11 Gather the shields! The *L*
51:11 it is the vengeance of the *L*,
51:12 For the *L* has both devised
51:14 The *L* of hosts has sworn by
51:19 The *L* of hosts is His name.
51:24 in your sight," says the *L*.
51:25 all the earth," says the *L*.
51:26 desolate forever," says the *L*.
51:29 For every purpose of the *L*
51:33 For thus says the *L* of hosts,
51:36 Therefore thus says the *L*:
51:39 And not awake," says the *L*.
51:45 from the fierce anger of the *L*.
51:48 from the north," says the *L*.
51:50 stand still! Remember the *L*
51:52 days are coming," says the *L*,
51:53 come to her," says the *L*.
51:55 Because the *L* is plundering
51:56 For the *L* is the God of
51:57 Whose name is the *L* of
51:58 Thus says the *L* of hosts:
51:62 "then you shall say, 'O *L*,
52: 2 did evil in the sight of the *L*,
52: 3 because of the anger of the *L*
52:13 He burned the house of the *L*
52:17 were in the house of the *L*,
52:17 were in the house of the *L*,
52:20 made for the house of the *L*—
Lam 1: 5 For the *L* has afflicted her
1: 9 She had no comforter. "O *L*,
1:11 to restore life. "See, O *L*,
1:12 Which the *L* has inflicted In
1:14 The *L* delivered me into the
1:15 The *L* has trampled underfoot all
1:15 The *L* trampled as in a
1:17 The *L* has commanded
1:18 The *L* is righteous, For I
1:20 'See, O *L*, that I am in
2: 1 How the *L* has covered the
2: 2 The *L* has swallowed up and has
2: 5 The *L* was like an enemy.
2: 6 The *L* has caused The
2: 7 The *L* has spurned His altar,
2: 7 a noise in the house of the *L*
2: 8 The *L* has purposed to destroy
2: 9 find no vision from the *L*.
2:17 The *L* has done what He
2:18 heart cried out to the *L*,
2:19 water before the face of the *L*.
2:20 See, O *L*, and consider!
2:20 In the sanctuary of the *L*?
3:18 Have perished from the *L*."
3:24 The *L* is my portion," says my
3:25 The *L* is good to those who
3:26 For the salvation of the *L*.
3:31 For the *L* will not cast off
3:36 The *L* does not approve.
3:37 When the *L* has not commanded
3:40 ways, And turn back to the *L*;
3:50 Till the *L* from heaven Looks
3:55 I called on Your name, O *L*,
3:58 O *L*, You have pleaded the
3:59 O *L*, You have seen how
3:61 have heard their reproach, O *L*,
3:64 Repay them, O *L*,
3:66 under the heavens of the *L*.
4:11 The *L* has fulfilled His fury,
4:16 The face of the *L* scattered
4:20 the anointed of the *L*,
5: 1 Remember, O *L*, what has
5:19 You, O *L*, remain forever;
5:21 Turn us back to You, O *L*,
Ezek 1: 3 the word of the *L* came
1: 3 and the hand of the *L* was upon
1:28 likeness of the glory of the *L*.
2: 4 Thus says the *L* GOD.'
3:11 Thus says the *L* GOD,' whether
3:12 is the glory of the *L* from
3:14 but the hand of the *L* was
3:16 days that the word of the *L*
3:22 Then the hand of the *L* was
3:23 the glory of the *L* stood
3:27 Thus says the *L* GOD.' He who
4:13 Then the *L* said, "So shall the
4:14 *L* GOD! Indeed I have never
5: 5 Thus says the *L* GOD: 'This is
5: 7 Therefore thus says the *L* GOD:
5: 8 therefore thus says the *L* GOD:
5:11 says the *L* GOD, 'surely,
5:13 they shall know that I, the *L*,
5:15 in furious rebukes. I, the *L*,
5:17 sword against you. I, the *L*,
6: 1 Now the word of the *L* came to
6: 3 hear the word of the *L* GOD!'
6: 3 the Lord GOD!' Thus says the *L*
6: 7 shall know that I am the *L*.
6:10 shall know that I am the *L*;
6:11 Thus says the *L* GOD: "Pound
6:13 shall know that I am the *L*,
6:14 shall know that I am the *L*.
7: 1 Moreover the word of the *L* came
7: 2 thus says the *L* GOD to the
7: 4 shall know that I am the *L*!'
7: 5 Thus says the *L* GOD: 'A
7: 9 shall know that I am the *L*
7:19 the day of the wrath of the *L*;
7:27 shall know that I am the *L*!'
8: 1 that the hand of the *L* GOD
8:12 The *L* does not see us, the
8:12 the *L* has forsaken the land.'
8:16 door of the temple of the *L*,
8:16 toward the temple of the *L*
9: 4 and the *L* said to him, "Go
9: 8 *L* GOD! Will You destroy all
9: 9 The *L* has forsaken the land,
9: 9 and the *L* does not see!'
10: 4 Then the glory of the *L* went up
10:18 Then the glory of the *L*
11: 5 Then the Spirit of the *L* fell
11: 5 me, "Speak! 'Thus says the *L*:
11: 7 Therefore thus says the *L* GOD:
11: 8 upon you," says the *L* GOD.
11:10 shall know that I am the *L*.
11:12 shall know that I am the *L*;
11:13 *L* GOD! Will You make a
11:14 Again the word of the *L* came
11:15 said, 'Get far away from the *L*;
11:16 Thus says the *L* GOD: "Although
11:17 Thus says the *L* GOD: "I will
11:21 own heads," says the *L* GOD.
11:23 And the glory of the *L* went up
11:25 of all the things the *L* had
12: 1 Now the word of the *L* came to
12: 8 the morning the word of the *L*
12:10 Thus says the *L* GOD: "This
12:15 shall know that I am the *L*,
12:16 shall know that I am the *L*.
12:17 Moreover the word of the *L*
12:19 Thus says the *L* GOD to the
12:20 shall know that I am the *L*.
12:21 And the word of the *L* came to
12:23 Thus says the *L* GOD: "I will
12:25 "For I am the *L*.
12:25 says the *L* GOD.'"
12:26 Again the word of the *L* came
12:28 Thus says the *L* GOD: "None of
12:28 be done," says the *L* GOD.'
13: 1 And the word of the *L* came to
13: 2 Hear the word of the *L*!'"
13: 3 Thus says the *L* GOD: "Woe to
13: 5 in battle on the day of the *L*.
13: 6 Thus says the *L*!' But the LORD
13: 6 says the LORD!' But the *L*
13: 7 The *L* says,' but I have not
13: 8 Therefore thus says the *L* GOD:
13: 8 against you," says the *L* GOD.
13: 9 you shall know that I am the *L*
13:13 Therefore thus says the *L* GOD:
13:14 shall know that I am the *L*.
13:16 no peace,'" says the *L* GOD.
13:18 Thus says the *L* GOD: "Woe to
13:20 Therefore thus says the *L* GOD:
13:21 shall know that I am the *L*.
13:23 shall know that I am the *L*.
14: 2 And the word of the *L* came to
14: 4 Thus says the *L* GOD: "Everyone
14: 4 I the *L* will answer him who
14: 6 Thus says the *L* GOD: "Repent,
14: 7 I the *L* will answer him by
14: 8 shall know that I am the *L*.
14: 9 I the *L* have induced that
14:11 their God," says the *L* GOD.'
14:12 The word of the *L* came again
14:14 says the *L* GOD.
14:16 says the *L* GOD, "they would
14:18 says the *L* GOD, "they would
14:20 says the *L* GOD, "they would
14:21 For thus says the *L* GOD: "How
14:23 in it," says the *L* GOD.
15: 1 Then the word of the *L* came to
15: 6 Therefore thus says the *L* GOD:
15: 7 shall know that I am the *L*,
15: 8 says the *L* GOD."
16: 1 Again the word of the *L* came to
16: 3 Thus says the *L* GOD to
16: 8 Mine," says the *L* GOD.
16:14 on you," says the *L* GOD.
16:19 it was," says the *L* GOD.
16:23 woe to you!' says the *L* GOD—
16:30 is your heart!" says the *L*
16:35 hear the word of the *L*!
16:36 Thus says the *L* GOD: "Because
16:43 says the *L* GOD. "And you
16:48 says the *L* GOD, "neither
16:58 abominations," says the *L*.
16:59 For thus says the *L* GOD: "I
16:62 shall know that I am the *L*,
16:63 have done," says the *L* GOD.'
17: 1 And the word of the *L* came to
17: 3 Thus says the *L* GOD: "A
17: 9 Thus says the *L* GOD: "Will
17:11 Moreover the word of the *L*
17:16 says the *L* GOD, 'surely in
17:19 Therefore thus says the *L* GOD:

17:21 you shall know that I, the *L*,
17:22 Thus says the *L* GOD: "I will
17:24 field shall know that I, the *L*,
17:24 dry tree flourish; I, the *L*,
18: 1 The word of the *L* came to me
18: 3 says the *L* GOD, "you shall
18: 9 surely live!" Says the *L*
18:23 says the *L* GOD, "and not
18:25 The way of the *L* is not fair.'
18:29 'The way of the *L* is not fair.'
18:30 says the *L* GOD. "Repent,
18:32 says the *L* GOD. "Therefore
20: 1 came to inquire of the *L*,
20: 2 Then the word of the *L* came to
20: 3 Thus says the *L* GOD: "Have you
20: 3 says the *L* GOD, "I will not
20: 5 Thus says the *L* GOD: "On the
20: 5 I am the *L* your God.'
20: 7 I am the *L* your God.'
20:12 might know that I am the *L*
20:19 I am the *L* your God: Walk in
20:20 you may know that I am the *L*
20:26 might know that I am the *L*.
20:27 Thus says the *L* GOD: "In this
20:30 Thus says the *L* GOD: "Are you
20:31 says the *L* GOD, "I will not
20:33 says the *L* GOD, "surely
20:36 with you," says the *L* GOD.
20:38 you will know that I am the *L*.
20:39 thus says the *L* GOD: "Go,
20:40 says the *L* GOD, "there all
20:42 shall know that I am the *L*,
20:44 shall know that I am the *L*,
20:44 of Israel," says the *L* GOD.'
20:45 the word of the *L* came to me,
20:47 'Hear the word of the *L*!
20:47 of the LORD! Thus says the *L*
20:48 flesh shall see that I, the *L*,
20:49 *L* GOD! They say of me, 'Does
21: 1 And the word of the *L* came to
21: 3 of Israel, 'Thus says the *L*:
21: 5 flesh may know that I, the *L*,
21: 7 to pass,' says the *L* GOD."
21: 8 Again the word of the *L* came
21: 9 Thus says the *L*!' Say: 'A
21:13 no more," says the *L* GOD.
21:17 My fury to rest; I, the *L*,
21:18 The word of the *L* came to me
21:24 Therefore thus says the *L* GOD:
21:26 thus says the *L* GOD: "Remove
21:28 Thus says the *L* GOD concerning
21:32 For I the *L* have spoken.'"
22: 1 Moreover the word of the *L* came
22: 3 Thus says the *L* GOD: "The city
22:12 Me," says the *L* GOD.
22:14 shall deal with you? I, the *L*,
22:16 shall know that I am the *L*.
22:17 The word of the *L* came to me,
22:19 Therefore thus says the *L* GOD:
22:22 you shall know that I, the *L*,
22:23 And the word of the *L* came to
22:28 Thus says the *L* GOD,' when the
22:28 when the *L* had not spoken.
22:31 own heads," says the *L* GOD.
23: 1 The word of the *L* came again to
23:22 thus says the *L* GOD:
23:28 For thus says the *L* GOD:
23:32 Thus says the *L* GOD: 'You
23:34 spoken,' Says the *L* GOD.
23:35 Therefore thus says the *L* GOD:
23:36 The *L* also said to me: "Son
23:46 For thus says the *L* GOD:
23:49 you shall know that I am the *L*
24: 1 the word of the *L* came to me,
24: 3 Thus says the *L* GOD: "Put on
24: 6 Therefore thus says the *L* GOD:
24: 9 Therefore thus says the *L* GOD:
24:14 I, the *L*, have spoken it;
24:14 Says the *L* GOD.'
24:15 Also the word of the *L* came to
24:20 The word of the *L* came to me,
24:21 Thus says the *L* GOD: 'Behold, I
24:24 you shall know that I am the *L*
24:27 shall know that I am the *L*.
25: 1 The word of the *L* came to me,
25: 3 Hear the word of the *L* GOD!
25: 3 the Lord GOD! Thus says the *L*
25: 5 shall know that I am the *L*.
25: 6 For thus says the *L* GOD:
25: 7 shall know that I am the *L*.
25: 8 Thus says the *L* GOD: "Because
25:11 shall know that I am the *L*.
25:12 Thus says the *L* GOD: "Because
25:13 therefore thus says the *L* GOD:
25:14 vengeance," says the *L* GOD.
25:15 Thus says the *L* GOD: "Because
25:16 therefore thus says the *L* GOD:
25:17 shall know that I am the *L*,
26: 1 that the word of the *L* came
26: 3 Therefore thus says the *L* GOD:
26: 5 says the *L* GOD; 'it shall
26: 6 shall know that I am the *L*.
26: 7 For thus says the *L* GOD:
26:14 for I the *L* have spoken,' says
26:14 spoken,' says the *L* GOD.
26:15 Thus says the *L* GOD to Tyre:
26:19 For thus says the *L* GOD: 'When
26:21 again,' says the *L* GOD."
27: 1 The word of the *L* came again to
27: 3 thus says the *L* GOD: "O
28: 1 The word of the *L* came to me
28: 2 Thus says the *L* GOD:
28: 6 Therefore thus says the *L* GOD:
28:10 spoken," says the *L* GOD.'
28:11 Moreover the word of the *L*
28:12 Thus says the *L* GOD: "You
28:20 Then the word of the *L* came to
28:22 Thus says the *L* GOD:
28:22 shall know that I am the *L*,
28:23 shall know that I am the *L*.
28:24 shall know that I am the *L*
28:25 Thus says the *L* GOD: "When I
28:26 shall know that I am the *L*
29: 1 the word of the *L* came to me,
29: 3 Thus says the *L* GOD:
29: 6 Shall know that I am the *L*,
29: 8 Therefore thus says the *L* GOD:
29: 9 will know that I am the *L*.
29:13 thus says the *L* GOD: "At the
29:16 shall know that I am the *L*
29:17 that the word of the *L* came to
29:19 Therefore thus says the *L* GOD:
29:20 for Me,' says the *L* GOD.
29:21 shall know that I am the *L*.
30: 1 The word of the *L* came to me
30: 2 Thus says the *L* GOD: "Wail,
30: 3 Even the day of the *L* is
30: 6 'Thus says the *L*:
30: 6 sword," Says the *L* GOD.
30: 8 will know that I am the *L*,
30:10 Thus says the *L* GOD: "I
30:12 the hand of aliens. I, the *L*,
30:13 Thus says the *L* GOD: "I
30:19 shall know that I am the *L*.
30:20 that the word of the *L* came
30:22 Therefore thus says the *L* GOD:
30:25 shall know that I am the *L*,
30:26 shall know that I am the *L*.
31: 1 that the word of the *L* came
31:10 Therefore thus says the *L* GOD:
31:15 Thus says the *L* GOD: 'In the
31:18 multitude,' says the *L* GOD."
32: 1 that the word of the *L* came
32: 3 Thus says the *L* GOD: 'I will
32: 8 your land,' Says the *L* GOD.
32:11 For thus says the *L* GOD: 'The
32:14 like oil,' Says the *L* GOD.
32:15 shall know that I am the *L*.
32:16 Says the *L* GOD."
32:17 that the word of the *L* came to
32:31 sword," Says the *L* GOD.
32:32 multitude," Says the *L* GOD.
33: 1 Again the word of the *L* came to
33:11 says the *L* GOD, 'I have no
33:17 The way of the *L* is not fair.'
33:20 The way of the *L* is not fair.'
33:22 Now the hand of the *L* had been
33:23 Then the word of the *L* came to
33:25 Thus says the *L* GOD: "You eat
33:27 Thus says the *L* GOD: "As I
33:29 shall know that I am the *L*,
33:30 word is that comes from the *L*.
34: 1 And the word of the *L* came to
34: 2 Thus says the *L* GOD to the
34: 7 hear the word of the *L*:
34: 8 says the *L* GOD, "surely
34: 9 hear the word of the *L*!
34:10 Thus says the *L* GOD: "Behold,
34:11 For thus says the *L* GOD:
34:15 lie down," says the *L* GOD.
34:17 thus says the *L* GOD: "Behold,
34:20 Therefore thus says the *L* GOD
34:24 'And I, the *L*, will be their
34:24 a prince among them; I, the *L*,
34:27 shall know that I am the *L*,
34:30 the *L* their God, am with
34:30 people," says the *L* GOD.'
34:31 your God," says the *L* GOD.
35: 1 Moreover the word of the *L* came
35: 3 Thus says the *L* GOD:
35: 4 shall know that I am the *L*.
35: 6 says the *L* GOD, "I will
35: 9 shall know that I am the *L*.
35:10 although the *L* was there,
35:11 says the *L* GOD, "I will do
35:12 shall know that I am the *L*.
35:14 Thus says the *L* GOD: "The
35:15 shall know that I am the *L*.
36: 1 hear the word of the *L*!
36: 2 Thus says the *L* GOD: "Because
36: 3 Thus says the *L* GOD: "Because
36: 4 hear the word of the *L* GOD!
36: 4 the Lord GOD! Thus says the *L*
36: 5 therefore thus says the *L* GOD:
36: 6 Thus says the *L* GOD: "Behold,
36: 7 Therefore thus says the *L* GOD:
36:11 shall know that I am the *L*.
36:13 Thus says the *L* GOD: "Because
36:14 anymore," says the *L* GOD.
36:15 anymore," says the *L* GOD.'
36:16 Moreover the word of the *L*
36:20 are the people of the *L*,
36:22 Thus says the *L* GOD: "I do not
36:23 shall know that I am the *L*,
36:23 says the *L* GOD, "when I am
36:32 says the *L* GOD, "let it be
36:33 Thus says the *L* GOD: "On the
36:36 you shall know that I, the *L*,
36:36 what was desolate. I, the *L*,
36:37 Thus says the *L* GOD: "I will
36:38 shall know that I am the *L*.
37: 1 The hand of the *L* came upon me
37: 1 me out in the Spirit of the *L*,
37: 3 O *L* GOD, You know."
37: 4 hear the word of the *L*!
37: 5 Thus says the *L* GOD to these
37: 6 shall know that I am the *L*.
37: 9 Thus says the *L* GOD: "Come
37:12 Thus says the *L* GOD: "Behold,
37:13 shall know that I am the *L*,
37:14 you shall know that I, the *L*,
37:14 performed it," says the *L*.
37:15 Again the word of the *L* came
37:19 Thus says the *L* GOD: "Surely I
37:21 Thus says the *L* GOD: "Surely I
37:28 also will know that I, the *L*,
38: 1 Now the word of the *L* came to
38: 3 Thus says the *L* GOD: "Behold,
38:10 Thus says the *L* GOD: "On that
38:14 Thus says the *L* GOD: "On that
38:17 Thus says the *L* GOD: "Are you
38:18 says the *L* GOD, "that My
38:21 says the *L* GOD. "Every
38:23 shall know that I am the *L*.
39: 1 Thus says the *L* GOD: "Behold,
39: 5 spoken," says the *L* GOD.
39: 6 shall know that I am the *L*.
39: 7 shall know that I am the *L*,
39: 8 says the *L* GOD. "This is
39:10 them," says the *L* GOD.
39:13 glorified," says the *L* GOD.
39:17 thus says the *L* GOD, 'Speak to
39:20 of war," says the *L* GOD.
39:22 shall know that I am the *L*
39:25 Therefore thus says the *L* GOD:
39:28 shall know that I am the *L*
39:29 of Israel,' says the *L* GOD."
40: 1 same day the hand of the *L*
40:46 who come near the *L* to
41:22 table that is before the *L*.
42:13 the priests who approach the *L*
43: 4 And the glory of the *L* came
43: 5 the glory of the *L* filled the
43:18 thus says the *L* GOD: 'These
43:19 to Me,' says the *L* GOD.
43:24 you offer them before the *L*,
43:24 as a burnt offering to the *L*.
43:27 accept you,' says the *L* GOD."
44: 2 And the *L* said to me, "This
44: 2 because the *L* God of Israel
44: 3 it to eat bread before the *L*;
44: 4 the glory of the *L* filled the
44: 4 filled the house of the *L*;
44: 5 And the *L* said to me, "Son of
44: 5 of the house of the *L* and all
44: 6 Thus says the *L* GOD: "O house
44: 9 Thus says the *L* GOD: "No
44:12 says the *L* GOD, "that they
44:15 the blood," says the *L* GOD.
44:27 court," says the *L* GOD.
45: 1 set apart a district for the *L*,
45: 4 come near to minister to the *L*;
45: 9 Thus says the *L* GOD: "Enough,
45: 9 My people," says the *L* GOD.
45:15 for them," says the *L* GOD.
45:18 Thus says the *L* GOD: "In the
45:23 a burnt offering to the *L*,
46: 1 Thus says the *L* GOD: "The
46: 3 to this gateway before the *L*
46: 4 the prince offers to the *L* on
46: 9 of the land come before the *L*
46:12 peace offering to the *L*,
46:13 a burnt offering to the *L* of
46:14 to be made regularly to the *L*.
46:16 Thus says the *L* GOD: "If the
47:13 Thus says the *L* GOD: "These
47:23 inheritance," says the *L* GOD.
48: 9 you shall set apart for the *L*
48:10 The sanctuary of the *L* shall
48:14 for it is holy to the *L*.
48:29 portions," says the *L* GOD.
48:35 THE *L* IS THERE."
Dan 1: 2 And the *L* gave Jehoiakim king of
1:10 I fear my *l* the king, who has
2:10 therefore no king, *l*,
2:47 the *L* of kings, and a revealer
4:19 answered and said, "My *l*,
4:24 which has come upon my *l* the
5:23 yourself up against the *L* of
9: 2 by the word of the *L* through
9: 3 I set my face toward the *L* God
9: 4 And I prayed to the *L* my God,
9: 4 confession, and said, "O *L*,
9: 7 'O *L*, righteousness belongs
9: 8 'O *L*, to us belongs shame
9: 9 To the *L* our God belong mercy
9:10 not obeyed the voice of the *L*
9:13 made our prayer before the *L*
9:14 Therefore the *L* has kept the
9:14 for the *L* our God is
9:15 O *L* our God, who brought Your
9:16 O *L*, according to all Your
9:19 'O *L*, hear! O Lord,
9:19 "O Lord, hear! O *L*,
9:19 hear! O Lord, forgive! O *L*,
9:20 my supplication before the *L*
10:16 him who stood before me, "My *l*,
10:17 how can this servant of my *l*
10:17 of my lord talk with you, my *l*?
10:19 Let my *l* speak, for you have
12: 8 understand. Then I said, "My *l*,
Hos 1: 1 The word of the *L* that came to
1: 2 When the *L* began to speak by
1: 2 the *L* said to Hosea: "Go,
1: 2 By departing from the *L*.
1: 4 Then the *L* said to him:

L

1: 7 Will save them by the *L* their
2:13 Me she forgot," says the *L*.
2:16 be, in that day," Says the *L*,
2:20 And you shall know the *L*.
2:21 I will answer," says the *L*;
3: 1 Then the *L* said to me, "Go
3: 1 just like the love of the *L*
3: 5 shall return and seek the *L*
3: 5 They shall fear the *L* and His
4: 1 Hear the word of the *L*,
4: 1 For the *L* brings a charge
4:10 they have ceased obeying the *L*.
4:15 saying, 'As the *L* lives'—
4:16 Now the *L* will let them
5: 4 And they do not know the *L*.
5: 6 They shall go to seek the *L*,
5: 7 dealt treacherously with the *L*,
6: 1 and let us return to the *L*;
6: 3 pursue the knowledge of the *L*.
7:10 they do not return to the *L*
8: 1 against the house of the *L*,
8:13 But the *L* does not accept
9: 4 offer wine offerings to the *L*,
9: 4 come into the house of the *L*.
9: 5 the day of the feast of the *L*?
9:14 Give them, O *L*—What will You
10: 3 Because we did not fear the *L*.
10:12 it is time to seek the *L*,
11:10 "They shall walk after the *L*.
11:11 in their houses," Says the *L*.
12: 2 The *L* also brings a charge
12: 5 the *L* God of hosts. The LORD
12: 5 The *L* is His memorable name.
12: 9 But I am the *L* your God,
12:13 By a prophet the *L* brought
12:14 Therefore his *L* will leave the
13: 4 Yet I am the *L* your God
13:15 The wind of the *L* shall come
14: 1 return to the *L* your God,
14: 2 with you, And return to the *L*.
14: 9 For the ways of the *L* are
Joel 1: 1 The word of the *L* that came to
1: 9 off from the house of the *L*;
1: 9 mourn, who minister to the *L*.
1:14 Into the house of the *L* your
1:14 God, And cry out to the *L*.
1:15 the day! For the day of the *L*
1:19 O *L*, to You I cry out;
2: 1 For the day of the *L* is
2:11 The *L* gives voice before His
2:11 For the day of the *L* is
2:12 therefore," says the *L*,
2:13 Return to the *L* your God,
2:14 a drink offering For the *L*
2:17 priests, who minister to the *L*,
2:17 say, "Spare Your people, O *L*,
2:18 Then the *L* will be zealous
2:19 The *L* will answer and say to
2:21 For the *L* has done marvelous
2:23 And rejoice in the *L* your
2:26 And praise the name of the *L*
2:27 I am the *L* your God
2:31 great and awesome day of the *L*.
2:32 calls on the name of the *L*
2:32 As the *L* has said, Among the
2:32 Among the remnant whom the *L*
3: 8 For the *L* has spoken."
3:11 ones to go down there, O *L*.
3:14 For the day of the *L* is
3:16 The *L* also will roar from
3:16 But the *L* will be a shelter
3:17 shall know that I am the *L*
3:18 flow from the house of the *L*
3:21 For the *L* dwells in Zion."
Am 1: 2 'The *L* roars from Zion,
1: 3 Thus says the *L*: "For three
1: 5 captive to Kir," Says the *L*.
1: 6 Thus says the *L*: "For three
1: 8 perish," Says the *L* GOD.
1: 9 Thus says the *L*: "For three
1:11 Thus says the *L*: "For three
1:13 Thus says the *L*: "For three
1:15 together," Says the *L*.
2: 1 Thus says the *L*: "For three
2: 3 with him," Says the *L*.
2: 4 Thus says the *L*: "For three
2: 4 have despised the law of the *L*,
2: 6 Thus says the *L*: "For three
2:11 of Israel?" Says the *L*.
2:16 in that day," Says the *L*.
3: 1 Hear this word that the *L* has
3: 6 will not the *L* have done it?
3: 7 Surely the *L* GOD does nothing,
3: 8 The *L* GOD has spoken!
3:10 know to do right,' Says the *L*,
3:11 Therefore thus says the *L* GOD:
3:12 Thus says the *L*: "As a
3:13 Says the *L* GOD, the God of
3:15 have an end," Says the *L*.
4: 2 The *L* GOD has sworn by His
4: 3 into Harmon," Says the *L*.
4: 5 of Israel!" Says the *L* GOD.
4: 6 returned to Me," Says the *L*.
4: 8 returned to Me," Says the *L*.
4: 9 returned to Me," Says the *L*.
4:10 returned to Me," Says the *L*.
4:11 returned to Me," Says the *L*.
4:13 The *L* God of hosts is His
5: 3 For thus says the *L* GOD:
5: 4 For thus says the *L* to the
5: 6 Seek the *L* and live, Lest He
5: 8 The *L* is His name.
5:14 So the *L* God of hosts will be
5:15 It may be that the *L* God of
5:16 Therefore the *L* God of hosts,
5:16 the LORD God of hosts, the *L*,
5:17 through you," Says the *L*.
5:18 who desire the day of the *L*!
5:18 good is the day of the *L* to
5:20 Is not the day of the *L*
5:27 beyond Damascus," Says the *L*,
6: 8 The *L* GOD has sworn by
6: 8 The *L* God of hosts says: "I
6:10 not mention the name of the *L*.
6:11 the *L* gives a command: He
6:14 Says the *L* God of hosts;
7: 1 Thus the *L* GOD showed me:
7: 2 'O *L* GOD, forgive, I pray!
7: 3 So the *L* relented concerning
7: 3 shall not be," said the *L*.
7: 4 Thus the *L* GOD showed me:
7: 4 the *L* GOD called for conflict
7: 5 'O *L* GOD, cease, I pray!
7: 6 So the *L* relented concerning
7: 6 not be," said the *L* GOD.
7: 7 the *L* stood on a wall made
7: 8 And the *L* said to me, "Amos,
7: 8 Then the *L* said: "Behold,
7:15 Then the *L* took me as I
7:15 And the *L* said to me, 'Go,
7:16 hear the word of the *L*:
7:17 "Therefore thus says the *L*:
8: 1 Thus the *L* GOD showed me:
8: 2 Then the *L* said to me:
8: 3 Says the *L* GOD—"MANY dead
8: 7 The *L* has sworn by the pride
8: 9 says the *L* GOD, "That I
8:11 says the *L* GOD, "That I
8:11 of hearing the words of the *L*.
8:12 fro, seeking the word of the *L*,
9: 1 I saw the *L* standing by the
9: 5 The *L* GOD of hosts, He who
9: 6 The *L* is His name.
9: 7 of Israel?" says the *L*.
9: 8 the eyes of the *L* GOD are on
9: 8 house of Jacob," Says the *L*.
9:12 Says the *L* who does this
9:13 days are coming," says the *L*,
9:15 Says the *L* your God.
Ob 1 Thus says the *L* GOD concerning
1 have heard a report from the *L*,
4 bring you down," says the *L*.
8 not in that day," says the *L*,
15 For the day of the *L* upon all
18 For the *L* has spoken.
Jon 1: 1 Now the word of the *L* came to
1: 3 from the presence of the *L*.
1: 3 from the presence of the *L*.
1: 4 But the *L* sent out a great
1: 9 am a Hebrew; and I fear the *L*,
1:10 from the presence of the *L*,
1:14 they cried out to the *L* and
1:14 LORD and said, "We pray, O *L*,
1:14 innocent blood; for You, O *L*,
1:16 Then the men feared the *L*
1:16 offered a sacrifice to the *L*
1:17 Now the *L* had prepared a great
2: 1 Then Jonah prayed to the *L* his
2: 2 I cried out to the *L* because of
2: 6 up my life from the pit, O *L*,
2: 7 within me, I remembered the *L*;
2: 9 Salvation is of the *L*."
2:10 So the *L* spoke to the fish,
3: 1 Now the word of the *L* came to
3: 3 according to the word of the *L*.
4: 2 So he prayed to the *L*,
4: 2 the LORD, and said, "Ah, *L*,
4: 3 'Therefore now, O *L*, please
4: 4 Then the *L* said, "Is it
4: 6 And the *L* God prepared a plant
4:10 But the *L* said, "You have had
Mic 1: 1 The word of the *L* that came to
1: 2 all that is in it! Let the *L*
1: 2 The *L* from His holy temple.
1: 3 the *L* is coming out of His
1:12 disaster came down from the *L*
2: 3 Therefore thus says the *L*:
2: 5 In the assembly of the *L*.
2: 7 Is the Spirit of the *L*
2:13 With the *L* at their head."
3: 4 Then they will cry to the *L*,
3: 5 Thus says the *L* concerning
3: 8 power by the Spirit of the *L*,
3:11 Yet they lean on the *L*,
3:11 Is not the *L* among us? No harm
4: 2 go up to the mountain of the *L*,
4: 2 And the word of the *L* from
4: 4 For the mouth of the *L* of
4: 5 walk in the name of the *L* our
4: 6 "In that day," says the *L*,
4: 7 So the *L* will reign over them
4:10 There the *L* will redeem you
4:12 not know the thoughts of the *L*,
4:13 consecrate their gain to the *L*,
4:13 And their substance to the *L*
5: 4 In the strength of the *L*,
5: 4 majesty of the name of the *L*
5: 7 peoples, Like dew from the *L*,
5:10 be in that day," says the *L*,
6: 1 Hear now what the *L* says:
6: 2 For the *L* has a complaint
6: 5 the righteousness of the *L*.
6: 6 what shall I come before the *L*,
6: 7 Will the *L* be pleased with
6: 8 And what does the *L* require
7: 7 I will look to the *L*;
7: 8 The *L* will be a light to
7: 9 bear the indignation of the *L*,
7:10 'Where is the *L* your God?"
7:17 shall be afraid of the *L* our
Nah 1: 2 and the *L* avenges; The LORD
1: 2 The *L* avenges and is
1: 2 The *L* will take vengeance on
1: 3 The *L* is slow to anger and
1: 3 The *L* has His way In the
1: 7 The *L* is good, A stronghold
1: 9 do you conspire against the *L*?
1:11 Who plots evil against the *L*,
1:12 Thus says the *L*: "Though
1:14 The *L* has given a command
2: 2 For the *L* will restore the
2:13 says the *L* of hosts, "I
3: 5 says the *L* of hosts; "I
Hab 1: 2 *L*, how long shall I cry,
1:12 O *L* my God, my Holy One? We
1:12 We shall not die. O *L*,
2: 2 Then the *L* answered me and
2:13 is it not of the *L* of hosts
2:14 of the glory of the *L*,
2:20 But the *L* is in His holy
3: 2 O *L*, I have heard your
3: 2 speech and was afraid; O *L*,
3: 8 O *L*, were You displeased
3:18 Yet I will rejoice in the *L*,
3:19 The *L* God is my strength;
Zeph 1: 1 The word of the *L* which came
1: 2 of the land," Says the *L*;
1: 3 of the land," Says the *L*.
1: 5 and swear oaths by the *L*,
1: 6 back from following the *L*,
1: 6 And have not sought the *L*,
1: 7 in the presence of the *L* GOD;
1: 7 For the day of the *L* is at
1: 7 For the *L* has prepared a
1:10 be on that day," says the *L*,
1:12 The *L* will not do good, Nor
1:14 The great day of the *L* is
1:14 noise of the day of the *L* is
1:17 they have sinned against the *L*;
2: 3 Seek the *L*, all you meek
2: 5 The word of the *L* is
2: 7 For the *L* their God will
2: 9 Says the *L* of hosts, the
2:10 Against the people of the *L*
2:11 The *L* will be awesome to
3: 2 She has not trusted in the *L*,
3: 5 The *L* is righteous in her
3: 8 wait for Me," says the *L*,
3: 9 may call on the name of the *L*,
3:12 trust in the name of the *L*.
3:15 The *L* has taken away your
3:15 The King of Israel, the *L*,
3:17 The *L* your God in your midst,
3:20 your eyes," Says the *L*.
Hag 1: 1 the word of the *L* came by
1: 2 Thus speaks the *L* of hosts,
1: 3 Then the word of the *L* came by
1: 5 thus says the *L* of hosts:
1: 7 Thus says the *L* of hosts:
1: 8 and be glorified," says the *L*.
1: 9 says the *L* of hosts.
1:12 obeyed the voice of the *L*
1:12 as the *L* their God had sent
1:12 feared the presence of the *L*.
1:13 "I am with you, says the *L*.
1:14 So the *L* stirred up the spirit
1:14 worked on the house of the *L*
2: 1 the word of the *L* came by
2: 4 Zerubbabel,' says the *L*;
2: 4 of the land,' says the *L*,
2: 4 says the *L* of hosts.
2: 6 For thus says the *L* of hosts:
2: 7 says the *L* of hosts.
2: 8 says the *L* of hosts.
2: 9 says the *L* of hosts. 'And in
2: 9 says the *L* of hosts."
2:10 the word of the *L* came by
2:11 Thus says the *L* of hosts: 'Now,
2:14 nation before Me,' says the *L*,
2:15 stone in the temple of the *L*—
2:17 not turn to Me,' says the *L*.
2:20 And again the word of the *L*
2:23 says the *L* of hosts, 'I will
2:23 son of Shealtiel,' says the *L*,
2:23 says the *L* of hosts."
Zech 1: 1 the word of the *L* came to
1: 2 The *L* has been very angry with
1: 3 Thus says the *L* of hosts:
1: 3 says the *L* of hosts, "and I
1: 3 says the *L* of hosts.
1: 4 Thus says the *L* of hosts:
1: 4 hear nor heed Me," says the *L*.
1: 6 Just as the *L* of hosts
1: 7 the word of the *L* came to
1: 9 Then I said, "My *l*,
1:10 are the ones whom the *L*
1:11 answered the Angel of the *L*,
1:12 Then the Angel of the *L*
1:12 O *L* of hosts, how long will You
1:13 And the *L* answered the angel
1:14 Thus says the *L* of hosts: "I
1:16 'Therefore thus says the *L*:
1:16 says the *L* of hosts, "And
1:17 Thus says the *L* of hosts:
1:17 The *L* will again comfort
1:20 Then the *L* showed me four

2: 5 'For I,' says the *L*,
2: 6 of the north," says the *L*;
2: 6 winds of heaven," says the *L*.
2: 8 For thus says the *L* of hosts:
2: 9 Then you will know that the *L*
2:10 in your midst," says the *L*.
2:11 shall be joined to the *L* in
2:11 Then you will know that the *L*
2:12 And the *L* will take possession
2:13 all flesh, before the *L*,
3: 1 before the Angel of the *L*,
3: 2 And the *L* said to Satan, "The
3: 2 'The *L* rebuke you, Satan!
3: 2 Satan! The *L* who has chosen
3: 5 And the Angel of the *L* stood
3: 6 Then the Angel of the *L*
3: 7 Thus says the *L* of hosts: 'If
3: 9 Says the *L* of hosts, 'And I
3:10 says the *L* of hosts,
4: 4 saying, "What are these, my *l*?
4: 5 And I said, "No, my *l*."
4: 6 This is the word of the *L* to
4: 6 Says the *L* of hosts.
4: 8 Moreover the word of the *L*
4: 9 you will know That the *L* of
4:10 They are the eyes of the *L*,
4:13 And I said, "No, my *l*."
4:14 who stand beside the *L* of the
5: 4 says the *L* of hosts; "It
6: 4 'What are these, my *l*?"
6: 5 their station before the *L* of
6: 9 Then the word of the *L* came to
6:12 Thus says the *L* of hosts,
6:12 build the temple of the *L*;
6:13 build the temple of the *L*.
6:14 in the temple of the *L* for
6:15 and build the temple of the *L*.
6:15 you shall know that the *L* of
6:15 obey the voice of the *L* your
7: 1 pass that the word of the *L*
7: 2 of God, to pray before the *L*,
7: 3 were in the house of the *L*
7: 4 Then the word of the *L* of
7: 7 obeyed the words which the *L*
7: 8 Then the word of the *L* came to
7: 9 Thus says the *L* of hosts:
7:12 law and the words which the *L*
7:12 great wrath came from the *L*
7:13 says the *L* of hosts.
8: 1 Again the word of the *L* of
8: 2 Thus says the *L* of hosts: 'I
8: 3 'Thus says the *L*: 'I will
8: 3 The Mountain of the *L* of
8: 4 Thus says the *L* of hosts:
8: 6 Thus says the *L* of hosts: 'If
8: 6 Says the *L* of hosts.
8: 7 Thus says the *L* of hosts:
8: 9 Thus says the *L* of hosts:
8: 9 For the house of the *L* of
8:11 says the *L* of hosts.
8:14 For thus says the *L* of hosts:
8:14 Says the *L* of hosts, 'And I
8:17 that I hate,' Says the *L*.
8:18 Then the word of the *L* of
8:19 Thus says the *L* of hosts:
8:20 Thus says the *L* of hosts:
8:21 to go and pray before the *L*,
8:21 And seek the *L* of hosts.
8:22 Shall come to seek the *L* of
8:22 And to pray before the *L*.
8:23 Thus says the *L* of hosts: 'In
9: 1 burden of the word of the *L*
9: 1 of Israel Are on the *L*);
9: 4 the *L* will cast her out;
9:14 Then the *L* will be seen over
9:14 The *L* GOD will blow the
9:15 The *L* of hosts will defend
9:16 The *L* their God will save them
10: 1 Ask the *L* for rain In the
10: 1 The *L* will make flashing
10: 3 For the *L* of hosts will visit
10: 5 shall fight because the *L* is
10: 6 For I am the *L* their God,
10: 7 heart shall rejoice in the *L*.
10:12 will strengthen them in the *L*,
10:12 in His name," Says the *L*.
11: 4 Thus says the *L* my God, "Feed
11: 5 them say, 'Blessed be the *L*,
11: 6 of the land," says the *L*.
11:11 that it was the word of the *L*.
11:13 And the *L* said to me, "Throw
11:13 them into the house of the *L*
11:15 And the *L* said to me, "Next,
12: 1 burden of the word of the *L*
12: 1 Thus says the *L*,
12: 4 "In that day," says the *L*,
12: 5 are my strength in the *L* of
12: 7 The *L* will save the tents of
12: 8 In that day the *L* will defend
12: 8 like the Angel of the *L* before
13: 2 says the *L* of hosts, "that
13: 3 lies in the name of the *L*.
13: 7 Says the *L* of hosts.
13: 8 in all the land," Says the *L*,
13: 9 The *L* is my God.'"
14: 1 the day of the *L* is coming,
14: 3 Then the *L* will go forth
14: 5 Thus the *L* my God will come,
14: 7 day Which is known to the *L*—
14: 9 And the *L* shall be King over
14: 9 The *L* is one," And His name
14:12 be the plague with which the *L*
14:13 a great panic from the *L* will
14:16 the *L* of hosts, and to keep
14:17 the *L* of hosts, on them there
14:18 the plague with which the *L*
14:20 HOLINESS TO THE *L*" shall be
14:21 shall be holiness to the *L* of
14:21 in the house of the *L* of
Mal 1: 1 burden of the word of the *L*
1: 2 have loved you," says the *L*.
1: 2 Jacob's brother?" Says the *L*.
1: 4 Thus says the *L* of hosts:
1: 4 the people against whom the *L*
1: 5 The *L* is magnified beyond the
1: 6 Says the *L* of hosts To you
1: 7 The table of the *L* is
1: 8 Says the *L* of hosts.
1: 9 Says the *L* of hosts.
1:10 Says the *L* of hosts, "Nor
1:11 Says the *L* of hosts.
1:12 The table of the *L* is defiled;
1:13 Says the *L* of hosts.
1:13 from your hand?" Says the *L*.
1:14 But sacrifices to the *L* what
1:14 Says the *L* of hosts, "And
2: 2 Says the *L* of hosts, "I
2: 4 Says the *L* of hosts.
2: 7 he is the messenger of the *L*
2: 8 Says the *L* of hosts.
2:12 May the *L* cut off from the
2:12 brings an offering to the *L*
2:13 You cover the altar of the *L*
2:14 Because the *L* has been
2:16 For the *L* God of Israel says
2:16 Says the *L* of hosts.
2:17 You have wearied the *L* with
2:17 good in the sight of the *L*,
3: 1 the way before Me. And the *L*,
3: 1 Says the *L* of hosts.
3: 3 That they may offer to the *L*
3: 4 Will be pleasant to the *L*,
3: 5 Says the *L* of hosts.
3: 6 "For I am the *L*,
3: 7 Says the *L* of hosts.
3:10 Says the *L* of hosts, "If
3:11 Says the *L* of hosts;
3:12 Says the *L* of hosts.
3:13 against Me," Says the *L*,
3:14 as mourners Before the *L* of
3:16 Then those who feared the *L*
3:16 And the *L* listened and heard
3:16 For those who fear the *L* And
3:17 says the *L* of hosts, "On
4: 1 Says the *L* of hosts,
4: 3 Says the *L* of hosts.
4: 5 and dreadful day of the *L*.
Mt 1:20 an angel of the *L* appeared to
1:22 which was spoken by the *L*
1:24 did as the angel of the *L*
2:13 an angel of the *L* appeared to
2:15 which was spoken by the *L*
2:19 an angel of the *L* appeared in a
3: 3 the way of the *L*;
4: 7 shall not tempt the *L*
4:10 You shall worship the *L*
5:33 perform your oaths to the *L*.
7:21 everyone who says to Me, '*L*,
7:21 who says to Me, 'Lord, *L*,
7:22 will say to Me in that day, '*L*,
7:22 say to Me in that day, 'Lord, *L*,
8: 2 and worshiped Him, saying, "*L*,
8: 6 saying, "*L*, my servant is
8: 8 answered and said, "*L*,
8:21 His disciples said to Him, "*L*,
8:25 Him and awoke Him, saying, "*L*,
9:28 They said to Him, "Yes, *L*.
9:38 Therefore pray the *L* of the
11:25 *L* of heaven and earth, that You
12: 8 For the Son of Man is *L* even of
13:51 They said to Him, "Yes, *L*.
14:28 answered Him and said, "*L*,
14:30 sink he cried out, saying, "*L*,
15:22 saying, "Have mercy on me, O *L*,
15:25 and worshiped Him, saying, "*L*,
15:27 And she said, "Yes, *L*,
16:22 saying, "Far be it from You, *L*;
17: 4 answered and said to Jesus, "*L*,
17:15 '*L*, have mercy on my son,
18:21 Peter came to Him and said, "*L*,
20:25 the rulers of the Gentiles *l*
20:30 saying, "Have mercy on us, O *L*,
20:31 saying, "Have mercy on us, O *L*,
20:33 They said to Him, "*L*, that
21: 3 The *L* has need of them,' and
21: 9 in the name of the *L*!'
22:37 You shall love the *L* your
22:43 in the Spirit call Him '*L*,
22:44 The *L* said to my Lord,
22:44 'The LORD said to my *L*,
22:45 "If David then calls Him '*L*,
23:39 in the name of the *L*!'
24:42 do not know what hour your *L*
25:11 virgins came also, saying, '*L*,
25:11 came also, saying, 'Lord, *L*,
25:19 After a long time the *l* of those
25:20 five other talents, saying, '*L*,
25:21 His *l* said to him, 'Well done,
25:21 Enter into the joy of your *l*.
25:22 two talents came and said, '*L*,
25:23 His *l* said to him, 'Well done,
25:23 Enter into the joy of your *l*.
25:24 one talent came and said, '*L*,
25:26 But his *l* answered and said to
25:37 will answer Him, saying, '*L*,
25:44 will answer Him, saying, '*L*,
26:22 them began to say to Him, "*L*,
27:10 as the *L* directed me."
28: 2 for an angel of the *L* descended
28: 6 see the place where the *L* lay.
Mk 1: 3 the way of the *L*;
2:28 the Son of Man is also *L* of
5:19 them what great things the *L*
7:28 and said to Him, "Yes, *L*,
9:24 out and said with tears, "*L*,
10:42 rulers over the Gentiles *l* it
11: 3 The *L* has need of it,' and
11: 9 in the name of the *L*!'
11:10 comes in the name of the *L*!
12:29 the *L* our God, the LORD
12:29 LORD our God, the *L* is one.
12:30 you shall love the *L*
12:36 The *L* said to my Lord,
12:36 'The LORD said to my *L*,
12:37 David himself calls Him '*L*';
13:20 And unless the *L* had shortened
16:19 after the *L* had spoken to them,
16:20 the *L* working with them and
Lk 1: 6 and ordinances of the *L*
1: 9 went into the temple of the *L*.
1:11 Then an angel of the *L* appeared
1:15 be great in the sight of the *L*,
1:16 the children of Israel to the *L*
1:17 a people prepared for the *L*.
1:25 Thus the *L* has dealt with me, in
1:28 the *L* is with you; blessed
1:32 and the *L* God will give Him the
1:38 the maidservant of the *L*!
1:43 that the mother of my *L* should
1:45 which were told her from the *L*.
1:46 "My soul magnifies the *L*,
1:58 and relatives heard how the *L*
1:66 And the hand of the *L* was
1:68 Blessed is the *L* God of Israel,
1:76 go before the face of the *L* to
2: 9 an angel of the *L* stood before
2: 9 and the glory of the *L* shone
2:11 a Savior, who is Christ the *L*.
2:15 which the *L* has made known to
2:22 to present Him to the *L*
2:23 is written in the law of the *L*,
2:23 be called holy to the *L*'
2:24 is said in the law of the *L*,
2:29 '*L*, now You are letting
2:38 she gave thanks to the *L*,
2:39 according to the law of the *L*,
3: 4 the way of the *L*;
4: 8 You shall worship the *L*
4:12 shall not tempt the *L*
4:18 The Spirit of the *L* is
4:19 acceptable year of the *L*.
5: 8 for I am a sinful man, O *L*!"
5:12 and implored Him, saying, "*L*,
5:17 And the power of the *L* was
6: 5 The Son of Man is also *L* of the
6:46 "But why do you call Me '*L*,
6:46 why do you call Me 'Lord, *L*,
7: 6 to Him, saying to Him, "*L*,
7:13 When the *L* saw her, He had
7:31 And the *L* said, "To what then
9:54 John saw this, they said, "*L*,
9:57 that someone said to Him, "*L*,
9:59 "Follow Me." But he said, "*L*,
9:61 And another also said, "*L*,
10: 1 After these things the *L*
10: 2 therefore pray the *L* of the
10:17 returned with joy, saying, "*L*,
10:21 *L* of heaven and earth, that You
10:27 You shall love the *L* your
10:40 approached Him and said, "*L*,
11: 1 His disciples said to Him, "*L*,
11:39 Then the *L* said to him, "Now
12:41 Then Peter said to Him, "*L*,
12:42 And the *L* said, "Who then is
13:15 The *L* then answered him and
13:23 Then one said to Him, "*L*,
13:25 knock at the door, saying, '*L*,
13:25 at the door, saying, 'Lord, *L*,
13:35 in the name of the *L*!'
17: 5 And the apostles said to the *L*,
17: 6 So the *L* said, "If you have
17:37 and said to Him, "Where, *L*?
18: 6 Then the *L* said, "Hear what the
18:41 to do for you?" He said, "*L*,
19: 8 stood and said to the *L*,
19: 8 and said to the Lord, "Look, *L*,
19:31 Because the *L* has need of it.'
19:34 The *L* has need of him."
19:38 in the name of the *L*!'
20:37 when he called the *L* 'the God
20:42 The *L* said to my Lord,
20:42 'The LORD said to my *L*,
20:44 David calls Him '*L*';
22:31 And the *L* said, "Simon, Simon!
22:33 But he said to Him, "*L*,
22:38 So they said, "*L*, look, here
22:49 happen, they said to Him, "*L*,
22:61 And the *L* turned and looked at
22:61 remembered the word of the *L*,
23:42 Then he said to Jesus, "*L*,
24: 3 did not find the body of the *L*
24:34 The *L* is risen indeed, and has
Jn 1:23 the way of the *L*,
4: 1 when the *L* knew that the
6:23 they ate bread after the *L* had
6:34 Then they said to Him, "*L*,

6:68 Simon Peter answered Him, "*L*,
8:11 She said, "No one, *L*.
9:36 and said, "Who is He, *L*,
9:38 Then he said, "*L*, I believe!"
11: 2 that Mary who anointed the *L*
11: 3 sent to Him, saying, "*L*,
11:12 Then His disciples said, "*L*,
11:21 Then Martha said to Jesus, "*L*,
11:27 She said to Him, "Yes, *L*,
11:32 at His feet, saying to Him, "*L*,
11:34 They said to Him, "*L*, come
11:39 who was dead, said to Him, "*L*,
12:13 in the name of the *L*!'
12:38 which he spoke: "*L*,
12:38 has the arm of the *L*
13: 6 And Peter said to Him, "*L*,
13: 9 Simon Peter said to Him, "*L*,
13:13 "You call me Teacher and *L*,
13:14 your *L* and Teacher, have
13:25 breast, he said to Him, "*L*,
13:36 Simon Peter said to Him, "*L*,
13:37 Peter said to Him, "*L*,
14: 5 Thomas said to Him, "*L*,
14: 8 Philip said to Him, "*L*,
14:22 (not Iscariot) said to Him, "*L*,
20: 2 They have taken away the *L* out
20:13 they have taken away my *L*,
20:18 that she had seen the *L*,
20:20 were glad when they saw the *L*.
20:25 to him, "We have seen the *L*.
20:28 My *L* and my God!"
21: 7 It is the *L*!" Now when Simon
21: 7 Peter heard that it was the *L*,
21:12 that it was the *L*.
21:15 He said to Him, "Yes, *L*;
21:16 He said to Him, "Yes, *L*;
21:17 And he said to Him, "*L*,
21:20 at the supper, and said, "*L*,
21:21 him, said to Jesus, "But *L*,
Acts 1: 6 they asked Him, saying, "*L*,
1:21 us all the time that the *L*
1:24 prayed and said, "You, O *L*,
2:20 and awesome day of the *L*.
2:21 on the name of the *L*
2:25 I foresaw the *L* always
2:34 The *L* said to my Lord,
2:34 'The LORD said to my *L*,
2:36 both *L* and Christ."
2:39 as many as the *L* our God will
2:47 And the *L* added to the church
3:19 come from the presence of the *L*,
3:22 The *L* your God will raise
4:24 with one accord and said: "*L*,
4:26 together Against the *L*
4:29 'Now, *L*, look on their
4:33 to the resurrection of the *L*
5: 9 to test the Spirit of the *L*?
5:14 increasingly added to the *L*,
5:19 But at night an angel of the *L*
7:30 an Angel of the *L* appeared to
7:31 the voice of the *L* came to him,
7:33 Then the *L* said to him,
7:37 The *L* your God will raise
7:49 build for Me? says the *L*,
7:59 *L* Jesus, receive my spirit."
7:60 out with a loud voice, "*L*,
8:16 baptized in the name of the *L*
8:24 Pray to the *L* for me, that none
8:25 and preached the word of the *L*,
8:26 Now an angel of the *L* spoke to
8:39 the Spirit of the *L* caught
9: 1 against the disciples of the *L*,
9: 5 And he said, "Who are You, *L*?
9: 5 Then the *L* said, "I am
9: 6 and astonished, said, "*L*,
9: 6 Then the *L* said to him,
9:10 and to him the *L* said in a
9:10 And he said, "Here I am, *L*.
9:11 So the *L* said to him, "Arise
9:13 Then Ananias answered, "*L*,
9:15 But the *L* said to him, "Go, for
9:17 the *L* Jesus, who appeared to
9:27 to them how he had seen the *L*
9:29 boldly in the name of the *L*
9:31 walking in the fear of the *L*
9:35 saw him and turned to the *L*.
9:42 and many believed on the *L*.
10: 4 and said, "What is it, *l*?
10:14 *L*! For I have never eaten
10:36 He is *L* of all—
10:48 baptized in the name of the *L*.
11: 8 *L*! For nothing common or
11:16 I remembered the word of the *L*,
11:17 us when we believed on the *L*
11:20 preaching the *L* Jesus.
11:21 And the hand of the *L* was with
11:21 believed and turned to the *L*.
11:23 they should continue with the *L*.
11:24 many people were added to the *L*.
12: 7 an angel of the *L* stood by
12:11 I know for certain that the *L*
12:17 he declared to them how the *L*
12:23 immediately an angel of the *L*
13: 2 As they ministered to the *L* and
13:10 the straight ways of the *L*?
13:11 the hand of the *L* is upon you,
13:12 at the teaching of the *L*.
13:47 For so the *L* has commanded us:
13:48 and glorified the word of the *L*.
13:49 And the word of the *L* was being
14: 3 time, speaking boldly in the *L*,
14:23 they commended them to the *L* in
15:11 that through the grace of the *L*
15:17 mankind may seek the *L*,
15:17 Says the *L* who does all
15:26 lives for the name of our *L*
15:35 and preaching the word of the *L*,
15:36 have preached the word of the *L*,
16:10 concluding that the *L* had
16:14 The *L* opened her heart to heed
16:15 me to be faithful to the *L*,
16:31 Believe on the *L* Jesus Christ,
16:32 they spoke the word of the *L*
17:24 since He is *L* of heaven and
17:27 that they should seek the *L*,
18: 8 believed on the *L* with all his
18: 9 Now the *L* spoke to Paul in the
18:25 instructed in the way of the *L*;
18:25 accurately the things of the *L*,
19: 5 baptized in the name of the *L*
19:10 in Asia heard the word of the *L*
19:13 to call the name of the *L*
19:17 and the name of the *L* Jesus was
19:20 So the word of the *L* grew
20:19 serving the *L* with all humility,
20:21 God and faith toward our *L*
20:24 which I received from the *L*
20:35 And remember the words of the *L*
21:13 for the name of the *L* Jesus.
21:14 The will of the *L* be done."
21:20 heard it, they glorified the *L*.
22: 8 I answered, 'Who are You, *L*?
22:10 I said, 'What shall I do, *L*?
22:10 And the *L* said to me, 'Arise
22:16 calling on the name of the *L*.
22:19 'So I said, '*L*, they know
23:11 But the following night the *L*
25:26 certain to write to my *l*
26:15 "So I said, 'Who are You, *L*?
28:31 the things which concern the *L*
Rom 1: 3 His Son Jesus Christ our *L*,
1: 7 from God our Father and the *L*
4: 8 the man to whom the *L*
4:24 Him who raised up Jesus our *L*
5: 1 peace with God through our *L*
5:11 rejoice in God through our *L*
5:21 life through Jesus Christ our *L*.
6:11 to God in Christ Jesus our *L*.
6:23 life in Christ Jesus our *L*.
7:25 —through Jesus Christ our *L*!
8:39 which is in Christ Jesus our *L*.
9:28 Because the *L* will make
9:29 Unless the *L* of Sabaoth
10: 9 confess with your mouth the *L*
10:12 for the same *L* over all is rich
10:13 on the name of the *L*
10:16 For Isaiah says, "*L*,
11: 3 *L*, they have killed Your
11:34 known the mind of the *L*?
12:11 in spirit, serving the *L*;
12:19 I will repay," says the *L*.
13:14 But put on the *L* Jesus Christ,
14: 6 the day, observes it to the *L*;
14: 6 to the *L* he does not observe
14: 6 He who eats, eats to the *L*,
14: 6 to the *L* he does not eat, and
14: 8 if we live, we live to the *L*;
14: 8 and if we die, we die to the *L*.
14: 9 that He might be *L* of both the
14:11 I live, says the *L*,
14:14 know and am convinced by the *L*
15: 6 the God and Father of our *L*
15:11 And again: "Praise the *L*,
15:30 through the *L* Jesus Christ, and
16: 2 you may receive her in the *L*
16: 8 Amplias, my beloved in the *L*.
16:11 of Narcissus who are in the *L*.
16:12 who have labored in the *L*.
16:12 who labored much in the *L*.
16:13 Greet Rufus, chosen in the *L*,
16:18 who are such do not serve our *L*
16:20 The grace of our *L* Jesus Christ
16:22 epistle, greet you in the *L*.
16:24 The grace of our *L* Jesus Christ
1 Cor 1: 2 the name of Jesus Christ our *L*,
1: 3 from God our Father and the *L*
1: 7 for the revelation of our *L*
1: 8 blameless in the day of our *L*
1: 9 of His Son, Jesus Christ our *L*.
1:10 by the name of our *L* Jesus
1:31 let him glory in the *L*.
2: 8 would not have crucified the *L*
2:16 known the mind of the *L*
3: 5 as the *L* gave to each one?
3:20 The *L* knows the thoughts
4: 4 but He who judges me is the *L*.
4: 5 until the *L* comes, who will
4:17 and faithful son in the *L*,
4:19 if the *L* wills, and I will
5: 4 In the name of our *L* Jesus
5: 4 with the power of our *L* Jesus
5: 5 be saved in the day of the *L*
6:11 justified in the name of the *L*
6:13 sexual immorality but for the *L*,
6:13 and the *L* for the body.
6:14 And God both raised up the *L* and
6:17 But he who is joined to the *L* is
7:10 I command, yet not I but the *L*:
7:12 But to the rest I, not the *L*,
7:17 as the *L* has called each one,
7:22 For he who is called in the *L*
7:25 have no commandment from the *L*;
7:25 judgment as one whom the *L* in
7:32 cares for the things of the *L*—
7:32 Lord—how he may please the *L*.
7:34 cares about the things of the *L*,
7:35 and that you may serve the *L*
7:39 whom she wishes, only in the *L*.
8: 6 and one *L* Jesus Christ, through
9: 1 I not seen Jesus Christ our *L*?
9: 1 Are you not my work in the *L*?
9: 2 seal of my apostleship in the *L*.
9: 5 apostles, the brothers of the *L*,
9:14 Even so the *L* has commanded that
10:21 cannot drink the cup of the *L*
10:22 Or do we provoke the *L* to
11:11 independent of man, in the *L*.
11:23 For I received from the *L* that
11:23 that the *L* Jesus on the same
11:27 or drinks this cup of the *L*
11:27 of the body and blood of the *L*.
11:32 we are chastened by the *L*,
12: 3 no one can say that Jesus is *L*
12: 5 of ministries, but the same *L*.
14:21 not hear Me," says the *L*.
14:37 are the commandments of the *L*.
15:31 I have in Christ Jesus our *L*,
15:47 the second Man is the *L* from
15:57 us the victory through our *L*
15:58 abounding in the work of the *L*,
15:58 labor is not in vain in the *L*.
16: 7 with you, if the *L* permits.
16:10 for he does the work of the *L*,
16:19 greet you heartily in the *L*,
16:22 If anyone does not love the *L*
16:22 let him be accursed. O *L*,
16:23 The grace of our *L* Jesus Christ
2 Cor 1: 2 from God our Father and the *L*
1: 3 be the God and Father of our *L*
1:14 in the day of the *L* Jesus.
2:12 door was opened to me by the *L*,
3:16 when one turns to the *L*,
3:17 Now the *L* is the Spirit;
3:17 and where the Spirit of the *L*
3:18 in a mirror the glory of the *L*,
3:18 just as by the Spirit of the *L*.
4: 5 but Christ Jesus the *L*,
4:10 in the body the dying of the *L*
4:14 that He who raised up the *L*
5: 6 body we are absent from the *L*.
5: 8 and to be present with the *L*.
5:11 therefore, the terror of the *L*,
6:17 be separate, says the *L*.
6:18 Says the *L* Almighty."
8: 5 first gave themselves to the *L*,
8: 9 For you know the grace of our *L*
8:19 by us to the glory of the *L*
8:21 not only in the sight of the *L*,
10: 8 which the *L* gave us for
10:17 let him glory in the *L*.
10:18 but whom the *L* commends.
11:17 I speak not according to the *L*,
11:31 The God and Father of our *L*
12: 1 and revelations of the *L*:
12: 8 this thing I pleaded with the *L*
13:10 to the authority which the *L*
13:14 The grace of the *L* Jesus Christ,
Gal 1: 3 from God the Father and our *L*
5:10 confidence in you, in the *L*,
6:14 except in the cross of our *L*
6:17 in my body the marks of the *L*
6:18 the grace of our *L* Jesus Christ
Eph 1: 2 from God our Father and the *L*
1: 3 be the God and Father of our *L*
1:15 I heard of your faith in the *L*
1:17 that the God of our *L* Jesus
2:21 into a holy temple in the *L*,
3:11 in Christ Jesus our *L*,
3:14 my knees to the Father of our *L*
4: 1 the prisoner of the *L*,
4: 5 one *L*, one faith, one baptism;
4:17 therefore, and testify in the *L*,
5: 8 now you are light in the *L*.
5:10 out what is acceptable to the *L*.
5:17 what the will of the *L* is.
5:19 melody in your heart to the *L*,
5:20 the Father in the name of our *L*
5:22 your own husbands, as to the *L*.
5:29 just as the *L* does the church.
6: 1 obey your parents in the *L*,
6: 4 and admonition of the *L*.
6: 7 doing service, as to the *L*,
6: 8 receive the same from the *L*,
6:10 be strong in the *L* and in the
6:21 and faithful minister in the *L*,
6:23 from God the Father and the *L*
6:24 with all those who love our *L*
Phil 1: 2 from God our Father and the *L*
1:14 most of the brethren in the *L*,
2:11 confess that Jesus Christ is *L*,
2:19 But I trust in the *L* Jesus to
2:24 But I trust in the *L* that I
2:29 Receive him therefore in the *L*
3: 1 my brethren, rejoice in the *L*.
3: 8 knowledge of Christ Jesus my *L*,
3:20 Savior, the *L* Jesus Christ,
4: 1 crown, so stand fast in the *L*,
4: 2 to be of the same mind in the *L*.
4: 4 Rejoice in the *L* always. Again I
4: 5 to all men. The *L* is at hand.
4:10 But I rejoiced in the *L* greatly
4:23 The grace of our *L* Jesus Christ
Col 1: 2 from God our Father and the *L*
1: 3 to the God and Father of our *L*
1:10 you may walk worthy of the *L*,
2: 6 received Christ Jesus the *L*,

3:16 grace in your hearts to the *L*.
3:17 do all in the name of the *L*
3:18 as is fitting in the *L*.
3:20 this is well pleasing to the *L*.
3:23 as to the *L* and not to men,
3:24 knowing that from the *L* you will
3:24 for you serve the *L* Christ.
4: 7 and fellow servant in the *L*,
4:17 you have received in the *L*,
1 Th 1: 1 in God the Father and the *L*
1: 1 from God our Father and the *L*
1: 3 and patience of hope in our *L*
1: 6 followers of us and of the *L*,
1: 8 For from you the word of the *L*
2:15 who killed both the *L* Jesus and
2:19 you in the presence of our *L*
3: 8 if you stand fast in the *L*.
3:11 and our *L* Jesus Christ, direct
3:12 And may the *L* make you increase
3:13 Father at the coming of our *L*
4: 1 we urge and exhort in the *L*
4: 2 we gave you through the *L*
4: 6 because the *L* is the avenger
4:15 say to you by the word of the *L*,
4:15 until the coming of the *L* will
4:16 For the *L* Himself will descend
4:17 in the clouds to meet the *L* in
4:17 we shall always be with the *L*.
5: 2 that the day of the *L* so comes
5: 9 obtain salvation through our *L*
5:12 and are over you in the *L* and
5:23 at the coming of our *L* Jesus
5:27 I charge you by the *L* that this
5:28 The grace of our *L* Jesus Christ
2 Th 1: 1 in God our Father and the *L*
1: 2 from God our Father and the *L*
1: 7 rest with us when the *L* Jesus
1: 8 do not obey the gospel of our *L*
1: 9 from the presence of the *L* and
1:12 that the name of our *L* Jesus
1:12 the grace of our God and the *L*
2: 1 concerning the coming of our *L*
2: 8 whom the *L* will consume with
2:13 you, brethren beloved by the *L*,
2:14 of the glory of our *L* Jesus
2:16 Now may our *L* Jesus Christ
3: 1 that the word of the *L* may run
3: 3 But the *L* is faithful, who will
3: 4 And we have confidence in the *L*
3: 5 Now may the *L* direct your hearts
3: 6 in the name of our *L* Jesus
3:12 and exhort through our *L* Jesus
3:16 Now may the *L* of peace Himself
3:16 The *L* be with you all.
3:18 The grace of our *L* Jesus Christ
1 Tim 1: 1 of God our Savior and the *L*
1: 2 Father and Jesus Christ our *L*.
1:12 I thank Christ Jesus our *L* who
1:14 And the grace of our *L* was
5:21 you before God and the *L*
6: 3 even the words of our *L* Jesus
6:14 blameless until our *L* Jesus
6:15 the King of kings and *L* of
2 Tim 1: 2 Father and Christ Jesus our *L*.
1: 8 of the testimony of our *L*,
1:16 The *L* grant mercy to the
1:18 The *L* grant to him that he may
1:18 he may find mercy from the *L*
2: 7 and may the *L* give you
2:14 charging them before the *L* not
2:19 The *L* knows those who are His,"
2:22 with those who call on the *L*
2:24 And a servant of the *L* must not
3:11 And out of them all the *L*
4: 1 therefore before God and the *L*
4: 8 of righteousness, which the *L*,
4:14 May the *L* repay him according
4:17 But the *L* stood with me and
4:18 And the *L* will deliver me from
4:22 The *L* Jesus Christ be with your
Titus 1: 4 from God the Father and the *L*
Phm 1: 3 from God our Father and the *L*
1: 5 which you have toward the *L*
1:16 both in the flesh and in the *L*.
1:20 me have joy from you in the *L*;
1:20 Lord; refresh my heart in the *L*.
1:25 The grace of our *L* Jesus Christ
Heb 1:10 And: "You, *L*, in the
2: 3 began to be spoken by the *L*,
7:14 For it is evident that our *L*
7:21 The *L* has sworn And will
8: 2 the true tabernacle which the *L*
8: 8 are coming, says the *L*,
8: 9 them, says the *L*.
8:10 those days, says the *L*:
8:11 saying, 'Know the *L*,
10:16 those days, says the *L*:
10:30 I will repay," says the *L*.
10:30 The *L* will judge His
12: 5 the chastening of the *L*,
12: 6 For whom the *L* loves He
12:14 which no one will see the *L*:
13: 6 The *L* is my helper; I
13:20 of peace who brought up our *L*
Jas 1: 1 of God and of the *L* Jesus
1: 7 receive anything from the *L*;
1:12 the crown of life which the *L*
2: 1 do not hold the faith of our *L*
2: 1 the *L* of glory, with
4:10 in the sight of the *L*,
4:15 If the *L* wills, we shall live
5: 4 have reached the ears of the *L*
5: 7 until the coming of the *L*.
5: 8 for the coming of the *L* is at
5:10 who spoke in the name of the *L*,
5:11 the end intended by the *L*—
5:11 that the *L* is very compassionate
5:14 with oil in the name of the *L*.
5:15 and the *L* will raise him up.
1 Pe 1: 3 be the God and Father of our *L*
1:25 But the word of the *L*
2: 3 you have tasted that the *L* is
3: 6 obeyed Abraham, calling him *l*,
3:12 For the eyes of the *L*
3:12 But the face of the *L*
3:15 But sanctify the *L* God in your
2 Pe 1: 2 of God and of Jesus our *L*,
1: 8 in the knowledge of our *L*
1:11 everlasting kingdom of our *L*
1:14 just as our *L* Jesus Christ
1:16 the power and coming of our *L*
2: 1 even denying the *L* who bought
2: 9 then the *L* knows how to deliver
2:11 against them before the *L*.
2:20 through the knowledge of the *L*
3: 2 the apostles of the *L* and
3: 8 that with the *L* one day is as
3: 9 The *L* is not slack concerning
3:10 But the day of the *L* will come
3:15 the longsuffering of our *L* is
3:18 grace and knowledge of our *L*
2 Jn 3 God the Father and from the *L*
Jude 4 lewdness and deny the only *L*
4 the only Lord God and our *L*
5 you once knew this, that the *L*,
9 but said, "The *L* rebuke you!"
14 the *L* comes with ten thousands
17 by the apostles of our *L* Jesus
21 looking for the mercy of our *L*
Rev 1: 8 and the End," says the *L*,
4: 8 *L* God Almighty, Who was and
4:11 "You are worthy, O *L*,
6:10 voice, saying, "How long, O *L*,
11: 8 where also our *L* was crucified.
11:15 become the kingdoms of our *L*
11:17 O *L* God Almighty, The One who
14:13 are the dead who die in the *L*
15: 3 *L* God Almighty! Just and true
15: 4 Who shall not fear You, O *L*,
16: 5 "You are righteous, O *L*,
16: 7 *L* God Almighty, true and
17:14 for He is *L* of lords and King
18: 8 for strong is the *L* God who
19: 1 and power belong to the *L* our
19: 6 Alleluia! For the *L* God
19:16 KING OF KINGS AND *L* OF
21:22 for the *L* God Almighty and the
22: 5 for the *L* God gives them light.
22: 6 And the *L* God of the holy
22:20 Even so, come, *L* Jesus!
22:21 The grace of our *L* Jesus Christ

LORD'S (139/134) LORD

Gen 40: 7 him in the custody of his *l*
44: 8 silver or gold from your *l*
44: 9 and we also will be my *l*
44:16 my *l* slaves, both we and he
44:18 servant speak a word in my *l*
Ex 9:29 know that the earth is the *L*.
12:11 It is the *L* Passover.
13: 9 that the *L* law may be in your
13:12 the males shall be the *L*.
32:26 Whoever is on the *L* side—come
35:21 and they brought the *L*
35:24 silver or bronze brought the *L*
Lev 3:16 aroma; all the fat is the *L*.
16: 9 bring the goat on which the *L*
23: 5 month at twilight is the *L*
27:26 which should be the *L*
27:26 an ox or sheep, it is the *L*.
27:30 fruit of the tree, is the *L*.
Num 9:10 he may still keep the *L*
9:14 and would keep the *L* Passover,
11:23 Has the *L* arm been shortened?
11:29 that all the *L* people were
18:28 and you shall give the *L* heave
31:37 and the *L* tribute of the sheep
31:38 of which the *L* tribute was
31:39 of which the *L* tribute was
31:40 of which the *L* tribute was
31:41 the tribute which was the *L*
32:10 So the *L* anger was aroused on
32:13 So the *L* anger was aroused
Deut 11:17 lest the *L* anger be aroused
15: 2 because it is called the *L*
32: 9 For the *L* portion is His
Josh 1:15 which Moses the *L* servant gave
5:15 Then the Commander of the *L*
22:19 where the *L* tabernacle stands,
Judg 11:31 Ammon, shall surely be the *L*,
1 Sam 2: 8 of the earth are the *L*,
2:24 You make the *L* people
14: 3 the *L* priest in Shiloh, was
16: 6 Surely the *L* anointed is
17:47 for the battle is the *L*,
18:17 and fight the *L* battles."
22:21 that Saul had killed the *L*
24: 6 the *L* anointed, to stretch out
24:10 for he is the *L* anointed.'
26: 9 out his hand against the *L*
26:11 out my hand against the *L*
26:16 the *L* anointed. And now see
26:23 out my hand against the *L*
2 Sam 1:14 your hand to destroy the *L*
1:16 I have killed the *L* anointed.'
6: 8 became angry because of the *L*
19:21 because he cursed the *L*
20: 6 Take your *l* servants and pursue
21: 7 because of the *L* oath that
1 Ki 18:13 I hid one hundred men of the *L*
2 Ki 11:17 that they should be the *L*
13:17 The arrow of the *L* deliverance
1 Chr 13:11 became angry because of the *L*
21: 3 are they not all my *l*
2 Chr 7: 2 of the LORD had filled the *L*
23:16 that they should be the *L*
Ps 11: 4 The *L* throne is in heaven;
22:28 For the kingdom is the *L*,
24: 1 The earth is the *L*,
109:20 Let this be the *L* reward to
113: 3 sun to its going down The *L*
115:16 even the heavens, are the *L*;
116:19 In the courts of the *L* house,
118:23 This was the *L* doing; It is
137: 4 How shall we sing the *L* song
Prov 16:11 weights and scales are the *L*;
19:21 the *L* counsel—that will stand.
Isa 2: 2 That the mountain of the *L*
34: 8 For it is the day of the *L*
40: 2 she has received from the *L*
42:19 And blind as the *L* servant?
44: 5 One will say, 'I am the *L*';
44: 5 write with his hand, 'The *L*,'
59: 1 the *L* hand is not shortened,
Jer 5:10 For they are not the *L*.
7: 2 Stand in the gate of the *L*
13:17 Because the *L* flock has been
19:14 he stood in the court of the *L*
25:17 Then I took the cup from the *L*
26: 2 Stand in the court of the *L*
26: 2 come to worship in the *L*
26:10 entry of the New Gate of the *L*
26:19 fear the LORD and seek the *L*
27:16 the vessels of the *L* house
28: 3 place all the vessels of the *L*
28: 6 back the vessels of the *L*
36: 6 of the people in the *L* house
36: 8 words of the LORD in the *L*
36:10 entry of the New Gate of the *L*
51: 6 this is the time of the *L*
51: 7 was a golden cup in the *L*
51:51 into the sanctuaries of the *L*
Lam 2:22 In the day of the *L* anger
3:22 Through the *L* mercies we are
Ezek 8:14 of the north gate of the *L*
8:16 into the inner court of the *L*
10: 4 of the brightness of the *L*
10:19 door of the east gate of the *L*
11: 1 me to the East Gate of the *L*
Dan 9:17 and for the *L* sake cause Your
Hos 9: 3 shall not dwell in the *L* land,
Ob 21 the kingdom shall be the *L*.
Mic 4: 1 That the mountain of the *L*
6: 2 the *L* complaint, And you
6: 9 The *L* voice cries to the
Hab 2:16 The cup of the *L* right hand
Zeph 1: 8 In the day of the *L*
1:18 them In the day of the *L*
2: 2 Before the *L* fierce anger
2: 2 Before the day of the *L* anger
2: 3 be hidden In the day of the *L*
Hag 1: 2 the time that the *L* house
1:13 the *L* messenger, spoke the
1:13 spoke the *L* message to the
2:18 that the foundation of the *L*
Zech 14:20 The pots in the *L* house shall
Mal 2:11 For Judah has profaned The *L*
Mt 21:42 This was the *L* doing,
25:18 and hid his *l* money.
Mk 12:11 This was the *L* doing,
Lk 2:26 death before he had seen the *L*
Rom 14: 8 we live or die, we are the *L*.
1 Cor 7:22 Lord while a slave is the *L*
10:21 you cannot partake of the *L*
10:26 for "the earth is the *L*,
10:28 for "the earth is the *L*,
11:20 it is not to eat the *L* Supper.
11:26 you proclaim the *L* death till
11:29 not discerning the *L* body.
Gal 1:19 except James, the *L* brother.
1 Pe 2:13 ordinance of man for the *L*
Rev 1:10 I was in the Spirit on the *L*

LORDLY (1/1) LORD

Judg 5:25 She brought out cream in a *l*

LORDS (40/38) LORD

Gen 19: 2 And he said, "Here now, my *l*,
19:18 to them, "Please, no, my *l*!
Num 21:28 The *l* of the heights of the
Deut 10:17 is God of gods and Lord of *l*,
Josh 13: 3 the five *l* of the
Judg 3: 3 five *l* of the Philistines, all
16: 5 And the *l* of the Philistines
16: 8 So the *l* of the Philistines
16:18 she sent and called for the *l*
16:18 So the *l* of the Philistines
16:23 Now the *l* of the Philistines
16:27 All the *l* of the Philistines
16:30 and the temple fell on the *l*
1 Sam 5: 8 to themselves all the *l* of the
5:11 gathered together all the *l* of

6: 4 to the number of the *l* of the
6: 4 on all of you and on your *l*.
6:12 And the *l* of the Philistines
6:16 So when the five *l* of the
6:18 belonging to the five *l*,
7: 7 the *l* of the Philistines went
29: 2 And the *l* of the Philistines
29: 6 Nevertheless the *l* do not favor
29: 7 you may not displease the *l* of
1 Chr 12:19 for the *l* of the Philistines
Ps 136: 3 give thanks to the Lord of *l*!
Isa 16: 8 The *l* of the nations have
Jer 2:31 do My people say, 'We are *l*;
Dan 5: 1 feast for a thousand of his *l*,
5: 2 that the king and his *l*,
5: 3 and the king and his *l*,
5: 9 and his *l* were astonished.
5:10 the words of the king and his *l*,
5:23 before you, and you and your *l*,
6:17 and with the signets of his *l*,
1 Cor 8: 5 there are many gods and many *l*)
1 Tim 6:15 the King of kings and Lord of *l*,
1 Pe 5: 3 nor as being *l* over those
Rev 17:14 for He is Lord of *l* and King of
19:16 KING OF KINGS AND LORD OF *L*.

LORDSHIP (1/1) LORD

Lk 22:25 of the Gentiles exercise *l*

LOSE (18/18) LOSES, LOSS, LOST

Judg 18:25 and you *l* your life, with the
Job 31:39 Or caused its owners to *l*
Eccl 3: 6 time to gain, And a time to *l*;
Mt 10:39 He who finds his life will *l* it,
10:42 he shall by no means *l* his
16:25 to save his life will *l* it,
Mk 8:35 to save his life will *l* it,
9:41 he will by no means *l* his
Lk 9:24 to save his life will *l* it,
17:33 seeks to save his life will *l*
18: 1 always ought to pray and not *l*
Jn 6:39 all He has given Me I should *l*
12:25 He who loves his life will *l* it,
2 Cor 4: 1 we do not *l* heart.
4:16 Therefore we do not *l* heart.
Gal 6: 9 we shall reap if we do not *l*
Eph 3:13 I ask that you do not *l* heart
2 Jn 8 that we do not *l* those things

LOSES (11/11) LOSE

Mt 5:13 but if the salt *l* its flavor,
10:39 and he who *l* his life for My
16:25 but whoever *l* his life for My
16:26 and *l* his own soul? Or what
Mk 8:35 but whoever *l* his life for My
8:36 and *l* his own soul?
9:50 but if the salt *l* its flavor,
Lk 9:24 but whoever *l* his life for My
15: 4 if he *l* one of them, does not
15: 8 if she *l* one coin, does not
17:33 and whoever *l* his life will

LOSS (15/14) LOSE

Gen 31:39 I bore the *l* of it. You
Ex 21:19 He shall only pay for the *l* of
Esth 7: 4 compensate for the king's *l*.
Job 11:20 their hope—*l* of life!"
Isa 47: 8 Nor shall I know the *l* of
47: 9 The *l* of children, and
Dan 6: 2 that the king would suffer no *l*.
Acts 27:10 end with disaster and much *l*,
27:21 incurred this disaster and *l*.
27:22 for there will be no *l* of life
1 Cor 3:15 is burned, he will suffer *l*;
2 Cor 7: 9 that you might suffer *l* from us
Phil 3: 7 these I have counted *l* for
3: 8 I also count all things *l* for
3: 8 for whom I have suffered the *l*

LOSSES (1/1)

Job 42:10 And the LORD restored Job's *l*

LOST (34/33) LOSE

Ex 22: 9 or for any kind of *l* thing
Lev 6: 3 or if he has found what was *l*
6: 4 or the *l* thing which he found,
Num 6:12 but the former days shall be *l*,
Deut 22: 3 with any *l* thing of your
22: 3 which he has *l* and you have
1 Sam 9: 3 of Kish, Saul's father, were *l*.
9:20 as for your donkeys that were *l*
2 Sam 4: 1 he *l* heart, and all Israel was
1 Ki 20:25 like the army that you have *l*,
Ps 27:13 I would have *l* heart,
119:176 I have gone astray like a *l*
Isa 49:20 After you have *l* the others,
49:21 Since I have *l* my children and
Jer 50: 6 My people have been *l* sheep.
Ezek 19: 5 waited, that her hope was *l*,
34: 4 away, nor sought what was *l*;
34:16 I will seek what was *l* and bring
37:11 bones are dry, our hope is *l*,
Mt 10: 6 But go rather to the *l* sheep of
15:24 was not sent except to the *l*
18:11 come to save that which was *l*.
Lk 9:25 and is himself destroyed or *l*?
14:34 but if the salt has *l* its
15: 4 and go after the one which is *l*
15: 6 found my sheep which was *l*!'
15: 9 have found the piece which I *l*!
15:24 he was *l* and is found.'
15:32 and was *l* and is found.'"
19:10 and to save that which was *l*.
21:18 a hair of your head shall be *l*.
Jn 6:12 remain, so that nothing is *l*.
17:12 and none of them is *l* except
18: 9 whom You gave Me I have *l* none.

LOT (100/92) LOT'S, LOTS

Gen 11:27 Nahor, and Haran. Haran begot *L*.
11:31 son Abram and his grandson *L*,
12: 4 and *L* went with him. And Abram
12: 5 took Sarai his wife and *L* his
13: 1 and *L* with him, to the South.
13: 5 *L* also, who went with Abram,
13: 8 So Abram said to *L*, "Please
13:10 And *L* lifted his eyes and saw
13:11 Then *L* chose for himself all the
13:11 and *L* journeyed east. And they
13:12 and *L* dwelt in the cities of
13:14 after *L* had separated from him:
14:12 They also took *L*, Abram's
14:16 brought back his brother *L* and
19: 1 and *L* was sitting in the gate
19: 1 When *L* saw them, he rose to
19: 5 And they called to *L* and said to
19: 6 So *L* went out to them through
19: 9 pressed hard against the man *L*,
19:10 out their hands and pulled *L*
19:12 Then the men said to *L*,
19:14 So *L* went out and spoke to his
19:15 the angels urged *L* to hurry,
19:18 Then *L* said to them, "Please,
19:23 had risen upon the earth when *L*
19:29 and sent *L* out of the midst of
19:29 the cities in which *L* had
19:30 Then *L* went up out of Zoar and
19:36 Thus both the daughters of *L*
Lev 16: 8 one *l* for the LORD and the
16: 8 for the LORD and the other *l*
16: 9 the goat on which the LORD's *l*
16:10 But the goat on which the *l* fell
Num 26:55 the land shall be divided by *l*;
26:56 According to the *l* their
33:54 you shall divide the land by *l*
33:54 be whatever falls to him by *l*.
34:13 which you shall inherit by *l*,
36: 2 land as an inheritance by *l* to
36: 3 so it will be taken from the *l*
Deut 2: 9 Ar to the descendants of *L* as
2:19 it to the descendants of *L* as
Josh 13: 6 only divide it by *l* to Israel
14: 2 Their inheritance was by *l*,
15: 1 So this was the *l* of the tribe
16: 1 The *l* fell to the children of
17: 1 There was also a *l* for the tribe
17: 2 And there was a *l* for the rest
17:14 have you given us only one *l*
17:17 you shall not have only one *l*,
18:11 Now the *l* of the tribe of the
18:11 and the territory of their *l*
19: 1 The second *l* came out for
19:10 The third *l* came out for the
19:17 The fourth *l* came out to
19:24 The fifth *l* came out for the
19:32 The sixth *l* came out to the
19:40 The seventh *l* came out for the
19:51 divided as an inheritance by *l*
21: 4 Now the *l* came out for the
21: 4 had thirteen cities by *l* from
21: 5 of Kohath had ten cities by *l*
21: 6 had thirteen cities by *l* from
21: 8 with their common-lands by *l*
21:10 for the *l* was theirs first.
21:20 they had the cities of their *l*
21:40 were by their *l* twelve cities.
23: 4 I have divided to you by *l*
Judg 20: 9 will go up against it by *l*.
1 Sam 14:41 of Israel, "Give a perfect *l*.
1 Chr 6:54 for they were given by *l* to
6:61 the Kohathites they gave by *l*
6:65 And they gave by *l* from the
24: 5 Thus they were divided by *l*,
24: 7 Now the first *l* fell to
25: 9 Now the first *l* for Asaph came
26:14 The *l* for the East Gate fell to
26:14 and his *l* came out for the
26:16 To Shuppim and Hosah the *l*
Esth 3: 7 they cast Pur (that is, the *l*),
9:24 had cast Pur (that is, the *l*),
Ps 16: 5 and my cup; You maintain my *l*.
83: 8 have helped the children of *L*.
Prov 1:14 Cast in your *l* among us,
16:33 The *l* is cast into the lap,
Isa 17:14 And the *l* of those who rob us.
34:17 He has cast the *l* for them,
57: 6 are your *l*! Even to them you
Jer 13:25 This is your *l*, The portion
Ezek 24: 6 On which no *l* has fallen.
45: 1 when you divide the land by *l*
47:22 be that you will divide it by *l*
48:29 which you shall divide by *l* as
Jon 1: 7 and the *l* fell on Jonah.
Mic 2: 5 to determine boundaries by *l*
Lk 1: 9 his *l* fell to burn incense when
17:28 as it was also in the days of *L*:
17:29 but on the day that *L* went out
Acts 1:26 and the *l* fell on Matthias.
2 Pe 2: 7 and delivered righteous *L*,

LOT'S (2/2) LOT

Gen 13: 7 livestock and the herdsmen of *L*
Lk 17:32 Remember *L* wife.

LOTAN (5/5)

Gen 36:20 who inhabited the land: *L*,
36:22 And the sons of *L* were Hori and
36:29 chiefs of the Horites: Chief *L*,
1 Chr 1:38 The sons of Seir were *L*,
1:39 And the sons of *L* were Hori and

LOTAN'S (2/2)

Gen 36:22 *L* sister was Timna.
1 Chr 1:39 *L* sister was Timna.

LOTHE (KJV) See LOATHE

LOTS (25/22) LOT

Lev 16: 8 Then Aaron shall cast *l* for the
Josh 18: 6 that I may cast *l* for you here
18: 8 that I may cast *l* for you here
18:10 Then Joshua cast *l* for them in
1 Sam 14:42 Cast *l* between my son Jonathan
1 Chr 24:31 These also cast *l* just as their
25: 8 And they cast *l* for their duty,
26:13 And they cast *l* for each gate,
26:14 Then they cast *l* for his son
Neh 10:34 We cast *l* among the priests, the
11: 1 the rest of the people cast *l*
Ps 22:18 for My clothing they cast *l*.
Prov 18:18 Casting *l* causes contentions to
Joel 3: 3 They have cast *l* for My people,
Ob 11 entered his gates And cast *l*
Jon 1: 7 another, "Come, let us cast *l*,
1: 7 come upon us." So they cast *l*,
Nah 3:10 They cast *l* for her honorable
Mt 27:35 divided His garments, casting *l*,
27:35 My clothing they cast *l*.
Mk 15:24 casting *l* for them to determine
Lk 23:34 divided His garments and cast *l*.
Jn 19:24 but cast *l* for it, whose it
19:24 My clothing they cast *l*.
Acts 1:26 And they cast their *l*,

LOTUS (2/2)

Job 40:21 He lies under the *l* trees,
40:22 The *l* trees cover him with

LOUD (72/72) HIGH, LOUDER, LOUDLY

Gen 39:14 and I cried out with a *l* voice.
Ex 19:16 sound of the trumpet was very *l*,
Deut 5:22 with a *l* voice; and He added no
27:14 Levites shall speak with a *l*
1 Sam 7:10 the LORD thundered with a *l*
28:12 she cried out with a *l* voice.
2 Sam 15:23 all the country wept with a *l*
19: 4 and the king cried out with a *l*
1 Ki 8:55 the assembly of Israel with a *l*
2 Ki 18:28 stood and called out with a *l*
2 Chr 15:14 oath before the LORD with a *l*
20:19 God of Israel with voices *l*
30:21 accompanied by *l* instruments.
32:18 Then they called out with a *l*
Ezra 3:12 wept with a *l* voice when the
3:13 for the people shouted with a *l*
10:12 answered and said with a *l*
Neh 9: 4 Levites and cried out with a *l*
Esth 4: 1 He cried out with a *l* and
Ps 150: 5 Praise Him with *l* cymbals;
Prov 7:11 She was *l* and rebellious,
27:14 who blesses his friend with a *l*
Isa 36:13 stood and called out with a *l*
Jer 51:55 Babylon And silencing her *l*
Ezek 8:18 they cry in My ears with a *l*
9: 1 out in my hearing with a *l*
11:13 on my face and cried with a *l*
Mic 2:12 They shall make a *l* noise
Zeph 1:10 And a *l* crashing from the
Mt 27:46 hour Jesus cried out with a *l*
27:50 Jesus cried out again with a *l*
Mk 1:26 him and cried out with a *l*
5: 7 And he cried out with a *l* voice
15:34 hour Jesus cried out with a *l*
15:37 And Jesus cried out with a *l*
Lk 1:42 Then she spoke out with a *l*
4:33 And he cried out with a *l*
8:28 and with a *l* voice said, "What
17:15 and with a *l* voice glorified
19:37 and praise God with a *l* voice
23:23 demanding with *l* voices that He
23:46 Jesus had cried out with a *l*
Jn 11:43 He cried with a *l* voice,
Acts 7:57 Then they cried out with a *l*
7:60 down and cried out with a *l*
8: 7 crying with a *l* voice, came out
14:10 said with a *l* voice, "Stand up
16:28 But Paul called with a *l* voice,
23: 9 Then there arose a *l* outcry.
26:24 Festus said with a *l* voice,
Rev 1:10 and I heard behind me a *l*
5: 2 angel proclaiming with a *l*
5:12 saying with a *l* voice:
6:10 And they cried with a *l* voice,
7: 2 And he cried with a *l* voice to

7:10 and crying out with a *l* voice,
8:13 saying with a *l* voice, "Woe,
10: 3 and cried with a *l* voice, as
11:12 And they heard a *l* voice from
11:15 And there were *l* voices in
12:10 Then I heard a *l* voice saying in
14: 2 and like the voice of *l*
14: 7 saying with a *l* voice, "Fear
14: 9 saying with a *l* voice, "If
14:15 crying with a *l* voice to Him
14:18 and he cried with a *l* cry to
16: 1 Then I heard a *l* voice from the
16:17 and a *l* voice came out of the
18: 2 And he cried mightily with a *l*
19: 1 After these things I heard a *l*
19:17 and he cried with a *l* voice,
21: 3 And I heard a *l* voice from

LOUDER (2/1) LOUD

Ex 19:19 sounded long and became *l* and
19:19 long and became louder and *l*,

LOUDLY (3/3) LOUD

1 Sam 4: 5 all Israel shouted so *l* that
Neh 12:42 The singers sang *l* with
Mk 5:38 and those who wept and wailed *l*.

LOVE (361/322) LOVED, LOVER, LOVES, LOVESICK, LOVING, LOVINGKINDNESS, UNLOVED

Gen 22: 2 only son Isaac, whom you *l*,
27: 4 me savory food, such as I *l*,
29:20 days to him because of the *l*
29:32 my husband will *l* me."
Ex 20: 6 to those who *l* Me and keep My
21: 5 I *l* my master, my wife, and my
Lev 19:18 but you shall *l* your neighbor
19:34 and you shall *l* him as
Deut 5:10 to those who *l* Me and keep My
6: 5 You shall *l* the LORD your God
7: 7 The LORD did not set His *l* on
7: 9 generations with those who *l*
7:13 And He will *l* you and bless you
10:12 walk in all His ways and to *l*
10:15 to *l* them; and He chose their
10:19 Therefore *l* the stranger, for
11: 1 Therefore you shall *l* the LORD
11:13 to *l* the LORD your God and
11:22 to *l* the LORD your God, to walk
13: 3 you to know whether you *l* the
19: 9 to *l* the LORD your God and to
30: 6 to *l* the LORD your God with
30:16 that I command you today to *l*
30:20 that you may *l* the LORD your
Josh 22: 5 to *l* the LORD your God, to
23:11 that you *l* the LORD your God.
Judg 5:31 O LORD! But let those who *l*
14:16 only hate me! You do not *l*
16:15 I *l* you,' when your heart is
1 Sam 18:22 and all his servants *l* you.
2 Sam 1:26 Your *l* to me was wonderful,
1:26 Surpassing the *l* of women.
13: 4 I *l* Tamar, my brother Absalom's
13:15 her was greater than the *l*
19: 6 in that you *l* your enemies and
1 Ki 11: 2 Solomon clung to these in *l*.
2 Chr 19: 2 you help the wicked and *l*
Neh 1: 5 and mercy with those who *l* You
Job 19:19 And those whom I *l* have turned
Ps 4: 2 How long will you *l*
5:11 Let those also who *l* Your name
18: 1 I will *l* You, O LORD, my
31:23 *l* the LORD, all you His
40:16 Let such as *l* Your salvation
45: the sons of Korah. A Song of *L*.
45: 7 You *l* righteousness and hate
52: 3 You *l* evil more than good,
52: 4 You *l* all devouring words,
69:36 And those who *l* His name shall
70: 4 And let those who *l* Your
91:14 Because he has set his *l* upon
97:10 You who *l* the LORD, hate evil!
109: 4 In return for my *l* they are my
109: 5 for good, And hatred for my *l*.
116: 1 I *l* the LORD, because He has
119:47 Your commandments, Which I *l*.
119:48 Your commandments, Which I *l*,
119:97 how I *l* Your law! It is my
119:113 But I *l* Your law.
119:119 Therefore I *l* Your testimonies
119:127 Therefore I *l* Your commandments
119:132 custom is toward those who *l*
119:159 Consider how I *l* Your precepts;
119:163 But I *l* Your law.
119:165 Great peace have those who *l*
119:167 And I *l* them exceedingly.
122: 6 May they prosper who *l* you.
145:20 The LORD preserves all who *l*
Prov 1:22 will you *l* simplicity?
4: 6 *L* her, and she will keep you.
5:19 always be enraptured with her *l*.
7:18 let us take our fill of *l* until
7:18 us delight ourselves with *l*.
8:17 I *l* those who love me,
8:17 I love those who *l* me,
8:21 That I may cause those who *l* me
8:36 All those who hate me *l*
9: 8 and he will *l* you.
10:12 But *l* covers all sins.
15:12 A scoffer does not *l* one who
15:17 is a dinner of herbs where *l*
16:13 And they *l* him who speaks
17: 9 covers a transgression seeks *l*,
18:21 And those who *l* it will eat
20:13 Do not *l* sleep, lest you come
27: 5 Open rebuke is better Than *l*
Eccl 3: 8 A time to *l*, And a time to
9: 1 People know neither *l* nor
9: 6 Also their *l*, their hatred,
9: 9 with the wife whom you *l* all
Song 1: 2 For your *l* is better than
1: 3 Therefore the virgins *l* you.
1: 4 We will remember your *l* more
1: 4 SHULAMITE Rightly do they *l*
1: 7 Tell me, O you whom I *l*,
1: 9 I have compared you, my *l*,
1:15 my *l*! Behold, you are fair!
2: 2 So is my *l* among the
2: 4 And his banner over me was *l*.
2: 7 Do not stir up nor awaken *l*
2:10 said to me: "Rise up, my *l*,
2:13 a good smell. Rise up, my *l*,
3: 1 on my bed I sought the one I *l*;
3: 2 I will seek the one I *l*.
3: 3 "Have you seen the one I *l*?
3: 4 When I found the one I *l*.
3: 5 Do not stir up nor awaken *l*
3:10 Its interior paved with *l* By
4: 1 my *l*! Behold, you are fair!
4: 7 You are all fair, my *l*,
4:10 How fair is your *l*,
4:10 much better than wine is your *l*,
5: 2 "Open for me, my sister, my *l*,
6: 4 O my *l*, you are as beautiful
7: 6 and how pleasant you are, O *l*,
7:12 There I will give you my *l*.
8: 4 Do not stir up nor awaken *l*
8: 6 For *l* is as strong as death,
8: 7 Many waters cannot quench *l*,
8: 7 If a man would give for *l* All
Isa 56: 6 And to *l* the name of the
61: 8 *l* justice; I hate robbery for
63: 9 In His *l* and in His pity He
66:10 all you who *l* her; Rejoice for
Jer 2: 2 The *l* of your betrothal,
2:33 you beautify your way to seek *l*?
5:31 And My people *l* to have it
31: 3 loved you with an everlasting *l*;
Ezek 16: 8 your time was the time of *l*;
23:17 came to her, into the bed of *l*,
33:31 their mouth they show much *l*,
Dan 9: 4 and mercy with those who *l* Him,
Hos 3: 1 *l* a woman who is loved by a
3: 1 just like the *l* of the LORD
3: 1 who look to other gods and *l*
4:18 Her rulers dearly *l* dishonor.
9: 1 You have made *l* for hire on
9:15 I will *l* them no more.
11: 4 gentle cords, With bands of *l*,
14: 4 I will *l* them freely, For My
Am 4: 5 offerings; For this you *l*,
5:15 *l* good; Establish justice in
Mic 3: 2 You who hate good and *l* evil;
6: 8 To *l* mercy, And to walk
Zeph 3:17 He will quiet you with His *l*,
Zech 8:17 And do not *l* a false oath.
8:19 Therefore *l* truth and peace.'
Mt 5:43 You shall *l* your neighbor
5:44 *l* your enemies, bless those who
5:46 For if you *l* those who love you,
5:46 For if you love those who *l* you,
6: 5 For they *l* to pray standing in
6:24 he will hate the one and *l* the
19:19 You shall *l* your neighbor
22:37 You shall *l* the LORD your
22:39 You shall *l* your neighbor
23: 6 They *l* the best places at
24:12 the *l* of many will grow cold.
Mk 12:30 And you shall *l* the LORD
12:31 You shall *l* your neighbor
12:33 And to *l* Him with all the heart,
12:33 and to *l* one's neighbor as
12:38 *l* greetings in the
Lk 6:27 *L* your enemies, do good to
6:32 But if you *l* those who love you,
6:32 But if you love those who *l* you,
6:32 For even sinners *l* those who
6:32 even sinners love those who *l*
6:35 But *l* your enemies, do good, and
7:42 which of them will *l* him
10:27 You shall *l* the LORD your
11:42 and pass by justice and the *l*
11:43 to you Pharisees! For you *l*
16:13 he will hate the one and *l* the
20:46 *l* greetings in the marketplace
Jn 5:42 that you do not have the *l* of
8:42 you would *l* Me, for I proceeded
11: 3 he whom You *l* is sick."
13:34 that you *l* one another; as I
13:34 that you also *l* one another.
13:35 if you have *l* for one
14:15 If you *l* Me, keep My
14:21 and I will *l* him and manifest
14:23 and My Father will *l* him, and
14:24 He who does not *l* Me does not
14:31 the world may know that I *l*
15: 9 have loved you; abide in My *l*.
15:10 you will abide in My *l*,
15:10 commandments and abide in His *l*.
15:12 that you *l* one another as I
15:13 Greater *l* has no one than this,
15:17 that you *l* one another.
15:19 the world would *l* its own.
17:26 that the *l* with which You loved
21:15 do you *l* Me more than these?"
21:15 You know that I *l* You."
21:16 do you *l* Me?" He said to Him,
21:16 You know that I *l* You."
21:17 do you *l* Me?" Peter was
21:17 Do you *l* Me?" And he said to
21:17 You know that I *l* You."
Rom 5: 5 because the *l* of God has been
5: 8 But God demonstrates His own *l*
8:28 for good to those who *l* God,
8:35 shall separate us from the *l*
8:39 able to separate us from the *l*
12: 9 Let *l* be without hypocrisy.
12:10 to one another with brotherly *l*,
13: 8 no one anything except to *l*
13: 9 You shall *l* your neighbor
13:10 *L* does no harm to a neighbor;
13:10 therefore *l* is the fulfillment
14:15 you are no longer walking in *l*.
15:30 and through the *l* of the
1 Cor 2: 9 prepared for those who *l*
4:21 or in *l* and a spirit of
8: 1 puffs up, but *l* edifies.
13: 1 and of angels, but have not *l*,
13: 2 mountains, but have not *l*,
13: 3 to be burned, but have not *l*,
13: 4 *L* suffers long and is kind;
13: 4 *l* does not envy; love does not
13: 4 *l* does not parade itself, is
13: 8 *L* never fails. But whether
13:13 And now abide faith, hope, *l*,
13:13 but the greatest of these is *l*.
14: 1 Pursue *l*, and desire
16:14 that you do be done with *l*.
16:22 If anyone does not *l* the Lord
16:24 My *l* be with you all in Christ
2 Cor 2: 4 but that you might know the *l*
2: 8 I urge you to reaffirm your *l*
5:14 For the *l* of Christ compels us,
6: 6 the Holy Spirit, by sincere *l*,
8: 7 and in your *l* for us—see that
8: 8 the sincerity of your *l* by the
8:24 churches the proof of your *l*
11:11 Because I do not *l* you?
12:15 though the more abundantly I *l*
13:11 and the God of *l* and peace will
13:14 and the *l* of God, and the
Gal 5: 6 but faith working through *l*.
5:13 but through *l* serve one
5:14 You shall *l* your neighbor
5:22 the fruit of the Spirit is *l*,
Eph 1: 4 without blame before Him in *l*,
1:15 in the Lord Jesus and your *l*
2: 4 because of His great *l* with
3:17 being rooted and grounded in *l*,
3:19 to know the *l* of Christ which
4: 2 bearing with one another in *l*,
4:15 but, speaking the truth in *l*,
4:16 for the edifying of itself in *l*.
5: 2 And walk in *l*, as Christ also
5:25 *l* your wives, just as Christ
5:28 So husbands ought to *l* their own
5:33 one of you in particular so *l*
6:23 and *l* with faith, from God the
6:24 Grace be with all those who *l*
Phil 1: 9 that your *l* may abound still
1:17 but the latter out of *l*,
2: 1 in Christ, if any comfort of *l*,
2: 2 like-minded, having the same *l*,
Col 1: 4 in Christ Jesus and of your *l*
1: 8 who also declared to us your *l*
1:13 the kingdom of the Son of His *l*,
2: 2 being knit together in *l*,
3:14 above all these things put on *l*,
3:19 *l* your wives and do not be
1 Th 1: 3 your work of faith, labor of *l*,
3: 6 good news of your faith and *l*,
3:12 you increase and abound in *l*
4: 9 But concerning brotherly *l* you
4: 9 are taught by God to *l* one
5: 8 the breastplate of faith and *l*,
5:13 to esteem them very highly in *l*
2 Th 1: 3 and the *l* of every one of you
2:10 they did not receive the *l* of
3: 5 direct your hearts into the *l*
1 Tim 1: 5 of the commandment is *l* from a
1:14 with faith and *l* which are in
2:15 if they continue in faith, *l*,
4:12 in word, in conduct, in *l*,
6:10 For the *l* of money is a root of
6:11 godliness, faith, *l*,
2 Tim 1: 7 but of power and of *l* and of a
1:13 in faith and *l* which are in
2:22 pursue righteousness, faith, *l*,
3:10 faith, longsuffering, *l*,
Titus 2: 2 temperate, sound in faith, in *l*,
2: 4 admonish the young women to *l*
2: 4 to *l* their children,
3: 4 when the kindness and the *l* of
3:15 Greet those who *l* us in the
Phm 1: 5 hearing of your *l* and faith
1: 7 joy and consolation in your *l*,
Heb 6:10 your work and labor of *l* which
10:24 another in order to stir up *l*
13: 1 Let brotherly *l* continue.
Jas 1:12 has promised to those who *l*
2: 5 He promised to those who *l* Him?
2: 8 You shall *l* your neighbor
1 Pe 1: 8 whom having not seen you *l*.

1:22 the Spirit in sincere *l* of the
1:22 *l* one another fervently with a
2:17 *L* the brotherhood. Fear God.
3: 8 *l* as brothers, be
3:10 He who would *l* life And
4: 8 all things have fervent *l* for
4: 8 *l* will cover a multitude of
5:14 one another with a kiss of *l*.
2 Pe 1: 7 and to brotherly kindness *l*.
1 Jn 2: 5 truly the *l* of God is perfected
2:15 Do not *l* the world or the
2:15 the *l* of the Father is not in
3: 1 Behold what manner of *l* the
3:10 nor is he who does not *l* his
3:11 that we should *l* one another,
3:14 because we *l* the brethren.
3:14 He who does not *l* his brother
3:16 By this we know *l*, because He
3:17 how does the *l* of God abide in
3:18 let us not *l* in word or in
3:23 of His Son Jesus Christ and *l*
4: 7 let us *l* one another, for love
4: 7 for *l* is of God; and everyone
4: 8 He who does not *l* does not know
4: 8 does not know God, for God is *l*.
4: 9 In this the *l* of God was
4:10 In this is *l*, not that we
4:11 we also ought to *l* one another.
4:12 If we *l* one another, God abides
4:12 and His *l* has been perfected in
4:16 have known and believed the *l*
4:16 that God has for us. God is *l*,
4:16 and he who abides in *l* abides
4:17 *L* has been perfected among us
4:18 There is no fear in *l*;
4:18 but perfect *l* casts out fear,
4:18 has not been made perfect in *l*.
4:19 We *l* Him because He first loved
4:20 I *l* God," and hates his
4:20 for he who does not *l* his
4:20 how can he *l* God whom he has
4:21 that he who loves God must *l*
5: 2 By this we know that we *l* the
5: 2 when we *l* God and keep His
5: 3 For this is the *l* of God, that
2 Jn 1 whom I *l* in truth, and not only
3 of the Father, in truth and *l*.
5 that we *l* one another.
6 This is *l*, that we walk
3 Jn 1 Gaius, whom I *l* in truth:
6 have borne witness of your *l*
Jude 2 and *l* be multiplied to you.
12 These are spots in your *l*
21 keep yourselves in the *l* of God,
Rev 2: 4 that you have left your first *l*.
2:19 "I know your works, *l*,
3:19 'As many as I *l*, I rebuke
12:11 and they did not *l* their lives

LOVE ONE ANOTHER (13/12)

Jn 13:34 I give to you, that you *l*;
13:34 have loved you, that you also *l*.
15:12 that you *l* as I have loved you.
15:17 I command you, that you *l*.
Rom 13: 8 no one anything except to *l*,
1 Th 4: 9 are taught by God to *l*;
1 Pe 1:22 *l* fervently with a pure heart,
1 Jn 3:11 the beginning, that we should *l*,
3:23 of His Son Jesus Christ and *l*,
4: 7 Beloved, let us *l*, for love
4:11 so loved us, we also ought to *l*.
4:12 seen God at any time. If we *l*,
2 Jn 5 from the beginning: that we *l*.

LOVE THE LORD YOUR GOD (14/14)

Deut 6: 5 You shall *l* with all your heart,
11: 1 "Therefore you shall *l*,
11:13 to *l* and serve Him with all
11:22 which I command you to do—to *l*,
13: 3 you to know whether you *l* with
19: 9 to *l* and to walk always in His
30: 6 to *l* with all your heart and
30:16 that I command you today to *l*,
30:20 'that you may *l*, that you may
Josh 22: 5 the LORD commanded you, to *l*,
23:11 heed to yourselves, that you *l*.
Mt 22:37 You shall *l* with all your
Mk 12:30 And you shall *l* with all
Lk 10:27 You shall *l* with all your

LOVE YOUR NEIGHBOR (8/8)

Lev 19:18 but you shall *l* as yourself:
Mt 5:43 You shall *l* and hate your
19:19 You shall *l* as yourself.'"
22:39 You shall *l* as yourself.'
Mk 12:31 You shall *l* as yourself.'
Rom 13: 9 You shall *l* as yourself."
Gal 5:14 You shall *l* as yourself."
Jas 2: 8 You shall *l* as yourself,"

LOVE'S (1/1)

Phm 1: 9 yet for *l* sake I rather appeal

LOVED (96/86) LOVE

Gen 24:67 and he *l* her. So Isaac was
25:28 And Isaac *l* Esau because he ate
25:28 but Rebekah *l* Jacob.
27:14 food, such as his father *l*.
29:18 Now Jacob *l* Rachel; so he said,
29:30 and he also *l* Rachel more than
34: 3 and he *l* the young woman and
37: 3 Now Israel *l* Joseph more than
37: 4 saw that their father *l* him
Deut 4:37 And because He *l* your fathers,
21:15 one *l* and the other unloved,
21:15 both the *l* and the unloved,
21:16 status on the son of the *l*
Judg 16: 4 it happened that he *l* a woman
1 Sam 1: 5 for he *l* Hannah, although the
16:21 And he *l* him greatly, and he
18: 1 and Jonathan *l* him as his own
18: 3 because he *l* him as his own
18:16 But all Israel and Judah *l*
18:20 *l* David. And they told Saul,
18:28 Saul's daughter, *l* him;
20:17 because he *l* him; for he loved
20:17 for he *l* him as he loved his
20:17 for he loved him as he *l* his
2 Sam 12:24 Now the LORD *l* him,
13: 1 and Amnon the son of David *l*
13:15 the love with which he had *l*
1 Ki 3: 3 And Solomon *l* the LORD, walking
5: 1 for Hiram had always *l* David.
10: 9 Because the LORD has *l* Israel
11: 1 But King Solomon *l* many foreign
2 Chr 9: 8 God! Because your God has *l*
11:21 Now Rehoboam *l* Maachah the
26:10 for he *l* the soil.
Esth 2:17 The king *l* Esther more than all
Ps 26: 8 I have *l* the habitation of Your
38:11 My *l* ones and my friends stand
78:68 Judah, Mount Zion which He *l*.
88:18 *L* one and friend You have put
109:17 As he *l* cursing, so let it come
Isa 43: 4 And I have *l* you; Therefore I
57: 8 You have *l* their bed, Where
Jer 2:25 No! For I have *l* aliens, and
8: 2 which they have *l* and which
14:10 Thus they have *l* to wander;
31: 3 I have *l* you with an
Ezek 16:37 took pleasure, all those you *l*,
Hos 3: 1 love a woman who is *l* by a
9:10 like the thing they *l*.
11: 1 I *l* him, And out of Egypt I
Mal 1: 2 I have *l* you," says the LORD.
1: 2 In what way have You *l* us?'
1: 2 'Yet Jacob I have *l*;
Mk 10:21 *l* him, and said to him, "One
Lk 7:47 for she *l* much. But to whom
Jn 3:16 For God so *l* the world that He
3:19 and men *l* darkness rather than
11: 5 Now Jesus *l* Martha and her
11:36 See how He *l* him!"
12:43 for they *l* the praise of men
13: 1 having *l* His own who were in
13: 1 He *l* them to the end.
13:23 of His disciples, whom Jesus *l*.
13:34 as I have *l* you, that you also
14:21 And he who loves Me will be *l*
14:28 If you *l* Me, you would rejoice
15: 9 As the Father *l* Me, I also have
15: 9 I also have *l* you; abide in My
15:12 love one another as I have *l*
16:27 because you have *l* Me, and have
17:23 and have *l* them as You have
17:23 have loved them as You have *l*
17:24 for You *l* Me before the
17:26 that the love with which You *l*
19:26 and the disciple whom He *l*
20: 2 other disciple, whom Jesus *l*,
21: 7 that disciple whom Jesus *l*
21:20 saw the disciple whom Jesus *l*
Rom 8:37 conquerors through Him who *l*
9:13 written, "Jacob I have *l*,
2 Cor 12:15 I love you, the less I am *l*.
Gal 2:20 who *l* me and gave Himself for
Eph 2: 4 His great love with which He *l*
5: 2 as Christ also has *l* us and
5:25 just as Christ also *l* the
2 Th 2:16 who has *l* us and given us
2 Tim 4: 8 but also to all who have *l* His
4:10 having *l* this present world,
Heb 1: 9 You have *l* righteousness
2 Pe 2:15 who *l* the wages of
1 Jn 4:10 not that we *l* God, but that He
4:10 but that He *l* us and sent His
4:11 if God so *l* us, we also ought
4:19 We love Him because He first *l*
Rev 1: 5 To Him who *l* us and washed us
3: 9 and to know that I have *l* you.

LOVELIEST (1/1)

1 Ki 20: 3 your *l* wives and children are

LOVELINESS (1/1) LOVELY

Isa 40: 6 And all its *l* is like the

LOVELY (19/19) LOVELINESS

Num 24: 5 How *l* are your tents, O Jacob!
2 Sam 13: 1 the son of David had a *l*
1 Ki 1: 3 So they sought for a *l* young
1: 4 The young woman was very *l*;
Esth 2: 7 The young woman was *l* and
Ps 84: 1 How *l* is Your tabernacle,
Prov 11:22 So is a *l* woman who lacks
Song 1: 5 I am dark, but *l*,
1:10 Your cheeks are *l* with
2:14 is sweet, And your face is *l*.
4: 3 scarlet, And your mouth is *l*.
5:16 Yes, he is altogether *l*.
6: 4 *L* as Jerusalem, Awesome as
Jer 6: 2 the daughter of Zion To a *l*
11:16 *L* and of Good Fruit. With the
Ezek 33:32 you are to them as a very *l*
Dan 4:12 Its leaves were *l*,
4:21 whose leaves were *l* and its
Phil 4: 8 pure, whatever things are *l*,

LOVER (2/2) LOVE, LOVERS

Hos 3: 1 a woman who is loved by a *l*
Titus 1: 8 a *l* of what is good,

LOVERS (25/23) LOVER

Jer 3: 1 played the harlot with many *l*;
4:30 Your *l* will despise you;
22:20 For all your *l* are destroyed.
22:22 And your *l* shall go into
30:14 All your *l* have forgotten you;
Lam 1: 2 Among all her *l* She has none
1:19 "I called for my *l*,
Ezek 16:33 your payments to all your *l*,
16:36 in your harlotry with your *l*,
16:37 I will gather all your *l* with
16:41 and you shall no longer hire *l*.
23: 5 And she lusted for her *l*,
23: 9 her Into the hand of her *l*,
23:22 I will stir up your *l* against
Hos 2: 5 she said, 'I will go after my *l*,
2: 7 She will chase her *l*,
2:10 lewdness in the sight of her *l*,
2:12 These are my wages that my *l*
2:13 jewelry, And went after her *l*;
8: 9 by itself; Ephraim has hired *l*.
Lk 16:14 who were *l* of money, also heard
2 Tim 3: 2 For men will be *l* of themselves,
3: 2 *l* of money, boasters, proud,
3: 4 *l* of pleasure rather than
3: 4 of pleasure rather than *l* of

LOVES (65/57) LOVE

Gen 27: 9 for your father, such as he *l*.
44:20 and his father *l* him.'
Deut 7: 8 but because the LORD *l* you, and
10:18 and *l* the stranger, giving him
15:16 because he *l* you and your
23: 5 because the LORD your God *l*
33: 3 He *l* the people; All His
Ruth 4:15 who *l* you, who is better to you
2 Chr 2:11 Because the LORD *l* His people,
Ps 11: 5 the wicked and the one who *l*
11: 7 He *l* righteousness;
33: 5 He *l* righteousness and justice;
34:12 And *l* many days, that he may
37:28 For the LORD *l* justice,
47: 4 excellence of Jacob whom He *l*.
87: 2 The LORD *l* the gates of Zion
99: 4 The King's strength also *l*
119:140 Therefore Your servant *l* it.
146: 8 The LORD *l* the righteous.
Prov 3:12 For whom the LORD *l* He
12: 1 Whoever *l* instruction loves
12: 1 Whoever loves instruction *l*
13:24 But he who *l* him disciplines
15: 9 But He *l* him who follows
17:17 A friend *l* at all times, And a
17:19 He who *l* transgression loves
17:19 He who loves transgression *l*
19: 8 He who gets wisdom *l* his own
21:17 He who *l* pleasure will be a
21:17 He who *l* wine and oil will not
22:11 He who *l* purity of heart
29: 3 Whoever *l* wisdom makes his
Eccl 5:10 He who *l* silver will not be
5:10 Nor he who *l* abundance, with
Isa 1:23 Everyone *l* bribes, And
48:14 The LORD *l* him; He shall do
Hos 10:11 is a trained heifer That *l*
12: 7 his hand; He *l* to oppress.
Mal 2:11 holy institution which He *l*:
Mt 10:37 He who *l* father or mother more
10:37 And he who *l* son or daughter
Lk 7: 5 for he *l* our nation, and has
7:47 the same *l* little."
Jn 3:35 The Father *l* the Son, and has
5:20 For the Father *l* the Son, and
10:17 Therefore My Father *l* Me,
12:25 He who *l* his life will lose it,
14:21 it is he who *l* Me. And he who
14:21 And he who *l* Me will be loved
14:23 If anyone *l* Me, he will keep My
16:27 for the Father Himself *l* you,
Rom 13: 8 for he who *l* another has
1 Cor 8: 3 But if anyone *l* God, this one is
2 Cor 9: 7 for God *l* a cheerful giver.
Eph 5:28 he who *l* his wife loves
5:28 he who loves his wife *l*
Heb 12: 6 For whom the LORD *l* He
1 Jn 2:10 He who *l* his brother abides in
2:15 If anyone *l* the world, the love
4: 7 and everyone who *l* is born of
4:21 that he who *l* God must love
5: 1 and everyone who *l* Him who
5: 1 who loves Him who begot also *l*
3 Jn 9 who *l* to have the preeminence

Rev 22:15 and whoever *l* and practices a

LOVESICK (2/2) LOVE
Song 2: 5 me with apples, For I am *l*.
5: 8 That you tell him I am *l*!

LOVING (3/3) LOVE
Prov 5:19 As a *l* deer and a graceful
22: 1 *L* favor rather than silver and
Isa 56:10 lying down, *l* to slumber.

LOVINGKINDNESS (29/29) LOVE, LOVINGKINDNESSES
Ps 17: 7 Show Your marvelous *l* by Your
26: 3 For Your *l* is before my eyes,
36: 7 How precious is Your *l*,
36:10 continue Your *l* to those who
40:10 I have not concealed Your *l*
40:11 Let Your *l* and Your truth
42: 8 The LORD will command His *l* in
48: 9 have thought, O God, on Your *l*,
51: 1 me, O God, According to Your *l*;
63: 3 Because Your *l* is better than
69:16 for Your *l* is good; Turn to
88:11 Shall Your *l* be declared in the
89:33 Nevertheless My *l* I will not
92: 2 To declare Your *l* in the
103: 4 Who crowns you with *l* and
107:43 they will understand the *l* of
119:88 Revive me according to Your *l*,
119:149 my voice according to Your *l*;
119:159 O LORD, according to Your *l*.
138: 2 praise Your name For Your *l*
143: 8 Cause me to hear Your *l* in the
144: 2 My *l* and my fortress, My high
Prov 20:28 And by *l* he upholds his
Jer 9:24 I am the LORD, exercising *l*,
16: 5 LORD, "*l* and mercies.
31: 3 Therefore with *l* I have drawn
32:18 You show *l* to thousands, and
Hos 2:19 and justice, In *l* and mercy;
Jon 4: 2 slow to anger and abundant in *l*,

LOVINGKINDNESSES (4/3) LOVINGKINDNESS
Ps 25: 6 Your tender mercies and Your *l*,
89:49 Lord, where are Your former *l*,
Isa 63: 7 I will mention the *l* of the
63: 7 to the multitude of His *l*.

LOVINGLY (1/1)
Isa 38:17 But You have *l* delivered my

LOW (32/30)
Judg 11:35 You have brought me very *l*!
16: 3 And Samson lay *l* till midnight;
1 Sam 2: 7 He brings *l* and lifts up.
2 Chr 28:19 For the LORD brought Judah *l*
Job 6: 5 Or does the ox *l* over its
14:21 know it; They are brought *l*,
24:24 are gone. They are brought *l*;
40:12 is proud, and bring him *l*;
Ps 10:10 So he crouches, he lies *l*,
49: 2 Both *l* and high, Rich and poor
62: 9 Surely men of *l* degree are a
79: 8 we have been brought very *l*.
106:43 And were brought *l* for their
107:39 are diminished and brought *l*
116: 6 the simple; I was brought *l*,
142: 6 For I am brought very *l*;
Prov 29:23 A man's pride will bring him *l*,
Eccl 12: 4 And the sound of grinding is *l*;
12: 4 of music are brought *l*;
Isa 2:12 up—And it shall be brought *l*—
2:17 of men shall be brought *l*;
13:11 And will lay *l* the haughtiness
25:12 He will bring down, lay *l*,
26: 5 The lofty city; He lays it *l*,
26: 5 He lays it *l* to the ground,
29: 4 Your speech shall be *l*,
32:19 And the city is brought *l* in
40: 4 mountain and hill brought *l*;
Ezek 17: 6 became a spreading vine of *l*
17:14 the kingdom might be brought *l*
17:24 the high tree and exalted the *l*
Lk 3: 5 and hill brought *l*;

LOWER (29/28)
Gen 6:16 You shall make it with *l*,
Deut 24: 6 No man shall take the *l* or the
28:43 and you shall come down *l* and
28:43 you shall come down lower and *l*.
Josh 15:19 her the upper springs and the *l*
16: 3 as far as the boundary of *L*
18:13 lies on the south side of *L*
Judg 1:15 her the upper springs and the *l*
1 Ki 9:17 built Gezer, *L* Beth Horon,
1 Chr 7:24 who built *L* and Upper Beth
2 Chr 8: 5 He built Upper Beth Horon and *L*
Neh 4:13 I positioned men behind the *l*
Job 41: 1 tongue with a line which you *l*?
41:24 Even as hard as the *l*
Ps 8: 5 You have made him a little *l*
63: 9 Shall go into the *l* parts of
Prov 25: 7 Than that you should be put *l*
Isa 22: 9 together the waters of the *l*
44:23 you *l* parts of the earth;
Ezek 32:24 down uncircumcised to the *l*
40:18 this was the *l* pavement.
40:19 width from the front of the *l*
42: 5 from them more than from the *l*
42: 6 was shortened more than the *l*
42: 9 At the *l* chambers was the
43:14 the base on the ground to the *l*
Eph 4: 9 also first descended into the *l*
Heb 2: 7 have made him a little *l*
2: 9 who was made a little *l* than

LOWEST (12/12)
Deut 32:22 And shall burn to the *l* hell;
1 Ki 6: 6 The *l* chamber was five cubits
Ps 88: 6 You have laid me in the *l* pit,
139:15 wrought in the *l* parts
Isa 14:15 To the *l* depths of the Pit.
Lam 3:55 O LORD, From the *l* pit.
Ezek 26:20 I will make you dwell in the *l*
41: 7 one went up from the *l* stories
Dan 4:17 And sets over it the *l* of
Jon 1: 5 Jonah had gone down into the *l*
Lk 14: 9 begin with shame to take the *l*
14:10 go and sit down in the *l* place,

LOWING (2/2)
1 Sam 6:12 *l* as they went, and did not
15:14 and the *l* of the oxen which I

LOWLAND (17/17) LOWLANDS
Deut 1: 7 in the mountains and in the *l*,
Josh 9: 1 in the hills and in the *l* and
10:40 and the South and the *l* and
11: 2 south of Chinneroth, in the *l*,
11:16 all the land of Goshen, the *l*,
15:33 In the *l*: Eshtaol, Zorah,
Judg 1: 9 in the South, and in the *l*.
1:19 out the inhabitants of the *l*,
1 Ki 10:27 sycamores which are in the *l*.
2 Chr 1:15 sycamores which are in the *l*.
9:27 sycamores which are in the *l*.
28:18 had invaded the cities of the *l*
Jer 17:26 land of Benjamin and from the *l*,
32:44 in the cities of the *l*,
33:13 in the cities of the *l*,
Ob 19 And the *L* shall possess
Zech 7: 7 and the South and the *L* were

LOWLANDS (4/4) LOWLAND
Josh 11:16 mountains of Israel and its *l*,
12: 8 the mountain country, in the *l*,
1 Chr 27:28 trees that were in the *l*,
2 Chr 26:10 both in the *l* and in the

LOWLIEST (1/1)
Ezek 29:15 It shall be the *l* of kingdoms;

LOWLINESS (2/2) LOWLY
Eph 4: 2 with all *l* and gentleness, with
Phil 2: 3 but in *l* of mind let each

LOWLY (14/14) LOWLINESS
Job 5:11 sets on high those who are *l*,
Ps 136:23 Who remembered us in our *l*
138: 6 on high, Yet He regards the *l*;
Prov 16:19 of a humble spirit with the *l*,
Eccl 10: 6 While the rich sit in a *l*
Ezek 29:14 and there they shall be a *l*
Zech 9: 9 *L* and riding on a donkey,
Mt 11:29 for I am gentle and *l* in heart,
21: 5 King is coming to you, *L*,
Lk 1:48 For He has regarded the *l* state
1:52 thrones, And exalted the *l*.
2 Cor 10: 1 who in presence am *l* among you,
Phil 3:21 who will transform our *l* body
Jas 1: 9 Let the *l* brother glory in his

LOWRING (KJV) See THREATENING

LOYAL (18/18) LOYALTY
2 Sam 20: 2 remained *l* to their king.
1 Ki 8:61 Let your heart therefore be *l* to
11: 4 and his heart was not *l* to the
15: 3 his heart was not *l* to the
15:14 Nevertheless Asa's heart was *l*
2 Ki 20: 3 You in truth and with a *l*
1 Chr 12:29 part of them had remained *l* to
12:38 came to Hebron with a *l* heart,
28: 9 and serve Him with a *l* heart
29: 9 because with a *l* heart they had
29:19 And give my son Solomon a *l*
2 Chr 15:17 the heart of Asa was *l* all his
16: 9 of those whose heart is *l* to
19: 9 faithfully and with a *l* heart:
25: 2 but not with a *l* heart.
Isa 38: 3 You in truth and with a *l*
Mt 6:24 or else he will be *l* to the one
Lk 16:13 or else he will be *l* to the one

LOYALTY (2/2) LOYAL
2 Sam 3: 8 Today I show *l* to the house of
16:17 Is this your *l* to your friend?

LUBIM (3/3)
2 Chr 12: 3 the *L* and the Sukkiim and the
16: 8 Were the Ethiopians and the *L*
Nah 3: 9 Put and *L* were your helpers.

LUBIMS (KJV) See LUBIM

LUCAS (KJV) See LUKE

LUCIFER (1/1)
Isa 14:12 are fallen from heaven, O *L*,

LUCIUS (2/2)
Acts 13: 1 *L* of Cyrene, Manaen who had
Rom 16:21 my fellow worker, and *L*,

LUCRE (KJV) See GAIN, MONEY

LUD (3/3)
Gen 10:22 were Elam, Asshur, Arphaxad, *L*,
1 Chr 1:17 were Elam, Asshur, Arphaxad, *L*,
Isa 66:19 to Tarshish and Pul and *L*,

LUDIM (2/2)
Gen 10:13 Mizraim begot *L*, Anamim,
1 Chr 1:11 Mizraim begot *L*, Anamim,

LUHITH (2/2)
Isa 15: 5 For by the Ascent of *L* They
Jer 48: 5 For in the Ascent of *L* they

LUKE (3/3)
Col 4:14 *L* the beloved physician and
2 Tim 4:11 Only *L* is with me. Get Mark and
Phm 1:24 do Mark, Aristarchus, Demas, *L*,

LUKEWARM (1/1)
Rev 3:16 "So then, because you are *l*,

LULLED (1/1)
Judg 16:19 Then she *l* him to sleep on her

LUMP (7/7)
2 Ki 20: 7 Take a *l* of figs." So they took
Isa 38:21 Let them take a *l* of figs, and
Rom 9:21 from the same *l* to make one
11:16 the *l* is also holy; and if
1 Cor 5: 6 leaven leavens the whole *l*?
5: 7 leaven, that you may be a new *l*,
Gal 5: 9 leaven leavens the whole *l*.

LUNATICK (KJV) See DEMON-POSSESSED, EPILEPTIC

LUNGE (1/1)
Joel 2: 8 Though they *l* between the

LURK (4/4)
Job 38:40 Or *l* in their lairs to lie in
Prov 1:11 Let us *l* secretly for the
1:18 They *l* secretly for their own
Hos 13: 7 a leopard by the road I will *l*;

LURKED (1/1)
Job 31: 9 Or if I have *l* at my

LURKING (4/4)
1 Sam 23:23 and take knowledge of all the *l*
Ps 10: 8 He sits in the *l* places of the
17:12 And like a young lion *l* in
Prov 7:12 *L* at every corner.

LUST (15/14) LUSTED, LUSTFUL, LUSTS, LUSTY
Prov 6:25 Do not *l* after her beauty in
11: 6 will be caught by their *l*.
Ezek 23:11 became more corrupt in her *l*
Mt 5:28 whoever looks at a woman to *l*
Rom 1:27 burned in their *l* for one
13:13 not in lewdness and *l*,
1 Cor 10: 6 the intent that we should not *l*
Gal 5:16 you shall not fulfill the *l* of
1 Th 4: 5 not in passion of *l*,
Jas 4: 2 You *l* and do not have. You
2 Pe 1: 4 is in the world through *l*.
2:10 to the flesh in the *l* of
1 Jn 2:16 the *l* of the flesh, the lust of
2:16 the *l* of the eyes, and the
2:17 and the *l* of it; but he who

LUSTED (8/8) LUST
Ps 106:14 But *l* exceedingly in the
Ezek 23: 5 And she *l* for her lovers, the
23: 7 And with all for whom she *l*,
23: 9 the Assyrians, For whom she *l*.
23:12 She *l* for the neighboring

23:16 She *l* for them And sent
23:20 For she *l* for her paramours,
1 Cor 10: 6 evil things as they also *l*.

LUSTFUL (1/1) LUST

Jer 13:27 your adulteries And your *l*

LUSTS (19/19) LUST

Rom 1:24 in the *l* of their hearts, to
6:12 you should obey it in its *l*.
13:14 the flesh, to fulfill its *l*.
Gal 5:17 For the flesh *l* against the
Eph 2: 3 conducted ourselves in the *l*
4:22 according to the deceitful *l*,
1 Tim 6: 9 many foolish and harmful *l*
2 Tim 2:22 Flee also youthful *l*;
3: 6 sins, led away by various *l*,
Titus 2:12 ungodliness and worldly *l*,
3: 3 serving various *l* and
1 Pe 1:14 yourselves to the former *l*,
2:11 abstain from fleshly *l* which
4: 2 time in the flesh for the *l* of
4: 3 we walked in lewdness, *l*,
2 Pe 2:18 they allure through the *l* of
3: 3 according to their own *l*,
Jude 16 according to their own *l*;
18 to their own ungodly *l*.

LUSTY (1/1) LUST

Jer 5: 8 They were like well-fed *l*

LUTE (6/6)

Ps 57: 8 *l* and harp! I will awaken the
71:22 Also with the *l* I will praise
81: 2 The pleasant harp with the *l*.
92: 3 of ten strings, On the *l*,
108: 2 *l* and harp! I will awaken the
150: 3 Praise Him with the *l* and

LUXURIOUSLY (2/2)

Rev 18: 7 glorified herself and lived *l*,
18: 9 fornication and lived *l* with

LUXURY (8/8)

2 Sam 1:24 clothed you in scarlet, with *l*;
Prov 19:10 *L* is not fitting for a fool,
Ezek 27:12 because of your many *l* goods.
27:18 because of your many *l* items,
27:33 of the earth With your many *l*
Lk 7:25 appareled and live in *l* are in
Jas 5: 5 on the earth in pleasure and *l*;
Rev 18: 3 through the abundance of her *l*.

LUZ (8/7)

Gen 28:19 name of that city had been *L*
35: 6 So Jacob came to *L* (that is,
48: 3 Almighty appeared to me at *L*
Josh 16: 2 then went out from Bethel to *L*,
18:13 went over from there toward *L*,
18:13 to the side of *L* (which is
Judg 1:23 of the city was formerly *L*.
1:26 a city, and called its name *L*,

LYCAONIA (1/1)

Acts 14: 6 Lystra and Derbe, cities of *L*,

LYCAONIAN (1/1)

Acts 14:11 saying in the *L* language,

LYCIA (1/1)

Acts 27: 5 we came to Myra, a city of *L*.

LYDDA (3/3)

Acts 9:32 to the saints who dwelt in *L*.
9:35 So all who dwelt at *L* and Sharon
9:38 And since *L* was near Joppa, and

LYDIA (4/4)

Ezek 27:10 "Those from Persia, *L*,
30: 5 'Ethiopia, Libya, *L*,
Acts 16:14 Now a certain woman named *L*
16:40 and entered the house of *L*;

LYDIANS (1/1)

Jer 46: 9 And the *L* who handle and bend

LYE (1/1)

Jer 2:22 though you wash yourself with *l*,

LYING (76/76) LIE

Gen 29: 2 were three flocks of sheep *l*
34: 7 thing in Israel by *l* with
49:14 *L* down between two burdens;
Ex 23: 5 donkey of one who hates you *l*
Lev 6: 2 against the LORD by *l* to his
Num 35:20 while *l* in wait, hurls
35:22 anything at him without *l* in
Deut 21: 1 *l* in the field in the land
22:22 If a man is found *l* with a
33:13 And the deep *l* beneath,
Judg 7:12 were *l* in the valley as
9:35 who were with him rose from *l*
16: 9 Now men were *l* in wait,
16:12 And men were *l* in
Ruth 3: 8 a woman was *l* at his feet.
1 Sam 3: 2 while Eli was *l* down in his
3: 3 and while Samuel was *l* down,
2 Sam 4: 5 who was *l* on his bed at noon.
4: 7 he was *l* on his bed in his
13: 8 and he was *l* down. Then she
1 Ki 13:18 (He was *l* to him.)
22:22 I will go out and be a *l* spirit
22:23 look! The LORD has put a *l*
2 Ki 4:32 the child, *l* dead on his bed.
2 Chr 18:21 I will go out and be a *l* spirit
18:22 The LORD has put a *l* spirit
Ps 31:18 Let the *l* lips be put to
52: 3 *L* rather than speaking
59:12 And for the cursing and *l*
109: 2 have spoken against me with a *l*
119:29 Remove from me the way of *l*,
119:163 hate and abhor *l*, But I love
120: 2 from *l* lips And from a
139: 3 comprehend my path and my *l*
144:11 Whose mouth speaks *l* words,
Prov 6:17 A *l* tongue, Hands that shed
10:18 Whoever hides hatred has *l*
12:19 But a *l* tongue is but for a
12:22 *L* lips are an abomination to
13: 5 A righteous man hates *l*,
17: 7 Much less *l* lips to a prince.
21: 6 Getting treasures by a *l* tongue
26:28 A *l* tongue hates those who
Isa 30: 9 *L* children, Children who
32: 7 To destroy the poor with *l*
56:10 *l* down, loving to slumber.
59:13 In transgressing and *l* against
Jer 7: 4 Do not trust in these *l* words,
7: 8 you trust in *l* words that
29:23 and have spoken *l* words in My
Lam 3:10 He has been to me a bear *l* in
Ezek 13:19 by your *l* to My people who
36:34 shall be tilled instead of *l*
Dan 2: 9 For you have agreed to speak *l*
Hos 4: 2 By swearing and *l*, Killing
Mt 8: 6 my servant is *l* at home
8:14 He saw his wife's mother *l* sick
9: 2 brought to Him a paralytic *l*
Mk 2: 4 on which the paralytic was *l*.
5:40 entered where the child was *l*.
7:30 and her daughter *l* on the bed.
Lk 2:12 cloths, *l* in a manger."
2:16 and the Babe *l* in a manger.
5:25 took up what he had been *l* on,
11:54 *l* in wait for Him, and seeking
24:12 he saw the linen cloths *l* by
Jn 5: 6 When Jesus saw him *l* there, and
11:41 place where the dead man was *l*.
20: 5 saw the linen cloths *l* there;
20: 6 and he saw the linen cloths *l*
20: 7 not *l* with the linen cloths,
Rom 9: 1 the truth in Christ, I am not *l*,
2 Cor 11:31 forever, knows that I am not *l*.
Eph 4:25 Therefore, putting away *l*,
2 Th 2: 9 power, signs, and *l* wonders,
1 Tim 2: 7 the truth in Christ and not *l*—

LYRE (4/4)

Dan 3: 5 of the horn, flute, harp, *l*,
3: 7 the horn, flute, harp, and *l*,
3:10 of the horn, flute, harp, *l*,
3:15 of the horn, flute, harp, *l*,

LYSANIAS (1/1)

Lk 3: 1 and *L* tetrarch of Abilene,

LYSIAS (3/3)

Acts 23:26 Claudius *L*, to the most
24: 7 But the commander *L* came by and
24:22 When *L* the commander comes

LYSTRA (6/6)

Acts 14: 6 aware of it and fled to *L* and
14: 8 And in *L* a certain man without
14:21 disciples, they returned to *L*,
16: 1 Then he came to Derbe and *L*.
16: 2 by the brethren who were at *L*
2 Tim 3:11 me at Antioch, at Iconium, at *L*—

M

MAACAH (7/7)

2 Sam 3: 3 the third, Absalom the son of *M*,
10: 6 and from the king of *M* one
10: 8 and *M* were by themselves in
1 Chr 3: 2 the third, Absalom the son of *M*,
8:29 whose wife's name was *M*,
9:35 whose wife's name was *M*,
2 Chr 11:20 After her he took *M* the

MAACHAH (19/19)

Gen 22:24 Tebah, Gaham, Thahash, and *M*.
1 Ki 2:39 ran away to Achish the son of *M*,
15: 2 His mother's name was *M* the
15:10 His grandmother's name was *M*
15:13 Also he removed *M* his
1 Chr 2:48 *M*, Caleb's concubine, bore
7:15 and Shuppim, whose name was *M*.
7:16 (*M* the wife of Machir bore a
11:43 Hanan the son of *M*,
19: 6 from Mesopotamia, from Syrian *M*,
19: 7 with the king of *M* and his
27:16 Shephatiah the son of *M*;
2 Chr 11:21 Now Rehoboam loved *M* the
11:22 appointed Abijah the son of *M*
15:16 Also he removed *M*, the mother

MAACHATHI (KJV) See MAACHATHITES

MAACHATHITE (4/4)

2 Sam 23:34 of Ahasbai, the son of the *M*,
2 Ki 25:23 and Jaazaniah the son of a *M*,
1 Chr 4:19 Garmite and of Eshtemoa the *M*.
Jer 40: 8 and Jezaniah the son of a *M*,

MAACHATHITES (5/4)

Deut 3:14 of the Geshurites and the *M*,
Josh 12: 5 of the Geshurites and the *M*,
13:11 border of the Geshurites and *M*,
13:13 out the Geshurites or the *M*,
13:13 but the Geshurites and the *M*

MAADAI (1/1)

Ezra 10:34 of the sons of Bani: *M*,

MAADIAH (1/1)

Neh 12: 5 Mijamin, *M*, Bilgah,

MAAI (1/1)

Neh 12:36 Azarel, Milalai, Gilalai, *M*,

MAALEH-ACRABBIM (KJV) See (ASCENT OF) AKRABBIM

MAARATH (1/1)

Josh 15:59 *M*, Beth Anoth, and Eltekon:

MAASAI (1/1)

1 Chr 9:12 *M* the son of Adiel, the son of

MAASEIAH (23/23)

1 Chr 15:18 Jehiel, Unni, Eliab, Benaiah, *M*,
15:20 Jehiel, Unni, Eliab, *M*,
2 Chr 23: 1 *M* the son of Adaiah, and
26:11 by Jeiel the scribe and *M* the
28: 7 killed *M* the king's son,
34: 8 *M* the governor of the city, and
Ezra 10:18 of Jozadak, and his brothers: *M*,
10:21 of the sons of Harim: *M*,
10:22 sons of Pashhur: Elioenai, *M*,
10:30 Adna, Chelal, Benaiah, *M*,
Neh 3:23 After them Azariah the son of *M*,
8: 4 Anaiah, Urijah, Hilkiah, and *M*;
8: 7 Akkub, Shabbethai, Hodijah, *M*,
10:25 Rehum, Hashabnah, *M*,
11: 5 and *M* the son of Baruch, the son
11: 7 son of Kolaiah, the son of *M*,
12:41 and the priests, Eliakim, *M*,
12:42 also *M*, Shemaiah, Eleazar,
Jer 21: 1 and Zephaniah the son of *M*,
29:21 and Zedekiah the son of *M*,
29:25 to Zephaniah the son of *M* the
35: 4 above the chamber of *M* the son
37: 3 and Zephaniah the son of *M*,

MAASIAI (KJV) See MAASAI

MAATH (1/1)

Lk 3:26 the son of *M*, the son of

MAAZ (1/1)

1 Chr 2:27 firstborn of Jerahmeel, were *M*,

MAAZIAH (2/2)

1 Chr 24:18 Delaiah, the twenty-fourth to *M*.
Neh 10: 8 *M*, Bilgai, and Shemaiah.

MACEDONIA (23/20)

Acts 16: 9 A man of *M* stood and pleaded
16: 9 Come over to *M* and help us."
16:10 we sought to go to *M*,
16:12 foremost city of that part of *M*,
18: 5 and Timothy had come from *M*,
19:21 when he had passed through *M*
19:22 So he sent into *M* two of those
20: 1 them, and departed to go to *M*.
20: 3 he decided to return through *M*.
Rom 15:26 For it pleased those from *M* and
1 Cor 16: 5 to you when I pass through *M*
16: 5 (for I am passing through *M*).
2 Cor 1:16 to pass by way of you to *M*,
1:16 to come again from *M* to you,
2:13 leave of them, I departed for *M*.

7: 5 For indeed, when we came to ***M***,
8: 1 bestowed on the churches of ***M***:
11: 9 the brethren who came from ***M***
Phil 4:15 gospel, when I departed from ***M***,
1 Th 1: 7 you became examples to all in ***M***
1: 8 not only in ***M*** and Achaia, but
4:10 the brethren who are in all ***M***.
1 Tim 1: 3 I urged you when I went into ***M***—

MACEDONIAN (1/1)

Acts 27: 2 a ***M*** of Thessalonica, was with

MACEDONIANS (3/3)

Acts 19:29 seized Gaius and Aristarchus, ***M***,
2 Cor 9: 2 which I boast of you to the ***M***,
9: 4 lest if some ***M*** come with me and

MACHBANAI (1/1)

1 Chr 12:13 the tenth, and ***M*** the eleventh.

MACHBENAH (1/1)

1 Chr 2:49 Sheva the father of ***M*** and the

MACHI (1/1)

Num 13:15 of Gad, Geuel the son of ***M***.

MACHIR (22/20)

Gen 50:23 The children of ***M***,
Num 26:29 The sons of Manasseh: of ***M***,
26:29 and ***M*** begot Gilead; of Gilead,
27: 1 the son of Gilead, the son of ***M***,
32:39 And the children of ***M*** the son of
32:40 So Moses gave Gilead to ***M*** the
36: 1 children of Gilead the son of ***M***,
Deut 3:15 "Also I gave Gilead to ***M***.
Josh 13:31 were for the children of ***M*** the
13:31 for half of the children of ***M***
17: 1 namely for ***M*** the firstborn of
17: 3 the son of Gilead, the son of ***M***,
Judg 5:14 From ***M*** rulers came down,
2 Sam 9: 4 he is in the house of ***M*** the
9: 5 him out of the house of ***M*** the
17:27 ***M*** the son of Ammiel from Lo
1 Chr 2:21 went in to the daughter of ***M***
2:23 belonged to the sons of ***M***
7:14 his Syrian concubine bore him ***M***
7:15 ***M*** took as his wife the sister
7:16 (Maachah the wife of ***M*** bore a
7:17 of Gilead the son of ***M***,

MACHIRITES (1/1)

Num 26:29 of Machir, the family of the ***M***;

MACHNADEBAI (1/1)

Ezra 10:40 ***M***, Shashai, Sharai,

MACHPELAH (6/6)

Gen 23: 9 he may give me the cave of ***M***
23:17 field of Ephron which was in ***M***,
23:19 in the cave of the field of ***M***,
25: 9 buried him in the cave of ***M***,
49:30 cave that is in the field of ***M***,
50:13 in the cave of the field of ***M***,

MAD (6/6) MADMAN, MADNESS

Deut 28:34 So you shall be driven ***m*** because
Isa 44:25 And drives diviners ***m***;
Jer 25:16 will drink and stagger and go ***m***
Jn 10:20 said, "He has a demon and is ***m***.
Acts 26:24 Much learning is driving you ***m***!
26:25 But he said, "I am not ***m***,

MADAI (2/2)

Gen 10: 2 Japheth were Gomer, Magog, ***M***,
1 Chr 1: 5 Japheth were Gomer, Magog, ***M***,

MADE (1316/1236) ESTABLISHED, MAKE, TOOK

Gen 1: 7 Thus God ***m*** the firmament, and
1:16 Then God ***m*** two great lights:
1:16 He ***m*** the stars also.
1:25 And God ***m*** the beast of the earth
1:31 saw everything that He had ***m***,
2: 3 which God had created and ***m***.
2: 4 in the day that the LORD God ***m***
2: 9 of the ground the LORD God ***m***
2:22 God had taken from man He ***m***
3: 1 field which the LORD God had ***m***.
3: 7 sewed fig leaves together and ***m***
3:21 and his wife the LORD God ***m***
5: 1 He ***m*** him in the likeness of
6: 6 LORD was sorry that He had ***m***
6: 7 for I am sorry that I have ***m***
7: 4 all living things that I have ***m***.
8: 1 And God ***m*** a wind to pass over
8: 6 of the ark which he had ***m***.
9: 6 For in the image of God He ***m***
13: 4 of the altar which he had ***m***
14: 2 that they ***m*** war with Bera king
14:23 I have ***m*** Abram rich'—
15:18 On the same day the LORD ***m*** a
17: 5 for I have ***m*** you a father of
19: 3 Then he ***m*** them a feast, and
19:33 So they ***m*** their father drink
19:35 Then they ***m*** their father drink
21: 6 God has ***m*** me laugh, and all who
21: 8 And Abraham ***m*** a great feast on
21:27 and the two of them ***m*** a
21:32 Thus they ***m*** a covenant at
24:11 And he ***m*** his camels kneel down
24:21 to know whether the LORD had ***m***
24:37 Now my master ***m*** me swear,
24:46 And she ***m*** haste and let her
26:22 For now the LORD has ***m*** room for
26:30 So he ***m*** them a feast, and they
27:14 and his mother ***m*** savory food,
27:31 He also had ***m*** savory food, and
27:37 Indeed I have ***m*** him your master,
28:20 Then Jacob ***m*** a vow, saying, "If
29:22 all the men of the place and ***m***
30:40 and ***m*** the flocks face toward
31:13 the pillar and where you ***m*** a
31:46 And they took stones and ***m*** a
33:17 and ***m*** booths for his livestock.
37: 3 Also he ***m*** him a tunic of many
39: 3 with him and that the LORD ***m***
39: 4 Then he ***m*** him overseer of his
39: 5 from the time that he had ***m***
39:23 the LORD ***m*** it prosper.
40:20 that he ***m*** a feast for all his
41:51 For God has ***m*** me forget all my
43:25 Then they ***m*** the present ready
43:30 so Joseph ***m*** haste and sought
45: 1 stood with him while Joseph ***m***
45: 8 and He has ***m*** me a father to
45: 9 God has ***m*** me lord of all Egypt;
46:29 So Joseph ***m*** ready his chariot
47:26 And Joseph ***m*** it a law over the
49:24 the arms of his hands were ***m***
50: 5 My father ***m*** me swear, saying,
50: 6 father, as he ***m*** you swear."
Ex 1:13 So the Egyptians ***m*** the children
1:14 And they ***m*** their lives bitter
1:14 their service in which they ***m***
2:14 Who ***m*** you a prince and a judge
4:11 Who has ***m*** man's mouth? Or who
5: 8 quota of bricks which they ***m***
5:21 because you have ***m*** us abhorrent
7: 1 I have ***m*** you as God to
9:20 the servants of Pharaoh ***m*** his
14: 6 So he ***m*** ready his chariot and
14:21 and ***m*** the sea into dry land,
15:17 which You have ***m*** For Your own
15:25 the waters were ***m*** sweet.
15:25 There He ***m*** a statute and an
16:31 of it was like wafers ***m*** with
18:25 and ***m*** them heads over the
20:11 For in six days the LORD ***m*** the
21:29 and it has been ***m*** known to his
24: 8 covenant which the LORD has ***m***
25:33 Three bowls shall be ***m*** like
25:33 and three bowls ***m*** like almond
25:34 itself four bowls shall be ***m***
25:39 It shall be ***m*** of a talent of
26:36 woven linen, ***m*** by a weaver.
27: 9 be hangings for the court ***m***
27:16 ***m*** by a weaver. It shall have
27:18 ***m*** of fine woven linen, and
28: 8 ***m*** of gold, blue, purple, and
29:18 an offering ***m*** by fire to the
29:23 one cake ***m*** with oil, and one
29:25 It is an offering ***m*** by fire to
29:33 with which the atonement was ***m***,
29:41 an offering ***m*** by fire to the
30:20 to burn an offering ***m*** by fire
31:17 for in six days the LORD ***m***
31:18 And when He had ***m*** an end of
32: 4 and ***m*** a molded calf. Then they
32: 5 And Aaron ***m*** a proclamation and
32: 8 They have ***m*** themselves a molded
32:20 took the calf which they had ***m***,
32:20 it on the water and ***m*** the
32:31 and have ***m*** for themselves a god
32:35 did with the calf which Aaron ***m***.
34: 8 So Moses ***m*** haste and bowed his
34:27 tenor of these words I have ***m***
35:22 every man who ***m*** an offering of
36: 8 who worked on the tabernacle ***m***
36: 8 designs of cherubim they ***m***
36:11 He ***m*** loops of blue yarn on the
36:12 Fifty loops he ***m*** on one curtain,
36:12 and fifty loops he ***m*** on the
36:13 And he ***m*** fifty clasps of gold,
36:14 He ***m*** curtains of goats' hair
36:14 he ***m*** eleven curtains.
36:17 And he ***m*** fifty loops on the edge
36:17 and fifty loops he ***m*** on the
36:18 He also ***m*** fifty bronze clasps to
36:19 Then he ***m*** a covering for the
36:20 For the tabernacle he ***m*** boards
36:22 Thus he ***m*** for all the boards of
36:23 And he ***m*** boards for the
36:24 Forty sockets of silver he ***m*** to
36:25 side, he ***m*** twenty boards
36:27 side of the tabernacle he ***m***
36:28 He also ***m*** two boards for the two
36:29 Thus he ***m*** both of them for the
36:31 And he ***m*** bars of acacia wood:
36:33 And he ***m*** the middle bar to pass
36:34 ***m*** their rings of gold to be
36:35 And he ***m*** a veil of blue,
36:36 He ***m*** for it four pillars of
36:37 He also ***m*** a screen for the
36:37 ***m*** by a weaver,
37: 1 Then Bezalel ***m*** the ark of acacia
37: 2 and ***m*** a molding of gold all
37: 4 He ***m*** poles of acacia wood, and
37: 6 He also ***m*** the mercy seat of pure
37: 7 He ***m*** two cherubim of beaten
37: 7 he ***m*** them of one piece at the
37: 8 He ***m*** the cherubim at the two
37:10 He ***m*** the table of acacia wood;
37:11 and ***m*** a molding of gold all
37:12 Also he ***m*** a frame of a
37:12 and ***m*** a molding of gold for the
37:15 And he ***m*** the poles of acacia
37:16 He ***m*** of pure gold the utensils
37:17 He also ***m*** the lampstand of pure
37:17 of hammered work he ***m*** the
37:19 There were three bowls ***m*** like
37:19 and three bowls ***m*** like almond
37:20 itself were four bowls ***m*** like
37:23 And he ***m*** its seven lamps, its
37:24 Of a talent of pure gold he ***m***
37:25 He ***m*** the incense altar of
37:26 He also ***m*** for it a molding of
37:27 He ***m*** two rings of gold for it
37:28 And he ***m*** the poles of acacia
37:29 He also ***m*** the holy anointing
38: 1 He ***m*** the altar of burnt offering
38: 2 He ***m*** its horns on its four
38: 3 He ***m*** all the utensils for the
38: 3 all its utensils he ***m*** of
38: 4 And he ***m*** a grate of bronze
38: 6 And he ***m*** the poles of acacia
38: 7 He ***m*** the altar hollow with
38: 8 He ***m*** the laver of bronze and
38: 9 Then he ***m*** the court on the
38:22 ***m*** all that the LORD had
38:28 and seventy-five shekels he ***m***
38:28 and ***m*** bands for them.
38:30 And with it he ***m*** the sockets for
39: 1 and scarlet thread they ***m***
39: 1 and ***m*** the holy garments for
39: 2 He ***m*** the ephod of gold, blue,
39: 4 They ***m*** shoulder straps for it to
39: 8 And he ***m*** the breastplate,
39: 9 They ***m*** the breastplate square by
39:15 And they ***m*** chains for the
39:16 They also ***m*** two settings of gold
39:19 And they ***m*** two rings of gold and
39:20 They ***m*** two other gold rings and
39:22 He ***m*** the robe of the ephod of
39:24 They ***m*** on the hem of the robe
39:25 And they ***m*** bells of pure gold,
39:27 They ***m*** tunics, artistically
39:29 ***m*** by a weaver, as the LORD had
39:30 Then they ***m*** the plate of the
Lev 1: 9 an offering ***m*** by fire, a sweet
1:13 an offering ***m*** by fire, a sweet
1:17 an offering ***m*** by fire, a sweet
2: 2 an offering ***m*** by fire, a sweet
2: 3 of the offerings to the LORD ***m***
2: 7 it shall be ***m*** of fine flour
2: 8 the grain offering that is ***m***
2: 9 It is an offering ***m*** by fire,
2:10 of the offerings to the LORD ***m***
2:11 bring to the LORD shall be ***m***
2:11 in any offering to the LORD ***m***
2:16 as an offering ***m*** by fire to the
3: 3 peace offering an offering ***m***
3: 5 as an offering ***m*** by fire, a
3: 9 as an offering ***m*** by fire to the
3:11 an offering ***m*** by fire to the
3:14 as an offering ***m*** by fire to the
3:16 an offering ***m*** by fire for a
4:35 according to the offerings ***m*** by
5:12 according to the offerings ***m***
6:17 portion of My offerings ***m*** by
6:18 concerning the offerings ***m*** by
6:21 It shall be ***m*** in a pan with oil.
7: 5 on the altar as an offering ***m***
7:25 which men offer an offering ***m***
7:30 shall bring the offerings ***m*** by
7:35 from the offerings ***m*** by fire to
8:21 an offering ***m*** by fire to the
8:28 That was an offering ***m*** by fire
10:12 remains of the offerings ***m*** by
10:13 of the sacrifices ***m*** by fire to
10:15 with the offerings of fat ***m*** by
10:16 Then Moses ***m*** careful inquiry
13:48 in leather or in anything ***m*** of
13:49 or in anything ***m*** of leather, it
13:51 the leather or in anything ***m***
13:53 or in anything ***m*** of leather,
13:57 or in anything ***m*** of leather, it
13:58 or whatever is ***m*** of leather, if
13:59 or in anything ***m*** of leather, to
14:11 present the man who is to be ***m***
14:36 is in the house may not be ***m***
16:20 And when he has ***m*** an end of
21: 6 the offerings of the LORD ***m***
21:21 near to offer the offerings ***m***
22: 4 And whoever touches anything ***m***
22: 5 thing by which he would be ***m***
22:27 be accepted as an offering ***m***
23: 8 you shall offer an offering ***m***
23:13 an offering ***m*** by fire to the
23:18 an offering ***m*** by fire for a
23:25 you shall offer an offering ***m***
23:27 and offer an offering ***m*** by fire
23:36 you shall offer an offering ***m***
23:36 you shall offer an offering ***m***
23:37 to offer an offering ***m*** by fire
23:43 generations may know that I ***m***
24: 7 an offering ***m*** by fire to the

24: 9 the offerings of the LORD *m*
26:13 the bands of your yoke and *m*
26:46 and laws which the LORD *m*
Num 4:26 service and all that is *m* for
5: 8 to whom restitution may be *m*
5: 8 with which atonement is *m* for
5:27 When he has *m* her drink the
6: 3 shall drink neither vinegar *m*
6: 3 made from wine nor vinegar *m*
7: 2 were numbered, *m* an offering.
8: 4 so he *m* the lampstand.
8:21 and Aaron *m* atonement for them
11: 8 and *m* cakes of it; and its
14:36 who returned and *m* all the
15:10 a hin of wine as an offering *m*
15:13 in presenting an offering *m* by
15:14 would present an offering *m* by
15:25 an offering *m* by fire to the
16:38 let them be *m* into hammered
16:47 So he put in the incense and *m*
18:17 their fat as an offering *m* by
20: 5 And why have you *m* us come up
21: 2 So Israel *m* a vow to the LORD,
21: 9 So Moses *m* a bronze serpent, and
25:13 and *m* atonement for the
28: 2 My food for My offerings *m* by
28: 3 This is the offering *m* by fire
28: 6 an offering *m* by fire to the
28: 8 offer it as an offering *m* by
28:13 an offering *m* by fire to the
28:19 shall present an offering *m* by
28:24 the food of the offering *m* by
29: 6 an offering *m* by fire to the
29:13 an offering *m* by fire as a
29:36 an offering *m* by fire as a
30:11 and *m* no response to her and
30:12 But if her husband truly *m* them
30:12 her husband has *m* them void,
30:14 because he *m* no response to her
31:20 everything *m* of leather,
31:20 and everything *m* of wood."
32:13 and He *m* them wander in the
35:33 and no atonement can be *m* for
Deut 1:15 and *m* them heads over you,
2:30 God hardened his spirit and *m*
4:23 the LORD your God which He *m*
5: 2 The LORD our God *m* a covenant
9: 9 the covenant which the LORD *m*
9:12 they have *m* themselves a molded
9:16 had *m* for yourselves a molded
9:21 sin, the calf which you had *m*,
10: 3 So I *m* an ark of acacia wood,
10: 5 in the ark which I had *m*;
10:22 now the LORD your God has *m*
11: 4 how He *m* the waters of the Red
18: 1 the offerings of the LORD *m*
26:19 all nations which He has *m*,
29: 1 the covenant which He *m* with
29:25 which He *m* with them when He
31:16 My covenant which I have *m*
32: 6 Has He not *m* you and
32:13 He *m* him ride in the heights of
32:13 He *m* him draw honey from the
32:15 Then he forsook God who *m*
Josh 2:17 oath of yours which you have *m*
2:20 from your oath which you *m* us
5: 3 So Joshua *m* flint knives for
8:15 And Joshua and all Israel *m* as
8:24 came to pass when Israel had *m*
8:28 So Joshua burned Ai and *m* it a
9:15 So Joshua *m* peace with them, and
9:15 and *m* a covenant with them to
9:16 after they had *m* a covenant
9:27 And that day Joshua *m* them
10: 1 the inhabitants of Gibeon had *m*
10: 4 for it has *m* peace with Joshua
10: 5 and camped before Gibeon and *m*
10:20 and the children of Israel *m*
11:18 Joshua *m* war a long time with
11:19 There was not a city that *m*
13:14 of the LORD God of Israel *m*
14: 8 brethren who went up with me *m*
19:49 When they had *m* an end of
19:51 So they *m* an end of dividing
22:25 For the LORD has *m* the Jordan a
22:28 the LORD which our fathers *m*,
24:25 So Joshua *m* a covenant with the
24:25 and *m* for them a statute and an
Judg 3:16 Now Ehud *m* himself a dagger (it
6: 2 the children of Israel *m* for
8:27 Then Gideon *m* it into an ephod
8:33 and *m* Baal-Berith their god.
9: 6 and they went and *m* Abimelech
9:18 and *m* Abimelech, the son of his
9:27 and *m* merry. And they went into
11: 4 that the people of Ammon *m* war
11: 5 when the people of Ammon *m* war
11:11 and the people *m* him head and
11:30 And Jephthah *m* a vow to the
17: 4 and he *m* it into a carved image
17: 5 and *m* an ephod and household
18:24 taken away my gods which I *m*,
18:27 took the things Micah had *m*,
18:31 Micah's carved image which he *m*,
21: 5 For they had *m* a great oath
21:15 because the LORD had *m* a void
1 Sam 1:11 Then she *m* a vow and said, "O
2:28 of the children of Israel *m* by
3:13 because his sons *m* themselves
4:18 when he *m* mention of the ark of
6:15 offered burnt offerings and *m*
8: 1 when Samuel was old that he *m*

11:15 and there they *m* Saul king
11:15 There they *m* sacrifices of
12: 1 and have *m* a king over you.
12: 8 your fathers out of Egypt and *m*
13:12 and I have not *m* supplication
14:14 Jonathan and his armorbearer *m*
15:33 As your sword has *m* women
15:35 LORD regretted that He had *m*
16: 8 and *m* him pass before Samuel.
16: 9 Then Jesse *m* Shammah pass by.
16:10 Thus Jesse *m* seven of his sons
18: 3 Then Jonathan and David *m* a
18:13 and *m* him his captain over a
20:16 So Jonathan *m* a covenant with
22: 8 to me that my son has *m* a
23:18 So the two of them *m* a covenant
23:26 So David *m* haste to get away
25:18 Then Abigail *m* haste and took
27:10 Where have you *m* a raid today?"
27:12 He has *m* his people Israel
30:14 We *m* an invasion of the southern
30:21 whom they also had *m* to stay at
30:25 he *m* it a statute and an
2 Sam 2: 9 and he *m* him king over Gilead,
3:20 And David *m* a feast for Abner
4: 4 as she *m* haste to flee, that he
5: 3 and King David *m* a covenant
7: 9 and have *m* you a great name,
7:24 For You have *m* Your people
8:13 And David *m* himself a name when
10: 6 of Ammon saw that they had *m*
10:19 they *m* peace with Israel and
11:13 and he *m* him drunk. And at
12:31 and *m* them cross over to the
13: 8 *m* cakes in his sight, and baked
13:10 took the cakes which she had *m*,
14:15 king because the people have *m*
15: 4 that I were *m* judge in the
15: 7 and pay the vow which I *m* to
17:25 And Absalom *m* Amasa captain of
22: 5 The floods of ungodliness *m* me
22:12 He *m* darkness canopies around
22:36 Your gentleness has *m* me
23: 5 Yet He has *m* with me an
1 Ki 1:43 No! Our lord King David has *m*
1:44 and they have *m* him ride on the
3: 1 Now Solomon *m* a treaty with
3: 7 You have *m* Your servant king
3:15 and *m* a feast for all his
4: 7 each one *m* provision for one
5:12 and the two of them *m* a treaty
6: 4 And he *m* for the house windows
6: 5 Thus he *m* side chambers all
6: 6 for he *m* narrow ledges around
6:23 the inner sanctuary he *m* two
6:31 of the inner sanctuary he *m*
6:33 door of the sanctuary he also *m*
7: 6 He also *m* the Hall of Pillars:
7: 7 Then he *m* a hall for the throne,
7: 8 Solomon also *m* a house like
7:16 Then he *m* two capitals of cast
7:17 He *m* a lattice network, with
7:18 So he *m* the pillars, and two
7:23 And he *m* the Sea of cast
7:27 He also *m* ten carts of bronze;
7:37 Thus he *m* the ten carts. All of
7:38 Then he *m* ten lavers of bronze;
7:40 Huram *m* the lavers and the
7:45 these articles which Huram *m*
7:48 had all the furnishings *m* for
8: 9 when the LORD *m* a covenant
8:21 And there I have *m* a place for
8:21 of the LORD which He *m* with
8:38 whatever supplication is *m* by
8:59 with which I have *m*
9: 3 supplication that you have *m*
9:22 children of Israel Solomon *m*
10: 9 therefore He *m* you king, to do
10:12 And the king *m* steps of the
10:16 And King Solomon *m* two hundred
10:17 He also *m* three hundred shields
10:18 Moreover the king *m* a great
10:20 nothing like this had been *m*
10:27 The king *m* silver as common in
10:27 and he *m* cedar trees as
11:28 *m* him the officer over all the
11:34 because I have *m* him ruler all
12: 4 Your father *m* our yoke heavy;
12:10 Your father *m* our yoke heavy,
12:14 My father *m* your yoke heavy, but
12:20 and *m* him king over all Israel.
12:28 *m* two calves of gold, and said
12:31 He *m* shrines on the high places,
12:31 and *m* priests from every class
12:32 to the calves that he had *m*.
12:32 the high places which he had *m*.
12:33 So he *m* offerings on the altar
12:33 on the altar which he had *m* at
13:33 but again he *m* priests from
14: 7 and *m* you ruler over My people
14: 9 for you have gone and *m* for
14:15 because they have *m* their
14:16 who sinned and who *m* Israel
14:19 how he *m* war and how he
14:26 shields which Solomon had *m*.
14:27 Then King Rehoboam *m* bronze
15:12 idols that his fathers had *m*.
15:13 because she had *m* an obscene
15:22 Then King Asa *m* a proclamation
15:26 in his sin by which he had *m*
15:30 sinned and by which he had *m*
15:34 in his sin by which he had *m*

16: 2 you out of the dust and *m* you
16: 2 and have *m* My people Israel
16:13 sinned and by which they had *m*
16:16 So all Israel *m* Omri, the
16:26 in his sin by which he had *m*
16:33 And Ahab *m* a wooden image.
18:26 the altar which they had *m*.
18:32 and he *m* a trench around the
20: 1 and *m* war against it.
20:34 So he *m* a treaty with him and
21:22 to anger, and *m* Israel sin.'
22:11 the son of Chenaanah had *m*
22:44 Also Jehoshaphat *m* peace with
22:45 and how he *m* war, are they not
22:48 Jehoshaphat *m* merchant ships to
22:52 who had *m* Israel sin;
2 Ki 3: 2 of Baal that his father had *m*.
3: 3 who had *m* Israel sin; he did
6: 6 and he *m* the iron float.
8:20 and *m* a king over themselves.
9:21 And his chariot was *m* ready.
10:25 as soon as he had *m* an end of
10:27 down the temple of Baal and *m*
10:29 who had *m* Israel sin, that
10:31 who had *m* Israel sin.
11: 4 And he *m* a covenant with them
11:12 they *m* him king and anointed
11:17 Then Jehoiada *m* a covenant
12:13 However there were not *m* for the
13: 2 who had *m* Israel sin. He did
13: 6 who had *m* Israel sin, but
13: 7 Syria had destroyed them and *m*
13:11 who *m* Israel sin, but walked
14:21 and *m* him king instead of his
14:24 who had *m* Israel sin.
14:28 how he *m* war, and how he
15: 9 who had *m* Israel sin.
15:18 who had *m* Israel sin.
15:24 who had *m* Israel sin.
15:28 who had *m* Israel sin.
16: 3 indeed he *m* his son pass
16:11 So Urijah the priest *m* it
16:12 king approached the altar and *m*
17: 8 of Israel, which they had *m*.
17:15 and His covenant that He had *m*
17:16 *m* for themselves a molded image
17:16 *m* a wooden image and worshiped
17:19 statutes of Israel which they *m*.
17:21 and they *m* Jeroboam the son of
17:21 and *m* them commit a great sin.
17:29 which the Samaritans had *m*,
17:30 The men of Babylon *m* Succoth
17:30 the men of Cuth *m* Nergal, the
17:30 the men of Hamath *m* Ashima,
17:31 and the Avites *m* Nibhaz and
17:35 with whom the LORD had *m* a
17:38 the covenant that I have *m*
18: 4 bronze serpent that Moses had *m*;
19:15 You have *m* heaven and earth.
19:25 not hear long ago How I *m* it,
20:20 and how he *m* a pool and a
21: 3 and *m* a wooden image, as Ahab
21: 6 Also he *m* his son pass through
21: 7 image of Asherah that he had *m*,
21:11 and has also *m* Judah sin with
21:16 besides his sin by which he *m*
21:24 Then the people of the land *m*
22: 7 there need be no accounting *m*
23: 3 king stood by a pillar and *m* a
23: 4 all the articles that were *m*
23:12 which the kings of Judah had *m*,
23:12 altars which Manasseh had *m* in
23:15 who *m* Israel sin, had made,
23:15 who made Israel sin, had *m*,
23:19 the kings of Israel had *m* to
23:30 and *m* him king in his father's
23:34 Then Pharaoh Necho *m* Eliakim the
24:13 Solomon king of Israel had *m*
24:17 Then the king of Babylon *m*
25:16 which Solomon had *m* for the
25:22 Then he *m* Gedaliah the son of
25:23 that the king of Babylon had *m*
1 Chr 5:10 Now in the days of Saul they *m*
5:19 They *m* war with the Hagrites,
9:30 of the sons of the priests *m*
11: 3 and David *m* a covenant with
12:18 and *m* them captains of the
14: 9 the Philistines went and *m* a
14:13 the Philistines once again *m* a
16: 5 but Asaph *m* music with cymbals;
16:16 The covenant which He *m* with
16:26 But the LORD *m* the heavens.
17: 8 and have *m* you a name like the
17:22 For You have *m* Your people
18: 8 with which Solomon *m* the bronze
19: 6 of Ammon saw that they had *m*
19:19 they *m* peace with David and
21:29 which Moses had *m* in the
22: 5 So David *m* abundant
22: 8 have shed much blood and have *m*
23: 1 he *m* his son Solomon king over
23: 5 instruments, "which I *m*,
26:10 his father *m* him the first),
26:32 whom King David *m* officials
28: 2 and had *m* preparations to build
28:19 the LORD *m* me understand in
29: 2 gold for things to be *m* of
29:19 the temple for which I have *m*
29:21 And they *m* sacrifices to the
29:22 And they *m* Solomon the son of
2 Chr 1: 3 the servant of the LORD had *m*
1: 5 of Uri, the son of Hur, had *m*,

1: 8 and have ***m*** me king in his
1: 9 for You have ***m*** me king over a
1:11 My people over whom I have ***m***
1:15 Also the king ***m*** silver and gold
1:15 and he ***m*** cedars as abundant as
2:11 He has ***m*** you king over them.
2:12 who ***m*** heaven and earth, for He
2:18 And he ***m*** seventy thousand of
3: 8 And he ***m*** the Most Holy Place.
3:10 In the Most Holy Place he ***m*** two
3:14 And he ***m*** the veil of blue,
3:15 Also he ***m*** in front of the
3:16 He ***m*** wreaths of chainwork, as in
3:16 and he ***m*** one hundred
4: 1 Moreover he ***m*** a bronze altar:
4: 2 Then he ***m*** the Sea of cast
4: 6 He also ***m*** ten lavers, and put
4: 7 And he ***m*** ten lampstands of gold
4: 8 He also ***m*** ten tables, and placed
4: 8 And he ***m*** one hundred bowls of
4: 9 Furthermore he ***m*** the court of
4:11 Then Huram ***m*** the pots and the
4:14 he also ***m*** carts and the lavers
4:16 Huram his master craftsman ***m***
4:18 had all these articles ***m*** in
4:19 had all the furnishings ***m*** for
5:10 when the LORD ***m*** a covenant
6:11 of the LORD which He ***m*** with
6:13 (for Solomon had ***m*** a bronze
6:29 whatever supplication is ***m*** by
6:40 be attentive to the prayer ***m***
7: 6 which King David had ***m*** to
7: 7 altar which Solomon had ***m*** was
7:15 My ears attentive to prayer ***m***
9: 8 therefore He ***m*** you king over
9:11 And the king ***m*** walkways of the
9:15 And King Solomon ***m*** two hundred
9:16 He also ***m*** three hundred
9:17 Moreover the king ***m*** a great
9:19 nothing like this had been ***m***
9:27 The king ***m*** silver as common in
9:27 and he ***m*** cedar trees as
10: 4 Your father ***m*** our yoke heavy;
10:10 Your father ***m*** our yoke heavy,
10:14 My father ***m*** your yoke heavy, but
11:12 and ***m*** them very strong, having
11:15 the calf idols which he had ***m***.
11:17 and ***m*** Rehoboam the son of
12: 9 shields which Solomon had ***m***.
12:10 Then King Rehoboam ***m*** bronze
13: 8 gold calves which Jeroboam ***m***
13: 9 and ***m*** for yourselves priests,
15:16 because she had ***m*** an obscene
16:14 which he had ***m*** for himself in
16:14 They ***m*** a very great burning for
18:10 the son of Chenaanah had ***m***
20:23 And when they had ***m*** an end of
20:27 for the LORD had ***m*** them
20:36 and they ***m*** the ships in Ezion
21: 7 of the covenant that He had ***m***
21: 8 and ***m*** a king over themselves.
21:11 Moreover he ***m*** high places in the
21:13 and have ***m*** Judah and the
21:19 And his people ***m*** no burning for
22: 1 the inhabitants of Jerusalem ***m***
23: 1 and ***m*** a covenant with the
23: 3 Then all the assembly ***m*** a
23:11 and ***m*** him king. Then Jehoiada
23:16 Then Jehoiada ***m*** a covenant
24: 8 at the king's command they ***m*** a
24: 9 And they ***m*** a proclamation
24:14 they ***m*** from it articles for the
25:16 Have we ***m*** you the king's
25:27 they ***m*** a conspiracy against him
26: 1 and ***m*** him king instead of his
26: 5 the LORD, God ***m*** him prosper.
26: 6 Now he went out and ***m*** war
26:13 that ***m*** war with mighty power,
26:15 And he ***m*** devices in Jerusalem,
28: 2 and ***m*** molded images for the
28:24 and ***m*** for himself altars in
28:25 single city of Judah he ***m*** high
29:24 and the sin offering be ***m***
32: 5 and ***m*** weapons and shields in
32:27 And he ***m*** himself treasuries for
33: 3 and ***m*** wooden images; and he
33: 7 image, the idol which he had ***m***,
33:22 which his father Manasseh had ***m***,
33:25 Then the people of the land ***m***
34: 4 and ***m*** dust of them and
34:31 king stood in his place and ***m***
34:32 And he ***m*** all who were present in
34:33 and ***m*** all who were present in
35:25 They ***m*** it a custom in Israel;
36: 1 and ***m*** him king in his father's
36: 4 Then the king of Egypt ***m***
36:10 and ***m*** Zedekiah, Jehoiakim's
36:13 who had ***m*** him swear an oath
36:22 so that he ***m*** a proclamation
Ezra 1: 1 so that he ***m*** a proclamation
4:15 that search may be ***m*** in the book
4:19 and a search has been ***m***,
4:23 and by force of arms ***m*** them
5:14 whom he had ***m*** governor.
5:17 let a search be ***m*** in the king's
6: 1 and a search was ***m*** in the
6:11 and let his house be ***m*** a refuse
6:22 for the LORD ***m*** them joyful,
10: 5 and ***m*** the leaders of the
Neh 3: 4 ***m*** repairs. Next to them
3: 4 ***m*** repairs. Next to them Zadok
3: 4 them Zadok the son of Baana ***m***
3: 5 Next to them the Tekoites ***m***
3: 8 ***m*** repairs. Also next to him
3: 8 ***m*** repairs; and they fortified
3: 9 of Jerusalem, ***m*** repairs.
3:10 Jedaiah the son of Harumaph ***m***
3:10 Hattush the son of Hashabniah ***m***
3:12 he and his daughters ***m*** repairs.
3:16 ***m*** repairs as far as the place
3:17 ***m*** repairs. Next to him
3:17 ***m*** repairs for his district.
3:18 of Keilah, ***m*** repairs.
3:22 of the plain, ***m*** repairs.
3:23 him Benjamin and Hasshub ***m***
3:23 ***m*** repairs by his house.
3:25 Palal the son of Uzai ***m***
3:25 Pedaiah the son of Parosh ***m***
3:26 Nethinim who dwelt in Ophel ***m***
3:28 the Horse Gate the priests ***m***
3:29 them Zadok the son of Immer ***m***
3:29 East Gate, ***m*** repairs.
3:30 the son of Berechiah ***m*** repairs
3:31 ***m*** repairs as far as the house
3:32 goldsmiths and the merchants ***m***
4: 9 Nevertheless we ***m*** our prayer to
6:14 the prophets who would have ***m***
8: 4 of wood which they had ***m*** for
8:16 out and brought them and ***m***
8:17 returned from the captivity ***m***
9: 6 You have ***m*** heaven, The heaven
9: 8 And ***m*** a covenant with him
9:10 So You ***m*** a name for Yourself,
9:14 You ***m*** known to them Your holy
9:18 Even when they ***m*** a molded calf
10:32 Also we ***m*** ordinances for
10:35 And we ***m*** ordinances to bring
12:43 for God had ***m*** them rejoice with
13:25 and ***m*** them swear by God,
13:26 and God ***m*** him king over all
Esth 1: 3 third year of his reign he ***m*** a
1: 5 the king ***m*** a feast lasting
1: 9 Queen Vashti also ***m*** a feast for
2:17 crown upon her head and ***m*** her
2:18 Then the king ***m*** a great feast,
2:23 And when an inquiry was ***m*** into
5:14 to him, "Let a gallows be ***m***,
5:14 Haman; so he had the gallows ***m***.
7: 9 which Haman ***m*** for Mordecai, who
9:17 the month they rested and ***m***
9:18 and ***m*** it a day of feasting and
Job 1:10 Have You not ***m*** a hedge around
2:11 For they had ***m*** an appointment
4:14 Which ***m*** all my bones shake.
9: 9 He ***m*** the Bear, Orion, and the
10: 8 Your hands have ***m*** me and
10: 9 that You have ***m*** me like clay.
12: 5 It is ***m*** ready for those
15: 7 Or were you ***m*** before the
15:27 And ***m*** his waist heavy with
16: 7 You have ***m*** desolate all my
17: 6 But He has ***m*** me a byword of the
23:16 For God ***m*** my heart weak,
27: 2 who has ***m*** my soul bitter,
28:18 No mention shall be ***m*** of coral
28:26 When He ***m*** a law for the rain,
31: 1 I have ***m*** a covenant with my
31:15 Did not He who ***m*** me in the womb
31:24 'If I have ***m*** gold my hope,
33: 4 The Spirit of God has ***m*** me,
38: 9 When I ***m*** the clouds its
39: 6 Whose home I have ***m*** the
40:15 which I ***m*** along with you;
40:19 Only He who ***m*** him can bring
41:33 Which is ***m*** without fear.
Ps 7:15 He ***m*** a pit and dug it out,
7:15 into the ditch which he ***m***.
8: 5 For You have ***m*** him a little
8: 6 You have ***m*** him to have dominion
9:15 down in the pit which they ***m***;
18: 4 the floods of ungodliness ***m*** me
18:11 He ***m*** darkness His secret place;
18:35 Your gentleness has ***m*** me
18:43 You have ***m*** me the head of the
21: 6 For You have ***m*** him most blessed
21: 6 You have ***m*** him exceedingly
22: 9 You ***m*** Me trust while on My
30: 7 by Your favor You have ***m*** my
30: 8 And to the LORD I ***m***
33: 6 of the LORD the heavens were ***m***,
39: 5 You have ***m*** my days as
45: 8 by which they have ***m*** You glad.
46: 8 Who has ***m*** desolations in the
50: 5 Those who have ***m*** a covenant
56:12 Vows ***m*** to You are binding
60: 2 You have ***m*** the earth tremble;
60: 3 You have ***m*** us drink the wine
69:11 I also ***m*** sackcloth my garment;
72:15 Prayer also will be ***m*** for Him
74:17 You have ***m*** summer and winter.
78:13 And He ***m*** the waters stand up
78:50 He ***m*** a path for His anger;
78:52 But He ***m*** His own people go
78:55 And ***m*** the tribes of Israel
78:64 And their widows ***m*** no
80: 6 You have ***m*** us a strife to our
80:15 And the branch that You ***m***
80:17 the son of man whom You ***m***
86: 9 All nations whom You have ***m***
88: 8 You have ***m*** me an abomination
89: 3 I have ***m*** a covenant with My
89:42 You have ***m*** all his enemies
89:44 You have ***m*** his glory cease,
91: 9 Because you have ***m*** the LORD,
92: 4 have ***m*** me glad through Your
95: 5 for He ***m*** it; And His hands
96: 5 But the LORD ***m*** the heavens.
98: 2 The LORD has ***m*** known His
100: 3 It is He who has ***m*** us, and
103: 7 He ***m*** known His ways to Moses,
104:24 In wisdom You have ***m*** them
104:26 Leviathan Which You have ***m*** to
105: 9 The covenant which He ***m*** with
105:21 He ***m*** him lord of his house,
105:24 And ***m*** them stronger than their
105:28 and ***m*** it dark; And they did
106:19 They ***m*** a calf in Horeb,
106:28 And ate sacrifices ***m*** to the
106:46 He also ***m*** them to be pitied
111: 4 He has ***m*** His wonderful works to
115:15 Who ***m*** heaven and earth.
118:24 is the day the LORD has ***m***;
119:60 I ***m*** haste, and did not delay
119:73 Your hands have ***m*** me and
119:87 They almost ***m*** an end of me on
121: 2 Who ***m*** heaven and earth.
124: 8 Who ***m*** heaven and earth.
129: 3 They ***m*** their furrows long."
134: 3 The LORD who ***m*** heaven and
136: 5 To Him who by wisdom ***m*** the
136: 7 To Him who ***m*** great lights,
136:14 And ***m*** Israel pass through the
138: 3 And ***m*** me bold with strength
139:14 am fearfully and wonderfully ***m***;
139:15 When I was ***m*** in secret,
143: 3 He has ***m*** me dwell in darkness,
146: 6 Who ***m*** heaven and earth,
148: 6 He ***m*** a decree which shall not
Prov 8:26 While as yet He had not ***m*** the
11:25 The generous soul will be ***m***
13: 4 soul of the diligent shall be ***m***
14:33 is in the heart of fools is ***m***
16: 4 The LORD has ***m*** all for
20: 9 I have ***m*** my heart clean, I am
20:12 The LORD has ***m*** them both.
21:11 the simple is ***m*** wise; But when
Eccl 1:15 What is crooked cannot be ***m***
2: 4 I ***m*** my works great, I built
2: 5 I ***m*** myself gardens and orchards,
2: 6 I ***m*** myself water pools from
3:11 He has ***m*** everything beautiful in
4:16 the people over whom he was ***m***
7: 3 sad countenance the heart is ***m***
7:13 can make straight what He has ***m***
7:29 That God ***m*** man upright,
10:19 A feast is ***m*** for laughter,
Song 1: 6 They ***m*** me the keeper of the
3: 9 of Lebanon Solomon the King ***M***
3:10 He ***m*** its pillars of silver,
6:12 My soul had ***m*** me As the
Isa 1: 9 We would have been ***m*** like
2: 8 which their own fingers have ***m***.
2:20 idols of gold, Which they ***m***,
5: 2 And also ***m*** a winepress in it;
14: 3 bondage in which you were ***m*** to
14:16 Is this the man who ***m*** the earth
14:17 Who ***m*** the world as a wilderness
16:10 I have ***m*** their shouting cease.
17: 8 respect what his fingers have ***m***,
21: 2 All its sighing I have ***m*** to
22:11 You also ***m*** a reservoir between
25: 2 For You have ***m*** a city a ruin,
26:14 And ***m*** all their memory to
27:11 Therefore He who ***m*** them will
28:15 We have ***m*** a covenant with death,
28:15 For we have ***m*** lies our refuge,
28:22 Lest your bonds be ***m*** strong;
29:16 For shall the thing ***m*** say of
29:16 thing made say of him who ***m*** it,
30:33 He has ***m*** it deep and large;
31: 7 which your own hands have ***m*** for
34: 6 It is ***m*** overflowing with
37:16 You have ***m*** heaven and earth.
37:26 not hear long ago How I ***m*** it,
40: 4 The crooked places shall be ***m***
41: 2 And ***m*** him rule over kings?
43: 7 him, yes, I have ***m*** him."
44: 2 Thus says the LORD who ***m*** you
45:12 I have ***m*** the earth,
45:18 Who formed the earth and ***m*** it,
46: 4 I will carry you! I have ***m***,
48: 6 I have ***m*** you hear new things
49: 1 matrix of My mother He has ***m***
49: 2 And He has ***m*** My mouth like a
49: 2 And ***m*** Me a polished shaft;
51:10 That ***m*** the depths of the sea a
51:12 the son of a man who will be ***m***
52:10 The LORD has ***m*** bare His holy
53: 9 And they ***m*** His grave with the
53:12 And ***m*** intercession for the
57: 8 have enlarged your bed And ***m***
57:16 And the souls which I have ***m***.
59: 8 They have ***m*** themselves crooked
63: 6 ***M*** them drunk in My fury,
63:17 why have You ***m*** us stray from
66: 2 all those things My hand has ***m***,
66: 8 Shall the earth be ***m*** to give
Jer 1:18 I have ***m*** you this day A
2: 7 you defiled My land And ***m*** My
2:15 They ***m*** his land waste;
2:28 are your gods that you have ***m***
3:16 nor shall it be ***m*** anymore.
5: 3 They have ***m*** their faces harder
10:11 The gods that have not ***m*** the
10:12 He has ***m*** the earth by His
10:25 And ***m*** his dwelling place

11:10 broken My covenant which I ***m***
12:10 They have ***m*** My pleasant
12:11 They have ***m*** it desolate;
12:11 The whole land is ***m*** desolate,
13:22 Your heels ***m*** bare.
13:27 Will you still not be ***m*** clean?
14:22 Since You have ***m*** all these.
17:23 but ***m*** their neck stiff, that
18: 4 And the vessel that he ***m*** of clay
18: 4 so he ***m*** it again into another
19: 4 they have forsaken Me and ***m***
19:11 which cannot be ***m*** whole again;
20: 8 the word of the LORD was ***m*** to
25:17 and ***m*** all the nations drink, to
26: 8 when Jeremiah had ***m*** an end of
27: 5 I have ***m*** the earth, the man and
28:13 but you have ***m*** in their place
29:26 The LORD has ***m*** you priest
31:32 to the covenant that I ***m*** with
32:17 You have ***m*** the heavens and the
32:20 and You have ***m*** Yourself a name,
33: 2 Thus says the LORD who ***m*** it,
34: 8 after King Zedekiah had ***m*** a
34:11 they changed their minds and ***m***
34:13 I ***m*** a covenant with your fathers
34:15 and you ***m*** a covenant before Me
34:18 of the covenant which they ***m***
37: 1 king of Babylon ***m*** king in the
37:15 For they had ***m*** that the prison.
38:16 who ***m*** our very souls, I will
40: 5 whom the king of Babylon has ***m***
40: 7 that the king of Babylon had ***m***
41: 2 whom the king of Babylon had ***m***
41: 9 the same one Asa the king had ***m***
41:18 whom the king of Babylon had ***m***
44:25 keep our vows that we have ***m***,
46:10 It shall be satiated and ***m***
46:16 He ***m*** many fall; Yes, one fell
48:30 His lies have ***m*** nothing right.
49:10 But I have ***m*** Esau bare; I have
51: 7 That ***m*** all the earth drunk.
51:15 He has ***m*** the earth by His
51:34 He has ***m*** me an empty vessel,
52:20 which King Solomon had ***m*** for
Lam 1:13 He has ***m*** me desolate And
1:14 He ***m*** my strength fail;
2: 7 They have ***m*** a noise in the
3: 2 He has led me and ***m*** me walk
3: 7 He has ***m*** my chain heavy.
3: 9 He has ***m*** my paths crooked.
3:11 He has ***m*** me desolate.
3:15 He has ***m*** me drink wormwood.
3:45 You have ***m*** us an offscouring
Ezek 3: 8 I have ***m*** your face strong
3: 9 I have ***m*** your forehead; do not
3:17 I have ***m*** you a watchman for the
6: 6 altars may be laid waste and ***m***
6: 6 your idols may be broken and ***m***
7:14 have blown the trumpet and ***m***
7:20 But they ***m*** from it The images
7:20 Therefore I have ***m*** it Like
12: 6 for I have ***m*** you a sign to the
13:22 Because with lies you have ***m*** the
13:22 whom I have not ***m*** sad; and you
15: 5 no object could be ***m*** from it.
16: 7 I ***m*** you thrive like a plant in
16:17 and ***m*** for yourself male images
16:24 and ***m*** a high place for yourself
16:25 and ***m*** your beauty to be
16:33 but you ***m*** your payments to all
17:13 ***m*** a covenant with him, and put
17:16 where the king dwells who ***m***
17:24 dried up the green tree and ***m***
19: 5 another of her cubs and ***m*** him
20: 5 and ***m*** Myself known to them in
20: 9 in whose sight I had ***m*** Myself
20:10 Therefore I ***m*** them go out of
21:15 Ah! It is ***m*** bright; It is
21:24 Because you have ***m*** your iniquity
22: 4 with the idols which you have ***m***.
22: 4 therefore I have ***m*** you a
22: 7 In you they have ***m*** light of
22:12 you have ***m*** profit from your
22:13 profit which you have ***m***,
22:25 they have ***m*** many widows in her
22:26 nor have they ***m*** known the
26:15 when slaughter is ***m*** in the
27: 5 They ***m*** all your planks of fir
27: 6 Of oaks from Bashan they ***m***
27:11 They ***m*** your beauty perfect.
27:16 of the abundance of goods you ***m***.
27:18 of the abundance of goods you ***m***,
29: 3 I have ***m*** it for myself.'
29: 7 You broke and ***m*** all their
29: 9 is mine, and I have ***m*** it.'
29:18 every head was ***m*** bald, and
31: 4 The waters ***m*** it grow;
31: 6 All the birds of the heavens ***m***
31: 6 its shadow all great nations ***m***
31: 9 I ***m*** it beautiful with a
31:16 I ***m*** the nations shake at the
33: 7 I have ***m*** you a watchman for the
33:29 when I have ***m*** the land most
36: 3 Because they ***m*** you desolate and
39:26 in their own land and no one ***m***
40:17 chambers and a pavement ***m*** all
41:18 And it was ***m*** with cherubim
41:19 thus it was ***m*** throughout the
43:18 altar on the day when it is ***m***,
46:14 to be ***m*** regularly to the LORD.
46:23 and cooking hearths were ***m***
Dan 2: 5 and your houses shall be ***m*** an
2:15 Then Arioch ***m*** the decision
2:17 and ***m*** the decision known to
2:23 And have now ***m*** known to me
2:23 For You have ***m*** known to us the
2:28 and He has ***m*** known to King
2:29 He who reveals secrets has ***m***
2:38 and has ***m*** you ruler over them
2:45 the great God has ***m*** known to the
2:48 and he ***m*** him ruler over the
3: 1 Nebuchadnezzar the king ***m*** an
3:10 have ***m*** a decree that everyone
3:15 the image which I have ***m***,
3:29 and their houses shall be ***m*** an
4: 5 I saw a dream which ***m*** me afraid,
5: 1 Belshazzar the king ***m*** a great
5:11 ***m*** him chief of the magicians,
5:21 his heart was ***m*** like the
5:29 and ***m*** a proclamation concerning
7: 4 lifted up from the earth and ***m***
7:16 So he told me and ***m*** known to me
7:22 and a judgment was ***m*** in favor
9: 1 who was ***m*** king over the realm
9: 4 and ***m*** confession, and said, "O
9:13 yet we have not ***m*** our prayer
9:15 and ***m*** Yourself a name, as it
10:10 which ***m*** me tremble on my knees
11:23 And after the league is ***m*** with
12:10 ***m*** white, and refined, but the
Hos 7: 5 day of our king Princes have ***m***
8: 4 They ***m*** princes, but I did not
8: 4 their silver and gold They ***m***
8: 6 A workman ***m*** it, and it is not
8:11 Because Ephraim has ***m*** many
9: 1 You have ***m*** love for hire on
13: 2 And have ***m*** for themselves
Joel 1: 7 Its branches are ***m*** white.
Am 4: 7 I ***m*** it rain on one city,
4:10 I ***m*** the stench of your camps
5: 8 He ***m*** the Pleiades and Orion;
5:26 Which you ***m*** for yourselves.
7: 7 the Lord stood on a wall ***m***
Jon 1: 9 who ***m*** the sea and the dry
4: 5 There he ***m*** himself a shelter
4: 6 God prepared a plant and ***m*** it
4:10 nor ***m*** it grow, which came up in
Nah 2: 3 of his mighty men are ***m*** red,
2:11 And no one ***m*** them afraid?
Hab 2:17 the plunder of beasts which ***m***
3: 9 Your bow was ***m*** quite ready;
Zeph 2: 8 And ***m*** arrogant threats against
2:10 they have reproached and ***m***
3: 6 I have ***m*** their streets
Zech 7:12 they ***m*** their hearts like flint,
7:14 for they ***m*** the pleasant land
9:13 And ***m*** you like the sword of a
11:10 the covenant which I had ***m***
Mal 2: 9 Therefore I also have ***m*** you
Mt 9:16 and the tear is ***m*** worse.
9:21 I shall be ***m*** well."
9:22 your faith has ***m*** you well."
9:22 And the woman was ***m*** well from
14:22 Immediately Jesus ***m*** His
14:36 as many as touched it were ***m***
15: 6 Thus you have ***m*** the
15:31 the maimed ***m*** whole, the lame
18:25 he had, and that payment be ***m***.
19: 4 you not read that He who ***m***
19: 4 ***m*** them male and female,'
19:12 there are eunuchs who were ***m***
19:12 there are eunuchs who have ***m***
20:12 and you ***m*** them equal to us who
21:13 but you have ***m*** it a 'den of
22: 5 But they ***m*** light of it and went
24:45 whom his master ***m*** ruler over
25:16 and ***m*** another five talents.
26:31 All of you will be ***m*** to stumble
26:33 Even if all are ***m*** to stumble
26:33 I will never be ***m*** to stumble."
27:64 command that the tomb be ***m***
27:66 So they went and ***m*** the tomb
Mk 2:21 and the tear is ***m*** worse.
2:27 The Sabbath was ***m*** for man, and
5:28 I shall be ***m*** well."
5:34 your faith has ***m*** you well.
6:45 Immediately He ***m*** His disciples
6:56 as many as touched Him were ***m***
8:25 hands on his eyes again and ***m***
10: 6 ***m*** them male and female.'
10:52 your faith has ***m*** you well."
11:17 But you have ***m*** it a 'den of
14:27 All of you will be ***m*** to stumble
14:29 Even if all are ***m*** to stumble,
14:58 I will destroy this temple ***m***
14:58 days I will build another ***m***
Lk 1:62 So they ***m*** signs to his
2:15 which the Lord has ***m*** known to
2:17 they ***m*** widely known the saying
3: 5 crooked places shall be ***m***
4:38 and they ***m*** request of Him
8:48 your faith has ***m*** you well.
8:50 and she will be ***m*** well."
9:15 and ***m*** them all sit down.
11:40 ones! Did not He who ***m***
12:14 who ***m*** Me a judge or an
13:13 and immediately she was ***m***
17:19 Your faith has ***m*** you well."
18:42 your faith has ***m*** you well."
19: 6 So he ***m*** haste and came down, and
19:46 but you have ***m*** it a 'den of
23:19 for a certain rebellion ***m*** in
Jn 1: 3 All things were ***m*** through Him,
1: 3 and without Him nothing was ***m***
1: 3 Him nothing was made that was ***m***.
1:10 and the world was ***m*** through
2: 9 had tasted the water that was ***m***
2:15 When He had ***m*** a whip of cords,
4: 1 had heard that Jesus ***m*** and
4:46 Cana of Galilee where He had ***m***
5: 4 was ***m*** well of whatever disease
5: 6 Do you want to be ***m*** well?"
5: 9 And immediately the man was ***m***
5:11 He who ***m*** me well said to me,
5:14 you have been ***m*** well. Sin no
5:15 that it was Jesus who had ***m***
7:23 you angry with Me because I ***m***
8:33 You will be ***m*** free'?"
9: 6 He spat on the ground and ***m***
9:11 A Man called Jesus ***m*** clay and
9:14 it was a Sabbath when Jesus ***m***
9:39 and that those who see may be ***m***
12: 2 There they ***m*** Him a supper;
15:15 I heard from My Father I have ***m***
16: 1 that you should not be ***m*** to
17:23 that they may be ***m*** perfect in
18:18 and officers who had ***m*** a fire
19: 7 because He ***m*** Himself the Son of
19:23 took His garments and ***m*** four
Acts 1: 1 The former account I ***m***,
2:28 You have ***m*** known to me
2:36 know assuredly that God has ***m***
3:12 own power or godliness we had ***m***
3:16 has ***m*** this man strong, whom you
3:25 and of the covenant which God ***m***
4: 9 by what means he has been ***m***
4:24 who ***m*** heaven and earth and the
7:10 and he ***m*** him governor over
7:13 the second time Joseph was ***m***
7:27 Who ***m*** you a ruler and a
7:35 Who ***m*** you a ruler and a
7:41 And they ***m*** a calf in those days,
7:43 Images which you ***m*** to
7:48 does not dwell in temples ***m***
7:50 Has My hand not ***m*** all
8: 2 and ***m*** great lamentation over
8: 3 he ***m*** havoc of the church,
9:39 and garments which Dorcas had ***m***
10:10 but while they ***m*** ready, he fell
10:17 been sent from Cornelius had ***m***
12:20 and having ***m*** Blastus the king's
13:32 that promise which was ***m*** to the
14: 5 when a violent attempt was ***m***
14:15 who ***m*** the heaven, the earth,
14:21 the gospel to that city and ***m***
15: 9 and ***m*** no distinction between us
16:13 where prayer was customarily ***m***;
17:24 who ***m*** the world and everything
17:24 does not dwell in temples ***m***
17:26 And He has ***m*** from one blood
19:24 who ***m*** silver shrines of Diana,
19:26 they are not gods which are ***m***
20:28 which the Holy Spirit has ***m***
21:26 time an offering should be ***m***
26: 6 for the hope of the promise ***m***
26:24 Now as he thus ***m*** his defense,
27:40 the mainsail to the wind and ***m***
28: 2 for they kindled a fire and ***m***
Rom 1:20 by the things that are ***m***,
1:23 God into an image ***m*** like
4:14 faith is ***m*** void and the promise
4:14 is made void and the promise ***m***
4:17 I have ***m*** you a father of
5:19 man's disobedience many were ***m***
5:19 Man's obedience many will be ***m***
8: 2 of life in Christ Jesus has ***m***
9:20 Why have you ***m*** me like this?"
9:29 And we would have been ***m***
10:10 with the mouth confession is ***m***
10:20 I was ***m*** manifest to
14: 4 he will be ***m*** to stand, for God
14:21 or is offended or is ***m*** weak.
15: 8 to confirm the promises ***m*** to
15:20 And so I have ***m*** it my aim to
16:26 but now has been ***m*** manifest, and
16:26 Scriptures has been ***m*** known to
1 Cor 1:17 cross of Christ should be ***m*** of
1:20 Has not God ***m*** foolish the
4: 9 for we have been ***m*** a spectacle
4:13 We have been ***m*** as the filth of
7:21 but if you can be ***m*** free,
7:25 the Lord in His mercy has ***m***
9:19 I have ***m*** myself a servant to
12:13 and have all been ***m*** to drink
15:22 so in Christ all shall be ***m***
15:28 Now when all things are ***m***
15:36 what you sow is not ***m*** alive
15:47 ***m*** of dust; the second Man is
15:48 so also are those who are ***m***
2 Cor 2: 2 me glad but the one who is ***m***
3: 6 who also ***m*** us sufficient as
3:10 For even what was ***m*** glorious had
5: 1 a house not ***m*** with hands,
5:21 For He ***m*** Him who knew no sin to
7: 8 For even if I ***m*** you sorry with
7: 8 that the same epistle ***m*** you
7: 9 not that you were ***m*** sorry, but
7: 9 For you were ***m*** sorry in a godly
11:29 Who is ***m*** to stumble, and I do
12: 9 for My strength is ***m*** perfect in
13: 9 that you may be ***m*** complete.
Gal 3: 3 are you now being ***m*** perfect by
3:16 his Seed were the promises ***m***.
3:19 come to whom the promise was ***m***;
5: 1 liberty by which Christ has ***m***
Eph 1: 6 by which He has ***m*** us accepted

1: 8 which He **m** to abound toward us
1: 9 having **m** known to us the mystery
2: 1 And you He **m** alive, who were
2: 5 **m** us alive together with Christ
2: 6 and **m** us sit together in the
2:11 is called the Circumcision **m**
2:14 who has **m** both one, and has
3: 3 how that by revelation He **m**
3: 5 which in other ages was not **m**
3:10 wisdom of God might be **m** known
5:13 things that are exposed are **m**
Phil 2: 7 but **m** Himself of no reputation,
4: 6 let your requests be **m** known to
Col 1:20 having **m** peace through the
2:11 with the circumcision **m**
2:13 He has **m** alive together with
2:15 He **m** a public spectacle of
1 Th 2: 6 when we might have **m** demands as
1 Tim 1: 9 that the law is not **m** for a
1:18 to the prophecies previously **m**
2: 1 and giving of thanks be **m** for
Heb 1: 2 through whom also He **m** the
2: 7 You have **m** him a little
2: 9 who was **m** a little lower than
2:17 in all things He had to be **m**
6:13 For when God **m** a promise to
7: 3 but **m** like the Son of God,
7:19 for the law **m** nothing perfect;
7:20 inasmuch as He was not **m**
8: 9 to the covenant that I **m**
8:13 He has **m** the first obsolete.
9: 8 Holiest of All was not yet **m**
9:11 more perfect tabernacle not **m**
9:24 not entered the holy places **m**
10:13 waiting till His enemies are **m**
10:33 partly while you were **m** a
11: 3 which are seen were not **m** of
11:22 **m** mention of the departure of
11:34 out of weakness were **m** strong,
11:40 that they should not be **m**
12:23 to the spirits of just men **m**
12:27 shaken, as of things that are **m**,
Jas 2:22 and by works faith was **m**
3: 9 who have been **m** in the
1 Pe 3:18 put to death in the flesh but **m**
3:22 and powers having been **m**
2 Pe 1:16 devised fables when we **m** known
2:12 like natural brute beasts **m** to
1 Jn 2:19 went out that they might be **m**
4:18 But he who fears has not been **m**
5:10 who does not believe God has **m**
Rev 1: 6 and has **m** us kings and priests
5:10 And have **m** us kings and priests
7:14 and washed their robes and **m**
8:11 because it was **m** bitter.
14: 7 and worship Him who **m** heaven
14: 8 because she has **m** all nations
17: 2 of the earth were **m** drunk with
18:19 For in one hour she is **m**
19: 7 and His wife has **m** herself

MADIAN (KJV) See MIDIAN

MADMAN (3/3) MAD, MADMEN

1 Sam 21:15 this fellow to play the **m** in
2 Ki 9:11 Why did this **m** come to you?"
Prov 26:18 Like a **m** who throws firebrands,

MADMANNAH (2/2)

Josh 15:31 Ziklag, **M**, Sansannah,
1 Chr 2:49 bore Shaaph the father of **M**,

MADMEN (2/2) MADMAN

1 Sam 21:15 'Have I need of **m**, that you
Jer 48: 2 O **M**! The sword shall pursue

MADMENAH (1/1)

Isa 10:31 **M** has fled, The inhabitants of

MADNESS (11/11) MAD

Deut 28:28 LORD will strike you with **m**
1 Sam 21:13 feigned **m** in their hands,
Ps 34: of David when he pretended **m**
Eccl 1:17 to know wisdom and to know **m**
2: 2 **M**!"; and of mirth, "What does
2:12 to consider wisdom and **m** and
7:25 Even of foolishness and **m**.
9: 3 **m** is in their hearts while
10:13 end of his talk is raving **m**.
Zech 12: 4 confusion, and its rider with **m**;
2 Pe 2:16 a man's voice restrained the **m**

MADON (2/2)

Josh 11: 1 that he sent to Jobab king of **M**,
12:19 the king of **M**, one; the king

MAGBISH (1/1)

Ezra 2:30 the people of **M**, one hundred

MAGDALA (1/1) MAGDALENE

Mt 15:39 and came to the region of **M**.

MAGDALENE (12/12) MAGDALA

Mt 27:56 among whom were Mary **M**,
27:61 And Mary **M** was there, and the
28: 1 Mary **M** and the other Mary came
Mk 15:40 afar, among whom were Mary **M**,
15:47 And Mary **M** and Mary the mother
16: 1 the Sabbath was past, Mary **M**,
16: 9 He appeared first to Mary **M**,
Lk 8: 2 and infirmities—Mary called **M**,
24:10 It was Mary **M**, Joanna, Mary
Jn 19:25 the wife of Clopas, and Mary **M**.
20: 1 first day of the week Mary **M**
20:18 Mary **M** came and told the

MAGDIEL (2/2)

Gen 36:43 Chief **M**, and Chief Iram.
1 Chr 1:54 Chief **M**, and Chief Iram.

MAGGOT (2/2)

Job 25: 6 much less man, who is a **m**,
Isa 14:11 The **m** is spread under you,

MAGIC (3/3) MAGICIAN

Ezek 13:18 Woe to the women who sew **m**
13:20 I am against your **m** charms by
Acts 19:19 of those who had practiced **m**

MAGICIAN (1/1) MAGIC, MAGICIANS

Dan 2:10 asked such things of any **m**,

MAGICIANS (15/14) MAGICIAN

Gen 41: 8 sent and called for all the **m**
41:24 So I told this to the **m**,
Ex 7:11 so the **m** of Egypt, they also
7:22 Then the **m** of Egypt did so with
8: 7 And the **m** did so with their
8:18 Now the **m** so worked with their
8:19 Then the **m** said to Pharaoh,
9:11 And the **m** could not stand before
9:11 for the boils were on the **m** and
Dan 1:20 ten times better than all the **m**
2: 2 gave the command to call the **m**,
2:27 men, the astrologers, the **m**,
4: 7 Then the **m**, the astrologers,
4: 9 "Belteshazzar, chief of the **m**,
5:11 king—made him chief of the **m**,

MAGISTRATE (1/1) MAGISTRATES

Lk 12:58 go with your adversary to the **m**,

MAGISTRATES (10/10) MAGISTRATE

Ezra 7:25 set **m** and judges who may judge
Isa 60:17 And your **m** righteousness.
Dan 3: 2 treasurers, the judges, the **m**,
3: 3 treasurers, the judges, the **m**,
Lk 12:11 you to the synagogues and **m**
Acts 16:20 And they brought them to the **m**,
16:22 and the **m** tore off their
16:35 the **m** sent the officers,
16:36 The **m** have sent to let you go.
16:38 told these words to the **m**,

MAGNIFICENCE (2/2)

Job 31:23 And because of His **m** I cannot
Acts 19:27 Diana may be despised and her **m**

MAGNIFICENT (1/1)

1 Chr 22: 5 LORD must be exceedingly **m**,

MAGNIFIED (9/9) EXALTED, MAGNIFY

2 Sam 7:26 So let Your name be **m** forever,
1 Chr 17:24 that Your name may be **m**
Ps 35:27 "Let the LORD be **m**,
40:16 The LORD be **m**!"
70: 4 Let God be **m**!"
138: 2 For You have **m** Your word above
Mal 1: 5 The LORD is **m** beyond the border
Acts 19:17 name of the Lord Jesus was **m**.
Phil 1:20 so now also Christ will be **m** in

MAGNIFIES (1/1) MAGNIFY

Lk 1:46 'My soul **m** the Lord,

MAGNIFY (7/7) EXALT, MAGNIFIED, MAGNIFIES

Job 36:24 Remember to **m** His work,
Ps 34: 3 **m** the LORD with me, And let
69:30 And will **m** Him with
Ezek 38:23 Thus I will **m** Myself and
Dan 11:36 he shall exalt and **m** himself
Acts 10:46 them speak with tongues and **m**
Rom 11:13 Gentiles, I **m** my ministry,

MAGOG (5/5) GOG

Gen 10: 2 sons of Japheth were Gomer, **M**,
1 Chr 1: 5 sons of Japheth were Gomer, **M**,
Ezek 38: 2 against Gog, of the land of **M**,
39: 6 And I will send fire on **M** and on
Rev 20: 8 corners of the earth, Gog and **M**,

MAGOR-MISSABIB (1/1)

Jer 20: 3 called your name Pashhur, but **M**.

MAGPIASH (1/1)

Neh 10:20 **M**, Meshullam, Hezir,

MAHALAH (KJV) See MAHLI

MAHALALEL (8/8)

Gen 5:12 seventy years, and begot **M**.
5:13 After he begot **M**, Cainan
5:15 **M** lived sixty-five years, and
5:16 **M** lived eight hundred and
5:17 So all the days of **M** were eight
1 Chr 1: 2 Cainan, **M**, Jared,
Neh 11: 4 son of Shephatiah, the son of **M**,
Lk 3:37 son of Jared, the son of **M**,

MAHALATH (4/4)

Gen 28: 9 went to Ishmael and took **M** the
2 Chr 11:18 took for himself as wife **M** the
Ps 53: the Chief Musician. Set to "**M**.
88: **M** Leannoth." A Contemplation of

MAHALI (1/1)

Ex 6:19 The sons of Merari were **M** and

MAHANAIM (13/13)

Gen 32: 2 called the name of that place **M**.
Josh 13:26 and from **M** to the border of
13:30 Their territory was from **M**,
21:38 **M** with its common-land,
2 Sam 2: 8 Saul and brought him over to **M**;
2:12 went out from **M** to Gibeon.
2:29 all Bithron; and they came to **M**.
17:24 Then David went to **M**.
17:27 when David had come to **M**,
19:32 supplies while he stayed at **M**,
1 Ki 2: 8 in the day when I went to **M**.
4:14 Ahinadab the son of Iddo, in **M**;
1 Chr 6:80 **M** with its common-lands,

MAHANEH DAN (2/2)

Judg 13:25 began to move upon him at **M**
18:12 they call that place **M** to this

M

MAHARAI (3/3)

2 Sam 23:28 **M** the Netophathite,
1 Chr 11:30 **M** the Netophathite, Heled the
27:13 for the tenth month was **M** the

MAHATH (3/3)

1 Chr 6:35 son of Elkanah, the son of **M**,
2 Chr 29:12 **M** the son of Amasai and Joel
31:13 Jozabad, Eliel, Ismachiah, **M**,

MAHAVITE (1/1)

1 Chr 11:46 Eliel the **M**, Jeribai and

MAHAZIOTH (2/2)

1 Chr 25: 4 Mallothi, Hothir, and **M**.
25:30 the twenty-third for **M**,

MAHER-SHALAL-HASH-BAZ (2/2)

Isa 8: 1 with a man's pen concerning **M**.
8: 3 said to me, "Call his name **M**;

MAHLAH (5/5)

Num 26:33 daughters of Zelophehad were **M**,
27: 1 the names of his daughters: **M**,
36:11 for **M**, Tirzah, Hoglah,
Josh 17: 3 the names of his daughters: **M**,
1 Chr 7:18 bore Ishhod, Abiezer, and **M**.

MAHLI (11/10)

Num 3:20 **M** and Mushi. These are the
1 Chr 6:19 The sons of Merari were **M** and
6:29 The sons of Merari were **M**,
6:47 the son of **M**, the son of
23:21 The sons of Merari were **M** and
23:21 The sons of **M** were Eleazar and
23:23 The sons of Mushi were **M**,
24:26 The sons of Merari were **M** and
24:28 Of **M**: Eleazar, who had no
24:30 Also the sons of Mushi were **M**,
Ezra 8:18 of the sons of **M** the son of

MAHLITES (2/2)

Num 3:33 came the family of the **M** and
26:58 Hebronites, the family of the **M**,

MAHLON (3/3)

Ruth 1: 2 names of his two sons were **M**
1: 5 Then both **M** and Chilion also
4:10 the Moabitess, the widow of **M**,

MAHLON'S (1/1)

Ruth 4: 9 all that was Chilion's and **M**,

MAHOL (1/1)

1 Ki 4:31 and Darda, the sons of ***M***;

MAHSEIAH (2/2)

Jer 32:12 the son of Neriah, son of ***M***,
51:59 the son of Neriah, the son of ***M***,

MAID (19/17) MAIDEN, MAIDS

Gen 16: 2 Please, go in to my ***m***;
16: 3 Abram's wife, took Hagar her ***m***,
16: 5 be upon you! I gave my ***m*** into
16: 6 Indeed your ***m*** is in your hand;
16: 8 And He said, "Hagar, Sarai's ***m***,
29:24 And Laban gave his ***m*** Zilpah to
29:24 to his daughter Leah as a ***m***.
29:29 And Laban gave his ***m*** Bilhah to
29:29 to his daughter Rachel as a ***m***.
30: 3 Here is my ***m*** Bilhah; go in to
30: 4 Then she gave him Bilhah her ***m***
30: 7 And Rachel's ***m*** Bilhah conceived
30: 9 she took Zilpah her ***m*** and gave
30:10 And Leah's ***m*** Zilpah bore Jacob a
30:12 And Leah's ***m*** Zilpah bore Jacob a
30:18 because I have given my ***m*** to my
Ex 2: 5 she sent her ***m*** to get it.
Ps 123: 2 As the eyes of a ***m*** to the hand
Isa 24: 2 with his master; As with the ***m***,

MAIDEN (2/2) MAID, MAIDENS

Ex 2: 8 So the ***m*** went and called the
Jer 51:22 pieces the young man and the ***m***;

MAIDENS (9/9) MAIDEN

Ex 2: 5 And her ***m*** walked along the
1 Sam 25:42 attended by five of her ***m***;
Job 41: 5 will you leash him for your ***m***?
Ps 68:25 Among them were the ***m***
78:63 And their ***m*** were not given in
148:12 Both young men and ***m***;
Prov 9: 3 She has sent out her ***m***,
Lam 5:11 The ***m*** in the cities of Judah.
Ezek 9: 6 ***m*** and little children and

MAIDS (5/5) MAID

Gen 24:61 Then Rebekah and her ***m*** arose,
2 Sam 6:20 today in the eyes of the ***m*** of
Esth 4: 4 So Esther's ***m*** and eunuchs came
4:16 My ***m*** and I will fast likewise.
Isa 14: 2 them for servants and ***m*** in the

MAIDS' (1/1)

Gen 31:33 and into the two ***m*** tents, but

MAIDSERVANT (40/35) FEMALE, MAIDSERVANTS, SERVANT

Gen 16: 1 And she had an Egyptian ***m*** whose
25:12 Hagar the Egyptian, Sarah's ***m***,
35:25 the sons of Bilhah, Rachel's ***m***,
35:26 the sons of Zilpah, Leah's ***m***,
Ruth 2:13 have spoken kindly to your ***m***,
3: 9 answered, "I am Ruth, your ***m***.
3: 9 Take your ***m*** under your wing,
1 Sam 1:11 on the affliction of Your ***m***
1:11 me, and not forget Your ***m***,
1:11 but will give Your ***m*** a male
1:16 Do not consider your ***m*** a wicked
1:18 Let your ***m*** find favor in your
25:24 And please let your ***m*** speak
25:24 and hear the words of your ***m***.
25:25 is with him. But I, your ***m***,
25:27 now this present which your ***m***
25:28 forgive the trespass of your ***m***.
25:31 my lord, then remember your ***m***.
25:41 and said, "Here is your ***m***,
28:21 your ***m*** has obeyed your voice,
28:22 heed also the voice of your ***m***,
2 Sam 14: 6 Now your ***m*** had two sons; and the
14: 7 has risen up against your ***m***,
14:12 let your ***m*** speak another word
14:15 And your ***m*** said, 'I will now
14:15 perform the request of his ***m***.
14:16 will hear and deliver his ***m***
14:17 Your ***m*** said, 'The word of my
14:19 words in the mouth of your ***m***.
20:17 him, "Hear the words of your ***m***.
1 Ki 1:13 lord, O king, swear to your ***m***,
1:17 by the LORD your God to your ***m***,
3:20 while your ***m*** slept, and laid
2 Ki 4: 2 Your ***m*** has nothing in the house
4:16 do not lie to your ***m***!"
Ps 86:16 And save the son of Your ***m***.
116:16 Your servant, the son of Your ***m***;
Prov 30:23 And a ***m*** who succeeds her
Lk 1:38 Behold the ***m*** of the Lord! Let it
1:48 the lowly state of His ***m***;

MAIDSERVANTS (13/12) FEMALE, MAIDSERVANT

Gen 33: 1 Leah, Rachel, and the two ***m***.
33: 2 And he put the ***m*** and their
33: 6 Then the ***m*** came near, they and
Ruth 2:13 I am not like one of your ***m***.
2 Sam 6:22 But as for the ***m*** of whom you
Esth 2: 9 Then seven choice ***m*** were
2: 9 and he moved her and her ***m*** to
Job 19:15 who dwell in my house, and my ***m***,
Prov 27:27 And the nourishment of your ***m***.
31:15 And a portion for her ***m***.
Joel 2:29 on My menservants and on My ***m***
Nah 2: 7 And her ***m*** shall lead her as
Acts 2:18 menservants and on My ***m***

MAIL (4/4)

Ex 28:32 like the opening in a coat of ***m***,
39:23 like the opening in a coat of ***m***,
1 Sam 17: 5 he was armed with a coat of ***m***,
17:38 clothed him with a coat of ***m***.

MAIMED (7/7)

Lev 22:22 that are blind or broken or ***m***,
Mt 15:30 them the lame, blind, mute, ***m***,
15:31 the ***m*** made whole, the lame
18: 8 to enter into life lame or ***m***,
Mk 9:43 for you to enter into life ***m***,
Lk 14:13 feast, invite the poor, the ***m***,
14:21 in here the poor and the ***m***

MAIN (4/4)

1 Ki 7:50 and for the doors of the ***m***
2 Chr 4:22 and the doors of the ***m*** hall of
Dan 7: 1 telling the ***m*** facts.
Heb 8: 1 Now this is the ***m*** point of the

MAINSAIL (1/1)

Acts 27:40 and they hoisted the ***m*** to the

MAINSTAY (1/1)

Isa 19:13 Those who are the ***m*** of its

MAINTAIN (10/10) MAINTAINED

1 Ki 8:45 and ***m*** their cause.
8:49 and ***m*** their cause,
8:59 that He may ***m*** the cause of His
1 Chr 26:27 in battles they dedicated to ***m***
2 Chr 6:35 and ***m*** their cause.
6:39 and ***m*** their cause, and forgive
Ps 16: 5 my cup; You ***m*** my lot.
140:12 I know that the LORD will ***m***
Titus 3: 8 in God should be careful to ***m***
3:14 let our people also learn to ***m***

MAINTAINED (2/2) MAINTAIN

1 Chr 4:33 and they ***m*** their genealogy:
Ps 9: 4 For You have ***m*** my right and my

MAINTAINING (1/1)

Acts 24: 9 ***m*** that these things were so.

MAJESTIC (7/6) MAJESTY

Job 37: 4 He thunders with His ***m*** voice,
39:20 His ***m*** snorting strikes terror.
Prov 30:29 are three things which are ***m***
Isa 33:21 But there the ***m*** LORD will be
33:21 Nor ***m*** ships pass by
Ezek 17: 8 And become a ***m*** vine." '
17:23 and be a ***m*** cedar. Under it will

MAJESTY (32/32) MAJESTIC

Deut 33:29 And the sword of your ***m***!
1 Chr 16:27 Honor and ***m*** are before Him;
29:11 The victory and the ***m***;
29:25 bestowed on him such royal ***m***
Esth 1: 4 the splendor of his excellent ***m***
Job 37:22 With God is awesome ***m***.
40:10 Then adorn yourself with ***m*** and
Ps 21: 5 Honor and ***m*** You have placed
29: 4 of the LORD is full of ***m***.
45: 3 With Your glory and Your ***m***.
45: 4 And in Your ***m*** ride prosperously
93: 1 reigns, He is clothed with ***m***;
96: 6 Honor and ***m*** are before Him;
104: 1 are clothed with honor and ***m***,
145: 5 the glorious splendor of Your ***m***,
145:12 And the glorious ***m*** of His
Isa 2:10 LORD And the glory of His ***m***.
2:19 LORD And the glory of His ***m***,
2:21 LORD And the glory of His ***m***,
24:14 For the ***m*** of the LORD
26:10 And will not behold the ***m*** of
Ezek 7:20 his ornaments, He set it in ***m***;
Dan 4:30 power and for the honor of my ***m***?
4:36 and excellent ***m*** was added to
5:18 your father a kingdom and ***m***,
5:19 And because of the ***m*** that He
Mic 5: 4 In the ***m*** of the name of the
Lk 9:43 they were all amazed at the ***m***
Heb 1: 3 at the right hand of the ***M*** on
8: 1 hand of the throne of the ***M*** in
2 Pe 1:16 but were eyewitnesses of His ***m***.
Jude 25 alone is wise, Be glory and ***m***,

MAJORITY (3/3)

Acts 27:12 the ***m*** advised to set sail from
2 Cor 2: 6 which was inflicted by the ***m***
9: 2 your zeal has stirred up the ***m***.

MAKAZ (1/1)

1 Ki 4: 9 Ben-Deker, in ***M***, Shaalbim,

MAKE (1012/947) MADE, MAKER, MAKES, MAKING

Gen 1:26 Let Us ***m*** man in Our image,
2:18 I will ***m*** him a helper
3: 6 and a tree desirable to ***m*** one
6:14 ***M*** yourself an ark of
6:14 ***m*** rooms in the ark, and cover
6:15 And this is how you shall ***m*** it:
6:16 You shall ***m*** a window for the
6:16 You shall ***m*** it with lower,
9:12 sign of the covenant which I ***m***
11: 3 let us ***m*** bricks and bake them
11: 4 let us ***m*** a name for ourselves,
12: 2 I will ***m*** you a great nation;
12: 2 I will bless you And ***m*** your
13:16 And I will ***m*** your descendants as
17: 2 And I will ***m*** My covenant between
17: 6 I will ***m*** you exceedingly
17: 6 and I will ***m*** nations of you,
17:20 and will ***m*** him fruitful, and
17:20 and I will ***m*** him a great
18: 6 ***m*** ready three measures of fine
18: 6 knead it and ***m*** cakes."
19:32 let us ***m*** our father drink wine,
19:34 let us ***m*** him drink wine tonight
21:13 Yet I will also ***m*** a nation of
21:18 for I will ***m*** him a great
24: 3 and I will ***m*** you swear by the
26: 4 And I will ***m*** your descendants
26:28 and let us ***m*** a covenant with
27: 4 And ***m*** me savory food, such as I
27: 7 Bring me game and ***m*** savory food
27: 9 and I will ***m*** savory food from
28: 3 And ***m*** you fruitful and
31:44 let us ***m*** a covenant, you and I,
32:12 and ***m*** your descendants as the
34: 9 'And ***m*** marriages with us;
35: 1 and ***m*** an altar there to God,
35: 3 and I will ***m*** an altar there to
40:14 ***m*** mention of me to Pharaoh, and
43:16 and slaughter an animal and ***m***
43:18 so that he may ***m*** a case against
45: 1 '***M*** everyone go out from me!"
46: 3 for I will ***m*** of you a great
47: 6 then ***m*** them chief herdsmen over
48: 4 I will ***m*** you fruitful and
48: 4 and I will ***m*** of you a multitude
48:20 May God ***m*** you as Ephraim and as
Ex 5: 5 and you ***m*** them rest from their
5: 7 give the people straw to ***m***
5:16 ***M*** brick!' And indeed your
8:23 I will ***m*** a difference between My
9: 4 And the LORD will ***m*** a
11: 7 may know that the LORD does ***m***
12: 4 to each man's need you shall ***m***
16: 8 your complaints which you ***m***
18:16 and I ***m*** known the statutes of
20: 4 You shall not ***m*** for yourself a
20:23 You shall not ***m*** anything to
20:23 or gods of gold you shall not ***m***
20:24 An altar of earth you shall ***m***
20:25 And if you ***m*** Me an altar of
21:34 the owner of the pit shall ***m*** it
22: 3 He should ***m*** full restitution;
22: 5 he shall ***m*** restitution from the
22: 6 kindled the fire shall surely ***m***
22:11 and he shall not ***m*** it good.
22:12 he shall ***m*** restitution to the
22:13 and he shall not ***m*** good what
22:14 he shall surely ***m*** it good.
22:15 he shall not ***m*** it good; if it
23:13 be circumspect and ***m*** no mention
23:27 and will ***m*** all your enemies
23:32 You shall ***m*** no covenant with
23:33 lest they ***m*** you sin against Me.
25: 8 And let them ***m*** Me a sanctuary,
25: 9 just so you shall ***m*** it.
25:10 And they shall ***m*** an ark of
25:11 and shall ***m*** on it a molding of
25:13 And you shall ***m*** poles of acacia
25:17 You shall ***m*** a mercy seat of pure
25:18 And you shall ***m*** two cherubim of
25:18 of hammered work you shall ***m***
25:19 ***M*** one cherub at one end, and the
25:19 you shall ***m*** the cherubim at the
25:23 You shall also ***m*** a table of
25:24 and ***m*** a molding of gold all
25:25 You shall ***m*** for it a frame of a
25:25 and you shall ***m*** a gold molding
25:26 And you shall ***m*** for it four
25:28 And you shall ***m*** the poles of
25:29 You shall ***m*** its dishes, its
25:29 You shall ***m*** them of pure gold.
25:31 You shall also ***m*** a lampstand of
25:37 You shall ***m*** seven lamps for it,
25:40 And see to it that you ***m*** them
26: 1 Moreover you shall ***m*** the
26: 4 And you shall ***m*** loops of blue
26: 5 Fifty loops you shall ***m*** in the
26: 5 and fifty loops you shall ***m*** on
26: 6 And you shall ***m*** fifty clasps of
26: 7 You shall also ***m*** curtains of
26: 7 You shall ***m*** eleven curtains.
26:10 You shall ***m*** fifty loops on the
26:11 And you shall ***m*** fifty bronze
26:14 You shall also ***m*** a covering of
26:15 for the tabernacle you shall ***m***

26:17 Thus you shall ***m*** for all the
26:18 And you shall ***m*** the boards for
26:19 You shall ***m*** forty sockets of
26:22 you shall ***m*** six boards.
26:23 And you shall also ***m*** two boards
26:26 And you shall ***m*** bars of acacia
26:29 ***m*** their rings of gold as
26:31 You shall ***m*** a veil woven of
26:36 You shall ***m*** a screen for the
26:37 And you shall ***m*** for the screen
27: 1 You shall ***m*** an altar of acacia
27: 2 You shall ***m*** its horns on its
27: 3 Also you shall ***m*** its pans to
27: 3 you shall ***m*** all its utensils of
27: 4 You shall ***m*** a grate for it, a
27: 4 and on the network you shall ***m***
27: 6 And you shall ***m*** poles for the
27: 8 You shall ***m*** it hollow with
27: 8 so shall they ***m*** it.
27: 9 You shall also ***m*** the court of
28: 2 And you shall ***m*** holy garments
28: 3 that they may ***m*** Aaron's
28: 4 the garments which they shall ***m***:
28: 4 So they shall ***m*** holy garments
28: 6 and they shall ***m*** the ephod of
28:13 You shall also ***m*** settings of
28:14 and you shall ***m*** two chains of
28:15 You shall ***m*** the breastplate of
28:15 of the ephod you shall ***m*** it:
28:15 woven linen, you shall ***m*** it.
28:22 You shall ***m*** chains for the
28:23 And you shall ***m*** two rings of
28:26 You shall ***m*** two rings of gold,
28:27 rings of gold you shall ***m***,
28:31 You shall ***m*** the robe of the
28:33 And upon its hem you shall ***m***
28:36 You shall also ***m*** a plate of
28:39 you shall ***m*** the turban of fine
28:39 and you shall ***m*** the sash of
28:40 For Aaron's sons you shall ***m***
28:40 and you shall ***m*** sashes for
28:40 And you shall ***m*** hats for them,
28:42 And you shall ***m*** for them linen
29: 2 anointed with oil (you shall ***m***
29:36 cleanse the altar when you ***m***
29:37 Seven days you shall ***m*** atonement
30: 1 You shall ***m*** an altar to burn
30: 1 you shall ***m*** it of acacia wood.
30: 3 and you shall ***m*** for it a
30: 4 Two gold rings you shall ***m*** for
30: 5 You shall ***m*** the poles of acacia
30:10 And Aaron shall ***m*** atonement upon
30:10 once a year he shall ***m***
30:15 to ***m*** atonement for yourselves.
30:16 to ***m*** atonement for
30:18 You shall also ***m*** a laver of
30:25 And you shall ***m*** from these a
30:32 nor shall you ***m*** any other
30:35 You shall ***m*** of these an incense,
30:37 the incense which you shall ***m***,
30:37 you shall not ***m*** any for
31: 6 that they may ***m*** all that I have
32: 1 ***m*** us gods that shall go before
32:10 And I will ***m*** of you a great
32:23 ***M*** us gods that shall go before
32:30 perhaps I can ***m*** atonement for
33:19 I will ***m*** all My goodness pass
34:10 I ***m*** a covenant. Before all your
34:12 lest you ***m*** a covenant with the
34:15 lest you ***m*** a covenant with the
34:15 harlot with their gods and ***m***
34:16 harlot with their gods and ***m***
34:17 You shall ***m*** no molded gods for
35:10 among you shall come and ***m*** all
Lev 1: 4 be accepted on his behalf to ***m***
4:20 So the priest shall ***m*** atonement
4:26 So the priest shall ***m*** atonement
4:31 So the priest shall ***m*** atonement
4:35 So the priest shall ***m*** atonement
5: 6 So the priest shall ***m*** atonement
5:10 So the priest shall ***m*** atonement
5:13 The priest shall ***m*** atonement for
5:16 And he shall ***m*** restitution for
5:16 So the priest shall ***m*** atonement
5:18 So the priest shall ***m*** atonement
6: 7 So the priest shall ***m*** atonement
6:30 to ***m*** atonement in the holy
8:15 to ***m*** atonement for it.
8:34 to ***m*** atonement for you.
9: 7 and ***m*** atonement for yourself
9: 7 and ***m*** atonement for them, as
10:17 to ***m*** atonement for them before
11:43 You shall not ***m*** yourselves
11:43 nor shall you ***m*** yourselves
12: 7 and ***m*** atonement for her.
12: 8 So the priest shall ***m*** atonement
14:18 So the priest shall ***m*** atonement
14:19 and ***m*** atonement for him who is
14:20 So the priest shall ***m*** atonement
14:21 to ***m*** atonement for him,
14:29 to ***m*** atonement for him before
14:31 So the priest shall ***m*** atonement
14:53 and ***m*** atonement for the house,
15:15 So the priest shall ***m*** atonement
15:30 and the priest shall ***m***
16: 6 and ***m*** atonement for himself and
16:10 to ***m*** atonement upon it, and to
16:11 and ***m*** atonement for himself and
16:16 So he shall ***m*** atonement for the
16:17 of meeting when he goes in to ***m***
16:17 that he may ***m*** atonement for
16:18 and ***m*** atonement for it, and

16:24 and ***m*** atonement for himself and
16:27 whose blood was brought in to ***m***
16:30 that day the priest shall ***m***
16:32 shall ***m*** atonement, and put on
16:33 then he shall ***m*** atonement for
16:33 and he shall ***m*** atonement for
16:33 and he shall ***m*** atonement for
16:34 to ***m*** atonement for the children
17:11 it to you upon the altar to ***m***
19: 4 nor ***m*** for yourselves molded
19:22 The priest shall ***m*** atonement for
19:28 You shall not ***m*** any cuttings in
20:25 and you shall not ***m*** yourselves
21: 5 They shall not ***m*** any bald
21: 5 the edges of their beards nor ***m***
22:22 nor ***m*** an offering by fire of
22:24 nor shall you ***m*** any offering
23:28 to ***m*** atonement for you before
24: 2 to ***m*** the lamps burn
24:18 kills an animal shall ***m*** it
25: 9 Day of Atonement you shall ***m***
26: 1 You shall not ***m*** idols for
26: 6 and none will ***m*** you afraid;
26: 9 look on you favorably and ***m***
26:19 I will ***m*** your heavens like iron
26:22 and ***m*** you few in number;
Num 5: 7 He shall ***m*** restitution for his
5:21 the LORD ***m*** you a curse and an
5:22 and ***m*** your belly swell and
5:24 And he shall ***m*** the woman drink
5:26 and afterward ***m*** the woman drink
6: 7 He shall not ***m*** himself unclean
6:11 and ***m*** atonement for him,
6:25 The LORD ***m*** His face shine upon
8: 7 and so ***m*** themselves clean.
8:12 to ***m*** atonement for the Levites.
8:19 and to ***m*** atonement for the
10: 2 ***M*** two silver trumpets for
10: 2 you shall ***m*** them of hammered
12: 6 ***m*** Myself known to him in a
14:12 and I will ***m*** of you a nation
14:27 which the children of Israel ***m***
14:30 land which I swore I would ***m***
15: 3 and you ***m*** an offering by fire to
15: 3 to ***m*** a sweet aroma to the
15:25 So the priest shall ***m*** atonement
15:28 So the priest shall ***m*** atonement
15:28 to ***m*** atonement for him; and it
15:38 Tell them to ***m*** tassels on the
16:46 to the congregation and ***m***
17: 5 which they ***m*** against you."
21: 8 ***M*** a fiery serpent, and set it
23:19 and will He not ***m*** it good?
28:22 to ***m*** atonement for you.
28:30 to ***m*** atonement for you.
29: 5 to ***m*** atonement for you;
30: 8 he shall ***m*** void her vow which
30:13 or her husband may ***m*** it void.
30:15 But if he does ***m*** them void after
31:50 to ***m*** atonement for ourselves
Deut 1:11 the LORD God of your fathers ***m***
1:13 and I will ***m*** them heads over
4:16 lest you act corruptly and ***m*** for
4:23 and ***m*** for yourselves a carved
4:25 and act corruptly and ***m*** a
5: 3 The LORD did not ***m*** this
5: 8 You shall not ***m*** for yourself a
7: 2 You shall ***m*** no covenant with
7: 3 Nor shall you ***m*** marriages with
8: 3 that He might ***m*** you know that
9:14 and I will ***m*** of you a nation
10: 1 up to Me on the mountain and ***m***
12:11 the LORD your God chooses to ***m***
14:23 the place where He chooses to ***m***
16: 6 the LORD your God chooses to ***m***
16:11 the LORD your God chooses to ***m***
19:18 And the judges shall ***m*** careful
20: 9 that they shall ***m*** captains of
20:12 Now if the city will not ***m***
22: 8 then you shall ***m*** a parapet for
22:12 You shall ***m*** tassels on the four
23:21 When you ***m*** a vow to the LORD
26: 2 the LORD your God chooses to ***m***
28:13 And the LORD will ***m*** you the
28:21 The LORD will ***m*** the plague
29: 1 the LORD commanded Moses to ***m***
29:14 I ***m*** this covenant and this
30: 9 The LORD your God will ***m*** you
32:26 I will ***m*** the memory of them to
32:39 I kill and I ***m*** alive; I wound
32:42 I will ***m*** My arrows drunk with
Josh 1: 8 For then you will ***m*** your way
5: 2 ***M*** flint knives for yourself, and
6: 5 when they ***m*** a long blast with
6:10 You shall not shout or ***m*** any
6:18 and ***m*** the camp of Israel a
7:19 and ***m*** confession to Him, and
9: 6 ***m*** a covenant with us."
9: 7 so how can we ***m*** a covenant with
9:11 ***m*** a covenant with us." '
22:25 So your descendants would ***m***
23: 7 You shall not ***m*** mention of the
23:12 and ***m*** marriages with them, and
24: 9 arose to ***m*** war against Israel,
Judg 2: 2 And you shall ***m*** no covenant with
8:24 I would like to ***m*** a request of
9:48 ***m*** haste and do as I have
17: 3 to ***m*** a carved image and a
20:10 to ***m*** provisions for the people,
20:38 ambush was that they would ***m*** a
Ruth 3: 3 but do not ***m*** yourself known to
4:11 The LORD ***m*** the woman who is

1 Sam 1: 4 the time came for Elkanah to ***m***
1: 6 to ***m*** her miserable, because the
2: 8 set them among princes And ***m***
2:19 Moreover his mother used to ***m***
2:24 You ***m*** the LORD's people
2:29 to ***m*** yourselves fat with the
6: 5 Therefore you shall ***m*** images of
6: 7 ***m*** a new cart, take two milk
8: 5 Now ***m*** us a king to judge us
8:12 and some to ***m*** his weapons of
8:22 and ***m*** them a king." And Samuel
10: 8 to offer burnt offerings and ***m***
11: 1 ***M*** a covenant with us, and we
11: 2 On this condition I will ***m*** a
12:22 it has pleased the LORD to ***m***
13:19 Lest the Hebrews ***m*** swords or
18:25 But Saul thought to ***m*** David
20:38 ***M*** haste, hurry, do not delay!"
22: 7 and ***m*** you all captains of
25:28 For the LORD will certainly ***m***
28: 2 Therefore I will ***m*** you one of my
28:15 for the Philistines ***m*** war
29: 4 ***M*** this fellow return, that he
2 Sam 3:12 ***M*** your covenant with me, and
3:13 I will ***m*** a covenant with you.
3:21 that they may ***m*** a covenant with
7:11 LORD tells you that He will ***m***
7:21 to ***m*** Your servant know them.
7:23 to ***m*** for Himself a name—and to
13: 6 let Tamar my sister come and ***m***
15:14 ***M*** haste to depart, lest he
15:20 Should I ***m*** you wander up and
17: 2 and ***m*** him afraid. And all the
21: 3 And with what shall I ***m***
22:35 He teaches my hands to ***m*** war,
23: 5 Will He not ***m*** it increase?
1 Ki 1:37 and ***m*** his throne greater than
1:47 May God ***m*** the name of Solomon
1:47 and may He ***m*** his throne greater
2:42 Did I not ***m*** you swear by the
8:33 and pray and ***m*** supplication to
8:47 and ***m*** supplication to You in
12: 1 had gone to Shechem to ***m*** him
12:10 but you ***m*** it lighter on
16: 3 and I will ***m*** your house like
16:19 sin which he had committed to ***m***
16:21 to ***m*** him king, and half
17:13 but ***m*** me a small cake from it
17:13 and afterward ***m*** some for
19: 2 if I do not ***m*** your life as the
21:22 I will ***m*** your house like the
22:16 How many times shall I ***m*** you
2 Ki 3:16 ***M*** this valley full of ditches.'
4:10 let us ***m*** a small upper room on
5: 7 to kill and ***m*** alive, that this
6: 2 and let us ***m*** there a place
7: 2 if the LORD would ***m*** windows
7:19 if the LORD would ***m*** windows
8: 3 and she went to ***m*** an appeal to
9: 2 and go in and ***m*** him rise up
9: 9 So I will ***m*** the house of Ahab
9:21 ***M*** ready." And his chariot was
10: 5 but we will not ***m*** anyone king.
16: 5 came up to Jerusalem to ***m*** war;
17:29 every nation continued to ***m***
18:30 nor let Hezekiah ***m*** you trust in
18:31 ***M*** peace with me by a present
19: 9 he has come out to ***m*** war with
21: 8 and I will not ***m*** the feet of
23:10 that no man might ***m*** his son or
1 Chr 6:49 and to ***m*** atonement for Israel,
11:10 to ***m*** him king, according to the
12:31 by name to come and ***m*** David
12:38 to ***m*** David king over all
12:38 Israel were of one mind to ***m***
16: 8 ***M*** known His deeds among the
17:21 to ***m*** for Yourself a name by
21: 3 May the LORD ***m*** His people a
22: 5 I will now ***m*** preparation for
28: 4 He was pleased with me to ***m*** me
29:12 In Your hand it is to ***m***
2 Chr 2:14 and to ***m*** any engraving and to
2:18 six hundred overseers to ***m*** the
5:13 to ***m*** one sound to be heard in
6:24 and pray and ***m*** supplication
6:37 and ***m*** supplication to You in
7:11 that came into his heart to ***m***
7:20 and will ***m*** it a proverb and a
8: 9 But Solomon did not ***m*** the
10: 1 had gone to Shechem to ***m*** him
10:10 but you ***m*** it lighter on
11:22 for he intended to ***m*** him king.
14: 7 us build these cities and ***m***
17:10 so that they did not ***m*** war
18:15 How many times shall I ***m*** you
20:36 he allied himself with him to ***m***
25: 8 God shall ***m*** you fall before the
29:10 Now it is in my heart to ***m*** a
29:24 altar as a sin offering to ***m***
30: 5 So they resolved to ***m*** a
32: 2 and that his purpose was to ***m***
35:21 for God commanded me to ***m***
Ezra 4:21 Now give the command to ***m*** these
5: 5 so that they could not ***m*** them
10: 3 let us ***m*** a covenant with our
10:11 ***m*** confession to the LORD God
Neh 2: 8 he must give me timber to ***m***
6: 9 they all were trying to ***m***
8:15 to ***m*** booths, as it is
9:38 We ***m*** a sure covenant, and
10:33 for the sin offerings to ***m***
Esth 1:20 king's decree which he will ***m***

4: 8 her to go in to the king to ***m***
9:22 that they should ***m*** them days of
Job 5:18 but His hands ***m*** whole.
8: 5 earnestly seek God And ***m*** your
11: 3 Should your empty talk ***m*** men
11:19 and no one would ***m*** you afraid;
13:11 Will not His excellence ***m*** you
13:21 let not the dread of You ***m*** me
13:23 ***M*** me know my transgression and
13:26 And ***m*** me inherit the
15:24 Trouble and anguish ***m*** him
17:13 If I ***m*** my bed in the darkness,
20: 2 my anxious thoughts ***m*** me
22: 3 it gain to Him that you ***m***
22:27 You will ***m*** your prayer to Him,
23:13 and who can ***m*** Him change?
24:25 And ***m*** my speech worth
31:15 He who made me in the womb ***m***
34:29 who then can ***m*** trouble?
39:27 And ***m*** its nest on high?
41: 3 Will he ***m*** many supplications to
41: 4 Will he ***m*** a covenant with you?
41: 6 Will your companions ***m*** a
41:28 The arrow cannot ***m*** him flee;
Ps 4: 8 ***m*** me dwell in safety.
5: 8 ***M*** Your way straight before my
6: 6 All night I ***m*** my bed swim;
11: 2 They ***m*** ready their arrow on
18:34 He teaches my hands to ***m*** war,
21: 9 You shall ***m*** them as a fiery
21:12 Therefore You will ***m*** them turn
21:12 You will ***m*** ready Your arrows
31:16 ***M*** Your face shine upon Your
33: 2 ***M*** melody to Him with an
34: 2 My soul shall ***m*** its boast in
38:22 ***M*** haste to help me, O Lord, my
39: 4 ***m*** me to know my end, And what
39: 8 Do not ***m*** me the reproach of
39:11 You ***m*** his beauty melt away
40:13 ***m*** haste to help me!
44:10 You ***m*** us turn back from the
44:13 You ***m*** us a reproach to our
44:14 You ***m*** us a byword among the
45:16 Whom You shall ***m*** princes in
45:17 I will ***m*** Your name to be
46: 4 a river whose streams shall ***m***
51: 6 in the hidden part You will ***m***
51: 8 ***M*** me hear joy and gladness,
52: 7 is the man who did not ***m***
57: 1 shadow of Your wings I will ***m***
64: 8 So He will ***m*** them stumble over
65: 8 You ***m*** the outgoings of the
65:10 You ***m*** it soft with showers,
66: 1 ***M*** a joyful shout to God, all
66: 2 ***M*** His praise glorious.
66: 8 you peoples! And ***m*** the voice
69:23 And ***m*** their loins shake
70: 1 ***M*** haste, O God, to deliver me!
70: 1 to deliver me! ***M*** haste to help
70: 5 ***M*** haste to me, O God!
71:12 ***m*** haste to help me!
71:16 I will ***m*** mention of Your
76:11 ***M*** vows to the LORD your God,
78: 5 That they should ***m*** them known
81: 1 ***M*** a joyful shout to the God of
83: 2 Your enemies ***m*** a tumult;
83:11 ***M*** their nobles like Oreb and
83:13 ***m*** them like the whirling dust,
84: 6 They ***m*** it a spring; The rain
85:13 And shall ***m*** His footsteps our
87: 4 I will ***m*** mention of Rahab and
89: 1 With my mouth will I ***m*** known
89:27 Also I will ***m*** him My
89:29 His seed also I will ***m*** to
90:15 ***M*** us glad according to the days
100: 1 ***M*** a joyful shout to the LORD,
104:15 Oil to ***m*** his face shine,
104:17 Where the birds ***m*** their nests;
104:20 You ***m*** darkness, and it is
105: 1 ***M*** known His deeds among the
106: 8 That He might ***m*** His mighty
110: 1 Till I ***m*** Your enemies Your
115: 8 Those who ***m*** them are like them;
119:27 ***M*** me understand the way of Your
119:35 ***M*** me walk in the path of Your
119:98 ***m*** me wiser than my enemies;
119:135 ***M*** Your face shine upon Your
132:17 There I will ***m*** the horn of
135:18 Those who ***m*** them are like them;
139: 8 If I ***m*** my bed in hell, behold,
140: 4 Who have purposed to ***m*** my
141: 1 ***M*** haste to me! Give ear to my
142: 1 my voice to the LORD I ***m*** my
145:12 To ***m*** known to the sons of men
Prov 1:16 And they ***m*** haste to shed
1:23 I will ***m*** my words known to
4:16 is taken away unless they ***m***
22:21 That I may ***m*** you know the
22:24 ***M*** no friendship with an angry
23: 5 For riches certainly ***m***
24:27 ***M*** it fit for yourself in the
27:11 and ***m*** my heart glad, That I
30:26 Yet they ***m*** their homes in the
Eccl 5: 4 When you ***m*** a vow to God, do
7:13 For who can ***m*** straight what He
Song 1: 7 Where you ***m*** it rest at noon.
1:11 We will ***m*** you ornaments of gold
8:14 ***M*** haste, my beloved, And be
Isa 1:15 Even though you ***m*** many
1:16 ***m*** yourselves clean; Put away
3: 7 Do not ***m*** me a ruler of the
5:19 Let Him ***m*** speed and hasten His
6:10 ***M*** the heart of this people dull,
7: 1 went up to Jerusalem to ***m*** war
7: 6 and let us ***m*** a gap in its wall
10:23 the Lord GOD of hosts Will ***m***
11:15 And ***m*** men cross over
12: 4 ***M*** mention that His name is
13:12 I will ***m*** a mortal more rare
13:20 Nor will the shepherds ***m*** their
14:23 I will also ***m*** it a possession
16: 3 ***M*** your shadow like the night
17: 2 and no one will ***m*** them afraid.
17:11 In the day you will ***m*** your
17:11 And in the morning you will ***m***
17:12 of many people Who ***m*** a noise
17:12 rushing of nations That ***m*** a
19:10 All who ***m*** wages will be
19:21 and will ***m*** sacrifice and
19:21 they will ***m*** a vow to the LORD
23:16 ***M*** sweet melody, sing many
25: 6 The LORD of hosts will ***m*** for
26:13 But by You only we ***m*** mention
27: 5 That he may ***m*** peace with Me;
27: 5 And he shall ***m*** peace with
28: 9 And whom will he ***m*** to
28:17 Also I will ***m*** justice the
29:16 He did not ***m*** me"? Or shall the
29:21 Who ***m*** a man an offender by a
32:11 ***m*** yourselves bare, And gird
33: 1 When you ***m*** an end of dealing
34:15 There the arrow snake shall ***m***
35: 3 And ***m*** firm the feeble knees.
36:15 nor let Hezekiah ***m*** you trust in
36:16 ***M*** peace with me by a present
37: 9 He has come out to ***m*** war with
38:12 From day until night You ***m*** an
38:13 From day until night You ***m*** an
38:16 So You will restore me and ***m***
38:19 The father shall ***m*** known Your
40: 3 ***M*** straight in the desert
41:15 I will ***m*** you into a new
41:15 And ***m*** the hills like chaff.
41:18 I will ***m*** the wilderness a pool
42:15 I will ***m*** the rivers
42:16 I will ***m*** darkness light before
42:21 He will exalt the law and ***m***
43:19 I will even ***m*** a road in the
44: 9 Those who ***m*** an image, all of
44:19 And shall I ***m*** the rest of it
45: 2 I will go before you And ***m*** the
45: 7 I ***m*** peace and create calamity;
45:14 They will ***m*** supplication to
46: 5 and ***m*** Me equal And compare
48: 1 And ***m*** mention of the God of
49:11 I will ***m*** each of My mountains a
49:17 Your sons shall ***m*** haste;
50: 2 I ***m*** the rivers a wilderness;
50: 3 And I ***m*** sackcloth their
51: 3 He will ***m*** her wilderness like
51: 4 And I will ***m*** My justice rest
52: 5 Those who rule over them ***M***
53:10 When You ***m*** His soul an
54: 3 And ***m*** the desolate cities
54:12 I will ***m*** your pinnacles of
55: 3 And I will ***m*** an everlasting
55:10 And ***m*** it bring forth and bud,
56: 7 And ***m*** them joyful in My house
57: 4 Against whom do you ***m*** a wide
58: 4 To ***m*** your voice heard on high.
59: 7 And they ***m*** haste to shed
60:13 And I will ***m*** the place of My
60:15 I will ***m*** you an eternal
60:17 I will also ***m*** your officers
61: 8 And will ***m*** with them an
62: 6 You who ***m*** mention of the
63:12 the water before them To ***m***
63:14 To ***m*** Yourself a glorious name.
64: 2 To ***m*** Your name known to Your
66:22 the new earth Which I will ***m***
Jer 4: 7 gone forth from his place To ***m***
4:16 ***M*** mention to the nations, Yes,
4:27 Yet I will not ***m*** a full end.
4:30 In vain you will ***m*** yourself
5:10 But do not ***m*** a complete end.
5:14 I will ***m*** My words in your mouth
5:18 I will not ***m*** a complete end of
6: 8 Lest I ***m*** you desolate, A land
6:26 And roll about in ashes! ***M***
7:16 nor ***m*** intercession to Me; for I
7:18 to ***m*** cakes for the queen of
9:11 I will ***m*** Jerusalem a heap of
9:11 I will ***m*** the cities of Judah
9:18 Let them ***m*** haste And take up a
10:22 To ***m*** the cities of Judah
15:14 And I will ***m*** you cross over
15:20 And I will ***m*** you to this people
16: 6 nor ***m*** themselves bald for them.
16:20 Will a man ***m*** gods for himself,
18: 4 seemed good to the potter to ***m***.
18:11 and ***m*** your ways and your doings
18:16 To ***m*** their land desolate and a
19: 7 And I will ***m*** void the counsel of
19: 8 I will ***m*** this city desolate and
19:12 and ***m*** this city like Tophet.
20: 4 I will ***m*** you a terror to
20: 9 I will not ***m*** mention of Him,
22: 6 Yet I surely will ***m*** you a
23:15 And ***m*** them drink the water of
23:16 They ***m*** you worthless;
23:27 who try to ***m*** My people forget My
25: 9 and ***m*** them an astonishment, a
25:12 and I will ***m*** it a perpetual
25:18 to ***m*** them a desolation, an
26: 6 then I will ***m*** this house like
26: 6 and will ***m*** this city a curse to
27: 2 ***M*** for yourselves bonds and
27: 7 and great kings shall ***m*** him
27:18 let them now ***m*** intercession to
28:15 but you ***m*** this people trust in
29:17 and will ***m*** them like rotten
29:22 The LORD ***m*** you like Zedekiah
30:10 And no one shall ***m*** him
30:11 Though I ***m*** a full end of all
30:11 Yet I will not ***m*** a complete
30:16 all who prey upon you I will ***m***
30:19 And the voice of those who ***m***
31:13 And ***m*** them rejoice rather than
31:21 ***M*** landmarks; Set your heart
31:31 when I will ***m*** a new covenant
31:33 is the covenant that I will ***m***
32:40 And I will ***m*** an everlasting
34:22 and I will ***m*** the cities of
37:20 and do not ***m*** me return to the
38:26 that he would not ***m*** me return
44:19 did we ***m*** cakes for her, to
46:27 No one shall ***m*** him afraid.
46:28 For I will ***m*** a complete end of
46:28 But I will not ***m*** a complete
48:26 ***M*** him drunk, Because he
49:15 I will ***m*** you small among
49:16 of the hill! Though you ***m***
49:19 But I will suddenly ***m*** him run
49:20 Surely He shall ***m*** their
50: 3 Which shall ***m*** her land
50:44 But I will ***m*** them suddenly run
50:45 Surely He will ***m*** their
51:11 ***M*** the arrows bright!
51:12 ***M*** the guard strong, Set up
51:25 And ***m*** you a burnt mountain.
51:29 To ***m*** the land of Babylon a
51:36 I will dry up her sea and ***m***
51:39 I will ***m*** them drunk,
51:57 And I will ***m*** drunk Her princes
Lam 4:21 you shall become drunk and ***m***
Ezek 3:26 I will ***m*** your tongue cling to
4: 9 and ***m*** bread of them for
5:14 Moreover I will ***m*** you a waste
6:14 out My hand against them and ***m***
7:23 ***M*** a chain, For the land is
8: 6 to ***m*** Me go far away from My
11:13 Lord GOD! Will You ***m*** a
13:18 charms on their sleeves and ***m***
14: 8 My face against that man and ***m***
14:15 and ***m*** it so desolate that no
15: 3 Is wood taken from it to ***m*** any
15: 3 Or can men ***m*** a peg from it to
15: 8 Thus I will ***m*** the land desolate,
16:33 Men ***m*** payment to all harlots,
16:41 and I will ***m*** you cease playing
20: 4 Then ***m*** known to them the
20:17 I did not ***m*** an end of them in
20:26 that I might ***m*** them desolate
20:31 when you offer your gifts and ***m***
20:37 I will ***m*** you pass under the rod,
21:10 Sharpened to ***m*** a dreadful
21:10 Should we then ***m*** mirth?
21:19 ***M*** a sign; put it at the head
21:27 I will ***m*** it overthrown!
22:30 a man among them who would ***m*** a
23:27 Thus I will ***m*** you cease your
24: 5 ***M*** it boil well, And let the
24: 9 the bloody city! I too will ***m***
24:17 ***m*** no mourning for the dead;
25: 4 encampments among you and ***m***
25: 5 And I will ***m*** Rabbah a stable for
25:13 and ***m*** it desolate from Teman;
26: 4 and ***m*** her like the top of a
26:14 I will ***m*** you like the top of a
26:19 When I ***m*** you a desolate city,
26:20 and I will ***m*** you dwell in the
26:21 I will ***m*** you a terror, and you
27: 5 took a cedar from Lebanon to ***m***
27:30 They will ***m*** their voice heard
29:10 and I will ***m*** the land of Egypt
29:12 I will ***m*** the land of Egypt
30: 9 go forth from Me in ships To ***m***
30:10 I will also ***m*** a multitude of
30:12 I will ***m*** the rivers dry,
30:12 I will ***m*** the land waste, and
30:14 I will ***m*** Pathros desolate,
30:21 to ***m*** it strong enough to hold a
30:22 and I will ***m*** the sword fall out
32: 7 and ***m*** its stars dark; I will
32: 8 lights of the heavens I will ***m***
32:10 I will ***m*** many peoples
32:14 Then I will ***m*** their waters
32:14 And ***m*** their rivers run like
32:15 When I ***m*** the land of Egypt
33: 2 man from their territory and ***m***
33:28 For I will ***m*** the land most
34:15 and I will ***m*** them lie down,"
34:25 I will ***m*** a covenant of peace
34:26 I will ***m*** them and the places all
34:28 and no one shall ***m*** them
35: 3 And ***m*** you most desolate;
35: 7 Thus I will ***m*** Mount Seir most
35: 9 I will ***m*** you perpetually
35:11 and I will ***m*** Myself known among
35:14 earth will rejoice when I ***m***
36:11 I will ***m*** you inhabited as in
37:19 and ***m*** them one stick, and they
37:22 and I will ***m*** them one nation in
37:26 Moreover I will ***m*** a covenant of
38:10 and you will ***m*** an evil plan:
39: 7 So I will ***m*** My holy name known

39: 9 and they will ***m*** fires with them
39:10 because they will ***m*** fires with
39:14 of seven months they will ***m*** a
43:11 ***m*** known to them the design of
43:20 thus you shall cleanse it and ***m***
43:26 Seven days they shall ***m***
44:14 Nevertheless I will ***m*** them keep
45:15 to ***m*** atonement for them," says
45:17 and the peace offerings to ***m***
45:20 Thus you shall ***m*** atonement for
46:13 You shall daily ***m*** a burnt
Dan 2: 5 if you do not ***m*** known the dream
2: 9 if you do not ***m*** known the dream
2:25 who will ***m*** known to the king
2:26 Are you able to ***m*** known to me
2:30 but for our sakes who ***m*** known
3:29 Therefore I ***m*** a decree that any
4: 6 that they might ***m*** known to me
4: 7 but they did not ***m*** known to me
4:18 of my kingdom are not able to ***m***
4:25 and they shall ***m*** you eat grass
4:32 They shall ***m*** you eat grass like
5: 8 or ***m*** known to the king its
5:15 should read this writing and ***m***
5:16 you can read the writing and ***m***
5:17 and ***m*** known to him the
6: 7 a royal statute and to ***m*** a
6:26 I ***m*** a decree that in every
8:16 ***m*** this man understand the
9: 3 face toward the Lord God to ***m***
9:24 To ***m*** an end of sins, To make
9:24 To ***m*** reconciliation for
10:14 Now I have come to ***m*** you
11: 6 to the king of the North to ***m***
11:35 and ***m*** them white, until the
Hos 2: 3 And ***m*** her like a wilderness,
2:12 So I will ***m*** them a forest,
2:18 In that day I will ***m*** a covenant
2:18 To ***m*** them lie down safely.
5: 9 the tribes of Israel I ***m*** known
7: 3 They ***m*** a king glad with their
10:11 I will ***m*** Ephraim pull a
11: 8 How can I ***m*** you like Admah?
12: 1 Also they ***m*** a covenant with
12: 9 I will again ***m*** you dwell in
Joel 2:19 I will no longer ***m*** you a
Am 8: 4 And ***m*** the poor of the land
8: 9 That I will ***m*** the sun go down at
8:10 I will ***m*** it like mourning for
9:14 They shall also ***m*** gardens and
Ob 2 I will ***m*** you small among the
Mic 1: 6 Therefore I will ***m*** Samaria a
1: 8 I will ***m*** a wailing like the
1:16 ***M*** yourself bald and cut off
2:12 They shall ***m*** a loud noise
3: 5 concerning the prophets Who ***m***
4: 4 And no one shall ***m*** them
4: 7 I will ***m*** the lame a remnant,
4:13 For I will ***m*** your horn iron,
4:13 And I will ***m*** your hooves
6:13 Therefore I will also ***m*** you
6:15 And ***m*** sweet wine, but not
6:16 That I may ***m*** you a desolation,
Nah 1: 8 an overflowing flood He will ***m***
1: 9 He will ***m*** an utter end of
2: 5 They ***m*** haste to her walls,
3: 6 ***M*** you vile, And make you a
3: 6 And ***m*** you a spectacle.
3:14 clay and tread the mortar! ***M***
3:15 ***M*** yourself many—like the
3:15 like the locust! ***M*** yourself
Hab 1:14 Why do You ***m*** men like fish of
2: 2 Write the vision And ***m*** it
2:15 Even to ***m*** him drunk,
2:18 trust in it, To ***m*** mute idols?
3: 2 In the midst of the years ***m***
3:19 He will ***m*** my feet like deer's
3:19 And He will ***m*** me walk on my
Zeph 1:18 For He will ***m*** speedy riddance
2:13 And ***m*** Nineveh a desolation,
3:13 And no one shall ***m*** them
Hag 2:23 and will ***m*** you like a signet
Zech 6:11 ***m*** an elaborate crown, and set
9:17 its beauty! Grain shall ***m*** the
10: 1 The LORD will ***m*** flashing
10: 3 And will ***m*** them as His royal
12: 2 I will ***m*** Jerusalem a cup of
12: 3 in that day that I will ***m***
12: 6 In that day I will ***m*** the
Mal 2:15 But did He not ***m*** them one,
3:17 On the day that I ***m*** them My
Mt 1:19 and not wanting to ***m*** her a
3: 3 ***M*** His paths straight.'"
4:19 and I will ***m*** you fishers of
5:36 because you cannot ***m*** one hair
8: 2 You can ***m*** me clean."
9:24 ***M*** room, for the girl is not
12:16 Yet He warned them not to ***m*** Him
12:33 Either ***m*** the tree good and its
12:33 or else ***m*** the tree bad and its
17: 4 let us ***m*** here three
22:44 Till I ***m*** Your enemies
23: 5 They ***m*** their phylacteries broad
23:14 and for a pretense ***m*** long
23:15 you ***m*** him twice as much a son
24:47 I say to you that he will ***m*** him
25:21 I will ***m*** you ruler over many
25:23 I will ***m*** you ruler over many
27:65 ***m*** it as secure as you know
28:14 we will appease him and ***m*** you
28:19 Go therefore and ***m*** disciples of
Mk 1: 3 ***M*** His paths straight.'"
1:17 and I will ***m*** you become fishers
1:40 You can ***m*** me clean."
3:12 them that they should not ***m***
5:39 Why ***m*** this commotion and weep?
6:39 He commanded them to ***m*** them
9: 5 and let us ***m*** three tabernacles:
12:36 Till I ***m*** Your enemies
12:40 and for a pretense ***m*** long
12:42 two mites, which ***m*** a quadrans.
14:15 there ***m*** ready for us."
Lk 1:17 to ***m*** ready a people prepared
3: 4 ***M*** His paths straight.
5:12 You can ***m*** me clean."
5:14 and ***m*** an offering for your
5:33 of John fast often and ***m***
5:34 Can you ***m*** the friends of the
9:14 ***M*** them sit down in groups of
9:33 and let us ***m*** three tabernacles:
11:39 Now you Pharisees ***m*** the outside
11:40 not He who made the outside ***m***
12:42 whom his master will ***m*** ruler
12:44 I say to you that he will ***m*** him
12:58 ***m*** every effort along the way to
14:18 all with one accord began to ***m***
14:31 going to ***m*** war against another
15:19 ***M*** me like one of your hired
15:29 that I might ***m*** merry with my
15:32 It was right that we should ***m***
16: 9 ***m*** friends for yourselves by
19: 5 ***m*** haste and come down, for
19:42 the things that ***m*** for your
20:43 Till I ***m*** Your enemies
20:47 and for a pretense ***m*** long
22:12 upper room; there ***m*** ready."
Jn 1:23 ***M*** straight the way of the
2:16 these things away! Do not ***m*** My
6:10 '***M*** the people sit down."
6:15 and take Him by force to ***m*** Him
8:32 and the truth shall ***m*** you
8:53 Whom do You ***m*** Yourself out to
10:33 being a Man, ***m*** Yourself God."
14:23 and We will come to him and ***m***
Acts 2:28 You will ***m*** me full of
2:35 Till I ***m*** Your enemies
7:40 ***M*** us gods to go before us;
7:44 instructing Moses to ***m*** it
9:34 Arise and ***m*** your bed." Then he
19:33 and wanted to ***m*** his defense to
19:39 you have any other inquiry to ***m***,
22:18 ***M*** haste and get out of Jerusalem
23:15 as though you were going to ***m***
24:22 I will ***m*** a decision on your
26:16 to ***m*** you a minister and a
Rom 1: 9 that without ceasing I ***m***
2:17 and ***m*** your boast in God,
2:23 You who ***m*** your boast in the law,
3: 3 Will their unbelief ***m*** the
3:31 Do we then ***m*** void the law
9:21 from the same lump to ***m*** one
9:22 to show His wrath and to ***m***
9:23 and that He might ***m*** known the
9:28 Because the LORD will ***m***
13:14 and ***m*** no provision for the
14: 4 for God is able to ***m*** him stand.
14:19 us pursue the things which ***m***
15:18 to ***m*** the Gentiles obedient—
15:26 from Macedonia and Achaia to ***m***
1 Cor 6:15 the members of Christ and ***m***
8:13 lest I ***m*** my brother stumble.
9:15 die than that anyone should ***m***
10:13 the temptation will also ***m*** the
12: 3 Therefore I ***m*** known to you that
14: 7 when they ***m*** a sound, unless
14: 7 unless they ***m*** a distinction in
2 Cor 2: 2 For if I ***m*** you sorrowful, then
5: 9 Therefore we ***m*** it our aim,
8: 1 we ***m*** known to you the grace of
9: 8 And God is able to ***m*** all grace
Gal 1:11 But I ***m*** known to you, brethren,
2:18 I ***m*** myself a transgressor.
3:17 that it should ***m*** the promise of
6:12 As many as desire to ***m*** a good
Eph 3: 9 and to ***m*** all see what is the
6:19 I may open my mouth boldly to ***m***
6:21 will ***m*** all things known to you;
Col 1:27 To them God willed to ***m*** known
4: 4 that I may ***m*** it manifest, as I
4: 9 They will ***m*** known to you all
1 Th 3:12 And may the Lord ***m*** you increase
2 Th 3: 9 but to ***m*** ourselves an example
2 Tim 3: 6 who creep into households and ***m***
3:15 which are able to ***m*** you wise
Heb 1:13 Till I ***m*** Your enemies
2:10 to ***m*** the captain of their
2:17 to ***m*** propitiation for the sins
7:25 since He always lives to ***m***
8: 5 when he was about to ***m*** the
8: 5 See that you ***m*** all things
8: 8 when I will ***m*** a new
8:10 covenant that I will ***m***
9: 9 are offered which cannot ***m*** him
10: 1 ***m*** those who approach perfect.
10:16 covenant that I will ***m***
12:13 and ***m*** straight paths for your
13:21 ***m*** you complete in every good
Jas 3:18 is sown in peace by those who ***m***
4:13 and sell, and ***m*** a profit";
2 Pe 1:10 be even more diligent to ***m*** your
1 Jn 1:10 we ***m*** Him a liar, and His word
Rev 3: 9 Indeed I will ***m*** those of the
3: 9 indeed I will ***m*** them come and
3:12 I will ***m*** him a pillar in the
10: 9 and it will ***m*** your stomach
11: 7 of the bottomless pit will ***m***
11:10 ***m*** merry, and send gifts to one
12:17 and he went to ***m*** war with the
13: 4 Who is able to ***m*** war with
13: 7 It was granted to him to ***m*** war
13:14 who dwell on the earth to ***m*** an
17:14 These will ***m*** war with the Lamb,
17:16 ***m*** her desolate and naked, eat
19:19 gathered together to ***m*** war
21: 5 I ***m*** all things new." And He

MAKER (22/21) MAKE

Ex 35:35 the designer and the tapestry ***m***,
Job 4:17 a man be more pure than his ***M***?
32:22 Else my ***M*** would soon take me
35:10 one says, 'Where is God my ***M***,
36: 3 ascribe righteousness to my ***M***.
Ps 95: 6 us kneel before the LORD our ***M***.
149: 2 Let Israel rejoice in their ***M***;
Prov 14:31 the poor reproaches his ***M***,
17: 5 mocks the poor reproaches his ***M***;
22: 2 The LORD is the ***m*** of them
Isa 17: 7 day a man will look to his ***M***,
22:11 But you did not look to its ***M***,
45: 9 to him who strives with his ***M***!
45:11 Holy One of Israel, and his ***M***:
51:13 you forget the LORD your ***M***,
54: 5 For your ***M*** is your husband,
Jer 10:16 For He is the ***M*** of all
51:19 For He is the ***M*** of all
Hos 8:14 Israel has forgotten his ***M***,
Hab 2:18 that its ***m*** should carve it,
2:18 That the ***m*** of its mold should
Heb 11:10 whose builder and ***m*** is God.

MAKERS (1/1)

Isa 45:16 Who are ***m*** of idols.

MAKES (120/115) MAKE

Ex 4:11 Or who ***m*** the mute, the deaf,
30:38 Whoever ***m*** any like it, to smell
Lev 7: 7 the priest who ***m*** atonement with
14:11 Then the priest who ***m*** him clean
17:11 for it is the blood that ***m***
Num 5:21 when the LORD ***m*** your thigh rot
30: 2 If a man ***m*** a vow to the LORD,
30: 3 Or if a woman ***m*** a vow to the
30: 7 and ***m*** no response to her on the
30:14 Now if her husband ***m*** no response
Deut 18:10 found among you anyone who ***m***
20:12 but ***m*** war against you, then you
20:20 against the city that ***m*** war
27:15 Cursed is the one who ***m*** a
27:18 Cursed is the one who ***m*** the
29:12 which the LORD your God ***m*** with
1 Sam 2: 6 'The LORD kills and ***m*** alive;
2: 7 The LORD ***m*** poor and makes
2: 7 The LORD makes poor and ***m***
2 Sam 22:33 And He ***m*** my way perfect.
22:34 He ***m*** my feet like the feet of
1 Ki 8:29 the prayer which Your servant ***m***
Job 12:17 And ***m*** fools of the judges.
12:23 He ***m*** nations great, and
12:24 And ***m*** them wander in a
12:25 And He ***m*** them stagger like a
25: 2 He ***m*** peace in His high places.
27:18 a booth which a watchman ***m***.
34:11 And ***m*** man to find a reward
35:11 And ***m*** us wiser than the birds
41:31 He ***m*** the deep boil like a pot;
41:31 He ***m*** the sea like a pot of
Ps 7:12 He bends His bow and ***m*** it
7:13 He ***m*** His arrows into fiery
18:32 And ***m*** my way perfect.
18:33 He ***m*** my feet like the feet of
23: 2 He ***m*** me to lie down in green
29: 6 He ***m*** them also skip like a
29: 9 The voice of the LORD ***m*** the
33:10 He ***m*** the plans of the peoples
40: 4 Blessed is that man who ***m*** the
46: 9 He ***m*** wars cease to the end of
77: 6 And my spirit ***m*** diligent
104: 3 Who ***m*** the clouds His chariot,
104: 4 Who ***m*** His angels spirits,
104:15 And wine that ***m*** glad the heart
107:36 There He ***m*** the hungry dwell,
107:41 And ***m*** their families like a
135: 7 He ***m*** lightning for the rain;
147: 8 Who ***m*** grass to grow on the
147:14 He ***m*** peace in your borders,
Prov 4:19 They do not know what ***m*** them
10: 1 A wise son ***m*** a glad father,
10: 4 But the hand of the diligent ***m***
10:22 The blessing of the LORD ***m***
12:25 But a good word ***m*** it glad.
13: 7 There is one who ***m*** himself
13: 7 And one who ***m*** himself poor,
13:12 Hope deferred ***m*** the heart sick,
15:13 A merry heart ***m*** a cheerful
15:20 A wise son ***m*** a father glad,
15:30 And a good report ***m*** the bones
16: 7 He ***m*** even his enemies to be at
18:16 A man's gift ***m*** room for him,
19: 4 Wealth ***m*** many friends, But the
19:11 The discretion of a man ***m*** him
29: 3 Whoever loves wisdom ***m*** his
31:22 She ***m*** tapestry for herself;

31:24 She ***m*** linen garments and sells
Eccl 8: 1 A man's wisdom ***m*** his face
10:19 And wine ***m*** merry; But money
11: 5 not know the works of God who ***m***
Isa 19:17 everyone who ***m*** mention of it
24: 1 the LORD ***m*** the earth empty and
24: 1 makes the earth empty and ***m*** it
27: 9 When he ***m*** all the stones of
40:23 He ***m*** the judges of the earth
43:16 who ***m*** a way in the sea And a
44:13 And ***m*** it like the figure of a
44:15 Indeed he ***m*** a god and worships
44:15 He ***m*** it a carved image, and
44:17 And the rest of it he ***m*** into a
44:24 who ***m*** all things, Who
44:25 And ***m*** their knowledge
46: 6 and he ***m*** it a god;
59:15 he who departs from evil ***m***
62: 7 He establishes And till He ***m***
Jer 4:19 in my very heart! My heart ***m***
10:13 He ***m*** lightning for the rain,
13:16 the shadow of death And ***m***
17: 5 man who trusts in man And ***m***
21: 2 king of Babylon ***m*** war against
29:27 Jeremiah of Anathoth who ***m***
48:28 And be like the dove which ***m***
51:16 He ***m*** lightnings for the rain;
Ezek 22: 3 and she ***m*** idols within herself
46:12 Now when the prince ***m*** a
Dan 6:13 but ***m*** his petition three times
9:27 shall be one who ***m*** desolate,
Am 4:13 And ***m*** the morning darkness,
5: 8 of death into morning And ***m***
Nah 1: 4 He rebukes the sea and ***m*** it
Mt 5:45 for He ***m*** His sun rise on the
Mk 7:37 He ***m*** both the deaf to hear and
Lk 5:36 otherwise the new ***m*** a tear, and
Jn 8:36 Therefore if the Son ***m*** you free,
19:12 Whoever ***m*** himself a king speaks
Rom 8:26 but the Spirit Himself ***m***
8:27 because He ***m*** intercession for
8:34 who also ***m*** intercession for us.
1 Cor 4: 7 For who ***m*** you differ from
8:13 if food ***m*** my brother stumble, I
14: 8 For if the trumpet ***m*** an
2 Cor 2: 2 then who is he who ***m*** me glad
Gal 2: 6 it ***m*** no difference to me;
Eph 5:13 for whatever ***m*** manifest is
Heb 1: 7 Who ***m*** His angels spirits
Jas 4: 4 to be a friend of the world ***m***
Rev 13:13 so that he even ***m*** fire come
19:11 righteousness He judges and ***m***

MAKHELOTH (2/2)

Num 33:25 from Haradah and camped at ***M***.
33:26 They moved from ***M*** and camped at

MAKING (37/37) MAKE

Gen 34:30 You have troubled me by ***m*** me
Ex 5:14 not fulfilled your task in ***m***
36: 3 the work of the service of ***m***
Deut 20:19 while ***m*** war against it to take
Judg 9:16 in truth and sincerity in ***m***
21:22 ***m*** yourselves guilty of your
2 Ki 6: 8 Now the king of Syria was ***m*** war
1 Chr 15:28 ***m*** music with stringed
17:19 in ***m*** known all these great
2 Chr 30:22 offering peace offerings and ***m***
Ps 19: 7 ***m*** wise the simple;
Eccl 12:12 Of ***m*** many books there is no
Isa 3:16 ***M*** a jingling with their feet,
45: 9 who forms it, 'What are you ***m***?
Jer 18: 3 ***m*** something at the wheel.
20:15 has been born to you!" ***M*** him
22:23 ***M*** your nest in the cedars,
Dan 6:11 and found Daniel praying and ***m***
7:21 and the same horn was ***m*** war
8:19 I am ***m*** known to you what shall
Hos 10: 4 Swearing falsely in ***m*** a
Am 8: 5 ***M*** the ephah small and the
Mic 6:13 By ***m*** you desolate because of
Zech 14: 4 ***M*** a very large valley;
Mk 7:13 ***m*** the word of God of no effect
Jn 5:18 ***m*** Himself equal with God.
Acts 7:19 ***m*** them expose their babies, so
Rom 1:10 ***m*** request if, by some means, now
2 Cor 6:10 yet ***m*** many rich; as having
Eph 1:16 ***m*** mention of you in my prayers:
2:15 from the two, thus ***m*** peace,
5:19 singing and ***m*** melody in your
Phil 1: 4 in every prayer of mine ***m***
1 Th 1: 2 ***m*** mention of you in our
Phm 1: 4 ***m*** mention of you always in my
2 Pe 2: 6 ***m*** them an example to those who
Jude 22 compassion, ***m*** a distinction;

MAKKEDAH (9/8)

Josh 10:10 down as far as Azekah and ***M***.
10:16 themselves in a cave at ***M***.
10:17 found hidden in the cave at ***M***.
10:21 to the camp, to Joshua at ***M***,
10:28 On that day Joshua took ***M***,
10:28 He also did to the king of ***M*** as
10:29 Then Joshua passed from ***M***,
12:16 the king of ***M***, one; the king
15:41 Beth Dagon, Naamah, and ***M***:

MAKTESH (1/1)

Zeph 1:11 you inhabitants of ***M***! For all

MALACHI (1/1)

Mal 1: 1 of the LORD to Israel by ***M***.

MALADY (1/1)

2 Chr 16:12 and his ***m*** was severe; yet in

MALCAM (1/1)

1 Chr 8: 9 he begot Jobab, Zibia, Mesha, ***M***,

MALCHIAH (3/3)

Ezra 10:25 of Parosh: Ramiah, Jeziah, ***M***,
Jer 38: 1 and Pashhur the son of ***M*** heard
38: 6 cast him into the dungeon of ***M***

MALCHIEL (3/3)

Gen 46:17 of Beriah were Heber and ***M***.
Num 26:45 family of the Heberites; of ***M***,
1 Chr 7:31 of Beriah were Heber and ***M***,

MALCHIELITES (1/1)

Num 26:45 Malchiel, the family of the ***M***.

MALCHIJAH (12/12)

1 Chr 6:40 son of Baaseiah, the son of ***M***,
9:12 the son of Pashur, the son of ***M***;
24: 9 the fifth to ***M***, the sixth to
Ezra 10:25 Malchiah, Mijamin, Eleazar, ***M***,
10:31 of Harim: Eliezer, Ishijah, ***M***,
Neh 3:11 ***M*** the son of Harim and Hashub
3:14 ***M*** the son of Rechab, leader of
3:31 After him ***M***, one of the
8: 4 left hand Pedaiah, Mishael, ***M***,
10: 3 Pashhur, Amariah, ***M***,
11:12 son of Pashhur, the son of ***M***,
12:42 Eleazar, Uzzi, Jehohanan, ***M***,

MALCHIRAM (1/1)

1 Chr 3:18 and ***M***, Pedaiah, Shenazzar,

MALCHISHUA (5/5)

1 Sam 14:49 were Jonathan, Jishui and ***M***.
31: 2 Jonathan, Abinadab, and ***M***,
1 Chr 8:33 and Saul begot Jonathan, ***M***,
9:39 and Saul begot Jonathan, ***M***,
10: 2 Jonathan, Abinadab, and ***M***,

MALCHUS (1/1)

Jn 18:10 The servant's name was ***M***.

MALE (164/146) MALES

Gen 1:27 ***m*** and female He created them.
5: 2 He created them ***m*** and female,
6:19 they shall be ***m*** and female.
7: 2 a ***m*** and his female; two each of
7: 2 unclean, a ***m*** and his female;
7: 3 ***m*** and female, to keep the
7: 9 ***m*** and female, as God had
7:16 ***m*** and female of all flesh, went
12:16 ***m*** donkeys, male and female
12:16 ***m*** and female servants, female
17:10 Every ***m*** child among you shall
17:12 every ***m*** child in your
17:14 And the uncircumcised ***m*** child,
17:23 every ***m*** among the men of
20:14 and ***m*** and female servants, and
24:35 ***m*** and female servants, and
30:35 So he removed that day the ***m***
30:43 female and ***m*** servants, and
32: 5 and ***m*** and female servants;
32:14 female goats and twenty ***m***
34:15 if every ***m*** of you is
34:22 if every ***m*** among us is
34:24 every ***m*** was circumcised, all
Ex 1:17 but saved the ***m*** children alive.
1:18 and saved the ***m*** children
12: 5 a ***m*** of the first year. You may
20:10 nor your ***m*** servant, nor your
20:17 nor his ***m*** servant, nor his
21: 7 she shall not go out as the ***m***
21:20 And if a man beats his ***m*** or
21:26 a man strikes the eye of his ***m***
21:27 knocks out the tooth of his ***m***
21:32 If the ox gores a ***m*** or female
34:19 and every ***m*** firstborn among
Lev 1: 3 let him offer a ***m*** without
1:10 he shall bring a ***m*** without
3: 1 whether ***m*** or female, he shall
3: 6 whether ***m*** or female, he shall
4:23 a ***m*** without blemish.
7: 6 Every ***m*** among the priests may
12: 2 and borne a ***m*** child, then she
12: 7 law for her who has borne a ***m***
14:10 eighth day he shall take two ***m***
14:12 the priest shall take one ***m***
14:21 then he shall take one ***m*** lamb
18:22 You shall not lie with a ***m*** as
20:13 If a man lies with a ***m*** as he
22:19 of your own free will a ***m***
23:12 a ***m*** lamb of the first year,
23:19 and two ***m*** lambs of the first
25: 6 your ***m*** and female servants,
25:44 And as for your ***m*** and female
25:44 from them you may buy ***m*** and
27: 3 if your valuation is of a ***m*** from
27: 5 then your valuation for a ***m***
27: 6 then your valuation for a ***m***
27: 7 old and above, if it is a ***m***,
Num 1: 2 every ***m*** individually,
1:20 every ***m*** individually, from
1:22 every ***m*** individually, from
3:15 you shall number every ***m*** from a
5: 3 You shall put out both ***m*** and
6:12 and bring a ***m*** lamb in its first
6:14 one ***m*** lamb in its first year
7:15 and one ***m*** lamb in its first
7:17 five ***m*** goats, and five male
7:17 and five ***m*** lambs in their first
7:21 and one ***m*** lamb in its first
7:23 five ***m*** goats, and five male
7:23 and five ***m*** lambs in their first
7:27 and one ***m*** lamb in its first
7:29 five ***m*** goats, and five male
7:29 and five ***m*** lambs in their first
7:33 and one ***m*** lamb in its first
7:35 five ***m*** goats, and five male
7:35 and five ***m*** lambs in their first
7:39 and one ***m*** lamb in its first
7:41 five ***m*** goats, and five male
7:41 and five ***m*** lambs in their first
7:45 and one ***m*** lamb in its first
7:47 five ***m*** goats, and five male
7:47 and five ***m*** lambs in their first
7:51 and one ***m*** lamb in its first
7:53 five ***m*** goats, and five male
7:53 and five ***m*** lambs in their first
7:57 and one ***m*** lamb in its first
7:59 five ***m*** goats, and five male
7:59 and five ***m*** lambs in their first
7:63 and one ***m*** lamb in its first
7:65 five ***m*** goats, and five male
7:65 and five ***m*** lambs in their first
7:69 and one ***m*** lamb in its first
7:71 five ***m*** goats, and five male
7:71 and five ***m*** lambs in their first
7:75 and one ***m*** lamb in its first
7:77 five ***m*** goats, and five male
7:77 and five ***m*** lambs in their first
7:81 and one ***m*** lamb in its first
7:83 five ***m*** goats, and five male
7:83 and five ***m*** lambs in their first
7:87 the ***m*** lambs in their first year
7:88 the ***m*** goats sixty, and the
18:10 every ***m*** shall eat it. It shall
26:62 every ***m*** from a month old and
28: 3 two ***m*** lambs in their first year
31:17 kill every ***m*** among the little
Deut 4:16 the likeness of ***m*** or female,
5:14 nor your ***m*** servant, nor your
5:14 that your ***m*** servant and your
5:21 his ***m*** servant, his female
7:14 there shall not be a ***m*** or
12:12 your ***m*** and female servants, and
12:18 your ***m*** servant and your female
16:11 your ***m*** servant and your female
16:14 your ***m*** servant and your female
20:13 you shall strike every ***m*** in it
28:68 for sale to your enemies as ***m***
Josh 17: 2 these were the ***m*** children of
Judg 21:11 shall utterly destroy every ***m***,
1 Sam 1:11 will give Your maidservant a ***m***
8:16 And he will take your ***m***
25:22 if I leave one ***m*** of all who
1 Ki 11:15 after he had killed every ***m*** in
11:16 until he had cut down every ***m***
14:10 cut off from Jeroboam every ***m***
16:11 he did not leave him one ***m***,
21:21 will cut off from Ahab every ***m***
2 Ki 5:26 ***m*** and female servants?
2 Chr 17:11 seven thousand seven hundred ***m***
28:10 and Jerusalem to be your ***m*** and
29:21 and seven ***m*** goats for a sin
29:23 Then they brought out the ***m***
Ezra 2:65 besides their ***m*** and female
6:17 for all Israel twelve ***m*** goats,
8:35 and twelve ***m*** goats as a sin
Neh 7:67 besides their ***m*** and female
Esth 7: 4 Had we been sold as ***m*** and
Job 3: 3 A ***m*** child is conceived.'
31:13 despised the cause of my ***m*** or
Prov 30:31 A ***m*** goat also, And a king
Eccl 2: 7 I acquired ***m*** and female
2: 8 I acquired ***m*** and female
Isa 66: 7 She delivered a ***m*** child.
Jer 20:15 A ***m*** child has been born to
34: 9 man should set free his ***m*** and
34:10 everyone should set free his ***m***
34:11 their minds and made the ***m*** and
34:11 them into subjection as ***m*** and
34:16 one of you brought back his ***m***
34:16 to be your ***m*** and female
51:40 Like rams with ***m*** goats.
Ezek 16:17 and made for yourself ***m*** images
Dan 8: 5 suddenly a ***m*** goat came from the
8: 8 Therefore the ***m*** goat grew very
8:21 And the ***m*** goat is the kingdom
Mal 1:14 Who has in his flock a ***m***,
Mt 2:16 and put to death all the ***m***
19: 4 made them ***m*** and female,'
Mk 10: 6 made them ***m*** and female.'
Lk 2:23 Every ***m*** who opens the womb
12:45 and begins to beat the ***m*** and

Gal 3:28 there is neither ***m*** nor female;
Rev 12: 5 She bore a ***m*** Child who was to
12:13 woman who gave birth to the ***m***

MALEFACTOR, MALEFACTORS (KJV) See CRIMINALS, EVILDOER

MALELEEL (KJV) See MAHALALEL

MALES (34/34) MALE

Gen 34:25 the city and killed all the ***m***.
Ex 12:48 let all his ***m*** be circumcised,
13:12 the ***m*** shall be the LORD's.
13:15 I sacrifice to the LORD all ***m***
23:17 times in the year all your ***m***
Lev 6:18 All the ***m*** among the children of
6:29 All the ***m*** among the priests may
Num 3:22 to the number of all the ***m***
3:28 to the number of all the ***m***,
3:34 to the number of all the ***m***
3:39 all the ***m*** from a month old and
3:40 Number all the firstborn ***m*** of
3:43 And all the firstborn ***m***,
31: 7 and they killed all the ***m***.
Deut 15:19 All the firstborn ***m*** that come
16:16 Three times a year all your ***m***
Josh 5: 4 came out of Egypt who were ***m***,
1 Sam 25:34 surely by morning light no ***m***
2 Ki 9: 8 cut off from Ahab all the ***m*** in
1 Chr 23: 3 and the number of individual ***m***
2 Chr 31:16 Besides those ***m*** from three years
31:19 portions to all the ***m*** among
Ezra 8: 3 were one hundred and fifty ***m***;
8: 4 and with him two hundred ***m***;
8: 5 and with him three hundred ***m***;
8: 6 Jonathan, and with him fifty ***m***;
8: 7 and with him seventy ***m***;
8: 8 Michael, and with him eighty ***m***;
8: 9 him two hundred and eighteen ***m***;
8:10 him one hundred and sixty ***m***;
8:11 and with him twenty-eight ***m***;
8:12 with him one hundred and ten ***m***;
8:13 Shemaiah—and with them sixty ***m***;
8:14 Zabbud, and with them seventy ***m***.

MALICE (6/6)

1 Cor 5: 8 nor with the leaven of ***m*** and
14:20 in ***m*** be babes, but in
Eph 4:31 put away from you, with all ***m***.
Col 3: 8 off all these: anger, wrath, ***m***,
Titus 3: 3 living in ***m*** and envy, hateful
1 Pe 2: 1 Therefore, laying aside all ***m***,

MALICIOUS (2/2)

1 Ki 2: 8 who cursed me with a ***m*** curse in
3 Jn 10 prating against us with ***m***

MALICIOUSNESS (1/1)

Rom 1:29 wickedness, covetousness, ***m***;

MALIGN (1/1)

Prov 30:10 Do not ***m*** a servant to his

MALIGNITY (KJV) See EVIL-MINDEDNESS

MALLOTHI (2/2)

1 Chr 25: 4 Romamti-Ezer, Joshbekashah, ***M***,
25:26 the nineteenth for ***M***,

MALLOW (1/1)

Job 30: 4 Who pluck ***m*** by the bushes,

MALLOWS (KJV) See MALLOW

MALLUCH (6/6)

1 Chr 6:44 the son of Abdi, the son of ***M***,
Ezra 10:29 the sons of Bani: Meshullam, ***M***,
10:32 Benjamin, ***M***, and Shemariah;
Neh 10: 4 Hattush, Shebaniah, ***M***,
10:27 ***M***, Harim, and Baanah.
12: 2 Amariah, ***M***, Hattush,

MALTA (1/1)

Acts 28: 1 that the island was called ***M***.

MAMMON (4/4)

Mt 6:24 You cannot serve God and ***m***.
Lk 16: 9 for yourselves by unrighteous ***m***,
16:11 faithful in the unrighteous ***m***,
16:13 You cannot serve God and ***m***.

MAMRE (10/10)

Gen 13:18 by the terebinth trees of ***M***,
14:13 by the terebinth trees of ***M***
14:24 with me: Aner, Eshcol, and ***M***;
18: 1 him by the terebinth trees of ***M***,
23:17 Machpelah, which was before ***M***,
23:19 before ***M*** (that is, Hebron) in
25: 9 Machpelah, which is before ***M***,
35:27 came to his father Isaac at ***M***,
49:30 which is before ***M*** in the land
50:13 field of Machpelah, before ***M***,

MAN (2081/1872) MAN'S, MANKIND, MEN, SON

Gen 1:26 Let Us make ***m*** in Our image,
1:27 So God created ***m*** in His own
2: 5 and there was no ***m*** to till
2: 7 And the LORD God formed ***m*** of
2: 7 and ***m*** became a living being.
2: 8 and there He put the ***m*** whom He
2:15 Then the LORD God took the ***m***
2:16 the LORD God commanded the ***m***,
2:18 It is not good that ***m*** should
2:22 the LORD God had taken from ***m***
2:22 and He brought her to the ***m***.
2:23 Because she was taken out of ***M***.
2:24 Therefore a ***m*** shall leave his
2:25 the ***m*** and his wife, and were
3:12 Then the ***m*** said, "The woman
3:22 the ***m*** has become like one of
3:24 So He drove out the ***m***;
4: 1 I have acquired a ***m*** from the
4:23 speech! For I have killed a ***m***
4:23 Even a young ***m*** for hurting me.
5: 1 In the day that God created ***m***,
6: 3 Spirit shall not strive with ***m***
6: 5 saw that the wickedness of ***m***
6: 6 was sorry that He had made ***m***
6: 7 I will destroy ***m*** whom I have
6: 7 both ***m*** and beast, creeping
6: 9 of Noah. Noah was a just ***m***,
7:21 on the earth, and every ***m***.
7:23 both ***m*** and cattle, creeping
9: 5 it, and from the hand of ***m***.
9: 5 I will require the life of ***m***.
9: 6 By ***m*** his blood shall be shed;
9: 6 in the image of God He made ***m***.
13:16 so that if a ***m*** could number the
16:12 He shall be a wild ***m***;
16:12 hand shall be against every ***m***,
17:17 a child be born to a ***m***
18: 7 calf, gave it to a young ***m***,
19: 8 who have not known a ***m***;
19: 9 pressed hard against the ***m*** Lot,
19:31 and there is no ***m*** on the
20: 3 Indeed you are a dead ***m*** because
24:16 no ***m*** had known her. And she
24:21 And the ***m***, wondering at her,
24:22 that the ***m*** took a golden nose
24:26 Then the ***m*** bowed down his head
24:29 and Laban ran out to the ***m*** by
24:30 Thus the ***m*** spoke to me," that
24:30 to me," that he went to the ***m***.
24:32 Then the ***m*** came to the house.
24:58 'Will you go with this ***m***?"
24:61 the camels and followed the ***m***.
24:65 Who is this ***m*** walking in the
25: 8 an old ***m*** and full of years,
25:27 a ***m*** of the field; but Jacob was
25:27 but Jacob was a mild ***m***,
26:11 He who touches this ***m*** or his
26:13 The ***m*** began to prosper, and
27:11 Esau my brother is a hairy ***m***,
27:11 and I am a smooth-skinned ***m***.
29:19 I should give her to another ***m***.
30:43 Thus the ***m*** became exceedingly
31:50 although no ***m*** is with us—see,
32:24 and a ***M*** wrestled with him until
34:19 So the young ***m*** did not delay to
37:15 Now a certain ***m*** found him, and
37:15 And the ***m*** asked him, saying,
37:17 And the ***m*** said, "They have
38:25 'By the ***m*** to whom these belong,
39: 2 and he was a successful ***m***;
41:12 there was a young Hebrew ***m***
41:12 to each ***m*** he interpreted
41:33 select a discerning and wise ***m***,
41:38 a ***m*** in whom is the Spirit of
41:44 and without your consent no ***m***
42:13 the sons of one ***m*** in the land
42:30 The ***m*** who is lord of the land
42:33 'Then the ***m***, the lord of the
43: 3 The ***m*** solemnly warned us,
43: 5 for the ***m*** said to us, 'You
43: 6 with me as to tell the ***m***
43: 7 The ***m*** asked us pointedly about
43:11 carry down a present for the ***m***—
43:13 and arise, go back to the ***m***.
43:14 give you mercy before the ***m***,
43:17 Then the ***m*** did as Joseph
43:17 and the ***m*** brought the men into
43:24 So the ***m*** brought the men into
43:27 the old ***m*** of whom you spoke?
44:11 Then each ***m*** speedily let down
44:13 and each ***m*** loaded his donkey
44:15 Did you not know that such a ***m***
44:17 the ***m*** in whose hand the cup was
44:20 'We have a father, an old ***m***,
45:22 gave to all of them, to each ***m***,
47:20 for every ***m*** of the Egyptians
49: 6 in their anger they slew a ***m***,
Ex 1: 1 each ***m*** and his household came
2: 1 And a ***m*** of the house of Levi
2:20 it that you have left the ***m***?
2:21 was content to live with the ***m***,
7:12 For every ***m*** threw down his rod,
8:17 and it became lice on ***m*** and
8:18 So there were lice on ***m*** and
9: 9 that break out in sores on ***m***
9:10 that break out in sores on ***m***
9:19 shall come down on every ***m*** and
9:22 in all the land of Egypt—on ***m***,
9:25 both ***m*** and beast; and the hail
10: 7 How long shall this ***m*** be a snare
11: 2 and let every ***m*** ask from his
11: 3 Moreover the ***m*** Moses was very
11: 7 against ***m*** or beast, that you
12: 3 day of this month every ***m***
12:12 both ***m*** and beast; and against
13: 2 both of ***m*** and beast; it is
13:13 And all the firstborn of ***m***
13:15 both the firstborn of ***m*** and the
15: 3 The LORD is a ***m*** of war;
16:16 Let every ***m*** gather it according
16:16 let every ***m*** take for those who
16:18 Every ***m*** had gathered according
16:21 every ***m*** according to his need.
16:29 Let every ***m*** remain in his
16:29 let no ***m*** go out of his place on
19:13 whether ***m*** or beast, he shall
21: 7 And if a ***m*** sells his daughter
21:12 He who strikes a ***m*** so that he
21:14 But if a ***m*** acts with
21:16 He who kidnaps a ***m*** and sells
21:20 And if a ***m*** beats his male or
21:26 If a ***m*** strikes the eye of his
21:28 If an ox gores a ***m*** or a woman
21:29 so that it has killed a ***m*** or a
21:33 And if a ***m*** opens a pit, or if a
21:33 or if a ***m*** digs a pit and does
22: 1 If a ***m*** steals an ox or a sheep,
22: 5 If a ***m*** causes a field or
22: 7 If a ***m*** delivers to his neighbor
22:10 If a ***m*** delivers to his neighbor
22:14 And if a ***m*** borrows anything
22:16 If a ***m*** entices a virgin who is
23: 3 show partiality to a poor ***m*** in
24:14 If any ***m*** has a difficulty, let
30:12 then every ***m*** shall give a
32: 1 the ***m*** who brought us up out of
32:23 the ***m*** who brought us out of the
32:27 Let every ***m*** put his sword on his
32:27 and let every ***m*** kill his
32:27 every ***m*** his companion, and
32:27 and every ***m*** his neighbor.'"
32:29 for every ***m*** has opposed his son
33: 8 and each ***m*** stood at his tent
33:10 each ***m*** in his tent door.
33:11 as a ***m*** speaks to his friend.
33:11 the son of Nun, a young ***m***,
33:20 for no ***m*** shall see Me, and
34: 3 And no ***m*** shall come up with you,
34: 3 and let no ***m*** be seen throughout
34:24 neither will any ***m*** covet your
35:22 every ***m*** who made an offering
35:23 And every ***m***, with whom was
36: 6 Let neither ***m*** nor woman do any
38:26 a bekah for each ***m*** (that is,
Lev 5: 3 uncleanness with which a ***m*** may
5: 4 whatever it is that a ***m*** may
6: 3 one of these things that a ***m***
13: 2 When a ***m*** has on the skin of his
13:29 If a ***m*** or woman has a sore on
13:38 If a ***m*** or a woman has bright
13:40 As for the ***m*** whose hair has
13:44 "he is a leprous ***m***.
14:11 him clean shall present the ***m***
15: 2 When any ***m*** has a discharge from
15:16 If any ***m*** has an emission of
15:18 when a woman lies with a ***m***,
15:24 And if any ***m*** lies with her at
15:33 either ***m*** or woman, and for him
16:17 There shall be no ***m*** in the
16:21 by the hand of a suitable ***m***.
17: 3 Whatever ***m*** of the house of
17: 4 shall be imputed to that ***m***.
17: 4 and that ***m*** shall be cut off
17: 8 Whatever ***m*** of the house of
17: 9 that ***m*** shall be cut off from
17:10 And whatever ***m*** of the house of
17:13 Whatever ***m*** of the children of
18: 5 which if a ***m*** does, he shall
19:20 woman who is betrothed to a ***m***
19:32 honor the presence of an old ***m***,
20: 3 will set My face against that ***m***,
20: 4 way hide their eyes from the ***m***,
20: 5 set My face against that ***m*** and
20:10 The ***m*** who commits adultery with
20:11 The ***m*** who lies with his father's
20:12 If a ***m*** lies with his
20:13 If a ***m*** lies with a male as he
20:14 If a ***m*** marries a woman and her
20:15 If a ***m*** mates with an animal, he
20:17 If a ***m*** takes his sister, his
20:18 If a ***m*** lies with a woman during
20:20 If a ***m*** lies with his uncle's
20:21 If a ***m*** takes his brother's wife,
20:27 A ***m*** or a woman who is a medium,
21: 4 being a chief ***m*** among his
21:17 No ***m*** of your descendants in
21:18 For any ***m*** who has a defect shall
21:18 a ***m*** blind or lame, who has a
21:19 a ***m*** who has a broken foot or
21:20 or a ***m*** who has a defect in
21:21 No ***m*** of the descendants of Aaron
22: 4 Whatever ***m*** of the descendants of
22: 4 or a ***m*** who has had an emission
22:14 And if a ***m*** eats the holy
22:18 Whatever ***m*** of the house of
24:10 Israelite woman's son and a ***m***
24:17 Whoever kills any ***m*** shall

M

24:19 If a ***m*** causes disfigurement of
24:20 has caused disfigurement of a ***m***,
24:21 but whoever kills a ***m*** shall be
25: 6 female servants, your hired ***m***,
25:26 Or if the ***m*** has no one to redeem
25:27 restore the remainder to the ***m***
25:29 If a ***m*** sells a house in a walled
25:33 And if a ***m*** purchases a house
27: 2 When a ***m*** consecrates by a vow
27:14 And when a ***m*** dedicates his
27:16 If a ***m*** dedicates to the LORD
27:20 has sold the field to another ***m***,
27:22 And if a ***m*** dedicates to the
27:26 no ***m*** shall dedicate; whether
27:28 no devoted offering that a ***m***
27:28 both ***m*** and beast, or the field
27:31 If a ***m*** wants at all to redeem
Num 1: 4 with you there shall be a ***m***
3:13 both ***m*** and beast. They shall be
4:32 you shall assign to each ***m***
5: 6 When a ***m*** or woman commits any
5: 8 But if the ***m*** has no relative to
5:10 whatever any ***m*** gives the priest
5:13 and a ***m*** lies with her carnally,
5:15 then the ***m*** shall bring his wife
5:19 If no ***m*** has lain with you, and
5:20 defiled yourself and some ***m***
5:30 of jealousy comes upon a ***m***,
5:31 Then the ***m*** shall be free from
6: 2 When either a ***m*** or woman
7: 5 to every ***m*** according to his
8:17 both ***m*** and beast; on the day
9:13 But the ***m*** who is clean and is
9:13 that ***m*** shall bear his sin.
11:27 And a young ***m*** ran and told
12: 3 (Now the ***m*** Moses was very
13: 2 fathers you shall send a ***m***,
14:15 You kill these people as one ***m***,
15:32 they found a ***m*** gathering sticks
15:35 The ***m*** must surely be put to
16: 7 and it shall be that the ***m***
16:18 So every ***m*** took his censer, put
16:22 shall one ***m*** sin, and You be
17: 5 be that the rod of the ***m*** whom
17: 9 and each ***m*** took his rod.
18:15 whether ***m*** or beast, shall be
18:15 the firstborn of ***m*** you shall
19: 9 Then a ***m*** who is clean shall
19:14 This is the law when a ***m*** dies
19:16 who has died, or a bone of a ***m***,
19:20 But the ***m*** who is unclean and
23:19 'God is not a ***m***, that He
23:19 He should lie, Nor a son of ***m***,
24: 3 The utterance of the ***m*** whose
24:15 And the utterance of the ***m***
25: 8 and he went after the ***m*** of
25: 8 the ***m*** of Israel, and the woman
26:64 among these there was not a ***m***
26:65 So there was not left a ***m*** of
27: 8 If a ***m*** dies and has no son, then
27:16 set a ***m*** over the congregation,
27:18 a ***m*** in whom is the Spirit, and
30: 2 If a ***m*** makes a vow to the LORD,
30:16 between a ***m*** and his wife, and
31:11 the booty—of ***m*** and beast.
31:17 every woman who has known a ***m***
31:18 girls who have not known a ***m***
31:26 of ***m*** and beast—you and Eleazar
31:35 of women who had not known a ***m***
31:47 drawn from ***m*** and beast, and
31:49 and not a ***m*** of us is missing.
31:50 what every ***m*** found of ornaments
31:53 every ***m*** for himself.)
32:27 every ***m*** armed for war, before
32:29 every ***m*** armed for battle before
35:23 by which a ***m*** could die,
Deut 1:16 judge righteously between a ***m***
1:23 one ***m*** from each tribe.
1:31 as a ***m*** carries his son, in all
4:32 the day that God created ***m*** on
5:24 this day that God speaks with ***m***;
8: 3 He might make you know that ***m***
8: 3 but ***m*** lives by every word that
8: 5 know in your heart that as a ***m***
11:25 No ***m*** shall be able to stand
12: 8 every ***m*** doing whatever is right
15: 7 there is among you a poor ***m*** of
15:12 "If your brother, a Hebrew ***m***,
16:17 Every ***m*** shall give as he is
17: 2 a ***m*** or a woman who has been
17: 5 bring out to your gates that ***m***
17: 5 shall stone to death that ***m*** or
17:12 the ***m*** who acts presumptuously
17:12 that ***m*** shall die. So you shall
19: 5 as when a ***m*** goes to the woods
19:15 shall not rise against a ***m***
19:16 witness rises against any ***m*** to
20: 5 What ***m*** is there who has built
20: 5 die in the battle and another ***m***
20: 6 Also what ***m*** is there who has
20: 6 die in the battle and another ***m***
20: 7 And what ***m*** is there who is
20: 7 die in the battle and another ***m***
20: 8 What ***m*** is there who is
21: 2 distance from the slain ***m*** to
21: 3 the city nearest to the slain ***m***
21: 6 city nearest to the slain ***m***
21:15 If a ***m*** has two wives, one loved
21:18 If a ***m*** has a stubborn and
21:22 If a ***m*** has committed a sin
22: 5 anything that pertains to a ***m***,
22: 5 nor shall a ***m*** put on a woman's
22:13 If any ***m*** takes a wife, and goes
22:16 I gave my daughter to this ***m*** as
22:18 of that city shall take that ***m***
22:22 If a ***m*** is found lying with a
22:22 the ***m*** that lay with the woman,
22:23 and a ***m*** finds her in the city
22:24 and the ***m*** because he humbled
22:25 But if a ***m*** finds a betrothed
22:25 and the ***m*** forces her and lies
22:25 then only the ***m*** who lay with
22:26 for just as when a ***m*** rises
22:28 If a ***m*** finds a young woman who
22:29 then the ***m*** who lay with her
22:30 A ***m*** shall not take his father's
23:10 If there is any ***m*** among you who
24: 1 When a ***m*** takes a wife and
24: 5 When a ***m*** has taken a new wife,
24: 6 No ***m*** shall take the lower or
24: 7 If a ***m*** is found kidnapping any
24:11 and the ***m*** to whom you lend
24:12 And if the ***m*** is poor, you shall
25: 2 if the wicked ***m*** deserves to be
25: 5 the widow of the dead ***m*** shall
25: 7 But if the ***m*** does not want to
25: 9 So shall it be done to the ***m*** who
28:29 as a blind ***m*** gropes in
28:30 but another ***m*** shall lie with
28:54 sensitive and very refined ***m***
29:18 there may not be among you ***m***
29:20 would burn against that ***m***,
32:25 terror within For the young ***m***
32:25 The nursing child with the ***m***
33: 1 with which Moses the ***m*** of God
Josh 1: 5 No ***m*** shall be able to stand
3:12 one ***m*** from every tribe.
4: 2 one ***m*** from every tribe,
4: 4 one ***m*** from every tribe;
5:13 a ***M*** stood opposite him with His
6: 5 the people shall go up every ***m***
6:20 every ***m*** straight before him,
6:21 both ***m*** and woman, young and
6:26 Cursed be the ***m*** before the
7:14 the LORD takes shall come ***m***
7:14 LORD takes shall come man by ***m***.
7:17 the family of the Zarhites ***m***
7:17 family of the Zarhites man by ***m***,
7:18 he brought his household ***m*** by
7:18 brought his household man by ***m***,
8:17 There was not a ***m*** left in Ai or
8:31 of whole stones over which no ***m***
10: 8 not a ***m*** of them shall stand
10:14 LORD heeded the voice of a ***m***;
11:14 but they struck every ***m*** with
14: 6 the LORD said to Moses the ***m***
14:15 Arba (Arba was the greatest ***m***
17: 1 because he was a ***m*** of war;
21:44 And not a ***m*** of all their
22:20 And that ***m*** did not perish alone
23:10 One ***m*** of you shall chase a
Judg 1:24 And when the spies saw a ***m***
1:25 but they let the ***m*** and all his
1:26 And the ***m*** went to the land of
3:15 the Benjamite, a left-handed ***m***.
3:17 (Now Eglon was a very fat ***m***.
3:29 of valor; not a ***m*** escaped.
4:16 the sword; not a ***m*** was left.
4:20 and if any ***m*** comes and inquires
4:20 Is there any ***m*** here?' you shall
4:22 I will show you the ***m*** whom you
5:30 To every ***m*** a girl or two;
6:12 you mighty ***m*** of valor!"
6:16 defeat the Midianites as one ***m***.
7: 7 every ***m*** to his place."
7: 8 every ***m*** to his tent, and
7:13 there was a ***m*** telling a dream
7:14 a ***m*** of Israel! Into his hand
7:21 And every ***m*** stood in his place
8:14 And he caught a young ***m*** of the
8:21 for as a ***m*** is, so is his
8:25 and each ***m*** threw into it the
9:54 called quickly to the young ***m***,
9:54 " So his young ***m*** thrust him
9:55 every ***m*** to his place.
10: 1 a ***m*** of Issachar; and he dwelt
10:18 Who is the ***m*** who will begin the
11: 1 the Gileadite was a mighty ***m***
11:39 he had vowed. She knew no ***m***.
13: 2 Now there was a certain ***m*** from
13: 6 A ***M*** of God came to me, and His
13: 8 please let the ***M*** of God whom
13:10 the ***M*** who came to me the other
13:11 his wife. When he came to the ***M***,
13:11 Are You the ***M*** who spoke to this
14:20 who had been his best ***m***.
16: 7 weak, and be like any other ***m***.
16:11 weak, and be like any other ***m***.
16:17 weak, and be like any other ***m***.
16:19 and called for a ***m*** and had him
17: 1 Now there was a ***m*** from the
17: 5 The ***m*** Micah had a shrine, and
17: 7 Now there was a young ***m*** from
17: 8 The ***m*** departed from the city of
17:11 was content to dwell with the ***m***;
17:11 and the young ***m*** became like one
17:12 and the young ***m*** became his
18:15 the house of the young Levite ***m***—
18:19 to the household of one ***m***,
19: 6 woman's father said to the ***m***,
19: 7 And when the ***m*** stood to depart,
19: 9 And when the ***m*** stood to
19:10 the ***m*** was not willing to spend
19:16 Just then an old ***m*** came in from
19:17 and the old ***m*** said, "Where are
19:19 and for the young ***m*** who is
19:20 And the old ***m*** said, "Peace be
19:22 master of the house, the old ***m***,
19:22 Bring out the ***m*** who came to your
19:23 But the ***m***, the master of the
19:23 act so wickedly! Seeing this ***m***
19:24 but to this ***m*** do not do such a
19:25 So the ***m*** took his concubine and
19:28 So the ***m*** lifted her onto the
19:28 and the ***m*** got up and went to
20: 1 gathered together as one ***m***
20: 8 all the people arose as one ***m***,
20:11 city, united together as one ***m***.
21:11 every woman who has known a ***m***
21:12 virgins who had not known a ***m***
21:21 and every ***m*** catch a wife for
21:24 every ***m*** to his tribe and
21:24 every ***m*** to his inheritance.
Ruth 1: 1 And a certain ***m*** of Bethlehem,
1: 2 The name of the ***m*** was
2: 1 a ***m*** of great wealth, of the
2:20 This ***m*** is a relation of ours,
3: 3 make yourself known to the ***m***
3: 8 at midnight that the ***m*** was
3:16 she told her all that the ***m***
3:18 for the ***m*** will not rest until
4: 7 one ***m*** took off his sandal and
1 Sam 1: 1 Now there was a certain ***m*** of
1: 3 This ***m*** went up from his city
1:21 Now the ***m*** Elkanah and all his
2: 9 For by strength no ***m*** shall
2:13 people was that when any ***m***
2:15 would come and say to the ***m***
2:16 And if the ***m*** said to him,
2:25 If one ***m*** sins against another,
2:25 But if a ***m*** sins against the
2:27 Then a ***m*** of God came to Eli and
2:31 there will not be an old ***m*** in
2:32 there shall not be an old ***m*** in
4:10 and every ***m*** fled to his tent.
4:12 Then a ***m*** of Benjamin ran from
4:13 And when the ***m*** came into the
4:14 And the ***m*** came quickly and
4:16 Then the ***m*** said to Eli, "I am
4:18 for the ***m*** was old and heavy.
8:22 Every ***m*** go to his city."
9: 1 There was a ***m*** of Benjamin whose
9: 1 a mighty ***m*** of power.
9: 6 there is in this city a ***m*** of
9: 6 God, and he is an honorable ***m***;
9: 7 go, what shall we bring the ***m***?
9: 7 no present to bring to the ***m***
9: 8 I will give that to the ***m*** of
9: 9 when a ***m*** went to inquire of
9:10 went to the city where the ***m***
9:16 this time I will send you a ***m***
9:17 the ***m*** of whom I spoke to you.
10: 6 and be turned into another ***m***.
10:12 Then a ***m*** from there answered and
10:22 'Has the ***m*** come here yet?"
10:25 every ***m*** to his house.
10:27 'How can this ***m*** save us?"
11:13 Not a ***m*** shall be put to death
13: 2 every ***m*** to his tent.
13:14 has sought for Himself a ***m***
14: 1 son of Saul said to the young ***m***
14: 6 Jonathan said to the young ***m***
14:24 Cursed is the ***m*** who eats any
14:28 Cursed is the ***m*** who eats food
14:36 and let us not leave a ***m*** of
14:39 But not a ***m*** among all the
14:52 And when Saul saw any strong ***m***
14:52 any strong man or any valiant ***m***,
15: 3 But kill both ***m*** and woman,
15:29 nor relent. For He is not a ***m***,
16: 7 the LORD does not see as ***m***
16: 7 for ***m*** looks at the outward
16:16 to seek out a ***m*** who is
16:17 Provide me now a ***m*** who can play
16:18 a mighty ***m*** of valor, a man of
16:18 a ***m*** of war, prudent in speech,
17: 8 Choose a ***m*** for yourselves, and
17:10 of Israel this day; give me a ***m***,
17:12 And the ***m*** was old, advanced in
17:24 of Israel, when they saw the ***m***,
17:25 Have you seen this ***m*** who has
17:25 and it shall be that the ***m*** who
17:26 What shall be done for the ***m*** who
17:27 So shall it be done for the ***m***
17:33 and he a ***m*** of war from his
17:41 and the ***m*** who bore the shield
17:56 whose son this young ***m***
17:58 "Whose son are you, young ***m***?
18:23 a poor and lightly esteemed ***m***?
20:22 if I say thus to the young ***m***,
21: 7 Now a certain ***m*** of the servants
21:14 you see the ***m*** is insane.
24:19 For if a ***m*** finds his enemy, will
25: 2 Now there was a ***m*** in Maon
25: 2 and the ***m*** was very rich.
25: 3 The name of the ***m*** was Nabal,
25: 3 but the ***m*** was harsh and evil
25:13 'Every ***m*** gird on his sword."
25:13 So every ***m*** girded on his
25:29 Yet a ***m*** has risen to pursue you
26:12 and no ***m*** saw it or knew it or
26:15 to Abner, "Are you not a ***m***?
26:23 May the LORD repay every ***m*** for
27: 3 each ***m*** with his household, and
27: 9 he left neither ***m*** nor woman
27:11 David would save neither ***m*** nor

28:14 An old ***m*** is coming up, and he
30: 6 every ***m*** for his sons and his
30:13 I am a young ***m*** from Egypt,
30:17 Not a ***m*** of them escaped, except
2 Sam 1: 2 it happened that a ***m*** came from
1: 5 So David said to the young ***m*** who
1: 6 Then the young ***m*** who told him
1:13 Then David said to the young ***m***
2: 3 every ***m*** with his household.
3:34 As a ***m*** falls before wicked
3:38 that a prince and a great ***m***
7:19 Is this the manner of ***m***,
12: 2 The rich ***m*** had exceedingly many
12: 3 But the poor ***m*** had nothing,
12: 4 a traveler came to the rich ***m***,
12: 4 one for the wayfaring ***m*** who
12: 4 lamb and prepared it for the ***m***
12: 5 greatly aroused against the ***m***,
12: 5 the ***m*** who has done this shall
12: 7 You are the ***m***! Thus says the
13: 3 Jonadab was a very crafty ***m***.
13:34 And the young ***m*** who was keeping
14:16 from the hand of the ***m*** who
14:21 bring back the young ***m***
16: 5 there was a ***m*** from the family
16: 7 Come out! You bloodthirsty ***m***,
16: 8 you are a bloodthirsty ***m***!"
17: 3 When all return except the ***m***
17: 8 and your father is a ***m*** of war,
17:10 that your father is a mighty ***m***,
17:25 This Amasa was the son of a ***m***
18: 5 for my sake with the young ***m***
18:10 Now a certain ***m*** saw it and told
18:11 So Joab said to the ***m*** who told
18:12 But the ***m*** said to Joab, "Though
18:12 lest anyone touch the young ***m***
18:24 and looked, and there was a ***m***,
18:26 the watchman saw another ***m***
18:26 and said, "There is another ***m***,
18:27 king said, "He is a good ***m***,
18:29 Is the young ***m*** Absalom safe?"
18:32 Is the young ***m*** Absalom safe?"
18:32 be like that young ***m***!"
19:14 just as the heart of one ***m***,
19:22 Shall any ***m*** go be put to death
19:32 Now Barzillai was a very aged ***m***,
19:32 for he was a very rich ***m***.
20: 1 Every ***m*** to his tents,
20: 2 So every ***m*** of Israel deserted
20:12 And when the ***m*** saw that all the
20:21 But a ***m*** from the mountains of
20:22 every ***m*** to his tent. So Joab
21: 4 nor shall you kill any ***m*** in
21: 5 As for the ***m*** who consumed us and
21:20 where there was a ***m*** of great
22:26 With a blameless ***m*** You will
22:49 delivered me from the violent ***m***.
23: 1 Thus says the ***m*** raised up on
23: 7 But the ***m*** who touches them
23:20 the son of a valiant ***m*** from
23:21 an Egyptian, a spectacular ***m***.
24:14 let me fall into the hand of ***m***.
1 Ki 1:42 in, for you are a prominent ***m***,
1:52 he proves himself a worthy ***m***,
2: 2 and prove yourself a ***m***.
2: 4 you shall not lack a ***m*** on the
2: 9 for you are a wise ***m*** and know
4:25 each ***m*** under his vine and his
4:27 each ***m*** in his month, provided
4:28 each ***m*** according to his charge.
7:14 and his father was a ***m*** of
8:25 'You shall not fail to have a ***m***
9: 5 'You shall not fail to have a ***m***
10:25 Each ***m*** brought his present:
11:28 The ***m*** Jeroboam was a mighty man
11:28 man Jeroboam was a mighty ***m***
11:28 seeing that the young ***m*** was
12:22 of God came to Shemaiah the ***m***
12:24 Let every ***m*** return to his
13: 1 a ***m*** of God went from Judah to
13: 4 heard the saying of the ***m*** of
13: 5 to the sign which the ***m*** of God
13: 6 answered and said to the ***m*** of
13: 6 So the ***m*** of God entreated the
13: 7 Then the king said to the ***m*** of
13: 8 But the ***m*** of God said to the
13:11 him all the works that the ***m***
13:12 sons had seen which way the ***m***
13:14 and went after the ***m*** of God, and
13:14 Are you the ***m*** of God who came
13:21 and he cried out to the ***m*** of God
13:26 It is the ***m*** of God who was
13:29 took up the corpse of the ***m*** of
13:31 me in the tomb where the ***m*** of
17:18 O ***m*** of God? Have you come to me
17:24 this I know that you are a ***m***
20: 7 and see how this ***m*** seeks
20:20 And each one killed his ***m***;
20:28 Then a ***m*** of God came and spoke
20:35 Now a certain ***m*** of the sons of
20:35 And the ***m*** refused to strike
20:37 And he found another ***m***,
20:37 So the ***m*** struck him,
20:39 a ***m*** came over and brought a man
20:39 a man came over and brought a ***m***
20:39 to me, and said, 'Guard this ***m***;
20:42 let slip out of your hand a ***m***
22: 8 "There is still one ***m***,
22:34 Now a certain ***m*** drew a bow at
22:36 Every ***m*** to his city, and every
22:36 and every ***m*** to his own
2 Ki 1: 6 A ***m*** came up to meet us, and said
1: 7 What kind of ***m*** was it who came
1: 8 A hairy ***m*** wearing a leather belt
1: 9 ***M*** of God, the king has said,
1:10 If I am a ***m*** of God, then let
1:11 ***M*** of God, thus has the king
1:12 If I am a ***m*** of God, let fire
1:13 ***M*** of God, please let my life and
3:25 and each ***m*** threw a stone on
4: 7 Then she came and told the ***m*** of
4: 9 I know that this is a holy ***m***
4:16 ***M*** of God, do not lie to your
4:21 laid him on the bed of the ***m***
4:22 that I may run to the ***m*** of God
4:25 and went to the ***m*** of God at
4:25 when the ***m*** of God saw her afar
4:27 Now when she came to the ***m*** of
4:27 But the ***m*** of God said, "Let
4:40 ***M*** of God, there is death in
4:42 Then a ***m*** came from Baal
4:42 and brought the ***m*** of God bread
5: 1 was a great and honorable ***m*** in
5: 1 He was also a mighty ***m*** of
5: 7 that this ***m*** sends a man to me
5: 7 that this man sends a ***m*** to me
5: 8 when Elisha the ***m*** of God heard
5:14 to the saying of the ***m*** of God;
5:15 And he returned to the ***m*** of
5:20 the servant of Elisha the ***m*** of
5:26 heart go with you when the ***m***
6: 2 and let every ***m*** take a beam
6: 6 So the ***m*** of God said, "Where
6: 9 And the ***m*** of God sent to the
6:10 to the place of which the ***m*** of
6:15 And when the servant of the ***m*** of
6:17 opened the eyes of the young ***m***,
6:19 and I will bring you to the ***m***
6:32 And the king sent a ***m*** ahead
7: 2 the king leaned answered the ***m***
7:17 just as the ***m*** of God had said,
7:18 So it happened just as the ***m*** of
7:19 officer had answered the ***m*** of
8: 2 to the saying of the ***m*** of God,
8: 4 the servant of the ***m*** of God,
8: 7 The ***m*** of God has come here."
8: 8 and go to meet the ***m*** of God,
8:11 and the ***m*** of God wept.
9: 4 So the young ***m***, the servant
9:11 You know the ***m*** and his babble."
9:13 Then each ***m*** hastened to take his
10:21 so that there was not a ***m*** left
11: 8 every ***m*** with his weapons in his
11:11 every ***m*** with his weapons in his
12: 4 and all the money that a ***m***
13:19 And the ***m*** of God was angry with
13:21 was, as they were burying a ***m***,
13:21 and they put the ***m*** in the tomb
13:21 and when the ***m*** was let down and
14:12 and every ***m*** fled to his tent.
15:20 from each ***m*** fifty shekels of
18:21 on which if a ***m*** leans, it will
22:15 Tell the ***m*** who sent you to Me,
23:10 that no ***m*** might make his son or
23:16 word of the LORD which the ***m***
23:17 It is the tomb of the ***m*** of God
1 Chr 11:22 the son of a valiant ***m*** from
11:23 a ***m*** of GREAT height, five
12: 4 a mighty ***m*** among the thirty,
12:28 Zadok, a young ***m***, a valiant
16: 3 both ***m*** and woman, to everyone a
16:21 He permitted no ***m*** to do them
16:43 every ***m*** to his house; and David
17:17 me according to the rank of a ***m***
20: 6 where there was a ***m*** of great
21:13 let me fall into the hand of ***m***.
22: 9 who shall be a ***m*** of rest; and I
23:14 Now the sons of Moses the ***m*** of
27:32 was a counselor, a wise ***m***,
28: 3 because you have been a ***m*** of
29: 1 the temple is not for ***m*** but
2 Chr 2: 7 Therefore send me at once a ***m***
2:13 now I have sent a skillful ***m***,
2:14 and his father was a ***m*** of
6: 5 nor did I choose any ***m*** to be a
6:16 'You shall not fail to have a ***m***
7:18 shall not fail to have a ***m***
8:14 for so David the ***m*** of God had
9:24 Each ***m*** brought his present:
10:16 Every ***m*** to your tents,
11: 2 LORD came to Shemaiah the ***m***
11: 4 your brethren! Let every ***m***
14:11 do not let ***m*** prevail against
15:13 or great, whether ***m*** or woman.
17:17 Eliada a mighty ***m*** of valor, and
18: 7 There is still one ***m*** by whom
18:33 Now a certain ***m*** drew a bow at
19: 6 for you do not judge for ***m*** but
20:27 every ***m*** of Judah and Jerusalem,
23: 7 every ***m*** with his weapons in his
23: 8 And each ***m*** took his men who
23:10 every ***m*** with his weapon in his
25: 7 But a ***m*** of God came to him,
25: 9 Then Amaziah said to the ***m*** of
25: 9 And the ***m*** of God answered,
25:22 and every ***m*** fled to his tent.
28: 7 a mighty ***m*** of Ephraim, killed
30:16 to the Law of Moses the ***m*** of
31: 1 every ***m*** to his possession.
31: 2 each ***m*** according to his
32:21 who cut down every mighty ***m*** of
34:23 Tell the ***m*** who sent you to Me,
36:17 had no compassion on young ***m***
Ezra 3: 1 gathered together as one ***m*** to
3: 2 in the Law of Moses the ***m*** of
8:17 a command for Iddo the chief ***m***
8:18 they brought us a ***m*** of
Neh 1:11 mercy in the sight of this ***m***.
2:10 were deeply disturbed that a ***m***
4:22 Let each ***m*** and his servant stay
5:13 So may God shake out each ***m*** from
6:11 'Should such a ***m*** as I flee?
7: 2 for he was a faithful ***m*** and
8: 1 gathered together as one ***m*** in
9:29 Which if a ***m*** does, he shall live
12:24 to the command of David the ***m***
12:36 instruments of David the ***m*** of
Esth 1:22 that each ***m*** should be master in
4:11 provinces know that any ***m*** or
6: 6 What shall be done for the ***m***
6: 7 For the ***m*** whom the king
6: 9 that he may array the ***m*** whom
6: 9 'Thus shall it be done to the ***m***
6:11 shall it be done to the ***m***
9: 4 for this ***m*** Mordecai became
Job 1: 1 There was a ***m*** in the land of
1: 1 and that ***m*** was blameless and
1: 3 so that this ***m*** was the greatest
1: 8 a blameless and upright ***m***,
2: 3 a blameless and upright ***m***,
2: 4 all that a ***m*** has he will give
3:23 Why is light given to a ***m***
4:17 Can a ***m*** be more pure than his
5: 2 For wrath kills a foolish ***m***,
5: 7 Yet ***m*** is born to trouble,
5:17 happy is the ***m*** whom God
7: 1 a time of hard service for ***m***
7: 1 also like the days of a hired ***m***?
7: 2 And like a hired ***m*** who eagerly
7:17 'What is ***m***, that You should
9: 2 But how can a ***m*** be righteous
9:32 "For He is not a ***m***,
10: 4 Or do You see as ***m*** sees?
10: 5 like the days of a mortal ***m***?
10: 5 like the days of a mighty ***m***,
11: 2 And should a ***m*** full of talk be
11:12 For an empty-headed ***m*** will be
11:12 wild donkey's colt is born a ***m***.
12:14 If He imprisons a ***m***,
12:25 them stagger like a drunken ***m***.
13: 9 you mock Him as one mocks a ***m***?
13:28 ***M*** decays like a rotten thing,
14: 1 ***M*** who is born of woman Is of
14: 6 Till like a hired ***m*** he
14:10 But ***m*** dies and is laid away;
14:12 So ***m*** lies down and does not
14:14 If a ***m*** dies, shall he live
14:19 So You destroy the hope of ***m***.
15: 2 Should a wise ***m*** answer with
15: 7 Are you the first ***m*** who was
15:14 'What is ***m***, that he could
15:16 How much less ***m***, who is
15:20 The wicked ***m*** writhes with pain
16:21 that one might plead for a ***m***
16:21 As a ***m*** pleads for his
17:10 I shall not find one wise ***m***
20: 4 Since ***m*** was placed on earth,
20:29 portion from God for a wicked ***m***,
21: 4 me, is my complaint against ***m***?
21:25 Another ***m*** dies in the
22: 2 Can a ***m*** be profitable to God,
22: 8 But the mighty ***m*** possessed the
22: 8 And the honorable ***m*** dwelt in
24:22 but no ***m*** is sure of life.
25: 4 How then can ***m*** be righteous
25: 6 How much less ***m***, who is
25: 6 is a maggot, And a son of ***m***,
27:13 is the portion of a wicked ***m***
27:19 The rich ***m*** will lie down,
28: 3 ***M*** puts an end to darkness,
28:13 ***M*** does not know its value,
28:28 And to ***m*** He said, 'Behold, the
29:13 The blessing of a perishing ***m***
31:19 Or any poor ***m*** without
32: 8 But there is a spirit in ***m***,
32:13 God will vanquish him, not ***m***.
32:21 Nor let me flatter any ***m***.
33:12 For God is greater than ***m***.
33:14 Yet ***m*** does not perceive it.
33:17 In order to turn ***m*** from his
33:17 And conceal pride from ***m***,
33:19 ***M*** is also chastened with pain
33:23 To show ***m*** His uprightness,
33:26 For He restores to ***m*** His
33:29 fact, three times with a ***m***,
34: 7 What ***m*** is like Job, Who
34: 9 It profits a ***m*** nothing That he
34:11 For He repays ***m*** according to
34:11 And makes ***m*** to find a reward
34:15 And ***m*** would return to dust.
34:21 His eyes are on the ways of ***m***,
34:23 need not further consider a ***m***,
34:29 it is against a nation or a ***m***
35: 8 Your wickedness affects a ***m***
35: 8 your righteousness a son of ***m***.
36:25 ***M*** looks on it from afar.
36:28 And pour abundantly on ***m***.
37: 7 He seals the hand of every ***m***,
37:20 If a ***m*** were to speak, surely
38: 3 Now prepare yourself like a ***m***;
38:26 in which there is no ***m***;
40: 7 prepare yourself like a ***m***;
Ps 1: 1 Blessed is the ***m*** Who walks
5: 6 bloodthirsty and deceitful ***m***.
8: 4 What is ***m*** that You are mindful
8: 4 And the son of ***m*** that You

9:19 Do not let ***m*** prevail; Let the
10:15 of the wicked and the evil ***m***;
10:18 That the ***m*** of the earth may
12: 1 for the godly ***m*** ceases!
18:25 With a blameless ***m*** You will
18:48 delivered me from the violent ***m***.
19: 5 And rejoices like a strong ***m***
22: 6 But I am a worm, and no ***m***;
25:12 Who is the ***m*** that fears the
31:12 I am forgotten like a dead ***m***,
31:20 presence From the plots of ***m***;
32: 2 Blessed is the ***m*** to whom the
33:16 A mighty ***m*** is not delivered by
34: 6 This poor ***m*** cried out, and the
34: 8 Blessed is the ***m*** who trusts
34:12 Who is the ***m*** who desires
36: 6 You preserve ***m*** and beast.
37: 7 Because of the ***m*** who brings
37:16 A little that a righteous ***m*** has
37:23 The steps of a good ***m*** are
37:37 Mark the blameless ***m***,
37:37 For the future of that ***m*** is
38:13 But I, like a deaf ***m***,
38:14 Thus I am like a ***m*** who does not
39: 5 Certainly every ***m*** at his best
39: 6 Surely every ***m*** walks about like
39:11 with rebukes You correct ***m*** for
39:11 Surely every ***m*** is vapor.
40: 4 Blessed is that ***m*** who makes
43: 1 the deceitful and unjust ***m***!
49:12 Nevertheless ***m***, though in
49:20 A ***m*** who is in honor, yet does
52: 1 you boast in evil, O mighty ***m***?
52: 7 Here is the ***m*** who did not make
55:13 a ***m*** my equal, My companion and
56: 1 for ***m*** would swallow me up;
56:11 What can ***m*** do to me?
60:11 For the help of ***m*** is useless.
62: 3 How long will you attack a ***m***?
64: 6 thought and the heart of ***m*** are
65: 4 Blessed is the ***m*** You choose,
71: 4 of the unrighteous and cruel ***m***.
74:22 Remember how the foolish ***m***
76:10 Surely the wrath of ***m*** shall
78:65 Like a mighty ***m*** who shouts
80:17 Let Your hand be upon the ***m*** of
80:17 Upon the son of ***m*** whom You
84: 5 Blessed is the ***m*** whose
84:12 Blessed is the ***m*** who trusts
88: 4 I am like a ***m*** who has no
89:48 What ***m*** can live and not see
90: A Prayer of Moses the ***m*** of God.
90: 3 You turn ***m*** to destruction,
92: 6 A senseless ***m*** does not know,
94:10 He who teaches ***m*** knowledge?
94:11 LORD knows the thoughts of ***m***,
94:12 Blessed is the ***m*** whom You
103:15 As for ***m***, his days are
104:14 vegetation for the service of ***m***,
104:15 that makes glad the heart of ***m***,
104:23 ***M*** goes out to his work And to
105:17 a ***m*** before them—Joseph—who
107:27 and stagger like a drunken ***m***,
108:12 For the help of ***m*** is useless.
109: 6 Set a wicked ***m*** over him,
109:16 persecuted the poor and needy ***m***,
112: 1 the LORD! Blessed is the ***m***
112: 5 A good ***m*** deals graciously and
118: 6 What can ***m*** do to me?
118: 8 Than to put confidence in ***m***.
119: 9 How can a young ***m*** cleanse his
119:134 me from the oppression of ***m***,
127: 5 Happy is the ***m*** who has his
128: 4 thus shall the ***m*** be blessed
135: 8 Both of ***m*** and beast.
140:11 Let evil hunt the violent ***m*** to
144: 3 LORD, what is ***m***, that You
144: 3 of him? Or the son of ***m***,
144: 4 ***M*** is like a breath; His days
146: 3 in princes, Nor in a son of ***m***,
147:10 no pleasure in the legs of a ***m***.
Prov 1: 4 To the young ***m*** knowledge and
1: 5 A wise ***m*** will hear and
1: 5 And a ***m*** of understanding will
2:12 From the ***m*** who speaks perverse
3: 4 In the sight of God and ***m***.
3:13 Happy is the ***m*** who finds
3:13 And the ***m*** who gains
3:30 Do not strive with a ***m*** without
5:21 For the ways of ***m*** are before
5:22 iniquities entrap the wicked ***m***,
6:11 And your need like an armed ***m***.
6:12 worthless person, a wicked ***m***,
6:26 by means of a harlot A ***m***
6:27 Can a ***m*** take fire to his bosom,
7: 7 A young ***m*** devoid of
8:34 Blessed is the ***m*** who listens to
9: 7 And he who rebukes a wicked ***m***
9: 8 he hate you; Rebuke a wise ***m***,
9: 9 Give instruction to a wise ***m***,
9: 9 still wiser; Teach a just ***m***,
10:23 But a ***m*** of understanding has
10:26 So is the lazy ***m*** to those
11: 7 When a wicked ***m*** dies, his
11:12 But a ***m*** of understanding holds
11:17 The merciful ***m*** does good for
11:18 The wicked ***m*** does deceptive
12: 2 A good ***m*** obtains favor from
12: 2 But a ***m*** of wicked intentions
12: 3 A ***m*** is not established by
12: 8 A ***m*** will be commended according
12:10 A righteous ***m*** regards the life
12:14 A ***m*** will be satisifed with good
12:16 But a prudent ***m*** covers shame.
12:23 A prudent ***m*** conceals knowledge,
12:24 But the lazy ***m*** will be put to
12:25 Anxiety in the heart of ***m***
12:27 The lazy ***m*** does not roast what
13: 2 A ***m*** shall eat well by the fruit
13: 4 The soul of a lazy ***m*** desires,
13: 5 A righteous ***m*** hates lying,
13: 5 But a wicked ***m*** is loathsome
13:16 Every prudent ***m*** acts with
13:22 A good ***m*** leaves an inheritance
14: 7 the presence of a foolish ***m***,
14:12 a way that seems right to a ***m***,
14:14 But a good ***m*** will be
14:16 A wise ***m*** fears and departs
14:17 A quick-tempered ***m*** acts
14:17 And a ***m*** of wicked intentions
14:20 The poor ***m*** is hated even by
15:18 A wrathful ***m*** stirs up strife,
15:19 The way of the lazy ***m*** is like
15:20 But a foolish ***m*** despises his
15:21 But a ***m*** of understanding walks
15:23 A ***m*** has joy by the answer of
16: 1 of the heart belong to ***m***,
16: 2 All the ways of a ***m*** are pure
16:14 But a wise ***m*** will appease it.
16:25 a way that seems right to a ***m***,
16:27 An ungodly ***m*** digs up evil,
16:28 A perverse ***m*** sows strife,
16:29 A violent ***m*** entices his
17:10 is more effective for a wise ***m***
17:11 An evil ***m*** seeks only
17:12 Let a ***m*** meet a bear robbed of
17:18 A ***m*** devoid of understanding
17:23 A wicked ***m*** accepts a bribe
17:27 And a ***m*** of understanding is
18: 1 A ***m*** who isolates himself seeks
18:12 destruction the heart of a ***m***
18:14 The spirit of a ***m*** will sustain
18:23 The poor ***m*** uses entreaties,
18:24 A ***m*** who has friends must
19: 3 The foolishness of a ***m*** twists
19: 6 And every ***m*** is a friend to
19:11 The discretion of a ***m*** makes him
19:19 A ***m*** of great wrath will
19:22 What is desired in a ***m*** is
19:22 And a poor ***m*** is better than a
19:24 A lazy ***m*** buries his hand in
20: 3 It is honorable for a ***m*** to
20: 4 The lazy ***m*** will not plow
20: 5 Counsel in the heart of ***m*** is
20: 5 But a ***m*** of understanding will
20: 6 But who can find a faithful ***m***?
20: 7 The righteous ***m*** walks in his
20:17 by deceit is sweet to a ***m***,
20:24 How then can a ***m*** understand
20:25 It is a snare for a ***m*** to
20:27 The spirit of a ***m*** is the lamp
21: 2 Every way of a ***m*** is right in
21: 8 The way of a guilty ***m*** is
21:16 A ***m*** who wanders from the way of
21:17 pleasure will be a poor ***m***;
21:20 But a foolish ***m*** squanders it.
21:22 A wise ***m*** scales the city of
21:24 A proud and haughty ***m***—
21:25 The desire of the lazy ***m*** kills
21:28 But the ***m*** who hears him will
21:29 A wicked ***m*** hardens his face,
22: 3 A prudent ***m*** foresees evil and
22:13 The lazy ***m*** says, "There is
22:24 no friendship with an angry ***m***,
22:24 And with a furious ***m*** do not
22:29 Do you see a ***m*** who excels in
23: 2 to your throat If you are a ***m***
23:21 drowsiness will clothe a ***m***
24: 5 A wise ***m*** is strong, Yes, a
24: 5 a ***m*** of knowledge increases
24:12 will He not render to each ***m***
24:15 not lie in wait, O wicked ***m***,
24:16 For a righteous ***m*** may fall
24:20 be no prospect for the evil ***m***;
24:29 I will render to the ***m***
24:30 by the field of the lazy ***m***,
24:30 And by the vineyard of the ***m***
24:34 And your need like an armed ***m***.
25:18 A ***m*** who bears false witness
25:19 in an unfaithful ***m*** in time of
25:26 A righteous ***m*** who falters
26:12 Do you see a ***m*** wise in his own
26:13 The lazy ***m*** says, "There is
26:14 So does the lazy ***m*** on his
26:15 The lazy ***m*** buries his hand in
26:16 The lazy ***m*** is wiser in his
26:19 Is the ***m*** who deceives his
26:21 So is a contentious ***m*** to
27: 2 Let another ***m*** praise you, and
27: 8 wanders from its nest Is a ***m***
27:12 A prudent ***m*** foresees evil and
27:17 So a ***m*** sharpens the
27:19 a man's heart reveals the ***m***.
27:20 So the eyes of ***m*** are never
27:21 And a ***m*** is valued by what
28: 2 But by a ***m*** of understanding
28: 3 A poor ***m*** who oppresses the poor
28:11 The rich ***m*** is wise in his own
28:14 Happy is the ***m*** who is always
28:17 A ***m*** burdened with bloodshed
28:20 A faithful ***m*** will abound with
28:21 for a piece of bread a ***m*** will
28:22 A ***m*** with an evil eye hastens
28:23 He who rebukes a ***m*** will find
29: 2 But when a wicked ***m*** rules,
29: 5 A ***m*** who flatters his neighbor
29: 6 By transgression an evil ***m*** is
29: 9 If a wise ***m*** contends with a
29: 9 man contends with a foolish ***m***,
29:11 But a wise ***m*** holds them back.
29:13 The poor ***m*** and the oppressor
29:20 Do you see a ***m*** hasty in his
29:22 An angry ***m*** stirs up strife,
29:22 And a furious ***m*** abounds in
29:25 The fear of ***m*** brings a snare,
29:26 But justice for ***m*** comes from
29:27 An unjust ***m*** is an abomination
30: 1 This ***m*** declared to Ithiel—to
30: 2 I am more stupid than any ***m***,
30: 2 have the understanding of a ***m***.
30:19 And the way of a ***m*** with a
Eccl 1: 3 What profit has a ***m*** from all
1: 8 ***M*** cannot express it. The eye
1:13 God has given to the sons of ***m***,
2:12 For what can the ***m*** do who
2:16 And how does a wise ***m*** die?
2:18 I must leave it to the ***m*** who
2:21 For there is a ***m*** whose labor is
2:21 must leave his heritage to a ***m***
2:22 For what has ***m*** for all his
2:24 Nothing is better for a ***m***
2:26 and knowledge and joy to a ***m***
3:13 and also that every ***m*** should eat
3:19 ***m*** has no advantage over
3:22 is better than that a ***m***
4: 4 and every skillful work a ***m*** is
5:12 The sleep of a laboring ***m*** is
5:19 As for every ***m*** to whom God has
6: 2 A ***m*** to whom God has given riches
6: 3 If a ***m*** begets a hundred
6: 5 this has more rest than that ***m***,
6: 7 All the labor of ***m*** is for his
6: 8 For what more has the wise ***m***
6: 8 What does the poor ***m*** have,
6:10 For it is known that he is ***m***;
6:11 How is ***m*** the better?
6:12 who knows what is good for ***m***
6:12 Who can tell a ***m*** what will
7: 5 of the wise Than for a ***m*** to
7:14 So that ***m*** can find out nothing
7:15 There is a just ***m*** who perishes
7:15 And there is a wicked ***m*** who
7:20 For there is not a just ***m*** on
7:28 One ***m*** among a thousand I have
7:29 That God made ***m*** upright,
8: 1 Who is like a wise ***m***?
8: 6 Though the misery of ***m***
8: 9 is a time in which one ***m***
8:15 because a ***m*** has nothing better
8:17 that a ***m*** cannot find out the
8:17 For though a ***m*** labors to
8:17 though a wise ***m*** attempts to
9:12 For ***m*** also does not know his
9:15 was found in it a poor wise ***m***,
9:15 one remembered that same poor ***m***.
10:14 No ***m*** knows what is to be;
11: 8 But if a ***m*** lives many years
11: 9 Rejoice, O young ***m***,
12: 5 For ***m*** goes to his eternal
Song 3: 8 Every ***m*** has his sword on his
8: 7 If a ***m*** would give for love
Isa 2: 9 And each ***m*** humbles himself;
2:11 The lofty looks of ***m*** shall be
2:17 The loftiness of ***m*** shall be
2:20 In that day a ***m*** will cast away
2:22 Sever yourselves from such a ***m***,
3: 2 The mighty ***m*** and the man of
3: 2 The mighty man and the ***m*** of
3: 3 of fifty and the honorable ***m***,
3: 6 When a ***m*** takes hold of his
4: 1 women shall take hold of one ***m***,
5:15 Each ***m*** shall be humbled,
5:23 justice from the righteous ***m***!
6: 5 I am undone! Because I am a ***m***
6:11 The houses are without a ***m***,
7:21 be in that day That a ***m*** will
9:19 No ***m*** shall spare his brother.
9:20 Every ***m*** shall eat the flesh of
10:13 inhabitants like a valiant ***m***.
10:18 they will be as when a sick ***m***
13:12 A ***m*** more than the golden wedge
13:14 And as a sheep that no ***m*** takes
13:14 Every ***m*** will turn to his own
14:16 Is this the ***m*** who made the
16:14 as the years of a hired ***m***,
17: 7 In that day a ***m*** will look to
19:14 As a drunken ***m*** staggers in his
21:16 to the year of a hired ***m***,
22:17 you away violently, O mighty ***m***,
29: 8 even be as when a hungry ***m***
29: 8 Or as when a thirsty ***m*** dreams,
29:21 Who make a ***m*** an offender by a
31: 7 For in that day every ***m*** shall
31: 8 shall fall by a sword not of ***m***,
32: 2 A ***m*** will be as a hiding place
32: 8 But a generous ***m*** devises
33: 8 The traveling ***m*** ceases.
33: 8 the cities, He regards no ***m***.
36: 6 on which if a ***m*** leans, it will
38:11 I shall observe ***m*** no more
38:19 The living, the living ***m***,
41:28 I looked, and there was no ***m***;
42:13 shall go forth like a mighty ***m***;
42:13 stir up His zeal like a ***m*** of
44:13 makes it like the figure of a ***m***,
44:13 According to the beauty of a ***m***,

44:15 Then it shall be for a **m** to
45:12 And created **m** on it. I—My
46:11 The **m** who executes My counsel,
47: 3 I will not arbitrate with a **m**.
49: 7 To Him whom **m** despises,
50: 2 when I came, was there no **m**?
51:12 you should be afraid Of a **m**
51:12 And of the son of a **m** who
52:14 was marred more than any **m**,
53: 3 A **M** of sorrows and acquainted
55: 7 And the unrighteous **m** his
56: 2 Blessed is the **m** who does
56: 2 And the son of **m** who lays
57: 1 And no **m** takes it to heart;
58: 5 A day for a **m** to afflict his
59:16 He saw that there was no **m**,
62: 5 For as a young **m** marries a
65:20 Nor an old **m** who has not
66: 3 a bull is as if he slays a **m**;
Jer 3: 1 If a **m** divorces his wife, And
4:25 and indeed there was no **m**,
4:29 And not a **m** shall dwell in it.
5: 1 places If you can find a **m**,
7: 5 execute judgment between a **m**
7:20 on **m** and on beast, on the trees
8: 6 No **m** repented of his
9:12 Who is the wise **m** who may
9:23 Let not the wise **m** glory in his
9:23 Let not the mighty **m** glory in
9:23 Nor let the rich **m** glory in
10:23 I know the way of **m** is not in
10:23 It is not in **m** who walks to
11: 3 Cursed is the **m** who does not
13:11 sash clings to the waist of a **m**,
14: 9 Why should You be like a **m**
15:10 A **m** of strife and a man of
15:10 A man of strife and a **m** of
16:20 Will a **m** make gods for himself,
17: 5 Cursed is the **m** who trusts in
17: 5 is the man who trusts in **m**
17: 7 Blessed is the **m** who trusts in
17:10 Even to give every **m** according
18:14 Will a **m** leave the snow water
20:15 Let the **m** be cursed Who
20:16 And let that **m** be like the
21: 6 both **m** and beast; they shall
22:28 Is this **m** Coniah a despised,
22:30 Write this **m** down as childless,
22:30 A **m** who shall not prosper in
23: 9 I am like a drunken **m**, And
23: 9 And like a **m** whom wine has
23:34 I will even punish that **m** and
26:11 This **m** deserves to die! For he
26:16 This **m** does not deserve to die.
26:20 Now there was also a **m** who
27: 5 the **m** and the beast that are
29:26 of the LORD over every **m** who
30: 6 Whether a **m** is ever in labor
30: 6 So why do I see every **m** with
31:22 woman shall encompass a **m**.
31:27 of Judah with the seed of **m**
31:30 every **m** who eats the sour
31:34 No more shall every **m** teach his
31:34 and every **m** his brother,
32:43 without **m** or beast; it has been
33:10 without **m** and without
33:10 without **m** and without
33:12 without **m** and without beast,
33:17 David shall never lack a **m** to
33:18 lack a **m** to offer burnt
34: 9 that every **m** should set free his
34: 9 a Hebrew **m** or woman—that no one
34:14 end of seven years let every **m**
34:15 every **m** proclaiming liberty to
35: 4 a **m** of God, which was by the
35:19 of Rechab shall not lack a **m**
36:29 and cause **m** and beast to cease
37:10 every **m** in his tent, and burn
38: 4 let this **m** be put to death, for
38: 4 For this **m** does not seek the
44: 7 to cut off from you **m** and
44:26 be named in the mouth of any **m**
46: 6 Nor the mighty **m** escape;
46:12 For the mighty **m** has stumbled
49:18 Nor shall a son of **m** dwell in
49:19 And who is a chosen **m** that
49:33 Nor son of **m** dwell in it."
50: 3 depart, Both **m** and beast.
50:40 Nor son of **m** dwell in it.
50:42 like a **m** for the battle,
50:44 And who is a chosen **m** that
51:22 also I will break in pieces **m**
51:22 break in pieces the young **m**
51:43 Through which no son of **m**
51:62 neither **m** nor beast, but it
Lam 3: 1 I am the **m** who has seen
3:27 It is good for a **m** to bear
3:35 turn aside the justice due a **m**
3:36 Or subvert a **m** in his
3:39 Why should a living **m** complain,
3:39 A **m** for the punishment of his
Ezek 1: 5 they had the likeness of a **m**.
1: 8 The hands of a **m** were under
1:10 each had the face of a **m**;
1:26 with the appearance of a **m**
2: 1 And He said to me, "Son of **m**,
2: 3 And He said to me: "Son of **m**,
2: 6 And you, son of **m**, do not be
2: 8 'But you, son of **m**, hear what
3: 1 He said to me, "Son of **m**, eat
3: 3 And He said to me, "Son of **m**,
3: 4 Then He said to me: "Son of **m**,
3:10 He said to me: "Son of **m**,
3:17 'Son of **m**, I have made you
3:18 that same wicked **m** shall die
3:20 when a righteous **m** turns from
3:21 if you warn the righteous **m**
3:25 'And you, O son of **m**, surely
4: 1 'You also, son of **m**, take a
4:16 He said to me, "Son of **m**,
5: 1 'And you, son of **m**, take a
6: 2 'Son of **m**, set your face
7: 2 'And you, son of **m**, thus
8: 5 Then He said to me, "Son of **m**,
8: 6 He said to me, "Son of **m**,
8: 8 Then He said to me, "Son of **m**,
8:11 Each **m** had a censer in his
8:12 Then He said to me, "Son of **m**,
8:12 every **m** in the room of his
8:15 you seen this, O son of **m**?
8:17 you seen this, O son of **m**?
9: 2 One **m** among them was clothed
9: 3 And He called to the **m** clothed
9:11 the **m** clothed with linen, who
10: 2 Then He spoke to the **m** clothed
10: 3 side of the temple when the **m**
10: 6 when He commanded the **m** clothed
10: 7 it into the hands of the **m**
10:14 the second face the face of a **m**,
10:21 likeness of the hands of a **m**
11: 2 And He said to me: "Son of **m**,
11: 4 prophesy, O son of **m**!"
11:15 'Son of **m**, your brethren,
12: 2 'Son of **m**, you dwell in
12: 3 "Therefore, son of **m**,
12: 9 'Son of **m**, has not the house
12:18 'Son of **m**, eat your bread
12:22 'Son of **m**, what is this
12:27 'Son of **m**, look, the house
13: 2 'Son of **m**, prophesy against
13:17 Likewise, son of **m**, set your
14: 3 'Son of **m**, these men have
14: 8 set My face against that **m** and
14:13 'Son of **m**, when a land
14:13 and cut off **m** and beast from
14:15 make it so desolate that no **m**
14:17 and I cut off **m** and beast from
14:19 and cut off from it **m** and
14:21 to cut off **m** and beast from it?
15: 2 'Son of **m**, how is the wood
16: 2 'Son of **m**, cause Jerusalem
17: 2 'Son of **m**, pose a riddle,
18: 5 But if a **m** is just And does
18: 8 true judgment between **m** and
18: 8 true judgment between man and **m**;
18:21 But if a wicked **m** turns from
18:24 But when a righteous **m** turns
18:24 that the wicked **m** does,
18:26 When a righteous **m** turns away
18:27 when a wicked **m** turns away
20: 3 'Son of **m**, speak to the
20: 4 "Will you judge them, son of **m**,
20:11 if a **m** does, he shall live by
20:13 if a **m** does, he shall live by
20:21 if a **m** does, he shall live by
20:27 "Therefore, son of **m**,
20:46 'Son of **m**, set your face
21: 2 'Son of **m**, set your face
21: 6 "Sigh therefore, son of **m**,
21: 9 'Son of **m**, prophesy and say,
21:12 "Cry and wail, son of **m**;
21:14 "You therefore, son of **m**,
21:19 'And son of **m**, appoint for
21:28 And you, son of **m**, prophesy
22: 2 'Now, son of **m**, will you
22:18 'Son of **m**, the house of
22:24 'Son of **m**, say to her:
22:30 So I sought for a **m** among them
23: 2 'Son of **m**, there were two
23:36 also said to me: "Son of **m**,
24: 2 'Son of **m**, write down the
24:16 'Son of **m**, behold, I take
24:25 And you, son of **m**—will it
25: 2 'Son of **m**, set your face
25:13 cut off **m** and beast from it,
26: 2 'Son of **m**, because Tyre
27: 2 'Now, son of **m**, take up a
28: 2 'Son of **m**, say to the prince
28: 2 of the seas,' Yet you are a **m**,
28: 9 a god'? But you shall be a **m**,
28:12 'Son of **m**, take up a
28:21 'Son of **m**, set your face
29: 2 'Son of **m**, set your face
29: 8 you and cut off from you **m** and
29:11 Neither foot of **m** shall pass
29:18 'Son of **m**, Nebuchadnezzar
30: 2 'Son of **m**, prophesy and
30:21 'Son of **m**, I have broken
30:24 of a mortally wounded **m**.
31: 2 'Son of **m**, say to Pharaoh
32: 2 'Son of **m**, take up a
32:10 every **m** for his own life, in
32:13 The foot of **m** shall muddy them
32:18 'Son of **m**, wail over the
33: 2 'Son of **m**, speak to the
33: 2 the people of the land take a **m**
33: 7 So you, son of **m**: I have
33: 8 say to the wicked, 'O wicked **m**,
33: 8 that wicked **m** shall die in his
33:10 "Therefore you, O son of **m**,
33:12 "Therefore you, O son of **m**,
33:12 of the righteous **m** shall not
33:22 me the evening before the **m**
33:24 'Son of **m**, they who
33:30 "As for you, son of **m**,
34: 2 'Son of **m**, prophesy against
35: 2 'Son of **m**, set your face
36: 1 'And you, son of **m**, prophesy
36:11 I will multiply upon you **m** and
36:17 'Son of **m**, when the house
37: 3 And He said to me, "Son of **m**,
37: 9 the breath, prophesy, son of **m**,
37:11 Then He said to me, "Son of **m**,
37:16 'As for you, son of **m**, take a
38: 2 'Son of **m**, set your face
38:14 "Therefore, son of **m**,
39: 1 'And you, son of **m**, prophesy
39:17 "And as for you, son of **m**,
40: 3 there was a **m** whose
40: 4 And the **m** said to me, "Son of
40: 4 the man said to me, "Son of **m**,
41:19 so that the face of a **m** was
43: 6 while a **m** stood beside me.
43: 7 And He said to me, "Son of **m**,
43:10 Son of **m**, describe the
43:18 And He said to me, "Son of **m**,
44: 2 and no **m** shall enter by it,
44: 5 LORD said to me, "Son of **m**,
47: 3 And when the **m** went out to the
47: 6 He said to me, "Son of **m**,
Dan 2:10 There is not a **m** on earth who
2:25 I have found a **m** of the captives
4:16 be changed from that of a **m**,
5:11 There is a **m** in your kingdom in
6: 7 whoever petitions any god or **m**
6:12 signed a decree that every **m**
6:12 man who petitions any god or **m**
7: 4 to stand on two feet like a **m**,
7: 8 were eyes like the eyes of a **m**,
7:13 behold, One like the Son of **M**,
8:15 having the appearance of a **m**.
8:16 make this **m** understand the
8:17 to me, "Understand, son of **m**,
9:21 the **m** Gabriel, whom I had seen
10: 5 a certain **m** clothed in linen,
10:11 **m** greatly beloved, understand
10:18 one having the likeness of a **m**
10:19 O **m** greatly beloved, fear not!
12: 6 And one said to the **m** clothed
12: 7 Then I heard the **m** clothed in
Hos 3: 3 harlot, nor shall you have a **m**—
4: 4 Now let no **m** contend, or rebuke
6: 9 of robbers lie in wait for a **m**,
9: 7 The spiritual **m** is insane,
9:12 will bereave them to the last **m**.
11: 9 For I am God, and not **m**,
Am 2: 7 A **m** and his father go in to
4:13 Who declares to **m** what his
5:19 It will be as though a **m** fled
Jon 1: 5 and every **m** cried out to his
3: 7 Let neither **m** nor beast, herd
3: 8 But let **m** and beast be covered
Mic 2: 2 So they oppress a **m** and his
2: 2 A **m** and his inheritance.
2:11 If a **m** should walk in a false
5: 7 That tarry for no **m** Nor wait
6: 8 He has shown you, O **m**,
7: 2 The faithful **m** has perished
7: 2 Every **m** hunts his brother with
7: 3 And the great **m** utters his
Nah 2: 1 **M** the fort! Watch the road!
Hab 2: 5 by wine, He is a proud **m**,
Zeph 1: 3 'I will consume **m** and beast;
1: 3 I will cut off **m** from the face
Zech 1: 8 a **m** riding on a red horse, and
1:10 And the **m** who stood among the
2: 1 a **m** with a measuring line in
2: 4 "Run, speak to this young **m**,
4: 1 as a **m** who is wakened out of
6:12 the **M** whose name is the
8:10 There were no wages for **m**
8:16 Speak each **m** the truth to his
8:23 grasp the sleeve of a Jewish **m**,
9:13 like the sword of a mighty **m**.
10: 7 shall be like a mighty **m**,
12: 1 and forms the spirit of **m**
13: 5 for a **m** taught me to keep
13: 7 Against the **M** who is My
Mal 2:12 from the tents of Jacob The **m**
3: 8 Will a **m** rob God? Yet you have
3:17 And I will spare them As a **m**
Mt 1:19 her husband, being a just **m**,
4: 4 **M** shall not live by bread
7: 9 Or what **m** is there among you
7:24 I will liken him to a wise **m**
7:26 will be like a foolish **m** who
8: 9 For I also am a **m** under
8:20 but the Son of **M** has nowhere to
9: 3 This **M** blasphemes!"
9: 6 you may know that the Son of **M**
9: 9 He saw a **m** named Matthew
9:32 behold, they brought to Him a **m**,
10:23 of Israel before the Son of **M**
10:35 set a **m** against his father,
10:41 he who receives a righteous **m**
10:41 in the name of a righteous **m**
11: 8 A **m** clothed in soft garments?
11:19 The Son of **M** came eating and
12: 8 For the Son of **M** is Lord even of
12:10 there was a **m** who had a
12:11 What **m** is there among you who
12:12 how much more value then is a **m**
12:13 Then He said to the **m**,
12:22 so that the blind and mute **m**
12:29 he first binds the strong **m**?
12:32 a word against the Son of **M**,

12:35 A good **m** out of the good
12:35 and an evil **m** out of the evil
12:40 so will the Son of **M** be three
12:43 unclean spirit goes out of a **m**,
12:45 and the last state of that **m**
13:24 kingdom of heaven is like a **m**
13:31 which a **m** took and sowed in his
13:37 the good seed is the Son of **M**.
13:41 The Son of **M** will send out His
13:44 which a **m** found and hid;
13:54 Where did this **M** get this
13:56 Where then did this **M** get all
15:11 goes into the mouth defiles a **m**;
15:11 of the mouth, this defiles a **m**.
15:18 the heart, and they defile a **m**.
15:20 the things which defile a **m**,
15:20 hands does not defile a **m**.
16:13 do men say that I, the Son of **M**,
16:26 For what profit is it to a **m** if
16:26 Or what will a **m** give in
16:27 For the Son of **M** will come in
16:28 till they see the Son of **M**
17: 9 to no one until the Son of **M**
17:12 Likewise the Son of **M** is also
17:14 a **m** came to Him, kneeling down
17:22 The Son of **M** is about to be
18: 7 but woe to that **m** by whom the
18:11 For the Son of **M** has come to
18:12 If a **m** has a hundred sheep, and
19: 3 Is it lawful for a **m** to divorce
19: 5 For this reason a **m** shall
19: 6 let not **m** separate."
19:10 If such is the case of the **m**
19:20 The young **m** said to Him, "All
19:22 But when the young **m** heard that
19:23 that it is hard for a rich **m**
19:24 of a needle than for a rich **m**
19:28 when the Son of **M** sits on the
20:14 I wish to give to this last **m**
20:18 and the Son of **M** will be
20:28 just as the Son of **M** did not
21:28 A **m** had two sons, and he came
22:11 he saw a **m** there who did not
22:24 Moses said that if a **m** dies,
24:27 the coming of the Son of **M** be.
24:30 Then the sign of the Son of **M**
24:30 and they will see the Son of **M**
24:37 the coming of the Son of **M** be.
24:39 the coming of the Son of **M** be.
24:44 for the Son of **M** is coming at
25:13 the hour in which the Son of **M**
25:14 of heaven is like a **m**
25:24 I knew you to be a hard **m**,
25:31 When the Son of **M** comes in His
26: 2 and the Son of **M** will be
26:18 into the city to a certain **m**,
26:24 The Son of **M** indeed goes just as
26:24 but woe to that **m** by whom the
26:24 that man by whom the Son of **M**
26:24 have been good for that **m** if
26:45 and the Son of **M** is being
26:64 you will see the Son of **M**
26:72 I do not know the **M**!"
26:74 I do not know the **M**!"
27:19 nothing to do with that just **M**,
27:32 they found a **m** of Cyrene, Simon
27:47 This **M** is calling for Elijah!"
27:57 there came a rich **m** from
27:58 This **m** went to Pilate and asked
Mk 1:23 Now there was a **m** in their
2: 7 Why does this **M** speak
2:10 you may know that the Son of **M**
2:27 "The Sabbath was made for **m**,
2:27 and not **m** for the Sabbath.
2:28 Therefore the Son of **M** is also
3: 1 and a **m** was there who had a
3: 3 And He said to the **m** who had the
3: 5 their hearts, He said to the **m**,
3:27 he first binds the strong **m**.
4:26 kingdom of God is as if a **m**
5: 2 met Him out of the tombs a **m**
5: 8 to him, "Come out of the **m**,
6: 2 Where did this **M** get these
6:20 that he was a just and holy **m**,
7:11 If a **m** says to his father or
7:15 is nothing that enters a **m**
7:15 are the things that defile a **m**.
7:18 that whatever enters a **m** from
7:20 said, "What comes out of a **m**,
7:20 out of a man, that defiles a **m**.
7:23 come from within and defile a **m**.
8:22 and they brought a blind **m** to
8:23 So He took the blind **m** by the
8:31 to teach them that the Son of **M**
8:36 For what will it profit a **m** if
8:37 Or what will a **m** give in
8:38 of him the Son of **M** also will
9: 9 till the Son of **M** had risen
9:12 written concerning the Son of **M**,
9:31 The Son of **M** is being betrayed
10: 2 Is it lawful for a **m** to divorce
10: 4 Moses permitted a **m** to write a
10: 7 For this reason a **m** shall
10: 9 let not **m** separate."
10:25 of a needle than for a rich **m**
10:33 and the Son of **M** will be
10:45 For even the Son of **M** did not
10:49 Then they called the blind **m**,
10:51 The blind **m** said to Him,
12: 1 A **m** planted a vineyard and set a
13:26 they will see the Son of **M**
13:34 It is like a **m** going to a far
14:13 and a **m** will meet you carrying
14:21 The Son of **M** indeed goes just as
14:21 but woe to that **m** by whom the
14:21 that man by whom the Son of **M**
14:21 have been good for that **m** if
14:41 the Son of **M** is being betrayed
14:51 Now a certain young **m** followed
14:62 And you will see the Son of **M**
14:71 I do not know this **M** of whom you
15:21 they compelled a certain **m**,
15:24 them to determine what every **m**
15:39 Truly this **M** was the Son of
16: 5 they saw a young **m** clothed in a
Lk 1:18 I know this? For I am an old **m**,
1:27 to a virgin betrothed to a **m**
1:34 be, since I do not know a **m**?
2:25 there was a **m** in Jerusalem
2:25 and this **m** was just and devout,
4: 4 **M** shall not live by bread
4:33 in the synagogue there was a **m**
5: 8 from me, for I am a sinful **m**,
5:12 a **m** who was full of leprosy saw
5:18 men brought on a bed a **m** who
5:20 faith, He said to him, "**M**,
5:24 you may know that the Son of **M**
5:24 He said to the **m** who was
6: 5 The Son of **M** is also Lord of the
6: 6 And a **m** was there whose right
6: 8 and said to the **m** who had the
6:10 at them all, He said to the **m**,
6:45 A good **m** out of the good
6:45 and an evil **m** out of the evil
6:48 He is like a **m** building a house,
6:49 and did nothing is like a **m**
7: 8 For I also am a **m** placed under
7:12 a dead **m** was being carried out,
7:14 And He said, "Young **m**,
7:25 A **m** clothed in soft garments?
7:34 The Son of **M** has come eating and
7:39 to himself, saying, "This **m**,
8:27 there met Him a certain **m** from
8:29 spirit to come out of the **m**.
8:33 the demons went out of the **m**
8:35 and found the **m** from whom the
8:38 Now the **m** from whom the demons
8:41 there came a **m** named Jairus,
9:22 The Son of **M** must suffer many
9:25 For what profit is it to a **m** if
9:26 of him the Son of **M** will be
9:38 Suddenly a **m** from the multitude
9:44 for the Son of **M** is about to be
9:56 For the Son of **M** did not come to
9:58 but the Son of **M** has nowhere to
10:30 A certain **m** went down from
11:21 'When a strong **m**, fully armed,
11:24 unclean spirit goes out of a **m**,
11:26 and the last state of that **m**
11:30 so also the Son of **M** will be to
12: 8 him the Son of **M** also will
12:10 a word against the Son of **M**,
12:14 But He said to him, "**M**,
12:16 ground of a certain rich **m**
12:40 for the Son of **M** is coming at
13: 6 A certain **m** had a fig tree
13:19 which a **m** took and put in his
14: 2 there was a certain **m** before
14: 9 to you, 'Give place to this **m**,
14:16 A certain **m** gave a great supper
14:30 This **m** began to build and was
15: 2 This **M** receives sinners and eats
15: 4 What **m** of you, having a hundred
15:11 A certain **m** had two sons.
16: 1 There was a certain rich **m** who
16: 1 was brought to him that this **m**
16:19 There was a certain rich **m** who
16:22 The rich **m** also died and was
17:22 one of the days of the Son of **M**,
17:24 so also the Son of **M** will be in
17:26 in the days of the Son of **M**:
17:30 be in the day when the Son of **M**
18: 2 did not fear God nor regard **m**.
18: 4 I do not fear God nor regard **m**,
18: 8 when the Son of **M** comes, will
18:14 this **m** went down to his house
18:25 of a needle than for a rich **m**
18:31 concerning the Son of **M** will
18:35 that a certain blind **m** sat by
19: 2 there was a **m** named Zacchaeus
19: 7 has gone to be a guest with a **m**
19:10 for the Son of **M** has come to
19:14 We will not have this **m** to
19:15 he might know how much every **m**
19:21 because you are an austere **m**.
19:22 knew that I was an austere **m**,
20: 9 A certain **m** planted a vineyard,
21:27 they will see the Son of **M**
21:36 to stand before the Son of **M**.
22:10 a **m** will meet you carrying a
22:22 And truly the Son of **M** goes as
22:22 but woe to that **m** by whom He is
22:48 are you betraying the Son of **M**
22:56 This **m** was also with Him."
22:58 of them." But Peter said, "**M**,
22:60 But Peter said, "**M**, I do not
22:69 Hereafter the Son of **M** will sit
23: 4 "I find no fault in this **M**.
23: 6 he asked if the **M** were a
23:14 You have brought this **M** to me,
23:14 I have found no fault in this **M**
23:18 saying, "Away with this **M**,
23:26 they laid hold of a certain **m**,
23:41 but this **M** has done nothing
23:47 this was a righteous **M**!"
23:50 there was a **m** named Joseph,
23:50 member, a good and just **m**.
23:52 This **m** went to Pilate and asked
24: 7 The Son of **M** must be delivered
Jn 1: 6 There was a **m** sent from God,
1: 7 This **m** came for a witness, to
1: 9 which gives light to every **m**
1:13 the flesh, nor of the will of **m**,
1:30 After me comes a **M** who is
1:51 descending upon the Son of **M**.
2:10 Every **m** at the beginning sets
2:25 that anyone should testify of **m**,
2:25 man, for He knew what was in **m**.
3: 1 There was a **m** of the Pharisees
3: 2 This **m** came to Jesus by night
3: 4 How can a **m** be born when he is
3:13 the Son of **M** who is in heaven.
3:14 even so must the Son of **M** be
3:27 A **m** can receive nothing unless
4:29 see a **M** who told me all things
4:50 So the **m** believed the word
5: 5 Now a certain **m** was there who
5: 7 The sick **m** answered Him, "Sir,
5: 7 I have no **m** to put me into the
5: 9 And immediately the **m** was made
5:12 Who is the **M** who said to you,
5:15 The **m** departed and told the Jews
5:27 because He is the Son of **M**.
5:34 do not receive testimony from **m**,
6:27 which the Son of **M** will give
6:52 How can this **M** give us His
6:53 eat the flesh of the Son of **M**
6:62 if you should see the Son of **M**
7:15 How does this **M** know letters,
7:22 and you circumcise a **m** on the
7:23 If a **m** receives circumcision on
7:23 with Me because I made a **m**
7:27 we know where this **M** is from;
7:31 signs than these which this **M**
7:46 No **m** ever spoke like this Man!"
7:46 No man ever spoke like this **M**!"
7:51 Does our law judge a **m** before it
8:28 "When you lift up the Son of **M**,
8:40 a **M** who has told you the truth
9: 1 He saw a **m** who was blind from
9: 2 this **m** or his parents, that he
9: 3 Neither this **m** nor his parents
9: 6 the eyes of the blind **m** with
9:11 A **M** called Jesus made clay and
9:16 This **M** is not from God, because
9:16 How can a **m** who is a sinner do
9:17 They said to the blind **m** again,
9:24 So they again called the **m** who
9:24 the glory! We know that this **M**
9:30 The **m** answered and said to them,
9:33 If this **M** were not from God, He
10:33 and because You, being a **M**,
10:41 that John spoke about this **M**
11: 1 Now a certain **m** was sick,
11:37 them said, "Could not this **M**,
11:37 also have kept this **m** from
11:41 the place where the dead **m**
11:47 For this **M** works many signs.
11:50 is expedient for us that one **m**
12:23 hour has come that the Son of **M**
12:34 The Son of **M** must be lifted up'?
12:34 Who is this Son of **M**?"
13:31 Now the Son of **M** is glorified,
18:14 it was expedient that one **m**
18:29 do you bring against this **M**?
18:40 again, saying, "Not this **M**,
19: 5 to them, "Behold the **M**!"
19:12 If you let this **M** go, you are
21:21 "But Lord, what about this **m**?
Acts 1:18 (Now this **m** purchased a field
2:22 a **M** attested by God to you by
3: 2 And a certain **m** lame from his
3:11 Now as the lame **m** who was
3:12 or godliness we had made this **m**
3:16 has made this **m** strong, whom
4: 9 good deed done to a helpless **m**,
4:10 by Him this **m** stands here
4:14 And seeing the **m** who had been
4:17 from now on they speak to no **m**
4:22 For the **m** was over forty years
5: 1 But a certain **m** named Ananias,
5:37 'After this **m**, Judas of
6: 5 a **m** full of faith and the Holy
6:13 This **m** does not cease to speak
7:19 This **m** dealt treacherously with
7:56 heavens opened and the Son of **M**
7:58 at the feet of a young **m** named
8: 9 But there was a certain **m**
8:10 This **m** is the great power of
8:27 a **m** of Ethiopia, a eunuch of
8:34 of himself or of some other **m**?
9:12 in a vision he has seen a **m**
9:13 heard from many about this **m**,
9:33 There he found a certain **m** named
10: 1 There was a certain **m** in
10: 2 a devout **m** and one who feared
10:22 the centurion, a just **m**,
10:26 I myself am also a **m**."
10:28 unlawful it is for a Jewish **m**
10:28 me that I should not call any **m**
10:30 a **m** stood before me in bright
11:24 For he was a good **m**,
12:22 voice of a god and not of a **m**!
13: 7 Paulus, an intelligent **m**.
13: 7 This **m** called for Barnabas and
13:21 a **m** of the tribe of Benjamin,

13:22 a **m** after My own heart,
13:38 that through this **M** is preached
14: 8 And in Lystra a certain **m**
14: 9 This **m** heard Paul speaking.
16: 9 A **m** of Macedonia stood and
17:31 in righteousness by the **M** whom
18: 7 the house of a certain **m**
18:24 an eloquent **m** and mighty in
18:25 This **m** had been instructed in
19:16 Then the **m** in whom the evil
19:24 For a certain **m** named Demetrius,
19:35 what **m** is there who does not
20: 9 a window sat a certain young **m**
20:12 And they brought the young **m** in
21: 9 Now this **m** had four virgin
21:11 Jews at Jerusalem bind the **m**
21:28 This is the **m** who teaches
22:12 a devout **m** according to the
22:25 lawful for you to scourge a **m**
22:26 for this **m** is a Roman."
23: 9 "We find no evil in this **m**;
23:17 Take this young **m** to the
23:18 me to bring this young **m** to
23:22 the commander let the young **m**
23:27 This **m** was seized by the Jews
23:30 the Jews lay in wait for the **m**,
24: 5 For we have found this **m** a
25: 5 down with me and accuse this **m**,
25:14 There is a certain **m** left a
25:16 of the Romans to deliver any **m**
25:17 seat and commanded the **m** to be
25:22 also would like to hear the **m**
25:24 you see this **m** about whom the
26:31 This **m** is doing nothing
26:32 This **m** might have been set free
28: 4 No doubt this **m** is a murderer,
Rom 1:23 image made like corruptible **m**—
2: 1 you are inexcusable, O **m**,
2: 3 And do you think this, O **m**,
2: 9 on every soul of **m** who does
2:21 You who preach that a **m** should
2:26 if an uncircumcised **m** keeps the
3: 4 let God be true but every **m** a
3: 5 inflicts wrath? (I speak as a **m**.
3:28 Therefore we conclude that a **m**
4: 6 the blessedness of the **m** to
4: 8 Blessed is the **m** to whom
5: 7 For scarcely for a righteous **m**
5: 7 yet perhaps for a good **m**
5:12 just as through one **m** sin
5:15 gift by the grace of the one **M**,
6: 6 that our old **m** was crucified
7: 1 the law has dominion over a **m**
7: 3 lives, she marries another **m**,
7: 3 she has married another **m**.
7:22 God according to the inward **m**.
7:24 O wretched **m** that I am! Who will
9:10 also had conceived by one **m**,
9:20 But indeed, O **m**, who are
10: 5 The **m** who does those things
14:20 but it is evil for the **m** who
1 Cor 2: 9 into the heart of **m** The
2:11 For what **m** knows the things of a
2:11 man knows the things of a **m**
2:11 man except the spirit of the **m**
2:14 But the natural **m** does not
4: 1 Let a **m** so consider us, as
5: 1 that a **m** has his father's wife!
6: 5 that there is not a wise **m**
6:18 Every sin that a **m** does is
7: 1 It is good for a **m** not to
7: 2 let each **m** have his own wife,
7:26 that it is good for a **m** to
7:36 But if any **m** thinks he is
9: 8 I say these things as a mere **m**?
10:13 except such as is common to **m**;
11: 3 know that the head of every **m**
11: 3 Christ, the head of woman is **m**,
11: 4 Every **m** praying or prophesying,
11: 7 For a **m** indeed ought not to
11: 7 but woman is the glory of **m**.
11: 8 For **m** is not from woman, but
11: 8 from woman, but woman from **m**.
11: 9 Nor was **m** created for the woman,
11: 9 the woman, but woman for the **m**.
11:11 neither is **m** independent of
11:11 nor woman independent of **m**,
11:12 For as woman came from **m**,
11:12 even so **m** also comes through
11:14 itself teach you that if a **m**
11:28 But let a **m** examine himself, and
13:11 a child; but when I became a **m**,
15:21 For since by **m** came death, by
15:21 by **M** also came the
15:45 The first **m** Adam became a
15:47 The first **m** was of the earth,
15:47 the second **M** is the Lord from
15:48 As was the **m** of dust, so also
15:48 and as is the heavenly **M**,
15:49 have borne the image of the **m**
15:49 the image of the heavenly **M**.
2 Cor 2: 6 is sufficient for such a **m**,
4:16 Even though our outward **m** is
4:16 yet the inward **m** is being
12: 2 I know a **m** in Christ who
12: 3 And I know such a **m**—
12: 4 which it is not lawful for a **m**
Gal 1: 1 (not from men nor through **m**,
1:11 by me is not according to **m**.
1:12 I neither received it from **m**,
2: 6 personal favoritism to no **m**—
2:16 knowing that a **m** is not
3:12 the **m** who does them shall
5: 3 And I testify again to every **m**
6: 1 if a **m** is overtaken in any
6: 7 for whatever a **m** sows, that he
Eph 2:15 to create in Himself one new **m**
3:16 His Spirit in the inner **m**,
4:13 the Son of God, to a perfect **m**,
4:22 the old **m** which grows corrupt
4:24 and that you put on the new **m**
5: 5 unclean person, nor covetous **m**,
5:31 For this reason a **m** shall
Phil 2: 8 found in appearance as a **m**,
Col 1:28 warning every **m** and teaching
1:28 every man and teaching every **m**
1:28 that we may present every **m**
3: 9 you have put off the old **m**
3:10 and have put on the new **m** who
1 Th 4: 8 rejects this does not reject **m**,
2 Th 2: 3 and the **m** of sin is revealed,
1 Tim 1:13 a persecutor, and an insolent **m**;
2: 5 and men, the **M** Christ Jesus,
2:12 or to have authority over a **m**,
3: 1 If a **m** desires the position of
3: 5 (for if a **m** does not know how to
5: 1 Do not rebuke an older **m**,
5: 9 she has been the wife of one **m**,
5:16 If any believing **m** or woman has
6:11 O **m** of God, flee these things
6:16 whom no **m** has seen or can see,
2 Tim 3:17 that the **m** of God may be
Titus 1: 6 if a **m** is blameless, the husband
3: 4 love of God our Savior toward **m**
3:10 Reject a divisive **m** after the
Heb 2: 6 What is **m** that You are
2: 6 Or the son of **m** that
5: 4 And no **m** takes this honor to
7: 4 Now consider how great this **m**
7:13 from which no **m** has officiated
8: 2 the Lord erected, and not **m**.
10:12 But this **M**, after He had
11:12 Therefore from one **m**,
13: 6 What can **m** do to me?"
Jas 1: 7 For let not that **m** suppose that
1: 8 he is a double-minded **m**,
1:11 So the rich **m** also will fade
1:12 Blessed is the **m** who endures
1:19 let every **m** be swift to hear,
1:20 for the wrath of **m** does not
1:23 he is like a **m** observing his
1:24 forgets what kind of **m** he was.
2: 2 come into your assembly a **m**
2: 2 should also come in a poor **m**
2: 3 place," and say to the poor **m**,
2: 6 you have dishonored the poor **m**.
2:20 you want to know, O foolish **m**,
2:24 You see then that a **m** is
3: 2 in word, he is a perfect **m**,
3: 8 But no **m** can tame the tongue.
5:16 prayer of a righteous **m** avails
5:17 Elijah was a **m** with a nature
1 Pe 1:24 And all the glory of **m**
2:13 to every ordinance of **m** for
2 Pe 1:21 never came by the will of **m**,
2: 8 (for that righteous **m**,
Rev 1:13 One like the Son of **M**,
4: 7 creature had a face like a **m**,
6:15 every slave and every free **m**,
9: 5 a scorpion when it strikes a **m**.
13:18 for it is the number of a **m**:
14:14 sat One like the Son of **M**,
16: 3 it became blood as of a dead **m**;
21:17 to the measure of a **m**,

MAN-MADE (1/1)

Neh 3:16 to the **m** pool, and as far as

MAN'S (113/107) MAN

Gen 8:21 curse the ground for **m** sake,
8:21 although the imagination of **m**
9: 5 the hand of every **m** brother
9: 6 Whoever sheds **m** blood, By man
16:12 And every **m** hand against him.
20: 3 for she is a **m** wife."
20: 7 restore the **m** wife; for he is
40: 5 each **m** dream in one night and
40: 5 dream in one night and each **m**
42:11 We are all one **m** sons; we are
42:25 to restore every **m** money to his
42:35 that surprisingly each **m** bundle
43:21 each **m** money was in the mouth
44: 1 and put each **m** money in the
44:26 for we may not see the **m** face
Ex 4:11 Who has made **m** mouth? Or who
12: 4 according to each **m** need you
12:44 But every **m** servant who is
21:35 If one **m** ox hurts another's, so
22: 5 and it feeds in another **m** field
22: 7 it is stolen out of the **m** house
30:32 shall not be poured on **m** flesh
Lev 20:10 adultery with another **m** wife,
Num 5:10 And every **m** holy things shall be
5:12 If any **m** wife goes astray and
17: 2 Write each **m** name on his rod.
Deut 1:17 not be afraid in any **m** presence
20:19 for the tree of the field is **m** food.
24: 2 and becomes another **m** wife,
Judg 7:16 he put a trumpet into every **m**
7:22 the LORD set every **m** sword
19:24 daughter and the **m** concubine;
19:26 down at the door of the **m** house
Ruth 2:19 The **m** name with whom I worked
1 Sam 12: 4 taken anything from any **m** hand.
13:20 Philistines to sharpen each **m**
14:20 and indeed every **m** sword was
14:34 Bring me here every **m** ox and
14:34 every man's ox and every **m** sheep,
17:32 Let no **m** heart fail because of
30:22 except for every **m** wife and
2 Sam 12: 4 but he took the poor **m** lamb and
17:18 away quickly and came to a **m**
1 Ki 18:44 as small as a **m** hand, rising
2 Ki 12: 4 each **m** census money, each man's
12: 4 each **m** assessment money—and
Esth 1: 8 do according to each **m** pleasure.
Ps 104:15 And bread which strengthens **m**
Prov 10:15 The rich **m** wealth is his
12:14 recompense of a **m** hands will
12:27 But diligence is **m** precious
13: 8 The ransom of a **m** life is his
16: 7 When a **m** ways please the LORD,
16: 9 A **m** heart plans his way,
18: 4 The words of a **m** mouth are
18:11 The rich **m** wealth is his
18:16 A **m** gift makes room for him,
18:20 A **m** stomach shall be satisfied
19:21 There are many plans in a **m**
20:24 A **m** steps are of the LORD;
27: 9 the sweetness of a **m** friend
27:19 So a **m** heart reveals the man.
29:23 A **m** pride will bring him low,
Eccl 2:14 The wise **m** eyes are in his
7: 7 oppression destroys a wise **m**
8: 1 A **m** wisdom makes his face
8: 5 And a wise **m** heart discerns
9:16 Nevertheless the poor **m** wisdom
10: 2 A wise **m** heart is at his right
10:12 The words of a wise **m** mouth
12:13 For this is **m** all.
Isa 8: 1 and write on it with a **m** pen
13: 7 Every **m** heart will melt,
Jer 3: 1 from him And becomes another **m**,
23:36 For every **m** word will be his
Ezek 10: 8 to have the form of a **m** hand
24:17 and do not eat **m** bread of
24:22 not cover your lips nor eat **m**
38:21 Every **m** sword will be against
39:15 and when anyone sees a **m** bone,
40: 5 In the **m** hand was a measuring
Dan 5: 5 hour the fingers of a **m** hand
7: 4 and a **m** heart was given to it.
8:16 And I heard a **m** voice between
Jon 1:14 do not let us perish for this **m**
Mic 7: 6 A **m** enemies are the men of
Mt 10:36 a **m** enemies will be those
10:41 man shall receive a righteous **m**
12:29 can one enter a strong **m** house
Mk 3:27 No one can enter a strong **m**
12:19 to us that if a **m** brother dies
Lk 6:22 For the Son of **M** sake.
16:12 faithful in what is another **m**,
16:21 fell from the rich **m** table.
20:28 wrote to us that if a **m** brother
Jn 18:17 not also one of this **M** disciples
Acts 5:28 intend to bring this **M** blood
11:12 and we entered the **m** house.
13:23 From this **m** seed, according to
17:29 something shaped by art and **m**
Rom 5:15 For if by the one **m** offense
5:17 For if by the one **m** offense
5:18 as through one **m** offense
5:18 even so through one **M** righteous
5:19 For as by one **m** disobedience
5:19 so also by one **M** obedience many
15:20 build on another **m** foundation,
1 Cor 2:13 not in words which **m** wisdom
10:29 judged by another **m** conscience?
2 Cor 4: 2 commending ourselves to every **m**
10:16 and not to boast in another **m**
Gal 3:15 Though it is only a **m** covenant,
2 Pe 2:16 a dumb donkey speaking with a **m**

MANAEN (1/1)

Acts 13: 1 **M** who had been brought up with

MANAGE (1/1)

1 Tim 5:14 **m** the house, give no

MANAHATH (3/3)

Gen 36:23 the sons of Shobal: Alvan, **M**,
1 Chr 1:40 sons of Shobal were Alian, **M**,
8: 6 who forced them to move to **M**:

MANAHETHITES (1/1)

1 Chr 2:54 Atroth Beth Joab, half of the **M**,

MANASSEH (147/135) MANASSEH'S

Gen 41:51 the name of the firstborn **M**:
46:20 the land of Egypt were born **M**
48: 1 two sons, **M** and Ephraim.
48: 5 your two sons, Ephraim and **M**,
48:13 and **M** with his left hand toward
48:14 for **M** was the firstborn.
48:20 make you as Ephraim and as **M**!'
48:20 thus he set Ephraim before **M**.
50:23 of Machir, the son of **M**,
Num 1:10 the son of Ammihud; from **M**,
1:34 From the children of **M**,
1:35 were numbered of the tribe of **M**

M

2:20 to him comes the tribe of **M**,
2:20 the leader of the children of **M**
7:54 leader of the children of **M**,
10:23 the tribe of the children of **M**
13:11 that is, from the tribe of **M**,
26:28 by **M** and Ephraim, were:
26:29 The sons of **M**: of Machir, the
26:34 These are the families of **M**;
27: 1 the son of Machir, the son of **M**,
27: 1 from the families of **M** the son
32:33 and to half the tribe of **M** the
32:39 of Machir the son of **M** went to
32:40 Gilead to Machir the son of **M**,
32:41 Also Jair the son of **M** went and
34:14 and the half-tribe of **M** has
34:23 the tribe of the children of **M**,
36: 1 the son of Machir, the son of **M**,
36:12 families of the children of **M**
Deut 3:13 I gave to half the tribe of **M**.
3:14 Jair the son of **M** took all the
29: 8 and to half the tribe of **M**.
33:17 they are the thousands of **M**.
34: 2 and the land of Ephraim and **M**,
Josh 1:12 and half the tribe of **M** Joshua
4:12 and half the tribe of **M** crossed
12: 6 and half the tribe of **M**.
13: 7 tribes and half the tribe of **M**.
13:29 to half the tribe of **M**;
13:29 the tribe of the children of **M**
13:31 children of Machir the son of **M**,
14: 4 **M** and Ephraim. And they gave no
16: 4 **M** and Ephraim, took their
16: 9 of the children of **M**,
17: 1 also a lot for the tribe of **M**,
17: 1 for Machir the firstborn of **M**,
17: 2 the rest of the children of **M**
17: 2 were the male children of **M**
17: 3 the son of Machir, the son of **M**,
17: 5 Ten shares fell to **M**,
17: 6 because the daughters of **M**
17: 7 And the territory of **M** was from
17: 8 **M** had the land of Tappuah, but
17: 8 but Tappuah on the border of **M**
17: 9 are among the cities of **M**.
17: 9 The border of **M** was on the
17:11 **M** had Beth Shean and its towns,
17:12 Yet the children of **M** could not
17:17 of Joseph—to Ephraim and **M**—
18: 7 and half the tribe of **M** have
20: 8 in Bashan, from the tribe of **M**.
21: 5 and from the half-tribe of **M**.
21: 6 and from the half-tribe of **M** in
21:25 and from the half-tribe of **M**,
21:27 from the other half-tribe of **M**,
22: 1 and half the tribe of **M**,
22: 7 Now to half the tribe of **M**
22: 9 and half the tribe of **M**
22:10 and half the tribe of **M** built
22:11 and half the tribe of **M** have
22:13 Gad, and to half the tribe of **M**,
22:15 Gad, and to half the tribe of **M**,
22:21 and half the tribe of **M**
22:30 and the children of **M** spoke, it
22:31 of Gad, and the children of **M**,
Judg 1:27 **M** did not drive out the
6:15 my clan is the weakest in **M**,
6:35 messengers throughout all **M**,
7:23 from Naphtali, Asher, and all **M**,
11:29 he passed through Gilead and **M**,
18:30 son of Gershom, the son of **M**,
1 Ki 4:13 the towns of Jair the son of **M**,
2 Ki 10:33 of Gilead—Gad, Reuben, and **M**—
20:21 Then **M** his son reigned in his
21: 1 **M** was twelve years old when he
21: 9 and **M** seduced them to do more
21:11 Because **M** king of Judah has done
21:16 Moreover **M** shed very much
21:17 Now the rest of the acts of **M**—
21:18 So **M** rested with his fathers,
21:20 as his father **M** had done.
23:12 and the altars which **M** had made
23:26 the provocations with which **M**
24: 3 sight because of the sins of **M**,
1 Chr 3:13 Hezekiah his son, **M** his son,
5:18 and half the tribe of **M** had
5:23 of the half-tribe of **M** dwelt
5:26 and the half-tribe of **M** into
6:61 cities from half the tribe of **M**.
6:62 and from the tribe of **M** in
6:70 And from the half-tribe of **M**:
6:71 family of the half-tribe of **M**
7:14 The descendants of **M**:
7:17 the son of Machir, the son of **M**.
7:29 borders of the children of **M**
9: 3 the children of Ephraim and **M**:
12:19 And some from **M** defected to
12:20 those of **M** who defected to him
12:20 the thousands who were from **M**.
12:31 of the half-tribe of **M** eighteen
12:37 Gadites and the half-tribe of **M**,
26:32 and the half-tribe of **M**,
27:20 over the half-tribe of **M**,
27:21 over the half-tribe of **M** in
2 Chr 15: 9 dwelt with them from Ephraim, **M**,
30: 1 wrote letters to Ephraim and **M**,
30:10 the country of Ephraim and **M**,
30:11 Nevertheless some from Asher, **M**,
30:18 people, many from Ephraim, **M**,
31: 1 Judah, Benjamin, Ephraim, and **M**—
32:33 Then **M** his son reigned in his
33: 1 **M** was twelve years old when he
33: 9 So **M** seduced Judah and the
33:10 And the LORD spoke to **M** and
33:11 who took **M** with hooks, bound
33:13 Then **M** knew that the LORD was
33:18 Now the rest of the acts of **M**,
33:20 So **M** rested with his fathers,
33:22 as his father **M** had done;
33:22 images which his father **M** had
33:23 as his father **M** had humbled
34: 6 so he did in the cities of **M**,
34: 9 had gathered from the hand of **M**
Ezra 10:30 Bezalel, Binnui, and **M**;
10:33 Zabad, Eliphelet, Jeremai, **M**,
Ps 60: 7 and **M** is Mine; Ephraim also
80: 2 Ephraim, Benjamin, and **M**,
108: 8 **M** is Mine; Ephraim also is
Isa 9:21 **M** shall devour Ephraim, and
9:21 devour Ephraim, and Ephraim **M**;
Jer 15: 4 because of **M** the son of
Ezek 48: 4 the west, one section for **M**;
48: 5 'by the border of **M**, from the
Mt 1:10 Hezekiah begot **M**,
1:10 **M** begot Amon, and Amon begot
Rev 7: 6 of the tribe of **M** twelve

MANASSEH'S (5/4) MANASSEH

Gen 48:14 and his left hand on **M** head,
48:17 it from Ephraim's head to **M**
Josh 17: 6 and the rest of **M** sons had the
17:10 Ephraim's, northward it was **M**,
17:10 **M** territory was adjoining Asher

MANASSES (KJV) See MANASSEH

MANASSITES (2/2)

Deut 4:43 and Golan in Bashan for the **M**.
Judg 12: 4 Ephraimites and among the **M**.

MANDRAKES (6/4)

Gen 30:14 of wheat harvest and found **m**
30:14 give me some of your son's **m**.
30:15 Would you take away my son's **m**
30:15 you tonight for your son's **m**.
30:16 hired you with my son's **m**.
Song 7:13 The **m** give off a fragrance,

MANEH (KJV) See MINA

MANGER (4/4)

Job 39: 9 Will he bed by your **m**?
Lk 2: 7 cloths, and laid Him in a **m**,
2:12 swaddling cloths, lying in a **m**.
2:16 and the Babe lying in a **m**.

MANIFEST (15/14) MANIFESTATION, MANIFESTED

Jn 14:21 and I will love him and **m**
14:22 how is it that You will **m**
Rom 1:19 what may be known of God is **m**
10:20 I was made **m** to those
16:26 but now has been made **m**,
Eph 5:13 that are exposed are made **m** by
5:13 for whatever makes **m** is light.
Col 4: 4 that I may make it **m**,
2 Th 1: 5 which is **m** evidence of the
1 Tim 6:15 which He will **m** in His own time,
2 Tim 3: 9 for their folly will be **m** to
Heb 9: 8 of All was not yet made **m**
1 Pe 1:20 but was **m** in these last times
1 Jn 2:19 out that they might be made **m**,
3:10 the children of the devil are **m**:

MANIFESTATION (3/3) MANIFEST

Lk 1:80 deserts till the day of his **m**
1 Cor 12: 7 But the **m** of the Spirit is given
2 Cor 4: 2 but by **m** of the truth

MANIFESTED (13/12) MANIFEST

Jn 2:11 and **m** His glory; and His
17: 6 I have **m** Your name to the men
2 Cor 4:10 life of Jesus also may be **m** in
4:11 life of Jesus also may be **m** in
11: 6 But we have been thoroughly **m**
1 Tim 3:16 God was **m** in the flesh,
Titus 1: 3 but has in due time **m** His word
1 Jn 1: 2 the life was **m**, and we have
1: 2 was with the Father and was **m**
3: 5 And you know that He was **m** to
3: 8 purpose the Son of God was **m**,
4: 9 In this the love of God was **m**
Rev 15: 4 For Your judgments have been **m**.

MANIFOLD (5/5)

Neh 9:19 Yet in Your **m** mercies You did
Ps 104:24 how **m** are Your works!
Am 5:12 For I know your **m**
Eph 3:10 to the intent that now the **m**
1 Pe 4:10 as good stewards of the **m** grace

MANKIND (8/8) MAN

Gen 5: 2 blessed them and called them **M**
Job 12:10 And the breath of all **m**?
Isa 31: 8 And a sword not of **m** shall
Acts 15:17 So that the rest of **m**
Jas 3: 7 tamed and has been tamed by **m**.
Rev 9:15 released to kill a third of **m**.
9:18 three plagues a third of **m**
9:20 But the rest of **m**, who were

MANNA (18/16)

Ex 16:31 of Israel called its name **M**.
16:33 a pot and put an omer of **m** in
16:35 the children of Israel ate **m**
16:35 they ate **m** until they came to
Num 11: 6 nothing at all except this **m**
11: 7 Now the **m** was like coriander
11: 9 the night, the **m** fell on it.
Deut 8: 3 and fed you with **m** which you
8:16 you in the wilderness with **m**,
Josh 5:12 Then the **m** ceased on the day
5:12 of Israel no longer had **m**,
Neh 9:20 And did not withhold Your **m**
Ps 78:24 Had rained down **m** on them to
Jn 6:31 Our fathers ate the **m** in the
6:49 Your fathers ate the **m** in the
6:58 as your fathers ate the **m**,
Heb 9: 4 the golden pot that had the **m**,
Rev 2:17 will give some of the hidden **m**

MANNER (94/91)

Gen 31:35 for the **m** of women is with
32:19 In this **m** you shall speak to
39:19 servant did to me after this **m**,
40:13 hand according to the former **m**,
42:15 In this **m** you shall be tested:
Ex 1:14 and in all **m** of service in the
7:11 they also did in like **m** with
12:16 No **m** of work shall be done on
23:11 In like **m** you shall do with
31: 3 and in all **m** of workmanship,
31: 5 and to work in all **m** of
35:31 in knowledge and all **m** of
35:33 and to work in all **m** of
35:35 them with skill to do all **m** of
36: 1 to know how to do all **m** of work
Lev 5:10 according to the prescribed **m**.
9:16 according to the prescribed **m**.
23:31 'You shall do no **m** of work;
Num 15:13 shall do these things in this **m**,
28:24 In this **m** you shall offer the
Josh 6:15 city seven times in the same **m**.
Judg 11:17 And in like **m** they sent to the
18: 7 in the **m** of the Sidonians,
1 Sam 17:27 people answered him in this **m**,
18:24 In this **m** David spoke."
19:24 before Samuel in like **m**,
2 Sam 7:19 Is this the **m** of man, O Lord
14: 3 king and speak to him in this **m**.
15: 6 In this **m** Absalom acted toward
17: 6 has spoken in this **m**.
1 Ki 22:20 So one spoke in this **m**,
22:20 and another spoke in that **m**.
2 Ki 22:18 in this **m** you shall speak to
1 Chr 28:21 will be with you for all **m**
2 Chr 4:20 to burn in the prescribed **m** in
18:19 Gilead?' So one spoke in this **m**,
18:19 and another spoke in that **m**.
30: 5 long time in the prescribed **m**.
34:26 in this **m** you shall speak to
Neh 6: 4 I answered them in the same **m**.
8:18 according to the prescribed **m**.
Esth 1:13 (for this was the king's **m**
Ps 107:18 Their soul abhorred all **m** of
Song 7:13 are pleasant fruits, All **m**,
Isa 10:24 you, in the **m** of Egypt.
10:26 so will He lift it up in the **m**
51: 6 dwell in it will die in like **m**;
Jer 13: 9 In this **m** I will ruin the pride
22:21 This has been your **m** from
Ezek 20:30 defiling yourselves in the **m**
23:15 In the **m** of the Babylonians of
23:45 will judge them after the **m** of
23:45 and after the **m** of women who
Am 4:10 among you a plague after the **m**
Nah 1:12 Yet in this **m** they will be cut
Mt 6: 9 'In this **m**, therefore, pray:
Mk 13: 1 see what **m** of stones and what
Lk 1:29 and considered what **m** of
6:23 For in like **m** their fathers
7:39 would know who and what **m** of
9:55 You do not know what **m** of spirit
11:42 tithe mint and rue and all **m**
20:31 and in like **m** the seven also;
Jn 2: 6 according to the **m** of
5:19 the Son also does in like **m**.
Acts 1:11 will so come in like **m** as you
15:11 we shall be saved in the same **m**
20:18 in what **m** I always lived among
23:25 a letter in the following **m**:
26: 4 My **m** of life from my youth,
Rom 7: 8 produced in me all **m** of evil
16: 2 receive her in the Lord in a **m**
1 Cor 7: 7 one in this **m** and another in
11:25 In the same **m** He also took the
11:27 of the Lord in an unworthy **m**
11:29 and drinks in an unworthy **m**
15:32 in the **m** of men, I have fought
2 Cor 7: 9 were made sorry in a godly **m**,
7:11 that you sorrowed in a godly **m**:
Gal 2:14 live in the **m** of Gentiles and
3:15 I speak in the **m** of men:
1 Th 1: 9 declare concerning us what **m**
2 Th 3:11 among you in a disorderly **m**,
1 Tim 2: 9 in like **m** also, that the women
2 Tim 3:10 **m** of life, purpose, faith,

Heb 6: 9 though we speak in this ***m***.
10:25 as is the ***m*** of some, but
1 Pe 1:11 or what ***m*** of time, the Spirit
3: 5 For in this ***m***, in former
2 Pe 3:11 what ***m*** of persons ought you
1 Jn 3: 1 Behold what ***m*** of love the Father
3 Jn 6 on their journey in a ***m*** worthy
Jude 7 around them in a similar ***m*** to
Rev 11: 5 he must be killed in this ***m***.

MANOAH (18/14)

Judg 13: 2 the Danites, whose name was ***M***;
13: 8 Then ***M*** prayed to the LORD, and
13: 9 God listened to the voice of ***M***,
13: 9 but ***M*** her husband was not with
13:11 So ***M*** arose and followed his
13:12 ***M*** said, "Now let Your words
13:13 Angel of the LORD said to ***M***,
13:15 Then ***M*** said to the Angel of the
13:16 Angel of the LORD said to ***M***,
13:16 (For ***M*** did not know He was
13:17 Then ***M*** said to the Angel of the
13:19 So ***M*** took the young goat with
13:19 He did a wondrous thing while ***M***
13:20 the flame of the altar! When ***M***
13:21 the LORD appeared no more to ***M***
13:21 then ***M*** knew that He was the
13:22 And ***M*** said to his wife, "We
16:31 in the tomb of his father ***M***.

MANSERVANT (KJV) See MALE, MENSERVANTS, SERVANT

MANSIONS (1/1)

Jn 14: 2 My Father's house are many ***m***;

MANSLAYER (12/12)

Num 35: 6 to which a ***m*** may flee. And to
35:11 that the ***m*** who kills any person
35:12 that the ***m*** may not die until he
35:24 shall judge between the ***m*** and
35:25 shall deliver the ***m*** from the
35:26 But if the ***m*** at any time goes
35:27 avenger of blood kills the ***m***,
35:28 death of the high priest the ***m***
Deut 4:42 that the ***m*** might flee there, who
19: 3 that any ***m*** may flee there.
19: 4 this is the case of the ***m*** who
19: 6 pursue the ***m*** and overtake him,

MANSLAYERS (1/1)

1 Tim 1: 9 and murderers of mothers, for ***m***,

MANTLE (7/7)

1 Sam 28:14 up, and he is covered with a ***m***.
1 Ki 19:13 he wrapped his face in his ***m***
19:19 passed by him and threw his ***m***
2 Ki 2: 8 Now Elijah took his ***m***,
2:13 He also took up the ***m*** of Elijah
2:14 Then he took the ***m*** of Elijah
Ps 109:29 their own disgrace as with a ***m***.

MANTLES (1/1)

Isa 3:22 the festal apparel, and the ***m***;

MANUHOTH (1/1)

1 Chr 2:52 half of the families of ***M***.

MANY (582/550)

Gen 17: 4 and you shall be a father of ***m***
17: 5 I have made you a father of ***m***
21:34 the land of the Philistines ***m***
37: 3 Also he made him a tunic of ***m***
37:23 the tunic of ***m*** colors that
37:32 Then they sent the tunic of ***m***
37:34 and mourned for his son ***m*** days.
50:20 to save ***m*** people alive.
Ex 5: 5 the people of the land are ***m***
19:21 and ***m*** of them perish.
23: 2 so as to turn aside after ***m*** to
35:22 as ***m*** as had a willing heart,
Lev 11:42 or whatever has ***m*** feet among
15:25 has a discharge of blood for ***m***
25:51 If there are still ***m*** years
Num 9:19 ***m*** days above the tabernacle,
10:36 To the ***m*** thousands of
13:18 are strong or weak, few or ***m***;
20:20 came out against them with ***m***
21: 6 and ***m*** of the people of Israel
22: 3 the people because they were ***m***,
24: 7 And his seed shall be in ***m***
35: 8 larger tribe you shall give ***m***,
Deut 1:46 So you remained in Kadesh ***m***
2: 1 and we skirted Mount Seir for ***m***
3: 5 besides a great ***m*** rural towns.
7: 1 and has cast out ***m*** nations
15: 6 you shall lend to ***m*** nations,
15: 6 you shall reign over ***m*** nations,
25: 3 this and beat him with ***m*** blows
28:12 You shall lend to ***m*** nations,
31:17 And ***m*** evils and troubles shall
31:21 when ***m*** evils and troubles have
32: 7 Consider the years of ***m***
Josh 11: 4 as ***m*** people as the sand that
11: 4 with very ***m*** horses and
22: 3 not left your brethren these ***m***
Judg 7: 2 who are with you are too ***m***
7: 4 "The people are still too ***m***;
8:30 for he had ***m*** wives.
9:40 and ***m*** fell wounded, to the
1 Sam 2: 5 And she who has ***m*** children has
14: 6 the LORD from saving by ***m*** or
25:10 There are ***m*** servants nowadays
2 Sam 1: 4 ***m*** of the people are fallen and
2:23 So it was that as ***m*** as came to
12: 2 rich man had exceedingly ***m***
13:18 Now she had on a robe of ***m***
13:19 and tore her robe of ***m*** colors
13:34 ***m*** people were coming from the
22:17 He drew me out of ***m*** waters.
23:20 who had done ***m*** deeds. He had
1 Ki 2:38 So Shimei dwelt in Jerusalem ***m***
7:47 because there were so ***m***;
11: 1 But King Solomon loved ***m*** foreign
17:15 he and her household ate for ***m***
18: 1 And it came to pass after ***m***
18:25 it first, for you are ***m***;
22:16 How ***m*** times shall I make you
2 Ki 9:22 and her witchcraft are so ***m***?
1 Chr 4:27 but his brothers did not have ***m***
5:22 for ***m*** fell dead, because the war
7: 4 for they had ***m*** wives and sons.
7:22 Ephraim their father mourned ***m***
8:40 They had ***m*** sons and grandsons,
11:22 who had done ***m*** deeds. He had
23:11 and Beriah did not have ***m*** sons;
23:17 sons of Rehabiah were very ***m***.
28: 5 (for the LORD has given me ***m***
2 Chr 11:23 He also sought ***m*** wives for
14:11 whether with ***m*** or with those
16: 8 not a huge army with very ***m***
18:15 How ***m*** times shall I make you
24:27 and the ***m*** oracles about him,
26:10 He dug ***m*** wells, for he had much
29:31 and as ***m*** as were of a willing
30:13 Now ***m*** people, a very great
30:17 For there were ***m*** in the
30:18 ***m*** from Ephraim, Manasseh,
32: 4 Thus ***m*** people gathered together
32:23 And ***m*** brought gifts to the LORD
Ezra 3:12 But ***m*** of the priests and
3:12 Yet ***m*** shouted aloud for joy,
5:11 the temple that was built ***m***
10:13 'But there are ***m*** people;
10:13 for there are ***m*** of us who
Neh 1: 4 and mourned for ***m*** days; I was
5: 2 sons, and our daughters are ***m***;
6:17 days the nobles of Judah sent ***m***
6:18 For ***m*** in Judah were pledged to
7: 2 man and feared God more than ***m***.
9:28 And ***m*** times You delivered them
9:30 Yet for ***m*** years You had
9:35 Or in the ***m*** good things that
13:26 Yet among ***m*** nations there was
Esth 1: 4 of his excellent majesty for ***m***
2: 8 and when ***m*** young women were
4: 3 and ***m*** lay in sackcloth and
8:17 Then ***m*** of the people of the
Job 4: 3 Surely you have instructed ***m***,
5:25 your descendants shall be ***m***,
11:19 ***m*** would court your favor.
13:23 How ***m*** are my iniquities and
16: 2 I have heard ***m*** such things;
23:14 And ***m*** such things are with
26: 3 you declared sound advice to ***m***?
33:19 And with strong pain in ***m*** of
41: 3 Will he make ***m*** supplications to
Ps 3: 1 increased who trouble me! ***M***
3: 2 ***M*** are they who say of me,
4: 6 There are ***m*** who say, "Who
18:16 He drew me out of ***m*** waters.
22:12 ***M*** bulls have surrounded Me
25:19 my enemies, for they are ***m***;
29: 3 The LORD is over ***m*** waters.
31:13 For I hear the slander of ***m***;
32:10 ***M*** sorrows shall be to the
34:12 And loves ***m*** days, that he may
34:19 ***M*** are the afflictions of the
35:18 I will praise You among ***m***
37:16 better than the riches of ***m***
40: 3 ***M*** will see it and fear,
40: 5 ***M***, O LORD my God, are Your
45:14 to the King in robes of ***m***
55:18 For there were ***m*** against me.
56: 2 For there are ***m*** who fight
61: 6 His years as ***m*** generations.
68:15 A mountain of ***m*** peaks is
68:16 you mountains of ***m*** peaks?
71: 7 I have become as a wonder to ***m***,
78:38 ***m*** a time He turned His anger
89:50 the reproach of all the ***m***
93: 4 mightier Than the noise of ***m***
106:43 ***M*** times He delivered them
110: 6 shall execute the heads of ***m***
119:84 How ***m*** are the days of Your
119:157 ***M*** are my persecutors and my
129: 1 ***M*** a time they have afflicted me
129: 2 ***M*** a time they have afflicted me
135:10 He defeated ***m*** nations And slew
Prov 4:10 years of your life will be ***m***.
6:35 be appeased though you give ***m***
7:26 For she has cast down ***m***
10:21 lips of the righteous feed ***m***,
14:20 But the rich has ***m*** friends.
19: 4 Wealth makes ***m*** friends,
19: 6 ***M*** entreat the favor of the
19:21 There are ***m*** plans in a man's
28: 2 ***m*** are its princes; But by a
28:27 who hides his eyes will have ***m***
29:26 ***M*** seek the ruler's favor,
31:29 '***M*** daughters have done well,
Eccl 5: 3 voice is known by his ***m***
5: 7 the multitude of dreams and ***m***
6: 3 a hundred children and lives ***m***
6: 3 the days of his years are ***m***,
6:11 Since there are ***m*** things that
7:22 For ***m*** times, also, your own
7:29 But they have sought out ***m***
11: 1 For you will find it after ***m***
11: 8 But if a man lives ***m*** years
11: 8 For they will be ***m***.
12: 9 sought out and set in order ***m***
12:12 Of making ***m*** books there is no
Song 8: 7 ***M*** waters cannot quench love,
Isa 1:15 Even though you make ***m***
2: 3 ***M*** people shall come and say,
2: 4 And rebuke ***m*** people;
5: 9 ***m*** houses shall be desolate,
6:12 the forsaken places are ***m*** in
8:15 And ***m*** among them shall stumble;
13: 4 Like that of ***m*** people!
17:12 Woe to the multitude of ***m***
17:13 will rush like the rushing of ***m***
23:16 sing ***m*** songs, That you may be
24:22 After ***m*** days they will be
31: 1 chariots because they are ***m***,
42:20 Seeing ***m*** things, but you do not
52:14 Just as ***m*** were astonished at
52:15 So shall He sprinkle ***m*** nations.
53:11 Servant shall justify ***m***,
53:12 And He bore the sin of ***m***,
58:12 raise up the foundations of ***m***
60:15 A joy of ***m*** generations.
61: 4 The desolations of ***m***
66:16 slain of the LORD shall be ***m***.
Jer 3: 1 have played the harlot with ***m***
5: 6 their transgressions are ***m***;
11:15 Having done lewd deeds with ***m***?
12:10 ***M*** rulers have destroyed My
13: 6 Now it came to pass after ***m*** days
14: 7 For our backslidings are ***m***,
16:16 I will send for ***m*** fishermen,"
16:16 and afterward I will send for ***m***
20:10 For I heard ***m*** mocking: "Fear
22: 8 And ***m*** nations will pass by this
25:14 (For ***m*** nations and great kings
27: 7 and then ***m*** nations and great
28: 8 you of old prophesied against ***m***
32:14 that they may last ***m*** days."
35: 7 that you may live ***m*** days in the
36:32 there were added to them ***m***
37:16 Jeremiah had remained there ***m***
42: 2 we are left but a few of ***m***,
46:11 In vain you will use ***m***
46:16 He made ***m*** fall; Yes, one fell
50:41 And a great nation and ***m*** kings
51:13 O you who dwell by ***m*** waters,
Lam 1:22 For my sighs are ***m***,
Ezek 1:24 like the noise of ***m*** waters,
3: 6 not to ***m*** people of unfamiliar
12:27 vision that he sees is for ***m***
16:41 on you in the sight of ***m*** women;
17: 7 eagle with large wings and ***m***
17: 8 was planted in good soil by ***m***
17: 9 And no great power or ***m*** people
17:15 might give him horses and ***m***
17:17 and build a wall to cut off ***m***
19:10 full of branches Because of ***m***
21:15 That the heart may melt and ***m***
22:25 they have made ***m*** widows in her
26: 3 and will cause ***m*** nations to
26: 7 and an army with ***m*** people.
27: 3 merchant of the peoples on ***m***
27:12 your merchant because of your ***m***
27:15 ***m*** isles were the market of
27:18 because of your ***m*** luxury items,
27:26 oarsmen brought you into ***m***
27:33 You satisfied ***m*** people;
27:33 kings of the earth With your ***m***
32: 3 over you with a company of ***m***
32: 9 also trouble the hearts of ***m***
32:10 I will make ***m*** peoples
33:24 the land. But we are ***m***;
37: 2 there were very ***m*** in the open
38: 6 ***m*** people are with you.
38: 8 After ***m*** days you will be
38: 8 the sword and gathered from ***m***
38: 9 you and all your troops and ***m***
38:15 you and ***m*** peoples with you, all
38:22 and on the ***m*** peoples who are
38:23 will be known in the eyes of ***m***
39:27 in them in the sight of ***m***
43: 2 voice was like the sound of ***m***
47: 7 were very ***m*** trees on one side
47:10 of the Great Sea, exceedingly ***m***.
Dan 2:48 promoted Daniel and gave him ***m***
8:25 He shall destroy ***m*** in their
8:26 For it refers to ***m*** days in
9:27 confirm a covenant with ***m*** for
10:14 for the vision refers to ***m***
11:14 Now in those times ***m*** shall rise
11:18 coastlands, and shall take ***m***.
11:26 and ***m*** shall fall down slain.
11:33 who understand shall instruct ***m***;
11:33 yet for ***m*** days they shall
11:34 but ***m*** shall join with them by
11:39 shall cause them to rule over ***m***,
11:40 and with ***m*** ships; and he shall
11:41 and ***m*** countries shall be

11:44 to destroy and annihilate **m**.
12: 2 And **m** of those who sleep in the
12: 3 And those who turn **m** to
12: 4 **m** shall run to and fro, and
12:10 **M** shall be purified, made white,
Hos 3: 3 You shall stay with me **m** days;
3: 4 of Israel shall abide **m** days
8:11 Because Ephraim has made **m**
Joel 2: 2 Even for **m** successive
Am 8: 3 '**M** dead bodies everywhere,
Mic 2:12 a loud noise because of so **m**
4: 2 **M** nations shall come and say,
4: 3 He shall judge between **m**
4:11 Now also **m** nations have
4:13 You shall beat in pieces **m**
5: 7 Shall be in the midst of **m**
5: 8 In the midst of **m** peoples,
Nah 1:12 they are safe, and likewise **m**,
3:15 like a locust. Make yourself **m**—
3:15 the locust! Make yourself **m**—
Hab 2: 6 to him who loads himself with **m**
2: 8 Because you have plundered **m**
2:10 Cutting off **m** peoples,
Zech 2:11 **M** nations shall be joined to the
7: 3 fast as I have done for so **m**
8:20 Inhabitants of **m** cities;
8:22 **m** peoples and strong nations
Mal 2: 6 And turned **m** away from
2: 8 You have caused **m** to stumble
Mt 3: 7 But when he saw **m** of the
6: 7 they will be heard for their **m**
7:13 and there are **m** who go in by
7:22 **M** will say to Me in that day,
7:22 and done **m** wonders in Your
8:11 And I say to you that **m** will
8:16 they brought to Him **m** who were
8:30 from them there was a herd of **m**
9:10 **m** tax collectors and sinners
10:31 you are of more value than **m**
13: 3 Then He spoke **m** things to them
13:17 I say to you that **m** prophets
13:58 Now He did not do **m** mighty works
14:36 And as **m** as touched it were
15:30 and **m** others; and they laid
15:34 'How **m** loaves do you have?"
16: 9 of the five thousand and how **m**
16:10 of the four thousand and how **m**
16:21 and suffer **m** things from the
19:30 But **m** who are first will be
20:16 For **m** are called, but few
20:28 to give His life a ransom for **m**.
22: 9 and as **m** as you find, invite to
22:14 For **m** are called, but few are
24: 5 For **m** will come in My name,
24: 5 the Christ,' and will deceive **m**.
24:10 And then **m** will be offended,
24:11 Then **m** false prophets will rise
24:11 will rise up and deceive **m**.
24:12 the love of **m** will grow cold.
25:21 I will make you ruler over **m**
25:23 I will make you ruler over **m**
26:28 which is shed for **m** for the
26:60 Even though **m** false witnesses
27:13 Do You not hear how **m** things
27:19 for I have suffered **m** things
27:52 and **m** bodies of the saints who
27:53 the holy city and appeared to **m**.
27:55 And **m** women who followed Jesus
Mk 1:34 Then He healed **m** who were sick
1:34 and cast out **m** demons; and He
2: 2 Immediately **m** gathered together,
2:15 that **m** tax collectors and
2:15 His disciples; for there were **m**,
3: 8 when they heard how **m** things He
3:10 For He healed **m**, so that as
3:10 so that as **m** as had afflictions
4: 2 Then He taught them **m** things by
4:33 And with **m** such parables He
5: 9 name is Legion; for we are **m**.
5:26 and had suffered **m** things from
5:26 had suffered many things from **m**
6: 2 And **m** hearing Him were
6:13 And they cast out **m** demons, and
6:13 and anointed with oil **m** who
6:20 he did **m** things, and heard him
6:31 For there were **m** coming and
6:33 and **m** knew Him and ran there on
6:34 So He began to teach them **m**
6:38 How **m** loaves do you have? Go and
6:56 And as **m** as touched Him were
7: 4 And there are **m** other things
7: 8 and **m** other such things you
7:13 And **m** such things you do."
8: 5 'How **m** loaves do you have?"
8:19 how **m** baskets full of fragments
8:20 how **m** large baskets full of
8:31 the Son of Man must suffer **m**
9:12 that He must suffer **m** things
9:26 so that **m** said, "He is dead."
10:31 But **m** who are first will be
10:45 to give His life a ransom for **m**.
10:48 Then **m** warned him to be quiet;
11: 8 And **m** spread their clothes on
12: 5 and **m** others, beating some and
12:41 And **m** who were rich put in
13: 6 For **m** will come in My name,
13: 6 'I am He,' and will deceive **m**.
14:24 covenant, which is shed for **m**.
14:56 For **m** bore false witness against
15: 3 chief priests accused Him of **m**
15: 4 See how **m** things they testify
15:41 and **m** other women who came up
Lk 1: 1 Inasmuch as **m** have taken in
1:14 and **m** will rejoice at his
1:16 And he will turn **m** of the
2:34 for the fall and rising of **m**
2:35 that the thoughts of **m** hearts
3:18 And with **m** other exhortations he
4:25 **m** widows were in Israel in the
4:27 And **m** lepers were in Israel in
4:41 And demons also came out of **m**,
7:11 and **m** of His disciples went
7:21 And that very hour He cured **m** of
7:21 and to **m** blind He gave sight.
7:47 to you, her sins, which are **m**,
8: 3 and **m** others who provided for
8:30 because **m** demons had entered
8:32 Now a herd of **m** swine was
9:22 The Son of Man must suffer **m**
10:24 for I tell you that **m** prophets
10:41 worried and troubled about **m**
11: 8 he will rise and give him as **m**
11:53 to cross-examine Him about **m**
12: 7 you are of more value than **m**
12:19 you have **m** goods laid up for
12:19 have many goods laid up for **m**
12:47 shall be beaten with **m**
13:24 through the narrow gate, for **m**,
14:16 a great supper and invited **m**,
15:13 And not **m** days after, the
15:17 How **m** of my father's hired
15:29 these **m** years I have been
17:25 But first He must suffer **m**
18:30 who shall not receive **m** times
19:36 **m** spread their clothes on the
21: 8 For **m** will come in My name,
22:65 And **m** other things they
23: 8 because he had heard **m** things
23: 9 Then he questioned Him with **m**
Jn 1:12 But as **m** as received Him, to
2:12 and they did not stay there **m**
2:23 **m** believed in His name when
4:39 And **m** of the Samaritans of that
4:41 And **m** more believed because of
6: 9 but what are they among so **m**?
6:60 Therefore **m** of His disciples,
6:66 From that time **m** of His
7:31 And **m** of the people believed in
7:40 Therefore **m** from the crowd,
8:26 I have **m** things to say and to
8:30 words, **m** believed in Him.
10:20 And **m** of them said, "He has a
10:32 **M** good works I have shown you
10:41 Then **m** came to Him and said,
10:42 And **m** believed in Him there.
11:19 And **m** of the Jews had joined the
11:45 Then **m** of the Jews who had come
11:47 For this Man works **m** signs.
11:55 and **m** went from the country up
12: 9 Now a great **m** of the Jews knew
12:11 because on account of him **m** of
12:37 But although He had done so **m**
12:42 even among the rulers **m**
14: 2 In My Father's house are **m**
16:12 I still have **m** things to say to
17: 2 give eternal life to as **m** as
19:20 Then **m** of the Jews read this
20:30 And truly Jesus did **m** other
21:11 and although there were so **m**,
21:25 And there are also **m** other
Acts 1: 3 alive after His suffering by **m**
1: 5 with the Holy Spirit not **m**
2:39 as **m** as the Lord our God will
2:40 And with **m** other words he
2:43 and **m** wonders and signs were
3:24 as **m** as have spoken, have also
4: 4 **m** of those who heard the word
4: 6 and as **m** as were of the family
5:12 the hands of the apostles **m**
5:37 and drew away **m** people after
6: 7 and a great **m** of the priests
8: 7 came out of **m** who were
8: 7 and **m** who were paralyzed and
8:25 preaching the gospel in **m**
9:13 I have heard from **m** about this
9:16 For I will show him how **m** things
9:23 Now after **m** days were past, the
9:42 and **m** believed on the Lord.
9:43 So it was that he stayed **m** days
10:27 he went in and found **m** who had
10:45 as **m** as came with Peter,
11:24 And a great **m** people were added
11:26 the church and taught a great **m**
12:12 where **m** were gathered together
13:31 He was seen for **m** days by those
13:43 **m** of the Jews and devout
13:48 And as **m** as had been appointed
14:21 gospel to that city and made **m**
14:22 We must through **m** tribulations
15:12 and Paul declaring how **m**
15:21 Moses has had throughout **m**
15:32 the brethren with **m** words.
15:35 Lord, with **m** others also.
16:18 And this she did for **m** days.
16:23 And when they had laid **m** stripes
17:12 Therefore **m** of them believed,
18: 8 And **m** of the Corinthians,
18:10 for I have **m** people in this
19:18 And **m** who had believed came
19:19 **m** of those who had practiced
19:26 has persuaded and turned away **m**
20: 2 and encouraged them with **m**
20: 8 There were **m** lamps in the upper
20:19 with **m** tears and trials which
21:10 And as we stayed **m** days, a
21:20 how **m** myriads of Jews there are
24:10 I know that you have been for **m**
24:17 Now after **m** years I came to
25: 7 stood about and laid **m** serious
25:14 When they had been there **m** days,
26: 9 I myself thought I must do **m**
26:10 and **m** of the saints I shut up
27: 7 When we had sailed slowly **m**
27:20 sun nor stars appeared for **m**
28:10 They also honored us in **m** ways;
28:23 **m** came to him at his lodging,
Rom 2:12 For as **m** as have sinned without
2:12 and as **m** as have sinned in the
4:17 made you a father of **m**
4:18 that he became the father of **m**
5:15 if by the one man's offense **m**
5:15 Jesus Christ, abounded to **m**.
5:16 free gift which came from **m**
5:19 as by one man's disobedience **m**
5:19 also by one Man's obedience **m**
6: 3 Or do you not know that as **m** of
8:14 For as **m** as are led by the
8:29 might be the firstborn among **m**
12: 4 For as we have **m** members in one
12: 5 so we, being **m**, are one body
15:23 having a great desire these **m**
16: 2 she has been a helper of **m** and
1 Cor 1:26 that not **m** wise according to
1:26 not **m** mighty, not many noble,
1:26 not **m** noble, are called.
4:15 yet you do not have **m**
8: 5 or on earth (as there are **m**
8: 5 (as there are many gods and **m**
10:17 For we, though **m**, are one
10:33 profit, but the profit of **m**,
11:30 For this reason **m** are weak and
11:30 among you, and **m** sleep.
12:12 as the body is one and has **m**
12:12 of that one body, being **m**,
12:14 body is not one member but **m**.
12:20 But now indeed there are **m**
14:10 so **m** kinds of languages in the
16: 9 and there are **m** adversaries.
2 Cor 1:11 that thanks may be given by **m**
1:11 gift granted to us through **m**.
2: 4 with **m** tears, not that you
2:17 For we are not, as so **m**,
4:15 having spread through the **m**,
6:10 yet making **m** rich; as having
8:22 have often proved diligent in **m**
9:12 but also is abounding through **m**
11:18 Seeing that **m** boast according to
12:21 and I shall mourn for **m** who
Gal 1:14 I advanced in Judaism beyond **m**
3: 4 Have you suffered so **m** things in
3:10 For as **m** as are of the works of
3:16 say, "And to seeds," as of **m**,
3:27 For as **m** of you as were baptized
4:27 For the desolate has **m**
6:12 As **m** as desire to make a good
6:16 And as **m** as walk according to
Phil 3:15 as **m** as are mature, have this
3:18 For **m** walk, of whom I have told
Col 2: 1 and for as **m** as have not seen
1 Tim 6: 1 Let as **m** bondservants as are
6: 9 and into **m** foolish and harmful
6:10 themselves through with **m**
6:12 in the presence of **m** witnesses.
2 Tim 1:18 and you know very well how **m**
2: 2 you have heard from me among **m**
Titus 1:10 For there are **m** insubordinate,
Heb 2:10 in bringing **m** sons to glory, to
7:23 Also there were **m** priests,
9:28 once to bear the sins of **m**.
11:12 were born as **m** as the stars
12:15 and by this **m** become defiled;
Jas 3: 1 let not **m** of you become
3: 2 For we all stumble in **m** things.
2 Pe 2: 2 And **m** will follow their
1 Jn 2:18 even now **m** antichrists have
4: 1 because **m** false prophets have
2 Jn 7 For **m** deceivers have gone out
12 Having **m** things to write to
3 Jn 13 I had **m** things to write, but I
Rev 1:15 and His voice as the sound of **m**
2:24 as **m** as do not have this
3:19 As **m** as I love, I rebuke and
5:11 and I heard the voice of **m**
8:11 and **m** men died from the water,
9: 9 the sound of chariots with **m**
10:11 must prophesy again about **m**
13:15 both speak and cause as **m** as
14: 2 like the voice of **m** waters, and
17: 1 the great harlot who sits on **m**
18:17 and as **m** as trade on the sea,
19: 6 as the sound of **m** waters and as
19:12 and on His head were **m** crowns.

MAOCH (1/1)

1 Sam 27: 2 with him to Achish the son of **M**,

MAON (7/5)

Josh 15:55 **M**, Carmel, Ziph, Juttah,
1 Sam 23:24 were in the Wilderness of **M**,
23:25 stayed in the Wilderness of **M**.
23:25 David in the Wilderness of **M**.
25: 2 Now there was a man in **M**
1 Chr 2:45 And the son of Shammai was **M**,
2:45 and **M** was the father of Beth

MAONITES (1/1)
Judg 10:12 Sidonians and Amalekites and ***M***

MAR (KJV) See BREAK, DISFIGURE, RUIN

MARA (1/1)
Ruth 1:20 not call me Naomi; call me ***M***,

MARAH (5/3)
Ex 15:23 Now when they came to ***M***,
15:23 could not drink the waters of ***M***,
15:23 the name of it was called ***M***.
Num 33: 8 of Etham, and camped at ***M***.
33: 9 They moved from ***M*** and came to

MARALAH (1/1)
Josh 19:11 went toward the west and to ***M***,

MARANATHA (KJV) See ACCURSED

MARBLE (5/4)
1 Chr 29: 2 and ***m*** slabs in abundance.
Esth 1: 6 and purple on silver rods and ***m***
1: 6 and white and black ***m***.
Song 5:15 His legs are pillars of ***m*** Set
Rev 18:12 wood, bronze, iron, and ***m***;

MARCH (6/6) MARCHED, MARCHING
Num 10:28 Thus was the order of ***m*** of the
Josh 6: 3 You shall ***m*** around the city, all
6: 4 But the seventh day you shall ***m***
6: 7 and ***m*** around the city, and let
Judg 5:21 soul, ***m*** on in strength!
Jer 46:22 For they shall ***m*** with an army

MARCHED (9/8) MARCH
Ex 14:10 the Egyptians ***m*** after them.
Josh 6:14 And the second day they ***m*** around
6:15 and ***m*** around the city seven
6:15 On that day only they ***m*** around
10: 9 having ***m*** all night from Gilgal.
Judg 5: 4 When You ***m*** from the field of
2 Ki 3: 9 and they ***m*** on that roundabout
Ps 68: 7 When You ***m*** through the
Hab 3:12 You ***m*** through the land in

MARCHES (3/3)
Joel 2: 7 Every one ***m*** in formation,
2: 8 Every one ***m*** in his own column.
Hab 1: 6 and hasty nation Which ***m***

MARCHING (2/2) MARCH
2 Sam 5:24 when you hear the sound of ***m*** in
1 Chr 14:15 when you hear a sound of ***m*** in

MARCUS (KJV) See MARK

MARESHAH (8/8)
Josh 15:44 Keilah, Achzib, and ***M***:
1 Chr 2:42 and the sons of ***M*** the father of
4:21 Lecah, Laadah the father of ***M***,
2 Chr 11: 8 Gath, ***M***, Ziph,
14: 9 chariots, and he came to ***M***.
14:10 in the Valley of Zephathah at ***M***.
20:37 Eliezer the son of Dodavah of ***M***
Mic 1:15 heir to you, O inhabitant of ***M***;

MARINERS (3/3)
Ezek 27:27 Your ***m*** and pilots,
27:29 who handle the oar, The ***m***,
Jon 1: 5 Then the ***m*** were afraid;

MARISHES (KJV) See MARSHES

MARK (32/31) MARKED, MARKS
Gen 4:15 And the LORD set a ***m*** on
Num 34: 7 From the Great Sea you shall ***m***
34: 8 from Mount Hor you shall ***m*** out
34:10 You shall ***m*** out your eastern
Job 10:14 then You ***m*** me, And will not
31:35 one to hear me! Here is my ***m***.
39: 1 Or can you ***m*** when the deer
Ps 37:37 ***M*** the blameless man, and
48:13 ***M*** well her bulwarks
56: 6 they ***m*** my steps, When they lie
130: 3 should ***m*** iniquities, O Lord,
Ezek 9: 4 and put a ***m*** on the foreheads of
9: 6 near anyone on whom is the ***m***;
44: 5 ***m*** well, see with your eyes and
44: 5 ***M*** well who may enter the house
47:18 On the east side you shall ***m*** out
Acts 12:12 of John whose surname was ***M***,
12:25 them John whose surname was ***M***.
15:37 to take with them John called ***M***.
15:39 And so Barnabas took ***M*** and
Col 4:10 with ***M*** the cousin of Barnabas
2 Tim 4:11 Get ***M*** and bring him with you,
Phm 1:24 as do ***M***, Aristarchus,
1 Pe 5:13 and so does ***M*** my son.
Rev 13:16 to receive a ***m*** on their right
13:17 sell except one who has the ***m***
14: 9 and receives his ***m*** on his
14:11 and whoever receives the ***m*** of
15: 2 over his image and over his ***m***
16: 2 upon the men who had the ***m*** of
19:20 those who received the ***m*** of
20: 4 and had not received his ***m*** on

MARKED (6/6) MARK
Job 24:16 into houses Which they ***m*** for
Prov 8:29 When He ***m*** out the foundations
Jer 2:22 Yet your iniquity is ***m*** before
23:18 Who has ***m*** His word and heard
Hab 1:12 You have ***m*** them for correction.
Jude 4 who long ago were ***m*** out for

MARKER (1/1)
Ezek 39:15 he shall set up a ***m*** by it, till

MARKET (3/3) MARKETPLACE
Ezek 27: 9 oarsmen were in you To ***m*** your
27:15 many isles were the ***m*** of your
1 Cor 10:25 whatever is sold in the meat ***m***,

MARKETPLACE (8/8) MARKET, MARKETPLACES
Isa 23: 3 And she is a ***m*** for the
Ezek 27:24 cords, which were in your ***m***.
Mt 20: 3 others standing idle in the ***m***,
Mk 7: 4 When they come from the ***m***,
Lk 7:32 like children sitting in the ***m***
Acts 16:19 and dragged them into the ***m***
17: 5 some of the evil men from the ***m***,
17:17 and in the ***m*** daily with those

MARKETPLACES (7/7) MARKETPLACE
1 Ki 20:34 and you may set up ***m*** for
Mt 11:16 like children sitting in the ***m***
23: 7 "greetings in the ***m***,
Mk 6:56 they laid the sick in the ***m***,
12:38 robes, love greetings in the ***m***,
Lk 11:43 and greetings in the ***m***.
20:46 robes, love greetings in the ***m***,

MARKS (5/4) MARK
Lev 19:28 nor tattoo any ***m*** on you: I am
Job 41:30 He spreads pointed ***m*** in the
Isa 44:13 He ***m*** one out with chalk;
44:13 He ***m*** it out with the compass,
Gal 6:17 for I bear in my body the ***m*** of

MAROTH (1/1)
Mic 1:12 For the inhabitant of ***M*** pined

MARRED (3/3)
Lev 21:18 who has a ***m*** face or any limb
Isa 52:14 So His visage was ***m*** more than
Jer 18: 4 that he made of clay was ***m*** in

MARRIAGE (17/16) MARRIAGES, MARRY
Ex 21:10 clothing, and her ***m*** rights.
Judg 12: 9 gave away thirty daughters in ***m***,
2 Chr 18: 1 and by ***m*** he allied himself with
Ezra 9:14 and join in ***m*** with the people
Ps 78:63 maidens were not given in ***m***.
Mt 22: 2 a certain king who arranged a ***m***
22:30 marry nor are given in ***m***,
24:38 marrying and giving in ***m***,
Mk 12:25 marry nor are given in ***m***,
Lk 17:27 wives, they were given in ***m***,
20:34 age marry and are given in ***m***.
20:35 marry nor are given in ***m***;
1 Cor 7:38 So then he who gives her in ***m***
7:38 he who does not give her in ***m***
Heb 13: 4 ***M*** is honorable among all, and
Rev 19: 7 for the ***m*** of the Lamb has come,
19: 9 those who are called to the ***m***

MARRIAGES (3/3) MARRIAGE
Gen 34: 9 And make ***m*** with us; give your
Deut 7: 3 Nor shall you make ***m*** with them.
Josh 23:12 and make ***m*** with them, and go in

MARRIED (32/31) MARRY
Gen 19:14 who had ***m*** his daughters, and
38: 2 and he ***m*** her and went in to
Ex 21: 3 by himself; if he comes in ***m***,
Lev 22:12 If the priest's daughter is ***m*** to
Num 12: 1 Ethiopian woman whom he had ***m***;
12: 1 for he had ***m*** an Ethiopian
36: 3 Now if they are ***m*** to any of the
36:11 were ***m*** to the sons of their
36:12 They were ***m*** into the families of
Deut 20: 7 to a woman and has not ***m*** her?
22:22 is found lying with a woman ***m***
25: 5 of the dead man shall not be ***m***
1 Ki 3: 1 and ***m*** Pharaoh's daughter;
1 Chr 2:21 whom he ***m*** when he was sixty
2 Chr 13:21 ***m*** fourteen wives, and begot
Neh 6:18 and his son Jehohanan had ***m*** the
13:23 days I also saw Jews who had ***m***
Prov 30:23 A hateful woman when she is ***m***,
Isa 54: 1 Than the children of the ***m***
62: 4 And your land shall be ***m***.
Jer 3:14 for I am ***m*** to you. I will take
Mal 2:11 He has ***m*** the daughter of a
Mt 22:25 The first died after he had ***m***,
Mk 6:17 for he had ***m*** her.
Lk 14:20 I have ***m*** a wife, and therefore I
17:27 they ***m*** wives, they were given
Rom 7: 3 though she has ***m*** another man.
7: 4 that you may be ***m*** to another—
1 Cor 7:10 Now to the ***m*** I command, yet
7:33 But he who is ***m*** cares about the
7:34 But she who is ***m*** cares about
7:39 she is at liberty to be ***m*** to

MARRIES (12/10) MARRY
Lev 20:14 If a man ***m*** a woman and her
Deut 24: 1 When a man takes a wife and ***m***
Isa 62: 5 For as a young man ***m*** a virgin,
Mt 5:32 and whoever ***m*** a woman who is
19: 9 and ***m*** another, commits
19: 9 and whoever ***m*** her who is
Mk 10:11 divorces his wife and ***m***
10:12 divorces her husband and ***m***
Lk 16:18 divorces his wife and ***m***
16:18 and whoever ***m*** her who is
Rom 7: 3 she ***m*** another man, she will be
1 Cor 7:28 not sinned; and if a virgin ***m***,

MARROW (4/4)
Job 21:24 And the ***m*** of his bones is
Ps 63: 5 shall be satisfied as with ***m***
Isa 25: 6 Of fat things full of ***m***,
Heb 4:12 and spirit, and of joints and ***m***,

MARRY (21/19) MARRIAGE, MARRIED, MARRIES, MARRYING, UNMARRIED
Gen 38: 8 in to your brother's wife and ***m***
Lev 21:14 a harlot—these he shall not ***m***;
Num 36: 3 of the tribe into which they ***m***;
36: 4 of the tribe into which they ***m***;
36: 6 Let them ***m*** whom they think best,
36: 6 but they may ***m*** only within the
Deut 20: 7 in the battle and another man ***m***
Isa 62: 5 So shall your sons ***m*** you;
Mt 19:10 wife, it is better not to ***m***.
22:24 his brother shall ***m*** his wife
22:30 the resurrection they neither ***m***
Mk 12:25 they neither ***m*** nor are given in
Lk 20:34 The sons of this age ***m*** and are
20:35 neither ***m*** nor are given in
1 Cor 7: 9 self-control, let them ***m***.
7: 9 For it is better to ***m*** than to
7:28 But even if you do ***m***,
7:36 He does not sin; let them ***m***.
1 Tim 4: 3 forbidding to ***m***, and
5:11 Christ, they desire to ***m***,
5:14 that the younger widows ***m***,

MARRYING (2/2) MARRY
Neh 13:27 against our God by ***m*** pagan
Mt 24:38 ***m*** and giving in marriage, until

MARS' (KJV) See AREOPAGUS

MARSENA (1/1)
Esth 1:14 Admatha, Tarshish, Meres, ***M***,

MARSH (2/2)
Job 8:11 the papyrus grow up without a ***m***?
40:21 In a covert of reeds and ***m***.

MARSHES (2/2)
Isa 14:23 And ***m*** of muddy water; I will
Ezek 47:11 But its swamps and ***m*** will not be

MARTHA (13/12)
Lk 10:38 and a certain woman named ***M***
10:40 But ***M*** was distracted with much
10:41 answered and said to her, "***M***,
10:41 and said to her, "Martha, ***M***,
Jn 11: 1 town of Mary and her sister ***M***.
11: 5 Now Jesus loved ***M*** and her sister
11:19 had joined the women around ***M***
11:20 Then ***M***, as soon as she
11:21 Then ***M*** said to Jesus, "Lord, if
11:24 ***M*** said to Him, "I know that he
11:30 but was in the place where ***M***
11:39 "Take away the stone." ***M***,
12: 2 and ***M*** served, but Lazarus was

MARTYR (2/2) MARTYRS
Acts 22:20 And when the blood of Your ***m***
Rev 2:13 Antipas was My faithful ***m***,

MARTYRS (1/1) MARTYR
Rev 17: 6 and with the blood of the ***m*** of

MARVEL (11/11) MARVELED, MARVELOUS, MARVELS

Eccl 5: 8 do not ***m*** at the matter;
Jn 3: 7 Do not ***m*** that I said to you,
5:20 than these, that you may ***m***.
5:28 Do not ***m*** at this; for the hour
7:21 "I did one work, and you all ***m***.
Acts 3:12 why do you ***m*** at this? Or why
13:41 ***M*** and perish! For I
Gal 1: 6 I ***m*** that you are turning away
1 Jn 3:13 Do not ***m***, my brethren, if
Rev 17: 7 said to me, "Why did you ***m***?
17: 8 who dwell on the earth will ***m***,

MARVELED (34/34) MARVEL

Ps 48: 5 They saw it, and so they ***m***;
Mt 8:10 When Jesus heard it, He ***m***,
8:27 So the men ***m***, saying,
9: 8 they ***m*** and glorified God, who
9:33 spoke. And the multitudes ***m***,
15:31 So the multitude ***m*** when they saw
21:20 the disciples saw it, they ***m***,
22:22 had heard these words, they ***m***,
27:14 so that the governor ***m*** greatly.
Mk 5:20 had done for him; and all ***m***.
6: 6 And He ***m*** because of their
6:51 beyond measure, and ***m***.
12:17 And they ***m*** at Him.
15: 5 nothing, so that Pilate ***m***.
15:44 Pilate ***m*** that He was already
Lk 1:21 and ***m*** that he lingered so long
1:63 name is John." So they all ***m***.
2:18 And all those who heard it ***m*** at
2:33 And Joseph and His mother ***m*** at
4:22 and ***m*** at the gracious words
7: 9 He ***m*** at him, and turned around
8:25 And they were afraid, and ***m***,
9:43 But while everyone ***m*** at all the
11:14 and the multitudes ***m***.
11:38 he ***m*** that He had not first
20:26 And they ***m*** at His answer and
24:41 did not believe for joy, and ***m***,
Jn 4:27 and they ***m*** that He talked with
7:15 And the Jews ***m***, saying, "How
Acts 2: 7 Then they were all amazed and ***m***,
4:13 and untrained men, they ***m***.
7:31 he ***m*** at the sight; and as he
Rev 13: 3 And all the world ***m*** and
17: 6 I ***m*** with great amazement.

MARVELING (1/1)

Lk 24:12 ***m*** to himself at what had

MARVELOUS (21/19) MARVEL

1 Chr 16:12 Remember His ***m*** works which He
Job 5: 9 ***M*** things without number.
Ps 9: 1 I will tell of all Your ***m***
17: 7 Show Your ***m*** lovingkindness by
31:21 For He has shown me His ***m***
78:12 ***M*** things He did in the sight of
98: 1 a new song! For He has done ***m***
105: 5 Remember His ***m*** works which He
118:23 It is ***m*** in our eyes.
139:14 ***M*** are Your works, And that
Isa 29:14 I will again do a ***m*** work
29:14 A ***m*** work and a wonder;
Joel 2:21 For the LORD has done ***m***
Zech 8: 6 If it is ***m*** in the eyes of the
8: 6 Will it also be ***m*** in My eyes?'
Mt 21:42 And it is ***m*** in our
Mk 12:11 And it is ***m*** in our
Jn 9:30 this is a ***m*** thing, that you do
1 Pe 2: 9 you out of darkness into His ***m***
Rev 15: 1 sign in heaven, great and ***m***:
15: 3 Great and ***m*** are Your works,

MARVELOUSLY (2/2)

2 Chr 26:15 for he was ***m*** helped till he
Job 37: 5 God thunders ***m*** with His voice;

MARVELS (1/1) MARVEL

Ex 34:10 all your people I will do ***m***

MARY (54/46)

Mt 1:16 begot Joseph the husband of ***M***,
1:18 After His mother ***M*** was
1:20 not be afraid to take to you ***M***
2:11 saw the young Child with ***M*** His
13:55 Is not His mother called ***M***?
27:56 among whom were ***M*** Magdalene,
27:56 ***M*** the mother of James and
27:61 And ***M*** Magdalene was there, and
27:61 was there, and the other ***M***,
28: 1 ***M*** Magdalene and the other Mary
28: 1 Mary Magdalene and the other ***M***
Mk 6: 3 not the carpenter, the Son of ***M***,
15:40 among whom were ***M*** Magdalene,
15:40 ***M*** the mother of James the Less
15:47 And ***M*** Magdalene and Mary the
15:47 And Mary Magdalene and ***M*** the
16: 1 ***M*** Magdalene, Mary the mother
16: 1 ***M*** the mother of James, and
16: 9 He appeared first to ***M***
Lk 1:27 The virgin's name was ***M***.
1:30 to her, "Do not be afraid, ***M***,
1:34 Then ***M*** said to the angel, "How
1:38 Then ***M*** said, "Behold the
1:39 Now ***M*** arose in those days and
1:41 heard the greeting of ***M***,
1:46 And ***M*** said: "My soul
1:56 And ***M*** remained with her about
2: 5 to be registered with ***M***,
2:16 came with haste and found ***M***
2:19 But ***M*** kept all these things and
2:34 and said to ***M*** His mother,
8: 2 ***M*** called Magdalene, out of whom
10:39 And she had a sister called ***M***,
10:42 and ***M*** has chosen that good
24:10 It was ***M*** Magdalene, Joanna, Mary
24:10 ***M*** the mother of James, and
Jn 11: 1 the town of ***M*** and her sister
11: 2 It was that ***M*** who anointed the
11:19 the women around Martha and ***M***,
11:20 but ***M*** was sitting in the house.
11:28 her way and secretly called ***M***
11:31 when they saw that ***M*** rose up
11:32 when ***M*** came where Jesus was,
11:45 of the Jews who had come to ***M***,
12: 3 Then ***M*** took a pound of very
19:25 ***M*** the wife of Clopas, and Mary
19:25 of Clopas, and ***M*** Magdalene.
20: 1 on the first day of the week ***M***
20:11 But ***M*** stood outside by the tomb
20:16 ***M***!" She turned and said to Him,
20:18 ***M*** Magdalene came and told the
Acts 1:14 with the women and ***M*** the mother
12:12 he came to the house of ***M***,
Rom 16: 6 Greet ***M***, who labored much

MASH (1/1)

Gen 10:23 were Uz, Hul, Gether, and ***M***.

MASHAL (1/1)

1 Chr 6:74 ***M*** with its common-lands, Abdon

MASONS (7/7)

2 Sam 5:11 trees, and carpenters and ***m***.
2 Ki 12:12 and to ***m*** and stonecutters, and
22: 6 carpenters and builders and ***m***—
1 Chr 14: 1 with ***m*** and carpenters, to build
22: 2 and he appointed ***m*** to cut hewn
2 Chr 24:12 and they hired ***m*** and carpenters
Ezra 3: 7 They also gave money to the ***m***

MASREKAH (2/2)

Gen 36:36 Samlah of ***M*** reigned in his
1 Chr 1:47 Samlah of ***M*** reigned in his

MASSA (2/2)

Gen 25:14 Mishma, Dumah, ***M***,
1 Chr 1:30 Mishma, Dumah, ***M***,

MASSACRED (1/1)

1 Ki 18: 4 while Jezebel ***m*** the prophets of

MASSAH (4/4) MERIBAH

Ex 17: 7 called the name of the place ***M***
Deut 6:16 God as you tempted Him in ***M***.
9:22 Also at Taberah and ***M*** and
33: 8 holy one, Whom You tested at ***M***,

MAST (3/3)

Prov 23:34 who lies at the top of the ***m***,
Isa 33:23 could not strengthen their ***m***,
Ezek 27: 5 from Lebanon to make you a ***m***.

MASTER (159/148) MASTER'S, MASTERS

Gen 24: 9 the thigh of Abraham his ***m***,
24:12 O LORD God of my ***m*** Abraham,
24:12 and show kindness to my ***m***
24:14 You have shown kindness to my ***m***.
24:27 be the LORD God of my ***m***
24:27 mercy and His truth toward my ***m***.
24:35 The LORD has blessed my ***m***
24:36 wife bore a son to my ***m*** when
24:37 Now my ***m*** made me swear, saying,
24:39 "And I said to my ***m***,
24:42 O LORD God of my ***m*** Abraham, if
24:48 blessed the LORD God of my ***m***
24:49 deal kindly and truly with my ***m***,
24:54 he said, "Send me away to my ***m***.
24:56 away so that I may go to my ***m***.
24:65 The servant said, "It is my ***m***.
27:29 Be ***m*** over your brethren,
27:37 "Indeed I have made him your ***m***,
39: 2 he was in the house of his ***m***
39: 3 And his ***m*** saw that the LORD
39: 8 my ***m*** does not know what is
39:16 garment with her until his ***m***
39:19 when his ***m*** heard the words
39:20 Then Joseph's ***m*** took him and put
Ex 21: 4 If his ***m*** has given him a wife,
21: 5 plainly says, 'I love my ***m***,
21: 6 then his ***m*** shall bring him to
21: 6 and his ***m*** shall pierce his ear
21: 8 "If she does not please her ***m***,
21:32 he shall give to their ***m*** thirty
22: 8 then the ***m*** of the house shall
Deut 23:15 shall not give back to his ***m***
23:15 who has escaped from his ***m*** to
Judg 3:25 And there was their ***m***, fallen
19:11 and the servant said to his ***m***,
19:12 But his ***m*** said to him, "We will
19:22 They spoke to the ***m*** of the
19:23 the ***m*** of the house, went out to
19:26 of the man's house where her ***m***
19:27 When her ***m*** arose in the
1 Sam 16:16 Let our ***m*** now command your
20:38 arrows and came back to his ***m***.
24: 6 I should do this thing to my ***m***,
25:10 break away each one from his ***m***.
25:14 the wilderness to greet our ***m***;
25:17 is determined against our ***m***
26:16 you have not guarded your ***m***,
29: 4 he reconcile himself to his ***m***,
30:13 and my ***m*** left me behind,
30:15 me into the hands of my ***m***,
2 Sam 2: 7 for your ***m*** Saul is dead, and
1 Ki 18: 8 "It is I. Go, tell your ***m***,
18:10 no nation or kingdom where my ***m***
18:11 now you say, 'Go, tell your ***m***,
18:14 now you say, 'Go, tell your ***m***,
22:17 LORD said, 'These have no ***m***.
2 Ki 2: 3 the LORD will take away your ***m***
2: 5 the LORD will take away your ***m***
2:16 them go and search for your ***m***,
5: 1 man in the eyes of his ***m***,
5: 3 If only my ***m*** were with the
5: 4 Naaman went in and told his ***m***,
5:18 when my ***m*** goes into the temple
5:20 my ***m*** has spared Naaman this
5:22 My ***m*** has sent me, saying,
5:25 went in and stood before his ***m***.
6: 5 ***m***! For it was borrowed."
6:15 my ***m***! What shall we do?"
6:22 eat and drink and go to their ***m***.
6:23 away and they went to their ***m***.
8:14 from Elisha, and came to his ***m***,
9: 7 down the house of Ahab your ***m***,
9:11 out to the servants of his ***m***,
9:31 Zimri, murderer of your ***m***?
10: 9 I conspired against my ***m*** and
18:23 give a pledge to my ***m*** the king
18:27 Has my ***m*** sent me to your master
18:27 my master sent me to your ***m***
19: 4 whom his ***m*** the king of Assyria
19: 6 "Thus you shall say to your ***m***,
1 Chr 12:19 He may defect to his ***m*** Saul and
15:27 and Chenaniah the music ***m*** with
2 Chr 2:13 Huram my ***m*** craftsman
4:16 all their articles Huram his ***m***
18:16 LORD said, 'These have no ***m***.
Ezra 10: 3 to the advice of my ***m*** and of
Esth 1:22 that each man should be ***m*** in
Job 3:19 the servant is free from his ***m***.
Prov 8:30 Then I was beside Him as a ***m***
27:18 So he who waits on his ***m*** will
30:10 not malign a servant to his ***m***,
Isa 19: 4 Into the hand of a cruel ***m***,
24: 2 with the servant, so with his ***m***;
36: 8 give a pledge to my ***m*** the king
36:12 Has my ***m*** sent me to your master
36:12 my master sent me to your ***m***
37: 4 whom his ***m*** the king of Assyria
37: 6 "Thus shall you say to your ***m***,
Jer 22:18 ***m***!' or 'Alas, his glory!'
Lam 1: 5 adversaries have become the ***m***,
Dan 1: 3 the ***m*** of his eunuchs, to bring
Hos 2:16 And no longer call Me 'My ***M***,
Mal 1: 6 And a servant his ***m***.
1: 6 is My honor? And if I am a ***M***,
Mt 10:24 nor a servant above his ***m***.
10:25 and a servant like his ***m***.
10:25 If they have called the ***m*** of
18:25 his ***m*** commanded that he be
18:26 down before him, saying, '***M***,
18:27 Then the ***m*** of that servant was
18:31 and came and told their ***m*** all
18:32 'Then his ***m***, after he had
18:34 And his ***m*** was angry, and
24:43 that if the ***m*** of the house had
24:45 whom his ***m*** made ruler over his
24:46 is that servant whom his ***m***,
24:48 My ***m*** is delaying his coming,'
24:50 the ***m*** of that servant will come
Mk 13:35 for you do not know when the ***m***
14:14 say to the ***m*** of the house, 'The
Lk 5: 5 answered and said to Him, "***M***,
8:24 Him and awoke Him, saying, "***M***,
8:24 awoke Him, saying, "Master, ***M***,
8:45 and those with him said, "***M***,
9:33 that Peter said to Jesus, "***M***,
9:49 John answered and said, "***M***,
12:36 like men who wait for their ***m***,
12:37 are those servants whom the ***m***,
12:39 that if the ***m*** of the house had
12:42 whom his ***m*** will make ruler
12:43 is that servant whom his ***m***
12:45 My ***m*** is delaying his coming,'
12:46 the ***m*** of that servant will come
13:25 When once the ***M*** of the house has
14:21 reported these things to his ***m***.
14:21 Then the ***m*** of the house, being
14:22 "And the servant said, '***M***,
14:23 Then the ***m*** said to the servant,
16: 3 For my ***m*** is taking the
16: 5 'How much do you owe my ***m***?
16: 8 So the ***m*** commended the unjust
17:13 voices and said, "Jesus, ***M***,
19:16 came the first, saying, '***M***,
19:18 the second came, saying, '***M***,
19:20 "Then another came, saying, '***M***,

19:25 ("But they said to him, '**M**,
22:11 Then you shall say to the **m** of
Jn 2: 8 and take it to the **m** of the
2: 9 When the **m** of the feast had
2: 9 the **m** of the feast called the
13:16 is not greater than his **m**;
15:15 does not know what his **m** is
15:20 is not greater than his **m**.
Rom 14: 4 To his own **m** he stands or
1 Cor 3:10 as a wise **m** builder I have laid
Gal 4: 1 though he is **m** of all,
Eph 6: 9 knowing that your own **M** also is
Col 4: 1 knowing that you also have a **M**
2 Tim 2:21 sanctified and useful for the **M**,

MASTER'S (28/24) MASTER

Gen 24:10 servant took ten of his **m** camels
24:10 for all his **m** goods were in
24:27 led me to the house of my **m**
24:36 And Sarah my **m** wife bore a son
24:44 LORD has appointed for my **m** son.
24:48 the daughter of my **m** brother
24:51 and let her be your **m** son's
39: 7 these things that his **m** wife
39: 8 he refused and said to his **m**
Ex 21: 4 and her children shall be her **m**,
1 Sam 29:10 morning with your **m** servants
2 Sam 9: 9 I have given to your **m** son all
9:10 that your **m** son may have food
9:10 But Mephibosheth your **m** son
12: 8 I gave you your **m** house and your
12: 8 master's house and your **m** wives
16: 3 'And where is your **m** son?"
2 Ki 6:32 Is not the sound of his **m** feet
10: 2 since your **m** sons are with
10: 3 the best qualified of your **m**
10: 3 and fight for your **m** house.
10: 6 your **m** sons, and come to me at
18:24 of the least of my **m** servants,
Isa 1: 3 owner And the donkey its **m** crib;
22:18 be the shame of your **m** house.
36: 9 captain of the least of my **m**
Lk 12:47 servant who knew his **m** will,
16: 5 called every one of his **m** debtors

MASTERBUILDER (KJV) See (MASTER) BUILDER

MASTERS (17/16) MASTER, MASTERS', TASKMASTERS

Ps 123: 2 look to the hand of their **m**,
Prov 25:13 he refreshes the soul of his **m**.
Isa 26:13 **m** besides You Have had
Jer 27: 4 command them to say to their **m**,
27: 4 you shall say to your **m**:
Mt 6:24 "No one can serve two **m**;
Lk 16:13 "No servant can serve two **m**;
Acts 16:16 who brought her **m** much profit
16:19 But when her **m** saw that their
Eph 6: 5 to those who are your **m**
6: 9 And you, **m**, do the same
Col 3:22 obey in all things your **m**
4: 1 **M**, give your bondservants
1 Tim 6: 1 the yoke count their own **m**
6: 2 And those who have believing **m**,
Titus 2: 9 to be obedient to their own **m**,
1 Pe 2:18 be submissive to your **m** with

MASTERS' (2/2) MASTERS

Zeph 1: 9 Who fill their **m** houses with
Mt 15:27 crumbs which fall from their **m**

MATCH (1/1)

Lk 5:36 out of the new does not **m** the

MATE (4/3)

Lev 18:23 Nor shall you **m** with any animal,
18:23 stand before an animal to **m**
Isa 34:15 Every one with her **m**.
34:16 Not one shall lack her **m**.

MATERIAL (4/4)

Ex 35:29 were willing to bring **m** for
36: 7 for the **m** they had was
Rom 15:27 also to minister to them in **m**
1 Cor 9:11 a great thing if we reap your **m**

MATES (2/2)

Lev 20:15 If a man **m** with an animal, he
20:16 approaches any animal and **m**

MATHUSALA (KJV) See METHUSELAH

MATING (1/1)

Jer 2:24 her desire; In her time of **m**,

MATRED (2/2)

Gen 36:39 Mehetabel, the daughter of **M**,
1 Chr 1:50 was Mehetabel the daughter of **M**,

MATRI (1/1)

1 Sam 10:21 the family of **M** was chosen.

MATRIX (1/1)

Isa 49: 1 From the **m** of My mother He has

MATTAN (3/3)

2 Ki 11:18 and killed **M** the priest of Baal
2 Chr 23:17 and killed **M** the priest of Baal
Jer 38: 1 Now Shephatiah the son of **M**,

MATTANAH (2/2)

Num 21:18 the wilderness they went to **M**,
21:19 from **M** to Nahaliel, from

MATTANIAH (16/16) ZEDEKIAH

2 Ki 24:17 Then the king of Babylon made **M**,
1 Chr 9:15 and **M** the son of Micah, the son
25: 4 the sons of Heman: Bukkiah, **M**,
25:16 the ninth for **M**, his sons and
2 Chr 20:14 the son of Jeiel, the son of **M**,
29:13 sons of Asaph, Zechariah and **M**;
Ezra 10:26 of the sons of Elam: **M**,
10:27 of Zattu: Elioenai, Eliashib, **M**,
10:30 Chelal, Benaiah, Maaseiah, **M**,
10:37 **M**, Mattenai, Jaasai,
Neh 11:17 **M** the son of Micha, the son of
11:22 son of Hashabiah, the son of **M**,
12: 8 and **M** who led the
12:25 **M**, Bakbukiah, Obadiah,
12:35 son of Shemaiah, the son of **M**,
13:13 the son of Zaccur, the son of **M**;

MATTATHAH (1/1)

Lk 3:31 son of Menan, the son of **M**,

MATTATHIAH (2/2)

Lk 3:25 the son of **M**, the son of
3:26 son of Maath, the son of **M**,

MATTATTAH (1/1)

Ezra 10:33 the sons of Hashum: Mattenai, **M**,

MATTENAI (3/3)

Ezra 10:33 of the sons of Hashum: **M**,
10:37 Mattaniah, **M**, Jaasai,
Neh 12:19 of Joiarib, **M**; of Jedaiah,

MATTER (68/64)

Gen 21:11 And the **m** was very displeasing
24: 9 swore to him concerning this **m**.
30:15 Is it a small **m** that you have
37:11 but his father kept the **m** in
Ex 2:15 When Pharaoh heard of this **m**,
18:22 it will be that every great **m**
18:22 but every small **m** they
23: 7 yourself far from a false **m**;
Lev 5: 1 has seen or known of the **m**—
Num 25:18 they seduced you in the **m** of
25:18 matter of Peor and in the **m** of
Deut 3:26 Speak no more to Me of this **m**.
17: 8 If a **m** arises which is too hard
19:15 of two or three witnesses the **m**
22:26 kills him, even so is this **m**.
Ruth 3:18 until you know how the **m** will
3:18 until he has concluded the **m**
1 Sam 10:16 But about the **m** of the
20:23 And as for the **m** which you and I
20:39 and David knew of the **m**.
30:24 who will heed you in this **m**?
2 Sam 1: 4 How did the **m** go? Please tell
19:42 then are you angry over this **m**?
1 Ki 15: 5 except in the **m** of Uriah the
2 Ki 3:18 And this is a simple **m** in the
1 Chr 26:32 for every **m** pertaining to God
27: 1 served the king in every **m** of
2 Chr 8:15 and Levites concerning any **m**
30: 4 And the **m** pleased the king and
Ezra 5: 5 was returned concerning this **m**.
5:17 his pleasure concerning this **m**.
10: 4 for this **m** is your
10: 9 trembling because of this **m**
10:13 who have transgressed in this **m**.
10:14 turned away from us in this **m**.
10:16 tenth month to examine the **m**.
Esth 2:22 So the **m** became known to
2:23 an inquiry was made into the **m**,
9:26 they had seen concerning this **m**,
Job 9:19 If it is a **m** of strength,
19:28 Since the root of the **m** is
Ps 64: 5 themselves in an evil **m**;
Prov 11:13 a faithful spirit conceals a **m**.
17: 9 But he who repeats a **m**
18:13 He who answers a **m** before he
25: 2 the glory of God to conceal a **m**,
25: 2 of kings is to search out a **m**.
Eccl 5: 8 do not marvel at the **m**;
8: 6 Because for every **m** there is a
10:20 a bird in flight may tell the **m**.
12:13 the conclusion of the whole **m**:
Ezek 16:20 acts of harlotry a small **m**,
Dan 1:14 consented with them in this **m**,
2:10 earth who can tell the king's **m**;
3:16 no need to answer you in this **m**.
7:28 but I kept the **m** in my heart."
9:23 therefore consider the **m**,
Mk 1:45 it freely, and to spread the **m**,
10:10 Him again about the same **m**.
Acts 8:21 part nor portion in this **m**,
15: 6 together to consider this **m**.
17:32 will hear you again on this **m**.
18:14 If it were a **m** of wrongdoing or
1 Cor 6: 1 having a **m** against another, go
2 Cor 7:11 to be clear in this **m**.
9: 5 that it may be ready as a **m**
1 Th 4: 6 defraud his brother in this **m**,
1 Pe 4:16 let him glorify God in this **m**.

MATTERS (21/20)

Lev 5: 4 be guilty in any of these **m**.
5: 5 he is guilty in any of these **m**,
5:13 has committed in any of these **m**;
Deut 17: 8 **m** of controversy within your
2 Sam 11:19 have finished telling the **m** of
19:29 do you speak anymore of your **m**?
2 Chr 19:11 priest is over you in all **m**
19:11 of Judah, for all the king's **m**;
Neh 6: 7 a king in Judah!' Now these **m**
11:24 was the king's deputy in all **m**
Esth 9:31 their descendants concerning **m**
9:32 of Esther confirmed these **m** of
Ps 35:20 But they devise deceitful **m**
131: 1 I concern myself with great **m**,
Dan 1:20 And in all **m** of wisdom and
Mt 23:23 neglected the weightier **m** of
Acts 18:15 want to be a judge of such **m**.
25:20 be judged concerning these **m**.
1 Cor 6: 2 to judge the smallest **m**?
7:19 of God is what **m**.
1 Pe 4:15 a busybody in other people's **m**.

MATTHAN (2/1)

Mt 1:15 begot Eleazar, Eleazar begot **M**,
1:15 and **M** begot Jacob.

MATTHAT (2/2)

Lk 3:24 the son of **M**, the son of
3:29 son of Jorim, the son of **M**,

MATTHEW (5/5) LEVI

Mt 9: 9 He saw a man named **M** sitting at
10: 3 Thomas and **M** the tax collector;
Mk 3:18 Andrew, Philip, Bartholomew, **M**,
Lk 6:15 **M** and Thomas; James the son of
Acts 1:13 and Thomas; Bartholomew and **M**;

MATTHIAS (2/2)

Acts 1:23 who was surnamed Justus, and **M**.
1:26 and the lot fell on **M**.

MATTITHIAH (8/8)

1 Chr 9:31 **M** of the Levites, the firstborn
15:18 Eliab, Benaiah, Maaseiah, **M**,
15:21 **M**, Elipheleh, Mikneiah,
16: 5 Jeiel, Shemiramoth, Jehiel, **M**,
25: 3 Shimei, Hashabiah, and **M**,
25:21 the fourteenth for **M**,
Ezra 10:43 of the sons of Nebo: Jeiel, **M**,
Neh 8: 4 him, at his right hand, stood **M**,

MATTOCK (1/1)

1 Sam 13:20 each man's plowshare, his **m**,

MATTOCKS (1/1)

1 Sam 13:21 a pim for the plowshares, the **m**,

MATURE (3/3) MATURITY

1 Cor 2: 6 wisdom among those who are **m**,
14:20 but in understanding be **m**.
Phil 3:15 let us, as many as are **m**,

MATURED (1/1)

Ezek 16: 7 in the field; and you grew, **m**,

MATURITY (1/1) MATURE

Lk 8:14 life, and bring no fruit to **m**.

MAULED (1/1)

2 Ki 2:24 came out of the woods and **m**

MAW (KJV) See STOMACH

MAY (1491/1306) See APPENDIX

MAZZAROTH (1/1)

Job 38:32 Can you bring out **M** in its

ME (4065/3061) See APPENDIX

MEADOW (2/2)

Gen 41: 2 and fat; and they fed in the **m**.
41:18 and fat; and they fed in the **m**.

MEADOWS (1/1)

Ps 37:20 Like the splendor of the **m**,

MEAH (KJV) See HUNDRED

MEAL (14/13) GRAIN, MEALTIME

Gen 18: 6 ready three measures of fine **m**;
37:25 And they sat down to eat a **m**.
Num 5:15 of an EPHAH of barley **m**;
15:20 of the first of your ground **m**
15:21 Of the first of your ground **m**
1 Ki 4:22 of fine flour, sixty kors of **m**,
Isa 47: 2 the millstones and grind **m**.
Ezek 39:17 all sides to My sacrificial **m**
39:17 A great sacrificial **m** on the
39:19 At My sacrificial **m** Which I
44:30 the first of your ground **m**,
Hos 8: 7 It shall never produce **m**.
Mt 13:33 and hid in three measures of **m**
Lk 13:21 and hid in three measures of **m**

MEALTIME (1/1) MEAL

Ruth 2:14 Now Boaz said to her at **m**,

MEAN (22/22) MEANING, MEANS, MEANT

Gen 33: 8 What do you **m** by all this
Ex 12:26 What do you **m** by this service?'
Deut 29:24 the heat of this great anger **m**?
Josh 4: 6 What do these stones **m** to you?'
1 Sam 4: 6 in the camp of the Hebrews **m**?
4:14 the sound of this tumult **m**?
2 Sam 16: 2 What do you **m** to do with
Isa 3:15 What do you **m** by crushing My
10: 7 Yet he does not **m** so, Nor does
Ezek 17:12 not know what these things **m**?
18: 2 What do you **m** when you use this
37:18 you not show us what you **m** by
Jon 1: 6 said to him, "What do you **m**,
Lk 8: 9 "What does this parable **m**?
Acts 2:12 "Whatever could this **m**?
17:20 to know what these things **m**.
21:13 What do you **m** by weeping and
21:39 a citizen of no **m** city; and I
1 Cor 5:10 Yet I certainly did not **m**
2 Cor 8:13 For I do not **m** that others
Eph 4: 9 what does it **m** but that He also
Phil 1:22 this will **m** fruit from my

MEANING (6/6) MEAN

Gen 21:29 What is the **m** of these seven
Deut 6:20 What is the **m** of the
Dan 8:15 vision and was seeking the **m**,
Acts 27: 2 **m** to sail along the coasts of
1 Cor 14:11 if I do not know the **m** of the
Heb 7: 2 and then also king of Salem, **m** '

MEANS (59/59) MEAN

Ex 28:28 bind the breastplate by **m** of
34: 7 by no **m** clearing the guilty,
39:21 bound the breastplate by **m** of
Lev 7:24 but you shall by no **m** eat it.
Num 14:18 but He by no **m** clears the
14:30 you shall by no **m** enter the
Deut 8:19 if you by any **m** forget the
Josh 6:18 by all **m** abstain from the
Judg 16: 5 and by what **m** we may overpower
1 Sam 6: 3 but by all **m** return it to Him
20: 2 By no **m**! You shall not die!
2 Sam 14:14 away a life; but He devises **m**,
1 Ki 3:26 and by no **m** kill him!" But the
3:27 and by no **m** kill him; she is
20:39 if by any **m** he is missing, your
Ps 49: 7 None of them can by any **m**
Prov 6:26 For by **m** of a harlot A man
Dan 8:25 be broken without human **m**.
Mt 5:18 jot or one tittle will by no **m**
5:20 you will by no **m** enter the
5:26 you will by no **m** get out of
9:13 "But go and learn what this **m**:
10:42 he shall by no **m** lose his
12: 7 if you had known what this **m**,
18: 3 you will by no **m** enter the
24:34 this generation will by no **m**
24:35 but My words will by no **m** pass
Mk 9:41 he will by no **m** lose his
10:15 as a little child will by no **m**
13:30 this generation will by no **m**
13:31 but My words will by no **m** pass
16:18 it will by no **m** hurt them;
Lk 8:36 seen it told them by what **m**
10:19 and nothing shall by any **m** hurt
18:17 as a little child will by no **m**
21:32 this generation will by no **m**
21:33 but My words will by no **m** pass
22:67 you will by no **m** believe.
22:68 you will by no **m** answer Me or
Jn 4:48 you will by no **m** believe."
6:37 who comes to Me I will by no **m**
9:21 but by what **m** he now sees we do
10: 5 Yet they will by no **m** follow a
Acts 4: 9 by what **m** he has been made
13:41 which you will by no **m**
18:21 I must by all **m** keep this coming
27:12 if by any **m** they could reach
Rom 1:10 making request if, by some **m**,
11:14 if by any **m** I may provoke to
1 Cor 9:22 that I might by all **m** save
Gal 2: 2 lest by any **m** I might run,
Phil 3:11 if, by any **m**, I may attain
1 Th 3: 5 lest by some **m** the tempter had
4:15 coming of the Lord will by no **m**
2 Th 2: 3 Let no one deceive you by any **m**;
1 Tim 6: 5 suppose that godliness is a **m**
Heb 9:15 by **m** of death, for the
1 Pe 2: 6 on Him will by no **m** be
Rev 21:27 But there shall by no **m** enter it

MEANT (6/5) MEAN

Gen 50:20 you **m** evil against me; but God
50:20 but God **m** it for good,
Mk 9:10 what the rising from the dead **m**.
Lk 15:26 and asked what these things **m**.
18:36 passing by, he asked what it **m**.
Acts 10:17 this vision which he had seen **m**,

MEANTIME (3/3)

1 Ki 18:45 Now it happened in the **m** that
Lk 12: 1 In the **m**, when an
Jn 4:31 In the **m** His disciples urged

MEANWHILE (10/10)

1 Sam 2:21 **M** the child Samuel grew before
2 Sam 16:15 **M** Absalom and all the people,
20:11 **M** one of Joab's men stood near
1 Ki 3: 2 **M** the people sacrificed at the
20:16 **M** Ben-Hadad and the thirty-two
Jer 39:15 **M** the word of the LORD had
Acts 24:26 **M** he also hoped that money would
27:40 **m** loosing the rudder ropes;
Col 4: 3 **m** praying also for us, that God
Phm 1:22 But, **m**, also prepare a guest

MEARAH (1/1)

Josh 13: 4 and **M** that belongs to the

MEASURE (57/53) MEASURED, MEASURES, MEASURING

Num 35: 5 And you shall **m** outside the city
Deut 21: 2 your judges shall go out and **m**
25:15 weight, a perfect and just **m**,
Josh 3: 4 about two thousand cubits by **m**.
1 Ki 7:37 were of the same mold, one **m**,
2 Ki 25:16 all these articles was beyond **m**.
1 Chr 22: 3 bronze in abundance beyond **m**,
22:14 and bronze and iron beyond **m**,
2 Chr 3: 3 according to the former **m**) and
Ezra 9: 8 our eyes and give us a **m** of
Job 11: 9 Their **m** is longer than the
28:25 And apportion the waters by **m**.
Ps 39: 4 And what is the **m** of my days,
60: 6 I will divide Shechem And **m**
80: 5 them tears to drink in great **m**.
108: 7 I will divide Shechem And **m**
Isa 5:14 And opened its mouth beyond **m**;
27: 8 In **m**, by sending it away,
40:12 the dust of the earth in a **m**?
65: 7 Therefore I will **m** their
Jer 51:13 The **m** of your covetousness.
52:20 all these articles was beyond **m**.
52:21 line of twelve cubits could **m**
Ezek 4:11 shall also drink water by **m**,
4:16 and shall drink water by **m** and
41:17 inside and outside, by **m**.
43:10 and let them **m** the pattern.
45: 3 is the district you shall **m**:
45:11 the bath shall be of the same **m**,
45:11 their **m** shall be according to
Mic 6:10 And the short **m** that is an
Zech 2: 2 To **m** Jerusalem, to see what is
Mt 7: 2 and with the **m** you use, it will
23:32 the **m** of your fathers' guilt.
Mk 4:24 With the same **m** you use, it
6:51 amazed in themselves beyond **m**,
7:37 they were astonished beyond **m**,
Lk 6:38 it will be given to you: good **m**,
6:38 For with the same **m** that you
Jn 3:34 does not give the Spirit by **m**.
Rom 12: 3 God has dealt to each one a **m**
2 Cor 1: 8 that we were burdened beyond **m**,
10:13 will not boast beyond **m**,
10:15 not boasting of things beyond **m**,
11:23 abundant, in stripes above **m**,
12: 7 I should be exalted above **m** by
12: 7 me, lest I be exalted above **m**.
Gal 1:13 the church of God beyond **m** and
Eph 4: 7 was given according to the **m**
4:13 to the **m** of the stature of the
1 Th 2:16 so as always to fill up the **m**
Rev 11: 1 Rise and **m** the temple of God,
11: 2 and do not **m** it, for it has
18: 7 In the **m** that she glorified
18: 7 in the same **m** give her torment
21:15 with me had a gold reed to **m**
21:17 according to the **m** of a man,

MEASURED (52/49) MEASURE

Ex 16:18 So when they **m** it by omers, he
Ruth 3:15 he **m** six ephahs of barley, and
2 Sam 8: 2 he **m** them off with a line.
8: 2 With two lines he **m** off those
1 Ki 7:15 and a line of twelve cubits **m**
7:23 and a line of thirty cubits **m**
2 Chr 4: 2 and a line of thirty cubits **m**
Isa 40:12 Who has **m** the waters in the
40:12 **M** heaven with a span
Jer 31:37 "If heaven above can be **m**,
33:22 nor the sand of the sea **m**,
Ezek 40: 5 and he **m** the width of the wall
40: 6 and he went up its stairs and **m**
40: 8 He also **m** the vestibule of the
40: 9 Then he **m** the vestibule of the
40:11 He **m** the width of the entrance
40:13 Then he **m** the gateway from the
40:14 He **m** the gateposts, sixty cubits
40:19 Then he **m** the width from the
40:20 and he **m** its length and its
40:23 and he **m** from gateway to
40:24 and he **m** its gateposts and
40:27 and he **m** from gateway to
40:28 he **m** the southern gateway
40:32 he **m** the gateway according to
40:35 me to the north gateway and **m**
40:47 And he **m** the court, one hundred
40:48 vestibule of the temple and **m**
41: 1 me into the sanctuary and **m**
41: 2 and he **m** its length, forty
41: 3 Also he went inside and **m** the
41: 4 He **m** the length, twenty cubits;
41: 5 he **m** the wall of the temple,
41:13 So he **m** the temple, one hundred
41:15 He **m** the length of the building
42:15 and **m** it all around.
42:16 He **m** the east side with the
42:17 He **m** the north side, five
42:18 He **m** the south side, five
42:19 around to the west side and **m**
42:20 He **m** it on the four sides; it
47: 3 he **m** one thousand cubits, and
47: 4 Again he **m** one thousand and
47: 4 Again he **m** one thousand and
47: 5 Again he **m** one thousand, and
Hos 1:10 Which cannot be **m** or numbered.
Hab 3: 6 He stood and **m** the earth;
Mt 7: 2 it will be **m** back to you.
Mk 4:24 it will be **m** to you; and to you
Lk 6:38 it will be **m** back to you."
Rev 21:16 And he **m** the city with the
21:17 Then he **m** its wall: one hundred

MEASUREMENT (1/1)

Lev 19:35 in **m** of length, weight, or

MEASUREMENTS (13/13)

Ex 26: 2 curtains shall have the same **m**.
26: 8 shall all have the same **m**.
Job 38: 5 Who determined its **m**?
Ezek 40:21 had the same **m** as the first
40:22 had the same **m** as the gateway
40:24 according to these same **m**.
40:28 according to these same **m**.
40:29 were according to these same **m**;
40:32 according to these same **m**.
40:33 were according to these same **m**;
40:35 it according to these same **m**—
43:13 These are the **m** of the altar in
48:16 "These shall be its **m**:

MEASURES (9/9) MEASURE

Gen 18: 6 make ready three **m** of fine
Deut 25:14 have in your house differing **m**,
1 Chr 23:29 mixed and with all kinds of **m**
Prov 20:10 Diverse weights and diverse **m**,
Jer 13:25 The portion of your **m** from
Mt 13:33 a woman took and hid in three **m**
Lk 13:21 a woman took and hid in three **m**
16: 6 A hundred **m** of oil.' So he said
16: 7 A hundred **m** of wheat.' And he

MEASURING (17/16) MEASURE

2 Ki 21:13 stretch over Jerusalem the **m**
Isa 28:17 I will make justice the **m** line,
34:17 divided it among them with a **m**
Jer 52:21 a **m** line of twelve cubits could
Ezek 40: 3 He had a line of flax and a **m**
40: 5 In the man's hand was a **m** rod
42:15 Now when he had finished **m** the
42:16 the east side with the **m** rod,
42:16 five hundred rods by the **m** rod
42:17 five hundred rods by the **m** rod
42:18 five hundred rods by the **m** rod.
42:19 five hundred rods by the **m** rod.
48:30 **m** four thousand five hundred
48:33 **m** four thousand five hundred
Zech 2: 1 a man with a **m** line in his
2 Cor 10:12 **m** themselves by themselves,
Rev 11: 1 I was given a reed like a **m**

MEAT (56/47)

Ex 16: 3 when we sat by the pots of **m**
16: 8 when the LORD gives you **m** to
16:12 'At twilight you shall eat **m**,
22:31 you shall not eat **m** torn by
Num 11: 4 Who will give us **m** to eat?
11:13 Where am I to get **m** to give to
11:13 all over me, saying, 'Give us **m**,
11:18 tomorrow, and you shall eat **m**;
11:18 'Who will give us **m** to eat?
11:18 the LORD will give you **m**,
11:21 have said, 'I will give them **m**,
11:33 But while the **m** was still

Deut 12:15 you may slaughter and eat **m**
12:20 you, and you say, 'Let me eat **m**,
12:20 because you long to eat **m**,
12:20 you may eat as much **m** as your
12:23 may not eat the life with the **m**.
12:27 the **m** and the blood, on the
12:27 God, and you shall eat the **m**.
16: 4 nor shall any of the **m** which
Judg 6:19 The **m** he put in a basket, and
6:20 Take the **m** and the unleavened
6:21 and touched the **m** and the
6:21 of the rock and consumed the **m**
1 Sam 2:13 in his hand while the **m** was
2:15 Give **m** for roasting to the
2:15 for he will not take boiled **m**
25:11 my bread and my water and my **m**
2 Sam 6:19 a loaf of bread, a piece of **m**,
1 Ki 17: 6 ravens brought him bread and **m**
17: 6 and bread and **m** in the evening;
1 Chr 16: 3 a loaf of bread, a piece of **m**,
Job 31:31 not been satisfied with his **m**?
Ps 78:20 Can He provide **m** for His
78:27 He also rained **m** on them like
Prov 9: 2 She has slaughtered her **m**,
23:20 with gluttonous eaters of **m**;
Isa 22:13 Eating **m** and drinking wine:
44:16 With this half he eats **m**;
44:19 I have roasted **m** and eaten
Jer 7:21 to your sacrifices and eat **m**.
16: 4 and their corpses shall be **m**
19: 7 their corpses I will give as **m**
34:20 dead bodies shall be for **m** for
Ezek 11: 3 the caldron, and we are the **m**.
11: 7 in its midst, they are the **m**,
11:11 nor shall you be the **m** in its
24: 4 Gather pieces of **m** in it,
24:10 Cook the **m** well, Mix in the
33:25 You eat **m** with blood, you lift
Dan 10: 3 no **m** or wine came into my
Mic 3: 3 chop them in pieces Like **m**
Hag 2:12 If one carries holy **m** in the
Rom 14:21 It is good neither to eat **m**
1 Cor 8:13 I will never again eat **m**,
10:25 Eat whatever is sold in the **m**

MEBUNNAI (1/1)

2 Sam 23:27 **M** the Hushathite,

MECHERATHITE (1/1)

1 Chr 11:36 Hepher the **M**, Ahijah the

MECONAH (1/1)

Neh 11:28 in Ziklag and **M** and its

MEDAD (2/2)

Num 11:26 and the name of the other **M**.
11:27 Eldad and **M** are prophesying in

MEDAN (2/2)

Gen 25: 2 she bore him Zimran, Jokshan, **M**,
1 Chr 1:32 were Zimran, Jokshan, **M**,

MEDDLE (4/4)

Deut 2: 5 Do not **m** with them, for I will
2:19 do not harass them or **m** with
2 Ki 14:10 for why should you **m** with
2 Chr 25:19 why should you **m** with trouble,

MEDDLES (1/1)

Prov 26:17 He who passes by and **m** in a

MEDDLING (1/1)

2 Chr 35:21 Refrain from **m** with God,

MEDE (2/2) MEDES, MEDIA

Dan 5:31 And Darius the **M** received the
11: 1 the first year of Darius the **M**,

MEDEBA (5/5)

Num 21:30 as Nophah, Which reaches to **M**.
Josh 13: 9 and all the plain of **M** as far
13:16 ravine, and all the plain by **M**;
1 Chr 19: 7 who came and encamped before **M**.
Isa 15: 2 will wail over Nebo and over **M**;

MEDES (13/13) MEDE

2 Ki 17: 6 and in the cities of the **M**.
18:11 and in the cities of the **M**,
Esth 1:19 laws of the Persians and the **M**,
Isa 13:17 I will stir up the **M** against
Jer 25:25 and all the kings of the **M**;
51:11 spirit of the kings of the **M**.
51:28 With the kings of the **M**,
Dan 5:28 and given to the **M** and
6: 8 according to the law of the **M**
6:12 according to the law of the **M**
6:15 that it is the law of the **M**
9: 1 of the lineage of the **M**,
Acts 2: 9 Parthians and **M** and Elamites,

MEDIA (7/7) MEDE

Ezra 6: 2 that is in the province of **M**,
Esth 1: 3 powers of Persia and **M**,
1:14 seven princes of Persia and **M**,
1:18 noble ladies of Persia and **M**
10: 2 chronicles of the kings of **M**
Isa 21: 2 O **M**! All its sighing I have
Dan 8:20 they are the kings of **M** and

MEDIATE (1/1)

Gal 3:20 Now a mediator does not **m** for

MEDIATOR (8/8)

Job 9:33 Nor is there any **m** between us,
33:23 is a messenger for him, A **m**,
Gal 3:19 angels by the hand of a **m**.
3:20 Now a **m** does not mediate for
1 Tim 2: 5 there is one God and one **M**
Heb 8: 6 inasmuch as He is also **M** of a
9:15 for this reason He is the **M** of
12:24 to Jesus the **M** of the new

MEDIATORS (1/1)

Isa 43:27 And your **m** have transgressed

MEDICINE (2/2)

Prov 17:22 merry heart does good, like **m**,
Ezek 47:12 food, and their leaves for **m**.

MEDICINES (2/2)

Jer 30:13 You have no healing **m**.
46:11 In vain you will use many **m**;

MEDITATE (18/18) MEDITATES, MEDITATING, MEDITATION

Gen 24:63 And Isaac went out to **m** in the
Josh 1: 8 but you shall **m** in it day and
Ps 4: 4 **M** within your heart on your
63: 6 I **m** on You in the night
77: 6 I **m** within my heart, And my
77:12 I will also **m** on all Your work,
119:15 I will **m** on Your precepts,
119:27 So shall I **m** on Your wondrous
119:48 And I will **m** on Your statutes.
119:78 But I will **m** on Your
119:148 That I may **m** on Your word.
143: 5 I **m** on all Your works; I muse
145: 5 I will **m** on the glorious
Isa 33:18 Your heart will **m** on terror:
Mal 3:16 who fear the LORD And who **m**
Lk 21:14 it in your hearts not to **m**
Phil 4: 8 **m** on these things.
1 Tim 4:15 **M** on these things; give yourself

MEDITATES (2/2) MEDITATE

Ps 1: 2 And in His law he **m** day and
119:23 But Your servant **m** on Your

MEDITATING (1/1) MEDITATE

1 Ki 18:27 he is a god; either he is **m**,

MEDITATION (9/9) MEDITATE

Ps 5: 1 words, O LORD, Consider my **m**.
7: A **M** of David, which he sang to
9:16 the work of his own hands. **M**.
19:14 words of my mouth and the **m** of
49: 3 And the **m** of my heart shall
64: 1 Hear my voice, O God, in my **m**;
104:34 May my **m** be sweet to Him;
119:97 I love Your law! It is my **m**
119:99 For Your testimonies are my **m**.

MEDIUM (5/4) MEDIUMS

Lev 20:27 'A man or a woman who is a **m**,
Deut 18:11 one who conjures spells, or a **m**,
1 Sam 28: 7 "Find me a woman who is a **m**,
28: 7 there is a woman who is a **m**
1 Chr 10:13 also because he consulted a **m**

MEDIUM'S (1/1)

Isa 29: 4 Your voice shall be like a **m**,

MEDIUMS (9/9) MEDIUM

Lev 19:31 Give no regard to **m** and
20: 6 'And the person who turns to **m**
1 Sam 28: 3 And Saul had put the **m** and the
28: 9 how he has cut off the **m** and
2 Ki 21: 6 and consulted spiritists and **m**.
23:24 put away those who consulted **m**
2 Chr 33: 6 and consulted **m** and spiritists.
Isa 8:19 Seek those who are **m** and
19: 3 The **m** and the sorcerers.

MEEK (5/5) MEEKNESS

Ps 37:11 But the **m** shall inherit the
Isa 11: 4 decide with equity for the **m**
Zeph 2: 3 all you **m** of the earth,
3:12 will leave in your midst A **m**
Mt 5: 5 Blessed are the **m**, For they

MEEKNESS (5/5) MEEK

2 Cor 10: 1 am pleading with you by the **m**
Col 3:12 mercies, kindness, humility, **m**,
Jas 1:21 and receive with **m** the
3:13 his works are done in the **m**
1 Pe 3:15 is in you, with **m** and fear;

MEET (115/111) MEETING, MEETS, MET

Gen 14:17 the king of Sodom went out to **m**
18: 2 he ran from the tent door to **m**
19: 1 he rose to **m** them, and he bowed
23: 8 and **m** with Ephron the son of
24:17 And the servant ran to **m** her and
24:65 man walking in the field to **m**
29:13 that he ran to **m** him, and
30:16 Leah went out to **m** him and
32: 6 and he also is coming to **m** you,
33: 4 But Esau ran to **m** him, and
46:29 and went up to Goshen to **m** his
Ex 4:14 he is also coming out to **m** you.
4:27 Go into the wilderness to **m**
5:20 and Aaron who stood there to **m**
7:15 stand by the river's bank to **m**
18: 7 So Moses went out to **m** his
19:17 the people out of the camp to **m**
23: 4 If you **m** your enemy's ox or his
25:22 And there I will **m** with you, and
29:42 where I will **m** you to speak
29:43 And there I will **m** with the
30: 6 where I will **m** with you.
30:36 of meeting where I will **m** with
Num 3:38 to **m** the needs of the children
17: 4 where I **m** with you.
22:36 he went out to **m** him at the
23: 3 the LORD will come to **m** me,
23:15 your burnt offering while I **m**
31:13 went to **m** them outside the
Deut 23: 4 because they did not **m** you with
Josh 2:16 lest the pursuers **m** you. Hide
9:11 and go to **m** them, and say to
Judg 4:18 And Jael went out to **m** Sisera,
4:22 Jael came out to **m** him, and
6:35 and they came up to **m** them.
11:31 of the doors of my house to **m**
11:34 coming out to **m** him with
19: 3 he was glad to **m** him.
Ruth 2:22 and that people do not **m** you in
1 Sam 10: 3 up to God at Bethel will **m** you,
10: 5 that you will **m** a group of
10:10 was a group of prophets to **m**
13:10 and Saul went out to **m** him,
15:12 rose early in the morning to **m**
17:48 and came and drew near to **m**
17:48 and ran toward the army to **m**
18: 6 to **m** King Saul, with
25:32 who sent you this day to **m** me!
25:34 you had hastened and come to **m**
30:21 So they went out to **m** David and
30:21 out to meet David and to **m** the
2 Sam 6:20 daughter of Saul came out to **m**
10: 5 he sent to **m** them, because the
15:32 Hushai the Archite coming to **m**
19:15 to go to **m** the king, to escort
19:16 down with the men of Judah to **m**
19:20 of Joseph to go down to **m** my
19:24 the son of Saul came down to **m**
19:25 he had come to Jerusalem to **m**
1 Ki 2: 8 But he came down to **m** me at the
2:19 And the king rose up to **m** her
18:16 So Obadiah went to **m** Ahab, and
18:16 and Ahab went to **m** Elijah.
21:18 go down to **m** Ahab king of
2 Ki 1: 3 go up to **m** the messengers of
1: 6 A man came up to **m** us, and said
1: 7 man was it who came up to **m**
2:15 And they came to **m** him, and
4:26 Please run now to **m** her, and say
4:29 If you **m** anyone, do not greet
4:31 Therefore he went back to **m**
5:21 got down from the chariot to **m**
5:26 back from his chariot to **m** you?
8: 8 and go to **m** the man of God, and
8: 9 So Hazael went to **m** him and took
9:17 a horseman and send him to **m**
9:18 So the horseman went to **m** him,
9:21 and they went out to **m** Jehu,
10:15 coming to **m** him; and he
16:10 King Ahaz went to Damascus to **m**
1 Chr 12:17 And David went out to **m** them,
19: 5 and he sent to **m** them, because
2 Chr 15: 2 And he went out to **m** Asa, and
19: 2 Hanani the seer went out to **m**
Neh 6: 2 let us **m** together among the
6:10 Let us **m** together in the house
Job 5:14 They **m** with darkness in the
Ps 21: 3 For You **m** him with the
59:10 God of mercy shall come to **m**
79: 8 mercies come speedily to **m** us,
Prov 7:15 So I came out to **m** you,
8: 2 the way, where the paths **m**.
17:12 Let a man **m** a bear robbed of
Isa 7: 3 Go out now to **m** Ahaz, you and
14: 9 To **m** you at your coming;
34:14 of the desert shall also **m**
64: 5 You **m** him who rejoices and does
Jer 41: 6 went out from Mizpah to **m** them,
51:31 One runner will run to **m**
51:31 And one messenger to **m**
Hos 13: 8 I will **m** them like a bear
Am 4:12 Prepare to **m** your God,
Zech 2: 3 angel was coming out to **m** him,
Mt 8:34 the whole city came out to **m**
25: 1 their lamps and went out to **m**

25: 6 go out to *m* him!'
Mk 14:13 and a man will *m* you carrying a
Lk 14:31 is able with ten thousand to *m*
22:10 a man will *m* you carrying a
Jn 12:13 of palm trees and went out to *m*
18:20 temple, where the Jews always *m*,
Acts 21:22 The assembly must certainly *m*,
28:15 they came to *m* us as far as
1 Th 4:17 with them in the clouds to *m*
Titus 3:14 to *m* urgent needs, that they

MEETING (149/143) MEET

Ex 27:21 "In the tabernacle of *m*,
28:43 come into the tabernacle of *m*,
29: 4 the door of the tabernacle of *m*,
29:10 before the tabernacle of *m*,
29:11 the door of the tabernacle of *m*.
29:30 he enters the tabernacle of *m*
29:32 the door of the tabernacle of *m*.
29:42 the door of the tabernacle of *m*
29:44 consecrate the tabernacle of *m*
30:16 service of the tabernacle of *m*,
30:18 it between the tabernacle of *m*
30:20 go into the tabernacle of *m*,
30:26 anoint the tabernacle of *m* and
30:36 in the tabernacle of *m* where I
31: 7 "the tabernacle of *m*,
33: 7 called it the tabernacle of *m*.
33: 7 went out to the tabernacle of *m*
35:21 the work of the tabernacle of *m*,
38: 8 the door of the tabernacle of *m*.
38:30 the door of the tabernacle of *m*,
39:32 the tabernacle of the tent of *m*
39:40 tabernacle, for the tent of *m*;
40: 2 the tabernacle of the tent of *m*.
40: 6 the tabernacle of the tent of *m*.
40: 7 between the tabernacle of *m*
40:12 the door of the tabernacle of *m*
40:22 table in the tabernacle of *m*,
40:24 in the tabernacle of *m*,
40:26 altar in the tabernacle of *m*
40:29 the tabernacle of the tent of *m*,
40:30 between the tabernacle of *m*
40:32 went into the tabernacle of *m*,
40:34 covered the tabernacle of *m*,
40:35 to enter the tabernacle of *m*,
Lev 1: 1 to him from the tabernacle of *m*,
1: 3 the door of the tabernacle of *m*
1: 5 the door of the tabernacle of *m*.
3: 2 the door of the tabernacle of *m*;
3: 8 it before the tabernacle of *m*;
3:13 it before the tabernacle of *m*;
4: 4 the door of the tabernacle of *m*
4: 5 bring it to the tabernacle of *m*.
4: 7 which is in the tabernacle of *m*;
4: 7 the door of the tabernacle of *m*.
4:14 it before the tabernacle of *m*.
4:16 blood to the tabernacle of *m*.
4:18 is in the tabernacle of *m*;
4:18 the door of the tabernacle of *m*.
6:16 court of the tabernacle of *m*
6:26 court of the tabernacle of *m*.
6:30 into the tabernacle of *m*,
8: 3 the door of the tabernacle of *m*.
8: 4 the door of the tabernacle of *m*.
8:31 the door of the tabernacle of *m*,
8:33 the door of the tabernacle of *m*
8:35 the door of the tabernacle of *m*
9: 5 before the tabernacle of *m*.
9:23 went into the tabernacle of *m*,
10: 7 the door of the tabernacle of *m*,
10: 9 you go into the tabernacle of *m*,
12: 6 the door of the tabernacle of *m*.
14:11 the door of the tabernacle of *m*.
14:23 the door of the tabernacle of *m*,
15:14 the door of the tabernacle of *m*,
15:29 the door of the tabernacle of *m*.
16: 7 the door of the tabernacle of *m*.
16:16 do for the tabernacle of *m*
16:17 no man in the tabernacle of *m*
16:20 Place, the tabernacle of *m*,
16:23 come into the tabernacle of *m*,
16:33 for the tabernacle of *m* and
17: 4 door of the tabernacle of *m* to
17: 5 the door of the tabernacle of *m*,
17: 6 the door of the tabernacle of *m*,
17: 9 the door of the tabernacle of *m*,
19:21 the door of the tabernacle of *m*,
24: 3 in the tabernacle of *m*,
Num 1: 1 Sinai, in the tabernacle of *m*,
2: 2 from the tabernacle of *m*.
2:17 And the tabernacle of *m* shall
3: 7 before the tabernacle of *m*,
3: 8 of the tabernacle of *m*,
3:25 Gershon in the tabernacle of *m*
3:25 the door of the tabernacle of *m*,
3:38 before the tabernacle of *m*,
4: 3 the work in the tabernacle of *m*.
4: 4 Kohath in the tabernacle of *m*,
4:15 things in the tabernacle of *m*
4:23 the work in the tabernacle of *m*.
4:25 and the tabernacle of *m* with
4:25 the door of the tabernacle of *m*,
4:28 Gershon in the tabernacle of *m*.
4:30 the work of the tabernacle of *m*.
4:31 service for the tabernacle of *m*:
4:33 service for the tabernacle of *m*,
4:35 for work in the tabernacle of *m*;
4:37 serve in the tabernacle of *m*,
4:39 for work in the tabernacle of *m*—
4:41 serve in the tabernacle of *m*,
4:43 for work in the tabernacle of *m*—
4:47 burdens in the tabernacle of *m*—
6:10 the door of the tabernacle of *m*;
6:13 the door of the tabernacle of *m*.
6:18 the door of the tabernacle of *m*,
7: 5 the work of the tabernacle of *m*;
7:89 went into the tabernacle of *m*
8: 9 before the tabernacle of *m*,
8:15 to service the tabernacle of *m*.
8:19 Israel in the tabernacle of *m*,
8:22 work in the tabernacle of *m*
8:24 the work of the tabernacle of *m*;
8:26 brethren in the tabernacle of *m*,
10: 3 the door of the tabernacle of *m*.
11:16 them to the tabernacle of *m*,
12: 4 to the tabernacle of *m*!"
14:10 in the tabernacle of *m* before
16:18 the door of the tabernacle of *m*
16:19 the door of the tabernacle of *m*.
16:42 toward the tabernacle of *m*;
16:43 came before the tabernacle of *m*.
16:50 the door of the tabernacle of *m*,
17: 4 them in the tabernacle of *m*
18: 4 needs of the tabernacle of *m*,
18: 6 the work of the tabernacle of *m*.
18:21 the work of the tabernacle of *m*.
18:22 come near the tabernacle of *m*,
18:23 the work of the tabernacle of *m*,
18:31 work in the tabernacle of *m*.
19: 4 in front of the tabernacle of *m*.
20: 6 the door of the tabernacle of *m*,
25: 6 the door of the tabernacle of *m*.
27: 2 doorway of the tabernacle of *m*,
31:54 it into the tabernacle of *m* as
Deut 31:14 in the tabernacle of *m*,
31:14 in the tabernacle of *m*.
Josh 18: 1 and set up the tabernacle of *m*
19:51 the door of the tabernacle of *m*.
1 Sam 2:22 the door of the tabernacle of *m*.
1 Ki 8: 4 the LORD, the tabernacle of *m*,
1 Chr 6:32 place of the tabernacle of *m*,
9:21 the door of the tabernacle of *m*.
23:32 needs of the tabernacle of *m*,
2 Chr 1: 3 for the tabernacle of *m* with
1: 6 was at the tabernacle of *m*,
1:13 from before the tabernacle of *m*,
5: 5 up the ark, the tabernacle of *m*,
Ps 74: 4 roar in the midst of Your *m*
74: 8 They have burned up all the *m*
Isa 1:13 iniquity and the sacred *m*.

MEETINGS (1/1)

Ezek 44:24 statutes in all My appointed *m*,

MEETS (4/4) MEET

Gen 32:17 When Esau my brother *m* you and
Num 35:19 when he *m* him, he shall put him
35:21 the murderer to death when he *m*
Acts 25:16 before the accused *m* the

MEGIDDO (12/12)

Josh 12:21 of Taanach, one; the king of *M*,
17:11 and the inhabitants of *M* and
Judg 1:27 or the inhabitants of *M* and its
5:19 In Taanach, by the waters of *M*;
1 Ki 4:12 son of Ahilud, in Taanach, *M*,
9:15 the wall of Jerusalem, Hazor, *M*,
2 Ki 9:27 is by Ibleam. Then he fled to *M*,
23:29 Necho killed him at *M* when he
23:30 his body in a chariot from *M*,
1 Chr 7:29 *M* and its towns, Dor and its
2 Chr 35:22 to fight in the Valley of *M*.
Zech 12:11 Hadad Rimmon in the plain of *M*.

MEGIDDON (KJV) See MEGIDDO

MEHETABEL (3/3)

Gen 36:39 His wife's name was *M*,
1 Chr 1:50 His wife's name was *M* the
Neh 6:10 son of Delaiah, the son of *M*,

MEHIDA (2/2)

Ezra 2:52 sons of Bazluth, the sons of *M*,
Neh 7:54 sons of Bazlith, the sons of *M*,

MEHIR (1/1)

1 Chr 4:11 the brother of Shuhah begot *M*,

MEHOLATHITE (2/2)

1 Sam 18:19 she was given to Adriel the *M*
2 Sam 21: 8 the son of Barzillai the *M*;

MEHUJAEL (2/1)

Gen 4:18 was born Irad; and Irad begot *M*,
4:18 and *M* begot Methushael, and

MEHUMAN (1/1)

Esth 1:10 merry with wine, he commanded *M*,

MEHUNIM (KJV) See MEUNIM

MEHUNIMS (KJV) See MEUNITES

MEKONAH (KJV) See MECONAH

MELATIAH (1/1)

Neh 3: 7 And next to them *M* the

MELCHI (2/2)

Lk 3:24 son of Levi, the son of *M*,
3:28 the son of *M*, the son of

MELCHIAH (1/1)

Jer 21: 1 to him Pashhur the son of *M*,

MELCHISEDEC (KJV) See MELCHIZEDEK

MELCHI-SHUA (KJV) See MALCHISHUA

MELCHIZEDEK (11/11)

Gen 14:18 Then *M* king of Salem brought
Ps 110: 4 According to the order of *M*.
Heb 5: 6 to the order of *M*";
5:10 to the order of *M*,
6:20 according to the order of *M*.
7: 1 For this *M*, king of Salem,
7:10 the loins of his father when *M*
7:11 according to the order of *M*,
7:15 in the likeness of *M*,
7:17 to the order of *M*.
7:21 to the order of *M*"),

MELEA (1/1)

Lk 3:31 the son of *M*, the son of

MELECH (2/2)

1 Chr 8:35 sons of Micah were Pithon, *M*,
9:41 sons of Micah were Pithon, *M*,

MELICHU (1/1)

Neh 12:14 of *M*, Jonathan;

MELICU (KJV) See MELICHU

MELITA (KJV) See MALTA

MELODY (5/5)

Ps 33: 2 Make *m* to Him with an
Isa 23:16 forgotten harlot; Make sweet *m*,
51: 3 and the voice of *m*.
Am 5:23 For I will not hear the *m* of
Eph 5:19 singing and making *m* in your

MELONS (1/1)

Num 11: 5 in Egypt, the cucumbers, the *m*,

MELT (16/15) MELTED, MELTS

Ex 15:15 inhabitants of Canaan will *m*
Josh 14: 8 made the heart of the people *m*,
2 Sam 17:10 will *m* completely. For all
Ps 39:11 You make his beauty *m* away
97: 5 The mountains *m* like wax at the
112:10 He will gnash his teeth and *m*
Isa 13: 7 Every man's heart will *m*,
19: 1 And the heart of Egypt will *m*
Ezek 21: 7 it comes, every heart will *m*,
21:15 That the heart may *m* and many
22:20 to *m* it; so I will gather you
22:20 I will leave you there and *m*
Mic 1: 4 The mountains will *m* under Him,
Nah 1: 5 quake before Him, The hills *m*,
2 Pe 3:10 and the elements will *m* with
3:12 and the elements will *m* with

MELTED (11/10) MELT

Ex 16:21 when the sun became hot, it *m*.
Josh 2:11 these things, our hearts *m*;
5: 1 over, that their heart *m*;
7: 5 the hearts of the people *m* and
Ps 22:14 It has *m* within Me.
46: 6 uttered His voice, the earth *m*.
Isa 34: 3 And the mountains shall be *m*
Ezek 22:21 and you shall be *m* in its
22:22 As silver is *m* in the midst of a
22:22 so shall you be *m* in its midst;
24:11 That its filthiness may be *m*

MELTING (1/1)

1 Sam 14:16 *m* away; and they went here and

MELTS (7/7) MELT

Ps 58: 8 them be like a snail which *m*
68: 2 As wax *m* before the fire,
107:26 Their soul *m* because of
119:28 My soul *m* from heaviness;
147:18 He sends out His word and *m*
Am 9: 5 who touches the earth and it *m*,

Nah 2:10 and waste! The heart **m**,

MELZAR (KJV) See STEWARD

MEMBER (8/7) MEMBERS

Lev 25:47 or to a **m** of the stranger's
Mk 15:43 a prominent council **m**,
Lk 23:50 a man named Joseph, a council **m**,
1 Cor 12:14 in fact the body is not one **m**
12:19 And if they were all one **m**,
12:26 And if one **m** suffers, all the
12:26 or if one **m** is honored, all the
Jas 3: 5 so the tongue is a little **m**

MEMBERS (32/24) MEMBER

Job 17: 7 And all my **m** are like
Mt 5:29 for you that one of your **m**
5:30 for you that one of your **m**
Rom 6:13 And do not present your **m** as
6:13 and your **m** as instruments of
6:19 just as you presented your **m**
6:19 so now present your **m** as
7: 5 the law were at work in our **m**
7:23 But I see another law in my **m**,
7:23 the law of sin which is in my **m**.
12: 4 For as we have many **m** in one
12: 4 but all the **m** do not have the
12: 5 and individually **m** of one
1 Cor 6:15 know that your bodies are **m** of
6:15 Shall I then take the **m** of
6:15 of Christ and make them **m** of
12:12 the body is one and has many **m**,
12:12 but all the **m** of that one body,
12:18 But now God has set the **m**,
12:20 now indeed there are many **m**,
12:22 those **m** of the body which seem
12:23 And those **m** of the body which
12:25 but that the **m** should have the
12:26 all the **m** suffer with it;
12:26 all the **m** rejoice with it.
12:27 of Christ, and **m** individually.
Eph 2:19 citizens with the saints and **m**
4:25 for we are **m** of one another.
5:30 For we are **m** of His body, of His
Col 3: 5 Therefore put to death your **m**
Jas 3: 6 tongue is so set among our **m**
4: 1 pleasure that war in your **m**?

MEMORABLE (1/1)

Hos 12: 5 The LORD is His **m** name.

MEMORIAL (26/25) MEMORY

Ex 3:15 and this is My **m** to all
12:14 this day shall be to you a **m**;
13: 9 to you on your hand and as a **m**
17:14 Write this for a **m** in the book
28:12 shoulders of the ephod as **m**
28:12 on his two shoulders as a **m**.
28:29 as a **m** before the LORD
30:16 that it may be a **m** for the
39: 7 shoulders of the ephod as **m**
Lev 2: 2 priest shall burn it as a **m**
2: 9 from the grain offering a **m**
2:16 the priest shall burn the **m**
5:12 take his handful of it as a **m**
6:15 as a **m** to the LORD.
23:24 a **m** of blowing of trumpets,
24: 7 it may be on the bread for a **m**,
Num 5:26 as its **m** portion, burn it on
10:10 and they shall be a **m** for you
16:40 to be a **m** to the children of
31:54 tabernacle of meeting as a **m**
Josh 4: 7 these stones shall be for a **m**
Neh 2:20 have no heritage or right or **m**
Zech 6:14 crown shall be for a **m** in the
Mt 26:13 done will also be told as a **m**
Mk 14: 9 done will also be told as a **m**
Acts 10: 4 your alms have come up for a **m**

MEMORY (9/9) MEMORIAL

Deut 32:26 I will make the **m** of them to
Esth 9:28 and that the **m** of them should
Job 18:17 The **m** of him perishes from the
Ps 9: 6 Even their **m** has perished.
109:15 That He may cut off the **m** of
145: 7 They shall utter the **m** of Your
Prov 10: 7 The **m** of the righteous is
Eccl 9: 5 For the **m** of them is
Isa 26:14 And made all their **m** to

MEMPHIS (1/1) NOPH

Hos 9: 6 **M** shall bury them. Nettles

MEMUCAN (4/4)

Esth 1:14 Tarshish, Meres, Marsena, and **M**,
1:16 And **M** answered before the king
1:21 did according to the word of **M**.
Mk 11:32 From **m**'"—they feared the

MEN (1592/1428) MAN, MEN-PLEASERS, MEN'S, PEOPLE

Gen 4:26 Then **m** began to call on the
6: 1 when **m** began to multiply on the
6: 2 of God saw the daughters of **m**,
6: 4 came in to the daughters of **m**
6: 4 Those were the mighty **m** who
6: 4 were of old, **m** of renown.
11: 5 the tower which the sons of **m**
12:20 So Pharaoh commanded his **m**
13:13 But the **m** of Sodom were
14:24 except only what the young **m**
14:24 and the portion of the **m** who
17:23 every male among the **m** of
17:27 and all the **m** of his house, born
18: 2 three **m** were standing by him;
18:16 Then the **m** rose from there and
18:22 Then the **m** turned away from
19: 4 the **m** of the city, the men of
19: 4 the **m** of Sodom, both old and
19: 5 Where are the **m** who came to you
19: 8 only do nothing to these **m**,
19:10 But the **m** reached out their
19:11 And they struck the **m** who were
19:12 Then the **m** said to Lot, "Have
19:16 the **m** took hold of his hand,
20: 8 and the **m** were very much
22: 3 and took two of his young **m**
22: 5 And Abraham said to his young **m**,
22:19 Abraham returned to his young **m**,
24:13 and the daughters of the **m** of
24:32 his feet and the feet of the **m**
24:54 And he and the **m** who were with
24:59 and Abraham's servant and his **m**.
26: 7 And the **m** of the place asked
26: 7 lest the **m** of the place kill me
29:22 gathered together all the **m** of
32: 6 and four hundred **m** are with
32:28 struggled with God and with **m**,
33: 1 with him were four hundred **m**.
33:13 And if the **m** should drive them
34: 7 and the **m** were grieved and very
34:20 and spoke with the **m** of their
34:21 These **m** are at peace with us.
34:22 on this condition will the **m**
38:21 Then he asked the **m** of that
38:22 the **m** of the place said there
39:11 and none of the **m** of the house
39:14 that she called to the **m** of her
41: 8 of Egypt and all its wise **m**.
42:11 man's sons; we are honest **m**;
42:19 "If you are honest **m**,
42:31 said to him, 'We are honest **m**;
42:33 know that you are honest **m**:
42:34 but that you are honest **m**.
43:15 So the **m** took that present and
43:16 Take these **m** to my home, and
43:16 for these **m** will dine with me
43:17 and the man brought the **m** into
43:18 Now the **m** were afraid because
43:24 So the man brought the **m** into
43:33 and the **m** looked in
44: 3 the **m** were sent away, they and
44: 4 steward, "Get up, follow the **m**;
46:32 And the **m** are shepherds, for
47: 2 And he took five **m** from among
47: 6 if you know any competent **m**
Ex 2:13 two Hebrew **m** were fighting, and
4:19 for all the **m** who sought your
5: 9 more work be laid on the **m**,
7:11 Pharaoh also called the wise **m**
10: 7 Let the **m** go, that they may
10:11 so! Go now, you who are **m**,
12:37 about six hundred thousand **m** on
15:15 The mighty **m** of Moab,
17: 9 Choose us some **m** and go out,
18:21 from all the people able **m**,
18:21 **m** of truth, hating
18:25 And Moses chose able **m** out of
21:18 If **m** contend with each other,
21:22 If **m** fight, and hurt a woman
22:31 And you shall be holy **m** to Me:
24: 5 Then he sent young **m** of the
32:28 And about three thousand **m** of
34:23 times in the year all your **m**
35:22 both **m** and women, as many as
35:29 all the **m** and women whose
38:26 five hundred and fifty **m**.
Lev 7:25 fat of the animal of which **m**
18:27 all these abominations the **m**
27: 9 If it is an animal that **m** may
27:29 doomed to destruction among **m**,
Num 1: 5 These are the names of the **m**
1:17 Moses and Aaron took these **m**
1:44 the leaders of Israel, twelve **m**,
5: 6 or woman commits any sin that **m**
9: 6 Now there were certain **m** who
9: 7 And those **m** said to him, "We
11:16 Gather to Me seventy **m** of the
11:21 are six hundred thousand **m** on
11:24 and he gathered the seventy **m**
11:26 But two **m** had remained in the
11:28 assistant, one of his choice **m**,
12: 3 more than all **m** who were on
13: 2 Send **m** to spy out the land of
13: 3 all of them **m** who were heads
13:16 These are the names of the **m**
13:24 of the cluster which the **m** of
13:31 But the **m** who had gone up with
13:32 whom we saw in it are **m** of
14:22 because all these **m** who have
14:36 Now the **m** whom Moses sent to spy
14:37 those very **m** who brought the
14:38 of the **m** who went to spy out
16: 1 Peleth, sons of Reuben, took **m**;
16: 2 congregation, **m** of renown.
16:14 you put out the eyes of these **m**?
16:26 the tents of these wicked **m**!
16:29 If these **m** die naturally like
16:29 men die naturally like all **m**,
16:29 by the common fate of all **m**,
16:30 will understand that these **m**
16:32 their households and all the **m**
16:35 the two hundred and fifty **m**
16:38 The censers of these **m** who
20:20 out against them with many **m**
22: 9 Who are these **m** with you?"
22:20 If the **m** come to call you, rise
22:35 said to Balaam, "Go with the **m**,
25: 5 Every one of you kill his **m** who
26:10 two hundred and fifty **m**;
31:21 the priest said to the **m** of
31:28 tribute for the LORD on the **m**
31:32 which the **m** of war had taken,
31:42 Moses separated from the **m** who
31:49 have taken a count of the **m** of
31:53 (The **m** of war had taken spoil,
32:11 Surely none of the **m** who came up
32:14 place, a brood of sinful **m**,
32:21 and all your armed **m** cross over
34:17 These are the names of the **m**
34:19 "These are the names of the **m**:
Deut 1:13 and knowledgeable **m** from among
1:15 wise and knowledgeable **m**,
1:22 Let us send **m** before us, and let
1:23 so I took twelve of your **m**,
1:35 Surely not one of these **m** of
2:14 all the generation of the **m** of
2:16 when all the **m** of war had
2:34 and we utterly destroyed the **m**,
3: 6 utterly destroying the **m**,
3:18 All you **m** of valor shall cross
4: 3 from among you all the **m** who
13:13 Corrupt **m** have gone out from
19:14 which the **m** of old have set, in
19:17 then both **m** in the controversy
21:21 Then all the **m** of his city shall
22:21 and the **m** of her city shall
25: 1 there is a dispute between **m**,
25:11 If two **m** fight together, and
27:14 voice and say to all the **m** of
29:10 all the **m** of Israel,
31:12 **m** and women and little ones,
32:26 of them to cease from among **m**,
33: 6 Nor let his **m** be few."
Josh 1:14 all your mighty **m** of valor, and
2: 1 the son of Nun sent out two **m**
2: 2 **m** have come here tonight from
2: 3 Bring out the **m** who have come to
2: 4 Then the woman took the two **m**
2: 4 the **m** came to me, but I did not
2: 5 that the **m** went out. Where the
2: 5 Where the **m** went I do not know;
2: 7 Then the **m** pursued them by the
2: 9 and said to the **m**:
2:14 So the **m** answered her, "Our
2:17 So the **m** said to her: "We will
2:23 So the two **m** returned, descended
3:12 take for yourselves twelve **m**
4: 2 Take for yourselves twelve **m**
4: 4 Then Joshua called the twelve **m**
4:12 And the **m** of Reuben, the men of
4:12 the **m** of Gad, and half the
5: 4 all the **m** of war, had died in
5: 6 all the people who were **m** of
6: 2 and the mighty **m** of valor.
6: 3 all you **m** of war; you shall go
6: 9 The armed **m** went before the
6:13 And the armed **m** went before
6:22 Joshua had said to the two **m**
6:23 And the young **m** who had been
7: 2 Now Joshua sent **m** from Jericho
7: 2 So the **m** went up and spied
7: 3 about two or three thousand **m**
7: 4 So about three thousand **m** went
7: 4 but they fled before the **m** of
7: 5 And the **m** of Ai struck down
7: 5 struck down about thirty-six **m**,
8: 3 chose thirty thousand mighty **m**
8:12 he took about five thousand **m**
8:14 that the **m** of the city hurried
8:20 And when the **m** of Ai looked
8:21 back and struck down the **m** of
8:25 both **m** and women, were twelve
9: 6 and said to him and to the **m** of
9: 7 Then the **m** of Israel said to the
9:14 Then the **m** of Israel took some
10: 2 and all its **m** were mighty.
10: 6 And the **m** of Gibeon sent to
10: 7 and all the mighty **m** of valor.
10:18 and set **m** by it to guard them.
10:24 Joshua called for all the **m** of
10:24 said to the captains of the **m**
18: 4 out from among you three **m** for
18: 8 Then the **m** arose to go away;
18: 9 So the **m** went, passed through
24:11 And the **m** of Jericho fought
Judg 1: 4 and they killed ten thousand **m**
1:23 So the house of Joseph sent **m** to
3:29 killed about ten thousand **m** of
3:29 all stout **m** of valor; not a man
3:31 who killed six hundred **m** of the
4: 6 take with you ten thousand **m** of
4:10 he went up with ten thousand **m**
4:14 Mount Tabor with ten thousand **m**
6:27 So Gideon took ten **m** from among
6:27 father's household and the **m**
6:28 And when the **m** of the city
6:30 Then the **m** of the city said to
7: 6 mouth, was three hundred **m**;

M

7: 7 By the three hundred **m** who
7: 8 retained those three hundred **m**.
7:11 to the outpost of the armed **m**
7:16 he divided the three hundred **m**
7:19 So Gideon and the hundred **m** who
7:23 And the **m** of Israel gathered
7:24 Then all the **m** of Ephraim
8: 1 Now the **m** of Ephraim said to
8: 4 he and the three hundred **m** who
8: 5 Then he said to the **m** of
8: 8 And the **m** of Penuel answered
8: 8 of Penuel answered him as the **m**
8: 9 So he also spoke to the **m** of
8:10 hundred and twenty thousand **m**
8:14 he caught a young man of the **m**
8:14 and its elders, seventy-seven **m**.
8:15 Then he came to the **m** of Succoth
8:15 give bread to your weary **m**?
8:16 and with them he taught the **m**
8:17 of Penuel and killed the **m** of
8:18 What kind of **m** were they whom
8:22 Then the **m** of Israel said to
9: 2 in the hearing of all the **m** of
9: 3 in the hearing of all the **m** of
9: 4 hired worthless and reckless **m**;
9: 6 And all the **m** of Shechem
9: 7 you **m** of Shechem, That God may
9: 9 which they honor God and **m**,
9:13 Which cheers both God and **m**,
9:18 king over the **m** of Shechem,
9:20 Abimelech and devour the **m** of
9:20 and let fire come from the **m** of
9:23 between Abimelech and the **m** of
9:23 and the **m** of Shechem dealt
9:24 and on the **m** of Shechem, who
9:25 And the **m** of Shechem set men in
9:25 And the men of Shechem set **m** in
9:26 and the **m** of Shechem put their
9:28 Serve the **m** of Hamor the father
9:36 mountains as if they were **m**.
9:39 leading the **m** of Shechem, and
9:46 Now when all the **m** of the tower
9:47 told Abimelech that all the **m**
9:49 about a thousand **m** and women.
9:51 and all the **m** and women—all the
9:54 lest **m** say of me, 'A woman
9:55 And when the **m** of Israel saw
9:57 And all the evil of the **m** of
11: 3 and worthless **m** banded together
12: 1 Then the **m** of Ephraim gathered
12: 4 gathered together all the **m** of
12: 4 And the **m** of Gilead defeated
12: 5 the **m** of Gilead would say to
14:10 for young **m** used to do so.
14:18 So the **m** of the city said to him
14:19 and killed thirty of their **m**,
15:10 And the **m** of Judah said, "Why
15:11 Then three thousand **m** of Judah
15:15 and killed a thousand **m** with
15:16 I have slain a thousand **m**!"
16: 9 Now **m** were lying in wait,
16:12 Samson!" And **m** were lying in
16:27 Now the temple was full of **m** and
16:27 about three thousand **m** and women
18: 2 children of Dan sent five **m** of
18: 2 **m** of valor from Zorah and
18: 7 So the five **m** departed and went
18:11 And six hundred **m** of the family
18:14 Then the five **m** who had gone to
18:16 The six hundred **m** armed with
18:17 Then the five **m** who had gone to
18:17 the gate with the six hundred **m**
18:22 the **m** who were in the houses
18:25 lest angry **m** fall upon you, and
19:16 whereas the **m** of the place
19:22 suddenly certain **m** of the city,
19:22 men of the city, perverted **m**,
19:25 But the **m** would not heed him.
20: 5 And the **m** of Gibeah rose against
20:10 We will take ten **m** out of every
20:11 So all the **m** of Israel were
20:12 the tribes of Israel sent **m**
20:13 therefore, deliver up the **m**,
20:13 the perverted **m** who are in
20:15 numbered twenty-six thousand **m**
20:15 numbered seven hundred select **m**.
20:16 were seven hundred select **m**
20:17 the **m** of Israel numbered four
20:17 four hundred thousand **m** who
20:17 all of these were **m** of war.
20:20 And the **m** of Israel went out to
20:20 and the **m** of Israel put
20:21 ground twenty-two thousand **m**
20:22 the **m** of Israel, encouraged
20:29 Then Israel set **m** in ambush all
20:31 about thirty **m** of Israel.
20:33 So all the **m** of Israel rose from
20:33 Then Israel's **m** in ambush burst
20:34 And ten thousand select **m** from
20:36 The **m** of Israel had given
20:36 because they relied on the **m** in
20:37 And the **m** in ambush quickly
20:37 the **m** in ambush spread out and
20:38 appointed signal between the **m**
20:38 the men of Israel and the **m** in
20:39 whereupon the **m** of Israel would
20:39 kill about thirty of the **m** of
20:41 And when the **m** of Israel turned
20:41 the **m** of Benjamin panicked, for
20:42 their backs before the **m** of
20:44 And eighteen thousand **m** of
20:44 all these were **m** of valor.
20:46 day were twenty-five thousand **m**
20:46 all these were **m** of valor.
20:47 But six hundred **m** turned and
20:48 And the **m** of Israel turned back
20:48 **m** and beasts, all who were
21: 1 Now the **m** of Israel had sworn an
21:10 of their most valiant **m**,
Ruth 2: 9 I not commanded the young **m**
2: 9 and drink from what the young **m**
2:15 Boaz commanded his young **m**,
2:21 shall stay close by my young **m**
3:10 you did not go after young **m**,
4: 2 And he took ten **m** of the elders
1 Sam 2: 4 The bows of the mighty **m** are
2:17 the sin of the young **m** was
2:17 for **m** abhorred the offering of
2:26 favor both with the LORD and **m**.
2:33 But any of your **m** whom I do not
4: 2 killed about four thousand **m**
4: 9 and conduct yourselves like **m**,
4: 9 Conduct yourselves like **m**,
5: 7 And when the **m** of Ashdod saw how
5: 9 and He struck the **m** of the
5:12 And the **m** who did not die were
6:10 Then the **m** did so; they took
6:15 Then the **m** of Beth Shemesh
6:19 Then He struck the **m** of Beth
6:19 fifty thousand and seventy **m**
6:20 And the **m** of Beth Shemesh said,
7: 1 Then the **m** of Kirjath Jearim
7:11 And the **m** of Israel went out of
8:16 servants, your finest young **m**,
8:22 And Samuel said to the **m** of
10: 2 you will find two **m** by Rachel's
10: 3 There three **m** going up to God
10:26 and valiant **m** went with him,
11: 1 and all the **m** of Jabesh said to
11: 5 told him the words of the **m** of
11: 8 and the **m** of Judah thirty
11: 9 Thus you shall say to the **m** of
11: 9 came and reported it to the **m**
11:10 Therefore the **m** of Jabesh said,
11:12 reign over us?' Bring the **m**,
11:15 and there Saul and all the **m** of
13: 2 for himself three thousand **m**
13: 6 When the **m** of Israel saw that
13:15 with him, about six hundred **m**.
14: 2 him were about six hundred **m**.
14: 8 let us cross over to these **m**,
14:12 Then the **m** of the garrison
14:14 made was about twenty **m** within
14:22 Likewise all the **m** of Israel who
14:24 And the **m** of Israel were
15: 4 soldiers and ten thousand **m** of
16:11 'Are all the young **m** here?"
17: 2 And Saul and the **m** of Israel
17:19 Saul and they and all the **m** of
17:24 And all the **m** of Israel, when
17:25 So the **m** of Israel said, "Have
17:26 Then David spoke to the **m** who
17:28 heard when he spoke to the **m**;
17:52 Now the **m** of Israel and Judah
18: 5 And Saul set him over the **m** of
18:27 arose and went, he and his **m**,
18:27 and killed two hundred **m** of the
21: 2 I have directed my young **m** to
21: 4 if the young **m** have at least
21: 5 And the vessels of the young **m**
22: 2 were about four hundred **m** with
22: 6 heard that David and the **m** who
22:18 on that day eighty-five **m** who
22:19 both **m** and women, children and
23: 3 But David's **m** said to him,
23: 5 And David and his **m** went to
23: 8 to besiege David and his **m**.
23:11 Will the **m** of Keilah deliver me
23:12 Will the **m** of Keilah deliver me
23:12 of Keilah deliver me and my **m**
23:13 So David and his **m**, about
23:24 But David and his **m** were in
23:25 When Saul and his **m** went to seek
23:26 and David and his **m** on the
23:26 for Saul and his **m** were
23:26 encircling David and his **m** to
24: 2 took three thousand chosen **m**
24: 2 went to seek David and his **m**
24: 3 (David and his **m** were staying
24: 4 Then the **m** of David said to him,
24: 6 And he said to his **m**,
24: 9 do you listen to the words of **m**
24:22 but David and his **m** went up to
25: 5 David sent ten young **m**;
25: 5 and David said to the young **m**,
25: 8 'Ask your young **m**, and they
25: 8 Therefore let my young **m** find
25: 9 So when David's young **m** came,
25:11 and give it to **m** when I do not
25:12 So David's young **m** turned on
25:13 Then David said to his **m**,
25:13 And about four hundred **m** went
25:14 Now one of the young **m** told
25:15 But the **m** were very good to us,
25:20 and there were David and his **m**,
25:25 did not see the young **m** of my
25:27 let it be given to the young **m**
26: 2 having three thousand chosen **m**
26:19 if it is the children of **m**,
26:22 Let one of the young **m** come
27: 2 over with the six hundred **m**
27: 3 Achish at Gath, he and his **m**,
27: 8 And David and his **m** went up and
28: 1 me to battle, you and your **m**.
28: 8 and two **m** with him; and they
29: 2 but David and his **m** passed in
29: 4 not with the heads of these **m**?
29:11 So David and his **m** rose early to
30: 1 when David and his **m** came to
30: 3 So David and his **m** came to the
30: 9 he and the six hundred **m** who
30:10 pursued, he and four hundred **m**;
30:17 except four hundred young **m** who
30:21 came to the two hundred **m** who
30:22 all the wicked and worthless **m**
30:31 where David himself and his **m**
31: 1 and the **m** of Israel fled from
31: 4 lest these uncircumcised **m** come
31: 6 and all his **m** died together
31: 7 And when the **m** of Israel who
31: 7 saw that the **m** of Israel had
31:12 all the valiant **m** arose and
2 Sam 1:11 and so did all the **m** who
1:15 called one of the young **m** and
2: 3 And David brought up the **m** who
2: 4 Then the **m** of Judah came, and
2: 4 The **m** of Jabesh Gilead were
2: 5 David sent messengers to the **m**
2:14 Let the young **m** now arise and
2:17 and Abner and the **m** of Israel
2:21 lay hold on one of the young **m**
2:29 Then Abner and his **m** went on all
2:30 of David's servants nineteen **m**
2:31 down, of Benjamin and Abner's **m**,
2:31 three hundred and sixty **m** who
2:32 And Joab and his **m** went all
3:20 So Abner and twenty **m** with him
3:20 a feast for Abner and the **m**
3:34 As a man falls before wicked **m**,
3:39 anointed king; and these **m**,
4: 2 Now Saul's son had two **m** who
4:11 when wicked **m** have killed a
4:12 So David commanded his young **m**,
5: 6 And the king and his **m** went to
5:21 and David and his **m** carried
6: 1 gathered all the choice **m** of
6:19 both the women and the **m**,
7: 9 like the name of the great **m**
7:14 chasten him with the rod of **m**
7:14 with the blows of the sons of **m**.
10: 5 because the **m** were greatly
10: 6 king of Maacah one thousand **m**,
10: 6 from Ish-Tob twelve thousand **m**.
10: 7 all the army of the mighty **m**.
11:16 he knew there were valiant **m**.
11:17 Then the **m** of the city came out
11:23 Surely the **m** prevailed against
12: 1 There were two **m** in one city,
13:32 have killed all the young **m**,
15: 1 and fifty **m** to run before him.
15: 6 stole the hearts of the **m** of
15:11 with Absalom went two hundred **m**
15:13 The hearts of the **m** of Israel
15:18 six hundred **m** who had followed
15:22 the Gittite and all his **m** and
16: 2 summer fruit for the young **m**
16: 6 the people and all the mighty **m**
16:13 And as David and his **m** went
16:15 the **m** of Israel, came to
16:18 and this people and all the **m**
17: 1 let me choose twelve thousand **m**,
17: 8 know your father and his **m**,
17: 8 men, that they are mighty **m**,
17:10 are with him are valiant **m**.
17:12 And of him and all the **m** who
17:14 So Absalom and all the **m** of
17:24 he and all the **m** of Israel with
18:15 And ten young **m** who bore Joab's
18:28 who has delivered up the **m** who
19:14 swayed the hearts of all the **m**
19:16 and came down with the **m** of
19:17 There were a thousand **m** of
19:28 father's house were but dead **m**
19:35 longer the voice of singing **m**
19:41 Just then all the **m** of Israel
19:41 the **m** of Judah, stolen you away
19:41 and all David's **m** with him
19:42 So all the **m** of Judah answered
19:42 men of Judah answered the **m** of
19:43 And the **m** of Israel answered the
19:43 men of Israel answered the **m**
19:43 Yet the words of the **m** of
19:43 than the words of the **m** of
20: 2 But the **m** of Judah, from the
20: 4 Assemble the **m** of Judah for me
20: 5 Amasa went to assemble the **m**
20: 7 So Joab's **m**, with the
20: 7 and all the mighty **m**,
20:11 Meanwhile one of Joab's **m** stood
21: 6 let seven **m** of his descendants
21:12 from the **m** of Jabesh Gilead who
21:17 Then the **m** of David swore to
23: 3 He who rules over **m** must be
23: 8 are the names of the mighty **m**
23: 8 he had killed eight hundred **m**
23: 9 one of the three mighty **m** with
23: 9 and the **m** of Israel had
23:13 three of the thirty chief **m**
23:16 So the three mighty **m** broke
23:17 this not the blood of the **m**
23:17 were done by the three mighty **m**.
23:18 spear against three hundred **m**,
23:22 won a name among three mighty **m**.
24: 9 hundred thousand valiant **m** who
24: 9 and the **m** of Judah were five
24: 9 were five hundred thousand **m**.

24:15 to Beersheba seventy thousand ***m***
1 Ki 1: 5 and fifty ***m*** to run before him.
1: 8 and the mighty ***m*** who belonged
1: 9 and all the ***m*** of Judah, the
1:10 prophet, Benaiah, the mighty ***m***,
2:32 because he struck down two ***m***
4:30 the wisdom of all the ***m*** of the
4:31 For he was wiser than all ***m***—
4:34 And ***m*** of all nations, from all
5:13 force was thirty thousand ***m***.
8: 2 Therefore all the ***m*** of Israel
8:39 hearts of all the sons of ***m***),
9:22 because they were ***m*** of war and
10: 8 Happy are your ***m*** and happy are
11:18 and they took ***m*** with them from
11:24 So he gathered ***m*** to him and
12: 8 and consulted the young ***m*** who
12:10 Then the young ***m*** who had grown
12:14 to the advice of the young ***m***,
12:21 and eighty thousand chosen ***m***
13:25 ***m*** passed by and saw the corpse
18:13 how I hid one hundred ***m*** of the
18:22 are four hundred and fifty ***m***.
20:17 ***M*** are coming out of Samaria!"
20:30 twenty-seven thousand of the ***m***
20:33 Now the ***m*** were watching closely
21:10 and seat two ***m***, scoundrels,
21:11 So the ***m*** of his city, the
21:13 And two ***m***, scoundrels,
22: 6 together, about four hundred ***m***,
2 Ki 1: 9 of fifty with his fifty ***m***.
1:10 consume you and your fifty ***m***.
1:11 of fifty with his fifty ***m***.
1:12 consume you and your fifty ***m***.
1:13 of fifty with his fifty ***m***.
2: 7 And fifty ***m*** of the sons of the
2:16 there are fifty strong ***m*** with
2:17 Therefore they sent fifty ***m***,
2:19 Then the ***m*** of the city said to
3:26 took with him seven hundred ***m***
4:22 send me one of the young ***m*** and
4:40 Then they served it to the ***m*** to
4:43 I set this before one hundred ***m***?
5:22 just now two young ***m*** of the
5:24 then he let the ***m*** go, and they
6:20 open the eyes of these ***m***,
7: 3 Now there were four leprous ***m***
7:13 let several ***m*** take five of the
8:12 and their young ***m*** you will kill
9:17 said, "I see a company of ***m***.
10: 6 voice, take the heads of the ***m***,
10: 6 were with the great ***m*** of the
10:11 and all his great ***m*** and his
10:14 well of Beth Eked, forty-two ***m***;
10:24 appointed for himself eighty ***m***
10:24 If any of the ***m*** whom I have
11: 9 Each of them took his ***m*** who
12:15 require an account from the ***m***
15:25 and with him were fifty ***m*** of
16: 6 and drove the ***m*** of Judah from
17:30 The ***m*** of Babylon made Succoth
17:30 the ***m*** of Cuth made Nergal, the
17:30 the ***m*** of Hamath made Ashima,
18:27 and not to the ***m*** who sit on the
20:14 What did these ***m*** say, and from
23: 2 of the LORD with all the ***m*** of
23:14 places with the bones of ***m***.
23:17 So the ***m*** of the city told
24:14 captains and all the mighty ***m***
24:16 All the valiant ***m***, seven
25: 4 and all the ***m*** of war fled at
25:19 who had charge of the ***m*** of war,
25:19 five ***m*** of the king's close
25:19 and sixty ***m*** of the people of
25:23 the armies, they and their ***m***,
25:23 a Maachathite, they and their ***m***.
25:24 an oath before them and their ***m***,
25:25 came with ten ***m*** and struck and
1 Chr 4:12 These were the ***m*** of Rechah.
4:22 the ***m*** of Chozeba, and Joash;
4:42 five hundred ***m*** of the sons of
5:18 hundred and sixty valiant ***m***,
5:18 ***m*** able to bear shield and
5:21 one hundred thousand of their ***m***;
5:24 They were mighty ***m*** of valor,
5:24 mighty men of valor, famous ***m***,
6:31 Now these are the ***m*** whom David
7: 2 sons of Tola were mighty ***m***
7: 3 All five of them were chief ***m***.
7: 5 of Issachar were mighty ***m*** of
7: 7 and thirty-four mighty ***m*** of
7: 9 thousand two hundred mighty ***m***
7:11 thousand two hundred mighty ***m***
7:21 The ***m*** of Gath who were born in
7:40 fathers' houses, choice ***m***,
7:40 mighty ***m*** of valor, chief
8:28 by their generations, chief ***m***.
8:40 The sons of Ulam were mighty ***m***
9: 9 All these ***m*** were heads of a
9:13 They were very able ***m*** for the
10: 1 and the ***m*** of Israel fled from
10: 4 lest these uncircumcised ***m*** come
10: 7 And when all the ***m*** of Israel who
10:12 all the valiant ***m*** arose and took
11:10 the heads of the mighty ***m*** whom
11:11 is the number of the mighty ***m***
11:12 was one of the three mighty ***m***.
11:15 three of the thirty chief ***m***
11:19 I drink the blood of these ***m***
11:19 were done by the three mighty ***m***.
11:20 spear against three hundred ***m***,
11:21 honored than the other two ***m***.
11:24 won a name among three mighty ***m***.
12: 1 Now these were the ***m*** who came
12: 1 they were among the mighty ***m***,
12: 8 mighty ***m*** of valor, men trained
12: 8 ***m*** trained for battle, who could
12:21 for they were all mighty ***m*** of
12:25 mighty ***m*** of valor fit for war,
12:30 mighty ***m*** of valor, famous men
12:30 famous ***m*** throughout their
12:33 stouthearted ***m*** who could keep
12:38 All these ***m*** of war, who could
17: 8 like the name of the great ***m***
19: 5 went and told David about the ***m***;
19: 5 because the ***m*** were greatly
19: 8 all the army of the mighty ***m***.
21: 5 million one hundred thousand ***m***
21: 5 hundred and seventy thousand ***m***
21:14 and seventy thousand ***m*** of
22:15 and all types of skillful ***m*** for
25: 1 And the number of the skilled ***m***
26: 6 because they were ***m*** of great
26: 7 and Semachiah were able ***m***.
26: 8 able ***m*** with strength for the
26: 9 and brethren, eighteen able ***m***.
26:12 gatekeepers, among the chief ***m***,
26:30 thousand seven hundred able ***m***,
26:31 found among them capable ***m*** at
26:32 thousand seven hundred able ***m***,
28: 1 the officials, the valiant ***m***,
28: 1 and all the mighty ***m*** of valor.
29:24 the leaders and the mighty ***m***,
2 Chr 2: 2 selected seventy thousand ***m*** to
2: 7 to engrave with the skillful ***m***
2:14 with your skillful ***m*** and with
2:14 men and with the skillful ***m*** of
5: 3 Therefore all the ***m*** of Israel
6:18 will God indeed dwell with ***m***
6:30 the hearts of the sons of ***m***),
8: 9 Some were ***m*** of war, captains
9: 7 Happy are your ***m*** and happy are
10: 8 and consulted the young ***m*** who
10:10 Then the young ***m*** who had grown
10:14 to the advice of the young ***m***,
11: 1 and eighty thousand chosen ***m***
13: 3 four hundred thousand choice ***m***.
13: 3 eight hundred thousand choice ***m***,
13: 3 men, mighty ***m*** of valor.
13:15 Then the ***m*** of Judah gave a
13:15 and as the ***m*** of Judah shouted,
13:17 five hundred thousand choice ***m***
14: 8 hundred and eighty thousand ***m***
14: 8 all these were mighty ***m*** of
14: 9 with an army of a million ***m***
17:13 and the ***m*** of war, mighty men of
17:13 mighty ***m*** of valor, were in
17:14 hundred thousand mighty ***m*** of
17:16 two hundred thousand mighty ***m***
17:17 with him two hundred thousand ***m***
18: 5 together, four hundred ***m***,
23: 8 And each man took his ***m*** who
24:24 came with a small company of ***m***;
25: 5 hundred thousand choice ***m***,
25: 6 one hundred thousand mighty ***m***
26:11 had an army of fighting ***m*** who
26:12 chief officers of the mighty ***m***
26:15 invented by skillful ***m***,
26:17 priests of the LORD—VALIANT ***m***.
28: 6 Judah in one day, all valiant ***m***,
28:14 So the armed ***m*** left the captives
28:15 Then the ***m*** who were designated
31:19 there were ***m*** who were
34:12 And the ***m*** did the work
34:30 with all the ***m*** of Judah and the
35:25 to this day all the singing ***m***
36:17 who killed their young ***m*** with
Ezra 1: 4 let the ***m*** of his place help him
2: 2 The number of the ***m*** of the
2:22 the ***m*** of Netophah, fifty-six;
2:23 the ***m*** of Anathoth, one hundred
2:27 the ***m*** of Michmas, one hundred
2:28 the ***m*** of Bethel and Ai, two
2:65 and they had two hundred ***m*** and
3:12 old ***m*** who had seen the first
4:11 the ***m*** of the region beyond
4:21 the command to make these ***m***
5: 4 we told them the names of the ***m***
5:10 might write the names of the ***m***
6: 8 be given immediately to these ***m***,
7:28 and I gathered leading ***m*** of
8:16 ***m*** of understanding.
8:18 sons and brothers, eighteen ***m***;
8:19 and their sons, twenty ***m***;
10: 1 God, a very large assembly of ***m***,
10: 9 So all the ***m*** of Judah and
10:17 questioning all the ***m*** who had
Neh 1: 2 one of my brethren came with ***m***
2:12 I and a few ***m*** with me; I told
3: 2 Next to Eliashib the ***m*** of
3: 7 the ***m*** of Gibeon and Mizpah,
3:22 the ***m*** of the plain, made
4:13 Therefore I positioned ***m***
4:21 and half of the ***m*** held the
4:23 nor the ***m*** of the guard who
5: 5 for other ***m*** have our lands and
7: 7 The number of the ***m*** of the
7:26 the ***m*** of Bethlehem and Netophah,
7:27 the ***m*** of Anathoth, one hundred
7:28 the ***m*** of Beth Azmaveth,
7:29 the ***m*** of Kirjath Jearim,
7:30 the ***m*** of Ramah and Geba, six
7:31 the ***m*** of Michmas, one hundred
7:32 the ***m*** of Bethel and Ai, one
7:33 the ***m*** of the other Nebo,
7:67 two hundred and forty-five ***m***
8: 2 Law before the assembly of ***m***
8: 3 before the ***m*** and women and
11: 2 the people blessed all the ***m***
11: 6 and sixty-eight valiant ***m***.
11:14 mighty ***m*** of valor, were one
11:14 the son of one of the great ***m***.
13:16 ***M*** of Tyre dwelt there also, who
Esth 1:13 the king said to the wise ***m***
6:13 his wise ***m*** and his wife Zeresh
9: 6 and destroyed five hundred ***m***.
9:12 and destroyed five hundred ***m***
9:15 and killed three hundred ***m*** at
Job 4:13 When deep sleep falls on ***m***,
7:20 I done to You, O watcher of ***m***?
11: 3 Should your empty talk make ***m***
11:11 For He knows deceitful ***m***;
12:12 Wisdom is with aged ***m***,
15:18 What wise ***m*** have told,
17: 6 have become one in whose face ***m***
17: 8 Upright ***m*** are astonished at
22:15 to the old way Which wicked ***m***
27:23 ***M*** shall clap their hands at
28: 4 They hang far away from ***m***;
29: 8 The young ***m*** saw me and hid,
29:21 ***M*** listened to me and waited,
30: 1 ***m*** younger than I, Whose
30: 5 were driven out from among ***m***,
30: 8 of fools, Yes, sons of vile ***m***;
31:31 If the ***m*** of my tent have not
32: 1 So these three ***m*** ceased
32: 5 in the mouth of these three ***m***,
32: 9 Great ***m*** are not always wise,
33:15 When deep sleep falls upon ***m***,
33:16 Then He opens the ears of ***m***,
33:27 Then he looks at ***m*** and says,
34: 2 "Hear my words, you wise ***m***;
34: 8 And walks with wicked ***m***?
34:10 you ***m*** of understanding: Far be
34:24 He breaks in pieces mighty ***m***
34:26 He strikes them as wicked ***m***
34:34 ***M*** of understanding say to me,
34:34 Wise ***m*** who listen to me:
34:36 are like those of wicked ***m***!
35:12 Because of the pride of evil ***m***.
36:24 Of which ***m*** have sung.
37: 7 That all ***m*** may know His work.
37:21 Even now ***m*** cannot look at the
37:24 Therefore ***m*** fear Him; He shows
Ps 4: 2 How long, O you sons of ***m***,
9:20 know themselves to be but ***m***.
11: 4 His eyelids test the sons of ***m***.
12: 1 from among the sons of ***m***.
12: 8 is exalted among the sons of ***m***.
14: 2 heaven upon the children of ***m***,
17: 4 Concerning the works of ***m***,
17:14 With Your hand from ***m***,
17:14 From ***m*** of the world who have
21:10 from among the sons of ***m***.
22: 6 and no man; A reproach of ***m***,
26: 9 my life with bloodthirsty ***m***,
31:19 the presence of the sons of ***m***!
33:13 He sees all the sons of ***m***.
36: 7 Therefore the children of ***m***
45: 2 are fairer than the sons of ***m***;
49:10 For he sees wise ***m*** die;
49:18 he blesses himself (For ***m***
53: 2 heaven upon the children of ***m***,
55:23 Bloodthirsty and deceitful ***m***
57: 4 I lie among the sons of ***m***
58: 1 judge uprightly, you sons of ***m***?
58:11 So that ***m*** will say, "Surely
59: of David when Saul sent ***m***,
59: 2 save me from bloodthirsty ***m***.
62: 9 Surely ***m*** of low degree are a
62: 9 ***M*** of high degree are a lie;
64: 9 All ***m*** shall fear, And shall
66: 5 His doing toward the sons of ***m***.
66:12 You have caused ***m*** to ride over
68:18 have received gifts among ***m***,
72:17 And ***m*** shall be blessed in
73: 5 not in trouble as other ***m***,
73: 5 are they plagued like other ***m***.
74: 5 They seem like ***m*** who lift up
76: 5 And none of the mighty ***m*** have
78:25 ***M*** ate angels' food; He sent
78:31 And struck down the choice ***m***
78:60 The tent He had placed among ***m***,
78:63 fire consumed their young ***m***,
82: 7 But you shall die like ***m***,
86:14 And a mob of violent ***m*** have
89:47 created all the children of ***m***?
90: 3 say, "Return, O children of ***m***.
107: 8 that ***m*** would give thanks to
107: 8 works to the children of ***m***!
107:15 that ***m*** would give thanks to
107:15 works to the children of ***m***!
107:21 that ***m*** would give thanks to
107:21 works to the children of ***m***!
107:31 that ***m*** would give thanks to
107:31 works to the children of ***m***!
115:16 has given to the children of ***m***.
116:11 'All ***m*** are liars.'
119:136 Because ***m*** do not keep Your
124: 2 When ***m*** rose up against us,
139:19 therefore, you bloodthirsty ***m***.
140: 1 me, O LORD, from evil ***m***;
140: 1 Preserve me from violent ***m***,
140: 4 Preserve me from violent ***m***,
141: 4 practice wicked works With ***m***
145: 6 ***M*** shall speak of the might of

145:12 To make known to the sons of ***m***
148:12 Both young ***m*** and maidens;
148:12 Old ***m*** and children.
Prov 7:26 slain by her were strong ***m***.
8: 4 'To you, O ***m***, I call,
8: 4 my voice is to the sons of ***m***.
8:31 delight was with the sons of ***m***.
11:16 But ruthless ***m*** retain riches.
12:12 covet the catch of evil ***m***,
13:20 He who walks with wise ***m*** will
15:11 the hearts of the sons of ***m***.
17: 6 are the crown of old ***m***,
18:16 And brings him before great ***m***.
20: 6 Most ***m*** will proclaim each his
20:29 The glory of young ***m*** is their
20:29 And the splendor of old ***m*** is
22:29 not stand before unknown ***m***.
23:28 the unfaithful among ***m***.
24: 1 Do not be envious of evil ***m***,
24: 9 scoffer is an abomination to ***m***.
25: 1 of Solomon which the ***m*** of
26:16 in his own eyes Than seven ***m***
28: 5 Evil ***m*** do not understand
28:12 arise, ***m*** hide themselves.
28:28 ***m*** hide themselves; But when
29: 8 But wise ***m*** turn away wrath.
30:14 And the needy from among ***m***.
Eccl 2: 3 was good for the sons of ***m*** to
2: 8 the delights of the sons of ***m***,
3:10 task with which the sons of ***m***
3:14 that ***m*** should fear before Him.
3:18 the condition of the sons of ***m***,
3:19 what happens to the sons of ***m***
3:21 the spirit of the sons of ***m***,
6: 1 sun, and it is common among ***m***:
7: 2 For that is the end of all ***m***;
8:11 the heart of the sons of ***m*** is
8:14 that there are just ***m*** to whom
8:14 there are wicked ***m*** to whom it
9: 3 the hearts of the sons of ***m***
9:11 Nor riches to ***m*** of
9:11 Nor favor to ***m*** of skill;
9:12 So the sons of ***m*** are snared
9:14 was a little city with few ***m***
12: 3 And the strong ***m*** bow down;
Song 3: 7 With sixty valiant ***m*** around
4: 4 All shields of mighty ***m***.
Isa 2:11 The haughtiness of ***m*** shall be
2:17 And the haughtiness of ***m*** shall
3:25 Your ***m*** shall fall by the sword,
5: 3 inhabitants of Jerusalem and ***m***
5: 7 And the ***m*** of Judah are His
5:13 Their honorable ***m*** are
5:22 Woe to ***m*** mighty at drinking
5:22 Woe to ***m*** valiant for mixing
6:12 The LORD has removed ***m*** far
7:13 small thing for you to weary ***m***,
7:24 With arrows and bows ***m*** will
9: 3 As ***m*** rejoice when they divide
9:17 have no joy in their young ***m***,
11:15 And make ***m*** cross over
13:18 bows will dash the young ***m*** to
19:12 Where are your wise ***m***?
21: 9 here comes a chariot of ***m*** with
21:17 the mighty ***m*** of the people of
22: 2 Your slain ***m*** are not slain
22: 6 the quiver With chariots of ***m***
23: 4 Neither do I rear young ***m***,
24: 6 And few ***m*** are left.
28:14 of the LORD, you scornful ***m***,
29:11 which ***m*** deliver to one who is
29:13 taught by the commandment of ***m***,
29:14 the wisdom of their wise ***m***
29:14 of their prudent ***m*** shall be
29:19 And the poor among ***m*** shall
31: 3 Now the Egyptians are ***m***,
31: 8 And his young ***m*** shall become
36:12 and not to the ***m*** who sit on the
38:16 by these things ***m*** live;
39: 3 What did these ***m*** say, and from
40:30 And the young ***m*** shall utterly
41:14 You ***m*** of Israel! I will help
43: 4 Therefore I will give ***m*** for
44:11 the workmen, they are mere ***m***.
44:25 Who turns wise ***m*** backward,
45:14 ***m*** of stature, Shall come over
45:24 To Him ***m*** shall come, And all
46: 8 this, and show yourselves ***m***;
51: 7 Do not fear the reproach of ***m***,
52:14 form more than the sons of ***m***;
53: 3 is despised and rejected by ***m***,
57: 1 Merciful ***m*** are taken away,
59:10 We are as dead ***m*** in
60:11 That ***m*** may bring to you the
64: 4 the beginning of the world ***M***
66:24 Upon the corpses of the ***m*** Who
Jer 3: 2 have you not lain with ***m***?
4: 3 thus says the LORD to the ***m***
4: 4 You ***m*** of Judah and inhabitants
5: 5 I will go to the great ***m*** and
5:16 They are all mighty ***m***.
5:26 My people are found wicked ***m***;
5:26 They set a trap; They catch ***m***.
6:11 And on the assembly of young ***m***
6:23 As ***m*** of war set in array
8: 9 The wise ***m*** are ashamed,
9: 2 An assembly of treacherous ***m***.
9:10 Nor can ***m*** hear the voice of
9:21 be outside! And the young ***m***—
9:22 Even the carcasses of ***m*** shall
10: 7 For among all the wise ***m*** of
10: 9 all the work of skillful ***m***.
11: 2 and speak to the ***m*** of Judah and
11: 9 has been found among the ***m*** of
11:21 the LORD concerning the ***m*** of
11:22 The young ***m*** shall die by the
11:23 bring catastrophe on the ***m*** of
15: 8 the mother of the young ***m***,
15:10 Nor have ***m*** lent to me for
16: 6 neither shall ***m*** lament for
16: 7 Nor shall ***m*** break bread in
16: 7 nor shall ***m*** give them the cup
17:25 accompanied by the ***m*** of Judah
18:11 speak to the ***m*** of Judah and to
18:21 Let their ***m*** be put to death,
18:21 Their young ***m*** be slain
19:10 the flask in the sight of the ***m***
26:21 with all his mighty ***m*** and all
26:22 Then Jehoiakim the king sent ***m***
26:22 and other ***m*** who went with
31:13 And the young ***m*** and the old,
32:19 all the ways of the sons of ***m***,
32:20 in Israel and among other ***m***;
32:32 the ***m*** of Judah, and the
32:44 ***M*** will buy fields for money,
33: 5 with the dead bodies of ***m*** whom
34:18 And I will give the ***m*** who have
35:13 Go and tell the ***m*** of Judah and
36:31 and on the ***m*** of Judah all the
37:10 there remained only wounded ***m***
38: 4 he weakens the hands of the ***m***
38: 9 these ***m*** have done evil in all
38:10 Take from here thirty ***m*** with
38:11 So Ebed-Melech took the ***m*** with
38:16 you into the hand of these ***m***
39: 4 king of Judah and all the ***m*** of
39:17 be given into the hand of the ***m***
40: 7 in the fields, they and their ***m***,
40: 7 and had committed to him ***m***,
40: 8 a Maachathite, they and their ***m***.
40: 9 an oath before them and their ***m***,
41: 1 came with ten ***m*** to Gedaliah the
41: 2 and the ten ***m*** who were with
41: 3 found there, the ***m*** of war.
41: 5 that certain ***m*** came from
41: 5 eighty ***m*** with their beards
41: 7 he and the ***m*** who were with him.
41: 8 But ten ***m*** were found among them
41: 9 all the dead bodies of the ***m***
41:12 they took all the ***m*** and went to
41:15 from Johanan with eight ***m*** and
41:16 the mighty ***m*** of war and the
42:17 So shall it be with all the ***m***
43: 2 and all the proud ***m*** spoke,
43: 6 ***m***, women, children, the
43: 9 them in the sight of the ***m*** of
44:15 Then all the ***m*** who knew that
44:20 spoke to all the people—the ***m***,
44:27 And all the ***m*** of Judah who are
46: 9 And let the mighty ***m*** come
46:15 Why are your valiant ***m*** swept
47: 2 Then the ***m*** shall cry, And all
48:14 We are mighty And strong ***m*** for
48:15 Her chosen young ***m*** have gone
48:31 I will mourn for the ***m*** of Kir
48:36 My heart shall wail For the ***m***
49:15 nations, Despised among ***m***.
49:22 The heart of the mighty ***m*** of
49:26 Therefore her young ***m*** shall
49:26 And all the ***m*** of war shall be
49:28 And devastate the ***m*** of the
50:30 Therefore her young ***m*** shall
50:30 And all her ***m*** of war shall be
50:35 her princes and her wise ***m***.
50:36 sword is against her mighty ***m***,
51: 3 Do not spare her young ***m***;
51:14 I will fill you with ***m***,
51:30 The mighty ***m*** of Babylon have
51:32 And the ***m*** of war are
51:56 And her mighty ***m*** are taken.
51:57 Her princes and wise ***m***,
51:57 her deputies, and her mighty ***m***.
52: 7 and all the ***m*** of war fled and
52:25 who had charge of the ***m*** of war,
52:25 seven ***m*** of the king's close
52:25 and sixty ***m*** of the people of
Lam 1:15 underfoot all my mighty ***m*** in
1:15 against me To crush my young ***m***;
1:18 My virgins and my young ***m***
2:21 My virgins and my young ***m***
3:33 Nor grieve the children of ***m***.
5:13 Young ***m*** ground at the
5:14 And the young ***m*** from their
Ezek 6: 4 I will cast down your slain ***m***
8:11 stood before them seventy ***m*** of
8:16 were about twenty-five ***m*** with
9: 2 And suddenly six ***m*** came from the
9: 4 mark on the foreheads of the ***m***
9: 6 "Utterly slay old and young ***m***,
11: 1 of the gate were twenty-five ***m***,
11: 2 these are the ***m*** who devise
12:16 I will spare a few of their ***m***
14: 3 these ***m*** have set up their idols
14:14 "Even if these three ***m***,
14:16 even though these three ***m*** were
14:18 even though these three ***m*** were
15: 3 Or can ***m*** make a peg from it to
16:33 ***M*** make payment to all harlots,
19: 3 catch prey, And he devoured ***m***.
19: 6 to catch prey; He devoured ***m***.
21:14 sword that slays the great ***m***,
21:31 you into the hands of brutal ***m***
22: 9 In you are ***m*** who slander to
22:10 In you ***m*** uncover their fathers'
22:20 As ***m*** gather silver, bronze,
23: 6 All of them desirable young ***m***,
23: 7 All of them choice ***m*** of
23:12 All of them desirable young ***m***.
23:14 She looked at ***m*** portrayed on
23:23 All of them desirable young ***m***,
23:23 Captains and ***m*** of renown,
23:40 Furthermore you sent for ***m*** to
23:42 from the wilderness with ***m*** of
23:44 as ***m*** go in to a woman who plays
23:45 But righteous ***m*** will judge them
25: 4 you as a possession to the ***m***
25:10 To the ***m*** of the East I will give
26:10 as ***m*** enter a city that has been
26:17 O one inhabited by seafaring ***m***,
27: 8 were your oarsmen; Your wise ***m***,
27: 9 of Gebal and its wise ***m*** Were
27:10 Libya Were in your army as ***m***
27:11 ***M*** of Arvad with your army were
27:11 And the ***m*** of Gammad were in
27:15 The ***m*** of Dedan were your
27:27 All your ***m*** of war who are in
30: 5 and the ***m*** of the lands who are
30:17 The young ***m*** of Aven and Pi
31:14 Among the children of ***m*** who go
34:31 flock of My pasture; you are ***m***,
36:10 I will multiply ***m*** upon you, all
36:12 I will cause ***m*** to walk on you,
36:13 You devour ***m*** and bereave your
36:14 therefore you shall devour ***m*** no
36:37 I will increase their ***m*** like a
36:38 be filled with flocks of ***m***.
38:20 and all ***m*** who are on the face
39:14 They will set apart ***m*** regularly
39:20 With mighty ***m*** And with all
39:20 mighty men And with all the ***m***
Dan 1: 4 young ***m*** in whom there was no
1:10 looking worse than the young ***m***
1:13 the appearance of the young ***m***
1:15 in flesh than all the young ***m***
1:17 As for these four young ***m***,
2:12 to destroy all the wise ***m*** of
2:13 they began killing the wise ***m***;
2:14 gone out to kill the wise ***m***
2:18 with the rest of the wise ***m***
2:24 to destroy the wise ***m*** of
2:24 Do not destroy the wise ***m*** of
2:27 king has demanded, the wise ***m***,
2:38 wherever the children of ***m***
2:43 will mingle with the seed of ***m***;
2:48 over all the wise ***m*** of
3:12 Meshach, and Abed-Nego; these ***m***,
3:13 So they brought these ***m*** before
3:20 he commanded certain mighty ***m***
3:21 Then these ***m*** were bound in their
3:22 of the fire killed those ***m*** who
3:23 And these three ***m***, Shadrach,
3:24 Did we not cast three ***m*** bound
3:25 I see four ***m*** loose, walking in
3:27 and they saw these ***m*** on whose
4: 6 to bring in all the wise ***m*** of
4:17 High rules in the kingdom of ***m***,
4:17 sets over it the lowest of ***m***.
4:18 since all the wise ***m*** of my
4:25 They shall drive you from ***m***,
4:25 High rules in the kingdom of ***m***,
4:32 And they shall drive you from ***m***,
4:32 High rules in the kingdom of ***m***,
4:33 he was driven from ***m*** and ate
5: 7 saying to the wise ***m*** of
5: 8 Now all the king's wise ***m*** came,
5:15 'Now the wise ***m***,
5:21 was driven from the sons of ***m***,
5:21 God rules in the kingdom of ***m***,
6: 5 Then these ***m*** said, "We shall
6:11 Then these ***m*** assembled and found
6:15 Then these ***m*** approached the
6:24 and they brought those ***m*** who
6:26 every dominion of my kingdom ***m***
9: 7 to the ***m*** of Judah, to the
10: 7 for the ***m*** who were with me did
10:16 the likeness of the sons of ***m***
11:14 violent ***m*** of your people shall
Hos 4:14 For the ***m*** themselves go
6: 7 But like ***m*** they transgressed the
10:13 the multitude of your mighty ***m***.
13: 2 Let the ***m*** who sacrifice kiss the
Joel 1:12 away from the sons of ***m***.
2: 7 They run like mighty ***m***,
2: 7 They climb the wall like ***m*** of
2:28 Your old ***m*** shall dream dreams,
2:28 Your young ***m*** shall see
3: 9 for war! Wake up the mighty ***m***,
3: 9 Let all the ***m*** of war draw
Am 2:11 And some of your young ***m*** as
2:16 The most courageous ***m*** of might
4:10 Your young ***m*** I killed with a
6: 9 that if ten ***m*** remain in one
8:13 virgins And strong young ***m***
Ob 7 All the ***m*** in your confederacy
7 The ***m*** at peace with you Shall
8 Even destroy the wise ***m*** from
9 Then your mighty ***m***,
Jon 1:10 Then the ***m*** were exceedingly
1:10 For the ***m*** knew that he fled
1:13 Nevertheless the ***m*** rowed hard to
1:16 Then the ***m*** feared the LORD
Mic 2: 8 Like ***m*** returned from war.
5: 5 shepherds and eight princely ***m***.
5: 7 Nor wait for the sons of ***m***.
6:12 For her rich ***m*** are full of
7: 2 is no one upright among ***m***.

7: 6 A man's enemies are the ***m*** of
Nah 2: 3 The shields of his mighty ***m***
2: 3 The valiant ***m*** are in scarlet.
3:10 cast lots for her honorable ***m***,
3:10 And all her great ***m*** were bound
Hab 1:14 Why do You make ***m*** like fish of
Zeph 1:12 And punish the ***m*** Who are
1:14 There the mighty ***m*** shall cry
1:17 "I will bring distress upon ***m***,
1:17 they shall walk like blind ***m***,
Hag 1:11 on ***m*** and livestock, and on all
Zech 2: 4 because of the multitude of ***m***
7: 2 with Regem-Melech and his ***m***,
8: 4 Old ***m*** and old women shall again
8:10 or came in; For I set all ***m***,
8:23 In those days ten ***m*** from every
9: 1 place (For the eyes of ***m*** And
9:17 Grain shall make the young ***m***
10: 5 They shall be like mighty ***m***,
Mt 2: 1 wise ***m*** from the East came to
2: 7 had secretly called the wise ***m***,
2:16 he was deceived by the wise ***m***,
2:16 had determined from the wise ***m***.
4:19 I will make you fishers of ***m***.
5:13 out and trampled underfoot by ***m***.
5:16 your light so shine before ***m***,
5:19 and teaches ***m*** so, shall be
6: 1 your charitable deeds before ***m***,
6: 2 that they may have glory from ***m***.
6: 5 that they may be seen by ***m***.
6:14 For if you forgive ***m*** their
6:15 But if you do not forgive ***m***
6:16 that they may appear to ***m*** to
6:18 that you do not appear to ***m***
7:12 whatever you want ***m*** to do to
7:16 Do ***m*** gather grapes from
8:27 So the ***m*** marveled, saying, "Who
8:28 met Him two demon-possessed ***m***,
8:33 to the demon-possessed ***m***.
9: 8 who had given such power to ***m***.
9:27 two blind ***m*** followed Him,
9:28 the blind ***m*** came to Him. And
10:17 'But beware of ***m***, for they
10:32 whoever confesses Me before ***m***,
10:33 whoever denies Me before ***m***,
12:31 blasphemy will be forgiven ***m***,
12:31 Spirit will not be forgiven ***m***.
12:36 you that for every idle word ***m***
12:41 The ***m*** of Nineveh will rise up in
13:17 many prophets and righteous ***m***
13:25 but while ***m*** slept, his enemy
14:21 were about five thousand ***m***,
14:35 And when the ***m*** of that place
15: 9 the commandments of ***m***.
15:38 who ate were four thousand ***m***,
16:13 Who do ***m*** say that I, the Son of
16:23 of God, but the things of ***m***.
17:22 be betrayed into the hands of ***m***,
19:12 who were made eunuchs by ***m***,
19:26 With ***m*** this is impossible, but
20:12 These last ***m*** have worked only
20:30 two blind ***m*** sitting by the
21:25 it from? From heaven or from ***m***?
21:26 "But if we say, 'From ***m***,
21:41 will destroy those wicked ***m***
22:16 do not regard the person of ***m***.
23: 5 works they do to be seen by ***m***.
23: 7 and to be called by ***m***, 'Rabbi,
23:13 the kingdom of heaven against ***m***;
23:28 outwardly appear righteous to ***m***,
23:34 I send you prophets, wise ***m***,
24:40 Then two ***m*** will be in the
26:62 What is it these ***m*** testify
28: 4 of him, and became like dead ***m***.
Mk 1:17 make you become fishers of ***m***.
2: 3 who was carried by four ***m***.
3:28 will be forgiven the sons of ***m***,
6:21 and the chief ***m*** of Galilee.
6:44 were about five thousand ***m***.
7: 7 the commandments of ***m***.
7: 8 you hold the tradition of ***m***—
7:21 within, out of the heart of ***m***,
8:24 I see ***m*** like trees, walking."
8:27 Who do ***m*** say that I am?"
8:33 of God, but the things of ***m***.
9:31 betrayed into the hands of ***m***,
10:27 With ***m*** it is impossible, but
11:30 it from heaven or from ***m***?
12:14 do not regard the person of ***m***,
14:51 And the young ***m*** laid hold of
14:60 What is it these ***m*** testify
Lk 2:14 goodwill toward ***m***!"
2:52 and in favor with God and ***m***.
5:10 From now on you will catch ***m***.
5:18 ***m*** brought on a bed a man who
6:22 Blessed are you when ***m*** hate
6:26 Woe to you when all ***m*** speak
6:31 And just as you want ***m*** to do to
6:44 For ***m*** do not gather figs from
7:20 When the ***m*** had come to Him, they
7:31 what then shall I liken the ***m***
9:14 were about five thousand ***m***.
9:30 two ***m*** talked with Him, who were
9:32 saw His glory and the two ***m***
9:44 be betrayed into the hands of ***m***.
11:31 up in the judgment with the ***m***
11:32 The ***m*** of Nineveh will rise up in
11:44 and the ***m*** who walk over them
11:46 For you load ***m*** with
12: 8 whoever confesses Me before ***m***,
12: 9 But he who denies Me before ***m***
12:36 and you yourselves be like ***m*** who
13: 4 sinners than all other ***m*** who
13:14 There are six days on which ***m***
14:24 say to you that none of those ***m***
14:35 but ***m*** throw it out. He who has
16:15 who justify yourselves before ***m***,
16:15 is highly esteemed among ***m*** is
17:12 there met Him ten ***m*** who were
17:34 night there will be two ***m*** in
17:36 'Two ***m*** will be in the field:
18: 1 that ***m*** always ought to pray and
18:10 Two ***m*** went up to the temple to
18:11 You that I am not like other ***m***—
18:27 which are impossible with ***m***
20: 4 it from heaven or from ***m***?
20: 6 "But if we say, 'From ***m***,
22:63 Now the ***m*** who held Jesus mocked
23:11 with his ***m*** of war, treated Him
23:23 And the voices of these ***m*** and
24: 4 two ***m*** stood by them in shining
24: 7 into the hands of sinful ***m***,
Jn 1: 4 and the life was the light of ***m***.
2:24 to them, because He knew all ***m***,
3:19 and ***m*** loved darkness rather
4:28 the city, and said to the ***m***,
5:41 "I do not receive honor from ***m***.
6:10 So the ***m*** sat down, in number
6:14 Then those ***m***, when they had
8:17 that the testimony of two ***m*** is
12:43 for they loved the praise of ***m***
17: 6 manifested Your name to the ***m***
Acts 1:10 two ***m*** stood by them in white
1:11 ***M*** of Galilee, why do you stand
1:16 ***M*** and brethren, this Scripture
1:21 of these ***m*** who have accompanied
2: 5 in Jerusalem Jews, devout ***m***,
2:14 ***M*** of Judea and all who dwell in
2:17 Your young ***m*** shall see
2:17 Your old ***m*** shall dream
2:22 ***M*** of Israel, hear these words:
2:29 ***M*** and brethren, let me speak
2:37 ***M*** and brethren, what shall we
3:12 ***M*** of Israel, why do you marvel
4: 4 and the number of the ***m*** came to
4:12 under heaven given among ***m*** by
4:13 were uneducated and untrained ***m***,
4:16 "What shall we do to these ***m***?
5: 4 You have not lied to ***m*** but to
5: 6 And the young ***m*** arose and
5:10 And the young ***m*** came in and
5:14 multitudes of both ***m*** and women,
5:25 the ***m*** whom you put in prison
5:29 ought to obey God rather than ***m***.
5:35 ***M*** of Israel, take heed to
5:35 intend to do regarding these ***m***.
5:36 to be somebody. A number of ***m***,
5:38 keep away from these ***m*** and let
5:38 this plan or this work is of ***m***,
6: 3 out from among you seven ***m*** of
6:11 Then they secretly induced ***m*** to
7:26 to reconcile them, saying, '***M***,
8: 2 And devout ***m*** carried Stephen to
8: 3 and dragging off ***m*** and women,
8:12 both ***m*** and women were baptized.
9: 2 whether ***m*** or women, he might
9: 7 And the ***m*** who journeyed with him
9:38 they sent two ***m*** to him,
10: 5 Now send ***m*** to Joppa, and send
10:17 the ***m*** who had been sent from
10:19 three ***m*** are seeking you.
10:21 Then Peter went down to the ***m***
11: 3 went in to uncircumcised ***m***
11:11 three ***m*** stood before the house
11:13 Send ***m*** to Joppa, and call for
11:20 But some of them were ***m*** from
13:15 ***M*** and brethren, if you have any
13:16 ***M*** of Israel, and you who fear
13:26 ***M*** and brethren, sons of the
13:50 women and the chief ***m*** of the
14:11 to us in the likeness of ***m***!"
14:15 and saying, "***M***, why are you
14:15 We also are ***m*** with the same
15: 1 And certain ***m*** came down from
15: 7 ***M*** and brethren, you know that a
15:13 ***M*** and brethren, listen to me:
15:22 to send chosen ***m*** of their own
15:22 leading ***m*** among the brethren.
15:25 to send chosen ***m*** to you with
15:26 ***m*** who have risked their lives
16:17 These ***m*** are the servants of the
16:20 and said, "These ***m***, being
16:35 saying, "Let those ***m*** go."
17: 5 took some of the evil ***m*** from
17:12 prominent women as well as ***m***.
17:22 ***M*** of Athens, I perceive that in
17:26 one blood every nation of ***m*** to
17:30 but now commands all ***m***
17:34 some ***m*** joined him and believed,
18:13 This fellow persuades ***m*** to
19: 7 Now the ***m*** were about twelve in
19:25 occupation, and said: "***M***,
19:35 ***M*** of Ephesus, what man is there
19:37 For you have brought these ***m***
20: 5 These ***m***, going ahead, waited
20:26 innocent of the blood of all ***m***.
20:30 Also from among yourselves ***m***
21:23 We have four ***m*** who have taken a
21:26 Then Paul took the ***m***,
21:28 ***M*** of Israel, help! This is the
21:28 is the man who teaches all ***m***
22: 4 delivering into prisons both ***m***
22:15 will be His witness to all ***m***
23: 1 ***M*** and brethren, I have lived in
23: 6 ***M*** and brethren, I am a
23:21 ***m*** who have bound themselves by
24:16 offense toward God and ***m***.
25: 2 high priest and the chief ***m*** of
25:11 these things of which these ***m***
25:23 commanders and the prominent ***m***
25:24 King Agrippa and all the ***m*** who
27:10 saying, "***M***, I perceive that
27:21 the midst of them and said, "***M***,
27:25 "Therefore take heart, ***m***,
27:31 Unless these ***m*** stay in the ship,
28:17 ***M*** and brethren, though I have
Rom 1:18 and unrighteousness of ***m***,
1:27 Likewise also the ***m***,
1:27 ***m*** with men committing what is
1:27 men with ***m*** committing what is
2:16 will judge the secrets of ***m*** by
2:29 whose praise is not from ***m*** but
5:12 and thus death spread to all ***m***,
5:18 offense judgment came to all ***m***,
5:18 the free gift came to all ***m***,
11: 4 Myself seven thousand ***m***
12:17 things in the sight of all ***m***.
12:18 you, live peaceably with all ***m***.
14:18 to God and approved by ***m***.
1 Cor 1:25 of God is wiser than ***m***,
1:25 of God is stronger than ***m***.
2: 5 not be in the wisdom of ***m*** but
3: 3 and behaving like mere ***m***?
3:21 Therefore let no one boast in ***m***.
4: 9 as ***m*** condemned to death; for we
4: 9 world, both to angels and to ***m***.
7: 7 For I wish that all ***m*** were even
7:23 do not become slaves of ***m***.
9:19 though I am free from all ***m***,
9:22 become all things to all ***m***,
10:15 I speak as to wise ***m***;
10:33 just as I also please all ***m*** in
13: 1 I speak with the tongues of ***m***
14: 2 in a tongue does not speak to ***m***
14: 3 exhortation and comfort to ***m***.
14:21 With ***m*** of other tongues and
15:19 we are of all ***m*** the most
15:32 If, in the manner of ***m***,
15:39 is one kind of flesh of ***m***,
16:18 Therefore acknowledge such ***m***.
2 Cor 3: 2 hearts, known and read by all ***m***;
5:11 of the Lord, we persuade ***m***;
8:21 but also in the sight of ***m***.
9:13 sharing with them and all ***m***,
Gal 1: 1 an apostle (not from ***m*** nor
1:10 For do I now persuade ***m***,
1:10 Or do I seek to please ***m***?
1:10 For if I still pleased ***m***,
2:12 for before certain ***m*** came from
3:15 I speak in the manner of ***m***:
Eph 3: 5 not made known to the sons of ***m***,
4: 8 And gave gifts to ***m***.
4:14 doctrine, by the trickery of ***m***,
6: 7 as to the Lord, and not to ***m***,
Phil 2: 7 coming in the likeness of ***m***.
2:29 and hold such ***m*** in esteem;
4: 5 gentleness be known to all ***m***.
Col 2: 8 according to the tradition of ***m***,
2:22 commandments and doctrines of ***m***?
3:23 as to the Lord and not to ***m***,
1 Th 1: 5 as you know what kind of ***m*** we
2: 4 so we speak, not as pleasing ***m***,
2: 6 Nor did we seek glory from ***m***,
2:13 it not as the word of ***m***,
2:15 God and are contrary to all ***m***,
2 Th 3: 2 from unreasonable and wicked ***m***;
1 Tim 2: 1 of thanks be made for all ***m***,
2: 4 who desires all ***m*** to be saved
2: 5 one Mediator between God and ***m***,
2: 8 I desire therefore that the ***m***
4:10 who is the Savior of all ***m***,
5: 1 younger ***m*** as brothers,
5:24 but those of some ***m*** follow
6: 5 useless wranglings of ***m*** of
6: 9 harmful lusts which drown ***m*** in
2 Tim 2: 2 commit these to faithful ***m*** who
3: 2 For ***m*** will be lovers of
3: 8 ***m*** of corrupt minds, disapproved
3:13 But evil ***m*** and impostors will
Titus 1:14 fables and commandments of ***m***
2: 2 that the older ***m*** be sober,
2: 6 Likewise exhort the young ***m*** to
2:11 salvation has appeared to all ***m***,
3: 2 showing all humility to all ***m***.
3: 8 are good and profitable to ***m***.
Heb 5: 1 high priest taken from among ***m***
5: 1 among men is appointed for ***m***
6:16 For ***m*** indeed swear by the
7: 8 Here mortal ***m*** receive tithes,
7:28 law appoints as high priests ***m***
9:17 testament is in force after ***m***
9:27 And as it is appointed for ***m*** to
12:23 to the spirits of just ***m*** made
Jas 3: 9 Father, and with it we curse ***m***,
1 Pe 2: 4 stone, rejected indeed by ***m***,
2:15 the ignorance of foolish ***m***—
4: 2 in the flesh for the lusts of ***m***,
4: 6 might be judged according to ***m***
2 Pe 1:21 but holy ***m*** of God spoke as
3: 7 and perdition of ungodly ***m***.
1 Jn 2:13 I write to you, young ***m***,
2:14 I have written to you, young ***m***,
5: 9 If we receive the witness of ***m***,
Jude 4 For certain ***m*** have crept in
4 this condemnation, ungodly ***m***,
14 prophesied about these ***m*** also,

Rev 6:15 kings of the earth, the great **m**,
6:15 the great men, the rich **m**,
6:15 the commanders, the mighty **m**,
8:11 and many **m** died from the water,
9: 4 but only those **m** who do not
9: 6 In those days **m** will seek death
9: 7 faces were like the faces of **m**.
9:10 Their power was to hurt **m** five
13:13 on the earth in the sight of **m**.
14: 4 were redeemed from among **m**,
16: 2 loathsome sore came upon the **m**
16: 8 was given to him to scorch **m**
16: 9 And **m** were scorched with great
16:18 as had not occurred since **m**
16:21 hail from heaven fell upon **m**,
16:21 **M** blasphemed God because of the
18:13 and bodies and souls of **m**.
18:23 merchants were the great **m** of
19:18 captains, the flesh of mighty **m**,
21: 3 tabernacle of God is with **m**,

MEN-PLEASERS (2/2) MEN

Eph 6: 6 not with eyeservice, as **m**,
Col 3:22 not with eyeservice, as **m**,

MEN'S (19/19) MEN

Gen 44: 1 Fill the **m** sacks with food, as
Deut 4:28 the work of **m** hands, wood and
1 Ki 13: 2 and **m** bones shall be burned on
2 Ki 19:18 but the work of **m** hands—wood
23:20 and burned **m** bones on them;
2 Chr 32:19 the work of **m** hands.
Ps 115: 4 The work of **m** hands.
135:15 The work of **m** hands.
Isa 37:19 but the work of **m** hands—wood
Jer 48:41 The mighty **m** hearts in Moab on
Hab 2: 8 Because of **m** blood And the
2:17 Because of **m** blood And the
Mt 23: 4 and lay them on **m** shoulders;
23:27 but inside are full of dead **m**
Lk 9:56 Man did not come to destroy **m**
21:26 **m** hearts failing them from fear
Acts 17:25 Nor is He worshiped with **m**
2 Cor 10:15 in other **m** labors, but having
1 Tim 5:24 Some **m** sins are clearly evident,

MENAHEM (8/8)

2 Ki 15:14 For **M** the son of Gadi went up
15:16 **M** attacked Tiphsah, all who
15:17 **M** the son of Gadi became king
15:19 and **M** gave Pul a thousand
15:20 And **M** exacted the money from
15:21 Now the rest of the acts of **M**,
15:22 So **M** rested with his fathers.
15:23 Pekahiah the son of **M** became

MENAN (1/1)

Lk 3:31 son of Melea, the son of **M**,

MENDED (1/1)

Josh 9: 4 old wineskins torn and **m**,

MENDING (2/2)

Mt 4:21 **m** their nets. He called them,
Mk 1:19 who also were in the boat **m**

MENE (3/2)

Dan 5:25 inscription that was written: **M**,
5:25 that was written: MENE, **M**,
5:26 of each word. **M**:

MENI (1/1)

Isa 65:11 furnish a drink offering for **M**.

MENSERVANTS (2/2) MALE, MANSERVANT

Joel 2:29 And also on My **m** and on My
Acts 2:18 And on My **m** and on My

MENSTEALERS (KJV) See KIDNAPPERS

MENTION (25/25) MENTIONED

Gen 40:14 make **m** of me to Pharaoh, and
Ex 23:13 be circumspect and make no **m** of
Josh 23: 7 You shall not make **m** of the
1 Sam 4:18 when he made **m** of the ark of
Job 28:18 No **m** shall be made of coral or
Ps 71:16 I will make **m** of Your
87: 4 I will make **m** of Rahab and
Isa 12: 4 Make **m** that His name is
19:17 everyone who makes **m** of it will
26:13 But by You only we make **m** of
48: 1 And make **m** of the God of
49: 1 of My mother He has made **m** of
62: 6 You who make **m** of the LORD,
63: 7 I will **m** the lovingkindnesses
Jer 4:16 Make **m** to the nations, Yes,
20: 9 'I will not make **m** of Him,
23:36 of the LORD you shall **m** no
Am 6:10 your tongue! For we dare not **m**
Rom 1: 9 that without ceasing I make **m**
2 Cor 9: 4 we (not to **m** you!) should be
Eph 1:16 making **m** of you in my prayers:
1 Th 1: 2 making **m** of you in our prayers,
Phm 1: 4 making **m** of you always in my
1:19 not to **m** to you that you owe me
Heb 11:22 made **m** of the departure of the

MENTIONED (3/3) MENTION

Num 1:17 took these men who had been **m**
1 Chr 4:38 these **m** by name were leaders in
2 Chr 20:34 which is **m** in the book of the

MEONOTHAI (1/1)

1 Chr 4:14 and **M** who begot Ophrah.

MEPHAATH (4/4)

Josh 13:18 Jahaza, Kedemoth, **M**,
21:37 and **M** with its common-land:
1 Chr 6:79 and **M** with its common-lands.
Jer 48:21 On Holon and Jahzah and **M**,

MEPHIBOSHETH (15/13) MERIB-BAAL

2 Sam 4: 4 became lame. His name was **M**.
9: 6 Now when **M** the son of Jonathan,
9: 6 Then David said, "**M**?"
9:10 But **M** your master's son shall
9:11 your servant do." "As for **M**,
9:12 **M** had a young son whose name
9:12 of Ziba were servants of **M**.
9:13 So **M** dwelt in Jerusalem, for he
16: 1 there was Ziba the servant of **M**,
16: 4 all that belongs to **M** is
19:24 Now **M** the son of Saul came down
19:25 "Why did you not go with me, **M**?
19:30 Then **M** said to the king,
21: 7 But the king spared **M** the son
21: 8 So the king took Armoni and **M**,

MERAB (3/3)

1 Sam 14:49 the name of the firstborn **M**,
18:17 "Here is my older daughter **M**;
18:19 it happened at the time when **M**,

MERAIAH (1/1)

Neh 12:12 houses were: of Seraiah, **M**;

MERAIOTH (7/7)

1 Chr 6: 6 Zerahiah, and Zerahiah begot **M**;
6: 7 **M** begot Amariah, and Amariah
6:52 **M** his son, Amariah his son,
9:11 the son of Zadok, the son of **M**,
Ezra 7: 3 son of Azariah, the son of **M**,
Neh 11:11 the son of Zadok, the son of **M**,
12:15 of Harim, Adna; of **M**,

MERARI (39/38)

Gen 46:11 were Gershon, Kohath, and **M**.
Ex 6:16 Gershon, Kohath, and **M**.
6:19 The sons of **M** were Mahali and
Num 3:17 names: Gershon, Kohath, and **M**.
3:20 And the sons of **M** by their
3:33 From **M** came the family of the
3:33 these were the families of **M**.
3:35 house of the families of **M**
3:36 duty of the children of **M**
4:29 "As for the sons of **M**,
4:33 the families of the sons of **M**,
4:42 the families of the sons of **M**
4:45 the families of the sons of **M**,
7: 8 oxen he gave to the sons of **M**,
10:17 of Gershon and the sons of **M**
26:57 family of the Kohathites; of **M**,
Josh 21: 7 The children of **M** according to
21:34 families of the children of **M**,
21:40 cities for the children of **M**
1 Chr 6: 1 were Gershon, Kohath, and **M**.
6:16 were Gershon, Kohath, and **M**.
6:19 The sons of **M** were Mahli and
6:29 The sons of **M** were Mahli, Libni
6:44 Their brethren, the sons of **M**,
6:47 the son of Mushi, the son of **M**,
6:63 To the sons of **M**, throughout
6:77 the rest of the children of **M**
9:14 of Hashabiah, of the sons of **M**;
15: 6 of the sons of **M**, Asaiah the
15:17 their brethren, the sons of **M**,
23: 6 of Levi: Gershon, Kohath, and **M**.
23:21 The sons of **M** were Mahli and
24:26 The sons of **M** were Mahli and
24:27 The sons of **M** by Jaaziah were
26:10 Hosah, of the children of **M**,
26:19 Korah and among the sons of **M**.
2 Chr 29:12 Kohathites; of the sons of **M**,
34:12 the Levites, of the sons of **M**,
Ezra 8:19 him Jeshaiah of the sons of **M**,

MERARITES (1/1)

Num 26:57 of Merari, the family of the **M**.

MERATHAIM (1/1)

Jer 50:21 "Go up against the land of **M**,

MERCENARIES (1/1)

Jer 46:21 Also her **m** are in her midst

MERCHANDISE (14/14)

Prov 31:18 She perceives that her **m** is
Isa 45:14 The labor of Egypt and **m** of Cush
Ezek 26:12 your riches and pillage your **m**;
27: 9 were in you To market your **m**.
27:13 vessels of bronze for your **m**.
27:17 They traded for your **m** wheat of
27:19 and cane were among your **m**.
27:25 were carriers of your **m**.
27:27 "Your riches, wares, and **m**,
27:33 many luxury goods and your **m**.
27:34 Your **m** and the entire company
Jn 2:16 My Father's house a house of **m**!
Rev 18:11 for no one buys their **m**
18:12 **m** of gold and silver, precious

MERCHANDISERS (1/1)

Ezek 27:27 pilots, Your caulkers and **m**,

MERCHANT (12/11) MERCHANTS

1 Ki 10:22 For the king had **m** ships at sea
10:22 Once every three years the **m**
22:48 Jehoshaphat made **m** ships to go
2 Chr 9:21 Once every three years the **m**
Prov 31:14 She is like the **m** ships,
Ezek 27: 3 **m** of the peoples on many
27:12 Tarshish was your **m** because of
27:16 Syria was your **m** because of the
27:18 Damascus was your **m** because of
27:20 Dedan was your **m** in
Zeph 1:11 of Maktesh! For all the **m**
Mt 13:45 kingdom of heaven is like a **m**

MERCHANT'S (1/1)

Song 3: 6 With all the **m** fragrant

MERCHANTMEN (KJV) See MERCHANTS, TRADERS

MERCHANTS (27/25) MERCHANT

Gen 23:16 of silver, currency of the **m**.
1 Ki 10:15 that from the traveling **m**,
10:28 the king's **m** bought them in
2 Chr 1:16 the king's **m** bought them in
9:14 besides what the traveling **m**
Neh 3:31 of the Nethinim and of the **m**,
3:32 the goldsmiths and the **m** made
13:20 Now the **m** and sellers of all
Job 41: 6 they apportion him among the **m**?
Prov 31:24 And supplies sashes for the **m**.
Isa 23: 2 You **m** of Sidon, Whom those
23: 8 Whose **m** are princes,
47:15 Your **m** from your youth;
Ezek 17: 4 He set it in a city of **m**.
27:21 of Kedar were your regular **m**.
27:22 The **m** of Sheba and Raamah were
27:22 Sheba and Raamah were your **m**.
27:23 the **m** of Sheba, Assyria, and
27:23 and Chilmad were your **m**.
27:24 These were your **m** in choice
27:36 The **m** among the peoples will
38:13 the **m** of Tarshish, and all
Nah 3:16 You have multiplied your **m** more
Rev 18: 3 and the **m** of the earth have
18:11 And the **m** of the earth will weep
18:15 The **m** of these things, who
18:23 For your **m** were the great men

MERCIES (35/35) MERCIES', MERCY

Gen 32:10 of the least of all the **m** and
2 Sam 24:14 for His **m** are great; but do
1 Chr 21:13 for His **m** are very great; but
2 Chr 6:42 Remember the **m** of Your servant
Neh 9:19 Yet in Your manifold **m** You did
9:27 according to Your abundant **m**
9:28 them according to Your **m**,
Ps 25: 6 Your tender **m** and Your
40:11 Do not withhold Your tender **m**
51: 1 the multitude of Your tender **m**,
69:16 the multitude of Your tender **m**.
77: 9 in anger shut up His tender **m**?
79: 8 against us! Let Your tender **m**
89: 1 I will sing of the **m** of the
103: 4 lovingkindness and tender **m**,
106: 7 the multitude of Your **m**,
106:45 to the multitude of His **m**.
119:41 Let Your **m** come also to me,
119:77 Let Your tender **m** come to me,
119:156 Great are Your tender **m**,
145: 9 And His tender **m** are over all
Prov 12:10 But the tender **m** of the wicked
Isa 54: 7 But with great **m** I will gather
55: 3 The sure **m** of David.
63: 7 on them according to His **m**,
63:15 of Your heart and Your **m**
Jer 16: 5 LORD, "lovingkindness and **m**.
Lam 3:22 Through the LORD's **m** we are
3:32 to the multitude of His **m**.
Dan 2:18 that they might seek **m** from the
9:18 but because of Your great **m**.
Acts 13:34 will give you the sure **m**
Rom 12: 1 by the **m** of God, that you
2 Cor 1: 3 the Father of **m** and God of all
Col 3:12 and beloved, put on tender **m**,

MERCIES' (3/3) MERCIES, MERCY

Ps 6: 4 save me for Your ***m*** sake!
31:16 Save me for Your ***m*** sake.
44:26 And redeem us for Your ***m*** sake.

MERCIFUL (39/35) MERCY, UNMERCIFUL

Gen 19:16 the LORD being ***m*** to him, and
Ex 34: 6 ***m*** and gracious, longsuffering,
Deut 4:31 the LORD your God is a ***m***
2 Sam 22:26 With the ***m*** You will show
22:26 You will show Yourself ***m***;
1 Ki 20:31 of the house of Israel are ***m***
2 Chr 30: 9 your God is gracious and ***m***,
Neh 9:17 to pardon, Gracious and ***m***,
9:31 You are God, gracious and ***m***.
Ps 18:25 With the ***m*** You will show
18:25 You will show Yourself ***m***;
26:11 Redeem me and be ***m*** to me.
37:26 He is ever ***m***, and lends;
41: 4 be ***m*** to me; Heal my soul, for
41:10 be ***m*** to me, and raise me up,
56: 1 Be ***m*** to me, O God, for man
57: 1 Be ***m*** to me, O God, be merciful
57: 1 be ***m*** to me! For my soul trusts
59: 5 Do not be ***m*** to any wicked
67: 1 God be ***m*** to us and bless us,
86: 3 Be ***m*** to me, O Lord, For I cry
103: 8 The LORD is ***m*** and gracious,
116: 5 righteous; Yes, our God is ***m***.
117: 2 For His ***m*** kindness is great
119:58 Be ***m*** to me according to Your
119:76 Your ***m*** kindness be for my
119:132 Look upon me and be ***m*** to me,
Prov 11:17 The ***m*** man does good for his own
Isa 57: 1 ***M*** men are taken away,
Jer 3:12 to fall on you. For I am ***m***,
Joel 2:13 God, For He is gracious and ***m***,
Jon 4: 2 that You are a gracious and ***m***
Mt 5: 7 Blessed are the ***m***, For they
Lk 6:36 'Therefore be ***m***, just as
6:36 just as your Father also is ***m***.
18:13 be ***m*** to me a sinner!'
Heb 2:17 that He might be a ***m*** and
8:12 For I will be ***m*** to their
Jas 5:11 is very compassionate and ***m***.

MERCURIUS (KJV) See HERMES

MERCY (282/269) MERCIES, MERCIES', MERCIFUL

Gen 19:19 and you have increased your ***m***
24:27 who has not forsaken His ***m*** and
39:21 with Joseph and showed him ***m***,
43:14 may God Almighty give you ***m***
Ex 15:13 You in Your ***m*** have led forth
20: 6 but showing ***m*** to thousands, to
25:17 You shall make a ***m*** seat of pure
25:18 them at the two ends of the ***m***
25:19 it of one piece with the ***m***
25:20 covering the ***m*** seat with their
25:20 shall be toward the ***m*** seat.
25:21 You shall put the ***m*** seat on top
25:22 with you from above the ***m*** seat,
26:34 You shall put the ***m*** seat upon
30: 6 before the ***m*** seat that is over
31: 7 ark of the Testimony and the ***m***
34: 7 keeping ***m*** for thousands,
35:12 with the ***m*** seat, and the veil
37: 6 He also made the ***m*** seat of pure
37: 7 piece at the two ends of the ***m***
37: 8 ends of one piece with the ***m***
37: 9 and covered the ***m*** seat with
37: 9 the cherubim were toward the ***m***
39:35 its poles, and the ***m*** seat;
40:20 and put the ***m*** seat on top of
Lev 16: 2 before the ***m*** seat which is on
16: 2 in the cloud above the ***m*** seat.
16:13 of incense may cover the ***m***
16:14 it with his finger on the ***m***
16:14 and before the ***m*** seat he shall
16:15 and sprinkle it on the ***m*** seat
16:15 the mercy seat and before the ***m***
Num 7:89 to him from above the ***m*** seat
14:18 longsuffering and abundant in ***m***,
14:19 to the greatness of Your ***m***,
Deut 5:10 but showing ***m*** to thousands, to
7: 2 covenant with them nor show ***m***
7: 9 God who keeps covenant and ***m***
7:12 with you the covenant and the ***m***
13:17 of His anger and show you ***m***,
Josh 11:20 that they might receive no ***m***,
Judg 1:24 city, and we will show you ***m***.
2 Sam 7:15 But My ***m*** shall not depart from
15:20 ***M*** and truth be with you."
22:51 And shows ***m*** to His anointed,
1 Ki 3: 6 You have shown great ***m*** to Your
8:23 who keep Your covenant and ***m***
20:33 see whether any sign of ***m***
1 Chr 16:34 for He is good! For His ***m***
16:41 because His ***m*** endures forever;
17:13 and I will not take My ***m*** away
28:11 and the place of the ***m*** seat;
2 Chr 1: 8 You have shown great ***m*** to David
5:13 For His ***m*** endures forever,"
6:14 who keep Your covenant and ***m***
7: 3 For His ***m*** endures forever."
7: 6 For His ***m*** endures forever,"
20:21 For His ***m*** endures forever."
Ezra 3:11 For His ***m*** endures forever
7:28 and has extended ***m*** to me before
9: 9 but He extended ***m*** to us in the
Neh 1: 5 who keep Your covenant and ***m***
1:11 and grant him ***m*** in the sight of
9:31 Nevertheless in Your great ***m***
9:32 God, Who keeps covenant and ***m***:
13:22 to the greatness of Your ***m***!
Job 9:15 I would beg ***m*** of my Judge.
37:13 Or for His land, Or for ***m***.
Ps 4: 1 Have ***m*** on me, and hear my
5: 7 in the multitude of Your ***m***;
6: 2 Have ***m*** on me, O LORD, for I
9:13 Have ***m*** on me, O LORD!
13: 5 But I have trusted in Your ***m***;
18:50 And shows ***m*** to His anointed,
21: 7 And through the ***m*** of the Most
23: 6 Surely goodness and ***m*** shall
25: 7 According to Your ***m*** remember
25:10 the paths of the LORD are ***m***
25:16 and have ***m*** on me, For I am
27: 7 I cry with my voice! Have ***m***
30:10 and have ***m*** on me; LORD, be my
31: 7 be glad and rejoice in Your ***m***,
31: 9 Have ***m*** on me, O LORD, for I am
32:10 ***m*** shall surround him.
33:18 On those who hope in His ***m***,
33:22 Let Your ***m***, O LORD, be upon
36: 5 Your ***m***, O LORD, is in the
37:21 But the righteous shows ***m*** and
51: 1 Have ***m*** upon me, O God,
52: 8 I trust in the ***m*** of God
57: 3 God shall send forth His ***m***
57:10 For Your ***m*** reaches unto the
59:10 My God of ***m*** shall come to meet
59:16 I will sing aloud of Your ***m*** in
59:17 is my defense, My God of ***m***.
61: 7 prepare ***m*** and truth, which may
62:12 to You, O Lord, belongs ***m***;
66:20 Nor His ***m*** from me!
69:13 God, in the multitude of Your ***m***,
77: 8 Has His ***m*** ceased forever?
85: 7 Show us Your ***m***, LORD, And
85:10 ***M*** and truth have met together
86: 5 And abundant in ***m*** to all those
86:13 For great is Your ***m*** toward me,
86:15 and abundant in ***m*** and truth.
86:16 and have ***m*** on me! Give Your
89: 2 ***M*** shall be built up forever;
89:14 ***M*** and truth go before Your
89:24 But My faithfulness and My ***m***
89:28 My ***m*** I will keep for him
90:14 satisfy us early with Your ***m***,
94:18 say, "My foot slips," Your ***m***,
98: 3 He has remembered His ***m*** and His
100: 5 His ***m*** is everlasting,
101: 1 I will sing of ***m*** and justice;
102:13 You will arise and have ***m*** on
103: 8 to anger, and abounding in ***m***.
103:11 So great is His ***m*** toward
103:17 But the ***m*** of the LORD is from
106: 1 for He is good! For His ***m***
107: 1 for He is good! For His ***m***
108: 4 For Your ***m*** is great above the
109:12 Let there be none to extend ***m***
109:16 he did not remember to show ***m***,
109:21 Because Your ***m*** is good,
109:26 save me according to Your ***m***,
115: 1 give glory, Because of Your ***m***,
118: 1 for He is good! For His ***m***
118: 2 His ***m*** endures forever."
118: 3 His ***m*** endures forever."
118: 4 His ***m*** endures forever."
118:29 for He is good! For His ***m***
119:64 O LORD, is full of Your ***m***;
119:124 servant according to Your ***m***,
123: 2 Until He has ***m*** on us.
123: 3 Have ***m*** on us, O LORD, have
123: 3 have ***m*** on us! For we are
130: 7 with the LORD there is ***m***,
136: 1 for He is good! For His ***m***
136: 2 to the God of gods! For His ***m***
136: 3 the Lord of lords! For His ***m***
136: 4 For His ***m*** endures forever;
136: 5 For His ***m*** endures forever;
136: 6 For His ***m*** endures forever;
136: 7 For His ***m*** endures forever—
136: 8 For His ***m*** endures forever;
136: 9 For His ***m*** endures forever.
136:10 For His ***m*** endures forever;
136:11 For His ***m*** endures forever;
136:12 For His ***m*** endures forever;
136:13 For His ***m*** endures forever;
136:14 For His ***m*** endures forever;
136:15 For His ***m*** endures forever;
136:16 For His ***m*** endures forever;
136:17 For His ***m*** endures forever;
136:18 For His ***m*** endures forever—
136:19 For His ***m*** endures forever;
136:20 For His ***m*** endures forever—
136:21 For His ***m*** endures forever;
136:22 For His ***m*** endures forever.
136:23 For His ***m*** endures forever;
136:24 For His ***m*** endures forever;
136:25 For His ***m*** endures forever.
136:26 the God of heaven! For His ***m***
138: 8 which concerns me; Your ***m***,
143:12 In Your ***m*** cut off my enemies,
145: 8 Slow to anger and great in ***m***.
147:11 In those who hope in His ***m***.
Prov 3: 3 Let not ***m*** and truth forsake
14:21 But he who has ***m*** on the poor,
14:22 But ***m*** and truth belong to
14:31 But he who honors Him has ***m*** on
16: 6 In ***m*** and truth Atonement is
20:28 ***M*** and truth preserve the king,
21:21 who follows righteousness and ***m***
28:13 and forsakes them will have ***m***.
Isa 9:17 Nor have ***m*** on their fatherless
14: 1 For the LORD will have ***m*** on
16: 5 In ***m*** the throne will be
27:11 who made them will not have ***m***
30:18 that He may have ***m*** on you.
47: 6 You showed them no ***m***;
49:10 For He who has ***m*** on them will
49:13 And will have ***m*** on His
54: 8 kindness I will have ***m*** on you,
54:10 the LORD, who has ***m*** on you.
55: 7 And He will have ***m*** on him;
60:10 But in My favor I have had ***m***
Jer 6:23 They are cruel and have no ***m***;
13:14 not pity nor spare nor have ***m***,
21: 7 spare them, or have pity or ***m***.
30:18 And have ***m*** on his dwelling
31:20 I will surely have ***m*** on him,
33:11 For His ***m*** endures
33:26 and will have ***m*** on them.'"
42:12 'And I will show you ***m***,
42:12 that he may have ***m*** on you and
50:42 are cruel and shall not show ***m***.
Ezek 39:25 and have ***m*** on the whole house
Dan 4:27 your iniquities by showing ***m***
9: 4 who keeps His covenant and ***m***
9: 9 To the Lord our God belong ***m***
Hos 1: 6 For I will no longer have ***m*** on
1: 7 Yet I will have ***m*** on the house
2: 1 your sisters, '***M*** is shown.'
2: 4 I will not have ***m*** on her
2:19 In lovingkindness and ***m***;
2:23 And I will have ***m*** on her who
2:23 her who had not obtained ***m***;
4: 1 There is no truth or ***m*** Or
6: 6 For I desire ***m*** and not
10:12 righteousness; Reap in ***m***;
12: 6 Observe ***m*** and justice,
14: 3 in You the fatherless finds ***m***.
Jon 2: 8 Forsake their own ***M***.
Mic 6: 8 But to do justly, To love ***m***,
7:18 Because He delights in ***m***.
7:20 give truth to Jacob And ***m*** to
Hab 3: 2 it known; In wrath remember ***m***.
Zech 1:12 how long will You not have ***m*** on
1:16 returning to Jerusalem with ***m***;
7: 9 Show ***m*** and compassion
10: 6 Because I have ***m*** on them.
Mt 5: 7 For they shall obtain ***m***.
9:13 I desire ***m*** and not
9:27 'Son of David, have ***m*** on us!"
12: 7 I desire ***m*** and not
15:22 Have ***m*** on me, O Lord, Son of
17:15 have ***m*** on my son, for he is an
20:30 Have ***m*** on us, O Lord, Son of
20:31 Have ***m*** on us, O Lord, Son of
23:23 justice and ***m*** and faith.
Mk 10:47 Son of David, have ***m*** on me!"
10:48 'Son of David, have ***m*** on me!"
Lk 1:50 And His ***m*** is on those who fear
1:54 In remembrance of His ***m***,
1:58 how the Lord had shown great ***m***
1:72 To perform the ***m*** promised to
1:78 Through the tender ***m*** of our
10:37 'He who showed ***m*** on him."
16:24 have ***m*** on me, and send Lazarus
17:13 Master, have ***m*** on us!"
18:38 Son of David, have ***m*** on me!"
18:39 'Son of David, have ***m*** on me!"
Rom 9:15 I will have ***m*** on whomever
9:15 on whomever I will have ***m***,
9:16 runs, but of God who shows ***m***.
9:18 Therefore He has ***m*** on whom He
9:23 His glory on the vessels of ***m***,
11:30 yet have now obtained ***m*** through
11:31 that through the ***m*** shown you
11:31 you they also may obtain ***m***.
11:32 that He might have ***m*** on all.
12: 8 with diligence; he who shows ***m***,
15: 9 might glorify God for His ***m***,
1 Cor 7:25 as one whom the Lord in His ***m***
2 Cor 4: 1 ministry, as we have received ***m***,
Gal 6:16 peace and ***m*** be upon them, and
Eph 2: 4 But God, who is rich in ***m***,
Phil 2: 1 Spirit, if any affection and ***m***,
2:27 but God had ***m*** on him, and not
1 Tim 1: 2 son in the faith: Grace, ***m***,
1:13 but I obtained ***m*** because I did
1:16 for this reason I obtained ***m***,
2 Tim 1: 2 a beloved son: Grace, ***m***,
1:16 The Lord grant ***m*** to the
1:18 to him that he may find ***m*** from
Titus 1: 4 in our common faith: Grace, ***m***,
3: 5 but according to His ***m*** He saved
Heb 4:16 that we may obtain ***m*** and find
9: 5 of glory overshadowing the ***m***
10:28 Moses' law dies without ***m*** on
Jas 2:13 For judgment is without ***m*** to the
2:13 to the one who has shown no ***m***.
2:13 ***M*** triumphs over judgment.
3:17 full of ***m*** and good fruits,
1 Pe 1: 3 who according to His abundant ***m***
2:10 who had not obtained ***m*** but now
2:10 mercy but now have obtained ***m***.
2 Jn 3 Grace, ***m***, and peace will be
Jude 2 ***M***, peace, and love be

21 looking for the *m* of our Lord

MERCY SEAT (28/23)

Ex 25:17 You shall make a *m* of pure gold;
25:18 them at the two ends of the *m*.
25:19 it of one piece with the *m*.
25:20 covering the *m* with their
25:20 shall be toward the *m*.
25:21 You shall put the *m* on top of
25:22 speak with you from above the *m*,
26:34 You shall put the *m* upon the ark
30: 6 before the *m* that is over the
31: 7 ark of the Testimony and the *m*
35:12 ark and its poles, with the *m*,
37: 6 He also made the *m* of pure gold;
37: 7 piece at the two ends of the *m*:
37: 8 ends of one piece with the *m*.
37: 9 and covered the *m* with their
37: 9 the cherubim were toward the *m*.
39:35 with its poles, and the *m*;
40:20 and put the *m* on top of the
Lev 16: 2 before the *m* which is on the
16: 2 appear in the cloud above the *m*.
16:13 of incense may cover the *m*
16:14 it with his finger on the *m*
16:14 and before the *m* he shall
16:15 and sprinkle it on the *m* and
16:15 the mercy seat and before the *m*.
Num 7:89 to him from above the *m* that
1 Chr 28:11 and the place of the *m*;
Heb 9: 5 of glory overshadowing the *m*.

MERCYSEAT (KJV) See MERCY SEAT

MERE (9/9)

2 Ki 18:20 but they are *m* words. And in
Job 26:14 Indeed these are the *m* edges
Prov 29:19 will not be corrected by *m*
Isa 36: 5 but they are *m* words. Now in
44:11 they are *m* men. Let them all
54: 7 For a *m* moment I have forsaken
1 Cor 3: 3 not carnal and behaving like *m*
9: 8 Do I say these things as a *m*
15:37 but *m* grain—perhaps wheat or

MERED (2/2)

1 Chr 4:17 sons of Ezrah were Jether, *M*,
4:18 of Pharaoh, whom *M* took.

MERED'S (1/1)

1 Chr 4:17 And *M* wife bore Miriam,

MERELY (1/1)

1 Pe 3: 3 Do not let your adornment be *m*

MEREMOTH (6/6)

Ezra 8:33 of our God by the hand of *M*
10:36 Vaniah, *M*, Eliashib,
Neh 3: 4 And next to them *M* the son of
3:21 After him *M* the son of Urijah,
10: 5 Harim, *M*, Obadiah,
12: 3 Shechaniah, Rehum, *M*,

MERES (1/1)

Esth 1:14 Shethar, Admatha, Tarshish, *M*,

MERIB-BAAL (4/2) MEPHIBOSHETH

1 Chr 8:34 The son of Jonathan was *M*,
8:34 and *M* begot Micah.
9:40 The son of Jonathan was *M*,
9:40 and *M* begot Micah.

MERIBAH (9/9) MASSAH

Ex 17: 7 name of the place Massah and *M*,
Num 20:13 This was the water of *M*,
20:24 My word at the water of *M*.
27:14 (These are the waters of *M*,
Deut 32:51 of Israel at the waters of *M*
33: 8 contended at the waters of *M*,
Ps 81: 7 tested you at the waters of *M*.
Ezek 47:19 from Tamar to the waters of *M*
48:28 from Tamar to the waters of *M*

MERODACH (1/1)

Jer 50: 2 *M* is broken in pieces;

MERODACH-BALADAN (1/1)

Isa 39: 1 At that time *M* the son of

MEROM (2/2)

Josh 11: 5 together at the waters of *M* to
11: 7 suddenly by the waters of *M*,

MERONOTHITE (2/2)

1 Chr 27:30 Jehdeiah the *M* was over the
Neh 3: 7 the Gibeonite, Jadon the *M*,

MEROZ (1/1)

Judg 5:23 'Curse *M*,' said the angel of

MERRILY (1/1)

Esth 5:14 then go *m* with the king to the

MERRY (21/21)

Gen 43:34 So they drank and were *m* with
Judg 9:27 and trod them, and made *m*.
16:25 when their hearts were *m*,
19: 6 night, and let your heart be *m*.
19: 9 here, that your heart may be *m*.
1 Sam 25:36 And Nabal's heart was *m* within
2 Sam 13:28 when Amnon's heart is *m* with
Esth 1:10 the heart of the king was *m*
Prov 15:13 A *m* heart makes a cheerful
15:15 But he who is of a *m* heart
17:22 A *m* heart does good, like
Eccl 8:15 than to eat, drink, and be *m*;
9: 7 And drink your wine with a *m*
10:19 for laughter, And wine makes *m*;
Jer 30:19 the voice of those who make *m*;
Lk 12:19 eat, drink, and be *m*."
15:23 it, and let us eat and be *m*;
15:24 And they began to be *m*.
15:29 that I might make *m* with my
15:32 was right that we should make *m*
Rev 11:10 will rejoice over them, make *m*,

MERRY-HEARTED (1/1)

Isa 24: 7 All the *m* sigh.

MESECH (KJV) See MESHECH

MESHA (4/4)

Gen 10:30 dwelling place was from *M* as
2 Ki 3: 4 Now *M* king of Moab was a
1 Chr 2:42 brother of Jerahmeel were *M*,
8: 9 wife he begot Jobab, Zibia, *M*,

MESHACH (15/14) MISHAEL

Dan 1: 7 Shadrach; to Mishael, *M*;
2:49 king, and he set Shadrach, *M*,
3:12 of Babylon: Shadrach, *M*,
3:13 command to bring Shadrach, *M*,
3:14 "Is it true, Shadrach, *M*,
3:16 Shadrach, *M*, and Abed-Nego
3:19 face changed toward Shadrach, *M*,
3:20 in his army to bind Shadrach, *M*,
3:22 men who took up Shadrach, *M*,
3:23 these three men, Shadrach, *M*,
3:26 spoke, saying, "Shadrach, *M*,
3:26 come here." Then Shadrach, *M*,
3:28 be the God of Shadrach, *M*,
3:29 against the God of Shadrach, *M*,
3:30 the king promoted Shadrach, *M*,

MESHECH (9/9)

Gen 10: 2 Magog, Madai, Javan, Tubal, *M*,
1 Chr 1: 5 Magog, Madai, Javan, Tubal, *M*,
1:17 Aram, Uz, Hul, Gether, and *M*.
Ps 120: 5 Woe is me, that I dwell in *M*,
Ezek 27:13 and *M* were your traders.
32:26 There are *M* and Tubal and all
38: 2 of Magog, the prince of Rosh, *M*,
38: 3 O Gog, the prince of Rosh, *M*,
39: 1 O Gog, the prince of Rosh, *M*,

MESHELEMIAH (4/4)

1 Chr 9:21 Zechariah the son of *M* was
26: 1 *M* the son of Kore, of the sons
26: 2 And the sons of *M* were
26: 9 And *M* had sons and brethren,

MESHEZABEL (3/3)

Neh 3: 4 son of Berechiah, the son of *M*,
10:21 *M*, Zadok, Jaddua,
11:24 Pethahiah the son of *M*,

MESHILLEMITH (1/1)

1 Chr 9:12 son of Meshullam, the son of *M*,

MESHILLEMOTH (2/2)

2 Chr 28:12 Johanan, Berechiah the son of *M*,
Neh 11:13 the son of Ahzai, the son of *M*,

MESHOBAB (1/1)

1 Chr 4:34 *M*, Jamlech, and Joshah

MESHULLAM (25/25)

2 Ki 22: 3 son of Azaliah, the son of *M*,
1 Chr 3:19 The sons of Zerubbabel were *M*,
5:13 father's house: Michael, *M*,
8:17 Zebadiah, *M*, Hizki, Heber,
9: 7 of Benjamin: Sallu the son of *M*,
9: 8 *M* the son of Shephatiah, the
9:11 son of Hilkiah, the son of *M*,
9:12 son of Jahzerah, the son of *M*,
2 Chr 34:12 of Merari, and Zechariah and *M*,
Ezra 8:16 Nathan, Zechariah, and *M*,
10:15 and *M* and Shabbethai the Levite
10:29 of the sons of Bani: *M*,
Neh 3: 4 Next to them *M* the son of
3: 6 the son of Paseah and *M* the
3:30 After him *M* the son of
6:18 had married the daughter of *M*
8: 4 Hashbadana, Zechariah, and *M*.
10: 7 *M*, Abijah, Mijamin,
10:20 Magpiash, *M*, Hezir,
11: 7 of Benjamin: Sallu the son of *M*,
11:11 son of Hilkiah, the son of *M*,
12:13 of Ezra, *M*; of Amariah,
12:16 Zechariah; of Ginnethon, *M*;
12:25 Bakbukiah, Obadiah, *M*,
12:33 and Azariah, Ezra, *M*,

MESHULLEMETH (1/1)

2 Ki 21:19 His mother's name was *M* the

MESOBAITE (KJV) See MEZOBAITE

MESOPOTAMIA (8/8) ARAM

Gen 24:10 And he arose and went to *M*,
Deut 23: 4 son of Beor from Pethor of *M*,
Judg 3: 8 of Cushan-Rishathaim king of *M*;
3:10 Cushan-Rishathaim king of *M*
1 Chr 19: 6 chariots and horsemen from *M*,
Ps 60: When he fought against *M* and
Acts 2: 9 Elamites, those dwelling in *M*,
7: 2 father Abraham when he was in *M*,

MESS (KJV) See SERVING

MESSAGE (23/20) MESSENGER

Ex 4: 8 nor heed the *m* of the first
4: 8 that they may believe the *m* of
Judg 3:19 'I have a secret *m* for you,
3:20 I have a *m* from God for you."
1 Ki 5: 8 I have considered the *m* which
20:12 when Ben-Hadad heard this *m*,
2 Ki 9: 5 I have a *m* for you, Commander."
Neh 6: 4 But they sent me this *m* four
Prov 26: 6 He who sends a *m* by the hand of
Isa 28: 9 he make to understand the *m*?
Jer 49:14 I have heard a *m* from the
Dan 10: 1 of Cyrus king of Persia a *m*
10: 1 The *m* was true, but the
10: 1 and he understood the *m*,
Jon 3: 2 and preach to it the *m* that I
Hag 1:13 spoke the LORD's *m* to the
Acts 20: 7 to them and continued his *m*
1 Cor 1:18 For the *m* of the cross is
1:21 the foolishness of the *m*
2 Tim 2:17 And their *m* will spread like
4:17 so that the *m* might be preached
1 Jn 1: 5 This is the *m* which we have
3:11 For this is the *m* that you heard

MESSENGER (35/33) MESSAGE, MESSENGERS

1 Sam 4:17 So the *m* answered and said,
23:27 But a *m* came to Saul, saying,
2 Sam 11:19 and charged the *m*,
11:22 So the *m* went, and came and
11:23 And the *m* said to David,
11:25 Then David said to the *m*,
15:13 Now a *m* came to David, saying,
1 Ki 19: 2 Then Jezebel sent a *m* to Elijah,
22:13 Then the *m* who had gone to call
2 Ki 5:10 And Elisha sent a *m* to him,
6:32 but before the *m* came to him,
6:32 when the *m* comes, shut the
6:33 with them, there was the *m*,
9:18 The *m* went to them, but is not
10: 8 Then a *m* came and told him,
2 Chr 18:12 Then the *m* who had gone to call
Job 1:14 and a *m* came to Job and said,
33:23 If there is a *m* for him,
Prov 13:17 A wicked *m* falls into trouble,
17:11 Therefore a cruel *m* will be
25:13 of harvest Is a faithful *m*
Eccl 5: 6 nor say before the *m* of God
Isa 42:19 Or deaf as My *m* whom I send?
Jer 51:31 And one *m* to meet another,
Ezek 23:40 to whom a *m* was sent;
Ob 1 And a *m* has been sent among
Hag 1:13 Then Haggai, the LORD's *m*,
Mal 2: 7 For he is the *m* of the LORD
3: 1 "Behold, I send My *m*,
3: 1 Even the *M* of the covenant,
Mt 11:10 I send My *m* before Your
Mk 1: 2 I send My *m* before Your
Lk 7:27 I send My *m* before Your
2 Cor 12: 7 a *m* of Satan to buffet me, lest
Phil 2:25 but your *m* and the one who

MESSENGERS (81/76) MESSENGER

Gen 32: 3 Then Jacob sent *m* before him to
32: 6 Then the *m* returned to Jacob,
50:16 So they sent *m* to Joseph,
Num 20:14 Now Moses sent *m* from Kadesh to
21:21 Then Israel sent *m* to Sihon
22: 5 Then he sent *m* to Balaam the son
24:12 I not also speak to your *m*
Deut 2:26 And I sent *m* from the
Josh 6:17 because she hid the *m* that we
6:25 because she hid the *m* whom
7:22 So Joshua sent *m*, and they
Judg 6:35 And he sent *m* throughout all
6:35 He also sent *m* to Asher,
7:24 Then Gideon sent *m* throughout

9:31 And he sent *m* to Abimelech
11:12 Now Jephthah sent *m* to the king
11:13 people of Ammon answered the *m*
11:14 So Jephthah again sent *m* to the
11:17 Then Israel sent *m* to the king
11:19 Then Israel sent *m* to Sihon king
1 Sam 6:21 So they sent *m* to the
11: 3 that we may send *m* to all the
11: 4 So the *m* came to Gibeah of Saul
11: 7 of Israel by the hands of *m*,
11: 9 And they said to the *m* who came,
11: 9 Then the *m* came and
16:19 Therefore Saul sent *m* to Jesse,
19:11 Saul also sent *m* to David's
19:14 So when Saul sent *m* to take
19:15 Then Saul sent the *m* back to
19:16 And when the *m* had come in,
19:20 Then Saul sent *m* to take David.
19:20 Spirit of God came upon the *m*
19:21 Saul was told, he sent other *m*,
19:21 Then Saul sent *m* again the
25:14 David sent *m* from the
25:42 and she followed the *m* of
2 Sam 2: 5 So David sent *m* to the men of
3:12 Then Abner sent *m* on his behalf
3:14 So David sent *m* to Ishbosheth,
3:26 he sent *m* after Abner, who
5:11 Hiram king of Tyre sent *m* to
11: 4 Then David sent *m*, and took
12:27 And Joab sent *m* to David, and
1 Ki 20: 2 Then he sent *m* into the city to
20: 5 Then the *m* came back and said,
20: 9 Therefore he said to the *m* of
20: 9 And the *m* departed and
2 Ki 1: 2 so he sent *m* and said to them,
1: 3 go up to meet the *m* of the king
1: 5 And when the *m* returned to him,
1:16 Because you have sent *m* to
7:15 So the *m* returned and told the
14: 8 Then Amaziah sent *m* to Jehoash
16: 7 So Ahaz sent *m* to
17: 4 for he had sent *m* to So, king
19: 9 So he again sent *m* to
19:14 letter from the hand of the *m*,
19:23 By your *m* you have reproached
1 Chr 14: 1 Now Hiram king of Tyre sent *m* to
19: 2 So David sent *m* to comfort
19:16 they sent *m* and brought the
2 Chr 35:21 But he sent *m* to him, saying,
36:15 sent warnings to them by His *m*,
36:16 But they mocked the *m* of God,
Neh 6: 3 So I sent *m* to them, saying, "I
Prov 16:14 As *m* of death is the king's
Isa 14:32 What will they answer the *m* of
18: 2 waters, saying, "Go, swift *m*,
37: 9 he sent *m* to Hezekiah, saying,
37:14 letter from the hand of the *m*,
44:26 performs the counsel of His *m*;
57: 9 You sent your *m* far off,
Jer 27: 3 by the hand of the *m* who come
Ezek 23:16 lusted for them And sent *m* to
30: 9 On that day *m* shall go forth
Nah 2:13 and the voice of your *m* shall
Lk 7:24 When the *m* of John had departed,
9:52 and sent *m* before His face.
2 Cor 8:23 they are *m* of the churches,
Jas 2:25 works when she received the *m*

MESSIAH (4/4)

Dan 9:25 and build Jerusalem Until *M*
9:26 after the sixty-two weeks *M*
Jn 1:41 We have found the *M*" (which is
4:25 'I know that *M* is coming"

MESSIAS (KJV) See MESSIAH

MET (47/47) MEET

Gen 32: 1 and the angels of God *m* him.
33: 8 by all this company which I *m*?
Ex 3:18 LORD God of the Hebrews has *m*
4:24 that the LORD *m* him and sought
4:27 So he went and *m* him on the
5: 3 The God of the Hebrews has *m*
5:20 they *m* Moses and Aaron who
Num 23: 4 And God *m* Balaam, and he said to
23:16 Then the LORD *m* Balaam, and put
Deut 25:18 how he *m* you on the way and
Josh 11: 5 And when all these kings had *m*
1 Sam 9:11 they *m* some young women going
21: 1 Ahimelech was afraid when he *m*
25:20 toward her, and she *m* them.
2 Sam 2:13 went out and *m* them by the pool
16: 1 who *m* him with a couple of
18: 9 Then Absalom *m* the servants of
1 Ki 11:29 prophet Ahijah the Shilonite *m*
13:24 a lion *m* him on the road and
18: 7 suddenly Elijah *m* him; and he
2 Ki 9:21 and *m* him on the property of
10:13 Jehu *m* with the brothers of
10:15 he *m* Jehonadab the son of
Neh 13: 2 because they had not *m* the
Ps 85:10 Mercy and truth have *m*
Prov 7:10 And there a woman *m* him,
Isa 21:14 With their bread they *m* him
Jer 41: 6 and it happened as he *m* them
Am 5:19 And a bear *m* him! Or as
Mt 8:28 there *m* Him two demon-possessed
28: 9 Jesus *m* them, saying,
Mk 5: 2 immediately there *m* Him out of
Lk 8:27 there *m* Him a certain man from
9:37 that a great multitude *m* Him.
17:12 there *m* Him ten men who were
Jn 4:51 his servants *m* him and told
11:20 went and *m* Him, but Mary was
11:30 was in the place where Martha *m*
12:18 this reason the people also *m*
18: 2 for Jesus often *m* there with
Acts 10:25 Cornelius *m* him and fell down
16:13 and spoke to the women who *m*
16:16 with a spirit of divination *m*
20:14 And when he *m* us at Assos, we
27:41 a place where two seas *m*,
Heb 7: 1 who *m* Abraham returning from
7:10 his father when Melchizedek *m*

METAL (1/1)

Job 37:18 Strong as a cast *m* mirror?

METALSMITH (3/3)

Jer 10: 9 And of the hands of the *m*;
10:14 Every *m* is put to shame by an
51:17 Every *m* is put to shame by the

METEYARD (KJV) See MEASUREMENT

METHEG AMMAH (1/1)

2 Sam 8: 1 And David took *M* from the hand

METHUSAEL (KJV) See METHUSHAEL

METHUSELAH (7/7)

Gen 5:21 sixty-five years, and begot *M*.
5:22 After he begot *M*,
5:25 *M* lived one hundred and
5:26 *M* lived seven hundred and
5:27 So all the days of *M* were nine
1 Chr 1: 3 Enoch, *M*, Lamech,
Lk 3:37 the son of *M*, the son of

METHUSHAEL (2/1)

Gen 4:18 Mehujael, and Mehujael begot *M*,
4:18 and *M* begot Lamech.

MEUNIM (2/2)

Ezra 2:50 sons of Asnah, the sons of *M*,
Neh 7:52 sons of Besai, the sons of *M*,

MEUNITES (2/2)

1 Chr 4:41 attacked their tents and the *M*
2 Chr 26: 7 in Gur Baal, and against the *M*.

MEZAHAB (2/2)

Gen 36:39 of Matred, the daughter of *M*.
1 Chr 1:50 of Matred, the daughter of *M*.

MEZOBAITE (1/1)

1 Chr 11:47 Eliel, Obed, and Jaasiel the *M*.

MIAMIN (KJV) See MIJAMIN

MIBHAR (1/1)

1 Chr 11:38 *M* the son of Hagri,

MIBSAM (3/3)

Gen 25:13 Nebajoth; then Kedar, Adbeel, *M*,
1 Chr 1:29 Nebajoth; then Kedar, Adbeel, *M*,
4:25 *M* his son, and Mishma his son.

MIBZAR (2/2)

Gen 36:42 Kenaz, Chief Teman, Chief *M*,
1 Chr 1:53 Kenaz, Chief Teman, Chief *M*,

MICAH (27/26) MICAIAH

Judg 17: 1 of Ephraim, whose name was *M*.
17: 4 and they were in the house of *M*.
17: 5 The man *M* had a shrine, and made
17: 8 of Ephraim, to the house of *M*,
17: 9 And *M* said to him, "Where do
17:10 *M* said to him, "Dwell with me,
17:12 So *M* consecrated the Levite, and
17:12 and lived in the house of *M*.
17:13 Then *M* said, "Now I know that
18: 2 of Ephraim, to the house of *M*,
18: 3 they were at the house of *M*,
18: 4 Thus and so *M* did for me. He has
18:13 and came to the house of *M*.
18:15 Levite man—to the house of *M*—
18:22 a good way from the house of *M*,
18:23 turned around and said to *M*,
18:26 And when *M* saw that they were
18:27 So they took the things *M* had
1 Chr 5: 5 *M* his son, Reaiah his son, Baal
8:34 and Merib-Baal begot *M*.
8:35 The sons of *M* were Pithon,
9:15 and Mattaniah the son of *M*,
9:40 and Merib-Baal begot *M*.
9:41 The sons of *M* were Pithon,
2 Chr 34:20 of Shaphan, Abdon the son of *M*,
Jer 26:18 *M* of Moresheth prophesied in the
Mic 1: 1 of the LORD that came to *M* of

MICAH'S (3/3)

Judg 18:18 When these went into *M* house and
18:22 who were in the houses near *M*
18:31 So they set up for themselves *M*

MICAIAH (20/20) MICAH

1 Ki 22: 8 *M* the son of Imlah, by whom we
22: 9 Bring *M* the son of Imlah
22:13 who had gone to call *M* spoke
22:14 And *M* said, "As the LORD
22:15 and the king said to him, "*M*,
22:19 Then *M* said, "Therefore hear
22:24 went near and struck *M* on the
22:25 And *M* said, "Indeed, you shall
22:26 king of Israel said, "Take *M*,
22:28 But *M* said, "If you ever return
2 Chr 18: 7 He is *M* the son of Imla."
18: 8 Bring *M* the son of Imla
18:12 who had gone to call *M* spoke
18:13 And *M* said, "As the LORD
18:14 and the king said to him, "*M*,
18:18 Then *M* said, "Therefore hear
18:23 went near and struck *M* on the
18:24 And *M* said, "Indeed you shall
18:25 king of Israel said, "Take *M*,
18:27 Then *M* said, "If you ever

MICE (KJV) See RATS

MICHA (4/4)

2 Sam 9:12 a young son whose name was *M*.
Neh 10:11 *M*, Rehob, Hashabiah,
11:17 Mattaniah the son of *M*,
11:22 son of Mattaniah, the son of *M*,

MICHAEL (15/15)

Num 13:13 of Asher, Sethur the son of *M*;
1 Chr 5:13 of their father's house: *M*,
5:14 the son of Gilead, the son of *M*,
6:40 the son of *M*, the son of
7: 3 the sons of Izrahiah were *M*,
8:16 *M*, Ispah, and Joha were
12:20 were Adnah, Jozabad, Jediael, *M*,
27:18 Issachar, Omri the son of *M*;
2 Chr 21: 2 Jehiel, Zechariah, Azaryahu, *M*,
Ezra 8: 8 Zebadiah the son of *M*,
Dan 10:13 twenty-one days; and behold, *M*,
10:21 except *M* your prince.
12: 1 At that time *M* shall stand up,
Jude 9 Yet *M* the archangel, in
Rev 12: 7 *M* and his angels fought with

MICHAH (4/3)

1 Chr 23:20 *M* was the first and Jesshiah
24:24 Of the sons of Uzziel, *M*;
24:24 Michah; of the sons of *M*,
24:25 The brother of *M*, Isshiah;

MICHAIAH (7/7)

2 Ki 22:12 of Shaphan, Achbor the son of *M*,
2 Chr 13: 2 His mother's name was *M* the
17: 7 Zechariah, Nethanel, and *M*,
Neh 12:35 son of Mattaniah, the son of *M*,
12:41 Eliakim, Maaseiah, Minjamin, *M*,
Jer 36:11 When *M* the son of Gemariah, the
36:13 Then *M* declared to them all the

MICHAL (18/17)

1 Sam 14:49 and the name of the younger *M*.
18:20 Now *M*, Saul's daughter,
18:27 Then Saul gave him *M* his
18:28 was with David, and that *M*,
19:11 kill him in the morning. And *M*,
19:12 So *M* let David down through a
19:13 And *M* took an image and laid it
19:17 Then Saul said to *M*, "Why
19:17 And *M* answered Saul, "He
25:44 But Saul had given *M* his
2 Sam 3:13 face unless you first bring *M*,
3:14 saying, "Give me my wife *M*,
6:16 came into the City of David, *M*,
6:20 And *M* the daughter of Saul came
6:21 So David said to *M*, "It was
6:23 Therefore *M* the daughter of Saul
21: 8 and the five sons of *M* the
1 Chr 15:29 to the City of David, that *M*,

MICHMAS (2/2)

Ezra 2:27 the men of *M*, one hundred and
Neh 7:31 the men of *M*, one hundred and

MICHMASH (9/9)

1 Sam 13: 2 thousand were with Saul in *M*
13: 5 they came up and encamped in *M*,
13:11 gathered together at *M*,
13:16 the Philistines encamped in *M*.
13:23 went out to the pass of *M*.
14: 5 one faced northward opposite *M*,
14:31 Philistines that day from *M* to
Neh 11:31 Benjamin from Geba dwelt in *M*,
Isa 10:28 At *M* he has attended to his

M

MICHMETHATH (2/2)

Josh 16: 6 the sea on the north side of **M**;
17: 7 of Manasseh was from Asher to **M**,

MICHRI (1/1)

1 Chr 9: 8 the son of Uzzi, the son of **M**;

MICHTAM (6/6)

Ps 16: A **M** of David.
56: A **M** of David when the
57: A **M** of David when he fled
58: A **M** of David.
59: A **M** of David when Saul sent
60: A **M** of David. For teaching.

MIDDAY (3/3)

1 Ki 18:29 And when **m** was past, they
Neh 8: 3 Water Gate from morning until **m**,
Acts 26:13 'at **m**, O king, along the road

MIDDIN (1/1)

Josh 15:61 the wilderness: Beth Arabah, **M**,

MIDDLE (42/40)

Gen 15:10 and cut them in two, down the **m**,
Ex 26:28 The **m** bar shall pass through the
28:32 opening for his head in the **m**
36:33 And he made the **m** bar to pass
39:23 an opening in the **m** of the robe,
Num 2:17 camp of the Levites in the **m**
35: 5 The city shall be in the **m**.
Deut 3:16 the **m** of the river as the
13:16 into the **m** of the street,
Josh 12: 2 from the **m** of that river, even
Judg 7:19 at the beginning of the **m** watch,
16:29 took hold of the two **m** pillars
2 Sam 10: 4 cut off their garments in the **m**,
20:12 blood in the **m** of the highway.
23:12 he stationed himself in the **m**
1 Ki 3:20 she arose in the **m** of the night
6: 6 the **m** was six cubits wide, and
6: 8 The doorway for the **m** story was
6: 8 They went up by stairs to the **m**
6: 8 and from the **m** to the third.
6:27 other in the **m** of the room.
8:64 consecrated the **m** of the court
2 Ki 20: 4 Isaiah had gone out into the **m**
1 Chr 11:14 in the **m** of that field,
19: 4 cut off their garments in the **m**,
2 Chr 7: 7 Solomon consecrated the **m** of
Job 34:20 in the **m** of the night;
Isa 16: 3 the night in the **m** of the day;
Jer 39: 3 came in and sat in the **M** Gate:
Ezek 1:16 a wheel in the **m** of a wheel.
10:10 a wheel in the **m** of a wheel.
15: 4 and its **m** is burned. Is it
41: 7 highest by way of the **m** one.
42: 5 more than from the lower and **m**
42: 6 than the lower and **m** levels
Dan 9:27 But in the **m** of the week
Mt 14:24 was now in the **m** of the sea,
Mk 6:47 boat was in the **m** of the sea;
Jn 7:14 Now about the **m** of the feast
Acts 1:18 he burst open in the **m** and all
Eph 2:14 and has broken down the **m** wall
Rev 22: 2 In the **m** of its street, and on

MIDIAN (41/40) MIDIANITE

Gen 25: 2 him Zimran, Jokshan, Medan, **M**,
25: 4 And the sons of **M** were Ephah,
36:35 who attacked **M** in the field of
Ex 2:15 and dwelt in the land of **M**;
2:16 Now the priest of **M** had seven
3: 1 father-in-law, the priest of **M**.
4:19 the LORD said to Moses in **M**,
18: 1 And Jethro, the priest of **M**,
Num 22: 4 So Moab said to the elders of **M**,
22: 7 of Moab and the elders of **M**
25:15 people of a father's house in **M**.
25:18 the daughter of a leader of **M**,
31: 3 vengeance for the LORD on **M**.
31: 8 They killed the kings of **M** with
31: 8 and Reba, the five kings of **M**.
31: 9 of Israel took the women of **M**
Josh 13:21 struck with the princes of **M**:
Judg 6: 1 them into the hand of **M** for
6: 2 and the hand of **M** prevailed
7: 8 Now the camp of **M** was below him
7:13 tumbled into the camp of **M**;
7:14 his hand God has delivered **M**
7:15 has delivered the camp of **M**
7:25 They pursued **M** and brought the
8: 3 your hands the princes of **M**,
8: 5 Zebah and Zalmunna, kings of **M**.
8:12 and he took the two kings of **M**,
8:22 delivered us from the hand of **M**.
8:26 which were on the kings of **M**,
8:28 Thus **M** was subdued before the
9:17 you out of the hand of **M**;
1 Ki 11:18 Then they arose from **M** and came
1 Chr 1:32 were Zimran, Jokshan, Medan, **M**,
1:33 The sons of **M** were Ephah,
1:46 who attacked **M** in the field of
Ps 83: 9 Deal with them as with **M**,
Isa 9: 4 oppressor, As in the day of **M**.
10:26 him like the slaughter of **M** at
60: 6 The dromedaries of **M** and
Hab 3: 7 The curtains of the land of **M**
Acts 7:29 a dweller in the land of **M**,

MIDIANITE (5/5) MIDIAN, MIDIANITES

Gen 37:28 Then **M** traders passed by;
Num 10:29 to Hobab the son of Reuel the **M**,
25: 6 presented to his brethren a **M**
25:14 who was killed with the **M**
25:15 And the name of the **M** woman who

MIDIANITES (22/22) KENITES, MIDIANITE

Gen 37:36 Now the **M** had sold him in Egypt
Num 25:17 'Harass the **M**, and attack
31: 2 Take vengeance on the **M** for the
31: 3 and let them go against the **M**
31: 7 And they warred against the **M**,
Judg 6: 2 Because of the **M**, the children
6: 3 **M** would come up; also
6: 6 impoverished because of the **M**,
6: 7 to the LORD because of the **M**,
6:11 in order to hide it from the **M**.
6:13 us into the hands of the **M**.
6:14 Israel from the hand of the **M**.
6:16 and you shall defeat the **M** as
6:33 Then all the **M** and Amalekites,
7: 1 so that the camp of the **M** was
7: 2 too many for Me to give the **M**
7: 7 and deliver the **M** into your
7:12 Now the **M** and Amalekites, all
7:23 all Manasseh, and pursued the **M**.
7:24 "Come down against the **M**,
7:25 captured two princes of the **M**,
8: 1 you went to fight with the **M**?

MIDIANITISH (KJV) See MIDIANITE

MIDNIGHT (12/11)

Ex 11: 4 About **m** I will go out into the
12:29 And it came to pass at **m** that
Judg 16: 3 And Samson lay low till **m**;
16: 3 midnight; then he arose at **m**,
Ruth 3: 8 Now it happened at **m** that the
Ps 119:62 At **m** I will rise to give thanks
Mt 25: 6 And at **m** a cry was heard:
Mk 13:35 is coming—in the evening, at **m**,
Lk 11: 5 and go to him at **m** and say to
Acts 16:25 But at **m** Paul and Silas were
20: 7 continued his message until **m**.
27:27 about **m** the sailors sensed that

MIDST (313/302)

Gen 1: 6 there be a firmament in the **m**
2: 9 of life was also in the **m** of
3: 3 of the tree which is in the **m**
19:29 and sent Lot out of the **m** of
48:16 grow into a multitude in the **m**
Ex 3: 2 in a flame of fire from the **m**
3: 4 God called to him from the **m** of
3:20 which I will do in its **m**;
8:22 that I am the LORD in the **m**
11: 4 I will go out into the **m** of
14:16 go on dry ground through the **m**
14:22 of Israel went into the **m** of
14:23 and went after them into the **m**
14:27 the Egyptians in the **m** of the
14:29 walked on dry land in the **m**
15:19 went on dry land in the **m** of
23:25 take sickness away from the **m**
24:16 He called to Moses out of the **m**
24:18 So Moses went into the **m** of the
26:28 bar shall pass through the **m**
33: 3 for I will not go up in your **m**,
33: 5 I could come up into your **m** in
34:12 lest it be a snare in your **m**.
Lev 16:16 remains among them in the **m** of
Num 5: 3 defile their camps in the **m** of
16:47 and ran into the **m** of the
19: 6 and cast them into the **m** of
33: 8 and passed through the **m** of
35:34 in the **m** of which I dwell;
Deut 2:14 of war was consumed from the **m**
2:15 to destroy them from the **m** of
4:11 burned with fire to the **m** of
4:12 spoke to you out of the **m** of
4:15 to you at Horeb out of the **m**
4:33 of God speaking out of the **m**
4:34 Himself a nation from the **m** of
4:36 heard His words out of the **m**
5: 4 on the mountain from the **m** of
5:22 in the mountain from the **m** of
5:23 you heard the voice from the **m**
5:24 heard His voice from the **m** of
5:26 living God speaking from the **m**
9:10 you on the mountain from the **m**
10: 4 you in the mountain from the **m**
11: 3 His acts which He did in the **m**
11: 6 in the **m** of all Israel—
13: 5 put away the evil from your **m**.
17:20 he and his children in the **m** of
18:15 a Prophet like me from your **m**,
19: 2 cities for yourself in the **m**
19:10 blood be shed in the **m** of your
23:14 LORD your God walks in the **m**
23:16 may dwell with you in your **m**,
32:51 you did not hallow Me in the **m**
Josh 3:17 firm on dry ground in the **m** of
4: 3 out of the **m** of the Jordan,
4: 5 the LORD your God into the **m**
4: 8 up twelve stones from the **m** of
4: 9 set up twelve stones in the **m**
4:10 bore the ark stood in the **m** of
4:18 the LORD had come from the **m**
7:13 is an accursed thing in your **m**,
7:21 hidden in the earth in the **m** of
7:23 And they took them from the **m** of
8:13 went that night into the **m** of
8:22 so they were caught in the **m**
10:13 So the sun stood still in the **m**
13: 9 and the town that is in the **m**
13:16 and the city that is in the **m**
Judg 20:42 they destroyed in their **m**.
1 Sam 11:11 and they came into the **m** of the
16:13 oil and anointed him in the **m**
2 Sam 1:25 mighty have fallen in the **m** of
6:17 set it in its place in the **m**
18:14 he was still alive in the **m**
23:20 and killed a lion in the **m** of
24: 5 of the town which is in the **m**
1 Ki 3: 8 And Your servant is in the **m** of
20:39 servant went out into the **m** of
1 Chr 11:22 and killed a lion in the **m** of
16: 1 and set it in the **m** of the
2 Chr 6:13 and had set it in the **m** of the
20:14 in the **m** of the assembly.
Neh 4:11 till we come into their **m** and
9:11 that they went through the **m**
Esth 4: 1 and went out into the **m** of the
Job 2: 8 himself while he sat in the **m**
Ps 22:22 In the **m** of the assembly I
46: 2 be carried into the **m** of the
46: 5 God is in the **m** of her, she
48: 9 In the **m** of Your temple.
55:10 and trouble are also in the **m**
55:11 Destruction is in its **m**;
57: 6 Into the **m** of it they
74: 4 Your enemies roar in the **m** of
74:12 Working salvation in the **m** of
78:28 He let them fall in the **m** of
102:24 Do not take me away in the **m**
110: 2 Rule in the **m** of Your enemies!
116:19 In the **m** of you, O Jerusalem.
135: 9 signs and wonders into the **m**
136:14 made Israel pass through the **m**
137: 2 Upon the willows in the **m** of
138: 7 Though I walk in the **m** of
Prov 4:21 Keep them in the **m** of your
5:14 In the **m** of the assembly and
8:20 In the **m** of the paths of
23:34 one who lies down in the **m** of
30:19 The way of a ship in the **m** of
Isa 4: 4 blood of Jerusalem from her **m**,
5: 2 He built a tower in its **m**,
5: 8 they may dwell alone in the **m**
5:25 were as refuse in the **m** of
6: 5 And I dwell in the **m** of a
6:12 places are many in the **m** of
10:23 a determined end In the **m** of
12: 6 Holy One of Israel in your **m**!
19: 1 of Egypt will melt in its **m**.
19: 3 of Egypt will fail in its **m**;
19:14 a perverse spirit in her **m**;
19:19 an altar to the LORD in the **m**
19:24 a blessing in the **m** of the
24:13 it shall be thus in the **m** of
24:18 he who comes up from the **m** of
25:11 out His hands in their **m** As a
29:23 The work of My hands, in his **m**,
41:18 And fountains in the **m** of the
52:11 Go out from the **m** of her,
58: 9 take away the yoke from your **m**,
66:17 After an idol in the **m**,
Jer 6: 1 yourselves to flee from the **m**
6: 6 is full of oppression in her **m**.
9: 6 dwelling place is in the **m** of
12:16 shall be established in the **m**
14: 9 You, O LORD, are in our **m**,
17:11 It will leave him in the **m** of
21: 4 I will assemble them in the **m**
29: 8 your diviners who are in your **m**
30:21 shall come from their **m**;
41: 7 when they came into the **m** of
41: 7 and cast them into the **m** of
46:21 her mercenaries are in her **m**
48:45 A flame from the **m** of Sihon,
50: 8 Move from the **m** of Babylon,
50:37 mixed peoples who are in her **m**;
51: 6 Flee from the **m** of Babylon,
51:45 go out of the **m** of her!
51:47 her slain shall fall in her **m**.
52:25 land who were found in the **m**
Lam 1:15 all my mighty men in my **m**;
3:45 and refuse In the **m** of the
4:13 Who shed in her **m** The blood
Ezek 1: 4 it and radiating out of its **m**
1: 4 out of the **m** of the fire.
5: 2 with fire one-third in the **m**
5: 4 and throw them into the **m** of
5: 5 I have set her in the **m** of the
5: 8 execute judgments in your **m** in
5:10 shall eat their sons in your **m**,
5:12 consumed with famine in your **m**;
6: 7 slain shall fall in your **m**,
7: 4 abominations will be in your **m**;
7: 9 abominations will be in your **m**.
8:11 and in their **m** stood Jaazaniah
9: 4 Go through the **m** of the city,
9: 4 through the **m** of Jerusalem, and
11: 7 whom you have laid in its **m**,

11: 7 I shall bring you out of the *m*
11: 9 I will bring you out of its *m*,
11:11 shall you be the meat in its *m*.
11:23 of the LORD went up from the *m*
12: 2 you dwell in the *m* of a
13:14 you shall be consumed in the *m*
14: 8 I will cut him off from the *m*
17:16 with him in the *m* of Babylon he
20: 8 My anger against them in the *m*
21:32 Your blood shall be in the *m*
22: 3 city sheds blood in her own *m*,
22: 7 in your *m* they have oppressed
22: 9 in your *m* they commit lewdness.
22:13 which has been in your *m*.
22:18 in the *m* of a furnace;
22:19 I will gather you into the *m* of
22:20 and tin into the *m* of a
22:21 you shall be melted in its *m*.
22:22 As silver is melted in the *m* of
22:22 so shall you be melted in its *m*;
22:25 of her prophets in her *m* is
22:25 have made many widows in her *m*.
22:27 Her princes in her *m* are like
23:39 thus they have done in the *m*
24: 7 For her blood is in her *m*;
26: 5 for spreading nets in the *m*
26:12 and your soil in the *m* of the
26:15 slaughter is made in the *m* of
27: 4 Your borders are in the *m* of
27:25 and very glorious in the *m* of
27:26 east wind broke you in the *m*
27:27 company which is in your *m*,
27:27 Will fall into the *m* of the
27:32 Destroyed in the *m* of the sea?
27:34 company will fall in your *m*.
28: 2 In the *m* of the seas,'
28: 8 death of the slain In the *m*
28:14 walked back and forth in the *m*
28:16 From the *m* of the fiery
28:18 I brought fire from your *m*;
28:22 I will be glorified in your *m*;
28:23 shall be judged in her *m* By
29: 3 monster who lies in the *m* of
29: 4 will bring you up out of the *m*
29:12 of Egypt desolate in the *m* of
29:21 your mouth to speak in their *m*.
30: 7 shall be desolate in the *m* of
30: 7 her cities shall be in the *m*
31:18 you shall lie in the *m* of the
32:20 They shall fall in the *m* of
32:21 speak to him out of the *m* of
32:25 have set her bed in the *m* of
32:25 It was put in the *m* of the
32:28 you shall be broken in the *m* of
32:32 he shall be placed in the *m* of
36:23 you have profaned in their *m*;
37: 1 and set me down in the *m* of the
37:26 set My sanctuary in their *m*
37:28 when My sanctuary is in their *m*
38:12 who dwell in the *m* of the land.
39: 7 My holy name known in the *m* of
43: 7 where I will dwell in the *m* of
43: 9 and I will dwell in their *m*
46:10 prince shall then be in their *m*.
48:22 the city which are in the *m*
Dan 3: 6 be cast immediately into the *m*
3:11 shall be cast into the *m* of a
3:15 be cast immediately into the *m*
3:21 and were cast into the *m* of the
3:23 fell down bound into the *m* of
3:24 three men bound into the *m* of
3:25 walking in the *m* of the fire;
3:26 and Abed-Nego came from the *m*
4:10 A tree in the *m* of the earth,
Hos 5: 4 of harlotry is in their *m*,
11: 9 The Holy One in your *m*;
Joel 2:27 shall know that I am in the *m*
Am 2: 3 cut off the judge from its *m*,
3: 9 See great tumults in her *m*,
6: 4 And calves from the *m* of
7: 8 setting a plumb line In the *m*
7:10 conspired against you in the *m*
Mic 2:12 Like a flock in the *m* of their
4: 9 Is there no king in your *m*?
5: 7 of Jacob Shall be in the *m* of
5: 8 In the *m* of many peoples,
5:10 cut off your horses from your *m*
5:13 your sacred pillars from your *m*;
5:14 your wooden images from your *m*;
6:14 Hunger shall be in your *m*.
7:14 In the *m* of Carmel; Let them
Nah 3:13 your people in your *m* are
Hab 3: 2 revive Your work in the *m* of
3: 2 midst of the years! In the *m*
Zeph 2:14 herds shall lie down in her *m*,
3: 3 Her princes in her *m* are
3: 5 LORD is righteous in her *m*,
3:11 I will take away from your *m*
3:12 I will leave in your *m* A meek
3:15 the LORD, is in your *m*;
3:17 The LORD your God in your *m*,
Zech 2: 5 I will be the glory in her *m*.
2:10 and I will dwell in your *m*,
2:11 And I will dwell in your *m*.
5: 4 It shall remain in the *m* of
8: 3 And dwell in the *m* of
8: 8 And they shall dwell in the *m*
14: 1 spoil will be divided in your *m*.
Mt 10:16 send you out as sheep in the *m*
18: 2 set him in the *m* of them,
18:20 I am there in the *m* of them."
Mk 7:31 He came through the *m* of the
9:36 child and set him in the *m* of
14:60 high priest stood up in the *m*
Lk 2:46 sitting in the *m* of the
4:30 Then passing through the *m* of
4:35 had thrown him in their *m*,
5:19 through the tiling into the *m*
17:11 that He passed through the *m*
21:21 let those who are in the *m* of
22:55 had kindled a fire in the *m* of
24:36 Jesus Himself stood in the *m* of
Jn 8: 3 when they had set her in the *m*,
8: 9 and the woman standing in the *m*.
8:59 going through the *m* of them,
20:19 Jesus came and stood in the *m*,
20:26 being shut, and stood in the *m*,
Acts 1:15 days Peter stood up in the *m*
2:22 God did through Him in your *m*,
4: 7 when they had set them in the *m*,
17:22 Then Paul stood in the *m* of the
24:18 in the *m* of which some Jews from
27:21 then Paul stood in the *m* of
Phil 2:15 of God without fault in the *m*
Heb 2:12 In the *m* of the assembly
Rev 1:13 and in the *m* of the seven
2: 1 who walks in the *m* of the seven
2: 7 which is in the *m* of the
4: 6 And in the *m* of the throne, and
5: 6 in the *m* of the throne and of
5: 6 and in the *m* of the elders,
6: 6 And I heard a voice in the *m* of
7:17 for the Lamb who is in the *m* of
8:13 an angel flying through the *m*
14: 6 another angel flying in the *m*
19:17 the birds that fly in the *m* of

MIDWAY (2/2)

Ex 27: 5 that the network may be *m* up
38: 4 *m* from the bottom.

MIDWIFE (3/3) MIDWIVES

Gen 35:17 that the *m* said to her, "Do
38:28 and the *m* took a scarlet
Ex 1:16 When you do the duties of a *m*

MIDWIVES (7/6) MIDWIFE

Ex 1:15 of Egypt spoke to the Hebrew *m*,
1:17 But the *m* feared God, and did
1:18 king of Egypt called for the *m*
1:19 And the *m* said to Pharaoh,
1:19 and give birth before the *m*
1:20 God dealt well with the *m*,
1:21 because the *m* feared God, that

MIGDAL EL (1/1)

Josh 19:38 Iron, *M*, Horem, Beth Anath, and

MIGDAL GAD (1/1)

Josh 15:37 Zenan, Hadashah, *M*,

MIGDOL (6/6)

Ex 14: 2 between *M* and the sea, opposite
Num 33: 7 and they camped near *M*.
Jer 44: 1 land of Egypt, who dwell at *M*,
46:14 in Egypt, and proclaim in *M*;
Ezek 29:10 from *M* to Syene, as far as the
30: 6 From *M* to Syene Those within

MIGHT (364/343) MIGHTIER, MIGHTILY, MIGHTY, STRENGTH

Gen 12:19 I *m* have taken her as my wife.
13: 6 that they *m* dwell together, for
17:18 that Ishmael *m* live before
26:10 One of the people *m* soon have
30:41 that they *m* conceive among the
31: 6 you know that with all my *m* I
31:27 for I *m* have sent you away with
37:22 that he *m* deliver him out of
49: 3 My *m* and the beginning of my
Ex 12:33 that they *m* send them out of
36:13 that it *m* be one tabernacle.
36:18 that it *m* be one.
Lev 24:12 that the mind of the LORD *m* be
26:45 that I *m* be their God: I am
Num 4:37 all who *m* serve in the
4:41 of all who *m* serve in the
14:13 for by Your *m* You brought these
16:40 that he *m* not become like Korah
22:41 that from tnere he *m* observe
Deut 2:30 that He *m* deliver him into your
4:14 that you *m* observe them in the
4:35 that you *m* know that the LORD
4:36 that He *m* instruct you;
4:42 that the manslayer *m* flee there,
4:42 to one of these cities he *m*
5:29 that it *m* be well with them and
6:23 that He *m* bring us in, to give
6:24 that He *m* preserve us alive, as
8: 3 that He *m* make you know that
8:16 that He *m* humble you and that
8:16 might humble you and that He *m*
8:17 My power and the *m* of my hand
32:13 That he *m* eat the produce of
Josh 11:20 that He *m* utterly destroy them,
11:20 and that they *m* receive no
11:20 but that He *m* destroy them, as
20: 9 killed a person accidentally *m*
22:16 that you *m* rebel this day
24: 8 that you *m* possess their land,
Judg 3: 1 that He *m* test Israel by them,
3: 2 of the children of Israel *m* be
3: 4 that He *m* test Israel by
6:14 Go in this *m* of yours, and you
9:24 seventy sons of Jerubbaal *m* be
16:30 And he pushed with all his *m*,
18: 7 no rulers in the land who *m*
Ruth 1: 6 her daughters-in-law that she *m*
1 Sam 4: 4 that they *m* bring from there
6: 6 that they *m* depart?
13:10 that he *m* greet him.
18:27 that he *m* become the king's
20: 6 permission of me that he *m*
2 Sam 6:14 the LORD with all his *m*;
10:10 that he *m* set them in battle
17:14 to the intent that the LORD *m*
1 Ki 2:27 that he *m* fulfill the word of
7: 7 where he *m* judge; and it was
8: 1 that they *m* bring up the ark of
8:16 that My name *m* be there; but I
12:15 that He *m* fulfill His word,
12:21 that he *m* restore the kingdom
15:17 that he *m* let none go out or
15:23 all the acts of Asa, all his *m*,
16: 5 Baasha, what he did, and his *m*,
16:27 and the *m* that he showed, are
19: 4 And he prayed that he *m* die,
22:45 the *m* that he showed, and how
2 Ki 10:34 all that he did, and all his *m*,
13: 8 all that he did, and his *m*,
13:12 and his *m* with which he fought
14:15 of Jehoash which he did—his *m*,
14:28 and all that he did—his *m*,
15:19 that his hand *m* be with him to
20:20 the acts of Hezekiah—all his *m*,
22:17 that they *m* provoke Me to anger
23:10 that no man *m* make his son or
23:24 that he *m* perform the words of
23:25 his soul, and with all his *m*,
23:33 that he *m* not reign in
1 Chr 13: 8 before God with all their *m*,
29: 2 I have prepared with all my *m*:
29:12 In Your hand is power and *m*;
29:30 with all his reign and his *m*,
2 Chr 5: 2 that they *m* bring the ark of
6: 5 that My name *m* be there, nor
10:15 that the LORD *m* fulfill His
11: 1 that he *m* restore the kingdom
16: 1 that he *m* let none go out or
20: 6 is there not power and *m*,
25:20 that He *m* give them into the
31: 4 that they *m* devote themselves
32:18 that they *m* take the city.
32:31 that He *m* know all that was
34:25 that they *m* provoke Me to anger
35:12 burnt offerings that they *m*
35:22 disguised himself so that he *m*
36:22 by the mouth of Jeremiah *m* be
Ezra 1: 1 by the mouth of Jeremiah *m* be
5:10 that we *m* write the names of
8:21 that we *m* humble ourselves
Neh 5: 3 that we *m* buy grain because of
6:13 so that they *m* have cause for
6:13 that they *m* reproach me.
7: 5 that they *m* be registered by
9:24 That they *m* do with them as
9:29 That You *m* bring them back to
Esth 4: 2 for no one *m* enter the king's
4: 8 that he *m* show it to Esther and
4: 8 and that he *m* command her to go
10: 2 the acts of his power and his *m*,
Job 6: 8 that I *m* have my request,
16:21 that one *m* plead for a man with
23: 3 that I knew where I *m* find Him,
23: 3 That I *m* come to His seat!
38:13 That it *m* take hold of the ends
Ps 68:18 That the LORD God *m* dwell
78: 6 That the generation to come *m*
105:45 That they *m* observe His
106: 8 That He *m* make His mighty
107: 7 That they *m* go to a city for a
109:16 That he *m* even slay the broken
118:13 that I *m* fall, But the LORD
119:11 That I *m* not sin against You!
145: 6 Men shall speak of the *m* of
Eccl 2: 3 till I *m* see what was good for
9:10 finds to do, do it with your *m*;
Isa 11: 2 The Spirit of counsel and *m*,
28:13 That they *m* go and fall
33:13 are near, acknowledge My *m*.
40:26 By the greatness of His *m* And
40:29 And to those who have no *m*
41: 7 That it *m* not totter.
63:13 That they *m* not stumble?"
64: 1 That the mountains *m* shake
Jer 9: 1 That I *m* weep day and night
9: 2 That I *m* leave my people,
9:23 the mighty man glory in his *m*,
10: 6 and Your name is great in *m*),
16:21 them to know My hand and My *m*;
17:23 that they *m* not hear nor
19:15 their necks that they *m* not
20:17 That my mother *m* have been my
23:10 And their *m* is not right.
25: 7 that you *m* provoke Me to anger
49:35 The foremost of their *m*.
51:30 Their *m* has failed,
Ezek 17: 7 That he *m* water it.
17:14 that the kingdom *m* be brought
17:14 by keeping his covenant it *m*
17:15 that they *m* give him horses and

M

20:12 that they **m** know that I am the
20:26 that I **m** make them desolate and
20:26 them desolate and that they **m**
28:17 That they **m** gaze at you.
32:29 Who despite their **m** Are laid
32:30 which they caused by their **m**;
40: 4 were brought here so that I **m**
41: 6 that they **m** be supported, but
Dan 1: 4 and whom they **m** teach the
1: 5 the end of that time they **m**
1: 8 chief of the eunuchs that he **m**
2:16 that he **m** tell the king the
2:18 that they **m** seek mercies from
2:18 Daniel and his companions **m**
2:20 For wisdom and **m** are His.
2:23 You have given me wisdom and **m**,
4: 6 that they **m** make known to me
5: 2 and his concubines **m** drink from
6: 2 that the satraps **m** give account
6:17 the purpose concerning Daniel **m**
9:13 that we **m** turn from our
Hos 8: 4 That they **m** be cut off.
Am 1:13 That they **m** enlarge their
2:16 The most courageous men of **m**
Jon 4: 5 till he **m** see what would become
4: 6 that it **m** be shade for his head
Mic 3: 8 LORD, And of justice and **m**,
7:16 and be ashamed of all their **m**;
Hab 3:16 That I **m** rest in the day of
Zech 4: 6 Not by **m** nor by power, but by My
6: 7 that they **m** walk to and fro
8: 9 That the temple **m** be built.
11:10 that I **m** break the covenant
11:14 that I **m** break the brotherhood
Mal 2: 5 I gave them to him that he **m**
Mt 1:22 So all this was done that it **m**
2:15 that it **m** be fulfilled which
2:23 that it **m** be fulfilled which
4:14 that it **m** be fulfilled which was
8:17 that it **m** be fulfilled which was
12:10 that they **m** accuse Him.
12:14 how they **m** destroy Him.
12:17 that it **m** be fulfilled which was
13:35 that it **m** be fulfilled which was
14: 7 to give her whatever she **m** ask.
14:36 and begged Him that they **m** only
15: 5 Whatever profit you **m** have
19:13 were brought to Him that He **m**
21: 4 All this was done that it **m** be
21:34 that they **m** receive its fruit.
22:15 went and plotted how they **m**
26: 9 For this fragrant oil **m** have
26:56 Scriptures of the prophets **m**
27:35 that it **m** be fulfilled which
Mk 3: 2 so that they **m** accuse Him.
3: 6 how they **m** destroy Him.
3:14 that they **m** be with Him and
3:14 be with Him and that He **m** send
5:18 begged Him that he **m** be with
6:56 and begged Him that they **m** just
7:11 Whatever profit you **m** have
10:13 that He **m** touch them; but the
11:18 heard it and sought how they **m**
12: 2 that he **m** receive some of the
14: 1 the scribes sought how they **m**
14: 5 For it **m** have been sold for more
14:11 So he sought how he **m**
14:35 the hour **m** pass from Him.
16: 1 that they **m** come and anoint
Lk 1:74 ***M*** serve Him without fear,
4:29 that they **m** throw Him down over
5:19 they could not find how they **m**
6: 7 that they **m** find an accusation
6:11 with one another what they **m**
8:38 departed begged Him that he **m**
11:54 to catch Him in something He **m**
11:54 that they **m** accuse Him.
15:29 that I **m** make merry with my
18:15 infants to Him that He **m** touch
19:15 that he **m** know how much every
19:23 that at my coming I **m** have
20:10 that they **m** give him some of
20:20 that they **m** seize on His words,
22: 2 the scribes sought how they **m**
22: 4 how he **m** betray Him to them.
23:26 they laid the cross that he **m**
24:45 that they **m** comprehend the
Jn 1: 7 that all through him **m** believe.
3:17 that the world through Him **m**
8: 6 that they **m** have something of
11:57 that they **m** seize Him.
12: 9 but that they **m** also see
12:38 word of Isaiah the prophet **m**
15:25 happened that the word **m** be
17:12 that the Scripture **m** be
18: 9 that the saying **m** be fulfilled
18:28 but that they **m** eat the
18:32 that the saying of Jesus **m** be
19:24 that the Scripture **m** be
19:28 that the Scripture **m** be
19:31 asked Pilate that their legs **m**
19:31 and that they **m** be taken away.
19:38 asked Pilate that he **m** take
Acts 1:25 that he **m** go to his own
5:15 shadow of Peter passing by **m**
7:19 so that they **m** not live.
8:15 prayed for them that they **m**
9: 2 he **m** bring them bound to
9:12 so that he **m** receive his
9:21 so that he **m** bring them bound
13:42 begged that these words **m** be
17:27 in the hope that they **m** grope
22:24 so that he **m** know why they
23:10 fearing lest Paul **m** be pulled
24:26 that he **m** release him.
26:29 **m** become both almost and
26:32 This man **m** have been set free if
Rom 1:13 that I **m** have some fruit among
3:26 that He **m** be just and the
4:11 that he **m** be the father of all
4:11 that righteousness **m** be imputed
4:16 it is of faith that it **m**
4:16 so that the promise **m** be sure
5:20 law entered that the offense **m**
5:21 even so grace **m** reign through
6: 6 that the body of sin **m** be done
7:13 that it **m** appear sin, was
7:13 sin through the commandment **m**
8: 4 requirement of the law **m** be
8:29 that He **m** be the firstborn
9:11 of God according to election **m**
9:23 and that He **m** make known the
11:19 were broken off that I **m** be
11:32 that He **m** have mercy on all.
14: 9 that He **m** be Lord of both the
15: 4 and comfort of the Scriptures **m**
15: 9 and that the Gentiles **m** glorify
15:16 that I **m** be a minister of Jesus
15:16 the offering of the Gentiles **m**
1 Cor 2:12 that we **m** know the things that
4: 8 that we also **m** reign with you!
4:15 For though you **m** have ten
5: 2 he who has done this deed **m** be
9:19 that I **m** win the more;
9:20 that I **m** win Jews; to those
9:20 that I **m** win those who are
9:21 that I **m** win those who are
9:22 that I **m** win the weak. I have
9:22 that I **m** by all means save
2 Cor 1:15 that you **m** have a second
2: 4 but that you **m** know the love
2: 9 that I **m** put you to the test,
5:21 that we **m** become the
7: 9 that you **m** suffer loss from us
7:12 for you in the sight of God **m**
8: 9 that you through His poverty **m**
11: 7 in humbling myself that you **m**
12: 6 For though I **m** desire to boast,
12: 8 the Lord three times that it **m**
Gal 1: 4 that He **m** deliver us from this
1:16 that I **m** preach Him among the
2: 2 lest by any means I **m** run, or
2: 4 that they **m** bring us into
2: 5 that the truth of the gospel **m**
2:16 that we **m** be justified by faith
2:19 law died to the law that I **m**
3:14 that the blessing of Abraham **m**
3:14 that we **m** receive the promise
3:22 by faith in Jesus Christ **m** be
3:24 that we **m** be justified by
4: 5 that we **m** receive the adoption
Eph 1:10 the fullness of the times He **m**
1:21 principality and power and **m**
2: 7 that in the ages to come He **m**
2:16 and that He **m** reconcile them
3:10 the manifold wisdom of God **m**
3:16 to be strengthened with **m**
4:10 that He **m** fill all things.)
5:26 that He **m** sanctify and cleanse
5:27 that He **m** present her to Himself
6:10 Lord and in the power of His **m**.
Phil 3: 4 though I also **m** have confidence
Col 1:11 strengthened with all **m**,
1 Th 2: 6 when we **m** have made demands as
2: 9 that we **m** not be a burden to
3: 5 and our labor **m** be in vain.
2 Th 2:10 that they **m** be saved.
3: 8 that we **m** not be a burden to
1 Tim 1:16 that in me first Jesus Christ **m**
2 Tim 4:17 so that the message **m** be
4:17 and that all the Gentiles **m**
Titus 2:14 that He **m** redeem us from every
Phm 1: 8 though I **m** be very bold in
1:13 that on your behalf he **m**
1:14 that your good deed **m** not be by
1:15 that you **m** receive him forever,
Heb 2: 9 **m** taste death for everyone.
2:14 that through death He **m** destroy
2:17 that He **m** be a merciful and
6:18 we **m** have strong consolation,
11:35 that they **m** obtain a better
13:12 that He **m** sanctify the people
Jas 1:18 that we **m** be a kind of
1 Pe 2:24 **m** live for righteousness—by
3:18 that He **m** bring us to God,
4: 6 that they **m** be judged according
2 Pe 2:11 who are greater in power and **m**,
1 Jn 2:19 they went out that they **m**
3: 8 that He **m** destroy the works of
4: 9 that we **m** live through Him.
Rev 7:12 and honor and power and **m**,
12:14 that she **m** fly into the
12:15 that he **m** cause her to be
16:12 of the kings from the east **m**

MIGHTIER (13/13) MIGHT, MIGHTY

Gen 26:16 for you are much **m** than we."
Ex 1: 9 of Israel are more and **m** than
Num 14:12 of you a nation greater and **m**
Deut 4:38 you nations greater and **m** than
7: 1 seven nations greater and **m**
9: 1 nations greater and **m** than
9:14 I will make of you a nation **m**
11:23 will dispossess greater and **m**
Ps 93: 4 The LORD on high is **m** Than
Eccl 6:10 contend with Him who is **m** than
Mt 3:11 He who is coming after me is **m**
Mk 1: 7 comes One after me who is **m**
Lk 3:16 but One **m** than I is coming,

MIGHTILY (11/11) MIGHT

Judg 14: 6 the Spirit of the LORD came **m**
14:19 of the LORD came upon him **m**,
15:14 the Spirit of the LORD came **m**
Isa 2:19 He arises to shake the earth **m**.
2:21 He arises to shake the earth **m**.
Jer 25:30 He will roar **m** against His
Jon 3: 8 and cry **m** to God; yes, let
Nah 2: 1 Fortify your power **m**.
Acts 19:20 So the word of the Lord grew **m**
Col 1:29 His working which works in me **m**.
Rev 18: 2 And he cried **m** with a loud

MIGHTY (286/278) MIGHT, MIGHTIER

Gen 6: 4 Those were the **m** men who were
10: 8 he began to be a **m** one on the
10: 9 He was a **m** hunter before the
10: 9 Like Nimrod the **m** hunter before
18:18 surely become a great and **m**
23: 6 You are a **m** prince among us;
49:24 By the hands of the ***M*** God
Ex 1: 7 and grew exceedingly **m**;
1:20 multiplied and grew very **m**.
3:19 not even by a **m** hand.
9:28 may be no more **m** thundering
10: 2 and your son's son the **m** things
15:10 sank like lead in the **m** waters.
15:15 The **m** men of Moab, Trembling
32:11 great power and with a **m** hand?
Lev 19:15 nor honor the person of the **m**.
Num 22: 6 for they are too **m** for me.
Deut 3:24 Your greatness and Your **m** hand,
3:24 Your works and Your **m** deeds?
4:34 by a **m** hand and an outstretched
4:37 with His **m** power,
5:15 you out from there by a **m** hand
6:21 us out of Egypt with a **m** hand;
7: 8 brought you out with a **m** hand,
7:19 the **m** hand and the outstretched
9:26 brought out of Egypt with a **m**
9:29 You brought out by Your **m** power
10:17 **m** and awesome, who shows no
11: 2 His greatness and His **m** hand
26: 5 he became a nation, great, **m**,
26: 8 us out of Egypt with a **m** hand
34:12 and by all that **m** power and all
Josh 1:14 all your **m** men of valor, and
4:24 of the LORD, that it is **m**,
6: 2 and the **m** men of valor.
8: 3 Joshua chose thirty thousand **m**
10: 2 Ai, and all its men were **m**.
10: 7 and all the **m** men of valor.
Judg 5:13 came down for me against the **m**.
5:23 help of the LORD against the **m**.
6:12 you **m** man of valor!"
11: 1 the Gileadite was a **m** man
1 Sam 2: 4 The bows of the **m** men are
4: 8 from the hand of these **m** gods?
6: 6 When He did **m** things among
9: 1 a **m** man of power.
16:18 a **m** man of valor, a man of war,
19: 8 and struck them with a **m** blow,
23: 5 struck them with a **m** blow, and
2 Sam 1:19 places! How the **m** have fallen!
1:21 For the shield of the **m** is
1:22 slain, From the fat of the **m**,
1:25 How the **m** have fallen in the
1:27 How the **m** have fallen, And the
10: 7 Joab and all the army of the **m**
16: 6 the people and all the **m** men
17: 8 that they are **m** men, and they
17:10 knows that your father is a **m**
20: 7 and all the **m** men, went out
23: 8 These are the names of the **m** men
23: 9 one of the three **m** men with
23:16 So the three **m** men broke through
23:17 were done by the three **m** men.
23:22 won a name among three **m** men.
1 Ki 1: 8 and the **m** men who belonged to
1:10 the **m** men, or Solomon his
11:28 The man Jeroboam was a **m** man of
2 Ki 5: 1 He was also a **m** man of valor,
24:14 all the captains and all the **m**
24:15 and the **m** of the land he
1 Chr 1:10 he began to be a **m** one on the
5:24 They were **m** men of valor,
7: 2 The sons of Tola were **m** men
7: 5 families of Issachar were **m**
7: 7 thousand and thirty-four **m** men
7: 9 thousand two hundred **m** men
7:11 thousand two hundred **m** men of
7:40 **m** men of valor, chief leaders.
8:40 The sons of Ulam were **m** men of
11:10 were the heads of the **m** men
11:11 this is the number of the **m** men
11:12 who was one of the three **m** men.
11:19 were done by the three **m** men.
11:24 and won a name among three **m**
11:26 Also the **m** warriors were
12: 1 and they were among the **m** men,
12: 4 a **m** man among the thirty, and
12: 8 **m** men of valor, men trained for
12:21 for they were all **m** men of

12:25 **m** men of valor fit for war,
12:30 **m** men of valor, famous men
19: 8 Joab and all the army of the **m**
27: 6 was the Benaiah who was **m**
28: 1 and all the **m** men of valor.
29:24 All the leaders and the **m** men,
2 Chr 6:32 of Your great name and Your **m**
13: 3 choice men, **m** men of valor.
13:21 But Abijah grew **m**,
14: 8 all these were **m** men of valor.
17:13 **m** men of valor, were in
17:14 him three hundred thousand **m**
17:16 him two hundred thousand **m** men
17:17 Eliada a **m** man of valor, and
25: 6 hired one hundred thousand **m**
26:12 of chief officers of the **m** men
26:13 that made war with **m** power, to
27: 6 So Jotham became **m**, because
28: 7 a **m** man of Ephraim, killed
32:21 angel who cut down every **m** man
Ezra 4:20 There have also been **m** kings
7:28 before all the king's **m** princes.
Neh 3:16 as far as the House of the **M**.
9:11 As a stone into the **m** waters.
9:32 our God, The great, the **m**,
11:14 **m** men of valor, were one
Job 5:15 sword, From the mouth of the **m**,
9: 4 God is wise in heart and **m** in
10: 5 years like the days of a **m** man,
12:19 And overthrows the **m**.
12:21 on princes, And disarms the **m**.
21: 7 Yes, become **m** in power?
22: 8 But the **m** man possessed the
24:22 But God draws the **m** away with
34:20 The **m** are taken away without a
34:24 He breaks in pieces **m** men
35: 9 because of the arm of the **m**.
36: 5 "Behold, God is **m**,
36: 5 He is **m** in strength of
36:19 Or all the **m** forces, Keep you
41:12 His **m** power, or his graceful
41:25 the **m** are afraid; Because of
Ps 24: 8 The LORD strong and **m**,
24: 8 The LORD **m** in battle.
29: 1 O you **m** ones, Give unto the
33:16 A **m** man is not delivered by
45: 3 O **M** One, With Your glory and
50: 1 The **M** One, God the LORD,
52: 1 O **m** man? The goodness of God
59: 3 The **m** gather against me,
68:33 out His voice, a **m** voice.
69: 4 They are **m** who would destroy
74:15 You dried up **m** rivers.
76: 5 And none of the **m** men have
78:65 Like a **m** man who shouts
80:10 And the **m** cedars with its
82: 1 in the congregation of the **m**;
89: 6 Who among the sons of the **m**
89: 8 Who is **m** like You, O LORD?
89:10 Your enemies with Your **m** arm.
89:13 You have a **m** arm; Strong is
89:19 given help to one who is **m**;
93: 4 Than the **m** waves of the sea.
106: 2 Who can utter the **m** acts of the
106: 8 That He might make His **m** power
112: 2 His descendants will be **m** on
132: 2 And vowed to the **M** One of
132: 5 A dwelling place for the **M** One
135:10 many nations And slew **m** kings—
145: 4 And shall declare Your **m** acts.
145:12 to the sons of men His **m** acts,
147: 5 our Lord, and **m** in power;
150: 1 Praise Him in His **m** firmament!
150: 2 Praise Him for His **m** acts;
Prov 16:32 to anger is better than the **m**,
18:18 And keeps the **m** apart.
21:22 man scales the city of the **m**,
23:11 For their Redeemer is **m**;
30:30 which is **m** among beasts And
Song 4: 4 All shields of **m** men.
Isa 1:24 the **M** One of Israel, "Ah, I
3: 2 The **m** man and the man of war,
3:25 And your **m** in the war.
5:22 Woe to men **m** at drinking wine,
8: 7 of the River, strong and **m**—
9: 6 **M** God, Everlasting Father,
10:21 of Jacob, To the **M** God.
10:34 Lebanon will fall by the **M** One.
11:15 With His **m** wind He will shake
13: 3 I have also called My **m** ones
17:12 like the rushing of **m** waters!
19:20 send them a Savior and a **M** One,
21:17 the **m** men of the people of
22:17 O **m** man, And will surely
28: 2 the Lord has a **m** and strong
28: 2 Like a flood of **m** waters
30:29 To the **M** One of Israel.
34: 7 young bulls with the **m** bulls;
42:13 shall go forth like a **m** man;
43:16 And a path through the **m** waters,
49:24 the prey be taken from the **m**,
49:25 Even the captives of the **m** shall
49:26 the **M** One of Jacob."
60:16 the **M** One of Jacob.
63: 1 in righteousness, **m** to save."
Jer 5:15 It is a **m** nation, It is an
5:16 They are all **m** men.
9:23 Let not the **m** man glory in
14: 9 Like a **m** one who cannot save?
14:17 been broken with a **m** stroke,
20:11 the LORD is with me as a **m**,
26:21 with all his **m** men and all the
32:18 the **M** God, whose name is the
32:19 great in counsel and **m** in work,
33: 3 show you great and **m** things,
41:16 the **m** men of war and the women
46: 5 Their **m** ones are beaten down;
46: 6 Nor the **m** man escape;
46: 9 O chariots! And let the **m** men
46:12 For the **m** man has stumbled
46:12 man has stumbled against the **m**;
48:14 We are **m** And strong men for
48:41 The **m** men's hearts in Moab on
49:22 The heart of the **m** men of Edom
50:36 A sword is against her **m** men,
51:30 The **m** men of Babylon have
51:56 And her **m** men are taken.
51:57 and her **m** men. And they shall
Lam 1:15 has trampled underfoot all my **m**
Ezek 17:13 He also took away the **m** of the
17:17 will Pharaoh with his **m** army
20:33 surely with a **m** hand, with an
20:34 with a **m** hand, with an
31:11 it into the hand of the **m** one
32:12 By the swords of the **m** warriors,
32:21 The strong among the **m** Shall
32:27 They do not lie with the **m**
32:27 of the terror of the **m** in the
38:15 a great company and a **m** army.
39:18 shall eat the flesh of the **m**,
39:20 With **m** men And with all the
Dan 3:20 And he commanded certain **m** men
4: 3 And how **m** His wonders!
4:30 a royal dwelling by my **m** power
8:24 His power shall be **m**,
8:24 He shall destroy the **m**,
9:15 land of Egypt with a **m** hand,
11: 3 Then a **m** king shall arise, who
11:25 battle with a very great and **m**
Hos 10:13 In the multitude of your **m** men.
Joel 2: 7 They run like **m** men,
3: 9 for war! Wake up the **m** men,
3:11 Cause Your **m** ones to go down
Am 2:14 Nor shall the **m** deliver
5:12 transgressions And your **m** sins:
5:24 And righteousness like a **m**
Ob 9 Then your **m** men, O Teman, shall
Jon 1: 4 and there was a **m** tempest on
Nah 2: 3 The shields of his **m** men are
Zeph 1:14 There the **m** men shall cry out.
3:17 The **M** One, will save; He will
Zech 9:13 you like the sword of a **m** man.
10: 5 They shall be like **m** men,
10: 7 Ephraim shall be like a **m** man,
11: 2 Because the **m** trees are
Mt 11:20 in which most of His **m** works
11:21 Bethsaida! For if the **m** works
11:23 for if the **m** works which were
13:54 get this wisdom and these **m**
13:58 Now He did not do many **m** works
Mk 6: 2 that such **m** works are performed
6: 5 Now He could do no **m** work there,
Lk 1:49 For He who is **m** has done great
1:52 He has put down the **m** from
10:13 Bethsaida! For if the **m** works
19:37 a loud voice for all the **m** works
24:19 who was a Prophet **m** in deed and
Acts 2: 2 as of a rushing **m** wind, and it
7:22 and was **m** in words and deeds.
18:24 an eloquent man and **m** in the
Rom 15:19 in **m** signs and wonders, by the
1 Cor 1:26 to the flesh, not many **m**,
1:27 to shame the things which are **m**;
2 Cor 10: 4 warfare are not carnal but **m**
12:12 signs and wonders and **m** deeds.
13: 3 toward you, but **m** in you.
Eph 1:19 to the working of His **m** power
2 Th 1: 7 from heaven with His **m** angels,
1 Pe 5: 6 humble yourselves under the **m**
Rev 6:13 when it is shaken by a **m** wind.
6:15 the **m** men, every slave and
10: 1 I saw still another **m** angel
16:18 such a **m** and great earthquake
18:10 that **m** city! For in one hour
18:21 Then a **m** angel took up a stone
19: 6 as the sound of **m** thunderings,
19:18 the flesh of **m** men, the flesh

MIGRON (2/2)

1 Sam 14: 2 pomegranate tree which is in **M**.
Isa 10:28 come to Aiath, He has passed **M**;

MIJAMIN (4/4)

1 Chr 24: 9 to Malchijah, the sixth to **M**,
Ezra 10:25 Ramiah, Jeziah, Malchiah, **M**,
Neh 10: 7 Meshullam, Abijah, **M**,
12: 5 **M**, Maadiah, Bilgah,

MIKLOTH (4/4)

1 Chr 8:32 and **M**, who begot Shimeah.
9:37 Gedor, Ahio, Zechariah, and **M**.
9:38 And **M** begot Shimeam. They also
27: 4 and of his division **M** also was

MIKNEIAH (2/2)

1 Chr 15:18 Mattithiah, Elipheleh, **M**,
15:21 Mattithiah, Elipheleh, **M**,

MILALAI (1/1)

Neh 12:36 brethren, Shemaiah, Azarel, **M**,

MILCAH (10/9)

Gen 11:29 and the name of Nahor's wife, **M**,
11:29 of Haran the father of **M** and
22:20 Indeed **M** also has borne children
22:23 These eight **M** bore to Nahor,
24:15 was born to Bethuel, son of **M**,
24:47 whom **M** bore to him.' So I put
Num 26:33 were Mahlah, Noah, Hoglah, **M**,
27: 1 Mahlah, Noah, Hoglah, **M**,
36:11 for Mahlah, Tirzah, Hoglah, **M**,
Josh 17: 3 Mahlah, Noah, Hoglah, **M**,

MILCAH'S (1/1)

Gen 24:24 **M** son, whom she bore to

MILCH (KJV) See MILK

MILCOM (6/6) MOLECH, MOLOCH

1 Ki 11: 5 and after **M** the abomination of
11:33 and **M** the god of the people of
2 Ki 23:13 and for **M** the abomination of
Jer 49: 1 Why then does **M** inherit Gad,
49: 3 For **M** shall go into captivity
Zeph 1: 5 But who also swear by **M**;

MILD (1/1)

Gen 25:27 but Jacob was a **m** man, dwelling

MILDEW (5/5)

Deut 28:22 with scorching, and with **m**;
1 Ki 8:37 pestilence or blight or **m**,
2 Chr 6:28 land, pestilence or blight or **m**,
Am 4: 9 blasted you with blight and **m**.
Hag 2:17 'I struck you with blight and **m**

MILE (1/1) MILES

Mt 5:41 whoever compels you to go one **m**,

MILES (3/3) MILE

Lk 24:13 which was seven **m** from
Jn 6:19 had rowed about three or four **m**,
11:18 about two **m** away.

MILETUS (3/3)

Acts 20:15 The next day we came to **M**.
20:17 From **M** he sent to Ephesus and
2 Tim 4:20 but Trophimus I have left in **M**

MILITARY (3/3)

1 Chr 27: 1 king in every matter of the **m**
2 Chr 32: 6 Then he set **m** captains over the
33:14 Then he put **m** captains in all

MILK (51/50)

Gen 18: 8 So he took butter and **m** and the
32:15 thirty **m** camels with their
49:12 And his teeth whiter than **m**.
Ex 3: 8 to a land flowing with **m** and
3:17 to a land flowing with **m** and
13: 5 a land flowing with **m** and
23:19 a young goat in its mother's **m**.
33: 3 up to a land flowing with **m**
34:26 a young goat in its mother's **m**.
Lev 20:24 a land flowing with **m** and
Num 13:27 It truly flows with **m** and
14: 8 a land which flows with **m** and
16:13 up out of a land flowing with **m**
16:14 us into a land flowing with **m**
Deut 6: 3 a land flowing with **m** and
11: 9 a land flowing with **m** and
14:21 a young goat in its mother's **m**.
26: 9 a land flowing with **m** and
26:15 a land flowing with **m** and
27: 3 a land flowing with **m** and
31:20 to the land flowing with **m** and
32:14 and **m** of the flock, With fat
Josh 5: 6 a land flowing with **m** and
Judg 4:19 So she opened a jug of **m**,
5:25 He asked for water, she gave **m**;
1 Sam 6: 7 take two **m** cows which have
6:10 they took two **m** cows and
Job 10:10 Did you not pour me out like **m**,
21:24 His pails are full of **m**,
Prov 27:27 shall have enough goats' **m**
30:33 For as the churning of **m**
Song 4:11 Honey and **m** are under your
5: 1 I have drunk my wine with my **m**.
5:12 of waters, Washed with **m**,
Isa 7:22 from the abundance of **m** they
28: 9 Those just weaned from **m**?
55: 1 buy wine and **m** Without money
60:16 You shall drink the **m** of the
60:16 And **m** the breast of kings;
Jer 11: 5 a land flowing with **m** and
32:22 a land flowing with **m** and
Lam 4: 7 than snow And whiter than **m**;
Ezek 20: 6 flowing with **m** and honey,' the
20:15 flowing with **m** and honey,' the
25: 4 and they shall drink your **m**.
Joel 3:18 The hills shall flow with **m**,
1 Cor 3: 2 I fed you with **m** and not with
9: 7 and does not drink of the **m** of
Heb 5:12 and you have come to need **m** and

5:13 who partakes only of *m* is
1 Pe 2: 2 desire the pure *m* of the word,

MILL (1/1)

Mt 24:41 will be grinding at the *m*:

MILLET (2/2)

Ezek 4: 9 barley, beans, lentils, *m*,
27:17 merchandise wheat of Minnith, *m*,

MILLION (4/4)

1 Chr 21: 5 All Israel had one *m* one
22:14 talents of gold and one *m*
2 Chr 14: 9 them with an army of a *m* men
Rev 9:16 the horsemen was two hundred *m*;

MILLO (10/9)

2 Sam 5: 9 built all around from the *M*
1 Ki 9:15 the LORD, his own house, the *M*,
9:24 for her. Then he built the *M*.
11:27 Solomon had built the *M* and
2 Ki 12:20 Joash in the house of the *M*,
1 Chr 11: 8 from the *M* to the surrounding
2 Chr 32: 5 also he repaired the *M* in the

MILLSTONE (9/9) MILLSTONES

Deut 24: 6 take the lower or the upper *m*
Judg 9:53 woman dropped an upper *m* on
2 Sam 11:21 a woman who cast a piece of a *m*
Job 41:24 Even as hard as the lower *m*.
Mt 18: 6 would be better for him if a *m*
Mk 9:42 would be better for him if a *m*
Lk 17: 2 would be better for him if a *m*
Rev 18:21 took up a stone like a great *m*
18:22 and the sound of a *m* shall not

MILLSTONES (4/4) MILLSTONE

Num 11: 8 ground it on *m* or beat it in
Isa 47: 2 Take the *m* and grind meal.
Jer 25:10 the sound of the *m* and the
Lam 5:13 Young men ground at the *m*;

MINA (5/5)

Ezek 45:12 fifteen shekels shall be your *m*.
Lk 19:16 your *m* has earned ten minas.'
19:18 your *m* has earned five minas.'
19:20 saying, 'Master, here is your *m*,
19:24 Take the *m* from him, and give

MINAS (9/9)

1 Ki 10:17 three *m* of gold went into each
Ezra 2:69 five thousand *m* of silver, and
Neh 7:71 thousand two hundred silver *m*.
7:72 drachmas, two thousand silver *m*,
Lk 19:13 delivered to them ten *m*,
19:16 your mina has earned ten *m*.
19:18 your mina has earned five *m*.
19:24 give it to him who has ten *m*.
19:25 to him, 'Master, he has ten *m*.

MINCING (1/1)

Isa 3:16 Walking and *m* as they go,

MIND (90/88) MINDED, MINDFUL, MINDS, UNMINDFUL

Gen 26:35 And they were a grief of *m* to
37:11 father kept the matter in *m*.
Lev 24:12 that the *m* of the LORD might
Deut 18: 6 with all the desire of his *m*
30: 1 and you call them to *m* among
1 Sam 2:35 is in My heart and in My *m*.
1 Chr 12:38 rest of Israel were of one *m*
22: 7 it was in my *m* to build a house
28: 9 heart and with a willing *m*;
Neh 4: 6 for the people had a *m* to work.
Job 38:36 Who has put wisdom in the *m*?
Ps 26: 2 Try my *m* and my heart.
31:12 like a dead man, out of *m*;
73:21 And I was vexed in my *m*.
Isa 26: 3 Whose *m* is stayed on You,
46: 8 yourselves men; Recall to *m*,
65:17 not be remembered or come to *m*.
Jer 3:16 It shall not come to *m*,
11:20 Testing the *m* and the heart,
12: 2 But far from their *m*.
15: 1 My *m* would not be favorable
17:10 the heart, I test the *m*,
19: 5 nor did it come into My *m*),
20:12 And see the *m* and heart,
32:35 nor did it come into My *m* that
44:21 and did it not come into His *m*?
51:50 let Jerusalem come to your *m*.
Lam 3:21 This I recall to my *m*,
Ezek 11: 5 things that come into your *m*.
20:32 What you have in your *m* shall
38:10 thoughts will arise in your *m*,
40: 4 and fix your *m* on everything I
Dan 2:29 thoughts came to your *m*
9:14 has kept the disaster in *m*,
Hab 1:11 Then his *m* changes, and he
Mt 22:37 soul, and with all your *m*.
Mk 3:21 they said, "He is out of His *m*.
5:15 and clothed and in his right *m*.
12:30 soul, with all your *m*,
14:72 Then Peter called to *m* the word
Lk 8:35 clothed and in his right *m*.
10:27 and with all your *m*,
12:29 drink, nor have an anxious *m*.
Rom 1:28 gave them over to a debased *m*,
7:23 warring against the law of my *m*,
7:25 with the *m* I myself serve the
8: 7 Because the carnal *m* is enmity
8:27 the hearts knows what the *m* of
11:34 For who has known the *m* of
12: 2 by the renewing of your *m*,
12:16 Be of the same *m* toward one
12:16 Do not set your *m* on high
14: 5 be fully convinced in his own *m*.
15: 6 that you may with one *m* and one
1 Cor 1:10 joined together in the same *m*
2:16 who has known the *m* of the
2:16 But we have the *m* of Christ.
14:23 say that you are out of your *m*?
2 Cor 5:13 or if we are of sound *m*,
8:12 if there is first a willing *m*,
8:19 and to show your ready *m*,
13:11 Be of good comfort, be of one *m*,
Gal 5:10 that you will have no other *m*;
Eph 2: 3 of the flesh and of the *m*,
4:17 in the futility of their *m*,
4:23 renewed in the spirit of your *m*,
Phil 1:27 with one *m* striving together
2: 2 being of one accord, of one *m*.
2: 3 but in lowliness of *m* let each
2: 5 Let this *m* be in you which was
3:15 many as are mature, have this *m*;
3:16 rule, let us be of the same *m*.
3:19 who set their *m* on earthly
4: 2 Syntyche to be of the same *m*
Col 1:21 and enemies in your *m* by
2:18 puffed up by his fleshly *m*,
3: 2 Set your *m* on things above, not
1 Th 4:11 to *m* your own business, and to
2 Th 2: 2 not to be soon shaken in *m* or
2 Tim 1: 7 and of love and of a sound *m*.
Titus 1:15 but even their *m* and conscience
Heb 8:10 put My laws in their *m*
11:15 truly if they had called to *m*
1 Pe 1:13 gird up the loins of your *m*,
3: 8 all of you be of one *m*,
4: 1 yourselves also with the same *m*,
3 Jn 10 I will call to *m* his deeds
Rev 17: 9 Here is the *m* which has wisdom:
17:13 "These are of one *m*,
17:17 His purpose, to be of one *m*,

MINDED (4/3) MIND

2 Ki 9:15 Jehu said, "If you are so *m*,
Mt 1:19 was *m* to put her away secretly.
Rom 8: 6 For to be carnally *m* is death,
8: 6 but to be spiritually *m* is

MINDFUL (11/11) MIND

Neh 9:17 And they were not *m* of Your
Ps 8: 4 What is man that You are *m* of
111: 5 He will ever be *m* of His
115:12 The LORD has been *m* of us;
144: 3 that You are *m* of him?
Isa 17:10 And have not been *m* of the
Mt 16:23 for you are not *m* of the things
Mk 8:33 Satan! For you are not *m* of the
2 Tim 1: 4 being *m* of your tears, that I
Heb 2: 6 is man that You are *m*
2 Pe 3: 2 that you may be *m* of the words

MINDS (19/19) MIND

Ex 13:17 the people change their *m* when
2 Sam 17: 8 they are enraged in their *m*,
Ps 7: 9 God tests the hearts and *m*.
Jer 31:33 I will put My law in their *m*,
34:11 afterward they changed their *m*
Ezek 24:25 that on which they set their *m*,
36: 5 joy and spiteful *m*,
Acts 14: 2 Gentiles and poisoned their *m*
28: 6 they changed their *m* and said
Rom 8: 5 to the flesh set their *m* on
2 Cor 3:14 But their *m* were blinded.
4: 4 whose *m* the god of this age has
11: 3 so your *m* may be corrupted from
Phil 4: 7 will guard your hearts and *m*
1 Tim 6: 5 wranglings of men of corrupt *m*
2 Tim 3: 8 the truth: men of corrupt *m*,
Heb 10:16 and in their *m* I will
2 Pe 3: 1 which I stir up your pure *m* by
Rev 2:23 I am He who searches the *m* and

MINE (69/60)

Gen 31:43 flock; all that you see is *m*.
48: 5 I came to you in Egypt, are *m*;
48: 5 and Simeon, they shall be *m*.
Ex 10: 1 I may show these signs of *M*
13: 2 both of man and beast; it is *M*.
19: 5 for all the earth is *M*.
34:19 "All that open the womb are *M*,
Lev 20:26 peoples, that you should be *M*.
25:23 permanently, for the land is *M*;
Num 3:12 the Levites shall be *M*,
3:13 all the firstborn are *M*.
3:13 man and beast. They shall be *M*:
3:45 The Levites shall be *M*:
8:14 and the Levites shall be *M*.
8:17 the children of Israel are *M*,
Deut 11:18 shall lay up these words of *m*
32:35 Vengeance is *M*,
2 Sam 14:30 "See, Joab's field is near *m*,
1 Ki 2:15 know that the kingdom was *m*,
3:26 Let him be neither *m* nor yours,
8:59 "And may these words of *m*,
20: 3 silver and your gold are *m*;
20: 3 wives and children are *m*.
Job 28: 1 Surely there is a *m* for silver,
41:11 Everything under heaven is *M*.
Ps 50:10 every beast of the forest is *M*,
50:11 wild beasts of the field are *M*.
50:12 tell you; For the world is *M*,
59: 4 through no fault of *m*.
60: 7 Gilead is *M*, and Manasseh
60: 7 is Mine, and Manasseh is *M*;
108: 8 is *M*; Manasseh is Mine;
108: 8 is Mine; Manasseh is *M*;
119:56 This has become *m*,
Prov 8:14 Counsel is *m*, and sound
Song 2:16 My beloved is *m*,
6: 3 And my beloved is *m*.
Isa 43: 1 you by your name; You are *M*.
Jer 44:28 will stand, *M* or theirs.
Ezek 16: 8 with you, and you became *M*,
18: 4 "Behold, all souls are *M*;
18: 4 as the soul of the son is *M*;
23: 4 her sister; They were *M*,
23: 5 harlot even though she was *M*;
29: 9 he said, 'The River is *m*,
35:10 these two countries shall be *m*,
Hag 2: 8 The silver is *M*, and the
2: 8 is Mine, and the gold is *M*,
Mal 3:17 'They shall be *M*,' says the
Mt 7:24 hears these sayings of *M*,
7:26 who hears these sayings of *M*,
20:21 that these two sons of *m*
20:23 hand and on My left is not *M*
Mk 10:40 hand and on My left is not *M*
Lk 11: 6 for a friend of *m* has come to me
19:27 bring here those enemies of *m*,
Jn 3:29 Therefore this joy of *m* is
7:16 said, "My doctrine is not *M*,
14:24 word which you hear is not *M*
16:14 for He will take of what is *M*
16:15 that the Father has are *M*.
16:15 I said that He will take of *M*
17:10 And all *M* are Yours, and Yours
17:10 Mine are Yours, and Yours are *M*,
Acts 9:15 for he is a chosen vessel of *M*
Rom 12:19 is written, "Vengeance is *M*,
16:13 the Lord, and his mother and *m*.
Phil 1: 4 always in every prayer of *m*
Heb 10:30 who said, "Vengeance is *M*,

MINGLE (1/1)

Dan 2:43 they will *m* with the seed of

MINGLED (10/10)

Ex 9:24 and fire *m* with the hail, so
Ps 102: 9 And *m* my drink with weeping,
106:35 But they *m* with the Gentiles
Isa 19:14 The LORD has *m* a perverse
Ezek 30: 5 all the *m* people, Chub, and the
Mt 27:34 they gave Him sour wine *m* with
Mk 15:23 Then they gave Him wine *m* with
Lk 13: 1 whose blood Pilate had *m* with
Rev 8: 7 *m* with blood, and they were
15: 2 like a sea of glass *m* with

MINIAMIN (1/1)

2 Chr 31:15 And under him were Eden, *M*,

MINISH, MINISHED (KJV) See DIMINISHED, REDUCE

MINISTER (75/72) MINISTERED, MINISTERING, MINISTERS, MINISTRY

Ex 28: 1 that he may *m* to Me as priest,
28: 3 that he may *m* to Me as priest.
28: 4 that he may *m* to Me as priest.
28:41 that they may *m* to Me as
28:43 they come near the altar to *m*
29:30 the tabernacle of meeting to *m*
29:44 both Aaron and his sons to *m*
30:20 they come near the altar to *m*,
30:30 that they may *m* to Me as
31:10 his sons, to *m* as priests,
35:19 his sons, to *m* as priests.'
39:26 the hem of the robe to *m* in,
39:41 to *m* in the holy place:
39:41 garments, to *m* as priests.
40:13 that he may *m* to Me as priest.
40:15 that they may *m* to Me as
Lev 7:35 Moses presented them to *m* to
16:32 anointed and consecrated to *m*
Num 3: 3 whom he consecrated to *m* as
4:12 of service with which they *m*
4:14 implements with which they *m*
8:26 They may *m* with their brethren
Deut 10: 8 to stand before the LORD to *m*
17:12 heed the priest who stands to *m*
18: 5 all your tribes to stand to *m*
21: 5 your God has chosen them to *m*
2 Sam 20:26 Ira the Jairite was a chief *m*
1 Chr 15: 2 carry the ark of God and to *m*

16: 4 some of the Levites to ***m***
16:37 the covenant of the LORD to ***m***
23:13 to ***m*** to Him, and to give the
2 Chr 13:10 and the priests who ***m*** to the
29:11 and that you should ***m*** to Him
Neh 10:36 to the priests who ***m*** in the
10:39 where the priests who ***m*** and
Isa 60: 7 The rams of Nebaioth shall ***m***
60:10 And their kings shall ***m*** to
Jer 33:22 servant and the Levites who ***m***
Ezek 40:46 who come near the LORD to ***m*** to
42:14 their garments in which they ***m***,
43:19 who approach Me to ***m*** to Me,'
44:11 shall stand before them to ***m***
44:13 shall not come near Me to ***m*** to
44:15 they shall come near Me to ***m*** to
44:16 shall come near My table to ***m***
44:17 come upon them while they ***m***
44:27 he goes to the sanctuary to ***m***
45: 4 who come near to ***m*** to the
Joel 1: 9 who ***m*** to the LORD.
1:13 you who ***m*** before the altar;
1:13 You who ***m*** to my God; For the
2:17 who ***m*** to the LORD, Weep
Mt 25:44 and did not ***m*** to You?'
Acts 26:16 to make you a ***m*** and a witness
Rom 13: 4 For he is God's ***m*** to you for
13: 4 in vain; for he is God's ***m***,
15:16 that I might be a ***m*** of Jesus
15:25 I am going to Jerusalem to ***m***
15:27 their duty is also to ***m*** to them
1 Cor 9:13 you not know that those who ***m***
2 Cor 11: 8 taking wages from them to ***m***
Gal 2:17 is Christ therefore a ***m*** of
Eph 3: 7 of which I became a ***m*** according
6:21 beloved brother and faithful ***m***
Col 1: 7 who is a faithful ***m*** of Christ
1:23 of which I, Paul, became a ***m***.
1:25 of which I became a ***m*** according
4: 7 a beloved brother, faithful ***m***,
1 Th 3: 2 our brother and ***m*** of God, and
1 Tim 4: 6 you will be a good ***m*** of Jesus
Phm 1:13 that on your behalf he might ***m***
Heb 1:14 spirits sent forth to ***m*** for
6:10 to the saints, and do ***m***.
8: 2 a ***M*** of the sanctuary and of the
1 Pe 4:10 ***m*** it to one another, as good

MINISTERED (24/24) MINISTER

Num 3: 4 So Eleazar and Ithamar ***m*** as
3:31 the sanctuary with which they ***m***,
Deut 10: 6 and Eleazar his son ***m*** as priest
1 Sam 2:11 But the child ***m*** to the LORD
2:18 But Samuel ***m*** before the LORD,
3: 1 Then the boy Samuel ***m*** to the
2 Ki 25:14 with which the priests ***m***.
1 Chr 6:10 begot Azariah (it was he who ***m***
6:33 And these are the ones who ***m***
24: 2 Eleazar and Ithamar ***m*** as
Neh 12:44 the priests and Levites who ***m***.
Jer 52:18 with which the priests ***m***.
Ezek 44:12 Because they ***m*** to them before
44:19 garments in which they have ***m***,
Dan 7:10 A thousand thousands ***m*** to Him;
Mt 4:11 angels came and ***m*** to Him.
Mk 1:13 and the angels ***m*** to Him.
15:41 who also followed Him and ***m*** to
Acts 13: 2 As they ***m*** to the Lord and
19:22 Macedonia two of those who ***m***
2 Cor 3: 3 ***m*** by us, written not with ink
Phil 2:25 messenger and the one who ***m*** to
2 Tim 1:18 very well how many ways he ***m***
Heb 6:10 in that you have ***m*** to the

MINISTERING (14/14) MINISTER

Ex 29: 1 do to them to hallow them for ***m***
35:19 for ***m*** in the holy place—the
39: 1 for ***m*** in the holy place, and
1 Ki 8:11 priests could not continue ***m***
1 Chr 6:32 They were ***m*** with music before
2 Chr 5:14 priests could not continue ***m***
Mt 27:55 ***m*** to Him, were there looking on
Rom 12: 7 let us use it in our ***m***;
15:16 ***m*** the gospel of God, that the
2 Cor 8: 4 and the fellowship of the ***m*** to
9: 1 Now concerning the ***m*** to the
Heb 1:14 Are they not all ***m*** spirits sent
10:11 And every priest stands ***m*** daily
1 Pe 1:12 but to us they were ***m*** the

MINISTERS (21/19) MINISTER

Ex 28:35 shall be upon Aaron when he ***m***,
2 Sam 8:18 and David's sons were chief ***m***.
1 Chr 18:17 and David's sons were chief ***m***
Ps 103:21 You ***m*** of His, who do His
104: 4 His ***m*** a flame of fire.
Jer 33:21 the Levites, the priests, My ***m***.
Ezek 44:11 Yet they shall be ***m*** in My
44:11 gatekeepers of the house and ***m***
45: 4 the ***m*** of the sanctuary, who
45: 5 the ***m*** of the temple; they shall
46:24 are the kitchens where the ***m***
Lk 1: 2 were eyewitnesses and ***m*** of the
Rom 13: 6 for they are God's ***m*** attending
1 Cor 3: 5 but ***m*** through whom you
2 Cor 3: 6 also made us sufficient as ***m***
6: 4 we commend ourselves as ***m*** of
11:15 it is no great thing if his ***m***
11:15 transform themselves into ***m*** of
11:23 Are they ***m*** of Christ?—I speak as
Heb 1: 7 angels spirits And His ***m***
1 Pe 4:11 the oracles of God. If anyone ***m***,

MINISTRATION (KJV) See DISTRIBUTION, MINISTRY, SERVICE

MINISTRIES (1/1) MINISTRY

1 Cor 12: 5 There are differences of ***m***,

MINISTRY (30/29) MINISTER, MINISTRIES

Ex 31:10 'the garments of ***m***, the holy
35:19 'the garments of ***m***,
39: 1 thread they made garments of ***m***,
39:41 and the garments of ***m***,
2 Chr 7: 6 David offered praise by their ***m***.
Lk 3:23 Jesus Himself began His ***m***
Acts 1:17 and obtained a part in this ***m***.
1:25 to take part in this ***m*** and
6: 4 to prayer and to the ***m*** of the
12:25 they had fulfilled their ***m***,
20:24 and the ***m*** which I received from
21:19 the Gentiles through his ***m***.
Rom 11:13 to the Gentiles, I magnify my ***m***,
12: 7 or ***m***, let us use it in our
1 Cor 16:15 devoted themselves to the ***m*** of
2 Cor 3: 7 But if the ***m*** of death, written
3: 8 how will the ***m*** of the Spirit not
3: 9 For if the ***m*** of condemnation
3: 9 the ***m*** of righteousness exceeds
4: 1 Therefore, since we have this ***m***,
5:18 and has given us the ***m*** of
6: 3 that our ***m*** may not be blamed.
9:13 through the proof of this ***m***,
Eph 4:12 of the saints for the work of ***m***,
Col 4:17 Take heed to the ***m*** which you
1 Tim 1:12 putting me into the ***m***,
2 Tim 4: 5 an evangelist, fulfill your ***m***.
4:11 for he is useful to me for ***m***.
Heb 8: 6 has obtained a more excellent ***m***,
9:21 and all the vessels of the ***m***.

MINJAMIN (2/2)

Neh 12:17 Abijah, Zichri; the son of ***M***;
12:41 priests, Eliakim, Maaseiah, ***M***,

MINNI (1/1)

Jer 51:27 against her: Ararat, ***M***,

MINNITH (2/2)

Judg 11:33 them from Aroer as far as ***M***—
Ezek 27:17 for your merchandise wheat of ***M***,

MINSTREL (KJV) See MUSICIAN

MINT (2/2)

Mt 23:23 For you pay tithe of ***m*** and
Lk 11:42 you Pharisees! For you tithe ***m***

MINUS (1/1)

2 Cor 11:24 I received forty stripes ***m***

MIPHKAD (1/1)

Neh 3:31 in front of the ***M*** Gate, and as

MIRACLE (5/5) MIRACLES

Ex 7: 9 Show a ***m*** for yourselves,' then
Mk 9:39 for no one who works a ***m*** in My
Lk 23: 8 and he hoped to see some ***m*** done
Acts 4:16 that a notable ***m*** has been done
4:22 forty years old on whom this ***m***

MIRACLES (11/11) MIRACLE, SIGNS

Judg 6:13 And where are all His ***m*** which
Acts 2:22 Man attested by God to you by ***m***,
8: 6 hearing and seeing the ***m*** which
8:13 seeing the ***m*** and signs which
15:12 and Paul declaring how many ***m***
19:11 Now God worked unusual ***m*** by the
1 Cor 12:10 to another the working of ***m***,
12:28 third teachers, after that ***m***,
12:29 Are all workers of ***m***?
Gal 3: 5 the Spirit to you and works ***m***
Heb 2: 4 and wonders, with various ***m***,

MIRE (12/11) MIRY

Job 30:19 He has cast me into the ***m***,
41:30 spreads pointed marks in the ***m***.
Ps 69: 2 I sink in deep ***m***, Where
69:14 Deliver me out of the ***m***,
Isa 10: 6 to tread them down like the ***m***
57:20 Whose waters cast up ***m*** and
Jer 38: 6 there was no water, but ***m***.
38: 6 So Jeremiah sank in the ***m***.
38:22 Your feet have sunk in the ***m***,
Zech 9: 3 And gold like the ***m*** of the
10: 5 down their enemies In the ***m***
2 Pe 2:22 to her wallowing in the ***m***.

MIRIAM (15/13)

Ex 15:20 Then ***M*** the prophetess, the
15:21 And ***M*** answered them: "Sing to
Num 12: 1 Then ***M*** and Aaron spoke against
12: 4 said to Moses, Aaron, and ***M***,
12: 5 and called Aaron and ***M***.
12:10 suddenly ***M*** became leprous, as
12:10 Then Aaron turned toward ***M***,
12:15 So ***M*** was shut out of the camp
12:15 people did not journey till ***M***
20: 1 and ***M*** died there and was buried
26:59 and Moses and their sister ***M***.
Deut 24: 9 the LORD your God did to ***M*** on
1 Chr 4:17 And Mered's wife bore ***M***,
6: 3 Amram were Aaron, Moses, and ***M***.
Mic 6: 4 before you Moses, Aaron, and ***M***.

MIRMAH (1/1)

1 Chr 8:10 Jeuz, Sachiah, and ***M***.

MIRROR (4/4) MIRRORS

Job 37:18 Strong as a cast metal ***m***?
1 Cor 13:12 For now we see in a ***m***,
2 Cor 3:18 beholding as in a ***m*** the glory
Jas 1:23 his natural face in a ***m***;

MIRRORS (2/2) MIRROR

Ex 38: 8 from the bronze ***m*** of the
Isa 3:23 and the ***m***; The fine linen,

MIRTH (12/12)

Ps 137: 3 who plundered us requested ***m***,
Prov 14:13 And the end of ***m*** may be
Eccl 2: 1 now, I will test you with ***m***;
2: 2 laughter—"Madness!"; and of ***m***,
7: 4 of fools is in the house of ***m***.
Isa 24: 8 The ***m*** of the tambourine ceases,
24:11 The ***m*** of the land is gone.
Jer 7:34 of Jerusalem the voice of ***m***
16: 9 the voice of ***m*** and the voice of
25:10 take from them the voice of ***m***
Ezek 21:10 Should we then make ***m***?
Hos 2:11 I will also cause all her ***m*** to

MIRY (1/1) MIRE

Ps 40: 2 Out of the ***m*** clay, And set my

M

MISCARRIAGE (2/2) MISCARRYING

Ex 23:26 No one shall suffer ***m*** or be
Job 21:10 Their cow calves without ***m***.

MISCARRIED (1/1)

Gen 31:38 your female goats have not ***m***

MISCARRYING (1/1) MISCARRIAGE

Hos 9:14 Give them a ***m*** womb And dry

MISCHIEF, MISCHIEFS (KJV) See CALAMITY, EVIL, FRAUD, HARM, PUNISHMENT, TROUBLE, WICKEDNESS

MISER (2/2)

Prov 23: 6 Do not eat the bread of a ***m***,
Isa 32: 5 Nor the ***m*** said to be

MISERABLE (3/3) MISERY

1 Sam 1: 6 her severely, to make her ***m***,
Job 16: 2 ***M*** comforters are you all!
Rev 3:17 know that you are wretched, ***m***,

MISERABLY (1/1)

Mt 21:41 will destroy those wicked men ***m***,

MISERIES (1/1)

Jas 5: 1 weep and howl for your ***m*** that

MISERY (9/9) MISERABLE

Judg 10:16 could no longer endure the ***m***
Job 3:20 light given to him who is in ***m***,
10:15 full of disgrace; See my ***m***!
11:16 you would forget your ***m***,
20:22 Every hand of ***m*** will come
Prov 31: 7 And remember his ***m*** no more.
Eccl 8: 6 Though the ***m*** of man increases
Jon 4: 6 head to deliver him from his ***m***.
Rom 3:16 Destruction and ***m*** are in

MISFORTUNE (3/3)

Eccl 4: 8 also is vanity and a grave ***m***.
5:14 those riches perish through ***m***;
Isa 10: 1 decrees, Who write ***m***,

MISHAEL (8/8) MESHACH

Ex 6:22 And the sons of Uzziel were ***M***,
Lev 10: 4 And Moses called ***M*** and
Neh 8: 4 and at his left hand Pedaiah, ***M***,
Dan 1: 6 Judah were Daniel, Hananiah, ***M***,

1: 7 to Hananiah, Shadrach; to *M*,
1:11 set over Daniel, Hananiah, *M*,
1:19 found like Daniel, Hananiah, *M*,
2:17 decision known to Hananiah, *M*,

MISHAL (2/2)

Josh 19:26 Alammelech, Amad, and *M*;
21:30 *M* with its common-land, Abdon

MISHAM (1/1)

1 Chr 8:12 sons of Elpaal were Eber, *M*,

MISHMA (4/4)

Gen 25:14 *M*, Dumah, Massa,
1 Chr 1:30 *M*, Dumah, Massa, Hadad,
4:25 and *M* his son.
4:26 And the sons of *M* were Hamuel

MISHMANNAH (1/1)

1 Chr 12:10 *M* the fourth, Jeremiah the

MISHRAITES (1/1)

1 Chr 2:53 the Shumathites, and the *M*.

MISLEADS (1/1)

Lk 23:14 as one who *m* the people.

MISPAR (1/1)

Ezra 2: 2 Reelaiah, Mordecai, Bilshan, *M*,

MISPERETH (1/1)

Neh 7: 7 Nahamani, Mordecai, Bilshan, *M*,

MISREPHOTH (2/2)

Josh 11: 8 Greater Sidon, to the Brook *M*,
13: 6 Lebanon as far as the Brook *M*,

MISS (2/2) MISSED, MISSING

Judg 20:16 at a hair's breadth and not *m*.
1 Sam 25:15 nor did we *m* anything as long

MISSED (2/2) MISS

1 Sam 20:18 the New Moon; and you will be *m*,
25:21 so that nothing was *m* of all

MISSES (1/1)

1 Sam 20: 6 If your father *m* me at all, then

MISSING (8/7) MISS

Num 31:49 and not a man of us is *m*.
Judg 21: 3 there should be one tribe *m*
1 Sam 25: 7 nor was there anything *m* from
2 Sam 2:30 there were *m* of David's
1 Ki 20:39 if by any means he is *m*,
2 Ki 10:19 his priests. Let no one be *m*,
10:19 Whoever is *m* shall not live."
Isa 40:26 of His power; Not one is *m*.

MISSION (2/2)

1 Sam 15:18 "Now the LORD sent you on a *m*,
15:20 and gone on the *m* on which the

MIST (3/3)

Gen 2: 6 but a *m* went up from the earth
Job 36:27 distill as rain from the *m*,
Acts 13:11 And immediately a dark *m* fell

MISTAKEN (3/3)

Mt 22:29 and said to them, "You are *m*,
Mk 12:24 them, "Are you not therefore *m*,
12:27 You are therefore greatly *m*.

MISTREAT (2/2) MISTREATED

Ex 22:21 You shall neither *m* a stranger
Lev 19:33 you shall not *m* him.

MISTREATED (4/4) MISTREAT

Deut 26: 6 But the Egyptians *m* us,
Ezek 22: 7 in you they have *m* the
22:29 and *m* the poor and needy;
Heb 13: 3 with them—those who are *m*—

MISTREATS (2/2)

Deut 24: 7 and *m* him or sells him, then
Prov 19:26 He who *m* his father and

MISTRESS (8/8)

Gen 16: 4 her *m* became despised in her
16: 8 from the presence of my *m*
16: 9 said to her, "Return to your *m*,
2 Ki 5: 3 Then she said to her *m*,
Ps 123: 2 of a maid to the hand of her *m*,
Prov 30:23 maidservant who succeeds her *m*.
Isa 24: 2 with the maid, so with her *m*;
Nah 3: 4 The *m* of sorceries, Who sells

MISUNDERSTAND (1/1)

Deut 32:27 their adversaries should *m*,

MISUSING (1/1)

1 Cor 7:31 who use this world as not *m*

MITE (1/1) MITES

Lk 12:59 you have paid the very last *m*.

MITES (2/2) MITE

Mk 12:42 widow came and threw in two *m*,
Lk 21: 2 poor widow putting in two *m*.

MITHKAH (2/2)

Num 33:28 from Terah and camped at *M*.
33:29 They went from *M* and camped at

MITHNITE (1/1)

1 Chr 11:43 son of Maachah, Joshaphat the *M*,

MITHREDATH (2/2)

Ezra 1: 8 them out by the hand of *M* the
4: 7 of Artaxerxes also, Bishlam, *M*,

MITRE (KJV) See TURBAN

MITYLENE (1/1)

Acts 20:14 took him on board and came to *M*.

MIX (4/4) MIXED, MIXTURE

Prov 23:20 Do not *m* with winebibbers,
Ezek 24:10 *M* in the spices, And let the
Dan 2:43 just as iron does not *m* with
Rev 18: 6 has mixed, *m* double for her.

MIXED (61/58) MIX

Ex 12:38 A *m* multitude went up with them
29: 2 unleavened cakes *m* with oil,
29:40 of an ephah of flour *m* with
Lev 2: 4 cakes of fine flour *m* with oil,
2: 5 unleavened, *m* with oil.
6:21 a pan with oil. When it is *m*,
7:10 whether *m* with oil, or dry,
7:12 unleavened cakes *m* with oil,
7:12 or cakes of blended flour *m*
9: 4 and a grain offering *m* with
14:10 of an ephah of fine flour *m*
14:21 of an ephah of fine flour *m*
19:19 not sow your field with *m* seed.
19:19 Nor shall a garment of *m* linen
23:13 of an ephah of fine flour *m*
Num 6:15 cakes of fine flour *m* with oil,
7:13 of them full of fine flour *m*
7:19 of them full of fine flour *m*
7:25 of them full of fine flour *m*
7:31 of them full of fine flour *m*
7:37 of them full of fine flour *m*
7:43 of them full of fine flour *m*
7:49 of them full of fine flour *m*
7:55 of them full of fine flour *m*
7:61 of them full of fine flour *m*
7:67 of them full of fine flour *m*
7:73 of them full of fine flour *m*
7:79 of them full of fine flour *m*
8: 8 grain offering of fine flour *m*
11: 4 Now the *m* multitude who were
15: 4 of an ephah of fine flour *m*
15: 6 of an ephah of fine flour *m*
15: 9 of an ephah of fine flour *m*
28: 5 flour as a grain offering *m*
28: 9 *m* with oil, with its drink
28:12 *m* with oil, for each bull;
28:12 *m* with oil, for the one ram;
28:13 *m* with oil, as a grain offering
28:20 shall be of fine flour *m* with
28:28 grain offering of fine flour *m*
29: 3 shall be fine flour *m* with
29: 9 shall be of fine flour *m*
29:14 shall be of fine flour *m*
Deut 22:11 such as wool and linen *m*
1 Chr 23:29 with what is *m* and with all
Ezra 9: 2 so that the holy seed is *m* with
Neh 13: 3 that they separated all the *m*
Ps 75: 8 the wine is red; It is fully *m*,
Prov 9: 2 She has *m* her wine, She has
9: 5 And drink of the wine I have *m*.
23:30 Those who go in search of *m*
Isa 1:22 Your wine *m* with water.
Jer 25:20 all the *m* multitude, all the
25:24 and all the kings of the *m*
50:37 And against all the *m* peoples
Dan 2:41 just as you saw the iron *m* with
2:43 As you saw iron *m* with ceramic
Hos 7: 8 Ephraim has *m* himself among the
Zech 9: 6 A *m* race shall settle in Ashdod,
Heb 4: 2 not being *m* with faith in those
Rev 18: 6 in the cup which she has *m*,

MIXING (1/1)

Isa 5:22 Woe to men valiant for *m*

MIXTURE (2/2) MIX

2 Chr 16:14 ingredients prepared in a *m* of
Jn 19:39 bringing a *m* of myrrh and

MIZAR (1/1)

Ps 42: 6 of Hermon, From the Hill *M*.

MIZPAH (47/43)

Gen 31:49 also *M*, because he said,
Josh 11: 3 below Hermon in the land of *M*.
11: 8 and to the Valley of *M*
15:38 Dilean, *M*, Joktheel,
18:26 *M*, Chephirah, Mozah,
Judg 10:17 together and encamped in *M*.
11:11 his words before the LORD in *M*.
11:29 and passed through *M* of Gilead;
11:29 and from *M* of Gilead he
11:34 Jephthah came to his house at *M*,
20: 1 one man before the LORD at *M*.
20: 3 of Israel had gone up to *M*.
21: 1 Israel had sworn an oath at *M*,
21: 5 not come up to the LORD at *M*,
21: 8 who did not come up to *M* to
1 Sam 7: 5 said, "Gather all Israel to *M*,
7: 6 So they gathered together at *M*,
7: 6 the children of Israel at *M*.
7: 7 had gathered together at *M*,
7:11 the men of Israel went out of *M*
7:12 stone and set it up between *M*
7:16 to Bethel, Gilgal, and *M*,
10:17 together to the LORD at *M*,
22: 3 David went from there to *M* of
1 Ki 15:22 built Geba of Benjamin, and *M*.
2 Ki 25:23 they came to Gedaliah at *M*—
25:25 who were with him at *M*.
2 Chr 16: 6 with them he built Geba and *M*.
Neh 3: 7 the men of Gibeon and *M*,
3:15 leader of the district of *M*,
3:19 son of Jeshua, the leader of *M*,
Jer 40: 6 the son of Ahikam, to *M*,
40: 8 then they came to Gedaliah at *M*—
40:10 I will indeed dwell at *M* and
40:12 land of Judah, to Gedaliah at *M*,
40:13 fields came to Gedaliah at *M*,
40:15 spoke secretly to Gedaliah in *M*,
41: 1 the son of Ahikam, at *M*.
41: 1 they ate bread together in *M*.
41: 3 that is, with Gedaliah at *M*,
41: 6 of Nethaniah went out from *M*
41:10 of the people who were in *M*,
41:10 the people who remained in *M*,
41:14 had carried away captive from *M*
41:16 took from *M* all the rest of the
Hos 5: 1 you have been a snare to *M*

MIZPAR (KJV) See MISPAR

MIZPEH (KJV) See MIZPAH

MIZRAIM (5/5) ABEL MIZRAIM, EGYPT

Gen 10: 6 The sons of Ham were Cush, *M*,
10:13 *M* begot Ludim, Anamim, Lehabim,
1 Chr 1: 8 The sons of Ham were Cush, *M*,
1:11 *M* begot Ludim, Anamim, Lehabim,

MIZZAH (3/3)

Gen 36:13 Nahath, Zerah, Shammah, and *M*.
36:17 Chief Shammah, and Chief *M*.
1 Chr 1:37 Nahath, Zerah, Shammah, and *M*.

MNASON (1/1)

Acts 21:16 brought with them a certain *M*

MOAB (170/153) MOABITE, MOABITESS

Gen 19:37 a son and called his name *M*;
36:35 Midian in the field of *M*,
Ex 15:15 The mighty men of *M*,
Num 21:11 wilderness which is east of *M*,
21:13 the Arnon is the border of *M*,
21:13 between *M* and the Amorites.
21:15 And lies on the border of *M*.
21:20 that is in the country of *M*,
21:26 against the former king of *M*,
21:28 of Sihon; It consumed Ar of *M*,
21:29 *M*! You have perished, O people
22: 1 and camped in the plains of *M*
22: 3 And *M* was exceedingly afraid of
22: 3 and *M* was sick with dread
22: 4 So *M* said to the elders of
22: 7 So the elders of *M* and the
22: 8 So the princes of *M* stayed
22:10 the son of Zippor, king of *M*,
22:14 And the princes of *M* rose and
22:21 and went with the princes of *M*.
22:36 to meet him at the city of *M*,
23: 6 he and all the princes of *M*.
23: 7 Balak the king of *M* has brought
23:17 and the princes of *M* were with
24:17 And batter the brow of *M*,
25: 1 harlotry with the women of *M*.
26: 3 with them in the plains of *M*
26:63 of Israel in the plains of *M*
31:12 to the camp in the plains of *M*
33:44 Ije Abarim, at the border of *M*.
33:48 and camped in the plains of *M*

33:49 Acacia Grove in the plains of ***M***.
33:50 to Moses in the plains of ***M*** by
35: 1 to Moses in the plains of ***M*** by
36:13 of Moses in the plains of ***M*** by
Deut 1: 5 of the Jordan in the land of ***M***,
2: 8 by way of the Wilderness of ***M***.
2: 9 said to me, 'Do not harass ***M***,
2:18 over at Ar, the boundary of ***M***.
29: 1 of Israel in the land of ***M***,
32:49 which is in the land of ***M***,
34: 1 went up from the plains of ***M***
34: 5 died there in the land of ***M***,
34: 6 in a valley in the land of ***M***,
34: 8 for Moses in the plains of ***M***
Josh 13:32 inheritance in the plains of ***M***
24: 9 the son of Zippor, king of ***M***,
Judg 3:12 strengthened Eglon king of ***M***
3:14 Israel served Eglon king of ***M***
3:15 sent tribute to Eglon king of ***M***.
3:17 the tribute to Eglon king of ***M***.
3:28 of the Jordan leading to ***M***,
3:29 about ten thousand men of ***M***,
3:30 So ***M*** was subdued that day under
10: 6 gods of Sidon, the gods of ***M***,
11:15 did not take away the land of ***M***,
11:17 they sent to the king of ***M***,
11:18 land of Edom and the land of ***M***,
11:18 the east side of the land of ***M***,
11:18 did not enter the border of ***M***,
11:18 the Arnon was the border of ***M***.
11:25 the son of Zippor, king of ***M***?
Ruth 1: 1 to dwell in the country of ***M***,
1: 2 they went to the country of ***M***
1: 4 took wives of the women of ***M***:
1: 6 return from the country of ***M***,
1: 6 had heard in the country of ***M***
1:22 returned from the country of ***M***.
2: 6 Naomi from the country of ***M***.
4: 3 come back from the country of ***M***,
1 Sam 12: 9 into the hand of the king of ***M***;
14:47 on every side, against ***M***,
22: 3 went from there to Mizpah of ***M***;
22: 3 and he said to the king of ***M***,
22: 4 them before the king of ***M***,
2 Sam 8: 2 Then he defeated ***M***.
8:12 from Syria, from ***M***,
23:20 two lion-like heroes of ***M***.
1 Ki 11: 7 Chemosh the abomination of ***M***,
2 Ki 1: 1 ***M*** rebelled against Israel after
3: 4 Now Mesha king of ***M*** was a
3: 5 that the king of ***M*** rebelled
3: 7 The king of ***M*** has rebelled
3: 7 go with me to fight against ***M***?
3:10 deliver them into the hand of ***M***.
3:13 deliver them into the hand of ***M***.
3:23 one another; now therefore, ***M***,
3:26 And when the king of ***M*** saw that
13:20 And the raiding bands from ***M***
1 Chr 1:46 Midian in the field of ***M***,
4:22 Joash; Saraph, who ruled in ***M***,
8: 8 children in the country of ***M***,
11:22 two lion-like heroes of ***M***.
18: 2 Then he defeated ***M***,
18:11 nations—from Edom, from ***M***,
2 Chr 20: 1 this that the people of ***M***
20:10 here are the people of Ammon, ***M***,
20:22 against the people of Ammon, ***M***,
20:23 For the people of Ammon and ***M***
Neh 13:23 women of Ashdod, Ammon, and ***M***.
Ps 60: 8 ***M*** is My washpot
83: 6 ***M*** and the Hagrites;
108: 9 ***M*** is My washpot
Isa 11:14 lay their hand on Edom and ***M***;
15: 1 The burden against ***M***.
15: 1 Because in the night Ar of ***M*** is
15: 1 Because in the night Kir of ***M***
15: 2 ***M*** will wail over Nebo and over
15: 4 the armed soldiers of ***M*** will
15: 5 "My heart will cry out for ***M***;
15: 8 all around the borders of ***M***,
15: 9 upon him who escapes from ***M***,
16: 2 shall be the daughters of ***M*** at
16: 4 My outcasts dwell with you, O ***M***;
16: 6 have heard of the pride of ***M***—
16: 7 Therefore ***M*** shall wail for
16: 7 Moab shall wail for ***M***;
16:11 shall resound like a harp for ***M***,
16:12 When it is seen that ***M*** is
16:13 LORD has spoken concerning ***M***
16:14 the glory of ***M*** will be despised
25:10 And ***M*** shall be trampled down
Jer 9:26 Edom, the people of Ammon, ***M***,
25:21 Edom, ***M***, and the people of
27: 3 the king of Edom, the king of ***M***,
40:11 all the Jews who were in ***M***,
48: 1 Against ***M***. Thus says the
48: 2 No more praise of ***M***.
48: 4 ***M*** is destroyed; Her little ones
48: 9 'Give wings to ***M***, That she
48:11 ***M*** has been at ease from his
48:13 ***M*** shall be ashamed of Chemosh,
48:15 ***M*** is plundered and gone up
48:16 The calamity of ***M*** is near at
48:18 For the plunderer of ***M*** has
48:20 ***M*** is shamed, for he is broken
48:20 that ***M*** is plundered.
48:24 all the cities of the land of ***M***,
48:25 The horn of ***M*** is cut off,
48:26 ***M*** shall wallow in his vomit,
48:28 You who dwell in ***M***,
48:29 We have heard the pride of ***M***
48:31 Therefore I will wail for ***M***,
48:31 And I will cry out for all ***M***;
48:33 field And from the land of ***M***;
48:35 'I will cause to cease in ***M*** The
48:36 shall wail like flutes for ***M***,
48:38 On all the housetops of ***M***,
48:38 For I have broken ***M*** like a
48:39 she is broken down! How ***M***
48:39 her back with shame!' So ***M***
48:40 And spread his wings over ***M***.
48:41 The mighty men's hearts in ***M***
48:42 And ***M*** shall be destroyed as a
48:43 upon you, O inhabitant of ***M***,
48:44 in the snare. For upon ***M***,
48:45 And shall devour the brow of ***M***,
48:46 O ***M***! The people of Chemosh
48:47 bring back the captives of ***M***
48:47 Thus far is the judgment of ***M***.
Ezek 25: 8 Because ***M*** and Seir say, 'Look!
25: 9 I will clear the territory of ***M***
25:11 I will execute judgments upon ***M***,
Dan 11:41 escape from his hand: Edom, ***M***,
Am 2: 1 three transgressions of ***M***,
2: 2 But I will send a fire upon ***M***,
2: 2 ***M*** shall die with tumult,
Mic 6: 5 now What Balak king of ***M***
Zeph 2: 8 have heard the reproach of ***M***,
2: 9 Surely ***M*** shall be like Sodom,

MOABITE (4/4) MOAB, MOABITES

Deut 23: 3 An Ammonite or ***M*** shall not
Ruth 2: 6 It is the young ***M*** woman who
1 Chr 11:46 sons of Elnaam, Ithmah the ***M***,
Neh 13: 1 written that no Ammonite or ***M***

MOABITES (17/16) MOABITE

Gen 19:37 he is the father of the ***M*** to
Num 22: 4 of Zippor was king of the ***M***
Deut 2:11 but the ***M*** call them Emim.
2:29 who dwell in Seir and the ***M***
Judg 3:28 delivered your enemies the ***M***
2 Sam 8: 2 So the ***M*** became David's
1 Ki 11: 1 of Pharaoh: women of the ***M***,
11:33 Chemosh the god of the ***M***,
2 Ki 3:18 He will also deliver the ***M*** into
3:21 And when all the ***M*** heard that
3:22 and the ***M*** saw the water on the
3:24 rose up and attacked the ***M***,
3:24 their land, killing the ***M***.
23:13 the abomination of the ***M***,
24: 2 bands of Syrians, bands of ***M***,
1 Chr 18: 2 and the ***M*** became David's
Ezra 9: 1 Jebusites, the Ammonites, the ***M***,

MOABITESS (6/6) MOAB

Ruth 1:22 and Ruth the ***M*** her
2: 2 So Ruth the ***M*** said to Naomi,
2:21 Ruth the ***M*** said, "He also said
4: 5 also buy it from Ruth the ***M***,
4:10 "Moreover, Ruth the ***M***,
2 Chr 24:26 the son of Shimrith the ***M***.

MOABITISH (KJV) See MOABITE

MOADIAH (1/1)

Neh 12:17 the son of Minjamin; of ***M***,

MOAN (2/2)

Ps 55: 2 my complaint, and ***m*** noisily,
Isa 59:11 And ***m*** sadly like doves;

MOB (4/4)

Ps 86:14 And a ***m*** of violent men have
Acts 17: 5 marketplace, and gathering a ***m***,
21:35 of the violence of the ***m***.
24:18 neither with a ***m*** nor with

MOCK (11/11) MOCKED, MOCKER, MOCKING, MOCKS

Gen 39:14 brought in to us a Hebrew to ***m***
39:17 to us came in to me to ***m*** me;
Job 11: 3 their peace? And when you ***m***,
13: 9 Or can you ***m*** Him as one mocks
30: 1 But now they ***m*** at me, men
Prov 1:26 I will ***m*** when your terror
14: 9 Fools ***m*** at sin, But among the
Ezek 22: 5 and those far from you will ***m***
Mt 20:19 Him to the Gentiles to ***m*** and
Mk 10:34 and they will ***m*** Him, and scourge
Lk 14:29 all who see it begin to ***m*** him,

MOCKED (20/20) MOCK

Judg 16:10 you have ***m*** me and told me lies.
16:13 Until now you have ***m*** me and told
16:15 You have ***m*** me these three
1 Ki 18:27 that Elijah ***m*** them and said,
2 Ki 2:23 came from the city and ***m*** him,
2 Chr 30:10 but they laughed at them and ***m***
36:16 But they ***m*** the messengers of
Neh 4: 1 indignant, and ***m*** the Jews.
Job 12: 4 'I am one ***m*** by his friends,
29:24 If I ***m*** at them, they did not
Lam 1: 7 adversaries saw her And ***m*** at
Mt 27:29 the knee before Him and ***m*** Him,
27:31 And when they had ***m*** Him, they
Mk 15:20 And when they had ***m*** Him, they
Lk 18:32 to the Gentiles and will be ***m***
22:63 Now the men who held Jesus ***m***
23:11 Him with contempt and ***m*** Him,
23:36 The soldiers also ***m*** Him, coming
Acts 17:32 of the dead, some ***m***,
Gal 6: 7 not be deceived, God is not ***m***;

MOCKER (1/1) MOCK, MOCKERS

Prov 20: 1 Wine is a ***m***, Strong drink

MOCKERS (5/5) MOCKER

Job 17: 2 Are not ***m*** with me? And does
Ps 35:16 With ungodly ***m*** at feasts
Isa 28:22 Now therefore, do not be ***m***,
Jer 15:17 sit in the assembly of the ***m***,
Jude 18 told you that there would be ***m***

MOCKERY (2/2)

Ezek 22: 4 and a ***m*** to all countries.
36: 4 which became plunder and ***m*** to

MOCKING (5/5) MOCK

Job 21: 3 after I have spoken, keep ***m***.
Jer 20:10 For I heard many ***m***: "Fear on
Mt 27:41 ***m*** with the scribes and elders,
Mk 15:31 ***m*** among themselves with the
Acts 2:13 Others ***m*** said, "They are full

MOCKINGS (1/1)

Heb 11:36 Still others had trial of ***m*** and

MOCKS (5/5) MOCK

Job 13: 9 Or can you mock Him as one ***m***
39:22 He ***m*** at fear, and is not
Prov 17: 5 He who ***m*** the poor reproaches
30:17 The eye that ***m*** his father,
Jer 20: 7 Everyone ***m*** me.

MODERATION (1/1)

1 Tim 2: 9 apparel, with propriety and ***m***,

MODEST (1/1) MODESTY

1 Tim 2: 9 adorn themselves in ***m*** apparel,

MODESTY (1/1) MODEST

1 Cor 12:23 parts have greater ***m***,

MOIST (1/1) MOISTURE

Job 21:24 the marrow of his bones is ***m***.

MOISTEN (1/1)

Ezek 46:14 a third of a hin of oil to ***m***

MOISTURE (2/2) MOIST

Job 37:11 Also with ***m*** He saturates the
Lk 8: 6 away because it lacked ***m***.

MOLADAH (4/4)

Josh 15:26 Amam, Shema, ***M***,
19: 2 Beersheba (Sheba), ***M***,
1 Chr 4:28 They dwelt at Beersheba, ***M***,
Neh 11:26 in Jeshua, ***M***, Beth Pelet,

MOLD (3/3)

1 Ki 7:37 All of them were of the same ***m***,
Isa 44:10 Who would form a god or ***m*** an
Hab 2:18 That the maker of its ***m*** should

MOLDED (29/29) MOLDS

Ex 32: 4 and made a ***m*** calf. Then they
32: 8 They have made themselves a ***m***
34:17 You shall make no ***m*** gods for
Lev 19: 4 nor make for yourselves ***m*** gods:
Num 33:52 destroy all their ***m*** images, and
Deut 9:12 they have made themselves a ***m***
9:16 had made for yourselves a ***m***
27:15 the one who makes a carved or ***m***
Judg 17: 3 to make a carved image and a ***m***
17: 4 it into a carved image and a ***m***
18:14 and a ***m*** image? Now therefore,
18:17 and the ***m*** image. The priest
18:18 and the ***m*** image, the priest
1 Ki 14: 9 for yourself other gods and ***m***
2 Ki 17:16 made for themselves a ***m*** image
2 Chr 28: 2 and made ***m*** images for the
34: 3 and the ***m*** images.
34: 4 and the ***m*** images he broke in
Neh 9:18 Even when they made a ***m*** calf for
Ps 106:19 And worshiped the ***m*** image.
Isa 30:22 And the ornament of your ***m***
41:29 Their ***m*** images are wind and
42:17 Who say to the ***m*** images, 'You
48: 5 And my carved image and my ***m***
Jer 10:14 For his ***m*** image is falsehood,
51:17 For his ***m*** image is falsehood,
Hos 13: 2 And have made for themselves ***m***
Nah 1:14 off the carved image and the ***m***
Hab 2:18 The ***m*** image, a teacher of

M

MOLDING (10/10)

Ex 25:11 and shall make on it a ***m*** of
25:24 and make a ***m*** of gold all
25:25 and you shall make a gold ***m*** for
30: 3 and you shall make for it a ***m***
30: 4 under the ***m*** on both its sides.
37: 2 and made a ***m*** of gold all around
37:11 and made a ***m*** of gold all around
37:12 and made a ***m*** of gold for the
37:26 He also made for it a ***m*** of gold
37:27 of gold for it under its ***m***,

MOLDS (3/3) MOLDED

1 Ki 7:46 king had them cast in clay ***m***,
2 Chr 4:17 king had them cast in clay ***m***,
Isa 40:19 The workman ***m*** an image,

MOLDY (2/2)

Josh 9: 5 their provision was dry and ***m***.
9:12 But now look, it is dry and ***m***.

MOLE (KJV) See CHAMELEON

MOLE (1/1)

Lev 11:29 that creep on the earth: the ***m***,

MOLECH (8/8) MILCOM, MOLOCH

Lev 18:21 pass through the fire to ***M***,
20: 2 any of his descendants to ***M***,
20: 3 some of his descendants to ***M***,
20: 4 some of his descendants to ***M***,
20: 5 him to commit harlotry with ***M***.
1 Ki 11: 7 and for ***M*** the abomination of
2 Ki 23:10 pass through the fire to ***M***.
Jer 32:35 to pass through the fire to ***M***,

MOLES (1/1)

Isa 2:20 To the ***m*** and bats,

MOLID (1/1)

1 Chr 2:29 and she bore him Ahban and ***M***.

MOLLIFIED (KJV) See SOOTHED

MOLOCH (1/1) MILCOM, MOLECH

Acts 7:43 up the tabernacle of ***M***,

MOLTEN (KJV) See CAST, MOLDED

MOMENT (24/24)

Ex 33: 5 up into your midst in one ***m***
Num 16:21 that I may consume them in a ***m***.
16:45 that I may consume them in a ***m***.
2 Sam 3:22 At that ***m*** the servants of David
Job 7:18 And test him every ***m***?
20: 5 the hypocrite is but for a ***m***?
21:13 And in a ***m*** go down to the
34:20 In a ***m*** they die, in the middle
Ps 30: 5 His anger is but for a ***m***,
73:19 as in a ***m***! They are utterly
Prov 12:19 a lying tongue is but for a ***m***.
Isa 26:20 as it were, for a little ***m***,
27: 3 keep it, I water it every ***m***;
47: 9 shall come to you In a ***m***,
54: 7 For a mere ***m*** I have forsaken
54: 8 I hid My face from you for a ***m***;
Jer 4:20 And my curtains in a ***m***.
Lam 4: 6 Which was overthrown in a ***m***,
Ezek 26:16 on the ground, tremble every ***m***,
32:10 and they shall tremble every ***m***,
Lk 4: 5 kingdoms of the world in a ***m***
Acts 11:11 'At that very ***m***, three men
1 Cor 15:52 in a ***m***, in the twinkling of an
2 Cor 4:17 which is but for a ***m***,

MONEY (148/131) MONEYCHANGERS

Gen 17:12 in your house or bought with ***m***
17:13 he who is bought with your ***m***
17:23 all who were bought with his ***m***,
17:27 in the house or bought with ***m***
23:13 I will give you ***m*** for the
31:15 also completely consumed our ***m***.
33:19 for one hundred pieces of ***m***.
42:25 to restore every man's ***m*** to his
42:27 at the encampment, he saw his ***m***;
42:28 My ***m*** has been restored, and
42:35 each man's bundle of ***m*** was in
42:35 father saw the bundles of ***m***,
43:12 Take double ***m*** in your hand, and
43:12 take back in your hand the ***m***
43:15 and they took double ***m*** in their
43:18 "It is because of the ***m***,
43:21 each man's ***m*** was in the mouth
43:21 our ***m*** in full weight; so we
43:22 we have brought down other ***m***
43:22 We do not know who put our ***m*** in
43:23 in your sacks; I had your ***m***.
44: 1 and put each man's ***m*** in the
44: 2 the youngest, and his grain ***m***.
44: 8 from the land of Canaan the ***m***
47:14 Joseph gathered up all the ***m***
47:14 and Joseph brought the ***m*** into
47:15 So when the ***m*** failed in the land
47:15 For the ***m*** has failed."
47:16 if the ***m*** is gone."
47:18 hide from my lord that our ***m***
Ex 12:44 servant who is bought for ***m***,
21:11 go out free, without paying ***m***.
21:30 is imposed on him a sum of ***m***,
21:34 he shall give ***m*** to their owner,
21:35 the live ox and divide the ***m***
22: 7 man delivers to his neighbor ***m***
22:17 he shall pay ***m*** according to the
22:25 If you lend ***m*** to any of My
30:16 you shall take the atonement ***m***
Lev 22:11 priest buys a person with his ***m***,
25:37 You shall not lend him your ***m***
25:51 of his redemption from the ***m***
27:15 he must add one-fifth of the ***m***
27:18 shall reckon to him the ***m*** due
27:19 he must add one-fifth of the ***m***
Num 3:48 "And you shall give the ***m***,
3:49 So Moses took the redemption ***m***
3:50 of Israel he took the ***m***,
3:51 Moses gave their redemption ***m***
Deut 2: 6 shall buy food from them with ***m***,
2: 6 also buy water from them with ***m***,
2:28 'You shall sell me food for ***m***,
2:28 eat, and give me water for ***m***,
14:25 you shall exchange it for ***m***,
14:25 take the ***m*** in your hand, and go
14:26 And you shall spend that ***m*** for
21:14 shall not sell her for ***m***;
23:19 interest on ***m*** or food or
Judg 16:18 up to her and brought the ***m*** in
1 Ki 21: 2 I will give you its worth in ***m***.
21: 6 'Give me your vineyard for ***m***;
21:15 he refused to give you for ***m***;
2 Ki 5:26 Is it time to receive ***m*** and
12: 4 All the ***m*** of the dedicated gifts
12: 4 the LORD—EACH man's census ***m***,
12: 4 money, each man's assessment ***m***—
12: 4 and all the ***m*** that a man
12: 7 do not take more ***m*** from your
12: 8 would neither receive more ***m***
12: 9 the door put there all the ***m***
12:10 saw that there was much ***m*** in
12:10 and counted the ***m*** that was
12:11 Then they gave the ***m***,
12:13 from the ***m*** brought into the
12:15 hand they delivered the ***m*** to
12:16 The ***m*** from the trespass
12:16 trespass offerings and the ***m***
15:20 And Menahem exacted the ***m*** from
17: 3 vassal, and paid him tribute ***m***.
22: 4 that he may count the ***m*** which
22: 7 made with them of the ***m***
22: 9 servants have gathered the ***m***
23:35 but he taxed the land to give ***m***
2 Chr 24: 5 and gather from all Israel ***m*** to
24:11 saw that there was much ***m***,
24:11 and gathered ***m*** in abundance.
24:14 they brought the rest of the ***m***
34: 9 they delivered the ***m*** that was
34:14 when they brought out the ***m***
34:17 And they have gathered the ***m***
Ezra 3: 7 They also gave ***m*** to the masons
7:17 be careful to buy with this ***m***
Neh 5: 4 We have borrowed ***m*** for the
5:10 am lending them ***m*** and grain.
5:11 also a hundredth of the ***m*** and
Esth 3:11 The ***m*** and the people are given
4: 7 and the sum of ***m*** that Haman had
Job 31:39 have eaten its fruit without ***m***,
Ps 15: 5 who does not put out his ***m*** at
Prov 7:20 He has taken a bag of ***m*** with
Eccl 7:12 wisdom is a defense as ***m*** is
10:19 But ***m*** answers everything.
Isa 43:24 bought Me no sweet cane with ***m***,
52: 3 you shall be redeemed without ***m***.
55: 1 And you who have no ***m***,
55: 1 buy wine and milk Without ***m***
55: 2 Why do you spend ***m*** for what
Jer 32: 9 and weighed out to him the ***m***—
32:10 and weighed the ***m*** on the
32:25 GOD, "Buy the field for ***m***,
32:44 'Men will buy fields for ***m***,
Mic 3:11 And her prophets divine for ***m***.
Zeph 1:11 All those who handle ***m*** are cut
Mt 10: 9 nor silver nor copper in your ***m***
17:27 you will find a piece of ***m***;
21:12 overturned the tables of the ***m***
22:19 "Show Me the tax ***m***."
25:18 ground, and hid his lord's ***m***.
25:27 ought to have deposited my ***m***
28:12 they gave a large sum of ***m*** to
28:15 So they took the ***m*** and did as
Mk 6: 8 no copper in their ***m*** belts—
11:15 overturned the tables of the ***m***
12:41 and saw how the people put ***m***
14:11 and promised to give him ***m***.
Lk 9: 3 staffs nor bag nor bread nor ***m***;
10: 4 Carry neither ***m*** bag, knapsack,
12:33 provide yourselves ***m*** bags which
16:14 Pharisees, who were lovers of ***m***,
19:15 to whom he had given the ***m***,
19:23 Why then did you not put my ***m*** in
22: 5 glad, and agreed to give him ***m***.
22:35 When I sent you without ***m*** bag,
22:36 he who has a ***m*** bag, let him
Jn 2:15 and poured out the changers' ***m***
12: 6 and had the ***m*** box; and he used
13:29 because Judas had the ***m*** box,
Acts 4:37 and brought the ***m*** and laid it
7:16 Abraham bought for a sum of ***m***
8:18 was given, he offered them ***m***,
8:20 Your ***m*** perish with you, because
8:20 God could be purchased with ***m***!
24:26 Meanwhile he also hoped that ***m***
1 Tim 3: 3 not violent, not greedy for ***m***,
3: 8 to much wine, not greedy for ***m***,
6:10 For the love of ***m*** is a root of
2 Tim 3: 2 of themselves, lovers of ***m***,
Titus 1: 7 not violent, not greedy for ***m***,

MONEYCHANGERS (1/1) MONEY

Jn 2:14 and the ***m*** doing business.

MONEYLENDER (1/1)

Ex 22:25 you shall not be like a ***m*** to

MONITOR (1/1)

Lev 11:30 the ***m*** lizard, the sand reptile,

MONKEYS (2/2)

1 Ki 10:22 silver, ivory, apes, and ***m***.
2 Chr 9:21 silver, ivory, apes, and ***m***.

MONSTER (3/3)

Jer 51:34 has swallowed me up like a ***m***;
Ezek 29: 3 O great ***m*** who lies in the
32: 2 And you are like a ***m*** in the

MONSTERS (KJV) See JACKALS

MONSTROUS (1/1)

Joel 2:20 he has done ***m*** things."

MONTH (247/185) MONTHS

Gen 7:11 of Noah's life, in the second ***m***,
7:11 the seventeenth day of the ***m***,
8: 4 the ark rested in the seventh ***m***,
8: 4 the seventeenth day of the ***m***,
8: 5 continually until the tenth ***m***.
8: 5 tenth month. In the tenth ***m***,
8: 5 on the first day of the ***m***,
8:13 and first year, in the first ***m***,
8:13 month, the first day of the ***m***,
8:14 And in the second ***m***,
8:14 the twenty-seventh day of the ***m***,
29:14 And he stayed with him for a ***m***.
Ex 12: 2 This ***m*** shall be your beginning
12: 2 it shall be the first ***m*** of
12: 3 On the tenth day of this ***m***
12: 6 fourteenth day of the same ***m***.
12:18 'In the first ***m***,
12:18 on the fourteenth day of the ***m***
12:18 the twenty-first day of the ***m***
13: 4 are going out, in the ***m*** Abib.
13: 5 keep this service in this ***m***.
16: 1 fifteenth day of the second ***m***
19: 1 In the third ***m*** after the
23:15 at the time appointed in the ***m***
34:18 in the appointed time of the ***m***
34:18 for in the ***m*** of Abib you came
40: 2 the first day of the first ***m***
40:17 it came to pass in the first ***m***
40:17 on the first day of the ***m***,
Lev 16:29 for you: In the seventh ***m***,
16:29 on the tenth day of the ***m***,
23: 5 fourteenth day of the first ***m***
23: 6 the fifteenth day of the same ***m***
23:24 saying: 'In the seventh ***m***,
23:24 on the first day of the ***m***,
23:27 tenth day of this seventh ***m***
23:32 on the ninth day of the ***m*** at
23:34 day of this seventh ***m*** shall
23:39 fifteenth day of the seventh ***m***,
23:41 celebrate it in the seventh ***m***.
25: 9 the tenth day of the seventh ***m***;
27: 6 and if from a ***m*** old up to five
Num 1: 1 the first day of the second ***m***,
1:18 the first day of the second ***m***;
3:15 number every male from a ***m*** old
3:22 of all the males from a ***m*** old
3:28 from a ***m*** old and above, there
3:34 of all the males from a ***m*** old
3:39 all the males from a ***m*** old and
3:40 the children of Israel from a ***m***
3:43 to the number of names from a ***m***
9: 1 in the first ***m*** of the second
9: 3 the fourteenth day of this ***m***,
9: 5 fourteenth day of the first ***m***,
9:11 fourteenth day of the second ***m***,
9:22 Whether it was two days, a ***m***,
10:11 twentieth day of the second ***m***,
11:20 'but for a whole ***m***,
11:21 they may eat for a whole ***m***.
18:16 you shall redeem when one ***m***
20: 1 of Zin in the first ***m***,
26:62 every male from a ***m*** old and
28:14 the burnt offering for each ***m***
28:16 fourteenth day of the first ***m***
28:17 on the fifteenth day of this ***m***
29: 1 'And in the seventh ***m***,
29: 1 on the first day of the ***m***,
29: 7 tenth day of this seventh ***m***
29:12 fifteenth day of the seventh ***m***
33: 3 from Rameses in the first ***m***,

33: 3 fifteenth day of the first **m**;
33:38 the first day of the fifth **m**.
Deut 1: 3 year, in the eleventh **m**,
1: 3 on the first day of the **m**,
16: 1 Observe the **m** of Abib, and keep
16: 1 for in the **m** of Abib the LORD
21:13 father and her mother a full **m**;
Josh 4:19 the tenth day of the first **m**,
5:10 on the fourteenth day of the **m**
1 Sam 20:27 day, the second day of the **m**,
20:34 no food the second day of the **m**,
1 Ki 4: 7 one made provision for one **m**
4:27 governors, each man in his **m**,
5:14 ten thousand a **m** in shifts:
5:14 they were one **m** in Lebanon and
6: 1 in the **m** of Ziv, which is the
6: 1 of Ziv, which is the second **m**,
6:37 was laid, in the **m** of Ziv.
6:38 in the **m** of Bul, which is the
6:38 of Bul, which is the eighth **m**,
8: 2 Solomon at the feast in the **m**
8: 2 which is the seventh **m**.
12:32 fifteenth day of the eighth **m**,
12:33 fifteenth day of the eighth **m**,
12:33 in the **m** which he had devised
2 Ki 15:13 and he reigned a full **m** in
25: 1 of his reign, in the tenth **m**,
25: 1 on the tenth day of the **m**,
25: 3 the ninth day of the fourth **m**
25: 8 And in the fifth **m**,
25: 8 on the seventh day of the **m**
25:25 it happened in the seventh **m**
25:27 king of Judah, in the twelfth **m**,
25:27 twenty-seventh day of the **m**,
1 Chr 12:15 the Jordan in the first **m**,
27: 1 came in and went out **m** by
27: 1 came in and went out month by **m**
27: 2 first division for the first **m**
27: 3 of the army for the first **m**.
27: 4 the division of the second **m**
27: 5 of the army for the third **m**
27: 7 captain for the fourth **m** was
27: 8 fifth captain for the fifth **m**
27: 9 sixth captain for the sixth **m**
27:10 captain for the seventh **m**
27:11 captain for the eighth **m** was
27:12 ninth captain for the ninth **m**
27:13 tenth captain for the tenth **m**
27:14 captain for the eleventh **m**
27:15 captain for the twelfth **m**
2 Chr 3: 2 second day of the second **m** in
5: 3 which was in the seventh **m**.
7:10 day of the seventh **m** he sent
15:10 at Jerusalem in the third **m**,
29: 3 of his reign, in the first **m**,
29:17 the first day of the first **m**,
29:17 and on the eighth day of the **m**
29:17 sixteenth day of the first **m**
30: 2 the Passover in the second **m**.
30:13 Bread in the second **m**.
30:15 fourteenth day of the second **m**.
31: 7 In the third **m** they began
31: 7 they finished in the seventh **m**.
35: 1 fourteenth day of the first **m**.
Ezra 3: 1 And when the seventh **m** had come,
3: 6 the first day of the seventh **m**
3: 8 Now in the second **m** of the
6:15 on the third day of the **m** of
6:19 fourteenth day of the first **m**.
7: 8 to Jerusalem in the fifth **m**,
7: 9 the first day of the first **m**
7: 9 the first day of the fifth **m**
8:31 the twelfth day of the first **m**,
10: 9 three days. It was the ninth **m**,
10: 9 on the twentieth of the **m**;
10:16 on the first day of the tenth **m**
10:17 By the first day of the first **m**
Neh 1: 1 It came to pass in the **m** of
2: 1 And it came to pass in the **m** of
7:73 When the seventh **m** came, the
8: 2 the first day of the seventh **m**.
8:14 the feast of the seventh **m**,
9: 1 the twenty-fourth day of this **m**
Esth 2:16 royal palace, in the tenth **m**,
2:16 which is the **m** of Tebeth, in
3: 7 In the first **m**, which is the
3: 7 which is the **m** of Nisan, in the
3: 7 to determine the day and the **m**,
3: 7 it fell on the twelfth **m**,
3: 7 which is the **m** of Adar.
3:12 thirteenth day of the first **m**,
3:13 day of the twelfth **m**,
3:13 which is the **m** of Adar, and to
8: 9 at that time, in the third **m**,
8: 9 which is the **m** of Sivan, on
8:12 day of the twelfth **m**,
8:12 which is the **m** of Adar.
9: 1 Now in the twelfth **m**,
9: 1 the **m** of Adar, on the
9:15 on the fourteenth day of the **m**
9:17 on the thirteenth day of the **m**
9:17 the fourteenth day of the **m**
9:18 and on the fifteenth of the **m**
9:19 the fourteenth day of the **m** of
9:21 and fifteenth days of the **m** of
9:22 as the **m** which was turned from
Jer 1: 3 captive in the fifth **m**.
2:24 In her **m** they will find her.
28: 1 fourth year and in the fifth **m**,
28:17 the same year in the seventh **m**.
36: 9 king of Judah, in the ninth **m**,
36:22 the winter house in the ninth **m**,
39: 1 king of Judah, in the tenth **m**,
39: 2 of Zedekiah, in the fourth **m**,
39: 2 on the ninth day of the **m**,
41: 1 came to pass in the seventh **m**
52: 4 of his reign, in the tenth **m**,
52: 4 on the tenth day of the **m**,
52: 6 By the fourth **m**, on the ninth
52: 6 on the ninth day of the **m**,
52:12 Now in the fifth **m**,
52:12 on the tenth day of the **m**
52:31 king of Judah, in the twelfth **m**,
52:31 the twenty-fifth day of the **m**,
Ezek 1: 1 year, in the fourth **m**,
1: 1 on the fifth day of the **m**,
1: 2 On the fifth day of the **m**,
8: 1 the sixth year, in the sixth **m**,
8: 1 on the fifth day of the **m**,
20: 1 seventh year, in the fifth **m**,
20: 1 on the tenth day of the **m**,
24: 1 the ninth year, in the tenth **m**,
24: 1 on the tenth day of the **m**,
26: 1 on the first day of the **m**,
29: 1 the tenth year, in the tenth **m**,
29: 1 on the twelfth day of the **m**,
29:17 year, in the first **m**,
29:17 on the first day of the **m**,
30:20 eleventh year, in the first **m**,
30:20 on the seventh day of the **m**,
31: 1 eleventh year, in the third **m**,
31: 1 on the first day of the **m**,
32: 1 twelfth year, in the twelfth **m**,
32: 1 on the first day of the **m**,
32:17 on the fifteenth day of the **m**,
33:21 our captivity, in the tenth **m**,
33:21 on the fifth day of the **m**,
40: 1 on the tenth day of the **m**,
45:18 Lord GOD: "In the first **m**,
45:18 on the first day of the **m**,
45:20 do on the seventh day of the **m**
45:21 "In the first **m**,
45:21 on the fourteenth day of the **m**,
45:25 "In the seventh **m**,
45:25 on the fifteenth day of the **m**,
47:12 They will bear fruit every **m**,
Dan 10: 4 day of the first **m**,
Joel 2:23 the latter rain in the first **m**.
Hag 1: 1 of King Darius, in the sixth **m**,
1: 1 on the first day of the **m**,
1:15 day of the sixth **m**,
2: 1 In the seventh **m**,
2: 1 on the twenty-first of the **m**,
2:10 day of the ninth **m**,
2:18 day of the ninth **m**,
2:20 the twenty-fourth day of the **m**,
Zech 1: 1 In the eighth **m** of the second
1: 7 day of the eleventh **m**,
1: 7 which is the **m** Shebat, in the
7: 1 the fourth day of the ninth **m**,
7: 3 Should I weep in the fifth **m** and
8:19 'The fast of the fourth **m**,
11: 8 the three shepherds in one **m**.
Lk 1:26 Now in the sixth **m** the angel
1:36 and this is now the sixth **m** for
Rev 9:15 for the hour and day and **m** and
22: 2 yielding its fruit every **m**.

MONTHLY (1/1)

Isa 47:13 And the **m** prognosticators

MONTHS (59/58) MONTH

Gen 38:24 about three **m** after, that Judah
Ex 2: 2 child, she hid him three **m**.
12: 2 shall be your beginning of **m**;
Num 10:10 and at the beginning of your **m**,
28:11 At the beginnings of your **m** you
28:14 each month throughout the **m** of
Deut 33:14 the precious produce of the **m**,
Judg 11:37 for me: let me alone for two **m**,
11:38 And he sent her away for two **m**;
11:39 it was so at the end of two **m**
19: 2 and was there four whole **m**.
20:47 the rock of Rimmon for four **m**.
1 Sam 6: 1 of the Philistines seven **m**.
27: 7 was one full year and four **m**.
2 Sam 2:11 Judah was seven years and six **m**.
5: 5 Judah seven years and six **m**,
6:11 Obed-Edom the Gittite three **m**.
24: 8 Jerusalem at the end of nine **m**
24:13 Or shall you flee three **m**
1 Ki 5:14 month in Lebanon and two **m** at
11:16 (because for six **m** Joab remained
2 Ki 15: 8 over Israel in Samaria six **m**.
23:31 and he reigned three **m** in
24: 8 he reigned in Jerusalem three **m**.
1 Chr 3: 4 reigned seven years and six **m**.
13:14 Obed-Edom in his house three **m**.
21:12 or three **m** to be defeated by
27: 1 by month throughout all the **m**
2 Chr 36: 2 and he reigned three **m** in
36: 9 he reigned in Jerusalem three **m**
Esth 2:12 six **m** with oil of myrrh, and
2:12 and six **m** with perfumes and
Job 3: 6 come into the number of the **m**.
7: 3 So I have been allotted **m** of
14: 5 The number of his **m** is with
21:21 When the number of his **m** is
29: 2 that I were as in **m** past,
39: 2 Can you number the **m** that they
Ezek 39:12 For seven **m** the house of Israel
39:14 At the end of seven **m** they will
Dan 4:29 At the end of the twelve **m** he
Am 4: 7 there were still three **m** to
Zech 7: 5 in the fifth and seventh **m**
Lk 1:24 and she hid herself five **m**,
1:56 remained with her about three **m**,
4:25 shut up three years and six **m**,
Jn 4:35 There are still four **m** and then
Acts 7:20 his father's house for three **m**.
18:11 there a year and six **m**,
19: 8 and spoke boldly for three **m**,
20: 3 and stayed three **m**.
28:11 After three **m** we sailed in an
Gal 4:10 You observe days and **m** and
Heb 11:23 was hidden three **m** by his
Jas 5:17 land for three years and six **m**.
Rev 9: 5 but to torment them for five **m**.
9:10 power was to hurt men five **m**.
11: 2 city underfoot for forty-two **m**.
13: 5 to continue for forty-two **m**.

MONTHS' (1/1)

Esth 2:12 completed twelve **m** preparation,

MONUMENT (2/2)

1 Sam 15:12 he set up a **m** for himself;
2 Sam 18:18 day it is called Absalom's **M**.

MONUMENTS (1/1)

Mt 23:29 of the prophets and adorn the **m**

MOON (52/51) MOONS

Gen 37: 9 And this time, the sun, the **m**,
Num 29: 6 grain offering for the New **M**,
Deut 4:19 when you see the sun, the **m**,
17: 3 either the sun or **m** or any of
Josh 10:12 stand still over Gibeon; And **M**,
10:13 And the **m** stopped, Till the
1 Sam 20: 5 "Indeed tomorrow is the New **M**,
20:18 David, "Tomorrow is the New **M**;
20:24 And when the New **M** had come,
2 Ki 4:23 It is neither the New **M** nor
23: 5 to Baal, to the sun, to the **m**,
Job 25: 5 If even the **m** does not shine,
31:26 Or the **m** moving in
Ps 8: 3 The **m** and the stars, which You
72: 5 as the sun and **m** endure,
72: 7 Until the **m** is no more.
81: 3 at the time of the New **M**,
81: 3 of the New Moon, At the full **m**,
89:37 established forever like the **m**,
104:19 He appointed the **m** for seasons;
121: 6 Nor the **m** by night.
136: 9 The **m** and stars to rule by
148: 3 Praise Him, sun and **m**;
Eccl 12: 2 The **m** and the stars, Are not
Song 6:10 as the morning, Fair as the **m**,
Isa 13:10 And the **m** will not cause its
24:23 Then the **m** will be disgraced
30:26 Moreover the light of the **m**
60:19 Nor for brightness shall the **m**
60:20 Nor shall your **m** withdraw
66:23 to pass That from one New **M**
Jer 8: 2 them before the sun and the **m**
31:35 The ordinances of the **m** and
Ezek 32: 7 And the **m** shall not give her
46: 1 and on the day of the New **M** it
46: 6 On the day of the New **M** it
Hos 5: 7 Now a New **M** shall devour them
Joel 2:10 The sun and **m** grow dark,
2:31 And the **m** into blood, Before
3:15 The sun and **m** will grow dark,
Am 8: 5 When will the New **M** be past,
Hab 3:11 The sun and **m** stood still in
Mt 24:29 and the **m** will not give its
Mk 13:24 and the **m** will not give its
Lk 21:25 be signs in the sun, in the **m**,
Acts 2:20 And the **m** into blood,
1 Cor 15:41 the sun, another glory of the **m**,
Col 2:16 a festival or a new **m** or
Rev 6:12 and the **m** became like blood.
8:12 was struck, a third of the **m**,
12: 1 with the **m** under her feet, and
21:23 no need of the sun or of the **m**

MOONS (11/11) MOON

1 Chr 23:31 the Sabbaths and on the New **M**
2 Chr 2: 4 on the Sabbaths, on the New **M**,
8:13 for the Sabbaths, the New **M**,
31: 3 for the Sabbaths and the New **M**
Ezra 3: 5 and those for New **M** and for
Neh 10:33 of the Sabbaths, the New **M**,
Isa 1:13 abomination to Me. The New **M**,
1:14 Your New **M** and your appointed
Ezek 45:17 at the feasts, the New **M**,
46: 3 on the Sabbaths and the New **M**.
Hos 2:11 Her feast days, Her New **M**,

MOORINGS (1/1)

Jon 2: 6 I went down to the **m** of the

MORAL (1/1)

2 Chr 28:19 for he had encouraged **m** decline

MORASTHITE (KJV) See MORESHETH

M

MORDECAI (60/53) MORDECAI'S

Ezra 2: 2 Nehemiah, Seraiah, Reelaiah, **M**,
Neh 7: 7 Azariah, Raamiah, Nahamani, **M**,
Esth 2: 5 a certain Jew whose name was **M**
2: 7 And **M** had brought up Hadassah,
2: 7 **M** took her as his own daughter.
2:10 for **M** had charged her not to
2:11 And every day **M** paced in front
2:15 of Abihail the uncle of **M**,
2:19 **M** sat within the king's gate.
2:20 just as **M** had charged her,
2:20 Esther obeyed the command of **M**
2:21 while **M** sat within the king's
2:22 So the matter became known to **M**,
3: 2 But **M** would not bow or pay
3: 3 the king's gate said to **M**,
3: 4 for **M** had told them that he
3: 5 When Haman saw that **M** did not
3: 6 he disdained to lay hands on **M**
3: 6 had told him of the people of **M**.
3: 6 of Ahasuerus—the people of **M**.
4: 1 When **M** learned all that had
4: 4 she sent garments to clothe **M**
4: 5 gave him a command concerning **M**,
4: 6 So Hathach went out to **M** in the
4: 7 And **M** told him all that had
4: 9 and told Esther the words of **M**.
4:10 and gave him a command for **M**:
4:12 So they told **M** Esther's words.
4:13 And **M** told them to answer
4:15 Esther told them to reply to **M**:
4:17 So **M** went his way and did
5: 9 but when Haman saw **M** in the
5: 9 with indignation against **M**.
5:13 so long as I see **M** the Jew
5:14 suggest to the king that **M** be
6: 2 And it was found written that **M**
6: 3 dignity has been bestowed on **M**
6: 4 to suggest that the king hang **M**
6:10 and do so for **M** the Jew who
6:11 arrayed **M** and led him on
6:12 Afterward **M** went back to the
6:13 wife Zeresh said to him, "If **M**,
7: 9 high, which Haman made for **M**,
7:10 that he had prepared for **M**.
8: 1 And **M** came before the king,
8: 2 from Haman, and gave it to **M**;
8: 2 and Esther appointed **M** over the
8: 7 said to Queen Esther and **M** the
8: 9 according to all that **M**
8:15 So **M** went out from the presence
9: 3 because the fear of **M** fell upon
9: 4 For **M** was great in the king's
9: 4 for this man **M** became
9:20 And **M** wrote these things and
9:23 as **M** had written to them,
9:29 with **M** the Jew, wrote with full
9:30 And **M** sent letters to all the
9:31 as **M** the Jew and Queen Esther
10: 2 account of the greatness of **M**,
10: 3 For **M** the Jew was second to

MORDECAI'S (2/2) MORDECAI

Esth 2:22 informed the king in **M** name.
3: 4 to see whether **M** words would

MORE (552/514)

Gen 3: 1 Now the serpent was **m** cunning
3:14 You are cursed **m** than all
3:14 And **m** than every beast of the
7: 4 For after seven **m** days I will
18:32 and I will speak but once **m**:
29:30 and he also loved Rachel **m** than
34:19 He was **m** honorable than all
37: 3 Now Israel loved Joseph **m** than
37: 4 that their father loved him **m**
37: 5 and they hated him even **m**.
37: 8 So they hated him even **m** for
37:30 and said, "The lad is no **m**;
38:26 She has been **m** righteous than I,
42:13 father today, and one is no **m**.
42:32 of our father; one is no **m**,
42:36 bereaved me: Joseph is no **m**,
42:36 is no more, Simeon is no **m**,
44:23 you, you shall see my face no **m**.
Ex 1: 9 the children of Israel are **m**
1:12 But the **m** they afflicted them,
1:12 the **m** they multiplied and grew.
5: 9 Let **m** work be laid on the men,
9:28 that there may be no **m** mighty
9:29 and there will be no **m** hail,
9:34 had ceased, he sinned yet **m**;
10:28 yourself and see my face no **m**!
11: 1 I will bring yet one **m** plague
14:13 you shall see again no **m**
16:17 did so and gathered, some **m**,
30:15 The rich shall not give **m** and
36: 5 The people bring much **m** than
36: 6 neither man nor woman do any **m**
Lev 6: 5 add one-fifth **m** to it, and
17: 7 They shall no **m** offer their
26:18 I will punish you seven times **m**
26:21 will bring on you seven times **m**
Num 3:46 who are **m** than the number of
8:25 this work, and shall work no **m**.
12: 3 **m** than all men who were on the
18: 5 that there may be no **m** wrath
20:19 through on foot, nothing **m**.
22:15 **m** numerous and more honorable
22:15 more numerous and **m** honorable
22:18 LORD my God, to do less or **m**.
22:19 I may know what **m** the LORD
32:14 to increase still **m** the fierce
Deut 1:11 a thousand times **m** numerous
3:26 Enough of that! Speak no **m** to Me
5:22 a loud voice; and He added no **m**.
7: 7 because you were **m** in number
19: 9 then you shall add three **m**
20: 1 chariots and people **m** numerous
25: 3 blows he may give him and no **m**,
30: 5 prosper you and multiply you **m**
31:27 then how much **m** after my death?
Josh 2:11 neither did there remain any **m**
10:11 There were **m** who died from
22:33 they spoke no **m** of going
Judg 2:19 reverted and behaved **m** corruptly
6:39 but let me speak just once **m**:
6:39 just once **m** with the fleece;
8:28 they lifted their heads no **m**.
10:13 I will deliver you no **m**.
13:21 of the LORD appeared no **m** to
16:18 saying, "Come up once **m**,
16:30 he killed at his death were **m**
18:24 Now what **m** do I have? How can
20:25 the ground eighteen thousand **m**
Ruth 1:17 and **m** also, If anything but
3:10 For you have shown **m** kindness
1 Sam 2: 3 'Talk no **m** so very proudly;
2:29 and honor your sons **m** than Me,
3:17 and **m** also, if you hide
9: 2 There was not a **m** handsome
14:44 God do so and **m** also; for you
15:35 And Samuel went no **m** to see Saul
18: 8 Now what **m** can he have but the
18:29 and Saul was still **m** afraid of
18:30 that David behaved **m** wisely
20:13 the LORD do so and much **m**
20:41 wept together, but David **m** so.
23: 3 How much **m** then if we go to
24:17 'You are **m** righteous than I;
25:22 and **m** also, to the enemies of
26:21 For I will harm you no **m**,
27: 4 to Gath; so he sought him no **m**.
30: 4 until they had no **m** power to
2 Sam 3: 9 and **m** also, if I do not do for
3:35 and **m** also, if I taste bread or
4:11 'How much **m**, when wicked men
5:13 And David took **m** concubines and
5:13 Also **m** sons and daughters were
6:22 And I will be even **m** undignified
7:10 of their own and move no **m**;
7:20 Now what **m** can David say to You?
12: 8 would have given you much **m**!
16:11 How much **m** now may this
18: 3 For you are now **m** help to us in
18: 8 and the woods devoured **m** people
19:13 and **m** also, if you are not
19:43 therefore we also have **m** right
20: 6 son of Bichri will do us **m** harm
21:17 You shall go out no **m** with us to
23:23 He was **m** honored than the
24: 3 to the people a hundred times **m**
1 Ki 2:23 and **m** also, if Adonijah has not
2:32 he struck down two men **m**
8:65 seven days and seven **m**
10: 5 there was no **m** spirit in her.
14: 9 but you have done **m** evil than
14:22 **m** than all that their fathers
16:30 **m** than all who were before
16:33 Ahab did **m** to provoke the LORD
19: 2 and **m** also, if I do not make
20:10 and **m** also, if enough dust is
2 Ki 2:12 So he saw him no **m**.
2:21 from it there shall be no **m**
5:13 How much **m** then, when he says
6:16 those who are with us are **m**
6:23 of Syrian raiders came no **m**
6:31 God do so to me and **m** also, if
9:35 but they found no **m** of her than
12: 7 do not take **m** money from your
12: 8 would neither receive **m** money
21: 9 Manasseh seduced them to do **m**
21:11 (he has acted **m** wickedly than
25:28 and gave him a **m** prominent seat
1 Chr 4: 9 Now Jabez was **m** honorable than
11:21 Of the three he was **m** honored
11:25 Indeed he was **m** honored than the
14: 3 Then David took **m** wives in
14: 3 and David begot **m** sons and
17: 9 of their own and move no **m**;
17:18 What **m** can David say to You for
21: 3 His people a hundred times **m**
24: 4 There were **m** leaders found of
2 Chr 9: 4 there was no **m** spirit in her.
9:12 much **m** than she had brought
11:21 the granddaughter of Absalom **m**
20:25 **m** than they could carry away;
25: 9 is able to give you much **m**
29:34 for the Levites were **m** diligent
32: 7 for there are **m** with us than
33: 9 of Jerusalem to do **m** evil than
33:23 but Amon trespassed **m** and more.
33:23 but Amon trespassed more and **m**.
36:14 and the people transgressed **m**
36:14 people transgressed more and **m**,
Ezra 7:20 And whatever **m** may be needed for
Neh 7: 2 a faithful man and feared God **m**
13:21 that time on they came no **m**
Esth 1:19 that Vashti shall come no **m**
2:17 The king loved Esther **m** than all
2:17 grace and favor in his sight **m**
4:13 in the king's palace any **m**
6: 6 the king delight to honor **m**
Job 3:21 And search for it **m** than
4:17 Can a mortal be **m** righteous than
4:17 Can a man be **m** pure than his
4:19 How much **m** those who dwell in
7: 8 who sees me will see me no **m**;
14:12 Till the heavens are no **m**,
20: 9 saw him will see him no **m**,
23:12 the words of His mouth **M** than
24:20 He should be remembered no **m**,
27:19 his eyes, And he is no **m**.
32:15 are dismayed and answer no **m**;
32:16 stood still and answered no **m**.
34:19 Nor does He regard the rich **m**
34:31 I will offend no **m**;
34:32 done iniquity, I will do no **m**'?
35: 2 My righteousness is **m** than
35: 3 **m** than if I had sinned?'
35:11 Who teaches us **m** than the
42:12 the latter days of Job **m** than
Ps 4: 7 **M** than in the season that
10:18 of the earth may oppress no **m**.
19:10 **M** to be desired are they than
37:10 and the wicked shall be no **m**;
37:10 But it shall be no **m**.
37:36 away, and behold, he was no **m**;
39:13 Before I go away and am no **m**.
40: 5 They are **m** than can be
40:12 They are **m** than the hairs of
41: 8 lies down, he will rise up no **m**.
45: 7 With the oil of gladness **m** than
52: 3 You love evil **m** than good,
68:35 You are **m** awesome than Your
69: 4 hate me without a cause Are **m**
71:14 And will praise You yet **m** and
71:14 will praise You yet more and **m**.
72: 7 Until the moon is no **m**.
73: 7 They have **m** than heart could
76: 4 You are **m** glorious and
77: 7 And will He be favorable no **m**?
78:17 But they sinned even **m** against
83: 4 Israel may be remembered no **m**.
87: 2 loves the gates of Zion **M**
88: 5 Whom You remember no **m**,
103:16 its place remembers it no **m**.
104:35 And the wicked be no **m**.
115:14 the LORD give you increase **m**
115:14 give you increase more and **m**,
119:99 I have **m** understanding than all
119:100 I understand **m** than the
119:127 I love Your commandments **M**
130: 6 My soul waits for the Lord **M**
130: 6 **m** than those who watch for
139:18 they would be **m** in number than
Prov 3:15 She is **m** precious than rubies,
10:25 passes by, the wicked is no **m**,
11:24 who scatters, yet increases **m**;
11:24 there is one who withholds **m**
11:31 How much **m** the ungodly and the
12: 7 are overthrown and are no **m**,
15:11 So how much **m** the hearts of
17:10 Rebuke is **m** effective for a
19: 7 How much **m** do his friends go
21: 3 and justice Is **m** acceptable
21:27 How much **m** when he brings it
26:12 There is **m** hope for a fool
28:23 rebukes a man will find **m** favor
29:20 There is **m** hope for a fool
30: 2 Surely I am **m** stupid than any
31: 7 And remember his misery no **m**.
Eccl 1:16 and have gained **m** wisdom than
2: 9 I became great and excelled **m**
2:15 And why was I then **m** wise?"
2:16 For there is no **m** remembrance
2:25 have enjoyment, **m** than I?
4: 2 **M** than the living who are
4:13 who will be admonished no **m**.
6: 5 this has **m** rest than that man,
6: 8 For what **m** has the wise man
7:19 strengthens the wise **M** than
7:26 And I find **m** bitter than death
9: 5 And they have no **m** reward,
10:10 Then he must use **m** strength;
Song 1: 4 We will remember your love **m**
5: 9 What is your beloved **M** than
5: 9 What is your beloved **M** than
Isa 1: 5 You will revolt **m** and more.
1: 5 You will revolt more and **m**.
1:13 Bring no **m** futile sacrifices;
5: 4 What **m** could have been done to
9: 1 And afterward **m** heavily
13:12 I will make a mortal **m** rare
13:12 A man **m** than the golden wedge
15: 9 Because I will bring **m** upon
17:14 before the morning, he is no **m**.
19: 7 be driven away, and be no **m**.
23:10 There is no **m** strength.
23:12 said, "You will rejoice no **m**,
25: 2 of foreigners to be a city no **m**;
26:21 And will no **m** cover her slain.
30:19 You shall weep no **m**.
38:11 I shall observe man no **m** among
47: 1 For you shall no **m** be called
52:14 So His visage was marred **m**
52:14 And His form **m** than the sons
54: 1 For **m** are the children of the
56:12 And much **m** abundant."
62: 4 Nor shall your land any **m** be
65:20 No **m** shall an infant from there
Jer 2:31 We will come no **m** to You'?
3:11 has shown herself **m** righteous

3:16 "that they will say no ***m***,
3:17 No ***m*** shall they follow the
7:32 when it will no ***m*** be called
10:20 from me, And they are no ***m***.
11:19 his name may be remembered no ***m***.
15: 8 will be increased to Me ***m*** than
16:14 that it shall no ***m*** be said, 'The
19: 6 that this place shall no ***m*** be
22:10 For he shall return no ***m***,
22:12 and shall see this land no ***m***.
23: 4 and they shall fear no ***m***,
23:36 LORD you shall mention no ***m***.
25:27 and vomit! Fall and rise no ***m***,
30: 8 Foreigners shall no ***m*** enslave
31:12 And they shall sorrow no ***m*** at
31:15 Because they are no ***m***.
31:29 those days they shall say no ***m***:
31:34 No ***m*** shall every man teach his
31:34 their sin I will remember no ***m***.
33:24 as if they should no ***m*** be a
38: 9 For there is no ***m*** bread in
42:18 you shall see this place no ***m***.
44:26 that My name shall no ***m*** be named
46:23 ***m*** numerous than grasshoppers.
48: 2 No ***m*** praise of Moab.
49: 7 Is wisdom no ***m*** in Teman?
49:10 his neighbors, And he is no ***m***.
50:39 It shall be inhabited no ***m***
52:32 him and gave him a ***m*** prominent
Lam 2: 9 the nations; The Law is no ***m***,
4: 7 They were ***m*** ruddy in body than
5: 7 fathers sinned and are no ***m***,
Ezek 5: 6 by doing wickedness ***m*** than the
5: 6 and against My statutes ***m*** than
5: 7 disobedience ***m*** than the nations
6:14 ***m*** desolate than the wilderness
12:23 and they shall no ***m*** use it as a
12:24 For no ***m*** shall there be any
12:25 it will no ***m*** be postponed;
12:28 words will be postponed any ***m***,
13:15 say to you, 'The wall is no ***m***,
14:21 How much ***m*** it shall be when I
16:42 be quiet, and be angry no ***m***.
16:47 you became ***m*** corrupt than they
16:51 multiplied your abominations ***m***
16:52 you committed were ***m*** abominable
16:52 they are ***m*** righteous than you.
20:39 but profane My holy name no ***m***
21:13 The scepter shall be no ***m***,
23:11 she became ***m*** corrupt in her
23:11 and in her harlotry ***m*** corrupt
26:13 your harps shall be heard no ***m***.
26:21 and you shall be no ***m***;
27:36 and be no ***m*** forever.'" '"
28:19 And shall be no ***m*** forever."
32:13 of man shall muddy them no ***m***,
34:10 shall feed themselves no ***m***;
36:12 no ***m*** shall you bereave them of
36:14 you shall devour men no ***m***,
42: 5 took away space from them ***m***
42: 6 upper level was shortened ***m***
43: 7 No ***m*** shall the house of Israel
44: 6 let us have no ***m*** of all your
45: 8 My princes shall no ***m*** oppress
Dan 2:30 to me because I have ***m*** wisdom
3:19 heat the furnace seven times ***m***
11: 2 three ***m*** kings will arise in
11: 8 and he shall continue ***m*** years
Hos 2:17 remembered by their name no ***m***.
4: 7 The ***m*** they increased, The more
4: 7 The ***m*** they sinned against Me;
6: 6 God ***m*** than burnt offerings.
9:15 I will love them no ***m***.
13: 2 Now they sin ***m*** and more,
13: 2 Now they sin more and ***m***,
Am 5: 2 has fallen; She will rise no ***m***.
6:10 Are there any ***m*** with you?"
Jon 1:11 sea was growing ***m*** tempestuous.
1:13 for the sea continued to grow ***m***
4:11 in which are ***m*** than one hundred
Mic 4: 3 shall they learn war any ***m***.
5:13 You shall no ***m*** worship the
Nah 1:12 I will afflict you no ***m***;
1:15 shall no ***m*** pass through you;
2:13 messengers shall be heard no ***m***.
3:16 multiplied your merchants ***m***
Hab 1: 8 And ***m*** fierce than evening
1:13 devours A person ***m*** righteous
Zeph 3:15 You shall see disaster no ***m***.
Hag 2: 6 Once ***m*** (it is a little while) I
Zech 9: 8 No ***m*** shall an oppressor pass
10:10 Until no ***m*** room is found for
Mt 2:18 Because they are no ***m***.
5:29 for it is ***m*** profitable for you
5:30 for it is ***m*** profitable for you
5:37 For whatever is ***m*** than these
5:47 what do you do ***m*** than others?
6:25 Is not life ***m*** than food and the
6:25 and the body ***m*** than clothing?
6:26 Are you not of ***m*** value than
6:30 will He not much ***m*** clothe
7:11 how much ***m*** will your Father who
10:15 it will be ***m*** tolerable for the
10:25 how much ***m*** will they call
10:31 you are of ***m*** value than many
10:37 who loves father or mother ***m***
10:37 loves son or daughter ***m*** than Me
11: 9 and ***m*** than a prophet.
11:22 it will be ***m*** tolerable for Tyre
11:24 that it shall be ***m*** tolerable
12:12 Of how much ***m*** value then is a
12:45 seven other spirits ***m*** wicked
13:12 to him ***m*** will be given, and he
18:13 he rejoices ***m*** over that sheep
18:16 take with you one or two ***m***,
20:10 that they would receive ***m***;
20:31 but they cried out all the ***m***,
21:36 ***m*** than the first, and they did
23:39 you shall see Me no ***m*** till you
25:17 had received two gained two ***m***
25:20 I have gained five ***m*** talents
25:22 I have gained two ***m*** talents
25:29 ***m*** will be given, and he will
26:53 and He will provide Me with ***m***
27:23 But they cried out all the ***m***,
Mk 4:24 you who hear, ***m*** will be given.
4:25 to him ***m*** will be given;
6:11 it will be ***m*** tolerable for
7:36 but the ***m*** He commanded them,
7:36 the ***m*** widely they proclaimed
8:14 and they did not have ***m*** than
9:25 out of him and enter him no ***m***!
10:48 but he cried out all the ***m***,
12:33 is ***m*** than all the whole burnt
12:43 this poor widow has put in ***m***
14: 5 it might have been sold for ***m***
14:31 But he spoke ***m*** vehemently, "If
15:14 But they cried out all the ***m***,
Lk 3:13 Collect no ***m*** than what is
5:15 around concerning Him all the ***m***;
7:26 and ***m*** than a prophet.
7:42 which of them will love him ***m***?
7:43 the one whom he forgave ***m***.
8:18 to him ***m*** will be given;
9:13 We have no ***m*** than five loaves
10:12 you that it will be ***m*** tolerable
10:14 But it will be ***m*** tolerable for
10:35 and whatever ***m*** you spend, when
11:13 how much ***m*** will your heavenly
11:26 seven other spirits ***m*** wicked
11:28 ***M*** than that, blessed are those
12: 4 and after that have no ***m*** that
12: 7 you are of ***m*** value than many
12:23 Life is ***m*** than food, and the
12:23 and the body is ***m*** than
12:24 Of how much ***m*** value are you
12:28 how much ***m*** will He clothe
12:48 of him they will ask the ***m***.
14: 8 lest one ***m*** honorable than you
15: 7 likewise there will be ***m*** joy
16: 8 sons of this world are ***m*** shrewd
18:30 shall not receive many times ***m***
18:39 but he cried out all the ***m***,
21: 3 this poor widow has put in ***m***
22:44 He prayed ***m*** earnestly. Then His
23: 5 But they were the ***m*** fierce,
Jn 4: 1 made and baptized ***m*** disciples
4:41 And many ***m*** believed because of
5:14 have been made well. Sin no ***m***,
5:18 Jews sought all the ***m*** to kill
6:66 back and walked with Him no ***m***.
7:31 will He do ***m*** signs than these
8:11 I condemn you; go and sin no ***m***.
10:10 they may have it ***m*** abundantly.
11: 6 He stayed two ***m*** days in the
12:43 they loved the praise of men ***m***
14:19 and the world will see Me no ***m***,
15: 2 that it may bear ***m*** fruit.
16:10 My Father and you see Me no ***m***;
19: 8 he was the ***m*** afraid,
21:15 do you love Me ***m*** than these?"
Acts 4:19 of God to listen to you ***m*** than
8:39 so that the eunuch saw him no ***m***;
9:22 increased all the ***m*** in strength
13:34 no ***m*** to return to corruption,
17:11 These were ***m*** fair-minded than
18:26 the way of God ***m*** accurately.
20:25 of God, will see my face no ***m***.
20:35 It is ***m*** blessed to give than to
20:38 they would see his face no ***m***.
22: 2 they kept all the ***m*** silent.
23:13 Now there were ***m*** than forty who
23:20 they were going to inquire ***m***
23:21 for ***m*** than forty of them lie in
24:10 I do the ***m*** cheerfully answer
24:11 may ascertain that it is no ***m***
24:22 having ***m*** accurate knowledge of
24:26 he sent for him ***m*** often
25: 6 he had remained among them ***m***
27:11 the centurion was ***m*** persuaded
Rom 5: 9 Much ***m*** then, having now been
5:10 the death of His Son, much ***m***,
5:15 much ***m*** the grace of God and the
5:17 much ***m*** those who receive
5:20 abounded, grace abounded much ***m***,
6: 9 raised from the dead, dies no ***m***.
6:19 of lawlessness leading to ***m***
8:37 things we are ***m*** than conquerors
11:12 how much ***m*** their fullness!
11:24 how much ***m*** will these, who are
12: 3 to think of himself ***m*** highly
15:15 I have written ***m*** boldly to you
1 Cor 6: 3 shall judge angels? How much ***m***,
9:12 over you, are we not even ***m***?
9:19 to all, that I might win the ***m***;
12:31 I show you a ***m*** excellent way.
14: 5 but even ***m*** that you prophesied;
14:18 my God I speak with tongues ***m***
15:10 but I labored ***m*** abundantly than
2 Cor 1:12 and ***m*** abundantly toward you.
1:23 that to spare you I came no ***m***
3: 8 the Spirit not be ***m*** glorious?
3: 9 exceeds much ***m*** in glory.
3:11 remains is much ***m*** glorious.
4:17 is working for us a far ***m***
7: 7 me, so that I rejoiced even ***m***.
7:13 And we rejoiced exceedingly ***m***
8:17 but being ***m*** diligent, he went
8:22 but now much ***m*** diligent,
10: 8 somewhat ***m*** about our authority,
11:23 speak as a fool—I am ***m***:
11:23 in labors ***m*** abundant, in
11:23 in prisons ***m*** frequently, in
12:15 though the ***m*** abundantly I love
Gal 1:14 being ***m*** exceedingly zealous for
4:27 desolate has many ***m*** children
Phil 1: 9 your love may abound still ***m***
1: 9 still more and ***m*** in knowledge
1:14 are much ***m*** bold to speak the
1:24 in the flesh is ***m*** needful
1:26 your rejoicing for me may be ***m***
2:12 but now much ***m*** in my absence,
2:28 I sent him the ***m*** eagerly,
3: 4 in the flesh, I ***m*** so:
1 Th 2:17 endeavored ***m*** eagerly to see
4: 1 Jesus that you should abound ***m***
4: 1 you should abound more and ***m***,
4:10 that you increase ***m*** and more;
4:10 that you increase more and ***m***;
2 Tim 2:16 will increase to ***m*** ungodliness.
Phm 1:16 no longer as a slave but ***m*** than
1:16 to me but how much ***m*** to you,
1:21 that you will do even ***m*** than I
Heb 1: 4 obtained a ***m*** excellent name
1: 9 the oil of gladness ***m*** than
2: 1 we must give the ***m*** earnest heed
3: 3 been counted worthy of ***m*** glory
3: 3 who built the house has ***m*** honor
6:17 determining to show ***m***
7:15 And it is yet far ***m*** evident if,
7:22 by so much ***m*** Jesus has become a
8: 6 a ***m*** excellent ministry,
8:12 I will remember no ***m***.
9:11 with the greater and ***m*** perfect
9:14 how much ***m*** shall the blood of
10: 2 no ***m*** consciousness of sins.
10:17 I will remember no ***m***.
10:25 and so much the ***m*** as you see
11: 4 to God a ***m*** excellent sacrifice
11:32 And what ***m*** shall I say? For the
12: 9 Shall we not much ***m*** readily be
12:25 much ***m*** shall we not escape
12:26 Yet once ***m*** I shake not
12:27 Now this, "Yet once ***m***,
Jas 4: 6 But He gives ***m*** grace.
1 Pe 1: 7 being much ***m*** precious than
2 Pe 1:10 be even ***m*** diligent to make your
Rev 2:19 the last are ***m*** than the first.
3:12 God, and he shall go out no ***m***.
9:12 still two ***m*** woes are coming
18:14 and you shall find them no ***m*** at
20: 3 deceive the nations no ***m*** till
21: 1 Also there was no ***m*** sea.
21: 4 there shall be no ***m*** death, nor
21: 4 There shall be no ***m*** pain, for
22: 3 And there shall be no ***m*** curse,

MOREH (3/3)

Gen 12: 6 far as the terebinth tree of ***M***.
Deut 11:30 beside the terebinth trees of ***M***?
Judg 7: 1 side of them by the hill of ***M***

MOREOVER (144/144)

Gen 24:25 ***M*** she said to him, "We have
45:15 ***M*** he kissed all his brothers and
48:22 ***M*** I have given to you one
Ex 3: 6 ***M*** He said, "I am the God of
3:15 ***M*** God said to Moses, "Thus you
11: 3 ***M*** the man Moses was very great
18:21 ***M*** you shall select from all the
26: 1 ***M*** you shall make the tabernacle
30:22 ***M*** the LORD spoke to Moses,
Lev 7:21 ***M*** the person who touches any
7:26 ***M*** you shall not eat any blood in
14:46 ***M*** he who goes into the house at
18:20 ***M*** you shall not lie carnally
25:45 ***M*** you may buy the children of
Num 3:38 ***M*** those who were to camp before
13:28 ***m*** we saw the descendants of
16:14 ***M*** you have not brought us into a
33:56 ***M*** it shall be that I will do to
35:31 ***M*** you shall take no ransom for
Deut 1:28 ***m*** we have seen the sons of the
1:39 ***M*** your little ones and your
7:20 ***M*** the LORD your God will send
28:45 ***M*** all these curses shall come
28:60 ***M*** He will bring back on you all
Judg 10: 9 ***M*** the people of Ammon crossed
Ruth 4:10 '***M***, Ruth the Moabitess,
1 Sam 2:19 ***M*** his mother used to make him a
12:23 '***M***, as for me, far be it from
14:21 ***M*** the Hebrews who were with the
17:37 ***M*** David said, "The LORD, who
24:11 '***M***, my father, see!
28:19 ***M*** the LORD will also deliver
2 Sam 7:10 ***M*** I will appoint a place for My
15: 4 ***M*** Absalom would say, "Oh, that
17: 1 ***M*** Ahithophel said to Absalom,
17:13 '***M***, if he has withdrawn into
1 Ki 1:47 And ***m*** the king's servants have
2: 5 ***M*** you know also what Joab the
2:14 ***M*** he said, "I have something
2:44 The king said ***m*** to Shimei, "You
8:41 ***M***, concerning a foreigner,

10:18 *M* the king made a great throne
14:14 *M* the LORD will raise up for
2 Ki 12:15 *M* they did not require an
21:16 *M* Manasseh shed very much
23:15 *M* the altar that was at
23:24 *M* Josiah put away those who
1 Chr 12:40 *M* those who were near to them,
17: 9 *M* I will appoint a place for My
18:12 *M* Abishai the son of Zeruiah
22:15 *M* there are workmen with you
25: 1 *M* David and the captains of the
26: 4 *M* the sons of Obed-Edom were
28: 7 *M* I will establish his kingdom
29: 3 '*M*, because I have set my
2 Chr 4: 1 *M* he made a bronze altar: twenty
6:32 *M*, concerning a foreigner,
9:17 *M* the king made a great throne
17: 6 *m* he removed the high places
19: 8 *M* in Jerusalem, for the
21:11 *M* he made high places in the
21:16 *M* the LORD stirred up against
25: 5 *M* Amaziah gathered Judah
26:11 *M* Uzziah had an army of
27: 4 *M* he built cities in the
29:19 *M* all the articles which King
29:30 *M* King Hezekiah and the leaders
31: 4 *M* he commanded the people who
32:29 *M* he provided cities for
36:14 *M* all the leaders of the priests
Ezra 6: 8 *M* I issue a decree as to what
Neh 3: 6 *M* Jehoiada the son of Paseah
3:26 *M* the Nethinim who dwelt in
5:14 *M*, from the time that I
9:12 *M* You led them by day with a
9:22 *M* You gave them kingdoms and
11:19 *M* the gatekeepers, Akkub,
12: 8 *M* the Levites were Jeshua,
Esth 5:12 *M* Haman said, "Besides, Queen
Job 27: 1 *M* Job continued his discourse,
35: 1 *M* Elihu answered and said:
40: 1 *M* the LORD answered Job, and
Ps 19:11 *M* by them Your servant is
78:67 *M* He rejected the tent of
105:16 *M* He called for a famine in the
Eccl 3:16 *M* I saw under the sun
5: 9 *M* the profit of the land is for
8:17 yet he will not find it; *m*,
12: 9 And *m*, because the Preacher
Isa 3:16 *M* the LORD says
7:10 *M* the LORD spoke again to
8: 1 *M* the LORD said to me, "Take a
19: 9 *M* those who work in fine flax
29: 5 *M* the multitude of your foes
30:26 *M* the light of the moon will be
Jer 1:11 *M* the word of the LORD came to
2: 1 *M* the word of the LORD came to
8: 4 *M* you shall say to them, 'Thus
20: 5 *M* I will deliver all the wealth
25:10 *M* I will take from them the
33: 1 *M* the word of the LORD came to
33:23 *M* the word of the LORD came to
37:18 *M* Jeremiah said to King
39: 7 *M* he put out Zedekiah's eyes,
40:13 *M* Johanan the son of Kareah and
44:24 *M* Jeremiah said to all the
48:35 '*M*,' says the LORD,
Ezek 3: 1 *M* He said to me, "Son of man,
3:10 *M* He said to me: "Son of man,
4: 3 *M* take for yourself an iron
4:16 *M* He said to me, "Son of man,
5:14 *M* I will make you a waste and a
7: 1 *M* the word of the LORD came to
12:17 *M* the word of the LORD came to
16:20 *M* you took your sons and your
16:29 *M* you multiplied your acts of
17:11 *M* the word of the LORD came to
19: 1 *M* take up a lamentation for the
20:12 *M* I also gave them My Sabbaths,
22: 1 *M* the word of the LORD came to
23:38 *M* they have done this to Me:
28:11 *M* the word of the LORD came to
35: 1 *M* the word of the LORD came to
36:16 *M* the word of the LORD came to
37:26 *M* I will make a covenant of
45: 1 '*M*, when you divide the land
46:18 *M* the prince shall not take any
48:22 '*M*, apart from the possession
Zech 4: 8 *M* the word of the LORD came to
Mt 6:16 *M*, when you fast, do not
18:15 *M* if your brother sins against
Lk 16:21 *M* the dogs came and licked his
Acts 2:26 *M* my flesh also will
11:12 *M* these six brethren
19:26 *M* you see and hear that not only
Rom 5:20 *M* the law entered that the
8:30 *M* whom He predestined, these He
1 Cor 4: 2 *M* it is required in stewards
10: 1 *M*, brethren, I do not want you
15: 1 *M*, brethren, I declare to you
2 Cor 1:23 *M* I call God as witness against
8: 1 *M*, brethren, we make known
1 Tim 3: 7 *M* he must have a good testimony
2 Pe 1:15 *M* I will be careful to ensure

MORESHETH (3/3)

Jer 26:18 Micah of *M* prophesied in the
Mic 1: 1 LORD that came to Micah of *M*

MORESHETH GATH (1/1)

Mic 1:14 you shall give presents to *M*;

MORIAH (2/2)

Gen 22: 2 love, and go to the land of *M*,
2 Chr 3: 1 LORD at Jerusalem on Mount *M*,

MORNING (231/218)

Gen 1: 5 So the evening and the *m* were
1: 8 So the evening and the *m* were
1:13 So the evening and the *m* were
1:19 So the evening and the *m* were
1:23 So the evening and the *m* were
1:31 So the evening and the *m* were
19:15 When the *m* dawned, the angels
19:27 Abraham went early in the *m* to
20: 8 Abimelech rose early in the *m*,
21:14 So Abraham rose early in the *m*,
22: 3 So Abraham rose early in the *m*
24:54 night. Then they arose in the *m*,
26:31 Then they arose early in the *m*
28:18 Then Jacob rose early in the *m*,
29:25 So it came to pass in the *m*,
31:55 And early in the *m* Laban arose,
40: 6 came in to them in the *m* and
41: 8 Now it came to pass in the *m*
44: 3 As soon as the *m* dawned, the men
49:27 In the *m* he shall devour the
Ex 7:15 "Go to Pharaoh in the *m*,
8:20 Rise early in the *m* and stand
9:13 Rise early in the *m* and stand
10:13 all that night. When it was *m*,
12:10 let none of it remain until *m*,
12:10 and what remains of it until *m*
12:22 the door of his house until *m*.
14:24 in the *m* watch, that the LORD
14:27 and when the *m* appeared,
16: 7 And in the *m* you shall see the
16: 8 and in the *m* bread to the full;
16:12 and in the *m* you shall be
16:13 and in the *m* the dew lay all
16:19 no one leave any of it till *m*.
16:20 of them left part of it until *m*,
16:21 So they gathered it every *m*,
16:23 remains, to be kept until *m*.
16:24 So they laid it up till *m*,
18:13 stood before Moses from *m*
18:14 people stand before you from *m*
19:16 pass on the third day, in the *m*,
23:18 of My sacrifice remain until *m*.
24: 4 And he rose early in the *m*,
27:21 tend it from evening until *m*
29:34 the bread, remains until the *m*,
29:39 lamb you shall offer in the *m*,
29:41 the drink offering, as in the *m*,
30: 7 on it sweet incense every *m*;
34: 2 "So be ready in the *m*,
34: 2 and come up in the *m* to Mount
34: 4 Then Moses rose early in the *m*
34:25 of the Passover be left until *m*.
36: 3 him freewill offerings every *m*.
Lev 6: 9 the altar all night until *m*,
6:12 shall burn wood on it every *m*,
6:20 half of it in the *m* and half of
7:15 not leave any of it until *m*.
9:17 the burnt sacrifice of the *m*.
19:13 with you all night until *m*.
22:30 shall leave none of it until *m*:
24: 3 of it from evening until *m*
Num 9:12 shall leave none of it until *m*,
9:15 from evening until *m* it was
9:21 only from evening until *m*:
9:21 the cloud was taken up in the *m*,
14:40 And they rose early in the *m* and
16: 5 Tomorrow *m* the LORD will show
22:13 So Balaam rose in the *m* and said
22:21 So Balaam rose in the *m*,
28: 4 lamb you shall offer in the *m*,
28: 8 as the *m* grain offering and its
28:23 the burnt offering of the *m*,
Deut 16: 4 remain overnight until *m*.
16: 7 and in the *m* you shall turn and
28:67 In the *m* you shall say, 'Oh,
28:67 that it were *m*!' because of the
Josh 3: 1 Then Joshua rose early in the *m*;
6:12 And Joshua rose early in the *m*,
7:14 In the *m* therefore you shall be
7:16 So Joshua rose early in the *m*
8:10 Joshua rose up early in the *m*
Judg 6:28 the city arose early in the *m*,
6:31 for him be put to death by *m*!
6:38 When he rose early the next *m*
9:33 soon as the sun is up in the *m*,
16: 2 all night, saying, "In the *m*,
19: 5 that they arose early in the *m*,
19: 8 Then he arose early in the *m* on
19:25 abused her all night until *m*;
19:27 When her master arose in the *m*,
20:19 of Israel rose in the *m* and
21: 4 So it was, on the next *m*,
Ruth 2: 7 came and has continued from *m*
3:13 and in the *m* it shall be that
3:13 LORD lives! Lie down until *m*.
3:14 So she lay at his feet until *m*,
1 Sam 1:19 Then they rose early in the *m*
3:15 So Samuel lay down until *m*,
5: 3 of Ashdod arose early in the *m*,
5: 4 they arose early the next *m*,
11:11 the midst of the camp in the *m*
14:36 and plunder them until the *m*
15:12 Samuel rose early in the *m* to
17:16 forty days, *m* and evening.
17:20 So David rose early in the *m*,
19: 2 please be on your guard until *m*,
19:11 him and to kill him in the *m*.
20:35 And so it was, in the *m*,
25:22 of all who belong to him by *m*
25:34 surely by *m* light no males
25:36 little or much, until *m* light.
25:37 So it was, in the *m*,
29:10 rise early in the *m* with your
29:10 as you are up early in the *m*
29:11 rose early to depart in the *m*,
2 Sam 2:27 surely then by *m* all the people
11:14 In the *m* it happened that David
17:22 By *m* light not one of them was
23: 4 be like the light of the *m*
23: 4 A *m* without clouds, Like the
24:11 Now when David arose in the *m*,
24:15 a plague upon Israel from the *m*
1 Ki 3:21 And when I rose in the *m* to
3:21 I had examined him in the *m*,
17: 6 him bread and meat in the *m*,
18:26 on the name of Baal from *m*
2 Ki 3:20 Now it happened in the *m*,
3:22 they rose up early in the *m*,
7: 9 If we wait until *m* light, some
10: 8 entrance of the gate until *m*.
10: 9 So it was, in the *m*,
16:15 the great new altar burn the *m*
19:35 people arose early in the *m*,
1 Chr 9:27 charge of opening it every *m*.
16:40 of burnt offering regularly *m*
23:30 to stand every *m* to thank and
2 Chr 2: 4 for the burnt offerings *m* and
13:11 they burn to the LORD every *m*
20:20 So they rose early in the *m* and
31: 3 for the *m* and evening burnt
Ezra 3: 3 both the *m* and evening burnt
Neh 8: 3 front of the Water Gate from *m*
Esth 2:14 and in the *m* she returned to
5:14 and in the *m* suggest to the
Job 1: 5 he would rise early in the *m*
3: 9 May the stars of its *m* be dark;
4:20 are broken in pieces from *m*
7:18 You should visit him every *m*,
11:17 dark, you would be like the *m*.
24:17 For the *m* is the same to them
38: 7 When the *m* stars sang together,
38:12 Have you commanded the *m* since
41:18 are like the eyelids of the *m*.
Ps 5: 3 voice You shall hear in the *m*,
5: 3 In the *m* I will direct it to
30: 5 But joy comes in the *m*.
49:14 dominion over them in the *m*;
55:17 and *m* and at noon
59:16 aloud of Your mercy in the *m*;
65: 8 make the outgoings of the *m*
73:14 And chastened every *m*.
88:13 And in the *m* my prayer comes
90: 5 In the *m* they are like grass
90: 6 In the *m* it flourishes and
92: 2 Your lovingkindness in the *m*,
110: 3 from the womb of the *m*,
119:147 before the dawning of the *m*,
130: 6 than those who watch for the *m*—
130: 6 than those who watch for the *m*.
139: 9 If I take the wings of the *m*,
143: 8 Your lovingkindness in the *m*,
Prov 7:18 take our fill of love until *m*;
27:14 voice, rising early in the *m*,
Eccl 10:16 your princes feast in the *m*!
11: 6 In the *m* sow your seed, And in
Song 6:10 is she who looks forth as the *m*,
Isa 5:11 those who rise early in the *m*,
14:12 son of the *m*! How you are cut
17:11 And in the *m* you will make
17:14 And before the *m*,
21:12 The *m* comes, and also the night.
28:19 For *m* by morning it will pass
28:19 For morning by *m* it will pass
33: 2 for You. Be their arm every *m*,
37:36 people arose early in the *m*,
38:13 I have considered until *m*—
50: 4 He awakens Me *m* by morning,
50: 4 He awakens Me morning by *m*,
58: 8 shall break forth like the *m*,
Jer 20:16 Let him hear the cry in the *m*
21:12 "Execute judgment in the *m*;
Lam 3:23 They are new every *m*;
Ezek 12: 8 And in the *m* the word of the
24:18 I spoke to the people in the *m*,
24:18 and the next *m* I did as I was
33:22 so when he came to me in the *m*,
46:13 you shall prepare it every *m*.
46:14 grain offering with it every *m*,
46:15 regular burnt offering every *m*.
Dan 6:19 king arose very early in the *m*
Hos 6: 3 forth is established as the *m*;
6: 4 your faithfulness is like a *m*
7: 6 In the *m* it burns like a
13: 3 they shall be like the *m* cloud
Joel 2: 2 Like the *m* clouds spread over
Am 4: 4 Bring your sacrifices every *m*,
4:13 And makes the *m* darkness,
5: 8 the shadow of death into *m*
Jon 4: 7 But as *m* dawned the next day God
Mic 2: 1 out evil on their beds! At *m*
Zeph 3: 3 That leave not a bone till *m*.
3: 5 Every *m* He brings His justice
Mt 16: 3 'and in the *m*, 'It will be
20: 1 who went out early in the *m* to
21:18 Now in the *m*, as He returned
27: 1 When *m* came, all the chief
Mk 1:35 Now in the *m*, having risen

11:20 Now in the **m**, as they passed
13:35 of the rooster, or in the **m**—
15: 1 Immediately, in the **m**,
16: 2 Very early in the **m**,
Lk 21:38 Then early in the **m** all the
24: 1 the week, very early in the **m**,
Jn 8: 2 Now early in the **m** He came again
18:28 Praetorium, and it was early **m**.
21: 4 But when the **m** had now come,
Acts 5:21 the temple early in the **m** and
28:23 from **m** till evening.
2 Pe 1:19 until the day dawns and the **m**
Rev 2:28 and I will give him the **m** star.
22:16 the Bright and **M** Star."

MORNINGS (1/1)

Dan 8:26 vision of the evenings and **m**

MORROW (KJV) See (NEXT) DAY, MORNING, TOMORROW

MORSEL (8/8)

Gen 18: 5 And I will bring a **m** of bread,
Judg 19: 5 Refresh your heart with a **m** of
1 Sam 2:36 for a piece of silver and a **m**
1 Ki 17:11 Please bring me a **m** of bread in
Job 31:17 Or eaten my **m** by myself,
Prov 17: 1 Better is a dry **m** with
23: 8 The **m** you have eaten, you will
Heb 12:16 who for one **m** of food sold his

MORSELS (1/1)

Ps 147:17 He casts out His hail like **m**;

MORTAL (9/9) MORTALITY, MORTALLY

Job 4:17 Can a **m** be more righteous than
10: 5 Your days like the days of a **m**
Isa 13:12 I will make a **m** more rare than
Rom 6:12 do not let sin reign in your **m**
8:11 will also give life to your **m**
1 Cor 15:53 and this **m** must put on
15:54 and this **m** has put on
2 Cor 4:11 also may be manifested in our **m**
Heb 7: 8 Here **m** men receive tithes, but

MORTALITY (1/1) MORTAL

2 Cor 5: 4 that **m** may be swallowed up by

MORTALLY (3/3) MORTAL

Deut 19:11 against him and strikes him **m**,
Ezek 30:24 groanings of a **m** wounded man.
Rev 13: 3 as if it had been **m** wounded,

MORTALS (1/1)

Ps 26: 4 have not sat with idolatrous **m**,

MORTAR (13/13)

Gen 11: 3 and they had asphalt for **m**.
Ex 1:14 bitter with hard bondage—in **m**,
Lev 14:42 and he shall take other **m** and
Num 11: 8 millstones or beat it in the **m**,
Prov 27:22 you grind a fool in a **m** with a
Isa 41:25 against princes as though **m**,
Ezek 13:10 plaster it with untempered **m**—
13:11 plaster it with untempered **m**,
13:12 Where is the **m** with which you
13:14 plastered with untempered **m**,
13:15 plastered it with untempered **m**;
22:28 them with untempered **m**,
Nah 3:14 into the clay and tread the **m**!

MORTER (KJV) See MORTAR

MORTGAGED (1/1)

Neh 5: 3 We have **m** our lands and

MORTIFY (KJV) See (PUT TO) DEATH

MOSAIC (1/1)

Esth 1: 6 of gold and silver on a **m**

MOSERAH (1/1)

Deut 10: 6 the wells of Bene Jaakan to **M**,

MOSEROTH (2/2)

Num 33:30 from Hashmonah and camped at **M**.
33:31 They departed from **M** and camped

MOSES (830/777) MOSES'

Ex 2:10 So she called his name **M**,
2:11 when **M** was grown, that he went
2:14 So **M** feared and said,
2:15 matter, he sought to kill **M**.
2:15 But **M** fled from the face of
2:17 but **M** stood up and helped them,
2:21 Then **M** was content to live with
2:21 gave Zipporah his daughter to **M**.
3: 1 Now **M** was tending the flock of
3: 3 Then **M** said, "I will now turn
3: 4 midst of the bush and said, "**M**,
3: 4 **M**!" And he said, "Here I
3: 6 And **M** hid his face, for he
3:11 But **M** said to God, "Who am I
3:13 Then **M** said to God, "Indeed,
3:14 And God said to **M**,
3:15 Moreover God said to **M**,
4: 1 Then **M** answered and said, "But
4: 3 and **M** fled from it.
4: 4 Then the LORD said to **M**,
4:10 Then **M** said to the LORD, "O
4:14 the LORD was kindled against **M**,
4:18 So **M** went and returned to
4:18 And Jethro said to **M**,
4:19 And the LORD said to **M** in
4:20 Then **M** took his wife and his
4:20 And **M** took the rod of God in
4:21 And the LORD said to **M**,
4:27 into the wilderness to meet **M**.
4:28 So **M** told Aaron all the words of
4:29 Then **M** and Aaron went and
4:30 which the LORD had spoken to **M**.
5: 1 Afterward **M** and Aaron went in
5: 4 **M** and Aaron, why do you take the
5:20 they met **M** and Aaron who stood
5:22 So **M** returned to the LORD and
6: 1 Then the LORD said to **M**,
6: 2 And God spoke to **M** and said to
6: 9 So **M** spoke thus to the children
6: 9 but they did not heed **M**,
6:10 And the LORD spoke to **M**,
6:12 And **M** spoke before the LORD,
6:13 Then the LORD spoke to **M** and
6:20 and she bore him Aaron and **M**.
6:26 are the same Aaron and **M** to
6:27 These are the same **M** and
6:28 on the day the LORD spoke to **M**
6:29 that the LORD spoke to **M**,
6:30 But **M** said before the LORD,
7: 1 So the LORD said to **M**:
7: 6 Then **M** and Aaron did so;
7: 7 And **M** was eighty years old and
7: 8 Then the LORD spoke to **M** and
7:10 So **M** and Aaron went in to
7:14 So the LORD said to **M**:
7:19 Then the LORD spoke to **M**,
7:20 And **M** and Aaron did so, just as
8: 1 And the LORD spoke to **M**,
8: 5 Then the LORD spoke to **M**,
8: 8 Then Pharaoh called for **M** and
8: 9 And **M** said to Pharaoh, "Accept
8:12 Then **M** and Aaron went out from
8:12 And **M** cried out to the LORD
8:13 did according to the word of **M**.
8:16 So the LORD said to **M**,
8:20 And the LORD said to **M**,
8:25 Then Pharaoh called for **M** and
8:26 And **M** said, "It is not right to
8:29 Then **M** said, "Indeed I am going
8:30 So **M** went out from Pharaoh and
8:31 did according to the word of **M**;
9: 1 Then the LORD said to **M**,
9: 8 So the LORD said to **M** and
9: 8 and let **M** scatter it toward the
9:10 and **M** scattered them toward
9:11 could not stand before **M**
9:12 as the LORD had spoken to **M**.
9:13 Then the LORD said to **M**,
9:22 Then the LORD said to **M**,
9:23 And **M** stretched out his rod
9:27 Pharaoh sent and called for **M**
9:29 So **M** said to him, "As soon as I
9:33 So **M** went out of the city from
9:35 as the LORD had spoken by **M**.
10: 1 Now the LORD said to **M**,
10: 3 So **M** and Aaron came in to
10: 8 So **M** and Aaron were brought
10: 9 And **M** said, "We will go with
10:12 Then the LORD said to **M**,
10:13 So **M** stretched out his rod over
10:16 Then Pharaoh called for **M** and
10:21 Then the LORD said to **M**,
10:22 So **M** stretched out his hand
10:24 Then Pharaoh called to **M** and
10:25 But **M** said, "You must also give
10:29 And **M** said, "You have spoken
11: 1 And the LORD said to **M**,
11: 3 Moreover the man **M** was very
11: 4 Then **M** said, "Thus says the
11: 9 But the LORD said to **M**,
11:10 So **M** and Aaron did all these
12: 1 Now the LORD spoke to **M** and
12:21 Then **M** called for all the
12:28 as the LORD had commanded **M**
12:31 Then he called for **M** and Aaron
12:35 done according to the word of **M**,
12:43 And the LORD said to **M** and
12:50 as the LORD commanded **M** and
13: 1 Then the LORD spoke to **M**,
13: 3 And **M** said to the people:
13:19 And **M** took the bones of Joseph
14: 1 Now the LORD spoke to **M**,
14:11 Then they said to **M**,
14:13 And **M** said to the people, "Do
14:15 And the LORD said to **M**,
14:21 Then **M** stretched out his hand
14:26 Then the LORD said to **M**,
14:27 And **M** stretched out his hand
14:31 the LORD and His servant **M**.
15: 1 Then **M** and the children of
15:22 So **M** brought Israel from the
15:24 the people complained against **M**,
16: 2 of Israel complained against **M**
16: 4 Then the LORD said to **M**,
16: 6 Then **M** and Aaron said to all the
16: 8 Also **M** said, "This shall be
16: 9 Then **M** spoke to Aaron, "Say to
16:11 And the LORD spoke to **M**,
16:15 And **M** said to them, "This is
16:19 And **M** said, "Let no one leave
16:20 they did not heed **M**.
16:20 And **M** was angry with them.
16:22 congregation came and told **M**.
16:24 as **M** commanded; and it did not
16:25 Then **M** said, "Eat that today,
16:28 And the LORD said to **M**,
16:32 Then **M** said, "This is the
16:33 And **M** said to Aaron, "Take a
16:34 As the LORD commanded **M**,
17: 2 the people contended with **M**,
17: 2 And **M** said to them, "Why do
17: 3 the people complained against **M**,
17: 4 So **M** cried out to the LORD,
17: 5 And the LORD said to **M**,
17: 6 And **M** did so in the sight of
17: 9 And **M** said to Joshua, "Choose
17:10 So Joshua did as **M** said to him,
17:10 and fought with Amalek. And **M**,
17:11 when **M** held up his hand, that
17:14 Then the LORD said to **M**,
17:15 And **M** built an altar and called
18: 1 of all that God had done for **M**
18: 5 his sons and his wife to **M** in
18: 6 Now he had said to **M**,
18: 7 So **M** went out to meet his
18: 8 And **M** told his father-in-law all
18:13 that **M** sat to judge the people;
18:13 and the people stood before **M**
18:15 And **M** said to his father-in-law,
18:24 So **M** heeded the voice of his
18:25 And **M** chose able men out of all
18:26 hard cases they brought to **M**,
18:27 Then **M** let his father-in-law
19: 3 And **M** went up to God, and the
19: 7 So **M** came and called for the
19: 8 So **M** brought back the words
19: 9 And the LORD said to **M**,
19: 9 So **M** told the words of the
19:10 Then the LORD said to **M**,
19:14 So **M** went down from the
19:17 And **M** brought the people out of
19:19 **M** spoke, and God answered him
19:20 And the LORD called **M** to the
19:20 the mountain, and **M** went up.
19:21 And the LORD said to **M**,
19:23 But **M** said to the LORD, "The
19:25 So **M** went down to the people and
20:19 Then they said to **M**,
20:20 And **M** said to the people, "Do
20:21 but **M** drew near the thick
20:22 Then the LORD said to **M**,
24: 1 Now He said to **M**, "Come up to
24: 2 And **M** alone shall come near the
24: 3 So **M** came and told the people
24: 4 And **M** wrote all the words of the
24: 6 And **M** took half the blood and
24: 8 And **M** took the blood, sprinkled
24: 9 Then **M** went up, also Aaron,
24:12 Then the LORD said to **M**,
24:13 So **M** arose with his assistant
24:13 and **M** went up to the mountain
24:15 Then **M** went up into the
24:16 the seventh day He called to **M**
24:18 So **M** went into the midst of the
24:18 And **M** was on the mountain forty
25: 1 Then the LORD spoke to **M**,
30:11 Then the LORD spoke to **M**,
30:17 Then the LORD spoke to **M**,
30:22 Moreover the LORD spoke to **M**,
30:34 And the LORD said to **M**:
31: 1 Then the LORD spoke to **M**,
31:12 And the LORD spoke to **M**,
31:18 He gave **M** two tablets of the
32: 1 Now when the people saw that **M**
32: 1 before us; for as for this **M**,
32: 7 And the LORD said to **M**,
32: 9 And the LORD said to **M**,
32:11 Then **M** pleaded with the LORD
32:15 And **M** turned and went down from
32:17 as they shouted, he said to **M**,
32:21 And **M** said to Aaron, "What did
32:23 go before us; as for this **M**,
32:25 Now when **M** saw that the people
32:26 then **M** stood in the entrance of
32:28 did according to the word of **M**.
32:29 Then **M** said, "Consecrate
32:30 to pass on the next day that **M**
32:31 Then **M** returned to the LORD and
32:33 And the LORD said to **M**,
33: 1 Then the LORD said to **M**,
33: 5 For the LORD had said to **M**,
33: 7 **M** took his tent and pitched it
33: 8 whenever **M** went out to the
33: 8 at his tent door and watched **M**
33: 9 when **M** entered the tabernacle,
33: 9 and the LORD talked with **M**.
33:11 So the LORD spoke to **M** face to
33:12 Then **M** said to the LORD,
33:17 So the LORD said to **M**,
34: 1 And the LORD said to **M**,
34: 4 Then **M** rose early in the
34: 8 So **M** made haste and bowed his
34:27 Then the LORD said to **M**,
34:29 when **M** came down from Mount
34:29 that **M** did not know that the

34:30 the children of Israel saw **M**,
34:31 Then **M** called to them, and Aaron
34:31 and **M** talked with them.
34:33 And when **M** had finished speaking
34:34 But whenever **M** went in before
34:35 of Israel saw the face of **M**,
34:35 then **M** would put the veil on
35: 1 Then **M** gathered all the
35: 4 And **M** spoke to all the
35:20 departed from the presence of **M**.
35:29 the LORD, by the hand of **M**,
35:30 And **M** said to the children of
36: 2 Then **M** called Bezalel and
36: 3 And they received from **M** all the
36: 5 and they spoke to **M**,
36: 6 So **M** gave a commandment, and
38:21 to the commandment of **M**,
38:22 that the LORD had commanded **M**.
39: 1 as the LORD had commanded **M**.
39: 5 as the LORD had commanded **M**.
39: 7 as the LORD had commanded **M**.
39:21 as the LORD had commanded **M**.
39:26 as the LORD had commanded **M**.
39:29 as the LORD had commanded **M**.
39:31 as the LORD had commanded **M**.
39:32 that the LORD had commanded **M**;
39:33 brought the tabernacle to **M**,
39:42 that the LORD had commanded **M**,
39:43 Then **M** looked over all the work,
39:43 And **M** blessed them.
40: 1 Then the LORD spoke to **M**,
40:16 Thus **M** did; according to all
40:18 So **M** raised up the tabernacle,
40:19 as the LORD had commanded **M**.
40:21 as the LORD had commanded **M**.
40:23 as the LORD had commanded **M**.
40:25 as the LORD had commanded **M**.
40:27 as the LORD had commanded **M**.
40:29 as the LORD had commanded **M**.
40:31 and **M**, Aaron, and his sons
40:32 as the LORD had commanded **M**.
40:33 So **M** finished the work.
40:35 And **M** was not able to enter the
Lev 1: 1 Now the LORD called to **M**,
4: 1 Now the LORD spoke to **M**,
5:14 Then the LORD spoke to **M**,
6: 1 And the LORD spoke to **M**,
6: 8 Then the LORD spoke to **M**,
6:19 And the LORD spoke to **M**,
6:24 And the LORD spoke to **M**,
7:22 And the LORD spoke to **M**,
7:28 Then the LORD spoke to **M**,
7:35 on the day when **M** presented
7:38 which the LORD commanded **M** on
8: 1 And the LORD spoke to **M**,
8: 4 So **M** did as the LORD commanded
8: 5 And **M** said to the congregation,
8: 6 Then **M** brought Aaron and his
8: 9 as the LORD had commanded **M**.
8:10 Also **M** took the anointing oil,
8:13 Then **M** brought Aaron's sons and
8:13 as the LORD had commanded **M**.
8:15 and **M** killed it. Then he took
8:16 and **M** burned them on the
8:17 as the LORD had commanded **M**.
8:19 and **M** killed it. Then he
8:20 and **M** burned the head,
8:21 And **M** burned the whole ram on
8:21 as the LORD had commanded **M**.
8:23 and **M** killed it. Also he took
8:24 And **M** put some of the blood on
8:24 And **M** sprinkled the blood all
8:28 Then **M** took them from their
8:29 And **M** took the breast and waved
8:29 as the LORD had commanded **M**.
8:30 Then **M** took some of the
8:31 And **M** said to Aaron and his
8:36 had commanded by the hand of **M**.
9: 1 pass on the eighth day that **M**
9: 5 So they brought what **M**
9: 6 Then **M** said, "This is the
9: 7 And **M** said to Aaron, "Go to the
9:10 as the LORD had commanded **M**.
9:21 as **M** had commanded.
9:23 And **M** and Aaron went into the
10: 3 And **M** said to Aaron, "This is
10: 4 And **M** called Mishael and
10: 5 out of the camp, as **M** had said.
10: 6 And **M** said to Aaron, and to
10: 7 did according to the word of **M**.
10:11 spoken to them by the hand of **M**.
10:12 And **M** spoke to Aaron, and to
10:16 Then **M** made careful inquiry
10:19 And Aaron said to **M**,
10:20 So when **M** heard that, he was
11: 1 Now the LORD spoke to **M** and
12: 1 Then the LORD spoke to **M**,
13: 1 And the LORD spoke to **M** and
14: 1 Then the LORD spoke to **M**,
14:33 And the LORD spoke to **M** and
15: 1 And the LORD spoke to **M** and
16: 1 Now the LORD spoke to **M** after
16: 2 and the LORD said to **M**:
16:34 he did as the LORD commanded **M**.
17: 1 And the LORD spoke to **M**,
18: 1 Then the LORD spoke to **M**,
19: 1 And the LORD spoke to **M**,
20: 1 Then the LORD spoke to **M**,
21: 1 And the LORD said to **M**,
21:16 And the LORD spoke to **M**,
21:24 And **M** told it to Aaron and his
22: 1 Then the LORD spoke to **M**,
22:17 And the LORD spoke to **M**,
22:26 And the LORD spoke to **M**,
23: 1 And the LORD spoke to **M**,
23: 9 And the LORD spoke to **M**,
23:23 Then the LORD spoke to **M**,
23:26 And the LORD spoke to **M**,
23:33 Then the LORD spoke to **M**,
23:44 So **M** declared to the children
24: 1 Then the LORD spoke to **M**,
24:11 and so they brought him to **M**.
24:13 And the LORD spoke to **M**,
24:23 Then **M** spoke to the children of
24:23 did as the LORD commanded **M**.
25: 1 And the LORD spoke to **M** on
26:46 on Mount Sinai by the hand of **M**.
27: 1 Now the LORD spoke to **M**,
27:34 which the LORD commanded **M**
Num 1: 1 Now the LORD spoke to **M** in the
1:17 Then **M** and Aaron took these men
1:19 As the LORD commanded **M**,
1:44 whom **M** and Aaron numbered, with
1:48 for the LORD had spoken to **M**,
1:54 all that the LORD commanded **M**,
2: 1 And the LORD spoke to **M** and
2:33 just as the LORD commanded **M**.
2:34 all that the LORD commanded **M**;
3: 1 are the records of Aaron and **M**
3: 1 when the LORD spoke with **M** on
3: 5 And the LORD spoke to **M**,
3:11 Then the LORD spoke to **M**,
3:14 Then the LORD spoke to **M** in
3:16 So **M** numbered them according to
3:38 tabernacle of meeting, were **M**,
3:39 whom **M** and Aaron numbered at
3:40 Then the LORD said to **M**:
3:42 So **M** numbered all the firstborn
3:44 Then the LORD spoke to **M**,
3:49 So **M** took the redemption money
3:51 And **M** gave their redemption
3:51 LORD, as the LORD commanded **M**.
4: 1 Then the LORD spoke to **M** and
4:17 Then the LORD spoke to **M** and
4:21 Then the LORD spoke to **M**,
4:34 And **M**, Aaron, and the leaders
4:37 whom **M** and Aaron numbered
4:37 of the LORD by the hand of **M**.
4:41 whom **M** and Aaron numbered
4:45 whom **M** and Aaron numbered
4:45 of the LORD by the hand of **M**.
4:46 numbered of the Levites, whom **M**,
4:49 were numbered by the hand of **M**,
4:49 him, as the LORD commanded **M**.
5: 1 And the LORD spoke to **M**,
5: 4 as the LORD spoke to **M**,
5: 5 Then the LORD spoke to **M**,
5:11 And the LORD spoke to **M**,
6: 1 Then the LORD spoke to **M**,
6:22 And the LORD spoke to **M**,
7: 1 when **M** had finished setting up
7: 4 Then the LORD spoke to **M**,
7: 6 So **M** took the carts and the
7:11 For the LORD said to **M**,
7:89 Now when **M** went into the
8: 1 And the LORD spoke to **M**,
8: 3 as the LORD commanded **M**.
8: 4 which the LORD had shown **M**,
8: 5 Then the LORD spoke to **M**,
8:20 Thus **M** and Aaron and all the
8:20 all that the LORD commanded **M**
8:22 as the LORD commanded **M**
8:23 Then the LORD spoke to **M**,
9: 1 Now the LORD spoke to **M** in the
9: 4 So **M** told the children of Israel
9: 5 all that the LORD commanded **M**,
9: 6 and they came before **M** and
9: 8 And **M** said to them, "Stand
9: 9 Then the LORD spoke to **M**,
9:23 of the LORD by the hand of **M**.
10: 1 And the LORD spoke to **M**,
10:13 of the LORD by the hand of **M**.
10:29 Now **M** said to Hobab the son of
10:31 So **M** said, "Please do not
10:35 that **M** said: "Rise up, O
11: 2 Then the people cried out to **M**,
11: 2 and when **M** prayed to the LORD,
11:10 Then **M** heard the people weeping
11:10 **M** also was displeased.
11:11 So **M** said to the LORD, "Why
11:16 So the LORD said to **M**:
11:21 And **M** said, "The people whom I
11:23 And the LORD said to **M**,
11:24 So **M** went out and told the
11:27 And a young man ran and told **M**,
11:28 **M** my lord, forbid them!"
11:29 Then **M** said to him, "Are you
11:30 And **M** returned to the camp,
12: 1 and Aaron spoke against **M**
12: 2 indeed spoken only through **M**?
12: 3 (Now the man **M** was very humble,
12: 4 Suddenly the LORD said to **M**,
12: 7 Not so with My servant **M**;
12: 8 To speak against My servant **M**?
12:11 So Aaron said to **M**,
12:13 So **M** cried out to the LORD,
12:14 Then the LORD said to **M**,
13: 1 And the LORD spoke to **M**,
13: 3 So **M** sent them from the
13:16 the names of the men whom **M**
13:16 And **M** called Hoshea the son of
13:17 Then **M** sent them to spy out the
13:26 departed and came back to **M**
13:30 quieted the people before **M**,
14: 2 of Israel complained against **M**
14: 5 Then **M** and Aaron fell on their
14:11 Then the LORD said to **M**:
14:13 And **M** said to the LORD: "Then
14:26 And the LORD spoke to **M** and
14:36 Now the men whom **M** sent to spy
14:39 Then **M** told these words to all
14:41 And **M** said, "Now why do you
14:44 the covenant of the LORD nor **M**
15: 1 And the LORD spoke to **M**,
15:17 Again the LORD spoke to **M**,
15:22 which the LORD has spoken to **M**—
15:23 commanded you by the hand of **M**,
15:33 sticks brought him to **M** and
15:35 Then the LORD said to **M**,
15:36 So, as the LORD commanded **M**,
15:37 Again the LORD spoke to **M**,
16: 2 and they rose up before **M** with
16: 3 gathered together against **M**
16: 4 So when **M** heard it, he fell on
16: 8 Then **M** said to Korah, "Hear
16:12 And **M** sent to call Dathan and
16:15 Then **M** was very angry, and said
16:16 And **M** said to Korah, "Tomorrow,
16:18 tabernacle of meeting with **M**
16:20 And the LORD spoke to **M** and
16:23 So the LORD spoke to **M**,
16:25 Then **M** rose and went to Dathan
16:28 And **M** said: "By this you shall
16:36 Then the LORD spoke to **M**,
16:40 LORD had said to him through **M**.
16:41 of Israel murmured against **M**
16:42 had gathered against **M** and
16:43 Then **M** and Aaron came before the
16:44 And the LORD spoke to **M**,
16:46 So **M** said to Aaron, "Take a
16:47 Then Aaron took it as **M**
16:50 So Aaron returned to **M** at the
17: 1 And the LORD spoke to **M**,
17: 6 So **M** spoke to the children of
17: 7 And **M** placed the rods before the
17: 8 to pass on the next day that **M**
17: 9 Then **M** brought out all the rods
17:10 And the LORD said to **M**,
17:11 Thus did **M**; just as the LORD
17:12 children of Israel spoke to **M**,
18:25 Then the LORD spoke to **M**,
19: 1 Now the LORD spoke to **M** and
20: 2 gathered together against **M**
20: 3 And the people contended with **M**
20: 6 So **M** and Aaron went from the
20: 7 Then the LORD spoke to **M**,
20: 9 So **M** took the rod from before
20:10 And **M** and Aaron gathered the
20:11 Then **M** lifted his hand and
20:12 Then the LORD spoke to **M** and
20:14 Now **M** sent messengers from
20:23 And the LORD spoke to **M** and
20:27 So **M** did just as the LORD
20:28 **M** stripped Aaron of his garments
20:28 Then **M** and Eleazar came down
21: 5 spoke against God and against **M**:
21: 7 Therefore the people came to **M**,
21: 7 So **M** prayed for the people.
21: 8 Then the LORD said to **M**,
21: 9 So **M** made a bronze serpent, and
21:16 well where the LORD said to **M**,
21:32 Then **M** sent to spy out Jazer;
21:34 Then the LORD said to **M**,
25: 4 Then the LORD said to **M**,
25: 5 So **M** said to the judges of
25: 6 woman in the sight of **M** and in
25:10 Then the LORD spoke to **M**,
25:16 Then the LORD spoke to **M**,
26: 1 that the LORD spoke to **M** and
26: 3 So **M** and Eleazar the priest
26: 4 just as the LORD commanded **M**
26: 9 who contended against **M** and
26:52 Then the LORD spoke to **M**,
26:59 to Amram she bore Aaron and **M**
26:63 those who were numbered by **M**
26:64 of those who were numbered by **M**
27: 2 And they stood before **M**,
27: 5 So **M** brought their case before
27: 6 And the LORD spoke to **M**,
27:11 just as the LORD commanded **M**.
27:12 Now the LORD said to **M**,
27:15 Then **M** spoke to the LORD,
27:18 And the LORD said to **M**:
27:22 So **M** did as the LORD commanded
27:23 commanded by the hand of **M**.
28: 1 Now the LORD spoke to **M**,
29:40 So **M** told the children of
29:40 just as the LORD commanded **M**.
30: 1 Then **M** spoke to the heads of the
30:16 which the LORD commanded **M**,
31: 1 And the LORD spoke to **M**,
31: 3 So **M** spoke to the people,
31: 6 Then **M** sent them to the war, one
31: 7 just as the LORD commanded **M**,
31:12 the booty, and the spoil to **M**,
31:13 And **M**, Eleazar the priest,
31:14 But **M** was angry with the
31:15 And **M** said to them: "Have you
31:21 law which the LORD commanded **M**:
31:25 Now the LORD spoke to **M**,
31:31 So **M** and Eleazar the priest did
31:31 did as the LORD commanded **M**.
31:41 So **M** gave the tribute which
31:41 as the LORD commanded **M**.
31:42 which **M** separated from the men
31:47 the children of Israel's half **M**

31:47 LORD, as the LORD commanded **M**.
31:48 of hundreds, came near to **M**;
31:49 and they said to **M**,
31:51 So **M** and Eleazar the priest
31:54 And **M** and Eleazar the priest
32: 2 of Reuben came and spoke to **M**,
32: 6 And **M** said to the children of
32:20 Then **M** said to them: "If you
32:25 children of Reuben spoke to **M**,
32:28 So **M** gave command concerning
32:29 And **M** said to them: "If the
32:33 So **M** gave to the children of
32:40 So **M** gave Gilead to Machir the
33: 1 armies under the hand of **M** and
33: 2 Now **M** wrote down the starting
33:50 Now the LORD spoke to **M** in the
34: 1 Then the LORD spoke to **M**,
34:13 Then **M** commanded the children
34:16 And the LORD spoke to **M**,
35: 1 And the LORD spoke to **M** in the
35: 9 Then the LORD spoke to **M**,
36: 1 came near and spoke before **M**
36: 2 LORD commanded my lord **M**
36: 5 Then **M** commanded the children
36:10 Just as the LORD commanded **M**,
36:13 of Israel by the hand of **M** in
Deut 1: 1 These are the words which **M**
1: 3 that **M** spoke to the children
1: 5 **M** began to explain this law,
4:41 Then **M** set apart three cities
4:44 Now this is the law which **M**
4:45 and the judgments which **M** spoke
4:46 whom **M** and the children of
5: 1 And **M** called all Israel, and
27: 1 Now **M**, with the elders
27: 9 Then **M** and the priests, the
27:11 And **M** commanded the people on
29: 1 which the LORD commanded **M** to
29: 2 Now **M** called all Israel and
31: 1 Then **M** went and spoke these
31: 7 Then **M** called Joshua and said
31: 9 So **M** wrote this law and
31:10 And **M** commanded them, saying:
31:14 Then the LORD said to **M**,
31:14 So **M** and Joshua went and
31:16 And the LORD said to **M**:
31:22 Therefore **M** wrote this song the
31:24 when **M** had completed writing
31:25 that **M** commanded the Levites,
31:30 Then **M** spoke in the hearing of
32:44 So **M** came with Joshua the son
32:45 **M** finished speaking all these
32:48 Then the LORD spoke to **M** that
33: 1 is the blessing with which **M**
33: 4 **M** commanded a law for us,
34: 1 Then **M** went up from the plains
34: 5 So **M** the servant of the LORD
34: 7 **M** was one hundred and twenty
34: 8 children of Israel wept for **M**
34: 8 of weeping and mourning for **M**
34: 9 for **M** had laid his hands on
34: 9 as the LORD had commanded **M**.
34:10 in Israel a prophet like **M**,
34:12 all the great terror which **M**
Josh 1: 1 After the death of **M** the
1: 2 **M** My servant is dead. Now
1: 3 have given you, as I said to **M**.
1: 5 of your life; as I was with **M**,
1: 7 to all the law which **M** My
1:13 Remember the word which **M** the
1:14 remain in the land which **M**
1:15 which **M** the LORD's servant
1:17 Just as we heeded **M** in all
1:17 be with you, as He was with **M**.
3: 7 may know that, as I was with **M**,
4:10 according to all that **M** had
4:12 as **M** had spoken to them.
4:14 him, as they had feared **M**,
8:31 as **M** the servant of the LORD
8:31 in the Book of the Law of **M**:
8:32 stones a copy of the law of **M**,
8:33 as **M** the servant of the LORD
8:35 was not a word of all that **M**
9:24 God commanded His servant **M** to
11:12 as **M** the servant of the LORD
11:15 As the LORD had commanded **M** his
11:15 so **M** commanded Joshua, and so
11:15 that the LORD had commanded **M**.
11:20 as the LORD had commanded **M**.
11:23 that the LORD had said to **M**;
12: 6 These **M** the servant of the LORD
12: 6 and **M** the servant of the LORD
13: 8 which **M** had given them, beyond
13: 8 as **M** the servant of the LORD
13:12 for **M** had defeated and cast out
13:15 And **M** had given to the tribe of
13:21 whom **M** had struck with the
13:24 **M** also had given an
13:29 **M** also had given an
13:32 These are the areas which **M**
13:33 But to the tribe of Levi **M** had
14: 2 had commanded by the hand of **M**,
14: 3 For **M** had given the inheritance
14: 5 As the LORD had commanded **M**,
14: 6 word which the LORD said to **M**
14: 7 I was forty years old when **M**
14: 9 So **M** swore on that day, saying,
14:10 the LORD spoke this word to **M**
14:11 this day as on the day that **M**
17: 4 The LORD commanded **M** to give us
18: 7 which **M** the servant of the
20: 2 which I spoke to you through **M**,
21: 2 The LORD commanded through **M** to
21: 8 had commanded by the hand of **M**.
22: 2 You have kept all that **M** the
22: 4 which **M** the servant of the
22: 5 and the law which **M** the
22: 7 to half the tribe of Manasseh **M**
22: 9 of the LORD by the hand of **M**.
23: 6 in the Book of the Law of **M**,
24: 5 Also I sent **M** and Aaron, and I
Judg 1:20 as **M** had said. Then he expelled
3: 4 their fathers by the hand of **M**.
4:11 of Hobab the father-in-law of **M**,
1 Sam 12: 6 is the LORD who raised up **M**
12: 8 then the LORD sent **M** and
1 Ki 2: 3 it is written in the Law of **M**,
8: 9 two tablets of stone which **M**
8:53 as You spoke by Your servant **M**,
8:56 promised through His servant **M**.
2 Ki 14: 6 in the Book of the Law of **M**,
18: 4 the bronze serpent that **M** had
18: 6 which the LORD had commanded **M**.
18:12 His covenant and all that **M**
21: 8 all the law that My servant **M**
23:25 according to all the Law of **M**;
1 Chr 6: 3 of Amram were Aaron, **M**,
6:49 according to all that **M** the
15:15 as **M** had commanded according to
21:29 offering, which **M** had made
22:13 with which the LORD charged **M**
23:13 The sons of Amram: Aaron and **M**;
23:14 Now the sons of **M** the man of God
23:15 The sons of **M** were Gershon and
26:24 son of Gershom, the son of **M**,
2 Chr 1: 3 which **M** the servant of the
5:10 except the two tablets which **M**
8:13 to the commandment of **M**,
23:18 it is written in the Law of **M**,
24: 6 to the commandment of **M** the
24: 9 LORD the collection that **M**
25: 4 in the Law in the Book of **M**,
30:16 according to the Law of **M** the
33: 8 the ordinances by the hand of **M**.
34:14 Law of the LORD given by **M**.
35: 6 of the LORD by the hand of **M**.
35:12 is written in the Book of **M**.
Ezra 3: 2 it is written in the Law of **M**
6:18 it is written in the Book of **M**.
7: 6 skilled scribe in the Law of **M**,
Neh 1: 7 You commanded Your servant **M**.
1: 8 You commanded Your servant **M**,
8: 1 bring the Book of the Law of **M**,
8:14 the LORD had commanded by **M**,
9:14 By the hand of **M** Your servant.
10:29 which was given by **M** the
13: 1 they read from the Book of **M**
Ps 77:20 like a flock By the hand of **M**
90: A Prayer of **M** the man of God.
99: 6 **M** and Aaron were among His
103: 7 He made known His ways to **M**,
105:26 He sent **M** His servant,
106:16 When they envied **M** in the camp,
106:23 Had not **M** His chosen one stood
106:32 So that it went ill with **M** on
Isa 63:11 **M** and his people, saying:
63:12 them by the right hand of **M**,
Jer 15: 1 Even if **M** and Samuel stood
Dan 9:11 oath written in the Law of **M**
9:13 it is written in the Law of **M**,
Mic 6: 4 And I sent before you **M**,
Mal 4: 4 "Remember the Law of **M**,
Mt 8: 4 and offer the gift that **M**
17: 3 **M** and Elijah appeared to them,
17: 4 one for You, one for **M**,
19: 7 Why then did **M** command to give a
19: 8 '**M**, because of the hardness of
22:24 **M** said that if a man dies,
Mk 1:44 cleansing those things which **M**
7:10 For **M** said, 'Honor your
9: 4 Elijah appeared to them with **M**,
9: 5 one for You, one for **M**,
10: 3 What did **M** command you?"
10: 4 **M** permitted a man to write a
12:19 **M** wrote to us that if a man's
12:26 you not read in the book of **M**,
Lk 2:22 according to the law of **M** were
5:14 just as **M** commanded."
9:30 who were **M** and Elijah,
9:33 one for You, one for **M**,
16:29 They have **M** and the prophets;
16:31 If they do not hear **M** and the
20:28 **M** wrote to us that if a man's
20:37 But even **M** showed in the
24:27 And beginning at **M** and all the
24:44 were written in the Law of **M**
Jn 1:17 For the law was given through **M**,
1:45 We have found Him of whom **M** in
3:14 And as **M** lifted up the serpent
5:45 there is one who accuses you—**M**,
5:46 "For if you believed **M**,
6:32 **M** did not give you the bread
7:19 Did not **M** give you the law, yet
7:22 **M** therefore gave you
7:22 (not that it is from **M**,
7:23 so that the law of **M** should not
8: 5 'Now **M**, in the law, commanded
9:29 "We know that God spoke to **M**;
Acts 3:22 For **M** truly said to the fathers,
6:11 blasphemous words against **M**
6:14 and change the customs which **M**
7:20 At this time **M** was born, and was
7:22 And **M** was learned in all the
7:29 **M** fled and became a dweller in
7:31 When **M** saw it, he marveled at
7:32 And **M** trembled and dared not
7:35 This **M** whom they rejected,
7:37 This is that **M** who said to the
7:40 as for this **M** who brought
7:44 instructing **M** to make it
13:39 be justified by the law of **M**.
15: 1 according to the custom of **M**,
15: 5 them to keep the law of **M**.
15:21 For **M** has had throughout many
21:21 among the Gentiles to forsake **M**,
26:22 those which the prophets and **M**
28:23 Jesus from both the Law of **M**
Rom 5:14 death reigned from Adam to **M**,
9:15 For He says to **M**, "I will
10: 5 For **M** writes about the
10:19 First **M** says: "I will
1 Cor 9: 9 it is written in the law of **M**,
10: 2 all were baptized into **M** in the
2 Cor 3: 7 look steadily at the face of **M**
3:13 unlike **M**, who put a veil
3:15 when **M** is read, a veil lies on
2 Tim 3: 8 Jannes and Jambres resisted **M**,
Heb 3: 2 as **M** also was faithful in all
3: 3 worthy of more glory than **M**,
3: 5 And **M** indeed was faithful in
3:16 came out of Egypt, led by **M**?
7:14 of which tribe **M** spoke nothing
8: 5 as **M** was divinely instructed
9:19 For when **M** had spoken every
11:23 By faith **M**, when he was born,
11:24 By faith **M**, when he became of
12:21 was the sight that **M** said,
Jude 9 he disputed about the body of **M**,
Rev 15: 3 They sing the song of **M**,

MOSES' (21/19) MOSES

Ex 4:25 of her son and cast it at **M** feet
17:12 But **M** hands became heavy; so
18: 1 **M** father-in-law, heard of all
18: 2 **M** father-in-law, took Zipporah,
18: 2 **M** wife, after he had sent her
18: 5 **M** father-in-law, came with his
18:12 **M** father-in-law, took a burnt
18:12 of Israel to eat bread with **M**
18:14 So when **M** father-in-law saw all
18:17 So **M** father-in-law said to him,
32:19 So **M** anger became hot, and he
34:29 of the Testimony were in **M**
34:35 that the skin of **M** face shone,
Lev 8:29 It was **M** part of the ram of
Num 10:29 **M** father-in-law, "We are
11:28 **M** assistant, one of his choice
Josh 1: 1 **M** assistant, saying:
Judg 1:16 **M** father-in-law, went up from
Mt 23: 2 and the Pharisees sit in **M**
Jn 9:28 but we are **M** disciples.
Heb 10:28 Anyone who has rejected **M** law

MOST (171/168)

Gen 14:18 he was the priest of God **M**
14:19 Blessed be Abram of God **M** High,
14:20 And blessed be God **M** High,
14:22 God **M** High, the Possessor of
Ex 26:33 the holy place and the **M** Holy.
26:34 ark of the Testimony in the **M**
29:37 And the altar shall be **m** holy.
30:10 It is **m** holy to the LORD."
30:29 that they may be **m** holy;
30:36 It shall be **m** holy to you.
40:10 The altar shall be **m** holy.
Lev 2: 3 It is **m** holy of the offerings
2:10 It is **m** holy of the offerings
6:17 it is **m** holy, like the sin
6:25 the LORD. It is **m** holy.
6:29 eat it. It is **m** holy.
7: 1 trespass offering (it is **m** holy)
7: 6 holy place. It is **m** holy.
10:12 for it is **m** holy.
10:17 since it is **m** holy, and God
14:13 offering. It is **m** holy.
21:22 both the **m** holy and the holy;
24: 9 for it is **m** holy to him from
27:28 devoted offering is **m** holy to
Num 4: 4 relating to the **m** holy
4:19 die when they approach the **m**
18: 9 shall be yours of the **m** holy
18: 9 shall be **m** holy for you and
18:10 In a **m** holy place you shall eat
24:16 the knowledge of the **M** High,
Deut 32: 8 When the **M** High divided their
33:24 Asher is **m** blessed of sons;
Judg 5:24 **M** blessed among women is Jael,
21:10 of their **m** valiant men,
2 Sam 22:14 And the **M** High uttered His
23:19 Was he not the **m** honored of
1 Ki 6:16 as the **M** Holy Place.
7:50 room (the **M** Holy Place)
8: 6 to the **M** Holy Place, under the
1 Chr 6:49 for all the work of the **M** Holy
23:13 sanctify the **m** holy things,
2 Chr 3: 8 And he made the **M** Holy Place.
3:10 In the **M** Holy Place he made two
4:22 inner doors to the **M** Holy Place,
5: 7 to the **M** Holy Place, under the
5:11 came out of the **M** Holy Place
31:14 LORD and the **m** holy things.
Ezra 2:63 not eat of the **m** holy things
Neh 7:65 they should not eat of the **m**
Esth 6: 9 of the king's **m** noble princes,

M

Job 34:17 condemn Him who is ***m*** just?
Ps 7:17 to the name of the LORD ***M*** High.
9: 2 praise to Your name, O ***M*** High.
18:13 And the ***M*** High uttered His
21: 6 For You have made him ***m*** blessed
21: 7 through the mercy of the ***M*** High
46: 4 of the tabernacle of the ***M*** High
47: 2 For the LORD ***M*** High is
50:14 pay your vows to the ***M*** High.
56: 2 fight against me, O ***M*** High.
57: 2 I will cry out to God ***M*** High,
73:11 there knowledge in the ***M*** High?
77:10 of the right hand of the ***M*** High.
78:17 By rebelling against the ***M*** High
78:35 And the ***M*** High God their
78:56 and provoked the ***M*** High God,
82: 6 of you are children of the ***M*** High.
83:18 Are the ***M*** High over all the
87: 5 And the ***M*** High Himself shall
91: 1 in the secret place of the ***M*** High
91: 9 Even the ***M*** High, your
92: 1 praises to Your name, O ***M*** High;
97: 9 are ***m*** high above all the
107:11 the counsel of the ***M*** High,
Prov 20: 6 ***M*** men will proclaim each his
Song 5:16 His mouth is ***m*** sweet, Yes, he
8: 6 A ***m*** vehement flame.
Isa 14:14 I will be like the ***M*** High.'
17: 6 five in its ***m*** fruitful branches,
26: 7 O ***M*** Upright, You weigh the
Jer 6:26 ***m*** bitter lamentation; For the
50:31 O ***m*** haughty one!" says the
50:32 The ***m*** proud shall stumble and
Lam 3:35 Before the face of the ***M*** High,
3:38 it not from the mouth of the ***M***
Ezek 23:12 Clothed ***m*** gorgeously,
28: 7 The ***m*** terrible of the nations;
30:11 the ***m*** terrible of the nations,
31:12 the ***m*** terrible of the nations,
32:12 all of them the ***m*** terrible of
33:28 will make the land ***m*** desolate,
33:29 when I have made the land ***m***
35: 3 And make you ***m*** desolate;
35: 7 make Mount Seir ***m*** desolate,
41: 4 This is the ***M*** Holy Place."
42:13 the LORD shall eat the ***m*** holy
42:13 There they shall lay the ***m*** holy
43:12 the mountaintop is ***m*** holy.
44:13 nor into the ***M*** Holy Place;
45: 3 the ***M*** Holy Place.
48:12 shall be to them a thing ***m*** holy
Dan 3:26 servants of the ***M*** High God,
4: 2 and wonders that the ***M*** High God
4:17 the living may know That the ***M***
4:24 this is the decree of the ***M*** High,
4:25 till you know that the ***M*** High
4:32 until you know that the ***M*** High
4:34 and I blessed the ***M*** High and
5:18 the ***M*** High God gave
5:21 till he knew that the ***M*** High
7:18 But the saints of the ***M*** High
7:22 of the saints of the ***M*** High,
7:25 words against the ***M*** High,
7:25 the saints of the ***M*** High,
7:27 the saints of the ***M*** High.
9:24 And to anoint the ***M*** Holy.
Hos 7:16 but not to the ***M*** High;
11: 7 Though they call to the ***M*** High
12:14 Him to anger ***m*** bitterly;
Am 2:16 The ***m*** courageous men of might
Mic 7: 4 The ***m*** upright is sharper
Mt 11:20 in which ***m*** of His mighty works
Mk 5: 7 Son of the ***M*** High God?
Lk 1: 3 ***m*** excellent Theophilus,
6:35 you will be sons of the ***M*** High.
8:28 Son of the ***M*** High God? I beg
Jn 1:51 ***M*** assuredly, I say to you,
3: 3 ***M*** assuredly, I say to you,
3: 5 ***M*** assuredly, I say to you,
3:11 ***M*** assuredly, I say to you, We
5:19 ***M*** assuredly, I say to you, the
5:24 ***M*** assuredly, I say to you, he
5:25 ***M*** assuredly, I say to you, the
6:26 ***M*** assuredly, I say to you, you
6:32 ***M*** assuredly, I say to you, Moses
6:47 ***M*** assuredly, I say to you, he
6:53 ***M*** assuredly, I say to you,
8:34 ***M*** assuredly, I say to you,
8:51 ***M*** assuredly, I say to you, if
8:58 ***M*** assuredly, I say to you,
10: 1 ***M*** assuredly, I say to you, he
10: 7 ***M*** assuredly, I say to you, I am
12:24 ***M*** assuredly, I say to you,
13:16 ***M*** assuredly, I say to you, a
13:20 ***M*** assuredly, I say to you, he
13:21 ***M*** assuredly, I say to you, one
13:38 ***M*** assuredly, I say to you, the
14:12 ***M*** assuredly, I say to you, he
16:20 ***M*** assuredly, I say to you that
16:23 ***M*** assuredly, I say to you,
21:18 ***M*** assuredly, I say to you, when
Acts 7:48 the ***M*** High does not dwell in
16:17 the servants of the ***M*** High God,
19:32 and ***m*** of them did not know why
20:38 sorrowing ***m*** of all for the words
23:26 to the ***m*** excellent governor
24: 3 ***m*** noble Felix, with all
26:25 ***m*** noble Festus, but speak the
1 Cor 10: 5 But with ***m*** of them God was not
14:27 let there be two or at the ***m***
15:19 are of all men the ***m*** pitiable.
2 Cor 11: 5 to the ***m*** eminent apostles.
12: 9 Therefore ***m*** gladly I will
12:11 in nothing was I behind the ***m***
Phil 1:14 and ***m*** of the brethren in the
Heb 7: 1 priest of the ***M*** High God, who
9:12 He entered the ***M*** Holy Place
9:25 priest enters the ***M*** Holy Place
Jude 20 yourselves up on your ***m*** holy
Rev 18:12 of object of ***m*** precious wood,
21:11 was like a ***m*** precious stone,

MOTE (KJV) See SPECK

MOTH (9/9) MOTH-EATEN

Job 4:19 Who are crushed before a ***m***?
27:18 He builds his house like a ***m***,
Ps 39:11 his beauty melt away like a ***m***;
Isa 50: 9 The ***m*** will eat them up.
51: 8 For the ***m*** will eat them up like
Hos 5:12 I will be to Ephraim like a ***m***,
Mt 6:19 where ***m*** and rust destroy and
6:20 where neither ***m*** nor rust
Lk 12:33 where no thief approaches nor ***m***

MOTH-EATEN (2/2) MOTH

Job 13:28 Like a garment that is ***m***.
Jas 5: 2 and your garments are ***m***.

MOTHER (240/225) GRANDMOTHER, MOTHER-IN-LAW, MOTHER'S, MOTHERS

Gen 2:24 shall leave his father and ***m***
3:20 because she was the ***m*** of all
17:16 and she shall be a ***m*** of
20:12 but not the daughter of my ***m***;
21:21 and his ***m*** took a wife for him
24:53 to her brother and to her ***m***.
24:55 But her brother and her ***m*** said,
24:60 may you become The ***m*** of
24:67 Isaac brought her into his ***m***
27:11 And Jacob said to Rebekah his ***m***,
27:13 But his ***m*** said to him, "Let
27:14 and brought them to his ***m***,
27:14 and his ***m*** made savory food,
28: 5 the ***m*** of Jacob and Esau.
28: 7 had obeyed his father and his ***m***
30:14 and brought them to his ***m*** Leah.
32:11 come and attack me and the ***m***
37:10 Shall your ***m*** and I and your
Ex 2: 8 went and called the child's ***m***.
20:12 "Honor your father and your ***m***,
21:15 who strikes his father or his ***m***
21:17 who curses his father or his ***m***
22:30 It shall be with its ***m*** seven
Lev 18: 7 or the nakedness of your ***m*** you
18: 7 not uncover. She is your ***m***;
18: 9 or the daughter of your ***m***,
18:13 she is near of kin to your ***m***.
19: 3 one of you shall revere his ***m***
20: 9 who curses his father or his ***m***
20: 9 has cursed his father or his ***m***.
20:14 a man marries a woman and her ***m***,
21: 2 who are nearest to him: his ***m***,
21:11 himself for his father or his ***m***;
22:27 shall be seven days with its ***m***;
Num 6: 7 even for his father or his ***m***,
Deut 5:16 'Honor your father and your ***m***,
13: 6 your brother, the son of your ***m***,
21:13 and mourn her father and her ***m***
21:18 father or the voice of his ***m***,
21:19 then his father and his ***m*** shall
22: 6 with the ***m*** sitting on the young
22: 6 you shall not take the ***m*** with
22: 7 you shall surely let the ***m*** go,
22:15 then the father and ***m*** of the
27:16 who treats his father or his ***m***
27:22 father or the daughter of his ***m***.
33: 9 Who says of his father and ***m***,
Josh 2:13 "and spare my father, my ***m***,
2:18 you bring your father, your ***m***,
6:23 out Rahab, her father, her ***m***,
Judg 5: 7 Arose a ***m*** in Israel.
5:28 The ***m*** of Sisera looked through
8:19 my brothers, the sons of my ***m***.
14: 2 up and told his father and ***m***,
14: 3 Then his father and ***m*** said to
14: 4 But his father and ***m*** did not
14: 5 to Timnah with his father and ***m***,
14: 6 not tell his father or his ***m***
14: 9 he came to his father and ***m***,
14:16 it to my father or my ***m***;
17: 2 And he said to his ***m***,
17: 2 And his ***m*** said, "May you
17: 3 shekels of silver to his ***m***,
17: 3 his ***m*** said, "I had wholly
17: 4 he returned the silver to his ***m***.
17: 4 Then his ***m*** took two hundred
Ruth 2:11 left your father and your ***m***
1 Sam 2:19 Moreover his ***m*** used to make him
15:33 so shall your ***m*** be childless
22: 3 Please let my father and ***m*** come
2 Sam 17:25 sister of Zeruiah, Joab's ***m***.
19:37 the grave of my father and ***m***.
20:19 seek to destroy a city and a ***m***
1 Ki 1: 6 His ***m*** had borne him after
1:11 spoke to Bathsheba the ***m*** of
2:13 came to Bathsheba the ***m*** of
2:19 a throne set for the king's ***m***;
2:20 said to her, "Ask it, my ***m***,
2:22 answered and said to his ***m***,
3:27 means kill him; she is his ***m***.
15:13 grandmother from being queen ***m***,
17:23 house, and gave him to his ***m***.
19:20 let me kiss my father and my ***m***,
22:52 father and in the way of his ***m***
2 Ki 3: 2 but not like his father and ***m***;
3:13 and the prophets of your ***m***.
4:19 a servant, "Carry him to his ***m***.
4:20 him and brought him to his ***m***,
4:30 And the ***m*** of the child said,
9:22 as the harlotries of your ***m***
10:13 and the sons of the queen ***m***.
11: 1 When Athaliah the ***m*** of Ahaziah
24:12 Jehoiachin king of Judah, his ***m***,
24:15 to Babylon. The king's ***m***,
1 Chr 2:26 she was the ***m*** of Onam.
4: 9 and his ***m*** called his name
2 Chr 15:16 the ***m*** of Asa the king, from
15:16 the king, from being queen ***m***,
22: 3 for his ***m*** advised him to do
22:10 Now when Athaliah the ***m*** of
Esth 2: 7 she had neither father nor ***m***.
2: 7 When her father and ***m*** died,
Job 17:14 You are my ***m*** and my sister,'
Ps 27:10 When my father and my ***m*** forsake
35:14 as one who mourns for his ***m***.
51: 5 And in sin my ***m*** conceived me.
109:14 And let not the sin of his ***m***
113: 9 Like a joyful ***m*** of children.
131: 2 Like a weaned child with his ***m***;
Prov 1: 8 not forsake the law of your ***m***;
4: 3 only one in the sight of my ***m***,
6:20 not forsake the law of your ***m***.
10: 1 son is the grief of his ***m***.
15:20 a foolish man despises his ***m***.
19:26 father and chases away his ***m***
20:20 curses his father or his ***m***,
23:22 And do not despise your ***m*** when
23:25 Let your father and your ***m*** be
28:24 robs his father or his ***m***,
29:15 himself brings shame to his ***m***.
30:11 And does not bless its ***m***.
30:17 And scorns obedience to his ***m***,
31: 1 the utterance which his ***m***
Song 3: 4 him to the house of my ***m***,
3:11 the crown With which his ***m***
6: 9 The only one of her ***m***,
8: 2 Into the house of my ***m***,
8: 5 There your ***m*** brought you
Isa 8: 4 to cry 'My father' and 'My ***m***,
49: 1 From the matrix of My ***m*** He has
50: 1 for your transgressions your ***m***
66:13 As one whom his ***m*** comforts,
Jer 13:18 to the king and to the queen ***m***,
15: 8 Against the ***m*** of the young
15:10 Woe is me, my ***m***,
16: 7 for their father or their ***m***.
20:14 not be blessed in which my ***m***
20:17 That my ***m*** might have been my
22:26 and your ***m*** who bore you, into
29: 2 Jeconiah the king, the queen ***m***,
50:12 Your ***m*** shall be deeply ashamed;
Ezek 16: 3 was an Amorite and your ***m*** a
16:44 proverb against you: 'Like ***m***,
16:45 your ***m*** was a Hittite and your
19: 2 "and say: 'What is your ***m***?
19:10 Your ***m*** was like a vine in your
22: 7 have made light of father and ***m***;
23: 2 The daughters of one ***m***.
44:25 person. Only for father or ***m***,
Hos 2: 2 charges against your ***m***,
2: 5 For their ***m*** has played the
4: 5 And I will destroy your ***m***.
10:14 A ***m*** dashed in pieces upon her
Mic 7: 6 Daughter rises against her ***m***,
Zech 13: 3 then his father and ***m*** who begot
13: 3 And his father and ***m*** who begot
Mt 1:18 After His ***m*** Mary was betrothed
2:11 the young Child with Mary His ***m***,
2:13 take the young Child and His ***m***,
2:14 took the young Child and His ***m***
2:20 take the young Child and His ***m***,
2:21 took the young Child and His ***m***,
8:14 He saw his wife's ***m*** lying sick
10:35 a daughter against her ***m***,
10:37 He who loves father or ***m*** more
12:46 His ***m*** and brothers stood
12:47 Your ***m*** and Your brothers are
12:48 Who is My ***m*** and who are My
12:49 Here are My ***m*** and My brothers!
12:50 is My brother and sister and ***m***.
13:55 Is not His ***m*** called Mary?
14: 8 having been prompted by her ***m***,
14:11 and she brought it to her ***m***.
15: 4 your father and your ***m***';
15: 4 who curses father or ***m***,
15: 5 says to his father or ***m***,
15: 6 need not honor his father or ***m***.
19: 5 leave his father and ***m***
19:19 your father and your ***m***,
19:29 or sisters or father or ***m*** or
20:20 Then the ***m*** of Zebedee's sons
27:56 Mary the ***m*** of James and Joses,
27:56 and the ***m*** of Zebedee's sons.
Mk 1:30 But Simon's wife's ***m*** lay sick
3:31 Then His brothers and His ***m***
3:32 Your ***m*** and Your brothers are
3:33 them, saying, "Who is My ***m***,
3:34 Here are My ***m*** and My brothers!
3:35 My brother and My sister and ***m***.
5:40 He took the father and the ***m*** of
6:24 she went out and said to her ***m***,

6:28 and the girl gave it to her **m**.
7:10 your father and your **m**';
7:10 who curses father or **m**,
7:11 a man says to his father or **m**,
7:12 for his father or his **m**,
10: 7 leave his father and **m**
10:19 your father and your **m**.
10:29 or sisters or father or **m** or
15:40 Mary the **m** of James the Less
15:47 Magdalene and Mary the **m** of
16: 1 Mary the **m** of James, and
Lk 1:43 that the **m** of my Lord should
1:60 His **m** answered and said, "No;
2:33 And Joseph and His **m** marveled at
2:34 them, and said to Mary His **m**,
2:43 And Joseph and His **m** did not
2:48 and His **m** said to Him, "Son,
2:51 but His **m** kept all these things
4:38 But Simon's wife's **m** was sick
7:12 out, the only son of his **m**;
7:15 And He presented him to his **m**.
8:19 Then His **m** and brothers came to
8:20 Your **m** and Your brothers are
8:21 My **m** and My brothers are these
8:51 and the father and **m** of the
12:53 **m** against daughter and daughter
12:53 daughter and daughter against **m**,
14:26 does not hate his father and **m**,
18:20 your father and your **m**.
24:10 Mary the **m** of James, and the
Jn 2: 1 and the **m** of Jesus was there.
2: 3 the **m** of Jesus said to Him,
2: 5 His **m** said to the servants,
2:12 down to Capernaum, He, His **m**,
6:42 whose father and **m** we know?
19:25 by the cross of Jesus His **m**,
19:26 When Jesus therefore saw His **m**,
19:26 standing by, He said to His **m**,
19:27 Behold your **m**!" And from that
Acts 1:14 with the women and Mary the **m**
12:12 the **m** of John whose surname was
Rom 16:13 and his **m** and mine.
Gal 4:26 which is the **m** of us all.
Eph 5:31 leave his father and **m**
6: 2 "Honor your father and **m**,
1 Th 2: 7 just as a nursing **m** cherishes
2 Tim 1: 5 grandmother Lois and your **m**
Heb 7: 3 without father, without **m**,
Rev 17: 5 THE **M** OF HARLOTS AND OF THE

MOTHER-IN-LAW (15/13) MOTHER

Deut 27:23 is the one who lies with his **m**.
Ruth 1:14 again; and Orpah kissed her **m**,
2:11 that you have done for your **m**
2:18 and her **m** saw what she had
2:19 And her **m** said to her, "Where
2:19 So she told her **m** with whom
2:23 and she dwelt with her **m**.
3: 1 Then Naomi her **m** said to her,
3: 6 did according to all that her **m**
3:16 So when she came to her **m**,
3:17 not go empty-handed to your **m**.
Mic 7: 6 Daughter-in-law against her **m**;
Mt 10:35 against her **m**';
Lk 12:53 **m** against her daughter-in-law
12:53 daughter-in-law against her **m**.

MOTHER'S (73/69) MOTHER

Gen 24:28 ran and told her **m** household
24:67 comforted after his **m** death.
27:29 And let your **m** sons bow down
28: 2 house of Bethuel your **m** father;
28: 2 of Laban your **m** brother.
29:10 of Laban his **m** brother,
29:10 and the sheep of Laban his **m**
29:10 flock of Laban his **m** brother.
43:29 his **m** son, and said, "Is this
44:20 alone is left of his **m** children,
Ex 23:19 boil a young goat in its **m** milk.
34:26 not boil a young goat in its **m** milk.
Lev 18:13 the nakedness of your **m** sister,
20:17 his father's daughter or his **m**
20:19 the nakedness of your **m** sister
24:11 (His **m** name was Shelomith the
Num 12:12 he comes out of his **m** womb!
Deut 14:21 boil a young goat in its **m** milk.
Judg 9: 1 to his **m** brothers, and spoke
9: 1 of the house of his **m** father,
9: 3 And his **m** brothers spoke all
16:17 Nazirite to God from my **m** womb.
Ruth 1: 8 return each to her **m** house. The
1 Sam 20:30 the shame of your **m** nakedness?
1 Ki 11:26 whose **m** name was Zeruah, a
14:21 His **m** name was Naamah, an
14:31 His **m** name was Naamah, an
15: 2 His **m** name was Maachah the
22:42 His **m** name was Azubah the
2 Ki 8:26 His **m** name was Athaliah the
12: 1 His **m** name was Zibiah of
14: 2 His **m** name was Jehoaddan of
15: 2 His **m** name was Jecholiah of
15:33 His **m** name was Jerusha the
18: 2 His **m** name was Abi the
21: 1 His **m** name was Hephzibah.
21:19 His **m** name was Meshullemeth
22: 1 His **m** name was Jedidah the
23:31 His **m** name was Hamutal the
23:36 His **m** name was Zebudah the
24: 8 His **m** name was Nehushta the
24:18 His **m** name was Hamutal the
2 Chr 12:13 His **m** name was Naamah, an
13: 2 His **m** name was Michaiah the
20:31 His **m** name was Azubah the
22: 2 His **m** name was Athaliah the
24: 1 His **m** name was Zibiah of
25: 1 His **m** name was Jehoaddan of
26: 3 His **m** name was Jecholiah of
27: 1 His **m** name was Jerushah the
29: 1 His **m** name was Abijah the
Job 1:21 Naked I came from my **m** womb,
3:10 shut up the doors of my **m** womb,
31:18 And from my **m** womb I guided
Ps 22: 9 Me trust while on My **m** breasts.
22:10 From My **m** womb You have
50:20 You slander your own **m** son.
69: 8 And an alien to my **m** children;
71: 6 He who took me out of my **m** womb.
139:13 You covered me in my **m** womb.
Eccl 5:15 As he came from his **m** womb,
Song 1: 6 My **m** sons were angry with me;
8: 1 Who nursed at my **m** breasts!
Isa 50: 1 certificate of your **m** divorce,
Jer 52: 1 His **m** name was Hamutal the
Ezek 16:45 You are your **m** daughter,
Mt 19:12 were born thus from their **m**
Lk 1:15 even from his **m** womb.
Jn 3: 4 a second time into his **m** womb
19:25 and His **m** sister, Mary the
Acts 3: 2 man lame from his **m** womb
14: 8 a cripple from his **m** womb, who
Gal 1:15 who separated me from my **m** womb

MOTHERS (7/7) MOTHER

Isa 49:23 their queens your nursing **m**;
Jer 16: 3 and concerning their **m** who bore
Lam 2:12 They say to their **m**,
5: 3 Our **m** are like widows.
Mk 10:30 and brothers and sisters and **m**
1 Tim 1: 9 of fathers and murderers of **m**,
5: 2 older women as **m**,

MOTHERS' (1/1)

Lam 2:12 life is poured out In their **m**

MOTIONED (3/3)

Jn 13:24 Simon Peter therefore **m** to him
Acts 19:33 And Alexander **m** with his hand,
21:40 Paul stood on the stairs and **m**

MOTIONING (2/2)

Acts 12:17 But **m** to them with his hand to
13:16 and **m** with his hand said,

MOUND (12/12) MOUNDS

2 Sam 20:15 and they cast up a siege **m**
2 Ki 19:32 Nor build a siege **m** against
Isa 29: 3 lay siege against you with a **m**,
37:33 Nor build a siege **m** against
Jer 6: 6 And build a **m** against
30:18 shall be built upon its own **m**,
49: 2 It shall be a desolate **m**,
Ezek 4: 2 and heap up a **m** against it; set
17:17 when they heap up a siege **m** and
21:22 gates, to heap up a siege **m**,
26: 8 he will heap up a siege **m**
Dan 11:15 shall come and build a siege **m**,

MOUNDS (4/4) MOUND

Josh 11:13 cities that stood on their **m**,
Jer 32:24 the siege **m**! They have come to
33: 4 fortify against the siege **m**
Hab 1:10 For they heap up earthen **m**

MOUNT (154/148) MOUNTAIN

Gen 22:14 In the **M** of The LORD it shall
36: 8 So Esau dwelt in **M** Seir.
36: 9 of the Edomites in **M** Seir.
Ex 19:11 will come down upon **M** Sinai
19:18 Now **M** Sinai was completely in
19:20 LORD came down upon **M** Sinai
19:23 cannot come up to **M** Sinai
24:16 of the LORD rested on **M** Sinai
31:18 speaking with him on **M** Sinai
33: 6 of their ornaments by **M** Horeb.
34: 2 up in the morning to **M** Sinai
34: 4 morning and went up **M** Sinai
34:29 Moses came down from **M** Sinai
34:32 spoken with him on **M** Sinai
Lev 7:38 commanded Moses on **M** Sinai
25: 1 spoke to Moses on **M** Sinai
26:46 children of Israel on **M** Sinai
27:34 children of Israel on **M** Sinai
Num 3: 1 spoke with Moses on **M** Sinai
20:22 from Kadesh and came to **M** Hor.
20:23 to Moses and Aaron in **M** Hor
20:25 and bring them up to **M** Hor;
20:27 and they went up to **M** Hor in
21: 4 Then they journeyed from **M** Hor
27:12 Go up into this **M** Abarim, and
28: 6 which was ordained at **M** Sinai
33:23 and camped at **M** Shepher.
33:24 They moved from **M** Shepher and
33:37 Kadesh and camped at **M** Hor
33:38 the priest went up to **M** Hor
33:39 old when he died on **M** Hor.
33:41 So they departed from **M** Hor and
34: 7 out your border line to **M** Hor;
34: 8 from **M** Hor you shall mark out
Deut 1: 2 from Horeb by way of **M** Seir to
2: 1 and we skirted **M** Seir for many
2: 5 because I have given **M** Seir to
3: 8 the River Arnon to **M** Hermon
4:48 even to **M** Sion (that is,
11:29 put the blessing on **M** Gerizim
11:29 and the curse on **M** Ebal.
27: 4 that on **M** Ebal you shall set
27:12 These shall stand on **M** Gerizim
27:13 and these shall stand on **M** Ebal
32:49 **M** Nebo, which is in the land
32:50 your brother died on **M** Hor
33: 2 He shone forth from **M** Paran,
34: 1 the plains of Moab to **M** Nebo
Josh 8:30 LORD God of Israel in **M** Ebal,
8:33 were in front of **M** Gerizim
8:33 half of them in front of **M** Ebal
11:17 from **M** Halak and the ascent to
11:17 of Lebanon below **M** Hermon.
12: 1 River Arnon to **M** Hermon,
12: 5 and reigned over **M** Hermon, over
12: 7 of Lebanon as far as **M** Halak
13: 5 from Baal Gad below **M** Hermon as
13:11 all **M** Hermon, and all Bashan as
15: 9 to the cities of **M** Ephron.
15:10 westward from Baalah to **M** Seir,
15:10 along to the side of **M** Jearim
15:11 passed along to **M** Baalah, and
19:26 it reached to **M** Carmel
24:30 on the north side of **M** Gaash.
Judg 1:35 determined to dwell in **M** Heres,
2: 9 on the north side of **M** Gaash.
3: 3 Hivites who dwelt in **M** Lebanon
3: 3 from **M** Baal Hermon to the
4: 6 and deploy troops at **M** Tabor;
4:12 Abinoam had gone up to **M** Tabor
4:14 Barak went down from **M** Tabor
7: 3 depart at once from **M** Gilead
9: 7 and stood on top of **M** Gerizim
9:48 Abimelech went up to **M** Zalmon
1 Sam 31: 1 and fell slain on **M** Gilboa.
31: 8 three sons fallen on **M** Gilboa
2 Sam 1: 6 by chance to be on **M** Gilboa,
15:30 the Ascent of the **M** of Olives
1 Ki 18:19 all Israel to me on **M** Carmel
18:20 prophets together on **M** Carmel
2 Ki 2:25 went from there to **M** Carmel
4:25 to the man of God at **M** Carmel
19:31 those who escape from **M** Zion
23:13 south of the **M** of Corruption
1 Chr 4:42 went to **M** Seir, having as their
5:23 that is, to Senir, or **M** Hermon.
10: 1 and fell slain on **M** Gilboa.
10: 8 and his sons fallen on **M** Gilboa
2 Chr 3: 1 LORD at Jerusalem on **M** Moriah,
13: 4 Abijah stood on **M** Zemaraim
20:10 and **M** Seir—whom You would not
20:22 and **M** Seir, who had come
20:23 the inhabitants of **M** Seir
33:15 that he had built in the **m** of
Neh 9:13 You came down also on **M** Sinai,
Job 39:27 Does the eagle **m** up at your
Ps 48: 2 Is **M** Zion on the sides of
48:11 Let **M** Zion rejoice, Let the
74: 2 This **M** Zion where You have
78:68 **M** Zion which He loved.
107:26 They **m** up to the heavens,
125: 1 in the LORD Are like **M** Zion,
Song 4: 1 Going down from **M** Gilead.
7: 5 head crowns you like **M** Carmel
Isa 4: 5 every dwelling place of **M** Zion,
8:18 Who dwells in **M** Zion.
9:18 They shall **m** up like rising
10:12 performed all His work on **M** Zion
10:32 will shake his fist at the **m**
14:13 I will also sit on the **m** of
16: 1 To the **m** of the daughter of
18: 7 of hosts, To **M** Zion.
24:23 of hosts will reign On **M** Zion
27:13 the LORD in the holy **m** at
28:21 will rise up as at **M** Perazim,
29: 8 Who fight against **M** Zion."
31: 4 come down To fight for **M** Zion
37:32 those who escape from **M** Zion
40:31 They shall **m** up with wings
Jer 4:15 affliction from **M** Ephraim:
31: 6 will cry on **M** Ephraim,
46: 4 And **m** up, you horsemen!
50:19 be satisfied on **M** Ephraim
51:53 Though Babylon were to **m** up to
Lam 5:18 Because of **M** Zion which is
Ezek 10:16 lifted their wings to **m** up
35: 2 set your face against **M** Seir
35: 3 O **M** Seir, I am against you;
35: 7 Thus I will make **M** Seir most
35:15 O **M** Seir, as well as all of
Joel 2:32 For in **M** Zion and in Jerusalem
Am 6: 1 And trust in **M** Samaria,
Ob 17 But on **M** Zion there shall be
21 saviors shall come to **M** Zion
Mic 4: 7 will reign over them in **M** Zion
Hab 3: 3 The Holy One from **M** Paran.
Zech 14: 4 will stand on the **M** of Olives
14: 4 And the **M** of Olives shall be
Mt 21: 1 at the **M** of Olives, then Jesus
24: 3 He sat on the **M** of Olives
26:30 out to the **M** of Olives
Mk 11: 1 at the **M** of Olives, He sent two
13: 3 He sat on the **M** of Olives
14:26 went out to the **M** of Olives.

Lk	19:37	descent of the ***M*** of Olives,
	22:39	He went to the ***M*** of Olives, as
Jn	8: 1	Jesus went to the ***M*** of Olives.
Acts	1:12	from the ***m*** called Olivet,
	7:30	in the wilderness of ***M*** Sinai.
	7:38	who spoke to him on ***M*** Sinai
Gal	4:24	the one from ***M*** Sinai which
	4:25	for this Hagar is ***M*** Sinai in
Heb	12:22	But you have come to ***M*** Zion and
Rev	14: 1	a Lamb standing on ***M*** Zion, and

MOUNTAIN (202/181) MOUNT, MOUNTAINS

Gen	10:30	the ***m*** of the east.
	12: 8	he moved from there to the ***m***
	14: 6	and the Horites in their ***m*** of
	31:54	offered a sacrifice on the ***m***,
	31:54	and stayed all night on the ***m***.
Ex	3: 1	to Horeb, the ***m*** of God.
	3:12	you shall serve God on this ***m***.
	4:27	So he went and met him on the ***m***
	15:17	in and plant them In the ***m*** of
	18: 5	where he was encamped at the ***m***
	19: 2	camped there before the ***m***.
	19: 3	LORD called to him from the ***m***,
	19:12	you do not go up to the ***m*** or
	19:12	Whoever touches the ***m*** shall
	19:13	they shall come near the ***m***.
	19:14	So Moses went down from the ***m***
	19:16	and a thick cloud on the ***m***;
	19:17	they stood at the foot of the ***m***.
	19:18	and the whole ***m*** quaked greatly.
	19:20	Sinai, on the top of the ***m***.
	19:20	Moses to the top of the ***m***,
	19:23	Set bounds around the ***m*** and
	20:18	and the ***m*** smoking; and when the
	24: 4	an altar at the foot of the ***m***,
	24:12	Come up to Me on the ***m*** and be
	24:13	and Moses went up to the ***m*** of
	24:15	Then Moses went up into the ***m***,
	24:15	and a cloud covered the ***m***.
	24:17	fire on the top of the ***m*** in
	24:18	cloud and went up into the ***m***.
	24:18	And Moses was on the ***m*** forty
	25:40	which was shown you on the ***m***.
	26:30	which you were shown on the ***m***.
	27: 8	as it was shown you on the ***m***,
	32: 1	delayed coming down from the ***m***,
	32:15	turned and went down from the ***m***,
	32:19	broke them at the foot of the ***m***.
	34: 2	to Me there on the top of the ***m***.
	34: 3	be seen throughout all the ***m***;
	34: 3	nor herds feed before that ***m***.
	34:29	when he came down from the ***m***),
Num	10:33	So they departed from the ***m*** of
	14:40	and went up to the top of the ***m***,
	14:45	Canaanites who dwelt in that ***m***
	20:28	died there on the top of the ***m***.
	20:28	Eleazar came down from the ***m***.
Deut	1: 6	dwelt long enough at this ***m***.
	1:41	were ready to go up into the ***m***.
	1:43	went up into the ***m***.
	1:44	Amorites who dwelt in that ***m***
	2: 3	You have skirted this ***m*** long
	4:11	and stood at the foot of the ***m***,
	4:11	and the ***m*** burned with fire to
	5: 4	with you face to face on the ***m***
	5: 5	and you did not go up the ***m***.
	5:22	in the ***m*** from the midst of the
	5:23	while the ***m*** was burning with
	9: 9	When I went up into the ***m*** to
	9: 9	then I stayed on the ***m*** forty
	9:10	had spoken to you on the ***m***
	9:15	turned and came down from the ***m***,
	9:15	and the ***m*** burned with fire;
	9:21	brook that descended from the ***m***.
	10: 1	and come up to Me on the ***m*** and
	10: 3	the first, and went up the ***m***,
	10: 4	had spoken to you in the ***m***
	10: 5	turned and came down from the ***m***,
	10:10	I stayed in the ***m*** forty days
	14: 5	the ***m*** goat, the antelope, and
	14: 5	and the ***m*** sheep.
	32:49	Go up this ***m*** of the Abarim,
	32:50	and die on the ***m*** which you
	33:19	call the peoples to the ***m***;
Josh	2:16	said to them, "Get to the ***m***,
	2:22	departed and went to the ***m***,
	2:23	returned, descended from the ***m***,
	10:40	the ***m*** country and the South and
	11:16	the ***m*** country, all the South,
	12: 8	in the ***m*** country, in the
	13:19	Zereth Shahar on the ***m*** of the
	14:12	give me this ***m*** of which the
	15: 8	went up to the top of the ***m***
	15:48	And in the ***m*** country: Shamir,
	17:16	The ***m*** country is not enough for
	17:18	but the ***m*** country shall be
	18:16	came down to the end of the ***m***
1 Sam	17: 3	The Philistines stood on a ***m*** on
	17: 3	and Israel stood on a ***m*** on the
	23:26	Saul went on one side of the ***m***,
	23:26	men on the other side of the ***m***.
2 Sam	15:32	had come to the top of the ***m***,
	16: 1	little past the top of the ***m***,
1 Ki	19: 8	far as Horeb, the ***m*** of God.
	19:11	and stand on the ***m*** before the
2 Ki	2:16	up and cast him upon some ***m*** or
	6:17	the ***m*** was full of horses and
	23:16	tombs that were there on the ***m***.
2 Chr	2:18	thousand stonecutters in the ***m***,
Neh	8:15	saying, "Go out to the ***m***,
Job	14:18	But as a ***m*** falls and crumbles
	39: 1	know the time when the wild ***m***
Ps	11: 1	Flee as a bird to your ***m***"?
	30: 7	Your favor You have made my ***m***
	48: 1	of our God, In His holy ***m***.
	68:15	A ***m*** of God is the mountain of
	68:15	A mountain of God is the ***m*** of
	68:15	A ***m*** of many peaks is the
	68:15	of many peaks is the ***m*** of
	68:16	This is the ***m*** which God
	78:54	This ***m*** which His right hand
Song	4: 6	I will go my way to the ***m*** of
Isa	2: 2	in the latter days That the ***m***
	2: 3	and let us go up to the ***m*** of
	11: 9	nor destroy in all My holy ***m***,
	13: 2	up a banner on the high ***m***,
	18: 6	will be left together for the ***m***
	22: 5	And of crying to the ***m***.
	25: 6	And in this ***m*** The LORD of
	25: 7	And He will destroy on this ***m***
	25:10	For on this ***m*** the hand of the
	30:17	left as a pole on top of a ***m***
	30:25	There will be on every high ***m***
	30:29	To come into the ***m*** of the
	40: 4	shall be exalted And every ***m***
	40: 9	Get up into the high ***m***;
	56: 7	them I will bring to My holy ***m***,
	57: 7	On a lofty and high ***m*** You have
	57:13	And shall inherit My holy ***m***.
	65:11	LORD, Who forget My holy ***m***,
	65:25	nor destroy in all My holy ***m***,
	66:20	to My holy ***m*** Jerusalem," says
Jer	3: 6	She has gone up on every high ***m***
	16:16	shall hunt them from every ***m***
	17: 3	O My ***m*** in the field, I will
	26:18	And the ***m*** of the temple Like
	31:23	and ***m*** of holiness!'
	50: 6	They have gone from ***m*** to hill;
	51:25	am against you, O destroying ***m***,
	51:25	rocks, And make you a burnt ***m***.
Ezek	11:23	of the city and stood on the ***m***,
	17:22	it on a high and prominent ***m***.
	17:23	On the ***m*** height of Israel I will
	20:40	"For on My holy ***m***,
	20:40	on the ***m*** height of Israel,"
	28:14	You were on the holy ***m*** of God;
	28:16	a profane thing Out of the ***m***
	40: 2	and set me on a very high ***m***;
Dan	2:35	the image became a great ***m*** and
	2:45	the stone was cut out of the ***m***
	9:16	city Jerusalem, Your holy ***m***;
	9:20	LORD my God for the holy ***m*** of
	11:45	seas and the glorious holy ***m***;
Joel	2: 1	sound an alarm in My holy ***m***!
	3:17	Dwelling in Zion My holy ***m***.
Am	4: 1	who are on the ***m*** of Samaria,
Ob	16	For as you drank on my holy ***m***,
Mic	3:12	And the ***m*** of the temple Like
	4: 1	in the latter days That the ***m***
	4: 2	and let us go up to the ***m*** of
	7:12	And ***m*** to mountain.
	7:12	sea to sea, And mountain to ***m***.
Zeph	3:11	longer be haughty In My holy ***m***.
Zech	4: 7	'Who are you, O great ***m***?
	8: 3	The ***M*** of the LORD of hosts,
	8: 3	the LORD of hosts, The Holy ***M***.
	14: 4	Half of the ***m*** shall move
	14: 5	you shall flee through My ***m***
	14: 5	For the ***m*** valley shall reach
Mt	4: 8	Him up on an exceedingly high ***m***,
	5: 1	multitudes, He went up on a ***m***,
	8: 1	He had come down from the ***m***,
	14:23	He went up on the ***m*** by Himself
	15:29	and went up on the ***m*** and sat
	17: 1	led them up on a high ***m*** by
	17: 9	as they came down from the ***m***,
	17:20	seed, you will say to this ***m***,
	21:21	but also if you say to this ***m***,
	28:16	to the ***m*** which Jesus had
Mk	3:13	And He went up on the ***m*** and
	6:46	He departed to the ***m*** to pray.
	9: 2	and led them up on a high ***m***
	9: 9	as they came down from the ***m***,
	11:23	to you, whoever says to this ***m***,
Lk	3: 5	be filled And every ***m***
	4: 5	taking Him up on a high ***m***,
	6:12	days that He went out to the ***m***
	8:32	was feeding there on the ***m***.
	9:28	and James and went up on the ***m***
	9:37	they had come down from the ***m***,
	19:29	at the ***m*** called Olivet, that
	21:37	He went out and stayed on the ***m***
Jn	4:20	fathers worshiped on this ***m***,
	4:21	when you will neither on this ***m***,
	6: 3	And Jesus went up on the ***m***,
	6:15	He departed again to the ***m*** by
Heb	8: 5	shown you on the ***m***.
	12:18	For you have not come to the ***m***
	12:20	as a beast touches the ***m***,
2 Pe	1:18	we were with Him on the holy ***m***.
Rev	6:14	and every ***m*** and island was
	8: 8	And something like a great ***m***
	21:10	Spirit to a great and high ***m***,

MOUNTAINEERS (1/1)

Judg	1:19	Judah. And they drove out the ***m***,

MOUNTAINS (235/221) MOUNTAIN

Gen	7:20	and the ***m*** were covered.
	8: 4	on the ***m*** of Ararat.
	8: 5	the tops of the ***m*** were seen.
	14:10	and the remainder fled to the ***m***.
	19:17	in the plain. Escape to the ***m***,
	19:19	but I cannot escape to the ***m***,
	19:30	out of Zoar and dwelt in the ***m***,
	22: 2	burnt offering on one of the ***m***
	31:21	and headed toward the ***m*** of
	31:23	and he overtook him in the ***m*** of
	31:25	had pitched his tent in the ***m***,
	31:25	his brethren pitched in the ***m***
Ex	32:12	them, to kill them in the ***m***,
Num	13:17	the South, and go up to the ***m***,
	13:29	and the Amorites dwell in the ***m***;
	23: 7	From the ***m*** of the east.
	33:47	Diblathaim and camped in the ***m***
	33:48	They departed from the ***m*** of
Deut	1: 7	and go to the ***m*** of the
	1: 7	in the ***m*** and in the lowland, in
	1:19	you saw on the way to the ***m*** of
	1:20	You have come to the ***m*** of the
	1:24	departed and went up into the ***m***,
	2:37	or to the cities of the ***m***,
	3:12	and half the ***m*** of Gilead and
	3:25	the Jordan, those pleasant ***m***,
	12: 2	on the high ***m*** and on the hills
	32:22	fire the foundations of the ***m***.
	33:15	best things of the ancient ***m***,
Josh	10: 6	the Amorites who dwell in the ***m***
	11: 2	were from the north, in the ***m***,
	11: 3	the Jebusite in the ***m***,
	11:16	the ***m*** of Israel and its
	11:21	cut off the Anakim from the ***m***:
	11:21	from all the ***m*** of Judah, and
	11:21	and from all the ***m*** of Israel;
	13: 6	all the inhabitants of the ***m***
	16: 1	up from Jericho through the ***m***
	17:15	since the ***m*** of Ephraim are too
	18:12	and went up through the ***m***
	19:50	Timnath Serah in the ***m*** of
	20: 7	in the ***m*** of Naphtali, Shechem
	20: 7	Shechem in the ***m*** of Ephraim,
	20: 7	(which is Hebron) in the ***m*** of
	21:11	in the ***m*** of Judah, with the
	21:21	with its common-land in the ***m***
	24: 4	To Esau I gave the ***m*** of Seir to
	24:30	which is in the ***m*** of Ephraim,
	24:33	was given to him in the ***m*** of
Judg	1: 9	Canaanites who dwelt in the ***m***,
	1:34	the children of Dan into the ***m***,
	2: 9	in the ***m*** of Ephraim, on the
	3:27	he blew the trumpet in the ***m***
	3:27	went down with him from the ***m***;
	4: 5	Ramah and Bethel in the ***m*** of
	5: 5	The ***m*** gushed before the LORD,
	6: 2	strongholds which are in the ***m***.
	7:24	throughout all the ***m*** of
	9:25	him on the tops of the ***m***,
	9:36	down from the tops of the ***m***!"
	9:36	You see the shadows of the ***m*** as
	10: 1	he dwelt in Shamir in the ***m*** of
	11:37	I may go and wander on the ***m***
	11:38	bewailed her virginity on the ***m***.
	12:15	in the ***m*** of the Amalekites.
	17: 1	Now there was a man from the ***m***
	17: 8	Then he came to the ***m*** of
	18: 2	So they went to the ***m*** of
	18:13	passed from there to the ***m*** of
	19: 1	Levite staying in the remote ***m***
	19:16	who also was from the ***m*** of
	19:18	in Judah toward the remote ***m***
1 Sam	1: 1	of the ***m*** of Ephraim, and his
	9: 4	So he passed through the ***m*** of
	13: 2	Saul in Michmash and in the ***m***
	14:22	Israel who had hidden in the ***m***
	23:14	and remained in the ***m*** in the
	26:20	one hunts a partridge in the ***m***.
2 Sam	1:21	O ***m*** of Gilboa, Let there be
	20:21	But a man from the ***m*** of
1 Ki	4: 8	in the ***m*** of Ephraim;
	5:15	who quarried stone in the ***m***,
	12:25	built Shechem in the ***m*** of
	19:11	and strong wind tore into the ***m***
	22:17	all Israel scattered on the ***m***,
2 Ki	5:22	have come to me from the ***m*** of
	19:23	come up to the height of the ***m***,
1 Chr	6:67	in the ***m*** of Ephraim, also Gezer
	12: 8	as swift as gazelles on the ***m***:
2 Chr	2: 2	to quarry stone in the ***m***,
	13: 4	which is in the ***m*** of Ephraim,
	15: 8	which he had taken in the ***m*** of
	18:16	all Israel scattered on the ***m***,
	19: 4	people from Beersheba to the ***m***
	21:11	he made high places in the ***m***
	26:10	and vinedressers in the ***m*** and
	27: 4	he built cities in the ***m*** of
Job	9: 5	He removes the ***m***,
	24: 8	wet with the showers of the ***m***,
	28: 9	He overturns the ***m*** at the
	39: 8	The range of the ***m*** is his
	40:20	Surely the ***m*** yield food for
Ps	36: 6	is like the great ***m***;
	46: 2	And though the ***m*** be carried
	46: 3	Though the ***m*** shake with its
	50:11	I know all the birds of the ***m***,
	65: 6	Who established the ***m*** by His
	68:16	you ***m*** of many peaks? This
	72: 3	The ***m*** will bring peace to the
	72:16	the earth, On the top of the ***m***;
	76: 4	and excellent Than the ***m*** of
	83:14	And as the flame sets the ***m*** on
	87: 1	foundation is in the holy ***m***.

90: 2 Before the ***m*** were brought
97: 5 The ***m*** melt like wax at the
104: 6 The waters stood above the ***m***.
104: 8 They went up over the ***m***;
114: 4 The ***m*** skipped like rams,
114: 6 O ***m***, that you skipped
125: 2 As the ***m*** surround Jerusalem,
133: 3 Descending upon the ***m*** of Zion;
144: 5 and come down; Touch the ***m***,
147: 8 makes grass to grow on the ***m***.
148: 9 ***M*** and all hills
Prov 8:25 Before the ***m*** were settled,
27:25 And the herbs of the ***m*** are
Song 2: 8 he comes Leaping upon the ***m***,
2:17 Or a young stag Upon the ***m***
4: 8 From the ***m*** of the leopards.
8:14 Or a young stag On the ***m*** of
Isa 2: 2 established on the top of the ***m***,
2:14 Upon all the high ***m***,
13: 4 noise of a multitude in the ***m***,
14:25 And on My ***m*** tread him
17:13 chased like the chaff of the ***m***
18: 3 he lifts up a banner on the ***m***,
34: 3 And the ***m*** shall be melted with
37:24 come up to the height of the ***m***,
40:12 Weighed the ***m*** in scales
41:15 You shall thresh the ***m*** and
42:11 shout from the top of the ***m***.
42:15 I will lay waste the ***m*** and
44:23 forth into singing, you ***m***,
49:11 I will make each of My ***m*** a
49:13 O ***m***! For the LORD has
52: 7 How beautiful upon the ***m*** Are
54:10 For the ***m*** shall depart And the
55:12 The ***m*** and the hills Shall
64: 1 would come down! That the ***m***
64: 3 The ***m*** shook at Your presence.
65: 7 have burned incense on the ***m***
65: 9 And from Judah an heir of My ***m***;
Jer 3:23 And from the multitude of ***m***;
4:24 I beheld the ***m***,
9:10 a weeping and wailing for the ***m***,
13:16 feet stumble On the dark ***m***,
17:26 from the ***m*** and from the South,
31: 5 shall yet plant vines on the ***m***
32:44 Judah, in the cities of the ***m***,
33:13 'In the cities of the ***m***,
46:18 as Tabor is among the ***m*** And
50: 6 have turned them away on the ***m***.
Lam 4:19 They pursued us on the ***m*** And
Ezek 6: 2 set your face toward the ***m*** of
6: 3 O ***m*** of Israel, hear the word of
6: 3 says the Lord GOD to the ***m***,
7: 7 And not of rejoicing in the ***m***.
7:16 will escape and be on the ***m***
18: 6 If he has not eaten on the ***m***,
18:11 But has eaten on the ***m*** Or
18:15 Who has not eaten on the ***m***,
19: 9 no longer be heard on the ***m*** of
22: 9 you are those who eat on the ***m***;
31:12 branches have fallen on the ***m***
32: 5 I will lay your flesh on the ***m***,
32: 6 of your blood, Even to the ***m***;
33:28 and the ***m*** of Israel shall be so
34: 6 wandered through all the ***m***,
34:13 I will feed them on the ***m*** of
34:14 fold shall be on the high ***m*** of
34:14 feed in rich pasture on the ***m***
35: 8 And I will fill its ***m*** with the
35:12 you have spoken against the ***m***
36: 1 prophesy to the ***m*** of Israel,
36: 1 O ***m*** of Israel, hear the word of
36: 4 O ***m*** of Israel, hear the word of
36: 4 says the Lord GOD to the ***m***,
36: 6 of Israel, and say to the ***m***,
36: 8 O ***m*** of Israel, you shall shoot
37:22 on the ***m*** of Israel; and one
38: 8 from many people on the ***m*** of
38:20 The ***m*** shall be thrown down, the
38:21 against Gog throughout all My ***m***,
39: 2 and bring you against the ***m*** of
39: 4 You shall fall upon the ***m*** of
39:17 sacrificial meal on the ***m*** of
Hos 10: 8 They shall say to the ***m***,
Joel 2: 2 clouds spread over the ***m***.
3:18 pass in that day That the ***m***
Am 3: 9 Assemble on the ***m*** of Samaria;
4:13 For behold, He who forms ***m***,
9:13 The ***m*** shall drip with sweet
Ob 8 And understanding from the ***m***
9 end that everyone from the ***m***
19 South shall possess the ***m*** of
21 to Mount Zion To judge the ***m***
Jon 2: 6 down to the moorings of the ***m***;
Mic 1: 4 The ***m*** will melt under Him,
4: 1 established on the top of the ***m***,
6: 1 plead your case before the ***m***,
6: 2 Hear, O you ***m***, the LORD's
Nah 1: 5 The ***m*** quake before Him, The
1:15 on the ***m*** The feet of him who
3:18 people are scattered on the ***m***,
Hab 3: 6 And the everlasting ***m*** were
3:10 The ***m*** saw You and trembled;
Hag 1: 8 Go up to the ***m*** and bring wood
1:11 a drought on the land and the ***m***,
Zech 6: 1 were coming from between two ***m***,
6: 1 and the ***m*** were mountains of
6: 1 and the mountains were ***m*** of
Mal 1: 3 And laid waste his ***m*** and his
Mt 18:12 ninety-nine and go to the ***m*** to
24:16 who are in Judea flee to the ***m***.
Mk 5: 5 he was in the ***m*** and in the
5:11 was feeding there near the ***m***.
13:14 who are in Judea flee to the ***m***.
Lk 21:21 who are in Judea flee to the ***m***,
23:30 begin 'to say to the ***m***,
1 Cor 13: 2 faith, so that I could remove ***m***,
Heb 11:38 They wandered in deserts and ***m***,
Rev 6:15 caves and in the rocks of the ***m***,
6:16 and said to the ***m*** and rocks,
16:20 and the ***m*** were not found.
17: 9 The seven heads are seven ***m*** on

MOUNTAINTOP (2/2)

Num 14:44 they presumed to go up to the ***m***;
Ezek 43:12 whole area surrounding the ***m***

MOUNTAINTOPS (3/3)

Ezek 6:13 every high hill, on all the ***m***,
Hos 4:13 They offer sacrifices on the ***m***,
Joel 2: 5 a noise like chariots Over ***m***

MOUNTED (3/3)

1 Ki 12:18 Therefore King Rehoboam ***m*** his
2 Chr 10:18 Therefore King Rehoboam ***m*** his
Ezek 10:19 lifted their wings and ***m*** up

MOUNTINGS (1/1)

Ex 39:13 in settings of gold in their ***m***.

MOUNTS (2/2)

Job 20: 6 Though his haughtiness ***m*** up to
Acts 23:24 and provide ***m*** to set Paul on,

MOURN (46/45) MOURNED, MOURNER, MOURNING, MOURNS

Gen 23: 2 and Abraham came to ***m*** for Sarah
Deut 21:13 and ***m*** her father and her mother
1 Sam 16: 1 How long will you ***m*** for Saul,
2 Sam 3:31 and ***m*** for Abner." And King
1 Ki 13:29 prophet came to the city to ***m***,
14:13 And all Israel shall ***m*** for him
Neh 8: 9 do not ***m*** nor weep." For all
Job 2:11 together to come and ***m*** with
5:11 And those who ***m*** are lifted to
14:22 And his soul will ***m*** over
Prov 5:11 And you ***m*** at last, When your
Eccl 3: 4 a time to laugh; A time to ***m***,
Isa 3:26 Her gates shall lament and ***m***,
16: 7 of Kir Hareseth you shall ***m***;
19: 8 The fishermen also will ***m***;
32:12 People shall ***m*** upon their
61: 2 our God; To comfort all who ***m***,
61: 3 To console those who ***m*** in Zion,
66:10 all you who ***m*** for her;
Jer 4:28 For this shall the earth ***m***,
12: 4 How long will the land ***m***,
14: 2 They ***m*** for the land, And the
48:31 I will ***m*** for the men of Kir
Lam 1: 4 The roads to Zion ***m*** Because no
Ezek 7:12 rejoice, Nor the seller ***m***,
7:27 'The king will ***m***,
24:16 yet you shall neither ***m*** nor
24:23 you shall neither ***m*** nor weep,
24:23 away in your iniquities and ***m***
31:15 I caused Lebanon to ***m*** for it,
Hos 4: 3 Therefore the land will ***m***;
10: 5 For its people ***m*** for it,
Joel 1: 9 of the LORD; The priests ***m***,
Am 1: 2 pastures of the shepherds ***m***,
8: 8 And everyone ***m*** who dwells in
9: 5 And all who dwell there ***m***;
Zech 12:10 they will ***m*** for Him as one
12:12 "And the land shall ***m***,
Mt 5: 4 Blessed are those who ***m***,
9:15 friends of the bridegroom ***m*** as
24:30 the tribes of the earth will ***m***,
Lk 6:25 For you shall ***m*** and weep.
2 Cor 12:21 and I shall ***m*** for many who have
Jas 4: 9 Lament and ***m*** and weep! Let your
Rev 1: 7 the tribes of the earth will ***m***
18:11 of the earth will weep and ***m***

MOURNED (24/24) MOURN

Gen 37:34 and ***m*** for his son many days.
50: 3 and the Egyptians ***m*** for him
50:10 and they ***m*** there with a great
Ex 33: 4 heard this bad news, they ***m***,
Num 14:39 and the people ***m*** greatly.
20:29 all the house of Israel ***m*** for
1 Sam 15:35 Nevertheless Samuel ***m*** for Saul,
2 Sam 1:12 And they ***m*** and wept and fasted
11:26 she ***m*** for her husband.
13:37 And David ***m*** for his son every
1 Ki 13:30 and they ***m*** over him, saying,
14:18 and all Israel ***m*** for him,
1 Chr 7:22 Then Ephraim their father ***m*** many
2 Chr 35:24 And all Judah and Jerusalem ***m***
Ezra 10: 6 for he ***m*** because of the guilt
Neh 1: 4 and ***m*** for many days; I was
Isa 38:14 I ***m*** like a dove; My eyes fail
Zech 7: 5 When you fasted and ***m*** in the
Mt 11:17 We ***m*** to you, And you did not
Mk 16:10 as they ***m*** and wept.
Lk 7:32 We ***m*** to you, And you did not
8:52 Now all wept and ***m*** for her; but
23:27 and women who also ***m*** and
1 Cor 5: 2 up, and have not rather ***m***,

MOURNER (1/1) MOURN, MOURNERS

2 Sam 14: 2 her, "Please pretend to be a ***m***,

MOURNERS (5/5) MOURNER

Job 29:25 As one who comforts ***m***.
Eccl 12: 5 And the ***m*** go about the
Isa 57:18 comforts to him And to his ***m***.
Hos 9: 4 shall be like bread of ***m*** to
Mal 3:14 And that we have walked as ***m***

MOURNFUL (1/1)

Zeph 1:10 The sound of a ***m*** cry from the

MOURNING (52/48) MOURN

Gen 27:41 The days of ***m*** for my father are
37:35 into the grave to my son in ***m***.
50: 4 And when the days of his ***m*** were
50:10 He observed seven days of ***m*** for
50:11 saw the ***m*** at the threshing
50:11 This is a deep ***m*** of the
Deut 26:14 not eaten any of it when in ***m***,
34: 8 So the days of weeping and ***m***
2 Sam 11:27 And when her ***m*** was over, David
14: 2 and put on ***m*** apparel; do not
14: 2 like a woman who has been ***m*** a
19: 1 the king is weeping and ***m*** for
19: 2 that day was turned into ***m***
1 Ki 21:27 in sackcloth, and went about ***m***.
Esth 4: 3 there was great ***m*** among the
6:12 ***m*** and with his head covered.
9:22 and from ***m*** to a holiday; that
Job 30:28 I go about ***m***, but not
30:31 My harp is turned to ***m***,
Ps 30:11 You have turned for me my ***m***
38: 6 I go ***m*** all the day long.
42: 9 Why do I go ***m*** because of the
43: 2 Why do I go ***m*** because of the
Eccl 7: 2 to go to the house of ***m*** Than
7: 4 the wise is in the house of ***m***,
Isa 22:12 Called for weeping and for ***m***,
60:20 And the days of your ***m*** shall
61: 3 The oil of joy for ***m***,
Jer 6:26 roll about in ashes! Make ***m***
8:21 of my people I am hurt. I am ***m***;
9:17 Consider and call for the ***m***
16: 5 "Do not enter the house of ***m***,
16: 7 shall men break bread in ***m***
31:13 For I will turn their ***m*** to
Lam 2: 5 And has increased ***m*** and
5:15 Our dance has turned into ***m***.
Ezek 2:10 on it were lamentations and ***m***
7:16 of the valleys, All of them ***m***,
24:17 make no ***m*** for the dead; bind
31:15 went down to hell, I caused ***m***.
Dan 10: 2 was ***m*** three full weeks.
Joel 2:12 with weeping, and with ***m***.
Am 5:16 shall call the farmer to ***m***,
8:10 I will turn your feasts into ***m***,
8:10 I will make it like ***m*** for an
Mic 1: 8 like the jackals And a ***m*** like
Zech 12:11 day there shall be a great ***m***
12:11 like the ***m*** at Hadad Rimmon in
Mt 2:18 weeping, and great ***m***,
2 Cor 7: 7 of your earnest desire, your ***m***,
Jas 4: 9 your laughter be turned to ***m***
Rev 18: 8 —death and ***m*** and famine.

MOURNS (9/9) MOURN

Ps 35:14 as one who ***m*** for his mother.
Isa 24: 4 The earth ***m*** and fades away,
33: 9 The earth ***m*** and languishes,
Jer 12:11 it ***m*** to Me; The whole land is
14: 2 'Judah ***m***, And her gates
23:10 because of a curse the land ***m***.
Joel 1:10 field is wasted, The land ***m***;
Mic 1:11 does not go out. Beth Ezel ***m***;
Zech 12:10 will mourn for Him as one ***m***

MOUSE (2/2)

Lev 11:29 on the earth: the mole, the ***m***,
Isa 66:17 and the abomination and the ***m***,

MOUTH (394/374) MOUTHS

Gen 4:11 which has opened its ***m*** to
8:11 olive leaf was in her ***m***;
29: 2 stone was on the well's ***m***.
29: 3 the stone from the well's ***m***,
29: 3 in its place on the well's ***m***.
29: 8 the stone from the well's ***m***;
29:10 the stone from the well's ***m***,
42:27 in the ***m*** of his sack.
43:12 that was returned in the ***m*** of
43:21 man's money was in the ***m*** of
44: 1 put each man's money in the ***m***
44: 2 in the ***m*** of the sack of the
44: 8 money which we found in the ***m***
45:12 Benjamin see that it is my ***m***
Ex 4:11 to him, "Who has made man's ***m***?
4:12 and I will be with your ***m*** and
4:15 him and put the words in his ***m***.
4:15 And I will be with your ***m*** and
4:15 with your mouth and with his ***m***,
4:16 And he himself shall be as a ***m***
13: 9 LORD's law may be in your ***m***;
23:13 nor let it be heard from your ***m***.
Num 16:30 and the earth opens its ***m*** and

16:32 and the earth opened its **m** and
22:28 Then the LORD opened the **m** of
22:38 The word that God puts in my **m**,
23: 5 LORD put a word in Balaam's **m**,
23:12 what the LORD has put in my **m**?
23:16 Balaam, and put a word in his **m**,
26:10 and the earth opened its **m** and
30: 2 all that proceeds out of his **m**.
32:24 has proceeded out of your **m**.
Deut 8: 3 word that proceeds from the **m**
11: 6 how the earth opened its **m** and
18:18 and will put My words in His **m**,
19:15 by the **m** of two or three
23:23 you have promised with your **m**.
30:14 in your **m** and in your heart,
32: 1 O earth, the words of my **m**.
Josh 1: 8 shall not depart from your **m**,
6:10 a word proceed out of your **m**,
10:18 large stones against the **m** of
10:22 Open the **m** of the cave, and
10:27 stones against the cave's **m**,
15: 5 the Salt Sea as far as the **m**
15: 5 at the bay of the sea at the **m**
Judg 7: 6 putting their hand to their **m**,
9:38 Where indeed is your **m** now,
11:36 to what has gone out of your **m**,
18:19 put your hand over your **m**,
1 Sam 1:12 LORD, that Eli watched her **m**.
2: 3 no arrogance come from your **m**,
14:26 no one put his hand to his **m**,
14:27 and put his hand to his **m**;
17:35 delivered the lamb from its **m**;
2 Sam 1:16 for your own **m** has testified
14: 3 So Joab put the words in her **m**.
14:19 he put all these words in the **m**
17:19 a covering over the well's **m**,
18:25 alone, there is news in his **m**.
22: 9 And devouring fire from His **m**;
1 Ki 8:15 who spoke with His **m** to my
8:24 have both spoken with Your **m**
17:24 the word of the LORD in your **m**
19:18 and every **m** that has not kissed
22:22 and be a lying spirit in the **m**
22:23 put a lying spirit in the **m** of
2 Ki 4:34 and put his **m** on his mouth, his
4:34 and put his mouth on his **m**,
1 Chr 16:12 and the judgments of His **m**,
2 Chr 6: 4 what He spoke with His **m** to
6:15 have both spoken with Your **m**
18:21 and be a lying spirit in the **m**
18:22 put a lying spirit in the **m** of
35:22 the words of Necho from the **m**
36:12 who spoke from the **m** of the
36:21 the word of the LORD by the **m**
36:22 the word of the LORD by the **m**
Ezra 1: 1 the word of the LORD by the **m**
Neh 9:20 Your manna from their **m**,
Esth 7: 8 As the word left the king's **m**,
Job 3: 1 After this Job opened his **m** and
5:15 From the **m** of the mighty,
5:16 And injustice shuts her **m**.
7:11 I will not restrain my **m**;
8: 2 And the words of your **m** be
8:21 He will yet fill your **m** with
9:20 my own **m** would condemn me;
12:11 the ear test words And the **m**
15: 5 your iniquity teaches your **m**,
15: 6 Your own **m** condemns you, and
15:13 such words go out of your **m**?
15:30 And by the breath of His **m** he
16: 5 would strengthen you with my **m**,
16:10 They gape at me with their **m**,
19:16 no answer; I beg him with my **m**.
20:12 evil is sweet in his **m**,
20:13 But still keeps it in his **m**,
21: 5 Put your hand over your **m**.
22:22 please, instruction from His **m**,
23: 4 And fill my **m** with arguments.
23:12 treasured the words of His **m**
29: 9 And put their hand on their **m**;
29:10 stuck to the roof of their **m**.
29:23 And they opened their **m** wide
31:27 And my **m** has kissed my hand;
31:30 I have not allowed my **m** to sin
32: 5 there was no answer in the **m**
33: 2 Now, I open my **m**;
33: 2 My tongue speaks in my **m**.
35:16 Therefore Job opens his **m** in
37: 2 rumbling that comes from His **m**.
40: 4 I lay my hand over my **m**.
40:23 the Jordan gushes into his **m**,
41:19 Out of his **m** go burning lights;
41:21 And a flame goes out of his **m**.
Ps 5: 9 is no faithfulness in their **m**;
8: 2 Out of the **m** of babes and
10: 7 His **m** is full of cursing and
17: 3 I have purposed that my **m**
18: 8 And devouring fire from His **m**;
19:14 Let the words of my **m** and the
22:21 Save Me from the lion's **m** And
33: 6 of them by the breath of His **m**.
34: 1 shall continually be in my **m**.
35:21 They also opened their **m** wide
36: 3 The words of his **m** are
37:30 The **m** of the righteous speaks
38:13 a mute who does not open his **m**.
38:14 And in whose **m** is no
39: 1 I will restrain my **m** with a
39: 9 was mute, I did not open my **m**,
40: 3 He has put a new song in my **m**—
49: 3 My **m** shall speak wisdom,
50:16 Or take My covenant in your **m**,
50:19 You give your **m** to evil,
51:15 And my **m** shall show forth Your
54: 2 Give ear to the words of my **m**.
55:21 The words of his **m** were
58: 6 Break their teeth in their **m**,
59: 7 they belch with their **m**;
59:12 For the sin of their **m** and
62: 4 They bless with their **m**,
63: 5 And my **m** shall praise You with
63:11 But the **m** of those who speak
66:14 my lips have uttered And my **m**
66:17 I cried to Him with my **m**,
69:15 let not the pit shut its **m** on
71: 8 Let my **m** be filled with Your
71:15 My **m** shall tell of Your
73: 9 They set their **m** against the
78: 1 your ears to the words of my **m**.
78: 2 I will open my **m** in a parable;
78:36 they flattered Him with their **m**,
81:10 Open your **m** wide, and I will
89: 1 With my **m** will I make known
103: 5 Who satisfies your **m** with good
105: 5 and the judgments of His **m**,
107:42 And all iniquity stops its **m**.
109: 2 For the **m** of the wicked and the
109: 2 mouth of the wicked and the **m**
109:30 praise the LORD with my **m**;
119:13 All the judgments of Your **m**.
119:43 of truth utterly out of my **m**,
119:72 The law of Your **m** is better to
119:88 keep the testimony of Your **m**.
119:103 Sweeter than honey to my **m**!
119:108 the freewill offerings of my **m**,
119:131 I opened my **m** and panted,
126: 2 Then our **m** was filled with
137: 6 cling to the roof of my **m**—
138: 4 they hear the words of Your **m**.
141: 3 a guard, O LORD, over my **m**;
141: 7 bones are scattered at the **m**
144: 8 Whose **m** speaks vain words,
144:11 Whose **m** speaks lying words,
145:21 My **m** shall speak the praise of
149: 6 praises of God be in their **m**,
Prov 2: 6 From His **m** come knowledge and
4: 5 away from the words of my **m**.
4:24 away from you a deceitful **m**,
5: 3 And her **m** is smoother than
5: 7 depart from the words of my **m**.
6: 2 snared by the words of your **m**;
6: 2 taken by the words of your **m**.
6:12 Walks with a perverse **m**;
7:24 attention to the words of my **m**:
8: 7 For my **m** will speak truth;
8: 8 All the words of my **m** are with
8:13 evil way And the perverse **m** I
10: 6 But violence covers the **m** of
10:11 The **m** of the righteous is a
10:11 But violence covers the **m** of
10:14 But the **m** of the foolish is
10:31 The **m** of the righteous brings
10:32 But the **m** of the wicked what
11: 9 The hypocrite with his **m**
11:11 But it is overthrown by the **m**
12: 6 But the **m** of the upright
12:14 good by the fruit of his **m**,
13: 2 eat well by the fruit of his **m**,
13: 3 He who guards his **m** preserves
14: 3 In the **m** of a fool is a rod of
15: 2 But the **m** of fools pours forth
15:14 But the **m** of fools feeds on
15:23 has joy by the answer of his **m**,
15:28 But the **m** of the wicked pours
16:10 His **m** must not transgress in
16:23 heart of the wise teaches his **m**,
16:26 For his hungry **m** drives him
18: 4 The words of a man's **m** are
18: 6 And his **m** calls for blows.
18: 7 A fool's **m** is his destruction,
18:20 from the fruit of his **m**,
19:24 so much as bring it to his **m**
19:28 And the **m** of the wicked
20:17 But afterward his **m** will be
21:23 Whoever guards his **m** and tongue
22:14 The **m** of an immoral woman is a
24: 7 He does not open his **m** in the
26: 7 Is a proverb in the **m** of
26: 9 Is a proverb in the **m** of
26:15 him to bring it back to his **m**.
26:28 And a flattering **m** works ruin.
27: 2 praise you, and not your own **m**;
30:20 She eats and wipes her **m**,
30:32 put your hand on your **m**.
31: 8 Open your **m** for the
31: 9 Open your **m**, judge
31:26 She opens her **m** with wisdom,
Eccl 5: 2 Do not be rash with your **m**,
5: 6 Do not let your **m** cause your
6: 7 the labor of man is for his **m**,
10:12 The words of a wise man's **m**
10:13 The words of his **m** begin with
Song 1: 2 me with the kisses of his **m**—
4: 3 And your **m** is lovely. Your
5:16 His **m** is most sweet, Yes, he
7: 9 And the roof of your **m** like the
Isa 1:20 For the **m** of the LORD has
5:14 itself And opened its **m**
6: 7 And he touched my **m** with it,
9:12 devour Israel with an open **m**.
9:17 And every **m** speaks folly. For
10:14 Nor opened his **m** with even a
11: 4 the earth with the rod of His **m**,
19: 7 by the **m** of the River,
34:16 For My **m** has commanded it, and
40: 5 For the **m** of the LORD has
45:23 The word has gone out of My **m**
48: 3 They went forth from My **m**,
49: 2 And He has made My **m** like a
51:16 I have put My words in your **m**;
53: 7 Yet He opened not His **m**;
53: 7 So He opened not His **m**.
53: 9 Nor was any deceit in His **m**.
55:11 be that goes forth from My **m**;
57: 4 whom do you make a wide **m**
58:14 The **m** of the LORD has
59:21 which I have put in your **m**,
59:21 shall not depart from your **m**,
59:21 nor from the **m** of your
59:21 nor from the **m** of your
62: 2 Which the **m** of the LORD will
Jer 1: 9 forth His hand and touched my **m**,
1: 9 I have put My words in your **m**.
5:14 I will make My words in your **m**
7:28 has been cut off from their **m**.
9: 8 to his neighbor with his **m**,
9:12 And who is he to whom the **m**
9:20 ear receive the word of His **m**;
12: 2 You are near in their **m** But
15:19 the vile, You shall be as My **m**.
23:16 Not from the **m** of the LORD.
36:18 He proclaimed with his **m** all
44:17 has gone out of our own **m**,
44:26 no more be named in the **m** of
48:28 In the sides of the cave's **m**.
51:44 And I will bring out of his **m**
Lam 2:16 enemies have opened their **m**
3:29 Let him put his **m** in the
3:38 Is it not from the **m** of the
4: 4 To the roof of its **m** for
Ezek 2: 8 open your **m** and eat what I give
3: 2 So I opened my **m**,
3: 3 and it was in my **m** like honey
3:17 therefore hear a word from My **m**,
3:26 cling to the roof of your **m**,
3:27 with you, I will open your **m**,
4:14 flesh ever come into my **m**.
16:56 was not a byword in your **m** in
16:63 and never open your **m** anymore
24:27 on that day your **m** will be
29:21 and I will open your **m** to speak
33: 7 you shall hear a word from My **m**
33:22 escaped. And He had opened my **m**;
33:22 my **m** was opened, and I was no
33:31 for with their **m** they show much
35:13 Thus with your **m** you have
Dan 3:26 Nebuchadnezzar went near the **m**
4:31 was still in the king's **m**,
6:17 was brought and laid on the **m**
7: 5 and had three ribs in its **m**
7: 8 and a **m** speaking pompous words.
7:20 horn which had eyes and a **m**
10: 3 no meat or wine came into my **m**,
10:16 then I opened my **m** and spoke,
Hos 2:17 For I will take from her **m** the
6: 5 slain them by the words of My **m**;
8: 1 Set the trumpet to your **m**! He
Joel 1: 5 it has been cut off from your **m**.
Am 3:12 a shepherd takes from the **m**
Mic 4: 4 For the **m** of the LORD of
6:12 tongue is deceitful in their **m**.
7: 5 Guard the doors of your **m**
7:16 put their hand over their **m**;
Nah 3:12 They fall into the **m** of the
Zeph 3:13 tongue be found in their **m**;
Zech 5: 8 threw the lead cover over its **m**.
8: 9 These words by the **m** of
9: 7 take away the blood from his **m**,
Mal 2: 6 The law of truth was in his **m**,
2: 7 should seek the law from his **m**;
Mt 4: 4 that proceeds from the **m**
5: 2 Then He opened His **m** and taught
12:34 abundance of the heart the **m**
13:35 I will open My **m** in
15: 8 near to Me with their **m**,
15:11 Not what goes into the **m** defiles
15:11 but what comes out of the **m**,
15:17 that whatever enters the **m**
15:18 which proceed out of the **m**
17:27 And when you have opened its **m**,
18:16 by the **m** of two or three
21:16 Out of the **m** of babes and
Mk 9:18 him down; he foams at the **m**,
9:20 and wallowed, foaming at the **m**.
Lk 1:64 Immediately his **m** was opened and
1:70 As He spoke by the **m** of His
4:22 which proceeded out of His **m**.
6:45 abundance of the heart his **m**
9:39 so that he foams at the **m**,
19:22 Out of your own **m** I will judge
21:15 for I will give you a **m** and
22:71 it ourselves from His own **m**.
Jn 19:29 on hyssop, and put it to His **m**.
Acts 1:16 Spirit spoke before by the **m**
3:18 which God foretold by the **m** of
3:21 which God has spoken by the **m**
4:25 who by the **m** of Your servant
8:32 So He opened not His **m**.
8:35 Then Philip opened his **m**,
10:34 Then Peter opened his **m** and
11: 8 has at any time entered my **m**.
15: 7 that by my **m** the Gentiles
15:27 the same things by word of **m**.
18:14 Paul was about to open his **m**,
22:14 and hear the voice of His **m**.
23: 2 by him to strike him on the **m**.

Rom 3:14 Whose **m** is full of cursing
3:19 that every **m** may be stopped,
10: 8 in your **m** and in your
10: 9 if you confess with your **m** the
10:10 and with the **m** confession is
15: 6 may with one mind and one **m**
2 Cor 13: 1 By the **m** of two or three
Eph 4:29 word proceed out of your **m**,
6:19 that I may open my **m** boldly to
Col 3: 8 filthy language out of your **m**.
2 Th 2: 8 with the breath of His **m** and
2 Tim 4:17 I was delivered out of the **m**
Jas 3:10 Out of the same **m** proceed
1 Pe 2:22 deceit found in His **m**";
Jude 16 and they **m** great swelling
Rev 1:16 out of His **m** went a sharp
2:16 them with the sword of My **m**.
3:16 I will vomit you out of My **m**.
9:19 For their power is in their **m**
10: 9 be as sweet as honey in your **m**.
10:10 was as sweet as honey in my **m**.
11: 5 fire proceeds from their **m** and
12:15 spewed water out of his **m** like
12:16 and the earth opened its **m** and
12:16 dragon had spewed out of his **m**.
13: 2 and his **m** like the mouth of a
13: 2 and his mouth like the **m** of a
13: 5 And he was given a **m** speaking
13: 6 Then he opened his **m** in
14: 5 And in their **m** was found no
16:13 frogs coming out of the **m** of
16:13 out of the **m** of the beast, and
16:13 and out of the **m** of the false
19:15 Now out of His **m** goes a sharp
19:21 which proceeded from the **m** of

MOUTHS (21/21) MOUTH

Deut 31:19 of Israel; put it in their **m**,
31:21 will not be forgotten in the **m**
Ps 17:10 With their **m** they speak
22:13 They gape at Me with their **m**,
78:30 food was still in their **m**,
115: 5 They have **m**, but they do not
135:16 They have **m**, but they do not
135:17 is there any breath in their **m**.
Isa 29:13 people draw near with their **m**
52:15 Kings shall shut their **m** at
Jer 44:25 wives have spoken with your **m**
Lam 3:46 enemies Have opened their **m**
Ezek 34:10 deliver My flock from their **m**,
Dan 6:22 His angel and shut the lions' **m**,
Mic 3: 5 Who puts nothing into their **m**:
Zech 14:12 shall dissolve in their **m**.
Titus 1:11 whose **m** must be stopped, who
Heb 11:33 stopped the **m** of lions,
Jas 3: 3 we put bits in horses' **m** that
Rev 9:17 and out of their **m** came fire,
9:18 which came out of their **m**.

MOVE (29/27) MOVED, MOVES, MOVING

Gen 9: 2 on all that **m** on the earth,
Ex 11: 7 of Israel shall a dog **m** its
Lev 11:10 all that **m** in the water or any
Num 2:17 tabernacle of meeting shall **m**
2:17 so they shall **m** out, everyone
14:25 tomorrow turn and **m** out into
Deut 32:21 I will **m** them to anger by a
Judg 13:25 Spirit of the LORD began to **m**
14: 4 He was seeking an occasion to **m**
2 Sam 6:10 So David would not **m** the ark of
7:10 in a place of their own and **m**
2 Ki 23:18 let no one **m** his bones." So
1 Chr 8: 6 and who forced them to **m** to
8: 7 and Gera who forced them to **m**.
13:13 So David would not **m** the ark
17: 9 in a place of their own and **m**
Isa 13:13 And the earth will **m** out of
46: 7 From its place it shall not **m**.
Jer 46: 7 Whose waters **m** like the
46: 8 And its waters **m** like the
50: 3 dwell therein. They shall **m**,
50: 8 **M** from the midst of Babylon,
Zech 14: 4 Half of the mountain shall **m**
Mt 17:20 **M** from here to there,' and it
17:20 here to there,' and it will **m**;
23: 4 but they themselves will not **m**
Acts 17:28 for in Him we live and **m** and
20:24 But none of these things **m** me;
Rom 10:19 I will **m** you to anger

MOVEABLE (KJV) See UNSTABLE

MOVED (92/91) MOVE

Gen 7:18 and the ark **m** about on the
7:21 And all flesh died that **m** on the
12: 8 And he **m** from there to the
13:18 Then Abram **m** his tent, and went
26:22 And he **m** from there and dug
47:21 he **m** them into the cities, from
Ex 7:23 Neither was his heart **m** by
14:19 **m** and went behind them; and the
Num 11:35 Kibroth Hattaavah the people **m**
12:16 And afterward the people **m** from
21:10 Now the children of Israel **m** on
21:12 From there they **m** and camped in
21:13 From there they **m** and camped on
22: 1 Then the children of Israel **m**,
33: 5 Then the children of Israel **m**
33: 7 They **m** from Etham and turned
33: 9 They **m** from Marah and came to
33:10 They **m** from Elim and camped by
33:11 They **m** from the Red Sea and
33:14 They **m** from Alush and camped at
33:16 They **m** from the Wilderness of
33:21 They **m** from Libnah and camped at
33:24 They **m** from Mount Shepher and
33:25 They **m** from Haradah and camped
33:26 They **m** from Makheloth and
33:28 They **m** from Terah and camped at
33:32 They **m** from Bene Jaakan and
33:34 They **m** from Jotbathah and camped
33:36 They **m** from Ezion Geber and
33:37 They **m** from Kadesh and camped at
33:46 They **m** from Dibon Gad and
33:47 They **m** from Almon Diblathaim and
Deut 32:21 They have **m** Me to anger by
Josh 10:21 No one **m** his tongue against any
Judg 2:18 for the LORD was **m** to pity by
1 Sam 1:13 in her heart; only her lips **m**,
2 Sam 7: 6 but have **m** about in a tent and
7: 7 Wherever I have **m** about with all
18:33 Then the king was deeply **m**,
20:12 he **m** Amasa from the highway to
24: 1 and He **m** David against them to
2 Ki 23:30 Then his servants **m** his body in
1 Chr 16:30 established, It shall not be **m**.
17: 6 Wherever I have **m** about with all
21: 1 and **m** David to number Israel.
Ezra 1: 5 all whose spirits God had **m**,
Esth 2: 9 and he **m** her and her
Job 14:18 And as a rock is **m** from its
41:23 are firm on him and cannot be **m**.
Ps 10: 6 his heart, "I shall not be **m**;
13: 4 trouble me rejoice when I am **m**.
15: 5 these things shall never be **m**.
16: 8 my right hand I shall not be **m**.
21: 7 the Most High he shall not be **m**.
30: 6 I said, "I shall never be **m**.
46: 5 of her, she shall not be **m**;
46: 6 raged, the kingdoms were **m**;
55:22 permit the righteous to be **m**.
62: 2 I shall not be greatly **m**.
62: 6 my defense; I shall not be **m**.
66: 9 does not allow our feet to be **m**.
68: 8 Sinai itself was **m** at the
78:58 And **m** Him to jealousy with
93: 1 so that it cannot be **m**.
96:10 established, It shall not be **m**;
99: 1 Let the earth be **m**!
104: 5 So that it should not be **m**
121: 3 not allow your foot to be **m**;
125: 1 Mount Zion, Which cannot be **m**,
Prov 12: 3 of the righteous cannot be **m**.
Isa 7: 2 the heart of his people were **m**
7: 2 as the trees of the woods are **m**
10:14 And there was no one who **m**
30:20 your teachers will not be **m**
Jer 4: 1 Then you shall not be **m**.
4:24 And all the hills **m** back and
Lam 3:17 You have **m** my soul far from
Ezek 1:17 When they **m**, they went toward
Dan 8: 7 he was **m** with rage against him,
11:11 king of the South shall be **m**
11:28 his heart shall be **m** against
Mt 9:36 He was **m** with compassion for
14:14 and He was **m** with compassion
18:27 master of that servant was **m**
21:10 Jerusalem, all the city was **m**,
Mk 1:41 **m** with compassion, stretched
6:34 saw a great multitude and was **m**
Acts 7: 4 He **m** him to this land in which
Col 1:23 and are not **m** away from the
Heb 11: 7 **m** with godly fear, prepared an
2 Pe 1:21 of God spoke as they were **m**
Rev 6:14 mountain and island was **m** out

MOVEMENT (1/1)

Num 10: 2 and for directing the **m** of the

MOVER (KJV) See CREATOR (OF DISSENSION)

MOVES (8/8) MOVE

Gen 1:21 and every living thing that **m**,
1:28 over every living thing that **m**
Lev 11:46 every living creature that **m**
Deut 27:17 Cursed is the one who **m** his
Job 9:11 If He **m** past, I do not
40:17 He **m** his tail like a cedar;
Ps 69:34 seas and everything that **m** in
Ezek 47: 9 that every living thing that **m**,

MOVING (4/4) MOVE

Gen 9: 3 Every **m** thing that lives shall
Job 31:26 Or the moon **m** in brightness,
Song 7: 9 **M** gently the lips of sleepers.
Jn 5: 3 waiting for the **m** of the water.

MOWED (1/1)

Jas 5: 4 the wages of the laborers who **m**

MOWING (1/1)

Ps 72: 6 rain upon the grass before **m**,

MOWINGS (1/1)

Am 7: 1 late crop after the king's **m**.

MOZA (5/5)

1 Chr 2:46 concubine, bore Haran, **M**,
8:36 and Zimri; and Zimri begot **M**.
8:37 **M** begot Binea, Raphah his son,
9:42 and Zimri; and Zimri begot **M**;
9:43 **M** begot Binea, Rephaiah his son,

MOZAH (1/1)

Josh 18:26 Mizpah, Chephirah, **M**,

MUCH (218/208)

Gen 20: 8 and the men were very **m** afraid.
26:16 for you are **m** mightier than
34:12 Ask me ever so **m** dowry and gift,
41:49 Joseph gathered very **m** grain, as
43:34 serving was five times as **m** as
44: 1 as **m** as they can carry, and put
Ex 14:28 Not so **m** as one of them
16: 5 and it shall be twice as **m** as
16:18 he who gathered **m** had nothing
16:22 that they gathered twice as **m**
18:18 For this thing is too **m** for
30:23 half as **m** sweet-smelling
36: 5 The people bring **m** more than
36: 7 work to be done—indeed too **m**.
Lev 7:10 to one as **m** as the other.
Num 16: 3 You take too **m** upon
16: 7 You take too **m** upon
Deut 2: 5 not so **m** as one footstep,
3:19 know that you have **m** livestock)
12:20 you may eat as **m** meat as your
12:21 may eat within your gates as **m**
28:38 You shall carry **m** seed out to
31:27 then how **m** more after my death?
Josh 9:24 therefore we were very **m** afraid
13: 1 and there remains very **m** land
19: 9 of Judah was too **m** for them.
22: 8 Return with **m** riches to your
22: 8 with very **m** livestock, with
22: 8 and with very **m** clothing.
Judg 6:27 and the men of the city too **m**
14:17 because she pressed him so **m**.
Ruth 1:13 for it grieves me very **m** for
1 Sam 2:16 then you may take as **m** as
14:30 How **m** better if the people had
14:30 have been a **m** greater slaughter
20:13 may the LORD do so and **m** more
21:12 and was very **m** afraid of Achish
22:15 of all this, little or **m**.
23: 3 How **m** more then if we go to
25:36 told him nothing, little or **m**,
26:24 as your life was valued **m** this
26:24 so let my life be valued **m** in
2 Sam 3:22 from a raid and brought **m** spoil
4:11 How **m** more, when wicked men have
12: 8 I also would have given you **m**
14:25 no one who was praised as **m** as
16:11 How **m** more now may this
17:12 shall not be left so **m** as one.
1 Ki 8:27 How **m** less this temple which I
9:11 as **m** as he desired), that King
10: 2 very **m** gold, and precious
12:28 It is too **m** for you to go up to
2 Ki 5:13 How **m** more then, when he says
10:18 a little, Jehu will serve him **m**.
12:10 they saw that there was **m** money
21: 6 He did **m** evil in the sight of
21:16 shed very **m** innocent blood
1 Chr 4:27 multiply as **m** as the children
22: 4 from Tyre brought **m** cedar wood
22: 8 You have shed **m** blood and have
22: 8 because you have shed **m** blood
22:14 Indeed I have taken **m** trouble to
2 Chr 2:16 as **m** as you need; we will bring
6:18 How **m** less this temple which I
9:12 **m** more than she had brought
14:13 they carried away very **m** spoil.
14:14 there was exceedingly **m** spoil
17:13 He had **m** property in the cities
20:25 spoil because there was so **m**.
24:11 saw that there was **m** money,
25: 9 is able to give you **m** more
25:13 and took **m** spoil.
26:10 for he had **m** livestock, both in
28: 8 and they also took away **m** spoil
32: 4 Assyria come and find **m** water?
32:15 How **m** less will your God
32:29 had given him very **m** property.
33: 6 He did **m** evil in the sight of
Neh 4:10 and there is so **m** rubbish
9:37 And it yields **m** increase to the
Job 4:19 How **m** more those who dwell in
15:10 **M** older than your father.
15:16 How **m** less man, who is
25: 6 How **m** less man, who is a
27: 8 Though he may gain **m**,
31:25 because my hand had gained **m**;
35:15 Nor taken **m** notice of folly,
42:10 the LORD gave Job twice as **m**
Ps 19:10 than **m** fine gold; Sweeter also
119:14 As **m** as in all riches.
119:107 I am afflicted very **m**;
Prov 11:31 How **m** more the ungodly and the
13:23 **M** food is in the fallow
14: 4 But **m** increase comes by the

15: 6 righteous there is ***m*** treasure,
15:11 So how ***m*** more the hearts of
16:16 How ***m*** better to get wisdom than
17: 7 ***M*** less lying lips to a prince.
19: 7 How ***m*** more do his friends go
19:10 ***M*** less for a servant to rule
19:24 And will not so ***m*** as bring it
21:27 How ***m*** more when he brings it
25:16 Eat only as ***m*** as you need,
25:27 It is not good to eat ***m*** honey;
Eccl 1:18 For in ***m*** wisdom is much grief,
1:18 For in much wisdom is ***m*** grief,
5: 3 dream comes through ***m*** activity,
5:12 Whether he eats little or ***m***;
5:17 And he has ***m*** sorrow and
9:18 But one sinner destroys ***m*** good.
12:12 and ***m*** study is wearisome to
Song 4:10 my spouse! How ***m*** better than
Isa 30:33 Its pyre is fire with ***m*** wood;
56:12 And ***m*** more abundant."
Jer 2:22 and use ***m*** soap, Yet your
2:36 Why do you gad about so ***m*** to
Ezek 14:21 How ***m*** more it shall be when I
15: 5 How ***m*** less will it be useful
23:32 in derision; It contains ***m***.
33:31 their mouth they show ***m*** love
46: 5 as ***m*** as he wants to give, as
46: 7 as ***m*** as he wants to give for
46:11 as ***m*** as he wants to give for
Dan 7: 5 'Arise, devour ***m*** flesh!'
11:13 a great army and ***m*** equipment.
Jon 4:11 and ***m*** livestock?"
Nah 2:10 ***M*** pain is in every side,
Hag 1: 6 "You have sown ***m***,
1: 9 "You looked for ***m***,
Mt 6:30 will He not ***m*** more clothe
7:11 how ***m*** more will your Father who
10:25 how ***m*** more will they call
12:12 Of how ***m*** more value then is a
13: 5 they did not have ***m*** earth;
23:15 you make him twice as ***m*** a son
26: 9 oil might have been sold for ***m***
Mk 3:20 so that they could not so ***m*** as
4: 5 where it did not have ***m*** earth;
12:41 many who were rich put in ***m***.
Lk 6:34 to sinners to receive as ***m*** back.
7:47 are forgiven, for she loved ***m***.
10:40 Martha was distracted with ***m***
11:13 how ***m*** more will your heavenly
12:24 Of how ***m*** more value are you
12:28 how ***m*** more will He clothe
12:48 For everyone to whom ***m*** is
12:48 from him ***m*** will be required;
12:48 and to whom ***m*** has been
16: 5 How ***m*** do you owe my master?'
16: 7 And how ***m*** do you owe?' So he
16:10 is least is faithful also in ***m***;
16:10 is least is unjust also in ***m***.
18:13 would not so ***m*** as raise his
19:15 that he might know how ***m*** every
Jn 3:23 because there was ***m*** water
6:10 Now there was ***m*** grass in the
6:11 as ***m*** as they wanted.
7:12 And there was ***m*** complaining
12:24 it produces ***m*** grain.
14:30 I will no longer talk ***m*** with
15: 5 bears ***m*** fruit; for without Me
15: 8 that you bear ***m*** fruit; so you
Acts 5: 8 you sold the land for so ***m***?
5: 8 She said, "Yes, for so ***m***.
9:13 how ***m*** harm he has done to Your
15: 7 when there had been ***m*** dispute,
16:16 brought her masters ***m*** profit
19: 2 We have not so ***m*** as heard
26:24 ***M*** learning is driving you mad!
27: 9 Now when ***m*** time had been spent,
27:10 end with disaster and ***m*** loss,
Rom 1:15 as ***m*** as is in me, I am ready
3: 2 ***M*** in every way! Chiefly because
5: 9 ***M*** more then, having now been
5:10 ***m*** more, having been reconciled,
5:15 ***m*** more the grace of God and the
5:17 ***m*** more those who receive
5:20 grace abounded ***m*** more,
9:22 endured with ***m*** longsuffering
11:12 how ***m*** more their fullness!
11:24 how ***m*** more will these, who are
12:18 as ***m*** as depends on you, live
15:22 this reason I also have been ***m***
16: 6 who labored ***m*** for us.
16:12 who labored ***m*** in the Lord.
1 Cor 2: 3 in fear, and in ***m*** trembling.
6: 3 How ***m*** more, things that pertain
12:22 ***m*** rather, those members of the
2 Cor 2: 4 For out of ***m*** affliction and
2: 7 swallowed up with too ***m*** sorrow.
3: 9 exceeds ***m*** more in glory.
3:11 remains is ***m*** more glorious.
6: 4 in ***m*** patience, in tribulations,
8: 4 imploring us with ***m*** urgency that
8:15 He who gathered ***m*** had
8:22 but now ***m*** more diligent,
Phil 1:14 are ***m*** more bold to speak the
2:12 but now ***m*** more in my absence,
1 Th 1: 5 Holy Spirit and in ***m*** assurance,
1: 6 the word in ***m*** affliction
2: 2 gospel of God in ***m*** conflict.
1 Tim 3: 8 not given to ***m*** wine, not greedy
2 Tim 4:14 the coppersmith did me ***m*** harm.
Titus 2: 3 not given to ***m*** wine, teachers
Phm 1:16 especially to me but how ***m*** more
Heb 1: 4 having become so ***m*** better than
5:11 of whom we have ***m*** to say, and
7:22 by so ***m*** more Jesus has become a
9:14 how ***m*** more shall the blood of
10:25 and so ***m*** the more as you see
10:29 Of how ***m*** worse punishment, do
12: 9 Shall we not ***m*** more readily be
12:20 And if so ***m*** as a beast
12:25 ***m*** more shall we not escape
Jas 5:16 of a righteous man avails ***m***.
1 Pe 1: 7 being ***m*** more precious than
Rev 5: 4 So I wept ***m***, because no one
8: 3 He was given ***m*** incense, that he

MUD (1/1)

Mic 7:10 will be trampled down Like ***m***

MUDDY (3/2)

Isa 14:23 And marshes of ***m*** water;
Ezek 32:13 The foot of man shall ***m*** them
32:13 shall the hooves of animals ***m***

MUFFLERS (KJV) See VEILS

MULBERRY (5/5)

2 Sam 5:23 upon them in front of the ***m***
5:24 marching in the tops of the ***m***
1 Chr 14:14 upon them in front of the ***m***
14:15 marching in the tops of the ***m***
Lk 17: 6 you can say to this ***m*** tree, 'Be

MULE (9/7) MULE-LOADS, MULES

2 Sam 13:29 and each one got on his ***m*** and
18: 9 of David. Absalom rode on a ***m***.
18: 9 The ***m*** went under the thick
18: 9 And the ***m*** which was under him
1 Ki 1:33 Solomon my son ride on my own ***m***,
1:38 Solomon ride on King David's ***m***,
1:44 made him ride on the king's ***m***.
Ps 32: 9 like the horse or like the ***m***,
Zech 14:15 plague On the horse and the ***m***,

MULE-LOADS (1/1) MULE

2 Ki 5:17 your servant be given two ***m*** of

MULES (8/8) MULE

1 Ki 10:25 armor, spices, horses, and ***m***,
18: 5 grass to keep the horses and ***m***
1 Chr 12:40 on ***m*** and oxen—provisions of
2 Chr 9:24 armor, spices, horses, and ***m***,
Ezra 2:66 their ***m*** two hundred and
Neh 7:68 their ***m*** two hundred and
Isa 66:20 on ***m*** and on camels, to My holy
Ezek 27:14 with horses, steeds, and ***m***.

MULTICOLORED (2/2)

Ezek 16:16 of your garments and adorned ***m***
27:24 in chests of ***m*** apparel, in

MULTIPLIED (43/42) MULTIPLY

Gen 47:27 there and grew and ***m***
Ex 1: 7 ***m*** and grew exceedingly mighty;
1:12 the more they ***m*** and grew.
1:20 and the people ***m*** and grew very
11: 9 so that My wonders may be ***m*** in
Deut 1:10 The LORD your God has ***m*** you,
8:13 your silver and your gold are ***m***,
8:13 and all that you have is ***m***;
11:21 days of your children may be ***m***
Josh 24: 3 and ***m*** his descendants and gave
Judg 16:24 And the one who ***m*** our dead."
1 Chr 5: 9 because their cattle had ***m*** in
Neh 9:23 You also ***m*** their children as
Job 27:14 If his children are ***m***,
35: 6 if your transgressions are ***m***,
Ps 16: 4 Their sorrows shall be ***m*** who
38:19 who hate me wrongfully have ***m***.
Prov 9:11 For by me your days will be ***m***,
29:16 When the wicked are ***m***,
Isa 9: 3 You have ***m*** the nation
59:12 For our transgressions are ***m***
Jer 3:16 when you are ***m*** and increased in
Ezek 5: 7 Because you have ***m*** disobedience
11: 6 You have ***m*** your slain in this
16:25 and ***m*** your acts of harlotry.
16:29 Moreover you ***m*** your acts of
16:51 but you have ***m*** your
23:19 'Yet she ***m*** her harlotry
31: 5 the field; Its boughs were ***m***,
35:13 have boasted against Me and ***m***
Dan 4: 1 Peace be ***m*** to you.
6:25 Peace be ***m*** to you.
Hos 2: 8 And ***m*** her silver and
8:14 Judah also has ***m*** fortified
12:10 And have ***m*** visions; I have
Nah 3:16 You have ***m*** your merchants more
Acts 6: 7 the number of the disciples ***m***
7:17 the people grew and ***m*** in Egypt
9:31 of the Holy Spirit, they were ***m***.
12:24 But the word of God grew and ***m***.
1 Pe 1: 2 Grace to you and peace be ***m***.
2 Pe 1: 2 Grace and peace be ***m*** to you in
Jude 2 and love be ***m*** to you.

MULTIPLIES (4/4) MULTIPLY

Job 9:17 And ***m*** my wounds without cause.
34:37 And ***m*** his words against
35:16 He ***m*** words without
Eccl 10:14 A fool also ***m*** words. No man

MULTIPLY (48/44) MULTIPLIED, MULTIPLIES, MULTIPLYING

Gen 1:22 saying, "Be fruitful and ***m***,
1:22 and let birds ***m*** on the earth."
1:28 to them, "Be fruitful and ***m***;
3:16 I will greatly ***m*** your sorrow and
6: 1 when men began to ***m*** on the face
8:17 and be fruitful and ***m*** on the
9: 1 to them: "Be fruitful and ***m***,
9: 7 as for you, be fruitful and ***m***;
9: 7 abundantly in the earth And ***m***
16:10 I will ***m*** your descendants
17: 2 and will ***m*** you exceedingly."
17:20 and will ***m*** him exceedingly. He
22:17 and multiplying I will ***m*** your
26: 4 I will make your descendants ***m***
26:24 I will bless you and ***m*** your
28: 3 And make you fruitful and ***m***
35:11 God Almighty. Be fruitful and ***m***;
48: 4 I will make you fruitful and ***m***
Ex 1:10 shrewdly with them, lest they ***m***,
7: 3 and ***m*** My signs and My wonders
32:13 I will ***m*** your descendants as the
Lev 26: 9 ***m*** you and confirm My covenant
Deut 6: 3 and that you may ***m*** greatly as
7:13 love you and bless you and ***m***
8: 1 that you may live and ***m***,
8:13 your herds and your flocks ***m***,
13:17 have compassion on you and ***m***
17:16 But he shall not ***m*** horses for
17:16 people to return to Egypt to ***m***
17:17 Neither shall he ***m*** wives for
17:17 nor shall he greatly ***m*** silver
28:63 over you to do you good and ***m***
30: 5 He will prosper you and ***m*** you
30:16 that you may live and ***m***;
1 Chr 4:27 did any of their families ***m*** as
27:23 the LORD had said He would ***m***
Job 29:18 And ***m*** my days as the sand.
Ps 107:38 and they ***m*** greatly; And He
Jer 30:19 I will ***m*** them, and they shall
33:22 so will I ***m*** the descendants of
Ezek 36:10 I will ***m*** men upon you, all the
36:11 I will ***m*** upon you man and beast;
36:29 I will call for the grain and ***m***
36:30 And I will ***m*** the fruit of your
37:26 I will establish them and ***m***
Am 4: 4 At Gilgal ***m*** transgression;
2 Cor 9:10 supply and ***m*** the seed you have
Heb 6:14 and multiplying I will ***m***

MULTIPLYING (3/3) MULTIPLY

Gen 22:17 and ***m*** I will multiply your
Acts 6: 1 number of the disciples was ***m***,
Heb 6:14 and ***m*** I will multiply

MULTITUDE (222/215) MULTITUDES

Gen 16:10 they shall not be counted for ***m***.
32:12 which cannot be numbered for ***m***.
48: 4 and I will make of you a ***m*** of
48:16 And let them grow into a ***m*** in
48:19 descendants shall become a ***m***
Ex 12:38 A mixed ***m*** went up with them
Lev 25:16 According to the ***m*** of years you
Num 11: 4 Now the mixed ***m*** who were among
32: 1 of Gad had a very great ***m*** of
Deut 1:10 as the stars of heaven in ***m***.
10:22 you as the stars of heaven in ***m***.
28:62 as the stars of heaven in ***m***,
Josh 11: 4 that is on the seashore in ***m***,
Judg 4: 7 with his chariots and his ***m*** at
7:12 the sand by the seashore in ***m***.
1 Sam 13: 5 which is on the seashore in ***m***.
14:16 looked, and there was the ***m***,
2 Sam 6:19 among the whole ***m*** of Israel,
17:11 sand that is by the sea for ***m***,
1 Ki 4:20 as the sand by the sea in ***m***,
8: 5 be counted or numbered for ***m***.
20:13 'Have you seen all this great ***m***?
20:28 I will deliver all this great ***m***
2 Ki 7:13 either become like all the ***m***
7:13 may become like all the ***m*** of
19:23 By the ***m*** of my chariots I have
25:11 Babylon, with the rest of the ***m***.
2 Chr 1: 9 like the dust of the earth in ***m***.
5: 6 be counted or numbered for ***m***.
13: 8 David; and you are a great ***m***,
14:11 Your name we go against this ***m***.
20: 2 A great ***m*** is coming against you
20:12 no power against this great ***m***
20:15 because of this great ***m***,
20:24 they looked toward the ***m***;
28: 5 and carried away a great ***m*** of
30:18 For a ***m*** of the people, many from
32: 7 nor before all the ***m*** that is
Neh 13: 3 they separated all the mixed ***m***
Esth 5:11 the ***m*** of his children,
10: 3 and well received by the ***m*** of
Job 11: 2 Should not the ***m*** of words be
31:34 Because I feared the great ***m***,
32: 7 And ***m*** of years should teach
35: 9 Because of the ***m*** of oppressions

Ps 5:7 come into Your house in the ***m***
5:10 Cast them out in the ***m*** of
33:16 No king is saved by the ***m*** of
42:4 For I used to go with the ***m***;
42:4 With a ***m*** that kept a pilgrim
49:6 And boast in the ***m*** of
51:1 According to the ***m*** of Your
69:13 in the ***m*** of Your mercy, Hear
69:16 Turn to me according to the ***m***
94:19 In the ***m*** of my anxieties within
97:1 Let the ***m*** of isles be glad!
106:7 They did not remember the ***m*** of
106:45 relented according to the ***m*** of
109:30 I will praise Him among the ***m***.
Prov 10:19 In the ***m*** of words sin is not
11:14 But in the ***m*** of counselors
14:28 In a ***m*** of people is a king's
15:22 But in the ***m*** of counselors
20:15 There is gold and a ***m*** of
24:6 And in a ***m*** of counselors
Eccl 5:7 For in the ***m*** of dreams and many
Isa 1:11 To what purpose is the ***m*** of
5:13 And their ***m*** dried up with
5:14 Their glory and their ***m*** and
13:4 The noise of a ***m*** in the
16:14 despised with all that great ***m***,
17:12 Woe to the ***m*** of many people
29:5 Moreover the ***m*** of your foes
29:5 And the ***m*** of the terrible ones
29:7 The ***m*** of all the nations who
29:8 So the ***m*** of all the nations
31:4 lion over his prey (When a ***m***
37:24 By the ***m*** of my chariots I have
47:9 fullness Because of the ***m*** of
47:12 your enchantments And the ***m***
47:13 You are wearied in the ***m*** of
60:6 The ***m*** of camels shall cover
63:7 According to the ***m*** of His
Jer 3:23 And from the ***m*** of mountains;
10:13 There is a ***m*** of waters in
12:6 they have called a ***m*** after you.
25:20 all the mixed ***m***,
25:24 all the kings of the mixed ***m***
30:14 For the ***m*** of your iniquities,
30:15 Because of the ***m*** of your
44:15 women who stood by, a great ***m***,
49:32 And the ***m*** of their cattle for
51:16 There is a ***m*** of waters in the
51:42 She is covered with the ***m*** of
Lam 1:5 her Because of the ***m*** of her
3:32 compassion According to the ***m***
Ezek 7:11 remain, None of their ***m***,
7:12 For wrath is on their whole ***m***.
7:13 the vision concerns the whole ***m***,
7:14 My wrath is on all their ***m***.
14:4 according to the ***m*** of his
23:42 The sound of a carefree ***m*** was
28:18 your sanctuaries By the ***m*** of
30:10 I will also make a ***m*** of Egypt to
30:15 I will cut off the ***m*** of No,
31:2 king of Egypt and to his ***m***:
31:9 I made it beautiful with a ***m*** of
31:18 This is Pharaoh and all his ***m***,
32:12 I will cause your ***m*** to fall.
32:12 And all its ***m*** shall be
32:16 for Egypt, And for all her ***m***,
32:18 wail over the ***m*** of Egypt, And
32:24 is Elam and all her ***m***,
32:25 of the slain, With all her ***m***,
32:31 be comforted over all his ***m***,
32:32 Pharaoh and all his ***m***,"
39:11 will bury Gog and all his ***m***.
47:9 There will be a very great ***m*** of
Dan 10:6 his words like the voice of a ***m***.
11:10 and assemble a ***m*** of great
11:11 who shall muster a great ***m***;
11:11 but the ***m*** shall be given into
11:12 "When he has taken away the ***m***,
11:13 will return and muster a ***m***
Hos 10:1 According to the ***m*** of his
10:13 In the ***m*** of your mighty men.
Nah 3:3 There is a ***m*** of slain,
3:4 Because of the ***m*** of harlotries
Zech 2:4 because of the ***m*** of men and
Mt 13:2 and the whole ***m*** stood on the
13:34 things Jesus spoke to the ***m*** in
13:36 Then Jesus sent the ***m*** away and
14:5 him to death, he feared the ***m***,
14:14 Jesus went out He saw a great ***m***;
15:10 When He had called the ***m*** to
15:31 So the ***m*** marveled when they saw
15:32 "I have compassion on the ***m***,
15:33 to fill such a great ***m***?
15:35 So He commanded the ***m*** to sit
15:36 the disciples gave to the ***m***.
15:39 And He sent away the ***m***,
17:14 when they had come to the ***m***,
20:29 a great ***m*** followed Him.
20:31 Then the ***m*** warned them that they
21:8 And a very great ***m*** spread their
21:26 say, 'From men,' we fear the ***m***,
26:47 with a great ***m*** with swords and
27:15 to releasing to the ***m*** one
27:24 washed his hands before the ***m***,
Mk 2:13 and all the ***m*** came to Him, and
3:7 And a great ***m*** from Galilee
3:8 from Tyre and Sidon, a great ***m***,
3:9 ready for Him because of the ***m***,
3:20 Then the ***m*** came together again,
3:32 And a ***m*** was sitting around Him;
4:1 And a great ***m*** was gathered to
4:1 and the whole ***m*** was on the land
4:36 Now when they had left the ***m***,
5:21 a great ***m*** gathered to Him;
5:24 and a great ***m*** followed Him and
5:31 You see the ***m*** thronging You, and
6:34 saw a great ***m*** and was moved
6:45 while He sent the ***m*** away.
7:14 When He had called all the ***m*** to
7:33 He took him aside from the ***m***,
8:1 the ***m*** being very great and
8:2 "I have compassion on the ***m***,
8:6 So He commanded the ***m*** to sit
8:6 and they set them before the ***m***.
9:14 He saw a great ***m*** around them,
10:46 His disciples and a great ***m***,
12:12 hands on Him, but feared the ***m***,
14:43 with a great ***m*** with swords and
15:8 Then the ***m***, crying aloud,
Lk 1:10 And the whole ***m*** of the people
2:13 there was with the angel a ***m***
5:1 as the ***m*** pressed about Him to
6:17 of His disciples and a great ***m***
6:19 And the whole ***m*** sought to touch
8:4 And when a great ***m*** had
8:37 Then the whole ***m*** of the
8:40 that the ***m*** welcomed Him, for
9:12 Send the ***m*** away, that they may
9:16 disciples to set before the ***m***.
9:37 that a great ***m*** met Him.
9:38 Suddenly a man from the ***m*** cried
12:1 when an innumerable ***m*** of people
13:17 and all the ***m*** rejoiced for all
18:36 And hearing a ***m*** passing by, he
19:37 the whole ***m*** of the disciples
22:6 to them in the absence of the ***m***.
22:47 was still speaking, behold, a ***m***;
23:1 Then the whole ***m*** of them arose
23:27 And a great ***m*** of the people
Jn 5:3 In these lay a great ***m*** of sick
5:13 a ***m*** being in that place.
6:2 Then a great ***m*** followed Him,
6:5 and seeing a great ***m*** coming
12:12 The next day a great ***m*** that had
21:6 to draw it in because of the ***m***
Acts 2:6 the ***m*** came together, and were
4:32 Now the ***m*** of those who believed
5:16 Also a ***m*** gathered from the
6:2 Then the twelve summoned the ***m***
6:5 the saying pleased the whole ***m***.
14:1 and so spoke that a great ***m***
14:4 But the ***m*** of the city was
14:14 clothes and ran in among the ***m***,
15:12 Then all the ***m*** kept silent and
15:30 when they had gathered the ***m***
16:22 Then the ***m*** rose up together
17:4 and a great ***m*** of the devout
19:9 evil of the Way before the ***m***,
19:33 drew Alexander out of the ***m***,
21:34 And some among the ***m*** cried one
21:36 For the ***m*** of the people followed
Heb 11:12 as the stars of the sky in ***m***—
Jas 5:20 a soul from death and cover a ***m***
1 Pe 4:8 love will cover a ***m*** of
Rev 7:9 a great ***m*** which no one could
19:1 a loud voice of a great ***m*** in
19:6 it were, the voice of a great ***m***,

MULTITUDES (50/48) MULTITUDE

Ezek 32:20 Drawing her and all her ***m***.
32:26 and Tubal and all their ***m***,
Joel 3:14 ***M***, multitudes in the valley
3:14 ***m*** in the valley of decision!
Mt 4:25 Great ***m*** followed Him—from
5:1 And seeing the ***m***, He went up
8:1 great ***m*** followed Him.
8:18 And when Jesus saw great ***m***
9:8 Now when the ***m*** saw it, they
9:33 And the ***m*** marveled, saying,
9:36 But when He saw the ***m***,
11:7 Jesus began to say to the ***m***
12:15 And great ***m*** followed Him, and
12:23 And all the ***m*** were amazed and
12:46 He was still talking to the ***m***,
13:2 And great ***m*** were gathered
14:13 But when the ***m*** heard it, they
14:15 Send the ***m*** away, that they may
14:19 Then He commanded the ***m*** to sit
14:19 and the disciples gave to the ***m***.
14:22 while He sent the ***m*** away.
14:23 And when He had sent the ***m*** away,
15:30 Then great ***m*** came to Him, having
19:2 And great ***m*** followed Him, and He
21:9 Then the ***m*** who went before and
21:11 So the ***m*** said, "This is Jesus,
21:46 hands on Him, they feared the ***m***,
22:33 And when the ***m*** heard this, they
23:1 Then Jesus spoke to the ***m*** and to
26:55 that hour Jesus said to the ***m***,
27:20 and elders persuaded the ***m***
Mk 6:33 But the ***m*** saw them departing,
10:1 And ***m*** gathered to Him again,
Lk 3:7 Then he said to the ***m*** that came
5:3 He sat down and taught the ***m***
5:15 and great ***m*** came together to
7:24 He began to speak to the ***m***
8:42 the ***m*** thronged Him.
8:45 the ***m*** throng and press You, and
9:11 But when the ***m*** knew it, they
11:14 and the ***m*** marveled.
12:54 Then He also said to the ***m***,
14:25 Now great ***m*** went with Him. And
Acts 5:14 ***m*** of both men and women,
8:6 And the ***m*** with one accord heeded
13:45 But when the Jews saw the ***m***,
14:13 to sacrifice with the ***m***.
14:18 could scarcely restrain the ***m***
14:19 and having persuaded the ***m***,
Rev 17:15 the harlot sits, are peoples, ***m***,

MUNITION (KJV) See FORT, FORTRESS

MUPPIM (1/1)

Gen 46:21 Gera, Naaman, Ehi, Rosh, ***M***,

MURDER (21/20) MURDERED, MURDERER, MURDERS

Ex 20:13 "You shall not ***m***.
Deut 5:17 'You shall not ***m***.
Ps 94:6 And ***m*** the fatherless.
Jer 7:9 "Will you steal, ***m***,
40:14 the son of Nethaniah to ***m*** you?
40:15 Why should he ***m*** you, so that
Hos 6:9 So the company of priests ***m***
Mt 5:21 of old, 'You shall not ***m***,
19:18 said, " 'You shall not ***m***,
Mk 10:19 adultery,' 'Do not ***m***,
15:7 they had committed ***m*** in the
Lk 18:20 adultery,' 'Do not ***m***,
23:19 made in the city, and for ***m***.
23:25 who for rebellion and ***m*** had
Acts 9:1 still breathing threats and ***m***
Rom 1:29 maliciousness; full of envy, ***m***,
13:9 "You shall not ***m***,
Jas 2:11 also said, "Do not ***m***.
2:11 commit adultery, but you do ***m***,
4:2 You ***m*** and covet and cannot
1 Jn 3:12 And why did he ***m*** him? Because

MURDERED (13/13) MURDER

Judg 20:4 husband of the woman who was ***m***,
1 Ki 21:19 Have you ***m*** and also taken
2 Ki 11:2 king's sons who were being ***m***;
14:5 his servants who had ***m*** his
2 Chr 22:11 king's sons who were being ***m***,
25:3 his servants who had ***m*** his
Jer 41:16 son of Nethaniah after he had ***m***
41:18 the son of Nethaniah had ***m***
Mt 23:31 you are sons of those who ***m***
23:35 whom you ***m*** between the temple
Acts 5:30 raised up Jesus whom you ***m*** by
Jas 5:6 you have ***m*** the just; he does
1 Jn 3:12 was of the wicked one and ***m***

MURDERER (21/16) MURDER, MURDERERS

Num 35:16 so that he dies, he is a ***m***;
35:16 the ***m*** shall surely be put to
35:17 and he does die, he is a ***m***;
35:17 the ***m*** shall surely be put to
35:18 and he does die, he is a ***m***;
35:18 the ***m*** shall surely be put to
35:19 blood himself shall put the ***m***
35:21 be put to death. He is a ***m***.
35:21 of blood shall put the ***m*** to
35:30 the ***m*** shall be put to death on
35:31 no ransom for the life of a ***m***
2 Ki 6:32 you see how this son of a ***m***
9:31 Zimri, ***m*** of your master?"
Job 24:14 The ***m*** rises with the light;
Hos 9:13 bring out his children to the ***m***.
Jn 8:44 He was a ***m*** from the beginning,
Acts 3:14 and asked for a ***m*** to be granted
28:4 "No doubt this man is a ***m***,
1 Pe 4:15 let none of you suffer as a ***m***,
1 Jn 3:15 hates his brother is a ***m***,
3:15 and you know that no ***m*** has

MURDERERS (9/8) MURDERER

2 Ki 14:6 But the children of the ***m*** he did
Isa 1:21 lodged in it, But now ***m***.
Jer 4:31 my soul is weary Because of ***m***!
Mt 22:7 his armies, destroyed those ***m***,
Acts 7:52 have become the betrayers and ***m***,
1 Tim 1:9 for ***m*** of fathers and murderers
1:9 for murderers of fathers and ***m***
Rev 21:8 unbelieving, abominable, ***m***,
22:15 and sexually immoral and ***m*** and

MURDERS (6/6) MURDER

Ps 10:8 In the secret places he ***m*** the
Mt 5:21 and whoever ***m*** will be in danger
15:19 heart proceed evil thoughts, ***m***,
Mk 7:21 adulteries, fornications, ***m***,
Gal 5:21 envy, ***m***, drunkenness, revelries,
Rev 9:21 they did not repent of their ***m***

MURKY (1/1)

Prov 25:26 the wicked Is like a ***m***

MURMUR (1/1) MURMURED, MURMURING

Jn 6:43 Do not ***m*** among yourselves.

MURMURED (1/1) MURMUR

Num 16:41 of the children of Israel ***m***

MURMURERS, MURMURINGS
(KJV) See COMPLAINING, COMPLAINTS, GRUMBLERS

MURMURING (1/1) MURMUR, MURMURINGS
Jn 7:32 Pharisees heard the crowd ***m***

MURRAIN (KJV) See PESTILENCE

MUSCLE (2/1)
Gen 32:32 of Israel do not eat the ***m***
32:32 socket of Jacob's hip in the ***m***

MUSCLES (1/1)
Job 40:16 his power is in his stomach ***m***.

MUSE (1/1)
Ps 143: 5 I ***m*** on the work of Your hands.

MUSHI (8/8)
Ex 6:19 of Merari were Mahali and ***M***.
Num 3:20 by their families: Mahli and ***M***.
1 Chr 6:19 of Merari were Mahli and ***M***.
6:47 the son of Mahli, the son of ***M***,
23:21 of Merari were Mahli and ***M***.
23:23 The sons of ***M*** were Mahli, Eder,
24:26 of Merari were Mahli and ***M***;
24:30 Also the sons of ***M*** were Mahli,

MUSHITES (2/2)
Num 3:33 and the family of the ***M***;
26:58 Mahlites, the family of the ***M***,

MUSIC (23/23) MUSICAL, MUSICIAN
1 Sam 18:10 So David played ***m*** with his
19: 9 And David was playing ***m*** with
2 Sam 6: 5 the house of Israel played ***m***
6:21 Therefore I will play ***m*** before
1 Chr 6:32 They were ministering with ***m***
13: 8 David and all Israel played ***m***
15:16 accompanied by instruments of ***m***,
15:22 in charge of the ***m***,
15:27 and Chenaniah the ***m*** master
15:28 making ***m*** with stringed
15:29 David whirling and playing ***m***;
16: 5 but Asaph made ***m*** with cymbals;
25: 6 of their father for the ***m*** in
2 Chr 5:13 cymbals and instruments of ***m***,
7: 6 also with instruments of the ***m***
34:12 skillful with instruments of ***m***,
Eccl 12: 4 And all the daughters of ***m*** are
Lam 5:14 And the young men from their ***m***.
Dan 3: 5 in symphony with all kinds of ***m***,
3: 7 in symphony with all kinds of ***m***,
3:10 in symphony with all kinds of ***m***,
3:15 in symphony with all kinds of ***m***,
Lk 15:25 he heard ***m*** and dancing.

MUSICAL (7/7) MUSIC
1 Sam 18: 6 and with ***m*** instruments.
1 Chr 16:42 trumpets and cymbals and the ***m***
23: 5 praised the LORD with ***m***
2 Chr 23:13 also the singers with ***m***
Neh 12:36 with the ***m*** instruments of David
Eccl 2: 8 and ***m*** instruments of all
Am 6: 5 And invent for yourselves ***m***

MUSICIAN (58/57) MUSIC, MUSICIANS
2 Ki 3:15 "But now bring me a ***m***.
3:15 when the ***m*** played, that the
Ps 4: To the Chief ***M***.
5: To the Chief ***M***.
6: To the Chief ***M***.
8: To the Chief ***M***.
9: To the Chief ***M***.
11: To the Chief ***M***.
12: To the Chief ***M***.
13: To the Chief ***M***.
14: To the Chief ***M***.
18: To the Chief ***M***.
19: To the Chief ***M***.
20: To the Chief ***M***.
21: To the Chief ***M***.
22: To the Chief ***M***.
31: To the Chief ***M***.
36: To the Chief ***M***.
39: To the Chief ***M***.
40: To the Chief ***M***.
41: To the Chief ***M***.
42: To the Chief ***M***.
44: To the Chief ***M***.
45: To the Chief ***M***.
46: To the Chief ***M***.
47: To the Chief ***M***.
49: To the Chief ***M***.
51: To the Chief ***M***.
52: To the Chief ***M***.
53: To the Chief ***M***.
54: To the Chief ***M***.
55: To the Chief ***M***.
56: To the Chief ***M***.
57: To the Chief ***M***.
58: To the Chief ***M***.
59: To the Chief ***M***.
60: To the Chief ***M***.
61: To the Chief ***M***.
62: To the Chief ***M***.
64: To the Chief ***M***.
65: To the Chief ***M***.
66: To the Chief ***M***.
67: To the Chief ***M***.
68: To the Chief ***M***.
69: To the Chief ***M***.
70: To the Chief ***M***.
75: To the Chief ***M***.
76: To the Chief ***M***.
77: To the Chief ***M***.
80: To the Chief ***M***.
81: To the Chief ***M***.
84: To the Chief ***M***.
85: To the Chief ***M***.
88: sons of Korah. To the Chief ***M***.
109: To the Chief ***M***.
139: For the Chief ***M***.
140: To the Chief ***M***.
Hab 3:19 my high hills. To the Chief ***M***.

MUSICIANS (2/2) MUSICIAN
Dan 6:18 and no ***m*** were brought before
Rev 18:22 "The sound of harpists, ***m***,

MUSICK (KJV) See MUSIC, SONG

MUSING (1/1)
Ps 39: 3 hot within me; While I was ***m***,

MUST (186/179)
Gen 17:13 is bought with your money ***m*** be
24: 5 ***M*** I take your son back to the
29:26 It ***m*** not be done so in our
30:16 You ***m*** come in to me, for I have
43:11 If it ***m*** be so, then do this:
47:29 time drew near that Israel ***m***
Ex 10: 9 for we ***m*** hold a feast to the
10:25 You ***m*** also give us sacrifices
10:26 For we ***m*** take some of them to
10:26 we do not know with what we ***m***
12:16 but that which everyone ***m***
18:20 them the way in which they ***m***
18:20 must walk and the work they ***m***
29:37 Whatever touches the altar ***m*** be
30:29 whatever touches them ***m*** be
Lev 6:18 Everyone who touches them ***m*** be
6:27 who touches its flesh ***m*** be
7:17 sacrifice on the third day ***m***
10: 3 those who come near Me I ***m***
10: 3 before all the people I ***m*** be
11:32 it ***m*** be put in water. And it
22:21 it ***m*** be perfect to be accepted;
23: 6 seven days you ***m*** eat unleavened
27:13 then he ***m*** add one-fifth to your
27:15 then he ***m*** add one-fifth of the
27:19 then he ***m*** add one-fifth of the
Num 4:31 And this is what they ***m*** carry
4:32 man by name the items he ***m***
5: 8 restitution for the wrong ***m***
6:21 so he ***m*** do according to the law
8:25 the age of fifty years they ***m***
9:14 he ***m*** do so according to the
15:35 The man ***m*** surely be put to
17:13 the tabernacle of the LORD ***m***
20:10 you rebels! ***M*** we bring water
22:38 my mouth, that I ***m*** speak."
23:12 ***M*** I not take heed to speak what
23:23 It now ***m*** be said of Jacob
23:26 LORD speaks, that I ***m*** do'?"
24:13 LORD says, that I ***m*** speak'?
Deut 3:22 You ***m*** not fear them, for the
4:22 But I ***m*** die in this land, I must
4:22 I ***m*** not cross over the Jordan;
8: 1 I command you today you ***m*** be
12:18 But you ***m*** eat them before the
21:16 that he ***m*** not bestow firstborn
22: 3 you ***m*** not hide yourself.
24: 4 husband who divorced her ***m*** not
31: 7 for you ***m*** go with this people
31:14 the days approach when you ***m***
Josh 3: 4 know the way by which you ***m*** go,
22:18 but that you ***m*** turn away this
Judg 13:16 you ***m*** offer it to the LORD."
14: 3 that you ***m*** go and get a wife
21:17 There ***m*** be an inheritance for
Ruth 4: 5 you ***m*** also buy it from Ruth
1 Sam 2:16 but you ***m*** give it now; and if
3: 9 that you ***m*** say, 'Speak, LORD,
5: 7 ark of the God of Israel ***m***
9:13 because he ***m*** bless the
14:43 So now I ***m*** die!"
2 Sam 23: 3 He who rules over men ***m*** be
23: 7 the man who touches them ***M***
1 Ki 18:27 perhaps he is sleeping and ***m***
2 Ki 13:17 for you ***m*** strike the Syrians at
1 Chr 17:11 when you ***m*** go to be with your
22: 5 to be built for the LORD ***m***
Ezra 10: 7 that they ***m*** gather at
10:12 As you have said, so we ***m*** do.
Neh 2: 7 that they ***m*** permit me to pass
2: 8 that he ***m*** give me timber to
13:19 and charged that they ***m*** not be
Job 32:20 I ***m*** open my lips and answer.
34:33 You ***m*** choose, and not I;
35:14 and you ***m*** wait for Him.
38:11 And here your proud waves ***m***
Ps 32: 9 Which ***m*** be harnessed with bit
69: 4 I still ***m*** restore it.
Prov 6:31 he ***m*** restore sevenfold; He may
16:10 His mouth ***m*** not transgress in
18:24 A man who has friends ***m***
Eccl 2:18 because I ***m*** leave it to the man
2:21 yet he ***m*** leave his heritage to
10:10 Then he ***m*** use more strength;
Isa 28:10 For precept ***m*** be upon
28:28 Bread flour ***m*** be ground;
Jer 10: 5 They ***m*** be carried, Because
10:19 And I ***m*** bear it."
15:19 But you ***m*** not return to them.
Ezek 34:18 that you ***m*** tread down with your
34:18 that you ***m*** foul the residue
44:27 he ***m*** offer his sin offering in
47: 5 water in which one ***m*** swim, a
Dan 6:26 dominion of my kingdom men ***m***
10:20 And now I ***m*** return to fight
Mt 16:21 to His disciples that He ***m*** go
17:10 the scribes say that Elijah ***m***
18: 7 of offenses! For offenses ***m***
24: 6 for all these things ***m*** come
26:54 that it ***m*** happen thus?"
Mk 2:22 But new wine ***m*** be put into new
8:31 them that the Son of Man ***m***
9:11 the scribes say that Elijah ***m***
9:12 that He ***m*** suffer many things
13: 7 for such things ***m*** happen, but
13:10 And the gospel ***m*** first be
14:49 But the Scriptures ***m*** be
Lk 2:49 Did you not know that I ***m*** be
4:43 I ***m*** preach the kingdom of God to
5:38 But new wine ***m*** be put into new
9:22 The Son of Man ***m*** suffer many
13:33 Nevertheless I ***m*** journey today,
14:18 and I ***m*** go and see it. I ask
17:25 But first He ***m*** suffer many
19: 5 for today I ***m*** stay at your
21: 9 for these things ***m*** come to pass
22: 7 when the Passover ***m*** be killed.
22:37 that this which is written ***m***
24: 7 The Son of Man ***m*** be delivered
24:44 that all things ***m*** be fulfilled
Jn 3: 7 You ***m*** be born again.'
3:14 even so ***m*** the Son of Man be
3:30 He ***m*** increase, but I must
3:30 but I ***m*** decrease.
4:24 and those who worship Him ***m***
9: 4 I ***m*** work the works of Him who
10:16 them also I ***m*** bring, and they
12:34 The Son of Man ***m*** be lifted up'?
20: 9 that He ***m*** rise again from the
Acts 1:22 one of these ***m*** become a witness
3:21 whom heaven ***m*** receive until the
4:12 given among men by which we ***m***
9: 6 you will be told what you ***m*** do.
9:16 show him how many things he ***m***
10: 6 He will tell you what you ***m***
10:15 What God has cleansed you ***m*** not
11: 9 What God has cleansed you ***m*** not
14:22 We ***m*** through many tribulations
15:24 You ***m*** be circumcised and keep
16:30 what ***m*** I do to be saved?"
18:21 I ***m*** by all means keep this
19:21 I ***m*** also see Rome."
20:35 that you ***m*** support the weak.
21:22 The assembly ***m*** certainly meet,
23:11 so you ***m*** also bear witness at
26: 9 I myself thought I ***m*** do many
27:24 you ***m*** be brought before Caesar;
27:26 we ***m*** run aground on a certain
Rom 13: 5 Therefore you ***m*** be subject, not
1 Cor 7:36 and thus it ***m*** be, let him do
11:19 For there ***m*** also be factions
15:25 For He ***m*** reign till He has put
15:53 For this corruptible ***m*** put on
15:53 and this mortal ***m*** put on
16: 1 so you ***m*** do also:
2 Cor 5:10 For we ***m*** all appear before the
8:11 but now you also ***m*** complete the
11:30 If I ***m*** boast, I will boast in
Col 3:13 so you also ***m*** do.
1 Tim 3: 2 A bishop then ***m*** be blameless,
3: 7 Moreover he ***m*** have a good
3: 8 Likewise deacons ***m*** be
3:11 Likewise their wives ***m*** be
2 Tim 2: 3 You therefore ***m*** endure hardship
2: 6 The hard-working farmer ***m*** be
2:24 And a servant of the Lord ***m*** not
3:14 But you ***m*** continue in the things
4:15 You also ***m*** beware of him, for he
Titus 1: 7 For a bishop ***m*** be blameless, as
1:11 whose mouths ***m*** be stopped, who
Heb 2: 1 Therefore we ***m*** give the more
4: 6 it remains that some ***m*** enter
4:13 the eyes of Him to whom we ***m***
9:16 there ***m*** also of necessity be
11: 6 for he who comes to God ***m***
13:17 as those who ***m*** give account.
2 Pe 1:14 knowing that shortly I ***m*** put
1 Jn 4:21 that he who loves God ***m*** love
Rev 1: 1 things which ***m*** shortly take
4: 1 I will show you things which ***m***
10:11 You ***m*** prophesy again about many
11: 5 he ***m*** be killed in this manner.
13:10 he who kills with the sword ***m***
17:10 he ***m*** continue a short time.
20: 3 But after these things he ***m*** be
22: 6 His servants the things which ***m***

MUSTACHE (2/2)

Lev 13:45 and he shall cover his ***m***,
2 Sam 19:24 for his feet, nor trimmed his ***m***,

MUSTARD (5/5)

Mt 13:31 kingdom of heaven is like a ***m***
17:20 if you have faith as a ***m*** seed,
Mk 4:31 It is like a ***m*** seed which,
Lk 13:19 It is like a ***m*** seed, which a man
17: 6 If you have faith as a ***m*** seed,

MUSTER (3/3)

1 Ki 20:25 and you shall ***m*** an army like the
Dan 11:11 who shall ***m*** a great multitude;
11:13 of the North will return and ***m***

MUSTERED (9/8)

Josh 8:10 up early in the morning and ***m***
1 Ki 20:15 Then he ***m*** the young leaders of
20:15 and after them he ***m*** all the
20:26 that Ben-Hadad ***m*** the Syrians
20:27 the children of Israel were ***m***
2 Ki 3: 6 of Samaria at that time and ***m***
25:19 who ***m*** the people of the land,
Jer 52:25 scribe of the army who ***m*** the
Dan 11:31 And forces shall be ***m*** by him,

MUSTERS (1/1)

Isa 13: 4 The LORD of hosts ***m*** The

MUTE (19/17)

Ex 4:11 man's mouth? Or who makes the ***m***,
Ps 38:13 And I am like a ***m*** who does
39: 2 I was ***m*** with silence, I held
39: 9 I was ***m***, I did not open my
Ezek 3:26 so that you shall be ***m*** and not
24:27 shall speak and no longer be ***m***.
33:22 opened, and I was no longer ***m***.
Hab 2:18 To make ***m*** idols?
Mt 9:32 ***m*** and demon-possessed.
9:33 the ***m*** spoke. And the multitudes
12:22 demon-possessed, blind and ***m***;
12:22 so that the blind and ***m*** man
15:30 with them the lame, blind, ***m***,
15:31 marveled when they saw the ***m***
Mk 7:37 the deaf to hear and the ***m*** to
9:17 who has a ***m*** spirit.
Lk 1:20 you will be ***m*** and not able to
11:14 out a demon, and it was ***m***.
11:14 that the ***m*** spoke; and the

MUTILATION (2/2)

Deut 23: 1 is emasculated by crushing or ***m***
Phil 3: 2 beware of the ***m***!

MUTTER (2/2)

Ps 115: 7 Nor do they ***m*** through their
Isa 8:19 and wizards, who whisper and ***m***,

MUTTERED (1/1)

Isa 59: 3 Your tongue has ***m*** perversity.

MUTUAL (3/3)

Ps 35:26 be ashamed and brought to ***m***
40:14 be ashamed and brought to ***m***
Rom 1:12 together with you by the ***m***

MUZZLE (4/4)

Deut 25: 4 You shall not ***m*** an ox while it
Ps 39: 1 will restrain my mouth with a ***m***,
1 Cor 9: 9 You shall not ***m*** an ox
1 Tim 5:18 You shall not ***m*** an ox

MY (4909/3361) See APPENDIX

MYRA (1/1)

Acts 27: 5 and Pamphylia, we came to ***M***,

MYRIADS (1/1)

Acts 21:20 how many ***m*** of Jews there are

MYRRH (17/16)

Gen 37:25 bearing spices, balm, and ***m***,
43:11 a little honey, spices and ***m***,
Ex 30:23 hundred shekels of liquid ***m***,
Esth 2:12 six months with oil of ***m***,
Ps 45: 8 garments are scented with ***m***
Prov 7:17 I have perfumed my bed With ***m***,
Song 1:13 A bundle of ***m*** is my beloved to
3: 6 Perfumed with ***m*** and
4: 6 go my way to the mountain of ***m***
4:14 ***M*** and aloes, With all the
5: 1 I have gathered my ***m*** with my
5: 5 And my hands dripped with ***m***,
5: 5 My fingers with liquid ***m***,
5:13 are lilies, Dripping liquid ***m***.
Mt 2:11 gold, frankincense, and ***m***.
Mk 15:23 gave Him wine mingled with ***m***
Jn 19:39 bringing a mixture of ***m*** and

MYRTLE (6/6)

Neh 8:15 ***m*** branches, palm branches, and
Isa 41:19 The ***m*** and the oil tree;
55:13 the brier shall come up the ***m***
Zech 1: 8 and it stood among the ***m*** trees
1:10 the man who stood among the ***m***
1:11 who stood among the ***m*** trees,

MYSELF (146/140) See APPENDIX

MYSIA (2/2)

Acts 16: 7 After they had come to ***M***,
16: 8 So passing by ***M***,

MYSTERIES (5/5) MYSTERY

Mt 13:11 given to you to know the ***m*** of
Lk 8:10 it has been given to know the ***m***
1 Cor 4: 1 of Christ and stewards of the ***m***
13: 2 and understand all ***m*** and all
14: 2 in the spirit he speaks ***m***.

MYSTERIOUS (1/1)

Deut 30:11 you today is not too ***m*** for

MYSTERY (22/22) MYSTERIES

Mk 4:11 it has been given to know the ***m***
Rom 11:25 should be ignorant of this ***m***,
16:25 to the revelation of the ***m***
1 Cor 2: 7 speak the wisdom of God in a ***m***,
15:51 Behold, I tell you a ***m***:
Eph 1: 9 having made known to us the ***m*** of
3: 3 He made known to me the ***m*** (as
3: 4 my knowledge in the ***m*** of
3: 9 is the fellowship of the ***m***,
5:32 This is a great ***m***,
6:19 boldly to make known the ***m*** of
Col 1:26 the ***m*** which has been hidden from
1:27 riches of the glory of this ***m***
2: 2 to the knowledge of the ***m*** of
4: 3 to speak the ***m*** of Christ, for
2 Th 2: 7 For the ***m*** of lawlessness is
1 Tim 3: 9 holding the ***m*** of the faith with
3:16 controversy great is the ***m*** of
Rev 1:20 The ***m*** of the seven stars which
10: 7 the ***m*** of God would be finished,
17: 5 forehead a name was written: ***M***,
17: 7 I will tell you the ***m*** of the

N

NAAM (1/1)

1 Chr 4:15 were Iru, Elah, and ***N***.

NAAMAH (5/5)

Gen 4:22 the sister of Tubal-Cain was ***N***.
Josh 15:41 Gederoth, Beth Dagon, ***N***,
1 Ki 14:21 His mother's name was ***N***,
14:31 His mother's name was ***N***,
2 Chr 12:13 His mother's name was ***N***,

NAAMAN (17/15)

Gen 46:21 Belah, Becher, Ashbel, Gera, ***N***,
Num 26:40 the sons of Bela were Ard and ***N***:
26:40 the family of the Ardites; of ***N***,
2 Ki 5: 1 Now ***N***, commander of the army
5: 4 And ***N*** went in and told his
5: 6 that I have sent ***N*** my servant
5: 9 Then ***N*** went with his horses and
5:11 But ***N*** became furious, and went
5:17 So ***N*** said, "Then, if not,
5:20 my master has spared ***N*** this
5:21 So Gehazi pursued ***N***.
5:21 When ***N*** saw him running after
5:23 So ***N*** said, "Please, take two
5:27 Therefore the leprosy of ***N*** shall
1 Chr 8: 4 Abishua, ***N***, Ahoah,
8: 7 ***N***, Ahijah, and Gera who forced
Lk 4:27 of them was cleansed except ***N***

NAAMAN'S (1/1)

2 Ki 5: 2 She waited on ***N*** wife.

NAAMATHITE (4/4)

Job 2:11 the Shuhite, and Zophar the ***N***.
11: 1 Then Zophar the ***N*** answered and
20: 1 Then Zophar the ***N*** answered and
42: 9 the Shuhite and Zophar the ***N***

NAAMITES (1/1)

Num 26:40 of Naaman, the family of the ***N***.

NAARAH (4/3)

Josh 16: 7 from Janohah to Ataroth and ***N***,
1 Chr 4: 5 had two wives, Helah and ***N***.
4: 6 ***N*** bore him Ahuzzam, Hepher,
4: 6 These were the sons of ***N***.

NAARAI (1/1)

1 Chr 11:37 ***N*** the son of Ezbai,

NAARAN (1/1)

1 Chr 7:28 and its towns: to the east ***N***,

NAARATH (KJV) See NAARAH

NAASHON, NAASSON (KJV) See NAHSHON

NABAL (19/16) NABAL'S

1 Sam 25: 3 The name of the man was ***N***.
25: 4 heard in the wilderness that ***N***
25: 5 men, "Go up to Carmel, go to ***N***,
25: 9 they spoke to ***N*** according to
25:10 Then ***N*** answered David's
25:19 she did not tell her husband ***N***.
25:25 my lord regard this scoundrel ***N***.
25:25 ***N*** is his name, and folly is
25:26 seek harm for my lord be as ***N***.
25:34 would have been left to ***N***!"
25:36 Now Abigail went to ***N***,
25:37 when the wine had gone from ***N***,
25:38 days, that the LORD struck ***N***,
25:39 So when David heard that ***N*** was
25:39 my reproach from the hand of ***N***,
25:39 returned the wickedness of ***N***
30: 5 and Abigail the widow of ***N*** the
2 Sam 2: 2 and Abigail the widow of ***N*** the
3: 3 by Abigail the widow of ***N*** the

NABAL'S (3/3) NABAL

1 Sam 25:14 ***N*** wife, saying, "Look, David
25:36 And ***N*** heart was merry within
27: 3 the Carmelitess, ***N*** widow.

NABOTH (22/18)

1 Ki 21: 1 after these things that ***N*** the
21: 2 So Ahab spoke to ***N***,
21: 3 But ***N*** said to Ahab, "The LORD
21: 4 because of the word which ***N***
21: 6 Because I spoke to ***N*** the
21: 7 give you the vineyard of ***N*** the
21: 8 dwelling in the city with ***N***.
21: 9 and seat ***N*** with high honor
21:12 and seated ***N*** with high honor
21:13 against him, against ***N***,
21:13 ***N*** has blasphemed God and the
21:14 ***N*** has been stoned and is dead."
21:15 when Jezebel heard that ***N*** had
21:15 of the vineyard of ***N*** the
21:15 for ***N*** is not alive, but dead."
21:16 when Ahab heard that ***N*** was
21:16 of the vineyard of ***N*** the
21:18 he is, in the vineyard of ***N***,
21:19 dogs licked the blood of ***N***,
2 Ki 9:21 met him on the property of ***N***
9:25 the tract of the field of ***N***
9:26 I saw yesterday the blood of ***N***

NACHON'S (1/1)

2 Sam 6: 6 And when they came to ***N***

NACHOR (KJV) See NAHOR

NADAB (20/20)

Ex 6:23 as wife; and she bore him ***N***,
24: 1 ***N*** and Abihu, and seventy of the
24: 9 Moses went up, also Aaron, ***N***,
28: 1 Aaron and Aaron's sons: ***N***,
Lev 10: 1 Then ***N*** and Abihu, the sons of
Num 3: 2 names of the sons of Aaron: ***N***,
3: 4 ***N*** and Abihu had died before the
26:60 To Aaron were born ***N*** and Abihu,
26:61 And ***N*** and Abihu died when they
1 Ki 14:20 Then ***N*** his son reigned in his
15:25 Now ***N*** the son of Jeroboam
15:27 while ***N*** and all Israel laid
15:31 Now the rest of the acts of ***N***,
1 Chr 2:28 The sons of Shammai were ***N*** and
2:30 The sons of ***N*** were Seled and
6: 3 And the sons of Aaron were ***N***,
8:30 Abdon, then Zur, Kish, Baal, ***N***,
9:36 then Zur, Kish, Baal, Ner, ***N***,
24: 1 The sons of Aaron were ***N***,
24: 2 And ***N*** and Abihu died before

NAGGAI (1/1)

Lk 3:25 son of Esli, the son of ***N***,

NAHALAL (1/1)

Josh 21:35 and ***N*** with its common-land:

NAHALIEL (2/1)

Num 21:19 from Mattanah to ***N***,
21:19 from ***N*** to Bamoth,

NAHALLAL (1/1)

Josh 19:15 Included were Kattath, ***N***,

N

NAHALOL (1/1)

Judg 1:30 Kitron or the inhabitants of *N*;

NAHAM (1/1)

1 Chr 4:19 Hodiah's wife, the sister of *N*,

NAHAMANI (1/1)

Neh 7: 7 Nehemiah, Azariah, Raamiah, *N*,

NAHARAI (2/2)

2 Sam 23:37 *N* the Beerothite (armorbearer
1 Chr 11:39 *N* the Berothite (the

NAHASH (9/8)

1 Sam 11: 1 Then *N* the Ammonite came up and
11: 1 all the men of Jabesh said to *N*,
11: 2 And *N* the Ammonite answered
12:12 And when you saw that *N* king of
2 Sam 10: 2 kindness to Hanun the son of *N*,
17:25 in to Abigail the daughter of *N*,
17:27 that Shobi the son of *N* from
1 Chr 19: 1 It happened after this that *N*
19: 2 kindness to Hanun the son of *N*,

NAHATH (5/5)

Gen 36:13 were the sons of Reuel: *N*,
36:17 of Reuel, Esau's son: Chief *N*,
1 Chr 1:37 The sons of Reuel were *N*,
6:26 his son, *N* his son,
2 Chr 31:13 Jehiel, Azaziah, *N*,

NAHBI (1/1)

Num 13:14 *N* the son of Vophsi;

NAHOR (17/17)

Gen 11:22 lived thirty years, and begot *N*.
11:23 After he begot *N*,
11:24 *N* lived twenty-nine years, and
11:25 *N* lived one hundred and
11:26 years, and begot Abram, *N*,
11:27 of Terah: Terah begot Abram, *N*,
11:29 Then Abram and *N* took wives:
22:20 children to your brother *N*:
22:23 These eight Milcah bore to *N*,
24:10 Mesopotamia, to the city of *N*.
24:15 son of Milcah, the wife of *N*,
24:24 son, whom she bore to *N*.
29: 5 you know Laban the son of *N*?
31:53 God of Abraham, the God of *N*,
Josh 24: 2 of Abraham and the father of *N*,
1 Chr 1:26 Serug, *N*, Terah,
Lk 3:34 son of Terah, the son of *N*,

NAHOR'S (2/2)

Gen 11:29 and the name of *N* wife, Milcah,
24:47 *N* son, whom Milcah bore to

NAHSHON (13/11)

Ex 6:23 of Amminadab, sister of *N*,
Num 1: 7 *N* the son of Amminadab;
2: 3 and *N* the son of Amminadab
7:12 on the first day was *N* the
7:17 This was the offering of *N* the
10:14 over their army was *N* the son
Ruth 4:20 Amminadab begot *N*,
4:20 and *N* begot Salmon;
1 Chr 2:10 and Amminadab begot *N*,
2:11 *N* begot Salma, and Salma begot
Mt 1: 4 Amminadab, Amminadab begot *N*,
1: 4 and *N* begot Salmon.
Lk 3:32 son of Salmon, the son of *N*,

NAHUM (2/2)

Nah 1: 1 The book of the vision of *N* the
Lk 3:25 son of Amos, the son of *N*,

NAILED (1/1) NAILS

Col 2:14 having **n** it to the cross.

NAILS (9/8) NAILED

Deut 21:12 shave her head and trim her **n**.
1 Chr 22: 3 iron in abundance for the **n** of
2 Chr 3: 9 The weight of the **n** was fifty
Eccl 12:11 scholars are like well-driven **n**,
Jer 10: 4 They fasten it with **n** and
Dan 4:33 eagles' feathers and his **n**
7:19 its teeth of iron and its **n** of
Jn 20:25 in His hands the print of the **n**,
20:25 finger into the print of the **n**,

NAIN (1/1)

Lk 7:11 He went into a city called *N*;

NAIOTH (6/5)

1 Sam 19:18 and Samuel went and stayed in *N*.
19:19 David is at *N* in Ramah!"
19:22 Indeed they are at *N* in
19:23 So he went there to *N* in Ramah.
19:23 prophesied until he came to *N*
20: 1 Then David fled from *N* in Ramah,

NAKED (41/40) NAKEDNESS

Gen 2:25 And they were both **n**,
3: 7 and they knew that they were **n**;
3:10 I was afraid because I was **n**;
3:11 "Who told you that you were **n**?
1 Sam 19:24 and lay down **n** all that day and
2 Chr 28:15 they clothed all who were **n**
Job 1:21 *N* I came from my mother's womb,
1:21 And **n** shall I return there.
22: 6 And stripped the **n** of their
24: 7 They spend the night **n**,
24:10 They cause the poor to go **n**,
26: 6 Sheol is **n** before Him,
Eccl 5:15 **n** shall he return, To go as he
Isa 20: 2 walking **n** and barefoot.
20: 3 My servant Isaiah has walked **n**
20: 4 **n** and barefoot, with their
58: 7 cast out; When you see the **n**,
Lam 4:21 drunk and make yourself **n**.
Ezek 16: 7 but you were **n** and bare.
16:22 when you were **n** and bare,
16:39 and leave you **n** and bare.
18: 7 the hungry And covered the **n**
18:16 the hungry And covered the **n**
23:29 and leave you **n** and bare.
Hos 2: 3 Lest I strip her **n** And expose
Am 2:16 men of might Shall flee **n** in
Mic 1: 8 I will go stripped and **n**;
1:11 Pass by in **n** shame, you
Mt 25:36 'I was **n** and you clothed Me;
25:38 or **n** and clothe You?
25:43 **n** and you did not clothe Me,
25:44 or thirsty or a stranger or **n**
Mk 14:51 cloth thrown around his **n**
14:52 cloth and fled from them **n**.
Acts 19:16 they fled out of that house **n**
2 Cor 5: 3 we shall not be found **n**.
Heb 4:13 but all things are **n** and open
Jas 2:15 If a brother or sister is **n** and
Rev 3:17 miserable, poor, blind, and **n**—
16:15 lest he walk **n** and they see his
17:16 harlot, make her desolate and **n**,

NAKEDNESS (57/43) NAKED

Gen 9:22 saw the **n** of his father, and
9:23 backward and covered the **n** of
9:23 did not see their father's **n**.
42: 9 You have come to see the **n** of
42:12 but you have come to see the **n**
Ex 20:26 that your **n** may not be exposed
28:42 linen trousers to cover their **n**;
Lev 18: 6 of kin to him, to uncover his **n**:
18: 7 The **n** of your father or the
18: 7 of your father or the **n** of
18: 7 you shall not uncover her **n**.
18: 8 The **n** of your father's wife you
18: 8 uncover; it is your father's **n**.
18: 9 The **n** of your sister, the
18: 9 their **n** you shall not uncover.
18:10 The **n** of your son's daughter or
18:10 their **n** you shall not uncover;
18:10 for theirs is your own **n**.
18:11 The **n** of your father's wife's
18:11 shall not uncover her **n**.
18:12 You shall not uncover the **n** of
18:13 You shall not uncover the **n** of
18:14 You shall not uncover the **n** of
18:15 You shall not uncover the **n** of
18:15 shall not uncover her **n**.
18:16 You shall not uncover the **n** of
18:16 it is your brother's **n**.
18:17 You shall not uncover the **n** of a
18:17 daughter, to uncover her **n**.
18:18 to uncover her **n** while the
18:19 a woman to uncover her **n** as
20:11 has uncovered his father's **n**;
20:17 and sees her **n** and she sees his
20:17 nakedness and she sees his **n**,
20:17 He has uncovered his sister's **n**.
20:18 her sickness and uncovers her **n**,
20:19 You shall not uncover the **n** of
20:20 he has uncovered his uncle's **n**.
20:21 has uncovered his brother's **n**.
Deut 28:48 you, in hunger, in thirst, in **n**,
1 Sam 20:30 to the shame of your mother's **n**?
Isa 47: 3 Your **n** shall be uncovered,
Lam 1: 8 Because they have seen her **n**;
Ezek 16: 8 over you and covered your **n**.
16:36 was poured out and your **n**
16:37 you and will uncover your **n** to
16:37 that they may see all your **n**.
22:10 men uncover their fathers' **n**;
23:10 They uncovered her **n**,
23:18 harlotry and uncovered her **n**.
23:29 The **n** of your harlotry shall be
Hos 2: 9 linen, Given to cover her **n**.
Nah 3: 5 I will show the nations your **n**,
Hab 2:15 That you may look on his **n**!
Rom 8:35 or persecution, or famine, or **n**,
2 Cor 11:27 fastings often, in cold and **n**—
Rev 3:18 that the shame of your **n** may

NAME (930/835) NAME'S, NAMED, NAMES

Gen 2:11 The **n** of the first is Pishon;
2:13 The **n** of the second river is
2:14 The **n** of the third river is
2:19 creature, that was its **n**.
3:20 And Adam called his wife's **n**
4:17 and called the **n** of the city
4:17 name of the city after the **n**
4:19 the **n** of one was Adah, and the
4:19 and the **n** of the second was
4:21 His brother's **n** was Jubal.
4:26 men began to call on the **n** of
5:29 And he called his **n** Noah,
10:25 the **n** of one was Peleg, for in
10:25 and his brother's **n** was
11: 4 let us make a **n** for ourselves,
11: 9 Therefore its **n** is called Babel,
11:29 the **n** of Abram's wife was
11:29 and the **n** of Nahor's wife,
12: 2 will bless you And make your **n**
12: 8 the LORD and called on the **n**
13: 4 there Abram called on the **n** of
16: 1 an Egyptian maidservant whose **n**
16:11 You shall call his **n** Ishmael,
16:13 Then she called the **n** of the
17: 5 No longer shall your **n** be called
17: 5 but your **n** shall be Abraham;
17:15 you shall not call her **n** Sarai,
17:15 but Sarah shall be her **n**.
17:19 and you shall call his **n** Isaac;
19:22 Therefore the **n** of the city
19:37 bore a son and called his **n**
19:38 bore a son and called his **n**
21: 3 And Abraham called the **n** of his
21:33 and there called on the **n** of
22:14 And Abraham called the **n** of the
22:24 whose **n** was Reumah, also bore
24:29 Rebekah had a brother whose **n**
25: 1 and her **n** was Keturah.
25:25 so they called his **n** Esau.
25:26 so his **n** was called Jacob.
25:30 Therefore his **n** was called
26:20 So he called the **n** of the
26:21 So he called its **n** Sitnah.
26:22 So he called its **n** Rehoboth,
26:25 there and called on the **n** of
26:33 Therefore the **n** of the city is
28:19 And he called the **n** of that
28:19 but the **n** of that city had been
29:16 the **n** of the elder was Leah,
29:16 and the **n** of the younger was
29:32 and she called his **n** Reuben;
29:33 And she called his **n** Simeon.
29:34 Therefore his **n** was called
29:35 Therefore she called his **n**
30: 6 Therefore she called his **n**
30: 8 So she called his **n** Naphtali.
30:11 comes!" So she called his **n**
30:13 So she called his **n** Asher.
30:18 So she called his **n** Issachar.
30:20 So she called his **n** Zebulun.
30:21 and called her **n** Dinah.
30:24 So she called his **n** Joseph, and
30:28 *N* me your wages, and I will give
31:48 Therefore its **n** was called
32: 2 And he called the **n** of that
32:27 said to him, "What is your **n**?
32:28 Your **n** shall no longer be called
32:29 saying, "Tell me Your **n**,
32:29 is it that you ask about My **n**?
32:30 And Jacob called the **n** of the
33:17 Therefore the **n** of the place is
35: 8 So the **n** of it was called Allon
35:10 Your **n** is Jacob; your name
35:10 your **n** shall not be called
35:10 but Israel shall be your **n**.
35:10 So He called his **n** Israel.
35:15 And Jacob called the **n** of the
35:18 that she called his **n** Ben-Oni;
36:32 and the **n** of his city was
36:35 And the **n** of his city was
36:39 and the **n** of his city was Pau.
36:39 His wife's **n** was Mehetabel,
38: 1 a certain Adullamite whose **n**
38: 2 of a certain Canaanite whose **n**
38: 3 and he called his **n** Er.
38: 4 and she called his **n** Onan.
38: 5 and called his **n** Shelah. He was
38: 6 and her **n** was Tamar.
38:29 be upon you!" Therefore his **n**
38:30 And his **n** was called Zerah.
41:45 And Pharaoh called Joseph's **n**
41:51 Joseph called the **n** of the
41:52 And the **n** of the second he
48: 6 they will be called by the **n** of
48:16 Let my **n** be named upon them,
48:16 And the **n** of my fathers
50:11 Therefore its **n** was called
Ex 1:15 of whom the **n** of one was
1:15 of one was Shiphrah and the **n**
2:10 So she called his **n** Moses,
2:22 and he called his **n** Gershom;
3:13 they say to me, 'What is His **n**?
3:15 This is My **n** forever, and this
5:23 to Pharaoh to speak in Your **n**,
6: 3 but by My **n** LORD I was not
9:16 and that My **n** may be declared
15: 3 of war; The LORD is His **n**.
15:23 Therefore the **n** of it was
16:31 house of Israel called its **n**
17: 7 So he called the **n** of the place
17:15 built an altar and called its **n**,
18: 3 of whom the **n** of one was
18: 4 and the **n** of the other was
20: 7 You shall not take the **n** of the
20: 7 him guiltless who takes His **n**

20:24 place where I record My **n** I
23:13 and make no mention of the **n**
23:21 for My **n** is in Him.
28:21 signet, each one with its own **n**;
31: 2 I have called by **n** Bezalel the
33:12 You have said, 'I know you by **n**,
33:17 My sight, and I know you by **n**.
33:19 and I will proclaim the **n** of
34: 5 and proclaimed the **n** of the
34:14 whose **n** is Jealous, is a
35:30 the LORD has called by **n**
39:14 each one with its own **n**
Lev 18:21 nor shall you profane the **n** of
19:12 you shall not swear by My **n**
19:12 nor shall you profane the **n** of
20: 3 sanctuary and profane My holy **n**.
21: 6 God and not profane the **n** of
22: 2 they do not profane My holy **n**
22:32 shall not profane My holy **n**,
24:11 woman's son blasphemed the **n**
24:11 (His mother's **n** was Shelomith
24:16 And whoever blasphemes the **n** of
24:16 When he blasphemes the **n** of
Num 1:17 men who had been mentioned by **n**,
4:32 assign to each man by **n** the
6:27 So they shall put My **n** on the
11: 3 So he called the **n** of the place
11:26 the **n** of one was Eldad, and
11:26 and the **n** of the other Medad.
11:34 So he called the **n** of that place
17: 2 Write each man's **n** on his rod.
17: 3 And you shall write Aaron's **n** on
21: 3 So the **n** of that place was
25:14 Now the **n** of the Israelite who
25:15 And the **n** of the Midianite woman
26:46 And the **n** of the daughter of
26:59 The **n** of Amram's wife was
27: 4 Why should the **n** of our father
32:42 it Nobah, after his own **n**.
Deut 3:14 called Bashan after his own **n**,
5:11 You shall not take the **n** of the
5:11 him guiltless who takes His **n**
6:13 and shall take oaths in His **n**.
7:24 and you will destroy their **n**
9:14 them and blot out their **n** from
10: 8 to Him and to bless in His **n**,
10:20 fast, and take oaths in His **n**.
12: 5 to put His **n** for His dwelling
12:11 your God chooses to make His **n**
12:21 your God chooses to put His **n**
14:23 where He chooses to make His **n**
14:24 your God chooses to put His **n**
16: 2 the LORD chooses to put His **n**.
16: 6 your God chooses to make His **n**
16:11 your God chooses to make His **n**
18: 5 to stand to minister in the **n**
18: 7 then he may serve in the **n** of
18:19 words, which He speaks in My **n**,
18:20 to speak a word in My **n**,
18:20 or who speaks in the **n** of other
18:22 a prophet speaks in the **n**
21: 5 to Him and to bless in the **n**
22:14 and brings a bad **n** on her, and
22:19 because he has brought a bad **n**
25: 6 bears will succeed to the **n** of
25: 6 that his **n** may not be blotted
25: 7 refuses to raise up a **n** to his
25:10 And his **n** shall be called in
26: 2 your God chooses to make His **n**
26:19 He has made, in praise, in **n**,
28:10 that you are called by the **n**
28:58 this glorious and awesome **n**,
29:20 the LORD would blot out his **n**
32: 3 For I proclaim the **n** of the
Josh 5: 9 Therefore the **n** of the place
7: 9 and cut off our **n** from the
7: 9 will You do for Your great **n**?
7:26 Therefore the **n** of that place
9: 9 because of the **n** of the LORD
14:15 And the **n** of Hebron formerly was
15:15 of Debir (formerly the **n** of
19:47 after the **n** of Dan their
21: 9 which are designated by **n**,
23: 7 not make mention of the **n** of
Judg 1:10 (Now the **n** of Hebron was
1:11 (The **n** of Debir was formerly
1:17 So the **n** of the city was called
1:23 (The **n** of the city was
1:26 and called its **n** Luz, which is
1:26 which is its **n** to this day.
2: 5 Then they called the **n** of that
8:31 whose **n** he called Abimelech.
13: 2 whose **n** was Manoah; and his
13: 6 and He did not tell me His **n**.
13:17 of the LORD, "What is Your **n**,
13:18 to him, "Why do you ask My **n**,
13:24 bore a son and called his **n**
15:19 Therefore he called its **n** En
16: 4 whose **n** was Delilah.
17: 1 whose **n** was Micah.
18:29 And they called the **n** of the
18:29 after the **n** of Dan their
18:29 the **n** of the city formerly was
Ruth 1: 2 The **n** of the man was Elimelech,
1: 2 the **n** of his wife was Naomi,
1: 4 the **n** of the one was Orpah,
1: 4 and the **n** of the other Ruth.
2: 1 His **n** was Boaz.
2:19 The man's **n** with whom I worked
4: 5 to perpetuate the **n** of the dead
4:10 to perpetuate the **n** of the dead
4:10 that the **n** of the dead may not

4:14 and may his **n** be famous in
4:17 the neighbor women gave him a **n**,
4:17 And they called his **n** Obed.
1 Sam 1: 1 and his **n** was Elkanah the son
1: 2 the **n** of one was Hannah, and
1: 2 and the **n** of the other
1:20 and called his **n** Samuel,
7:12 and called its **n** Ebenezer,
8: 2 The **n** of his firstborn was Joel,
8: 2 and the **n** of his second,
9: 1 was a man of Benjamin whose **n**
9: 2 and handsome son whose **n** was
14: 4 And the **n** of one was Bozez,
14: 4 and the **n** of the other Seneh.
14:49 the **n** of the firstborn Merab,
14:49 and the **n** of the younger
14:50 The **n** of Saul's wife was
14:50 And the **n** of the commander of
16: 3 anoint for Me the one I **n** to
17:12 whose **n** was Jesse, and who had
17:23 of Gath, Goliath by **n**,
17:45 But I come to you in the **n** of
18:30 so that his **n** became highly
20:42 we have both sworn in the **n** of
21: 7 And his **n** was Doeg, an
24:21 that you will not destroy my **n**
25: 3 The **n** of the man was Nabal, and
25: 3 and the **n** of his wife Abigail.
25: 5 to Nabal, and greet him in my **n**.
25: 9 to all these words in the **n** of
25:25 For as his **n** is, so is he:
25:25 is, so is he: Nabal is his **n**,
28: 8 up for me the one I shall **n** to
2 Sam 3: 7 whose **n** was Rizpah, the
4: 2 The **n** of one was Baanah and
4: 2 of one was Baanah and the **n**
4: 4 His **n** was Mephibosheth.
5:20 Therefore he called the **n** of
6: 2 whose **n** is called by the Name,
6: 2 whose name is called by the *N*,
6: 8 and he called the **n** of the
6:18 he blessed the people in the **n**
7: 9 and have made you a great **n**,
7: 9 like the **n** of the great men who
7:13 shall build a house for My **n**,
7:23 people, to make for Himself a **n**—
7:26 So let Your **n** be magnified
8:13 And David made himself a **n** when
9: 2 of the house of Saul whose **n**
9:12 had a young son whose **n** was
12:24 and he called his **n** Solomon.
12:25 So he called his **n** Jedidiah,
12:28 and it be called after my **n**.
13: 1 whose **n** was Tamar; and Amnon
13: 3 But Amnon had a friend whose **n**
14: 7 leave to my husband neither **n**
14:27 and one daughter whose **n** was
16: 5 whose **n** was Shimei the son of
17:25 was the son of a man whose **n**
18:18 I have no son to keep my **n** in
18:18 the pillar after his own **n**.
20: 1 whose **n** was Sheba the son of
20:21 Sheba the son of Bichri by **n**,
22:50 And sing praises to Your **n**.
23:18 and won a **n** among these three.
23:22 and won a **n** among three mighty
1 Ki 1:47 May God make the **n** of Solomon
1:47 of Solomon better than your **n**,
3: 2 was no house built for the **n**
5: 3 not build a house for the **n** of
5: 5 to build a house for the **n** of
5: 5 shall build the house for My **n**.
7:21 on the right and called its **n**
7:21 on the left and called its **n**
8:16 that My **n** might be there; but I
8:17 to build a temple for the **n** of
8:18 to build a temple for My **n**,
8:19 shall build the temple for My **n**.
8:20 I have built a temple for the **n**
8:29 My **n** shall be there,' that You
8:33 back to You and confess Your **n**,
8:35 this place and confess Your **n**,
8:42 they will hear of Your great **n**
8:43 of the earth may know Your **n**
8:43 have built is called by Your **n**.
8:44 which I have built for Your **n**,
8:48 which I have built for Your **n**:
9: 3 you have built to put My **n**
9: 7 I have consecrated for My **n** I
10: 1 of Solomon concerning the **n** of
11:26 whose mother's **n** was Zeruah, a
11:36 to put My **n** there.
13: 2 'Behold, a child, Josiah by **n**,
14:21 to put His **n** there.
14:21 His mother's **n** was Naamah, an
14:31 His mother's **n** was Naamah, an
15: 2 His mother's **n** was Maachah the
15:10 His grandmother's **n** was
16:24 and called the **n** of the city
16:24 after the **n** of Shemer, owner of
18:24 Then you call on the **n** of your
18:24 and I will call on the **n** of the
18:25 and call on the **n** of your god,
18:26 and called on the **n** of Baal
18:31 "Israel shall be your **n**.
18:32 he built an altar in the **n** of
21: 8 she wrote letters in Ahab's **n**,
22:16 nothing but the truth in the **n**
22:42 His mother's **n** was Azubah the
2 Ki 2:24 a curse on them in the **n** of
5:11 and stand and call on the **n** of
8:26 His mother's **n** was Athaliah

12: 1 His mother's **n** was Zibiah of
14: 2 His mother's **n** was Jehoaddan of
14: 7 and called its **n** Joktheel to
14:27 that He would blot out the **n**
15: 2 His mother's **n** was Jecholiah
15:33 His mother's **n** was Jerusha the
18: 2 His mother's **n** was Abi the
21: 1 His mother's **n** was Hephzibah.
21: 4 "In Jerusalem I will put My **n**.
21: 7 I will put My **n** forever;
21:19 His mother's **n** was
22: 1 His mother's **n** was Jedidah the
23:27 My **n** shall be there.'"
23:31 His mother's **n** was Hamutal the
23:34 and changed his **n** to Jehoiakim.
23:36 His mother's **n** was Zebudah the
24: 8 His mother's **n** was Nehushta
24:17 and changed his **n** to Zedekiah.
24:18 His mother's **n** was Hamutal the
1 Chr 1:19 the **n** of one was Peleg, for in
1:19 and his brother's **n** was
1:43 and the **n** of his city was
1:46 The **n** of his city was Avith.
1:50 and the **n** of his city was Pai.
1:50 His wife's **n** was Mehetabel the
2:26 whose **n** was Atarah; she was the
2:29 And the **n** of the wife of Abishur
2:34 had an Egyptian servant whose **n**
4: 3 and the **n** of their sister was
4: 9 and his mother called his **n**
4:38 these mentioned by **n** were
4:41 These recorded by **n** came in the
7:15 whose **n** was Maachah. The name
7:15 The **n** of Gilead's grandson
7:16 and she called his **n** Peresh.
7:16 The **n** of his brother was
7:23 and he called his **n** Beriah,
8:29 whose wife's **n** was Maacah,
9:35 whose wife's **n** was Maacah,
11:20 and won a **n** among these three.
11:24 and won a **n** among three mighty
12:31 who were designated by **n** to
13: 6 where His **n** is proclaimed.
14:11 Therefore they called the **n**
16: 2 he blessed the people in the **n**
16: 8 to the LORD! Call upon His **n**;
16:10 Glory in His holy **n**;
16:29 the LORD the glory due His **n**;
16:35 To give thanks to Your holy **n**,
16:41 who were designated by **n**,
17: 8 and have made you a **n** like the
17: 8 made you a name like the **n** of
17:21 to make for Yourself a **n** by
17:24 that Your **n** may be magnified
21:19 which he had spoken in the **n** of
22: 7 mind to build a house to the **n**
22: 8 not build a house for My **n**,
22: 9 His **n** shall be Solomon, for I
22:10 shall build a house for My **n**,
22:19 that is to be built for the **n**
23:13 to give the blessing in His **n**
28: 3 not build a house for My **n**,
29:13 And praise Your glorious **n**.
29:16 You a house for Your holy **n** is
2 Chr 2: 1 to build a temple for the **n** of
2: 4 am building a temple for the **n**
3:17 he called the **n** of the one on
3:17 and the **n** of the one on the
6: 5 that My **n** might be there, nor
6: 6 that My **n** may be there; and I
6: 7 to build a temple for the **n** of
6: 8 to build a temple for My **n**,
6: 9 shall build the temple for My **n**.
6:10 built the temple for the **n** of
6:20 said You would put Your **n**,
6:24 and return and confess Your **n**,
6:26 this place and confess Your **n**,
6:32 for the sake of Your great **n**
6:33 of the earth may know Your **n**
6:33 have built is called by Your **n**.
6:34 which I have built for Your **n**,
6:38 which I have built for Your **n**:
7:14 people who are called by My **n**
7:16 that My **n** may be there forever;
7:20 I have sanctified for My **n** I
12:13 to put His **n** there. His
12:13 His mother's **n** was Naamah, an
13: 2 His mother's **n** was Michaiah
14:11 and in Your **n** we go against
18:15 nothing but the truth in the **n**
20: 8 a sanctuary in it for Your **n**,
20: 9 in Your presence (for Your **n**
20:26 therefore the **n** of that place
20:31 His mother's **n** was Azubah the
22: 2 His mother's **n** was Athaliah
24: 1 His mother's **n** was Zibiah of
25: 1 His mother's **n** was Jehoaddan
26: 3 His mother's **n** was Jecholiah of
27: 1 His mother's **n** was Jerushah
28: 9 whose **n** was Oded; and he went
28:15 men who were designated by **n**
29: 1 His mother's **n** was Abijah the
31:19 men who were designated by **n**
33: 4 In Jerusalem shall My **n** be
33: 7 I will put My **n** forever;
33:18 who spoke to him in the **n** of
36: 4 and changed his **n** to Jehoiakim.
Ezra 2:61 and was called by their **n**.
5: 1 in the **n** of the God of Israel,
6:12 may the God who causes His **n**
8:20 of them were designated by **n**.
10:16 households, each of them by **n**;

Neh 1: 9 chosen as a dwelling for My ***n***.
1:11 who desire to fear Your ***n***;
7:63 and was called by their ***n***.
9: 5 "Blessed be Your glorious ***n***,
9: 7 And gave him the ***n*** Abraham;
9:10 So You made a ***n*** for Yourself,
Esth 2: 5 was a certain Jew whose ***n*** was
2:14 in her and called for her by ***n***.
2:22 the king in Mordecai's ***n***.
3:12 In the ***n*** of King Ahasuerus it
8: 8 as you please, in the king's ***n***,
8: 8 is written in the king's ***n*** and
8:10 And he wrote in the ***n*** of King
9:26 after the ***n*** Pur. Therefore,
Job 1: 1 whose ***n*** was Job; and that man
1:21 Blessed be the ***n*** of the
18:17 And he has no ***n*** among the
42:14 And he called the ***n*** of the first
42:14 the ***n*** of the second Keziah, and
42:14 and the ***n*** of the third
Ps 5:11 those also who love Your ***n***
7:17 And will sing praise to the ***n***
8: 1 How excellent is Your ***n*** in
8: 9 How excellent is Your ***n*** in
9: 2 I will sing praise to Your ***n***,
9: 5 You have blotted out their ***n***
9:10 And those who know Your ***n*** will
18:49 And sing praises to Your ***n***.
20: 1 May the ***n*** of the God of Jacob
20: 5 And in the ***n*** of our God we
20: 7 But we will remember the ***n*** of
22:22 I will declare Your ***n*** to My
29: 2 LORD the glory due to His ***n***;
30: 4 the remembrance of His holy ***n***.
33:21 we have trusted in His holy ***n***.
34: 3 And let us exalt His ***n***
41: 5 and his ***n*** perish?"
44: 5 Through Your ***n*** we will trample
44: 8 And praise Your ***n*** forever.
44:20 If we had forgotten the ***n*** of
45:17 I will make Your ***n*** to be
48:10 According to Your ***n***,
52: 9 I will wait on Your ***n***,
54: 1 Save me, O God, by Your ***n***,
54: 6 to You; I will praise Your ***n***,
61: 5 of those who fear Your ***n***.
61: 8 I will sing praise to Your ***n***
63: 4 will lift up my hands in Your ***n***.
66: 2 Sing out the honor of His ***n***;
66: 4 shall sing praises to Your ***n***.
68: 4 to God, sing praises to His ***n***;
68: 4 By His ***n*** YAH, And rejoice
69:30 I will praise the ***n*** of God with
69:36 And those who love His ***n*** shall
72:17 His ***n*** shall endure forever;
72:17 His ***n*** shall continue as long
72:19 And blessed be His glorious ***n***
74: 7 the dwelling place of Your ***n***
74:10 the enemy blaspheme Your ***n***
74:18 people has blasphemed Your ***n***.
74:21 poor and needy praise Your ***n***.
75: 1 works declare that Your ***n*** is
76: 1 His ***n*** is great in Israel.
79: 6 that do not call on Your ***n***.
79: 9 For the glory of Your ***n***;
80:18 and we will call upon Your ***n***.
83: 4 That the ***n*** of Israel may be
83:16 That they may seek Your ***n***,
83:18 whose ***n*** alone is the LORD,
86: 9 And shall glorify Your ***n***.
86:11 Unite my heart to fear Your ***n***.
86:12 And I will glorify Your ***n***
89:12 and Hermon rejoice in Your ***n***.
89:16 In Your ***n*** they rejoice all day
89:24 And in My ***n*** his horn shall be
91:14 high, because he has known My ***n***.
92: 1 And to sing praises to Your ***n***,
96: 2 Sing to the LORD, bless His ***n***;
96: 8 the LORD the glory due His ***n***;
97:12 the remembrance of His holy ***n***.
99: 3 praise Your great and awesome ***n***—
99: 6 those who called upon His ***n***;
100: 4 to Him, and bless His ***n***.
102:12 And the remembrance of Your ***n***
102:15 the nations shall fear the ***n***
102:21 To declare the ***n*** of the LORD
103: 1 bless His holy ***n***!
105: 1 to the LORD! Call upon His ***n***;
105: 3 Glory in His holy ***n***;
106:47 To give thanks to Your holy ***n***,
109:13 following let their ***n*** be
111: 9 Holy and awesome is His ***n***.
113: 1 Praise the ***n*** of the LORD!
113: 2 Blessed be the ***n*** of the LORD
113: 3 its going down The LORD's ***n***
115: 1 But to Your ***n*** give glory,
116: 4 Then I called upon the ***n*** of the
116:13 And call upon the ***n*** of the
116:17 And will call upon the ***n*** of
118:10 But in the ***n*** of the LORD
118:11 But in the ***n*** of the LORD I
118:12 For in the ***n*** of the LORD I
118:26 is he who comes in the ***n*** of
119:55 I remember Your ***n*** in the night,
119:132 toward those who love Your ***n***.
122: 4 To give thanks to the ***n*** of the
124: 8 Our help is in the ***n*** of the
129: 8 We bless you in the ***n*** of the
135: 1 the LORD! Praise the ***n*** of
135: 3 good; Sing praises to His ***n***,
135:13 Your ***n***, O LORD, endures
138: 2 And praise Your ***n*** For Your
138: 2 Your word above all Your ***n***.
139:20 Your enemies take Your ***n*** in
140:13 shall give thanks to Your ***n***;
142: 7 That I may praise Your ***n***;
145: 1 And I will bless Your ***n***
145: 2 And I will praise Your ***n***
145:21 flesh shall bless His holy ***n***
147: 4 He calls them all by ***n***.
148: 5 Let them praise the ***n*** of the
148:13 Let them praise the ***n*** of the
148:13 For His ***n*** alone is exalted;
149: 3 Let them praise His ***n*** with the
Prov 10: 7 But the ***n*** of the wicked will
18:10 The ***n*** of the LORD is a strong
21:24 man—Scoffer" is his ***n***;
22: 1 A good ***n*** is to be chosen
30: 4 of the earth? What is His ***n***,
30: 4 name, and what is His Son's ***n***,
30: 9 And profane the ***n*** of my God.
Eccl 6: 4 and its ***n*** is covered with
7: 1 A good ***n*** is better than
Song 1: 3 Your ***n*** is ointment poured
Isa 4: 1 let us be called by your ***n***,
7:14 and shall call His ***n*** Immanuel.
8: 3 "Call his ***n*** Maher-Shalal-Hash-Baz;
9: 6 And His ***n*** will be called
12: 4 the LORD, call upon His ***n***;
12: 4 Make mention that His ***n*** is
14:22 cut off from Babylon the ***n***
18: 7 To the place of the ***n*** of the
24:15 The ***n*** of the LORD God of
25: 1 You, I will praise Your ***n***,
26: 8 of our soul is for Your ***n***
26:13 only we make mention of Your ***n***.
29:23 They will hallow My ***n***,
30:27 the ***n*** of the LORD comes from
40:26 He calls them all by ***n***,
41:25 the sun he shall call on My ***n***;
42: 8 I am the LORD, that is My ***n***;
43: 1 I have called you by your ***n***;
43: 7 Everyone who is called by My ***n***,
44: 5 will call himself by the ***n*** of
44: 5 And ***n*** himself by the name of
44: 5 And name himself by the ***n*** of
45: 3 Who call you by your ***n***,
45: 4 have even called you by your ***n***;
47: 4 the LORD of hosts is His ***n***,
48: 1 Who are called by the ***n*** of
48: 1 Who swear by the ***n*** of the
48: 2 The LORD of hosts is His ***n***:
48:11 For how should My ***n*** be
48:19 His ***n*** would not have been cut
49: 1 He has made mention of My ***n***.
50:10 Let him trust in the ***n*** of the
51:15 LORD of hosts is His ***n***.
52: 5 And My ***n*** is blasphemed
52: 6 My people shall know My ***n***;
54: 5 The LORD of hosts is His ***n***;
55:13 shall be to the LORD for a ***n***,
56: 5 within My walls a place and a ***n***
56: 5 will give them an everlasting ***n***
56: 6 And to love the ***n*** of the
57:15 whose ***n*** is Holy: "I dwell in
59:19 So shall they fear The ***n*** of
60: 9 To the ***n*** of the LORD your
62: 2 You shall be called by a new ***n***,
62: 2 the mouth of the LORD will ***n***.
63:12 for Himself an everlasting ***n***,
63:14 To make Yourself a glorious ***n***.
63:16 from Everlasting is Your ***n***.
63:19 who were never called by Your ***n***.
64: 2 To make Your ***n*** known to Your
64: 7 is no one who calls on Your ***n***,
65: 1 that was not called by My ***n***.
65:15 You shall leave your ***n*** as a
65:15 call His servants by another ***n***;
66:22 your descendants and your ***n***
Jer 3:17 to the ***n*** of the LORD, to
7:10 house which is called by My ***n***,
7:11 house, which is called by My ***n***,
7:12 where I set My ***n*** at the first,
7:14 house which is called by My ***n***,
7:30 house which is called by My ***n***,
10: 6 and Your ***n*** is great in might),
10:16 The LORD of hosts is His ***n***.
10:25 who do not call on Your ***n***;
11:16 The LORD called your ***n***,
11:19 that his ***n*** may be remembered no
11:21 Do not prophesy in the ***n*** of the
12:16 of My people, to swear by My ***n***,
14: 9 And we are called by Your ***n***;
14:14 prophets prophesy lies in My ***n***.
14:15 prophets who prophesy in My ***n***,
15:16 For I am called by Your ***n***,
16:21 And they shall know that My ***n***
20: 3 LORD has not called your ***n***
20: 9 Nor speak anymore in His ***n***.
23: 6 Now this is His ***n*** by which He
23:25 said who prophesy lies in My ***n***,
23:27 to make My people forget My ***n***
23:27 as their fathers forgot My ***n***
25:29 city which is called by My ***n***,
26: 9 have you prophesied in the ***n***
26:16 he has spoken to us in the ***n***
26:20 a man who prophesied in the ***n***
27:15 they prophesy a lie in My ***n***,
29: 9 prophesy falsely to you in My ***n***,
29:21 prophesy a lie to you in My ***n***:
29:23 have spoken lying words in My ***n***,
29:25 have sent letters in your ***n*** to
31:35 (The LORD of hosts is His ***n***)
32:18 whose ***n*** is the LORD of hosts.
32:20 and You have made Yourself a ***n***,
32:34 house which is called by My ***n***,
33: 2 it (the LORD is His ***n***):
33: 9 Then it shall be to Me a ***n*** of
33:16 And this is the ***n*** by which
34:15 house which is called by My ***n***.
34:16 turned around and profaned My ***n***,
37:13 of the guard was there whose ***n***
44:16 you have spoken to us in the ***n***
44:26 I have sworn by My great ***n***,
44:26 that My ***n*** shall no more be named
46:18 Whose ***n*** is the LORD of
48:15 Whose ***n*** is the LORD of
48:17 And all you who know his ***n***,
50:34 The LORD of hosts is His ***n***.
51:19 The LORD of hosts is His ***n***.
51:57 Whose ***n*** is the LORD of
52: 1 His mother's ***n*** was Hamutal the
Lam 3:55 I called on Your ***n***,
Ezek 20:29 So its ***n*** is called Bamah to
20:39 but profane My holy ***n*** no more
24: 2 write down the ***n*** of the day,
36:20 went, they profaned My holy ***n***—
36:21 I had concern for My holy ***n***,
36:23 I will sanctify My great ***n***,
39: 7 So I will make My holy ***n*** known
39: 7 let them profane My holy ***n***
39:16 The ***n*** of the city will also
39:25 I will be jealous for My holy ***n***—
43: 7 of Israel defile My holy ***n***,
43: 8 they defiled My holy ***n*** by the
48:35 and the ***n*** of the city from
Dan 1: 7 he gave Daniel the ***n***
2:20 Blessed be the ***n*** of God forever
2:26 whose ***n*** was Belteshazzar,
4: 8 Daniel came before me (his ***n***
4: 8 according to the ***n*** of my god;
4:19 whose ***n*** was Belteshazzar, was
9: 6 who spoke in Your ***n*** to our
9:15 hand, and made Yourself a ***n***,
9:18 city which is called by Your ***n***;
9:19 people are called by Your ***n***.
10: 1 whose ***n*** was called
Hos 1: 4 Call his ***n*** Jezreel, For in a
1: 6 Call her ***n*** Lo-Ruhamah, For I
1: 9 Call his ***n*** Lo-Ammi, For you
2:17 shall be remembered by their ***n***
12: 5 The LORD is His memorable ***n***.
Joel 2:26 And praise the ***n*** of the LORD
2:32 That whoever calls on the ***n***
Am 2: 7 To defile My holy ***n***.
4:13 LORD God of hosts is His ***n***.
5: 8 the earth; The LORD is His ***n***.
5:27 whose ***n*** is the God of hosts.
6:10 For we dare not mention the ***n***
9: 6 the earth—The LORD is His ***n***.
9:12 Gentiles who are called by My ***n***,
Mic 4: 5 all people walk each in the ***n***
4: 5 But we will walk in the ***n*** of
5: 4 In the majesty of the ***n*** of the
6: 9 Wisdom shall see Your ***n***:
Nah 1:14 Your ***n*** shall be perpetuated no
Zeph 3: 9 they all may call on the ***n*** of
3:12 And they shall trust in the ***n***
Zech 5: 4 one who swears falsely by My ***n***.
6:12 the Man whose ***n*** is the BRANCH!
10:12 shall walk up and down in His ***n***,
13: 3 you have spoken lies in the ***n***
13: 9 tested. They will call on My ***n***,
14: 9 And His ***n*** one.
Mal 1: 6 you priests who despise My ***n***.
1: 6 way have we despised Your ***n***?
1:11 My ***n*** shall be great among
1:11 shall be offered to My ***n***,
1:11 For My ***n*** shall be great among
1:14 And My ***n*** is to be feared
2: 2 heart, To give glory to My ***n***,
2: 5 And was reverent before My ***n***.
3:16 And who meditate on His ***n***.
4: 2 But to you who fear My ***n*** The
Mt 1:21 and you shall call His ***n***
1:23 and they shall call His ***n***
1:25 And he called His ***n*** JESUS.
6: 9 in heaven, Hallowed be Your ***n***.
7:22 we not prophesied in Your ***n***,
7:22 name, cast out demons in Your ***n***,
7:22 and done many wonders in Your ***n***?
10:41 receives a prophet in the ***n*** of
10:41 a righteous man in the ***n*** of a
10:42 a cup of cold water in the ***n***
12:21 And in His ***n*** Gentiles
18: 5 little child like this in My ***n***
18:20 are gathered together in My ***n***,
21: 9 is He who comes in the ***n***
23:39 is He who comes in the ***n***
24: 5 "For many will come in My ***n***,
27:32 a man of Cyrene, Simon by ***n***.
28:19 baptizing them in the ***n*** of the
Mk 3:16 to whom He gave the ***n*** Peter;
3:17 to whom He gave the ***n***
5: 9 He asked him, "What is your ***n***?
5: 9 My ***n*** is Legion; for we are
5:22 the synagogue came, Jairus by ***n***.
6:14 for His ***n*** had become well
9:37 these little children in My ***n***
9:38 us casting out demons in Your ***n***,
9:39 one who works a miracle in My ***n***
9:41 a cup of water to drink in My ***n***,
11: 9 is He who comes in the ***n***
11:10 David That comes in the ***n*** of
13: 6 "For many will come in My ***n***,

16:17 In My ***n*** they will cast out
Lk 1: 5 and her ***n*** was Elizabeth.
1:13 and you shall call his ***n*** John.
1:27 betrothed to a man whose ***n*** was
1:27 The virgin's ***n*** was Mary.
1:31 and shall call His ***n*** JESUS.
1:49 for me, And holy is His ***n***.
1:59 would have called him by the ***n***
1:61 who is called by this ***n***.
1:63 His ***n*** is John." So they all
2:21 His ***n*** was called JESUS, the
2:21 the ***n*** given by the angel before
2:25 was a man in Jerusalem whose ***n***
6:22 and cast out your ***n*** as evil,
8:30 him, saying, "What is your ***n***?
9:48 this little child in My ***n***
9:49 casting out demons in Your ***n***,
10:17 are subject to us in Your ***n***.
11: 2 in heaven, Hallowed be Your ***n***.
13:35 is He who comes in the ***n***
19:38 King who comes in the ***n***
21: 8 For many will come in My ***n***,
24:18 Then the one whose ***n*** was Cleopas
24:47 should be preached in His ***n*** to
Jn 1: 6 whose ***n*** was John.
1:12 to those who believe in His ***n***:
2:23 many believed in His ***n*** when
3:18 he has not believed in the ***n***
5:43 "I have come in My Father's ***n***,
5:43 if another comes in his own ***n***,
10: 3 and he calls his own sheep by ***n***
10:25 that I do in My Father's ***n***,
12:13 is He who comes in the ***n***
12:28 "Father, glorify Your ***n***.
14:13 "And whatever you ask in My ***n***,
14:14 "If you ask anything in My ***n***,
14:26 the Father will send in My ***n***,
15:16 you ask the Father in My ***n*** He
16:23 you ask the Father in My ***n*** He
16:24 you have asked nothing in My ***n***.
16:26 that day you will ask in My ***n***,
17: 6 I have manifested Your ***n*** to the
17:11 keep through Your ***n*** those whom
17:12 world, I kept them in Your ***n***.
17:26 I have declared to them Your ***n***,
18:10 The servant's ***n*** was Malchus.
20:31 you may have life in His ***n***.
Acts 2:21 whoever calls on the ***n***
2:38 of you be baptized in the ***n*** of
3: 6 In the ***n*** of Jesus Christ of
3:16 'And His ***n***, through faith in
3:16 name, through faith in His ***n***,
4: 7 By what power or by what ***n*** have
4:10 that by the ***n*** of Jesus Christ
4:12 for there is no other ***n*** under
4:17 they speak to no man in this ***n***.
4:18 at all nor teach in the ***n*** of
4:30 may be done through the ***n*** of
5:28 you not to teach in this ***n***?
5:40 they should not speak in the ***n***
5:41 to suffer shame for His ***n***.
8:12 the kingdom of God and the ***n***
8:16 only been baptized in the ***n*** of
9:14 to bind all who call on Your ***n***.
9:15 vessel of Mine to bear My ***n***
9:21 those who called on this ***n*** in
9:27 boldly at Damascus in the ***n*** of
9:29 And he spoke boldly in the ***n*** of
10:43 witness that, through His ***n***,
10:48 them to be baptized in the ***n***
13: 6 a Jew whose ***n*** was Bar-Jesus,
13: 8 the sorcerer (for so his ***n*** is
15:14 out of them a people for His ***n***.
15:17 who are called by My ***n***,
15:26 risked their lives for the ***n***
16:18 I command you in the ***n*** of Jesus
19: 5 they were baptized in the ***n*** of
19:13 upon themselves to call the ***n***
19:17 and the ***n*** of the Lord Jesus was
21:13 to die at Jerusalem for the ***n***
22:16 calling on the ***n*** of the Lord.'
26: 9 many things contrary to the ***n***
28: 7 whose ***n*** was Publius, who
Rom 1: 5 among all nations for His ***n***,
2:24 the ***n*** of God is blasphemed
9:17 and that My ***n*** may be
10:13 whoever calls on the ***n*** of
15: 9 And sing to Your ***n***.
1 Cor 1: 2 in every place call on the ***n***
1:10 by the ***n*** of our Lord Jesus
1:13 Or were you baptized in the ***n***
1:15 that I had baptized in my own ***n***.
5: 4 In the ***n*** of our Lord Jesus
6:11 you were justified in the ***n*** of
Eph 1:21 and every ***n*** that is named, not
5:20 to God the Father in the ***n*** of
Phil 2: 9 Him and given Him the ***n*** which
2: 9 the name which is above every ***n***,
2:10 that at the ***n*** of Jesus every
Col 3:17 do all in the ***n*** of the Lord
2 Th 1:12 that the ***n*** of our Lord Jesus
3: 6 in the ***n*** of our Lord Jesus
1 Tim 6: 1 so that the ***n*** of God and His
2 Tim 2:19 Let everyone who names the ***n*** of
Heb 1: 4 obtained a more excellent ***n***
2:12 I will declare Your ***n*** to
6:10 you have shown toward His ***n***,
13:15 lips, giving thanks to His ***n***.
Jas 2: 7 not blaspheme that noble ***n*** by
5:10 who spoke in the ***n*** of the Lord,
5:14 him with oil in the ***n*** of the
1 Pe 4:14 If you are reproached for the ***n***
1 Jn 3:23 we should believe on the ***n*** of
5:13 to you who believe in the ***n*** of
5:13 continue to believe in the ***n***
3 Jn 14 Greet the friends by ***n***.
Rev 2:13 And you hold fast to My ***n***,
2:17 and on the stone a new ***n***
3: 1 that you have a ***n*** that you are
3: 5 and I will not blot out his ***n***
3: 5 but I will confess his ***n*** before
3: 8 word, and have not denied My ***n***.
3:12 And I will write on him the ***n***
3:12 the name of My God and the ***n***
3:12 will write on him My new ***n***.
6: 8 And the ***n*** of him who sat on it
8:11 The ***n*** of the star is Wormwood. A
9:11 whose ***n*** in Hebrew is Abaddon,
9:11 but in Greek he has the ***n***
11:18 And those who fear Your ***n***,
13: 1 on his heads a blasphemous ***n***.
13: 6 against God, to blaspheme His ***n***,
13:17 one who has the mark or the ***n***
13:17 beast, or the number of his ***n***.
14: 1 having His Father's ***n*** written
14:11 receives the mark of his ***n***.
15: 2 and over the number of his ***n***,
15: 4 You, O Lord, and glorify Your ***n***?
16: 9 and they blasphemed the ***n*** of
17: 5 And on her forehead a ***n*** was
19:12 He had a ***n*** written that no one
19:13 and His ***n*** is called The Word of
19:16 His robe and on His thigh a ***n***
22: 4 and His ***n*** shall be on their

NAME'S (29/29) NAME

1 Sam 12:22 for His great ***n*** sake, because
1 Ki 8:41 from a far country for Your ***n***
Ps 23: 3 of righteousness For His ***n***
25:11 For Your ***n*** sake, O LORD,
31: 3 for Your ***n*** sake, Lead me and
79: 9 For Your ***n*** sake!
106: 8 He saved them for His ***n*** sake,
109:21 Deal with me for Your ***n*** sake;
143:11 for Your ***n*** sake! For Your
Isa 48: 9 For My ***n*** sake I will defer My
66: 5 Who cast you out for My ***n***
Jer 14: 7 Do it for Your ***n*** sake;
14:21 for Your ***n*** sake; Do not
Ezek 20: 9 But I acted for My ***n*** sake, that
20:14 But I acted for My ***n*** sake, that
20:22 My hand and acted for My ***n***
20:44 I have dealt with you for My ***n***
36:22 but for My holy ***n*** sake, which
Mt 10:22 will be hated by all for My ***n***
19:29 for My ***n*** sake, shall receive a
24: 9 hated by all nations for My ***n***
Mk 13:13 will be hated by all for My ***n***
Lk 21:12 kings and rulers for My ***n*** sake.
21:17 will be hated by all for My ***n***
Jn 15:21 they will do to you for My ***n***
Acts 9:16 things he must suffer for My ***n***
1 Jn 2:12 sins are forgiven you for His ***n***
3 Jn 7 they went forth for His ***n*** sake,
Rev 2: 3 and have labored for My ***n*** sake

NAMED (64/64) NAME

Gen 4:25 and she bore a son and ***n*** him
4:26 and he ***n*** him Enosh. Then men
5: 3 and ***n*** him Seth.
16:15 and Abram ***n*** his son, whom Hagar
23:16 for Ephron which he had ***n*** in
27:36 Is he not rightly ***n*** Jacob? For
48:16 Let my name be ***n*** upon them,
Josh 2: 1 came to the house of a harlot ***n***
1 Sam 4:21 Then she ***n*** the child Ichabod,
17: 4 ***n*** Goliath, from Gath, whose
22:20 ***n*** Abiathar, escaped and fled
2 Ki 17:34 whom He ***n*** Israel,
Ezra 5:14 and they were given to one ***n***
Eccl 6:10 he has been ***n*** already, For it
Isa 14:20 of evildoers shall never be ***n***.
45: 4 I have ***n*** you, though you have
61: 6 But you shall be ***n*** the priests
Jer 44:26 My name shall no more be ***n*** in
Ezek 48:31 gates of the city shall be ***n***
Dan 5:12 whom the king ***n*** Belteshazzar,
Mic 2: 7 You who are ***n*** the house of
Mt 9: 9 He saw a man ***n*** Matthew sitting
27:57 ***n*** Joseph, who himself had also
Mk 14:32 came to a place which was ***n***
15: 7 And there was one ***n*** Barabbas,
Lk 1: 5 a certain priest ***n*** Zacharias,
1:26 by God to a city of Galilee ***n***
5:27 out and saw a tax collector ***n***
6:13 He chose twelve whom He also ***n***
6:14 whom He also ***n*** Peter, and
8:41 there came a man ***n*** Jairus, and
10:38 and a certain woman ***n*** Martha
16:20 there was a certain beggar ***n***
19: 2 there was a man ***n*** Zacchaeus
23:50 there was a man ***n*** Joseph, a
Jn 3: 1 was a man of the Pharisees ***n***
Acts 4:36 who was also ***n*** Barnabas by the
5: 1 But a certain man ***n*** Ananias,
5:34 a Pharisee ***n*** Gamaliel, a
7:58 at the feet of a young man ***n***
9:10 certain disciple at Damascus ***n***
9:12 in a vision he has seen a man ***n***
9:33 There he found a certain man ***n***
9:36 there was a certain disciple ***n***
11:28 ***n*** Agabus, stood up and showed
12:13 a girl ***n*** Rhoda came to answer.
15:22 Judas who was also ***n*** Barsabas,
16: 1 ***n*** Timothy, the son of a
16:14 Now a certain woman ***n*** Lydia
17:34 a woman ***n*** Damaris, and others
18: 2 And he found a certain Jew ***n***
18: 7 the house of a certain man ***n***
18:24 Now a certain Jew ***n*** Apollos,
19:24 For a certain man ***n*** Demetrius, a
20: 9 sat a certain young man ***n***
21:10 a certain prophet ***n*** Agabus came
24: 1 elders and a certain orator ***n***
27: 1 some other prisoners to one ***n***
Rom 15:20 gospel, not where Christ was ***n***,
1 Cor 5: 1 immorality as is not even ***n***
5:11 to keep company with anyone ***n***
Eph 1:21 and every name that is ***n***,
3:15 family in heaven and earth is ***n***,
5: 3 let it not even be ***n*** among you,

NAMELY (14/13)

Gen 21:10 ***n*** with Isaac."
Ex 3:22 shall ask of her neighbor, ***n***,
Num 14:34 ***n*** forty years, and you shall
Josh 15:13 of the LORD to Joshua, ***n***,
17: 1 ***n*** for Machir the firstborn of
Judg 3: 3 ***n***, five lords of the
1 Ki 4:24 ***n*** over all the kings on this
Ezra 8:18 ***n*** Sherebiah, with his sons and
Isa 29:10 And has closed your eyes, ***n***,
29:10 He has covered your heads, ***n***,
Jer 25:20 the land of the Philistines (***n***,
Dan 7:20 up, before which three fell, ***n***,
Acts 15:22 with Paul and Barnabas, ***n***,
Rom 13: 9 summed up in this saying, ***n***,

NAMES (93/84) NAME

Gen 2:20 So Adam gave ***n*** to all cattle, to
25:13 And these were the ***n*** of the
25:13 the sons of Ishmael, by their ***n***,
25:16 Ishmael and these were their ***n***,
26:18 He called them by the ***n*** which
36:10 These were the ***n*** of Esau's
36:40 And these were the ***n*** of the
36:40 and their places, by their ***n***:
46: 8 Now these were the ***n*** of the
Ex 1: 1 Now these are the ***n*** of the
6:16 These are the ***n*** of the sons of
28: 9 and engrave on them the ***n*** of
28:10 six of their ***n*** on one stone, and
28:10 and six ***n*** on the other stone,
28:11 the two stones with the ***n*** of
28:12 So Aaron shall bear their ***n***
28:21 the stones shall have the ***n*** of
28:21 twelve according to their ***n***,
28:29 So Aaron shall bear the ***n*** of the
39: 6 with the ***n*** of the sons of
39:14 stones according to the ***n*** of
39:14 of Israel: according to their ***n***,
Num 1: 2 according to the number of ***n***,
1: 5 These are the ***n*** of the men who
1:18 according to the number of ***n***,
1:20 according to the number of ***n***,
1:22 according to the number of ***n***,
1:24 according to the number of ***n***,
1:26 according to the number of ***n***,
1:28 according to the number of ***n***,
1:30 according to the number of ***n***,
1:32 according to the number of ***n***,
1:34 according to the number of ***n***,
1:36 according to the number of ***n***,
1:38 according to the number of ***n***,
1:40 according to the number of ***n***,
1:42 according to the number of ***n***,
3: 2 And these are the ***n*** of the sons
3: 3 These are the ***n*** of the sons of
3:17 the sons of Levi by their ***n***:
3:18 And these are the ***n*** of the sons
3:40 and take the number of their ***n***.
3:43 according to the number of ***n***
13: 4 Now these were their ***n***:
13:16 These are the ***n*** of the men whom
26:33 and the ***n*** of the daughters of
26:53 according to the number of ***n***.
26:55 inherit according to the ***n*** of
27: 1 and these were the ***n*** of his
32:38 Nebo and Baal Meon (their ***n***
32:38 and they gave other ***n*** to the
34:17 These are the ***n*** of the men who
34:19 These are the ***n*** of the men:
Deut 12: 3 their gods and destroy their ***n***
Josh 17: 3 And these are the ***n*** of his
Ruth 1: 2 and the ***n*** of his two sons were
1 Sam 14:49 And the ***n*** of his two daughters
17:13 The ***n*** of his three sons who
2 Sam 5:14 Now these are the ***n*** of those
23: 8 These are the ***n*** of the mighty
1 Ki 4: 8 These are their ***n***:
1 Chr 6:17 These are the ***n*** of the sons of
6:65 which are called by their ***n***.
8:38 Azel had six sons whose ***n*** were
9:44 And Azel had six sons whose ***n***
14: 4 And these are the ***n*** of his
23:24 by the number of their ***n***,
Ezra 5: 4 we told them the ***n*** of the men
5:10 We also asked them their ***n*** to
5:10 that we might write the ***n*** of
8:13 whose ***n*** are these—Eliphelet,
Ps 16: 4 Nor take up their ***n*** on my
49:11 their lands after their own ***n***.

N

Ezek 23: 4 Their ***n***: Oholah the elder
23: 4 daughters. As for their ***n***,
48: 1 Now these are the ***n*** of the
Dan 1: 7 the chief of the eunuchs gave ***n***:
Hos 2:17 will take from her mouth the ***n***
Zeph 1: 4 The ***n*** of the idolatrous
Zech 13: 2 that I will cut off the ***n*** of
Mt 10: 2 Now the ***n*** of the twelve apostles
Lk 10:20 rather rejoice because your ***n***
Acts 1:15 (altogether the number of ***n***
18:15 it is a question of words and ***n***
Phil 4: 3 whose ***n*** are in the Book of
2 Tim 2:19 Let everyone who ***n*** the name of
Rev 3: 4 You have a few ***n*** even in Sardis
13: 8 whose ***n*** have not been written
17: 3 beast which was full of ***n*** of
17: 8 whose ***n*** are not written in the
21:12 and ***n*** written on them, which
21:12 which are the ***n*** of the twelve
21:14 and on them were the ***n*** of the

NAOMI (19/18) NAOMI'S

Ruth 1: 2 the name of his wife was *N*,
1: 8 And *N* said to her two
1:11 But *N* said, "Turn back, my
1:19 the women said, "Is this *N*?
1:20 to them, "Do not call me *N*;
1:21 empty. Why do you call me *N*,
1:22 So *N* returned, and Ruth the
2: 2 So Ruth the Moabitess said to *N*,
2: 6 woman who came back with *N*
2:20 Then *N* said to her
2:20 living and the dead!" And *N*
2:22 And *N* said to Ruth her
3: 1 Then *N* her mother-in-law said to
4: 3 said to the close relative, "*N*,
4: 5 the field from the hand of *N*,
4: 9 Mahlon's, from the hand of *N*.
4:14 Then the women said to *N*,
4:16 Then *N* took the child and laid
4:17 "There is a son born to *N*.

NAOMI'S (2/2) NAOMI

Ruth 1: 3 *N* husband, died; and she was
2: 1 There was a relative of *N*

NAPHISH (3/3)

Gen 25:15 Hadar, Tema, Jetur, *N*,
1 Chr 1:31 Jetur, *N*, and Kedemah.
5:19 war with the Hagrites, Jetur, *N*,

NAPHTALI (54/50)

Gen 30: 8 So she called his name *N*.
35:25 maidservant, were Dan and *N*;
46:24 The sons of *N* were Jahzeel,
49:21 *N* is a deer let loose; He uses
Ex 1: 4 Dan, *N*, Gad, and Asher.
Num 1:15 'from *N*, Ahira the son of
1:42 From the children of *N*,
1:43 were numbered of the tribe of *N*
2:29 "Then comes the tribe of *N*,
2:29 the leader of the children of *N*
7:78 leader of the children of *N*,
10:27 the tribe of the children of *N*
13:14 from the tribe of *N*,
26:48 The sons of *N* according to
26:50 These are the families of *N*
34:28 the tribe of the children of *N*,
Deut 27:13 Gad, Asher, Zebulun, Dan, and *N*.
33:23 And of *N* he said: "O
33:23 of Naphtali he said: "O *N*,
34: 2 all *N* and the land of Ephraim
Josh 19:32 came out to the children of *N*,
19:32 for the children of *N* according
19:39 the tribe of the children of *N*
20: 7 Galilee, in the mountains of *N*,
21: 6 of Asher, from the tribe of *N*,
21:32 and from the tribe of *N*,
Judg 1:33 Nor did *N* drive out the
4: 6 son of Abinoam from Kedesh in *N*,
4: 6 thousand men of the sons of *N*
4:10 And Barak called Zebulun and *N*
5:18 *N* also, on the heights of the
6:35 to Asher, Zebulun, and *N*;
7:23 Israel gathered together from *N*,
1 Ki 4:15 Ahimaaz, in *N*; he also took
7:14 of a widow from the tribe of *N*,
15:20 with all the land of *N*.
2 Ki 15:29 and Galilee, all the land of *N*;
1 Chr 2: 2 Dan, Joseph, Benjamin, *N*,
6:62 of Asher, from the tribe of *N*,
6:76 And from the tribe of *N*:
7:13 The sons of *N* were Jahziel,
12:34 of *N* one thousand captains, and
12:40 as Issachar and Zebulun and *N*,
27:19 the son of Obadiah; over *N*,
2 Chr 16: 4 and all the storage cities of *N*.
34: 6 as far as *N* and all around,
Ps 68:27 Zebulun and the princes of *N*.
Isa 9: 1 of Zebulun and the land of *N*,
Ezek 48: 3 the west, one section for *N*;
48: 4 "by the border of *N*,
48:34 for Asher, and one gate for *N*.
Mt 4:13 in the regions of Zebulun and *N*,
4:15 Zebulun and the land of *N*,
Rev 7: 6 of the tribe of *N* twelve

NAPHTUHIM (2/2)

Gen 10:13 begot Ludim, Anamim, Lehabim, *N*,
1 Chr 1:11 begot Ludim, Anamim, Lehabim, *N*,

NAPKIN (KJV) See HANDKERCHIEF

NARCISSUS (1/1)

Rom 16:11 who are of the household of *N*

NARRATIVE (1/1)

Lk 1: 1 in hand to set in order a ***n*** of

NARROW (8/8)

Num 22:24 of the LORD stood in a ***n*** path
22:26 and stood in a ***n*** place where
1 Ki 6: 6 for he made ***n*** ledges around the
Prov 23:27 And a seductress is a ***n*** well.
Isa 28:20 And the covering so ***n*** that one
Mt 7:13 Enter by the ***n*** gate; for wide
7:14 Because ***n*** is the gate and
Lk 13:24 Strive to enter through the ***n***

NATHAN (43/40)

2 Sam 5:14 Jerusalem: Shammua, Shobab, *N*,
7: 2 that the king said to *N* the
7: 3 Then *N* said to the king, "Go,
7: 4 the word of the LORD came to *N*,
7:17 so *N* spoke to David.
12: 1 Then the LORD sent *N* to David.
12: 5 the man, and he said to *N*,
12: 7 Then *N* said to David, "You
12:13 So David said to *N*,
12:13 And *N* said to David, "The
12:15 Then *N* departed to his house.
12:25 He sent word by the hand of *N*
23:36 Igal the son of *N* of Zobah, Bani
1 Ki 1: 8 *N* the prophet, Shimei, Rei, and
1:10 But he did not invite *N* the
1:11 So *N* spoke to Bathsheba the
1:22 *N* the prophet also came in.
1:23 Here is *N* the prophet." And
1:24 And *N* said, "My lord, O king,
1:32 *N* the prophet, and Benaiah the
1:34 let Zadok the priest and *N* the
1:38 *N* the prophet, Benaiah the son
1:44 *N* the prophet, Benaiah the son
1:45 So Zadok the priest and *N* the
4: 5 Azariah the son of *N*,
4: 5 officers; Zabud the son of *N*,
1 Chr 2:36 Attai begot *N*,
2:36 and *N* begot Zabad;
3: 5 in Jerusalem: Shimea, Shobab, *N*,
11:38 Joel the brother of *N*,
14: 4 Jerusalem: Shammua, Shobab, *N*,
17: 1 that David said to *N* the
17: 2 Then *N* said to David, "Do all
17: 3 that the word of God came to *N*,
17:15 so *N* spoke to David.
29:29 in the book of *N* the prophet,
2 Chr 9:29 not written in the book of *N*
29:25 and of *N* the prophet; for thus
Ezra 8:16 Elnathan, Jarib, Elnathan, *N*,
10:39 Shelemiah, *N*, Adaiah,
Ps 51: A Psalm of David when *N* the
Zech 12:12 the family of the house of *N* by
Lk 3:31 of Mattathah, the son of *N*,

NATHAN-MELECH (1/1)

2 Ki 23:11 the LORD, by the chamber of *N*,

NATHANAEL (6/6) BARTHOLOMEW

Jn 1:45 Philip found *N* and said to him,
1:46 And *N* said to him, "Can
1:47 Jesus saw *N* coming toward Him,
1:48 *N* said to Him, "How do You know
1:49 *N* answered and said to Him,
21: 2 *N* of Cana in Galilee, the sons

NATION (151/132) NATIONS

Gen 12: 2 I will make you a great ***n***;
15:14 And also the ***n*** whom they serve I
17:20 and I will make him a great ***n***.
18:18 become a great and mighty ***n***,
20: 4 will You slay a righteous ***n***
21:13 Yet I will also make a ***n*** of the
21:18 for I will make him a great ***n***.
35:11 a ***n*** and a company of nations
46: 3 I will make of you a great ***n***
Ex 9:24 of Egypt since it became a ***n***.
19: 6 kingdom of priests and a holy ***n***.
32:10 I will make of you a great ***n***.
33:13 And consider that this ***n*** is
34:10 in all the earth, nor in any ***n***;
Lev 18:26 either any of your own ***n*** or
20:23 walk in the statutes of the ***n***
Num 14:12 and I will make of you a ***n***
Deut 4: 6 Surely this great ***n*** is a wise
4: 7 For what great ***n*** is there that
4: 8 And what great ***n*** is there that
4:34 to go and take for Himself a ***n***
4:34 from the midst of another ***n***,
9:14 and I will make of you a ***n***
26: 5 number; and there he became a ***n***,
28:33 A ***n*** whom you have not known
28:36 whom you set over you to a ***n***
28:49 The LORD will bring a ***n*** against
28:49 a ***n*** whose language you will not
28:50 a ***n*** of fierce countenance, which
32:21 by those who are not a ***n***;
32:21 them to anger by a foolish ***n***.
32:28 For they are a ***n*** void of
Judg 2:20 Because this ***n*** has transgressed
2 Sam 7:23 the one ***n*** on the earth whom God
1 Ki 18:10 there is no ***n*** or kingdom where
18:10 an oath from the kingdom or ***n***
2 Ki 17:29 However every ***n*** continued to
17:29 every ***n*** in the cities where
1 Chr 16:20 When they went from one ***n*** to
17:21 the one ***n*** on the earth whom God
2 Chr 15: 6 So ***n*** was destroyed by nation,
15: 6 "So nation was destroyed by ***n***,
32:15 for no god of any ***n*** or kingdom
Job 34:29 Whether it is against a ***n*** or
Ps 33:12 Blessed is the ***n*** whose God is
43: 1 my cause against an ungodly ***n***;
83: 4 us cut them off from being a ***n***,
105:13 When they went from one ***n*** to
106: 5 in the gladness of Your ***n***,
147:20 has not dealt thus with any ***n***;
Prov 14:34 Righteousness exalts a ***n***,
Isa 1: 4 Alas, sinful ***n***, A people
2: 4 *N* shall not lift up sword
2: 4 not lift up sword against ***n***,
9: 3 You have multiplied the ***n***
10: 6 send him against an ungodly ***n***,
14:32 answer the messengers of the ***n***?
18: 2 to a ***n*** tall and smooth of
18: 2 A ***n*** powerful and treading
18: 7 A ***n*** powerful and treading
26: 2 That the righteous ***n*** which
26:15 You have increased the ***n***,
26:15 You have increased the ***n***;
49: 7 To Him whom the ***n*** abhors,
51: 4 And give ear to Me, O My ***n***:
55: 5 Surely you shall call a ***n*** you
58: 2 As a ***n*** that did righteousness,
60:12 For the ***n*** and kingdom which
60:22 And a small one a strong ***n***.
65: 1 To a ***n*** that was not called
66: 8 Or shall a ***n*** be born at once?
Jer 2:11 Has a ***n*** changed its gods,
5: 9 I not avenge Myself on such a ***n***
5:15 I will bring a ***n*** against you
5:15 the LORD. "It is a mighty ***n***,
5:15 nation, It is an ancient ***n***,
5:15 A ***n*** whose language you do not
5:29 I not avenge Myself on such a ***n***
6:22 And a great ***n*** will be raised
7:28 This is a ***n*** that does not obey
9: 9 I not avenge Myself on such a ***n***
12:17 pluck up and destroy that ***n***,
18: 7 instant I speak concerning a ***n***
18: 8 if that ***n*** against whom I have
18: 9 instant I speak concerning a ***n***
25:12 the king of Babylon and that ***n***,
25:32 shall go forth From ***n*** to
25:32 go forth From nation to ***n***,
27: 8 that the ***n*** and kingdom which
27: 8 that ***n*** I will punish,' says the
27:13 LORD has spoken against the ***n***
31:36 also cease From being a ***n***
33:24 if they should no more be a ***n***
48: 2 and let us cut her off as a ***n***.
49:31 go up to the wealthy ***n*** that
50: 3 For out of the north a ***n*** comes
50:41 And a great ***n*** and many kings
51:20 with you I will break the ***n*** in
Lam 4:17 watching we watched For a ***n***
Ezek 2: 3 to a rebellious ***n*** that has
36:13 devour men and bereave your ***n***
36:14 nor bereave your ***n*** anymore,'
36:15 nor shall you cause your ***n*** to
37:22 and I will make them one ***n*** in
Dan 3:29 a decree that any people, ***n***,
8:22 shall arise out of that ***n***,
12: 1 never was since there was a ***n***,
Joel 1: 6 For a ***n*** has come up against My
Am 6: 1 Notable persons in the chief ***n***,
6:14 I will raise up a ***n*** against
Mic 4: 3 *N* shall not lift up sword
4: 3 not lift up sword against ***n***,
4: 7 And the outcast a strong ***n***;
Hab 1: 6 A bitter and hasty ***n*** Which
Zeph 2: 1 together, O undesirable ***n***,
2: 5 The ***n*** of the Cherethites!
2:14 midst, Every beast of the ***n***.
Hag 2:14 and so is this ***n*** before Me,'
Mal 3: 9 robbed Me, Even this whole ***n***.
Mt 21:43 taken from you and given to a ***n***
24: 7 For ***n*** will rise against nation,
24: 7 nation will rise against ***n***,
Mk 13: 8 For ***n*** will rise against nation,
13: 8 nation will rise against ***n***,
Lk 7: 5 "for he loves our ***n***,
21:10 *N* will rise against nation, and
21:10 "Nation will rise against ***n***,
23: 2 this fellow perverting the ***n***,
Jn 11:48 take away both our place and ***n***.
11:50 and not that the whole ***n*** should
11:51 that Jesus would die for the ***n***,
11:52 and not for that ***n*** only, but
18:35 Your own ***n*** and the chief
Acts 2: 5 from every ***n*** under heaven.
7: 7 And the ***n*** to whom they
10:22 reputation among all the ***n*** of
10:28 with or go to one of another ***n***.
10:35 But in every ***n*** whoever fears Him

17:26 made from one blood every ***n*** of
24: 2 is being brought to this ***n*** by
24:10 many years a judge of this ***n***,
24:17 alms and offerings to my ***n***,
26: 4 the beginning among my own ***n***
28:19 of which to accuse my ***n***.
Rom 10:19 by those who are not a ***n***,
10:19 to anger by a foolish ***n***.
Gal 1:14 my contemporaries in my own ***n***,
1 Pe 2: 9 a royal priesthood, a holy ***n***,
Rev 5: 9 and tongue and people and ***n***,
13: 7 over every tribe, tongue, and ***n***.
14: 6 dwell on the earth—to every ***n***,

NATION'S (1/1)

Num 21:18 Dug by the ***n*** nobles, By the

NATIONS (445/426) NATION

Gen 10: 5 to their families, into their ***n***.
10:20 in their lands and in their ***n***.
10:31 lands, according to their ***n***.
10:32 their generations, in their ***n***;
10:32 and from these the ***n*** were
14: 1 of Elam, and Tidal king of ***n***,
14: 9 king of Elam, Tidal king of ***n***,
17: 4 you shall be a father of many ***n***.
17: 5 made you a father of many ***n***.
17: 6 and I will make ***n*** of you, and
17:16 she shall be a mother of ***n***;
18:18 and all the ***n*** of the earth
22:18 In your seed all the ***n*** of the
25:16 princes according to their ***n***.
25:23 'Two ***n*** are in your womb,
26: 4 and in your seed all the ***n*** of
27:29 And ***n*** bow down to you.
35:11 a nation and a company of ***n***
48:19 shall become a multitude of ***n***.
Ex 34:24 For I will cast out the ***n*** before
Lev 18:24 for by all these the ***n*** are
18:28 as it vomited out the ***n*** that
25:44 from the ***n*** that are around you,
26:33 I will scatter you among the ***n***
26:38 You shall perish among the ***n***,
26:45 of Egypt in the sight of the ***n***,
Num 14:15 then the ***n*** which have heard of
23: 9 reckoning itself among the ***n***.
24: 8 He shall consume the ***n***,
24:20 was first among the ***n***,
Deut 2:25 and fear of you upon the ***n***
4:27 left few in number among the ***n***
4:38 driving out from before you ***n***
7: 1 and has cast out many ***n*** before
7: 1 seven ***n*** greater and mightier
7:17 'These ***n*** are greater than I;
7:22 your God will drive out those ***n***
8:20 As the ***n*** which the LORD
9: 1 and go in to dispossess ***n***
9: 4 of the wickedness of these ***n***
9: 5 of the wickedness of these ***n***
11:23 will drive out all these ***n***
11:23 greater and mightier ***n*** than
12: 2 all the places where the ***n***
12:29 cuts off from before you the ***n***
12:30 How did these ***n*** serve their
15: 6 you shall lend to many ***n***,
15: 6 you shall reign over many ***n***,
17:14 a king over me like all the ***n***
18: 9 the abominations of those ***n***.
18:14 For these ***n*** which you will
19: 1 your God has cut off the ***n***
20:15 not of the cities of these ***n***.
26:19 will set you high above all ***n***
28: 1 will set you high above all ***n***
28:12 You shall lend to many ***n***,
28:37 and a byword among all ***n*** where
28:65 And among those ***n*** you shall find
29:16 and that we came through the ***n***
29:18 and serve the gods of these ***n***,
29:24 All ***n*** would say, 'Why has the
30: 1 them to mind among all the ***n***
30: 3 you again from all the ***n*** where
31: 3 He will destroy these ***n*** from
32: 8 their inheritance to the ***n***,
Josh 23: 3 God has done to all these ***n***
23: 4 divided to you by lot these ***n***
23: 4 with all the ***n*** that I have cut
23: 7 lest you go among these ***n***,
23: 9 before you great and strong ***n***;
23:12 cling to the remnant of these ***n***—
23:13 no longer drive out these ***n***
Judg 2:21 out before them any of the ***n***
2:23 the LORD left those ***n***,
3: 1 Now these are the ***n*** which the
1 Sam 8: 5 king to judge us like all the ***n***.
8:20 we also may be like all the ***n***,
27: 8 For those ***n*** were the
2 Sam 7:23 for Yourself from Egypt, the ***n***,
8:11 he had dedicated from all the ***n***
22:44 kept me as the head of the ***n***.
1 Ki 4:31 was in all the surrounding ***n***.
4:34 And men of all ***n***, from all
11: 2 from the ***n*** of whom the LORD had
14:24 all the abominations of the ***n***
2 Ki 16: 3 to the abominations of the ***n***
17: 8 in the statutes of the ***n*** whom
17:11 like the ***n*** whom the LORD had
17:15 and went after the ***n*** who were
17:26 The ***n*** whom you have removed and
17:33 to the rituals of the ***n*** from
17:41 So these ***n*** feared the LORD, yet
18:33 Has any of the gods of the ***n*** at
19:12 Have the gods of the ***n*** delivered
19:17 Assyria have laid waste the ***n***
21: 2 to the abominations of the ***n***
21: 9 them to do more evil than the ***n***
1 Chr 14:17 the fear of him upon all ***n***.
16:24 Declare His glory among the ***n***,
16:31 And let them say among the ***n***,
17:21 by driving out ***n*** from before
18:11 had brought from all these ***n***—
2 Chr 12: 8 of the kingdoms of the ***n***.
20: 6 over all the kingdoms of the ***n***,
28: 3 to the abominations of the ***n***
32:13 Were the gods of the ***n*** of those
32:14 among all the gods of those ***n***
32:17 As the gods of the ***n*** of other
32:23 exalted in the sight of all ***n***
33: 2 to the abominations of the ***n***
33: 9 to do more evil than the ***n***
36:14 all the abominations of the ***n***,
Ezra 4:10 and the rest of the ***n*** whom the
6:21 from the filth of the ***n*** of the
Neh 1: 8 I will scatter you among the ***n***;
5: 8 brethren who were sold to the ***n***.
5: 9 of the reproach of the ***n***,
5:17 those who came to us from the ***n***
6: 6 It is reported among the ***n***,
6:16 and all the ***n*** around us saw
9:22 You gave them kingdoms and ***n***,
13:26 Yet among many ***n*** there was no
Job 12:23 He makes ***n*** great, and destroys
12:23 destroys them; He enlarges ***n***,
Ps 2: 1 Why do the ***n*** rage, And the
2: 8 and I will give You The ***n***
9: 5 You have rebuked the ***n***,
9:15 The ***n*** have sunk down in the pit
9:17 And all the ***n*** that forget
9:19 Let the ***n*** be judged in Your
9:20 That the ***n*** may know
10:16 The ***n*** have perished out of His
18:43 have made me the head of the ***n***;
22:27 And all the families of the ***n***
22:28 And He rules over the ***n***.
33:10 brings the counsel of the ***n*** to
44: 2 You drove out the ***n*** with Your
44:11 have scattered us among the ***n***.
44:14 make us a byword among the ***n***,
46: 6 The ***n*** raged, the kingdoms were
46:10 I will be exalted among the ***n***,
47: 3 And the ***n*** under our feet.
47: 8 God reigns over the ***n***;
57: 9 I will sing to You among the ***n***.
59: 5 Awake to punish all the ***n***;
59: 8 You shall have all the ***n*** in
66: 7 His eyes observe the ***n***;
67: 2 Your salvation among all ***n***.
67: 4 let the ***n*** be glad and sing for
67: 4 And govern the ***n*** on earth.
72:11 All ***n*** shall serve Him.
72:17 All ***n*** shall call Him blessed.
78:55 He also drove out the ***n*** before
79: 1 the ***n*** have come into Your
79: 6 Pour out Your wrath on the ***n***
79:10 Why should the ***n*** say, "Where
79:10 there be known among the ***n*** in
80: 8 Egypt; You have cast out the ***n***,
82: 8 For You shall inherit all ***n***.
86: 9 All ***n*** whom You have made Shall
94:10 He who instructs the ***n***,
96: 3 Declare His glory among the ***n***,
96:10 Say among the ***n***,
98: 2 revealed in the sight of the ***n***.
102:15 So the ***n*** shall fear the name of
105:44 inherited the labor of the ***n***,
106:27 their descendants among the ***n***,
108: 3 sing praises to You among the ***n***.
110: 6 He shall judge among the ***n***,
111: 6 them the heritage of the ***n***.
113: 4 The LORD is high above all ***n***,
118:10 All ***n*** surrounded me, But in
126: 2 Then they said among the ***n***,
135:10 He defeated many ***n*** And slew
135:15 The idols of the ***n*** are silver
149: 7 To execute vengeance on the ***n***,
Prov 24:24 ***N*** will abhor him.
Isa 2: 2 And all ***n*** shall flow to it.
2: 4 He shall judge between the ***n***,
5:26 will lift up a banner to the ***n***
10: 7 And cut off not a few ***n***.
11:12 will set up a banner for the ***n***,
13: 4 noise of the kingdoms of ***n***
14: 6 He who ruled the ***n*** in anger,
14: 9 All the kings of the ***n***.
14:12 You who weakened the ***n***!
14:18 "All the kings of the ***n***,
14:26 is stretched out over all the ***n***.
16: 8 The lords of the ***n*** have broken
17:12 And to the rushing of ***n*** That
17:13 The ***n*** will rush like the
23: 3 she is a marketplace for the ***n***.
25: 3 The city of the terrible ***n***
25: 7 veil that is spread over all ***n***.
29: 7 The multitude of all the ***n*** who
29: 8 So the multitude of all the ***n***
30:28 To sift the ***n*** with the sieve
33: 3 the ***n*** shall be scattered;
34: 1 Come near, you ***n***,
34: 2 of the LORD is against all ***n***,
36:18 any one of the gods of the ***n***
37:12 Have the gods of the ***n*** delivered
37:18 have laid waste all the ***n*** and
40:15 the ***n*** are as a drop in a
40:17 All ***n*** before Him are as
41: 2 Who gave the ***n*** before him,
43: 9 Let all the ***n*** be gathered
45: 1 To subdue ***n*** before him
45:20 who have escaped from the ***n***.
49:22 My hand in an oath to the ***n***,
52:10 In the eyes of all the ***n***;
52:15 So shall He sprinkle many ***n***.
54: 3 descendants will inherit the ***n***,
55: 5 And ***n*** who do not know you
56: 7 a house of prayer for all ***n***.
60:12 And those ***n*** shall be utterly
61:11 spring forth before all the ***n***.
64: 2 That the ***n*** may tremble at
66:18 be that I will gather all ***n***
66:19 who escape I will send to the ***n***:
66:20 to the LORD out of all ***n***,
Jer 1: 5 ordained you a prophet to the ***n***.
1:10 this day set you over the ***n***
3:17 and all the ***n*** shall be gathered
3:19 heritage of the hosts of ***n***?
4: 2 The ***n*** shall bless themselves
4: 7 And the destroyer of ***n*** is on
4:16 "Make mention to the ***n***,
6:18 Therefore hear, you ***n***,
9:26 For all these ***n*** are
10: 7 not fear You, O King of the ***n***?
10: 7 all the wise men of the ***n***,
10:10 And the ***n*** will not be able to
14:22 any among the idols of the ***n***
22: 8 And many ***n*** will pass by this
25: 9 and against these ***n*** all around,
25:11 and these ***n*** shall serve the
25:13 prophesied concerning all the ***n***.
25:14 (For many ***n*** and great kings
25:15 My hand, and cause all the ***n***,
25:17 and made all the ***n*** drink, to
25:31 has a controversy with the ***n***;
26: 6 this city a curse to all the ***n***
27: 7 So all ***n*** shall serve him and his
27: 7 and then many ***n*** and great kings
27:11 But the ***n*** that bring their necks
28:11 Babylon from the neck of all ***n***
28:14 iron on the neck of all these ***n***,
29:14 will gather you from all the ***n***
29:18 and a reproach among all the ***n***
30:11 I make a full end of all ***n***
31: 7 shout among the chief of the ***n***;
31:10 the word of the LORD, O ***n***,
33: 9 and an honor before all ***n*** of
36: 2 Judah, and against all the ***n***,
43: 5 from all ***n*** where they had been
44: 8 and a reproach among all the ***n***
46: 1 the prophet against the ***n***.
46:12 The ***n*** have heard of your shame,
46:28 a complete end of all the ***n***
49:14 has been sent to the ***n***:
49:15 I will make you small among ***n***,
49:36 There shall be no ***n*** where the
50: 2 "Declare among the ***n***,
50: 9 An assembly of great ***n*** from
50:12 the least of the ***n*** shall be a
50:23 a desolation among the ***n***!
50:46 the cry is heard among the ***n***.
51: 7 The ***n*** drank her wine;
51: 7 Therefore the ***n*** are deranged.
51:27 Blow the trumpet among the ***n***!
51:27 the nations! Prepare the ***n***
51:28 Prepare against her the ***n***,
51:41 become desolate among the ***n***!
51:44 And the ***n*** shall not stream to
51:58 will labor in vain, And the ***n***,
Lam 1: 1 Who was great among the ***n***!
1: 3 She dwells among the ***n***,
1:10 For she has seen the ***n*** enter
2: 9 her princes are among the ***n***;
4:15 Those among the ***n*** said,
4:20 We shall live among the ***n***.
Ezek 5: 5 set her in the midst of the ***n***
5: 6 wickedness more than the ***n***,
5: 7 disobedience more than the ***n***
5: 7 to the judgments of the ***n*** that
5: 8 midst in the sight of the ***n***.
5:14 and a reproach among the ***n***
5:15 and an astonishment to the ***n***
6: 8 escape the sword among the ***n***
6: 9 will remember Me among the ***n***
12:15 I scatter them among the ***n*** and
16:14 fame went out among the ***n***
19: 4 The ***n*** also heard of him;
19: 8 Then the ***n*** set against him from
22: 4 made you a reproach to the ***n***,
22:15 will scatter you among the ***n***,
22:16 yourself in the sight of the ***n***;
25: 7 give you as plunder to the ***n***;
25: 8 of Judah is like all the ***n***,
25:10 not be remembered among the ***n***.
26: 3 and will cause many ***n*** to come
26: 5 shall become plunder for the ***n***.
28: 7 The most terrible of the ***n***;
29:12 the Egyptians among the ***n*** and
29:15 again exalt itself above the ***n***,
29:15 they will not rule over the ***n***
30:11 him, the most terrible of the ***n***,
30:23 the Egyptians among the ***n***,
30:26 the Egyptians among the ***n*** and
31: 6 And in its shadow all great ***n***
31:11 hand of the mighty one of the ***n***,
31:12 the most terrible of the ***n***,
31:16 I made the ***n*** shake at the sound
31:17 in its shadows among the ***n***.
32: 2 like a young lion among the ***n***,

32: 9 your destruction among the *n*,
32:12 them the most terrible of the *n*,
32:16 The daughters of the *n* shall
32:18 the daughters of the famous *n*,
34:28 no longer be a prey for the *n*,
35:10 These two *n* and these two
36: 3 possession of the rest of the *n*,
36: 4 mockery to the rest of the *n*
36: 5 against the rest of the *n* and
36: 6 have borne the shame of the *n*.
36: 7 in an oath that surely the *n*
36:15 you hear the taunts of the *n*
36:19 I scattered them among the *n*,
36:20 "When they came to the *n*,
36:21 Israel had profaned among the *n*
36:22 you have profaned among the *n*
36:23 has been profaned among the *n*,
36:23 and the *n* shall know that I am
36:24 will take you from among the *n*,
36:30 reproach of famine among the *n*.
36:36 Then the *n* which are left all
37:21 of Israel from among the *n*,
37:22 they shall no longer be two *n*,
37:28 The *n* also will know that I, the
38: 8 they were brought out of the *n*,
38:12 a people gathered from the *n*,
38:16 so that the *n* may know Me, when
38:23 be known in the eyes of many *n*.
39: 7 Then the *n* shall know that I
39:21 will set My glory among the *n*;
39:21 all the *n* shall see My judgment
39:27 in them in the sight of many *n*,
39:28 them into captivity among the *n*,
Dan 3: 4 it is commanded, O peoples, *n*,
3: 7 of music, all the people, *n*,
4: 1 the king, To all peoples, *n*,
5:19 He gave him, all peoples, *n*,
6:25 Darius wrote: To all peoples, *n*,
7:14 a kingdom, That all peoples, *n*,
Hos 8:10 they have hired among the *n*,
9:17 shall be wanderers among the *n*.
Joel 2:17 That the *n* should rule over
2:19 make you a reproach among the *n*.
3: 2 I will also gather all *n*,
3: 2 they have scattered among the *n*;
3: 9 Proclaim this among the *n*:
3:11 Assemble and come, all you *n*,
3:12 Let the *n* be wakened, and come
3:12 to judge all the surrounding *n*.
Am 9: 9 the house of Israel among all *n*,
Ob 1 has been sent among the *n*,
2 will make you small among the *n*;
15 day of the LORD upon all the *n*
16 So shall all the *n* drink
Mic 4: 2 Many *n* shall come and say,
4: 3 And rebuke strong *n* afar off;
4:11 Now also many *n* have gathered
5:15 in anger and fury On the *n*
7:16 The *n* shall see and be ashamed
Nah 3: 4 Who sells *n* through her
3: 5 I will show the *n* your
Hab 1: 5 Look among the *n* and watch—Be
1:17 And continue to slay *n* without
2: 5 He gathers to himself all *n*
2: 8 you have plundered many *n*,
2:13 And *n* weary themselves in
3: 6 He looked and startled the *n*.
3:12 You trampled the *n* in anger.
Zeph 2:11 Indeed all the shores of the *n*.
3: 6 "I have cut off *n*,
3: 8 is to gather the *n* To My
Hag 2: 7 'and I will shake all *n*,
2: 7 come to the Desire of All *N*,
Zech 1:15 am exceedingly angry with the *n*
1:21 to cast out the horns of the *n*
2: 8 to the *n* which plunder you;
2:11 Many *n* shall be joined to the
7:14 a whirlwind among all the *n*
8:13 as you were a curse among the *n*,
8:22 many peoples and strong *n*
8:23 from every language of the *n*
9:10 He shall speak peace to the *n*;
12: 3 though all *n* of the earth are
12: 9 will seek to destroy all the *n*
14: 2 For I will gather all the *n* to
14: 3 And fight against those *n*,
14:14 wealth of all the surrounding *n*
14:16 who is left of all the *n* which
14:18 which the LORD strikes the *n*
14:19 and the punishment of all the *n*
Mal 1:11 name shall be great among the *n*,
1:14 is to be feared among the *n*.
3:12 And all *n* will call you blessed,
Mt 24: 9 and you will be hated by all *n*
24:14 world as a witness to all the *n*,
25:32 All the *n* will be gathered
28:19 and make disciples of all the *n*,
Mk 11:17 of prayer for all *n*'?
13:10 first be preached to all the *n*.
Lk 12:30 For all these things the *n* of
21:24 be led away captive into all *n*.
21:25 and on the earth distress of *n*,
24:47 preached in His name to all *n*,
Acts 4:25 'Why did the *n* rage,
13:19 when He had destroyed seven *n*
14:16 generations allowed all *n* to
Rom 1: 5 to the faith among all *n* for
4:17 you a father of many *n*'
4:18 he became the father of many *n*,
16:26 has been made known to all *n*,
Gal 3: 8 In you all the *n* shall be
Rev 2:26 I will give power over the *n*—
7: 9 no one could number, of all *n*,
10:11 again about many peoples, *n*,
11: 9 and *n* will see their dead
11:18 The *n* were angry, and Your
12: 5 Child who was to rule all *n*
14: 8 because she has made all *n*
15: 4 For all *n* shall come and
16:19 and the cities of the *n* fell.
17:15 are peoples, multitudes, *n*,
18: 3 For all the *n* have drunk of the
18:23 for by your sorcery all the *n*
19:15 with it He should strike the *n*.
20: 3 so that he should deceive the *n*
20: 8 will go out to deceive the *n*
21:24 And the *n* of those who are saved
21:26 glory and the honor of the *n*
22: 2 were for the healing of the *n*.

NATIVE (9/9) NATIVE-BORN

Gen 11:28 his father Terah in his *n* land,
Ex 12:19 he is a stranger or a *n* of
12:48 and he shall be as a *n* of the
Lev 16:29 whether a *n* of your own
17:15 whether he is a *n* of your
23:42 All who are *n* Israelites shall
Num 9:14 for the stranger and the *n* of
Ps 37:35 And spreading himself like a *n*
Jer 22:10 Nor see his *n* country.

NATIVE-BORN (5/5) NATIVE

Ex 12:49 One law shall be for the *n* and
Num 15:13 All who are *n* shall do these
15:29 for him who is *n* among the
15:30 whether he is *n* or a
Ezek 47:22 They shall be to you as *n* among

NATIVES (2/2)

Acts 28: 2 And the *n* showed us unusual
28: 4 So when the *n* saw the creature

NATIVITY (5/5)

Jer 46:16 And to the land of our *n*
Ezek 16: 3 Your birth and your *n* are from
16: 4 "As for your *n*,
21:30 In the land of your *n*.
23:15 The land of their *n*.

NATURAL (11/10) NATURALLY, NATURE

Deut 34: 7 His eyes were not dim nor his *n*
Rom 1:26 their women exchanged the *n*
1:27 leaving the *n* use of the woman,
11:21 For if God did not spare the *n*
11:24 who are *n* branches, be
1 Cor 2:14 But the *n* man does not receive
15:44 It is sown a *n* body, it is
15:44 There is a *n* body, and there is
15:46 is not first, but the *n*,
Jas 1:23 is like a man observing his *n*
2 Pe 2:12 like *n* brute beasts made to be

NATURALLY (6/6) NATURAL

Lev 7:24 fat of an animal that dies *n*,
17:15 person who eats what died *n*
22: 8 Whatever dies *n* or is torn by
Num 16:29 If these men die *n* like all men,
Ezek 44:31 that died *n* or was torn by
Jude 10 and whatever they know *n*,

NATURE (13/12) NATURAL

Acts 14:15 We also are men with the same *n*
17:29 not to think that the Divine *N*
Rom 1:26 use for what is against *n*.
2:14 by *n* do the things in the law,
11:24 olive tree which is wild by *n*,
11:24 and were grafted contrary to *n*
1 Cor 11:14 Does not even *n* itself teach you
Gal 2:15 "We who are Jews by *n*,
4: 8 you served those which by *n* are
Eph 2: 3 and were by *n* children of
Jas 3: 6 sets on fire the course of *n*;
5:17 Elijah was a man with a *n* like
2 Pe 1: 4 be partakers of the divine *n*,

NAUGHTINESS, NAUGHTY (KJV)

See BAD, FALSE, INSOLENCE, LUST, WICKEDNESS, WORTHLESS

NAUM (KJV) See NAHUM

NAVEL (2/2)

Song 7: 2 Your *n* is a rounded goblet;
Ezek 16: 4 on the day you were born your *n*

NAVES (KJV) See RIMS

NAVY (KJV) See FLEET

NAY (KJV) See NO, (CERTAINLY) NOT, YET

NAZARENE (1/1) NAZARENES, NAZARETH

Mt 2:23 "He shall be called a *N*.

NAZARENES (1/1) NAZARENE

Acts 24: 5 ringleader of the sect of the *N*.

NAZARETH (29/29) NAZARENE

Mt 2:23 and dwelt in a city called *N*,
4:13 And leaving *N*, He came
21:11 the prophet from *N* of
26:71 also was with Jesus of *N*.
Mk 1: 9 days that Jesus came from *N*
1:24 we to do with You, Jesus of *N*?
10:47 he heard that it was Jesus of *N*,
14:67 "You also were with Jesus of *N*.
16: 6 be alarmed. You seek Jesus of *N*,
Lk 1:26 to a city of Galilee named *N*,
2: 4 Galilee, out of the city of *N*,
2:39 Galilee, to their own city, *N*.
2:51 down with them and came to *N*,
4:16 So He came to *N*, where He
4:34 we to do with You, Jesus of *N*?
18:37 they told him that Jesus of *N*
24:19 things concerning Jesus of *N*,
Jn 1:45 the prophets, wrote—Jesus of *N*,
1:46 anything good come out of *N*?
18: 5 They answered Him, "Jesus of *N*.
18: 7 And they said, "Jesus of *N*.
19:19 And the writing was: JESUS OF *N*,
Acts 2:22 hear these words: Jesus of *N*,
3: 6 the name of Jesus Christ of *N*,
4:10 the name of Jesus Christ of *N*,
6:14 him say that this Jesus of *N*
10:38 how God anointed Jesus of *N* with
22: 8 He said to me, 'I am Jesus of *N*,
26: 9 to the name of Jesus of *N*.

NAZIRITE (9/9) NAZIRITES

Num 6: 2 offering to take the vow of a *N*,
6:13 'Now this is the law of the *N*:
6:18 Then the *N* shall shave his
6:19 them upon the hands of the *N*
6:20 After that the *N* may drink
6:21 This is the law of the *N* who
Judg 13: 5 for the child shall be a *N* to
13: 7 for the child shall be a *N* to
16:17 for I have been a *N* to God

NAZIRITES (3/3) NAZIRITE

Lam 4: 7 Her *N* were brighter than snow
Am 2:11 some of your young men as *N*.
2:12 But you gave the *N* wine to

NEAH (1/1)

Josh 19:13 to Rimmon, which borders on *N*.

NEAPOLIS (1/1)

Acts 16:11 and the next day came to *N*,

NEAR (309/295)

Gen 18:23 And Abraham came *n* and said,
19: 9 and came *n* to break down the
19:20 this city is *n* enough to flee
20: 4 But Abimelech had not come *n*
27:21 said to Jacob, "Please come *n*,
27:22 So Jacob went *n* to Isaac his
27:25 Bring it *n* to me, and I will
27:25 So he brought it *n* to him,
27:26 Come *n* now and kiss me, my
27:27 And he came *n* and kissed him;
29:10 that Jacob went *n* and rolled
33: 3 until he came *n* to his brother.
33: 6 Then the maidservants came *n*,
33: 7 And Leah also came *n* with her
33: 7 Joseph and Rachel came *n*,
37:18 even before he came *n* them,
43:19 When they drew *n* to the steward
44:18 Then Judah came *n* to him and
45: 4 Please come *n* to me." So they
45: 4 near to me." So they came *n*.
45:10 and you shall be *n* to me, you
47:29 When the time drew *n* that Israel
48:10 Then Joseph brought them *n* him,
48:13 and brought them *n* him.
Ex 3: 5 Do not draw *n* this place. Take
3:22 of her who dwells *n* her house,
12:48 and then let him come *n* and
13:17 although that was *n*;
14:10 And when Pharaoh drew *n*,
14:20 so that the one did not come *n*
16: 9 Come *n* before the LORD, for He
19:13 they shall come *n* the
19:15 do not come *n* your wives."
19:22 let the priests who come *n* the
20:21 but Moses drew *n* the thick
24: 2 And Moses alone shall come *n* the
24: 2 but they shall not come *n*;
28:43 or when they come *n* the altar
30:20 or when they come *n* the altar
32:19 as soon as he came *n* the camp,
34:30 and they were afraid to come *n*
34:32 the children of Israel came *n*,
40:32 and when they came *n* the altar,
Lev 9: 5 And all the congregation drew *n*

10: 3 By those who come ***n*** Me I must
10: 4 and said to them, "Come ***n***,
10: 5 So they went ***n*** and carried them
18: 6 shall approach anyone who is ***n***
18:12 she is ***n*** of kin to your
18:13 for she is ***n*** of kin to your
18:17 They are ***n*** of kin to her. It
20:19 for that would uncover his ***n*** of
21: 3 his virgin sister who is ***n*** to
21:11 nor shall he go ***n*** any dead body,
21:21 shall come ***n*** to offer the
21:21 he shall not come ***n*** to offer
21:23 only he shall not go ***n*** the veil
22: 3 who goes ***n*** the holy things
25:49 or anyone who is ***n*** of kin to
Num 1:51 The outsider who comes ***n*** shall
3: 6 "Bring the tribe of Levi ***n***,
3:10 but the outsider who comes ***n***
3:38 but the outsider who came ***n*** was
5:16 the priest shall bring her ***n***,
6: 6 to the LORD he shall not go ***n***
8:19 the children of Israel come ***n***
11:31 sea and left them fluttering ***n***
13:21 ***n*** the entrance of Hamath.
16: 5 and will cause him to come ***n***
16: 5 He will cause to come ***n*** to Him.
16: 9 to bring you ***n*** to Himself, to
16:10 and that He has brought you ***n***
16:40 should come ***n*** to offer incense
17:13 Whoever even comes ***n*** the
18: 3 but they shall not come ***n*** the
18: 4 an outsider shall not come ***n***
18: 7 but the outsider who comes ***n***
18:22 of Israel shall not come ***n*** the
22: 5 which is ***n*** the River in the
24:17 now; I behold Him, but not ***n***;
31:48 hundreds, came ***n*** to Moses;
32:16 Then they came ***n*** to him and
33: 7 and they camped ***n*** Migdol.
36: 1 came ***n*** and spoke before Moses
Deut 1:22 And everyone of you came ***n*** to me
2:19 And when you come ***n*** the people
2:37 Only you did not go ***n*** the land
4: 7 is there that has God so ***n***
4:11 Then you came ***n*** and stood at the
5:23 that you came ***n*** to me, all the
5:27 You go ***n*** and hear all that the
13: 7 ***n*** to you or far off from you,
16:21 ***n*** the altar which you build for
20:10 When you go ***n*** a city to fight
21: 5 the sons of Levi, shall come ***n***,
22: 2 And if your brother is not ***n***
25:11 and the wife of one draws ***n*** to
30:14 But the word is very ***n*** you, in
Josh 3: 4 Do not come ***n*** it, that you may
8:11 with him went up and drew ***n***;
9:16 their neighbors who dwelt ***n***
9:22 when you dwell ***n*** us?
10:24 war who went with him, "Come ***n***,
10:24 And they drew ***n*** and put their
15:46 all that lay ***n*** Ashdod, with
17: 4 And they came ***n*** before Eleazar
18:13 ***n*** the hill that lies on the
19:46 with the region ***n*** Joppa.
21: 1 houses of the Levites came ***n***
Judg 1:16 which lies in the South ***n***
4:11 Kenites and pitched his tent ***n***
9:52 and he drew ***n*** the door of the
18:22 men who were in the houses ***n***
19:11 They were ***n*** Jebus, and the day
19:13 let us draw ***n*** to one of these
19:14 and the sun went down on them ***n***
20:23 Shall I again draw ***n*** for battle
1 Sam 7:10 the Philistines drew ***n*** to
9:18 Then Saul drew ***n*** to Samuel in
10:20 the tribes of Israel to come ***n***,
10:21 tribe of Benjamin to come ***n*** by
14:36 Let us draw ***n*** to God here."
17:16 And the Philistine drew ***n*** and
17:40 And he drew ***n*** to the
17:41 and began drawing ***n*** to David,
17:48 arose and came and drew ***n*** to
30:21 And when David came ***n*** the
2 Sam 1:15 the young men and said, "Go ***n***,
10:13 who were with him drew ***n*** for
11:20 Why did you approach so ***n*** to the
11:21 did you go ***n*** the wall?'—then
13:23 which is ***n*** Ephraim; so Absalom
14:30 Joab's field is ***n*** mine, and he
15: 5 whenever anyone came ***n*** to bow
18:25 And he came rapidly and drew ***n***.
19:37 ***n*** the grave of my father and
20:11 one of Joab's men stood ***n***
20:17 When he had come ***n*** to her, the
1 Ki 2: 1 Now the days of David drew ***n***
8:46 the land of the enemy, far or ***n***;
8:59 be ***n*** the LORD our God day and
9:26 which is ***n*** Elath on the shore
18:30 Come ***n*** to me." So all the
18:30 So all the people came ***n*** to
18:36 that Elijah the prophet came ***n***
21: 2 garden, because it is ***n***,
22:24 the son of Chenaanah went ***n***
2 Ki 4:27 but Gehazi came ***n*** to push her
5:13 And his servants came ***n*** and
20: 1 days Hezekiah was sick and ***n***
1 Chr 12:40 Moreover those who were ***n*** to
19:14 who were with him drew ***n*** for
2 Chr 6:36 them captive to a land far or ***n***;
18:23 the son of Chenaanah went ***n***
21:16 and the Arabians who were ***n***
29:31 yourselves to the LORD, come ***n***,
32:24 days Hezekiah was sick and ***n***
Neh 4:12 when the Jews who dwelt ***n*** them
Esth 5: 2 Then Esther went ***n*** and touched
9:20 ***n*** and far, who were in all the
Job 17:12 into day; 'The light is ***n***,
33:22 his soul draws ***n*** the Pit,
40:19 He who made him can bring ***n***
41:16 One is so ***n*** another That no
Ps 22:11 far from Me, For trouble is ***n***;
32: 6 waters They shall not come ***n***
32: 9 Else they will not come ***n*** you.
34:18 The LORD is ***n*** to those who
69:18 Draw ***n*** to my soul, and redeem
73:28 it is good for me to draw ***n***
75: 1 declare that Your name is ***n***.
85: 9 Surely His salvation is ***n*** to
88: 3 And my life draws ***n*** to the
91: 7 But it shall not come ***n*** you.
91:10 Nor shall any plague come ***n***
107:18 And they drew ***n*** to the gates
119:150 They draw ***n*** who follow after
119:151 You are ***n***, O LORD,
145:18 The LORD is ***n*** to all who call
148:14 A people ***n*** to Him. Praise the
Prov 5: 8 And do not go ***n*** the door of
7: 8 Passing along the street ***n*** her
10:14 the mouth of the foolish is ***n***
Eccl 5: 1 and draw ***n*** to hear rather than
12: 1 And the years draw ***n*** when you
Isa 5:19 the Holy One of Israel draw ***n***
13:22 Her time is ***n*** to come,
26:17 When she draws ***n*** the time of
29:13 as these people draw ***n*** with
33:13 have done; And you who are ***n***,
34: 1 Come ***n***, you nations, to hear;
38: 1 days Hezekiah was sick and ***n***
41: 1 strength! Let them come ***n***,
41: 1 Let us come ***n*** together for
41: 5 They drew ***n*** and came.
45:20 Draw ***n*** together, You who
46:13 I bring My righteousness ***n***,
48:16 Come ***n*** to Me, hear this: I have
50: 8 He is ***n*** who justifies Me;
50: 8 Let him come ***n*** Me.
51: 5 My righteousness is ***n***,
54:14 for it shall not come ***n*** you.
55: 6 Call upon Him while He is ***n***.
57:19 far off and to him who is ***n***,
65: 5 Do not come ***n*** me, For I am
Jer 12: 2 You are ***n*** in their mouth
23:23 Am I a God ***n*** at hand," says
25:26 kings of the north, far and ***n***,
30:21 I will cause him to draw ***n***,
41:17 which is ***n*** Bethlehem, as they
42: 1 least to the greatest, came ***n***
46: 3 And draw ***n*** to battle!
48:16 The calamity of Moab is ***n*** at
48:24 of the land of Moab, Far or ***n***.
52: 7 though the Chaldeans were ***n***
Lam 3:57 You drew ***n*** on the day I called
4:18 in our streets. Our end was ***n***;
Ezek 6:12 he who is ***n*** shall fall by the
7: 7 A day of trouble is ***n***,
7:12 time has come, The day draws ***n***.
9: 1 charge over the city draw ***n***,
9: 6 but do not come ***n*** anyone on
11: 3 The time is not ***n*** to build
22: 4 have caused your days to draw ***n***,
22: 5 Those ***n*** and those far from you
30: 3 For the day is ***n***,
30: 3 the day of the LORD is ***n***;
40:46 who come ***n*** the LORD to
44:13 And they shall not come ***n*** Me to
44:13 nor come ***n*** any of My holy
44:15 they shall come ***n*** Me to
44:16 and they shall come ***n*** My table
44:25 defile themselves by coming ***n***
45: 4 who come ***n*** to minister to the
Dan 3:26 Then Nebuchadnezzar went ***n*** the
7:13 And they brought Him ***n*** before
7:16 I came ***n*** to one of those who
8:17 So he came ***n*** where I stood, and
9: 7 those ***n*** and those far off in
Joel 3: 9 Let all the men of war draw ***n***,
3:14 the day of the LORD is ***n*** in
Am 6: 3 the seat of violence to come ***n***;
Ob 15 upon all the nations is ***n***;
Zeph 1:14 great day of the LORD is ***n***;
1:14 It is ***n*** and hastens quickly.
3: 2 She has not drawn ***n*** to her
Mal 3: 5 And I will come ***n*** you for
Mt 15: 8 These people draw ***n*** to Me
21: 1 Now when they drew ***n*** Jerusalem,
21:34 "Now when vintage-time drew ***n***,
24:32 you know that summer is ***n***.
24:33 these things, know that it is ***n***—
Mk 2: 2 not even ***n*** the door. And He
2: 4 And when they could not come ***n***
5:11 of swine was feeding there ***n***
11: 1 Now when they drew ***n*** Jerusalem,
13:28 you know that summer is ***n***.
13:29 happening, know that it is ***n***—
Lk 7:12 And when He came ***n*** the gate of
10: 9 The kingdom of God has come ***n*** to
10:11 the kingdom of God has come ***n***
15: 1 and the sinners drew ***n*** to Him
15:25 And as he came and drew ***n*** to
18:35 as He was coming ***n*** Jericho,
18:40 to Him. And when he had come ***n***,
19:11 because He was ***n*** Jerusalem and
19:29 when He came ***n*** to Bethphage and
19:37 as He was now drawing ***n*** the
19:41 Now as He drew ***n***,
21: 8 'The time has drawn ***n***.'
21:20 know that its desolation is ***n***.
21:28 because your redemption draws ***n***.
21:30 yourselves that summer is now ***n***.
21:31 that the kingdom of God is ***n***.
22: 1 of Unleavened Bread drew ***n***,
22:47 went before them and drew ***n*** to
23:54 and the Sabbath drew ***n***.
24:15 that Jesus Himself drew ***n*** and
24:28 Then they drew ***n*** to the village
Jn 3:23 also was baptizing in Aenon ***n***
4: 5 ***n*** the plot of ground that Jacob
6: 4 a feast of the Jews, was ***n***.
6:19 on the sea and drawing ***n*** the
6:23 ***n*** the place where they ate
11:18 Now Bethany was ***n*** Jerusalem,
11:54 from there into the country ***n***
11:55 the Passover of the Jews was ***n***,
19:20 Jesus was crucified was ***n*** the
Acts 1:12 which is ***n*** Jerusalem, a Sabbath
7:17 the time of the promise drew ***n***
7:31 and as he drew ***n*** to observe,
8:29 Go ***n*** and overtake this
9: 3 As he journeyed he came ***n***
9:38 And since Lydda was ***n*** Joppa, and
10: 9 on their journey and drew ***n***
21:33 Then the commander came ***n*** and
22: 6 as I journeyed and came ***n***
23:15 to kill him before he comes ***n***.
27: 8 ***n*** the city of Lasea.
27:27 that they were drawing ***n*** some
Rom 10: 8 The word is ***n*** you, in your
Eph 2:13 far off have been brought ***n*** by
2:17 off and to those who were ***n***.
Heb 6: 8 it is rejected and ***n*** to being
7:19 through which we draw ***n*** to God.
10:22 let us draw ***n*** with a true heart
Jas 4: 8 Draw ***n*** to God and He will draw
4: 8 near to God and He will draw ***n***
Rev 1: 3 in it; for the time is ***n***.

NEARBY (3/3)

2 Sam 20:16 Please say to Joab, 'Come ***n***,
Prov 27:10 Better is a neighbor ***n*** than a
Jn 19:42 Day, for the tomb was ***n***.

NEARER (1/1)

Rom 13:11 for now our salvation is ***n***

NEAREST (4/4)

Lev 21: 2 for his relatives who are ***n*** to
Deut 21: 3 that the elders of the city ***n***
21: 6 all the elders of that city ***n***
Prov 7: 4 call understanding your ***n*** kin,

NEARIAH (3/3)

1 Chr 3:22 were Hattush, Igal, Bariah, *N*,
3:23 The sons of *N* were Elioenai,
4:42 as their captains Pelatiah, *N*,

NEARLY (1/1)

Ps 73: 2 My steps had ***n*** slipped.

NEBAI (1/1)

Neh 10:19 Hariph, Anathoth, *N*,

NEBAIOTH (1/1)

Isa 60: 7 The rams of *N* shall minister

NEBAJOTH (4/4)

Gen 25:13 The firstborn of Ishmael, *N*;
28: 9 Abraham's son, the sister of *N*,
36: 3 Ishmael's daughter, sister of *N*.
1 Chr 1:29 The firstborn of Ishmael was *N*;

NEBALLAT (1/1)

Neh 11:34 in Hadid, Zeboim, *N*;

NEBAT (25/25)

1 Ki 11:26 servant, Jeroboam the son of *N*,
12: 2 when Jeroboam the son of *N*
12:15 to Jeroboam the son of *N*.
15: 1 of King Jeroboam the son of *N*,
16: 3 house of Jeroboam the son of *N*.
16:26 ways of Jeroboam the son of *N*,
16:31 sins of Jeroboam the son of *N*,
21:22 house of Jeroboam the son of *N*,
22:52 way of Jeroboam the son of *N*,
2 Ki 3: 3 sins of Jeroboam the son of *N*,
9: 9 house of Jeroboam the son of *N*,
10:29 sins of Jeroboam the son of *N*,
13: 2 sins of Jeroboam the son of *N*,
13:11 sins of Jeroboam the son of *N*,
14:24 sins of Jeroboam the son of *N*,
15: 9 sins of Jeroboam the son of *N*,
15:18 sins of Jeroboam the son of *N*,
15:24 sins of Jeroboam the son of *N*,
15:28 sins of Jeroboam the son of *N*,
17:21 they made Jeroboam the son of *N*
23:15 which Jeroboam the son of *N*,
2 Chr 9:29 Jeroboam the son of *N*?
10: 2 when Jeroboam the son of *N*
10:15 to Jeroboam the son of *N*.

13: 6 "Yet Jeroboam the son of *N*,

NEBO (13/13) PISGAH

Num 32: 3 Heshbon, Elealeh, Shebam, *N*,
32:38 *N* and Baal Meon (their names
33:47 mountains of Abarim, before *N*.
Deut 32:49 mountain of the Abarim, Mount *N*,
34: 1 the plains of Moab to Mount *N*,
1 Chr 5: 8 as far as *N* and Baal Meon.
Ezra 2:29 the people of *N*,
10:43 of the sons of *N*:
Neh 7:33 the men of the other *N*,
Isa 15: 2 Moab will wail over *N* and over
46: 1 *N* stoops; Their idols were on
Jer 48: 1 Woe to *N*! For it is plundered,
48:22 On Dibon and *N* and Beth

NEBUCHADNEZZAR (90/88)

2 Ki 24: 1 In his days *N* king of Babylon
24:10 At that time the servants of *N*
24:11 And *N* king of Babylon came
25: 1 that *N* king of Babylon and all
25: 8 the nineteenth year of King *N*
25:22 whom *N* king of Babylon had
1 Chr 6:15 into captivity by the hand of *N*.
2 Chr 36: 6 *N* king of Babylon came up
36: 7 *N* also carried off some of the
36:10 At the turn of the year King *N*
36:13 he also rebelled against King *N*,
Ezra 1: 7 which *N* had taken from
2: 1 whom *N* the king of Babylon had
5:12 He gave them into the hand of *N*
5:14 which *N* had taken from the
6: 5 which *N* took from the temple
Neh 7: 6 whom *N* the king of Babylon had
Esth 2: 6 whom *N* the king of Babylon had
Jer 21: 2 for *N* king of Babylon makes war
21: 7 into the hand of *N* king of
22:25 the hand of *N* king of Babylon
24: 1 after *N* king of Babylon had
25: 1 was the first year of *N* king
25: 9 and *N* the king of Babylon, My
27: 6 these lands into the hand of *N*
27: 8 kingdom which will not serve *N*
27:20 which *N* king of Babylon did not
28: 3 that *N* king of Babylon took
28:11 so I will break the yoke of *N*
28:14 that they may serve *N* king of
29: 1 and all the people whom *N* had
29: 3 to *N* king of Babylon, saying,
29:21 them into the hand of *N* king
32: 1 was the eighteenth year of *N*.
32:28 into the hand of *N* king of
34: 1 when *N* king of Babylon and all
35:11 when *N* king of Babylon came up
37: 1 whom *N* king of Babylon made
39: 1 *N* king of Babylon and all his
39: 5 they brought him up to *N* king
39:11 Now *N* king of Babylon gave
43:10 I will send and bring *N* the
44:30 of Judah into the hand of *N*
46: 2 and which *N* king of Babylon
46:13 how *N* king of Babylon would
46:26 into the hand of *N* king of
49:28 which *N* king of Babylon shall
49:30 For *N* king of Babylon has taken
50:17 Now at last this *N* king of
51:34 *N* the king of Babylon
52: 4 that *N* king of Babylon and all
52:12 the nineteenth year of King *N*
52:28 These are the people whom *N*
52:29 in the eighteenth year of *N* he
52:30 in the twenty-third year of *N*,
Ezek 26: 7 against Tyre from the north *N*
29:18 *N* king of Babylon caused his
29:19 give the land of Egypt to *N*
30:10 to cease By the hand of *N*
Dan 1: 1 *N* king of Babylon came to
1:18 brought them in before *N*.
2: 1 *N* had dreams; and his spirit
2:28 and He has made known to King *N*
2:46 Then King *N* fell on his face,
3: 1 *N* the king made an image of
3: 2 And King *N* sent word to gather
3: 2 of the image which King *N* had
3: 3 of the image that King *N* had
3: 3 stood before the image that *N*
3: 5 the gold image that King *N* has
3: 7 the gold image which King *N*
3: 9 They spoke and said to King *N*,
3:13 Then *N*, in rage and fury,
3:14 *N* spoke, saying to them, "Is
3:16 and said to the king, "O *N*,
3:19 Then *N* was full of fury, and
3:24 Then King *N* was astonished; and
3:26 Then *N* went near the mouth of
3:28 *N* spoke, saying, "Blessed be
4: 1 *N* the king, To all peoples,
4: 4 I, *N*, was at rest in my house,
4:18 "This dream I, King *N*,
4:28 All this came upon King *N*.
4:31 fell from heaven: "King *N*,
4:33 word was fulfilled concerning *N*;
4:34 at the end of the time I, *N*,
4:37 Now I, *N*, praise and extol
5: 2 vessels which his father *N* had
5:11 and King *N* your father—your
5:18 the Most High God gave *N* your

NEBUCHADNEZZAR'S (1/1)

Dan 2: 1 Now in the second year of *N*

NEBUSHASBAN (1/1)

Jer 39:13 the captain of the guard sent *N*,

NEBUZARADAN (16/16)

2 Ki 25: 8 *N* the captain of the guard, a
25:11 Then *N* the captain of the guard
25:20 So *N*, captain of the guard,
Jer 39: 9 Then *N* the captain of the guard
39:10 But *N* the captain of the guard
39:11 concerning Jeremiah to *N* the
39:13 So *N* the captain of the guard
40: 1 from the LORD after *N* the
40: 5 *N* said, "Go back to Gedaliah
41:10 whom *N* the captain of the guard
43: 6 and every person whom *N* the
52:12 king of Babylon), *N*,
52:15 Then *N* the captain of the guard
52:16 But *N* the captain of the guard
52:26 And *N* the captain of the guard
52:30 *N* the captain of the guard

NECESSARY (14/14)

Job 23:12 of His mouth More than my **n**
Lk 23:17 (for it was **n** for him to release
24:46 and thus it was **n** for the
Acts 13:46 It was **n** that the word of God
15: 5 It is **n** to circumcise them, and
15:28 no greater burden than these **n**
28:10 provided such things as were **n**.
1 Cor 12:22 which seem to be weaker are **n**.
2 Cor 9: 5 Therefore I thought it **n** to
Eph 4:29 but what is good for **n**
Phil 2:25 Yet I considered it **n** to send
Heb 8: 3 Therefore it is **n** that this
9:23 Therefore it was **n** that the
Jude 3 I found it **n** to write to you

NECESSITIES (2/2) NECESSITY

Acts 20:34 hands have provided for my **n**,
Phil 4:16 aid once and again for my **n**.

NECESSITY (5/5) NECESSITIES

1 Cor 7:37 in his heart, having no **n**,
9:16 for **n** is laid upon me; yes, woe
2 Cor 9: 7 heart, not grudgingly or of **n**;
Heb 7:12 of **n** there is also a change of
9:16 there must also of **n** be the

NECHO (9/8) PHARAOH

2 Ki 23:29 In his days Pharaoh *N* king of
23:29 And Pharaoh *N* killed him at
23:33 Now Pharaoh *N* put him in prison
23:34 Then Pharaoh *N* made Eliakim the
23:35 to give it to Pharaoh *N*.
2 Chr 35:20 *N* king of Egypt came up to
35:22 and did not heed the words of *N*
36: 4 And *N* took Jehoahaz his brother
Jer 46: 2 the army of Pharaoh *N*,

NECK (61/59) NECKS

Gen 27:16 and on the smooth part of his **n**.
27:40 break his yoke from your **n**.
33: 4 and fell on his **n** and kissed
41:42 put a gold chain around his **n**.
45:14 on his brother Benjamin's **n**
45:14 and Benjamin wept on his **n**.
46:29 and fell on his **n** and wept on
46:29 on his neck and wept on his **n**
49: 8 Your hand shall be on the **n**
Ex 13:13 it, then you shall break its **n**.
34:20 then you shall break his **n**.
Lev 5: 8 wring off its head from its **n**,
Deut 21: 4 they shall break the heifer's **n**
21: 6 hands over the heifer whose **n**
28:48 put a yoke of iron on your **n**
31:27 your rebellion and your stiff **n**.
Judg 5:30 of dyed embroidery for the **n**
1 Sam 4:18 and his **n** was broken and he
2 Chr 36:13 but he stiffened his **n** and
Job 16:12 He also has taken me by my **n**,
39:19 Have you clothed his **n** with
41:22 Strength dwells in his **n**,
Ps 69: 1 waters have come up to my **n**.
75: 5 Do not speak with a stiff **n**.
Prov 1: 9 And chains about your **n**.
3: 3 Bind them around your **n**,
3:22 your soul And grace to your **n**.
6:21 Tie them around your **n**.
29: 1 rebuked, and hardens his **n**,
Song 1:10 Your **n** with chains of gold.
4: 4 Your **n** is like the tower of
7: 4 Your **n** is like an ivory tower,
Isa 8: 8 He will reach up to the **n**;
10:27 And his yoke from your **n**,
30:28 Which reaches up to the **n**,
48: 4 And your **n** was an iron sinew,
52: 2 from the bonds of your **n**,
66: 3 as if he breaks a dog's **n**;
Jer 7:26 ear, but stiffened their **n**.
17:23 but made their **n** stiff, that
27: 2 yokes, and put them on your **n**,
27: 8 and which will not put its **n**
28:10 off the prophet Jeremiah's **n**
28:11 king of Babylon from the **n** of
28:12 had broken the yoke from the **n**
28:14 put a yoke of iron on the **n** of
30: 8 will break his yoke from your **n**,
Lam 1:14 And thrust upon my **n**.
Ezek 16:11 wrists, and a chain on your **n**.
Dan 5: 7 a chain of gold around his **n**;
5:16 a chain of gold around your **n**,
5:29 a chain of gold around his **n**,
Hos 10:11 But I harnessed her fair **n**,
11: 4 who take the yoke from their **n**.
Hab 3:13 bare from foundation to **n**.
Mt 18: 6 were hung around his **n**,
Mk 9:42 were hung around his **n**,
Lk 15:20 and ran and fell on his **n** and
17: 2 were hung around his **n**,
Acts 15:10 God by putting a yoke on the **n**
20:37 and fell on Paul's **n** and kissed

NECKLACE (2/2)

Ps 73: 6 pride serves as their **n**;
Song 4: 9 With one link of your **n**.

NECKLACES (2/2)

Ex 35:22 and nose rings, rings and **n**,
Num 31:50 signet rings and earrings and **n**,

NECKS (18/16) NECK

Josh 10:24 put your feet on the **n** of these
10:24 and put their feet on their **n**.
Judg 8:21 that were on their camels' **n**.
8:26 were around their camels' **n**.
2 Sam 22:41 You have also given me the **n** of
2 Ki 17:14 not hear, but stiffened their **n**,
17:14 like the **n** of their fathers,
Neh 9:16 proudly, Hardened their **n**,
9:17 But they hardened their **n**,
9:29 shoulders, Stiffened their **n**,
Ps 18:40 You have also given me the **n** of
Isa 3:16 And walk with outstretched **n**
Jer 19:15 they have stiffened their **n**
27:11 the nations that bring their **n**
27:12 Bring your **n** under the yoke of
Ezek 21:29 To bring you on the **n** of the
Mic 2: 3 which you cannot remove your **n**;
Rom 16: 4 who risked their own **n** for my

NECROMANCER (KJV) See SPIRITIST

NEDABIAH (1/1)

1 Chr 3:18 Jecamiah, Hoshama, and *N*.

NEED (72/70) NEEDED, NEEDFUL, NEEDS, NEEDY

Gen 33:15 What **n** is there? Let me find
Ex 12: 4 according to each man's **n** you
16:16 it according to each one's **n**,
16:18 according to each one's **n**.
16:21 every man according to his **n**.
Lev 13:36 the priest **n** not seek for
Deut 15: 8 lend him sufficient for his **n**,
28:48 and in **n** of everything; and He
1 Sam 21:15 Have I **n** of madmen, that you
2 Ki 22: 7 However there **n** be no accounting
2 Chr 2:16 from Lebanon, as much as you **n**;
20:17 You will not **n** to fight in this
Ezra 6: 9 And whatever they **n**—
Job 34:23 For He **n** not further consider a
Prov 6:11 And your **n** like an armed man.
24:34 And your **n** like an armed man.
25:16 Eat only as much as you **n**,
Isa 64: 5 And we **n** to be saved.
Ezek 36:30 so that you **n** never again bear
Dan 3:16 we have no **n** to answer you in
Mt 3:14 I **n** to be baptized by You, and
6: 8 knows the things you have **n** of
6:32 Father knows that you **n** all
9:12 Those who are well have no **n** of
14:16 They do not **n** to go away. You
15: 6 then he **n** not honor his father
21: 3 The Lord has **n** of them,' and
26:65 blasphemy! What further **n** do
Mk 2:17 Those who are well have no **n** of
2:25 David did when he was in **n** and
11: 3 The Lord has **n** of it,' and
14:63 What further **n** do we have of
Lk 5:31 Those who are well have no **n** of
9:11 and healed those who had **n** of
12:30 your Father knows that you **n**
15: 7 ninety-nine just persons who **n**
19:31 Because the Lord has **n** of it.'
19:34 The Lord has **n** of him."
22:71 further testimony do we **n**?
Jn 2:25 and had no **n** that anyone should
13:29 Buy those things we **n** for the
16:30 and have no **n** that anyone
Acts 2:45 them among all, as anyone had **n**.
4:35 to each as anyone had **n**.
Rom 16: 2 in whatever business she has **n**
1 Cor 5:10 since then you would **n** to go
12:21 I have no **n** of you"; nor again
12:21 I have no **n** of you."
12:24 presentable parts have no **n**.
2 Cor 3: 1 commend ourselves? Or do we **n**,
11: 9 was present with you, and in **n**,

Eph 4:28 something to give him who has ***n***.
Phil 2:25 the one who ministered to my ***n***;
4:11 Not that I speak in regard to ***n***,
4:12 both to abound and to suffer ***n***.
4:19 my God shall supply all your ***n***
1 Th 1: 8 so that we do not ***n*** to say
4: 9 brotherly love you have no ***n***
5: 1 you have no ***n*** that I should
2 Tim 2:15 a worker who does not ***n*** to be
Heb 4:16 find grace to help in time of ***n***.
5:12 you ***n*** someone to teach you
5:12 and you have come to ***n*** milk and
7:11 what further ***n*** was there that
7:27 who does not ***n*** daily, as those
10:36 For you have ***n*** of endurance, so
1 Pe 1: 6 if ***n*** be, you have been grieved
1 Jn 2:27 and you do not ***n*** that anyone
3:17 and sees his brother in ***n***,
Rev 3:17 and have ***n*** of nothing'—and do
21:23 The city had no ***n*** of the sun or
22: 5 They ***n*** no lamp nor light of the

NEEDED (6/6) NEED

Ezra 7:20 And whatever more may be ***n*** for
Ezek 17: 9 or many people Will be ***n*** to
Lk 10:42 "But one thing is ***n***,
Jn 4: 4 But He ***n*** to go through Samaria.
Acts 17:25 as though He ***n*** anything, since
Jas 2:16 them the things which are ***n***

NEEDFUL (1/1) NEED

Phil 1:24 remain in the flesh is more ***n***

NEEDLE (3/3)

Mt 19:24 to go through the eye of a ***n***
Mk 10:25 to go through the eye of a ***n***
Lk 18:25 to go through the eye of a ***n***

NEEDS (22/18) NEED

Num 3: 7 they shall attend to his ***n***
3: 7 attend to his needs and the ***n***
3: 8 and to the ***n*** of the children of
3:38 to meet the ***n*** of the children
8:26 of meeting, to attend to ***n***,
18: 3 They shall attend to your ***n*** and
18: 3 to your needs and all the ***n*** of
18: 4 with you and attend to the ***n***
Deut 15: 8 for his need, whatever he ***n***.
Judg 3:24 is probably attending to his ***n***
19:20 let all your ***n*** be my
1 Sam 24: 3 Saul went in to attend to his ***n***.
1 Chr 23:32 they should attend to the ***n*** of
23:32 the ***n*** of the holy place, and
23:32 and the ***n*** of the sons of Aaron
Lk 11: 8 and give him as many as he ***n***.
Jn 13:10 He who is bathed ***n*** only to wash
Rom 12:13 distributing to the ***n*** of the
2 Cor 6: 4 patience, in tribulations, in ***n***,
9:12 not only supplies the ***n*** of the
12:10 in reproaches, in ***n***,
Titus 3:14 good works, to meet urgent ***n***,

NEEDY (40/39) NEED

Deut 15:11 to your poor and your ***n***,
24:14 servant who is poor and ***n***,
Job 5:15 But He saves the ***n*** from the
24: 4 They push the ***n*** off the road;
24:14 light; He kills the poor and ***n***;
Ps 9:18 For the ***n*** shall not always be
12: 5 poor, for the sighing of the ***n***,
35:10 the poor and the ***n*** from him who
37:14 To cast down the poor and ***n***,
40:17 But I am poor and ***n***;
70: 5 But I am poor and ***n***;
72: 4 will save the children of the ***n***,
72:12 For He will deliver the ***n*** when
72:13 He will spare the poor and ***n***,
72:13 will save the souls of the ***n***.
74:21 ashamed! Let the poor and ***n***
82: 3 justice to the afflicted and ***n***.
82: 4 Deliver the poor and ***n***;
86: 1 hear me; For I am poor and ***n***.
109:16 But persecuted the poor and ***n***
109:22 For I am poor and ***n***,
113: 7 And lifts the ***n*** out of the
Prov 14:31 honors Him has mercy on the ***n***.
30:14 And the ***n*** from among men.
31: 9 the cause of the poor and ***n***.
31:20 reaches out her hands to the ***n***.
Isa 10: 2 To rob the ***n*** of justice,
14:30 And the ***n*** will lie down in
25: 4 A strength to the ***n*** in his
26: 6 poor And the steps of the ***n***.
32: 7 Even when the ***n*** speaks
41:17 The poor and ***n*** seek water, but
Jer 5:28 And the right of the ***n*** they do
22:16 the cause of the poor and ***n***;
Ezek 16:49 the hand of the poor and ***n***.
18:12 he has oppressed the poor and ***n***,
22:29 and mistreated the poor and ***n***;
Am 4: 1 the poor, Who crush the ***n***,
8: 4 this, you who swallow up the ***n***,
8: 6 And the ***n*** for a pair of

NEGLECT (5/5) NEGLECTED

Josh 18: 3 How long will you ***n*** to go and
Neh 10:39 and we will not ***n*** the house of
Col 2:23 and ***n*** of the body, but are of
1 Tim 4:14 Do not ***n*** the gift that is in
Heb 2: 3 how shall we escape if we ***n*** so

NEGLECTED (2/2) NEGLECT

Mt 23:23 and have ***n*** the weightier
Acts 6: 1 because their widows were ***n*** in

NEGLIGENT (2/2)

2 Chr 29:11 do not be ***n*** now, for the LORD
2 Pe 1:12 this reason I will not be ***n*** to

NEHELAMITE (3/3)

Jer 29:24 also speak to Shemaiah the ***N***,
29:31 LORD concerning Shemaiah the ***N***:
29:32 I will punish Shemaiah the ***N***

NEHEMIAH (8/8)

Ezra 2: 2 with Zerubbabel were Jeshua, ***N***,
Neh 1: 1 The words of ***N*** the son of
3:16 After him ***N*** the son of Azbuk,
7: 7 with Zerubbabel were Jeshua, ***N***,
8: 9 And ***N***, who was the governor,
10: 1 ***N*** the governor, the son of
12:26 and in the days of ***N*** the
12:47 and in the days of ***N*** all

NEHUM (1/1)

Neh 7: 7 Bilshan, Mispereth, Bigvai, ***N***,

NEHUSHTA (1/1)

2 Ki 24: 8 His mother's name was ***N*** the

NEHUSHTAN (1/1)

2 Ki 18: 4 incense to it, and called it ***N***.

NEIEL (1/1)

Josh 19:27 beyond Beth Emek and ***N***,

NEIGHBOR (100/95) NEIGHBOR'S, NEIGHBORS

Ex 3:22 every woman shall ask of her ***n***,
11: 2 let every man ask from his ***n***
11: 2 and every woman from her ***n***,
12: 4 let him and his ***n*** next to his
20:16 false witness against your ***n***.
21:14 premeditation against his ***n***,
22: 7 If a man delivers to his ***n***
22: 9 shall pay double to his ***n***.
22:10 If a man delivers to his ***n*** a
22:14 borrows anything from his ***n***,
32:27 companion, and every man his ***n***.
Lev 6: 2 the LORD by lying to his ***n***
6: 2 if he has extorted from his ***n***,
19:13 'You shall not cheat your ***n***,
19:15 you shall judge your ***n***.
19:16 against the life of your ***n***:
19:17 You shall surely rebuke your ***n***,
19:18 but you shall love your ***n*** as
24:19 causes disfigurement of his ***n***,
25:14 if you sell anything to your ***n***
25:15 you shall buy from your ***n***,
Deut 4:42 who kills his ***n*** unintentionally,
5:20 false witness against your ***n***.
15: 2 who has lent anything to his ***n***
15: 2 shall not require it of his ***n***
19: 4 Whoever kills his ***n***
19: 5 goes to the woods with his ***n***
19: 5 the handle and strikes his ***n***
19:11 "But if anyone hates his ***n***,
22:26 when a man rises against his ***n***
27:24 is the one who attacks his ***n***
Josh 20: 5 because he struck his ***n***
Ruth 4:17 Also the ***n*** women gave him a
1 Sam 14:20 man's sword was against his ***n***,
15:28 and has given it to a ***n*** of
28:17 hand and given it to your ***n***,
2 Sam 12:11 eyes and give them to your ***n***,
1 Ki 8:31 anyone sins against his ***n***,
20:35 of the prophets said to his ***n***
2 Chr 6:22 "If anyone sins against his ***n***,
Job 16:21 As a man pleads for his ***n***!
Ps 12: 2 speak idly everyone with his ***n***;
15: 3 tongue, Nor does evil to his ***n***,
101: 5 secretly slanders his ***n***,
Prov 3:28 Do not say to your ***n***,
3:29 not devise evil against your ***n***,
11: 9 with his mouth destroys his ***n***,
11:12 devoid of wisdom despises his ***n***,
14:20 man is hated even by his own ***n***,
14:21 He who despises his ***n*** sins;
16:29 A violent man entices his ***n***,
18:17 Until his ***n*** comes and examines
21:10 His ***n*** finds no favor in his
24:28 not be a witness against your ***n***
25: 8 When your ***n*** has put you to
25: 9 Debate your case with your ***n***,
25:18 false witness against his ***n***
26:19 the man who deceives his ***n***,
27:10 Better is a ***n*** nearby than a
29: 5 A man who flatters his ***n***
Eccl 4: 4 work a man is envied by his ***n***.
Isa 3: 5 another and every one by his ***n***;
19: 2 And everyone against his ***n***,
41: 6 Everyone helped his ***n***,
Jer 6:21 The ***n*** and his friend shall
7: 5 between a man and his ***n***,
9: 4 "Everyone take heed to his ***n***,
9: 4 And every ***n*** will walk with
9: 5 Everyone will deceive his ***n***,
9: 8 speaks peaceably to his ***n*** with
9:20 And everyone her ***n*** a
22: 8 and everyone will say to his ***n***,
23:27 which everyone tells his ***n***,
23:30 My words every one from his ***n***.
23:35 one of you shall say to his ***n***,
31:34 shall every man teach his ***n***,
34:15 proclaiming liberty to his ***n***;
34:17 brother and every one to his ***n***.
Hab 2:15 to him who gives drink to his ***n***,
Zech 3:10 Everyone will invite his ***n***
8:10 men, everyone, against his ***n***.
8:16 each man the truth to his ***n***;
8:17 in your heart against your ***n***;
14:13 will seize the hand of his ***n***,
Mt 5:43 You shall love your ***n*** and
19:19 You shall love your ***n*** as
22:39 You shall love your ***n*** as
Mk 12:31 You shall love your ***n*** as
12:33 and to love one's ***n*** as oneself,
Lk 10:27 your ***n*** as yourself.'"
10:29 to Jesus, "And who is my ***n***?
10:36 these three do you think was ***n***
Acts 7:27 But he who did his ***n*** wrong
Rom 13: 9 You shall love your ***n*** as
13:10 Love does no harm to a ***n***;
15: 2 Let each of us please his ***n*** for
Gal 5:14 You shall love your ***n*** as
Eph 4:25 speak truth with his ***n***,
Heb 8:11 of them shall teach his ***n***,
Jas 2: 8 You shall love your ***n*** as

NEIGHBOR'S (29/24) NEIGHBOR

Ex 20:17 shall not covet your ***n*** house;
20:17 shall not covet your ***n*** wife,
20:17 nor anything that is your ***n***.
22: 8 put his hand into his ***n*** goods.
22:11 put his hand into his ***n*** goods;
22:26 If you ever take your ***n*** garment
Lev 18:20 not lie carnally with your ***n***
20:10 adultery with his ***n*** wife,
25:14 or buy from your ***n*** hand,
Deut 5:21 shall not covet your ***n*** wife;
5:21 shall not desire your ***n*** house,
5:21 or anything that is your ***n***.
19:14 not remove your ***n*** landmark
22:24 because he humbled his ***n*** wife
23:24 you come into your ***n*** vineyard,
23:25 into your ***n*** standing grain,
23:25 not use a sickle on your ***n***
27:17 one who moves his ***n*** landmark.
Job 31: 9 I have lurked at my ***n*** door,
Prov 6:29 he who goes in to his ***n*** wife;
25:17 set foot in your ***n*** house,
Jer 5: 8 one neighed after his ***n*** wife.
22:13 Who uses his ***n*** service
Ezek 18: 6 Nor defiled his ***n*** wife,
18:11 Or defiled his ***n*** wife;
18:15 Nor defiled his ***n*** wife;
22:11 abomination with his ***n*** wife;
Zech 11: 6 give everyone into his ***n*** hand
14:13 his hand against his ***n*** hand;

NEIGHBORING (3/3)

Deut 1: 7 to all the ***n*** places in the
Ezek 23: 5 the ***n*** Assyrians,
23:12 She lusted for the ***n*** Assyrians,

NEIGHBORS (20/20) NEIGHBOR

Josh 9:16 heard that they were their ***n***
2 Ki 4: 3 everywhere, from all your ***n***—
Ps 28: 3 Who speak peace to their ***n***,
31:11 But especially among my ***n***,
44:13 make us a reproach to our ***n***,
79: 4 have become a reproach to our ***n***,
79:12 And return to our ***n*** sevenfold
80: 6 have made us a strife to our ***n***,
89:41 He is a reproach to his ***n***.
Jer 12:14 Against all My evil ***n*** who touch
49:10 His brethren and his ***n***,
49:18 Sodom and Gomorrah And their ***n***,
50:40 Sodom and Gomorrah And their ***n***,
Ezek 16:26 Egyptians, your very fleshly ***n***,
22:12 have made profit from your ***n***
Lk 1:58 When her ***n*** and relatives heard
14:12 your relatives, nor rich ***n***,
15: 6 together his friends and ***n***,
15: 9 she calls her friends and ***n***
Jn 9: 8 Therefore the ***n*** and those who

NEIGHBORS' (1/1)

Jer 29:23 adultery with their ***n*** wives,

NEIGHED (1/1)

Jer 5: 8 Every one ***n*** after his

NEIGHING (1/1)

Jer 8:16 trembled at the sound of the ***n***

N

NEIGHINGS (1/1)
Jer 13:27 adulteries And your lustful **n**,

NEITHER (195/190)
Gen 31:24 that you speak to Jacob **n** good
31:29 that you speak to Jacob **n** good
45: 6 in which there will be **n**
Ex 4:10 **n** before nor since You have
5:23 **n** have You delivered Your
7:23 **N** was his heart moved by this.
8:32 **n** would he let the people go.
9:35 **n** would he let the children of
10: 6 which **n** your fathers nor your
22:21 You shall **n** mistreat a stranger
34: 3 let **n** flocks nor herds feed
34:24 **n** will any man covet your land
34:28 he **n** ate bread nor drank water.
36: 6 Let **n** man nor woman do any more
Lev 3:17 you shall eat **n** fat nor blood.'
11:44 **N** shall you defile yourselves
23:14 You shall eat **n** bread nor
25: 4 You shall **n** sow your field nor
25:11 in it you shall **n** sow nor reap
26: 1 **n** a carved image nor a sacred
Num 6: 3 he shall drink **n** vinegar made
6: 3 **n** shall he drink any grape
14:44 **n** the ark of the covenant of
23:25 **N** curse them at all, nor bless
Deut 2:27 and I will turn **n** to the right
4:28 which **n** see nor hear nor eat
9: 9 I **n** ate bread nor drank water.
9:18 I **n** ate bread nor drank water,
13: 6 **n** you nor your fathers,
17:17 **N** shall he multiply wives for
21: 4 which is **n** plowed nor sown, and
28:36 over you to a nation which **n**
28:39 but you shall **n** drink of the
28:64 which **n** you nor your fathers
Josh 2:11 **n** did there remain any more
7:12 **N** will I be with you anymore,
Judg 6: 4 **n** sheep nor ox nor donkey.
11:34 Besides her he had **n** son nor
1 Sam 1:15 I have drunk **n** wine nor
5: 5 Therefore **n** the priests of Dagon
13:22 that there was **n** sword nor
16: 8 **N** has the LORD chosen this
16: 9 **N** has the LORD chosen this
21: 8 For I have brought **n** my sword
24:11 know and see that there is **n**
27: 9 he left **n** man nor woman alive,
27:11 David would save **n** man nor woman
28:15 **n** by prophets nor by dreams.
30:15 to me by God that you will **n**
2 Sam 13:22 spoke to his brother Amnon **n**
14: 7 and leave to my husband **n** name
19: 6 today that you regard **n**
22:38 **N** did I turn back again till
1 Ki 3:26 Let him be **n** mine nor yours,
5: 4 there is **n** adversary nor evil
13:16 **n** can I eat bread nor drink
16:11 **n** of his relatives nor of his
2 Ki 4:23 It is **n** the New Moon nor the
4:31 but there was **n** voice nor
12: 8 agreed that they would **n**
18:12 and they would **n** hear nor do
Neh 4:11 They will **n** know nor see
4:23 So **n** I, my brethren, my
5:14 **n** I nor my brothers ate the
9:34 **N** our kings nor our princes,
Esth 2: 7 for she had **n** father nor
4:16 **n** eat nor drink for three days,
Job 18:19 He has **n** son nor posterity
21: 9 **N** is the rod of God upon
28:17 **N** gold nor crystal can equal
Ps 18:37 **N** did I turn back again till
33:17 **N** shall it deliver any by its
75: 6 For exaltation comes **n** from
121: 4 He who keeps Israel Shall **n**
129: 8 **N** let those who pass by them
131: 1 **N** do I concern myself with
Prov 30: 3 I **n** learned wisdom Nor have
30: 8 Give me **n** poverty nor
Eccl 4: 8 He has **n** son nor brother.
9: 1 People know **n** love nor hatred
Isa 2: 4 **N** shall they learn war
3: 7 For in my house is **n** food nor
19:15 **N** will there be any work for
23: 4 **N** do I rear young men,
40:28 **N** faints nor is weary.
44: 9 They **n** see nor know, that they
49:10 They shall **n** hunger nor thirst,
49:10 **N** heat nor sun shall strike
54: 4 **N** be disgraced, for you will
60:18 **N** wasting nor destruction
Jer 2: 6 **N** did they say, 'Where is the
5:12 **N** will evil come upon us,
9:16 whom **n** they nor their fathers
15:10 to the whole earth! I have **n**
16: 6 **n** shall men lament for them,
16:13 **n** you nor your fathers;
19: 4 in it to other gods whom **n**
29:19 **n** would you heed, says the
37: 2 But **n** he nor his servants nor
49:31 Which has **n** gates nor bars,
51:62 **n** man nor beast, but it shall
Ezek 9:10 My eye will **n** spare, nor will I
14:16 they would deliver **n** sons nor
14:18 they would deliver **n** sons nor
14:20 they would deliver **n** son nor
16:48 **n** your sister Sodom nor her
16:49 **n** did she strengthen the hand
24:16 yet you shall **n** mourn nor weep,
24:23 you shall **n** mourn nor weep, but
29:11 **N** foot of man shall pass through
29:18 yet **n** he nor his army received
38:11 and having **n** bars nor gates'—
44:20 They shall **n** shave their heads
Dan 9: 6 **N** have we heeded Your servants
11: 6 and **n** he nor his authority
11:37 He shall regard **n** the God of his
Jon 3: 7 Let **n** man nor beast, herd nor
Mic 4: 3 **N** shall they learn war any
Zeph 1:18 **N** their silver nor their gold
Zech 14: 7 **N** day nor night. But at
Mal 4: 1 That will leave them **n** root nor
Mt 5:34 **n** by heaven, for it is God's
6:15 **n** will your Father forgive your
6:20 where **n** moth nor rust destroys
6:26 for they **n** sow nor reap nor
6:28 they **n** toil nor spin;
10: 9 Provide **n** gold nor silver nor
11:18 For John came **n** eating nor
21:27 **N** will I tell you by what
22:30 in the resurrection they **n**
23:13 for you **n** go in yourselves,
25:13 for you know **n** the day nor the
Mk 5: 4 **n** could anyone tame him.
8:26 **N** go into the town, nor tell
11:26 **n** will your Father in heaven
11:33 **N** will I tell you by what
12:25 they **n** marry nor are given in
14:68 I **n** know nor understand what you
Lk 1:15 and shall drink **n** wine nor
7:33 For John the Baptist came **n**
9: 3 **n** staffs nor bag nor bread nor
10: 4 Carry **n** money bag, knapsack, nor
12:24 for they **n** sow nor reap, which
12:24 which have **n** storehouse nor
12:27 they **n** toil nor spin; and yet I
14:35 It is **n** fit for the land nor for
16:31 **n** will they be persuaded though
20: 8 **N** will I tell you by what
20:35 **n** marry nor are given in
23:15 **n** did Herod, for I sent you
Jn 4:21 hour is coming when you will **n**
5:37 You have **n** heard His voice at
8:11 **N** do I condemn you; go and sin
8:19 'You know **n** Me nor My Father.
9: 3 **N** this man nor his parents
10:28 **n** shall anyone snatch them out
14:17 because it **n** sees Him nor knows
14:27 **n** let it be afraid.
15: 4 **n** can you, unless you abide in
Acts 4:32 **n** did anyone say that any of
8:21 You have **n** part nor portion in
9: 9 and **n** ate nor drank.
15:10 neck of the disciples which **n**
19:37 these men here who are **n**
23:12 saying that they would **n** eat
23:21 by an oath that they will **n**
24:12 And they **n** found me in the
24:18 **n** with a mob nor with tumult.
25: 8 **N** against the law of the Jews,
27:20 Now when **n** sun nor stars
28:21 We **n** received letters from Judea
Rom 8:38 For I am persuaded that **n** death
14:21 It is good **n** to eat meat nor
1 Cor 3: 7 So then **n** he who plants is
6: 9 **N** fornicators, nor idolaters,
8: 8 for **n** if we eat are we the
11:11 **n** is man independent of woman,
Gal 1:12 For I **n** received it from man,
3:28 There is **n** Jew nor Greek, there
3:28 there is **n** slave nor free,
3:28 there is **n** male nor female;
5: 6 For in Christ Jesus **n**
6:15 For in Christ Jesus **n**
Eph 5: 4 **n** filthiness, nor foolish
Col 3:11 where there is **n** Greek nor Jew,
1 Th 2: 5 For **n** at any time did we use
2 Th 3:10 will not work, **n** shall he eat.
1 Tim 1: 7 understanding **n** what they say
Heb 7: 3 having **n** beginning of days nor
2 Pe 1: 8 you will be **n** barren nor
1 Jn 3: 6 Whoever sins has **n** seen Him nor
Rev 3:15 that you are **n** cold nor hot.
3:16 and **n** cold nor hot, I will
7:16 They shall **n** hunger anymore nor
9:20 which can **n** see nor hear nor

NEKEB (1/1)
Josh 19:33 tree in Zaanannim, Adami **N**,

NEKODA (4/4)
Ezra 2:48 sons of Rezin, the sons of **N**,
2:60 of Tobiah, and the sons of **N**,
Neh 7:50 sons of Rezin, the sons of **N**,
7:62 sons of Tobiah, the sons of **N**,

NEMUEL (3/3)
Num 26: 9 The sons of Eliab were **N**,
26:12 to their families were: of **N**,
1 Chr 4:24 The sons of Simeon were **N**,

NEMUELITES (1/1)
Num 26:12 of Nemuel, the family of the **N**;

NEPHEG (4/4)
Ex 6:21 sons of Izhar were Korah, **N**,
2 Sam 5:15 Ibhar, Elishua, **N**,
1 Chr 3: 7 Nogah, **N**, Japhia,
14: 6 Nogah, **N**, Japhia,

NEPHISH (KJV) See NAPHISH

NEPHISHESIM (1/1)
Neh 7:52 sons of Meunim, the sons of **N**,

NEPHTHALIM, NEPTHALIM (KJV) See NAPHTALI

NEPHTOAH (2/2)
Josh 15: 9 the fountain of the water of **N**,
18:15 the spring of the waters of **N**.

NEPHUSIM (1/1)
Ezra 2:50 sons of Meunim, the sons of **N**,

NER (16/16)
1 Sam 14:50 army was Abner the son of **N**,
14:51 and **N** the father of Abner was
26: 5 lay, and Abner the son of **N**,
26:14 and to Abner the son of **N**,
2 Sam 2: 8 But Abner the son of **N**,
2:12 Now Abner the son of **N**,
3:23 Abner the son of **N** came to the
3:25 that Abner the son of **N** came
3:28 the blood of Abner the son of **N**.
3:37 to kill Abner the son of **N**.
1 Ki 2: 5 to Abner the son of **N** and Amasa
2:32 the sword—Abner the son of **N**,
1 Chr 8:33 **N** begot Kish, Kish begot Saul,
9:36 Abdon, then Zur, Kish, Baal, **N**,
9:39 **N** begot Kish, Kish begot Saul,
26:28 son of Kish, Abner the son of **N**,

NEREUS (1/1)
Rom 16:15 **N** and his sister, and Olympas,

NERGAL (1/1)
2 Ki 17:30 Benoth, the men of Cuth made **N**,

NERGAL-SAREZER (1/1)
Jer 39: 3 Sarsechim, Rabsaris, **N**,

NERGAL-SHAREZER (2/2)
Jer 39: 3 and sat in the Middle Gate: **N**,
39:13 sent Nebushasban, Rabsaris, **N**,

NERI (1/1)
Lk 3:27 of Shealtiel, the son of **N**,

NERIAH (10/10)
Jer 32:12 deed to Baruch the son of **N**,
32:16 deed to Baruch the son of **N**,
36: 4 called Baruch the son of **N**;
36: 8 And Baruch the son of **N** did
36:14 So Baruch the son of **N** took
36:32 Baruch the scribe, the son of **N**,
43: 3 But Baruch the son of **N** has set
43: 6 prophet and Baruch the son of **N**.
45: 1 spoke to Baruch the son of **N**,
51:59 commanded Seraiah the son of **N**,

NEST (17/17) NESTED, NESTS
Num 24:21 And your **n** is set in the rock;
Deut 22: 6 If a bird's **n** happens to be
32:11 As an eagle stirs up its **n**,
Job 29:18 I said, 'I shall die in my **n**,
39:27 And make its **n** on high?
Ps 84: 3 And the swallow a **n** for
Prov 27: 8 a bird that wanders from its **n**
Isa 10:14 My hand has found like a **n** the
16: 2 bird thrown out of the **n**;
34:15 arrow snake shall make her **n**
Jer 22:23 Making your **n** in the cedars,
48:28 the dove which makes her **n**
49:16 Though you make your **n** as
Ob 4 And though you set your **n**
Hab 2: 9 That he may set his **n** on high,
Mt 13:32 birds of the air come and **n** in
Mk 4:32 that the birds of the air may **n**

NESTED (1/1) NEST
Lk 13:19 and the birds of the air **n** in

NESTLED (1/1)
Job 30: 7 Under the nettles they **n**.

NESTS (4/4) NEST
Ps 104:17 Where the birds make their **n**;
Ezek 31: 6 of the heavens made their **n** in
Mt 8:20 and birds of the air have **n**,
Lk 9:58 and birds of the air have **n**,

NET (36/34) NETS

Job 18: 8 For he is cast into a *n* by his
18: 9 The *n* takes him by the heel,
19: 6 has surrounded me with His *n*.
Ps 9:15 In the *n* which they hid, their
10: 9 when he draws him into his *n*.
25:15 pluck my feet out of the *n*.
31: 4 Pull me out of the *n* which they
35: 7 cause they have hidden their *n*
35: 8 And let his *n* that he has
57: 6 They have prepared a *n* for my
66:11 You brought us into the *n*;
140: 5 They have spread a *n* by the
Prov 1:17 in vain the *n* is spread In the
29: 5 his neighbor Spreads a *n* for
Eccl 9:12 Like fish taken in a cruel *n*,
Isa 51:20 Like an antelope in a *n*;
Lam 1:13 He has spread a *n* for my feet
Ezek 12:13 I will also spread My *n* over
17:20 I will spread My *n* over him, and
19: 8 And spread their *n* over him;
32: 3 I will therefore spread My *n*
32: 3 they will draw you up in My *n*.
Hos 5: 1 been a snare to Mizpah And a *n*
7:12 I will spread My *n* on them;
Mic 7: 2 man hunts his brother with a *n*.
Hab 1:15 They catch them in their *n*,
1:16 they sacrifice to their *n*,
1:17 they therefore empty their *n*,
Mt 4:18 casting a *n* into the sea;
Mk 1:16 Andrew his brother casting a *n*
Lk 5: 5 Your word I will let down the *n*.
5: 6 and their *n* was breaking.
Jn 21: 6 Cast the *n* on the right side of
21: 8 dragging the *n* with fish.
21:11 went up and dragged the *n* to
21:11 the *n* was not broken.

NETAIM (1/1)

1 Chr 4:23 and those who dwell at *N* and

NETHANEL (14/14)

Num 1: 8 *N* the son of Zuar;
2: 5 and *N* the son of Zuar shall
7:18 On the second day *N* the son of
7:23 This was the offering of *N* the
10:15 the children of Issachar was *N*
1 Chr 2:14 *N* the fourth, Raddai the fifth,
15:24 Shebaniah, Joshaphat, *N*,
24: 6 scribe, Shemaiah the son of *N*,
26: 4 the fourth, *N* the fifth,
2 Chr 17: 7 Ben-Hail, Obadiah, Zechariah, *N*,
35: 9 his brothers Shemaiah and *N*,
Ezra 10:22 Elioenai, Maaseiah, Ishmael, *N*,
Neh 12:21 Hashabiah; and of Jedaiah, *N*.
12:36 Milalai, Gilalai, Maai, *N*,

NETHANIAH (20/20)

2 Ki 25:23 at Mizpah—Ishmael the son of *N*,
25:25 month that Ishmael the son of *N*,
1 Chr 25: 2 of Asaph: Zaccur, Joseph, *N*,
25:12 the fifth for *N*, his sons
2 Chr 17: 8 he sent Levites: Shemaiah, *N*,
Jer 36:14 sent Jehudi the son of *N*,
40: 8 at Mizpah—Ishmael the son of *N*,
40:14 has sent Ishmael the son of *N*
40:15 will kill Ishmael the son of *N*,
41: 1 that Ishmael the son of *N*,
41: 2 Then Ishmael the son of *N*,
41: 6 Now Ishmael the son of *N* went
41: 7 that Ishmael the son of *N*
41: 9 Ishmael the son of *N* filled it
41:10 And Ishmael the son of *N*
41:11 evil that Ishmael the son of *N*
41:12 fight with Ishmael the son of *N*;
41:15 But Ishmael the son of *N* escaped
41:16 from Ishmael the son of *N*
41:18 because Ishmael the son of *N*

NETHER, NETHERMOST (KJV)

See FOOT, LOWER, LOWEST

NETHINIM (18/16)

1 Chr 9: 2 priests, Levites, and the *N*.
Ezra 2:43 The *N*: the sons of Ziha,
2:58 All the *N* and the children of
2:70 the gatekeepers, and the *N*,
7: 7 and the *N* came up to Jerusalem
7:24 singers, gatekeepers, *N*,
8:17 to Iddo and his brethren the *N*
8:20 also of the *N*, whom David
8:20 two hundred and twenty *N*.
Neh 3:26 Moreover the *N* who dwelt in
3:31 as far as the house of the *N*
7:46 The *N*: the sons of Ziha,
7:60 All the *N*, and the sons of
7:73 some of the people, the *N*,
10:28 gatekeepers, the singers, the *N*,
11: 3 priests, Levites, *N*,
11:21 But the *N* dwelt in Ophel. And
11:21 and Gishpa were over the *N*.

NETHINIMS (KJV) See NETHINIM

NETOPHAH (2/2)

Ezra 2:22 the men of *N*, fifty-six;
Neh 7:26 the men of Bethlehem and *N*,

NETOPHATHITE (8/7)

2 Sam 23:28 the Ahohite, Maharai the *N*,
23:29 Heleb the son of Baanah (the *N*),
2 Ki 25:23 the son of Tanhumeth the *N*,
1 Chr 11:30 Maharai the *N*, Heled the son
11:30 Heled the son of Baanah the *N*,
27:13 tenth month was Maharai the *N*,
27:15 twelfth month was Heldai the *N*,
Jer 40: 8 the sons of Ephai the *N*,

NETOPHATHITES (3/3)

1 Chr 2:54 of Salma were Bethlehem, the *N*,
9:16 lived in the villages of the *N*.
Neh 12:28 from the villages of the *N*,

NETS (13/13) NET

Ps 141:10 wicked fall into their own *n*,
Eccl 7:26 whose heart is snares and *n*,
Isa 19: 8 will languish who spread *n* on
Ezek 19: 9 Babylon; They brought him in *n*,
26: 5 be a place for spreading *n*
26:14 be a place for spreading *n*,
47:10 places for spreading their *n*.
Mt 4:20 They immediately left their *n*
4:21 their father, mending their *n*.
Mk 1:18 They immediately left their *n*
1:19 in the boat mending their *n*.
Lk 5: 2 them and were washing their *n*.
5: 4 the deep and let down your *n*

NETTLES (4/4)

Job 30: 7 Under the *n* they nestled.
Prov 24:31 Its surface was covered with *n*;
Isa 34:13 *N* and brambles in its
Hos 9: 6 *N* shall possess their

NETWORK (13/11)

Ex 27: 4 a *n* of bronze; and on the
27: 4 and on the *n* you shall make
27: 5 that the *n* may be midway up the
38: 4 And he made a grate of bronze *n*
1 Ki 7:17 He made a lattice *n*,
7:18 of pomegranates above the *n*
7:20 which was next to the *n*;
7:42 rows of pomegranates for each *n*,
2 Ki 25:17 and the *n* and pomegranates all
25:17 pillar was the same, with a *n*.
2 Chr 4:13 rows of pomegranates for each *n*,
Jer 52:22 with a *n* and pomegranates all
52:23 all around on the *n*,

NETWORKS (4/4)

1 Ki 7:41 the two *n* covering the two
7:42 pomegranates for the two *n*
2 Chr 4:12 the two *n* covering the two
4:13 pomegranates for the two *n*

NEVER (123/114)

Gen 8:21 I will *n* again curse the ground
9:11 *N* again shall all flesh be cut
9:11 *n* again shall there be a flood
9:15 the waters shall *n* again become
38:26 And he *n* knew her again.
41:19 such ugliness as I have *n* seen
Ex 10:29 I will *n* see your face again."
Lev 6:13 it shall *n* go out.
Num 11:25 although they *n* did so again.
19: 2 and on which a yoke has *n*
Deut 15:11 For the poor will *n* cease from
28:68 You shall *n* see it again.' And
Judg 2: 1 I will *n* break My covenant with
16:11 with new ropes that have *n*
1 Sam 4: 7 to us! For such a thing has *n*
6: 7 take two milk cows which have *n*
2 Sam 3:29 and let there *n* fail to be in
12:10 the sword shall *n* depart from
1 Ki 10:10 There *n* again came such
10:12 There *n* again came such almug
22:48 but they *n* sailed, for the
2 Ki 23:22 Such a Passover surely had *n*
2 Chr 9: 9 there *n* were any spices such as
18: 7 because he *n* prophesies good
Ezra 9:12 and *n* seek their peace or
Neh 2: 1 Now I had *n* been sad in his
Esth 7: 4 although the enemy could *n*
Job 3:16 Like infants who *n* saw light?
6:28 For I would *n* lie to your
7: 7 is a breath! My eye will *n*
7:10 He shall *n* return to his house,
21:25 *N* having eaten with pleasure.
34:12 Surely God will *n* do wickedly,
41: 8 the battle—*N* do it again!
Ps 10: 6 I shall *n* be in adversity."
10:11 He will *n* see."
15: 5 who does these things shall *n*
30: 6 I shall *n* be moved."
31: 1 Let me *n* be ashamed; Deliver
49:19 They shall *n* see light.
55:22 He shall *n* permit the
71: 1 Let me *n* be put to shame.
112: 6 Surely he will *n* be shaken;
119:93 I will *n* forget Your precepts,
Prov 10:30 The righteous will *n* be
27:20 Hell and Destruction are *n*
27:20 So the eyes of man are *n*
30:15 are three things that are *n*
30:15 Four *n* say, "Enough!":
30:16 And the fire *n* says,
Eccl 4: 3 than both is he who has *n*
4: 8 But he *n* asks, "For whom
Isa 10:20 Will *n* again depend on him who
13:20 It will *n* be inhabited,
14:20 brood of evildoers shall *n* be
25: 2 It will *n* be rebuilt.
56:11 are greedy dogs Which *n*
62: 6 They shall *n* hold their peace
63:19 over whom You *n* ruled, Those
63:19 Those who were *n* called by
Jer 20:11 everlasting confusion will *n*
33:17 David shall *n* lack a man to sit
Ezek 4:14 Lord GOD! Indeed I have *n*
4:14 I have *n* eaten what died of
5: 9 will do among you what I have *n*
5: 9 and the like of which I will *n*
16:63 and *n* open your mouth anymore
20:32 you have in your mind shall *n*
23: 8 She has *n* given up her harlotry
26:14 and you shall *n* be rebuilt, for
26:20 so that you may *n* be inhabited;
26:21 you will *n* be found again,'
29:15 it shall *n* again exalt itself
36:30 so that you need *n* again bear
Dan 2:44 set up a kingdom which shall *n*
9:12 the whole heaven such has *n*
12: 1 Such as *n* was since there was
Hos 8: 7 It shall *n* produce meal.
Joel 2: 2 The like of whom has *n* been;
2:26 And My people shall *n* be put
2:27 My people shall *n* be put to
Am 7:13 But *n* again prophesy at Bethel,
8: 7 Surely I will *n* forget any of
8:14 lives!' They shall fall and *n*
Ob 16 shall be as though they had *n*
Nah 3: 1 Its victim *n* departs.
Hab 1: 4 And justice *n* goes forth.
Zeph 3: 5 He *n* fails, But the unjust
Mt 7:23 I *n* knew you; depart from Me,
9:33 It was *n* seen like this in
21:16 Have you *n* read, 'Out of
21:42 Have you *n* read in the
26:33 I will *n* be made to stumble."
Mk 2:12 We *n* saw anything like this!"
2:25 Have you *n* read what David did
3:29 against the Holy Spirit *n* has
9:43 into the fire that shall *n* be
9:45 into the fire that shall *n* be
14:21 good for that man if he had *n*
Lk 15:29 I *n* transgressed your
15:29 and yet you *n* gave me a young
23:29 wombs that *n* bore, and breasts
23:29 and breasts which *n* nursed!'
Jn 4:14 that I shall give him will *n*
6:35 He who comes to Me shall *n*
6:35 he who believes in Me shall *n*
7:15 having *n* studied?"
8:33 and have *n* been in bondage to
8:51 keeps My word he shall *n* see
8:52 keeps My word he shall *n* taste
10:28 and they shall *n* perish;
11:26 and believes in Me shall *n* die.
13: 8 You shall *n* wash my feet!"
Acts 10:14 Lord! For I have *n* eaten
14: 8 who had *n* walked.
1 Cor 8:13 I will *n* again eat meat, lest I
13: 8 Love *n* fails. But whether there
2 Tim 3: 7 always learning and *n* able to
Heb 10: 1 can *n* with these same
10:11 which can *n* take away sins.
13: 5 I will *n* leave you nor
2 Pe 1:10 you do these things you will *n*
1:21 for prophecy *n* came by the will

NEVERMORE (1/1)

Eccl 9: 6 *N* will they have a share

NEVERTHELESS (117/117)

Ex 32:34 My Angel shall go before you. *N*,
Lev 11: 4 *N* these you shall not eat among
11:36 *N* a spring or a cistern, in
25:32 *N* the cities of the Levites,
27:28 *N* no devoted offering that a
Num 13:28 *N* the people who dwell in the
14:44 to go up to the mountaintop; *n*,
18:15 *n* the firstborn of man you
24:22 *N* Kain shall be burned
26:11 *N* the children of Korah did not
Deut 1:26 *N* you would not go up, but
14: 7 "*N*, of those that chew the
23: 5 *N* the LORD your God would not
Josh 13:13 *N* the children of Israel did not
14: 8 *N* my brethren who went up with
22:19 '*N*, if the land of your
Judg 1:33 *N* the inhabitants of Beth
2:16 *N*, the LORD raised up
4: 9 *n* there will be no glory for
1 Sam 2:25 *N* they did not heed the voice
8:19 *N* the people refused to obey
15:35 *N* Samuel mourned for Saul, and
20: 8 *N*, if there is iniquity in me
20:26 *N* Saul did not say anything that
29: 6 *N* the lords do not favor you.
29: 9 *n* the princes of the
2 Sam 5: 7 *N* David took the stronghold of
17:18 *N* a lad saw them, and told

N

23:16 ***N*** he would not drink it, but
24: 4 ***N*** the king's word prevailed
1 Ki 8:19 ***N*** you shall not build the
11:12 ***N*** I will not do it in your days,
15: 4 ***N*** for David's sake the LORD his
15:14 ***N*** Asa's heart was loyal to the
22:43 ***N*** the high places were not
2 Ki 2:10 have asked a hard thing. ***N***,
3: 3 ***N*** he persisted in the sins of
13: 6 ***N*** they did not depart from the
17:14 ***N*** they would not hear, but
23: 9 ***N*** the priests of the high places
23:26 ***N*** the LORD did not turn from
1 Chr 11: 5 shall not come in here!" ***N***
11:18 ***N*** David would not drink it, but
21: 4 ***N*** the king's word prevailed
2 Chr 6: 9 ***N*** you shall not build the
12: 8 ***N*** they will be his servants,
15:17 ***N*** the heart of Asa was loyal
19: 3 ***N*** good things are found in you,
20:33 ***N*** the high places were not taken
30:11 ***N*** some from Asher, Manasseh, and
33:17 ***N*** the people still sacrificed on
35:22 ***N*** Josiah would not turn his face
Neh 4: 9 ***N*** we made our prayer to our God,
9:26 ***N*** they were disobedient
9:31 ***N*** in Your great mercy You did
13:26 ***N*** pagan women caused even him
Esth 5:10 ***N*** Haman restrained himself and
Ps 31:22 ***N*** You heard the voice of my
49:12 ***N*** man, though in honor, does
73:23 ***N*** I am continually with You
78:36 ***N*** they flattered Him with their
89:33 ***N*** My lovingkindness I will not
106: 8 ***N*** He saved them for His name's
106:44 ***N*** He regarded their affliction,
Prov 19:21 ***N*** the LORD's counsel—that
Eccl 9:16 ***N*** the poor man's wisdom is
Isa 9: 1 ***N*** the gloom will not be upon
Jer 5:18 ***N*** in those days," says the
26:24 ***N*** the hand of Ahikam the son of
28: 7 ***N*** hear now this word that I
36:25 ***N*** Elnathan, Delaiah, and
Ezek 3:21 ***N*** if you warn the righteous man
16:60 ***N*** I will remember My covenant
20:17 ***N*** My eye spared them from
20:22 ***N*** I withdrew My hand and acted
33: 9 ***N*** if you warn the wicked to turn
44:14 ***N*** I will make them keep charge
Dan 4:15 ***N*** leave the stump and roots in
Jon 1:13 ***N*** the men rowed hard to return
Mt 14: 9 And the king was sorry; ***n***,
17:27 '***N***, lest we offend them, go
26:39 let this cup pass from Me; ***n***,
26:64 It is as you said. ***N***,
Mk 14:36 Take this cup away from Me; ***n***,
Lk 5: 5 ***n*** at Your word I will let down
10:11 ***N*** know this, that the kingdom
10:20 ***N*** do not rejoice in this, that
13:33 ***N*** I must journey today,
18: 8 He will avenge them speedily. ***N***,
22:42 ***n*** not My will, but Yours, be
Jn 11:15 ***N*** let us go to him."
12:42 ***N*** even among the rulers many
16: 7 ***N*** I tell you the truth. It is to
Acts 14:17 ***N*** He did not leave Himself
24: 4 '***N***, not to be tedious to you
27:11 ***N*** the centurion was more
Rom 5:14 ***N*** death reigned from Adam to
15:15 ***N***, brethren, I have written
1 Cor 7: 2 ***N***, because of sexual
7:28 ***N*** such will have trouble in the
7:37 ***N*** he who stands steadfast in his
9:12 ***N*** we have not used this right,
11:11 ***N***, neither is man independent
2 Cor 3:16 ***N*** when one turns to the Lord,
7: 6 ***N*** God, who comforts the
12:16 may, I did not burden you. ***N***,
Gal 4:30 ***N*** what does the Scripture say?
Eph 5:33 ***N*** let each one of you in
Phil 1:24 ***N*** to remain in the flesh is
3:16 ***N***, to the degree that we have
4:14 ***N*** you have done well that you
1 Tim 2:15 ***N*** she will be saved in
2 Tim 1:12 ***n*** I am not ashamed, for I know
2:19 ***N*** the solid foundation of God
Heb 12:11 for the present, but painful; ***n***,
2 Pe 3:13 ***N*** we, according to His promise,
Rev 2: 4 ***N*** I have this against you, that
2:20 ***N*** I have a few things against

NEW (173/153) NEWBORN, NEWNESS, NEWS

Ex 1: 8 Now there arose a ***n*** king over
Lev 23:16 then you shall offer a ***n*** grain
26:10 out the old because of the ***n***.
Num 16:30 if the LORD creates a ***n*** thing,
18:12 all the best of the ***n*** wine and
28:26 when you bring a ***n*** grain
29: 6 grain offering for the ***N*** Moon,
Deut 7:13 your grain and your ***n*** wine and
11:14 your ***n*** wine, and your oil.
12:17 of your grain or your ***n*** wine
14:23 of your grain and your ***n*** wine
18: 4 of your grain and your ***n*** wine
20: 5 there who has built a ***n*** house
22: 8 When you build a ***n*** house, then
24: 5 When a man has taken a ***n*** wife,
28:51 not leave you grain or ***n*** wine
32:17 To ***n*** gods, new arrivals
32:17 ***n*** arrivals That your fathers
33:28 In a land of grain and ***n*** wine;
Josh 9:13 which we filled were ***n***,
Judg 5: 8 They chose ***n*** gods; Then there
9:13 'Should I cease my ***n*** wine,
15:13 they bound him with two ***n*** ropes
16:11 bind me securely with ***n*** ropes
16:12 Therefore Delilah took ***n*** ropes
1 Sam 6: 7 make a ***n*** cart, take two milk
20: 5 Indeed tomorrow is the ***N*** Moon,
20:18 Tomorrow is the ***N*** Moon; and you
20:24 And when the ***N*** Moon had come,
2 Sam 6: 3 set the ark of God on a ***n*** cart,
6: 3 drove the ***n*** cart.
21:16 who was bearing a ***n*** sword,
1 Ki 11:29 himself with a ***n*** garment
11:30 took hold of the ***n*** garment
2 Ki 2:20 Bring me a ***n*** bowl, and put salt
4:23 It is neither the ***N*** Moon nor
16:14 from between the ***n*** altar and
16:14 the north side of the ***n*** altar.
16:15 On the great ***n*** altar burn the
18:32 a land of grain and ***n*** wine, a
1 Chr 13: 7 the ark of God on a ***n*** cart
23:31 Sabbaths and on the ***N*** Moons
2 Chr 2: 4 on the ***N*** Moons, and on the set
8:13 the ***N*** Moons, and the three
20: 5 before the ***n*** court,
31: 3 Sabbaths and the ***N*** Moons
Ezra 3: 5 and those for ***N*** Moons and for
6: 4 stones and one row of ***n*** timber.
Neh 5:11 the ***n*** wine and the oil, that
10:33 the ***N*** Moons, and the set
10:37 the ***n*** wine and oil, to the
10:39 of the ***n*** wine and the oil, to
13: 5 the ***n*** wine and oil, which were
13:12 of the grain and the ***n*** wine
Job 32:19 ready to burst like ***n*** wineskins.
Ps 33: 3 Sing to Him a ***n*** song; Play
40: 3 He has put a ***n*** song in my
81: 3 at the time of the ***N*** Moon,
96: 1 sing to the LORD a ***n*** song!
98: 1 sing to the LORD a ***n*** song!
144: 9 I will sing a ***n*** song to You, O
149: 1 LORD! Sing to the LORD a ***n***
Prov 3:10 vats will overflow with ***n*** wine.
Eccl 1: 9 And there is nothing ***n*** under
1:10 this is ***n***"? It has already
Song 7:13 ***n*** and old, Which I have laid
Isa 1:13 The ***N*** Moons, the Sabbaths, and
1:14 Your ***N*** Moons and your appointed
24: 7 The ***n*** wine fails, the vine
36:17 a land of grain and ***n*** wine, a
41:15 you into a ***n*** threshing sledge
42: 9 And ***n*** things I declare;
42:10 Sing to the LORD a ***n*** song,
43:19 I will do a ***n*** thing, Now it
48: 6 I have made you hear ***n*** things
62: 2 shall be called by a ***n*** name,
62: 8 shall not drink your ***n*** wine,
65: 8 As the ***n*** wine is found in the
65:17 I create ***n*** heavens and a new
65:17 I create new heavens and a ***n***
66:22 For as the ***n*** heavens and the
66:22 new heavens and the ***n*** earth
66:23 to pass That from one ***N*** Moon
Jer 26:10 down in the entry of the ***N*** Gate
31:12 For wheat and ***n*** wine and oil,
31:22 LORD has created a ***n*** thing
31:31 when I will make a ***n*** covenant
36:10 at the entry of the ***N*** Gate
Lam 3:23 They are ***n*** every morning;
Ezek 11:19 and I will put a ***n*** spirit
18:31 and get yourselves a ***n*** heart
18:31 a new heart and a ***n*** spirit.
36:26 I will give you a ***n*** heart and
36:26 you a new heart and put a ***n***
45:17 the ***N*** Moons, the Sabbaths, and
46: 1 and on the day of the ***N*** Moon it
46: 3 on the Sabbaths and the ***N*** Moons.
46: 6 On the day of the ***N*** Moon it
Hos 2: 8 ***n*** wine, and oil, And
2: 9 grain in its time And My ***n*** wine
2:11 Her ***N*** Moons, Her Sabbaths—All
2:22 With ***n*** wine, And with oil;
4:11 and ***n*** wine enslave the heart.
5: 7 Now a ***N*** Moon shall devour them
7:14 together for grain and ***n*** wine,
9: 2 And the ***n*** wine shall fail in
Joel 1: 5 Because of the ***n*** wine, For it
1:10 The ***n*** wine is dried up,
2:19 I will send you grain and ***n***
2:24 vats shall overflow with ***n*** wine
3:18 mountains shall drip with ***n*** wine
Am 8: 5 When will the ***N*** Moon be past,
Hag 1:11 on the grain and the ***n*** wine and
Zech 9:17 And ***n*** wine the young women.
Mt 9:17 Nor do they put ***n*** wine into old
9:17 But they put ***n*** wine into new
9:17 But they put new wine into ***n***
13:52 his treasure things ***n*** and old.
26:28 is My blood of the ***n*** covenant,
26:29 that day when I drink it ***n***
27:60 and laid it in his ***n*** tomb which
Mk 1:27 What ***n*** doctrine is this?
2:21 or else the ***n*** piece pulls away
2:22 And no one puts ***n*** wine into old
2:22 or else the ***n*** wine bursts the
2:22 But ***n*** wine must be put into new
2:22 must be put into ***n*** wineskins
14:24 is My blood of the ***n*** covenant,
14:25 that day when I drink it ***n*** in
16:17 they will speak with ***n*** tongues;
Lk 5:36 puts a piece from a ***n*** garment
5:36 otherwise the ***n*** makes a tear,
5:36 that was taken out of the ***n***
5:37 And no one puts ***n*** wine into old
5:37 or else the ***n*** wine will burst
5:38 But ***n*** wine must be put into new
5:38 must be put into ***n*** wineskins
5:39 wine, immediately desires ***n***;
22:20 This cup is the ***n*** covenant in
Jn 13:34 A ***n*** commandment I give to you,
19:41 and in the garden a ***n*** tomb in
Acts 2:13 They are full of ***n*** wine."
17:19 May we know what this ***n*** doctrine
17:21 to tell or to hear some ***n***
1 Cor 5: 7 that you may be a ***n*** lump, since
11:25 This cup is the ***n*** covenant in My
2 Cor 3: 6 as ministers of the ***n*** covenant,
5:17 he is a ***n*** creation;
5:17 all things have become ***n***.
Gal 6:15 anything, but a ***n*** creation.
Eph 2:15 create in Himself one ***n*** man
4:24 and that you put on the ***n*** man
Col 2:16 a festival or a ***n*** moon
3:10 and have put on the ***n*** man who
Heb 8: 8 when I will make a ***n*** covenant
8:13 A ***n*** covenant," He has made
9:15 Mediator of the ***n*** covenant
10:20 by a ***n*** and living way which He
12:24 to Jesus the Mediator of the ***n***
2 Pe 3:13 look for ***n*** heavens and a new
3:13 for new heavens and a ***n*** earth
1 Jn 2: 7 I write no ***n*** commandment to
2: 8 a ***n*** commandment I write to you,
2 Jn 5 I wrote a ***n*** commandment to you,
Rev 2:17 and on the stone a ***n*** name
3:12 the ***N*** Jerusalem, which comes
3:12 I will write on him My ***n*** name.
5: 9 And they sang a ***n*** song, saying:
14: 3 They sang as it were a ***n*** song
21: 1 Now I saw a ***n*** heaven and a new
21: 1 Now I saw a new heaven and a ***n***
21: 2 ***N*** Jerusalem, coming down out of
21: 5 "Behold, I make all things ***n***.

NEWBORN (1/1) NEW

1 Pe 2: 2 as ***n*** babes, desire the pure milk

NEWLY (1/1)

2 Ki 4:42 and ***n*** ripened grain in his

NEWNESS (2/2) NEW

Rom 6: 4 so we also should walk in ***n*** of
7: 6 that we should serve in the ***n***

NEWS (41/38) NEW

Ex 33: 4 the people heard this bad ***n***,
1 Sam 4:19 and when she heard the ***n*** that
11: 4 Gibeah of Saul and told the ***n***
11: 6 upon Saul when he heard this ***n***,
17:18 and bring back ***n*** of them."
27:11 to bring ***n*** to Gath, saying,
2 Sam 4: 4 was five years old when the ***n***
4:10 thinking to have brought good ***n***,
4:10 give him a reward for his ***n***.
13:30 that ***n*** came to David, saying,
18:19 Let me run now and take the ***n*** to
18:20 You shall not take the ***n*** this
18:20 for you shall take the ***n***
18:20 But today you shall take no ***n***,
18:22 since you have no ***n*** ready?"
18:25 there is ***n*** in his mouth."
18:26 king said, "He also brings ***n***.
18:27 good man, and comes with good ***n***.
18:31 Cushite said, "There is good ***n***,
1 Ki 1:42 prominent man, and bring good ***n***.
2:28 Then ***n*** came to Joab, for Joab
14: 6 been sent to you with bad ***n***.
2 Ki 7: 9 This day is a day of good ***n***,
1 Chr 10: 9 Philistines to proclaim the ***n***
16:23 Proclaim the good ***n*** of His
Ps 40: 9 I have proclaimed the good ***n*** of
96: 2 Proclaim the good ***n*** of His
Prov 25:25 So is good ***n*** from a far
Isa 52: 7 feet of him who brings good ***n***,
Jer 20:15 man be cursed Who brought ***n***
37: 5 besieging Jerusalem heard ***n*** of
49:23 For they have heard bad ***n***.
Ezek 21: 7 shall answer, 'Because of the ***n***;
Dan 11:44 But ***n*** from the east and the
Nah 3:19 All who hear ***n*** of you
Mt 9:31 they spread the ***n*** about Him in
Lk 4:14 and ***n*** of Him went out through
Acts 11:22 Then ***n*** of these things came to
21:31 ***n*** came to the commander of the
Col 4: 7 will tell you all the ***n*** about
1 Th 3: 6 and brought us good ***n*** of your

NEXT (104/97)

Gen 17:21 bear to you at this set time ***n***
19:34 It happened on the ***n*** day that
47:18 they came to him the ***n*** year and
Ex 9: 6 LORD did this thing on the ***n***
12: 4 let him and his neighbor ***n*** to
18:13 on the ***n*** day, that Moses sat to
32: 6 Then they rose early on the ***n***
32:30 Now it came to pass on the ***n***
Lev 7:16 but on the ***n*** day the remainder
19: 6 and on the ***n*** day. And if any
Num 2: 5 Those who camp ***n*** to him shall

2:12 Those who camp ***n*** to him shall
2:20 ***N*** to him comes the tribe of
2:27 Those who camp ***n*** to him shall
11:32 and all the ***n*** day, and gathered
16:41 On the ***n*** day all the
17: 8 Now it came to pass on the ***n***
22: 5 and are settling ***n*** to me!
22:41 So it was the ***n*** day, that Balak
Judg 6:38 When he rose early the ***n***
9:42 And it came about on the ***n*** day
21: 4 on the ***n*** morning, that the
Ruth 4: 4 and I am ***n*** after you.'" And
1 Sam 5: 4 And when they arose early the ***n***
11:11 on the ***n*** day, that Saul put the
17:13 ***n*** to him Abinadab, and the
18:10 And it happened on the ***n*** day
20:27 And it happened the ***n*** day, the
23:17 and I shall be ***n*** to you. Even
30:17 until the evening of the ***n*** day.
31: 8 So it happened the ***n*** day, when
2 Sam 11:12 in Jerusalem that day and the ***n***.
1 Ki 7:20 convex surface which was ***n*** to
21: 1 ***n*** to the palace of Ahab king of
21: 2 ***n*** to my house; and for it I
2 Ki 4:16 About this time ***n*** year you shall
6:29 And I said to her on the ***n*** day,
8:15 But it happened on the ***n*** day
1 Chr 5:11 the children of Gad dwelt ***n*** to
5:12 was the chief, Shapham the ***n***,
10: 8 So it happened the ***n*** day, when
16: 5 and ***n*** to him Zechariah, then
29:21 to the LORD on the ***n*** day:
2 Chr 17:15 and ***n*** to him was Jehohanan the
17:16 and ***n*** to him was Amasiah the
17:18 and ***n*** to him was Jehozabad, and
31:12 Shimei his brother was the ***n***.
Neh 3: 2 ***N*** to Eliashib the men of
3: 2 And ***n*** to them Zaccur the son of
3: 4 And ***n*** to them Meremoth the son
3: 4 ***N*** to them Meshullam the son of
3: 4 ***N*** to them Zadok the son of
3: 5 ***N*** to them the Tekoites made
3: 7 And ***n*** to them Melatiah the
3: 8 ***N*** to him Uzziel the son of
3: 8 Also ***n*** to him Hananiah, one of
3: 9 And ***n*** to them Rephaiah the son
3:10 ***N*** to them Jedaiah the son of
3:10 And ***n*** to him Hattush the son of
3:12 And ***n*** to him was Shallum the son
3:17 ***N*** to him Hashabiah, leader of
3:19 And ***n*** to him Ezer the son of
3:27 ***n*** to the great projecting
13:13 and ***n*** to them was Hanan the
Ps 22:30 recounted of the Lord to the ***n***
44:12 You sell Your people for ***n*** to
Jer 20: 3 And it happened on the ***n*** day
Ezek 24:18 and the ***n*** morning I did as I
41: 5 ***N***, he measured the wall
48:21 ***n*** to the twenty-five thousand
48:21 and westward ***n*** to the
Jon 4: 7 But as morning dawned the ***n*** day
Zech 11:15 And the LORD said to me, "***N***,
Mt 27:62 On the ***n*** day, which followed
Mk 1:38 Let us go into the ***n*** towns, that
11:12 Now the ***n*** day, when they had
Lk 9:37 Now it happened on the ***n*** day,
10:35 On the ***n*** day, when he departed,
Jn 1:29 The ***n*** day John saw Jesus coming
1:35 the ***n*** day, John stood with two
12:12 The ***n*** day a great multitude
Acts 4: 3 them in custody until the ***n***
4: 5 on the ***n*** day, that their
7:26 And the ***n*** day he appeared to two
10: 9 The ***n*** day, as they went on
10:23 On the ***n*** day Peter went away
13:42 might be preached to them the ***n***
13:44 On the ***n*** Sabbath almost the
14:20 And the ***n*** day he departed with
16:11 and the ***n*** day came to
18: 7 whose house was ***n*** door to the
20: 7 ready to depart the ***n*** day,
20:15 and the ***n*** day came opposite
20:15 The ***n*** day we came to Miletus.
21: 8 On the ***n*** day we who were Paul's
21:26 and the ***n*** day, having been
22:30 The ***n*** day, because he wanted to
23:32 The ***n*** day they left the horsemen
25: 6 And the ***n*** day, sitting on the
25:17 the ***n*** day I sat on the judgment
25:23 So the ***n*** day, when Agrippa and
27: 3 And the ***n*** day we landed at
27:18 the ***n*** day they lightened the
28:13 and the ***n*** day we came to

NEZIAH (2/2)

Ezra 2:54 the sons of ***N***, and the sons
Neh 7:56 the sons of ***N***, and the sons

NEZIB (1/1)

Josh 15:43 Jiphtah, Ashnah, ***N***,

NIBHAZ (1/1)

2 Ki 17:31 and the Avites made ***N*** and

NIBSHAN (1/1)

Josh 15:62 ***N***, the City of Salt,

NICANOR (1/1)

Acts 6: 5 and Philip, Prochorus, ***N***,

NICODEMUS (5/5)

Jn 3: 1 a man of the Pharisees named ***N***,
3: 4 ***N*** said to Him, "How can a man
3: 9 ***N*** answered and said to Him,
7:50 ***N*** (he who came to Jesus by
19:39 And ***N***, who at first came to

NICOLAITANS (2/2)

Rev 2: 6 you hate the deeds of the ***N***,
2:15 who hold the doctrine of the ***N***,

NICOLAS (1/1)

Acts 6: 5 Nicanor, Timon, Parmenas, and ***N***,

NICOPOLIS (1/1)

Titus 3:12 be diligent to come to me at ***N***,

NIGER (1/1) SIMEON, SIMON

Acts 13: 1 Simeon who was called ***N***,

NIGH (KJV) See NEAR

NIGHT (305/293) NIGHTS

Gen 1: 5 and the darkness He called ***N***.
1:14 to divide the day from the ***n***;
1:16 the lesser light to rule the ***n***.
1:18 over the day and over the ***n***,
8:22 And day and ***n*** Shall not
14:15 his forces against them by ***n***,
19: 2 servant's house and spend the ***n***,
19: 2 but we will spend the ***n*** in the
19:33 their father drink wine that ***n***.
19:34 I lay with my father last ***n***;
19:35 their father drink wine that ***n***
20: 3 to Abimelech in a dream by ***n***,
24:54 ate and drank and stayed all ***n***.
26:24 appeared to him the same ***n*** and
28:11 place and stayed there all ***n***,
30:16 And he lay with her that ***n***.
31:24 the Syrian in a dream by ***n***,
31:29 your father spoke to me last ***n***,
31:39 stolen by day or stolen by ***n***.
31:40 consumed me, and the frost by ***n***,
31:42 hands, and rebuked you last ***n***.
31:54 ate bread and stayed all ***n*** on
32:13 So he lodged there that same ***n***,
32:21 but he himself lodged that ***n*** in
32:22 And he arose that ***n*** and took
40: 5 each man's dream in one ***n*** and
41:11 "we each had a dream in one ***n***,
46: 2 Israel in the visions of the ***n***,
49:27 And at ***n*** he shall divide the
Ex 10:13 all that day and all that ***n***.
12: 8 shall eat the flesh on that ***n***;
12:12 the land of Egypt on that ***n***,
12:30 So Pharaoh rose in the ***n***,
12:31 called for Moses and Aaron by ***n***,
12:42 It is a ***n*** of solemn observance
12:42 This is that ***n*** of the LORD, a
13:21 and by ***n*** in a pillar of fire to
13:21 light, so as to go by day and ***n***.
13:22 day or the pillar of fire by ***n***
14:20 and it gave light by ***n*** to the
14:20 come near the other all that ***n***.
14:21 a strong east wind all that ***n***,
40:38 day, and fire was over it by ***n***,
Lev 6: 9 the hearth upon the altar all ***n***
6:20 the morning and half of it at ***n***.
8:35 of meeting day and ***n*** for seven
19:13 shall not remain with you all ***n***
Num 9:16 and the appearance of fire by ***n***.
9:21 journey; whether by day or by ***n***,
11: 9 dew fell on the camp in the ***n***,
11:32 stayed up all that day, all ***n***,
14: 1 and the people wept that ***n***.
14:14 and in a pillar of fire by ***n***.
22:20 And God came to Balaam at ***n*** and
Deut 1:33 in the fire by ***n*** and in the
16: 1 brought you out of Egypt by ***n***.
23:10 by some occurrence in the ***n***,
28:66 you shall fear day and ***n***,
Josh 1: 8 shall meditate in it day and ***n***,
8: 3 valor and sent them away by ***n***,
8: 9 but Joshua lodged that ***n*** among
8:13 Joshua went that ***n*** into the
10: 9 having marched all ***n*** from
Judg 6:25 Now it came to pass the same ***n***
6:27 do it by day, he did it by ***n***.
6:40 And God did so that ***n***.
7: 9 It happened on the same ***n*** that
9:32 "Now therefore, get up by ***n***,
9:34 who were with him rose by ***n***,
16: 2 and lay in wait for him all ***n***
16: 2 the city. They were quiet all ***n***,
19: 6 be content to stay all ***n***,
19: 9 evening; please spend the ***n***.
19:10 was not willing to spend that ***n***;
19:13 and spend the ***n*** in Gibeah or in
19:15 into his house to spend the ***n***.
19:20 only do not spend the ***n*** in the
19:25 knew her and abused her all ***n***
20: 4 to Benjamin, to spend the ***n***.
20: 5 and surrounded the house at ***n***
Ruth 3:13 'Stay this ***n***, and in the
1 Sam 14:34 brought his ox with him that ***n***,
14:36 down after the Philistines by ***n***,
15:11 he cried out to the LORD all ***n***.
15:16 the LORD said to me last ***n***.
19:10 David fled and escaped that ***n***.
19:24 all that day and all that ***n***.
25:16 were a wall to us both by ***n***
26: 7 Abishai came to the people by ***n***;
28: 8 and they came to the woman by ***n***.
28:20 eaten no food all day or all ***n***.
28:25 they rose and went away that ***n***.
31:12 men arose and traveled all ***n***,
2 Sam 2:29 and his men went on all that ***n***
2:32 And Joab and his men went all ***n***,
4: 7 and were all ***n*** escaping through
7: 4 But it happened that ***n*** that the
12:16 and went in and lay all ***n*** on
17:16 Do not spend this ***n*** in the
19: 7 one will stay with you this ***n***.
21:10 the beasts of the field by ***n***.
1 Ki 3: 5 to Solomon in a dream by ***n***;
3:19 this woman's son died in the ***n***,
3:20 arose in the middle of the ***n***
8:29 be open toward this temple ***n***
8:59 the LORD our God day and ***n***,
19: 9 and spent the ***n*** in that place;
2 Ki 6:14 and they came by ***n*** and
7:12 So the king arose in the ***n*** and
8:21 Then he rose by ***n*** and attacked
19:35 it came to pass on a certain ***n***
25: 4 all the men of war fled at ***n***
1 Chr 9:33 in that work day and ***n***.
17: 3 But it happened that ***n*** that the
2 Chr 1: 7 On that ***n*** God appeared to
6:20 toward this temple day and ***n***,
7:12 LORD appeared to Solomon by ***n***,
21: 9 And he rose by ***n*** and attacked
35:14 burnt offerings and fat until ***n***;
Neh 1: 6 pray before You now, day and ***n***,
2:12 Then I arose in the ***n***,
2:13 And I went out by ***n*** through the
2:15 So I went up in the ***n*** by the
4: 9 a watch against them day and ***n***.
4:22 man and his servant stay at ***n***
4:22 they may be our guard by ***n*** and
6:10 at ***n*** they will come to kill
9:12 And by ***n*** with a pillar of
9:19 Nor the pillar of fire by ***n***,
13:21 Why do you spend the ***n*** around
Esth 4:16 ***n*** or day. My maids and I will
6: 1 That ***n*** the king could not sleep.
Job 3: 3 And the ***n*** in which it was
3: 6 As for that ***n***, may darkness
3: 7 may that ***n*** be barren! May no
4:13 from the visions of the ***n***,
5:14 grope at noontime as in the ***n***.
7: 4 And the ***n*** be ended?' For I
17:12 They change the ***n*** into day;
20: 8 away like a vision of the ***n***.
24: 7 They spend the ***n*** naked, without
24:14 And in the ***n*** he is like a
27:20 steals him away in the ***n***.
29:19 And the dew lies all ***n*** on my
30:17 bones are pierced in me at ***n***,
33:15 a dream, in a vision of the ***n***,
34:20 die, in the middle of the ***n***;
34:25 He overthrows them in the ***n***,
35:10 Who gives songs in the ***n***,
36:20 Do not desire the ***n***,
Ps 1: 2 His law he meditates day and ***n***.
6: 6 All ***n*** I make my bed swim;
16: 7 also instructs me in the ***n***
17: 3 You have visited me in the ***n***;
19: 2 And ***n*** unto night reveals
19: 2 And night unto ***n*** reveals
22: 2 And in the ***n*** season, and am
30: 5 Weeping may endure for a ***n***,
32: 4 For day and ***n*** Your hand was
42: 3 have been my food day and ***n***,
42: 8 And in the ***n*** His song shall
55:10 Day and ***n*** they go around it on
63: 6 I meditate on You in the ***n***
74:16 the ***n*** also is Yours; You have
77: 2 hand was stretched out in the ***n***
77: 6 to remembrance my song in the ***n***;
78:14 And all the ***n*** with a light of
88: 1 I have cried out day and ***n***
90: 4 And like a watch in the ***n***.
91: 5 be afraid of the terror by ***n***,
92: 2 And Your faithfulness every ***n***,
104:20 You make darkness, and it is ***n***,
105:39 fire to give light in the ***n***.
119:55 I remember Your name in the ***n***,
119:148 eyes are awake through the ***n***
121: 6 you by day, Nor the moon by ***n***.
134: 1 Who by ***n*** stand in the house of
136: 9 moon and stars to rule by ***n***,
139:11 Even the ***n*** shall be light
139:12 But the ***n*** shines as the day;
Prov 7: 9 In the black and dark ***n***.
31:15 also rises while it is yet ***n***,
31:18 her lamp does not go out by ***n***.
Eccl 2:23 even in the ***n*** his heart takes
8:16 one sees no sleep day or ***n***,
Song 1:13 That lies all ***n*** between my
3: 1 By ***n*** on my bed I sought the one
3: 8 thigh Because of fear in the ***n***.
5: 2 locks with the drops of the ***n***.
Isa 4: 5 shining of a flaming fire by ***n***.
5:11 Who continue until ***n***,

N

15: 1 Because in the ***n*** Ar of Moab is
15: 1 Because in the ***n*** Kir of Moab
16: 3 Make your shadow like the ***n*** in
21: 4 The ***n*** for which I longed He
21: 8 I have sat at my post every ***n***.
21:11 "Watchman, what of the ***n***?
21:11 night? Watchman, what of the ***n***?
21:12 morning comes, and also the ***n***.
26: 9 I have desired You in the ***n***,
27: 3 I keep it ***n*** and day.
28:19 pass over, And by day and by ***n***;
29: 7 Shall be as a dream of a ***n***
30:29 shall have a song As in the ***n***
34:10 It shall not be quenched ***n*** or
34:14 Also the ***n*** creature shall rest
38:12 From day until ***n*** You make an
38:13 From day until ***n*** You make an
60:11 shall not be shut day or ***n***,
62: 6 never hold their peace day or ***n***.
65: 4 And spend the ***n*** in the tombs;
Jer 6: 5 Arise, and let us go by ***n***,
9: 1 That I might weep day and ***n***
14: 8 turns aside to tarry for a ***n***?
14:17 Let my eyes flow with tears ***n***
16:13 serve other gods day and ***n***,
31:35 and the stars for a light by ***n***,
33:20 day and My covenant with the ***n***,
33:20 there will not be day and ***n*** in
33:25 covenant is not with day and ***n***,
36:30 the day and the frost of the ***n***.
39: 4 and went out of the city by ***n***,
49: 9 grapes? If thieves by ***n***,
52: 7 and went out of the city at ***n***
Lam 1: 2 She weeps bitterly in the ***n***,
2:18 run down like a river day and ***n***;
2:19 "Arise, cry out in the ***n***,
Dan 2:19 was revealed to Daniel in a ***n***
5:30 That very ***n*** Belshazzar, king of
6:18 to his palace and spent the ***n***
7: 2 "I saw in my vision by ***n***,
7: 7 After this I saw in the ***n***,
7:13 I was watching in the ***n***
Hos 4: 5 shall stumble with you in the ***n***;
7: 6 Their baker sleeps all ***n***;
Joel 1:13 lie all ***n*** in sackcloth, You
Am 5: 8 And makes the day dark as ***n***;
Ob 5 come to you, If robbers by ***n***—
Jon 4:10 which came up in a ***n*** and
4:10 in a night and perished in a ***n***.
Mic 3: 6 Therefore you shall have ***n***
Zech 1: 8 I saw by ***n***, and behold, a man
14: 7 to the LORD—NEITHER day nor ***n***.
Mt 2:14 Child and His mother by ***n*** and
14:25 in the fourth watch of the ***n***
26:31 to stumble because of Me this ***n***,
26:34 I say to you that this ***n***,
27:64 lest His disciples come by ***n***
28:13 His disciples came at ***n*** and
Mk 4:27 and should sleep by ***n*** and rise
5: 5 ***n*** and day, he was in the
6:48 the fourth watch of the ***n*** He
14:27 to stumble because of Me this ***n***,
14:30 to you that today, even this ***n***,
Lk 2: 8 watch over their flock by ***n***.
2:37 with fastings and prayers ***n***
5: 5 we have toiled all ***n*** and caught
6:12 and continued all ***n*** in prayer
12:20 Fool! This ***n*** your soul will be
17:34 in that ***n*** there will be two
18: 7 elect who cry out day and ***n*** to
21:37 but at ***n*** He went out and stayed
Jn 3: 2 This man came to Jesus by ***n*** and
7:50 (he who came to Jesus by ***n***,
9: 4 the ***n*** is coming when no one
11:10 "But if one walks in the ***n***,
13:30 out immediately. And it was ***n***.
19:39 who at first came to Jesus by ***n***,
21: 3 and that ***n*** they caught nothing.
Acts 5:19 But at ***n*** an angel of the Lord
9:24 watched the gates day and ***n***,
9:25 the disciples took him by ***n***
12: 6 that ***n*** Peter was sleeping,
16: 9 appeared to Paul in the ***n***.
16:33 them the same hour of the ***n***
17:10 sent Paul and Silas away by ***n***
18: 9 Lord spoke to Paul in the ***n*** by
20:31 not cease to warn everyone ***n***
23:11 But the following ***n*** the Lord
23:23 at the third hour of the ***n***;
23:31 Paul and brought him by ***n*** to
26: 7 earnestly serving God ***n*** and
27:23 For there stood by me this ***n*** an
27:27 Now when the fourteenth ***n*** had
Rom 13:12 The ***n*** is far spent, the day is
1 Cor 11:23 the Lord Jesus on the same ***n***
2 Cor 11:25 a ***n*** and a day I have been in
1 Th 2: 9 for laboring ***n*** and day, that we
3:10 ***n*** and day praying exceedingly
5: 2 so comes as a thief in the ***n***.
5: 5 We are not of the ***n*** nor of
5: 7 For those who sleep, sleep at ***n***,
5: 7 who get drunk are drunk at ***n***.
2 Th 3: 8 worked with labor and toil ***n***
1 Tim 5: 5 in supplications and prayers ***n***
2 Tim 1: 3 I remember you in my prayers ***n***
2 Pe 3:10 will come as a thief in the ***n***,
Rev 4: 8 And they do not rest day or ***n***,
7:15 and serve Him day and ***n*** in His
8:12 not shine, and likewise the ***n***.
12:10 them before our God day and ***n***,
14:11 and they have no rest day or ***n***,
20:10 will be tormented day and ***n***
21:25 all by day (there shall be no ***n***
22: 5 There shall be no ***n*** there:

NIGHTS (17/16) NIGHT

Gen 7: 4 earth forty days and forty ***n***,
7:12 earth forty days and forty ***n***.
Ex 24:18 mountain forty days and forty ***n***.
34:28 LORD forty days and forty ***n***;
Deut 9: 9 mountain forty days and forty ***n***.
9:11 end of forty days and forty ***n***,
9:18 first, forty days and forty ***n***;
9:25 forty days and forty ***n*** I kept
10:10 mountain forty days and forty ***n***;
1 Sam 30:12 for three days and three ***n***.
1 Ki 19: 8 food forty days and forty ***n*** as
Job 2:13 ground seven days and seven ***n***,
7: 3 And wearisome ***n*** have been
Jon 1:17 the fish three days and three ***n***.
Mt 4: 2 fasted forty days and forty ***n***,
12:40 was three days and three ***n*** in
12:40 Man be three days and three ***n***

NIMRAH (1/1)

Num 32: 3 "Ataroth, Dibon, Jazer, ***N***,

NIMRIM (2/2)

Isa 15: 6 For the waters of ***N*** will be
Jer 48:34 For the waters of ***N*** also shall

NIMROD (4/4)

Gen 10: 8 Cush begot ***N***; he began to
10: 9 Like ***N*** the mighty hunter before
1 Chr 1:10 Cush begot ***N***; he began to
Mic 5: 6 And the land of ***N*** at its

NIMSHI (5/5)

1 Ki 19:16 shall anoint Jehu the son of ***N***
2 Ki 9: 2 of Jehoshaphat, the son of ***N***,
9:14 of Jehoshaphat, the son of ***N***,
9:20 driving of Jehu the son of ***N***,
2 Chr 22: 7 against Jehu the son of ***N***,

NINE (28/28) NINTH

Gen 5: 5 the days that Adam lived were ***n***
5: 8 So all the days of Seth were ***n***
5:11 So all the days of Enosh were ***n***
5:14 all the days of Cainan were ***n***
5:20 So all the days of Jared were ***n***
5:27 the days of Methuselah were ***n***
9:29 So all the days of Noah were ***n***
11:19 Peleg lived two hundred and ***n***
Num 29:26 On the fifth day present ***n***
34:13 has commanded to give to the ***n***
Deut 3:11) ***N*** cubits is its length and
Josh 13: 7 land as an inheritance to the ***n***
14: 2 for the ***n*** tribes and the
15:44 ***n*** cities with their villages;
15:54 ***n*** cities with their villages;
21:16 ***n*** cities from those two tribes;
Judg 4: 3 for Jabin had ***n*** hundred
4:13 ***n*** hundred chariots of iron, and
2 Sam 24: 8 to Jerusalem at the end of ***n***
2 Ki 17: 1 and he reigned ***n*** years.
1 Chr 3: 8 and Eliphelet—***n*** in all.
9: 9 —***n*** hundred and fifty-six.
Ezra 2: 8 ***n*** hundred and forty-five;
2:36 ***n*** hundred and seventy-three;
Neh 7:38 three thousand ***n*** hundred and
7:39 ***n*** hundred and seventy-three;
11: 8 ***n*** hundred and twenty-eight.
Lk 17:17 cleansed? But where are the ***n***?

NINE-TENTHS (1/1)

Neh 11: 1 and ***n*** were to dwell in

NINETEEN (3/3)

Gen 11:25 Nahor lived one hundred and ***n***
Josh 19:38 ***n*** cities with their villages.
2 Sam 2:30 missing of David's servants ***n***

NINETEENTH (4/4)

2 Ki 25: 8 of the month (which was the ***n***
1 Chr 24:16 the ***n*** to Pethahiah, the
25:26 the ***n*** for Mallothi, his sons and
Jer 52:12 of the month (which was the ***n***

NINETY (7/7)

Gen 5: 9 Enosh lived ***n*** years, and begot
17:17 who is ***n*** years old, bear a
1 Chr 9: 6 brethren—six hundred and ***n***.
Ezek 4: 5 three hundred and ***n*** days;
4: 9 three hundred and ***n*** days, you
41:12 and its length ***n*** cubits.
Dan 12:11 one thousand two hundred and ***n***

NINETY-EIGHT (3/3)

1 Sam 4:15 Eli was ***n*** years old, and his
Ezra 2:16 people of Ater of Hezekiah, ***n***;
Neh 7:21 the sons of Ater of Hezekiah, ***n***;

NINETY-FIVE (4/4)

Gen 5:17 were eight hundred and ***n*** years;
5:30 lived five hundred and ***n*** years,
Ezra 2:20 the people of Gibbar, ***n***;
Neh 7:25 the sons of Gibeon, ***n***;

NINETY-NINE (6/6)

Gen 17: 1 When Abram was ***n*** years old, the
17:24 Abraham was ***n*** years old when he
Mt 18:12 does he not leave the ***n*** and go
18:13 that sheep than over the ***n***
Lk 15: 4 does not leave the ***n*** in the
15: 7 sinner who repents than over ***n***

NINETY-SIX (2/2)

Ezra 8:35 ***n*** rams, seventy-seven lambs,
Jer 52:23 There were ***n*** pomegranates on the

NINETY-TWO (2/2)

Ezra 2:58 were three hundred and ***n***.
Neh 7:60 were three hundred and ***n***.

NINEVEH (19/18)

Gen 10:11 he went to Assyria and built ***N***,
10:12 and Resen between ***N*** and Calah
2 Ki 19:36 home, and remained at ***N***.
Isa 37:37 home, and remained at ***N***.
Jon 1: 2 "Arise, go to ***N***,
3: 2 "Arise, go to ***N***,
3: 3 So Jonah arose and went to ***N***,
3: 3 Now ***N*** was an exceedingly great
3: 4 and ***N*** shall be overthrown!"
3: 5 So the people of ***N*** believed
3: 6 Then word came to the king of ***N***;
3: 7 and published throughout ***N*** by
4:11 "And should I not pity ***N***,
Nah 1: 1 The burden against ***N***.
2: 8 Though ***N*** of old was like a
3: 7 ***N*** is laid waste! Who will
Zeph 2:13 And make ***N*** a desolation,
Mt 12:41 The men of ***N*** will rise up in the
Lk 11:32 The men of ***N*** will rise up in the

NINEVITES (1/1)

Lk 11:30 as Jonah became a sign to the ***N***,

NINTH (33/32) NINE

Lev 23:32 on the ***n*** day of the month at
25:22 and eat old produce until the ***n***
Num 7:60 On the ***n*** day Abidan the son of
2 Ki 17: 6 In the ***n*** year of Hoshea, the
18:10 the ***n*** year of Hoshea king of
25: 1 Now it came to pass in the ***n***
25: 3 By the ***n*** day of the fourth
1 Chr 12:12 the eighth, Elzabad the ***n***,
24:11 the ***n*** to Jeshua, the tenth to
25:16 the ***n*** for Mattaniah, his sons
27:12 The ***n*** captain for the ninth
27:12 The ninth captain for the ***n***
Ezra 10: 9 It was the ***n*** month, on the
Jer 36: 9 in the ***n*** month, that they
36:22 in the winter house in the ***n***
39: 1 In the ***n*** year of Zedekiah king
39: 2 on the ***n*** day of the month, the
52: 4 Now it came to pass in the ***n***
52: 6 on the ***n*** day of the month, the
Ezek 24: 1 in the ***n*** year, in the tenth
Hag 2:10 the twenty-fourth day of the ***n***
2:18 the twenty-fourth day of the ***n***
Zech 7: 1 on the fourth day of the ***n***
Mt 20: 5 out about the sixth and the ***n***
27:45 from the sixth hour until the ***n***
27:46 And about the ***n*** hour Jesus cried
Mk 15:33 over the whole land until the ***n***
15:34 And at the ***n*** hour Jesus cried
Lk 23:44 over all the earth until the ***n***
Acts 3: 1 hour of prayer, the ***n*** hour.
10: 3 About the ***n*** hour of the day he
10:30 and at the ***n*** hour I prayed in
Rev 21:20 the ***n*** topaz, the tenth

NISAN (2/2) ABIB

Neh 2: 1 came to pass in the month of ***N***,
Esth 3: 7 month, which is the month of ***N***,

NISROCH (2/2)

2 Ki 19:37 worshiping in the temple of ***N***
Isa 37:38 worshiping in the house of ***N***

NITRE (KJV) See SODA

NO (1676/1556) See APPENDIX

NOADIAH (2/2)

Ezra 8:33 the son of Jeshua and ***N*** the
Neh 6:14 and the prophetess ***N*** and the

NOAH (55/50)

Gen 5:29 And he called his name ***N***,
5:30 After he begot ***N***,
5:32 And ***N*** was five hundred years
5:32 and ***N*** begot Shem, Ham, and
6: 8 But ***N*** found grace in the eyes of
6: 9 This is the genealogy of ***N***.
6: 9 ***N*** was a just man, perfect in

6: 9 *N* walked with God.
6:10 And *N* begot three sons:
6:13 And God said to *N*,
6:22 Thus *N* did; according to all
7: 1 Then the LORD said to *N*,
7: 5 And *N* did according to all that
7: 6 *N* was six hundred years old
7: 7 So *N*, with his sons, his wife,
7: 9 two they went into the ark to *N*,
7: 9 female, as God had commanded *N*.
7:13 On the very same day *N* and
7:15 And they went into the ark to *N*,
7:23 Only *N* and those who were with
8: 1 Then God remembered *N*,
8: 6 that *N* opened the window of the
8:11 and *N* knew that the waters had
8:13 and *N* removed the covering of
8:15 Then God spoke to *N*,
8:18 So *N* went out, and his sons and
8:20 Then *N* built an altar to the
9: 1 So God blessed *N* and his sons,
9: 8 Then God spoke to *N* and to his
9:17 And God said to *N*,
9:18 Now the sons of *N* who went out
9:19 These three were the sons of *N*,
9:20 And *N* began to be a farmer,
9:24 So *N* awoke from his wine, and
9:28 And *N* lived after the flood
9:29 So all the days of *N* were nine
10: 1 the genealogy of the sons of *N*:
10:32 the families of the sons of *N*,
Num 26:33 of Zelophehad were Mahlah, *N*,
27: 1 of his daughters: Mahlah, *N*,
36:11 Tirzah, Hoglah, Milcah, and *N*,
Josh 17: 3 of his daughters: Mahlah, *N*,
1 Chr 1: 4 *N*, Shem, Ham, and Japheth.
Isa 54: 9 this is like the waters of *N*
54: 9 sworn That the waters of *N*
Ezek 14:14 "Even if these three men, *N*,
14:20 'even though *N*, Daniel, and
Mt 24:37 But as the days of *N* were, so
24:38 until the day that *N* entered
Lk 3:36 son of Shem, the son of *N*,
17:26 as it was in the days of *N*,
17:27 until the day that *N* entered
Heb 11: 7 By faith *N*, being divinely
1 Pe 3:20 waited in the days of *N*,
2 Pe 2: 5 the ancient world, but saved *N*,

NOAH'S (3/2)

Gen 7:11 In the six hundredth year of *N*
7:13 the very same day Noah and *N*
7:13 and *N* wife and the three wives

NOB (6/6)

1 Sam 21: 1 Now David came to *N*,
22: 9 saw the son of Jesse going to *N*,
22:11 the priests who were in *N*.
22:19 Also *N*, the city of the priests,
Neh 11:32 in Anathoth, *N*, Ananiah;
Isa 10:32 As yet he will remain at *N* that

NOBAH (3/2)

Num 32:42 Then *N* went and took Kenath and
32:42 villages, and he called it *N*,
Judg 8:11 in tents on the east of *N* and

NOBILITY (1/1)

Prov 19: 6 entreat the favor of the ***n***,

NOBLE (11/11) NOBLEMAN, NOBLES

Ezra 4:10 nations whom the great and ***n***
Esth 1:18 This very day the ***n*** ladies of
6: 9 of one of the king's most ***n***
Song 6:12 As the chariots of my ***n*** people.
Jer 2:21 Yet I had planted you a ***n*** vine,
Lk 8:15 having heard the word with a ***n***
Acts 24: 3 most ***n*** Felix, with all
26:25 most ***n*** Festus, but speak the
1 Cor 1:26 not many mighty, not many ***n***,
Phil 4: 8 true, whatever things are ***n***,
Jas 2: 7 Do they not blaspheme that ***n***

NOBLEMAN (3/3) NOBLE

Lk 19:12 A certain ***n*** went into a far
Jn 4:46 And there was a certain ***n*** whose
4:49 The ***n*** said to Him, "Sir, come

NOBLES (34/34) NOBLE

Ex 24:11 But on the ***n*** of the children of
Num 21:18 Dug by the nation's ***n***,
Judg 5:13 down, the people against the ***n***;
1 Ki 21: 8 to the elders and the ***n*** who
21:11 the elders and ***n*** who were
2 Chr 23:20 the captains of hundreds, the ***n***,
Neh 2:16 the Jews, the priests, the ***n***,
3: 5 but their ***n*** did not put their
4:14 and arose and said to the ***n***,
4:19 Then I said to the ***n***,
5: 7 I rebuked the ***n*** and rulers, and
6:17 Also in those days the ***n*** of
7: 5 into my heart to gather the ***n***,
10:29 with their brethren, their ***n***,
13:17 Then I contended with the ***n*** of
Esth 1: 3 of Persia and Media, the ***n***,
Job 29:10 The voice of ***n*** was hushed,
34:18 are worthless,' And to ***n***,
Ps 83:11 Make their ***n*** like Oreb and like
149: 8 And their ***n*** with fetters of
Prov 8:16 By me princes rule, and ***n***,
Eccl 10:17 when your king is the son of ***n***,
Isa 13: 2 may enter the gates of the ***n***.
34:12 They shall call its ***n*** to the
Jer 14: 3 Their ***n*** have sent their lads
27:20 and all the ***n*** of Judah and
30:21 Their ***n*** shall be from among
39: 6 Babylon also killed all the ***n***
Dan 1: 3 descendants and some of the ***n***,
4:36 My counselors and ***n*** resorted to
Jon 3: 7 decree of the king and his ***n***,
Nah 2: 5 He remembers his ***n***;
3:18 Your ***n*** rest in the dust.
Mk 6:21 birthday gave a feast for his ***n***,

NOD (1/1)

Gen 4:16 and dwelt in the land of *N* on

NODAB (1/1)

1 Chr 5:19 Hagrites, Jetur, Naphish, and *N*.

NODDED (1/1)

Acts 24:10 after the governor had ***n*** to him

NOE (KJV) See NOAH

NOGAH (2/2)

1 Chr 3: 7 *N*, Nepheg, Japhia,
14: 6 *N*, Nepheg, Japhia,

NOHAH (1/1)

1 Chr 8: 2 *N* the fourth, and Rapha the

NOISE (62/48) NOISES

Ex 32:17 And when Joshua heard the ***n*** of
32:17 There is a ***n*** of war in the
32:18 It is not the ***n*** of the shout
32:18 Nor the ***n*** of the cry of
Josh 6:10 shall not shout or make any ***n***
Judg 5:11 Far from the ***n*** of the archers,
1 Sam 4: 6 the Philistines heard the ***n*** of
4:14 When Eli heard the ***n*** of the
14:19 that the ***n*** which was in the
1 Ki 1:45 This is the ***n*** that you have
2 Ki 7: 6 of the Syrians to hear the ***n***
7: 6 noise of chariots and the ***n*** of
7: 6 the ***n*** of a great army; so they
11:13 Now when Athaliah heard the ***n***
2 Chr 23:12 Now when Athaliah heard the ***n***
Ezra 3:13 people could not discern the ***n***
3:13 of the shout of joy from the ***n***
Ps 42: 7 Deep calls unto deep at the ***n***
65: 7 You who still the ***n*** of the
65: 7 The ***n*** of their waves, And the
93: 4 high is mightier Than the ***n***
Isa 13: 4 The ***n*** of a multitude in the
13: 4 of many people! A tumultuous ***n***
17:12 of many people Who make a ***n***
22: 2 You who are full of ***n***,
24: 8 The ***n*** of the jubilant ends,
24:18 That he who flees from the ***n***
25: 5 You will reduce the ***n*** of
29: 6 and earthquake and great ***n***,
31: 4 Nor be disturbed by their ***n***),
33: 3 At the ***n*** of the tumult the
66: 6 The sound of ***n*** from the city!
Jer 4:19 heart! My heart makes a ***n*** in
4:29 city shall flee from the ***n*** of
10:22 the ***n*** of the report has come,
11:16 With the ***n*** of a great tumult
25:31 A ***n*** will come to the ends of
46:17 king of Egypt, is but a ***n***.
46:22 Her ***n*** shall go like a serpent,
47: 3 At the ***n*** of the stamping hooves
49:21 The earth shakes at the ***n*** of
49:21 At the cry its ***n*** is heard at
50:46 At the ***n*** of the taking of
51:55 And the ***n*** of their voice is
Lam 2: 7 They have made a ***n*** in the
Ezek 1:24 I heard the ***n*** of their wings,
1:24 like the ***n*** of many waters, like
1:24 a tumult like the ***n*** of an army;
3:13 I also heard the ***n*** of the
3:13 and the ***n*** of the wheels beside
3:13 them, and a great thunderous ***n***.
19: 7 was desolated By the ***n*** of his
26:10 your walls will shake at the ***n***
37: 7 as I prophesied, there was a ***n***,
Joel 2: 5 With a ***n*** like chariots
2: 5 Like the ***n*** of a flaming fire
Am 5:23 Take away from Me the ***n*** of your
Mic 2:12 They shall make a loud ***n***
Nah 3: 2 The ***n*** of a whip And the noise
3: 2 noise of a whip And the ***n*** of
Zeph 1:14 The ***n*** of the day of the LORD
2 Pe 3:10 will pass away with a great ***n***,

NOISED (KJV) See DISCUSSED, HEARD, SPREAD

NOISES (3/3) NOISE

Rev 8: 5 to the earth. And there were ***n***,
11:19 And there were lightnings, ***n***,
16:18 And there were ***n*** and thunderings

NOISILY (1/1)

Ps 55: 2 in my complaint, and moan ***n***,

NOISOME (KJV) See FOUL, PERILOUS, WILD

NOISY (3/3)

1 Ki 1:41 the city in such a ***n*** uproar?"
Isa 9: 5 sandal from the ***n*** battle,
Mt 9:23 flute players and the ***n*** crowd

NON (KJV) See NUN

NONE (187/179)

Gen 23: 6 *N* of us will withhold from you
28:17 is this place! This is ***n***
39:11 and ***n*** of the men of the house
Ex 5:11 yet ***n*** of your work will be
9:14 you may know that there is ***n***
9:24 so very heavy that there was ***n***
11: 7 But against ***n*** of the children of
12:10 You shall let ***n*** of it remain
12:22 And ***n*** of you shall go out of
15:26 I will put ***n*** of the diseases on
16:26 the Sabbath, there will be ***n***.
16:27 day to gather, but they found ***n***.
23:15 ***n*** shall appear before Me
34:20 And ***n*** shall appear before Me
Lev 18: 6 *N* of you shall approach anyone
21: 1 *N* shall defile himself for the
22:30 you shall leave ***n*** of it until
26: 6 and ***n*** will make you afraid;
Num 7: 9 to the sons of Kohath he gave ***n***,
9:12 They shall leave ***n*** of it until
30: 5 then ***n*** of her vows nor her
32:11 Surely ***n*** of the men who came up
Deut 2:34 we left ***n*** remaining.
4:35 there is ***n*** other besides Him.
7:15 and will afflict you with ***n*** of
13:17 So ***n*** of the accursed things
23: 2 even to the tenth generation ***n***
23: 3 even to the tenth generation ***n***
Josh 2:14 if ***n*** of you tell this business
6: 1 ***n*** went out, and none came in.
6: 1 and ***n*** came in.
8:22 so that they let ***n*** of them
9:23 and ***n*** of you shall be freed
10:28 He let ***n*** remain. He also did to
10:30 He let ***n*** remain in it, but did
10:33 until he left him ***n*** remaining.
10:37 he left ***n*** remaining, according
10:39 He left ***n*** remaining; as he had
10:40 he left ***n*** remaining, but
11: 8 them until they left ***n*** of them
11:11 There was ***n*** left breathing.
11:13 Israel burned ***n*** of them, except
11:14 and they left ***n*** breathing.
11:22 *N* of the Anakim were left in the
Judg 20: 8 *N* of us will go to his tent,
21: 1 *N* of us shall give his daughter
1 Sam 2: 2 For there is ***n*** besides You,
3:19 LORD was with him and let ***n***
14:24 So ***n*** of the people tasted
21: 9 There is ***n*** like it; give it to
2 Sam 7:22 For there is ***n*** like You, nor
22:42 but there was ***n*** to save;
1 Ki 5: 6 For you know there is ***n*** among
12:20 There was ***n*** who followed the
15:17 that he might let ***n*** go out or
15:22 ***n*** was exempted. And they took
2 Ki 6:12 one of his servants said, "*N*,
9:10 and there shall be ***n*** to bury
10:11 until he left him ***n*** remaining.
10:14 and he left ***n*** of them.
17:18 there was ***n*** left but the tribe
18: 5 so that after him was ***n*** like
24:14 *N* remained except the poorest
1 Chr 17:20 there is ***n*** like You, nor is
2 Chr 1:12 such as ***n*** of the kings have had
9:11 and there were ***n*** such as
16: 1 that he might let ***n*** go out or
35:18 and ***n*** of the kings of Israel
Ezra 8:15 and found ***n*** of the sons of Levi
Job 1: 8 that there is ***n*** like him on
2: 3 that there is ***n*** like him on
3: 9 it look for light, but have ***n***,
18:15 dwell in his tent who are ***n***
Ps 7: 2 while there is ***n*** to deliver.
10: 4 God is in ***n*** of his thoughts.
10:15 wickedness until You find ***n***.
14: 1 There is ***n*** who does good.
14: 3 There is ***n*** who does good,
18:41 but there was ***n*** to save;
22:11 For there is ***n*** to help.
34:22 And ***n*** of those who trust in
37:31 *N* of his steps shall slide.
49: 7 *N* of them can by any means
50:22 And there be ***n*** to deliver:
53: 1 There is ***n*** who does good.
53: 3 There is ***n*** who does good,
69:20 to take pity, but there was ***n***;
69:20 for comforters, but I found ***n***.
71:11 for there is ***n*** to deliver
73:25 And there is ***n*** upon earth
76: 5 And ***n*** of the mighty men have

81:11 And Israel would have *n* of
86: 8 Among the gods there is *n*
105:37 And there was *n* feeble among
107:12 and there was *n* to help.
109:12 Let there be *n* to extend mercy
139:16 When as yet there were *n*
Prov 1:25 And would have *n* of my rebuke,
1:30 They would have *n* of my counsel
2:19 *N* who go to her return, Nor do
3:31 And choose *n* of his ways;
16: 5 *n* will go unpunished.
Song 4: 2 And *n* is barren among them.
6: 6 And *n* is barren among them.
Isa 24:10 so that *n* may go in.
34:12 But *n* shall be there, and
41:17 seek water, but there is *n*,
45: 6 its setting That there is *n*
45:21 There is *n* besides Me.
46: 9 and there is *n* like Me,
50: 2 was there *n* to answer? Is My
59:11 for justice, but there is *n*;
Jer 10: 6 Inasmuch as there is *n* like
10: 7 There is *n* like You.
22:30 For *n* of his descendants shall
30: 7 So that *n* is like it; And it
35:14 for to this day they drink *n*,
42:17 And *n* of them shall remain or
44: 7 leaving *n* to remain,
44:14 so that *n* of the remnant of
44:14 For *n* shall return except those
50: 9 *N* shall return in vain.
50:20 sought, but there shall be *n*;
50:29 Let *n* of them escape. Repay
51:62 so that *n* shall remain in it,
Lam 1: 2 all her lovers She has *n* to
5: 8 There is *n* to deliver us
Ezek 7:11 *N* of them shall remain,
7:11 *N* of their multitude, None of
7:11 *N* of them; Nor shall there
7:25 peace, but there shall be *n*.
12:28 *N* of My words will be postponed
18:11 And does *n* of those duties,
18:22 *N* of the transgressions which he
33:13 *n* of his righteous works shall
33:16 *N* of his sins which he has
39:28 and left *n* of them captive any
46:18 so that *n* of My people may be
Dan 1:19 and among them all *n* was found
12:10 and *n* of the wicked shall
Hos 7: 7 *N* among them calls upon Me.
11: 7 *N* at all exalt Him.
Am 6:10 Then someone will say, "*N*.
Mic 5: 8 And *n* can deliver.
Zeph 2:15 and there is *n* besides me."
3: 6 With *n* passing by. Their
Zech 7:10 Let *n* of you plan evil in his
8:17 Let *n* of you think evil in your
Mal 2:15 And let *n* deal treacherously
Mt 12:43 seeking rest, and finds *n*.
26:60 but found *n*. Even though
26:60 came forward, they found *n*.
Mk 14:55 put Him to death, but found *n*.
Lk 3:11 let him give to him who has *n*;
4:26 but to *n* of them was Elijah sent
4:27 and *n* of them was cleansed
11:24 seeking rest; and finding *n*,
13: 6 seeking fruit on it and found *n*.
13: 7 on this fig tree and find *n*.
14:24 For I say to you that *n* of those
18:34 But they understood *n* of these
Jn 7:19 yet *n* of you keeps the law? Why
16: 5 and *n* of you asks Me, 'Where
17:12 and *n* of them is lost except
18: 9 whom You gave Me I have lost *n*.
21:12 Yet *n* of the disciples dared
Acts 5:13 Yet *n* of the rest dared join
8:16 as yet He had fallen upon *n* of
8:24 that *n* of the things which you
20:24 But *n* of these things move me;
26:26 for I am convinced that *n* of
Rom 3:10 There is *n* righteous, no,
3:11 There is *n* who
3:11 There is *n* who seeks
3:12 There is *n* who does
14: 7 For *n* of us lives to himself,
1 Cor 1:14 I thank God that I baptized *n* of
2: 8 which *n* of the rulers of this
4: 6 that *n* of you may be puffed up
7:29 should be as though they had *n*,
9:15 But I have used *n* of these
14:10 and *n* of them is without
Gal 1:19 But I saw *n* of the other
Heb 8:11 *N* of them shall teach his
8:11 and *n* his brother, saying,
1 Pe 4:15 But let *n* of you suffer as a
1 Jn 2:19 that *n* of them were of us.

NONEXISTENT (1/1)

Isa 41:12 nothing, As a *n* thing.

NONSENSE (2/2)

Job 27:12 do you behave with complete *n*?
Ezek 13: 8 Because you have spoken *n* and

NOON (13/13) NOONDAY

Gen 43:16 men will dine with me at *n*.
43:25 ready for Joseph's coming at *n*,
2 Sam 4: 5 who was lying on his bed at *n*.
1 Ki 18:26 Baal from morning even till *n*,
18:27 And so it was, at *n*,
20:16 So they went out at *n*.
2 Ki 4:20 he sat on her knees till *n*,
Ps 55:17 Evening and morning and at *n* I
Song 1: 7 Where you make it rest at *n*.
Jer 6: 4 Arise, and let us go up at *n*.
20:16 morning And the shouting at *n*,
Am 8: 9 will make the sun go down at *n*,
Acts 22: 6 came near Damascus at about *n*,

NOONDAY (8/8) NOON

Deut 28:29 "And you shall grope at *n*,
Job 11:17 life would be brighter than *n*.
Ps 37: 6 And your justice as the *n*.
91: 6 that lays waste at *n*.
Isa 58:10 darkness shall be as the *n*.
59:10 We stumble at *n* as at
Jer 15: 8 young men, A plunderer at *n*;
Zeph 2: 4 shall drive out Ashdod at *n*,

NOONTIME (1/1)

Job 5:14 And grope at *n* as in the

NOOSE (1/1)

Job 18:10 A *n* is hidden for him on the

NOPH (7/7) MEMPHIS

Isa 19:13 The princes of *N* are deceived;
Jer 2:16 Also the people of *N* and
44: 1 at Migdol, at Tahpanhes, at *N*,
46:14 Proclaim in *N* and in
46:19 to go into captivity! For *N*
Ezek 30:13 the images to cease from *N*;
30:16 And *N* shall be in distress

NOPHAH (1/1)

Num 21:30 Then we laid waste as far as *N*,

NOR (1027/863)

Gen 3: 3 *n* shall you touch it, lest you
8:21 *n* will I again destroy every
19:17 life! Do not look behind you *n*
21:26 *n* had I heard of it until
31:24 speak to Jacob neither good *n*
31:29 speak to Jacob neither good *n*
39: 9 *n* has he kept back anything
45: 6 will be neither plowing *n*
49:10 *N* a lawgiver from between his
Ex 4: 8 *n* heed the message of the first
4:10 neither before *n* since You have
5: 2 *n* will I let Israel go."
10: 6 which neither your fathers *n*
10:14 *n* shall there be such after
10:23 *n* did anyone rise from his
11: 6 *n* shall be like it again.
12: 9 *n* boiled at all with water, but
12:39 *n* had they prepared provisions
12:46 *n* shall you break one of its
13: 7 *n* shall leaven be seen among
16:24 *n* were there any worms in it.
20: 5 shall not bow down to them *n*
20:10 *n* your son, nor your daughter,
20:10 *n* your daughter, nor your male
20:10 *n* your male servant, nor your
20:10 *n* your female servant, nor your
20:10 *n* your cattle, nor your
20:10 *n* your stranger who is within
20:17 *n* his male servant, nor his
20:17 *n* his female servant, nor his
20:17 *n* his ox, nor his donkey, nor
20:17 *n* his donkey, nor anything that
20:17 *n* anything that is your
20:26 *N* shall you go up by steps to My
22:21 neither mistreat a stranger *n*
22:28 *n* curse a ruler of your people.
23: 2 *n* shall you testify in a
23:13 *n* let it be heard from your
23:18 *n* shall the fat of My sacrifice
23:24 *n* serve them, nor do according
23:24 *n* do according to their works;
23:32 *n* with their gods.
24: 2 *n* shall the people go up with
30: 9 *n* shall you pour a drink
30:32 *n* shall you make any other
32:18 *N* the noise of the cry of
34: 3 let neither flocks *n* herds feed
34:10 *n* in any nation; and all the
34:25 *n* shall the sacrifice of the
34:28 he neither ate bread *n* drank
36: 6 Let neither man *n* woman do any
Lev 2:11 for you shall burn no leaven *n*
3:17 you shall eat neither fat *n*
5:11 *n* shall he put frankincense on
7:18 *n* shall it be imputed to him;
10: 6 Do not uncover your heads *n* tear
10: 9 *n* your sons with you, when you
11:43 *n* shall you make yourselves
12: 4 *n* come into the sanctuary until
17:12 *n* shall any stranger who dwells
18: 3 *n* shall you walk in their
18:17 *n* shall you take her son's
18:18 *N* shall you take a woman as a
18:21 *n* shall you profane the name of
18:23 *N* shall you mate with any
18:23 *N* shall any woman stand before
19: 4 *n* make for yourselves molded
19: 9 *n* shall you gather the
19:10 *n* shall you gather every grape
19:11 *n* deal falsely, nor lie to one
19:11 *n* lie to one another.
19:12 *n* shall you profane the name of
19:13 *n* rob him. The wages of him
19:14 *n* put a stumbling block before
19:15 *n* honor the person of the
19:16 *n* shall you take a stand
19:18 *n* bear any grudge against the
19:19 *N* shall a garment of mixed
19:20 has not at all been redeemed *n*
19:26 *n* shall you practice divination
19:27 *n* shall you disfigure the edges
19:28 *n* tattoo any marks on you:
20:19 of your mother's sister *n* of
21: 5 *n* shall they shave the edges of
21: 5 the edges of their beards *n*
21: 7 *n* shall they take a woman
21:10 shall not uncover his head *n*
21:11 *n* shall he go near any dead
21:11 *n* defile himself for his father
21:12 *n* shall he go out of the
21:12 *n* profane the sanctuary of his
21:15 *N* shall he profane his posterity
22:22 *n* make an offering by fire of
22:24 *n* shall you make any offering
22:25 *N* from a foreigner's hand shall
23:14 You shall eat neither bread *n*
23:14 bread nor parched grain *n*
23:22 *n* shall you gather any gleaning
25: 4 shall neither sow your field *n*
25: 5 *n* gather the grapes of your
25:11 in it you shall neither sow *n*
25:11 *n* gather the grapes of your
25:20 since we shall not sow *n* gather
25:37 *n* lend him your food at a
26: 1 neither a carved image *n* a
26: 1 *n* shall you set up an engraved
26:20 *n* shall the trees of the land
26:44 *n* shall I abhor them, to
27:33 *n* shall he exchange it; and if
Num 1:49 *n* take a census of them among
5:13 *n* was she caught—
6: 3 vinegar made from wine *n*
6: 3 *n* eat fresh grapes or raisins.
9:12 *n* break one of its bones.
11:19 *n* two days, nor five days, nor
11:19 *n* five days, nor ten days, nor
11:19 *n* ten days, nor twenty days,
11:19 *n* twenty days,
14: 9 *n* fear the people of the land,
14:23 *n* shall any of those who
14:44 of the covenant of the LORD *n*
16:14 *n* given us inheritance of
16:15 *n* have I hurt one of them."
18:20 *n* shall you have any portion
20: 5 *n* is there any water to
20:17 *n* will we drink water from
23:19 *N* a son of man, that He should
23:21 *N* has He seen wickedness in
23:23 *N* any divination against
23:25 *n* bless them at all!"
30: 5 then none of her vows *n* her
Deut 1:42 Do not go up *n* fight, for I am
1:45 not listen to your voice *n*
2: 9 *n* contend with them in battle,
2:27 turn neither to the right *n* to
4: 2 *n* take from it, that you may
4:28 which neither see *n* hear nor
4:28 which neither see nor hear *n*
4:28 neither see nor hear nor eat *n*
4:31 He will not forsake you *n*
4:31 *n* forget the covenant of your
5: 9 shall not bow down to them *n*
5:14 *n* your son, nor your daughter,
5:14 *n* your daughter, nor your male
5:14 *n* your male servant, nor your
5:14 *n* your female servant, nor your
5:14 *n* your ox, nor your donkey, nor
5:14 *n* your donkey, nor any of your
5:14 *n* any of your cattle, nor your
5:14 *n* your stranger who is within
7: 2 make no covenant with them *n*
7: 3 *N* shall you make marriages with
7: 3 *n* take their daughter for your
7: 7 did not set His love on you *n*
7:16 *n* shall you serve their gods,
7:25 *n* take it for yourselves, lest
7:26 *N* shall you bring an abomination
8: 3 manna which you did not know *n*
8: 4 *n* did your foot swell these
9: 9 I neither ate bread *n* drank
9:18 I neither ate bread *n* drank
9:23 and you did not believe Him *n*
10: 9 Therefore Levi has no portion *n*
10:17 who shows no partiality *n* takes
12:12 since he has no portion *n*
12:32 you shall not add to it *n* take
13: 6 neither you *n* your fathers,
13: 8 *n* shall your eye pity him, nor
13: 8 *n* shall you spare him or
14: 1 you shall not cut yourselves *n*
14:27 for he has no part *n*
14:29 because he has no portion *n*
15: 7 shall not harden your heart *n*
15:19 *n* shear the firstborn of your
16: 4 *n* shall any of the meat which
16:19 *n* take a bribe, for a bribe
17:16 *n* cause the people to return to
17:17 *n* shall he greatly multiply
18: 1 shall have no part *n* inheritance
18:16 *n* let me see this great fire

21: 4 which is neither plowed ***n*** sown,
21: 7 ***n*** have our eyes seen it.
22: 5 ***n*** shall a man put on a woman's
22:30 ***n*** uncover his father's bed.
23: 6 shall not seek their peace ***n***
24:16 ***n*** shall the children be put to
24:17 ***n*** take a widow's garment as a
26:13 ***n*** have I forgotten them.
26:14 ***n*** have I removed any of it for
26:14 ***n*** given any of it for the
28:36 to a nation which neither you ***n***
28:39 neither drink of the wine ***n***
28:50 does not respect the elderly ***n***
28:64 which neither you ***n*** your
28:65 ***n*** shall the sole of your foot
29: 6 ***n*** have you drunk wine or
29:23 ***n*** does it bear, nor does any
29:23 ***n*** does any grass grow there,
30:11 ***n*** is it far off.
30:13 ***N*** is it beyond the sea, that
31: 6 do not fear ***n*** be afraid of
31: 6 He will not leave you ***n*** forsake
31: 8 He will not leave you ***n*** forsake
31: 8 do not fear ***n*** be dismayed."
32:28 ***N*** is there any
32:39 ***N*** is there any who can
33: 6 ***N*** let his men be few."
33: 9 ***N*** did he acknowledge his
34: 7 His eyes were not dim ***n*** his
Josh 1: 5 I will not leave you ***n*** forsake
1: 9 ***n*** be dismayed, for the LORD
6:10 ***n*** shall a word proceed out of
8: 1 ***n*** be dismayed; take all the
10:25 ***n*** be dismayed; be strong and of
22:19 ***n*** rebel against us, by building
22:26 not for burnt offering ***n*** for
22:28 not for burnt offerings ***n*** for
23: 7 ***n*** cause anyone to swear by
23: 7 you shall not serve them ***n*** bow
24:19 forgive your transgressions ***n***
Judg 1:29 ***N*** did Ephraim drive out the
1:30 ***N*** did Zebulun drive out the
1:31 ***N*** did Asher drive out the
1:33 ***N*** did Naphtali drive out the
2:10 who did not know the LORD ***n***
2:19 cease from their own doings ***n***
2:23 ***n*** did He deliver them into the
6: 4 neither sheep ***n*** ox nor donkey.
6: 4 neither sheep nor ox ***n*** donkey.
8:23 ***n*** shall my son rule over you;
8:35 ***n*** did they show kindness to the
11:15 ***n*** the land of the people of
11:34 her he had neither son ***n***
13: 7 ***n*** eat anything unclean, for the
13:14 ***n*** may she drink wine or
13:14 ***n*** eat anything unclean. All
13:23 ***n*** would He have shown us all
13:23 ***n*** would He have told us such
20: 8 ***n*** will any turn back to his
Ruth 2: 8 ***n*** go from here, but stay close
1 Sam 1:15 I have drunk neither wine ***n***
2: 2 ***N*** is there any rock like our
3: 7 ***n*** was the word of the LORD yet
4:20 ***n*** did she regard it.
5: 5 neither the priests of Dagon ***n***
12: 4 ***n*** have you taken anything from
13:22 that there was neither sword ***n***
15:29 of Israel will not lie ***n***
20:31 ***n*** your kingdom. Now therefore,
21: 8 brought neither my sword ***n*** my
24:11 that there is neither evil ***n***
25: 7 ***n*** was there anything missing
25:15 ***n*** did we miss anything as long
25:31 ***n*** offense of heart to my lord,
27: 9 he left neither man ***n*** woman
27:11 David would save neither man ***n***
28:15 neither by prophets ***n*** by
28:18 obey the voice of the LORD ***n***
30:12 for he had eaten no bread ***n***
30:15 that you will neither kill me ***n***
2 Sam 1:21 Let there be no dew ***n*** rain
1:21 ***N*** fields of offerings.
2:28 ***n*** did they fight anymore.
3:34 Your hands were not bound ***N***
7:10 ***n*** shall the sons of wickedness
7:22 ***n*** is there any God besides
12:17 ***n*** did he eat food with them.
13:22 brother Amnon neither good ***n***
14: 7 to my husband neither name ***n***
18: 3 ***n*** if half of us die, will they
19: 6 you regard neither princes ***n***
19:24 ***n*** trimmed his mustache, nor
19:24 ***n*** washed his clothes, from the
20: 1 ***N*** do we have inheritance in
21: 4 ***n*** shall you kill any man in
21:10 air to rest on them by day ***n***
24:24 ***n*** will I offer burnt offerings
1 Ki 1:26 ***n*** Zadok the priest, nor Benaiah
1:26 ***n*** Benaiah the son of Jehoiada,
1:26 ***n*** your servant Solomon.
3:11 ***n*** have asked riches for
3:11 ***n*** have asked the life of your
3:12 ***n*** shall any like you arise
3:26 Let him be neither mine ***n*** yours,
5: 4 there is neither adversary ***n***
8:57 May He not leave us ***n*** forsake
10:12 ***n*** has the like been seen to
11: 2 ***n*** they with you. Surely they
12:24 You shall not go up ***n*** fight
13: 8 ***n*** would I eat bread nor drink
13: 8 nor would I eat bread ***n*** drink
13: 9 ***n*** drink water, nor return by
13: 9 ***n*** return by the same way you
13:16 I cannot return with you ***n*** go in
13:16 neither can I eat bread ***n*** drink
13:17 You shall not eat bread ***n*** drink
13:17 ***n*** return by going the way you
13:28 lion had not eaten the corpse ***n***
16:11 neither of his relatives ***n*** of
17: 1 there shall not be dew ***n*** rain
17:14 ***n*** shall the jar of oil run dry,
17:16 ***n*** did the jar of oil run dry,
2 Ki 3: 9 ***n*** for the animals that followed
3:14 not look at you, ***n*** see you.
3:17 ***n*** shall you see rain; yet that
4:23 It is neither the New Moon ***n***
4:31 but there was neither voice ***n***
6:19 ***n*** is this the city. Follow me,
12: 8 ***n*** repair the damages of the
14: 6 ***n*** shall children be put to
17:34 ***n*** do they follow their statutes
17:35 ***n*** bow down to them nor serve
17:35 nor bow down to them ***n*** serve
17:35 down to them nor serve them ***n***
17:38 ***n*** shall you fear other gods.
18: 5 ***n*** who were before him.
18:12 and they would neither hear ***n***
18:30 ***n*** let Hezekiah make you trust in
19:32 ***N*** shoot an arrow there,
19:32 ***N*** come before it with shield,
19:32 ***N*** build a siege mound against
23:22 ***n*** in all the days of the kings
23:25 ***n*** after him did any arise like
1 Chr 4:27 ***n*** did any of their families
17: 9 ***n*** shall the sons of wickedness
17:20 ***n*** is there any God besides
21:24 ***n*** offer burnt offerings with
22:13 do not fear ***n*** be dismayed.
27:24 ***n*** was the number recorded in
28:20 do not fear ***n*** be dismayed, for
28:20 He will not leave you ***n*** forsake
2 Chr 1:11 ***n*** have you asked long life—but
1:12 ***n*** shall any after you have the
6: 5 ***n*** did I choose any man to be a
15: 5 ***n*** to the one who came in, but
19: 7 ***n*** taking of bribes."
20:12 ***n*** do we know what to do, but
20:15 Do not be afraid ***n*** dismayed
25: 4 ***n*** shall the children be put to
30: 3 ***n*** had the people gathered
32: 7 do not be afraid ***n*** dismayed
32: 7 ***n*** before all the multitude that
Ezra 9:12 ***n*** take their daughters to your
10:13 ***N*** is this the work of one or
Neh 1: 7 ***n*** the ordinances which You
2:12 ***n*** was there any animal with me,
4:11 They will neither know ***n*** see
4:23 ***n*** the men of the guard who
5:14 neither I ***n*** my brothers ate the
7:61 their father's house ***n*** their
8: 9 do not mourn ***n*** weep." For all
9:19 ***N*** the pillar of fire by night,
9:31 did not utterly consume them ***n***
9:34 Neither our kings ***n*** our
9:34 Our priests ***n*** our fathers,
9:34 ***N*** heeded Your commandments and
9:35 ***N*** did they turn from their
10:30 ***n*** take their daughters for our
13:25 ***n*** take their daughters for your
Esth 2: 7 for she had neither father ***n***
4:16 neither eat ***n*** drink for three
Job 1:22 In all this Job did not sin ***n***
3: 4 ***N*** the light shine upon it.
3:10 ***N*** hide sorrow from my eyes.
3:26 ***n*** am I quiet; I have no rest,
5: 6 ***N*** does trouble spring from the
7:10 ***N*** shall his place know him
8:20 ***N*** will He uphold the
9:33 ***N*** is there any mediator between
14:12 They will not awake ***N*** be
15:29 ***N*** will his wealth continue,
15:29 ***N*** will his possessions
18:19 He has neither son ***n*** posterity
18:19 ***N*** any remaining in his
20: 9 ***N*** will his place behold him
24:13 They do not know its ways ***N***
27: 4 ***N*** my tongue utter deceit.
28: 7 ***N*** has the falcon's eye seen
28: 8 ***N*** has the fierce lion passed
28:13 ***N*** is it found in the land of
28:15 ***N*** can silver be weighed for
28:17 Neither gold ***n*** crystal can
28:17 ***N*** can it be exchanged for
28:19 ***N*** can it be valued in pure
32: 9 ***N*** do the aged always
32:21 ***N*** let me flatter any man.
33: 7 ***N*** will my hand be heavy on
34:12 ***N*** will the Almighty pervert
34:19 ***N*** does He regard the rich more
34:22 There is no darkness ***n*** shadow
35:13 ***N*** will the Almighty regard it.
35:15 ***N*** taken much notice of folly,
36:26 ***N*** can the number of His years
39:22 ***N*** does he turn back from the
39:24 ***N*** does he come to a halt
41:26 ***N*** does spear, dart, or
Ps 1: 1 ***N*** stands in the path of
1: 1 ***N*** sits in the seat of the
1: 5 ***N*** sinners in the congregation
5: 4 ***N*** shall evil dwell with You.
6: 1 ***N*** chasten me in Your hot
15: 3 ***N*** does evil to his neighbor,
15: 3 ***N*** does he take up a reproach
15: 5 ***N*** does he take a bribe against
16: 4 ***N*** take up their names on my
16:10 ***N*** will You allow Your Holy One
19: 3 There is no speech ***n*** language
22:24 For He has not despised ***n***
22:24 ***N*** has He hidden His face from
24: 4 ***N*** sworn deceitfully.
25: 7 ***n*** my transgressions; According
26: 4 ***N*** will I go in with
26: 9 ***N*** my life with bloodthirsty
27: 9 Do not leave me ***n*** forsake me,
28: 5 ***N*** the operation of His hands,
35:19 ***N*** let them wink with the eye
37: 1 ***N*** be envious of the workers of
37:25 ***N*** his descendants begging
37:33 ***N*** condemn him when he is
38: 1 ***N*** chasten me in Your hot
38: 3 ***N*** any health in my bones
40: 4 ***n*** such as turn aside to lies.
44: 3 ***N*** did their own arm save them;
44: 6 ***N*** shall my sword save me.
44:17 ***N*** have we dealt falsely with
44:18 ***N*** have our steps departed from
49: 7 ***N*** give to God a ransom for
50: 9 ***N*** goats out of your folds.
55:12 ***N*** is it one who hates me
59: 3 Not for my transgression ***n***
62:10 ***N*** vainly hope in robbery;
66:20 ***N*** His mercy from me!
69:15 ***N*** let the deep swallow me up;
73: 5 ***N*** are they plagued like other
74: 9 ***N*** is there any among us who
75: 6 neither from the east ***N*** from
75: 6 the east Nor from the west ***n***
78:37 ***N*** were they faithful in His
81: 9 ***N*** shall you worship any
82: 5 ***n*** do they understand; They
86: 8 ***N*** are there any works like
89:22 ***N*** the son of wickedness
89:33 ***N*** allow My faithfulness to
89:34 ***N*** alter the word that has gone
91: 5 ***N*** of the arrow that flies by
91: 6 ***N*** of the pestilence that
91: 6 ***N*** of the destruction that
91:10 ***N*** shall any plague come near
92: 6 ***N*** does a fool understand this.
94: 7 ***N*** does the God of Jacob
94:14 ***N*** will He forsake His
103: 9 ***N*** will He keep His anger
103:10 ***N*** punished us according to our
109:12 ***N*** let there be any to favor
115: 7 ***N*** do they mutter through their
115:17 ***N*** any who go down into
121: 4 Shall neither slumber ***n*** sleep.
121: 6 ***N*** the moon by night.
129: 7 ***N*** he who binds sheaves, his
131: 1 ***N*** my eyes lofty. Neither do I
131: 1 ***N*** with things too profound for
135:17 ***N*** is there any breath in
146: 3 ***N*** in a son of man, in whom
Prov 2:19 ***N*** do they regain the paths of
3:11 ***N*** detest His correction;
3:25 ***N*** of trouble from the wicked
4: 5 ***n*** turn away from the words of
5:13 ***N*** inclined my ear to those who
6: 4 ***N*** slumber to your eyelids.
6:25 ***N*** let her allure you with her
6:35 ***N*** will he be appeased though
15:12 ***N*** will he go to the wise.
17:26 ***N*** to strike princes for
22:22 ***N*** oppress the afflicted at the
23: 6 ***N*** desire his delicacies;
23:10 ***N*** enter the fields of the
24: 1 ***N*** desire to be with them;
24:19 ***N*** be envious of the wicked;
27:10 ***N*** go to your brother's house
27:24 ***N*** does a crown endure to all
30: 3 I neither learned wisdom ***N***
30: 8 Give me neither poverty ***n***
31: 3 ***N*** your ways to that which
31: 4 ***N*** for princes intoxicating
Eccl 1: 8 ***N*** the ear filled with hearing.
1:11 ***N*** will there be any
4: 8 He has neither son ***n*** brother.
4: 8 ***N*** is his eye satisfied with
5: 6 ***n*** say before the messenger of
5:10 ***N*** he who loves abundance, with
7:16 ***N*** be overly wise: Why should
7:17 ***N*** be foolish: Why should you
8:13 ***n*** will he prolong his days,
9: 1 People know neither love ***n***
9:11 ***N*** the battle to the strong,
9:11 ***N*** bread to the wise, Nor
9:11 ***N*** riches to men of
9:11 ***N*** favor to men of skill;
Song 2: 7 Do not stir up ***n*** awaken love
3: 5 Do not stir up ***n*** awaken love
8: 4 Do not stir up ***n*** awaken love
8: 7 ***N*** can the floods drown it.
Isa 1:23 ***N*** does the cause of the widow
3: 7 in my house is neither food ***n***
5:12 ***N*** consider the operation of
5:27 ***N*** will the belt on their loins
5:27 ***N*** the strap of their sandals
7: 7 ***N*** shall it come to pass.
7:12 ***n*** will I test the LORD!"
8:12 ***N*** be afraid of their threats,
8:12 threats, ***n*** be troubled.
9:13 ***N*** do they seek the LORD of
9:17 ***N*** have mercy on their
10: 7 ***N*** does his heart think so;
10:14 ***N*** opened his mouth with even
11: 3 ***N*** decide by the hearing of His

11: 9 They shall not hurt ***n*** destroy
13:20 ***N*** will it be settled from
13:20 ***N*** will the Arabian pitch tents
13:20 ***N*** will the shepherds make
16:10 ***N*** will there be shouting;
17: 8 ***N*** the wooden images nor the
17: 8 Nor the wooden images ***n*** the
22: 2 ***N*** dead in battle.
22:11 ***N*** did you have respect for Him
23: 4 ***n*** bring forth children;
23: 4 ***N*** bring up virgins."
23:18 it will not be treasured ***n*** laid
26:18 ***N*** have the inhabitants of the
28:27 ***N*** is a cartwheel rolled over
29:22 ***N*** shall his face now grow
31: 1 ***N*** seek the LORD!
31: 4 be afraid of their voice ***N*** be
32: 5 ***N*** the miser said to be
33:20 ***N*** will any of its cords be
33:21 ***N*** majestic ships pass by
35: 9 ***N*** shall any ravenous beast go
36:15 ***n*** let Hezekiah make you trust in
37:33 ***N*** shoot an arrow there, Nor
37:33 ***N*** come before it with shield,
37:33 ***N*** build a siege mound against
40:16 ***N*** its beasts sufficient for a
40:28 Neither faints ***n*** is weary.
42: 2 ***n*** raise His voice, Nor cause
42: 2 ***N*** cause His voice to be heard
42: 4 He will not fail ***n*** be
42: 8 ***N*** My praise to carved images.
42:24 ***N*** were they obedient to His
43: 2 ***N*** shall the flame scorch you.
43:10 ***N*** shall there be after Me.
43:18 ***N*** consider the things of old.
43:23 ***N*** have you honored Me with
43:23 ***N*** wearied you with incense.
43:24 ***N*** have you satisfied Me with
44: 8 ***n*** be afraid; Have I not told
44: 9 They neither see ***n*** know, that
44:18 They do not know ***n*** understand;
44:19 ***N*** is there knowledge nor
44:19 Nor is there knowledge ***n***
44:20 ***N*** say, "Is there not a lie
45:13 Not for price ***n*** reward,"
46: 7 yet it cannot answer ***N*** save
47: 7 ***N*** remember the latter end of
47: 8 ***N*** shall I know the loss of
47:14 ***N*** a fire to sit before!
48:19 would not have been cut off ***N***
49:10 They shall neither hunger ***n***
49:10 Neither heat ***n*** sun shall
50: 5 ***N*** did I turn away.
51: 7 ***N*** be afraid of their insults.
51:18 ***N*** is there any who takes
52:12 ***N*** go by flight; For the LORD
53: 9 ***N*** was any deceit in His
54: 9 angry with you, ***n*** rebuke you.
54:10 ***N*** shall My covenant of peace
55: 8 ***N*** are your ways My ways,"
56: 3 ***N*** let the eunuch say, "Here
57:11 ***N*** taken it to your heart?
57:16 ***N*** will I always be angry;
58:13 ***N*** finding your own pleasure,
58:13 ***N*** speaking your own words,
59: 1 ***N*** His ear heavy, That it
59: 4 ***N*** does any plead for truth.
59: 6 ***N*** will they cover themselves
59: 9 ***N*** does righteousness overtake
59:21 ***n*** from the mouth of your
59:21 ***n*** from the mouth of your
60:18 Neither wasting ***n*** destruction
60:19 ***N*** for brightness shall the
60:20 ***N*** shall your moon withdraw
62: 4 ***N*** shall your land any more be
64: 4 world Men have not heard ***n***
64: 4 ***N*** has the eye seen any God
64: 9 ***N*** remember iniquity forever;
65:19 ***N*** the voice of crying.
65:20 ***N*** an old man who has not
65:23 ***N*** bring forth children for
65:25 They shall not hurt ***n*** destroy
66:19 who have not heard My fame ***n***
Jer 3:16 ***n*** shall they remember it, nor
3:16 ***n*** shall they visit it, nor
3:16 ***n*** shall it be made anymore.
4:28 ***N*** will I turn back from it.
5:12 ***N*** shall we see sword or
5:15 ***N*** can you understand what they
6:15 ***N*** did they know how to blush.
6:19 ***N*** My law, but rejected it.
6:20 ***N*** your sacrifices sweet to
6:25 ***N*** walk by the way. Because of
7:16 ***n*** lift up a cry or prayer for
7:16 ***n*** make intercession to Me; for
7:28 voice of the LORD their God ***n***
7:31 ***n*** did it come into My heart.
8: 2 They shall not be gathered ***n***
8:12 ***N*** did they know how to blush.
8:13 ***N*** figs on the fig tree,
9:10 ***N*** can men hear the voice of
9:13 ***n*** walked according to it,
9:16 whom neither they ***n*** their
9:23 ***N*** let the rich man glory in
10: 5 ***N*** can they do any good."
13:14 I will not pity ***n*** spare nor have
13:14 I will not pity nor spare ***n*** have
14:13 ***n*** shall you have famine, but I
14:14 ***n*** spoken to them; they prophesy
14:16 them ***n*** their wives, their sons
14:16 their sons ***n*** their
15:10 ***N*** have men lent to me for
15:17 ***N*** did I rejoice; I sat alone
16: 2 ***n*** shall you have sons or
16: 4 they shall not be lamented ***n***
16: 5 ***n*** go to lament or bemoan them;
16: 6 ***n*** make themselves bald for
16: 7 ***N*** shall men break bread in
16: 7 ***n*** shall men give them the cup
16:13 neither you ***n*** your fathers; and
16:17 ***n*** is their iniquity hidden from
17: 8 ***N*** will cease from yielding
17:16 ***N*** have I desired the woeful
17:21 ***n*** bring it in by the gates of
17:22 ***n*** carry a burden out of your
17:22 ***n*** do any work, but hallow the
17:23 But they did not obey ***n*** incline
17:23 that they might not hear ***n***
18:18 ***n*** counsel from the wise, nor
18:18 ***n*** the word from the prophet.
18:23 ***N*** blot out their sin from Your
19: 4 ***n*** the kings of Judah have
19: 5 ***n*** did it come into My mind),
20: 9 ***N*** speak anymore in His name."
22: 3 ***n*** shed innocent blood in this
22:10 ***n*** bemoan him; Weep bitterly
22:10 ***N*** see his native country.
23: 4 ***n*** be dismayed, nor shall they
23: 4 ***n*** shall they be lacking," says
25: 4 but you have not listened ***n***
25:35 ***N*** the leaders of the flock to
29: 8 ***n*** listen to your dreams which
29:32 ***n*** shall he see the good that I
30:10 '***N*** be dismayed, O Israel;
32:35 ***n*** did it come into My mind that
33:18 ***n*** shall the priests, the
33:22 ***n*** the sand of the sea measured,
34:14 your fathers did not obey Me ***n***
35: 6 you ***n*** your sons, forever.
35: 7 ***n*** have any of these; but all
35: 9 ***n*** to build ourselves houses to
35: 9 ***n*** do we have vineyard, field,
35:15 inclined your ear, ***n*** obeyed Me.
36:24 ***n*** did they tear their garments,
36:24 the king ***n*** any of his servants
37: 2 But neither he ***n*** his servants
37: 2 neither he nor his servants ***n***
38:16 ***n*** will I give you into the hand
42:14 ***n*** hear the sound of the
42:14 ***n*** be hungry for bread, and
44: 3 they ***n*** you nor your fathers.
44: 3 they nor you ***n*** your fathers.
44:10 ***n*** have they feared; they have
46: 6 ***N*** the mighty man escape; They
48:11 ***N*** has he gone into captivity.
49:18 ***N*** shall a son of man dwell in
49:31 Which has neither gates ***n*** bars,
49:33 ***N*** son of man dwell in it."
50:39 ***N*** shall it be dwelt in from
50:40 ***N*** son of man dwell in it.
51: 5 ***N*** Judah, By his God, the LORD
51:26 you a stone for a corner ***N*** a
51:62 neither man ***n*** beast, but it
Lam 3:33 ***N*** grieve the children of men.
4:16 do not respect the priests ***N***
Ezek 2: 6 do not be afraid of them ***n*** be
3: 9 ***n*** be dismayed at their looks,
3:18 ***n*** speak to warn the wicked from
3:19 ***n*** from his wicked way, he shall
4:14 ***n*** has abominable flesh ever
5: 7 not walked in My statutes ***n***
5: 7 ***n*** even done according to the
5:11 ***n*** will I have any pity.
7: 4 ***N*** will I have pity; But I
7: 9 ***N*** will I have pity; I will
7:11 ***N*** shall there be wailing
7:12 ***N*** the seller mourn, For wrath
7:19 ***N*** fill their stomachs,
8:18 My eye will not spare ***n*** will I
9: 5 ***n*** have any pity.
9:10 ***n*** will I have pity, but I will
11:11 ***n*** shall you be the meat in its
11:12 not walked in My statutes ***n***
13: 9 ***n*** be written in the record of
13: 9 ***n*** shall they enter into the
13:15 ***n*** those who plastered it,
13:23 no longer envision futility ***n***
14:11 ***n*** be profaned anymore with all
14:16 would deliver neither sons ***n***
14:18 would deliver neither sons ***n***
14:20 would deliver neither son ***n***
16: 4 ***n*** were you washed in water to
16: 4 you were not rubbed with salt ***n***
16:16 should not happen, ***n*** be.
16:47 did not walk in their ways ***n***
16:48 neither your sister Sodom ***n*** her
17:17 ***N*** will Pharaoh with his mighty
18: 6 ***N*** lifted up his eyes to the
18: 6 ***N*** defiled his neighbor's wife,
18: 6 ***N*** approached a woman during
18: 8 If he has not exacted usury ***N***
18:15 ***N*** lifted his eyes to the idols
18:15 ***N*** defiled his neighbor's wife;
18:16 ***N*** withheld a pledge,
18:16 ***N*** robbed by violence,
18:20 ***n*** the father bear the guilt of
20: 8 ***n*** did they forsake the idols of
20:18 ***n*** observe their judgments, nor
20:18 ***n*** defile yourselves with their
20:44 according to your wicked ways ***n***
22:26 ***n*** have they made known the
23:27 ***N*** remember Egypt anymore.'
24:14 ***N*** will I spare, Nor will I
24:14 ***N*** will I relent; According to
24:16 yet you shall neither mourn ***n***
24:16 ***n*** shall your tears run down.
24:22 shall not cover your lips ***n***
24:23 you shall neither mourn ***n*** weep,
29:11 of man shall pass through it ***n***
29:18 yet neither he ***n*** his army
30:21 ***n*** a splint put on to bind it,
31:14 ***n*** set their tops among the
32:13 ***N*** shall the hooves of animals
33:12 ***n*** shall the righteous be able
34: 4 ***n*** have you healed those who
34: 4 ***n*** bound up the broken, nor
34: 4 ***n*** brought back what was driven
34: 4 ***n*** sought what was lost;
34: 8 ***n*** did My shepherds search for
34:28 ***n*** shall beasts of the land
34:29 ***n*** bear the shame of the
36:14 ***n*** bereave your nation
36:15 ***N*** will I let you hear the taunts
36:15 ***n*** bear the reproach of the
36:15 ***n*** shall you cause your nation
37:22 ***n*** shall they ever be divided
37:23 ***n*** with their detestable things,
37:23 ***n*** with any of their
38:11 and having neither bars ***n***
39:10 not take wood from the field ***n***
43: 7 they ***n*** their kings, by their
44:13 ***n*** come near any of My holy
44:13 ***n*** into the Most Holy Place;
44:20 neither shave their heads ***n***
Dan 1: 8 ***n*** with the wine which he drank;
3:18 ***n*** will we worship the gold
3:27 of their head was not singed ***n***
3:28 that they should not serve ***n***
5:10 ***n*** let your countenance change.
6: 4 ***n*** was there any error or fault
8: 4 ***n*** was there any that could
10: 3 ***n*** did I anoint myself at all,
10:17 ***n*** is any breath left in me."
11: 4 but not among his posterity ***n***
11: 6 and neither he ***n*** his authority
11:24 ***n*** his forefathers: he shall
11:37 the God of his fathers ***n*** the
11:37 ***n*** regard any god; for he shall
Hos 1: 7 ***N*** by sword or battle,
2: 2 ***n*** am I her Husband! Let her
3: 3 ***n*** shall you have a man—so, too,
4:14 ***N*** your brides when they commit
4:15 ***N*** go up to Beth Aven, Nor
4:15 ***N*** swear an oath, saying, 'As
5:13 ***N*** heal you of your wound.
7:10 ***N*** seek Him for all this.
9: 4 ***N*** shall their sacrifices be
14: 3 ***N*** will we say anymore to the
Joel 2: 2 ***N*** will there ever be any such
Am 2:14 ***N*** shall the mighty deliver
2:15 ***N*** shall he who rides a horse
5: 5 ***N*** enter Gilgal, Nor pass over
5: 5 ***N*** pass over to Beersheba;
5:22 ***N*** will I regard your fattened
7:14 ***N*** was I a son of a prophet,
8:11 ***N*** a thirst for water, But of
9:10 calamity shall not overtake ***n***
Ob 12 ***N*** should you have rejoiced
12 ***N*** should you have spoken
13 ***N*** laid hands on their
14 ***N*** should you have delivered up
Jon 3: 7 Let neither man ***n*** beast, herd
3: 7 herd ***n*** flock, taste anything;
4:10 ***n*** made it grow, which came up
Mic 2: 3 ***N*** shall you walk haughtily,
4:12 ***N*** do they understand His
5: 7 That tarry for no man ***N*** wait
Hab 3:17 ***N*** fruit be on the vines;
Zeph 1: 6 ***n*** inquired of Him."
1:12 ***N*** will He do evil.'
1:18 Neither their silver ***n*** their
3:13 ***N*** shall a deceitful tongue be
Zech 1: 4 they did not hear ***n*** heed Me,"
4: 6 Not by might ***n*** by power, but by
8:10 were no wages for man ***n*** any
11:16 ***n*** seek the young, nor heal
11:16 ***n*** heal those that are broken,
11:16 ***n*** feed those that still stand.
14: 7 Neither day ***n*** night. But at
Mal 1:10 ***N*** will I accept an offering from
2:13 ***N*** receive it with goodwill
3:11 ***N*** shall the vine fail to bear
4: 1 will leave them neither root ***n***
Mt 5:15 ***N*** do they light a lamp and put
5:35 ***n*** by the earth, for it is His
5:35 ***n*** by Jerusalem, for it is the
5:36 ***N*** shall you swear by your head,
6:20 where neither moth ***n*** rust
6:25 ***n*** about your body, what you
6:26 for they neither sow ***n*** reap nor
6:26 for they neither sow nor reap ***n***
6:28 they neither toil ***n*** spin;
7: 6 ***n*** cast your pearls before
7:18 ***n*** can a bad tree bear good
9:17 ***N*** do they put new wine into old
10: 9 Provide neither gold ***n*** silver
10: 9 neither gold nor silver ***n***
10:10 ***n*** bag for your journey, nor two
10:10 ***n*** two tunics, nor sandals, nor
10:10 ***n*** sandals, nor staffs; for a
10:10 ***n*** staffs; for a worker is
10:14 whoever will not receive you ***n***
10:24 ***n*** a servant above his master.
11:18 John came neither eating ***n***
11:27 ***N*** does anyone know the Father
12: 4 ***n*** for those who were with him,

12:19 He will not quarrel **n** cry
12:19 **N** will anyone hear His
13:13 **n** do they understand.
16:10 **N** the seven loaves of the four
22:16 **n** do You care about anyone, for
22:29 not knowing the Scriptures **n**
22:30 they neither marry **n** are given
22:46 **n** from that day on did anyone
23:13 **n** do you allow those who are
24:21 **n** ever shall be.
25:13 for you know neither the day **n**
Mk 4:22 **n** has anything been kept secret
6:11 whoever will not receive you **n**
8:17 Do you not yet perceive **n**
8:26 **n** tell anyone in the town."
12:21 **n** did he leave any offspring.
12:24 do not know the Scriptures **n**
12:25 they neither marry **n** are given
13:15 **n** enter to take anything out of
13:19 **n** ever shall be.
13:32 **n** the Son, but only the Father.
14:68 I neither know **n** understand what
Lk 1:15 and shall drink neither wine **n**
6:43 **n** does a bad tree bear good
6:44 **n** do they gather grapes from a
7:33 came neither eating bread **n**
8:17 **n** anything hidden that will
8:27 **n** did he live in a house but in
9: 3 neither staffs **n** bag nor bread
9: 3 neither staffs nor bag **n** bread
9: 3 staffs nor bag nor bread **n**
10: 4 **n** sandals; and greet no one
12: 2 **n** hidden that will not be
12:22 **n** about the body, what you will
12:24 for they neither sow **n** reap,
12:24 have neither storehouse **n** barn;
12:27 they neither toil **n** spin;
12:29 **n** have an anxious mind.
12:33 where no thief approaches **n**
14:12 **n** rich neighbors, lest they
14:35 is neither fit for the land **n**
16:26 **n** can those from there pass to
17:21 **n** will they say, 'See here!' or
18: 2 a judge who did not fear God **n**
18: 4 Though I do not fear God **n**
20:35 neither marry **n** are given in
20:36 **n** can they die anymore, for they
Jn 1:13 **n** of the will of the flesh, nor
1:13 **n** of the will of man, but of
1:25 **n** Elijah, nor the Prophet?"
1:25 **n** the Prophet?"
4:15 **n** come here to draw."
4:21 **n** in Jerusalem, worship the
5:37 **n** seen His form.
6:24 **n** His disciples, they also got
8:19 You know neither Me **n** My Father.
8:42 **n** have I come of Myself, but He
9: 3 Neither this man **n** his parents
11:50 **n** do you consider that it is
13:16 **n** is he who is sent greater
14:17 because it neither sees Him **n**
16: 3 have not known the Father **n** Me.
Acts 2:27 **N** will You allow Your
2:31 **n** did His flesh see corruption.
4:12 **N** is there salvation in any
4:18 them not to speak at all **n**
4:34 **N** was there anyone among them
8:21 You have neither part **n** portion
9: 9 and neither ate **n** drank.
13:27 **n** even the voices of the
15:10 which neither our fathers **n** we
17:25 **N** is He worshiped with men's
19:37 neither robbers of temples **n**
20:24 **n** do I count my life dear to
21:21 to circumcise their children **n**
23:12 that they would neither eat **n**
23:21 that they will neither eat **n**
24:12 temple disputing with anyone **n**
24:13 **N** can they prove the things of
24:18 neither with a mob **n** with
25: 8 **n** against the temple, nor
25: 8 **n** against Caesar have I
27:20 Now when neither sun **n** stars
28:21 **n** have any of the brethren who
Rom 1:21 **n** were thankful, but became
2:28 **n** is circumcision that which
8: 7 **n** indeed can be.
8:38 persuaded that neither death **n**
8:38 **n** angels nor principalities nor
8:38 nor angels **n** principalities nor
8:38 nor angels nor principalities **n**
8:38 **n** things present nor things to
8:38 nor things present **n** things to
8:39 **n** height nor depth, nor any
8:39 nor height **n** depth, nor any
8:39 **n** any other created thing,
9: 7 **n** are they all children
9:11 **n** having done any good or evil,
9:16 **n** of him who runs, but of God
14:21 is good neither to eat meat **n**
14:21 to eat meat nor drink wine **n**
1 Cor 2: 6 **n** of the rulers of this age,
2: 9 **n** ear heard, Nor have
2: 9 **N** have entered into the
2:14 **n** can he know them, because
3: 7 **n** he who waters, but God who
5: 8 **n** with the leaven of malice and
6: 9 **n** idolaters, nor adulterers,
6: 9 **n** adulterers, nor homosexuals,
6: 9 **n** homosexuals, nor sodomites,
6: 9 nor homosexuals, **n** sodomites,
6:10 **n** thieves, nor covetous, nor
6:10 **n** covetous, nor drunkards, nor
6:10 **n** drunkards, nor revilers, nor
6:10 **n** revilers, nor extortioners
6:10 **n** extortioners will inherit the
8: 8 **n** if we do not eat are we the
9:15 **n** have I written these things
10: 8 **N** let us commit sexual
10: 9 **n** let us tempt Christ, as some
10:10 **n** complain, as some of them also
11: 9 **N** was man created for the woman,
11:11 **n** woman independent of man, in
11:16 **n** do the churches of God.
12:21 **n** again the head to the feet,
15:50 **n** does corruption inherit
2 Cor 4: 2 not walking in craftiness **n**
7:12 **n** for the sake of him who
Gal 1: 1 an apostle (not from men **n**
1:12 **n** was I taught it, but it
1:17 **n** did I go up to Jerusalem to
3:28 There is neither Jew **n** Greek,
3:28 there is neither slave **n** free,
3:28 there is neither male **n** female;
5: 6 Jesus neither circumcision **n**
6:15 Jesus neither circumcision **n**
Eph 4:27 **n** give place to the devil.
5: 4 **n** foolish talking, nor coarse
5: 4 **n** coarse jesting, which are not
5: 5 **n** covetous man, who is an
Col 3:11 where there is neither Greek **n**
3:11 circumcised **n** uncircumcised,
3:11 slave **n** free, but Christ is
1 Th 2: 3 **n** was it in deceit.
2: 5 **n** a cloak for covetousness—God
2: 6 **N** did we seek glory from men,
5: 5 We are not of the night **n** of
2 Th 3: 8 **n** did we eat anyone's bread free
1 Tim 1: 4 **n** give heed to fables and
1: 7 neither what they say **n** the
5:22 **n** share in other people's sins;
6:17 **n** to trust in uncertain riches
2 Tim 1: 8 **n** of me His prisoner, but share
Heb 7: 3 neither beginning of days **n**
10: 8 **n** had pleasure in them"
12: 5 **N** be discouraged when you
13: 5 I will never leave you **n**
Jas 1:13 **n** does He Himself tempt anyone.
1 Pe 2:22 **N** was deceit found in
3:14 **n** be troubled."
5: 3 **n** as being lords over those
2 Pe 1: 8 you will be neither barren **n**
1 Jn 3: 6 sins has neither seen Him **n**
3:10 **n** is he who does not love his
2 Jn 10 receive him into your house **n**
Rev 3:15 that you are neither cold **n**
3:16 and neither cold **n** hot, I will
7:16 shall neither hunger anymore **n**
7:16 not strike them, **n** any heat;
9:20 which can neither see **n** hear
9:20 can neither see nor hear **n**
12: 8 **n** was a place found for them in
21: 4 more death **n** sorrow, nor crying
21: 4 **n** crying. There shall be no
22: 5 They need no lamp **n** light of

NORTH (137/129) NORTHERN, NORTHWARD

Gen 14:15 which is **n** of Damascus.
28:14 to the **n** and the south; and in
Ex 26:20 the **n** side, there shall be
26:35 shall put the table on the **n**
27:11 along the length of the **n** side
36:25 the **n** side, he made twenty
38:11 On the **n** side the hangings
40:22 on the **n** side of the
Lev 1:11 He shall kill it on the **n** side
Num 2:25 with Dan shall be on the **n**
3:35 These were to camp on the **n**
35: 5 and on the **n** side two thousand
Deut 3:27 eyes toward the west, the **n**,
Josh 8:11 the city and camped on the **n**
8:13 the army that was on the **n** of
11: 2 the kings who were from the **n**,
15: 6 up to Beth Hoglah and passed **n**
15:10 side of Mount Jearim on the **n**
16: 6 out toward the sea on the **n**
17: 9 of Manasseh was on the **n** side
17:10 was adjoining Asher on the **n**
18: 5 in their territory on the **n**.
18:12 Their border on the **n** side began
18:12 to the side of Jericho on the **n**,
18:16 Valley of the Rephaim on the **n**,
18:17 And it went around from the **n**,
18:18 it passed along toward the **n**
18:19 border passed along to the **n**
18:19 then the border ended at the **n**
19:14 border went around it on the **n**
24:30 on the **n** side of Mount Gaash.
Judg 2: 9 on the **n** side of Mount Gaash.
7: 1 of the Midianites was on the **n**
21:19 which is **n** of Bethel, on the
1 Ki 7:25 three looking toward the **n**,
2 Ki 16:14 and put it on the **n** side of the
1 Chr 9:24 directions: the east, west, **n**,
26:14 and his lot came out for the **N**
26:17 on the **n** four each day, on the
2 Chr 4: 4 three looking toward the **n**,
Job 26: 7 He stretches out the **n** over
37: 9 scattering winds of the **n**.
37:22 He comes from the **n** as golden
Ps 48: 2 Zion on the sides of the **n**,
89:12 The **n** and the south, You have
107: 3 From the **n** and from the south.
Prov 25:23 The **n** wind brings forth rain,
Eccl 1: 6 And turns around to the **n**;
11: 3 falls to the south or the **n**,
Song 4:16 O **n** wind, And come, O south!
Isa 14:13 On the farthest sides of the **n**;
14:31 For smoke will come from the **n**,
41:25 have raised up one from the **n**,
43: 6 I will say to the **n**,
49:12 Look! Those from the **n** and the
Jer 1:13 it is facing away from the **n**.
1:14 Out of the **n** calamity shall
1:15 of the kingdoms of the **n**,
3:12 these words toward the **n**,
3:18 out of the land of the **n** to
4: 6 will bring disaster from the **n**,
6: 1 disaster appears out of the **n**,
6:22 a people comes from the **n**
10:22 a great commotion out of the **n**
13:20 Those who come from the **n**.
16:15 Israel from the land of the **n**
23: 8 the house of Israel from the **n**
25: 9 take all the families of the **n**,
25:26 all the kings of the **n**,
31: 8 I will bring them from the **n**
46: 6 stumble and fall Toward the **n**,
46:10 hosts has a sacrifice In the **n**
46:20 comes, it comes from the **n**.
46:24 hand Of the people of the **n**.
47: 2 waters rise out of the **n**,
50: 3 For out of the **n** a nation comes
50: 9 of great nations from the **n**
50:41 a people shall come from the **n**,
51:48 shall come to her from the **n**,
Ezek 1: 4 was coming out of the **n**,
8: 3 to the door of the **n** gate of
8: 5 lift your eyes now toward the **n**.
8: 5 I lifted my eyes toward the **n**,
8: 5 **n** of the altar gate, was this
8:14 me to the door of the **n** gate
9: 2 the upper gate, which faces **n**,
16:46 with her daughters to the **n** of
20:47 faces from the south to the **n**
21: 4 all flesh from south to **n**,
26: 7 bring against Tyre from the **n**
32:30 are the princes of the **n**,
38: 6 of Togarmah from the far **n**
38:15 your place out of the far **n**,
39: 2 bringing you up from the far **n**,
40:19 toward the east and the **n**.
40:20 was also a gateway facing **n**,
40:35 Then he brought me to the **n**
40:44 and the other facing **n** at the
40:46 The chamber which faces **n** is
41:11 one door toward the **n** and
42: 1 court, by the way toward the **n**;
42: 1 the building toward the **n**.
42: 2 fifty cubits), was the **n** door.
42: 4 cubit; and their doors faced **n**.
42:11 which were toward the **n**;
42:13 The **n** chambers and the south
42:17 He measured the **n** side, five
44: 4 He brought me by way of the **n**
46: 9 whoever enters by way of the **n**
46: 9 shall go out by way of the **n**
46:19 priests which face toward the **n**;
47: 2 brought me out by way of the **n**
47:15 the border of the land on the **n**:
47:17 of Damascus; and as for the **n**,
47:17 This is the **n** side.
48:10 on the **n** twenty-five thousand
48:16 the **n** side four thousand five
48:17 to the **n** two hundred and fifty
48:30 On the **n** side, measuring four
Dan 11: 6 shall go to the king of the **N**
11: 7 fortress of the king of the **N**,
11: 8 years than the king of the **N**.
11: 9 Also the king of the **N**
11:11 him, with the king of the **N**,
11:13 For the king of the **N** will
11:15 So the king of the **N** shall come
11:40 and the king of the **N** shall
11:44 news from the east and the **n**
Am 8:12 And from **n** to east; They
Zeph 2:13 out His hand against the **n**,
Zech 2: 6 up! Flee from the land of the **n**,
6: 6 black horses is going to the **n**
6: 8 those who go toward the **n**
6: 8 rest to My Spirit in the **n**
14: 4 shall move toward the **n**
Lk 13:29 from the **n** and the south, and
Rev 21:13 the east, three gates on the **n**,

NORTHERN (9/9) NORTH

Num 34: 7 And this shall be your **n**
34: 9 This shall be your **n** border.
Josh 15: 5 And the border on the **n** quarter
Jer 15:12 The **n** iron and the bronze?
Ezek 40:23 inner court was opposite the **n**
40:40 up to the entrance of the **n**
40:44 south at the side of the **n**
48: 1 From the **n** border along the
Joel 2:20 will remove far from you the **n**

NORTHWARD (13/13) NORTH

Gen 13:14 from the place where you are—**n**,
Deut 2: 3 mountain long enough; turn **n**.
Josh 13: 3 as far as the border of Ekron **n**
15: 7 and it turned **n** toward Gilgal,
15: 8 end of the Valley of Rephaim **n**.

N

15:11 went out to the side of Ekron ***n***.
17:10 ***n*** it was Manasseh's, and the
19:27 then ***n*** beyond Beth Emek and
1 Sam 14: 5 The front of one faced ***n***
Ezek 47:17 and as for the north, ***n***,
48: 1 Enan, the border of Damascus ***n***,
48:31 of Israel), the three gates ***n***:
Dan 8: 4 saw the ram pushing westward, ***n***,

NORTHWEST (1/1)

Acts 27:12 toward the southwest and ***n***,

NOSE (15/14) NOSES

Gen 24:22 that the man took a golden ***n***
24:30 when he saw the ***n*** ring, and the
24:47 So I put the ***n*** ring on her
24:47 So I put the nose ring on her ***n***
Ex 35:22 and brought earrings and ***n***
2 Ki 19:28 I will put My hook in your ***n***
Job 40:24 Or one pierces his ***n*** with a
41: 2 you put a reed through his ***n***,
Prov 30:33 And wringing the ***n*** produces
Song 7: 4 Your ***n*** is like the tower of
Isa 3:21 the rings; The ***n*** jewels,
37:29 I will put My hook in your ***n***
Ezek 8:17 they put the branch to their ***n***.
16:12 "And I put a jewel in your ***n***,
23:25 They shall remove your ***n*** and

NOSES (1/1) NOSE

Ps 115: 6 *N* they have, but they do not

NOSTRILS (14/14)

Gen 2: 7 and breathed into his ***n*** the
7:22 All in whose ***n*** was the breath
Ex 15: 8 And with the blast of Your ***n***
Num 11:20 until it comes out of your ***n***
2 Sam 22: 9 Smoke went up from His ***n***,
22:16 blast of the breath of His ***n***.
Job 27: 3 And the breath of God in my ***n***,
41:20 Smoke goes out of his ***n***,
Ps 18: 8 Smoke went up from His ***n***,
18:15 blast of the breath of Your ***n***.
Isa 2:22 Whose breath is in his ***n***;
65: 5 These are smoke in My ***n***,
Lam 4:20 The breath of our ***n***,
Am 4:10 your camps come up into your ***n***;

NOT (6474/5488) See APPENDIX

NOTABLE (5/5) NOTE

2 Ki 4: 8 where there was a ***n*** woman, and
Dan 8: 5 and the goat had a ***n*** horn
8: 8 and in place of it four ***n*** ones
Am 6: 1 *N* persons in the chief nation,
Acts 4:16 that a ***n*** miracle has been done

NOTE (15/15) NOTABLE, NOTICE

Num 32:23 you do not do so, then take ***n***,
Judg 9:31 Take ***n***! Gaal the son of Ebed and
1 Sam 12:13 you have desired. And take ***n***,
19:19 was told Saul, saying, "Take ***n***,
24: 1 Take ***n***! David is in the
2 Sam 3:36 Now all the people took ***n*** of
13:24 the king and said, "Kindly ***n***,
1 Ki 20:22 strengthen yourself; take ***n***,
2 Chr 16:11 *N* that the acts of Asa, first
Job 23: 6 No! But He would take ***n*** of
Isa 30: 8 And ***n*** it on a scroll, That it
Rom 16: 7 who are of ***n*** among the
16:17 ***n*** those who cause divisions and
Phil 3:17 and ***n*** those who so walk, as you
2 Th 3:14 ***n*** that person and do not keep

NOTED (2/2)

Dan 10:21 But I will tell you what is ***n*** in
Lk 14: 7 when He ***n*** how they chose the

NOTHING (286/280)

Gen 11: 6 now ***n*** that they propose to do
14:23 "that I will take ***n***,
19: 8 only do ***n*** to these men, since
26:29 and since we have done ***n*** to you
29:15 you therefore serve me for ***n***?
40:15 and also I have done ***n*** here
47:18 There is ***n*** left in the sight of
Ex 9: 4 So ***n*** shall die of all that
10:15 So there remained ***n*** green on
12:20 You shall eat ***n*** leavened; in all
16:18 he who gathered much had ***n*** left
21: 2 he shall go out free and pay ***n***.
22: 3 full restitution; if he has ***n***,
Num 6: 4 his separation he shall eat ***n***
11: 6 there is ***n*** at all except this
16:26 of these wicked men! Touch ***n***
20:19 through on foot, ***n*** more."
22:16 Please let ***n*** hinder you from
Deut 2: 7 with you; you have lacked ***n***.
8: 9 in which you will lack ***n***;
15: 9 poor brother and you give him ***n***,
20:16 you shall let ***n*** that breathes
22:26 But you shall do ***n*** to the young
28:55 because he has ***n*** left in the
28:63 destroy you and bring you to ***n***;
Josh 11:15 He left ***n*** undone of all that

Judg 7:14 This is ***n*** else but the sword of
14: 6 though he had ***n*** in his hand.
18: 9 is very good. Would you do ***n***?
1 Sam 3:18 and hid ***n*** from him. And he
12:21 or deliver, for they are ***n***.
14: 6 For ***n*** restrains the LORD from
20: 2 my father will do ***n*** either
22:15 For your servant knew ***n*** of all
25:21 so that ***n*** was missed of all
25:36 drunk; therefore she told him ***n***,
27: 1 There is ***n*** better for me than
30:19 And ***n*** of theirs was lacking,
2 Sam 12: 3 "But the poor man had ***n***,
18:13 For there is ***n*** hidden from the
19:10 why do you say ***n*** about bringing
24:24 God with that which costs me ***n***.
1 Ki 8: 9 *N* was in the ark except the two
10: 3 there was ***n*** so difficult for
10:20 ***n*** like this had been made for
10:21 for this was accounted as ***n*** in
11:22 country?" So he answered, "*N*,
18:43 and said, "There is ***n***.
22:16 you swear that you tell me ***n***
2 Ki 4: 2 Your maidservant has ***n*** in the
4:41 And there was ***n*** harmful in
5:16 whom I stand, I will receive ***n***.
10:10 Know now that ***n*** shall fall to
20:13 There was ***n*** in his house or in
20:15 there is ***n*** among my treasures
20:17 ***n*** shall be left,' says the
1 Chr 21:24 with that which costs me ***n***.
2 Chr 5:10 *N* was in the ark except the two
9: 2 there was ***n*** so difficult for
9:19 ***n*** like this had been made for
9:20 for this was accounted as ***n*** in
14:11 it is ***n*** for You to help,
18:15 you swear that you tell me ***n***
30:26 there had been ***n*** like this in
Ezra 4: 3 You may do ***n*** with us to build a
Neh 2: 2 This is ***n*** but sorrow of
4:15 God had brought their plot to ***n***,
5: 8 they were silenced and found ***n***
5:12 and will require ***n*** from them;
8:10 portions to those for whom ***n***
9:21 the wilderness, They lacked ***n***;
Esth 2:15 she requested ***n*** but what Hegai
5:13 "Yet all this avails me ***n***,
6: 3 *N* has been done for him."
6:10 within the king's gate! Leave ***n***
Job 1: 9 said, "Does Job fear God for ***n***?
5:24 visit your dwelling and find ***n***
6:21 For now you are ***n***,
8: 9 born yesterday, and know ***n***,
8:22 of the wicked will come to ***n***.
20:21 *N* is left for him to eat
24:25 And make my speech worth ***n***?
26: 7 He hangs the earth on ***n***.
34: 9 It profits a man ***n*** That he
37:19 For we can prepare ***n*** because
41:33 On earth there is ***n*** like him,
Ps 16: 2 My goodness is ***n*** apart from
17: 3 have tried me and have found ***n***;
19: 6 And there is ***n*** hidden from its
33:10 the counsel of the nations to ***n***;
39: 5 And my age is as ***n*** before
44:12 Your people for next to ***n***,
49:17 when he dies he shall carry ***n***
69: 4 Though I have stolen ***n***,
101: 3 I will set ***n*** wicked before my
119:165 And ***n*** causes them to stumble.
Prov 8: 8 *N* crooked or perverse is in
9:13 She is simple, and knows ***n***.
10: 2 of wickedness profit ***n***,
13: 4 a lazy man desires, and has ***n***;
13: 7 makes himself rich, yet has ***n***;
13:10 By pride comes ***n*** but strife,
20: 4 beg during harvest and have ***n***.
20:14 "It is good for ***n***,
22:27 If you have ***n*** with which to
29:24 tell the truth, but reveals ***n***.
Eccl 1: 9 And there is ***n*** new under the
2:24 *N* is better for a man than
3:12 I know that ***n*** is better for
3:14 *N* can be added to it,
3:14 And ***n*** taken from it. God does
3:22 So I perceived that ***n*** is better
5:14 there is ***n*** in his hand.
5:15 And he shall take ***n*** from his
6: 2 so that he lacks ***n*** for himself
7:14 So that man can find out ***n***
8: 5 his command will experience ***n***
8:15 because a man has ***n*** better
9: 5 will die; But the dead know ***n***,
Isa 8:10 together, but it will come to ***n***;
15: 6 there is ***n*** green.
29:20 terrible one is brought to ***n***,
34:12 and all its princes shall be ***n***.
39: 2 There was ***n*** in his house or in
39: 4 there is ***n*** among my treasures
39: 6 ***n*** shall be left,' says the
40:17 nations before Him are as ***n***,
40:17 are counted by Him less than ***n***
40:23 He brings the princes to ***n***;
41:11 disgraced; They shall be as ***n***,
41:12 war against you Shall be as ***n***,
41:24 Indeed you are ***n***,
41:24 nothing, And your work is ***n***;
41:29 worthless; Their works are ***n***;
44:10 an image That profits him ***n***?
49: 4 I have spent my strength for ***n***
52: 3 have sold yourselves for ***n***,
52: 5 My people are taken away for ***n***?

Jer 10:24 anger, lest You bring me to ***n***.
13: 7 ruined. It was profitable for ***n***.
13:10 sash which is profitable for ***n***.
22:13 without wages And gives him ***n***
22:17 eyes and your heart are for ***n***
32:17 There is ***n*** too hard for You.
32:23 They have done ***n*** of all that
38: 5 For the king can do ***n*** against
38:14 Hide ***n*** from me."
39:10 the poor people, who had ***n***,
42: 4 I will keep ***n*** back from you."
48:30 His lies have made ***n*** right.
50:26 Let ***n*** of her be left.
Lam 1:12 Is it ***n*** to you, all you who
Ezek 13: 3 own spirit and have seen ***n***!
14:23 shall know that I have done ***n***
21:26 *N* shall remain the same.
Dan 4:35 of the earth are reputed as ***n***;
Joel 2: 3 Surely ***n*** shall escape them.
Am 3: 4 of his den, if he has caught ***n***?
3: 5 if it has caught ***n*** at all?
3: 7 Surely the Lord GOD does ***n***,
5: 5 And Bethel shall come to ***n***.
Mic 3: 5 war against him Who puts ***n***
Zeph 2:11 For He will reduce to ***n*** all
Hag 2: 3 is this not in your eyes as ***n***?
Mt 5:13 It is then good for ***n*** but to be
10:26 For there is ***n*** covered that
15:32 with Me three days and have ***n***
17:20 and ***n*** will be impossible for
21:19 He came to it and found ***n*** on it
23:16 swears by the temple, it is ***n***;
23:18 swears by the altar, it is ***n***;
26:62 said to Him, "Do You answer ***n***?
27:12 and elders, He answered ***n***.
27:19 Have ***n*** to do with that just Man,
Mk 1:44 See that you say ***n*** to anyone;
4:22 For there is ***n*** hidden which will
6: 8 He commanded them to take ***n*** for
6:36 for they have ***n*** to eat."
7:15 There is ***n*** that enters a man
8: 1 being very great and having ***n***
8: 2 with Me three days and have ***n***
9:29 This kind can come out by ***n*** but
11:13 He found ***n*** but leaves, for it
14:60 saying, "Do You answer ***n***?
14:61 He kept silent and answered ***n***.
15: 3 many things, but He answered ***n***.
15: 4 saying, "Do You answer ***n***?
15: 5 But Jesus still answered ***n***,
16: 8 And they said ***n*** to anyone, for
Lk 1:37 For with God ***n*** will be
4: 2 And in those days He ate ***n***,
5: 5 toiled all night and caught ***n***;
6:35 hoping for ***n*** in return; and
6:49 But he who heard and did ***n*** is
7:42 And when they had ***n*** with which
8:17 For ***n*** is secret that will not be
9: 3 Take ***n*** for the journey, neither
10:19 and ***n*** shall by any means hurt
11: 6 and I have ***n*** to set before
12: 2 For there is ***n*** covered that will
22:35 anything?" So they said, "*N*.
23: 9 words, but He answered him ***n***.
23:15 and indeed ***n*** deserving of death
23:41 but this Man has done ***n***
Jn 1: 3 and without Him ***n*** was made that
3:27 A man can receive ***n*** unless it
4:11 You have ***n*** to draw with, and
5:19 the Son can do ***n*** of Himself,
5:30 "I can of Myself do ***n***.
6:12 so that ***n*** is lost."
6:39 He has given Me I should lose ***n***,
6:63 gives life; the flesh profits ***n***.
7:26 and they say ***n*** to Him. Do the
8:28 and that I do ***n*** of Myself; but
8:54 I honor Myself, My honor is ***n***.
9:33 not from God, He could do ***n***.
11:49 You know ***n*** at all,
12:19 that you are accomplishing ***n***.
14:30 and he has ***n*** in Me.
15: 5 for without Me you can do ***n***.
16:23 in that day you will ask Me ***n***.
16:24 Until now you have asked ***n*** in My
18:20 and in secret I have said ***n***.
21: 3 and that night they caught ***n***.
Acts 4:14 they could say ***n*** against it.
5:36 were scattered and came to ***n***.
5:38 is of men, it will come to ***n***;
10:20 and go with them, doubting ***n***;
11: 8 Lord! For ***n*** common or unclean
11:12 me to go with them, doubting ***n***.
17:21 there spent their time in ***n***
19:36 you ought to be quiet and do ***n***
20:20 how I kept back ***n*** that was
21:24 informed concerning you are ***n***,
23:14 a great oath that we will eat ***n***
23:29 but had ***n*** charged against him
25:11 but if there is ***n*** in these
25:25 I found that he had committed ***n***
25:26 I have ***n*** certain to write to my
26:31 This man is doing ***n*** deserving of
27:33 without food, and eaten ***n***.
28:17 though I have done ***n*** against
Rom 7:18 in my flesh) ***n*** good dwells;
14:14 Lord Jesus that there is ***n***
1 Cor 1:19 And bring to ***n*** the
1:28 to bring to ***n*** the things that
2: 6 this age, who are coming to ***n***.
4: 4 For I know ***n*** against myself, yet
4: 5 Therefore judge ***n*** before the
7:19 Circumcision is ***n*** and

7:19 nothing and uncircumcision is **n**,
8: 2 he knows **n** yet as he ought to
8: 4 we know that an idol is **n** in
9:16 I have **n** to boast of, for
11:22 God and shame those who have **n**?
13: 2 but have not love, I am **n**.
13: 3 have not love, it profits me **n**.
2 Cor 6:10 making many rich; as having **n**,
7: 9 might suffer loss from us in **n**.
8:15 who gathered much had **n**
12:11 for in **n** was I behind the most
12:11 eminent apostles, though I am **n**.
13: 8 For we can do **n** against the
Gal 2: 6 to be something added **n** to
5: 2 Christ will profit you **n**.
6: 3 to be something, when he is **n**,
Phil 1:20 expectation and hope that in **n**
2: 3 Let **n** be done through selfish
4: 6 Be anxious for **n**,
1 Th 4:12 and that you may lack **n**.
1 Tim 4: 4 and **n** is to be refused if it is
5:21 doing **n** with partiality.
6: 4 he is proud, knowing **n**,
6: 7 For we brought **n** into this
6: 7 it is certain we can carry **n**
Titus 1:15 are defiled and unbelieving **n**
2: 8 having **n** evil to say of you.
3:13 haste, that they may lack **n**.
Phm 1:14 your consent I wanted to do **n**,
Heb 2: 8 He left **n** that is not put
7:14 of which tribe Moses spoke **n**
7:19 for the law made **n** perfect;
Jas 1: 4 perfect and complete, lacking **n**.
3 Jn 7 taking **n** from the Gentiles.
Rev 3:17 wealthy, and have need of **n**'—
18:17 such great riches came to **n**.

NOTICE (10/10) NOTE, UNNOTICED

Ruth 2:10 that you should take **n** of me,
2:19 Blessed be the one who took **n**
3: 4 that you shall **n** the place
2 Sam 20:10 But Amasa did not **n** the sword
1 Ki 20: 7 of the land, and said, "**N**,
2 Ki 2:19 city said to Elisha, "Please **n**,
2 Chr 19:11 'And take **n**: Amariah the
Job 35:15 Nor taken much **n** of folly,
Isa 58: 3 our souls, and You take no **n**?
Acts 18:17 But Gallio took no **n** of these

NOTORIOUS (1/1)

Mt 27:16 And at that time they had a **n**

NOTWITHSTANDING (3/3)

Ex 16:20 **N** they did not heed Moses.
21:21 '**N**, if he remains alive
Ezek 20:21 '**N**, the children rebelled

NOUGHT (KJV) See DISREPUTE, FREE (OF CHARGE), NOTHING

NOURISHED (6/6) NOURISHES

2 Sam 12: 3 lamb which he had bought and **n**;
Isa 1: 2 I have **n** and brought up
Ezek 19: 2 Among the young lions she **n**
Col 2:19 **n** and knit together by joints
1 Tim 4: 6 **n** in the words of faith and of
Rev 12:14 where she is **n** for a time and

NOURISHER (1/1) NOURISHES

Ruth 4:15 you a restorer of life and a **n**

NOURISHES (2/2) NOURISHED, NOURISHER

Isa 44:14 and the rain **n** it.
Eph 5:29 but **n** and cherishes it, just as

NOURISHMENT (2/2)

Prov 27:27 And the **n** of your
Acts 27:34 I urge you to take **n**,

NOVICE (1/1)

1 Tim 3: 6 not a **n**, lest being puffed up

NOW (2142/2106) See APPENDIX

NOWADAYS (1/1)

1 Sam 25:10 There are many servants **n** who

NOWHERE (4/4)

1 Sam 10:14 When we saw that they were **n**
Job 6:18 They go **n** and perish.
Mt 8:20 but the Son of Man has **n** to lay
Lk 9:58 but the Son of Man has **n** to lay

NUDITY (1/1)

Isa 57: 8 Where you saw their **n**.

NUMBER (174/162) NUMBERED, NUMEROUS

Gen 13:16 so that if a man could **n** the
15: 5 the stars if you are able to **n**
26:14 of herds and a great **n** of
34:30 and since I am few in **n**,
47:12 according to the **n** in their
Ex 12: 4 take it according to the **n** of
16:16 according to the **n** of
23:26 I will fulfill the **n** of your
30:12 children of Israel for their **n**,
30:12 when you **n** them, that there may
30:12 plague among them when you **n**
Lev 25:15 According to the **n** of years
25:15 and according to the **n** of years
25:16 and according to the fewer **n** of
25:16 to you according to the **n** of
25:50 shall be according to the **n** of
26:22 and make you few in **n**;
Num 1: 2 according to the **n** of names,
1: 3 You and Aaron shall **n** them by
1:18 according to the **n** of names,
1:20 according to the **n** of names,
1:22 according to the **n** of names,
1:24 according to the **n** of names,
1:26 according to the **n** of names,
1:28 according to the **n** of names,
1:30 according to the **n** of names,
1:32 according to the **n** of names,
1:34 according to the **n** of names,
1:36 according to the **n** of names,
1:38 according to the **n** of names,
1:40 according to the **n** of names,
1:42 according to the **n** of names,
1:49 tribe of Levi you shall not **n**,
3:15 **N** the children of Levi by their
3:15 you shall **n** every male from a
3:22 according to the **n** of all the
3:28 According to the **n** of all the
3:34 according to the **n** of all the
3:40 **N** all the firstborn males of the
3:40 and take the **n** of their names.
3:43 according to the **n** of names
3:46 who are more than the **n** of the
3:48 with which the excess **n** of them
4:23 you shall **n** them, all who enter
4:29 you shall **n** them by their
4:30 you shall **n** them, everyone who
14:29 according to your entire **n**,
14:34 According to the **n** of the days
15:12 According to the **n** that you
15:12 everyone according to their **n**.
23:10 Or **n** one-fourth of Israel?
26:53 according to the **n** of names.
29:18 and for the lambs, by their **n**,
29:21 and for the lambs, by their **n**,
29:24 and for the lambs, by their **n**,
29:27 and for the lambs, by their **n**,
29:30 and for the lambs, by their **n**,
29:33 and for the lambs, by their **n**,
29:37 and for the lambs, by their **n**,
31:36 was in **n** three hundred and
Deut 4:27 and you will be left few in **n**
7: 7 you because you were more in **n**
25: 2 with a certain **n** of blows.
26: 5 Egypt and dwelt there, few in **n**;
28:62 "You shall be left few in **n**,
32: 8 peoples According to the **n** of
Josh 4: 5 according to the **n** of the
4: 8 according to the **n** of the
Judg 6: 5 and their camels were without **n**;
7: 6 And the **n** of those who lapped,
7:12 their camels were without **n**,
21:23 took enough wives for their **n**
1 Sam 6: 4 according to the **n** of the
6:18 according to the **n** of all the
2 Sam 2:15 they arose and went over by **n**,
15:12 continually increased in **n**.
21:20 on each foot, twenty-four in **n**;
24: 1 **n** Israel and Judah."
24: 2 that I may know the **n** of the
24: 9 Joab gave the sum of the **n** of
1 Ki 18:31 according to the **n** of the
1 Chr 7: 2 their **n** in the days of David
7:40 their **n** was twenty-six
11:11 And this is the **n** of the mighty
16:19 When you were few in **n**,
21: 1 and moved David to **n** Israel.
21: 2 **n** Israel from Beersheba to Dan,
21: 2 and bring the **n** of them to me
21: 5 Joab gave the sum of the **n** of
23: 3 and the **n** of individual males
23:24 counted individually by the **n**
23:31 by **n** according to the ordinance
25: 1 And the **n** of the skilled men
25: 7 So the **n** of them, with their
27: 1 of Israel, according to their **n**,
27:23 But David did not take the **n** of
27:24 nor was the **n** recorded in the
2 Chr 12: 3 and people without **n** who came
26:11 according to the **n** on their
26:12 The total **n** of chief officers of
29:32 And the **n** of the burnt offerings
30: 3 because a sufficient **n** of
30:24 and a great **n** of priests
35: 7 to the **n** of thirty thousand, as
Ezra 1: 9 This is the **n** of them: thirty
2: 2 The **n** of the men of the people
3: 4 daily burnt offerings in the **n**
6:17 according to the **n** of the
8:34 with the **n** and weight of
Neh 7: 7 The **n** of the men of the people
Esth 9:11 On that day the **n** of those who
Job 1: 5 offerings according to the **n**
3: 6 May it not come into the **n** of
5: 9 Marvelous things without **n**.
9:10 Yes, wonders without **n**.
14: 5 The **n** of his months is with
14:16 For now You **n** my steps, But do
15:20 And the **n** of years is hidden
21:21 When the **n** of his months is
25: 3 Is there any **n** to His armies?
31:37 I would declare to Him the **n** of
36:26 Nor can the **n** of His years be
38:21 Or because the **n** of your days
38:37 Who can **n** the clouds by wisdom?
39: 2 Can you **n** the months that they
Ps 56: 8 You **n** my wanderings; Put my
90:12 So teach us to **n** our days,
105:12 When they were few in **n**,
105:34 came, Young locusts without **n**,
139:18 they would be more in **n** than
147: 4 He counts the **n** of the stars;
Song 6: 8 And virgins without **n**.
Isa 10:19 his forest Will be so few in **n**
21:17 and the remainder of the **n** of
40:26 Who brings out their host by **n**;
65:12 Therefore I will **n** you for the
Jer 2:28 For according to the **n** of
2:32 forgotten Me days without **n**.
11:13 For according to the **n** of your
11:13 and according to the **n** of the
44:28 Yet a small **n** who escape the
Ezek 4: 4 According to the **n** of the days
4: 5 according to the **n** of the days,
4: 9 During the **n** of days that you
5: 3 You shall also take a small **n** of
Dan 9: 2 understood by the books the **n**
11:23 become strong with a small **n**
Hos 1:10 Yet the **n** of the children of
Joel 1: 6 My land, Strong, and without **n**;
Nah 3: 3 A great **n** of bodies,
Lk 5: 6 they caught a great **n** of fish,
5:29 And there were a great **n** of tax
Jn 6:10 in **n** about five thousand.
Acts 1:15 disciples (altogether the **n** of
4: 4 and the **n** of the men came to be
5:36 A **n** of men, about four hundred,
6: 1 when the **n** of the disciples
6: 7 and the **n** of the disciples
11:21 and a great **n** believed and
16: 5 and increased in **n** daily.
Rom 9:27 Though the **n** of the
1 Tim 5: 9 years old be taken into the **n**,
Rev 5:11 and the **n** of them was ten
6:11 until both the **n** of their
7: 4 And I heard the **n** of those who
7: 9 multitude which no one could **n**,
9:16 Now the **n** of the army of the
9:16 I heard the **n** of them.
13:17 or the **n** of his name.
13:18 understanding calculate the **n**
13:18 for it is the **n** of a man: His
13:18 His **n** is 666.
15: 2 over his mark and over the **n**
20: 8 whose **n** is as the sand of the

NUMBERED (121/107) NUMBER

Gen 13:16 descendants also could be **n**.
32:12 which cannot be **n** for
Ex 30:13 everyone among those who are **n**
30:14 included among those who are **n**,
38:25 silver from those who were **n**
Num 1:19 so he **n** them in the Wilderness
1:21 those who were **n** of the tribe of
1:22 house, of those who were **n**,
1:23 those who were **n** of the tribe of
1:25 those who were **n** of the tribe of
1:27 those who were **n** of the tribe of
1:29 those who were **n** of the tribe of
1:31 those who were **n** of the tribe of
1:33 those who were **n** of the tribe of
1:35 those who were **n** of the tribe of
1:37 those who were **n** of the tribe of
1:39 those who were **n** of the tribe of
1:41 those who were **n** of the tribe of
1:43 those who were **n** of the tribe of
1:44 These are the ones who were **n**,
1:44 whom Moses and Aaron **n**,
1:45 So all who were **n** of the
1:46 all who were **n** were six hundred
1:47 But the Levites were not **n**
2: 4 And his army was **n** at
2: 6 And his army was **n** at fifty-four
2: 8 And his army was **n** at
2: 9 All who were **n** according to
2:11 And his army was **n** at forty-six
2:13 And his army was **n** at fifty-nine
2:15 And his army was **n** at forty-five
2:16 All who were **n** according to
2:19 And his army was **n** at forty
2:21 And his army was **n** at thirty-two
2:23 And his army was **n** at
2:24 All who were **n** according to
2:26 And his army was **n** at sixty-two
2:28 And his army was **n** at forty-one
2:30 And his army was **n** at
2:31 All who were **n** of the forces
2:32 are the ones who were **n** of
2:32 All who were **n** according to
2:33 But the Levites were not **n** among
3:16 So Moses **n** them according to the
3:22 Those who were **n**, according
3:22 of those who were **n** there were
3:34 And those who were **n**,
3:39 All who were **n** of the Levites,
3:39 whom Moses and Aaron **n** at the

3:42 So Moses **n** all the firstborn
3:43 of those who were **n** of them,
4:34 leaders of the congregation **n**
4:36 and those who were **n** by their
4:37 were the ones who were **n** of
4:37 whom Moses and Aaron **n**
4:38 And those who were **n** of the
4:40 those who were **n** by their
4:41 These are the ones who were **n**
4:41 whom Moses and Aaron **n**
4:42 the sons of Merari who were **n**,
4:44 those who were **n** by their
4:45 These are the ones who were **n**
4:45 whom Moses and Aaron **n**
4:46 All who were **n** of the Levites,
4:46 and the leaders of Israel **n**,
4:48 those who were **n** were eight
4:49 of the LORD they were **n** by
4:49 thus were they **n** by him, as the
7: 2 and over those who were **n**,
14:29 all of you who were **n**,
26: 7 those who were **n** of them were
26:18 according to those who were **n**
26:22 according to those who were **n**
26:25 according to those who were **n**
26:27 according to those who were **n**
26:34 and those who were **n** of them
26:37 according to those who were **n**
26:41 and those who were **n** of them
26:43 according to those who were **n**
26:47 according to those who were **n**
26:50 and those who were **n** of them
26:51 These are those who were **n** of
26:54 according to those who were **n**
26:57 these are those who were **n** of
26:62 Now those who were **n** of them
26:62 for they were not **n** among the
26:63 These are those who were **n** by
26:63 who **n** the children of Israel in
26:64 not a man of those who were **n**
26:64 Aaron the priest when they **n**
Judg 20:15 time the children of Benjamin **n**
20:15 who **n** seven hundred select men.
20:17 the men of Israel **n** four
1 Sam 11: 8 When he **n** them in Bezek, the
13:15 And Saul **n** the people present
15: 4 the people together and **n** them
2 Sam 18: 1 And David **n** the people who were
24:10 condemned him after he had **n**
1 Ki 3: 8 too numerous to be **n** or
8: 5 that could not be counted or **n**
1 Chr 21:17 commanded the people to be **n**?
23: 3 Now the Levites were **n** from the
23:27 of David the Levites were **n**
2 Chr 2:17 Then Solomon **n** all the aliens
2:17 in which David his father had **n**
5: 6 that could not be counted or **n**
25: 5 and he **n** them from twenty years
Ps 40: 5 They are more than can be **n**.
Eccl 1:15 what is lacking cannot be **n**.
Isa 22:10 You **n** the houses of Jerusalem,
53:12 And He was **n** with the
Jer 33:22 the host of heaven cannot be **n**,
Dan 5:26 God has **n** your kingdom, and
Hos 1:10 Which cannot be measured or **n**.
Mt 10:30 hairs of your head are all **n**.
Mk 15:28 And He was **n** with the
Lk 12: 7 hairs of your head are all **n**.
22: 3 who was **n** among the twelve.
22:37 And He was **n** with the
Acts 1:17 for he was **n** with us and
1:26 And he was **n** with the eleven

NUMBERING (1/1)

Ex 38:26 for everyone included in the **n**

NUMBERS (4/4)

1 Chr 5:23 Their **n** increased from Bashan
12:23 Now these were the **n** of the
2 Chr 15: 9 came over to him in great **n**
17:14 These are their **n**,

NUMEROUS (12/12) NUMBER

Ex 23:29 of the field become too **n** for
Num 22:15 more **n** and more honorable than
Deut 1:11 you a thousand times more **n**
2:10 a people as great and **n** and
2:21 a people as great and **n** and tall
7:22 of the field become too **n** for
20: 1 and chariots and people more **n**
Judg 6: 5 coming in as **n** as locusts;
7:12 were lying in the valley as **n**
1 Ki 3: 8 too **n** to be numbered or
4:20 Judah and Israel were as **n** as
Jer 46:23 And more **n** than grasshoppers.

NUN (30/30)

Ex 33:11 his servant Joshua the son of **N**,
Num 11:28 So Joshua the son of **N**,
13: 8 of Ephraim, Hoshea the son of **N**;
13:16 called Hoshea the son of **N**,
14: 6 But Joshua the son of **N** and
14:30 and Joshua the son of **N**,
14:38 But Joshua the son of **N** and
26:65 and Joshua the son of **N**.
27:18 Take Joshua the son of **N** with
32:12 and Joshua the son of **N**,
32:28 priest, to Joshua the son of **N**,
34:17 priest and Joshua the son of **N**.
Deut 1:38 Joshua the son of **N**,
31:23 inaugurated Joshua the son of **N**,
32:44 came with Joshua the son of **N**
34: 9 Now Joshua the son of **N** was
Josh 1: 1 spoke to Joshua the son of **N**,
2: 1 Now Joshua the son of **N** sent out
2:23 came to Joshua the son of **N**,
6: 6 Then Joshua the son of **N** called
14: 1 the priest, Joshua the son of **N**,
17: 4 before Joshua the son of **N**,
19:49 them to Joshua the son of **N**.
19:51 the priest, Joshua the son of **N**,
21: 1 priest, to Joshua the son of **N**,
24:29 things that Joshua the son of **N**,
Judg 2: 8 Now Joshua the son of **N**,
1 Ki 16:34 through Joshua the son of **N**.
1 Chr 7:27 **N** his son, and Joshua his son.
Neh 8:17 the days of Joshua the son of **N**

NURSE (13/12) NURSED, NURSING

Gen 21: 7 to Abraham that Sarah would **n**
24:59 Rebekah their sister and her **n**,
35: 8 Now Deborah, Rebekah's **n**,
Ex 2: 7 Shall I go and call a **n** for you
2: 7 that she may **n** the child for
2: 9 Take this child away and **n** him
Ruth 4:16 and became a **n** to him.
2 Sam 4: 4 and his **n** took him up and fled.
1 Ki 3:21 I rose in the morning to **n** my
2 Ki 11: 2 and they hid him and his **n** in
2 Chr 22:11 and put him and his **n** in a
Job 3:12 the breasts, that I should **n**?
Lam 4: 3 present their breasts To **n**

NURSED (6/6) NURSE

Ex 2: 9 the woman took the child and **n**
1 Sam 1:23 So the woman stayed and **n** her
Song 8: 1 Who **n** at my mother's breasts!
Isa 60: 4 And your daughters shall be **n**
Lk 11:27 and the breasts which **n** You!"
23:29 and breasts which never **n**!'

NURSING (15/15) NURSE

Gen 33:13 flocks and herds which are **n**
Num 11:12 as a guardian carries a **n**
Deut 32:25 The **n** child with the man of
1 Sam 15: 3 infant and **n** child, ox and
22:19 children and **n** infants, oxen
Ps 8: 2 of the mouth of babes and **n**
Isa 11: 8 The **n** child shall play by the
49:15 Can a woman forget her **n** child,
49:23 And their queens your **n**
Joel 2:16 Gather the children and **n**
Mt 21:16 the mouth of babes and **n**
24:19 and to those who are **n** babies
Mk 13:17 and to those who are **n** babies
Lk 21:23 and to those who are **n** babies
1 Th 2: 7 just as a **n** mother cherishes

NUTS (2/2)

Gen 43:11 pistachio **n** and almonds.
Song 6:11 I went down to the garden of **n**

NYMPHAS (1/1)

Col 4:15 and **N** and the church that is

O

O (996/903) See APPENDIX

OAK (5/5) OAKS

Josh 24:26 and set it up there under the **o**
1 Ki 13:14 found him sitting under an **o**.
Isa 6:13 As a terebinth tree or as an **o**,
44:14 takes the cypress and the **o**;
Ezek 6:13 tree, and under every thick **o**,

OAKS (5/5) OAK

Isa 2:13 And upon all the **o** of Bashan;
Ezek 27: 6 Of **o** from Bashan they made
Hos 4:13 incense on the hills, Under **o**,
Am 2: 9 he was as strong as the **o**;
Zech 11: 2 O **o** of Bashan, For the thick

OAR (1/1)

Ezek 27:29 "All who handle the **o**,

OARS (2/2)

Isa 33:21 In which no galley with **o** will
Ezek 27: 6 from Bashan they made your **o**;

OARSMEN (3/3)

Ezek 27: 8 of Sidon and Arvad were your **o**;
27: 9 ships of the sea And their **o**
27:26 Your **o** brought you into many

OATH (100/92) OATHS

Gen 21:31 the two of them swore an **o**
24: 8 will be released from this **o**;
24:41 You will be clear from this **o**
24:41 you will be released from my **o**.
26: 3 and I will perform the **o** which
26:28 Let there now be an **o** between
26:31 in the morning and swore an **o**
50:25 Then Joseph took an **o** from the
Ex 13:19 of Israel under solemn **o**,
22:11 then an **o** of the LORD shall be
Lev 5: 1 hearing the utterance of an **o**,
5: 4 a man may pronounce by an **o**,
Num 5:19 priest shall put her under **o**,
5:21 put the woman under the **o** of
5:21 LORD make you a curse and an **o**
30: 2 or swears an **o** to bind himself
30:10 by an agreement with an **o**,
30:13 Every vow and every binding **o** to
32:10 on that day, and He swore an **o**,
Deut 1:34 and was angry, and took an **o**,
7: 8 and because He would keep the **o**
29:12 LORD your God, and into His **o**,
29:14 make this covenant and this **o**,
Josh 2:17 will be blameless of this **o**
2:20 we will be free from your **o**
9:20 be upon us because of the **o**
Judg 21: 1 men of Israel had sworn an **o**
21: 5 For they had made a great **o**
21:18 of Israel have sworn an **o**,
21:22 yourselves guilty of your **o**.
1 Sam 14:24 had placed the people under **o**,
14:26 for the people feared the **o**.
14:27 charge the people with the **o**;
14:28 charged the people with an **o**,
20: 3 Then David took an **o** again, and
2 Sam 3:35 was still day, David took an **o**,
21: 7 because of the LORD's **o** that
1 Ki 1:29 And the king took an **o** and said,
2:43 then have you not kept the **o**
8:31 and is forced to take an **o**,
8:31 and comes and takes an **o**
18:10 he took an **o** from the kingdom
2 Ki 11: 4 with them and took an **o** from
25:24 And Gedaliah took an **o** before
1 Chr 16:16 And His **o** to Isaac,
2 Chr 6:22 and is forced to take an **o**,
6:22 and comes and takes an **o**
15:14 Then they took an **o** before the
15:15 And all Judah rejoiced at the **o**,
36:13 who had made him swear an **o**
Ezra 10: 5 and all Israel swear an **o** that
10: 5 this word. So they swore an **o**.
Neh 5:12 and required an **o** from them
10:29 entered into a curse and an **o**
Ps 102: 8 Those who deride me swear an **o**
105: 9 And His **o** to Isaac,
106:26 raised up His hand in an **o**
Eccl 8: 2 for the sake of your **o** to God.
9: 2 He who takes an **o** as he who
9: 2 an oath as he who fears an **o**.
Isa 45:23 Every tongue shall take an **o**.
49:22 I will lift My hand in an **o** to
Jer 11: 5 that I may establish the **o** which
40: 9 took an **o** before them and their
42:18 And you shall be an **o**,
44:12 famine; and they shall be an **o**,
Ezek 16: 8 I swore an **o** to you and entered
16:59 who despised the **o** by breaking
17:13 with him, and put him under **o**.
17:16 whose **o** he despised and whose
17:18 Since he despised the **o** by
17:19 surely My **o** which he despised,
20: 5 and raised My hand in an **o** to
20: 5 I raised My hand in an **o** to
20: 6 day I raised My hand in an **o**
20:15 I also raised My hand in an **o**
20:23 Also I raised My hand in an **o** to
20:28 I had raised My hand in an **o**
20:42 which I raised My hand in an **o**
36: 7 I have raised My hand in an **o**
44:12 I have raised My hand in an **o**
47:14 for I raised My hand in an **o** to
Dan 9:11 therefore the curse and the **o**
Hos 4:15 to Beth Aven, Nor swear an **o**,
Zech 8:17 And do not love a false **o**.
Mt 14: 7 he promised with an **o** to give
26:63 I put You under **o** by the living
26:72 But again he denied with an **o**,
Lk 1:73 The **o** which He swore to our
Acts 2:30 that God had sworn with an **o**
23:12 and bound themselves under an **o**,
23:14 ourselves under a great **o** that
23:21 have bound themselves by an **o**
Heb 6:16 and an **o** for confirmation is
6:17 counsel, confirmed it by an **o**,
7:20 not made priest without an **o**
7:21 become priests without an **o**,
7:21 but He with an **o** by Him who
7:28 weakness, but the word of the **o**,
Jas 5:12 or by earth or with any other **o**.

OATHS (8/8) OATH

Deut 6:13 and shall take **o** in His name.
10:20 and take **o** in His name.
Ezek 21:23 eyes of those who have sworn **o**
Hab 3: 9 **O** were sworn over Your
Zeph 1: 5 who worship and swear **o** by
Mt 5:33 but shall perform your **o** to the
14: 9 because of the **o** and because of
Mk 6:26 because of the **o** and because of

OBADIAH (20/19)

1 Ki 18: 3 And Ahab had called ***O***,
18: 3 (Now ***O*** feared the LORD
18: 4 that ***O*** had taken one hundred
18: 5 And Ahab had said to ***O***,
18: 6 and ***O*** went another way by
18: 7 Now as ***O*** was on his way,
18:16 So ***O*** went to meet Ahab, and told
1 Chr 3:21 sons of Arnan, the sons of ***O***,
7: 3 of Izrahiah were Michael, ***O***,
8:38 Bocheru, Ishmael, Sheariah, ***O***,
9:16 ***O*** the son of Shemaiah, the son
9:44 Bocheru, Ishmael, Sheariah, ***O***,
12: 9 ***O*** the second, Eliab the third,
27:19 Zebulun, Ishmaiah the son of ***O***;
2 Chr 17: 7 sent his leaders, Ben-Hail, ***O***,
34:12 overseers were Jahath and ***O***
Ezra 8: 9 ***O*** the son of Jehiel, and with
Neh 10: 5 Harim, Meremoth, ***O***,
12:25 Mattaniah, Bakbukiah, ***O***,
Ob 1 The vision of ***O***.

OBAL (1/1)

Gen 10:28 ***O***, Abimael, Sheba,

OBED (13/11) OBED-EDOM

Ruth 4:17 And they called his name ***O***.
4:21 begot Boaz, and Boaz begot ***O***;
4:22 ***O*** begot Jesse, and Jesse begot
1 Chr 2:12 Boaz begot ***O***, and Obed
2:12 and ***O*** begot Jesse;
2:37 Ephlal, and Ephlal begot ***O***;
2:38 ***O*** begot Jehu, and Jehu begot
11:47 Eliel, ***O***, and Jaasiel
26: 7 were Othni, Rephael, ***O***,
2 Chr 23: 1 Jehohanan, Azariah the son of ***O***,
Mt 1: 5 Boaz by Rahab, Boaz begot ***O*** by
1: 5 Obed by Ruth, ***O*** begot Jesse,
Lk 3:32 son of Jesse, the son of ***O***,

OBED-EDOM (20/15) EDOM, OBED

2 Sam 6:10 it aside into the house of ***O***
6:11 remained in the house of ***O*** the
6:11 And the LORD blessed ***O*** and all
6:12 has blessed the house of ***O*** and
6:12 ark of God from the house of ***O***
1 Chr 13:13 it aside into the house of ***O***
13:14 remained with the family of ***O***
13:14 LORD blessed the house of ***O***
15:18 Elipheleh, Mikneiah, ***O***,
15:21 Elipheleh, Mikneiah, ***O***,
15:24 and ***O*** and Jehiah, doorkeepers
15:25 the LORD from the house of ***O***
16: 5 Eliab, Benaiah, and ***O***:
16:38 and ***O*** with his sixty-eight
16:38 including ***O*** the son of
26: 4 Moreover the sons of ***O*** were
26: 8 these were of the sons of ***O***,
26: 8 for the work: sixty-two of ***O***.
26:15 to ***O*** the South Gate, and to his
2 Chr 25:24 in the house of God with ***O***,

OBEDIENCE (14/14) OBEDIENT

Gen 49:10 be the ***o*** of the people.
Prov 30:17 And scorns ***o*** to his mother,
Rom 1: 5 for ***o*** to the faith among all
5:19 so also by one Man's ***o*** many
6:16 or of ***o*** leading to
16:19 For your ***o*** has become known to
16:26 for ***o*** to the faith—
2 Cor 7:15 he remembers the ***o*** of you all,
9:13 for the ***o*** of your confession
10: 5 captivity to the ***o*** of Christ,
10: 6 all disobedience when your ***o***
Phm 1:21 Having confidence in your ***o***,
Heb 5: 8 yet He learned ***o*** by the things
1 Pe 1: 2 for ***o*** and sprinkling of the

OBEDIENT (14/14) OBEDIENCE, OBEY

Ex 24: 7 has said we will do, and be ***o***.
Num 27:20 the children of Israel may be ***o***.
Deut 8:20 because you would not be ***o*** to
Prov 25:12 Is a wise rebuker to an ***o***
Isa 1:19 If you are willing and ***o***,
42:24 Nor were they ***o*** to His law.
Acts 6: 7 many of the priests were ***o*** to
Rom 15:18 deed, to make the Gentiles ***o***—
2 Cor 2: 9 whether you are ***o*** in all
Eph 6: 5 be ***o*** to those who are your
Phil 2: 8 He humbled Himself and became ***o***
Titus 2: 5 ***o*** to their own husbands, that
2: 9 Exhort bondservants to be ***o*** to
1 Pe 1:14 as ***o*** children, not conforming

OBEISANCE (KJV) See BOWED (DOWN)

OBESE (1/1)

Deut 32:15 You are ***o***! Then he forsook

OBEY (108/104) OBEDIENT, OBEYED, OBEYING

Gen 27: 8 ***o*** my voice according to what I
27:13 only ***o*** my voice, and go, get
27:43 ***o*** my voice: arise, flee to my
Ex 5: 2 that I should ***o*** His voice to
19: 5 if you will indeed ***o*** My voice
23:21 Beware of Him and ***o*** His voice;
23:22 But if you indeed ***o*** His voice
Lev 26:14 But if you do not ***o*** Me, and do
26:18 if you do not ***o*** Me, then I will
26:21 and are not willing to ***o*** Me, I
26:27 if you do not ***o*** Me, but walk
Deut 4:30 to the LORD your God and ***o***
9:23 you did not believe Him nor ***o***
11:13 be that if you earnestly ***o*** My
11:27 if you ***o*** the commandments of
11:28 if you do not ***o*** the
12:28 Observe and ***o*** all these words
13: 4 and keep His commandments and ***o***
15: 5 only if you carefully ***o*** the
21:18 rebellious son who will not ***o***
21:20 he will not ***o*** our voice; he is
26:17 and that you will ***o*** His voice.
27:10 Therefore you shall ***o*** the voice
28: 1 if you diligently ***o*** the voice
28: 2 because you ***o*** the voice of the
28:15 if you do not ***o*** the voice of
28:45 because you did not ***o*** the voice
28:62 because you would not ***o*** the
30: 2 to the LORD your God and ***o***
30: 8 And you will again ***o*** the voice
30:10 if you ***o*** the voice of the LORD
30:20 that you may ***o*** His voice, and
Josh 5: 6 because they did not ***o*** the
24:24 and His voice we will ***o***!"
Judg 3: 4 to know whether they would ***o***
1 Sam 8:19 the people refused to ***o*** the
12:14 the LORD and serve Him and ***o***
12:15 if you do not ***o*** the voice of
15:19 Why then did you not ***o*** the voice
15:22 to ***o*** is better than sacrifice,
28:18 Because you did not ***o*** the voice
2 Sam 22:45 soon as they hear, they ***o*** me.
2 Ki 10: 6 If you are for me and will ***o***
17:40 However they did not ***o***,
18:12 because they did not ***o*** the voice
2 Chr 30:12 them singleness of heart to ***o***
Neh 9:17 They refused to ***o***,
Esth 1:15 because she did not ***o*** the
Job 36:11 If they ***o*** and serve Him, They
36:12 But if they do not ***o***,
Ps 18:44 soon as they hear of me they ***o***
Isa 11:14 the people of Ammon shall ***o***
Jer 7:23 ***O*** My voice, and I will be your
7:24 Yet they did not ***o*** or incline
7:26 Yet they did not ***o*** Me or incline
7:27 but they will not ***o*** you.
7:28 is a nation that does not ***o***
11: 3 is the man who does not ***o*** the
11: 4 ***O*** My voice, and do according to
11: 7 saying, "***O*** My voice."
11: 8 Yet they did not ***o*** or incline
12:17 "But if they do not ***o***,
17:23 But they did not ***o*** nor incline
18:10 My sight so that it does not ***o***
18:12 and we will every one ***o*** the
22:21 That you did not ***o*** My voice.
26:13 and ***o*** the voice of the LORD
34:14 But your fathers did not ***o*** Me
35:13 not receive instruction to ***o***
35:14 and ***o*** their father's
35:14 speaking, you did not ***o*** Me.
38:20 ***o*** the voice of the LORD which
42: 6 we will ***o*** the voice of the
42: 6 may be well with us when we ***o***
43: 4 and all the people would not ***o***
43: 7 for they did not ***o*** the voice of
Ezek 20: 8 against Me and would not ***o*** Me.
20:39 —if you will not ***o*** me;
Dan 7:27 all dominions shall serve and ***o***
9:11 and has departed so as not to ***o***
Hos 9:17 Because they did not ***o*** Him;
Zech 6:15 to pass if you diligently ***o***
Mt 8:27 even the winds and the sea ***o***
Mk 1:27 spirits, and they ***o*** Him."
4:41 even the wind and the sea ***o***
Lk 8:25 water, and they ***o*** Him!"
17: 6 and it would ***o*** you.
Acts 5:29 We ought to ***o*** God rather than
5:32 God has given to those who ***o***
7:39 "whom our fathers would not ***o***,
Rom 2: 8 are self-seeking and do not ***o***
2: 8 ***o*** unrighteousness—indignation
6:12 that you should ***o*** it in its
6:16 present yourselves slaves to ***o***,
6:16 that one's slaves whom you ***o***,
Gal 3: 1 you that you should not ***o*** the
Eph 6: 1 ***o*** your parents in the Lord, for
Col 3:20 ***o*** your parents in all things,
3:22 ***o*** in all things your masters
2 Th 1: 8 and on those who do not ***o*** the
3:14 And if anyone does not ***o*** our
Titus 3: 1 to rulers and authorities, to ***o***,
Heb 3:18 but to those who did not ***o***?
5: 9 eternal salvation to all who ***o***
13:17 ***O*** those who rule over you, and
Jas 3: 3 horses' mouths that they may ***o***
1 Pe 3: 1 that even if some do not ***o*** the
4:17 the end of those who do not ***o***

OBEYED (43/43) OBEY

Gen 22:18 because you have ***o*** My voice."
26: 5 because Abraham ***o*** My voice and
28: 7 and that Jacob had ***o*** his father
Deut 26:14 I have ***o*** the voice of the LORD
Josh 22: 2 and have ***o*** my voice in all that
Judg 2: 2 But you have not ***o*** My voice.
6:10 But you have not ***o*** My voice.'
1 Sam 15:20 But I have ***o*** the voice of the
15:24 I feared the people and ***o***
28:21 your maidservant has ***o*** your
1 Ki 12:24 Therefore they ***o*** the
20:36 Because you have not ***o*** the voice
2 Ki 22:13 because our fathers have not ***o***
1 Chr 29:23 and all Israel ***o*** him.
2 Chr 11: 4 Therefore they ***o*** the
Esth 2:20 for Esther ***o*** the command of
Prov 5:13 I have not ***o*** the voice of my
Jer 3:13 And you have not ***o*** My voice,'
3:25 And have not ***o*** the voice of
9:13 and have not ***o*** My voice, nor
32:23 but they have not ***o*** Your voice
34:10 they ***o*** and let them go.
34:17 You have not ***o*** Me in proclaiming
35: 8 Thus we have ***o*** the voice of
35:10 and have ***o*** and done according
35:15 inclined your ear, nor ***o*** Me.
35:16 but this people has not ***o*** Me."
35:18 Because you have ***o*** the
40: 3 and not ***o*** His voice, therefore
42:21 but you have not ***o*** the voice of
44:23 and have not ***o*** the voice of the
Dan 9:10 We have not ***o*** the voice of the
9:14 though we have not ***o*** His voice.
Zeph 3: 2 She has not ***o*** His voice, She
Hag 1:12 ***o*** the voice of the LORD their
Zech 7: 7 Should you not have ***o*** the
Acts 5:36 and all who ***o*** him were
5:37 and all who ***o*** him were
Rom 6:17 yet you ***o*** from the heart that
10:16 But they have not all ***o*** the
Phil 2:12 beloved, as you have always ***o***,
Heb 11: 8 By faith Abraham ***o*** when he was
1 Pe 3: 6 as Sarah ***o*** Abraham, calling him

OBEYING (5/5) OBEY

Judg 2:17 in ***o*** the commandments of the
1 Sam 15:22 As in ***o*** the voice of the
Hos 4:10 Because they have ceased ***o*** the
Gal 5: 7 Who hindered you from ***o*** the
1 Pe 1:22 have purified your souls in ***o***

OBEYS (1/1)

Isa 50:10 Who ***o*** the voice of His

OBIL (1/1)

1 Chr 27:30 ***O*** the Ishmaelite was over the

OBJECT (9/8) OBJECTS

Ezek 15: 3 taken from it to make any ***o***?
15: 5 no ***o*** could be made from it.
Acts 10:11 and saw heaven opened and an ***o***
10:16 And the ***o*** was taken up into
11: 5 an ***o*** descending like a great
24:19 have been here before you to ***o***
25:11 I do not ***o*** to dying; but if
Rev 18:12 every kind of ***o*** of ivory, every
18:12 every kind of ***o*** of most

OBJECTION (1/1)

Acts 10:29 Therefore I came without ***o*** as

OBJECTS (1/1) OBJECT

Acts 17:23 through and considering the ***o***

OBLATION, OBLATIONS (KJV) See DISTRICT, OFFERING, OFFERINGS, SACRIFICES

OBLIGATION (1/1)

2 Cor 9: 5 and not as a grudging ***o***.

OBLIGED (2/2)

Mt 23:16 he is ***o*** to perform it.'
23:18 he is ***o*** to perform it.'

OBNOXIOUS (1/1)

Gen 34:30 have troubled me by making me ***o***

OBOTH (4/4)

Num 21:10 Israel moved on and camped in ***O***.
21:11 And they journeyed from ***O*** and
33:43 from Punon and camped at ***O***.
33:44 They departed from ***O*** and camped

OBSCENE (4/2)

1 Ki 15:13 because she had made an ***o*** image
15:13 And Asa cut down her ***o*** image
2 Chr 15:16 because she had made an ***o*** image
15:16 and Asa cut down her ***o*** image,

OBSCURE (1/1)

Isa 33:19 A people of ***o*** speech, beyond

OBSCURITY (1/1)

Isa 29:18 of the blind shall see out of **o**

OBSERVANCE (2/1) OBSERVE

Ex 12:42 It is a night of solemn **o** to
12:42 a solemn **o** for all the children

OBSERVATION (1/1) OBSERVE

Lk 17:20 of God does not come with **o**;

OBSERVE (85/81) OBSERVANCE, OBSERVATION, OBSERVED, OBSERVES, OBSERVING

Gen 16:14 **o**, it is between Kadesh and
Ex 12:17 So you shall **o** the Feast of
12:17 Therefore you shall **o** this day
12:24 And you shall **o** this thing as an
31:16 to **o** the Sabbath throughout
34:11 ***O*** what I command you this day.
34:22 And you shall **o** the Feast of
Lev 18: 4 You shall **o** My judgments and
19:37 Therefore you shall **o** all My
25:18 So you shall **o** My statutes and
26:14 and do not **o** all these
Num 15:22 and do not **o** all these
22:41 that from there he might **o** the
Deut 4: 1 which I teach you to **o**,
4: 6 Therefore be careful to **o** them;
4:14 that you might **o** them in the
5: 1 learn them and be careful to **o**
5:12 ***O*** the Sabbath day, to keep it
5:31 that they may **o** them in the
6: 1 that you may **o** them in the
6: 3 and be careful to **o** it, that
6:24 the LORD commanded us to **o**
6:25 if we are careful to **o** all
7:11 you today, to **o** them.
8: 1 today you must be careful to **o**,
11:32 And you shall be careful to **o**
12: 1 you shall be careful to **o** in
12:28 ***O*** and obey all these words which
12:32 be careful to **o** it; you shall
15: 5 to **o** with care all these
16: 1 ***O*** the month of Abib, and keep
16:12 and you shall be careful to **o**
16:13 You shall **o** the Feast of
17:19 his God and be careful to **o**
24: 8 that you carefully **o** and do
26:16 your God commands you to **o**
26:16 you shall be careful to **o** them
27:10 and **o** His commandments and His
28: 1 to **o** carefully all His
28:13 and are careful to **o** them.
28:15 to **o** carefully all His
28:58 If you do not carefully **o** all
31:12 LORD your God and carefully **o**
32:46 children to be careful to **o**—
Josh 1: 7 that you may **o** to do according
1: 8 that you may **o** to do according
Judg 13:14 that I commanded her let her **o**.
1 Sam 19: 3 Then what I **o**, I will tell
2 Ki 17:37 you shall be careful to **o**
1 Chr 28: 7 if he is steadfast to **o** My
2 Chr 14: 4 and to **o** the law and the
Ezra 7:26 Whoever will not **o** the law of
Neh 1: 5 with those who love You and **o**
10:29 and to **o** and do all the
Job 39:29 Its eyes **o** from afar.
Ps 10:14 for You **o** trouble and grief,
37:37 and **o** the upright; For the
66: 7 His eyes **o** the nations;
105:45 That they might **o** His statutes
107:43 Whoever is wise will **o** these
119:34 I shall **o** it with my whole
119:117 And I shall **o** Your statutes
Prov 23:26 And let your eyes **o** my ways.
Isa 38:11 I shall **o** man no more among
42:20 many things, but you do not **o**;
Jer 8: 7 and the swallow ***O*** the time of
Ezek 20:18 nor **o** their judgments, nor
20:21 and were not careful to **o** My
37:24 walk in My judgments and **o** My
45:21 you shall **o** the Passover, a
Hos 12: 6 ***O*** mercy and justice, And wait
Mt 23: 3 whatever they tell you to **o**,
23: 3 that **o** and do, but do not do
28:20 teaching them to **o** all things
Acts 7:31 and as he drew near to **o**,
16:21 being Romans, to receive or **o**.
21:25 decided that they should **o** no
Rom 14: 6 and he who does not **o** the day,
14: 6 to the Lord he does not **o** it.
1 Cor 10:18 ***O*** Israel after the flesh:
2 Cor 7:11 For **o** this very thing, that you
Gal 4:10 You **o** days and months and
1 Tim 5:21 and the elect angels that you **o**
1 Pe 2:12 your good works which they **o**,
3: 2 when they **o** your chaste conduct

OBSERVED (13/13) KEPT, OBSERVE

Gen 50:10 He **o** seven days of mourning for
Num 23:21 He has not **o** iniquity in Jacob,
Deut 33: 9 For they have **o** Your word And
2 Chr 7: 9 for they **o** the dedication of
Esth 9:28 should not fail to be **o**
Job 31:26 If I have **o** the sun when it
Ezek 18:19 has kept all My statutes and **o**
Hos 14: 8 I have heard and **o** him.
Mk 15:47 Mary the mother of Joses **o**
Lk 23:55 and they **o** the tomb and how His
Acts 10: 4 And when he **o** him, he was
11: 6 When I **o** it intently and
27:39 but they **o** a bay with a beach,

OBSERVER (1/1)

Isa 28: 4 Which an **o** sees; He eats it

OBSERVES (4/3) OBSERVE

Eccl 11: 4 He who **o** the wind will not sow,
Rom 14: 6 He who **o** the day, observes it
14: 6 **o** it to the Lord; and he who
Jas 1:24 for he **o** himself, goes away, and

OBSERVING (2/2) OBSERVE

Acts 14: 9 **o** him intently and seeing that
Jas 1:23 he is like a man **o** his natural

OBSESSED (1/1)

1 Tim 6: 4 but is **o** with disputes and

OBSOLETE (2/1)

Heb 8:13 He has made the first **o**.
8:13 Now what is becoming **o** and

OBSTINATE (2/2)

Deut 2:30 his spirit and made his heart **o**,
Isa 48: 4 I knew that you were **o**,

OBSTRUCT (1/1)

Ezek 39:11 and it will **o** travelers,

OBTAIN (13/13) OBTAINED, OBTAINS

Gen 16: 2 perhaps I shall **o** children by
Isa 35:10 They shall **o** joy and gladness,
51:11 They shall **o** joy and gladness;
Mt 5: 7 For they shall **o** mercy.
Rom 11:31 you they also may **o** mercy.
1 Cor 9:24 a way that you may **o** it.
9:25 Now they do it to **o** a
1 Th 5: 9 but to **o** salvation through our
1 Tim 3:13 as deacons **o** for themselves
2 Tim 2:10 that they also may **o** the
Heb 4:16 that we may **o** mercy and find
11:35 that they might **o** a better
Jas 4: 2 murder and covet and cannot **o**.

OBTAINED (27/25) OBTAIN

Josh 22: 9 which they had **o** according to
Neh 13: 6 certain days I **o** leave
Esth 2: 9 and she **o** his favor; so he
2:15 And Esther **o** favor in the sight
2:17 and she **o** grace and favor in
Hos 2:23 her who had not **o** mercy;
Acts 1:17 numbered with us and **o** a part
22:28 With a large sum I **o** this
26:22 having **o** help from God, to this
27:13 they had **o** their desire,
Rom 11: 7 Israel has not **o** what it seeks;
11: 7 but the elect have **o** it, and
11:30 yet have now **o** mercy through
Eph 1:11 In Him also we have **o** an
1 Tim 1:13 but I **o** mercy because I did it
1:16 for this reason I **o** mercy, that
Heb 1: 4 as He has by inheritance **o** a
6:15 endured, he **o** the promise.
8: 6 But now He has **o** a more
9:12 having **o** eternal redemption.
11: 2 For by it the elders **o** a good
11: 4 through which he **o** witness that
11:33 **o** promises, stopped the mouths
11:39 having **o** a good testimony
1 Pe 2:10 who had not **o** mercy but now
2:10 mercy but now have **o** mercy.
2 Pe 1: 1 To those who have **o** like

OBTAINING (1/1)

2 Th 2:14 for the **o** of the glory of our

OBTAINS (3/3) OBTAIN

Prov 8:35 And **o** favor from the LORD;
12: 2 A good man **o** favor from the
18:22 And **o** favor from the LORD.

OBVIOUSLY (1/1)

Gen 26: 9 'Quite **o** she is your wife;

OCCASION (7/7)

Judg 14: 4 that He was seeking an **o** to move
1 Sam 10: 7 that you do as the **o** demands;
2 Sam 12:14 deed you have given great **o** to
2 Chr 22: 7 going to Joram was God's **o** for
Ezra 7:20 which you may have **o** to
Lk 21:13 will turn out for you as an **o**
Rom 7:11 taking **o** by the commandment,

OCCASIONALLY (1/1)

1 Sam 17:15 But David **o** went and returned

OCCASIONED (KJV) See CAUSED

OCCASIONS (1/1)

Job 33:10 Yet He finds **o** against me,

OCCUPATION (7/7)

Gen 46:32 for their **o** has been to feed
46:33 you and says, 'What is your **o**?
46:34 Your servants' **o** has been with
47: 3 his brothers, "What is your **o**?
Jon 1: 8 trouble upon us? What is your **o**?
Acts 18: 3 for by **o** they were tentmakers.
19:25 with the workers of similar **o**,

OCCUPIED (3/3)

Eccl 3:10 the sons of men are to be **o**.
Acts 26:12 While thus **o**, as I
Heb 13: 9 profited those who have been **o**

OCCUPIES (1/1)

1 Cor 14:16 how will he who **o** the place of

OCCUPY (1/1)

Neh 2: 8 and for the house that I will **o**.

OCCUR (2/2)

Eccl 8: 7 who can tell him when it will **o**?
Zech 14: 8 summer and winter it shall **o**.

OCCURRED (5/5) OCCURS

Judg 20:12 is this wickedness that has **o**
Esth 9: 1 overpower them, the opposite **o**,
Acts 2: 6 And when this sound **o**,
Gal 2: 4 And this **o** because of false
Rev 16:18 great earthquake as had not **o**

OCCURRENCE (2/2)

Deut 23:10 who becomes unclean by some **o**
1 Ki 5: 4 neither adversary nor evil **o**.

OCCURS (1/1) OCCURRED

Eccl 8:14 There is a vanity which **o** on

OCRAN (5/5)

Num 1:13 Asher, Pagiel the son of ***O***;
2:27 shall be Pagiel the son of ***O***.
7:72 day Pagiel the son of ***O***,
7:77 offering of Pagiel the son of ***O***.
10:26 Asher was Pagiel the son of ***O***.

ODD (KJV) See EXCESS

ODED (3/3)

2 Chr 15: 1 came upon Azariah the son of ***O***.
15: 8 words and the prophecy of ***O***
28: 9 was there, whose name was ***O***;

ODOR (2/2)

Eccl 10: 1 cause it to give off a foul **o**;
Joel 2:20 And his foul **o** will rise,

ODOUR (KJV) See FRAGRANCE

OF (31661/17357) See APPENDIX

OFF (397/383)

Gen 9:11 again shall all flesh be cut **o**
17:14 that person shall be cut **o** from
22: 4 eyes and saw the place afar **o**.
37:18 Now when they saw him afar **o**,
38:14 So she took **o** her widow's
40:19 three days Pharaoh will lift **o**
41:42 Pharaoh took his signet ring **o**
44: 4 city, and were not yet far **o**,
44:12 with the oldest and left **o**
Ex 2: 4 And his sister stood afar **o**,
3: 5 Take your sandals **o** your feet,
4:25 took a sharp stone and cut **o**
9:15 then you would have been cut **o**
12:15 that person shall be cut **o** from
12:19 that same person shall be cut **o**
14:25 And He took **o** their chariot
20:18 they trembled and stood afar **o**.
20:21 So the people stood afar **o**,
23:23 and I will cut them **o**.
30:33 shall be cut **o** from his
30:38 he shall be cut **o** from his
31:14 that person shall be cut **o** from
32: 2 Break **o** the golden earrings
32: 3 So all the people broke **o** the
32:24 any gold, let them break it **o**.
33: 5 take **o** your ornaments, that I
34:34 he would take the veil **o** until
40: 3 and partition **o** the ark with
40:21 and partitioned **o** the ark of
Lev 1:15 wring **o** its head, and burn it

5: 8 and wring o its head from its
6:11 Then he shall take o his
7:20 that person shall be cut o from
7:21 that person shall be cut o from
7:25 who eats it shall be cut o;
7:27 that person shall be cut o from
14: 8 shave o all his hair, and wash
14: 9 he shall shave all the hair o
14: 9 his hair he shall shave o.
14:41 and the dust that they scrape o
16:23 shall take o the linen garments
17: 4 and that man shall be cut o
17: 9 that man shall be cut o from
17:10 and will cut him o from among
17:14 Whoever eats it shall be cut o.
18:29 who commit them shall be cut o
19: 8 and that person shall be cut o
20: 3 and will cut him o from his
20: 5 and I will cut him o from his
20: 6 that person and cut him o from
20:17 And they shall be cut o in the
20:18 Both of them shall be cut o
22: 3 that person shall be cut o from
23:29 on that same day shall be cut o
26:26 When I have cut o your supply of
Num 4:18 Do not cut o the tribe of the
5:23 and he shall scrape them o
9:13 that same person shall be cut o
15:30 and he shall be cut o from
15:31 shall be completely cut o;
19:13 That person shall be cut o from
19:20 that person shall be cut o from
Deut 12:29 the LORD your God cuts o from
13: 7 near to you or far o from you,
19: 1 the LORD your God has cut o
21:13 She shall put o the clothes of
25:12 then you shall cut o her hand;
27:18 who makes the blind to wander o
28:40 for your olives shall drop o.
28:63 and you shall be plucked from o
30:11 for you, nor is it far o.
Josh 3:13 of the Jordan shall be cut o,
3:16 Sea, failed, and were cut o;
4: 7 waters of the Jordan were cut o
4: 7 waters of the Jordan were cut o.
5:15 Take your sandal o your foot,
7: 9 and cut o our name from the
11:21 time Joshua came and cut o the
23: 4 the nations that I have cut o,
Judg 1: 6 him and caught him and cut o
1: 7 thumbs and big toes cut o used
16:12 But he broke them o his arms
16:19 for a man and had him shave o
21: 6 One tribe is cut o from Israel
Ruth 4: 7 one man took o his sandal and
4: 8 So he took o his sandal.
4:10 of the dead may not be cut o
1 Sam 2:31 are coming that I will cut o
2:33 your men whom I do not cut o
4:18 that Eli fell o the seat
5: 4 of its hands were broken o on
11: 3 Hold o for seven days, that we
17:39 So David took them o.
17:51 and cut o his head with it.
18: 4 And Jonathan took o the robe
19:24 And he also stripped o his
20:15 but you shall not cut o your
20:15 not when the LORD has cut o
24: 4 David arose and secretly cut o
24:11 in my hand! For in that I cut o
24:21 LORD that you will not cut o
26:13 on the top of a hill afar o,
28: 9 how he has cut o the mediums
31: 9 And they cut o his head and
31: 9 cut off his head and stripped o
2 Sam 4:12 cut o their hands and feet, and
7: 9 and have cut o all your enemies
8: 2 he measured them o with a line.
8: 2 With two lines he measured o
10: 4 shaved o half of their beards,
10: 4 cut o their garments in the
16: 9 let me go over and take o his
20:22 And they cut o the head of
1 Ki 9: 7 then I will cut o Israel from
14:10 and will cut o from Jeroboam
14:14 over Israel who shall cut o
20:11 like the one who takes it o.
21:21 and will cut o from Ahab every
2 Ki 4:25 the man of God saw her afar o,
6: 6 So he cut o a stick, and threw
9: 8 and I will cut o from Ahab all
10:32 days the LORD began to cut o
11: 7 two contingents of you who go o
11: 9 with those who were going o
16:17 And King Ahaz cut o the panels
23:27 and will cast o this city
1 Chr 17: 8 and have cut o all your enemies
19: 4 and cut o their garments in the
28: 9 He will cast you o forever.
2 Chr 14:15 and carried o sheep and camels
20:25 which they stripped o for
22: 7 the LORD had anointed to cut o
23: 8 with those who were going o
26:21 for he was cut o from the house
33:11 and carried him o to Babylon.
36: 4 his brother and carried him o
36: 6 bronze fetters to carry him o
36: 7 Nebuchadnezzar also carried o
Ezra 3:13 and the sound was heard afar o.
Neh 4:23 guard who followed me took o
4:23 that everyone took them o for
12:43 of Jerusalem was heard afar o.
Esth 8: 2 So the king took o his signet
Job 4: 7 were the upright ever cut o?
6: 9 loose His hand and cut me o!
8:14 confidence shall be cut o,
9: 7 He seals o the stars;
9:27 I will put o my sad face and
15: 4 you cast o fear, And restrain
15:33 He will shake o his unripe
15:33 And cast o his blossom like an
17:11 past, My purposes are broken o,
23:17 Because I was not cut o from
24: 4 They push the needy o the road;
30:11 They have cast o restraint
36:20 When people are cut o in their
Ps 10: 1 Why do You stand afar o,
12: 3 May the LORD cut o all
30:11 You have put o my sackcloth
31:22 I am cut o from before Your
34:16 To cut o the remembrance of
37: 9 For evildoers shall be cut o;
37:22 cursed by Him shall be cut o.
37:28 of the wicked shall be cut o.
37:34 When the wicked are cut o,
37:38 of the wicked shall be cut o.
38:11 And my relatives stand afar o.
43: 2 strength; Why do You cast me o?
44: 9 But You have cast us o and put
44:23 Arise! Do not cast us o
54: 5 Cut them o in Your truth.
55: 7 Indeed, I would wander far o,
60: 1 O God, You have cast us o;
60:10 not You, O God, who cast us o?
71: 9 Do not cast me o in the time of
74: 1 why have You cast us o
75:10 of the wicked I will also cut o,
76:12 He shall cut o the spirit of
77: 7 Will the Lord cast o forever?
83: 4 and let us cut them o from
88: 5 And who are cut o from Your
88:14 why do You cast o my soul?
88:16 Your terrors have cut me o.
89:38 But You have cast o and
90:10 For it is soon cut o,
94:14 For the LORD will not cast o
94:23 And shall cut them o in their
94:23 LORD our God shall cut them o.
101: 8 That I may cut o all the
108:11 not You, O God, who cast us o?
109:13 Let his posterity be cut o,
109:15 That He may cut o the memory
109:23 I am shaken o like a locust.
139: 2 understand my thought afar o.
143:12 In Your mercy cut o my enemies,
Prov 2:22 But the wicked will be cut o
23:18 your hope will not be cut o.
24:14 your hope will not be cut o.
26: 6 by the hand of a fool Cuts o
29:18 the people cast o restraint;
30:14 To devour the poor from o the
Eccl 7:24 As for that which is far o and
10: 1 And cause it to give o a foul
Song 5: 3 I have taken o my robe;
7:13 The mandrakes give o a
Isa 9:14 the LORD will cut o head and
10: 7 And cut o not a few nations.
10:33 Will lop o the bough with
11:13 of Judah shall be cut o;
14:22 And cut o from Babylon the name
15: 2 And every beard cut o.
18: 5 He will both cut o the sprigs
20: 2 and take your sandals o your
22:25 that was on it will be cut o;
23: 7 Whose feet carried her far o
27:11 withered, they will be broken o;
29:20 watch for iniquity are cut o—
33: 9 And Bashan and Carmel shake o
33:13 Hear, you who are afar o,
33:17 see the land that is very far o.
38:12 I have cut o my life like a
38:12 He cuts me o from the loom;
46:13 near, it shall not be far o;
47: 2 Take o the skirt, Uncover the
47:11 will not be able to put it o.
48: 9 So that I do not cut you o.
48:19 name would not have been cut o
53: 8 For He was cut o from the land
55:13 sign that shall not be cut o.
56: 5 name That shall not be cut o.
57: 9 You sent your messengers far o,
57:19 peace to him who is far o
59:14 righteousness stands afar o;
66:19 to the coastlands afar o who
Jer 6:29 For the wicked are not drawn o.
7:28 has perished and has been cut o
7:29 Cut o your hair and cast it
9:21 To kill o the children—no
11:19 and let us cut him o from the
22:24 hand, yet I would pluck you o;
23:23 LORD, "And not a God afar o?
28:10 the prophet took the yoke o
31:10 declare it in the isles afar o,
31:37 I will also cast o all the
33:24 He has also cast them o'?
39: 7 bronze fetters to carry him o
44: 7 to cut o from you man and
44: 8 that you may cut yourselves o
44:11 catastrophe and for cutting o
47: 4 To cut o from Tyre and Sidon
47: 5 Ashkelon is cut o With the
48: 2 and let us cut her o as a
48:25 The horn of Moab is cut o,
49: 5 will gather those who wander o.
49:26 the men of war shall be cut o
50:16 Cut o the sower from Babylon,
50:30 her men of war shall be cut o
51: 6 his life! Do not be cut o in
51:50 Remember the LORD afar o,
51:62 against this place to cut it o,
Lam 2: 3 He has cut o in fierce anger
3:31 For the Lord will not cast o
3:54 I said, "I am cut o!"
4: 9 slain by the sword are better o
Ezek 4:16 surely I will cut o the supply
5:16 the famine upon you and cut o
6:12 He who is far o shall die by the
11:16 I have cast them far o among
12:27 he prophesies of times far o.
13:21 I will also tear o your veils
14: 8 and I will cut him o from the
14:13 I will cut o its supply of
14:13 and cut o man and beast from
14:17 and I cut o man and beast from
14:19 and cut o from it man and
14:21 to cut o man and beast from it?
16: 9 I thoroughly washed o your
17: 4 He cropped o its topmost young
17: 9 Cut o its fruit, And leave it
17:17 and build a wall to cut o many
17:22 I will crop o from the topmost
21: 3 out of its sheath and cut o
21: 4 Because I will cut o both
21:26 turban, and take o the crown;
25: 7 I will cut you o from the
25:13 cut o man and beast from it,
25:16 and I will cut o the
26:16 and take o their embroidered
29: 8 a sword upon you and cut o
29:19 carry o her spoil, and remove
30:15 I will cut o the multitude of
35: 7 and cut o from it the one who
37:11 and we ourselves are cut o!'
44:19 they shall take o their
Dan 4:14 Chop down the tree and cut o its
4:14 Strip o its leaves and scatter
4:27 break o your sins by being
7: 4 till its wings were plucked o;
9: 7 those near and those far o in
9:26 weeks Messiah shall be cut o,
Hos 8: 4 they might be cut o.
10: 7 her king is cut o Like a twig
10:15 king of Israel Shall be cut o
13: 3 Like chaff blown o from a
Joel 1: 5 For it has been cut o from
1: 9 offering Have been cut o from
1:16 Is not the food cut o before
3: 8 the Sabeans, To a people far o;
Am 1: 5 And cut o the inhabitant from
1: 8 I will cut o the inhabitant
1:11 And cast o all pity;
2: 3 And I will cut o the judge from
3:14 of the altar shall be cut o
6: 3 Woe to you who put far o the
Ob 5 how you will be cut o!—
9 of Esau May be cut o by
10 And you shall be cut o
14 at the crossroads To cut o
Mic 1:16 Make yourself bald and cut o
2: 8 You pull o the robe with the
4: 3 rebuke strong nations afar o;
5: 9 all your enemies shall be cut o.
5:10 That I will cut o your horses
5:11 I will cut o the cities of your
5:12 I will cut o sorceries from
5:13 carved images I will also cut o,
Nah 1:13 For now I will break o his yoke
1:14 of your gods I will cut o the
1:15 He is utterly cut o.
2:13 I will cut o your prey from the
3:15 you, The sword will cut you o;
Hab 2:10 Cutting o many peoples, And
3:17 Though the flock may be cut o
Zeph 1: 3 I will cut o man from the face
1: 4 I will cut o every trace of
1:11 who handle money are cut o.
3: 6 I have cut o nations, Their
3: 7 her dwelling would not be cut o,
Zech 9: 6 And I will cut o the pride of
9:10 I will cut o the chariot from
9:10 The battle bow shall be cut o.
11:16 care for those who are cut o,
13: 2 that I will cut o the names of
13: 8 in it shall be cut o and die,
14: 2 the people shall not be cut o
Mal 2:12 May the LORD cut o from the
Mt 5:30 cut it o and cast it from you;
8:30 Now a good way o from them there
10:14 shake o the dust from your
18: 8 cut it o and cast it from you.
26:51 and cut o his ear.
27:31 they took the robe o Him, put
Mk 6:11 shake o the dust under your
9:43 causes you to sin, cut it o.
9:45 causes you to sin, cut it o.
14:47 and cut o his ear.
15:20 they took the purple o Him, put
Lk 9: 5 shake o the very dust from your
10:11 which clings to us we wipe o
14:32 other is still a great way o,
15:20 when he was still a great way o,
16:23 his eyes and saw Abraham afar o,
17:12 were lepers, who stood afar o.
18:13 tax collector, standing afar o,
22:50 of the high priest and cut o
Jn 18:10 and cut o his right ear.

O

18:26 of him whose ear Peter cut o,
Acts 2:39 and to all who are afar o,
7:33 Take your sandals o your
8: 3 and dragging o men and women,
12: 7 And his chains fell o his
13:51 But they shook o the dust from
15:30 So when they were sent o,
16:22 and the magistrates tore o
18:18 He had his hair cut o at
22:23 as they cried out and tore o
27: 5 the sea which is o Cilicia
27: 7 with difficulty o Cnidus,
27: 7 under the shelter of Crete o
27:32 of the skiff and let it fall o.
28: 5 But he shook o the creature into
Rom 11:17 of the branches were broken o,
11:19 Branches were broken o that I
11:20 of unbelief they were broken o,
11:22 you also will be cut o.
13:12 Therefore let us cast o the
2 Cor 11:12 that I may cut o the
Gal 5:12 would even cut themselves o!
Eph 2:13 Jesus you who once were far o
2:17 peace to you who were afar o
4:22 that you put o, concerning
Col 2:11 by putting o the body of the
3: 8 now you yourselves are to put o
3: 9 since you have put o the old
1 Tim 5:12 because they have cast o their
Heb 11:13 but having seen them afar o
2 Pe 1:14 that shortly I must put o my

OFFAL (5/5)

Ex 29:14 bull, with its skin and its o,
Lev 4:11 and legs, its entrails and o—
8:17 its hide, its flesh, and its o,
16:27 skins, their flesh, and their o.
Num 19: 5 and its o shall be burned.

OFFEND (7/7) OFFENDED, OFFENSE, OFFENSIVE

Job 34:31 I will o no more;
Jer 2: 3 All that devour him will o;
Hos 4:15 the harlot, Let not Judah o.
Mt 13:41 His kingdom all things that o,
17:27 lest we o them, go to the sea,
Lk 17: 2 than that he should o one of
Jn 6:61 to them, "Does this o you?

OFFENDED (15/15) OFFEND

Gen 20: 9 How have I o you, that you have
40: 1 baker of the king of Egypt o
2 Chr 28:13 for we already have o the
Prov 18:19 A brother o is harder to
Jer 50: 7 said, 'We have not o,
Ezek 25:12 and has greatly o by avenging
Hos 13: 1 But when he o through Baal
Mt 11: 6 blessed is he who is not o
13:57 So they were o at Him. But Jesus
15:12 know that the Pharisees were o
24:10 "And then many will be o,
Mk 6: 3 And they were o at Him.
Lk 7:23 blessed is he who is not o
Acts 25: 8 nor against Caesar have I o in
Rom 14:21 your brother stumbles or is o

OFFENDER (2/2)

Isa 29:21 Who make a man an o by a word,
Acts 25:11 'For if I am an o, or have

OFFENDERS (2/2)

Num 25: 4 of the people and hang the o
1 Ki 1:21 Solomon will be counted as o.

OFFENSE (21/20) OFFEND, OFFENSES

1 Sam 25:31 nor o of heart to my lord,
Isa 8:14 of stumbling and a rock of o
Jer 37:18 What o have I committed against
Hos 5:15 Till they acknowledge their o.
Hab 1:11 he transgresses; He commits o,
Mt 16:23 You are an o to Me, for you
18: 7 woe to that man by whom the o
Acts 24:16 to have a conscience without o
Rom 5:15 free gift is not like the o.
5:15 For if by the one man's o many
5:16 which came from one o
5:17 For if by the one man's o death
5:18 as through one man's o
5:20 the law entered that the o
9:33 stone and rock of o,
14:20 for the man who eats with o.
1 Cor 10:32 Give no o, either to the
2 Cor 6: 3 We give no o in anything, that
Gal 5:11 Then the o of the cross has
Phil 1:10 may be sincere and without o
1 Pe 2: 8 And a rock of o.

OFFENSES (8/7) OFFENSE

2 Chr 19:10 whether of bloodshed or o
Eccl 10: 4 conciliation pacifies great o.
Mt 18: 7 Woe to the world because of o!
18: 7 For o must come, but woe to
Lk 17: 1 It is impossible that no o
Rom 4:25 delivered up because of our o,
5:16 gift which came from many o
16:17 those who cause divisions and o,

OFFENSIVE (1/1) OFFEND

Job 19:17 My breath is o to my wife,

OFFER (217/196) OFFERED, OFFERING, OFFERS

Gen 22: 2 and o him there as a burnt
Ex 18:12 sacrifices to o to God.
22:29 You shall not delay to o the
23:18 You shall not o the blood of My
29:36 And you shall o a bull every day
29:38 what you shall o on the altar:
29:39 One lamb you shall o in the
29:39 and the other lamb you shall o
29:41 the other lamb you shall o
29:41 and you shall o with it the
30: 9 You shall not o strange incense
34:25 You shall not o the blood of My
Lev 1: 3 let him o a male without
1: 3 he shall o it of his own free
2:12 you shall o them to the LORD,
2:13 offerings you shall o salt.
2:14 If you o a grain offering of
2:14 you shall o for the grain
3: 1 he shall o it without blemish
3: 3 Then he shall o from the
3: 6 he shall o it without blemish.
3: 7 then he shall o it before the
3: 9 Then he shall o from the
3:12 then he shall o it before the
3:14 Then he shall o from it his
4: 3 then let him o to the LORD for
4:14 then the assembly shall o a
5: 8 who shall o that which is for
5:10 And he shall o the second as a
6:14 The sons of Aaron shall o it on
6:20 which they shall o to the
6:21 you shall o for a sweet aroma
6:22 shall o it. It is a statute
7: 3 And he shall o from it all its
7:11 offerings which he shall o to
7:12 a thanksgiving, then he shall o,
7:13 as his offering he shall o
7:14 And from it he shall o one cake
7:25 of which men o an offering
7:38 Israel to o their offerings
9: 2 and o them before the LORD.
9: 7 o your sin offering and your
9: 7 O the offering of the people,
10:15 to o as a wave offering before
12: 7 Then he shall o it before the
14:12 take one male lamb and o it as
14:19 Then the priest shall o the sin
14:20 And the priest shall o the burnt
14:30 And he shall o one of the
15:15 Then the priest shall o them,
15:30 Then the priest shall o the one
16: 6 Aaron shall o the bull as a sin
16: 9 and o it as a sin offering.
16:24 come out and o his burnt
17: 4 of meeting to o an offering
17: 5 their sacrifices which they o
17: 5 and o them as peace offerings
17: 7 They shall no more o their
17: 9 to o it to the LORD, that man
19: 5 And if you o a sacrifice of a
19: 5 you shall o it of your own free
19: 6 eaten the same day you o it,
21: 6 for they o the offerings of the
21:17 may approach to o the bread of
21:21 shall come near to o the
21:21 he shall not come near to o the
22:15 which they o to the LORD,
22:18 which they o to the LORD as a
22:19 you shall o of your own free
22:20 has a defect, you shall not o,
22:22 you shall not o to the LORD,
22:23 may o as a freewill offering,
22:24 You shall not o to the LORD
22:25 hand shall you o any of these
22:29 And when you o a sacrifice of
22:29 o it of your own free will.
23: 8 But you shall o an offering made
23:12 And you shall o on that day,
23:16 then you shall o a new grain
23:18 And you shall o with the bread
23:25 and you shall o an offering
23:27 and o an offering made by fire
23:36 For seven days you shall o an
23:36 and you shall o an offering
23:37 to o an offering made by fire
27:11 animal which they do not o as
Num 6:11 and the priest shall o one as a
6:16 LORD and o his sin offering
6:17 and he shall o the ram as a
6:17 the priest shall also o its
7:11 They shall o their offering, one
8:11 and Aaron shall o the Levites
8:12 and you shall o one as a sin
8:13 and then o them like a wave
8:15 shall cleanse them and o them,
15: 7 offering you shall o one-third
15:19 that you shall o up a heave
15:20 You shall o up a cake of the
15:20 so shall you o it up.
15:24 shall o one young bull as a
16:40 should come near to o incense
18:12 their firstfruits which they o
18:19 which the children of Israel o
18:24 which they o up as a heave
18:26 then you shall o up a heave
18:28 Thus you shall also o a heave
18:29 Of all your gifts you shall o up
28: 2 you shall be careful to o to Me
28: 3 made by fire which you shall o
28: 4 The one lamb you shall o in the
28: 4 the other lamb you shall o in
28: 8 The other lamb you shall o in
28: 8 you shall o it as an offering
28:20 of an ephah you shall o for
28:21 you shall o one-tenth of an
28:23 You shall o these besides the
28:24 In this manner you shall o the
29: 2 You shall o a burnt offering as
Deut 12:13 do not o your burnt offerings
12:14 there you shall o your burnt
12:27 And you shall o your burnt
18: 3 from those who o a sacrifice,
20:10 then proclaim an o of peace to
20:11 they accept your o of peace,
27: 6 and o burnt offerings on it to
27: 7 You shall o peace offerings, and
33:19 There they shall o sacrifices
Josh 22:23 or if to o on it burnt
22:23 or if to o peace offerings on
Judg 5: 2 people willingly o themselves,
6:26 and take the second bull and o
11:31 and I will o it up as a burnt
13:16 But if you o a burnt offering,
13:16 you must o it to the LORD."
16:23 gathered together to o a great
1 Sam 1:21 and all his house went up to o
2:19 to o the yearly sacrifice.
2:28 to o upon My altar, to burn
10: 8 I will come down to you to o
2 Sam 24:12 'I o you three things;
24:22 my lord the king take and o up
24:24 nor will I o burnt offerings to
1 Ki 12:27 If these people go up to o
2 Ki 5:17 longer o either burnt offering
10:24 So they went in to o sacrifices
17:36 to Him you shall o sacrifice.
1 Chr 16:40 to o burnt offerings to the
21:10 'I o you three things;
21:24 nor o burnt offerings with
29:14 That we should be able to o so
29:17 present here to o willingly
2 Chr 23:18 to o the burnt offerings of the
29:21 to o them on the altar of the
29:27 Hezekiah commanded them to o
35:12 to o to the LORD, as it is
35:16 and to o burnt offerings on
Ezra 3: 2 to o burnt offerings on it, as
3: 6 began to o burnt offerings to
6:10 that they may o sacrifices of
7:17 and o them on the altar of the
Neh 4: 2 Will they o sacrifices?
Job 1: 5 morning and o burnt offerings
6:22 O a bribe for me from your
42: 8 and o up for yourselves a burnt
Ps 4: 5 O the sacrifices of
16: 4 offerings of blood I will not o,
27: 6 Therefore I will o sacrifices
50:14 O to God thanksgiving, And pay
51:19 Then they shall o bulls on
66:15 I will o You burnt sacrifices
66:15 I will o bulls with goats.
72:10 Sheba and Seba Will o gifts.
116:17 I will o to You the sacrifice
Isa 57: 7 you went up To o sacrifice.
Jer 11:12 gods to whom they o incense,
14:12 and when they o burnt offering
33:18 lack a man to o burnt offerings
Ezek 20:31 For when you o your gifts and
43:22 On the second day you shall o a
43:23 you shall o a young bull
43:24 When you o them before the
43:24 and they will o them up as a
43:27 that the priests shall o your
44:15 shall stand before Me to o to
44:27 he must o his sin offering in
45:13 the offering which you shall o:
Hos 4:13 They o sacrifices on the
4:14 And o sacrifices with a ritual
9: 4 They shall not o wine
14: 2 For we will o the sacrifices
Am 4: 5 O a sacrifice of thanksgiving
5:22 Though you o Me burnt offerings
5:25 Did you o Me sacrifices and
Hag 2:14 and what they o there is
Mal 1: 7 You o defiled food on My altar.
1: 8 And when you o the blind as a
1: 8 And when you o the lame and
1: 8 O it then to your governor!
3: 3 That they may o to the LORD
Mt 5:24 and then come and o your gift.
8: 4 and o the gift that Moses
Mk 1:44 and o for your cleansing those
Lk 2:24 and to o a sacrifice according
6:29 o the other also. And from him
11:12 will he o him a scorpion?
Acts 7:42 Did you o Me slaughtered
Heb 5: 1 that he may o both gifts and
5: 3 to o sacrifices for sins.
7:27 to o up sacrifices, first for
8: 3 priest is appointed to o both
8: 3 One also have something to o.
8: 4 are priests who o the gifts
9:25 not that He should o Himself
10: 1 which they o continually year
13:15 o the sacrifice of praise to
1 Pe 2: 5 to o up spiritual sacrifices
Rev 8: 3 that he should o it with the

OFFERED (129/123) OFFER

Gen 8:20 and **o** burnt offerings on the
22:13 and **o** it up for a burnt
31:54 Then Jacob **o** a sacrifice on the
46: 1 and **o** sacrifices to the God of
Ex 24: 5 who **o** burnt offerings and
32: 6 **o** burnt offerings, and brought
35:24 Everyone who **o** an offering of
40:29 and **o** upon it the burnt
Lev 7: 8 burnt offering which he has **o**.
7:15 be eaten the same day it is **o**.
9:15 and killed it and **o** it for sin,
9:16 the burnt offering and **o** it
10: 1 and **o** profane fire before the
10:19 this day they have **o** their sin
16: 1 when they **o** profane fire
Num 3: 4 when they **o** profane fire
7:10 the leaders **o** the dedication
7:10 so the leaders **o** their offering
7:12 And the one who **o** his offering
7:19 For his offering he **o** one
15: 9 then shall be **o** with the young
22:40 Then Balak **o** oxen and sheep, and
23: 2 and Balak and Balaam **o** a bull
23: 4 and I have **o** on each altar a
23:14 and **o** a bull and a ram on each
23:30 and **o** a bull and a ram on
26:61 died when they **o** profane fire
28:15 to the LORD shall be **o**,
28:24 it shall be **o** besides the
31:52 of the offering that they **o** to
Deut 28:68 And there you shall be **o** for
Josh 8:31 And they **o** on it burnt
Judg 5: 9 of Israel Who **o** themselves
6:28 the second bull was being **o** on
13:19 and **o** it upon the rock to the
20:26 and they **o** burnt offerings and
21: 4 and **o** burnt offerings and peace
1 Sam 2:13 when any man **o** a sacrifice,
6:14 of the cart and **o** the cows
6:15 Beth Shemesh **o** burnt offerings
7: 9 took a suckling lamb and **o** it
13: 9 And he **o** the burnt offering.
13:12 and **o** a burnt offering."
2 Sam 6:17 Then David **o** burnt offerings
15:12 —while he **o** sacrifices.
24:25 and **o** burnt offerings and peace
1 Ki 3: 4 Solomon **o** a thousand burnt
3:15 **o** up burnt offerings, offered
3:15 **o** peace offerings, and made a
8:62 Israel with him **o** sacrifices
8:63 And Solomon **o** a sacrifice of
8:63 which he **o** to the LORD,
8:64 for there he **o** burnt offerings,
9:25 three times a year Solomon **o**
12:32 and **o** sacrifices on the altar.
12:33 and **o** sacrifices on the altar
22:43 for the people **o** sacrifices
2 Ki 3:20 when the grain offering was **o**,
3:27 and **o** him as a burnt offering
1 Chr 6:49 and his sons **o** sacrifices
15:26 that they **o** seven bulls and
16: 1 Then they **o** burnt offerings and
21:26 and **o** burnt offerings and peace
29: 6 king's work, **o** willingly.
29: 9 for they had **o** willingly,
29: 9 heart they had **o** willingly
29:17 of my heart I have willingly **o**
29:21 LORD and **o** burnt offerings
2 Chr 1: 6 and **o** a thousand burnt
4: 6 such things as they **o** for the
7: 4 all the people **o** sacrifices
7: 5 King Solomon **o** a sacrifice of
7: 6 whenever David **o** praise by
7: 7 for there he **o** burnt offerings
8:12 Then Solomon **o** burnt offerings
15:11 And they **o** to the LORD at that
17:16 who willingly **o** himself to the
24:14 And they **o** burnt offerings in
29: 7 incense or **o** burnt offerings
Ezra 1: 6 all that was willingly **o**.
2:68 **o** freely for the house of God,
3: 3 and they **o** burnt offerings on
3: 4 and **o** the daily burnt
3: 5 Afterwards they **o** the regular
3: 5 **o** a freewill offering to the
6: 3 where they **o** sacrifices;
6:17 And they **o** sacrifices at the
7:15 his counselors have freely **o**
7:16 are to be freely **o** for the
8:25 who were present, had **o**.
8:35 **o** burnt offerings to the God of
Neh 11: 2 all the men who willingly **o**
12:43 Also that day they **o** great
Isa 57: 6 You have **o** a grain offering.
Jer 32:29 roofs they have **o** incense
Ezek 6:13 wherever they **o** sweet incense
16:21 My children and **o** them up
16:25 You **o** yourself to everyone who
20:28 there they **o** their sacrifices
36:38 Like a flock **o** as holy
44: 7 and when you **o** My food, the fat
Jon 1:16 and **o** a sacrifice to the LORD
Mal 1:11 place incense shall be **o** to
Mt 27:48 and **o** it to Him to drink.
Mk 15:36 and **o** it to Him to drink,
Acts 7:41 **o** sacrifices to the idol, and
8:18 was given, he **o** them money,
12: 5 but constant prayer was **o** to
15:29 that you abstain from things **o**
21:25 keep themselves from things **o**
1 Cor 8: 1 Now concerning things **o** to
8: 4 the eating of things **o** to
8: 7 until now eat it as a thing **o**
8:10 to eat those things **o** to idols?
10:19 or what is **o** to idols is
10:28 This was **o** to idols," do not
Heb 5: 7 when He had **o** up prayers and
7:27 for all when He **o** up Himself.
9: 7 which he **o** for himself and for
9: 9 sacrifices are **o** which cannot
9:14 eternal Spirit **o** Himself
9:28 so Christ was **o** once to bear the
10: 2 they not have ceased to be **o**?
10: 8 (which are **o** according to
10:12 after He had **o** one sacrifice
11: 4 By faith Abel **o** to God a more
11:17 **o** up Isaac, and he who had
11:17 had received the promises **o** up
Jas 2:21 by works when he **o** Isaac

OFFERING (803/547) OFFER, OFFERINGS

Gen 4: 3 to pass that Cain brought an **o**
4: 4 LORD respected Abel and his **o**,
4: 5 did not respect Cain and his **o**.
22: 2 offer him there as a burnt **o**
22: 3 split the wood for the burnt **o**,
22: 6 took the wood of the burnt **o**
22: 7 is the lamb for a burnt **o**?
22: 8 Himself the lamb for a burnt **o**.
22:13 and offered it up for a burnt **o**
35:14 and he poured a drink **o** on it,
Ex 18:12 took a burnt **o** and other
25: 2 Israel, that they bring Me an **o**.
25: 2 his heart you shall take My **o**.
25: 3 And this is the **o** which you
29:14 the camp. It is a sin **o**.
29:18 It is a burnt **o** to the LORD;
29:18 an **o** made by fire to the LORD.
29:24 shall wave them as a wave **o**
29:25 them on the altar as a burnt **o**,
29:25 It is an **o** made by fire to the
29:26 and wave it as a wave **o**
29:27 the breast of the wave **o** which
29:27 and the thigh of the heave **o**
29:28 For it is a heave **o**;
29:28 it shall be a heave **o** from the
29:28 their heave **o** to the LORD.
29:36 a bull every day as a sin **o**
29:40 of a hin of wine as a drink **o**.
29:41 offer with it the grain **o** and
29:41 grain offering and the drink **o**,
29:41 an **o** made by fire to the LORD.
29:42 shall be a continual burnt **o**
30: 9 incense on it, or a burnt **o**,
30: 9 a burnt offering, or a grain **o**;
30: 9 nor shall you pour a drink **o** on
30:10 with the blood of the sin **o** of
30:13 half-shekel shall be an **o** to
30:14 shall give an **o** to the LORD.
30:15 when you give an **o** to the
30:20 to burn an **o** made by fire to
30:28 the altar of burnt **o** with all
31: 9 the altar of burnt **o** with all
35: 5 Take from among you an **o** to the
35: 5 let him bring it as an **o** to the
35:16 the altar of burnt **o** with its
35:21 they brought the LORD's **o** for
35:22 every man who made an **o** of
35:24 Everyone who offered an **o** of
35:24 or bronze brought the LORD's **o**.
35:29 of Israel brought a freewill **o**
36: 3 received from Moses all the **o**
36: 6 do any more work for the **o** of
38: 1 He made the altar of burnt **o** of
38:24 that is, the gold of the **o**,
38:29 The **o** of bronze was seventy
40: 6 set the altar of the burnt **o**
40:10 the altar of the burnt **o** and
40:29 And he put the altar of burnt **o**
40:29 and offered upon it the burnt **o**
40:29 burnt offering and the grain **o**,
Lev 1: 2 any one of you brings an **o** to
1: 2 you shall bring your **o** of the
1: 3 If his **o** is a burnt sacrifice
1: 4 hand on the head of the burnt **o**,
1: 6 And he shall skin the burnt **o**
1: 9 an **o** made by fire, a sweet
1:10 If his **o** is of the flocks—of
1:13 an **o** made by fire, a sweet
1:14 if the burnt sacrifice of his **o**
1:14 then he shall bring his **o** of
1:17 an **o** made by fire, a sweet
2: 1 When anyone offers a grain **o** to
2: 1 his **o** shall be of fine flour.
2: 2 an **o** made by fire, a sweet
2: 3 The rest of the grain **o** shall
2: 4 And if you bring as an **o** a
2: 4 bring as an offering a grain **o**
2: 5 But if your **o** is a grain
2: 5 if your offering is a grain **o**
2: 6 oil on it; it is a grain **o**.
2: 7 If your **o** is a grain offering
2: 7 your offering is a grain **o**
2: 8 You shall bring the grain **o** that
2: 9 shall take from the grain **o** a
2: 9 It is an **o** made by fire, a
2:10 what is left of the grain **o**
2:11 No grain **o** which you bring to
2:11 leaven nor any honey in any **o**
2:12 As for the **o** of the firstfruits,
2:13 And every **o** of your grain
2:13 every offering of your grain **o**
2:13 to be lacking from your grain **o**.
2:14 If you offer a grain **o** of your
2:14 shall offer for the grain **o** of
2:15 on it. It is a grain **o**.
2:16 as an **o** made by fire to the
3: 1 When his **o** is a sacrifice of a
3: 1 is a sacrifice of a peace **o**,
3: 2 his hand on the head of his **o**,
3: 3 the sacrifice of the peace **o**
3: 3 of the peace offering an **o**
3: 5 as an **o** made by fire, a sweet
3: 6 If his **o** as a sacrifice of a
3: 6 as a sacrifice of a peace **o** to
3: 7 'If he offers a lamb as his **o**,
3: 8 his hand on the head of his **o**,
3: 9 the sacrifice of the peace **o**,
3: 9 as an **o** made by fire to the
3:11 an **o** made by fire to the LORD.
3:12 And if his **o** is a goat, then
3:14 he shall offer from it his **o**,
3:14 as an **o** made by fire to the
3:16 an **o** made by fire for a sweet
4: 3 bull without blemish as a sin **o**.
4: 7 of the altar of the burnt **o**,
4: 8 fat of the bull as the sin **o**.
4:10 of the sacrifice of the peace **o**;
4:10 on the altar of the burnt **o**.
4:18 base of the altar of burnt **o**,
4:20 he did with the bull as a sin **o**;
4:21 It is a sin **o** for the
4:23 he shall bring as his **o** a kid
4:24 where they kill the burnt **o**
4:24 the LORD. It is a sin **o**.
4:25 some of the blood of the sin **o**
4:25 horns of the altar of burnt **o**,
4:25 base of the altar of burnt **o**.
4:26 of the sacrifice of the peace **o**.
4:28 then he shall bring as his **o** a
4:29 hand on the head of the sin **o**,
4:29 and kill the sin **o** at the place
4:29 at the place of the burnt **o**.
4:30 horns of the altar of burnt **o**,
4:31 the sacrifice of the peace **o**;
4:32 he brings a lamb as his sin **o**,
4:33 hand on the head of the sin **o**,
4:33 and kill it as a sin **o** at the
4:33 where they kill the burnt **o**.
4:34 of the blood of the sin **o** with
4:34 horns of the altar of burnt **o**,
4:35 the sacrifice of the peace **o**.
5: 6 he shall bring his trespass **o**
5: 6 a kid of the goats as a sin **o**.
5: 7 one as a sin **o** and the other as
5: 7 and the other as a burnt **o**.
5: 8 that which is for the sin **o**
5: 9 of the blood of the sin **o** on
5: 9 of the altar. It is a sin **o**.
5:10 offer the second as a burnt **o**
5:11 sinned shall bring for his **o**
5:11 ephah of fine flour as a sin **o**.
5:11 on it, for it is a sin **o**.
5:12 to the LORD. It is a sin **o**.
5:13 be the priest's as a grain **o**.
5:15 to the LORD as his trespass **o**
5:15 the sanctuary, as a trespass **o**.
5:16 with the ram of the trespass **o**,
5:18 your valuation, as a trespass **o**.
5:19 "It is a trespass **o**;
6: 5 on the day of his trespass **o**.
6: 6 he shall bring his trespass **o**
6: 6 your valuation, as a trespass **o**,
6: 9 is the law of the burnt **o**:
6: 9 The burnt **o** shall be on the
6:10 up the ashes of the burnt **o**
6:12 and lay the burnt **o** in order on
6:14 is the law of the grain **o**:
6:15 the fine flour of the grain **o**,
6:15 which is on the grain **o**,
6:17 like the sin **o** and the trespass
6:17 sin offering and the trespass **o**.
6:20 This is the **o** of Aaron and his
6:20 fine flour as a daily grain **o**,
6:21 The baked pieces of the grain **o**
6:23 For every grain **o** for the priest
6:25 'This is the law of the sin **o**:
6:25 In the place where the burnt **o**
6:25 the sin **o** shall be killed
6:30 But no sin **o** from which any of
7: 1 is the law of the trespass **o**
7: 2 where they kill the burnt **o**
7: 2 they shall kill the trespass **o**.
7: 5 burn them on the altar as an **o**
7: 5 the LORD. It is a trespass **o**.
7: 7 The trespass **o** is like the sin
7: 7 offering is like the sin **o**;
7: 8 who offers anyone's burnt **o**,
7: 8 the skin of the burnt **o** which
7: 9 Also every grain **o** that is baked
7:10 'Every grain **o**, whether mixed
7:13 as his **o** he shall offer
7:13 of thanksgiving of his peace **o**.
7:14 offer one cake from each **o** as
7:14 each offering as a heave **o** to
7:14 the blood of the peace **o**.
7:15 of the sacrifice of his peace **o**
7:16 But if the sacrifice of his **o**
7:16 is a vow or a voluntary **o**,
7:18 of the sacrifice of his peace **o**
7:20 of the sacrifice of the peace **o**
7:21 of the sacrifice of the peace **o**
7:25 animal of which men offer an **o**

O

7:29 the sacrifice of his peace **o**
7:29 to the LORD shall bring his **o**
7:29 the sacrifice of his peace **o**.
7:30 may be waved as a wave **o**
7:32 to the priest as a heave **o**
7:33 the blood of the peace **o** and
7:34 For the breast of the wave **o** and
7:34 and the thigh of the heave **o** I
7:37 is the law of the burnt **o**,
7:37 the burnt offering, the grain **o**,
7:37 the grain offering, the sin **o**,
7:37 sin offering, the trespass **o**,
7:37 the sacrifice of the peace **o**,
8: 2 oil, a bull as the sin **o**,
8:14 brought the bull for the sin **o**.
8:14 head of the bull for the sin **o**,
8:18 brought the ram as the burnt **o**.
8:21 an **o** made by fire to the LORD,
8:27 and waved them as a wave **o**
8:28 on the altar, on the burnt **o**.
8:28 That was an **o** made by fire to
8:29 and waved it as a wave **o**
9: 2 a young bull as a sin **o** and a
9: 2 offering and a ram as a burnt **o**,
9: 3 a kid of the goats as a sin **o**,
9: 3 without blemish, as a burnt **o**,
9: 4 and a grain **o** mixed with oil;
9: 7 offer your sin **o** and your burnt
9: 7 sin offering and your burnt **o**,
9: 7 Offer the **o** of the people, and
9: 8 killed the calf of the sin **o**,
9:10 from the liver of the sin **o** he
9:12 And he killed the burnt **o**;
9:13 they presented the burnt **o** to
9:14 burned them with the burnt **o**
9:15 Then he brought the people's **o**,
9:15 which was the sin **o** for the
9:16 And he brought the burnt **o** and
9:17 Then he brought the grain **o**,
9:21 thigh Aaron waved as a wave **o**
9:22 and came down from **o** the sin
9:22 down from offering the sin **o**,
9:22 the sin offering, the burnt **o**,
9:24 LORD and consumed the burnt **o**
10:12 Take the grain **o** that remains of
10:14 The breast of the wave **o** and the
10:14 and the thigh of the heave **o**
10:15 The thigh of the heave **o** and the
10:15 and the breast of the wave **o**
10:15 to offer as a wave **o** before
10:16 about the goat of the sin **o**,
10:17 have you not eaten the sin **o**
10:19 they have offered their sin **o**
10:19 sin offering and their burnt **o**
10:19 If I had eaten the sin **o** today,
12: 6 of the first year as a burnt **o**,
12: 6 or a turtledove as a sin **o**,
12: 8 one as a burnt **o** and the other
12: 8 and the other as a sin **o**.
14:10 mixed with oil as a grain **o**,
14:12 and offer it as a trespass **o**,
14:12 and wave them as a wave **o**
14:13 place where he kills the sin **o**
14:13 sin offering and the burnt **o**,
14:13 for as the sin **o** is the
14:13 priest's, so is the trespass **o**.
14:14 of the blood of the trespass **o**,
14:17 on the blood of the trespass **o**.
14:19 priest shall offer the sin **o**,
14:19 he shall kill the burnt **o**.
14:20 priest shall offer the burnt **o**
14:20 burnt offering and the grain **o**
14:21 one male lamb as a trespass **o**
14:21 mixed with oil as a grain **o**,
14:22 one shall be a sin **o** and the
14:22 and the other a burnt **o**.
14:24 the lamb of the trespass **o** and
14:24 shall wave them as a wave **o**
14:25 kill the lamb of the trespass **o**,
14:25 of the blood of the trespass **o**
14:28 of the blood of the trespass **o**.
14:31 the one as a sin **o** and the
14:31 and the other as a burnt **o**,
14:31 offering, with the grain **o**.
15:15 the one as a sin **o** and the
15:15 and the other as a burnt **o**.
15:30 offer the one as a sin **o** and
15:30 and the other as a burnt **o**,
16: 3 of a young bull as a sin **o**,
16: 3 and of a ram as a burnt **o**.
16: 5 kids of the goats as a sin **o**,
16: 5 and one ram as a burnt **o**.
16: 6 shall offer the bull as a sin **o**,
16: 9 fell, and offer it as a sin **o**.
16:11 bring the bull of the sin **o**,
16:11 kill the bull as the sin **o**
16:15 kill the goat of the sin **o**,
16:24 come out and offer his burnt **o**
16:24 burnt offering and the burnt **o**
16:25 The fat of the sin **o** he shall
16:27 The bull for the sin **o** and the
16:27 and the goat for the sin **o**,
17: 4 of meeting to offer an **o** to
17: 8 who offers a burnt **o** or
19: 5 offer a sacrifice of a peace **o**
19: 8 he has profaned the hallowed **o**
19:21 he shall bring his trespass **o**
19:21 meeting, a ram as a trespass **o**.
19:22 with the ram of the trespass **o**
22:10 outsider shall eat the holy **o**;
22:14 'And if a man eats the holy **o**
22:14 he shall restore a holy **o** to
22:18 offer to the LORD as a burnt **o**—
22:21 a sacrifice of a peace **o** to
22:21 or a freewill **o** from the cattle
22:22 nor make an **o** by fire of them
22:23 you may offer as a freewill **o**,
22:24 nor shall you make any **o** of
22:27 it shall be accepted as an **o**
23: 8 But you shall offer an **o** made by
23:12 as a burnt **o** to the LORD.
23:13 Its grain **o** shall be
23:13 an **o** made by fire to the LORD,
23:13 and its drink **o** shall be of
23:14 day that you have brought an **o**
23:15 brought the sheaf of the wave **o**:
23:16 you shall offer a new grain **o**
23:18 They shall be as a burnt **o** to
23:18 with their grain **o** and their
23:18 an **o** made by fire for a sweet
23:19 one kid of the goats as a sin **o**,
23:19 as a sacrifice of a peace **o**.
23:20 of the firstfruits as a wave **o**
23:25 and you shall offer an **o** made
23:27 and offer an **o** made by fire to
23:36 days you shall offer an **o** made
23:36 and you shall offer an **o** made
23:37 to offer an **o** made by fire to
23:37 a burnt **o** and a grain offering,
23:37 a burnt offering and a grain **o**,
24: 7 an **o** made by fire to the LORD.
27: 9 that men may bring as an **o** to
27:23 on that day as a holy **o** to
27:28 Nevertheless no devoted **o** that
27:28 every devoted **o** is most holy
Num 4:16 incense, the daily grain **o**,
5: 9 Every **o** of all the holy things
5:15 He shall bring the **o** required
5:15 because it is a grain **o** of
5:15 an **o** for remembering, for
5:18 and put the **o** for remembering
5:18 which is the grain **o** of
5:25 priest shall take the grain **o**
5:25 shall wave the **o** before the
5:26 shall take a handful of the **o**,
6: 2 a man or woman consecrates an **o**
6:11 shall offer one as a sin **o** and
6:11 and the other as a burnt **o**,
6:12 its first year as a trespass **o**;
6:14 And he shall present his **o** to
6:14 without blemish as a burnt **o**,
6:14 year without blemish as a sin **o**,
6:14 without blemish as a peace **o**,
6:15 and their grain **o** with their
6:16 the LORD and offer his sin **o**
6:16 sin offering and his burnt **o**;
6:17 ram as a sacrifice of peace **o**
6:17 shall also offer its grain **o**
6:17 grain offering and its drink **o**.
6:18 the sacrifice of the peace **o**.
6:20 shall wave them as a wave **o**
6:20 with the breast of the wave **o**
6:20 and the thigh of the heave **o**.
6:21 who vows to the LORD the **o**
7: 2 who were numbered, made an **o**.
7: 3 And they brought their **o** before
7:10 offered the dedication **o** for
7:10 so the leaders offered their **o**
7:11 "They shall offer their **o**,
7:12 And the one who offered his **o**
7:13 His **o** was one silver platter,
7:13 mixed with oil as a grain **o**;
7:15 in its first year, as a burnt **o**;
7:16 one kid of the goats as a sin **o**;
7:17 This was the **o** of Nahshon the
7:18 of Issachar, presented an **o**.
7:19 For his **o** he offered one silver
7:19 mixed with oil as a grain **o**;
7:21 in its first year, as a burnt **o**;
7:22 one kid of the goats as a sin **o**;
7:23 This was the **o** of Nethanel the
7:24 of Zebulun, presented an **o**.
7:25 His **o** was one silver platter,
7:25 mixed with oil as a grain **o**;
7:27 in its first year, as a burnt **o**;
7:28 one kid of the goats as a sin **o**;
7:29 This was the **o** of Eliab the
7:30 of Reuben, presented an **o**.
7:31 His **o** was one silver platter,
7:31 mixed with oil as a grain **o**;
7:33 in its first year, as a burnt **o**;
7:34 one kid of the goats as a sin **o**;
7:35 This was the **o** of Elizur the
7:36 of Simeon, presented an **o**.
7:37 His **o** was one silver platter,
7:37 mixed with oil as a grain **o**;
7:39 in its first year, as a burnt **o**;
7:40 one kid of the goats as a sin **o**;
7:41 This was the **o** of Shelumiel
7:42 of Gad, presented an **o**.
7:43 His **o** was one silver platter,
7:43 mixed with oil as a grain **o**;
7:45 in its first year, as a burnt **o**;
7:46 one kid of the goats as a sin **o**;
7:47 This was the **o** of Eliasaph the
7:48 of Ephraim, presented an **o**.
7:49 His **o** was one silver platter,
7:49 mixed with oil as a grain **o**;
7:51 in its first year, as a burnt **o**;
7:52 one kid of the goats as a sin **o**;
7:53 This was the **o** of Elishama the
7:54 of Manasseh, presented an **o**.
7:55 His **o** was one silver platter,
7:55 mixed with oil as a grain **o**;
7:57 in its first year, as a burnt **o**;
7:58 one kid of the goats as a sin **o**;
7:59 This was the **o** of Gamaliel the
7:60 of Benjamin, presented an **o**.
7:61 His **o** was one silver platter,
7:61 mixed with oil as a grain **o**;
7:63 in its first year, as a burnt **o**;
7:64 one kid of the goats as a sin **o**;
7:65 This was the **o** of Abidan the
7:66 of Dan, presented an **o**.
7:67 His **o** was one silver platter,
7:67 mixed with oil as a grain **o**;
7:69 in its first year, as a burnt **o**;
7:70 one kid of the goats as a sin **o**;
7:71 This was the **o** of Ahiezer the
7:72 of Asher, presented an **o**.
7:73 His **o** was one silver platter,
7:73 mixed with oil as a grain **o**;
7:75 in its first year, as a burnt **o**;
7:76 one kid of the goats as a sin **o**;
7:77 This was the **o** of Pagiel the
7:78 of Naphtali, presented an **o**.
7:79 His **o** was one silver platter,
7:79 mixed with oil as a grain **o**;
7:81 in its first year, as a burnt **o**;
7:82 one kid of the goats as a sin **o**;
7:83 This was the **o** of Ahira the
7:84 This was the dedication **o** for
7:87 All the oxen for the burnt **o**
7:87 year twelve, with their grain **o**,
7:87 kids of the goats as a sin **o**
7:88 This was the dedication **o** for
8: 8 a young bull with its grain **o**
8: 8 another young bull as a sin **o**.
8:11 like a wave **o** from the
8:12 you shall offer one as a sin **o**
8:12 and the other as a burnt **o** to
8:13 then offer them like a wave **o**
8:15 and offer them, like a wave **o**.
8:21 like a wave **o** before the
9: 7 we kept from presenting the **o**
9:13 because he did not bring the **o**
15: 3 and you make an **o** by fire to the
15: 3 a burnt **o** or a sacrifice, to
15: 3 a vow or as a freewill **o** or in
15: 4 then he who presents his **o** to
15: 4 LORD shall bring a grain **o** of
15: 5 of a HIN of wine as a drink **o**
15: 5 shall prepare with the burnt **o**
15: 6 you shall prepare as a grain **o**
15: 7 and as a drink **o** you shall offer
15: 8 a young bull as a burnt **o**,
15: 8 or as a peace **o** to the LORD,
15: 9 with the young bull a grain **o**
15:10 you shall bring as the drink **o**
15:10 half a hin of wine as an **o**
15:13 in presenting an **o** made by
15:14 and would present an **o** made by
15:19 you shall offer up a heave **o**
15:20 your ground meal as a heave **o**;
15:20 as a heave **o** of the threshing
15:21 give to the LORD a heave **o**
15:24 one young bull as a burnt **o**,
15:24 with its grain **o** and its drink
15:24 grain offering and its drink **o**,
15:24 one kid of the goats as a sin **o**.
15:25 they shall bring their **o**,
15:25 an **o** made by fire to the LORD,
15:25 and their sin **o** before the
15:27 in its first year as a sin **o**.
16:15 LORD, "Do not respect their **o**.
16:35 and fifty men who were **o**
18: 9 every **o** of theirs, every grain
18: 9 every grain **o** and every sin
18: 9 grain offering and every sin **o**
18: 9 offering and every trespass **o**
18:11 the heave **o** of their gift, with
18:17 and burn their fat as an **o**
18:24 they offer up as a heave **o** to
18:26 you shall offer up a heave **o**
18:27 And your heave **o** shall be
18:28 you shall also offer a heave **o**
18:28 shall give the LORD's heave **o**
18:29 shall offer up every heave **o**
23: 3 Balak, "Stand by your burnt **o**,
23: 6 he was, standing by his burnt **o**,
23:15 Stand here by your burnt **o** while
23:17 he was, standing by his burnt **o**,
28: 2 Israel, and say to them, 'My **o**,
28: 3 This is the **o** made by fire
28: 3 by day, as a regular burnt **o**.
28: 5 of fine flour as a grain **o**
28: 6 It is a regular burnt **o** which
28: 6 an **o** made by fire to the LORD.
28: 7 And its drink **o** shall be
28: 7 the drink to the LORD as an **o**.
28: 8 as the morning grain **o** and its
28: 8 grain offering and its drink **o**,
28: 8 you shall offer it as an **o**
28: 9 of fine flour as a grain **o**,
28: 9 with oil, with its drink **o**—
28:10 this is the burnt **o** for every
28:10 besides the regular burnt **o**
28:10 burnt offering with its drink **o**.
28:11 you shall present a burnt **o** to
28:12 of fine flour as a grain **o**,
28:12 of fine flour as a grain **o**,
28:13 as a grain **o** for each lamb, as
28:13 as a burnt **o** of sweet aroma, an
28:13 an **o** made by fire to the LORD.
28:14 Their drink **o** shall be half a
28:14 this is the burnt **o** for each

28:15 kid of the goats as a sin **o** to
28:15 besides the regular burnt **o** and
28:15 burnt offering and its drink **o**.
28:19 And you shall present an **o** made
28:19 made by fire as a burnt **o** to
28:20 Their grain **o** shall be of fine
28:22 'also one goat as a sin **o**,
28:23 these besides the burnt **o** of
28:23 which is for a regular burnt **o**.
28:24 shall offer the food of the **o**
28:24 besides the regular burnt **o**
28:24 burnt offering and its drink **o**.
28:26 when you bring a new grain **o** to
28:27 You shall present a burnt **o** as a
28:28 with their grain **o** of fine flour
28:31 besides the regular burnt **o**
28:31 burnt offering with its grain **o**.
29: 2 You shall offer a burnt **o** as a
29: 3 Their grain **o** shall be fine
29: 5 kid of the goats as a sin **o**,
29: 6 besides the burnt **o** with its
29: 6 offering with its grain **o** for
29: 6 the regular burnt **o** with its
29: 6 burnt offering with its grain **o**,
29: 6 an **o** made by fire to the LORD.
29: 8 You shall present a burnt **o** to
29: 9 Their grain **o** shall be of
29:11 kid of the goats as a sin **o**,
29:11 besides the sin **o** for
29:11 the regular burnt **o** with its
29:11 burnt offering with its grain **o**,
29:13 'You shall present a burnt **o**,
29:13 an **o** made by fire as a sweet
29:14 Their grain **o** shall be of
29:16 kid of the goats as a sin **o**,
29:16 besides the regular burnt **o**,
29:16 burnt offering, its grain **o**,
29:16 grain offering, and its drink **o**.
29:18 and their grain **o** and their
29:19 kid of the goats as a sin **o**,
29:19 besides the regular burnt **o**
29:19 burnt offering with its grain **o**,
29:21 and their grain **o** and their
29:22 'also one goat as a sin **o**,
29:22 besides the regular burnt **o**,
29:22 burnt offering, its grain **o**,
29:22 grain offering, and its drink **o**.
29:24 and their grain **o** and their
29:25 kid of the goats as a sin **o**,
29:25 besides the regular burnt **o**,
29:25 burnt offering, its grain **o**,
29:25 grain offering, and its drink **o**.
29:27 and their grain **o** and their
29:28 'also one goat as a sin **o**,
29:28 besides the regular burnt **o**,
29:28 burnt offering, its grain **o**,
29:28 grain offering, and its drink **o**.
29:30 and their grain **o** and their
29:31 'also one goat as a sin **o**,
29:31 besides the regular burnt **o**,
29:31 burnt offering, its grain **o**,
29:31 grain offering, and its drink **o**.
29:33 and their grain **o** and their
29:34 'also one goat as a sin **o**,
29:34 besides the regular burnt **o**,
29:34 burnt offering, its grain **o**,
29:34 grain offering, and its drink **o**.
29:36 'You shall present a burnt **o**,
29:36 an **o** made by fire as a sweet
29:37 and their grain **o** and their
29:38 'also one goat as a sin **o**,
29:38 besides the regular burnt **o**,
29:38 burnt offering, its grain **o**,
29:38 grain offering, and its drink **o**.
31:29 the priest as a heave **o** to the
31:41 was the LORD's heave **o** to
31:50 we have brought an **o**
31:52 And all the gold of the **o** that
Deut 12:17 or of the heave **o** of your hand.
16:10 the tribute of a freewill **o**
23:18 LORD your God for any vowed **o**,
32:38 drank the wine of their drink **o**?
Josh 22:26 not for burnt **o** nor for
Judg 6:18 come to You and bring out my **o**
11:31 I will offer it up as a burnt **o**.
13:16 But if you offer a burnt **o**,
13:19 the young goat with the grain **o**,
13:23 not have accepted a burnt **o**
13:23 a burnt offering and a grain **o**
1 Sam 1: 4 came for Elkanah to make an **o**,
2:17 for men abhorred the **o** of the
2:29 kick at My sacrifice and My **o**
3:14 be atoned for by sacrifice or **o**
6: 3 it to Him with a trespass **o**.
6: 4 What is the trespass **o** which we
6: 8 to Him as a trespass **o** in a
6:14 offered the cows as a burnt **o**
6:17 returned as a trespass **o** to
7: 9 it as a whole burnt **o** to the
7:10 Now as Samuel was **o** up the burnt
7:10 was offering up the burnt **o**,
13: 9 Bring a burnt **o** and peace
13: 9 And he offered the burnt **o**.
13:10 finished presenting the burnt **o**,
13:12 and offered a burnt **o**.
26:19 against me, let Him accept an **o**.
2 Sam 6:18 And when David had finished **o**
1 Ki 18:29 until the time of the **o** of
18:36 at the time of the **o** of the
2 Ki 3:20 when the grain **o** was offered,
3:27 and offered him as a burnt **o**
5:17 no longer offer either burnt **o**
10:25 as he had made an end of **o** the
10:25 an end of offering the burnt **o**,
16:13 So he burned his burnt **o** and his
16:13 burnt offering and his grain **o**;
16:13 and he poured his drink **o** and
16:15 altar burn the morning burnt **o**,
16:15 offering, the evening grain **o**,
16:15 sacrifice, and his grain **o**,
16:15 with the burnt **o** of all the
16:15 of the land, their grain **o**,
16:15 it all the blood of the burnt **o**
1 Chr 6:49 on the altar of burnt **o** and on
16: 2 And when David had finished **o**
16:29 due His name; Bring an **o**,
16:40 LORD on the altar of burnt **o**
21:23 and the wheat for the grain **o**;
21:26 by fire on the altar of burnt **o**.
21:29 and the altar of the burnt **o**,
22: 1 this is the altar of burnt **o**
23:29 the fine flour for the grain **o**,
23:31 presentation of a burnt **o** to
2 Chr 4: 6 as they offered for the burnt **o**
7: 1 and consumed the burnt **o** and
8:13 **o** according to the commandment
24:14 articles for serving and **o**,
29:21 seven male goats for a sin **o**
29:23 the male goats for the sin **o**
29:24 blood on the altar as a sin **o**
29:24 commanded that the burnt **o**
29:24 burnt offering and the sin **o**
29:27 them to offer the burnt **o** on
29:27 And when the burnt **o** began, the
29:28 continued until the burnt **o**
29:29 And when they had finished **o**,
29:32 all these were for a burnt **o**
29:35 offerings for every burnt **o**.
30:22 **o** peace offerings and making
35:14 were busy in **o** burnt
Ezra 3: 5 offered the regular burnt **o**,
3: 5 willingly offered a freewill **o**
6:17 and as a sin **o** for all Israel
7:16 along with the freewill **o** of
8:25 the **o** for the house of our God
8:28 and the gold are a freewill **o**
8:35 twelve male goats as a sin **o**.
8:35 All this was a burnt **o** to the
10:19 the flock as their trespass **o**.
Neh 10:33 for the regular grain **o**,
10:33 for the regular burnt **o** of the
10:34 for bringing the wood **o** into
10:39 of Levi shall bring the **o** of
13: 9 with the grain **o** and the
13:31 and to bringing the wood **o** and
Job 42: 8 up for yourselves a burnt **o**;
Ps 40: 6 Sacrifice and **o** You did not
40: 6 Burnt **o** and sin offering You
40: 6 Burnt offering and sin **o** You
51:16 You do not delight in burnt **o**.
51:19 With burnt **o** and whole burnt
51:19 offering and whole burnt **o**;
96: 8 due His name; Bring an **o**,
Isa 19:21 and will make sacrifice and **o**;
40:16 beasts sufficient for a burnt **o**.
53:10 When You make His soul an **o**
57: 6 them you have poured a drink **o**,
57: 6 You have offered a grain **o**.
61: 8 I hate robbery for burnt **o**;
65:11 And who furnish a drink **o** for
66: 3 He who offers a grain **o**,
66:20 all your brethren for an **o** to
66:20 children of Israel bring an **o**
Jer 11:17 to provoke Me to anger in **o**
14:12 and when they offer burnt **o** and
14:12 burnt offering and grain **o**,
Ezek 40:38 where they washed the burnt **o**.
40:39 on which to slay the burnt **o**,
40:39 the burnt offering, the sin **o**,
40:39 offering, and the trespass **o**.
40:42 of hewn stone for the burnt **o**,
40:42 they slaughtered the burnt **o**
42:13 most holy offerings—the grain **o**,
42:13 grain offering, the sin **o**,
42:13 offering, and the trespass **o**—
43:19 give a young bull for a sin **o**
43:21 also take the bull of the sin **o**
43:22 without blemish for a sin **o**;
43:24 offer them up as a burnt **o** to
43:25 prepare a goat for a sin **o**;
44:11 they shall slay the burnt **o** and
44:27 he must offer his sin **o** in the
44:29 "They shall eat the grain **o**,
44:29 the grain offering, the sin **o**,
44:29 offering, and the trespass **o**;
45:13 This is the **o** which you shall
45:16 of the land shall give this **o**
45:17 He shall prepare the sin **o**,
45:17 the sin offering, the grain **o**,
45:17 the grain offering, the burnt **o**,
45:19 some of the blood of the sin **o**
45:22 of the land a bull for a sin **o**.
45:23 he shall prepare a burnt **o** to
45:23 of the goats daily for a sin **o**.
45:24 he shall prepare a grain **o**
45:25 days, according to the sin **o**,
45:25 the sin offering, the burnt **o**,
45:25 the burnt offering, the grain **o**,
46: 2 shall prepare his burnt **o** and
46: 4 The burnt **o** that the prince
46: 5 and the grain **o** shall be one
46: 5 and the grain **o** for the lambs,
46: 7 He shall prepare a grain **o** of an
46:11 feast days the grain **o** shall
46:12 makes a voluntary burnt **o** or
46:12 offering or voluntary peace **o**
46:12 he shall prepare his burnt **o**
46:13 shall daily make a burnt **o**
46:14 you shall prepare a grain **o**
46:14 This grain **o** is a perpetual
46:15 prepare the lamb, the grain **o**,
46:15 as a regular burnt **o** every
46:20 shall boil the trespass **o** and
46:20 trespass offering and the sin **o**,
46:20 they shall bake the grain **o**,
Dan 2:46 that they should present an **o**
9:21 about the time of the evening **o**.
9:27 bring an end to sacrifice and **o**.
Joel 1: 9 The grain **o** and the drink
1: 9 grain offering and the drink **o**
1:13 For the grain **o** and the drink
1:13 grain offering and the drink **o**
2:14 A grain **o** and a drink offering
2:14 grain offering and a drink **o**
Zeph 3:10 ones, Shall bring My **o**.
Mal 1:10 Nor will I accept an **o** from your
1:11 to My name, And a pure **o**;
1:13 Thus you bring an **o**! Should I
2:12 Yet who brings an **o** to the
2:13 So He does not regard the **o**
3: 3 may offer to the LORD An **o**
3: 4 Then the **o** of Judah and
Lk 5:14 and make an **o** for your
23:36 coming and **o** Him sour wine,
Acts 21:26 at which time an **o** should be
Rom 15:16 that the **o** of the Gentiles
Eph 5: 2 an **o** and a sacrifice to God for
Phil 2:17 poured out as a drink **o** on
2 Tim 4: 6 being poured out as a drink **o**,
Heb 10: 5 Sacrifice and **o** You did not
10: 8 saying, "Sacrifice and **o**,
10:10 been sanctified through the **o**
10:11 stands ministering daily and **o**
10:14 For by one **o** He has perfected
10:18 there is no longer an **o** for

OFFERINGS (279/210) OFFERING

Gen 8:20 and offered burnt **o** on the
Ex 10:25 give us sacrifices and burnt **o**,
20:24 sacrifice on it your burnt **o**
20:24 offerings and your peace **o**,
24: 5 who offered burnt **o** and
24: 5 and sacrificed peace **o** of oxen
29:28 the sacrifices of their peace **o**,
29:34 the flesh of the consecration **o**,
32: 6 the next day, offered burnt **o**,
32: 6 offerings, and brought peace **o**;
36: 3 bringing to him freewill **o**
Lev 2: 3 It is most holy of the **o** to
2:10 It is most holy of the **o** to
2:13 With all your **o** you shall offer
4:35 according to the **o** made by fire
5:12 on the altar according to the **o**
6:12 on it the fat of the peace **o**.
6:17 it as their portion of My **o**
6:18 generations concerning the **o**
7:11 law of the sacrifice of peace **o**
7:30 own hands shall bring the **o**
7:32 the sacrifices of your peace **o**.
7:34 the sacrifices of their peace **o**,
7:35 from the **o** made by fire to the
7:38 of Israel to offer their **o** to
8:28 They were consecration **o** for a
8:31 in the basket of consecration **o**,
9: 4 a bull and a ram as peace **o**,
9:18 ram as sacrifices of peace **o**,
9:22 the burnt offering, and peace **o**.
10:12 offering that remains of the **o**
10:14 from the sacrifices of peace **o**
10:15 they shall bring with the **o** of
17: 5 and offer them as peace **o** to
21: 6 for they offer the **o** of the
21:21 shall come near to offer the **o**
22: 4 shall not eat the holy **o** until
22: 6 and shall not eat the holy **o**
22: 7 he may eat the holy **o**,
22:12 she may not eat of the holy **o**.
22:15 shall not profane the holy **o**
22:16 when they eat their holy **o**;
22:18 or for any of his freewill **o**,
23:18 offering and their drink **o**,
23:37 a sacrifice and drink **o**,
23:38 and besides all your freewill **o**
24: 9 most holy to him from the **o** of
Num 6:15 offering with their drink **o**.
7:17 for the sacrifice of peace **o**:
7:23 and as the sacrifice of peace **o**:
7:29 for the sacrifice of peace **o**:
7:35 and as the sacrifice of peace **o**:
7:41 and as the sacrifice of peace **o**:
7:47 and as the sacrifice of peace **o**:
7:53 and as the sacrifice of peace **o**:
7:59 and as the sacrifice of peace **o**:
7:65 and as the sacrifice of peace **o**:
7:71 and as the sacrifice of peace **o**:
7:77 and as the sacrifice of peace **o**:
7:83 and as the sacrifice of peace **o**:
7:88 for the sacrifice of peace **o**
10:10 the trumpets over your burnt **o**
10:10 the sacrifices of your peace **o**;
18: 8 given you charge of My heave **o**,
18:11 with all the wave **o** of the
18:19 All the heave **o** of the holy
28: 2 My food for My **o** made by fire
28:31 them with their drink **o**,

29: 6 offering, and their drink **o**,
29:11 offering, and their drink **o**.
29:18 offering and their drink **o** for
29:19 offering, and their drink **o**.
29:21 offering and their drink **o** for
29:24 offering and their drink **o** for
29:27 offering and their drink **o** for
29:30 offering and their drink **o** for
29:33 offering and their drink **o** for
29:37 offering and their drink **o** for
29:39 feasts (besides your vowed **o**
29:39 offerings and your freewill **o**)
29:39 as your burnt **o** and your
29:39 offerings and your grain **o**,
29:39 as your drink **o** and your peace
29:39 offerings and your peace **o**.
Deut 12: 6 you shall take your burnt **o**,
12: 6 the heave **o** of your hand, your
12: 6 of your hand, your vowed **o**,
12: 6 offerings, your freewill **o**,
12:11 I command you: your burnt **o**,
12:11 the heave **o** of your hand, and
12:11 and all your choice **o** which you
12:13 you do not offer your burnt **o**
12:14 you shall offer your burnt **o**,
12:17 of any of your **o** which you vow,
12:17 you vow, of your freewill **o**,
12:26 you have, and your vowed **o**,
12:27 you shall offer your burnt **o**,
18: 1 they shall eat the **o** of the
27: 6 and offer burnt **o** on it to the
27: 7 "You shall offer peace **o**,
Josh 8:31 And they offered on it burnt **o**
8:31 LORD, and sacrificed peace **o**.
22:23 or if to offer on it burnt **o** or
22:23 it burnt offerings or grain **o**,
22:23 or if to offer peace **o** on it,
22:27 before Him with our burnt **o**,
22:27 and with our peace **o**;
22:28 though not for burnt **o** nor for
22:29 to build an altar for burnt **o**,
22:29 burnt offerings, for grain **o**,
Judg 20:26 and they offered burnt **o** and
20:26 burnt offerings and peace **o**,
21: 4 and offered burnt **o** and peace
21: 4 burnt offerings and peace **o**.
1 Sam 2:28 house of your father all the **o**
2:29 fat with the best of all the **o**
6:15 of Beth Shemesh offered burnt **o**
10: 8 down to you to offer burnt **o**
10: 8 and make sacrifices of peace **o**.
11:15 they made sacrifices of peace **o**
13: 9 a burnt offering and peace **o**
15:22 as great delight in burnt **o**
2 Sam 1:21 rain upon you, Nor fields of **o**.
6:17 Then David offered burnt **o** and
6:17 burnt offerings and peace **o**
6:18 had finished offering burnt **o**
6:18 burnt offerings and peace **o**,
24:24 nor will I offer burnt **o** to the
24:25 and offered burnt **o** and peace
24:25 burnt offerings and peace **o**.
1 Ki 3: 4 offered a thousand burnt **o** on
3:15 the LORD, offered up burnt **o**,
3:15 offerings, offered peace **o**,
8:63 offered a sacrifice of peace **o**,
8:64 for there he offered burnt **o**,
8:64 burnt offerings, grain **o**,
8:64 and the fat of the peace **o**,
8:64 small to receive the burnt **o**,
8:64 burnt offerings, the grain **o**,
8:64 and the fat of the peace **o**.
9:25 a year Solomon offered burnt **o**
9:25 burnt offerings and peace **o** on
12:33 So he made **o** on the altar which
2 Ki 10:24 to offer sacrifices and burnt **o**.
12:16 The money from the trespass **o**
12:16 and the money from the sin **o**
16:12 the altar and made **o** on it.
16:13 the blood of his peace **o** on
16:15 offering, and their drink **o**;
1 Chr 16: 1 Then they offered burnt **o** and
16: 1 burnt offerings and peace **o**
16: 2 finished offering the burnt **o**
16: 2 burnt offerings and the peace **o**,
16:40 to offer burnt **o** to the LORD on
21:23 give you the oxen for burnt **o**,
21:24 nor offer burnt **o** with that
21:26 and offered burnt **o** and peace
21:26 burnt offerings and peace **o**,
29:21 the LORD and offered burnt **o**
29:21 lambs, with their drink **o**,
2 Chr 1: 6 and offered a thousand burnt **o**
2: 4 for the burnt **o** morning and
7: 7 for there he offered burnt **o**
7: 7 and the fat of the peace **o**,
7: 7 not able to receive the burnt **o**,
7: 7 burnt offerings, the grain **o**,
8:12 Then Solomon offered burnt **o** to
23:18 to offer the burnt **o** of the
24:14 And they offered burnt **o** in the
29: 7 incense or offered burnt **o** in
29:18 the altar of burnt **o** with all
29:31 bring sacrifices and thank **o**
29:31 in sacrifices and thank **o**,
29:31 willing heart brought burnt **o**.
29:32 And the number of the burnt **o**
29:34 could not skin all the burnt **o**;
29:35 Also the burnt **o** were in
29:35 with the fat of the peace **o** and
29:35 and with the drink **o** for
30:15 and brought the burnt **o** to the
30:22 offering peace **o** and making
31: 2 and Levites for burnt **o** and
31: 2 for burnt offerings and peace **o**,
31: 3 his possessions for the burnt **o**:
31: 3 the morning and evening burnt **o**,
31: 3 the burnt **o** for the Sabbaths
31:10 people began to bring the **o**
31:12 faithfully brought in the **o**,
31:14 was over the freewill **o** to
31:14 to distribute the **o** of the
33:16 sacrificed peace **o** and thank
33:16 peace offerings and thank **o** on
35: 6 "So slaughter the Passover **o**,
35: 7 all for Passover **o** for all who
35: 8 the priests for the Passover **o**
35: 9 to the Levites for Passover **o**
35:11 slaughtered the Passover **o**;
35:12 Then they removed the burnt **o**
35:13 they roasted the Passover **o**
35:13 but the other holy **o** they
35:14 busy in offering burnt **o** and
35:16 Passover and to offer burnt **o**
Ezra 1: 4 besides the freewill **o** for the
3: 2 to offer burnt **o** on it, as it
3: 3 and they offered burnt **o** on it
3: 3 the morning and evening burnt **o**.
3: 4 and offered the daily burnt **o**
3: 6 they began to offer burnt **o** to
6: 9 and lambs for the burnt **o** of
7:17 with their grain **o** and their
7:17 offerings and their drink **o**,
8:35 offered burnt **o** to the God of
Neh 10:33 for the sin **o** to make atonement
10:37 firstfruits of our dough, our **o**,
12:44 of the storehouse for the **o**,
13: 5 they had stored the grain **o**,
13: 5 and the **o** for the priests.
Job 1: 5 the morning and offer burnt **o**
Ps 16: 4 Their drink **o** of blood I will
20: 3 May He remember all your **o**,
50: 8 sacrifices Or your burnt **o**,
66:13 go into Your house with burnt **o**;
119:108 the freewill **o** of my mouth,
Prov 7:14 I have peace **o** with me;
Isa 1:11 I have had enough of burnt **o** of
43:23 Me the sheep for your burnt **o**,
43:23 you to serve with grain **o**,
56: 7 Their burnt **o** and their
Jer 6:20 Your burnt **o** are not
7:18 and they pour out drink **o** to
7:21 Add your burnt **o** to your
7:22 concerning burnt **o** or
17:26 bringing burnt **o** and
17:26 grain **o** and incense, bringing
19: 5 sons with fire for burnt **o** to
19:13 and poured out drink **o** to other
32:29 to Baal and poured out drink **o**
33:18 lack a man to offer burnt **o**
33:18 before Me, to kindle grain **o**,
41: 5 with **o** and incense in their
44:17 of heaven and pour out drink **o**
44:18 heaven and pouring out drink **o**
44:19 heaven and poured out drink **o**
44:19 and pour out drink **o** to her
44:25 of heaven and pour out drink **o**
Ezek 20:28 and provoked Me with their **o**.
20:28 and poured out their drink **o**.
20:40 and there I will require your **o**
42:13 LORD shall eat the most holy **o**.
42:13 they shall lay the most holy **o**—
43:18 for sacrificing burnt **o** on it,
43:27 shall offer your burnt **o** and
43:27 offerings and your peace **o** on
45:15 These shall be for grain **o**,
45:15 be for grain offerings, burnt **o**,
45:15 burnt offerings, and peace **o**,
45:17 prince's part to give burnt **o**,
45:17 give burnt offerings, grain **o**,
45:17 grain offerings, and drink **o**,
45:17 and the peace **o** to make
46: 2 burnt offering and his peace **o**.
46:12 burnt offering and his peace **o**
Hos 6: 6 of God more than burnt **o**.
8:13 For the sacrifices of My **o**
9: 4 They shall not offer wine **o** to
Am 4: 5 and announce the freewill **o**;
5:22 Though you offer Me burnt **o** and
5:22 offerings and your grain **o**,
5:22 I regard your fattened peace **o**.
5:25 you offer Me sacrifices and **o**
Mic 6: 6 I come before Him with burnt **o**,
Mal 3: 8 robbed You?' In tithes and **o**.
Mk 12:33 than all the whole burnt **o** and
Lk 21: 4 their abundance have put in **o**
Acts 24:17 I came to bring alms and **o** to
1 Cor 9:13 at the altar partake of the **o**
Heb 10: 6 In burnt **o** and sacrifices
10: 8 and offering, burnt **o**,
10: 8 and **o** for sin You did

OFFERS (21/20) OFFER

Lev 2: 1 When anyone **o** a grain offering
3: 1 if he **o** it of the herd,
3: 7 If he **o** a lamb as his offering,
6:26 The priest who **o** it for sin
7: 8 And the priest who **o** anyone's
7: 9 shall be the priest's who **o** it
7:12 If he **o** it for a thanksgiving,
7:16 be eaten the same day that he **o**
7:18 be an abomination to him who **o**
7:29 He who **o** the sacrifice of his
7:33 who **o** the blood of the peace
17: 8 who **o** a burnt offering or
21: 8 for he **o** the bread of your God.
22:18 who **o** his sacrifice for any of
22:21 And whoever **o** a sacrifice of a
Ps 50:23 Whoever **o** praise glorifies Me;
Isa 66: 3 He who **o** a grain offering, as
66: 3 as if he **o** swine's blood;
Jer 48:35 to cease in Moab The one who **o**
Ezek 46: 4 offering that the prince **o** to
Jn 16: 2 kills you will think that he **o**

OFFICE (11/11) OFFICER

Gen 41:13 He restored me to my **o**,
1 Chr 6:32 and they served in their **o**
9:22 them to their trusted **o**.
9:26 For in this trusted **o** were four
9:31 had the trusted **o** over the
Ps 109: 8 And let another take his **o**.
Isa 22:19 I will drive you out of your **o**,
Mt 9: 9 Matthew sitting at the tax **o**.
Mk 2:14 Alphaeus sitting at the tax **o**.
Lk 5:27 Levi, sitting at the tax **o**.
Acts 1:20 'Let another take his **o**.

OFFICER (23/21) OFFICE, OFFICERS

Gen 37:36 an **o** of Pharaoh and captain of
39: 1 an **o** of Pharaoh, captain of the
Judg 9:28 and is not Zebul his **o**?
1 Ki 11:28 made him the **o** over all the
22: 9 the king of Israel called an **o**
2 Ki 7: 2 So an **o** on whose hand the king
7:17 the king had appointed the **o**
7:19 Then that **o** had answered the man
8: 6 the king appointed a certain **o**
15:25 an **o** of his, conspired against
23:11 the **o** who was in the court;
25:19 also took out of the city an **o**
25:19 the chief recruiting **o** of the
1 Chr 9:11 the **o** over the house of God;
9:20 son of Eleazar had been the **o**
27:16 the **o** over the Reubenites was
2 Chr 24:11 scribe and the high priest's **o**
26:11 the scribe and Maaseiah the **o**,
28: 7 Azrikam the **o** over the house,
Jer 52:25 also took out of the city an **o**
Mt 5:25 judge hand you over to the **o**,
Lk 12:58 the judge deliver you to the **o**,
12:58 and the **o** throw you into

OFFICERS (60/60) OFFICER

Gen 40: 2 was angry with his two **o**,
40: 7 So he asked Pharaoh's **o** who
41:34 and let him appoint **o** over the
Ex 5: 6 of the people and their **o**,
5:10 of the people and their **o** went
5:14 Also the **o** of the children of
5:15 Then the **o** of the children of
5:19 And the **o** of the children of
Num 11:16 the elders of the people and **o**
31:14 But Moses was angry with the **o**
31:48 Then the **o** who were over
Deut 1:15 and **o** for your tribes.
16:18 shall appoint judges and **o** in
20: 5 Then the **o** shall speak to the
20: 8 The **o** shall speak further to the
20: 9 when the **o** have finished
29:10 and your elders and your **o**,
31:28 of your tribes, and your **o**,
Josh 1:10 Then Joshua commanded the **o** of
3: 2 that the **o** went through the
8:33 with their elders and **o** and
23: 2 their judges, and for their **o**,
24: 1 their judges, and for their **o**;
1 Sam 8:15 and give it to his **o** and
1 Ki 4: 5 the son of Nathan, over the **o**;
9:22 of war and his servants: his **o**,
2 Ki 10:25 then the guards and the **o** threw
11:15 the **o** of the army, and said to
11:18 And the priest appointed **o** over
24:12 and his **o** went out to the king
24:15 mother, the king's wives, his **o**,
1 Chr 23: 4 six thousand were **o** and
27: 1 and hundreds and their **o**,
28: 1 the **o** of the tribes and the
29: 6 with the **o** over the king's
2 Chr 8: 9 men of war, captains of his **o**,
18: 8 of Israel called one of his **o**
21: 9 So Jehoram went out with his **o**,
26:12 The total number of chief **o** of
34:13 of the Levites were scribes, **o**,
Esth 1: 8 the king had ordered all the **o**
2: 3 and let the king appoint **o** in
Isa 60:17 I will also make your **o** peace,
Jer 29:26 so that there should be **o** in
39:13 the king of Babylon's chief **o**;
41: 1 the royal family and of the **o**
Mk 6:21 for his nobles, the high **o**,
14:65 And the **o** struck Him with
Jn 7:32 and the chief priests sent **o**
7:45 Then the **o** came to the chief
7:46 The **o** answered, "No man ever
18: 3 and **o** from the chief priests
18:12 and the captain and the **o** of
18:18 Now the servants and **o** who had
18:22 one of the **o** who stood by
19: 6 when the chief priests and **o**
Acts 5:22 But when the **o** came and did not
5:26 the captain went with the **o**

16:35 day, the magistrates sent the **o**,
16:38 And the **o** told these words to

OFFICIAL (5/4)

2 Chr 24:11 was brought to the king's **o** by
Neh 2:10 and Tobiah the Ammonite **o**
2:19 Horonite, Tobiah the Ammonite **o**,
Eccl 5: 8 for high **o** watches over high
5: 8 official watches over high **o**,

OFFICIALS (23/21)

1 Ki 4: 2 And these were his **o**:
9:23 Others were chiefs of the **o**
1 Chr 24: 5 for there were **o** of the
24: 5 of the sanctuary and **o** of
26:29 his sons performed duties as **o**
26:32 whom King David made **o** over the
27:31 All these were the **o** over King
28: 1 and of his sons, with the **o**,
2 Chr 8:10 others were chiefs of the **o**
19:11 also the Levites will be **o**
Neh 2:16 And the **o** did not know where I
2:16 the priests, the nobles, the **o**,
Esth 1: 3 he made a feast for all his **o**
1:11 beauty to the people and the **o**,
1:18 will say to all the king's **o**
2:18 for all his **o** and servants;
3:12 to the **o** of all people, to
5:11 he had advanced him above the **o**
9: 3 And all the **o** of the provinces,
Eccl 5: 8 and higher **o** are over them.
Dan 3: 2 and all the **o** of the provinces,
3: 3 and all the **o** of the provinces
Acts 19:31 Then some of the **o** of Asia, who

OFFICIATED (1/1)

Heb 7:13 from which no man has **o** at the

OFFSCOURING (2/2)

Lam 3:45 You have made us an **o** and
1 Cor 4:13 the **o** of all things until now.

OFFSPRING (41/41)

Gen 15: 3 "Look, You have given me no **o**;
21:23 deal falsely with me, with my **o**,
48: 6 Your **o** whom you beget after them
48:11 God has also shown me your **o**!"
Deut 7:13 of your cattle and the **o** of
28: 4 of your cattle and the **o** of
28:18 of your cattle and the **o** of
28:51 of your cattle or the **o** of
Judg 8:30 seventy sons who were his own **o**,
Ruth 4:12 because of the **o** which the
2 Chr 32:21 some of his own **o** struck him
Job 5:25 And your **o** like the grass of
21: 8 And their **o** before their eyes.
27:14 And his **o** shall not be
39: 3 young, They deliver their **o**.
Ps 21:10 Their **o** You shall destroy from
22:23 all you **o** of Israel!
Isa 14:22 And **o** and posterity," says
14:29 And its **o** will be a fiery
22:24 the **o** and the posterity, all
44: 3 And My blessing on your **o**;
48:19 And the **o** of your body like
57: 3 You **o** of the adulterer and the
57: 4 **O** of falsehood,
61: 9 And their **o** among the people.
65:23 And their **o** with them.
Jer 46:27 And your **o** from the land of
Lam 2:20 Should the women eat their **o**,
Ezek 17:13 'And he took the king's **o**,
Mal 2:15 And why one? He seeks godly **o**.
Mt 22:24 marry his wife and raise up **o**
22:25 he had married, and having no **o**,
Mk 12:19 take his wife and raise up **o**
12:20 a wife; and dying, he left no **o**.
12:21 he died; nor did he leave any **o**.
12:22 the seven had her and left no **o**.
Lk 20:28 take his wife and raise up **o**
Acts 17:28 said, 'For we are also His **o**.
17:29 since we are the **o** of God, we
Rev 12:17 make war with the rest of her **o**,
22:16 I am the Root and the **O** of

OFTEN (34/31)

2 Ki 4: 8 as **o** as he passed by, he would
Job 21:17 How **o** is the lamp of the wicked
21:17 How **o** does their destruction
Ps 78:40 How **o** they provoked Him in the
Prov 29: 1 He who is **o** rebuked, and
Isa 28:19 As **o** as it goes out it will
Mt 9:14 do we and the Pharisees fast **o**,
17:15 for he **o** falls into the fire
17:15 falls into the fire and **o** into
18:21 how **o** shall my brother sin
23:37 How **o** I wanted to gather
Mk 5: 4 because he had **o** been bound with
9:22 And **o** he has thrown him both
Lk 5:16 So He Himself **o** withdrew into
5:33 do the disciples of John fast **o**
8:29 For it had **o** seized him, and he
13:34 How **o** I wanted to gather
Jn 18: 2 for Jesus **o** met there with His
Acts 24:26 he sent for him more **o** and
26:11 And I punished them **o** in every
Rom 1:13 that I **o** planned to come to you
1 Cor 11:25 as **o** as you drink it, in
11:26 For as **o** as you eat this bread
2 Cor 8:22 them our brother whom we have **o**
11:23 more frequently, in deaths **o**.
11:26 in journeys **o**, in perils
11:27 and toil, in sleeplessness **o**,
11:27 and thirst, in fastings **o**,
Phil 3:18 walk, of whom I have told you **o**,
2 Tim 1:16 for he **o** refreshed me, and was
Heb 6: 7 which drinks in the rain that **o**
9:25 that He should offer Himself **o**,
9:26 then would have had to suffer **o**
Rev 11: 6 as **o** as they desire.

OG (22/22)

Num 21:33 So **O** king of Bashan went out
32:33 Amorites and the kingdom of **O**
Deut 1: 4 and **O** king of Bashan, who dwelt
3: 1 and **O** king of Bashan came out
3: 3 our hands **O** king of Bashan,
3: 4 the kingdom of **O** in Bashan.
3:10 cities of the kingdom of **O** in
3:11 For only **O** king of Bashan
3:13 all Bashan, the kingdom of **O**,
4:47 of his land and the land of **O**
29: 7 Sihon king of Heshbon and **O**
31: 4 them as He did to Sihon and **O**,
Josh 2:10 side of the Jordan, Sihon and **O**,
9:10 and **O** king of Bashan, who was
12: 4 The other king was **O** king of
13:12 all the kingdom of **O** in Bashan,
13:30 all the kingdom of **O** king of
13:31 cities of the kingdom of **O** in
1 Ki 4:19 and of **O** king of Bashan.
Neh 9:22 And the land of **O** king of
Ps 135:11 **O** king of Bashan, And all the
136:20 And **O** king of Bashan, For His

OH (104/100) See APPENDIX

OHAD (2/2)

Gen 46:10 Simeon were Jemuel, Jamin, **O**,
Ex 6:15 Simeon were Jemuel, Jamin, **O**,

OHEL (1/1)

1 Chr 3:20 and Hashubah, **O**, Berechiah,

OHOLAH (5/4)

Ezek 23: 4 **O** the elder and Oholibah her
23: 4 their names, Samaria is **O**,
23: 5 **O** played the harlot even though
23:36 will you judge **O** and Oholibah?
23:44 thus they went in to **O** and

OHOLIBAH (6/5)

Ezek 23: 4 Oholah the elder and **O** her
23: 4 is Oholah, and Jerusalem is **O**.
23:11 Now although her sister **O** saw
23:22 Therefore, **O**, thus says
23:36 will you judge Oholah and **O**?
23:44 they went in to Oholah and **O**,

OIL (222/204) OILS

Gen 28:18 and poured **o** on top of it.
35:14 and he poured **o** on it.
Ex 25: 6 **o** for the light, and spices for
25: 6 and spices for the anointing **o**
27:20 that they bring you pure **o** of
29: 2 unleavened cakes mixed with **o**,
29: 2 wafers anointed with **o** (you
29: 7 you shall take the anointing **o**,
29:21 and some of the anointing **o**,
29:23 bread, one cake made with **o**,
29:40 of a hin of pressed **o**,
30:24 sanctuary, and a hin of olive **o**.
30:25 from these a holy anointing **o**,
30:25 It shall be a holy anointing **o**.
30:31 shall be a holy anointing **o** to
31:11 and the anointing **o** and sweet
35: 8 **o** for the light, and spices for
35: 8 and spices for the anointing **o**
35:14 and the **o** for the light;
35:15 its poles, the anointing **o**,
35:28 and spices and **o** for the light,
35:28 the light, for the anointing **o**,
37:29 also made the holy anointing **o**
39:37 and the **o** for light;
39:38 the gold altar, the anointing **o**,
40: 9 you shall take the anointing **o**,
Lev 2: 1 And he shall pour **o** on it, and
2: 2 his handful of fine flour and **o**
2: 4 of fine flour mixed with **o**,
2: 4 wafers anointed with **o**.
2: 5 flour, unleavened, mixed with **o**.
2: 6 break it in pieces and pour **o**
2: 7 be made of fine flour with **o**.
2:15 And you shall put **o** on it, and
2:16 beaten grain and part of its **o**,
5:11 He shall put no **o** on it, nor
6:15 the grain offering, with its **o**,
6:21 shall be made in a pan with **o**.
7:10 offering, whether mixed with **o**,
7:12 unleavened cakes mixed with **o**,
7:12 wafers anointed with **o**,
7:12 of blended flour mixed with **o**.
8: 2 the garments, the anointing **o**,
8:10 Moses took the anointing **o**,
8:12 poured some of the anointing **o**
8:26 cake of bread anointed with **o**,
8:30 took some of the anointing **o**
9: 4 a grain offering mixed with **o**;
10: 7 for the anointing **o** of the
14:10 of fine flour mixed with **o** as
14:10 offering, and one log of **o**.
14:12 offering, and the log of **o**,
14:15 take some of the log of **o**,
14:16 dip his right finger in the **o**
14:16 shall sprinkle some of the **o**
14:17 And of the rest of the **o** in his
14:18 The rest of the **o** that is in
14:21 of fine flour mixed with **o** as
14:21 as a grain offering, a log of **o**,
14:24 offering and the log of **o**,
14:26 shall pour some of the **o** into
14:27 his right finger some of the **o**
14:28 shall put some of the **o** that
14:29 The rest of the **o** that is in
21:10 on whose head the anointing **o**
21:12 of the anointing **o** of his God
23:13 of fine flour mixed with **o**,
24: 2 that they bring to you pure **o**
Num 4: 9 and all its **o** vessels, with
4:16 of Aaron the priest is the **o**
4:16 grain offering, the anointing **o**,
5:15 he shall pour no **o** on it and
6:15 of fine flour mixed with **o**,
6:15 wafers anointed with **o**,
7:13 of fine flour mixed with **o** as
7:19 of fine flour mixed with **o** as
7:25 of fine flour mixed with **o** as
7:31 of fine flour mixed with **o** as
7:37 of fine flour mixed with **o** as
7:43 of fine flour mixed with **o** as
7:49 of fine flour mixed with **o** as
7:55 of fine flour mixed with **o** as
7:61 of fine flour mixed with **o** as
7:67 of fine flour mixed with **o** as
7:73 of fine flour mixed with **o** as
7:79 of fine flour mixed with **o** as
8: 8 of fine flour mixed with **o**,
11: 8 taste of pastry prepared with **o**.
15: 4 with one-fourth of a HIN of **o**;
15: 6 with one-third of a HIN of **o**;
15: 9 mixed with half a HIN of **o**;
18:12 "All the best of the **o**,
28: 5 of a hin of pressed **o**.
28: 9 a grain offering, mixed with **o**,
28:12 a grain offering, mixed with **o**,
28:12 a grain offering, mixed with **o**,
28:13 of fine flour, mixed with **o**,
28:20 be of fine flour mixed with **o**:
28:28 of fine flour mixed with **o**:
29: 3 be fine flour mixed with **o**:
29: 9 be of fine flour mixed with **o**:
29:14 be of fine flour mixed with **o**:
35:25 was anointed with the holy **o**.
Deut 7:13 and your new wine and your **o**,
8: 8 a land of olive **o** and honey;
11:14 your new wine, and your **o**.
12:17 or your new wine or your **o**,
14:23 and your new wine and your **o**,
18: 4 and your new wine and your **o**,
28:40 not anoint yourself with the **o**;
28:51 you grain or new wine or **o**,
32:13 And **o** from the flinty rock;
33:24 And let him dip his foot in **o**.
Judg 9: 9 'Should I cease giving my **o**,
1 Sam 10: 1 Then Samuel took a flask of **o**
16: 1 your horn with **o**, and go;
16:13 Then Samuel took the horn of **o**
2 Sam 1:21 of Saul, not anointed with **o**.
14: 2 do not anoint yourself with **o**,
1 Ki 1:39 the priest took a horn of **o**
5:11 and twenty kors of pressed **o**.
17:12 and a little **o** in a jar;
17:14 nor shall the jar of **o** run dry,
17:16 nor did the jar of **o** run dry,
2 Ki 4: 2 in the house but a jar of **o**.
4: 6 So the **o** ceased.
4: 7 sell the **o** and pay your debt;
9: 1 take this flask of **o** in your
9: 3 "Then take the flask of **o**,
9: 6 And he poured the **o** on his
1 Chr 9:29 flour and the wine and the **o**
12:40 wine and **o** and oxen and sheep
27:28 Joash was over the store of **o**.
2 Chr 2:10 and twenty thousand baths of **o**.
2:15 the wheat, the barley, the **o**,
11:11 in them, and stores of food, **o**,
31: 5 **o** and honey, and of all the
32:28 harvest of grain, wine, and **o**;
Ezra 3: 7 and **o** to the people of Sidon
6: 9 wheat, salt, wine, and **o**,
7:22 of wine, one hundred baths of **o**,
Neh 5:11 grain, the new wine and the **o**,
8:15 branches of **o** trees, myrtle
10:37 of trees, the new wine and **o**,
10:39 of the new wine and the **o**,
13: 5 of grain, the new wine and **o**,
13:12 and the new wine and the **o** to
Esth 2:12 six months with **o** of myrrh, and
Job 24:11 They press out **o** within their
29: 6 the rock poured out rivers of **o**
Ps 23: 5 You anoint my head with **o**;
45: 7 has anointed You With the **o** of
55:21 His words were softer than **o**,
89:20 With My holy **o** I have anointed
92:10 have been anointed with fresh **o**.

104:15 ***O*** to make his face shine,
109:18 And like **o** into his bones.
133: 2 It is like the precious **o**
141: 5 It shall be as excellent **o**;
Prov 5: 3 her mouth is smoother than **o**;
21:17 He who loves wine and **o** will
21:20 And **o** in the dwelling of the
27:16 And grasps **o** with his right
Eccl 9: 8 And let your head lack no **o**.
Isa 10:27 because of the anointing **o**.
41:19 The myrtle and the **o** tree;
61: 3 The **o** of joy for mourning,
Jer 31:12 wheat and new wine and **o**,
40:10 wine and summer fruit and **o**,
41: 8 treasures of wheat, barley, **o**,
Ezek 16: 9 and I anointed you with **o**.
16:13 of fine flour, honey, and **o**.
16:18 and you set My **o** and My incense
16:19 you—the pastry of fine flour, **o**,
23:41 you had set My incense and My **o**.
27:17 of Minnith, millet, honey, **o**,
32:14 make their rivers run like **o**,
45:14 "The ordinance concerning **o**,
45:14 concerning oil, the bath of **o**,
45:24 together with a hin of **o** for
45:25 the grain offering, and the **o**.
46: 5 as well as a hin of **o** with
46: 7 and a hin of **o** with every
46:11 and a hin of **o** with every
46:14 and a third of a hin of **o** to
46:15 the grain offering, and the **o**,
Hos 2: 5 My **o** and my drink.'
2: 8 gave her grain, new wine, and **o**,
2:22 With new wine, And with **o**;
12: 1 And **o** is carried to Egypt.
Joel 1:10 is dried up, The **o** fails.
2:19 you grain and new wine and **o**,
2:24 overflow with new wine and **o**.
Mic 6: 7 rams, Ten thousand rivers of **o**?
6:15 not anoint yourselves with **o**;
Hag 1:11 and the new wine and the **o**,
2:12 bread or stew, wine or **o**,
Zech 4:12 pipes from which the golden **o**
Mt 25: 3 took their lamps and took no **o**
25: 4 but the wise took **o** in their
25: 8 wise, 'Give us some of your **o**,
26: 7 flask of very costly fragrant **o**,
26: 9 For this fragrant **o** might have
26:12 in pouring this fragrant **o**
Mk 6:13 and anointed with **o** many who
14: 3 flask of very costly **o** of
14: 4 Why was this fragrant **o** wasted?
Lk 7:37 alabaster flask of fragrant **o**,
7:38 them with the fragrant **o**.
7:46 did not anoint My head with **o**,
7:46 My feet with fragrant **o**.
10:34 pouring on **o** and wine; and he
16: 6 said, 'A hundred measures of **o**.'
Jn 11: 2 the Lord with fragrant **o** and
12: 3 took a pound of very costly **o**
12: 3 with the fragrance of the **o**.
12: 5 Why was this fragrant **o** not sold
Heb 1: 9 anointed You With the **o**
Jas 5:14 anointing him with **o** in the
Rev 6: 6 and do not harm the **o** and the
18:13 fragrant **o** and frankincense,
18:13 and frankincense, wine and **o**,

OILS (1/1) OIL

Lk 23:56 prepared spices and fragrant **o**.

OINTMENT (11/11) OINTMENTS

Ex 30:25 an **o** compounded according to
2 Ki 20:13 gold, the spices and precious **o**,
1 Chr 9:30 sons of the priests made the **o**
Job 41:31 makes the sea like a pot of **o**.
Prov 27: 9 ***O*** and perfume delight the
Eccl 7: 1 name is better than precious **o**,
10: 1 flies putrefy the perfumer's **o**,
Song 1: 3 Your name is **o** poured forth;
Isa 1: 6 or bound up, Or soothed with **o**.
39: 2 gold, the spices and precious **o**,
57: 9 You went to the king with **o**,

OINTMENTS (3/3) OINTMENT

2 Chr 16:14 prepared in a mixture of **o**.
Song 1: 3 of the fragrance of your good **o**,
Am 6: 6 yourselves with the best **o**,

OLD (339/310) ELDEST, OLDER, OLDEST, OLDNESS

Gen 5:32 Noah was five hundred years **o**,
6: 4 the mighty men who were of **o**,
7: 6 Noah was six hundred years **o**
11:10 Shem was one hundred years **o**,
12: 4 was seventy-five years **o** when
15:15 be buried at a good **o** age.
16:16 Abram was eighty-six years **o**
17: 1 Abram was ninety-nine years **o**,
17:12 He who is eight days **o** among you
17:17 man who is one hundred years **o**?
17:17 Sarah, who is ninety years **o**,
17:24 was ninety-nine years **o** when
17:25 his son was thirteen years **o**
18:11 Now Abraham and Sarah were **o**,
18:12 saying, "After I have grown **o**,
18:12 my lord being **o** also?"
18:13 bear a child, since I am **o**?
19: 4 both **o** and young, all the
19:31 the younger, "Our father is **o**,
21: 2 Abraham a son in his **o** age,
21: 4 Isaac when he was eight days **o**,
21: 5 was one hundred years **o** when
21: 7 him a son in his **o** age."
24: 1 Now Abraham was **o**,
24:36 son to my master when she was **o**;
25: 8 last and died in a good **o** age,
25: 8 an **o** man and full of years,
25:20 Isaac was forty years **o** when he
25:26 Isaac was sixty years **o** when
26:34 When Esau was forty years **o**,
27: 1 when Isaac was **o** and his eyes
27: 2 he said, "Behold now, I am **o**.
35:29 being **o** and full of days.
37: 2 being seventeen years **o**,
37: 3 he was the son of his **o** age.
41:46 Joseph was thirty years **o** when
43:27 the **o** man of whom you spoke?
44:20 an **o** man, and a child of his
44:20 and a child of his **o** age, who
47: 8 Jacob, "How **o** are you?"
50:26 one hundred and ten years **o**;
Ex 7: 7 And Moses was eighty years **o**
7: 7 and Aaron eighty-three years **o**
10: 9 go with our young and our **o**;
30:14 from twenty years **o** and above,
38:26 numbering from twenty years **o**
Lev 13:11 it is an **o** leprosy on the skin
19:32 the presence of an **o** man,
25:22 and eat **o** produce until the
25:22 eat of the **o** harvest.
26:10 You shall eat the **o** harvest, and
26:10 and clear out the **o** because of
27: 3 of a male from twenty years **o**
27: 3 years old up to sixty years **o**,
27: 5 and if from five years **o** up to
27: 5 years old up to twenty years **o**,
27: 6 and if from a month **o** up to five
27: 6 a month old up to five years **o**,
27: 7 and if from sixty years **o** and
Num 1: 3 from twenty years **o** and
1:18 from twenty years **o** and above,
1:20 from twenty years **o** and above,
1:22 from twenty years **o** and above,
1:24 from twenty years **o** and above,
1:26 from twenty years **o** and above,
1:28 from twenty years **o** and above,
1:30 from twenty years **o** and above,
1:32 from twenty years **o** and above,
1:34 from twenty years **o** and above,
1:36 from twenty years **o** and above,
1:38 from twenty years **o** and above,
1:40 from twenty years **o** and above,
1:42 from twenty years **o** and above,
1:45 from twenty years **o** and above,
3:15 every male from a month **o** and
3:22 of all the males from a month **o**
3:28 from a month **o** and above,
3:34 of all the males from a month **o**
3:39 all the males from a month **o**
3:40 of Israel from a month **o** and
3:43 number of names from a month **o**
4: 3 from thirty years **o** and above,
4: 3 above, even to fifty years **o**,
4:23 From thirty years **o** and above,
4:23 above, even to fifty years **o**,
4:30 From thirty years **o** and above,
4:30 above, even to fifty years **o**,
4:35 from thirty years **o** and above,
4:35 above, even to fifty years **o**,
4:39 from thirty years **o** and above,
4:39 above, even to fifty years **o**,
4:43 from thirty years **o** and above,
4:43 above, even to fifty years **o**,
4:47 from thirty years **o** and above,
4:47 above, even to fifty years **o**,
8:24 From twenty-five years **o** and
14:29 from twenty years **o** and above.
18:16 shall redeem when one month **o**,
26: 2 of Israel from twenty years **o**
26: 4 people from twenty years **o**
26:62 every male from a month **o** and
32:11 from twenty years **o** and above,
33:39 and twenty-three years **o** when
Deut 4:25 grandchildren and have grown **o**
19:14 which the men of **o** have set, in
31: 2 one hundred and twenty years **o**
32: 7 "Remember the days of **o**,
34: 7 one hundred and twenty years **o**
Josh 6:21 both man and woman, young and **o**,
9: 4 And they took **o** sacks on their
9: 4 **o** wineskins torn and mended,
9: 5 **o** and patched sandals on their
9: 5 and **o** garments on themselves;
9:13 and our sandals have become **o**
13: 1 Now Joshua was **o**, advanced
13: 1 LORD said to him: "You are **o**,
14: 7 I was forty years **o** when Moses
14:10 this day, eighty-five years **o**.
23: 1 round about, that Joshua was **o**,
23: 2 and said to them: "I am **o**,
24: 2 of the River in **o** times;
24:29 one hundred and ten years **o**.
Judg 2: 8 one hundred and ten years **o**.
6:25 second bull of seven years **o**,
8:32 Joash died at a good **o** age,
19:16 Just then an **o** man came in from
19:17 and the **o** man said, "Where are
19:20 And the **o** man said, "Peace be
19:22 the **o** man, saying, "Bring out
Ruth 1:12 for I am too **o** to have a
4:15 and a nourisher of your **o** age;
1 Sam 2:22 Now Eli was very **o**;
2:31 so that there will not be an **o**
2:32 And there shall not be an **o** man
4:15 Eli was ninety-eight years **o**,
4:18 for the man was **o** and heavy.
8: 1 came to pass when Samuel was **o**
8: 5 said to him, "Look, you are **o**,
12: 2 and I am **o** and grayheaded, and
17:12 eight sons. And the man was **o**,
27: 8 of the land from of **o**,
28:14 An **o** man is coming up, and he
2 Sam 2:10 was forty years **o** when he
4: 4 He was five years **o** when the
5: 4 David was thirty years **o** when
19:32 a very aged man, eighty years **o**.
19:35 "I am today eighty years **o**.
1 Ki 1: 1 Now King David was **o**,
1:15 (Now the king was very **o**,
11: 4 it was so, when Solomon was **o**,
13:11 Now an **o** prophet dwelt in
13:25 the city where the **o** prophet
13:29 So the **o** prophet came to the
14:21 was forty-one years **o** when he
15:23 But in the time of his **o** age he
22:42 was thirty-five years **o** when
2 Ki 4:14 no son, and her husband is **o**.
8:17 He was thirty-two years **o** when
8:26 was twenty-two years **o** when
11:21 Jehoash was seven years **o** when
14: 2 He was twenty-five years **o** when
14:21 who was sixteen years **o**,
15: 2 He was sixteen years **o** when he
15:33 He was twenty-five years **o** when
16: 2 Ahaz was twenty years **o** when he
18: 2 He was twenty-five years **o** when
21: 1 Manasseh was twelve years **o**
21:19 Amon was twenty-two years **o**
22: 1 Josiah was eight years **o** when
23:31 was twenty-three years **o** when
23:36 was twenty-five years **o** when
24: 8 was eighteen years **o** when he
24:18 was twenty-one years **o** when
1 Chr 2:21 when he was sixty years **o**;
23: 1 So when David was **o** and full of
23:27 numbered from twenty years **o**
27:23 number of those twenty years **o**
29:28 So he died in a good **o** age, full
2 Chr 12:13 was forty-one years **o** when he
20:31 He was thirty-five years **o**
21: 5 was thirty-two years **o** when
21:20 He was thirty-two years **o** when
22: 2 Ahaziah was forty-two years **o**
24: 1 Joash was seven years **o** when he
24:15 But Jehoiada grew **o** and was
24:15 one hundred and thirty years **o**
25: 1 was twenty-five years **o** when
25: 5 them from twenty years **o** and
26: 1 who was sixteen years **o**,
26: 3 Uzziah was sixteen years **o** when
27: 1 was twenty-five years **o** when
27: 8 He was twenty-five years **o** when
28: 1 Ahaz was twenty years **o** when he
29: 1 he was twenty-five years **o**,
31:16 those males from three years **o**
31:17 the Levites from twenty years **o**
33: 1 Manasseh was twelve years **o**
33:21 Amon was twenty-two years **o**
34: 1 Josiah was eight years **o** when
36: 2 was twenty-three years **o** when
36: 5 was twenty-five years **o** when
36: 9 Jehoiachin was eight years **o**
36:11 was twenty-one years **o** when
Ezra 3: 8 the Levites from twenty years **o**
3:12 **o** men who had seen the first
Neh 3: 6 Besodeiah repaired the ***O*** Gate;
12:39 above the ***O*** Gate, above the
12:46 days of David and Asaph of **o**
Esth 3:13 all the Jews, both young and **o**,
Job 4:11 The **o** lion perishes for lack of
14: 8 Though its root may grow **o** in
20: 4 "Do you not know this of **o**,
21: 7 the wicked live and become **o**,
22:15 Will you keep to the **o** way
32: 6 in years, and you are very **o**;
42:17 **o** and full of days.
Ps 6: 7 It grows **o** because of all my
25: 6 For they are from of **o**.
32: 3 my bones grew **o** Through my
37:25 have been young, and now am **o**;
44: 1 in their days, In days of **o**:
55:19 Even He who abides from of **o**.
68:33 which were of **o**! Indeed, He
71: 9 me off in the time of **o** age;
71:18 Now also when I am **o** and
74: 2 which You have purchased of **o**,
74:12 For God is my King from of **o**,
77: 5 have considered the days of **o**,
77:11 will remember Your wonders of **o**.
78: 2 I will utter dark sayings of **o**,
92:14 still bear fruit in **o** age;
93: 2 is established from of **o**;
102:25 Of **o** You laid the foundation of
102:26 they will all grow **o** like a
119:52 remembered Your judgments of **o**,
119:152 I have known of **o** that You
143: 5 I remember the days of **o**;
148:12 ***O*** men and children.
Prov 8:22 His way, Before His works of **o**.
17: 6 are the crown of **o** men,
20:29 And the splendor of **o** men is

22: 6 And when he is o he will not
23:22 your mother when she is o.
Eccl 4:13 Than an o and foolish king
Song 7:13 fruits, All manner, new and o,
Isa 20: 4 as captives, young and o,
22:11 walls For the water of the o
25: 1 Your counsels of o are
30:33 Tophet was established of o,
43:18 Nor consider the things of o.
46: 4 Even to your o age, I am He,
46: 9 the former things of o,
50: 9 Indeed they will all grow o
51: 6 The earth will grow o like a
51: 9 days, In the generations of o.
57:11 I have held My peace from of o
58:12 build the o waste places;
61: 4 shall rebuild the o ruins,
63: 9 carried them All the days of o.
63:11 he remembered the days of o,
63:19 have become like those of o,
65:20 Nor an o man who has not
65:20 shall die one hundred years o,
65:20 being one hundred years o
Jer 2:20 For of o I have broken your
6:16 And ask for the o paths, where
28: 8 before me and before you of o
31: 3 The LORD has appeared of o to
31:13 And the young men and the o,
38:11 and took from there o clothes
38:11 there old clothes and o rags,
38:12 Please put these o clothes and
46:26 inhabited as in the days of o,
51:22 you I will break in pieces o
52: 1 was twenty-one years o when
Lam 1: 7 That she had in the days of o.
2:17 He commanded in days of o.
2:21 Young and o lie On the ground
5:21 Renew our days as of o,
Ezek 9: 6 Utterly slay o and young men,
23:43 her who had grown o in
25:15 because of the o hatred,"
26:20 the Pit, to the people of o,
Dan 5:31 being about sixty-two years o.
Joel 2:28 Your o men shall dream dreams,
Am 9:11 rebuild it as in the days of o;
Mic 5: 2 goings forth are from of o,
6: 6 With calves a year o?
7:14 and Gilead, As in days of o.
7:20 to our fathers From days of o.
Nah 2: 8 Though Nineveh of o was like
Zech 8: 4 O men and old women shall again
8: 4 Old men and o women shall again
Mal 3: 4 the LORD, As in the days of o,
Mt 2:16 from two years o and under,
5:21 that it was said to those of o,
5:27 that it was said to those of o,
5:33 that it was said to those of o,
9:16 cloth on an o garment;
9:17 new wine into o wineskins,
13:52 his treasure things new and o.
Mk 2:21 cloth on an o garment;
2:21 piece pulls away from the o,
2:22 new wine into o wineskins;
Lk 1:18 For I am an o man, and my wife
1:36 conceived a son in her o age;
2:42 And when He was twelve years o,
5:36 from a new garment on an o one;
5:36 of the new does not match the o.
5:37 new wine into o wineskins;
5:39 having drunk o wine,
5:39 says, 'The o is better.'
9: 8 that one of the o prophets
9:19 that one of the o prophets
12:33 money bags which do not grow o,
Jn 3: 4 can a man be born when he is o?
8:57 "You are not yet fifty years o,
21:18 you wished; but when you are o,
Acts 2:17 Your o men shall dream
4:22 the man was over forty years o
7:23 "Now when he was forty years o,
Rom 4:19 he was about a hundred years o)
6: 6 that our o man was crucified
1 Cor 5: 7 purge out the o leaven,
5: 8 not with o leaven, nor with the
2 Cor 3:14 reading of the O Testament,
5:17 o things have passed away;
Eph 4:22 the o man which grows corrupt
Col 3: 9 you have put off the o man
1 Tim 4: 7 But reject profane and o wives'
5: 9 a widow under sixty years o be
Heb 1:11 And they will all grow o
8:13 obsolete and growing o is
2 Pe 1: 9 was cleansed from his o sins.
3: 5 of God the heavens were of o,
1 Jn 2: 7 but an o commandment which you
2: 7 The o commandment is the word
Rev 12: 9 was cast out, that serpent of o,
20: 2 the dragon, that serpent of o,

OLDER (16/16) OLD

Gen 25:23 And the o shall serve the
27: 1 that he called Esau his o son
27:42 And the words of Esau her o son
1 Sam 18:17 'Here is my o daughter Merab;
1 Ki 2:22 for he is my o brother—for him,
2 Ki 3:21 were able to bear arms and o
2 Chr 22: 1 had killed all the o sons.
Job 15:10 Much o than your father.
32: 4 Now because they were years o
Ezek 16:61 when you receive your o and
Lk 15:25 Now his o son was in the field.
Rom 9:12 The o shall serve the
1 Tim 5: 1 Do not rebuke an o man, but
5: 2 o women as mothers, younger as
Titus 2: 2 that the o men be sober,
2: 3 the o women likewise, that they

OLDEST (9/9) OLD

Gen 24: 2 So Abraham said to the o servant
44:12 He began with the o and left
Num 1:20 Israel's o son, their
1 Sam 17:13 The three o sons of Jesse had
17:14 And the three o followed Saul.
17:28 Now Eliab his o brother heard
Job 1:13 in their o brother's house;
1:18 in their o brother's house,
Jn 8: 9 beginning with the o even to

OLDNESS (1/1) OLD

Rom 7: 6 of the Spirit and not in the o

OLIVE (41/38) OLIVES

Gen 8:11 a freshly plucked o leaf was
Ex 23:11 vineyard and your o grove.
30:24 and a hin of o oil.
Deut 6:11 vineyards and o trees which you
8: 8 a land of o oil and honey;
24:20 When you beat your o trees, you
28:40 You shall have o trees
Josh 24:13 of the vineyards and o groves
Judg 9: 8 And they said to the o tree,
9: 9 But the o tree said to them,
15: 5 as the vineyards and o groves.
1 Sam 8:14 and your o groves, and give
1 Ki 6:23 two cherubim of o wood,
6:31 he made doors of o wood;
6:32 The two doors were of o wood;
6:33 made doorposts of o wood,
2 Ki 5:26 o groves and vineyards, sheep
18:32 a land of o groves and honey,
1 Chr 27:28 Gederite was over the o trees
Neh 5:11 their o groves, and their
8:15 and bring o branches, branches
9:25 o groves, And fruit trees in
Job 15:33 his blossom like an o tree.
Ps 52: 8 But I am like a green o tree
128: 3 Your children like o plants
Isa 17: 6 Like the shaking of an o tree,
24:13 the shaking of an o tree,
Jer 11:16 Green O Tree, Lovely and of
Hos 14: 6 shall be like an o tree,
Am 4: 9 And your o trees, The locust
Hab 3:17 Though the labor of the o may
Hag 2:19 and the o tree have not yielded
Zech 4: 3 Two o trees are by it, one at
4:11 'What are these two o trees—at
4:12 What are these two o branches
Rom 11:17 being a wild o tree,
11:17 and fatness of the o tree,
11:24 were cut out of the o tree
11:24 into a cultivated o tree,
11:24 into their own o tree?
Rev 11: 4 These are the two o trees and

OLIVES (18/17) OLIVE

Ex 27:20 you pure oil of pressed o for
Lev 24: 2 to you pure oil of pressed o
Deut 28:40 for your o shall drop off.
2 Sam 15:30 the Ascent of the Mount of O,
Isa 17: 6 Two or three o at the top of
Mic 6:15 You shall tread the o,
Zech 14: 4 will stand on the Mount of O,
14: 4 And the Mount of O shall be
Mt 21: 1 to Bethphage, at the Mount of O,
24: 3 as He sat on the Mount of O,
26:30 they went out to the Mount of O.
Mk 11: 1 and Bethany, at the Mount of O,
13: 3 as He sat on the Mount of O
14:26 they went out to the Mount of O.
Lk 19:37 the descent of the Mount of O,
22:39 out, He went to the Mount of O,
Jn 8: 1 Jesus went to the Mount of O.
Jas 3:12 a fig tree, my brethren, bear o,

OLIVET (3/3)

Lk 19:29 at the mountain called O,
21:37 stayed on the mountain called O.
Acts 1:12 from the mount called O,

OLYMPAS (1/1)

Rom 16:15 Nereus and his sister, and O,

OMAR (3/3)

Gen 36:11 sons of Eliphaz were Teman, O,
36:15 Esau, were Chief Teman, Chief O,
1 Chr 1:36 sons of Eliphaz were Teman, O,

OMEGA (4/4)

Rev 1: 8 "I am the Alpha and the O,
1:11 "I am the Alpha and the O,
21: 6 I am the Alpha and the O,
22:13 "I am the Alpha and the O,

OMENS (1/1)

Deut 18:10 or one who interprets o,

OMER (4/4)

Ex 16:16 one o for each person,
16:32 Fill an o with it, to be kept
16:33 Take a pot and put an o of manna
16:36 Now an o is one-tenth of an

OMERS (2/2)

Ex 16:18 So when they measured it by o,
16:22 two o for each one. And all the

OMNIPOTENT (1/1)

Rev 19: 6 Alleluia! For the Lord God O

OMRI (18/16)

1 Ki 16:16 So all Israel made O,
16:17 Then O and all Israel with him
16:21 him king, and half followed O.
16:22 But the people who followed O
16:22 So Tibni died and O reigned.
16:23 O became king over Israel, and
16:25 O did evil in the eyes of the
16:27 Now the rest of the acts of O
16:28 So O rested with his fathers and
16:29 Ahab the son of O became king
16:29 and Ahab the son of O reigned
16:30 Now Ahab the son of O did evil
2 Ki 8:26 Athaliah the granddaughter of O,
1 Chr 7: 8 Joash, Eliezer, Elioenai, O,
9: 4 son of Ammihud, the son of O,
27:18 O the son of Michael;
2 Chr 22: 2 Athaliah the granddaughter of O.
Mic 6:16 For the statutes of O are kept;

ON (4/4) See APPENDIX

Gen 41:45 of Poti-Pherah priest of O.
41:50 of Poti-Pherah priest of O,
46:20 of Poti-Pherah priest of O,
Num 16: 1 and O the son of Peleth,

ONAGER (1/1)

Job 39: 5 Who loosed the bonds of the o,

ONAM (4/4)

Gen 36:23 Manahath, Ebal, Shepho, and O.
1 Chr 1:40 Manahath, Ebal, Shephi, and O.
2:26 she was the mother of O.
2:28 The sons of O were Shammai and

ONAN (8/6)

Gen 38: 4 son, and she called his name O.
38: 8 And Judah said to O,
38: 9 But O knew that the heir would
46:12 The sons of Judah were Er, O,
46:12 and Zerah (but Er and O died in
Num 26:19 sons of Judah were Er and O;
26:19 and Er and O died in the land
1 Chr 2: 3 The sons of Judah were Er, O,

ONCE (83/81) ONE

Gen 18:32 and I will speak but o more:
Ex 10:17 forgive my sin only this o,
30:10 atonement upon its horns o a
30:10 o a year he shall make
Lev 16:34 o a year." And he did as the
Num 13:30 Let us go up at o and take
22: 6 "Therefore please come at o,
32:15 He will o again leave them in
Deut 7:22 be unable to destroy them at o,
Josh 6: 3 shall go all around the city o.
6:11 the city, going around it o.
6:14 they marched around the city o
Judg 6:39 but let me speak just o more:
6:39 just o more with the fleece;
7: 3 let him turn and depart at o
9: 8 The trees o went forth to anoint
16:18 Come up o more, for he has told
16:28 me, I pray, just this o,
1 Sam 23: 4 David inquired of the LORD o
26: 8 let me strike him at o with the
2 Sam 5:22 Then the Philistines went up o
1 Ki 10:22 O every three years the
2 Ki 6:10 not just o or twice.
1 Chr 14:13 Then the Philistines o again
2 Chr 2: 7 Therefore send me at o a man
9:21 O every three years the
Neh 5:18 and o every ten days an
13:20 lodged outside Jerusalem o or
Job 33:21 his bones stick out which o
40: 5 O I have spoken, but I will not
Ps 62:11 God has spoken o,
74: 6 down its carved work, all at o,
76: 7 stand in Your presence When o
89:35 O I have sworn by My holiness
Prov 12:16 A fool's wrath is known at o,
Isa 42:14 I will pant and gasp at o.
66: 8 shall a nation be born at o?
Jer 16:21 I will this o cause them to
Ezek 32:15 is destitute of all that o
Hag 2: 6 O more (it is a little while) I
Zech 10: 8 they shall increase as they o
Mt 9: 3 And at o some of the scribes
Mk 1:30 they told Him about her at o.

1:43 him and sent him away at **o**,
5:13 And at **o** Jesus gave them
6:25 I want you to give me at **o** the
Lk 13:25 When **o** the Master of the house
17: 7 Come at **o** and sit down to eat'?
23:18 And they all cried out at **o**,
Acts 9:18 and he received his sight at **o**;
Rom 6:10 He died to sin **o** for all; but
7: 9 I was alive **o** without the law,
11:30 For as you were **o** disobedient to
1 Cor 15: 6 over five hundred brethren at **o**,
2 Cor 11:25 **o** I was stoned; three times I
Gal 1:23 preaches the faith which he **o**
Eph 2: 2 in which you **o** walked according
2: 3 among whom also we all **o**
2:11 **o** Gentiles in the flesh—who are
2:13 now in Christ Jesus you who **o**
5: 8 For you were **o** darkness, but
Phil 2:23 I hope to send him at **o**,
4:16 in Thessalonica you sent aid **o**
Col 1:21 who **o** were alienated and
3: 7 in which you yourselves **o** walked
Titus 3: 3 For we ourselves were also **o**
Phm 1:11 who **o** was unprofitable to you,
Heb 6: 4 impossible for those who were **o**
7:27 for this He did **o** for all when
9: 7 the high priest went alone **o**
9:12 entered the Most Holy Place **o**
9:26 **o** at the end of the ages, He
9:27 is appointed for men to die **o**,
9:28 so Christ was offered **o** to bear
10: 2 **o** purified, would have had no
10:10 of the body of Jesus Christ **o**
12:26 Yet **o** more I shake not
12:27 Yet **o** more," indicates the
1 Pe 2:10 who **o** were not a people but
3:18 For Christ also suffered **o** for
3:20 when **o** the Divine longsuffering
Jude 3 for the faith which was **o** for
5 though you **o** knew this, that

ONE (2611/2242) ONCE

Gen 1: 9 together into **o** place,
2:11 it is the **o** which skirts the
2:13 it is the **o** which goes around
2:14 it is the **o** which goes toward
2:21 and He took **o** of his ribs, and
2:24 and they shall become **o** flesh.
3: 6 tree desirable to make **o** wise,
3:22 the man has become like **o** of
4:19 the name of **o** was Adah, and
5: 3 And Adam lived **o** hundred and
5: 6 Seth lived **o** hundred and five
5:18 Jared lived **o** hundred and
5:25 Methuselah lived **o** hundred and
5:28 Lamech lived **o** hundred and
5:29 This **o** will comfort us
6: 3 yet his days shall be **o** hundred
7:24 waters prevailed on the earth **o**
10: 8 he began to be a mighty **o** on
10:25 the name of **o** was Peleg, for
11: 1 Now the whole earth had **o**
11: 1 earth had one language and **o**
11: 3 Then they said to **o** another,
11: 6 Indeed the people are **o** and
11: 6 are one and they all have **o**
11: 7 that they may not understand **o**
11:10 Shem was **o** hundred years old,
11:25 Nahor lived **o** hundred and
14:13 Then **o** who had escaped came and
15: 3 indeed **o** born in my house is my
15: 4 This **o** shall not be your heir,
15: 4 but **o** who will come from your
17:17 who is **o** hundred years old?
19: 9 This **o** came in to stay here,
19:20 flee to, and it is a little **o**;
19:20 there (is it not a little **o**?
21: 5 Now Abraham was **o** hundred years
21:15 and she placed the boy under **o**
22: 2 there as a burnt offering on **o**
23: 1 Sarah lived **o** hundred and
24:14 let her be the **o** You have
25: 7 **o** hundred and seventy-five
25:17 **o** hundred and thirty-seven
25:23 ***O*** people shall be stronger
26:10 ***O*** of the people might soon have
26:21 and they quarreled over that **o**
26:26 **o** of his friends, and Phichol
26:31 an oath with **o** another;
27:33 Where is the **o** who hunted game
27:38 Have you only **o** blessing, my
27:45 bereaved also of you both in **o**
28:11 And he took **o** of the stones of
29:27 and we will give you this **o**
30:33 every **o** that is not speckled
30:35 every **o** that had some white in
31:49 we are absent **o** from another.
32: 8 If Esau comes to the **o** company
32:17 And he commanded the first **o**,
33:13 men should drive them hard **o**
33:19 for **o** hundred pieces of money.
34:14 to give our sister to **o** who is
34:16 and we will become **o** people.
34:22 to be **o** people: if every male
35:28 days of Isaac were **o** hundred
37:19 Then they said to **o** another,
38:28 that the **o** put out his hand;
38:28 This **o** came out first."
39: 9 There is no **o** greater in this
40: 5 each man's dream in **o** night
41: 5 of grain came up on **o** stalk,
41: 8 but there was no **o** who could
41:11 we each had a dream in **o** night,
41:15 and there is no **o** who can
41:21 no **o** would have known that they
41:22 seven heads came up on **o** stalk,
41:24 but there was no **o** who could
41:25 "The dreams of Pharaoh are **o**;
41:26 seven years; the dreams are **o**.
41:38 Can we find such a **o** as this,
41:39 there is no **o** as discerning
42: 1 Why do you look at **o** another?"
42:11 'We are all **o** man's sons;
42:13 the sons of **o** man in the land
42:13 and **o** is no more."
42:16 Send **o** of you, and let him bring
42:19 let **o** of your brothers be
42:21 Then they said to **o** another,
42:27 But as **o** of them opened his
42:28 saying to **o** another, "What is
42:32 **o** is no more, and the
42:33 Leave **o** of your brothers here
43:33 in astonishment at **o** another.
44: 5 Is not this the **o** from which
44:28 and the **o** went out from me, and
44:29 But if you take this **o** also from
45: 1 So no **o** stood with him while
47: 9 pilgrimage are **o** hundred and
47:21 from **o** end of the borders of
47:28 length of Jacob's life was **o**
48:18 for this **o** is the firstborn;
48:22 have given to you **o** portion
49:16 people As **o** of the tribes
49:28 he blessed each **o** according to
50:22 And Joseph lived **o** hundred and
50:26 being **o** hundred and ten years
Ex 1:15 of whom the name of **o** was
2: 6 This is **o** of the Hebrews'
2:11 **o** of his brethren.
2:12 that way, and when he saw no **o**,
2:13 and he said to the **o** who did
6:16 of the life of Levi were **o**
6:18 of the life of Kohath were **o**
6:20 of the life of Amram were **o**
6:25 took for himself **o** of the
8:10 may know that there is no **o**
8:31 his people. Not **o** remained.
9: 6 of Israel, not **o** died.
9: 7 not even **o** of the livestock of
10: 5 so that no **o** will be able to
10:19 There remained not **o** locust in
10:23 They did not see **o** another;
11: 1 I will bring yet **o** more plague
12:30 where there was not **o** dead.
12:46 In **o** house it shall be eaten;
12:46 nor shall you break **o** of its
12:49 ***O*** law shall be for the
14: 7 with captains over every **o** of
14:20 cloud and darkness to the **o**,
14:20 so that the **o** did not come near
14:28 Not so much as **o** of them
16:15 they said to **o** another, "What
16:16 **o** omer for each person,
16:19 Let no **o** leave any of it till
16:22 bread, two omers for each **o**.
17:12 **o** on one side, and the other on
17:12 one on **o** side, and the other on
18: 3 of whom the name of **o** was
18:16 and I judge between **o** and
21:18 and **o** strikes the other with a
21:35 If **o** man's ox hurts another's,
22:10 away, no **o** seeing it,
23: 5 If you see the donkey of **o** who
23:26 No **o** shall suffer miscarriage or
23:29 from before you in **o** year,
24: 3 people answered with **o** voice
25:12 two rings shall be on **o** side,
25:19 'Make **o** cherub at one end, and
25:19 'Make one cherub at **o** end, and
25:19 two ends of it of **o** piece
25:20 and they shall face **o** another;
25:31 shall be of **o** piece.
25:32 of the lampstand out of **o** side,
25:33 almond blossoms on **o** branch,
25:36 shall be of **o** piece;
25:36 it shall be **o** hammered piece
26: 2 And every **o** of the curtains
26: 3 shall be coupled to **o** another,
26: 3 coupled to **o** another.
26: 4 on the selvedge of **o** set,
26: 5 shall make in the **o** curtain,
26: 5 may be clasped to **o** another.
26: 6 so that it may be **o** tabernacle.
26:10 that is outermost in **o** set,
26:11 tent together, that it may be **o**.
26:13 And a cubit on **o** side and a
26:17 in each board for binding **o** to
26:24 together at the top by **o** ring.
26:26 five for the boards on **o** side
27: 2 its horns shall be of **o** piece
27: 9 **o** hundred cubits long for one
27: 9 cubits long for **o** side.
27:11 be hangings **o** hundred cubits
27:14 The hangings on **o** side of the
27:18 shall be **o** hundred cubits,
28:10 six of their names on **o** stone,
28:21 each **o** with its own name;
29: 1 Take **o** young bull and two rams
29: 3 You shall put them in **o** basket
29:15 You shall also take **o** ram, and
29:23 **o** loaf of bread, one cake made
29:23 **o** cake made with oil, and one
29:23 and **o** wafer from the basket of
29:39 ***O*** lamb you shall offer in the
29:40 With the **o** lamb shall be
30: 2 Its horns shall be of **o** piece
32:15 on the **o** side and on the other
33: 4 and no **o** put on his ornaments.
33: 5 into your midst in **o** moment
34:15 and **o** of them invites you
36:10 five curtains to **o** another,
36:10 he coupled to **o** another.
36:11 on the selvedge of **o** set;
36:12 he made on **o** curtain,
36:12 the loops held **o** curtain to
36:13 the curtains to **o** another
36:13 that it might be **o** tabernacle.
36:17 that is outermost in **o** set,
36:18 together, that it might be **o**.
36:22 had two tenons for binding **o**
36:29 together at the top by **o** ring.
36:31 five for the boards on **o** side
36:33 through the boards from **o** end
37: 3 two rings on **o** side, and two
37: 7 he made them of **o** piece at the
37: 8 **o** cherub at one end on this
37: 8 one cherub at **o** end on this
37: 8 at the two ends of **o** piece
37: 9 They faced **o** another; the faces
37:18 of the lampstand out of **o** side,
37:19 almond blossoms on **o** branch,
37:22 branches were of **o** piece;
37:22 all of it was **o** hammered piece
37:25 Its horns were of **o** piece
38: 2 the horns were of **o** piece
38: 9 **o** hundred cubits long.
38:11 were **o** hundred cubits long,
38:14 The hangings of **o** side of the
38:25 was **o** hundred talents
38:25 hundred talents and **o** thousand
38:27 **o** hundred sockets from the
38:27 **o** talent for each socket.
38:28 Then from the **o** thousand seven
39:14 each **o** with its own name
Lev 1: 2 When any **o** of you brings an
2: 2 **o** of whom shall take from it
5: 7 **o** as a sin offering and the
6: 3 in any **o** of these things that a
6: 7 he shall be forgiven for any **o**
7: 7 there is **o** law for them both:
7:10 to **o** as much as the other.
7:14 it he shall offer **o** cake
8:26 he took **o** unleavened cake,
8:26 and **o** wafer, and put them on
9:15 it for sin, like the first **o**.
12: 8 **o** as a burnt offering and the
13: 2 to Aaron the priest or to **o** of
13: 4 priest shall isolate the **o**
13:12 covers all the skin of the **o**
13:23 bright spot stays in **o** place,
13:28 bright spot stays in **o** place,
13:31 priest shall isolate the **o**
13:33 priest shall isolate the **o**
14: 5 priest shall command that **o** of
14:10 **o** ewe lamb of the first year
14:10 and **o** log of oil.
14:12 And the priest shall take **o** male
14:21 then he shall take **o** male lamb
14:22 **o** shall be a sin offering and
14:30 And he shall offer **o** of the
14:31 the **o** as a sin offering and
14:32 This is the law for **o** who had
14:50 Then he shall kill **o** of the
15:11 And whomever the **o** who has the
15:15 the **o** as a sin offering and
15:30 the priest shall offer the **o**
15:32 This is the law for **o** who has a
15:33 and for **o** who has a discharge,
16: 5 and **o** ram as a burnt offering.
16: 8 **o** lot for the LORD and the
17:12 No **o** among you shall eat blood,
19: 3 Every **o** of you shall revere his
19:11 nor lie to **o** another.
19:34 among you shall be to you as **o**
22:10 **o** who dwells with the priest,
22:11 and **o** who is born in his house
23:18 **o** young bull, and two rams.
23:19 Then you shall sacrifice **o** kid
24:22 law for the stranger and for **o**
25:14 shall not oppress **o** another.
25:17 shall not oppress **o** another,
25:25 If **o** of your brethren becomes
25:26 Or if the man has no **o** to redeem
25:35 If **o** of your brethren becomes
25:39 And if **o** of your brethren
25:46 not rule over **o** another
25:47 and **o** of your brethren who
25:48 ***O*** of his brothers may redeem
26:17 and you shall flee when no **o**
26:26 bake your bread in **o** oven,
26:36 and they shall fall when no **o**
26:37 stumble over **o** another,
26:37 when no **o** pursues; and you
27:10 then both it and the **o**
27:24 to the **o** who owned the land as
27:32 the tenth **o** shall be holy to
27:33 then both it and the **o**
Num 1: 4 each **o** the head of his father's
1:18 each **o** individually.
1:44 each **o** representing his
2: 9 **o** hundred and eighty-six
2:16 **o** hundred and fifty-one
2:24 **o** hundred and eight thousand
2:24 hundred and eight thousand **o**
2:31 **o** hundred and fifty-seven

2:34 each **o** by his family, according
3:47 for each **o** individually;
3:50 **o** thousand three hundred and
5: 7 and give it to the **o** he has
6:11 and the priest shall offer **o** as
6:14 **o** male lamb in its first year
6:14 **o** ewe lamb in its first year
6:14 **o** ram without blemish as a
6:19 **o** unleavened cake from the
6:19 and **o** unleavened wafer, and put
7: 3 and for each **o** an ox; and they
7:11 **o** leader each day, for the
7:12 And the **o** who offered his
7:13 offering was **o** silver platter,
7:13 of which was **o** hundred
7:13 and **o** silver bowl of seventy
7:14 **o** gold pan of ten shekels, full
7:15 **o** young bull, one ram, and one
7:15 **o** ram, and one male lamb in its
7:15 and **o** male lamb in its first
7:16 **o** kid of the goats as a sin
7:19 he offered **o** silver platter,
7:19 of which was **o** hundred
7:19 and **o** silver bowl of seventy
7:20 **o** gold pan of ten shekels, full
7:21 **o** young bull, one ram, and one
7:21 **o** ram, and one male lamb in its
7:21 and **o** male lamb in its first
7:22 **o** kid of the goats as a sin
7:25 was **o** silver platter,
7:25 of which was **o** hundred
7:25 and **o** silver bowl of seventy
7:26 **o** gold pan of ten shekels, full
7:27 **o** young bull, one ram, and one
7:27 **o** ram, and one male lamb in its
7:27 and **o** male lamb in its first
7:28 **o** kid of the goats as a sin
7:31 was **o** silver platter,
7:31 of which was **o** hundred
7:31 and **o** silver bowl of seventy
7:32 **o** gold pan of ten shekels, full
7:33 **o** young bull, one ram, and one
7:33 **o** ram, and one male lamb in its
7:33 and **o** male lamb in its first
7:34 **o** kid of the goats as a sin
7:37 was **o** silver platter,
7:37 of which was **o** hundred
7:37 and **o** silver bowl of seventy
7:38 **o** gold pan of ten shekels, full
7:39 **o** young bull, one ram, and one
7:39 **o** ram, and one male lamb in its
7:39 and **o** male lamb in its first
7:40 **o** kid of the goats as a sin
7:43 was **o** silver platter,
7:43 of which was **o** hundred
7:43 and **o** silver bowl of seventy
7:44 **o** gold pan of ten shekels, full
7:45 **o** young bull, one ram, and one
7:45 **o** ram, and one male lamb in its
7:45 and **o** male lamb in its first
7:46 **o** kid of the goats as a sin
7:49 was **o** silver platter,
7:49 of which was **o** hundred
7:49 and **o** silver bowl of seventy
7:50 **o** gold pan of ten shekels, full
7:51 **o** young bull, one ram, and one
7:51 **o** ram, and one male lamb in its
7:51 and **o** male lamb in its first
7:52 **o** kid of the goats as a sin
7:55 was **o** silver platter,
7:55 of which was **o** hundred
7:55 and **o** silver bowl of seventy
7:56 **o** gold pan of ten shekels, full
7:57 **o** young bull, one ram, and one
7:57 **o** ram, and one male lamb in its
7:57 and **o** male lamb in its first
7:58 **o** kid of the goats as a sin
7:61 was **o** silver platter,
7:61 of which was **o** hundred
7:61 and **o** silver bowl of seventy
7:62 **o** gold pan of ten shekels, full
7:63 **o** young bull, one ram, and one
7:63 **o** ram, and one male lamb in its
7:63 and **o** male lamb in its first
7:64 **o** kid of the goats as a sin
7:67 was **o** silver platter,
7:67 of which was **o** hundred
7:67 and **o** silver bowl of seventy
7:68 **o** gold pan of ten shekels, full
7:69 **o** young bull, one ram, and one
7:69 **o** ram, and one male lamb in its
7:69 and **o** male lamb in its first
7:70 **o** kid of the goats as a sin
7:73 was **o** silver platter,
7:73 of which was **o** hundred
7:73 and **o** silver bowl of seventy
7:74 **o** gold pan of ten shekels, full
7:75 **o** young bull, one ram, and one
7:75 **o** ram, and one male lamb in its
7:75 and **o** male lamb in its first
7:76 **o** kid of the goats as a sin
7:79 was **o** silver platter,
7:79 of which was **o** hundred
7:79 and **o** silver bowl of seventy
7:80 **o** gold pan of ten shekels, full
7:81 **o** young bull, one ram, and one
7:81 **o** ram, and one male lamb in its
7:81 and **o** male lamb in its first
7:82 **o** kid of the goats as a sin
7:85 Each silver platter weighed **o**
7:86 the gold of the pans weighed **o**
7:89 he heard the voice of **O**
8:12 and you shall offer **o** as a sin
8:24 years old and above **o** may
9:12 nor break **o** of its bones.
9:14 you shall have **o** ordinance,
10: 4 "But if they blow only **o**,
11:19 not **o** day, nor two days, nor
11:26 the name of **o** was Eldad, and
11:28 **o** of his choice men, answered
12:12 do not let her be as **o** dead,
13: 2 every **o** a leader among them."
13:23 down a branch with **o** cluster
14: 4 So they said to **o** another, "Let
14:15 kill these people as **o** man,
14:34 shall bear your guilt **o** year,
15:15 **O** ordinance shall be for you
15:16 **O** law and one custom shall be
15:16 One law and **o** custom shall be
15:24 shall offer **o** young bull
15:24 and **o** kid of the goats as a sin
15:29 You shall have **o** law for him who
15:30 that **o** brings reproach on the
16: 3 every **o** of them, and the LORD
16: 5 That **o** whom He chooses He will
16: 7 LORD chooses is the holy **o**.
16:15 I have not taken **o** donkey from
16:15 nor have I hurt **o** of them."
16:22 shall **o** man sin, and You be
17: 3 For there shall be **o** rod for
18:16 shall redeem when **o** month old,
19: 8 And the **o** who burns it shall
19:10 And the **o** who gathers the ashes
19:16 in the open field touches **o**
19:18 or on the **o** who touched a bone,
24:19 Out of Jacob **O** shall have
25: 5 Every **o** of you kill his men who
25: 6 **o** of the children of Israel
26:51 six hundred and **o** thousand
28: 4 The **o** lamb you shall offer in
28:11 **o** ram, and seven lambs in their
28:12 with oil, for the **o** ram;
28:15 Also **o** kid of the goats as a sin
28:19 **o** ram, and seven lambs in their
28:22 also **o** goat as a sin offering,
28:27 **o** ram, and seven lambs in their
28:28 two-tenths for the **o** ram,
28:30 also **o** kid of the goats, to
29: 2 **o** young bull, one ram, and
29: 2 **o** ram, and seven lambs in
29: 5 also **o** kid of the goats as a
29: 8 **o** young bull, one ram, and
29: 8 **o** ram, and seven lambs in
29: 9 two-tenths for the **o** ram,
29:11 also **o** kid of the goats as a
29:16 also **o** kid of the goats as a
29:19 also **o** kid of the goats as a
29:22 also **o** goat as a sin offering,
29:25 also **o** kid of the goats as a
29:28 also **o** goat as a sin offering,
29:31 also **o** goat as a sin offering,
29:34 also **o** goat as a sin offering,
29:36 **o** bull, one ram, seven lambs in
29:36 **o** ram, seven lambs in their
29:38 also **o** goat as a sin offering,
31: 5 divisions of Israel **o** thousand
31: 6 **o** thousand from each tribe;
31:28 **o** of every five hundred of the
31:30 Israel's half you shall take **o**
31:47 Israel's half Moses took **o** of
32:18 to our homes until every **o** of
33:39 Aaron was **o** hundred and
34:18 And you shall take **o** leader of
35:17 by which **o** could die, and he
35:18 by which **o** could die, and he
35:21 the **o** who struck him shall
35:30 but **o** witness is not
36: 7 for every **o** of the children of
36: 8 Israel shall be the wife of **o**
36: 9 change hands from **o** tribe
Deut 1:23 **o** man from each tribe.
1:35 Surely not **o** of these men of
2: 5 not so much as **o** footstep,
2:36 there was not **o** city too strong
4: 4 alive today, every **o** of you.
4:32 and ask from **o** end of heaven
4:42 and that by fleeing to **o** of
6: 4 our God, the LORD is **o**!
7:24 no **o** shall be able to stand
12:14 in **o** of your tribes, there you
13: 7 from **o** end of the earth to the
13:12 If you hear someone in **o** of
17: 6 on the testimony of **o** witness.
17: 8 between **o** judgment or another,
17: 8 or between **o** punishment or
17:15 **o** from among your brethren you
17:18 from the **o** before the
18:10 or **o** who practices
18:10 or **o** who interprets omens, or a
18:11 or **o** who conjures spells, or a
18:11 or **o** who calls up the dead.
19: 5 he shall flee to **o** of these
19:11 and he flees to **o** of these
19:15 **O** witness shall not rise
21:15 **o** loved and the other unloved,
22:19 fine him **o** hundred shekels
22:27 but there was no **o** to save
23: 2 **O** of illegitimate birth shall
23:16 which he chooses within **o** of
23:17 or a perverted **o** of the sons of
24: 5 be free at home **o** year,
24:14 whether **o** of your brethren or
24:14 one of your brethren or **o** of
25: 5 and **o** of them dies and has no
25:11 and the wife of **o** draws near to
25:11 husband from the hand of the **o**
26: 3 And you shall go to the **o** who is
27:15 Cursed is the **o** who makes a
27:16 Cursed is the **o** who treats his
27:17 Cursed is the **o** who moves his
27:18 Cursed is the **o** who makes the
27:19 Cursed is the **o** who perverts
27:20 Cursed is the **o** who lies with
27:21 Cursed is the **o** who lies with
27:22 Cursed is the **o** who lies with
27:23 Cursed is the **o** who lies with
27:24 Cursed is the **o** who attacks his
27:25 Cursed is the **o** who takes a
27:26 Cursed is the **o** who does not
28: 7 shall come out against you **o**
28:25 you shall go out **o** way against
28:26 and no **o** shall frighten them
28:29 and no **o** shall save you.
28:31 and you shall have no **o** to
28:64 from **o** end of the earth to the
28:68 but no **o** will buy you."
29:11 from the **o** who cuts your wood
29:11 one who cuts your wood to the **o**
31: 2 I am **o** hundred and twenty years
31: 6 He is the **O** who goes with you.
31: 8 He is the **o** who goes before
32:30 How could **o** chase a thousand,
32:36 And there is no **o**
33: 8 Your Urim be with Your holy **o**,
33:26 There is no **o** like the God of
34: 6 but no **o** knows his grave to
34: 7 Moses was **o** hundred and twenty
Josh 3:12 **o** man from every tribe.
4: 2 **o** man from every tribe,
4: 4 **o** man from every tribe;
4: 5 and each **o** of you take up a
9: 2 and Israel with **o** accord.
10: 2 like **o** of the royal cities, and
10:21 No **o** moved his tongue against
10:42 land Joshua took at **o** time,
12: 2 **O** king was Sihon king of the
12: 9 the king of Jericho, **o**;
12: 9 Ai, which is beside Bethel, **o**;
12:10 the king of Jerusalem, **o**;
12:10 one; the king of Hebron, **o**;
12:11 the king of Jarmuth, **o**;
12:11 one; the king of Lachish, **o**;
12:12 the king of Eglon, **o**;
12:12 one; the king of Gezer, **o**;
12:13 the king of Debir, **o**;
12:13 one; the king of Geder, **o**;
12:14 the king of Hormah, **o**;
12:14 one; the king of Arad, **o**;
12:15 the king of Libnah, **o**;
12:15 one; the king of Adullam, **o**;
12:16 the king of Makkedah, **o**;
12:16 one; the king of Bethel, **o**;
12:17 the king of Tappuah, **o**;
12:17 one; the king of Hepher, **o**;
12:18 the king of Aphek, **o**;
12:18 one; the king of Lasharon, **o**;
12:19 the king of Madon, **o**;
12:19 one; the king of Hazor, **o**;
12:20 the king of Shimron Meron, **o**;
12:20 one; the king of Achshaph, **o**;
12:21 the king of Taanach, **o**;
12:21 one; the king of Megiddo, **o**;
12:22 the king of Kedesh, **o**;
12:22 king of Jokneam in Carmel, **o**;
12:23 of Dor in the heights of Dor, **o**;
12:23 king of the people of Gilgal, **o**;
12:24 the king of Tirzah, **o**—
17:14 have you given us only **o** lot
17:14 only one lot and **o** share
17:17 you shall not have only **o** lot,
20: 4 And when he flees to **o** of those
20: 4 take him into the city as **o** of
20: 6 and until the death of the **o**
21:10 **o** of the families of the
21:42 Every **o** of these cities had its
22:14 **o** ruler each from the chief
22:14 and each **o** was the head of the
23: 9 no **o** has been able to stand
23:10 **O** man of you shall chase a
23:14 your souls that not **o** thing
23:14 not **o** word of them has failed.
24:29 being **o** hundred and ten years
24:32 Shechem for **o** hundred pieces
Judg 2: 8 died when he was **o** hundred
6:16 defeat the Midianites as **o** man.
6:29 So they said to **o** another, "Who
6:31 Let the **o** who would plead for
7: 4 This **o** shall go with you,' the
7: 4 This **o** shall not go with you,'
8:10 for **o** hundred and twenty
8:18 each **o** resembled the son of a
8:26 he requested was **o** thousand
9: 2 or that **o** reign over you?'
9: 5 on **o** stone. But Jotham the
9:18 his seventy sons on **o** stone,
10:18 said to **o** another, "Who is
14: 6 and he tore the lion apart as **o**
16: 5 and every **o** of us will give you
16:24 And the **o** who multiplied our
16:28 that I may with **o** blow take
16:29 **o** on his right and the other on
17: 5 and he consecrated **o** of his
17:11 the young man became like **o** of
18:19 to the household of **o** man,
19:13 let us draw near to **o** of these
19:15 for no **o** would take them into

19:18 But there is no ***o*** who will
20: 1 gathered together as ***o*** man
20: 8 the people arose as ***o*** man,
20:11 united together as ***o*** man.
20:16 every ***o*** could sling a stone at
20:31 in the highways (***o*** of which
20:35 that day twenty-five thousand ***o***
21: 3 that today there should be ***o***
21: 6 ***O*** tribe is cut off from Israel
21: 8 What ***o*** is there from the
21: 8 no ***o*** had come to the camp from
21: 9 not ***o*** of the inhabitants of
21:18 Cursed be the ***o*** who gives a
Ruth 1: 4 the name of the ***o*** was Orpah,
2:13 though I am not like ***o*** of your
2:19 Blessed be the ***o*** who took
2:20 ***o*** of our close relatives."
3:14 and she arose before ***o*** could
4: 4 for there is no ***o*** but you to
4: 7 ***o*** man took off his sandal and
1 Sam 1: 2 the name of ***o*** was Hannah, and
1:24 ***o*** ephah of flour, and a skin of
2: 2 No ***o*** is holy like the LORD,
2:25 If ***o*** man sins against another,
2:34 in ***o*** day they shall die, both
2:36 put me in ***o*** of the priestly
6:17 ***o*** for Ashdod, one for Gaza, one
6:17 ***o*** for Gaza, one for Ashkelon,
6:17 ***o*** for Ashkelon, one for Gath,
6:17 ***o*** for Gath, one for Ekron;
6:17 one for Gath, ***o*** for Ekron;
9: 3 take ***o*** of the servants with
9: 8 I have here at hand ***o*** fourth of
9:17 This ***o*** shall reign over My
10: 3 ***o*** carrying three young goats,
10:11 that the people said to ***o***
10:24 that there is no ***o*** like him
11: 3 if there is no ***o*** to save us,
11: 7 and they came out with ***o***
13: 1 Saul reigned ***o*** year; and when he
13:17 ***O*** company turned to the road to
14: 1 Now it happened ***o*** day that
14: 4 was a sharp rock on ***o*** side
14: 4 And the name of ***o*** was Bozez,
14: 5 The front of ***o*** faced northward
14:26 but no ***o*** put his hand to his
14:28 Then ***o*** of the people said,
14:34 So every ***o*** of the people
14:40 You be on ***o*** side, and my son
14:45 not ***o*** hair of his head shall
16: 3 you shall anoint for Me the ***o***
16: 8 has the LORD chosen this ***o***.
16: 9 has the LORD chosen this ***o***.
16:12 for this is the ***o***!"
16:18 Then ***o*** of the servants answered
17: 3 stood on a mountain on ***o*** side,
17:36 Philistine will be like ***o*** of
18:25 but ***o*** hundred foreskins
20:15 the LORD has cut off every ***o***
20:41 And they kissed ***o*** another;
21: 1 and no ***o*** is with you?"
21: 9 is no other except that ***o***
21:11 not sing of him to ***o*** another
22: 7 the son of Jesse give every ***o***
22: 8 and there is no ***o*** who reveals
22: 8 and there is not ***o*** of you who
22:20 Now ***o*** of the sons of Ahimelech
23:26 Then Saul went on ***o*** side of the
25:10 nowadays who break away each ***o***
25:14 Now ***o*** of the young men told
25:17 is such a scoundrel that ***o***
25:18 ***o*** hundred clusters of raisins,
25:22 if I leave ***o*** male of all who
26:15 For ***o*** of the people came in to
26:20 as when ***o*** hunts a partridge in
26:22 Let ***o*** of the young men come
27: 7 of the Philistines was ***o*** full
28: 2 Therefore I will make you ***o*** of
28: 8 and bring up for me the ***o*** I
29: 5 of whom they sang to ***o*** another
2 Sam 1:15 Then David called ***o*** of the young
2:13 ***o*** on one side of the pool and
2:13 one on ***o*** side of the pool and
2:16 And each ***o*** grasped his opponent
2:21 and lay hold on ***o*** of the young
3:13 But ***o*** thing I require of you:
3:29 to be in the house of Joab ***o***
4: 2 The name of ***o*** was Baanah and
4:10 the ***o*** who thought I would give
5: 2 you were the ***o*** who led Israel
6:20 as ***o*** of the base fellows
7:23 the ***o*** nation on the earth whom
8: 2 and with ***o*** full line those to
8: 4 David took from him ***o*** thousand
8: 4 them for ***o*** hundred chariots.
9:11 shall eat at my table like ***o***
10: 6 the king of Maacah ***o*** thousand
11: 2 Then it happened ***o*** evening that
11:25 for the sword devours ***o*** as well
12: 1 There were two men in ***o*** city,
12: 1 ***o*** rich and the other poor.
12: 3 except ***o*** little ewe lamb which
12: 4 from his own herd to prepare ***o***
13:13 you would be like ***o*** of the
13:29 and each ***o*** got on his mule and
13:30 and not ***o*** of them is left!"
14: 6 and there was no ***o*** to part
14: 6 but the ***o*** struck the other and
14:11 not ***o*** hair of your son shall
14:13 the king speaks this thing as ***o***
14:13 does not bring his banished ***o***
14:19 no ***o*** can turn to the right hand

14:25 in all Israel there was no ***o***
14:27 and ***o*** daughter whose name was
16: 1 ***o*** hundred clusters of raisins,
16: 1 ***o*** hundred summer fruits, and a
16:23 was as if ***o*** had inquired at
17:12 shall not be left so much as ***o***.
17:13 until there is not ***o*** small
17:22 By morning light not ***o*** of them
18: 2 Then David sent out ***o*** third of
18: 2 ***o*** third under the hand of
18: 2 and ***o*** third under the hand of
19: 7 not ***o*** will stay with you this
19:14 just as the heart of ***o*** man,
20:11 Meanwhile ***o*** of Joab's men stood
21:16 who was ***o*** of the sons of the
21:18 who was ***o*** of the sons of the
23: 8 eight hundred men at ***o*** time.
23: 9 ***o*** of the three mighty men with
23:24 the brother of Joab was ***o*** of
24:12 choose ***o*** of them for yourself,
1 Ki 1:48 who has given ***o*** to sit on my
1:49 and each ***o*** went his way.
1:52 not ***o*** hair of him shall fall to
2:16 'Now I ask ***o*** petition of you;
2:20 I desire ***o*** small petition of
3:17 And ***o*** woman said, "O my lord,
3:18 no ***o*** was with us in the house,
3:22 No! But the living ***o*** is my son,
3:22 and the dead ***o*** is your son."
3:22 No! But the dead ***o*** is your son,
3:22 and the living ***o*** is my son."
3:23 The ***o*** says, 'This is my son,
3:23 and your son is the dead ***o***';
3:23 But your son is the dead ***o***,
3:23 and my son is the living ***o***.
3:25 in two, and give half to ***o***,
4: 7 each ***o*** made provision for one
4: 7 made provision for ***o*** month
4:22 Solomon's provision for ***o*** day
4:23 and ***o*** hundred sheep, besides
4:32 and his songs were ***o*** thousand
5:14 they were ***o*** month in Lebanon
6:24 ***O*** wing of the cherub was five
6:24 ten cubits from the tip of ***o***
6:26 The height of ***o*** cherub was ten
6:27 so that the wing of the ***o***
6:27 the wing of the one touched ***o***
6:34 two panels comprised ***o*** folding
7: 2 its length was ***o*** hundred
7:15 each ***o*** eighteen cubits high,
7:16 The height of ***o*** capital was
7:17 seven chains for ***o*** capital and
7:23 ten cubits from ***o*** brim to the
7:31 at the top was ***o*** cubit
7:31 ***o*** and a half cubits in outside
7:32 The height of a wheel was ***o***
7:37 ***o*** measure, and one shape.
7:37 one measure, and ***o*** shape.
7:44 ***o*** Sea, and twelve oxen under the
8:38 when each ***o*** knows the plague of
8:46 (for there is no ***o*** who
8:56 There has not failed ***o*** word of
8:63 thousand bulls and ***o*** hundred
9:14 sent the king ***o*** hundred
10:10 Then she gave the king ***o*** hundred
10:20 ***o*** on each side of the six
10:21 Not ***o*** was silver, for this
10:26 he had ***o*** thousand four hundred
10:29 and a horse ***o*** hundred and
11:13 I will give ***o*** tribe to your son
11:32 (but he shall have ***o*** tribe for
11:36 And to his son I will give ***o***
12:21 ***o*** hundred and eighty thousand
12:29 And he set up ***o*** in Bethel, and
12:30 went to worship before the ***o***
13:33 and he became ***o*** of the priests
14:10 as ***o*** takes away refuse until it
14:13 for he is the only ***o*** of
16:11 he did not leave him ***o*** male,
18: 4 had taken ***o*** hundred prophets
18: 6 Ahab went ***o*** way by himself, and
18:13 how I hid ***o*** hundred men of the
18:23 and let them choose ***o*** bull for
18:25 Choose ***o*** bull for yourselves and
18:26 no ***o*** answered. Then they leaped
18:29 no ***o*** answered, no one paid
18:29 no ***o*** paid attention.
18:40 prophets of Baal! Do not let ***o***
19: 2 your life as the life of ***o*** of
20:11 Let not the ***o*** who puts on his
20:11 on his armor boast like the ***o***
20:20 And each ***o*** killed his man;
20:29 killed ***o*** hundred thousand
20:29 soldiers of the Syrians in ***o***
20:41 of Israel recognized him as ***o***
21:25 But there was no ***o*** like Ahab
22: 8 There is still ***o*** man, Micaiah
22:13 words of the prophets with ***o***
22:13 word be like the word of ***o*** of
22:20 So ***o*** spoke in this manner, and
22:31 Fight with no ***o*** small or great,
2 Ki 3: 4 ***o*** hundred thousand lambs
3: 4 lambs and the wool of ***o***
3:11 So ***o*** of the servants of the
3:23 struck swords and have killed ***o***
4: 8 Now it happened ***o*** day that
4:11 And it happened ***o*** day that he
4:18 Now it happened ***o*** day that he
4:22 Please send me ***o*** of the young
4:22 me one of the young men and ***o***
4:39 So ***o*** went out into the field to
4:43 Shall I set this before ***o***

6: 3 Then ***o*** said, "Please consent to
6: 5 But as ***o*** was cutting down a
6:12 And ***o*** of his servants said,
7: 3 and they said to ***o*** another,
7: 5 to their surprise no ***o*** was
7: 6 so they said to ***o*** another,
7: 8 they went into ***o*** tent and ate
7: 9 Then they said to ***o*** another,
7:10 and surprisingly no ***o*** was
7:13 And ***o*** of his servants answered
8:26 and he reigned ***o*** year in
9: 1 Elisha the prophet called ***o*** of
9: 5 For which ***o*** of us?" And he
9:11 and ***o*** said to him, "Is all
9:15 let no ***o*** leave or escape from
10:19 Let no ***o*** be missing, for I have
10:21 of Baal was full from ***o*** end
10:22 And he said to the ***o*** in charge
10:25 let no ***o*** come out!" And they
12: 9 on the right side as ***o*** comes
14: 8 let us face ***o*** another in
14:11 king of Judah faced ***o*** another
17:27 Send there ***o*** of the priests whom
17:28 Then ***o*** of the priests whom they
18:24 will you repel ***o*** captain
18:31 and every ***o*** of you eat from his
18:31 from his own vine and every ***o***
18:31 and every ***o*** of you drink the
19:15 the ***O*** who dwells between the
19:22 Against the Holy ***O*** of Israel.
19:35 of the Assyrians ***o*** hundred
21:13 I will wipe Jerusalem as ***o***
21:16 he had filled Jerusalem from ***o***
23:18 let no ***o*** move his bones."
23:33 tribute of ***o*** hundred talents
23:35 from every ***o*** according to his
24:16 ***o*** thousand, all who were
25:16 ***o*** Sea, and the carts, which
25:17 The height of ***o*** pillar was
1 Chr 1:10 he began to be a mighty ***o*** on
1:19 the name of ***o*** was Peleg, for
5:21 also ***o*** hundred thousand of their
6:57 the sons of Aaron they gave ***o***
6:67 And they gave them ***o*** of the
8:40 ***o*** hundred and fifty in all.
9:13 ***o*** thousand seven hundred and
11: 2 you were the ***o*** who led Israel
11:11 killed by him at ***o*** time.
11:12 who was ***o*** of the three mighty
12:25 seven thousand ***o*** hundred;
12:34 of Naphtali ***o*** thousand captains,
12:37 ***o*** hundred and twenty thousand
12:38 of Israel were of ***o*** mind
15: 2 No ***o*** may carry the ark of God
15: 5 and ***o*** hundred and twenty of his
15: 7 and ***o*** hundred and thirty of his
15:10 and ***o*** hundred and twelve of his
16:20 When they went from ***o*** nation to
16:20 And from ***o*** kingdom to another
17: 5 and from ***o*** tabernacle to
17:21 the ***o*** nation on the earth whom
18: 4 David took from him ***o*** thousand
18: 4 them for ***o*** hundred chariots.
20: 4 who was ***o*** of the sons of the
21: 5 All Israel had ***o*** million one
21: 5 All Israel had one million ***o***
21:10 choose ***o*** of them for yourself,
21:17 I am the ***o*** who has sinned and
22:14 for the house of the LORD ***o***
22:14 gold and ***o*** million talents
23:11 they were assigned as ***o***
24: 5 ***o*** group as another, for there
24: 6 ***o*** of the Levites, wrote them
24: 6 ***o*** father's house taken for
24: 6 house taken for Eleazar and ***o***
26:30 ***o*** thousand seven hundred able
27:18 ***o*** of David's brothers;
29: 7 and ***o*** hundred thousand talents
2 Chr 1:14 he had ***o*** thousand four hundred
1:17 and a horse for ***o*** hundred and
2:17 were found to be ***o*** hundred
3: 4 and the height was ***o*** hundred
3:11 ***o*** wing of the one cherub
3:11 one wing of the ***o*** cherub
3:12 ***o*** wing of the other cherub was
3:16 and he made ***o*** hundred
3:17 ***o*** on the right hand and the
3:17 he called the name of the ***o*** on
3:17 and the name of the ***o*** on the
4: 2 ten cubits from ***o*** brim to the
4: 8 And he made ***o*** hundred bowls of
4:15 ***o*** Sea and twelve oxen under it;
5:12 and with them ***o*** hundred and
5:13 and singers were as ***o***,
5:13 to make ***o*** sound to be heard in
6:29 when each ***o*** knows his own
6:36 (for there is no ***o*** who
7: 5 thousand bulls and ***o*** hundred
9: 9 And she gave the king ***o*** hundred
9:19 ***o*** on each side of the six
9:20 Not ***o*** was silver, for this
11: 1 Judah and Benjamin ***o*** hundred
15: 5 there was no peace to the ***o***
15: 5 nor to the ***o*** who came in, but
17:18 and with him ***o*** hundred and
18: 7 There is still ***o*** man by whom
18: 8 the king of Israel called ***o***
18:12 the prophets with ***o*** accord
18:12 word be like the word of ***o***
18:19 So ***o*** spoke in this manner, and
18:30 Fight with no ***o*** small or great,
20: 6 so that no ***o*** is able to

20:23 helped to destroy **o** another.
20:24 the earth. No **o** had escaped.
22: 2 and he reigned **o** year in
22: 9 the house of Ahaziah had no **o**
23: 6 But let no **o** come into the house
23:19 so that no **o** who was in any
24:15 he was **o** hundred and thirty
25: 6 He also hired **o** hundred thousand
25: 6 from Israel for **o** hundred
25:17 let us face **o** another in
25:21 king of Judah faced **o** another
26:11 **o** of the king's captains.
27: 5 in that year **o** hundred talents
28: 6 the son of Remaliah killed **o**
28: 6 twenty thousand in Judah in **o** day,
29:32 **o** hundred rams, and two
32:12 You shall worship before **o** altar
35:24 and was buried in **o** of the
36: 3 tribute of **o** hundred talents
Ezra 1: 9 **o** thousand silver platters,
1:10 and **o** thousand other articles.
2: 3 two thousand **o** hundred and
2: 7 **o** thousand two hundred and
2:12 **o** thousand two hundred and
2:18 **o** hundred and twelve;
2:21 **o** hundred and twenty-three;
2:23 **o** hundred and twenty-eight;
2:27 **o** hundred and twenty-two;
2:30 **o** hundred and fifty-six;
2:31 **o** thousand two hundred and
2:37 **o** thousand and fifty-two;
2:38 **o** thousand two hundred and
2:39 **o** thousand and seventeen.
2:41 **o** hundred and twenty-eight.
2:42 **o** hundred and thirty-nine in
2:69 and **o** hundred priestly
3: 1 gathered together as **o** man
3: 9 arose as **o** to oversee those
5:14 and they were given to **o** named
6: 4 rows of heavy stones and **o** row
6:17 **o** hundred bulls, two hundred
7:22 up to **o** hundred talents of
7:22 **o** hundred kors of wheat, one
7:22 **o** hundred baths of wine, one
7:22 **o** hundred baths of oil, and
8: 3 with him were **o** hundred and
8:10 and with him **o** hundred and
8:12 and with him **o** hundred and ten
8:26 weighing **o** hundred talents,
8:26 **o** hundred talents of gold,
9:11 which have filled it from **o**
9:15 though no **o** can stand before
10: 2 **o** of the sons of Elam, spoke
10:13 Nor is this the work of **o** or
Neh 1: 2 that Hanani **o** of my brethren
2:12 I told no **o** what my God had put
2:12 except the **o** on which I rode.
3: 8 **o** of the goldsmiths, made
3: 8 **o** of the perfumers, made
3:31 **o** of the goldsmiths, made
4:17 themselves so that with **o** hand
4:18 Every **o** of the builders had his
4:18 And the **o** who sounded the
4:19 separated far from **o** another
5:17 And at my table were **o** hundred
5:18 was prepared daily was **o** ox
7: 3 **o** at his watch station and
7: 8 two thousand **o** hundred and
7:12 **o** thousand two hundred and
7:24 **o** hundred and twelve;
7:26 **o** hundred and eighty-eight;
7:27 **o** hundred and twenty-eight;
7:31 **o** hundred and twenty-two;
7:32 **o** hundred and twenty-three;
7:34 **o** thousand two hundred and
7:40 **o** thousand and fifty-two;
7:41 **o** thousand two hundred and
7:42 **o** thousand and seventeen.
7:44 **o** hundred and forty-eight.
7:45 **o** hundred and thirty-eight.
7:70 **o** thousand gold drachmas,
8: 1 gathered together as **o** man
8:16 each **o** on the roof of his
11: 1 the people cast lots to bring **o**
11:14 were **o** hundred and
11:14 was Zabdiel the son of **o** of
11:19 were **o** hundred and
12:31 ***O*** went to the right hand on
13:24 according to the language of **o**
13:28 And **o** of the sons of Joiada,
Esth 1: 1 who reigned over **o** hundred
1: 4 **o** hundred and eighty days in
3:13 in **o** day, on the thirteenth
4: 2 for no **o** might enter the
4: 5 **o** of the king's eunuchs whom
4:11 he has but **o** law: put all to
4:11 except the **o** to whom the king
5:12 Queen Esther invited no **o** but
6: 1 So **o** was commanded to bring the
6: 9 be delivered to the hand of **o**
7: 9 **o** of the eunuchs, said to the
8: 8 signet ring no **o** can revoke."
8: 9 **o** hundred and twenty-seven
8:12 on **o** day in all the provinces of
9: 2 And no **o** could withstand them,
9:19 sending presents to **o** another.
9:22 sending presents to **o** another
9:30 to the **o** hundred and
Job 1: 1 and **o** who feared God and
1: 8 **o** who fears God and shuns
2: 3 **o** who fears God and shuns evil?
2:10 You speak as **o** of the foolish

2:11 each **o** came from his own
2:12 and each **o** tore his robe and
2:13 and no **o** spoke a word to him,
4: 2 If **o** attempts a word with you,
4:20 forever, with no **o** regarding.
5: 2 man, And envy slays a simple **o**.
6:10 the words of the Holy ***O***.
6:26 the speeches of a desperate **o**,
9: 3 If **o** wished to contend with
9: 3 He could not answer Him **o** time
9:22 It is all **o** thing;
10: 7 And there is no **o** who can
11: 3 should no **o** rebuke you?
11:19 and no **o** would make you
12: 4 I am **o** mocked by his friends,
12: 5 is despised in the thought of **o**
13: 9 Or can you mock Him as **o** mocks
14: 3 You open Your eyes on such a **o**,
14: 4 out of an unclean? No **o**!
15:28 In houses which no **o** inhabits,
16:21 that **o** might plead for a man
17: 6 And I have become **o** in whose
17:10 For I shall not find **o** wise
19:11 And He counts me as **o** of His
21:23 ***O*** dies in his full strength,
22:30 He will even deliver **o** who is
24:18 So that no **o** would turn
26: 3 How have you counseled **o** who
29:12 The fatherless and the **o**
29:25 As **o** who comforts mourners.
31:15 Did not the same ***O*** fashion us
31:35 that I had **o** to hear me!
32:12 And surely not **o** of you
33:14 For God may speak in **o** way, or
33:23 **o** among a thousand, To show
34:17 Should **o** who hates justice
35:10 But no **o** says, 'Where is God
36: 4 ***O*** who is perfect in knowledge
36: 5 is mighty, but despises no **o**;
36:18 He take you away with **o** blow;
38:26 a land where there is no **o**,
40: 2 Shall the **o** who contends with
40:24 Or **o** pierces his nose with a
41: 9 Shall **o** not be overwhelmed
41:10 No **o** is so fierce that he
41:16 ***O*** is so near another That no
41:17 They are joined **o** to another,
41:32 ***O*** would think the deep had
42:11 Each **o** gave him a piece of
42:12 **o** thousand yoke of oxen, and
42:12 and **o** thousand female donkeys.
42:16 After this Job lived **o** hundred
Ps 3: 3 My glory and the ***O*** who lifts
11: 5 But the wicked and the **o** who
14: 3 none who does good, No, not **o**.
16:10 will You allow Your Holy ***O*** to
19: 6 Its rising is from **o** end of
25: 3 let no **o** who waits on You be
27: 4 ***O*** thing I have desired of the
34:20 Not **o** of them is broken.
35:14 as **o** who mourns for his
45: 3 upon Your thigh, O Mighty ***O***,
49:16 Do not be afraid when **o** becomes
50: 1 The Mighty ***O***, God the LORD,
53: 3 Every **o** of them has turned
53: 3 none who does good, No, not **o**.
55:12 Nor is it **o** who hates me
57: 3 He reproaches the **o** who would
62:12 For You render to each **o**
68:21 The hairy scalp of the **o** who
69:25 Let no **o** live in their tents.
71:22 O Holy ***O*** of Israel.
73:20 As a dream when **o** awakes,
75: 7 is the Judge: He puts down **o**,
78:41 And limited the Holy ***O*** of
79: 3 And there was no **o** to bury
82: 7 And fall like **o** of the
83: 5 together with **o** consent;
84: 7 Each **o** appears before God in
87: 4 This **o** was born there.'"
87: 5 This **o** and that one were born
87: 5 This one and that **o** were born
87: 6 This **o** was born there." Selah
88:18 Loved **o** and friend You have put
89:10 as **o** who is slain; You have
89:18 king to the Holy ***O*** of Israel.
89:19 in a vision to Your holy **o**,
89:19 I have given help to **o** who is
89:19 I have exalted **o** chosen from
101: 5 The **o** who has a haughty look
105:13 When they went from **o** nation to
105:13 From **o** kingdom to another
105:14 He permitted no **o** to do them
106:11 There was not **o** of them left.
106:23 Had not Moses His chosen **o**
119:160 And every **o** of Your righteous
119:162 I rejoice at Your word As **o**
120: 6 has dwelt too long With **o** who
128: 1 Blessed is every **o** who fears
132: 2 to the Mighty ***O*** of Jacob:
132: 5 the Mighty ***O*** of Jacob."
137: 3 Sing us **o** of the songs of
137: 8 Happy the **o** who repays you as
137: 9 Happy the **o** who takes and
141: 7 As when **o** plows and breaks up
142: 4 For there is no **o** who
142: 4 No **o** cares for my soul.
143: 2 For in Your sight no **o** living
144: 2 My shield and the ***O*** in whom
144:10 The ***O*** who gives salvation to
145: 4 ***O*** generation shall praise Your
Prov 1:14 Let us all have **o** purse"—

1:24 out my hand and no **o** regarded,
4: 3 Tender and the only **o** in the
5: 9 And your years to the cruel **o**;
6:19 And **o** who sows discord among
6:28 Can **o** walk on hot coals, And
8:11 And all the things **o** may
9:10 the knowledge of the Holy ***O***
10:22 of the LORD makes **o** rich,
11:15 But **o** who hates being surety
11:24 There is **o** who scatters, yet
11:24 And there is **o** who withholds
12: 9 Better is the **o** who is
12:18 There is **o** who speaks like the
13: 7 There is **o** who makes himself
13: 7 And **o** who makes himself poor,
13:14 To turn **o** away from the
14:27 To turn **o** away from the
15:12 A scoffer does not love **o** who
16: 6 by the fear of the LORD **o**
18:17 The first **o** to plead his cause
19: 1 in his integrity Than **o** who
19: 6 every man is a friend to **o**
19:15 Laziness casts **o** into a deep
19:25 Rebuke **o** who has
20:16 Take the garment of **o** who is
20:19 do not associate with **o** who
22:26 Do not be **o** of those who shakes
22:26 ***O*** of those who is surety for
23:34 you will be like **o** who lies
23:34 Or like **o** who lies at the top
25:20 Like **o** who takes away a
25:20 Is **o** who sings songs to a
26: 8 Like **o** who binds a stone in a
26:17 not his own Is like **o** who
28: 1 flee when no **o** pursues,
28: 6 his integrity Than **o** perverse
28: 8 ***O*** who increases his possessions
28: 9 ***O*** who turns away his ear from
28:17 Let no **o** help him.
30: 3 have knowledge of the Holy ***O***.
Eccl 1: 4 ***O*** generation passes away, and
3:11 except that no **o** can find out
3:19 **o** thing befalls them: as one
3:19 as **o** dies, so dies the other.
3:19 they all have **o** breath; man has
3:20 All go to **o** place: all are from
4: 8 There is **o** alone, without
4: 9 Two are better than **o**,
4:10 **o** will lift up his companion.
4:10 For he has no **o** to help him
4:11 But how can **o** be warm alone?
4:12 Though **o** may be overpowered by
5:18 is good and fitting for **o**
6: 6 Do not all go to **o** place?
6:10 Whatever **o** is, he has been
7:14 God has appointed the **o** as
7:27 Adding **o** thing to the other to
7:28 ***O*** man among a thousand I have
8: 8 No **o** has power over the spirit
8: 8 And no **o** has power in the day
8: 9 is a time in which **o** man
8:16 even though **o** sees no sleep day
9: 2 ***O***e event happens to the
9: 3 that **o** thing happens to all.
9:15 Yet no **o** remembered that same
9:18 But **o** sinner destroys much
10: 1 a little folly to **o** respected
10:10 And **o** does not sharpen the
12: 4 When **o** rises up at the sound
12:11 given by **o** Shepherd.
Song 1: 7 For why should I be as **o** who
2:10 "Rise up, my love, my fair **o**,
2:13 Rise up, my love, my fair **o**,
3: 1 my bed I sought the **o** I love;
3: 2 I will seek the **o** I love."
3: 3 Have you seen the **o** I love?"
3: 4 When I found the **o** I love.
4: 2 Every **o** of which bears twins,
4: 9 have ravished my heart With **o**
4: 9 With **o** link of your necklace.
5: 2 my love, My dove, my perfect **o**;
6: 6 Every **o** bears twins, And none
6: 9 My dove, my perfect **o**,
6: 9 my perfect one, Is the only **o**,
6: 9 The only **o** of her mother, The
6: 9 The favorite of the **o** who bore
8:10 I became in his eyes As **o** who
Isa 1: 4 provoked to anger The Holy ***O***
1:24 the Mighty ***O*** of Israel, "Ah,
1:31 And no **o** shall quench them.
3: 5 Every **o** by another and every
3: 5 one by another and every **o** by
4: 1 women shall take hold of **o** man,
5:10 of vineyard shall yield **o** bath,
5:10 of seed shall yield **o** ephah."
5:19 let the counsel of the Holy ***O***
5:24 the word of the Holy ***O*** of
5:27 No **o** will be weary or stumble
5:27 No **o** will slumber or sleep;
5:29 And no **o** will deliver.
5:30 And if **o** looks to the land,
6: 2 each **o** had six wings: with two
6: 3 And **o** cried to another and said:
6: 6 Then **o** of the seraphim flew to
9:14 branch and bulrush in **o** day.
10:14 And as **o** gathers eggs that
10:14 And there was no **o** who moved
10:17 And his Holy ***O*** for a flame;
10:17 thorns and his briers in **o** day.
10:20 the Holy ***O*** of Israel, in truth.
10:34 will fall by the Mighty ***O***.
12: 6 For great is the Holy ***O*** of

O

13: 8 be amazed at **o** another;
14: 6 persecuted and no **o** hinders.
14:31 And no **o** will be alone in
16: 5 And **O** will sit on it in truth,
17: 2 and no **o** will make them
17: 7 have respect for the Holy **O** of
19:18 **o** will be called the City of
19:20 them a Savior and a Mighty **O**,
19:24 In that day Israel will be **o** of
22:22 and no **o** shall shut; And he
22:22 and no **o** shall open.
23:15 to the days of **o** king.
27:12 And you will be gathered **o** by
27:12 you will be gathered one by **o**,
28: 2 Lord has a mighty and strong **o**,
28:20 the covering so narrow that **o**
29:11 which men deliver to **o** who is
29:12 the book is delivered to **o** who
29:19 shall rejoice In the Holy **O**
29:20 For the terrible **o** is brought
29:20 The scornful **o** is consumed,
29:23 And hallow the Holy **O** of
30:11 Cause the Holy **O** of Israel To
30:12 thus says the Holy **O** of Israel:
30:15 the Holy **O** of Israel: "In
30:17 **O** thousand shall flee at the
30:17 shall flee at the threat of **o**,
30:29 gladness of heart as when **o**
30:29 To the Mighty **O** of Israel.
31: 1 who do not look to the Holy **O**
33:20 Not **o** of its stakes will ever
34:10 No **o** shall pass through it
34:15 Every **o** with her mate.
34:16 Not **o** of these shall fail;
34:16 Not **o** shall lack her mate.
36: 9 will you repel **o** captain
36:16 and every **o** of you eat from his
36:16 from his own vine and every **o**
36:16 and every **o** of you drink the
36:18 Has any **o** of the gods of the
37:16 the **O** who dwells between the
37:23 Against the Holy **O** of Israel.
37:36 of the Assyrians **o** hundred
40: 3 The voice of **o** crying in the
40:25 I be equal?" says the Holy **O**.
40:26 Not **o** is missing.
41: 2 Who raised up **o** from the east?
41:14 the Holy **O** of Israel.
41:16 And glory in the Holy **O** of
41:20 And the Holy **O** of Israel has
41:25 I have raised up **o** from the
41:26 Surely there is no **o** who
41:26 Surely there is no **o** who
41:26 Surely there is no **o** who
41:27 I will give to Jerusalem **o** who
42: 1 My Elect **O** in whom My soul
42:22 and no **o** delivers;
42:22 and no **o** says, "Restore!"
43: 3 The Holy **O** of Israel, your
43:13 And there is no **o** who can
43:14 The Holy **O** of Israel: "For
43:15 I am the LORD, your Holy **O**,
44: 5 **O** will say, 'I am the LORD's'
44: 8 no other Rock; I know not **o**.
44:12 with the tongs works **o** in the
44:13 He marks **o** out with chalk;
44:19 And no **o** considers in his
45:11 The Holy **O** of Israel, and his
46: 7 Though **o** cries out to it, yet
47: 4 The Holy **O** of Israel.
47: 8 and there is no **o** else
47: 9 in **o** day: The loss of
47:10 No **o** sees me'; Your wisdom and
47:10 and there is no **o** else
47:15 They shall wander each **o** to
47:15 No **o** shall save you.
48:17 The Holy **O** of Israel: "I am
49: 7 of Israel, their Holy **O**,
49: 7 The Holy **O** of Israel; And He
49:26 the Mighty **O** of Jacob."
51:10 Are You not the **O** who dried
51:18 There is no **o** to guide her
53: 6 We have turned, every **o**,
54: 5 your Redeemer is the Holy **O**
54:11 "O you afflicted **o**,
55: 5 And the Holy **O** of Israel;
56:11 Every **o** for his own gain,
56:12 **o** says, "I will bring
57: 1 While no **o** considers That the
57: 2 Each **o** walking in his
57:14 And **o** shall say, "Heap it
57:15 thus says the High and Lofty **O**
59: 4 No **o** calls for justice, Nor
60: 9 And to the Holy **O** of Israel,
60:14 Zion of the Holy **O** of Israel.
60:15 So that no **o** went through
60:16 the Mighty **O** of Jacob.
60:22 A little **o** shall become a
60:22 And a small **o** a strong nation.
63: 1 This **O** who is glorious in
63: 2 And Your garments like **o** who
63: 3 And from the peoples no **o** was
63: 5 but there was no **o** to help,
63: 5 That there was no **o** to
64: 4 Who acts for the **o** who waits
64: 7 And there is no **o** who calls
65: 8 And **o** says, 'Do not destroy
65:20 shall die **o** hundred years old,
65:20 being **o** hundred years old
66: 2 'But on this **o** will I look:
66: 4 no **o** answered, When I spoke
66: 8 be made to give birth in **o** day?
66:13 As **o** whom his mother comforts,
66:23 to pass That from **o** New Moon
66:23 And from **o** Sabbath to another,

Jer 1:15 They shall come and each **o** set
2: 6 a land that no **o** crossed
2: 6 crossed And where no **o** dwelt?'
3:14 **o** from a city and two from a
4: 4 And burn so that no **o** can
5: 8 Every **o** neighed after his
5:26 They lie in wait as **o** who sets
6: 3 Each **o** shall pasture in his
7:33 And no **o** will frighten them
8: 4 Will **o** turn away and not
9: 8 **O** speaks peaceably to his
9:10 So that no **o** can pass through;
9:12 so that no **o** can pass through?
9:22 And no **o** shall gather them.'
10: 3 For **o** cuts a tree from the
10:20 There is no **o** to pitch my
12:11 Because no **o** takes it to
12:12 LORD shall devour From **o** end
13:14 And I will dash them **o** against
13:19 And no **o** shall open them;
14: 9 Like a mighty **o** who cannot
14:16 they will have no **o** to bury
15:10 Every **o** of them curses me.
16:12 each **o** follows the dictates of
16:12 so that no **o** listens to Me.
18:11 Return now every **o** from his
18:12 and we will every **o** obey the
19:11 as **o** breaks a potter's vessel,
20:11 with me as a mighty, awesome **O**.
21:12 fire And burn so that no **o**
23:14 So that no **o** turns back from
23:30 who steal My words every **o** from
23:35 Thus every **o** of you shall say to
23:35 and every **o** to his brother,
24: 2 **O** basket had very good figs,
25:26 **o** with another; and all the
25:33 of the LORD shall be from **o**
28: 9 the prophet will be known as **o**
30:10 And no **o** shall make him
30:13 There is no **o** to plead your
30:14 the chastisement of a cruel **o**,
30:16 every **o** of them, shall go into
30:17 No **o** seeks her." '
31: 8 woman with child And the **o**
31:11 him from the hand of **o** stronger
31:30 But every **o** shall die for his
32:39 then I will give them **o** heart
32:39 them one heart and **o** way,
34: 9 that no **o** should keep a Jewish
34:10 that no **o** should keep them in
34:16 and every **o** of you brought back
34:17 every **o** to his brother and
34:17 one to his brother and every **o**
35: 2 into **o** of the chambers, and
36:16 they looked in fear from **o** to
36:19 and let no **o** know where you
36:30 He shall have no **o** to sit on the
38: 7 **o** of the eunuchs, who was in
38:24 Let no **o** know of these words,
40:15 and no **o** will know it.
41: 4 when as yet no **o** knew it,
41: 9 was the same **o** Asa the king
44: 2 and no **o** dwells in them,
46:16 **o** fell upon another. And they
46:27 No **o** shall make him afraid.
48: 8 No **o** shall escape. The valley
48:33 No **o** will tread with joyous
48:35 The **o** who offers sacrifices
48:40 **o** shall fly like an eagle,
49: 5 And no **o** will gather those who
49:12 And are you the **o** who will
49:18 'No **o** shall remain there,
49:33 No **o** shall reside there,
50: 3 And no **o** shall dwell therein.
50:29 Against the Holy **O** of Israel.
50:31 O most haughty **o**!" says the
50:32 And no **o** will raise him up;
50:40 So no **o** shall reside there,
51: 5 with sin against the Holy **O** of
51: 6 And every **o** save his life!
51:31 **O** runner will run to meet
51:31 And **o** messenger to meet
51:43 A land where no **o** dwells,
51:46 (A rumor will come **o** year,
51:56 Every **o** of their bows is
52:20 **o** Sea, the twelve bronze bulls
52:21 the height of **o** pillar was
52:22 and the height of **o** capital
52:23 the network, were **o** hundred.

Lam 1: 4 mourn Because no **o** comes
1: 7 With no **o** to help her,
1:17 But no **o** comforts her;
1:21 But no **o** comforts me. All my
3:26 It is good that **o** should
3:30 him give his cheek to the **o**
4: 4 But no **o** breaks it for them.
4:14 So that no **o** would touch their

Ezek 1: 6 Each **o** had four faces, and each
1: 6 and each **o** had four wings.
1: 9 Their wings touched **o** another.
1: 9 but each **o** went straight
1:11 two wings of each **o** touched
1:11 each one touched **o** another,
1:12 And each **o** went straight
1:17 they went toward any **o** of four
1:23 **o** toward another. Each one had
1:23 Each **o** had two which covered
1:23 two which covered **o** side,
1:23 and each **o** had two which
1:28 and I heard a voice of **O**
3:13 that touched **o** another,
3:26 you shall be mute and not be **o**
4: 8 you cannot turn from **o** side
4: 9 put them into **o** vessel, and
4:17 and be dismayed with **o** another,
7:13 No **o** will strengthen himself
7:14 But no **o** goes to battle;
9: 2 **O** man among them was clothed
10: 9 **o** wheel by one cherub and
10: 9 one wheel by **o** cherub and
10:14 Each **o** had four faces: the first
10:17 and when **o** was lifted up, the
10:21 Each **o** had four faces and each
10:21 one had four faces and each **o**
11:19 Then I will give them **o** heart,
13:10 and **o** builds a wall, and they
14:10 as the punishment of the **o** who
15: 7 They will go out from **o** fire,
16:34 because no **o** solicited you to
17:22 I will take also **o** of the
17:22 of its young twigs a tender **o**,
18: 7 Has robbed no **o** by violence,
18:30 every **o** according to his
18:32 no pleasure in the death of **o**
19: 3 She brought up **o** of her cubs,
20:39 serve every **o** of you his
22: 6 each **o** has used his power to
22:11 **O** commits abomination with his
22:30 destroy it; but I found no **o**.
23: 2 The daughters of **o** mother.
23:32 cup, The deep and wide **o**;
24:16 of your eyes with **o** stroke;
24:23 and mourn with **o** another.
24:26 on that day **o** who escapes will
26:17 O **o** inhabited by seafaring
30:22 both the strong **o** and the one
30:22 both the strong one and the **o**
31:11 into the hand of the mighty **o**
33:20 I will judge every **o** of you
33:21 that **o** who had escaped from
33:24 are saying, 'Abraham was only **o**,
33:26 and you defile **o** another's
33:27 and the **o** who is in the open
33:28 shall be so desolate that no **o**
33:30 and they speak to **o** another,
33:32 as a very lovely song of **o** who
34: 6 and no **o** was seeking or
34:23 I will establish **o** shepherd over
34:28 and no **o** shall make them
35: 7 and cut off from it the **o** who
35: 7 it the one who leaves and the **o**
37:17 Then join them **o** to another for
37:17 for yourself into **o** stick,
37:17 and they will become **o** in your
37:19 and make them **o** stick, and they
37:19 and they will be **o** in My
37:22 and I will make them **o** nation in
37:22 and **o** king shall be king over
37:24 shall all have **o** shepherd;
39: 7 the Holy **O** in Israel.
39:26 in their own land and no **o**
40: 5 wall structure, **o** rod;
40: 5 and the height, **o** rod.
40: 6 which was **o** rod wide, and the
40: 6 the other threshold was **o** rod
40: 7 Each gate chamber was **o** rod
40: 7 was one rod long and **o** rod
40: 7 of the inside gate was **o** rod.
40: 8 inside gate, **o** rod.
40:10 three gate chambers on **o** side
40:12 **o** cubit on this side and one
40:12 on this side and **o** cubit
40:13 the roof of **o** gate chamber
40:19 **o** hundred cubits toward the
40:23 **o** hundred cubits.
40:26 **o** on this side and one on that
40:26 one on this side and **o** on that
40:27 south, **o** hundred cubits.
40:40 as **o** goes up to the entrance of
40:42 **o** cubit and a half long, one
40:42 **o** cubit and a half wide, and
40:42 and **o** cubit high; on these they
40:44 **o** facing south at the side of
40:47 **o** hundred cubits long and one
40:47 long and **o** hundred cubits
40:49 **o** on this side and another on
41: 1 six cubits wide on **o** side and
41: 6 **o** above the other, thirty
41: 7 As **o** went up from story to
41: 7 of the structure increased as **o**
41: 7 highest by way of the middle **o**.
41:11 **o** door toward the north and
41:13 **o** hundred cubits long; and the
41:13 walls was **o** hundred cubits
41:14 was **o** hundred cubits.
41:15 its galleries on the **o** side
41:15 **o** hundred cubits, as well as
41:19 a palm tree on **o** side,
41:24 two panels for **o** door and two
41:26 and palm trees on **o** side
42: 2 which was **o** hundred cubits
42: 4 at a distance of **o** cubit;
42: 8 temple was **o** hundred cubits.
42: 9 as **o** goes into them from the
42:12 as **o** enters them, there was a
43:13 (the cubit is **o** cubit
43:13 the base **o** cubit high and one
43:13 one cubit high and **o** cubit
43:13 all around its edge of **o** span.
43:14 **o** cubit; from the smaller ledge
43:14 of the ledge, **o** cubit.

43:17 **o** cubit all around; and its
45: 7 have a section on **o** side
45: 7 shall be side by side with **o**
45:15 And **o** lamb shall be given from a
45:24 a grain offering of **o** ephah
45:24 ephah for each bull and **o** ephah
46: 5 offering shall be **o** ephah
46:17 of some of his inheritance to **o**
47: 3 he measured **o** thousand cubits,
47: 4 Again he measured **o** thousand and
47: 4 Again he measured **o** thousand
47: 5 Again he measured **o** thousand,
47: 5 water in which **o** must swim, a
47: 7 were very many trees on **o** side
47:14 it equally with **o** another;
47:15 as **o** goes to Zedad,
47:20 the southern boundary until **o**
48: 1 there shall be **o** section
48: 2 **o** section for Asher;
48: 3 **o** section for Naphtali;
48: 4 **o** section for Manasseh;
48: 5 **o** section for Ephraim;
48: 6 **o** section for Reuben;
48: 7 **o** section for Judah;
48: 8 and in length the same as **o** of
48:21 on **o** side and on the other of
48:23 shall have **o** section;
48:24 Simeon shall have **o** section;
48:25 shall have **o** section;
48:26 shall have **o** section;
48:27 Gad shall have **o** section;
48:31 **o** gate for Reuben, one gate for
48:31 **o** gate for Judah, and one gate
48:31 and **o** gate for Levi;
48:32 **o** gate for Joseph, one gate for
48:32 **o** gate for Benjamin, and one
48:32 and **o** gate for Dan;
48:33 **o** gate for Simeon, one gate for
48:33 **o** gate for Issachar, and one
48:33 and **o** gate for Zebulun;
48:34 **o** gate for Gad, one gate for
48:34 **o** gate for Asher, and one gate
48:34 and **o** gate for Naphtali.
Dan 2: 9 there is only **o** decree for
2:43 will not adhere to **o** another,
4:13 there was a watcher, a holy **o**,
4:23 king saw a watcher, a holy **o**,
4:35 No **o** can restrain His hand Or
5:13 Are you that Daniel who is **o** of
6: 1 over the kingdom **o** hundred
6: 2 of whom Daniel was **o**,
6:13 who is **o** of the captives from
6:26 His kingdom is the **o** which
7: 5 It was raised up on **o** side, and
7: 8 was another horn, a little **o**,
7:13 **O** like the Son of Man, Coming
7:14 And His kingdom the **o** Which
7:16 I came near to **o** of those who
8: 1 after the **o** that appeared to me
8: 3 but **o** was higher than the
8: 3 and the higher **o** came up last.
8: 7 and there was no **o** that could
8: 9 And out of **o** of them came a
8:13 Then I heard a holy **o** speaking;
8:13 and another holy **o** said to
8:13 one said to that certain **o**
8:15 there stood before me **o** having
8:27 but no **o** understood it.
9:27 with many for **o** week;
9:27 of abominations shall be **o** who
10:13 **o** of the chief princes, came to
10:16 **o** having the likeness of the
10:18 the **o** having the likeness of
10:21 (No **o** upholds me against these,
11: 5 as well as **o** of his princes;
11: 7 from a branch of her roots **o**
11:10 and **o** shall certainly come and
11:16 and no **o** shall stand against
11:20 shall arise in his place **o** who
11:45 and no **o** will help him.
12: 1 Every **o** who is found written
12: 5 **o** on this riverbank and the
12: 6 And **o** said to the man clothed
12:11 there shall be **o** thousand
12:12 and comes to the **o** thousand
Hos 1:11 appoint for themselves **o** head;
2:10 And no **o** shall deliver her
3: 2 and **o** and one-half homers of
5:14 and no **o** shall rescue.
11: 9 The Holy **O** in your midst;
11:12 Even with the Holy **O** who is
Joel 2: 7 Every **o** marches in formation,
2: 8 They do not push **o** another;
2: 8 Every **o** marches in his own
2:11 For strong is the **O** who
Am 1: 5 And the **o** who holds the
1: 8 And the **o** who holds the
4: 3 Each **o** straight ahead of her,
4: 7 I made it rain on **o** city, I
4: 7 **O** part was rained upon,
5: 2 There is no **o** to raise her
5: 6 With no **o** to quench it in
5:10 They hate the **o** who rebukes in
5:10 And they abhor the **o** who
6: 9 if ten men remain in **o** house,
6:10 with **o** who will burn the
6:10 he will say to **o** inside the
6:12 Does **o** plow there with oxen?
Ob 7 No **o** is aware of it.
11 Even you were as **o** of them.
Jon 1: 7 And they said to **o** another,
3: 8 let every **o** turn from his evil
4: 2 **O** who relents from doing harm.
4:11 are more than **o** hundred
Mic 2: 4 In that day **o** shall take up a
2: 5 Therefore you will have no **o** to
2:13 The **o** who breaks open will come
4: 4 And no **o** shall make them
5: 2 shall come forth to Me The **O**
5: 5 And this **O** shall be peace.
7: 2 And there is no **o** upright
Nah 1:11 From you comes forth **o** Who
1:15 For the wicked **o** shall no more
2: 4 They jostle **o** another in the
2: 8 But no **o** turns back.
2:11 And no **o** made them afraid?
3:18 And no **o** gathers them.
Hab 1:12 O LORD my God, my Holy **O**?
3: 3 The Holy **O** from Mount Paran.
Zeph 2:11 Each **o** from his place, Indeed
3: 6 are destroyed; There is no **o**,
3: 9 To serve Him with **o** accord.
3:13 And no **o** shall make them
3:17 in your midst, The Mighty **O**,
Hag 1: 6 but no **o** is warm; And he who
1: 9 while every **o** of you runs to
2:12 If **o** carries holy meat in the
2:13 If **o** who is unclean because
2:16 when **o** came to a heap of
2:16 when **o** came to the wine vat to
2:22 Every **o** by the sword of his
Zech 1:21 so that no **o** could lift up his
3: 9 of that land in **o** day.
4: 3 **o** at the right of the bowl and
5: 4 thief And the house of the **o**
6: 6 The **o** with the black horses is
7:14 so that no **o** passed through or
8: 4 Each **o** with his staff in his
8:21 The inhabitants of **o** city
11: 7 the **o** I called Beauty, and the
11: 8 the three shepherds in **o** month.
12: 8 the **o** who is feeble among them
12:10 mourn for Him as **o** mourns
12:10 and grieve for Him as **o** grieves
13: 6 And **o** will say to him, 'What
13: 9 And each **o** will say, 'The
14: 7 It shall be **o** day Which is
14: 9 it shall be—"The LORD is **o**,
14: 9 is one," And His name **o**.
Mal 2: 3 And **o** will take you away with
2: 5 **o** of life and peace, And I
2:10 Have we not all **o** Father?
2:10 Has not **o** God created us?
2:10 treacherously with **o** another
2:15 But did He not make them **o**,
2:15 of the Spirit? And why **o**?
3:16 the LORD spoke to **o** another,
3:18 Between **o** who serves God And
3:18 one who serves God And **o** who
Mt 3: 3 The voice of **o** crying in
5:18 **o** jot or one tittle will by no
5:18 one jot or **o** tittle will by no
5:19 Whoever therefore breaks **o** of
5:29 more profitable for you that **o**
5:30 more profitable for you that **o**
5:36 because you cannot make **o** hair
5:37 than these is from the evil **o**.
5:41 compels you to go **o** mile,
6:13 But deliver us from the evil **o**.
6:24 No **o** can serve two masters;
6:24 for either he will hate the **o**
6:24 else he will be loyal to the **o**
6:27 by worrying can add **o** cubit
6:29 glory was not arrayed like **o**
7:29 for He taught them as **o** having
8: 4 him, "See that you tell no **o**;
8: 9 under me. And I say to this **o**,
8:28 so that no **o** could pass that
9:16 No **o** puts a piece of unshrunk
9:30 See that no **o** knows it."
10:29 And not **o** of them falls to the
10:42 And whoever gives **o** of these
11: 3 to Him, "Are You the Coming **O**,
11:11 of women there has not risen **o**
11:27 and no **o** knows the Son except
11:27 and the **o** to whom the Son
12: 6 that in this place there is **O**
12:11 among you who has **o** sheep,
12:22 Then **o** was brought to Him who
12:29 Or how can **o** enter a strong
12:47 Then **o** said to Him, "Look, Your
12:48 He answered and said to the **o**
13:19 then the wicked **o** comes and
13:38 are the sons of the wicked **o**.
13:46 when he had found **o** pearl of
16:14 and others Jeremiah or **o** of the
16:20 that they should tell no **o**
17: 4 **o** for You, one for Moses, and
17: 4 **o** for Moses, and one for
17: 4 and **o** for Elijah."
17: 8 they saw no **o** but Jesus only.
17: 9 Tell the vision to no **o** until
18: 5 Whoever receives **o** little child
18: 6 But whoever causes **o** of these
18: 9 enter into life with **o** eye,
18:10 heed that you do not despise **o**
18:12 and **o** of them goes astray, does
18:12 to the mountains to seek the **o**
18:14 Father who is in heaven that **o**
18:16 take with you **o** or two more,
18:24 **o** was brought to him who owed
18:28 servant went out and found **o**
19: 5 shall become **o** flesh'?
19: 6 no longer two but **o** flesh.
19:16 **o** came and said to Him, "Good
19:17 No **o** is good but One, that
19:17 Me good? No one is good but **O**,
20: 7 Because no **o** hired us.' He said
20:12 have worked only **o** hour,
20:13 But he answered **o** of them and
20:21 **o** on Your right hand and the
21:24 I also will ask you **o** thing,
21:35 took his servants, beat **o**,
21:35 servants, beat one, killed **o**,
22: 5 **o** to his own farm, another to
22:35 Then **o** of them, a lawyer, asked
22:46 And no **o** was able to answer Him
23: 4 will not move them with **o** of
23: 8 for **O** is your Teacher, the
23: 9 for **O** is your Father, He who is
23:10 for **O** is your Teacher, the
23:15 and sea to win **o** proselyte,
23:37 the **o** who kills the prophets
24: 2 not **o** stone shall be left here
24: 4 Take heed that no **o** deceives
24:10 will betray **o** another, and will
24:10 and will hate **o** another.
24:31 from **o** end of heaven to the
24:36 that day and hour no **o** knows,
24:40 **o** will be taken and the other
24:41 **o** will be taken and the other
25:15 And to **o** he gave five talents,
25:15 another two, and to another **o**,
25:18 But he who had received **o** went
25:24 had received the **o** talent
25:32 separate them **o** from another,
25:40 inasmuch as you did it to **o** of
25:45 as you did not do it to **o** of
26:14 Then **o** of the twelve, called
26:21 **o** of you will betray Me."
26:40 you not watch with Me **o** hour?
26:47 **o** of the twelve, with a great
26:48 "Whomever I kiss, He is the **O**;
26:51 **o** of those who were with
26:68 Christ! Who is the **o** who struck
26:73 Surely you also are **o** of them,
27:14 But He answered him not **o** word,
27:15 to the multitude **o** prisoner
27:38 **o** on the right and another on
27:48 Immediately **o** of them ran and
Mk 1: 3 The voice of **o** crying in
1: 7 There comes **O** after me who is
1:22 for He taught them as **o** having
1:24 the Holy **O** of God!"
2:21 No **o** sews a piece of unshrunk
2:22 And no **o** puts new wine into old
3:27 No **o** can enter a strong man's
4:41 and said to **o** another, "Who
5: 3 and no **o** could bind him, not
5:15 and saw the **o** who had been
5:22 **o** of the rulers of the
5:37 And He permitted no **o** to follow
5:43 them strictly that no **o** should
6:15 or like **o** of the prophets."
7:24 a house and wanted no **o** to
7:32 Then they brought to Him **o** who
7:36 them that they should tell no **o**;
8: 4 How can **o** satisfy these people
8:14 did not have more than **o** loaf
8:28 **o** of the prophets."
8:30 them that they should tell no **o**
9: 5 **o** for You, one for Moses, and
9: 5 **o** for Moses, and one for
9: 5 and **o** for Elijah"—
9: 8 they saw no **o** anymore, but only
9: 9 that they should tell no **o** the
9:17 Then **o** of the crowd answered and
9:26 And he became as **o** dead, so
9:37 Whoever receives **o** of these
9:39 for no **o** who works a miracle in
9:42 But whoever causes **o** of these
9:47 the kingdom of God with **o** eye,
9:50 and have peace with **o**
10: 8 shall become **o** flesh';
10: 8 no longer two, but **o** flesh.
10:17 **o** came running, knelt before
10:18 No **o** is good but One, that
10:18 Me good? No one is good but **O**,
10:21 **O** thing you lack: Go your way,
10:29 there is no **o** who has left
10:37 **o** on Your right hand and the
11: 2 on which no **o** has sat. Loose it
11:14 Let no **o** eat fruit from you ever
11:29 I also will ask you **o** question;
12: 6 Therefore still having **o** son,
12:14 are true, and care about no **o**;
12:28 Then **o** of the scribes came, and
12:29 our God, the LORD is **o**.
12:32 for there is **o** God, and there
12:34 But after that no **o** dared
12:42 Then **o** poor widow came and threw
13: 1 **o** of His disciples said to Him,
13: 2 Not **o** stone shall be left upon
13: 5 Take heed that no **o** deceives
13:32 day and hour no **o** knows,
14:10 **o** of the twelve, went to the
14:18 **o** of you who eats with Me will
14:19 and to say to Him **o** by one,
14:19 and to say to Him one by **o**,
14:20 It is **o** of the twelve, who
14:37 Could you not watch **o** hour?
14:43 **o** of the twelve, with a great
14:44 "Whomever I kiss, He is the **O**;
14:47 And **o** of those who stood by drew
14:66 **o** of the servant girls of the
14:69 This is **o** of them."

O

14:70 'Surely you are **o** of them;
15: 6 to releasing **o** prisoner
15: 7 And there was **o** named Barabbas,
15:27 **o** on His right and the other on
Lk 1:28 "Rejoice, highly favored **o**,
1:35 that Holy **O** who is to be born
1:61 There is no **o** among your
2:15 shepherds said to **o** another,
2:36 Now there was **o**, Anna,
3: 4 The voice of **o** crying in
3:16 but **O** mightier than I is
4:34 the Holy **O** of God!"
4:40 He laid His hands on every **o**
5: 3 Then He got into **o** of the boats,
5:14 And He charged him to tell no **o**,
5:36 No **o** puts a piece from a new
5:36 from a new garment on an old **o**;
5:37 And no **o** puts new wine into old
5:39 'And no **o**, having drunk old
6: 9 I will ask you **o** thing: Is it
6:11 and discussed with **o** another
6:29 strikes you on the **o** cheek,
7: 4 saying that the **o** for whom He
7: 8 under me. And I say to **o**,
7:19 saying, "Are You the Coming **O**,
7:20 saying, 'Are You the Coming **O**,
7:32 and calling to **o** another,
7:36 Then **o** of the Pharisees asked
7:41 **O** owed five hundred denarii,
7:43 I suppose the **o** whom he forgave
8:16 No **o**, when he has lit
8:25 saying to **o** another, "Who can
8:51 He permitted no **o** to go in
8:56 He charged them to tell no **o**
9: 8 and by others that **o** of the old
9:19 and others say that **o** of the
9:21 them to tell this to no **o**,
9:33 **o** for You, one for Moses, and
9:33 **o** for Moses, and one for
9:33 and **o** for Elijah"—not knowing
9:36 and told no **o** in those days any
9:62 But Jesus said to him, "No **o**,
10: 4 and greet no **o** along the road.
10:22 and no **o** knows who the Son is
10:22 and the **o** to whom the Son
10:42 But **o** thing is needed, and Mary
11: 1 that **o** of His disciples said
11: 4 But deliver us from the evil **o**.
11:33 No **o**, when he has lit
11:45 Then **o** of the lawyers answered
11:46 do not touch the burdens with **o**
12: 1 that they trampled **o** another,
12: 6 And not **o** of them is forgotten
12:13 Then **o** from the crowd said to
12:25 by worrying can add **o** cubit
12:27 glory was not arrayed like **o**
12:52 For from now on five in **o** house
13:10 Now He was teaching in **o** of the
13:15 Hypocrite! Does not each **o** of
13:23 Then **o** said to Him, "Lord, are
13:34 the **o** who kills the prophets
14: 1 as He went into the house of **o**
14: 8 lest **o** more honorable than you
14:15 Now when **o** of those who sat at
14:18 But they all with **o** accord
15: 4 if he loses **o** of them, does not
15: 4 and go after the **o** which is
15: 7 be more joy in heaven over **o**
15: 8 if she loses **o** coin, does not
15:10 angels of God over **o** sinner
15:16 and no **o** gave him anything.
15:19 Make me like **o** of your hired
15:26 So he called **o** of the servants
16: 5 So he called every **o** of his
16:13 for either he will hate the **o**
16:13 else he will be loyal to the **o**
16:17 earth to pass away than for **o**
16:30 but if **o** goes to them from the
16:31 will they be persuaded though **o**
17: 2 than that he should offend **o** of
17:15 And **o** of them, when he saw that
17:22 when you will desire to see **o**
17:24 that flashes out of **o** part
17:31 And likewise the **o** who is in
17:34 will be two men in **o** bed:
17:34 the **o** will be taken and the
17:35 the **o** will be taken and the
17:36 the **o** will be taken and the
18:10 **o** a Pharisee and the other a
18:19 No **o** is good but One, that
18:19 Me good? No one is good but **O**,
18:22 You still lack **o** thing. Sell all
18:29 there is no **o** who has left
19:30 on which no **o** has ever sat.
19:44 not leave in you **o** stone
20: 1 Now it happened on **o** of those
20: 3 I also will ask you **o** thing, and
21: 6 come in which not **o** stone
22:27 Yet I am among you as the **O** who
22:29 just as My Father bestowed **o**
22:36 him sell his garment and buy **o**.
22:47 **o** of the twelve, went before
22:50 And **o** of them struck the servant
22:64 Prophesy! Who is the **o** who
23:14 as **o** who misleads the people.
23:17 necessary for him to release **o**
23:25 And he released to them the **o**
23:33 **o** on the right hand and the
23:39 Then **o** of the criminals who were
23:53 where no **o** had ever lain
24:17 that you have with **o** another
24:18 Then the **o** whose name was
24:32 And they said to **o** another,
Jn 1:18 No **o** has seen God at any time.
1:23 The voice of **o** crying in
1:26 but there stands **O** among you
1:40 **O** of the two who heard John
3: 2 for no **o** can do these signs
3: 3 unless **o** is born again, he
3: 5 unless **o** is born of water and
3:13 No **o** has ascended to heaven but
3:32 and no **o** receives His
4:18 and the **o** whom you now have is
4:20 Jerusalem is the place where **o**
4:27 yet no **o** said, "What do You
4:33 the disciples said to **o**
4:37 **O** sows and another reaps.'
5:13 But the **o** who was healed did not
5:22 "For the Father judges no **o**,
5:44 receive honor from **o** another,
5:45 there is **o** who accuses
6: 7 that every **o** of them may have a
6: 8 **O** of His disciples, Andrew,
6:22 except that **o** which His
6:37 and the **o** who comes to Me I
6:44 No **o** can come to Me unless the
6:50 that **o** may eat of it and not
6:65 I have said to you that no **o**
6:70 and **o** of you is a devil?"
6:71 being **o** of the twelve.
7: 4 For no **o** does anything in secret
7:13 no **o** spoke openly of Him for
7:18 He who seeks the glory of the **O**
7:21 I did **o** work, and you all
7:27 no **o** knows where He is from."
7:30 but no **o** laid a hand on Him,
7:44 but no **o** laid hands on Him.
7:50 being **o** of them) said to them,
8: 9 went out **o** by one, beginning
8: 9 conscience, went out one by **o**,
8:10 raised Himself up and saw no **o**
8:10 Has no **o** condemned you?"
8:11 She said, "No **o**, Lord."
8:15 to the flesh; I judge no **o**.
8:18 I am **O** who bears witness of
8:20 and no **o** laid hands on Him, for
8:41 we have **o** Father—God."
8:50 there is **O** who seeks and
9: 4 the night is coming when no **o**
9:25 **O** thing I know: that though I
9:32 anyone opened the eyes of **o**
10:12 **o** who does not own the sheep,
10:16 and there will be **o** flock and
10:16 be one flock and **o** shepherd.
10:18 No **o** takes it from Me, but I lay
10:21 These are not the words of **o** who
10:29 and no **o** is able to snatch
10:30 "I and My Father are **o**.
11:10 But if **o** walks in the night, he
11:49 And **o** of them, Caiaphas, being
11:50 expedient for us that **o** man
11:52 He would gather together in **o**
12: 2 but Lazarus was **o** of those who
12: 4 Then **o** of His disciples, Judas
13:14 to wash **o** another's feet.
13:21 **o** of you will betray Me."
13:22 disciples looked at **o** another,
13:23 was leaning on Jesus' bosom **o**
13:28 But no **o** at the table knew for
13:34 that you love **o** another; as I
13:34 that you also love **o** another.
13:35 have love for **o** another."
14: 6 No **o** comes to the Father except
15:12 that you love **o** another as I
15:13 Greater love has no **o** than this,
15:17 that you love **o** another.
15:24 them the works which no **o** else
16:22 and your joy no **o** will take
17:11 that they may be **o** as We are.
17:15 keep them from the evil **o**.
17:21 "that they all may be **o**,
17:21 that they also may be **o** in Us,
17:22 that they may be **o** just as We
17:22 may be one just as We are **o**:
17:23 they may be made perfect in **o**,
18:14 it was expedient that **o** man
18:17 You are not also **o** of this
18:22 **o** of the officers who stood by
18:25 You are not also **o** of His
18:26 **O** of the servants of the high
19:11 Therefore the **o** who delivered
19:18 **o** on either side, and Jesus in
19:23 woven from the top in **o** piece.
19:34 But **o** of the soldiers pierced
19:36 Not **o** of His bones shall
19:41 a new tomb in which no **o** had
20:12 **o** at the head and the other at
20:24 **o** of the twelve, was not with
21:11 **o** hundred and fifty-three;
21:20 who is the **o** who betrays You?"
21:25 which if they were written **o** by
21:25 if they were written one by **o**,
Acts 1:14 These all continued with **o**
1:20 And let no **o** live in
1:22 **o** of these must become a
2: 1 they were all with **o** accord in
2: 1 were all with one accord in **o**
2: 3 and **o** sat upon each of them.
2: 7 saying to **o** another, "Look,
2:12 saying to **o** another, "Whatever
2:27 You allow Your Holy **O** to
2:38 and let every **o** of you be
2:46 daily with **o** accord
3:14 But you denied the Holy **O** and
3:26 in turning away every **o** of
4:24 voice to God with **o** accord
4:32 who believed were of **o** heart
4:32 were of one heart and **o** soul;
5:12 And they were all with **o** accord
5:23 we found no **o** inside!"
5:25 So **o** came and told them, saying,
5:34 Then **o** in the council stood up,
7:24 And seeing **o** of them suffer
7:26 why do you wrong **o** another?'
7:35 is the **o** God sent to be a
7:38 the **o** who received the living
7:52 the coming of the Just **O**,
7:57 and ran at him with **o** accord;
8: 6 And the multitudes with **o** accord
9: 7 hearing a voice but seeing no **o**.
9: 8 eyes were opened he saw no **o**.
9:11 at the house of Judas for **o**
10: 2 a devout man and **o** who feared
10:22 **o** who fears God and has a good
10:28 to keep company with or go to **o**
11:19 preaching the word to no **o** but
11:28 Then **o** of them, named Agabus,
12:10 out and went down **o** street,
12:20 came to him with **o** accord,
13:25 there comes **O** after me, the
13:35 not allow Your Holy **O** to
13:41 Though **o** were to declare
15:25 being assembled with **o** accord,
15:38 not take with them the **o** who
15:39 they parted from **o** another.
17:23 the **O** whom you worship without
17:26 And He has made from **o** blood
17:27 He is not far from each **o** of
18: 7 **o** who worshiped God, whose
18:10 and no **o** will attack you to
18:12 the Jews with **o** accord rose up
19:29 the theater with **o** accord,
19:32 Some therefore cried **o** thing and
19:34 all with **o** voice cried out for
19:38 charges against **o** another.
21: 6 our leave of **o** another,
21: 7 and stayed with them **o** day.
21: 8 who was **o** of the seven, and
21:26 should be made for each **o** of
21:34 the multitude cried **o** thing
22:14 His will, and see the Just **O**,
23: 6 Paul perceived that **o** part
23:17 Then Paul called **o** of the
23:22 Tell no **o** that you have revealed
24:21 it is for this **o** statement
25:11 no **o** can deliver me to them. I
27: 1 prisoners to **o** named Julius,
28: 4 they said to **o** another, "No
28:13 And after **o** day the south wind
28:25 after Paul had said **o** word:
28:31 no **o** forbidding him.
Rom 1:27 in their lust for **o** another,
2: 6 will render to each **o**
2:28 not a Jew who is **o** outwardly,
2:29 but he is a Jew who is **o**
3:10 none righteous, no, not **o**;
3:12 who does good, no, not **o**.
3:26 and the justifier of the **o** who
3:30 since there is **o** God who will
5: 7 for a righteous man will **o** die;
5:12 just as through **o** man sin
5:15 For if by the **o** man's offense
5:15 the gift by the grace of the **o**
5:16 which came through the **o** who
5:16 which came from **o** offense
5:17 For if by the **o** man's offense
5:17 death reigned through the **o**,
5:17 reign in life through the **O**,
5:18 as through **o** man's offense
5:18 even so through **o** Man's
5:19 For as by **o** man's disobedience
5:19 so also by **o** Man's obedience
7:21 the **o** who wills to do good.
8:24 for why does **o** still hope for
9:10 also had conceived by **o** man,
9:21 same lump to make **o** vessel
10:10 For with the heart **o** believes
12: 3 as God has dealt to each **o** a
12: 4 have many members in **o** body,
12: 5 are **o** body in Christ, and
12: 5 members of **o** another.
12:10 affectionate to **o** another
12:10 giving preference to **o** another;
12:16 Be of the same mind toward **o**
12:17 Repay no **o** evil for evil.
13: 8 Owe no **o** anything except to
13: 8 except to love **o** another,
14: 1 Receive **o** who is weak in the
14: 2 For **o** believes he may eat all
14: 5 **O** person esteems one day above
14: 5 One person esteems **o** day above
14: 7 and no **o** dies to himself.
14:13 let us not judge **o** another
14:15 destroy with your food the **o**
14:19 and the things by which **o** may
15: 5 like-minded toward **o** another,
15: 6 that you may with **o** mind and
15: 6 with one mind and **o** mouth
15: 7 Therefore receive **o** another,
15:14 also to admonish **o** another.
16:16 Greet **o** another with a holy
1 Cor 2:11 Even so no **o** knows the things
2:15 is rightly judged by no **o**.
3: 4 For when **o** says, "I am of
3: 5 as the Lord gave to each **o**?
3: 8 plants and he who waters are **o**,

3: 8 and each **o** will receive his own
3:10 But let each **o** take heed how he
3:18 Let no **o** deceive himself.
3:21 Therefore let no **o** boast in men.
4: 2 is required in stewards that **o**
4: 6 may be puffed up on behalf of **o**
5: 5 deliver such a **o** to Satan for
6: 5 wise man among you, not even **o**,
6: 7 that you go to law against **o**
6:16 joined to a harlot is **o** body
6:16 shall become **o** flesh."
6:17 joined to the Lord is **o** spirit
7: 5 Do not deprive **o** another except
7: 7 But each **o** has his own gift
7: 7 **o** in this manner and another in
7:17 God has distributed to each **o**,
7:17 as the Lord has called each **o**,
7:20 Let each **o** remain in the same
7:24 let each **o** remain with God in
7:25 yet I give judgment as **o** whom
8: 3 this **o** is known by Him.
8: 4 there is no other God but **o**.
8: 6 yet for us there is **o** God, the
8: 6 and **o** Lord Jesus Christ,
9:24 but **o** receives the prize?
9:26 not as **o** who beats the air.
10: 8 and in **o** day twenty-three
10:17 are **o** bread and one body;
10:17 are one bread and **o** body;
10:17 all partake of that **o** bread.
10:24 Let no **o** seek his own, but each
10:24 but each **o** the other's
10:28 eat it for the sake of the **o**
11: 5 for that is **o** and the same as
11:20 come together in **o** place,
11:21 each **o** takes his own supper
11:21 and **o** is hungry and another is
11:33 wait for **o** another.
12: 3 I make known to you that no **o**
12: 3 and no **o** can say that Jesus is
12: 7 the Spirit is given to each **o**
12: 8 for to **o** is given the word of
12:11 But **o** and the same Spirit works
12:11 distributing to each **o**
12:12 For as the body is **o** and has
12:12 the members of that **o** body,
12:12 are **o** body, so also is Christ.
12:13 For by **o** Spirit we were all
12:13 baptized into **o** body—whether
12:13 made to drink into **o** Spirit.
12:14 fact the body is not **o** member
12:18 each **o** of them, in the body
12:19 And if they were all **o** member,
12:20 many members, yet **o** body.
12:25 should have the same care for **o**
12:26 And if **o** member suffers, all the
12:26 or if **o** member is honored, all
14: 2 for no **o** understands him;
14:23 comes together in **o** place,
14:27 and let **o** interpret.
14:31 For you can all prophesy **o** by
14:31 you can all prophesy one by **o**,
15: 8 as by **o** born out of due time.
15:23 But each **o** in his own order:
15:36 Foolish **o**, what you sow
15:39 but there is **o** kind of
15:40 glory of the celestial is **o**,
15:41 There is **o** glory of the sun,
15:41 for **o** star differs from
16: 2 day of the week let each **o** of
16:11 Therefore let no **o** despise him.
16:20 Greet **o** another with a holy
2 Cor 2: 2 he who makes me glad but the **o**
2: 7 lest perhaps such a **o** be
2:10 I have forgiven that **o** for your
2:16 To the **o** we are the aroma of
3:16 Nevertheless when **o** turns to the
5:10 that each **o** may receive the
5:14 that if **O** died for all, then
5:16 we regard no **o** according to the
7: 2 to us. We have wronged no **o**,
7: 2 no one, we have corrupted no **o**,
7: 2 no one, we have cheated no **o**.
8:12 accepted according to what **o**
9: 7 So let each **o** give as he
11: 2 betrothed you to **o** husband,
11: 9 in need, I was a burden to no **o**,
11:10 no **o** shall stop me from this
11:16 let no **o** think me a fool.
11:20 For you put up with it if **o**
11:20 if **o** devours you, if one takes
11:20 if **o** takes from you, if one
11:20 if **o** exalts himself, if one
11:20 if **o** strikes you on the face.
11:24 received forty stripes minus **o**.
12: 2 such a **o** was caught up to the
12: 5 Of such a **o** I will boast; yet of
13:11 be of **o** mind, live in peace;
13:12 Greet **o** another with a holy
Gal 3:11 But that no **o** is justified by
3:15 no **o** annuls or adds to it.
3:16 as of many, but as of **o**,
3:20 does not mediate for **o** only,
3:20 for one only, but God is **o**.
3:28 for you are all **o** in Christ
4:22 the **o** by a bondwoman, the other
4:24 the **o** from Mount Sinai which
5:13 through love serve **o** another.
5:14 law is fulfilled in **o** word,
5:15 you bite and devour **o** another,
5:15 be consumed by **o** another!
5:17 are contrary to **o** another,
5:26 provoking **o** another, envying
5:26 envying **o** another.
6: 1 spiritual restore such a **o** in
6: 2 Bear **o** another's burdens, and so
6: 4 But let each **o** examine his own
6: 5 For each **o** shall bear his own
6:17 From now on let no **o** trouble me,
Eph 1:10 He might gather together in **o**
2:14 our peace, who has made both **o**,
2:15 to create in Himself **o** new man
2:16 them both to God in **o** body
2:18 both have access by **o** Spirit
4: 2 bearing with **o** another in love,
4: 4 There is **o** body and one
4: 4 is one body and **o** Spirit,
4: 4 as you were called in **o** hope
4: 5 **o** Lord, one faith, one baptism;
4: 5 **o** faith, one baptism;
4: 5 one faith, **o** baptism;
4: 6 **o** God and Father of all, who is
4: 7 But to each **o** of us grace was
4:10 He who descended is also the **O**
4:25 Let each **o** of you speak
4:25 are members of **o** another.
4:32 And be kind to **o** another,
4:32 forgiving **o** another, just as
5: 6 Let no **o** deceive you with empty
5:19 speaking to **o** another in psalms
5:21 submitting to **o** another in the
5:29 For no **o** ever hated his own
5:31 shall become **o** flesh."
5:33 Nevertheless let each **o** of you
6:16 the fiery darts of the wicked **o**.
Phil 1:27 that you stand fast in **o**
1:27 with **o** mind striving together
2: 2 being of **o** accord, of one
2: 2 one accord, of **o** mind.
2:20 For I have no **o** like-minded, who
2:25 but your messenger and the **o**
3:13 but **o** thing I do, forgetting
Col 2:16 So let no **o** judge you in food or
2:18 Let no **o** cheat you of your
3: 9 Do not lie to **o** another, since
3:13 bearing with **o** another, and
3:13 and forgiving **o** another, if
3:15 also you were called in **o** body;
3:16 and admonishing **o** another
4: 6 how you ought to answer each **o**.
4: 9 who is **o** of you. They will
4:12 who is **o** of you, a bondservant
1 Th 2:11 and charged every **o** of you, as
3: 3 that no **o** should be shaken by
3:12 abound in love to **o** another
4: 6 that no **o** should take advantage
4: 9 by God to love **o** another;
4:18 Therefore comfort **o** another with
5:11 each other and edify **o** another,
5:15 See that no **o** renders evil for
2 Th 1: 3 and the love of every **o** of you
2: 3 Let no **o** deceive you by any
2: 8 And then the lawless **o** will be
2: 9 The coming of the lawless **o** is
3: 3 and guard you from the evil **o**.
1 Tim 1: 8 know that the law is good if **o**
2: 5 For there is **o** God and one
2: 5 For there is one God and **o**
3: 2 the husband of **o** wife,
3: 4 **o** who rules his own house well,
3:12 be the husbands of **o** wife,
4:12 Let no **o** despise your youth,
5: 9 she has been the wife of **o** man,
2 Tim 2: 4 No **o** engaged in warfare
4:16 At my first defense no **o** stood
Titus 1: 6 the husband of **o** wife, having
1:12 **O** of them, a prophet of their
2: 8 that **o** who is an opponent may
2:15 Let no **o** despise you.
3: 2 to speak evil of no **o**,
3: 3 hateful and hating **o** another.
Phm 1: 9 being such a **o** as Paul, the
Heb 2: 6 But **o** testified in a certain
2:11 being sanctified are all of **o**,
3: 3 For this **O** has been counted
3:13 but exhort **o** another daily,
6:11 And we desire that each **o** of you
6:13 because He could swear by no **o**
7:18 For on the **o** hand there is an
8: 3 it is necessary that this **O**
10:12 after He had offered **o**
10:14 For by **o** offering He has
10:24 And let us consider **o** another in
10:25 but exhorting **o** another, and
11:12 Therefore from **o** man, and him as
12:14 without which no **o** will see the
12:16 who for **o** morsel of food sold
13:14 but we seek the **o** to come.
Jas 1:13 Let no **o** say when he is tempted,
1:14 But each **o** is tempted when he is
1:25 this **o** will be blessed in what
2: 3 and you pay attention to the **o**
2:10 and yet stumble in **o** point, he
2:13 is without mercy to the **o** who
2:16 and **o** of you says to them,
2:19 You believe that there is **o** God.
4:11 Do not speak evil of **o** another,
4:12 There is **o** Lawgiver, who is able
5: 9 Do not grumble against **o**
5:16 your trespasses to **o** another,
5:16 and pray for **o** another, that
1 Pe 1:22 love **o** another fervently with a
2:19 of conscience toward God **o**
3: 8 all of you be of **o** mind,
3: 8 compassion for **o** another;
4: 8 fervent love for **o** another,
4: 9 Be hospitable to **o** another
4:10 As each **o** has received a gift,
4:10 minister it to **o** another, as
4:18 If the righteous **o** is
5: 5 all of you be submissive to **o**
5:14 Greet **o** another with a kiss of
2 Pe 2: 5 **o** of eight people, a
3: 8 do not forget this **o** thing,
3: 8 that with the Lord **o** day is as
3: 8 and a thousand years as **o** day.
1 Jn 1: 7 we have fellowship with **o**
2:13 you have overcome the wicked **o**.
2:14 you have overcome the wicked **o**.
2:20 an anointing from the Holy **O**,
3: 7 let no **o** deceive you. He who
3:11 that we should love **o** another,
3:12 Cain who was of the wicked **o**
3:23 His Son Jesus Christ and love **o**
4: 7 let us love **o** another, for love
4:11 we also ought to love **o**
4:12 No **o** has seen God at any time.
4:12 If we love **o** another, God
5: 7 Spirit; and these three are **o**.
5: 8 and these three agree as **o**.
5:18 and the wicked **o** does not touch
5:19 the sway of the wicked **o**.
2 Jn 5 that we love **o** another.
Rev 1:13 of the seven lampstands **O**
2:17 a new name written which no **o**
2:23 And I will give to each **o** of
3: 7 He who opens and no **o**
3: 7 and shuts and no **o**
3: 8 and no **o** can shut it; for you
3:11 that no **o** may take your crown.
4: 2 and **O** sat on the throne.
5: 3 And no **o** in heaven or on the
5: 4 because no **o** was found worthy
5: 5 But **o** of the elders said to me,
6: 1 I saw when the Lamb opened **o**
6: 1 and I heard **o** of the four
6: 4 And it was granted to the **o** who
6: 4 people should kill **o** another;
7: 4 **O** hundred and forty-four
7: 9 a great multitude which no **o**
7:13 Then **o** of the elders answered,
9:12 **O** woe is past. Behold, still two
11: 3 will prophesy **o** thousand
11:10 and send gifts to **o** another,
11:17 The **O** who is and who was and
12: 6 feed her there **o** thousand
13: 3 And I saw **o** of his heads as if
13:17 and that no **o** may buy or sell
13:17 no one may buy or sell except **o**
14: 1 and with Him **o** hundred and
14: 3 and no **o** could learn that song
14:14 and on the cloud sat **O** like
14:20 for **o** thousand six hundred
15: 7 Then **o** of the four living
15: 8 and no **o** was able to enter the
16: 5 The **O** who is and who was and
17: 1 Then **o** of the seven angels who
17:10 **o** is, and the other has not
17:12 receive authority for **o** hour
17:13 These are of **o** mind, and they
17:17 to be of **o** mind, and to give
18: 8 her plagues will come in **o** day—
18:10 that mighty city! For in **o** hour
18:11 for no **o** buys their merchandise
18:17 For in **o** hour such great riches
18:19 by her wealth! For in **o** hour
19:12 He had a name written that no **o**
20:13 each **o** according to his works.
21: 9 Then **o** of the seven angels who
21:17 **o** hundred and forty-four
21:21 gate was of **o** pearl.
22:12 to give to every **o** according to

ONE-FIFTH (13/13)

Gen 41:34 to collect **o** of the produce
47:24 harvest that you shall give **o**
47:26 that Pharaoh should have **o**,
Lev 5:16 and shall add **o** to it and give
6: 5 add **o** more to it, and give it
22:14 the priest, and add **o** to it.
27:13 then he must add **o** to your
27:15 then he must add **o** of the money
27:19 then he must add **o** of the money
27:27 and shall add **o** to it; or if it
27:31 he shall add **o** to it.
Num 5: 7 plus **o** of it, and give it to
1 Ki 6:31 lintel and doorposts were **o**

ONE-FOURTH (12/11)

Ex 29:40 ephah of flour mixed with **o**
29:40 and **o** of a hin of wine as a
Lev 23:13 be of wine, **o** of a hin.
Num 15: 4 of fine flour mixed with **o** of
15: 5 and **o** of a HIN of wine as a
23:10 Or number **o** of Israel? Let me
28: 5 a grain offering mixed with **o**
28: 7 drink offering shall be **o** of
28:14 and **o** of a hin for a lamb;
1 Ki 6:33 wood, **o** of the wall.
2 Ki 6:25 and **o** of a kab of dove
Neh 9: 3 of the LORD their God for **o**

O

ONE-HALF (1/1)

Hos 3: 2 and one and **o** homers of barley.

ONE-SIXTH (3/2)

Ezek 4:11 **o** of a hin; from time to time
45:13 you shall give **o** of an ephah
45:13 and **o** of an ephah from a homer

ONE-TENTH (17/16)

Ex 16:36 Now an omer is **o** of an ephah.
29:40 With the one lamb shall be **o** of
Lev 5:11 shall bring for his offering **o**
6:20 **o** of an ephah of fine flour as
14:21 **o** of an ephah of fine flour
Num 5:15 **o** of an EPHAH of barley meal;
15: 4 bring a grain offering of **o**
28: 5 and **o** of an ephah of fine flour
28:13 and **o** of an ephah of fine
28:21 you shall offer **o** of an ephah
28:29 and **o** for each of the seven
29: 4 and **o** for each of the seven
29:10 and **o** for each of the seven
29:15 and **o** for each of the fourteen
Ezek 45:11 so that the bath contains **o** of
45:11 and the ephah **o** of a homer;
45:14 is **o** of a bath from a kor.

ONE-THIRD (17/12)

Num 15: 6 of fine flour mixed with **o** of
15: 7 offering you shall offer **o** of
28:14 **o** of a hin for a ram, and
2 Ki 11: 5 **O** of you who come on duty on
11: 6 **o** shall be at the gate of Sur,
11: 6 and **o** at the gate behind the
2 Chr 23: 4 **O** of you entering on the
23: 5 **o** shall be at the king's
23: 5 and **o** at the Gate of the
Neh 10:32 exact from ourselves yearly **o**
Ezek 5: 2 You shall burn with fire **o** in
5: 2 then you shall take **o** and
5: 2 and **o** you shall scatter in the
5:12 **O** of you shall die of the
5:12 and **o** shall fall by the sword
Zech 13: 8 But **o**d shall be left in it:
13: 9 I will bring the **o** through the

ONE'S (20/19)

Ex 16:16 it according to each **o** need,
16:18 according to each **o** need.
Deut 24: 6 for he takes **o** living in
2 Chr 21:20 to no **o** sorrow, departed.
Job 21:19 God lays up **o** iniquity for his
Ps 127: 4 the children of **o** youth.
Prov 25:27 So to seek **o** own glory is
Eccl 7: 1 death than the day of **o** birth;
Lam 3:34 To crush under **o** feet All the
Mal 2:16 For it covers **o** garment with
Mk 12:33 and to love **o** neighbor as
Lk 12:15 for **o** life does not consist in
Jn 15:13 than to lay down **o** life for his
Acts 20:33 I have coveted no **o** silver or
Rom 6:16 you are that **o** slaves whom you
1 Cor 3:13 each **o** work will become clear;
3:13 fire will test each **o** work,
4: 5 Then each **o** praise will come
Jas 1:26 this **o** religion is useless.
1 Pe 1:17 according to each **o** work,

ONES (126/123)

Gen 30:32 and all the brown **o** among the
30:35 and all the brown **o** among the
34:29 All their little **o** and their
43: 8 and you and also our little **o**.
45:19 of Egypt for your little **o** and
46: 5 father Jacob, their little **o**,
47:24 and as food for your little **o**.
50: 8 Only their little **o**,
50:21 for you and your little **o**.
Ex 6:27 These are the **o** who spoke to
10: 8 Who are the **o** that are
10:10 I let you and your little **o**
10:24 Let your little **o** also go with
34: 1 of stone like the first **o**,
34: 4 of stone like the first **o**.
Num 1:44 These are the **o** who were
2:32 These are the **o** who were
4:37 These were the **o** who were
4:41 These are the **o** who were
4:45 These are the **o** who were
14:31 'But your little **o**,
31: 9 captive, with their little **o**,
31:17 every male among the little **o**,
32:16 and cities for our little **o**,
32:17 and our little **o** will dwell in
32:24 cities for your little **o**
32:26 'Our little **o**, our wives,
34:29 These are the **o** the LORD
Deut 1:39 Moreover your little **o** and your
2:34 and little **o** of every city;
3:19 'But your wives, your little **o**,
20:14 "But the women, the little **o**,
22: 6 with young **o** or eggs, with the
29:11 your little **o** and your
31:12 men and women and little **o**,
Josh 1:14 "Your wives, your little **o**,
8:35 with the women, the little **o**,
Judg 18:21 departed, and put the little **o**,
1 Sam 17:30 answered him as the first **o**
2 Sam 2: 4 of Jabesh Gilead were the **o**
14:14 so that His banished **o** are not
15:22 his men and all the little **o**
2 Ki 4: 4 and set aside the full **o**.
1 Chr 6:33 And these are the **o** who
12:15 These are the **o** who crossed the
16:13 of Jacob, His chosen **o**!
16:22 "Do not touch My anointed **o**,
2 Chr 20:13 all Judah, with their little **o**,
24:26 These are the **o** who conspired
28:15 and they let all the feeble **o**
31:18 their little **o** and their wives,
Ezra 2:59 And these were the **o** who came
8:21 way for us and our little **o**
Neh 7:61 And these were the **o** who came
Job 5: 1 And to which of the holy **o**
12:20 He deprives the trusted **o** of
21:11 send forth their little **o** like
38:41 When its young **o** cry to God,
39: 4 Their young **o** are healthy,
39:30 Its young **o** suck up blood;
Ps 16: 3 "They are the excellent **o**,
29: 1 unto the LORD, O you mighty **o**,
35:20 matters Against the quiet **o**
38:11 My loved **o** and my friends stand
58: 1 righteousness, you silent **o**?
69:26 For they persecute the **o** You
83: 3 against Your sheltered **o**.
105: 6 of Jacob, His chosen **o**!
105:15 "Do not touch My anointed **o**,
105:43 His chosen **o** with gladness.
106: 5 the benefit of Your chosen **o**,
137: 9 takes and dashes Your little **o**
Prov 1:22 "How long, you simple **o**,
8: 5 O you simple **o**, understand
Song 5: 1 O beloved **o**! THE SHULAMITE
Isa 5: 9 Great and beautiful **o**,
5:17 the waste places of the fat **o**
10:16 send leanness among his fat **o**;
11: 7 Their young **o** shall lie down
13: 3 have commanded My sanctified **o**;
13: 3 I have also called My mighty **o**
14: 9 All the chief **o** of the earth;
24:21 on high the host of exalted **o**,
25: 4 the blast of the terrible **o**
25: 5 The song of the terrible **o**
29: 5 the multitude of the terrible **o**
32:11 Be troubled, you complacent **o**;
33: 7 Surely their valiant **o** shall
49: 6 to restore the preserved **o** of
57:15 the heart of the contrite **o**.
Jer 8:16 of the neighing of His strong **o**;
46: 5 Their mighty **o** are beaten
48: 4 Her little **o** have caused a cry
Ezek 34:21 butted all the weak **o** with your
Dan 4:17 by the word of the holy **o**,
7:24 be different from the first **o**,
8: 8 in place of it four notable **o**
11:17 and upright **o** with him;
Joel 3:11 Cause Your mighty **o** to go down
Zeph 3:10 The daughter of My dispersed **o**,
Zech 1:10 These are the **o** whom the
4:14 "These are the two anointed **o**,
13: 7 My hand against the little **o**.
Mt 10:42 gives one of these little **o**
18: 6 causes one of these little **o**
18:10 despise one of these little **o**,
18:14 that one of these little **o**
19:18 He said to Him, "Which **o**?
Mk 4:15 And these are the **o** by the
4:16 These likewise are the **o** sown on
4:18 Now these are the **o** sown among
4:18 they are the **o** who hear the
4:20 But these are the **o** sown on good
9:42 causes one of these little **o**
10:42 and their great **o** exercise
Lk 8:12 by the wayside are the **o**
8:13 But the **o** on the rock are
8:14 Now the **o** that fell among
8:15 But the **o** that fell on the good
11:40 Foolish **o**! Did not He who made
17: 2 offend one of these little **o**.
24:25 He said to them, "O foolish **o**,
2 Pe 2:18 the **o** who have actually escaped
Rev 7:14 These are the **o** who come out of
14: 4 These are the **o** who were not
14: 4 These are the **o** who follow the

ONESELF (2/2)

Mk 12:33 and to love one's neighbor as **o**,
Jas 1:27 and to keep **o** unspotted from

ONESIMUS (2/2)

Col 4: 9 with **O**, a faithful and
Phm 1:10 I appeal to you for my son **O**,

ONESIPHORUS (2/2)

2 Tim 1:16 mercy to the household of **O**,
4:19 Aquila, and the household of **O**.

ONIONS (1/1)

Num 11: 5 the melons, the leeks, the **o**,

ONLY (289/285)

Gen 6: 5 thoughts of his heart was **o**
7:23 **O** Noah and those who were with
14:24 except **o** what the young men have
19: 8 **o** do nothing to these men,
22: 2 your **o** son Isaac, whom you
22:12 your **o** son, from Me."
22:16 your son, your **o** son—
24: 8 **o** do not take my son back
27:13 **o** obey my voice, and go, get
27:38 Have you **o** one blessing, my
29:20 and they seemed **o** a few days
34:22 **O** on this condition will the
34:23 **O** let us consent to them, and
41:40 **o** in regard to the throne will
47:22 **O** the land of the priests he did
47:26 for the land of the priests **o**,
50: 8 **O** their little ones, their
Ex 8: 9 they may remain in the river **o**.
8:11 shall remain in the river **o**.
8:28 **o** you shall not go very far
9:26 **O** in the land of Goshen, where
10:17 please forgive my sin **o** this
10:17 take away from me this death **o**.
10:24 **o** let your flocks and your
12:16 that **o** may be prepared by you.
21:19 He shall **o** pay for the loss of
22:20 any god, except to the LORD **o**,
22:27 For that is his **o** covering, it
Lev 13: 6 it is **o** a scab, and he shall
21:23 **o** he shall not go near the veil
Num 1:49 **O** the tribe of Levi you shall
9:21 when the cloud remained **o** from
10: 4 But if they blow **o** one, then
12: 2 Has the LORD indeed spoken **o**
14: 2 If **o** we had died in the land of
14: 2 in the land of Egypt! Or if **o**
14: 9 **O** do not rebel against the
20: 3 If **o** we had died when our
20:19 let me **o** pass through on foot,
22:20 but **o** the word which I speak to
22:35 but **o** the word that I speak to
23:13 you shall see **o** the outer part
31:22 **O** the gold, the silver, the
36: 6 but they may marry **o** within the
Deut 2:28 **o** let me pass through on foot,
2:35 We took **o** the livestock as
2:37 **O** you did not go near the land
3:11 For **o** Og king of Bashan remained
4: 9 **O** take heed to yourself, and
4:12 you **o** heard a voice.
10:15 The LORD delighted **o** in your
12:16 **O** you shall not eat the blood;
12:23 **O** be sure that you do not eat
12:26 **O** the holy things which you
15: 5 **o** if you carefully obey the
15:23 **O** you shall not eat its blood;
20:20 **O** the trees which you know are
22:25 then **o** the man who lay with her
28:13 the tail; you shall be above **o**,
28:29 you shall be **o** oppressed and
28:33 and you shall be **o** oppressed
Josh 1: 7 **O** be strong and very courageous,
1:17 **O** the LORD your God be with
1:18 **O** be strong and of good
6:15 On that day **o** they marched
6:17 **O** Rahab the harlot shall live,
6:24 **O** the silver and gold, and the
8: 2 **O** its spoil and its cattle you
8:27 **O** the livestock and the spoil of
11:13 none of them, except Hazor **o**,
11:22 they remained **o** in Gaza, in
13: 6 **o** divide it by lot to Israel as
13:14 **O** to the tribe of Levi he had
17: 3 but **o** daughters. And these are
17:14 Why have you given us **o** one lot
17:17 you shall not have **o** one lot,
Judg 3: 2 (this was **o** so that the
6:37 if there is dew on the fleece **o**,
6:39 let it now be dry **o** on the
6:40 It was dry on the fleece **o**,
9:29 If **o** this people were under my
10:15 **o** deliver us this day, we
11:34 and she was his **o** child.
14:16 You **o** hate me! You do not love
19:20 **o** do not spend the night in the
1 Sam 1:13 **o** her lips moved, but her voice
1:23 **O** let the LORD establish His
5: 4 **o** Dagon's torso was left of it.
7: 3 for the LORD, and serve Him **o**;
7: 4 and served the LORD **o**.
12:24 **O** fear the LORD, and serve Him
14:43 I **o** tasted a little honey with
17:42 for he was **o** a youth, ruddy
18: 8 have ascribed **o** thousands.
18:17 **O** be valiant for me, and fight
20:14 And you shall not **o** show me the
20:39 **O** Jonathan and David knew of
2 Sam 2:10 **O** the house of Judah followed
13:32 for **o** Amnon is dead. For by the
13:33 For **o** Amnon is dead."
15:20 you came **o** yesterday. Should I
17: 2 and I will strike **o** the king.
18:33 —if **o** I had died in your place!
20:21 against David. Deliver him **o**,
23:10 people returned after him **o** to
1 Ki 4:19 He was the **o** governor who
8:25 **o** if your sons take heed to
12:20 David, but the tribe of Judah **o**.
14: 8 to do **o** what was right in My
14:13 for he is the **o** one of Jeroboam
17:12 **o** a handful of flour in a bin,
22:31 but **o** with the king of
22:47 **o** a deputy of the king.
2 Ki 5: 3 If **o** my master were with the
7: 4 kill us, we shall **o** die."

7:10 **o** horses and donkeys tied, and
10:23 but **o** the worshipers of Baal."
13: 7 left of the army of Jehoahaz **o**
13:19 now you will strike Syria **o**
21: 8 **o** if they are careful to do
1 Chr 2:34 **o** daughters. And Sheshan had an
7:15 but Zelophehad begot **o**
22:12 ***O*** may the LORD give you wisdom
23:22 but **o** daughters; and their
2 Chr 6:16 **o** if your sons take heed to
18:30 but **o** with the king of
33: 8 **o** if they are careful to do all
33:17 but **o** to the LORD their God.
Ezra 10:15 ***O*** Jonathan the son of Asahel and
Esth 1:16 Queen Vashti has not **o** wronged
Job 1:12 **o** do not lay a hand on his
13:20 ***O*** two things do not do to me,
40:19 ***O*** He who made him can bring
Ps 37: 8 it **o** causes harm.
51: 4 Against You, You **o**,
62: 2 He **o** is my rock and my
62: 4 They **o** consult to cast him
62: 6 He **o** is my rock and my
71:16 Your righteousness, of Yours **o**.
72:18 Who **o** does wondrous things!
90:10 Yet their boast is **o** labor
91: 8 ***O*** with your eyes shall you
Prov 4: 3 Tender and the **o** one in the
5:17 Let them be **o** your own, And
9: 7 he who rebukes a wicked man **o**
11:23 desire of the righteous is **o**
14:23 But idle chatter leads **o** to
17:11 An evil man seeks **o** rebellion;
25:16 Eat **o** as much as you need,
26:19 says, "I was **o** joking!"
Eccl 2:12 ***O*** what he has already done.
7:29 this **o** I have found: That God
Song 6: 9 Is the **o** one, The only one of
6: 9 The **o** one of her mother, The
Isa 4: 1 ***O*** let us be called by your
26:13 But by You **o** we make mention
Jer 3:13 ***O*** acknowledge your iniquity,
6:26 mourning as for an **o** son,
32:30 children of Judah have done **o**
32:30 of Israel have provoked Me **o**
33: 5 but **o** to fill their places
34: 7 for **o** these fortified cities
37:10 and there remained **o** wounded
Ezek 14:14 would deliver **o** themselves
14:16 **o** they would be delivered, and
14:18 but **o** they themselves would be
14:20 would deliver **o** themselves
33:24 Abraham was **o** one, and he
44:25 ***O*** for father or mother, for son
Dan 2: 9 there is **o** one decree for
11:24 but **o** for a time.
Am 3: 2 You **o** have I known of all the
8:10 make it like mourning for an **o**
Zech 12:10 Him as one mourns for his **o**
Mt 4:10 and Him **o** you shall
5:47 if you greet your brethren **o**,
8: 8 But **o** speak a word, and my
9:21 If **o** I may touch His garment, I
10:42 one of these little ones **o** a
12: 4 but **o** for the priests?
13:21 but endures **o** for a while.
14:17 We have here **o** five loaves and
14:36 begged Him that they might **o**
17: 8 they saw no one but Jesus **o**.
19:11 but **o** those to whom it has
20:12 'These last men have worked **o**
21:21 you will not **o** do what was done
24:36 of heaven, but My Father **o**.
Mk 4:17 and so endure **o** for a time.
5:28 If **o** I may touch His clothes, I
5:36 not be afraid; **o** believe."
9: 8 but **o** Jesus with themselves.
13:32 the Son, but **o** the Father.
Lk 4: 8 and Him **o** you shall
7:12 the **o** son of his mother;
8:42 for he had an **o** daughter about
8:50 **o** believe, and she will be made
9:38 for he is my **o** child.
12:41 do You speak this parable **o** to
24:18 Are You the **o** stranger in
Jn 1:14 the glory as of the **o** begotten
1:18 The **o** begotten Son, who is in
3:16 the world that He gave His **o**
3:18 believed in the name of the **o**
5:18 because He not **o** broke the
5:44 that comes from the **o** God?
11:52 and not for that nation **o**,
12: 9 came, not for Jesus' sake **o**,
13: 9 to Him, "Lord, not my feet **o**,
13:10 He who is bathed needs **o** to wash
17: 3 the **o** true God, and Jesus
Acts 2:15 since it is **o** the third hour
8:16 They had **o** been baptized in the
11:19 word to no one but the Jews **o**.
18:25 though he knew **o** the baptism of
19:26 you see and hear that not **o** at
19:27 So not **o** is this trade of ours
21:13 For I am ready not **o** to be
26:29 I would to God that not **o** you,
27:10 not **o** of the cargo and ship,
27:22 but **o** of the ship.
Rom 1:32 not **o** do the same but also
3:29 is He the God of the Jews **o**?
4: 9 come upon the circumcised **o**,
4:12 to those who not **o** are of the
4:16 not **o** to those who are of the
5: 3 And not **o** that, but we also
5:11 And not **o** that, but we also
8:23 Not **o** that, but we also who
9:10 And not **o** this, but when
9:24 He called, not of the Jews **o**,
13: 5 not **o** because of wrath but also
14: 2 is weak eats **o** vegetables.
16: 4 to whom not **o** I give thanks,
1 Cor 7:39 she wishes, **o** in the Lord.
9: 6 Or is it **o** Barnabas and I who
14:36 Or was it you **o** that it
15:19 If in this life **o** we have hope
2 Cor 7: 7 and not **o** by his coming, but
7: 8 though **o** for a while.
8: 5 And not **o** as we had hoped, but
8:10 It is to your advantage not **o**
8:17 For he not **o** accepted the
8:19 and not **o** that, but who was
8:21 not **o** in the sight of the Lord,
9:12 of this service not **o** supplies
Gal 1:23 But they were hearing **o**,
2:10 They desired **o** that we should
3: 2 This **o** I want to learn from you:
3: 7 Therefore know that **o** those who
3:15 Though it is **o** a man's
3:20 does not mediate for one **o**,
4:18 and not **o** when I am present
5:13 **o** do not use liberty as an
6:12 **o** that they may not suffer
Eph 1:21 not **o** in this age but also in
Phil 1:18 ***O*** that in every way, whether
1:27 ***O*** let your conduct be worthy of
1:29 not **o** to believe in Him, but
2: 4 Let each of you look out not **o**
2:12 obeyed, not as in my presence **o**,
2:27 and not **o** on him but on me
4:15 giving and receiving but you **o**.
Col 4:11 These are my **o** fellow workers
1 Th 1: 5 did not come to you in word **o**,
1: 8 not **o** in Macedonia and Achaia,
2: 8 pleased to impart to you not **o**
2 Th 2: 7 **o** He who now restrains will
1 Tim 5:13 and not **o** idle but also gossips
5:23 No longer drink **o** water, but use
6:15 the blessed and **o** Potentate,
2 Tim 2:20 a great house there are not **o**
4: 8 and not to me **o** but also to all
4:11 ***O*** Luke is with me. Get Mark and
Heb 5:13 For everyone who partakes **o** of
9:10 concerned **o** with foods and
11:17 offered up his **o** begotten son,
12:26 once more I shake not **o**
Jas 1:22 of the word, and not hearers **o**,
2:24 by works, and not by faith **o**.
1 Pe 2:18 not **o** to the good and gentle,
1 Jn 2: 2 and not for ours **o** but also for
4: 9 has sent His **o** begotten Son
5: 6 not **o** by water, but by water
2 Jn 1 and not **o** I, but also all those
Jude 4 into lewdness and deny the **o**
12 serving **o** themselves.
Rev 9: 4 but **o** those men who do not have
21:27 but **o** those who are written in

ONLY SON (7/7)

Gen 22: 2 your **o** Isaac, whom you love,
22:12 not withheld your son, your **o**,
22:16 not withheld your son, your **o**—
Jer 6:26 Make mourning as for an **o**,
Am 8:10 make it like mourning for an **o**,
Zech 12:10 Him as one mourns for his **o**,
Lk 7:12 the **o** of his mother; and she

ONO (5/5)

1 Chr 8:12 who built ***O*** and Lod with its
Ezra 2:33 the people of Lod, Hadid, and ***O***,
Neh 6: 2 the villages in the plain of ***O***.
7:37 the sons of Lod, Hadid, and ***O***,
11:35 in Lod, ***O***, and the Valley

ONTO (5/5)

Num 22:23 the donkey to turn her back **o**
Judg 19:28 So the man lifted her **o** the
1 Ki 22:35 blood ran out from the wound **o**
Jon 2:10 and it vomited Jonah **o** dry
Acts 27:39 **o** which they planned to run the

ONWARD (4/4)

Ex 40:36 children of Israel would go **o**
Num 15:23 LORD gave commandment and **o**
Isa 18: 2 terrible from their beginning **o**,
18: 7 terrible from their beginning **o**,

ONYCHA (1/1)

Ex 30:34 stacte and **o** and galbanum, and

ONYX (11/11)

Gen 2:12 Bdellium and the **o** stone are
Ex 25: 7 **o** stones, and stones to be set
28: 9 Then you shall take two **o** stones
28:20 the fourth row, a beryl, an **o**,
35: 9 **o** stones, and stones to be set
35:27 The rulers brought **o** stones, and
39: 6 And they set **o** stones, enclosed
39:13 the fourth row, a beryl, an **o**,
1 Chr 29: 2 **o** stones, stones to be set,
Job 28:16 In precious **o** or sapphire.
Ezek 28:13 topaz, and diamond, Beryl, **o**,

OPEN (160/158) OPENED, OPENING, OPENLY, OPENS

Gen 19: 2 will spend the night in the **o**
38:14 and sat in an **o** place which
Ex 13:12 apart to the LORD all that **o**
13:15 to the LORD all males that **o**
34:19 All that **o** the womb are Mine,
Lev 14: 7 the living bird loose in the **o**
14:53 loose outside the city in the **o**
17: 5 which they offer in the **o**
Num 8:16 for Myself instead of all who **o**
19:15 and every **o** vessel, which has no
19:16 Whoever in the **o** field touches
24: 4 falls down, with eyes wide **o**:
24:16 falls down, with eyes wide **o**:
Deut 15: 8 but you shall **o** your hand wide
15:11 You shall **o** your hand wide to
20:11 and **o** to you, then all the
28:12 The LORD will **o** to you His good
Josh 8:17 So they left the city **o** and
10:22 ***O*** the mouth of the cave, and
Judg 19:15 he sat down in the **o** square of
19:17 he saw the traveler in the **o**
19:20 do not spend the night in the **o**
2 Sam 11:11 my lord are encamped in the **o**
1 Ki 6:18 with ornamental buds and **o**
6:29 palm trees, and **o** flowers.
6:32 and **o** flowers, and overlaid
6:35 and **o** flowers on them, and
8:29 that Your eyes may be **o** toward
8:52 that Your eyes may be **o** to the
2 Ki 6:17 **o** his eyes that he may see."
6:20 **o** the eyes of these men, that
8:12 and rip **o** their women with
9: 3 ' Then **o** the door and flee,
13:17 ***O*** the east window"; and he
15:16 who were with child he ripped **o**.
19:16 **o** Your eyes, O LORD, and see;
2 Chr 6:20 that Your eyes may be **o** toward
6:40 let Your eyes be **o** and let
7:15 Now My eyes will be **o** and My
32: 6 them together to him in the **o**
Ezra 10: 9 and all the people sat in the **o**
Neh 1: 6 be attentive and Your eyes **o**,
6: 5 with an **o** letter in his hand.
8: 1 together as one man in the **o**
8: 3 Then he read from it in the **o**
8:16 and in the **o** square of the
8:16 of the Water Gate and in the **o**
Job 11: 5 And **o** His lips against you,
14: 3 And do You **o** Your eyes on such
28: 4 He breaks **o** a shaft away from
29: 7 When I took my seat in the **o**
32:20 I must **o** my lips and answer.
33: 2 I **o** my mouth; My tongue speaks
34:26 them as wicked men In the **o**
41:14 Who can **o** the doors of his
Ps 5: 9 Their throat is an **o** tomb;
34:15 And His ears are **o** to their
38:13 am like a mute who does not **o**
39: 9 I did not **o** my mouth, Because
51:15 **o** my lips, And my mouth shall
74:15 You broke **o** the fountain and
77: 4 You hold my eyelids **o**;
78: 2 I will **o** my mouth in a parable;
81:10 ***O*** your mouth wide, and I will
104:28 You **o** Your hand, they are
118:19 ***O*** to me the gates of
119:18 ***O*** my eyes, that I may see
145:16 You **o** Your hand And satisfy
Prov 1:20 She raises her voice in the **o**
7:12 at times in the **o** square,
13:16 But a fool lays **o** his folly.
20:13 ***O*** your eyes, and you will be
24: 7 He does not **o** his mouth in the
27: 5 ***O*** rebuke is better Than love
31: 8 ***O*** your mouth for the
31: 9 ***O*** your mouth, judge
Song 5: 2 ***O*** for me, my sister, my love,
5: 5 I arose to **o** for my beloved,
7:12 the grape blossoms are **o**,
Isa 9:12 shall devour Israel with an **o**
14:17 Who did not **o** the house of
22:22 on his shoulder; So he shall **o**,
22:22 shall shut, and no one shall **o**.
24:18 the windows from on high are **o**,
24:19 broken, The earth is split **o**,
26: 2 ***O*** the gates, That the
37:17 **o** Your eyes, O LORD, and see;
41:18 I will **o** rivers in desolate
42: 7 To **o** blind eyes, To bring out
45: 1 To **o** before him the double
45: 8 righteousness; Let the earth **o**,
60:11 your gates shall be **o**
Jer 5: 1 And seek in her **o** places If
5:16 Their quiver is like an **o**
9:22 shall fall as refuse on the **o**
13:19 And no one shall **o** them;
32:11 custom, and that which was **o**;
32:14 sealed and this deed which is **o**,
32:19 for your eyes are **o** to all the
50:26 ***O*** her storehouses; Cast her
Ezek 2: 8 **o** your mouth and eat what I
3:27 I will **o** your mouth, and you
16: 5 you were thrown out into the **o**
16:63 and never **o** your mouth anymore
29: 5 You shall fall on the **o** field;
29:21 and I will **o** your mouth to
30:16 pain, No shall be split **o**,
32: 4 I will cast you out on the **o**

33:27 and the one who is in the **o**
36: 5 in order to plunder its **o**
37: 2 there were very many in the **o**
37:12 I will **o** your graves and cause
39: 5 You shall fall on the **o** field;
45: 2 fifty cubits around it for an **o**
Dan 6:10 with his windows **o** toward
9:18 **o** Your eyes and see our
Hos 4:16 them forage Like a lamb in **o**
13: 8 I will tear **o** their rib cage,
13:16 their women with child ripped **o**.
Joel 1:19 For fire has devoured the **o**
1:20 And fire has devoured the **o**
2:22 For the **o** pastures are
Am 1:13 Because they ripped **o** the
Mic 2:13 The one who breaks **o** will come
Nah 3:13 gates of your land are wide **o**
Zech 11: 1 **O** your doors, O Lebanon, That
12: 4 I will **o** My eyes on the house
Mal 3:10 If I will not **o** for you the
Mt 13:35 I will **o** My mouth in
25:11 'Lord, Lord, **o** to us!'
Lk 7:14 Then He came and touched the **o**
12:36 he comes and knocks they may **o**
13:25 **o** for us,' and He will answer
Jn 1:51 you shall see heaven **o**,
9:26 How did He **o** your eyes?"
10:21 Can a demon **o** the eyes of the
Acts 1:18 he burst **o** in the middle and
12:14 of her gladness she did not **o**
16:27 and seeing the prison doors **o**,
18:14 And when Paul was about to **o**
19:38 the courts are **o** and there are
26:18 to **o** their eyes, in order to
Rom 3:13 Their throat is an **o** tomb;
2 Cor 6:11 to you, our heart is wide **o**.
6:13 as to children), you also be **o**.
7: 2 **O** your hearts to us
Eph 6:19 that I may **o** my mouth boldly to
Col 4: 3 that God would **o** to us a door
Heb 4:13 all things are naked and **o** to
6: 6 and put Him to an **o** shame.
1 Pe 3:12 And His ears are **o** to
Rev 3: 8 I have set before you an **o**
4: 1 a door standing **o** in heaven.
5: 2 Who is worthy to **o** the scroll
5: 3 under the earth was able to **o**
5: 4 no one was found worthy to **o**
5: 5 has prevailed to **o** the scroll
5: 9 And to **o** its seals; For You
10: 2 He had a little book **o** in his
10: 8 the little book which is **o** in

OPENED (128/122) OPEN

Gen 3: 5 eat of it your eyes will be **o**,
3: 7 the eyes of both of them were **o**,
4:11 which has **o** its mouth to
7:11 the windows of heaven were **o**.
8: 6 that Noah **o** the window of the
21:19 Then God **o** her eyes, and she saw
29:31 He **o** her womb; but Rachel was
30:22 and God listened to her and **o**
41:56 and Joseph **o** all the
42:27 But as one of them **o** his sack
43:21 that we **o** our sacks, and there,
44:11 and each **o** his sack.
Ex 2: 6 And when she had **o** it, she saw
Num 16:32 and the earth **o** its mouth and
22:28 Then the LORD **o** the mouth of
22:31 Then the LORD **o** Balaam's eyes,
24: 3 of the man whose eyes are **o**,
24:15 of the man whose eyes are **o**;
26:10 and the earth **o** its mouth and
Deut 11: 6 how the earth **o** its mouth and
Judg 3:25 and still he had not **o** the
3:25 they took the key and **o** them.
4:19 So she **o** a jug of milk, gave
19:27 and **o** the doors of the house
1 Sam 3:15 and **o** the doors of the house of
2 Ki 4:35 and the child **o** his eyes.
6:17 Then the LORD **o** the eyes of
6:20 And the LORD **o** their eyes,
9:10 And he **o** the door and fled.
13:17 and he **o** it. Then Elisha said,
2 Chr 29: 3 he **o** the doors of the house of
Neh 7: 3 let the gates of Jerusalem be **o**
8: 5 And Ezra **o** the book in the sight
8: 5 and when he **o** it, all the
13:19 that they must not be **o** till
Job 3: 1 After this Job **o** his mouth and
29:23 And they **o** their mouth wide
31:32 For I have **o** my doors to the
Ps 35:21 They also **o** their mouth wide
40: 6 not desire; My ears You have **o**.
78:23 And **o** the doors of heaven,
105:41 He **o** the rock, and water gushed
106:17 The earth **o** up and swallowed
109: 2 mouth of the deceitful Have **o**
119:131 I **o** my mouth and panted, For I
Song 5: 6 I **o** for my beloved, But my
Isa 5:14 has enlarged itself And **o** its
10:14 Nor **o** his mouth with even a
35: 5 eyes of the blind shall be **o**,
48: 8 long ago your ear was not **o**.
50: 5 The Lord GOD has **o** My ear;
53: 7 Yet He **o** not His mouth;
53: 7 So He **o** not His mouth.
Jer 50:25 The LORD has **o** His armory,
Lam 2:16 All your enemies have **o** their
3:46 All our enemies Have **o** their
Ezek 1: 1 that the heavens were **o** and I
3: 2 So I **o** my mouth, and He caused
24:27 that day your mouth will be **o**
33:22 And He had **o** my mouth; so when
33:22 in the morning, my mouth was **o**,
37:13 when I have **o** your graves, O My
41:11 doors of the side chambers **o**
44: 2 be shut; it shall not be **o**,
46: 1 on the Sabbath it shall be **o**,
46: 1 of the New Moon it shall be **o**.
46:12 the east shall then be **o** for
Dan 7:10 seated, And the books were **o**.
10:16 then I **o** my mouth and spoke,
Nah 2: 6 The gates of the rivers are **o**,
Zech 13: 1 that day a fountain shall be **o**
Mt 2:11 And when they had **o** their
3:16 the heavens were **o** to Him, and
5: 2 Then He **o** His mouth and taught
7: 7 and it will be **o** to you.
7: 8 to him who knocks it will be **o**.
9:30 And their eyes were **o**.
17:27 And when you have **o** its mouth,
20:33 "Lord, that our eyes may be **o**.
27:52 and the graves were **o**;
Mk 7:34 "Ephphatha," that is, "Be **o**.
7:35 Immediately his ears were **o**,
Lk 1:64 Immediately his mouth was **o** and
3:21 He prayed, the heaven was **o**.
4:17 And when He had **o** the book, He
11: 9 and it will be **o** to you.
11:10 to him who knocks it will be **o**.
24:31 Then their eyes were **o** and they
24:32 and while He **o** the Scriptures
24:45 And He **o** their understanding,
Jn 9:10 to him, "How were your eyes **o**?
9:14 when Jesus made the clay and **o**
9:17 you say about Him because He **o**
9:21 or who **o** his eyes we do not
9:30 yet He has **o** my eyes!
9:32 been unheard of that anyone **o**
11:37 who **o** the eyes of the blind,
Acts 5:19 at night an angel of the Lord **o**
5:23 but when we **o** them, we found no
7:56 Look! I see the heavens **o** and
8:32 So He **o** not His mouth.
8:35 Then Philip **o** his mouth, and
9: 8 and when his eyes were **o** he saw
9:40 And she **o** her eyes, and when
10:11 and saw heaven **o** and an object
10:34 Then Peter **o** his mouth and
12:10 which **o** to them of its own
12:16 and when they **o** the door and
14:27 and that He had **o** the door of
16:14 The Lord **o** her heart to heed
16:26 all the doors were **o** and
1 Cor 16: 9 great and effective door has **o**
2 Cor 2:12 and a door was **o** to me by the
Rev 6: 1 Now I saw when the Lamb **o** one of
6: 3 When He **o** the second seal, I
6: 5 When He **o** the third seal, I
6: 7 When He **o** the fourth seal, I
6: 9 When He **o** the fifth seal, I saw
6:12 I looked when He **o** the sixth
8: 1 When He **o** the seventh seal,
9: 2 And he **o** the bottomless pit, and
11:19 Then the temple of God was **o** in
12:16 and the earth **o** its mouth and
13: 6 Then he **o** his mouth in blasphemy
15: 5 the testimony in heaven was **o**.
19:11 Now I saw heaven **o**,
20:12 before God, and books were **o**.
20:12 And another book was **o**,

OPENING (15/9) OPEN

Ex 28:32 There shall be an **o** for his head
28:32 woven binding all around its **o**,
28:32 like the **o** in a coat of mail,
39:23 And there was an **o** in the
39:23 like the **o** in a coat of mail,
39:23 woven binding all around the **o**,
1 Ki 7:31 Its **o** inside the crown at the
7:31 and the **o** was round, shaped
7:31 and also on the **o** were
1 Chr 9:27 and they were in charge of **o**
Prov 8: 6 And from the **o** of my lips
Isa 42:20 **O** the ears, but he does not
61: 1 And the **o** of the prison to
Acts 27:12 a harbor of Crete **o** toward the
Jas 3:11 and bitter from the same **o**?

OPENINGS (2/2)

Neh 4:13 parts of the wall, at the **o**;
Prov 1:21 At the **o** of the gates in the

OPENLY (14/14) OPEN

Gen 38:21 is the harlot who was **o**
Mt 6: 4 will Himself reward you **o**.
6: 6 in secret will reward you **o**.
6:18 in secret will reward you **o**.
Mk 1:45 so that Jesus could no longer **o**
8:32 He spoke this word **o**.
Jn 7: 4 he himself seeks to be known **o**.
7:10 went up to the feast, not **o**,
7:13 no one spoke **o** of Him for fear
11:54 Jesus no longer walked **o** among
18:20 I spoke **o** to the world. I always
Acts 10:40 the third day, and showed Him **o**,
16:37 them, "They have beaten us **o**,
2 Cor 6:11 Corinthians! We have spoken **o**

OPENS (18/17) OPEN

Ex 13: 2 whatever **o** the womb among the
21:33 And if a man **o** a pit, or if a
Num 3:12 of every firstborn who **o** the
16:30 and the earth **o** its mouth and
18:15 Everything that first **o** the womb
Job 27:19 He **o** his eyes, And he is no
33:16 Then He **o** the ears of men, And
35:16 Therefore Job **o** his mouth in
36:10 He also **o** their ear to
36:15 And **o** their ears in
Ps 146: 8 The LORD **o** the eyes of the
Prov 13: 3 But he who **o** wide his lips
31:26 She **o** her mouth with wisdom,
Lk 2:23 Every male who **o** the womb
Jn 10: 3 "To him the doorkeeper **o**,
Rev 3: 7 He who **o** and no one
3: 7 and shuts and no one **o**":
3:20 If anyone hears My voice and **o**

OPERATION (2/2)

Ps 28: 5 Nor the **o** of His hands,
Isa 5:12 Nor consider the **o** of His

OPHEL (5/5)

2 Chr 27: 3 extensively on the wall of **O**.
33:14 Fish Gate; and it enclosed **O**,
Neh 3:26 the Nethinim who dwelt in **O**
3:27 and as far as the wall of **O**.
11:21 But the Nethinim dwelt in **O**.

OPHIR (13/12)

Gen 10:29 **O**, Havilah, and Jobab.
1 Ki 9:28 And they went to **O**,
10:11 which brought gold from **O**,
10:11 wood and precious stones from **O**.
22:48 made merchant ships to go to **O**
1 Chr 1:23 **O**, Havilah, and Jobab.
29: 4 of gold, of the gold of **O**,
2 Chr 8:18 the servants of Solomon to **O**,
9:10 who brought gold from **O**,
Job 22:24 And the gold of **O** among the
28:16 be valued in the gold of **O**,
Ps 45: 9 stands the queen in gold from **O**.
Isa 13:12 more than the golden wedge of **O**.

OPHNI (1/1)

Josh 18:24 Chephar Haammoni, **O**,

OPHRAH (8/8)

Josh 18:23 Avim, Parah, **O**,
Judg 6:11 terebinth tree which was in **O**,
6:24 To this day it is still in **O**
8:27 and set it up in his city, **O**.
8:32 in **O** of the Abiezrites.
9: 5 to his father's house at **O** and
1 Sam 13:17 company turned to the road to **O**,
1 Chr 4:14 and Meonothai who begot **O**.

OPINION (5/5) OPINIONS

Job 32: 6 And dared not declare my **o** to
32:10 me, I also will declare my **o**.
32:17 part, I too will declare my **o**.
Rom 11:25 should be wise in your own **o**,
12:16 Do not be wise in your own **o**.

OPINIONS (1/1) OPINION

1 Ki 18:21 will you falter between two **o**?

OPPONENT (2/2)

2 Sam 2:16 And each one grasped his **o** by
Titus 2: 8 that one who is an **o** may be

OPPONENT'S (1/1)

2 Sam 2:16 thrust his sword in his **o** side;

OPPORTUNE (2/2) OPPORTUNITY

Mk 6:21 Then an **o** day came when Herod on
Lk 4:13 he departed from Him until an **o**

OPPORTUNITY (13/12) OPPORTUNE

Judg 9:33 then do to them as you find **o**.
Mt 26:16 So from that time he sought **o** to
Lk 22: 6 So he promised and sought **o** to
Acts 25:16 and has **o** to answer for himself
Rom 7: 8 taking **o** by the commandment,
2 Cor 5:12 but give you **o** to boast on our
11:12 that I may cut off the **o** from
11:12 from those who desire an **o** to
Gal 5:13 do not use liberty as an **o**
6:10 Therefore, as we have **o**,
Phil 4:10 did care, but you lacked **o**.
1 Tim 5:14 give no **o** to the adversary to
Heb 11:15 they would have had **o** to

OPPOSE (3/3) OPPOSES

Job 30:21 strength of Your hand You **o** me.
Dan 8:12 given over to the horn to **o**
Zech 3: 1 at his right hand to **o** him.

OPPOSED (4/4)

Ex 32:29 for every man has **o** his son and
Ezra 10:15 Jahaziah the son of Tikvah **o**
Acts 13:45 they **o** the things spoken by
18: 6 But when they **o** him and

OPPOSES (1/1) OPPOSE

2 Th 2: 4 who **o** and exalts himself above

OPPOSITE (49/44)

Gen 15:10 and placed each piece **o** the
21:16 So she sat **o** him, and lifted
Ex 14: 2 **o** Baal Zephon; you shall camp
Deut 1: 1 in the plain **o** Suph, between
3:29 So we stayed in the valley **o**
4:46 in the valley **o** Beth Peor, in
11:30 who dwell in the plain **o**
34: 6 **o** Beth Peor; but no one knows
Josh 3:16 and the people crossed over **o**
5:13 a Man stood **o** him with His
Judg 19:10 and came to **o** Jebus (that is,
1 Sam 14: 5 front of one faced northward **o**
14: 5 and the other southward **o**
26: 1 Hachilah, **o** Jeshimon?"
26: 3 which is **o** Jeshimon, by the
2 Sam 16:13 went along the hillside **o** him
1 Ki 7: 4 and window was **o** window in
7: 5 and window was **o** window in
20:29 And they encamped **o** each other
1 Chr 26:16 watchman **o** watchman.
2 Chr 7: 6 The priests sounded trumpets **o**
Neh 3:23 and Hasshub made repairs **o**
3:25 son of Uzai made repairs **o**
12:38 thanksgiving choir went the **o**
Esth 9: 1 the **o** occurred, in that the
Ezek 16:34 You are the **o** of other women in
16:34 you, therefore you are the **o**.
40:23 A gate of the inner court was **o**
41:16 around their three stories **o**
42: 1 into the chamber which was **o**
42: 1 and which was **o** the building
42: 3 ***O*** the inner court of twenty
42: 3 and **o** the pavement of the outer
42:10 **o** the separating courtyard and
42:10 the separating courtyard and **o**
42:13 which are **o** the separating
46: 9 but shall go out through the **o**
47:20 until one comes to a point **o**
48:13 ***O*** the border of the priests,
Dan 5: 5 hand appeared and wrote **o** the
Mt 21: 2 Go into the village **o** you, and
27:61 sitting **o** the tomb.
Mk 11: 2 'Go into the village **o** you;
12:41 Now Jesus sat **o** the treasury
13: 3 He sat on the Mount of Olives **o**
15:39 who stood **o** Him, saw that He
Lk 8:26 which is **o** Galilee.
19:30 Go into the village **o** you,
Acts 20:15 and the next day came **o** Chios.

OPPOSITION (1/1)

2 Tim 2:25 correcting those who are in **o**,

OPPRESS (27/27) OPPRESSED, OPPRESSES, OPPRESSION, OPPRESSOR

Ex 3: 9 with which the Egyptians **o**
22:21 mistreat a stranger nor **o** him,
23: 9 Also you shall not **o** a stranger,
Lev 25:14 you shall not **o** one another.
25:17 Therefore you shall not **o** one
Deut 23:16 you shall not **o** him.
24:14 You shall not **o** a hired servant
2 Sam 7:10 shall the sons of wickedness **o**
1 Chr 17: 9 shall the sons of wickedness **o**
Job 10: 3 good to You that You should **o**,
37:23 justice; He does not **o**.
Ps 10:18 the man of the earth may **o** no
17: 9 From the wicked who **o** me,
119:122 Do not let the proud **o** me.
Prov 22:22 Nor **o** the afflicted at the
Isa 49:26 I will feed those who **o** you
Jer 7: 6 if you do not **o** the stranger,
30:20 And I will punish all who **o**
Ezek 22:29 and they wrongfully **o** the
45: 8 and My princes shall no more **o**
Hos 12: 7 in his hand; He loves to **o**.
Am 4: 1 Who **o** the poor, Who crush the
Mic 2: 2 So they **o** a man and his house,
Hab 2: 7 Will they not awaken who **o**
Zech 7:10 Do not **o** the widow or the
Acts 7: 6 bring them into bondage and **o**
Jas 2: 6 Do not the rich **o** you and drag

OPPRESSED (44/44) OPPRESS

Deut 28:29 you shall be only **o** and
28:33 and you shall be only **o** and
Judg 2:18 because of those who **o** them
4: 3 for twenty years he harshly **o**
6: 9 out of the hand of all who **o**
10: 8 that year they harassed and **o**
10:12 and Amalekites and Maonites **o**
1 Sam 10:18 kingdoms and from those who **o**
12: 3 have I cheated? Whom have I **o**,
12: 4 You have not cheated us or **o** us,
2 Ki 13: 4 because the king of Syria **o**
13:22 And Hazael king of Syria **o**
2 Chr 16:10 And Asa **o** some of the people
Neh 9:27 Who **o** them; And in the time
Job 20:19 For he has **o** and forsaken the
36: 6 But gives justice to the **o**.
Ps 9: 9 also will be a refuge for the **o**,
10:18 to the fatherless and the **o**,
74:21 do not let the **o** return
76: 9 To deliver all the **o** of the
103: 6 And justice for all who are **o**.
106:42 Their enemies also **o** them,
146: 7 Who executes justice for the **o**,
Eccl 4: 1 And look! The tears of the **o**,
Isa 3: 5 The people will be **o**,
9: 1 And afterward more heavily **o**
23:12 O you **o** virgin daughter of
38:14 O LORD, I am **o**;
52: 4 Then the Assyrian **o** them
53: 7 He was **o** and He was afflicted,
58: 6 To let the **o** go free,
Jer 50:33 children of Israel were **o**,
Ezek 18: 7 If he has not **o** anyone,
18:12 If he has **o** the poor and needy,
18:16 Has not **o** anyone, Nor withheld
18:18 father, Because he cruelly **o**,
22: 7 in your midst they have **o** the
Hos 5:11 Ephraim is **o** and broken in
Am 3: 9 And the **o** within her.
Lk 4:18 liberty those who are **o**;
Acts 7:19 and **o** our forefathers, making
7:24 and avenged him who was **o**,
10:38 and healing all who were **o** by
2 Pe 2: 7 who was **o** by the filthy

OPPRESSES (5/5) OPPRESS

Num 10: 9 land against the enemy who **o**
Ps 56: 1 Fighting all day he **o** me.
Prov 14:31 He who **o** the poor reproaches
22:16 He who **o** the poor to increase
28: 3 A poor man who **o** the poor Is

OPPRESSING (3/3)

Jer 46:16 of our nativity From the **o**
50:16 For fear of the **o** sword
Zeph 3: 1 To the **o** city!

OPPRESSION (27/27) OPPRESS

Ex 3: 7 I have surely seen the **o** of My
3: 9 and I have also seen the **o** with
Deut 26: 7 and our labor and our **o**.
2 Ki 13: 4 for He saw the **o** of Israel,
Job 36:15 And opens their ears in **o**.
Ps 10: 7 of cursing and deceit and **o**;
12: 5 For the **o** of the poor, for the
42: 9 I go mourning because of the **o**
43: 2 I go mourning because of the **o**
44:24 forget our affliction and our **o**?
55: 3 Because of the **o** of the
55:11 ***O*** and deceit do not depart
62:10 Do not trust in **o**,
72:14 will redeem their life from **o**
73: 8 speak wickedly concerning **o**;
107:39 and brought low Through **o**,
119:134 Redeem me from the **o** of man,
Eccl 4: 1 and considered all the **o** that
5: 8 If you see the **o** of the poor,
7: 7 Surely **o** destroys a wise man's
Isa 5: 7 for justice, but behold, **o**;
30:12 And trust in **o** and perversity,
54:14 You shall be far from **o**,
59:13 Speaking **o** and revolt,
Jer 6: 6 She is full of **o** in her
22:17 And practicing **o** and
Acts 7:34 I have surely seen the **o**

OPPRESSIONS (3/3)

Job 35: 9 Because of the multitude of **o**
Isa 33:15 He who despises the gain of **o**,
Ezek 22:29 people of the land have used **o**,

OPPRESSOR (15/14) OPPRESS, OPPRESSORS

Job 3:18 do not hear the voice of the **o**.
15:20 of years is hidden from the **o**.
Ps 72: 4 And will break in pieces the **o**.
Prov 3:31 Do not envy the **o**,
28:16 understanding is a great **o**,
29:13 The poor man and the **o** have
Isa 1:17 Seek justice, Rebuke the **o**;
9: 4 his shoulder, The rod of his **o**,
14: 4 'How the **o** has ceased,
51:13 Because of the fury of the **o**,
51:13 where is the fury of the **o**?
Jer 21:12 Out of the hand of the **o**,
22: 3 out of the hand of the **o**.
25:38 of the fierceness of the ***O***,
Zech 9: 8 No more shall an **o** pass

OPPRESSORS (9/9) OPPRESSOR

Job 6:23 'Redeem me from the hand of **o**'?
27:13 God, And the heritage of **o**,
Ps 54: 3 And **o** have sought after my
119:121 Do not leave me to my **o**.
Eccl 4: 1 On the side of their **o** there
Isa 3:12 people, children are their **o**,
14: 2 were, and rule over their **o**.
16: 4 The **o** are consumed out of the
19:20 to the LORD because of the **o**,

OR (1407/1104) See APPENDIX

ORACLE (17/13) ORACLES

Num 23: 7 And he took up his **o** and said:
23:18 Then he took up his **o** and said:
24: 3 Then he took up his **o** and said:
24:15 So he took up his **o** and said:
24:20 and he took up his **o** and said:
24:21 and he took up his **o** and said:
24:23 Then he took up his **o** and said:
2 Sam 16:23 as if one had inquired at the **o**
Ps 36: 1 An **o** within my heart concerning
Jer 23:33 'What is the **o** of the LORD?'
23:33 shall then say to them, 'What **o**?
23:34 The **o** of the LORD!' I will even
23:36 And the **o** of the LORD you shall
23:36 every man's word will be his **o**,
23:38 The **o** of the LORD!' therefore
23:38 The **o** of the LORD!" and I have
23:38 The **o** of the LORD!'"

ORACLES (5/5) ORACLE

2 Chr 24:27 and the many **o** about him, and
Acts 7:38 one who received the living **o**
Rom 3: 2 to them were committed the **o**
Heb 5:12 the first principles of the **o**
1 Pe 4:11 let him speak as the **o** of

ORATION (1/1)

Acts 12:21 on his throne and gave an **o** to

ORATOR (1/1)

Acts 24: 1 with the elders and a certain **o**

ORCHARD (1/1)

Song 4:13 Your plants are an **o** of

ORCHARDS (1/1)

Eccl 2: 5 I made myself gardens and **o**,

ORDAIN (1/1) ORDAINED

1 Cor 7:17 And so I **o** in all the churches.

ORDAINED (10/10) ORDAIN

Num 28: 6 burnt offering which was **o** at
1 Ki 12:32 Jeroboam **o** a feast on the
12:33 And he **o** a feast for the
2 Ki 23: 5 whom the kings of Judah had **o**
Ps 8: 2 and nursing infants You have **o**
8: 3 and the stars, which You have **o**,
Jer 1: 5 I **o** you a prophet to the
Acts 10:42 that it is He who was **o** by God
17:31 by the Man whom He has **o**.
1 Cor 2: 7 the hidden wisdom which God **o**

ORDER (73/72) ORDERED, ORDERLY, ORDERS, WELL-ORDERED

Gen 18:19 in **o** that he may command his
22: 9 there and placed the wood in **o**;
50:20 in **o** to bring it about as it
Ex 8:22 in **o** that you may know that I
28:10 in **o** of their birth.
39:37 its lamps (the lamps set in **o**),
40: 4 things that are to be set in **o**
40:23 and he set the bread in **o** upon
Lev 1: 7 and lay the wood in **o** on the
1: 8 and the fat in **o** on the wood
1:12 the priest shall lay them in **o**
6:12 lay the burnt offering in **o** on
24: 8 Sabbath he shall set it in **o**
Num 10:28 Thus was the **o** of march of the
Deut 13: 5 because he has spoken in **o** to
17:10 do according to all that they **o**
Josh 2: 6 which she had laid in **o** on the
Judg 6:11 in **o** to hide it from the
14:15 Have you invited us in **o** to
1 Sam 21: 6 in **o** to put hot bread in its
2 Sam 17:23 Then he put his household in **o**,
1 Ki 18:33 And he put the wood in **o**,
20:14 "Who will set the battle in **o**?
2 Ki 20: 1 the LORD: 'Set your house in **o**,
23: 4 the priests of the second **o**,
1 Chr 6:32 office according to their **o**.
15:13 consult Him about the proper **o**.
25: 2 prophesied according to the **o**
2 Chr 8:14 according to the **o** of David his
13: 3 Abijah set the battle in **o** with
13:11 also set the showbread in **o**
29:35 house of the LORD was set in **o**.
32:31 in **o** to test him, that He might
Ezra 6:21 of the nations of the land in **o**
Neh 8:13 in **o** to understand the words of
Esth 1:11 in **o** to show her beauty to the
Job 10:22 shadow of death, without any **o**,
33: 5 Set your words in **o** before
33:17 In **o** to turn man from his
Ps 40: 5 be recounted to You in **o**;
50:21 And set them in **o** before your
59: watched the house in **o** to
110: 4 forever According to the **o** of
Eccl 12: 9 and sought out and set in **o**
Isa 9: 7 To **o** it and establish it with

38: 1 the LORD: 'Set your house in **o**,
44: 7 him declare it and set it in **o**
Jer 46: 3 **O** the buckler and shield, And
Ezek 36: 5 in **o** to plunder its open
39:12 in **o** to cleanse the land.
39:14 in **o** to cleanse it. At the end
Dan 4:17 In **o** that the living may know
Mt 12:44 it empty, swept, and put in **o**.
Lk 1: 1 have taken in hand to set in **o**
1: 8 as priest before God in the **o**
11:25 he finds it swept and put in **o**.
20:20 in **o** to deliver Him to the
Acts 11: 4 explained it to them in **o**
18:23 of Galatia and Phrygia in **o**,
26:18 in **o** to turn them from
1 Cor 11:34 And the rest I will set in **o**
14:40 be done decently and in **o**.
15:23 But each one in his own **o**:
Col 2: 5 rejoicing to see your good **o**
Titus 1: 5 that you should set in **o** the
Heb 5: 6 According to the **o** of
5:10 according to the **o** of
6:20 forever according to the **o** of
7:11 should rise according to the **o**
7:11 be called according to the **o**
7:17 According to the **o** of
7:21 According to the **o** of
10:24 us consider one another in **o**

ORDERED (8/8) ORDER

Gen 43:17 Then the man did as Joseph **o**,
1 Sam 21: 2 The king has **o** me on some
2 Sam 16:11 for so the LORD has **o** him.
23: 5 **O** in all things and secure.
Esth 1: 8 for so the king had **o** all the
Ps 37:23 steps of a good man are **o** by
Ezek 21:16 Wherever your edge is **o**!
Acts 22:24 the commander **o** him to be

ORDERLY (3/3) ORDER

Ex 13:18 of Israel went up in **o** ranks
Lk 1: 3 to write to you an **o** account,
Acts 21:24 that you yourself also walk **o**

ORDERS (6/6) ORDER

2 Sam 14: 8 and I will give **o** concerning
18: 5 king gave all the captains **o**
Ezra 8:36 they delivered the king's **o** to
Ps 50:23 And to him who **o** his conduct
Acts 20:13 on board; for so he had given **o**,
1 Cor 16: 1 as I have given **o** to the

ORDINANCE (42/41) ORDINANCES

Ex 12:14 as a feast by an everlasting **o**.
12:17 generations as an everlasting **o**.
12:24 observe this thing as an **o** for
12:43 This is the **o** of the Passover:
13:10 shall therefore keep this **o** in
15:25 He made a statute and an **o** for
Lev 18:30 'Therefore you shall keep My **o**,
22: 9 'They shall therefore keep My **o**,
Num 9:14 you shall have one **o**, both
10: 8 these shall be to you as an **o**
15:15 One **o** shall be for you of the
15:15 an **o** forever throughout your
15:24 offering, according to the **o**,
18: 8 your sons, as an **o** forever.
18:11 as an **o** forever. Everyone who
18:19 and daughters with you as an **o**
19: 2 This is the **o** of the law which
29: 6 offerings, according to their **o**,
29:18 number, according to the **o**;
29:21 number, according to the **o**;
29:24 number, according to the **o**;
29:27 number, according to the **o**;
29:30 number, according to the **o**;
29:33 number, according to the **o**;
29:37 number, according to the **o**;
31:21 This is the **o** of the law which
Josh 24:25 for them a statute and an **o** in
1 Sam 30:25 he made it a statute and an **o**
1 Chr 23:31 by number according to the **o**
24:19 the LORD according to their **o**
2 Chr 2: 4 This is an **o** forever to
35:13 with fire according to the **o**;
Ezra 3: 4 in the number required by **o**
3:10 according to the **o** of David
Ps 99: 7 kept His testimonies and the **o**
Isa 24: 5 the laws, Changed the **o**,
58: 2 And did not forsake the **o** of
Ezek 45:14 The **o** concerning oil, the bath
46:14 grain offering is a perpetual **o**,
Mal 3:14 is it that we have kept His **o**,
Rom 13: 2 the authority resists the **o** of
1 Pe 2:13 submit yourselves to every **o**

ORDINANCES (29/28) ORDINANCE

Lev 18: 3 nor shall you walk in their **o**.
18: 4 My judgments and keep My **o**,
Num 9:12 According to all the **o** of the
2 Ki 17:34 their statutes or their **o**,
17:37 "And the statutes, the **o**,
2 Chr 19:10 against statutes or **o**,
33: 8 law and the statutes and the **o**
Ezra 7:10 and to teach statutes and **o** in
Neh 1: 7 nor the **o** which You commanded
9:13 And gave them just **o** and true
10:29 and His **o** and His statutes:
10:32 Also we made **o** for ourselves,
10:35 And we made **o** to bring the
Job 38:33 Do you know the **o** of the
Ps 119:43 For I have hoped in Your **o**.
119:91 this day according to Your **o**,
Isa 58: 2 They ask of Me the **o** of
Jer 31:35 The **o** of the moon and the
31:36 If those **o** depart From before
33:25 if I have not appointed the **o**
Ezek 43:11 its entire design and all its **o**,
43:11 its whole design and all its **o**,
43:18 These are the **o** for the altar
44: 5 to you concerning all the **o** of
Mal 3: 7 You have gone away from My **o**
Lk 1: 6 in all the commandments and **o**
Eph 2:15 of commandments contained in **o**,
Heb 9: 1 even the first covenant had **o**
9:10 and fleshly **o** imposed until the

ORDINARY (1/1)

Jer 31: 5 shall plant and eat them as **o**

ORE (2/2)

Job 28: 2 And copper is smelted from **o**.
28: 3 searches every recess For **o**

OREB (7/4)

Judg 7:25 **O** and Zeeb. They killed Oreb at
7:25 They killed **O** at the rock of
7:25 killed Oreb at the rock of **O**,
7:25 and brought the heads of **O** and
8: 3 **O** and Zeeb. And what was I able
Ps 83:11 Make their nobles like **O** and
Isa 10:26 of Midian at the rock of **O**;

OREN (1/1)

1 Chr 2:25 the firstborn, and Bunah, **O**,

ORGAN (KJV) See FLUTE

ORIGIN (1/1)

Ezek 29:14 Pathros, to the land of their **o**,

ORIGINAL (1/1)

2 Chr 24:13 house of God to its **o** condition

ORIGINALLY (1/1)

1 Cor 14:36 Or did the word of God come **o**

ORION (3/3)

Job 9: 9 He made the Bear, **O**,
38:31 Or loose the belt of **O**?
Am 5: 8 He made the Pleiades and **O**;

ORNAMENT (5/5) ORNAMENTS

Prov 1: 9 they will be a graceful **o** on
4: 9 will place on your head an **o**
25:12 an earring of gold and an **o** of
Isa 30:22 And the **o** of your molded
49:18 with them all as an **o**,

ORNAMENTAL (11/8)

Ex 25:31 its **o** knobs, and flowers shall
25:33 with an **o** knob and a flower,
25:33 with an **o** knob and a
25:34 each with its **o** knob and
37:17 its **o** knobs, and its flowers
37:19 with an **o** knob and a flower,
37:19 with an **o** knob and a
37:20 each with its **o** knob and
1 Ki 6:18 carved with **o** buds and open
7:24 Below its brim were **o** buds
7:24 The **o** buds were cast in two

ORNAMENTS (17/17) ORNAMENT

Ex 33: 4 and no one put on his **o**.
33: 5 Now therefore, take off your **o**,
33: 6 stripped themselves of their **o**
Num 31:50 what every man found of **o** of
31:51 from them, all the fashioned **o**.
Judg 8:21 and took the crescent **o** that
8:26 of gold, besides the crescent **o**,
2 Sam 1:24 Who put **o** of gold on your
Song 1:10 Your cheeks are lovely with **o**,
1:11 We will make you **o** of gold
Isa 3:20 The headdresses, the leg **o**,
61:10 decks himself with **o**,
Jer 2:32 Can a virgin forget her **o**,
4:30 you adorn yourself with **o** of
Ezek 7:20 'As for the beauty of his **o**,
16:11 "I adorned you with **o**,
23:40 and adorned yourself with **o**.

ORNAN (12/10) ARAUNAH

1 Chr 21:15 by the threshing floor of **O**
21:18 on the threshing floor of **O**
21:20 Now **O** turned and saw the angel;
21:20 but **O** continued threshing
21:21 Then David came to **O**,
21:21 and **O** looked and saw David.
21:22 Then David said to **O**,
21:23 And **O** said to David, "Take it
21:24 Then King David said to **O**,
21:25 So David gave **O** six hundred
21:28 him on the threshing floor of **O**
2 Chr 3: 1 on the threshing floor of **O**

ORPAH (2/2)

Ruth 1: 4 the name of the one was **O**,
1:14 and **O** kissed her mother-in-law,

ORPHANS (4/4)

Lam 5: 3 We have become **o** and waifs,
Mal 3: 5 wage earners and widows and **o**,
Jn 14:18 "I will not leave you **o**;
Jas 1:27 to visit **o** and widows in their

OSEE (KJV) See HOSEA

OSHEA (KJV) See HOSHEA

OSNAPPER (1/1)

Ezra 4:10 whom the great and noble **O**

OSPRAY (KJV) See BUZZARD

OSSIFRAGE (KJV) See VULTURE

OSTRICH (3/3)

Lev 11:16 'the **o**, the short-eared owl,
Deut 14:15 'the **o**, the short-eared owl,
Job 39:13 The wings of the **o** wave proudly,

OSTRICHES (7/7)

Job 30:29 jackals, And a companion of **o**.
Isa 13:21 **O** will dwell there, And wild
34:13 of jackals, A courtyard for **o**.
43:20 Me, The jackals and the **o**,
Jer 50:39 And the **o** shall dwell in it.
Lam 4: 3 Like **o** in the wilderness.
Mic 1: 8 And a mourning like the **o**,

OTHER (468/440)

Gen 13:11 And they separated from each **o**.
15:10 each piece opposite the **o**;
25:23 shall be stronger than the **o**,
28:17 is this place! This is none **o**
31:50 or if you take **o** wives besides
32: 8 then the **o** company which is
41: 3 seven **o** cows came up after them
41: 3 and stood by the **o** cows on the
41:19 seven **o** cows came up after
43:14 may release your **o** brother
43:22 And we have brought down **o** money
47:21 of Egypt to the **o** end.
Ex 1:15 and the name of the **o** Puah;
4: 7 it was restored like his **o**
14:20 gave light by night to the **o**,
14:20 the one did not come near the **o**
17:12 and the **o** on the other side;
17:12 and the other on the **o** side;
18: 4 and the name of the **o** was
18: 7 And they asked each **o** about
18:12 offering and **o** sacrifices
20: 3 You shall have no **o** gods before
21:18 "If men contend with each **o**,
21:18 and one strikes the **o** with a
23:13 mention of the name of **o** gods,
25:12 and two rings on the **o** side.
25:19 and the **o** cherub at the other
25:19 other cherub at the **o** end;
25:32 of the lampstand out of the **o**
25:33 like almond blossoms on the **o**
26: 3 and the **o** five curtains
26: 4 do on the outer edge of the **o**
26:13 and a cubit on the **o** side,
26:27 bars for the boards on the **o**
27:15 And on the **o** side shall be
28:10 and six names on the **o** stone,
28:25 and the **o** two ends of the two
28:27 And two **o** rings of gold you
29:19 You shall also take the **o** ram,
29:39 and the **o** lamb you shall offer
29:41 And the **o** lamb you shall offer
30:32 nor shall you make any **o** like
32:15 one side and on the **o** they
34:14 (for you shall worship no **o** god,
36:10 and the **o** five curtains he
36:11 outer edge of the **o** curtain
36:25 And for the **o** side of the
36:32 bars for the boards on the **o**
36:33 boards from one end to the **o**.
37: 3 and two rings on the **o** side of
37: 8 **o** cherub at the other end
37: 8 and the other cherub at the **o**
37:18 of the lampstand out of the **o**
37:19 blossoms on the **o** branch,
38:15 and the same for the **o** side of
39:20 They made two **o** gold rings and
Lev 5: 7 as a sin offering and the **o** as
6:11 put on **o** garments, and carry
7:10 to one as much as the **o**.
7:24 may be used in any **o** way;
11:23 But all **o** flying insects which
12: 8 as a burnt offering and the **o**
14:22 be a sin offering and the **o** a
14:31 as a sin offering and the **o**

14:42 Then they shall take **o** stones
14:42 and he shall take **o** mortar and
15:15 as a sin offering and the **o**
15:25 **o** than at the time of her
15:30 as a sin offering and the **o**
16: 8 lot for the LORD and the **o** lot
18:18 her nakedness while the **o** is
24:10 a man of Israel fought each **o**
Num 5:20 yourself and some man **o** than
6:11 as a sin offering and the **o**
8:12 as a sin offering and the **o** as
11:26 and the name of the **o** Medad.
11:31 a day's journey on the **o** side,
21:13 they moved and camped on the **o**
24: 1 he did not go as at **o** times, to
26:62 numbered among the **o** children
28: 4 the **o** lamb you shall offer in
28: 8 The **o** lamb you shall offer in
32:19 not inherit with them on the **o**
32:38 and they gave **o** names to the
36: 3 to any of the sons of the **o**
Deut 4:32 from one end of heaven to the **o**,
4:35 there is none **o** besides Him.
4:39 earth beneath; there is no **o**.
5: 7 You shall have no **o** gods before
6:14 You shall not go after **o** gods,
7: 4 to serve **o** gods; so the anger
7: 7 in number than any **o** people,
8:19 and follow **o** gods, and serve
11:16 turn aside and serve **o** gods
11:28 to go after **o** gods which you
11:30 Are they not on the **o** side of
13: 2 Let us go after **o** gods'—which
13: 6 Let us go and serve **o** gods,'
13: 7 end of the earth to the **o** end
13:13 Let us go and serve **o** gods"
17: 3 who has gone and served **o** gods
18:20 speaks in the name of **o** gods,
21:15 one loved and the **o** unloved,
28:14 to go after **o** gods to serve
28:36 you shall serve **o** gods—wood
28:64 one end of the earth to the **o**,
28:64 and there you shall serve **o**
29:26 for they went and served **o** gods
30:17 and worship **o** gods and serve
31:18 they have turned to **o** gods.
31:20 then they will turn to **o** gods
Josh 2:10 who were on the **o** side
7: 7 and dwelt on the **o** side of the
12: 1 land they possessed on the **o**
12: 4 The **o** king was Og king of
13: 8 With the **o** half tribe the
13:27 on the **o** side of the Jordan
13:32 plains of Moab on the **o** side
14: 3 and the half-tribe on the **o**
17: 5 which were on the **o** side of
20: 8 And on the **o** side of the Jordan,
21:27 from the **o** half-tribe of
22: 4 LORD gave you on the **o** side
22: 7 but to the **o** half of it Joshua
23:16 and have gone and served **o**
24: 2 dwelt on the **o** side of the
24: 2 and they served **o** gods.
24: 3 father Abraham from the **o** side
24: 8 who dwelt on the **o** side of the
24:14 fathers served on the **o** side
24:15 that were on the **o** side
24:16 forsake the LORD to serve **o**
Judg 2:12 and they followed **o** gods from
2:17 played the harlot with **o** gods,
2:19 by following **o** gods, to serve
7: 7 Let all the **o** people go, every
7:25 to Gideon on the **o** side
9:44 and the **o** two companies rushed
10: 8 of Israel who were on the **o**
10:13 have forsaken Me and served **o**
11:18 and encamped on the **o** side of
13:10 Man who came to me the **o** day
16: 7 and be like any **o** man."
16:11 and be like any **o** man."
16:17 and be like any **o** man."
16:20 at **o** times, and shake myself
16:29 one on his right and the **o** on
20:30 Gibeah as at the **o** times.
20:31 as at the **o** times, in the
20:31 goes up to Bethel and the **o** to
Ruth 1: 4 and the name of the **o** Ruth.
2:22 do not meet you in any **o** field.
4: 7 sandal and gave it to the **o**,
1 Sam 1: 2 and the name of the **o** Peninnah.
3:10 and called as at **o** times,
8: 8 served **o** gods—so they are doing
14: 1 garrison that is on the **o**
14: 4 a sharp rock on the **o** side.
14: 4 and the name of the **o** Seneh.
14: 5 and the **o** southward opposite
14:40 and I will be on the **o** side.
17: 3 on a mountain on the **o** side,
18:10 as at **o** times; but there was
19:21 he sent **o** messengers, and they
20:25 as at **o** times, on a seat by the
21: 9 For there is no **o** except that
23:26 David and his men on the **o** side
26:13 David went over to the **o** side,
26:19 saying, 'Go, serve **o** gods.'
28: 8 himself and put on **o** clothes,
30:20 they had driven before those **o**
31: 7 who were on the **o** side
31: 7 who were on the **o** side
2 Sam 2:13 and the **o** on the other side
2:13 and the other on the **o** side
4: 2 Baanah and the name of the **o**
12: 1 one rich and the **o** poor.
13:16 me away is worse than the **o**
14: 6 and the two fought with each **o**
14: 6 but the one struck the **o** and
17: 9 or in some **o** place. And it
1 Ki 3:22 Then the **o** woman said, "No!
3:23 and the **o** says, 'No! But your
3:25 half to one, and half to the **o**.
3:26 kill him!" But the **o** said,
4:12 as far as the **o** side of
6:24 and the **o** wing of the cherub
6:24 of one wing to the tip of the **o**.
6:25 And the **o** cherub was ten
6:26 and so was the **o** cherub.
6:27 and the wing of the **o** cherub
6:27 cherub touched the **o** wall.
6:27 And their wings touched each **o**
6:34 comprised the **o** folding door.
7:16 and the height of the **o** capital
7:17 and seven for the **o** capital.
7:18 and thus he did for the **o**
7:23 cubits from one brim to the **o**;
8:60 LORD is God; there is no **o**.
9: 6 but go and serve **o** gods and
9: 9 and have embraced **o** gods, and
10:20 been made for any **o** kingdom.
11: 4 turned his heart after **o** gods;
11:10 that he should not go after **o**
12:29 and the **o** he put in Dan.
14: 9 and made for yourself **o** gods
18:23 and I will prepare the **o** bull,
20:29 they encamped opposite each **o**
2 Ki 3:22 saw the water on the **o** side
5:17 or sacrifice to **o** gods,
10:21 was full from one end to the **o**.
10:24 his life for the life of the **o**.
12: 7 Jehoiada the priest and the **o**
17: 7 and they had feared **o** gods,
17:35 You shall not fear **o** gods, nor
17:37 you shall not fear **o** gods.
17:38 nor shall you fear **o** gods.
22:17 burned incense to **o** gods,
1 Chr 6:78 And on the **o** side of the Jordan,
9:33 were free from **o** duties;
11:21 honored than the **o** two men.
12:37 from the **o** side of the Jordan,
23:17 And Eliezer had no **o** sons, but
2 Chr 3:11 and the **o** wing was five
3:11 the wing of the **o** cherub;
3:12 one wing of the **o** cherub was
3:12 and the **o** wing also was five
3:12 the wing of the **o** cherub.
3:17 on the right hand and the **o** on
4: 2 cubits from one brim to the **o**;
7:19 and go and serve **o** gods, and
7:22 and embraced **o** gods, and
9:19 been made for any **o** kingdom.
13: 9 like the peoples of **o** lands?
28:25 to burn incense to **o** gods,
29:34 work was ended and until the **o**
32:13 all the peoples of **o** lands?
32:17 the gods of the nations of **o**
34:25 burned incense to **o** gods,
35:13 but the **o** holy offerings they
Ezra 1:10 and one thousand **o** articles.
2:31 the people of the **o** Elam, one
Neh 3:18 leader of the **o** half of the
3:20 repaired the **o** section,
4:16 while the **o** half held the
4:17 and with the **o** held a weapon.
5: 5 for **o** men have our lands and
7:33 the men of the **o** Nebo,
7:34 the sons of the **o** Elam, one
11: 1 were to dwell in **o** cities.
12:38 The **o** thanksgiving choir went
13:24 of one or the **o** people.
Esth 1: 7 being different from the **o**,
2:17 more than all the **o** women,
3: 8 different from all **o** people's,
4:13 any more than all the **o** Jews.
Job 8:12 It withers before any **o**
Ps 19: 6 And its circuit to the **o** end;
73: 5 are not in trouble as **o** men,
73: 5 are they plagued like **o** men.
Eccl 3:19 as one dies, so dies the **o**.
7:14 the one as well as the **o**,
7:18 not remove your hand from the **o**;
7:27 Adding one thing to the **o** to
Isa 44: 8 Indeed there is no **o** Rock;
45: 5 the LORD, and there is no **o**;
45: 6 the LORD, and there is no **o**;
45:14 in you, And there is no **o**;
45:14 There is no **o** God.'"
45:18 the LORD, and there is no **o**.
45:21 And there is no **o** God
45:22 I am God, and there is no **o**.
46: 9 I am God, and there is no **o**;
57: 8 yourself to those **o** than Me,
Jer 1:16 Burned incense to **o** gods, And
7: 6 or walk after **o** gods to your
7: 9 and walk after **o** gods whom you
7:18 drink offerings to **o** gods,
11:10 and they have gone after **o** gods
12:12 end of the land to the **o** end
13:10 and walk after **o** gods to serve
16:11 they have walked after **o** gods
16:13 there you shall serve **o** gods
19: 4 have burned incense in it to **o**
19:13 out drink offerings to **o** gods.
22: 9 and worshiped **o** gods and served
24: 2 and the **o** basket had very bad
25: 6 Do not go after **o** gods to serve
25:33 the earth even to the **o** end
26:22 and **o** men who went with him
32:20 and in Israel and among **o** men;
32:29 out drink offerings to **o** gods,
35:15 and do not go after **o** gods to
44: 3 incense and to serve **o** gods
44: 5 to burn no incense to **o** gods.
44: 8 burning incense to **o** gods in
44:15 had burned incense to **o** gods,
Ezek 1:23 one had two which covered the **o**
10: 9 wheel by each **o** cherub;
10:17 the **o** lifted itself up, for
15: 2 of the vine better than any **o**
16:34 You are the opposite of **o** women
20:32 the families in **o** countries,
40: 6 and the **o** threshold was one
40:10 on one side and three on the **o**;
40:13 chamber to the roof of the **o**;
40:40 and on the **o** side of the
40:44 and the **o** facing north at the
41: 1 cubits wide on the **o** side—the
41: 2 five cubits on the **o** side;
41: 6 three stories, one above the **o**,
41:15 one side and on the **o** side,
41:19 toward a palm tree on the **o**
41:24 two panels for the **o** door.
41:26 trees on one side and on the **o**,
42:14 They shall put on **o** garments;
44:19 and put on **o** garments; and in
45: 7 section on one side and the **o**
47: 7 trees on one side and the **o**.
48: 8 one of the **o** portions,
48:21 on one side and on the **o** of the
Dan 2:11 and there is no **o** who can tell
2:44 shall not be left to **o** people;
3:21 and their **o** garments, and were
3:29 because there is no **o** God who
5: 6 knees knocked against each **o**.
7: 3 sea, each different from the **o**.
7:20 and the **o** horn which came up,
7:23 from all **o** kingdoms,
8: 3 but one was higher than the **o**,
12: 5 on this riverbank and the **o** on
Hos 3: 1 who look to **o** gods and love
9: 1 with joy like **o** peoples, For
13:10 your King; Where is any **o**,
Joel 2:27 your God And there is no **o**.
Ob 11 you stood on the **o** side—In
Zech 4: 3 right of the bowl and the **o** at
11: 7 and the **o** I called Bonds; and I
11:14 Then I cut in two my **o** staff,
Mt 4:21 He saw two **o** brothers, James
5:39 turn the **o** to him also.
6:24 hate the one and love the **o**,
6:24 to the one and despise the **o**.
8:18 to depart to the **o** side.
8:28 When He had come to the **o** side,
12:13 was restored as whole as the **o**.
12:45 takes with him seven **o** spirits
14:22 go before Him to the **o** side,
16: 5 had come to the **o** side,
20:21 on Your right hand and the **o**
21:36 Again he sent **o** servants, more
21:41 vineyard to **o** vinedressers
22: 4 he sent out **o** servants, saying,
24:31 from one end of heaven to the **o**.
24:40 one will be taken and the **o**
24:41 one will be taken and the **o**
25:11 Afterward the **o** virgins came
25:20 and brought five **o** talents,
27:61 and the **o** Mary, sitting
28: 1 Mary Magdalene and the **o** Mary
Mk 3: 5 was restored as whole as the **o**.
4: 8 But **o** seed fell on good ground
4:19 and the desires for **o** things
4:35 cross over to the **o** side."
4:36 And **o** little boats were also
5: 1 Then they came to the **o** side of
5:21 again by boat to the **o** side,
6:45 boat and go before Him to the **o**
7: 4 And there are many **o** things
7: 8 and many **o** such things you
8:13 departed to the **o** side.
10: 1 region of Judea by the **o** side
10:37 hand and the **o** on Your left,
12:31 There is no **o** commandment
12:32 and there is no **o** but He.
15:27 one on His right and the **o** on
15:41 and many **o** women who came up
Lk 3:18 And with many **o** exhortations he
4:43 of God to the **o** cities
5: 7 partners in the **o** boat
6:10 was restored as whole as the **o**.
6:29 offer the **o** also. And from him
7:41 denarii, and the **o** fifty.
8:22 Let us cross over to the **o** side
10:31 he passed by on the **o** side.
10:32 and passed by on the **o** side.
11:26 and takes with him seven **o**
13: 2 sinners than all **o** Galileans,
13: 4 worse sinners than all **o** men
14:32 while the **o** is still a great
16:13 hate the one and love the **o**,
16:13 to the one and despise the **o**.
17:24 under heaven shines to the **o**
17:34 taken and the **o** will be left.
17:35 will be taken and the **o** left.
17:36 will be taken and the **o** left."
18:10 one a Pharisee and the **o** a tax
18:11 thank You that I am not like **o**
18:14 justified rather than the **o**;
22:65 And many **o** things they

23:12 became friends with each **o**,
23:12 had been at enmity with each **o**.
23:33 on the right hand and the **o** on
23:40 But the **o**, answering,
24: 1 and certain **o** women with
24:10 and the **o** women with them, who
Jn 6:22 standing on the **o** side
6:22 saw that there was no **o** boat
6:23 **o** boats came from Tiberias,
6:25 they found Him on the **o** side
10: 1 but climbs up some **o** way, the
10:16 And **o** sheep I have which are not
18:16 Then the **o** disciple, who was
19:32 first and of the **o** who was
20: 2 and to the **o** disciple, whom
20: 3 and the **o** disciple, and were
20: 4 and the **o** disciple outran Peter
20: 8 Then the **o** disciple, who came to
20:12 one at the head and the **o** at
20:25 The **o** disciples therefore said
20:30 Jesus did many **o** signs
21: 8 But the **o** disciples came in the
21:25 And there are also many **o** things
Acts 2: 4 to speak with **o** tongues,
2:40 And with many **o** words he
4:12 is there salvation in any **o**,
4:12 for there is no **o** name under
5:29 But Peter and the **o** apostles
8:34 of himself or of some **o** man?"
19:39 But if you have any **o** inquiry to
23: 6 Sadducees and the **o** Pharisees,
26:22 saying no **o** things than those
27: 1 Paul and some **o** prisoners
Rom 1:13 just as among the **o** Gentiles.
8:39 nor any **o** created thing, shall
13: 9 is any **o** commandment,
1 Cor 1:16 know whether I baptized any **o**.
3:11 For no **o** foundation can anyone
4: 6 on behalf of one against the **o**.
8: 4 and that there is no **o** God
9: 5 as do also the **o** apostles, the
10:29 not your own, but that of the **o**.
14:17 but the **o** is not edified.
14:21 **o** tongues and other lips
14:21 of other tongues and **o**
15:37 perhaps wheat or some **o** grain.
2 Cor 1:13 are not writing any **o** things
2:16 and to the **o** the aroma of life
10:15 in **o** men's labors, but having
11: 8 I robbed **o** churches, taking
11:28 besides the **o** things, what comes
12:13 in which you were inferior to **o**
Gal 1: 8 preach any **o** gospel to you than
1: 9 if anyone preaches any **o** gospel
1:19 But I saw none of the **o** apostles
4:22 the **o** by a freewoman.
5:10 that you will have no **o** mind;
Eph 3: 5 which in **o** ages was not made
1 Th 5:11 Therefore comfort each **o** and
2 Th 1: 3 you all abounds toward each **o**,
1 Tim 1: 3 they teach no **o** doctrine,
1:10 and if there is any **o** thing
5:22 nor share in **o** people's sins;
Heb 7:19 on the **o** hand, there is the
Jas 5:12 or by earth or with any **o** oath.
1 Pe 4:15 or as a busybody in **o** people's
Rev 2:24 I will put on you no **o** burden.
17:10 and the **o** has not yet come.

OTHER'S (2/2)

Zech 11: 9 are left eat each **o** flesh."
1 Cor 10:24 but each one the **o** well-being.

OTHERS (95/94)

Josh 8:22 Then the **o** came out of the city
11:19 All the **o** they took in
1 Ki 9:23 ***O*** were chiefs of the officials
2 Chr 8:10 And **o** were chiefs of the
20: 1 and **o** with them besides the
21: 4 and also **o** of the princes of
32:22 and from the hand of all **o**,
34:12 ***O*** of the Levites, all of whom
Ezra 10:25 And **o** of Israel: of the sons of
Neh 2:16 or the **o** who did the work.
Job 8:19 And out of the earth **o** will
24:24 out of the way like all **o**;
31:10 And let **o** bow down over her.
34:24 And sets **o** in their place.
34:26 men In the open sight of **o**,
Ps 49:10 And leave their wealth to **o**.
Prov 5: 9 Lest you give your honor to **o**,
27:21 a man is valued by what **o**
Eccl 7:22 That even you have cursed **o**.
Isa 35: 8 But it shall be for **o**.
49:20 After you have lost the **o**,
56: 8 to him ***O*** besides those who
Jer 6:12 shall be turned over to **o**,
8:10 I will give their wives to **o**,
Ezek 9: 5 To the **o** He said in my hearing,
42:11 as long and as wide as the **o**,
44: 8 but you have set **o** to keep
Dan 2:40 in pieces and crush all the **o**.
7:19 was different from all the **o**,
11: 4 even for **o** besides these.
12: 5 and there stood two **o**,
Mt 5:47 what do you do more than **o**?
13: 8 But **o** fell on good ground and
15:30 blind, mute, maimed, and many **o**;
16:14 and **o** Jeremiah or one of the
20: 3 about the third hour and saw **o**
20: 6 hour he went out and found **o**
21: 8 **o** cut down branches from the
23:23 without leaving the **o** undone.
26:67 and **o** struck Him with the
27:42 'He saved **o**; Himself He
Mk 6:15 ***O*** said, "It is Elijah."
6:15 And **o** said, "It is the
8:28 but some say, Elijah; and **o**,
11: 8 and **o** cut down leafy branches
12: 5 and him they killed; and many **o**,
12: 9 and give the vineyard to **o**.
15:31 the scribes, said, "He saved **o**;
Lk 5:29 number of tax collectors and **o**
8: 3 and many **o** who provided for Him
8: 8 But **o** fell on good ground,
9: 8 and by **o** that one of the old
9:19 and **o** say that one of the old
10: 1 the Lord appointed seventy **o**
11:16 ***O***, testing Him, sought from
11:42 without leaving the **o** undone.
18: 9 were righteous, and despised **o**:
20:16 and give the vineyard to **o**.
23:32 There were also two **o**,
23:35 sneered, saying, "He saved **o**;
Jn 4:38 **o** have labored, and you have
7:12 **o** said, "No, on the contrary,
7:41 ***O*** said, "This is the Christ."
9: 9 ***O*** said, "He is like him."
9:16 ***O*** said, "How can a man who
10:21 ***O*** said, "These are not the
12:29 ***O*** said, "An angel has spoken
18:34 or did **o** tell you this
19:18 and two **o** with Him, one on
21: 2 and two **o** of His disciples were
Acts 2:13 ***O*** mocking said, "They are full
15: 2 and Barnabas and certain **o** of
15:35 with many **o** also.
17:18 ***O*** said, "He seems to be a
17:32 while **o** said, "We will hear
17:34 Damaris, and **o** with them.
1 Cor 9: 2 If I am not an apostle to **o**,
9:12 If **o** are partakers of this
9:27 lest, when I have preached to **o**,
11:21 his own supper ahead of **o**;
14:19 that I may teach **o** also, than
14:29 and let the **o** judge.
2 Cor 3: 1 Or do we need, as some **o**,
8: 8 your love by the diligence of **o**.
8:13 For I do not mean that **o**
Eph 2: 3 of wrath, just as the **o**.
Phil 2: 3 of mind let each esteem **o**
2: 4 but also for the interests of **o**.
1 Th 2: 6 men, either from you or from **o**,
4:13 lest you sorrow as **o** who have
5: 6 as **o** do, but let us watch and
2 Tim 2: 2 men who will be able to teach **o**
Heb 11:35 And **o** were tortured, not
11:36 Still **o** had trial of mockings
Jude 23 but **o** save with fear, pulling

OTHERWISE (15/14)

Lev 21: 4 ***O*** he shall not defile himself,
2 Sam 18:13 ***O*** I would have dealt falsely
1 Ki 1:21 ***O*** it will happen, when my lord
Mt 6: 1 ***O*** you have no reward from your
Lk 5:36 **o** the new makes a tear, and
Rom 11: 6 **o** grace is no longer grace.
11: 6 **o** work is no longer work.
11:22 ***O*** you also will be cut off.
1 Cor 7:14 **o** your children would be
14:16 ***O***, if you bless with
15:29 ***O***, what will they do
2 Cor 11:16 If **o**, at least receive me
Phil 3:15 and if in anything you think **o**,
1 Tim 5:25 and those that are **o** cannot be
6: 3 If anyone teaches **o** and does

OTHNI (1/1)

1 Chr 26: 7 The sons of Shemaiah were ***O***,

OTHNIEL (7/6)

Josh 15:17 So ***O*** the son of Kenaz, the
Judg 1:13 And ***O*** the son of Kenaz, Caleb's
3: 9 ***O*** the son of Kenaz, Caleb's
3:11 Then ***O*** the son of Kenaz died.
1 Chr 4:13 The sons of Kenaz were ***O*** and
4:13 The sons of ***O*** were Hathath,
27:15 Heldai the Netophathite, of ***O***;

OUCHES (KJV) See SETTINGS

OUGHT (52/52)

Gen 20: 9 have done deeds to me that **o**
34: 7 a thing which **o** not to be done.
Lev 4: 2 the LORD in anything which **o**
4:27 the LORD in anything which **o**
1 Ki 2: 9 a wise man and know what you **o**
1 Chr 12:32 to know what Israel **o** to do,
Ps 76:11 bring presents to Him who **o** to
Mt 23:23 These you **o** to have done,
25:27 So you **o** to have deposited my
Mk 13:14 standing where it **o** not"
Lk 11:42 These you **o** to have done,
12:12 in that very hour what you **o**
13:14 are six days on which men **o** to
13:16 So **o** not this woman, being a
18: 1 that men always **o** to pray and
24:26 ***O*** not the Christ to have
Jn 4:20 is the place where one **o** to
13:14 you also **o** to wash one
19: 7 and according to our law He **o**
Acts 5:29 We **o** to obey God rather than
17:29 we **o** not to think that the
19:36 you **o** to be quiet and do
21:21 saying that they **o** not to
24:19 They **o** to have been here before
25:10 where I **o** to be judged. To the
Rom 8:26 what we should pray for as we **o**,
12: 3 himself more highly than he **o**
15: 1 We then who are strong **o** to bear
1 Cor 8: 2 he knows nothing yet as he **o** to
11: 7 For a man indeed **o** not to cover
11:10 For this reason the woman **o** to
2 Cor 2: 3 over those from whom I **o** to
2: 7 you **o** rather to forgive and
12:11 For I **o** to have been commended
12:14 For the children **o** not to lay
Eph 5:28 So husbands **o** to love their own
6:20 boldly, as I **o** to speak.
Col 4: 4 it manifest, as I **o** to speak.
4: 6 that you may know how you **o** to
1 Th 4: 1 you received from us how you **o**
2 Th 3: 7 you yourselves know how you **o**
1 Tim 3:15 so that you may know how you **o**
5:13 saying things which they **o** not.
Titus 1:11 teaching things which they **o**
Heb 5:12 For though by this time you **o**
Jas 3:10 these things **o** not to be so.
4:15 Instead you **o** to say, "If the
2 Pe 3:11 what manner of persons **o** you
1 Jn 2: 6 He who says he abides in Him **o**
3:16 And we also **o** to lay down our
4:11 we also **o** to love one another.
3 Jn 8 We therefore **o** to receive such,

OUR (1158/896) See APPENDIX

OURS (18/18) See APPENDIX

OURSELVES (62/54) See APPENDIX

OUT (2498/2294) See APPENDIX

OUTBREAK (3/3)

Deut 24: 8 Take heed in an **o** of leprosy,
2 Sam 6: 8 angry because of the LORD's **o**
1 Chr 13:11 angry because of the LORD's **o**

OUTBURSTS (2/2)

2 Cor 12:20 **o** of wrath, selfish ambitions,
Gal 5:20 **o** of wrath, selfish ambitions,

OUTCAST (3/3) OUTCASTS

Jer 30:17 Because they called you an **o**
Mic 4: 6 I will gather the **o** And those
4: 7 And the **o** a strong nation;

OUTCASTS (7/7) OUTCAST

Ps 147: 2 He gathers together the **o** of
Isa 11:12 And will assemble the **o** of
16: 3 middle of the day; Hide the **o**,
16: 4 Let My **o** dwell with you, O
27:13 And they who are **o** in the land
56: 8 who gathers the **o** of Israel,
Jer 49:36 be no nations where the **o** of

OUTCOME (2/2)

Acts 5:24 they wondered what the **o** would
Heb 13: 7 considering the **o** of their

OUTCRY (8/8)

Gen 18:20 Because the **o** against Sodom and
18:21 altogether according to the **o**
19:13 because the **o** against them has
1 Sam 4:14 Eli heard the noise of the **o**,
Neh 5: 1 And there was a great **o** of the
5: 6 angry when I heard their **o** and
Ps 144:14 That there be no **o** in our
Acts 23: 9 Then there arose a loud **o**.

OUTER (33/32)

Ex 26: 4 you shall do on the **o** edge
36:11 likewise he did on the **o** edge
Num 23:13 you shall see only the **o** part
1 Ki 6:29 the inner and **o** sanctuaries,
6:30 the inner and **o** sanctuaries.
2 Ki 16:18 removed the king's **o** entrance
Esth 6: 4 had just entered the **o** court
Job 41:13 Who can remove his **o** coat?
Isa 3:22 The **o** garments, the purses,
Ezek 10: 5 was heard even in the **o** court,
40:17 brought me into the **o** court;
40:20 On the **o** court was also a
40:31 Its archways faced the **o** court,
40:34 Its archways faced the **o** court,
40:37 Its gateposts faced the **o** court,
40:40 At the **o** side of the vestibule,
41: 9 The thickness of the **o** wall of
42: 1 me out into the **o** court,
42: 3 the pavement of the **o** court,
42: 7 toward the **o** court; its length
42: 8 chambers toward the **o** court
42: 9 into them from the **o** court.

42:14 holy chamber into the o court;
44: 1 brought me back to the o gate
44:19 When they go out to the o court,
44:19 to the o court to the people,
46:20 them out into the o court
46:21 me out into the o court
47: 2 outside to the o gateway
Mt 8:12 be cast out into o darkness.
22:13 and cast him into o darkness;
25:30 servant into the o darkness.
Jn 21: 7 he put on his o garment

OUTERMOST (2/2)

Ex 26:10 edge of the curtain that is o
36:17 edge of the curtain that is o

OUTGOINGS (1/1)

Ps 65: 8 You make the o of the morning

OUTLANDISH (KJV) See PAGAN

OUTLET (1/1)

2 Chr 32:30 also stopped the water o of

OUTLIVED (2/2)

Josh 24:31 the days of the elders who o
Judg 2: 7 the days of the elders who o

OUTMOST (KJV) See SECOND

OUTPOST (2/2)

Judg 7:11 Purah his servant to the o of
7:19 were with him came to the o

OUTRAGE (2/2)

Judg 19:23 my house, do not commit this o.
20: 6 they committed lewdness and o

OUTRAN (2/2)

2 Sam 18:23 and o the Cushite.
Jn 20: 4 and the other disciple o Peter

OUTSIDE (138/136)

Gen 6:14 and cover it inside and o with
9:22 and told his two brothers o.
15: 5 Then He brought him o and said,
19:16 brought him out and set him o
19:17 when they had brought them o,
24:11 he made his camels kneel down o
24:31 the LORD! Why do you stand o?
39:12 in her hand, and fled and ran o.
39:13 garment in her hand and fled o,
39:15 with me, and fled and went o.
39:18 his garment with me and fled o.
Ex 12:46 not carry any of the flesh o
21:19 rises again and walks about o
26:35 You shall set the table o the
27:21 o the veil which is before the
29:14 you shall burn with fire o the
33: 7 took his tent and pitched it o
33: 7 of meeting which was o the
37: 2 it with pure gold inside and o,
40:22 tabernacle, o the veil;
Lev 4:12 whole bull he shall carry o
4:21 'Then he shall carry the bull o
6:11 and carry the ashes o the camp
8:17 he burned with fire o the camp,
8:33 And you shall not go o the door
9:11 the hide he burned with fire o
13:46 his dwelling shall be o the
13:55 whether the damage is o or
14: 8 and shall stay o his tent seven
14:40 them into an unclean place o
14:41 pour out in an unclean place o
14:45 and he shall carry them o the
14:53 let the living bird loose o
16:27 shall be carried o the camp.
17: 3 or who kills it o the camp,
24: 3 O the veil of the Testimony, in
24:14 Take o the camp him who has
24:23 and they took o the camp him
Num 5: 3 you shall put them o the camp,
5: 4 and put them o the camp; as the
15:35 shall stone him with stones o
15:36 the congregation brought him o
19: 3 that he may take it o the camp,
19: 9 and store them o the camp in a
31:13 went to meet them o the camp.
31:19 remain o the camp seven days;
35: 5 And you shall measure o the city
35:26 manslayer at any time goes o
35:27 avenger of blood finds him o
Deut 23:10 then he shall go o the camp;
23:12 Also you shall have a place o
23:13 and when you sit down o,
24:11 "You shall stand o,
25: 5 not be married to a stranger o
32:25 The sword shall destroy o;
Josh 2:19 shall be that whoever goes o
6:23 her relatives and left them o
1 Sam 9:26 arose, and both of them went o,
1 Ki 6: 6 narrow ledges around the o of
7: 9 and also on the o to the great
7:31 one and a half cubits in o
8: 8 they could not be seen from o.
21:13 Then they took him o the
2 Ki 10:24 for himself eighty men on the o,
11:15 Take her o under guard, and slay
23: 4 and he burned them o Jerusalem
23: 6 to the Brook Kidron o
1 Chr 26:29 and judges over Israel o
2 Chr 5: 9 they could not be seen from o.
23:14 Take her o under guard, and slay
24: 8 and set it o at the gate of the
32: 3 from the springs which were o
32: 5 and built another wall o;
33:14 After this he built a wall o
Ezra 10:13 and we are not able to stand o.
Neh 11:16 oversight of the business o of
13:20 of all kinds of wares lodged o
Ps 31:11 Those who see me o flee from
Prov 1:20 Wisdom calls aloud o;
7:12 At times she was o,
22:13 There is a lion o! I shall be
24:27 Prepare your o work, Make it
Song 8: 1 If I should find you o,
Isa 33: 7 their valiant ones shall cry o,
Jer 6:11 pour it out on the children o,
9:21 no longer to be o! And the
21: 4 the Chaldeans who besiege you o
Lam 1:20 O the sword bereaves, At home
Ezek 2:10 on the inside and on the o,
7:15 The sword is o, And the
40: 5 was a wall all around the o of
40:44 O the inner gate were the
41:17 to the inner room, as well as o,
41:17 wall all around, inside and o,
41:25 on the front of the vestibule o.
42: 7 And a wall which was o ran
43:21 temple, o the sanctuary.
46: 2 of the gateway from the o,
47: 2 and led me around on the o to
Hos 7: 1 band of robbers takes spoil o.
Mt 9:25 But when the crowd was put o,
12:46 His mother and brothers stood o,
12:47 Your brothers are standing o,
23:25 For you cleanse the o of the
23:26 that the o of them may be clean
26:69 Now Peter sat o in the
Mk 1:45 but was o in deserted places;
3:31 and standing o they sent to
3:32 mother and Your brothers are o
4:11 of God; but to those who are o,
5:40 But when He had put them all o,
7:15 that enters a man from o which
7:18 whatever enters a man from o
11: 4 the colt tied by the door o on
Lk 1:10 of the people was praying o at
8:20 Your brothers are standing o,
8:54 But He put them all o,
11:39 Now you Pharisees make the o of
11:40 Did not He who made the o make
13:25 and you begin to stand o and
13:33 that a prophet should perish o
Jn 18:16 But Peter stood at the door o.
20:11 But Mary stood o by the tomb
Acts 5:23 and the guards standing o
5:34 them to put the apostles o for
1 Cor 5:12 judging those also who are o?
5:13 But those who are o God judges.
6:18 Every sin that a man does is o
2 Cor 7: 5 O were conflicts, inside were
Col 4: 5 wisdom toward those who are o,
1 Th 4:12 properly toward those who are o,
1 Tim 3: 7 testimony among those who are o,
Heb 13:11 are burned o the camp.
13:12 suffered o the gate.
13:13 o the camp, bearing His
Rev 11: 2 leave out the court which is o
14:20 the winepress was trampled o
22:15 But o are dogs and sorcerers

OUTSIDER (11/11) FOREIGNER

Ex 29:33 but an o shall not eat them,
30:33 whoever puts any of it on an o,
Lev 22:10 No o shall eat the holy
22:12 daughter is married to an o,
22:13 but no o shall eat it.
Num 1:51 The o who comes near shall be
3:10 but the o who comes near shall
3:38 but the o who came near was to
16:40 children of Israel that no o,
18: 4 but an o shall not come near
18: 7 but the o who comes near shall

OUTSKIRTS (6/6)

Num 11: 1 and consumed some in the o of
1 Sam 9:27 they were going down to the o
14: 2 And Saul was sitting in the o of
2 Sam 15:17 after him, and stopped at the o.
2 Ki 7: 5 when they had come to the o of
7: 8 these lepers came to the o of

OUTSTRETCHED (18/18)

Ex 6: 6 and I will redeem you with an o
Deut 4:34 by a mighty hand and an o arm,
5:15 by a mighty hand and by an o
7:19 the mighty hand and the o arm,
9:29 mighty power and by Your o arm.
11: 2 and His mighty hand and His o
26: 8 a mighty hand and with an o
1 Ki 8:42 and Your strong hand and Your o
2 Ki 17:36 with great power and an o arm,
2 Chr 6:32 and Your mighty hand and Your o
Ps 136:12 and with an o arm, For His
Isa 3:16 And walk with o necks And
Jer 21: 5 fight against you with an o
27: 5 by My great power and by My o
32:17 by Your great power and o arm.
32:21 with a strong hand and an o
Ezek 20:33 with an o arm, and with fury
20:34 with an o arm, and with fury

OUTWARD (6/6) OUTWARDLY

Num 35: 4 from the wall of the city o a
1 Sam 16: 7 for man looks at the o
Rom 2:28 circumcision that which is o
2 Cor 4:16 Even though our o man is
10: 7 at things according to the o
1 Pe 3: 3 let your adornment be merely o—

OUTWARDLY (3/3) OUTWARD

Mt 23:27 which indeed appear beautiful o,
23:28 Even so you also o appear
Rom 2:28 he is not a Jew who is one o,

OUTWENT (KJV) See ARRIVED (BEFORE)

OUTWIT (1/1)

Ps 89:22 The enemy shall not o him,

OVEN (13/13)

Gen 15:17 there appeared a smoking o and
Lev 2: 4 a grain offering baked in the o,
7: 9 that is baked in the o and all
11:35 whether it is an o or
26:26 shall bake your bread in one o,
Ps 21: 9 shall make them as a fiery o
Lam 5:10 Our skin is hot as an o,
Hos 7: 4 Like an o heated by a
7: 6 prepare their heart like an o,
7: 7 They are all hot, like an o,
Mal 4: 1 is coming, Burning like an o,
Mt 6:30 tomorrow is thrown into the o,
Lk 12:28 tomorrow is thrown into the o,

OVENS (3/3)

Ex 8: 3 on your people, into your o,
Neh 3:11 as well as the Tower of the O.
12:38 going past the Tower of the O

OVER (1022/895) See APPENDIX

OVERALL (2/2)

2 Chr 3:11 twenty cubits in o length:
3:13 spanned twenty cubits o.

OVERBOARD (2/2)

Acts 27:19 we threw the ship's tackle o
27:43 who could swim should jump o

OVERCAME (2/2) OVERCOME

Rev 3:21 as I also o and sat down with
12:11 And they o him by the blood of

OVERCHARGE (KJV) See SEVERE

OVERCOME (21/20) OVERCAME, OVERCOMES

Num 13:30 for we are well able to o it."
1 Sam 7:10 confused them that they were o
2 Ki 16: 5 besieged Ahaz but could not o
Song 6: 5 For they have o me. Your hair
Isa 28: 1 To those who are o with wine!
Jer 23: 9 And like a man whom wine has o,
Mk 5:42 And they were o with great
Jn 16:33 I have o the world."
Acts 20: 9 He was o by sleep; and as Paul
Rom 3: 4 And may o when You are
12:21 Do not be o by evil, but
12:21 but o evil with good.
2 Pe 2:19 for by whom a person is o,
2:20 again entangled in them and o,
1 Jn 2:13 Because you have o the wicked
2:14 And you have o the wicked
4: 4 and have o them, because He who
5: 4 this is the victory that has o
Rev 11: 7 o them, and kill them.
13: 7 war with the saints and to o
17:14 and the Lamb will o them, for

OVERCOMES (11/11) OVERCOME

Lk 11:22 than he comes upon him and o
1 Jn 5: 4 For whatever is born of God o
5: 5 Who is he who o the world, but
Rev 2: 7 To him who o I will give to eat
2:11 He who o shall not be hurt by
2:17 To him who o I will give some
2:26 'And he who o, and keeps
3: 5 He who o shall be clothed in
3:12 'He who o, I will make
3:21 To him who o I will grant to sit
21: 7 He who o shall inherit all

O

OVERCOMING (1/1)

Job 41: 9 any hope of **o** him is false;

OVERDRIVE (KJV) See DRIVE

OVEREXTENDING (1/1)

2 Cor 10:14 For we are not **o** ourselves

OVERFLOW (14/14) OVERFLOWING, OVERFLOWS

Deut 11: 4 the waters of the Red Sea **o**
Ps 69: 2 Where the floods **o** me.
69:15 Let not the floodwater **o** me,
Prov 3:10 And your vats will **o** with new
Isa 8: 8 He will **o** and pass over,
10:22 destruction decreed shall **o**
23:10 ***O*** through your land like the
28:17 And the waters will **o** the
43: 2 they shall not **o** you. When you
Jer 47: 2 They shall **o** the land and all
Lam 3:48 My eyes **o** with rivers of water
Joel 2:24 And the vats shall **o** with new
3:13 winepress is full, The vats **o**—
Jas 1:21 lay aside all filthiness and **o**

OVERFLOWED (3/3)

Josh 4:18 returned to their place and **o**
1 Chr 12:15 when it had **o** all its banks;
Ps 78:20 gushed out, And the streams **o**.

OVERFLOWING (10/10) OVERFLOW

Job 38:25 has divided a channel for the **o**
Ps 45: 1 My heart is **o** with a good
Isa 28: 2 a flood of mighty waters **o**,
28:15 When the **o** scourge passes
28:18 When the **o** scourge passes
30:28 His breath is like an **o** stream,
34: 6 It is made **o** with fatness,
Jer 47: 2 And shall be an **o** flood;
Nah 1: 8 But with an **o** flood He will
Hab 3:10 The **o** of the water passed by.

OVERFLOWS (2/2) OVERFLOW

Josh 3:15 of the water (for the Jordan **o**
Lam 1:16 my eye **o** with water; Because

OVERGROWN (1/1)

Prov 24:31 all **o** with thorns; Its surface

OVERLAID (36/32)

Ex 26:32 four pillars of acacia wood **o**
36:34 He **o** the boards with gold, made
36:34 and **o** the bars with gold.
36:36 and **o** them with gold, with
36:38 And he **o** their capitals and
37: 2 He **o** it with pure gold inside
37: 4 and **o** them with gold.
37:11 And he **o** it with pure gold, and
37:15 and **o** them with gold.
37:26 And he **o** it with pure gold:
37:28 and **o** them with gold.
38: 2 And he **o** it with bronze.
38: 6 and **o** them with bronze.
38:28 **o** their capitals, and made
1 Ki 6:20 He **o** it with pure gold, and
6:20 and **o** the altar of cedar.
6:21 So Solomon **o** the inside of the
6:21 and **o** it with gold.
6:22 The whole temple he **o** with gold,
6:22 also he **o** with gold the entire
6:28 Also he **o** the cherubim with
6:30 the floor of the temple he **o**
6:32 and **o** them with gold; and he
6:35 and **o** them with gold applied
10:18 and **o** it with pure gold.
2 Ki 18:16 Hezekiah king of Judah had **o**,
2 Chr 3: 4 He **o** the inside with pure gold.
3: 5 with cypress which he **o** with
3: 7 He also **o** the house—the beams
3: 8 He **o** it with six hundred
3: 9 and he **o** the upper area with
3:10 and **o** them with gold.
4: 9 and he **o** these doors with
9:17 and **o** it with pure gold.
Hab 2:19 it is **o** with gold and silver,
Heb 9: 4 and the ark of the covenant **o**

OVERLAY (15/13)

Ex 25:11 And you shall **o** it with pure
25:11 inside and out you shall **o** it,
25:13 and **o** them with gold.
25:24 And you shall **o** it with pure
25:28 and **o** them with gold, that the
26:29 You shall **o** the boards with
26:29 and **o** the bars with gold.
26:37 and **o** them with gold; their
27: 2 And you shall **o** it with bronze.
27: 6 and **o** them with bronze.
30: 3 And you shall **o** its top, its
30: 5 and **o** them with gold.
38:17 and the **o** of their capitals
38:19 and the **o** of their capitals and

1 Chr 29: 4 to **o** the walls of the houses;

OVERLIVED (KJV) See (OUT) LIVED

OVERLOOK (1/1) OVERLOOKED

Prov 19:11 And his glory is to **o** a

OVERLOOKED (1/1) OVERLOOK

Acts 17:30 these times of ignorance God **o**,

OVERLOOKING (1/1)

2 Chr 20:24 to a place **o** the wilderness,

OVERLOOKS (2/2)

Num 23:28 that **o** the wasteland.
1 Sam 13:18 the road of the border that **o**

OVERLY (3/2)

Eccl 7:16 Do not be **o** righteous, Nor be
7:16 Nor be **o** wise: Why should you
7:17 Do not be **o** wicked, Nor be

OVERMUCH (KJV) See (TOO) MUCH

OVERNIGHT (3/3)

Deut 16: 4 first day at twilight remain **o**
21:23 his body shall not remain **o** on
24:12 you shall not keep his pledge **o**.

OVERPASS (KJV) See SURPASS

OVERPAST (KJV) See PASSED

OVERPLUS (KJV) See REMAINDER

OVERPOWER (4/4) OVERPOWERED

Num 22:11 perhaps I shall be able to **o**
Judg 16: 5 and by what means we may **o**
Esth 9: 1 of the Jews had hoped to **o**
Job 15:24 They **o** him, like a king ready

OVERPOWERED (5/5) OVERPOWER

Esth 9: 1 in that the Jews themselves **o**
Eccl 4:12 Though one may be **o** by another,
Lam 1:13 And it **o** them; He has spread
Dan 6:24 and the lions **o** them, and broke
Acts 19:16 **o** them, and prevailed against

OVERRULE (1/1)

Num 30:11 response to her and did not **o**

OVERRULED (1/1)

Num 30: 5 because her father **o** her.

OVERRULES (2/2)

Num 30: 5 But if her father **o** her on the
30: 8 But if her husband **o** her on the

OVERRUN (1/1)

Zeph 2: 9 ***O*** with weeds and saltpits,

OVERSEE (4/4) OVERSEER, OVERSIGHT

2 Ki 22: 9 who **o** the house of the LORD."
2 Chr 2: 2 thousand six hundred to **o** them.
Ezra 3: 8 years old and above to **o** the
3: 9 arose as one to **o** those working

OVERSEER (8/8) OVERSEE

Gen 39: 4 Then he made him **o** of his
39: 5 time that he had made him **o**
1 Chr 26:24 was **o** of the treasuries.
Neh 11: 9 the son of Zichri was their **o**,
11:14 Their **o** was Zabdiel the son of
11:22 Also the **o** of the Levites at
Prov 6: 7 captain, ***O*** or ruler,
1 Pe 2:25 returned to the Shepherd and ***O***

OVERSEERS (8/8)

2 Ki 22: 5 who are the **o** in the house of
2 Chr 2:18 three thousand six hundred **o**
31:13 and Benaiah were **o** under the
34:12 Their **o** were Jahath and
34:13 the burden bearers and were **o**
34:17 it into the hand of the **o** and
Acts 20:28 the Holy Spirit has made you **o**,
1 Pe 5: 2 is among you, serving as **o**,

OVERSHADOW (1/1) OVERSHADOWED, OVERSHADOWING

Lk 1:35 the power of the Highest will **o**

OVERSHADOWED (6/6) OVERSHADOW

1 Ki 8: 7 and the cherubim **o** the ark and
1 Chr 28:18 spread their wings and **o** the
2 Chr 5: 8 and the cherubim **o** the ark and
Mt 17: 5 a bright cloud **o** them;
Mk 9: 7 And a cloud came and **o** them;
Lk 9:34 a cloud came and **o** them;

OVERSHADOWING (1/1) OVERSHADOW

Heb 9: 5 it were the cherubim of glory **o**

OVERSIGHT (8/8) OVERSEE

Gen 43:12 your sacks; perhaps it was an **o**.
Num 3:32 with **o** of those who kept
4:16 the **o** of all the tabernacle, of
2 Ki 12:11 who had the **o** of the house of
1 Chr 26:30 had the **o** of Israel on the west
2 Chr 23:18 Also Jehoiada appointed the **o** of
34:10 of the foremen who had the **o**
Neh 11:16 had the **o** of the business

OVERSPREAD (1/1)

Job 15:29 Nor will his possessions **o** the

OVERSPREADS (1/1)

Isa 40:19 The goldsmith **o** it with gold,

OVERTAKE (25/24) OVERTAKEN, OVERTOOK

Gen 19:19 lest some evil **o** me and I die.
44: 4 and when you **o** them, say to
Ex 15: 9 said, 'I will pursue, I will **o**,
Deut 19: 6 pursue the manslayer and **o** him,
28: 2 shall come upon you and **o** you,
28:15 will come upon you and **o** you:
28:45 come upon you and pursue and **o**
Josh 2: 5 for you may **o** them."
1 Sam 30: 8 Shall I **o** them?" And He
30: 8 for you shall surely **o** them
2 Sam 15:14 lest he **o** us suddenly and bring
Job 27:20 Terrors **o** him like a flood;
Ps 7: 5 Let the enemy pursue me and **o**
Prov 12:21 No grave trouble will **o** the
Isa 59: 9 Nor does righteousness **o** us;
Jer 42:16 sword which you feared shall **o**
Lam 1: 3 All her persecutors **o** her in
Hos 2: 7 But not **o** them; Yes, she will
10: 9 of iniquity Did not **o** them.
Am 9:10 The calamity shall not **o** nor
9:13 When the plowman shall **o** the
Zech 1: 6 Did they not **o** your fathers?
Jn 12:35 lest darkness **o** you; he who
Acts 8:29 Go near and **o** this chariot."
1 Th 5: 4 so that this Day should **o** you

OVERTAKEN (5/5) OVERTAKE

Ps 18:37 have pursued my enemies and **o**
40:12 My iniquities have **o** me, so
119:143 Trouble and anguish have **o** me,
1 Cor 10:13 No temptation has **o** you except
Gal 6: 1 if a man is **o** in any trespass,

OVERTAKING (1/1)

1 Chr 21:12 sword of your enemies **o** you,

OVERTHREW (11/10) OVERTHROW

Gen 19:25 So He **o** those cities, all the
19:29 when He **o** the cities in which
Ex 14:27 So the LORD **o** the Egyptians in
Deut 29:23 which the LORD **o** in His anger
1 Chr 20: 1 And Joab defeated Rabbah and **o**
Ps 136:15 But **o** Pharaoh and his army in
Isa 13:19 Will be as when God **o** Sodom
Jer 20:16 the cities Which the LORD **o**,
50:40 As God **o** Sodom and Gomorrah
Am 4:11 I **o** some of you, As God
4:11 As God **o** Sodom and Gomorrah,

OVERTHROW (17/16) OVERTHREW, OVERTHROWN, OVERTHROWS

Gen 19:21 in that I will not **o** this city
19:29 Lot out of the midst of the **o**,
Ex 23:24 but you shall utterly **o** them
Deut 29:23 like the **o** of Sodom and
2 Sam 10: 3 spy it out, and to **o** it?"
11:25 and **o** it.' So encourage him."
1 Chr 19: 3 come to you to search and to **o**
2 Chr 25: 8 God has power to help and to **o**.
Ps 106:26 To **o** them in the wilderness,
106:27 To **o** their descendants among
140:11 evil hunt the violent man to **o**
Prov 18: 5 Or to **o** the righteous in
Jer 49:18 As in the **o** of Sodom and
Hag 2:22 I will **o** the throne of
2:22 I will **o** the chariots And
Acts 5:39 you cannot **o** it—lest you even
2 Tim 2:18 and they **o** the faith of some.

OVERTHROWING (1/1)

Prov 21:12 ***O*** the wicked for their

OVERTHROWN (16/14) OVERTHROW

Ex 15: 7 of Your excellence You have **o**

2 Sam 17: 9 when some of them are o at the
18: 7 The people of Israel were o
2 Chr 14:13 So the Ethiopians were o,
Ps 141: 6 Their judges are o by the sides
Prov 11:11 But it is o by the mouth of
12: 7 The wicked are o and are no
14:11 house of the wicked will be o,
Isa 1: 7 desolate, as o by strangers.
Jer 18:23 But let them be o before You.
Lam 4: 6 Which was o in a moment,
Ezek 21:27 O, overthrown, I will
21:27 Overthrown, o, I will
21:27 I will make it o! It shall be
Dan 11:41 and many countries shall be o;
Jon 3: 4 and Nineveh shall be o!"

OVERTHROWS (5/5) OVERTHROW

Job 12:19 And o the mighty.
34:25 He o them in the night,
Prov 13: 6 But wickedness o the sinner.
22:12 But He o the words of the
29: 4 he who receives bribes o it.

OVERTOOK (9/9) OVERTAKE

Gen 31:23 and he o him in the mountains
31:25 So Laban o Jacob. Now Jacob had
44: 6 So he o them, and he spoke to
Ex 14: 9 and o them camping by the sea
Judg 18:22 house gathered together and o
20:42 but the battle o them, and
2 Ki 25: 5 and they o him in the plains of
Jer 39: 5 army pursued them and o
52: 8 and they o Zedekiah in the

OVERTURNED (5/5) OVERTURNS

Judg 7:13 struck it so that it fell and o,
Lam 1:20 My heart is o within me,
Mt 21:12 and o the tables of the money
Mk 11:15 and o the tables of the money
Jn 2:15 out the changers' money and o

OVERTURNS (2/2) OVERTURNED

Job 9: 5 and they do not know When He o
28: 9 He o the mountains at the

OVERWHELM (4/4)

Job 6:27 you o the fatherless, And you
12:15 they o the earth.
Dan 11:10 shall certainly come and o and
11:40 o them, and pass through.

OVERWHELMED (10/10)

Job 41: 9 Shall one not be o at the
Ps 55: 5 And horror has o me.
61: 2 cry to You, When my heart is o;
77: 3 complained, and my spirit was o.
78:53 But the sea o their enemies.
102: of the afflicted when he is o
124: 4 Then the waters would have o
142: 3 When my spirit was o within me,
143: 4 Therefore my spirit is o within
Dan 10:16 of the vision my sorrows have o

OVERWORK (1/1)

Prov 23: 4 Do not o to be rich;

OWE (5/5) OWED, OWES

Mt 18:28 Pay me what you o!'
Lk 16: 5 How much do you o my master?'
16: 7 another, 'And how much do you o?
Rom 13: 8 O no one anything except to
Phm 1:19 to mention to you that you o

OWED (4/4) OWE

Deut 15: 3 up your claim to what is o by
Mt 18:24 one was brought to him who o
18:28 of his fellow servants who o
Lk 7:41 One o five hundred denarii, and

OWES (1/1) OWE

Phm 1:18 But if he has wronged you or o

OWL (12/8)

Lev 11:16 'the ostrich, the short-eared o,
11:17 'the little o, the fisher
11:17 'the little owl, the fisher o,
11:17 fisher owl, and the screech o;
11:18 'the white o, the jackdaw,
Deut 14:15 ostrich, the short-eared o,
14:16 'the little o, the screech owl,
14:16 "the little owl, the screech o,
14:16 the screech owl, the white o,
14:17 carrion vulture, the fisher o,
Ps 102: 6 I am like an o of the desert.
Isa 34:11 Also the o and the raven shall

OWLS (1/1)

Isa 13:21 their houses will be full of o;

OWN (652/591) OWNER

Gen 1:27 created man in His o image;
5: 3 a son in his o likeness,
14:14 who were born in his o house,
15: 4 will come from your o body
30:25 that I may go to my o place and
30:30 shall I also provide for my o
30:40 but he put his o flocks by
40: 5 with its o interpretation.
41:11 interpretation of his o dream.
41:12 according to his o dream.
47:24 Four-fifths shall be your o,
49:28 according to his o blessing.
Ex 5:16 but the fault is in your o
15:17 You have made For Your o
18:27 went his way to his o land.
21:36 the dead animal shall be his o.
22: 5 from the best of his o field
22: 5 and the best of his o vineyard.
28:21 each one with its o name;
32:13 You swore by Your o self,
39:14 each one with its o name
Lev 1: 3 he shall offer it of his o free
7:30 His o hands shall bring the
14:15 the palm of his o left hand.
14:26 the palm of his o left hand.
16:29 whether a native of your o
17:15 a native of your o country
18:10 theirs is your o nakedness.
18:26 either any of your o nation or
19: 5 offer it of your o free will.
21:14 take a virgin of his o people
22:19 offer of your o free will
22:29 offer it of your o free will.
24:22 for one from your o country;
25: 5 What grows of its o accord of
25:11 what grows of its o accord,
25:41 return to his o family.
Num 1:52 everyone by his o camp,
1:52 everyone by his o standard,
2: 2 camp by his o standard,
10:30 but I will depart to my o land
13:33 grasshoppers in our o sight,
15:39 to which your o heart
15:39 your own heart and your o eyes
16:28 not done them of my o will.
16:38 sinned against their o souls,
24:13 to do good or bad of my o will.
27: 3 but he died in his o sin;
32:42 after his o name.
36: 9 keep its o inheritance."
Deut 3:14 Bashan after his o name,
12: 8 whatever is right in his o eyes
13: 6 friend who is as your o soul,
22: 2 bring it to your o house,
24:13 may sleep in his o garment
24:16 be put to death for his o sin.
28:53 eat the fruit of your o body,
33: 9 Or know his o children;
Josh 2:18 household to your o home.
2:19 shall be on his o head,
7:11 put it among their o stuff.
20: 6 return and come to his o city
20: 6 his own city and his o house,
24:28 each to his o inheritance.
Judg 2: 6 went each to his o inheritance
2:19 not cease from their o doings
7: 2 My o hand has saved me.'
8:29 and dwelt in his o house.
8:30 sons who were his o offspring,
9: 2 that I am your o flesh
9:49 likewise cut down his o bough
9:57 God returned on their o heads,
17: 6 was right in his o eyes.
21:25 was right in his o eyes.
Ruth 4: 6 lest I ruin my o inheritance.
1 Sam 2:20 would go to their o home.
5:11 it go back to its o place,
6: 9 the road to its o territory,
8:11 them for his o chariots
13:14 a man after His o heart,
14:46 went to their o place.
15:17 you were little in your o eyes,
18: 1 and Jonathan loved him as his o
18: 3 he loved him as his o soul.
20:17 him as he loved his o soul.
20:30 of Jesse to your o shame
23:18 Jonathan went to his o house.
25:26 yourself with your o hand,
25:33 myself with my o hand.
25:39 of Nabal on his o head.
28: 3 in his o city. And Saul had put
2 Sam 1:11 took hold of his o clothes
1:16 Your blood is on your o head,
1:16 for your o mouth has testified
4:11 person in his o house
6:22 be humble in my o sight.
7:10 may dwell in a place of their o
7:21 and according to Your o heart,
7:24 Israel Your very o people
12: 3 It ate of his o food and drank
12: 3 food and drank from his o cup
12: 4 to take from his o flock
12: 4 flock and from his o herd
12:11 against you from your o house;
12:20 Then he went to his o house;
14:24 Let him return to his o house,
14:24 returned to his o house,
15:19 an exile from your o place.
16: 8 you are caught in your o evil,
16:11 son who came from my o body
18:13 dealt falsely against my o life.
18:18 the pillar after his o name.
19:28 among those who eat at your o
19:30 back in peace to his o house."
19:37 that I may die in my o city,
19:39 and he returned to his o place.
23:21 him with his o spear.
1 Ki 1:12 that you may save your o life
1:33 my son ride on my o mule,
2:23 this word against his o life!
2:26 to your o fields, for you are
2:34 was buried in his o house
2:37 blood shall be on your o head.
2:44 your wickedness on your o head.
3: 1 finished building his o house,
7: 1 years to build his o house;
8:38 the plague of his o heart,
9:15 his o house, the Millo, the
10: 6 which I heard in my o land
10: 7 until I came and saw with my o
10:13 and went to her o country,
11:19 as wife the sister of his o wife,
11:21 I may go to my o country."
11:22 to go to your o country?"
12:16 see to your o house,
12:33 he had devised in his o heart.
13:30 the corpse in his o tomb;
14:12 go to your o house. When your
17:19 and laid him on his o bed.
22:36 every man to his o country!"
2 Ki 2:12 took hold of his o clothes
3:27 and returned to their o land.
4:13 I dwell among my o people."
12:18 and his o sacred things, and
14: 6 be put to death for his o sin.
17:23 away from their o land
17:29 continued to make gods of its o,
17:33 their o gods—according to
18:27 eat and drink their o waste
18:31 one of you eat from his o vine
18:31 every one from his o fig tree,
18:31 the waters of his o cistern;
18:32 to a land like your o land,
19: 7 rumor and return to his o land;
19: 7 by the sword in his o land."
19:34 to save it For My o sake and
20: 6 this city for My o sake,
21:18 in the garden of his o house,
21:23 the king in his o house.
23:30 and buried him in his o tomb.
25:21 away captive from its o land.
1 Chr 11:23 killed him with his o spear.
17: 9 may dwell in a place of their o
17:19 and according to Your o heart,
17:22 Israel Your very o people
29: 3 my o special treasure of gold
29:14 And of Your o we have given
29:16 Your hand, and is all Your o.
2 Chr 6:23 his way on his o head,
6:29 one knows his o burden
6:29 own burden and his o grief,
7:11 of the LORD and in his o house.
8: 1 of the LORD and his o house,
9: 5 which I heard in my o land
9: 6 I came and saw with my o eyes;
9:12 and went to her o country,
10:16 Now see to your o house,
16:14 They buried him in his o tomb,
24:25 his o servants conspired
25: 4 shall die for his o sin."
25:15 could not rescue their o people
31: 1 returned to their o cities
32:21 shamefaced to his o land.
32:21 some of his o offspring struck
33:20 they buried him in his o house.
33:24 and killed him in his o house.
Ezra 2: 1 everyone to his o city.
Neh 3:28 each in front of his o house.
3:29 in front of his o house.
4: 4 their reproach on their o heads,
6: 8 invent them in your o heart."
6:16 disheartened in their o eyes;
7: 3 in front of his o house."
11: 3 dwelt in his o possession in
Esth 1:22 province in its o script,
1:22 people in their o language,
1:22 be master in his o house,
1:22 the language of his o people.
2: 7 took her as his o daughter.
8: 9 province in its o script,
8: 9 people in their o language,
8: 9 the Jews in their o script
9:25 should return on his o head,
Job 2:11 from his o place—Eliphaz
4:21 Does not their o excellence go
5:13 the wise in their o craftiness,
9:20 my o mouth would condemn me;
9:31 And my o clothes will abhor
13:15 I will defend my o ways before
15: 6 Your o mouth condemns you, and
15: 6 your o lips testify against
18: 7 And his o counsel casts him
18: 8 cast into a net by his o feet,
19:17 to the children of my o body.
20: 7 forever like his o refuse;
32: 1 he was righteous in his o eyes.
40:14 you That your o right hand
Ps 5:10 them fall by their o counsels;
7:16 shall return upon his o head,
7:16 shall come down on his o crown.
9:15 their o foot is caught.
9:16 in the work of his o hands.
12: 4 prevail; Our lips are our o;
15: 4 He who swears to his o hurt
21:13 in Your o strength! We will

33:12 chosen as His **o** inheritance.
35:13 would return to my **o** heart.
36: 2 flatters himself in his **o** eyes,
37:15 shall enter their **o** heart,
41: 9 Even my **o** familiar friend in
44: 3 of the land by their **o** sword,
44: 3 Nor did their **o** arm save them;
45:10 Forget your **o** people also, and
49:11 lands after their **o** names.
50:20 You slander your **o** mother's
64: 8 stumble over their **o** tongue;
67: 6 our **o** God, shall bless us.
74:22 plead Your **o** cause; Remember
78:29 gave them their **o** desire.
78:52 But He made His **o** people go
81:12 over to their **o** stubborn hearts,
81:12 To walk in their **o** counsels.
94:23 on them their **o** iniquity,
94:23 off in their **o** wickedness;
106:39 were defiled by their **o** works,
106:39 the harlot by their **o** deeds.
106:40 He abhorred His **o** inheritance.
109:29 themselves with their **o** disgrace
141:10 wicked fall into their **o** nets,
Prov 1:18 in wait for their **o** blood,
1:18 secretly for their **o** lives.
1:31 the fruit of their **o** way,
1:31 the full with their **o** fancies.
3: 5 not on your **o** understanding;
3: 7 Do not be wise in your **o** eyes;
5:15 water from your **o** cistern,
5:15 running water from your **o** well.
5:17 Let them be only your **o**,
5:22 His **o** iniquities entrap the
6:32 does so destroys his **o** soul.
8:36 me wrongs his **o** soul;
11: 5 will fall by his **o** wickedness.
11:17 man does good for his **o** soul,
11:17 cruel troubles his **o** flesh.
11:19 pursues it to his **o** death.
11:29 He who troubles his **o** house
12:15 is right in his **o** eyes,
14:10 heart knows its **o** bitterness,
14:14 will be filled with his **o** ways,
14:20 hated even by his **o** neighbor,
15:27 for gain troubles his **o** house,
15:32 despises his **o** soul,
16: 2 man are pure in his **o** eyes,
18: 1 himself seeks his **o** desire;
18: 2 But in expressing his **o** heart.
18:11 a high wall in his **o** esteem.
19: 8 gets wisdom loves his **o** soul;
20: 2 sins against his **o** life.
20: 6 proclaim each his **o** goodness,
20:24 can a man understand his **o** way?
21: 2 a man is right in his **o** eyes,
23: 4 of your **o** understanding,
24: 6 you will wage your **o** war,
25:27 So to seek one's **o** glory is
25:28 has no rule over his **o** spirit
26: 5 Lest he be wise in his **o** eyes.
26: 6 fool Cuts off his **o** feet
26:11 As a dog returns to his **o**
26:12 see a man wise in his **o** eyes?
26:16 lazy man is wiser in his **o**
26:17 meddles in a quarrel not his **o**
27: 2 and not your **o** mouth;
27: 2 and not your **o** lips.
27:10 Do not forsake your **o** friend or
28:10 will fall into his **o** pit;
28:11 rich man is wise in his **o** eyes,
28:26 He who trusts in his **o** heart is
29:24 with a thief hates his **o** life;
30:12 that is pure in its **o** eyes,
31:31 And let her **o** works praise her
Eccl 3:22 should rejoice in his **o** works,
4: 5 And consumes his **o** flesh.
7:22 your **o** heart has known That
8: 9 over another to his **o** hurt.
Song 1: 6 But my **o** vineyard I have not
8:12 My **o** vineyard is before me.
Isa 2: 8 the work of their **o** hands,
2: 8 That which their **o** fingers
4: 1 We will eat our **o** food and wear
4: 1 food and wear our **o** apparel;
5:21 who are wise in their **o** eyes,
5:21 And prudent in their **o** sight!
9:20 shall eat the flesh of his **o**
13:14 man will turn to his **o** people,
13:14 will flee to his **o** land.
14: 1 settle them in their **o** land.
14:18 Everyone in his **o** house;
31: 7 which your **o** hands have made
36:12 eat and drink their **o** waste
36:16 one of you eat from his **o** vine
36:16 every one from his **o** fig tree
36:16 the waters of his **o** cistern;
36:17 away to a land like your **o** land
37: 7 and return to his **o** land
37: 7 by the sword in his **o** land.
37:35 to save it For My **o** sake and
38:17 Indeed it was for my **o** peace
43:25 transgressions for My **o** sake;
44: 9 They are their **o** witnesses;
48:11 For My **o** sake, for My own sake,
48:11 for My **o** sake, I will do it;
49:26 you with their **o** flesh,
49:26 be drunk with their **o** blood
53: 6 to his **o** way; And the LORD
56:11 They all look to their **o** way,
56:11 Every one for his **o** gain,
56:11 From his **o** territory.
58: 7 yourself from your **o** flesh?
58:13 not doing your **o** ways, Nor
58:13 Nor finding your **o** pleasure,
58:13 Nor speaking your **o** words,
59:16 Therefore His **o** arm brought
59:16 And His **o** righteousness, it
63: 5 Therefore My **o** arm brought
63: 5 And My **o** fury, it sustained
65: 2 According to their **o** thoughts;
66: 3 they have chosen their **o** ways,
Jer 1:16 the works of their **o** hands.
2:19 Your **o** wickedness will correct
5:31 the priests rule by their **o**
6: 3 shall pasture in his **o** place.
7:19 to the shame of their **o** faces?
8: 6 turned to his **o** course,
9:14 the dictates of their **o** hearts
10:23 walks to direct his **o** steps.
16:12 dictates of his **o** evil heart,
18:12 walk according to our **o** plans
23: 8 shall dwell in their **o** land.
23:16 They speak a vision of their **o**
23:17 to the dictates of his **o** heart,
23:26 of the deceit of their **o** heart,
24: 5 this place for their **o** good,
25: 7 of your hands to your **o** hurt.
25:14 to the works of their **o** hands.
27:11 them remain in their **o** land,
30:18 be built upon its **o** mound,
30:18 remain according to its **o** plan.
31:17 come back to their **o** border.
31:30 shall die for his **o** iniquity;
37: 7 to their **o** land.
42:12 cause you to return to your **o**
44: 9 your **o** wickedness, and the
44:17 has gone out of our **o** mouth,
46:16 Let us go back to our **o** people
50:16 shall turn to his **o** people,
50:16 shall flee to his **o** land.
51: 9 go everyone to his **o** country;
52:27 away captive from its **o** land.
Lam 4:10 Have cooked their **o** children;
Ezek 9:10 their deeds on their **o** head.
11:21 their deeds on their **o** heads,
13: 2 prophesy out of their **o** heart,
13: 3 who follow their **o** spirit and
13:17 who prophesy out of their **o**
16: 6 struggling in your **o** blood,
16:15 you trusted in your **o** beauty,
16:43 your deeds on your **o** head,
16:52 bear your **o** shame also, because
16:52 and bear your **o** shame, because
16:54 that you may bear your **o** shame
17:19 I will recompense on his **o** head
20:43 yourselves in your **o** sight
22: 3 The city sheds blood in her **o**
22:31 their deeds on their **o** heads,
23:34 And tear at your **o** breasts;
28:25 they will dwell in their **o** land
29: 3 has said, 'My River is my **o**;
32:10 every man for his **o** life, in
33: 4 blood shall be on his **o** head
33:13 he trusts in his **o** righteousness
33:20 of you according to his **o** ways
33:31 hearts pursue their **o** gain
34:13 will bring them to their **o** land
36: 7 around you shall bear their **o**
36:17 of Israel dwelt in their **o** land
36:17 they defiled it by their **o** ways
36:24 and bring you into your **o** land.
36:31 loathe yourselves in your **o**
36:32 and confounded for your **o** ways,
37:14 I will place you in your **o** land
37:21 and bring them into their **o**
39:26 they dwelt safely in their **o**
46:18 for his sons from his **o** property
Dan 3:28 worship any god except their **o**
6:17 the king sealed it with his **o**
8:24 but not by his **o** power;
9:19 Do not delay for Your **o** sake
11: 9 but shall return to his **o** land.
11:16 shall do according to his **o** will
11:19 the fortress of his **o** land
11:28 do damage and return to his **o**
11:36 shall do according to his **o** will
Hos 7: 2 Now their **o** deeds have
9: 4 bread shall be for their **o**
10: 6 be ashamed of his **o** counsel
10:13 Because you trusted in your **o**
11: 6 Because of their **o** counsels.
Joel 2: 8 Every one marches in his **o**
3: 4 retaliation upon your **o** head
3: 7 your retaliation upon your **o**
Am 6:13 for ourselves By our **o** strength
7:11 away captive From their **o** land
7:17 away captive From his **o** land
Ob 15 shall return upon your **o** head.
Jon 2: 8 idols Forsake their **o** Mercy.
Mic 7: 6 enemies are the men of his **o**
Hab 3:14 through with his **o** arrows
Hag 1: 9 one of you runs to his **o** house
Zech 12: 6 inhabited again in her **o** place
Mal 3:17 As a man spares his **o** son
Mt 2:12 they departed for their **o** country
6:34 will worry about its **o** things.
6:34 for the day is its **o** trouble.
7: 3 consider the plank in your **o**
7: 4 a plank is in your **o** eye?
7: 5 remove the plank from your **o**
8:22 and let the dead bury their **o**
9: 1 and came to His **o** city.
10:36 be those of his **o** household
13:54 He had come to His **o** country
13:57 without honor except in his **o**
13:57 own country and in his **o** house
16:26 and loses his **o** soul? Or what
20:15 do what I wish with my **o** things
22: 5 one to his **o** farm, another to
25:14 who called his **o** servants and
25:15 each according to his **o** ability
25:27 I would have received back my **o**
27:31 put His **o** clothes on Him, and
Mk 3:21 But when His **o** people heard
6: 1 there and came to His **o** country
6: 4 honor except in his **o** country
6: 4 among his **o** relatives, and in
6: 4 and in his **o** house."
8: 3 away hungry to their **o** houses
8:36 and loses his **o** soul?
15:20 put His **o** clothes on Him, and
Lk 1:20 will be fulfilled in their **o** time
1:23 that he departed to his **o** house
2: 3 everyone to his **o** city.
2:35 will pierce through your **o** soul
2:39 to their **o** city, Nazareth.
4:24 no prophet is accepted in his **o**
5:25 and departed to his **o** house,
5:29 a great feast in his **o** house
6:41 perceive the plank in your **o**
6:42 the plank that is in your **o** eye
6:42 remove the plank from your **o**
6:44 tree is known by its **o** fruit
8:39 Return to your **o** house, and tell
9:26 when He comes in His **o** glory,
9:60 Let the dead bury their **o** dead,
10:34 and he set him on his **o** animal,
11:21 guards his **o** palace, his goods
14:26 and his **o** life also, he cannot
16:12 will give you what is your **o**?
18: 7 God not avenge His **o** elect
19:22 Out of your **o** mouth I will judge
19:35 And they threw their **o** clothes
22:71 it ourselves from His **o** mouth
Jn 1:11 He came to His **o**,
1:11 and His **o** did not receive Him.
1:41 He first found his **o** brother
4:41 believed because of His **o** word
4:44 a prophet has no honor in his **o**
5:30 because I do not seek My **o** will
5:43 if another comes in his **o** name,
6:38 not to do My **o** will, but the
7:17 God or whether I speak on My **o**
7:18 from himself seeks his **o** glory;
7:53 And everyone went to his **o**
8:44 he speaks from his **o** resources
8:50 And I do not seek My **o** glory;
10: 3 and he calls his **o** sheep by
10: 4 when he brings out his **o** sheep
10:12 one who does not **o** the sheep,
10:14 My sheep, and am known by My **o**.
11:51 this he did not say on his **o**
12:49 For I have not spoken on My **o**
13: 1 having loved His **o** who were in
14:10 to you I do not speak on My **o**
15:19 the world would love its **o**.
16:13 for He will not speak on His **o**
16:32 be scattered, each to his **o**,
18:35 Your **o** nation and the chief
19:27 that disciple took her to his **o**
20:10 away again to their **o** homes
Acts 1: 7 the Father has put in His **o**
1:19 that field is called in their **o**
1:25 he might go to his **o** place
2: 6 heard them speak in his **o**
2: 8 each in our **o** language in which
2:11 them speaking in our **o** tongues
3:12 as though by our **o** power or
4:23 they went to their **o** companions
4:32 things he possessed was his **o**,
5: 4 it remained, was it not your **o**?
5: 4 was it not in your **o** control?
7:21 brought him up as her **o** son
7:41 in the works of their **o** hands.
12:10 which opened to them of its **o**
13:22 a man after My **o** heart,
13:36 he had served his **o** generation
14:16 all nations to walk in their **o**
15:22 to send chosen men of their **o**
17:28 as also some of your **o** poets
18: 6 Your blood be upon your **o** heads
18:15 words and names and your **o** law
20:28 which He purchased with His **o**
21:11 bound his **o** hands and feet,
25:19 him about their **o** religion
26: 4 the beginning among my **o** nation
27:19 overboard with our **o** hands
28:30 dwelt two whole years in his **o**
Rom 4:19 he did not consider his **o** body,
5: 8 But God demonstrates His **o** love
8: 3 God did by sending His **o** Son
8:32 He who did not spare His **o** Son,
10: 3 establish their **o** righteousness
11:24 be grafted into their **o** olive
11:25 you should be wise in your **o**
12:16 not be wise in your **o** opinion
14: 4 To his **o** master he stands or
14: 5 fully convinced in his **o** mind
16: 4 who risked their **o** necks for my
16:18 but their **o** belly, and by
1 Cor 1:15 I had baptized in my **o** name
3: 8 and each one will receive his **o**
3: 8 reward according to his **o** labor
3:19 the wise in their **o** craftiness
4:12 working with our **o** hands.

6:18 immorality sins against his **o**
6:19 God, and you are not your **o**?
7: 2 let each man have his **o** wife,
7: 2 each woman have her **o** husband
7: 4 have authority over her **o** body
7: 4 not have authority over his **o**
7: 7 But each one has his **o** gift
7:35 this I say for your **o** profit
7:37 but has power over his **o** will,
9: 7 goes to war at his **o** expense?
10:24 Let no one seek his **o**,
10:29 I say, not your **o**, but that of
10:33 not seeking my **o** profit, but
11:21 each one takes his **o** supper
13: 5 rudely, does not seek its **o**,
14:35 let them ask their **o** husbands
15:23 But each one in his **o** order:
15:38 and to each seed its **o** body.
16:21 The salutation with my **o**
2 Cor 6:12 you are restricted by your **o**
8:17 he went to you of his **o** accord.
11:26 in perils of my **o** countrymen
Gal 1:14 of my contemporaries in my **o**
4:15 have plucked out your **o** eyes
6: 4 each one examine his **o** work
6: 5 each one shall bear his **o** load
6:11 written to you with my **o** hand
Eph 5:22 submit to your **o** husbands, as
5:24 let the wives be to their **o**
5:28 husbands ought to love their **o**
5:28 love their own wives as their **o**
5:29 For no one ever hated his **o**
5:33 particular so love his **o** wife
6: 9 knowing that your **o** Master also
Phil 2: 4 you look out not only for his **o**
2:12 work out your **o** salvation with
2:21 For all seek their **o**,
3: 9 not having my **o** righteousness,
Col 3:18 submit to your **o** husbands, as
4:18 This salutation by my **o** hand
1 Th 2: 7 nursing mother cherishes her **o**
2: 8 but also our **o** lives, because
2:11 a father does his **o** children
2:12 who calls you into His **o** kingdom
2:14 the same things from your **o**
2:15 Lord Jesus and their **o** prophets
4: 4 how to possess his **o** vessel
4:11 to mind your **o** business, and to
4:11 and to work with your **o** hands,
2 Th 2: 6 may be revealed in his **o** time
3:12 quietness and eat their **o** bread
3:17 salutation of Paul with my **o**
1 Tim 3: 4 one who rules his **o** house well,
3: 5 does not know how to rule his **o**
3:12 children and their **o** houses
4: 2 having their **o** conscience
5: 8 does not provide for his **o**,
6: 1 the yoke count their **o** masters
6:15 He will manifest in His **o** time,
2 Tim 1: 9 but according to His **o** purpose
4: 3 according to their **o** desires
Titus 1:12 of them, a prophet of their **o**,
2: 5 obedient to their **o** husbands,
2: 9 be obedient to their **o** masters
2:14 and purify for Himself His **o**
Phm 1:12 that is, my **o** heart,
1:19 am writing with my **o** hand.
1:19 you owe me even your **o** self
Heb 2: 4 according to His **o** will?
3: 6 as a Son over His **o** house
7:27 first for His **o** sins and then
9:12 but with His **o** blood He entered
13:12 sanctify the people with His **o**
Jas 1:14 is drawn away by his **o** desires
1:18 Of His **o** will He brought us
1:26 tongue but deceives his **o** heart
1 Pe 2: 9 His **o** special people, that you
2:24 bore our sins in His **o** body
3: 1 submissive to your **o** husbands
3: 5 being submissive to their **o**
2 Pe 2:12 perish in their **o** corruption
2:13 carousing in their **o** deceptions
2:22 A dog returns to his **o** vomit
3: 3 walking according to their **o**
3:16 twist to their **o** destruction
3:17 lest you also fall from your **o**
Jude 6 but left their **o** abode, He has
13 foaming up their **o** shame;
16 according to their **o** lusts
18 would walk according to their **o**
Rev 1: 5 us from our sins in His **o** blood

OWNED (2/2)

Lev 27:24 to the one who **o** the land as a
1 Ki 17:17 the son of the woman who **o** the

OWNER (20/18) OWN

Ex 21:28 but the **o** of the ox shall be
21:29 it has been made known to his **o**,
21:29 ox shall be stoned and its **o**
21:34 the **o** of the pit shall make it
21:34 he shall give money to their **o**,
21:36 and its **o** has not kept it
22:11 and the **o** of it shall accept
22:12 make restitution to the **o** of
22:14 the **o** of it not being with it,
22:15 If its **o** was with it, he shall
1 Ki 16:24 Shemer, **o** of the hill.
Eccl 5:13 Riches kept for their **o** to his
Isa 1: 3 The ox knows its **o** And the
Mt 13:27 So the servants of the **o** came
20: 8 the **o** of the vineyard said to
21:40 when the **o** of the vineyard
Mk 12: 9 Therefore what will the **o** of the
Lk 20:13 Then the **o** of the vineyard said,
20:15 Therefore what will the **o** of
Acts 27:11 by the helmsman and the **o** of

OWNERS (5/5)

Job 31:39 Or caused its **o** to lose their
Prov 1:19 takes away the life of its **o**.
Eccl 5:11 So what profit have the **o**
Zech 11: 5 whose **o** slaughter them and feel
Lk 19:33 the **o** of it said to them, "Why

OWNS (3/3)

Lev 14:35 and he who **o** the house comes and
Dan 5:23 your breath in His hand and **o**
Acts 21:11 at Jerusalem bind the man who **o**

OX (68/58) OXEN

Gen 49: 6 self-will they hamstrung an **o**.
Ex 20:17 his female servant, nor his **o**,
21:28 If an **o** gores a man or a woman
21:28 then the **o** shall surely be
21:28 but the owner of the **o** shall
21:29 But if the **o** tended to thrust
21:29 the **o** shall be stoned and its
21:32 If the **o** gores a male or female
21:32 and the **o** shall be stoned.
21:33 and an **o** or a donkey falls in
21:35 If one man's **o** hurts another's,
21:35 they shall sell the live **o** and
21:35 and the dead **o** they shall also
21:36 Or if it was known that the **o**
21:36 he shall surely pay **o** for ox,
21:36 he shall surely pay ox for **o**,
22: 1 If a man steals an **o** or a sheep,
22: 1 restore five oxen for an **o** and
22: 4 whether it is an **o** or donkey or
22: 9 whether it concerns an **o**,
22:10 to his neighbor a donkey, an **o**,
23: 4 If you meet your enemy's **o** or
23:12 that your **o** and your donkey may
34:19 whether **o** or sheep.
Lev 7:23 of **o** or sheep or goat.
17: 3 house of Israel who kills an **o**
27:26 whether it is an **o** or sheep,
Num 7: 3 leaders, and for each one an **o**;
22: 4 as an **o** licks up the grass of
23:22 He has strength like a wild **o**.
24: 8 He has strength like a wild **o**;
Deut 5:14 your female servant, nor your **o**,
5:21 his female servant, his **o**,
14: 4 which you may eat: the **o**,
22: 1 shall not see your brother's **o**
22: 4 your brother's donkey or his **o**
22:10 You shall not plow with an **o**
25: 4 You shall not muzzle an **o** while
28:31 Your **o** shall be slaughtered
33:17 like the horns of the wild **o**;
Josh 6:21 **o** and sheep and donkey, with
Judg 3:31 of the Philistines with an **o**
6: 4 neither sheep nor **o** nor donkey.
1 Sam 12: 3 Whose **o** have I taken, or whose
14:34 Bring me here every man's **o** and
14:34 one of the people brought his **o**
15: 3 **o** and sheep, camel and donkey.'
Neh 5:18 was prepared daily was one **o**
Job 6: 5 Or does the **o** low over its
24: 3 They take the widow's **o** as a
39: 9 Will the wild **o** be willing to
39:10 Can you bind the wild **o** in the
40:15 He eats grass like an **o**.
Ps 29: 6 and Sirion like a young wild **o**.
69:31 the LORD better than an **o** or
92:10 You have exalted like a wild **o**;
106:20 glory Into the image of an **o**
Prov 7:22 as an **o** goes to the slaughter,
14: 4 comes by the strength of an **o**.
Isa 1: 3 The **o** knows its owner And the
11: 7 lion shall eat straw like the **o**.
32:20 out freely the feet of the **o**
65:25 lion shall eat straw like the **o**,
Ezek 1:10 the four had the face of an **o**
Lk 13:15 you on the Sabbath loose his **o**
14: 5 having a donkey or an **o** that
1 Cor 9: 9 shall not muzzle an **o**
1 Tim 5:18 shall not muzzle an **o**

OXEN (94/88) OX

Gen 12:16 for her sake. He had sheep, **o**,
20:14 Then Abimelech took sheep, **o**,
21:27 So Abraham took sheep and **o** and
32: 5 'I have **o**, donkeys, flocks,
34:28 They took their sheep, their **o**,
Ex 9: 3 on the camels, on the **o**,
20:24 your sheep and your **o**.
22: 1 he shall restore five **o** for an
22:30 you shall do with your **o** and
24: 5 peace offerings of **o** to the
Num 7: 3 six covered carts and twelve **o**,
7: 6 Moses took the carts and the **o**,
7: 7 Two carts and four **o** he gave to
7: 8 and four carts and eight **o** he
7:17 of peace offerings: two **o**,
7:23 of peace offerings: two **o**,
7:29 of peace offerings: two **o**,
7:35 of peace offerings: two **o**,
7:41 of peace offerings: two **o**,
7:47 of peace offerings: two **o**,
7:53 of peace offerings: two **o**,
7:59 of peace offerings: two **o**,
7:65 of peace offerings: two **o**,
7:71 of peace offerings: two **o**,
7:77 of peace offerings: two **o**,
7:83 of peace offerings: two **o**,
7:87 All the **o** for the burnt offering
7:88 And all the **o** for the sacrifice
22:40 Then Balak offered **o** and sheep,
Deut 14:26 for **o** or sheep, for wine or
Josh 7:24 his sons, his daughters, his **o**,
1 Sam 11: 7 So he took a yoke of **o** and cut
11: 7 so it shall be done to his **o**.
14:32 on the spoil, and took sheep, **o**,
15: 9 the best of the sheep, the **o**,
15:14 and the lowing of the **o** which I
15:15 the best of the sheep and the **o**,
15:21 of the plunder, sheep and **o**,
22:19 **o** and donkeys and sheep—with
27: 9 but took away the sheep, the **o**,
2 Sam 6: 6 for the **o** stumbled.
6:13 that he sacrificed **o** and fatted
24:22 here are **o** for burnt
24:22 and the yokes of the **o** for
24:24 the threshing floor and the **o**
1 Ki 1: 9 sacrificed sheep and **o** and
1:19 He has sacrificed **o** and fattened
1:25 and has sacrificed **o** and
4:23 ten fatted **o**, twenty oxen
4:23 twenty **o** from the pastures, and
7:25 It stood on twelve **o**:
7:29 the frames were lions, **o**,
7:29 Below the lions and **o** were
7:44 and twelve **o** under the Sea;
8: 5 sacrificing sheep and **o** that
19:19 with twelve yoke of **o**
19:20 And he left the **o** and ran after
19:21 and took a yoke of **o** and
2 Ki 5:26 and vineyards, sheep and **o**,
16:17 down the Sea from the bronze **o**
1 Chr 12:40 and camels, on mules and **o**—
12:40 wine and oil and **o** and sheep
13: 9 for the **o** stumbled.
21:23 I also give you the **o** for
2 Chr 4: 3 under it was the likeness of **o**
4: 3 The **o** were cast in two rows,
4: 4 It stood on twelve **o**:
4:15 one Sea and twelve **o** under it;
5: 6 were sacrificing sheep and **o**
18: 2 and Ahab killed sheep and **o** in
31: 6 brought the tithe of **o** and
Job 1: 3 camels, five hundred yoke of **o**,
1:14 The **o** were plowing and the
42:12 camels, one thousand yoke of **o**,
Ps 8: 7 All sheep and **o**—
22:21 from the horns of the wild **o**!
144:14 That our **o** may be
Prov 14: 4 Where no **o** are, the trough is
Isa 7:25 it will become a range for **o**
22:13 Slaying **o** and killing sheep,
30:24 Likewise the **o** and the young
34: 7 The wild **o** shall come down with
Jer 51:23 the farmer and his yoke of **o**;
Dan 4:25 shall make you eat grass like **o**.
4:32 shall make you eat grass like **o**;
4:33 from men and ate grass like **o**;
5:21 They fed him with grass like **o**,
Am 6:12 Does one plow there with **o**?
Mt 22: 4 my **o** and fatted cattle are
Lk 14:19 'I have bought five yoke of **o**,
Jn 2:14 in the temple those who sold **o**
2:15 with the sheep and the **o**,
Acts 14:13 brought **o** and garlands to the
1 Cor 9: 9 Is it **o** God is concerned

OXEN'S (1/1)

1 Ki 19:21 using the **o** equipment, and gave

OZEM (2/2)

1 Chr 2:15 ***O*** the sixth, and David the
2:25 firstborn, and Bunah, Oren, ***O***,

OZIAS (KJV) See UZZIAH

OZNI (1/1)

Num 26:16 of ***O***, the family of

OZNITES (1/1)

Num 26:16 of Ozni, the family of the ***O***;

P

PAARAI (1/1)

2 Sam 23:35 Carmelite, ***P*** the Arbite,

PACE (3/3)

Gen 33:14 I will lead on slowly at a ***p***
2 Ki 4:24 do not slacken the ***p*** for me
Prov 30:29 which are majestic in ***p***,

PACED (2/2)
Esth 2:11 And every day Mordecai **p** in
Ps 35:14 I **p** about as though he were

PACES (1/1)
2 Sam 6:13 ark of the LORD had gone six **p**,

PACIFIES (2/2)
Prov 21:14 A gift in secret **p** anger,
Eccl 10: 4 For conciliation **p** great

PACKED (1/1)
Acts 21:15 And after those days we **p** and

PADAN (1/1)
Gen 48: 7 as for me, when I came from **P**,

PADAN ARAM (10/10)
Gen 25:20 of Bethuel the Syrian of **P**,
28: 2 'Arise, go to **P**, to the house
28: 5 Jacob away, and he went to **P**,
28: 6 Jacob and sent him away to **P**
28: 7 his mother and had gone to **P**.
31:18 which he had gained in **P**,
33:18 of Canaan, when he came from **P**;
35: 9 again, when he came from **P**,
35:26 Jacob who were born to him in **P**.
46:15 whom she bore to Jacob in **P**,

PADANARAM (KJV) See PADAN ARAM

PADON (2/2)
Ezra 2:44 sons of Siaha, the sons of **P**,
Neh 7:47 the sons of Sia, the sons of **P**,

PAGAN (12/12)
Ezra 10: 2 and have taken **p** wives from the
10:10 transgressed and have taken **p**
10:11 and from the **p** wives."
10:14 in our cities who have taken **p**
10:17 all the men who had taken **p**
10:18 of the priests who had taken **p**
10:44 All these had taken **p** wives, and
Neh 13:26 Nevertheless **p** women caused
13:27 against our God by marrying **p**
13:30 I cleansed them of everything **p**.
Hos 5: 7 For they have begotten **p**
Zeph 1: 4 idolatrous priests with the **p**

PAGANS (1/1)
Hos 3: 1 the raisin cakes of the **p**.

PAGIEL (5/5)
Num 1:13 **P** the son of Ocran;
2:27 children of Asher shall be **P**
7:72 On the eleventh day **P** the son
7:77 This was the offering of **P** the
10:26 of the children of Asher was **P**

PAHATH-MOAB (6/6)
Ezra 2: 6 the people of **P**,
8: 4 of the sons of **P**,
10:30 of the sons of **P**:
Neh 3:11 Harim and Hashub the son of **P**
7:11 the sons of **P**, of the sons
10:14 of the people: Parosh, **P**,

PAI (1/1)
1 Chr 1:50 and the name of his city was **P**.

PAID (23/23) PAY
1 Ki 1:31 and **p** homage to the king, and
18:29 no one **p** attention.
2 Ki 3: 4 and he regularly **p** the king of
12:11 and they **p** it out to the
12:12 and for all that was **p** out to
12:15 delivered the money to be **p** to
17: 3 and **p** him tribute money.
21: 9 But they **p** no attention, and
2 Chr 27: 5 The people of Ammon **p** this to
Ezra 4:20 and custom were **p** to them.
6: 4 Let the expenses be **p** from the
6: 8 Let the cost be **p** at the king's
Esth 3: 2 the king's gate bowed and **p**
Job 32:12 I **p** close attention to you;
Prov 7:14 Today I have **p** my vows.
Ezek 16:58 You have **p** for your lewdness and
27:19 Dan and Javan **p** for your wares,
Dan 3:12 have not **p** due regard to you.
Jon 1: 3 so he **p** the fare, and went down
Mt 5:26 out of there till you have **p**
Lk 12:59 from there till you have **p** the
Heb 7: 9 **p** tithes through Abraham, so to
12: 9 and we **p** them respect.

PAILS (1/1)
Job 21:24 His **p** are full of milk,

PAIN (28/27) PAINED, PAINFUL, PAINS
Gen 3:16 In **p** you shall bring forth
34:25 third day, when they were in **p**,
1 Chr 4: 9 "Because I bore him in **p**.
4:10 that I may not cause **p**!"
2 Chr 21:19 so he died in severe **p**.
Job 14:22 But his flesh will be in **p** over
15:20 The wicked man writhes with **p**
33:19 Man is also chastened with **p** on
33:19 And with strong **p** in many of
Ps 25:18 Look on my affliction and my **p**,
48: 6 hold of them there, And **p**,
Isa 13: 8 They will be in **p** as a woman
21: 3 my loins are filled with **p**;
26:17 As a woman with child Is in **p**
26:18 with child, we have been in **p**;
66: 7 Before her **p** came, She
Jer 6:24 **P** as of a woman in labor.
12:13 They have put themselves to **p**
15:18 Why is my **p** perpetual And my
22:23 Like the **p** of a woman in
51: 8 for her! Take balm for her **p**;
Ezek 30:16 Egypt; Sin shall have great **p**,
Joel 2: 6 them the people writhe in **p**;
Mic 4:10 Be in **p**, and labor to bring
Nah 2:10 Much **p** is in every side,
Rev 12: 2 cried out in labor and in **p** to
16:10 their tongues because of the **p**.
21: 4 There shall be no more **p**,

PAINED (2/2) PAIN
Ps 55: 4 My heart is severely **p** within
Jer 4:19 my soul! I am **p** in my very

PAINFUL (4/4) PAIN
Job 2: 7 and struck Job with **p** boils
Ps 73:16 It was too **p** for me—
Ezek 28:24 be a pricking brier or a **p**
Heb 12:11 joyful for the present, but **p**;

PAINS (6/6) PAIN
1 Sam 4:19 for her labor **p** came upon her.
Job 30:17 And my gnawing **p** take no rest.
Ps 116: 3 The **p** of death surrounded me,
Acts 2:24 having loosed the **p** of death,
1 Th 5: 3 as labor **p** upon a pregnant
Rev 16:11 of heaven because of their **p**

PAINT (2/2)
2 Ki 9:30 and she put **p** on her eyes and
Jer 4:30 you enlarge your eyes with **p**,

PAINTED (1/1)
Ezek 23:40 **p** your eyes, and adorned

PAINTING (1/1)
Jer 22:14 it with cedar And **p** it with

PAIR (7/7)
Judg 15: 4 and put a torch between each **p**
Isa 21: 7 he saw a chariot with a **p** of
21: 9 a chariot of men with a **p** of
Am 2: 6 And the poor for a **p** of
8: 6 And the needy for a **p** of
Lk 2:24 A **p** of turtledoves or two
Rev 6: 5 and he who sat on it had a **p** of

PALACE (32/32) PALACES
1 Ki 21: 1 next to the **p** of Ahab king of
2 Ki 20:18 they shall be eunuchs in the **p**
Ezra 4:14 we receive support from the **p**,
6: 2 in the **p** that is in the
Esth 1: 5 of the garden of the king's **p**.
1: 9 for the women in the royal **p**
2: 8 also was taken to the king's **p**,
2: 9 for her from the king's **p**,
2:13 quarters to the king's **p**.
2:16 Ahasuerus, into his royal **p**,
4:13 you will escape in the king's **p**
5: 1 the inner court of the king's **p**,
6: 4 outer court of the king's **p** to
7: 7 of wine and went into the **p**
7: 8 the king returned from the **p**
9: 4 was great in the king's **p**,
Ps 45:13 is all glorious within the **p**;
45:15 They shall enter the King's **p**.
144:12 Sculptured in **p** style;
Isa 25: 2 A **p** of foreigners to be a city
39: 7 they shall be eunuchs in the **p**
Jer 30:18 And the **p** shall remain
Dan 1: 4 to serve in the king's **p**,
4: 4 house, and flourishing in my **p**.
4:29 was walking about the royal **p**
5: 5 of the wall of the king's **p**;
6:18 Now the king went to his **p** and
11:45 shall plant the tents of his **p**
Nah 2: 6 And the **p** is dissolved.
Mt 26: 3 the people assembled at the **p**
Lk 11:21 fully armed, guards his own **p**,
Phil 1:13 become evident to the whole **p**

PALACES (30/29) PALACE
2 Chr 36:19 burned all its **p** with fire, and
Ps 45: 8 cassia, Out of the ivory **p**,
48: 3 God is in her **p**;
48:13 her bulwarks; Consider her **p**;
122: 7 Prosperity within your **p**.
Prov 30:28 hands, And it is in kings' **p**.
Isa 13:22 jackals in their pleasant **p**.
23:13 towers, They raised up its **p**,
32:14 Because the **p** will be forsaken,
34:13 thorns shall come up in its **p**,
Jer 6: 5 And let us destroy her **p**.
9:21 our windows, Has entered our **p**,
17:27 and it shall devour the **p** of
49:27 consume the **p** of Ben-Hadad."
Lam 2: 5 He has swallowed up all her **p**;
2: 7 has given up the walls of her **p**
Hos 8:14 And it shall devour his **p**.
Am 1: 4 devour the **p** of Ben-Hadad.
1: 7 Which shall devour its **p**.
1:10 Which shall devour its **p**."
1:12 devour the **p** of Bozrah."
1:14 And it shall devour its **p**,
2: 2 devour the **p** of Kerioth;
2: 5 devour the **p** of Jerusalem."
3: 9 Proclaim in the **p** at Ashdod,
3: 9 And in the **p** in the land of
3:10 violence and robbery in their **p**.
3:11 And your **p** shall be
6: 8 pride of Jacob, And hate his **p**;
Mic 5: 5 And when he treads in our **p**,

PALAL (1/1)
Neh 3:25 **P** the son of Uzai made repairs

PALANQUIN (1/1)
Song 3: 9 the King Made himself a **p**:

PALATE (1/1)
Job 34: 3 the ear tests words As the **p**

PALE (3/3)
Isa 29:22 Nor shall his face now grow **p**;
Jer 30: 6 labor, And all faces turned **p**?
Rev 6: 8 and behold, a **p** horse.

PALESTINA, PALESTINE (KJV) See PHILISTIA

PALLU (5/5)
Gen 46: 9 sons of Reuben were Hanoch, **P**,
Ex 6:14 of Israel, were Hanoch, **P**,
Num 26: 5 family of the Hanochites; of **P**,
26: 8 And the son of **P** was Eliab.
1 Chr 5: 3 of Israel were Hanoch, **P**,

PALLUITES (1/1)
Num 26: 5 of Pallu, the family of the **P**;

PALM (38/35) PALMS
Ex 15:27 water and seventy **p** trees;
Lev 14:15 and pour it into the **p** of his
14:26 the **p** of his own left hand.
23:40 branches of **p** trees, the boughs
Num 33: 9 of water and seventy **p** trees;
Deut 34: 3 the city of **p** trees, as far as
Judg 4: 5 would sit under the **p** tree
1 Ki 6:29 **p** trees, and open flowers.
6:32 **p** trees, and open flowers, and
6:32 cherubim and on the **p** trees.
6:35 **p** trees, and open flowers on
7:36 and **p** trees, wherever there was
2 Chr 3: 5 and he carved **p** trees and
28:15 the city of **p** trees. Then they
Neh 8:15 **p** branches, and branches of
Ps 92:12 shall flourish like a **p** tree,
Song 7: 7 of yours is like a **p** tree,
7: 8 'I will go up to the **p** tree,
Isa 9:14 **P** branch and bulrush in one
19:15 **P** branch or bulrush, may do.
Jer 10: 5 like a **p** tree, And they cannot
Ezek 40:16 each gatepost were **p** trees.
40:22 and also its **p** trees, had the
40:26 and it had **p** trees on its
40:31 **p** trees were on its gateposts,
40:34 and **p** trees were on its
40:37 **p** trees were on its gateposts
41:18 with cherubim and **p** trees,
41:18 a **p** tree between cherub and
41:19 of a man was toward a **p** tree
41:19 of a young lion toward a **p** tree
41:20 cherubim and **p** trees were
41:25 Cherubim and **p** trees were
41:26 window frames and **p** trees
Joel 1:12 The **p** tree also, And the
Jn 12:13 took branches of **p** trees and
18:22 by struck Jesus with the **p** of
Rev 7: 9 with **p** branches in their hands,

PALMERWORM (KJV) See LOCUST

PALMS (8/8) PALM
Judg 1:16 went up from the City of **P** with
3:13 possession of the City of **P**.
1 Sam 5: 4 head of Dagon and both the **p**
2 Ki 9:35 skull and the feet and the **p**

Isa 49:16 I have inscribed you on the **p**
Dan 10:10 on my knees and on the **p** of
Mt 26:67 others struck Him with the **p**
Mk 14:65 officers struck Him with the **p**

PALSY (KJV) See PARALYTIC

PALTI (2/2)

Num 13: 9 ***P*** the son of Raphu;
1 Sam 25:44 to ***P*** the son of Laish, who was

PALTIEL (2/2)

Num 34:26 ***P*** the son of Azzan;
2 Sam 3:15 from ***P*** the son of Laish.

PALTITE (1/1)

2 Sam 23:26 Helez the *P*, Ira the son

PAMPERS (1/1)

Prov 29:21 He who **p** his servant from

PAMPHYLIA (5/5)

Acts 2:10 'Phrygia and *P*, Egypt and
13:13 Paphos, they came to Perga in *P*;
14:24 through Pisidia, they came to *P*.
15:38 who had departed from them in *P*,
27: 5 sea which is off Cilicia and *P*,

PAN (20/19)

Lev 2: 5 a grain offering baked in a **p**,
2: 7 offering baked in a covered **p**,
6:21 It shall be made in a **p** with
7: 9 is prepared in the covered **p**,
7: 9 in the covered pan, or in a **p**,
Num 7:14 one gold **p** of ten shekels, full
7:20 one gold **p** of ten shekels, full
7:26 one gold **p** of ten shekels, full
7:32 one gold **p** of ten shekels, full
7:38 one gold **p** of ten shekels, full
7:44 one gold **p** of ten shekels, full
7:50 one gold **p** of ten shekels, full
7:56 one gold **p** of ten shekels, full
7:62 one gold **p** of ten shekels, full
7:68 one gold **p** of ten shekels, full
7:74 one gold **p** of ten shekels, full
7:80 one gold **p** of ten shekels, full
1 Sam 2:14 he would thrust it into the **p**,
2 Sam 13: 9 And she took the **p** and placed
1 Chr 23:29 and what is baked in the **p**,

PANELED (7/7) PANELING

1 Ki 6: 9 and he **p** the temple with beams
6:15 the temple to the ceiling he **p**
7: 3 And it was **p** with cedar above
7: 7 and it was **p** with cedar from
2 Chr 3: 5 The larger room he **p** with
Ezek 41:16 the threshold were **p** with
Hag 1: 4 to dwell in your **p** houses,

PANELING (1/1) PANELED

Jer 22:14 ***P*** it with cedar And painting

PANELS (14/9)

1 Ki 6:34 two **p** comprised one folding
6:34 and two **p** comprised the other
7:28 design of the carts: They had **p**,
7:28 and the **p** were between frames;
7:29 on the **p** that were between the
7:31 but the **p** were square, not
7:32 Under the **p** were the four
7:35 its flanges and its **p** were of
7:36 of its flanges and on its **p** he
2 Ki 16:17 And King Ahaz cut off the **p** of
Ezek 41:24 The doors had two **p** apiece, two
41:24 panels apiece, two folding **p**:
41:24 two **p** for one door and two
41:24 panels for one door and two **p**

PANGS (16/15)

Ps 18: 4 The **p** of death surrounded me,
48: 6 pain, as of a woman in birth **p**,
73: 4 For there are no **p** in their
116: 3 And the **p** of Sheol laid hold
Isa 13: 8 ***P*** and sorrows will take hold
21: 3 ***P*** have taken hold of me, like
21: 3 like the **p** of a woman in labor.
26:17 in pain and cries out in her **p**,
Jer 13:21 Will not **p** seize you, Like a
22:23 you be when **p** come upon you,
48:41 the heart of a woman in birth **p**.
49:22 the heart of a woman in birth **p**.
50:43 ***P*** as of a woman in childbirth.
Mic 4: 9 For **p** have seized you like a
4:10 Like a woman in birth **p**.
Rom 8:22 groans and labors with birth **p**

PANIC (1/1)

Zech 14:13 in that day That a great **p**

PANICKED (1/1)

Judg 20:41 back, the men of Benjamin **p**,

PANS (10/9)

Ex 25:29 shall make its dishes, its **p**,
27: 3 Also you shall make its **p** to
38: 3 utensils for the altar: the **p**,
Num 4: 7 and put on it the dishes, the **p**,
7:84 silver bowls, and twelve gold **p**.
7:86 The twelve gold **p** full of
7:86 all the gold of the **p** weighed
11: 8 in the mortar, cooked it in **p**,
1 Chr 9:31 things that were baked in the **p**.
2 Chr 35:13 in pots, in caldrons, and in **p**,

PANT (2/2)

Isa 42:14 I will **p** and gasp at once.
Am 2: 7 They **p** after the dust of the

PANTED (1/1)

Ps 119:131 I opened my mouth and **p**,

PANTETH (KJV) See PANTS

PANTS (3/2)

Ps 38:10 My heart **p**, my strength
42: 1 As the deer **p** for the water
42: 1 So **p** my soul for You, O God.

PAPER (1/1)

2 Jn 12 did not wish to do so with **p**

PAPHOS (2/2)

Acts 13: 6 gone through the island to *P*,
13:13 and his party set sail from *P*,

PAPYRUS (2/2)

Job 8:11 Can the **p** grow up without a
Isa 19: 7 The **p** reeds by the River, by

PARABLE (35/35) PARABLES

Ps 78: 2 I will open my mouth in a **p**;
Ezek 17: 2 and speak a **p** to the house of
24: 3 And utter a **p** to the rebellious
Mt 13:18 Therefore hear the **p** of the
13:24 Another **p** He put forth to them,
13:31 Another **p** He put forth to them,
13:33 Another **p** He spoke to them:
13:34 and without a **p** He did not
13:36 Explain to us the **p** of the tares
15:15 Explain this **p** to us."
21:33 Hear another **p**: There was
24:32 Now learn this **p** from the fig
Mk 4:10 twelve asked Him about the **p**.
4:13 "Do you not understand this **p**?
4:30 Or with what **p** shall we picture
4:34 But without a **p** He did not speak
7:17 asked Him concerning the **p**.
12:12 they knew He had spoken the **p**
13:28 Now learn this **p** from the fig
Lk 5:36 Then He spoke a **p** to them: "No
6:39 And He spoke a **p** to them: "Can
8: 4 every city, He spoke by a **p**:
8: 9 What does this **p** mean?"
8:11 Now the **p** is this: The seed is
12:16 Then He spoke a **p** to them,
12:41 do You speak this **p** only to
13: 6 He also spoke this **p**:
14: 7 So He told a **p** to those who
15: 3 So He spoke this **p** to them,
18: 1 Then He spoke a **p** to them, that
18: 9 Also He spoke this **p** to some
19:11 things, He spoke another **p**,
20: 9 began to tell the people this **p**:
20:19 they knew He had spoken this **p**
21:29 Then He spoke to them a **p**:

PARABLES (16/16) PARABLE

Ezek 20:49 say of me, 'Does he not speak **p**?
Mt 13: 3 spoke many things to them in **p**,
13:10 "Why do You speak to them in **p**?
13:13 I speak to them in **p**,
13:34 spoke to the multitude in **p**;
13:35 will open My mouth in **p**;
13:53 when Jesus had finished these **p**,
21:45 and Pharisees heard His **p**,
22: 1 and spoke to them again by **p**
Mk 3:23 Himself and said to them in **p**:
4: 2 He taught them many things by **p**,
4:11 outside, all things come in **p**,
4:13 will you understand all the **p**?
4:33 And with many such **p** He spoke
12: 1 He began to speak to them in **p**:
Lk 8:10 to the rest it is given in **p**,

PARADE (3/3)

Esth 6: 9 Then **p** him on horseback through
Job 18:14 And they **p** him before the king
1 Cor 13: 4 love does not **p** itself, is not

PARADISE (3/3)

Lk 23:43 today you will be with Me in *P*.
2 Cor 12: 4 how he was caught up into ***P*** and
Rev 2: 7 which is in the midst of the ***P***

PARAH (1/1)

Josh 18:23 Avim, *P*, Ophrah,

PARALLEL (1/1)

Ezek 42: 7 a wall which was outside ran **p**

PARALYTIC (8/7) PARALYTICS, PARALYZED

Mt 9: 2 they brought to Him a **p** lying
9: 2 their faith, He said to the **p**,
9: 6 He said to the **p**, "Arise,
Mk 2: 3 bringing a **p** who was carried by
2: 4 let down the bed on which the **p**
2: 5 their faith, He said to the **p**,
2: 9 is easier, to say to the **p**,
2:10 forgive sins"—He said to the **p**,

PARALYTICS (1/1) PARALYTIC

Mt 4:24 epileptics, and **p**; and He

PARALYZED (6/6) PARALYTIC

Mt 8: 6 my servant is lying at home **p**,
Lk 5:18 on a bed a man who was **p**,
5:24 said to the man who was **p**,
Jn 5: 3 of sick people, blind, lame, **p**,
Acts 8: 7 and many who were **p** and lame
9:33 bedridden eight years and was **p**.

PARAMOURS (1/1)

Ezek 23:20 For she lusted for her **p**,

PARAN (12/11) EL PARAN

Gen 21:21 He dwelt in the Wilderness of *P*;
Num 10:12 down in the Wilderness of *P*.
12:16 camped in the Wilderness of *P*.
13: 3 them from the Wilderness of ***P***
13:26 Israel in the Wilderness of *P*,
Deut 1: 1 plain opposite Suph, between *P*,
33: 2 He shone forth from Mount *P*,
1 Sam 25: 1 down to the Wilderness of *P*.
1 Ki 11:18 arose from Midian and came to *P*;
11:18 they took men with them from ***P***
Hab 3: 3 The Holy One from Mount *P*.

PARAPET (1/1)

Deut 22: 8 then you shall make a **p** for

PARBAR (2/1)

1 Chr 26:18 As for the ***P*** on the west, there
26:18 the highway and two at the *P*.

PARCEL (1/1)

Gen 33:19 And he bought the **p** of land,

P

PARCHED (9/8)

Lev 23:14 eat neither bread nor **p** grain
Josh 5:11 unleavened bread and **p** grain,
Ruth 2:14 and he passed **p** grain to her;
2 Sam 17:28 **p** grain and beans, lentils and
17:28 lentils and **p** seeds,
Job 14:11 And a river becomes **p** and
Isa 35: 7 The **p** ground shall become a
Jer 14: 4 Because the ground is **p**,
17: 6 But shall inhabit the **p** places

PARCHMENTS (1/1)

2 Tim 4:13 the books, especially the **p**.

PARDON (15/14) PARDONED, PARDONING

Ex 23:21 for He will not **p** your
34: 9 and **p** our iniquity and our sin,
Num 14:19 ***P*** the iniquity of this people, I
1 Sam 15:25 please **p** my sin, and return
2 Ki 5:18 in this thing may the LORD **p**
5:18 may the LORD please **p** your
24: 4 which the LORD would not **p**.
Neh 9:17 But You are God, Ready to **p**,
Job 7:21 Why then do You not **p** my
Ps 25:11 ***P*** my iniquity, for it is
Isa 55: 7 For He will abundantly **p**.
Jer 5: 1 And I will **p** her.
5: 7 How shall I **p** you for this?
33: 8 and I will **p** all their
50:20 For I will **p** those whom I

PARDONED (3/3) PARDON

Num 14:20 the LORD said: "I have **p**,
Isa 40: 2 ended, That her iniquity is **p**;
Lam 3:42 and rebelled; You have not **p**.

PARDONING (1/1) PARDON

Mic 7:18 ***P*** iniquity And passing over

PARENTS (21/20)

Mt 10:21 will rise up against **p** and
Mk 13:12 will rise up against **p** and
Lk 2:27 And when the **p** brought in the

2:41 His **p** went to Jerusalem every
8:56 And her **p** were astonished, but
18:29 no one who has left house or **p**
21:16 will be betrayed even by **p**
Jn 9: 2 who sinned, this man or his **p**,
9: 3 Neither this man nor his **p**
9:18 until they called the **p** of him
9:20 His **p** answered them and said,
9:22 His **p** said these things because
9:23 Therefore his **p** said, "He is of
Rom 1:30 evil things, disobedient to **p**,
2 Cor 12:14 ought not to lay up for the **p**,
12:14 but the **p** for the children.
Eph 6: 1 obey your **p** in the Lord, for
Col 3:20 obey your **p** in all things, for
1 Tim 5: 4 at home and to repay their **p**;
2 Tim 3: 2 blasphemers, disobedient to **p**,
Heb 11:23 hidden three months by his **p**,

PARMASHTA (1/1)

Esth 9: 9 *P*, Arisai, Aridai,

PARMENAS (1/1)

Acts 6: 5 Prochorus, Nicanor, Timon, *P*,

PARNACH (1/1)

Num 34:25 Zebulun, Elizaphan the son of *P*;

PAROSH (6/6)

Ezra 2: 3 the people of *P*,
8: 3 of Shecaniah, of the sons of *P*,
10:25 of Israel: of the sons of *P*:
Neh 3:25 After him Pedaiah the son of *P*
7: 8 the sons of *P*, two thousand
10:14 The leaders of the people: *P*,

PARSHANDATHA (1/1)

Esth 9: 7 Also *P*, Dalphon, Aspatha,

PART (88/79) PARTED, PARTING, PARTLY, PARTS, SHARE

Gen 27:16 his hands and on the smooth **p**
31:37 what **p** of your household things
Ex 16:20 But some of them left **p** of it
Lev 2:16 **p** of its beaten grain and
2:16 of its beaten grain and **p** of
7:33 have the right thigh for his **p**.
8:29 It was Moses' **p** of the ram of
11:25 whoever carries **p** of the carcass
11:35 And everything on which a **p** of
11:37 And if a **p** of any such carcass
11:38 and if a **p** of any such
27:16 a man dedicates to the LORD **p**
Num 18:29 the consecrated **p** of them.'
23:13 you shall see only the outer **p**
31:27 between those who took **p** in the
Deut 14:27 for he has no **p** nor inheritance
18: 1 shall have no **p** nor inheritance
33:21 He provided the first **p** for
Josh 14: 4 And they gave no **p** to the
18: 7 But the Levites have no **p** among
22:25 You have no **p** in the LORD."
22:27 You have no **p** in the LORD." '
Ruth 2: 3 she happened to come to the **p**
1 Sam 9:24 up the thigh with its upper **p**
23:20 and our **p** shall be to deliver
27: 1 to seek me anymore in any **p** of
30:24 But as his **p** is who goes down
30:24 so shall his **p** be who stays
2 Sam 4: 2 (For Beeroth also was **p** of
14: 6 and there was no one to **p**
1 Ki 7:34 its supports were **p** of the
2 Ki 18:23 if you are able on your **p** to put
1 Chr 12:29 (until then the greatest **p** of
2 Chr 28:21 For Ahaz took **p** of the
29:16 priests went into the inner **p**
Neh 1: 9 cast out to the farthest **p** of
Job 32:17 I also will answer my **p**,
Ps 5: 9 Their inward **p** is
51: 6 And in the hidden **p** You will
Isa 7:18 That is in the farthest **p** of
36: 8 if you are able on your **p** to put
Ezek 26:20 make you dwell in the lowest **p**
45:17 it shall be the prince's **p** to
48:14 may not alienate this best **p**
Dan 5: 5 and the king saw the **p** of the
Am 4: 7 One **p** was rained upon,
4: 7 where it did not rain the **p**
Mk 13:27 from the farthest **p** of earth to
13:27 of earth to the farthest **p** of
Lk 10:42 and Mary has chosen that good **p**,
11:36 having no **p** dark, the whole
11:39 but your inward **p** is full of
17:24 that flashes out of one **p**
17:24 heaven shines to the other **p**
Jn 13: 8 you have no **p** with Me."
19:23 four parts, to each soldier a **p**,
Acts 1:17 with us and obtained a **p** in
1:25 to take **p** in this ministry and
5: 2 And he kept back **p** of the
5: 2 and brought a certain **p** and
5: 3 Holy Spirit and keep back **p**
8:21 You have neither **p** nor portion
14: 4 **p** sided with the Jews, and part
14: 4 and **p** with the apostles.
16:12 is the foremost city of that **p**
23: 6 when Paul perceived that one **p**
Rom 11:25 that blindness in **p** has
1 Cor 11:18 and in **p** I believe it.
12:24 given greater honor to that **p**
13: 9 For we know in **p** and we prophesy
13: 9 in part and we prophesy in **p**.
13:10 then that which is in **p** will be
13:12 face to face. Now I know in **p**,
15: 6 of whom the greater **p** remain to
16:17 for what was lacking on your **p**
2 Cor 1:14 you have understood us in **p**),
6:15 Or what **p** has a believer with
Eph 4:16 working by which every **p** does
Heb 7: 2 also Abraham gave a tenth **p** of
9: 2 was prepared: the first **p**,
9: 3 the **p** of the tabernacle which
9: 6 always went into the first **p**
9: 7 But into the second **p** the high
1 Pe 4:14 On their **p** He is blasphemed,
4:14 but on your **p** He is glorified.
Rev 20: 6 and holy is he who has **p** in
21: 8 all liars shall have their **p**
22:19 God shall take away his **p** from

PARTAKE (8/8) PARTAKER

Deut 33:19 For they shall **p** of the
1 Cor 9:13 those who serve at the altar **p**
10:17 for we all **p** of that one bread.
10:21 you cannot **p** of the Lord's
10:30 But if I **p** with thanks, why am I
2 Cor 1: 7 so also you will **p** of the
2 Tim 2: 6 farmer must be first to **p** of
1 Pe 4:13 to the extent that you **p** of

PARTAKEN (1/1)

Heb 2:14 then as the children have **p** of

PARTAKER (5/5) PARTAKE, PARTAKERS

Ps 50:18 And have been a **p** with
Rom 11:17 and with them became a **p** of the
1 Cor 9:10 threshes in hope should be **p**
9:23 that I may be **p** of it with
1 Pe 5: 1 and also a **p** of the glory that

PARTAKERS (15/15) PARTAKER

Mt 23:30 we would not have been **p** with
Rom 15:27 if the Gentiles have been **p** of
1 Cor 9:12 If others are **p** of this right
10:18 who eat of the sacrifices **p** of
2 Cor 1: 7 we know that as you are **p** of
Eph 3: 6 and **p** of His promise in Christ
5: 7 Therefore do not be **p** with them.
Phil 1: 7 you all are **p** with me of grace.
Col 1:12 who has qualified us to be **p**
Heb 3: 1 **p** of the heavenly calling,
3:14 For we have become **p** of Christ
6: 4 and have become **p** of the Holy
12: 8 of which all have become **p**,
12:10 that we may be **p** of His
2 Pe 1: 4 through these you may be **p** of

PARTAKES (1/1)

Heb 5:13 For everyone who **p** only of milk

PARTED (4/4) PART

Gen 2:10 and from there it **p** and became
Job 41:17 stick together and cannot be **p**.
Lk 24:51 that He was **p** from them and
Acts 15:39 became so sharp that they **p**

PARTHIANS (1/1)

Acts 2: 9 **P** and Medes and Elamites, those

PARTIAL (2/2)

Lev 19:15 You shall not be **p** to the poor,
Job 34:19 Yet He is not **p** to princes,

PARTIALITY (24/24)

Ex 23: 3 You shall not show **p** to a poor
Deut 1:17 You shall not show **p** in
10:17 who shows no **p** nor takes a
16:19 justice; you shall not show **p**,
2 Chr 19: 7 with the LORD our God, no **p**,
Job 13: 8 Will you show **p** for Him?
13:10 If you secretly show **p**.
32:21 show **p** to anyone; Nor let me
37:24 He shows no **p** to any who are
Ps 82: 2 And show **p** to the wicked?
Prov 18: 5 It is not good to show **p** to
24:23 It is not good to show **p** in
28:21 To show **p** is not good,
Mal 2: 9 kept My ways But have shown **p**
Acts 10:34 I perceive that God shows no **p**.
Rom 2:11 For there is no **p** with God.
Eph 6: 9 and there is no **p** with Him.
Col 3:25 he has done, and there is no **p**.
1 Tim 5:21 prejudice, doing nothing with **p**.
Jas 2: 1 the Lord of glory, with **p**.
2: 4 have you not shown **p** among
2: 9 but if you show **p**,
3:17 without **p** and without
1 Pe 1:17 who without **p** judges according

PARTICULAR (2/2)

Zech 11: 7 in **p** the poor of the flock.
Eph 5:33 let each one of you in **p** so

PARTIES (2/2)

Ex 22: 9 the cause of both **p** shall come
1 Pe 4: 3 revelries, drinking **p**,

PARTING (3/3) PART

Ezek 21:21 of Babylon stands at the **p** of
Mk 1:10 He saw the heavens **p** and the
Lk 9:33 as they were **p** from Him, that

PARTITION (1/1)

Ex 40: 3 and **p** off the ark with the

PARTITIONED (1/1)

Ex 40:21 and **p** off the ark of the

PARTLY (10/4) PART

Dan 2:33 its feet **p** of iron and partly
2:33 its feet partly of iron and **p**
2:41 **p** of potter's clay and partly
2:41 partly of potter's clay and **p**
2:42 the toes of the feet were **p**
2:42 were partly of iron and **p** of
2:42 so the kingdom shall be **p**
2:42 shall be partly strong and **p**
Heb 10:33 **p** while you were made a
10:33 and **p** while you became

PARTNER (3/3)

Prov 29:24 Whoever is a **p** with a thief
2 Cor 8:23 he is my **p** and fellow worker
Phm 1:17 If then you count me as a **p**,

PARTNERS (2/2)

Lk 5: 7 So they signaled to their **p** in
5:10 who were **p** with Simon.

PARTRIDGE (2/2)

1 Sam 26:20 as when one hunts a **p** in the
Jer 17:11 As a **p** that broods but does

PARTS (37/37) PART

Lev 1: 8 Aaron's sons, shall lay the **p**,
Num 31:27 divide the plunder into two **p**,
Deut 14: 6 the hoof split into two **p**,
19: 3 and divide into three **p** the
30: 4 driven out to the farthest **p**
Josh 18: 5 shall divide it into seven **p**.
18: 6 survey the land in seven **p** and
18: 9 survey in a book in seven **p** by
Ruth 1:17 If anything but death **p** you
1 Ki 7:25 and all their back **p** pointed
16:21 Israel were divided into two **p**:
2 Ki 10:32 the LORD began to cut off **p**
2 Chr 4: 4 and all their back **p** pointed
Neh 4:13 men behind the lower **p** of the
Ps 51: 6 desire truth in the inward **p**,
63: 9 Shall go into the lower **p** of
65: 8 who dwell in the farthest **p**
139: 9 And dwell in the uttermost **p**
139:13 For You formed my inward **p**;
139:15 wrought in the lowest **p** of the
Isa 3:17 will uncover their secret **p**.
44:23 you lower **p** of the earth;
Jer 6:22 be raised from the farthest **p**
25:32 raised up From the farthest **p**
34:18 in two and passed between the **p**
34:19 land who passed between the **p**
Ezek 32:24 uncircumcised to the lower **p**
Jon 1: 5 gone down into the lowest **p** of
Jn 19:23 His garments and made four **p**,
Acts 2:10 Egypt and the **p** of Libya
9:32 as Peter went through all **p**
27:44 some on boards and some on **p**
Rom 15:23 having a place in these **p**,
1 Cor 12:23 and our unpresentable **p** have
12:24 but our presentable **p** have no
Eph 4: 9 descended into the lower **p** of
Rev 16:19 city was divided into three **p**,

PARTY (5/5)

Neh 4:22 guard by night and a working **p**
Ezek 39:14 with the help of a search **p**,
39:15 The search **p** will pass through
Acts 13:13 Now when Paul and his **p** set
23: 9 the scribes of the Pharisees' **p**

PARUAH (1/1)

1 Ki 4:17 Jehoshaphat the son of *P*,

PARVAIM (1/1)

2 Chr 3: 6 and the gold was gold from *P*.

PARZITES (1/1)

Num 26:20 of Perez, the family of the *P*;

PASACH (1/1)

1 Chr 7:33 The sons of Japhlet were *P*,

PASDAMMIM (1/1)

1 Chr 11:13 He was with David at **P**.

PASEAH (4/4)

1 Chr 4:12 And Eshton begot Beth-Rapha, **P**,
Ezra 2:49 the sons of Uzza, the sons of **P**,
Neh 3: 6 Jehoiada the son of **P** and
7:51 the sons of Uzza, the sons of **P**,

PASHHUR (13/11)

Ezra 2:38 the sons of **P**, one thousand
10:22 of the sons of **P**:
Neh 7:41 the sons of **P**, one
10: 3 **P**, Amariah, Malchijah,
11:12 son of Zechariah, the son of **P**,
Jer 20: 1 Now **P** the son of Immer, the
20: 2 Then **P** struck Jeremiah the
20: 3 on the next day that **P** brought
20: 3 has not called your name **P**,
20: 6 'And you, **P**, and all who
21: 1 King Zedekiah sent to him **P**
38: 1 Mattan, Gedaliah the son of **P**,
38: 1 and **P** the son of Malchiah heard

PASHUR (1/1)

1 Chr 9:12 son of Jeroham, the son of **P**,

PASS (426/410) PASSED, PASSES, PASSING

Gen 4: 3 process of time it came to **p**
4: 8 his brother; and it came to **p**,
6: 1 Now it came to **p**, when men
7:10 And it came to **p** after seven
8: 1 And God made a wind to **p** over
8: 6 So it came to **p**, at the end
8:13 And it came to **p** in the six
11: 2 And it came to **p**, as they
12:11 And it came to **p**, when he
14: 1 And it came to **p** in the days of
15:17 came to **p**, when the sun
18: 3 do not **p** on by Your servant.
18: 5 After that you may **p** by,
19:17 So it came to **p**, when they
19:29 And it came to **p**, when God
20:13 'And it came to **p**, when God
21:22 And it came to **p** at that time
22: 1 came to **p** after these things
22:20 Now it came to **p** after these
24:30 So it came to **p**, when he
24:43 and it shall come to **p** that
24:52 And it came to **p**, when
25:11 And it came to **p**, after the
26: 8 Now it came to **p**, when he
26:32 It came to **p** the same day that
27: 1 Now it came to **p**, when Isaac
27:40 And it shall come to **p**,
29:10 And it came to **p**, when Jacob
29:13 Then it came to **p**, when
29:23 Now it came to **p** in the evening,
29:25 So it came to **p** in the morning,
30:25 And it came to **p**, when
30:32 Let me **p** through all your flock
30:41 And it came to **p**, whenever
31:52 that I will not **p** beyond this
31:52 and you will not **p** beyond this
32:16 **P** over before me, and put some
34:25 Now it came to **p** on the third
35:17 Now it came to **p**, when she
37:23 So it came to **p**, when
38: 1 It came to **p** at that time that
38: 9 not be his; and it came to **p**,
38:24 And it came to **p**, about
38:27 Now it came to **p**, at the
39: 7 And it came to **p** after these
40: 1 It came to **p** after these things
40:20 Now it came to **p** on the third
41: 1 Then it came to **p**, at the
41: 8 Now it came to **p** in the morning
41:13 'And it came to **p**, just as
41:32 God will shortly bring it to **p**.
43: 2 And it came to **p**, when they
47:24 And it shall come to **p** in the
48: 1 Now it came to **p** after these
Ex 2:11 Now it came to **p** in those days,
4:24 And it came to **p** on the way, at
6:28 And it came to **p**, on the day
12:12 For I will **p** through the land of
12:13 I will **p** over you; and the
12:23 For the LORD will **p** through to
12:23 the LORD will **p** over the door
12:25 It will come to **p** when you come
12:29 And it came to **p** at midnight
12:41 And it came to **p** at the end of
12:41 it came to **p** that all the armies
12:51 And it came to **p**, on that
13:15 'And it came to **p**, when
13:17 Then it came to **p**, when
14:24 Now it came to **p**, in the
15:16 Till Your people **p** over,
15:16 Till the people **p** over
16:10 Now it came to **p**, as Aaron
19:16 Then it came to **p** on the third
26:28 The middle bar shall **p** through
32:30 Now it came to **p** on the next
33: 7 And it came to **p** that everyone
33: 9 And it came to **p**, when Moses
33:19 I will make all My goodness **p**
33:22 you with My hand while I **p** by.
36:33 And he made the middle bar to **p**
40:17 And it came to **p** in the first
Lev 9: 1 It came to **p** on the eighth day
18:21 let any of your descendants **p**
Num 7: 1 Now it came to **p**, when Moses
10:11 Now it came to **p** on the
16:31 Now it came to **p**, as he
17: 8 Now it came to **p** on the next
20:17 Please let us **p** through your
20:17 We will not **p** through fields or
20:18 You shall not **p** through my
20:19 let me only **p** through on foot,
20:20 'You shall not **p** through."
21:22 'Let me **p** through your land.
21:23 would not allow Israel to **p**
26: 1 And it came to **p**, after the
27: 7 of their father to **p** to them.
27: 8 cause his inheritance to **p** to
Deut 1: 3 Now it came to **p** in the fortieth
2: 4 You are about to **p** through
2:27 'Let me **p** through your land;
2:28 only let me **p** through on foot,
2:30 of Heshbon would not let us **p**
3:21 kingdoms through which you **p**.
7:12 "Then it shall come to **p**,
9:11 'And it came to **p**, at the
13: 2 sign or the wonder comes to **p**,
18:10 makes his son or his daughter **p**
18:22 does not happen or come to **p**,
28: 1 "Now it shall come to **p**,
28:15 "But it shall come to **p**,
30: 1 "Now it shall come to **p**,
Josh 1: 1 it came to **p** that the LORD
1:11 **P** through the camp and command
1:14 But you shall **p** before your
3:13 "And it shall come to **p**,
4: 1 And it came to **p**, when all
4:11 Then it came to **p**,
4:18 And it came to **p**, when the
5:13 And it came to **p**,
6: 5 "It shall come to **p**,
6:15 But it came to **p** on the seventh
8:24 And it came to **p** when Israel
9: 1 And it came to **p** when all the
10: 1 Now it came to **p** when
11: 1 And it came to **p**, when Jabin
21:45 house of Israel. All came to **p**.
23: 1 Now it came to **p**, a long
23:14 All have come to **p** for you;
23:15 "Therefore it shall come to **p**,
24:29 Now it came to **p** after these
Judg 1: 1 death of Joshua it came to **p**
1:28 And it came to **p**, when Israel
2:19 And it came to **p**, when the
6: 7 And it came to **p**, when the
6:25 Now it came to **p** the same night
11: 4 It came to **p** after a time that
11:17 Please let me **p** through your
11:19 Please let us **p** through your
11:20 Sihon did not trust Israel to **p**
11:35 And it came to **p**, when he
13:12 let Your words come to **p**!
13:17 when Your words come to **p** we
14:15 But it came to **p** on the seventh
16:16 And it came to **p**, when she
19: 1 And it came to **p** in those days,
19: 5 Then it came to **p** on the fourth
21: 3 why has this come to **p** in
Ruth 1: 1 Now it came to **p**, in the days
1 Sam 1:20 So it came to **p** in the process
2:36 And it shall come to **p** that
3: 2 And it came to **p** at that time,
8: 1 Now it came to **p** when Samuel was
9: 6 that he says surely comes to **p**.
10: 9 and all those signs came to **p**
13:23 Philistines went out to the **p**
16: 8 and made him **p** before Samuel.
16: 9 Then Jesse made Shammah **p** by.
16:10 Jesse made seven of his sons **p**
25:30 "And it shall come to **p**,
2 Sam 1: 1 Now it came to **p** after the
7: 1 Now it came to **p** when the king
8: 1 After this it came to **p** that
12:18 on the seventh day it came to **p**
13:23 And it came to **p**, after two
13:30 And it came to **p**, while they
15: 7 Now it came to **p** after forty
17:21 Now it came to **p**, after they
1 Ki 6: 1 And it came to **p** in the four
8:10 And it came to **p**, when the
9: 1 And it came to **p**, when
12:20 Now it came to **p** when all Israel
13: 4 So it came to **p** when King
13:32 Samaria, will surely come to **p**.
16:11 Then it came to **p**, when he
16:31 And it came to **p**, as though
18: 1 And it came to **p** after many
18:12 "And it shall come to **p**,
18:36 And it came to **p**, at the
18:44 Then it came to **p** the seventh
21: 1 And it came to **p** after these
21:15 And it came to **p**, when
22: 2 Then it came to **p**, in the
2 Ki 2: 1 And it came to **p**, when the
4: 6 Now it came to **p**, when the
6: 9 Beware that you do not **p** this
8: 3 It came to **p**, at the end of
16: 3 indeed he made his son **p**
17:17 their sons and daughters to **p**
18: 1 Now it came to **p** in the third
18: 9 Now it came to **p** in the fourth
19:25 Now I have brought it to **p**,
19:35 And it came to **p** on a certain
19:37 Now it came to **p**, as he was
21: 6 Also he made his son **p** through
22: 3 Now it came to **p**, in the
23:10 make his son or his daughter **p**
25: 1 Now it came to **p** in the ninth
25:27 Now it came to **p** in the
1 Chr 17: 1 Now it came to **p**, when David
18: 1 After this it came to **p** that
2 Chr 5:11 And it came to **p** when the
5:13 indeed it came to **p**,
8: 1 It came to **p** at the end of
12: 1 Now it came to **p**, when
33: 6 Also he caused his sons to **p**
Neh 1: 1 It came to **p** in the month of
2: 1 And it came to **p** in the month of
2: 7 that they must permit me to **p**
2:14 for the animal under me to **p**.
Esth 1: 1 Now it came to **p** in the days of
Job 6:15 streams of the brooks that **p**
9:26 They **p** by like swift ships,
14: 5 his limits, so that he cannot **p**.
19: 8 up my way, so that I cannot **p**;
34:20 The people are shaken and **p**
Ps 8: 8 the fish of the sea That **p**
37: 5 And He shall bring it to **p**.
37: 7 who brings wicked schemes to **p**.
78:13 the sea and caused them to **p**
80:12 So that all who **p** by the way
84: 6 As they **p** through the Valley
89:41 All who **p** by the way plunder
104: 9 a boundary that they may not **p**
105:19 time that his word came to **p**,
129: 8 Neither let those who **p** by them
136:14 And made Israel **p** through the
148: 6 made a decree which shall not **p**
Prov 4:15 Turn away from it and **p** on.
9:15 To call to those who **p** by,
22: 3 But the simple **p** on and are
27:12 The simple **p** on and are
Isa 2: 2 Now it shall come to **p** in the
4: 3 And it shall come to **p** that he
7: 1 Now it came to **p** in the days of
7: 7 Nor shall it come to **p**.
7:18 And it shall come to **p** in that
8: 8 He will **p** through Judah,
8: 8 He will overflow and **p** over,
8:21 They will **p** through it hard
10:12 Therefore it shall come to **p**,
10:20 And it shall come to **p** in that
10:27 It shall come to **p** in that day
11:11 It shall come to **p** in that day
14: 3 It shall come to **p** in the day
14:24 thought, so it shall come to **p**,
16:12 And it shall come to **p**,
17: 4 that day it shall come to **p**
21: 1 As whirlwinds in the South **p**
22: 7 It shall come to **p** that your
23:15 Now it shall come to **p** in that
24:21 It shall come to **p** in that day
27:12 And it shall come to **p** in that
28:19 morning by morning it will **p**
28:21 And bring to **p** His act, His
33:21 Nor majestic ships **p** by
34:10 No one shall **p** through it
35: 8 The unclean shall not **p** over
36: 1 Now it came to **p** in the
37:26 Now I have brought it to **p**,
37:38 Now it came to **p**, as he was
42: 9 former things have come to **p**,
43: 2 When you **p** through the waters,
46:11 I will also bring it to **p**.
47: 2 **P** through the rivers.
48: 3 I did them, and they came to **p**.
48: 5 Before it came to **p** I
65:24 It shall come to **p** That before
66:23 And it shall come to **p** That
Jer 2:10 For **p** beyond the coasts of
3: 9 'So it came to **p**, through her
3:16 "Then it shall come to **p**,
4: 9 And it shall come to **p** in that
5:22 that it cannot **p** beyond it?
5:22 yet they cannot **p** over it.
8:13 I have given them shall **p** away
9:10 So that no one can **p** through;
9:12 so that no one can **p** through?
13: 6 Now it came to **p** after many days
22: 8 And many nations will **p** by this
25:12 'Then it will come to **p**,
28: 9 word of the prophet comes to **p**,
30: 8 For it shall come to **p** in that
31:28 "And it shall come to **p**,
32:35 sons and their daughters to **p**
33:13 the flocks shall again **p** under
35:11 "But it came to **p**,
36: 1 Now it came to **p** in the fourth
36: 9 Now it came to **p** in the fifth
41: 1 Now it came to **p** in the seventh
49:39 But it shall come to **p** in the
52: 4 Now it came to **p** in the ninth
52:31 Now it came to **p** in the
Lam 1:12 all you who **p** by? Behold and
2:15 All who **p** by clap their hands
3:37 who speaks and it comes to **p**,
3:44 That prayer should not **p**
4:21 of Uz! The cup shall also **p**
Ezek 1: 1 Now it came to **p** in the
3:16 Now it came to **p** at the end of
5: 1 and **p** it over your head and
5:14 in the sight of all who **p** by.
5:17 Pestilence and blood shall **p**
8: 1 And it came to **p** in the sixth

12:25 which I speak will come to **p**;
14:15 If I cause wild beasts to **p**
14:15 so desolate that no man may **p**
16:21 up to them by causing them to **p**
20: 1 It came to **p** in the seventh
20:26 caused all their firstborn to **p**
20:31 your gifts and make your sons **p**
20:37 I will make you **p** under the rod,
21: 7 and shall be brought to **p**,
24:14 spoken it; It shall come to **p**,
26: 1 And it came to **p** in the eleventh
29:11 Neither foot of man shall **p**
29:11 through it nor foot of beast **p**
29:17 And it came to **p** in the
30:20 And it came to **p** in the
31: 1 Now it came to **p** in the eleventh
32: 1 And it came to **p** in the twelfth
32:17 It came to **p** also in the
33:21 And it came to **p** in the twelfth
33:28 so desolate that no one will **p**
33:33 "And when this comes to **p**—
36:34 in the sight of all who **p** by.
37: 2 Then He caused me to **p** by them
38:10 that day it shall come to **p**
38:18 And it will come to **p** at the
39:11 It will come to **p** in that day
39:11 the valley of those who **p** by
39:14 to **p** through the land and bury
39:15 The search party will **p** through
46:21 outer court and caused me to **p**
Dan 2:29 about what would come to **p**
2:45 to the king what will come to **p**
4:16 And let seven times **p** over
4:23 till seven times **p** over him';
4:25 and seven times shall **p** over
4:32 and seven times shall **p** over
7:14 Which shall not **p** away,
11:10 come and overwhelm and **p**
11:40 them, and **p** through.
Hos 1: 5 It shall come to **p** in that day
1:10 And it shall come to **p** In the
2:21 It shall come to **p** in that day
Joel 2:28 And it shall come to **p**
2:32 And it shall come to **p** That
3:17 And no aliens shall ever **p**
3:18 And it will come to **p** in that
Am 5: 5 Nor **p** over to Beersheba;
5:17 For I will **p** through you,"
6: 9 Then it shall come to **p**,
7: 8 I will not **p** by them anymore.
8: 2 I will not **p** by them anymore.
8: 9 And it shall come to **p** in that
Mic 1:11 **P** by in naked shame, you
2: 8 as they **p** by, Like men
2:13 **P** through the gate, And go
2:13 Their king will **p** before them,
4: 1 Now it shall come to **p** in the
Nah 1:15 the wicked one shall no more **p**
3: 7 It shall come to **p** that all
Zeph 1:12 And it shall come to **p** at that
Zech 6:15 And this shall come to **p** if
7: 1 of King Darius it came to **p**
8:13 And it shall come to **p** That
9: 8 No more shall an oppressor **p**
10:11 He shall **p** through the sea with
13: 3 It shall come to **p** that if
13: 8 And it shall come to **p** in all
14: 6 It shall come to **p** in that day
14:13 It shall come to **p** in that day
14:16 And it shall come to **p** that
Mt 5:18 till heaven and earth **p** away,
5:18 one tittle will by no means **p**
8:28 so that no one could **p** that
11: 1 Now it came to **p**, when Jesus
13:53 Now it came to **p**, when Jesus
19: 1 Now it came to **p**, when Jesus
24: 6 these things must come to **p**,
24:34 generation will by no means **p**
24:35 Heaven and earth will **p** away,
24:35 but My words will by no means **p**
26: 1 Now it came to **p**, when Jesus
26:39 let this cup **p** from Me;
26:42 if this cup cannot **p** away from
Mk 1: 9 It came to **p** in those days
13:30 generation will by no means **p**
13:31 Heaven and earth will **p** away,
13:31 but My words will by no means **p**
14:35 the hour might **p** from Him.
Lk 2: 1 And it came to **p** in those days
2:15 this thing that has come to **p**,
3:21 it came to **p** that Jesus also
6:12 Now it came to **p** in those days
8: 1 Now it came to **p**, afterward,
9:28 Now it came to **p**, about eight
9:51 Now it came to **p**, when the
11: 1 Now it came to **p**, as He was
11:42 and **p** by justice and the love
16:17 for heaven and earth to **p** away
16:26 so that those who want to **p**
16:26 nor can those from there **p** to
19: 4 for He was going to **p** that
19:29 And it came to **p**, when He
21: 9 for these things must come to **p**
21:32 generation will by no means **p**
21:33 Heaven and earth will **p** away,
21:33 but My words will by no means **p**
21:36 things that will come to **p**,
24:30 Now it came to **p**, as He sat
24:51 Now it came to **p**, while He
Jn 13:19 that when it does come to **p**,
14:29 that when it does come to **p**,
Acts 2:17 And it shall come to **p** in
2:21 And it shall come to **p**
4: 5 And it came to **p**, on the next
9:32 Now it came to **p**, as Peter
21: 1 Now it came to **p**, that when
28:17 And it came to **p** after three
Rom 9:26 And it shall come to **p** in
1 Cor 15:54 then shall be brought to **p** the
16: 5 I will come to you when I **p**
2 Cor 1:16 to **p** by way of you to Macedonia,
Jas 1:10 a flower of the field he will **p**
2 Pe 3:10 in which the heavens will **p**

PASSAGE (3/3)

Num 20:21 Edom refused to give Israel **p**
Mk 12:26 Moses, in the burning bush **p**,
Lk 20:37 showed in the burning bush **p**

PASSAGES (1/1)

Jer 51:32 The **p** are blocked, The reeds

PASSED (113/105) PASS

Gen 12: 6 Abram **p** through the land to the
15:17 oven and a burning torch that **p**
18:11 and Sarah had **p** the age of
37:28 Then Midianite traders **p** by;
Ex 7:25 And seven days **p** after the LORD
12:27 who **p** over the houses of the
34: 6 And the LORD **p** before him and
Num 14: 7 The land we **p** through to spy out
20:17 or to the left until we have **p**
21:22 King's Highway until we have **p**
33: 8 from before Hahiroth and **p**
Deut 2: 8 And when we **p** beyond our
2: 8 we turned and **p** by way of the
29:16 the nations which you **p** by,
Josh 3: 4 for you have not **p** this way
10:29 Then Joshua **p** from Makkedah,
10:31 Then Joshua **p** from Libnah, and
10:34 From Lachish Joshua **p** to Eglon,
15: 3 **p** along to Zin, ascended on the
15: 3 **p** along to Hezron, went up to
15: 4 From there it **p** toward Azmon
15: 6 went up to Beth Hoglah and **p**
15:10 **p** along to the side of Mount
15:10 and **p** on to Timnah.
15:11 **p** along to Mount Baalah, and
16: 2 **p** along to the border of the
16: 6 and **p** by it on the east of
18: 9 **p** through the land, and wrote
18:18 Then it **p** along toward the north
18:19 And the border **p** along to the
19:13 And from there it **p** along on the
24:17 the people through whom we **p**.
Judg 3:26 and **p** beyond the stone images
9:25 and they robbed all who **p** by
11:29 and he **p** through Gilead and
11:29 and **p** through Mizpah of Gilead;
18:13 And they **p** from there to the
19:14 And they **p** by and went their
Ruth 2:14 and he **p** parched grain to her;
1 Sam 9: 4 So he **p** through the mountains of
9: 4 Then they **p** through the land of
9: 4 Then he **p** through the land of
15:12 **p** by, and gone down to
29: 2 the lords of the Philistines **p**
29: 2 but David and his men **p** in
2 Sam 15:18 Then all his servants **p** before
15:18 Gath, **p** before the king.
1 Ki 13:25 men **p** by and saw the corpse
19:11 the LORD **p** by, and a great and
19:19 Then Elijah **p** by him and threw
20:39 Now as the king **p** by, he cried
22: 1 Now three years **p** without war
2 Ki 4: 8 as often as he **p** by, he would
6:30 and as he **p** by on the wall, the
14: 9 beast that was in Lebanon **p**
2 Chr 25:18 beast that was in Lebanon **p**
30:10 So the runners **p** from city to
Job 4:15 Then a spirit **p** before my face;
11:16 it as waters that have **p**
15:19 And no alien **p** among them:
28: 8 Nor has the fierce lion **p** over
30:15 And my prosperity has **p** like a
37:21 When the wind has **p** and
Ps 18:12 His thick clouds **p** with
37:36 Yet he **p** away, and behold, he
48: 4 They **p** by together.
57: 1 these calamities have **p** by.
90: 9 For all our days have **p** away in
Song 3: 4 Scarcely had I **p** by them,
Isa 10:28 He has **p** Migron; At Michmash
40:27 And my just claim is **p** over by
41: 3 and **p** safely By the way that
Jer 11:15 And the holy flesh has **p** from
34:18 they cut the calf in two and **p**
34:19 the people of the land who **p**
46:17 He has **p** by the appointed
Ezek 16: 6 And when I **p** by you and saw you
16: 8 When I **p** by you again and looked
16:25 yourself to everyone who **p** by,
Jon 2: 3 Your billows and Your waves **p**
Nah 3:19 whom has not your wickedness **p**
Hab 3:10 overflowing of the water **p** by.
Zech 7:14 so that no one **p** through or
Mt 9: 9 As Jesus **p** on from there, He
27:39 And those who **p** by blasphemed
Mk 2:14 As He **p** by, He saw Levi the son
6:48 and would have **p** them by.
9:30 they departed from there and **p**
11:20 as they **p** by, they saw the fig
15:29 And those who **p** by blasphemed
Lk 10:31 he **p** by on the other side.
10:32 and **p** by on the other side.
17:11 He went to Jerusalem that He **p**
19: 1 Then Jesus entered and **p**
22:59 Then after about an hour had **p**,
Jn 5:24 but has **p** from death into life.
8:59 midst of them, and so **p** by.
9: 1 Now as Jesus **p** by, He saw a man
Acts 7:30 "And when forty years had **p**,
14:24 And after they had **p** through
15: 3 they **p** through Phoenicia and
17: 1 Now when they had **p** through
19: 1 having **p** through the upper
19:21 when he had **p** through Macedonia
21: 3 we **p** it on the left, sailed to
Rom 3:25 in His forbearance God had **p**
1 Cor 10: 1 all **p** through the sea,
2 Cor 5:17 old things have **p** away;
Heb 4:14 a great High Priest who has **p**
11:29 By faith they **p** through the Red
1 Jn 3:14 We know that we have **p** from
Rev 21: 1 and the first earth had **p** away.
21: 4 for the former things have **p**

PASSES (29/29) PASS

Ex 33:22 while My glory **p** by, that I
Lev 27:32 of whatever **p** under the rod,
1 Sam 14: 4 Between the **p**, by which
1 Ki 9: 8 everyone who **p** by it will be
2 Ki 4: 9 who **p** by us regularly.
2 Chr 7:21 everyone who **p** by it will be
Job 11:10 If He **p** by, imprisons, and
14:20 and he **p** on; You change his
Ps 78:39 A breath that **p** away and does
103:16 For the wind **p** over it, and it
Prov 10:25 When the whirlwind **p** by, the
26:17 He who **p** by and meddles in a
Eccl 1: 4 One generation **p** away, and
6:12 of his vain life which he **p**
Isa 28:15 When the overflowing scourge **p**
28:18 When the overflowing scourge **p**
29: 5 Like chaff that **p** away;
30:32 where the staff of punishment **p**,
Jer 13:24 them like stubble That **p** away
18:16 Everyone who **p** by it will be
19: 8 everyone who **p** by it will be
51:43 Through which no son of man **p**.
Hos 13: 3 And like the early dew that **p**
Mic 5: 8 if he **p** through, Both treads
Nah 1:12 will be cut down When he **p**
Zeph 2: 2 Or the day **p** like chaff,
2:15 to lie down! Everyone who **p**
Zech 9: 8 Because of him who **p** by and
Eph 3:19 know the love of Christ which **p**

PASSING (28/28) PASS

Judg 19:18 We are **p** from Bethlehem in
2 Ki 6:26 as the king of Israel was **p** by
Ps 144: 4 His days are like a **p** shadow.
Prov 7: 8 **P** along the street near her
31:30 is deceitful and beauty is **p**,
Isa 31: 5 **P** over, He will preserve
Ezek 16:15 your harlotry on everyone **p** by
23:37 **p** them through the fire, to
Mic 7:18 Pardoning iniquity And **p** over
Zeph 3: 6 With none **p** by. Their cities
Mt 20:30 they heard that Jesus was **p** by,
Mk 15:21 out of the country and **p** by,
Lk 4:30 Then **p** through the midst of
18:36 And hearing a multitude **p** by, he
18:37 that Jesus of Nazareth was **p**
Acts 5:15 at least the shadow of Peter **p**
8:40 And **p** through, he preached in
16: 8 So **p** by Mysia, they came down to
17:23 for as I was **p** through and
27: 8 **P** it with difficulty, we came to
1 Cor 7:31 For the form of this world is **p**
16: 5 through Macedonia (for I am **p**
2 Cor 3: 7 which glory was **p** away,
3:11 For if what is **p** away was
3:13 at the end of what was **p** away.
Heb 11:25 of God than to enjoy the **p**
1 Jn 2: 8 because the darkness is **p** away,
2:17 And the world is **p** away, and the

PASSION (3/3) PASSIONS

1 Cor 7: 9 to marry than to burn with **p**.
Col 3: 5 fornication, uncleanness, **p**,
1 Th 4: 5 not in **p** of lust, like the

PASSIONS (3/3) PASSION

Rom 1:26 God gave them up to vile **p**.
7: 5 the sinful **p** which were aroused
Gal 5:24 crucified the flesh with its **p**

PASSOVER (78/73)

Ex 12:11 in haste. It is the LORD's **P**.
12:21 and kill the **P** lamb.
12:27 It is the **P** sacrifice of the
12:43 is the ordinance of the **P**:
12:48 you and wants to keep the **P**
34:25 of the Feast of the **P** be left
Lev 23: 5 at twilight is the LORD's **P**.
Num 9: 2 children of Israel keep the **P**
9: 4 that they should keep the **P**.
9: 5 And they kept the **P** on the

9: 6 that they could not keep the **P**
9:10 he may still keep the LORD's **P**.
9:12 to all the ordinances of the **P**
9:13 and ceases to keep the **P**,
9:14 and would keep the LORD's **P**,
9:14 according to the rite of the **P**
28:16 of the first month is the **P**
33: 3 on the day after the **P** the
Deut 16: 1 and keep the **P** to the LORD
16: 2 you shall sacrifice the **P** to
16: 5 You may not sacrifice the **P**
16: 6 you shall sacrifice the **P** at
Josh 5:10 and kept the **P** on the
5:11 the land on the day after the **P**,
2 Ki 23:21 Keep the **P** to the LORD your
23:22 Such a **P** surely had never been
23:23 year of King Josiah this **P** was
2 Chr 30: 1 to keep the **P** to the LORD God
30: 2 had agreed to keep the **P** in
30: 5 they should come to keep the **P**
30:15 Then they slaughtered the **P**
30:17 of the slaughter of the **P**
30:18 yet they ate the **P** contrary to
35: 1 Now Josiah kept a **P** to the LORD
35: 1 and they slaughtered the **P**
35: 6 So slaughter the **P** offerings,
35: 7 all for **P** offerings for all
35: 8 gave to the priests for the **P**
35: 9 gave to the Levites for **P**
35:11 And they slaughtered the **P**
35:13 Also they roasted the **P**
35:16 to keep the **P** and to offer
35:17 who were present kept the **P** at
35:18 There had been no **P** kept in
35:18 of Israel had kept such a **P** as
35:19 of the reign of Josiah this **P**
Ezra 6:19 of the captivity kept the **P** on
6:20 And they slaughtered the **P**
Ezek 45:21 month, you shall observe the **P**,
Mt 26: 2 that after two days is the **P**,
26:17 to prepare for You to eat the **P**?
26:18 I will keep the **P** at your house
26:19 and they prepared the **P**.
Mk 14: 1 After two days it was the **P** and
14:12 when they killed the **P** lamb,
14:12 prepare, that You may eat the **P**?
14:14 room in which I may eat the **P**
14:16 and they prepared the **P**.
Lk 2:41 year at the Feast of the **P**.
22: 1 drew near, which is called **P**.
22: 7 when the **P** must be killed.
22: 8 Go and prepare the **P** for us,
22:11 room where I may eat the **P**
22:13 them, and they prepared the **P**.
22:15 I have desired to eat this **P**
Jn 2:13 Now the **P** of the Jews was at
2:23 He was in Jerusalem at the **P**,
6: 4 Now the **P**, a feast of
11:55 And the **P** of the Jews was near,
11:55 up to Jerusalem before the **P**,
12: 1 Then, six days before the **P**,
13: 1 Now before the feast of the **P**,
18:28 but that they might eat the **P**.
18:39 release someone to you at the **P**.
19:14 the Preparation Day of the **P**,
Acts 12: 4 him before the people after **P**.
1 Cor 5: 7 For indeed Christ, our **P**,
Heb 11:28 By faith he kept the **P** and the

PAST (42/42)

Gen 50: 4 the days of his mourning were **p**,
Ex 21:29 thrust with its horn in times **p**,
21:36 ox tended to thrust in time **p**,
Deut 2:10 Emim had dwelt there in times **p**,
4:32 concerning the days that are **p**,
4:42 having hated him in time **p**,
19: 4 not having hated him in time **p**—
19: 6 not hated the victim in time **p**.
1 Sam 15:32 the bitterness of death is **p**.
19: 7 in his presence as in times **p**.
2 Sam 3:17 In time **p** you were seeking for
5: 2 'Also, in time **p**, when Saul
16: 1 When David was a little **p** the
1 Ki 18:29 And when midday was **p**,
1 Chr 9:20 the officer over them in time **p**;
11: 2 'Also, in time **p**, even when
Neh 12:38 going **p** the Tower of the Ovens
Job 9:10 He does great things **p** finding
9:11 do not see Him; If He moves **p**,
14:13 me until Your wrath is **p**,
17:11 My days are **p**, My purposes
29: 2 that I were as in months **p**,
Ps 90: 4 like yesterday when it is **p**,
Eccl 3:15 an account of what is **p**.
Song 2:11 For lo, the winter is **p**,
Isa 26:20 Until the indignation is **p**.
Jer 8:20 "The harvest is **p**,
Am 8: 5 "When will the New Moon be **p**,
Mk 16: 1 Now when the Sabbath was **p**,
Acts 9:23 Now after many days were **p**,
12:10 When they were **p** the first and
20:16 For Paul had decided to sail **p**
Rom 11:33 His judgments and His ways **p**
1 Cor 7:36 if she is **p** the flower of
Gal 5:21 as I also told you in time **p**,
Eph 4:19 being **p** feeling, have given
2 Tim 2:18 the resurrection is already **p**;
Heb 1: 1 in various ways spoke in time **p**
11:11 she bore a child when she was **p**
1 Pe 4: 3 we have spent enough of our **p**
Rev 9:12 One woe is **p**. Behold, still
11:14 The second woe is **p**.

PASTOR (KJV) See SHEPHERD

PASTORS (1/1)

Eph 4:11 and some **p** and teachers,

PASTRY (3/3)

Num 11: 8 taste was like the taste of **p**
Ezek 16:13 You ate **p** of fine flour,
16:19 the **p** of fine flour, oil, and

PASTURE (24/22) PASTURES

Gen 47: 4 your servants have no **p** for
1 Chr 4:39 to seek **p** for their flocks.
4:40 And they found rich, good **p**,
4:41 because there was **p** for their
Job 39: 8 of the mountains is his **p**,
Ps 74: 1 against the sheep of Your **p**?
79:13 Your people and sheep of Your **p**,
95: 7 we are the people of His **p**,
100: 3 people and the sheep of His **p**.
Isa 5:17 the lambs shall feed in their **p**,
32:14 wild donkeys, a **p** of flocks—
Jer 6: 3 Each one shall **p** in his own
23: 1 and scatter the sheep of My **p**!
25:36 the LORD has plundered their **p**,
Lam 1: 6 like deer That find no **p**,
Ezek 34:14 "I will feed them in good **p**,
34:14 a good fold and feed in rich **p**
34:18 you to have eaten up the good **p**,
34:18 your feet the residue of your **p**—
34:31 are My flock, the flock of My **p**;
Hos 13: 6 When they had **p**, they were
Joel 1:18 Because they have no **p**;
Mic 2:12 a flock in the midst of their **p**;
Jn 10: 9 will go in and out and find **p**.

PASTURED (1/1)

Gen 36:24 in the wilderness as he **p** the

PASTURES (14/14) PASTURE

1 Ki 4:23 oxen, twenty oxen from the **p**,
Ps 23: 2 makes me to lie down in green **p**;
65:12 They drop on the **p** of the
65:13 The **p** are clothed with flocks;
83:12 us take for ourselves The **p**
Isa 7:19 And on all thorns and in all **p**.
30:23 cattle will feed In large **p**.
49: 9 And their **p** shall be on all
Ezek 45:15 from the rich **p** of Israel.
Joel 1:19 fire has devoured the open **p**,
1:20 fire has devoured the open **p**.
2:22 For the open **p** are springing
Am 1: 2 The **p** of the shepherds mourn,
Zeph 2: 6 The seacoast shall be **p**,

PATARA (1/1)

Acts 21: 1 to Rhodes, and from there to **P**.

PATCH (1/1) PATCHED

Mt 9:16 for the **p** pulls away from the

PATCHED (1/1) PATCH

Josh 9: 5 old and **p** sandals on their feet,

PATCHES (1/1)

Job 18:13 It devours **p** of his skin;

PATH (28/28) PATHS, PATHWAY

Gen 49:17 by the way, A viper by the **p**,
Num 22:24 the LORD stood in a narrow **p**
2 Sam 22:37 You enlarged my **p** under me;
Job 28: 7 That **p** no bird knows, Nor has
28:26 And a **p** for the thunderbolt,
30:13 They break up my **p**,
38:25 Or a **p** for the thunderbolt,
Ps 1: 1 Nor stands in the **p** of
16:11 You will show me the **p** of life;
18:36 You enlarged my **p** under me,
27:11 And lead me in a smooth **p**,
77:19 Your **p** in the great waters,
78:50 He made a **p** for His anger;
119:35 Make me walk in the **p** of Your
119:105 to my feet And a light to my **p**.
139: 3 You comprehend my **p** and my
142: 3 within me, Then You knew my **p**.
Prov 1:15 Keep your foot from their **p**;
2: 9 Equity and every good **p**.
4:14 Do not enter the **p** of the
4:18 But the **p** of the just is like
4:26 Ponder the **p** of your feet,
5: 6 Lest you ponder her **p** of
7: 8 And he took the **p** to her house
Isa 26: 7 You weigh the **p** of the just.
30:11 the way, Turn aside from the **p**,
40:14 And taught Him in the **p** of
43:16 makes a way in the sea And a **p**

PATHLESS (1/1)

Job 12:24 them wander in a **p** wilderness.

PATHROS (5/5)

Isa 11:11 From **P** and Cush, From Elam
Jer 44: 1 Noph, and in the country of **P**,
44:15 in the land of Egypt, in **P**,
Ezek 29:14 them to return to the land of **P**,
30:14 I will make **P** desolate,

PATHRUSIM (2/2)

Gen 10:14 **P**, and Casluhim
1 Chr 1:12 **P**, Casluhim (from whom

PATHS (41/41) PATH

Job 6:18 The **p** of their way turn aside,
8:13 So are the **p** of all who forget
13:27 And watch closely all my **p**.
19: 8 He has set darkness in my **p**.
24:13 its ways Nor abide in its **p**.
33:11 stocks, He watches all my **p**.
38:20 That you may know the **p** to
Ps 8: 8 sea That pass through the **p**
17: 4 I have kept away from the **p** of
17: 5 Uphold my steps in Your **p**,
23: 3 He leads me in the **p** of
25: 4 ways, O LORD; Teach me Your **p**.
25:10 All the **p** of the LORD are
65:11 And Your **p** drip with
Prov 2: 8 He guards the **p** of justice,
2:13 From those who leave the **p** of
2:15 who are devious in their **p**;
2:18 And her **p** to the dead;
2:19 Nor do they regain the **p** of
2:20 And keep to the **p** of
3: 6 And He shall direct your **p**.
3:17 And all her **p** are peace.
4:11 I have led you in right **p**.
5:21 And He ponders all his **p**.
7:25 Do not stray into her **p**;
8: 2 the way, where the **p** meet.
8:20 In the midst of the **p** of
Isa 2: 3 And we shall walk in His **p**.
3:12 And destroy the way of your **p**.
42:16 I will lead them in **p** they
59: 7 and destruction are in their **p**.
59: 8 have made themselves crooked **p**;
Jer 6:16 and see, And ask for the old **p**,
18:15 ways, From the ancient **p**,
Lam 3: 9 He has made my **p** crooked.
Hos 2: 6 So that she cannot find her **p**.
Mic 4: 2 And we shall walk in His **p**.
Mt 3: 3 Make His **p** straight.'"
Mk 1: 3 Make His **p** straight.'"
Lk 3: 4 Make His **p** straight.
Heb 12:13 and make straight **p** for your

PATHWAY (2/2) PATH, PATHWAYS

Ps 85:13 shall make His footsteps our **p**.
Prov 12:28 And in its **p** there is no

PATHWAYS (1/1) PATHWAY

Jer 18:15 To walk in **p** and not on a

PATIENCE (25/25) PATIENT

Neh 9:30 Yet for many years You had **p**
Jer 15:15 In Your enduring **p**,
Mt 18:26 have **p** with me, and I will pay
18:29 Have **p** with me, and I will pay
Lk 8:15 keep it and bear fruit with **p**.
21:19 By your **p** possess your souls.
Rom 15: 4 that we through the **p** and
15: 5 Now may the God of **p** and comfort
2 Cor 6: 4 as ministers of God: in much **p**,
Col 1:11 for all **p** and longsuffering
1 Th 1: 3 and **p** of hope in our Lord Jesus
2 Th 1: 4 the churches of God for your **p**
3: 5 the love of God and into the **p**
1 Tim 6:11 godliness, faith, love, **p**,
Titus 2: 2 sound in faith, in love, in **p**;
Heb 6:12 those who through faith and **p**
Jas 1: 3 of your faith produces **p**.
1: 4 But let **p** have its perfect
5:10 an example of suffering and **p**.
Rev 1: 9 tribulation and kingdom and **p**
2: 2 your works, your labor, your **p**,
2: 3 you have persevered and have **p**,
2:19 service, faith, and your **p**;
13:10 Here is the **p** and the faith of
14:12 Here is the **p** of the saints;

PATIENT (7/7) PATIENCE, PATIENTLY

Eccl 7: 8 The **p** in spirit is better
Rom 2: 7 eternal life to those who by **p**
12:12 **p** in tribulation, continuing
1 Th 5:14 the weak, be **p** with all.
2 Tim 2:24 gentle to all, able to teach, **p**,
Jas 5: 7 Therefore be **p**,
5: 8 You also be **p**. Establish your

PATIENTLY (7/6) PATIENT

Ps 37: 7 and wait **p** for Him; Do not
40: 1 I waited **p** for the LORD;
Acts 26: 3 I beg you to hear me **p**.
Heb 6:15 after he had **p** endured, he
Jas 5: 7 waiting **p** for it until it
1 Pe 2:20 for your faults, you take it **p**?
2:20 and suffer, if you take it **p**,

PATMOS (1/1)

Rev 1: 9 on the island that is called **P**

PATRIARCH (2/2) PATRIARCHS

Acts 2:29 speak freely to you of the **p**
Heb 7: 4 to whom even the **p** Abraham gave

PATRIARCHS (2/2) PATRIARCH

Acts 7: 8 and Jacob begot the twelve **p**.
7: 9 And the **p**, becoming

PATROBAS (1/1)

Rom 16:14 Asyncritus, Phlegon, Hermas, **P**,

PATROL (1/1)

1 Ki 20:17 And Ben-Hadad sent out a **p**,

PATTERN (13/12)

Ex 25: 9 the **p** of the tabernacle and the
25: 9 of the tabernacle and the **p** of
25:40 make them according to the **p**
26:30 tabernacle according to its **p**
Num 8: 4 According to the **p** which the
2 Ki 16:10 design of the altar and its **p**,
Ezek 43:10 and let them measure the **p**.
Acts 7:44 to make it according to the **p**
Phil 3:17 so walk, as you have us for a **p**.
1 Tim 1:16 as a **p** to those who are going
2 Tim 1:13 Hold fast the **p** of sound words
Titus 2: 7 showing yourself to be a **p**
Heb 8: 5 things according to the **p**

PAU (1/1)

Gen 36:39 and the name of his city was **P**.

PAUL (156/152) PAUL'S, SAUL

Acts 13: 9 Saul, who also is called **P**,
13:13 Now when **P** and his party set
13:16 Then **P** stood up, and motioning
13:43 devout proselytes followed **P**
13:45 opposed the things spoken by **P**.
13:46 Then **P** and Barnabas grew bold
13:50 up persecution against **P** and
14: 9 This man heard **P** speaking.
14: 9 **P**, observing him intently
14:11 Now when the people saw what **P**
14:12 they called Zeus, and **P**,
14:14 the apostles Barnabas and **P**
14:19 they stoned **P** and dragged him
15: 2 when **P** and Barnabas had no
15: 2 they determined that **P** and
15:12 and listened to Barnabas and **P**
15:22 own company to Antioch with **P**
15:25 with our beloved Barnabas and **P**,
15:35 **P** and Barnabas also remained in
15:36 Then after some days **P** said to
15:38 But **P** insisted that they should
15:40 but **P** chose Silas and departed,
16: 3 **P** wanted to have him go on with
16: 9 And a vision appeared to **P** in
16:14 to heed the things spoken by **P**.
16:17 This girl followed **P** and us, and
16:18 But **P**, greatly annoyed, turned
16:19 they seized **P** and Silas and
16:25 But at midnight **P** and Silas
16:28 But **P** called with a loud voice,
16:29 fell down trembling before **P**
16:36 reported these words to **P**,
16:37 But **P** said to them, "They have
17: 2 Then **P**, as his custom was,
17: 4 joined **P** and Silas.
17:10 the brethren immediately sent **P**
17:13 word of God was preached by **P**
17:14 the brethren sent **P** away,
17:15 So those who conducted **P** brought
17:16 Now while **P** waited for them at
17:22 Then **P** stood in the midst of
17:33 So **P** departed from among them.
18: 1 After these things **P** departed
18: 5 **P** was compelled by the Spirit,
18: 9 Now the Lord spoke to **P** in the
18:12 one accord rose up against **P**
18:14 And when **P** was about to open
18:18 So **P** still remained a good
19: 1 Apollos was at Corinth, that **P**,
19: 4 Then **P** said, "John indeed
19: 6 And when **P** had laid hands on
19:11 miracles by the hands of **P**,
19:13 you by the Jesus whom **P**
19:15 and **P** I know; but who are
19:21 **P** purposed in the Spirit, when
19:26 this **P** has persuaded and turned
19:30 And when **P** wanted to go in to
20: 1 **P** called the disciples to
20: 7 bread, **P**, ready to depart
20: 9 and as **P** continued speaking, he
20:10 But **P** went down, fell on him,
20:13 there intending to take **P** on
20:16 For **P** had decided to sail past
21: 4 They told **P** through the Spirit
21:13 Then **P** answered, "What do you
21:18 On the following day **P** went in
21:26 Then **P** took the men, and the
21:29 whom they supposed that **P** had
21:30 people ran together, seized **P**,
21:32 they stopped beating **P**.
21:37 Then as **P** was about to be led
21:39 But **P** said, "I am a Jew from
21:40 **P** stood on the stairs and
22:25 **P** said to the centurion who
22:28 And **P** said, "But I was born
22:30 and brought **P** down and set him
23: 1 Then **P**, looking earnestly at
23: 3 Then **P** said to him, "God will
23: 5 Then **P** said, "I did not know,
23: 6 But when **P** perceived that one
23:10 fearing lest **P** might be pulled
23:11 and said, "Be of good cheer, **P**;
23:12 drink till they had killed **P**.
23:14 nothing until we have killed **P**.
23:16 entered the barracks and told **P**.
23:17 Then **P** called one of the
23:18 **P** the prisoner called me to him
23:20 agreed to ask that you bring **P**
23:24 and provide mounts to set **P** on,
23:31 took **P** and brought him by
23:33 they also presented **P** to him.
24: 1 to the governor against **P**.
24:10 Then **P**, after the governor
24:23 the centurion to keep **P** and to
24:24 he sent for **P** and heard him
24:26 money would be given him by **P**,
24:27 Jews a favor, left **P** bound.
25: 2 the Jews informed him against **P**;
25: 4 But Festus answered that **P**
25: 6 he commanded **P** to be brought.
25: 7 serious complaints against **P**,
25: 9 answered **P** and said, "Are you
25:10 So **P** said, "I stand at Caesar's
25:19 whom **P** affirmed to be alive.
25:21 But when **P** appealed to be
25:23 at Festus' command **P** was
26: 1 Then Agrippa said to **P**,
26: 1 So **P** stretched out his hand
26:24 '**P**, you are beside yourself!
26:28 Then Agrippa said to **P**,
26:29 And **P** said, "I would to God
27: 1 they delivered **P** and some other
27: 3 And Julius treated **P** kindly and
27: 9 already over, **P** advised them,
27:11 than by the things spoken by **P**.
27:21 then **P** stood in the midst of
27:24 "saying, 'Do not be afraid, **P**;
27:31 **P** said to the centurion and the
27:33 **P** implored them all to take
27:43 centurion, wanting to save **P**,
28: 3 But when **P** had gathered a bundle
28: 8 **P** went in to him and prayed,
28:15 When **P** saw them, he thanked God
28:16 but **P** was permitted to dwell by
28:17 to pass after three days that **P**
28:25 they departed after **P** had said
28:30 Then **P** dwelt two whole years in
Rom 1: 1 **P**, a bondservant of Jesus
1 Cor 1: 1 **P**, called to be an apostle
1:12 each of you says, "I am of **P**,
1:13 Was **P** crucified for you?
1:13 you baptized in the name of **P**?
3: 4 For when one says, "I am of **P**,
3: 5 Who then is **P**, and who is
3:22 whether **P** or Apollos or Cephas,
2 Cor 1: 1 **P**, an apostle of Jesus
10: 1 Now I, **P**, myself am pleading
Gal 1: 1 **P**, an apostle (not from
5: 2 Indeed I, **P**, say to you that
Eph 1: 1 **P**, an apostle of Jesus
3: 1 For this reason I, **P**,
Phil 1: 1 **P** and Timothy, bondservants of
Col 1: 1 **P**, an apostle of Jesus
1:23 under heaven, of which I, **P**,
4:18 salutation by my own hand—**P**.
1 Th 1: 1 **P**, Silvanus, and Timothy,
2:18 wanted to come to you—even I, **P**,
2 Th 1: 1 **P**, Silvanus, and Timothy,
3:17 The salutation of **P** with my own
1 Tim 1: 1 **P**, an apostle of Jesus
2 Tim 1: 1 **P**, an apostle of Jesus
Titus 1: 1 **P**, a bondservant of God
Phm 1: 1 **P**, a prisoner of Christ
1: 9 to you—being such a one as **P**,
1:19 I, **P**, am writing with
2 Pe 3:15 also our beloved brother **P**,

PAUL'S (7/7)

Acts 19:29 **P** travel companions.
20:37 and fell on **P** neck and kissed
21: 8 day we who were **P** companions
21:11 he took **P** belt, bound his own
23:16 So when **P** sister's son heard of
25:14 Festus laid **P** case before the
1 Cor 16:21 salutation with my own hand—**P**.

PAULUS (1/1)

Acts 13: 7 with the proconsul, Sergius **P**,

PAUSE (1/1)

Isa 29: 9 **P** and wonder! Blind

PAUSED (1/1)

Ezek 10: 4 and **p** over the threshold of

PAVED (2/2)

Ex 24:10 under His feet as it were a **p**
Song 3:10 Its interior **p** with love

PAVEMENT (9/7)

2 Ki 16:17 and put it on a **p** of stones.
2 Chr 7: 3 faces to the ground on the **p**,
Esth 1: 6 gold and silver on a mosaic **p**
Ezek 40:17 there were chambers and a **p**
40:17 thirty chambers faced the **p**.
40:18 The **p** was by the side of the
40:18 this was the lower **p**.
42: 3 and opposite the **p** of the outer
Jn 19:13 a place that is called The **P**,

PAVILION (4/4)

2 Ki 16:18 Also he removed the Sabbath **p**
Ps 27: 5 He shall hide me in His **p**;
31:20 shall keep them secretly in a **p**
Jer 43:10 And he will spread his royal **p**

PAW (2/1)

1 Sam 17:37 who delivered me from the **p** of
17:37 paw of the lion and from the **p**

PAWS (2/2)

Lev 11:27 'And whatever goes on its **p**,
Job 39:21 He **p** in the valley, and

PAY (63/59) PAID

Ex 21: 2 he shall go out free and **p**
21:19 He shall only **p** for the loss
21:22 and he shall **p** as the judges
21:30 then he shall **p** to redeem his
21:36 he shall surely **p** ox for ox,
22: 7 he shall **p** double.
22: 9 the judges condemn shall **p**
22:16 he shall surely **p** the
22:17 he shall **p** money according to
Lev 27: 8 But if he is too poor to **p** your
Num 20:19 then I will **p** for it; let me
Deut 23:21 you shall not delay to **p** it;
2 Sam 15: 7 let me go to Hebron and **p** the
1 Ki 5: 6 and I will **p** you wages for your
20:39 or else you shall **p** a talent of
2 Ki 4: 7 sell the oil and **p** your debt;
18:14 you impose on me I will **p**.
Ezra 4:13 they will not **p** tax, tribute,
7:20 **p** for it from the king's
Esth 3: 2 But Mordecai would not bow or **p**
3: 5 that Mordecai did not bow or **p**
3: 9 and I will **p** ten thousand
4: 7 that Haman had promised to **p**
Job 22:27 And you will **p** your vows.
41:11 that I should **p** him?
Ps 22:25 I will **p** My vows before those
50:14 And **p** your vows to the Most
66:13 I will **p** You my vows,
76:11 and **p** them; Let all who are
116:14 I will **p** my vows to the LORD
116:18 I will **p** my vows to the LORD
Prov 5: 1 **p** attention to my wisdom;
7:24 **P** attention to the words of my
19:17 And He will **p** back what he has
22:27 have nothing with which to **p**,
Eccl 5: 4 do not delay to **p** it; For He
5: 4 **P** what you have vowed—
5: 5 to vow than to vow and not **p**.
Isa 23:18 Her gain and her **p** will be set
Lam 5: 4 We **p** for the water we drink,
Ezek 23:49 and you shall **p** for your
Jon 2: 9 I will **p** what I have vowed.
Mic 1: 7 And all her **p** as a harlot
1: 7 she gathered it from the **p** of
1: 7 they shall return to the **p** of
3:11 bribe, Her priests teach for **p**,
Mt 17:24 Does your Teacher not **p** the
18:25 "But as he was not able to **p**,
18:26 and I will **p** you all.'
18:28 **P** me what you owe!'
18:29 and I will **p** you all.'
18:30 into prison till he should **p**
18:34 the torturers until he should **p**
22:17 Is it lawful to **p** taxes to
23:23 hypocrites! For you **p** tithe of
Mk 12:14 Is it lawful to **p** taxes to
12:15 'Shall we **p**, or shall we not
12:15 we pay, or shall we not **p**?
Lk 20:22 Is it lawful for us to **p** taxes
23: 2 and forbidding to **p** taxes to
Acts 21:24 and **p** their expenses so that
Rom 13: 6 For because of this you also **p**
Jas 2: 3 and you **p** attention to the one

PAYING (1/1)

Ex 21:11 out free, without **p** money.

PAYMENT (7/6)

Ezek 16:31 a harlot, because you scorned **p**.
16:33 Men make **p** to all harlots, but
16:34 In that you gave **p** but no
16:34 that you gave payment but no **p**
27:15 you ivory tusks and ebony as **p**.
Joel 3: 3 Have given a boy as **p** for a
Mt 18:25 and that **p** be made.

PAYMENTS (1/1)

Ezek 16:33 but you made your ***p*** to all your

PAYS (1/1)

Prov 29:12 If a ruler ***p*** attention to lies,

PEACE (396/368) PEACEABLE, PEACEMAKERS, PEACETIME

Gen 15:15 shall go to your fathers in ***p***;
26:29 and have sent you away in ***p***.
26:31 and they departed from him in ***p***.
28:21 back to my father's house in ***p***,
34: 5 so Jacob held his ***p*** until they
34:21 These men are at ***p*** with us.
41:16 give Pharaoh an answer of ***p***.
43:23 ***P*** be with you, do not be
44:17 go up in ***p*** to your father."
Ex 4:18 Jethro said to Moses, "Go in ***p***.
14:14 you, and you shall hold your ***p***.
18:23 also go to their place in ***p***.
20:24 your burnt offerings and your ***p***
24: 5 offerings and sacrificed ***p***
29:28 from the sacrifices of their ***p***
32: 6 and brought ***p*** offerings;
Lev 3: 1 offering is a sacrifice of a ***p***
3: 3 from the sacrifice of the ***p***
3: 6 offering as a sacrifice of a ***p***
3: 9 from the sacrifice of the ***p***
4:10 bull of the sacrifice of the ***p***
4:26 fat of the sacrifice of the ***p***
4:31 from the sacrifice of the ***p***
4:35 from the sacrifice of the ***p***
6:12 burn on it the fat of the ***p***
7:11 the law of the sacrifice of ***p***
7:13 of thanksgiving of his ***p***
7:14 sprinkles the blood of the ***p***
7:15 flesh of the sacrifice of his ***p***
7:18 flesh of the sacrifice of his ***p***
7:20 flesh of the sacrifice of the ***p***
7:21 flesh of the sacrifice of the ***p***
7:29 offers the sacrifice of his ***p***
7:29 from the sacrifice of his ***p***
7:32 from the sacrifices of your ***p***
7:33 who offers the blood of the ***p***
7:34 from the sacrifices of their ***p***
7:37 and the sacrifice of the ***p***
9: 4 also a bull and a ram as ***p***
9:18 and the ram as sacrifices of ***p***
9:22 and ***p*** offerings.
10: 3 ' So Aaron held his ***p***.
10:14 given from the sacrifices of ***p***
17: 5 and offer them as ***p*** offerings
19: 5 if you offer a sacrifice of a ***p***
22:21 offers a sacrifice of a ***p***
23:19 year as a sacrifice of a ***p***
26: 6 I will give ***p*** in the land, and
Num 6:14 one ram without blemish as a ***p***
6:17 the ram as a sacrifice of ***p***
6:18 is under the sacrifice of the ***p***
6:26 upon you, And give you ***p***.
7:17 and for the sacrifice of ***p***
7:23 and as the sacrifice of ***p***
7:29 and for the sacrifice of ***p***
7:35 and as the sacrifice of ***p***
7:41 and as the sacrifice of ***p***
7:47 and as the sacrifice of ***p***
7:53 and as the sacrifice of ***p***
7:59 and as the sacrifice of ***p***
7:65 and as the sacrifice of ***p***
7:71 and as the sacrifice of ***p***
7:77 and as the sacrifice of ***p***
7:83 and as the sacrifice of ***p***
7:88 the oxen for the sacrifice of ***p***
10:10 over the sacrifices of your ***p***
15: 8 or as a ***p*** offering to the
25:12 I give to him My covenant of ***p***;
29:39 your drink offerings and your ***p***
30: 4 and her father holds his ***p***,
Deut 2:26 of Heshbon, with words of ***p***,
20:10 then proclaim an offer of ***p*** to
20:11 if they accept your offer of ***p***,
20:12 if the city will not make ***p***
23: 6 You shall not seek their ***p*** nor
27: 7 You shall offer ***p*** offerings, and
29:19 heart, saying, 'I shall have ***p***,
Josh 8:31 and sacrificed ***p*** offerings.
9:15 So Joshua made ***p*** with them, and
10: 1 of Gibeon had made ***p*** with
10: 4 for it has made ***p*** with Joshua
10:21 to Joshua at Makkedah, in ***p***.
11:19 was not a city that made ***p***
22:23 or if to offer ***p*** offerings on
22:27 and with our ***p*** offerings; that
Judg 4:17 for there was ***p*** between Jabin
6:23 ***P*** be with you; do not fear, you
8: 9 saying, "When I come back in ***p***,
11:31 when I return in ***p*** from the
18: 6 priest said to them, "Go in ***p***.
19:20 ***P*** be with you! However, let
20:26 offered burnt offerings and ***p***
21: 4 offered burnt offerings and ***p***
21:13 and announced ***p*** to them.
1 Sam 1:17 answered and said, "Go in ***p***,
7:14 Also there was ***p*** between Israel
10: 8 and make sacrifices of ***p***
10:27 no presents. But he held his ***p***.
11:15 There they made sacrifices of ***p***
13: 9 Bring a burnt offering and ***p***
20:42 said to David, "Go in ***p***,
25: 6 ***P*** be to you, peace to your
25: 6 ***p*** to your house, and peace to
25: 6 and ***p*** to all that you have!
25:35 Go up in ***p*** to your house. See, I
29: 7 return now, and go in ***p***,
2 Sam 3:21 Abner away, and he went in ***p***.
3:22 him away, and he had gone in ***p***.
3:23 him away, and he has gone in ***p***.
6:17 offered burnt offerings and ***p***
6:18 offering burnt offerings and ***p***
10:19 they made ***p*** with Israel and
13:20 with you? But now hold your ***p***,
15: 9 the king said to him, "Go in ***p***.
15:27 a seer? Return to the city in ***p***,
17: 3 all the people will be at ***p***.
19:24 until the day he returned in ***p***.
19:30 the king has come back in ***p*** to
24:25 offered burnt offerings and ***p***
1 Ki 2: 6 hair go down to the grave in ***p***.
2:33 there shall be ***p*** forever from
3:15 offered ***p*** offerings, and made a
4:24 and he had ***p*** on every side all
5:12 and there was ***p*** between Hiram
8:63 offered a sacrifice of ***p***
8:64 and the fat of the ***p*** offerings,
8:64 and the fat of the ***p*** offerings.
9:25 offered burnt offerings and ***p***
20:18 "If they have come out for ***p***,
22:17 each return to his house in ***p***.
22:27 affliction, until I come in ***p***.
22:28 said, "If you ever return in ***p***,
22:44 Also Jehoshaphat made ***p*** with the
2 Ki 5:19 Then he said to him, "Go in ***p***.
9:17 and let him say, 'Is it ***p***?
9:18 says the king: 'Is it ***p***?
9:18 "What have you to do with ***p***?
9:19 says the king: 'Is it ***p***?
9:19 "What have you to do with ***p***?
9:22 Jehu, that he said, "Is it ***p***,
9:22 So he answered, "What ***p***,
9:31 the gate, she said, "Is it ***p***,
16:13 sprinkled the blood of his ***p***
18:31 Make ***p*** with me by a present and
18:36 But the people held their ***p*** and
20:19 Will there not be ***p*** and truth at
22:20 be gathered to your grave in ***p***;
1 Chr 12:18 your side, O son of Jesse! ***P***,
12:18 ***p*** to you, And peace to your
12:18 And ***p*** to your helpers!
16: 1 offered burnt offerings and ***p***
16: 2 the burnt offerings and the ***p***
19:19 they made ***p*** with David and
21:26 offered burnt offerings and ***p***
22: 9 for I will give ***p*** and quietness
2 Chr 7: 7 offerings and the fat of the ***p***
15: 5 in those times there was no ***p***
18:16 each return to his house in ***p***.
18:26 affliction until I return in ***p***.
18:27 said, "If you ever return in ***p***,
29:35 with the fat of the ***p*** offerings
30:22 offering ***p*** offerings and making
31: 2 for burnt offerings and ***p***
33:16 sacrificed ***p*** offerings and
34:28 be gathered to your grave in ***p***;
Ezra 4:17 remainder beyond the River: ***P***,
5: 7 thus—To Darius the king: All ***p***.
7:12 the God of heaven: Perfect ***p***,
9:12 and never seek their ***p*** or
Esth 9:30 with words of ***p*** and truth,
10: 3 of his people and speaking ***p***
Job 5:23 of the field shall be at ***p***
5:24 know that your tent is in ***p***;
11: 3 talk make men hold their ***p***?
13:13 Hold your ***p*** with me, and let me
22:21 yourself with Him, and be at ***p***;
25: 2 He makes ***p*** in His high places.
33:31 Job, listen to me; Hold your ***p***,
33:33 not, listen to me; Hold your ***p***,
Ps 4: 8 I will both lie down in ***p***,
7: 4 evil to him who was at ***p*** with
28: 3 Who speak ***p*** to their
29:11 will bless His people with ***p***.
34:14 Seek ***p*** and pursue it.
35:20 For they do not speak ***p***,
37:11 in the abundance of ***p***.
37:37 the future of that man is ***p***.
39: 2 I held my ***p*** even from good;
55:18 He has redeemed my soul in ***p***
55:20 against those who were at ***p***
72: 3 The mountains will bring ***p*** to
72: 7 flourish, And abundance of ***p***,
83: 1 O God! Do not hold Your ***p***,
85: 8 For He will speak ***p*** To His
85:10 Righteousness and ***p*** have
119:165 Great ***p*** have those who love
120: 6 too long With one who hates ***p***.
120: 7 I am for ***p***; But when I
122: 6 Pray for the ***p*** of Jerusalem:
122: 7 ***P*** be within your walls,
122: 8 ***P*** be within you."
125: 5 ***P*** be upon Israel!
128: 6 ***P*** be upon Israel!
147:14 He makes ***p*** in your borders,
Prov 3: 2 of days and long life And ***p***
3:17 And all her paths are ***p***.
7:14 I have ***p*** offerings with me;
11:12 of understanding holds his ***p***.
12:20 But counselors of ***p*** have joy.
16: 7 even his enemies to be at ***p***
17:28 wise when he holds his ***p***;
29: 9 or laughs, there is no ***p***.
Eccl 3: 8 time of war, And a time of ***p***.
Song 8:10 in his eyes As one who found ***p***.
Isa 9: 6 Father, Prince of ***P***.
9: 7 of His government and ***p***
26: 3 will keep him in perfect ***p***,
26:12 You will establish ***p*** for us,
27: 5 That he may make ***p*** with Me;
27: 5 And he shall make ***p*** with
32:17 work of righteousness will be ***p***,
33: 7 The ambassadors of ***p*** shall
36:16 Make ***p*** with me by a present
36:21 But they held their ***p*** and
38:17 it was for my own ***p*** That
39: 8 At least there will be ***p*** and
42:14 I have held My ***p*** a long time,
45: 7 I make ***p*** and create calamity;
48:18 My commandments! Then your ***p***
48:22 "There is no ***p***,
52: 7 good news, Who proclaims ***p***,
53: 5 The chastisement for our ***p***
54:10 Nor shall My covenant of ***p*** be
54:13 And great shall be the ***p*** of
55:12 And be led out with ***p***;
57: 2 He shall enter into ***p***;
57:11 it not because I have held My ***p***
57:19 the fruit of the lips: ***P***,
57:19 ***p*** to him who is far off and
57:21 "There is no ***p***,
59: 8 The way of ***p*** they have not
59: 8 takes that way shall not know ***p***.
60:17 will also make your officers ***p***,
62: 1 sake I will not hold My ***p***,
62: 6 They shall never hold their ***p***
64:12 O LORD? Will You hold Your ***p***,
66:12 I will extend ***p*** to her like a
Jer 4:10 Saying, 'You shall have ***p***,
4:19 in me; I cannot hold my ***p***,
6:14 people slightly, Saying, '***P***,
6:14 slightly, Saying, 'Peace, ***p***!'
6:14 When there is no ***p***.
8:11 people slightly, Saying, '***P***,
8:11 slightly, Saying, 'Peace, ***p***!'
8:11 When there is no ***p***.
8:15 "We looked for ***p***,
12: 5 And if in the land of ***p***,
12:12 land; No flesh shall have ***p***.
14:13 but I will give you assured ***p***
14:19 for us? We looked for ***p***,
16: 5 for I have taken away My ***p*** from
23:17 You shall have ***p***" '; And to
28: 9 the prophet who prophesies of ***p***,
29: 7 And seek the ***p*** of the city where
29: 7 for in its ***p*** you will have
29: 7 in its peace you will have ***p***.
29:11 thoughts of ***p*** and not of evil,
30: 5 Of fear, and not of ***p***.
33: 6 to them the abundance of ***p*** and
34: 5 'You shall die in ***p***;
43:12 he shall go out from there in ***p***.
Lam 3:17 have moved my soul far from ***p***;
Ezek 7:25 They will seek ***p***,
13:10 ***P***!' when there is no peace—and
13:10 'Peace!' when there is no ***p***—
13:16 and who see visions of ***p*** for
13:16 for her when there is no ***p***,
34:25 I will make a covenant of ***p***
37:26 I will make a covenant of ***p***
43:27 your burnt offerings and your ***p***
45:15 and ***p*** offerings, to make
45:17 and the ***p*** offerings to make
46: 2 his burnt offering and his ***p***
46:12 burnt offering or voluntary ***p***
46:12 his burnt offering and his ***p***
Dan 4: 1 ***P*** be multiplied to you.
6:25 ***P*** be multiplied to you.
10:19 fear not! ***P*** be to you;
Am 5:22 will I regard your fattened ***p***
Ob 7 The men at ***p*** with you Shall
Mic 3: 5 Who chant "***P***" While they
5: 5 And this One shall be ***p***.
Nah 1:15 Who proclaims ***p***! O Judah,
Hag 2: 9 in this place I will give ***p***,
Zech 6:13 And the counsel of ***p*** shall be
8:10 There was no ***p*** from the
8:16 gates for truth, justice, and ***p***;
8:19 Therefore love truth and ***p***.
9:10 He shall speak ***p*** to the
Mal 2: 5 with him, one of life and ***p***,
2: 6 He walked with Me in ***p*** and
Mt 10:13 let your ***p*** come upon it. But if
10:13 let your ***p*** return to you.
10:34 think that I came to bring ***p***
10:34 I did not come to bring ***p*** but a
Mk 4:39 to the sea, "***P***, be still!"
5:34 has made you well. Go in ***p***,
9:50 and have ***p*** with one another."
Lk 1:79 our feet into the way of ***p***.
2:14 in the highest, And on earth ***p***,
2:29 Your servant depart in ***p***,
7:50 faith has saved you. Go in ***p***.
8:48 has made you well. Go in ***p***.
10: 5 first say, '***P*** to this house.'
10: 6 And if a son of ***p*** is there, your
10: 6 your ***p*** will rest on it; if not,
11:21 own palace, his goods are in ***p***.
12:51 suppose that I came to give ***p***
14:32 and asks conditions of ***p***.
19:38 ***P*** in heaven and glory in the
19:42 things that make for your ***p***!
24:36 said to them, "***P*** to you."
Jn 14:27 ***P*** I leave with you, My peace I
14:27 My ***p*** I give to you; not as the
16:33 you, that in Me you may have ***p***.

P

20:19 to them, "*P* be with you."
20:21 *P* to you! As the Father has sent
20:26 and said, "*P* to you!"
Acts 9:31 and Samaria had *p* and were
10:36 preaching *p* through Jesus
12:20 their friend, they asked for *p*,
16:36 therefore depart, and go in *p*.
24: 2 through you we enjoy great *p*,
Rom 1: 7 Grace to you and *p* from God
2:10 and *p* to everyone who works
3:17 And the way of *p* they
5: 1 we have *p* with God through our
8: 6 minded is life and *p*.
10:15 preach the gospel of *p*,
14:17 but righteousness and *p* and joy
14:19 the things which make for *p*
15:13 fill you with all joy and *p* in
15:33 Now the God of *p* be with you
16:20 And the God of *p* will crush
1 Cor 1: 3 Grace to you and *p* from God our
7:15 But God has called us to *p*.
14:33 author of confusion but of *p*,
16:11 send him on his journey in *p*,
2 Cor 1: 2 Grace to you and *p* from God our
13:11 be of one mind, live in *p*;
13:11 and the God of love and *p* will
Gal 1: 3 Grace to you and *p* from God the
5:22 of the Spirit is love, joy, *p*,
6:16 *p* and mercy be upon them, and
Eph 1: 2 Grace to you and *p* from God our
2:14 For He Himself is our *p*,
2:15 from the two, thus making *p*,
2:17 And He came and preached *p* to
4: 3 of the Spirit in the bond of *p*.
6:15 preparation of the gospel of *p*;
6:23 *P* to the brethren, and love with
Phil 1: 2 Grace to you and *p* from God our
4: 7 and the *p* of God, which
4: 9 and the God of *p* will be with
Col 1: 2 Grace to you and *p* from God
1:20 having made *p* through the blood
3:15 And let the *p* of God rule in
1 Th 1: 1 Grace to you and *p* from God
5: 3 *P* and safety!" then sudden
5:13 Be at *p* among yourselves.
5:23 Now may the God of *p* Himself
2 Th 1: 2 Grace to you and *p* from God our
3:16 Now may the Lord of *p* Himself
3:16 of peace Himself give you *p*
1 Tim 1: 2 and *p* from God our Father and
2 Tim 1: 2 and *p* from God the Father and
2:22 *p* with those who call on the
Titus 1: 4 and *p* from God the Father and
Phm 1: 3 Grace to you and *p* from God our
Heb 7: 2 of Salem, meaning "king of *p*,
11:31 had received the spies with *p*.
12:14 Pursue *p* with all people, and
13:20 Now may the God of *p* who
Jas 2:16 you says to them, "Depart in *p*,
3:18 of righteousness is sown in *p*
3:18 in peace by those who make *p*.
1 Pe 1: 2 Grace to you and *p* be
3:11 Let him seek *p* and
5:14 *P* to you all who are in Christ
2 Pe 1: 2 Grace and *p* be multiplied to you
3:14 to be found by Him in *p*,
2 Jn 3 and *p* will be with you from
3 Jn 14 *P* to you. Our friends greet
Jude 2 Mercy, *p*, and love be
Rev 1: 4 Grace to you and *p* from Him
6: 4 the one who sat on it to take *p*

PEACEABLE (5/5) PEACE, PEACEABLY

2 Sam 20:19 I am among the *p* and
1 Tim 2: 2 we may lead a quiet and *p* life
Titus 3: 2 speak evil of no one, to be *p*,
Heb 12:11 afterward it yields the *p* fruit
Jas 3:17 above is first pure, then *p*,

PEACEABLY (11/10) PEACEABLE

Gen 37: 4 him and could not speak *p* to
Judg 11:13 restore those lands *p*.
1 Sam 16: 4 and said, "Do you come *p*?
16: 5 And he said, "*P*;
1 Ki 2:13 So she said, "Do you come *p*?"
2:13 And he said, "*P*."
1 Chr 12:17 If you have come *p* to me to help
Jer 9: 8 One speaks *p* to his neighbor
Dan 11:21 royalty; but he shall come in *p*,
11:24 'He shall enter *p*, even into
Rom 12:18 live *p* with all men.

PEACEFUL (4/4)

1 Chr 4:40 land was broad, quiet, and *p*;
Isa 32:18 My people will dwell in a *p*
Jer 25:37 And the *p* dwellings are cut
Ezek 38:11 I will go to a *p* people, who

PEACEMAKERS (1/1) PEACE

Mt 5: 9 Blessed are the *p*, For they

PEACETIME (1/1) PEACE

1 Ki 2: 5 he shed the blood of war in *p*,

PEACOCKS (KJV) See MONKEYS, OSTRICHES

PEAKS (2/2)

Ps 68:15 A mountain of many *p* is the
68:16 envy, you mountains of many *p*?

PEARL (2/2) PEARLS

Mt 13:46 when he had found one *p* of
Rev 21:21 individual gate was of one *p*.

PEARLS (7/7) PEARL

Mt 7: 6 nor cast your *p* before swine,
13:45 a merchant seeking beautiful *p*,
1 Tim 2: 9 with braided hair or gold or *p*
Rev 17: 4 gold and precious stones and *p*,
18:12 silver, precious stones and *p*,
18:16 gold and precious stones and *p*!
21:21 The twelve gates were twelve *p*:

PEDAHEL (1/1)

Num 34:28 *P* the son of Ammihud."

PEDAHZUR (5/5)

Num 1:10 Manasseh, Gamaliel the son of *P*;
2:20 be Gamaliel the son of *P*.
7:54 day Gamaliel the son of *P*,
7:59 of Gamaliel the son of *P*.
10:23 was Gamaliel the son of *P*.

PEDAIAH (8/8)

2 Ki 23:36 was Zebudah the daughter of *P*
1 Chr 3:18 and Malchiram, *P*,
3:19 The sons of *P* were Zerubbabel
27:20 of Manasseh, Joel the son of *P*;
Neh 3:25 After him *P* the son of Parosh
8: 4 and at his left hand *P*,
11: 7 the son of Joed, the son of *P*,
13:13 scribe, and of the Levites, *P*;

PEDDLING (1/1)

2 Cor 2:17 *p* the word of God; but as of

PEDESTAL (2/2)

1 Ki 7:29 And on the frames was a *p* on
7:31 was round, shaped like a *p*,

PEELED (2/2)

Gen 30:37 *p* white strips in them, and
30:38 And the rods which he had *p*,

PEEP (1/1)

Isa 10:14 opened his mouth with even a *p*.

PEG (9/8)

Judg 4:21 took a tent *p* and took a hammer
4:21 softly to him and drove the *p*
4:22 dead with the *p* in his temple.
5:26 her hand to the tent *p*,
Ezra 9: 8 and to give us a *p* in His holy
Isa 22:23 I will fasten him as a *p* in a
22:25 the *p* that is fastened in the
Ezek 15: 3 Or can men make a *p* from it to
Zech 10: 4 From him the tent *p*, From him

PEGS (11/8)

Ex 27:19 for all its service, all its *p*,
27:19 and all the *p* of the court,
35:18 the *p* of the tabernacle, the
35:18 the *p* of the court, and their
38:20 All the *p* of the tabernacle, and
38:31 all the *p* for the tabernacle,
38:31 and all the *p* for the court all
39:40 gate, its cords, and its *p*;
Num 3:37 with their sockets, their *p*,
4:32 the court with their sockets, *p*,
Isa 41: 7 Then he fastened it with *p*,

PEKAH (11/11)

2 Ki 15:25 Then *P* the son of Remaliah, an
15:27 *P* the son of Remaliah became
15:29 In the days of *P* king of Israel,
15:30 led a conspiracy against *P* the
15:31 Now the rest of the acts of *P*,
15:32 In the second year of *P* the son
15:37 send Rezin king of Syria and *P*
16: 1 In the seventeenth year of *P* the
16: 5 Rezin king of Syria and *P* the
2 Chr 28: 6 For *P* the son of Remaliah killed
Isa 7: 1 Rezin king of Syria and *P* the

PEKAHIAH (3/3)

2 Ki 15:22 Then *P* his son reigned in his
15:23 *P* the son of Menahem became
15:26 Now the rest of the acts of *P*,

PEKOD (2/2)

Jer 50:21 against the inhabitants of *P*.
Ezek 23:23 All the Chaldeans, *P*,

PELAIAH (3/3)

1 Chr 3:24 were Hodaviah, Eliashib, *P*,
Neh 8: 7 Azariah, Jozabad, Hanan, *P*,
10:10 Shebaniah, Hodijah, Kelita, *P*,

PELALIAH (1/1)

Neh 11:12 son of Jeroham, the son of *P*,

PELATIAH (5/5)

1 Chr 3:21 The sons of Hananiah were *P* and
4:42 having as their captains *P*,
Neh 10:22 *P*, Hanan, Anaiah,
Ezek 11: 1 and *P* the son of Benaiah,
11:13 that *P* the son of Benaiah died.

PELEG (8/8)

Gen 10:25 sons: the name of one was *P*,
11:16 thirty-four years, and begot *P*.
11:17 After he begot *P*, Eber lived
11:18 *P* lived thirty years, and begot
11:19 *P* lived two hundred and nine
1 Chr 1:19 sons: the name of one was *P*,
1:25 Eber, *P*, Reu,
Lk 3:35 son of Reu, the son of *P*,

PELET (4/4)

1 Chr 2:47 were Regem, Jotham, Geshan, *P*,
12: 3 Jeziel and *P* the sons of

PELETH (2/2)

Num 16: 1 of Eliab, and On the son of *P*,
1 Chr 2:33 The sons of Jonathan were *P* and

PELETHITES (7/7)

2 Sam 8:18 both the Cherethites and the *P*;
15:18 all the Cherethites, all the *P*,
20: 7 with the Cherethites, the *P*,
20:23 over the Cherethites and the *P*;
1 Ki 1:38 and the *P* went down and had
1:44 the Cherethites, and the *P*;
1 Chr 18:17 over the Cherethites and the *P*;

PELICAN (3/3) JACKDAW

Ps 102: 6 I am like a *p* of the
Isa 34:11 But the *p* and the porcupine
Zeph 2:14 Both the *p* and the bittern

PELONITE (3/3)

1 Chr 11:27 the Harorite, Helez the *P*,
11:36 the Mecherathite, Ahijah the *P*,
27:10 seventh month was Helez the *P*,

PEN (6/6)

Job 19:24 on a rock With an iron *p* and
Ps 45: 1 My tongue is the *p* of a ready
Isa 8: 1 and write on it with a man's *p*
Jer 8: 8 the false *p* of the scribe
17: 1 of Judah is written with a *p*
3 Jn 13 not wish to write to you with *p*

PENALTY (3/3)

Num 35:30 a person for the death *p*.
Ezek 23:35 you shall bear the *p* Of
Rom 1:27 receiving in themselves the *p*

PENCE (KJV) See DENARII

PENDANTS (2/2)

Judg 8:26 the crescent ornaments, *p*,
Isa 3:19 The *p*, the bracelets,

PENETRATED (1/1)

Jer 39: 2 of the month, the city was *p*.

PENIEL (1/1) PENUEL

Gen 32:30 called the name of the place *P*:

PENINNAH (3/2)

1 Sam 1: 2 and the name of the other *P*.
1: 2 *P* had children, but Hannah had
1: 4 he would give portions to *P* his

PENITENTS (1/1)

Isa 1:27 And her *p* with righteousness.

PENNY (1/1)

Mt 5:26 till you have paid the last *p*.

PENNYWORTH (KJV) See DENARII

PENTECOST (3/3)

Acts 2: 1 When the Day of *P* had fully
20:16 if possible, on the Day of *P*.
1 Cor 16: 8 I will tarry in Ephesus until *P*.

PENUEL (8/7) PENIEL

Gen 32:31 Just as he crossed over *P* the
Judg 8: 8 he went up from there to *P* and

8: 8 And the men of ***P*** answered him
8: 9 he also spoke to the men of ***P***,
8:17 he tore down the tower of ***P***
1 Ki 12:25 went out from there and built ***P***.
1 Chr 4: 4 and ***P*** was the father of Gedor,
8:25 and ***P*** were the sons of

PEOPLE (2136/1908) PEOPLE'S, PEOPLES

Gen 11: 6 Indeed the ***p*** are one and they
12: 5 and the ***p*** whom they had
14:16 as well as the women and the ***p***.
17:14 shall be cut off from his ***p***;
19: 4 all the ***p*** from every quarter,
19:38 he is the father of the ***p*** of
23: 7 up and bowed himself to the ***p***
23:11 presence of the sons of my ***p***.
23:12 himself down before the ***p*** of
23:13 Ephron in the hearing of the ***p***
25: 8 and was gathered to his ***p***.
25:17 died, and was gathered to his ***p***.
25:23 One ***p*** shall be stronger than
26:10 One of the ***p*** might soon have
26:11 So Abimelech charged all his ***p***,
29: 1 and came to the land of the ***p***
32: 7 and he divided the ***p*** that were
33:15 leave with you some of the ***p***
34:16 you, and we will become one ***p***.
34:22 to dwell with us, to be one ***p***:
35: 6 he and all the ***p*** who were with
35:29 died, and was gathered to his ***p***,
41:40 and all my ***p*** shall be ruled
41:55 the ***p*** cried to Pharaoh for
42: 6 it was he who sold to all the ***p***
47:21 And as for the ***p***, he moved
47:23 Then Joseph said to the ***p***,
48: 4 make of you a multitude of ***p***,
48:19 He also shall become a ***p***,
49:10 be the obedience of the ***p***.
49:16 Dan shall judge his ***p*** As one of
49:29 "I am to be gathered to my ***p***;
49:33 last, and was gathered to his ***p***.
50:20 to save many ***p*** alive.
Ex 1: 9 And he said to his ***p***,
1: 9 the ***p*** of the children of Israel
1:20 and the ***p*** multiplied and grew
1:22 So Pharaoh commanded all his ***p***,
3: 7 seen the oppression of My ***p***
3:10 Pharaoh that you may bring My ***p***,
3:12 When you have brought the ***p*** out
3:21 And I will give this ***p*** favor in
4:16 be your spokesman to the ***p***.
4:21 so that he will not let the ***p***
4:30 the signs in the sight of the ***p***.
4:31 So the ***p*** believed; and when they
5: 1 Let My ***p*** go, that they may hold
5: 4 why do you take the ***p*** from
5: 5 the ***p*** of the land are many
5: 6 the taskmasters of the ***p*** and
5: 7 shall no longer give the ***p***
5:10 And the taskmasters of the ***p***
5:10 went out and spoke to the ***p***,
5:12 So the ***p*** were scattered abroad
5:16 the fault is in your own ***p***.
5:22 You brought trouble on this ***p***?
5:23 he has done evil to this ***p***;
5:23 have You delivered Your ***p*** at
6: 7 'I will take you as My ***p***,
7: 4 and bring My armies and My ***p***,
7:14 he refuses to let the ***p*** go.
7:16 Let My ***p*** go, that they may serve
8: 1 Let My ***p*** go, that they may serve
8: 3 of your servants, on your ***p***,
8: 4 shall come up on you, on your ***p***,
8: 8 the frogs from me and from my ***p***;
8: 8 and I will let the ***p*** go, that
8: 9 your servants, and for your ***p***,
8:11 your servants, and from your ***p***.
8:20 Let My ***p*** go, that they may serve
8:21 if you will not let My ***p*** go,
8:21 on your ***p*** and into your houses.
8:22 in which My ***p*** dwell, that no
8:23 make a difference between My ***p***
8:23 between My people and your ***p***.
8:29 his servants, and from his ***p***.
8:29 anymore in not letting the ***p***
8:31 his servants, and from his ***p***.
8:32 neither would he let the ***p*** go.
9: 1 Let My ***p*** go, that they may serve
9: 7 and he did not let the ***p*** go.
9:13 Let My ***p*** go, that they may serve
9:14 on your servants and on your ***p***,
9:15 hand and struck you and your ***p***
9:17 exalt yourself against My ***p*** in
9:27 and my ***p*** and I are wicked.
10: 3 Let My ***p*** go, that they may
10: 4 if you refuse to let My ***p*** go,
11: 2 now in the hearing of the ***p***,
11: 3 And the LORD gave the ***p*** favor
11: 3 and in the sight of the ***p***.
11: 8 and all the ***p*** who follow you!'
12:27 So the ***p*** bowed their heads
12:31 "Rise, go out from among my ***p***,
12:33 And the Egyptians urged the ***p***,
12:34 So the ***p*** took their dough before
12:36 And the LORD had given the ***p***
13: 3 And Moses said to the ***p***:
13:17 when Pharaoh had let the ***p*** go,
13:17 Lest perhaps the ***p*** change their
13:18 So God led the ***p*** around by way
13:22 by night from before the ***p***.
14: 5 the king of Egypt that the ***p***
14: 5 was turned against the ***p***;
14: 6 his chariot and took his ***p***
14:13 And Moses said to the ***p***,
14:31 so the ***p*** feared the LORD, and
15:13 mercy have led forth The ***p***
15:14 The ***p*** will hear and be afraid;
15:16 Till Your ***p*** pass over,
15:16 Till the ***p*** pass over Whom You
15:24 And the ***p*** complained against
16: 4 And the ***p*** shall go out and
16:27 happened that some of the ***p***
16:30 So the ***p*** rested on the seventh
17: 1 there was no water for the ***p***
17: 2 Therefore the ***p*** contended with
17: 3 And the ***p*** thirsted there for
17: 3 and the ***p*** complained against
17: 4 "What shall I do with this ***p***?
17: 5 to Moses, "Go on before the ***p***,
17: 6 that the ***p*** may drink."
17:13 defeated Amalek and his ***p*** with
18: 1 for Moses and for Israel His ***p***—
18:10 and who has delivered the ***p***
18:13 that Moses sat to judge the ***p***;
18:13 and the ***p*** stood before Moses
18:14 saw all that he did for the ***p***,
18:14 that you are doing for the ***p***?
18:14 and all the ***p*** stand before you
18:15 Because the ***p*** come to me to
18:18 Both you and these ***p*** who are
18:19 Stand before God for the ***p***,
18:21 you shall select from all the ***p***
18:22 And let them judge the ***p*** at all
18:23 and all this ***p*** will also go to
18:25 and made them heads over the ***p***:
18:26 So they judged the ***p*** at all
19: 5 treasure to Me above all ***p***;
19: 7 called for the elders of the ***p***,
19: 8 Then all the ***p*** answered together
19: 8 back the words of the ***p*** to the
19: 9 that the ***p*** may hear when I
19: 9 Moses told the words of the ***p***
19:10 Go to the ***p*** and consecrate them
19:11 Sinai in the sight of all the ***p***.
19:12 shall set bounds for the ***p***
19:14 from the mountain to the ***p*** and
19:14 the people and sanctified the ***p***,
19:15 And he said to the ***p***,
19:16 so that all the ***p*** who were in
19:17 And Moses brought the ***p*** out of
19:21 Moses, "Go down and warn the ***p***,
19:23 The ***p*** cannot come up to Mount
19:24 not let the priests and the ***p***
19:25 So Moses went down to the ***p*** and
20:18 Now all the ***p*** witnessed the
20:18 and when the ***p*** saw it, they
20:20 And Moses said to the ***p***,
20:21 So the ***p*** stood afar off, but
21: 8 to sell her to a foreign ***p***,
22:25 you lend money to any of My ***p***
22:28 nor curse a ruler of your ***p***.
23:11 that the poor of your ***p*** may
23:27 confusion among all the ***p*** to
24: 2 nor shall the ***p*** go up with
24: 3 So Moses came and told the ***p***
24: 3 And all the ***p*** answered with one
24: 7 read in the hearing of the ***p***.
24: 8 blood, sprinkled it on the ***p***,
30:33 shall be cut off from his ***p***.
30:38 he shall be cut off from his ***p***.
31:14 be cut off from among his ***p***.
32: 1 Now when the ***p*** saw that Moses
32: 1 the ***p*** gathered together to
32: 3 So all the ***p*** broke off the
32: 6 and the ***p*** sat down to eat and
32: 7 get down! For your ***p*** whom you
32: 9 to Moses, "I have seen this ***p***,
32: 9 indeed it is a stiff-necked ***p***!
32:11 wrath burn hot against Your ***p***
32:12 relent from this harm to Your ***p***.
32:14 He said He would do to His ***p***.
32:17 heard the noise of the ***p*** as
32:21 What did this ***p*** do to you that
32:22 lord become hot. You know the ***p***,
32:25 Now when Moses saw that the ***p***
32:28 three thousand men of the ***p***
32:30 day that Moses said to the ***p***,
32:31 these ***p*** have committed a great
32:34 lead the ***p*** to the place of
32:35 So the LORD plagued the ***p***
33: 1 you and the ***p*** whom you have
33: 3 for you are a stiff-necked ***p***.
33: 4 And when the ***p*** heard this bad
33: 5 'You are a stiff-necked ***p***.
33: 8 that all the ***p*** rose, and each
33:10 All the ***p*** saw the pillar of
33:10 and all the ***p*** rose and
33:12 You say to me, 'Bring up this ***p***.
33:13 that this nation is Your ***p***.
33:16 will it be known that Your ***p***
33:16 Your ***p*** and I, from all the
33:16 from all the ***p*** who are upon
34: 9 though we are a stiff-necked ***p***;
34:10 Before all your ***p*** I will do
34:10 and all the ***p*** among whom you
36: 5 The ***p*** bring much more than
36: 6 And the ***p*** were restrained
Lev 4: 3 sins, bringing guilt on the ***p***,
4:27 If anyone of the common ***p*** sins
7:20 shall be cut off from his ***p***.
7:21 shall be cut off from his ***p***.
7:25 it shall be cut off from his ***p***.
7:27 shall be cut off from his ***p***.
9: 7 for yourself and for the ***p***.
9: 7 Offer the offering of the ***p***,
9:15 was the sin offering for the ***p***,
9:18 which were for the ***p***.
9:22 lifted his hand toward the ***p***,
9:23 and came out and blessed the ***p***.
9:23 the LORD appeared to all the ***p***,
9:24 When all the ***p*** saw it, they
10: 3 And before all the ***p*** I must
10: 6 and wrath come upon all the ***p***.
16:15 offering, which is for the ***p***,
16:24 and the burnt offering of the ***p***,
16:24 for himself and for the ***p***.
16:33 the priests and for all the ***p***
17: 4 be cut off from among his ***p***,
17: 9 be cut off from among his ***p***.
17:10 cut him off from among his ***p***.
18:29 be cut off from among their ***p***.
19: 8 shall be cut off from his ***p***.
19:16 as a talebearer among your ***p***;
19:18 against the children of your ***p***,
20: 2 The ***p*** of the land shall stone
20: 3 and will cut him off from his ***p***,
20: 4 And if the ***p*** of the land should
20: 5 I will cut him off from his ***p***,
20: 6 and cut him off from his ***p***.
20:17 cut off in the sight of their ***p***.
20:18 shall be cut off from their ***p***.
21: 1 for the dead among his ***p***,
21: 4 being a chief man among his ***p***,
21:14 take a virgin of his own ***p*** as
21:15 his posterity among his ***p***,
23:29 day shall be cut off from his ***p***.
23:30 I will destroy from among his ***p***.
26:12 your God, and you shall be My ***p***.
Num 5:21 curse and an oath among your ***p***,
5:27 will become a curse among her ***p***.
9:13 be cut off from among his ***p***,
11: 1 Now when the ***p*** complained, it
11: 2 Then the ***p*** cried out to Moses,
11: 8 The ***p*** went about and gathered
11:10 Then Moses heard the ***p*** weeping
11:11 laid the burden of all these ***p***
11:12 "Did I conceive all these ***p***?
11:13 get meat to give to all these ***p***?
11:14 am not able to bear all these ***p***
11:16 know to be the elders of the ***p***
11:17 shall bear the burden of the ***p***
11:18 "Then you shall say to the ***p***,
11:21 The ***p*** whom I am among are six
11:24 Moses went out and told the ***p***
11:24 men of the elders of the ***p*** and
11:29 that all the LORD's ***p*** were
11:32 And the ***p*** stayed up all that
11:33 LORD was aroused against the ***p***,
11:33 and the LORD struck the ***p*** with
11:34 there they buried the ***p*** who
11:35 From Kibroth Hattaavah the ***p***
12:15 and the ***p*** did not journey till
12:16 And afterward the ***p*** moved from
13:18 whether the ***p*** who dwell in it
13:28 Nevertheless the ***p*** who dwell in
13:30 Then Caleb quieted the ***p*** before
13:31 not able to go up against the ***p***,
13:32 and all the ***p*** whom we saw in it
14: 1 and the ***p*** wept that night.
14: 9 nor fear the ***p*** of the land, for
14:11 How long will these ***p*** reject Me?
14:13 Your might You brought these ***p***
14:14 You, LORD, are among these ***p***;
14:15 Now if You kill these ***p*** as one
14:16 was not able to bring this ***p***
14:19 "Pardon the iniquity of this ***p***,
14:19 as You have forgiven this ***p***,
14:39 and the ***p*** mourned greatly.
15:26 because all the ***p*** did it
15:30 be cut off from among his ***p***.
16:41 You have killed the ***p*** of the
16:47 plague had begun among the ***p***.
16:47 and made atonement for the ***p***.
20: 1 and the ***p*** stayed in Kadesh;
20: 3 And the ***p*** contended with Moses
20:24 shall be gathered to his ***p***,
20:26 shall be gathered to his ***p***
21: 2 You will indeed deliver this ***p***
21: 4 and the soul of the ***p*** became
21: 5 And the ***p*** spoke against God and
21: 6 sent fiery serpents among the ***p***,
21: 6 the people, and they bit the ***p***;
21: 6 and many of the ***p*** of Israel
21: 7 Therefore the ***p*** came to Moses,
21: 7 So Moses prayed for the ***p***.
21:16 Gather the ***p*** together, and I
21:23 So Sihon gathered all his ***p***
21:24 as far as the ***p*** of Ammon;
21:24 for the border of the ***p*** of
21:29 O ***p*** of Chemosh! He has given
21:33 against them, he and all his ***p***,
21:34 with all his ***p*** and his land;
21:35 him, his sons, and all his ***p***,
22: 3 was exceedingly afraid of the ***p***
22: 5 the land of the sons of his ***p***,
22: 5 a ***p*** has come from Egypt.
22: 6 curse this ***p*** for me, for they
22:11 a ***p*** has come out of Egypt, and
22:12 you shall not curse the ***p***,
22:17 curse this ***p*** for me.'"
22:41 observe the extent of the ***p***.
23: 9 There! A ***p*** dwelling alone,
23:24 a ***p*** rises like a lioness,
24:14 now, indeed, I am going to my ***p***.
24:14 I will advise you what this ***p***

P

24:14 this people will do to your **p**
25: 1 and the **p** began to commit
25: 2 They invited the **p** to the
25: 2 and the **p** ate and bowed down to
25: 4 Take all the leaders of the **p**
25:15 he was head of the **p** of a
26: 4 Take a census of the **p**
27:13 shall be gathered to your **p**,
31: 2 you shall be gathered to your **p**.
31: 3 So Moses spoke to the **p**,
32:15 you will destroy all these **p**.
33:14 there was no water for the **p**
Deut 1:28 The **p** are greater and taller
2: 4 'And command the **p**,
2:10 a **p** as great and numerous and
2:16 perished from among the **p**,
2:19 And when you come near the **p** of
2:19 you any of the land of the **p**
2:21 a **p** as great and numerous and
2:32 Then Sihon and all his **p** came
2:33 him, his sons, and all his **p**.
2:37 not go near the land of the **p**
3: 1 against us, he and all his **p**,
3: 2 delivered him and all his **p**
3: 3 king of Bashan, with all his **p**,
3:11 (Is it not in Rabbah of the **p**
3:16 the border of the **p** of Ammon;
3:28 he shall go over before this **p**,
4: 6 is a wise and understanding **p**.
4:10 Gather the **p** to Me, and I will
4:20 out of Egypt, to be His **p**,
4:33 Did any **p** ever hear the voice
5:28 voice of the words of this **p**
7: 6 For you are a holy **p** to the
7: 6 God has chosen you to be a **p**
7: 7 more in number than any other **p**,
9: 2 a **p** great and tall, the
9: 6 for you are a stiff-necked **p**.
9:12 for your **p** whom you brought out
9:13 me, saying, 'I have seen this **p**,
9:13 they are a stiff-necked **p**.
9:26 do not destroy Your **p** and Your
9:27 on the stubbornness of this **p**,
9:29 Yet they are Your **p** and Your
10:11 your journey before the **p**,
13: 7 of the gods of the **p** which are
13: 9 afterward the hand of all the **p**.
14: 2 For you are a holy **p** to the
14: 2 LORD has chosen you to be a **p**
14:21 for you are a holy **p** to the
16:18 and they shall judge the **p** with
17: 7 the hands of all the **p**.
17:13 And all the **p** shall hear and
17:16 nor cause the **p** to return to
18: 3 be the priest's due from the **p**,
20: 1 see horses and chariots and **p**
20: 2 approach and speak to the **p**.
20: 5 officers shall speak to the **p**,
20: 8 shall speak further to the **p**,
20: 9 have finished speaking to the **p**,
20: 9 of the armies to lead the **p**.
20:11 then all the **p** who are found
21: 8 for Your **p** Israel, whom You
21: 8 blood to the charge of Your **p**
26:15 and bless Your **p** Israel and the
26:18 you to be His special **p**,
26:19 and that you may be a holy **p** to
27: 1 of Israel, commanded the **p**,
27: 9 This day you have become the **p**
27:11 And Moses commanded the **p** on
27:12 on Mount Gerizim to bless the **p**,
27:15 And all the **p** shall answer
27:16 And all the **p** shall say,
27:17 And all the **p** shall say,
27:18 And all the **p** shall say,
27:19 And all the **p** shall say,
27:20 And all the **p** shall say,
27:21 And all the **p** shall say,
27:22 And all the **p** shall say,
27:23 And all the **p** shall say,
27:24 And all the **p** shall say,
27:25 And all the **p** shall say,
27:26 And all the **p** shall say,
28: 9 will establish you as a holy **p**
28:32 shall be given to another **p**,
29:13 may establish you today as a **p**
29:25 Then **p** would say: 'Because they
31: 7 for you must go with this **p** to
31:12 Gather the **p** together, men and
31:16 and this **p** will rise and play
32: 6 LORD, O foolish and unwise **p**?
32: 9 the LORD's portion is His **p**;
32:36 the LORD will judge His **p**
32:43 O Gentiles, with His **p**;
32:43 for His land and His **p**.
32:44 song in the hearing of the **p**.
32:50 and be gathered to your **p**,
32:50 Hor and was gathered to his **p**;
33: 3 Yes, He loves the **p**;
33: 5 When the leaders of the **p** were
33: 7 Judah, And bring him to his **p**;
33:21 came with the heads of the **p**;
33:29 a **p** saved by the LORD,
Josh 1: 2 this Jordan, you and all this **p**,
1: 6 for to this **p** you shall divide
1:10 commanded the officers of the **p**,
1:11 the camp and command the **p**,
3: 3 and they commanded the **p**,
3: 5 And Joshua said to the **p**,
3: 6 and cross over before the **p**.
3: 6 covenant and went before the **p**.
3:14 when the **p** set out from their
3:14 of the covenant before the **p**,
3:16 and the **p** crossed over opposite
3:17 until all the **p** had crossed
4: 1 when all the **p** had completely
4: 2 twelve men from the **p**,
4:10 Joshua to speak to the **p**,
4:10 and the **p** hurried and crossed
4:11 when all the **p** had completely
4:11 over in the presence of the **p**.
4:19 Now the **p** came up from the
5: 4 All the **p** who came out of Egypt
5: 5 For all the **p** who came out had
5: 5 but all the **p** born in the
5: 6 till all the **p** who were men
5: 8 finished circumcising all the **p**,
6: 5 that all the **p** shall shout with
6: 5 And the **p** shall go up every man
6: 7 And he said to the **p**,
6: 8 when Joshua had spoken to the **p**,
6:10 Now Joshua had commanded the **p**,
6:16 that Joshua said to the **p**:
6:20 So the **p** shouted when the
6:20 And it happened when the **p**
6:20 and the **p** shouted with a great
6:20 Then the **p** went up into the
7: 3 Do not let all the **p** go up, but
7: 3 Do not weary all the **p** there,
7: 3 for the **p** of Ai are few."
7: 4 men went up there from the **p**,
7: 5 therefore the hearts of the **p**
7: 7 why have You brought this **p**
7:13 "Get up, sanctify the **p**,
8: 1 take all the **p** of war with you,
8: 1 your hand the king of Ai, his **p**,
8: 3 and all the **p** of war, to go up
8: 5 Then I and all the **p** who are
8: 9 lodged that night among the **p**.
8:10 the morning and mustered the **p**,
8:10 before the **p** to Ai.
8:11 And all the **p** of war who were
8:13 And when they had set the **p**,
8:14 to battle, he and all his **p**,
8:16 So all the **p** who were in Ai
8:20 and the **p** who had fled to the
8:25 all the **p** of Ai.
8:33 that they should bless the **p** of
10: 7 he and all the **p** of war with
10:13 Till the **p** had revenge Upon
10:21 And all the **p** returned to the
10:28 —all the **p** who were in it.
10:30 he struck it and all the **p** who
10:32 and struck it and all the **p** who
10:33 and Joshua struck him and his **p**,
10:35 all the **p** who were in it he
10:37 and all the **p** who were in it;
10:37 destroyed it and all the **p** who
10:39 and utterly destroyed all the **p**
11: 4 as many **p** as the sand that
11: 7 So Joshua and all the **p** of war
11:11 And they struck all the **p** who
12:23 the king of the **p** of Gilgal,
14: 8 with me made the heart of the **p**
17:14 since we are a great **p**,
17:15 them, "If you are a great **p**,
17:17 You are a great **p** and have
19: 9 the inheritance of that **p**.
24: 2 And Joshua said to all the **p**,
24:16 So the **p** answered and said:
24:17 we went and among all the **p**
24:18 out from before us all the **p**,
24:19 But Joshua said to the **p**,
24:21 And the **p** said to Joshua, "No,
24:22 So Joshua said to the **p**,
24:24 And the **p** said to Joshua, "The
24:25 made a covenant with the **p**
24:27 And Joshua said to all the **p**,
24:28 So Joshua let the **p** depart, each
Judg 1:16 they went and dwelt among the **p**.
2: 4 that the **p** lifted up their
2: 6 when Joshua had dismissed the **p**,
2: 7 So the **p** served the LORD all
2:12 from among the gods of the **p**
3:13 he gathered to himself the **p**
3:18 he sent away the **p** who had
4:13 and all the **p** who were with
5: 2 When the **p** willingly offer
5: 9 themselves willingly with the **p**.
5:11 Then the **p** of the LORD shall
5:13 the **p** against the nobles;
5:18 Zebulun is a **p** who
6: 3 also Amalekites and the **p** of
6:33 the **p** of the East, gathered
7: 1 and all the **p** who were
7: 2 The **p** who are with you are too
7: 3 in the hearing of the **p**,
7: 3 twenty-two thousand of the **p**
7: 4 The **p** are still too many;
7: 5 So he brought the **p** down to the
7: 6 but all the rest of the **p** got
7: 7 Let all the other **p** go, every
7: 8 So the **p** took provisions and
7:12 all the **p** of the East, were
8: 5 give loaves of bread to the **p**
8:10 left of all the army of the **p**
9:29 If only this **p** were under my
9:32 you and the **p** who are with
9:33 and when he and the **p** who are
9:34 So Abimelech and all the **p** who
9:35 Abimelech and the **p** who were
9:36 And when Gaal saw the **p**,
9:36 **p** are coming down from the tops
9:37 **p** are coming down from the
9:38 Are not these the **p** whom you
9:42 on the next day that the **p**
9:43 So he took his **p**, divided
9:43 he looked, and there were the **p**,
9:45 took the city and killed the **p**
9:48 he and all the **p** who were with
9:48 then he said to the **p** who were
9:49 So each of the **p** likewise cut
9:49 so that all the **p** of the tower
9:51 all the **p** of the city—fled there
10: 6 the gods of the **p** of Ammon, and
10: 7 and into the hands of the **p** of
10: 9 Moreover the **p** of Ammon crossed
10:11 the Amorites and from the **p** of
10:17 Then the **p** of Ammon gathered
10:18 And the **p**, the leaders of
10:18 begin the fight against the **p**
11: 4 to pass after a time that the **p**
11: 5 when the **p** of Ammon made war
11: 6 we may fight against the **p** of
11: 8 us and fight against the **p** of
11: 9 home to fight against the **p** of
11:11 and the **p** made him head and
11:12 to the king of the **p** of Ammon,
11:13 And the king of the **p** of Ammon
11:14 to the king of the **p** of Ammon,
11:15 nor the land of the **p** of Ammon;
11:20 So Sihon gathered all his **p**
11:21 delivered Sihon and all his **p**
11:23 the Amorites from before His **p**
11:27 children of Israel and the **p**
11:28 the king of the **p** of Ammon did
11:29 he advanced toward the **p** of
11:30 You will indeed deliver the **p**
11:31 I return in peace from the **p**
11:32 Jephthah advanced toward the **p**
11:33 Thus the **p** of Ammon were
11:36 the **p** of Ammon."
12: 1 over to fight against the **p** of
12: 2 My **p** and I were in a great
12: 2 in a great struggle with the **p**
12: 3 and crossed over against the **p**
14: 3 brethren, or among all my **p**,
14:16 a riddle to the sons of my **p**,
14:17 the riddle to the sons of her **p**.
16:24 When the **p** saw him, they praised
16:30 on the lords and all the **p** who
18: 7 They saw the **p** who were there,
18:10 you will come to a secure **p** and
18:20 and took his place among the **p**.
18:27 to a **p** quiet and secure;
20: 2 And the leaders of all the **p**,
20: 2 in the assembly of the **p** of
20: 8 So all the **p** arose as one man,
20:10 to make provisions for the **p**,
20:16 Among all this **p** were seven
20:22 And the **p**, that is, the men
20:26 of Israel, that is, all the **p**,
20:31 Benjamin went out against the **p**,
20:31 down and kill some of the **p**,
21: 2 Then the **p** came to the house of
21: 4 that the **p** rose early and built
21: 9 For when the **p** were counted,
21:15 And the **p** grieved for Benjamin,
Ruth 1: 6 the LORD had visited His **p** by
1:10 will return with you to your **p**.
1:15 has gone back to her **p** and to
1:16 Your **p** shall be my people,
1:16 Your people shall be my **p**,
2:11 and have come to a **p** whom you
2:22 and that **p** do not meet you in
3:11 for all the **p** of my town know
4: 4 and the elders of my **p**.
4: 9 to the elders and all the **p**,
4:11 And all the **p** who were at the
1 Sam 2:13 the priests' custom with the **p**
2:23 evil dealings from all the **p**.
2:24 You make the LORD's **p**
2:29 the offerings of Israel My **p**?
4: 3 And when the **p** had come into the
4: 4 So the **p** sent to Shiloh, that
4:17 a great slaughter among the **p**.
5: 3 And when the **p** of Ashdod arose
5: 6 of the LORD was heavy on the **p**
5:10 to kill us and our **p**!"
5:11 it does not kill us and our **p**.
6: 6 did they not let the **p** go, that
6:13 Now the **p** of Beth Shemesh
6:19 and seventy men of the **p**,
6:19 and the **p** lamented because the
6:19 the LORD had struck the **p**
8: 7 Heed the voice of the **p** in all
8:10 the words of the LORD to the **p**
8:19 Nevertheless the **p** refused to
8:21 heard all the words of the **p**,
9: 2 was taller than any of the **p**.
9:12 there is a sacrifice of the **p**
9:13 For the **p** will not eat until he
9:16 anoint him commander over My **p**
9:16 that he may save My **p** from the
9:16 for I have looked upon My **p**,
9:17 This one shall reign over My **p**.
9:24 since I said I invited the **p**.
10:11 that the **p** said to one another,
10:17 Then Samuel called the **p**
10:23 and when he stood among the **p**,
10:23 he was taller than any of the **p**
10:24 And Samuel said to all the **p**,
10:24 no one like him among all the **p**?
10:24 So all the **p** shouted and
10:25 Samuel explained to the **p** the
10:25 And Samuel sent all the **p** away,

11: 4 news in the hearing of the ***p***.
11: 4 And all the ***p*** lifted up their
11: 5 said, "What troubles the ***p***,
11: 7 fear of the LORD fell on the ***p***,
11:11 that Saul put the ***p*** in three
11:12 Then the ***p*** said to Samuel,
11:14 Then Samuel said to the ***p***,
11:15 So all the ***p*** went to Gilgal, and
12: 6 Then Samuel said to the ***p***,
12:18 and all the ***p*** greatly feared
12:19 And all the ***p*** said to Samuel,
12:20 Then Samuel said to the ***p***,
12:22 LORD will not forsake His ***p***,
12:22 the LORD to make you His ***p***.
13: 2 The rest of the ***p*** he sent away,
13: 4 And the ***p*** were called together
13: 5 and ***p*** as the sand which is on
13: 6 (for the ***p*** were distressed),
13: 6 then the ***p*** hid in caves, in
13: 7 and all the ***p*** followed him
13: 8 and the ***p*** were scattered from
13:11 When I saw that the ***p*** were
13:14 to be commander over His ***p***,
13:15 And Saul numbered the ***p*** present
13:16 and the ***p*** present with them
13:22 in the hand of any of the ***p***
14: 2 The ***p*** who were with him were
14: 3 But the ***p*** did not know that
14:15 the field, and among all the ***p***.
14:17 Then Saul said to the ***p*** who
14:20 Then Saul and all the ***p*** who
14:24 for Saul had placed the ***p*** under
14:24 So none of the ***p*** tasted food.
14:25 Now all the ***p*** of the land came
14:26 And when the ***p*** had come into the
14:26 for the ***p*** feared the oath.
14:27 heard his father charge the ***p***
14:28 Then one of the ***p*** said, "Your
14:28 father strictly charged the ***p***
14:28 And the ***p*** were faint.
14:30 How much better if the ***p*** had
14:31 So the ***p*** were very faint.
14:32 And the ***p*** rushed on the spoil,
14:32 and the ***p*** ate them with the
14:33 the ***p*** are sinning against the
14:34 yourselves among the ***p***,
14:34 So every one of the ***p*** brought
14:38 here, all you chiefs of the ***p***,
14:39 But not a man among all the ***p***
14:40 And the ***p*** said to Saul, "Do
14:41 but the ***p*** escaped.
14:45 But the ***p*** said to Saul, "Shall
14:45 So the ***p*** rescued Jonathan,
14:47 against the ***p*** of Ammon, against
15: 1 to anoint you king over His ***p***,
15: 4 So Saul gathered the ***p*** together
15: 8 and utterly destroyed all the ***p***
15: 9 But Saul and the ***p*** spared Agag
15:15 for the ***p*** spared the best of
15:21 But the ***p*** took of the plunder,
15:24 because I feared the ***p*** and
15:30 before the elders of my ***p*** and
17:27 And the ***p*** answered him in this
17:30 and these ***p*** answered him as the
18: 5 in the sight of all the ***p*** and
18:13 out and came in before the ***p***.
23: 8 Then Saul called all the ***p***
26: 5 with the ***p*** encamped all around
26: 7 and Abishai came to the ***p*** by
26: 7 And Abner and the ***p*** lay all
26:14 And David called out to the ***p***
26:15 For one of the ***p*** came in to
27:12 He has made his ***p*** Israel utterly
30: 4 Then David and the ***p*** who were
30: 6 for the ***p*** spoke of stoning him,
30: 6 because the soul of all the ***p***
30:21 to meet David and to meet the ***p***
30:21 And when David came near the ***p***,
31: 9 of their idols and among the ***p***.
2 Sam 1: 4 The ***p*** have fled from the battle,
1: 4 many of the ***p*** are fallen and
1:12 for the ***p*** of the LORD and for
2:26 it be then until you tell the ***p***
2:27 then by morning all the ***p***
2:28 and all the ***p*** stood still and
2:30 when he had gathered all the ***p***
3:18 I will save My ***p*** Israel from
3:31 said to Joab and to all the ***p***
3:32 and all the ***p*** wept.
3:34 Then all the ***p*** wept over him
3:35 And when all the ***p*** came to
3:36 Now all the ***p*** took note of it,
3:36 the king did pleased all the ***p***.
3:37 For all the ***p*** and all Israel
5: 2 You shall shepherd My ***p*** Israel,
5:12 kingdom for the sake of His ***p***
6: 2 arose and went with all the ***p***
6:18 he blessed the ***p*** in the name of
6:19 he distributed among all the ***p***,
6:19 So all the ***p*** departed, everyone
6:21 to appoint me ruler over the ***p***
7: 7 I commanded to shepherd My ***p***
7: 8 sheep, to be ruler over My ***p***,
7:10 I will appoint a place for My ***p***
7:11 judges to be over My ***p***
7:23 "And who is like Your ***p***,
7:23 to redeem for Himself as a ***p***,
7:23 before Your ***p*** whom You redeemed
7:24 For You have made Your ***p*** Israel
7:24 people Israel Your very own ***p***
8:12 from the ***p*** of Ammon, from the
8:15 and justice to all his ***p***.
10: 1 this that the king of the ***p*** of
10: 2 came into the land of the ***p*** of
10: 3 And the princes of the ***p*** of
10: 6 When the ***p*** of Ammon saw that
10: 6 the ***p*** of Ammon sent and hired
10: 8 Then the ***p*** of Ammon came out and
10:10 And the rest of the ***p*** he put
10:10 in battle array against the ***p***
10:11 but if the ***p*** of Ammon are too
10:12 and let us be strong for our ***p***
10:13 So Joab and the ***p*** who were with
10:14 When the ***p*** of Ammon saw that the
10:14 So Joab returned from the ***p*** of
10:19 were afraid to help the ***p*** of
11: 1 and they destroyed the ***p*** of
11: 7 and how the ***p*** were doing, and
11:17 And some of the ***p*** of the
12: 9 him with the sword of the ***p*** of
12:26 fought against Rabbah of the ***p***
12:28 gather the rest of the ***p***
12:29 So David gathered all the ***p***
12:31 And he brought out the ***p*** who
12:31 did to all the cities of the ***p***
12:31 Then David and all the ***p***
13:34 many ***p*** were coming from the
14:13 such a thing against the ***p*** of
14:15 my lord the king because the ***p***
15:12 for the ***p*** with Absalom
15:17 king went out with all the ***p***
15:23 and all the ***p*** crossed over.
15:23 and all the ***p*** crossed over
15:24 went up until all the ***p*** had
15:30 And all the ***p*** who were with
16: 6 And all the ***p*** and all the
16:14 Now the king and all the ***p*** who
16:15 Absalom and all the ***p***,
16:18 but whom the LORD and this ***p***
17: 2 And all the ***p*** who are with him
17: 3 I will bring back all the ***p*** to
17: 3 all the ***p*** will be at peace."
17: 8 and will not camp with the ***p***.
17: 9 is a slaughter among the ***p*** who
17:16 lest the king and all the ***p*** who
17:22 So David and all the ***p*** who were
17:27 of Nahash from Rabbah of the ***p***
17:29 for David and the ***p*** who were
17:29 The ***p*** are hungry and weary and
18: 1 And David numbered the ***p*** who
18: 2 sent out one third of the ***p***
18: 2 And the king said to the ***p***,
18: 3 But the ***p*** answered, "You shall
18: 4 and all the ***p*** went out by
18: 5 And all the ***p*** heard when the
18: 6 So the ***p*** went out into the
18: 7 The ***p*** of Israel were overthrown
18: 8 and the woods devoured more ***p***
18:16 and the ***p*** returned from
18:16 For Joab held back the ***p***.
19: 2 into mourning for all the ***p***.
19: 2 For the ***p*** heard it said that
19: 3 And the ***p*** stole back into the
19: 3 as ***p*** who are ashamed steal away
19: 8 And they told all the ***p***,
19: 8 So all the ***p*** came before the
19: 9 Now all the ***p*** were in a dispute
19:39 Then all the ***p*** went over the
19:40 And all the ***p*** of Judah escorted
19:40 and also half the ***p*** of Israel.
20:12 when the man saw that all the ***p***
20:13 all the ***p*** went on after Joab to
20:15 And all the ***p*** who were with
20:22 in her wisdom went to all the ***p***.
22:28 You will save the humble ***p***;
22:44 me from the strivings of my ***p***;
22:44 A ***p*** I have not known shall
23:10 and the ***p*** returned after him
23:11 Then the ***p*** fled from the
24: 2 to Beersheba, and count the ***p***,
24: 2 I may know the number of the ***p***.
24: 3 LORD your God add to the ***p*** a
24: 4 of the king to count the ***p*** of
24: 9 the sum of the number of the ***p***
24:10 him after he had numbered the ***p***.
24:15 seventy thousand men of the ***p***
24:16 angel who was destroying the ***p***,
24:17 angel who was striking the ***p***,
24:21 may be withdrawn from the ***p***.
1 Ki 1:39 and all the ***p*** said, "Long
1:40 And all the ***p*** went up after him;
1:40 and the ***p*** played the flutes and
3: 2 Meanwhile the ***p*** sacrificed at
3: 8 is in the midst of Your ***p***
3: 8 whom You have chosen, a great ***p***,
3: 9 heart to judge Your ***p***,
3: 9 is able to judge this great ***p***
5: 7 a wise son over this great ***p***!
5:16 who supervised the ***p*** who
6:13 and will not forsake My ***p***
8:16 the day that I brought My ***p***
8:16 I chose David to be over My ***p***
8:30 of Your servant and of Your ***p***
8:33 When Your ***p*** Israel are defeated
8:34 and forgive the sin of Your ***p***
8:36 Your ***p*** Israel, that You may
8:36 which You have given to Your ***p***
8:38 or by all Your ***p*** Israel, when
8:41 who is not of Your ***p*** Israel,
8:43 as do Your ***p*** Israel, and that
8:44 When Your ***p*** go out to battle
8:50 and forgive Your ***p*** who have
8:51 (for they are Your ***p*** and Your
8:52 and the supplication of Your ***p***
8:56 who has given rest to His ***p***
8:59 servant and the cause of His ***p***
8:66 On the eighth day he sent the ***p***
8:66 David, and for Israel His ***p***.
9:20 All the ***p*** who were left of
9:23 who ruled over the ***p*** who did
11: 7 the abomination of the ***p*** of
11:33 and Milcom the god of the ***p*** of
12: 5 And the ***p*** departed.
12: 6 advise me to answer these ***p***?
12: 7 will be a servant to these ***p***
12: 9 How should we answer this ***p*** who
12:10 you should speak to this ***p*** who
12:12 So Jeroboam and all the ***p*** came
12:13 Then the king answered the ***p***
12:15 king did not listen to the ***p***;
12:16 the ***p*** answered the king,
12:23 and to the rest of the ***p***,
12:27 If these ***p*** go up to offer
12:27 then the heart of this ***p*** will
12:28 of gold, and said to the ***p***,
12:30 for the ***p*** went to worship
12:31 priests from every class of ***p***,
13:33 priests from every class of ***p***
14: 2 I would be king over this ***p***.
14: 7 I exalted you from among the ***p***,
14: 7 and made you ruler over My ***p***
16: 2 and made you ruler over My ***p***
16: 2 and have made My ***p*** Israel sin,
16:15 And the ***p*** were encamped
16:16 Now the ***p*** who were encamped
16:21 Then the ***p*** of Israel were
16:21 half of the ***p*** followed Tibni
16:22 But the ***p*** who followed Omri
16:22 Omri prevailed over the ***p*** who
18:21 And Elijah came to all the ***p***,
18:21 But the ***p*** answered him not a
18:22 Then Elijah said to the ***p***,
18:24 So all the ***p*** answered and
18:30 Then Elijah said to all the ***p***,
18:30 So all the ***p*** came near to
18:37 that this ***p*** may know that You
18:39 Now when all the ***p*** saw it, they
19:21 equipment, and gave it to the ***p***,
20: 8 all the elders and all the ***p***
20:10 for a handful for each of the ***p***
20:15 them he mustered all the ***p***,
20:42 and your ***p*** for his people.'"
20:42 life, and your people for his ***p***.
21: 9 with high honor among the ***p***;
21:12 with high honor among the ***p***.
21:13 in the presence of the ***p***,
22: 4 my ***p*** as your people, my horses
22: 4 you are, my people as your ***p***,
22:28 'Take heed, all you ***p***!"
22:43 for the ***p*** offered sacrifices
2 Ki 3: 7 my ***p*** as your people, my horses
3: 7 you are, my people as your ***p***,
4:13 "I dwell among my own ***p***.
4:41 and said, "Serve it to the ***p***,
4:42 he said, "Give it to the ***p***,
4:43 said again, "Give it to the ***p***,
6:18 and said, "Strike this ***p***,
6:30 the ***p*** looked, and there
7:16 Then the ***p*** went out and
7:17 But the ***p*** trampled him in the
7:20 for the ***p*** trampled him in the
9: 6 anointed you king over the ***p***
10: 9 stood, and said to all the ***p***,
10:18 Then Jehu gathered all the ***p***
11:13 noise of the escorts and the ***p***,
11:13 she came to the ***p*** in the
11:14 All the ***p*** of the land were
11:17 the LORD, the king, and the ***p***,
11:17 they should be the LORD's ***p***,
11:17 between the king and the ***p***.
11:18 And all the ***p*** of the land went
11:19 and all the ***p*** of the land; and
11:20 So all the ***p*** of the land
12: 3 the ***p*** still sacrificed and
12: 8 receive more money from the ***p***,
14: 4 and the ***p*** still sacrificed and
14:21 And all the ***p*** of Judah took
15: 4 the ***p*** still sacrificed and
15: 5 judging the ***p*** of the land.
15:10 killed him in front of the ***p***;
15:35 the ***p*** still sacrificed and
16: 9 carried its ***p*** captive to Kir,
16:15 burnt offering of all the ***p*** of
17:24 the king of Assyria brought ***p***
18:26 Hebrew in the hearing of the ***p***
18:36 But the ***p*** held their peace and
19:12 and the ***p*** of Eden who were in
19:35 and when ***p*** arose early in the
20: 5 Hezekiah the leader of My ***p***,
21:24 But the ***p*** of the land executed
21:24 Then the ***p*** of the land made his
22: 4 have gathered from the ***p***.
22:13 for the ***p*** and for all Judah,
23: 2 and the prophets and all the ***p***,
23: 3 And all the ***p*** took a stand for
23: 6 on the graves of the common ***p***.
23:13 the abomination of the ***p*** of
23:21 the king commanded all the ***p***,
23:30 And the ***p*** of the land took
23:35 the silver and gold from the ***p***
24: 2 and bands of the ***p*** of Ammon;
24:14 remained except the poorest ***p***
25: 3 there was no food for the ***p*** of
25:11 away captive the rest of the ***p***
25:19 who mustered the ***p*** of the land,
25:19 and sixty men of the ***p*** of the

25:22 governor over the **p** who
25:26 And all the **p**, small and
1 Chr 10: 9 of their idols and among the **p**.
11: 2 You shall shepherd My **p** Israel,
11: 2 be ruler over My **p** Israel.'
11:13 And the **p** fled from the
13: 4 right in the eyes of all the **p**.
14: 2 exalted for the sake of His **p**
16: 2 he blessed the **p** in the name of
16:20 from one kingdom to another **p**,
16:36 And all the **p** said, "Amen!"
16:43 Then all the **p** departed, every
17: 6 I commanded to shepherd My **p**,
17: 7 to be ruler over My **p** Israel.
17: 9 I will appoint a place for My **p**
17:10 judges to be over My **p**
17:21 And who is like Your **p** Israel,
17:21 to redeem for Himself as a **p**—
17:21 out nations from before Your **p**
17:22 For You have made Your **p** Israel
17:22 people Israel Your very own **p**
18:11 from the **p** of Ammon, from the
18:14 and justice to all his **p**.
19: 1 that Nahash the king of the **p**
19: 2 to Hanun in the land of the **p**
19: 3 And the princes of the **p** of
19: 6 When the **p** of Ammon saw that
19: 6 Hanun and the **p** of Ammon sent a
19: 7 the king of Maachah and his **p**,
19: 7 Also the **p** of Ammon gathered
19: 9 Then the **p** of Ammon came out and
19:11 And the rest of the **p** he put
19:11 in battle array against the **p**
19:12 but if the **p** of Ammon are too
19:13 and let us be strong for our **p**
19:14 So Joab and the **p** who were with
19:15 When the **p** of Ammon saw that the
19:19 were not willing to help the **p**
20: 1 ravaged the country of the **p**
20: 3 And he brought out the **p** who
20: 3 did to all the cities of the **p**
20: 3 Then David and all the **p**
21: 2 and to the leaders of the **p**,
21: 3 May the LORD make His **p** a
21: 5 the sum of the number of the **p**
21:17 it not I who commanded the **p**
21:17 but not against Your **p** that
21:22 may be withdrawn from the **p**.
22:18 the LORD and before His **p**.
23:25 Israel has given rest to His **p**,
28: 2 "Hear me, my brethren and my **p**:
28:21 also the leaders and all the **p**
29: 9 Then the **p** rejoiced, for they
29:14 who am I, and who are my **p**,
29:17 now with joy I have seen Your **p**,
29:18 thoughts of the heart of Your **p**,
2 Chr 1: 9 You have made me king over a **p**
1:10 out and come in before this **p**;
1:10 for who can judge this great **p**
1:11 that you may judge My **p** over
2:11 Because the LORD loves His **p**,
2:18 overseers to make the **p** work.
6: 5 the day that I brought My **p**
6: 5 any man to be a ruler over My **p**
6: 6 chosen David to be over My **p**
6:21 of Your servant and of Your **p**
6:24 Or if Your **p** Israel are
6:25 and forgive the sin of Your **p**
6:27 Your **p** Israel, that You may
6:27 which You have given to Your **p**
6:29 or by all Your **p** Israel, when
6:32 who is not of Your **p** Israel,
6:33 as do Your **p** Israel, and that
6:34 When Your **p** go out to battle
6:39 and forgive Your **p** who have
7: 4 Then the king and all the **p**
7: 5 So the king and all the **p**
7:10 the seventh month he sent the **p**
7:10 and for His **p** Israel.
7:13 or send pestilence among My **p**,
7:14 if My **p** who are called by My
8: 7 All the **p** who were left of
8:10 and fifty, who ruled over the **p**.
10: 5 And the **p** departed.
10: 6 advise me to answer these **p**?
10: 7 "If you are kind to these **p**,
10: 9 How should we answer this **p** who
10:10 you should speak to the **p**
10:12 So Jeroboam and all the **p** came
10:15 king did not listen to the **p**;
10:16 the **p** answered the king,
12: 3 and **p** without number who came
13:17 Then Abijah and his **p** struck
14:13 And Asa and the **p** who were with
16:10 Asa oppressed some of the **p**
17: 9 of Judah and taught the **p**.
18: 2 in abundance for him and the **p**
18: 3 and my **p** as your people;
18: 3 are, and my people as your **p**;
18:27 'Take heed, all you **p**!"
19: 4 he went out again among the **p**
20: 1 after this that the **p** of Moab
20: 1 the people of Moab with the **p**
20: 7 of this land before Your **p**
20:10 here are the **p** of Ammon, Moab,
20:21 he had consulted with the **p**,
20:22 set ambushes against the **p** of
20:23 For the **p** of Ammon and Moab
20:25 When Jehoshaphat and his **p** came
20:33 for as yet the **p** had not
21:14 the LORD will strike your **p**
21:19 And his **p** made no burning for
23: 5 All the **p** shall be in the
23: 6 but all the **p** shall keep the
23:10 Then he set all the **p**,
23:12 heard the noise of the **p**
23:12 she came to the **p** in the
23:13 All the **p** of the land were
23:16 covenant between himself, the **p**,
23:16 they should be the LORD's **p**.
23:17 And all the **p** went to the temple
23:20 nobles, the governors of the **p**,
23:20 and all the **p** of the land, and
23:21 So all the **p** of the land
24:10 all the leaders and all the **p**
24:20 priest, who stood above the **p**,
24:23 all the leaders of the **p** from
24:23 of the people from among the **p**,
25:11 himself, and leading his **p**,
25:11 killed ten thousand of the **p**
25:14 he brought the gods of the **p**
25:15 you sought the gods of the **p**,
25:15 could not rescue their own **p**
26: 1 Now all the **p** of Judah took
26:21 judging the **p** of the land.
27: 2 But still the **p** acted
27: 5 And the **p** of Ammon gave him in
27: 5 The **p** of Ammon paid this to him
29:36 Then Hezekiah and all the **p**
29:36 that God had prepared the **p**,
30: 3 nor had the **p** gathered together
30:13 Now many **p**, a very great
30:18 For a multitude of the **p**,
30:20 to Hezekiah and healed the **p**.
30:27 arose and blessed the **p**,
31: 4 Moreover he commanded the **p** who
31: 8 blessed the LORD and His **p**
31:10 Since the **p** began to bring the
31:10 for the LORD has blessed His **p**;
32: 4 Thus many **p** gathered together
32: 6 military captains over the **p**,
32: 8 And the **p** were strengthened
32:14 that could deliver his **p** from
32:15 was able to deliver his **p** from
32:17 have not delivered their **p**
32:17 will not deliver His **p** from my
32:18 a loud voice in Hebrew to the **p**
32:19 as against the gods of the **p** of
33:10 spoke to Manasseh and his **p**,
33:17 Nevertheless the **p** still
33:25 But the **p** of the land executed
33:25 Then the **p** of the land made his
34:30 and the Levites, and all the **p**,
35: 3 the LORD your God and His **p**
35: 5 of your brethren the lay **p**,
35: 7 Then Josiah gave the lay **p**
35: 8 leaders gave willingly to the **p**,
35:12 fathers' houses of the lay **p**,
35:13 quickly among all the lay **p**.
36: 1 Then the **p** of the land took
36:14 of the priests and the **p**
36:15 He had compassion on His **p** and
36:16 the LORD arose against His **p**,
36:23 Who is among you of all His **p**?
Ezra 1: 3 Who is among you of all His **p**?
2: 1 Now these are the **p** of the
2: 2 The number of the men of the **p**
2: 3 the **p** of Parosh, two thousand
2: 4 the **p** of Shephatiah, three
2: 5 the **p** of Arah, seven hundred and
2: 6 the **p** of Pahath-Moab, of the
2: 6 of the **p** of Jeshua and Joab,
2: 7 the **p** of Elam, one thousand two
2: 8 the **p** of Zattu, nine hundred and
2: 9 the **p** of Zaccai, seven hundred
2:10 the **p** of Bani, six hundred and
2:11 the **p** of Bebai, six hundred and
2:12 the **p** of Azgad, one thousand two
2:13 the **p** of Adonikam, six hundred
2:14 the **p** of Bigvai, two thousand
2:15 the **p** of Adin, four hundred and
2:16 the **p** of Ater of Hezekiah,
2:17 the **p** of Bezai, three hundred
2:18 the **p** of Jorah, one hundred and
2:19 the **p** of Hashum, two hundred and
2:20 the **p** of Gibbar, ninety-five;
2:21 the **p** of Bethlehem, one hundred
2:24 the **p** of Azmaveth, forty-two;
2:25 the **p** of Kirjath Arim,
2:26 the **p** of Ramah and Geba, six
2:29 the **p** of Nebo, fifty-two;
2:30 the **p** of Magbish, one hundred
2:31 the **p** of the other Elam, one
2:32 the **p** of Harim, three hundred
2:33 the **p** of Lod, Hadid, and Ono,
2:34 the **p** of Jericho, three hundred
2:35 the **p** of Senaah, three thousand
2:70 and the Levites, some of the **p**,
3: 1 the **p** gathered together as one
3: 3 upon them because of the **p** of
3: 7 and oil to the **p** of Sidon and
3:11 Then all the **p** shouted with a
3:13 so that the **p** could not discern
3:13 noise of the weeping of the **p**,
3:13 for the **p** shouted with a loud
4: 4 Then the **p** of the land tried to
4: 4 land tried to discourage the **p**
4: 9 the **p** of Persia and Erech and
5:12 this temple and carried the **p**
6:12 there destroy any king or **p**
7:13 decree that all those of the **p**
7:16 the freewill offering of the **p**
7:25 judges who may judge all the **p**
8:15 And I looked among the **p** and
8:36 So they gave support to the **p**
9: 1 The **p** of Israel and the priests
9:14 and join in marriage with the **p**
10: 1 for the **p** wept very bitterly.
10: 9 and all the **p** sat in the open
10:13 "But there are many **p**;
Neh 1:10 are Your servants and Your **p**,
4: 6 for the **p** had a mind to work.
4:13 and I set the **p** according to
4:14 and to the rest of the **p**,
4:19 rulers, and the rest of the **p**,
4:22 same time I also said to the **p**,
5: 1 was a great outcry of the **p**
5:13 Then the **p** did according to
5:15 before me laid burdens on the **p**,
5:15 servants bore rule over the **p**,
5:18 the bondage was heavy on this **p**.
5:19 all that I have done for this **p**.
7: 4 but the **p** in it were few, and
7: 5 nobles, the rulers, and the **p**,
7: 6 These are the **p** of the province
7: 7 number of the men of the **p** of
7:72 that which the rest of the **p**
7:73 the singers, some of the **p**,
8: 1 Now all the **p** gathered together
8: 3 and the ears of all the **p** were
8: 5 book in the sight of all the **p**,
8: 5 was standing above all the **p**;
8: 5 all the **p** stood up.
8: 6 Then all the **p** answered,
8: 7 helped the **p** to understand the
8: 7 and the **p** stood in their
8: 9 the Levites who taught the **p**
8: 9 the people said to all the **p**,
8: 9 For all the **p** wept, when they
8:11 the Levites quieted all the **p**,
8:12 And all the **p** went their way to
8:13 fathers' houses of all the **p**,
8:16 Then the **p** went out and brought
9:10 And against all the **p** of his
9:24 So the **p** went in And possessed
9:24 With their kings And the **p** of
9:32 Our fathers and on all Your **p**,
10:14 The leaders of the **p**:
10:28 Now the rest of the **p**—
10:34 priests, the Levites, and the **p**,
11: 1 Now the leaders of the **p** dwelt
11: 1 the rest of the **p** cast lots to
11: 2 And the **p** blessed all the men
11:24 in all matters concerning the **p**.
12:30 themselves, and purified the **p**,
12:38 behind them with half of the **p**
13: 1 Moses in the hearing of the **p**,
13:15 In those days I saw **p** in Judah
13:24 language of one or the other **p**.
Esth 1: 5 seven days for all the **p** who
1:11 to show her beauty to the **p**
1:16 and all the **p** who are in all
1:22 and to every **p** in their own
1:22 in the language of his own **p**.
2:10 Esther had not revealed her **p** or
2:20 revealed her family and her **p**,
3: 6 for they had told him of the **p**
3: 6 the **p** of Mordecai.
3: 8 There is a certain **p** scattered
3: 8 and dispersed among the **p** in
3:11 The money and the **p** are given
3:12 to the officials of all **p**,
3:12 and to every **p** in their
3:14 being published for all **p**,
4: 8 and plead before him for her **p**.
4:11 the king's servants and the **p**
7: 3 and my **p** at my request.
7: 4 my **p** and I, to be destroyed, to
8: 6 the evil that will come to my **p**?
8: 9 to every **p** in their own
8:11 all the forces of any **p** or
8:13 and published for all **p**,
8:17 Then many of the **p** of the land
9: 2 fear of them fell upon all **p**.
10: 3 seeking the good of his **p** and
Job 1: 3 was the greatest of all the **p**
1:19 and it fell on the young **p**,
12: 2 "No doubt you are the **p**,
12:24 of the chiefs of the **p** of the
17: 6 has made me a byword of the **p**,
18:19 son nor posterity among his **p**,
28: 4 breaks open a shaft away from **p**;
34:20 The **p** are shaken and pass
34:30 Lest the **p** be ensnared.
36:20 When **p** are cut off in their
Ps 2: 1 And the **p** plot a vain thing?
3: 6 be afraid of ten thousands of **p**
3: 8 Your blessing is upon Your **p**.
9:11 Declare His deeds among the **p**.
14: 4 Who eat up my **p** as they eat
14: 7 back the captivity of His **p**,
18:27 For You will save the humble **p**,
18:43 me from the strivings of the **p**;
18:43 A **p** I have not known shall
22: 6 of men, and despised by the **p**.
22:31 His righteousness to a **p** who
28: 9 Save Your **p**, And bless Your
29:11 will give strength to His **p**;
29:11 The LORD will bless His **p**
33:12 The **p** He has chosen as His own
35:18 I will praise You among many **p**.
44:12 You sell Your **p** for next to
45:10 Forget your own **p** also, and
45:12 The rich among the **p** will seek
45:17 Therefore the **p** shall praise
47: 9 The princes of the **p** have

47: 9 The **p** of the God of Abraham.
50: 4 earth, that He may judge His **p**:
50: 7 'Hear, O My **p**, and I will
53: 4 Who eat up my **p** as they eat
53: 6 back the captivity of His **p**,
59:11 lest my **p** forget; Scatter them
60: 3 You have shown Your **p** hard
62: 8 in Him at all times, you **p**;
67: 4 For You shall judge the **p** righteously,
68: 7 when You went out before Your **p**,
68:35 strength and power to His **p**.
72: 2 He will judge Your **p** with
72: 3 will bring peace to the **p**,
72: 4 justice to the poor of the **p**;
73:10 Therefore his **p** return here,
74:14 gave him as food to the **p**
74:18 And that a foolish **p** has
77:15 with Your arm redeemed Your **p**,
77:20 You led Your **p** like a flock
78: 1 Give ear, O my **p**,
78:20 Can He provide meat for His **p**?
78:52 But He made His own **p** go forth
78:62 He also gave His **p** over to the
78:71 To shepherd Jacob His **p**,
79:13 Your **p** and sheep of Your
80: 4 Against the prayer of Your **p**?
81: 8 'Hear, O My **p**, and I will
81:11 But My **p** would not heed My
81:13 that My **p** would listen to Me,
83: 3 crafty counsel against Your **p**,
85: 2 forgiven the iniquity of Your **p**;
85: 6 That Your **p** may rejoice in
85: 8 He will speak peace To His **p**
89:15 Blessed are the **p** who know the
89:19 exalted one chosen from the **p**.
94: 5 They break in pieces Your **p**,
94: 8 you senseless among the **p**;
94:14 LORD will not cast off His **p**,
95: 7 And we are the **p** of His
95:10 It is a **p** who go astray in
100: 3 We are His **p** and the sheep
102:18 That a **p** yet to be created may
105:13 From one kingdom to another **p**,
105:20 The ruler of the **p** let him go
105:24 He increased His **p** greatly,
105:25 their heart to hate His **p**,
105:40 The **p** asked, and He brought
105:43 He brought out His **p** with joy,
106: 4 favor You have toward Your **p**;
106:40 LORD was kindled against His **p**,
106:48 And let all the **p** say,
107:32 also in the assembly of the **p**,
110: 3 Your **p** shall be volunteers
111: 6 He has declared to His **p** the
111: 9 has sent redemption to His **p**;
113: 8 the princes of His **p**.
114: 1 The house of Jacob from a **p** of
116:14 in the presence of all His **p**.
116:18 in the presence of all His **p**,
125: 2 So the LORD surrounds His **p**
135:12 A heritage to Israel His **p**.
135:14 For the LORD will judge His **p**,
136:16 To Him who led His **p** through
144: 2 Who subdues my **p** under me.
144:15 Happy are the **p** who are in
144:15 Happy are the **p** whose God is
148:14 has exalted the horn of His **p**,
148:14 A **p** near to Him. Praise the
149: 4 LORD takes pleasure in His **p**;
Prov 6:30 **P** do not despise a thief
10:14 Wise **p** store up knowledge,
11:14 the **p** fall; But in the
11:26 The **p** will curse him who
14:28 In a multitude of **p** is a
14:28 But in the lack of **p** is the
14:34 sin is a reproach to any **p**.
24:24 Him the **p** will curse;
28:15 Is a wicked ruler over poor **p**.
29: 2 the **p** rejoice; But when a
29: 2 man rules, the **p** groan.
29:18 the **p** cast off restraint;
30:25 The ants are a **p** not strong,
Eccl 4:16 was no end of all the **p** over
7:21 not take to heart everything **p**
9: 1 **P** know neither love nor hatred
12: 9 he still taught the **p**
Song 6:12 As the chariots of my noble **p**.
Isa 1: 3 My **p** do not consider."
1: 4 A **p** laden with iniquity,
1:10 You **p** of Gomorrah:
2: 3 Many **p** shall come and say,
2: 4 the nations, And rebuke many **p**;
2: 6 For You have forsaken Your **p**,
2: 9 **P** bow down, And each man
3: 5 The **p** will be oppressed, Every
3: 7 not make me a ruler of the **p**.
3:12 As for My **p**, children are
3:12 O My **p**! Those who lead you
3:13 And stands to judge the **p**.
3:14 With the elders of His **p** And
3:15 do you mean by crushing My **p**
5:13 Therefore my **p** have gone into
5:15 **P** shall be brought down, Each
5:25 LORD is aroused against His **p**;
6: 5 I dwell in the midst of a **p** of
6: 9 He said, "Go, and tell this **p**:
6:10 Make the heart of this **p** dull,
7: 2 heart and the heart of his **p**
7: 8 that it will not be a **p**.
7:17 of Assyria upon you and your **p**
8: 6 'Inasmuch as these **p** refused
8:11 not walk in the way of this **p**,
8:12 Concerning all that this **p**
8:19 should not a **p** seek their
9: 2 The **p** who walked in darkness
9: 9 All the **p** will know—Ephraim
9:13 For the **p** do not turn to Him
9:16 For the leaders of this **p** cause
9:19 And the **p** shall be as fuel for
10: 2 is right from the poor of My **p**,
10: 6 And against the **p** of My wrath
10:13 removed the boundaries of the **p**,
10:14 like a nest the riches of the **p**,
10:22 For though your **p**, O Israel,
10:24 Lord GOD of hosts: "O My **p**,
11:10 stand as a banner to the **p**;
11:11 recover the remnant of His **p**
11:14 they shall plunder the **p** of
11:14 And the **p** of Ammon shall obey
11:16 for the remnant of His **p** Who
13: 4 Like that of many **p**!
13:14 man will turn to his own **p**,
14: 2 Then **p** will take them and bring
14: 6 He who struck the **p** in wrath
14:20 your land And slain your **p**.
14:32 And the poor of His **p** shall
17:12 to the multitude of many **p**
18: 2 To a **p** terrible from their
18: 7 to the LORD of hosts From a **p**
18: 7 And from a **p** terrible from
19:25 "Blessed is Egypt My **p**,
21:17 the mighty men of the **p** of
22: 4 of the daughter of my **p**.
23:13 This **p** which was not;
24: 2 it shall be: As with the **p**,
24: 4 The haughty **p** of the earth
24:13 midst of the land among the **p**,
25: 3 Therefore the strong **p** will
25: 6 of hosts will make for all **p**
25: 7 of the covering cast over all **p**,
25: 8 The rebuke of His **p** He will
26:11 ashamed For their envy of **p**;
26:20 Come, my **p**, enter your
27:11 For it is a **p** of no
28: 5 beauty To the remnant of His **p**,
28:11 tongue He will speak to this **p**,
28:14 Who rule this **p** who are in
29:13 Inasmuch as these **p** draw near
29:14 a marvelous work Among this **p**,
30: 5 They were all ashamed of a **p**
30: 6 To a **p** who shall not profit;
30: 9 That this is a rebellious **p**,
30:19 For the **p** shall dwell in Zion
30:26 binds up the bruise of His **p**
30:28 a bridle in the jaws of the **p**,
32:12 **P** shall mourn upon their
32:13 On the land of my **p** will come
32:18 My **p** will dwell in a peaceful
33: 3 the noise of the tumult the **p**
33:12 And the **p** shall be like the
33:19 You will not see a fierce **p**,
33:19 A **p** of obscure speech, beyond
33:24 The **p** who dwell in it will
34: 1 you **p**! Let the earth hear, and
34: 5 And on the **p** of My curse, for
36:11 Hebrew in the hearing of the **p**
37:12 and the **p** of Eden who were in
37:36 and when **p** arose early in the
40: 1 comfort My **p**!" Says your God.
40: 7 Surely the **p** are grass.
41: 1 And let the **p** renew their
42: 5 Who gives breath to the **p** on
42: 6 give You as a covenant to the **p**,
42:22 But this is a **p** robbed and
43: 4 And **p** for your life.
43: 8 Bring out the blind **p** who have
43: 9 And let the **p** be assembled.
43:20 desert, To give drink to My **p**,
43:21 This **p** I have formed for
44: 7 I appointed the ancient **p**.
47: 6 I was angry with My **p**;
49: 8 You As a covenant to the **p**,
49:13 the LORD has comforted His **p**,
51: 4 "Listen to Me, My **p**;
51: 7 You **p** in whose heart is My
51:16 say to Zion, 'You are My **p**.
51:22 Who pleads the cause of His **p**:
52: 4 My **p** went down at first Into
52: 5 That My **p** are taken away for
52: 6 Therefore My **p** shall know My
52: 9 the LORD has comforted His **p**,
53: 8 the transgressions of My **p** He
55: 4 him as a witness to the **p**,
55: 4 leader and commander for the **p**.
56: 3 separated me from His **p**";
57:14 block out of the way of My **p**.
58: 1 Tell My **p** their transgression,
60: 2 earth, And deep darkness the **p**;
60:21 Also your **p** shall all be
61: 9 their offspring among the **p**.
62:10 Prepare the way for the **p**;
62:12 they shall call them The Holy **P**,
63: 8 said, "Surely they are My **p**,
63:11 days of old, Moses and his **p**,
63:14 to rest, So You lead Your **p**,
63:18 Your holy **p** have possessed it
64: 9 we all are Your **p**!
65: 2 all day long to a rebellious **p**,
65: 3 A **p** who provoke Me to anger
65:10 For My **p** who have sought Me.
65:18 And her **p** a joy.
65:19 in Jerusalem, And joy in My **p**;
65:22 so shall be the days of My **p**,
Jer 1:18 And against the **p** of the land.
2:11 But My **p** have changed their
2:13 For My **p** have committed two
2:16 Also the **p** of Noph and
2:31 Why do My **p** say, 'We are
2:32 Yet My **p** have forgotten Me
4:10 have greatly deceived this **p**
4:11 it will be said To this **p** and
4:11 Toward the daughter of My **p**—
4:22 For My **p** are foolish, They
5:14 And this **p** wood, And it shall
5:21 'Hear this now, O foolish **p**,
5:23 But this **p** has a defiant and
5:26 For among My **p** are found wicked
5:31 And My **p** love to have it
6:14 also healed the hurt of My **p**
6:19 bring calamity on this **p**—
6:21 stumbling blocks before this **p**,
6:22 a **p** comes from the north
6:26 O daughter of my **p**,
6:27 and a fortress among My **p**,
6:30 **P** will call them rejected
7:12 of the wickedness of My **p**
7:16 do not pray for this **p**,
7:23 your God, and you shall be My **p**.
7:33 The corpses of this **p** will be
8: 5 Why has this **p** slidden back,
8: 7 But My **p** do not know the
8:11 hurt of the daughter of My **p**
8:19 cry of the daughter of my **p**
8:21 hurt of the daughter of my **p** I
8:22 health of the daughter of my **p**?
9: 1 slain of the daughter of my **p**!
9: 2 That I might leave my **p**,
9: 7 deal with the daughter of My **p**?
9:15 I will feed them, this **p**,
9:26 the **p** of Ammon, Moab, and all
11: 4 you; so shall you be My **p**,
11:14 "So do not pray for this **p**,
12:14 which I have caused My **p**
12:16 carefully the ways of My **p**,
12:16 as they taught My **p** to swear
12:16 in the midst of My **p**.
13:10 'This evil **p**, who refuse to
13:11 'that they may become My **p**,
14:10 Thus says the LORD to this **p**:
14:11 to me, "Do not pray for this **p**,
14:16 And the **p** to whom they prophesy
14:17 the virgin daughter of my **p**
15: 1 not be favorable toward this **p**.
15: 7 I will destroy My **p**, Since
15:20 And I will make you to this **p**
16: 5 taken away My peace from this **p**,
16:10 when you show this **p** all these
17:19 gate of the children of the **p**,
18:15 Because My **p** have forgotten Me,
19: 1 some of the elders of the **p**
19:11 Even so I will break this **p** and
19:14 house and said to all the **p**,
21: 7 Judah, his servants and the **p**,
21: 8 "Now you shall say to this **p**,
22: 2 and your servants and your **p**
22: 4 accompanied by servants and **p**,
23: 2 the shepherds who feed My **p**:
23:13 by Baal And caused My **p**
23:22 And had caused My **p** to hear My
23:27 who try to make My **p** forget My
23:32 and cause My **p** to err by their
23:32 they shall not profit this **p**
23:33 So when these **p** or the prophet
23:34 and the priest and the **p** who
24: 7 and they shall be My **p**,
25: 1 Jeremiah concerning all the **p**
25: 2 the prophet spoke to all the **p**
25:19 his princes, and all his **p**;
25:21 and the **p** of Ammon;
26: 7 and the prophets and all the **p**
26: 8 him to speak to all the **p**,
26: 8 and the prophets and all the **p**
26: 9 And all the **p** were gathered
26:11 to the princes and all the **p**,
26:12 all the princes and all the **p**,
26:16 So the princes and all the **p**
26:17 to all the assembly of the **p**,
26:18 and spoke to all the **p** of
26:23 into the graves of the common **p**.
26:24 him into the hand of the **p** to
27:12 and serve him and his **p**,
27:13 will you die, you and your **p**,
27:16 the priests and to all this **p**,
28: 1 of the priests and of all the **p**,
28: 5 in the presence of all the **p**
28: 7 and in the hearing of all the **p**:
28:11 in the presence of all the **p**,
28:15 but you make this **p** trust in a
29: 1 and all the **p** whom
29:16 concerning all the **p** who dwell
29:25 in your name to all the **p** who
29:32 anyone to dwell among this **p**,
29:32 good that I will do for My **p**,
30: 3 bring back from captivity My **p**
30:22 'You shall be My **p**,
31: 1 Israel, and they shall be My **p**.
31: 2 The **p** who survived the sword
31: 7 and say, 'O LORD, save Your **p**,
31:14 And My **p** shall be satisfied
31:33 God, and they shall be My **p**.
32:21 You have brought Your **p** Israel
32:38 'They shall be My **p**,
32:42 this great calamity on this **p**,
33:24 you not considered what these **p**
33:24 Thus they have despised My **p**,
34: 1 his dominion, and all the **p**,

34: 8 made a covenant with all the **p**
34:10 all the princes and all the **p**,
34:19 and all the **p** of the land who
35:16 but this **p** has not obeyed Me."
36: 6 in the hearing of the **p** in the
36: 7 has pronounced against this **p**.
36: 9 before the LORD to all the **p**
36: 9 and to all the **p** who came from
36:10 in the hearing of all the **p**.
36:13 book in the hearing of the **p**.
36:14 read in the hearing of the **p**,
37: 2 he nor his servants nor the **p**
37: 4 coming and going among the **p**,
37:12 his property there among the **p**.
37:18 servants, or against this **p**,
38: 1 had spoken to all the **p**,
38: 4 and the hands of all the **p**,
38: 4 not seek the welfare of this **p**,
39: 8 house and the houses of the **p**
39: 9 to Babylon the remnant of the **p**
39: 9 with the rest of the **p** who
39:10 in the land of Judah the poor **p**,
39:14 home. So he dwelt among the **p**.
40: 3 Because you **p** have sinned
40: 5 and dwell with him among the **p**.
40: 6 and dwelt with him among the **p**
41:10 captive all the rest of the **p**
41:10 king's daughters and all the **p**
41:13 when all the **p** who were with
41:14 Then all the **p** whom Ishmael had
41:16 Mizpah all the rest of the **p**
42: 1 son of Hoshaiah, and all the **p**,
42: 8 and all the **p** from the least
43: 1 stopped speaking to all the **p**
43: 4 and all the **p** would not obey
44:15 and all the **p** who dwelt in the
44:20 Jeremiah spoke to all the **p**—
44:20 and all the **p** who had given him
44:21 and the **p** of the land, did not
44:24 Jeremiah said to all the **p** and
46:16 Let us go back to our own **p**
46:24 into the hand Of the **p** of the
48:42 Moab shall be destroyed as a **p**,
48:46 O Moab! The **p** of Chemosh
49: 1 And his **p** dwell in its cities?
49: 6 The captives of the **p** of
50: 6 My **p** have been lost sheep.
50:16 shall turn to his own **p**,
50:41 a **p** shall come from the north,
51:45 My **p**, go out of the midst
51:58 The **p** will labor in vain, And
52: 6 there was no food for the **p** of
52:15 captive some of the poor **p**,
52:15 the rest of the **p** who remained
52:25 of the army who mustered the **p**
52:25 and sixty men of the **p** of the
52:28 These are the **p** whom
Lam 1: 1 the city That was full of **p**!
1: 7 When her **p** fell into the hand
1:11 All her **p** sigh, They seek
2:11 of the daughter of my **p**,
3:14 become the ridicule of all my **p**—
3:48 of the daughter of my **p**.
4: 3 But the daughter of my **p** is
4: 6 of the daughter of my **p** Is
4:10 of the daughter of my **p**.
4:16 The **p** do not respect the
Ezek 3: 5 For you are not sent to a **p** of
3: 6 not to many **p** of unfamiliar
3:11 to the children of your **p**,
7:27 And the hands of the common **p**
11: 1 of Benaiah, princes of the **p**.
11:20 do them; and they shall be My **p**,
12:19 And say to the **p** of the land,
12:22 is this proverb that you **p**
13: 9 not be in the assembly of My **p**,
13:10 because they have seduced My **p**,
13:17 against the daughters of your **p**,
13:18 make veils for the heads of **p**
13:18 Will you hunt the souls of My **p**,
13:19 will you profane Me among My **p**
13:19 killing **p** who should not die,
13:19 and keeping **p** alive who should
13:19 by your lying to My **p** who
13:21 off your veils and deliver My **p**
13:23 for I will deliver My **p** out of
14: 8 him off from the midst of My **p**.
14: 9 and destroy him from among My **p**
14:11 but that they may be My **p** and I
17: 9 And no great power or many **p**
17:15 give him horses and many **p**.
18:18 what is not good among his **p**,
21:12 For it will be against My **p**,
21:12 the sword will be against My **p**;
22:25 the prey; they have devoured **p**;
22:27 to shed blood, to destroy **p**,
22:29 The **p** of the land have used
23:24 war-horses, With a horde of **p**.
24:18 So I spoke to the **p** in the
24:19 And the **p** said to me, "Will
25:14 on Edom by the hand of My **p**
26: 7 and an army with many **p**.
26:11 he will slay your **p** by the
26:20 to the **p** of old, and I will
27:33 by sea, You satisfied many **p**;
30: 5 Libya, Lydia, all the mingled **p**,
30:11 He and his **p** with him, the most
32: 3 you with a company of many **p**,
33: 2 speak to the children of your **p**,
33: 2 and the **p** of the land take a
33: 3 the trumpet and warns the **p**,
33: 6 and the **p** are not warned, and
33:12 say to the children of your **p**:
33:17 Yet the children of your **p** say,
33:30 the children of your **p** are
33:31 So they come to you as **p** do,
33:31 they sit before you as My **p**,
34:30 the house of Israel, are My **p**,
36: 3 talkers and slandered by the **p**'
36: 8 and yield your fruit to My **p**
36:12 My **p** Israel; they shall take
36:20 These are the **p** of the LORD,
36:28 your fathers; you shall be My **p**,
37:12 the Lord GOD: "Behold, O My **p**,
37:13 have opened your graves, O My **p**,
37:18 when the children of your **p**
37:23 them. Then they shall be My **p**,
37:27 God, and they shall be My **p**.
38: 6 many **p** are with you.
38: 8 and gathered from many **p** on
38:11 I will go to a peaceful **p**,
38:12 and against a **p** gathered from
38:14 On that day when My **p** Israel
38:16 You will come up against My **p**
39: 7 name known in the midst of My **p**
39:13 Indeed all the **p** of the land
42:14 that which is for the **p**.
44:11 and the sacrifice for the **p**,
44:19 to the outer court to the **p**,
44:19 they shall not sanctify the **p**.
44:23 And they shall teach My **p** the
45: 8 shall no more oppress My **p**,
45: 9 and stop dispossessing My **p**,
45:16 All the **p** of the land shall give
45:22 for himself and for all the **p**
46: 3 Likewise the **p** of the land shall
46: 9 But when the **p** of the land come
46:18 so that none of My **p** may be
46:20 outer court to sanctify the **p**.
46:24 boil the sacrifices of the **p**.
Dan 2:44 shall not be left to other **p**;
3: 7 when all the **p** heard the sound
3: 7 all kinds of music, all the **p**,
3:29 I make a decree that any **p**,
7:27 Shall be given to the **p**,
8:24 mighty, and also the holy **p**.
9: 6 to our fathers and all the **p** of
9:15 who brought Your **p** out of the
9:16 Jerusalem and Your **p** are a
9:19 for Your city and Your **p** are
9:20 my sin and the sin of my **p**
9:24 are determined For your **p** and
9:26 And the **p** of the prince who is
10:14 what will happen to your **p** in
11:14 violent men of your **p** shall
11:23 with a small number of **p**.
11:32 but the **p** who know their God
11:33 And those of the **p** who
11:41 and the prominent **p** of Ammon.
12: 1 watch over the sons of your **p**;
12: 1 And at that time your **p** shall
12: 7 when the power of the holy **p**
Hos 1: 9 Lo-Ammi, For you are not My **p**,
1:10 to them, 'You are not My **p**,
2: 1 Say to your brethren, 'My **p**,
2:23 to those who were not My **p**,
2:23 You are My **p**!' And they shall
4: 4 For your **p** are like those who
4: 6 My **p** are destroyed for lack of
4: 8 They eat up the sin of My **p**;
4: 9 And it shall be: like **p**,
4:12 My **p** ask counsel from their
4:14 Therefore **p** who do not
6:11 I return the captives of My **p**.
10: 5 For its **p** mourn for it,
10:14 tumult shall arise among your **p**,
11: 7 My **p** are bent on backsliding
Joel 2: 2 A **p** come, great and strong,
2: 5 Like a strong **p** set in battle
2: 6 Before them the **p** writhe in
2:16 Gather the **p**, Sanctify the
2:17 Let them say, "Spare Your **p**,
2:18 for His land, And pity His **p**.
2:19 will answer and say to His **p**,
2:26 And My **p** shall never be put to
2:27 My **p** shall never be put to
3: 2 them there On account of My **p**,
3: 3 They have cast lots for My **p**,
3: 6 Also the **p** of Judah and the
3: 6 the people of Judah and the **p**
3: 8 Into the hand of the **p** of
3: 8 To a **p** far off; For the LORD
3:16 will be a shelter for His **p**,
3:19 of violence against the **p** of
Am 1: 5 The **p** of Syria shall go
1:13 three transgressions of the **p**
3: 6 will not the **p** be afraid?
7: 8 line In the midst of My **p**
7:15 prophesy to My **p** Israel.'
8: 2 The end has come upon My **p**
9: 7 Are you not like the **p** of
9:10 All the sinners of My **p** shall
9:14 bring back the captives of My **p**
Ob 13 have entered the gate of My **p**
Jon 1: 8 And of what **p** are you?"
3: 5 So the **p** of Nineveh believed
Mic 1: 9 has come to the gate of My **p**—
2: 4 changed the heritage of my **p**;
2: 8 Lately My **p** have risen up as an
2: 9 The women of My **p** you cast out
2:11 would be the prattler of this **p**.
2:12 noise because of so many **p**.
3: 2 Who strip the skin from My **p**,
3: 3 Who also eat the flesh of My **p**,
3: 5 the prophets Who make my **p**
4: 5 For all **p** walk each in the name
6: 2 has a complaint against His **p**,
6: 3 'O My **p**, what have I done
6: 5 O My **p**, remember now
6:16 shall bear the reproach of My **p**.
7:14 Shepherd Your **p** with Your
Nah 3:13 your **p** in your midst are
3:18 Your **p** are scattered on the
Hab 2: 8 All the remnant of the **p** shall
3:13 for the salvation of Your **p**,
3:16 When he comes up to the **p**,
Zeph 1:11 For all the merchant **p** are
2: 8 And the insults of the **p** of
2: 8 which they have reproached My **p**,
2: 9 And the **p** of Ammon like
2: 9 The residue of My **p** shall
2: 9 And the remnant of My **p** shall
2:10 threats Against the **p** of the
2:11 **P** shall worship Him, Each
3: 4 are insolent, treacherous **p**;
3:12 your midst A meek and humble **p**,
Hag 1: 2 This **p** says, "The time has not
1:12 with all the remnant of the **p**,
1:12 and the **p** feared the presence
1:13 the LORD's message to the **p**,
1:14 of all the remnant of the **p**;
2: 2 and to the remnant of the **p**,
2: 4 all you **p** of the land,' says
2:14 and said, "'So is this **p**,
Zech 2:11 day, and they shall become My **p**.
7: 2 when the **p** sent Sherezer, with
7: 5 Say to all the **p** of the land,
8: 6 eyes of the remnant of this **p**
8: 7 I will save My **p** from the land
8: 8 They shall be My **p** And I will
8:11 treat the remnant of this **p**
8:12 cause the remnant of this **p**
9:16 As the flock of His **p**.
10: 2 Therefore the **p** wend their
13: 9 I will say, 'This is My **p**';
14: 2 But the remnant of the **p** shall
14:11 The **p** shall dwell in it;
14:12 the LORD will strike all the **p**
Mal 1: 4 And the **p** against whom the
2: 7 And **p** should seek the law
2: 9 and base Before all the **p**,
Mt 1:21 for He will save His **p** from
2: 4 priests and scribes of the **p**
2: 6 Who will shepherd My **p**
4:16 The **p** who sat in darkness
4:23 kinds of disease among the **p**.
4:24 they brought to Him all sick **p**
7:28 that the **p** were astonished at
9:35 and every disease among the **p**.
13:15 For the hearts of this **p**
15: 8 These **p** draw near to Me
21:23 priests and the elders of the **p**
26: 3 and the elders of the **p**
26: 5 there be an uproar among the **p**.
26:47 priests and elders of the **p**.
27: 1 priests and elders of the **p**
27:25 And all the **p** answered and said,
27:64 Him away, and say to the **p**,
Mk 3:21 But when His own **p** heard about
6: 5 laid His hands on a few sick **p**
6:12 went out and preached that **p**
6:54 immediately the **p** recognized
7: 6 This **p** honors Me with their
8: 4 How can one satisfy these **p** with
8:34 When He had called the **p** to
9:15 all the **p** were greatly amazed,
9:25 When Jesus saw that the **p** came
11:18 because all the **p** were
11:32 'From men'"—they feared the **p**,
12:37 And the common **p** heard Him
12:41 the treasury and saw how the **p**
14: 2 there be an uproar of the **p**.
Lk 1:10 the whole multitude of the **p**
1:17 to make ready a **p** prepared for
1:21 And the **p** waited for Zacharias,
1:25 take away my reproach among **p**.
1:68 has visited and redeemed His **p**,
1:77 of salvation to His **p** By the
2:10 joy which will be to all **p**.
2:32 And the glory of Your **p**
3:10 So the **p** asked Him, saying,
3:15 Now as the **p** were in
3:18 he preached to the **p**.
3:21 When all the **p** were baptized,
6:17 and a great multitude of **p**
7: 1 sayings in the hearing of the **p**,
7:16 and, "God has visited His **p**.
7:29 And when all the **p** heard Him,
8:47 in the presence of all the **p**
9:13 go and buy food for all these **p**.
12: 1 an innumerable multitude of **p**
12:41 only to us, or to all **p**?
18:43 glorifying God. And all the **p**,
19:47 and the leaders of the **p** sought
19:48 for all the **p** were very
20: 1 as He taught the **p** in the
20: 6 all the **p** will stone us, for
20: 9 Then He began to tell the **p**
20:19 on Him, but they feared the **p**—
20:26 words in the presence of the **p**.
20:45 in the hearing of all the **p**,
21:23 the land and wrath upon this **p**.
21:38 early in the morning all the **p**
22: 2 kill Him, for they feared the **p**.
22:66 it was day, the elders of the **p**,
23: 5 saying, "He stirs up the **p**,

23:13 priests, the rulers, and the **p**,
23:14 me, as one who misleads the **p**.
23:27 And a great multitude of the **p**
23:35 And the **p** stood looking on.
24:19 word before God and all the **p**,
Jn 4:48 Unless you **p** see signs and
5: 3 lay a great multitude of sick **p**,
6:10 Make the **p** sit down." Now there
6:22 when the **p** who were standing on
6:24 when the **p** therefore saw that
7:12 much complaining among the **p**
7:12 the contrary, He deceives the **p**.
7:20 The **p** answered and said, "You
7:31 And many of the **p** believed in
7:43 was a division among the **p**
8: 2 and all the **p** came to Him;
11:42 but because of the **p** who are
11:50 one man should die for the **p**,
12:17 Therefore the **p**, who were
12:18 For this reason the **p** also met
12:29 Therefore the **p** who stood by and
12:34 The **p** answered Him, "We have
18:14 one man should die for the **p**.
Acts 2:47 and having favor with all the **p**.
3: 9 And all the **p** saw him walking
3:11 all the **p** ran together to them
3:12 saw it, he responded to the **p**:
3:23 destroyed from among the **p**.
4: 1 Now as they spoke to the **p**,
4: 2 that they taught the **p** and
4: 8 Rulers of the **p** and elders of
4:10 and to all the **p** of Israel,
4:17 spreads no further among the **p**,
4:21 them, because of the **p**,
4:25 And the **p** plot vain
4:27 with the Gentiles and the **p** of
5:12 wonders were done among the **p**.
5:13 but the **p** esteemed them highly.
5:16 bringing sick **p** and those who
5:20 the temple and speak to the **p**
5:25 the temple and teaching the **p**!
5:26 violence, for they feared the **p**,
5:34 held in respect by all the **p**,
5:37 and drew away many **p** after him.
6: 8 wonders and signs among the **p**.
6:12 And they stirred up the **p**,
7:14 to him, seventy-five **p**.
7:17 the **p** grew and multiplied in
7:19 dealt treacherously with our **p**,
7:34 the oppression of my **p**
8: 9 the city and astonished the **p**
10: 2 gave alms generously to the **p**,
10:41 'not to all the **p**, but to
10:42 commanded us to preach to the **p**,
11:24 And a great many **p** were added
11:26 and taught a great many **p**.
12: 4 to bring him before the **p**
12:11 the expectation of the Jewish **p**.
12:20 had been very angry with the **p**
12:22 And the **p** kept shouting, "The
13:15 word of exhortation for the **p**,
13:17 The God of this **p** Israel chose
13:17 and exalted the **p** when they
13:24 of repentance to all the **p** of
13:31 who are His witnesses to the **p**.
14:11 Now when the **p** saw what Paul had
15:14 to take out of them a **p** for
17: 5 to bring them out to the **p**.
18:10 for I have many **p** in this
19: 4 saying to the **p** that they
19:26 and turned away many **p**,
19:30 Paul wanted to go in to the **p**,
19:33 to make his defense to the **p**.
21:28 men everywhere against the **p**,
21:30 and the **p** ran together, seized
21:36 For the multitude of the **p**
21:39 permit me to speak to the **p**.
21:40 motioned with his hand to the **p**.
23: 5 of a ruler of your **p**.
26:17 deliver you from the Jewish **p**,
26:23 light to the Jewish **p** and to
28:17 done nothing against our **p** or
28:26 Go to this **p** and say:
28:27 For the hearts of this **p**
Rom 9:25 "I will call them My **p**,
9:25 people, who were not My **p**,
9:26 them, You are not My **p**,
10:21 disobedient and contrary **p**.
11: 1 then, has God cast away His **p**?
11: 2 God has not cast away His **p** whom
15:10 Gentiles, with His **p**!"
1 Cor 3: 1 to you as to spiritual **p** but
5: 9 company with sexually immoral **p**.
5:10 with the sexually immoral **p** of
10: 7 The **p** sat down to eat and
14:21 I will speak to this **p**;
2 Cor 6:16 And they shall be My **p**.
2 Tim 3: 5 And from such **p** turn away!
Titus 2:14 for Himself His own special **p**,
3:14 And let our **p** also learn to
Heb 2:17 for the sins of the **p**.
4: 9 therefore a rest for the **p** of
5: 3 he is required as for the **p**,
7: 5 to receive tithes from the **p**
7:11 (for under it the **p** received
8:10 and they shall be My **p**.
9:19 every precept to all the **p**
9:19 the book itself and all the **p**,
10:30 LORD will judge His **p**.
11:25 to suffer affliction with the **p**
12:14 Pursue peace with all **p**,
13:12 that He might sanctify the **p**
1 Pe 2: 9 holy nation, His own special **p**,
2:10 who once were not a **p** but are
2:10 a people but are now the **p** of
2:17 Honor all **p**. Love the
5: 5 Likewise you younger **p**,
2 Pe 2: 1 also false prophets among the **p**,
2: 5 saved Noah, one of eight **p**,
3:16 which untaught and unstable **p**
Jude 5 having saved the **p** out of the
16 flattering **p** to gain advantage.
Rev 5: 9 of every tribe and tongue and **p**
6: 4 and that **p** should kill one
11:13 the earthquake seven thousand **p**
14: 6 nation, tribe, tongue, and **p**—
18: 4 saying, "Come out of her, my **p**,
19:18 them, and the flesh of all **p**,
21: 3 them, and they shall be His **p**.

PEOPLE'S (7/7) PEOPLE

Lev 9:15 Then he brought the **p** offering,
Esth 3: 8 different from all other **p**,
Ezek 46:18 take any of the **p** inheritance
1 Tim 5:22 nor share in other **p** sins;
Heb 7:27 His own sins and then for the **p**,
9: 7 himself and for the **p** sins
1 Pe 4:15 busybody in other **p** matters.

PEOPLES (159/156) PEOPLE

Gen 10: 5 From these the coastland **p** of
17:16 kings of **p** shall be from her."
25:23 Two **p** shall be separated from
27:29 Let **p** serve you, And nations
28: 3 you may be an assembly of **p**;
Lev 20:24 has separated you from the **p**.
20:26 have separated you from the **p**,
Deut 4: 6 in the sight of the **p** who will
4:19 your God has given to all the **p**
4:27 will scatter you among the **p**,
6:14 the gods of the **p** who are all
7: 6 treasure above all the **p** on
7: 7 for you were the least of all **p**;
7:14 shall be blessed above all **p**;
7:16 you shall destroy all the **p**
7:19 LORD your God do to all the **p**
10:15 after them, you above all **p**,
14: 2 treasure above all the **p** who
20:16 But of the cities of these **p**
28:10 Then all **p** of the earth shall
28:64 will scatter you among all **p**,
32: 8 He set the boundaries of the **p**
33:17 with them He shall push the **p**
33:19 They shall call the **p** to the
Josh 4:24 that all the **p** of the earth may
Judg 5:14 you, Benjamin, with your **p**,
2 Sam 22:48 And subdues the **p** under me;
1 Ki 8:43 that all **p** of the earth may
8:53 them from among all the **p** of
8:60 that all the **p** of the earth may
9: 7 and a byword among all **p**.
1 Chr 5:25 harlot after the gods of the **p**
16: 8 known His deeds among the **p**!
16:24 His wonders among all **p**.
16:26 For all the gods of the **p** are
16:28 the LORD, O families of the **p**,
2 Chr 6:33 that all **p** of the earth may
7:20 and a byword among all **p**.
13: 9 like the **p** of other lands, so
32:13 fathers have done to all the **p**
Ezra 9: 1 themselves from the **p** of the
9: 2 holy seed is mixed with the **p**
9:11 with the uncleanness of the **p**
10: 2 taken pagan wives from the **p**
10:11 separate yourselves from the **p**
Neh 9:30 them into the hand of the **p** of
10:28 themselves from the **p** of the
10:30 daughters as wives to the **p** of
10:31 if the **p** of the land brought
Job 36:31 For by these He judges the **p**;
Ps 7: 7 So the congregation of the **p**
7: 8 The LORD shall judge the **p**;
9: 8 administer judgment for the **p**
18:47 And subdues the **p** under me;
33:10 He makes the plans of the **p** of
44: 2 planted; You afflicted the **p**,
44:14 shaking of the head among the **p**.
45: 5 The **p** fall under You.
47: 1 clap your hands, all you **p**!
47: 3 He will subdue the **p** under us,
49: 1 Hear this, all **p**;
56: 7 In anger cast down the **p**,
57: 9 praise You, O Lord, among the **p**;
65: 7 waves, And the tumult of the **p**.
66: 8 Oh, bless our God, you **p**!
67: 3 Let the **p** praise You, O God;
67: 3 Let all the **p** praise You.
67: 5 Let the **p** praise You, O God;
67: 5 Let all the **p** praise You.
68:30 bulls with the calves of the **p**,
68:30 Scatter the **p** who delight in
77:14 Your strength among the **p**.
87: 6 When He registers the **p**:
89:50 reproach of all the many **p**,
96: 3 His wonders among all **p**.
96: 5 For all the gods of the **p** are
96: 7 the LORD, O families of the **p**,
96:10 He shall judge the **p**
96:13 And the **p** with His truth.
97: 6 And all the **p** see His glory.
98: 9 And the **p** with equity.
99: 1 Let the **p** tremble! He dwells
99: 2 He is high above all the **p**.
102:22 When the **p** are gathered
105: 1 known His deeds among the **p**!
106:34 They did not destroy the **p**,
108: 3 You, O LORD, among the **p**,
117: 1 Laud Him, all you **p**!
148:11 Kings of the earth and all **p**;
149: 7 And punishments on the **p**;
Isa 8: 9 "Be shattered, O you **p**,
12: 4 Declare His deeds among the **p**,
49: 1 you **p** from afar! The LORD has
49:22 set up My standard for the **p**;
51: 4 rest As a light of the **p**.
51: 5 And My arms will judge the **p**;
62:10 Lift up a banner for the **p**!
63: 3 And from the **p** no one was
63: 6 I have trodden down the **p** in My
Jer 10: 3 For the customs of the **p** are
50:37 And against all the mixed **p**
Lam 1:18 Hear now, all **p**, And behold
3:45 refuse In the midst of the **p**.
Ezek 11:17 "I will gather you from the **p**,
20:34 will bring you out from the **p**
20:35 into the wilderness of the **p**,
20:41 I bring you out from the **p** and
25: 7 I will cut you off from the **p**,
26: 2 who was the gateway of the **p**;
27: 3 merchant of the **p** on many
27:36 The merchants among the **p** will
28:19 All who knew you among the **p**
28:25 the house of Israel from the **p**
29:13 the Egyptians from the **p** among
31:12 and all the **p** of the earth have
32: 9 trouble the hearts of many **p**,
32:10 I will make many **p** astonished
34:13 will bring them out from the **p**
36:15 nor bear the reproach of the **p**
38: 9 and all your troops and many **p**
38:15 you and many **p** with you, all of
38:22 and on the many **p** who are with
39: 4 and all your troops and the **p**
39:27 brought them back from the **p**
Dan 3: 4 "To you it is commanded, O **p**,
4: 1 the king, To all **p**,
5:19 majesty that He gave him, all **p**,
6:25 King Darius wrote: To all **p**,
7:14 and a kingdom, That all **p**,
Hos 7: 8 has mixed himself among the **p**;
9: 1 Israel, with joy like other **p**,
10:10 **P** shall be gathered against
Joel 2:17 should they say among the **p**,
Mic 1: 2 all you **p**! Listen, O earth,
4: 1 And **p** shall flow to it.
4: 3 He shall judge between many **p**,
4:13 shall beat in pieces many **p**;
5: 7 be in the midst of many **p**,
5: 8 In the midst of many **p**,
Hab 2: 5 And heaps up for himself all **p**.
2:10 your house, Cutting off many **p**,
2:13 the LORD of hosts That the **p**
Zeph 3: 9 then I will restore to the **p** a
3:20 and praise Among all the **p** of
Zech 8:20 **P** shall yet come, Inhabitants
8:22 many **p** and strong nations
10: 9 "I will sow them among the **p**,
11:10 which I had made with all the **p**.
12: 2 to all the surrounding **p**,
12: 3 a very heavy stone for all **p**;
12: 4 strike every horse of the **p**
12: 6 devour all the surrounding **p**
Lk 2:31 before the face of all **p**,
Jn 12:32 will draw all **p** to Myself."
Rom 15:11 Laud Him, all you **p**!"
Rev 7: 9 of all nations, tribes, **p**,
10:11 prophesy again about many **p**,
11: 9 Then those from the **p**,
17:15 where the harlot sits, are **p**,

PEOR (15/13)

Num 23:28 took Balaam to the top of **P**,
25: 3 Israel was joined to Baal of **P**,
25: 5 who were joined to Baal of **P**.
25:18 seduced you in the matter of **P**
25:18 day of the plague because of **P**.
31:16 the LORD in the incident of **P**,
Deut 4: 3 the men who followed Baal of **P**.
Josh 22:17 Is the iniquity of **P** not enough
Ps 106:28 themselves also to Baal of **P**,

PER (1/1)

Judg 17:10 shekels of silver **p** year,

PERAZIM (5/3)

Isa 28:21 will rise up as at Mount **P**,

PERCEIVE (23/23) PERCEIVED, PERCEIVES

Deut 29: 4 has not given you a heart to **p**
Josh 22:31 This day we **p** that the LORD is
1 Sam 12:17 that you may **p** and see that
2 Sam 19: 6 for today I **p** that if Absalom
Job 9:11 moves past, I do not **p** Him;
14:21 and he does not **p** it.
23: 8 but I cannot **p** Him;
33:14 Yet man does not **p** it.
Prov 1: 2 To **p** the words of
14: 7 When you do not **p** in him the
Isa 6: 9 Keep on seeing, but do not **p**.

P

Mt 13:14 you will see and not **p**;
Mk 4:12 they may see and not **p**,
7:18 Do you not **p** that whatever
8:17 Do you not yet **p** nor
Lk 6:41 but do not **p** the plank in your
9:45 them so that they did not **p** it;
Jn 4:19 I **p** that You are a prophet.
Acts 10:34 In truth I **p** that God shows no
17:22 I **p** that in all things you are
27:10 I **p** that this voyage will end
28:26 you will see, and not **p**;
2 Cor 7: 8 For I **p** that the same epistle

PERCEIVED (24/24) PERCEIVE

Judg 6:22 Now Gideon **p** that He was the
1 Sam 3: 8 Then Eli **p** that the LORD had
28:14 And Saul **p** that it was
2 Sam 12:19 David **p** that the child was
14: 1 So Joab the son of Zeruiah **p**
Neh 6:12 Then I **p** that God had not sent
6:16 for they **p** that this work was
Prov 7: 7 I **p** among the youths, A young
Eccl 1:17 I **p** that this also is grasping
2:14 Yet I myself **p** That the same
3:22 So I **p** that nothing is better
Isa 64: 4 Men have not heard nor **p** by
Jer 23:18 And has **p** and heard His word?
Mt 21:45 they **p** that He was speaking of
22:18 But Jesus **p** their wickedness,
Mk 2: 8 when Jesus **p** in His spirit that
Lk 1:22 and they **p** that he had seen a
5:22 But when Jesus **p** their thoughts,
8:46 for I **p** power going out from
20:23 But He **p** their craftiness, and
Jn 6:15 Therefore when Jesus **p** that
Acts 4:13 and **p** that they were uneducated
23: 6 But when Paul **p** that one part
Gal 2: 9 **p** the grace that had been given

PERCEIVES (1/1) PERCEIVE

Prov 31:18 She **p** that her merchandise is

PERCEIVING (2/2)

Mk 12:28 **p** that He had answered them
Lk 9:47 **p** the thought of their heart,

PERCEPTION (1/1)

Isa 33:19 of obscure speech, beyond **p**,

PERCEPTIVE (1/1)

Prov 17:28 his lips, he is considered **p**.

PERDITION (8/8)

Jn 17:12 is lost except the son of **p**,
Phil 1:28 which is to them a proof of **p**,
2 Th 2: 3 sin is revealed, the son of **p**,
1 Tim 6: 9 drown men in destruction and **p**.
Heb 10:39 not of those who draw back to **p**,
2 Pe 3: 7 the day of judgment and **p** of
Rev 17: 8 the bottomless pit and go to **p**.
17:11 of the seven, and is going to **p**.

PERES (1/1) UPHARSIN

Dan 5:28 **P**: Your kingdom has been

PERESH (1/1)

1 Chr 7:16 son, and she called his name **P**.

PEREZ (22/19)

Gen 38:29 Therefore his name was called **P**.
46:12 Judah were Er, Onan, Shelah, **P**,
46:12 The sons of **P** were Hezron and
Num 26:20 family of the Shelanites; of **P**,
26:21 And the sons of **P** were: of
Ruth 4:12 house be like the house of **P**,
4:18 this is the genealogy of **P**:
4:18 **P** begot Hezron;
1 Chr 2: 4 bore him **P** and Zerah. All the
2: 5 The sons of **P** were Hezron and
4: 1 The sons of Judah were **P**,
9: 4 Bani, of the descendants of **P**,
27: 3 he was of the children of **P**,
Neh 11: 4 Mahalalel, of the children of **P**;
11: 6 All the sons of **P** who dwelt at
Mt 1: 3 Judah begot **P** and Zerah by
1: 3 **P** begot Hezron, and Hezron
Lk 3:33 son of Hezron, the son of **P**,

PEREZ UZZA (1/1)

1 Chr 13:11 that place is called **P** to this day

PEREZ UZZAH (1/1)

2 Sam 6: 8 called the name of the place **P**

PERFECT (61/56) PERFECTED, PERFECTING, PERFECTION, PERFECTLY

Gen 6: 9 **p** in his generations. Noah
Lev 22:21 it must be **p** to be accepted;
Deut 25:15 You shall have a **p** and just
25:15 a **p** and just measure, that your
32: 4 is the Rock, His work is **p**;
1 Sam 14:41 Give a **p** lot." So Saul and
2 Sam 22:31 As for God, His way is **p**;
22:33 power, And He makes my way **p**.
Ezra 7:12 **P** peace, and so forth.
Job 36: 4 One who is **p** in knowledge is
37:16 wondrous works of Him who is **p**
Ps 18:30 As for God, His way is **p**;
18:32 strength, And makes my way **p**.
19: 7 The law of the LORD is **p**,
101: 2 I will behave wisely in a **p**
101: 2 walk within my house with a **p**
101: 6 He who walks in a **p** way,
138: 8 The LORD will **p** that which
139:22 I hate them with **p** hatred;
Prov 4:18 ever brighter unto the **p** day.
Song 5: 2 my **p** one; For my head is
6: 9 my **p** one, Is the only one,
Isa 18: 5 when the bud is **p** And the sour
26: 3 You will keep him in **p** peace,
42:19 is blind as he who is **p**,
Ezek 16:14 for it was **p** through My
27: 3 I am **p** in beauty.'
27:11 They made your beauty **p**.
28:12 Full of wisdom and **p** in
28:15 You were **p** in your ways from
Mt 5:48 "Therefore you shall be **p**,
5:48 as your Father in heaven is **p**.
19:21 to him, "If you want to be **p**,
Lk 1: 3 having had **p** understanding of
Jn 17:23 that they may be made **p** in one,
Acts 3:16 Him has given him this **p**
Rom 12: 2 that good and acceptable and **p**
1 Cor 13:10 But when that which is **p** has
2 Cor 12: 9 for My strength is made **p** in
Gal 3: 3 are you now being made **p** by the
Eph 4:13 to a **p** man, to the measure of
Col 1:28 we may present every man **p** in
4:12 that you may stand **p** and
1 Th 3:10 that we may see your face and **p**
Heb 2:10 captain of their salvation **p**
7:19 for the law made nothing **p**;
9: 9 who performed the service **p** in
9:11 with the greater and more **p**
10: 1 year, make those who approach **p**.
11:40 that they should not be made **p**
12:23 the spirits of just men made **p**,
Jas 1: 4 But let patience have its **p**
1: 4 that you may be **p** and complete,
1:17 Every good gift and every **p** gift
1:25 But he who looks into the **p** law
2:22 and by works faith was made **p**?
3: 2 he is a **p** man, able also to
1 Pe 5:10 you have suffered a while, **p**,
1 Jn 4:18 but **p** love casts out fear,
4:18 who fears has not been made **p**
Rev 3: 2 I have not found your works **p**

PERFECTED (11/11) PERFECT

Ps 64: 6 We have **p** a shrewd scheme."
Ezek 27: 4 Your builders have **p** your
Mt 21:16 infants You have **p**
Lk 13:32 and the third day I shall be **p**.
Phil 3:12 attained, or am already **p**;
Heb 5: 9 And having been **p**,
7:28 the Son who has been **p** forever.
10:14 For by one offering He has **p**
1 Jn 2: 5 truly the love of God is **p** in
4:12 and His love has been **p** in us.
4:17 Love has been **p** among us in

PERFECTING (1/1) PERFECT

2 Cor 7: 1 **p** holiness in the fear of God.

PERFECTION (7/7) PERFECT

Ps 50: 2 the **p** of beauty, God will
119:96 seen the consummation of all **p**,
Lam 2:15 The **p** of beauty, The joy of the
Ezek 28:12 "You were the seal of **p**,
Col 3:14 on love, which is the bond of **p**.
Heb 6: 1 of Christ, let us go on to **p**,
7:11 if **p** were through the Levitical

PERFECTLY (6/6) PERFECT

1 Ki 7:35 it was **p** round. And on the
Jer 23:20 days you will understand it **p**.
Mt 14:36 many as touched it were made **p**
Lk 6:40 but everyone who is **p** trained
1 Cor 1:10 but that you be **p** joined
1 Th 5: 2 For you yourselves know **p** that

PERFORM (54/52) PERFORMED

Gen 26: 3 and I will **p** the oath which I
Ex 18:18 you are not able to **p** it by
Lev 19:37 and **p** them: I am the LORD.'
20: 8 and **p** them: I am the LORD who
20:22 and **p** them, that the land where
22:31 and **p** them: I am the LORD.
25:18 and **p** them; and you will dwell
26: 3 commandments, and **p** them,
26:15 so that you do not **p** all My
Num 4:23 all who enter to **p** the service,
8:11 that they may **p** the work of the
8:24 and above one may enter to **p**
18:21 for the work which they **p**,
18:23 But the Levites shall **p** the work
Deut 4:13 which He commanded you to **p**,
23:23 your lips you shall keep and **p**,
25: 5 and **p** the duty of a husband's
25: 7 he will not **p** the duty of my
Josh 22:27 that we may **p** the service of
Judg 16:25 that he may **p** for us." So they
21:21 of Shiloh come out to **p** their
Ruth 3:13 it shall be that if he will **p**
3:13 But if he does not want to **p**
3:13 then I will **p** the duty for you,
1 Sam 3:12 In that day I will **p** against Eli
2 Sam 14:15 it may be that the king will **p**
1 Ki 6:12 then I will **p** My word with you,
2 Ki 23: 3 to **p** the words of this covenant
23:24 that he might **p** the words of
2 Chr 34:31 to **p** the words of the covenant
Neh 5:13 who does not **p** this promise.
Ps 21:11 which they are not able to **p**.
61: 8 That I may daily **p** my vows.
119:112 I have inclined my heart to **p**
Eccl 9: 9 and in the labor which you **p**
Isa 9: 7 of the LORD of hosts will **p**
19:21 make a vow to the LORD and **p**
44:28 And he shall **p** all My
Jer 1:12 for I am ready to **p** My word."
28: 6 the LORD **p** your words which
29:10 I will visit you and **p** My good
33:14 that I will **p** that good thing
44:25 your vows and **p** your vows!'
Ezek 12:25 I will say the word and **p** it,"
43:11 ordinances, and **p** them.
Nah 1:15 **P** your vows. For the wicked
Mt 5:33 but shall **p** your oaths to the
23:16 he is obliged to **p** it.'
23:18 he is obliged to **p** it.'
Lk 1:72 To **p** the mercy promised to our
13:32 I cast out demons and **p** cures
Jn 6:30 What sign will You **p** then, that
Rom 4:21 promised He was also able to **p**.
7:18 but how to **p** what is good I do

PERFORMED (28/28) PERFORM

Num 14:11 all the signs which I have **p**
Deut 34:12 the great terror which Moses **p**
Judg 16:25 and he **p** for them. And they
16:27 roof watching while Samson **p**.
1 Sam 15:11 and has not **p** My
15:13 you of the LORD! I have **p** the
2 Sam 21:14 So they **p** all that the king
1 Chr 26:29 Chenaniah and his sons **p**
Neh 9: 8 You have **p** Your words, For
Ps 65: 1 And to You the vow shall be **p**.
105:27 They **p** His signs among them,
Isa 10:12 when the LORD has **p** all His
41: 4 Who has **p** and done it,
Jer 23:20 Until He has executed and **p**
30:24 And until He has **p** the intents
34:18 who have not **p** the words of the
35:14 sons, not to drink wine, are **p**;
35:16 the son of Rechab have **p** the
39:16 and they shall be **p** in that
51:29 purpose of the LORD shall be **p**
Ezek 37:14 have spoken it and **p** it,"
Mk 6: 2 that such mighty works are **p** by
Lk 2:39 So when they had **p** all things
Jn 6: 2 they saw His signs which He **p**
10:41 John **p** no sign, but all the
Acts 4:22 miracle of healing had been **p**.
Rom 15:28 when I have **p** this and have
Heb 9: 9 which cannot make him who **p**

PERFORMING (4/4)

Num 8:25 fifty years they must cease **p**
1 Chr 25: 1 the number of the skilled men **p**
Heb 9: 6 **p** the services.
Rev 16:14 **p** signs, which go out to the

PERFORMS (4/4)

Job 23:14 For He **p** what is appointed
Ps 57: 2 To God who **p** all things for
Isa 44:26 And **p** the counsel of His
Rev 13:13 He **p** great signs, so that he

PERFUME (2/2)

Prov 27: 9 Ointment and **p** delight the
Isa 3:20 The **p** boxes, the charms,

PERFUMED (2/2) PERFUMES

Prov 7:17 I have **p** my bed With myrrh,
Song 3: 6 **P** with myrrh and frankincense,

PERFUMER (3/3)

Ex 30:25 according to the art of the **p**.
30:35 according to the art of the **p**,
37:29 according to the work of the **p**.

PERFUMER'S (1/1) PERFUMERS

Eccl 10: 1 putrefy the **p** ointment,

PERFUMERS (2/2) PERFUMER'S, PERFUMES

1 Sam 8:13 take your daughters to be **p**,
Neh 3: 8 to him Hananiah, one of the **p**,

PERFUMES (3/3) PERFUMED

Esth 2:12 and six months with **p** and
Song 4:10 And the scent of your **p** Than

Isa 57: 9 ointment, And increased your **p**;

PERGA (3/3)

Acts 13:13 they came to **P** in Pamphylia;
13:14 But when they departed from **P**,
14:25 they had preached the word in **P**,

PERGAMOS (2/2)

Rev 1:11 to Ephesus, to Smyrna, to **P**,
2:12 to the angel of the church in **P**

PERHAPS (37/36)

Gen 16: 2 **p** I shall obtain children by
24: 5 **P** the woman will not be willing
24:39 **P** the woman will not follow me.'
27:12 **P** my father will feel me, and I
31:31 **P** you would take your daughters
32:20 **p** he will accept me."
43:12 **p** it was an oversight.
44:34 lest **p** I see the evil that
50:15 **P** Joseph will hate us, and may
Ex 13:17 Lest **p** the people change their
32:30 **p** I can make atonement for your
Num 22: 6 **P** I shall be able to defeat
22:11 **p** I shall be able to overpower
23: 3 **p** the LORD will come to meet
23:27 **p** it will please God that you
Josh 9: 7 **P** you dwell among us; so how can
1 Sam 6: 5 **p** He will lighten His hand from
9: 6 **p** he can show us the way that
1 Ki 18: 5 **p** we may find grass to keep the
18:27 or **p** he is sleeping and must
20:31 **p** he will spare your life."
2 Ki 2:16 lest **p** the Spirit of the LORD
Isa 47:12 **P** you will be able to profit,
47:12 **P** you will prevail.
Jer 20:10 **P** he can be induced; Then we
21: 2 **P** the LORD will deal with us
26: 3 **P** everyone will listen and turn
51: 8 **P** she may be healed.
Dan 4:27 **P** there may be a lengthening of
Jon 1: 6 **p** your God will consider us, so
Mk 11:13 He went to see if **p** He would
Acts 8:22 and pray God if **p** the thought
Rom 5: 7 yet **p** for a good man someone
1 Cor 15:37 **p** wheat or some other grain.
2 Cor 2: 7 lest **p** such a one be swallowed
2 Tim 2:25 if God **p** will grant them
Phm 1:15 For **p** he departed for a while

PERIDA (1/1)

Neh 7:57 of Sophereth, the sons of **P**,

PERIL (1/1) PERILOUS, PERILS

Rom 8:35 or famine, or nakedness, or **p**,

PERILOUS (2/2) PERIL

Ps 91: 3 And from the **p** pestilence.
2 Tim 3: 1 that in the last days **p** times

PERILS (8/1) PERIL

2 Cor 11:26 in **p** of waters, in perils of
11:26 in **p** of robbers, in perils of
11:26 in **p** of my own countrymen,
11:26 in **p** of the Gentiles, in
11:26 in **p** in the city, in perils
11:26 in **p** in the wilderness, in
11:26 in **p** in the sea, in perils
11:26 in **p** among false brethren;

PERIOD (5/5)

1 Ki 2:11 The **p** that David reigned over
11:42 And the **p** that Solomon reigned
14:20 The **p** that Jeroboam reigned was
2 Ki 10:36 And the **p** that Jehu reigned over
1 Chr 29:27 And the **p** that he reigned over

PERISH (110/108) PERISHABLE, PERISHED, PERISHES, PERISHING

Gen 41:36 that the land may not **p** during
Ex 19:21 the LORD, and many of them **p**.
Lev 26:38 You shall **p** among the nations,
Num 17:12 saying, "Surely we die, we **p**,
17:12 we die, we perish, we all **p**!
Deut 4:26 that you will soon utterly **p**
8:19 day that you shall surely **p**.
8:20 before you, so you shall **p**,
11:17 and you **p** quickly from the good
26: 5 was a Syrian, about to **p**,
28:20 are destroyed and until you **p**
28:22 shall pursue you until you **p**.
30:18 today that you shall surely **p**;
Josh 22:20 And that man did not **p** alone in
23:13 until you **p** from this good land
23:16 and you shall **p** quickly from
Judg 5:31 "Thus let all Your enemies **p**,
1 Sam 26:10 he shall go out to battle and **p**.
27: 1 Now I shall **p** someday by the
2 Ki 9: 8 the whole house of Ahab shall **p**;
Esth 4:14 and your father's house will **p**.
4:16 is against the law; and if I **p**,
4:16 if I perish, I **p**!"
9:28 the memory of them should not **p**
Job 3: 3 May the day **p** on which I was
3:11 Why did I not **p** when I came
4: 9 By the blast of God they **p**,
4:20 They **p** forever, with no one
6:18 aside, They go nowhere and **p**.
8:13 hope of the hypocrite shall **p**,
13:19 If now I hold my tongue, I **p**.
20: 7 Yet he will **p** forever like his
31:19 If I have seen anyone **p** for
34:15 All flesh would **p** together,
36:12 They shall **p** by the sword,
Ps 1: 6 the way of the ungodly shall **p**.
2:12 And you **p** in the way, When
9: 3 They shall fall and **p** at Your
9:18 of the poor shall not **p**
37:20 But the wicked shall **p**;
41: 5 will he die, and his name **p**?
49:10 fool and the senseless person **p**,
49:12 He is like the beasts that **p**.
49:20 Is like the beasts that **p**.
68: 2 So let the wicked **p** at the
73:27 who are far from You shall **p**;
80:16 They **p** at the rebuke of Your
83:17 let them be put to shame and **p**,
92: 9 behold, Your enemies shall **p**;
102:26 They will **p**, but You will
112:10 desire of the wicked shall **p**.
146: 4 In that very day his plans **p**.
Prov 10:28 of the wicked will **p**.
11: 7 dies, his expectation will **p**,
11:10 And when the wicked **p**,
19: 9 he who speaks lies shall **p**.
21:28 A false witness shall **p**,
28:28 themselves; But when they **p**,
Eccl 5:14 But those riches **p** through
Isa 26:14 And made all their memory to **p**.
27:13 who are about to **p** in the land
29:14 of their wise men shall **p**,
31: 3 They all will **p** together.
41:11 who strive with you shall **p**.
60:12 will not serve you shall **p**,
Jer 4: 9 the heart of the king shall **p**,
6:21 neighbor and his friend shall **p**.
9:12 Why does the land **p** and burn
10:11 heavens and the earth shall **p**
10:15 their punishment they shall **p**.
18:18 for the law shall not **p** from
27:10 drive you out, and you will **p**.
27:15 you out, and that you may **p**,
40:15 and the remnant in Judah **p**?
48: 8 The valley also shall **p**,
48:46 The people of Chemosh **p**;
51:18 their punishment they shall **p**.
Ezek 7:26 But the law will **p** from the
25: 7 and I will cause you to **p** from
Dan 2:18 and his companions might not **p**
Am 1: 8 of the Philistines shall **p**,
2:14 Therefore flight shall **p** from
3:15 The houses of ivory shall **p**,
Jon 1: 6 us, so that we may not **p**.
1:14 please do not let us **p** for this
3: 9 anger, so that we may not **p**?
Zech 9: 5 The king shall **p** from Gaza,
11: 9 die, and what is perishing **p**.
Mt 5:29 you that one of your members **p**,
5:30 you that one of your members **p**,
18:14 of these little ones should **p**.
26:52 all who take the sword will **p**
Lk 13: 3 repent you will all likewise **p**.
13: 5 repent you will all likewise **p**.
13:33 be that a prophet should **p**
15:17 and I **p** with hunger!
Jn 3:15 believes in Him should not **p**
3:16 believes in Him should not **p**
10:28 life, and they shall never **p**;
11:50 that the whole nation should **p**.
Acts 8:20 Your money **p** with you, because
13:41 Marvel and **p**! For I
Rom 2:12 sinned without law will also **p**
1 Cor 8:11 shall the weak brother **p**,
Col 2:22 all concern things which **p**
2 Th 2:10 deception among those who **p**,
Heb 1:11 They will **p**, but You
11:31 the harlot Rahab did not **p**
2 Pe 2:12 and will utterly **p** in their own
3: 9 not willing that any should **p**

PERISHABLE (1/1) PERISH

1 Cor 9:25 do it to obtain a **p** crown,

PERISHED (28/28) PERISH

Num 16:33 and they **p** from among the
21:29 Woe to you, Moab! You have **p**,
21:30 Heshbon has **p** as far as Dibon.
Deut 2:16 the men of war had finally **p**
2 Sam 1:27 And the weapons of war **p**!"
Job 4: 7 who ever **p** being innocent?
10:18 that I had **p** and no eye had
30: 2 hands to me? Their vigor has **p**.
Ps 9: 6 Even their memory has **p**.
10:16 The nations have **p** out of His
83:10 Who **p** at En Dor, Who became
119:92 I would then have **p** in my
Eccl 9: 6 and their envy have now **p**;
Jer 7:28 Truth has **p** and has been cut
48:36 they have acquired have **p**.
49: 7 Has counsel **p** from the
Lam 3:18 strength and my hope Have **p**
Ezek 26:17 say to you: "How you have **p**,
Joel 1:11 the harvest of the field has **p**.
Jon 4:10 which came up in a night and **p**
Mic 4: 9 midst? Has your counselor **p**?
7: 2 The faithful man has **p** from
Mt 8:32 and **p** in the water.
Lk 11:51 to the blood of Zechariah who **p**
Acts 5:37 people after him. He also **p**,
1 Cor 15:18 fallen asleep in Christ have **p**.
2 Pe 3: 6 the world that then existed **p**,
Jude 11 and **p** in the rebellion of

PERISHES (10/10) PERISH

Num 24:20 But shall be last until he **p**.
24:24 so shall Amalek, until he **p**.
Job 4:11 The old lion **p** for lack of
18:17 The memory of him **p** from the
Prov 11: 7 And the hope of the unjust **p**.
Eccl 7:15 There is a just man who **p** in
Isa 57: 1 The righteous **p**, And no man
Jn 6:27 not labor for the food which **p**,
Jas 1:11 and its beautiful appearance **p**.
1 Pe 1: 7 more precious than gold that **p**,

PERISHING (11/11) PERISH

Job 29:13 The blessing of a **p** man came
33:18 And his life from **p** by the
Prov 31: 6 strong drink to him who is **p**,
Zech 11: 9 and what is **p** perish. Let those
Mt 8:25 save us! We are **p**!"
Mk 4:38 do You not care that we are **p**?
Lk 8:24 'Master, Master, we are **p**!"
1 Cor 1:18 foolishness to those who are **p**,
2 Cor 2:15 saved and among those who are **p**.
4: 3 it is veiled to those who are **p**,
4:16 though our outward man is **p**,

PERIZZITE (5/5) PERIZZITES

Ex 33: 2 and the Hittite and the **P** and
34:11 and the Hittite and the **P** and
Deut 20:17 and the Canaanite and the **P**
Josh 9: 1 Amorite, the Canaanite, the **P**,
11: 3 the Amorite, the Hittite, the **P**,

PERIZZITES (18/18) PERIZZITE

Gen 13: 7 The Canaanites and the **P** then
15:20 "the Hittites, the **P**,
34:30 among the Canaanites and the **P**;
Ex 3: 8 and the Amorites and the **P** and
3:17 and the Amorites and the **P** and
23:23 and the Hittites and the **P** and
Deut 7: 1 and the Canaanites and the **P**
Josh 3:10 and the Hivites and the **P** and
12: 8 Amorites, the Canaanites, the **P**,
17:15 there in the land of the **P** and
24:11 you—also the Amorites, the **P**,
Judg 1: 4 the Canaanites and the **P** into
1: 5 the Canaanites and the **P**.
3: 5 Hittites, the Amorites, the **P**,
1 Ki 9:20 of the Amorites, Hittites, **P**,
2 Chr 8: 7 of the Hittites, Amorites, **P**,
Ezra 9: 1 Canaanites, the Hittites, the **P**,
Neh 9: 8 Hittites, the Amorites, the **P**,

PERJURER (1/1)

Zech 5: 3 Every **p** shall be expelled,'

PERJURERS (2/2)

Mal 3: 5 Against adulterers, Against **p**,
1 Tim 1:10 kidnappers, for liars, for **p**,

PERMANENT (1/1)

Lev 25:46 they shall be your **p** slaves.

PERMANENTLY (2/2)

Lev 25:23 'The land shall not be sold **p**,
25:30 the walled city shall belong **p**

PERMISSION (8/8) PERMIT

Num 22:13 LORD has refused to give me **p**
1 Sam 20: 6 David earnestly asked **p** of me
20:28 David earnestly asked **p** of me
Ezra 3: 7 according to the **p** which they
Jer 44:19 to her without our husbands' **p**?
Mk 5:13 And at once Jesus gave them **p**.
Jn 19:38 Jesus; and Pilate gave him **p**.
Acts 21:40 So when he had given him **p**,

PERMIT (14/14) PERMISSION, PERMITS, PERMITTED

Ex 22:18 You shall not **p** a sorceress to
Judg 15: 1 But her father would not **p**
2 Sam 14:11 and do not **p** the avenger of
Neh 2: 7 that they must **p** me to pass
Ps 55:22 He shall never **p** the righteous
Eccl 5:12 of the rich will not **p** him to
Mt 3:15 **P** it to be so now, for thus
8:31 **p** us to go away into the herd
Mk 5:19 Jesus did not **p** him, but said
Lk 8:32 they begged Him that He would **p**
22:51 and said, "**P** even this."
Acts 16: 7 but the Spirit did not **p** them.
21:39 **p** me to speak to the people."
1 Tim 2:12 And I do not **p** a woman to teach

P

PERMITS (2/2) PERMIT

1 Cor 16: 7 a while with you, if the Lord **p**.
Heb 6: 3 And this we will do if God **p**.

PERMITTED (12/12) PERMIT

Deut 22:29 he shall not be **p** to divorce
1 Chr 16:21 He **p** no man to do them wrong;
Esth 8:11 By these letters the king **p** the
Ps 105:14 He **p** no one to do them wrong;
Mt 19: 8 **p** you to divorce your wives,
Mk 5:37 And He **p** no one to follow Him
10: 4 Moses **p** a man to write a
Lk 8:32 enter them. And He **p** them.
8:51 He **p** no one to go in except
Acts 26: 1 You are **p** to speak for
28:16 but Paul was **p** to dwell by
1 Cor 14:34 for they are not **p** to speak;

PERMITTING (1/1)

Acts 27: 7 the wind not **p** us to proceed,

PERPETUAL (24/24) PERPETUALLY

Gen 9:12 with you, for **p** generations:
Ex 29: 9 theirs for a **p** statute.
30: 8 a **p** incense before the LORD
31:16 generations as a **p** covenant.
Lev 3:17 This shall be a **p** statute
24: 9 by fire, by a **p** statute."
25:34 for it is their **p** possession.
Num 19:21 It shall be a **p** statute for
Ps 74: 3 feet to the **p** desolations.
78:66 He put them to a **p** reproach.
Jer 5:22 By a **p** decree, that it cannot
8: 5 in a **p** backsliding? They hold
15:18 Why is my pain **p** And my wound
18:16 desolate and a **p** hissing;
23:40 and a **p** shame, which shall not
25: 9 a hissing, and **p** desolations.
25:12 will make it a **p** desolation.
49:13 cities shall be **p** wastes."
50: 5 to the LORD In a **p** covenant
51:39 And sleep a **p** sleep And not
51:57 And they shall sleep a **p** sleep
Ezek 46:14 offering is a **p** ordinance,
Hab 3: 6 The **p** hills bowed. His ways
Zeph 2: 9 And a **p** desolation.

PERPETUALLY (4/4) PERPETUAL

1 Ki 9: 3 and My heart will be there **p**.
2 Chr 7:16 and My heart will be there **p**.
Ezek 35: 9 I will make you **p** desolate, and
Am 1:11 off all pity; His anger tore **p**,

PERPETUATE (2/2)

Ruth 4: 5 to **p** the name of the dead
4:10 to **p** the name of the dead

PERPETUATED (1/1)

Nah 1:14 Your name shall be **p** no longer.

PERPLEXED (6/6)

Esth 3:15 but the city of Shushan was **p**.
Lk 9: 7 was done by Him; and he was **p**,
24: 4 as they were greatly **p** about
Jn 13:22 **p** about whom He spoke.
Acts 2:12 So they were all amazed and **p**,
2 Cor 4: 8 yet not crushed; we are **p**,

PERPLEXITY (3/3)

Isa 22: 5 and treading down and **p**
Mic 7: 4 Now shall be their **p**.
Lk 21:25 distress of nations, with **p**,

PERSECUTE (19/19) PERSECUTED, PERSECUTING, PERSECUTION, PERSECUTOR

Job 19:22 Why do you **p** me as God does,
19:28 How shall we **p** him?'— Since the
Ps 7: 1 me from all those who **p** me;
31:15 And from those who **p** me.
69:26 For they **p** the ones You have
119:84 judgment on those who **p** me?
119:86 They **p** me wrongfully;
119:161 Princes **p** me without a cause,
Jer 17:18 Let them be ashamed who **p** me,
Dan 7:25 Shall **p** the saints of the Most
Mt 5:11 you when they revile and **p** you,
5:44 spitefully use you and **p** you,
10:23 When they **p** you in this city,
23:34 in your synagogues and **p** from
Lk 11:49 of them they will kill and **p**,
21:12 lay their hands on you and **p**
Jn 15:20 they will also **p** you. If they
Acts 7:52 prophets did your fathers not **p**?
Rom 12:14 Bless those who **p** you; bless and

PERSECUTED (18/18) PERSECUTE

Deut 30: 7 who hate you, who **p** you.
Ps 109:16 But **p** the poor and needy man,
143: 3 For the enemy has **p** my soul;
Isa 14: 6 Is **p** and no one hinders.
Mt 5:10 Blessed are those who are **p** for
5:12 for so they **p** the prophets who
Jn 5:16 reason the Jews **p** Jesus,
15:20 If they **p** Me, they will also
Acts 22: 4 I **p** this Way to the death,
26:11 I **p** them even to foreign
1 Cor 4:12 reviled, we bless; being **p**,
15: 9 because I **p** the church of God.
2 Cor 4: 9 **p**, but not forsaken;
Gal 1:13 how I **p** the church of God
1:23 He who formerly **p** us now
4:29 to the flesh then **p** him who
1 Th 2:15 and have **p** us; and they do not
Rev 12:13 he **p** the woman who gave birth

PERSECUTES (1/1)

Ps 10: 2 The wicked in his pride **p** the

PERSECUTING (7/7) PERSECUTE

Acts 9: 4 why are you **p** Me?"
9: 5 "I am Jesus, whom you are **p**.
22: 7 why are you **p** Me?'
22: 8 of Nazareth, whom you are **p**.
26:14 why are you **p** Me? It is hard
26:15 'I am Jesus, whom you are **p**.
Phil 3: 6 **p** the church; concerning the

PERSECUTION (9/9) PERSECUTE, PERSECUTIONS

Mt 13:21 For when tribulation or **p**
Mk 4:17 when tribulation or **p** arises
Acts 8: 1 At that time a great **p** arose
11:19 who were scattered after the **p**
13:50 raised up **p** against Paul and
Rom 8:35 tribulation, or distress, or **p**,
Gal 5:11 why do I still suffer **p**?
6:12 that they may not suffer **p** for
2 Tim 3:12 in Christ Jesus will suffer **p**.

PERSECUTIONS (5/4) PERSECUTION

Mk 10:30 and children and lands, with **p**—
2 Cor 12:10 in reproaches, in needs, in **p**,
2 Th 1: 4 and faith in all your **p** and
2 Tim 3:11 **p**, afflictions, which
3:11 what **p** I endured. And out of

PERSECUTOR (1/1) PERSECUTE, PERSECUTORS

1 Tim 1:13 was formerly a blasphemer, a **p**,

PERSECUTORS (6/6) PERSECUTOR

Neh 9:11 And their **p** You threw into the
Ps 119:157 Many are my **p** and my enemies,
142: 6 very low; Deliver me from my **p**,
Jer 15:15 take vengeance for me on my **p**.
20:11 Therefore my **p** will stumble,
Lam 1: 3 All her **p** overtake her in dire

PERSEVERANCE (9/8) PERSEVERE

Rom 5: 3 that tribulation produces **p**;
5: 4 and **p**, character;
8:25 we eagerly wait for it with **p**.
2 Cor 12:12 among you with all **p**,
Eph 6:18 to this end with all **p** and
2 Tim 3:10 faith, longsuffering, love, **p**,
Jas 5:11 You have heard of the **p** of Job
2 Pe 1: 6 self-control, to self-control **p**,
1: 6 perseverance, to **p** godliness,

PERSEVERE (1/1) PERSEVERANCE, PERSEVERED

Rev 3:10 you have kept My command to **p**,

PERSEVERED (1/1) PERSEVERE

Rev 2: 3 and you have **p** and have

PERSIA (30/26) ELAM, PERSIAN

2 Chr 36:20 the rule of the kingdom of **P**,
36:22 first year of Cyrus king of **P**,
36:22 the spirit of Cyrus king of **P**,
36:23 Thus says Cyrus king of **P**:
Ezra 1: 1 first year of Cyrus king of **P**,
1: 1 the spirit of Cyrus king of **P**,
1: 2 Thus says Cyrus king of **P**:
1: 8 and Cyrus king of **P** brought them
3: 7 they had from Cyrus king of **P**.
4: 3 as King Cyrus the king of **P** has
4: 5 all the days of Cyrus king of **P**,
4: 5 the reign of Darius king of **P**.
4: 7 wrote to Artaxerxes king of **P**;
4: 9 the people of **P** and Erech and
4:24 the reign of Darius king of **P**.
6:14 and Artaxerxes king of **P**.
7: 1 reign of Artaxerxes king of **P**,
9: 9 in the sight of the kings of **P**,
Esth 1: 3 the powers of **P** and Media, the
1:14 the seven princes of **P** and
1:18 day the noble ladies of **P** and
10: 2 of the kings of Media and **P**?
Ezek 27:10 Those from **P**, Lydia,
38: 5 '**P**, Ethiopia, and Libya
Dan 8:20 are the kings of Media and **P**.
10: 1 third year of Cyrus king of **P**
10:13 the prince of the kingdom of **P**
10:13 alone there with the kings of **P**.
10:20 to fight with the prince of **P**;
11: 2 more kings will arise in **P**,

PERSIAN (2/2) ELAMITES, PERSIA, PERSIANS

Neh 12:22 the reign of Darius the **P**,
Dan 6:28 and in the reign of Cyrus the **P**.

PERSIANS (7/7) PERSIAN

Ezra 5: 6 the **P** who were in the
6: 6 and your companions the **P** who
Esth 1:19 recorded in the laws of the **P**
Dan 5:28 and given to the Medes and **P**.
6: 8 to the law of the Medes and **P**,
6:12 to the law of the Medes and **P**,
6:15 is the law of the Medes and **P**

PERSIS (1/1)

Rom 16:12 Greet the beloved **P**, who

PERSISTED (2/2)

2 Ki 3: 3 Nevertheless he **p** in the sins of
Ezek 15: 8 because they have **p** in

PERSISTENCE (1/1)

Lk 11: 8 yet because of his **p** he will

PERSISTENT (1/1)

Ezek 14:13 Me by **p** unfaithfulness,

PERSON (100/94) PERSONAL, PERSONS

Gen 17:14 that **p** shall be cut off from
Ex 12:15 that **p** shall be cut off from
12:19 that same **p** shall be cut off
12:48 For no uncircumcised **p** shall
16:16 one's need, one omer for each **p**,
31:14 that **p** shall be cut off from
Lev 4: 2 If a **p** sins unintentionally
5: 1 If a **p** sins in hearing the
5: 2 Or if a **p** touches any unclean
5: 4 Or if a **p** swears, speaking
5:15 If a **p** commits a trespass, and
5:17 If a **p** sins, and commits any of
6: 2 If a **p** sins and commits a
7:18 and the **p** who eats of it shall
7:20 But the **p** who eats the flesh of
7:20 that **p** shall be cut off from
7:21 Moreover the **p** who touches any
7:21 that **p** shall be cut off from
7:25 the **p** who eats it shall be cut
7:27 that **p** shall be cut off from
13: 9 the leprous sore is on a **p**,
17:10 set My face against that **p** who
17:15 And every **p** who eats what died
19: 8 and that **p** shall be cut off
19:15 nor honor the **p** of the mighty.
20: 6 And the **p** who turns to mediums
20: 6 set My face against that **p** and
22: 3 that **p** shall be cut off from My
22: 5 or any **p** by whom he would
22: 6 the **p** who has touched any such
22:11 But if the priest buys a **p** with
23:29 For any **p** who is not afflicted
23:30 And any **p** who does any work on
23:30 that **p** I will destroy from
27:29 No **p** under the ban, who may
Num 5: 6 and that **p** is guilty,
9:13 that same **p** shall be cut off
15:27 And if a **p** sins
15:28 shall make atonement for the **p**
15:30 But the **p** who does anything
15:31 that **p** shall be completely cut
19:13 That **p** shall be cut off from
19:17 And for an unclean **p** they shall
19:18 A clean **p** shall take hyssop and
19:19 The clean **p** shall sprinkle the
19:20 that **p** shall be cut off from
19:22 Whatever the unclean **p** touches
19:22 and the **p** who touches it shall
31:19 whoever has killed any **p**,
35:11 the manslayer who kills any **p**
35:15 that anyone who kills a **p**
35:30 'Whoever kills a **p**,
35:30 testimony against a **p** for the
Deut 15:22 the unclean and the clean **p**
24:16 a **p** shall be put to death for
27:25 a bribe to slay an innocent **p**.
Josh 20: 3 that the slayer who kills a **p**
20: 9 that whoever killed a **p**
1 Sam 9: 2 was not a more handsome **p**
16:18 in speech, and a handsome **p**;
25:35 your voice and respected your **p**.
2 Sam 4:11 men have killed a righteous **p**
17:11 and that you go to battle in **p**.
1 Ki 14: 6 you pretend to be another **p**?
2 Ki 14: 6 but a **p** shall be put to death
2 Chr 25: 4 but a **p** shall die for his own
Job 1:12 do not lay a hand on his **p**.
22:29 He will save the humble **p**.
Ps 15: 4 In whose eyes a vile **p** is
31:23 And fully repays the proud **p**.
49:10 the fool and the senseless **p**
109:20 who speak evil against my **p**.
Prov 3:32 For the perverse **p** is an
6:12 A worthless **p**, a wicked

16:26 The **p** who labors, labors for
19:15 And an idle **p** will suffer
Isa 32: 5 The foolish **p** will no longer be
32: 6 For the foolish **p** will speak
Jer 43: 6 and every **p** whom Nebuzaradan
Ezek 33: 6 sword comes and takes any **p**
44:25 by coming near a dead **p**.
Dan 11:21 his place shall arise a vile **p**,
Hab 1:13 when the wicked devours A **p**
Mt 5:39 you not to resist an evil **p**.
22:16 for You do not regard the **p** of
27:24 of the blood of this just **P**.
Mk 12:14 for You do not regard the **p** of
Rom 14: 5 One **p** esteems one day above
1 Cor 5:11 even to eat with such a **p**.
5:13 from yourselves the evil **p**.
14:24 unbeliever or an uninformed **p**
2 Cor 10:11 Let such a **p** consider this, that
Eph 5: 5 that no fornicator, unclean **p**,
2 Th 3:14 note that **p** and do not keep
1 Tim 1: 9 is not made for a righteous **p**,
Titus 3:11 knowing that such a **p** is warped
Heb 1: 3 and the express image of His **p**,
12:16 be any fornicator or profane **p**
1 Pe 3: 4 let it be the hidden **p** of
2 Pe 2:19 for by whom a **p** is overcome, by

PERSONAL (3/3) PERSON, PERSONALLY

Lk 20:21 You do not show **p** favoritism,
Acts 12:20 made Blastus the king's **p** aide
Gal 2: 6 God shows **p** favoritism to no

PERSONALLY (1/1)

Gen 24:57 the young woman and ask her **p**.

PERSONS (44/40) PERSON

Gen 14:21 said to Abram, "Give me the **p**,
36: 6 and all the **p** of his household,
46:15 his daughter Dinah. All the **p**,
46:18 she bore to Jacob: sixteen **p**.
46:22 fourteen **p** in all.
46:25 to Jacob: seven **p** in all.
46:26 All the **p** who went with Jacob
46:26 were sixty-six **p** in all.
46:27 to him in Egypt were two **p**.
46:27 All the **p** of the house of Jacob
Ex 1: 5 of Jacob were seventy **p** (for
12: 4 to the number of the **p**;
16:16 according to the number of **p**;
Lev 18:29 the **p** who commit them shall be
27: 2 consecrates by a vow certain **p**
Num 19:18 on the **p** who were there, or on
31:28 of every five hundred of the **p**,
31:30 every fifty, drawn from the **p**,
31:35 and thirty-two thousand **p** in
31:40 The **p** were sixteen thousand, of
31:40 tribute was thirty-two **p**.
31:46 and sixteen thousand **p**—
Deut 10:22 down to Egypt with seventy **p**,
1 Sam 9:22 there were about thirty **p**.
22:22 the death of all the **p** of
1 Ki 14:24 there were also perverted **p** in
15:12 And he banished the perverted **p**
22:46 And the rest of the perverted **p**,
2 Ki 10: 6 Now the king's sons, seventy **p**,
10: 7 sons and slaughtered seventy **p**,
23: 7 booths of the perverted **p** that
Job 36:14 ends among the perverted **p**.
Jer 52:29 eight hundred and thirty-two **p**;
52:30 seven hundred and forty-five **p**.
52:30 All the **p** were four thousand
Ezek 10:22 their appearance and their **p**.
17:17 build a wall to cut off many **p**.
Am 6: 1 Notable **p** in the chief nation,
Jon 4:11 hundred and twenty thousand **p**
Lk 15: 7 than over ninety-nine just **p**
Acts 27:37 two hundred and seventy-six **p**
2 Cor 1:11 thanks may be given by many **p**
2 Pe 3:11 what manner of **p** ought you to
Jude 19 These are sensual **p**,

PERSUADE (14/14) PERSUADED, PERSUASIVE

2 Sam 3:35 when all the people came to **p**
1 Ki 22:20 Who will **p** Ahab to go up, that
22:21 and said, 'I will **p** him.'
22:22 You shall **p** him, and also
2 Ki 18:32 lest he **p** you, saying, "The
2 Chr 18:19 Who will **p** Ahab king of Israel
18:20 I will **p** him.' The LORD said to
18:21 You shall **p** him and also
32:11 Does not Hezekiah **p** you to give
32:15 let Hezekiah deceive you or **p**
Isa 36:18 Beware lest Hezekiah **p** you,
Acts 26:28 You almost **p** me to become a
2 Cor 5:11 we **p** men; but we are well known
Gal 1:10 For do I now **p** men, or God?

PERSUADED (21/21) PERSUADE

Josh 15:18 that she **p** him to ask her
2 Ki 4: 8 and she **p** him to eat some food.
2 Chr 18: 2 and **p** him to go up with him
Prov 25:15 long forbearance a ruler is **p**,
Jer 20: 7 You induced me, and I was **p**;
Mt 27:20 the chief priests and elders **p**
Lk 16:31 neither will they be **p** though
20: 6 for they are **p** that John was a
Acts 13:43 **p** them to continue in the grace
14:19 and having **p** the multitudes,
16:15 and stay." So she **p** us.
17: 4 And some of them were **p**;
17: 5 But the Jews who were not **p**,
18: 4 and **p** both Jews and Greeks.
19:26 this Paul has **p** and turned away
21:14 So when he would not be **p**,
27:11 the centurion was more **p** by
28:24 And some were **p** by the things
Rom 8:38 For I am **p** that neither death
2 Tim 1: 5 and I am **p** is in you also.
1:12 whom I have believed and am **p**

PERSUADES (1/1)

Acts 18:13 This fellow **p** men to worship

PERSUADING (2/2)

Acts 19: 8 reasoning and **p** concerning the
28:23 **p** them concerning Jesus from

PERSUASION (1/1)

Gal 5: 8 This **p** does not come from Him

PERSUASIVE (2/2) PERSUADE

1 Cor 2: 4 were not with **p** words of
Col 2: 4 deceive you with **p** words.

PERTAIN (4/4) PERTAINING

Rom 9: 4 to whom **p** the adoption, the
15:17 Jesus in the things which **p**
1 Cor 6: 3 things that **p** to this life?
2 Pe 1: 3 given to us all things that **p**

PERTAINING (5/5) PERTAIN

1 Chr 26:32 for every matter **p** to God and
Acts 1: 3 and speaking of the things **p**
1 Cor 6: 4 judgments concerning things **p**
Heb 2:17 High Priest in things **p** to
5: 1 appointed for men in things **p**

PERTAINS (3/3)

Num 8:24 This is what **p** to the Levites:
Deut 22: 5 shall not wear anything that **p**
Neh 2: 8 gates of the citadel which **p**

PERTURBED (1/1)

Prov 30:21 three things the earth is **p**,

PERUDA (1/1)

Ezra 2:55 of Sophereth, the sons of **P**,

PERVERSE (33/33) PERVERT

Num 22:32 because your way is **p** before
Deut 32: 5 A **p** and crooked generation.
32:20 For they are a **p** generation,
1 Sam 20:30 said to him, "You son of a **p**,
Job 9:20 blameless, it would prove me **p**.
Ps 101: 4 A **p** heart shall depart from me;
Prov 2:12 the man who speaks **p** things,
3:32 For the **p** person is an
4:24 And put **p** lips far from you.
6:12 Walks with a **p** mouth;
8: 8 Nothing crooked or **p** is in
8:13 evil way And the **p** mouth
10:31 But the **p** tongue will be cut
10:32 mouth of the wicked what is **p**.
11:20 Those who are of a **p** heart are
12: 8 But he who is of a **p** heart
14: 2 But he who is **p** in his ways
16:28 A **p** man sows strife, And a
16:30 his eye to devise **p** things;
17:20 And he who has a **p** tongue
19: 1 Than one who is **p** in his
21: 8 The way of a guilty man is **p**;
22: 5 snares are in the way of the **p**;
23:33 heart will utter **p** things.
28: 6 in his integrity Than one **p**
28:18 But he who is **p** in his
Isa 19:14 The LORD has mingled a **p**
Hab 1: 4 Therefore **p** judgment proceeds.
Mt 17:17 O faithless and **p** generation,
Lk 9:41 O faithless and **p** generation,
Acts 2:40 from this **p** generation."
20:30 speaking **p** things, to draw away
Phil 2:15 of a crooked and **p** generation,

PERVERSENESS (1/1)

Prov 15: 4 But **p** in it breaks the spirit.

PERVERSION (3/3)

Lev 18:23 to mate with it. It is **p**.
20:12 to death. They have committed **p**.
Eccl 5: 8 and the violent **p** of justice

PERVERSITY (6/6)

Prov 2:14 And delight in the **p** of the
6:14 **P** is in his heart, He devises
11: 3 But the **p** of the unfaithful
Isa 30:12 And trust in oppression and **p**,
59: 3 Your tongue has muttered **p**.
Ezek 9: 9 and the city full of **p**;

PERVERT (11/11) PERVERSE, PERVERTED, PERVERTING, PERVERTS

Ex 23: 2 to turn aside after many to **p**
23: 6 You shall not **p** the judgment of
Deut 16:19 'You shall not **p** justice;
24:17 You shall not **p** justice due the
Job 8: 3 Or does the Almighty **p**
34:12 Nor will the Almighty **p**
Prov 17:23 a bribe behind the back To **p**
31: 5 And **p** the justice of all the
Am 2: 7 And **p** the way of the humble.
Mic 3: 9 Who abhor justice And **p** all
Gal 1: 7 who trouble you and want to **p**

PERVERTED (12/12) PERVERT

Deut 23:17 or a **p** one of the sons of
Judg 19:22 **p** men, surrounded the house
20:13 the **p** men who are in Gibeah,
1 Sam 8: 3 took bribes, and **p** justice.
1 Ki 14:24 And there were also **p** persons in
15:12 And he banished the **p** persons
22:46 And the rest of the **p** persons,
2 Ki 23: 7 the ritual booths of the **p**
Job 33:27 and **p** what was right, And it
36:14 their life ends among the **p**
Jer 3:21 For they have **p** their way;
23:36 for you have **p** the words of the

PERVERTING (2/2) PERVERT

Lk 23: 2 We found this fellow **p** the
Acts 13:10 will you not cease **p** the

PERVERTS (3/3) PERVERT

Ex 23: 8 blinds the discerning and **p**
Deut 27:19 Cursed is the one who **p** the
Prov 10: 9 But he who **p** his ways will

PESTERED (1/1)

Judg 16:16 when she **p** him daily with her

PESTILENCE (42/41) PESTILENCES

Ex 5: 3 lest He fall upon us with **p** or
9: 3 on the sheep—a very severe **p**.
9:15 you and your people with **p**,
Lev 26:25 your cities I will send **p**
Num 14:12 I will strike them with the **p**
Deut 32:24 Devoured by **p** and bitter
1 Ki 8:37 **p** or blight or mildew,
2 Chr 6:28 **p** or blight or mildew, locusts
7:13 or send **p** among My people,
20: 9 upon us—sword, judgment, **p**,
Ps 91: 3 And from the perilous **p**
91: 6 Nor of the **p** that walks in
Jer 14:12 by the famine, and by the **p**.
21: 6 they shall die of a great **p**.
21: 7 left in this city from the **p**
21: 9 the sword, by famine, and by **p**;
24:10 and the **p** among them, till they
27: 8 sword, the famine, and the **p**,
27:13 by the famine, and by the **p**,
28: 8 war and disaster and **p**.
29:17 sword, the famine, and the **p**,
29:18 sword, with famine, and with **p**;
32:24 of the sword and famine and **p**.
32:36 by the famine, and by the **p**':
34:17 the LORD—'to the sword, to **p**,
38: 2 the sword, by famine, and by **p**;
42:17 the sword, by famine, and by **p**.
42:22 and by **p** in the place where you
44:13 the sword, by famine, and by **p**,
Ezek 5:12 of you shall die of the **p**,
5:17 **P** and blood shall pass through
6:11 the sword, by famine, and by **p**.
6:12 is far off shall die by the **p**,
7:15 And the **p** and famine within.
7:15 Famine and **p** will devour him.
12:16 sword, from famine, and from **p**,
14:19 Or if I send a **p** into that
14:21 famine and wild beasts and **p**—
28:23 For I will send **p** upon her,
33:27 and caves shall die of the **p**.
38:22 bring him to judgment with **p**
Hab 3: 5 Before Him went **p**,

PESTILENCES (2/2) PESTILENCE

Mt 24: 7 And there will be famines, **p**,
Lk 21:11 places, and famines and **p**;

PESTILENT (KJV) See PLAGUE

PESTLE (1/1)

Prov 27:22 a fool in a mortar with a **p**

PETER (158/153) CEPHAS, PETER'S, SIMON

Mt 4:18 two brothers, Simon called **P**,
10: 2 first, Simon, who is called **P**,
14:28 And **P** answered Him and said,
14:29 And when **P** had come down out
15:15 Then **P** answered and said to Him,
16:16 Simon **P** answered and said, "You

16:18 also say to you that you are **P**,
16:22 Then **P** took Him aside and began
16:23 But He turned and said to **P**,
17: 1 Now after six days Jesus took **P**,
17: 4 Then **P** answered and said to
17:24 the temple tax came to **P** and
17:26 **P** said to Him, "From
18:21 Then **P** came to Him and said,
19:27 Then **P** answered and said to Him,
26:33 **P** answered and said to Him,
26:35 **P** said to Him, "Even if I have
26:37 And He took with Him **P** and the
26:40 them asleep, and said to **P**,
26:58 But **P** followed Him at a distance
26:69 Now **P** sat outside in the
26:73 stood by came up and said to **P**,
26:75 And **P** remembered the word of
Mk 3:16 to whom He gave the name **P**;
5:37 no one to follow Him except **P**,
8:29 **P** answered and said to Him,
8:32 And **P** took Him aside and began
8:33 at His disciples, He rebuked **P**,
9: 2 after six days Jesus took **P**,
9: 5 Then **P** answered and said to
10:28 Then **P** began to say to Him,
11:21 And **P**, remembering, said
13: 3 Olives opposite the temple, **P**,
14:29 **P** said to Him, "Even if all are
14:33 And He took **P**, James,
14:37 them sleeping, and said to **P**,
14:54 But **P** followed Him at a
14:66 Now as **P** was below in the
14:67 And when she saw **P** warming
14:70 those who stood by said to **P**
14:72 Then **P** called to mind the word
16: 7 go, tell His disciples—and **P**
Lk 5: 8 When Simon **P** saw it, he fell
6:14 Simon, whom He also named **P**,
8:45 **P** and those with him said,
8:51 no one to go in except **P**,
9:20 **P** answered and said, "The
9:28 these sayings, that He took **P**,
9:32 But **P** and those with him were
9:33 that **P** said to Jesus,
12:41 Then **P** said to Him, "Lord, do
18:28 Then **P** said, "See, we have left
22: 8 And He sent **P** and John, saying,
22:34 Then He said, "I tell you, **P**,
22:54 But **P** followed at a distance.
22:55 **P** sat among them.
22:58 But **P** said, "Man, I am
22:60 But **P** said, "Man, I do not know
22:61 the Lord turned and looked at **P**.
22:61 And **P** remembered the word of
22:62 So **P** went out and wept bitterly.
24:12 But **P** arose and ran to the tomb;
Jn 1:44 the city of Andrew and **P**.
6:68 But Simon **P** answered Him,
13: 6 Then He came to Simon **P**.
13: 6 And **P** said to Him, "Lord, are
13: 8 **P** said to Him, "You shall never
13: 9 Simon **P** said to Him, "Lord, not
13:24 Simon **P** therefore motioned to
13:36 Simon **P** said to Him, "Lord,
13:37 **P** said to Him, "Lord, why can I
18:10 Then Simon **P**, having a sword,
18:11 So Jesus said to **P**,
18:15 And Simon **P** followed Jesus, and
18:16 But **P** stood at the door outside.
18:16 the door, and brought **P** in.
18:17 who kept the door said to **P**,
18:18 And **P** stood with them and
18:25 Now Simon **P** stood and warmed
18:26 a relative of him whose ear **P**
18:27 **P** then denied again;
20: 2 she ran and came to Simon **P**,
20: 3 **P** therefore went out, and the
20: 4 and the other disciple outran **P**
20: 6 Then Simon **P** came, following
21: 2 Simon **P**, Thomas called the
21: 3 Simon **P** said to them, "I am
21: 7 whom Jesus loved said to **P**,
21: 7 is the Lord!" Now when Simon **P**
21:11 Simon **P** went up and dragged the
21:15 Jesus said to Simon **P**,
21:17 **P** was grieved because He said
21:20 Then **P**, turning around, saw
21:21 **P**, seeing him, said to Jesus,
Acts 1:13 room where they were staying: **P**,
1:15 And in those days **P** stood up in
2:14 But **P**, standing up with
2:37 and said to **P** and the rest of
2:38 Then **P** said to them, "Repent,
3: 1 Now **P** and John went up together
3: 3 seeing **P** and John about to go
3: 4 **P** said, "Look at us."
3: 6 Then **P** said, "Silver and gold I
3:11 man who was healed held on to **P**
3:12 So when **P** saw it, he responded
4: 8 Then **P**, filled with the Holy
4:13 they saw the boldness of **P** and
4:19 But **P** and John answered and said
5: 3 But **P** said, "Ananias, why has
5: 8 And **P** answered her, "Tell me
5: 9 Then **P** said to her, "How is it
5:15 that at least the shadow of **P**
5:29 But **P** and the other apostles
8:14 they sent **P** and John to them,
8:20 But **P** said to him, "Your money
9:32 as **P** went through all parts
9:34 And **P** said to him, "Aeneas,
9:38 the disciples had heard that **P**
9:39 Then **P** arose and went with them.
9:40 But **P** put them all out, and
9:40 and when she saw **P** she sat up.
10: 5 for Simon whose surname is **P**.
10: 9 **P** went up on the housetop to
10:13 a voice came to him, "Rise, **P**;
10:14 But **P** said, "Not so, Lord!
10:17 Now while **P** wondered within
10:18 Simon, whose surname was **P**,
10:19 While **P** thought about the
10:21 Then **P** went down to the men who
10:23 On the next day **P** went away
10:25 As **P** was coming in, Cornelius
10:26 But **P** lifted him up, saying,
10:32 Simon here, whose surname is **P**.
10:34 Then **P** opened his mouth and
10:44 While **P** was still speaking
10:45 as many as came with **P**,
10:46 Then **P** answered,
11: 2 And when **P** came up to Jerusalem,
11: 4 But **P** explained it to them in
11: 7 a voice saying to me, 'Rise, **P**;
11:13 for Simon whose surname is **P**,
12: 3 he proceeded further to seize **P**
12: 5 **P** was therefore kept in prison,
12: 6 that night **P** was sleeping,
12: 7 and he struck **P** on the side and
12:11 And when **P** had come to himself,
12:13 And as **P** knocked at the door of
12:14 but ran in and announced that **P**
12:16 Now **P** continued knocking;
12:18 about what had become of **P**.
15: 7 **P** rose up and said to them:
Gal 1:18 I went up to Jerusalem to see **P**,
2: 7 for the circumcised was to **P**
2: 8 He who worked effectively in **P**
2:11 Now when **P** had come to Antioch,
2:14 I said to **P** before them all,
1 Pe 1: 1 **P**, an apostle of Jesus
2 Pe 1: 1 Simon **P**, a bondservant and

PETER'S (4/4) PETER

Mt 8:14 Jesus had come into **P** house,
Jn 1:40 was Andrew, Simon **P** brother.
6: 8 Simon **P** brother, said to Him,
Acts 12:14 When she recognized **P** voice,

PETHAHIAH (4/4)

1 Chr 24:16 the nineteenth to **P**,
Ezra 10:23 (the same is Kelita), **P**,
Neh 9: 5 Hodijah, Shebaniah, and **P**,
11:24 **P** the son of Meshezabel, of the

PETHOR (2/2)

Num 22: 5 to Balaam the son of Beor at **P**,
Deut 23: 4 Balaam the son of Beor from **P**

PETHUEL (1/1)

Joel 1: 1 that came to Joel the son of **P**.

PETITION (14/14) PETITIONED, PETITIONS

1 Sam 1:17 the God of Israel grant your **p**
1:27 the LORD has granted me my **p**
1 Ki 2:16 Now I ask one **p** of you; do not
2:20 'I desire one small **p** of you;
Esth 5: 6 to Esther, "What is your **p**?
5: 7 My **p** and request is this:
5: 8 pleases the king to grant my **p**
7: 2 to Esther, "What is your **p**,
7: 3 let my life be given me at my **p**,
9:12 provinces? Now what is your **p**?
Jer 37:20 let my **p** be accepted before
42: 2 let our **p** be acceptable to you,
42: 9 you sent me to present your **p**
Dan 6:13 but makes his **p** three times a

PETITIONED (3/3) PETITION

Dan 2:49 Also Daniel **p** the king, and he
Acts 25: 2 and they **p** him,
25:24 whole assembly of the Jews **p**

PETITIONS (4/4) PETITION

Ps 20: 5 the LORD fulfill all your **p**.
Dan 6: 7 that whoever **p** any god or man
6:12 a decree that every man who **p**
1 Jn 5:15 we know that we have the **p** that

PEULTHAI (1/1)

1 Chr 26: 5 **P** the eighth; for God blessed

PHALEC (KJV) See PELEG

PHALLU (KJV) See PALLU

PHALTI, PHALTIEL (KJV) See PALTI, PALTIEL

PHANUEL (1/1)

Lk 2:36 a prophetess, the daughter of **P**,

PHARAOH (234/207) HOPHRA, NECHO, PHARAOH'S

Gen 12:15 The princes of **P** also saw her
12:15 saw her and commended her to **P**.
12:17 But the LORD plagued **P** and his
12:18 And **P** called Abram and said,
12:20 So **P** commanded his men
37:36 an officer of **P** and captain of
39: 1 And Potiphar, an officer of **P**,
40: 2 And **P** was angry with his two
40:13 Now within three days **P** will
40:14 to me; make mention of me to **P**,
40:17 all kinds of baked goods for **P**,
40:19 Within three days **P** will lift
41: 1 that **P** had a dream; and behold,
41: 4 and fat cows. So **P** awoke.
41: 7 So **P** awoke, and indeed, it
41: 8 And **P** told them his dreams, but
41: 8 who could interpret them for **P**.
41: 9 the chief butler spoke to **P**,
41:10 When **P** was angry with his
41:14 Then **P** sent and called Joseph,
41:14 his clothing, and came to **P**.
41:15 And **P** said to Joseph, "I have
41:16 So Joseph answered **P**,
41:16 God will give **P** an answer of
41:17 Then **P** said to Joseph: "Behold,
41:25 Then Joseph said to **P**,
41:25 'The dreams of **P** are one;
41:25 God has shown **P** what He is
41:28 thing which I have spoken to **P**.
41:28 God has shown **P** what He is
41:32 the dream was repeated to **P**
41:33 let **P** select a discerning and
41:34 Let **P** do this, and let him
41:35 grain under the authority of **P**,
41:37 was good in the eyes of **P** and
41:38 And **P** said to his servants,
41:39 Then **P** said to Joseph,
41:41 And **P** said to Joseph, "See, I
41:42 Then **P** took his signet ring off
41:44 **P** also said to Joseph, "I am
41:44 also said to Joseph, "I am **P**,
41:45 And **P** called Joseph's name
41:46 old when he stood before **P**
41:46 went out from the presence of **P**,
41:55 the people cried to **P** for
41:55 Then **P** said to all the
42:15 be tested: By the life of **P**,
42:16 or else, by the life of **P**,
44:18 for you are even like **P**.
45: 2 Egyptians and the house of **P**
45: 8 He has made me a father to **P**,
45:16 So it pleased **P** and his
45:17 And **P** said to Joseph, "Say to
45:21 according to the command of **P**,
46: 5 in the carts which **P** had sent
46:31 "I will go up and tell **P**,
46:33 when **P** calls you and says,
47: 1 Then Joseph went and told **P**,
47: 2 and presented them to **P**.
47: 3 Then **P** said to his brothers,
47: 3 And they said to **P**,
47: 4 said to **P**, "We have come
47: 5 Then **P** spoke to Joseph, saying,
47: 7 Jacob and set him before **P**;
47: 7 Pharaoh; and Jacob blessed **P**.
47: 8 **P** said to Jacob, "How old are
47: 9 And Jacob said to **P**,
47:10 So Jacob blessed **P**,
47:10 and went out from before **P**.
47:11 as **P** had commanded.
47:19 our land will be servants of **P**;
47:20 all the land of Egypt for **P**;
47:22 allotted to them by **P**,
47:22 they ate their rations which **P**
47:23 and your land this day for **P**.
47:24 you shall give one-fifth to **P**.
47:26 that **P** should have one-fifth,
50: 4 spoke to the household of **P**,
50: 4 speak in the hearing of **P**,
50: 6 And **P** said, "Go up and bury
50: 7 went up all the servants of **P**,
Ex 1:11 And they built for **P** supply
1:19 And the midwives said to **P**,
1:22 So **P** commanded all his people,
2: 5 Then the daughter of **P** came
2:15 When **P** heard of this matter, he
2:15 Moses fled from the face of **P**
3:10 and I will send you to **P** that
3:11 am I that I should go to **P**,
4:21 do all those wonders before **P**
4:22 "Then you shall say to **P**,
5: 1 and Aaron went in and told **P**,
5: 2 And **P** said, "Who is the LORD,
5: 5 And **P** said, "Look, the people
5: 6 So the same day **P** commanded the
5:10 people, saying, "Thus says **P**:
5:15 Israel came and cried out to **P**,
5:20 Then, as they came out from **P**,
5:21 us abhorrent in the sight of **P**
5:23 For since I came to **P** to speak
6: 1 shall see what I will do to **P**.
6:11 tell **P** king of Egypt to let the
6:12 How then shall **P** heed me, for I
6:13 children of Israel and for **P**
6:27 are the ones who spoke to **P**
6:29 Speak to **P** king of Egypt all
6:30 and how shall **P** heed me?"
7: 1 I have made you as God to **P**,

7: 2 your brother shall speak to **P**
7: 4 But **P** will not heed you, so that
7: 7 years old when they spoke to **P**.
7: 9 When **P** speaks to you, saying,
7: 9 your rod and cast it before **P**,
7:10 So Moses and Aaron went in to **P**,
7:10 cast down his rod before **P** and
7:11 But **P** also called the wise men
7:15 Go to **P** in the morning, when he
7:20 in the sight of **P** and in the
7:23 And **P** turned and went into his
8: 1 Go to **P** and say to him, 'Thus
8: 8 Then **P** called for Moses and
8: 9 And Moses said to **P**,
8:12 Moses and Aaron went out from **P**.
8:12 which He had brought against **P**.
8:15 But when **P** saw that there was
8:19 Then the magicians said to **P**,
8:20 the morning and stand before **P**
8:24 flies came into the house of **P**,
8:25 Then **P** called for Moses and
8:28 And **P** said, "I will let you go,
8:29 may depart tomorrow from **P**,
8:29 But let **P** not deal deceitfully
8:30 So Moses went out from **P** and
8:31 the swarms of flies from **P**,
8:32 But **P** hardened his heart at this
9: 1 Go in to **P** and tell him, 'Thus
9: 7 Then **P** sent, and indeed, not
9: 7 But the heart of **P** became hard,
9: 8 the heavens in the sight of **P**.
9:10 the furnace and stood before **P**,
9:12 LORD hardened the heart of **P**;
9:13 the morning and stand before **P**,
9:20 LORD among the servants of **P**
9:27 And **P** sent and called for Moses
9:33 went out of the city from **P**
9:34 And when **P** saw that the rain,
9:35 So the heart of **P** was hard;
10: 1 said to Moses, "Go in to **P**;
10: 3 Moses and Aaron came in to **P**
10: 6 he turned and went out from **P**.
10: 8 Aaron were brought again to **P**,
10:16 Then **P** called for Moses and
10:18 So he went out from **P** and
10:24 Then **P** called to Moses and
10:28 Then **P** said to him, "Get away
11: 1 yet one more plague on **P** and
11: 5 from the firstborn of **P** who
11: 8 Then he went out from **P** in
11: 9 **P** will not heed you, so that My
11:10 did all these wonders before **P**;
12:29 from the firstborn of **P** who sat
12:30 So **P** rose in the night, he, all
13:15 when **P** was stubborn about
13:17 when **P** had let the people go,
14: 3 For **P** will say of the children
14: 4 and I will gain honor over **P**
14: 5 and the heart of **P** and his
14: 8 LORD hardened the heart of **P**
14: 9 the horses and chariots of **P**,
14:10 And when **P** drew near, the
14:17 So I will gain honor over **P** and
14:18 gained honor for Myself over **P**,
14:28 and all the army of **P** that
15:19 For the horses of **P** went with
18: 4 me from the sword of **P**");
18: 8 that the LORD had done to **P**
18:10 and out of the hand of **P**,
Deut 6:21 We were slaves of **P** in Egypt,
6:22 and severe, against Egypt, **P**,
7: 8 from the hand of **P** king of
7:18 the LORD your God did to **P**
11: 3 to **P** king of Egypt, and to all
29: 2 to **P** and to all his servants
34:11 in the land of Egypt, before **P**,
1 Sam 6: 6 hearts as the Egyptians and **P**
1 Ki 3: 1 Solomon made a treaty with **P**
9:16 (**P** king of Egypt had gone up and
11: 1 as well as the daughter of **P**:
11:18 to **P** king of Egypt, who gave
11:19 great favor in the sight of **P**,
11:20 household among the sons of **P**.
11:21 army was dead, Hadad said to **P**,
11:22 Then **P** said to him, "But what
2 Ki 17: 7 from under the hand of **P** king
18:21 So is **P** king of Egypt to all
23:29 In his days **P** Necho king of
23:29 And **P** Necho killed him at
23:33 Now **P** Necho put him in prison at
23:34 Then **P** Necho made Eliakim the
23:34 And **P** took Jehoahaz and went
23:35 according to the command of **P**;
23:35 to give it to **P** Necho.
1 Chr 4:18 of Bithiah the daughter of **P**,
2 Chr 8:11 brought the daughter of **P** up
Neh 9:10 signs and wonders against **P**,
Ps 135: 9 Upon **P** and all his servants.
136:15 But overthrew **P** and his army in
Isa 19:11 How do you say to **P**,
30: 2 themselves in the strength of **P**,
30: 3 Therefore the strength of **P**
36: 6 So is **P** king of Egypt to all
Jer 25:19 **P** king of Egypt, his servants,
44:30 I will give **P** Hophra king of
46: 2 Concerning the army of **P** Necho,
46:17 They cried there, '**P**,
46:25 and **P** and Egypt, with their
46:25 **P** and those who trust in him.
47: 1 before **P** attacked Gaza.
Ezek 17:17 Nor will **P** with his mighty army
29: 2 set your face against **P** king of
29: 3 O **P** king of Egypt, O great
30:21 I have broken the arm of **P** king
30:22 Surely I am against **P** king of
30:25 but the arms of **P** shall fall
31: 2 say to **P** king of Egypt and to
31:18 This is **P** and all his
32: 2 take up a lamentation for **P**
32:31 **P** will see them And be
32:31 **P** and all his army, Slain by
32:32 **P** and all his multitude,"
Acts 7:10 and wisdom in the presence of **P**,
7:13 family became known to the **P**.
Rom 9:17 For the Scripture says to **P**,

PHARAOH'S (47/44) PHARAOH

Gen 12:15 woman was taken to **P** house.
40: 7 So he asked **P** officers who were
40:11 'Then **P** cup was in my hand;
40:11 and pressed them into **P** cup,
40:11 and placed the cup in **P** hand."
40:13 and you will put **P** cup in his
40:20 which was **P** birthday, that he
40:21 he placed the cup in **P** hand.
45:16 of it was heard in **P** house,
47:14 brought the money into **P** house.
47:20 upon them. So the land became **P**.
47:25 and we will be **P** servants."
47:26 only, which did not become **P**.
Ex 2: 7 sister said to **P** daughter,
2: 8 And **P** daughter said to her,
2: 9 Then **P** daughter said to her,
2:10 brought him to **P** daughter,
5:14 whom **P** taskmasters had set over
7: 3 And I will harden **P** heart, and
7:13 And **P** heart grew hard, and he
7:14 **P** heart is hard; he refuses to
7:22 and **P** heart grew hard, and he
8:19 But **P** heart grew hard, and he
10: 7 Then **P** servants said to him,
10:11 driven out from **P** presence.
10:20 But the LORD hardened **P** heart,
10:27 But the LORD hardened **P** heart,
11: 3 in the sight of **P** servants and
11:10 and the LORD hardened **P** heart,
14: 4 Then I will harden **P** heart, so
14:23 all **P** horses, his chariots, and
15: 4 **P** chariots and his army He has
1 Sam 2:27 were in Egypt in **P** house?
1 Ki 3: 1 and married **P** daughter; then he
7: 8 this hall for **P** daughter,
9:24 But **P** daughter came up from the
11:20 Tahpenes weaned in **P** house.
11:20 And Genubath was in **P** household
Song 1: 9 To my filly among **P** chariots.
Isa 19:11 **P** wise counselors give foolish
Jer 37: 5 Then **P** army came up from Egypt;
37: 7 **P** army which has come up to
37:11 Jerusalem for fear of **P** army,
43: 9 at the entrance to **P** house
Ezek 30:24 but I will break **P** arms, and he
Acts 7:21 **P** daughter took him away and
Heb 11:24 called the son of **P** daughter,

PHARAOH-NECHO, PHARAOH-NECHOH (KJV) See PHARAOH (NECHO)

PHARES, PHAREZ (KJV) See PEREZ

PHARISEE (11/10) PHARISEES

Mt 23:26 'Blind **P**, first cleanse the
Lk 7:39 Now when the **P** who had invited
11:37 a certain **P** asked Him to dine
11:38 When the **P** saw it, he marveled
18:10 one a **P** and the other a tax
18:11 The **P** stood and prayed thus with
Acts 5:34 a **P** named Gamaliel, a teacher
23: 6 "Men and brethren, I am a **P**,
23: 6 I am a Pharisee, the son of a **P**;
26: 5 of our religion I lived a **P**.
Phil 3: 5 concerning the law, a **P**;

PHARISEE'S (2/2)

Lk 7:36 And He went to the **P** house, and
7:37 at the table in the **P** house,

PHARISEES (86/84) PHARISEE, PHARISEES'

Mt 3: 7 But when he saw many of the **P**
5:20 of the scribes and **P**,
9:11 And when the **P** saw it, they
9:14 Why do we and the **P** fast often,
9:34 But the **P** said, "He casts out
12: 2 And when the **P** saw it, they
12:14 Then the **P** went out and plotted
12:24 Now when the **P** heard it they
12:38 Then some of the scribes and **P**
15: 1 Then the scribes and **P** who were
15:12 Do You know that the **P** were
16: 1 Then the **P** and Sadducees came,
16: 6 beware of the leaven of the **P**
16:11 beware of the leaven of the **P**
16:12 but of the doctrine of the **P**
19: 3 The **P** also came to Him, testing
21:45 when the chief priests and **P**
22:15 Then the **P** went and plotted how
22:34 But when the **P** heard that He
22:41 While the **P** were gathered
23: 2 The scribes and the **P** sit in
23:13 "But woe to you, scribes and **P**,
23:14 "Woe to you, scribes and **P**,
23:15 "Woe to you, scribes and **P**,
23:23 "Woe to you, scribes and **P**,
23:25 "Woe to you, scribes and **P**,
23:27 "Woe to you, scribes and **P**,
23:29 "Woe to you, scribes and **P**,
27:62 the chief priests and **P**
Mk 2:16 And when the scribes and **P** saw
2:18 disciples of John and of the **P**
2:18 disciples of John and of the **P**
2:24 And the **P** said to Him, "Look,
3: 6 Then the **P** went out and
7: 1 Then the **P** and some of the
7: 3 For the **P** and all the Jews do
7: 5 Then the **P** and scribes asked
8:11 Then the **P** came out and began
8:15 beware of the leaven of the **P**
10: 2 The **P** came and asked Him, "Is
12:13 they sent to Him some of the **P**
Lk 5:17 that there were **P** and teachers
5:21 And the scribes and the **P** began
5:30 And their scribes and the **P**
5:33 and likewise those of the **P**,
6: 2 And some of the **P** said to them,
6: 7 So the scribes and **P** watched Him
7:30 But the **P** and lawyers rejected
7:36 Then one of the **P** asked Him to
11:39 Now you **P** make the outside of
11:42 But woe to you **P**! For you tithe
11:43 Woe to you **P**! For you love the
11:44 "Woe to you, scribes and **P**,
11:53 the scribes and the **P** began to
12: 1 "Beware of the leaven of the **P**,
13:31 On that very day some **P** came,
14: 1 of one of the rulers of the **P**
14: 3 spoke to the lawyers and **P**,
15: 2 And the **P** and scribes
16:14 Now the **P**, who were lovers
17:20 Now when He was asked by the **P**
19:39 And some of the **P** called to Him
Jn 1:24 who were sent were from the **P**
3: 1 There was a man of the **P** named
4: 1 when the Lord knew that the **P**
7:32 The **P** heard the crowd murmuring
7:32 and the **P** and the chief priests
7:45 came to the chief priests and **P**,
7:47 Then the **P** answered them, "Are
7:48 any of the rulers or the **P**
8: 3 Then the scribes and **P** brought
8:13 The **P** therefore said to Him,
9:13 who formerly was blind to the **P**.
9:15 Then the **P** also asked him again
9:16 Therefore some of the **P** said,
9:40 Then some of the **P** who were
11:46 of them went away to the **P** and
11:47 the chief priests and the **P**
11:57 the chief priests and the **P**
12:19 The **P** therefore said among
12:42 but because of the **P** they did
18: 3 from the chief priests and **P**,
Acts 15: 5 But some of the sect of the **P**
23: 6 were Sadducees and the other **P**,
23: 7 dissension arose between the **P**
23: 8 but the **P** confess both.

PHARISEES' (1/1)

Acts 23: 9 And the scribes of the **P** party

PHAROSH (KJV) See PAROSH

PHARPAR (1/1)

2 Ki 5:12 "Are not the Abanah and the **P**,

PHARZITES (KJV) See PARZITES

PHASEAH (KJV) See PASEAH

PHEBE (KJV) See PHOEBE

PHENICE (KJV) See PHOENICIA

PHENICIA (KJV) See PHOENICIA

PHICHOL (3/3)

Gen 21:22 that time that Abimelech and **P**,
21:32 So Abimelech rose with **P**,
26:26 and **P** the commander of his

PHILADELPHIA (2/2)

Rev 1:11 to Thyatira, to Sardis, to **P**,
3: 7 to the angel of the church in **P**

PHILEMON (1/1)

Phm 1: 1 To **P** our beloved friend and

PHILETUS (1/1)

2 Tim 2:17 Hymenaeus and **P** are of this

PHILIP (33/32) PHILIP'S

Mt 10: 3 **P** and Bartholomew; Thomas and
Mk 3:18 Andrew, **P**, Bartholomew,

P

Lk 3: 1 his brother **P** tetrarch of
6:14 and John; **P** and Bartholomew;
Jn 1:43 and He found **P** and said to him,
1:44 Now **P** was from Bethsaida, the
1:45 **P** found Nathanael and said to
1:46 **P** said to him, "Come and
1:48 Before **P** called you, when you
6: 5 coming toward Him, He said to **P**,
6: 7 **P** answered Him, "Two hundred
12:21 Then they came to **P**,
12:22 **P** came and told Andrew, and in
12:22 and in turn Andrew and **P** told
14: 8 **P** said to Him, "Lord, show us
14: 9 yet you have not known Me, **P**?
Acts 1:13 **P** and Thomas; Bartholomew and
6: 5 and the Holy Spirit, and **P**,
8: 5 Then **P** went down to the city of
8: 6 heeded the things spoken by **P**,
8:12 But when they believed **P** as he
8:13 baptized he continued with **P**,
8:26 an angel of the Lord spoke to **P**,
8:29 Then the Spirit said to **P**,
8:30 So **P** ran to him, and heard him
8:31 And he asked **P** to come up and
8:34 So the eunuch answered **P** and
8:35 Then **P** opened his mouth, and
8:37 Then **P** said, "If you believe
8:38 And both **P** and the eunuch went
8:39 the Spirit of the Lord caught **P**
8:40 But **P** was found at Azotus.
21: 8 and entered the house of **P** the

PHILIP'S (3/3) PHILIP

Mt 14: 3 Herodias, his brother **P** wife.
Mk 6:17 his brother **P** wife; for he had
Lk 3:19 his brother **P** wife, and for all

PHILIPPI (6/6) PHILIPPIANS

Acts 16:12 and from there to **P**,
20: 6 But we sailed away from **P** after
Phil 1: 1 in Christ Jesus who are in **P**,
1 Th 2: 2 were spitefully treated at **P**,

PHILIPPIANS (1/1) PHILIPPI

Phil 4:15 Now you **P** know also that in the

PHILISTIA (10/10) PHILISTINE

Ex 15:14 hold of the inhabitants of **P**.
23:31 from the Red Sea to the sea, **P**,
Ps 60: 8 **P**, shout in triumph because
83: 7 **P** with the inhabitants of
87: 4 O **P** and Tyre, with Ethiopia:
108: 9 Over **P** I will triumph."
Isa 14:29 not rejoice, all you of **P**,
14:31 O city! All you of **P** are
Joel 3: 4 Sidon, and all the coasts of **P**?
Ob 19 the Lowland shall possess **P**.

PHILISTINE (34/29) PHILISTIA, PHILISTINES

1 Sam 10: 5 to the hill of God where the **P**
17: 8 up for battle? Am I not a **P**,
17:10 And the **P** said, "I defy the
17:11 heard these words of the **P**,
17:16 And the **P** drew near and
17:23 the **P** of Gath, Goliath by name,
17:26 for the man who kills this **P**
17:26 who is this uncircumcised **P**,
17:32 will go and fight with this **P**.
17:33 not able to go against this **P**
17:36 and this uncircumcised **P** will
17:37 me from the hand of this **P**.
17:40 hand. And he drew near to the **P**.
17:41 So the **P** came, and began drawing
17:42 And when the **P** looked about and
17:43 So the **P** said to David, "Am I
17:43 And the **P** cursed David by his
17:44 And the **P** said to David, "Come
17:45 Then David said to the **P**,
17:48 when the **P** arose and came and
17:48 toward the army to meet the **P**.
17:49 he slung it and struck the **P**
17:50 So David prevailed over the **P**
17:50 and struck the **P** and killed
17:51 David ran and stood over the **P**,
17:54 David took the head of the **P**
17:55 David going out against the **P**,
17:57 from the slaughter of the **P**,
17:57 Saul with the head of the **P** in
18: 6 from the slaughter of the **P**,
19: 5 in his hands and killed the **P**,
21: 9 "The sword of Goliath the **P**,
22:10 him the sword of Goliath the **P**.
2 Sam 21:17 and struck the **P** and killed

PHILISTINES (250/213) PHILISTINE

Gen 10:14 Casluhim (from whom came the **P**
21:32 returned to the land of the **P**.
21:34 stayed in the land of the **P**
26: 1 went to Abimelech king of the **P**,
26: 8 that Abimelech king of the **P**
26:14 So the **P** envied him.
26:15 Now the **P** had stopped up all the
26:18 for the **P** had stopped them up
Ex 13:17 by way of the land of the **P**,
Josh 13: 2 all the territory of the **P** and
13: 3 the five lords of the **P**—
Judg 3: 3 namely, five lords of the **P**,
3:31 six hundred men of the **P** with
10: 6 of Ammon, and the gods of the **P**;
10: 7 them into the hands of the **P**
10:11 people of Ammon and from the **P**?
13: 1 them into the hand of the **P**
13: 5 Israel out of the hand of the **P**.
14: 1 of the daughters of the **P**.
14: 2 of the daughters of the **P**;
14: 3 a wife from the uncircumcised **P**?
14: 4 occasion to move against the **P**.
14: 4 For at that time the **P** had
15: 3 be blameless regarding the **P**
15: 5 the standing grain of the **P**,
15: 6 Then the **P** said, "Who has done
15: 6 So the **P** came up and burned
15: 9 Now the **P** went up, encamped in
15:11 Do you not know that the **P** rule
15:12 you into the hand of the **P**.
15:14 the **P** came shouting against
15:20 years in the days of the **P**.
16: 5 And the lords of the **P** came up
16: 8 So the lords of the **P** brought up
16: 9 The **P** are upon you, Samson!"
16:12 The **P** are upon you, Samson!"
16:14 The **P** are upon you, Samson!"
16:18 called for the lords of the **P**,
16:18 So the lords of the **P** came up
16:20 The **P** are upon you, Samson!"
16:21 Then the **P** took him and put out
16:23 Now the lords of the **P** gathered
16:27 All the lords of the **P** were
16:28 blow take vengeance on the **P**
16:30 Let me die with the **P**!" And he
1 Sam 4: 1 out to battle against the **P**,
4: 1 and the **P** encamped in Aphek.
4: 2 Then the **P** put themselves in
4: 2 Israel was defeated by the **P**,
4: 3 defeated us today before the **P**?
4: 6 Now when the **P** heard the noise
4: 7 So the **P** were afraid, for they
4: 9 yourselves like men, you **P**,
4:10 So the **P** fought, and Israel was
4:17 "Israel has fled before the **P**,
5: 1 Then the **P** took the ark of God
5: 2 When the **P** took the ark of God,
5: 8 all the lords of the **P**,
5:11 together all the lords of the **P**,
6: 1 was in the country of the **P**
6: 2 And the **P** called for the priests
6: 4 number of the lords of the **P**.
6:12 And the lords of the **P** went
6:16 So when the five lords of the **P**
6:17 the golden tumors which the **P**
6:18 of all the cities of the **P**
6:21 The **P** have brought back the ark
7: 3 you from the hand of the **P**.
7: 7 Now when the **P** heard that the
7: 7 the lords of the **P** went up
7: 7 it, they were afraid of the **P**.
7: 8 save us from the hand of the **P**.
7:10 the **P** drew near to battle
7:10 with a loud thunder upon the **P**
7:11 out of Mizpah and pursued the **P**,
7:13 So the **P** were subdued, and they
7:13 of the LORD was against the **P**
7:14 Then the cities which the **P** had
7:14 from the hands of the **P**.
9:16 people from the hand of the **P**;
12: 9 Hazor, into the hand of the **P**,
13: 3 attacked the garrison of the **P**
13: 3 and the **P** heard of it. Then
13: 4 attacked a garrison of the **P**,
13: 4 become an abomination to the **P**.
13: 5 Then the **P** gathered together to
13:11 and that the **P** gathered
13:12 The **P** will now come down on me
13:16 But the **P** encamped in Michmash.
13:17 came out of the camp of the **P**
13:19 for the **P** said, "Lest the
13:20 would go down to the **P** to
13:23 And the garrison of the **P** went
14:11 to the garrison of the **P**.
14:11 And the **P** said, "Look, the
14:19 which was in the camp of the **P**
14:21 Hebrews who were with the **P**
14:22 when they heard that the **P**
14:30 greater slaughter among the **P**?
14:31 Now they had driven back the **P**
14:36 Let us go down after the **P** by
14:37 "Shall I go down after the **P**?
14:46 returned from pursuing the **P**,
14:46 and the **P** went to their own
14:47 of Zobah, and against the **P**.
14:52 was fierce war with the **P** all
17: 1 Now the **P** gathered their armies
17: 2 in battle array against the **P**.
17: 3 The **P** stood on a mountain on one
17: 4 went out from the camp of the **P**,
17:19 of Elah, fighting with the **P**.
17:21 For Israel and the **P** had drawn
17:23 up from the armies of the **P**;
17:46 carcasses of the camp of the **P**
17:51 And when the **P** saw that their
17:52 and pursued the **P** as far as the
17:52 And the wounded of the **P** fell
17:53 returned from chasing the **P**,
18:17 but let the hand of the **P** be
18:21 and that the hand of the **P** may
18:25 one hundred foreskins of the **P**,
18:25 David fall by the hand of the **P**.
18:27 killed two hundred men of the **P**.
18:30 Then the princes of the **P** went
19: 8 went out and fought with the **P**,
23: 1 the **P** are fighting against
23: 2 "Shall I go and attack these **P**?
23: 2 to David, "Go and attack the **P**,
23: 3 against the armies of the **P**?
23: 4 For I will deliver the **P** into
23: 5 to Keilah and fought with the **P**,
23:27 for the **P** have invaded the
23:28 David, and went against the **P**;
24: 1 returned from following the **P**,
27: 1 escape to the land of the **P**;
27: 7 dwelt in the country of the **P**
27:11 dwelt in the country of the **P**.
28: 1 in those days that the **P**
28: 4 Then the **P** gathered together,
28: 5 When Saul saw the army of the **P**,
28:15 for the **P** make war against me,
28:19 with you into the hand of the **P**.
28:19 Israel into the hand of the **P**.
29: 1 Then the **P** gathered together all
29: 2 And the lords of the **P** passed in
29: 3 Then the princes of the **P** said,
29: 3 said to the princes of the **P**,
29: 4 But the princes of the **P** were
29: 4 so the princes of the **P** said to
29: 7 displease the lords of the **P**.
29: 9 the princes of the **P** have said,
29:11 to return to the land of the **P**.
29:11 And the **P** went up to Jezreel.
30:16 taken from the land of the **P**
31: 1 Now the **P** fought against Israel;
31: 1 Israel fled from before the **P**,
31: 2 Then the **P** followed hard after
31: 2 And the **P** killed Jonathan,
31: 7 and the **P** came and dwelt in
31: 8 when the **P** came to strip the
31: 9 throughout the land of the **P**,
31:11 Jabesh Gilead heard what the **P**
2 Sam 1:20 Lest the daughters of the **P**
3:14 a hundred foreskins of the **P**.
3:18 Israel from the hand of the **P**
5:17 Now when the **P** heard that they
5:17 all the **P** went up to search for
5:18 The **P** also went and deployed
5:19 "Shall I go up against the **P**?
5:19 I will doubtless deliver the **P**
5:22 Then the **P** went up once again
5:24 you to strike the camp of the **P**.
5:25 and he drove back the **P** from
8: 1 pass that David attacked the **P**
8: 1 Ammah from the hand of the **P**.
8:12 the people of Ammon, from the **P**,
19: 9 us from the hand of the **P**,
21:12 where the **P** had hung them up,
21:12 after the **P** had struck down
21:15 When the **P** were at war again
21:15 down and fought against the **P**;
21:18 was again a battle with the **P**
21:19 there was war at Gob with the **P**,
23: 9 David when they defied the **P**
23:10 He arose and attacked the **P**
23:11 The **P** had gathered together
23:11 Then the people fled from the **P**.
23:12 defended it, and killed the **P**.
23:13 And the troop of **P** encamped in
23:14 and the garrison of the **P** was
23:16 broke through the camp of the **P**,
1 Ki 4:21 the River to the land of the **P**,
15:27 which belonged to the **P**,
16:15 which belonged to the **P**.
2 Ki 8: 2 and dwelt in the land of the **P**
8: 3 returned from the land of the **P**;
18: 8 He subdued the **P**,
1 Chr 1:12 Casluhim (from whom came the **P**
10: 1 Now the **P** fought against Israel;
10: 1 Israel fled from before the **P**,
10: 2 Then the **P** followed hard after
10: 2 And the **P** killed Jonathan,
10: 7 then the **P** came and dwelt in
10: 8 when the **P** came to strip the
10: 9 throughout the land of the **P**
10:11 Gilead heard all that the **P**
11:13 Now there the **P** were gathered
11:13 And the people fled from the **P**.
11:14 defended it, and killed the **P**.
11:15 and the army of the **P** encamped
11:16 and the garrison of the **P** was
11:18 broke through the camp of the **P**,
12:19 when he was going with the **P**
12:19 for the lords of the **P** sent him
14: 8 Now when the **P** heard that David
14: 8 all the **P** went up to search for
14: 9 Then the **P** went and made a raid
14:10 "Shall I go up against the **P**?
14:13 Then the **P** once again made a
14:15 you to strike the camp of the **P**.
14:16 drove back the army of the **P**
18: 1 pass that David attacked the **P**,
18: 1 towns from the hand of the **P**.
18:11 the people of Ammon, from the **P**,
20: 4 broke out at Gezer with the **P**,
20: 5 Again there was war with the **P**,
2 Chr 9:26 the River to the land of the **P**,
17:11 Also some of the **P** brought
21:16 Jehoram the spirit of the **P**
26: 6 out and made war against the **P**,
26: 6 around Ashdod and among the **P**.
26: 7 God helped him against the **P**,
28:18 The **P** also had invaded the
Ps 56: A Michtam of David when the **P**
Isa 2: 6 are soothsayers like the **P**,

9:12 The Syrians before and the **P**
11:14 down upon the shoulder of the **P**
Jer 25:20 the kings of the land of the **P**
47: 1 the prophet against the **P**,
47: 4 that comes to plunder all the **P**,
47: 4 the LORD shall plunder the **P**,
Ezek 16:27 you, the daughters of the **P**,
16:57 and of the daughters of the **P**,
25:15 Because the **P** dealt vengefully
25:16 out My hand against the **P**,
Am 1: 8 And the remnant of the **P** shall
6: 2 Then go down to Gath of the **P**.
9: 7 The **P** from Caphtor, And the
Zeph 2: 5 O Canaan, land of the **P**:
Zech 9: 6 will cut off the pride of the **P**.

PHILISTINES' (2/2)

1 Sam 14: 1 us go over to the **P** garrison
14: 4 to go over to the **P** garrison,

PHILOLOGUS (1/1)

Rom 16:15 Greet **P** and Julia, Nereus and

PHILOSOPHERS (1/1) PHILOSOPHY

Acts 17:18 certain Epicurean and Stoic **p**

PHILOSOPHY (1/1) PHILOSOPHERS

Col 2: 8 anyone cheat you through **p** and

PHINEHAS (24/23)

Ex 6:25 as wife; and she bore him **P**.
Num 25: 7 Now when **P** the son of Eleazar,
25:11 **P** the son of Eleazar, the son of
31: 6 he sent them to the war with **P**
Josh 22:13 the children of Israel sent **P**
22:30 Now when **P** the priest and the
22:31 Then **P** the son of Eleazar the
22:32 And **P** the son of Eleazar the
24:33 him in a hill belonging to **P**
Judg 20:28 and **P** the son of Eleazar, the
1 Sam 1: 3 two sons of Eli, Hophni and **P**,
2:34 your two sons, on Hophni and **P**:
4: 4 two sons of Eli, Hophni and **P**,
4:11 two sons of Eli, Hophni and **P**,
4:17 your two sons, Hophni and **P**,
14: 3 Ichabod's brother, the son of **P**,
1 Chr 6: 4 Eleazar begot **P**, and Phinehas
6: 4 and **P** begot Abishua;
6:50 **P** his son, Abishua his son,
9:20 And **P** the son of Eleazar had
Ezra 7: 5 son of Abishua, the son of **P**,
8: 2 of the sons of **P**, Gershom;
8:33 him was Eleazar the son of **P**;
Ps 106:30 Then **P** stood up and intervened,

PHINEHAS' (1/1)

1 Sam 4:19 **P** wife, was with child, due to

PHLEGON (1/1)

Rom 16:14 Greet Asyncritus, **P**,

PHOEBE (1/1)

Rom 16: 1 I commend to you **P** our sister,

PHOENICIA (3/3)

Acts 11:19 Stephen traveled as far as **P**,
15: 3 they passed through **P** and
21: 2 a ship sailing over to **P**,

PHOENIX (1/1)

Acts 27:12 by any means they could reach **P**,

PHRYGIA (3/3)

Acts 2:10 **P** and Pamphylia, Egypt and the
16: 6 when they had gone through **P**
18:23 the region of Galatia and **P** in

PHURAH (KJV) See PURAH

PHUT (KJV) See PUT

PHUVAH (KJV) See PUVAH

PHYGELLUS (1/1)

2 Tim 1:15 among whom are **P** and

PHYLACTERIES (1/1)

Mt 23: 5 They make their **p** broad and

PHYSICAL (1/1) PHYSICALLY

Gal 4:13 You know that because of **p**

PHYSICALLY (1/1)

Rom 2:27 And will not the **p**

PHYSICIAN (6/6) PHYSICIANS

Jer 8:22 Is there no **p** there?
Mt 9:12 are well have no need of a **p**,
Mk 2:17 are well have no need of a **p**,
Lk 4:23 say this proverb to Me, '**P**,
5:31 are well have no need of a **p**,
Col 4:14 Luke the beloved **p** and Demas

PHYSICIANS (6/5) PHYSICIAN

Gen 50: 2 commanded his servants the **p**
50: 2 So the **p** embalmed Israel.
2 Chr 16:12 not seek the LORD, but the **p**.
Job 13: 4 lies, You are all worthless **p**.
Mk 5:26 many things from many **p**.
Lk 8:43 spent all her livelihood on **p**

PI BESETH (1/1)

Ezek 30:17 men of Aven and **P** shall fall

PI HAHIROTH (3/3)

Ex 14: 2 turn and camp before **P**
Ex 14: 9 camping by the sea beside **P**
Num 33: 7 turned back to **P**, which is east

PI-BESETH (KJV) See PI BESETH

PICK (8/8) PICKED

Ex 12:21 **P** out and take lambs for
Num 16:37 to **p** up the censers out of the
Josh 18: 4 **P** out from among you three men
2 Ki 4:36 he said, "**P** up your son."
6: 7 **P** it up for yourself." So he
9:25 **P** him up, and throw him into
Prov 30:17 ravens of the valley will **p** it
Jon 1:12 **P** me up and throw me into the

PICKED (3/3) PICK

2 Ki 4:37 then she **p** up her son and went
Ezek 29: 5 You shall not be **p** up or
Jon 1:15 So they **p** up Jonah and threw him

PICKS (3/3)

2 Sam 12:31 to work with saws and iron **p**
1 Chr 20: 3 to work with saws, with iron **p**,
Am 6:10 **p** up the bodies to take them

PICTURE (1/1)

Mk 4:30 Or with what parable shall we **p**

PIECE (49/43) PIECES

Gen 15:10 and placed each **p** opposite the
Ex 25:19 the two ends of it of one **p**
25:31 flowers shall be of one **p**.
25:36 branches shall be of one **p**;
25:36 of it shall be one hammered **p**
27: 2 its horns shall be of one **p**
30: 2 Its horns shall be of one **p**
37: 7 he made them of one **p** at the
37: 8 at the two ends of one **p**
37:17 its flowers were of the same **p**.
37:22 their branches were of one **p**;
37:22 all of it was one hammered **p**
37:25 Its horns were of one **p** with
38: 2 the horns were of one **p** with
Ruth 2:14 and dip your **p** of bread in the
4: 3 sold the **p** of land which
1 Sam 2:36 and bow down to him for a **p**
2:36 that I may eat a **p** of bread."
28:22 and let me set a **p** of bread
30:12 And they gave him a **p** of a cake
2 Sam 6:19 a **p** of meat, and a cake of
11:21 it not a woman who cast a **p** of
23:11 a troop where there was a **p** of
2 Ki 3:19 and ruin every good **p** of land
3:25 threw a stone on every good **p**
1 Chr 11:13 and there was a **p** of ground
16: 3 a **p** of meat, and a cake of
Job 42:11 Each one gave him a **p** of silver
Prov 28:21 Because for a **p** of bread a man
Song 4: 3 your veil Are like a **p** of
6: 7 Like a **p** of pomegranate Are
Jer 37:21 they should give him daily a **p**
Ezek 24: 4 of meat in it, Every good **p**,
24: 6 gone from it! Bring it out **p**
24: 6 Bring it out piece by **p**,
Am 3:12 of a lion Two legs or a **p** of
Mt 9:16 No one puts a **p** of unshrunk
17:27 you will find a **p** of money;
Mk 2:21 No one sews a **p** of unshrunk
2:21 or else the new **p** pulls away
Lk 5:36 No one puts a **p** from a new
5:36 and also the **p** that was taken
14:18 I have bought a **p** of ground, and
15: 9 for I have found the **p** which I
24:42 So they gave Him a **p** of a
Jn 13:26 is he to whom I shall give a **p**
13:27 Now after the **p** of bread, Satan
13:30 Having received the **p** of bread,
19:23 woven from the top in one **p**.

PIECES (118/107) PIECE

Gen 15:17 that passed between those **p**.
20:16 your brother a thousand **p** of
33:19 for one hundred **p** of money.
37:33 doubt Joseph is torn to **p**.
44:28 Surely he is torn to **p**"; and I
45:22 he gave three hundred **p** of
Ex 15: 6 has dashed the enemy in **p**.
22:13 If it is torn to **p** by a
29:17 you shall cut the ram in **p**,
29:17 and put them with its **p** and
Lev 1: 6 offering and cut it into its **p**.
1:12 'And he shall cut it into its **p**,
2: 6 You shall break it in **p** and pour
6:21 The baked **p** of the grain
8:20 And he cut the ram into **p**;
8:20 Moses burned the head, the **p**,
9:13 with its **p** and head, and he
Deut 32:26 said, "I will dash them in **p**,
Josh 24:32 of Shechem for one hundred **p**
Judg 5:30 Two **p** of dyed embroidery for
16: 5 give you eleven hundred **p** of
19:29 and divided her into twelve **p**,
20: 6 of my concubine, cut her in **p**,
1 Sam 2:10 the LORD shall be broken in **p**;
11: 7 yoke of oxen and cut them in **p**,
15:33 And Samuel hacked Agag in **p**
1 Ki 11:30 him, and tore it into twelve **p**.
11:31 "Take for yourself ten **p**,
18:23 for themselves, cut it in **p**,
18:33 in order, cut the bull in **p**,
19:11 and broke the rocks in **p**
2 Ki 2:12 and tore them into two **p**.
11:18 They thoroughly broke in **p** its
18: 4 the wooden image and broke in **p**
23:14 And he broke in **p** the sacred
24:13 and he cut in **p** all the
25:13 LORD, the Chaldeans broke in **p**,
2 Chr 23:17 They broke in **p** its altars and
25:12 that they all were dashed in **p**.
28:24 cut in **p** the articles of the
31: 1 broke the sacred pillars in **p**,
34: 4 the molded images he broke in **p**,
Job 4:20 They are broken in **p** from
16:12 by my neck, and shaken me to **p**;
19: 2 And break me in **p** with words?
34:24 He breaks in **p** mighty men
Ps 2: 3 Let us break Their bonds in **p**
2: 9 You shall dash them to **p** like
7: 2 like a lion, Rending me in **p**,
50:22 God, Lest I tear you in **p**,
58: 7 his arrows be as if cut in **p**.
68:30 submits himself with **p** of
72: 4 And will break in **p** the
74:14 the heads of Leviathan in **p**,
89:10 You have broken Rahab in **p**,
94: 5 They break in **p** Your people,
107:14 And broke their chains in **p**.
129: 4 He has cut in **p** the cords of
Isa 8: 9 and be broken in **p**! Give ear,
8: 9 yourselves, but be broken in **p**;
8: 9 yourselves, but be broken in **p**.
13:16 also will be dashed to **p**
13:18 will dash the young men to **p**,
25: 6 all people A feast of choice **p**,
30:14 vessel, Which is broken in **p**;
45: 2 I will break in **p** the gates of
Jer 5: 6 from there shall be torn in **p**,
23:29 that breaks the rock in **p**?
50: 2 Merodach is broken in **p**;
50: 2 Her images are broken in **p**.
51:20 I will break the nation in **p**;
51:21 With you I will break in **p** the
51:21 With you I will break in **p** the
51:22 you also I will break in **p** man
51:22 With you I will break in **p** old
51:22 With you I will break in **p** the
51:23 you also I will break in **p** the
51:23 With you I will break in **p** the
51:23 And with you I will break in **p**
52:17 LORD, the Chaldeans broke in **p**,
Lam 3:11 aside my ways and torn me in **p**;
Ezek 13:19 handfuls of barley and for **p**
24: 4 Gather **p** of meat in it,
Dan 2: 5 you shall be cut in **p**,
2:34 and clay, and broke them in **p**.
2:40 inasmuch as iron breaks in **p**
2:40 that kingdom will break in **p**
2:44 it shall break in **p** and consume
2:45 and that it broke in **p** the
3:29 and Abed-Nego shall be cut in **p**,
6:24 and broke all their bones in **p**
7: 7 it was devouring, breaking in **p**,
7:19 which devoured, broke in **p**,
7:23 Trample it and break it in **p**.
Hos 8: 6 of Samaria shall be broken to **p**.
10:14 A mother dashed in **p** upon her
13:16 infants shall be dashed in **p**,
Am 6:11 And the little house into **p**.
Mic 1: 7 images shall be beaten to **p**,
3: 3 And chop them in **p** Like
4:13 You shall beat in **p** many
5: 8 treads down and tears in **p**,
Nah 2:12 The lion tore in **p** enough for
3:10 children also were dashed to **p**
Zech 11:12 out for my wages thirty **p** of
11:13 So I took the thirty **p** of
11:16 fat and tear their hooves in **p**.
12: 3 it away will surely be cut in **p**,
Mt 7: 6 and turn and tear you in **p**.
26:15 counted out to him thirty **p** of
27: 3 and brought back the thirty **p**
27: 5 Then he threw down the **p** of
27: 6 priests took the silver **p** and
27: 9 they took the thirty **p**
Mk 5: 4 and the shackles broken in **p**;
Acts 19:19 it totaled fifty thousand **p**
23:10 lest Paul might be pulled to **p**
Rev 2:27 shall be dashed to **p**

P

PIERCE (9/9) PIERCED, PIERCING

Ex 21: 6 and his master shall **p** his ear
Num 24: 8 break their bones And **p** them
2 Ki 18:21 go into his hand and **p** it.
Job 20:24 A bronze bow will **p** him
41: 2 Or **p** his jaw with a hook?
Ps 38: 2 For Your arrows **p** me deeply,
Isa 36: 6 go into his hand and **p** it.
Lam 3:13 His quiver To **p** my loins.
Lk 2:35 a sword will **p** through your own

PIERCED (9/9) PIERCE

Judg 5:26 she **p** his head, She split and
Job 26:13 His hand **p** the fleeing
30:17 My bones are **p** in me at night,
Ps 22:16 They **p** My hands and My feet;
Zech 12:10 will look on Me whom they **p**.
Jn 19:34 But one of the soldiers **p** His
19:37 look on Him whom they **p**.
1 Tim 6:10 and **p** themselves through with
Rev 1: 7 even they who **p** Him. And all

PIERCES (2/2)

Job 16:13 He **p** my heart and does not
40:24 Or one **p** his nose with a

PIERCING (1/1) PIERCE

Heb 4:12 **p** even to the division of soul

PIERCINGS (1/1)

Prov 12:18 is one who speaks like the **p**

PIETY (1/1)

1 Tim 5: 4 let them first learn to show **p**

PIGEON (2/2) PIGEONS

Gen 15: 9 a turtledove, and a young **p**.
Lev 12: 6 and a young **p** or a turtledove

PIGEONS (10/10) PIGEON

Lev 1:14 of turtledoves or young **p**.
5: 7 two turtledoves or two young **p**:
5:11 two turtledoves or two young **p**,
12: 8 two turtledoves or two young **p**—
14:22 two turtledoves or two young **p**,
14:30 of the turtledoves or young **p**,
15:14 two turtledoves or two young **p**,
15:29 two turtledoves or two young **p**,
Num 6:10 two turtledoves or two young **p**
Lk 2:24 turtledoves or two young **p**.

PILATE (56/54) PONTIUS

Mt 27: 2 and delivered Him to Pontius **P** the
27:13 Then **P** said to Him, "Do You not
27:17 **P** said to them, "Whom do you
27:22 **P** said to them, "What then
27:24 When **P** saw that he could not
27:58 This man went to **P** and asked for
27:58 Then **P** commanded the body to be
27:62 gathered together to **P**,
27:65 **P** said to them, "You have a
Mk 15: 1 away, and delivered Him to **P**.
15: 2 Then **P** asked Him, "Are You the
15: 4 Then **P** asked Him again, saying,
15: 5 so that **P** marveled.
15: 9 But **P** answered them, saying,
15:12 **P** answered and said to them
15:14 Then **P** said to them, "Why, what
15:15 So **P**, wanting to gratify the
15:43 went in to **P** and asked for the
15:44 **P** marveled that He was already
Lk 3: 1 Pontius **P** being governor of
13: 1 the Galileans whose blood **P**
23: 1 of them arose and led Him to **P**.
23: 3 Then **P** asked Him, saying, "Are
23: 4 So **P** said to the chief priests
23: 6 When **P** heard of Galilee, he
23:11 robe, and sent Him back to **P**.
23:12 That very day **P** and Herod became
23:13 Then **P**, when he had called
23:20 **P**, therefore, wishing to
23:24 So **P** gave sentence that it
23:52 This man went to **P** and asked for
Jn 18:29 **P** then went out to them and
18:31 Then **P** said to them, "You take
18:33 Then **P** entered the Praetorium
18:35 **P** answered, "Am I a Jew?
18:37 **P** therefore said to Him, "Are
18:38 **P** said to Him, "What is
19: 1 So then **P** took Jesus and
19: 4 **P** then went out again, and said
19: 5 And **P** said to them, "Behold
19: 6 crucify Him!" **P** said to them,
19: 8 when **P** heard that saying, he
19:10 Then **P** said to Him, "Are You
19:12 From then on **P** sought to release
19:13 When **P** therefore heard that
19:15 **P** said to them, "Shall I
19:19 Now **P** wrote a title and put it
19:21 priests of the Jews said to **P**,
19:22 **P** answered, "What I have
19:31 the Jews asked **P** that their
19:38 asked **P** that he might take away
19:38 and **P** gave him permission.
Acts 3:13 and denied in the presence of **P**,
4:27 both Herod and Pontius **P**,
13:28 they asked **P** that He should be
1 Tim 6:13 confession before Pontius **P**,

PILDASH (1/1)

Gen 22:22 "Chesed, Hazo, **P**,

PILE (2/2)

Job 27:17 He may **p** it up, but the just
Ezek 24: 5 Also **p** fuel bones under it,

PILEHA (KJV) See PILHA

PILES (1/1)

Job 27:16 And **p** up clothing like clay—

PILFERING (1/1)

Titus 2:10 not **p**, but showing all good

PILGRIM (1/1)

Ps 42: 4 With a multitude that kept a **p**

PILGRIMAGE (5/4) PILGRIMS

Gen 47: 9 The days of the years of my **p**
47: 9 fathers in the days of their **p**.
Ex 6: 4 of Canaan, the land of their **p**,
Ps 84: 5 You, Whose heart is set on **p**.
119:54 my songs In the house of my **p**.

PILGRIMS (4/4) PILGRIMAGE

1 Chr 29:15 For we are aliens and **p** before
Heb 11:13 that they were strangers and **p**
1 Pe 1: 1 To the **p** of the Dispersion in
2:11 I beg you as sojourners and **p**,

PILHA (1/1)

Neh 10:24 Hallohesh, **P**, Shobek,

PILLAGE (3/3)

Ezek 26:12 will plunder your riches and **p**
29:19 off her spoil, and remove her **p**;
39:10 and **p** those who pillaged

PILLAGED (1/1)

Ezek 39:10 and pillage those who **p** them,"

PILLAR (51/39) PILLARS

Gen 19:26 and she became a **p** of salt.
28:18 at his head, set it up as a **p**,
28:22 stone which I have set as a **p**
31:13 where you anointed the **p** and
31:45 a stone and set it up as a **p**.
31:51 this heap and here is this **p**,
31:52 and this **p** is a witness, that
31:52 beyond this heap and this **p** to
35:14 So Jacob set up a **p** in the place
35:14 a **p** of stone; and he poured a
35:20 And Jacob set a **p** on her grave,
35:20 which is the **p** of Rachel's
Ex 13:21 went before them by day in a **p**
13:21 and by night in a **p** of fire to
13:22 He did not take away the **p** of
13:22 of cloud by day or the **p** of
14:19 and the **p** of cloud went from
14:24 of the Egyptians through the **p**
33: 9 that the **p** of cloud descended
33:10 All the people saw the **p** of
Lev 26: 1 a carved image nor a sacred **p**
Num 12: 5 the LORD came down in the **p**
14:14 and You go before them in a **p**
14:14 of cloud by day and in a **p** of
Deut 16:22 shall not set up a sacred **p**,
31:15 at the tabernacle in a **p** of
31:15 and the **p** of cloud stood above
Judg 9: 6 the terebinth tree at the **p**
2 Sam 18:18 had taken and set up a **p** for
18:18 He called the **p** after his own
1 Ki 7:21 he set up the **p** on the right
7:21 and he set up the **p** on the left
2 Ki 3: 2 for he put away the sacred **p**
10:27 they broke down the sacred **p**
11:14 was the king standing by a **p**
23: 3 Then the king stood by a **p** and
25:17 The height of one **p** was
25:17 The second **p** was the same, with
2 Chr 23:13 was the king standing by his **p**
Neh 9:12 led them by day with a cloudy **p**,
9:12 And by night with a **p** of fire,
9:19 The **p** of the cloud did not
9:19 Nor the **p** of fire by night,
Ps 99: 7 spoke to them in the cloudy **p**;
Isa 19:19 and a **p** to the LORD at its
Jer 1:18 A fortified city and an iron **p**,
52:21 the height of one **p** was
52:22 all of bronze. The second **p**,
Hos 3: 4 without sacrifice or sacred **p**,
1 Tim 3:15 the **p** and ground of the truth.
Rev 3:12 I will make him a **p** in the

PILLARS (105/90) PILLAR

Ex 23:24 break down their sacred **p**.
24: 4 and twelve **p** according to the
26:32 shall hang it upon the four **p**
26:37 make for the screen five **p** of
27:10 And its twenty **p** and their
27:10 The hooks of the **p** and their
27:11 with its twenty **p** and their
27:11 and the hooks of the **p** and
27:12 with their ten **p** and their ten
27:14 with their three **p** and their
27:15 with their three **p** and their
27:16 It shall have four **p** and four
27:17 All the **p** around the court shall
34:13 altars, break their sacred **p**,
35:11 its boards, its bars, its **p**,
35:17 hangings of the court, its **p**,
36:36 He made for it four **p** of acacia
36:38 and its five **p** with their hooks.
38:10 There were twenty **p** for them,
38:10 The hooks of the **p** and their
38:11 with twenty **p** and their twenty
38:11 The hooks of the **p** and their
38:12 with ten **p** and their ten
38:12 The hooks of the **p** and their
38:14 with their three **p** and their
38:15 with their three **p** and their
38:17 The sockets for the **p** were
38:17 the hooks of the **p** and their
38:17 and all the **p** of the court had
38:19 And there were four **p** with
38:28 he made hooks for the **p**,
39:33 its boards, its bars, its **p**,
39:40 its **p** and its sockets, the
40:18 its bars, and raised up its **p**.
Num 3:36 the tabernacle, its bars, its **p**,
3:37 and the **p** of the court all
4:31 the tabernacle, its bars, its **p**,
4:32 and the **p** around the court with
Deut 7: 5 and break down their sacred **p**,
12: 3 altars, break their sacred **p**,
Judg 16:25 stationed him between the **p**.
16:26 Let me feel the **p** which support
16:29 took hold of the two middle **p**
1 Sam 2: 8 For the **p** of the earth are the
1 Ki 7: 2 with four rows of cedar **p**,
7: 2 and cedar beams on the **p**.
7: 3 that were on forty-five **p**,
7: 6 He also made the Hall of **P**:
7: 6 of them was a portico with **p**,
7:15 And he cast two **p** of bronze,
7:16 to set on the tops of the **p**.
7:17 which were on top of the **p**:
7:18 So he made the **p**, and two
7:19 which were on top of the **p** in
7:20 The capitals on the two **p** also
7:21 Then he set up the **p** by the
7:22 The tops of the **p** were in the
7:22 So the work of the **p** was
7:41 the two **p**, the two
7:41 that were on top of the two **p**;
7:41 which were on top of the **p**;
7:42 that were on top of the **p**);
14:23 high places, sacred **p**,
2 Ki 10:26 And they brought the sacred **p**
17:10 set up for themselves sacred **p**
18: 4 places and broke the sacred **p**,
18:16 and from the **p** which Hezekiah
23:14 broke in pieces the sacred **p**
25:13 The bronze **p** that were in the
25:16 The two **p**, one Sea,
1 Chr 18: 8 made the bronze Sea, the **p**,
2 Chr 3:15 in front of the temple two **p**
3:16 and put them on top of the **p**;
3:17 Then he set up the **p** before the
4:12 the two **p** and the bowl-shaped
4:12 that were on top of the two **p**;
4:12 which were on top of the **p**;
4:13 capitals that were on the **p**);
14: 3 and broke down the sacred **p**
31: 1 of Judah and broke the sacred **p**
Esth 1: 6 on silver rods and marble **p**;
Job 9: 6 And its **p** tremble;
26:11 The **p** of heaven tremble, And
Ps 75: 3 I set up its **p** firmly. Selah
144:12 our daughters may be as **p**,
Prov 9: 1 She has hewn out her seven **p**;
Song 3: 6 out of the wilderness Like **p**
3:10 He made its **p** of silver,
5:15 His legs are **p** of marble
Jer 27:19 LORD of hosts concerning the **p**,
43:13 shall also break the sacred **p**
52:17 The bronze **p** that were in the
52:20 The two **p**, one Sea,
52:21 Now concerning the **p**:
Ezek 26:11 and your strong **p** will fall to
40:49 led up to it there were **p** by
42: 6 stories and did not have **p**
42: 6 not have pillars like the **p** of
Hos 10: 1 have embellished his sacred **p**.
10: 2 He will ruin their sacred **p**.
Joel 2:30 Blood and fire and **p** of smoke.
Mic 5:13 And your sacred **p** from your
Zeph 2:14 on the capitals of her **p**;
Gal 2: 9 and John, who seemed to be **p**,
Rev 10: 1 and his feet like **p** of fire.

PILLED (KJV) See PEELED

PILLOW (1/1)

Mk 4:38 was in the stern, asleep on a **p**.

PILOT (1/1)

Jas 3: 4 small rudder wherever the ***p***

PILOTS (4/4)

Ezek 27: 8 in you; They became your ***p***.
27:27 Your mariners and ***p***,
27:28 the sound of the cry of your ***p***.
27:29 All the ***p*** of the sea Will

PILTAI (1/1)

Neh 12:17 son of Minjamin; of Moadiah, ***P***;

PIM (1/1)

1 Sam 13:21 for a sharpening was a ***p*** for

PIN (2/2)

1 Sam 18:11 I will ***p*** David to the wall!"
19:10 Then Saul sought to ***p*** David to

PINE (6/6)

Isa 41:19 the cypress tree and the ***p***
44:14 of the forest. He plants a ***p***,
60:13 to you, The cypress, the ***p***,
Lam 4: 9 For these ***p*** away, Stricken
Ezek 24:23 but you shall ***p*** away in your
33:10 and we ***p*** away in them, how can

PINED (1/1)

Mic 1:12 the inhabitant of Maroth ***p*** for

PINIONS (2/2)

Job 39:13 But are her wings and ***p*** like
Ezek 17: 3 with large wings and long ***p***,

PINNACLE (2/2)

Mt 4: 5 set Him on the ***p*** of the temple,
Lk 4: 9 set Him on the ***p*** of the temple,

PINNACLES (1/1)

Isa 54:12 I will make your ***p*** of rubies,

PINON (2/2)

Gen 36:41 Aholibamah, Chief Elah, Chief ***P***,
1 Chr 1:52 Aholibamah, Chief Elah, Chief ***P***,

PINS (1/1)

1 Ki 7:33 a chariot wheel; their axle ***p***,

PIPED (1/1)

1 Cor 14: 7 how will it be known what is ***p***

PIPES (3/3)

Ezek 28:13 of your timbrels and ***p*** Was
Zech 4: 2 seven lamps with seven ***p*** to
4:12 receptacles of the two gold ***p***

PIPINGS (1/1)

Judg 5:16 To hear the ***p*** for the flocks?

PIRAM (1/1)

Josh 10: 3 ***P*** king of Jarmuth, Japhia king

PIRATHON (1/1)

Judg 12:15 died and was buried in ***P*** in

PIRATHONITE (5/5)

Judg 12:13 Abdon the son of Hillel the ***P***
12:15 Abdon the son of Hillel the ***P***
2 Sam 23:30 Benaiah a ***P***, Hiddai from
1 Chr 11:31 sons of Benjamin, Benaiah the ***P***,
27:14 month was Benaiah the ***P***,

PISGAH (8/8) NEBO

Num 21:20 to the top of ***P*** which looks
23:14 of Zophim, to the top of ***P***,
Deut 3:17 below the slopes of ***P***.
3:27 'Go up to the top of ***P***,
4:49 Arabah, below the slopes of ***P***.
34: 1 to Mount Nebo, to the top of ***P***,
Josh 12: 3 southward below the slopes of ***P***.
13:20 Beth Peor, the slopes of ***P***,

PISHON (1/1)

Gen 2:11 The name of the first is ***P***;

PISIDIA (2/2)

Acts 13:14 they came to Antioch in ***P***,
14:24 after they had passed through ***P***,

PISON (KJV) See PISHON

PISPAH (1/1)

1 Chr 7:38 of Jether were Jephunneh, ***P***,

PISS (KJV) See WASTE

PISSETH (KJV) See MALE, MALES

PISTACHIO (1/1)

Gen 43:11 ***p*** nuts and almonds.

PIT (89/81) PITS

Gen 37:20 him and cast him into some ***p***;
37:22 but cast him into this ***p*** which
37:24 took him and cast him into a ***p***.
37:24 And the ***p*** was empty;
37:28 up and lifted him out of the ***p***,
37:29 Then Reuben returned to the ***p***,
37:29 indeed Joseph was not in the ***p***;
Ex 21:33 "And if a man opens a ***p***,
21:33 or if a man digs a ***p*** and does
21:34 the owner of the ***p*** shall make
Num 16:30 they go down alive into the ***p***,
16:33 them went down alive into the ***p***;
2 Sam 17: 9 by now he is hidden in some ***p***,
18:17 and cast him into a large ***p*** in
23:20 a lion in the midst of a ***p*** on
1 Chr 11:22 a lion in the midst of a ***p*** on
Job 9:31 You will plunge me into the ***p***,
33:18 keeps back his soul from the ***P***,
33:22 Yes, his soul draws near the ***P***,
33:24 him from going down to the ***P***;
33:28 soul from going down to the ***P***,
33:30 bring back his soul from the ***P***,
Ps 7:15 He made a ***p*** and dug it out,
9:15 have sunk down in the ***p*** which
28: 1 like those who go down to the ***p***.
30: 3 I should not go down to the ***p***.
30: 9 blood, When I go down to the ***p***?
35: 7 hidden their net for me in a ***p***,
40: 2 me up out of a horrible ***p***,
49: 9 eternally, And not see the ***P***.
55:23 shall bring them down to the ***p***
57: 6 They have dug a ***p*** before me;
69:15 And let not the ***p*** shut its
88: 4 with those who go down to the ***p***;
88: 6 have laid me in the lowest ***p***,
94:13 Until the ***p*** is dug for the
143: 7 those who go down into the ***p***.
Prov 1:12 like those who go down to the ***P***;
22:14 an immoral woman is a deep ***p***;
23:27 For a harlot is a deep ***p***,
26:27 Whoever digs a ***p*** will fall into
28:10 will fall into his own ***p***;
28:17 bloodshed will flee into a ***p***;
Eccl 10: 8 He who digs a ***p*** will fall into
Isa 14:15 To the lowest depths of the ***P***.
14:19 go down to the stones of the ***p***,
24:17 Fear and the ***p*** and the snare
24:18 the fear Shall fall into the ***p***,
24:18 up from the midst of the ***p***
24:22 prisoners are gathered in the ***p***,
38:17 delivered my soul from the ***p***
38:18 Those who go down to the ***p***
51: 1 And to the hole of the ***p*** from
51:14 he should not die in the ***p***,
Jer 18:20 For they have dug a ***p*** for my
18:22 For they have dug a ***p*** to take
41: 7 them into the midst of a ***p***,
41: 9 Now the ***p*** into which Ishmael had
48:43 Fear and the ***p*** and the snare
48:44 the fear shall fall into the ***p***,
48:44 And he who gets out of the ***p***
Lam 3:53 silenced my life in the ***p*** And
3:55 O LORD, From the lowest ***p***.
Ezek 19: 4 him; He was trapped in their ***p***,
19: 8 him; He was trapped in their ***p***.
26:20 those who descend into the ***P***,
26:20 with those who go down to the ***P***,
28: 8 shall throw you down into the ***P***,
31:14 of men who go down to the ***P***.
31:16 those who descend into the ***P***;
32:18 those who go down to the ***P***:
32:23 set in the recesses of the ***P***,
32:24 with those who go down to the ***P***.
32:25 those who go down to the ***P***;
32:29 with those who go down to the ***P***.
32:30 with those who go down to the ***P***.
Jon 2: 6 brought up my life from the ***p***,
Zech 9:11 free from the waterless ***p***.
Mt 12:11 and if it falls into a ***p*** on the
Lk 14: 5 an ox that has fallen into a ***p***,
Rev 9: 1 the key to the bottomless ***p***.
9: 2 And he opened the bottomless ***p***,
9: 2 and smoke arose out of the ***p***
9: 2 because of the smoke of the ***p***.
9:11 the angel of the bottomless ***p***,
11: 7 out of the bottomless ***p*** will
17: 8 ascend out of the bottomless ***p***
20: 1 the key to the bottomless ***p***
20: 3 cast him into the bottomless ***p***,

PITCH (10/9) PITCHED

Gen 6:14 it inside and outside with ***p***.
Ex 2: 3 daubed it with asphalt and ***p***,
Num 1:52 children of Israel shall ***p***
9:17 the children of Israel would ***p***
Deut 1:33 out a place for you to ***p*** your
Isa 13:20 Nor will the Arabian ***p*** tents
34: 9 streams shall be turned into ***p***,
34: 9 land shall become burning ***p***.
Jer 6: 3 They shall ***p*** their tents
10:20 There is no one to ***p*** my tent

PITCHED (14/13) PITCH

Gen 12: 8 and he ***p*** his tent with Bethel
13:12 of the plain and ***p*** his tent
26:17 departed from there and ***p*** his
26:25 and he ***p*** his tent there;
31:25 Now Jacob had ***p*** his tent in the
31:25 with his brethren ***p*** in the
33:18 and he ***p*** his tent before the
33:19 where he had ***p*** his tent, from
35:21 Israel journeyed and ***p*** his tent
Ex 33: 7 Moses took his tent and ***p*** it
Judg 4:11 the Kenites and ***p*** his tent
2 Sam 16:22 So they ***p*** a tent for Absalom on
1 Chr 15: 1 and ***p*** a tent for it.
2 Chr 1: 4 for he had ***p*** a tent for it at

PITCHER (12/12) PITCHERS

Gen 24:14 Please let down your ***p*** that I
24:15 came out with her ***p*** on her
24:16 down to the well, filled her ***p***,
24:17 a little water from your ***p***.
24:18 Then she quickly let her ***p***
24:20 Then she quickly emptied her ***p***
24:43 me a little water from your ***p***
24:45 coming out with her ***p*** on her
24:46 she made haste and let her ***p***
Eccl 12: 6 Or the ***p*** shattered at the
Mk 14:13 man will meet you carrying a ***p***
Lk 22:10 man will meet you carrying a ***p***

PITCHERS (12/11) PITCHER

Ex 7:19 in buckets of wood and ***p***
25:29 its dishes, its pans, its ***p***,
37:16 and its ***p*** for pouring.
Num 4: 7 and the ***p*** for pouring; and the
Judg 7:16 every man's hand, with empty ***p***,
7:16 and torches inside the ***p***.
7:19 the trumpets and broke the ***p***
7:20 the trumpets and broke the ***p***—
1 Chr 28:17 the ***p*** of pure gold, and the
Isa 22:24 from the cups to all the ***p***.
Mk 7: 4 like the washing of cups, ***p***,
7: 8 the washing of ***p*** and cups, and

PITHOM (1/1)

Ex 1:11 supply cities, ***P*** and Raamses.

PITHON (2/2)

1 Chr 8:35 The sons of Micah were ***P***,
9:41 The sons of Micah were ***P***,

PITIABLE (1/1) PITY

1 Cor 15:19 we are of all men the most ***p***.

PITIED (6/6)

Ps 106:46 He also made them to be ***p***
Lam 2: 2 has swallowed up and has not ***p***
2:17 has thrown down and has not ***p***,
2:21 have slaughtered and not ***p***.
3:43 You have slain and not ***p***.
Ezek 16: 5 No eye ***p*** you, to do any of these

PITIES (2/1) PITY

Ps 103:13 As a father ***p*** his children,
103:13 So the LORD ***p*** those who fear

PITS (6/6) PIT

Gen 14:10 Siddim was full of asphalt ***p***;
1 Sam 13: 6 in rocks, in holes, and in ***p***.
Ps 119:85 The proud have dug ***p*** for me,
140:10 into the fire, Into deep ***p***,
Jer 2: 6 a land of deserts and ***p***,
Lam 4:20 LORD, Was caught in their ***p***,

PITY (33/32) PITIABLE, PITIES

Deut 7:16 your eye shall have no ***p*** on
13: 8 nor shall your eye ***p*** him, nor
19:13 Your eye shall not ***p*** him, but
19:21 "Your eye shall not ***p***:
25:12 your eye shall not ***p*** her.
Judg 2:18 for the LORD was moved to ***p*** by
2 Sam 12: 6 thing and because he had no ***p***.
Job 16:13 pierces my heart and does not ***p***;
19:21 Have ***p*** on me, have pity on me,
19:21 have ***p*** on me, O you my friends,
Ps 69:20 looked for someone to take ***p***,
Prov 19:17 He who has ***p*** on the poor lends
28: 8 Gathers it for him who will ***p***
Isa 13:18 And they will have no ***p*** on the
63: 9 In His love and in His ***p*** He
Jer 13:14 I will not ***p*** nor spare nor have
15: 5 For who will have ***p*** on you,
21: 7 or have ***p*** or mercy." '
Ezek 5:11 spare, nor will I have any ***p***.
7: 4 spare you, Nor will I have ***p***;
7: 9 not spare, Nor will I have ***p***;
8:18 not spare nor will I have ***p***;
9: 5 your eye spare, nor have any ***p***.
9:10 spare, nor will I have ***p***,
Hos 13:14 I will be your destruction! ***P***
Joel 2:18 And ***p*** His people.
Am 1:11 the sword, And cast off all ***p***;

P

Jon 4:10 You have had ***p*** on the plant for
4:11 And should I not ***p*** Nineveh, that
Hab 1:17 to slay nations without ***p***?
Zech 11: 5 and their shepherds do not ***p***
11: 6 For I will no longer ***p*** the
Mt 18:33 just as I had ***p*** on you?'

PLACE (845/798)

Gen 1: 9 be gathered together into one ***p***,
2:21 closed up the flesh in its ***p***.
8: 9 But the dove found no resting ***p***
10:30 And their dwelling ***p*** was from
12: 6 through the land to the ***p*** of
13: 3 to the ***p*** where his tent had
13: 4 to the ***p*** of the altar which he
13:14 eyes now and look from the ***p***
18:24 would You also destroy the ***p***
18:26 then I will spare all the ***p*** for
18:33 and Abraham returned to his ***p***.
19:12 take them out of this ***p***!
19:13 "For we will destroy this ***p***,
19:14 "Get up, get out of this ***p***;
19:27 early in the morning to the ***p***
20:11 fear of God is not in this ***p***;
20:13 should do for me: in every ***p***,
21:31 Therefore he called that ***p***
22: 3 and arose and went to the ***p*** of
22: 4 lifted his eyes and saw the ***p***
22: 9 Then they came to the ***p*** of
22:14 called the name of the ***p***,
23: 4 Give me property for a burial ***p***
23: 6 withhold from you his burial ***p***,
23: 9 as property for a burial ***p***
23:20 Heth as property for a burial ***p***.
24:31 and a ***p*** for the camels."
26: 7 And the men of the ***p*** asked about
26: 7 lest the men of the ***p*** kill me
28:11 So he came to a certain ***p*** and
28:11 one of the stones of that ***p***
28:11 and he lay down in that ***p*** to
28:16 "Surely the LORD is in this ***p***,
28:17 How awesome is this ***p***! This is
28:19 he called the name of that ***p***
29: 3 put the stone back in its ***p*** on
29:22 together all the men of the ***p***
30: 2 Am I in the ***p*** of God, who has
30:25 that I may go to my own ***p*** and
31:55 departed and returned to his ***p***.
32: 2 he called the name of that ***p***
32:30 Jacob called the name of the ***p***
33:17 Therefore the name of the ***p*** is
35: 7 an altar there and called the ***p***
35:13 God went up from him in the ***p***
35:14 Jacob set up a pillar in the ***p***
35:15 Jacob called the name of the ***p***
36:33 of Bozrah reigned in his ***p***.
36:34 the Temanites reigned in his ***p***.
36:35 field of Moab, reigned in his ***p***.
36:36 of Masrekah reigned in his ***p***.
36:37 reigned in his ***p***.
36:38 son of Achbor reigned in his ***p***.
36:39 died, Hadar reigned in his ***p***;
38:14 and sat in an open ***p*** which was
38:21 Then he asked the men of that ***p***,
38:21 was no harlot in this ***p***.
38:22 the men of the ***p*** said there was
38:22 there was no harlot in this ***p***.
39:20 a ***p*** where the king's prisoners
40: 3 the ***p*** where Joseph was
40:13 head and restore you to your ***p***,
42: 2 go down to that ***p*** and buy for
42:15 you shall not leave this ***p***
43:32 So they set him a ***p*** by himself,
47:30 and bury me in their burial ***p***.
48: 9 God has given me in this ***p***.
49: 5 are in their dwelling ***p***.
49:30 as a possession for a burial ***p***.
50:13 as property for a burial ***p***.
50:19 for am I in the ***p*** of God?
Ex 3: 5 said, "Do not draw near this ***p***.
3: 5 for the ***p*** where you stand is
3: 8 to the ***p*** of the Canaanites and
10:23 nor did anyone rise from his ***p***
13: 3 brought you out of this ***p***.
15:17 of Your inheritance, In the ***p***,
16:29 Let every man remain in his ***p***;
16:29 let no man go out of his ***p*** on
17: 7 So he called the name of the ***p***
18:21 and ***p*** such over them to be
18:23 people will also go to their ***p***
20:24 In every ***p*** where I record My
21:13 then I will appoint for you a ***p***
23:20 way and to bring you into the ***p***
26:33 for you between the holy ***p***
28:29 when he goes into the holy ***p***,
28:35 when he goes into the holy ***p***
28:43 to minister in the holy ***p***,
29:30 son who becomes priest in his ***p***
29:30 to minister in the holy ***p***.
29:31 boil its flesh in the holy ***p***.
30: 4 You shall ***p*** them on its two
31:11 sweet incense for the holy ***p***.
32:34 lead the people to the ***p*** of
33:21 Here is a ***p*** by Me, and you shall
35:19 for ministering in the holy ***p***—
38:24 in all the work of the holy ***p***,
39: 1 for ministering in the holy ***p***,
39:41 to minister in the holy ***p***:
Lev 1:16 into the ***p*** for ashes.
4:12 outside the camp to a clean ***p***,
4:24 and kill it at the ***p*** where they
4:29 kill the sin offering at the ***p***
4:33 it as a sin offering at the ***p***
6:11 outside the camp to a clean ***p***.
6:16 it shall be eaten in a holy ***p***;
6:22 sons, who is anointed in his ***p***,
6:25 In the ***p*** where the burnt
6:26 In a holy ***p*** it shall be eaten,
6:27 it was sprinkled, in a holy ***p***.
6:30 make atonement in the holy ***p***,
7: 2 In the ***p*** where they kill the
7: 6 It shall be eaten in a holy ***p***.
10:13 "You shall eat it in a holy ***p***,
10:14 you shall eat in a clean ***p***,
10:17 the sin offering in a holy ***p***,
10:18 not brought inside the holy ***p***;
10:18 have eaten it in a holy ***p***,
13:19 and in the ***p*** of the boil there
13:23 the bright spot stays in one ***p***,
13:28 the bright spot stays in one ***p***,
14:13 he shall kill the lamb in the ***p***
14:13 the burnt offering, in a holy ***p***;
14:28 on the ***p*** of the blood of the
14:40 cast them into an unclean ***p***
14:41 shall pour out in an unclean ***p***
14:42 stones and put them in the ***p***
14:45 the city to an unclean ***p***.
16: 2 just any time into the Holy ***P***
16: 3 shall come into the Holy ***P***:
16:16 make atonement for the Holy ***P***,
16:17 make atonement in the Holy ***P***,
16:20 end of atoning for the Holy ***P***,
16:23 when he went into the Holy ***P***,
16:24 his body with water in a holy ***p***,
16:27 make atonement in the Holy ***P***,
16:32 as priest in his father's ***p***,
21: 5 shall not make any bald ***p*** on
24: 9 they shall eat it in a holy ***p***;
Num 2:17 move out, everyone in his ***p***,
9:17 and in the ***p*** where the cloud
10:29 We are setting out for the ***p*** of
10:33 to search out a resting ***p*** for
11: 3 So he called the name of the ***p***
11:34 So he called the name of that ***p***
13:24 The ***p*** was called the Valley of
14:40 and we will go up to the ***p***
17: 4 Then you shall ***p*** them in the
18:10 In a most holy ***p*** you shall eat
18:31 'You may eat it in any ***p***,
19: 9 outside the camp in a clean ***p***;
20: 5 to bring us to this evil ***p***?
20: 5 It is not a ***p*** of grain or figs
21: 3 So the name of that ***p*** was
22:26 and stood in a narrow ***p*** where
23:13 come with me to another ***p*** from
23:27 I will take you to another ***p***;
24:11 "Now therefore, flee to your ***p***.
24:21 "Firm is your dwelling ***p***,
24:25 departed and returned to his ***p***;
28: 7 in a holy ***p*** you shall pour out
32: 1 indeed the region was a ***p*** for
32:14 have risen in your father's ***p***,
32:17 we have brought them to their ***p***;
Deut 1:31 went until you came to this ***p***.
1:33 before you to search out a ***p***
2:12 them, and dwelt in their ***p***,
2:21 them and dwelt in their ***p***,
2:22 them and dwelt in their ***p***,
2:23 them and dwelt in their ***p***.
9: 7 Egypt until you came to this ***p***,
11: 5 until you came to this ***p***;
11:24 Every ***p*** on which the sole of
12: 3 destroy their names from that ***p***.
12: 5 But you shall seek the ***p*** where
12: 5 put His name for His dwelling ***p***;
12:11 then there will be the ***p*** where
12:13 your burnt offerings in every ***p***
12:14 but in the ***p*** which the LORD
12:18 the LORD your God in the ***p***
12:21 If the ***p*** where the LORD your
12:26 you shall take and go to the ***p***
14:23 in the ***p*** where He chooses to
14:24 or if the ***p*** where the LORD
14:25 and go to the ***p*** which the LORD
15:20 your God year by year in the ***p***
16: 2 in the ***p*** where the LORD
16: 6 but at the ***p*** where the LORD
16: 7 roast and eat it in the ***p***
16:11 at the ***p*** where the LORD your
16:15 to the LORD your God in the ***p***
16:16 the LORD your God in the ***p***
17: 8 shall arise and go up to the ***p***
17:10 pronounce upon you in that ***p***
18: 6 the desire of his mind to the ***p***
23:12 Also you shall have a ***p*** outside
23:16 in the ***p*** which he chooses
26: 2 it in a basket and go to the ***p***
26: 9 He has brought us to this ***p*** and
28:65 of your foot have a resting ***p***;
29: 7 "And when you came to this ***p***,
31:11 the LORD your God in the ***p***
32: 9 Jacob is the ***p*** of His
Josh 1: 3 Every ***p*** that the sole of your
3: 3 you shall set out from your ***p***
4: 3 from the ***p*** where the priests'
4: 3 and leave them in the lodging ***p***
4: 8 them over with them to the ***p***
4: 9 in the ***p*** where the feet of the
4:18 the Jordan returned to their ***p***
5: 7 whom He raised up in their ***p***;
5: 9 Therefore the name of the ***p***
5:15 for the ***p*** where you stand is
7:26 Therefore the name of that ***p***
8:14 at an appointed ***p*** before the
8:19 arose quickly out of their ***p***;
9:27 in the ***p*** which He would choose,
17:15 forest country and clear a ***p***
20: 4 one of them, and give him a ***p***,
Judg 2: 5 they called the name of that ***p***
7: 7 people go, every man to his ***p***.
7:21 And every man stood in his ***p*** all
9:55 departed, every man to his ***p***.
11:19 through your land into our ***p***.
15:17 and called that ***p*** Ramath Lehi.
15:19 So God split the hollow ***p*** that
16: 2 they surrounded the ***p*** and
17: 8 wherever he could find a ***p***.
17: 9 I am on my way to find a ***p***
18: 3 What are you doing in this ***p***?
18:10 a ***p*** where there is no lack of
18:12 (Therefore they call that ***p***
18:20 and took his ***p*** among the
19:16 whereas the men of the ***p*** were
19:28 man got up and went to his ***p***.
20:22 the battle line at the ***p*** where
20:33 men of Israel rose from their ***p***
Ruth 1: 7 she went out from the ***p*** where
3: 4 that you shall notice the ***p***
1 Sam 2:29 commanded in My dwelling ***p***,
2:32 see an enemy in My dwelling ***p***,
3: 2 Eli was lying down in his ***p***,
3: 9 went and lay down in his ***p***.
5: 3 took Dagon and set it in its ***p***
5:11 and let it go back to its own ***p***,
6: 2 how we should send it to its ***p***.
9:12 the people today on the high ***p***.
9:13 he goes up to the high ***p*** to
9:14 on his way up to the high ***p***.
9:19 Go up before me to the high ***p***,
9:22 and had them sit in the ***p*** of
9:25 had come down from the high ***p***
10: 5 coming down from the high ***p***
10:13 he went to the high ***p***.
12: 8 and made them dwell in this ***p***.
14: 9 we will stand still in our ***p***
14:46 Philistines went to their own ***p***.
19: 2 and stay in a secret ***p*** and
20:19 down quickly and come to the ***p***
20:25 but David's ***p*** was empty.
20:27 that David's ***p*** was empty.
20:37 When the lad had come to the ***p***
20:41 David arose from a ***p*** toward
21: 2 young men to such and such a ***p***.
21: 6 to put hot bread in its ***p***
23:22 and see the ***p*** where his hideout
23:28 so they called that ***p*** the Rock
26: 5 David arose and came to the ***p***
26: 5 And David saw the ***p*** where Saul
26:25 way, and Saul returned to his ***p***.
27: 5 let them give me a ***p*** in some
29: 4 that he may go back to the ***p***
2 Sam 2:16 Therefore that ***p*** was called the
2:23 that as many as came to the ***p***
5:20 he called the name of that ***p***
6: 8 and he called the name of the ***p***
6:17 and set it in its ***p*** in the
7:10 Moreover I will appoint a ***p*** for
7:10 that they may dwell in a ***p*** of
10: 1 Hanun his son reigned in his ***p***.
11:16 that he assigned Uriah to a ***p***
15:19 also an exile from your own ***p***.
15:21 surely in whatever ***p*** my lord
15:25 me both it and His dwelling ***p***.
16: 8 in whose ***p*** you have reigned;
17: 9 some pit, or in some other ***p***.
17:12 we will come upon him in some ***p***
18: 7 of twenty thousand took ***p***
18:33 —if only I had died in your ***p***!
19:13 before me continually in ***p*** of
19:39 and he returned to his own ***p***.
22:20 brought me out into a broad ***p***;
23: 7 burned with fire in their ***p***.
1 Ki 1:30 shall sit on my throne in my ***p***,
1:35 and he shall be king in my ***p***.
2:35 the son of Jehoiada in his ***p***
2:35 put Zadok the priest in the ***p***
3: 4 for that was the great high ***p***:
4:28 and straw to the proper ***p***,
5: 1 had anointed him king in ***p*** of
5: 5 set on your throne in your ***p***,
5: 9 them in rafts by sea to the ***p***
6:16 sanctuary, as the Most Holy ***P***.
7:50 inner room (the Most Holy ***P***)
8: 6 covenant of the LORD to its ***p***,
8: 6 the temple, to the Most Holy ***P***,
8: 7 their two wings over the ***p*** of
8: 8 could be seen from the holy ***p***,
8:10 priests came out of the holy ***p***,
8:13 And a ***p*** for You to dwell in
8:21 And there I have made a ***p*** for
8:29 toward the ***p*** of which You said,
8:29 servant makes toward this ***p***.
8:30 when they pray toward this ***p***.
8:30 Hear in heaven Your dwelling ***p***;
8:35 when they pray toward this ***p***
8:39 hear in heaven Your dwelling ***p***,
8:43 in heaven Your dwelling ***p***,
8:49 hear in heaven Your dwelling ***p***
10:19 on either side of the ***p*** of the
11: 7 Then Solomon built a high ***p*** for
11:43 his son reigned in his ***p***.
13: 8 bread nor drink water in this ***p***.
13:16 drink water with you in this ***p***.
13:22 and drank water in the ***p*** of
14:20 Nadab his son reigned in his ***p***.

14:27 made bronze shields in their ***p***,
14:31 Abijam his son reigned in his ***p***.
15: 8 Asa his son reigned in his ***p***.
15:24 his son reigned in his ***p***.
15:28 of Judah, and reigned in his ***p***.
16: 6 Elah his son reigned in his ***p***.
16:10 of Judah, and reigned in his ***p***.
16:28 Ahab his son reigned in his ***p***.
18:12 LORD will carry you to a ***p*** I
19: 9 and spent the night in that ***p***;
19:16 anoint as prophet in your ***p***.
21:19 In the ***p*** where dogs licked the
22:40 his son reigned in his ***p***.
22:50 his son reigned in his ***p***.
2 Ki 1:17 Jehoram became king in his ***p***,
3:27 who would have reigned in his ***p***,
5:11 and wave his hand over the ***p***,
6: 1 the ***p*** where we dwell with you
6: 2 and let us make there a ***p*** where
6: 6 And he showed him the ***p***.
6: 8 will be in such and such a ***p***.
6: 9 that you do not pass this ***p***,
6:10 Israel sent someone to the ***p***
8:15 and Hazael reigned in his ***p***.
8:24 his son reigned in his ***p***.
9: 2 "Now when you arrive at that ***p***,
10:35 his son reigned in his ***p***.
12:21 his son reigned in his ***p***.
13: 9 Joash his son reigned in his ***p***.
13:24 his son reigned in his ***p***.
14:16 his son reigned in his ***p***.
14:29 his son reigned in his ***p***.
15: 7 Jotham his son reigned in his ***p***.
15:10 people; and he reigned in his ***p***.
15:14 him; and he reigned in his ***p***.
15:22 his son reigned in his ***p***.
15:25 killed him and reigned in his ***p***.
15:30 so he reigned in his ***p*** in the
15:38 Ahaz his son reigned in his ***p***.
16:20 his son reigned in his ***p***.
18:25 the LORD against this ***p*** to
19:27 'But I know your dwelling ***p***,
19:37 his son reigned in his ***p***.
20:21 his son reigned in his ***p***.
21:18 his son Amon reigned in his ***p***.
21:24 his son Josiah king in his ***p***.
21:26 Josiah his son reigned in his ***p***.
22:16 I will bring calamity on this ***p***
22:17 be aroused against this ***p*** and
22:19 what I spoke against this ***p***
22:20 which I will bring on this ***p***.
23:15 and the high ***p*** which Jeroboam
23:15 both that altar and the high ***p***
23:15 and he burned the high ***p*** and
23:30 made him king in his father's ***p***.
23:34 the son of Josiah king in ***p*** of
24: 6 his son reigned in his ***p***.
24:17 uncle, king in his ***p***,
1 Chr 1:44 of Bozrah reigned in his ***p***.
1:45 the Temanites reigned in his ***p***.
1:46 field of Moab, reigned in his ***p***.
1:47 of Masrekah reigned in his ***p***.
1:48 reigned in his ***p***.
1:49 son of Achbor reigned in his ***p***.
1:50 died, Hadad reigned in his ***p***;
4:41 day. So they dwelt in their ***p***,
5:22 And they dwelt in their ***p*** until
6:32 music before the dwelling ***p*** of
6:49 the work of the Most Holy ***P***,
13:11 therefore that ***p*** is called
14:11 they called the name of that ***p***
15: 1 and he prepared a ***p*** for the ark
15: 3 the ark of the LORD to its ***p***,
15:12 LORD God of Israel to the ***p***
16:27 and gladness are in His ***p***.
16:39 of the LORD at the high ***p***
17: 9 Moreover I will appoint a ***p*** for
17: 9 that they may dwell in a ***p*** of
19: 1 and his son reigned in his ***p***.
21:22 Grant me the ***p*** of this
21:25 of gold by weight for the ***p***.
21:29 at that time at the high ***p*** in
23:32 the needs of the holy ***p***,
28:11 and the ***p*** of the mercy seat;
29:28 his son reigned in his ***p***.
2 Chr 1: 3 went to the high ***p*** that was at
1: 4 from Kirjath Jearim to the ***p***
1: 8 and have made me king in his ***p***.
1:13 to Jerusalem from the high ***p***
3: 1 at the ***p*** that David had
3: 8 And he made the Most Holy ***P***.
3:10 In the Most Holy ***P*** he made two
4:22 inner doors to the Most Holy ***P***,
5: 7 covenant of the LORD to its ***p***,
5: 7 the temple, to the Most Holy ***P***,
5: 8 spread their wings over the ***p***
5: 9 be seen from the holy ***p***,
5:11 came out of the Most Holy ***P***
6: 2 And a ***p*** for You to dwell in
6:20 toward the ***p*** where You said
6:20 servant prays toward this ***p***.
6:21 when they pray toward this ***p***.
6:21 from heaven Your dwelling ***p***,
6:26 when they pray toward this ***p***
6:30 from heaven Your dwelling ***p***,
6:33 from heaven Your dwelling ***p***,
6:39 from heaven Your dwelling ***p***
6:40 to the prayer made in this ***p***.
6:41 O LORD God, to Your resting ***p***,
7:12 and have chosen this ***p*** for
7:15 to prayer made in this ***p***.
9:18 on either side of the ***p*** of the
9:31 his son reigned in his ***p***.
12:10 made bronze shields in their ***p***,
12:16 Abijah his son reigned in his ***p***.
14: 1 Asa his son reigned in his ***p***.
17: 1 his son reigned in his ***p***,
20:24 So when Judah came to a ***p***
20:26 therefore the name of that ***p***
21: 1 his son reigned in his ***p***.
22: 1 his youngest son king in his ***p***,
24:11 it and returned it to its ***p***.
24:27 his son reigned in his ***p***.
26:20 they thrust him out of that ***p***.
26:23 Jotham his son reigned in his ***p***.
27: 9 Ahaz his son reigned in his ***p***.
28:27 his son reigned in his ***p***.
29: 5 the rubbish from the holy ***p***.
29: 6 faces away from the dwelling ***p***
29: 7 burnt offerings in the holy ***p***
29:36 since the events took ***p*** so
30:16 They stood in their ***p*** according
30:27 came up to His holy dwelling ***p***,
32:33 his son reigned in his ***p***.
33:20 his son Amon reigned in his ***p***.
33:25 his son Josiah king in his ***p***.
34:24 I will bring calamity on this ***p***
34:25 will be poured out on this ***p***,
34:27 heard His words against this ***p***
34:28 which I will bring on this ***p***
34:31 Then the king stood in his ***p*** and
35: 5 And stand in the holy ***p***
36: 1 him king in his father's ***p*** in
36: 8 his son reigned in his ***p***.
36:15 people and on His dwelling ***p***.
Ezra 1: 4 And whoever is left in any ***p***
1: 4 let the men of his ***p*** help him
2:68 of God, to erect it in its ***p***:
6: 3 the ***p*** where they offered
6: 5 in Jerusalem, each to its ***p***;
8:17 for Iddo the chief man at the ***p***
8:17 brethren the Nethinim at the ***p***
9: 8 to give us a peg in His holy ***p***,
Neh 1: 9 and bring them to the ***p*** which I
2: 3 the ***p*** of my fathers' tombs,
3:16 made repairs as far as the ***p***
3:26 repairs as far as the ***p*** in
4:12 From whatever ***p*** you turn, they
8: 7 the people stood in their ***p***.
9: 3 And they stood up in their ***p*** and
13:11 and set them in their ***p***.
Esth 2: 9 maidservants to the best ***p*** in
4:14 for the Jews from another ***p***,
7: 8 the palace garden to the ***p*** of
Job 2:11 each one came from his own ***p***—
5: 3 I cursed his dwelling ***p***.
6:17 hot, they vanish from their ***p***.
7:10 Nor shall his ***p*** know him
8: 6 your rightful dwelling ***p***.
8:17 And look for a ***p*** in the
8:18 If he is destroyed from his ***p***,
8:22 And the dwelling ***p*** of the
9: 6 shakes the earth out of its ***p***,
10:21 Before I go to the ***p*** from
14:18 as a rock is moved from its ***p***;
16: 4 your soul were in my soul's ***p***.
16:18 let my cry have no resting ***p***!
18: 4 the rock be removed from its ***p***?
18:21 And this is the ***p*** of him
20: 9 Nor will his ***p*** behold him
21:28 The dwelling ***p*** of the wicked?'
27:21 It sweeps him out of his ***p***.
27:23 shall hiss him out of his ***p***.
28: 1 And a ***p*** where gold is
28:12 And where is the ***p*** of
28:20 And where is the ***p*** of
28:23 its way, And He knows its ***p***.
34:24 And sets others in their ***p***.
36:16 Into a broad ***p*** where there
36:20 people are cut off in their ***p***.
37: 1 trembles, And leaps from its ***p***.
38:12 caused the dawn to know its ***p***,
38:19 And darkness, where is its ***p***,
40:12 down the wicked in their ***p***.
Ps 18:11 He made darkness His secret ***p***;
18:19 brought me out into a broad ***p***;
24: 3 Or who may stand in His holy ***p***?
26: 8 And the ***p*** where Your glory
26:12 My foot stands in an even ***p***;
27: 5 In the secret ***p*** of His
31: 8 have set my feet in a wide ***p***.
31:20 hide them in the secret ***p*** of
32: 7 You are my hiding ***p***;
33:14 From the ***p*** of His dwelling He
37:10 will look carefully for his ***p***,
44:19 severely broken us in the ***p*** of
46: 4 The holy ***p*** of the tabernacle
52: 5 you out of your dwelling ***p***,
68:17 as in Sinai, in the Holy ***P***.
69:25 Let their dwelling ***p*** be
74: 4 in the midst of Your meeting ***p***;
74: 7 have defiled the dwelling ***p*** of
76: 2 And His dwelling ***p*** in Zion.
79: 7 And laid waste his dwelling ***p***.
81: 7 I answered you in the secret ***p***
88:11 Your faithfulness in the ***p*** of
90: 1 You have been our dwelling ***p*** in
91: 1 He who dwells in the secret ***p***
91: 9 the Most High, your dwelling ***p***,
103:16 And its ***p*** remembers it no
104: 8 To the ***p*** which You founded for
107: 7 go to a city for a dwelling ***p***.
107:36 a city for a dwelling ***p***,
118: 5 me and set me in a broad ***p***.
119:114 You are my hiding ***p*** and my
132: 5 Until I find a ***p*** for the LORD,
132: 5 A dwelling ***p*** for the Mighty
132: 8 O LORD, to Your resting ***p***,
132:13 desired it for His dwelling ***p***:
132:14 This is My resting ***p*** forever;
Prov 4: 9 She will ***p*** on your head an
14:26 His children will have a ***p*** of
15: 3 of the LORD are in every ***p***,
24:15 Do not plunder his resting ***p***;
25: 6 And do not stand in the ***p*** of
27: 8 a man who wanders from his ***p***.
Eccl 1: 5 And hastens to the ***p*** where it
1: 7 To the ***p*** from which the rivers
3:16 In the ***p*** of judgment,
3:16 And in the ***p*** of
3:20 All go to one ***p***:
4:15 youth who stands in his ***p***.
6: 6 Do not all go to one ***p***?
8:10 had come and gone from the ***p***
10: 6 the rich sit in a lowly ***p***.
11: 3 In the ***p*** where the tree falls,
Isa 4: 5 create above every dwelling ***p***
4: 6 for a ***p*** of refuge, and for a
5: 8 Till there is no ***p*** Where
7:25 a range for oxen And a ***p*** for
11:10 And His resting ***p*** shall be
13:13 earth will move out of her ***p***,
14: 2 them and bring them to their ***p***,
16:12 Moab is weary on the high ***p***,
18: 4 I will look from My dwelling ***p***
18: 7 To the ***p*** of the name of the
22:23 him as a peg in a secure ***p***,
22:25 is fastened in the secure ***p***
25: 5 of aliens, As heat in a dry ***p***;
26:21 the LORD comes out of His ***p***
28: 8 and filth; No ***p*** is clean.
28:17 will overflow the hiding ***p***.
28:25 The barley in the appointed ***p***,
28:25 place, And the spelt in its ***p***?
30:32 And in every ***p*** where the staff
32: 2 A man will be as a hiding ***p***
32: 2 As rivers of water in a dry ***p***,
33:16 His ***p*** of defense will be the
33:21 LORD will be for us A ***p*** of
34:14 And find for herself a ***p*** of
37:28 "But I know your dwelling ***p***,
37:38 his son reigned in his ***p***.
43: 3 Ethiopia and Seba in your ***p***.
45:19 In a dark ***p*** of the earth;
46: 7 carry it And set it in its ***p***,
46: 7 From its ***p*** it shall not move.
46:13 And I will ***p*** salvation in
49:20 The ***p*** is too small for me;
49:20 Give me a ***p*** where I may
54: 2 'Enlarge the ***p*** of your tent,
56: 5 house And within My walls a ***p***
57:15 dwell in the high and holy ***p***,
60:13 To beautify the ***p*** of My
60:13 And I will make the ***p*** of My
65:10 And the Valley of Achor a ***p***
66: 1 And where is the ***p*** of My
Jer 4: 7 He has gone forth from his ***p***
6: 3 one shall pasture in his own ***p***.
7: 3 cause you to dwell in this ***p***.
7: 6 shed innocent blood in this ***p***,
7: 7 cause you to dwell in this ***p***,
7:12 But go now to My ***p*** which was
7:14 and to this ***p*** which I gave to
7:20 will be poured out on this ***p***—
9: 2 in the wilderness A lodging ***p***
9: 6 Your dwelling ***p*** is in the
10:25 And made his dwelling ***p***
13: 7 and I took the sash from the ***p***
14:13 you assured peace in this ***p***.
16: 2 sons or daughters in this ***p***.
16: 3 who are born in this ***p***,
16: 9 will cause to cease from this ***p***,
17:12 from the beginning Is the ***p***
19: 3 such a catastrophe on this ***p***,
19: 4 Me and made this an alien ***p***,
19: 4 and have filled this ***p*** with the
19: 6 that this ***p*** shall no more be
19: 7 Judah and Jerusalem in this ***p***,
19:11 in Tophet till there is no ***p***
19:12 "Thus I will do to this ***p***,
19:13 shall be defiled like the ***p*** of
22: 3 shed innocent blood in this ***p***.
22:11 father, who went from this ***p***:
22:12 but he shall die in the ***p*** where
24: 5 whom I have sent out of this ***p***
27:22 up and restore them to this ***p***.
28: 3 I will bring back to this ***p***
28: 3 Babylon took away from this ***p***
28: 4 I will bring back to this ***p***
28: 6 captive, from Babylon to this ***p***.
28:13 but you have made in their ***p***
29:10 cause you to return to this ***p***.
29:14 and I will bring you to the ***p***
32:37 will bring them back to this ***p***,
33:10 there shall be heard in this ***p***—
33:12 In this ***p*** which is desolate,
33:12 shall again be a dwelling ***p*** of
38: 9 to die from hunger in the ***p***
40: 2 pronounced this doom on this ***p***.
42:18 and you shall see this ***p*** no
42:22 and by pestilence in the ***p***
44:29 I will punish you in this ***p***,
49:19 Jordan Against the dwelling ***p***
50: 6 have forgotten their resting ***p***.
50:44 Jordan Against the dwelling ***p***
50:45 He will make their dwelling ***p***

51:37 A dwelling **p** for jackals,
51:62 You have spoken against this **p**
Lam 2: 6 He has destroyed His **p** of
Ezek 3:12 glory of the LORD from His **p**!
4: 2 and **p** battering rams against it
7:22 they will defile My secret **p**;
12: 3 You shall go from your **p** into
12: 3 into captivity to another **p** in
16:24 and made a high **p** for yourself
16:31 and built your high **p** in every
17:16 surely in the **p** where the king
20:29 What is this high **p** to which
21:30 I will judge you In the **p**
25: 5 camels and Ammon a resting **p**
26: 5 It shall be a **p** for spreading
26:14 you shall be a **p** for
31: 4 rivers running around the **p**
37:14 and I will **p** you in your own
38:15 you will come from your **p**
39:11 I will give Gog a burial **p**
41: 4 me, "This is the Most Holy **P**.
41: 9 the remaining terrace by the **p**
42:13 for the **p** is holy.
43: 7 this is the **p** of My throne
43: 7 place of My throne and the **p**
43:21 and burn it in the appointed **p**
44:13 nor into the Most Holy **P**;
45: 3 the sanctuary, the Most Holy **P**.
45: 4 it shall be a **p** for their
45: 4 for their houses and a holy **p**
46:19 and there a **p** was situated at
46:20 This is the **p** where the priests
Dan 7: 9 till thrones were put in **p**,
8: 8 and in **p** of it four notable
8:11 and the **p** of His sanctuary was
8:22 the four that stood up in its **p**,
11: 7 roots one shall arise in his **p**,
11:20 There shall arise in his **p** one
11:21 And in his **p** shall arise a vile
11:31 and **p** there the abomination of
11:38 But in their **p** he shall honor a
Hos 1:10 it shall come to pass In the **p**
5:15 I will return again to My **p**
9:13 Tyre, planted in a pleasant **p**,
Joel 3: 7 I will raise them Out of the **p**
Mic 1: 3 LORD is coming out of His **p**;
1: 4 waters poured down a steep **p**.
1:11 Its **p** to stand is taken away
Nah 1: 8 will make an utter end of its **p**,
2:11 And the feeding **p** of the young
3:17 And the **p** where they are is
Zeph 1: 4 every trace of Baal from this **p**,
2:11 Him, Each one from his **p**,
2:15 A **p** for beasts to lie down!
Hag 2: 9 And in this **p** I will give
Zech 6:12 is the BRANCH! From His **p** He
9: 1 And Damascus its resting **p**
12: 6 be inhabited again in her own **p**—
14:10 up and inhabited in her **p** from
14:10 from Benjamin's Gate to the **p**
Mal 1:11 In every **p** incense shall be
Mt 6: 6 Father who is in the secret **p**;
6:18 Father who is in the secret **p**;
8:32 ran violently down the steep **p**
12: 6 I say to you that in this **p**
14:13 there by boat to a deserted **p**
14:15 saying, "This is a deserted **p**,
14:35 And when the men of that **p**
24:15 standing in the holy **p**"
24:34 till all these things take **p**.
26:36 Jesus came with them to a **p**
26:52 him, "Put your sword in its **p**,
27:33 And when they had come to a **p**
27:33 is to say, **P** of a Skull,
28: 6 see the **p** where the Lord lay.
Mk 1:35 and departed to a solitary **p**;
5:13 ran violently down the steep **p**
6:10 In whatever **p** you enter a house,
6:10 till you depart from that **p**.
6:31 by yourselves to a deserted **p**
6:32 they departed to a deserted **p**
6:35 said, "This is a deserted **p**,
12: 1 dug a **p** for the wine vat and
13:30 till all these things take **p**.
14:32 Then they came to a **p** which was
15:22 And they brought Him to the **p**
15:22 translated, **P** of a Skull.
16: 6 See the **p** where they laid Him.
Lk 1:20 the day these things take **p**,
2: 2 This census first took **p** while
4:17 He found the **p** where it was
4:37 Him went out into every **p** in
4:42 and went into a deserted **p**.
6:17 them and stood on a level **p**
8:33 ran violently down the steep **p**
9:10 privately into a deserted **p**
9:12 for we are in a deserted **p**
10: 1 His face into every city and **p**
10:32 when he arrived at the **p**,
11: 1 He was praying in a certain **p**,
11:33 puts it in a secret **p** or under
14: 8 do not sit down in the best **p**,
14: 9 Give **p** to this man,' and then
14: 9 with shame to take the lowest **p**.
14:10 go and sit down in the lowest **p**,
16:28 lest they also come to this **p**
19: 5 And when Jesus came to the **p**,
21: 7 things are about to take **p**?
21:32 away till all things take **p**.
22:40 When He came to the **p**,
23: 5 from Galilee to this **p**.
23:33 And when they had come to the **p**

Jn 4:20 say that in Jerusalem is the **p**
5:13 a multitude being in that **p**.
6:10 there was much grass in the **p**.
6:23 near the **p** where they ate bread
8:37 because My word has no **p** in
10:40 beyond the Jordan to the **p**
11: 6 stayed two more days in the **p**
11:30 but was in the **p** where Martha
11:41 away the stone from the **p**
11:48 come and take away both our **p**
14: 2 I go to prepare a **p** for you.
14: 3 And if I go and prepare a **p** for
18: 2 betrayed Him, also knew the **p**;
19:13 in the judgment seat in a **p**
19:17 went out to a **p** called the
19:17 out to a place called the **P**
19:20 for the **p** where Jesus was
19:41 Now in the **p** where He was
20: 7 but folded together in a **p** by
Acts 1:20 Let his dwelling **p** be
1:25 that he might go to his own **p**.
2: 1 all with one accord in one **p**.
4:31 the **p** where they were assembled
6:13 words against this holy **p** and
6:14 of Nazareth will destroy this **p**
7: 7 and serve Me in this **p**.
7:33 for the **p** where you stand
7:49 Or what is the **p** of My
8:32 The **p** in the Scripture which he
12:17 departed and went to another **p**.
21:12 both we and those from that **p**
21:28 the people, the law, and this **p**;
21:28 and has defiled this holy **p**.
25:26 the examination has taken **p** I
27: 8 we came to a **p** called Fair
27:41 But striking a **p** where two seas
Rom 9:26 come to pass in the **p**
12:19 but rather give **p** to wrath;
15:23 But now no longer having a **p** in
1 Cor 1: 2 with all who in every **p** call on
11:20 when you come together in one **p**,
14:16 how will he who occupies the **p**
14:23 church comes together in one **p**,
2 Cor 2:14 of His knowledge in every **p**.
Eph 2:22 together for a dwelling **p** of
4:27 nor give **p** to the devil.
1 Th 1: 8 and Achaia, but also in every **p**.
Heb 2: 6 one testified in a certain **p**,
4: 4 He has spoken in a certain **p**
4: 5 and again in this **p**:
5: 6 As He also says in another **p**:
8: 7 then no **p** would have been
9:12 He entered the Most Holy **P**
9:25 priest enters the Most Holy **P**
11: 8 was called to go out to the **p**
12:17 for he found no **p** for
Jas 2: 3 him, "You sit here in a good **p**,
2 Pe 1:19 a light that shines in a dark **p**,
Rev 1: 1 which must shortly take **p**.
1:19 the things which will take **p**
2: 5 your lampstand from its **p**—
4: 1 you things which must take **p**
6:14 island was moved out of its **p**.
12: 6 where she has a **p** prepared by
12: 8 nor was a **p** found for them in
12:14 into the wilderness to her **p**,
16:16 them together to the **p** called
18: 2 and has become a dwelling **p** of
20:11 And there was found no **p** for
22: 6 which must shortly take **p**.

PLACED (30/30)

Gen 3:24 and He **p** cherubim at the east
15:10 and **p** each piece opposite the
21:15 and she **p** the boy under one of
22: 9 built an altar there and **p** the
30:41 that Jacob **p** the rods before
31:51 which I have **p** between you and
40:11 and **p** the cup in Pharaoh's
40:21 and he **p** the cup in Pharaoh's
Ex 13:19 for he had **p** the children of
Num 11:24 the elders of the people and **p**
11:25 and **p** the same upon the
17: 7 And Moses **p** the rods before the
Deut 20:11 are found in it shall be **p**
1 Sam 14:24 for Saul had **p** the people under
2 Sam 13: 9 And she took the pan and **p** them
2 Ki 17: 6 and **p** them in Halah and by the
17:24 and **p** them in the cities of
17:26 whom you have removed and **p** in
2 Chr 4: 8 and **p** them in the temple, five
17: 2 And he **p** troops in all the
Neh 10: 1 Now those who **p** their seal on
Esth 6: 8 which has a royal crest **p** on
Job 20: 4 Since man was **p** on earth,
Ps 21: 5 Honor and majesty You have **p**
78:60 The tent He had **p** among men,
Jer 5:22 Who have **p** the sand as the
Ezek 17: 5 He **p** it by abundant waters
32:19 be **p** with the uncircumcised.'
32:32 And he shall be **p** in the midst
Lk 7: 8 For I also am a man **p** under

PLACENTA (1/1)

Deut 28:57 her **p** which comes out from

PLACES (196/183)

Gen 23: 6 in the choicest of our burial **p**.
36:40 to their families and their **p**,
36:43 according to their dwelling **p**
Lev 26:30 I will destroy your high **p**,
Num 22:41 brought him up to the high **p**
33:52 and demolish all their high **p**;
Deut 1: 7 to all the neighboring **p** in
12: 2 shall utterly destroy all the **p**
33:29 shall tread down their high **p**.
Josh 5: 8 that they stayed in their **p** in
Judg 5:11 archers, among the watering **p**,
7:24 seize from them the watering **p**
7:24 and seized the watering **p** as
19:13 us draw near to one of these **p**,
1 Sam 7:16 judged Israel in all those **p**.
23:23 knowledge of all the lurking **p**
30:31 and to all the **p** where David
2 Sam 1:19 Israel is slain on your high **p**!
1:25 was slain in your high **p**.
22:34 deer, And sets me on my high **p**.
1 Ki 3: 2 people sacrificed at the high **p**,
3: 3 burned incense at the high **p**.
12:31 He made shrines on the high **p**,
12:32 the priests of the high **p**
13: 2 the priests of the high **p** who
13:32 all the shrines on the high **p**
13:33 class of people for the high **p**;
13:33 of the priests of the high **p**.
14:23 built for themselves high **p**,
15:14 But the high **p** were not removed.
20:24 and put captains in their **p**;
22:43 Nevertheless the high **p** were
22:43 burned incense on the high **p**.
2 Ki 12: 3 But the high **p** were not taken
12: 3 burned incense on the high **p**.
14: 4 However the high **p** were not
14: 4 burned incense on the high **p**.
15: 4 except that the high **p** were not
15: 4 burned incense on the high **p**.
15:35 However the high **p** were not
15:35 burned incense on the high **p**.
16: 4 burned incense on the high **p**,
17: 9 built for themselves high **p** in
17:11 incense on all the high **p**,
17:29 in the shrines on the high **p**
17:32 priests of the high **p**,
17:32 in the shrines of the high **p**.
18: 4 He removed the high **p** and broke
18:22 is it not He whose high **p** and
21: 3 For he rebuilt the high **p** which
23: 5 to burn incense on the high **p**
23: 5 cities of Judah and in the **p**
23: 8 and defiled the high **p** where
23: 8 also he broke down the high **p**
23: 9 the priests of the high **p** did
23:13 the king defiled the high **p**
23:14 and filled their **p** with the
23:19 all the shrines of the high **p**
23:20 all the priests of the high **p**
1 Chr 4:33 These were their dwelling **p**,
6:54 these are their dwelling **p**
7:28 possessions and dwelling **p**
2 Chr 8:11 because the **p** to which the
11:15 himself priests for the high **p**,
14: 3 foreign gods and the high **p**,
14: 5 He also removed the high **p** and
15:17 But the high **p** were not removed
17: 6 moreover he removed the high **p**
20:33 Nevertheless the high **p** were not
21:11 Moreover he made high **p** in the
28: 4 burned incense on the high **p**,
28:25 city of Judah he made high **p**
31: 1 and threw down the high **p** and
32:12 Hezekiah taken away His high **p**
33: 3 For he rebuilt the high **p** which
33:17 still sacrificed on the high **p**,
33:19 the sites where he built high **p**
34: 3 and Jerusalem of the high **p**,
35:10 the priests stood in their **p**,
35:15 sons of Asaph, were in their **p**,
Neh 12:27 out the Levites in all their **p**,
Job 25: 2 He makes peace in His high **p**.
28: 4 In **p** forgotten by feet They
Ps 10: 8 He sits in the lurking **p** of the
10: 8 In the secret **p** he murders the
16: 6 fallen to me in pleasant **p**;
17:12 young lion lurking in secret **p**.
18:33 deer, And sets me on my high **p**.
49:11 Their dwelling **p** to all
68:35 more awesome than Your holy **p**.
73:18 You set them in slippery **p**;
74: 8 burned up all the meeting **p** of
74:20 For the dark **p** of the earth
78:58 Him to anger with their high **p**,
95: 4 In His hand are the deep **p** of
103:22 In all **p** of His dominion.
105:41 It ran in the dry **p** like a
109:10 also from their desolate **p**.
110: 6 He shall fill the **p** with
135: 6 In the seas and in all deep **p**.
Prov 9: 3 cries out from the highest **p**
9:14 On a seat by the highest **p** of
Song 2:14 In the secret **p** of the cliff,
Isa 5:17 And in the waste **p** of the fat
6:12 And the forsaken **p** are many
15: 2 To the high **p** to weep.
32:18 and in quiet resting **p**,
36: 7 is it not He whose high **p**
40: 4 The crooked **p** shall be made
40: 4 made straight And the rough **p**
42:16 And crooked **p** straight.
44:26 I will raise up her waste **p**;
45: 2 you And make the crooked **p**
45: 3 And hidden riches of secret **p**,

49:19 your waste and desolate **p**,
51: 3 will comfort all her waste **p**;
52: 9 You waste **p** of Jerusalem!
58:12 Shall build the old waste **p**;
59:10 are as dead men in desolate **p**.
Jer 5: 1 And seek in her open **p** If you
7:31 they have built the high **p**
8: 3 who remain in all the **p** where I
9:10 And for the dwelling **p** of the
17: 3 And your high **p** of sin within
17: 6 shall inhabit the parched **p** in
17:26 cities of Judah and from the **p**
19: 5 have also built the high **p** of
23:10 The pleasant **p** of the
23:24 anyone hide himself in secret **p**,
24: 9 in all **p** where I shall drive
29:14 the nations and from all the **p**
30:18 have mercy on his dwelling **p**;
32:35 And they built the high **p** of
32:44 in the **p** around Jerusalem, in
33: 5 but only to fill their **p** with
33: 7 and will rebuild those **p** as at
33:13 in the **p** around Jerusalem, and
40:12 the Jews returned out of all **p**
45: 5 life to you as a prize in all **p**,
48:35 sacrifices in the high **p** And
49:10 I have uncovered his secret **p**,
49:20 He shall make their dwelling **p**
51:30 have burned her dwelling **p**,
Lam 2: 2 not pitied All the dwelling **p**
3: 6 He has set me in dark **p** Like
Ezek 6: 3 and I will destroy your high **p**.
6: 6 In all your dwelling **p** the
6: 6 and the high **p** shall be
6:14 Diblah, in all their dwelling **p**.
7:24 And their holy **p** shall be
16:16 and adorned multicolored high **p**
16:25 You built your high **p** at the
16:39 and break down your high **p**.
19: 7 He knew their desolate **p**,
21: 2 preach against the holy **p**,
26:20 in **p** desolate from antiquity,
34:12 and deliver them from all the **p**
34:13 and in all the inhabited **p** of
34:26 I will make them and the **p** all
36:36 have rebuilt the ruined **p** and
37:23 them from all their dwelling **p**
38:12 your hand against the waste **p**
38:20 the steep **p** shall fall, and
43: 7 of their kings on their high **p**.
47:10 they will be **p** for spreading
Dan 11:24 even into the richest **p** of the
Hos 10: 8 Also the high **p** of Aven, the
Am 4: 6 lack of bread in all your **p**;
4:13 Who treads the high **p** of the
7: 9 The high **p** of Isaac shall be
Mic 1: 3 down And tread on the high **p**
1: 5 And what are the high **p** of
1: 6 **P** for planting a vineyard;
Hab 1: 6 To possess dwelling **p** that
Zech 3: 7 I will give you **p** to walk
Mal 1: 4 return and build the desolate **p**,
Mt 12:43 of a man, he goes through dry **p**,
13: 5 "Some fell on stony **p**,
13:20 received the seed on stony **p**,
23: 6 They love the best **p** at feasts,
24: 7 and earthquakes in various **p**.
Mk 1:45 but was outside in deserted **p**;
12:39 and the best **p** at feasts,
13: 8 be earthquakes in various **p**,
Lk 3: 5 The crooked **p** shall be
11:24 of a man, he goes through dry **p**,
14: 7 noted how they chose the best **p**,
20:46 and the best **p** at feasts,
21:11 great earthquakes in various **p**,
Acts 24: 3 accept it always and in all **p**,
Eph 1: 3 blessing in the heavenly **p** in
1:20 right hand in the heavenly **p**,
2: 6 together in the heavenly **p** in
3:10 and powers in the heavenly **p**,
6:12 wickedness in the heavenly **p**.
Heb 9:24 has not entered the holy **p**

PLAGUE (75/64) PLAGUES

Ex 11: 1 I will bring yet one more **p** on
12:13 and the **p** shall not be on you
30:12 that there may be no **p** among
Lev 13:47 if a garment has a leprous **p** in
13:49 and if the **p** is greenish or
13:49 it is a leprous **p** and shall be
13:50 priest shall examine the **p**
13:50 that which has the **p** seven
13:51 'And he shall examine the **p** on
13:51 If the **p** has spread in the
13:51 the **p** is an active leprosy.
13:52 that garment in which is the **p**,
13:53 and indeed the **p** has not spread
13:54 the thing in which is the **p**;
13:55 the priest shall examine the **p**
13:55 and indeed if the **p** has not
13:55 though the **p** has not spread, it
13:56 and indeed the **p** has faded
13:57 leather, it is a spreading **p**;
13:57 fire that in which is the **p**.
13:58 if the **p** has disappeared from
13:59 is the law of the leprous **p**
14:34 and I put the leprous **p** in a
14:35 to me that there is some **p**
14:36 goes into it to examine the **p**,
14:37 "And he shall examine the **p**;
14:37 and indeed if the **p** is on the
14:39 and indeed if the **p** has spread
14:40 the stones in which is the **p**,
14:43 Now if the **p** comes back and
14:44 and indeed if the **p** has spread
14:48 and indeed the **p** has not spread
14:48 because the **p** is healed.
Num 8:19 that there be no **p** among the
11:33 the people with a very great **p**.
14:37 died by the **p** before the LORD.
16:46 The **p** has begun."
16:47 and already the **p** had begun
16:48 so the **p** was stopped.
16:49 Now those who died in the **p** were
16:50 for the **p** had stopped.
25: 8 So the **p** was stopped among the
25: 9 And those who died in the **p** were
25:18 was killed in the day of the **p**
26: 1 it came to pass, after the **p**,
31:16 and there was a **p** among the
Deut 28:21 The LORD will make the **p** cling
28:61 every sickness and every **p**,
Josh 22:17 although there was a **p** in the
1 Sam 6: 4 For the same **p** was on all of
2 Sam 24:13 Or shall there be three days' **p**
24:15 So the LORD sent a **p** upon
24:21 that the **p** may be withdrawn
24:25 and the **p** was withdrawn from
1 Ki 8:37 whatever **p** or whatever sickness
8:38 when each one knows the **p** of
1 Chr 21:12 the **p** in the land, with the
21:14 So the LORD sent a **p** upon
21:22 that the **p** may be withdrawn
2 Chr 6:28 whatever **p** or whatever sickness
Ps 38:11 friends stand aloof from my **p**,
39:10 Remove Your **p** from me; I am
78:50 gave their life over to the **p**,
89:23 And **p** those who hate him.
91:10 Nor shall any **p** come near your
106:29 And the **p** broke out among
106:30 And the **p** was stopped.
Am 4:10 I sent among you a **p** after the
Zech 14:12 And this shall be the **p** with
14:15 Such also shall be the **p** On
14:15 So shall this **p** be.
14:18 they shall receive the **p** with
Acts 24: 5 we have found this man a **p**,
Rev 16:21 God because of the **p** of the
16:21 since that **p** was exceedingly

PLAGUED (6/6)

Gen 12:17 But the LORD **p** Pharaoh and his
Ex 32:35 So the LORD **p** the people
Josh 24: 5 and I **p** Egypt, according to
1 Chr 21:17 people that they should be **p**.
Ps 73: 5 Nor are they **p** like other
73:14 For all day long I have been **p**,

PLAGUES (22/21) PLAGUE

Gen 12:17 and his house with great **p**
Ex 9:14 this time I will send all My **p**
Lev 26:21 bring on you seven times more **p**,
Deut 28:59 descendants extraordinary **p**—
28:59 plagues—great and prolonged **p**—
29:22 when they see the **p** of that
1 Sam 4: 8 the Egyptians with all the **p**
Jer 19: 8 and hiss because of all its **p**.
49:17 And will hiss at all its **p**.
50:13 And hiss at all her **p**.
Hos 13:14 I will be your **p**! O Grave, I
Rev 9:18 By these three **p** a third of
9:20 who were not killed by these **p**,
11: 6 to strike the earth with all **p**,
15: 1 angels having the seven last **p**,
15: 6 seven angels having the seven **p**,
15: 8 the temple till the seven **p** of
16: 9 God who has power over these **p**;
18: 4 and lest you receive of her **p**.
18: 8 Therefore her **p** will come in one
21: 9 filled with the seven last **p**
22:18 God will add to him the **p** that

PLAIN (53/53) PLAINLY, PLAINS

Gen 11: 2 that they found a **p** in the land
13:10 his eyes and saw all the **p** of
13:11 chose for himself all the **p** of
13:12 dwelt in the cities of the **p**
19:17 you nor stay anywhere in the **p**.
19:25 those cities, all the **p**,
19:28 toward all the land of the **p**;
19:29 destroyed the cities of the **p**,
Deut 1: 1 in the **p** opposite Suph, between
1: 7 neighboring places in the **p**,
2: 8 away from the road of the **p**,
3:10 "all the cities of the **p**,
3:17 the **p** also, with the Jordan as
4:49 and all the **p** on the east side
11:30 Canaanites who dwell in the **p**
34: 3 and the **p** of the Valley of
Josh 8:14 an appointed place before the **p**.
11: 2 in the **p** south of Chinneroth,
11:16 the lowland, and the Jordan **p**—
12: 1 and all the eastern Jordan **p**:
12: 3 and the eastern Jordan **p** from
12: 8 the lowlands, in the Jordan **p**,
13: 9 and all the **p** of Medeba as far
13:16 and all the **p** by Medeba;
13:17 its cities that are in the **p**:
13:21 all the cities of the **p** and all
20: 8 in the wilderness on the **p**,
Judg 20:33 from their position in the **p**
1 Sam 23:24 in the **p** on the south of
2 Sam 2:29 on all that night through the **p**,
4: 7 night escaping through the **p**.
18:23 Ahimaaz ran by way of the **p**,
1 Ki 7:46 In the **p** of Jordan the king had
20:23 we fight against them in the **p**,
20:25 fight against them in the **p**;
2 Ki 25: 4 the king went by way of the **p**.
2 Chr 4:17 In the **p** of Jordan the king had
Neh 3:22 the priests, the men of the **p**,
6: 2 among the villages in the **p** of
Prov 8: 9 They are all **p** to him who
Jer 21:13 the valley, And rock of the **p**,
39: 4 And he went out by way of the **p**.
48: 8 And the **p** shall be destroyed,
48:21 judgment has come on the **p**
52: 7 And they went by way of the **p**.
Ezek 3:22 me, "Arise, go out into the **p**,
3:23 I arose and went out into the **p**,
8: 4 the vision that I saw in the **p**.
Dan 3: 1 He set it up in the **p** of Dura,
Hab 2: 2 the vision And make it **p** on
Zech 4: 7 you shall become a **p**! And
12:11 at Hadad Rimmon in the **p** of
14:10 land shall be turned into a **p**

PLAINLY (12/12) PLAIN

Ex 21: 5 But if the servant **p** says, 'I
Num 12: 8 with him face to face, Even **p**,
Deut 27: 8 And you shall write very **p** on
1 Sam 10:16 He told us **p** that the donkeys
Isa 32: 4 will be ready to speak **p**.
Jer 2:34 But **p** on all these things.
Mk 7:35 was loosed, and he spoke **p**.
Jn 10:24 You are the Christ, tell us **p**.
11:14 Then Jesus said to them **p**,
16:25 but I will tell you **p** about the
16:29 "See, now You are speaking **p**,
Heb 11:14 who say such things declare **p**

PLAINS (20/20) PLAIN

Num 22: 1 and camped in the **p** of Moab on
26: 3 spoke with them in the **p** of
26:63 children of Israel in the **p** of
31:12 to the camp in the **p** of Moab by
33:48 of Abarim and camped in the **p**
33:49 the Abel Acacia Grove in the **p**
33:50 LORD spoke to Moses in the **p**
35: 1 LORD spoke to Moses in the **p**
36:13 by the hand of Moses in the **p**
Deut 34: 1 Then Moses went up from the **p** of
34: 8 Israel wept for Moses in the **p**
Josh 4:13 to the **p** of Jericho.
5:10 the month at twilight on the **p**
13:32 as an inheritance in the **p** of
2 Sam 15:28 I will wait in the **p** of the
17:16 not spend this night in the **p**
2 Ki 25: 5 and they overtook him in the **p**
2 Chr 26:10 in the lowlands and in the **p**;
Jer 39: 5 and overtook Zedekiah in the **p**
52: 8 overtook Zedekiah in the **p** of

PLAITED (1/1)

1 Ki 7:29 and oxen were wreaths of **p**

PLAITING (KJV) See ARRANGING

PLAN (16/15) PLANNED, PLANS

Deut 1:23 The **p** pleased me well; so I took
2 Chr 2:14 and to accomplish any **p** which
Neh 6: 6 that you and the Jews **p** to
Ps 38:12 And **p** deception all the day
140: 2 Who **p** evil things in their
Jer 18:11 a disaster and devising a **p**
30:18 remain according to its own **p**.
49:30 And has conceived a **p** against
51:11 For His **p** is against Babylon
Ezek 38:10 and you will make an evil **p**:
42:11 entrances were according to **p**.
Zech 7:10 Let none of you **p** evil in his
Acts 5:38 for if this **p** or this work is
27:42 And the soldiers' **p** was to kill
2 Cor 1:17 it lightly? Or the things I **p**,
1:17 do I **p** according to the flesh,

PLANE (1/1)

Isa 44:13 He fashions it with a **p**,

PLANES (KJV) See PLANE

PLANK (6/5)

Mt 7: 3 but do not consider the **p** in
7: 4 a **p** is in your own eye?
7: 5 Hypocrite! First remove the **p**
Lk 6:41 but do not perceive the **p** in
6:42 you yourself do not see the **p**
6:42 Hypocrite! First remove the **p**

PLANKS (3/3)

1 Ki 6:15 the floor of the temple with **p**
Ezek 27: 5 They made all your **p** of fir
27: 6 of Ashurites have inlaid your **p**

PLANNED (2/2) PLAN

Acts 27:39 onto which they ***p*** to run the
Rom 1:13 that I often ***p*** to come to you

PLANNING (1/1)

2 Cor 1:17 when I was ***p*** this, did I do it

PLANS (22/22) PLAN

1 Ki 6:38 and according to all its ***p***.
2 Ki 18:20 You speak of having ***p*** and power
1 Chr 28:11 gave his son Solomon the ***p*** for
28:12 and the ***p*** for all that he had by
28:19 me, all the works of these ***p***.
Job 5:12 hands cannot carry out their ***p***.
Ps 33:10 He makes the ***p*** of the peoples
33:11 The ***p*** of His heart to all
146: 4 In that very day his ***p*** perish.
Prov 6:18 A heart that devises wicked ***p***,
15:22 ***p*** go awry, But in the
16: 9 A man's heart ***p*** his way, But
19:21 There are many ***p*** in a man's
20:18 ***P*** are established by counsel
21: 5 The ***p*** of the diligent lead
Isa 30: 1 not of Me, And who devise ***p***,
32: 7 He devises wicked ***p*** To
36: 5 I say you speak of having ***p*** and
Jer 18:12 walk according to our own ***p***,
18:18 Come and let us devise ***p*** against
Dan 11:24 and he shall devise his ***p***
11:25 for they shall devise ***p*** against

PLANT (50/48) PLANTED, PLANTS

Gen 2: 5 before any ***p*** of the field was in
Ex 15:17 You will bring them in and ***p***
Deut 6:11 olive trees which you did not ***p***—
16:21 You shall not ***p*** for yourself
28:30 you shall ***p*** a vineyard, but
28:39 You shall ***p*** vineyards and tend
Josh 24:13 groves which you did not ***p***.
2 Sam 7:10 and will ***p*** them, that they may
2 Ki 19:29 ***P*** vineyards and eat the fruit
1 Chr 17: 9 and will ***p*** them, that they may
Job 8:12 It withers before any other ***p***.
14: 9 bring forth branches like a ***p***.
Ps 107:37 And sow fields and ***p*** vineyards,
Eccl 3: 2 a time to die; A time to ***p***,
Isa 5: 7 men of Judah are His pleasant ***p***.
17:10 Therefore you will ***p*** pleasant
17:11 the day you will make your ***p***
28:25 ***P*** the wheat in rows, The
37:30 ***P*** vineyards and eat the fruit
41:19 I will ***p*** in the wilderness the
51:16 That I may ***p*** the heavens,
53: 2 up before Him as a tender ***p***,
65:21 They shall ***p*** vineyards and eat
65:22 They shall not ***p*** and another
Jer 1:10 throw down, To build and to ***p***.
2:21 Into the degenerate ***p*** of
18: 9 to build and to ***p*** it,
24: 6 and I will ***p*** them and not pluck
29: 5 ***p*** gardens and eat their fruit.
29:28 and ***p*** gardens and eat their
31: 5 You shall yet ***p*** vines on the
31: 5 The planters shall ***p*** and eat
31:28 over them to build and to ***p***,
32:41 and I will assuredly ***p*** them in
35: 7 ***p*** a vineyard, nor have any of
42:10 and I will ***p*** you and not pluck
Ezek 16: 7 I made you thrive like a ***p*** in
17:22 and will ***p*** it on a high and
17:23 height of Israel I will ***p*** it;
28:26 and ***p*** vineyards; yes, they will
Dan 11:45 And he shall ***p*** the tents of his
Am 9:14 They shall ***p*** vineyards and
9:15 I will ***p*** them in their land,
Jon 4: 6 And the LORD God prepared a ***p***
4: 6 was very grateful for the ***p***.
4: 7 and it so damaged the ***p*** that
4: 9 for you to be angry about the ***p***?
4:10 You have had pity on the ***p*** for
Zeph 1:13 They shall ***p*** vineyards, but
Mt 15:13 Every ***p*** which My heavenly Father

PLANTED (41/41) PLANT

Gen 2: 8 The LORD God ***p*** a garden
9:20 and he ***p*** a vineyard.
21:33 Then Abraham ***p*** a tamarisk tree
Lev 19:23 and have ***p*** all kinds of trees
Num 24: 6 Like aloes ***p*** by the LORD,
Deut 20: 6 what man is there who has ***p***
Ps 1: 3 He shall be like a tree ***P*** by
44: 2 with Your hand, But them You ***p***;
80: 8 out the nations, and ***p*** it.
80:15 which Your right hand has ***p***,
92:13 Those who are ***p*** in the house of
94: 9 He who ***p*** the ear, shall He not
104:16 cedars of Lebanon which He ***p***,
Eccl 2: 4 and ***p*** myself vineyards.
2: 5 and I ***p*** all kinds of fruit
3: 2 a time to pluck what is ***p***;
Isa 5: 2 And ***p*** it with the choicest
40:24 Scarcely shall they be ***p***,
Jer 2:21 Yet I had ***p*** you a noble vine, a
11:17 who ***p*** you, has pronounced doom
12: 2 You have ***p*** them, yes, they have
17: 8 For he shall be like a tree ***p***
45: 4 and what I have ***p*** I will pluck
Ezek 17: 5 of the seed of the land And ***p***
17: 7 terrace where it had been ***p***.
17: 8 It was ***p*** in good soil by many
17:10 Behold, it is ***p***,
19:10 ***P*** by the waters, Fruitful and
19:13 And now she is ***p*** in the
31: 4 around the place where it was ***p***,
36:36 the ruined places and ***p*** what
Hos 9:13 ***p*** in a pleasant place, So
Am 5:11 You have ***p*** pleasant vineyards,
Mt 15:13 My heavenly Father has not ***p***
21:33 was a certain landowner who ***p***
Mk 12: 1 A man ***p*** a vineyard and set a
Lk 13: 6 certain man had a fig tree ***p***
17: 6 up by the roots and be ***p*** in
17:28 they bought, they sold, they ***p***,
20: 9 A certain man ***p*** a vineyard,
1 Cor 3: 6 I ***p***, Apollos watered, but God

PLANTERS (1/1)

Jer 31: 5 The ***p*** shall plant and eat

PLANTING (4/4)

Lev 11:37 such carcass falls on any ***p***
Isa 60:21 forever, The branch of My ***p***,
61: 3 The ***p*** of the LORD, that He
Mic 1: 6 Places for ***p*** a vineyard;

PLANTS (12/12) PLANT

Ex 10:15 green on the trees or on the ***p***
Ps 128: 3 Your children like olive ***p***
144:12 That our sons may be as ***p***
Prov 31:16 From her profits she ***p*** a
Song 4:13 Your ***p*** are an orchard of
Isa 16: 8 have broken down its choice ***p***,
17:10 you will plant pleasant ***p*** And
44:14 He ***p*** a pine, and the rain
Jer 48:32 Your ***p*** have gone over the sea,
1 Cor 3: 7 So then neither he who ***p*** is
3: 8 Now he who ***p*** and he who waters
9: 7 Who ***p*** a vineyard and does not

PLASTER (5/5)

Lev 14:42 shall take other mortar and ***p***
14:45 and all the ***p*** of the house, and
Ezek 13:10 and they ***p*** it with untempered
13:11 say to those who ***p*** it with
Dan 5: 5 the lampstand on the ***p*** of the

PLASTERED (7/6)

Lev 14:43 the house, and after it is ***p***,
14:48 the house after the house was ***p***,
Ezek 13:12 is the mortar with which you ***p***
13:14 break down the wall you have ***p***
13:15 wall and on those who have ***p***
13:15 nor those who ***p*** it,
22:28 Her prophets ***p*** them with

PLATE (4/4)

Ex 28:36 You shall also make a ***p*** of pure
39:30 Then they made the ***p*** of the
Lev 8: 9 its front, he put the golden ***p***,
Ezek 4: 3 take for yourself an iron ***p***,

PLATEAU (1/1)

Deut 4:43 in the wilderness on the ***p*** for

PLATES (3/3)

Num 16:38 them be made into hammered ***p***
1 Ki 7:36 On the ***p*** of its flanges and on
Jer 10: 9 Silver is beaten into ***p***;

PLATFORM (2/2)

2 Chr 6:13 Solomon had made a bronze ***p***
Neh 8: 4 So Ezra the scribe stood on a ***p***

PLATITUDES (1/1)

Job 13:12 Your ***p*** are proverbs of ashes,

PLATTED (KJV) See TWISTED

PLATTER (17/17)

Num 7:13 His offering was one silver ***p***,
7:19 he offered one silver ***p***,
7:25 His offering was one silver ***p***,
7:31 His offering was one silver ***p***,
7:37 His offering was one silver ***p***,
7:43 His offering was one silver ***p***,
7:49 His offering was one silver ***p***,
7:55 His offering was one silver ***p***,
7:61 His offering was one silver ***p***,
7:67 His offering was one silver ***p***,
7:73 His offering was one silver ***p***,
7:79 His offering was one silver ***p***,
7:85 Each silver ***p*** weighed one
Mt 14: 8 the Baptist's head here on a ***p***.
14:11 And his head was brought on a ***p***
Mk 6:25 head of John the Baptist on a ***p***.
6:28 brought his head on a ***p***,

PLATTERS (3/2)

Num 7:84 was anointed: twelve silver ***p***,
Ezra 1: 9 number of them: thirty gold ***p***,
1: 9 platters, one thousand silver ***p***,

PLAY (23/22) PLAYED, PLAYING

Gen 4:21 the father of all those who ***p***
Ex 32: 6 eat and drink, and rose up to ***p***.
34:15 and they ***p*** the harlot with
34:16 and his daughters ***p*** the harlot
34:16 gods and make your sons ***p*** the
Deut 22:21 to ***p*** the harlot in her father's
31:16 and this people will rise and ***p***
1 Sam 16:16 and it shall be that he will ***p***
16:17 me now a man who can ***p***
16:23 David would take a harp and ***p***
21:15 have brought this fellow to ***p***
2 Sam 6:21 Therefore I will ***p*** music
2 Chr 21:13 inhabitants of Jerusalem to ***p***
Job 40:20 all the beasts of the field ***p***
41: 5 Will you ***p*** with him as with a
Ps 33: 3 ***P*** skillfully with a shout of
104:26 Which You have made to ***p***
Isa 11: 8 The nursing child shall ***p*** by
Ezek 6: 9 and by their eyes which ***p*** the
33:32 has a pleasant voice and can ***p***
Hos 3: 3 you shall not ***p*** the harlot, nor
4:15 ***p*** the harlot, Let not Judah
1 Cor 10: 7 drink, and rose up to ***p***.

PLAYED (31/30) PLAY

Gen 38:24 your daughter-in-law has ***p*** the
Lev 17: 7 after whom they have ***p*** the
Judg 2:17 but they ***p*** the harlot with
8:27 And all Israel ***p*** the harlot
8:33 the children of Israel again ***p***
19: 2 But his concubine ***p*** the harlot
1 Sam 18:10 So David ***p*** music with his
26:21 Indeed I have ***p*** the fool and
2 Sam 6: 5 and all the house of Israel ***p***
1 Ki 1:40 and the people ***p*** the flutes and
2 Ki 3:15 happened, when the musician ***p***,
1 Chr 5:25 and ***p*** the harlot after the gods
13: 8 Then David and all Israel ***p***
Ps 106:39 And ***p*** the harlot by their own
Jer 3: 1 But you have ***p*** the harlot with
3: 6 and there ***p*** the harlot.
3: 8 but went and ***p*** the harlot also.
Ezek 16:15 ***p*** the harlot because of your
16:16 and ***p*** the harlot on them.
16:17 for yourself male images and ***p***
16:28 You also ***p*** the harlot with the
16:28 indeed you ***p*** the harlot with
23: 5 Oholah ***p*** the harlot even though
23:19 When she had ***p*** the harlot in
Hos 2: 5 For their mother has ***p*** the
4:12 And they have ***p*** the harlot
9: 1 For you have ***p*** the harlot
Mt 11:17 We ***p*** the flute for you, And you
Lk 7:32 We ***p*** the flute for you, And you
1 Cor 14: 7 it be known what is piped or ***p***?
Gal 2:13 And the rest of the Jews also ***p***

PLAYER (1/1)

1 Sam 16:16 a man who is a skillful ***p*** on

PLAYERS (3/3)

Ps 68:25 the ***p*** on instruments followed
87: 7 Both the singers and the ***p*** on
Mt 9:23 and saw the flute ***p*** and the

PLAYING (9/9) PLAY

Lev 21: 9 if she profanes herself by ***p***
1 Sam 16:18 who is skillful in ***p***,
19: 9 And David was ***p*** music with
1 Chr 15:29 saw King David whirling and ***p***
Ps 68:25 them were the maidens ***p***
Jer 2:20 You lay down, ***p*** the harlot.
Ezek 16:41 and I will make you cease ***p*** the
Zech 8: 5 be full of boys and girls ***P***
Rev 14: 2 I heard the sound of harpists ***p***

PLAYS (1/1)

Ezek 23:44 as men go in to a woman who ***p***

PLEA (1/1)

Gen 25:21 and the LORD granted his ***p***,

PLEAD (35/33) PLEADED, PLEADING, PLEADS

Judg 6:31 Would you ***p*** for Baal? Would you
6:31 Let the one who would ***p*** for him
6:31 let him ***p*** for himself, because
6:32 Let Baal ***p*** against him, because
1 Sam 24:15 and see and ***p*** my case, and
Esth 4: 8 make supplication to him and ***p***
Job 16:21 that one might ***p*** for a man with
19: 5 And ***p*** my disgrace against me,
Ps 35: 1 ***P*** my cause, O LORD, with
43: 1 And ***p*** my cause against an
74:22 ***p*** Your own cause; Remember how
119:154 ***P*** my cause and redeem me
Prov 6: 3 ***P*** with your friend.
18:17 The first one to ***p*** his cause
22:23 For the LORD will ***p*** their
23:11 He will ***p*** their cause against
31: 9 And ***p*** the cause of the poor

Isa 1:17 **P** for the widow.
3:13 The LORD stands up to **p**,
59: 4 Nor does any **p** for truth.
Jer 2:29 Why will you **p** with Me?
2:35 I will **p** My case against you,
5:28 They do not **p** the cause,
12: 1 when I **p** with You; Yet let me
25:31 He will **p** His case with all
30:13 There is no one to **p** your
50:34 He will thoroughly **p** their
51:36 I will **p** your case and take
Ezek 20:35 and there I will **p** My case with
20:36 so I will **p** My case with you,"
Mic 6: 1 **p** your case before the
Mk 5:17 Then they began to **p** with Him to
1 Cor 1:10 Now I **p** with you, brethren, by
2 Cor 6: 1 together with Him also **p**
2 Jn 5 And now I **p** with you, lady, not

PLEADED (16/16) PLEAD

Gen 25:21 Now Isaac **p** with the LORD for
42:21 anguish of his soul when he **p**
Ex 32:11 Then Moses **p** with the LORD his
Deut 3:23 Then I **p** with the LORD at that
1 Sam 25:39 who has **p** the cause of my
2 Sam 12:16 David therefore **p** with God for
2 Ki 1:13 and **p** with him, and said to
13: 4 So Jehoahaz **p** with the LORD,
Jer 20:12 For I have **p** my cause before
Lam 3:58 You have **p** the case for my
Ezek 20:36 Just as I **p** My case with your
Lk 15:28 his father came out and **p** with
Acts 16: 9 A man of Macedonia stood and **p**
16:39 Then they came and **p** with them
21:12 we and those from that place **p**
2 Cor 12: 8 Concerning this thing I **p** with

PLEADING (6/6) PLEAD

Esth 7: 7 **p** for his life, for he saw that
Mt 8: 5 came to Him, **p** with Him,
Lk 7: 3 **p** with Him to come and heal his
Acts 19:31 sent to him **p** that he would not
2 Cor 5:20 as though God were **p** through
10: 1 myself am **p** with you by the

PLEADINGS (1/1)

Job 13: 6 And heed the **p** of my lips.

PLEADS (4/4) PLEAD

Job 16:21 As a man **p** for his neighbor!
Isa 51:22 Who **p** the cause of His
Mic 7: 9 Until He **p** my case And
Rom 11: 2 how he **p** with God against

PLEASANT (47/47) PLEASANTNESS

Gen 2: 9 made every tree grow that is **p**
3: 6 that it was **p** to the eyes, and
49:15 And that the land was **p**;
Deut 3:25 those **p** mountains, and
2 Sam 1:23 Jonathan were beloved and **p**
1:26 You have been very **p** to me;
1 Ki 20: 6 that whatever is **p** in your
2 Ki 2:19 situation of this city is **p**,
Ps 16: 6 lines have fallen to me in **p**
81: 2 The **p** harp with the lute.
106:24 Then they despised the **p** land;
133: 1 how good and how **p** it is
135: 3 to His name, for it is **p**.
147: 1 to our God; For it is **p**,
Prov 2:10 And knowledge is **p** to your
9:17 bread eaten in secret is **p**.
15:26 the words of the pure are **p**.
16:24 **P** words are like a honeycomb,
22:18 For it is a **p** thing if you
23: 8 And waste your **p** words.
24: 4 filled With all precious and **p**
Eccl 11: 7 And it is **p** for the eyes to
Song 1:16 **p**! Also our bed is green.
4:13 of pomegranates With **p** fruits,
4:16 to his garden And eat its **p**
7: 6 How fair and how **p** you are,
7:13 And at our gates are **p**
Isa 5: 7 And the men of Judah are His **p**
13:22 And jackals in their **p**
17:10 Therefore you will plant **p**
32:12 upon their breasts For the **p**
64:11 And all our **p** things are laid
Jer 3:19 the children And give you a **p**
12:10 They have made My **p** portion a
23:10 The **p** places of the wilderness
31:20 Is he a **p** child? For though
Lam 1: 7 Jerusalem remembers all her **p**
1:10 spread his hand Over all her **p**
Ezek 26:12 your walls and destroy your **p**
33:32 lovely song of one who has a **p**
Dan 10: 3 I ate no **p** food, no meat or wine
11:38 with precious stones and **p**
Hos 9:13 planted in a **p** place,
Am 5:11 You have planted **p** vineyards,
Mic 2: 9 you cast out From their **p**
Zech 7:14 for they made the **p** land
Mal 3: 4 Judah and Jerusalem Will be **p**

PLEASANTNESS (1/1) PLEASANT

Prov 3:17 Her ways are ways of **p**,

PLEASE (220/214) PLEASED, PLEASES, PLEASING

Gen 12:13 **P** say you are my sister, that
13: 8 **P** let there be no strife between
13: 9 **P** separate from me. If you
16: 2 **P**, go in to my maid;
16: 6 your hand; do to her as you **p**.
18: 4 **P** let a little water be brought,
19: 2 **p** turn in to your servant's
19: 7 and said, "**P**, my brethren,
19: 8 **p**, let me bring them out
19:18 to them, "**P**, no, my lords!
19:20 **p** let me escape there (is it
23:13 **p** hear me. I will give you
24: 2 '**P**, put your hand under my
24:12 **p** give me success this day, and
24:14 **P** let down your pitcher that I
24:17 **P** let me drink a little water
24:23 daughter are you? Tell me, **p**,
24:43 **P** give me a little water from
24:45 said to her, '**P** let me drink.'
25:30 **P** feed me with that same red
27: 3 **p** take your weapons, your
27:19 **p** arise, sit and eat of my
27:21 **P** come near, that I may feel
28: 8 daughters of Canaan did not **p**
30:14 **P** give me some of your son's
30:27 **P** stay, if I have found favor
33:10 And Jacob said, "No, **p**,
33:11 '**P**, take my blessing
33:14 **P** let my lord go on ahead before
34: 8 **P** give her to him as a wife.
37: 6 **P** hear this dream which I have
37:14 **P** go and see if it is well with
37:16 **P** tell me where they are
38:16 '**P** let me come in to you";
38:25 **P** determine whose these are—the
40: 8 to God? Tell them to me, **p**.
40:14 and **p** show kindness to me;
44:18 **p** let your servant speak a word
44:33 **p** let your servant remain
45: 4 **P** come near to me." So they
47: 4 **p** let your servants dwell in
47:29 **p** put your hand under my thigh,
47:29 **P** do not bury me in Egypt,
48: 9 **P** bring them to me, and I will
50: 4 **p** speak in the hearing of
50: 5 **p** let me go up and bury my
50:17 **p** forgive the trespass of your
50:17 did evil to you." ' Now, **p**,
Ex 3:18 now, **p**, let us go three days'
4:13 **p** send by the hand of whomever
4:18 **P** let me go and return to my
5: 3 has met with us. **P**, let us
10:17 **p** forgive my sin only this
21: 8 If she does not **p** her master,
33:18 And he said, "**P**, show me
Num 10:31 **P** do not leave, inasmuch as you
11:15 **p** kill me here and now—if I
12:11 my lord! **P** do not lay this sin
12:12 **P** do not let her be as one dead,
12:13 **P** heal her, O God, I pray!"
20:17 **P** let us pass through your
22: 6 Therefore **p** come at once, curse
22:16 **P** let nothing hinder you from
22:17 Therefore **p** come, curse this
22:19 'Now therefore, **p**, you also
23:13 **P** come with me to another place
23:27 **P** come, I will take you to
23:27 perhaps it will **p** God that you
Judg 1:24 **P** show us the entrance to the
4:19 **P** give me a little water to
8: 5 **P** give loaves of bread to the
9: 2 **P** speak in the hearing of all
11:17 **P** let me pass through your
11:19 **P** let us pass through your land
13: 4 **p** be careful not to drink wine
13: 8 **p** let the Man of God whom You
13:15 **P** let us detain You, and we will
15: 2 **P**, take her instead."
16: 6 **P** tell me where your great
16:10 **p** tell me what you may be bound
18: 5 **P** inquire of God, that we may
19: 6 **P** be content to stay all night,
19: 8 **P** refresh your heart." So they
19: 9 **p** spend the night. See, the day
19:11 said to his master, "Come, **p**,
19:24 them, and do with them as you **p**;
Ruth 2: 2 **P** let me go to the field, and
2: 7 **P** let me glean and gather after
1 Sam 2:36 '**P**, put me in one of the
3:17 **P** do not hide it from me.
9: 3 Kish said to his son Saul, "**P**,
9:18 **P** tell me, where is the seer's
10:15 Saul's uncle said, "Tell me, **p**,
15:25 **p** pardon my sin, and return
15:30 sinned; yet honor me now, **p**,
16:22 **P** let David stand before me, for
19: 2 Therefore **p** be on your guard
20:29 **P** let me go, for our family has
20:29 **p** let me get away and see my
22: 3 **P** let my father and mother come
23:22 **P** go and find out for sure, and
25: 8 **P** give whatever comes to your
25:24 let this iniquity be! And **p**
25:25 '**P**, let not my lord
25:28 **P** forgive the trespass of your
26: 8 **p**, let me strike him at once
26:11 the LORD's anointed. But **p**,
26:19 'Now therefore, **p**, let my
28: 8 **P** conduct a seance for me, and
28:22 'Now therefore, **p**, heed also
30: 7 **P** bring the ephod here to me."
2 Sam 1: 4 **P** tell me." And he answered,
1: 9 **P** stand over me and kill me, for
7:29 let it **p** You to bless the house
13: 5 **P** let my sister Tamar come and
13: 6 **P** let Tamar my sister come and
13:13 **p** speak to the king; for he
13:24 **p**, let the king and his
13:26 **p** let my brother Amnon go with
14: 2 **P** pretend to be a mourner, and
14:11 **P** let the king remember the
14:12 Therefore the woman said, "**P**,
14:18 **P** do not hide from me anything
14:18 And the woman said, "**P**,
15: 7 Absalom said to the king, "**P**,
16: 9 **P**, let me go over and take
18:22 **p** let me also run after the
19:37 **P** let your servant turn back
20:16 Hear! **P** say to Joab, 'Come
24:14 **P** let us fall into the hand of
1 Ki 1:12 'Come, **p**, let me now give
2:17 **P** speak to King Solomon, for he
9:12 but they did not **p** him.
13: 6 **P** entreat the favor of the LORD
14: 2 **P** arise, and disguise yourself,
17:10 **P** bring me a little water in a
17:11 **P** bring me a morsel of bread in
19:20 **P** let me kiss my father and my
20: 7 the land, and said, "Notice, **p**,
20:31 **P**, let us put sackcloth
20:32 **P** let me live.'" And he said,
20:35 of the LORD, "Strike me, **p**.
20:37 man, and said, "Strike me, **p**.
22: 5 **P** inquire for the word of the
22:13 **P**, let your word be like the
2 Ki 1:13 **p** let my life and the life of
2: 2 said to Elisha, "Stay here, **p**,
2: 4 to him, "Elisha, stay here, **p**,
2: 6 said to him, "Stay here, **p**,
2: 9 **P** let a double portion of your
2:16 **P** let them go and search for
2:19 **P** notice, the situation of this
4:10 '**P**, let us make a small
4:22 **P** send me one of the young men
4:26 **P** run now to meet her, and say
5: 7 Therefore **p** consider, and see
5: 8 **P** let him come to me, and he
5:15 **p** take a gift from your
5:17 **p** let your servant be given two
5:18 may the LORD **p** pardon your
5:22 **P** give them a talent of silver
5:23 So Naaman said, "**P**,
6: 2 '**P**, let us go to the Jordan,
6: 3 **P** consent to go with your
7:13 servants answered and said, "**P**,
8: 4 of God, saying, "Tell me, **p**,
18:26 **P** speak to your servants in
1 Chr 21:13 **P** let me fall into the hand of
2 Chr 10: 7 and **p** them, and speak good
18: 4 **P** inquire for the word of the
18:12 Therefore **p** let your word be
Ezra 10:14 '**P**, let the leaders of our
Neh 1: 6 **p** let Your ear be attentive and
1:11 **p** let Your ear be attentive to
5:10 **P**, let us stop this usury!
Esth 8: 8 concerning the Jews, as you **p**,
Job 6: 9 That it would **p** God to crush
8: 8 "For inquire, **p**,
17:10 But **p**, come back again,
22:22 Receive, **p**, instruction from
33: 1 'But **p**, Job, hear my
42: 4 Listen, **p**, and let me speak;
Ps 69:31 This also shall **p** the LORD
Prov 16: 7 When a man's ways **p** the LORD,
Isa 5: 3 and men of Judah, Judge, **p**,
5: 5 **p** let Me tell you what I will
29:11 saying, "Read this, **p**.
29:12 saying, "Read this, **p**.
36:11 **P** speak to your servants in the
51:21 Therefore **p** hear this, you
55:11 it shall accomplish what I **p**,
64: 9 **p** look—we all are Your people!
Jer 21: 2 **P** inquire of the LORD for us,
32: 8 **P** buy my field that is in
37:20 'Therefore **p** hear now, O my lord
37:20 **P**, let my petition be
38: 4 princes said to the king, "**P**,
38:12 **P** put these old clothes and rags
38:20 **P**, obey the voice of the LORD
40:15 Mizpah, saying, "Let me go, **p**,
42: 2 to Jeremiah the prophet, "**P**,
Ezek 33:30 **P** come and hear what the word is
Dan 1:12 **P** test your servants for ten
Jon 1: 8 **P** tell us! For whose cause is
1:14 **p** do not let us perish for this
4: 3 **p** take my life from me, for it
Jn 8:29 I always do those things that **p**
Rom 8: 8 who are in the flesh cannot **p**
15: 1 and not to **p** ourselves.
15: 2 Let each of us **p** his neighbor
15: 3 For even Christ did not **p**
1 Cor 7:32 how he may **p** the Lord.
7:33 how he may **p** his wife.
7:34 how she may **p** her husband.
10:33 just as I also **p** all men in all
Gal 1:10 Or do I seek to **p** men? For if I
1 Th 2:15 and they do not **p** God and are
4: 1 how you ought to walk and to **p**
2 Tim 2: 4 that he may **p** him who enlisted
Heb 11: 6 faith it is impossible to **p**

PLEASED (60/59) PLEASE

Gen 33:10 and you were **p** with me.
34:18 And their words **p** Hamor and
45:16 So it **p** Pharaoh and his
Num 24: 1 Now when Balaam saw that it **p**
Deut 1:23 The plan **p** me well; so I took
Josh 22:30 Manasseh spoke, it **p** them.
22:33 So the thing **p** the children of
Judg 14: 7 and she **p** Samson well.
1 Sam 12:22 because it has **p** the LORD to
18:20 and the thing **p** him.
18:26 it **p** David well to become the
2 Sam 3:36 and it **p** them, since whatever
3:36 since whatever the king did **p**
17: 4 And the saying **p** Absalom and all
19: 6 then it would have **p** you well.
1 Ki 3:10 The speech **p** the LORD, that
1 Chr 17:27 Now You have been **p** to bless the
28: 4 He was **p** with me to make me
2 Chr 30: 4 And the matter **p** the king and
Neh 2: 6 So it **p** the king to send me;
Esth 1:21 And the reply **p** the king and the
2: 4 This thing **p** the king, and he
2: 9 Now the young woman **p** him, and
5:14 And the thing **p** Haman; so he
9: 5 and did what they **p** with those
Job 6:28 be **p** to look at me; For I
Ps 40:13 Be **p**, O LORD, to deliver
41:11 this I know that You are well **p**
51:19 Then You shall be **p** with the
Isa 2: 6 And they are **p** with the
39: 2 And Hezekiah was **p** with them,
42:21 The LORD is well **p** for His
53:10 Yet it **p** the LORD to bruise
Dan 6: 1 It **p** Darius to set over the
Jon 1:14 have done as it **p** You."
Mic 6: 7 Will the LORD be **p** with
Mal 1: 8 your governor! Would he be **p**
Mt 3:17 Son, in whom I am well **p**.
12:18 whom My soul is well **p**!
14: 6 danced before them and **p** Herod.
17: 5 Son, in whom I am well **p**.
Mk 1:11 Son, in whom I am well **p**.
6:22 and **p** Herod and those who sat
Lk 3:22 beloved Son; in You I am well **p**.
Acts 6: 5 And the saying **p** the whole
12: 3 And because he saw that it **p** the
15:22 Then it **p** the apostles and
Rom 15:26 For it **p** those from Macedonia
15:27 It **p** them indeed, and they are
1 Cor 1:21 it **p** God through the
10: 5 most of them God was not well **p**,
12:18 them, in the body just as He **p**.
2 Cor 5: 8 well **p** rather to be absent from
Gal 1:10 For if I still **p** men, I would
1:15 But when it **p** God, who separated
Col 1:19 For it **p** the Father that in
1 Th 2: 8 we were well **p** to impart to you
Heb 11: 5 testimony, that he **p** God.
13:16 such sacrifices God is well **p**.
2 Pe 1:17 Son, in whom I am well **p**.

PLEASES (23/23) PLEASE

Gen 20:15 dwell where it **p** you."
Judg 14: 3 for she **p** me well."
1 Sam 20:13 But if it **p** my father to do
1 Ki 21: 6 if it **p** you, I will give you
Neh 2: 5 If it **p** the king, and if your
2: 7 If it **p** the king, let letters be
Esth 1:19 If it **p** the king, let a royal
2: 4 let the young woman who **p**
3: 9 If it **p** the king, let a decree
5: 4 If it **p** the king, let the king
5: 8 and if it **p** the king to grant
7: 3 and if it **p** the king, let my
8: 5 If it **p** the king, and if I have
9:13 If it **p** the king, let it be
Ps 115: 3 He does whatever He **p**.
135: 6 Whatever the LORD **p** He does,
Eccl 7:26 He who **p** God shall escape from
8: 3 for he does whatever **p** him."
Song 2: 7 up nor awaken love Until it **p**.
3: 5 up nor awaken love Until it **p**.
8: 4 up nor awaken love Until it **p**.
Isa 56: 4 And choose what **p** Me,
1 Cor 15:38 But God gives it a body as He **p**,

PLEASING (13/13) PLEASE

Esth 8: 5 right to the king and I am **p**
Jer 42: 6 Whether it is **p** or
Lam 2: 4 He has slain all who were **p**
Hos 9: 4 shall their sacrifices be **p** to
Acts 7:20 and was well **p** to God; and he
2 Cor 5: 9 to be well **p** to Him.
Phil 4:18 sacrifice, well **p** to God.
Col 1:10 fully **p** Him, being fruitful in
3:20 for this is well **p** to the Lord.
1 Th 2: 4 not as **p** men, but God who tests
Titus 2: 9 to be well **p** in all things,
Heb 13:21 working in you what is well **p**
1 Jn 3:22 and do those things that are **p**

PLEASURE (55/54) PLEASURES

Gen 18:12 have grown old, shall I have **p**,
Deut 23:24 your fill of grapes at your **p**,
1 Chr 29:17 You test the heart and have **p**
Ezra 5:17 and let the king send us his **p**
Neh 9:37 and our cattle At their **p**;
Esth 1: 8 do according to each man's **p**.
Job 21:25 Never having eaten with **p**.
22: 3 Is it any **p** to the Almighty
Ps 5: 4 You are not a God who takes **p**
35:27 Who has **p** in the prosperity of
51:18 Do good in Your good **p** to Zion;
102:14 For Your servants take **p** in her
103:21 ministers of His, who do His **p**.
105:22 To bind his princes at his **p**,
111: 2 Studied by all who have **p** in
147:10 He takes no **p** in the legs of a
147:11 The LORD takes **p** in those who
149: 4 For the LORD takes **p** in His
Prov 21:17 He who loves **p** will be a poor
Eccl 2: 1 therefore enjoy **p**"; but
2:10 withhold my heart from any **p**,
5: 4 For He has no **p** in fools.
12: 1 I have no **p** in them":
Isa 44:28 And he shall perform all My **p**,
46:10 And I will do all My **p**,'
48:14 He shall do His **p** on Babylon,
53:10 And the **p** of the LORD shall
58: 3 the day of your fast you find **p**,
58:13 From doing your **p** on My holy
58:13 Nor finding your own **p**,
Jer 22:28 vessel in which is no **p**?
34:16 had set at liberty, at their **p**,
48:38 like a vessel in which is no **p**,
Ezek 16:37 lovers with whom you took **p**,
18:23 Do I have any **p** at all that the
18:32 For I have no **p** in the death of
33:11 I have no **p** in the death of the
Hos 8: 8 a vessel in which is no **p**.
Hag 1: 8 that I may take **p** in it and be
Mal 1:10 I have no **p** in you,"
Lk 12:32 for it is your Father's good **p**
2 Cor 12:10 Therefore I take **p** in
Eph 1: 5 according to the good **p** of His
1: 9 according to His good **p** which
Phil 2:13 will and to do for His good **p**.
2 Th 1:11 and fulfill all the good **p** of
2:12 believe the truth but had **p** in
1 Tim 5: 6 But she who lives in **p** is dead
2 Tim 3: 4 lovers of **p** rather than lovers
Heb 10: 6 for sin You had no **p**.
10: 8 nor had **p** in them" (which
10:38 My soul has no **p** in
Jas 4: 1 from your desires for **p** that
5: 5 have lived on the earth in **p**
2 Pe 2:13 as those who count it **p** to

PLEASURES (8/8) PLEASURE

Job 36:11 And their years in **p**.
Ps 16:11 At Your right hand are **p**
36: 8 drink from the river of Your **p**.
Isa 47: 8 now, you who are given to **p**,
Lk 8:14 and **p** of life, and bring no
Titus 3: 3 serving various lusts and **p**,
Heb 11:25 than to enjoy the passing **p** of
Jas 4: 3 you may spend it on your **p**.

PLEDGE (27/26)

Gen 38:17 Will you give me a **p** till you
38:18 'What **p** shall I give you?"
38:20 to receive his **p** from the
Ex 22:26 your neighbor's garment as a **p**,
Lev 6: 2 for safekeeping, or about a **p**,
Deut 24: 6 or the upper millstone in **p**,
24: 6 for he takes one's living in **p**.
24:10 go into his house to get his **p**.
24:11 you lend shall bring the **p** out
24:12 you shall not keep his **p**
24:13 shall in any case return the **p**
24:17 take a widow's garment as a **p**.
2 Ki 18:23 give a **p** to my master the king
Job 17: 3 Now put down a **p** for me with
24: 3 take the widow's ox as a **p**.
24: 9 And take a **p** from the poor.
Prov 6: 1 you have shaken hands in **p** for
17:18 shakes hands in a **p**,
20:16 And hold it as a **p** when it
22:26 those who shakes hands in a **p**,
27:13 And hold it in **p** when he is
Isa 36: 8 give a **p** to my master the king
Ezek 18: 7 restored to the debtor his **p**;
18:12 violence, Not restored the **p**,
18:16 anyone, Nor withheld a **p**,
33:15 "if the wicked restores the **p**,
Am 2: 8 altar on clothes taken in **p**,

PLEDGED (2/2)

Neh 6:18 For many in Judah were **p** to him,
Jer 30:21 For who is this who **p** his

PLEDGES (2/2)

Job 22: 6 For you have taken **p** from your
Hab 2: 6 who loads himself with many **p**'?

PLEIADES (3/3)

Job 9: 9 made the Bear, Orion, and the **P**,
38:31 you bind the cluster of the **P**,
Am 5: 8 He made the **P** and Orion;

PLENTIFUL (8/8) PLENTY

Gen 41:34 land of Egypt in the seven **p**
41:47 Now in the seven **p** years the
Ps 68: 9 sent a **p** rain, Whereby You
Isa 16:10 And joy from the **p** field;
30:23 It will be fat and **p**.
Jer 48:33 gladness are taken From the **p**
Hab 1:16 is sumptuous And their food **p**.
Mt 9:37 "The harvest truly is **p**,

PLENTIFULLY (1/1)

Lk 12:16 of a certain rich man yielded **p**.

PLENTY (13/13) PLENTIFUL

Gen 27:28 And **p** of grain and wine.
41:29 Indeed seven years of great **p**
41:30 and all the **p** will be forgotten
41:31 So the **p** will not be known in
41:53 Then the seven years of **p** which
Lev 11:36 in which there is **p** of
Deut 28:11 the LORD will grant you **p**
2 Chr 31:10 had enough to eat and have **p**
Prov 3:10 barns will be filled with **p**,
21: 5 the diligent lead surely to **p**,
28:19 who tills his land will have **p**
Jer 44:17 For then we had **p** of food,
Joel 2:26 You shall eat in **p** and be

PLIGHT (2/2)

Job 9:23 He laughs at the **p** of the
30:16 is poured out because of my **p**;

PLOT (15/14) PLOTS, PLOTTED

Josh 24:32 in the **p** of ground which Jacob
2 Ki 9:10 shall eat Jezebel on the **p** of
9:26 'and I will repay you in this **p**,
9:26 take and throw him on the **p**
9:36 On the **p** of ground at Jezreel
9:37 in the **p** at Jezreel, so that
Neh 4:15 that God had brought their **p**
Esth 9:25 by letter that this wicked **p**
Ps 2: 1 And the people **p** a vain thing?
21:11 They devised a **p** which they
35: 4 brought to confusion Who **p** my
Ezek 45: 2 this there shall be a square **p**
Jn 4: 5 near the **p** of ground that Jacob
Acts 4:25 And the people **p** vain
9:24 But their **p** became known to

PLOTS (6/6) PLOT

Ps 10: 2 Let them be caught in the **p**
31:20 of Your presence From the **p**
37:12 The wicked **p** against the just,
64: 2 Hide me from the secret **p** of
Prov 24: 8 He who **p** to do evil Will be
Nah 1:11 you comes forth one Who **p**

PLOTTED (14/14) PLOT

1 Sam 23: 9 When David knew that Saul **p**
2 Sam 21: 5 the man who consumed us and **p**
Esth 9:24 had **p** against the Jews to
Isa 7: 5 and the son of Remaliah have **p**
Mt 12:14 the Pharisees went out and **p**
22:15 Then the Pharisees went and **p**
26: 4 and **p** to take Jesus by trickery
27: 1 and elders of the people **p**
Mk 3: 6 went out and immediately **p**
Jn 11:53 they **p** to put Him to death.
12:10 But the chief priests **p** to put
Acts 5:33 they were furious and **p** to kill
9:23 the Jews **p** to kill him.
20: 3 And when the Jews **p** against him

PLOTTING (2/2)

Acts 20:19 which happened to me by the **p**
Eph 4:14 craftiness of deceitful **p**,

PLOUGH (KJV) See PLOW

PLOW (10/9) PLOWED, PLOWING, PLOWMAN, PLOWSHARE

Deut 22:10 You shall not **p** with an ox and
1 Sam 8:12 will set some to **p** his
Job 4: 8 Those who **p** iniquity And sow
39:10 Or will he **p** the valleys
Prov 20: 4 The lazy man will not **p**
Hos 10:11 I will make Ephraim pull a **p**.
10:11 pull a plow. Judah shall **p**;
Am 6:12 Does one **p** there with oxen?
Lk 9:62 having put his hand to the **p**,
1 Cor 9:10 that he who plows should **p** in

PLOWED (6/6) PLOW

Deut 21: 4 which is neither **p** nor sown,
Judg 14:18 If you had not **p** with my heifer,
Ps 129: 3 The plowers **p** on my back;
Jer 26:18 Zion shall be **p** like a field,
Hos 10:13 You have **p** wickedness;
Mic 3:12 of you Zion shall be **p** like

PLOWERS (1/1)

Ps 129: 3 The **p** plowed on my back;

PLOWING (7/7) PLOW

Gen 45: 6 there will be neither **p** nor
Ex 34:21 in **p** time and in harvest you

1 Ki 19:19 who was **p** with twelve yoke
Job 1:14 The oxen were **p** and the donkeys
Prov 21: 4 And the **p** of the wicked are
Isa 28:24 Does the plowman keep **p** all day
Lk 17: 7 having a servant **p** or tending

PLOWMAN (2/2) PLOW

Isa 28:24 Does the **p** keep plowing all day
Am 9:13 When the **p** shall overtake the

PLOWMEN (2/2)

Isa 61: 5 foreigner Shall be your **p**
Jer 14: 4 The **p** were ashamed;

PLOWS (2/2)

Ps 141: 7 As when one **p** and breaks up
1 Cor 9:10 that he who **p** should plow in

PLOWSHARE (1/1) PLOW, PLOWSHARES

1 Sam 13:20 to sharpen each man's **p**,

PLOWSHARES (4/4) PLOWSHARE

1 Sam 13:21 sharpening was a pim for the **p**,
Isa 2: 4 shall beat their swords into **p**,
Joel 3:10 Beat your **p** into swords
Mic 4: 3 shall beat their swords into **p**,

PLUCK (22/21) PLUCKED

Deut 23:25 you may **p** the heads with your
Job 30: 4 Who **p** mallow by the bushes,
Ps 25:15 For He shall **p** my feet out of
52: 5 and **p** you out of your dwelling
80:12 that all who pass by the way **p**
Eccl 3: 2 And a time to **p** what is
Jer 12:14 I will **p** them out of their land
12:14 them out of their land and **p**
12:17 I will utterly **p** up and destroy
18: 7 to **p** up, to pull down, and to
22:24 yet I would **p** you off;
24: 6 and I will plant them and not **p**
31:28 I have watched over them to **p**
42:10 and I will plant you and not **p**
45: 4 what I have planted I will **p**
Ezek 17: 9 people Will be needed to **p** it
Mic 5:14 I will **p** your wooden images
Mt 5:29 **p** it out and cast it from you;
12: 1 and began to **p** heads of grain
18: 9 **p** it out and cast it from you.
Mk 2:23 went His disciples began to **p**
9:47 **p** it out. It is better for you

PLUCKED (14/14) PLUCK

Gen 8:11 a freshly **p** olive leaf was in
Deut 28:63 and you shall be **p** from off the
Ezra 9: 3 and **p** out some of the hair of
Job 29:17 And **p** the victim from his
Isa 50: 6 And My cheeks to those who **p**
Jer 12:15 after I have **p** them out, that I
31:40 It shall not be **p** up or thrown
Ezek 19:12 But she was **p** up in fury,
Dan 7: 4 I watched till its wings were **p**
7: 8 of the first horns were **p** out
Am 4:11 you were like a firebrand **p**
Zech 3: 2 you! Is this not a brand **p**
Lk 6: 1 And His disciples **p** the heads
Gal 4:15 you would have **p** out your own

PLUMB (5/3)

Am 7: 7 stood on a wall made with a **p**
7: 7 with a **p** line in His hand.
7: 8 A **p** line." Then the Lord said:
7: 8 I am setting a **p** line In the
Zech 4:10 seven rejoice to see The **p**

PLUMMET (2/2)

2 Ki 21:13 line of Samaria and the **p** of
Isa 28:17 line, And righteousness the **p**;

PLUMP (2/2)

Gen 41: 5 on one stalk, **p** and good.
41: 7 heads devoured the seven **p** and

PLUNDER (71/61) PLUNDERED, PLUNDERERS, PLUNDERING

Ex 3:22 So you shall **p** the Egyptians."
Num 31:26 Count up the **p** that was taken—of
31:27 and divide the **p** into two parts,
31:32 The booty remaining from the **p**,
Deut 2:35 took only the livestock as **p**
13:16 you shall gather all its **p**
13:16 fire the city and all its **p**,
20:14 you shall **p** for yourself;
20:14 you shall eat the enemies' **p**
Judg 5:30 **p** of dyed garments, Plunder of
5:30 **P** of garments embroidered and
8:24 give me the earrings from his **p**.
8:25 into it the earrings from his **p**.
1 Sam 14:36 and **p** them until the morning
15:21 "But the people took of the **p**,
2 Sam 23:10 returned after him only to **p**.
2 Ki 21:14 they shall become victims of **p**
Ezra 9: 7 the sword, to captivity, to **p**,
Neh 4: 4 and give them as **p** to a land of
Esth 3:13 and to **p** their possessions.
8:11 and to **p** their possessions,
9:10 did not lay a hand on the **p**.
9:15 did not lay a hand on the **p**.
9:16 did not lay a hand on the **p**.
Ps 89:41 All who pass by the way **p** him;
109:11 And let strangers **p** his labor.
Prov 22:23 And **p** the soul of those who
22:23 the soul of those who **p** them.
24:15 Do not **p** his resting place;
Isa 3:14 The **p** of the poor is in your
11:14 Together they shall **p** the
17:14 is the portion of those who **p**
33: 1 Woe to you who **p**,
33: 4 And Your **p** shall be gathered
33:23 Then the prey of great **p** is
42:22 and no one delivers; For **p**,
42:24 Who gave Jacob for **p**,
Jer 15:13 treasures I will give as **p**
17: 3 I will give as **p** your wealth,
20: 5 who will **p** them, seize them,
20: 8 Violence and **p**!" Because the
30:16 Those who **p** you shall become
30:16 who plunder you shall become **p**,
47: 4 of the day that comes to **p** all
47: 4 For the LORD shall **p** the
49:32 multitude of their cattle for **p**.
50:10 And Chaldea shall become **p**;
50:10 All who **p** her shall be
Ezek 7:21 I will give it as **p** Into the
23:46 give them up to trouble and **p**.
25: 7 and give you as **p** to the
26: 5 it shall become **p** for the
26:12 They will **p** your riches and
32:12 They shall **p** the pomp of Egypt,
36: 4 which became **p** and mockery to
36: 5 in order to **p** its open
38:12 to take **p** and to take booty, to
38:13 you, 'Have you come to take **p**?
38:13 and goods, to take great **p**?
39:10 and they will **p** those who
Dan 11:24 shall disperse among them the **p**,
Hos 13:15 He shall **p** the treasury of
Hab 2: 8 remnant of the people shall **p**
2:17 And the **p** of beasts which
Zeph 2: 9 residue of My people shall **p**
3: 8 the day I rise up for **p**;
Zech 2: 8 to the nations which **p** you;
Mt 12:29 a strong man's house and **p** his
12:29 And then he will **p** his house.
Mk 3:27 a strong man's house and **p** his
3:27 And then he will **p** his house.

PLUNDERED (39/36) PLUNDER

Gen 34:27 and **p** the city, because their
34:29 and they **p** even all that was
Ex 12:36 Thus they **p** the Egyptians.
Deut 28:29 shall be only oppressed and **p**
Judg 2:16 out of the hand of those who **p**
1 Sam 14:48 from the hands of those who **p**
17:53 and they **p** their tents.
2 Ki 7:16 Then the people went out and **p**
2 Chr 14:14 and they **p** all the cities, for
Job 12:17 He leads counselors away **p**,
12:19 He leads princes away **p**,
Ps 7: 4 Or have **p** my enemy without
76: 5 The stouthearted were **p**;
137: 3 And those who **p** us requested
Isa 13:16 Their houses will be **p** And
24: 3 entirely emptied and utterly **p**,
33: 1 though you have not been **p**;
33: 1 plundering, You will be **p**;
42:22 this is a people robbed and **p**;
Jer 2:14 a homeborn slave? Why is he **p**?
4:13 Woe to us, for we are **p**!"
4:20 For the whole land is **p**.
4:20 Suddenly my tents are **p**,
4:30 "And when you are **p**,
9:19 How we are **p**! We are greatly
10:20 My tent is **p**, And all my
21:12 And deliver him who is **p**
22: 3 and deliver the **p** out of the
25:36 For the LORD has **p** their
48: 1 "Woe to Nebo! For it is **p**,
48:15 Moab is **p** and gone up from her
48:20 it in Arnon, that Moab is **p**.
49: 3 for Ai is **p**! Cry, you
49:10 himself. His descendants are **p**,
Ezek 39:10 they will plunder those who **p**
Hos 10:14 all your fortresses shall be **p**
10:14 be plundered As Shalman **p**
Am 3:11 And your palaces shall be **p**.
Hab 2: 8 Because you have **p** many

PLUNDERER (7/7)

Isa 21: 2 And the **p** plunders. Go up,
Jer 6:26 For the **p** will suddenly come
15: 8 A **p** at noonday; I will cause
48: 8 And the **p** shall come against
48:18 For the **p** of Moab has come
48:32 The **p** has fallen on your
51:56 Because the **p** comes against

PLUNDERERS (5/5) PLUNDER

Judg 2:14 them into the hands of **p** who
2 Ki 17:20 them into the hand of **p**,
Jer 12:12 The **p** have come On all the
51:48 For the **p** shall come to her
51:53 Yet from Me **p** would come to

PLUNDERING (9/9) PLUNDER

Isa 22: 4 to comfort me Because of the **p**
33: 1 with you! When you cease **p**,
Jer 6: 7 Violence and **p** are heard in
48: 3 **P** and great destruction!'
51:55 Because the LORD is **p** Babylon
Ezek 45: 9 Remove violence and **p**,
Dan 11:33 and flame, by captivity and **p**.
Hab 1: 3 For **p** and violence are before
Heb 10:34 and joyfully accepted the **p** of

PLUNDERS (3/3)

Ps 35:10 and the needy from him who **p**
Isa 21: 2 And the plunderer **p**.
Nah 3:16 The locust **p** and flies away.

PLUNGE (1/1)

Job 9:31 Yet You will **p** me into the pit,

PLUNGED (1/1)

Jn 21: 7 and **p** into the sea.

PLUS (1/1)

Num 5: 7 **p** one-fifth of it, and give it

POCHERETH (2/2)

Ezra 2:57 the sons of **P** of Zebaim, and
Neh 7:59 the sons of **P** of Zebaim, and

POCKET (1/1)

1 Sam 25:29 as from the **p** of a sling.

PODS (1/1)

Lk 15:16 filled his stomach with the **p**

POETS (1/1)

Acts 17:28 as also some of your own **p** have

POINT (13/13) POINTS

Gen 46:28 to **p** out before him the way
Judg 5:18 their lives to the **p** of death,
Job 20:25 the glittering **p** comes out of
Jer 17: 1 With the **p** of a diamond it
Ezek 21:15 I have set the **p** of the sword
47:20 boundary until one comes to a **p**
Mk 5:23 little daughter lies at the **p**
Jn 4:27 And at this **p** His disciples
4:47 for he was at the **p** of death.
Phil 2: 8 and became obedient to the **p**
2 Tim 2: 9 even to the **p** of chains;
Heb 8: 1 Now this is the main **p** of the
Jas 2:10 law, and yet stumble in one **p**,

POINTED (3/3)

1 Ki 7:25 and all their back parts **p**
2 Chr 4: 4 and all their back parts **p**
Job 41:30 He spreads **p** marks in the

POINTEDLY (1/1)

Gen 43: 7 The man asked us **p** about

POINTING (1/1)

Isa 58: 9 The **p** of the finger, and

POINTS (6/5) POINT

Num 33: 2 wrote down the starting **p** of
33: 2 according to their starting **p**:
1 Sam 13:21 and to set the **p** of the goads.
Prov 6:13 He **p** with his fingers;
Rom 15:15 more boldly to you on some **p**,
Heb 4:15 but was in all **p** tempted as

POISON (9/8)

Deut 32:24 With the **p** of serpents of the
32:33 Their wine is the **p** of
Job 6: 4 My spirit drinks in their **p**;
20:16 He will suck the **p** of cobras;
Ps 58: 4 Their **p** is like the poison of
58: 4 Their poison is like the **p** of
140: 3 The **p** of asps is under their
Rom 3:13 The **p** of asps is under
Jas 3: 8 unruly evil, full of deadly **p**.

POISONED (2/2)

Acts 8:23 For I see that you are **p** by
14: 2 stirred up the Gentiles and **p**

POLE (4/4)

Num 13:23 it between two of them on a **p**.
21: 8 serpent, and set it on a **p**;
21: 9 serpent, and put it on a **p**;
Isa 30:17 Till you are left as a **p** on

POLES (38/34)

Ex 25:13 And you shall make **p** of acacia

25:14 You shall put the **p** into the
25:15 The **p** shall be in the rings of
25:27 as holders for the **p** to bear
25:28 And you shall make the **p** of
27: 6 And you shall make **p** for the
27: 6 **p** of acacia wood, and overlay
27: 7 The **p** shall be put in the rings,
27: 7 and the **p** shall be on the two
30: 4 they will be holders for the **p**
30: 5 You shall make the **p** of acacia
35:12 'the ark and its **p**,
35:13 'the table and its **p**,
35:15 'the incense altar, its **p**,
35:16 with its bronze grating, its **p**,
37: 4 He made **p** of acacia wood, and
37: 5 And he put the **p** into the rings
37:14 as holders for the **p** to bear
37:15 And he made the **p** of acacia wood
37:27 as holders for the **p** with which
37:28 And he made the **p** of acacia
38: 5 grating, as holders for the **p**.
38: 6 And he made the **p** of acacia
38: 7 Then he put the **p** into the rings
39:35 ark of the Testimony with its **p**,
39:39 its grate of bronze, its **p**,
40:20 inserted the **p** through the
Num 4: 6 and they shall insert its **p**.
4: 8 and they shall insert its **p**.
4:11 and they shall insert its **p**.
4:14 badger skins, and insert its **p**.
1 Ki 8: 7 overshadowed the ark and its **p**.
8: 8 The **p** extended so that the ends
8: 8 so that the ends of the **p**
1 Chr 15:15 on their shoulders, by its **p**,
2 Chr 5: 8 overshadowed the ark and its **p**.
5: 9 And the **p** extended so that the
5: 9 so that the ends of the **p** of

POLISH (1/1)

Jer 46: 4 **P** the spears, Put on the

POLISHED (7/6)

Ezra 8:27 and two vessels of fine **p**
Isa 49: 2 And made Me a **p** shaft; In His
Ezek 21: 9 sword is sharpened And also **p**!
21:10 **P** to flash like lightning!
21:11 And He has given it to be **p**,
21:11 and it is **p** To be given into
21:28 **P** for slaughter, For

POLLUTE (2/2)

Num 35:33 So you shall not **p** the land
Jer 7:30 by My name, to **p** it.

POLLUTED (8/8)

Ps 106:38 And the land was **p** with blood.
Prov 25:26 like a murky spring and a **p**
Jer 2:23 "How can you say, 'I am not **p**,
3: 1 not that land be greatly **p**?
3: 2 And you have **p** the land With
Zeph 3: 1 to her who is rebellious and **p**,
3: 4 Her priests have **p** the
Acts 15:20 them to abstain from things **p**

POLLUTIONS (1/1)

2 Pe 2:20 after they have escaped the **p**

POMEGRANATE (10/8) POMEGRANATES

Ex 28:34 "a golden bell and a **p**,
28:34 a golden bell and a **p**,
39:26 a bell and a **p**,
39:26 a pomegranate, a bell and a **p**,
1 Sam 14: 2 outskirts of Gibeah under a **p**
Song 4: 3 veil Are like a piece of **p**.
6: 7 Like a piece of **p** Are your
8: 2 wine, Of the juice of my **p**.
Joel 1:12 The **p** tree, The palm tree
Hag 2:19 the vine, the fig tree, the **p**,

POMEGRANATES (23/17) POMEGRANATE

Ex 28:33 upon its hem you shall make **p**
39:24 made on the hem of the robe **p**
39:25 put the bells between the **p** on
39:25 robe all around between the **p**:
Num 13:23 also brought some of the **p**
20: 5 of grain or figs or vines or **p**;
Deut 8: 8 of vines and fig trees and **p**,
1 Ki 7:18 and two rows of **p** above the
7:20 on the two pillars also had **p**
7:20 there were two hundred such **p**
7:42 four hundred **p** for the two
7:42 the two networks (two rows of **p**
2 Ki 25:17 and the network and **p** all
2 Chr 3:16 and he made one hundred **p**,
4:13 four hundred **p** for the two
4:13 the two networks (two rows of **p**
Song 4:13 plants are an orchard of **p**
6:11 the vine had budded And the **p**
7:12 And the **p** are in bloom.
Jer 52:22 with a network and **p** all around
52:22 with **p** was the same.
52:23 There were ninety-six **p** on the
52:23 on the sides; all the **p**,

POMP (5/5) POMPOUS

Isa 5:14 and their multitude and their **p**,
14:11 Your **p** is brought down to
Ezek 7:24 I will cause the **p** of the
32:12 They shall plunder the **p** of
Acts 25:23 Bernice had come with great **p**,

POMPOUS (4/4) POMP

Dan 7: 8 and a mouth speaking **p** words.
7:11 because of the sound of the **p**
7:20 eyes and a mouth which spoke **p**
7:25 He shall speak **p** words against

PONDER (2/2) PONDERED

Prov 4:26 **P** the path of your feet,
5: 6 Lest you **p** her path of

PONDERED (2/2) PONDER

Eccl 12: 9 he **p** and sought out and set in
Lk 2:19 kept all these things and **p**

PONDERS (1/1)

Prov 5:21 And He **p** all his paths.

PONDS (2/2)

Ex 7:19 over their rivers, over their **p**,
8: 5 over the rivers, and over the **p**,

PONTIUS (4/4) PILATE

Mt 27: 2 away and delivered Him to **P** Pilate
Lk 3: 1 **P** Pilate being governor of
Acts 4:27 both Herod and **P** Pilate, with
1 Tim 6:13 the good confession before **P** Pilate,

PONTUS (3/3)

Acts 2: 9 Cappadocia, **P** and Asia,
18: 2 Jew named Aquila, born in **P**,
1 Pe 1: 1 pilgrims of the Dispersion in **P**,

POOL (24/22) POOLS, WATERPOOLS

2 Sam 2:13 went out and met them by the **p**
2:13 one on one side of the **p** and
2:13 on the other side of the **p**.
4:12 and hanged them by the **p** in
1 Ki 22:38 washed the chariot at a **p** in
2 Ki 18:17 the aqueduct from the upper **p**,
20:20 and how he made a **p** and a
Neh 2:14 Gate and to the King's **P**,
3:15 and repaired the wall of the **P**
3:16 of David, to the man-made **p**,
Ps 114: 8 Who turned the rock into a **p**
Isa 7: 3 the aqueduct from the upper **p**,
22: 9 the waters of the lower **p**.
22:11 For the water of the old **p**.
35: 7 parched ground shall become a **p**,
36: 2 the aqueduct from the upper **p**,
41:18 I will make the wilderness a **p**
Jer 41:12 they found him by the great **p**
Nah 2: 8 Nineveh of old was like a **p**
Jn 5: 2 by the Sheep Gate a **p**,
5: 4 at a certain time into the **p**
5: 7 no man to put me into the **p**
9: 7 wash in the **p** of Siloam"
9:11 Go to the **p** of Siloam and wash.'

POOLS (6/6) POOL

Ex 7:19 and over all their **p** of water,
Ps 84: 6 The rain also covers it with **p**.
107:35 He turns a wilderness into **p** of
Eccl 2: 6 I made myself water **p** from which
Song 7: 4 Your eyes like the **p** in
Isa 42:15 And I will dry up the **p**.

POOR (201/194) POOREST

Gen 41:19 **p** and very ugly and gaunt, such
Ex 22:25 any of My people who are **p**
23: 3 not show partiality to a **p** man
23: 6 pervert the judgment of your **p**
23:11 that the **p** of your people may
30:15 shall not give more and the **p**
Lev 14:21 But if he is **p** and cannot
19:10 you shall leave them for the **p**
19:15 shall not be partial to the **p**,
23:22 You shall leave them for the **p**
25:25 one of your brethren becomes **p**,
25:35 one of your brethren becomes **p**,
25:39 who dwells by you becomes **p**,
25:47 who dwells by him becomes **p**,
27: 8 But if he is too **p** to pay your
Num 13:20 the land is rich or **p**;
Deut 15: 4 except when there may be no **p**
15: 7 If there is among you a **p** man
15: 7 nor shut your hand from your **p**
15: 9 your eye be evil against your **p**
15:11 For the **p** will never cease from
15:11 to your **p** and your needy, in
24:12 "And if the man is **p**,
24:14 a hired servant who is **p** and
24:15 for he is **p** and has set his
Ruth 3:10 whether **p** or rich.
1 Sam 2: 7 The LORD makes **p** and makes
2: 8 He raises the **p** from the dust
18:23 seeing I am a **p** and lightly
2 Sam 12: 1 city, one rich and the other **p**.
12: 3 But the **p** man had nothing,
12: 4 but he took the **p** man's lamb
2 Ki 25:12 the guard left some of the **p**
Esth 9:22 one another and gifts to the **p**.
Job 5:16 So the **p** have hope, And
20:10 will seek the favor of the **p**,
20:19 oppressed and forsaken the **p**,
24: 4 All the **p** of the land are
24: 9 And take a pledge from the **p**.
24:10 They cause the **p** to go naked,
24:14 He kills the **p** and needy;
29:12 Because I delivered the **p** who
29:16 I was a father to the **p**,
30:25 not my soul grieved for the **p**?
31:16 If I have kept the **p** from their
31:19 Or any **p** man without
34:19 regard the rich more than the **p**;
34:28 they caused the cry of the **p**
36:15 He delivers the **p** in their
Ps 9:18 The expectation of the **p** shall
10: 2 in his pride persecutes the **p**;
10: 9 He lies in wait to catch the **p**;
10: 9 He catches the **p** when he draws
12: 5 "For the oppression of the **p**,
14: 6 You shame the counsel of the **p**,
22:26 The **p** shall eat and be
34: 6 This **p** man cried out, and the
35:10 Delivering the **p** from him who
35:10 the **p** and the needy from him
37:14 To cast down the **p** and needy,
40:17 But I am **p** and needy;
41: 1 is he who considers the **p**;
49: 2 Rich and **p** together.
68:10 from Your goodness for the **p**.
69:29 But I am **p** and sorrowful;
69:33 For the LORD hears the **p**,
70: 5 But I am **p** and needy;
72: 2 And Your **p** with justice.
72: 4 will bring justice to the **p** of
72:12 The **p** also, and him who has
72:13 He will spare the **p** and needy,
74:19 not forget the life of Your **p**
74:21 return ashamed! Let the **p** and
82: 3 Defend the **p** and fatherless;
82: 4 Deliver the **p** and needy;
86: 1 For I am **p** and needy.
107:41 Yet He sets the **p** on high, far
109:16 But persecuted the **p** and needy
109:22 For I am **p** and needy, And my
109:31 at the right hand of the **p**,
112: 9 abroad, He has given to the **p**;
113: 7 He raises the **p** out of the
132:15 I will satisfy her **p** with
140:12 And justice for the **p**.
Prov 10: 4 who has a slack hand becomes **p**,
10:15 The destruction of the **p** is
13: 7 And one who makes himself **p**,
13: 8 But the **p** does not hear
13:23 in the fallow ground of the **p**,
14:20 The **p** man is hated even by his
14:21 But he who has mercy on the **p**,
14:31 He who oppresses the **p**
17: 5 He who mocks the **p** reproaches
18:23 The **p** man uses entreaties,
19: 1 Better is the **p** who walks in
19: 4 But the **p** is separated from
19: 7 All the brothers of the **p** hate
19:17 He who has pity on the **p** lends
19:22 And a **p** man is better than a
21:13 his ears to the cry of the **p**
21:17 loves pleasure will be a **p**
22: 2 The rich and the **p** have this in
22: 7 The rich rules over the **p**,
22: 9 he gives of his bread to the **p**.
22:16 He who oppresses the **p** to
22:22 Do not rob the **p** because he
22:22 rob the poor because he is **p**,
28: 3 A **p** man who oppresses the poor
28: 3 A poor man who oppresses the **p**
28: 6 Better is the **p** who walks in
28: 8 it for him who will pity the **p**.
28:11 But the **p** who has
28:15 bear Is a wicked ruler over **p**
28:27 He who gives to the **p** will not
29: 7 considers the cause of the **p**,
29:13 The **p** man and the oppressor
29:14 The king who judges the **p** with
30: 9 Or lest I be **p** and steal,
30:14 To devour the **p** from off the
31: 9 And plead the cause of the **p**
31:20 She extends her hand to the **p**,
Eccl 4:13 Better a **p** and wise youth
4:14 Although he was born **p** in his
5: 8 you see the oppression of the **p**,
6: 8 What does the **p** man have, Who
9:15 Now there was found in it a **p**
9:15 no one remembered that same **p**
9:16 Nevertheless the **p** man's
Isa 3:14 The plunder of the **p** is in
3:15 grinding the faces of the **p**?
10: 2 take what is right from the **p**
10:30 far as Laish—O **p** Anathoth!
11: 4 He shall judge the **p**,
14:30 The firstborn of the **p** will
14:32 And the **p** of His people shall
25: 4 have been a strength to the **p**,
26: 6 The feet of the **p** And the
29:19 And the **p** among men shall
32: 7 wicked plans To destroy the **p**
41:17 The **p** and needy seek water, but
58: 7 you bring to your house the **p**

61: 1 preach good tidings to the **p**;
66: 2 On him who is **p** and of a
Jer 2:34 blood of the lives of the **p**
5: 4 I said, "Surely these are **p**.
20:13 has delivered the life of the **p**
22:16 He judged the cause of the **p**
39:10 left in the land of Judah the **p**
52:15 away captive some of the **p**
52:16 the guard left some of the **p**
Ezek 16:49 strengthen the hand of the **p**
18:12 If he has oppressed the **p** and
18:17 withdrawn his hand from the **p**
22:29 and mistreated the **p** and needy;
Dan 4:27 by showing mercy to the **p**.
Am 2: 6 And the **p** for a pair of
2: 7 which is on the head of the **p**,
4: 1 of Samaria, Who oppress the **p**,
5:11 because you tread down the **p**
5:12 Diverting the **p** from justice
8: 4 And make the **p** of the land
8: 6 That we may buy the **p** for
Hab 3:14 was like feasting on the **p** in
Zech 7:10 fatherless, The alien or the **p**.
11: 7 in particular the **p** of the
11:11 Thus the **p** of the flock, who
Mt 5: 3 Blessed are the **p** in spirit,
11: 5 dead are raised up and the **p**
19:21 what you have and give to the **p**,
26: 9 for much and given to the **p**.
26:11 For you have the **p** with you
Mk 10:21 you have and give to the **p**,
12:42 Then one **p** widow came and threw
12:43 I say to you that this **p** widow
14: 5 denarii and given to the **p**.
14: 7 For you have the **p** with you
Lk 4:18 the gospel to the **p**;
6:20 said: "Blessed are you **p**,
7:22 the **p** have the gospel preached
14:13 you give a feast, invite the **p**,
14:21 and bring in here the **p** and
18:22 have and distribute to the **p**,
19: 8 give half of my goods to the **p**;
21: 2 and He saw also a certain **p**
21: 3 I say to you that this **p**
Jn 12: 5 denarii and given to the **p**?
12: 6 not that he cared for the **p**,
12: 8 For the **p** you have with you
13:29 should give something to the **p**.
Rom 15:26 certain contribution for the **p**
1 Cor 13: 3 all my goods to feed the **p**,
2 Cor 6:10 yet always rejoicing; as **p**,
8: 9 yet for your sakes He became **p**,
9: 9 He has given to the **p**;
Gal 2:10 that we should remember the **p**,
Jas 2: 2 there should also come in a **p**
2: 3 and say to the **p** man, "You
2: 5 Has God not chosen the **p** of
2: 6 But you have dishonored the **p**
Rev 3:17 you are wretched, miserable, **p**,
13:16 small and great, rich and **p**,

POOREST (2/2) POOR

2 Ki 24:14 None remained except the **p**
Jer 40: 7 and the **p** of the land who had

POORLY (1/1)

1 Cor 4:11 and we are **p** clothed, and

POPLAR (1/1)

Gen 30:37 for himself rods of green **p**

POPLARS (1/1)

Hos 4:13 on the hills, Under oaks, **p**,

POPULATED (1/1)

Gen 9:19 these the whole earth was **p**.

POPULOUS (1/1)

Deut 26: 5 a nation, great, mighty, and **p**.

PORATHA (1/1)

Esth 9: 8 **P**, Adalia, Aridatha,

PORCH (7/7) PORCHES

Judg 3:23 Ehud went out through the **p**
Ezek 8:16 between the **p** and the altar,
Joel 2:17 Weep between the **p** and the
Mk 14:68 And he went out on the **p**,
Jn 10:23 in the temple, in Solomon's **p**.
Acts 3:11 ran together to them in the **p**
5:12 with one accord in Solomon's **P**.

PORCHES (2/2) PORCH

Ezek 41:15 as the inner temple and the **p**
Jn 5: 2 Hebrew, Bethesda, having five **p**.

PORCIUS (1/1)

Acts 24:27 But after two years **P** Festus

PORCUPINE (2/2)

Isa 14:23 make it a possession for the **p**,
34:11 But the pelican and the **p** shall

PORTICO (1/1)

1 Ki 7: 6 and in front of them was a **p**

PORTION (64/61) PORTIONS, SHARE

Gen 14:24 and the **p** of the men who went
14:24 Mamre; let them take their **p**.
31:14 Is there still any **p** or
48:22 I have given to you one **p**
Ex 29:26 LORD; and it shall be your **p**.
Lev 2: 9 the grain offering a memorial **p**,
2:16 shall burn the memorial **p**:
5:12 handful of it as a memorial **p**,
6:17 I have given it as their **p** of
7:35 This is the consecrated **p** for
Num 5:26 the offering, as its memorial **p**,
18: 8 I have given them as a **p** to you
18:20 nor shall you have any **p** among
18:20 I am your **p** and your
31:36 the **p** for those who had gone
Deut 10: 9 Therefore Levi has no **p** nor
12:12 since he has no **p** nor
14:29 because he has no **p** nor
18: 1 LORD made by fire, and His **p**.
21:17 by giving him a double **p** of
32: 9 For the LORD's **p** is His
33:21 Because a lawgiver's **p** was
1 Sam 1: 5 Hannah he would give a double **p**,
9:23 Bring the **p** which I gave you, of
2 Ki 2: 9 Please let a double **p** of your
25:30 a **p** for each day, all the days
2 Chr 31: 3 The king also appointed a **p** of
31:16 house of the LORD his daily **p**
Neh 11:23 them that a certain **p** should
12:47 a **p** for each day. They also
Job 20:29 This is the **p** from God for a
24:18 Their **p** should be cursed in
27:13 This is the **p** of a wicked man
Ps 11: 6 burning wind Shall be the **p**
16: 5 You are the **p** of my
17:14 of the world who have their **p**
63:10 They shall be a **p** for jackals.
68:23 of your dogs may have their **p**
73:26 strength of my heart and my **p**
119:57 You are my **p**,
142: 5 My **p** in the land of the
Prov 31:15 And a **p** for her maidservants.
Eccl 9: 9 for that is your **p** in life,
Isa 17:14 This is the **p** of those who
53:12 I will divide Him a **p** with the
57: 6 of the stream Is your **p**;
61: 7 they shall rejoice in their **p**.
Jer 10:16 The **P** of Jacob is not like
12:10 They have trodden My **p**
12:10 They have made My pleasant **p**
13:25 The **p** of your measures from
51:19 The **P** of Jacob is not like
52:34 a **p** for each day until the day
Lam 3:24 "The LORD is my **p**,
Dan 1: 8 not defile himself with the **p**
1:13 of the young men who eat the **p**
1:15 the young men who ate the **p** of
1:16 the steward took away their **p**
11:26 those who eat of the **p** of his
Mt 24:51 in two and appoint him his **p**
Lk 12:42 to give them their **p** of food
12:46 in two and appoint him his **p**
15:12 give me the **p** of goods that
Acts 8:21 You have neither part nor **p** in

PORTIONS (16/15) PORTION

Deut 18: 8 They shall have equal **p** to eat,
1 Sam 1: 4 he would give **p** to Peninnah his
2 Chr 31:19 by name to distribute **p** to all
35:14 Then afterward they prepared **p**
35:14 the Levites prepared **p** for
35:15 the Levites prepared **p** for
Neh 8:10 and send **p** to those for whom
8:12 to send **p** and rejoice greatly,
12:44 the fields of the cities the **p**
12:47 Nehemiah all Israel gave the **p**
13:10 I also realized that the **p** for
Ezek 45: 7 side with one of the tribal **p**,
47:13 Joseph shall have two **p**.
48: 8 the same as one of the other **p**,
48:21 adjacent to the tribal **p**;
48:29 Israel, and these are their **p**,

PORTRAY (1/1)

Ezek 4: 1 and **p** on it a city, Jerusalem.

PORTRAYED (4/3)

Ezek 8:10 **p** all around on the walls.
23:14 She looked at men **p** on the
23:14 Images of Chaldeans **p** in
Gal 3: 1 eyes Jesus Christ was clearly **p**

POSE (3/3)

Judg 14:12 Let me **p** a riddle to you. If you
14:13 **P** your riddle, that we may hear
Ezek 17: 2 **p** a riddle, and speak a parable

POSED (1/1)

Judg 14:16 You do not love me! You have **p**

POSITION (11/11)

Judg 20:33 burst forth from their **p** in
Ruth 4:10 his brethren and from his **p** at
1 Ki 8:20 and I have filled the **p** of my
20:24 the kings, each from his **p**,
2 Chr 6:10 and I have filled the **p** of my
20:17 **P** yourselves, stand still and
35:15 did not have to leave their **p**,
Esth 1:19 let the king give her royal **p**
Ps 62: 4 cast him down from his high **p**;
Isa 22:19 And from your **p** he will pull
1 Tim 3: 1 If a man desires the **p** of a

POSITIONED (1/1)

Neh 4:13 Therefore I **p** men behind the

POSITIONS (1/1)

1 Sam 2:36 put me in one of the priestly **p**,

POSSESS (101/92) POSSESSED, POSSESSES, POSSESSING, POSSESSION, POSSESSOR

Gen 22:17 and your descendants shall **p**
24:60 And may your descendants **p**
47: 1 their herds and all that they **p**,
Lev 20:24 and I will give it to you to **p**,
Num 27:11 and he shall **p** it.'" And it
33:53 I have given you the land to **p**.
36: 8 children of Israel each may **p**
Deut 1: 8 go in and **p** the land which the
1:21 go up and **p** it, as the LORD
1:39 and they shall **p** it.
2:24 Begin to **p** it, and engage him
2:31 Begin to **p** it, that you may
3:18 has given you this land to **p**.
3:20 and they also **p** the land which
4: 1 and go in and **p** the land which
4: 5 in the land which you go to **p**.
4:14 land which you cross over to **p**.
4:22 but you shall cross over and **p**
4:26 you cross over the Jordan to **p**;
5:31 which I am giving them to **p**.
5:33 in the land which you shall **p**.
6: 1 you are crossing over to **p**,
6:18 and that you may go in and **p**
7: 1 into the land which you go to **p**,
8: 1 and go in and **p** the land of
9: 4 LORD has brought me in to **p**
9: 5 your heart that you go in to **p**
9: 6 giving you this good land to **p**
9:23 Go up and **p** the land which I
10:11 that they may go in and **p** the
11: 8 and go in and **p** the land which
11: 8 land which you cross over to **p**,
11:10 the land which you go to **p**
11:11 land which you cross over to **p**
11:29 into the land which you go to **p**,
11:31 over the Jordan and go in to **p**
11:31 and you will **p** it and dwell in
12: 1 your fathers is giving you to **p**,
15: 4 your God is giving you to **p**
17:14 and **p** it and dwell in it, and
19: 2 your God is giving you to **p**.
19:14 your God is giving you to **p**.
21: 1 your God is giving you to **p**,
23:20 which you are entering to **p**.
25:19 your God is giving you to **p**
26: 1 and you **p** it and dwell in it,
28:21 land which you are going to **p**.
28:63 off the land which you go to **p**.
30: 5 and you shall **p** it. He will
30:16 in the land which you go to **p**.
30:18 over the Jordan to go in and **p**.
31:13 which you cross the Jordan to **p**.
32:47 you cross over the Jordan to **p**.
33:23 **P** the west and the south."
Josh 1:11 to go in to **p** the land which
1:11 your God is giving you to **p**.
18: 3 will you neglect to go and **p**
23: 5 So you shall **p** their land, as
24: 4 gave the mountains of Seir to **p**,
24: 8 that you might **p** their land,
Judg 2: 6 to his own inheritance to **p**
11:23 should you then **p** it?
11:24 Will you not **p** whatever Chemosh
11:24 Chemosh your god gives you to **p**?
11:24 of before us, we will **p**.
18: 9 and enter to **p** the land.
1 Chr 28: 8 that you may **p** this good land,
Ezra 9:11 which you are entering to **p** is
Neh 9:15 And told them to go in to **p**
9:23 their fathers To go in and **p**.
Ps 69:35 they may dwell there and **p** it.
Isa 14: 2 and the house of Israel will **p**
14:21 Lest they rise up and **p** the
34:11 and the porcupine shall **p** it,
34:17 They shall **p** it forever;
57:13 puts his trust in Me shall **p**
61: 7 in their land they shall **p**
Jer 30: 3 and they shall **p** it.'"
Ezek 7:24 And they will **p** their houses;
33:25 Should you then **p** the land?
33:26 Should you then **p** the land?" '
35:10 and we will **p** them,' although
Dan 7:18 and **p** the kingdom forever, even
7:22 time came for the saints to **p**
Hos 9: 6 Nettles shall **p** their
Am 2:10 To **p** the land of the Amorite.

9:12 That they may ***p*** the remnant of
Ob 17 The house of Jacob shall ***p***
19 The South shall ***p*** the
19 And the Lowland shall ***p***
19 They shall ***p*** the fields of
19 Benjamin shall ***p*** Gilead.
20 children of Israel Shall ***p***
20 who are in Sepharad Shall ***p***
Hab 1: 6 To ***p*** dwelling places that
Zeph 2: 9 remnant of My people shall ***p***
Zech 8:12 remnant of this people To ***p***
Lk 18:12 I give tithes of all that I ***p***.
21:19 By your patience ***p*** your souls.
1 Cor 7:30 buy as though they did not ***p***,
1 Th 4: 4 of you should know how to ***p***

POSSESSED (14/14) POSSESS

Deut 3:12 which we ***p*** at that time, from
30: 5 the land which your fathers ***p***,
Josh 12: 1 and whose land they ***p*** on the
13: 1 very much land yet to be ***p***.
Neh 9:24 So the people went in And ***p***
9:25 And ***p*** houses full of all
Job 22: 8 But the mighty man ***p*** the land,
Prov 8:22 The LORD ***p*** me at the beginning
Isa 63:18 Your holy people have ***p*** it but
Jer 32:15 and vineyards shall be ***p*** again
Acts 4:32 say that any of the things he ***p***
7:45 with Joshua into the land ***p*** by
8: 7 came out of many who were ***p***;
16:16 that a certain slave girl ***p***

POSSESSES (2/2) POSSESS

Num 36: 8 And every daughter who ***p*** an
Lk 12:15 abundance of the things he ***p***.

POSSESSING (2/2) POSSESS

Dan 1: 4 ***p*** knowledge and quick to
2 Cor 6:10 and yet ***p*** all things.

POSSESSION (105/94) POSSESS, POSSESSIONS

Gen 17: 8 of Canaan, as an everlasting ***p***;
23:18 to Abraham as a ***p*** in the
36:43 places in the land of their ***p***.
47:11 and gave them a ***p*** in the land
48: 4 after you as an everlasting ***p***.
49:30 of Ephron the Hittite as a ***p***
Lev 14:34 Canaan, which I give you as a ***p***,
14:34 a house in the land of your ***p***,
25:10 of you shall return to his ***p***,
25:13 of you shall return to his ***p***.
25:24 And in all the land of your ***p***
25:25 and has sold some of his ***p***,
25:27 it, that he may return to his ***p***.
25:28 and he shall return to his ***p***.
25:32 houses in the cities of their ***p***,
25:33 was sold in the city of his ***p***
25:33 of the Levites are their ***p***
25:34 for it is their perpetual ***p***.
25:41 He shall return to the ***p*** of his
25:46 you, to inherit them as a ***p***;
27:16 LORD part of a field of his ***p***,
27:21 it shall be the ***p*** of the
27:22 which is not the field of his ***p***,
27:24 one who owned the land as a ***p***.
27:28 beast, or the field of his ***p***,
Num 13:30 us go up at once and take ***p***,
21:24 and took ***p*** of his land from the
21:35 and they took ***p*** of his land.
24:18 "And Edom shall be a ***p***;
24:18 also, his enemies, shall be a ***p***,
27: 4 Give us a ***p*** among our father's
27: 7 you shall surely give them a ***p***
32: 5 given to your servants as a ***p***.
32:22 and this land shall be your ***p***
32:29 them the land of Gilead as a ***p***.
32:32 but the ***p*** of our inheritance
35: 2 from the inheritance of their ***p***,
35: 8 give shall be from the ***p*** of
35:28 may return to the land of his ***p***.
Deut 2: 5 Mount Seir to Esau as a ***p***.
2: 9 you any of their land as a ***p***,
2: 9 the descendants of Lot as a ***p***.
2:12 did to the land of their ***p***
2:19 of the people of Ammon as a ***p***,
2:19 the descendants of Lot as a ***p***.
3:20 each of you may return to his ***p***
4:47 And they took ***p*** of his land and
11: 6 substance that was in their ***p***,
32:49 the children of Israel as a ***p***;
Josh 1:15 and they also have taken ***p*** of
1:15 return to the land of your ***p***
12: 6 the LORD had given it as a ***p***
12: 7 to the tribes of Israel as a ***p***
19:47 took ***p*** of it, and dwelt in it.
21:12 the son of Jephunneh as his ***p***.
21:41 of the Levites within the ***p*** of
21:43 and they took ***p*** of it and dwelt
22: 4 and to the land of your ***p***,
22: 7 of Manasseh Moses had given a ***p***
22: 7 half of it Joshua gave a ***p***
22: 9 Gilead, to the land of their ***p***,
22:19 if the land of your ***p*** is
22:19 over to the land of the ***p*** of
22:19 and take ***p*** among us; but do not
Judg 3:13 and took ***p*** of the City of
11:21 Thus Israel gained ***p*** of all the
11:22 They took ***p*** of all the territory
11:24 the LORD our God takes ***p*** of
1 Ki 21:15 take ***p*** of the vineyard of
21:16 got up and went down to take ***p***
21:18 he has gone down to take ***p*** of
21:19 you murdered and also taken ***p***?
2 Ki 17:24 and they took ***p*** of Samaria and
2 Chr 20:11 to throw us out of Your ***p***
31: 1 own cities, every man to his ***p***.
Neh 9:22 So they took ***p*** of the land of
11: 3 everyone dwelt in his own ***p*** in
Ps 2: 8 ends of the earth for Your ***p***.
17:14 leave the rest of their ***p*** for
44: 3 For they did not gain ***p*** of the
83:12 The pastures of God for a ***p***.
Prov 12:27 diligence is man's precious ***p***.
Isa 14:23 I will also make it a ***p*** for the
Jer 32:23 And they came in and took ***p*** of
49: 2 Then Israel shall take ***p*** of
Ezek 11:15 has been given to us as a ***p***.
25: 4 I will deliver you as a ***p*** to
25:10 the East I will give it as a ***p***,
33:24 has been given to us as a ***p***.
36: 2 heights have become our ***p***,
36: 3 so that you became the ***p*** of the
36: 5 My land to themselves as a ***p***,
36:12 they shall take ***p*** of you, and
44:28 You shall give them no ***p*** in
44:28 in Israel, for I am their ***p***.
45: 5 have twenty chambers as a ***p***.
45: 8 The land shall be his ***p*** in
46:16 it is their ***p*** by inheritance.
48:22 apart from the ***p*** of the Levites
48:22 of the Levites and the ***p*** of
Zech 2:12 And the LORD will take ***p*** of
Acts 5: 1 Sapphira his wife, sold a ***p***
7: 5 to give it to him for a ***p***,
Eph 1:14 redemption of the purchased ***p***,
Heb 10:34 a better and an enduring ***p*** for

POSSESSIONS (39/38) POSSESSION

Gen 12: 5 and all their ***p*** that they had
13: 6 for their ***p*** were so great that
15:14 shall come out with great ***p***.
26:14 for he had ***p*** of flocks and
26:14 possessions of flocks and ***p*** of
31:18 all his livestock and all his ***p***
34:10 and acquire ***p*** for yourselves in
36: 7 For their ***p*** were too great for
47:27 and they had ***p*** there and grew
Num 32:30 they shall have ***p*** among you in
Deut 21:16 on the day he bequeaths his ***p***
1 Chr 7:28 Now their ***p*** and dwelling places
9: 2 who dwelt in their ***p*** in their
28: 1 over all the substance and ***p***
2 Chr 11:14 their common-lands and their ***p***
21:14 your wives, and all your ***p***;
21:17 and carried away all the ***p*** that
31: 3 appointed a portion of his ***p***
32:29 and ***p*** of flocks and herds in
35: 7 these were from the king's ***p***.
36:19 destroyed all its precious ***p***.
Ezra 8:21 our little ones and all our ***p***.
Esth 3:13 of Adar, and to plunder their ***p***.
8:11 women, and to plunder their ***p***,
Job 1: 3 his ***p*** were seven thousand
1:10 and his ***p*** have increased in the
15:29 Nor will his ***p*** overspread the
Ps 104:24 The earth is full of Your ***p***—
105:21 And ruler of all his ***p***,
Prov 1:13 find all kinds of precious ***p***,
3: 9 Honor the LORD with your ***p***,
28: 8 One who increases his ***p*** by
Eccl 2: 7 I had greater ***p*** of herds and
Joel 3: 5 into your temples My prized ***p***.
Ob 17 of Jacob shall possess their ***p***.
Mt 19:22 sorrowful, for he had great ***p***.
Mk 10:22 sorrowful, for he had great ***p***.
Lk 15:13 and there wasted his ***p*** with
Acts 2:45 and sold their ***p*** and goods, and

POSSESSOR (3/3) POSSESS

Gen 14:19 ***P*** of heaven and earth;
14:22 the ***P*** of heaven and earth,
Prov 17: 8 stone in the eyes of its ***p***;

POSSESSORS (1/1)

Acts 4:34 for all who were ***p*** of lands or

POSSIBLE (15/15)

Mt 19:26 but with God all things are ***p***.
24:24 and wonders to deceive, if ***p***,
26:39 "O My Father, if it is ***p***,
Mk 9:23 all things are ***p*** to him who
10:27 for with God all things are ***p***.
13:22 and wonders to deceive, if ***p***,
14:35 and prayed that if it were ***p***,
14:36 all things are ***p*** for You.
Lk 18:27 are impossible with men are ***p***
Acts 2:24 because it was not ***p*** that He
20:16 to be at Jerusalem, if ***p***,
27:39 planned to run the ship if ***p***.
Rom 12:18 If it is ***p***, as much as
Gal 4:15 I bear you witness that, if ***p***,
Heb 10: 4 For it is not ***p*** that the blood

POSSIBLY (1/1)

Gen 43: 7 Could we ***p*** have known that he

POST (4/4)

1 Ki 20:12 were drinking at the command ***p***,
20:16 getting drunk at the command ***p***.
Eccl 10: 4 Do not leave your ***p***;
Isa 21: 8 I have sat at my ***p*** every

POSTED (2/2)

Judg 7:19 just as they had ***p*** the watch;
Neh 13:19 Then I ***p*** some of my servants

POSTERITY (18/17) ISSUE

Gen 21:23 with my offspring, or with my ***p***;
45: 7 me before you to preserve a ***p***
Lev 21:15 Nor shall he profane his ***p*** among
Num 9:10 If anyone of you or your ***p*** is
1 Ki 16: 3 surely I will take away the ***p*** of
16: 3 posterity of Baasha and the ***p***
21:21 on you. I will take away your ***p***,
Job 18:19 He has neither son nor ***p*** among
Ps 22:30 A ***p*** shall serve Him. It will
49:13 And of their ***p*** who approve
109:13 Let his ***p*** be cut off, And in
Prov 11:21 But the ***p*** of the righteous
Isa 14:22 remnant, And offspring and ***p***,
22:24 house, the offspring and the ***p***,
61: 9 That they are the ***p*** whom the
Jer 7:15 the whole ***p*** of Ephraim.
Dan 11: 4 but not among his ***p*** nor
Am 4: 2 And your ***p*** with fishhooks.

POSTPONED (2/2)

Ezek 12:25 to pass; it will no more be ***p***;
12:28 None of My words will be ***p*** any

POSTS (4/4)

Prov 8:34 Waiting at the ***p*** of my doors.
Isa 6: 4 And the ***p*** of the door were
57: 8 behind the doors and their ***p***
Acts 12:10 first and the second guard ***p***,

POT (22/20) POTS, POTSHERD, WASHPOT, WATERPOT

Ex 16:33 Take a ***p*** and put an omer of
Lev 6:28 if it is boiled in a bronze ***p***,
Judg 6:19 and he put the broth in a ***p***;
1 Sam 2:14 or kettle, or caldron, or ***p***;
2 Ki 4:38 servant, "Put on the large ***p***,
4:39 and sliced them into the ***p*** of
4:40 there is death in the ***p***!"
4:41 And he put it into the ***p***,
4:41 was nothing harmful in the ***p***.
Job 41:20 As from a boiling ***p*** and
41:31 makes the deep boil like a ***p***;
41:31 He makes the sea like a ***p*** of
Prov 17: 3 The refining ***p*** is for silver
27:21 The refining ***p*** is for silver
Eccl 7: 6 crackling of thorns under a ***p***,
Jer 1:13 And I said, "I see a boiling ***p***,
Ezek 24: 3 the Lord GOD: "Put on a ***p***,
24: 6 To the ***p*** whose scum is in it,
24:11 Then set the ***p*** empty on the
Mic 3: 3 in pieces Like meat for the ***p***,
Zech 14:21 every ***p*** in Jerusalem and Judah
Heb 9: 4 in which were the golden ***p***

POTENTATE (1/1)

1 Tim 6:15 who is the blessed and only ***P***,

POTI-PHERAH (3/3)

Gen 41:45 the daughter of ***P*** priest of On.
41:50 the daughter of ***P*** priest of On,
46:20 the daughter of ***P*** priest of On,

POTIPHAR (2/2)

Gen 37:36 had sold him in Egypt to ***P***,
39: 1 been taken down to Egypt. And ***P***,

POTS (11/11) POT

Ex 16: 3 when we sat by the ***p*** of meat
1 Ki 7:45 the ***p***, the shovels, and the
2 Ki 25:14 They also took away the ***p***,
2 Chr 4:11 Then Huram made the ***p*** and the
4:16 also the ***p***, the shovels,
35:13 offerings they boiled in ***p***,
Ps 58: 9 Before your ***p*** can feel the
Jer 52:18 They also took away the ***p***,
52:19 the firepans, the bowls, the ***p***,
Lam 4: 2 they are regarded as clay ***p***,
Zech 14:20 The ***p*** in the LORD's house

POTSHERD (4/4) POT

Job 2: 8 And he took for himself a ***p*** with
Ps 22:15 strength is dried up like a ***p***,
Isa 45: 9 with his Maker! Let the ***p***
Jer 19: 2 is by the entry of the ***P*** Gate;

POTSHERDS (2/2)

Job 41:30 undersides are like sharp ***p***;
Isa 45: 9 potsherd strive with the ***p*** of

POTTAGE (KJV) See STEW

POTTER (10/8) POTTER'S

Isa 29:16 turned around! Shall the **p** be
41:25 As the **p** treads clay.
64: 8 are the clay, and You our **p**;
Jer 18: 4 was marred in the hand of the **p**;
18: 4 as it seemed good to the **p** to
18: 6 can I not do with you as this **p**?
Lam 4: 2 work of the hands of the **p**!
Zech 11:13 Throw it to the **p**"—that
11:13 house of the LORD for the **p**.
Rom 9:21 Does not the **p** have power over

POTTER'S (11/11) POTTER

Ps 2: 9 dash them to pieces like a **p**
Isa 30:14 it like the breaking of the **p**
Jer 18: 2 Arise and go down to the **p**
18: 3 Then I went down to the **p** house,
18: 6 as the clay is in the **p** hand,
19: 1 Go and get a **p** earthen flask,
19:11 as one breaks a **p** vessel,
Dan 2:41 partly of **p** clay and partly of
Mt 27: 7 and bought with them the **p**
27:10 and gave them for the **p**
Rev 2:27 to pieces like the **p**

POTTERS (1/1)

1 Chr 4:23 These were the **p** and those who

POUCH (1/1)

1 Sam 17:40 in a **p** which he had, and his

POULTICE (1/1)

Isa 38:21 and apply it as a **p** on the

POUND (2/2) POUNDS

Ezek 6:11 **P** your fists and stamp your
Jn 12: 3 Then Mary took a **p** of very

POUNDED (2/2)

Judg 5:22 Then the horses' hooves **p**,
5:26 She **p** Sisera, she pierced his

POUNDS (1/1) POUND

Jn 19:39 and aloes, about a hundred **p**.

POUR (67/66) POURED, POURING

Ex 4: 9 water from the river and **p** it
29: 7 **p** it on his head, and anoint
29:12 and **p** all the blood beside the
30: 9 nor shall you **p** a drink
Lev 2: 1 And he shall **p** oil on it, and
2: 6 shall break it in pieces and **p**
4: 7 and he shall **p** the remaining
4:18 and he shall **p** the remaining
4:25 and **p** its blood at the base of
4:30 and **p** all the remaining blood
4:34 and **p** all the remaining blood
14:15 and **p** it into the palm of his
14:26 And the priest shall **p** some of
14:41 they scrape off they shall **p**
17:13 he shall **p** out its blood and
Num 5:15 he shall **p** no oil on it and put
24: 7 He shall **p** water from his
28: 7 in a holy place you shall **p**
Deut 12:16 you shall **p** it on the earth
12:24 you shall **p** it on the earth
15:23 you shall **p** it on the ground
Judg 6:20 and **p** out the broth." And he
1 Ki 18:33 and **p** it on the burnt
2 Ki 4: 4 then **p** it into all those
9: 3 and **p** it on his head, and say,
Job 3:24 And my groanings **p** out like
10:10 Did you not **p** me out like milk,
16:20 My eyes **p** out tears to God.
36:28 the clouds drop down And **p**
38:37 Or who can **p** out the bottles
Ps 42: 4 I **p** out my soul within me.
62: 8 **P** out your heart before Him;
69:24 **P** out Your indignation upon
79: 6 **P** out Your wrath on the nations
142: 2 I **p** out my complaint before
Prov 1:23 Surely I will **p** out my spirit
Isa 44: 3 For I will **p** water on him who
44: 3 I will **p** My Spirit on your
45: 8 And let the skies **p** down
Jer 6:11 I will **p** it out on the children
7:18 and they **p** out drink offerings
10:25 **P** out Your fury on the
14:16 for I will **p** their wickedness on
18:21 And **p** out their blood By the
44:17 to the queen of heaven and **p**
44:19 and **p** out drink offerings to
44:25 to the queen of heaven and **p**
Lam 2:19 **P** out your heart like water
Ezek 7: 8 Now upon you I will soon **p** out
14:19 into that land and **p** out My
20: 8 I will **p** out My fury on them and
20:13 Then I said I would **p** out My
20:21 Then I said I would **p** out My
21:31 I will **p** out My indignation on
24: 3 And also **p** water into it.
24: 7 She did not **p** it on the
30:15 I will **p** My fury on Sin, the
Hos 5:10 I will **p** out my wrath on them
Joel 2:28 pass afterward That I will **p**
2:29 on My maidservants I will **p**
Mic 1: 6 I will **p** down her stones into
Zeph 3: 8 To **p** on them My indignation,
Zech 12:10 And I will **p** on the house of
Mal 3:10 the windows of heaven And **p**
Acts 2:17 That I will **p** out of My
2:18 My maidservants I will **p**
Rev 16: 1 Go and **p** out the bowls of the

POURED (86/82) POUR

Gen 28:18 and **p** oil on top of it.
35:14 and he **p** a drink offering on
35:14 and he **p** oil on it.
Ex 9:33 and the rain was not **p** on the
30:32 It shall not be **p** on man's
Lev 4:12 where the ashes are **p** out, and
4:12 where the ashes are **p** out it
8:12 And he **p** some of the anointing
8:15 And he **p** the blood at the base
9: 9 and **p** the blood at the base of
21:10 head the anointing oil was **p**
Deut 12:27 of your sacrifices shall be **p**
Judg 5: 4 trembled and the heavens **p**,
5: 4 The clouds also **p** water;
1 Sam 1:15 but have **p** out my soul before
7: 6 and **p** it out before the LORD.
10: 1 took a flask of oil and **p** it
2 Sam 20:10 and his entrails **p** out on the
21:10 harvest until the late rains **p**
23:16 but **p** it out to the LORD.
1 Ki 13: 3 and the ashes on it shall be **p**
13: 5 and the ashes **p** out from the
2 Ki 3:11 who **p** water on the hands of
4: 5 and she **p** it out.
9: 6 And he **p** the oil on his head,
16:13 and he **p** his drink offering and
1 Chr 11:18 but **p** it out to the LORD.
2 Chr 12: 7 My wrath shall not be **p** out on
34:21 wrath of the LORD that is **p**
34:25 Therefore My wrath will be **p**
Job 29: 6 And the rock **p** out rivers of
30:16 And now my soul is **p** out because
Ps 22:14 I am **p** out like water, And all
45: 2 Grace is **p** upon Your lips;
77:17 The clouds **p** out water;
Song 1: 3 Your name is ointment **p**
Isa 26:16 They **p** out a prayer when Your
29:10 For the LORD has **p** out on you
32:15 Until the Spirit is **p** upon us
42:25 Therefore He has **p** on him the
53:12 Because He **p** out His soul unto
57: 6 Even to them you have **p** a
Jer 7:20 My anger and My fury will be **p**
19:13 and **p** out drink offerings to
32:29 offered incense to Baal and **p**
42:18 anger and My fury have been **p**
42:18 so will My fury be **p** out on you
44: 6 'So My fury and My anger were **p**
44:19 to the queen of heaven and **p**
Lam 2: 4 He has **p** out His fury like
2:11 My bile is **p** on the ground
2:12 As their life is **p** out
4:11 He has **p** out His fierce anger.
Ezek 16:15 and **p** out your harlotry on
16:36 Because your filthiness was **p**
20:28 up their sweet aroma and **p** out
20:33 and with fury **p** out, I will
20:34 and with fury **p** out.
22:22 have **p** out My fury on you.'"
22:31 Therefore I have **p** out My
23: 8 And **p** out their immorality
36:18 Therefore I **p** out My fury on
39:29 for I shall have **p** out My
Dan 9:11 the servant of God have been **p**
9:27 Is **p** out on the desolate."
Mic 1: 4 Like waters **p** down a steep
Nah 1: 6 His fury is **p** out like fire,
Zeph 1:17 Their blood shall be **p** out
Mt 26: 7 and she **p** it on His head as He
Mk 14: 3 Then she broke the flask and **p**
Jn 2:15 and **p** out the changers' money
13: 5 He **p** water into a basin and
Acts 2:33 He **p** out this which you now see
10:45 of the Holy Spirit had been **p**
Rom 5: 5 the love of God has been **p** out
Phil 2:17 and if I am being **p** out as a
2 Tim 4: 6 For I am already being **p** out as
Titus 3: 6 whom He **p** out on us abundantly
Rev 14:10 which is **p** out full strength
16: 2 So the first went and **p** out his
16: 3 Then the second angel **p** out his
16: 4 Then the third angel **p** out his
16: 8 Then the fourth angel **p** out his
16:10 Then the fifth angel **p** out his
16:12 Then the sixth angel **p** out his
16:17 Then the seventh angel **p** out

POURING (7/7) POUR

Ex 25:29 pitchers, and its bowls for **p**.
37:16 bowls, and its pitchers for **p**.
Num 4: 7 bowls, and the pitchers for **p**;
Jer 44:18 queen of heaven and **p** out drink
Ezek 9: 8 of Israel in **p** out Your fury
Mt 26:12 For in **p** this fragrant oil on My
Lk 10:34 **p** on oil and wine; and he set

POURS (9/9)

Job 12:21 He **p** contempt on princes,
16:13 He **p** out my gall on the
Ps 75: 8 and He **p** it out; Surely its
102: when he is overwhelmed and **p**
107:40 He **p** contempt on princes,
Prov 15: 2 But the mouth of fools **p** forth
15:28 But the mouth of the wicked **p**
Am 5: 8 the waters of the sea And **p**
9: 6 And **p** them out on the face of

POURTRAY (KJV) See PORTRAY

POVERTY (21/21)

Gen 45:11 all that you have, come to **p**;
Lev 25:35 and falls into **p** among you,
Prov 6:11 So shall your **p** come on you
10:15 of the poor is their **p**.
11:24 is right, But it leads to **p**.
13:18 **P** and shame will come to him
14:23 idle chatter leads only to **p**.
20:13 love sleep, lest you come to **p**;
21: 5 who is hasty, surely to **p**.
22:16 rich, will surely come to **p**.
23:21 and the glutton will come to **p**,
24:34 So shall your **p** come like a
28:19 follows frivolity will have **p**
28:22 And does not consider that **p**
30: 8 Give me neither **p** nor
31: 7 Let him drink and forget his **p**,
Mk 12:44 but she out of her **p** put in all
Lk 21: 4 but she out of her **p** put in all
2 Cor 8: 2 of their joy and their deep **p**
8: 9 that you through His **p** might
Rev 2: 9 and **p** (but you are rich);

POWDER (6/6)

Ex 32:20 the fire, and ground it to **p**;
Deut 28:24 the rain of your land to **p** and
2 Ki 23:15 place and crushed it to **p**,
2 Chr 34: 7 beaten the carved images into **p**,
Mt 21:44 falls, it will grind him to **p**.
Lk 20:18 falls, it will grind him to **p**.

POWDERS (1/1)

Song 3: 6 all the merchant's fragrant **p**?

POWER (245/237) POWERFUL, POWERLESS, POWERS

Gen 31:29 It is in my **p** to do you harm,
49: 3 dignity and the excellency of **p**.
Ex 9:16 that I may show My **p** in you,
15: 6 LORD, has become glorious in **p**;
32:11 the land of Egypt with great **p**
Lev 26:19 will break the pride of your **p**;
26:37 and you shall have no **p** to
Num 14:17 let the **p** of my LORD be great,
22:38 have I any **p** at all to say
Deut 4:37 His Presence, with His mighty **p**,
8:17 My **p** and the might of my hand
8:18 for it is He who gives you **p**
9:29 brought out by Your mighty **p**
32:36 When He sees that their **p** is
34:12 and by all that mighty **p** and all
Josh 8:20 So they had no **p** to flee this
17:17 a great people and have great **p**;
1 Sam 9: 1 a Benjamite, a mighty man of **p**.
30: 4 until they had no more **p** to
2 Sam 22:33 God is my strength and **p**,
2 Ki 17:36 the land of Egypt with great **p**
18:20 speak of having plans and **p**
19:26 their inhabitants had little **p**;
1 Chr 18: 3 as he went to establish his **p**
29:11 The **p** and the glory,
29:12 In Your hand is **p** and might;
2 Chr 14:11 or with those who have no **p**;
20: 6 in Your hand is there not **p**
20:12 For we have no **p** against this
22: 9 Ahaziah had no one to assume **p**
25: 8 for God has **p** to help and to
26:13 that made war with mighty **p**,
Ezra 8:22 but His **p** and His wrath are
Neh 1:10 have redeemed by Your great **p**,
5: 5 It is not in our **p** to
Esth 10: 2 Now all the acts of his **p** and
Job 1:12 all that he has is in your **p**;
5:20 And in war from the **p** of the
21: 7 Yes, become mighty in **p**?
23: 6 contend with me in His great **p**?
24:22 the mighty away with His **p**;
26: 2 helped him who is without **p**?
26:12 He stirs up the sea with His **p**,
26:14 But the thunder of His **p** who
27:22 flees desperately from its **p**.
36:22 God is exalted by His **p**;
37:23 He is excellent in **p**,
40:16 And his **p** is in his stomach
41:12 his limbs, His mighty **p**,
Ps 21:13 We will sing and praise Your **p**.
22:20 My precious life from the **p**
37:35 have seen the wicked in great **p**,
49:15 will redeem my soul from the **p**
59:11 Scatter them by Your **p**,
59:16 But I will sing of Your **p**;
62:11 That **p** belongs to God.
63: 2 To see Your **p** and Your glory.
65: 6 Being clothed with **p**;
66: 3 the greatness of Your **p** Your
66: 7 He rules by His **p** forever;
68:35 He who gives strength and **p** to

P

71:18 Your p to everyone who is to
78:26 And by His p He brought in the
78:42 They did not remember His p:
79:11 to the greatness of Your p
89:48 he deliver his life from the p
90:11 Who knows the p of Your anger?
106: 8 He might make His mighty p
110: 3 In the day of Your p;
111: 6 declared to His people the p
145:11 kingdom, And talk of Your p,
147: 5 is our Lord, and mighty in p;
Prov 3:27 When it is in the p of your
18:21 Death and life are in the p of
Eccl 4: 1 their oppressors there is p,
5:19 and given him p to eat of it,
6: 2 yet God does not give him p to
8: 4 of a king is, there is p;
8: 8 No one has p over the spirit to
8: 8 And no one has p in the day of
Isa 3: 6 these ruins be under your p,
36: 5 you speak of having plans and p
37:27 their inhabitants had little p;
40:26 And the strength of His p;
40:29 He gives p to the weak, And to
43:17 The army and the p (They
47:14 deliver themselves From the p
50: 2 Or have I no p to deliver?
Jer 5:31 priests rule by their own p;
10:12 has made the earth by His p,
27: 5 by My great p and by My
32:17 and the earth by Your great p
51:15 has made the earth by His p;
Ezek 17: 9 And no great p or many people
22: 6 each one has used his p to shed
30: 6 And the pride of her p shall
35: 5 children of Israel by the p of
Dan 2:37 has given you a kingdom, p,
3:27 whose bodies the fire had no p;
4:30 a royal dwelling by my mighty p
6:27 delivered Daniel from the p of
8: 6 and ran at him with furious p.
8: 7 There was no p in the ram to
8:22 that nation, but not with its p.
8:24 His p shall be mighty, but not
8:24 be mighty, but not by his own p;
11: 5 and he shall gain p over him
11: 6 but she shall not retain the p
11:16 Land with destruction in his p.
11:25 He shall stir up his p and his
11:43 He shall have p over the
12: 7 and when the p of the holy
Hos 13:14 I will ransom them from the p of
Am 2:14 shall not strengthen his p,
Mic 2: 1 Because it is in the p of
3: 8 But truly I am full of p by
Nah 1: 3 slow to anger and great in p,
2: 1 your flanks! Fortify your p
Hab 1:11 Ascribing this p to his
2: 9 he may be delivered from the p
3: 4 And there His p was hidden.
Zech 4: 6 'Not by might nor by p,
9: 4 He will destroy her p in the
Mt 6:13 Yours is the kingdom and the p
9: 6 know that the Son of Man has p
9: 8 who had given such p to men.
10: 1 He gave them p over unclean
22:29 the Scriptures nor the p of
24:30 on the clouds of heaven with p
26:64 at the right hand of the P,
Mk 2:10 know that the Son of Man has p
3:15 and to have p to heal sicknesses
5:30 knowing in Himself that p had
6: 7 and gave them p over unclean
9: 1 kingdom of God present with p.
12:24 know the Scriptures nor the p
13:26 in the clouds with great p and
14:62 at the right hand of the P,
Lk 1:17 before Him in the spirit and p
1:35 and the p of the Highest will
4:14 Then Jesus returned in the p of
4:36 is! For with authority and p
5:17 And the p of the Lord was
5:24 know that the Son of Man has p
6:19 for p went out from Him and
8:46 for I perceived p going out
9: 1 together and gave them p and
10:19 and over all the p of the
12: 5 has p to cast into hell; yes, I
20:20 order to deliver Him to the p
21:27 of Man coming in a cloud with p
22:53 and the p of darkness."
22:69 sit on the right hand of the p
24:49 until you are endued with p
Jn 10:18 I have p to lay it down, and I
10:18 and I have p to take it again.
19:10 Do You not know that I have p
19:10 and p to release You?"
19:11 You could have no p at all
Acts 1: 8 But you shall receive p when the
3:12 as though by our own p or
4: 7 By what p or by what name have
4:33 And with great p the apostles
6: 8 Stephen, full of faith and p,
8:10 This man is the great p of
8:19 Give me this p also, that anyone
10:38 with the Holy Spirit and with p,
26:18 and from the p of Satan to
Rom 1: 4 to be the Son of God with p
1:16 for it is the p of God to
1:20 even His eternal p and
9:17 that I may show My p in
9:21 Does not the potter have p over
9:22 His wrath and to make His p
15:13 may abound in hope by the p of
15:19 by the p of the Spirit of God,
1 Cor 1:18 are being saved it is the p of
1:24 Christ the p of God and the
2: 4 of the Spirit and of p,
2: 5 the wisdom of men but in the p
4:19 who are puffed up, but the p.
4:20 of God is not in word but in p.
5: 4 with the p of our Lord Jesus
6:12 not be brought under the p of
6:14 will also raise us up by His p.
7:37 but has p over his own will,
15:24 rule and all authority and p.
15:43 in weakness, it is raised in p.
2 Cor 4: 7 that the excellence of the p
6: 7 by the p of God, by the armor
12: 9 that the p of Christ may rest
13: 4 yet He lives by the p of God.
13: 4 we shall live with Him by the p
Eph 1:19 exceeding greatness of His p
1:19 to the working of His mighty p
1:21 above all principality and p
2: 2 to the prince of the p of the
3: 7 the effective working of His p.
3:20 according to the p that works
6:10 in the Lord and in the p of
Phil 3:10 that I may know Him and the p of
Col 1:11 according to His glorious p,
1:13 He has delivered us from the p
2:10 head of all principality and p.
1 Th 1: 5 you in word only, but also in p,
2 Th 1: 9 and from the glory of His p,
1:11 and the work of faith with p,
2: 9 working of Satan, with all p,
1 Tim 6:16 be honor and everlasting p.
2 Tim 1: 7 but of p and of love and of a
1: 8 the gospel according to the p
3: 5 of godliness but denying its p.
Heb 1: 3 all things by the word of His p,
2:14 destroy him who had the p of
7:16 but according to the p of an
9:17 since it has no p at all while
1 Pe 1: 5 who are kept by the p of God
2 Pe 1: 3 as His divine p has given to us
1:16 we made known to you the p and
2:11 who are greater in p and might,
Jude 25 and majesty, Dominion and p,
Rev 2:26 to him I will give p over the
4:11 receive glory and honor and p;
5:12 who was slain To receive p
5:13 and honor and glory and p Be
6: 8 And p was given to them over a
7:12 Thanksgiving and honor and p
9: 3 And to them was given p,
9: 3 scorpions of the earth have p.
9:10 Their p was to hurt men five
9:19 For their p is in their mouth
11: 3 And I will give p to my two
11: 6 These have p to shut heaven, so
11: 6 and they have p over waters to
11:17 You have taken Your great p
12:10 and the p of His Christ have
13: 2 The dragon gave him his p,
13:15 He was granted p to give breath
14:18 who had p over fire, and he
15: 8 the glory of God and from His p,
16: 8 and p was given to him to
16: 9 the name of God who has p over
17:13 and they will give their p and
19: 1 and glory and honor and p
20: 6 such the second death has no p,

POWERFUL (6/6) POWER

2 Chr 17:12 became increasingly p,
Ps 29: 4 The voice of the LORD is p;
Isa 18: 2 A nation p and treading down,
18: 7 A nation p and treading down,
2 Cor 10:10 they say, "are weighty and p,
Heb 4:12 word of God is living and p,

POWERLESS (1/1) POWER

Hab 1: 4 Therefore the law is p,

POWERS (13/13) POWER

Esth 1: 3 the p of Persia and Media, the
Mt 14: 2 and therefore these p are at
24:29 and the p of the heavens will
Mk 6:14 and therefore these p are at
13:25 and the p in the heavens will
Lk 21:26 for the p of heaven will be
Rom 8:38 angels nor principalities nor p,
Eph 3:10 to the principalities and p in
6:12 principalities, against p,
Col 1:16 or principalities or p.
2:15 disarmed principalities and p,
Heb 6: 5 the good word of God and the p
1 Pe 3:22 angels and authorities and p

PRACTICE (18/17) PRACTICED, PRACTICES, PRACTICING

Gen 44:15 such a man as I can certainly p
Lev 19:26 nor shall you p divination or
Ps 141: 4 To p wicked works With men
Isa 32: 6 To p ungodliness, To utter
Ezek 13:23 longer envision futility nor p
23:48 women may be taught not to p
Mic 2: 1 At morning light they p it,
Mt 7:23 you who p lawlessness!'
13:41 and those who p lawlessness,
Rom 1:32 that those who p such things
1:32 but also approve of those who p
2: 1 for you who judge p the same
2: 2 to truth against those who p
7:15 I will to do, that I do not p;
7:19 I will not to do, that I p.
Gal 5:21 that those who p such things
1 Jn 1: 6 we lie and do not p the truth.
3:10 Whoever does not p

PRACTICED (7/7) PRACTICE

2 Ki 17:17 p witchcraft and soothsaying,
21: 6 p soothsaying, used witchcraft,
2 Chr 33: 6 he p soothsaying, used
Acts 8: 9 who previously p sorcery in the
19:19 many of those who had p magic
Rom 3:13 their tongues they have p
2 Cor 12:21 and lewdness which they have p.

PRACTICES (7/7) PRACTICE

Gen 44: 5 and with which he indeed p
Deut 18:10 or one who p witchcraft, or
Rom 13: 4 to execute wrath on him who p
2 Pe 2:14 a heart trained in covetous p,
1 Jn 2:29 you know that everyone who p
3: 7 He who p righteousness is
Rev 22:15 and whoever loves and p a lie.

PRACTICING (4/4) PRACTICE

2 Ki 17:34 To this day they continue p the
Jer 22:17 And p oppression and
Jn 3:20 For everyone p evil hates the
Rom 2: 3 you who judge those p such

PRAETORIUM (7/6)

Mt 27:27 governor took Jesus into the P
Mk 15:16 Him away into the hall called P,
Jn 18:28 Jesus from Caiaphas to the P,
18:28 did not go into the P,
18:33 Then Pilate entered the P again,
19: 9 and went again into the P,
Acts 23:35 him to be kept in Herod's P.

PRAISE (236/205) PRAISED, PRAISES, PRAISEWORTHY, PRAISING, THANK

Gen 29:35 Now I will p the LORD."
49: 8 he whom your brothers shall p;
Ex 15: 2 and I will p Him; My father's
Lev 19:24 a p to the LORD.
Deut 10:21 "He is your p,
26:19 nations which He has made, in p,
Judg 5: 3 I will sing p to the LORD God
1 Chr 16: 4 and to p the LORD God of
16:35 To triumph in Your p."
23: 5 said David, "for giving p.
23:30 every morning to thank and p
25: 3 a harp to give thanks and to p
29:13 We thank You And p Your
2 Chr 7: 6 which King David had made to p
7: 6 whenever David offered p by
8:14 Levites for their duties (to p
20:19 of the Korahites stood up to p
20:21 and who should p the beauty of
20:21 P the LORD, For His mercy
20:22 they began to sing and to p,
23:13 and those who led in p.
29:30 the Levites to sing p to the
31: 2 and to p in the gates of the
Ezra 3:10 to p the LORD, according to
Neh 9: 5 above all blessing and p!
12:24 to p and give thanks, group
12:46 and songs of p and thanksgiving
Ps 7:17 I will p the LORD according to
7:17 And will sing p to the name of
9: 1 I will p You, O LORD, with my
9: 2 I will sing p to Your name,
9:14 That I may tell of all Your p
21:13 strength! We will sing and p
22:22 midst of the assembly I will p
22:23 p Him! All you descendants of
22:25 My p shall be of You in the
22:26 Those who seek Him will p the
28: 7 And with my song I will p Him.
30: 4 Sing p to the LORD, You saints
30: 9 Will the dust p You? Will it
30:12 end that my glory may sing p
33: 1 O you righteous! For p from
33: 2 P the LORD with the harp
34: 1 His p shall continually be
35:18 I will p You among many
35:28 righteousness And of Your p
40: 3 P to our God; Many will see
42: 4 With the voice of joy and p,
42: 5 for I shall yet p Him For the
42:11 For I shall yet p Him,
43: 4 And on the harp I will p You,
43: 5 For I shall yet p Him,
44: 8 And p Your name forever. Selah
45:17 Therefore the people shall p
48:10 So is Your p to the ends of
49:18 himself (For men will p you
50:23 Whoever offers p glorifies Me;
51:15 mouth shall show forth Your p.
52: 9 I will p You forever, Because

54: 6 I will ***p*** Your name, O LORD,
56: 4 In God (I will ***p*** His word),
56:10 In God (I will ***p*** His word),
56:10 In the LORD (I will ***p*** His
57: 7 I will sing and give ***p***.
57: 9 I will ***p*** You, O Lord, among the
61: 8 So I will sing ***p*** to Your name
63: 3 My lips shall ***p*** You.
63: 5 And my mouth shall ***p*** You with
65: 1 ***P*** is awaiting You, O God, in
66: 2 Make His ***p*** glorious.
66: 8 And make the voice of His ***p***
67: 3 Let the peoples ***p*** You, O God;
67: 3 Let all the peoples ***p*** You.
67: 5 Let the peoples ***p*** You, O God;
67: 5 Let all the peoples ***p*** You.
69:30 I will ***p*** the name of God with a
69:34 Let heaven and earth ***p*** Him,
71: 6 My ***p*** shall be continually of
71: 8 my mouth be filled with Your ***p***
71:14 And will ***p*** You yet more and
71:22 Also with the lute I will ***p***
74:21 Let the poor and needy ***p*** Your
76:10 the wrath of man shall ***p*** You;
79:13 We will show forth Your ***p*** to
86:12 I will ***p*** You, O Lord my God,
88:10 Shall the dead arise and ***p***
89: 5 And the heavens will ***p*** Your
99: 3 Let them ***p*** Your great and
100: 4 And into His courts with ***p***.
102:18 people yet to be created may ***p***
102:21 And His ***p*** in Jerusalem,
104:33 I will sing ***p*** to my God while
104:35 O my soul! ***P*** the LORD!
105:45 keep His laws. ***P*** the LORD!
106: 1 ***P*** the LORD! Oh, give thanks
106: 2 Who can declare all His ***p***?
106:12 His words; They sang His ***p***.
106:47 To triumph in Your ***p***.
106:48 Amen!" ***P*** the LORD!
107:32 And ***p*** Him in the company of
108: 1 I will sing and give ***p***,
108: 3 I will ***p*** You, O LORD, among
109: 1 keep silent, O God of my ***p***!
109:30 I will greatly ***p*** the LORD with
109:30 I will ***p*** Him among the
111: 1 ***P*** the LORD! I will praise the
111: 1 Praise the LORD! I will ***p*** the
111:10 His ***p*** endures forever.
112: 1 ***P*** the LORD! Blessed is the
113: 1 ***P*** the LORD! Praise,
113: 1 Praise the LORD! ***P***,
113: 1 ***P*** the name of the LORD!
113: 9 of children. ***P*** the LORD!
115:17 The dead do not ***p*** the LORD,
115:18 and forevermore. ***P*** the LORD!
116:19 O Jerusalem. ***P*** the LORD!
117: 1 ***P*** the LORD, all you Gentiles!
117: 2 endures forever. ***P*** the LORD!
118:19 And I will ***p*** the LORD.
118:21 I will ***p*** You, For You have
118:28 and I will ***p*** You; You are my
119: 7 I will ***p*** You with uprightness
119:164 Seven times a day I ***p*** You,
119:171 My lips shall utter ***p***,
119:175 and it shall ***p*** You; And let
135: 1 ***P*** the LORD! Praise the name
135: 1 Praise the LORD! ***P*** the name
135: 1 ***P*** Him, O you servants of the
135: 3 ***P*** the LORD, for the LORD is
135:21 Who dwells in Jerusalem! ***P***
138: 1 I will ***p*** You with my whole
138: 2 And ***p*** Your name For Your
138: 4 the kings of the earth shall ***p***
139:14 I will ***p*** You, for I am
142: 7 That I may ***p*** Your name;
145: 2 And I will ***p*** Your name forever
145: 4 One generation shall ***p*** Your
145:10 All Your works shall ***p*** You,
145:21 My mouth shall speak the ***p*** of
146: 1 ***P*** the LORD! Praise the LORD,
146: 1 Praise the LORD! ***P*** the LORD,
146: 2 While I live I will ***p*** the
146:10 all generations. ***P*** the LORD!
147: 1 ***P*** the LORD! For it is good
147: 1 and ***p*** is beautiful.
147:12 ***P*** the LORD, O Jerusalem!
147:12 O Jerusalem! ***P*** your God,
147:20 known them. ***P*** the LORD!
148: 1 ***P*** the LORD! Praise the LORD
148: 1 Praise the LORD! ***P*** the LORD
148: 1 ***P*** Him in the heights!
148: 2 ***P*** Him, all His angels
148: 2 ***P*** Him, all His hosts!
148: 3 ***P*** Him, sun and moon
148: 3 ***P*** Him, all you stars of light!
148: 4 ***P*** Him, you heavens of heavens,
148: 5 Let them ***p*** the name of the
148: 7 ***P*** the LORD from the earth,
148:13 Let them ***p*** the name of the
148:14 The ***p*** of all His saints—Of
148:14 to Him. ***P*** the LORD!
149: 1 ***P*** the LORD! Sing to the LORD
149: 1 And His ***p*** in the assembly of
149: 3 Let them ***p*** His name with the
149: 9 His saints. ***P*** the LORD!
150: 1 ***P*** the LORD! Praise God in His
150: 1 Praise the LORD! ***P*** God in His
150: 1 ***P*** Him in His mighty firmament!
150: 2 ***P*** Him for His mighty acts
150: 2 ***P*** Him according to His
150: 3 ***P*** Him with the sound of the
150: 3 ***P*** Him with the lute and harp!
150: 4 ***P*** Him with the timbrel and
150: 4 ***P*** Him with stringed
150: 5 ***P*** Him with loud cymbals
150: 5 ***P*** Him with clashing cymbals!
150: 6 everything that has breath ***p***
150: 6 the LORD. ***P*** the LORD!
Prov 27: 2 Let another man ***p*** you, and not
28: 4 Those who forsake the law ***p*** the
31:31 And let her own works ***p*** her in
Isa 12: 1 I will ***p*** You; Though You were
12: 4 ***P*** the LORD, call upon His name;
25: 1 I will ***p*** Your name, For You
38:18 Death cannot ***p*** You; Those who
38:19 he shall ***p*** You, As I do this
42: 8 Nor My ***p*** to carved images.
42:10 And His ***p*** from the ends of
42:12 And declare His ***p*** in the
43:21 They shall declare My ***p***.
48: 9 And for My ***p*** I will restrain
60:18 Salvation, And your gates ***P***.
61: 3 The garment of ***p*** for the
61:11 will cause righteousness and ***p***
62: 7 till He makes Jerusalem a ***p*** in
62: 9 And ***p*** the LORD; Those who
Jer 13:11 My people, for renown, for ***p***,
17:14 be saved, For You are my ***p***.
17:26 bringing sacrifices of ***p*** to the
20:13 Sing to the LORD! ***P*** the
31: 7 the nations; Proclaim, give ***p***,
33: 9 be to Me a name of joy, a ***p***,
33:11 ***P*** the LORD of hosts, For the
33:11 will bring the sacrifice of ***p***
48: 2 No more ***p*** of Moab. In Heshbon
49:25 Why is the city of ***p*** not
51:41 how the ***p*** of the whole earth is
Dan 2:23 I thank You and ***p*** You, O God of
4:37 ***p*** and extol and honor the King
Joel 2:26 And ***p*** the name of the LORD
Hab 3: 3 the earth was full of His ***p***.
Zeph 3:19 I will appoint them for ***p*** and
3:20 For I will give you fame and ***p***
Mt 21:16 You have perfected ***p***'?
Lk 18:43 saw it, gave ***p*** to God.
19:37 began to rejoice and ***p*** God
Jn 12:43 for they loved the ***p*** of men more
12:43 praise of men more than the ***p***
Rom 2:29 whose ***p*** is not from men but
13: 3 and you will have ***p*** from the
15:11 ***P*** the LORD, all you
1 Cor 4: 5 Then each one's ***p*** will come
11: 2 Now I ***p*** you, brethren, that you
11:17 these instructions I do not ***p***
11:22 Shall I ***p*** you in this? I do not
11:22 I do not ***p*** you.
2 Cor 8:18 with him the brother whose ***p***
Eph 1: 6 to the ***p*** of the glory of His
1:12 in Christ should be to the ***p***
1:14 to the ***p*** of His glory.
Phil 1:11 to the glory and ***p*** of God.
Heb 2:12 assembly I will sing ***p***
13:15 offer the sacrifice of ***p*** to
1 Pe 1: 7 by fire, may be found to ***p***,
2:14 of evildoers and for the ***p***
Rev 19: 5 ***P*** our God, all you His servants

PRAISED (24/24) PRAISE

Judg 16:24 they ***p*** their god; for they
2 Sam 14:25 there was no one who was ***p*** as
22: 4 LORD, who is worthy to be ***p***;
1 Chr 16:25 is great and greatly to be ***p***;
16:36 Amen!" and ***p*** the LORD.
23: 5 and four thousand ***p*** the LORD
2 Chr 5:13 and ***p*** the LORD, saying:
7: 3 and worshiped and ***p*** the LORD,
30:21 the Levites and the priests ***p***
Ezra 3:11 when they ***p*** the LORD, because
Neh 5:13 'Amen!" and ***p*** the LORD.
Ps 18: 3 LORD, who is worthy to be ***p***;
48: 1 and greatly to be ***p*** In the
72:15 And daily He shall be ***p***.
96: 4 is great and greatly to be ***p***;
113: 3 The LORD's name is to be ***p***.
145: 3 the LORD, and greatly to be ***p***;
Prov 31:30 fears the LORD, she shall be ***p***.
Eccl 4: 2 Therefore I ***p*** the dead who were
Song 6: 9 And they ***p*** her.
Isa 64:11 Where our fathers ***p*** You,
Dan 4:34 I blessed the Most High and ***p***
5: 4 and ***p*** the gods of gold and
5:23 And you have ***p*** the gods of

PRAISES (36/32) PRAISE

Ex 15:11 in holiness, Fearful in ***p***,
2 Sam 22:50 And sing ***p*** to Your name.
2 Chr 29:30 So they sang ***p*** with gladness,
Ps 9:11 Sing ***p*** to the LORD, who dwells
18:49 And sing ***p*** to Your name.
22: 3 Enthroned in the ***p*** of Israel.
27: 6 I will sing ***p*** to the LORD.
47: 6 Sing ***p*** to God, sing praises!
47: 6 sing ***p***! Sing praises to our
47: 6 sing praises! Sing ***p*** to our
47: 6 to our King, sing ***p***!
47: 7 Sing ***p*** with understanding.
56:12 I will render ***p*** to You,
59:17 O my Strength, I will sing ***p***;
66: 4 shall worship You And sing ***p***
66: 4 They shall sing ***p*** to Your
68: 4 sing ***p*** to His name; Extol Him
68:32 sing ***p*** to the Lord, Selah
75: 9 I will sing ***p*** to the God of
78: 4 to the generation to come the ***p***
92: 1 And to sing ***p*** to Your name,
98: 4 in song, rejoice, and sing ***p***.
101: 1 To You, O LORD, I will sing ***p***.
108: 3 And I will sing ***p*** to You among
135: 3 Sing ***p*** to His name, for it
138: 1 Before the gods I will sing ***p***
144: 9 of ten strings I will sing ***p***
146: 2 I will sing ***p*** to my God while
147: 1 For it is good to sing ***p*** to
147: 7 Sing ***p*** on the harp to our God,
149: 3 Let them sing ***p*** to Him with
149: 6 Let the high ***p*** of God be in
Prov 31:28 husband also, and he ***p*** her:
Isa 60: 6 And they shall proclaim the ***p***
63: 7 of the LORD And the ***p*** of
1 Pe 2: 9 that you may proclaim the ***p*** of

PRAISEWORTHY (1/1) PRAISE

Phil 4: 8 and if there is anything ***p***—

PRAISING (11/11) PRAISE

2 Chr 5:13 one sound to be heard in ***p*** and
23:12 of the people running and ***p***
Ezra 3:11 ***p*** and giving thanks to the
Ps 84: 4 They will still be ***p*** You.
Lk 1:64 and he spoke, ***p*** God.
2:13 of the heavenly host ***p*** God and
2:20 glorifying and ***p*** God for all
24:53 continually in the temple ***p***
Acts 2:47 ***p*** God and having favor with all
3: 8 —walking, leaping, and ***p*** God.
3: 9 people saw him walking and ***p***

PRATING (3/3)

Prov 10: 8 But a ***p*** fool will fall.
10:10 But a ***p*** fool will fall.
3 Jn 10 ***p*** against us with malicious

PRATTLE (1/1)

Mic 2: 6 Do not ***p***," you say

PRATTLER (1/1)

Mic 2:11 Even he would be the ***p*** of

PRAY (146/139) PRAYED, PRAYER, PRAYING, PRAYS

Gen 20: 7 and he will ***p*** for you and you
32:11 "Deliver me, I ***p***,
32:29 "Tell me Your name, I ***p***.
Ex 32:32 their sin—but if not, I ***p***,
33:13 "Now therefore, I ***p***,
34: 9 sight, O Lord, let my Lord, I ***p***,
Num 12:13 heal her, O God, I ***p***!"
14:17 'And now, I ***p***, let the power
14:19 iniquity of this people, I ***p***,
21: 7 ***p*** to the LORD that He take
Deut 3:25 'I ***p***, let me cross over
Judg 6:18 "Do not depart from here, I ***p***,
6:39 once more: Let me test, I ***p***,
10:15 only deliver us this day, we ***p***.
16:28 I ***p***! Strengthen me, I pray,
16:28 me, I pray! Strengthen me, I ***p***,
1 Sam 7: 5 and I will ***p*** to the LORD for
12:19 ***P*** for your servants to the LORD
12:23 the LORD in ceasing to ***p*** for
23:11 O LORD God of Israel, I ***p***,
2 Sam 7:27 has found it in his heart to ***p***
15:31 And David said, "O LORD, I ***p***,
24:10 what I have done; but now, I ***p***,
24:17 they done? Let Your hand, I ***p***,
1 Ki 8:26 'And now I ***p***, O God
8:30 when they ***p*** toward this place.
8:33 and ***p*** and make supplication to
8:35 when they ***p*** toward this place
8:44 and when they ***p*** to the LORD
8:48 and ***p*** to You toward their land
13: 6 and ***p*** for me, that my hand may
17:21 and said, "O LORD my God, I ***p***,
2 Ki 6:17 prayed, and said, "LORD, I ***p***,
6:18 said, "Strike this people, I ***p***,
19:19 therefore, O LORD our God, I ***p***,
20: 3 "Remember now, O LORD, I ***p***,
1 Chr 17:25 found it in his heart to ***p***
21: 8 done this thing; but now, I ***p***,
21:17 they done? Let Your hand, I ***p***,
2 Chr 6:21 when they ***p*** toward this place.
6:24 and ***p*** and make supplication
6:26 when they ***p*** toward this place
6:32 when they come and ***p*** in this
6:34 and when they ***p*** to You toward
6:38 and ***p*** toward their land which
6:40 "Now, my God, I ***p***,
7:14 and ***p*** and seek My face, and
Ezra 6:10 and ***p*** for the life of the king
Neh 1: 5 And I said: "I ***p***,
1: 6 of Your servant which I ***p***
1: 8 'Remember, I ***p***, the word that
1:11 'O Lord, I ***p***, please let Your
1:11 servant prosper this day, I ***p***,
Job 10: 9 Remember, I ***p***, that You have
21:15 what profit do we have if we ***p***
32:21 Let me not, I ***p***,
33:26 He shall ***p*** to God, and He will
42: 8 and My servant Job shall ***p*** for

Ps 5: 2 my God, For to You I will **p**.
32: 6 everyone who is godly shall **p**
55:17 morning and at noon I will **p**,
118:25 Save now, I **p**,
118:25 I pray, O LORD; O LORD, I **p**,
119:76 Let, I **p**, Your merciful
119:108 Accept, I **p**, the freewill
122: 6 **P** for the peace of Jerusalem
Isa 16:12 will come to his sanctuary to **p**;
38: 3 "Remember now, O LORD, I **p**,
45:20 And **p** to a god that cannot
Jer 7:16 Therefore do not **p** for this
11:14 So do not **p** for this people, or
14:11 Do not **p** for this people, for
29: 7 and **p** to the LORD for it;
29:12 will call upon Me and go and **p**
37: 3 **P** now to the LORD our God for
42: 2 and **p** for us to the LORD your
42: 4 I will **p** to the LORD your God
42:20 **P** for us to the LORD our God,
Dan 9:16 to all Your righteousness, I **p**,
Am 7: 2 I **p**! Oh, that Jacob may stand,
7: 5 I **p**! Oh, that Jacob may stand,
Jon 1:14 to the LORD and said, "We **p**,
Zech 7: 2 to **p** before the LORD,
8:21 Let us continue to go and **p**
8:22 And to **p** before the LORD.'
Mt 5:44 and **p** for those who spitefully
6: 5 "And when you **p**,
6: 5 For they love to **p** standing in
6: 6 "But you, when you **p**,
6: 6 **p** to your Father who is in the
6: 7 "And when you **p**,
6: 9 "In this manner, therefore, **p**:
9:38 Therefore **p** the Lord of the
14:23 on the mountain by Himself to **p**.
19:13 put His hands on them and **p**,
24:20 And **p** that your flight may not
26:36 Sit here while I go and **p** over
26:41 'Watch and **p**, lest you enter
26:53 you think that I cannot now **p**
Mk 6:46 departed to the mountain to **p**.
11:24 things you ask when you **p**,
13:18 And **p** that your flight may not
13:33 "Take heed, watch and **p**;
14:32 disciples, "Sit here while I **p**.
14:38 'Watch and **p**, lest you enter
Lk 6:12 went out to the mountain to **p**,
6:28 and **p** for those who spitefully
9:28 went up on the mountain to **p**.
10: 2 therefore **p** the Lord of the
11: 1 to Him, "Lord, teach us to **p**,
11: 2 He said to them, "When you **p**,
18: 1 that men always ought to **p** and
18:10 men went up to the temple to **p**,
21:36 and **p** always that you may be
22:40 **P** that you may not enter into
22:46 "Why do you sleep? Rise and **p**,
Jn 14:16 And I will **p** the Father, and He
16:26 not say to you that I shall **p**
17: 9 I **p** for them. I do not pray for
17: 9 I do not **p** for the world but
17:15 I do not **p** that You should take
17:20 I do not **p** for these alone, but
Acts 8:22 and **p** God if perhaps the
8:24 **P** to the Lord for me, that none
10: 9 went up on the housetop to **p**,
Rom 8:26 we do not know what we should **p**
1 Cor 11:13 Is it proper for a woman to **p**
14:13 him who speaks in a tongue **p**
14:14 For if I **p** in a tongue, my
14:15 I will **p** with the spirit, and I
14:15 and I will also **p** with the
2 Cor 13: 7 Now I **p** to God that you do no
13: 9 are strong. And this also we **p**,
Phil 1: 9 And this I **p**, that your love
Col 1: 9 do not cease to **p** for you, and
1 Th 5:17 **p** without ceasing,
5:25 Brethren, **p** for us.
2 Th 1:11 Therefore we also **p** always for
3: 1 **p** for us, that the word of the
1 Tim 2: 8 desire therefore that the men **p**
Heb 13:18 **P** for us; for we are
Jas 5:13 among you suffering? Let him **p**.
5:14 and let them **p** over him,
5:16 and **p** for one another, that you
1 Jn 5:16 I do not say that he should **p**
3 Jn 2 I **p** that you may prosper in all

PRAYED (59/59) PRAY

Gen 20:17 So Abraham **p** to God; and God
Num 11: 2 and when Moses **p** to the LORD,
21: 7 So Moses **p** for the people.
Deut 9:20 so I **p** for Aaron also at the
9:26 Therefore I **p** to the LORD, and
Judg 13: 8 Then Manoah **p** to the LORD, and
1 Sam 1:10 and **p** to the LORD and wept in
1:27 "For this child I **p**,
2: 1 And Hannah **p** and said: "My
8: 6 So Samuel **p** to the LORD.
1 Ki 19: 4 And he **p** that he might die, and
2 Ki 4:33 and **p** to the LORD.
6:17 And Elisha **p**, and said,
6:18 Elisha **p** to the LORD, and
19:15 Then Hezekiah **p** before the
19:20 Because you have **p** to Me against
20: 2 and **p** to the LORD, saying,
2 Chr 30:18 But Hezekiah **p** for them,
32:20 **p** and cried out to heaven.
32:24 and he **p** to the LORD; and He
33:13 and **p** to Him; and He received
Neh 2: 4 So I **p** to the God of heaven.
Job 42:10 Job's losses when he **p** for his
Isa 37:15 Then Hezekiah **p** to the LORD,
37:21 Because you have **p** to Me against
38: 2 and **p** to the LORD,
Jer 32:16 I **p** to the LORD, saying:
Dan 6:10 and **p** and gave thanks before
9: 4 And I **p** to the LORD my God, and
Jon 2: 1 Then Jonah **p** to the LORD his
4: 2 So he **p** to the LORD, and said,
Mt 26:39 and fell on His face, and **p**,
26:42 second time, He went away and **p**,
26:44 and **p** the third time, saying
Mk 1:35 solitary place; and there He **p**.
14:35 and **p** that if it were possible,
14:39 Again He went away and **p**,
Lk 3:21 was baptized; and while He **p**,
5:16 into the wilderness and **p**.
9:29 As He **p**, the appearance
18:11 The Pharisee stood and **p** thus
22:32 But I have **p** for you, that your
22:41 throw, and He knelt down and **p**,
22:44 He **p** more earnestly. Then His
Acts 1:24 And they **p** and said, "You, O
4:31 And when they had **p**,
6: 6 apostles; and when they had **p**,
8:15 **p** for them that they might
9:40 all out, and knelt down and **p**.
10: 2 and **p** to God always.
10:30 and at the ninth hour I **p** in my
13: 3 Then, having fasted and **p**,
14:23 and **p** with fasting, they
20:36 he knelt down and **p** with them
21: 5 knelt down on the shore and **p**.
27:29 and **p** for day to come.
28: 8 Paul went in to him and **p**,
Jas 5:17 and he **p** earnestly that it
5:18 And he **p** again, and the heaven

PRAYER (113/108) PRAY, PRAYERS

2 Sam 7:27 it in his heart to pray this **p**
21:14 And after that God heeded the **p**
1 Ki 8:28 Yet regard the **p** of Your servant
8:28 and listen to the cry and the **p**
8:29 that You may hear the **p** which
8:38 'whatever **p**, whatever
8:45 then hear in heaven their **p** and
8:49 Your dwelling place their **p**
8:54 had finished praying all this **p**
9: 3 I have heard your **p** and your
2 Ki 19: 4 Therefore lift up your **p** for
20: 5 father: "I have heard your **p**,
1 Chr 5:20 the battle. He heeded their **p**,
2 Chr 6:19 Yet regard the **p** of Your servant
6:19 and listen to the cry and the **p**
6:20 that You may hear the **p** which
6:29 'whatever **p**, whatever
6:35 then hear from heaven their **p**
6:39 Your dwelling place their **p**
6:40 ears be attentive to the **p**
7:12 to him: "I have heard your **p**,
7:15 open and My ears attentive to **p**
30:27 and their **p** came up to His
33:18 his **p** to his God, and the words
33:19 Also his **p** and how God
Ezra 8:23 for this, and He answered our **p**.
Neh 1: 6 that You may hear the **p** of Your
1:11 Your ear be attentive to the **p**
1:11 and to the **p** of Your servants
4: 9 Nevertheless we made our **p** to
11:17 began the thanksgiving with **p**;
Job 15: 4 And restrain **p** before God.
16:17 And my **p** is pure.
22:27 You will make your **p** to Him,
Ps 4: 1 mercy on me, and hear my **p**.
6: 9 The LORD will receive my **p**.
17: A **P** of David.
17: 1 Give ear to my **p** which is
35:13 And my **p** would return to my
39:12 'Hear my **p**, O LORD,
42: 8 A **p** to the God of my life.
54: 2 Hear my **p**, O God; Give ear
55: 1 Give ear to my **p**,
61: 1 my cry, O God; Attend to my **p**.
65: 2 O You who hear **p**,
66:19 attended to the voice of my **p**.
66:20 Who has not turned away my **p**,
69:13 my **p** is to You, O LORD, in
72:15 **P** also will be made for Him
80: 4 You be angry Against the **p** of
84: 8 LORD God of hosts, hear my **p**;
86: A **P** of David
86: 6 Give ear, O LORD, to my **p**;
88: 2 Let my **p** come before You;
88:13 And in the morning my **p** comes
90: A **P** of Moses the man of God.
102: A **P** of the afflicted when he is
102: 1 Hear my **p**, O LORD, And let
102:17 He shall regard the **p** of the
102:17 And shall not despise their **p**.
109: 4 But I give myself to **p**.
109: 7 And let his **p** become sin.
141: 2 Let my **p** be set before You as
141: 5 For still my **p** is against the
142: A **P** when he was in the cave.
143: 1 Hear my **p**, O LORD,
Prov 15: 8 But the **p** of the upright is
15:29 But He hears the **p** of the
28: 9 Even his **p** is an abomination.
Isa 26:16 They poured out a **p** when Your
37: 4 Therefore lift up your **p** for
38: 5 father: "I have heard your **p**,
56: 7 them joyful in My house of **p**.
56: 7 shall be called a house of **p**
Jer 7:16 nor lift up a cry or **p** for
11:14 or lift up a cry or **p** for them;
Lam 3: 8 and shout, He shuts out my **p**.
3:44 That **p** should not pass
Dan 9: 3 Lord God to make request by **p**
9:13 yet we have not made our **p**
9:17 hear the **p** of Your servant, and
9:21 yes, while I was speaking in **p**,
Jon 2: 7 And my **p** went up to You,
Hab 3: 1 A **p** of Habakkuk the prophet, on
Mt 17:21 does not go out except by **p**
21:13 be called a house of **p**,
21:22 whatever things you ask in **p**,
Mk 9:29 can come out by nothing but **p**
11:17 be called a house of **p**
Lk 1:13 for your **p** is heard; and your
6:12 and continued all night in **p** to
19:46 house is a house of **p**,
22:45 When He rose up from **p**,
Acts 1:14 continued with one accord in **p**
3: 1 to the temple at the hour of **p**,
6: 4 ourselves continually to **p** and
10:31 your **p** has been heard, and your
12: 5 but constant **p** was offered to
16:13 where **p** was customarily made;
16:16 it happened, as we went to **p**,
Rom 10: 1 my heart's desire and **p** to God
12:12 continuing steadfastly in **p**;
1 Cor 7: 5 yourselves to fasting and **p**;
2 Cor 1:11 you also helping together in **p**
9:14 and by their **p** for you, who long
Eph 6:18 praying always with all **p** and
Phil 1: 4 always in every **p** of mine making
1:19 my deliverance through your **p**
4: 6 but in everything by **p** and
Col 4: 2 Continue earnestly in **p**,
1 Tim 4: 5 by the word of God and **p**.
Jas 5:15 And the **p** of faith will save the
5:16 fervent **p** of a righteous man

PRAYERS (27/27) PRAYER

2 Sam 24:25 So the LORD heeded the **p** for
Ps 72:20 The **p** of David the son of Jesse
Isa 1:15 Even though you make many **p**,
Mt 23:14 and for a pretense make long **p**.
Mk 12:40 and for a pretense make long **p**.
Lk 2:37 God with fastings and **p** night
5:33 of John fast often and make **p**,
20:47 and for a pretense make long **p**.
Acts 2:42 the breaking of bread, and in **p**.
10: 4 Your **p** and your alms have come
Rom 1: 9 mention of you always in my **p**,
15:30 strive together with me in **p**
Eph 1:16 making mention of you in my **p**:
Col 4:12 laboring fervently for you in **p**,
1 Th 1: 2 making mention of you in our **p**,
1 Tim 2: 1 of all that supplications, **p**,
5: 5 in supplications and **p** night
2 Tim 1: 3 ceasing I remember you in my **p**
Phm 1: 4 mention of you always in my **p**,
1:22 I trust that through your **p** I
Heb 5: 7 when He had offered up **p** and
1 Pe 3: 7 that your **p** may not be
3:12 ears are open to their **p**;
4: 7 serious and watchful in your **p**.
Rev 5: 8 which are the **p** of the saints.
8: 3 he should offer it with the **p**
8: 4 with the **p** of the saints,

PRAYING (25/25) PRAY

1 Sam 1:12 as she continued **p** before the
1:26 by you here, **p** to the LORD.
1 Ki 8:28 prayer which Your servant is **p**
8:54 when Solomon had finished **p** all
2 Chr 6:19 prayer which Your servant is **p**
7: 1 When Solomon had finished **p**,
Ezra 10: 1 Now while Ezra was **p**,
Neh 1: 4 I was fasting and **p** before the
Dan 6:11 assembled and found Daniel **p**
9:20 Now while I was speaking, **p**,
Mk 11:25 "And whenever you stand **p**,
Lk 1:10 multitude of the people was **p**
9:18 it happened, as He was alone **p**,
11: 1 as He was **p** in a certain place,
Acts 9:11 of Tarsus, for behold, he is **p**.
11: 5 "I was in the city of Joppa **p**;
12:12 many were gathered together **p**.
16:25 midnight Paul and Silas were **p**
22:17 to Jerusalem and was **p** in the
1 Cor 11: 4 Every man **p** or prophesying,
Eph 6:18 **p** always with all prayer and
Col 1: 3 **p** always for you,
4: 3 meanwhile **p** also for us, that
1 Th 3:10 night and day **p** exceedingly that
Jude 20 **p** in the Holy Spirit,

PRAYS (5/5) PRAY

1 Ki 8:42 when he comes and **p** toward this
2 Chr 6:20 the prayer which Your servant **p**
Isa 44:17 **P** to it and says, "Deliver
1 Cor 11: 5 But every woman who **p** or
14:14 I pray in a tongue, my spirit **p**,

PREACH (47/45) PREACHED, PREACHER, PREACHES, PREACHING, PROCLAIM

Isa 61: 1 the LORD has anointed Me To **p**
Ezek 20:46 **p** against the south and
21: 2 **p** against the holy places, and
Jon 3: 2 and **p** to it the message that I
Mt 4:17 that time Jesus began to **p** and
10: 7 "And as you go, **p**,
10:27 **p** on the housetops.
11: 1 from there to teach and to **p**
Mk 1:38 that I may **p** there also,
3:14 He might send them out to **p**,
16:15 Go into all the world and **p** the
Lk 4:18 He has anointed Me To **p**
4:43 I must **p** the kingdom of God to
9: 2 He sent them to **p** the kingdom of
9:60 but you go and **p** the kingdom of
Acts 10:42 And He commanded us to **p** to the
14:15 and **p** to you that you should
15:21 many generations those who **p**
16: 6 by the Holy Spirit to **p** the
16:10 the Lord had called us to **p**
17: 3 This Jesus whom I **p** to you is
Rom 1:15 I am ready to **p** the gospel to
2:21 You who **p** that a man should not
10: 8 the word of faith which we **p**):
10:15 And how shall they **p** unless they
10:15 the feet of those who **p**
15:20 so I have made it my aim to **p**
1 Cor 1:17 but to **p** the gospel, not with
1:23 but we **p** Christ crucified, to
9:14 has commanded that those who **p**
9:16 For if I **p** the gospel, I have
9:16 woe is me if I do not **p** the
9:18 That when I **p** the gospel, I may
15:11 so we **p** and so you believed.
2 Cor 2:12 when I came to Troas to **p**
4: 5 For we do not **p** ourselves, but
10:16 to **p** the gospel in the regions
Gal 1: 8 **p** any other gospel to you than
1:16 that I might **p** Him among the
2: 2 to them that gospel which I **p**
5:11 if I still **p** circumcision, why
Eph 3: 8 that I should **p** among the
Phil 1:15 Some indeed **p** Christ even from
1:16 The former **p** Christ from selfish
Col 1:28 Him we **p**, warning every man
2 Tim 4: 2 **P** the word! Be ready in season
Rev 14: 6 the everlasting gospel to **p** to

PREACHED (59/59) PREACH

Zech 1: 4 to whom the former prophets **p**,
Mt 11: 5 the poor have the gospel **p** to
24:14 of the kingdom will be **p** in
26:13 wherever this gospel is **p** in
Mk 1: 7 And he **p**, saying, "There comes
2: 2 And He **p** the word to them.
6:12 So they went out and **p** that
13:10 the gospel must first be **p**
14: 9 wherever this gospel is **p** in
16:20 And they went out and **p**
Lk 3:18 many other exhortations he **p**
7:22 the poor have the gospel **p** to
16:16 the kingdom of God has been **p**,
20: 1 the people in the temple and **p**
24:47 remission of sins should be **p**
Acts 3:20 who was **p** to you before,
4: 2 they taught the people and **p**
8: 5 to the city of Samaria and **p**
8:12 they believed Philip as he **p**
8:25 when they had testified and **p**
8:35 Scripture, **p** Jesus to him.
8:40 he **p** in all the cities till he
9:20 Immediately he **p** the Christ in
9:27 and how he had **p** boldly at
10:37 after the baptism which John **p**:
13: 5 they **p** the word of God in the
13:24 "after John had first **p**,
13:38 that through this Man is **p** to
13:42 that these words might be **p** to
14:21 And when they had **p** the gospel
14:25 Now when they had **p** the word in
15:36 in every city where we have **p**
17:13 that the word of God was **p** by
17:18 because he **p** to them Jesus
Rom 15:19 to Illyricum I have fully **p**
1 Cor 1:21 foolishness of the message **p**
9:27 when I have **p** to others, I
15: 1 to you the gospel which I **p** to
15: 2 hold fast that word which I **p**
15:12 Now if Christ is **p** that He has
2 Cor 1:19 who was **p** among you by us—by
11: 4 Jesus whom we have not **p**,
11: 7 because I **p** the gospel of God
Gal 1: 8 to you than what we have **p** to
1:11 that the gospel which was **p** by
3: 8 **p** the gospel to Abraham
4:13 of physical infirmity I **p** the
Eph 2:17 And He came and **p** peace to you
Phil 1:18 or in truth, Christ is **p**;
Col 1:23 which was **p** to every creature
1 Th 2: 9 we **p** to you the gospel of God.
1 Tim 3:16 **P** among the Gentiles,
2 Tim 4:17 so that the message might be **p**
Heb 4: 2 For indeed the gospel was **p** to
4: 6 those to whom it was first **p**
1 Pe 1:12 to you through those who have **p**
1:25 word which by the gospel was **p**
3:19 by whom also He went and **p** to
4: 6 this reason the gospel was **p**

PREACHER (11/11) PREACH

Eccl 1: 1 The words of the **P**,
1: 2 of vanities," says the **P**;
1:12 I, the **P**, was king over
7:27 what I have found," says the **P**,
12: 8 of vanities," says the **P**,
12: 9 because the **P** was wise, he
12:10 The **P** sought to find acceptable
Rom 10:14 how shall they hear without a **p**?
1 Tim 2: 7 for which I was appointed a **p**
2 Tim 1:11 to which I was appointed a **p**,
2 Pe 2: 5 a **p** of righteousness, bringing

PREACHES (4/4) PREACH

Acts 19:13 you by the Jesus whom Paul **p**.
2 Cor 11: 4 For if he who comes **p** another
Gal 1: 9 if anyone **p** any other gospel to
1:23 formerly persecuted us now **p**

PREACHING (26/26) PREACH

Mt 3: 1 days John the Baptist came **p**
4:23 **p** the gospel of the kingdom,
9:35 **p** the gospel of the kingdom,
12:41 because they repented at the **p**
Mk 1: 4 in the wilderness and **p** a
1:14 **p** the gospel of the kingdom of
1:39 And He was **p** in their synagogues
Lk 3: 3 **p** a baptism of repentance for
4:44 And He was **p** in the synagogues
8: 1 **p** and bringing the glad tidings
9: 6 **p** the gospel and healing
11:32 for they repented at the **p** of
Acts 5:42 did not cease teaching and **p**
8: 4 scattered went everywhere **p**
8:25 **p** the gospel in many villages
10:36 **p** peace through Jesus Christ—He
11:19 **p** the word to no one but the
11:20 **p** the Lord Jesus.
14: 7 And they were **p** the gospel
15:35 teaching and **p** the word of the
20:25 among whom I have gone **p** the
28:31 **p** the kingdom of God and
Rom 16:25 to my gospel and the **p** of
1 Cor 2: 4 And my speech and my **p** were not
15:14 then our **p** is empty and your
Titus 1: 3 manifested His word through **p**,

PREAPPOINTED (1/1)

Acts 17:26 has determined their **p** times

PRECEDE (1/1)

1 Th 4:15 of the Lord will by no means **p**

PRECEDED (1/1)

Job 41:11 Who has **p** Me, that I should pay

PRECEDING (1/1)

1 Tim 5:24 **p** them to judgment, but those

PRECEPT (11/5) PRECEPTS

Isa 28:10 For **p** must be upon precept,
28:10 For precept must be upon **p**,
28:10 **p** upon precept, Line upon
28:10 upon precept, precept upon **p**,
28:13 **P** upon precept, precept upon
28:13 was to them, "Precept upon **p**,
28:13 **p** upon precept, Line upon
28:13 upon precept, precept upon **p**,
Hos 5:11 he willingly walked by human **p**.
Mk 10: 5 your heart he wrote you this **p**.
Heb 9:19 when Moses had spoken every **p**

PRECEPTS (25/25) PRECEPT

Neh 9:14 Sabbath, And commanded them **p**,
Ps 111: 7 All His **p** are sure.
119: 4 commanded us To keep Your **p**
119:15 I will meditate on Your **p**,
119:27 me understand the way of Your **p**;
119:40 Behold, I long for Your **p**;
119:45 at liberty, For I seek Your **p**.
119:56 Because I kept Your **p**.
119:63 And of those who keep Your **p**.
119:69 But I will keep Your **p** with
119:78 But I will meditate on Your **p**.
119:87 But I did not forsake Your **p**.
119:93 I will never forget Your **p**,
119:94 For I have sought Your **p**.
119:100 Because I keep Your **p**.
119:104 Through Your **p** I get
119:110 I have not strayed from Your **p**.
119:128 Therefore all Your **p**
119:134 of man, That I may keep Your **p**.
119:141 Yet I do not forget Your **p**.
119:159 Consider how I love Your **p**;
119:168 I keep Your **p** and Your
119:173 For I have chosen Your **p**.
Jer 35:18 and kept all his **p** and done
Dan 9: 5 even by departing from Your **p**

PRECIOUS (77/75)

Gen 24:53 He also gave **p** things to her
Deut 33:13 With the **p** things of heaven,
33:14 With the **p** fruits of the sun,
33:14 With the **p** produce of the
33:15 With the **p** things of the
33:16 With the **p** things of the earth
1 Sam 26:21 because my life was **p** in your
2 Sam 12:30 with **p** stones. And it was set
1 Ki 10: 2 and **p** stones; and when she came
10:10 and **p** stones. There never again
10:11 of almug wood and **p** stones
2 Ki 1:13 fifty servants of yours be **p**
1:14 But let my life now be **p** in
20:13 the spices and **p** ointment, and
1 Chr 20: 2 and there were **p** stones in
29: 2 all kinds of **p** stones, and
29: 8 And whoever had **p** stones gave
2 Chr 3: 6 the house with **p** stones
9: 1 and **p** stones; and when she came
9: 9 and **p** stones; there never were
9:10 algum wood and **p** stones.
20:25 and **p** jewelry, which they
21: 3 silver and gold and **p** things,
32:27 for **p** stones, for spices, for
36:19 all its **p** possessions.
Ezra 1: 6 and with **p** things, besides all
8:27 polished bronze, **p** as gold.
Job 22:25 your gold And your **p** silver;
28:10 his eye sees every **p** thing.
28:16 In **p** onyx or sapphire.
Ps 22:20 My **p** life from the power of
35:17 My **p** life from the lions.
36: 7 How **p** is Your lovingkindness,
72:14 And **p** shall be their blood in
116:15 **P** in the sight of the LORD
133: 2 It is like the **p** oil upon the
139:17 How **p** also are Your thoughts to
Prov 1:13 all kinds of **p** possessions,
3:15 She is more **p** than rubies,
6:26 will prey upon his **p** life.
12:27 is man's **p** possession.
17: 8 A present is a **p** stone in the
20:15 of knowledge are a **p** jewel.
24: 4 With all **p** and pleasant riches.
Eccl 7: 1 is better than **p** ointment,
Isa 28:16 a **p** cornerstone, a sure
39: 2 the spices and **p** ointment, and
43: 4 Since you were **p** in My sight,
44: 9 And their **p** things shall not
54:12 all your walls of **p** stones.
Jer 15:19 If you take out the **p** from the
20: 5 and all its **p** things; all the
25:34 shall fall like a **p** vessel.
Lam 4: 2 The **p** sons of Zion, Valuable
Ezek 22:25 taken treasure and **p** things;
27:22 all kinds of **p** stones, and
28:13 Every **p** stone was your
Dan 11: 8 princes and their **p** articles
11:38 with **p** stones and pleasant
11:43 and over all the **p** things of
Mic 1:16 Because of your **p** children;
1 Cor 3:12 **p** stones, wood, hay, straw,
Jas 5: 7 farmer waits for the **p** fruit
1 Pe 1: 7 being much more **p** than gold
1:19 but with the **p** blood of Christ,
2: 4 men, but chosen by God and **p**,
2: 6 chief cornerstone, elect, **p**,
2: 7 to you who believe, He is **p**;
3: 4 which is very **p** in the sight of
2 Pe 1: 1 who have obtained like **p** faith
1: 4 to us exceedingly great and **p**
Rev 17: 4 adorned with gold and **p** stones
18:12 **p** stones and pearls, fine linen
18:12 object of most **p** wood, bronze,
18:16 with gold and **p** stones
21:11 light was like a most **p** stone,
21:19 all kinds of **p** stones:

PREDESTINATE, PREDESTINATED (KJV)

See PREDESTINED

PREDESTINED (4/4)

Rom 8:29 He also **p** to be conformed to
8:30 Moreover whom He **p**,
Eph 1: 5 having **p** us to adoption as sons
1:11 being **p** according to the

PREEMINENCE (2/2)

Col 1:18 in all things He may have the **p**.
3 Jn 9 who loves to have the **p** among

PREFERENCE (2/2) PREFERRED

Deut 21:16 the son of the loved wife in **p**
Rom 12:10 in honor giving **p** to one

PREFERRED (3/3) PREFERENCE

Jn 1:15 He who comes after me is **p**
1:27 is **p** before me, whose sandal
1:30 After me comes a Man who is **p**

PREGNANCY (1/1)

Hos 9:11 like a bird—No birth, no **p**,

PREGNANT (4/4)

Mt 24:19 But woe to those who are **p** and
Mk 13:17 But woe to those who are **p** and
Lk 21:23 But woe to those who are **p** and

P

1 Th 5: 3 as labor pains upon a *p* woman.

PREJUDICE (1/1)
1 Tim 5:21 observe these things without *p*,

PREMATURELY (1/1)
Ex 21:22 so that she gives birth *p*,

PREMEDITATE (1/1)
Mk 13:11 or *p* what you will speak.

PREMEDITATION (1/1)
Ex 21:14 But if a man acts with *p*

PREPARATION (11/10) PREPARE
1 Chr 22: 5 I will now make *p* for it."
Esth 2:12 had completed twelve months' *p*,
2:12 thus were the days of their *p*
Nah 2: 3 torches In the day of his *p*,
Mt 27:62 which followed the Day of *P*,
Mk 15:42 because it was the *P* Day, that
Lk 23:54 That day was the *P*,
Jn 19:14 Now it was the *P* Day of the
19:31 because it was the *P* Day, that
19:42 because of the Jews' *P* Day,
Eph 6:15 shod your feet with the *p* of

PREPARATIONS (6/6)
1 Chr 22: 5 So David made abundant *p*
28: 2 and had made *p* to build it.
Esth 2: 3 And let beauty *p* be given
2: 9 so he readily gave beauty *p* to
2:12 six months with perfumes and *p*
Prov 16: 1 The *p* of the heart belong to

PREPARE (97/96) PREPARATION, PREPARED
Gen 18: 7 and he hastened to *p* it.
Ex 16: 5 the sixth day that they shall *p*
Num 15: 5 as a drink offering you shall *p*
15: 6 Or for a ram you shall *p* as a
15: 8 And when you *p* a young bull as a
15:12 to the number that you *p*,
23: 1 and *p* for me here seven bulls
23:29 and *p* for me here seven bulls
Deut 19: 3 You shall *p* roads for yourself,
Josh 1:11 *P* provisions for yourselves, for
22:26 Let us now *p* to build ourselves
Judg 13:15 and we will *p* a young goat for
1 Sam 7: 3 and *p* your hearts for the
2 Sam 12: 4 and from his own herd to *p* one
13: 5 and *p* the food in my sight,
13: 7 and *p* food for him."
1 Ki 17:12 sticks that I may go in and *p*
18:23 and I will *p* the other bull,
18:25 one bull for yourselves and *p*
18:44 *P* your chariot, and go down
1 Chr 22:14 I have taken much trouble to *p*
2 Chr 2: 9 to *p* timber for me in abundance,
12:14 because he did not *p* his heart
31:11 Hezekiah commanded them to *p*
35: 4 *P* yourselves according to your
35: 6 and *p* them for your brethren,
Esth 5: 8 to the banquet which I will *p*
Job 11:13 'If you would *p* your heart,
37:19 For we can *p* nothing because
38: 3 Now *p* yourself like a man;
40: 7 'Now *p* yourself like a man;
Ps 10:17 You will *p* their heart;
23: 5 You *p* a table before me in the
59: 4 They run and *p* themselves
61: 7 *p* mercy and truth, which may
78:19 Can God *p* a table in the
132:17 I will *p* a lamp for My
Prov 24:27 *P* your outside work, Make it
30:25 Yet they *p* their food in the
Isa 14:21 *P* slaughter for his children
21: 5 *P* the table, Set a watchman in
40: 3 '*P* the way of the LORD;
40:20 a skillful workman To *p* a
57:14 Heap it up! Heap it up! *P* the
62:10 Go through the gates! *P* the
65:11 Who *p* a table for Gad,
Jer 1:17 Therefore *p* yourself and arise,
6: 4 *P* war against her; Arise, and
12: 3 And *p* them for the day of
22: 7 I will *p* destroyers against
46:14 Stand fast and *p* yourselves,
46:19 *P* yourself to go into
51:12 *P* the ambushes. For the LORD
51:27 *P* the nations against her,
51:28 *P* against her the nations,
51:39 In their excitement I will *p*
Ezek 4:15 and you shall *p* your bread over
12: 3 *p* your belongings for
35: 6 I will *p* you for blood, and
38: 7 *P* yourself and be ready, you
43:25 day for seven days you shall *p*
43:25 they shall also *p* a young bull
45:17 He shall *p* the sin offering,
45:22 on that day the prince shall *p*
45:23 days of the feast he shall *p* a
45:24 And he shall *p* a grain offering
46: 2 The priests shall *p* his burnt
46: 7 He shall *p* a grain offering of
46:12 and he shall *p* his burnt
46:13 you shall *p* it every morning.
46:14 And you shall *p* a grain offering
46:15 Thus they shall *p* the lamb, the
Hos 7: 6 They *p* their heart like an
Joel 3: 9 *P* for war! Wake up the mighty
Am 4:12 *P* to meet your God, O
Mic 3: 5 But who *p* war against him
Mal 3: 1 And he will *p* the way before
Mt 3: 3 *P* the way of the LORD;
11:10 Who will *p* Your way
26:17 Where do You want us to *p* for
Mk 1: 2 Who will *p* Your way
1: 3 *P* the way of the LORD;
14:12 do You want us to go and *p*,
Lk 1:76 the face of the Lord to *p* His
3: 4 *P* the way of the LORD;
7:27 Who will *p* Your way
9:52 Samaritans, to *p* for Him.
12:47 and did not *p* himself or do
17: 8 *P* something for my supper, and
22: 8 Go and *p* the Passover for us,
22: 9 "Where do You want us to *p*?
Jn 14: 2 I go to *p* a place for you.
14: 3 And if I go and *p* a place for
Acts 23:23 *P* two hundred soldiers, seventy
1 Cor 14: 8 who will *p* himself for battle?
2 Cor 9: 5 and *p* your generous gift
Phm 1:22 also *p* a guest room for me, for

PREPARED (109/107) PREPARE
Gen 18: 8 and the calf which he had *p*,
24:31 For I have *p* the house, and a
27:17 and the bread, which she had *p*,
Ex 12:16 that only may be *p* by you.
12:39 nor had they *p* provisions for
23:20 into the place which I have *p*.
Lev 7: 9 in the oven and all that is *p*
Num 10:21 (The tabernacle would be *p* for
11: 8 was like the taste of pastry *p*
23: 4 I have *p* the seven altars, and I
Josh 4:13 About forty thousand *p* for war
Judg 6:19 So Gideon went in and *p* a young
2 Sam 12: 4 took the poor man's lamb and *p*
1 Ki 1: 5 and he *p* for himself chariots
5:18 and they *p* timber and stones to
6:19 And he *p* the inner sanctuary
18:26 and they *p* it, and called on
2 Ki 6:23 Then he *p* a great feast for
1 Chr 12:39 for their brethren had *p* for
15: 1 and he *p* a place for the ark of
15: 3 which he had *p* for it.
15:12 Israel to the place I have *p*
22: 3 And David *p* iron in abundance
22:14 I have *p* timber and stone also,
29: 2 the house of my God I have *p*
29: 3 and above all that I have *p*
29:16 this abundance that we have *p*
2 Chr 1: 4 to the place David had *p* for
3: 1 at the place that David had *p*
16:14 and various ingredients *p* in a
17:18 hundred and eighty thousand *p*
19: 3 and have *p* your heart to seek
26:11 the number on their roll as *p*
26:14 Then Uzziah *p* for them, for the
27: 6 because he *p* his ways before
29:19 in his transgression we have *p*
29:36 people rejoiced that God had *p*
31:11 and they *p* them.
35:10 So the service was *p*,
35:14 Then afterward they *p* portions
35:14 therefore the Levites *p*
35:15 their brethren the Levites *p*
35:16 the service of the LORD was *p*
35:20 when Josiah had *p* the temple,
Ezra 7:10 For Ezra had *p* his heart to seek
Neh 5:18 Now that which was *p* daily was
5:18 Also fowl were *p* for me, and
8:10 to those for whom nothing is *p*;
13: 5 And he had *p* for him a large
Esth 2:13 Thus *p*, each young woman
5: 4 to the banquet that I have *p*
5: 5 the banquet that Esther had *p*.
5:12 king to the banquet that she *p*;
6: 4 on the gallows that he had *p*
6:14 the banquet which Esther had *p*.
7:10 on the gallows that he had *p*
Job 13:18 I have *p* my case, I know that
28:27 He *p* it, indeed, He searched
Ps 9: 7 He has *p* His throne for
31:19 Which You have *p* for those
57: 6 They have *p* a net for my steps;
65: 9 For so You have *p* it.
74:16 You have *p* the light and the
80: 9 You *p* room for it, And caused
Prov 8:27 When He *p* the heavens, I was
19:29 Judgments are *p* for scoffers,
21:31 The horse is *p* for the day of
Isa 30:33 Yes, for the king it is *p*.
51:13 When he has *p* to destroy.
Ezek 23:41 with a table *p* before it, on
28:13 Was *p* for you on the day
Hos 2: 8 Which they *p* for Baal.
Jon 1:17 Now the LORD had *p* a great
4: 6 And the LORD God *p* a plant and
4: 7 dawned the next day God *p* a
4: 8 that God *p* a vehement east
Nah 2: 5 walls, And the defense is *p*.
Zeph 1: 7 For the LORD has *p* a
Mt 20:23 for those for whom it is *p*
22: 4 I have *p* my dinner; my oxen and
25:34 inherit the kingdom *p* for you
25:41 into the everlasting fire *p* for
26:19 and they *p* the Passover.
Mk 10:40 for those for whom it is *p*.
14:15 upper room, furnished and *p*;
14:16 and they *p* the Passover.
Lk 1:17 to make ready a people *p* for
2:31 Which You have *p* before the
22:13 and they *p* the Passover.
23:56 Then they returned and *p* spices
24: 1 the spices which they had *p*.
Rom 9:22 the vessels of wrath *p* for
9:23 which He had *p* beforehand for
1 Cor 2: 9 things which God has *p*
2 Cor 5: 5 Now He who has *p* us for this
Eph 2:10 which God *p* beforehand that we
2 Tim 2:21 *p* for every good work.
Heb 9: 2 For a tabernacle was *p*:
9: 6 these things had been thus *p*,
10: 5 But a body You have *p*
11: 7 *p* an ark for the saving of his
11:16 for He has *p* a city for them.
1 Pe 3:20 while the ark was being *p*,
Rev 8: 6 who had the seven trumpets *p*
9: 7 the locusts was like horses *p*
9:15 who had been *p* for the hour and
12: 6 where she has a place *p* by God,
16:12 kings from the east might be *p*.
21: 2 *p* as a bride adorned for her

PREPARES (5/5)
Num 4: 5 When the camp *p* to journey,
2 Chr 30:19 who *p* his heart to seek God,
Job 15:35 Their womb *p* deceit."
Ps 7:13 He also *p* for Himself
147: 8 Who *p* rain for the earth,

PREPARING (2/2)
1 Chr 9:32 were in charge of *p* the
Neh 13: 7 in *p* a room for him in the

PRESBYTERY (KJV) See ELDERSHIP

PRESCRIBED (9/9)
Lev 5:10 offering according to the *p*
9:16 offered it according to the *p*
2 Chr 4:20 to burn in the *p* manner in
30: 5 it for a long time in the *p*
Ezra 7:22 and salt without *p* limit.
Neh 8:18 according to the *p* manner.
Esth 9:27 and according to the *p* time,
9:31 the Jew and Queen Esther had *p*
Isa 10: 1 Which they have *p*

PRESENCE (156/147) PRESENT
Gen 3: 8 wife hid themselves from the *p*
4:16 Then Cain went out from the *p*
16: 6 with her, she fled from her *p*.
16: 8 I am fleeing from the *p* of my
16:12 And he shall dwell in the *p* of
23:10 answered Abraham in the *p* of
23:11 I give it to you in the *p* of
23:18 as a possession in the *p* of
25:18 He died in the *p* of all his
27: 7 eat it and bless you in the *p*
27:30 scarcely gone out from the *p*
31:32 In the *p* of our brethren,
36: 6 to a country away from the *p*
41:46 And Joseph went out from the *p*
45: 3 for they were dismayed in his *p*.
47:15 for why should we die in your *p*?
Ex 10:11 driven out from Pharaoh's *p*.
33:14 My *P* will go with you, and I
33:15 If Your *P* does not go with us,
35:20 of Israel departed from the *p*
Lev 19:32 gray headed and honor the *p* of
22: 3 shall be cut off from My *p*:
Num 3: 4 ministered as priests in the *p*
20: 6 and Aaron went from the *p* of the
Deut 1:17 not be afraid in any man's *p*,
4:37 you out of Egypt with His *P*,
25: 2 lie down and be beaten in his *p*,
25: 9 shall come to him in the *p* of
Josh 4:11 priests crossed over in the *p*
8:32 in the *p* of the children of
Judg 4:23 Jabin king of Canaan in the *p*
18: 6 The *p* of the LORD be with you
Ruth 4: 4 Buy it back in the *p* of the
1 Sam 18:11 But David escaped his *p* twice.
18:13 Saul removed him from his *p*,
19: 7 and he was in his *p* as in times
19:10 he slipped away from Saul's *p*;
21:15 to play the madman in my *p*?
2 Sam 3:26 Joab had gone from David's *p*,
16:19 Should I not serve in the *p*
16:19 have served in your father's *p*,
16:19 so will I be in your *p*.
24: 4 of the army went out from the *p*
1 Ki 1:28 So she came into the king's *p*
8:22 altar of the LORD in the *p* of
10:24 all the earth sought the *p* of
12: 2 for he had fled from the *p* of
21:13 in the *p* of the people, saying,
2 Ki 3:14 it not that I regard the *p* of
5:27 And he went out from his *p*
13:23 them or cast them from His *p*.
24:20 cast them out from His *p*.
1 Chr 24:31 in the *p* of King David, Zadok,

2 Chr 6:12 altar of the LORD in the **p** of
9:23 of the earth sought the **p** of
10: 2 where he had fled from the **p** of
20: 9 this temple and in Your **p** (for
34: 4 altars of the Baals in his **p**,
Neh 2: 1 I had never been sad in his **p**
Esth 1:10 eunuchs who served in the **p** of
1:14 who had access to the king's **p**,
2:23 of the chronicles in the **p** of
8:15 Mordecai went out from the **p**
Job 1:12 So Satan went out from the **p**
2: 7 So Satan went out from the **p** of
23:15 I am terrified at His **p**;
23:17 I was not cut off from the **p**
Ps 9: 3 shall fall and perish at Your **p**.
16:11 In Your **p** is fullness of joy;
17: 2 my vindication come from Your **p**;
21: 6 exceedingly glad with Your **p**.
23: 5 a table before me in the **p** of
31:19 who trust in You In the **p** of
31:20 in the secret place of Your **p**
51:11 not cast me away from Your **p**,
52: 9 And in the **p** of Your saints
68: 2 let the wicked perish at the **p**
68: 8 also dropped rain at the **p** of
68: 8 itself was moved at the **p** of
76: 7 And who may stand in Your **p**
95: 2 Let us come before His **p** with
97: 5 melt like wax at the **p** of the
97: 5 At the **p** of the Lord of the
100: 2 Come before His **p** with
101: 7 lies shall not continue in my **p**.
114: 7 at the **p** of the Lord, At the
114: 7 At the **p** of the God of Jacob,
116:14 to the LORD Now in the **p** of
116:18 to the LORD Now in the **p** of
139: 7 where can I flee from Your **p**?
140:13 upright shall dwell in Your **p**.
Prov 14: 7 Go from the **p** of a foolish man,
25: 6 not exalt yourself in the **p** of
25: 7 should be put lower in the **p**
Eccl 8: 3 not be hasty to go from his **p**.
Isa 1: 7 devour your land in your **p**;
19: 1 of Egypt will totter at His **p**,
63: 9 And the Angel of His **P** saved
64: 1 mountains might shake at Your **p**—
64: 2 nations may tremble at Your **p**!
64: 3 The mountains shook at Your **p**.
Jer 4:26 were broken down At the **p** of
5:22 'Will you not tremble at My **p**,
23:39 will cast you out of My **p**.
28: 1 house of the LORD in the **p** of
28: 5 the prophet Hananiah in the **p**
28: 5 of the priests and in the **p** of
28:11 And Hananiah spoke in the **p** of
32:12 in the **p** of Hanamel my uncle's
32:12 and in the **p** of the witnesses
52: 3 cast them out from His **p**.
Ezek 38:20 the earth shall shake at My **p**.
Dan 2:27 Daniel answered in the **p** of the
5: 1 and drank wine in the **p** of the
Jon 1: 3 to flee to Tarshish from the **p**
1: 3 them to Tarshish from the **p** of
1:10 knew that he fled from the **p**
Nah 1: 5 And the earth heaves at His **p**,
Zeph 1: 7 Be silent in the **p** of the Lord
Hag 1:12 and the people feared the **p** of
Mk 2:12 and went out in the **p** of them
Lk 1:19 who stands in the **p** of God, and
8:47 she declared to Him in the **p** of
13:26 'We ate and drank in Your **p**,
14:10 you will have glory in the **p**
15:10 there is joy in the **p** of the
20:26 Him in His words in the **p** of
23:14 having examined Him in your **p**,
24:43 He took it and ate in their **p**.
Jn 20:30 did many other signs in the **p**
Acts 2:28 me full of joy in Your **p**.
3:13 up and denied in the **p** of
3:16 perfect soundness in the **p** of
3:19 refreshing may come from the **p**
5:41 So they departed from the **p** of
7:10 him favor and wisdom in the **p**
27:35 gave thanks to God in the **p** of
Rom 4:17 of many nations") in the **p**
1 Cor 1:29 no flesh should glory in His **p**.
2 Cor 2:10 one for your sakes in the **p** of
10: 1 who in **p** am lowly among you,
10:10 but his bodily **p** is weak, and
Phil 2:12 not as in my **p** only, but now
1 Th 2:17 from you for a short time in **p**,
2:19 Is it not even you in the **p**
2 Th 1: 9 destruction from the **p** of the
1 Tim 5:20 are sinning rebuke in the **p** of
6:12 the good confession in the **p**
Heb 6:19 and which enters the **P** behind
9:24 now to appear in the **p** of God
Jude 24 you faultless Before the **p** of
Rev 12:14 from the **p** of the serpent.
13:12 of the first beast in his **p**,
14:10 fire and brimstone in the **p** of
14:10 of the holy angels and in the **p**
19:20 who worked signs in his **p**,

PRESENT (130/127) PRESENCE, PRESENTABLE, PRESENTED, PRESENTS, UNPRESENTABLE

Gen 32:13 what came to his hand as a **p**
32:18 It is a **p** sent to my lord
32:20 I will appease him with the **p**
32:21 So the **p** went on over before
33:10 then receive my **p** from my hand,
43:11 vessels and carry down a **p** for
43:15 So the men took that **p** and
43:25 Then they made the **p** ready for
43:26 they brought him the **p** which
Ex 34: 2 and **p** yourself to Me there on
Lev 14:11 who makes him clean shall **p**
16: 7 shall take the two goats and **p**
27: 8 then he shall **p** himself before
27:11 then he shall **p** the animal
Num 3: 6 and **p** them before Aaron the
6:14 And he shall **p** his offering to
15:14 and would **p** an offering made by
16:16 you and all your company be **p**
28:11 of your months you shall **p** a
28:19 And you shall **p** an offering made
28:27 You shall **p** a burnt offering as
28:31 You shall **p** them with their
29: 8 You shall **p** a burnt offering to
29:13 You shall **p** a burnt offering, an
29:17 On the second day **p** twelve
29:20 On the third day **p** eleven
29:23 On the fourth day **p** ten bulls,
29:26 On the fifth day **p** nine bulls,
29:29 On the sixth day **p** eight
29:32 On the seventh day **p** seven
29:36 You shall **p** a burnt offering, an
29:39 These you shall **p** to the LORD
Deut 31:14 and **p** yourselves in the
1 Sam 9: 7 and there is no **p** to bring to
10:19 **p** yourselves before the LORD
13:15 And Saul numbered the people **p**
13:16 and the people **p** with them
25:27 And now this **p** which your
30:26 Here is a **p** for you from the
2 Sam 20: 4 and be **p** here yourself."
1 Ki 10:25 Each man brought his **p**:
15:19 I have sent you a **p** of silver
18: 1 **p** yourself to Ahab, and I will
18: 2 So Elijah went to **p** himself to
18:15 I will surely **p** myself to him
2 Ki 8: 8 Take a **p** in your hand, and go to
8: 9 went to meet him and took a **p**
16: 8 and sent it as a **p** to the
18:31 Make peace with me by a **p** and
20:12 sent letters and a **p** to
1 Chr 29:17 who are **p** here to offer
2 Chr 5:11 all the priests who were **p**
9:24 Each man brought his **p**:
29:29 the king and all who were **p**
30:21 children of Israel who were **p**
31: 1 all Israel who were **p** went out
34:32 And he made all who were **p** in
34:33 and made all who were **p** in
35: 7 offerings for all who were **p**,
35:17 children of Israel who were **p**
35:18 all Judah and Israel who were **p**,
Ezra 8:25 and all Israel who were **p**,
Esth 1: 5 for all the people who were **p**
4:16 gather all the Jews who are **p**
Job 1: 6 when the sons of God came to **p**
2: 1 when the sons of God came to **p**
2: 1 Satan came also among them to **p**
23: 4 I would **p** my case before Him,
Ps 46: 1 A very **p** help in trouble.
Prov 17: 8 A **p** is a precious stone in the
Isa 18: 7 In that time a **p** will be
36:16 Make peace with me by a **p** and
39: 1 sent letters and a **p** to
41:21 **P** your case," says the LORD.
Jer 36: 7 It may be that they will **p** their
42: 9 to whom you sent me to **p** your
Lam 4: 3 Even the jackals **p** their
Dan 2:46 commanded that they should **p**
9:18 for we do not **p** our
Hos 10: 6 be carried to Assyria As a **p**
Mk 9: 1 they see the kingdom of God **p**
Lk 2:22 brought Him to Jerusalem to **p**
5:17 the power of the Lord was **p**
13: 1 There were **p** at that season some
18:30 many times more in this **p** time,
Jn 14:25 spoken to you while being **p**
Acts 10:33 we are all **p** before God, to
21:18 and all the elders were **p**.
25:24 and all the men who are here **p**
Rom 3:26 to demonstrate at the **p** time His
6:13 And do not **p** your members as
6:13 but **p** yourselves to God as
6:16 you not know that to whom you **p**
6:19 so now **p** your members as
7:18 for to will is **p** with me, but
7:21 that evil is **p** with me, the one
8:18 that the sufferings of this **p**
8:38 nor things **p** nor things to
11: 5 at this **p** time there is a
12: 1 that you **p** your bodies a living
1 Cor 3:22 or things **p** or things to
4:11 To the **p** hour we both hunger and
5: 3 as absent in body but **p** in
5: 3 judged (as though I were **p**)
7:26 this is good because of the **p**
9:18 I may **p** the gospel of Christ
15: 6 greater part remain to the **p**,
2 Cor 4:14 and will **p** us with you.
5: 8 from the body and to be **p** with
5: 9 whether **p** or absent, to be well
10: 2 I beg you that when I am **p** I
10:11 also be in deed when we are **p**.
11: 2 that I may **p** you as a chaste
11: 9 And when I was **p** with you, and
13: 2 and foretell as if I were **p** the
13:10 lest being **p** I should use
Gal 1: 4 He might deliver us from this **p**
4:18 and not only when I am **p** with
4:20 I would like to be **p** with you
Eph 5:27 that He might **p** her to Himself a
Col 1:22 to **p** you holy, and blameless,
1:28 that we may **p** every man perfect
1 Tim 6:17 those who are rich in this **p**
2 Tim 2:15 Be diligent to **p** yourself
4:10 having loved this **p** world, and
Titus 2:12 and godly in the **p** age,
Heb 9: 9 It was symbolic for the **p** time
12:11 seems to be joyful for the **p**,
2 Pe 1:12 and are established in the **p**
Jude 24 And to **p** you faultless

PRESENTABLE (1/1) PRESENT

1 Cor 12:24 but our **p** parts have no need.

PRESENTATION (1/1)

1 Chr 23:31 and at every **p** of a burnt

PRESENTED (39/39) PRESENT

Gen 46:29 and he **p** himself to him, and
47: 2 from among his brothers and **p**
Lev 2: 8 And when it is **p** to the priest,
7:35 on the day when Moses **p** them
9:12 and Aaron's sons **p** to him the
9:13 Then they **p** the burnt offering
9:18 And Aaron's sons **p** to him the
16:10 to be the scapegoat shall be **p**
Num 7: 3 and they **p** them before the
7:18 Issachar, **p** an offering.
7:24 **p** an offering.
7:30 **p** an offering.
7:36 **p** an offering.
7:42 **p** an offering.
7:48 **p** an offering.
7:54 **p** an offering.
7:60 **p** an offering.
7:66 **p** an offering.
7:72 **p** an offering.
7:78 **p** an offering.
8:21 then Aaron **p** them, like a wave
16:38 Because they **p** them before the
16:39 those who were burned up had **p**,
25: 6 children of Israel came and **p**
Deut 31:14 So Moses and Joshua went and **p**
Josh 24: 1 and they **p** themselves before
Judg 6:19 under the terebinth tree and **p**
20: 2 **p** themselves in the assembly of
1 Sam 17:16 the Philistine drew near and **p**
2 Chr 24: 7 and had also **p** all the
29:24 and they **p** their blood on the
Ezra 10:19 they **p** a ram of the flock as
Jer 38:26 I **p** my request before the king,
Mt 2:11 they **p** gifts to Him: gold,
Lk 7:15 And He **p** him to his mother.
Acts 1: 3 to whom He also **p** Himself alive
9:41 and widows, he **p** her alive.
23:33 they also **p** Paul to him.
Rom 6:19 For just as you **p** your members

PRESENTING (5/5)

Num 9: 7 Why are we kept from **p** the
15:13 in **p** an offering made by fire,
Judg 3:18 And when he had finished **p** the
1 Sam 13:10 as soon as he had finished **p**
Dan 9:20 and **p** my supplication before

PRESENTS (11/11) PRESENT

Num 15: 4 then he who **p** his offering to
1 Sam 10:27 him, and brought him no **p**.
2 Chr 17: 5 and all Judah gave **p** to
17:11 brought Jehoshaphat **p** and
32:23 and **p** to Hezekiah king of
Esth 9:19 and for sending **p** to one
9:22 of sending **p** to one another and
Ps 68:29 Kings will bring **p** to You.
72:10 and of the isles Will bring **p**;
76:11 all who are around Him bring **p**
Mic 1:14 Therefore you shall give **p** to

PRESERVE (35/34) PRESERVED, PRESERVES

Gen 19:32 that we may **p** the lineage of
19:34 that we may **p** the lineage of
45: 5 for God sent me before you to **p**
45: 7 God sent me before you to **p** a
Deut 6:24 that He might **p** us alive, as
Neh 9: 6 And You **p** them all. The host
Job 36: 6 He does not **p** the life of the
Ps 12: 7 You shall **p** them from this
16: 1 **P** me, O God, for in You I put
25:21 integrity and uprightness **p** me,
32: 7 You shall **p** me from trouble;
36: 6 You **p** man and beast.
40:11 and Your truth continually **p**
41: 2 The LORD will **p** him and keep
61: 7 which may **p** him!
64: 1 **P** my life from fear of the
79:11 the greatness of Your power **P**
86: 2 **P** my life, for I am holy
121: 7 The LORD shall **p** you from all
121: 7 He shall **p** your soul.
121: 8 The LORD shall **p** your going
140: 1 **P** me from violent men,
140: 4 **P** me from violent men,

P

Prov 2:11 Discretion will **p** you;
4: 6 and she will **p** you; Love her,
5: 2 That you may **p** discretion,
14: 3 the lips of the wise will **p**
20:28 Mercy and truth **p** the king,
22:12 The eyes of the LORD **p**
Isa 31: 5 He will **p** it."
49: 8 I will **p** You and give You
Jer 49:11 I will **p** them alive; And let
50:20 I will pardon those whom I **p**.
Lk 17:33 whoever loses his life will **p**
2 Tim 4:18 me from every evil work and **p**

PRESERVED (16/16) PRESERVE

Gen 32:30 face to face, and my life is **p**.
Josh 24:17 and **p** us in all the way that we
1 Sam 30:23 who has **p** us and delivered into
2 Sam 8: 6 The LORD **p** David wherever he
8:14 And the LORD **p** David wherever
1 Chr 18: 6 So the LORD **p** David wherever
18:13 And the LORD **p** David wherever
Job 10:12 And Your care has **p** my spirit.
Ps 37:28 They are **p** forever, But the
Isa 49: 6 And to restore the **p** ones of
Hos 12:13 And by a prophet he was **p**.
Mt 9:17 new wineskins, and both are **p**.
Lk 5:38 new wineskins, and both are **p**.
1 Th 5:23 and body be **p** blameless at the
2 Pe 3: 7 and the earth which are now **p**
Jude 1 and **p** in Jesus Christ:

PRESERVES (8/8) PRESERVE

Ps 31:23 His saints! For the LORD **p**
97:10 hate evil! He **p** the souls of
116: 6 The LORD **p** the simple; I was
145:20 The LORD **p** all who love Him,
Prov 2: 8 And **p** the way of His saints.
13: 3 He who guards his mouth **p** his
16:17 He who keeps his way **p** his
Ezek 18:27 he **p** himself alive.

PRESIDENTS (KJV) See GOVERNORS

PRESS (5/5) PRESSED, PRESSES, PRESSING

Job 24:11 They **p** out oil within their
Hag 2:16 draw out fifty baths from the **p**,
Lk 8:45 the multitudes throng and **p**
Phil 3:12 but I **p** on, that I may lay hold
3:14 I **p** toward the goal for the

PRESSED (19/19) PRESS

Gen 19: 9 So they **p** hard against the
40:11 and I took the grapes and **p**
Ex 27:20 they bring you pure oil of **p**
29:40 with one-fourth of a hin of **p**
Lev 24: 2 they bring to you pure oil of **p**
Num 28: 5 with one-fourth of a hin of **p**
Judg 14:17 because she **p** him so much. Then
16:16 him daily with her words and **p**
1 Ki 5:11 and twenty kors of **p** oil.
Esth 8:14 hastened and **p** on by the king's
Isa 8:21 will pass through it hard **p**
Ezek 23: 3 Their virgin bosom was there **p**.
23: 8 **P** her virgin bosom,
23:21 When the Egyptians **p** your
Mk 3:10 as many as had afflictions **p**
Lk 5: 1 as the multitude **p** about Him to
6:38 **p** down, shaken together, and
2 Cor 4: 8 We are hard **p** on every side,
Phil 1:23 For I am hard **p** between the two,

PRESSES (3/3) PRESS

Neh 13:15 in Judah treading wine **p** on
Ps 38: 2 And Your hand **p** me down.
Isa 16:10 will tread out wine in the **p**;

PRESSING (2/2) PRESS

Hab 2:15 **P** him to your bottle,
Lk 16:16 and everyone is **p** into it.

PRESUME (1/1)

Esth 7: 5 who would dare **p** in his heart

PRESUMED (1/1)

Num 14:44 But they **p** to go up to the

PRESUMES (1/1)

Deut 18:20 But the prophet who **p** to speak a

PRESUMPTUOUS (2/2) PRESUMPTUOUSLY

Ps 19:13 back Your servant also from **p**
2 Pe 2:10 despise authority. They are **p**,

PRESUMPTUOUSLY (5/5) PRESUMPTUOUS

Num 15:30 the person who does anything **p**,
Deut 1:43 and **p** went up into the
17:12 Now the man who acts **p** and will
17:13 and fear, and no longer act **p**.
18:22 the prophet has spoken it **p**;

PRETEND (5/5)

2 Sam 13: 5 Lie down on your bed and **p** to be
14: 2 Please **p** to be a mourner, and
1 Ki 14: 5 that she will **p** to be another
14: 6 Why do you **p** to be another
Ps 81:15 haters of the LORD would **p**

PRETENDED (4/4)

Josh 9: 4 and went and **p** to be
2 Sam 13: 6 Then Amnon lay down and **p** to be
Ps 34: A Psalm of David when he **p**
Lk 20:20 and sent spies who **p** to be

PRETENSE (6/6)

Jer 3:10 with her whole heart, but in **p**,
Mt 23:14 and for a **p** make long prayers.
Mk 12:40 and for a **p** make long prayers.
Lk 20:47 and for a **p** make long prayers.
Acts 27:30 under **p** of putting out anchors
Phil 1:18 whether in **p** or in truth,

PRETTY (1/1)

Jer 46:20 Egypt is a very **p** heifer,

PREVAIL (27/27) PREVAILED

Gen 32:25 when He saw that He did not **p**
1 Sam 2: 9 by strength no man shall **p**.
17: 9 But if I **p** against him and kill
26:25 great things and also still **p**.
1 Ki 22:22 shall persuade him, and also **p**.
2 Chr 14:11 do not let man **p** against You!"
18:21 shall persuade him and also **p**;
Esth 6:13 you will not **p** against him but
Job 14:20 You **p** forever against him, and
Ps 9:19 O LORD, Do not let man **p**;
12: 4 "With our tongue we will **p**;
65: 3 Iniquities **p** against me;
Isa 7: 1 but could not **p** against it.
16:12 to pray; But he will not **p**.
42:13 He shall **p** against His
47:12 to profit, Perhaps you will **p**.
Jer 1:19 But they shall not **p** against
5:22 to and fro, Yet they cannot **p**;
15:20 But they shall not **p** against
20:10 Then we will **p** against him,
20:11 will stumble, and will not **p**.
Dan 11: 7 North, and deal with them and **p**.
11:12 of thousands, but he will not **p**.
Ob 7 Shall deceive you and **p** against
Mt 16:18 the gates of Hades shall not **p**
27:24 Pilate saw that he could not **p**
Rev 12: 8 but they did not **p**,

PREVAILED (27/26) PREVAIL

Gen 7:18 The waters **p** and greatly
7:19 And the waters **p** exceedingly on
7:20 The waters **p** fifteen cubits
7:24 And the waters **p** on the earth
30: 8 my sister, and indeed I have **p**.
32:28 God and with men, and have **p**.
Ex 17:11 held up his hand, that Israel **p**;
17:11 he let down his hand, Amalek **p**.
Judg 3:10 and his hand **p** over
6: 2 and the hand of Midian **p** against
1 Sam 17:50 So David **p** over the Philistine
2 Sam 11:23 Surely the men **p** against us and
24: 4 Nevertheless the king's word **p**
1 Ki 16:22 the people who followed Omri **p**
1 Chr 5: 2 yet Judah **p** over his brothers,
21: 4 Nevertheless the king's word **p**
2 Chr 13:18 and the children of Judah **p**,
Ps 13: 4 'I have **p** against him";
129: 2 Yet they have not **p** against
Jer 20: 7 are stronger than I, and have **p**.
38:22 have set upon you And **p**
Lam 1:16 desolate Because the enemy **p**.
Hos 12: 4 struggled with the Angel and **p**;
Lk 23:23 men and of the chief priests **p**.
Acts 19:16 and **p** against them, so that
19:20 of the Lord grew mightily and **p**.
Rev 5: 5 has **p** to open the scroll and to

PREVAILING (1/1)

Dan 7:21 and **p** against them,

PREVENT (1/1) PREVENTED

Mt 3:14 And John tried to **p** Him,

PREVENTED (1/1) PREVENT

Heb 7:23 because they were **p** by death

PREVIOUSLY (16/16)

Gen 28:19 of that city had been Luz **p**.
Ex 10:14 **p** there had been no such
2 Sam 7:10 oppress them anymore, as **p**,
15:34 I was your father's servant **p**,
1 Chr 17: 9 oppress them anymore, as **p**,
Neh 13: 5 where **p** they had stored the
Jon 4: 2 Therefore I fled **p** to Tarshish;
Lk 23:12 for **p** they had been at enmity
Jn 9: 8 and those who **p** had seen
Acts 8: 9 who **p** practiced sorcery in the
21:29 (For they had **p** seen Trophimus

Rom 3: 9 For we have **p** charged both Jews
3:25 sins that were **p** committed,
2 Cor 9: 5 which you had **p** promised,
1 Tim 1:18 to the prophecies **p** made
Heb 10: 8 **P** saying, "Sacrifice and

PREY (39/36)

Gen 49: 9 is a lion's whelp; From the **p**,
49:27 morning he shall devour the **p**,
Num 23:24 lie down until it devours the **p**,
Job 4:11 old lion perishes for lack of **p**,
9:26 an eagle swooping on its **p**.
38:39 Can you hunt the **p** for the
39:29 From there it spies out the **p**;
Ps 17:12 a lion is eager to tear his **p**,
76: 4 Than the mountains of **p**.
104:21 young lions roar after their **p**,
124: 6 Who has not given us as **p** to
Prov 6:26 And an adulteress will **p** upon
Isa 5:29 And lay hold of the **p**;
10: 2 That widows may be their **p**,
10: 6 seize the spoil, to take the **p**,
18: 6 for the mountain birds of **p**
18: 6 The birds of **p** will summer on
31: 4 And a young lion over his **p**
33:23 Then the **p** of great plunder is
33:23 divided; The lame take the **p**.
42:22 prison houses; They are for **p**,
46:11 Calling a bird of **p** from the
49:24 Shall the **p** be taken from the
49:25 And the **p** of the terrible be
59:15 from evil makes himself a **p**.
Jer 30:16 And all who **p** upon you I will
30:16 prey upon you I will make a **p**.
Ezek 13:21 they shall no longer be as **p**
19: 3 He learned to catch **p**,
19: 6 He learned to catch **p**;
22:25 a roaring lion tearing the **p**;
22:27 are like wolves tearing the **p**,
34: 8 because My flock became a **p**,
34:22 and they shall no longer be a **p**;
34:28 they shall no longer be a **p**
39: 4 I will give you to birds of **p**
Am 3: 4 in the forest, when he has no **p**?
Nah 2:12 Filled his caves with **p**,
2:13 I will cut off your **p** from the

PREYS (1/1)

Job 24:21 For he **p** on the barren who do

PRICE (26/25) PRICED

Gen 23: 9 him give it to me at the full **p**,
Lev 25:16 years you shall increase its **p**,
25:16 years you shall diminish its **p**;
25:50 The **p** of his release shall be
25:51 to them he shall repay the **p**
25:52 years he shall repay him the **p**
Deut 23:18 the wages of a harlot or the **p**
2 Sam 24:24 surely buy it from you for a **p**;
1 Ki 10:28 them in Keveh at the current **p**.
1 Chr 21:22 grant it to me at the full **p**,
21:24 surely buy it for the full **p**,
2 Chr 1:16 them in Keveh at the current **p**.
Job 28:15 silver be weighed for its **p**.
28:18 For the **p** of wisdom is above
Prov 17:16 hand of a fool the purchase **p**
27:26 And the goats the **p** of a
Isa 45:13 Not for **p** nor reward,"
55: 1 Without money and without **p**.
Jer 15:13 will give as plunder without **p**,
Lam 5: 4 And our wood comes at a **p**.
Zech 11:13 that princely **p** they set on me.
Mt 13:46 had found one pearl of great **p**,
27: 6 because they are the **p** of
Acts 5: 3 and keep back part of the **p**
1 Cor 6:20 For you were bought at a **p**;
7:23 You were bought at a **p**;

PRICED (2/1) PRICE

Mt 27: 9 value of Him who was **p**,
27: 9 of the children of Israel **p**,

PRICKING (1/1)

Ezek 28:24 there shall no longer be a **p**

PRICKS (KJV) See GOADS, IRRITANTS

PRIDE (51/48) PROUD

Lev 26:19 I will break the **p** of your
1 Sam 17:28 I know your **p** and the insolence
2 Chr 32:26 humbled himself for the **p** of
Job 33:17 And conceal **p** from man,
35:12 Because of the **p** of evil men.
41:15 His rows of scales are his **p**,
41:34 king over all the children of **p**.
Ps 10: 2 The wicked in his **p** persecutes
36:11 Let not the foot of **p** come
59:12 them even be taken in their **p**,
73: 6 Therefore **p** serves as their
Prov 8:13 **P** and arrogance and the evil
11: 2 When **p** comes, then comes shame;
13:10 By **p** comes nothing but strife,
14: 3 mouth of a fool is a rod of **p**,
16:18 **P** goes before destruction,
21:24 He acts with arrogant **p**.
29:23 A man's **p** will bring him low,

Isa 9: 9 Who say in **p** and arrogance of
13:19 The beauty of the Chaldeans' **p**,
16: 6 We have heard of the **p** of
16: 6 Of his haughtiness and his **p**
23: 9 To bring to dishonor the **p** of
25:11 And He will bring down their **p**
28: 1 Woe to the crown of **p**,
28: 3 The crown of **p**,
Jer 13: 9 this manner I will ruin the **p**
13: 9 pride of Judah and the great **p**
13:17 will weep in secret for your **p**;
48:29 'We have heard the **p** of Moab
48:29 loftiness and arrogance and **p**,
49:16 The **p** of your heart, O you
Ezek 7:10 **P** has budded.
16:49 She and her daughter had **p**,
16:56 mouth in the days of your **p**,
30: 6 And the **p** of her power shall
Dan 4:37 And those who walk in **p** He is
5:20 his spirit was hardened in **p**,
Hos 5: 5 The **p** of Israel testifies to
7:10 And the **p** of Israel testifies
Am 6: 8 'I abhor the **p** of Jacob,
8: 7 The LORD has sworn by the **p**
Ob 3 The **p** of your heart has
Zeph 2:10 they shall have for their **p**,
3:11 Those who rejoice in your **p**,
Zech 9: 6 And I will cut off the **p** of
10:11 Then the **p** of Assyria shall be
11: 3 of roaring lions! For the **p**
Mk 7:22 an evil eye, blasphemy, **p**,
1 Tim 3: 6 lest being puffed up with **p** he
1 Jn 2:16 and the **p** of life—is not of the

PRIEST (510/456) PRIESTHOOD, PRIEST'S, PRIESTS

Gen 14:18 he was the **p** of God Most High.
41:45 the daughter of Poti-Pherah **p**
41:50 the daughter of Poti-Pherah **p**
46:20 the daughter of Poti-Pherah **p**
Ex 2:16 Now the **p** of Midian had seven
3: 1 the **p** of Midian. And he led the
18: 1 the **p** of Midian, Moses'
28: 1 that he may minister to Me as **p**,
28: 3 that he may minister to Me as **p**.
28: 4 that he may minister to Me as **p**.
29:30 That son who becomes **p** in his
31:10 holy garments for Aaron the **p**
35:19 holy garments for Aaron the **p**
38:21 of Ithamar, son of Aaron the **p**.
39:41 holy garments for Aaron the **p**,
40:13 that he may minister to Me as **p**.
Lev 1: 7 The sons of Aaron the **p** shall
1: 9 And the **p** shall burn all on the
1:12 and the **p** shall lay them in
1:13 Then the **p** shall bring it all
1:15 The **p** shall bring it to the
1:17 and the **p** shall burn it on the
2: 2 And the **p** shall burn it as a
2: 8 when it is presented to the **p**,
2: 9 Then the **p** shall take from the
2:16 Then the **p** shall burn the
3:11 and the **p** shall burn them on
3:16 and the **p** shall burn them on the
4: 3 if the anointed **p** sins, bringing
4: 5 Then the anointed **p** shall take
4: 6 The **p** shall dip his finger in
4: 7 And the **p** shall put some of the
4:10 and the **p** shall burn them on
4:16 The anointed **p** shall bring some
4:17 Then the **p** shall dip his finger
4:20 So the **p** shall make atonement
4:25 The **p** shall take some of the
4:26 So the **p** shall make atonement
4:30 Then the **p** shall take some of
4:31 and the **p** shall burn it on the
4:31 So the **p** shall make atonement
4:34 The **p** shall take some of the
4:35 Then the **p** shall burn it on the
4:35 So the **p** shall make atonement
5: 6 So the **p** shall make atonement
5: 8 he shall bring them to the **p**,
5:10 So the **p** shall make atonement
5:12 he shall bring it to the **p**,
5:12 and the **p** shall take his
5:13 The **p** shall make atonement for
5:16 to it and give it to the **p**.
5:16 So the **p** shall make atonement
5:18 And he shall bring to the **p** a
5:18 So the **p** shall make atonement
6: 6 a trespass offering, to the **p**.
6: 7 So the **p** shall make atonement
6:10 And the **p** shall put on his linen
6:12 And the **p** shall burn wood on it
6:22 The **p** from among his sons, who
6:23 every grain offering for the **p**
6:26 The **p** who offers it for sin
7: 5 and the **p** shall burn them on the
7: 7 the **p** who makes atonement with
7: 8 And the **p** who offers anyone's
7: 8 that **p** shall have for himself
7:14 It shall belong to the **p** who
7:31 And the **p** shall burn the fat on
7:32 thigh you shall give to the **p**
7:34 have given them to Aaron the **p**
12: 6 she shall bring to the **p** a lamb
12: 8 So the **p** shall make atonement
13: 2 be brought to Aaron the **p** or
13: 3 The **p** shall examine the sore on
13: 3 Then the **p** shall examine him,
13: 4 then the **p** shall isolate the
13: 5 And the **p** shall examine him on
13: 5 then the **p** shall isolate him
13: 6 Then the **p** shall examine him
13: 6 then the **p** shall pronounce him
13: 7 he has been seen by the **p** for
13: 7 he shall be seen by the **p**
13: 8 And if the **p** sees that the scab
13: 8 then the **p** shall pronounce him
13: 9 he shall be brought to the **p**.
13:10 And the **p** shall examine him;
13:11 The **p** shall pronounce him
13:12 wherever the **p** looks,
13:13 'then the **p** shall consider;
13:15 And the **p** shall examine the raw
13:16 again, he shall come to the **p**.
13:17 And the **p** shall examine him; and
13:17 then the **p** shall pronounce him
13:19 then it shall be shown to the **p**;
13:20 when the **p** sees it, it indeed
13:20 the **p** shall pronounce him
13:21 But if the **p** examines it, and
13:21 then the **p** shall isolate him
13:22 then the **p** shall pronounce him
13:23 and the **p** shall pronounce him
13:25 'then the **p** shall examine it;
13:25 Therefore the **p** shall pronounce
13:26 But if the **p** examines it, and
13:26 then the **p** shall isolate him
13:27 And the **p** shall examine him on
13:27 then the **p** shall pronounce him
13:28 The **p** shall pronounce him
13:30 then the **p** shall examine the
13:30 then the **p** shall pronounce him
13:31 But if the **p** examines the scaly
13:31 then the **p** shall isolate the
13:32 And on the seventh day the **p**
13:33 And the **p** shall isolate the
13:34 On the seventh day the **p** shall
13:34 then the **p** shall pronounce him
13:36 then the **p** shall examine him;
13:36 the **p** need not seek for yellow
13:37 and the **p** shall pronounce him
13:39 then the **p** shall look; and
13:43 'Then the **p** shall examine it;
13:44 The **p** shall surely pronounce
13:49 and shall be shown to the **p**.
13:50 The **p** shall examine the plague
13:53 But if the **p** examines it, and
13:54 then the **p** shall command that
13:55 Then the **p** shall examine the
13:56 If the **p** examines it, and
14: 2 He shall be brought to the **p**.
14: 3 And the **p** shall go out of the
14: 3 and the **p** shall examine him;
14: 4 then the **p** shall command to take
14: 5 And the **p** shall command that one
14:11 Then the **p** who makes him clean
14:12 And the **p** shall take one male
14:14 The **p** shall take some of the
14:14 and the **p** shall put it on the
14:15 And the **p** shall take some of
14:16 Then the **p** shall dip his right
14:17 the **p** shall put some on the
14:18 So the **p** shall make atonement
14:19 Then the **p** shall offer the sin
14:20 And the **p** shall offer the burnt
14:20 So the **p** shall make atonement
14:23 He shall bring them to the **p** on
14:24 And the **p** shall take the lamb of
14:24 and the **p** shall wave them as a
14:25 and the **p** shall take some of
14:26 And the **p** shall pour some of the
14:27 Then the **p** shall sprinkle with
14:28 And the **p** shall put some of the
14:31 So the **p** shall make atonement
14:35 the house comes and tells the **p**,
14:36 then the **p** shall command that
14:36 before the **p** goes into it to
14:36 and afterward the **p** shall go in
14:38 then the **p** shall go out of the
14:39 And the **p** shall come again on
14:40 then the **p** shall command that
14:44 then the **p** shall come and look;
14:48 But if the **p** comes in and
14:48 then the **p** shall pronounce the
15:14 meeting, and give them to the **p**.
15:15 Then the **p** shall offer them, the
15:15 So the **p** shall make atonement
15:29 and bring them to the **p**,
15:30 Then the **p** shall offer the one
15:30 and the **p** shall make atonement
16:30 For on that day the **p** shall
16:32 'And the **p**, who is anointed
16:32 consecrated to minister as **p**
17: 5 tabernacle of meeting, to the **p**,
17: 6 And the **p** shall sprinkle the
19:22 The **p** shall make atonement for
21: 7 for the **p** is holy to his God.
21: 9 'The daughter of any **p**,
21:10 He who is the high **p** among
21:21 the descendants of Aaron the **p**,
22:10 one who dwells with the **p**,
22:11 But if the **p** buys a person with
22:14 a holy offering to the **p**,
23:10 of your harvest to the **p**.
23:11 the day after the Sabbath the **p**
23:20 The **p** shall wave them with the
23:20 be holy to the LORD for the **p**.
27: 8 present himself before the **p**,
27: 8 and the **p** shall set a value for
27: 8 the **p** shall value him.
27:11 present the animal before the **p**;
27:12 and the **p** shall set a value for
27:12 is good or bad; as you, the **p**,
27:14 then the **p** shall set a value
27:14 as the **p** values it, so it shall
27:18 then the **p** shall reckon to him
27:21 be the possession of the **p**.
27:23 then the **p** shall reckon to him
Num 3: 6 present them before Aaron the **p**,
3:32 Eleazar the son of Aaron the **p**
4:16 Eleazar the son of Aaron the **p**
4:28 Ithamar the son of Aaron the **p**.
4:33 Ithamar the son of Aaron the **p**.
5: 8 go to the LORD for the **p**,
5: 9 which they bring to the **p**,
5:10 whatever any man gives the **p**
5:15 shall bring his wife to the **p**.
5:16 And the **p** shall bring her near,
5:17 The **p** shall take holy water in
5:18 Then the **p** shall stand the woman
5:18 And the **p** shall have in his
5:19 And the **p** shall put her under
5:21 then the **p** shall put the woman
5:23 Then the **p** shall write these
5:25 Then the **p** shall take the grain
5:26 and the **p** shall take a handful
5:30 and the **p** shall execute all
6:10 or two young pigeons to the **p**,
6:11 and the **p** shall offer one as a
6:16 Then the **p** shall bring them
6:17 the **p** shall also offer its
6:19 And the **p** shall take the boiled
6:20 and the **p** shall wave them as a
6:20 they are holy for the **p**,
7: 8 Ithamar the son of Aaron the **p**.
15:25 So the **p** shall make atonement
15:28 So the **p** shall make atonement
16:37 Eleazar, the son of Aaron the **p**,
16:39 So Eleazar the **p** took the bronze
18:28 offering from it to Aaron the **p**.
19: 3 shall give it to Eleazar the **p**,
19: 4 and Eleazar the **p** shall take
19: 6 And the **p** shall take cedar wood
19: 7 Then the **p** shall wash his
19: 7 the **p** shall be unclean until
25: 7 Eleazar, the son of Aaron the **p**,
25:11 Eleazar, the son of Aaron the **p**,
26: 1 Eleazar the son of Aaron the **p**,
26: 3 So Moses and Eleazar the **p** spoke
26:63 by Moses and Eleazar the **p**,
26:64 by Moses and Aaron the **p** when
27: 2 Moses, before Eleazar the **p**,
27:19 set him before Eleazar the **p** and
27:21 stand before Eleazar the **p**,
27:22 set him before Eleazar the **p**
31: 6 the son of Eleazar the **p**,
31:12 to Moses, to Eleazar the **p**,
31:13 And Moses, Eleazar the **p**,
31:21 Then Eleazar the **p** said to the
31:26 you and Eleazar the **p** and the
31:29 and give it to Eleazar the **p**
31:31 So Moses and Eleazar the **p** did
31:41 heave offering to Eleazar the **p**,
31:51 So Moses and Eleazar the **p**
31:54 And Moses and Eleazar the **p**
32: 2 to Moses, to Eleazar the **p**,
32:28 them to Eleazar the **p**,
33:38 Then Aaron the **p** went up to
34:17 Eleazar the **p** and Joshua the
35:25 until the death of the high **p**
35:28 until the death of the high **p**,
35:28 after the death of the high **p**
35:32 land before the death of the **p**.
Deut 10: 6 his son ministered as **p** in his
17:12 and will not heed the **p** who
18: 3 they shall give to the **p** the
20: 2 that the **p** shall approach and
26: 3 shall go to the one who is **p**
26: 4 Then the **p** shall take the basket
Josh 14: 1 of Canaan, which Eleazar the **p**,
17: 4 came near before Eleazar the **p**,
19:51 which Eleazar the **p**,
20: 6 death of the one who is high **p**
21: 1 came near to Eleazar the **p**,
21: 4 And the children of Aaron the **p**,
21:13 to the children of Aaron the **p**
22:13 the son of Eleazar the **p** to
22:30 Now when Phinehas the **p** and the
22:31 the son of Eleazar the **p** said
22:32 the son of Eleazar the **p**,
Judg 17: 5 of his sons, who became his **p**.
17:10 and be a father and a **p** to me,
17:12 and the young man became his **p**,
17:13 since I have a Levite as **p**!"
18: 4 me, and I have become his **p**.
18: 6 And the **p** said to them, "Go in
18:17 The **p** stood at the entrance of
18:18 the **p** said to them, "What are
18:19 be a father and a **p** to us.
18:19 it better for you to be a **p**
18:19 or that you be a **p** to a tribe
18:24 my gods which I made, and the **p**,
18:27 and the **p** who had belonged to
1 Sam 1: 9 Now Eli the **p** was sitting on
2:11 to the LORD before Eli the **p**.
2:14 and the **p** would take for
2:15 meat for roasting to the **p**,
2:28 tribes of Israel to be My **p**,
2:35 up for Myself a faithful **p**
14: 3 the LORD's **p** in Shiloh, was
14:19 while Saul talked to the **p**,
14:19 increase; so Saul said to the **p**,
14:36 Then the **p** said, "Let us

P

21: 1 came to Nob, to Ahimelech the ***p***.
21: 2 David said to Ahimelech the ***p***,
21: 4 And the ***p*** answered David and
21: 5 Then David answered the ***p***,
21: 6 So the ***p*** gave him holy bread;
21: 9 So the ***p*** said, "The sword of
22:11 sent to call Ahimelech the ***p***,
23: 9 him, he said to Abiathar the ***p***,
30: 7 David said to Abiathar the ***p***,
2 Sam 15:27 king also said to Zadok the ***p***,
1 Ki 1: 7 Zeruiah and with Abiathar the ***p***,
1: 8 But Zadok the ***p***,
1:19 of the king, Abiathar the ***p***,
1:25 of the army, and Abiathar the ***p***;
1:26 your servant—nor Zadok the ***p***,
1:32 said, "Call to me Zadok the ***p***,
1:34 There let Zadok the ***p*** and Nathan
1:38 So Zadok the ***p***,
1:39 Then Zadok the ***p*** took a horn of
1:42 the son of Abiathar the ***p***.
1:44 has sent with him Zadok the ***p***,
1:45 So Zadok the ***p*** and Nathan the
2:22 him, and for Abiathar the ***p***,
2:26 And to Abiathar the ***p*** the king
2:27 removed Abiathar from being ***p***
2:35 and the king put Zadok the ***p*** in
4: 2 Azariah the son of Zadok, the ***p***;
4: 5 a ***p*** and the king's friend;
2 Ki 11: 9 to all that Jehoiada the ***p***
11: 9 and came to Jehoiada the ***p***.
11:10 And the ***p*** gave the captains of
11:15 And Jehoiada the ***p*** commanded the
11:15 For the ***p*** had said, "Do not
11:18 and killed Mattan the ***p*** of Baal
11:18 And the ***p*** appointed officers
12: 2 days in which Jehoiada the ***p***
12: 7 Jehoash called Jehoiada the ***p***
12: 9 Then Jehoiada the ***p*** took a
12:10 king's scribe and the high ***p***
16:10 King Ahaz sent to Urijah the ***p***
16:11 Then Urijah the ***p*** built an altar
16:11 So Urijah the ***p*** made it before
16:15 Ahaz commanded Urijah the ***p***,
16:16 Thus did Urijah the ***p***,
22: 4 "Go up to Hilkiah the high ***p***,
22: 8 Then Hilkiah the high ***p*** said to
22:10 Hilkiah the ***p*** has given me a
22:12 king commanded Hilkiah the ***p***,
22:14 So Hilkiah the ***p***,
23: 4 commanded Hilkiah the high ***p***,
23:24 in the book that Hilkiah the ***p***
25:18 guard took Seraiah the chief ***p***,
25:18 priest, Zephaniah the second ***p***,
1 Chr 6:10 (it was he who ministered as ***p***
16:39 and Zadok the ***p*** and his brethren
24: 6 king, the leaders, Zadok the ***p***,
27: 5 the son of Jehoiada the ***p***,
29:22 the leader, and Zadok to be ***p***.
2 Chr 13: 9 bull and seven rams may be a ***p***
15: 3 true God, without a teaching ***p***,
19:11 Amariah the chief ***p*** is over
22:11 the wife of Jehoiada the ***p*** (for
23: 8 to all that Jehoiada the ***p***
23: 8 for Jehoiada the ***p*** had not
23: 9 And Jehoiada the ***p*** gave to the
23:14 And Jehoiada the ***p*** brought out
23:14 For the ***p*** had said, "Do not
23:17 and killed Mattan the ***p*** of Baal
24: 2 all the days of Jehoiada the ***p***.
24: 6 called Jehoiada the chief ***p***,
24:20 the son of Jehoiada the ***p***,
24:25 of the sons of Jehoiada the ***p***,
26:17 So Azariah the ***p*** went in after
26:20 And Azariah the chief ***p*** and all
31:10 And Azariah the chief ***p***,
34: 9 they came to Hilkiah the high ***p***,
34:14 Hilkiah the ***p*** found the Book of
34:18 Hilkiah the ***p*** has given me a
Ezra 2:63 the most holy things till a ***p***
7: 5 the son of Aaron the chief ***p***—
7:11 King Artaxerxes gave Ezra the ***p***,
7:12 king of kings, To Ezra the ***p***,
7:21 River, that whatever Ezra the ***p***,
8:33 Meremoth the son of Uriah the ***p***,
10:10 Then Ezra the ***p*** stood up and
10:16 did so. And Ezra the ***p***,
Neh 3: 1 Then Eliashib the high ***p*** rose up
3:20 house of Eliashib the high ***p***.
7:65 the most holy things till a ***p***
8: 2 So Ezra the ***p*** brought the Law
8: 9 Ezra the ***p*** and scribe, and the
10:38 And the ***p***, the descendant of
12:26 the governor, and of Ezra the ***p***,
13: 4 before this, Eliashib the ***p***,
13:13 the storehouse Shelemiah the ***p***
13:28 the son of Eliashib the high ***p***,
Ps 110: 4 You are a ***p*** forever According
Isa 8: 2 Uriah the ***p*** and Zechariah the
24: 2 with the people, so with the ***p***;
28: 7 The ***p*** and the prophet have
Jer 6:13 from the prophet even to the ***p***,
8:10 From the prophet even to the ***p***
14:18 both prophet and ***p*** go about in
18:18 law shall not perish from the ***p***,
20: 1 the ***p*** who was also chief
21: 1 the son of Maaseiah, the ***p***,
23:11 For both prophet and ***p*** are
23:33 people or the prophet or the ***p***
23:34 as for the prophet and the ***p***
29:25 the son of Maaseiah the ***p***,
29:26 The LORD has made you ***p*** instead
29:26 instead of Jehoiada the ***p***,
29:29 Now Zephaniah the ***p*** read this
37: 3 the son of Maaseiah, the ***p***,
52:24 guard took Seraiah the chief ***p***,
52:24 priest, Zephaniah the second ***p***,
Lam 2: 6 has spurned the king and the ***p***.
2:20 Should the ***p*** and prophet be
Ezek 1: 3 came expressly to Ezekiel the ***p***,
7:26 the law will perish from the ***p***,
44:13 near Me to minister to Me as ***p***,
44:21 No ***p*** shall drink wine when he
44:30 also you shall give to the ***p***
45:19 The ***p*** shall take some of the
Hos 4: 4 those who contend with the ***p***.
4: 6 will reject you from being ***p***
4: 9 shall be: like people, like ***p***.
Am 7:10 Then Amaziah the ***p*** of Bethel
Hag 1: 1 son of Jehozadak, the high ***p***,
1:12 son of Jehozadak, the high ***p***,
1:14 son of Jehozadak, the high ***p***,
2: 2 son of Jehozadak, the high ***p***,
2: 4 son of Jehozadak, the high ***p***;
Zech 3: 1 he showed me Joshua the high ***p***
3: 8 'Hear, O Joshua, the high ***p***,
6:11 son of Jehozadak, the high ***p***.
6:13 So He shall be a ***p*** on His
Mal 2: 7 For the lips of a ***p*** should keep
Mt 8: 4 way, show yourself to the ***p***,
26: 3 at the palace of the high ***p***,
26:51 the servant of the high ***p***,
26:57 away to Caiaphas the high ***p***,
26:62 And the high ***p*** arose and said to
26:63 And the high ***p*** answered and
26:65 Then the high ***p*** tore his
Mk 1:44 way, show yourself to the ***p***,
2:26 days of Abiathar the high ***p***,
14:47 the servant of the high ***p***,
14:53 led Jesus away to the high ***p***;
14:54 the courtyard of the high ***p***.
14:60 And the high ***p*** stood up in the
14:61 Again the high ***p*** asked Him,
14:63 Then the high ***p*** tore his clothes
14:66 the servant girls of the high ***p***
Lk 1: 5 a certain ***p*** named Zacharias, of
1: 8 that while he was serving as ***p***
5:14 go and show yourself to the ***p***,
10:31 Now by chance a certain ***p*** came
22:50 the servant of the high ***p*** and
Jn 11:49 being high ***p*** that year, said to
11:51 but being high ***p*** that year he
18:13 of Caiaphas who was high ***p***
18:15 was known to the high ***p***,
18:15 the courtyard of the high ***p***.
18:16 who was known to the high ***p***,
18:19 The high ***p*** then asked Jesus
18:22 Do You answer the high ***p*** like
18:24 bound to Caiaphas the high ***p***.
18:26 of the servants of the high ***p***,
Acts 4: 6 as well as Annas the high ***p***,
4: 6 of the family of the high ***p***,
5:17 Then the high ***p*** rose up, and
5:21 But the high ***p*** and those with
5:24 Now when the high ***p***,
5:27 And the high ***p*** asked them,
7: 1 Then the high ***p*** said, "Are
9: 1 went to the high ***p***
14:13 Then the ***p*** of Zeus, whose temple
19:14 sons of Sceva, a Jewish chief ***p***,
22: 5 as also the high ***p*** bears me
23: 2 And the high ***p*** Ananias commanded
23: 4 "Do you revile God's high ***p***?
23: 5 that he was the high ***p***;
24: 1 five days Ananias the high ***p***
25: 2 Then the high ***p*** and the chief
Heb 2:17 a merciful and faithful High ***P***
3: 1 the Apostle and High ***P*** of our
4:14 that we have a great High ***P***
4:15 For we do not have a High ***P*** who
5: 1 For every high ***p*** taken from
5: 5 Himself to become High ***P***,
5: 6 You are a ***p*** forever
5:10 called by God as High ***P***
6:20 having become High ***P*** forever
7: 1 ***p*** of the Most High God, who met
7: 3 remains a ***p*** continually.
7:11 need was there that another ***p***
7:15 there arises another ***p***
7:17 You are a ***p*** forever
7:20 as He was not made ***p***
7:21 You are a ***p*** forever
7:26 For such a High ***P*** was fitting
8: 1 We have such a High ***P***,
8: 3 For every high ***p*** is appointed to
8: 4 on earth, He would not be a ***p***,
9: 7 into the second part the high ***p***
9:11 But Christ came as High ***P*** of
9:25 as the high ***p*** enters the Most
10:11 And every ***p*** stands ministering
10:21 and having a High ***P*** over the
13:11 the sanctuary by the high ***p***

PRIEST'S (16/16) PRIEST

Lev 5:13 The rest shall be the ***p*** as a
7: 9 shall be the ***p*** who offers it.
14:13 as the sin offering is the ***p***,
14:18 of the oil that is in the ***p***
14:29 of the oil that is in the ***p***
22:12 If the ***p*** daughter is married to
22:13 But if the ***p*** daughter is a widow
Deut 18: 3 And this shall be the ***p*** due
Judg 18:20 So the ***p*** heart was glad; and he
1 Sam 2:13 the ***p*** servant would come with a
2:15 the ***p*** servant would come and
2 Chr 24:11 king's scribe and the high ***p***
Ezek 44:30 your sacrifices, shall be the ***p***;
Mt 26:58 Him at a distance to the high ***p***
Lk 22:54 and brought Him into the high ***p***
Jn 18:10 drew it and struck the high ***p***

PRIESTHOOD (21/19) PRIEST

Ex 29: 9 The ***p*** shall be theirs for a
40:15 surely be an everlasting ***p***
Num 3:10 they shall attend to their ***p***;
16:10 And are you seeking the ***p*** also?
18: 1 associated with your ***p***.
18: 7 you shall attend to your ***p*** for
18: 7 I give your ***p*** to you as a
25:13 a covenant of an everlasting ***p***,
Josh 18: 7 for the ***p*** of the LORD is
Ezra 2:62 were excluded from the ***p*** as
Neh 7:64 they were excluded from the ***p***
13:29 they have defiled the ***p*** and
13:29 and the covenant of the ***p*** and
Lk 1: 9 to the custom of the ***p***,
Heb 7: 5 sons of Levi, who receive the ***p***,
7:11 were through the Levitical ***p***
7:12 For the ***p*** being changed, of
7:14 spoke nothing concerning ***p***.
7:24 forever, has an unchangeable ***p***.
1 Pe 2: 5 up a spiritual house, a holy ***p***,
2: 9 a chosen generation, a royal ***p***,

PRIESTLY (4/4)

1 Sam 2:36 me in one of the ***p*** positions,
Ezra 2:69 and one hundred ***p*** garments.
Neh 7:70 hundred and thirty ***p*** garments.
7:72 and sixty-seven ***p*** garments.

PRIESTS (409/383) PRIEST

Gen 47:22 Only the land of the ***p*** he did
47:22 for the ***p*** had rations allotted
47:26 except for the land of the ***p***
Ex 19: 6 shall be to Me a kingdom of ***p***
19:22 Also let the ***p*** who come near the
19:24 But do not let the ***p*** and the
28:41 they may minister to Me as ***p***.
29: 1 them for ministering to Me as ***p***:
29:44 his sons to minister to Me as ***p***.
30:30 they may minister to Me as ***p***.
31:10 of his sons, to minister as ***p***,
35:19 of his sons, to minister as ***p***.
39:41 garments, to minister as ***p***.
40:15 they may minister to Me as ***p***;
Lev 1: 5 before the LORD; and the ***p***,
1: 8 'Then the ***p***, Aaron's sons,
1:11 before the LORD; and the ***p***,
2: 2 bring it to Aaron's sons, the ***p***,
3: 2 and Aaron's sons, the ***p***,
6:29 All the males among the ***p*** may
7: 6 Every male among the ***p*** may eat
7:35 to minister to the LORD as ***p***.
13: 2 or to one of his sons the ***p***.
16:33 shall make atonement for the ***p***
21: 1 said to Moses, "Speak to the ***p***,
Num 3: 3 sons of Aaron, the anointed ***p***,
3: 3 he consecrated to minister as ***p***.
3: 4 and Ithamar ministered as ***p*** in
10: 8 "The sons of Aaron, the ***p***,
Deut 17: 9 "And you shall come to the ***p***,
17:18 from the one before the ***p***,
18: 1 'The ***p***, the Levites—all
19:17 before the ***p*** and the judges who
21: 5 'Then the ***p***, the sons of
24: 8 do according to all that the ***p***,
27: 9 Then Moses and the ***p***,
31: 9 law and delivered it to the ***p***,
Josh 3: 3 the LORD your God, and the ***p***,
3: 6 Then Joshua spoke to the ***p***,
3: 8 You shall command the ***p*** who bear
3:13 the soles of the feet of the ***p***
3:14 with the ***p*** bearing the ark of
3:15 and the feet of the ***p*** who bore
3:17 Then the ***p*** who bore the ark of
4: 9 place where the feet of the ***p***
4:10 So the ***p*** who bore the ark stood
4:11 the ark of the LORD and the ***p***
4:16 Command the ***p*** who bear the ark
4:17 therefore commanded the ***p***,
4:18 when the ***p*** who bore the ark of
6: 4 And seven ***p*** shall bear seven
6: 4 and the ***p*** shall blow the
6: 6 the son of Nun called the ***p***
6: 6 and let seven ***p*** bear seven
6: 8 that the seven ***p*** bearing the
6: 9 The armed men went before the ***p***
6: 9 while the ***p*** continued blowing
6:12 and the ***p*** took up the ark of
6:13 Then seven ***p*** bearing seven
6:13 while the ***p*** continued blowing
6:16 when the ***p*** blew the trumpets,
6:20 the people shouted when the ***p***
8:33 side of the ark before the ***p***,
21:19 of the children of Aaron, the ***p***,
Judg 18:30 and his sons were ***p*** to the
1 Sam 1: 3 the ***p*** of the LORD, were
5: 5 Therefore neither the ***p*** of Dagon
6: 2 Philistines called for the ***p***
22:11 the ***p*** who were in Nob.
22:17 Turn and kill the ***p*** of the
22:17 their hands to strike the ***p*** of
22:18 You turn and kill the ***p***!" So

22:18 Edomite turned and struck the **p**,
22:19 Also Nob, the city of the **p**,
22:21 Saul had killed the LORD's **p**.
2 Sam 8:17 the son of Abiathar were the **p**;
15:35 have Zadok and Abiathar the **p**
15:35 to Zadok and Abiathar the **p**.
17:15 to Zadok and Abiathar the **p**,
19:11 to Zadok and Abiathar the **p**,
20:25 Zadok and Abiathar were the **p**;
1 Ki 4: 4 Zadok and Abiathar, the **p**;
8: 3 and the **p** took up the ark.
8: 4 The **p** and the Levites brought
8: 6 Then the **p** brought in the ark of
8:10 when the **p** came out of the holy
8:11 so that the **p** could not continue
12:31 and made **p** from every class of
12:32 at Bethel he installed the **p**
13: 2 on you he shall sacrifice the **p**
13:33 but again he made **p** from every
13:33 and he became one of the **p** of
2 Ki 10:11 close acquaintances and his **p**,
10:19 all his servants, and all his **p**.
12: 4 And Jehoash said to the **p**,
12: 5 let the **p** take it themselves,
12: 6 that the **p** had not repaired
12: 7 the priest and the other **p**,
12: 8 And the **p** agreed that they would
12: 9 and the **p** who kept the door put
12:16 the LORD. It belonged to the **p**.
17:27 Send there one of the **p** whom you
17:28 Then one of the **p** whom they had
17:32 appointed for themselves **p** of
19: 2 scribe, and the elders of the **p**,
23: 2 the **p** and the prophets and all
23: 4 the **p** of the second order, and
23: 5 he removed the idolatrous **p**
23: 8 And he brought all the **p** from
23: 8 the high places where the **p**
23: 9 Nevertheless the **p** of the high
23:20 He executed all the **p** of the
25:14 utensils with which the **p**
1 Chr 9: 2 cities were Israelites, **p**,
9:10 Of the **p**: Jedaiah,
9:30 And some of the sons of the **p**
13: 2 and with them to the **p** and
15:11 for Zadok and Abiathar the **p**,
15:14 So the **p** and the Levites
15:24 Benaiah, and Eliezer, the **p**,
16: 6 Benaiah and Jahaziel the **p**
16:39 priest and his brethren the **p**,
18:16 the son of Abiathar were the **p**;
23: 2 with the **p** and the Levites.
24: 2 and Ithamar ministered as **p**.
24: 6 the fathers' houses of the **p**
24:31 the fathers' houses of the **p**
28:13 also for the division of the **p**
28:21 are the divisions of the **p**
2 Chr 4: 6 but the Sea was for the **p** to
4: 9 he made the court of the **p**,
5: 5 The **p** and the Levites brought
5: 7 Then the **p** brought in the ark of
5:11 And it came to pass when the **p**
5:11 Holy Place (for all the **p** who
5:12 them one hundred and twenty **p**
5:14 so that the **p** could not continue
6:41 of Your strength. Let Your **p**,
7: 2 And the **p** could not enter the
7: 6 And the **p** attended to their
7: 6 The **p** sounded trumpets opposite
8:14 the divisions of the **p** for
8:14 praise and serve before the **p**)
8:15 command of the king to the **p**
11:13 all their territories the **p**
11:14 them from serving as **p** to the
11:15 he appointed for himself **p** for
13: 9 Have you not cast out the **p** of
13: 9 and made for yourselves **p**,
13:10 and the **p** who minister to the
13:12 and His **p** with sounding
13:14 and the **p** sounded the trumpets.
17: 8 Elishama and Jehoram, the **p**.
19: 8 some of the Levites and **p**,
23: 4 of the **p** and the Levites,
23: 6 of the LORD except the **p** and
23:18 the LORD to the hand of the **p**,
24: 5 Then he gathered the **p** and the
26:17 and with him were eighty **p** of
26:18 to the LORD, but for the **p**,
26:19 while he was angry with the **p**,
26:19 before the **p** in the house of
26:20 the chief priest and all the **p**
29: 4 Then he brought in the **p** and the
29:16 Then the **p** went into the inner
29:21 Then he commanded the **p**,
29:22 and the **p** received the blood
29:24 And the **p** killed them; and they
29:26 and the **p** with the trumpets.
29:34 But the **p** were too few, so that
29:34 ended and until the other **p**
29:34 themselves than the **p**.
30: 3 a sufficient number of **p** had
30:15 The **p** and the Levites were
30:16 the **p** sprinkled the blood
30:21 and the Levites and the **p**
30:24 and a great number of **p**
30:25 also the **p** and Levites, all the
30:27 Then the **p**, the Levites,
31: 2 the divisions of the **p** and the
31: 2 the **p** and Levites for burnt
31: 4 to contribute support for the **p**
31: 9 Then Hezekiah questioned the **p**
31:15 in the cities of the **p**,
31:17 and to the **p** who were written in
31:19 for the sons of Aaron the **p**,
31:19 to all the males among the **p**
34: 5 also burned the bones of the **p**
34:30 the **p** and the Levites, and all
35: 2 And he set the **p** in their duties
35: 8 to the people, to the **p**,
35: 8 gave to the **p** for the Passover
35:10 and the **p** stood in their
35:11 and the **p** sprinkled the blood
35:14 for themselves and for the **p**,
35:14 for the priests, because the **p**,
35:14 for themselves and for the **p**,
35:18 with the **p** and the Levites, all
36:14 all the leaders of the **p** and
Ezra 1: 5 and the **p** and the Levites, with
2:36 The **p**: the sons of Jedaiah,
2:61 and of the sons of the **p**:
2:70 So the **p** and the Levites, some
3: 2 Jozadak and his brethren the **p**,
3: 8 rest of their brethren the **p**
3:10 the **p** stood in their apparel
3:12 But many of the **p** and Levites
6: 9 to the request of the **p** who
6:16 the **p** and the Levites and the
6:18 They assigned the **p** to their
6:20 For the **p** and the Levites had
6:20 for their brethren the **p**,
7: 7 the children of Israel, the **p**,
7:13 the people of Israel and the **p**
7:16 of the people and the **p**,
7:24 or custom on any of the **p**,
8:15 among the people and the **p**,
8:24 twelve of the leaders of the **p**—
8:29 before the leaders of the **p**
8:30 So the **p** and the Levites
9: 1 people of Israel and the **p**
9: 7 and our **p** have been delivered
10: 5 and made the leaders of the **p**,
10:18 And among the sons of the **p** who
Neh 2:16 not yet told the Jews, the **p**,
3: 1 up with his brethren the **p** and
3:22 And after him the **p**,
3:28 Beyond the Horse Gate the **p**
5:12 you say." Then I called the **p**,
7:39 The **p**: the sons of Jedaiah,
7:63 and of the **p**: the sons of
7:73 So the **p**, the Levites,
8:13 with the **p** and Levites, were
9:32 Our **p** and our prophets,
9:34 Our **p** nor our fathers,
9:38 and our **p** seal it."
10: 8 Shemaiah. These were the **p**.
10:28 the rest of the people—the **p**,
10:34 We cast lots among the **p**,
10:36 to the **p** who minister in the
10:37 the new wine and oil, to the **p**,
10:39 where the **p** who minister and
11: 3 in their cities—Israelites, **p**,
11:10 Of the **p**: Jedaiah the son
11:20 of the **p** and Levites, were in
12: 1 Now these are the **p** and the
12: 7 These were the heads of the **p**
12:12 in the days of Joiakim, the **p**,
12:22 kept of the Levites and **p**
12:30 Then the **p** and Levites purified
12:41 and the **p**, Eliakim, Maaseiah,
12:44 specified by the Law for the **p**
12:44 for Judah rejoiced over the **p**
13: 5 and the offerings for the **p**.
13:30 I also assigned duties to the **p**
Ps 78:64 Their **p** fell by the sword,
99: 6 and Aaron were among His **p**,
132: 9 Let Your **p** be clothed with
132:16 I will also clothe her **p** with
Isa 37: 2 scribe, and the elders of the **p**,
61: 6 But you shall be named the **p** of
66:21 also take some of them for **p**
Jer 1: 1 of the **p** who were in Anathoth
1:18 its princes, Against its **p**,
2: 8 The **p** did not say, 'Where is
2:26 and their **p** and their prophets,
4: 9 The **p** shall be astonished,
5:31 And the **p** rule by their own
8: 1 princes, and the bones of the **p**,
13:13 sit on David's throne, the **p**,
19: 1 and some of the elders of the **p**.
26: 7 So the **p** and the prophets and
26: 8 that the **p** and the prophets and
26:11 And the **p** and the prophets spoke
26:16 all the people said to the **p**
27:16 Also I spoke to the **p** and to
28: 1 LORD in the presence of the **p**
28: 5 in the presence of the **p** and
29: 1 carried away captive—to the **p**,
29:25 the priest, and to all the **p**,
31:14 will satiate the soul of the **p**
32:32 kings, their princes, their **p**,
33:18 'nor shall the **p**,
33:21 and with the Levites, the **p**,
34:19 Jerusalem, the eunuchs, the **p**,
48: 7 His **p** and his princes
49: 3 go into captivity With his **p**
52:18 utensils with which the **p**
Lam 1: 4 Her **p** sigh, Her virgins are
1:19 My **p** and my elders Breathed
4:13 And the iniquities of her **p**,
4:16 people do not respect the **p**
Ezek 22:26 Her **p** have violated My law and
40:45 faces south is for the **p** who
40:46 faces north is for the **p** who
42:13 the holy chambers where the **p**
42:14 When the **p** enter them, they
43:19 for a sin offering to the **p**,
43:24 the **p** shall throw salt on them,
43:27 that the **p** shall offer your
44:15 But the **p**, the Levites,
44:22 house of Israel, or widows of **p**.
44:31 The **p** shall not eat anything,
45: 4 of the land, belonging to the **p**,
46: 2 The **p** shall prepare his burnt
46:19 into the holy chambers of the **p**
46:20 is the place where the **p**
48:10 "To these—to the **p**—
48:11 It shall be for the **p** of the
48:13 "Opposite the border of the **p**,
Hos 5: 1 O **p**! Take heed, O house of
6: 9 So the company of **p** murder on
10: 5 And its **p** shriek for
Joel 1: 9 The **p** mourn, who minister to
1:13 yourselves and lament, you **p**;
2:17 Let the **p**, who minister to
Mic 3:11 Her **p** teach for pay, And her
Zeph 1: 4 The names of the idolatrous **p**
1: 4 priests with the pagan **p**—
3: 4 Her **p** have polluted the
Hag 2:11 ask the **p** concerning the law,
2:12 Then the **p** answered and said,
2:13 So the **p** answered and said,
Zech 7: 3 and to ask the **p** who were in
7: 5 of the land, and to the **p**:
Mal 1: 6 the LORD of hosts To you **p**
2: 1 "And now, O **p**,
Mt 2: 4 he had gathered all the chief **p**
12: 4 with him, but only for the **p**?
12: 5 law that on the Sabbath the **p**
16:21 from the elders and chief **p**
20:18 be betrayed to the chief **p** and
21:15 But when the chief **p** and scribes
21:23 the chief **p** and the elders of
21:45 Now when the chief **p** and
26: 3 Then the chief **p**,
26:14 went to the chief **p**
26:47 came from the chief **p** and
26:59 Now the chief **p**,
27: 1 all the chief **p** and elders of
27: 3 of silver to the chief **p** and
27: 6 But the chief **p** took the silver
27:12 being accused by the chief **p**
27:20 But the chief **p** and elders
27:41 Likewise the chief **p** also,
27:62 the chief **p** and Pharisees
28:11 and reported to the chief **p**
Mk 2:26 lawful to eat, except for the **p**,
8:31 by the elders and chief **p** and
10:33 be betrayed to the chief **p** and
11:18 And the scribes and chief **p**
11:27 in the temple, the chief **p**,
14: 1 And the chief **p** and the scribes
14:10 went to the chief **p** to betray
14:43 came from the chief **p** and the
14:53 were assembled all the chief **p**,
14:55 Now the chief **p** and all the
15: 1 the chief **p** held a consultation
15: 3 And the chief **p** accused Him of
15:10 For he knew that the chief **p** had
15:11 But the chief **p** stirred up the
15:31 Likewise the chief **p** also,
Lk 3: 2 Annas and Caiaphas were high **p**,
6: 4 is not lawful for any but the **p**
9:22 by the elders and chief **p** and
17:14 "Go, show yourselves to the **p**.
19:47 in the temple. But the chief **p**,
20: 1 that the chief **p** and the
20:19 And the chief **p** and the scribes
22: 2 And the chief **p** and the scribes
22: 4 and conferred with the chief **p**
22:52 Then Jesus said to the chief **p**,
22:66 both chief **p** and scribes, came
23: 4 So Pilate said to the chief **p**
23:10 And the chief **p** and scribes
23:13 had called together the chief **p**,
23:23 of these men and of the chief **p**
24:20 and how the chief **p** and our
Jn 1:19 when the Jews sent **p** and
7:32 the Pharisees and the chief **p**
7:45 officers came to the chief **p**
11:47 Then the chief **p** and the
11:57 Now both the chief **p** and the
12:10 But the chief **p** plotted to put
18: 3 and officers from the chief **p**
18:35 Your own nation and the chief **p**
19: 6 when the chief **p** and officers
19:15 The chief **p** answered, "We
19:21 Therefore the chief **p** of the
Acts 4: 1 they spoke to the people, the **p**,
4:23 reported all that the chief **p**
5:24 and the chief **p** heard these
6: 7 and a great many of the **p** were
9:14 has authority from the chief **p**
9:21 bring them bound to the chief **p**?
22:30 and commanded the chief **p** and
23:14 They came to the chief **p** and
25:15 about whom the chief **p** and the
26:10 authority from the chief **p**;
26:12 and commission from the chief **p**,
Heb 7:21 (for they have become **p** without
7:23 Also there were many **p**,
7:27 not need daily, as those high **p**,
7:28 For the law appoints as high **p**
8: 4 since there are **p** who offer the
9: 6 the **p** always went into the
Rev 1: 6 and has made us kings and **p** to
5:10 And have made us kings and **p** to

20: 6 but they shall be ***p*** of God and

PRIESTS' (4/4)

Josh 4: 3 from the place where the ***p*** feet
4:18 and the soles of the ***p*** feet
1 Sam 2:13 And the ***p*** custom with the people
Neh 12:35 and some of the ***p*** sons with

PRIME (2/2)

Job 29: 4 as I was in the days of my ***p***,
Isa 38:10 In the ***p*** of my life I shall go

PRIMEVAL (1/1)

Prov 8:26 Or the ***p*** dust of the world.

PRINCE (54/50) PRINCELY, PRINCES

Gen 23: 6 You are a mighty ***p*** among us;
34: 2 ***p*** of the country, saw her, he
Ex 2:14 Who made you a ***p*** and a judge
Num 16:13 you should keep acting like a ***p***
2 Sam 3:38 Do you not know that a ***p*** and a
Ezra 1: 8 them out to Sheshbazzar the ***p***
Job 21:28 'Where is the house of the ***p***?
31:37 Like a ***p*** I would approach Him.
Prov 14:28 people is the downfall of a ***p***.
17: 7 Much less lying lips to a ***p***.
25: 7 lower in the presence of the ***p***,
Isa 9: 6 Father, ***P*** of Peace.
Ezek 7:27 The ***p*** will be clothed with
12:10 This burden concerns the ***p*** in
12:12 And the ***p*** who is among them
21:25 wicked ***p*** of Israel, whose day
28: 2 say to the ***p*** of Tyre, 'Thus
34:24 and My servant David a ***p*** among
37:25 David shall be their ***p***
38: 2 the ***p*** of Rosh, Meshech, and
38: 3 the ***p*** of Rosh, Meshech, and
39: 1 the ***p*** of Rosh, Meshech, and
44: 3 "As for the ***p***,
44: 3 prince, because he is the ***p***,
45: 7 The ***p*** shall have a section on
45:16 give this offering for the ***p***
45:22 And on that day the ***p*** shall
46: 2 The ***p*** shall enter by way of the
46: 4 The burnt offering that the ***p***
46: 8 When the ***p*** enters, he shall go
46:10 The ***p*** shall then be in their
46:12 Now when the ***p*** makes a
46:16 If the ***p*** gives a gift of some
46:17 which it shall return to the ***p***.
46:18 Moreover the ***p*** shall not take
48:21 rest shall belong to the ***p***,
48:21 it shall belong to the ***p***.
48:22 midst of what belongs to the ***p***,
48:22 Benjamin shall belong to the ***p***.
Dan 8:11 himself as high as the ***P*** of
8:25 shall even rise against the ***P***
9:25 Jerusalem Until Messiah the ***P***,
9:26 And the people of the ***p*** who is
10:13 But the ***p*** of the kingdom of
10:20 return to fight with the ***p*** of
10:20 indeed the ***p*** of Greece will
10:21 these, except Michael your ***p***.
11:22 and also the ***p*** of the covenant.
12: 1 The great ***p*** who stands watch
Hos 3: 4 many days without king or ***p***,
Mic 7: 3 The ***p*** asks for gifts,
Acts 3:15 and killed the ***P*** of life, whom
5:31 to His right hand to be ***P***
Eph 2: 2 according to the ***p*** of the power

PRINCE'S (2/2)

Song 7: 1 O ***p*** daughter! The curves of
Ezek 45:17 Then it shall be the ***p*** part to

PRINCELY (2/2) PRINCE

Mic 5: 5 shepherds and eight ***p*** men.
Zech 11:13 —that ***p*** price they set on me.

PRINCES (173/161) PRINCE

Gen 12:15 The ***p*** of Pharaoh also saw her
17:20 He shall beget twelve ***p***,
25:16 twelve ***p*** according to their
Num 22: 8 So the ***p*** of Moab stayed with
22:13 the morning and said to the ***p***
22:14 And the ***p*** of Moab rose and went
22:15 Then Balak again sent ***p***,
22:21 and went with the ***p*** of Moab.
22:35 So Balaam went with the ***p*** of
22:40 some to Balaam and to the ***p***
23: 6 he and all the ***p*** of Moab.
23:17 and the ***p*** of Moab were with
Josh 13:21 Moses had struck with the ***p*** of
13:21 who were ***p*** of Sihon dwelling
Judg 5: 3 O ***p***! I, even I, will sing to
5:15 And the ***p*** of Issachar were
7:25 And they captured two ***p*** of the
8: 3 into your hands the ***p*** of
1 Sam 2: 8 To set them among ***p*** And make
18:30 Then the ***p*** of the Philistines
29: 3 Then the ***p*** of the Philistines
29: 3 And Achish said to the ***p*** of
29: 4 But the ***p*** of the Philistines
29: 4 so the ***p*** of the Philistines
29: 9 nevertheless the ***p*** of the
2 Sam 10: 3 And the ***p*** of the people of Ammon
19: 6 that you regard neither ***p*** nor
2 Ki 24:12 his mother, his servants, his ***p***,
1 Chr 19: 3 And the ***p*** of the people of Ammon
2 Chr 21: 4 and also others of the ***p*** of
22: 8 and found the ***p*** of Judah and
32:31 the ambassadors of the ***p*** of
Ezra 7:28 before all the king's mighty ***p***.
8:25 and his counselors and his ***p***,
Neh 9:32 upon us, Our kings and our ***p***,
9:34 Neither our kings nor our ***p***,
Esth 1: 3 and the ***p*** of the provinces
1:14 the seven ***p*** of Persia and
1:16 before the king and the ***p***:
1:16 the king, but also all the ***p***,
1:21 pleased the king and the ***p***,
3: 1 set his seat above all the ***p***
6: 9 one of the king's most noble ***p***,
8: 9 and the ***p*** of the provinces from
Job 3:15 Or with ***p*** who had gold, Who
12:19 He leads ***p*** away plundered,
12:21 He pours contempt on ***p***,
29: 9 The ***p*** refrained from talking,
34:19 Yet He is not partial to ***p***,
Ps 45:16 Whom You shall make ***p*** in all
47: 9 The ***p*** of the people have
68:27 The ***p*** of Judah and their
68:27 The ***p*** of Zebulun and the
68:27 princes of Zebulun and the ***p***
76:12 shall cut off the spirit of ***p***;
82: 7 And fall like one of the ***p***.
83:11 all their ***p*** like Zebah and
105:22 To bind his ***p*** at his pleasure,
107:40 He pours contempt on ***p***,
113: 8 That He may seat him with ***p***—
113: 8 With the ***p*** of His people.
118: 9 Than to put confidence in ***p***.
119:23 ***P*** also sit and speak against
119:161 ***P*** persecute me without a
146: 3 Do not put your trust in ***p***,
148:11 ***P*** and all judges of the earth;
Prov 8:16 By me ***p*** rule, and nobles,
17:26 Nor to strike ***p*** for their
19:10 for a servant to rule over ***p***.
28: 2 of a land, many are its ***p***;
31: 4 Nor for ***p*** intoxicating drink;
Eccl 10: 7 While ***p*** walk on the ground
10:16 And your ***p*** feast in the
10:17 And your ***p*** feast at the proper
Isa 1:23 Your ***p*** are rebellious,
3: 4 give children to be their ***p***,
3:14 elders of His people And His ***p***:
10: 8 Are not my ***p*** altogether kings?
19:11 Surely the ***p*** of Zoan are
19:13 The ***p*** of Zoan have become
19:13 The ***p*** of Noph are deceived;
21: 5 Eat and drink. Arise, you ***p***,
23: 8 city, Whose merchants are ***p***,
30: 4 For his ***p*** were at Zoan,
31: 9 And his ***p*** shall be afraid of
32: 1 And ***p*** will rule with justice.
34:12 and all its ***p*** shall be nothing.
40:23 He brings the ***p*** to nothing;
41:25 And he shall come against ***p*** as
43:28 I will profane the ***p*** of the
49: 7 ***P*** also shall worship, Because
Jer 1:18 kings of Judah, Against its ***p***,
2:26 and their kings and their ***p***,
4: 9 perish, And the heart of the ***p***;
8: 1 Judah, and the bones of its ***p***,
17:25 gates of this city kings and ***p***
17:25 and on horses, they and their ***p***,
24: 1 and the ***p*** of Judah with the
24: 8 the king of Judah, his ***p***,
25:18 of Judah, its kings and its ***p***,
25:19 of Egypt, his servants, his ***p***,
26:10 When the ***p*** of Judah heard these
26:11 and the prophets spoke to the ***p***
26:12 Jeremiah spoke to all the ***p***
26:16 So the ***p*** and all the people
26:21 his mighty men and all the ***p***,
29: 2 the ***p*** of Judah and Jerusalem,
32:32 their kings, their ***p***,
34:10 Now when all the ***p*** and all the
34:19 the ***p*** of Judah, the princes of
34:19 the ***p*** of Jerusalem, the
34:21 king of Judah and his ***p*** into
35: 4 was by the chamber of the ***p***,
36:12 and there all the ***p*** were
36:12 son of Hananiah, and all the ***p***.
36:14 Therefore all the ***p*** sent Jehudi
36:19 Then the ***p*** said to Baruch, "Go
36:21 and in the hearing of all the ***p***
37:14 and brought him to the ***p***.
37:15 Therefore the ***p*** were angry with
38: 4 Therefore the ***p*** said to the
38:17 to the king of Babylon's ***p***,
38:18 to the king of Babylon's ***p***,
38:22 to the king of Babylon's ***p***,
38:25 But if the ***p*** hear that I have
38:27 Then all the ***p*** came to Jeremiah
39: 3 Then all the ***p*** of the king of
39: 3 with the rest of the ***p*** of the
44:17 fathers, our kings and our ***p***,
44:21 fathers, your kings and your ***p***,
48: 7 His priests and his ***p***
49: 3 With his priests and his ***p***
49:38 from there the king and the ***p***,
50:35 And against her ***p*** and her wise
51:57 And I will make drunk Her ***p*** and
52:10 And he killed all the ***p*** of
Lam 1: 6 Her ***p*** have become like deer
2: 2 profaned the kingdom and its ***p***.
2: 9 Her king and her ***p*** are among
5:12 ***P*** were hung up by their hands,
Ezek 11: 1 ***p*** of the people.
17:12 and took its king and ***p***,
19: 1 up a lamentation for the ***p*** of
21:12 Against all the ***p*** of Israel.
22: 6 the ***p*** of Israel: each one has
22:27 Her ***p*** in her midst are like
26:16 Then all the ***p*** of the sea will
27:21 Arabia and all the ***p*** of Kedar
30:13 There shall no longer be ***p***
32:29 Her kings and all her ***p***,
32:30 There are the ***p*** of the north,
39:18 Drink the blood of the ***p*** of
45: 8 and My ***p*** shall no more oppress
45: 9 O ***p*** of Israel! Remove violence
Dan 8:25 rise against the Prince of ***p***;
9: 6 name to our kings and our ***p***,
9: 8 of face, to our kings, our ***p***,
10:13 Michael, one of the chief ***p***,
11: 5 as well as one of his ***p***;
11: 8 with their ***p*** and their
Hos 5:10 The ***p*** of Judah are like those
7: 3 And ***p*** with their lies.
7: 5 In the day of our king ***P*** have
7:16 Their ***p*** shall fall by the
8: 4 but not by Me; They made ***p***,
8:10 of the burden of the king of ***p***.
9:15 All their ***p*** are rebellious.
13:10 said, 'Give me a king and ***p***'?
Am 1:15 He and his ***p*** together,"
2: 3 And slay all its ***p*** with him,"
Hab 1:10 And ***p*** are scorned by them.
Zeph 1: 8 That I will punish the ***p*** and
3: 3 Her ***p*** in her midst are roaring

PRINCESS (1/1) PRINCESSES

Lam 1: 1 great among the nations! The ***p***

PRINCESSES (1/1) PRINCESS

1 Ki 11: 3 he had seven hundred wives, ***p***,

PRINCIPAL (3/3) PRINCIPALITY

Gen 10:12 and Calah (that is the ***p***
Prov 4: 7 Wisdom is the ***p*** thing;
Jer 52:25 the ***p*** scribe of the army who

PRINCIPALITIES (5/5) PRINCIPALITY

Rom 8:38 nor angels nor ***p*** nor powers,
Eph 3:10 known by the church to the ***p***
6:12 flesh and blood, but against ***p***,
Col 1:16 thrones or dominions or ***p*** or
2:15 Having disarmed ***p*** and powers, He

PRINCIPALITY (2/2) PRINCIPAL, PRINCIPALITIES

Eph 1:21 far above all ***p*** and power and
Col 2:10 who is the head of all ***p*** and

PRINCIPLES (4/4)

Col 2: 8 according to the basic ***p*** of the
2:20 with Christ from the basic ***p***
Heb 5:12 to teach you again the first ***p***
6: 1 of the elementary ***p*** of Christ,

PRINT (2/1)

Jn 20:25 I see in His hands the ***p*** of
20:25 and put my finger into the ***p*** of

PRISCA (1/1) PRISCILLA

2 Tim 4:19 Greet ***P*** and Aquila, and the

PRISCILLA (5/5) PRISCA

Acts 18: 2 come from Italy with his wife ***P***
18:18 and ***P*** and Aquila were with
18:26 When Aquila and ***P*** heard him,
Rom 16: 3 Greet ***P*** and Aquila, my fellow
1 Cor 16:19 Aquila and ***P*** greet you heartily

PRISON (93/87) PRISONER, PRISONS

Gen 39:20 took him and put him into the ***p***,
39:20 And he was there in the ***p***.
39:21 sight of the keeper of the ***p***.
39:22 And the keeper of the ***p***
39:22 prisoners who were in the ***p***;
39:23 The keeper of the ***p*** did not look
40: 3 captain of the guard, in the ***p***,
40: 5 who were confined in the ***p***,
42:16 and you shall be kept in ***p***,
42:17 he put them all together in ***p***
42:19 brothers be confined to your ***p***
Judg 16:21 he became a grinder in the ***p***.
16:25 called for Samson from the ***p***,
1 Ki 22:27 king: "Put this fellow in ***p***,
2 Ki 17: 4 shut him up, and bound him in ***p***.
23:33 Now Pharaoh Necho put him in ***p***
25:27 Jehoiachin king of Judah from ***p***.
25:29 Jehoiachin changed from his ***p***
2 Chr 16:10 with the seer, and put him in ***p***,
18:26 king: "Put this fellow in ***p***,
Neh 3:25 that was by the court of the ***p***.
12:39 stopped by the Gate of the ***P***.
Ps 142: 7 Bring my soul out of ***p***,

Eccl 4:14 For he comes out of **p** to be
Isa 24:22 And will be shut up in the **p**;
42: 7 bring out prisoners from the **p**,
42: 7 who sit in darkness from the **p**
42:22 And they are hidden in **p**
53: 8 He was taken from **p** and from
61: 1 And the opening of the **p** to
Jer 29:26 that you should put him in **p**
32: 2 shut up in the court of the **p**,
32: 8 to me in the court of the **p**
32:12 who sat in the court of the **p**.
33: 1 shut up in the court of the **p**,
37: 4 they had not yet put him in **p**.
37:15 struck him and put him in **p** in
37:15 For they had made that the **p**.
37:18 that you have put me in **p**?
37:21 Jeremiah to the court of the **p**,
37:21 remained in the court of the **p**.
38: 6 was in the court of the **p**,
38:13 remained in the court of the **p**.
38:28 remained in the court of the **p**
39:14 from the court of the **p**,
39:15 shut up in the court of the **p**,
52:11 and put him in **p** till the day
52:31 Judah and brought him out of **p**.
52:33 Jehoiachin changed from his **p**
Mt 4:12 that John had been put in **p**,
5:25 and you be thrown into **p**.
11: 2 And when John had heard in **p**
14: 3 and put him in **p** for the sake
14:10 sent and had John beheaded in **p**.
18:30 but went and threw him into **p**
25:36 I was in **p** and you came to Me.'
25:39 did we see You sick, or in **p**,
25:43 sick and in **p** and you did not
25:44 or naked or sick or in **p**,
Mk 1:14 Now after John was put in **p**,
6:17 and bound him in **p** for the sake
6:27 he went and beheaded him in **p**,
Lk 3:20 all, that he shut John up in **p**.
12:58 the officer throw you into **p**.
22:33 both to **p** and to death."
23:19 who had been thrown into **p** for a
23:25 murder had been thrown into **p**;
Jn 3:24 had not yet been thrown into **p**.
Acts 5:18 and put them in the common **p**.
5:19 angel of the Lord opened the **p**
5:21 and sent to the **p** to have them
5:22 and did not find them in the **p**,
5:23 Indeed we found the **p** shut
5:25 the men whom you put in **p** are
8: 3 women, committing them to **p**.
12: 4 arrested him, he put him in **p**,
12: 5 Peter was therefore kept in **p**,
12: 6 the door were keeping the **p**.
12: 7 and a light shone in the **p**;
12:17 had brought him out of the **p**.
16:23 them, they threw them into **p**,
16:24 he put them into the inner **p**
16:26 that the foundations of the **p**
16:27 And the keeper of the **p**,
16:27 from sleep and seeing the **p**
16:36 So the keeper of the **p** reported
16:37 and have thrown us into **p**.
16:40 So they went out of the **p** and
26:10 of the saints I shut up in **p**,
1 Pe 3:19 preached to the spirits in **p**,
Rev 2:10 to throw some of you into **p**,
18: 2 a **p** for every foul spirit, and
20: 7 will be released from his **p**

PRISONER (17/17) PRISON, PRISONERS

2 Ki 24:12 year of his reign, took him **p**.
Ps 79:11 Let the groaning of the **p** come
102:20 To hear the groaning of the **p**,
Mt 27:15 to the multitude one **p** whom
27:16 time they had a notorious **p**
Mk 15: 6 accustomed to releasing one **p**
Acts 23:18 Paul the **p** called me to him and
25:14 is a certain man left a **p** by
25:27 to me unreasonable to send a **p**
28:17 yet I was delivered as a **p** from
Eph 3: 1 the **p** of Christ Jesus for you
4: 1 the **p** of the Lord, beseech you
Col 4:10 Aristarchus my fellow **p** greets
2 Tim 1: 8 of our Lord, nor of me His **p**,
Phm 1: 1 a **p** of Christ Jesus, and
1: 9 and now also a **p** of Jesus
1:23 my fellow **p** in Christ Jesus,

PRISONERS (22/22) PRISONER

Gen 39:20 a place where the king's **p**
39:22 to Joseph's hand all the **p** who
Num 21: 1 Israel and took some of them **p**.
Job 3:18 There the **p** rest together;
Ps 69:33 And does not despise His **p**.
146: 7 LORD gives freedom to the **p**.
Isa 10: 4 they shall bow down among the **p**,
14:17 did not open the house of his **p**?
20: 4 lead away the Egyptians as **p**
24:22 As **p** are gathered in the pit,
42: 7 To bring out **p** from the
49: 9 That You may say to the **p**,
Lam 3:34 under one's feet All the **p** of
Zech 9:11 I will set your **p** free from
9:12 You **p** of hope. Even today I
Acts 16:25 and the **p** were listening to
16:27 supposing the **p** had fled, drew
27: 1 Paul and some other **p** to one
27:42 plan was to kill the **p**,
28:16 the centurion delivered the **p**
Rom 16: 7 my countrymen and my fellow **p**,
Heb 13: 3 Remember the **p** as if chained

PRISONS (3/3) PRISON

Lk 21:12 you up to the synagogues and **p**.
Acts 22: 4 binding and delivering into **p**
2 Cor 11:23 in **p** more frequently, in deaths

PRIVATE (3/3) PRIVATELY

Judg 3:20 in his cool **p** chamber).
Ezek 21:14 That enters their **p** chambers.
2 Pe 1:20 is of any **p** interpretation,

PRIVATELY (9/9) PRIVATE

2 Sam 3:27 in the gate to speak with him **p**,
Mt 17:19 the disciples came to Jesus **p**
24: 3 the disciples came to Him **p**,
Mk 9:28 His disciples asked Him **p**,
13: 3 John, and Andrew asked Him **p**,
Lk 9:10 He took them and went aside **p**
10:23 to His disciples and said **p**,
Acts 23:19 hand, went aside and asked **p**,
Gal 2: 2 but **p** to those who were of

PRIZE (9/9)

Jer 21: 9 and his life shall be as a **p** to
38: 2 his life shall be as a **p** to
39:18 but your life shall be as a **p**
45: 5 give your life to you as a **p**
Hos 13:15 treasury of every desirable **p**.
Nah 2: 9 Or wealth of every desirable **p**.
1 Cor 9:24 all run, but one receives the **p**?
9:25 who competes for the **p** is
Phil 3:14 toward the goal for the **p** of

PRIZED (1/1)

Joel 3: 5 your temples My **p** possessions.

PROBABLY (2/2)

Judg 3:24 He is **p** attending to his needs
Lk 20:13 **P** they will respect him when

PROBLEMS (1/1)

Deut 1:12 How can I alone bear your **p** and

PROCEED (17/17) PROCEEDED, PROCEEDS

Gen 35:11 a company of nations shall **p**
Num 34: 9 the border shall **p** to Ziphron,
Josh 6: 7 And he said to the people, "**P**,
6:10 nor shall a word **p** out of your
Job 40: 5 but I will **p** no further."
Isa 22:15 **p** to this steward, To Shebna,
51: 4 For law will **p** from Me, And I
Jer 9: 3 For they **p** from evil to evil,
30:19 Then out of them shall **p**
Lam 3:38 That woe and well-being **p**?
Hab 1: 7 judgment and their dignity **p**
Mt 15:18 But those things which **p** out of
15:19 For out of the heart **p** evil
Mk 7:21 **p** evil thoughts, adulteries,
Acts 27: 7 the wind not permitting us to **p**,
Eph 4:29 Let no corrupt word **p** out of
Jas 3:10 Out of the same mouth **p** blessing

PROCEEDED (8/8) PROCEED

Num 30:12 then whatever **p** from her lips
32:24 and do what has **p** out of your
Job 36: 1 Elihu also **p** and said:
Lk 4:22 words which **p** out of His mouth.
Jn 8:42 for I **p** forth and came from
Acts 12: 3 he **p** further to seize Peter
Rev 4: 5 from the throne **p** lightnings,
19:21 the sword which **p** from the

PROCEEDING (2/2)

Eccl 10: 5 As an error **p** from the ruler:
Rev 22: 1 **p** from the throne of God and of

PROCEEDINGS (1/1)

Acts 24:22 he adjourned the **p** and said,

PROCEEDS (12/12) PROCEED

Num 30: 2 do according to all that **p** out
Deut 8: 3 man lives by every word that **p**
1 Sam 24:13 Wickedness **p** from the wicked.'
2 Ki 8: 6 and all the **p** of the field from
Job 20:18 From the **p** of business
Prov 3:14 For her **p** are better than the
Hab 1: 4 Therefore perverse judgment **p**.
Mt 4: 4 but by every word that **p**
Jn 15:26 the Spirit of truth who **p** from
Acts 4:34 and brought the **p** of the things
5: 2 And he kept back part of the **p**,
Rev 11: 5 fire **p** from their mouth and

PROCESS (4/4)

Gen 4: 3 And in the **p** of time it came to
38:12 Now in the **p** of time the
Ex 2:23 Now it happened in the **p** of
1 Sam 1:20 So it came to pass in the **p** of

PROCESSION (3/2)

Ps 68:24 They have seen Your **p**,
68:24 The **p** of my God, my King, into
Isa 60:11 Gentiles, And their kings in **p**.

PROCHORUS (1/1)

Acts 6: 5 the Holy Spirit, and Philip, **P**,

PROCLAIM (54/52) PROCLAIMED, PROCLAIMER, PROCLAIMS, PROCLAMATION

Ex 33:19 and I will **p** the name of the
Lev 23: 2 which you shall **p** to be holy
23: 4 convocations which you shall **p**
23:21 And you shall **p** on the same day
23:37 of the LORD which you shall **p**
25:10 and **p** liberty throughout all
Deut 20:10 then **p** an offer of peace to it.
32: 3 For I **p** the name of the LORD:
Judg 7: 3 **p** in the hearing of the people,
1 Sam 31: 9 to **p** it in the temple of
2 Sam 1:20 **P** it not in the streets of
1 Ki 21: 9 **P** a fast, and seat Naboth with
2 Ki 10:20 **P** a solemn assembly for Baal."
1 Chr 10: 9 land of the Philistines to **p**
16:23 **P** the good news of His
Neh 6: 7 also appointed prophets to **p**
8:15 they should announce and **p** in
Esth 6: 9 and **p** before him: 'Thus shall
Ps 26: 7 That I may **p** with the voice of
96: 2 **P** the good news of His
Prov 20: 6 Most men will **p** each his own
Isa 44: 7 And who can **p** as I do?
48:20 **p** this, Utter it to the end of
60: 6 And they shall **p** the praises
61: 1 To **p** liberty to the captives,
61: 2 To **p** the acceptable year of the
Jer 3:12 Go and **p** these words toward the
4: 5 Declare in Judah and **p** in
4:16 **p** against Jerusalem, That
5:20 in the house of Jacob And **p**
7: 2 and **p** there this word, and say,
11: 6 **P** all these words in the cities
19: 2 and **p** there the words that I
31: 7 the chief of the nations; **P**,
34: 8 who were at Jerusalem to **p**
34:17 I **p** liberty to you,' says the
46:14 and **p** in Migdol; Proclaim in
46:14 **P** in Noph and in Tahpanhes;
50: 2 among the nations, **P**,
50: 2 **P**—do not conceal it—Say,
Joel 3: 9 **P** this among the nations:
Am 3: 9 **P** in the palaces at Ashdod,
4: 5 **P** and announce the freewill
Zech 1:14 spoke with me said to me, "**P**,
1:17 'Again **p**, saying, 'Thus says
Mk 1:45 he went out and began to **p** it
5:20 And he departed and began to **p**
Lk 4:18 To **p** liberty to the
4:19 To **p** the acceptable year
Acts 16:17 who **p** to us the way of
17:23 Him I **p** to you:
26:23 and would **p** light to the
1 Cor 11:26 you **p** the Lord's death till He
1 Pe 2: 9 that you may **p** the praises of

PROCLAIMED (33/32) PROCLAIM

Ex 34: 5 and **p** the name of the LORD.
34: 6 LORD passed before him and **p**,
36: 6 and they caused it to be **p**
Deut 26:17 Today you have **p** the LORD to be
26:18 Also today the LORD has **p** you
1 Ki 21:12 They **p** a fast, and seated Naboth
2 Ki 10:20 for Baal." So they **p** it.
23:16 LORD which the man of God **p**,
23:16 who **p** these words.
23:17 God who came from Judah and **p**
1 Chr 13: 6 cherubim, where His name is **p**.
2 Chr 20: 3 and **p** a fast throughout all
Ezra 8:21 Then I **p** a fast there at the
Esth 1:20 decree which he will make is **p**
2:18 and he **p** a holiday in the
3:15 and the decree was **p** in Shushan
6:11 and **p** before him, "Thus shall
Ps 40: 9 I have **p** the good news of
68:11 the company of those who **p** it:
Isa 43:12 declared and saved, I have **p**,
48: 5 Before it came to pass I **p** it
62:11 Indeed the LORD has **p** To the
Jer 36: 9 that they **p** a fast before the
36:18 He **p** with his mouth all these
Jon 3: 5 **p** a fast, and put on sackcloth,
3: 7 And he caused it to be **p** and
Zech 7: 7 the words which the LORD **p**
7:13 that just as He **p** and they
Mk 7:36 the more widely they **p** it.
Lk 8:39 And he went his way and **p**
12: 3 ear in inner rooms will be **p**
Acts 10:37 which was **p** throughout all
20:20 but **p** it to you, and taught you

PROCLAIMER (1/1) PROCLAIM

Acts 17:18 He seems to be a **p** of foreign

P

PROCLAIMING (3/3)

Jer 34:15 every man **p** liberty to his
34:17 You have not obeyed Me in **p**
Rev 5: 2 Then I saw a strong angel **p** with

PROCLAIMS (5/4) PROCLAIM

Prov 12:23 heart of fools **p** foolishness.
Isa 52: 7 Who **p** peace, Who brings glad
52: 7 Who **p** salvation, Who says to
Jer 4:15 voice declares from Dan And **p**
Nah 1:15 Who **p** peace! O Judah, keep

PROCLAMATION (8/8) PROCLAIM

Ex 32: 5 And Aaron made a **p** and said,
1 Ki 15:22 Then King Asa made a **p**
2 Chr 24: 9 And they made a **p** throughout
30: 5 So they resolved to make a **p**
36:22 so that he made a **p** throughout
Ezra 1: 1 so that he made a **p** throughout
10: 7 And they issued a **p** throughout
Dan 5:29 and made a **p** concerning him

PROCONSUL (4/4)

Acts 13: 7 who was with the **p**,
13: 8 seeking to turn the **p** away from
13:12 Then the **p** believed, when he saw
18:12 When Gallio was **p** of Achaia, the

PROCONSULS (1/1)

Acts 19:38 courts are open and there are **p**.

PROCURED (1/1)

Jer 4:18 ways and your doings Have **p**

PRODIGAL (1/1)

Lk 15:13 his possessions with **p** living.

PRODUCE (40/37) PRODUCED, PRODUCES, PRODUCING

Gen 41:34 collect one-fifth of the **p**
Ex 22:29 the first of your ripe **p** and
23:10 your land and gather in its **p**,
Lev 25: 6 And the sabbath **p** of the land
25: 7 all its **p** shall be for food.
25:12 you shall eat its **p** from the
25:20 not sow nor gather in our **p**?
25:21 and it will bring forth **p**
25:22 and eat old **p** until the ninth
25:22 until its **p** comes in, you shall
26: 4 the land shall yield its **p**,
26:20 your land shall not yield its **p**,
Num 18:30 to the Levites as the **p** of the
18:30 threshing floor and as the **p**
Deut 11:17 rain, and the land yield no **p**,
14:28 bring out the tithe of your **p**
16:15 will bless you in all your **p**
26: 2 some of the first of all the **p**
28: 4 the **p** of your ground and the
28:11 and in the **p** of your ground, in
28:18 fruit of your body and the **p**
28:33 fruit of your land and the **p**
28:42 all your trees and the **p** of
28:51 of your livestock and the **p** of
30: 9 and in the **p** of your land for
32:13 That he might eat the **p** of the
33:14 With the precious **p** of the
Josh 5:11 And they ate of the **p** of the
5:12 day after they had eaten the **p**
Judg 6: 4 against them and destroy the **p**
1 Chr 27:27 the Shiphmite was over the **p**
2 Chr 31: 5 and of all the **p** of the field;
Neh 10:31 forego the seventh year's **p**
Ps 144:13 Supplying all kinds of **p**;
Prov 18:20 From the **p** of his lips he
Jer 20: 5 wealth of this city, all its **p**,
Ezek 48:18 and its **p** shall be food for the
Hos 8: 7 It shall never **p** meal. If it
8: 7 produce meal. If it should **p**,
Jas 1:20 for the wrath of man does not **p**

PRODUCED (7/7) PRODUCE

Num 6: 4 he shall eat nothing that is **p**
17: 8 had **p** blossoms and yielded ripe
Mt 13:26 the grain had sprouted and **p** a
Mk 4: 8 that sprang up, increased and **p**:
Rom 7: 8 **p** in me all manner of evil
2 Cor 7:11 What diligence it **p** in you,
Jas 5:18 and the earth **p** its fruit.

PRODUCES (10/7) PRODUCE

Deut 14:22 of your grain that the field **p**
Prov 30:33 For as the churning of milk **p**
30:33 And wringing the nose **p** blood,
30:33 So the forcing of wrath **p**
Mt 13:23 who indeed bears fruit and **p**:
Jn 12:24 it **p** much grain.
Rom 5: 3 knowing that tribulation **p**
2 Cor 7:10 For godly sorrow **p** repentance
7:10 but the sorrow of the world **p**
Jas 1: 3 the testing of your faith **p**

PRODUCING (1/1) PRODUCE

Rom 7:13 was **p** death in me through what

PROFANE (36/36) PROFANED, PROFANING

Lev 10: 1 and offered **p** fire before the
16: 1 when they offered **p** fire
18:21 nor shall you **p** the name of
19:12 nor shall you **p** the name of
20: 3 to defile My sanctuary and **p** My
21: 4 his people, to **p** himself.
21: 6 be holy to their God and not **p**
21:12 nor **p** the sanctuary of his God;
21:15 Nor shall he **p** his posterity
21:23 lest he **p** My sanctuaries; for I
22: 2 and that they do not **p** My holy
22: 9 if they **p** it: I the LORD
22:15 They shall not **p** the holy
22:32 You shall not **p** My holy name,
Num 3: 4 the LORD when they offered **p**
18:32 But you shall not **p** the holy
26:61 Abihu died when they offered **p**
Neh 13:17 by which you **p** the Sabbath day?
Prov 30: 9 And **p** the name of my God.
Isa 43:28 Therefore I will **p** the princes
Jer 23:11 both prophet and priest are **p**;
Ezek 13:19 And will you **p** Me among My
20:39 but **p** My holy name no more with
21:25 'Now to you, O **p**,
23:39 came into My sanctuary to **p** it;
24:21 I will **p** My sanctuary, your
28:16 Therefore I cast you as a **p**
39: 7 and I will not let them **p** My
Mal 1:12 But you **p** it, In that you say,
Mt 12: 5 the priests in the temple **p**
Acts 24: 6 He even tried to **p** the temple,
1 Tim 1: 9 sinners, for the unholy and **p**,
4: 7 But reject **p** and old wives'
6:20 avoiding the **p** and idle
2 Tim 2:16 But shun **p** and idle babblings,
Heb 12:16 there be any fornicator or **p**

PROFANED (25/23) PROFANE

Ex 20:25 tool on it, you have **p** it.
Lev 19: 8 because he has **p** the hallowed
Ps 89:39 You have **p** his crown by
Isa 47: 6 I have **p** My inheritance,
48:11 For how should My name be **p**?
Jer 34:16 Then you turned around and **p** My
Lam 2: 2 He has **p** the kingdom and its
Ezek 14:11 nor be **p** anymore with all their
20: 9 that it should not be **p** before
20:14 that it should not be **p** before
20:16 but **p** My Sabbaths; for their
20:21 but they **p** My Sabbaths. Then I
20:22 that it should not be **p** in the
20:24 **p** My Sabbaths, and their eyes
22: 8 despised My holy things and **p**
22:26 have violated My law and **p** My
22:26 so that I am **p** among them.
23:38 on the same day and **p** My
25: 3 My sanctuary when it was **p**,
36:20 they **p** My holy name—when they
36:21 which the house of Israel had **p**
36:22 which you have **p** among the
36:23 which has been **p** among the
36:23 which you have **p** in their
Mal 2:11 For Judah has **p** The LORD's

PROFANENESS (1/1)

Jer 23:15 the prophets of Jerusalem **P**

PROFANES (3/2)

Ex 31:14 Everyone who **p** it shall surely
Lev 21: 9 if she **p** herself by playing the
21: 9 she **p** her father. She shall be

PROFANING (2/2) PROFANE

Neh 13:18 added wrath on Israel by **p** the
Mal 2:10 with one another By **p** the

PROFESS (1/1) PROFESSING

Titus 1:16 They **p** to know God, but in works

PROFESSING (3/3) PROFESS

Rom 1:22 **P** to be wise, they became fools,
1 Tim 2:10 which is proper for women **p**
6:21 by **p** it some have strayed

PROFIT (53/52) PROFITABLE, PROFITED, PROFITS

Gen 37:26 What **p** is there if we kill our
Lev 25:37 nor lend him your food at a **p**.
1 Sam 12:21 empty things which cannot **p** or
Job 21:15 And what **p** do we have if we
30: 2 what **p** is the strength of
33:27 And it did not **p** me.'
35: 3 What **p** shall I have, more than
Ps 30: 9 What **p** is there in my blood,
Prov 10: 2 Treasures of wickedness **p**
11: 4 Riches do not **p** in the day of
14:23 In all labor there is **p**,
Eccl 1: 3 What **p** has a man from all his
2:11 There was no **p** under the
3: 9 What **p** has the worker from that
5: 9 Moreover the **p** of the land is
5:11 So what **p** have the owners
5:16 And what **p** has he who has
Isa 30: 6 To a people who shall not **p**;
44: 9 precious things shall not **p**;
47:12 you will be able to **p**,
48:17 your God, Who teaches you to **p**,
57:12 For they will not **p** you.
Jer 2: 8 after things that do not **p**.
2:11 For what does not **p**.
7: 8 in lying words that cannot **p**.
12:13 to pain but do not **p**.
23:32 therefore they shall not **p** this
Ezek 22:12 you have made **p** from your
22:13 My fists at the dishonest **p**
Hab 2:18 What **p** is the image, that its
Mal 3:14 What **p** is it that we have
Mt 15: 5 Whatever **p** you might have
16:26 For what **p** is it to a man if he
Mk 7:11 Whatever **p** you might have
8:36 For what will it **p** a man if he
Lk 9:25 For what **p** is it to a man if he
Acts 16:16 who brought her masters much **p**
16:19 saw that their hope of **p** was
19:24 brought no small **p** to the
Rom 3: 1 or what is the **p** of
1 Cor 7:35 And this I say for your own **p**,
10:33 things, not seeking my own **p**,
10:33 but the **p** of many, that they
12: 7 is given to each one for the **p**
14: 6 what shall I **p** you unless I
Gal 5: 2 Christ will **p** you nothing.
2 Tim 2:14 to strive about words to no **p**,
Heb 4: 2 word which they heard did not **p**
12:10 to them, but He for our **p**,
Jas 2:14 What does it **p**,
2:16 for the body, what does it **p**?
4:13 buy and sell, and make a **p**";
Jude 11 in the error of Balaam for **p**,

PROFITABLE (13/12) PROFIT, UNPROFITABLE

Job 22: 2 'Can a man be **p** to God,
22: 2 he who is wise may be **p** to
Eccl 7:11 And **p** to those who see the
Jer 13: 7 It was **p** for nothing.
13:10 just like this sash which is **p**
Mt 5:29 for it is more **p** for you that
5:30 for it is more **p** for you that
Rom 2:25 For circumcision is indeed **p** if
2 Cor 12: 1 It is doubtless not **p** for me to
1 Tim 4: 8 but godliness is **p** for all
2 Tim 3:16 and is **p** for doctrine, for
Titus 3: 8 These things are good and **p** to
Phm 1:11 but now is **p** to you and to me.

PROFITED (1/1) PROFIT

Heb 13: 9 not with foods which have not **p**

PROFITS (7/7) PROFIT

Job 34: 9 It **p** a man nothing That he
Prov 3:14 are better than the **p** of
31:16 From her **p** she plants a
Isa 44:10 a god or mold an image That **p**
Jn 6:63 the flesh **p** nothing. The words
1 Cor 13: 3 it **p** me nothing.
1 Tim 4: 8 For bodily exercise **p** a little,

PROFOUND (1/1)

Ps 131: 1 Nor with things too **p** for me.

PROGNOSTICATORS (1/1)

Isa 47:13 And the monthly **p** Stand up

PROGRESS (3/3)

Phil 1:25 with you all for your **p** and
1 Tim 4:15 that your **p** may be evident to
2 Tim 3: 9 but they will **p** no further, for

PROJECTING (2/2)

Neh 3:26 and on the **p** tower.
3:27 next to the great **p** tower, and

PROJECTS (1/1)

Neh 3:25 and on the tower which **p** from

PROLONG (14/14) PROLONGED

Deut 4:26 you will not **p** your days in
4:40 and that you may **p** your days
5:33 and that you may **p** your days
11: 9 and that you may **p** your days in
17:20 and that he may **p** his days in
22: 7 with you and that you may **p**
30:18 you shall not **p** your days in
32:47 and by this word you shall **p**
Job 6:11 that I should **p** my life?
Ps 61: 6 You will **p** the king's life,
85: 5 Will You **p** Your anger to all
Prov 28:16 who hates covetousness will **p**
Eccl 8:13 nor will he **p** his days, which
Isa 53:10 He shall **p** His days, And the

PROLONGED (8/7) PROLONG

Deut 6: 2 and that your days may be **p**.
28:59 great and **p** plagues—and serious
28:59 and serious and **p** sicknesses.
Prov 28: 2 and knowledge Right will be **p**.
Eccl 8:12 times, and his days are **p**,
Isa 13:22 And her days will not be **p**.
Ezek 12:22 which says, 'The days are **p**,
Dan 7:12 yet their lives were **p** for a

PROLONGS (2/2)

Prov 10:27 The fear of the LORD **p** days,
Eccl 7:15 there is a wicked man who **p**

PROMINENT (10/10)

1 Ki 1:42 for you are a **p** man, and bring
2 Ki 25:28 and gave him a more **p** seat than
Esth 9: 4 Mordecai became increasingly **p**.
Jer 52:32 to him and gave him a more **p**
Ezek 17:22 will plant it on a high and **p**
Dan 11:41 and the **p** people of Ammon.
Mk 15:43 a **p** council member, who was
Acts 13:50 stirred up the devout and **p**
17:12 **p** women as well as men.
25:23 with the commanders and the **p**

PROMISE (53/50) PROMISED, PROMISES

1 Ki 8:56 one word of all His good **p**,
2 Chr 1: 9 let Your **p** to David my father
Ezra 10:19 And they gave their **p** that they
Neh 5:12 would do according to this **p**.
5:13 who does not perform this **p**.
5:13 people did according to this **p**.
Ps 77: 8 Has His **p** failed forevermore?
105:42 For He remembered His holy **p**,
Lk 24:49 I send the **P** of My Father upon
Acts 1: 4 but to wait for the **P** of the
2:33 received from the Father the **p**
2:39 For the **p** is to you and to your
7:17 But when the time of the **p** drew
13:23 man's seed, according to the **p**,
13:32 that **p** which was made to the
23:21 waiting for the **p** from you."
26: 6 am judged for the hope of the **p**
26: 7 To this **p** our twelve tribes,
Rom 4:13 For the **p** that he would be the
4:14 faith is made void and the **p**
4:16 so that the **p** might be sure to
4:20 He did not waver at the **p** of God
9: 8 but the children of the **p** are
9: 9 For this is the word of **p**:
Gal 3:14 that we might receive the **p** of
3:17 that it should make the **p** of no
3:18 the law, it is no longer of **p**;
3:18 God gave it to Abraham by **p**.
3:19 Seed should come to whom the **p**
3:22 that the **p** by faith in Jesus
3:29 and heirs according to the **p**.
4:23 he of the freewoman through **p**,
4:28 Isaac was, are children of **p**.
Eph 1:13 with the Holy Spirit of **p**,
2:12 from the covenants of **p**,
3: 6 and partakers of His **p** in
6: 2 is the first commandment with **p**:
1 Tim 4: 8 having **p** of the life that now
2 Tim 1: 1 according to the **p** of life
Heb 4: 1 since a **p** remains of entering
6:13 For when God made a **p** to
6:15 endured, he obtained the **p**.
6:17 abundantly to the heirs of **p**
9:15 are called may receive the **p**
10:36 of God, you may receive the **p**:
11: 9 he dwelt in the land of **p** as
11: 9 heirs with him of the same **p**;
11:39 faith, did not receive the **p**,
2 Pe 2:19 While they **p** them liberty, they
3: 4 Where is the **p** of His coming?
3: 9 is not slack concerning His **p**,
3:13 we, according to His **p**,
1 Jn 2:25 And this is the **p** that He has

PROMISED (51/50) PROMISE

Ex 12:25 will give you, just as He **p**,
Num 10:29 for the LORD has **p** good things
14:40 the place which the LORD has **p**,
Deut 1:11 and bless you as He has **p** you!
6: 3 God of your fathers has **p** you—
9:28 them to the land which He **p**
10: 9 just as the LORD your God **p**
12:20 your border as He has **p** you,
15: 6 God will bless you just as He **p**
19: 8 gives you the land which He **p**
23:23 LORD your God what you have **p**
26:18 just as He **p** you, that you
27: 3 the LORD God of your fathers **p**
Josh 9:21 as the rulers had **p** them."
22: 4 as He **p** them; now therefore,
23: 5 as the LORD your God **p** you.
23:10 fights for you, as He **p** you.
23:15 you which the LORD your God **p**
2 Sam 7:28 and You have **p** this goodness to
1 Ki 2:24 a house for me, as He **p**,
5:12 as He had **p** him; and there was
8:20 of Israel, as the LORD **p**;
8:24 You have kept what You **p** Your
8:25 now keep what You **p** Your
8:56 according to all that He **p**.
8:56 which He **p** through His servant
9: 5 as I **p** David your father,
2 Ki 8:19 as He **p** him to give a lamp to
1 Chr 17:26 and have **p** this goodness to
2 Chr 6:10 of Israel, as the LORD **p**;
6:15 You have kept what You **p** Your
6:16 now keep what You **p** Your
21: 7 and since He had **p** to give a
Esth 4: 7 sum of money that Haman had **p**
Jer 32:42 them all the good that I have **p**
33:14 that good thing which I have **p**
Mt 14: 7 Therefore he **p** with an oath to
Mk 14:11 and **p** to give him money. So he
Lk 1:72 To perform the mercy **p** to our
22: 6 So he **p** and sought opportunity
Acts 7: 5 He **p** to give it to him for a
Rom 1: 2 which He **p** before through His
4:21 convinced that what He had **p**
2 Cor 9: 5 which you had previously **p**,
Titus 1: 2 **p** before time began,
Heb 10:23 for He who **p** is faithful.
11:11 judged Him faithful who had **p**.
12:26 the earth; but now He has **p**,
Jas 1:12 of life which the Lord has **p**
2: 5 of the kingdom which He **p** to
1 Jn 2:25 is the promise that He has **p**

PROMISES (13/13) PROMISE

Rom 9: 4 the service of God, and the **p**;
15: 8 to confirm the **p** made to the
2 Cor 1:20 For all the **p** of God in Him are
7: 1 Therefore, having these **p**,
Gal 3:16 and his Seed were the **p** made.
3:21 Is the law then against the **p**
Heb 6:12 and patience inherit the **p**.
7: 6 and blessed him who had the **p**.
8: 6 was established on better **p**.
11:13 not having received the **p**,
11:17 and he who had received the **p**
11:33 righteousness, obtained **p**,
2 Pe 1: 4 great and precious **p**,

PROMOTE (2/2)

Job 30:13 They **p** my calamity; They have
Prov 4: 8 and she will **p** you; She will

PROMOTED (4/4)

Esth 3: 1 these things King Ahasuerus **p**
5:11 in which the king had **p** him,
Dan 2:48 Then the king **p** Daniel and gave
3:30 Then the king **p** Shadrach,

PROMOTES (1/1)

Prov 12:18 tongue of the wise **p** health.

PROMPTED (1/1)

Mt 14: 8 having been **p** by her mother,

PROMPTLY (1/1)

Prov 13:24 who loves him disciplines him **p**.

PRONOUNCE (27/26) PRONOUNCED

Lev 5: 4 it is that a man may **p** by an
13: 3 and **p** him unclean.
13: 6 then the priest shall **p** him
13: 8 then the priest shall **p** him
13:11 The priest shall **p** him unclean,
13:13 he shall **p** him clean who has
13:15 examine the raw flesh and **p**
13:17 then the priest shall **p** him
13:20 the priest shall **p** him unclean.
13:22 then the priest shall **p** him
13:23 and the priest shall **p** him
13:25 Therefore the priest shall **p**
13:27 then the priest shall **p** him
13:28 The priest shall **p** him clean,
13:30 then the priest shall **p** him
13:34 then the priest shall **p** him
13:37 and the priest shall **p** him
13:44 The priest shall surely **p** him
13:59 to **p** it clean or to pronounce
13:59 to pronounce it clean or to **p**
14: 7 and shall **p** him clean, and
14:48 then the priest shall **p** the
Deut 17: 9 they shall **p** upon you the
17:10 to the sentence which they **p**
17:11 from the sentence which they **p**
Judg 12: 6 for he could not **p** it right.
Ps 5:10 **P** them guilty, O God! Let them

PRONOUNCED (17/17) PRONOUNCE

2 Ki 2:24 and **p** a curse on them in the
25: 6 and they **p** judgment on him.
Neh 6:12 but that he **p** this prophecy
Jer 11:17 has **p** doom against you for the
16:10 Why has the LORD **p** all this
19:15 all the doom that I have **p**
25:13 all My words which I have **p**
26:13 the doom that He has **p** against
26:19 the doom which He had **p**
34: 5 For I have **p** the word,
35:17 all the doom that I have **p**
36: 7 the fury that the LORD has **p**
36:31 all the doom that I have **p**
39: 5 where he **p** judgment on him.
40: 2 The LORD your God has **p** this
52: 9 and he **p** judgment on him.
Ezek 20:26 and I **p** them unclean because of

PROOF (4/4) PROOFS

2 Cor 8:24 and before the churches the **p**
9:13 through the **p** of this ministry,
13: 3 since you seek a **p** of Christ
Phil 1:28 which is to them a **p** of

PROOFS (1/1) PROOF

Acts 1: 3 suffering by many infallible **p**,

PROPER (13/13) PROPERLY

Judg 6:26 on top of this rock in the **p**
1 Ki 4:28 barley and straw to the **p**
1 Chr 15:13 did not consult Him about the **p**
Ezra 4:14 it was not **p** for us to see the
Ps 75: 2 'When I choose the **p** time,
Eccl 10:17 your princes feast at the **p**
Jer 26:14 do with me as seems good and **p**
27: 5 given it to whom it seemed **p**
1 Cor 7:35 leash on you, but for what is **p**,
11:13 Is it **p** for a woman to pray to
1 Tim 2:10 which is **p** for women professing
Titus 2: 1 speak the things which are **p**
Jude 6 angels who did not keep their **p**

PROPERLY (2/2) PROPER

Rom 13:13 Let us walk **p**, as in the day,
1 Th 4:12 that you may walk **p** toward those

PROPERTY (23/20)

Gen 23: 4 Give me **p** for a burial place
23: 9 as **p** for a burial place among
23:20 by the sons of Heth as **p** for a
34:23 not their livestock, their **p**,
50:13 from Ephron the Hittite as **p**
Ex 21:21 be punished; for he is his **p**.
Lev 25:45 and they shall become your **p**.
Josh 14: 4 for their livestock and their **p**.
2 Ki 9:21 and met him on the **p** of Naboth
1 Chr 27:31 officials over King David's **p**.
2 Chr 17:13 He had much **p** in the cities of
32:29 God had given him very much **p**.
Ezra 10: 8 all his **p** would be confiscated,
Neh 5:13 from his house, and from his **p**,
Jer 37:12 land of Benjamin to claim his **p**
Ezek 45: 6 You shall appoint as the **p** of
45: 7 holy district and the city's **p**;
45: 7 holy district and the city's **p**,
46:18 by evicting them from their **p**;
46:18 for his sons from his own **p**,
46:18 may be scattered from his **p**.
48:20 the holy district with the **p**
48:21 district and of the city's **p**,

PROPHECIES (4/4) PROPHECY

Lam 2:14 envisioned for you false **p** and
1 Cor 13: 8 But whether there are **p**,
1 Th 5:20 Do not despise **p**.
1 Tim 1:18 according to the **p** previously

PROPHECY (18/18) PROPHECIES, PROPHESY, PROPHETIC

2 Chr 9:29 in the **p** of Ahijah the
15: 8 heard these words and the **p** of
Neh 6:12 but that he pronounced this **p**
Dan 9:24 To seal up vision and **p**,
Mt 13:14 And in them the **p** of Isaiah is
Rom 12: 6 us, let us use them: if **p**,
1 Cor 12:10 of miracles, to another **p**,
13: 2 though I have the gift of **p**,
1 Tim 4:14 which was given to you by **p**
2 Pe 1:20 that no **p** of Scripture is of
1:21 for **p** never came by the will of
Rev 1: 3 who hear the words of this **p**,
11: 6 falls in the days of their **p**;
19:10 of Jesus is the spirit of **p**.
22: 7 he who keeps the words of the **p**
22:10 not seal the words of the **p**
22:18 who hears the words of the **p**
22:19 the words of the book of this **p**,

PROPHESIED (47/44) PROPHESY

Num 11:25 rested upon them, that they **p**,
11:26 yet they **p** in the camp.
1 Sam 10:10 and he **p** among them.
10:11 formerly saw that he indeed **p**
18:10 and he **p** inside the house.
19:20 of Saul, and they also **p**.
19:21 and they **p** likewise. Then Saul
19:21 and they **p** also.
19:23 and he went on and **p** until he
19:24 stripped off his clothes and **p**
1 Ki 18:29 they **p** until the time of the
22:10 and all the prophets **p** before
22:12 And all the prophets **p** so,
1 Chr 25: 2 who **p** according to the order of
25: 3 who **p** with a harp to give
2 Chr 18: 9 and all the prophets **p** before
18:11 And all the prophets **p** so,
20:37 son of Dodavah of Mareshah **p**
Ezra 5: 1 **p** to the Jews who were in
Jer 2: 8 The prophets **p** by Baal,

20: 1 heard that Jeremiah **p** these
20: 6 to whom you have **p** lies.'"
23:13 They **p** by Baal And caused My
23:21 not spoken to them, yet they **p**.
25:13 which Jeremiah has **p** concerning
26: 9 Why have you **p** in the name of
26:11 deserves to die! For he has **p**
26:18 Micah of Moresheth **p** in the days
26:20 there was also a man who **p** in
26:20 who **p** against this city and
28: 6 your words which you have **p**,
28: 8 me and before you of old **p**
29:31 Because Shemaiah has **p** to you,
37:19 now are your prophets who **p**
Ezek 37: 7 So I **p** as I was commanded;
37: 7 as I was commanded; and as I **p**,
37:10 So I **p** as He commanded me, and
38:17 who **p** for years in those days
Mt 7:22 have we not **p** in Your name,
11:13 all the prophets and the law **p**
Lk 1:67 with the Holy Spirit, and **p**,
Jn 11:51 high priest that year he **p**
Acts 19: 6 they spoke with tongues and **p**.
21: 9 had four virgin daughters who **p**.
1 Cor 14: 5 but even more that you **p**;
1 Pe 1:10 who **p** of the grace that would
Jude 14 **p** about these men also, saying,

PROPHESIES (10/9) PROPHESY

2 Chr 18: 7 because he never **p** good
Jer 28: 9 As for the prophet who **p** of
Ezek 12:27 and he **p** of times far off.'
Zech 13: 3 to pass that if anyone still **p**,
13: 3 thrust him through when he **p**.
13: 4 ashamed of his vision when he **p**;
1 Cor 11: 5 But every woman who prays or **p**
14: 3 But he who **p** speaks edification
14: 4 but he who **p** edifies the
14: 5 for he who **p** is greater than

PROPHESY (86/75) PROPHECY, PROPHESIED, PROPHESIES, PROPHESYING, PROPHET, PROPHETESS

1 Sam 10: 6 and you will **p** with them and be
1 Ki 22: 8 because he does not **p** good
22:18 I not tell you he would not **p**
1 Chr 25: 1 who should **p** with harps,
2 Chr 18:17 I not tell you he would not **p**
Isa 30:10 Do not **p** to us right things;
30:10 smooth things, **p** deceits.
Jer 5:31 The prophets **p** falsely,
11:21 Do not **p** in the name of the
14:14 The prophets **p** lies in My name.
14:14 they **p** to you a false vision,
14:15 concerning the prophets who **p**
14:16 And the people to whom they **p**
19:14 the LORD had sent him to **p**;
23:16 words of the prophets who **p** to
23:25 the prophets have said who **p**
23:26 the heart of the prophets who **p**
23:32 I am against those who **p** false
25:30 Therefore **p** against them all
26:12 The LORD sent me to **p** against
27:10 For they **p** a lie to you, to
27:14 for they **p** a lie to you;
27:15 yet they **p** a lie in My name,
27:15 you and the prophets who **p** to
27:16 words of your prophets who **p**
27:16 for they **p** a lie to you.
29: 9 For they **p** falsely to you in My
29:21 who **p** a lie to you in My name:
32: 3 Why do you **p** and say, 'Thus says
Ezek 4: 7 and you shall **p** against it.
6: 2 and **p** against them,
11: 4 Therefore **p** against them,
11: 4 prophesy against them, **p**,
13: 2 **p** against the prophets of
13: 2 the prophets of Israel who **p**,
13: 2 and say to those who **p** out of
13:16 the prophets of Israel who **p**
13:17 who **p** out of their own heart;
13:17 **p** against them,
20:46 preach against the south and **p**
21: 2 and **p** against the land of
21: 9 **p** and say, 'Thus says the
21:14 therefore, son of man, **p**,
21:28 **p** and say, 'Thus says the Lord
25: 2 and **p** against them.
28:21 and **p** against her,
29: 2 and **p** against him, and against
30: 2 **p** and say, 'Thus says the Lord
34: 2 **p** against the shepherds of
34: 2 **p** and say to them, 'Thus says
35: 2 face against Mount Seir and **p**
36: 1 **p** to the mountains of Israel,
36: 3 'therefore **p**, and say,
36: 6 Therefore **p** concerning the land
37: 4 **P** to these bones, and say to
37: 9 **P** to the breath, prophesy, son
37: 9 me, "Prophesy to the breath, **p**,
37:12 Therefore **p** and say to them,
38: 2 and **p** against him,
38:14 **p** and say to Gog, 'Thus says
39: 1 **p** against Gog, and say, 'Thus
Joel 2:28 sons and your daughters shall **p**,
Am 2:12 prophets saying, 'Do not **p**!'
3: 8 GOD has spoken! Who can but **p**?
7:12 There eat bread, And there **p**.
7:13 But never again **p** at Bethel,
7:15 **p** to My people Israel.'
7:16 Do not **p** against Israel, And do
Mic 2: 6 you say to those who **p**.
2: 6 So they shall not **p** to you;
2:11 I will **p** to you of wine and
Mt 15: 7 Hypocrites! Well did Isaiah **p**
26:68 **P** to us, Christ! Who is the one
Mk 7: 6 Well did Isaiah **p** of you
14:65 **P**!" And the officers struck Him
Lk 22:64 **P**! Who is the one who struck
Acts 2:17 and your daughters shall **p**,
2:18 And they shall **p**.
Rom 12: 6 let us **p** in proportion to
1 Cor 13: 9 For we know in part and we **p** in
14: 1 but especially that you may **p**.
14:24 But if all **p**, and an
14:31 For you can all **p** one by one,
14:39 brethren, desire earnestly to **p**,
Rev 10:11 You must **p** again about many
11: 3 and they will **p** one thousand

PROPHESYING (9/9) PROPHESY

Num 11:27 Eldad and Medad are **p** in the
1 Sam 10: 5 before them; and they will be **p**.
10:13 And when he had finished **p**,
19:20 saw the group of prophets **p**,
Ezra 6:14 they prospered through the **p**
Ezek 11:13 Now it happened, while I was **p**,
1 Cor 11: 4 Every man praying or **p**,
14: 6 revelation, by knowledge, by **p**,
14:22 but **p** is not for unbelievers

PROPHET (242/227) PROPHESY, PROPHET'S, PROPHETS

Gen 20: 7 the man's wife; for he is a **p**,
Ex 7: 1 your brother shall be your **p**.
Num 12: 6 If there is a **p** among you,
Deut 13: 1 If there arises among you a **p** or
13: 3 listen to the words of that **p**
13: 5 But that **p** or that dreamer of
18:15 God will raise up for you a **P**
18:18 I will raise up for them a **P**
18:20 But the **p** who presumes to speak
18:20 that **p** shall die.'
18:22 when a **p** speaks in the name of
18:22 the **p** has spoken it
34:10 has not arisen in Israel a **p**
Judg 6: 8 that the LORD sent a **p** to the
1 Sam 3:20 had been established as a **p**
9: 9 he who is now called a **p**
22: 5 Now the **p** Gad said to David,
2 Sam 7: 2 the king said to Nathan the **p**,
12:25 by the hand of Nathan the **p**:
24:11 of the LORD came to the **p** Gad,
1 Ki 1: 8 son of Jehoiada, Nathan the **p**,
1:10 he did not invite Nathan the **p**,
1:22 Nathan the **p** also came in.
1:23 saying, "Here is Nathan the **p**.
1:32 Zadok the priest, Nathan the **p**,
1:34 the priest and Nathan the **p**
1:38 Zadok the priest, Nathan the **p**,
1:44 Zadok the priest, Nathan the **p**,
1:45 the priest and Nathan the **p**
11:29 that the **p** Ahijah the Shilonite
13:11 Now an old **p** dwelt in Bethel,
13:18 I too am a **p** as you are, and
13:20 of the LORD came to the **p** who
13:23 the **p** whom he had brought back.
13:25 it in the city where the old **p**
13:26 Now when the **p** who had brought
13:29 And the **p** took up the corpse of
13:29 So the old **p** came to the city
14: 2 Ahijah the **p** is there, who
14:18 His servant Ahijah the **p**.
16: 7 word of the LORD came by the **p**
16:12 against Baasha by Jehu the **p**,
18:22 I alone am left a **p** of the
18:36 that Elijah the **p** came near and
19:16 Meholah you shall anoint as **p**
20:13 Suddenly a **p** approached Ahab
20:22 And the **p** came to the king of
20:38 Then the **p** departed and waited
22: 7 Is there not still a **p** of the
2 Ki 3:11 Is there no **p** of the LORD
5: 3 my master were with the **p** who
5: 8 he shall know that there is a **p**
5:13 if the **p** had told you to do
6:12 the **p** who is in Israel, tells
9: 1 And Elisha the **p** called one of
9: 4 young man, the servant of the **p**,
14:25 the **p** who was from Gath
19: 2 with sackcloth, to Isaiah the **p**,
20: 1 near death. And Isaiah the **p**,
20:11 So Isaiah the **p** cried out to the
20:14 Then Isaiah the **p** went to King
23:18 with the bones of the **p** who
1 Chr 17: 1 that David said to Nathan the **p**,
29:29 in the book of Nathan the **p**,
2 Chr 9:29 in the book of Nathan the **p**,
12: 5 Then Shemaiah the **p** came to
12:15 in the book of Shemaiah the **p**,
13:22 written in the annals of the **p**
15: 8 and the prophecy of Oded the **p**,
18: 6 Is there not still a **p** of the
21:12 came to him from Elijah the **p**,
25:15 and He sent him a **p** who said to
25:16 Then the **p** ceased, and said,
26:22 the **p** Isaiah the son of Amoz
28: 9 But a **p** of the LORD was there,
29:25 seer, and of Nathan the **p**;
32:20 of this King Hezekiah and the **p**
32:32 in the vision of Isaiah the **p**,
35:18 since the days of Samuel the **p**;
36:12 himself before Jeremiah the **p**,
Ezra 5: 1 Then the **p** Haggai and Zechariah
6:14 the prophesying of Haggai the **p**
Ps 51: of David when Nathan the **p**
74: 9 There is no longer any **p**;
Isa 3: 2 of war, The judge and the **p**,
9:15 The **p** who teaches lies, he is
28: 7 The priest and the **p** have
37: 2 with sackcloth, to Isaiah the **p**,
38: 1 near death. And Isaiah the **p**,
39: 3 Then Isaiah the **p** went to King
Jer 1: 5 I ordained you a **p** to the
6:13 And from the **p** even to the
8:10 From the **p** even to the priest
14:18 both **p** and priest go about in a
18:18 wise, nor the word from the **p**.
20: 2 Pashhur struck Jeremiah the **p**,
23:11 For both **p** and priest are
23:28 The **p** who has a dream, let him
23:33 when these people or the **p**
23:34 And as for the **p** and the
23:37 "Thus you shall say to the **p**,
25: 2 which Jeremiah the **p** spoke to
28: 1 Hananiah the son of Azur the **p**,
28: 5 Then the **p** Jeremiah spoke to
28: 5 prophet Jeremiah spoke to the **p**
28: 6 and the **p** Jeremiah said, "Amen!
28: 9 As for the **p** who prophesies of
28: 9 when the word of the **p** comes to
28: 9 the **p** will be known as one
28:10 Then Hananiah the **p** took the
28:10 prophet took the yoke off the **p**
28:11 And the **p** Jeremiah went his
28:12 after Hananiah the **p** had broken
28:12 the yoke from the neck of the **p**
28:15 Then the **p** Jeremiah said to
28:15 Jeremiah said to Hananiah the **p**,
28:17 So Hananiah the **p** died the same
29: 1 the letter that Jeremiah the **p**
29:26 and considers himself a **p**,
29:27 Anathoth who makes himself a **p**
29:29 the hearing of Jeremiah the **p**.
32: 2 and Jeremiah the **p** was shut up
34: 6 Then Jeremiah the **p** spoke all
36: 8 to all that Jeremiah the **p**
36:26 the scribe and Jeremiah the **p**,
37: 2 LORD which He spoke by the **p**
37: 3 to the **p** Jeremiah, saying,
37: 6 word of the LORD came to the **p**
37:13 and he seized Jeremiah the **p**,
38: 9 have done to Jeremiah the **p**,
38:10 and lift Jeremiah the **p** out of
38:14 sent and had Jeremiah the **p**
42: 2 and said to Jeremiah the **p**,
42: 4 Then Jeremiah the **p** said to
43: 6 and Jeremiah the **p** and Baruch
45: 1 The word that Jeremiah the **p**
46: 1 which came to Jeremiah the **p**
46:13 LORD spoke to Jeremiah the **p**,
47: 1 that came to Jeremiah the **p**
49:34 that came to Jeremiah the **p**
50: 1 the Chaldeans by Jeremiah the **p**.
51:59 The word which Jeremiah the **p**
Lam 2:20 Should the priest and **p** be
Ezek 2: 5 yet they will know that a **p** has
7:26 will seek a vision from a **p**;
14: 4 and then comes to the **p**,
14: 7 then comes to a **p** to inquire of
14: 9 And if the **p** is induced to speak
14: 9 I the LORD have induced that **p**,
14:10 the punishment of the **p** shall
33:33 then they will know that a **p** has
Dan 9: 2 LORD through Jeremiah the **p**,
Hos 4: 5 The **p** also shall stumble with
9: 7 Israel knows! The **p** is a
9: 8 But the **p** is a fowler's snare
12:13 By a **p** the LORD brought Israel
12:13 And by a **p** he was preserved.
Am 7:14 to Amaziah: "I was no **p**,
7:14 Nor was I a son of a **p**,
Hab 1: 1 The burden which the **p** Habakkuk
3: 1 A prayer of Habakkuk the **p**,
Hag 1: 1 the LORD came by Haggai the **p**
1: 3 the LORD came by Haggai the **p**,
1:12 and the words of Haggai the **p**,
2: 1 the LORD came by Haggai the **p**,
2:10 the LORD came by Haggai the **p**,
Zech 1: 1 the son of Iddo the **p**,
1: 7 the son of Iddo the **p**:
13: 4 be in that day that every **p**
13: 5 "But he will say, 'I am no **p**,
Mal 4: 5 I will send you Elijah the **p**
Mt 1:22 by the Lord through the **p**,
2: 5 for thus it is written by the **p**:
2:15 by the Lord through the **p**,
2:17 was spoken by Jeremiah the **p**,
3: 3 he who was spoken of by the **p**
4:14 was spoken by Isaiah the **p**,
8:17 was spoken by Isaiah the **p**,
10:41 He who receives a **p** in the name
10:41 a prophet in the name of a **p**
11: 9 what did you go out to see? A **p**?
11: 9 I say to you, and more than a **p**.
12:17 was spoken by Isaiah the **p**,
12:39 to it except the sign of the **p**
13:35 which was spoken by the **p**,
13:57 A **p** is not without honor except
14: 5 because they counted him as a **p**.
16: 4 to it except the sign of the **p**

21: 4 which was spoken by the ***p***,
21:11 the ***p*** from Nazareth of
21:26 for all count John as a ***p***.
21:46 because they took Him for a ***p***.
24:15 spoken of by Daniel the ***p***,
27: 9 was spoken by Jeremiah the ***p***,
27:35 which was spoken by the ***p***:
Mk 6: 4 A ***p*** is not without honor except
6:15 And others said, "It is the ***P***,
11:32 counted John to have been a ***p***
13:14 spoken of by Daniel the ***p***,
Lk 1:76 will be called the ***p*** of the
3: 4 of the words of Isaiah the ***p***,
4:17 He was handed the book of the ***p***
4:24 no ***p*** is accepted in his own
4:27 in the time of Elisha the ***p***,
7:16 A great ***p*** has risen up among
7:26 what did you go out to see? A ***p***?
7:26 I say to you, and more than a ***p***.
7:28 women there is not a greater ***p***
7:39 "This man, if He were a ***p***,
11:29 except the sign of Jonah the ***p***.
13:33 for it cannot be that a ***p***
20: 6 are persuaded that John was a ***p***.
24:19 who was a ***P*** mighty in deed and
Jn 1:21 "I am not." "Are you the ***P***?
1:23 as the ***p*** Isaiah said."
1:25 Christ, nor Elijah, nor the ***P***?
4:19 I perceive that You are a ***p***.
4:44 Himself testified that a ***p*** has
6:14 This is truly the ***P*** who is to
7:40 said, "Truly this is the ***P***.
7:52 for no ***p*** has arisen out of
9:17 eyes?" He said, "He is a ***p***.
12:38 that the word of Isaiah the ***p***
Acts 2:16 is what was spoken by the ***p***
2:30 "Therefore, being a ***p***,
3:22 raise up for you a ***P***
3:23 who will not hear that ***P***
7:37 raise up for you a ***P***
7:48 with hands, as the ***p*** says:
8:28 he was reading Isaiah the ***p***.
8:30 and heard him reading the ***p***
8:34 of whom does the ***p*** say this, of
13: 6 a certain sorcerer, a false ***p***,
13:20 fifty years, until Samuel the ***p***.
21:10 a certain ***p*** named Agabus came
28:25 rightly through Isaiah the ***p***
1 Cor 14:37 thinks himself to be a ***p*** or
Titus 1:12 a ***p*** of their own, said,
2 Pe 2:16 restrained the madness of the ***p***.
Rev 16:13 out of the mouth of the false ***p***.
19:20 and with him the false ***p*** who
20:10 the beast and the false ***p*** are.

PROPHET'S (1/1) PROPHET

Mt 10:41 shall receive a ***p*** reward.

PROPHETESS (8/8) PROPHESY

Ex 15:20 Then Miriam the ***p***,
Judg 4: 4 Now Deborah, a ***p***,
2 Ki 22:14 and Asaiah went to Huldah the ***p***,
2 Chr 34:22 appointed went to Huldah the ***p***,
Neh 6:14 and the ***p*** Noadiah and the rest
Isa 8: 3 Then I went to the ***p***,
Lk 2:36 Now there was one, Anna, a ***p***,
Rev 2:20 Jezebel, who calls herself a ***p***,

PROPHETIC (2/2) PROPHECY

Rom 16:26 and by the ***p*** Scriptures has
2 Pe 1:19 And so we have the ***p*** word

PROPHETS (237/225) PROPHET

Num 11:29 all the LORD's people were ***p***
1 Sam 10: 5 that you will meet a group of ***p***
10:10 there was a group of ***p*** to meet
10:11 indeed prophesied among the ***p***,
10:11 Is Saul also among the ***p***?"
10:12 "Is Saul also among the ***p***?
19:20 when they saw the group of ***p***
19:24 "Is Saul also among the ***p***?
28: 6 dreams or by Urim or by the ***p***.
28:15 neither by ***p*** nor by dreams.
1 Ki 18: 4 while Jezebel massacred the ***p***
18: 4 had taken one hundred ***p*** and
18:13 I did when Jezebel killed the ***p***
18:13 hundred men of the LORD's ***p***,
18:19 the four hundred and fifty ***p*** of
18:19 and the four hundred ***p*** of
18:20 and gathered the ***p*** together on
18:22 but Baal's ***p*** are four hundred
18:25 Now Elijah said to the ***p*** of
18:40 Seize the ***p*** of Baal! Do not let
19: 1 how he had executed all the ***p***
19:10 and killed Your ***p*** with the
19:14 and killed Your ***p*** with the
20:35 man of the sons of the ***p*** said
20:41 recognized him as one of the ***p***.
22: 6 king of Israel gathered the ***p***
22:10 and all the ***p*** prophesied before
22:12 And all the ***p*** prophesied so,
22:13 the words of the ***p*** with one
22:22 in the mouth of all his ***p***.
22:23 in the mouth of all these ***p*** of
2 Ki 2: 3 Now the sons of the ***p*** who were
2: 5 Now the sons of the ***p*** who were
2: 7 fifty men of the sons of the ***p***
2:15 Now when the sons of the ***p*** who
3:13 Go to the ***p*** of your father and
3:13 of your father and the ***p*** of
4: 1 the wives of the sons of the ***p***
4:38 Now the sons of the ***p*** were
4:38 boil stew for the sons of the ***p***.
5:22 young men of the sons of the ***p***
6: 1 And the sons of the ***p*** said to
9: 1 called one of the sons of the ***p***,
9: 7 the blood of My servants the ***p***,
10:19 call to me all the ***p*** of Baal,
17:13 against Judah, by all of His ***p***,
17:13 to you by My servants the ***p***.
17:23 said by all His servants the ***p***.
21:10 spoke by His servants the ***p***,
23: 2 the priests and the ***p*** and all
24: 2 spoken by His servants the ***p***.
1 Chr 16:22 And do My ***p*** no harm."
2 Chr 18: 5 king of Israel gathered the ***p***
18: 9 and all the ***p*** prophesied before
18:11 And all the ***p*** prophesied so,
18:12 the words of the ***p*** with one
18:21 in the mouth of all his ***p***.
18:22 spirit in the mouth of these ***p***
20:20 be established; believe His ***p***,
24:19 Yet He sent ***p*** to them, to bring
29:25 of the LORD by his ***p***.
36:16 His words, and scoffed at His ***p***,
Ezra 5: 1 Zechariah the son of Iddo, ***p***,
5: 2 and the ***p*** of God were with
9:11 by Your servants the ***p***,
Neh 6: 7 And you have also appointed ***p*** to
6:14 Noadiah and the rest of the ***p***
9:26 their backs And killed Your ***p***,
9:30 them by Your Spirit in Your ***p***.
9:32 princes, Our priests and our ***p***,
Ps 105:15 And do My ***p*** no harm."
Isa 29:10 closed your eyes, namely, the ***p***;
30:10 "Do not see," And to the ***p***,
Jer 2: 8 The ***p*** prophesied by Baal,
2:26 and their priests and their ***p***,
2:30 Your sword has devoured your ***p***
4: 9 And the ***p*** shall wonder."
5:13 And the ***p*** become wind, For the
5:31 The ***p*** prophesy falsely,
7:25 to you all My servants the ***p***,
8: 1 priests, and the bones of the ***p***,
13:13 throne, the priests, the ***p***,
14:13 the ***p*** say to them, 'You shall
14:14 The ***p*** prophesy lies in My name.
14:15 the LORD concerning the ***p*** who
14:15 By sword and famine those ***p***
23: 9 me is broken Because of the ***p***;
23:13 I have seen folly in the ***p***
23:14 seen a horrible thing in the ***p***
23:15 LORD of hosts concerning the ***p***:
23:15 For from the ***p*** of Jerusalem
23:16 listen to the words of the ***p***
23:21 "I have not sent these ***p***,
23:25 I have heard what the ***p*** have
23:26 this be in the heart of the ***p***
23:26 Indeed they are ***p*** of the
23:30 behold, I am against the ***p***,
23:31 "Behold, I am against the ***p***,
25: 4 to you all His servants the ***p***,
26: 5 the words of My servants the ***p***
26: 7 So the priests and the ***p*** and
26: 8 that the priests and the ***p*** and
26:11 And the priests and the ***p*** spoke
26:16 said to the priests and the ***p***,
27: 9 do not listen to your ***p***,
27:14 listen to the words of the ***p***
27:15 you and the ***p*** who prophesy to
27:16 listen to the words of your ***p***
27:18 'But if they are ***p***,
28: 8 The ***p*** who have been before me
29: 1 captive—to the priests, the ***p***,
29: 8 Do not let your ***p*** and your
29:15 The LORD has raised up ***p*** for us
29:19 to them by My servants the ***p***,
32:32 princes, their priests, their ***p***,
35:15 to you all My servants the ***p***,
37:19 Where now are your ***p*** who
44: 4 to you all My servants the ***p***,
Lam 2: 9 And her ***p*** find no vision from
2:14 Your ***p*** have seen for you
4:13 Because of the sins of her ***p***
Ezek 13: 2 prophesy against the ***p*** of
13: 3 GOD: "Woe to the foolish ***p***,
13: 4 your ***p*** are like foxes in the
13: 9 My hand will be against the ***p***
13:16 the ***p*** of Israel who prophesy
22:25 The conspiracy of her ***p*** in her
22:28 Her ***p*** plastered them with
38:17 days by My servants the ***p*** of
Dan 9: 6 we heeded Your servants the ***p***,
9:10 before us by His servants the ***p***.
Hos 6: 5 I have hewn them by the ***p***,
12:10 I have also spoken by the ***p***,
12:10 through the witness of the ***p***.
Am 2:11 up some of your sons as ***p***,
2:12 And commanded the ***p*** saying,
3: 7 secret to His servants the ***p***.
Mic 3: 5 says the LORD concerning the ***p***
3: 6 The sun shall go down on the ***p***,
3:11 And her ***p*** divine for money.
Zeph 3: 4 Her ***p*** are insolent, treacherous
Zech 1: 4 to whom the former ***p*** preached,
1: 5 where are they? And the ***p***,
1: 6 I commanded My servants the ***p***,
7: 3 the LORD of hosts, and the ***p***,
7: 7 through the former ***p*** when
7:12 His Spirit through the former ***p***.
8: 9 words by the mouth of the ***p***,
13: 2 I will also cause the ***p*** and the
Mt 2:23 which was spoken by the ***p***,
5:12 for so they persecuted the ***p***
5:17 to destroy the Law or the ***P***.
7:12 for this is the Law and the ***P***.
7:15 "Beware of false ***p***,
11:13 For all the ***p*** and the law
13:17 I say to you that many ***p*** and
16:14 others Jeremiah or one of the ***p***.
22:40 hang all the Law and the ***P***.
23:29 you build the tombs of the ***p***
23:30 with them in the blood of the ***p***.
23:31 of those who murdered the ***p***.
23:34 indeed, I send you ***p***,
23:37 the one who kills the ***p*** and
24:11 Then many false ***p*** will rise up
24:24 For false christs and false ***p***
26:56 that the Scriptures of the ***p***
Mk 1: 2 As it is written in the ***P***:
6:15 Prophet, or like one of the ***p***.
8:28 and others, one of the ***p***.
13:22 For false christs and false ***p***
Lk 1:70 by the mouth of His holy ***p***,
6:23 their fathers did to the ***p***.
6:26 their fathers to the false ***p***.
9: 8 by others that one of the old ***p***
9:19 say that one of the old ***p*** has
10:24 for I tell you that many ***p*** and
11:47 you build the tombs of the ***p***,
11:49 I will send them ***p*** and apostles,
11:50 that the blood of all the ***p***
13:28 Isaac and Jacob and all the ***p***
13:34 the one who kills the ***p*** and
16:16 The law and the ***p*** were until
16:29 him, 'They have Moses and the ***p***;
16:31 do not hear Moses and the ***p***,
18:31 that are written by the ***p***
24:25 to believe in all that the ***p***
24:27 at Moses and all the ***P***,
24:44 in the Law of Moses and the ***P***
Jn 1:45 in the law, and also the ***p***,
6:45 "It is written in the ***p***,
8:52 Abraham is dead, and the ***p***;
8:53 And the ***p*** are dead. Whom do You
Acts 3:18 by the mouth of all His ***p***,
3:21 by the mouth of all His holy ***p***
3:24 "Yes, and all the ***p***,
3:25 "You are sons of the ***p***,
7:42 is written in the book of the ***P***:
7:52 Which of the ***p*** did your fathers
10:43 To Him all the ***p*** witness that,
11:27 And in these days ***p*** came from
13: 1 at Antioch there were certain ***p***
13:15 reading of the Law and the ***P***,
13:27 nor even the voices of the ***P***
13:40 what has been spoken in the ***p***
15:15 with this the words of the ***p***
15:32 themselves being ***p*** also,
24:14 written in the Law and in the ***P***.
26:22 things than those which the ***p***
26:27 Agrippa, do you believe the ***p***?
28:23 both the Law of Moses and the ***P***,
Rom 1: 2 promised before through His ***p***
3:21 witnessed by the Law and the ***P***,
11: 3 they have killed Your ***p***
1 Cor 12:28 first apostles, second ***p***,
12:29 Are all apostles? Are all ***p***?
14:29 Let two or three ***p*** speak, and
14:32 And the spirits of the ***p*** are
14:32 prophets are subject to the ***p***.
Eph 2:20 of the apostles and ***p***,
3: 5 to His holy apostles and ***p***:
4:11 some to be apostles, some ***p***,
1 Th 2:15 the Lord Jesus and their own ***p***,
Heb 1: 1 past to the fathers by the ***p***,
11:32 of David and Samuel and the ***p***:
Jas 5:10 My brethren, take the ***p***,
1 Pe 1:10 Of this salvation the ***p*** have
2 Pe 2: 1 But there were also false ***p***
3: 2 spoken before by the holy ***p***,
1 Jn 4: 1 because many false ***p*** have gone
Rev 10: 7 declared to His servants the ***p***.
11:10 because these two ***p*** tormented
11:18 reward Your servants the ***p*** and
16: 6 shed the blood of saints and ***p***,
18:20 and you holy apostles and ***p***,
18:24 in her was found the blood of ***p***
22: 6 And the Lord God of the holy ***p***
22: 9 and of your brethren the ***p***,

PROPITIATION (4/4)

Rom 3:25 whom God set forth as a ***p*** by
Heb 2:17 to make ***p*** for the sins of the
1 Jn 2: 2 And He Himself is the ***p*** for our
4:10 and sent His Son to be the ***p***

PROPORTION (2/2)

Num 35: 8 in ***p*** to the inheritance that
Rom 12: 6 let us prophesy in ***p*** to our

PROPORTIONS (1/1)

Job 41:12 mighty power, or his graceful ***p***.

PROPOSE (3/3) PROPOSED

Gen 11: 6 now nothing that they ***p*** to do
1 Ki 5: 5 I ***p*** to build a house for the
2 Chr 28:10 And now you ***p*** to force the

PROPOSED (4/4) PROPOSE

1 Sam 25:39 And David sent and ***p*** to
Jer 49:20 And His purposes that He has ***p***
50:45 And His purposes that He has ***p***
Acts 1:23 And they ***p*** two: Joseph called

PROPPED (2/2)

1 Ki 22:35 and the king was ***p*** up in his
2 Chr 18:34 king of Israel ***p*** himself up

PROPRIETY (1/1)

1 Tim 2: 9 with ***p*** and moderation, not with

PROSECUTOR (1/1)

Job 31:35 That my ***P*** had written a book!

PROSELYTE (2/2) PROSELYTES

Mt 23:15 land and sea to win one ***p***,
Acts 6: 5 a ***p*** from Antioch,

PROSELYTES (2/2) PROSELYTE

Acts 2:10 from Rome, both Jews and ***p***,
13:43 many of the Jews and devout ***p***

PROSPECT (2/2)

Prov 24:14 have found it, there is a ***p***,
24:20 For there will be no ***p*** for the

PROSPER (49/48) PROSPERED, PROSPERITY, PROSPEROUS, PROSPERS

Gen 24:40 send His angel with you and ***p***
24:42 if You will now ***p*** the way in
26:13 The man began to ***p***,
39: 3 the LORD made all he did to ***p***
39:23 he did, the LORD made it ***p***.
Deut 28:29 you shall not ***p*** in your ways;
29: 9 that you may ***p*** in all that you
30: 5 He will ***p*** you and multiply you
Josh 1: 7 that you may ***p*** wherever you go.
Ruth 4:11 and may you ***p*** in Ephrathah and
1 Ki 2: 3 that you may ***p*** in all that you
22:12 "Go up to Ramoth Gilead and ***p***,
22:15 And he answered him, "Go and ***p***,
1 Chr 22:11 be with you; and may you ***p***,
22:13 "Then you will ***p***,
2 Chr 13:12 for you shall not ***p***!"
18:11 "Go up to Ramoth Gilead and ***p***,
18:14 And he said, "Go and ***p***,
20:20 His prophets, and you shall ***p***.
24:20 the LORD, so that you cannot ***p***?
26: 5 the LORD, God made him ***p***.
Neh 1:11 and let Your servant ***p*** this
2:20 God of heaven Himself will ***p***
Job 8: 6 And ***p*** your rightful dwelling
12: 6 The tents of robbers ***p***,
Ps 1: 3 And whatever he does shall ***p***.
122: 6 May they ***p*** who love you.
Prov 28:13 who covers his sins will not ***p***,
Eccl 11: 6 you do not know which will ***p***,
Isa 48:15 brought him, and his way will ***p***.
53:10 pleasure of the LORD shall ***p***
54:17 formed against you shall ***p***,
55:11 And it shall ***p*** in the thing
Jer 2:37 And you will not ***p*** by them.
5:28 of the fatherless; Yet they ***p***,
10:21 Therefore they shall not ***p***,
12: 1 does the way of the wicked ***p***?
20:11 ashamed, for they will not ***p***.
22:30 A man who shall not ***p*** in his
22:30 none of his descendants shall ***p***,
23: 5 A King shall reign and ***p***,
Lam 1: 5 the master, Her enemies ***p***;
Ezek 17:15 and many people. Will he ***p***?
Dan 8:24 And shall ***p*** and thrive;
8:25 He shall cause deceit to ***p***
11:27 same table; but it shall not ***p***,
11:36 and shall ***p*** till the wrath has
1 Cor 16: 2 aside, storing up as he may ***p***,
3 Jn 2 I pray that you may ***p*** in all

PROSPERED (12/12) PROSPER

Gen 24:56 since the LORD has ***p*** my way;
2 Sam 11: 7 were doing, and how the war ***p***.
2 Ki 18: 7 he ***p*** wherever he went. And he
1 Chr 29:23 of David his father, and ***p***;
2 Chr 14: 7 So they built and ***p***.
31:21 it with all his heart. So he ***p***.
32:30 Hezekiah ***p*** in all his works.
Ezra 6:14 and they ***p*** through the
Job 9: 4 himself against Him and ***p***?
Prov 28:25 trusts in the LORD will be ***p***.
Dan 6:28 So this Daniel ***p*** in the reign
8:12 He did all this and ***p***.

PROSPERING (2/2)

Gen 26:13 and continued ***p*** until he became
Ps 10: 5 His ways are always ***p***;

PROSPERITY (24/24) PROSPER

Deut 23: 6 seek their peace nor their ***p***
1 Sam 25: 6 say to him who lives in ***p***:
1 Ki 10: 7 Your wisdom and ***p*** exceed the
Ezra 9:12 and never seek their peace or ***p***,
Job 15:21 In ***p*** the destroyer comes upon
21:16 Indeed their ***p*** is not in their
30:15 And my ***p*** has passed like a
36:11 shall spend their days in ***p***,
Ps 25:13 He himself shall dwell in ***p***,
30: 6 Now in my ***p*** I said, "I shall
35:27 Who has pleasure in the ***p*** of
68: 6 out those who are bound into ***p***;
73: 3 When I saw the ***p*** of the
118:25 O LORD, I pray, send now ***p***.
122: 7 ***P*** within your palaces."
Eccl 7:14 In the day of ***p*** be joyful,
Jer 22:21 I spoke to you in your ***p***,
33: 9 all the goodness and all the ***p***
Lam 3:17 from peace; I have forgotten ***p***.
Dan 4:27 may be a lengthening of your ***p***.
8:25 shall destroy many in their ***p***.
Zech 1:17 again spread out through ***p***;
Acts 19:25 you know that we have our ***p*** by
24: 2 and ***p*** is being brought to this

PROSPEROUS (8/8) PROSPER

Gen 24:21 LORD had made his journey ***p***
26:13 until he became very ***p***;
30:43 the man became exceedingly ***p***,
Josh 1: 8 then you will make your way ***p***,
Judg 18: 5 on which we go will be ***p***.
Ps 22:29 All the ***p*** of the earth
Zech 7: 7 around it were inhabited and ***p***,
8:12 'For the seed shall be ***p***,

PROSPEROUSLY (1/1)

Ps 45: 4 And in Your majesty ride ***p***

PROSPERS (5/5) PROSPER

Deut 15:16 since he ***p*** with you,
Ezra 5: 8 work goes on diligently and ***p***
Ps 37: 7 not fret because of him who ***p***
Prov 17: 8 Wherever he turns, he ***p***.
3 Jn 2 in health, just as your soul ***p***.

PROSTITUTE (3/3)

Lev 19:29 Do not ***p*** your daughter, to
20: 5 and all who ***p*** themselves with
20: 6 to ***p*** himself with them, I will

PROSTRATE (4/4)

Job 9:13 The allies of the proud lie ***p***
Isa 46: 6 They ***p*** themselves, yes, they
60:14 who despised you shall fall ***p***
Dan 2:46 ***p*** before Daniel, and commanded

PROSTRATED (6/6)

Gen 43:28 bowed their heads down and ***p***
Deut 9:25 Thus I ***p*** myself before the
2 Sam 1: 2 he fell to the ground and ***p***
9: 6 he fell on his face and ***p***
14: 4 on her face to the ground and ***p***
1 Chr 29:20 and bowed their heads and ***p***

PROSTRATING (1/1)

Deut 9:25 days and forty nights I kept ***p***

PROTECT (1/1)

Esth 8:11 city to gather together and ***p***

PROTECTED (3/3)

1 Sam 25:21 Surely in vain I have ***p*** all that
Esth 9:16 gathered together and ***p*** their
Mk 6:20 and he ***p*** him. And when he heard

PROTECTION (3/3)

Num 14: 9 their ***p*** has departed from them,
2 Sam 21: 2 children of Israel had sworn ***p***
Isa 22: 8 He removed the ***p*** of Judah.

PROTEST (1/1)

Isa 3: 7 In that day he will ***p***,

PROTESTED (1/1)

Acts 23: 9 Pharisees' party arose and ***p***,

PROUD (47/47) PRIDE, PROUDLY

Job 9:13 The allies of the ***p*** lie
28: 8 The ***p*** lions have not trodden
38:11 And here your ***p*** waves must
40:11 Look on everyone who is ***p***,
40:12 Look on everyone who is ***p***,
Ps 10: 4 The wicked in his ***p*** countenance
12: 3 And the tongue that speaks ***p***
31:23 And fully repays the ***p*** person.
40: 4 And does not respect the ***p***,
86:14 the ***p*** have risen against me,
94: 2 Render punishment to the ***p***.
101: 5 who has a haughty look and a ***p***
119:21 You rebuke the ***p***—
119:51 The ***p*** have me in great
119:69 The ***p*** have forged a lie against
119:78 Let the ***p*** be ashamed, For they
119:85 The ***p*** have dug pits for me,
119:122 Do not let the ***p*** oppress me.
123: 4 With the contempt of the ***p***.
138: 6 But the ***p*** He knows from afar.
140: 5 The ***p*** have hidden a snare for
Prov 6:17 A ***p*** look, A lying tongue,
15:25 will destroy the house of the ***p***,
16: 5 Everyone ***p*** in heart is an
16:19 to divide the spoil with the ***p***.
21: 4 a ***p*** heart, And the plowing of
21:24 ***p*** and haughty man—Scoffer"
28:25 He who is of a ***p*** heart stirs up
Eccl 7: 8 in spirit is better than the ***p***
Isa 2:12 come upon everything ***p*** and
13:11 halt the arrogance of the ***p***,
16: 6 pride of Moab—He is very ***p***—
Jer 13:15 and give ear: Do not be ***p***,
43: 2 and all the ***p*** men spoke, saying
48:29 of Moab (He is exceedingly ***p***)
50:29 For she has been ***p*** against the
50:32 The most ***p*** shall stumble and
Hab 2: 4 "Behold the ***p***, His soul is not
2: 5 He is a ***p*** man, And he does
Mal 3:15 So now we call the ***p*** blessed,
4: 1 like an oven, And all the ***p***,
Lk 1:51 He has scattered the ***p*** in the
Rom 1:30 haters of God, violent, ***p***,
1 Tim 6: 4 he is ***p***, knowing nothing,
2 Tim 3: 2 lovers of money, boasters, ***p***,
Jas 4: 6 says: "God resists the ***p***,
1 Pe 5: 5 for "God resists the ***p***,

PROUDLY (9/9) PROUD

Ex 18:11 thing in which they behaved ***p***,
1 Sam 2: 3 "Talk no more so very ***p***,
Neh 9:10 For You knew that they acted ***p***
9:16 they and our fathers acted ***p***,
9:29 to Your law. Yet they acted ***p***,
Job 39:13 wings of the ostrich wave ***p***,
Ps 17:10 With their mouths they speak ***p***.
31:18 Which speak insolent things ***p***
Ob 12 Nor should you have spoken ***p***

PROVE (8/8) PROVED, PROVING, TEST, TRY

1 Ki 2: 2 and ***p*** yourself a man.
Job 6:25 But what does your arguing ***p***?
9:20 it would ***p*** me perverse.
24:25 who will ***p*** me a liar, And make
Ps 26: 2 and ***p*** me; Try my mind and my
Acts 24:13 Nor can they ***p*** the things of
25: 7 Paul, which they could not ***p***,
Rom 12: 2 that you may ***p*** what is that

PROVED (5/5) PROVE, TESTED

Eccl 7:23 All this I have ***p*** by wisdom.
2 Cor 7:11 In all things you ***p***
8:22 brother whom we have often ***p***
Col 4:11 they have ***p*** to be a comfort to
Heb 2: 2 word spoken through angels ***p***

PROVEN (3/3)

2 Sam 22:31 The word of the LORD is ***p***;
Ps 18:30 The word of the LORD is ***p***;
Phil 2:22 But you know his ***p*** character,

PROVENDER (KJV) See FEED

PROVERB (21/20) PROVERBS

Deut 28:37 become an astonishment, a ***p***,
1 Sam 10:12 Therefore it became a ***p***:
24:13 As the ***p*** of the ancients says,
1 Ki 9: 7 Israel will be a ***p*** and a byword
2 Chr 7:20 and will make it a ***p*** and a
Ps 49: 4 I will incline my ear to a ***p***;
Prov 1: 6 To understand a ***p*** and an
26: 7 lame that hang limp Is a ***p***
26: 9 hand of a drunkard Is a ***p*** in
Isa 14: 4 that you will take up this ***p***
Ezek 12:22 what is this ***p*** that you
12:23 I will lay this ***p*** to rest, and
12:23 shall no more use it as a ***p*** in
14: 8 man and make him a sign and a ***p***,
16:44 proverbs will use this ***p***
18: 2 do you mean when you use this ***p***
18: 3 shall no longer use this ***p***
Mic 2: 4 that day one shall take up a ***p***
Hab 2: 6 not all these take up a ***p***
Lk 4:23 You will surely say this ***p*** to
2 Pe 2:22 to them according to the true ***p***:

PROVERBS (8/8) PROVERB

Num 21:27 Therefore those who speak in ***p***
1 Ki 4:32 He spoke three thousand ***p***,
Job 13:12 Your platitudes are ***p*** of
Prov 1: 1 The ***p*** of Solomon the son of
10: 1 The ***P*** of Solomon: A wise son
25: 1 These also are ***p*** of Solomon
Eccl 12: 9 out and set in order many ***p***.
Ezek 16:44 Indeed everyone who quotes ***p***

PROVES (1/1)

1 Ki 1:52 If he ***p*** himself a worthy man,

PROVIDE (30/29) PROVIDED, PROVIDES, PROVISION

Gen 22: 8 God will **p** for Himself the lamb
30:30 when shall I also **p** for my own
45:11 There I will **p** for you, lest you
50:21 I will **p** for you and your
Ex 21:19 and shall **p** for him to be
Num 6:21 else his hand is able to **p**;
11:22 to **p** enough for them? Or shall
11:22 to **p** enough for them?"
Deut 21: 8 **P** atonement, O LORD, for Your
32:43 He will **p** atonement for His
1 Sam 16:17 **P** me now a man who can play
2 Sam 19:33 and I will **p** for you while you
1 Ki 17: 9 commanded a widow there to **p**
2 Chr 30:18 May the good LORD **p** atonement
Ezra 7:20 you may have occasion to **p**,
Ps 65: 3 You will **p** atonement for them.
65: 9 You **p** their grain, For so You
78:20 Can He **p** meat for His
79: 9 and **p** atonement for our sins,
Prov 27:26 The lambs will **p** your
Jer 18:23 **P** no atonement for their
33: 9 and all the prosperity that I **p**
Ezek 16:63 when I **p** you an atonement for
46:18 he shall **p** an inheritance for
Mt 10: 9 **P** neither gold nor silver nor
26:53 and He will **p** Me with more than
Lk 12:33 **p** yourselves money bags which
Acts 23:24 and **p** mounts to set Paul on, and
24:23 forbid any of his friends to **p**
1 Tim 5: 8 But if anyone does not **p** for his

PROVIDED (21/21) PROVIDE

Gen 22:14 of The LORD it shall be **p**.
24:32 and **p** straw and feed for the
47:12 Then Joseph **p** his father, his
Ex 1:21 that He **p** households for them.
Deut 21: 8 And atonement shall be **p** on
33:21 He **p** the first part for
1 Sam 16: 1 For I have **p** Myself a king
2 Sam 15: 1 this it happened that Absalom **p**
19:32 And he had **p** the king with
1 Ki 4: 7 who **p** food for the king and his
4:27 **p** food for King Solomon and for
2 Chr 2: 7 whom David my father **p**.
32:29 Moreover he **p** cities for
Esth 2: 9 choice maidservants were **p** for
Ps 68:10 **p** from Your goodness for the
Prov 16: 6 and truth Atonement is **p** for
Lk 8: 3 and many others who **p** for Him
12:20 things be which you have **p**?
Acts 20:34 know that these hands have **p**
28:10 they **p** such things as were
Heb 11:40 God having **p** something better

PROVIDES (4/4) PROVIDE

Job 12: 6 In what God **p** by His hand.
38:41 Who **p** food for the raven,
Prov 6: 8 **P** her supplies in the summer,
31:15 And **p** food for her household,

PROVIDING (1/1)

2 Cor 8:21 **p** honorable things, not only in

PROVINCE (27/26) PROVINCES

Ezra 2: 1 these are the people of the **p**
5: 8 king that we went into the **p**
6: 2 in the palace that is in the **p**
7:16 that you may find in all the **p**
Neh 1: 3 from the captivity in the **p**
7: 6 These are the people of the **p**
11: 3 These are the heads of the **p**
Esth 1:22 to each **p** in its own script,
3:12 governors who were over each **p**,
3:12 to every **p** according to its
3:14 to be issued as law in every **p**,
4: 3 And in every **p** where the king's
8: 9 to every **p** in its own script,
8:11 the forces of any people or **p**
8:13 issued as a decree in every **p**
8:17 And in every **p** and city,
9:28 every family, every **p**,
Eccl 5: 8 and righteousness in a **p**,
Dan 2:48 him ruler over the whole **p** of
2:49 over the affairs of the **p** of
3: 1 in the **p** of Babylon.
3:12 set over the affairs of the **p**
3:30 and Abed-Nego in the **p** of
8: 2 which is in the **p** of Elam;
11:24 the richest places of the **p**;
Acts 23:34 he asked what **p** he was from.
25: 1 when Festus had come to the **p**,

PROVINCES (30/29) PROVINCE, REGION

1 Ki 20:14 'By the young leaders of the **p**.
20:15 the young leaders of the **p**,
20:17 The young leaders of the **p** went
20:19 these young leaders of the **p**
Ezra 4:15 city, harmful to kings and **p**,
Esth 1: 1 one hundred and twenty-seven **p**,
1: 3 and the princes of the **p** being
1:16 people who are in all the **p**
1:22 letters to all the king's **p**,
2: 3 appoint officers in all the **p**
2:18 proclaimed a holiday in the **p**
3: 8 among the people in all the **p**
3:13 couriers into all the king's **p**,
4:11 and the people of the king's **p**
8: 5 who are in all the king's **p**.
8: 9 and the princes of the **p** from
8: 9 one hundred and twenty-seven **p**
8:12 on one day in all the **p** of King
9: 2 cities throughout all the **p** of
9: 3 And all the officials of the **p**,
9: 4 spread throughout all the **p**;
9:12 in the rest of the king's **p**?
9:16 of the Jews in the king's **p**
9:20 who were in all the **p** of King
9:30 one hundred and twenty-seven **p**
Eccl 2: 8 treasures of kings and of the **p**.
Lam 1: 1 princess among the **p**
Ezek 19: 8 set against him from the **p** on
Dan 3: 2 and all the officials of the **p**,
3: 3 and all the officials of the **p**

PROVING (1/1) PROVE

Acts 9:22 **p** that this Jesus is the

PROVISION (9/9) PROVIDE

Josh 9: 5 and all the bread of their **p**
9:12 of ours we took hot for our **p**
1 Ki 4: 7 each one made **p** for one month
4:22 Now Solomon's **p** for one day was
1 Chr 29:19 temple for which I have made **p**.
Ps 105:16 He destroyed all the **p** of
132:15 I will abundantly bless her **p**;
Dan 1: 5 appointed for them a daily **p**
Rom 13:14 and make no **p** for the flesh, to

PROVISIONS (19/19)

Gen 14:11 and Gomorrah, and all their **p**,
42:25 and to give them **p** for the
45:21 and he gave them **p** for the
Ex 12:39 nor had they prepared **p** for
Josh 1:11 Prepare **p** for yourselves, for
9:11 Take **p** with you for the journey,
9:14 of Israel took some of their **p**;
Judg 7: 8 So the people took **p** and their
20:10 to make **p** for the people, that
1 Sam 22:10 the LORD for him, gave him **p**,
1 Ki 20:27 were mustered and given **p**,
2 Ki 25:30 And as for his **p**,
1 Chr 12:40 **p** of flour and cakes of figs and
2 Chr 11:23 and he gave them **p** in
Neh 5:14 brothers ate the governor's **p**.
5:18 did not demand the governor's **p**,
13:15 on which they were selling **p**.
Jer 52:34 And as for his **p**,
Lk 9:12 country, and lodge and get **p**;

PROVOCATION (5/5)

Deut 32:19 Because of the **p** of His sons
1 Ki 15:30 because of his **p** with which he
21:22 because of the **p** with which you
Job 17: 2 not my eye dwell on their **p**?
Jer 32:31 this city has been to Me a **p**

PROVOCATIONS (3/3)

2 Ki 23:26 because of all the **p** with which
Neh 9:18 of Egypt,' And worked great **p**,
9:26 And they worked great **p**.

PROVOKE (37/36) PROVOKED, PROVOKING

Ex 23:21 do not **p** Him, for He will not
Deut 4:25 of the LORD your God to **p** Him
9:18 to **p** Him to anger.
31:20 and they will **p** Me and break My
31:29 to **p** Him to anger through the
32:21 But I will **p** them to jealousy
1 Ki 14: 9 gods and molded images to **p** Me
16: 2 to **p** Me to anger with their
16:33 Ahab did more to **p** the LORD
2 Ki 17:11 and they did wicked things to **p**
17:17 to **p** Him to anger.
21: 6 to **p** Him to anger.
22:17 that they might **p** Me to anger
23:19 kings of Israel had made to **p**
2 Chr 33: 6 to **p** Him to anger.
34:25 that they might **p** Me to anger
Job 12: 6 And those who **p** God are
Isa 3: 8 To **p** the eyes of His glory.
65: 3 A people who **p** Me to anger
Jer 7:18 that they may **p** Me to anger.
7:19 'Do they **p** Me to anger?"
7:19 Do they not **p** themselves, to
11:17 done against themselves to **p**
25: 6 and do not **p** Me to anger with
25: 7 that you might **p** Me to anger
32:29 to **p** Me to anger;
32:32 which they have done to **p** Me to
44: 3 which they have committed to **p**
44: 8 in that you **p** Me to wrath with
Ezek 8:17 then they have returned to **p** Me
16:26 your acts of harlotry to **p** Me
Rom 10:19 I will **p** you to jealousy
11:11 to **p** them to jealousy,
11:14 if by any means I may **p** to
1 Cor 10:22 Or do we **p** the Lord to jealousy?
Eph 6: 4 do not **p** your children to
Col 3:21 do not **p** your children, lest

PROVOKED (30/29) PROVOKE

Deut 9: 7 Do not forget how you **p** the
9: 8 Also in Horeb you **p** the LORD to
9:22 and Kibroth Hattaavah you **p**
32:16 They **p** Him to jealousy with
32:16 With abominations they **p** Him
32:21 They have **p** Me to jealousy by
Judg 2:12 and they **p** the LORD to anger.
1 Sam 1: 6 And her rival also **p** her
1: 7 that she **p** her; therefore she
1 Ki 14:22 and they **p** Him to jealousy with
15:30 with which he had **p** the LORD
21:22 with which you have **p** Me to
22:53 and **p** the LORD God of Israel
2 Ki 21:15 and have **p** Me to anger since
23:26 with which Manasseh had **p** Him.
2 Chr 28:25 and **p** to anger the LORD God of
Ezra 5:12 But because our fathers **p** the
Neh 4: 5 for they have **p** You to anger
Ps 78:40 How often they **p** Him in the
78:56 Yet they tested and **p** the Most
78:58 For they **p** Him to anger with
106:29 Thus they **p** Him to anger with
Isa 1: 4 They have **p** to anger The Holy
Jer 8:19 Why have they **p** Me to anger
32:30 the children of Israel have **p**
Ezek 20:28 offered their sacrifices and **p**
Hos 12:14 Ephraim **p** Him to anger most
Zech 8:14 When your fathers **p** Me to
Acts 17:16 his spirit was **p** within him
1 Cor 13: 5 does not seek its own, is not **p**,

PROVOKES (3/3)

Job 16: 3 Or what **p** you that you answer?
Prov 20: 2 Whoever **p** him to anger sins
Ezek 8: 3 which **p** to jealousy.

PROVOKING (5/5) PROVOKE

1 Ki 14:15 **p** the LORD to anger.
16: 7 the sight of the LORD in **p** Him
16:13 in **p** the LORD God of Israel to
16:26 **p** the LORD God of Israel to
Gal 5:26 **p** one another, envying one

PROW (2/2)

Acts 27:30 putting out anchors from the **p**,
27:41 and the **p** stuck fast and

PROWL (1/1)

Ps 12: 8 The wicked **p** on every side,

PROWLER (2/2)

Prov 6:11 poverty come on you like a **p**,
24:34 your poverty come like a **p**,

PRUDENCE (7/7) PRUDENT

2 Chr 2:12 endowed with **p** and
Job 11: 6 they would double your **p**.
12:16 With Him are strength and **p**.
Prov 1: 4 To give **p** to the simple,
8: 5 you simple ones, understand **p**,
8:12 "I, wisdom, dwell with **p**,
Eph 1: 8 toward us in all wisdom and **p**,

PRUDENT (22/22) PRUDENCE, PRUDENTLY

1 Sam 16:18 **p** in speech, and a handsome
Prov 12:16 But a **p** man covers shame.
12:23 A **p** man conceals knowledge,
13:16 Every **p** man acts with
14: 8 The wisdom of the **p** is to
14:15 But the **p** considers well his
14:18 But the **p** are crowned with
15: 5 he who receives correction is **p**.
16:21 wise in heart will be called **p**,
18:15 The heart of the **p** acquires
19:14 But a **p** wife is from the
22: 3 A **p** man foresees evil and
27:12 A **p** man foresees evil and
Isa 5:21 And **p** in their own sight!
10:13 And by my wisdom, for I am **p**;
29:14 the understanding of their **p**
Jer 49: 7 counsel perished from the **p**?
Hos 14: 9 these things. Who is **p**?
Am 5:13 Therefore the **p** keep silent at
Mt 11:25 things from the wise and **p**
Lk 10:21 things from the wise and **p**
1 Cor 1:19 the understanding of the **p**.

PRUDENTLY (2/2) PRUDENT

Eccl 5: 1 Walk **p** when you go to the house
Isa 52:13 My Servant shall deal **p**;

PRUNE (2/2)

Lev 25: 3 and six years you shall **p** your
25: 4 neither sow your field nor **p**

PRUNED (1/1) PRUNES

Isa 5: 6 It shall not be **p** or dug,

PRUNES (1/1) PRUNED, PRUNING, PRUNING (HOOKS)

Jn 15: 2 branch that bears fruit He **p**,

PRUNING (4/4) PRUNES, PRUNING (HOOKS)

Isa 2: 4 And their spears into **p** hooks;
18: 5 cut off the sprigs with **p** hooks
Joel 3:10 into swords And your **p** hooks
Mic 4: 3 And their spears into **p** hooks;

PRUNINGHOOKS (KJV) See PRUNING (HOOKS)

PSALM (83/83) PSALMIST, PSALMS, PSALTERY

1 Chr 16: 7 David first delivered this **p**
Ps 3: A **P** of David when he fled from
4: A **P** of David.
5: A **P** of David.
6: A **P** of David.
8: A **P** of David.
9: A **P** of David.
11: A **P** of David.
12: A **P** of David.
13: A **P** of David.
14: A **P** of David.
15: A **P** of David.
18: A **P** of David the servant of the
19: A **P** of David.
20: A **P** of David.
21: A **P** of David.
22: A **P** of David.
23: A **P** of David.
24: A **P** of David.
25: A **P** of David.
26: A **P** of David.
27: A **P** of David.
28: A **P** of David.
29: A **P** of David.
30: A **P**. A Song at the dedication
31: A **P** of David.
32: A **P** of David. A Contemplation.
34: A **P** of David when he pretended
35: A **P** of David.
36: A **P** of David the servant of the
37: A **P** of David.
38: A **P** of David. To bring to
39: A **P** of David.
40: A **P** of David.
41: A **P** of David.
46: A **P** of the sons of Korah.
47: A **P** of the sons of Korah.
48: A **P** of the sons of Korah.
49: A **P** of the sons of Korah.
50: A **P** of Asaph.
51: A **P** of David when Nathan the
61: A **P** of David.
62: A **P** of David.
63: A **P** of David when he was in the
64: A **P** of David.
65: A **P** of David. A Song.
66: the Chief Musician. A Song. A **P**.
67: On stringed instruments. A **P**.
68: A **P** of David. A Song.
69: A **P** of David.
70: A **P** of David. To bring to
72: A **P** of Solomon.
73: A **P** of Asaph.
75: A **P** of Asaph. A Song.
76: A **P** of Asaph. A Song.
77: A **P** of Asaph.
79: A **P** of Asaph.
80: A Testimony of Asaph. A **P**.
81: A **P** of Asaph.
82: A **P** of Asaph.
83: A **P** of Asaph.
84: A **P** of the sons of Korah.
85: A **P** of the sons of Korah.
87: A **P** of the sons of Korah.
88: A **P** of the sons of Korah.
92: A **P**. A Song for the Sabbath
98: A **P**.
98: 5 the harp and the sound of a **p**,
100: A **P** of Thanksgiving.
101: A **P** of David.
103: A **P** of David.
108: A **P** of David.
109: A **P** of David.
110: A **P** of David.
138: A **P** of David.
139: A **P** of David.
140: A **P** of David.
141: A **P** of David.
143: A **P** of David.
144: A **P** of David.
Acts 13:33 is also written in the second **P**:
13:35 He also says in another **P**:
1 Cor 14:26 together, each of you has a **p**,

PSALMIST (1/1) PSALM

2 Sam 23: 1 And the sweet **p** of Israel:

PSALMS (10/10) PSALM

1 Chr 16: 9 sing **p** to Him; Talk of all His
Neh 12: 8 who led the thanksgiving **p**,
Ps 95: 2 us shout joyfully to Him with **p**.
105: 2 sing **p** to Him; Talk of all His
Lk 20:42 himself said in the Book of **P**:
24:44 and the Prophets and the **P**
Acts 1:20 it is written in the book of **P**:
Eph 5:19 speaking to one another in **p** and
Col 3:16 admonishing one another in **p**
Jas 5:13 anyone cheerful? Let him sing **p**.

PSALTERY (3/3) PSALM

Dan 3: 5 horn, flute, harp, lyre, and **p**,
3:10 horn, flute, harp, lyre, and **p**,
3:15 horn, flute, harp, lyre, and **p**,

PTOLEMAIS (1/1)

Acts 21: 7 voyage from Tyre, we came to **P**,

PUAH (4/4)

Ex 1:15 and the name of the other **P**;
Num 26:23 family of the Tolaites; of **P**,
Judg 10: 1 save Israel Tola the son of **P**,
1 Chr 7: 1 sons of Issachar were Tola, **P**,

PUBLIC (2/2)

Mt 1:19 to make her a **p** example,
Col 2:15 He made a **p** spectacle of them,

PUBLICAN (KJV) See (TAX) COLLECTOR

PUBLICK (KJV) See PUBLIC

PUBLICLY (2/2)

Acts 18:28 vigorously refuted the Jews **p**,
20:20 and taught you **p** and from house

PUBLISHED (3/3)

Esth 3:14 being **p** for all people, that
8:13 decree in every province and **p**
Jon 3: 7 it to be proclaimed and **p**

PUBLIUS (2/2)

Acts 28: 7 of the island, whose name was **P**,
28: 8 happened that the father of **P**

PUDENS (1/1)

2 Tim 4:21 greets you, as well as **P**,

PUFFED (7/7) PUFFS

1 Cor 4: 6 that none of you may be **p** up on
4:18 Now some are **p** up, as though I
4:19 the word of those who are **p** up,
5: 2 And you are **p** up, and have not
13: 4 parade itself, is not **p** up;
Col 2:18 vainly **p** up by his fleshly
1 Tim 3: 6 lest being **p** up with pride he

PUFFS (1/1) PUFFED

1 Cor 8: 1 Knowledge **p** up, but love

PUL (4/3)

2 Ki 15:19 **P** king of Assyria came against
15:19 and Menahem gave **P** a thousand
1 Chr 5:26 stirred up the spirit of **P**
Isa 66:19 to Tarshish and **P** and Lud, who

PULL (14/14) PULLED, PULLING, PULLS

2 Sam 17:13 and we will **p** it into the
1 Ki 13: 4 so that he could not **p** it back
Ps 31: 4 **P** me out of the net which they
Isa 22:19 from your position he will **p**
Jer 1:10 To root out and to **p** down,
12: 3 **P** them out like sheep for the
18: 7 to **p** down, and to destroy it,
24: 6 I will build them and not **p**
42:10 then I will build you and not **p**
Ezek 17: 9 Will he not **p** up its roots,
Hos 10:11 I will make Ephraim **p** a
Mic 2: 8 You **p** off the robe with the
Lk 12:18 I will **p** down my barns and
14: 5 will not immediately **p** him out

PULLED (14/14) PULL

Gen 19:10 reached out their hands and **p**
37:28 so the brothers **p** Joseph up
Deut 21: 3 worked and which has not **p**
Judg 16: 3 **p** them up, bar and all, put
16:14 and **p** out the batten and the
Ezra 6:11 let a timber be **p** from his
Neh 13:25 struck some of them and **p** out
Jer 33: 4 which have been **p** down to
38:13 So they **p** Jeremiah up with ropes
Am 9:15 And no longer shall they be **p**
Mk 5: 4 And the chains had been **p** apart
Lk 17: 6 Be **p** up by the roots and be
Acts 23:10 fearing lest Paul might be **p** to
Jude 12 **p** up by the roots;

PULLING (2/2) PULL

2 Cor 10: 4 in God for **p** down strongholds,
Jude 23 **p** them out of the fire, hating

PULLS (3/3) PULL

Prov 14: 1 But the foolish **p** it down with
Mt 9:16 for the patch **p** away from the
Mk 2:21 or else the new piece **p** away

PULSE (KJV) See SEEDS, VEGETABLES

PULVERIZED (1/1)

2 Ki 23:12 king broke down and **p** there,

PUNISH (47/47) PUNISHED, PUNISHMENT, UNPUNISHED

Lev 26:18 then I will **p** you seven times
26:24 and I will **p** you yet seven
Deut 22:18 city shall take that man and **p**
1 Sam 15: 2 I will **p** Amalek for what he did
Ps 59: 5 Awake to **p** all the nations;
89:32 Then I will **p** their
Prov 17:26 to **p** the righteous is not
Isa 10:12 I will **p** the fruit of the
13:11 I will **p** the world for its
24:21 day That the LORD will **p** on
26:21 comes out of His place To **p**
27: 1 Will **p** Leviathan the fleeing
Jer 5: 9 Shall I not **p** them for these
5:29 Shall I not **p** them for these
6:15 At the time I **p** them,
9: 9 Shall I not **p** them for these
9:25 that I will **p** all who are
11:22 I will **p** them. The young men
14:10 And **p** their sins."
21:14 But I will **p** you according to
23:34 of the LORD!' I will even **p**
25:12 that I will **p** the king of
27: 8 Babylon, that nation I will **p**,
29:32 I will **p** Shemaiah the
30:20 And I will **p** all who oppress
36:31 I will **p** him, his family, and
44:13 For I will **p** those who dwell in
44:29 that I will **p** you in this place,
49: 8 The time that I will **p** him.
50:18 I will **p** the king of Babylon
50:31 The time that I will **p** you.
51:44 I will **p** Bel in Babylon, And I
Lam 4:22 He will **p** your iniquity,
Hos 2:13 I will **p** her For the days of
4: 9 So I will **p** them for their
4:14 I will not **p** your daughters when
8:13 remember their iniquity and **p**
9: 9 He will **p** their sins.
12: 2 And will **p** Jacob according to
Am 3: 2 Therefore I will **p** you for all
3:14 That in the day I **p** Israel for
Zeph 1: 8 That I will **p** the princes and
1: 9 In the same day I will **p** All
1:12 And **p** the men Who are settled
Zech 8:14 Just as I determined to **p** you
10: 3 And I will **p** the goatherds.
2 Cor 10: 6 and being ready to **p** all

PUNISHED (19/19) PUNISH

Ex 21:20 his hand, he shall surely be **p**.
21:21 a day or two, he shall not be **p**;
21:22 he shall surely be **p**
Ezra 9:13 since You our God have **p** us
Job 35:15 because He has not **p** in His
Ps 103:10 Nor **p** us according to our
Prov 21:11 When the scoffer is **p**,
22: 3 the simple pass on and are **p**.
27:12 The simple pass on and are **p**.
Isa 24:22 After many days they will be **p**.
26:14 Therefore You have **p** and
29: 6 You will be **p** by the LORD of
Jer 6: 6 This is the city to be **p**.
44:13 as I have **p** Jerusalem, by the
50:18 As I have **p** the king of
Zeph 3: 7 everything for which I **p** her.
Acts 22: 5 were there to Jerusalem to be **p**.
26:11 And I **p** them often in every
2 Th 1: 9 These shall be **p** with

PUNISHES (2/2)

Job 31:14 when God rises up? When He **p**,
Jer 13:21 What will you say when He **p**

PUNISHING (1/1)

Acts 4:21 finding no way of **p** them,

PUNISHMENT (46/42) PUNISH

Gen 4:13 My **p** is greater than I can
19:15 lest you be consumed in the **p**
Ex 32:34 in the day when I visit for **p**,
32:34 I will visit **p** upon them for
Lev 18:25 therefore I visit the **p** of its
Deut 17: 8 or between one **p** or another,
1 Sam 28:10 no **p** shall come upon you for
2 Ki 7: 9 some **p** will come upon us.
Job 19:29 For wrath brings the **p** of the
Ps 94: 2 Render **p** to the proud.
Prov 19:19 of great wrath will suffer **p**;
Isa 10: 3 will you do in the day of **p**,
30:32 place where the staff of **p**
Jer 8:12 In the time of their **p** They
10:15 In the time of their **p** they
11:23 even the year of their **p**.

23:12 on them, The year of their **p**,
46:21 upon them, The time of their **p**.
46:25 I will bring **p** on Amon of No,
48:44 will bring The year of their **p**,
50:27 has come, the time of their **p**.
51:18 In the time of their **p** they
Lam 3:39 A man for the **p** of his sins?
4: 6 The **p** of the iniquity of the
4: 6 people Is greater than the **p**
4:22 The **p** of your iniquity is
Ezek 14:10 the **p** of the prophet shall be
14:10 shall be the same as the **p** of
Hos 9: 7 The days of **p** have come;
Joel 1:18 the flocks of sheep suffer **p**.
Am 1: 3 I will not turn away its **p**,
1: 6 I will not turn away its **p**,
1: 9 I will not turn away its **p**,
1:11 I will not turn away its **p**,
1:13 I will not turn away its **p**,
2: 1 I will not turn away its **p**,
2: 4 I will not turn away its **p**,
2: 6 I will not turn away its **p**,
Mic 7: 4 day of your watchman and your **p**
Zech 14:19 This shall be the **p** of Egypt and
14:19 punishment of Egypt and the **p**
Mt 25:46 will go away into everlasting **p**,
2 Cor 2: 6 This **p** which was inflicted by
Heb 10:29 Of how much worse **p**,
1 Pe 2:14 who are sent by him for the **p**
2 Pe 2: 9 to reserve the unjust under **p**

PUNISHMENTS (1/1)

Ps 149: 7 And **p** on the peoples;

PUNITES (1/1)

Num 26:23 of Puah, the family of the **P**;

PUNON (2/2)

Num 33:42 from Zalmonah and camped at **P**.
33:43 They departed from **P** and camped

PUR (3/3) PURIM

Esth 3: 7 they cast **P** (that is, the
9:24 and had cast **P** (that is, the
9:26 days Purim, after the name **P**.

PURAH (2/2)

Judg 7:10 go down to the camp with **P** your
7:11 Then he went down with **P** his

PURCHASE (6/5) PURCHASED

Prov 17:16 in the hand of a fool the **p**
Jer 32:11 So I took the **p** deed, both that
32:12 and I gave the **p** deed to Baruch
32:12 the witnesses who signed the **p**
32:14 both this **p** deed which is
32:16 when I had delivered the **p**

PURCHASED (9/9) PURCHASE

Gen 25:10 the field which Abraham **p** from
49:32 the cave that is there were **p**
Ex 15:16 pass over Whom You have **p**.
Job 28:15 It cannot be **p** for gold,
Ps 74: 2 which You have **p** of old,
Acts 1:18 (Now this man **p** a field with the
8:20 that the gift of God could be **p**
20:28 the church of God which He **p**
Eph 1:14 redemption of the **p** possession,

PURCHASES (1/1)

Lev 25:33 And if a man **p** a house from the

PURE (102/97) PURER, PURIFY, PURITY

Ex 25:11 shall overlay it with **p** gold,
25:17 make a mercy seat of **p** gold;
25:24 shall overlay it with **p** gold,
25:29 You shall make them of **p** gold.
25:31 make a lampstand of **p** gold;
25:36 one hammered piece of **p** gold.
25:38 trays shall be of **p** gold.
25:39 be made of a talent of **p** gold,
27:20 that they bring you **p** oil
28:14 shall make two chains of **p** gold
28:22 like braided cords of **p** gold.
28:36 also make a plate of **p** gold
30: 3 and its horns with **p** gold;
30:34 and **p** frankincense with these
30:35 art of the perfumer, salted, **p**,
31: 8 the **p** gold lampstand with all
37: 2 He overlaid it with **p** gold
37: 6 made the mercy seat of **p** gold;
37:11 And he overlaid it with **p** gold,
37:16 He made of **p** gold the utensils
37:17 made the lampstand of **p** gold;
37:22 one hammered piece of **p** gold.
37:23 and its trays of **p** gold.
37:24 Of a talent of **p** gold he made
37:26 And he overlaid it with **p** gold:
37:29 anointing oil and the **p** incense
39:15 like braided cords of **p** gold.
39:25 And they made bells of **p** gold,
39:30 of the holy crown of **p** gold,
39:37 the **p** gold lampstand with its
Lev 24: 2 that they bring to you **p** oil
24: 4 lamps on the **p** gold lampstand
24: 6 on the **p** gold table before the
24: 7 And you shall put **p** frankincense
2 Sam 22:27 With the **p** You will show
22:27 pure You will show Yourself **p**;
1 Ki 6:20 He overlaid it with **p** gold, and
6:21 of the temple with **p** gold.
7:49 the lampstands of **p** gold, five
7:50 and the censers of **p** gold; and
10:18 and overlaid it with **p** gold.
10:21 the Forest of Lebanon were **p**
1 Chr 28:17 also **p** gold for the forks, the
28:17 the pitchers of **p** gold, and the
2 Chr 3: 4 the inside with **p** gold.
4:20 with their lamps of **p** gold,
4:22 and the censers of **p** gold.
9:17 and overlaid it with **p** gold.
9:20 Forest of Lebanon were **p** gold.
13:11 order on the **p** gold table,
Job 4:17 Can a man be more **p** than his
8: 6 If you were **p** and upright,
11: 4 have said, 'My doctrine is **p**,
15:14 is man, that he could be **p**?
15:15 And the heavens are not **p** in
16:17 my hands, And my prayer is **p**.
25: 4 Or how can he be **p** who is
25: 5 And the stars are not **p** in His
28:19 can it be valued in **p** gold.
33: 3 My lips utter **p** knowledge.
33: 9 am **p**, without transgression;
Ps 12: 6 The words of the LORD are **p**
18:26 With the **p** You will show
18:26 pure You will show Yourself **p**;
19: 8 commandment of the LORD is **p**,
21: 3 You set a crown of **p** gold upon
24: 4 has clean hands and a **p** heart,
73: 1 To such as are **p** in heart.
119:140 Your word is very **p**;
Prov 15:26 But the words of the **p** are
16: 2 All the ways of a man are **p** in
20: 9 I am **p** from my sin"?
20:11 Whether what he does is **p** and
21: 8 perverse; But as for the **p**,
30: 5 Every word of God is **p**;
30:12 is a generation that is **p**
Dan 7: 9 of His head was like **p** wool.
Mic 6:11 Shall I count **p** those with the
Zeph 3: 9 to the peoples a **p** language,
Mal 1:11 And a **p** offering; For My name
Mt 5: 8 Blessed are the **p** in heart,
Rom 14:20 All things indeed are **p**,
Phil 4: 8 just, whatever things are **p**,
1 Tim 1: 5 is love from a **p** heart,
3: 9 the faith with a **p** conscience.
5:22 people's sins; keep yourself **p**.
2 Tim 1: 3 I serve with a **p** conscience,
2:22 on the Lord out of a **p** heart.
Titus 1:15 To the **p** all things are pure,
1:15 To the pure all things are **p**,
1:15 and unbelieving nothing is **p**;
Heb 10:22 our bodies washed with **p** water.
Jas 1:27 **P** and undefiled religion before
3:17 that is from above is first **p**,
1 Pe 1:22 fervently with a **p** heart,
2: 2 desire the **p** milk of the word,
2 Pe 3: 1 which I stir up your **p** minds
1 Jn 3: 3 himself, just as He is **p**.
Rev 15: 6 clothed in **p** bright linen, and
21:18 and the city was **p** gold, like
21:21 the street of the city was **p**
22: 1 And he showed me a **p** river of

PURER (1/1) PURE

Hab 1:13 You are of **p** eyes than to

PUREST (1/1)

2 Chr 4:21 of gold, of **p** gold;

PURGE (6/6) PURGED

2 Chr 34: 3 the twelfth year he began to **p**
Ps 51: 7 **P** me with hyssop, and I shall
Isa 1:25 And thoroughly **p** away your
Ezek 20:38 I will **p** the rebels from among
Mal 3: 3 And **p** them as gold and silver,
1 Cor 5: 7 Therefore **p** out the old leaven,

PURGED (4/4) PURGE, PURIFIED

2 Chr 34: 8 when he had **p** the land and the
Isa 4: 4 and **p** the blood of Jerusalem
6: 7 is taken away, And your sin **p**.
Heb 1: 3 when He had by Himself **p** our

PURGETH (KJV) See PRUNE

PURIFICATION (18/16) PURIFY

Lev 12: 4 continue in the blood of her **p**
12: 4 until the days of her **p** are
12: 5 continue in the blood of her **p**
12: 6 When the days of her **p** are
Num 8: 7 Sprinkle water of **p** on them,
19: 9 of Israel for the water of **p**;
19:13 because the water of **p** was not
19:17 of the heifer burnt for **p** from
19:20 The water of **p** has not been
19:21 He who sprinkles the water of **p**
19:21 he who touches the water of **p**
31:23 be purified with the water of **p**.
2 Chr 30:19 cleansed according to the **p**
Neh 12:45 God and the charge of the **p**,
Lk 2:22 Now when the days of her **p**
Jn 2: 6 according to the manner of **p** of
3:25 disciples and the Jews about **p**.
Acts 21:26 the expiration of the days of **p**,

PURIFIED (15/14) PURIFY

Lev 8:15 and **p** the altar. And he poured
Num 8:21 And the Levites **p** themselves and
31:23 and it shall be **p** with the
Ezra 6:20 priests and the Levites had **p**
Neh 12:30 Then the priests and Levites **p**
12:30 and **p** the people, the gates,
Ps 12: 6 **P** seven times.
Dan 12:10 "Many shall be **p**,
Acts 21:24 Take them and be **p** with them,
21:26 having been **p** with them,
24:18 some Jews from Asia found me **p**
Heb 9:22 the law almost all things are **p**
9:23 in the heavens should be **p**
10: 2 For the worshipers, once **p**,
1 Pe 1:22 Since you have **p** your souls in

PURIFIER (1/1)

Mal 3: 3 will sit as a refiner and a **p**

PURIFIES (1/1) PURIFY

1 Jn 3: 3 who has this hope in Him **p**

PURIFY (15/14) PURE, PURIFICATION, PURIFIED, PURIFIES, PURIFYING

Gen 35: 2 **p** yourselves, and change your
Num 19:12 He shall **p** himself with the
19:12 But if he does not **p** himself on
19:13 and does not **p** himself, defiles
19:19 on the seventh day he shall **p**
19:20 who is unclean and does not **p**
31:19 **p** yourselves and your captives
31:20 **P** every garment, everything made
Isa 66:17 who sanctify themselves and **p**
Ezek 43:26 atonement for the altar and **p**
Dan 11:35 **p** them, and make them white,
Mal 3: 3 He will **p** the sons of Levi,
Jn 11:55 to **p** themselves.
Titus 2:14 from every lawless deed and **p**
Jas 4: 8 and **p** your hearts, you

PURIFYING (5/5) PURIFY

Num 19: 9 it is for **p** from sin.
1 Chr 23:28 in the **p** of all holy things and
Mk 7:19 thus **p** all foods?"
Acts 15: 9 **p** their hearts by faith.
Heb 9:13 sanctifies for the **p** of the

PURIM (5/5) PUR

Esth 9:26 So they called these days **P**,
9:28 that these days of **P** should not
9:29 this second letter about **P**.
9:31 to confirm these days of **P** at
9:32 confirmed these matters of **P**,

PURITY (5/5) PURE

Job 22:30 he will be delivered by the **p**
Prov 22:11 He who loves **p** of heart
2 Cor 6: 6 by **p**, by knowledge, by
1 Tim 4:12 love, in spirit, in faith, in **p**.
5: 2 younger as sisters, with all **p**.

PURLOINING (KJV) See PILFERING

PURPLE (53/53)

Ex 25: 4 'blue, **p**, and scarlet
26: 1 fine woven linen and blue, **p**,
26:31 make a veil woven of blue, **p**,
26:36 tabernacle, woven of blue, **p**,
27:16 cubits long, woven of blue, **p**,
28: 5 shall take the gold, blue, **p**,
28: 6 make the ephod of gold, blue, **p**,
28: 8 made of gold, blue, **p**,
28:15 shall make it: of gold, blue, **p**,
28:33 make pomegranates of blue, **p**,
35: 6 'blue, **p**, and scarlet
35:23 with whom was found blue, **p**,
35:25 what they had spun, of blue , **p**,
35:35 the tapestry maker, in blue, **p**,
36: 8 of fine linen, and of blue, **p**,
36:35 And he made a veil of blue, **p**,
36:37 the tabernacle door, of blue, **p**,
38:18 the court was woven of blue, **p**,
38:23 designer, a weaver of blue, **p**,
39: 1 Of the blue, **p**,
39: 2 made the ephod of gold, blue, **p**,
39: 3 work it in with the blue, **p**,
39: 5 woven of gold, blue, **p**,
39: 8 of the ephod, of gold, blue, **p**,
39:24 robe pomegranates of blue, **p**,
39:29 fine woven linen with blue, **p**,
Num 4:13 and spread a **p** cloth over it.
Judg 8:26 and **p** robes which were on the
2 Chr 2: 7 in **p** and crimson and blue, who
2:14 **p** and blue, fine linen and
3:14 And he made the veil of blue, **p**,
Esth 1: 6 with cords of fine linen and **p**

P

8:15 a garment of fine linen and **p**;
Prov 31:22 clothing is fine linen and **p**.
Song 3:10 of gold, Its seat of **p**,
7: 5 hair of your head is like **p**;
Jer 10: 9 Blue and **p** are their
Ezek 23: 6 Who were clothed in **p**,
27: 7 Blue and **p** from the coasts of
27:16 you for your wares emeralds, **p**,
27:24 in **p** clothes, in embroidered
Dan 5: 7 shall be clothed with **p** and
5:16 you shall be clothed with **p** and
5:29 and they clothed Daniel with **p**
Mk 15:17 And they clothed Him with **p**;
15:20 they took the **p** off Him, put
Lk 16:19 rich man who was clothed in **p**
Jn 19: 2 and they put on Him a **p** robe.
19: 5 crown of thorns and the **p** robe.
Acts 16:14 She was a seller of **p** from the
Rev 17: 4 The woman was arrayed in **p** and
18:12 and pearls, fine linen and **p**,
18:16 was clothed in fine linen, **p**,

PURPOSE (39/39) PURPOSED, PURPOSES

Ex 9:16 But indeed for this **p** I have
2 Chr 32: 2 and that his **p** was to make war
Ezra 4: 5 them to frustrate their **p** all
Neh 8: 4 which they had made for the **p**;
Job 42: 2 And that no **p** of Yours can
Ps 20: 4 And fulfill all your **p**.
Eccl 3: 1 A time for every **p** under
3:17 is a time there for every **p**
Isa 1:11 To what **p** is the multitude of
14:26 This is the **p** that is purposed
30: 7 shall help in vain and to no **p**.
Jer 6:20 For what **p** to Me Comes
26: 3 the calamity which I **p** to
36: 3 all the adversities which I **p**
51:29 For every **p** of the LORD shall
Dan 6:17 that the **p** concerning Daniel
Mk 1:38 because for this **p** I have come
Lk 4:43 because for this **p** I have been
Jn 12:27 But for this **p** I came to this
Acts 2:23 delivered by the determined **p**
4:28 whatever Your hand and Your **p**
9:21 and has come here for that **p**,
11:23 them all that with **p** of heart
26:16 have appeared to you for this **p**,
27:43 Paul, kept them from their **p**,
Rom 8:28 the called according to His **p**.
9:11 that the **p** of God according to
9:17 For this very **p** I have
Gal 3:19 What **p** then does the law
Eph 1:11 predestined according to the **p**
3:11 according to the eternal **p** which
6:22 sent to you for this very **p**,
Col 4: 8 him to you for this very **p**,
1 Tim 1: 5 Now the **p** of the commandment is
2 Tim 1: 9 but according to His own **p** and
3:10 my doctrine, manner of life, **p**,
Phm 1:15 for a while for this **p**,
1 Jn 3: 8 For this **p** the Son of God was
Rev 17:17 their hearts to fulfill His **p**,

PURPOSED (15/15) PURPOSE

2 Sam 17:14 For the LORD had **p** to defeat
Ps 17: 3 I have **p** that my mouth shall
140: 4 Who have **p** to make my steps
Isa 14:24 come to pass, And as I have **p**,
14:26 This is the purpose that is **p**
14:27 For the LORD of hosts has **p**,
19:12 what the LORD of hosts has **p**
23: 9 The LORD of hosts has **p** it,
46:11 I have **p** it; I will also do
Jer 4:28 I have **p** and will not relent,
Lam 2: 8 The LORD has **p** to destroy
2:17 The LORD has done what He **p**;
Dan 1: 8 But Daniel **p** in his heart that
Acts 19:21 Paul **p** in the Spirit, when he
Eph 1: 9 to His good pleasure which He **p**

PURPOSELY (1/1)

Ruth 2:16 grain from the bundles fall **p**

PURPOSES (5/5) PURPOSE

2 Ki 12: 4 all the money that a man **p** in
Job 17:11 My **p** are broken off, Even
Jer 49:20 And His **p** that He has proposed
50:45 And His **p** that He has proposed
2 Cor 9: 7 let each one give as he **p** in

PURSE (1/1)

Prov 1:14 Let us all have one **p**"—

PURSES (2/2)

Prov 16:30 He **p** his lips and brings
Isa 3:22 The outer garments, the **p**,

PURSUE (48/46) PURSUED, PURSUES, PURSUING, PURSUIT

Gen 35: 5 and they did not **p** the sons of
Ex 14: 4 so that he will **p** them; and I
15: 9 The enemy said, 'I will **p**,
Deut 19: 6 **p** the manslayer and overtake
28:22 they shall **p** you until you
28:45 shall come upon you and **p** and
Josh 2: 5 **p** them quickly, for you may
8:16 in Ai were called together to **p**
10:19 but **p** your enemies, and attack
1 Sam 24:14 Israel come out? Whom do you **p**?
25:29 Yet a man has risen to **p** you and
26:18 Why does my lord thus **p** his
30: 8 Shall I **p** this troop? Shall I
30: 8 And He answered him, "**P**,
2 Sam 2:28 stood still and did not **p**
17: 1 and I will arise and **p** David
20: 6 your lord's servants and **p** him,
20: 7 they went out of Jerusalem to **p**
20:13 people went on after Joab to **p**
24:13 while they **p** you? Or shall
Job 13:25 And will You **p** dry stubble?
30:15 They **p** my honor as the wind,
Ps 7: 5 Let the enemy **p** me and overtake
34:14 Seek peace and **p** it.
35: 3 And stop those who **p** me.
35: 6 let the angel of the LORD **p**
71:11 **P** and take him, for there is
83:15 So **p** them with Your tempest,
Prov 19: 7 go far from him! He may **p**
Isa 30:16 Therefore those who **p** you shall
Jer 29:18 And I will **p** them with the
48: 2 O Madmen! The sword shall **p**
Lam 3:66 **P** and destroy them From under
5: 5 They **p** at our heels; We labor
Ezek 33:31 but their hearts **p** their own
35: 6 and blood shall **p** you;
35: 6 therefore blood shall **p** you.
Hos 6: 3 Let us **p** the knowledge of the
8: 3 The enemy will **p** him.
Nah 1: 8 And darkness will **p** His
Rom 9:30 who did not **p** righteousness,
14:19 Therefore let us **p** the things
1 Cor 14: 1 **P** love, and desire spiritual
1 Th 5:15 but always **p** what is good both
1 Tim 6:11 flee these things and **p**
2 Tim 2:22 but **p** righteousness, faith,
Heb 12:14 **P** peace with all people, and
1 Pe 3:11 him seek peace and **p** it.

PURSUED (41/40) PURSUE

Gen 14:15 attacked them and **p** them
31:23 his brethren with him and **p** him
31:36 that you have so hotly **p** me?
Ex 14: 8 and he **p** the children of
14: 9 So the Egyptians **p** them, all the
14:23 And the Egyptians **p** and went
Deut 11: 4 overflow them as they **p** you,
Josh 2: 7 Then the men **p** them by the road
2: 7 And as soon as those who **p** them
8:16 And they **p** Joshua and were
8:17 the city open and **p** Israel.
8:24 wilderness where they **p** them,
24: 6 and the Egyptians **p** your
Judg 1: 6 and they **p** him and caught him
4:16 But Barak **p** the chariots and the
4:22 as Barak **p** Sisera, Jael came
7:23 and **p** the Midianites.
7:25 They **p** Midian and brought the
8:12 he **p** them; and he took the two
20:45 Then they **p** them relentlessly
1 Sam 7:11 went out of Mizpah and **p** the
17:52 and **p** the Philistines as far as
23:25 he **p** David in the Wilderness of
30:10 But David **p**, he and four
2 Sam 2:19 So Asahel **p** Abner, and in going
2:24 Joab and Abishai also **p** Abner.
20:10 and Abishai his brother **p** Sheba
22:38 I have **p** my enemies and
1 Ki 20:20 and Israel **p** them;
2 Ki 5:21 So Gehazi **p** Naaman.
9:27 So Jehu **p** him, and said,
25: 5 of the Chaldeans **p** the king,
2 Chr 13:19 And Abijah **p** Jeroboam and took
14:13 who were with him **p** them
Ps 18:37 I have **p** my enemies and
Isa 41: 3 Who **p** them, and passed safely
Jer 39: 5 But the Chaldean army **p** them and
52: 8 of the Chaldeans **p** the king,
Lam 3:43 Yourself with anger And **p** us;
4:19 They **p** us on the mountains
Am 1:11 Because he **p** his brother with

PURSUER (1/1)

Lam 1: 6 without strength Before the **p**.

PURSUERS (6/4)

Josh 2:16 lest the **p** meet you. Hide there
2:16 until the **p** have returned.
2:22 there three days until the **p**
2:22 The **p** sought them all along
8:20 wilderness turned back on the **p**.
Lam 4:19 Our **p** were swifter Than the

PURSUES (9/8) PURSUE

Lev 26:17 you shall flee when no one **p**
26:36 they shall fall when no one **p**.
26:37 before a sword, when no one **p**;
Josh 20: 5 'Then if the avenger of blood **p**
Prov 11:19 So he who **p** evil pursues it
11:19 So he who pursues evil **p** it
13:21 Evil **p** sinners, But to the
28: 1 The wicked flee when no one **p**,
Hos 12: 1 And **p** the east wind; He daily

PURSUING (10/10) PURSUE

Judg 8: 5 and I am **p** Zebah and Zalmunna,
1 Sam 14:46 Then Saul returned from **p** the
23:28 Therefore Saul returned from **p**
2 Sam 2:26 the people to return from **p**
2:27 people would have given up **p**
2:30 So Joab returned from **p** Abner.
18:16 and the people returned from **p**
1 Ki 22:33 that they turned back from **p**
2 Chr 18:32 that they turned back from **p**
Rom 9:31 **p** the law of righteousness, has

PURSUIT (2/2) PURSUE

Gen 14:14 and went in **p** as far as Dan.
Judg 8: 4 over, exhausted but still in **p**.

PURSUITS (1/1)

Jas 1:11 also will fade away in his **p**.

PUSH (6/6)

Deut 33:17 with them He shall **p** the
2 Ki 4:27 but Gehazi came near to **p** her
Job 24: 4 They **p** the needy off the road;
30:12 They **p** away my feet, And they
Ps 44: 5 Through You we will **p** down our
Joel 2: 8 They do not **p** one another;

PUSHED (5/5)

Num 22:25 she **p** herself against the wall
Judg 16:30 the Philistines!" And he **p**
Ps 118:13 You **p** me violently, that I
Ezek 34:21 Because you have **p** with side and
Acts 7:27 he who did his neighbor wrong **p**

PUSHES (2/2)

Num 35:20 If he **p** him out of hatred or,
35:22 if he **p** him suddenly without

PUSHING (1/1)

Dan 8: 4 I saw the ram **p** westward,

PUT (893/823)

Gen 2: 8 and there He **p** the man whom He
2:15 took the man and **p** him in the
3:15 And I will **p** enmity Between
3:22 lest he **p** out his hand and take
8: 9 So he **p** out his hand and took
10: 6 of Ham were Cush, Mizraim, **P**,
24: 2 **p** your hand under my thigh,
24: 9 So the servant **p** his hand under
24:47 So I **p** the nose ring on her
26:11 shall surely be **p** to death."
27:15 and **p** them on Jacob her younger
27:16 And she **p** the skins of the kids
28:11 stones of that place and **p** it
28:18 that he had **p** at his head,
28:20 to eat and clothing to **p** on,
29: 3 and **p** the stone back in its
30:36 Then he **p** three days' journey
30:40 but he **p** his own flocks by
30:40 themselves and did not **p** them
30:42 he did not **p** them in;
31:34 **p** them in the camel's saddle,
32:16 and **p** some distance between
33: 2 And he **p** the maidservants and
35: 2 **P** away the foreign gods that
37:34 **p** sackcloth on his waist, and
38:19 her veil and **p** on the garments
38:28 that the one **p** out his hand;
39: 4 and all that he had he **p** under
39:20 master took him and **p** him into
40: 3 So he **p** them in custody in the
40:13 and you will **p** Pharaoh's cup in
40:15 here that they should **p** me
41:10 and **p** me in custody in the
41:42 ring off his hand and **p** it on
41:42 garments of fine linen and **p** a
42:17 So he **p** them all together in
42:37 **p** him in my hands, and I will
43:22 We do not know who **p** our money
44: 1 and **p** each man's money in the
44: 2 Also **p** my cup, the silver cup,
46: 4 and Joseph will **p** his hand on
47:29 please **p** your hand under my
48:18 **p** your right hand on his
50:26 and he was **p** in a coffin in
Ex 2: 3 **p** the child in it, and laid it
3:22 and you shall **p** them on your
4: 6 Now **p** your hand in your bosom."
4: 6 And he **p** his hand in his
4: 7 **P** your hand in your bosom
4: 7 So he **p** his hand in his bosom
4:15 you shall speak to him and **p**
4:21 before Pharaoh which I have **p**
5:21 to **p** a sword in their hand to
12: 7 take some of the blood and **p**
15:26 I will **p** none of the diseases
16:33 Take a pot and **p** an omer of
17:12 so they took a stone and **p** it
19:12 the mountain shall surely be **p**
21:12 that he dies shall surely be **p**
21:15 or his mother shall surely be **p**
21:16 shall surely be **p** to death.
21:17 or his mother shall surely be **p**
21:29 and its owner also shall be **p**

22: 8 to see whether he has ***p*** his
22:11 that he has not ***p*** his hand into
22:19 an animal shall surely be ***p*** to
23: 1 Do not ***p*** your hand with the
24: 6 took half the blood and ***p*** it
25:12 and ***p*** them in its four
25:14 You shall ***p*** the poles into the
25:16 And you shall ***p*** into the ark the
25:21 You shall ***p*** the mercy seat on
25:21 and in the ark you shall ***p*** the
25:26 and ***p*** the rings on the four
26:11 ***p*** the clasps into the loops,
26:34 You shall ***p*** the mercy seat upon
26:35 and you shall ***p*** the table on
27: 5 You shall ***p*** it under the rim of
27: 7 The poles shall be ***p*** in the
28:12 And you shall ***p*** the two stones
28:17 And you shall ***p*** settings of
28:23 and ***p*** the two rings on the two
28:24 Then you shall ***p*** the two braided
28:25 and ***p*** them on the shoulder
28:26 and ***p*** them on the two ends of
28:27 and ***p*** them on the two shoulder
28:30 And you shall ***p*** in the
28:37 And you shall ***p*** it on a blue
28:41 So you shall ***p*** them on Aaron
29: 3 You shall ***p*** them in one basket
29: 5 ***p*** the tunic on Aaron, and the
29: 6 You shall ***p*** the turban on his
29: 6 and ***p*** the holy crown on the
29: 8 you shall bring his sons and ***p***
29: 9 and ***p*** the hats on them.
29:10 and Aaron and his sons shall ***p***
29:12 of the blood of the bull and ***p***
29:15 and Aaron and his sons shall ***p***
29:17 and ***p*** them with its pieces and
29:19 and Aaron and his sons shall ***p***
29:20 take some of its blood and ***p***
29:24 and you shall ***p*** all these in the
29:30 priest in his place shall ***p***
30: 6 And you shall ***p*** it before the
30:18 You shall ***p*** it between the
30:18 And you shall ***p*** water in it,
30:36 and ***p*** some of it before the
31: 6 and I have ***p*** wisdom in the
31:14 profanes it shall surely be ***p***
31:15 he shall surely be ***p*** to death.
32:27 Let every man ***p*** his sword on his
33: 4 and no one ***p*** on his ornaments.
33:22 that I will ***p*** you in the cleft
34:33 he ***p*** a veil on his face.
34:35 then Moses would ***p*** the veil on
35: 2 does any work on it shall be ***p***
35:34 And He has ***p*** in his heart the
36: 1 in whom the LORD has ***p*** wisdom
36: 2 in whose heart the LORD had ***p***
37: 5 And he ***p*** the poles into the
37:13 and ***p*** the rings on the four
38: 7 Then he ***p*** the poles into the
39: 7 He ***p*** them on the shoulders of
39:16 and ***p*** the two rings on the two
39:17 And they ***p*** the two braided
39:18 and ***p*** them on the shoulder
39:19 made two rings of gold and ***p***
39:20 two other gold rings and ***p***
39:25 and ***p*** the bells between the
40: 3 You shall ***p*** in it the ark of the
40: 5 and ***p*** up the screen for the
40: 7 and ***p*** water in it.
40:13 You shall ***p*** the holy garments on
40:18 ***p*** in its bars, and raised up
40:19 tent over the tabernacle and ***p***
40:20 He took the Testimony and ***p*** it
40:20 and ***p*** the mercy seat on top of
40:22 He ***p*** the table in the tabernacle
40:24 He ***p*** the lampstand in the
40:26 He ***p*** the gold altar in the
40:29 And he ***p*** the altar of burnt
40:30 and ***p*** water there for washing;
Lev 1: 4 Then he shall ***p*** his hand on the
1: 7 of Aaron the priest shall ***p***
2: 1 and ***p*** frankincense on it.
2:15 And you shall ***p*** oil on it, and
4: 7 And the priest shall ***p*** some of
4:18 And he shall ***p*** some of the
4:25 ***p*** it on the horns of the altar
4:30 ***p*** it on the horns of the altar
4:34 ***p*** it on the horns of the altar
5:11 He shall ***p*** no oil on it, nor
5:11 nor shall he ***p*** frankincense on
6:10 And the priest shall ***p*** on his
6:10 his linen trousers he shall ***p***
6:10 and he shall ***p*** them beside the
6:11 ***p*** on other garments, and carry
6:12 it; it shall not be ***p*** out.
8: 7 And he ***p*** the tunic on him,
8: 7 and ***p*** the ephod on him;
8: 8 Then he ***p*** the breastplate on
8: 8 and he ***p*** the Urim and the
8: 9 And he ***p*** the turban on his head.
8: 9 he ***p*** the golden plate, the holy
8:13 brought Aaron's sons and ***p***
8:13 and ***p*** hats on them, as the
8:15 and ***p*** some on the horns of the
8:23 took some of its blood and ***p***
8:24 And Moses ***p*** some of the blood
8:26 and ***p*** them on the fat and on
8:27 and he ***p*** all these in Aaron's
9: 9 ***p*** it on the horns of the
9:20 and they ***p*** the fat on the
10: 1 each took his censer and ***p*** fire
10: 1 ***p*** incense on it, and offered

11:32 it must be ***p*** in water.
11:38 But if water is ***p*** on the seed,
14:14 and the priest shall ***p*** it on
14:17 the priest shall ***p*** some on the
14:18 in the priest's hand he shall ***p***
14:25 of the trespass offering and ***p***
14:28 And the priest shall ***p*** some of
14:29 in the priest's hand he shall ***p***
14:34 and I ***p*** the leprous plague in a
14:42 shall take other stones and ***p***
16: 4 He shall ***p*** the holy linen tunic
16: 4 body in water, and ***p*** them on.
16:13 And he shall ***p*** the incense on
16:18 and ***p*** it on the horns of the
16:23 the linen garments which he ***p***
16:24 ***p*** on his garments, come out and
16:32 and ***p*** on the linen clothes,
19:14 nor ***p*** a stumbling block before
19:20 but they shall not be ***p*** to
20: 2 he shall surely be ***p*** to death.
20: 9 or his mother shall surely be ***p***
20:10 shall surely be ***p*** to death.
20:11 both of them shall surely be ***p***
20:12 both of them shall surely be ***p***
20:13 They shall surely be ***p*** to
20:15 he shall surely be ***p*** to death,
20:16 They shall surely be ***p*** to
20:27 shall surely be ***p*** to death;
24: 7 And you shall ***p*** pure
24:12 Then they ***p*** him in custody,
24:16 of the LORD shall surely be ***p***
24:16 he shall be ***p*** to death.
24:17 any man shall surely be ***p*** to
24:21 whoever kills a man shall be ***p***
26: 8 and a hundred of you shall ***p***
27:29 but shall surely be ***p*** to
Num 1:51 who comes near shall be ***p*** to
3:10 who comes near shall be ***p*** to
3:38 who came near was to be ***p*** to
4: 6 Then they shall ***p*** on it a
4: 7 and ***p*** on it the dishes, the
4:10 Then they shall ***p*** it with all
4:10 and ***p*** it on a carrying beam.
4:12 ***p*** them in a blue cloth, cover
4:12 and ***p*** them on a carrying beam.
4:14 They shall ***p*** on it all its
5: 2 that they ***p*** out of the camp
5: 3 You shall ***p*** out both male and
5: 3 you shall ***p*** them outside the
5: 4 and ***p*** them outside the camp;
5:15 shall pour no oil on it and ***p***
5:17 floor of the tabernacle and ***p***
5:18 and ***p*** the offering for
5:19 And the priest shall ***p*** her under
5:21 then the priest shall ***p*** the
6:18 his consecrated head and ***p*** it
6:19 and ***p*** them upon the hands of
6:27 So they shall ***p*** My name on the
11:17 that is upon you and will ***p***
11:29 and that the LORD would ***p***
14:22 and have ***p*** Me to the test now
15:34 They ***p*** him under guard, because
15:35 The man must surely be ***p*** to
15:38 and to ***p*** a blue thread in the
16: 7 ***p*** fire in them and put incense
16: 7 put fire in them and ***p*** incense
16:14 Will you ***p*** out the eyes of
16:17 each take his censer and ***p***
16:18 ***p*** fire in it, laid incense on
16:46 Take a censer and ***p*** fire in it
16:46 ***p*** incense on it, and take it
16:47 So he ***p*** in the incense and made
17: 8 had sprouted and ***p*** forth buds,
17:10 that you may ***p*** their complaints
18: 7 who comes near shall be ***p*** to
19:17 and running water shall be ***p*** on
20:26 Aaron of his garments and ***p***
20:28 Aaron of his garments and ***p***
21: 9 and ***p*** it on a pole; and so it
23: 5 Then the LORD ***p*** a word in
23:12 to speak what the LORD has ***p***
23:16 and ***p*** a word in his mouth, and
31:23 you shall ***p*** through the fire,
31:23 cannot endure fire you shall ***p***
35:16 the murderer shall surely be ***p***
35:17 the murderer shall surely be ***p***
35:18 the murderer shall surely be ***p***
35:19 of blood himself shall ***p*** the
35:19 he shall ***p*** him to death.
35:21 struck him shall surely be ***p***
35:21 The avenger of blood shall ***p***
35:30 the murderer shall be ***p*** to
35:31 but he shall surely be ***p*** to
Deut 2:25 This day I will begin to ***p*** the
10: 2 and you shall ***p*** them in the
10: 5 and ***p*** the tablets in the ark
11:25 the LORD your God will ***p*** the
11:29 that you shall ***p*** the blessing
12: 5 to ***p*** His name for His dwelling
12: 7 in all to which you have ***p***
12:18 your God in all to which you ***p***
12:21 the LORD your God chooses to ***p***
13: 5 dreamer of dreams shall be ***p***
13: 5 So you shall ***p*** away the evil
13: 9 be first against him to ***p*** him
14:24 the LORD your God chooses to ***p***
15:10 and in all to which you ***p*** your
16: 2 where the LORD chooses to ***p***
16: 9 the time you begin to ***p***
17: 6 deserving of death shall be ***p***
17: 6 he shall not be ***p*** to death on
17: 7 be the first against him to ***p***

17: 7 So you shall ***p*** away the evil
17:12 So you shall ***p*** away the evil
18:18 and will ***p*** My words in His
19:13 but you shall ***p*** away the
19:19 so you shall ***p*** away the evil
21: 9 So you shall ***p*** away the guilt
21:13 She shall ***p*** off the clothes of
21:21 so you shall ***p*** away the evil
21:22 and he is ***p*** to death, and you
22: 5 nor shall a man ***p*** on a woman's
22:21 So you shall ***p*** away the evil
22:22 so you shall ***p*** away the evil
22:24 so you shall ***p*** away the evil
23:24 but you shall not ***p*** any in
24: 7 and you shall ***p*** away the evil
24:16 Fathers shall not be ***p*** to death
24:16 nor shall the children be ***p*** to
24:16 a person shall be ***p*** to death
26: 2 and ***p*** it in a basket and go to
28:48 and He will ***p*** a yoke of iron on
30: 7 the LORD your God will ***p***
31:19 ***p*** it in their mouths, that this
31:26 and ***p*** it beside the ark of the
32:30 And two ***p*** ten thousand to
33:10 They shall ***p*** incense before
Josh 1:18 shall be ***p*** to death.
6:24 they ***p*** into the treasury of the
7: 6 and they ***p*** dust on their heads.
7:11 and they have also ***p*** it among
10:24 ***p*** your feet on the necks of
10:24 And they drew near and ***p***
17:13 that they ***p*** the Canaanites to
24: 7 and He ***p*** darkness between you
24:14 and ***p*** away the gods which your
24:23 ***p*** away the foreign gods which
Judg 1:28 that they ***p*** the Canaanites
1:30 and were ***p*** under tribute.
1:33 Shemesh and Beth Anath were ***p***
1:35 they were ***p*** under tribute.
6:19 The meat he ***p*** in a basket,
6:19 and he ***p*** the broth in a pot;
6:21 Then the Angel of the LORD ***p***
6:31 who would plead for him be ***p***
6:37 I shall ***p*** a fleece of wool on
7:16 and he ***p*** a trumpet into every
9:26 and the men of Shechem ***p*** their
9:49 ***p*** them against the stronghold,
10:16 So they ***p*** away the foreign gods
15: 4 and ***p*** a torch between each pair
16: 3 ***p*** them on his shoulders,
16:21 the Philistines took him and ***p***
17: 2 and on which you ***p*** a curse,
18: 7 rulers in the land who might ***p***
18:19 ***p*** your hand over your mouth,
18:21 and ***p*** the little ones,
20:13 that we may ***p*** them to death and
20:20 and the men of Israel ***p***
20:22 at the place where they had ***p***
20:30 and ***p*** themselves in battle
20:33 rose from their place and ***p***
21: 5 He shall surely be ***p*** to death."
Ruth 3: 3 ***p*** on your best garment and go
1 Sam 1:14 ***P*** your wine away from you!"
2:36 ***p*** me in one of the priestly
4: 2 Then the Philistines ***p***
6: 8 and ***p*** the articles of gold
6:15 and ***p*** them on the large stone.
7: 3 then ***p*** away the foreign gods
7: 4 So the children of Israel ***p*** away
8:16 and ***p*** them to his work.
11: 2 that I may ***p*** out all your right
11:11 that Saul ***p*** the people in three
11:12 that we may ***p*** them to death."
11:13 Not a man shall be ***p*** to death
14:26 but no one ***p*** his hand to his
14:27 and ***p*** his hand to his mouth;
17:38 and he ***p*** a bronze helmet on his
17:40 and ***p*** them in a shepherd's bag,
17:49 Then David ***p*** his hand in his bag
17:54 but he ***p*** his armor in his tent.
19:13 ***p*** a cover of goats' hair for
21: 6 in order to ***p*** hot bread in
28: 3 And Saul had ***p*** the mediums and
28: 8 So Saul disguised himself and ***p***
28:21 and I have ***p*** my life in my
31:10 Then they ***p*** his armor in the
2 Sam 1:14 was it you were not afraid to ***p***
1:24 Who ***p*** ornaments of gold on
3:34 were not bound Nor your feet ***p***
6: 6 Uzzah ***p*** out his hand to the
8: 2 he measured off those to be ***p***
8: 6 Then David ***p*** garrisons in Syria
8:14 He also ***p*** garrisons in Edom;
8:14 throughout all Edom he ***p***
10: 8 people of Ammon came out and ***p***
10: 9 some of Israel's best and ***p***
10:10 And the rest of the people he ***p***
12:13 The LORD also has ***p*** away your
12:31 and ***p*** them to work with saws
13:17 Here! ***P*** this woman out, away
13:18 And his servant ***p*** her out and
13:19 Then Tamar ***p*** ashes on her head,
14: 2 and ***p*** on mourning apparel;
14: 3 So Joab ***p*** the words in her
14:19 and he ***p*** all these words in the
15: 5 that he would ***p*** out his hand
17:23 Then he ***p*** his household in
19:21 Shall not Shimei be ***p*** to death
19:22 Shall any man be ***p*** to death
20: 3 and ***p*** them in seclusion and
21: 9 and were ***p*** to death in the days
1 Ki 1: 1 and they ***p*** covers on him, but

1:51 to me today that he will not ***p***
2: 5 and ***p*** the blood of war on his
2: 8 I will not ***p*** you to death with
2:24 Adonijah shall be ***p*** to death
2:26 but I will not ***p*** you to death
2:35 The king ***p*** Benaiah the son of
2:35 and the king ***p*** Zadok the priest
5: 3 until the LORD ***p*** his foes
7:39 And he ***p*** five carts on the right
7:51 He ***p*** them in the treasuries of
8: 9 tablets of stone which Moses ***p***
9: 3 which you have built to ***p*** My
10:17 The king ***p*** them in the House of
10:24 which God had ***p*** in his heart.
11:36 for Myself, to ***p*** My name there.
12: 4 and his heavy yoke which he ***p***
12: 9 the yoke which your father ***p***
12:11 whereas my father ***p*** a heavy
12:29 and the other he ***p*** in Dan.
14:21 to ***p*** His name there.
18:23 but ***p*** no fire under it; and I
18:23 wood, but ***p*** no fire under it.
18:25 but ***p*** no fire under it."
18:33 And he ***p*** the wood in order, cut
18:42 and ***p*** his face between his
20: 6 they will ***p*** it in their hands
20:24 and ***p*** captains in their places;
20:31 let us ***p*** sackcloth around our
20:32 around their waists and ***p***
21:27 that he tore his clothes and ***p***
22:10 having ***p*** on their robes, sat
22:23 The LORD has ***p*** a lying
22:27 ***P*** this fellow in prison, and
22:30 but you ***p*** on your robes."
2 Ki 2:20 a new bowl, and ***p*** salt in it."
3: 2 for he ***p*** away the sacred
4:10 and let us ***p*** a bed for him
4:34 and ***p*** his mouth on his mouth,
4:38 ***P*** on the large pot, and boil
4:41 And he ***p*** it into the pot,
9:13 to take his garment and ***p*** it
9:30 and she ***p*** paint on her eyes and
10: 7 ***p*** their heads in baskets and
11: 8 let him be ***p*** to death.
11:12 ***p*** the crown on him, and gave
12: 9 the priests who kept the door ***p***
12:10 the high priest came up and ***p***
13:16 '***P*** your hand on the bow."
13:16 So he ***p*** his hand on it, and
13:16 and Elisha ***p*** his hands on the
13:21 and they ***p*** the man in the tomb
14: 6 Fathers shall not be ***p*** to death
14: 6 nor shall children be ***p*** to
14: 6 but a person shall be ***p*** to
16:14 and ***p*** it on the north side of
16:17 and ***p*** it on a pavement of
17:29 and ***p*** them in the shrines on
18:11 and ***p*** them in Halah and by the
18:23 you are able on your part to ***p***
18:24 and ***p*** your trust in Egypt for
19:28 Therefore I will ***p*** My hook in
21: 4 In Jerusalem I will ***p*** My name."
21: 7 I will ***p*** My name forever;
23:24 Moreover Josiah ***p*** away those who
23:33 Now Pharaoh Necho ***p*** him in
25: 7 ***p*** out the eyes of Zedekiah,
25:21 of Babylon struck them and ***p***
1 Chr 1: 8 of Ham were Cush, Mizraim, ***P***,
5:20 because they ***p*** their trust in
10:10 Then they ***p*** his armor in the
11:19 of these men who have ***p***
12:15 and they ***p*** to flight all those
13: 9 Uzza ***p*** out his hand to hold the
13:10 and He struck him because he ***p***
18: 6 Then David ***p*** garrisons in Syria
18:13 He also ***p*** garrisons in Edom, and
19: 9 people of Ammon came out and ***p***
19:10 some of Israel's best and ***p***
19:11 And the rest of the people he ***p***
20: 3 and ***p*** them to work with saws,
2 Chr 1: 5 he ***p*** before the tabernacle of
3:16 and ***p*** them on top of the
3:16 and ***p*** them on the wreaths of
4: 6 and ***p*** five on the right side
5: 1 And he ***p*** them in the
5:10 the two tablets which Moses ***p***
6:11 And there I have ***p*** the ark, in
6:20 where You said You would ***p***
9:16 The king ***p*** them in the House of
9:23 which God had ***p*** in his heart.
10: 4 and his heavy yoke which he ***p***
10: 9 the yoke which your father ***p***
10:11 whereas my father ***p*** a heavy
11:11 and ***p*** captains in them, and
11:12 Also in every city he ***p***
12:13 to ***p*** His name there.
15:13 God of Israel was to be ***p*** to
16:10 and ***p*** him in prison, for he
17:19 besides those the king ***p*** in the
18:22 look! The LORD has ***p*** a lying
18:26 ***P*** this fellow in prison, and
18:29 but you ***p*** on your robes."
22:11 and ***p*** him and his nurse in a
23: 7 let him be ***p*** to death.
23:11 ***p*** the crown on him, gave him
24:10 and ***p*** them into the chest
25: 4 The fathers shall not be ***p*** to
25: 4 nor shall the children be ***p*** to
29: 7 ***p*** out the lamps, and have not
33: 7 I will ***p*** My name forever;
33:14 Then he ***p*** military captains in
34:10 Then they ***p*** it in the hand of

35: 3 ***P*** the holy ark in the house
35:24 him out of that chariot and ***p***
36: 7 and ***p*** them in his temple at
36:22 and also ***p*** it in writing,
Ezra 1: 1 and also ***p*** it in writing,
1: 7 had taken from Jerusalem and ***p***
6:12 any king or people who ***p*** their
7:27 who has ***p*** such a thing as
10: 3 a covenant with our God to ***p***
10:19 promise that they would ***p*** away
Neh 2:12 I told no one what my God had ***p***
3: 5 but their nobles did not ***p***
7: 5 Then my God ***p*** it into my heart
Esth 4: 1 he tore his clothes and ***p*** on
4:11 ***p*** all to death, except the one
5: 1 on the third day that Esther ***p***
Job 9:27 I will ***p*** off my sad face and
11:14 and you ***p*** it far away,
13:14 And ***p*** my life in my hands?
13:27 You ***p*** my feet in the stocks,
17: 3 Now ***p*** down a pledge for me with
18: 2 How long till you ***p*** an end to
18: 6 And his lamp beside him is ***p***
21: 5 ***P*** your hand over your mouth.
21:17 is the lamp of the wicked ***p***
27: 5 Till I die I will not ***p*** away
29: 9 And ***p*** their hand on their
29:14 I ***p*** on righteousness, and it
30: 1 fathers I disdained to ***p*** with
38:36 Who has ***p*** wisdom in the mind?
41: 2 Can you ***p*** a reed through his
Ps 2:12 Blessed are all those who ***p***
4: 5 And ***p*** your trust in the LORD.
4: 7 You have ***p*** gladness in my
5:11 let all those rejoice who ***p***
7: 1 in You I ***p*** my trust; Save me
8: 6 You have ***p*** all things under
9:10 those who know Your name will ***p***
9:20 ***P*** them in fear, O LORD,
11: 1 In the LORD I ***p*** my trust;
15: 5 He who does not ***p*** out his
16: 1 for in You I ***p*** my trust.
18:22 And I did not ***p*** away His
25:20 for I ***p*** my trust in You.
30:11 You have ***p*** off my sackcloth
31: 1 I ***p*** my trust; Let me never be
31:18 Let the lying lips be ***p*** to
35: 4 Let those be ***p*** to shame and
36: 7 the children of men ***p*** their
40: 3 He has ***p*** a new song in my
44: 7 And have ***p*** to shame those who
44: 9 You have cast us off and ***p*** us
53: 5 You have ***p*** them to shame,
55:20 He has ***p*** forth his hands
56: 4 In God I have ***p*** my trust;
56: 8 ***P*** my tears into Your bottle;
56:11 In God I have ***p*** my trust;
71: 1 I ***p*** my trust; Let me never be
71: 1 Let me never be ***p*** to shame.
73:28 I have ***p*** my trust in the Lord
78:66 He ***p*** them to a perpetual
83:17 let them be ***p*** to shame and
88: 8 You have ***p*** away my
88:18 one and friend You have ***p*** far
97: 7 Let all be ***p*** to shame who serve
118: 8 trust in the LORD Than to ***p***
118: 9 the LORD Than to ***p*** confidence
119:31 do not ***p*** me to shame!
119:119 You ***p*** away all the wicked of
129: 5 all those who hate Zion Be ***p***
146: 3 Do not ***p*** your trust in princes,
Prov 4:24 ***P*** away from you a deceitful
4:24 And ***p*** perverse lips far from
12:24 But the lazy man will be ***p*** to
13: 9 lamp of the wicked will be ***p***
20:20 His lamp will be ***p*** out in deep
23: 2 And ***p*** a knife to your throat
24:20 lamp of the wicked will be ***p***
25: 7 Than that you should be ***p***
25: 8 When your neighbor has ***p*** you
30: 5 He is a shield to those who ***p***
30:32 ***p*** your hand on your mouth.
Eccl 3:11 Also He has ***p*** eternity in their
11:10 And ***p*** away evil from your
Song 5: 3 How can I ***p*** it on again?
5: 4 My beloved ***p*** his hand By the
Isa 1:16 ***P*** away the evil of your doings
5:20 Who ***p*** darkness for light, and
5:20 Who ***p*** bitter for sweet, and
10:13 So I have ***p*** down the
11: 8 And the weaned child shall ***p***
36: 8 you are able on your part to ***p***
36: 9 and ***p*** your trust in Egypt for
37:29 Therefore I will ***p*** My hook in
42: 1 My soul delights! I have ***p*** My
43:26 ***P*** Me in remembrance
47:11 You will not be able to ***p*** it
50: 1 Whom I have ***p*** away? Or which
50: 1 your mother has been ***p*** away.
51: 9 ***p*** on strength, O arm of the
51:16 And I have ***p*** My words in your
51:23 But I will ***p*** it into the hand
52: 1 ***P*** on your strength,
52: 1 ***P*** on your beautiful garments,
53:10 He has ***p*** Him to grief.
54: 4 for you will not be ***p*** to shame;
59:17 For He ***p*** on righteousness as a
59:17 He ***p*** on the garments of
59:21 and My words which I have ***p*** in
63:11 Where is He who ***p*** His Holy
Jer 1: 9 Then the LORD ***p*** forth His hand
1: 9 I have ***p*** My words in your

3: 8 I had ***p*** her away and given her
3:19 How can I ***p*** you among the
4: 1 And if you will ***p*** away your
6: 9 ***p*** your hand back into the
8:14 For the LORD our God has ***p*** us
10:14 Every metalsmith is ***p*** to shame
12:13 They have ***p*** themselves to pain
13: 1 and ***p*** it around your waist, but
13: 1 but do not ***p*** it in water."
13: 2 and ***p*** it around my waist.
17:18 But do not let me be ***p*** to
18:21 Let their men be ***p*** to death,
20: 2 and ***p*** him in the stocks that
26:15 know for certain that if you ***p***
26:19 all Judah ever ***p*** him to death?
26:21 the king sought to ***p*** him to
26:24 the hand of the people to ***p***
27: 2 and ***p*** them on your neck,
27: 8 and which will not ***p*** its neck
28:14 I have ***p*** a yoke of iron on the
29:26 that you should ***p*** him in prison
31:33 I will ***p*** My law in their minds,
32:14 and ***p*** them in an earthen
32:40 but I will ***p*** My fear in their
37: 4 for they had not yet ***p*** him in
37:15 and they struck him and ***p*** him
37:18 that you have ***p*** me in prison?
38: 4 let this man be ***p*** to death, for
38: 7 heard that they had ***p*** Jeremiah
38:12 Please ***p*** these old clothes and
38:15 will you not surely ***p*** me to
38:16 I will not ***p*** you to death, nor
38:25 we will not ***p*** you to death,'
39: 7 Moreover he ***p*** out Zedekiah's
39:18 because you have ***p*** your trust
40:10 ***p*** them in your vessels, and
43: 3 that they may ***p*** us to death or
46: 4 ***P*** on the armor!
47: 6 ***P*** yourself up into your
50:14 ***P*** yourselves in array against
51:17 Every metalsmith is ***p*** to shame
52:11 He also ***p*** out the eyes of
52:11 and ***p*** him in prison till the
52:27 of Babylon struck them and ***p***
Lam 3:29 Let him ***p*** his mouth in the
Ezek 3:25 surely they will ***p*** ropes on you
4: 9 ***p*** them into one vessel, and
8:17 Indeed they ***p*** the branch to
9: 4 and ***p*** a mark on the foreheads
10: 7 and took some of it and ***p***
11:19 and I will ***p*** a new spirit
14: 3 and ***p*** before them that which
16:11 ***p*** bracelets on your wrists,
16:12 And I ***p*** a jewel in your nose,
17: 6 And ***p*** forth shoots.
17:13 and ***p*** him under oath.
19: 9 They ***p*** him in a cage with
21:19 ***p*** it at the head of the road
23:31 therefore I will ***p*** her cup in
23:42 who ***p*** bracelets on their wrists
24: 3 '***P*** on a pot, set it on,
24:17 and ***p*** your sandals on your
26:13 I will ***p*** an end to the sound of
29: 4 But I will ***p*** hooks in your
30:13 I will ***p*** fear in the land of
30:21 nor a splint ***p*** on to bind it,
30:24 of the king of Babylon and ***p***
30:25 when I ***p*** My sword into the hand
32: 7 When I ***p*** out your light,
32:25 It was ***p*** in the midst of the
36:26 give you a new heart and ***p*** a
36:27 I will ***p*** My Spirit within you
37: 6 I will ***p*** sinews on you and bring
37: 6 cover you with skin and ***p***
37:14 I will ***p*** My Spirit in you, and
38: 4 ***p*** hooks into your jaws, and
42:14 They shall ***p*** on other garments;
43: 9 Now let them ***p*** their harlotry
43:20 take some of its blood and ***p***
44:17 that they shall ***p*** on linen
44:19 and ***p*** on other garments;
45:19 of the sin offering and ***p*** it
Dan 4:37 walk in pride He is able to ***p***
5:19 whomever he wished, he ***p*** down.
5:29 Daniel with purple and ***p*** a
7: 9 watched till thrones were ***p***
Hos 2: 2 am I her Husband! Let her ***p***
Joel 2:26 My people shall never be ***p*** to
2:27 My people shall never be ***p*** to
3:13 ***P*** in the sickle, for the
Am 6: 3 Woe to you who ***p*** far off the
Jon 3: 5 and ***p*** on sackcloth, from the
Mic 2:12 I will ***p*** them together like
7: 5 Do not ***p*** your confidence in a
7:16 They shall ***p*** their hand over
Nah 3: 9 ***P*** and Lubim were your helpers.
Zeph 3:19 every land where they were ***p***
Hag 1: 6 Earns wages to ***p*** into a bag
Zech 3: 5 Let them ***p*** a clean turban on his
3: 5 So they ***p*** a clean turban on
3: 5 and they ***p*** the clothes on him.
10: 5 riders on horses shall be ***p*** to
Mt 1:19 was minded to ***p*** her away
2:16 and he sent forth and ***p*** to
4:12 heard that John had been ***p*** in
5:15 do they light a lamp and ***p***
6:25 what you will ***p*** on. Is not life
8: 3 Then Jesus ***p*** out His hand and
9:17 Nor do they ***p*** new wine into old
9:17 But they ***p*** new wine into new
9:25 But when the crowd was ***p***
10:21 parents and cause them to be ***p***

12:18 will ***p*** My Spirit upon Him,
12:44 empty, swept, and ***p*** in order.
13:24 Another parable He ***p*** forth to
13:31 parable He ***p*** forth to them,
14: 3 and ***p*** him in prison for the
14: 5 And although he wanted to ***p*** him
15: 4 let him be ***p*** to death.'
19: 7 divorce, and to ***p*** her away?"
19:13 brought to Him that He might ***p***
26:52 ***P*** your sword in its place, for
26:59 testimony against Jesus to ***p***
26:63 I ***p*** You under oath by the living
27: 1 plotted against Jesus to ***p*** Him
27: 6 It is not lawful to ***p*** them into
27:28 And they stripped Him and ***p*** a
27:29 they ***p*** it on His head, and a
27:31 ***p*** His own clothes on Him, and
27:37 And they ***p*** up over His head the
27:48 it with sour wine and ***p*** it
Mk 1:14 Now after John was ***p*** in prison,
2:22 But new wine must be ***p*** into new
4:21 Is a lamp brought to be ***p*** under
5:40 But when He had ***p*** them all
6: 9 and not to ***p*** on two tunics.
7:10 let him be ***p*** to death.'
7:32 and they begged Him to ***p*** His
7:33 and ***p*** His fingers in his ears,
8:23 He had spit on his eyes and ***p***
8:25 Then He ***p*** His hands on his eyes
10:16 ***p*** His hands on them, and
12:41 and saw how the people ***p*** money
12:41 And many who were rich ***p*** in
12:43 you that this poor widow has ***p***
12:44 for they all ***p*** in out of their
12:44 but she out of her poverty ***p*** in
13:12 parents and cause them to be ***p***
14: 1 take Him by trickery and ***p***
14:55 testimony against Jesus to ***p***
15:17 of thorns, ***p*** it on His head,
15:20 ***p*** His own clothes on Him, and
15:36 ***p*** it on a reed, and offered
Lk 1:52 He has ***p*** down the mighty from
5: 3 and asked him to ***p*** out a little
5:13 Then He ***p*** out His hand and
5:38 But new wine must be ***p*** into new
6:38 and running over will be ***p*** into
8:54 But He ***p*** them all outside, took
9:62 having ***p*** his hand to the plow,
11:25 he finds it swept and ***p*** in
12:22 the body, what you will ***p*** on.
13:17 all His adversaries were ***p*** to
13:19 which a man took and ***p*** in his
15:22 Bring out the best robe and ***p***
15:22 and ***p*** a ring on his hand and
16: 4 that when I am ***p*** out of the
19:20 which I have kept ***p*** away in a
19:23 Why then did you not ***p*** my money
21: 3 you that this poor widow has ***p***
21: 4 out of their abundance have ***p***
21: 4 but she out of her poverty ***p*** in
21:16 and they will ***p*** some of you to
23:32 led with Him to be ***p*** to death.
Jn 5: 7 I have no man to ***p*** me into the
9:15 He ***p*** clay on my eyes, and I
9:22 he would be ***p*** out of the
11:53 they plotted to ***p*** Him to death.
12: 6 and he used to take what was ***p***
12:10 the chief priests plotted to ***p***
12:42 lest they should be ***p*** out of
13: 2 the devil having already ***p*** it
16: 2 They will ***p*** you out of the
18:11 ***P*** your sword into the sheath.
18:31 It is not lawful for us to ***p***
19: 2 a crown of thorns and ***p*** it on
19: 2 and they ***p*** on Him a purple
19:19 Now Pilate wrote a title and ***p***
19:29 ***p*** it on hyssop, and put it to
19:29 and ***p*** it to His mouth.
20:25 and ***p*** my finger into the print
20:25 and ***p*** my hand into His side,
20:27 and ***p*** it into My side.
21: 7 he ***p*** on his outer garment (for
Acts 1: 7 seasons which the Father has ***p***
2:23 have crucified, and ***p*** to death;
4: 3 and ***p*** them in custody until
5:18 hands on the apostles and ***p***
5:25 the men whom you ***p*** in prison
5:34 and commanded them to ***p*** the
9:40 But Peter ***p*** them all out,
12: 4 he ***p*** him in prison,
12: 8 ***P*** on your garment and follow
12:19 that they should be ***p*** to
13:18 time of about forty years He ***p***
13:28 Pilate that He should be ***p*** to
16:24 he ***p*** them into the inner prison
16:37 And now do they ***p*** us out
26:10 and when they were ***p*** to death,
27: 2 we ***p*** to sea, meaning to sail
27: 4 When we had ***p*** to sea from there,
27: 6 and he ***p*** us on board.
Rom 8:13 but if by the Spirit you ***p*** to
9:33 will not be ***p*** to shame."
10:11 on Him will not be ***p*** to
13:12 and let us ***p*** on the armor of
13:14 But ***p*** on the Lord Jesus Christ,
14:13 not to ***p*** a stumbling block or a
1 Cor 1:27 things of the world to ***p*** to
1:27 weak things of the world to ***p***
5:13 ***p*** away from yourselves the
7:35 not that I may ***p*** a leash on
13:11 I ***p*** away childish things.
15:25 For He must reign till He has ***p***
15:27 He has ***p*** all things under
15:27 all things are ***p*** under Him,"
15:27 it is evident that He who ***p***
15:28 also be subject to Him who ***p***
15:53 For this corruptible must ***p*** on
15:53 and this mortal must ***p*** on
15:54 So when this corruptible has ***p***
15:54 and this mortal has ***p*** on
2 Cor 2: 9 that I might ***p*** you to the test,
3:13 who ***p*** a veil over his face so
11: 4 you may well ***p*** up with it!
11:19 For you ***p*** up with fools gladly,
11:20 For you ***p*** up with it if one
Gal 3:27 baptized into Christ have ***p*** on
Eph 1:22 And He ***p*** all things under His
4:22 that you ***p*** off, concerning your
4:24 and that you ***p*** on the new man
4:31 and evil speaking be ***p*** away
6:11 ***P*** on the whole armor of God,
6:14 having ***p*** on the breastplate of
Col 3: 5 Therefore ***p*** to death your
3: 8 But now you yourselves are to ***p***
3: 9 since you have ***p*** off the old
3:10 and have ***p*** on the new man who
3:12 ***p*** on tender mercies, kindness,
3:14 But above all these things ***p*** on
Phm 1:18 ***p*** that on my account.
Heb 2: 5 For He has not ***p*** the world to
2: 8 You have ***p*** all things in
2: 8 For in that He ***p*** all in
2: 8 He left nothing that is not ***p***
2: 8 we do not yet see all things ***p***
2:13 I will ***p*** My trust in
6: 6 and ***p*** Him to an open shame.
8:10 I will ***p*** My laws in
9:26 He has appeared to ***p*** away sin
10:16 I will ***p*** My laws into
Jas 3: 3 we ***p*** bits in horses' mouths
1 Pe 2: 6 will by no means be ***p***
2:15 that by doing good you may ***p*** to
3:18 being ***p*** to death in the flesh
2 Pe 1:14 knowing that shortly I must ***p***
Rev 2:14 who taught Balak to ***p*** a
2:24 I will ***p*** on you no other
11: 9 their dead bodies to be ***p*** into
17:17 For God has ***p*** it into their

PUTEOLI (1/1)

Acts 28:13 and the next day we came to ***P***,

PUTHITES (1/1)

1 Chr 2:53 were the Ithrites, the ***P***,

PUTIEL (1/1)

Ex 6:25 one of the daughters of ***P*** as

PUTREFY (1/1)

Eccl 10: 1 Dead flies ***p*** the perfumer's

PUTREFYING (1/1)

Isa 1: 6 But wounds and bruises and ***p***

PUTS (29/29)

Ex 30:33 or whoever ***p*** any of it on an
Num 22:38 The word that God ***p*** in my
Deut 24: 1 divorce, ***p*** it in her hand,
24: 3 ***p*** it in her hand, and sends
25:11 and ***p*** out her hand and seizes
1 Ki 20:11 Let not the one who ***p*** on his
Job 4:18 If He ***p*** no trust in His
15:15 If God ***p*** no trust in His
28: 3 Man ***p*** an end to darkness,
28: 9 He ***p*** his hand on the flint;
33:11 He ***p*** my feet in the stocks,
Ps 75: 7 He ***p*** down one, And exalts
Song 2:13 The fig tree ***p*** forth her green
Isa 57:13 But he who ***p*** his trust in Me
Jer 43:12 as a shepherd ***p*** on his garment,
Ezek 14: 4 and ***p*** before him what causes
14: 7 up his idols in his heart and ***p***
Mic 3: 5 prepare war against him Who ***p***
Mt 9:16 No one ***p*** a piece of unshrunk
24:32 has already become tender and ***p***
Mk 2:22 And no one ***p*** new wine into old
4:29 immediately he ***p*** in the sickle,
13:28 and ***p*** forth leaves, you know
Lk 5:36 No one ***p*** a piece from a new
5:37 And no one ***p*** new wine into old
8:16 covers it with a vessel or ***p***
11:33 ***p*** it in a secret place or
1 Cor 15:24 when He ***p*** an end to all rule
2 Cor 8:16 But thanks be to God who ***p*** the

PUTTING (18/18)

Gen 21:14 and ***p*** it on her shoulder, he
Lev 16:21 ***p*** them on the head of the goat,
Judg 7: 6 ***p*** their hand to their mouth,
Lk 21: 1 He looked up and saw the rich ***p***
21: 2 also a certain poor widow ***p*** in
Acts 9:12 named Ananias coming in and ***p***
15:10 why do you test God by ***p*** a yoke
19:33 the Jews ***p*** him forward.
27:13 ***p*** out to sea, they sailed close
27:30 under pretense of ***p*** out anchors
28:18 there was no cause for ***p*** me to
Eph 2:16 thereby ***p*** to death the enmity.
4:25 ***p*** away lying, Let each one
Col 2:11 by ***p*** off the body of the sins
1 Th 5: 8 ***p*** on the breastplate of faith
1 Tim 1:12 ***p*** me into the ministry,
1 Pe 3: 3 or ***p*** on fine apparel—
3 Jn 10 ***p*** them out of the church.

PUVAH (1/1)

Gen 46:13 sons of Issachar were Tola, ***P***,

PYGARG (KJV) See (ROE) DEER

PYRE (2/2)

Isa 30:33 Its ***p*** is fire with much wood;
Ezek 24: 9 I too will make the ***p*** great.

Q

QUADRANS (1/1)

Mk 12:42 in two mites, which make a ***q***.

QUAIL (3/3) QUAILS

Num 11:31 and it brought ***q*** from the sea
11:32 and gathered the ***q*** (he who
Ps 105:40 people asked, and He brought ***q***,

QUAILS (1/1) QUAIL

Ex 16:13 So it was that ***q*** came up at

QUAKE (1/1)

Nah 1: 5 The mountains ***q*** before Him,

QUAKED (5/5)

Ex 19:18 and the whole mountain ***q***
1 Sam 14:15 also trembled; and the earth ***q***,
2 Sam 22: 8 The foundations of heaven ***q***
Ps 18: 7 of the hills also ***q*** and were
Mt 27:51 top to bottom; and the earth ***q***,

QUAKES (1/1)

Joel 2:10 The earth ***q*** before them,

QUAKING (1/1)

Ezek 12:18 of man, eat your bread with ***q***,

QUALIFIED (2/2)

2 Ki 10: 3 choose the best ***q*** of your
Col 1:12 thanks to the Father who has ***q***

QUALITY (2/2)

Ex 30:23 take for yourself ***q*** spices—five
Jer 2:21 noble vine, a seed of highest ***q***.

QUANTITIES (1/1)

1 Ki 10:11 brought great ***q*** of almug wood

QUANTITY (2/2)

1 Ki 10:10 of gold, spices in great ***q***,
Isa 22:24 all vessels of small ***q***,

QUARREL (7/7) QUARRELED, QUARRELSOME

Gen 26:22 and they did not ***q*** over it.
2 Ki 5: 7 and see how he seeks a ***q*** with
Prov 17:14 stop contention before a ***q***
20: 3 Since any fool can start a ***q***.
26:17 passes by and meddles in a ***q***
Mt 12:19 He will not ***q*** nor cry
2 Tim 2:24 servant of the Lord must not ***q***

QUARRELED (4/3) QUARREL

Gen 26:20 But the herdsmen of Gerar ***q*** with
26:20 because they ***q*** with him.
26:21 and they ***q*** over that one also.
Jn 6:52 The Jews therefore ***q*** among

QUARRELSOME (1/1) QUARREL

1 Tim 3: 3 for money, but gentle, not ***q***,

QUARRIED (2/2)

1 Ki 5:15 and eighty thousand who ***q***
5:18 and the Gebalites ***q*** them;

QUARRIES (1/1)

Eccl 10: 9 He who ***q*** stones may be hurt by

QUARRY (3/3)

1 Ki 5:17 the king commanded them to ***q***
6: 7 with stone finished at the ***q***,
2 Chr 2: 2 eighty thousand to ***q*** stone in

QUART (1/1)
Rev 6: 6 'A *q* of wheat for a denarius,

QUARTER (6/6) QUARTERS
Gen 19: 4 all the people from every *q*,
Josh 15: 5 the border on the northern *q*
2 Ki 22:14 in Jerusalem in the Second *Q*.
2 Chr 34:22 in Jerusalem in the Second *Q*.
Isa 47:15 shall wander each one to his *q*.
Zeph 1:10 A wailing from the Second *Q*,

QUARTERMASTER (1/1)
Jer 51:59 And Seraiah was the *q*.

QUARTERNIONS (KJV) See SQUADS

QUARTERS (5/5) QUARTER
Ex 13: 7 be seen among you in all your *q*.
Esth 2: 3 the citadel, into the women's *q*,
2:11 of the court of the women's *q*,
2:13 with her from the women's *q* to
Jer 49:36 four winds From the four *q* of

QUARTS (1/1)
Rev 6: 6 and three *q* of barley for a

QUARTUS (1/1)
Rom 16:23 of the city, greets you, and *Q*,

QUARTZ (1/1)
Job 28:18 shall be made of coral or *q*,

QUEEN (53/52) QUEENS
1 Ki 10: 1 Now when the *q* of Sheba heard of
10: 4 And when the *q* of Sheba had seen
10:10 abundance of spices as the *q*
10:13 Now King Solomon gave the *q* of
11:19 the sister of *Q* Tahpenes.
15:13 his grandmother from being *q*
2 Ki 10:13 the king and the sons of the *q*
2 Chr 9: 1 Now when the *q* of Sheba heard
9: 3 And when the *q* of Sheba had seen
9: 9 any spices such as those the *q*
9:12 King Solomon gave to the *q* of
15:16 from being *q* mother, because
Neh 2: 6 Then the king said to me (the *q*
Esth 1: 9 *Q* Vashti also made a feast for
1:11 to bring *Q* Vashti before the
1:12 But *Q* Vashti refused to come at
1:15 What shall we do to *Q* Vashti,
1:16 *Q* Vashti has not only wronged
1:17 commanded *Q* Vashti to be
1:18 heard of the behavior of the *q*.
2: 4 woman who pleases the king be *q*
2:17 upon her head and made her *q*
2:22 who told *Q* Esther, and Esther
4: 4 and the *q* was deeply
5: 2 when the king saw *Q* Esther
5: 3 *Q* Esther? What is your
5:12 *Q* Esther invited no one but me
7: 1 went to dine with *Q* Esther.
7: 2 *Q* Esther? It shall be granted
7: 3 Then *Q* Esther answered and said,
7: 5 answered and said to *Q* Esther,
7: 6 terrified before the king and *q*.
7: 7 Haman stood before *Q* Esther,
7: 8 Will he also assault the *q* while
8: 1 *Q* Esther the house of Haman,
8: 7 King Ahasuerus said to *Q* Esther
9:12 And the king said to *Q* Esther,
9:29 Then *Q* Esther, the daughter of
9:31 Mordecai the Jew and *Q* Esther
Ps 45: 9 Your right hand stands the *q*
Jer 7:18 to make cakes for the *q* of
13:18 Say to the king and to the *q*
29: 2 the *q* mother, the eunuchs, the
44:17 to burn incense to the *q* of
44:18 burning incense to the *q* of
44:19 we burned incense to the *q* of
44:25 to burn incense to the *q* of
Dan 5:10 The *q*, because of
5:10 The *q* spoke, saying, "O king,
Mt 12:42 The *q* of the South will rise up
Lk 11:31 The *q* of the South will rise up
Acts 8:27 authority under Candace the *q*
Rev 18: 7 says in her heart, 'I sit as *q*,

QUEEN'S (1/1)
Esth 1:17 For the *q* behavior will become

QUEENS (3/3) QUEEN
Song 6: 8 There are sixty *q* And eighty
6: 9 The *q* and the concubines,
Isa 49:23 And their *q* your nursing

QUENCH (11/11) QUENCHED, UNQUENCHABLE
2 Sam 21:17 lest you *q* the lamp of
Ps 104:11 The wild donkeys *q* their
Song 8: 7 Many waters cannot *q* love,
Isa 1:31 And no one shall *q* them.
42: 3 And smoking flax He will not *q*;
Jer 4: 4 that no one can *q* it, Because
21:12 And burn so that no one can *q*
Am 5: 6 With no one to *q* it in
Mt 12:20 flax He will not *q*,
Eph 6:16 which you will be able to *q*
1 Th 5:19 Do not *q* the Spirit.

QUENCHED (17/17) QUENCH
Num 11: 2 to the LORD, the fire was *q*.
2 Ki 22:17 this place and shall not be *q*.
2 Chr 34:25 out on this place, and not be *q*.
Ps 118:12 They were *q* like a fire of
Isa 34:10 It shall not be *q* night or day;
43:17 they are *q* like a wick):
66:24 die, And their fire is not *q*.
Jer 7:20 And it will burn and not be *q*.
17:27 and it shall not be *q*.
Ezek 20:47 blazing flame shall not be *q*,
20:48 kindled it; it shall not be *q*.
Mk 9:43 the fire that shall never be *q*—
9:44 And the fire is not *q*.
9:45 the fire that shall never be *q*—
9:46 And the fire is not *q*.
9:48 And the fire is not *q*.
Heb 11:34 *q* the violence of fire,

QUESTION (14/14) QUESTIONED, QUESTIONS
Job 38: 3 like a man; I will *q* you,
40: 7 *q* you, and you shall answer Me:
42: 4 I will *q* you, and you shall
Mt 22:35 a lawyer, asked Him a *q*,
22:46 that day on did anyone dare *q*
Mk 11:29 "I also will ask you one *q*;
12:34 But after that no one dared *q*
Lk 20:40 But after that they dared not *q*
22:23 Then they began to *q* among
Jn 16:30 no need that anyone should *q*
Acts 15: 2 and elders, about this *q*.
18:15 But if it is a *q* of words and
19:40 in danger of being called in *q*
1 Cor 10:27 asking no *q* for conscience'

QUESTIONED (3/3) QUESTION
2 Chr 31: 9 Then Hezekiah *q* the priests and
Mk 1:27 amazed, so that they *q* among
Lk 23: 9 Then he *q* Him with many words,

QUESTIONING (2/2)
Ezra 10:17 first month they finished *q*
Mk 9:10 *q* what the rising from the dead

QUESTIONS (10/10) QUESTION
1 Ki 10: 1 came to test him with hard *q*.
10: 3 So Solomon answered all her *q*;
2 Chr 9: 1 to test Solomon with hard *q*,
9: 2 So Solomon answered all her *q*;
Lk 2:46 to them and asking them *q*.
Acts 23:29 he was accused concerning *q* of
25:19 but had some *q* against him about
25:20 I was uncertain of such *q*,
26: 3 are expert in all customs and *q*
1 Cor 10:25 asking no *q* for conscience'

QUICK (1/1) QUICKLY, QUICK-TEMPERED
Dan 1: 4 possessing knowledge and *q* to

QUICKEN (KJV) See GIVE (LIFE), REVIVE

QUICK-TEMPERED (2/2) QUICK
Prov 14:17 A *q* man acts foolishly,
Titus 1: 7 of God, not self-willed, not *q*,

QUICKLY (59/57) HASTENED, QUICK
Gen 18: 6 the tent to Sarah and said, "*Q*,
24:18 Then she *q* let her pitcher
24:20 Then she *q* emptied her pitcher
27:20 that you have found it so *q*,
41:14 and they brought him *q* out of
Ex 32: 8 They have turned aside *q* out of
Num 16:46 and take it *q* to the
Deut 9: 3 them out and destroy them *q*,
9:12 go down *q* from here, for your
9:12 they have *q* turned aside from
9:16 calf! You had turned aside *q*
11:17 and you perish *q* from the good
28:20 and until you perish *q*,
Josh 2: 5 I do not know; pursue them *q*,
8:19 So those in ambush arose *q* out
10: 6 your servants; come up to us *q*,
23:16 and you shall perish *q* from the
Judg 2:17 They turned *q* from the way in
9:54 Then he called *q* to the young
20:37 And the men in ambush *q* rushed
1 Sam 4:14 And the man came *q* and told
20:19 go down *q* and come to the place
2 Sam 5:24 trees, then you shall advance *q*.
17:16 send *q* and tell David, saying,
17:18 But both of them went away *q*
17:21 and cross over the water *q*.
1 Ki 20:33 and they *q* grasped at this
22: 9 Micaiah the son of Imlah *q*!"
2 Ki 1:11 the king said, 'Come down *q*!'
2 Chr 18: 8 Micaiah the son of Imla *q*!"
24: 5 year, and see that you do it *q*.
24: 5 the Levites did not do it *q*.
35:13 and divided them *q* among all
Esth 5: 5 the king said, "Bring Haman *q*,
Job 5:13 counsel of the cunning comes *q*
Ps 68:31 Ethiopia will *q* stretch out
Eccl 4:12 And a threefold cord is not *q*
Jer 48:16 And his affliction comes *q*.
Dan 2:25 Then Arioch *q* brought Daniel
Zeph 1:14 It is near and hastens *q*.
Mt 5:25 "Agree with your adversary *q*,
28: 7 And go *q* and tell His disciples
28: 8 So they went out *q* from the tomb
Mk 16: 8 So they went out *q* and fled from
Lk 14:21 Go out *q* into the streets and
16: 6 and sit down *q* and write
Jn 11:29 she arose *q* and came to Him.
11:31 they saw that Mary rose up *q*
13:27 to him, "What you do, do *q*.
Acts 12: 7 Arise *q*!" And his chains fell
22:18 and get out of Jerusalem *q*,
2 Tim 4: 9 Be diligent to come to me *q*;
Rev 2: 5 I will come to you *q* and remove
2:16 or else I will come to you *q*
3:11 I am coming *q*! Hold fast what
11:14 the third woe is coming *q*.
22: 7 I am coming *q*! Blessed is he
22:12 "And behold, I am coming *q*,
22:20 says, "Surely I am coming *q*.

QUIET (36/36) QUIETLY, QUIETNESS
Judg 8:28 And the country was *q* for forty
16: 2 They were *q* all night, saying,
18: 7 *q* and secure. There were no
18:19 And they said to him, "Be *q*,
18:27 to a people *q* and secure;
1 Sam 15:16 Be *q*! And I will tell you what
2 Ki 11:20 rejoiced; and the city was *q*,
1 Chr 4:40 and the land was broad, *q*,
2 Chr 14: 1 In his days the land was *q* for
14: 5 and the kingdom was *q* under
20:30 the realm of Jehoshaphat was *q*,
23:21 rejoiced; and the city was *q*,
Job 3:13 have lain still and been *q*,
3:26 I am not at ease, nor am I *q*;
Ps 35:20 matters Against the *q* ones
107:30 are glad because they are *q*;
Isa 7: 4 to him: 'Take heed, and be *q*;
14: 7 whole earth is at rest and *q*;
32:18 and in *q* resting places,
33:20 a *q* home, A tabernacle that
Jer 30:10 return, have rest and be *q*,
47: 6 How long until you are *q*?
47: 7 How can it be *q*,
49:23 on the sea; It cannot be *q*.
Ezek 16:42 I will be *q*, and be angry no
Zeph 3:17 He will *q* you with His love,
Mt 20:31 them that they should be *q*;
Mk 1:25 rebuked him, saying, "Be *q*,
10:48 Then many warned him to be *q*;
Lk 4:35 rebuked him, saying, "Be *q*,
9:36 they kept *q*, and told no one
18:39 warned him that he should be *q*;
Acts 19:36 you ought to be *q* and do
1 Th 4:11 also aspire to lead a *q* life,
1 Tim 2: 2 that we may lead a *q* and
1 Pe 3: 4 of a gentle and *q* spirit,

QUIETED (4/4)
Num 13:30 Then Caleb *q* the people before
Neh 8:11 So the Levites *q* all the people,
Ps 131: 2 Surely I have calmed and *q* my
Acts 19:35 And when the city clerk had *q*

QUIETLY (3/3) QUIET
Eccl 9:17 Words of the wise, spoken *q*,
Lam 3:26 one should hope and wait *q*
Zech 1:11 all the earth is resting *q*.

QUIETNESS (8/8) QUIET
1 Chr 22: 9 for I will give peace and *q* to
Job 20:20 Because he knows no *q* in his
34:29 When He gives *q*, who then can
Prov 17: 1 Better is a dry morsel with *q*,
Eccl 4: 6 Better a handful with *q* Than
Isa 30:15 In *q* and confidence shall be
32:17 *q* and assurance forever.
2 Th 3:12 Christ that they work in *q* and

QUIETS (1/1)
Job 37:17 When He *q* the earth by the

QUIRINIUS (1/1)
Lk 2: 2 first took place while *Q* was

QUITE (3/3)
Gen 26: 9 *Q* obviously she is your wife;
Hab 3: 9 Your bow was made *q* ready;
1 Cor 16:12 but he was *q* unwilling to come

QUIVER (8/8)
Gen 27: 3 your *q* and your bow, and go out
Job 39:23 The *q* rattles against him,
Ps 127: 5 is the man who has his *q* full
Isa 22: 6 Elam bore the *q* With chariots

49: 2 In His ***q*** He has hidden Me."
Jer 5:16 Their ***q*** is like an open tomb;
Lam 3:13 has caused the arrows of His ***q***
Ezek 29: 7 and made all their backs ***q***.

QUIVERED (1/1)

Hab 3:16 My lips ***q*** at the voice;

QUOTA (6/6)

Ex 5: 8 you shall lay on them the ***q*** of
5:13 your work, your daily ***q***,
5:18 yet you shall deliver the ***q*** of
5:19 any bricks from your daily ***q***.
16: 4 go out and gather a certain ***q***
Neh 11:23 the singers, a ***q*** day

QUOTES (1/1)

Ezek 16:44 Indeed everyone who ***q*** proverbs

R

RAAMA (2/1)

1 Chr 1: 9 were Seba, Havilah, Sabta, ***R***,
1: 9 The sons of ***R*** were Sheba and

RAAMAH (3/2)

Gen 10: 7 were Seba, Havilah, Sabtah, ***R***,
10: 7 and the sons of ***R*** were Sheba
Ezek 27:22 The merchants of Sheba and ***R***

RAAMIAH (1/1)

Neh 7: 7 Jeshua, Nehemiah, Azariah, ***R***,

RAAMSES (1/1) RAMESES

Ex 1:11 supply cities, Pithom and ***R***.

RABBAH (15/14)

Deut 3:11 (Is it not in ***R*** of the people
Josh 13:25 as Aroer, which is before ***R***,
15:60 is Kirjath Jearim) and ***R***:
2 Sam 11: 1 people of Ammon and besieged ***R***.
12:26 Now Joab fought against ***R*** of
12:27 said, "I have fought against ***R***,
12:29 people together and went to ***R***,
17:27 Shobi the son of Nahash from ***R***
1 Chr 20: 1 Ammon, and came and besieged ***R***.
20: 1 And Joab defeated ***R*** and
Jer 49: 2 be heard an alarm of war In ***R***
49: 3 Cry, you daughters of ***R***,
Ezek 21:20 a road for the sword to go to ***R***
25: 5 And I will make ***R*** a stable for
Am 1:14 kindle a fire in the wall of ***R***,

RABBATH (KJV) See RABBAH

RABBI (17/15) RABBONI

Mt 23: 7 and to be called by men, '***R***,
23: 7 to be called by men, 'Rabbi, ***R***.
23: 8 "But you, do not be called '***R***';
26:25 Him, answered and said, "***R***,
26:49 ***R***!" and kissed Him.
Mk 9: 5 answered and said to Jesus, "***R***,
11:21 remembering, said to Him, "***R***,
14:45 up to Him and said to Him, "***R***,
14:45 ***R***!" and kissed Him.
Jn 1:38 ***R***" (which is to say, when
1:49 answered and said to Him, "***R***,
3: 2 by night and said to Him, "***R***,
3:26 to John and said to him, "***R***,
4:31 urged Him, saying, "***R***,
6:25 the sea, they said to Him, "***R***,
9: 2 asked Him, saying, "***R***,
11: 8 The disciples said to Him, "***R***,

RABBIM (1/1)

Song 7: 4 By the gate of Bath ***R***.

RABBITH (1/1)

Josh 19:20 ***R***, Kishion, Abez,

RABBLE (1/1)

Job 30:12 At my right hand the ***r***

RABBONI (2/2) RABBI

Mk 10:51 The blind man said to Him, "***R***,
Jn 20:16 ***R***!" (which is to say, Teacher).

RABMAG (2/2)

Jer 39: 3 Rabsaris, Nergal-Sarezer, ***R***,
39:13 Rabsaris, Nergal-Sharezer, ***R***,

RABSARIS (3/3)

2 Ki 18:17 sent the Tartan, the ***R***,
Jer 39: 3 Samgar-Nebo, Sarsechim, ***R***,
39:13 the guard sent Nebushasban, ***R***,

RABSHAKEH (16/16)

2 Ki 18:17 and the ***R*** from Lachish, with
18:19 Then the ***R*** said to them, "Say
18:26 Shebna, and Joah said to the ***R***,
18:27 But the ***R*** said to them, "Has
18:28 Then the ***R*** stood and called out
18:37 told him the words of the ***R***.
19: 4 hear all the words of the ***R***,
19: 8 Then the ***R*** returned and found
Isa 36: 2 the king of Assyria sent the ***R***
36: 4 Then the ***R*** said to them, "Say
36:11 Shebna, and Joah said to the ***R***,
36:12 But the ***R*** said, "Has my master
36:13 Then the ***R*** stood and called
36:22 told him the words of the ***R***.
37: 4 will hear the words of the ***R***,
37: 8 Then the ***R*** returned, and found

RACA (1/1)

Mt 5:22 ***R***!' shall be in danger of the

RACE (7/7)

Ps 19: 5 like a strong man to run its ***r***.
Eccl 9:11 The ***r*** is not to the swift,
Zech 9: 6 A mixed ***r*** shall settle in
Acts 20:24 so that I may finish my ***r*** with
1 Cor 9:24 know that those who run in a ***r***
2 Tim 4: 7 fight, I have finished the ***r***,
Heb 12: 1 let us run with endurance the ***r***

RACHAB (KJV) See RAHAB

RACHAL (1/1)

1 Sam 30:29 those who were in ***R***,

RACHEL (43/40) RACHEL'S

Gen 29: 6 his daughter ***R*** is coming with
29: 9 ***R*** came with her father's sheep,
29:10 when Jacob saw ***R*** the daughter
29:11 Then Jacob kissed ***R***,
29:12 And Jacob told ***R*** that he was
29:16 the name of the younger was ***R***.
29:17 but ***R*** was beautiful of form and
29:18 Now Jacob loved ***R***;
29:18 serve you seven years for ***R***
29:20 Jacob served seven years for ***R***,
29:25 Was it not for ***R*** that I served
29:28 So he gave him his daughter ***R***
29:29 maid Bilhah to his daughter ***R***
29:30 Then Jacob also went in to ***R***,
29:30 and he also loved ***R*** more than
29:31 but ***R*** was barren.
30: 1 Now when ***R*** saw that she bore
30: 1 ***R*** envied her sister, and said
30: 2 anger was aroused against ***R***,
30: 6 Then ***R*** said, "God has judged my
30: 8 Then ***R*** said, "With great
30:14 Then ***R*** said to Leah, "Please
30:15 And ***R*** said, "Therefore he
30:22 Then God remembered ***R***,
30:25 when ***R*** had borne Joseph, that
31: 4 So Jacob sent and called ***R*** and
31:14 Then ***R*** and Leah answered and
31:19 and ***R*** had stolen the household
31:32 For Jacob did not know that ***R***
31:34 Now ***R*** had taken the household
33: 1 the children among Leah, ***R***,
33: 2 and ***R*** and Joseph last.
33: 7 Afterward Joseph and ***R*** came
35:16 ***R*** labored in childbirth, and
35:19 So ***R*** died and was buried on the
35:24 the sons of ***R*** were Joseph and
46:19 The sons of ***R***, Jacob's wife,
46:22 These were the sons of ***R***,
46:25 whom Laban gave to ***R*** his
48: 7 ***R*** died beside me in the land of
Ruth 4:11 is coming to your house like ***R***
Jer 31:15 ***R*** weeping for her children,
Mt 2:18 ***R*** weeping for her

RACHEL'S (5/5) RACHEL

Gen 30: 7 And ***R*** maid Bilhah conceived
31:33 Leah's tent and entered ***R*** tent.
35:20 which is the pillar of ***R*** grave
35:25 ***R*** maidservant, were Dan and
1 Sam 10: 2 you will find two men by ***R*** tomb

RADDAI (1/1)

1 Chr 2:14 the fourth, ***R*** the fifth,

RADIANT (2/2)

Ps 34: 5 They looked to Him and were ***r***,
Isa 60: 5 you shall see and become ***r***,

RADIATING (1/1)

Ezek 1: 4 was all around it and ***r*** out

RAFTERS (1/1)

Song 1:17 And our ***r*** of fir.

RAFTS (2/2)

1 Ki 5: 9 I will float them in ***r*** by sea
2 Chr 2:16 we will bring it to you in ***r*** by

RAGAU (KJV) See REU

RAGE (19/19) RAGED, RAGES, RAGING

2 Ki 5:12 he turned and went away in a ***r***.
19:27 And your ***r*** against Me.
19:28 Because your ***r*** against Me and
2 Chr 28: 9 but you have killed them in a ***r***
Job 39:24 distance with fierceness and ***r***;
40:11 Disperse the ***r*** of your wrath;
40:23 Indeed the river may ***r***,
Ps 2: 1 Why do the nations ***r***,
7: 6 Yourself up because of the ***r***
Isa 37:28 And your ***r*** against Me.
37:29 Because your ***r*** against Me and
Jer 46: 9 Come up, O horses, and ***r***,
Dan 3:13 in ***r*** and fury, gave the command
8: 7 he was moved with ***r*** against
11:11 the South shall be moved with ***r***,
11:30 and return in ***r*** against the
Nah 2: 4 The chariots ***r*** in the streets,
Lk 6:11 But they were filled with ***r***,
Acts 4:25 'Why did the nations ***r***,

RAGED (1/1) RAGE

Ps 46: 6 The nations ***r***, the kingdoms

RAGES (3/3) RAGE

Prov 14:16 But a fool ***r*** and is
18: 1 He ***r*** against all wise
29: 9 Whether the fool ***r*** or

RAGING (6/6) RAGE

Ps 22:13 Like a ***r*** and roaring lion.
89: 9 You rule the ***r*** of the sea;
Ezek 1: 4 a great cloud with ***r*** fire
Jon 1:15 and the sea ceased from its ***r***.
Lk 8:24 wind and the ***r*** of the water.
Jude 13 ***r*** waves of the sea, foaming up

RAGS (4/4)

Prov 23:21 will clothe a man with ***r***.
Isa 64: 6 are like filthy ***r***;
Jer 38:11 there old clothes and old ***r***,
38:12 put these old clothes and ***r***

RAGUEL (KJV) See REUEL

RAHAB (11/11)

Josh 2: 1 the house of a harlot named ***R***,
2: 3 the king of Jericho sent to ***R***,
6:17 Only ***R*** the harlot shall live,
6:23 spies went in and brought out ***R***,
6:25 And Joshua spared ***R*** the harlot,
Ps 87: 4 I will make mention of ***R*** and
89:10 You have broken ***R*** in pieces, as
Isa 51: 9 You not the arm that cut ***R***
Mt 1: 5 Salmon begot Boaz by ***R***,
Heb 11:31 By faith the harlot ***R*** did not
Jas 2:25 was not ***R*** the harlot also

RAHAB-HEM-SHEBETH (1/1)

Isa 30: 7 Therefore I have called her ***R***.

RAHAM (1/1)

1 Chr 2:44 Shema begot ***R*** the father of

RAHEL (KJV) See RACHEL

RAID (4/4) RAIDED, RAIDERS, RAIDING, RAIDS

1 Sam 27:10 Where have you made a ***r*** today?"
2 Sam 3:22 of David and Joab came from a ***r***
1 Chr 14: 9 Philistines went and made a ***r***
14:13 once again made a ***r*** on the

RAIDED (4/4) RAID

1 Sam 27: 8 and his men went up and ***r*** the
2 Chr 25:13 they ***r*** the cities of Judah from
Job 1:15 when the Sabeans ***r*** them and
1:17 ***r*** the camels and took them

RAIDERS (7/7) RAID

1 Sam 13:17 Then ***r*** came out of the camp of
14:15 The garrison and the ***r*** also
1 Ki 11:24 captain over a band of ***r***,
2 Ki 6:23 So the bands of Syrian ***r*** came
13:21 they spied a band of ***r***;
1 Chr 12:21 David against the bands of ***r***,
2 Chr 22: 1 for the ***r*** who came with the

RAIDING (3/3) RAID

Judg 11: 3 with Jephthah and went out ***r***
2 Ki 13:20 And the ***r*** bands from Moab
24: 2 the LORD sent against him ***r***

RAIDS (1/1) RAID

2 Ki 5: 2 the Syrians had gone out on ***r***,

R

RAIMENT (KJV) See CLOTHES, CLOTHING, GARMENT, GARMENTS

RAIN (105/89) RAINED, RAINS, RAINY

Gen 2: 5 God had not caused it to *r* on
7: 4 more days I will cause it to *r*
7:12 And the *r* was on the earth forty
8: 2 and the *r* from heaven was
Ex 9:18 will cause very heavy hail to *r*
9:33 and the *r* was not poured on the
9:34 And when Pharaoh saw that the *r*,
16: 4 I will *r* bread from heaven for
Lev 26: 4 then I will give you *r* in its
Deut 11:11 which drinks water from the *r*
11:14 then I will give you the *r* for
11:14 the early *r* and the latter
11:14 the early rain and the latter *r*,
11:17 heavens so that there be no *r*,
28:12 to give the *r* to your land in
28:24 The LORD will change the *r* of
32: 2 Let my teaching drop as the *r*,
1 Sam 12:17 and He will send thunder and *r*,
12:18 the LORD sent thunder and *r*
2 Sam 1:21 Let there be no dew nor *r*
23: 4 By clear shining after *r*,
1 Ki 8:35 are shut up and there is no *r*
8:36 and send *r* on Your land which
17: 1 there shall not be dew nor *r*
17: 7 because there had been no *r* in
17:14 the day the LORD sends *r* on
18: 1 and I will send *r* on the
18:41 is the sound of abundance of *r*.
18:44 and go down before the *r* stops
18:45 wind, and there was a heavy *r*.
2 Ki 3:17 see wind, nor shall you see *r*;
2 Chr 6:26 are shut up and there is no *r*
6:27 and send *r* on Your land which
7:13 up heaven and there is no *r*,
Ezra 10: 9 matter and because of heavy *r*.
10:13 it is the season for heavy *r*,
Job 5:10 He gives *r* on the earth,
20:23 And will *r* it on him while he
28:26 When He made a law for the *r*,
29:23 waited for me as for the *r*,
29:23 mouth wide as for the spring *r*.
36:27 Which distill as *r* from the
37: 6 Likewise to the gentle *r* and
37: 6 gentle rain and the heavy *r* of
38:26 To cause it to *r* on a land
38:28 Has the *r* a father?
Ps 11: 6 Upon the wicked He will *r*
68: 8 The heavens also dropped *r* at
68: 9 You, O God, sent a plentiful *r*,
72: 6 He shall come down like *r* upon
84: 6 The *r* also covers it with
105:32 He gave them hail for *r*,
135: 7 He makes lightning for the *r*;
147: 8 Who prepares *r* for the earth,
Prov 16:15 like a cloud of the latter *r*.
25:14 like clouds and wind without *r*.
25:23 The north wind brings forth *r*,
26: 1 As snow in summer and *r* in
28: 3 the poor Is like a driving *r*
Eccl 11: 3 If the clouds are full of *r*,
12: 2 do not return after the *r*;
Song 2:11 The *r* is over and gone.
Isa 4: 6 for a shelter from storm and *r*.
5: 6 the clouds That they *r* no
5: 6 clouds That they rain no *r* on
30:23 Then He will give the *r* for
44:14 and the *r* nourishes it.
45: 8 *R* down, you heavens, from
55:10 For as the *r* comes down, and the
Jer 3: 3 And there has been no latter *r*.
5:24 the LORD our God, Who gives *r*,
10:13 He makes lightning for the *r*,
14: 4 For there was no *r* in the
14:22 of the nations that can cause *r*?
51:16 He makes lightnings for the *r*;
Ezek 13:11 There will be flooding *r*,
13:13 there shall be a flooding *r* in
38:22 I will *r* down on him, on his
38:22 who are with him, flooding *r*,
Hos 6: 3 He will come to us like the *r*,
6: 3 Like the latter and former *r*
Joel 2:23 He has given you the former *r*
2:23 And He will cause the *r* to
2:23 come down for you—The former *r*,
2:23 And the latter *r* in the first
Am 4: 7 I also withheld *r* from you,
4: 7 I made it *r* on one city,
4: 7 I withheld *r* from another
4: 7 And where it did not *r* the
Zech 10: 1 Ask the LORD for *r* In the
10: 1 In the time of the latter *r*.
10: 1 He will give them showers of *r*,
14:17 on them there will be no *r*.
14:18 in, they shall have no *r*;
Mt 5:45 and sends *r* on the just and on
7:25 *r* descended, the floods came,
7:27 and the *r* descended, the floods
Acts 14:17 gave us *r* from heaven and
28: 2 because of the *r* that was
Heb 6: 7 the earth which drinks in the *r*
Jas 5: 7 receives the early and latter *r*.
5:17 earnestly that it would not *r*;
5:17 and it did not *r* on the land
5:18 again, and the heaven gave *r*,
Rev 11: 6 so that no *r* falls in the days

RAINBOW (6/6)

Gen 9:13 I set My *r* in the cloud, and it
9:14 that the *r* shall be seen in the
9:16 The *r* shall be in the cloud, and
Ezek 1:28 Like the appearance of a *r* in a
Rev 4: 3 and there was a *r* around the
10: 1 And a *r* was on his head, his

RAINDROPS (1/1)

Deut 32: 2 As *r* on the tender herb,

RAINED (7/7) RAIN

Gen 19:24 Then the LORD *r* brimstone and
Ex 9:23 And the LORD *r* hail on the
Ps 78:24 Had *r* down manna on them to
78:27 He also *r* meat on them like the
Ezek 22:24 land that is not cleansed or *r*
Am 4: 7 One part was *r* upon,
Lk 17:29 that Lot went out of Sodom it *r*

RAINS (3/3) RAIN

2 Sam 21:10 of harvest until the late *r*
Hos 10:12 Till He comes and *r*
Am 5: 9 He *r* ruin upon the strong,

RAINY (2/2) RAIN

Prov 27:15 dripping on a very *r* day
Ezek 1:28 rainbow in a cloud on a *r* day,

RAISE (63/62) PERPETUATE, RAISED, RAISES, RAISING

Gen 38: 8 and *r* up an heir to your
Ex 26:30 And you shall *r* up the
Deut 18:15 The LORD your God will *r* up
18:18 I will *r* up for them a Prophet
25: 7 husband's brother refuses to *r*
32:40 For I *r* My hand to heaven,
Josh 8:29 and *r* over it a great heap of
1 Sam 2:35 Then I will *r* up for Myself a
2 Sam 12:11 I will *r* up adversity against
12:17 to *r* him up from the ground.
18:12 I would not *r* my hand against
1 Ki 14:14 Moreover the LORD will *r* up for
Job 30:12 And they *r* against me their
Ps 41:10 and *r* me up, That I may repay
81: 2 *R* a song and strike the
Isa 13: 2 *R* your voice to them;
15: 5 They will *r* up a cry of
29: 3 And I will *r* siegeworks
42: 2 nor *r* His voice, Nor cause
44:26 And I will *r* up her waste
49: 6 You should be My Servant To *r*
58:12 You shall *r* up the foundations
61: 4 They shall *r* up the former
Jer 4:16 come from a far country And *r*
23: 5 That I will *r* to David a Branch
30: 9 Whom I will *r* up for them.
50: 9 I will *r* and cause to come up
50:32 And no one will *r* him up;
51: 1 I will *r* up against Babylon,
Ezek 24: 8 That it may *r* up fury and take
26: 8 and *r* a defense against you.
34:29 I will *r* up for them a garden of
Hos 6: 2 On the third day He will *r* us
Joel 3: 7 I will *r* them Out of the place
Am 5: 2 There is no one to *r* her
6:14 I will *r* up a nation against
9:11 On that day I will *r* up The
9:11 I will *r* up its ruins,
Mic 5: 5 Then we will *r* against him
Zech 11:16 For indeed I will *r* up a
14:13 And *r* his hand against his
Mt 3: 9 to you that God is able to *r*
10: 8 *r* the dead, cast out demons.
22:24 shall marry his wife and *r* up
Mk 12:19 should take his wife and *r* up
Lk 3: 8 to you that God is able to *r*
13:11 bent over and could in no way *r*
18:13 would not so much as *r* his
20:28 should take his wife and *r* up
Jn 2:19 and in three days I will *r* it
2:20 and will You *r* it up in three
6:39 but should *r* it up at the last
6:40 *r* him up at the last day."
6:44 will *r* him up at the last day.
6:54 will *r* him up at the last day.
Acts 2:30 He would *r* up the Christ to sit
3:22 LORD your God will *r* up
7:37 LORD your God will *r* up
1 Cor 6:14 up the Lord and will also *r* us
15:15 whom He did not *r* up—if in fact
2 Cor 4:14 up the Lord Jesus will also *r*
Heb 11:19 that God was able to *r* him
Jas 5:15 and the Lord will *r* him up.

RAISED (132/127) RAISE

Gen 14:22 I have *r* my hand to the LORD,
Ex 9:16 for this purpose I have *r* you
29:27 the heave offering which is *r*,
40:17 that the tabernacle was *r* up.
40:18 So Moses *r* up the tabernacle,
40:18 and *r* up its pillars.
40:33 And he *r* up the court all around
Num 9:15 day that the tabernacle was *r*
24: 2 And Balaam *r* his eyes, and saw
Josh 5: 7 their sons whom He *r* up in
7:26 Then they *r* over him a great
Judg 2:16 the LORD *r* up judges who
2:18 And when the LORD *r* up judges
3: 9 the LORD *r* up a deliverer for
3:15 the LORD *r* up a deliverer for
19:17 And when he *r* his eyes, he saw
1 Sam 12: 6 It is the LORD who *r* up Moses
2 Sam 18:28 has delivered up the men who *r*
20:21 has *r* his hand against the
23: 1 Thus says the man *r* up on
1 Ki 5:13 Then King Solomon *r* up a labor
9:15 force which King Solomon *r*:
9:21 from these Solomon *r* forced
11:14 Now the LORD *r* up an adversary
11:23 And God *r* up another adversary
2 Ki 19:22 Against whom have you *r* your
21: 3 he *r* up altars for Baal,
2 Chr 8: 8 from these Solomon *r* forced
32: 5 *r* it up to the towers, and
33: 3 he *r* up altars for the Baals,
33:14 and he *r* it to a very great
Job 2:12 And when they *r* their eyes from
31:21 If I have *r* my hand against the
Ps 106:26 Therefore He *r* up His hand in
Isa 14: 9 It has *r* up from their thrones
23:13 They *r* up its palaces,
37:23 Against whom have you *r* your
41: 2 'Who *r* up one from the east?
41:25 I have *r* up one from the north,
45:13 I have *r* him up in
Jer 6:22 And a great nation will be *r*
25:32 a great whirlwind shall be *r*
29:15 The LORD has *r* up prophets for
50:41 and many kings Shall be *r* up
51:11 The LORD has *r* up the spirit
Ezek 20: 5 day when I chose Israel and *r*
20: 5 I *r* My hand in an oath to them,
20: 6 On that day I *r* My hand in an
20:15 So I also *r* My hand in an oath
20:23 Also I *r* My hand in an oath to
20:28 land concerning which I had *r*
20:42 the country for which I *r* My
36: 7 I have *r* My hand in an oath that
44:12 therefore I have *r* My hand in
47:14 for I *r* My hand in an oath to
Dan 7: 5 It was *r* up on one side, and
Am 2:11 I *r* up some of your sons as
Zech 1:18 Then I *r* my eyes and looked,
2: 1 Then I *r* my eyes and looked, and
5: 1 Then I turned and *r* my eyes, and
5: 9 Then I *r* my eyes and looked, and
6: 1 Then I turned and *r* my eyes and
9:13 And *r* up your sons, O Zion,
14:10 Jerusalem shall be *r* up and
Mal 3:15 those who do wickedness are *r*
Mt 11: 5 the dead are *r* up and the
16:21 and be *r* the third day.
17:23 and the third day He will be *r*
26:32 "But after I have been *r*,
27:52 who had fallen asleep were *r*;
Mk 6:16 he has been *r* from the dead!"
14:28 "But after I have been *r*,
Lk 1:69 And has *r* up a horn of
7:22 the deaf hear, the dead are *r*,
9:22 and be *r* the third day."
11:27 certain woman from the crowd *r*
20:37 passage that the dead are *r*,
Jn 8: 7 He *r* Himself up and said to
8:10 When Jesus had *r* Himself up and
12: 1 whom He had *r* from the dead.
12: 9 whom He had *r* from the dead.
12:17 Lazarus out of his tomb and *r*
21:14 to His disciples after He was *r*
Acts 2:14 *r* his voice and said to them,
2:24 whom God *r* up, having loosed the
2:32 This Jesus God has *r* up, of
3:15 whom God *r* from the dead, of
3:26 having *r* up His Servant Jesus,
4:10 whom God *r* from the dead, by
4:24 they *r* their voice to God with
5:30 The God of our fathers *r* up
10:40 Him God *r* up on the third day,
12: 7 struck Peter on the side and *r*
13:22 He *r* up for them David as king,
13:23 *r* up for Israel a Savior—Jesus—
13:30 But God *r* Him from the dead.
13:33 in that He has *r* up Jesus.
13:34 And that He *r* Him from the dead,
13:37 but He whom God *r* up saw no
13:50 *r* up persecution against Paul
14:11 they *r* their voices, saying in
22:22 and then they *r* their voices
Rom 4:24 to us who believe in Him who *r*
4:25 and was *r* because of our
6: 4 that just as Christ was *r* from
6: 9 having been *r* from the dead,
7: 4 to Him who was *r* from the dead,
8:11 But if the Spirit of Him who *r*
8:11 He who *r* Christ from the dead
9:17 very purpose I have *r*
10: 9 in your heart that God has *r*
1 Cor 6:14 And God both *r* up the Lord and
15:12 is preached that He has been *r*
15:15 testified of God that He *r* up
15:35 'How are the dead *r* up?
15:42 it is *r* in incorruption.
15:43 it is *r* in glory. It is sown in
15:43 it is *r* in power.
15:44 it is *r* a spiritual body.
15:52 and the dead will be *r*
2 Cor 4:14 knowing that He who *r* up the
Gal 1: 1 and God the Father who *r* Him

Eph 1:20 He worked in Christ when He *r*
2: 6 and *r* us up together, and made
Col 2:12 in which you also were *r* with
2:12 who *r* Him from the dead.
3: 1 If then you were *r* with Christ,
1 Th 1:10 whom He *r* from the dead, even
2 Tim 2: 8 was *r* from the dead according
Heb 11:35 Women received their dead *r* to
1 Pe 1:21 who *r* Him from the dead and
Rev 10: 5 on the land *r* up his hand to

RAISES (11/11) RAISE

1 Sam 2: 8 He *r* the poor from the dust
Job 41:25 When he *r* himself up,
Ps 107:25 For He commands and *r* the
113: 7 He *r* the poor out of the dust,
145:14 And *r* up all who are bowed
146: 8 The LORD *r* those who are
Prov 1:20 She *r* her voice in the open
Dan 2:21 He removes kings and *r* up
Jn 5:21 For as the Father *r* the dead and
Acts 26: 8 incredible by you that God *r*
2 Cor 1: 9 in ourselves but in God who *r*

RAISIN (1/1) RAISINS

Hos 3: 1 to other gods and love the *r*

RAISING (3/3) RAISE

1 Chr 15:16 by *r* the voice with resounding
Hab 1: 6 For indeed I am *r* up the
Acts 17:31 assurance of this to all by *r*

RAISINS (8/8) RAISIN

Num 6: 3 nor eat fresh grapes or *r*.
1 Sam 25:18 one hundred clusters of *r*,
30:12 of figs and two clusters of *r*.
2 Sam 6:19 of meat, and a cake of *r*.
16: 1 one hundred clusters of *r*,
1 Chr 12:40 cakes of figs and cakes of *r*,
16: 3 of meat, and a cake of *r*.
Song 2: 5 Sustain me with cakes of *r*,

RAKEM (1/1)

1 Chr 7:16 and his sons were Ulam and *R*.

RAKKATH (1/1)

Josh 19:35 are Ziddim, Zer, Hammath, *R*,

RAKKON (1/1)

Josh 19:46 Me Jarkon, and *R*, with the

RALLY (1/1)

Neh 4:20 *r* to us there. Our God will

RAM (104/93) RAM'S, RAMS

Gen 15: 9 female goat, a three-year-old *r*,
22:13 and there behind him was a *r*
22:13 So Abraham went and took the *r*,
Ex 25: 5 *r* skins dyed red, badger skins,
26:14 shall also make a covering of *r*
29:15 "You shall also take one *r*,
29:15 hands on the head of the *r*;
29:16 "and you shall kill the *r*,
29:17 Then you shall cut the *r* in
29:18 you shall burn the whole *r*
29:19 shall also take the other *r*,
29:19 hands on the head of the *r*.
29:20 "Then you shall kill the *r*,
29:22 you shall take the fat of the *r*,
29:22 right thigh (for it is a *r* of
29:26 shall take the breast of the *r*
29:27 And from the *r* of the
29:31 And you shall take the *r* of the
29:32 shall eat the flesh of the *r*,
35: 7 *r* skins dyed red, badger skins,
36:19 a covering for the tent of *r*
39:34 the covering of *r* skins dyed
Lev 5:15 as his trespass offering a *r*
5:16 atonement for him with the *r*
5:18 shall bring to the priest a *r*
6: 6 a *r* without blemish from the
8:18 Then he brought the *r* as the
8:18 hands on the head of the *r*,
8:20 And he cut the *r* into pieces;
8:21 And Moses burned the whole *r* on
8:22 And he brought the second *r*,
8:22 the *r* of consecration.
8:22 hands on the head of the *r*,
8:29 It was Moses' part of the *r* of
9: 2 bull as a sin offering and a *r*
9: 4 also a bull and a *r* as peace
9:18 also killed the bull and the *r*
9:19 the fat from the bull and the *r*—
16: 3 and of a *r* as a burnt
16: 5 and one *r* as a burnt offering.
19:21 a *r* as a trespass offering.
19:22 atonement for him with the *r*
Num 5: 8 in addition to the *r* of the
6:14 one *r* without blemish as a
6:17 and he shall offer the *r* as a
6:19 the boiled shoulder of the *r*,
7:15 one young bull, one *r*,
7:21 one young bull, one *r*,
7:27 bull, one *r*, and one male lamb
7:33 one *r*, and one male lamb in its
7:39 one young bull, one *r*,
7:45 one young bull, one *r*,
7:51 one young bull, one *r*,
7:57 one young bull, one *r*,
7:63 one young bull, one *r*,
7:69 one young bull, one *r*,
7:75 one young bull, one *r*,
7:81 one young bull, one *r*,
15: 6 Or for a *r* you shall prepare as
15:11 for each young bull, for each *r*,
23: 2 Balaam offered a bull and a *r*
23: 4 on each altar a bull and a *r*.
23:14 and offered a bull and a *r* on
23:30 and offered a bull and a *r* on
28:11 LORD: two young bulls, one *r*,
28:12 mixed with oil, for the one *r*;
28:14 one-third of a hin for a *r*,
28:19 LORD: two young bulls, one *r*,
28:20 a bull, and two-tenths for a *r*;
28:27 LORD: two young bulls, one *r*,
28:28 bull, two-tenths for the one *r*,
29: 2 LORD: one young bull, one *r*,
29: 3 the bull, two-tenths for the *r*,
29: 8 aroma: one young bull, one *r*,
29: 9 bull, two-tenths for the one *r*,
29:36 to the LORD: one bull, one *r*,
29:37 for the bull, for the *r*,
Ruth 4:19 Hezron begot *R*, and Ram
4:19 and *R* begot Amminadab;
1 Chr 2: 9 born to him were Jerahmeel, *R*,
2:10 *R* begot Amminadab, and
2:25 firstborn of Hezron, were *R*,
2:27 The sons of *R*, the firstborn of
Ezra 10:19 they presented a *r* of the
Job 32: 2 the Buzite, of the family of *R*,
Ezek 43:23 and a *r* from the flock without
43:25 prepare a young bull and a *r*
45:24 bull and one ephah for each *r*,
46: 4 and a *r* without blemish;
46: 5 shall be one ephah for a *r*,
46: 6 blemish, six lambs, and a *r*;
46: 7 for a bull, an ephah for a *r*,
46:11 for a bull, an ephah for a *r*,
Dan 8: 3 was a *r* which had two horns,
8: 4 I saw the *r* pushing westward,
8: 6 Then he came to the *r* that had
8: 7 And I saw him confronting the *r*;
8: 7 against him, attacked the *r*,
8: 7 There was no power in the *r* to
8: 7 no one that could deliver the *r*
8:20 The *r* which you saw, having the
Mt 1: 3 Hezron, and Hezron begot *R*.
1: 4 *R* begot Amminadab, Amminadab
Lk 3:33 of Amminadab, the son of *R*,

RAM'S (2/2) RAM

Josh 6: 5 make a long blast with the *r*
Hos 5: 8 Blow the *r* horn in Gibeah,

RAMAH (38/36) RAMOTH

Josh 18:25 Gibeon, *R*, Beeroth,
19: 8 *R* of the South. This was the
19:29 And the border turned to *R* and
19:36 Adamah, *R*, Hazor,
Judg 4: 5 palm tree of Deborah between *R*
19:13 the night in Gibeah or in *R*.
1 Sam 1:19 and came to their house at *R*.
2:11 Elkanah went to his house at *R*.
7:17 But he always returned to *R*,
8: 4 and came to Samuel at *R*,
15:34 Then Samuel went to *R*,
16:13 So Samuel arose and went to *R*.
19:18 and went to Samuel at *R*,
19:19 David is at Naioth in *R*!"
19:22 Then he also went to *R*,
19:22 they are at Naioth in *R*.
19:23 So he went there to Naioth in *R*.
19:23 until he came to Naioth in *R*.
20: 1 David fled from Naioth in *R*,
22: 6 under a tamarisk tree in *R*,
25: 1 and buried him at his home in *R*.
28: 3 for him and buried him in *R*,
1 Ki 15:17 up against Judah, and built *R*,
15:21 it, that he stopped building *R*,
15:22 away the stones and timber of *R*,
2 Ki 8:29 had inflicted on him at *R*,
2 Chr 16: 1 up against Judah and built *R*,
16: 5 that he stopped building *R* and
16: 6 away the stones and timber of *R*,
22: 6 which he had received at *R*,
Ezra 2:26 the people of *R* and Geba, six
Neh 7:30 the men of *R* and Geba, six
11:33 in Hazor, *R*, Gittaim;
Isa 10:29 *R* is afraid, Gibeah of Saul
Jer 31:15 "A voice was heard in *R*,
40: 1 the guard had let him go from *R*,
Hos 5: 8 The trumpet in *R*! Cry aloud
Mt 2:18 voice was heard in *R*,

RAMATH LEHI (1/1)

Judg 15:17 hand and called that place *R*

RAMATH MIZPAH (1/1)

Josh 13:26 and from Heshbon to *R* and

RAMATHAIM ZOPHIM (1/1)

1 Sam 1: 1 there was a certain man of *R*,

RAMATHAIM-ZOPHIM (KJV) See RAMATHAIM ZOPHIM

RAMATHITE (1/1)

1 Chr 27:27 And Shimei the *R* was over the

RAMESES (4/4) RAAMSES

Gen 47:11 of the land, in the land of *R*,
Ex 12:37 of Israel journeyed from *R* to
Num 33: 3 They departed from *R* in the
33: 5 of Israel moved from *R* and

RAMIAH (1/1)

Ezra 10:25 of the sons of Parosh: *R*,

RAMOTH (27/27) JARMUTH, RAMAH

Deut 4:43 *R* in Gilead for the Gadites,
Josh 20: 8 *R* in Gilead, from the tribe of
21:38 *R* in Gilead with its
1 Sam 30:27 those who were in *R* of the
1 Ki 4:13 in *R* Gilead; to him belonged
22: 3 Do you know that *R* in Gilead is
22: 4 with me to fight at *R* Gilead?"
22: 6 Shall I go against *R* Gilead to
22:12 Go up to *R* Gilead and prosper,
22:15 we go to war against *R* Gilead,
22:20 that he may fall at *R* Gilead?'
22:29 of Judah went up to *R* Gilead.
2 Ki 8:28 king of Syria at *R* Gilead;
9: 1 and go to *R* Gilead.
9: 4 the prophet, went to *R* Gilead.
9:14 had been defending *R* Gilead,
1 Chr 6:73 *R* with its common-lands, and
6:80 *R* in Gilead with its
2 Chr 18: 2 go up with him to *R* Gilead.
18: 3 you go with me against *R*
18: 5 go to war against *R* Gilead,
18:11 Go up to *R* Gilead and prosper,
18:14 we go to war against *R* Gilead,
18:19 that he may fall at *R* Gilead?'
18:28 of Judah went up to *R* Gilead.
22: 5 king of Syria at *R* Gilead;
Ezra 10:29 Adaiah, Jashub, Sheal, and *R*;

RAMOTH GILEAD (19/19)

1 Ki 4:13 Ben-Geber, in Ramoth *G*;
22: 4 go with me to fight at Ramoth *G*?
22: 6 Shall I go against Ramoth *G* to
22:12 Go up to Ramoth *G* and prosper,
22:15 we go to war against Ramoth *G*,
22:20 that he may fall at Ramoth *G*?
22:29 of Judah went up to Ramoth *G*.
2 Ki 8:28 king of Syria at Ramoth *G*;
9: 1 your hand, and go to Ramoth *G*.
9: 4 the prophet, went to Ramoth *G*.
9:14 had been defending Ramoth *G*,
2 Chr 18: 2 to go up with him to Ramoth *G*.
18: 3 go with me against Ramoth *G*?
18: 5 we go to war against Ramoth *G*,
18:11 Go up to Ramoth *G* and prosper,
18:14 we go to war against Ramoth *G*,
18:19 that he may fall at Ramoth *G*?
18:28 of Judah went up to Ramoth *G*.
22: 5 king of Syria at Ramoth *G*;

RAMPART (4/4)

2 Sam 20:15 the city, and it stood by the *r*.
Lam 2: 8 Therefore He has caused the *r*
Nah 3: 8 Whose *r* was the sea,
Hab 2: 1 watch And set myself on the *r*,

RAMS (71/70) RAM, RAMS'

Gen 31:10 the *r* which leaped upon the
31:12 all the *r* which leap on the
31:38 and I have not eaten the *r* of
32:14 two hundred ewes and twenty *r*,
Ex 29: 1 Take one young bull and two *r*
29: 3 with the bull and the two *r*.
35:23 goats' hair, red skins of *r*,
Lev 8: 2 bull as the sin offering, two *r*,
23:18 one young bull, and two *r*.
Num 7:17 offerings: two oxen, five *r*,
7:23 offerings: two oxen, five *r*,
7:29 offerings: two oxen, five *r*,
7:35 offerings: two oxen, five *r*,
7:41 offerings: two oxen, five *r*,
7:47 offerings: two oxen, five *r*,
7:53 offerings: two oxen, five *r*,
7:59 offerings: two oxen, five *r*,
7:65 offerings: two oxen, five *r*,
7:71 offerings: two oxen, five *r*,
7:77 offerings: two oxen, five *r*,
7:83 offerings: two oxen, five *r*,
7:87 the *r* twelve, the male lambs in
7:88 the *r* sixty, the male goats
23: 1 me here seven bulls and seven *r*.
23:29 me here seven bulls and seven *r*.
29:13 thirteen young bulls, two *r*,
29:14 for each of the two *r*,
29:17 twelve young bulls, two *r*,
29:18 for the bulls, for the *r*,
29:20 present eleven bulls, two *r*,
29:21 for the bulls, for the *r*,
29:23 day present ten bulls, two *r*,
29:24 for the bulls, for the *r*,

R

29:26 day present nine bulls, two r,
29:27 for the bulls, for the r,
29:29 day present eight bulls, two r,
29:30 for the bulls, for the r,
29:32 day present seven bulls, two r,
29:33 for the bulls, for the r,
Deut 32:14 And r of the breed of Bashan,
1 Sam 15:22 And to heed than the fat of r.
2 Ki 3: 4 wool of one hundred thousand r.
1 Chr 15:26 offered seven bulls and seven r.
29:21 a thousand bulls, a thousand r,
2 Chr 13: 9 with a young bull and seven r
17:11 seven thousand seven hundred r
29:21 brought seven bulls, seven r,
29:22 Likewise they killed the r and
29:32 seventy bulls, one hundred r,
Ezra 6: 9 they need—young bulls, r,
6:17 hundred bulls, two hundred r,
7:17 to buy with this money bulls, r,
8:35 for all Israel, ninety-six r,
Job 42: 8 seven bulls and seven r,
Ps 66:15 With the sweet aroma of r;
114: 4 The mountains skipped like r,
114: 6 that you skipped like r?
Isa 1:11 enough of burnt offerings of r
34: 6 the fat of the kidneys of r.
60: 7 The r of Nebaioth shall
Jer 50: 8 And be like the r before the
51:40 Like r with male goats.
Ezek 4: 2 and place battering r against
21:22 to set up battering r,
21:22 to set battering r against the
26: 9 'He will direct his battering r
27:21 traded with you in lambs, r,
34:17 between r and goats.
39:18 Of r and lambs, Of goats and
45:23 seven bulls and seven r without
Mic 6: 7 be pleased with thousands of r,

RAMS' (5/5) RAMS

Josh 6: 4 bear seven trumpets of r horns
6: 6 bear seven trumpets of r horns
6: 8 the seven trumpets of r horns
6:13 seven trumpets of r horns
2 Chr 15:14 and trumpets and r horns.

RAN (64/64) RUN

Gen 18: 2 he r from the tent door to meet
18: 7 And Abraham r to the herd,
24:17 And the servant r to meet her
24:20 r back to the well to draw
24:28 So the young woman r and told
24:29 and Laban r out to the man by
29:12 So she r and told her father.
29:13 that he r to meet him, and
33: 4 But Esau r to meet him, and
39:12 and fled and r outside.
Num 11:27 And a young man r and told
16:47 and r into the midst of the
Josh 7:22 and they r to the tent;
8:19 they r as soon as he had
Judg 7:21 and the whole army r and cried
9:21 And Jotham r away and fled;
13:10 Then the woman r in haste and
1 Sam 3: 5 So he r to Eli and said, "Here
4:12 Then a man of Benjamin r from
10:23 So they r and brought him from
17:22 r to the army, and came and
17:48 that David hastened and r
17:51 Therefore David r and stood over
20:36 which I shoot." As the lad r,
2 Sam 18:21 bowed himself to Joab and r.
18:23 Then Ahimaaz r by way of the
1 Ki 2:39 that two slaves of Shimei r
18:35 So the water r all around the
18:46 he girded up his loins and r
19: 3 he arose and r for his life,
19:20 And he left the oxen and r after
22:35 The blood r out from the wound
2 Chr 32: 4 springs and the brook that r
Ps 105:41 It r in the dry places like a
Jer 23:21 sent these prophets, yet they r.
Ezek 1:14 And the living creatures r back
42: 7 And a wall which was outside r
Dan 8: 6 and r at him with furious
Mt 8:32 the whole herd of swine r
27:48 Immediately one of them r and
28: 8 and r to bring His disciples
Mk 5: 6 he r and worshiped Him.
5:13 and the herd r violently down
6:33 and many knew Him and r there
6:55 r through that whole surrounding
15:36 Then someone r and filled a
Lk 8:33 and the herd r violently down
15:20 and r and fell on his neck and
19: 4 So he r ahead and climbed up
24:12 But Peter arose and r to the
Jn 2: 3 And when they r out of wine,
20: 2 Then she r and came to Simon
20: 4 So they both r together, and the
Acts 3:11 all the people r together to
7:57 and r at him with one accord;
8:30 So Philip r to him, and heard
12:14 but r in and announced that
14:14 they tore their clothes and r
16:11 we r a straight course to
16:29 r in, and fell down trembling
21:30 and the people r together,
21:32 centurions, and r down to them.
27:41 they r the ship aground; and

Gal 5: 7 You r well. Who hindered you

RANDOM (2/2)

1 Ki 22:34 a certain man drew a bow at r,
2 Chr 18:33 bow at r, and struck the king

RANGE (3/3)

2 Ki 11: 8 and whoever comes within r,
Job 39: 8 The r of the mountains is his
Isa 7:25 But it will become a r for

RANGING (KJV) See CHARGING

RANK (2/2) RANKED

1 Chr 15:18 their brethren of the second r:
17:17 regarded me according to the r

RANKED (1/1) RANK

Esth 1:14 and who r highest in the

RANKS (7/7)

Ex 13:18 of Israel went up in orderly r
Deut 25:18 way and attacked your rear r,
1 Chr 12:33 men who could keep r;
12:38 men of war, who could keep r,
Prov 30:27 Yet they all advance in r;
Joel 2: 7 And they do not break r.
Mk 6:40 So they sat down in r,

RANSOM (13/13) RANSOMED

Ex 30:12 then every man shall give a r
Num 35:31 Moreover you shall take no r for
35:32 And you shall take no r for him
Job 33:24 to the Pit; I have found a r';
36:18 For a large r would not help
Ps 49: 7 Nor give to God a r for him—
Prov 13: 8 The r of a man's life is his
21:18 The wicked shall be a r for
Isa 43: 3 I gave Egypt for your r,
Hos 13:14 I will r them from the power of
Mt 20:28 and to give His life a r for
Mk 10:45 give His life a r for many."
1 Tim 2: 6 who gave Himself a r for all,

RANSOMED (3/3) RANSOM

Isa 35:10 And the r of the LORD shall
51:11 So the r of the LORD shall
Jer 31:11 And r him from the hand of one

RAPHA (1/1)

1 Chr 8: 2 and R the fifth.

RAPHAH (1/1)

1 Chr 8:37 R his son, Eleasah his son,

RAPHU (1/1)

Num 13: 9 of Benjamin, Palti the son of R;

RAPIDLY (1/1)

2 Sam 18:25 And he came r and drew near.

RARE (2/2)

1 Sam 3: 1 the word of the LORD was r in
Isa 13:12 I will make a mortal more r

RASE (KJV) See RAZE

RASH (4/4)

Num 30: 6 bound by her vows or by a r
Job 6: 3 my words have been r.
Eccl 5: 2 Do not be r with your mouth,
Isa 32: 4 Also the heart of the r will

RASHLY (3/3)

Ps 106:33 So that he spoke r with his
Prov 20:25 a snare for a man to devote r
Acts 19:36 to be quiet and do nothing r.

RATE (3/3)

1 Ki 10:25 at a set r year by year.
2 Chr 8:13 according to the daily r,
9:24 at a set r year by year.

RATHER (58/56)

2 Sam 10: 3 Has David not r sent his
19:30 said to the king, "R, let him
Job 7:15 strangling And death r than
32: 2 justified himself r than God.
36:21 chosen this r than affliction.
Ps 52: 3 Lying r than speaking
84:10 I would r be a doorkeeper in
Prov 8:10 And knowledge r than choice
16:16 is to be chosen r than silver.
17:12 R than a fool in his folly.
22: 1 be chosen r than great riches,
22: 1 Loving favor r than silver and
Eccl 5: 1 and draw near to hear r than to
9:17 should be heard R than the

Jer 8: 3 shall be chosen r than life
31:13 And make them rejoice r than
Mt 10: 6 But go r to the lost sheep of
10:28 But r fear Him who is able to
18: 8 r than having two hands or two
18: 9 r than having two eyes, to be
25: 9 but go r to those who sell, and
27:24 but r that a tumult was
Mk 5:26 no better, but r grew worse.
9:43 r than having two hands, to go
9:45 r than having two feet, to be
9:47 r than having two eyes, to be
15:11 so that he should r release
Lk 10:20 but r rejoice because your
11:41 But r give alms of such things
12:51 not at all, but r division.
17: 8 But will he not r say to him,
18:14 justified r than the other;
Jn 3:19 and men loved darkness r than
Acts 5:29 We ought to obey God r than men.
Rom 1:25 and served the creature r than
12:19 but r give place to wrath;
14:13 but r resolve this, not to put
1 Cor 5: 2 and have not r mourned, that he
6: 7 Why do you not r accept wrong?
6: 7 Why do you not r let
7:21 can be made free, r use it.
10:20 R, that the things which the
12:22 No, much r, those members of
14:19 in the church I would r speak
2 Cor 2: 7 you ought r to forgive and
5: 8 well pleased r to be absent
12: 9 most gladly I will r boast
Gal 4: 9 or r are known by God, how is
Eph 4:28 but r let him labor, working
5: 4 but r giving of thanks.
5:11 but r expose them.
1 Tim 1: 4 which cause disputes r than
6: 2 but r serve them because those
2 Tim 3: 4 lovers of pleasure r than
Phm 1: 9 yet for love's sake I r appeal
Heb 11:25 choosing r to suffer affliction
12:13 dislocated, but r be healed.
1 Pe 3: 4 r let it be the hidden person

RATION (2/2)

2 Ki 25:30 there was a regular r given
Jer 52:34 there was a regular r given him

RATIONS (3/2)

Gen 47:22 for the priests had r allotted
47:22 and they ate their r which
Jer 40: 5 of the guard gave him r and a

RATS (4/4)

1 Sam 6: 4 golden tumors and five golden r,
6: 5 tumors and images of your r
6:11 and the chest with the gold r
6:18 and the golden r,

RATTLES (1/1)

Job 39:23 The quiver r against him,

RATTLING (2/2)

Ezek 37: 7 was a noise, and suddenly a r;
Nah 3: 2 of a whip And the noise of r

RAVAGE (1/1) RAVAGED

1 Sam 6: 5 and images of your rats that r

RAVAGED (2/2) RAVAGE

1 Sam 5: 6 and He r them and struck them
1 Chr 20: 1 led out the armed forces and r

RAVEN (6/6) RAVENS

Gen 8: 7 Then he sent out a r,
Lev 11:15 every r after its kind,
Deut 14:14 'every r after its kind;
Job 38:41 Who provides food for the r,
Song 5:11 are wavy, And black as a r.
Isa 34:11 Also the owl and the r shall

RAVENOUS (3/3)

Gen 49:27 'Benjamin is a r wolf;
Isa 35: 9 Nor shall any r beast go up
Mt 7:15 but inwardly they are r wolves.

RAVENS (5/5) RAVEN

1 Ki 17: 4 and I have commanded the r to
17: 6 The r brought him bread and meat
Ps 147: 9 And to the young r that cry.
Prov 30:17 The r of the valley will pick
Lk 12:24 'Consider the r, for they

RAVIN (KJV) See FLESH, RAVENOUS

RAVINE (4/4) RAVINES

Deut 2:36 the city that is in the r,
Josh 13: 9 that is in the midst of the r,
13:16 the midst of the r, and all the
2 Sam 24: 5 is in the midst of the r of

RAVINES (2/2) RAVINE

Ezek 6: 3 to the hills, to the *r*,
35: 8 your valleys and in all your *r*

RAVING (1/1)

Eccl 10:13 And the end of his talk is *r*

RAVISHED (6/5)

Judg 20: 5 but instead they *r* my concubine
Song 4: 9 You have *r* my heart,
4: 9 You have *r* my heart With one
Isa 13:16 be plundered And their wives *r*.
Lam 5:11 They *r* the women in Zion,
Zech 14: 2 houses rifled, And the women *r*.

RAW (9/8)

Ex 12: 9 'Do not eat it *r*,
Lev 13:10 there is a spot of *r* flesh
13:14 But when *r* flesh appears on him,
13:15 shall examine the *r* flesh
13:15 for the *r* flesh is unclean.
13:16 Or if the *r* flesh changes and
13:24 and the *r* flesh of the burn
1 Sam 2:15 boiled meat from you, but *r*.
Ezek 29:18 and every shoulder rubbed *r*;

RAYS (1/1)

Hab 3: 4 He had *r* flashing from His

RAZE (2/1)

Ps 137: 7 *R* it, raze it, To its very
137: 7 *r* it, To its very

RAZOR (7/7)

Num 6: 5 the vow of his separation no *r*
Judg 13: 5 And no *r* shall come upon his
16:17 No *r* has ever come upon my head,
1 Sam 1:11 and no *r* shall come upon his
Ps 52: 2 destruction, Like a sharp *r*,
Isa 7:20 Lord will shave with a hired *r*,
Ezek 5: 1 sword, take it as a barber's *r*,

REACH (11/10) REACHED, REACHES, REACHING

Ex 4: 4 *R* out your hand and take it by
28:42 they shall *r* from the waist to
Num 34:11 the border shall go down and *r*
Ps 125: 3 Lest the righteous *r* out their
Isa 8: 8 He will *r* up to the neck;
Jer 48:32 They *r* to the sea of Jazer.
Ezek 31:14 may ever be high enough to *r*
Zech 14: 5 the mountain valley shall *r* to
Jn 20:27 *R* your finger here, and look at
20:27 and *r* your hand here, and put
Acts 27:12 if by any means they could *r*

REACHED (21/21) REACH

Gen 19:10 But the men *r* out their hands
28:12 and its top *r* to heaven;
Ex 4: 4 it by the tail" (and he *r*
Josh 16: 7 *r* to Jericho, and came out at
19:22 And the border *r* to Tabor,
19:26 it *r* to Mount Carmel westward,
19:27 and it *r* to Zebulun and to the
Judg 3:21 Then Ehud *r* with his left hand,
15:15 *r* out his hand and took it,
2 Ki 6: 7 So he *r* out his hand and took
Isa 16: 8 Which have *r* to Jazer And
Ezek 31: 7 Because its roots *r* to
Dan 4:11 Its height *r* to the heavens,
4:20 whose height *r* to the heavens
8:23 When the transgressors have *r*
9:21 *r* me about the time of the
Acts 21:35 When he *r* the stairs, he had to
28:13 there we circled round and *r*
1 Cor 14:36 Or was it you only that it *r*?
Jas 5: 4 the cries of the reapers have *r*
Rev 18: 5 For her sins have *r* to heaven,

REACHES (17/17) REACH

Num 21:15 slope of the brooks That *r* to
21:30 Which *r* to Medeba."
2 Chr 28: 9 killed them in a rage that *r*
Job 20: 6 And his head *r* to the clouds,
41:26 Though the sword *r* him, it
Ps 36: 5 Your faithfulness *r* to the
57:10 For Your mercy *r* unto the
108: 4 And Your truth *r* to the
Prov 31:20 she *r* out her hands to the
Isa 23: 5 When the report *r* Egypt,
25:11 in their midst As a swimmer *r*
30:28 Which *r* up to the neck,
Jer 4:10 Whereas the sword *r* to the
4:18 Because it *r* to your heart."
51: 9 For her judgment *r* to heaven
Ezek 47: 8 When it *r* the sea, its
Dan 4:22 your greatness has grown and *r*

REACHETH (KJV) See EXTENDED, EXTENDS, REACHES

REACHING (1/1) REACH

Phil 3:13 things which are behind and *r*

READ (67/63) READER, READING, READS

Ex 24: 7 the Book of the Covenant and *r*
Deut 17:19 and he shall *r* it all the days
31:11 you shall *r* this law before all
Josh 8:34 And afterward he *r* all the words
8:35 which Joshua did not *r* before
2 Ki 5: 7 when the king of Israel *r* the
19:14 and *r* it; and Hezekiah went up
22: 8 book to Shaphan, and he *r* it.
22:10 And Shaphan *r* it before the
22:16 which the king of Judah has *r*—
23: 2 And he *r* in their hearing all
2 Chr 34:18 And Shaphan *r* it before the
34:24 in the book which they have *r*
34:30 And he *r* in their hearing all
Ezra 4:18 sent to us has been clearly *r*
4:23 King Artaxerxes' letter was *r*
Neh 8: 3 Then he *r* from it in the open
8: 8 So they *r* distinctly from the
8:18 he *r* from the Book of the Law
9: 3 stood up in their place and *r*
13: 1 On that day they *r* from the Book
Esth 6: 1 and they were *r* before the
Isa 29:11 saying, "*R* this, please."
29:12 *R* this, please." And he says,
34:16 the book of the LORD, and *r*:
37:14 and *r* it; and Hezekiah went up
Jer 29:29 Now Zephaniah the priest *r* this
36: 6 and *r* from the scroll which you
36: 6 And you shall also *r* them in
36:10 Then Baruch *r* from the book the
36:13 he had heard when Baruch *r* the
36:14 scroll from which you have *r*
36:15 and *r* it in our hearing."
36:15 So Baruch *r* it in their
36:21 And Jehudi *r* it in the hearing
36:23 when Jehudi had *r* three or four
51:61 and *r* all these words,
Dan 5: 8 but they could not *r* the
5:15 that they should *r* this writing
5:16 Now if you can *r* the writing
5:17 yet I will *r* the writing to the
Mt 12: 3 Have you not *r* what David did
12: 5 Or have you not *r* in the law
19: 4 Have you not *r* that He who made
21:16 them, "Yes. Have you never *r*,
21:42 Have you never *r* in the
22:31 have you not *r* what was spoken
Mk 2:25 Have you never *r* what David did
12:10 Have you not even *r* this
12:26 have you not *r* in the book of
Lk 4:16 Sabbath day, and stood up to *r*.
6: 3 Have you not even *r* this, what
Jn 19:20 Then many of the Jews *r* this
Acts 8:32 in the Scripture which he *r*
13:27 of the Prophets which are *r*
15:21 being *r* in the synagogues every
15:31 When they had *r* it, they
23:34 And when the governor had *r* it,
2 Cor 1:13 things to you than what you *r*
3: 2 known and *r* by all men;
3:15 to this day, when Moses is *r*,
Eph 3: 4 by which, when you *r*,
Col 4:16 Now when this epistle is *r*
4:16 see that it is *r* also in the
4:16 and that you likewise *r* the
1 Th 5:27 Lord that this epistle be *r* to
Rev 5: 4 was found worthy to open and *r*

READER (1/1) READ

Mk 13:14 not" (let the *r* understand),

READILY (2/2)

Esth 2: 9 so he *r* gave beauty
Heb 12: 9 Shall we not much more *r* be in

READINESS (2/2) READY

Acts 17:11 received the word with all *r*,
2 Cor 8:11 that as there was a *r* to

READING (10/9) READ

Neh 8: 8 them to understand the *r*.
Jer 36: 8 *r* from the book the words of
51:63 when you have finished *r* this
Lk 10:26 What is your *r* of it?"
Acts 8:28 he was *r* Isaiah the prophet.
8:30 and heard him *r* the prophet
8:30 you understand what you are *r*?
13:15 And after the *r* of the Law and
2 Cor 3:14 veil remains unlifted in the *r*
1 Tim 4:13 I come, give attention to *r*,

READS (4/4) READ

Dan 5: 7 Whoever *r* this writing, and
Hab 2: 2 That he may run who *r* it.
Mt 24:15 holy place" (whoever *r*, let
Rev 1: 3 Blessed is he who *r* and those

READY (84/82) READINESS

Gen 18: 6 make *r* three measures of fine
43:16 slaughter an animal and make *r*;
43:25 Then they made the present *r* for
46:29 So Joseph made *r* his chariot and
Ex 14: 6 So he made *r* his chariot and
17: 4 They are almost *r* to stone
19:11 And let them be *r* for the third
19:15 Be *r* for the third day; do not
34: 2 So be *r* in the morning, and come
Num 32:17 *r* to go before the children
Deut 1:41 you were *r* to go up into the
Josh 8: 4 the city, but all of you be *r*.
2 Sam 15:15 *r* to do whatever my lord the
18:22 son, since you have no news *r*?
1 Ki 20:12 said to his servants, "Get *r*.
20:12 And they got *r* to attack the
2 Ki 4:29 to Gehazi, "Get yourself *r*,
9: 1 said to him, "Get yourself *r*,
9:21 Then Joram said, "Make *r*.
9:21 And his chariot was made *r*.
1 Chr 7: 4 thirty-six thousand troops *r*
Neh 9:17 *R* to pardon, Gracious and
Esth 3:14 that they should be *r* for that
8:13 so that the Jews would be *r* on
Job 3: 8 Those who are *r* to arouse
12: 5 It is made *r* for those whose
15:23 that a day of darkness is *r* at
15:24 like a king *r* for battle.
17: 1 The grave is *r* for me.
18:12 And destruction is *r* at his
32:19 It is *r* to burst like new
Ps 7:12 bends His bow and makes it *r*.
11: 2 They make *r* their arrow on the
21:12 You will make *r* Your arrows
38:17 For I am *r* to fall, And my
45: 1 My tongue is the pen of a *r*
86: 5 and *r* to forgive, And abundant
88:15 I have been afflicted and *r*
Isa 30:13 be to you Like a breach *r* to
32: 4 of the stammerers will be *r* to
38:20 The LORD was *r* to save me;
41: 7 It is *r* for the soldering";
Jer 1:12 for I am *r* to perform My
Ezek 7:14 the trumpet and made everyone *r*,
21:16 Swords at the *r*! Thrust right!
38: 7 "Prepare yourself and be *r*,
Dan 3:15 Now if you are *r* at the time you
Hab 3: 9 Your bow was made quite *r*;
Zech 5:11 land of Shinar; when it is *r*,
Mt 22: 4 killed, and all things are *r*.
22: 8 his servants, 'The wedding is *r*,
24:44 "Therefore you also be *r*,
25:10 and those who were *r* went in
Mk 3: 9 a small boat should be kept *r*
14:15 there make *r* for us."
Lk 1:17 to make *r* a people prepared for
7: 2 was sick and *r* to die.
12:40 "Therefore you also be *r*,
14:17 'Come, for all things are now *r*.
22:12 upper room; there make *r*.
22:33 I am *r* to go with You, both to
Jn 7: 6 come, but your time is always *r*.
Acts 10:10 but while they made *r*,
20: 7 *r* to depart the next day,
21:13 For I am *r* not only to be
23:15 but we are *r* to kill him before
23:21 killed him; and now they are *r*,
Rom 1:15 I am *r* to preach the gospel
2 Cor 8:19 Himself and to show your *r*
9: 2 that Achaia was *r* a year ago;
9: 3 that, as I said, you may be *r*;
9: 5 that it may be *r* as a matter
10: 6 and being *r* to punish all
12:14 for the third time I am *r* to
1 Tim 6:18 *r* to give, willing to share,
2 Tim 4: 2 Preach the word! Be *r* in season
Titus 3: 1 to be *r* for every good work,
Heb 8:13 obsolete and growing old is *r*
1 Pe 1: 5 through faith for salvation *r*
3:15 and always be *r* to give a
4: 5 an account to Him who is *r* to
Rev 3: 2 that are *r* to die, for I have
12: 4 before the woman who was *r* to
19: 7 and His wife has made herself *r*.

REAFFIRM (1/1)

2 Cor 2: 8 Therefore I urge you to *r* your

REAIAH (4/4)

1 Chr 4: 2 And *R* the son of Shobal begot
5: 5 *R* his son, Baal his son,
Ezra 2:47 sons of Gahar, the sons of *R*,
Neh 7:50 sons of *R*, the sons of Rezin,

REAL (1/1)

Acts 12: 9 was done by the angel was *r*,

REALIZE (1/1) REALIZED, REALIZES

2 Sam 3:25 Surely you *r* that Abner the son

REALIZED (2/2) REALIZE

Neh 13:10 I also *r* that the portions for
Acts 4:13 And they *r* that they had been

REALIZES (2/2) REALIZE

Lev 5: 3 when he *r* it, then he shall be
5: 4 *r* it, then he shall be guilty

R

REALLY (14/14) REAL

Gen 27:21 whether you are *r* my son Esau
27:24 Are you *r* my son Esau?"
31:16 from our father are *r* ours
Judg 15: 2 I *r* thought that you thoroughly
1 Sam 2:16 They should *r* burn the fat
2 Sam 10: 3 Do you think that David *r* honors
2 Ki 8:10 shown me that he will *r* die."
1 Chr 19: 3 Do you think that David *r* honors
Zech 7: 5 did you *r* fast for Me—for Me?
Lk 18: 8 will He *r* find faith on the
1 Tim 5: 3 Honor widows who are *r* widows.
5: 5 Now she who is *r* a widow, and
5:16 relieve those who are *r* widows.
Jas 2: 8 If you *r* fulfill the royal law

REALM (7/7)

2 Chr 20:30 Then the *r* of Jehoshaphat was
Ezra 7:13 the priests and Levites in my *r*,
7:23 there be wrath against the *r*
Dan 1:20 who were in all his *r*.
6: 3 to setting him over the whole *r*.
9: 1 who was made king over the *r* of
11: 2 stir up all against the *r* of

REAP (34/28) REAPED, REAPER, REAPING, REAPS

Lev 19: 9 When you *r* the harvest of your
19: 9 you shall not wholly *r* the
23:10 and *r* its harvest, then you
23:22 When you *r* the harvest of your
23:22 you shall not wholly *r* the
23:22 of your field when you *r*,
25: 5 of your harvest you shall not *r*,
25:11 it you shall neither sow nor *r*
Deut 24:19 When you *r* your harvest in your
Ruth 2: 9 be on the field which they *r*,
1 Sam 8:12 some to plow his ground and *r*
2 Ki 19:29 in the third year sow and *r*,
Job 4: 8 iniquity And sow trouble *r*
Ps 126: 5 who sow in tears Shall *r* in
Prov 22: 8 He who sows iniquity will *r*
Eccl 11: 4 regards the clouds will not *r*.
Isa 37:30 in the third year sow and *r*,
Hos 8: 7 And *r* the whirlwind.
10:12 righteousness; *R* in mercy;
Mic 6:15 "You shall sow, but not *r*;
Mt 6:26 for they neither sow nor *r* nor
25:26 you knew that I *r* where I have
Lk 12:24 for they neither sow nor *r*,
19:21 and *r* what you did not sow.'
Jn 4:38 I sent you to *r* that for which
1 Cor 9:11 is it a great thing if we *r*
2 Cor 9: 6 who sows sparingly will also *r*
9: 6 sows bountifully will also *r*
Gal 6: 7 a man sows, that he will also *r*.
6: 8 his flesh will of the flesh *r*
6: 8 the Spirit will of the Spirit *r*
6: 9 for in due season we shall *r* if
Rev 14:15 "Thrust in Your sickle and *r*,
14:15 the time has come for You to *r*,

REAPED (4/4) REAP

Gen 26:12 and *r* in the same year a
Jer 12:13 They have sown wheat but *r*
Hos 10:13 You have *r* iniquity.
Rev 14:16 the earth, and the earth was *r*.

REAPER (2/2) REAP, REAPERS

Ps 129: 7 With which the *r* does not fill
Am 9:13 plowman shall overtake the *r*,

REAPERS (10/10) REAPER

Ruth 2: 3 in the field after the *r*.
2: 4 Bethlehem, and said to the *r*,
2: 5 who was in charge of the *r*,
2: 6 who was in charge of the *r*
2: 7 me glean and gather after the *r*
2:14 So she sat beside the *r*,
2 Ki 4:18 out to his father, to the *r*.
Mt 13:30 of harvest I will say to the *r*,
13:39 and the *r* are the angels.
Jas 5: 4 and the cries of the *r* have

REAPING (3/3) REAP

1 Sam 6:13 of Beth Shemesh were *r* their
Mt 25:24 *r* where you have not sown, and
Lk 19:22 what I did not deposit and *r*

REAPS (4/3) REAP

Isa 17: 5 And *r* the heads with his arm;
Jn 4:36 And he who *r* receives wages, and
4:36 both he who sows and he who *r*
4:37 true: 'One sows and another *r*.

REAR (14/13) REARED, REARING

Lev 26: 1 a sacred pillar shall you *r*
Num 10:25 of the children of Dan (the *r*
Deut 25:18 on the way and attacked your *r*
25:18 all the stragglers at your *r*,
Josh 6: 9 and the *r* guard came after the
6:13 But the *r* guard came after the
8:13 and its *r* guard on the west of
10:19 and attack their *r* guard.
1 Sam 29: 2 men passed in review at the *r*
1 Ki 6:16 the twenty-cubit room at the *r*
2 Chr 13:14 line was at both front and *r*;
Isa 23: 4 Neither do I *r* young men,
52:12 God of Israel will be your *r*
58: 8 of the LORD shall be your *r*

REARED (3/3) REAR

2 Ki 10: 1 and to those who *r* Ahab's
10: 5 and those who *r* the sons,
Job 31:18 (But from my youth I *r* him as a

REARING (1/1) REAR

2 Ki 10: 6 of the city, who were *r* them.

REASON (67/67) REASONABLE, REASONED, REASONING

Gen 19: 8 since this is the *r* they have
Deut 4: 7 for whatever *r* we may call
Josh 5: 4 And this is the *r* why Joshua
22:24 have done it for fear, for a *r*,
1 Sam 12: 7 that I may *r* with you before
1 Ki 9:15 And this is the *r* for the
14: 4 for his eyes were glazed by *r*
2 Chr 21:15 your intestines come out by *r*
Neh 6:13 For this *r* he was hired,
Job 9:14 And choose my words to *r*
13: 3 And I desire to *r* with God.
15: 3 Should he *r* with unprofitable
22: 6 from your brother for no *r*,
23: 7 There the upright could *r* with
Ps 90:10 And if by *r* of strength they
Eccl 7: 7 destroys a wise man's *r*,
7:25 and seek out wisdom and the *r*
7:27 to the other to find out the *r*,
Isa 1:18 and let us *r* together,"
Dan 2:12 For this *r* the king was angry
4:36 At the same time my *r* returned
Mal 2:14 Yet you say, "For what *r*?
Mt 5:32 divorces his wife for any *r*
16: 8 why do you *r* among yourselves
19: 3 his wife for just any *r*?
19: 5 For this *r* a man shall
Mk 2: 8 Why do you *r* about these things
8:17 Why do you *r* because you have no
10: 7 For this *r* a man shall
Lk 5:21 and the Pharisees began to *r*,
8:47 of all the people the *r* she
23:22 I have found no *r* for death in
Jn 5:16 For this *r* the Jews persecuted
12:18 For this *r* the people also met
13:28 at the table knew for what *r*
Acts 10:21 For what *r* have you come?"
10:29 for what *r* have you sent for
18:14 there would be *r* why I should
19:40 there being no *r* which we may
23:28 And when I wanted to know the *r*
26:25 speak the words of truth and *r*.
28:20 For this *r* therefore I have
Rom 1:26 For this *r* God gave them up to
15: 9 For this *r* I will confess
15:17 Therefore I have *r* to glory in
15:22 For this *r* I also have been
1 Cor 4:17 For this *r* I have sent Timothy
11:10 For this *r* the woman ought to
11:30 For this *r* many are weak and
Eph 3: 1 For this *r* I, Paul, the prisoner
3:14 For this *r* I bow my knees to
5:31 For this *r* a man shall
Phil 2:18 For the same *r* you also be glad
Col 1: 9 For this *r* we also, since the
1 Th 2:13 For this *r* we also thank God
3: 5 For this *r*, when I could no
2 Th 2:11 And for this *r* God will send
1 Tim 1:16 for this *r* I obtained mercy,
2 Tim 1:12 For this *r* I also suffer these
Titus 1: 5 For this *r* I left you in Crete,
Heb 2:11 for which *r* He is not ashamed
5:14 those who by *r* of use have
9:15 And for this *r* He is the
1 Pe 3:15 to everyone who asks you a *r*
4: 6 For this *r* the gospel was
2 Pe 1: 5 But also for this very *r*,
1:12 For this *r* I will not be

REASONABLE (1/1) REASON

Rom 12: 1 which is your *r* service.

REASONED (14/14) REASON

Mt 16: 7 And they *r* among themselves,
21:25 they *r* among themselves,
Mk 2: 8 in His spirit that they *r* thus
8:16 And they *r* among themselves,
11:31 they *r* among themselves,
Lk 3:15 and all *r* in their hearts about
20: 5 And they *r* among themselves,
20:14 they *r* among themselves,
24:15 while they conversed and *r*,
Acts 17: 2 and for three Sabbaths *r* with
17:17 Therefore he *r* in the synagogue
18: 4 And he *r* in the synagogue every
18:19 entered the synagogue and *r*
24:25 Now as he *r* about righteousness,

REASONING (6/6) REASON, REASONINGS

Job 13: 6 Now hear my *r*, And heed
Mk 2: 6 were sitting there and *r* in
12:28 and having heard them *r*
Lk 5:22 Why are you *r* in your hearts?
Acts 19: 8 *r* and persuading concerning the
19: 9 *r* daily in the school of

REASONINGS (1/1) REASONING

Job 32:11 I listened to your *r*,

REASONS (2/2)

Isa 41:21 "Bring forth your strong *r*,
Acts 26:21 For these *r* the Jews seized me

REBA (2/2)

Num 31: 8 Rekem, Zur, Hur, and *R*,
Josh 13:21 Evi, Rekem, Zur, Hur, and *R*,

REBECCA (1/1) REBEKAH

Rom 9:10 but when *R* also had conceived

REBEKAH (28/27) REBECCA, REBEKAH'S

Gen 22:23 And Bethuel begot *R*.
24:15 speaking, that behold, *R*,
24:29 Now *R* had a brother whose name
24:30 heard the words of his sister *R*,
24:45 in my heart, there was *R*,
24:51 Here is *R* before you; take her
24:53 clothing, and gave them to *R*.
24:58 Then they called *R* and said to
24:59 So they sent away *R* their sister
24:60 And they blessed *R* and said to
24:61 Then *R* and her maids arose, and
24:61 So the servant took *R* and
24:64 Then *R* lifted her eyes, and when
24:67 and he took *R* and she became
25:20 forty years old when he took *R*
25:21 and *R* his wife conceived.
25:28 but *R* loved Jacob.
26: 7 men of the place kill me for *R*,
26: 8 showing endearment to *R* his
26:35 a grief of mind to Isaac and *R*.
27: 5 Now *R* was listening when Isaac
27: 6 So *R* spoke to Jacob her son,
27:11 And Jacob said to *R* his mother,
27:15 Then *R* took the choice clothes
27:42 her older son were told to *R*.
27:46 And *R* said to Isaac, "I am
28: 5 the Syrian, the brother of *R*,
49:31 there they buried Isaac and *R*

REBEKAH'S (2/2) REBEKAH

Gen 29:12 and that he was *R* son.
35: 8 *R* nurse, died, and she was

REBEL (18/17) REBELLED, REBELLING, REBELLION, REBELLIOUS

Num 14: 9 Only do not *r* against the LORD,
Josh 22:16 that you might *r* this day
22:18 if you *r* today against the
22:19 but do not *r* against the LORD,
22:19 nor *r* against us, by building
22:29 be it from us that we should *r*
1 Sam 12:14 and do not *r* against the
12:15 but *r* against the commandment
2 Sam 20: 1 there happened to be there a *r*,
1 Ki 11:27 this is what caused him to *r*
2 Ki 18:20 that you *r* against me?
Neh 2:19 Will you *r* against the king?"
6: 6 you and the Jews plan to *r*;
Job 24:13 There are those who *r* against
Ps 105:28 And they did not *r* against His
Isa 1:20 But if you refuse and *r*,
36: 5 that you *r* against me?
Hos 7:14 They *r* against Me;

REBELLED (37/37) REBEL

Gen 14: 4 in the thirteenth year they *r*.
Num 20:24 because you *r* against My word
27:14 you *r* against My command to
Deut 1:26 but *r* against the command of
1:43 but *r* against the command of
9:23 then you *r* against the
1 Ki 11:26 also *r* against the king.
2 Ki 1: 1 Moab *r* against Israel after the
3: 5 that the king of Moab *r* against
3: 7 The king of Moab has *r* against
18: 7 And he *r* against the king of
24: 1 Then he turned and *r* against
24:20 Then Zedekiah *r* against the
2 Chr 13: 6 rose up and *r* against his lord.
36:13 And he also *r* against King
Neh 9:26 they were disobedient And *r*
Ps 5:10 For they have *r* against You.
106: 7 But *r* by the sea—the Red Sea.
106:33 Because they *r* against His
106:43 But they *r* in their counsel,
107:11 Because they *r* against the
Isa 1: 2 And they have *r* against Me;
63:10 But they *r* and grieved His Holy
Jer 52: 3 Then Zedekiah *r* against the
Lam 1:18 For I *r* against His
3:42 We have transgressed and *r*;
Ezek 2: 3 a rebellious nation that has *r*
5: 6 She has *r* against My judgments

17:15 But he *r* against him by sending
20: 8 But they *r* against Me and would
20:13 Yet the house of Israel *r*
20:21 the children *r* against Me;
Dan 9: 5 we have done wickedly and *r*,
9: 9 though we have *r* against Him.
Hos 8: 1 My covenant And *r* against My
13:16 For she has *r* against her God.
Heb 3:16 For who, having heard, *r*?

REBELLING (1/1) REBEL

Ps 78:17 even more against Him By *r*

REBELLION (23/23) REBEL

Deut 31:27 for I know your *r* and your stiff
Josh 22:22 itself know—if it is in *r*,
1 Sam 15:23 For *r* is as the sin of
24:11 there is neither evil nor *r*
2 Sam 23: 6 But the sons of *r* shall all
1 Ki 12:19 So Israel has been in *r* against
2 Chr 10:19 So Israel has been in *r* against
Ezra 4:19 and *r* and sedition have been
Neh 9:17 And in their *r* They appointed
Job 34:37 For he adds *r* to his sin;
Ps 64: 2 From the *r* of the workers of
95: 8 harden your hearts, as in the *r*,
Prov 17:11 An evil man seeks only *r*;
Jer 28:16 because you have taught *r*
29:32 because he has taught *r* against
Hos 4:18 Their drink is *r*,
Mk 15: 7 had committed murder in the *r*.
Lk 23:19 into prison for a certain *r*
23:25 who for *r* and murder had been
Acts 21:38 some time ago stirred up a *r*
Heb 3: 8 your hearts as in the *r*,
3:15 your hearts as in the *r*.
Jude 11 and perished in the *r* of Korah.

REBELLIOUS (40/38) REBEL

Deut 9: 7 you have been *r* against the
9:24 been *r* against the LORD
21:18 a man has a stubborn and *r*
21:20 son of ours is stubborn and *r*;
31:27 you have been *r* against the
1 Sam 20:30 son of a perverse, *r* woman!
Ezra 4:12 and are building the *r* and evil
4:15 and know that this city is a *r*
Ps 66: 7 Do not let the *r* exalt
68: 6 But the *r* dwell in a dry
68:18 among men, Even from the *r*,
78: 8 A stubborn and *r* generation,
Prov 7:11 She was loud and *r*,
Isa 1:23 Your princes are *r*,
30: 1 Woe to the *r* children," says
30: 9 That this is a *r* people,
50: 5 opened My ear; And I was not *r*,
65: 2 My hands all day long to a *r*
Jer 4:17 Because she has been *r* against
5:23 this people has a defiant and *r*
Lam 1:20 For I have been very *r*.
Ezek 2: 3 to a *r* nation that has rebelled
2: 5 for they are a *r* house—yet they
2: 6 though they are a *r* house.
2: 7 they refuse, for they are *r*.
2: 8 Do not be *r* like that
2: 8 not be rebellious like that *r*
3: 9 though they are a *r* house."
3:26 them, for they are a *r* house.
3:27 for they are a *r* house.
12: 2 you dwell in the midst of a *r*
12: 2 hear; for they are a *r* house.
12: 3 though they are a *r* house.
12: 9 the *r* house, said to you, 'What
12:25 O *r* house, I will say the word
17:12 Say now to the *r* house: 'Do you
24: 3 And utter a parable to the *r*
44: 6 "Now say to the *r*,
Hos 9:15 All their princes are *r*.
Zeph 3: 1 Woe to her who is *r* and

REBELS (7/7)

Num 17:10 be kept as a sign against the *r*,
20:10 you *r*! Must we bring water for
Josh 1:18 Whoever *r* against your command
1 Sam 10:27 But some *r* said, "How can this
Jer 6:28 They are all stubborn *r*,
Ezek 20:38 I will purge the *r* from among
Mk 15: 7 was chained with his fellow *r*;

REBUILD (8/7) REBUILDING, REBUILT

Ezra 9: 9 to *r* its ruins, and to give us
Neh 2: 5 that I may *r* it."
Isa 9:10 But we will *r* with hewn
61: 4 And they shall *r* the old
Jer 33: 7 and will *r* those places as at
Am 9:11 And *r* it as in the days of
Acts 15:16 I will return And will *r*
15:16 I will *r* its ruins,

REBUILDING (3/3) REBUILD

Ezra 5:11 and we are *r* the temple that
Neh 4: 1 Sanballat heard that we were *r*
6: 6 you are *r* the wall, that you

REBUILT (16/16) REBUILD

Judg 18:28 So they *r* the city and dwelt
21:23 and they *r* the cities and dwelt
2 Ki 21: 3 For he *r* the high places which
2 Chr 33: 3 *r* the high places which
Ezra 4:16 the king that if this city is *r*
5:15 and let the house of God be *r*
6: 3 Jerusalem: "Let the house be *r*,
Neh 6: 1 our enemies heard that I had *r*
7: 4 few, and the houses were not *r*.
Job 12:14 a thing down, it cannot be *r*;
Isa 25: 2 no more; It will never be *r*.
Jer 31: 4 build you, and you shall be *r*,
Ezek 26:14 nets, and you shall never be *r*,
36:10 be inhabited and the ruins *r*.
36:33 and the ruins shall be *r*.
36:36 have *r* the ruined places and

REBUKE (70/69) REBUKED

Lev 19:17 You shall surely *r* your
Deut 28:20 and *r* in all that you set your
Ruth 2:16 and do not *r* her."
2 Sam 22:16 At the *r* of the LORD, At the
2 Ki 19: 3 day is a day of trouble, and *r*,
19: 4 and will *r* the words which the
Job 6:26 Do you intend to *r* my words,
11: 3 should no one *r* you?
13:10 He will surely *r* you If you
20: 3 I have heard the *r* that
26:11 And are astonished at His *r*.
Ps 6: 1 do not *r* me in Your anger,
18:15 world were uncovered At Your *r*,
38: 1 do not *r* me in Your wrath,
50: 8 I will not *r* you for your
50:21 But I will *r* you, And set
68:30 *R* the beasts of the reeds,
76: 6 At Your *r*, O God of Jacob,
80:16 They perish at the *r* of Your
104: 7 At Your *r* they fled; At the
119:21 You *r* the proud—the cursed,
141: 5 And let him *r* me; It shall
Prov 1:23 Turn at my *r*; Surely I will
1:25 And would have none of my *r*,
1:30 And despised my every *r*.
9: 8 *R* a wise man, and he will
13: 1 a scoffer does not listen to *r*.
13: 8 But the poor does not hear *r*.
13:18 But he who regards a *r* will be
15:32 But he who heeds *r* gets
17:10 *R* is more effective for a wise
19:25 *R* one who has understanding,
24:25 But those who *r* the wicked
27: 5 Open *r* is better Than love
29:15 The rod and *r* give wisdom,
30: 6 Lest He *r* you, and you be
Eccl 7: 5 It is better to hear the *r* of
Isa 1:17 *R* the oppressor; Defend the
2: 4 And *r* many people;
17:13 But God will *r* them and they
25: 8 The *r* of His people He will
37: 3 day is a day of trouble and *r*
37: 4 and will *r* the words which the
50: 2 Indeed with My *r* I dry up the
51:20 The *r* of your God.
54: 9 be angry with you, nor *r* you.
66:15 And His *r* with flames of fire.
Jer 2:19 And your backslidings will *r*
15:15 for Your sake I have suffered *r*.
Ezek 3:26 be mute and not be one to *r*
Hos 4: 4 contend, or *r* another;
5: 2 Though I *r* them all.
5: 9 be desolate in the day of *r*;
Mic 4: 3 And *r* strong nations afar off;
Zech 3: 2 'The LORD *r* you, Satan!
3: 2 who has chosen Jerusalem *r*
Mal 2: 3 I will *r* your descendants
3:11 And I will *r* the devourer for
Mt 11:20 Then He began to *r* the cities
16:22 took Him aside and began to *r*
Mk 8:32 Him aside and began to *r* Him.
Lk 17: 3 *r* him; and if he repents,
19:39 *r* Your disciples."
1 Tim 5: 1 Do not *r* an older man, but
5:20 Those who are sinning *r* in the
2 Tim 4: 2 Convince, *r*, exhort,
Titus 1:13 Therefore *r* them sharply, that
2:15 and *r* with all authority.
Jude 9 The Lord *r* you!"
Rev 3:19 I *r* and chasten. Therefore be

REBUKED (31/31) REBUKE

Gen 20:16 Thus she was *r*.
21:25 Then Abraham *r* Abimelech
31:36 Then Jacob was angry and *r*
31:42 and *r* you last night."
37:10 and his father *r* him and said
1 Ki 1: 6 (And his father had not *r* him at
1 Chr 16:21 He *r* kings for their sakes,
Neh 5: 7 I *r* the nobles and rulers, and
Ps 9: 5 You have *r* the nations,
105:14 He *r* kings for their sakes,
106: 9 He *r* the Red Sea also, and it
Prov 29: 1 He who is often *r*,
Mt 8:26 Then He arose and *r* the winds
17:18 And Jesus *r* the demon, and it
19:13 but the disciples *r* them.
Mk 1:25 But Jesus *r* him, saying, "Be
4:39 Then He arose and *r* the wind,
8:33 He *r* Peter, saying, "Get
9:25 He *r* the unclean spirit, saying
10:13 but the disciples *r* those who
16:14 and He *r* their unbelief and
Lk 3:19 being *r* by him concerning
4:35 But Jesus *r* him, saying, "Be
4:39 So He stood over her and *r* the
8:24 Then He arose and *r* the wind
9:42 Then Jesus *r* the unclean
9:55 But He turned and *r* them, and
18:15 disciples saw it, they *r* them.
23:40 *r* him, saying, "Do you not
Heb 12: 5 when you are *r* by Him;
2 Pe 2:16 but he was *r* for his iniquity:

REBUKER (1/1)

Prov 25:12 Is a wise *r* to an obedient ear.

REBUKES (9/9)

Job 40: 2 He who *r* God, let him answer
Ps 39:11 When with *r* You correct man for
Prov 9: 7 And he who *r* a wicked man
15:31 The ear that hears the *r* of
28:23 He who *r* a man will find more
Ezek 5:15 and in fury and in furious *r*.
25:17 on them with furious *r*;
Am 5:10 They hate the one who *r* in the
Nah 1: 4 He *r* the sea and makes it dry,

REBUKING (1/1)

Lk 4:41 *r* them, did not allow them to

RECALL (3/3)

Isa 46: 8 *R* to mind, O you transgressors.
Lam 3:21 This I *r* to my mind,
Heb 10:32 But *r* the former days in which,

RECAPTURED (3/2)

2 Ki 13:25 Jehoash the son of Jehoahaz *r*
13:25 times Joash defeated him and *r*
14:28 and how he *r* for Israel, from

RECEDED (4/4)

Gen 8: 3 And the waters *r* continually
8: 8 to see if the waters had *r* from
8:11 Noah knew that the waters had *r*
Rev 6:14 Then the sky *r* as a scroll when

RECEIPT OF CUSTOM (KJV) See (TAX) OFFICE

RECEIVE (173/167) RECEIVED, RECEIVES, RECEIVING

Gen 4:11 has opened its mouth to *r* your
33:10 then *r* my present from my hand,
38:20 to *r* his pledge from the
Ex 27: 3 you shall make its pans to *r*
29:25 You shall *r* them back from their
Num 18:28 all your tithes which you *r*
Deut 9: 9 went up into the mountain to *r*
Josh 11:20 and that they might *r* no
1 Sam 10: 4 which you shall *r* from their
2 Sam 18:12 Though I were to *r* a thousand
1 Ki 8:64 the LORD was too small to *r*
2 Ki 5:16 I stand, I will *r* nothing."
5:26 Is it time to *r* money and to
5:26 time to receive money and to *r*
12: 8 that they would neither *r*
2 Chr 7: 7 had made was not able to *r* the
Ezra 4:14 Now because we *r* support from
Neh 10:37 for the Levites should *r* the
10:38 the Levites when the Levites *r*
Job 3:12 Why did the knees *r* me? Or why
22:22 *R*, please, instruction
35: 7 Or what does He *r* from your
Ps 6: 9 The LORD will *r* my prayer.
24: 5 He shall *r* blessing from the
49:15 For He shall *r* me. Selah
73:24 And afterward *r* me to glory.
Prov 1: 3 To *r* the instruction of wisdom,
2: 1 if you *r* my words, And
4:10 Hear, my son, and *r* my sayings,
8:10 *R* my instruction, and not
10: 8 The wise in heart will *r*
19:20 Listen to counsel and *r*
Eccl 5:19 to *r* his heritage and rejoice
Isa 57: 6 Should I *r* comfort in these?
Jer 5: 3 But they have refused to *r*
7:28 of the LORD their God nor *r*
9:20 And let your ear *r* the word of
17:23 that they might not hear nor *r*
32:33 yet they have not listened to *r*
35:13 Will you not *r* instruction to
Ezek 3:10 *r* into your heart all My words
16:61 when you *r* your older and your
Dan 2: 6 you shall *r* from me gifts,
7:18 of the Most High shall *r* the
Hos 10: 6 Ephraim shall *r* shame,
14: 2 *R* us graciously, For we will
Zeph 3: 7 You will *r* instruction'—So
Zech 6:10 *R* the gift from the
14:18 they shall *r* the plague with
Mal 2:13 Nor *r* it with goodwill from
3:10 not be room enough to *r*
Mt 10:14 And whoever will not *r* you nor
10:41 the name of a prophet shall *r*
10:41 of a righteous man shall *r* a
11:14 And if you are willing to *r* it,
19:29 shall *r* a hundredfold, and

R

20: 7 whatever is right you will *r*.
20:10 they supposed that they would *r*
21:22 prayer, believing, you will *r*.
21:34 that they might *r* its fruit.
23:14 Therefore you will *r* greater
Mk 2: 2 there was no longer room to *r*
4:16 immediately *r* it with gladness;
6:11 And whoever will not *r* you nor
10:15 whoever does not *r* the kingdom
10:30 who shall not *r* a hundredfold
10:51 that I may *r* my sight."
11:24 believe that you *r* them, and
12: 2 that he might *r* some of the
12:40 will *r* greater condemnation."
Lk 6:34 those from whom you hope to *r*
6:34 sinners lend to sinners to *r*
8:13 *r* the word with joy;
9: 5 And whoever will not *r* you, when
9:53 But they did not *r* Him, because
10: 8 and they *r* you, eat such things
10:10 and they do not *r* you, go out
16: 4 they may *r* me into their
16: 9 they may *r* you into an
18:17 whoever does not *r* the kingdom
18:30 who shall not *r* many times more
18:41 that I may *r* my sight."
18:42 *R* your sight; your faith has
19:12 went into a far country to *r*
20:47 These will *r* greater
23:41 for we *r* the due reward of our
Jn 1:11 and His own did not *r* Him.
3:11 and you do not *r* Our witness.
3:27 A man can *r* nothing unless it
5:34 Yet I do not *r* testimony from
5:41 I do not *r* honor from men.
5:43 and you do not *r* Me;
5:43 in his own name, him you will *r*.
5:44 who *r* honor from one another,
7:39 those believing in Him would *r*;
12:48 and does not *r* My words, has
14: 3 I will come again and *r* you to
14:17 truth, whom the world cannot *r*,
16:24 in My name. Ask, and you will *r*,
20:22 *R* the Holy Spirit.
Acts 1: 8 But you shall *r* power when the
2:38 and you shall *r* the gift of the
3: 5 expecting to *r* something from
3:21 whom heaven must *r* until the
7:59 'Lord Jesus, *r* my spirit."
8:15 for them that they might *r* the
8:19 on whom I lay hands may *r* the
9:12 so that he might *r* his sight."
9:17 has sent me that you may *r* your
10:43 whoever believes in Him will *r*
16:21 Romans, to *r* or observe."
18:27 exhorting the disciples to *r*
19: 2 Did you *r* the Holy Spirit when
20:35 more blessed to give than to *r*.
22:13 Saul, *r* your sight.'
22:18 for they will not *r* your
26:18 that they may *r* forgiveness of
27: 3 to go to his friends and *r*
Rom 5:17 much more those who *r* abundance
8:15 For you did not *r* the spirit of
14: 1 *R* one who is weak in the faith,
15: 7 Therefore *r* one another, just
16: 2 that you may *r* her in the Lord
1 Cor 2:14 But the natural man does not *r*
3: 2 now you were not able to *r*
3: 8 and each one will *r* his own
3:14 he will *r* a reward.
4: 7 do you have that you did not *r*?
4: 7 Now if you did indeed *r* it,
14: 5 that the church may *r*
2 Cor 5:10 that each one may *r* the things
6: 1 also plead with you not to *r*
6:17 And I will *r* you."
8: 4 much urgency that we would *r*
11: 4 or if you *r* a different spirit
11:16 at least *r* me as a fool, that I
Gal 3: 2 Did you *r* the Spirit by the
3:14 that we might *r* the promise of
4: 5 that we might *r* the adoption as
Eph 6: 8 he will *r* the same from the
Phil 2:29 *R* him therefore in the Lord with
Col 3:24 that from the Lord you will *r*
2 Th 2:10 because they did not *r* the love
1 Tim 5:19 Do not *r* an accusation against
Phm 1:12 You therefore *r* him, that is,
1:15 that you might *r* him forever,
1:17 *r* him as you would me.
Heb 7: 5 who *r* the priesthood, have a
7: 5 have a commandment to *r* tithes
7: 8 Here mortal men *r* tithes, but
9:15 those who are called may *r* the
10:36 you may *r* the promise:
11: 8 to the place which he would *r*
11:39 did not *r* the promise,
Jas 1: 7 that man suppose that he will *r*
1:12 he will *r* the crown of life
1:21 and *r* with meekness the
3: 1 knowing that we shall *r* a
4: 3 You ask and do not *r*,
1 Pe 5: 4 you will *r* the crown of glory
2 Pe 2:13 and will *r* the wages of
1 Jn 3:22 And whatever we ask we *r* from
5: 9 If we *r* the witness of men,
2 Jn 8 but that we may *r* a full
10 do not *r* him into your house
3 Jn 8 We therefore ought to *r* such,
9 among them, does not *r* us.
10 he himself does not *r* the
Rev 4:11 To *r* glory and honor and
5:12 is the Lamb who was slain To *r*
13:16 to *r* a mark on their right hand
17:12 but they *r* authority for one
18: 4 and lest you *r* of her plagues.

RECEIVED (155/153) RECEIVE

Ex 32: 4 And he *r* the gold from their
36: 3 And they *r* from Moses all the
Num 12:14 and afterward she may be *r*
23:20 I have *r* a command to bless;
31:51 Moses and Eleazar the priest *r*
31:54 Eleazar the priest *r* the gold
32:18 of the children of Israel has *r*
34:14 have *r* their inheritance;
34:14 half-tribe of Manasseh has *r*
34:15 and the half-tribe have *r*
Josh 13: 8 Reubenites and the Gadites *r*
17: 6 the daughters of Manasseh *r* an
18: 2 tribes which had not yet *r*
18: 7 the tribe of Manasseh have *r*
1 Sam 12: 3 or from whose hand have I *r*
25:35 So David *r* from her hand what
2 Ki 19:14 And Hezekiah *r* the letter from
1 Chr 12:18 So David *r* them, and made them
2 Chr 22: 6 from the wounds which he had *r*
29:22 and the priests *r* the blood and
30:16 priests sprinkled the blood *r*
33:13 and He *r* his entreaty, heard
33:19 his prayer and how God *r* his
Ezra 8:30 the priests and the Levites *r*
Job 4:12 And my ear *r* a whisper of it.
15:18 Not hiding anything *r* from
27:13 *r* from the Almighty:
Ps 68:18 You have *r* gifts among men,
Prov 24:32 I looked on it and *r*
Isa 37:14 And Hezekiah *r* the letter from
40: 2 For she has *r* from the LORD's
Jer 2:30 They *r* no correction.
Ezek 18:17 hand from the poor And not *r*
29:18 yet neither he nor his army *r*
Dan 5:31 And Darius the Mede *r* the
Zeph 3: 2 She has not *r* correction;
Mt 10: 8 Freely you have *r*, freely give.
13:19 This is he who *r* seed by the
13:20 But he who *r* the seed on stony
13:22 Now he who *r* seed among the
13:23 But he who *r* seed on the good
15: 5 profit you might have *r* from
17:24 those who *r* the temple tax
20: 9 they each *r* a denarius.
20:10 and they likewise *r* each a
20:11 And when they had *r* it, they
20:34 And immediately their eyes *r*
25:16 Then he who had *r* the five
25:17 And likewise he who had *r* two
25:18 But he who had *r* one went and
25:20 So he who had *r* five talents
25:22 He also who had *r* two talents
25:24 Then he who had *r* the one talent
25:27 and at my coming I would have *r*
Mk 7: 4 other things which they have *r*
7:11 profit you might have *r* from
10:52 And immediately he *r* his
16:19 He was *r* up into heaven, and
Lk 6:24 For you have *r* your
9:11 and He *r* them and spoke to them
9:51 time had come for Him to be *r*
15:27 and because he has *r* him safe
16:25 that in your lifetime you *r*
18:43 And immediately he *r* his sight,
19: 6 and *r* Him joyfully.
19:15 having *r* the kingdom, he then
Jn 1:12 But as many as *r* Him, to them He
1:16 of His fullness we have all *r*,
3:33 He who has *r* His testimony has
4:45 the Galileans *r* Him, having
6:21 Then they willingly *r* Him into
9:11 and washed, and I *r* sight."
9:15 asked him again how he had *r*
9:18 that he had been blind and *r*
9:18 the parents of him who had *r*
10:18 This command I have *r* from My
13:30 Having *r* the piece of bread, he
17: 8 and they have *r* them, and have
18: 3 having *r* a detachment of
19:30 So when Jesus had *r* the sour
Acts 1: 9 and a cloud *r* Him out of their
2:33 and having *r* from the Father
2:41 Then those who gladly *r* his word
3: 7 his feet and ankle bones *r*
7:38 the one who *r* the living
7:45 having *r* it in turn, also
7:53 who have *r* the law by the
8:14 heard that Samaria had *r* the
8:17 and they *r* the Holy Spirit.
9:18 and he *r* his sight at once;
9:19 So when he had *r* food, he was
10:47 not be baptized who have *r* the
11: 1 that the Gentiles had also *r*
15: 4 they were *r* by the church and
16:24 Having *r* such a charge, he put
17:11 in that they *r* the word with
20:24 and the ministry which I *r* from
21:17 the brethren *r* us gladly.
22: 5 from whom I also *r* letters to
26:10 having *r* authority from the
28: 7 who *r* us and entertained us
28:21 We neither *r* letters from Judea
28:30 and *r* all who came to him,
Rom 1: 5 Through Him we have *r* grace and
4:11 And he *r* the sign of
5:11 through whom we have now *r* the
8:15 but you *r* the Spirit of
14: 3 for God has *r* him.
15: 7 just as Christ also *r* us, to
1 Cor 2:12 Now we have *r*, not the spirit
4: 7 you boast as if you had not *r*
11:23 For I *r* from the Lord that
15: 1 which also you *r* and in which
15: 3 of all that which I also *r*:
2 Cor 4: 1 as we have *r* mercy, we do not
7:15 with fear and trembling you *r*
11: 4 spirit which you have not *r*,
11:24 From the Jews five times I *r*
Gal 1: 9 to you than what you have *r*,
1:12 For I neither *r* it from man, nor
4:14 but you *r* me as an angel of
Phil 4: 9 things which you learned and *r*
4:18 having *r* from Epaphroditus the
Col 2: 6 As you have therefore *r* Christ
4:10 of Barnabas (about whom you *r*
4:17 the ministry which you have *r*
1 Th 1: 6 having *r* the word in much
2:13 because when you *r* the word of
4: 1 just as you *r* from us how you
2 Th 3: 6 to the tradition which he *r*
1 Tim 3:16 *R* up in glory.
4: 3 which God created to be *r* with
4: 4 is to be refused if it is *r*
Heb 2: 2 and disobedience *r* a just
7: 6 is not derived from them *r*
7:11 (for under it the people *r* the
10:26 sin willfully after we have *r*
11:11 By faith Sarah herself also *r*
11:13 not having *r* the promises, but
11:17 and he who had *r* the promises
11:19 from which he also *r* him in a
11:31 when she had *r* the spies with
11:35 Women *r* their dead raised to
Jas 2:25 justified by works when she *r*
1 Pe 1:18 from your aimless conduct *r* by
4:10 As each one has *r* a gift,
2 Pe 1:17 For He *r* from God the Father
1 Jn 2:27 the anointing which you have *r*
2 Jn 4 as we *r* commandment from the
Rev 2:27 as I also have *r* from My
3: 3 therefore how you have *r* and
17:12 saw are ten kings who have *r*
19:20 which he deceived those who *r*
20: 4 and had not *r* his mark on

RECEIVES (42/28) RECEIVE

Lev 13:24 Or if the body *r* a burn on its
Num 35: 8 to the inheritance that each *r*.
Deut 33: 3 Everyone *r* Your words.
Prov 15: 5 But he who *r* correction is
21:11 is instructed, he *r* knowledge.
29: 4 But he who *r* bribes overthrows
Mt 7: 8 "For everyone who asks *r*,
10:40 He who *r* you receives Me,
10:40 He who receives you *r* Me,
10:40 and he who *r* Me receives Him
10:40 and he who receives Me *r* Him
10:41 He who *r* a prophet in the name
10:41 And he who *r* a righteous man in
13:20 the word and immediately *r* it
18: 5 Whoever *r* one little child like
18: 5 child like this in My name *r*
Mk 9:37 Whoever *r* one of these little
9:37 little children in My name *r*
9:37 and whoever *r* Me, receives not
9:37 *r* not Me but Him who sent Me."
Lk 9:48 Whoever *r* this little child in
9:48 this little child in My name *r*
9:48 and whoever *r* Me receives Him
9:48 and whoever receives Me *r* Him
11:10 "For everyone who asks *r*,
15: 2 This Man *r* sinners and eats with
Jn 3:32 and no one *r* His testimony.
4:36 And he who reaps *r* wages, and
7:23 If a man *r* circumcision on the
13:20 he who *r* whomever I send
13:20 who receives whomever I send *r*
13:20 and he who *r* Me receives Him
13:20 and he who receives Me *r* Him
1 Cor 9:24 all run, but one *r* the prize?
Heb 6: 7 *r* blessing from God;
7: 8 but there he *r* them, of whom
7: 9 who *r* tithes, paid tithes
12: 6 every son whom He *r*.
Jas 5: 7 patiently for it until it *r*
Rev 2:17 no one knows except him who *r*
14: 9 and *r* his mark on his forehead
14:11 and whoever *r* the mark of his

RECEIVING (6/6) RECEIVE

2 Ki 5:20 while not *r* from his hands what
Acts 17:15 and *r* a command for Silas and
Rom 1:27 and *r* in themselves the penalty
Phil 4:15 me concerning giving and *r* but
Heb 12:28 since we are *r* a kingdom which
1 Pe 1: 9 *r* the end of your faith—the

RECENTLY (2/2)

Jer 34:15 Then you *r* turned and did what
Acts 18: 2 who had *r* come from Italy with

RECEPTACLES (1/1)

Zech 4:12 branches that drip into the *r*

RECESS (1/1)
Job 28: 3 And searches every ***r*** For ore

RECESSES (2/2)
1 Sam 24: 3 his men were staying in the ***r***
Ezek 32:23 Her graves are set in the ***r*** of

RECHAB (13/13) RECHABITES
2 Sam 4: 2 and the name of the other ***R***,
4: 5 ***R*** and Baanah, set out and came
4: 6 Then ***R*** and Baanah his brother
4: 9 But David answered ***R*** and Baanah
2 Ki 10:15 he met Jehonadab the son of ***R***,
10:23 Jehu and Jehonadab the son of ***R***
1 Chr 2:55 the father of the house of ***R***.
Neh 3:14 Malchijah the son of ***R***,
Jer 35: 6 wine, for Jonadab the son of ***R***,
35: 8 voice of Jonadab the son of ***R***,
35:14 words of Jonadab the son of ***R***,
35:16 sons of Jonadab the son of ***R***
35:19 Jonadab the son of ***R*** shall not

RECHABITES (4/4) RECHAB
Jer 35: 2 "Go to the house of the ***R***,
35: 3 and the whole house of the ***R***,
35: 5 the sons of the house of the ***R***
35:18 said to the house of the ***R***,

RECHAH (1/1)
1 Chr 4:12 These were the men of ***R***.

RECITE (1/1) RECITED
Ps 45: 1 I ***r*** my composition concerning

RECITED (1/1) RECITE
Num 1:18 and they ***r*** their ancestry by

RECKLESS (1/1)
Judg 9: 4 hired worthless and ***r*** men;

RECKLESSNESS (1/1)
Jer 23:32 by their lies and by their ***r***.

RECKON (5/5) RECKONED, RECKONING
Lev 25:50 Thus he shall ***r*** with him who
25:52 then he shall ***r*** with him, and
27:18 then the priest shall ***r*** to him
27:23 priest shall ***r*** to him the worth
Rom 6:11 ***r*** yourselves to be dead indeed

RECKONED (2/2) RECKON
Num 18:27 your heave offering shall be ***r***
1 Chr 23:14 of Moses the man of God were ***r***

RECKONING (2/2) RECKON
Gen 9: 5 lifeblood I will demand a ***r***;
Num 23: 9 Not ***r*** itself among the

RECLINE (1/1)
Am 6: 7 And those who ***r*** at banquets

RECOGNIZE (7/7) RECOGNIZED
Gen 27:23 And he did not ***r*** him, because
42: 8 but they did not ***r*** him.
Ruth 3:14 she arose before one could ***r***
1 Ki 14: 2 that they may not ***r*** you as the
Job 2:12 from afar, and did not ***r*** him,
Acts 27:39 they did not ***r*** the land; but
1 Th 5:12 to ***r*** those who labor among you,

RECOGNIZED (10/10) RECOGNIZE
Gen 37:33 And he ***r*** it and said, "It is
42: 7 Joseph saw his brothers and ***r***
42: 8 So Joseph ***r*** his brothers, but
Judg 18: 3 they ***r*** the voice of the young
1 Ki 18: 7 and he ***r*** him, and fell on his
20:41 and the king of Israel ***r*** him as
Mt 14:35 when the men of that place ***r***
Mk 6:54 immediately the people ***r*** Him,
Acts 12:14 When she ***r*** Peter's voice,
1 Cor 11:19 those who are approved may be ***r***

RECOGNIZES (1/1)
Job 24:17 If someone ***r*** them,

RECOMPENSE (17/17)
Deut 32:35 Vengeance is Mine, and ***r***;
Job 21:19 Let Him ***r*** him, that he may
Prov 6:35 He will accept no ***r***,
12:14 And the ***r*** of a man's hands
20:22 I will ***r*** evil"; Wait for the
Isa 34: 8 The year of ***r*** for the cause of
35: 4 With the ***r*** of God; He will
59:18 ***R*** to His enemies;
Jer 51: 6 vengeance; He shall ***r*** her.
51:56 For the LORD is the God of ***r***,
Ezek 9:10 but I will ***r*** their deeds on
11:21 I will ***r*** their deeds on their
16:43 surely I will also ***r*** your deeds
17:19 I will ***r*** on his own head.
Hos 9: 7 The days of ***r*** have come.
12: 2 to his deeds He will ***r*** him.
Rom 11: 9 block and a ***r*** to them.

RECOMPENSED (6/6)
2 Sam 22:21 of my hands He has ***r*** me.
22:25 Therefore the LORD has ***r*** me
Ps 18:20 of my hands He has ***r*** me.
18:24 Therefore the LORD has ***r*** me
Prov 11:31 If the righteous will be ***r*** on
Ezek 22:31 and I have ***r*** their deeds on

RECONCILE (4/4) RECONCILED, RECONCILIATION, RECONCILING
1 Sam 29: 4 For with what could he ***r***
Acts 7:26 and tried to ***r*** them, saying,
Eph 2:16 and that He might ***r*** them both to
Col 1:20 and by Him to ***r*** all things to

RECONCILED (7/6) RECONCILE
Mt 5:24 First be ***r*** to your brother, and
Rom 5:10 when we were enemies we were ***r***
5:10 Son, much more, having been ***r***,
1 Cor 7:11 her remain unmarried or be ***r***
2 Cor 5:18 who has ***r*** us to Himself through
5:20 Christ's behalf, be ***r*** to God.
Col 1:21 yet now He has ***r***

RECONCILIATION (4/4) RECONCILE
Dan 9:24 To make ***r*** for iniquity,
Rom 5:11 whom we have now received the ***r***.
2 Cor 5:18 has given us the ministry of ***r***,
5:19 committed to us the word of ***r***.

RECONCILING (2/2) RECONCILE
Rom 11:15 being cast away is the ***r*** of
2 Cor 5:19 that God was in Christ ***r*** the

RECONSIDER (1/1)
Prov 20:25 And afterward to ***r*** his vows.

RECORD (6/6) RECORDED, RECORDER, RECORDS
Ex 20:24 In every place where I ***r*** My
Ezra 6: 2 and in it a ***r*** was written
Neh 12:22 a ***r*** was also kept of the
Ps 87: 6 The LORD will ***r***,
Isa 8: 2 Myself faithful witnesses to ***r***,
Ezek 13: 9 nor be written in the ***r*** of the

RECORDED (8/8)
1 Chr 4:41 These ***r*** by name came in the days
7: 9 And they were ***r*** by genealogy
7:40 And they were ***r*** by genealogies
9: 1 So all Israel was ***r*** by
9:22 They were ***r*** by their genealogy,
27:24 nor was the number ***r*** in the
Esth 1:19 and let it be ***r*** in the laws of
Isa 4: 3 everyone who is ***r*** among the

RECORDER (9/9)
2 Sam 8:16 the son of Ahilud was ***r***;
20:24 the son of Ahilud was ***r***;
1 Ki 4: 3 the son of Ahilud, the ***r***;
2 Ki 18:18 Joah the son of Asaph, the ***r***,
18:37 Joah the son of Asaph, the ***r***,
1 Chr 18:15 the son of Ahilud was ***r***;
2 Chr 34: 8 Joah the son of Joahaz the ***r***,
Isa 36: 3 Joah the son of Asaph, the ***r***,
36:22 Joah the son of Asaph, the ***r***,

RECORDS (5/4)
Num 3: 1 Now these are the ***r*** of Aaron
1 Chr 4:22 Now the ***r*** are ancient.
Ezra 4:15 be made in the book of the ***r***
4:15 will find in the book of the ***r***
Esth 6: 1 to bring the book of the ***r*** of

RECOUNT (2/2) RECOUNTED
Ex 17:14 a memorial in the book and ***r***
Judg 5:11 There they shall ***r*** the

RECOUNTED (2/2) RECOUNT
Ps 22:30 It will be ***r*** of the Lord to
40: 5 toward us Cannot be ***r*** to You

RECOVER (16/16) RECOVERED, RECOVERY
Judg 11:26 why did you not ***r*** them within
1 Sam 30: 8 them and without fail ***r*** all.
2 Sam 8: 3 as he went to ***r*** his territory
2 Ki 1: 2 whether I shall ***r*** from this
8: 8 saying, 'Shall I ***r*** from this
8: 9 Shall I ***r*** from this disease?'"
8:10 to him, 'You shall certainly ***r***.
8:14 "He told me you would surely ***r***.
8:29 went back to Jezreel to ***r*** from
9:15 had returned to Jezreel to ***r***
2 Chr 13:20 So Jeroboam did not ***r*** strength
14:13 and they could not ***r***,
22: 6 he returned to Jezreel to ***r***
Isa 11:11 again the second time To ***r***
38:21 on the boil, and he shall ***r***.
Mk 16:18 on the sick, and they will ***r***.

RECOVERED (8/8) RECOVER
1 Sam 7:14 and Israel ***r*** its territory from
30:18 So David ***r*** all that the
30:19 taken from them; David ***r*** all.
30:22 of the spoil that we have ***r***,
2 Ki 20: 7 laid it on the boil, and he ***r***.
Isa 38: 9 when he had been sick and had ***r***
39: 1 that he had been sick and had ***r***.
Jer 41:16 of the people whom he had ***r***

RECOVERY (2/2) RECOVER
Jer 8:22 Why then is there no ***r*** For
Lk 4:18 to the captives And ***r***

RECRUITED (1/1)
Num 31: 5 So there were ***r*** from the

RECRUITER'S (1/1)
Judg 5:14 those who bear the ***r*** staff.

RECRUITING (1/1)
2 Ki 25:19 the chief ***r*** officer of the

RECTANGULAR (1/1)
1 Ki 7: 5 and doorposts had ***r*** frames;

RED (51/50) REDNESS
Gen 25:25 And the first came out ***r***.
25:30 feed me with that same ***r*** stew,
Ex 10:19 and blew them into the ***R*** Sea.
13:18 of the wilderness of the ***R*** Sea.
15: 4 also are drowned in the ***R*** Sea.
15:22 brought Israel from the ***R*** Sea;
23:31 set your bounds from the ***R*** Sea
25: 5 "ram skins dyed ***r***,
26:14 a covering of ram skins dyed ***r***
35: 7 'ram skins dyed ***r***,
35:23 ***r*** skins of rams, and badger
36:19 the tent of ram skins dyed ***r***,
39:34 covering of ram skins dyed ***r***,
Num 14:25 by the Way of the ***R*** Sea."
19: 2 that they bring you a ***r*** heifer
21: 4 by the Way of the ***R*** Sea,
33:10 Elim and camped by the ***R*** Sea.
33:11 They moved from the ***R*** Sea and
Deut 1:40 by the Way of the ***R*** Sea.'
2: 1 of the Way of the ***R*** Sea,
11: 4 He made the waters of the ***R*** Sea
14:13 the ***r*** kite, the falcon, and the
Josh 2:10 the water of the ***R*** Sea for
4:23 LORD your God did to the ***R*** Sea,
24: 6 and horsemen to the ***R*** Sea.
Judg 11:16 wilderness as far as the ***R*** Sea
1 Ki 9:26 on the shore of the ***R*** Sea,
2 Ki 3:22 water on the other side as ***r***
Neh 9: 9 heard their cry by the ***R*** Sea.
Ps 75: 8 is a cup, And the wine is ***r***;
106: 7 by the sea—the ***R*** Sea.
106: 9 He rebuked the ***R*** Sea also,
106:22 Awesome things by the ***R*** Sea.
136:13 To Him who divided the ***R*** Sea
136:15 and his army in the ***R*** Sea,
Prov 23:31 look on the wine when it is ***r***,
Isa 1:18 Though they are ***r*** like
27: 2 A vineyard of ***r*** wine!
63: 2 Why is Your apparel ***r***,
Jer 49:21 its noise is heard at the ***R*** Sea.
Nah 2: 3 of his mighty men are made ***r***,
Zech 1: 8 a man riding on a ***r*** horse, and
1: 8 were horses: ***r***, sorrel, and
6: 2 With the first chariot were ***r***
Mt 16: 2 fair weather, for the sky is ***r***';
16: 3 for the sky is ***r*** and
Acts 7:36 and in the ***R*** Sea, and in
Heb 11:29 they passed through the ***R*** Sea
Rev 6: 4 Another horse, fiery ***r***,
9:17 had breastplates of fiery ***r***,
12: 3 fiery ***r*** dragon having seven

REDDISH (2/2)
Lev 13:49 if the plague is greenish or ***r***
14:37 streaks, greenish or ***r***,

REDDISH-WHITE (4/4)
Lev 13:19 swelling or a bright spot, ***r***,
13:24 bright spot, ***r*** or white,
13:42 head or bald forehead a ***r*** sore,
13:43 the swelling of the sore is ***r***

REDEEM (62/46) REDEEMED, REDEEMER, REDEEMING, REDEEMS, REDEMPTION
Ex 6: 6 and I will ***r*** you with an
13:13 of a donkey you shall ***r*** with a
13:13 and if you will not ***r*** it, then
13:13 man among your sons you shall ***r***.
13:15 the firstborn of my sons I ***r***.
21:30 then he shall pay to ***r*** his
34:20 of a donkey you shall ***r*** with a
34:20 And if you will not ***r*** him,
34:20 of your sons you shall ***r***.
Lev 25:25 redeeming relative comes to ***r***
25:25 then he may ***r*** what his brother

25:26 Or if the man has no one to *r*
25:26 he himself becomes able to *r*
25:29 then he may *r* it within a whole
25:29 within a full year he may *r*
25:32 the Levites may *r* at any time.
25:48 One of his brothers may *r* him;
25:49 uncle or his uncle's son may *r*
25:49 kin to him in his family may *r*
25:49 or if he is able he may *r*
27:13 But if he wants at all to *r*
27:15 who dedicated it wants to *r*
27:19 the field ever wishes to *r* it,
27:20 But if he does not want to *r* the
27:27 then he shall *r* it according
27:31 If a man wants at all to *r* any
Num 18:15 of man you shall surely *r*,
18:15 of unclean animals you shall *r*.
18:16 the devoted things you shall *r*
18:17 of a goat you shall not *r*;
Ruth 4: 4 If you will *r* it, redeem it;
4: 4 *r* it; but if you will not
4: 4 but if you will not *r* it,
4: 4 there is no one but you to *r*
4: 4 And he said, "I will *r* it."
4: 6 I cannot *r* it for myself, lest
4: 6 You *r* my right of redemption
4: 6 for I cannot *r* it."
2 Sam 7:23 on the earth whom God went to *r*
1 Chr 17:21 on the earth whom God went to *r*
Neh 5: 5 It is not in our power to *r*
Job 5:20 In famine He shall *r* you from
6:23 *R* me from the hand of
33:28 He will *r* his soul from going
Ps 25:22 *R* Israel, O God, Out of all
26:11 *R* me and be merciful to me.
44:26 And *r* us for Your mercies'
49: 7 of them can by any means *r*
49:15 But God will *r* my soul from the
69:18 near to my soul, and *r* it;
72:14 He will *r* their life from
119:134 *R* me from the oppression of
119:154 Plead my cause and *r* me;
130: 8 And He shall *r* Israel From all
Isa 50: 2 at all that it cannot *r*?
Jer 15:21 And I will *r* you from the grip
Hos 13:14 I will *r* them from death.
Mic 4:10 There the LORD will *r* you
Zech 10: 8 For I will *r* them;
Lk 24:21 it was He who was going to *r*
Gal 4: 5 to *r* those who were under the
Titus 2:14 that He might *r* us from every

REDEEMED (60/59) REDEEM

Gen 48:16 The Angel who has *r* me from all
Ex 15:13 The people whom You have *r*;
21: 8 then he shall let her be *r*.
Lev 19:20 and who has not at all been *r*
25:30 But if it is not *r* within the
25:31 of the country. They may be *r*,
25:48 after he is sold he may be *r*
25:54 And if he is not *r* in these
27:20 it shall not be *r* anymore;
27:27 or if it is not *r*, then it
27:28 possession, shall be sold or *r*;
27:29 among men, shall be *r*,
27:33 be holy; it shall not be *r*.
Num 3:48 the excess number of them is *r*,
3:49 and above those who were *r* by
18:16 And those *r* of the devoted
Deut 7: 8 and *r* you from the house of
9:26 inheritance whom You have *r*
13: 5 out of the land of Egypt and *r*
15:15 and the LORD your God *r* you;
21: 8 people Israel, whom You have *r*,
24:18 and the LORD your God *r* you
2 Sam 4: 9 who has *r* my life from all
7:23 before Your people whom You *r*
1 Ki 1:29 who has *r* my life from every
1 Chr 17:21 before Your people whom You *r*
Neh 1:10 whom You have *r* by Your great
5: 8 to our ability we have *r* our
Ps 31: 5 You have *r* me, O LORD God of
55:18 He has *r* my soul in peace from
71:23 And my soul, which You have *r*.
74: 2 inheritance, which You have *r*—
77:15 You have with Your arm *r* Your
78:42 The day when He *r* them from
106:10 And *r* them from the hand of
107: 2 Let the *r* of the LORD say so,
107: 2 Whom He has *r* from the hand of
Isa 1:27 Zion shall be *r* with justice,
29:22 who *r* Abraham, concerning the
35: 9 But the *r* shall walk there,
43: 1 for I have *r* you; I have
44:22 for I have *r* you."
44:23 For the LORD has *r* Jacob,
48:20 The LORD has *r* His servant
51:10 of the sea a road For the *r*
52: 3 And you shall be *r* without
52: 9 He has *r* Jerusalem.
62:12 The *R* of the LORD;
63: 4 And the year of My *r* has come.
63: 9 His love and in His pity He *r*
Jer 31:11 For the LORD has *r* Jacob,
Lam 3:58 You have *r* my life.
Hos 7:13 against Me! Though I *r* them,
Mic 6: 4 I *r* you from the house of
Lk 1:68 For He has visited and *r* His
Gal 3:13 Christ has *r* us from the curse
1 Pe 1:18 knowing that you were not *r* with
Rev 5: 9 And have *r* us to God by Your

14: 3 forty-four thousand who were *r*
14: 4 These were *r* from among men,

REDEEMER (18/18) REDEEM

Job 19:25 For I know that my *R* lives,
Ps 19:14 O LORD, my strength and my *R*.
78:35 And the Most High God their *R*.
Prov 23:11 For their *R* is mighty;
Isa 41:14 says the LORD And your *R*,
43:14 Thus says the LORD, your *R*,
44: 6 the King of Israel, And his *R*,
44:24 Thus says the LORD, your *R*,
47: 4 As for our *R*, the LORD
48:17 Thus says the LORD, your *R*,
49: 7 The *R* of Israel, their Holy
49:26 am your Savior, And your *R*,
54: 5 And your *R* is the Holy One of
54: 8 Says the LORD, your *R*.
59:20 The *R* will come to Zion,
60:16 am your Savior And your *R*,
63:16 Our *R* from Everlasting is
Jer 50:34 Their *R* is strong;

REDEEMING (4/4) REDEEM

Ruth 4: 7 times in Israel concerning *r*
Eph 5:16 *r* the time, because the days are
Col 4: 5 who are outside, *r* the time.

REDEEMING RELATIVE (1/1)

Lev 25:25 and if his *r* comes to redeem

REDEEMS (2/2) REDEEM

Ps 34:22 The LORD *r* the soul of His
103: 4 Who *r* your life from

REDEMPTION (23/23) REDEEM

Lev 25:24 possession you shall grant *r*
25:51 shall repay the price of his *r*
25:52 repay him the price of his *r*.
Num 3:46 And for the *r* of the two hundred
3:49 So Moses took the *r* money from
3:51 And Moses gave their *r* money to
Ruth 4: 6 You redeem my right of *r* for
Ps 49: 8 For the *r* of their souls is
111: 9 He has sent *r* to His people;
130: 7 And with Him is abundant *r*.
Jer 32: 7 for the right of *r* is yours to
32: 8 and the *r* yours; buy it for
Lk 2:38 to all those who looked for *r*
21:28 because your *r* draws near."
Rom 3:24 by His grace through the *r*
8:23 the *r* of our body.
1 Cor 1:30 and sanctification and *r*—
Eph 1: 7 In Him we have *r* through His
1:14 of our inheritance until the *r*
4:30 were sealed for the day of *r*.
Col 1:14 in whom we have *r* through His
Heb 9:12 all, having obtained eternal *r*.
9:15 for the *r* of the transgressions

REDNESS (1/1) RED

Prov 23:29 Who has *r* of eyes?

REDOUND (KJV) See ABOUND

REDUCE (4/4) REDUCED

Ex 5: 8 You shall not *r* it.
5:19 You shall not *r* any bricks from
Isa 25: 5 You will *r* the noise of aliens,
Zeph 2:11 For He will *r* to nothing all

REDUCED (2/2) REDUCE

Ex 5:11 yet none of your work will be *r*.
Prov 6:26 of a harlot A man is *r* to

REED (18/18) REEDS

1 Ki 14:15 as a *r* is shaken in the water.
2 Ki 18:21 in the staff of this broken *r*,
Job 41: 2 Can you put a *r* through his
Isa 18: 2 Even in vessels of *r* on the
36: 6 in the staff of this broken *r*,
42: 3 A bruised *r* He will not break,
Ezek 29: 6 they have been a staff of *r* to
Mt 11: 7 A *r* shaken by the wind?
12:20 A bruised *r* He will not
27:29 and a *r* in His right hand.
27:30 and took the *r* and struck Him
27:48 sour wine and put it on a *r*,
Mk 15:19 Him on the head with a *r* and
15:36 of sour wine, put it on a *r*,
Lk 7:24 A *r* shaken by the wind?
Rev 11: 1 Then I was given a *r* like a
21:15 talked with me had a gold *r* to
21:16 he measured the city with the *r*:

REEDS (9/9) REED

Ex 2: 3 and laid it in the *r* by the
2: 5 she saw the ark among the *r*,
Job 8:11 Can the *r* flourish without
40:21 In a covert of *r* and marsh.
Ps 68:30 Rebuke the beasts of the *r*,
Isa 19: 6 The *r* and rushes will wither.
19: 7 The papyrus *r* by the River,

35: 7 shall be grass with *r* and
Jer 51:32 The *r* they have burned with

REEL (2/2)

Ps 107:27 They *r* to and fro, and stagger
Isa 24:20 The earth shall *r* to and fro

REELAIAH (1/1)

Ezra 2: 2 Jeshua, Nehemiah, Seraiah, *R*,

REFERS (3/3)

Dan 8:17 that the vision *r* to the time
8:26 For it *r* to many days in
10:14 for the vision *r* to many days

REFINE (3/3) REFINED, REFINES

Jer 9: 7 I will *r* them and try them;
Dan 11:35 to *r* them, purify them, and
Zech 13: 9 Will *r* them as silver is

REFINED (11/10) REFINE

Deut 28:54 The sensitive and very *r* man
1 Chr 28:18 and *r* gold by weight for the
29: 4 talents of *r* silver, to overlay
Job 28: 1 And a place where gold is *r*.
Ps 66:10 You have *r* us as silver is
66:10 have refined us as silver is *r*.
Isa 48:10 I have *r* you, but not as
Dan 12:10 be purified, made white, and *r*,
Zech 13: 9 refine them as silver is *r*,
Rev 1:15 as if *r* in a furnace, and His
3:18 you to buy from Me gold *r* in

REFINER (1/1)

Mal 3: 3 He will sit as a *r* and a

REFINER'S (1/1)

Mal 3: 2 For He is like a *r* fire

REFINES (1/1) REFINE

Jer 6:29 The smelter *r* in vain,

REFINING (2/2)

Prov 17: 3 The *r* pot is for silver and
27:21 The *r* pot is for silver

REFLECTS (1/1)

Prov 27:19 As in water face *r* face, So a

REFORMATION (1/1) REFORMED

Heb 9:10 imposed until the time of *r*.

REFORMED (1/1)

Lev 26:23 by these things you are not *r*

REFRAIN (12/12)

Ex 23: 5 and you would *r* from helping
1 Ki 22: 6 Gilead to fight, or shall I *r*?
22:15 Ramoth Gilead, or shall we *r*?
2 Chr 18: 5 Ramoth Gilead, or shall I *r*?
18:14 Ramoth Gilead, or shall I *r*?
35:21 *R* from meddling with God,
Eccl 3: 5 And a time to *r* from
Jer 31:16 '*R* your voice from weeping,
Zech 11:12 me my wages; and if not, *r*.
1 Cor 9: 6 and I who have no right to *r*
2 Cor 12: 6 But I *r*, lest anyone should
1 Pe 3:10 Let him *r* his tongue

REFRAINED (1/1)

Job 29: 9 The princes *r* from talking,

REFRAINETH (KJV) See RESTRAINS

REFRESH (6/6) REFRESHED, REFRESHING

Gen 18: 5 that you may *r* your hearts.
Judg 19: 5 *R* your heart with a morsel of
19: 8 'Please *r* your heart."
1 Ki 13: 7 Come home with me and *r*
Song 2: 5 *R* me with apples, For I am
Phm 1:20 *r* my heart in the Lord.

REFRESHED (9/9) REFRESH

Ex 23:12 and the stranger may be *r*.
31:17 seventh day He rested and was *r*.
1 Sam 16:23 Then Saul would become *r* and
2 Sam 16:14 so they *r* themselves there.
Rom 15:32 and may be *r* together with you.
1 Cor 16:18 For they *r* my spirit and yours.
2 Cor 7:13 because his spirit has been *r*
2 Tim 1:16 for he often *r* me, and was not
Phm 1: 7 of the saints have been *r* by

REFRESHES (1/1)

Prov 25:13 For he *r* the soul of his

REFRESHING (2/2) REFRESH

Isa 28:12 'This is the ***r***';
Acts 3:19 so that times of ***r*** may come

REFUGE (61/60)

Num 35: 6 shall appoint six cities of ***r***,
35:11 cities to be cities of ***r*** for
35:12 They shall be cities of ***r*** for
35:13 you shall have six cities of ***r***.
35:14 which will be cities of ***r***.
35:15 six cities shall be for ***r*** for
35:25 return him to the city of ***r***
35:26 the limits of the city of ***r***
35:27 the limits of his city of ***r***,
35:28 have remained in his city of ***r***
35:32 who has fled to his city of ***r***,
Deut 32:37 rock in which they sought ***r***?
32:38 and help you, And be your ***r***.
33:27 The eternal God is your ***r***,
Josh 20: 2 for yourselves cities of ***r***,
20: 3 and they shall be your ***r*** from
21:13 its common-land (a city of ***r***
21:21 of Ephraim (a city of ***r*** for
21:27 its common-land (a city of ***r***
21:32 its common-land (a city of ***r***
21:38 its common-land (a city of ***r***
Ruth 2:12 whose wings you have come for ***r***.
2 Sam 22: 3 My stronghold and my ***r***;
1 Chr 6:57 gave one of the cities of ***r***,
6:67 them one of the cities of ***r***,
Ps 9: 9 The LORD also will be a ***r*** for
9: 9 A ***r*** in times of trouble.
14: 6 But the LORD is his ***r***.
28: 8 And He is the saving ***r*** of His
31: 2 me speedily; Be my rock of ***r***,
46: 1 God is our ***r*** and strength,
46: 7 The God of Jacob is our ***r***.
46:11 The God of Jacob is our ***r***.
48: 3 He is known as her ***r***.
57: 1 of Your wings I will make my ***r***,
59:16 have been my defense And ***r*** in
62: 7 rock of my strength, And my ***r***,
62: 8 God is a ***r*** for us. Selah
71: 3 Be my strong ***r***, To which I
71: 7 But You are my strong ***r***.
91: 2 He is my ***r*** and my fortress;
91: 4 His wings you shall take ***r***;
91: 9 made the LORD, who is my ***r***,
94:22 And my God the rock of my ***r***.
104:18 The cliffs are a ***r*** for the
141: 8 GOD the Lord; In You I take ***r***;
142: 4 ***R*** has failed me; No one cares
142: 5 LORD: I said, "You are my ***r***,
144: 2 and the One in whom I take ***r***,
Prov 14:26 children will have a place of ***r***.
14:32 But the righteous has a ***r*** in
Isa 4: 6 from the heat, for a place of ***r***,
10:31 inhabitants of Gebim seek ***r***.
14:32 of His people shall take ***r*** in
25: 4 A ***r*** from the storm, A shade
28:15 For we have made lies our ***r***,
28:17 hail will sweep away the ***r*** of
Jer 4: 6 Take ***r***! Do not delay!
16:19 My ***r*** in the day of affliction,
Nah 3:11 You also will seek ***r*** from the
Heb 6:18 who have fled for ***r*** to lay hold

REFUGEE (1/1)

Lam 2:22 LORD's anger There was no ***r***

REFUSE (52/50) REFUSED, REFUSES, REFUSING

Ex 4:23 But if you ***r*** to let him go,
8: 2 But if you ***r*** to let them go,
9: 2 For if you ***r*** to let them go,
10: 3 How long will you ***r*** to humble
10: 4 if you ***r*** to let My people go,
16:28 How long do you ***r*** to keep My
Deut 23:13 it and turn and cover your ***r***.
28:56 will ***r*** to the husband of her
1 Ki 2:17 for he will not ***r*** you, that he
2:20 petition of you; do not ***r*** me."
2:20 for I will not ***r*** you."
14:10 as one takes away ***r*** until it is
2 Ki 9:37 of Jezebel shall be as ***r*** on
10:27 temple of Baal and made it a ***r***
Ezra 6:11 and let his house be made a ***r***
Neh 2:13 to the Serpent Well and the ***R***
3:13 of the wall as far as the ***R***
3:14 repaired the ***R*** Gate;
12:31 hand on the wall toward the ***R***
Job 20: 7 perish forever like his own ***r***;
Ps 83:10 Who became as ***r*** on the
141: 5 Let my head not ***r*** it.
Prov 21: 7 Because they ***r*** to do justice.
21:25 For his hands ***r*** to labor.
Isa 1:20 But if you ***r*** and rebel,
5:25 Their carcasses were as ***r*** in
7:15 that He may know to ***r*** the evil
7:16 the Child shall know to ***r*** the
25:10 is trampled down for the ***r***
Jer 3: 3 You ***r*** to be ashamed.
8: 2 they shall be like ***r*** on the
8: 5 They ***r*** to return.
9: 6 Through deceit they ***r*** to know
9:22 of men shall fall as ***r*** on the
13:10 who ***r*** to hear My words, who
16: 4 but they shall be like ***r*** on
25:28 if they ***r*** to take the cup from
25:33 they shall become ***r*** on the
38:21 'But if you ***r*** to surrender,
Lam 3:45 made us an offscouring and ***r***
Ezek 2: 5 they hear or whether they ***r***—
2: 7 they hear or whether they ***r***,
3:11 they hear, or whether they ***r***,
3:27 and he who refuses, let him ***r***;
7:19 And their gold will be like ***r***;
7:20 I have made it Like ***r*** to them.
Zeph 1:17 dust, And their flesh like ***r***.
Mal 2: 3 your descendants And spread ***r***
2: 3 The ***r*** of your solemn feasts;
Mk 6:26 he did not want to ***r*** her.
1 Tim 5:11 But ***r*** the younger widows;
Heb 12:25 See that you do not ***r*** Him who

REFUSED (31/30) REFUSE

Gen 37:35 but he ***r*** to be comforted, and
39: 8 But he ***r*** and said to his
48:19 But his father ***r*** and said, "I
Num 20:21 Thus Edom ***r*** to give Israel
22:13 for the LORD has ***r*** to give me
1 Sam 8:19 Nevertheless the people ***r*** to
16: 7 because I have ***r*** him.
28:23 But he ***r*** and said, "I will not
2 Sam 2:23 he ***r*** to turn aside.
12: 4 who ***r*** to take from his own
13: 9 but he ***r*** to eat. Then Amnon
1 Ki 20:35 And the man ***r*** to strike him.
21:15 which he ***r*** to give you for
2 Ki 5:16 urged him to take it, but he ***r***.
Neh 9:17 They ***r*** to obey, And they were
Esth 1:12 But Queen Vashti ***r*** to come at
Ps 77: 2 My soul ***r*** to be comforted.
78:10 They ***r*** to walk in His law,
Prov 1:24 I have called and you ***r***,
Isa 8: 6 Inasmuch as these people ***r*** The
54: 6 a youthful wife when you were ***r***,
Jer 5: 3 But they have ***r*** to receive
5: 3 They have ***r*** to return.
11:10 of their forefathers who ***r*** to
50:33 They have ***r*** to let them go.
Ezek 5: 6 for they have ***r*** My judgments,
Hos 11: 5 Because they ***r*** to repent.
Zech 7:11 But they ***r*** to heed, shrugged
1 Tim 4: 4 and nothing is to be ***r*** if it is
Heb 11:24 ***r*** to be called the son of
12:25 if they did not escape who ***r***

REFUSES (10/9) REFUSE

Ex 7:14 he ***r*** to let the people go.
22:17 If her father utterly ***r*** to give
Num 22:14 Balaam ***r*** to come with us."
Deut 25: 7 My husband's brother ***r*** to raise
Job 6: 7 My soul ***r*** to touch them;
Prov 10:17 But he who ***r*** correction goes
Jer 15:18 Which ***r*** to be healed?
Ezek 3:27 let him hear; and he who ***r***,
Mt 18:17 And if he ***r*** to hear them, tell
18:17 But if he ***r*** even to hear the

REFUSING (4/4) REFUSE

Isa 33:15 ***r*** bribes, Who stops his ears
Jer 31:15 ***R*** to be comforted for her
Zech 7:12 ***r*** to hear the law and the words
Mt 2:18 ***R*** to be comforted,

REFUTED (1/1)

Acts 18:28 for he vigorously ***r*** the Jews

REGAIN (2/2)

Ps 39:13 that I may ***r*** strength,
Prov 2:19 Nor do they ***r*** the paths of

REGARD (47/46) REGARDED, REGARDING, REGARDS

Gen 41:40 only in ***r*** to the throne will I
Ex 5: 9 and let them not ***r*** false
9:21 But he who did not ***r*** the word of
Lev 5:15 and sins unintentionally in ***r***
5:16 the harm that he has done in ***r***
11:11 but you shall ***r*** their carcasses
11:13 And these you shall ***r*** as an
15: 3 shall be his uncleanness in ***r***
19:31 Give no ***r*** to mediums and
Num 4:19 but do this in ***r*** to them, that
6:11 because he sinned in ***r*** to the
1 Sam 4:20 nor did she ***r*** it.
25:25 let not my lord ***r*** this
2 Sam 19: 6 ***r*** neither princes nor servants;
1 Ki 8:28 Yet ***r*** the prayer of Your servant
2 Ki 3:14 surely were it not that I ***r*** the
2 Chr 6:19 Yet ***r*** the prayer of Your servant
Ezra 7:14 with ***r*** to the Law of your God
Job 13:24 And ***r*** me as Your enemy?
30:20 I stand up, and You ***r*** me.
34:19 Nor does He ***r*** the rich more
35:13 Nor will the Almighty ***r*** it.
Ps 28: 5 Because they do not ***r*** the works
31: 6 I have hated those who ***r***
66:18 If I ***r*** iniquity in my heart,
102:17 He shall ***r*** the prayer of the
Isa 5:12 But they do not ***r*** the work of
13:17 Who will not ***r*** silver;
Ezek 44:28 in ***r*** to their inheritance,
Dan 3:12 have not paid due ***r*** to you.
6:13 does not show due ***r*** for you,
11:30 So he shall return and show ***r***
11:37 He shall ***r*** neither the God of
11:37 desire of women, nor ***r*** any god;
Am 5:22 Nor will I ***r*** your fattened
Jon 2: 8 Those who ***r*** worthless idols
Mal 2:13 So He does not ***r*** the offering
Mt 22:16 You do not ***r*** the person of men.
Mk 12:14 for You do not ***r*** the person of
Lk 18: 2 who did not fear God nor ***r*** man.
18: 4 I do not fear God nor ***r*** man,
Rom 6:20 you were free in ***r*** to
12:17 Have ***r*** for good things in the
2 Cor 5:16 we ***r*** no one according to the
Phil 4:11 Not that I speak in ***r*** to need,
Heb 9: 9 the service perfect in ***r*** to
1 Pe 4: 4 In ***r*** to these, they think it

REGARDED (13/13) REGARD

Lev 10: 3 who come near Me I must be ***r***
Deut 2:11 They were also ***r*** as giants,
2:20 (That was also ***r*** as a land of
2 Ki 13:23 and ***r*** them, because of His
1 Chr 17:17 and have ***r*** me according to the
Job 18: 3 And ***r*** as stupid in your
41:29 Darts are ***r*** as straw;
Ps 106:44 Nevertheless He ***r*** their
119:126 For they have ***r*** Your law as
Prov 1:24 out my hand and no one ***r***,
Lam 4: 2 How they are ***r*** as clay pots,
Lk 1:48 For He has ***r*** the lowly state of
2 Cor 11:12 desire an opportunity to be ***r***

REGARDING (13/13) REGARD

Lev 5:18 for him ***r*** his ignorance
25:46 But ***r*** your brethren,
Num 8:26 the Levites ***r*** their duties."
Josh 7: 1 trespass ***r*** the accursed things,
Judg 15: 3 be blameless ***r*** the Philistines
2 Chr 32:31 ***r*** the ambassadors of the
Job 4:20 perish forever, with no one ***r***.
Ps 119:80 be blameless ***r*** Your statutes,
Isa 5: 1 A song of my Beloved ***r*** His
Lk 14: 6 not answer Him ***r*** these things.
Acts 5:35 what you intend to do ***r*** these
Phil 2:30 not ***r*** his life, to supply what
Col 2:16 or ***r*** a festival or a new moon

REGARDS (7/7) REGARD

Job 41:27 He ***r*** iron as straw,
Ps 138: 6 Yet He ***r*** the lowly;
Prov 12:10 A righteous man ***r*** the life of
13:18 But he who ***r*** a rebuke will be
Eccl 11: 4 And he who ***r*** the clouds will
Isa 33: 8 the cities, He ***r*** no man.
Lam 4:16 He no longer ***r*** them.

REGEM (1/1)

1 Chr 2:47 And the sons of Jahdai were ***R***,

REGEM-MELECH (1/1)

Zech 7: 2 with ***R*** and his men, to the

REGENERATION (2/2)

Mt 19:28 I say to you, that in the ***r***,
Titus 3: 5 through the washing of ***r*** and

REGIMENT (2/2)

Acts 10: 1 what was called the Italian ***R***,
27: 1 a centurion of the Augustan ***R***.

REGION (59/57) PROVINCES, REGIONS

Num 32: 1 that indeed the ***r*** was a place
Deut 3: 4 all the ***r*** of Argob, the kingdom
3:13 (All the ***r*** of Argob, with all
3:14 son of Manasseh took all the ***r***
Josh 19:29 and ended at the sea by the ***r***
19:46 with the ***r*** near Joppa.
22:10 And when they came to the ***r*** of
22:11 in the ***r*** of the Jordan—on the
1 Ki 4:13 to him also belonged the ***r*** of
4:24 had dominion over all the ***r***
Ezra 4:11 the men of the ***r*** beyond the
4:20 who have ruled over all the ***r***
5: 3 the governor of the ***r*** beyond
5: 6 The governor of the ***r*** beyond
5: 6 Persians who were in the ***r***
6: 6 governor of the ***r*** beyond the
6: 8 expense from taxes on the ***r***
6:13 governor of the ***r*** beyond the
7:21 who are in the ***r*** beyond
7:25 the people who are in the ***r***
8:36 and the governors in the ***r***
Neh 2: 7 for the governors of the ***r***
2: 9 to the governors in the ***r***
3: 7 of the governor of the ***r***
Ezek 47: 8 flows toward the eastern ***r***,
Mt 2:22 he turned aside into the ***r*** of
3: 5 and all the ***r*** around the Jordan
4:16 those who sat in the ***r***
8:34 Him to depart from their ***r***.
14:35 out into all that surrounding ***r***,
15:21 there and departed to the ***r*** of
15:22 of Canaan came from that ***r*** and
15:39 and came to the ***r*** of Magdala.

16:13 When Jesus came into the *r* of
19: 1 from Galilee and came to the *r*
Mk 1:28 spread throughout all the *r*
5:17 with Him to depart from their *r*.
6:55 that whole surrounding *r*,
7:24 He arose and went to the *r* of
7:31 departing from the *r* of Tyre
7:31 through the midst of the *r* of
8:10 and came to the *r* of
10: 1 from there and came to the *r*
Lk 3: 1 tetrarch of Iturea and the *r*
3: 3 And he went into all the *r*
4:14 through all the surrounding *r*.
4:26 in the *r* of Sidon, to a
4:37 place in the surrounding *r*.
7:17 Judea and all the surrounding *r*.
8:37 multitude of the surrounding *r*
Acts 13:49 spread throughout all the *r*.
13:50 and expelled them from their *r*.
14: 6 and to the surrounding *r*.
16: 3 of the Jews who were in that *r*,
16: 6 gone through Phrygia and the *r*
18:23 he departed and went over the *r*
20: 2 when he had gone over that *r*
26:20 and throughout all the *r* of
28: 7 In that *r* there was an estate of

REGIONS (9/9) REGION

Josh 17:11 and its towns—three hilly *r*.
1 Ki 4:11 in all the *r* of Dor;
Isa 41: 9 And called from its farthest *r*,
Mt 4:13 in the *r* of Zebulun and
Acts 8: 1 all scattered throughout the *r*
19: 1 passed through the upper *r*,
2 Cor 10:16 to preach the gospel in the *r*
11:10 me from this boasting in the *r*
Gal 1:21 Afterward I went into the *r* of

REGISTER (1/1)

Neh 7: 5 And I found a *r* of the

REGISTERED (10/10)

1 Chr 5: 7 of their generations was *r*:
5:17 All these were *r* by genealogies
Ezra 2:62 among those who were *r* by
8: 3 and *r* with him were one
Neh 7: 5 that they might be *r* by
7:64 among those who were *r* by
Lk 2: 1 that all the world should be *r*.
2: 3 So all went to be *r*,
2: 5 to be *r* with Mary, his betrothed
Heb 12:23 of the firstborn who are *r*

REGISTERS (1/1)

Ps 87: 6 When He *r* the peoples:

REGRET (3/2)

1 Sam 15:11 I greatly *r* that I have set up
2 Cor 7: 8 I do not *r* it; though I did
7: 8 though I did *r* it.

REGRETTED (3/3)

1 Sam 15:35 and the LORD *r* that He had
Mt 21:29 but afterward he *r* it and
2 Cor 7:10 to salvation, not to be *r*;

REGULAR (25/24) REGULARLY

Num 28: 3 as a *r* burnt offering.
28: 6 It is a *r* burnt offering which
28:10 besides the *r* burnt offering
28:15 besides the *r* burnt offering
28:23 which is for a *r* burnt
28:24 besides the *r* burnt offering
28:31 besides the *r* burnt offering
29: 6 the *r* burnt offering with its
29:11 the *r* burnt offering with its
29:16 besides the *r* burnt offering,
29:19 besides the *r* burnt offering,
29:22 besides the *r* burnt offering,
29:25 besides the *r* burnt offering,
29:28 besides the *r* burnt offering,
29:31 besides the *r* burnt offering,
29:34 besides the *r* burnt offering,
29:38 besides the *r* burnt offering,
2 Ki 25:30 there was a *r* ration given
2 Chr 30: 3 not keep it at the *r* time,
Ezra 3: 5 they offered the *r* burnt
Neh 10:33 for the *r* grain offering, for
10:33 for the *r* burnt offering of the
Jer 52:34 there was a *r* ration given him
Ezek 27:21 princes of Kedar were your *r*
46:15 as a *r* burnt offering every

REGULARLY (11/11) REGULAR

2 Ki 3: 4 and he *r* paid the king of
4: 9 man of God, who passes by us *r*.
25:29 and he ate bread *r* before the
1 Chr 16: 6 and Jahaziel the priests *r*
16:37 to minister before the ark *r*,
16:40 the altar of burnt offering *r*
23:31 *r* before the LORD;
Job 1: 5 their hearts." Thus Job did *r*.
Jer 52:33 and he ate bread *r* before the
Ezek 39:14 They will set apart men *r*
46:14 to be made *r* to the LORD.

REGULATIONS (2/2)

Esth 2:12 according to the *r* for the
Col 2:20 do you subject yourselves to *r*—

REHABIAH (5/3)

1 Chr 23:17 *R* was the first. And Eliezer
23:17 but the sons of *R* were very
24:21 Concerning *R*, of the sons of
24:21 Rehabiah, of the sons of *R*,
26:25 his brethren by Eliezer were *R*

REHEARSE (KJV) See RECOUNT

REHOB (12/12)

Num 13:21 Wilderness of Zin as far as *R*,
Josh 19:28 including Ebron, *R*,
19:30 and *R* were included:
21:31 and *R* with its common-land:
Judg 1:31 Achzib, Helbah, Aphik, or *R*.
2 Sam 8: 3 defeated Hadadezer the son of *R*,
8:12 spoil of Hadadezer the son of *R*,
1 Chr 6:75 and *R* with its common-lands.
Neh 10:11 Micha, *R*, Hashabiah,

REHOBOAM (52/42)

1 Ki 11:43 And *R* his son reigned in his
12: 1 And *R* went to Shechem,
12: 3 of Israel came and spoke to *R*,
12: 6 Then King *R* consulted the
12:12 and all the people came to *R*
12:17 But *R* reigned over the children
12:18 Then King *R* sent Adoram, who
12:18 Therefore King *R* mounted his
12:21 And when *R* came to Jerusalem,
12:21 might restore the kingdom to *R*
12:23 Speak to *R* the son of Solomon,
12:27 *R* king of Judah, and they will
12:27 will kill me and go back to *R*
14:21 And *R* the son of Solomon
14:21 *R* was forty-one years old when
14:25 in the fifth year of King *R*
14:27 Then King *R* made bronze shields
14:29 Now the rest of the acts of *R*,
14:30 And there was war between *R* and
14:31 So *R* rested with his fathers,
15: 6 And there was war between *R* and
1 Chr 3:10 Solomon's son was *R*;
2 Chr 9:31 And *R* his son reigned in his
10: 1 And *R* went to Shechem,
10: 3 all Israel came and spoke to *R*,
10: 6 Then King *R* consulted the
10:12 and all the people came to *R*
10:13 King *R* rejected the advice of
10:17 But *R* reigned over the children
10:18 Then King *R* sent Hadoram, who
10:18 Therefore King *R* mounted his
11: 1 Now when *R* came to Jerusalem, he
11: 1 might restore the kingdom to *R*.
11: 3 Speak to *R* the son of Solomon,
11: 5 So *R* dwelt in Jerusalem, and
11:17 and made *R* the son of Solomon
11:18 Then *R* took for himself as wife
11:21 Now *R* loved Maachah the
11:22 And *R* appointed Abijah the son
12: 1 when *R* had established the
12: 2 in the fifth year of King *R*,
12: 5 Shemaiah the prophet came to *R*
12:10 Then King *R* made bronze shields
12:13 Thus *R* strengthened himself in
12:13 Now *R* was forty-one years old
12:15 The acts of *R*, first and last,
12:15 And there were wars between *R*
12:16 So *R* rested with his fathers,
13: 7 themselves against *R* the son
13: 7 when *R* was young and
Mt 1: 7 Solomon begot *R*,
1: 7 *R* begot Abijah, and Abijah

REHOBOTH (2/2)

Gen 26:22 So he called its name *R*,

REHOBOTH IR (1/1)

Gen 10:11 Assyria and built Nineveh, *R*,

REHOBOTH-BY-THE-RIVER (2/2)

Gen 36:37 Saul of *R* reigned in his place.
1 Chr 1:48 Samlah died, Saul of *R* reigned

REHUM (8/8)

Ezra 2: 2 Bilshan, Mispar, Bigvai, *R*,
4: 8 *R* the commander and Shimshai the
4: 9 From *R* the commander, Shimshai
4:17 To *R* the commander, to
4:23 letter was read before *R*,
Neh 3:17 under *R* the son of Bani, made
10:25 *R*, Hashabnah, Maaseiah,
12: 3 Shechaniah, *R*, Meremoth,

REI (1/1)

1 Ki 1: 8 Nathan the prophet, Shimei, *R*,

REIGN (102/97) REIGNED, REIGNS

Gen 37: 8 'Shall you indeed *r* over us?
Ex 15:18 The LORD shall *r* forever and
Lev 26:17 Those who hate you shall *r* over
Deut 15: 6 you shall *r* over many nations,
15: 6 but they shall not *r* over you.
Judg 9: 2 of the sons of Jerubbaal *r*
9: 2 or that one *r* over you?'
9: 8 the olive tree, '*R* over us!'
9:10 You come and *r* over us!'
9:12 You come and *r* over us!'
9:14 You come and *r* over us!'
1 Sam 8: 7 that I should not *r* over them.
8: 9 of the king who will *r* over
8:11 of the king who will *r* over
9:17 This one shall *r* over My
11:12 'Shall Saul *r* over us?'
12:12 but a king shall *r* over us,'
2 Sam 2:10 years old when he began to *r*
3:21 and that you may *r* over all
5: 4 years old when he began to *r*,
1 Ki 1:13 your son Solomon shall *r* after
1:17 Solomon your son shall *r* after
1:24 Adonijah shall *r* after me, and
2:15 on me, that I should *r*.
6: 1 the fourth year of Solomon's *r*
11:37 and you shall *r* over all your
16:11 to pass, when he began to *r*,
2 Ki 8:16 son of Jehoshaphat began to *r*
8:25 king of Judah, began to *r*.
15:32 king of Judah, began to *r*.
16: 1 king of Judah, began to *r*.
18: 1 Ahaz, king of Judah, began to *r*.
23:33 that he might not *r* in
24:12 in the eighth year of his *r*,
25: 1 pass in the ninth year of his *r*,
25:27 in the year that he began to *r*,
1 Chr 4:31 were their cities until the *r*
26:31 In the fortieth year of the *r*
29:12 And You *r* over all.
29:30 with all his *r* and his might,
2 Chr 3: 2 in the fourth year of his *r*.
15:10 in the fifteenth year of the *r*
15:19 the thirty-fifth year of the *r*
16: 1 the thirty-sixth year of the *r*
16:12 the thirty-ninth year of his *r*,
16:13 the forty-first year of his *r*.
17: 7 in the third year of his *r* he
23: 3 the king's son shall *r*,
29: 3 In the first year of his *r*,
29:19 which King Ahaz in his *r* had
34: 3 For in the eighth year of his *r*,
34: 8 the eighteenth year of his *r*,
35:19 In the eighteenth year of the *r*
Ezra 4: 5 even until the *r* of Darius king
4: 6 In the *r* of Ahasuerus, in the
4: 6 in the beginning of his *r*,
4:24 until the second year of the *r*
6:15 was in the sixth year of the *r*
7: 1 in the *r* of Artaxerxes king of
8: 1 in the *r* of King Artaxerxes:
Neh 12:22 During the *r* of Darius the
Esth 1: 3 in the third year of his *r* he
2:16 in the seventh year of his *r*.
Job 34:30 the hypocrite should not *r*,
Ps 146:10 The LORD shall *r* forever—Your
Prov 8:15 By me kings *r*, And rulers
Isa 24:23 For the LORD of hosts will *r*
32: 1 a king will *r* in righteousness,
Jer 1: 2 in the thirteenth year of his *r*.
22:15 Shall you *r* because you enclose
23: 5 A King shall *r* and prosper,
26: 1 In the beginning of the *r* of
27: 1 In the beginning of the *r* of
28: 1 at the beginning of the *r* of
33:21 he shall not have a son to *r*
49:34 in the beginning of the *r* of
51:59 in the fourth year of his *r*.
52: 4 pass in the ninth year of his *r*,
52:31 in the first year of his *r*,
Dan 1: 1 In the third year of the *r* of
2: 1 year of Nebuchadnezzar's *r*,
6:28 this Daniel prospered in the *r*
6:28 reign of Darius and in the *r*
8: 1 In the third year of the *r* of
9: 2 in the first year of his *r* I,
Mic 4: 7 So the LORD will *r* over them
Lk 1:33 And He will *r* over the house of
3: 1 in the fifteenth year of the *r*
19:14 will not have this man to *r*
19:27 who did not want me to *r* over
Rom 5:17 gift of righteousness will *r*
5:21 even so grace might *r* through
6:12 Therefore do not let sin *r* in
15:12 He who shall rise to *r*
1 Cor 4: 8 indeed I could wish you did *r*,
4: 8 that we also might *r* with you!
15:25 For He must *r* till He has put
2 Tim 2:12 We shall also *r* with Him.
Rev 5:10 And we shall *r* on the
11:15 and He shall *r* forever and
20: 6 and shall *r* with Him a thousand
22: 5 And they shall *r* forever and

REIGNED (177/164) REIGN

Gen 36:31 these were the kings who *r* in
36:31 land of Edom before any king *r*
36:32 Bela the son of Beor *r* in Edom,
36:33 the son of Zerah of Bozrah *r*
36:34 of the land of the Temanites *r*
36:35 of Moab, *r* in his place.
36:36 Samlah of Masrekah *r* in his
36:37 of Rehoboth-by-the-River *r* in

36:38 Baal-Hanan the son of Achbor *r*
36:39 Hadar *r* in his place;
Josh 12: 5 and *r* over Mount Hermon, over
13:10 who *r* in Heshbon, as far as the
13:12 who *r* in Ashtaroth and Edrei,
13:21 who *r* in Heshbon, whom Moses
Judg 4: 2 king of Canaan, who *r* in Hazor.
9:22 After Abimelech had *r* over
1 Sam 13: 1 Saul *r* one year; and when he had
13: 1 and when he had *r* two years
2 Sam 2:10 and he *r* two years.
5: 4 and he *r* forty years.
5: 5 In Hebron he *r* over Judah seven
5: 5 and in Jerusalem he *r*
8:15 So David *r* over all Israel;
10: 1 and Hanun his son *r* in his
16: 8 Saul, in whose place you have *r*;
1 Ki 2:11 The period that David *r* over
2:11 seven years he *r* in Hebron, and
2:11 and in Jerusalem he *r*
4:21 So Solomon *r* over all kingdoms
11:24 and *r* in Damascus.
11:25 and *r* over Syria.
11:42 And the period that Solomon *r* in
11:43 And Rehoboam his son *r* in his
12:17 But Rehoboam *r* over the children
14:19 how he made war and how he *r*,
14:20 The period that Jeroboam *r* was
14:20 Then Nadab his son *r* in his
14:21 Rehoboam the son of Solomon *r*
14:21 He *r* seventeen years in
14:31 Then Abijam his son *r* in his
15: 2 He *r* three years in Jerusalem.
15: 8 Then Asa his son *r* in his
15:10 And he *r* forty-one years in
15:24 Then Jehoshaphat his son *r* in
15:25 and he *r* over Israel two years.
15:28 and *r* in his place.
15:33 and *r* twenty-four years.
16: 6 Then Elah his son *r* in his
16: 8 and *r* two years in Tirzah.
16:10 and *r* in his place.
16:15 Zimri had *r* in Tirzah seven
16:22 So Tibni died and Omri *r*.
16:23 and *r* twelve years.
16:23 Six years he *r* in Tirzah.
16:28 Then Ahab his son *r* in his
16:29 and Ahab the son of Omri *r* over
22:40 Then Ahaziah his son *r* in his
22:42 and he *r* twenty-five years in
22:50 Then Jehoram his son *r* in his
22:51 and *r* two years over Israel.
2 Ki 3: 1 and *r* twelve years.
3:27 eldest son who would have *r* in
8:15 and Hazael *r* in his place.
8:17 and he *r* eight years in
8:24 Then Ahaziah his son *r* in his
8:26 and he *r* one year in Jerusalem.
10:35 Then Jehoahaz his son *r* in his
10:36 And the period that Jehu *r* over
11: 3 while Athaliah *r* over the land.
12: 1 and he *r* forty years in
12:21 Then Amaziah his son *r* in his
13: 1 and *r* seventeen years.
13: 9 Then Joash his son *r* in his
13:10 and *r* sixteen years.
13:24 Then Ben-Hadad his son *r* in his
14: 2 and he *r* twenty-nine years in
14:16 Then Jeroboam his son *r* in his
14:23 and *r* forty-one years.
14:29 Then Zechariah his son *r* in his
15: 2 and he *r* fifty-two years in
15: 7 Then Jotham his son *r* in his
15: 8 the son of Jeroboam *r* over
15:10 and he *r* in his place.
15:13 and he *r* a full month in
15:14 and he *r* in his place.
15:17 and *r* ten years in Samaria.
15:22 Then Pekahiah his son *r* in his
15:23 and *r* two years.
15:25 He killed him and *r* in his
15:27 and *r* twenty years.
15:30 so he *r* in his place in the
15:33 and he *r* sixteen years in
15:38 Then Ahaz his son *r* in his
16: 2 and he *r* sixteen years in
16:20 Then Hezekiah his son *r* in his
17: 1 and he *r* nine years.
18: 2 and he *r* twenty-nine years in
19:37 Then Esarhaddon his son *r* in
20:21 Then Manasseh his son *r* in his
21: 1 and he *r* fifty-five years in
21:18 Then his son Amon *r* in his
21:19 and he *r* two years in
21:26 Then Josiah his son *r* in his
22: 1 and he *r* thirty-one years in
23:31 and he *r* three months in
23:36 and he *r* eleven years in
24: 6 Then Jehoiachin his son *r* in
24: 8 and he *r* in Jerusalem three
24:18 and he *r* eleven years in
1 Chr 1:43 these were the kings who *r* in
1:43 land of Edom before a king *r*
1:44 the son of Zerah of Bozrah *r*
1:45 of the land of the Temanites *r*
1:46 *r* in his place. The name of his
1:47 Samlah of Masrekah *r* in his
1:48 of Rehoboth-by-the-River *r* in
1:49 Baal-Hanan the son of Achbor *r*
1:50 Hadad *r* in his place;
3: 4 There he *r* seven years and six
3: 4 and in Jerusalem he *r*
18:14 So David *r* over all Israel, and
19: 1 and his son *r* in his place.
29:26 Thus David the son of Jesse *r*
29:27 And the period that he *r* over
29:27 seven years he *r* in Hebron, and
29:27 and thirty-three years he *r* in
29:28 and Solomon his son *r* in his
2 Chr 1:13 and *r* over Israel.
9:26 So he *r* over all the kings from
9:30 Solomon *r* in Jerusalem over all
9:31 And Rehoboam his son *r* in his
10:17 But Rehoboam *r* over the children
12:13 himself in Jerusalem and *r*.
12:13 and he *r* seventeen years in
12:16 Then Abijah his son *r* in his
13: 2 He *r* three years in Jerusalem.
14: 1 Then Asa his son *r* in his
17: 1 Then Jehoshaphat his son *r* in
20:31 and he *r* twenty-five years in
21: 1 Then Jehoram his son *r* in his
21: 5 and he *r* eight years in
21:20 He *r* in Jerusalem eight years
22: 1 of Jehoram, king of Judah, *r*.
22: 2 and he *r* one year in Jerusalem.
22:12 while Athaliah *r* over the land.
24: 1 and he *r* forty years in
24:27 Then Amaziah his son *r* in his
25: 1 and he *r* twenty-nine years in
26: 3 and he *r* fifty-two years in
26:23 Then Jotham his son *r* in his
27: 1 and he *r* sixteen years in
27: 8 and he *r* sixteen years in
27: 9 Then Ahaz his son *r* in his
28: 1 and he *r* sixteen years in
28:27 Then Hezekiah his son *r* in his
29: 1 and he *r* twenty-nine years in
32:33 Then Manasseh his son *r* in his
33: 1 and he *r* fifty-five years in
33:20 Then his son Amon *r* in his
33:21 and he *r* two years in
34: 1 and he *r* thirty-one years in
36: 2 and he *r* three months in
36: 5 and he *r* eleven years in
36: 8 Then Jehoiachin his son *r* in
36: 9 and he *r* in Jerusalem three
36:11 and he *r* eleven years in
Esth 1: 1 (this was the Ahasuerus who *r*
Isa 37:38 Then Esarhaddon his son *r* in
Jer 22:11 who *r* instead of Josiah his
37: 1 Zedekiah the son of Josiah *r*
52: 1 and he *r* eleven years in
Rom 5:14 Nevertheless death *r* from Adam
5:17 the one man's offense death *r*
5:21 so that as sin *r* in death, even
1 Cor 4: 8 have *r* as kings without us—and
Rev 11:17 taken Your great power and *r*.
20: 4 And they lived and *r* with

REIGNING (2/2)

1 Sam 16: 1 I have rejected him from *r*
Mt 2:22 he heard that Archelaus was *r*

REIGNS (12/12) REIGN

1 Sam 12:14 both you and the king who *r*
2 Sam 15:10 Absalom *r* in Hebron!'"
1 Chr 16:31 the nations, "The LORD *r*.
Ps 47: 8 God *r* over the nations;
93: 1 The LORD *r*, He is clothed
96:10 the nations, "The LORD *r*;
97: 1 The LORD *r*; Let the earth
99: 1 The LORD *r*; Let the peoples
Prov 30:22 For a servant when he *r*,
Isa 52: 7 says to Zion, "Your God *r*!"
Rev 17:18 saw is that great city which *r*
19: 6 For the Lord God Omnipotent *r*!

REINFORCED (1/1)

2 Chr 24:13 to its original condition and *r*

REJECT (10/10) REJECTED, REJECTS

Num 14:11 How long will these people *r* Me?
Ps 119:118 You *r* all those who stray from
Hos 4: 6 I also will *r* you from being
Mk 7: 9 All too well you *r* the
Acts 13:46 but since you *r* it, and judge
Gal 4:14 flesh you did not despise or *r*,
1 Th 4: 8 he who rejects this does not *r*
1 Tim 4: 7 But *r* profane and old wives'
Titus 3:10 *R* a divisive man after the first
Jude 8 *r* authority, and speak evil of

REJECTED (48/44) REJECT

Num 14:23 nor shall any of those who *r* Me
16:30 that these men have *r* the
1 Sam 8: 7 for they have not *r* you,
8: 7 but they have *r* Me, that I
10:19 But you have today *r* your God,
15:23 Because you have *r* the word of
15:23 He also has *r* you from being
15:26 for you have *r* the word of the
15:26 and the LORD has *r* you from
16: 1 seeing I have *r* him from
1 Ki 12: 8 But he *r* the advice which the
12:13 and *r* the advice which the
2 Ki 17:15 And they *r* His statutes and His
17:20 And the LORD *r* all the
2 Chr 10: 8 But he *r* the advice which the
10:13 King Rehoboam *r* the advice of
11:14 for Jeroboam and his sons had *r*
Ps 78:67 Moreover He *r* the tent of
118:22 stone which the builders *r*
Isa 5:24 Because they have *r* the law of
53: 3 He is despised and *r* by men,
Jer 2:37 For the LORD has *r* your
6:19 Nor My law, but *r* it.
6:30 People will call them *r*
6:30 Because the LORD has *r*
7:29 for the LORD has *r* and
8: 9 they have *r* the word of the
14:19 Have You utterly *r* Judah?
Lam 5:22 Unless You have utterly *r* us,
Hos 4: 6 Because you have *r* knowledge,
8: 3 Israel has *r* the good;
8: 5 Your calf is *r*,
Mt 21:42 which the builders *r* Has
Mk 8:31 and be *r* by the elders and
12:10 which the builders *r* Has
Lk 7:30 But the Pharisees and lawyers *r*
9:22 and be *r* by the elders and
17:25 suffer many things and be *r* by
20:17 which the builders *r* Has
Acts 4:11 stone which was *r* by you
7:35 "This Moses whom they *r*,
7:39 fathers would not obey, but *r*.
1 Tim 1:19 conscience, which some having *r*,
Heb 6: 8 it is *r* and near to being
10:28 Anyone who has *r* Moses' law dies
12:17 inherit the blessing, he was *r*,
1 Pe 2: 4 *r* indeed by men, but chosen by
2: 7 which the builders *r* Has

REJECTION (1/1)

Num 14:34 years, and you shall know My *r*.

REJECTS (6/3) REJECT

Lk 10:16 he who *r* you rejects Me, and he
10:16 he who rejects you *r* Me, and he
10:16 and he who *r* Me rejects Him who
10:16 and he who rejects Me *r* Him who
Jn 12:48 He who *r* Me, and does not
1 Th 4: 8 Therefore he who *r* this does

REJOICE (199/187) REJOICED, REJOICES, REJOICING

Lev 23:40 and you shall *r* before the
Deut 12: 7 and you shall *r* in all to which
12:12 And you shall *r* before the LORD
12:18 and you shall *r* before the
14:26 LORD your God, and you shall *r*,
16:11 You shall *r* before the LORD
16:14 And you shall *r* in your feast,
16:15 hands, so that you surely *r*.
26:11 So you shall *r* in every good
27: 7 and *r* before the LORD your
28:63 so the LORD will *r* over you to
30: 9 For the LORD will again *r* over
32:43 '*R*, O Gentiles, with His
33:18 And of Zebulun he said: "*R*,
Judg 9:19 then *r* in Abimelech, and let
9:19 and let him also *r* in you.
16:23 to Dagon their god, and to *r*.
1 Sam 2: 1 Because I *r* in Your salvation.
2 Sam 1:20 daughters of the Philistines *r*,
1 Chr 16:10 Let the hearts of those *r* who
16:31 Let the heavens *r*,
16:32 its fullness; Let the field *r*,
16:33 the trees of the woods shall *r*
2 Chr 6:41 And let Your saints *r* in
20:27 for the LORD had made them *r*
Neh 8:12 to send portions and *r* greatly,
12:43 for God had made them *r* with
Job 3: 6 May it not *r* among the days of
3:22 Who *r* exceedingly, And are
21:12 And *r* to the sound of the
Ps 2:11 And *r* with trembling.
5:11 But let all those *r* who put
9: 2 I will be glad and *r* in You;
9:14 I will *r* in Your salvation.
13: 4 Lest those who trouble me *r*
13: 5 My heart shall *r* in Your
14: 7 Let Jacob *r* and Israel be
20: 5 We will *r* in your salvation,
21: 1 how greatly shall he *r*!
30: 1 And have not let my foes *r*
31: 7 I will be glad and *r* in Your
32:11 Be glad in the LORD and *r*,
33: 1 *R* in the LORD, O you
33:21 For our heart shall *r* in Him,
35: 9 It shall *r* in His salvation.
35:19 Let them not *r* over me who are
35:24 And let them not *r* over me.
35:26 to mutual confusion Who *r* at
38:16 lest they *r* over me,
40:16 Let all those who seek You *r*
48:11 Let Mount Zion *r*,
51: 8 the bones You have broken may *r*.
53: 6 Let Jacob *r* and Israel be
58:10 The righteous shall *r* when he
60: 6 in His holiness: "I will *r*;
63: 7 shadow of Your wings I will *r*.
63:11 But the king shall *r* in God;
65: 8 of the morning and evening *r*.
65:12 And the little hills *r* on
66: 6 There we will *r* in Him.
68: 3 Let them *r* before God;
68: 3 let them *r* exceedingly.
68: 4 And *r* before Him.

R

70: 4 Let all those who seek You *r*
71:23 My lips shall greatly *r* when I
85: 6 That Your people may *r* in You?
86: 4 *R* the soul of Your servant,
89:12 Tabor and Hermon *r* in Your
89:16 In Your name they *r* all day
89:42 have made all his enemies *r*.
90:14 That we may *r* and be glad all
96:11 Let the heavens *r*,
96:12 the trees of the woods will *r*
97: 1 LORD reigns; Let the earth *r*;
97: 8 And the daughters of Judah *r*
97:12 *R* in the LORD, you righteous,
98: 4 Break forth in song, *r*,
104:31 May the LORD *r* in His works.
105: 3 Let the hearts of those *r* who
106: 5 That I may *r* in the gladness
107:42 The righteous see it and *r*,
108: 7 in His holiness: "I will *r*;
109:28 But let Your servant *r*.
118:24 We will *r* and be glad in it.
119:162 I *r* at Your word As one who
149: 2 Let Israel *r* in their Maker;
Prov 2:14 Who *r* in doing evil,
5:18 And *r* with the wife of your
23:15 heart is wise, My heart will *r*—
23:16 my inmost being will *r* When
23:24 of the righteous will greatly *r*,
23:25 And let her who bore you *r*.
24:17 Do not *r* when your enemy falls,
28:12 When the righteous *r*,
29: 2 are in authority, the people *r*;
29: 3 loves wisdom makes his father *r*,
31:25 She shall *r* in time to come.
Eccl 3:12 is better for them than to *r*,
3:22 than that a man should *r* in
4:16 who come afterward will not *r*
5:19 to receive his heritage and *r*
11: 9 *R*, O young man, in your youth,
Song 1: 4 We will be glad and *r* in you.
Isa 8: 6 And *r* in Rezin and in
9: 3 They *r* before You According
9: 3 As men *r* when they divide the
13: 3 Those who *r* in My exaltation."
14: 8 Indeed the cypress trees *r* over
14:29 'Do not *r*, all you of
23:12 You will *r* no more, O you
25: 9 We will be glad and *r* in His
29:19 the poor among men shall *r* In
35: 1 And the desert shall *r* and
35: 2 shall blossom abundantly and *r*,
41:16 You shall *r* in the LORD,
43:14 who *r* in their ships.
61: 7 of confusion they shall *r* in
61:10 I will greatly *r* in the LORD,
62: 5 So shall your God *r* over you.
65:13 Behold, My servants shall *r*,
65:18 But be glad and *r* forever in
65:19 I will *r* in Jerusalem,
66:10 *R* with Jerusalem, And be glad
66:10 *R* for joy with her, all you
66:14 see this, your heart shall *r*,
Jer 11:15 When you do evil, then you *r*.
15:17 of the mockers, Nor did I *r*;
31: 4 in the dances of those who *r*.
31:13 Then shall the virgin *r* in the
31:13 And make them *r* rather than
32:41 I will *r* over them to do them
51:39 them drunk, That they may *r*,
Lam 2:17 He has caused an enemy to *r*
4:21 *R* and be glad, O daughter of
Ezek 7:12 'Let not the buyer *r*,
35:14 The whole earth will *r* when I
Hos 9: 1 Do not *r*, O Israel, with joy
Joel 2:21 O land; Be glad and *r*,
2:23 And *r* in the LORD your God;
Am 6:13 You who *r* over Lo Debar,
Mic 7: 8 Do not *r* over me, my enemy;
Hab 1:15 Therefore they *r* and are glad.
3:18 Yet I will *r* in the LORD,
Zeph 3:11 from your midst Those who *r*
3:14 O Israel! Be glad and *r* with
3:17 He will *r* over you with
3:17 He will *r* over you with
Zech 2:10 Sing and *r*, O daughter of
4:10 For these seven *r* to see The
9: 9 *R* greatly, O daughter of Zion!
10: 7 And their heart shall *r* as if
10: 7 Their heart shall *r* in the
Mt 5:12 *R* and be exceedingly glad, for
28: 9 *R*!" So they came and held Him
Lk 1:14 and many will *r* at his birth.
1:28 the angel said to her, "*R*,
6:23 *R* in that day and leap for joy!
10:20 Nevertheless do not *r* in this,
10:20 but rather *r* because your names
15: 6 *R* with me, for I have found my
15: 9 *R* with me, for I have found the
19:37 of the disciples began to *r*
Jn 4:36 who sows and he who reaps may *r*
5:35 were willing for a time to *r*
14:28 you would *r* because I said, 'I
16:20 lament, but the world will *r*;
16:22 you again and your heart will *r*,
Rom 5: 2 and *r* in hope of the glory of
5:11 but we also *r* in God through
12:15 *R* with those who rejoice, and
12:15 Rejoice with those who *r*,
15:10 And again he says: "*R*,
1 Cor 7:30 those who *r* as though they did
7:30 as though they did not *r*,
12:26 all the members *r* with it.
13: 6 does not *r* in iniquity, but
2 Cor 7: 9 Now I *r*, not that you were
7:16 Therefore I *r* that I have
Gal 4:27 For it is written: "*R*,
Phil 1:18 is preached; and in this I *r*,
1:18 this I rejoice, yes, and will *r*.
2:16 so that I may *r* in the day of
2:17 I am glad and *r* with you all.
2:18 reason you also be glad and *r*
2:28 you see him again you may *r*,
3: 1 my brethren, *r* in the Lord.
3: 3 *r* in Christ Jesus, and have no
4: 4 *R* in the Lord always.
4: 4 Again I will say, *r*!
Col 1:24 I now *r* in my sufferings for
1 Th 3: 9 for all the joy with which we *r*
5:16 *R* always,
1 Pe 1: 6 In this you greatly *r*,
1: 8 you *r* with joy inexpressible
4:13 but *r* to the extent that you
Rev 11:10 who dwell on the earth will *r*
12:12 'Therefore *r*, O heavens,
18:20 *R* over her, O heaven, and you
19: 7 Let us be glad and *r* and give

REJOICED (44/42) REJOICE

Ex 18: 9 Then Jethro *r* for all the good
Deut 28:63 that just as the LORD *r* over
30: 9 over you for good as He *r* over
1 Sam 6:13 and *r* to see it.
11:15 and all the men of Israel *r*
19: 5 all Israel. You saw it and *r*.
1 Ki 1:40 people played the flutes and *r*
5: 7 that he *r* greatly and said,
2 Ki 11:20 So all the people of the land *r*;
1 Chr 29: 9 Then the people *r*,
29: 9 and King David also *r* greatly.
2 Chr 15:15 And all Judah *r* at the oath, for
23:21 So all the people of the land *r*;
24:10 leaders and all the people *r*,
29:36 Hezekiah and all the people *r*
30:25 The whole assembly of Judah *r*,
Neh 12:43 offered great sacrifices, and *r*,
12:43 women and the children also *r*,
12:44 for Judah *r* over the priests
Esth 8:15 and the city of Shushan *r* and
Job 31:25 If I have *r* because my wealth
31:29 If I have *r* at the destruction
Ps 35:15 But in my adversity they *r* And
119:14 I have *r* in the way of Your
Eccl 2:10 For my heart *r* in all my
Jer 50:11 you were glad, because you *r*,
Ezek 25: 6 and *r* in heart with all your
35:15 As you *r* because the inheritance
Ob 12 Nor should you have *r* over the
Mt 2:10 they *r* with exceedingly great
Lk 1:47 And my spirit has *r* in God my
1:58 mercy to her, they *r* with her.
10:21 In that hour Jesus *r* in the
13:17 and all the multitude *r* for all
Jn 8:56 Your father Abraham *r* to see My
Acts 2:26 Therefore my heart *r*,
7:41 and *r* in the works of their own
15:31 they *r* over its encouragement.
16:34 set food before them; and he *r*,
2 Cor 7: 7 so that I *r* even more.
7:13 And we *r* exceedingly more for
Phil 4:10 But I *r* in the Lord greatly
2 Jn 4 I *r* greatly that I have found
3 Jn 3 For I *r* greatly when brethren

REJOICES (15/15) REJOICE

1 Sam 2: 1 'My heart *r* in the LORD;
Job 39:21 and *r* in his strength;
Ps 16: 9 heart is glad, and my glory *r*;
19: 5 And *r* like a strong man to
28: 7 Therefore my heart greatly *r*,
Prov 11:10 with the righteous, the city *r*;
13: 9 The light of the righteous *r*,
15:30 The light of the eyes *r* the
29: 6 But the righteous sings and *r*.
Eccl 11: 8 a man lives many years And *r*
Isa 62: 5 And as the bridegroom *r* over
64: 5 You meet him who *r* and does
Mt 18:13 he *r* more over that sheep than
Jn 3:29 *r* greatly because of the
1 Cor 13: 6 but *r* in the truth;

REJOICING (29/29) REJOICE

1 Ki 1:45 they have gone up from there *r*,
4:20 eating and drinking and *r*.
2 Ki 11:14 the people of the land were *r*
2 Chr 23:13 the people of the land were *r*
23:18 with *r* and with singing, as
Job 8:21 laughing, And your lips with *r*.
Ps 19: 8 LORD are right, *r* the heart;
45:15 With gladness and *r* they shall
107:22 And declare His works with *r*.
118:15 The voice of *r* and salvation
119:111 For they are the *r* of my
126: 6 doubtless come again with *r*,
Prov 8:30 *R* always before Him,
8:31 *R* in His inhabited world,
Isa 65:18 I create Jerusalem as a *r*,
Jer 15:16 word was to me the joy and *r*
Ezek 7: 7 And not of *r* in the mountains.
Hab 3:14 Their *r* was like feasting on
Zeph 2:15 This is the *r* city That dwelt
Lk 15: 5 he lays it on his shoulders, *r*.
Acts 5:41 *r* that they were counted worthy
8:39 and he went on his way *r*.
Rom 12:12 *r* in hope, patient in
2 Cor 6:10 as sorrowful, yet always *r*;
Gal 6: 4 and then he will have *r* in
Phil 1:26 that your *r* for me may be more
Col 2: 5 *r* to see your good order and
1 Th 2:19 our hope, or joy, or crown of *r*?
Heb 3: 6 fast the confidence and the *r*

REKEM (5/5)

Num 31: 8 those who were killed—Evi, *R*,
Josh 13:21 the princes of Midian: Evi, *R*,
18:27 *R*, Irpeel, Taralah,
1 Chr 2:43 Hebron were Korah, Tappuah, *R*,
2:44 and *R* begot Shammai.

RELATED (2/2)

Num 18: 1 you shall bear the iniquity *r*
Esth 8: 1 Esther had told how he was *r*

RELATING (4/4)

Num 3:26 according to all the work *r* to
3:31 and all the work *r* to them.
3:36 all the work *r* to them,
4: 4 *r* to the most holy things:

RELATION (1/1)

Ruth 2:20 'This man is a *r* of ours,

RELATIVE (21/20) RELATION, RELATIVES

Gen 29:12 that he was her father's *r*
29:15 Jacob, "Because you are my *r*,
Num 5: 8 But if the man has no *r* to whom
27:11 give his inheritance to the *r*
Ruth 2: 1 There was a *r* of Naomi's
3: 2 were with, is he not our *r*?
3: 9 for you are a close *r*."
3:12 it is true that I am a close *r*;
3:12 there is a *r* closer than I.
3:13 perform the duty of a close *r*
4: 1 the close *r* of whom Boaz had
4: 3 Then he said to the close *r*,
4: 6 And the close *r* said, "I cannot
4: 8 Therefore the close *r* said to
4:14 you this day without a close *r*;
2 Sam 19:42 the king is a close *r*
Am 6:10 And when a *r* of the dead,
Lk 1:36 Elizabeth your *r* has also
Jn 18:26 a *r* of him whose ear Peter

RELATIVES (20/20) RELATIVE

Lev 21: 2 except for his *r* who are nearest
Num 10:30 to my own land and to my *r*.
Josh 6:23 So they brought out all her *r*
Ruth 2:20 of ours, one of our close *r*.
1 Ki 16:11 neither of his *r* nor of his
1 Chr 8:32 also dwelt alongside their *r*
9:38 also dwelt alongside their *r*
12:29 *r* of Saul, three thousand
Job 19:14 My *r* have failed, And my close
Ps 38:11 And my *r* stand afar off.
Ezek 11:15 of man, your brethren, your *r*,
Mk 6: 4 own country, among his own *r*,
Lk 1:58 When her neighbors and *r* heard
1:61 There is no one among your *r* who
2:44 and sought Him among their *r*
14:12 friends, your brothers, your *r*,
21:16 and brothers, *r* and friends;
Acts 7: 3 country and from your *r*,
7:14 his father Jacob and all his *r*
10:24 and had called together his *r*

RELEASE (30/27) LOOSE, RELEASED, RELEASING

Gen 43:14 that he may *r* your other
Lev 16:22 and he shall *r* the goat in the
25:50 The price of his *r* shall be
Num 30: 5 and the LORD will *r* her,
30: 8 and the LORD will *r* her.
30:12 and the LORD will *r* her.
Deut 15: 1 years you shall grant a *r* of
15: 2 this is the form of the *r*:
15: 2 to his neighbor shall *r* it;
15: 2 it is called the LORD's *r*.
15: 9 seventh year, the year of *r*,
31:10 appointed time in the year of *r*,
Job 12:14 a man, there can be no *r*.
Ps 102:20 To *r* those appointed to death,
Eccl 8: 8 There is no *r* from that war,
Mt 27:17 Whom do you want me to *r* to you?
27:21 of the two do you want me to *r*
Mk 15: 9 Do you want me to *r* to you the
15:11 so that he should rather *r*
Lk 23:16 therefore chastise Him and *r*
23:17 was necessary for him to *r* one
23:18 and *r* to us Barabbas"—
23:20 wishing to *r* Jesus, again
Jn 18:39 custom that I should *r* someone
18:39 therefore want me to *r* to you
19:10 and power to *r* You?"
19:12 then on Pilate sought to *r* Him,
Acts 24:26 that he might *r* him.
Heb 2:15 and *r* those who through fear of
Rev 9:14 *R* the four angels who are bound

RELEASED (20/20) RELEASE

Gen 24: 8 then you will be *r* from this
24:41 then you will be *r* from my
Lev 16:26 And he who *r* the goat as the
25:28 in the Jubilee it shall be *r*,
25:30 It shall not be *r* in the
25:31 and they shall be *r* in the
25:33 of his possession shall be *r*
25:54 then he shall be *r* in the Year
27:21 when it is *r* in the Jubilee,
2 Ki 25:27 *r* Jehoiachin king of Judah from
Ps 105:20 The king sent and *r* him,
Mt 18:27 *r* him, and forgave him the
27:26 Then he *r* Barabbas to them;
Mk 15:15 *r* Barabbas to them;
Lk 23:25 And he *r* to them the one they
Acts 22:30 he *r* him from his bonds,
Rom 7: 2 she is *r* from the law of her
Rev 9:15 were *r* to kill a third of
20: 3 these things he must be *r* for
20: 7 Satan will be *r* from his prison

RELEASING (3/3) RELEASE

Prov 17:14 of strife is like *r* water;
Mt 27:15 to *r* to the multitude one
Mk 15: 6 accustomed to *r* one prisoner

RELENT (17/16) RELENTED, RELENTS

Ex 32:12 and *r* from this harm to Your
1 Sam 15:29 of Israel will not lie nor *r*.
15:29 is not a man, that He should *r*.
Ps 110: 4 LORD has sworn And will not *r*,
Jer 4:28 I have purposed and will not *r*,
18: 8 I will *r* of the disaster that I
18:10 then I will *r* concerning the
20:16 LORD overthrew, and did not *r*;
26: 3 that I may *r* concerning the
26:13 then the LORD will *r*
42:10 For I *r* concerning the disaster
Ezek 24:14 will I spare, Nor will I *r*;
Joel 2:14 knows if He will turn and *r*,
Jon 3: 9 tell if God will turn and *r*,
Zech 8:14 of hosts, 'And I would not *r*,
Mt 21:32 you did not afterward *r* and
Heb 7:21 has sworn And will not *r*,

RELENTED (8/8) RELENT

Ex 32:14 So the LORD *r* from the harm
2 Sam 24:16 the LORD *r* from the
1 Chr 21:15 the LORD looked and *r* of the
Ps 106:45 And *r* according to the
Jer 26:19 And the Lord *r* concerning the
Am 7: 3 So the LORD *r* concerning
7: 6 So the LORD *r* concerning
Jon 3:10 and God *r* from the disaster

RELENTING (1/1)

Jer 15: 6 I am weary of *r*!

RELENTLESSLY (1/1)

Judg 20:45 Then they pursued them *r* up to

RELENTS (2/2) RELENT

Joel 2:13 And He *r* from doing harm.
Jon 4: 2 One who *r* from doing harm.

RELIED (5/4) RELY

Judg 20:36 because they *r* on the men in
2 Chr 13:18 because they *r* on the LORD God
16: 7 Because you have *r* on the king
16: 7 and have not *r* on the LORD
16: 8 because you *r* on the LORD,

RELIEF (5/5) RELIEVE

Ex 8:15 Pharaoh saw that there was *r*,
Esth 4:14 *r* and deliverance will arise
Job 32:20 will speak, that I may find *r*;
Lam 2:18 and night; Give yourself no *r*;
Acts 11:29 determined to send *r* to the

RELIEVE (3/2) RELIEF, RELIEVED, RELIEVES

Job 16: 5 the comfort of my lips would *r*
1 Tim 5:16 let them *r* them, and do not let
5:16 that it may *r* those who are

RELIEVED (3/3) RELIEVE

Job 16: 6 I speak, my grief is not *r*;
Ps 4: 1 You have *r* me in my distress;
1 Tim 5:10 if she has *r* the afflicted,

RELIEVES (1/1) RELIEVE

Ps 146: 9 He *r* the fatherless and widow;

RELIGION (5/5) RELIGIOUS

Acts 25:19 against him about their own *r*
26: 5 to the strictest sect of our *r*
Col 2:23 of wisdom in self-imposed *r*,
Jas 1:26 this one's *r* is useless.
1:27 Pure and undefiled *r* before God

RELIGIOUS (2/2) RELIGION

Acts 17:22 in all things you are very *r*;
Jas 1:26 anyone among you thinks he is *r*,

RELY (5/5) RELIED

Job 24:23 and they *r* on it;
Isa 30:12 and perversity, And *r* on them,
31: 1 And *r* on horses, Who trust
50:10 in the name of the LORD And *r*
Ezek 33:26 You *r* on your sword, you commit

REMAIN (111/108) REMAINED, REMAINING, REMAINS, REMNANT

Gen 38:11 *R* a widow in your father's house
44:33 please let your servant *r*
Ex 8: 9 that they may *r* in the river
8:11 They shall *r* in the river
12:10 You shall let none of it *r* until
16:29 Let every man *r* in his place;
23:18 shall the fat of My sacrifice *r*
Lev 19:13 of him who is hired shall not *r*
25:28 then what was sold shall *r* in
25:52 And if there *r* but a few years
27:18 according to the years that *r*
Num 9:20 of the LORD they would *r*
9:22 the children of Israel would *r*
31:19 *r* outside the camp seven days;
32:32 of our inheritance shall *r*
33:55 be that those whom you let *r*
35:25 and he shall *r* there until the
Deut 13:17 of the accursed things shall *r*
16: 4 the first day at twilight *r*
19:20 And those who *r* shall hear and
20:16 let nothing that breathes *r*
21:13 *r* in your house, and mourn her
21:23 his body shall not *r* overnight
22: 2 and it shall *r* with you until
Josh 1:14 and your livestock shall *r* in
2:11 neither did there *r* any more
8:22 so that they let none of them *r*
10:27 which *r* until this very day.
10:28 who were in it. He let none *r*.
10:30 He let none *r* in it, but did to
18: 5 Judah shall *r* in their
18: 5 the house of Joseph shall *r* in
23: 4 you by lot these nations that *r*,
23: 7 these who *r* among you.
23:12 these that *r* among you—and make
Judg 5:17 And why did Dan *r* on ships?
21: 7 we do for wives for those who *r*,
21:16 we do for wives for those who *r*,
1 Sam 1:22 appear before the LORD and *r*
5: 7 of the God of Israel must not *r*
20:19 and *r* by the stone Ezel.
2 Sam 15:19 Return and *r* with the king.
16:18 will be, and with him I will *r*.
2 Ki 7: 9 good news, and we *r* silent.
2 Chr 32:10 that you *r* under siege in
Esth 3: 8 for the king to let them *r*.
4:14 For if you *r* completely silent
Job 16: 6 And if I *r* silent, how am I
37: 8 And *r* in their lairs.
Ps 49:12 though in honor, does not *r*;
55: 7 And *r* in the wilderness.
Prov 2:21 And the blameless will *r* in
Eccl 8:15 for this will *r* with him in his
Isa 10:32 As yet he will *r* at Nob that
32:16 And righteousness *r* in the
44:13 that it may *r* in the house.
66:22 Which I will make shall *r*
66:22 descendants and your name *r*.
Jer 3: 5 Will He *r* angry forever?
3:12 I will not *r* angry forever.
8: 3 all the residue of those who *r*
8: 3 who *r* in all the places where I
17:25 and this city shall *r* forever.
24: 8 the residue of Jerusalem who *r*
27:11 I will let them *r* in their own
27:19 of the vessels that *r* in this
27:21 concerning the vessels that *r*
30:18 And the palace shall *r*
38: 4 hands of the men of war who *r*
40: 4 with me to Babylon, *r* here.
42:10 If you will still *r* in this
42:17 And none of them shall *r* or
43: 4 to *r* in the land of Judah.
44: 7 out of Judah, leaving none to *r*,
49:18 No one shall *r* there, Nor shall
51:62 so that none shall *r* in it,
Lam 5:19 You, O LORD, *r* forever;
Ezek 5:10 and all of you who *r* I will
7:11 None of them shall *r*,
17:21 and those who *r* shall be
21:26 Nothing shall *r* the same.
22:14 or can your hands *r* strong, in
31:13 On its ruin will *r* all the birds
48:15 cubits in width that *r*,
Am 6: 9 that if ten men *r* in one house,
Ob 18 And no survivor shall *r* of
Zech 5: 4 It shall *r* in the midst of his
12:14 "all the families that *r*,
Lk 10: 7 And *r* in the same house, eating
Jn 6:12 up the fragments that *r*,
15:11 that My joy may *r* in you,
15:16 and that your fruit should *r*,
19:31 that the bodies should not *r* on
21:22 If I will that he *r* till I come,
21:23 If I will that he *r* till I come,
Acts 15:34 it seemed good to Silas to *r*
1 Cor 7: 8 It is good for them if they *r*
7:11 let her *r* unmarried or be
7:20 Let each one *r* in the same
7:24 let each one *r* with God in that
7:26 it is good for a man to *r* as
15: 6 of whom the greater part *r* to
16: 6 And it may be that I will *r*,
Phil 1:24 Nevertheless to *r* in the flesh
1:25 I know that I shall *r* and
1 Th 4:15 that we who are alive and *r*
4:17 Then we who are alive and *r*
1 Tim 1: 3 *r* in Ephesus that you may charge
Heb 1:11 will perish, but You *r*;
12:27 which cannot be shaken may *r*.
Rev 3: 2 strengthen the things which *r*,

REMAINDER (14/14)

Gen 14:10 and the *r* fled to the
Ex 29:34 then you shall burn the *r* with
Lev 6:16 And the *r* of it Aaron and his
7:16 but on the next day the *r* of it
7:17 the *r* of the flesh of the
25:27 and restore the *r* to the man to
Ezra 4:10 the cities of Samaria and the *r*
4:17 and to the *r* beyond the River:
Esth 9:16 The *r* of the Jews in the king's
Ps 76:10 With the *r* of wrath You shall
Isa 21:17 and the *r* of the number of
38:10 I am deprived of the *r* of my
Jer 27:19 and concerning the *r* of the
29: 1 sent from Jerusalem to the *r*

REMAINED (79/78) REMAIN

Gen 7:23 who were with him in the ark *r*
24:21 *r* silent so as to know whether
49:24 But his bow *r* in strength,
Ex 8:31 and from his people. Not one *r*.
10:15 So there *r* nothing green on the
10:19 There *r* not one locust in all
14:28 Not so much as one of them *r*.
Num 9:18 above the tabernacle they *r*
9:21 when the cloud *r* only from
9:22 or a year that the cloud *r*
9:23 the command of the LORD they *r*
11:26 But two men had *r* in the camp:
14:38 Caleb the son of Jephunneh *r*
25: 1 Now Israel *r* in Acacia Grove,
35:28 because he should have *r* in his
36:12 and their inheritance *r* in the
Deut 1:46 So you *r* in Kadesh many days,
3:11 For only Og king of Bashan *r* of
Josh 11:22 they *r* only in Gaza, in Gath,
13:12 who *r* of the remnant of the
18: 2 But there *r* among the children
Judg 7: 3 returned, and ten thousand *r*.
11:17 So Israel *r* in Kadesh.
21: 2 and *r* there before God till
Ruth 1: 2 to the country of Moab and *r*
1 Sam 7: 2 So it was that the ark *r* in
13:16 the people present with them *r*
23:14 and *r* in the mountains in the
2 Sam 6:11 The ark of the LORD *r* in the
11: 1 But David *r* at Jerusalem.
11:12 So Uriah *r* in Jerusalem that
13:20 So Tamar *r* desolate in her
15:29 And they *r* there.
20: 2 *r* loyal to their king.
1 Ki 11:16 (because for six months Joab *r*
15:21 and *r* in Tirzah.
22:46 who *r* in the days of his father
2 Ki 10:11 So Jehu killed all who *r* of the
10:17 he killed all who *r* to Ahab in
13: 6 and the wooden image also *r* in
19:36 and *r* at Nineveh.
24:14 None *r* except the poorest
25:11 the rest of the people who *r*
25:22 governor over the people who *r*
1 Chr 12:29 the greatest part of them had *r*
13:14 The ark of God *r* with the family
Eccl 2: 9 Also my wisdom *r* with me.
Isa 37:37 and *r* at Nineveh.
Jer 34: 7 only these fortified cities *r*
37:10 and there *r* only wounded men
37:16 and Jeremiah had *r* there many
37:21 Thus Jeremiah *r* in the court of
38:13 And Jeremiah *r* in the court of
38:28 Now Jeremiah *r* in the court of
39: 9 remnant of the people who *r* in
39: 9 the rest of the people who *r*.
41:10 and all the people who *r* in
48:11 Therefore his taste *r* in him,
51:30 They have *r* in their
52:15 the rest of the people who *r* in
Ezek 3:15 and *r* there astonished among
Dan 10: 8 and no strength *r* in me;
Ob 14 up those among them who *r* In
Mt 11:23 it would have *r* until this day.
14:20 full of the fragments that *r*.
Lk 1:22 for he beckoned to them and *r*
1:56 And Mary *r* with her about three
Jn 1:32 and He *r* upon Him.
1:39 and *r* with Him that day (now it
3:22 and there He *r* with them and
7: 9 He *r* in Galilee.
11:54 and there *r* with His disciples.
Acts 5: 4 'While it *r*, was it not your
15:35 Paul and Barnabas also *r* in
17:14 but both Silas and Timothy *r*
18:18 So Paul still *r* a good while.

25: 6 And when he had ***r*** among them
27:41 and the prow stuck fast and ***r***
Gal 1:18 and ***r*** with him fifteen days.

REMAINING (22/22) REMAIN

Lev 4: 7 and he shall pour the ***r*** blood
4:18 and he shall pour the ***r*** blood
4:30 and pour all the ***r*** blood at
4:34 and pour all the ***r*** blood at
25:51 there are still many years ***r***,
Num 31:32 The booty ***r*** from the plunder,
Deut 2:34 of every city; we left none ***r***.
3: 3 him until he had no survivors ***r***.
32:36 And there is no one ***r***,
Josh 10:33 until he left him none ***r***.
10:37 who were in it; he left none ***r***,
10:39 He left none ***r***; as he had done
10:40 all their kings; he left none ***r***,
11: 8 until they left none of them ***r***.
2 Sam 21: 5 we should be destroyed from ***r***
2 Ki 7:13 men take five of the ***r*** horses
10:11 until he left him none ***r***.
Job 18:19 Nor any ***r*** in his dwellings.
Ezek 39:14 land and bury those bodies ***r***
41: 9 and so also the ***r*** terrace by
Jn 1:33 and ***r*** on Him, this is He who
Rev 8:13 because of the ***r*** blasts of the

REMAINS (48/47) REMAIN

Gen 8:22 "While the earth ***r***,
Ex 10: 5 which ***r*** to you from the hail,
12:10 and what ***r*** of it until morning
16:23 up for yourselves all that ***r***,
21:21 if he ***r*** alive a day or two, he
26:12 The remnant that ***r*** of the
26:12 tent, the half curtain that ***r***,
26:13 of what ***r*** of the length of the
29:34 ***r*** until the morning, then you
Lev 8:32 What ***r*** of the flesh and of the
10:12 the grain offering that ***r***
11:37 is to be sown, it ***r*** clean.
16:16 tabernacle of meeting which ***r***
19: 6 And if any ***r*** until the third
Num 24:19 And destroy the ***r*** of the
Josh 8:29 a great heap of stones that ***r***
13: 1 and there ***r*** very much land yet
13: 2 "This is the land that yet ***r***:
1 Sam 6:18 which stone ***r*** to this day in
16:11 'There ***r*** yet the youngest,
2 Sam 1: 9 but my life still ***r*** in me.'
2 Ki 2:22 So the water ***r*** healed to this
6:31 of Elisha the son of Shaphat ***r***
Job 19: 4 My error ***r*** with me.
21:34 Since falsehood ***r*** in your
Ps 68:12 And she who ***r*** at home divides
Isa 4: 3 who is left in Zion and ***r*** in
6:13 Whose stump ***r*** when it is cut
Jer 21: 9 He who ***r*** in this city shall die
38: 2 He who ***r*** in this city shall die
47: 4 and Sidon every helper who ***r***;
Ezek 6:12 and he who ***r*** and is besieged
Dan 10:17 no strength ***r*** in me now,
Hag 2: 5 so My Spirit ***r*** among you; do
Zech 9: 7 But he who ***r***, even he shall
Jn 9:41 Therefore your sin ***r***.
12:24 it ***r*** alone; but if it dies, it
12:34 from the law that the Christ ***r***
1 Cor 7:40 But she is happier if she ***r*** as
2 Cor 3:11 what ***r*** is much more glorious.
3:14 until this day the same veil ***r***
2 Tim 2:13 He ***r*** faithful; He cannot deny
Heb 4: 1 since a promise ***r*** of entering
4: 6 Since therefore it ***r*** that some
4: 9 There ***r*** therefore a rest for the
7: 3 ***r*** a priest continually.
10:26 there no longer ***r*** a sacrifice
1 Jn 3: 9 for His seed ***r*** in him; and he

REMALIAH (11/11)

2 Ki 15:25 Then Pekah the son of ***R***,
15:27 Pekah the son of ***R*** became king
15:30 against Pekah the son of ***R***,
15:32 year of Pekah the son of ***R***,
15:37 of Syria and Pekah the son of ***R***
16: 1 year of Pekah the son of ***R***,
16: 5 of Syria and Pekah the son of ***R***,
2 Chr 28: 6 For Pekah the son of ***R*** killed
Isa 7: 1 of Syria and Pekah the son of ***R***,
7: 4 and Syria, and the son of ***R***.
7: 5 and the son of ***R*** have plotted

REMALIAH'S (2/2)

Isa 7: 9 the head of Samaria is ***R*** son.
8: 6 rejoice in Rezin and in ***R*** son;

REMEDY (3/3)

2 Chr 36:16 people, till there was no ***r***.
Prov 6:15 he shall be broken without ***r***.
29: 1 destroyed, and that without ***r***.

REMEMBER (164/160) REMEMBERED, REMEMBERING, REMEMBERS, REMEMBRANCE

Gen 9:15 and I will ***r*** My covenant which
9:16 and I will look on it to ***r*** the
40:14 But ***r*** me when it is well with
40:23 Yet the chief butler did not ***r***
41: 9 I ***r*** my faults this day.
Ex 13: 3 ***R*** this day in which you went out
20: 8 ***R*** the Sabbath day, to keep it
32:13 ***R*** Abraham, Isaac, and Israel,
Lev 26:42 then I will ***r*** My covenant with
26:42 covenant with Abraham I will ***r***;
26:42 I will ***r*** the land.
26:45 But for their sake I will ***r*** the
Num 11: 5 We ***r*** the fish which we ate
15:39 you may look upon it and ***r*** all
15:40 and that you may ***r*** and do all My
Deut 5:15 And ***r*** that you were a slave in
7:18 but you shall ***r*** well what the
8: 2 And you shall ***r*** that the LORD
8:18 And you shall ***r*** the LORD your
9: 7 ***R***! Do not forget how you
9:27 ***R*** Your servants, Abraham, Isaac,
15:15 You shall ***r*** that you were a
16: 3 that you may ***r*** the day in which
16:12 And you shall ***r*** that you were a
24: 9 ***R*** what the LORD your God did to
24:18 But you shall ***r*** that you were a
24:22 And you shall ***r*** that you were a
25:17 ***R*** what Amalek did to you on the
32: 7 ***R*** the days of old, Consider the
Josh 1:13 ***R*** the word which Moses the
Judg 8:34 children of Israel did not ***r***
9: 2 ***R*** that I am your own flesh
16:28 ***r*** me, I pray! Strengthen me, I
1 Sam 1:11 of Your maidservant and ***r*** me,
25:31 then ***r*** your maidservant."
2 Sam 14:11 Please let the king ***r*** the LORD
19:19 or ***r*** what wrong your servant
2 Ki 9:25 of Naboth the Jezreelite; for ***r***,
20: 3 ***R*** now, O LORD, I pray, how I
1 Chr 16:12 ***R*** His marvelous works which He
16:15 ***R*** His covenant forever,
2 Chr 6:42 ***R*** the mercies of Your servant
24:22 Thus Joash the king did not ***r***
Neh 1: 8 '***R***, I pray, the word that
4:14 ***R*** the Lord, great and awesome,
5:19 ***R*** me, my God, for good,
6:14 ***r*** Tobiah and Sanballat,
13:14 ***R*** me, O my God, concerning
13:22 ***R*** me, O my God, concerning
13:29 ***R*** them, O my God, because they
13:31 ***R*** me, O my God, for good!
Job 4: 7 ***R*** now, who ever perished being
7: 7 ***r*** that my life is a breath!
10: 9 ***R***, I pray, that You have made
11:16 And ***r*** it as waters that
14:13 a set time, and ***r*** me!
21: 6 Even when I ***r*** I am terrified,
36:24 ***R*** to magnify His work,
41: 8 ***R*** the battle—Never do it
Ps 20: 3 May He ***r*** all your offerings,
20: 7 But we will ***r*** the name of the
22:27 the ends of the world Shall ***r***
25: 6 ***R***, O LORD, Your tender
25: 7 Do not ***r*** the sins of my youth,
25: 7 According to Your mercy ***r*** me,
42: 4 When I ***r*** these things, I pour
42: 6 Therefore I will ***r*** You from
63: 6 When I ***r*** You on my bed,
74: 2 ***R*** Your congregation, which You
74:18 ***R*** this, that the enemy has
74:22 ***R*** how the foolish man
77:10 But I will ***r*** the years of
77:11 I will ***r*** the works of the
77:11 Surely I will ***r*** Your wonders
78:42 They did not ***r*** His power:
79: 8 do not ***r*** former iniquities
88: 5 Whom You ***r*** no more, And who
89:47 ***R*** how short my time is
89:50 ***R***, Lord, the reproach of Your
103:18 And to those who ***r*** His
105: 5 ***R*** His marvelous works which He
106: 4 ***R*** me, O LORD, with the favor
106: 7 They did not ***r*** the multitude
109:16 Because he did not ***r*** to show
119:49 ***R*** the word to Your servant,
119:55 I ***r*** Your name in the night,
132: 1 ***r*** David And all his
137: 6 If I do not ***r*** you, Let my
137: 7 ***R***, O LORD, against the sons
143: 5 I ***r*** the days of old;
Prov 31: 7 And ***r*** his misery no more.
Eccl 11: 8 Yet let him ***r*** the days of
12: 1 ***R*** now your Creator in the days
12: 6 ***R*** your Creator before the
Song 1: 4 We will ***r*** your love more than
Isa 38: 3 ***R*** now, O LORD, I pray, how I
43:18 'Do not ***r*** the former things,
43:25 And I will not ***r*** your sins.
44:21 ***R*** these, O Jacob, And Israel,
46: 8 ***R*** this, and show yourselves
46: 9 ***R*** the former things of old,
47: 7 Nor ***r*** the latter end of them.
54: 4 And will not ***r*** the reproach of
64: 9 Nor ***r*** iniquity forever;
Jer 2: 2 I ***r*** you, The kindness of your
3:16 nor shall they ***r*** it, nor shall
14:10 He will ***r*** their iniquity now,
14:21 ***R***, do not break Your covenant
15:15 ***R*** me and visit me, And take
17: 2 While their children ***r*** Their
18:20 ***R*** that I stood before You
31:20 I earnestly ***r*** him still;
31:34 and their sin I will ***r*** no
44:21 did not the LORD ***r*** them, and
51:50 Do not stand still! ***R*** the
Lam 2: 1 And did not ***r*** His footstool
3:19 ***R*** my affliction and roaming,
5: 1 ***R***, O LORD, what has come upon
Ezek 6: 9 those of you who escape will ***r***
16:22 acts of harlotry you did not ***r***
16:43 Because you did not ***r*** the days
16:60 Nevertheless I will ***r*** My
16:61 Then you will ***r*** your ways and be
16:63 that you may ***r*** and be ashamed,
20:43 And there you shall ***r*** your ways
23:27 Nor ***r*** Egypt anymore.'
36:31 Then you will ***r*** your evil ways
Hos 7: 2 in their hearts That I ***r*** all
8:13 Now He will ***r*** their iniquity
9: 9 He will ***r*** their iniquity;
Am 1: 9 And did not ***r*** the covenant of
Mic 6: 5 ***r*** now What Balak king of Moab
Hab 3: 2 In wrath ***r*** mercy.
Zech 10: 9 And they shall ***r*** Me in far
Mal 4: 4 ***R*** the Law of Moses, My servant,
Mt 5:23 and there ***r*** that your brother
16: 9 or ***r*** the five loaves of the
27:63 saying, "Sir, we ***r***,
Mk 8:18 you not hear? And do you not ***r***?
Lk 1:72 to our fathers And to ***r*** His
16:25 ***r*** that in your lifetime you
17:32 ***R*** Lot's wife.
23:42 ***r*** me when You come into Your
24: 6 ***R*** how He spoke to you when He
Jn 15:20 ***R*** the word that I said to you,
16: 4 you may ***r*** that I told you of
Acts 20:31 and ***r*** that for three years I
20:35 And ***r*** the words of the Lord
Rom 11:18 ***r*** that you do not support the
1 Cor 11: 2 that you ***r*** me in all things and
Gal 2:10 desired only that we should ***r***
Eph 2:11 Therefore ***r*** that you, once
Col 4:18 ***R*** my chains. Grace be with
1 Th 2: 9 For you ***r***, brethren, our labor
2 Th 2: 5 Do you not ***r*** that when I was
2 Tim 1: 3 as without ceasing I ***r*** you in
2: 8 ***R*** that Jesus Christ, of the seed
Heb 8:12 lawless deeds I will ***r***
10:17 deeds I will ***r*** no more."
13: 3 ***R*** the prisoners as if chained
13: 7 ***R*** those who rule over you, who
Jude 17 ***r*** the words which were spoken
Rev 2: 5 ***R*** therefore from where you have
3: 3 ***R*** therefore how you have

REMEMBERED (51/51) REMEMBER, REMEMBERS

Gen 8: 1 Then God ***r*** Noah, and every
19:29 that God ***r*** Abraham, and sent
30:22 Then God ***r*** Rachel, and God
42: 9 Then Joseph ***r*** the dreams which
Ex 2:24 and God ***r*** His covenant with
6: 5 and I have ***r*** My covenant.
Num 10: 9 and you will be ***r*** before the
1 Sam 1:19 and the LORD ***r*** her.
Esth 2: 1 he ***r*** Vashti, what she had done,
9:28 that these days should be ***r***
Job 24:20 He should be ***r*** no more,
Ps 45:17 I will make Your name to be ***r***
77: 3 I ***r*** God, and was troubled;
78:35 Then they ***r*** that God was their
78:39 For He ***r*** that they were but
83: 4 the name of Israel may be ***r*** no
98: 3 He has ***r*** His mercy and His
105:42 For He ***r*** His holy promise,
106:45 And for their sake He ***r*** His
109:14 iniquity of his fathers be ***r***
111: 4 His wonderful works to be ***r***;
119:52 I ***r*** Your judgments of old,
136:23 Who ***r*** us in our lowly state,
137: 1 we wept When we ***r*** Zion.
Eccl 9:15 Yet no one ***r*** that same poor
Isa 23:16 many songs, That you may be ***r***.
57:11 That you have lied And not ***r***
63:11 Then he ***r*** the days of old,
65:17 And the former shall not be ***r***
Jer 11:19 that his name may be ***r*** no
Ezek 3:20 he has done shall not be ***r***;
18:22 he has committed shall be ***r***
18:24 he has done shall not be ***r***;
21:24 have made your iniquity to be ***r***,
21:32 You shall not be ***r***,
25:10 that the Ammonites may not be ***r***
33:13 his righteous works shall be ***r***;
33:16 he has committed shall be ***r***
Hos 2:17 And they shall be ***r*** by their
Jon 2: 7 I ***r*** the LORD; And my prayer
Zech 13: 2 and they shall no longer be ***r***.
Mt 26:75 And Peter ***r*** the word of Jesus
Lk 22:61 And Peter ***r*** the word of the
24: 8 And they ***r*** His words.
Jn 2:17 Then His disciples ***r*** that it was
2:22 His disciples ***r*** that He had
12:16 then they ***r*** that these things
Acts 10:31 and your alms are ***r*** in the
11:16 Then I ***r*** the word of the Lord,
Rev 16:19 And great Babylon was ***r*** before
18: 5 and God has ***r*** her iniquities.

REMEMBERING (4/4) REMEMBER

Num 5:15 of jealousy, an offering for ***r***,
5:18 and put the offering for ***r*** in
Mk 11:21 And Peter, ***r***, said to Him,
1 Th 1: 3 ***r*** without ceasing your work of

REMEMBERS (10/10) REMEMBER

Ps 9:12 He *r* them; He does not forget
103:14 He *r* that we are dust.
103:16 And its place *r* it no more.
105: 8 He *r* His covenant forever,
Isa 64: 5 Who *r* You in Your ways.
Lam 1: 7 Jerusalem *r* all her pleasant
3:20 My soul still *r* And sinks
Nah 2: 5 He *r* his nobles; They stumble
Jn 16:21 she no longer *r* the anguish,
2 Cor 7:15 are greater for you as he *r*

REMEMBRANCE (33/32) REMEMBER

Ex 17:14 I will utterly blot out the *r*
Num 5:15 for bringing iniquity to *r*.
Deut 25:19 that you will blot out the *r*
2 Sam 18:18 no son to keep my name in *r*.
1 Ki 17:18 come to me to bring my sin to *r*,
Ps 6: 5 For in death there is no *r* of
30: 4 And give thanks at the *r* of
34:16 To cut off the *r* of them from
38: A Psalm of David. To bring to *r*.
70: Psalm of David. To bring to *r*.
77: 6 I call to *r* my song in the
97:12 And give thanks at the *r* of
102:12 And the *r* of Your name to all
112: 6 will be in everlasting *r*.
Eccl 1:11 There is no *r* of former
1:11 Nor will there be any *r* of
2:16 For there is no more *r* of the
Isa 26: 8 for Your name And for the *r*
43:26 Put Me in *r*; Let us contend
57: 8 You have set up your *r*;
Ezek 21:23 will bring their iniquity to *r*,
21:24 you have come to *r*,
23:19 her harlotry In calling to *r*
23:21 Thus you called to *r* the
Mal 3:16 So a book of *r* was written
Lk 1:54 In *r* of His mercy,
22:19 do this in *r* of Me."
Jn 14:26 and bring to your *r* all things
1 Cor 11:24 do this in *r* of Me."
11:25 as you drink it, in *r* of Me."
Phil 1: 3 I thank my God upon every *r* of
1 Th 3: 6 that you always have good *r* of
2 Tim 1: 5 when I call to *r* the genuine

REMETH (1/1)

Josh 19:21 *R*, En Gannim, En Haddah,

REMIND (7/7) REMINDER

Ezek 29:16 but will *r* them of their
1 Cor 4:17 who will *r* you of my ways in
2 Tim 1: 6 Therefore I *r* you to stir up the
2:14 *R* them of these things,
Titus 3: 1 *R* them to be subject to rulers
2 Pe 1:12 I will not be negligent to *r*
Jude 5 But I want to *r* you, though you

REMINDER (3/3) REMIND

Heb 10: 3 sacrifices there is a *r* of
2 Pe 1:15 that you always have a *r* of
3: 1 your pure minds by way of *r*),

REMINDING (2/2)

Rom 15:15 as *r* you, because of the grace
2 Pe 1:13 to stir you up by *r* you,

REMISSION (9/9)

Mt 26:28 for many for the *r* of sins.
Mk 1: 4 repentance for the *r* of sins.
Lk 1:77 By the *r* of their sins,
3: 3 repentance for the *r* of sins,
24:47 that repentance and *r* of sins
Acts 2:38 Jesus Christ for the *r* of sins;
10:43 Him will receive *r* of sins."
Heb 9:22 shedding of blood there is no *r*.
10:18 Now where there is *r* of these,

REMISSION OF SINS (6/6)

Mt 26:28 is shed for many for the *r*.
Mk 1: 4 baptism of repentance for the *r*.
Lk 3: 3 baptism of repentance for the *r*,
24:47 and that repentance and *r* should
Acts 2:38 name of Jesus Christ for the *r*;
10:43 believes in Him will receive *r*.

REMNANT (85/83) REMAIN

Ex 26:12 The *r* that remains of the
Deut 3:11 of Bashan remained of the *r* of
Josh 12: 4 who was of the *r* of the
13:12 who remained of the *r* of the
23:12 and cling to the *r* of these
2 Sam 14: 7 my husband neither name nor *r*
21: 2 but of the *r* of the Amorites;
1 Ki 14:10 I will take away the *r* of the
2 Ki 19: 4 lift up your prayer for the *r*
19:30 And the *r* who have escaped of
19:31 out of Jerusalem shall go a *r*,
21:14 So I will forsake the *r* of My
2 Chr 30: 6 then He will return to the *r* of
34: 9 from all the *r* of Israel,
Ezra 9: 8 to leave us a *r* to escape,
9:14 so that there would be no *r*
9:15 for we are left as a *r*,
Job 22:20 And the fire consumes their *r*.
Isa 1: 9 Had left to us a very small *r*,
10:20 pass in that day That the *r*
10:21 The *r* will return, the remnant
10:21 the *r* of Jacob, To the Mighty
10:22 A *r* of them will return;
11:11 second time To recover the *r*
11:16 will be a highway for the *r* of
14:22 off from Babylon the name and *r*,
14:30 And it will slay your *r*.
15: 9 And on the *r* of the land."
16:14 and the *r* will be very small
17: 3 And the *r* of Syria; They will
28: 5 a diadem of beauty To the *r*
37: 4 lift up your prayer for the *r*
37:31 And the *r* who have escaped of
37:32 out of Jerusalem shall go a *r*,
46: 3 And all the *r* of the house of
Jer 6: 9 glean as a vine the *r* of
11:23 and there shall be no *r* of them,
15: 9 And the *r* of them I will
15:11 it will be well with your *r*;
23: 3 But I will gather the *r* of My
25:20 and the *r* of Ashdod);
31: 7 Your people, The *r* of Israel!'
39: 9 to Babylon the *r* of the people
40:11 king of Babylon had left a *r*
40:15 and the *r* in Judah perish?"
42: 2 for all this *r* (since we are
42:15 O *r* of Judah! Thus says the
42:19 O *r* of Judah, 'Do not go to
43: 5 forces took all the *r* of Judah
44:12 And I will take the *r* of Judah
44:14 so that none of the *r* of Judah
44:28 and all the *r* of Judah, who
47: 4 The *r* of the country of
47: 5 is cut off With the *r* of
Ezek 6: 8 "Yet I will leave a *r*,
9: 8 Will You destroy all the *r* of
11:13 make a complete end of the *r*
14:22 there shall be left in it a *r*
23:25 And your *r* shall fall by the
23:25 And your *r* shall be devoured
25:16 Cherethites and destroy the *r*
Joel 2:32 Among the *r* whom the LORD
Am 1: 8 And the *r* of the Philistines
5:15 Will be gracious to the *r* of
9:12 That they may possess the *r* of
Mic 2:12 I will surely gather the *r* of
4: 7 I will make the lame a *r*,
5: 3 Then the *r* of His brethren
5: 7 Then the *r* of Jacob Shall be
5: 8 And the *r* of Jacob Shall be
7:18 the transgression of the *r* of
Hab 2: 8 All the *r* of the people shall
Zeph 2: 7 The coast shall be for the *r* of
2: 9 And the *r* of My people shall
3:13 The *r* of Israel shall do no
Hag 1:12 with all the *r* of the people,
1:14 and the spirit of all the *r* of
2: 2 and to the *r* of the people,
Zech 8: 6 marvelous in the eyes of the *r*
8:11 now I will not treat the *r*
8:12 I will cause the *r* of this
14: 2 But the *r* of the people shall
Mal 2:15 Having a *r* of the Spirit?
Rom 9:27 The *r* will be saved.
11: 5 this present time there is a *r*

REMORSEFUL (1/1)

Mt 27: 3 was *r* and brought back the

REMOTE (2/2)

Judg 19: 1 staying in the *r* mountains
19:18 Judah toward the *r* mountains

REMOVAL (2/2) REMOVE

Heb 12:27 indicates the *r* of those
1 Pe 3:21 baptism (not the *r* of the filth

REMOVE (56/53) REMOVAL, REMOVED, REMOVES, TAKE

Gen 48:17 hold of his father's hand to *r*
Ex 12:15 On the first day you shall *r*
Lev 1:16 And he shall *r* its crop with its
3: 4 above the kidneys, he shall *r*;
3: 9 whole fat tail which he shall *r*
3:10 above the kidneys, he shall *r*;
3:15 above the kidneys, he shall *r*;
4: 9 above the kidneys, he shall *r*,
4:31 He shall *r* all its fat, as fat
4:35 He shall *r* all its fat, as the
7: 4 above the kidneys, he shall *r*;
Deut 19:14 You shall not *r* your neighbor's
25: 9 *r* his sandal from his foot,
Judg 9:29 Then I would *r* Abimelech."
20:13 them to death and *r* the evil
2 Sam 4:11 blood at your hand and *r* you
2 Ki 23:27 I will also *r* Judah from My
24: 3 to *r* them from His sight
2 Chr 33: 8 and I will not again *r* the foot
Job 22:23 You will *r* iniquity far from
24: 2 Some *r* landmarks; They seize
41:13 Who can *r* his outer coat?
Ps 39:10 *R* Your plague from me
39:13 *R* Your gaze from me, that I may
119:22 *R* from me reproach and
119:29 *R* from me the way of lying,
Prov 4:27 *R* your foot from evil.
5: 8 *R* your way far from her,
22:28 Do not *r* the ancient landmark
23:10 Do not *r* the ancient landmark,
30: 8 *R* falsehood and lies far from
Eccl 7:18 And also not *r* your hand from
11:10 Therefore *r* sorrow from your
Isa 7:20 And will also *r* the beard.
20: 2 and *r* the sackcloth from your
47: 2 *R* your veil, Take off the
Jer 27:10 to *r* you far from your land;
32:31 so I will *r* it from before My
Ezek 21:26 *R* the turban, and take off the
22:15 and *r* your filthiness
23:25 They shall *r* your nose and
29:19 and *r* her pillage; and that
45: 9 O princes of Israel! *R* violence
Hos 5:10 like those who *r* a landmark;
Joel 2:20 But I will *r* far from you the
3: 6 That you may *r* them far from
Mic 2: 3 From which you cannot *r* your
Zech 3: 9 And I will *r* the iniquity of
Mt 7: 4 Let me *r* the speck from your
7: 5 Hypocrite! First *r* the plank
7: 5 will see clearly to *r* the speck
Lk 6:42 let me *r* the speck that is in
6:42 Hypocrite! First *r* the plank
6:42 see clearly to *r* the speck
1 Cor 13: 2 so that I could *r* mountains,
Rev 2: 5 quickly and *r* your lampstand

REMOVED (63/60) REMOVE

Gen 8:13 and Noah *r* the covering of the
30:35 So he *r* that day the male goats
Ex 8:31 He *r* the swarms of flies from
Lev 4:31 as fat is *r* from the sacrifice
4:35 as the fat of the lamb is *r*
Num 27: 4 the name of our father be *r*
Deut 25:10 of him who had his sandal *r*.
26:13 I have *r* the holy tithe from
26:14 nor have I *r* any of it for an
1 Sam 6: 3 to you why His hand is not *r*
18:13 Therefore Saul *r* him from his
2 Sam 7:15 whom I *r* from before you.
20:13 When he was *r* from the highway,
1 Ki 2:27 So Solomon *r* Abiathar from being
15:12 and *r* all the idols that his
15:13 Also he *r* Maachah his
15:14 But the high places were not *r*.
2 Ki 15: 4 that the high places were not *r*;
15:35 the high places were not *r*;
16:17 and *r* the lavers from them;
16:18 Also he *r* the Sabbath pavilion
16:18 and he *r* the king's outer
17:18 and *r* them from His sight;
17:23 until the LORD *r* Israel out of
17:26 The nations whom you have *r* and
18: 4 He *r* the high places and broke
23: 5 Then he *r* the idolatrous priests
23:11 Then he *r* the horses that the
23:27 as I have *r* Israel, and will
2 Chr 14: 3 for he *r* the altars of the
14: 5 He also *r* the high places and
15: 8 and *r* the abominable idols from
15:16 Also he *r* Maachah, the mother
15:17 But the high places were not *r*
17: 6 moreover he *r* the high places
19: 3 in that you have *r* the wooden
34:33 Thus Josiah *r* all the
35:12 Then they *r* the burnt offerings
Job 18: 4 Or shall the rock be *r* from
19:13 He has *r* my brothers far from
Ps 46: 2 Even though the earth be *r*,
81: 6 I *r* his shoulder from the
103:12 So far has He *r* our
Prov 10:30 The righteous will never be *r*,
27:25 When the hay is *r*,
Isa 6:12 The LORD has *r* men far away,
10:13 Also I have *r* the boundaries
14:25 Then his yoke shall be *r* from
14:25 And his burden *r* from their
22: 8 He *r* the protection of Judah.
22:25 in the secure place will be *r*
29:13 But have *r* their hearts far
33:20 of its stakes will ever be *r*,
54:10 depart And the hills be *r*,
54:10 shall My covenant of peace be *r*,
Dan 11:18 and with the reproach *r*,
Am 6: 7 recline at banquets shall be *r*.
Mic 2: 4 How He has *r* it from me!
Zech 3: 4 I have *r* your iniquity from
Mt 21:21 Be *r* and be cast into the sea,'
Mk 11:23 Be *r* and be cast into the sea,'
Jn 21: 7 outer garment (for he had *r*
Acts 13:22 And when He had *r* him, He raised

REMOVES (3/3) REMOVE

Job 9: 5 He *r* the mountains, and they do
Isa 27: 8 He *r* it by His rough wind
Dan 2:21 He *r* kings and raises up

REMOVING (1/1)

Gen 30:32 *r* from there all the speckled

REMMON (KJV) See RIMMON

R

REMMON-METHOAR (KJV) See RIMMON

REMPHAN (1/1)
Acts 7:43 the star of your god *R*,

REND (2/2)
Isa 64: 1 that You would *r* the heavens!
Joel 2:13 So *r* your heart, and not your

RENDER (22/22) RENDERS
Num 18: 9 trespass offering which they *r*
Deut 32:41 I will *r* vengeance to My
32:43 And *r* vengeance to His
Judg 11:27 *r* judgment this day between the
Ps 28: 4 *R* to them what they deserve.
38:20 Those also who *r* evil for good,
56:12 I will *r* praises to You,
62:12 For You *r* to each one
94: 2 *R* punishment to the proud.
116:12 What shall I *r* to the LORD
Prov 24:12 And will He not *r* to each
24:29 I will *r* to the man according
Isa 66:15 To *r* His anger with fury,
Mt 21:41 other vinedressers who will *r*
22:21 *R* therefore to Caesar the things
Mk 12:17 *R* to Caesar the things that are
Lk 20:25 *R* therefore to Caesar the things
Rom 2: 6 will *r* to each one
13: 7 *R* therefore to all their due:
1 Cor 7: 3 Let the husband *r* to his wife
1 Th 3: 9 For what thanks can we *r* to God
Rev 18: 6 *R* to her just as she rendered to

RENDERED (3/3)
1 Ki 3:28 judgment which the king had *r*;
Prov 12:14 of a man's hands will be *r* to
Rev 18: 6 Render to her just as she *r* to

RENDERS (1/1) RENDER
1 Th 5:15 See that no one *r* evil for evil

RENDING (1/1)
Ps 7: 2 *R* me in pieces, while there

RENEW (8/8) RENEWED, RENEWING
1 Sam 11:14 let us go to Gilgal and *r* the
Job 10:17 You *r* Your witnesses against
Ps 51:10 And *r* a steadfast spirit
104:30 And You *r* the face of the
Isa 40:31 who wait on the LORD Shall *r*
41: 1 And let the people *r* their
Lam 5:21 *R* our days as of old,
Heb 6: 6 to *r* them again to repentance,

RENEWED (5/5) RENEW
Job 29:20 And my bow is *r* in my hand.'
Ps 103: 5 So that your youth is *r* like
2 Cor 4:16 yet the inward man is being *r*
Eph 4:23 and be *r* in the spirit of your
Col 3:10 put on the new man who is *r*

RENEWING (2/2) RENEW
Rom 12: 2 but be transformed by the *r* of
Titus 3: 5 washing of regeneration and *r*

RENOUNCE (1/1)
Ps 10:13 Why do the wicked *r* God?

RENOUNCED (2/2)
Ps 89:39 You have *r* the covenant of Your
2 Cor 4: 2 But we have *r* the hidden things

RENOUNCES (1/1)
Ps 10: 3 the greedy and *r* the LORD.

RENOWN (6/6)
Gen 6: 4 men who were of old, men of *r*.
Num 16: 2 of the congregation, men of *r*.
Jer 13:11 may become My people, for *r*,
Ezek 23:23 rulers, Captains and men of *r*,
34:29 raise up for them a garden of *r*,
39:13 and they will gain *r* for it on

RENOWNED (2/2)
Job 18:17 And he has no name among the *r*.
Ezek 26:17 O *r* city, Who was strong at

RENTED (1/1)
Acts 28:30 whole years in his own *r* house,

REPAID (11/11) REPAY
Gen 44: 4 Why have you *r* evil for good?
Judg 1: 7 so God has *r* me." Then they
9:56 Thus God *r* the wickedness of
1 Sam 25:21 And he has *r* me evil for good.
Ps 7: 4 If I have *r* evil to him who was
Prov 13:21 the righteous, good shall be *r*.
Jer 18:20 Shall evil be *r* for good?
Lk 14:12 invite you back, and you be *r*.
14:14 for you shall be *r* at the
Rom 11:35 And it shall be *r* to
Col 3:25 But he who does wrong will be *r*

REPAIR (13/12) REPAIRED, REPAIRER, REPAIRS
2 Ki 12: 5 and let them *r* the damages of
12: 8 nor *r* the damages of the
12:12 to *r* the damage of the house of
12:12 for all that was paid out to *r*
22: 5 to *r* the damages of the house—
22: 6 buy timber and hewn stone to *r*
2 Chr 24: 5 from all Israel money to *r* the
24:12 masons and carpenters to *r* the
34: 8 to *r* the house of the LORD his
34:10 to *r* and restore the house.
Ezra 9: 9 to *r* the house of our God,
Isa 61: 4 And they shall *r* the ruined
Am 9:11 And *r* its damages; I will

REPAIRED (24/22) REPAIR
Num 21:27 Let the city of Sihon be *r*.
1 Ki 11:27 had built the Millo and *r* the
18:30 And he *r* the altar of the LORD
2 Ki 12: 6 that the priests had not *r* the
12: 7 Why have you not *r* the damages
12:14 and they *r* the house of the
1 Chr 11: 8 Joab *r* the rest of the city.
2 Chr 29: 3 of the house of the LORD and *r*
32: 5 also he *r* the Millo in the
33:16 He also *r* the altar of the
Neh 3: 6 the son of Besodeiah *r* the Old
3: 7 *r* the residence of the governor
3:11 Hashub the son of Pahath-Moab *r*
3:13 and the inhabitants of Zanoah *r*
3:13 and *r* a thousand cubits of the
3:14 *r* the Refuse Gate; he built it
3:15 *r* the Fountain Gate; he built
3:15 and *r* the wall of the Pool of
3:19 *r* another section in front of
3:20 the son of Zabbai carefully *r*
3:21 *r* another section, from the
3:24 him Binnui the son of Henadad *r*
3:27 After them the Tekoites *r*
3:30 of Zalaph, *r* another section.

REPAIRER (1/1) REPAIR
Isa 58:12 And you shall be called the *R*

REPAIRING (4/4)
2 Ki 12: 7 but deliver it for *r* the
2 Chr 24: 4 set his heart on *r* the house
24:27 and the *r* of the house of God,
Ezra 4:12 walls and *r* the foundations.

REPAIRS (26/18) REPAIR
Neh 3: 4 Urijah, the son of Koz, made *r*.
3: 4 the son of Meshezabel, made *r*.
3: 4 Zadok the son of Baana made *r*.
3: 5 to them the Tekoites made *r*;
3: 8 one of the goldsmiths, made *r*.
3: 8 one of the perfumers, made *r*;
3: 9 district of Jerusalem, made *r*.
3:10 the son of Harumaph made *r* in
3:10 the son of Hashabniah made *r*.
3:12 he and his daughters made *r*.
3:16 made *r* as far as the place in
3:17 Rehum the son of Bani, made *r*.
3:17 made *r* for his district.
3:18 the district of Keilah, made *r*.
3:22 the men of the plain, made *r*.
3:23 him Benjamin and Hasshub made *r*
3:23 made *r* by his house.
3:25 Palal the son of Uzai made *r*
3:25 the son of Parosh made *r*.
3:26 who dwelt in Ophel made *r* as
3:28 Horse Gate the priests made *r*,
3:29 Zadok the son of Immer made *r*
3:29 keeper of the East Gate, made *r*.
3:30 the son of Berechiah made *r* in
3:31 made *r* as far as the house of
3:32 and the merchants made *r*.

REPAY (47/45) REPAID, REPAYS
Gen 50:15 and may actually *r* us for all
Lev 25:51 according to them he shall *r*
25:52 to his years he shall *r* him
Deut 7:10 He will *r* him to his face.
32:41 And *r* those who hate Me.
Judg 20:10 they may *r* all the vileness
Ruth 2:12 'The LORD *r* your work,
1 Sam 26:23 May the LORD *r* every man for
2 Sam 2: 6 I also will *r* you this
3:39 The LORD shall *r* the evildoer
16:12 and that the LORD will *r* me
19:36 And why should the king *r* me
2 Ki 9:26 and I will *r* you in this plot,'
2 Chr 24:22 'The LORD look on it, and *r*!"
32:25 But Hezekiah did not *r* according
Job 34:33 Should He *r* it according to
Ps 10:14 To *r* it by Your hand.
37:21 wicked borrows and does not *r*,
41:10 That I may *r* them.
54: 5 He will *r* my enemies for their
Isa 59:18 deeds, accordingly He will *r*,
59:18 The coastlands He will fully *r*.
65: 6 not keep silence, but will *r*—
65: 6 Even *r* into their bosom—
Jer 16:18 And first I will *r* double for
25:14 and I will *r* them according to
32:18 and *r* the iniquity of the
50:29 *R* her according to her work;
51:24 And I will *r* Babylon And all
51:56 recompense, He will surely *r*.
Lam 3:64 *R* them, O LORD, According to
Ezek 7: 3 And I will *r* you for all your
7: 4 But I will *r* your ways,
7: 8 And I will *r* you for all your
7: 9 I will *r* you according to your
23:49 They shall *r* you for your
Lk 7:42 had nothing with which to *r*,
10:35 I come again, I will *r* you.'
14:14 because they cannot *r* you;
Rom 12:17 *R* no one evil for evil.
12:19 is Mine, I will *r*,
2 Th 1: 6 a righteous thing with God to *r*
1 Tim 5: 4 to show piety at home and to *r*
2 Tim 4:14 May the Lord *r* him according to
Phm 1:19 with my own hand. I will *r*—
Heb 10:30 is Mine, I will *r*,
Rev 18: 6 and *r* her double according to

REPAYS (6/6) REPAY
Deut 7:10 and He *r* those who hate Him to
Job 21:31 And who *r* him for what he
34:11 For He *r* man according to his
Ps 31:23 And fully *r* the proud person.
137: 8 Happy the one who *r* you as you
Isa 66: 6 Who fully *r* His enemies!

REPEATED (2/2) REPEATS, REPETITIONS
Gen 41:32 And the dream was *r* to Pharaoh
1 Sam 8:21 and he *r* them in the hearing of

REPEATEDLY (1/1)
Heb 10:11 daily and offering *r* the same

REPEATS (2/2) REPEATED
Prov 17: 9 But he who *r* a matter
26:11 So a fool *r* his folly.

REPEL (3/3)
2 Sam 5: 6 the blind and the lame will *r*
2 Ki 18:24 How then will you *r* one captain
Isa 36: 9 will you *r* one captain of the

REPENT (34/32) REPENTANCE, REPENTED, REPENTS
Num 23:19 a son of man, that He should *r*.
1 Ki 8:47 were carried captive, and *r*,
2 Chr 6:37 were carried captive, and *r*,
Job 42: 6 And *r* in dust and ashes."
Jer 25: 5 *R* now everyone of his evil way
Ezek 14: 6 'Thus says the Lord GOD: "*R*,
18:30 says the Lord GOD. "*R*,
Hos 11: 5 Because they refused to *r*.
Mt 3: 2 and saying, "*R*,
4:17 began to preach and to say, "*R*,
11:20 done, because they did not *r*:
Mk 1:15 kingdom of God is at hand. *R*,
6:12 preached that people should *r*.
Lk 13: 3 but unless you *r* you will all
13: 5 but unless you *r* you will all
16:30 them from the dead, they will *r*.
17: 4 returns to you, saying, 'I *r*,
Acts 2:38 Then Peter said to them, "*R*,
3:19 *R* therefore and be converted,
8:22 *R* therefore of this your
17:30 all men everywhere to *r*,
26:20 Gentiles, that they should *r*,
Rev 2: 5 *r* and do the first works, or
2: 5 from its place—unless you *r*.
2:16 '*R*, or else I will come to you
2:21 And I gave her time to *r* of her
2:21 immorality, and she did not *r*.
2:22 unless they *r* of their deeds.
3: 3 and heard; hold fast and *r*.
3:19 Therefore be zealous and *r*.
9:20 did not *r* of the works of their
9:21 And they did not *r* of their
16: 9 and they did not *r* and give Him
16:11 and did not *r* of their deeds.

REPENTANCE (24/24) REPENT
Mt 3: 8 bear fruits worthy of *r*,
3:11 baptize you with water unto *r*,
9:13 righteous, but sinners, to *r*.
Mk 1: 4 and preaching a baptism of *r*
2:17 righteous, but sinners, to *r*.
Lk 3: 3 preaching a baptism of *r* for
3: 8 bear fruits worthy of *r*,
5:32 righteous, but sinners, to *r*.
15: 7 just persons who need no *r*.
24:47 and that *r* and remission of sins
Acts 5:31 to give *r* to Israel and
11:18 also granted to the Gentiles *r*
13:24 the baptism of *r* to all the
19: 4 baptized with a baptism of *r*,
20:21 *r* toward God and faith toward
26:20 God, and do works befitting *r*.

Rom 2: 4 goodness of God leads you to *r*?
2 Cor 7: 9 but that your sorrow led to *r*.
7:10 For godly sorrow produces *r*
2 Tim 2:25 God perhaps will grant them *r*,
Heb 6: 1 again the foundation of *r* from
6: 6 away, to renew them again to *r*,
12:17 for he found no place for *r*,
2 Pe 3: 9 but that all should come to *r*.

REPENTED (7/7) REPENT

Jer 8: 6 No man *r* of his wickedness,
31:19 Surely, after my turning, I *r*;
Mt 11:21 they would have *r* long ago in
12:41 because they *r* at the preaching
Lk 10:13 they would have *r* long ago,
11:32 for they *r* at the preaching of
2 Cor 12:21 sinned before and have not *r*

REPENTS (3/3) REPENT

Lk 15: 7 in heaven over one sinner who *r*
15:10 of God over one sinner who *r*.
17: 3 you, rebuke him; and if he *r*,

REPETITIONS (1/1) REPEATED

Mt 6: 7 do not use vain *r* as the

REPHAEL (1/1)

1 Chr 26: 7 sons of Shemaiah were Othni, *R*,

REPHAH (1/1)

1 Chr 7:25 and *R* was his son, as well as

REPHAIAH (5/5)

1 Chr 3:21 and Jeshaiah, the sons of *R*,
4:42 captains Pelatiah, Neariah, *R*,
7: 2 The sons of Tola were Uzzi, *R*,
9:43 *R* his son, Eleasah his son, and
Neh 3: 9 And next to them *R* the son of

REPHAIM (10/10)

Gen 14: 5 him came and attacked the *R* in
15:20 Hittites, the Perizzites, the *R*,
Josh 15: 8 at the end of the Valley of *R*
18:16 is in the Valley of the *R* on
2 Sam 5:18 themselves in the Valley of *R*.
5:22 themselves in the Valley of *R*.
23:13 encamped in the Valley of *R*.
1 Chr 11:15 encamped in the Valley of *R*.
14: 9 made a raid on the Valley of *R*.
Isa 17: 5 of grain In the Valley of *R*.

REPHAIMS (KJV) See REPHAIM

REPHIDIM (5/5)

Ex 17: 1 of the LORD, and camped in *R*;
17: 8 and fought with Israel in *R*.
19: 2 For they had departed from *R*,
Num 33:14 from Alush and camped at *R*,
33:15 They departed from *R* and camped

REPLACE (1/1)

Isa 9:10 But we will *r* them with

REPLENISH (KJV) See FILL

REPLENISHED (1/1)

Jer 31:25 and I have *r* every sorrowful

REPLICA (1/1)

Josh 22:28 Here is the *r* of the altar of

REPLIED (1/1)

Acts 21:37 "May I speak to you?" He *r*,

REPLY (3/3)

Esth 1:21 And the *r* pleased the king and
4:15 Then Esther told them to *r* to
Rom 9:20 who are you to *r* against God?

REPORT (41/38) REPORTED

Gen 29:13 when Laban heard the *r* about
37: 2 and Joseph brought a bad *r* of
45:16 Now the *r* of it was heard in
Ex 23: 1 shall not circulate a false *r*.
Num 13:32 the children of Israel a bad *r*
14:36 him by bringing a bad *r* of the
14:37 very men who brought the evil *r*
Deut 2:25 who shall hear the *r* of you,
Judg 18: 8 to them, "What is your *r*?
1 Sam 2:24 For it is not a good *r* that
20:13 then I will *r* it to you and
1 Ki 10: 6 It was a true *r* which I heard in
2 Chr 9: 5 It was a true *r* which I heard
Ezra 5: 5 not make them cease till a *r*
Neh 6:13 might have cause for an evil *r*,
Esth 1:17 in their eyes, when they *r*,
Job 28:22 We have heard a *r* about it with
Prov 15:30 And a good *r* makes the bones
Isa 23: 5 When the *r* reaches Egypt,
23: 5 also will be in agony at the *r*
28:19 terror just to understand the *r*.
53: 1 Who has believed our *r*?
Jer 6:24 We have heard the *r* of it;
10:22 the noise of the *r* has come,
20:10 side!" "*R*," they say,
20:10 and we will *r* it!" All my
50:43 king of Babylon has heard the *r*
Ob 1 Edom (We have heard a *r* from
Mt 9:26 And the *r* of this went out into
14: 1 Herod the tetrarch heard the *r*
Lk 4:37 And the *r* about Him went out
5:15 the *r* went around concerning
7:17 And this *r* about Him went
Jn 11:57 he should *r* it, that they
12:38 who has believed our *r*?
Acts 15:27 who will also *r* the same things
Rom 10:16 who has believed our *r*?
1 Cor 14:25 he will worship God and *r* that
2 Cor 6: 8 by evil *r* and good report;
6: 8 by evil report and good *r*;
Phil 4: 8 whatever things are of good *r*,

REPORTED (26/25) REPORT

Judg 4:12 And they *r* to Sisera that Barak
Ruth 2:11 'It has been fully *r* to me,
1 Sam 11: 9 Then the messengers came and *r*
17:31 they *r* them to Saul; and he
1 Ki 18:13 Was it not *r* to my lord what I
2 Ki 9:18 So the watchman *r*, saying,
9:20 So the watchman *r*,
Neh 6: 6 It is *r* among the nations,
6: 7 Now these matters will be *r* to
6:19 Also they *r* his good deeds
6:19 and *r* my words to him.
Ezek 9:11 *r* back and said, "I have done
Mt 28:11 guard came into the city and *r*
28:15 and this saying is commonly *r*
Lk 7:18 Then the disciples of John *r* to
14:21 So that servant came and *r* these
Acts 4:23 their own companions and *r* all
5:22 the prison, they returned and *r*,
14:27 they *r* all that God had done
15: 4 and they *r* all things that God
16:36 So the keeper of the prison *r*
28:21 brethren who came *r* or spoken
Rom 3: 8 as we are slanderously *r* and as
1 Cor 5: 1 It is actually *r* that there
1 Tim 5:10 well *r* for good works: if she
1 Pe 1:12 things which now have been *r*

REPRESENTATIVES (3/3)

Num 16: 2 *r* of the congregation, men of
26: 9 *r* of the congregation, who
Ezra 4: 9 *r* of the Dinaites,

REPRESENTING (1/1)

Num 1:44 each one *r* his father's house.

REPRIMANDED (1/1)

Judg 8: 1 And they *r* him sharply.

REPRISAL (1/1)

Ob 15 Your *r* shall return upon your

REPROACH (89/87) REPROACHED, REPROACHES

Gen 30:23 said, "God has taken away my *r*.
34:14 for that would be a *r* to us.
Num 15:30 that one brings *r* on the LORD,
Josh 5: 9 day I have rolled away the *r*
Ruth 2:15 and do not *r* her.
1 Sam 11: 2 and bring *r* on all Israel."
17:26 and takes away the *r* from
25:39 has pleaded the cause of my *r*
2 Ki 19: 4 king of Assyria has sent to *r*
19:16 which he has sent to *r* the
Neh 1: 3 there in great distress and *r*.
2:17 that we may no longer be a *r*.
4: 4 turn their *r* on their own
5: 9 of our God because of the *r* of
6:13 that they might *r* me.
Job 27: 6 My heart shall not *r* me as
Ps 15: 3 Nor does he take up a *r*
22: 6 A *r* of men, and despised by
31:11 I am a *r* among all my enemies,
39: 8 Do not make me the *r* of the
42:10 My enemies *r* me, While they
44:13 You make us a *r* to our
69: 7 for Your sake I have borne *r*;
69: 9 the reproaches of those who *r*
69:10 with fasting, That became my *r*.
69:19 You know my *r*, my shame,
69:20 *R* has broken my heart,
71:13 Let them be covered with *r*
74:10 how long will the adversary *r*?
78:66 He put them to a perpetual *r*.
79: 4 We have become a *r* to our
79:12 into their bosom Their *r* with
89:41 He is a *r* to his neighbors.
89:50 the *r* of Your servants—How I
89:50 I bear in my bosom the *r* of
102: 8 My enemies *r* me all day long,
109:25 I also have become a *r* to them;
119:22 Remove from me *r* and contempt,
119:39 Turn away my *r* which I dread,
Prov 6:33 And his *r* will not be wiped
14:34 But sin is a *r* to any
18: 3 And with dishonor comes *r*.
19:26 who causes shame and brings *r*.
22:10 strife and *r* will cease.
Isa 4: 1 your name, To take away our *r*.
30: 5 But a shame and also a *r*.
37: 4 king of Assyria has sent to *r*
37:17 which he has sent to *r* the
51: 7 Do not fear the *r* of men,
54: 4 And will not remember the *r* of
Jer 3:25 And our *r* covers us.
6:10 the word of the LORD is a *r* to
20: 8 the LORD was made to me A *r*
23:40 I will bring an everlasting *r*
24: 9 to be a *r* and a byword,
29:18 and a *r* among all the nations
31:19 Because I bore the *r* of my
42:18 astonishment, a curse, and a *r*;
44: 8 off and be a curse and a *r*
44:12 a curse and a *r*!
49:13 shall become a desolation, a *r*,
51:51 ashamed because we have heard *r*.
Lam 3:30 strikes him, And be full of *r*.
3:61 You have heard their *r*,
5: 1 and behold our *r*!
Ezek 5:14 I will make you a waste and a *r*
5:15 'So it shall be a *r*,
16:57 It was like the time of the *r*
21:28 and concerning their *r*,
22: 4 therefore I have made you a *r*
36:15 nor bear the *r* of the peoples
36:30 need never again bear the *r* of
Dan 9:16 and Your people are a *r* to
11:18 But a ruler shall bring the *r*
11:18 and with the *r* removed, he
Hos 12:14 And return his *r* upon him.
Joel 2:17 do not give Your heritage to *r*,
2:19 I will no longer make you a *r*
Mic 6:16 you shall bear the *r* of My
Zeph 2: 8 I have heard the *r* of Moab,
3:18 To whom its *r* is a burden.
Lk 1:25 to take away my *r* among
11:45 by saying these things You *r* us
Col 1:22 and above *r* in His sight—
1 Tim 3: 7 lest he fall into *r* and the
4:10 end we both labor and suffer *r*,
Heb 11:26 esteeming the *r* of Christ
13:13 outside the camp, bearing His *r*.
Jas 1: 5 to all liberally and without *r*,

REPROACHED (13/12) REPROACH

2 Ki 19:22 Whom have you *r* and blasphemed?
19:23 By your messengers you have *r*
Job 19: 3 These ten times you have *r* me;
Ps 74:18 this, that the enemy has *r*,
79:12 with which they have *r* You,
89:51 With which Your enemies have *r*,
89:51 With which they have *r* the
Isa 37:23 Whom have you *r* and blasphemed?
37:24 By your servants you have *r* the
Zeph 2: 8 With which they have *r* My
2:10 Because they have *r* and made
Rom 15: 3 reproaches of those who *r*
1 Pe 4:14 If you are *r* for the name of

REPROACHES (14/14) REPROACH

Job 20: 3 I have heard the rebuke that *r*
Ps 44:16 of the voice of him who *r* and
55:12 it is not an enemy who *r* me;
57: 3 He *r* the one who would swallow
69: 9 And the *r* of those who
74:22 how the foolish man *r* You
119:42 I have an answer for him who *r*
Prov 14:31 He who oppresses the poor *r* his
17: 5 He who mocks the poor *r* his
27:11 That I may answer him who *r*
Isa 43:28 to the curse, And Israel to *r*.
Rom 15: 3 The *r* of those who
2 Cor 12:10 pleasure in infirmities, in *r*,
Heb 10:33 made a spectacle both by *r* and

REPROACHFULLY (2/2)

Job 16:10 They strike me *r* on the cheek,
1 Tim 5:14 to the adversary to speak *r*.

REPROBATE, REPROBATES (KJV) See DEBASED, DISQUALIFIED, REJECTED

REPROOF (1/1) REBUKE

2 Tim 3:16 profitable for doctrine, for *r*,

REPROOFS (1/1)

Prov 6:23 *R* of instruction are the way

REPROVE (KJV) See CONVICT, CONVINCE, EXPOSE, REBUKE

REPROVED (1/1) REBUKED

Jer 29:27 why have you not *r* Jeremiah of

REPROVES (1/1) REBUKES

Isa 29:21 And lay a snare for him who *r*

REPTILE (3/3)

Lev 11:30 the monitor lizard, the sand *r*,
Isa 27: 1 And He will slay the *r* that
Jas 3: 7 of *r* and creature of the sea,

REPULSIVE (4/4)

2 Sam 10: 6 they had made themselves *r* to
1 Chr 19: 6 they had made themselves *r* to
Job 19:17 And I am *r* to the children of
Ps 31:11 And am *r* to my acquaintances;

REPUTATION (5/5)

Prov 25:10 And your *r* be ruined.
Acts 6: 3 among you seven men of good *r*,
10:22 who fears God and has a good *r*
Gal 2: 2 to those who were of *r*,
Phil 2: 7 but made Himself of no *r*,

REPUTED (1/1)

Dan 4:35 of the earth are *r* as nothing;

REQUEST (26/26) REQUESTED, REQUESTS

Judg 8:24 I would like to make a *r* of you,
Ruth 3:11 will do for you all that you *r*,
2 Sam 14:15 the king will perform the *r* of
14:22 the king has fulfilled the *r*
19:38 Now whatever you *r* of me, I
Ezra 6: 9 according to the *r* of the
7: 6 The king granted him all his *r*,
8:22 For I was ashamed to *r* of the
Neh 2: 4 said to me, "What do you *r*?
Esth 5: 3 Queen Esther? What is your *r*?
5: 6 be granted you. What is your *r*,
5: 7 My petition and *r* is this:
5: 8 my petition and fulfill my *r*,
7: 2 And what is your *r*,
7: 3 petition, and my people at my *r*.
9:12 Or what is your further *r*?
Job 6: 8 "Oh, that I might have my *r*,
Ps 21: 2 And have not withheld the *r* of
106:15 And He gave them their *r*,
Prov 30: 7 Two things I *r* of You
Jer 38:26 I presented my *r* before the
Dan 9: 3 toward the Lord God to make *r*
Lk 4:38 and they made *r* of Him
Rom 1:10 making *r* if, by some means, now
1 Cor 1:22 For Jews *r* a sign, and Greeks
Phil 1: 4 every prayer of mine making *r*

REQUESTED (10/10) REQUEST

Ex 12:36 granted them what they *r*.
Judg 8:26 of the gold earrings that he *r*
2 Sam 12:20 to his own house; and when he *r*,
1 Chr 4:10 So God granted him what he *r*.
Esth 2:15 she *r* nothing but what Hegai
Ps 137: 3 And those who plundered us *r*
Dan 1: 8 therefore he *r* of the chief of
Mk 15: 6 to them, whomever they *r*.
Lk 23:24 that it should be as they *r*.
23:25 released to them the one they *r*,

REQUESTS (2/2) REQUEST

Dan 2:11 difficult thing that the king *r*,
Phil 4: 6 let your *r* be made known to

REQUIRE (26/25) REQUIRED, REQUIREMENT, REQUIRES

Gen 9: 5 hand of every beast I will *r*
9: 5 of every man's brother I will *r*
43: 9 from my hand you shall *r* him.
Deut 10:12 what does the LORD your God *r*
15: 2 he shall not *r* it of his
15: 3 Of a foreigner you may *r* it;
18:19 I will *r* it of him.
23:21 LORD your God will surely *r*
Josh 22:23 let the LORD Himself *r* an
1 Sam 20:16 Let the LORD *r* it at the hand
2 Sam 3:13 But one thing I *r* of you:
4:11 shall I not now *r* his blood at
1 Ki 8:59 Israel, as each day may *r*,
2 Ki 12:15 Moreover they did not *r* an
1 Chr 21: 3 Why then does my lord *r* this
Ezra 7:21 may *r* of you, let it be done
Neh 5:12 and will *r* nothing from them;
Ps 10:13 You will not *r* an account."
40: 6 and sin offering You did not *r*.
Ezek 3:18 but his blood I will *r* at your
3:20 but his blood I will *r* at your
20:40 and there I will *r* your
33: 6 but his blood I will *r* at the
33: 8 but his blood I will *r* at your
34:10 and I will *r* My flock at their
Mic 6: 8 And what does the LORD *r* of

REQUIRED (18/17) REQUIRE

Gen 31:39 You *r* it from my hand, whether
42:22 his blood is now *r* of us."
50: 3 Forty days were *r* for him,
50: 3 for such are the days *r* for
Num 5:15 He shall bring the offering *r*
1 Sam 21: 8 the king's business *r* haste."
1 Chr 16:37 as every day's work *r*;
2 Chr 8:14 as the duty of each day *r*,
24: 6 Why have you not *r* the Levites
Ezra 3: 4 offerings in the number *r* by
Neh 5:12 and *r* an oath from them that
Isa 1:12 Who has *r* this from your hand,
Lk 11:50 of the world may be *r* of this
11:51 it shall be *r* of this
12:20 This night your soul will be *r*
12:48 given, from him much will be *r*;
1 Cor 4: 2 Moreover it is *r* in stewards
Heb 5: 3 Because of this he is *r* as for

REQUIREMENT (1/1) REQUIRE, REQUIREMENTS

Rom 8: 4 that the righteous *r* of the law

REQUIREMENTS (2/2) REQUIREMENT

Rom 2:26 man keeps the righteous *r* of
Col 2:14 wiped out the handwriting of *r*

REQUIRES (1/1) REQUIRE

Eccl 3:15 And God *r* an account of what

REQUITE, REQUITED, REQUITING (KJV) See REPAY

RESCUE (11/11)

Ex 6: 6 I will *r* you from their
Deut 25:11 the wife of one draws near to *r*
28:31 and you shall have no one to *r*
2 Chr 25:15 which could not *r* their own
Ps 22: 8 let Him *r* Him; Let Him deliver
35:17 *R* me from their destructions,
144: 7 *R* me and deliver me out of
144:11 *R* me and deliver me from the
Prov 19:19 For if you *r* him, you will
Hos 5:14 them away, and no one shall *r*.
Mic 6:14 And what you do *r* I will give

RESCUED (4/4)

1 Sam 14:45 So the people *r* Jonathan,
30:18 and David *r* his two wives.
Ps 136:24 And *r* us from our enemies,
Acts 23:27 Coming with the troops I *r* him,

RESCUES (1/1)

Dan 6:27 He delivers and *r*,

REREWARD (KJV) See (REAR) GUARD

RESEMBLANCE (1/1)

Zech 5: 6 This is their *r* throughout the

RESEMBLED (1/1)

Judg 8:18 each one *r* the son of a king."

RESEN (1/1)

Gen 10:12 and *R* between Nineveh and Calah

RESERVE (2/2) RESERVED

Gen 41:36 that food shall be as a *r*
2 Pe 2: 9 out of temptations and to *r*

RESERVED (15/15) RESERVE

Gen 27:36 Have you not *r* a blessing for
Num 18: 9 of the most holy things *r*
Deut 33:21 a lawgiver's portion was *r*
1 Ki 19:18 Yet I have *r* seven thousand in
Job 20:26 Total darkness is *r* for his
21:30 For the wicked are *r* for the
38:23 Which I have *r* for the time of
Acts 25:21 when Paul appealed to be *r*
Rom 11: 4 I have *r* for Myself seven
1 Pe 1: 4 *r* in heaven for you,
2 Pe 2: 4 to be *r* for judgment;
2:17 for whom is *r* the blackness of
3: 7 are *r* for fire until the day of
Jude 6 He has *r* in everlasting chains
13 for whom is *r* the blackness

RESERVES (2/2)

Jer 5:24 He *r* for us the appointed
Nah 1: 2 And He *r* wrath for His

RESERVOIR (1/1)

Isa 22:11 You also made a *r* between the

RESHEPH (1/1)

1 Chr 7:25 was his son, as well as *R*,

RESIDE (2/2)

Jer 49:33 No one shall *r* there,
50:40 So no one shall *r* there,

RESIDENCE (2/2)

Neh 3: 7 repaired the *r* of the governor
Am 7:13 And it is the royal *r*.

RESIDES (1/1)

Job 39:28 On the rocks it dwells and *r*,

RESIDUE (8/7)

Ex 10: 5 and they shall eat the *r* of
Jer 8: 3 rather than life by all the *r*
24: 8 the *r* of Jerusalem who remain
Ezek 34:18 down with your feet the *r* of
34:18 that you must foul the *r* with
Dan 7: 7 and trampling the *r* with its
7:19 and trampled the *r* with its
Zeph 2: 9 The *r* of My people shall

RESIST (10/10) RESISTED, RESISTS

Dan 11:15 shall have no strength to *r*.
Mt 5:39 But I tell you not to *r* an evil
Lk 21:15 not be able to contradict or *r*.
Acts 6:10 And they were not able to *r* the
7:51 in heart and ears! You always *r*
Rom 13: 2 and those who *r* will bring
2 Tim 3: 8 so do these also *r* the truth:
Jas 4: 7 *R* the devil and he will flee
5: 6 he does not *r* you.
1 Pe 5: 9 *R* him, steadfast in the faith,

RESISTED (4/4) RESIST

Rom 9:19 For who has *r* His will?"
2 Tim 3: 8 Now as Jannes and Jambres *r*
4:15 for he has greatly *r* our words.
Heb 12: 4 You have not yet *r* to bloodshed,

RESISTS (4/3) RESIST

Rom 13: 2 Therefore whoever *r* the
13: 2 resists the authority *r* the
Jas 4: 6 God *r* the proud, But gives
1 Pe 5: 5 God *r* the proud, But gives

RESOLVE (1/1)

Rom 14:13 but rather *r* this, not to put a

RESOLVED (2/2)

2 Chr 30: 5 So they *r* to make a proclamation
Lk 16: 4 I have *r* what to do, that when I

RESOLVES (1/1)

Judg 5:15 There were great *r* of heart.

RESORT (1/1) RESORTED

Ps 71: 3 To which I may *r* continually;

RESORTED (1/1)

Dan 4:36 My counselors and nobles *r* to

RESOUND (1/1)

Isa 16:11 Therefore my heart shall *r* like

RESOUNDING (1/1)

1 Chr 15:16 raising the voice with *r* joy.

RESOURCES (1/1)

Jn 8:44 he speaks from his own *r*,

RESPECT (17/17) RESPECTED, RESPECTS

Gen 4: 5 but He did not *r* Cain and his
Num 16:15 'Do not *r* their offering.
Deut 28:50 which does not *r* the elderly
Ezra 9: 1 with *r* to the abominations of
Ps 40: 4 And does not *r* the proud,
74:20 Have *r* to the covenant;
Isa 17: 7 And his eyes will have *r* for
17: 8 He will not *r* what his fingers
22:11 Nor did you have *r* for Him who
Lam 4:16 The people do not *r* the
Mt 21:37 They will *r* my son.'
Mk 12: 6 They will *r* my son.'
Lk 20:13 Probably they will *r* him when
Acts 5:34 a teacher of the law held in *r*
2 Cor 3:10 glorious had no glory in this *r*,
9: 3 you should be in vain in this *r*,
Heb 12: 9 and we paid them *r*.

RESPECTED (4/4) RESPECT

Gen 4: 4 And the LORD *r* Abel and his
1 Sam 25:35 your voice and *r* your person."
Eccl 10: 1 folly to one *r* for wisdom
Lam 5:12 And elders were not *r*.

RESPECTER (KJV) See PARTIALITY

RESPECTS (1/1) RESPECT

Eph 5:33 see that she *r* her husband.

RESPOND (2/2)

Job 13:22 then You *r* to me.
Prov 29:19 he understands, he will not *r*.

RESPONDED (1/1)

Acts 3:12 he *r* to the people: "Men of

RESPONSE (7/6)

Num 30: 7 and makes no *r* to her on the
30:11 and made no *r* to her and did
30:14 her husband makes no *r* whatever
30:14 because he made no *r* to her on
Ps 38:14 And in whose mouth is no *r*.
Mk 11:14 In *r* Jesus said to it, "Let no
Rom 11: 4 But what does the divine *r* say

RESPONSIBILITY (4/4)

Judg 19:20 let all your needs be my *r*;
1 Chr 9:27 of God because they had the *r*,
Ezra 10: 4 for this matter is your *r*.
Isa 22:21 I will commit your *r* into his

RESPONSIVELY (1/1)

Ezra 3:11 And they sang *r*, praising and

REST (305/295) RESTED, RESTING, RESTS

Gen 18: 4 and *r* yourselves under the
30:36 and Jacob fed the *r* of Laban's
49:15 He saw that *r* was good,
Ex 5: 5 and you make them *r* from their
16:23 'Tomorrow is a Sabbath *r*,
23:11 year you shall let it *r* and
23:12 on the seventh day you shall *r*,
23:12 your ox and your donkey may *r*,
31:15 seventh is the Sabbath of *r*,
33:14 and I will give you *r*."
34:21 on the seventh day you shall *r*;
34:21 time and in harvest you shall *r*.
35: 2 a Sabbath of *r* to the LORD.
Lev 2: 3 The *r* of the grain offering
5: 9 and the *r* of the blood shall be
5:13 The *r* shall be the priest's
14:17 And of the *r* of the oil in his
14:18 The *r* of the oil that is in the
14:29 The *r* of the oil that is in the
16:31 It is a sabbath of solemn *r* for
23: 3 day is a Sabbath of solemn *r*,
23:32 to you a sabbath of solemn *r*,
25: 4 shall be a sabbath of solemn *r*
25: 5 for it is a year of *r* for the
26:34 then the land shall *r* and enjoy
26:35 as it lies desolate it shall *r*—
26:35 for the time it did not *r* on
Num 18:30 then the *r* shall be accounted
31: 8 kings of Midian with the *r*
Deut 3:13 The *r* of Gilead, and all Bashan,
3:20 until the LORD has given *r* to
5:14 and your female servant may *r*
12: 9 yet you have not come to the *r*
12:10 and He gives you *r* from all
25:19 LORD your God has given you *r*
28:54 and toward the *r* of his
28:65 nations you shall find no *r*,
31:16 you will *r* with your fathers;
Josh 1:13 LORD your God is giving you *r*
1:15 LORD has given your brethren *r*,
3:13 shall *r* in the waters of the
13:27 the *r* of the kingdom of Sihon
14:15 Then the land had *r* from war.
17: 2 there was a lot for the *r* of
17: 6 and the *r* of Manasseh's sons
21: 5 The *r* of the children of Kohath
21:20 the *r* of the children of
21:26 common-lands were for the *r* of
21:34 the *r* of the Levites, from the
21:40 the *r* of the families of the
21:44 The LORD gave them *r* all
22: 4 the LORD your God has given *r*
23: 1 after the LORD had given *r* to
Judg 3:11 So the land had *r* for forty
3:30 And the land had *r* for eighty
5:31 So the land had *r* for forty
7: 6 but all the *r* of the people got
7: 8 And he sent away all the *r*
Ruth 1: 9 LORD grant that you may find *r*,
3:18 for the man will not *r* until he
1 Sam 13: 2 The *r* of the people he sent
15:15 and the *r* we have utterly
2 Sam 3:29 Let it *r* on the head of Joab and
7: 1 and the LORD had given him *r*
7:11 and have caused you to *r* from
7:12 days are fulfilled and you *r*
10:10 And the *r* of the people he put
12:28 gather the *r* of the people
21:10 the birds of the air to *r* on
1 Ki 5: 4 LORD my God has given me *r* on
8:56 who has given *r* to His people
11:41 Now the *r* of the acts of
12:23 and to the *r* of the people,
14:19 Now the *r* of the acts of
14:29 Now the *r* of the acts of
15: 7 Now the *r* of the acts of Abijam,
15:23 The *r* of all the acts of Asa,
15:31 Now the *r* of the acts of Nadab,
16: 5 Now the *r* of the acts of
16:14 Now the *r* of the acts of Elah,
16:20 Now the *r* of the acts of Zimri,
16:27 Now the *r* of the acts of Omri
20:30 But the *r* fled to Aphek, into
22:39 Now the *r* of the acts of Ahab,
22:45 Now the *r* of the acts of
22:46 And the *r* of the perverted
2 Ki 1:18 Now the *r* of the acts of Ahaziah
4: 7 and your sons live on the *r*.
8:23 Now the *r* of the acts of Joram,
10:34 Now the *r* of the acts of Jehu,
12:19 Now the *r* of the acts of Joash,
13: 8 Now the *r* of the acts of
13:12 Now the *r* of the acts of Joash,
14:15 Now the *r* of the acts of
14:18 Now the *r* of the acts of
14:28 Now the *r* of the acts of
15: 6 Now the *r* of the acts of
15:11 Now the *r* of the acts of
15:15 Now the *r* of the acts of
15:21 Now the *r* of the acts of
15:26 Now the *r* of the acts of
15:31 Now the *r* of the acts of Pekah,
15:36 Now the *r* of the acts of
16:19 Now the *r* of the acts of Ahaz
20:20 Now the *r* of the acts of
21:17 Now the *r* of the acts of
21:25 Now the *r* of the acts of Amon
23:28 Now the *r* of the acts of
24: 5 Now the *r* of the acts of
25:11 carried away captive the *r* of
25:11 with the *r* of the multitude.
1 Chr 4:43 And they defeated the *r* of the
6:31 LORD, after the ark came to *r*.
6:61 To the *r* of the family of the
6:70 for the *r* of the family of the
6:77 the tribe of Zebulun the *r* of
11: 8 Joab repaired the *r* of the
12:38 and all the *r* of Israel were
16:41 Heman and Jeduthun and the *r*
19:11 And the *r* of the people he put
22: 9 to you, who shall be a man of *r*;
22: 9 and I will give him *r* from all
22:18 And has He not given you *r* on
23:25 God of Israel has given *r* to
24:20 And the *r* of the sons of Levi:
28: 2 my heart to build a house of *r*
2 Chr 9:29 Now the *r* of the acts of
13:22 Now the *r* of the acts of Abijah,
14: 6 in Judah, for the land had *r*;
14: 6 the LORD had given him *r*.
14: 7 and He has given us *r* on every
14:11 for we *r* on You, and in Your
15:15 and the LORD gave them *r* all
20:30 for his God gave him *r* all
20:34 Now the *r* of the acts of
24:14 they brought the *r* of the money
25:26 Now the *r* of the acts of
26:22 Now the *r* of the acts of
27: 7 Now the *r* of the acts of
28:26 Now the *r* of his acts and all
32:32 Now the *r* of the acts of
33:18 Now the *r* of the acts of
35:26 Now the *r* of the acts of Josiah
36: 8 Now the *r* of the acts of
Ezra 3: 8 and the *r* of their brethren the
4: 3 and Jeshua and the *r* of the
4: 7 and the *r* of their companions
4: 9 the scribe, and the *r* of their
4:10 and the *r* of the nations whom
4:17 to the *r* of their companions
6:16 and the Levites and the *r* of
7:18 your brethren to do with the *r*
Neh 4:14 and to the *r* of the people,
4:19 and the *r* of the people,
6: 1 and the *r* of our enemies heard
6:14 prophetess Noadiah and the *r*
7:72 And that which the *r* of the
9:28 "But after they had *r*,
10:28 Now the *r* of the people—the
11: 1 the *r* of the people cast lots
11:20 And the *r* of Israel, of the
Esth 9:12 What have they done in the *r* of
9:16 had *r* from their enemies,
9:22 days on which the Jews had *r*
Job 3:13 Then I would have been at *r*
3:17 And there the weary are at *r*.
3:18 There the prisoners *r*
3:26 nor am I quiet; I have no *r*,
11:18 and take your *r* in safety.
14: 6 away from him that he may *r*,
17:16 Shall we have *r* together in
30:17 And my gnawing pains take no *r*.
30:27 is in turmoil and cannot *r*;
Ps 16: 9 My flesh also will *r* in hope.
17:14 And leave the *r* of their
37: 7 *R* in the LORD, and wait
55: 6 I would fly away and be at *r*.
94:13 That You may give him *r* from
95:11 'They shall not enter My *r*.'
116: 7 Return to your *r*,
125: 3 of wickedness shall not *r* On
Prov 21:16 Will *r* in the assembly of the
24:33 folding of the hands to *r*;
29:17 son, and he will give you *r*;
Eccl 2:23 the night his heart takes no *r*.
6: 5 this has more *r* than that man,
Song 1: 7 Where you make it *r* at noon.
Isa 7:19 and all of them will *r* In the
10:19 Then the *r* of the trees of his
11: 2 Spirit of the LORD shall *r*
14: 3 the day the LORD gives you *r*
14: 7 The whole earth is at *r* and
18: 4 said to me, "I will take My *r*,
23:12 There also you will have no *r*.
25:10 the hand of the LORD will *r*,
28:12 'This is the *r* with which
28:12 You may cause the weary to *r*,
30:15 In returning and *r* you shall be
34:14 the night creature shall *r*
34:14 find for herself a place of *r*.
44:17 And the *r* of it he makes into a
44:19 And shall I make the *r* of it
51: 4 And I will make My justice *r*
57: 2 They shall *r* in their beds,
57:20 troubled sea, When it cannot *r*,
62: 1 Jerusalem's sake I will not *r*,
62: 7 And give Him no *r* till He
63:14 of the LORD causes him to *r*,
66: 1 where is the place of My *r*?
Jer 6:16 Then you will find *r* for your
30:10 have *r* and be quiet, And no
31: 2 when I went to give him *r*.
39: 3 with the *r* of the princes of
39: 9 with the *r* of the people who
41:10 carried away captive all the *r*
41:16 took from Mizpah all the *r* of
45: 3 in my sighing, and I find no *r*.
46:27 have *r* and be at ease;
47: 6 *R* and be still!
50:34 That He may give *r* to the
52:15 the *r* of the people who
52:15 and the *r* of the craftsmen.
Lam 1: 3 the nations, She finds no *r*;
2:18 no relief; Give your eyes no *r*.
5: 5 We labor and have no *r*.
Ezek 5:13 and I will cause My fury to *r*
12:23 "I will lay this proverb to *r*,
16:42 So I will lay to *r* My fury
21:17 And I will cause My fury to *r*;
24:13 I have caused My fury to *r*
36: 3 became the possession of the *r*
36: 4 plunder and mockery to the *r*
36: 5 burning jealousy against the *r*
44:30 to cause a blessing to *r* on
45: 8 but they shall give the *r* of
48:18 The *r* of the length, alongside
48:21 The *r* shall belong to the
48:23 As for the *r* of the tribes, from
Dan 2:18 might not perish with the *r* of
4: 4 was at *r* in my house,
7:12 As for the *r* of the beasts, they
12:13 till the end; for you shall *r*,
Am 5: 7 And lay righteousness to *r* in
Mic 2:10 For this is not your *r*;
Nah 3:18 Your nobles *r* in the dust.
Hab 3:16 That I might *r* in the day of
Zech 6: 8 the north country have given *r*
Mt 11:28 laden, and I will give you *r*.
11:29 and you will find *r* for your
12:43 through dry places, seeking *r*,
22: 6 And the *r* seized his servants,
27:49 The *r* said, "Let Him alone;
Mk 6:31 to a deserted place and *r* a
16:13 they went and told it to the *r*,
Lk 8:10 but to the *r* it is given in
10: 6 your peace will *r* on it;
11:24 through dry places, seeking *r*;
12:26 why are you anxious for the *r*?
24: 9 to the eleven and to all the *r*.
Jn 11:13 He was speaking about taking *r*
Acts 2:26 my flesh also will *r* in
2:37 and said to Peter and the *r* of
5:13 Yet none of the *r* dared join
7:49 is the place of My *r*?
15:17 So that the *r* of mankind
17: 9 security from Jason and the *r*,
27:44 and the *r*, some on boards and
28: 9 the *r* of those on the island
Rom 2:17 and *r* on the law, and make your
11: 7 and the *r* were blinded.
1 Cor 7:12 But to the *r* I, not the Lord,
11:34 And the *r* I will set in order
2 Cor 2:13 I had no *r* in my spirit, because
7: 5 Macedonia, our bodies had no *r*,
12: 9 that the power of Christ may *r*
13: 2 sinned before, and to all the *r*,
Gal 2:13 And the *r* of the Jews also
Eph 4:17 should no longer walk as the *r*
Phil 1:13 palace guard, and to all the *r*,
4: 3 and the *r* of my fellow workers,
2 Th 1: 7 to give you who are troubled *r*
1 Tim 5:20 that the *r* also may fear.
Heb 3:11 shall not enter My *r*.'
3:18 that they would not enter His *r*,
4: 1 remains of entering His *r*,
4: 3 have believed do enter that *r*,
4: 3 shall not enter My *r*,'
4: 5 shall not enter My *r*.'
4: 8 For if Joshua had given them *r*,
4: 9 There remains therefore a *r* for
4:10 For he who has entered His *r* has
4:11 be diligent to enter that *r*,
1 Pe 1:13 and *r* your hope fully upon the
4: 2 he no longer should live the *r*
2 Pe 3:16 as they do also the *r* of the
Rev 2:24 and to the *r* in Thyatira,
4: 8 And they do not *r* day or night,
6:11 to them that they should *r* a
9:20 But the *r* of mankind, who were
11:13 and the *r* were afraid and gave
12:17 he went to make war with the *r*
14:11 and they have no *r* day or
14:13 that they may *r* from their
19:21 And the *r* were killed with the
20: 5 But the *r* of the dead did not

RESTED (55/55) REST

Gen 2: 2 and He *r* on the seventh day

R

2: 3 because in it He *r* from all His
8: 4 Then the ark *r* in the seventh
Ex 10:14 all the land of Egypt and *r* on
16:30 So the people *r* on the seventh
20:11 and *r* the seventh day.
24:16 Now the glory of the LORD *r* on
31:17 and on the seventh day He *r* and
40:35 because the cloud *r* above it,
Num 10:36 And when it *r*, he said:
11:25 when the Spirit *r* upon them,
11:26 And the Spirit *r* upon them.
Josh 11:23 Then the land *r* from war.
Ruth 2: 7 though she *r* a little in the
1 Ki 2:10 So David *r* with his fathers,
11:21 that David *r* with his fathers,
11:43 Then Solomon *r* with his fathers,
14:20 So he *r* with his fathers.
14:31 So Rehoboam *r* with his fathers,
15: 8 So Abijam *r* with his fathers,
15:24 So Asa *r* with his fathers,
16: 6 So Baasha *r* with his fathers and
16:28 So Omri *r* with his fathers and
22:40 So Ahab *r* with his fathers.
22:50 And Jehoshaphat *r* with his
2 Ki 8:24 So Joram *r* with his fathers,
10:35 So Jehu *r* with his fathers,
13: 9 So Jehoahaz *r* with his fathers,
13:13 So Joash *r* with his fathers.
14:16 So Jehoash *r* with his fathers,
14:22 after the king *r* with his
14:29 So Jeroboam *r* with his fathers,
15: 7 So Azariah *r* with his fathers,
15:22 So Menahem *r* with his fathers.
15:38 So Jotham *r* with his fathers,
16:20 So Ahaz *r* with his fathers,
20:21 So Hezekiah *r* with his fathers.
21:18 So Manasseh *r* with his fathers,
24: 6 So Jehoiakim *r* with his fathers.
2 Chr 9:31 Then Solomon *r* with his fathers,
12:16 So Rehoboam *r* with his fathers,
14: 1 So Abijah *r* with his fathers,
16:13 So Asa *r* with his fathers;
21: 1 And Jehoshaphat *r* with his
26: 2 after the king *r* with his
26:23 So Uzziah *r* with his fathers,
27: 9 So Jotham *r* with his fathers,
28:27 So Ahaz *r* with his fathers,
32:33 So Hezekiah *r* with his fathers,
33:20 So Manasseh *r* with his fathers,
Esth 9:17 day of the month they *r* and
9:18 fifteenth of the month they *r*,
Ezek 41: 6 they *r* on ledges which were
Lk 23:56 And they *r* on the Sabbath
Heb 4: 4 And God *r* on the seventh

RESTING (16/16) REST

Gen 8: 9 But the dove found no *r* place
Num 10:33 to search out a *r* place for
Deut 28:65 your foot have a *r* place;
2 Chr 6:41 to Your *r* place, You and the
Job 16:18 let my cry have no *r* place!
Ps 132: 8 to Your *r* place, You and the
132:14 This is My *r* place forever;
Prov 24:15 Do not plunder his *r* place;
Isa 11:10 And His *r* place shall be
32:18 and in quiet *r* places,
Jer 50: 6 have forgotten their *r* place.
Ezek 25: 5 for camels and Ammon a *r* place
Zech 1:11 all the earth is *r* quietly."
9: 1 And Damascus its *r* place
Mt 26:45 "Are you still sleeping and *r*?
Mk 14:41 "Are you still sleeping and *r*?

RESTITUTION (8/7)

Ex 22: 3 He should make full *r*;
22: 5 he shall make *r* from the best
22: 6 the fire shall surely make *r*.
22:12 he shall make *r* to the owner of
Lev 5:16 And he shall make *r* for the harm
Num 5: 7 He shall make *r* for his
5: 8 relative to whom *r* may be made
5: 8 the *r* for the wrong must go

RESTLESS (3/3)

Gen 27:40 come to pass, when you become *r*,
Ps 55: 2 I am *r* in my complaint,
Joel 1:18 The herds of cattle are *r*,

RESTORATION (1/1) RESTORE

Acts 3:21 receive until the times of *r*

RESTORE (56/55) RESTORATION, RESTORED, RESTORER, RESTORES

Gen 20: 7 *r* the man's wife; for he is a
20: 7 But if you do not *r* her,
40:13 lift up your head and *r* you
42:25 to *r* every man's money to his
Ex 22: 1 he shall *r* five oxen for an ox
22: 4 he shall *r* double.
Lev 6: 4 that he shall *r* what he has
6: 5 He shall *r* its full value,
22:14 then he shall *r* a holy
24:21 kills an animal shall *r* it;
25:27 and *r* the remainder to the man
Deut 22: 2 then you shall *r* it to him.
Judg 11:13 *r* those lands peaceably."
1 Sam 12: 3 I will *r* it to you."
2 Sam 9: 7 and will *r* to you all the land
12: 6 And he shall *r* fourfold for the
16: 3 the house of Israel will *r* the
1 Ki 12:21 that he might *r* the kingdom to
20:34 took from your father I will *r*;
2 Ki 8: 6 *R* all that was hers, and all
2 Chr 11: 1 that he might *r* the kingdom to
24:12 iron and bronze to *r* the house
34:10 to repair and *r* the house.
Neh 5:11 *R* now to them, even this day,
5:12 We will *r* it, and will require
Job 20:10 And his hands will *r* his
20:18 He will *r* that for which he
Ps 51:12 *R* to me the joy of Your
60: 1 Oh, *r* us again!
69: 4 I still must *r* it.
80: 3 *R* us, O God; Cause Your face
80: 7 *R* us, O God of hosts
80:19 *R* us, O LORD God of hosts
85: 4 *R* us, O God of our salvation,
Prov 6:31 he must *r* sevenfold;
Isa 1:26 I will *r* your judges as at the
38:16 So You will *r* me and make me
42:22 no one says, "*R*!"
49: 6 And to *r* the preserved ones of
49: 8 To *r* the earth, To cause them
57:18 And *r* comforts to him And to
Jer 27:22 bring them up and *r* them
30:17 For I will *r* health to you
31:18 *R* me, and I will return,
Lam 1:11 valuables for food to *r* life.
1:16 who should *r* my life,
1:19 sought food To *r* their life.
Dan 9:25 forth of the command To *r* and
Joel 2:25 So I will *r* to you the years
Nah 2: 2 For the LORD will *r* the
Zeph 3: 9 For then I will *r* to the peoples
Zech 9:12 That I will *r* double to you.
Mt 17:11 is coming first and will *r* all
Lk 19: 8 accusation, I *r* fourfold."
Acts 1: 6 will You at this time *r* the
Gal 6: 1 you who are spiritual *r* such a

RESTORED (33/30) RESTORE

Gen 20:14 and he *r* Sarah his wife to him.
40:21 Then he *r* the chief butler to
41:13 He *r* me to my office, and he
42:28 brothers, "My money has been *r*,
Ex 4: 7 it was *r* like his other flesh.
Lev 25:28 able to have it *r* to himself,
Deut 28:31 and shall not be *r* to you;
1 Sam 7:14 had taken from Israel were *r*
1 Ki 13: 6 that my hand may be *r* to me."
13: 6 and the king's hand was *r* to
2 Ki 5:10 and your flesh shall be *r* to
5:14 and his flesh was *r* like the
8: 1 to the woman whose son he had *r*
8: 5 the king how he had *r* the dead
8: 5 the woman whose son he had *r*
8: 5 this is her son whom Elisha *r*
14:22 He built Elath and *r* it to
14:25 He *r* the territory of Israel
2 Chr 15: 8 and he *r* the altar of the LORD
24:13 they *r* the house of God to its
26: 2 He built Elath and *r* it to
Ezra 6: 5 be *r* and taken back to the
Neh 4: 7 of Jerusalem were being *r* and
Job 42:10 And the LORD *r* Job's losses
Lam 5:21 You, O LORD, and we will be *r*;
Ezek 18: 7 But has *r* to the debtor his
18:12 Not *r* the pledge,
Dan 4:36 I was *r* to my kingdom, and
Mt 12:13 and it was *r* as whole as the
Mk 3: 5 and his hand was *r* as whole as
8:25 And he was *r* and saw everyone
Lk 6:10 and his hand was *r* as whole as
Heb 13:19 that I may be *r* to you the

RESTORER (2/2) RESTORE

Ruth 4:15 And may he be to you a *r* of life
Isa 58:12 The *R* of Streets to Dwell In.

RESTORES (4/4) RESTORE

Job 33:26 For He *r* to man His
Ps 23: 3 He *r* my soul; He leads me in
Ezek 33:15 if the wicked *r* the pledge,
Mk 9:12 coming first and *r* all things.

RESTRAIN (15/15) RESTRAINED, RESTRAINING, RESTRAINS, RESTRAINT

Gen 45: 1 Then Joseph could not *r* himself
Ruth 1:13 Would you *r* yourselves from
1 Sam 3:13 and he did not *r* them.
2 Sam 24:16 is enough; now *r* your hand."
1 Chr 21:15 now *r* your hand." And the
Job 7:11 Therefore I will not *r* my
15: 4 And *r* prayer before God.
37: 4 And He does not *r* them when
Ps 39: 1 I will *r* my mouth with a
40: 9 I do not *r* my lips, O LORD,
Isa 48: 9 And for My praise I will *r* it
64:12 Will You *r* Yourself because of
Ezek 4: 8 And surely I will *r* you so that
Dan 4:35 No one can *r* His hand Or say
Acts 14:18 they could scarcely *r* the

RESTRAINED (14/14) RESTRAIN

Gen 8: 2 and the rain from heaven was *r*.
16: 2 the LORD has *r* me from bearing
43:31 and he *r* himself, and said,
Ex 32:25 (for Aaron had not *r* them,
36: 6 And the people were *r* from
1 Sam 24: 7 So David *r* his servants with
Esth 5:10 Nevertheless Haman *r* himself and
Ps 119:101 I have *r* my feet from every
Isa 42:14 have been still and *r* Myself.
63:15 mercies toward me? Are they *r*?
Jer 14:10 They have not *r* their feet.
Ezek 31:15 I *r* its rivers, and the great
Lk 24:16 But their eyes were *r*,
2 Pe 2:16 speaking with a man's voice *r*

RESTRAINING (1/1) RESTRAIN

2 Th 2: 6 And now you know what is *r*,

RESTRAINS (5/4) RESTRAIN

1 Sam 14: 6 For nothing *r* the LORD from
Prov 10:19 But he who *r* his lips is
27:16 Whoever *r* her restrains the
27:16 Whoever restrains her *r* the
2 Th 2: 7 only He who now *r* will do so

RESTRAINT (4/4) RESTRAIN

Job 30:11 They have cast off *r* before
36:16 place where there is no *r*;
Prov 29:18 the people cast off *r*;
Hos 4: 2 adultery, They break all *r*,

RESTRICTED (3/2)

Mic 2: 7 "Is the Spirit of the LORD *r*?
2 Cor 6:12 You are not *r* by us, but you are
6:12 but you are *r* by your own

RESTS (5/5) REST

1 Ki 1:21 when my lord the king *r* with
2 Ki 2:15 The spirit of Elijah *r* on
Prov 14:33 Wisdom *r* in the heart of him
Eccl 7: 9 For anger *r* in the bosom of
1 Pe 4:14 Spirit of glory and of God *r*

RESULT (1/1)

Ezra 4:16 the *r* will be that you will

RESULTED (2/1) RESULTING

Rom 5:16 came from one offense *r* in
5:16 came from many offenses *r* in

RESULTING (2/1) RESULTED

Rom 5:18 *r* in condemnation, even so
5:18 *r* in justification of life.

RESURRECTION (41/40)

Mt 22:23 who say there is no *r*,
22:28 "Therefore, in the *r*,
22:30 For in the *r* they neither marry
22:31 But concerning the *r* of the
27:53 out of the graves after His *r*,
Mk 12:18 who say there is no *r*,
12:23 "Therefore, in the *r*,
Lk 14:14 you shall be repaid at the *r*
20:27 who deny that there is a *r*,
20:33 "Therefore, in the *r*,
20:35 and the *r* from the dead,
20:36 of God, being sons of the *r*.
Jn 5:29 to the *r* of life, and those who
5:29 to the *r* of condemnation.
11:24 he will rise again in the *r* at
11:25 'I am the *r* and the life.
Acts 1:22 a witness with us of His *r*.
2:31 spoke concerning the *r* of the
4: 2 and preached in Jesus the *r*
4:33 apostles gave witness to the *r*
17:18 to them Jesus and the *r*.
17:32 And when they heard of the *r* of
23: 6 concerning the hope and *r* of
23: 8 say that there is no *r*—
24:15 that there will be a *r* of the
24:21 Concerning the *r* of the dead I
Rom 1: 4 by the *r* from the dead.
6: 5 be in the likeness of His *r*,
1 Cor 15:12 you say that there is no *r* of
15:13 But if there is no *r* of the
15:21 by Man also came the *r* of the
15:42 So also is the *r* of the dead.
Phil 3:10 know Him and the power of His *r*,
3:11 I may attain to the *r* from the
2 Tim 2:18 saying that the *r* is already
Heb 6: 2 of *r* of the dead, and of
11:35 they might obtain a better *r*.
1 Pe 1: 3 to a living hope through the *r*
3:21 through the *r* of Jesus Christ,
Rev 20: 5 This is the first *r*.
20: 6 he who has part in the first *r*.

RETAIN (9/9) RETAINED

Prov 3:18 And happy are all who *r* her.
4: 4 'Let your heart *r* my words;
11:16 But ruthless men *r* riches.
29:23 the humble in spirit will *r*

Eccl 8: 8 has power over the spirit to **r**
Dan 11: 6 but she shall not **r** the power
Mic 7:18 He does not **r** His anger
Jn 20:23 if you **r** the sins of any, they
Rom 1:28 even as they did not like to **r**

RETAINED (4/4) RETAIN

Judg 7: 8 and **r** those three hundred men.
Dan 10: 8 and I **r** no strength.
10:16 and I have **r** no strength.
Jn 20:23 the sins of any, they are **r**.

RETAINS (1/1)

Prov 11:16 A gracious woman **r** honor,

RETALIATE (2/1)

Joel 3: 4 Will you **r** against Me?
3: 4 But if you **r** against Me,

RETALIATION (2/2)

Joel 3: 4 speedily I will return your **r**
3: 7 And will return your **r** upon

RETINUE (2/2)

1 Ki 10: 2 Jerusalem with a very great **r**,
2 Chr 9: 1 having a very great **r**,

RETREAT (1/1)

2 Sam 11:15 and **r** from him, that he may be

RETREATED (1/1)

2 Sam 23: 9 and the men of Israel had **r**.

RETRIBUTION (1/1)

2 Chr 6:23 bringing **r** on the wicked by

RETURN (282/258) RETURNED, RETURNING, RETURNS

Gen 3:19 shall eat bread Till you **r** to
3:19 And to dust you shall **r**."
8:12 which did not **r** again to him
14:17 after his **r** from the defeat of
15:16 fourth generation they shall **r**
16: 9 **R** to your mistress, and submit
18:10 I will certainly **r** to you
18:14 At the appointed time I will **r**
31: 3 **R** to the land of your fathers
31:13 and **r** to the land of your
32: 9 **R** to your country and to your
Ex 4:18 Please let me go and **r** to my
4:19 **r** to Egypt; for all the men who
13:17 and **r** to Egypt."
22:26 you shall **r** it to him before
33:11 And he would **r** to the camp,
Lev 25:10 and each of you shall **r** to his
25:10 and each of you shall **r** to his
25:13 each of you shall **r** to his
25:27 that he may **r** to his
25:28 and he shall **r** to his
25:41 and shall **r** to his own family.
25:41 He shall **r** to the possession of
27:24 of Jubilee the field shall **r**
Num 10:36 when it rested, he said: "**R**,
14: 3 it not be better for us to **r**
14: 4 Let us select a leader and **r** to
18:21 Israel as an inheritance in **r**
23: 5 **R** to Balak, and thus you shall
32:18 We will not **r** to our homes until
32:22 then afterward you may **r** and be
35:25 and the congregation shall **r**
35:28 priest the manslayer may **r** to
35:32 that he may **r** to dwell in the
Deut 3:20 Then each of you may **r** to his
5:30 **R** to your tents.'
17:16 nor cause the people to **r** to
17:16 You shall not **r** that way again.'
20: 5 Let him go and **r** to his house,
20: 6 Let him go and **r** to his house,
20: 7 Let him go and **r** to his house,
20: 8 Let him go and **r** to his house,
24:13 You shall in any case **r** the
30: 2 and you **r** to the LORD your God
Josh 1:15 Then you shall **r** to the land of
20: 6 Then the slayer may **r** and come
22: 4 **r** and go to your tents and to
22: 8 **R** with much riches to your
Judg 11:31 when I **r** in peace from the
17: 3 I will **r** it to you."
Ruth 1: 6 that she might **r** from the
1: 7 and they went on the way to **r**
1: 8 **r** each to her mother's house.
1:10 Surely we will **r** with you to
1:15 **r** after your sister-in-law."
1 Sam 6: 3 but by all means **r** it to Him
6: 4 offering which we shall **r** to
7: 3 If you **r** to the LORD with all
9: 5 was with him, "Come, let us **r**,
15:25 and **r** with me, that I may
15:26 I will not **r** with you, for you
15:30 and **r** with me, that I may
26:21 'I have sinned. **R**, my son
29: 4 to him, "Make this fellow **r**,
29: 7 Therefore **r** now, and go in
29:11 to **r** to the land of the
2 Sam 1:22 the sword of Saul did not **r**
2:26 until you tell the people to **r**
3:16 **r**!" And he returned.
10: 5 beards have grown, and then **r**.
12:23 but he shall not **r** to me."
14:24 'Let him **r** to his own house,
15:19 **R** and remain with the king.
15:20 **R**, and take your brethren back.
15:27 **R** to the city in peace,
15:34 'But if you **r** to the city,
17: 3 When all **r** except the man whom
19:14 this word to the king: "**R**,
1 Ki 2:32 So the LORD will **r** his blood on
2:33 Their blood shall therefore **r**
2:44 therefore the LORD will **r** your
8:48 and when they **r** to You with all
12:24 Let every man **r** to his house,
12:26 Now the kingdom may **r** to the
13: 9 nor **r** by the same way you
13:10 went another way and did not **r**
13:16 I cannot **r** with you nor go in
13:17 nor **r** by going the way you
19:15 **r** on your way to the Wilderness
22:17 Let each **r** to his house in
22:26 and **r** him to Amon the governor
22:28 'If you ever **r** in peace,
2 Ki 1: 6 **r** to the king who sent you,
19: 7 he shall hear a rumor and **r** to
19:33 By the same shall he **r**;
20: 5 **R** and tell Hezekiah the leader
1 Chr 19: 5 beards have grown, and then **r**.
2 Chr 6:24 and **r** and confess Your name,
6:38 and when they **r** to You with all
11: 4 your brethren! Let every man **r**
18:16 Let each **r** to his house in
18:25 and **r** him to Amon the governor
18:26 water of affliction until I **r**
18:27 'If you ever **r** in peace,
28:11 and **r** the captives, whom you
30: 6 **r** to the LORD God of Abraham,
30: 6 then He will **r** to the remnant
30: 9 'For if you **r** to the LORD,
30: 9 His face from you if you **r** to
Neh 1: 9 but if you **r** to Me, and keep My
2: 6 And when will you **r**?"
7: 5 who had come up in the first **r**,
9:17 They appointed a leader To **r**
Esth 9:25 against the Jews should **r** on
Job 1:21 And naked shall I **r** there.
7:10 He shall never **r** to his house,
10:21 from which I shall not **r**,
15:22 does not believe that he will **r**
16:22 I shall go the way of no **r**.
22:23 If you **r** to the Almighty, you
33:25 He shall **r** to the days of his
34:15 And man would **r** to dust.
39: 4 They depart and do not **r** to
Ps 6: 4 **R**, O LORD, deliver me!
7: 7 sakes, therefore, **r** on high.
7:16 His trouble shall **r** upon his
35:13 And my prayer would **r** to my
59: 6 At evening they **r**,
59:14 And at evening they **r**,
73:10 Therefore his people **r** here,
74:21 do not let the oppressed **r**
79:12 And **r** to our neighbors
80:14 **R**, we beseech You, O God
90: 3 to destruction, And say, "**R**,
90:13 **R**, O LORD! How long?
94:15 But judgment will **r** to
104: 9 That they may not **r** to cover
104:29 they die and **r** to their dust.
109: 4 In **r** for my love they are my
116: 7 **R** to your rest, O my soul,
Prov 2:19 None who go to her **r**,
Eccl 1: 7 There they **r** again.
3:20 and all **r** to dust.
5:15 mother's womb, naked shall he **r**,
12: 2 And the clouds do not **r** after
12: 7 Then the dust will **r** to the
12: 7 And the spirit will **r** to God
Song 6:13 **R**, return, O Shulamite;
6:13 Return, **r**, O Shulamite;
6:13 return, O Shulamite; **R**,
6:13 return, O Shulamite; Return, **r**,
Isa 6:10 And **r** and be healed."
6:13 And will **r** and be for
10:21 The remnant will **r**,
10:22 A remnant of them will **r**;
19:22 they will **r** to the LORD, and
21:12 **R**! Come back!"
23:17 She will **r** to her hire, and
31: 6 **R** to Him against whom the
35:10 ransomed of the LORD shall **r**,
37: 7 he shall hear a rumor and **r** to
37:34 By the same shall he **r**;
44:22 **R** to Me, for I have redeemed
45:23 righteousness, And shall not **r**,
51:11 ransomed of the LORD shall **r**,
55: 7 Let him **r** to the LORD,
55:10 And do not **r** there,
55:11 It shall not **r** to Me void,
63:17 **R** for Your servants' sake,
Jer 3: 1 May he **r** to her again?'
3: 1 Yet **r** to Me," says the LORD.
3: 7 **R** to Me.' But she did not
3: 7 to Me.' But she did not **r**.
3:12 toward the north, and say: '**R**,
3:14 '**R**, O backsliding
3:22 '**R**, you backsliding
4: 1 'If you will **r**, O Israel,"
4: 1 **R** to Me; And if you will put
5: 3 They have refused to **r**.
8: 4 Will one turn away and not **r**?
8: 5 to deceit, They refuse to **r**.
12:15 that I will **r** and have
15: 7 Since they do not **r** from
15:19 says the LORD: "If you **r**,
15:19 Let them **r** to you, But you
15:19 But you must not **r** to them.
18:11 **R** now every one from his evil
22:10 For he shall **r** no more,
22:11 He shall not **r** here anymore,
22:27 land to which they desire to **r**,
22:27 return, there they shall not **r**.
24: 7 for they shall **r** to Me with
29:10 and cause you to **r** to this
30: 3 And I will cause them to **r** to
30:10 Jacob shall **r**, have rest and
30:24 anger of the LORD will not **r**
31: 8 A great throng shall **r** there.
31:18 Restore me, and I will **r**,
32:44 will cause their captives to **r**,
33: 7 and the captives of Israel to **r**,
33:11 the captives of the land to **r**
33:26 will cause their captives to **r**,
34:11 the male and female slaves **r**,
34:22 and cause them to **r** to this
37: 7 come up to help you will **r** to
37:20 and do not make me **r** to the
38:26 that he would not make me **r** to
42:12 on you and cause you to **r** to
44:14 lest they **r** to the land of
44:14 to which they desire to **r** and
44:14 For none shall **r** except those
44:28 the sword shall **r** from the land
46:27 their captivity; Jacob shall **r**,
50: 9 None shall **r** in vain.
Ezek 7:13 For the seller shall not **r** to
16:55 **r** to their former state, and
16:55 Samaria and her daughters **r** to
16:55 you and your daughters will **r**
21: 5 it shall not **r** anymore." '
21:30 '**R** it to its sheath.
29:14 of Egypt and cause them to **r** to
46: 9 He shall not **r** by way of the
46:17 after which it shall **r** to the
Dan 10:20 And now I must **r** to fight with
11: 9 but shall **r** to his own land.
11:10 then he shall **r** to his fortress
11:13 king of the North will **r** and
11:28 so he shall do damage and **r** to
11:29 appointed time he shall **r** and
11:30 and **r** in rage against the holy
11:30 So he shall **r** and show regard
Hos 2: 7 I will go and **r** to my first
2: 9 Therefore I will **r** and take
3: 5 children of Israel shall **r** and
5:15 I will **r** again to My place
6: 1 and let us **r** to the LORD;
6:11 When I **r** the captives of My
7:10 But they do not **r** to the LORD
7:16 They **r**, but not to the Most
8:13 They shall **r** to Egypt.
9: 3 But Ephraim shall **r** to Egypt,
11: 5 He shall not **r** to the land of
12: 6 by the help of your God, **r**;
12:14 And **r** his reproach upon him.
14: 1 **r** to the LORD your God,
14: 2 And **r** to the LORD.
14: 7 dwell under his shadow shall **r**;
Joel 2:13 **R** to the LORD your God,
3: 4 Swiftly and speedily I will **r**
3: 7 And will **r** your retaliation
Ob 15 Your reprisal shall **r** upon
Jon 1:13 the men rowed hard to **r** to
Mic 1: 7 And they shall **r** to the pay of
2: 6 They shall not **r** insult for
5: 3 of His brethren Shall **r** to
Zeph 2: 7 And **r** their captives.
3:20 When I **r** your captives before
Zech 1: 3 **R** to Me," says the LORD of
1: 3 and I will **r** to you," says the
8: 3 I will **r** to Zion, And dwell in
9:12 **R** to the stronghold,
10: 9 children, And they shall **r**.
Mal 1: 4 But we will **r** and build the
3: 7 **R** to Me, and I will return to
3: 7 and I will **r** to you,"
3: 7 'In what way shall we **r**?'
Mt 2:12 dream that they should not **r** to
10:13 let your peace **r** to you.
12:44 I will **r** to my house from which
Lk 6:35 lend, hoping for nothing in **r**;
8:39 **R** to your own house, and tell
10: 6 it will **r** to you.
11:24 I will **r** to my house from which
12:36 when he will **r** from the
19:12 for himself a kingdom and to **r**.
Acts 13:34 no more to **r** to corruption, He
15:16 After this I will **r** And
18:21 but I will **r** again to you, God
20: 3 he decided to **r** through
2 Cor 6:13 Now in **r** for the same (I speak
Heb 11:15 would have had opportunity to **r**.
1 Pe 2:23 reviled, did not revile in **r**;

RETURNED (187/185) RETURN

Gen 8: 9 and she **r** into the ark to him,
18:33 and Abraham **r** to his place.
21:32 and they **r** to the land of the
22:19 So Abraham **r** to his young men,
31:55 Then Laban departed and **r** to

32: 6 Then the messengers ***r*** to Jacob,
33:16 So Esau ***r*** that day on his way to
37:29 Then Reuben ***r*** to the pit, and
37:30 And he ***r*** to his brothers and
38:22 So he ***r*** to Judah and said, "I
42:24 Then he ***r*** to them again, and
43:10 surely by now we would have ***r***
43:12 your hand the money that was ***r***
43:18 which was ***r*** in our sacks the
44:13 man loaded his donkey and ***r*** to
50:14 Joseph ***r*** to Egypt, he and his
Ex 4:18 So Moses went and ***r*** to Jethro
4:20 and he ***r*** to the land of Egypt.
5:22 So Moses ***r*** to the LORD and
14:27 the sea ***r*** to its full depth,
14:28 Then the waters ***r*** and covered
32:31 Then Moses ***r*** to the LORD and
34:31 rulers of the congregation ***r***
Lev 22:13 and has ***r*** to her father's house
Num 11:30 And Moses ***r*** to the camp, both
13:25 And they ***r*** from spying out the
14:36 who ***r*** and made all the
16:50 So Aaron ***r*** to Moses at the door
23: 6 So he ***r*** to him, and there he
24:25 Balaam rose and departed and ***r***
Deut 1:45 Then you ***r*** and wept before the
Josh 2:16 days, until the pursuers have ***r***.
2:22 three days until the pursuers ***r***.
2:23 So the two men ***r***,
4:18 the waters of the Jordan ***r*** to
6:14 around the city once and ***r*** to
7: 3 And they ***r*** to Joshua and said to
8:24 that all the Israelites ***r*** to Ai
10:15 Then Joshua ***r***, and all Israel
10:21 And all the people ***r*** to the
10:38 Then Joshua ***r***, and all
10:43 Then Joshua ***r***, and all Israel
22: 9 half the tribe of Manasseh ***r***,
22:32 ***r*** from the children of Reuben
Judg 7: 3 thousand of the people ***r***,
7:15 He ***r*** to the camp of Israel, and
8:13 Gideon the son of Joash ***r*** from
9:57 of the men of Shechem God ***r*** on
11:39 end of two months that she ***r***
14: 8 when he ***r*** to get her, he turned
15:19 and he drank; and his spirit ***r***,
17: 3 So when he had ***r*** the eleven
17: 4 Thus he ***r*** the silver to his
21:23 Then they went and ***r*** to their
Ruth 1:22 So Naomi ***r***, and Ruth
1:22 who ***r*** from the country of Moab.
1 Sam 1:19 and ***r*** and came to their house
6:16 they ***r*** to Ekron the same day.
6:17 tumors which the Philistines ***r***
7:17 But he always ***r*** to Ramah, for
14:46 Then Saul ***r*** from pursuing the
17:15 David occasionally went and ***r***
17:53 Then the children of Israel ***r***
17:57 as David ***r*** from the slaughter
23:28 Therefore Saul ***r*** from pursuing
24: 1 when Saul had ***r*** from following
25:39 the LORD has ***r*** the wickedness
26:25 and Saul ***r*** to his place.
27: 9 and ***r*** and came to Achish.
2 Sam 1: 1 when David had ***r*** from the
2:30 So Joab ***r*** from pursuing Abner.
3:16 him, "Go, return!" And he ***r***.
3:27 Now when Abner had ***r*** to Hebron,
6:20 Then David ***r*** to bless his
8:13 made himself a name when he ***r***
10:14 So Joab ***r*** from the people of
11: 4 and she ***r*** to her house.
12:31 David and all the people ***r*** to
14:24 So Absalom ***r*** to his own
17:20 they ***r*** to Jerusalem.
18:16 and the people ***r*** from pursuing
19:15 Then the king ***r*** and came to the
19:24 departed until the day he ***r*** in
19:39 and he ***r*** to his own place.
20:22 So Joab ***r*** to the king at
23:10 and the people ***r*** after him only
2 Ki 1: 5 And when the messengers ***r*** to
2:25 and from there he ***r*** to Samaria.
3:27 they departed from him and ***r*** to
4:35 He ***r*** and walked back and forth
4:38 And Elisha ***r*** to Gilgal, and
5:15 And he ***r*** to the man of God, he
7:15 So the messengers ***r*** and told
8: 3 that the woman ***r*** from the land
9:15 But King Joram had ***r*** to Jezreel
14:14 hostages, and ***r*** to Samaria.
19: 8 Then the Rabshakeh ***r*** and found
19:36 ***r*** home, and remained at
23:20 and he ***r*** to Jerusalem.
1 Chr 16:43 and David ***r*** to bless his house.
20: 3 David and all the people ***r*** to
21:27 and he ***r*** his sword to its
2 Chr 10: 2 that Jeroboam ***r*** from Egypt.
14:15 and ***r*** to Jerusalem.
19: 1 the king of Judah ***r*** safely to
19: 8 when they ***r*** to Jerusalem.
20:27 Then they ***r***, every man of
22: 6 Then he ***r*** to Jezreel to recover
24:11 and took it and ***r*** it to its
25:10 and they ***r*** home in great anger.
25:24 and hostages, and ***r*** to Samaria.
28:15 Then they ***r*** to Samaria.
31: 1 all the children of Israel ***r***
32:21 So he ***r*** shamefaced to his own
34: 7 he ***r*** to Jerusalem.
Ezra 2: 1 and who ***r*** to Jerusalem and
5: 5 Then a written answer was ***r***
5:11 And thus they ***r*** us an answer,
6:21 children of Israel who had ***r***
Neh 2:15 by the Valley Gate, and so ***r***.
4:15 that all of us ***r*** to the wall,
7: 6 and who ***r*** to Jerusalem and
8:17 assembly of those who had ***r***
9:28 Yet when they ***r*** and cried out
13: 6 king of Babylon I had ***r*** to the
Esth 2:14 and in the morning she ***r*** to the
4: 9 So Hathach ***r*** and told Esther the
7: 8 When the king ***r*** from the palace
Ps 60: and Joab ***r*** and killed twelve
78:34 And they ***r*** and sought
Eccl 4: 1 Then I ***r*** and considered all the
4: 7 Then I ***r***, and I saw vanity
9:11 I ***r*** and saw under the sun
Isa 37: 8 Then the Rabshakeh ***r***,
37:37 ***r*** home, and remained at
38: 8 So the sun ***r*** ten degrees on
Jer 14: 3 They ***r*** with their vessels
40:12 then all the Jews ***r*** out of all
43: 5 the remnant of Judah who had ***r***
Ezek 8:17 then they have ***r*** to provoke Me
47: 6 Then he brought me and ***r*** me
47: 7 When I ***r***, there, along the bank
Dan 4:34 and my understanding ***r*** to me;
4:36 At the same time my reason ***r*** to
4:36 my honor and splendor ***r*** to me.
Am 4: 6 Yet you have not ***r*** to Me,"
4: 8 Yet you have not ***r*** to Me,"
4: 9 Yet you have not ***r*** to Me,"
4:10 Yet you have not ***r*** to Me,"
4:11 Yet you have not ***r*** to Me,"
Mic 2: 8 Like men ***r*** from war.
Zech 1: 6 So they ***r*** and said: 'Just as
7:14 that no one passed through or ***r***;
Mt 21:18 as He ***r*** to the city, He was
Mk 14:40 And when He ***r***, He found them
Lk 1:56 and ***r*** to her house.
2:20 Then the shepherds ***r***,
2:39 they ***r*** to Galilee, to their
2:43 finished the days, as they ***r***,
2:45 they ***r*** to Jerusalem, seeking
4: 1 ***r*** from the Jordan and was led
4:14 Then Jesus ***r*** in the power of
8:37 And He got into the boat and ***r***.
8:40 So it was, when Jesus ***r***,
8:55 Then her spirit ***r***,
9:10 the apostles, when they had ***r***,
10:17 Then the seventy ***r*** with joy,
17:15 he saw that he was healed, ***r***,
17:18 not any found who ***r*** to give
19:15 "And so it was that when he ***r***,
22:32 and when you have ***r*** to Me,
23:48 done, beat their breasts and ***r***.
23:56 Then they ***r*** and prepared spices
24: 9 Then they ***r*** from the tomb and
24:33 rose up that very hour and ***r***
24:52 and ***r*** to Jerusalem with great
Acts 1:12 Then they ***r*** to Jerusalem from
5:22 they ***r*** and reported,
8:25 they ***r*** to Jerusalem, preaching
12:25 And Barnabas and Saul ***r*** from
13:13 from them, ***r*** to Jerusalem.
14:21 they ***r*** to Lystra, Iconium, and
21: 6 the ship, and they ***r*** home.
22:17 when I ***r*** to Jerusalem and was
23:32 and ***r*** to the barracks.
Gal 1:17 and ***r*** again to Damascus.
1 Pe 2:25 but have now ***r*** to the Shepherd

RETURNING (9/9) RETURN

1 Sam 6: 8 of gold which you are ***r*** to Him
18: 6 when David was ***r*** from the
Isa 30:15 In ***r*** and rest you shall be
Dan 11:28 While ***r*** to his land with great
Zech 1:16 I am ***r*** to Jerusalem with mercy;
Lk 7:10 ***r*** to the house, found the
Acts 8:28 was ***r***. And sitting in his
Heb 7: 1 who met Abraham ***r*** from the
1 Pe 3: 9 not ***r*** evil for evil or reviling

RETURNS (6/6) RETURN

Ps 146: 4 he ***r*** to his earth;
Prov 26:11 As a dog ***r*** to his own vomit,
Ezek 35: 7 who leaves and the one who ***r***.
Zech 9: 8 him who passes by and him who ***r***.
Lk 17: 4 and seven times in a day ***r*** to
2 Pe 2:22 A dog ***r*** to his own

REU (6/6)

Gen 11:18 lived thirty years, and begot ***R***.
11:19 After he begot ***R***,
11:20 ***R*** lived thirty-two years, and
11:21 ***R*** lived two hundred and seven
1 Chr 1:25 Eber, Peleg, ***R***,
Lk 3:35 son of Serug, the son of ***R***,

REUBEN (75/71) REUBENITES

Gen 29:32 son, and she called his name ***R***;
30:14 Now ***R*** went in the days of wheat
35:22 that ***R*** went and lay with Bilhah
35:23 the sons of Leah were ***R***,
37:21 But ***R*** heard it, and he
37:22 And ***R*** said to them, "Shed no
37:29 Then ***R*** returned to the pit, and
42:22 And ***R*** answered them, saying,
42:37 Then ***R*** spoke to his father,
46: 8 ***R*** was Jacob's firstborn.
46: 9 The sons of ***R*** were Hanoch,
48: 5 as ***R*** and Simeon, they shall be
49: 3 '***R***, you are my firstborn,
Ex 1: 2 ***R***, Simeon, Levi, and Judah;
6:14 fathers' houses: The sons of ***R***,
6:14 These are the families of ***R***.
Num 1: 5 shall stand with you: from ***R***,
1:20 Now the children of ***R***,
1:21 were numbered of the tribe of ***R***
2:10 standard of the forces with ***R***
2:10 the leader of the children of ***R***
2:16 armies of the forces with ***R***,
7:30 leader of the children of ***R***,
10:18 the standard of the camp of ***R***
13: 4 names: from the tribe of ***R***,
16: 1 On the son of Peleth, sons of ***R***,
26: 5 ***R*** was the firstborn of Israel
26: 5 The children of ***R*** were:
32: 1 Now the children of ***R*** and the
32: 2 of Gad and the children of ***R***
32: 6 of Gad and to the children of ***R***:
32:25 of Gad and the children of ***R***
32:29 of Gad and the children of ***R***
32:31 of Gad and the children of ***R***
32:33 of Gad, to the children of ***R***,
32:37 And the children of ***R*** built
34:14 the tribe of the children of ***R***
Deut 11: 6 the sons of Eliab, the son of ***R***:
27:13 stand on Mount Ebal to curse: ***R***,
33: 6 Let ***R*** live, and not die,
Josh 4:12 And the men of ***R***,
13:15 the tribe of the children of ***R***
13:23 the border of the children of ***R***
13:23 of the children of ***R*** according
15: 6 the stone of Bohan the son of ***R***.
18: 7 their inheritance. And Gad, ***R***,
18:17 the stone of Bohan the son of ***R***.
20: 8 the plain, from the tribe of ***R***,
21: 7 cities from the tribe of ***R***,
21:36 and from the tribe of ***R***,
22: 9 So the children of ***R***,
22:10 of Canaan, the children of ***R***,
22:11 "Behold, the children of ***R***,
22:13 the priest to the children of ***R***,
22:15 they came to the children of ***R***,
22:21 Then the children of ***R***,
22:25 you children of ***R*** and children
22:30 words that the children of ***R***,
22:31 said to the children of ***R***,
22:32 from the children of ***R*** and the
22:33 land where the children of ***R***
22:34 The children of ***R*** and the
Judg 5:15 Among the divisions of ***R***
5:16 The divisions of ***R*** have great
2 Ki 10:33 all the land of Gilead—Gad, ***R***,
1 Chr 2: 1 were the sons of Israel: ***R***,
5: 1 Now the sons of ***R*** the firstborn
5: 3 the sons of ***R*** the firstborn of
5:18 The sons of ***R***, the Gadites,
6:63 cities from the tribe of ***R***,
6:78 given from the tribe of ***R***:
Ezek 48: 6 the west, one section for ***R***;
48: 7 "by the border of ***R***,
48:31 gates northward: one gate for ***R***,
Rev 7: 5 of the tribe of ***R*** twelve

REUBENITE (1/1)

1 Chr 11:42 Adina the son of Shiza the ***R*** (a

REUBENITES (15/15)

Num 26: 7 are the families of the ***R***:
Deut 3:12 I gave to the ***R*** and the
3:16 And to the ***R*** and the Gadites I
4:43 on the plateau for the ***R***,
29: 8 it as an inheritance to the ***R***,
Josh 1:12 And to the ***R***, the Gadites,
12: 6 it as a possession to the ***R***,
13: 8 the other half tribe the ***R*** and
22: 1 Then Joshua called the ***R***,
1 Chr 5: 6 He was leader of the ***R***.
5:26 of Assyria. He carried the ***R***,
11:42 Reubenite (a chief of the ***R***)
12:37 of the ***R*** and the Gadites and the
26:32 David made officials over the ***R***,
27:16 the officer over the ***R*** was

REUEL (11/10) JETHRO

Gen 36: 4 to Esau, and Basemath bore ***R***.
36:10 and ***R*** the son of Basemath the
36:13 These were the sons of ***R***:
36:17 These were the sons of ***R***,
36:17 These were the chiefs of ***R*** in
Ex 2:18 When they came to ***R*** their
Num 2:14 be Eliasaph the son of ***R***.
10:29 said to Hobab the son of ***R*** the
1 Chr 1:35 sons of Esau were Eliphaz, ***R***,
1:37 The sons of ***R*** were Nahath,
9: 8 son of Shephatiah, the son of ***R***,

REUMAH (1/1)

Gen 22:24 His concubine, whose name was ***R***,

REVEAL (12/12) REVEALED, REVEALS, REVELATION

1 Sam 2:27 Did I not clearly ***r*** Myself to
28:15 that you may ***r*** to me what I

Esth 2:10 had charged her not to **r** it.
Job 20:27 The heavens will **r** his
Jer 33: 6 I will heal them and **r** to them
Dan 2:47 since you could **r** this
Mt 11:27 whom the Son wills to **r** Him.
Lk 10:22 whom the Son wills to **r** Him."
Acts 26:16 things which I will yet **r** to
1 Cor 4: 5 things of darkness and **r** the
Gal 1:16 to **r** His Son in me, that I might
Phil 3:15 God will **r** even this to you.

REVEALED (58/57) REVEAL

Deut 29:29 but those things which are **r**
1 Sam 3: 7 the word of the LORD yet **r** to
3:21 For the LORD **r** Himself to
2 Sam 7:27 have **r** this to Your servant,
1 Chr 17:25 have **r** to Your servant that You
Esth 2:10 Esther had not **r** her people or
2:20 Now Esther had not **r** her family
Job 38:17 the gates of death been **r** to
Ps 98: 2 His righteousness He has **r** in
Prov 26:26 His wickedness will be **r**
Isa 22:14 Then it was **r** in my hearing by
23: 1 the land of Cyprus it is **r** to
40: 5 glory of the LORD shall be **r**,
53: 1 has the arm of the LORD been **r**?
56: 1 And My righteousness to be **r**.
Jer 11:20 For to You I have **r** my cause.
51:10 The LORD has **r** our
Ezek 23:18 She **r** her harlotry and
Dan 2:19 Then the secret was **r** to Daniel
2:30 this secret has not been **r** to
10: 1 king of Persia a message was **r**
Mt 10:26 covered that will not be **r**,
11:25 wise and prudent and have **r**
16:17 flesh and blood has not **r** this
Mk 4:22 hidden which will not be **r**,
Lk 2:26 And it had been **r** to him by the
2:35 of many hearts may be **r**.
8:17 is secret that will not be **r**,
10:21 wise and prudent and **r** them
12: 2 covered that will not be **r**,
17:30 day when the Son of Man is **r**.
Jn 1:31 but that He should be **r** to
9: 3 the works of God should be **r**
12:38 arm of the LORD been **r**?
Acts 23:22 Tell no one that you have **r**
Rom 1:17 the righteousness of God is **r**
1:18 For the wrath of God is **r** from
3:21 of God apart from the law is **r**,
8:18 the glory which shall be **r** in
1 Cor 2:10 But God has **r** them to us
3:13 because it will be **r** by fire;
14:25 the secrets of his heart are **r**;
14:30 But if anything is **r** to another
Gal 3:23 which would afterward be **r**.
Eph 3: 5 as it has now been **r** by the
Col 1:26 but now has been **r** to His
2 Th 1: 7 when the Lord Jesus is **r** from
2: 3 first, and the man of sin is **r**,
2: 6 that he may be **r** in his own
2: 8 then the lawless one will be **r**,
2 Tim 1:10 but has now been **r** by the
1 Pe 1: 5 for salvation ready to be **r** in
1:12 To them it was **r** that, not to
4:13 that when His glory is **r**,
5: 1 of the glory that will be **r**:
1 Jn 3: 2 and it has not yet been **r** what
3: 2 but we know that when He is **r**,
Rev 3:18 of your nakedness may not be **r**;

REVEALER (1/1)

Dan 2:47 and a **r** of secrets, since you

REVEALING (1/1)

Rom 8:19 eagerly waits for the **r** of the

REVEALS (11/10) REVEAL

1 Sam 22: 8 and there is no one who **r** to
22: 8 you who is sorry for me or **r** to
Ps 19: 2 And night unto night **r**
Prov 11:13 A talebearer **r** secrets, But he
20:19 goes about as a talebearer **r**
27:19 So a man's heart **r** the man.
29:24 tell the truth, but **r** nothing.
Dan 2:22 He **r** deep and secret things;
2:28 there is a God in heaven who **r**
2:29 and He who **r** secrets has made
Am 3: 7 Unless He **r** His secret to His

REVELATION (15/15) REVEAL

1 Sam 3: 1 there was no widespread **r**.
Prov 29:18 Where there is no **r**,
Lk 2:32 A light to bring **r** to the
Rom 2: 5 in the day of wrath and **r** of
16:25 according to the **r** of the
1 Cor 1: 7 eagerly waiting for the **r** of
14: 6 I speak to you either by **r**,
14:26 teaching, has a tongue, has a **r**,
Gal 1:12 but it came through the **r** of
2: 2 And I went up by **r**,
Eph 1:17 you the spirit of wisdom and **r**
3: 3 how that by **r** He made known to
1 Pe 1: 7 and glory at the **r** of Jesus
1:13 to be brought to you at the **r**
Rev 1: 1 The **R** of Jesus Christ, which

REVELATIONS (2/2)

2 Cor 12: 1 I will come to visions and **r** of
12: 7 by the abundance of the **r**,

REVELRIES (2/2) REVELRY

Gal 5:21 envy, murders, drunkenness, **r**,
1 Pe 4: 3 lewdness, lusts, drunkenness, **r**,

REVELRY (1/1) REVELRIES

Rom 13:13 not in **r** and drunkenness,

REVENGE (3/3)

Josh 10:13 Till the people had **r** Upon
Judg 15: 7 I will surely take **r** on you,
Jer 20:10 And we will take our **r** on

REVENUE (6/6)

2 Sam 20:24 Adoram was in charge of **r**;
1 Ki 12:18 who was in charge of the **r**;
2 Chr 10:18 who was in charge of **r**;
Prov 8:19 And my **r** than choice silver.
15: 6 But in the **r** of the wicked is
Isa 23: 3 harvest of the River, is her **r**;

REVENUES (1/1)

Prov 16: 8 Than vast **r** without justice.

REVERE (1/1) REVERENCE, REVERENT

Lev 19: 3 Every one of you shall **r** his

REVERENCE (9/9) REVERENT

Lev 19:30 shall keep My Sabbaths and **r**
26: 2 shall keep My Sabbaths and **r**
Job 4: 6 Is not your **r** your confidence?
Ps 89: 7 And to be held in **r** by all
Mal 1: 6 I am a Master, Where is My **r**?
1 Tim 2: 2 life in all godliness and **r**.
3: 4 in submission with all **r**
Titus 2: 7 doctrine showing integrity, **r**,
Heb 12:28 may serve God acceptably with **r**

REVERENT (6/6) REVERENCE

Prov 28:14 is the man who is always **r**,
Mal 2: 5 So he feared Me And was **r**
1 Tim 3: 8 Likewise deacons must be **r**,
3:11 their wives must be **r**,
Titus 2: 2 that the older men be sober, **r**,
2: 3 that they be **r** in behavior, not

REVERSE (2/2)

Num 23:20 and I cannot **r** it.
Isa 43:13 and who will **r** it?"

REVERTED (1/1)

Judg 2:19 that they **r** and behaved more

REVIEW (2/1)

1 Sam 29: 2 of the Philistines passed in **r**
29: 2 David and his men passed in **r**

REVILE (7/7) REVILED, REVILER, REVILERS, REVILING

Ex 22:28 You shall not **r** God, nor curse
2 Chr 32:17 He also wrote letters to **r** the
Mt 5:11 Blessed are you when they **r** and
Lk 6:22 And **r** you, and cast out your
Acts 23: 4 Do you **r** God's high priest?"
1 Pe 2:23 did not **r** in return; when He
3:16 those who **r** your good conduct

REVILED (6/6) REVILE

1 Sam 25:14 our master; and he **r** them.
Mt 27:44 who were crucified with Him **r**
Mk 15:32 who were crucified with Him **r**
Jn 9:28 Then they **r** him and said, "You
1 Cor 4:12 with our own hands. Being **r**,
1 Pe 2:23 who, when He was **r**,

REVILER (1/1) REVILE

1 Cor 5:11 or an idolater, or a **r**,

REVILERS (1/1) REVILE

1 Cor 6:10 covetous, nor drunkards, nor **r**,

REVILES (1/1)

Ps 44:16 of him who reproaches and **r**,

REVILING (5/4) REVILE

1 Tim 6: 4 from which come envy, strife, **r**,
1 Pe 3: 9 returning evil for evil or **r**
3: 9 evil for evil or reviling for **r**,
2 Pe 2:11 do not bring a **r** accusation
Jude 9 dared not bring against him a **r**

REVIVAL (1/1)

Ezra 9: 8 and give us a measure of **r** in

REVIVE (20/19) REVIVAL, REVIVED

Ezra 9: 9 to **r** us, to repair the house of
Neh 4: 2 Will they **r** the stones from the
Ps 71:20 Shall **r** me again, And bring
80:18 **R** us, and we will call upon
85: 6 Will You not **r** us again,
119:25 **R** me according to Your word.
119:37 And **r** me in Your way.
119:40 **R** me in Your righteousness.
119:88 **R** me according to Your
119:107 **R** me, O LORD, according to
119:149 **r** me according to Your justice.
119:154 **R** me according to Your word.
119:156 **R** me according to Your
119:159 **R** me, O LORD, according to
138: 7 You will **r** me; You will
143:11 **R** me, O LORD, for Your name's
Isa 57:15 To **r** the spirit of the humble,
57:15 And to **r** the heart of the
Hos 6: 2 After two days He will **r** us;
Hab 3: 2 **r** Your work in the midst of the

REVIVED (6/6) REVIVE

Gen 45:27 spirit of Jacob their father **r**.
Judg 15:19 his spirit returned, and he **r**.
1 Ki 17:22 came back to him, and he **r**.
2 Ki 13:21 he **r** and stood on his feet.
Hos 14: 7 They shall be **r** like grain,
Rom 7: 9 sin **r** and I died.

REVOKE (2/2)

Esth 8: 5 let it be written to **r** the
8: 8 king's signet ring no one can **r**.

REVOLT (4/4)

2 Ki 8:22 Thus Edom has been in **r** against
2 Chr 21:10 Thus Edom has been in **r** against
Isa 1: 5 You will **r** more and more.
59:13 Speaking oppression and **r**,

REVOLTED (7/7)

2 Ki 8:20 In his days Edom **r** against
8:22 And Libnah **r** at that time.
2 Chr 21: 8 his days the Edomites **r** against
21:10 At that time Libnah **r** against
Ezra 4:19 this city in former times has **r**
Isa 31: 6 of Israel have deeply **r**.
Jer 5:23 They have **r** and departed.

REVOLTERS (1/1)

Hos 5: 2 The **r** are deeply involved in

REWARD (55/54) REWARDED, REWARDER, REWARDS

Gen 15: 1 your exceedingly great **r**.
Num 18:31 for it is your **r** for your work
Ruth 2:12 and a full **r** be given you by
1 Sam 24:19 Therefore may the LORD **r** you
2 Sam 4:10 thought I would give him a **r**
19:36 king repay me with such a **r**?
1 Ki 13: 7 and I will give you a **r**.
Job 15:31 For futility will be his **r**.
34:11 And makes man to find a **r**
Ps 19:11 keeping them there is great **r**.
35:12 They **r** me evil for good,
58:11 Surely there is a **r** for the
91: 8 And see the **r** of the wicked.
109:20 Let this be the LORD's **r** to
127: 3 The fruit of the womb is a **r**.
Prov 11:18 will have a sure **r**.
25:22 And the LORD will **r** you.
Eccl 2:10 And this was my **r** from all my
4: 9 Because they have a good **r** for
9: 5 And they have no more **r**,
Isa 3:11 For the **r** of his hands shall
40:10 His **r** is with Him, And His
45:13 go free, Not for price nor **r**,
49: 4 Yet surely my just **r** is with
62:11 His **r** is with Him, And His
Hos 4: 9 And **r** them for their deeds.
Mt 5:12 for great is your **r** in heaven,
5:46 what **r** have you? Do not even
6: 1 Otherwise you have no **r** from
6: 2 I say to you, they have their **r**.
6: 4 in secret will Himself **r** you
6: 5 I say to you, they have their **r**.
6: 6 who sees in secret will **r** you
6:16 I say to you, they have their **r**.
6:18 who sees in secret will **r** you
10:41 shall receive a prophet's **r**.
10:41 receive a righteous man's **r**.
10:42 he shall by no means lose his **r**.
16:27 and then He will **r** each
Mk 9:41 he will by no means lose his **r**.
Lk 6:23 For indeed your **r** is great
6:35 and your **r** will be great, and
23:41 for we receive the due **r** of our
1 Cor 3: 8 each one will receive his own **r**
3:14 endures, he will receive a **r**.
9:17 I do this willingly, I have a **r**;
9:18 What is my **r** then? That when I
Col 2:18 Let no one cheat you of your **r**,
3:24 Lord you will receive the **r** of
Heb 2: 2 disobedience received a just **r**,
10:35 confidence, which has great **r**.
11:26 for he looked to the **r**.

2 Jn 8 that we may receive a full *r*.
Rev 11:18 And that You should *r* Your
22:12 and My *r* is with Me, to give

REWARDED (8/7) REWARD

1 Sam 24:17 for you have *r* me with good,
24:17 whereas I have *r* you with evil.
2 Sam 22:21 The LORD *r* me according to my
2 Chr 15: 7 for your work shall be *r*!"
Ps 18:20 The LORD *r* me according to my
109: 5 Thus they have *r* me evil for
Prov 13:13 fears the commandment will be *r*.
Jer 31:16 For your work shall be *r*,

REWARDER (1/1) REWARD

Heb 11: 6 and that He is a *r* of those

REWARDING (1/1)

2 Chr 20:11 *r* us by coming to throw us out

REWARDS (4/4) REWARD

Prov 17:13 Whoever *r* evil for good,
Isa 1:23 bribes, And follows after *r*.
Dan 2: 6 shall receive from me gifts, *r*,
5:17 and give your *r* to another;

REZEPH (2/2)

2 Ki 19:12 Gozan and Haran and *R*,
Isa 37:12 Gozan and Haran and *R*,

REZIA (KJV) See RIZIA

REZIN (11/11)

2 Ki 15:37 days the LORD began to send *R*
16: 5 Then *R* king of Syria and Pekah
16: 6 At that time *R* king of Syria
16: 9 captive to Kir, and killed *R*.
Ezra 2:48 the sons of *R*, the sons of
Neh 7:50 sons of Reaiah, the sons of *R*,
Isa 7: 1 that *R* king of Syria and Pekah
7: 4 for the fierce anger of *R* and
7: 8 And the head of Damascus is *R*.
8: 6 And rejoice in *R* and in
9:11 set up The adversaries of *R*

REZON (1/1)

1 Ki 11:23 *R* the son of Eliadah, who had

RHEGIUM (1/1)

Acts 28:13 we circled round and reached *R*.

RHESA (1/1)

Lk 3:27 son of Joannas, the son of *R*,

RHODA (1/1)

Acts 12:13 a girl named *R* came to answer.

RHODES (1/1)

Acts 21: 1 to Cos, the following day to *R*,

RIB (2/2) RIBS

Gen 2:22 Then the *r* which the LORD God
Hos 13: 8 I will tear open their *r* cage,

RIBAI (2/2)

2 Sam 23:29 Ittai the son of *R* from Gibeah
1 Chr 11:31 Ithai the son of *R* of Gibeah, of

RIBBAND (KJV) See THREAD

RIBLAH (11/11)

Num 34:11 go down from Shepham to *R* on
2 Ki 23:33 Necho put him in prison at *R*
25: 6 up to the king of Babylon at *R*,
25:20 to the king of Babylon at *R*.
25:21 and put them to death at *R* in
Jer 39: 5 to *R* in the land of Hamath,
39: 6 Zedekiah before his eyes in *R*;
52: 9 up to the king of Babylon at *R*
52:10 all the princes of Judah in *R*.
52:26 to the king of Babylon at *R*.
52:27 and put them to death at *R* in

RIBS (3/3) RIB

Gen 2:21 slept; and He took one of his *r*,
Job 40:18 His *r* like bars of iron.
Dan 7: 5 and had three *r* in its mouth

RICH (94/93) RICHES, RICHLY

Gen 13: 2 Abram was very *r* in livestock,
14:23 say, 'I have made Abram *r*'—
49:20 from Asher shall be *r*,
Ex 30:15 The *r* shall not give more and
Lev 25:47 stranger close to you becomes *r*,
Num 13:20 whether the land is *r* or poor;
Ruth 3:10 young men, whether poor or *r*.
1 Sam 2: 7 LORD makes poor and makes *r*;
25: 2 Carmel, and the man was very *r*.
2 Sam 12: 1 one *r* and the other poor.
12: 2 The *r* man had exceedingly many
12: 4 a traveler came to the *r* man,
19:32 for he was a very *r* man.
1 Chr 4:40 And they found *r*,
Neh 9:25 strong cities and a *r* land,
9:35 Or in the large and *r* land
Job 15:29 He will not be *r*,
27:19 The *r* man will lie down,
34:19 Nor does He regard the *r* more
Ps 45:12 The *r* among the people will
49: 2 *R* and poor together.
49:16 be afraid when one becomes *r*,
66:12 But You brought us out to *r*
Prov 10: 4 hand of the diligent makes *r*.
10:15 The *r* man's wealth is his
10:22 of the LORD makes one *r*,
11:25 generous soul will be made *r*,
13: 4 of the diligent shall be made *r*.
13: 7 is one who makes himself *r*,
14:20 But the *r* has many friends.
18:11 The *r* man's wealth is his
18:23 But the *r* answers roughly.
21:17 wine and oil will not be *r*.
22: 2 The *r* and the poor have this in
22: 7 The *r* rules over the poor,
22:16 And he who gives to the *r*,
23: 4 Do not overwork to be *r*;
28: 6 in his ways, though he be *r*.
28:11 The *r* man is wise in his own
28:20 he who hastens to be *r* will not
Eccl 5:12 the abundance of the *r* will not
10: 6 While the *r* sit in a lowly
10:20 Do not curse the *r*,
Isa 3:24 Instead of a *r* robe, a girding
53: 9 But with the *r* at His death,
Jer 5:27 have become great and grown *r*.
9:23 Nor let the *r* man glory in
Ezek 34:14 good fold and feed in *r* pasture
45:15 from the *r* pastures of Israel.
Hos 12: 8 'Surely I have become *r*,
Mic 6:12 For her *r* men are full of
Zech 3: 4 clothe you with *r* robes."
11: 5 be the LORD, for I am *r*';
Mt 19:23 it is hard for a *r* man to enter
19:24 than for a *r* man to enter
27:57 there came a *r* man from
Mk 10:25 than for a *r* man to enter
12:41 And many who were *r* put in
Lk 1:53 And the *r* He has sent away
6:24 "But woe to you who are *r*,
12:16 The ground of a certain *r* man
12:21 and is not *r* toward God."
14:12 nor *r* neighbors, lest they also
16: 1 There was a certain *r* man who
16:19 There was a certain *r* man who
16:21 which fell from the *r* man's
16:22 The *r* man also died and was
18:23 sorrowful, for he was very *r*.
18:25 than for a *r* man to enter
19: 2 tax collector, and he was *r*.
21: 1 looked up and saw the *r* putting
Rom 10:12 the same Lord over all is *r* to
1 Cor 4: 8 full! You are already *r*!
2 Cor 6:10 as poor, yet making many *r*;
8: 9 Christ, that though He was *r*,
8: 9 His poverty might become *r*.
Eph 2: 4 who is *r* in mercy, because of
1 Tim 6: 9 those who desire to be *r* fall
6:17 Command those who are *r* in this
6:18 that they be *r* in good works,
Jas 1:10 but the *r* in his humiliation,
1:11 So the *r* man also will fade
2: 5 poor of this world to be *r* in
2: 6 Do not the *r* oppress you and
5: 1 Come now, you *r*, weep and
Rev 2: 9 and poverty (but you are *r*);
3:17 "Because you say, 'I am *r*,
3:18 in the fire, that you may be *r*;
6:15 the *r* men, the commanders, the
13:16 *r* and poor, free and slave, to
18: 3 the earth have become *r* through
18:14 all the things which are *r* and
18:15 who became *r* by her, will stand
18:19 ships on the sea became *r* by

RICHER (1/1)

Dan 11: 2 and the fourth shall be far *r*

RICHES (92/89) RICH

Gen 31:16 For all these *r* which God has
Josh 22: 8 Return with much *r* to your
1 Sam 17:25 king will enrich with great *r*,
1 Ki 3:11 nor have asked *r* for yourself,
3:13 both *r* and honor, so that there
10:23 the kings of the earth in *r* and
1 Chr 29:12 Both *r* and honor come from
29:28 full of days and *r* and honor;
2 Chr 1:11 and you have not asked *r* or
1:12 and I will give you *r* and
9:22 the kings of the earth in *r* and
17: 5 and he had *r* and honor in
18: 1 Jehoshaphat had *r* and honor in
32:27 Hezekiah had very great *r* and
Esth 1: 4 when he showed the *r* of his
5:11 Haman told them of his great *r*,
Job 20:15 He swallows down *r* And vomits
36:19 Will your *r*, Or all the mighty
Ps 37:16 Is better than the *r* of many
39: 6 in vain; He heaps up *r*,
49: 6 in the multitude of their *r*,
52: 7 in the abundance of his *r*,
62:10 If *r* increase, Do not set
73:12 at ease; They increase in *r*.
112: 3 Wealth and *r* will be in his
119:14 As much as in all *r*.
Prov 3:16 In her left hand *r* and honor.
8:18 *R* and honor are with me,
8:18 Enduring *r* and righteousness.
11: 4 *R* do not profit in the day of
11:16 But ruthless men retain *r*.
11:28 He who trusts in his *r* will
13: 7 himself poor, yet has great *r*.
13: 8 of a man's life is his *r*,
14:24 crown of the wise is their *r*,
19:14 Houses and *r* are an
22: 1 be chosen rather than great *r*,
22: 4 Are *r* and honor and life.
22:16 the poor to increase his *r*,
23: 5 For *r* certainly make
24: 4 all precious and pleasant *r*.
27:24 For *r* are not forever,
28:22 an evil eye hastens after *r*,
30: 8 Give me neither poverty nor *r*—
Eccl 4: 8 is his eye satisfied with *r*.
5:13 *R* kept for their owner to his
5:14 But those *r* perish through
5:19 to whom God has given *r* and
6: 2 man to whom God has given *r* and
9:11 Nor *r* to men of understanding,
Isa 8: 4 the *r* of Damascus and the
10:14 has found like a nest the *r* of
30: 6 They will carry their *r* on the
45: 3 And hidden *r* of secret places,
61: 6 You shall eat the *r* of the
Jer 9:23 the rich man glory in his *r*;
17:11 So is he who gets *r*,
48:36 Therefore the *r* they have
Ezek 26:12 They will plunder your *r* and
27:27 Your *r*, wares, and
28: 4 You have gained *r* for
28: 5 trade you have increased your *r*,
28: 5 is lifted up because of your *r*)
Dan 11: 2 by his strength, through his *r*,
11:24 them the plunder, spoil, and *r*;
11:28 to his land with great *r*,
Mt 13:22 the deceitfulness of *r* choke
Mk 4:19 world, the deceitfulness of *r*,
10:23 it is for those who have *r* to
10:24 for those who trust in *r* to
Lk 8:14 and are choked with cares, *r*,
16:11 to your trust the true *r*?
18:24 it is for those who have *r* to
Rom 2: 4 Or do you despise the *r* of His
9:23 He might make known the *r* of
11:12 Now if their fall is *r* for the
11:12 and their failure *r* for the
11:33 the depth of the *r* both of the
2 Cor 8: 2 poverty abounded in the *r* of
Eph 1: 7 according to the *r* of His grace
1:18 what are the *r* of the glory of
2: 7 He might show the exceeding *r*
3: 8 Gentiles the unsearchable *r* of
3:16 according to the *r* of His
Phil 4:19 your need according to His *r* in
Col 1:27 to make known what are the *r* of
2: 2 and attaining to all *r* of the
1 Tim 6:17 nor to trust in uncertain *r* but
Heb 11:26 reproach of Christ greater *r*
Jas 5: 2 Your *r* are corrupted, and your
Rev 5:12 To receive power and *r* and
18:17 in one hour such great *r* came

RICHEST (1/1)

Dan 11:24 even into the *r* places of the

RICHLY (2/2) RICH

Col 3:16 word of Christ dwell in you *r*
1 Tim 6:17 who gives us *r* all things to

RICHNESS (1/1)

Job 36:16 your table would be full of *r*.

RID (3/3)

Lev 26: 6 I will *r* the land of evil
Num 17: 5 thus I will *r* Myself of the
Isa 1:24 I will *r* Myself of My

RIDDANCE (1/1)

Zeph 1:18 For He will make speedy *r* Of

RIDDEN (2/2)

Num 22:30 your donkey on which you have *r*,
Esth 6: 8 a horse on which the king has *r*,

RIDDLE (10/10) RIDDLES

Judg 14:12 'Let me pose a *r* to you.
14:13 they said to him, "Pose your *r*,
14:14 they could not explain the *r*.
14:15 that he may explain the *r* to
14:16 love me! You have posed a *r* to
14:17 Then she explained the *r* to the
14:18 would not have solved my *r*!"
14:19 those who had explained the *r*.
Ezek 17: 2 "Son of man, pose a *r*,
Hab 2: 6 And a taunting *r* against him,

RIDDLES (2/2) RIDDLE

Prov 1: 6 words of the wise and their r.
Dan 5:12 interpreting dreams, solving r,

RIDE (19/19) RIDER, RIDES, RIDING, RODE

Gen 41:43 And he had him r in the second
Deut 32:13 He made him r in the heights of
Judg 5:10 you who r on white donkeys,
2 Sam 16: 2 for the king's household to r
19:26 that I may r on it and go to
1 Ki 1:33 and have Solomon my son r on my
1:38 went down and had Solomon r on
1:44 and they have made him r on the
2 Ki 10:16 So they had him r in his
2 Chr 28:15 they let all the feeble ones r
Job 30:22 to the wind and cause me to r
Ps 45: 4 And in Your majesty r
66:12 You have caused men to r over
Isa 30:16 We will r on swift
58:14 And I will cause you to r on
Jer 6:23 And they r on horses, As men
50:42 They shall r on horses,
Hos 14: 3 We will not r on horses,
Hag 2:22 And those who r in them;

RIDER (7/6) RIDE, RIDERS

Gen 49:17 So that its r shall fall
Ex 15: 1 The horse and its r He has
15:21 The horse and its r He has
Job 39:18 She scorns the horse and its r.
Jer 51:21 in pieces the horse and its r;
51:21 in pieces the chariot and its r;
Zech 12: 4 and its r with madness;

RIDERS (5/5) RIDER

2 Ki 18:23 able on your part to put r on
Isa 36: 8 able on your part to put r on
Ezek 39:20 at My table With horses and r,
Hag 2:22 The horses and their r shall
Zech 10: 5 And the r on horses shall be

RIDES (6/6) RIDE

Lev 15: 9 who has the discharge r shall
Deut 33:26 Who r the heavens to help
Ps 68: 4 Extol Him who r on the clouds,
68:33 To Him who r on the heaven of
Isa 19: 1 the LORD r on a swift cloud,
Am 2:15 Nor shall he who r a horse

RIDGE (1/1)

Isa 10:29 They have gone along the r,

RIDGES (1/1)

Ps 65:10 You water its r abundantly,

RIDICULE (3/3) LAUGH

Ps 22: 7 All those who see Me r Me;
Isa 57: 4 Whom do you r?
Lam 3:14 I have become the r of all my

RIDICULED (5/5) LAUGHED

Judg 8:15 about whom you r me, saying,
Job 12: 4 just and blameless who is r.
Mt 9:24 but sleeping." And they r Him.
Mk 5:40 And they r Him. But when He had
Lk 8:53 And they r Him, knowing that she

RIDING (12/12) RIDE

Num 22:22 And he was r on his donkey, and
2 Ki 9:25 when you and I were r together
Esth 8:10 r on royal horses bred from
Jer 17:25 r in chariots and on horses,
22: 4 r on horses and in chariots,
Ezek 23: 6 Horsemen r on horses.
23:12 Horsemen r on horses,
23:23 All of them r on horses.
27:20 merchant in saddlecloths for r.
38:15 all of them r on horses,
Zech 1: 8 a man r on a red horse, and it
9: 9 Lowly and r on a donkey,

RIE (KJV) See SPELT

RIFLED (1/1)

Zech 14: 2 shall be taken, The houses r,

RIGHT (358/329) RIGHTLY

Gen 13: 9 left, then I will go to the r;
13: 9 or, if you go to the r,
18:25 the Judge of all the earth do r?
24:49 that I may turn to the r hand
48:13 Ephraim with his r hand toward
48:13 his left hand toward Israel's r
48:14 Israel stretched out his r hand
48:17 that his father laid his r hand
48:18 put your r hand on his head."
Ex 8:26 It is not r to do so, for we
14:22 a wall to them on their r hand
14:29 a wall to them on their r hand
15: 6 Your r hand, O LORD, has become
15: 6 Your r hand, O LORD, has
15:12 You stretched out Your r hand;
15:26 your God and do what is r in
21: 8 He shall have no r to sell her
28:27 r at the seam above the
29:20 put it on the tip of the r ear
29:20 and on the tip of the r ear
29:20 on the thumb of their r hand
29:20 on the big toe of their r foot,
29:22 the r thigh (for it is a ram
39:20 r at the seam above the
Lev 7:32 Also the r thigh you shall give
7:33 shall have the r thigh for his
8:23 it on the tip of Aaron's r ear,
8:23 on the thumb of his r hand, and
8:23 on the big toe of his r foot.
8:24 on the tips of their r ears,
8:24 on the thumbs of their r hands,
8:24 the big toes of their r feet.
8:25 and the r thigh;
8:26 on the fat and on the r thigh;
9:21 but the breasts and the r thigh
14:14 put it on the tip of the r
14:14 on the thumb of his r hand, and
14:14 on the big toe of his r foot.
14:16 priest shall dip his r finger
14:17 some on the tip of the r ear
14:17 on the thumb of his r hand, and
14:17 on the big toe of his r foot,
14:25 put it on the tip of the r ear
14:25 on the thumb of his r hand, and
14:25 on the big toe of his r foot.
14:27 sprinkle with his r finger
14:28 hand on the tip of the r ear
14:28 on the thumb of the r hand, and
14:28 on the big toe of his r foot,
Num 18:18 the wave breast and the r thigh
20:17 not turn aside to the r hand
22:26 to turn either to the r hand
27: 7 of Zelophehad speak what is r;
36: 5 the sons of Joseph speaks is r.
Deut 2:27 turn neither to the r nor to
5:28 They are r in all that they
5:32 turn aside to the r hand or to
6:18 And you shall do what is r and
12: 8 doing whatever is r in his
12:25 when you do what is r in the
12:28 you do what is good and r in
13:18 to do what is r in the eyes
17:11 turn aside to the r hand
17:20 the commandment to the r hand
21: 9 you when you do what is r in
21:17 the r of the firstborn is his.
28:14 to the r or the left, to go
33: 2 From His r hand Came a fiery
Josh 1: 7 turn from it to the r hand
9:25 as it seems good and r to do
23: 6 aside from it to the r hand
Judg 3:16 his clothes on his r thigh.
3:21 the dagger from his r thigh,
5:26 Her r hand to the workmen's
7:20 the trumpets in their r hands
12: 6 he could not pronounce it r.
16:29 one on his r and the other on
17: 6 everyone did what was r in
21:25 everyone did what was r in
Ruth 4: 6 You redeem my r of redemption
1 Sam 6:12 turn aside to the r hand
11: 2 I may put out all your r eyes,
12:23 you the good and the r way.
26: 8 with the spear, r to the earth;
2 Sam 2:19 he did not turn to the r hand
2:21 Turn aside to your r hand or to
14:19 no one can turn to the r hand
14:21 the king said to Joab, "All r,
15: 3 your case is good and r;
16: 6 mighty men were on his r hand
19:28 Therefore what r have I still
19:43 we also have more r to
20: 9 by the beard with his r hand
24: 5 on the r side of the town which
1 Ki 2:19 so she sat at his r hand.
6: 8 middle story was on the r side
7:21 set up the pillar on the r and
7:39 put five carts on the r side
7:39 He set the Sea on the r side of
7:49 five on the r side and five on
11:33 My ways to do what is r in
11:38 and do what is r in My sight,
14: 8 to do only what was r in My
15: 5 David did what was r in the
15:11 Asa did what was r in the eyes
22:19 on His r hand and on His left.
22:43 doing what was r in the eyes
2 Ki 7: 9 another, "We are not doing r.
10:15 said to him, "Is your heart r,
10:30 in doing what is r in My
11:11 from the r side of the temple
12: 2 Jehoash did what was r in the
12: 9 on the r side as one comes into
14: 3 And he did what was r in the
15: 3 And he did what was r in the
15:34 And he did what was r in the
16: 2 he did not do what was r in
17: 9 God things that were not r,
18: 3 And he did what was r in the
22: 2 And he did what was r in the
22: 2 not turn aside to the r hand
1 Chr 6:39 who stood at his r hand, was
12: 2 using both the r hand and the
13: 4 for the thing was r in the eyes
2 Chr 3:17 one on the r hand and the other
3:17 name of the one on the r hand
4: 6 and put five on the r side and
4: 7 five on the r side and five on
4: 8 five on the r side and five on
4:10 He set the Sea on the r side,
14: 2 Asa did what was good and r
18:18 heaven standing on His r hand
20:32 doing what was r in the sight
23:10 from the r side of the temple
24: 2 Joash did what was r in the
25: 2 And he did what was r in the
26: 4 And he did what was r in the
27: 2 And he did what was r in the
28: 1 and he did not do what was r
29: 2 And he did what was r in the
31:20 and he did what was good and r
34: 2 And he did what was r in the
34: 2 not turn aside to the r hand
Ezra 8:21 to seek from Him the r way for
Neh 2:20 but you have no heritage or r
8: 4 at his r hand, stood
12:31 One went to the r hand on the
Esth 8: 5 sight and the thing seems r to
Job 6:25 How forceful are r words!
23: 9 When He turns to the r hand, I
27: 5 That I should say you are r;
30:12 At my r hand the rabble
33:27 and perverted what was r,
34: 6 Should I lie concerning my r?
35: 2 "Do you think this is r?
40:14 to you That your own r hand
42: 7 not spoken of Me what is r,
42: 8 not spoken of Me what is r,
Ps 9: 4 For You have maintained my r
16: 8 Because He is at my r hand I
16:11 At Your r hand are pleasures
17: 7 lovingkindness by Your r hand,
18:35 Your r hand has held me up,
19: 8 statutes of the LORD are r,
20: 6 saving strength of His r hand.
21: 8 Your r hand will find those
26:10 And whose r hand is full of
33: 4 the word of the LORD is r,
44: 3 But it was Your r hand, Your
45: 4 And Your r hand shall teach
45: 9 At Your r hand stands the
48:10 Your r hand is full of
50:16 What r have you to declare My
60: 5 Save with Your r hand, and
63: 8 Your r hand upholds me.
73:23 You hold me by my r hand.
74:11 Your hand, even Your r hand?
77:10 the years of the r hand
78:54 mountain which His r hand
80:15 the vineyard which Your r hand
80:17 upon the man of Your r hand,
89:13 and high is Your r hand.
89:25 And his r hand over the
89:42 You have exalted the r hand of
91: 7 ten thousand at your r hand;
98: 1 His r hand and His holy arm
107: 7 He led them forth by the r way,
108: 6 Save with Your r hand, and
109: 6 accuser stand at his r hand.
109:31 He shall stand at the r hand
110: 1 Sit at My r hand, Till I make
110: 5 The Lord is at Your r hand;
118:15 The r hand of the LORD does
118:16 The r hand of the LORD is
118:16 The r hand of the LORD does
119:75 that Your judgments are r,
119:128 things I consider to be r;
121: 5 is your shade at your r hand.
137: 5 Let my r hand forget its
138: 7 And Your r hand will save me.
139:10 And Your r hand shall hold me.
142: 4 Look on my r hand and see,
144: 8 whose r hand is a right hand
144: 8 And whose right hand is a r
144:11 And whose r hand is a right
144:11 whose right hand is a r hand
Prov 3:16 of days is in her r hand,
4:11 I have led you in r paths.
4:25 And your eyelids look r before
4:27 Do not turn to the r or the
8: 6 my lips will come r things;
8: 9 And r to those who find
11:24 who withholds more than is r,
12: 5 of the righteous are r,
12:15 The way of a fool is r in his
14:12 There is a way that seems r
16:13 love him who speaks what is r.
16:25 There is a way that seems r
18:17 to plead his cause seems r,
20:11 what he does is pure and r.
21: 2 Every way of a man is r in his
21: 8 for the pure, his work is r.
23:16 When your lips speak r things.
24:26 He who gives a r answer kisses
27:16 grasps oil with his r hand.
28: 2 and knowledge R will be
Eccl 10: 2 man's heart is at his r hand,
Song 2: 6 And his r hand embraces me.
8: 3 And his r hand embraces me.
Isa 9:20 he shall snatch on the r hand
10: 2 And to take what is r from the
28:26 instructs him in r judgment,
30:10 Do not prophesy to us r things;
30:21 Whenever you turn to the r
41:10 you with My righteous r hand.'
41:13 will hold your r hand,
44:20 not a lie in my r hand?"
45: 1 whose r hand I have held—To

45:19 I declare things that are *r*.
48:13 And My *r* hand has stretched
54: 3 For you shall expand to the *r*
62: 8 LORD has sworn by His *r* hand
63:12 Who led them by the *r* hand of
Jer 5:28 And the *r* of the needy they do
17:11 who gets riches, but not by *r*;
17:16 It was *r* there before You.
22:24 were the signet on My *r* hand,
23:10 And their might is not *r*.
32: 7 for the *r* of redemption is
32: 8 for the *r* of inheritance is
34:15 turned and did what was *r* in
48:30 the LORD, "But it is not *r*;
48:30 His lies have made nothing *r*.
Lam 2: 3 He has drawn back His *r* hand
2: 4 With His *r* hand, like an
Ezek 1:10 face of a lion on the *r* side,
4: 6 lie again on your *r* side;
18: 5 And does what is lawful and *r*;
18:19 has done what is lawful and *r*,
18:21 and does what is lawful and *r*,
18:27 and does what is lawful and *r*,
21:16 at the ready! Thrust *r*!
21:22 In his *r* hand is the divination
21:27 Until He comes whose *r* it is,
33:14 and does what is lawful and *r*,
33:16 has done what is lawful and *r*;
33:19 and does what is lawful and *r*,
39: 3 to fall out of your *r* hand.
47: 1 flowing from under the *r* side
47: 2 running out on the *r* side.
Dan 12: 7 when he held up his *r* hand and
Hos 14: 9 the ways of the LORD are *r*;
Am 3:10 For they do not know to do *r*,
Jon 4: 4 Is it *r* for you to be angry?"
4: 9 Is it *r* for you to be angry
4: 9 It is *r* for me to be angry,
4:11 discern between their *r* hand
Hab 2:16 The cup of the LORD's *r* hand
Zech 3: 1 Satan standing at his *r* hand
4: 3 one at the *r* of the bowl and
4:11 at the *r* of the lampstand and at
11:17 his arm And against his *r* eye;
11:17 And his *r* eye shall be totally
12: 6 peoples on the *r* hand and
Mt 5:29 If your *r* eye causes you to sin,
5:30 And if your *r* hand causes you to
5:39 slaps you on your *r* cheek,
6: 3 know what your *r* hand is doing,
20: 4 and whatever is *r* I will give
20: 7 and whatever is *r* you will
20:21 one on Your *r* hand and the
20:23 but to sit on My *r* hand and on
22:44 Sit at My *r* hand, Till I
25:33 set the sheep on His *r* hand,
25:34 say to those on His *r* hand,
26:64 Man sitting at the *r* hand of
27:29 and a reed in His *r* hand.
27:38 one on the *r* and another on the
Mk 5:15 and clothed and in his *r* mind.
10:37 one on Your *r* hand and the
10:40 but to sit on My *r* hand and on
12:36 Sit at My *r* hand, Till I
14:54 *r* into the courtyard of the
14:62 Man sitting at the *r* hand of
15:27 one on His *r* and the other on
16: 5 robe sitting on the *r* side;
16:19 and sat down at the *r* hand of
Lk 1:11 standing on the *r* side of the
6: 6 a man was there whose *r* hand
8:35 clothed and in his *r* mind.
12:57 do you not judge what is *r*?
15:32 It was *r* that we should make
20:42 Sit at My *r* hand,
22:50 priest and cut off his *r* ear.
22:69 Man will sit on the *r* hand of
23:33 one on the *r* hand and the other
Jn 1:12 to them He gave the *r* to become
18:10 and cut off his *r* ear.
21: 6 Cast the net on the *r* side of
Acts 2:25 For He is at my *r* hand,
2:33 being exalted to the *r* hand of
2:34 Sit at My *r* hand,
3: 7 And he took him by the *r* hand
4:19 Whether it is *r* in the sight of
5:31 God has exalted to His *r* hand
7:55 Jesus standing at the *r* hand
7:56 Man standing at the *r* hand of
8:21 for your heart is not *r* in the
Rom 8:34 who is even at the *r* hand of
1 Cor 9: 4 Do we have no *r* to eat and
9: 5 Do we have no *r* to take along a
9: 6 Barnabas and I who have no *r*
9:12 are partakers of this *r* over
9:12 we have not used this *r*,
2 Cor 6: 7 of righteousness on the *r* hand
Gal 2: 9 they gave me and Barnabas the *r*
Eph 1:20 and seated Him at His *r* hand
6: 1 in the Lord, for this is *r*.
Phil 1: 7 just as it is *r* for me to think
Col 3: 1 sitting at the *r* hand of God.
Heb 1: 3 sat down at the *r* hand of the
1:13 Sit at My *r* hand, Till I
8: 1 who is seated at the *r* hand of
10:12 sat down at the *r* hand of God,
12: 2 and has sat down at the *r* hand
13:10 tabernacle have no *r* to eat.
1 Pe 3:22 heaven and is at the *r* hand
2 Pe 1:13 Yes, I think it is *r*,
2:15 They have forsaken the *r* way and
Rev 1:16 He had in His *r* hand seven
1:17 But He laid His *r* hand on me,
1:20 which you saw in My *r* hand,
2: 1 the seven stars in His *r* hand,
5: 1 And I saw in the *r* hand of Him
5: 7 the scroll out of the *r* hand
10: 2 And he set his *r* foot on the
13:16 receive a mark on their *r* hand
22:14 that they may have the *r* to the

RIGHTEOUS (262/248) RIGHTEOUSLY, RIGHTEOUSNESS, UNRIGHTEOUS

Gen 7: 1 I have seen that you are *r*
18:23 You also destroy the *r* with
18:24 Suppose there were fifty *r*
18:24 not spare it for the fifty *r*
18:25 to slay the *r* with the wicked,
18:25 so that the *r* should be as the
18:26 find in Sodom fifty *r* within
18:28 were five less than the fifty *r*;
20: 4 will You slay a *r* nation also?
38:26 She has been more *r* than I,
Ex 9:27 The LORD is *r*,
23: 7 do not kill the innocent and *r*.
23: 8 and perverts the words of the *r*.
Num 23:10 Let me die the death of the *r*,
Deut 4: 8 statutes and *r* judgments
16:19 and twists the words of the *r*.
25: 1 and they justify the *r* and
32: 4 *R* and upright is He.
Judg 5:11 they shall recount the *r* acts
5:11 The *r* acts for His villagers
1 Sam 12: 7 concerning all the *r* acts
24:17 'You are more *r* than I;
2 Sam 4:11 men have killed a *r* person
1 Ki 2:32 he struck down two men more *r*
8:32 and justifying the *r* by giving
2 Ki 10: 9 to all the people, "You are *r*.
2 Chr 6:23 and justifying the *r* by giving
12: 6 they said, "The LORD is *r*.
Ezra 9:15 LORD God of Israel, You are *r*,
Neh 9: 8 Your words, For You are *r*.
Job 4:17 Can a mortal be more *r* than God?
9: 2 But how can a man be *r* before
9:15 For though I were *r*,
9:20 Though I were *r*,
10:15 woe to me; Even if I am *r*,
15:14 of a woman, that he could be *r*?
17: 9 Yet the *r* will hold to his way,
22: 3 to the Almighty that you are *r*?
22:19 'The *r* see it and are glad,
25: 4 How then can man be *r* before
32: 1 because he was *r* in his own
33:12 in this you are not *r*.
34: 5 "For Job has said, 'I am *r*,
35: 7 If you are *r*, what do you give
36: 7 withdraw His eyes from the *r*;
Ps 1: 5 in the congregation of the *r*.
1: 6 LORD knows the way of the *r*,
5:12 You, O LORD, will bless the *r*;
7: 9 For the *r* God tests the hearts
11: 3 What can the *r* do?
11: 5 The LORD tests the *r*,
11: 7 For the LORD is *r*,
14: 5 with the generation of the *r*.
19: 9 of the LORD are true and *r*
31:18 contemptuously against the *r*.
32:11 in the LORD and rejoice, you *r*;
33: 1 O you *r*! For praise from the
34:15 eyes of the LORD are on the *r*,
34:17 The *r* cry out, and the LORD
34:19 are the afflictions of the *r*,
34:21 And those who hate the *r* shall
35:27 Who favor my *r* cause; And let
37:16 A little that a *r* man has Is
37:17 But the LORD upholds the *r*.
37:21 But the *r* shows mercy and
37:25 have not seen the *r* forsaken,
37:29 The *r* shall inherit the land,
37:30 The mouth of the *r* speaks
37:32 The wicked watches the *r*,
37:39 But the salvation of the *r* is
52: 6 The *r* also shall see and fear,
55:22 He shall never permit the *r* to
58:10 The *r* shall rejoice when he
58:11 there is a reward for the *r*;
64:10 The *r* shall be glad in the
68: 3 But let the *r* be glad;
69:28 And not be written with the *r*.
72: 7 In His days the *r* shall
75:10 But the horns of the *r* shall
92:12 The *r* shall flourish like a
94:21 against the life of the *r*,
97:11 Light is sown for the *r*,
97:12 Rejoice in the LORD, you *r*,
107:42 The *r* see it and rejoice,
112: 4 and full of compassion, and *r*.
112: 6 The *r* will be in everlasting
116: 5 Gracious is the LORD, and *r*;
118:15 Is in the tents of the *r*;
118:20 Through which the *r* shall
119: 7 When I learn Your *r* judgments.
119:62 Because of Your *r* judgments.
119:106 I will keep Your *r* judgments.
119:123 And Your *r* word.
119:137 *R* are You, O LORD,
119:138 Are *r* and very faithful.
119:160 every one of Your *r* judgments
119:164 Because of Your *r* judgments.
125: 3 On the land allotted to the *r*,
125: 3 Lest the *r* reach out their
129: 4 The LORD is *r*;
140:13 Surely the *r* shall give thanks
141: 5 Let the *r* strike me;
142: 7 The *r* shall surround me,
143: 2 Your sight no one living is *r*.
145:17 The LORD is *r* in all His
146: 8 down; The LORD loves the *r*.
Prov 10: 3 will not allow the *r* soul to
10: 6 are on the head of the *r*,
10: 7 The memory of the *r* is
10:11 The mouth of the *r* is a well
10:16 The labor of the *r* leads to
10:20 The tongue of the *r* is choice
10:21 The lips of the *r* feed many,
10:24 And the desire of the *r* will
10:25 But the *r* has an everlasting
10:28 The hope of the *r* will be
10:30 The *r* will never be removed,
10:31 The mouth of the *r* brings forth
10:32 The lips of the *r* know what is
11: 8 The *r* is delivered from
11: 9 through knowledge the *r* will
11:10 When it goes well with the *r*,
11:21 the posterity of the *r* will be
11:23 The desire of the *r* is only
11:28 But the *r* will flourish like
11:30 The fruit of the *r* is a tree
11:31 If the *r* will be recompensed on
12: 3 But the root of the *r* cannot
12: 5 The thoughts of the *r* are
12: 7 But the house of the *r* will
12:10 A *r* man regards the life of
12:12 But the root of the *r* yields
12:13 But the *r* will come through
12:21 trouble will overtake the *r*,
12:26 The *r* should choose his friends
13: 5 A *r* man hates lying,
13: 9 The light of the *r* rejoices,
13:21 But to the *r*, good shall be
13:22 sinner is stored up for the *r*.
13:25 The *r* eats to the satisfying of
14:19 wicked at the gates of the *r*.
14:32 But the *r* has a refuge in his
15: 6 In the house of the *r* there
15:28 The heart of the *r* studies how
15:29 He hears the prayer of the *r*.
16:13 *R* lips are the delight of
17:26 to punish the *r* is not good,
18: 5 Or to overthrow the *r* in
18:10 The *r* run to it and are safe.
20: 7 The *r* man walks in his
21:12 The *r* God wisely considers the
21:18 shall be a ransom for the *r*,
21:26 But the *r* gives and does not
23:24 The father of the *r* will
24:15 against the dwelling of the *r*;
24:16 For a *r* man may fall seven
24:24 to the wicked, "You are *r*,
25:26 A *r* man who falters before the
28: 1 But the *r* are bold as a lion.
28:12 When the *r* rejoice, there is
28:28 they perish, the *r* increase.
29: 2 When the *r* are in authority,
29: 6 But the *r* sings and rejoices.
29: 7 The *r* considers the cause of
29:16 But the *r* will see their fall.
29:27 man is an abomination to the *r*,
Eccl 3:17 God shall judge the *r* and the
7:16 Do not be overly *r*,
8:14 according to the work of the *r*.
9: 1 that the *r* and the wise and
9: 2 One event happens to the *r* and
Isa 3:10 Say to the *r* that it shall
5:23 take away justice from the *r*
24:16 Glory to the *r*!" But I said,
26: 2 That the *r* nation which keeps
41:10 I will uphold you with My *r*
41:26 that we may say, 'He is *r*'?
49:24 Or the captives of the *r* be
53:11 By His knowledge My *r* Servant
57: 1 The *r* perishes, And no man
57: 1 That the *r* is taken away
60:21 your people shall all be *r*;
Jer 3:11 has shown herself more *r* than
12: 1 *R* are You, O LORD, when I
20:12 of hosts, You who test the *r*,
Lam 1:18 "The LORD is *r*,
Ezek 3:20 when a *r* man turns from his
3:21 if you warn the *r* man
3:21 the righteous man that the *r*
13:22 made the heart of the *r* sad,
16:52 they are more *r* than you.
18:20 righteousness of the *r* shall
18:24 But when a *r* man turns away
18:26 When a *r* man turns away from
21: 3 sheath and cut off both *r* and
21: 4 I will cut off both *r* and
23:45 But *r* men will judge them after
33:12 The righteousness of the *r* man
33:12 nor shall the *r* be able to live
33:13 When I say to the *r* that he
33:13 none of his *r* works shall be
33:18 When the *r* turns from his
Dan 4:27 break off your sins by being *r*,
9:14 for the LORD our God is *r* in
9:18 You because of our *r* deeds,
Hos 14: 9 The *r* walk in them,
Am 2: 6 Because they sell the *r* for
Hab 1: 4 For the wicked surround the *r*;
1:13 devours A person more *r* than
Zeph 3: 5 The LORD is *r* in her midst,
Mal 3:18 discern Between the *r* and

Mt 9:13 I did not come to call the *r*,
10:41 And he who receives a *r* man in
10:41 man in the name of a *r* man
10:41 man shall receive a *r* man's
13:17 to you that many prophets and *r*
13:43 Then the *r* will shine forth as
23:28 so you also outwardly appear *r*
23:29 adorn the monuments of the *r*,
23:35 you may come all the *r* blood
23:35 from the blood of *r* Abel to the
25:37 Then the *r* will answer Him,
25:46 but the *r* into eternal life."
Mk 2:17 I did not come to call the *r*,
Lk 1: 6 And they were both *r* before God,
5:32 have not come to call the *r*,
18: 9 in themselves that they were *r*,
20:20 spies who pretended to be *r*,
23:47 Certainly this was a *r* Man!"
Jn 5:30 I judge; and My judgment is *r*,
7:24 but judge with *r* judgment."
17:25 O *r* Father! The world has not
Rom 1:32 knowing the *r* judgment of God,
2: 5 wrath and revelation of the *r*
2:26 uncircumcised man keeps the *r*
3:10 "There is none *r*,
5: 7 For scarcely for a *r* man will
5:18 even so through one Man's *r* act
5:19 obedience many will be made *r*.
8: 4 that the *r* requirement of the
2 Th 1: 5 is manifest evidence of the *r*
1: 6 since it is a *r* thing with God
1 Tim 1: 9 is not made for a *r* person,
2 Tim 4: 8 the *r* Judge, will give to me on
Heb 11: 4 obtained witness that he was *r*,
Jas 5:16 fervent prayer of a *r* man
1 Pe 3:12 the LORD are on the *r*,
4:18 If the *r* one is scarcely
2 Pe 2: 7 and delivered *r* Lot, who was
2: 8 (for that *r* man, dwelling among
2: 8 tormented his *r* soul from day
1 Jn 2: 1 the Father, Jesus Christ the *r*.
2:29 If you know that He is *r*,
3: 7 practices righteousness is *r*,
3: 7 is righteous, just as He is *r*.
3:12 were evil and his brother's *r*.
Rev 16: 5 waters saying: "You are *r*,
16: 7 true and *r* are Your
19: 2 For true and *r* are His
19: 8 the fine linen is the *r* acts
22:11 he who is *r*, let him be
22:11 let him be *r* still; he who is

RIGHTEOUSLY (8/8) RIGHTEOUS

Deut 1:16 and judge *r* between a man and
Ps 67: 4 You shall judge the people *r*,
96:10 He shall judge the peoples *r*.
Prov 31: 9 Open your mouth, judge *r*,
Isa 33:15 He who walks *r* and speaks
Jer 11:20 of hosts, You who judge *r*,
Titus 2:12 we should live soberly, *r*,
1 Pe 2:23 Himself to Him who judges *r*;

RIGHTEOUSNESS (311/292) RIGHTEOUS, RIGHTEOUSNESS', RIGHTEOUSNESSES

Gen 15: 6 He accounted it to him for *r*.
18:19 to do *r* and justice, that the
30:33 So my *r* will answer for me in
Lev 19:15 In *r* you shall judge your
Deut 6:25 Then it will be *r* for us, if we
9: 4 Because of my *r* the LORD has
9: 5 It is not because of your *r* or
9: 6 to possess because of your *r*,
24:13 and it shall be *r* to you before
33:19 shall offer sacrifices of *r*;
1 Sam 26:23 repay every man for his *r* and
2 Sam 22:21 rewarded me according to my *r*;
22:25 me according to my *r*,
1 Ki 3: 6 before You in truth, in *r*,
8:32 giving him according to his *r*.
10: 9 you king, to do justice and *r*.
2 Chr 6:23 giving him according to his *r*.
9: 8 over them, to do justice and *r*.
Job 6:29 my *r* still stands!
27: 6 My *r* I hold fast, and will not
29:14 I put on *r*, and it clothed me;
33:26 For He restores to man His *r*.
35: 2 My *r* is more than God's'?
35: 8 And your *r* a son of man.
36: 3 I will ascribe *r* to my Maker.
Ps 4: 1 O God of my *r*! You have
4: 5 Offer the sacrifices of *r*,
5: 8 in Your *r* because of my
7: 8 me, O LORD, according to my *r*,
7:17 the LORD according to His *r*,
9: 4 sat on the throne judging in *r*.
9: 8 He shall judge the world in *r*,
11: 7 is righteous, He loves *r*;
15: 2 walks uprightly, And works *r*,
17:15 I will see Your face in *r*;
18:20 rewarded me according to my *r*;
18:24 me according to my *r*,
22:31 will come and declare His *r* to
23: 3 He leads me in the paths of *r*
24: 5 And *r* from the God of his
31: 1 Deliver me in Your *r*.
33: 5 He loves *r* and justice;
35:24 my God, according to Your *r*;
35:28 my tongue shall speak of Your *r*
36: 6 Your *r* is like the great
36:10 And Your *r* to the upright in
37: 6 He shall bring forth your *r* as
40: 9 proclaimed the good news of *r*
40:10 I have not hidden Your *r* within
45: 4 of truth, humility, and *r*;
45: 6 A scepter of *r* is the scepter
45: 7 You love *r* and hate wickedness;
48:10 Your right hand is full of *r*.
50: 6 Let the heavens declare His *r*,
51:14 shall sing aloud of Your *r*.
51:19 with the sacrifices of *r*,
52: 3 Lying rather than speaking *r*.
58: 1 Do you indeed speak *r*,
65: 5 By awesome deeds in *r* You will
69:27 let them not come into Your *r*.
71: 2 Deliver me in Your *r*,
71:15 My mouth shall tell of Your *r*
71:16 I will make mention of Your *r*,
71:19 Also Your *r*, O God, is very
71:24 also shall talk of Your *r* all
72: 1 And Your *r* to the king's Son.
72: 2 will judge Your people with *r*,
72: 3 And the little hills, by *r*.
85:10 *R* and peace have kissed.
85:11 And *r* shall look down from
85:13 *R* will go before Him,
88:12 And Your *r* in the land of
89:14 *R* and justice are the
89:16 And in Your *r* they are
94:15 But judgment will return to *r*,
96:13 shall judge the world with *r*,
97: 2 *R* and justice are the
97: 6 The heavens declare His *r*,
98: 2 His *r* He has revealed in the
98: 9 With *r* He shall judge the
99: 4 have executed justice and *r* in
103: 6 The LORD executes *r* And
103:17 And His *r* to children's
106: 3 And he who does *r* at all
106:31 was accounted to him for *r* To
111: 3 And His *r* endures forever.
112: 3 And his *r* endures forever.
112: 9 His *r* endures forever;
118:19 Open to me the gates of *r*;
119:40 Revive me in Your *r*.
119:121 I have done justice and *r*;
119:142 Your *r* is an everlasting
119:142 is an everlasting *r*,
119:144 The *r* of Your testimonies is
119:172 all Your commandments are *r*.
132: 9 Your priests be clothed with *r*,
143: 1 answer me, And in Your *r*.
145: 7 And shall sing of Your *r*.
Prov 2: 9 Then you will understand *r* and
2:20 And keep to the paths of *r*.
8: 8 words of my mouth are with *r*;
8:18 with me, Enduring riches and *r*.
8:20 I traverse the way of *r*,
10: 2 But *r* delivers from death.
11: 4 But *r* delivers from death.
11: 5 The *r* of the blameless will
11: 6 The *r* of the upright will
11:18 But he who sows *r* will have
11:19 As *r* leads to life, So he who
12:17 who speaks truth declares *r*,
12:28 In the way of *r* is life,
13: 6 *R* guards him whose way is
14:34 *R* exalts a nation, But sin is
15: 9 But He loves him who follows *r*.
16: 8 Better is a little with *r*,
16:12 a throne is established by *r*.
16:31 it is found in the way of *r*.
21: 3 To do *r* and justice Is more
21:21 He who follows *r* and mercy
21:21 Finds life, *r* and honor.
25: 5 throne will be established in *r*.
Eccl 3:16 And in the place of *r*,
5: 8 perversion of justice and *r* in
7:15 just man who perishes in his *r*,
Isa 1:21 *R* lodged in it, But now
1:26 shall be called the city of *r*,
1:27 And her penitents with *r*.
5: 7 For *r*, but behold, a cry for
5:16 is holy shall be hallowed in *r*.
10:22 decreed shall overflow with *r*.
11: 4 But with *r* He shall judge the
11: 5 *R* shall be the belt of His
16: 5 seeking justice and hastening *r*.
26: 9 of the world will learn *r*.
26:10 Yet he will not learn *r*;
28:17 And *r* the plummet; The hail
32: 1 Behold, a king will reign in *r*,
32:16 And *r* remain in the fruitful
32:17 The work of *r* will be peace,
32:17 be peace, And the effect of *r*,
33: 5 filled Zion with justice and *r*.
41: 2 Who in *r* called him to His
42: 6 the LORD, have called You in *r*,
45: 8 And let the skies pour down *r*;
45: 8 And let *r* spring up together.
45:13 I have raised him up in *r*,
45:19 I, the LORD, speak *r*,
45:23 has gone out of My mouth in *r*,
45:24 Surely in the LORD I have *r* and
46:12 Who are far from *r*:
46:13 I bring My *r* near, it shall not
48: 1 But not in truth or in *r*;
48:18 And your *r* like the waves of
51: 1 to Me, you who follow after *r*,
51: 5 My *r* is near, My salvation
51: 6 And My *r* will not be
51: 7 to Me, you who know *r*,
51: 8 But My *r* will be forever,
54:14 In *r* you shall be established;
54:17 And their *r* is from Me,"
56: 1 "Keep justice, and do *r*,
56: 1 And My *r* to be revealed.
57:12 I will declare your *r* And your
58: 2 ways, As a nation that did *r*,
58: 8 And your *r* shall go before
59: 9 Nor does *r* overtake us;
59:14 And *r* stands afar off;
59:16 His own *r*, it sustained Him.
59:17 For He put on *r* as a
60:17 And your magistrates *r*.
61: 3 they may be called trees of *r*,
61:10 covered me with the robe of *r*,
61:11 So the Lord GOD will cause *r*
62: 1 Until her *r* goes forth as
62: 2 The Gentiles shall see your *r*,
63: 1 'I who speak in *r*, mighty to
64: 5 him who rejoices and does *r*,
Jer 4: 2 truth, in judgment, and in *r*;
9:24 and *r* in the earth. For in
22: 3 LORD: "Execute judgment and *r*,
22:15 And do justice and *r*?
23: 5 raise to David a Branch of *r*;
23: 5 And execute judgment and *r* in
23: 6 will be called: THE LORD OUR *R*.
33:15 grow up to David A Branch of *r*;
33:15 shall execute judgment and *r*
33:16 will be called: THE LORD OUR *R*.
51:10 The LORD has revealed our *r*.
Ezek 3:20 man turns from his *r* and
3:20 and his *r* which he has done
14:14 only themselves by their *r*,
14:20 only themselves by their *r*.
18:20 The *r* of the righteous shall be
18:22 because of the *r* which he has
18:24 man turns away from his *r* and
18:24 All the *r* which he has done
18:26 man turns away from his *r*,
33:12 The *r* of the righteous man shall
33:12 to live because of his *r* in
33:13 but he trusts in his own *r* and
33:18 the righteous turns from his *r*
45: 9 execute justice and *r*,
Dan 9: 7 *r* belongs to You, but to us
9:16 Lord, according to all Your *r*,
9:24 To bring in everlasting *r*,
12: 3 And those who turn many to *r*
Hos 2:19 I will betroth you to Me In *r*
10:12 Sow for yourselves *r*;
10:12 Till He comes and rains *r* on
Am 5: 7 And lay *r* to rest in the
5:24 And *r* like a mighty stream.
6:12 And the fruit of *r* into
Mic 6: 5 That you may know the *r* of the
7: 9 to the light; I will see His *r*.
Zeph 2: 3 upheld His justice. Seek *r*,
Zech 8: 8 be their God, In truth and *r*.
Mal 3: 3 to the LORD An offering in *r*.
4: 2 who fear My name The Sun of *R*
Mt 3:15 fitting for us to fulfill all *r*.
5: 6 who hunger and thirst for *r*,
5:20 that unless your *r* exceeds the
5:20 righteousness exceeds the *r*
6:33 the kingdom of God and His *r*,
21:32 came to you in the way of *r*,
Lk 1:75 In holiness and *r* before Him
Jn 16: 8 the world of sin, and of *r*,
16:10 'of *r*, because I go to My
Acts 10:35 whoever fears Him and works *r*
13:10 the devil, you enemy of all *r*,
17:31 He will judge the world in *r*
24:25 Now as he reasoned about *r*,
Rom 1:17 For in it the *r* of God is
3: 5 demonstrates the *r* of God,
3:21 But now the *r* of God apart from
3:22 even the *r* of God, through faith
3:25 faith, to demonstrate His *r*,
3:26 at the present time His *r*,
4: 3 accounted to him for *r*.
4: 5 his faith is accounted for *r*,
4: 6 the man to whom God imputes *r*
4: 9 was accounted to Abraham for *r*.
4:11 a seal of the *r* of the faith
4:11 that *r* might be imputed to them
4:13 but through the *r* of faith.
4:22 accounted to him for *r*.
5:17 of grace and of the gift of *r*
5:21 so grace might reign through *r*
6:13 members as instruments of *r*
6:16 or of obedience leading to *r*?
6:18 sin, you became slaves of *r*.
6:19 your members as slaves of *r*
6:20 you were free in regard to *r*.
8:10 Spirit is life because of *r*.
9:28 and cut it short in *r*,
9:30 Gentiles, who did not pursue *r*,
9:30 have attained to *r*,
9:30 even the *r* of faith;
9:31 Israel, pursuing the law of *r*,
9:31 not attained to the law of *r*.
10: 3 they being ignorant of God's *r*,
10: 3 to establish their own *r*,
10: 3 have not submitted to the *r* of
10: 4 is the end of the law for *r*
10: 5 For Moses writes about the *r*
10: 6 But the *r* of faith speaks in
10:10 the heart one believes unto *r*,
14:17 but *r* and peace and joy in the
1 Cor 1:30 and *r* and sanctification and

R

15:34 Awake to *r*, and do not sin;
2 Cor 3: 9 the ministry of *r* exceeds much
5:21 that we might become the *r* of
6: 7 by the armor of *r* on the right
6:14 For what fellowship has *r* with
9: 9 His *r* endures forever."
9:10 increase the fruits of your *r*,
11:15 themselves into ministers of *r*,
Gal 2:21 for if *r* comes through the
3: 6 accounted to him for *r*.
3:21 truly *r* would have been by the
5: 5 eagerly wait for the hope of *r*
Eph 4:24 in true *r* and holiness.
5: 9 Spirit is in all goodness, *r*,
6:14 put on the breastplate of *r*,
Phil 1:11 filled with the fruits of *r*
3: 6 concerning the *r* which is in
3: 9 in Him, not having my own *r*,
3: 9 the *r* which is from God by
1 Tim 6:11 flee these things and pursue *r*,
2 Tim 2:22 youthful lusts; but pursue *r*,
3:16 for instruction in *r*,
4: 8 laid up for me the crown of *r*,
Titus 3: 5 not by works of *r* which we have
Heb 1: 8 A scepter of *r* is the
1: 9 You have loved *r* and
5:13 is unskilled in the word of *r*,
7: 2 being translated "king of *r*,
11: 7 world and became heir of the *r*
11:33 subdued kingdoms, worked *r*,
12:11 the peaceable fruit of *r* to
Jas 1:20 of man does not produce the *r*
2:23 accounted to him for *r*.
3:18 Now the fruit of *r* is sown in
1 Pe 2:24 died to sins, might live for *r*—
2 Pe 1: 1 faith with us by the *r* of our
2: 5 eight people, a preacher of *r*,
2:21 not to have known the way of *r*,
3:13 and a new earth in which *r*
1 Jn 2:29 that everyone who practices *r*
3: 7 He who practices *r* is
3:10 Whoever does not practice *r* is
Rev 19:11 and in *r* He judges and makes

RIGHTEOUSNESS' (4/4) RIGHTEOUSNESS
Ps 143:11 For Your *r* sake bring my soul
Isa 42:21 is well pleased for His *r* sake;
Mt 5:10 those who are persecuted for *r*
1 Pe 3:14 even if you should suffer for *r*

RIGHTEOUSNESSES (1/1) RIGHTEOUSNESS
Isa 64: 6 And all our *r* are like filthy

RIGHTFUL (2/2)
Job 8: 6 And prosper your *r* dwelling
Jer 10: 7 For this is Your *r* due.

RIGHTLY (13/13) RIGHT
Gen 27:36 'Is he not *r* named Jacob?
Prov 15: 2 of the wise uses knowledge *r*,
Song 1: 4 THE SHULAMITE *R* do they
Jer 46:28 I will *r* correct you, For I
Lk 7:43 You have *r* judged."
10:28 to him, "You have answered *r*;
20:21 know that You say and teach *r*,
22:70 You *r* say that I am."
Jn 8:48 Do we not say *r* that You are a
18:37 'You say *r* that I am a king.
Acts 28:25 The Holy Spirit spoke *r* through
1 Cor 2:15 yet he himself is *r* judged by
2 Tim 2:15 *r* dividing the word of truth.

RIGHTS (1/1)
Ex 21:10 clothing, and her marriage *r*.

RIGID (1/1)
Mk 9:18 his teeth, and becomes *r*.

RIGOR (5/5)
Ex 1:13 children of Israel serve with *r*.
1:14 made them serve was with *r*.
Lev 25:43 shall not rule over him with *r*,
25:46 rule over one another with *r*.
25:53 and he shall not rule with *r*

RIGOUR (KJV) See RIGOR

RIM (5/5)
Ex 27: 5 You shall put it under the *r* of
38: 4 for the altar, under its *r*,
Ezek 43:13 with a *r* all around its edge of
43:17 with a *r* of half a cubit around
43:20 and on the *r* around it;

RIMMON (24/21)
Josh 15:32 Lebaoth, Shilhim, Ain, and *R*:
19: 7 Ain, *R*, Ether, and Ashan:
19:13 Eth Kazin, and extended to *R*,
Judg 20:45 the wilderness to the rock of *R*;
20:47 the wilderness to the rock of *R*,
20:47 they stayed at the rock of *R*
21:13 who were at the rock of *R*,
2 Sam 4: 2 the sons of *R* the Beerothite,
4: 5 Then the sons of *R* the
4: 9 the sons of *R* the Beerothite,
2 Ki 5:18 goes into the temple of *R* to
5:18 I bow down in the temple of *R*—
5:18 I bow down in the temple of *R*,
1 Chr 4:32 villages were Etam, Ain, *R*,
6:77 of Merari were given *R* with
Zech 14:10 into a plain from Geba to *R*

RIMMON PEREZ (2/2)
Num 33:19 from Rithmah and camped at *R*.
33:20 They departed from *R* and camped

RIMS (3/2)
1 Ki 7:33 wheel; their axle pins, their *r*,
Ezek 1:18 As for their *r*, they were so
1:18 and their *r* were full of eyes,

RING (17/16) RINGS
Gen 24:22 the man took a golden nose *r*
24:30 to pass, when he saw the nose *r*,
24:47 So I put the nose *r* on her
41:42 Then Pharaoh took his signet *r*
Ex 26:24 together at the top by one *r*.
36:29 together at the top by one *r*.
Esth 3:10 So the king took his signet *r*
3:12 sealed with the king's signet *r*.
8: 2 the king took off his signet *r*,
8: 8 it with the king's signet *r*;
8: 8 with the king's signet *r* no
8:10 it with the king's signet *r*,
Job 42:11 a piece of silver and each a *r*
Prov 11:22 As a *r* of gold in a swine's
Dan 6:17 it with his own signet *r* and
Hag 2:23 will make you like a signet *r*;
Lk 15:22 and put a *r* on his hand and

RINGLEADER (1/1)
Acts 24: 5 and a *r* of the sect of the

RINGS (44/33) RING
Ex 25:12 You shall cast four *r* of gold
25:12 two *r* shall be on one side,
25:12 and two *r* on the other side.
25:14 shall put the poles into the *r*
25:15 The poles shall be in the *r* of
25:26 you shall make for it four *r*
25:26 and put the *r* on the four
25:27 The *r* shall be close to the
26:29 make their *r* of gold as
27: 4 you shall make four bronze *r*
27: 7 poles shall be put in the *r*,
28:23 And you shall make two *r* of gold
28:23 and put the two *r* on the two
28:24 chains of gold in the two *r*
28:26 You shall make two *r* of gold,
28:27 And two other *r* of gold you
28:28 breastplate by means of its *r*
28:28 by means of its rings to the *r*
30: 4 Two gold *r* you shall make for
35:22 brought earrings and nose *r*,
35:22 *r* and necklaces, all jewelry of
36:34 made their *r* of gold to be
36:38 their capitals and their *r*
37: 3 And he cast for it four *r* of
37: 3 two *r* on one side, and two
37: 3 and two *r* on the other side of
37: 5 he put the poles into the *r* at
37:13 And he cast for it four *r* of
37:13 and put the *r* on the four
37:14 The *r* were close to the frame,
37:27 He made two *r* of gold for it
38: 5 He cast four *r* for the four
38: 7 he put the poles into the *r* on
39:16 settings of gold and two gold *r*,
39:16 and put the two *r* on the two
39:17 chains of gold in the two *r* on
39:19 And they made two *r* of gold and
39:20 They made two other gold *r* and
39:21 breastplate by means of its *r*
39:21 by means of its rings to the *r*
40:20 the poles through the *r* of the
Num 31:50 and bracelets and signet *r* and
Isa 3:21 and the *r*;
Jas 2: 2 your assembly a man with gold *r*,

RINGSTRAKED (KJV) See SPECKLED

RINNAH (1/1)
1 Chr 4:20 sons of Shimon were Amnon, *R*,

RINSED (3/3)
Lev 6:28 it shall be both scoured and *r*
15:11 and has not *r* his hands in
15:12 vessel of wood shall be *r* in

RIP (1/1) RIPPED
2 Ki 8:12 and *r* open their women with

RIPE (9/9) RIPENS
Gen 40:10 brought forth *r* grapes.
Ex 22:29 the first of your *r* produce
Num 13:20 season of the first *r* grapes.
17: 8 blossoms and yielded *r* almonds.
18:13 Whatever first *r* fruit is in
Jer 24: 2 the figs that are first *r*;
Joel 3:13 sickle, for the harvest is *r*.
Rev 14:15 the harvest of the earth is *r*.
14:18 for her grapes are fully *r*.

RIPENED (2/2)
2 Ki 4:42 and newly *r* grain in his
Nah 3:12 are fig trees with *r* figs:

RIPENING (1/1)
Isa 18: 5 And the sour grape is *r* in

RIPENS (2/2) RIPE
Job 5:26 As a sheaf of grain *r* in its
Mk 4:29 "But when the grain *r*,

RIPHATH (1/1)
Gen 10: 3 sons of Gomer were Ashkenaz, *R*,

RIPPED (3/3) RIP
2 Ki 15:16 were with child he *r* open.
Hos 13:16 their women with child *r* open.
Am 1:13 Because they *r* open the women

RISE (154/152) RISEN, RISES, RISING, ROSE
Gen 19: 2 then you may *r* early and go on
31:35 my lord that I cannot *r* before
Ex 8:20 *R* early in the morning and stand
9:13 *R* early in the morning and stand
10:23 nor did anyone *r* from his place
12:31 Aaron by night, and said, "*R*,
Lev 19:32 You shall *r* before the gray
Num 10:35 *R* up, O LORD! Let Your enemies
22:20 *r* and go with them; but only
23:18 '*R* up, Balak, and hear!
24:17 A Scepter shall *r* out of
Deut 2:13 Now *r* and cross over the Valley
2:24 *R*, take your journey, and
6: 7 lie down, and when you *r* up.
11:19 lie down, and when you *r* up.
19:15 One witness shall not *r* against
28: 7 your enemies who *r* against
28:43 is among you shall *r* higher
29:22 of your children who *r* up
31:16 and this people will *r* and play
32:38 Let them *r* and help you,
33:11 loins of those who *r* against
33:11 that they *r* not again."
Josh 8: 7 Then you shall *r* from the ambush
18: 4 they shall *r* and go through the
Judg 8:20 to Jether his firstborn, "*R*,
8:21 '*R* yourself, and kill us;
9:33 that you shall *r* early and
20:38 make a great cloud of smoke *r*
20:40 But when the cloud began to *r*
1 Sam 22:13 that he should *r* against me, to
24: 7 and did not allow them to *r*
29:10 *r* early in the morning with
2 Sam 15: 2 Now Absalom would *r* early and
18:32 and all who *r* against you to do
22:39 So that they could not *r*;
22:49 lift me up above those who *r*
2 Ki 9: 2 and go in and make him *r* up
16: 7 who *r* up against me."
Neh 2:18 'Let us *r* up and build."
Job 1: 5 and he would *r* early in the
9: 7 the sun, and it does not *r*;
14:12 man lies down and does not *r*.
20:27 And the earth will *r* up
25: 3 Upon whom does His light not *r*?
Ps 3: 1 Many are they who *r* up
7: 6 *R* up for me to the judgment
17: 7 in You From those who *r* up
18:38 So that they could not *r*;
18:48 lift me up above those who *r*
27: 3 Though war should *r* against
35:11 Fierce witnesses *r* up;
36:12 cast down and are not able to *r*.
41: 8 he will *r* up no more."
44: 5 we will trample those who *r* up
59: 1 Defend me from those who *r* up
74:23 The tumult of those who *r* up
89: 9 When its waves *r*, You still
92:11 desire on the wicked Who *r*
94: 2 *R* up, O Judge of the earth
94:16 Who will *r* up for me against
119:62 At midnight I will *r* to give
119:147 I *r* before the dawning of the
127: 2 It is vain for you to *r* up
139:21 do I not loathe those who *r* up
140:10 that they *r* not up again.
Prov 6: 9 When will you *r* from your
24:16 may fall seven times And *r*
24:22 For their calamity will *r*
31:28 Her children *r* up and call her
Song 2:10 '*R* up, my love, my fair one,
2:13 *R* up, my love, my fair one,
3: 2 'I will *r* now," I said,
Isa 5:11 Woe to those who *r* early in
14:21 Lest they *r* up and possess the
14:22 For I will *r* up against them,"
24:20 it will fall, and not *r* again.
26:14 are deceased, they will not *r*.
28:21 For the LORD will *r* up as at

32: 9 *R* up, you women who are at
33:10 Now I will *r*," says the LORD;
34: 3 Their stench shall *r* from
43:17 down together, they shall not *r*;
60: 1 A*r*, shine; For your light has
Jer 8: 4 "Will they fall and not *r*?
25:27 and vomit! Fall and *r* no more,
37:10 they would *r* up, every man in
47: 2 waters *r* out of the north,
49:14 And *r* up to battle!
51:64 Babylon shall sink and not *r*
Dan 7:24 And another shall *r* after
8:25 He shall even *r* against the
11:14 in those times many shall *r* up
Joel 2:20 And his foul odor will *r*,
Am 5: 2 She will *r* no more. She lies
7: 9 I will *r* with the sword
8:14 They shall fall and never *r*
Ob 1 and let us *r* up against her for
Nah 1: 9 Affliction will not *r* up a
Hab 2: 7 Will not your creditors *r* up
Zeph 3: 8 Until the day I *r* up for
Mt 5:45 for He makes His sun *r* on the
10:21 and children will *r* up against
12:41 The men of Nineveh will *r* up in
12:42 The queen of the South will *r* up
20:19 And the third day He will *r*
24: 7 For nation will *r* against
24:11 many false prophets will *r* up
24:24 and false prophets will *r* and
26:46 '*R*, let us be going.
27:63 'After three days I will *r*.
Mk 4:27 should sleep by night and *r* by
8:31 and after three days *r* again.
9:31 He will *r* the third day."
10:34 And the third day He will *r*
10:49 to him, "Be of good cheer. *R*,
12:23 the resurrection, when they *r*,
12:25 For when they *r* from the dead,
12:26 the dead, that they *r*,
13: 8 For nation will *r* against
13:12 and children will *r* up against
13:22 and false prophets will *r* and
14:42 '*R*, let us be going. See,
Lk 5:23 *R* up and walk'?
11: 7 I cannot *r* and give to you'?
11: 8 though he will not *r* and give
11: 8 of his persistence he will *r*
11:31 The queen of the South will *r* up
11:32 The men of Nineveh will *r* up in
16:31 be persuaded though one *r* from
18:33 And the third day He will *r*
21:10 Nation will *r* against nation,
22:46 *R* and pray, lest you enter into
24: 7 and the third day *r* again.'"
24:46 Christ to suffer and to *r* from
Jn 5: 8 Jesus said to him, "*R*,
11:23 Your brother will *r* again."
11:24 I know that he will *r* again in
20: 9 that He must *r* again from the
Acts 3: 6 Nazareth, *r* up and walk."
10:13 And a voice came to him, "*R*,
11: 7 heard a voice saying to me, '*R*,
17: 3 Christ had to suffer and *r* again
20:30 among yourselves men will *r* up,
26:16 But *r* and stand on your feet;
26:23 that He would be the first to *r*
Rom 15:12 And He who shall *r* to
1 Cor 15:15 up—if in fact the dead do not *r*.
15:16 For if the dead do not *r*,
15:29 if the dead do not *r* at all?
15:32 If the dead do not *r*,
1 Th 4:16 And the dead in Christ will *r*
Heb 7:11 that another priest should *r*
Rev 11: 1 *R* and measure the temple of God,

RISEN (42/42) RISE

Gen 19:23 The sun had *r* upon the earth
Ex 22: 3 'If the sun has *r* on him,
Num 32:14 And look! You have *r* in your
Judg 9:18 but you have *r* up against my
1 Sam 25:29 Yet a man has *r* to pursue you
2 Sam 14: 7 now the whole family has *r*
Ezra 9: 6 for our iniquities have *r*
Ps 20: 8 But we have *r* and stand
27:12 For false witnesses have *r*
54: 3 For strangers have *r* up against
86:14 the proud have *r* against me,
Isa 60: 1 the glory of the LORD is *r*
Ezek 7:11 Violence has *r* up into a rod of
Mic 2: 8 Lately My people have *r* up as an
Mt 11:11 born of women there has not *r*
14: 2 he is *r* from the dead,
17: 9 one until the Son of Man is *r*
27:64 'He has *r* from the dead.'
28: 6 "He is not here; for He is *r*,
28: 7 tell His disciples that He is *r*
Mk 1:35 having *r* a long while before
3:26 And if Satan has *r* up against
6:14 John the Baptist is *r* from the
9: 9 till the Son of Man had *r* from
16: 2 to the tomb when the sun had *r*.
16: 6 He is *r*! He is not here.
16:14 who had seen Him after He had *r*.
Lk 7:16 A great prophet has *r* up among
9: 7 said by some that John had *r*
9: 8 one of the old prophets had *r*
9:19 one of the old prophets has *r*
13:25 the Master of the house has *r*
24: 6 'He is not here, but is *r*!
24:34 The Lord is *r* indeed, and has
Jn 2:22 when He had *r* from the dead,
Rom 8:34 died, and furthermore is also *r*,
1 Cor 15:13 the dead, then Christ is not *r*.
15:14 And if Christ is not *r*,
15:16 not rise, then Christ is not *r*.
15:17 And if Christ is not *r*,
15:20 But now Christ is *r* from the
Jas 1:11 For no sooner has the sun *r* with

RISES (24/24) RISE

Ex 21:19 if he *r* again and walks about
Num 23:24 a people *r* like a lioness,
Deut 19:11 *r* against him and strikes him
19:16 If a false witness *r* against any
22:26 for just as when a man *r*
Josh 6:26 the man before the LORD who *r*
2 Sam 11:20 happens that the king's wrath *r*,
23: 4 of the morning when the sun *r*,
Job 16: 8 My leanness *r* up against me
24:14 The murderer *r* with the light;
24:22 He *r* up, but no man is sure
27: 7 And he who *r* up against me
31:14 then shall I do when God *r* up?
Ps 104:22 When the sun *r*, they gather
Prov 31:15 She also *r* while it is yet
Eccl 1: 5 The sun also *r*,
10: 4 If the spirit of the ruler *r*
12: 4 When one *r* up at the sound of
Isa 54:17 And every tongue which *r*
Jer 46: 8 Egypt *r* up like a flood,
Mic 7: 6 Daughter *r* against her mother,
Nah 3:17 When the sun *r* they flee away,
2 Pe 1:19 dawns and the morning star *r*
Rev 19: 3 Alleluia! Her smoke *r* up forever

RISING (35/35) RISE

Num 2: 3 toward the *r* of the sun, those
Deut 4:41 toward the *r* of the sun,
4:47 toward the *r* of the sun,
Josh 12: 1 of the Jordan toward the *r* of
1 Ki 18:44 man's hand, *r* out of the sea!"
2 Chr 36:15 *r* up early and sending them,
Job 36:33 concerning the *r* storm.
Ps 19: 6 Its *r* is from one end of
50: 1 called the earth From the *r*
113: 3 From the *r* of the sun to its
139: 2 know my sitting down and my *r*
Prov 27:14 *r* early in the morning,
Isa 9:18 shall mount up like *r* smoke.
41:25 From the *r* of the sun he shall
45: 6 they may know from the *r* of
59:19 And His glory from the *r* of
60: 3 to the brightness of your *r*.
Jer 7:13 *r* up early and speaking, but
7:25 daily *r* up early and sending
11: 7 *r* early and exhorting, saying,
25: 3 *r* early and speaking, but you
25: 4 *r* early and sending them, but
26: 5 both *r* up early and sending
29:19 *r* up early and sending them;
32:33 *r* up early and teaching them,
35:14 *r* early and speaking, you did
35:15 *r* up early and sending them,
44: 4 *r* early and sending them,
Lam 3:63 their sitting down and their *r*
Mal 1:11 For from the *r* of the sun, even
Mt 27:24 but rather that a tumult was *r*,
Mk 9:10 questioning what the *r* from the
Lk 2:34 is destined for the fall and *r*
12:54 Whenever you see a cloud *r* out
Rev 13: 1 And I saw a beast *r* up out of

RISK (2/2)

1 Chr 11:19 For at the *r* of their lives
Lam 5: 9 We get our bread at the *r* of

RISKED (3/3)

Judg 9:17 *r* his life, and delivered you
Acts 15:26 men who have *r* their lives for
Rom 16: 4 who *r* their own necks for my

RISSAH (2/2)

Num 33:21 from Libnah and camped at *R*.
33:22 They journeyed from *R* and camped

RITE (1/1)

Num 9:14 do so according to the *r* of

RITES (1/1)

Num 9: 3 According to all its *r* and

RITHMAH (2/2)

Num 33:18 from Hazeroth and camped at *R*.
33:19 They departed from *R* and camped

RITUAL (4/4)

Deut 23:17 There shall be no *r* harlot of
2 Ki 23: 7 Then he tore down the *r* booths
Ezek 20:26 them unclean because of their *r*
Hos 4:14 And offer sacrifices with a *r*

RITUALLY (1/1)

Ezra 6:20 all of them were *r* clean.

RITUALS (6/5)

2 Ki 17:26 of Samaria do not know the *r*
17:26 because they do not know the *r*
17:27 and let him teach them the *r* of
17:33 according to the *r* of the
17:34 practicing the former *r*;
17:40 they followed their former *r*.

RIVAL (2/2)

Lev 18:18 shall you take a woman as a *r*
1 Sam 1: 6 And her *r* also provoked her

RIVER (164/138) RIVERHEADS, RIVERS, RIVERSIDE

Gen 2:10 Now a *r* went out of Eden to
2:13 The name of the second *r* is
2:14 The name of the third *r* is
2:14 The fourth *r* is the Euphrates.
15:18 from the *r* of Egypt to the
15:18 river of Egypt to the great *r*,
15:18 the *R* Euphrates—
31:21 He arose and crossed the *r*,
41: 1 and behold, he stood by the *r*.
41: 2 there came up out of the *r*
41: 3 came up after them out of the *r*,
41: 3 cows on the bank of the *r*.
41:17 I stood on the bank of the *r*.
41:18 seven cows came up out of the *r*,
Ex 1:22 born you shall cast into the *r*,
2: 5 came down to bathe at the *r*.
4: 9 you shall take water from the *r*
4: 9 which you take from the *r* will
7:17 the waters which are in the *r*
7:18 the fish that are in the *r*
7:18 the *r* shall stink, and the
7:18 to drink the water of the *r*.
7:20 the waters that were in the *r*,
7:20 the waters that were in the *r*
7:21 The fish that were in the *r*
7:21 the *r* stank, and the Egyptians
7:21 not drink the water of the *r*.
7:24 Egyptians dug all around the *r*
7:24 not drink the water of the *r*.
7:25 the LORD had struck the *r*.
8: 3 So the *r* shall bring forth frogs
8: 9 that they may remain in the *r*
8:11 They shall remain in the *r*
17: 5 rod with which you struck the *r*,
23:31 and from the desert to the *R*.
Num 22: 5 which is near the *R* in the
Deut 1: 7 Lebanon, as far as the great *r*,
1: 7 the *R* Euphrates.
2:24 and cross over the *R* Arnon.
2:36 which is on the bank of the *R*
2:37 anywhere along the *R* Jabbok, or
3: 8 from the *R* Arnon to Mount
3:12 which is by the *R* Arnon, and
3:16 from Gilead as far as the *R*
3:16 the middle of the *r* as the
3:16 as far as the *R* Jabbok, the
4:48 which is on the bank of the *R*
11:24 and Lebanon, from the *r*,
11:24 the *R* Euphrates, even to the
Josh 1: 4 Lebanon as far as the great *r*,
1: 4 the *R* Euphrates, all the land
12: 1 from the *R* Arnon to Mount
12: 2 which is on the bank of the *R*
12: 2 from the middle of that *r*,
12: 2 even as far as the *R* Jabbok,
13: 9 which is on the bank of the *R*
13:16 which is on the bank of the *R*
24: 2 on the other side of the *R* in
24: 3 from the other side of the *R*,
24:14 on the other side of the *R* and
24:15 on the other side of the *R*,
Judg 4: 7 and his multitude at the *R*
4:13 from Harosheth Hagoyim to the *R*
2 Sam 8: 3 recover his territory at the *R*
10:16 Syrians who were beyond the *R*,
17:13 and we will pull it into the *r*,
1 Ki 4:21 over all kingdoms from the *R*
4:24 region on this side of the *R*
4:24 the kings on this side of the *R*;
14:15 will scatter them beyond the *R*,
2 Ki 10:33 which is by the *R* Arnon,
17: 6 the *R* of Gozan, and in the
18:11 the *R* of Gozan, and in the
23:29 to the *R* Euphrates; and King
24: 7 the Brook of Egypt to the *R*
1 Chr 5: 9 wilderness this side of the *R*
5:26 and the *r* of Gozan to this day.
18: 3 to establish his power by the *R*
19:16 Syrians who were beyond the *R*,
2 Chr 9:26 over all the kings from the *R*
Ezra 4:10 and the remainder beyond the *R*—
4:11 of the region beyond the *R*,
4:16 have no dominion beyond the *R*.
4:17 to the remainder beyond the *R*:
4:20 all the region beyond the *R*;
5: 3 of the region beyond the *R*,
5: 6 of the region beyond the *R*,
5: 6 in the region beyond the *R*,
6: 6 of the region beyond the *R*,
6: 6 Persians who are beyond the *R*,
6: 8 on the region beyond the *R*;
6:13 of the region beyond the *R*,
7:21 in the region beyond the *R*,
7:25 in the region beyond the *R*,
8:15 Now I gathered them by the *r*

R

8:21 a fast there at the *r* of Ahava,
8:31 Then we departed from the *r* of
8:36 in the region beyond the *R*.
Neh 2: 7 of the region beyond the *R*,
2: 9 in the region beyond the *R*,
3: 7 of the region beyond the *R*.
Job 14:11 And a *r* becomes parched and
40:23 Indeed the *r* may rage, Yet he
Ps 36: 8 You give them drink from the *r*
46: 4 There is a *r* whose streams
65: 9 The *r* of God is full of water;
66: 6 They went through the *r* on
72: 8 And from the *R* to the ends of
80:11 Sea, And her branches to the *R*.
105:41 ran in the dry places like a *r*.
Isa 7:20 With those from beyond the *R*,
8: 7 over them The waters of the *R*,
11:15 will shake His fist over the *R*,
19: 5 And the *r* will be wasted and
19: 7 The papyrus reeds by the *R*,
19: 7 River, by the mouth of the *R*,
19: 7 And everything sown by the *R*,
19: 8 who cast hooks into the *R*,
23: 3 The harvest of the *R*,
23:10 through your land like the *R*,
27:12 From the channel of the *R* to
48:18 peace would have been like a *r*,
66:12 extend peace to her like a *r*,
Jer 2:18 To drink the waters of the *R*?
17: 8 spreads out its roots by the *r*,
46: 2 which was by the *R* Euphrates in
46: 6 by the *R* Euphrates.
46:10 In the north country by the *R*
Lam 2:18 Let tears run down like a *r*
Ezek 1: 1 among the captives by the *R*
1: 3 land of the Chaldeans by the *R*
3:15 who dwelt by the *R* Chebar; and
3:23 the glory which I saw by the *R*
10:15 living creature I saw by the *R*
10:20 the God of Israel by the *R*
10:22 faces which I had seen by the *R*
29: 3 My *R* is my own; I have made
29: 9 The *R* is mine, and I have made
43: 3 the vision which I saw by the *R*
47: 5 and it was a *r* that I could
47: 5 a *r* that could not be crossed.
47: 6 me to the bank of the *r*.
47: 7 there, along the bank of the *r*,
47: 9 will live wherever the *r* goes.
47:12 "Along the bank of the *r*,
Dan 8: 2 the vision that I was by the *R*
8: 3 there, standing beside the *r*,
8: 6 had seen standing beside the *r*,
10: 4 was by the side of the great *r*,
12: 6 was above the waters of the *r*,
12: 7 was above the waters of the *r*,
Am 8: 8 of it shall swell like the *R*,
8: 8 Heave and subside Like the *R*
9: 5 of it shall swell like the *R*,
9: 5 And subside like the *R* of
Mic 7:12 From the fortress to the *R*,
Nah 3: 8 That was situated by the *R*,
Zech 9:10 And from the *R* to the ends of
10:11 All the depths of the *R* shall
Mk 1: 5 baptized by him in the Jordan *R*,
Rev 9:14 who are bound at the great *r*
16:12 out his bowl on the great *r*
22: 1 And he showed me a pure *r* of
22: 2 and on either side of the *r*,

RIVER'S (2/2)

Ex 2: 3 laid it in the reeds by the *r*
7:15 and you shall stand by the *r*

RIVERBANK (2/1)

Dan 12: 5 one on this *r* and the other on
12: 5 and the other on that *r*.

RIVERBEDS (1/1)

Ezek 32: 6 And the *r* will be full of you.

RIVERHEADS (1/1) RIVER

Gen 2:10 it parted and became four *r*.

RIVERS (67/62) RIVER

Ex 7:19 their streams, over their *r*,
8: 5 over the streams, over the *r*,
Lev 11: 9 whether in the seas or in the *r*—
11:10 all in the seas or in the *r*
Deut 10: 7 a land of *r* of water.
2 Ki 5:12 the *r* of Damascus, better than
Job 20:17 The *r* flowing with honey and
29: 6 And the rock poured out *r* of
Ps 1: 3 like a tree Planted by the *r*
74:15 You dried up mighty *r*.
78:16 waters to run down like *r*.
78:44 Turned their *r* into blood,
89:25 And his right hand over the *r*.
98: 8 Let the *r* clap their hands;
107:33 He turns *r* into a wilderness,
119:136 *R* of water run down from my
137: 1 By the *r* of Babylon, There we
Prov 21: 1 Like the *r* of water;
Eccl 1: 7 All the *r* run into the sea,
1: 7 To the place from which the *r*
Song 5:12 eyes are like doves By the *r*
Isa 7:18 in the farthest part of the *r*
18: 1 Which is beyond the *r* of
18: 2 Whose land the *r* divide."
18: 7 Whose land the *r* divide—To
19: 6 The *r* will turn foul;
30:25 And on every high hill *R*
32: 2 As *r* of water in a dry place,
33:21 be for us A place of broad *r*
41:18 I will open *r* in desolate
42:15 I will make the *r* coastlands,
43: 2 And through the *r*, they shall
43:19 road in the wilderness And *r*
43:20 in the wilderness And *r* in
44:27 And I will dry up your *r*';
47: 2 Pass through the *r*.
50: 2 I make the *r* a wilderness;
Jer 31: 9 cause them to walk by the *r* of
46: 7 Whose waters move like the *r*?
46: 8 its waters move like the *r*;
Lam 3:48 My eyes overflow with *r* of
Ezek 29: 3 who lies in the midst of his *r*,
29: 4 And cause the fish of your *r*
29: 4 up out of the midst of your *r*,
29: 4 And all the fish in your *r*
29: 5 You and all the fish of your *r*;
29:10 against you and against your *r*,
30:12 I will make the *r* dry, And
31: 4 With their *r* running around
31:12 boughs lie broken by all the *r*
31:15 I restrained its *r*,
32: 2 seas, Bursting forth in your *r*,
32: 2 And fouling their *r*.'
32:14 And make their *r* run like
36: 4 the mountains, the hills, the *r*,
36: 6 the mountains, the hills, the *r*,
47: 9 wherever the *r* go, will live.
Mic 6: 7 Ten thousand *r* of oil?
Nah 1: 4 And dries up all the *r*.
2: 6 The gates of the *r* are opened,
Hab 3: 8 were You displeased with the *r*,
3: 8 Was Your anger against the *r*,
3: 9 You divided the earth with *r*.
Zeph 3:10 From beyond the *r* of Ethiopia
Jn 7:38 out of his heart will flow *r* of
Rev 8:10 and it fell on a third of the *r*
16: 4 poured out his bowl on the *r*

RIVERSIDE (3/3) RIVER

Ex 2: 5 her maidens walked along the *r*;
Num 24: 6 Like gardens by the *r*,
Acts 16:13 went out of the city to the *r*,

RIVULETS (1/1)

Ezek 31: 4 And sent out *r* to all the

RIZIA (1/1)

1 Chr 7:39 Ulla were Arah, Haniel, and *R*.

RIZPAH (4/4)

2 Sam 3: 7 a concubine, whose name was *R*,
21: 8 the two sons of *R* the daughter
21:10 Now *R* the daughter of Aiah took
21:11 And David was told what *R* the

ROAD (85/79)

Num 21: 1 Israel was coming on the *r* to
22:23 to turn her back onto the *r*.
Deut 2: 8 away from the *r* of the plain,
2:27 I will keep strictly to the *r*,
3: 1 we turned and went up the *r* to
22: 4 or his ox fall down along the *r*,
23: 4 with bread and water on the *r*
27:18 the blind to wander off the *r*.
Josh 2: 7 the men pursued them by the *r*
10:10 chased them along the *r* that
12: 3 the *r* to Beth Jeshimoth,
Judg 5:10 And who walk along the *r*.
8:11 Then Gideon went up by the *r* of
1 Sam 6: 9 if it goes up the *r* to its own
6:12 cows headed straight for the *r*
13:17 One company turned to the *r* to
13:18 company turned to the *r* to
13:18 company turned to the *r* of
17:52 Philistines fell along the *r*
24: 3 came to the sheepfolds by the *r*,
26: 3 is opposite Jeshimon, by the *r*.
2 Sam 2:24 which is before Giah by the *r*
13:34 people were coming from the *r*
16:13 and his men went along the *r*,
1 Ki 13:24 a lion met him on the *r* and
13:24 his corpse was thrown on the *r*,
13:25 saw the corpse thrown on the *r*,
13:28 his corpse thrown on the *r*,
20:38 waited for the king by the *r*,
2 Ki 2:23 and as he was going up the *r*,
7:15 and indeed all the *r* was full
9:27 he fled by the *r* to Beth
Ezra 8:22 us against the enemy on the *r*,
8:31 and from ambush along the *r*.
Neh 9:12 To give them light on the *r*
9:19 To lead them on the *r*;
Job 18:10 And a trap for him in the *r*.
19:12 And build up their *r* against
21:29 asked those who travel the *r*?
24: 4 They push the needy off the *r*;
Prov 26:13 There is a lion in the *r*!
Isa 35: 8 highway shall be there, and a *r*,
35: 8 Whoever walks the *r*,
43:19 I will even make a *r* in the
49:11 make each of My mountains a *r*,
51:10 made the depths of the sea a *r*
Jer 2:18 And now why take the *r* to
2:18 Or why take the *r* to Assyria,
3: 2 By the *r* you have sat for them
Ezek 16:25 places at the head of every *r*,
16:31 shrine at the head of every *r*,
21:19 put it at the head of the *r* to
21:20 Appoint a *r* for the sword to go
21:21 stands at the parting of the *r*,
47:15 by the *r* to Hethlon, as one
48: 1 northern border along the *r* to
Hos 13: 7 Like a leopard by the *r* I will
Nah 2: 1 Man the fort! Watch the *r*!
Mt 20:17 disciples aside on the *r* and
20:30 two blind men sitting by the *r*,
21: 8 spread their clothes on the *r*;
21: 8 trees and spread them on the *r*.
21:19 And seeing a fig tree by the *r*,
Mk 8:27 and on the *r* He asked His
9:33 among yourselves on the *r*?
9:34 for on the *r* they had disputed
10:17 as He was going out on the *r*,
10:32 Now they were on the *r*,
10:46 sat by the *r* begging.
10:52 and followed Jesus on the *r*.
11: 8 spread their clothes on the *r*,
11: 8 trees and spread them on the *r*.
Lk 9:57 as they journeyed on the *r*,
10: 4 and greet no one along the *r*.
10:31 certain priest came down that *r*.
18:35 certain blind man sat by the *r*
19:36 spread their clothes on the *r*.
24:32 He talked with us on the *r*,
24:35 that had happened on the *r*,
Acts 8:26 go toward the south along the *r*
8:36 Now as they went down the *r*,
9:17 who appeared to you on the *r* as
9:27 he had seen the Lord on the *r*,
25: 3 lay in ambush along the *r* to
26:13 along the *r* I saw a light from

ROADS (5/5)

Deut 19: 3 You shall prepare *r* for
Isa 49: 9 "They shall feed along the *r*,
Lam 1: 4 The *r* to Zion mourn Because no
Ezek 21:21 road, at the fork of the two *r*,
Nah 2: 4 one another in the broad *r*;

ROADSIDE (1/1)

Gen 38:21 harlot who was openly by the *r*?

ROAM (2/2)

Prov 6:22 When you *r*, they will lead you;
Isa 7:25 And a place for sheep to *r*.

ROAMING (2/2)

Lam 1: 7 days of her affliction and *r*,
3:19 Remember my affliction and *r*,

ROAR (21/19) ROARED, ROARING, ROARS

1 Chr 16:32 Let the sea *r*, and all
Ps 46: 3 Though its waters *r* and be
74: 4 Your enemies *r* in the midst of
96:11 earth be glad; Let the sea *r*,
98: 7 Let the sea *r*, and all its
104:21 The young lions *r* after their
Isa 5:29 They will *r* like young lions;
5:29 they will *r* And lay hold of
5:30 In that day they will *r* against
17:12 Who make a noise like the *r*
Jer 5:22 cannot prevail; Though they *r*,
25:30 The LORD will *r* from on high,
25:30 He will *r* mightily against His
31:35 And its waves *r* (The LORD of
50:42 Their voice shall *r* like the
51:38 They shall *r* together like
51:55 Though her waves *r* like great
Hos 11:10 He will *r* like a lion.
Joel 3:16 The LORD also will *r* from
Am 3: 4 Will a lion *r* in the forest,
Zech 9:15 They shall drink and *r* as if

ROARED (3/3) ROAR

Isa 51:15 divided the sea whose waves *r*—
Jer 2:15 The young lions *r* at him, and
Am 3: 8 A lion has *r*! Who will not

ROARING (14/14) ROAR

Judg 14: 5 a young lion came *r* against
Job 4:10 The *r* of the lion, The voice
Ps 22:13 Like a raging and *r* lion.
Prov 19:12 king's wrath is like the *r* of
20: 2 of a king is like the *r* of
28:15 Like a *r* lion and a charging
Isa 5:29 Their *r* will be like a lion,
5:30 Like the *r* of the sea.
Ezek 19: 7 By the noise of his *r*.
22:25 in her midst is like a *r* lion
Zeph 3: 3 in her midst are *r* lions;
Zech 11: 3 is the sound of *r* lions!
Lk 21:25 the sea and the waves *r*;
1 Pe 5: 8 walks about like a *r* lion,

ROARS (6/6) ROAR

Job 37: 4 After it a voice *r*;

Isa 31: 4 spoken to me: "As a lion r,
Jer 6:23 Their voice r like the sea;
Hos 11:10 He r. Then His sons shall
Am 1: 2 'The LORD r from Zion,
Rev 10: 3 a loud voice, as when a lion r.

ROAST (3/3) ROASTED

Deut 16: 7 And you shall r and eat it in
Prov 12:27 The lazy man does not r what
Isa 44:16 he eats meat; He roasts a r,

ROASTED (7/7) ROAST

Ex 12: 8 r in fire, with unleavened
12: 9 but r in fire—its head with its
Lev 2:14 green heads of grain r on the
1 Sam 25:18 five seahs of r grain,
2 Chr 35:13 Also they r the Passover
Isa 44:19 I have r meat and eaten it;
Jer 29:22 whom the king of Babylon r in

ROASTING (1/1)

1 Sam 2:15 Give meat for r to the priest,

ROASTS (1/1)

Isa 44:16 He r a roast, and is

ROB (8/7) ROBBED, ROBBER, ROBBERY

Lev 19:13 your neighbor, nor r him.
26:22 which shall r you of your
Prov 22:22 Do not r the poor because he
Isa 10: 2 To r the needy of justice,
10: 2 And that they may r the
17:14 And the lot of those who r us.
Mal 3: 8 Will a man r God? Yet you have
Rom 2:22 do you r temples?

ROBBED (14/13) ROB

Judg 9:25 and they r all who passed by
2 Sam 17: 8 like a bear r of her cubs in
Prov 17:12 Let a man meet a bear r of her
Isa 10:13 And have r their treasuries;
42:22 But this is a people r and
Jer 50:37 treasures, and they will be r.
Ezek 18: 7 Has r no one by violence,
18:12 R by violence, Not restored
18:16 Nor r by violence, But has
18:18 R his brother by violence,
Mal 3: 8 Yet you have r Me!
3: 8 'In what way have we r You?'
3: 9 For you have r Me, Even this
2 Cor 11: 8 I r other churches, taking wages

ROBBER (6/6) PROWLER, ROB, ROBBERS

Ezek 18:10 he begets a son who is a r
Mt 26:55 you come out, as against a r,
Mk 14:48 you come out, as against a r,
Lk 22:52 you come out, as against a r,
Jn 10: 1 the same is a thief and a r.
18:40 Now Barabbas was a r.

ROBBERS (12/12) ROBBER

Job 12: 6 The tents of r prosper,
Isa 42:24 plunder, and Israel to the r?
Ezek 7:22 For r shall enter it and
Hos 6: 9 As bands of r lie in wait for a
7: 1 A band of r takes spoil
Ob 5 If r by night—Oh, how you
Mt 27:38 Then two r were crucified with
27:44 Even the r who were crucified
Mk 15:27 Him they also crucified two r,
Jn 10: 8 before Me are thieves and r,
Acts 19:37 men here who are neither r of
2 Cor 11:26 of waters, in perils of r,

ROBBERY (7/7) ROB

Lev 6: 2 or about a pledge, or about a r,
Ps 62:10 Nor vainly hope in r;
Isa 61: 8 I hate r for burnt offering;
Ezek 22:29 used oppressions, committed r,
Am 3:10 Who store up violence and r in
Nah 3: 1 It is all full of lies and r.
Phil 2: 6 did not consider it r to be

ROBBING (1/1)

1 Sam 23: 1 and they are r the threshing

ROBE (49/48) ROBES

Ex 28: 4 a breastplate, an ephod, a r,
28:31 You shall make the r of the
28:34 upon the hem of the r all
29: 5 and the r of the ephod,
39:22 He made the r of the ephod of
39:23 opening in the middle of the r,
39:24 They made on the hem of the r
39:25 on the hem of the r all around
39:26 all around the hem of the r to
Lev 8: 7 sash, clothed him with the r,
1 Sam 2:19 used to make him a little r,
15:27 Saul seized the edge of his r,
18: 4 And Jonathan took off the r that
24: 4 cut off a corner of Saul's r.
24: 5 because he had cut Saul's r.
24:11 see the corner of your r in my
24:11 I cut off the corner of your r,
2 Sam 13:18 Now she had on a r of many
13:19 and tore her r of many colors
15:32 coming to meet him with his r
1 Chr 15:27 David was clothed with a r of
Ezra 9: 3 I tore my garment and my r,
9: 5 having torn my garment and my r,
Esth 6: 8 let a royal r be brought which
6: 9 Then let this r and horse be
6:10 take the r and the horse,
6:11 So Haman took the r and the
Job 1:20 Then Job arose, tore his r,
2:12 and each one tore his r and
29:14 My justice was like a r and a
Song 5: 3 I have taken off my r;
Isa 3:24 Instead of a rich r,
6: 1 and the train of His r filled
22:21 I will clothe him with your r
61:10 He has covered me with the r
Jon 3: 6 his throne and laid aside his r,
Mic 2: 8 You pull off the r with the
Zech 13: 4 they will not wear a r of
Mt 27:28 Him and put a scarlet r on Him.
27:31 they took the r off Him, put
Mk 16: 5 man clothed in a long white r
Lk 9:29 and His r became white and
15:22 Bring out the best r and put it
23:11 arrayed Him in a gorgeous r,
Jn 19: 2 and they put on Him a purple r.
19: 5 of thorns and the purple r.
Rev 6:11 Then a white r was given to each
19:13 He was clothed with a r dipped
19:16 And He has on His r and on His

ROBES (17/17) ROBE

Judg 8:26 and purple r which were on the
1 Ki 22:10 Judah, having put on their r,
22:30 but you put on your r."
2 Chr 18: 9 of Judah, clothed in their r,
18:29 but you put on your r."
Esth 5: 1 Esther put on her royal r
Ps 45:14 be brought to the King in r of
Isa 3:23 linen, the turbans, and the r.
63: 3 And I have stained all My r.
Ezek 26:16 thrones, lay aside their r,
Zech 3: 4 I will clothe you with rich r.
Mk 12:38 desire to go around in long r,
Lk 20:46 desire to go around in long r,
Rev 4: 4 sitting, clothed in white r;
7: 9 the Lamb, clothed with white r,
7:13 are these arrayed in white r,
7:14 and washed their r and made

ROBOAM (KJV) See REHOBOAM

ROBS (1/1)

Prov 28:24 Whoever r his father or his

ROCK (123/111) ROCKS

Ex 17: 6 before you there on the r in
17: 6 and you shall strike the r,
33:21 and you shall stand on the r.
33:22 put you in the cleft of the r,
Lev 11: 5 the r hyrax, because it chews
Num 20: 8 Speak to the r before their
20: 8 water for them out of the r,
20:10 assembly together before the r;
20:10 water for you out of this r?
20:11 his hand and struck the r
24:21 And your nest is set in the r;
Deut 8:15 for you out of the flinty r;
14: 7 and the r hyrax; for they chew
32: 4 He is the R, His work is
32:13 made him draw honey from the r,
32:13 And oil from the flinty r;
32:15 And scornfully esteemed the R
32:18 Of the R who begot you,
32:30 Unless their R had sold them,
32:31 For their r is not like our
32:31 their rock is not like our R,
32:37 The r in which they sought
Judg 6:20 bread and lay them on this r,
6:21 and fire rose out of the r and
6:26 your God on top of this r in
7:25 They killed Oreb at the r of
13:19 and offered it upon the r to
15: 8 dwelt in the cleft of the r of
15:11 down to the cleft of the r of
15:13 and brought him up from the r.
20:45 toward the wilderness to the r
20:47 toward the wilderness to the r
20:47 and they stayed at the r of
21:13 of Benjamin who were at the r
1 Sam 2: 2 Nor is there any r like our
14: 4 there was a sharp r on one
14: 4 rock on one side and a sharp r
23:25 Therefore he went down to the r,
23:28 so they called that place the R
2 Sam 21:10 spread it for herself on the r,
22: 2 The LORD is my r and my
22:32 who is a r, except our God?
22:47 LORD lives! Blessed be my R!
22:47 The R of my salvation!
23: 3 The R of Israel spoke to me:
1 Chr 11:15 chief men went down to the r
2 Chr 25:12 them to the top of the r,
25:12 them down from the top of the r,
Neh 9:15 them water out of the r for
Job 8:17 His roots wrap around the r
14:18 And as a r is moved from its
18: 4 Or shall the r be removed from
19:24 That they were engraved on a r
24: 8 And huddle around the r for
29: 6 And the r poured out rivers of
39:28 On the crag of the r and the
Ps 18: 2 The LORD is my r and my
18:31 the LORD? And who is a r,
18:46 LORD lives! Blessed be my R!
27: 5 He shall set me high upon a r.
28: 1 You I will cry, O LORD my R:
31: 2 Be my r of refuge, A fortress
31: 3 For You are my r and my
40: 2 clay, And set my feet upon a r,
42: 9 I will say to God my R,
61: 2 Lead me to the r that is
62: 2 He only is my r and my
62: 6 He only is my r and my
62: 7 The r of my strength, And my
71: 3 For You are my r and my
78:16 brought streams out of the r,
78:20 Behold, He struck the r,
78:35 that God was their r,
81:16 And with honey from the r I
89:26 and the r of my salvation.'
92:15 LORD is upright; He is my r,
94:22 And my God the r of my refuge.
95: 1 us shout joyfully to the R of
104:18 cliffs are a refuge for the r
105:41 He opened the r, and water
114: 8 Who turned the r into a pool
137: 9 little ones against the r!
144: 1 Blessed be the LORD my R,
Prov 30:19 The way of a serpent on a r,
30:26 The r badgers are a feeble
Song 2:14 my dove, in the clefts of the r,
Isa 2:10 Enter into the r, and hide
8:14 a stone of stumbling and a r
10:26 slaughter of Midian at the r
17:10 have not been mindful of the R
22:16 a tomb for himself in a r?
32: 2 As the shadow of a great r in
44: 8 Indeed there is no other R;
48:21 the waters to flow from the r
48:21 for them; He also split the r,
51: 1 Look to the r from which you
Jer 5: 3 made their faces harder than r;
13: 4 it there in a hole in the r.
18:14 Which comes from the r of
21:13 And r of the plain," says
23:29 a hammer that breaks the r in
48:28 the cities and dwell in the r,
49:16 dwell in the clefts of the r,
Ezek 24: 7 She set it on top of a r;
24: 8 set her blood on top of a r,
26: 4 make her like the top of a r.
26:14 make you like the top of a r;
Ob 3 dwell in the clefts of the r,
Hab 1:12 O R, You have marked them
Mt 7:24 who built his house on the r:
7:25 for it was founded on the r.
16:18 and on this r I will build My
27:60 which he had hewn out of the r;
Mk 15:46 had been hewn out of the r,
Lk 6:48 laid the foundation on the r.
6:48 it, for it was founded on the r.
8: 6 'Some fell on r; and as soon
8:13 But the ones on the r are
23:53 that was hewn out of the r,
Rom 9:33 a stumbling stone and r
1 Cor 10: 4 they drank of that spiritual R
10: 4 and that R was Christ.
1 Pe 2: 8 And a r of offense."

ROCKS (23/22) ROCK

Num 23: 9 For from the top of the r I see
1 Sam 13: 6 hid in caves, in thickets, in r,
24: 2 David and his men on the R of
1 Ki 19:11 the mountains and broke the r
Job 28:10 He cuts out channels in the r,
30: 6 caves of the earth and the r.
39:28 On the r it dwells and resides,
Ps 78:15 He split the r in the
Isa 2:19 go into the holes of the r,
2:21 To go into the clefts of the r,
2:21 into the crags of the rugged r,
7:19 and in the clefts of the r,
33:16 will be the fortress of r;
57: 5 Under the clefts of the r?
Jer 4:29 thickets and climb up on the r.
16:16 and out of the holes of the r.
51:25 you, Roll you down from the r,
Am 6:12 Do horses run on r?
Nah 1: 6 And the r are thrown down by
Mt 27:51 and the r were split,
Acts 27:29 we should run aground on the r,
Rev 6:15 in the caves and in the r of
6:16 and said to the mountains and r,

ROD (93/83) RODS

Ex 4: 2 in your hand?" He said, "A r.
4: 4 and it became a r in his hand),
4:17 And you shall take this r in
4:20 And Moses took the r of God in
7: 9 Take your r and cast it before
7:10 And Aaron cast down his r
7:12 For every man threw down his r,
7:12 But Aaron's r swallowed up
7:15 and the r which was turned to a
7:17 are in the river with the r

R

7:19 Take your **r** and stretch out your
7:20 So he lifted up the **r** and
8: 5 out your hand with your **r** over
8:16 to Aaron, 'Stretch out your **r**,
8:17 out his hand with his **r** and
9:23 And Moses stretched out his **r**
10:13 So Moses stretched out his **r**
14:16 "But lift up your **r**,
17: 5 Also take in your hand your **r**
17: 9 the top of the hill with the **r**
21:20 male or female servant with a **r**,
Lev 27:32 of whatever passes under the **r**,
Num 17: 2 and get from them a **r** from each
17: 2 Write each man's name on his **r**.
17: 3 write Aaron's name on the **r** of
17: 3 For there shall be one **r** for
17: 5 And it shall be that the **r** of
17: 6 of their leaders gave him a **r**
17: 6 and the **r** of Aaron was among
17: 8 the **r** of Aaron, of the house of
17: 9 looked, and each man took his **r**.
17:10 Bring Aaron's **r** back before the
20: 8 'Take the **r**; you and your
20: 9 So Moses took the **r** from before
20:11 the rock twice with his **r**;
1 Sam 14:27 stretched out the end of the **r**
14:43 honey with the end of the **r**
2 Sam 7:14 I will chasten him with the **r**
Job 9:34 Let Him take His **r** away from
21: 9 Neither is the **r** of God upon
Ps 2: 9 You shall break them with a **r**
23: 4 Your **r** and Your staff, they
89:32 their transgression with the **r**,
110: 2 The LORD shall send the **r** of
Prov 10:13 But a **r** is for the back of
13:24 He who spares his **r** hates his
14: 3 the mouth of a fool is a **r** of
22: 8 And the **r** of his anger will
22:15 The **r** of correction will drive
23:13 For if you beat him with a **r**,
23:14 You shall beat him with a **r**,
26: 3 And a **r** for the fool's back.
29:15 The **r** and rebuke give wisdom,
Isa 9: 4 The **r** of his oppressor,
10: 5 the **r** of My anger And the
10:15 As if a **r** could wield itself
10:24 He shall strike you with a **r**
10:26 as His **r** was on the sea, so
11: 1 There shall come forth a **R** from
11: 4 strike the earth with the **r** of
14:29 Because the **r** that struck you
28:27 stick, And the cummin with a **r**.
30:31 As He strikes with the **r**.
Jer 48:17 The beautiful **r**!'
Lam 3: 1 has seen affliction by the **r**
Ezek 7:10 The **r** has blossomed, Pride
7:11 has risen up into a **r** of
19:14 Fire has come out from a **r** of
20:37 will make you pass under the **r**,
40: 3 line of flax and a measuring **r**
40: 5 man's hand was a measuring **r**
40: 5 of the wall structure, one **r**;
40: 5 one rod; and the height, one **r**.
40: 6 which was one **r** wide, and the
40: 6 the other threshold was one **r**
40: 7 Each gate chamber was one **r**
40: 7 was one rod long and one **r**
40: 7 of the inside gate was one **r**.
40: 8 of the inside gate, one **r**.
41: 8 of the side chambers, a full **r**,
42:16 east side with the measuring **r**,
42:16 rods by the measuring **r** all
42:17 rods by the measuring **r** all
42:18 hundred rods by the measuring **r**.
42:19 hundred rods by the measuring **r**.
Mic 5: 1 the judge of Israel with a **r**
6: 9 Hear the **R**! Who has appointed
1 Cor 4:21 Shall I come to you with a **r**,
Heb 9: 4 Aaron's **r** that budded, and the
Rev 2:27 shall rule them with a **r**
11: 1 given a reed like a measuring **r**.
12: 5 to rule all nations with a **r**
19:15 will rule them with a **r** of

RODANIM (1/1)

1 Chr 1: 7 Tarshishah, Kittim, and **R**.

RODE (15/15) RIDE

Gen 24:61 and they **r** on the camels and
Judg 10: 4 Now he had thirty sons who **r** on
12:14 who **r** on seventy young donkeys.
1 Sam 25:20 as she **r** on the donkey, that
25:42 Abigail rose in haste and **r** on
30:17 four hundred young men who **r** on
2 Sam 18: 9 Absalom **r** on a mule. The mule
22:11 He **r** upon a cherub, and flew;
1 Ki 13:13 donkey for him; and he **r** on it,
18:45 So Ahab **r** away and went to
2 Ki 9:16 So Jehu **r** in a chariot and went
Neh 2:12 me, except the one on which I **r**.
Esth 8:14 The couriers who **r** on royal
Ps 18:10 And He **r** upon a cherub, and
Hab 3: 8 That You **r** on Your horses,

RODS (21/18) ROD

Gen 30:37 Now Jacob took for himself **r** of
30:37 the white which was in the **r**.
30:38 And the **r** which he had peeled,
30:39 flocks conceived before the **r**,
30:41 that Jacob placed the **r** before
30:41 they might conceive among the **r**.
Ex 7:12 rod swallowed up their **r**.
Num 17: 2 their fathers' houses—twelve **r**.
17: 6 their fathers' houses, twelve **r**;
17: 6 rod of Aaron was among their **r**.
17: 7 And Moses placed the **r** before
17: 9 Moses brought out all the **r**
Esth 1: 6 linen and purple on silver **r**
Song 5:14 His hands are **r** of gold
Ezek 42:16 five hundred **r** by the measuring
42:17 five hundred **r** by the measuring
42:18 five hundred **r** by the measuring
42:19 and measured five hundred **r**
45: 2 five hundred by five hundred **r**,
Acts 16:22 them to be beaten with **r**.
2 Cor 11:25 Three times I was beaten with **r**;

ROE (1/1)

Deut 14: 5 the **r** deer, the wild goat, the

ROEBUCK (KJV) See ROEBUCKS

ROEBUCKS (1/1)

1 Ki 4:23 besides deer, gazelles, **r**,

ROES (KJV) See GAZELLES

ROGELIM (2/2)

2 Sam 17:27 Barzillai the Gileadite from **R**,
19:31 the Gileadite came down from **R**

ROGUE (1/1)

2 Sam 16: 7 You bloodthirsty man, you **r**!

ROGUES (1/1)

2 Chr 13: 7 Then worthless **r** gathered to

ROHGAH (1/1)

1 Chr 7:34 The sons of Shemer were Ahi, **R**,

ROI BEER LAHAI ROI

ROLL (14/13) ROLLED

Gen 29: 3 and they would **r** the stone from
Josh 10:18 **R** large stones against the mouth
1 Sam 14:17 Now call the **r** and see who has
14:17 And when they had called the **r**,
14:33 **r** a large stone to me this
2 Chr 26:11 to the number on their **r** as
Job 30:14 the ruinous storm they **r** along.
Prov 26:27 a stone will have it **r** back
Jer 6:26 in sackcloth And **r** about
25:34 and cry! **R** about in the
51:25 **R** you down from the rocks,
Ezek 27:30 They will **r** about in ashes;
Mic 1:10 In Beth Aphrah **R** yourself in
Mk 16: 3 Who will **r** away the stone from

ROLLED (13/13) ROLL

Gen 29: 8 and they have **r** the stone from
29:10 that Jacob went near and **r** the
Josh 5: 9 This day I have **r** away the
2 Ki 2: 8 **r** it up, and struck the water;
Isa 9: 5 And garments **r** in blood,
28:27 Nor is a cartwheel **r** over the
34: 4 And the heavens shall be **r** up
Mt 27:60 and he **r** a large stone against
28: 2 and came and **r** back the stone
Mk 15:46 and **r** a stone against the door
16: 4 saw that the stone had been **r**
Lk 24: 2 But they found the stone **r** away
Rev 6:14 as a scroll when it is **r** up,

ROLLER (KJV) See SPLINT

ROLLING (1/1)

Isa 17:13 Like a **r** thing before the

ROLLS (1/1)

Prov 26:27 And he who **r** a stone will have

ROMAMTI-EZER (2/2)

1 Chr 25: 4 Hanani, Eliathah, Giddalti, **R**,
25:31 the twenty-fourth for **R**,

ROMAN (5/5) ROMANS, ROME

Acts 22:25 you to scourge a man who is a **R**,
22:26 you do, for this man is a **R**.
22:27 to him, "Tell me, are you a **R**?
22:29 he found out that he was a **R**,
23:27 having learned that he was a **R**.

ROMANS (6/6) ROMAN

Jn 11:48 and the **R** will come and take
Acts 16:21 are not lawful for us, being **R**,
16:37 beaten us openly, uncondemned **R**,
16:38 they heard that they were **R**.
25:16 It is not the custom of the **R** to
28:17 into the hands of the **R**,

ROME (9/9) ROMAN

Acts 2:10 Cyrene, visitors from **R**,
18: 2 all the Jews to depart from **R**);
19:21 been there, I must also see **R**.
23:11 you must also bear witness at **R**.
28:14 And so we went toward **R**.
28:16 Now when we came to **R**,
Rom 1: 7 To all who are in **R**,
1:15 the gospel to you who are in **R**
2 Tim 1:17 but when he arrived in **R**,

ROOF (21/18) ROOFS

Gen 19: 8 come under the shadow of my **r**.
Deut 22: 8 shall make a parapet for your **r**,
Josh 2: 6 had brought them up to the **r**
2: 6 she had laid in order on the **r**.
2: 8 she came up to them on the **r**,
Judg 16:27 thousand men and women on the **r**
2 Sam 11: 2 his bed and walked on the **r** of
11: 2 And from the **r** he saw a woman
18:24 the watchman went up to the **r**
2 Ki 23:12 The altars that were on the **r**,
Neh 8:16 each one on the **r** of his house,
Job 29:10 their tongue stuck to the **r** of
Ps 137: 6 Let my tongue cling to the **r**
Song 7: 9 And the **r** of your mouth like
Lam 4: 4 of the infant clings To the **r**
Ezek 3:26 your tongue cling to the **r** of
40:13 the gateway from the **r** of one
40:13 of one gate chamber to the **r**
Mt 8: 8 that You should come under my **r**.
Mk 2: 4 they uncovered the **r** where He
Lk 7: 6 You should enter under my **r**.

ROOFS (2/2)

Jer 19:13 of all the houses on whose **r**
32:29 with the houses on whose **r** they

ROOM (53/52) ROOMS

Gen 24:23 is there **r** in your father's
24:25 and **r** to lodge."
26:22 For now the LORD has made **r** for
Judg 3:23 shut the doors of the upper **r**
3:24 the doors of the upper **r** were
3:25 opened the doors of the upper **r**.
15: 1 go in to my wife, into her **r**.
16: 9 wait, staying with her in the **r**.
16:12 lying in wait, staying in the **r**.
1 Ki 6:16 he built the twenty-cubit **r** at
6:27 the cherubim inside the inner **r**;
6:27 other in the middle of the **r**.
7:50 for the doors of the inner **r**
17:19 and carried him to the upper **r**
17:23 him down from the upper **r** into
2 Ki 1: 2 the lattice of his upper **r** in
4:10 let us make a small upper **r** on
4:11 and he turned in to the upper **r**
9: 2 and take him to an inner **r**.
10:25 and went into the inner **r** of
2 Chr 3: 5 The larger **r** he paneled with
3:11 touching the wall of the **r**,
3:12 touching the wall of the **r**,
Neh 2:14 but there was no **r** for the
3:31 and as far as the upper **r** at
3:32 And between the upper **r** at the
13: 5 had prepared for him a large **r**,
13: 7 in preparing a **r** for him in the
13: 8 goods of Tobiah out of the **r**.
Ps 80: 9 You prepared **r** for it,
Prov 18:16 A man's gift makes **r** for him,
Jer 7:32 in Tophet until there is no **r**.
Ezek 8:12 every man in the **r** of his
41:17 the door, even to the inner **r**,
Dan 6:10 And in his upper **r**, with his
Joel 2:16 the bride from her dressing **r**.
Zech 10:10 Until no more **r** is found for
Mal 3:10 That there will not be **r**
Mt 6: 6 when you pray, go into your **r**,
9:24 He said to them, "Make **r**,
Mk 2: 2 so that there was no longer **r**
14:14 Where is the guest **r** in which I
14:15 will show you a large upper **r**,
Lk 2: 7 because there was no **r** for them
12:17 since I have no **r** to store my
14:22 commanded, and still there is **r**.
22:11 Where is the guest **r** where I may
22:12 you a large, furnished upper **r**;
Acts 1:13 they went up into the upper **r**
9:37 they laid her in an upper **r**.
9:39 brought him to the upper **r**.
20: 8 were many lamps in the upper **r**
Phm 1:22 also prepare a guest **r** for me,

ROOMS (8/8) ROOM

Gen 6:14 make **r** in the ark, and cover it
2 Chr 31:11 commanded them to prepare **r**
Neh 10:38 to the **r** of the storehouse.
12:44 some were appointed over the **r**
13: 9 commanded them to cleanse the **r**;
Prov 24: 4 By knowledge the **r** are filled
Mt 24:26 He is in the inner **r**!' do not
Lk 12: 3 spoken in the ear in inner **r**

ROOSTER (13/12)

Mt 26:34 before the **r** crows, you will
26:74 Immediately a **r** crowed.
26:75 Before the **r** crows, you will

Mk 13:35 at the crowing of the *r*,
14:30 before the *r* crows twice, you
14:68 on the porch, and a *r* crowed.
14:72 A second time the *r* crowed.
14:72 Before the *r* crows twice, you
Lk 22:34 the *r* shall not crow this day
22:60 still speaking, the *r* crowed.
22:61 Before the *r* crows, you will
Jn 13:38 the *r* shall not crow till you
18:27 and immediately a *r* crowed.

ROOSTS (1/1)

Isa 60: 8 And like doves to their *r*?

ROOT (36/35) ROOTED, ROOTS

Deut 29:18 not be among you a *r* bearing
2 Ki 19:30 of Judah Shall again take *r*
Job 5: 3 have seen the foolish taking *r*,
14: 8 Though its *r* may grow old in
19:28 Since the *r* of the matter is
29:19 My *r* is spread out to the
31:12 And would *r* out all my
Ps 80: 9 And caused it to take deep *r*,
Prov 12: 3 But the *r* of the righteous
12:12 But the *r* of the righteous
Isa 5:24 So their *r* will be as
11:10 in that day there shall be a *R*
27: 6 come He shall cause to take *r*
37:31 of Judah Shall again take *r*
40:24 shall their stock take *r* in
53: 2 And as a *r* out of dry ground.
Jer 1:10 To *r* out and to pull down,
12: 2 them, yes, they have taken *r*;
Hos 9:16 Their *r* is dried up;
Mal 4: 1 leave them neither *r* nor
Mt 3:10 now the ax is laid to the *r* of
13: 6 and because they had no *r* they
13:21 yet he has no *r* in himself, but
Mk 4: 6 and because it had no *r* it
4:17 and they have no *r* in
Lk 3: 9 now the ax is laid to the *r* of
8:13 with joy; and these have no *r*,
Rom 11:16 and if the *r* is holy, so are
11:17 became a partaker of the *r* and
11:18 that you do not support the *r*,
11:18 but the *r* supports you.
15:12 There shall be a *r* of
1 Tim 6:10 For the love of money is a *r* of
Heb 12:15 lest any *r* of bitterness
Rev 5: 5 the *R* of David, has prevailed
22:16 I am the *R* and the Offspring of

ROOTED (3/3) ROOT

Job 31: 8 let my harvest be *r* out.
Eph 3:17 being *r* and grounded in love,
Col 2: 7 *r* and built up in Him and

ROOTS (24/23) ROOT

Judg 5:14 were those whose *r* were in
Job 8:17 His *r* wrap around the rock
18:16 His *r* are dried out below,
28: 9 the mountains at the *r*.
30: 4 And broom tree *r* for their
Isa 11: 1 Branch shall grow out of his *r*.
14:29 For out of the serpent's *r*
14:30 I will kill your *r* with
Jer 17: 8 Which spreads out its *r* by the
Ezek 17: 6 But its *r* were under it.
17: 7 this vine bent its *r* toward
17: 9 Will he not pull up its *r*,
17: 9 needed to pluck it up by its *r*.
31: 7 Because its *r* reached to
Dan 4:15 leave the stump and *r* in the
4:23 but leave its stump and *r* in
4:26 to leave the stump and *r* of
7: 8 horns were plucked out by the *r*.
11: 7 But from a branch of her *r* one
Hos 14: 5 And lengthen his *r* like
Am 2: 9 fruit above And his *r* beneath.
Mk 11:20 fig tree dried up from the *r*.
Lk 17: 6 Be pulled up by the *r* and be
Jude 12 twice dead, pulled up by the *r*;

ROPE (3/3) ROPES

Josh 2:15 Then she let them down by a *r*
Isa 3:24 Instead of a sash, a *r*;
5:18 And sin as if with a cart *r*;

ROPES (15/15) ROPE

Judg 15:13 they bound him with two new *r*
15:14 and the *r* that were on his
16:11 bind me securely with new *r*
16:12 Therefore Delilah took new *r* and
2 Sam 17:13 then all Israel shall bring *r*
1 Ki 20:31 around our waists and *r* around
20:32 their waists and put *r* around
Job 39:10 wild ox in the furrow with *r*?
Jer 38: 6 they let Jeremiah down with *r*.
38:11 and let them down by *r* into the
38:12 under your armpits, under the *r*.
38:13 they pulled Jeremiah up with *r*
Ezek 3:25 surely they will put *r* on you
Acts 27:32 the soldiers cut away the *r* of
27:40 meanwhile loosing the rudder *r*;

ROSE (100/99) RISE

Gen 4: 8 that Cain *r* up against Abel his
7:17 and it *r* high above the earth.
18:16 Then the men *r* from there and
19: 1 he *r* to meet them, and he bowed
20: 8 So Abimelech *r* early in the
21:14 So Abraham *r* early in the
21:32 So Abimelech *r* with Phichol,
22: 3 So Abraham *r* early in the
22:19 and they *r* and went together to
28:18 Then Jacob *r* early in the
31:17 Then Jacob *r* and set his sons
32:31 crossed over Penuel the sun *r*
Ex 12:30 So Pharaoh *r* in the night, he,
15: 7 have overthrown those who *r*
24: 4 And he *r* early in the morning,
32: 6 Then they *r* early on the next
32: 6 and *r* up to play.
33: 8 that all the people *r*,
33:10 and all the people *r* and
34: 4 Then Moses *r* early in the
Num 14:40 And they *r* early in the morning
16: 2 and they *r* up before Moses with
16:25 Then Moses *r* and went to Dathan
22:13 So Balaam *r* in the morning and
22:14 And the princes of Moab *r* and
22:21 So Balaam *r* in the morning,
24:25 So Balaam *r* and departed and
25: 7 he *r* from among the
Josh 3: 1 Then Joshua *r* early in the
3:16 and *r* in a heap very far away
6:12 And Joshua *r* early in the
6:15 seventh day that they *r* early,
7:16 So Joshua *r* early in the
8:10 Then Joshua *r* up early in the
8:14 the city hurried and *r* early
Judg 6:21 and fire *r* out of the rock and
6:38 When he *r* early the next
7: 1 the people who were with him *r*
9:34 people who were with him *r* by
9:35 the people who were with him *r*
9:43 and he *r* against them and
19:10 so he *r* and departed, and came
20: 5 And the men of Gibeah *r* against
20:19 So the children of Israel *r* in
20:33 So all the men of Israel *r* from
21: 4 that the people *r* early and
Ruth 2:15 And when she *r* up to glean, Boaz
1 Sam 1:19 Then they *r* early in the
15:12 So when Samuel *r* early in the
17:20 So David *r* early in the
25:42 So Abigail *r* in haste and rode
28:25 Then they *r* and went away that
29:11 So David and his men *r* early to
2 Sam 18:31 you this day of all those who *r*
22:40 subdued under me those who *r*
1 Ki 2:19 And the king *r* up to meet her
3:21 And when I *r* in the morning to
2 Ki 3:22 Then they *r* up early in the
3:24 Israel *r* up and attacked the
7: 5 And they *r* at twilight to go to
8:21 Then he *r* by night and attacked
1 Chr 28: 2 Then King David *r* to his feet
2 Chr 13: 6 *r* up and rebelled against his
20:20 So they *r* early in the morning
21: 9 And he *r* by night and attacked
28:15 who were designated by name *r*
29:20 Then King Hezekiah *r* early,
Ezra 5: 2 Jeshua the son of Jozadak *r* up
10: 6 Then Ezra *r* up from before the
Neh 3: 1 Eliashib the high priest *r* up
Ps 18:39 subdued under me those who *r*
124: 2 When men *r* up against us,
Song 2: 1 I am the *r* of Sharon,
Isa 35: 1 rejoice and blossom as the *r*;
Jer 26:17 of the elders of the land *r* up
Dan 3:24 and he *r* in haste and spoke,
Zeph 3: 7 But they *r* early and corrupted
Mk 10:50 he *r* and came to Jesus.
14:57 Then some *r* up and bore false
16: 9 Now when He *r* early on the
Lk 4:29 and *r* up and thrust Him out of
5:25 Immediately he *r* up before them,
5:28 *r* up, and followed Him.
22:45 When He *r* up from prayer, and
24:33 So they *r* up that very hour and
Jn 11:31 when they saw that Mary *r* up
13: 4 *r* from supper and laid aside His
Acts 5:17 Then the high priest *r* up, and
5:36 For some time ago Theudas *r* up,
5:37 Judas of Galilee *r* up in the
14:20 he *r* up and went into the city.
15: 5 Pharisees who believed *r* up,
15: 7 Peter *r* up and said to them:
16:22 Then the multitude *r* up together
18:12 the Jews with one accord *r* up
Rom 14: 9 to this end Christ died and *r*
1 Cor 10: 7 and *r* up to play."
15: 4 and that He *r* again the third
2 Cor 5:15 for Him who died for them and *r*
1 Th 4:14 believe that Jesus died and *r*

ROSH (4/4)

Gen 46:21 Ashbel, Gera, Naaman, Ehi, *R*,
Ezek 38: 2 land of Magog, the prince of *R*,
38: 3 you, O Gog, the prince of *R*,
39: 1 you, O Gog, the prince of *R*,

ROT (5/5) ROTTEN

Num 5:21 the LORD makes your thigh *r*
5:22 belly swell and your thigh *r*.
5:27 will swell, her thigh will *r*,
Prov 10: 7 the name of the wicked will *r*.
Isa 40:20 a tree that will not *r*;

ROTTEN (3/3) ROT, ROTTENNESS

Job 13:28 Man decays like a *r* thing,
41:27 And bronze as *r* wood.
Jer 29:17 and will make them like *r* figs

ROTTENNESS (5/5) ROTTEN

Prov 12: 4 who causes shame is like *r* in
14:30 But envy is *r* to the bones.
Isa 5:24 So their root will be as *r*,
Hos 5:12 to the house of Judah like *r*.
Hab 3:16 *R* entered my bones;

ROUGH (3/3) ROUGHLY

Isa 27: 8 He removes it by His *r* wind
40: 4 And the *r* places smooth;
Lk 3: 5 And the *r* ways smooth;

ROUGHLY (6/6) ROUGH

Gen 42: 7 a stranger to them and spoke *r*
42:30 is lord of the land spoke *r*
1 Sam 20:10 if your father answers you *r*?
1 Ki 12:13 the king answered the people *r*,
2 Chr 10:13 Then the king answered them *r*.
Prov 18:23 But the rich answers *r*.

ROUND (12/11) ROUNDED

Ex 16:14 was a small *r* substance, as
Deut 12:10 from all your enemies *r* about,
Josh 23: 1 from all their enemies *r* about,
1 Ki 7:23 it was completely *r*.
7:31 and the opening was *r*,
7:31 the panels were square, not *r*.
7:35 a cubit, it was perfectly *r*.
10:19 the top of the throne was *r*
2 Chr 4: 2 it was completely *r*.
Ps 97: 3 burns up His enemies *r* about.
Acts 28:13 From there we circled *r* and
Rom 15:19 from Jerusalem and *r* about

ROUNDABOUT (1/1)

2 Ki 3: 9 they marched on that *r* route

ROUNDED (1/1) ROUND

Song 7: 2 Your navel is a *r* goblet;

ROUSE (2/2)

Gen 49: 9 who shall *r* him?
Num 24: 9 who shall *r* him?' "Blessed

ROUSED (1/1)

Job 14:12 They will not awake Nor be *r*

ROUTE (1/1)

2 Ki 3: 9 marched on that roundabout *r*

ROUTED (3/3)

Josh 10:10 So the LORD *r* them before
Judg 4:15 And the LORD *r* Sisera and all
8:12 and *r* the whole army.

ROVE (1/1)

1 Sam 30:31 his men were accustomed to *r*.

ROVED (1/1)

Ezek 19: 6 He *r* among the lions,

ROVERS (KJV) See RAIDERS

ROW (17/15)

Ex 28:17 The first *r* shall be a
28:17 this shall be the first *r*;
28:18 the second *r* shall be a
28:19 'the third *r*, a jacinth,
28:20 "and the fourth *r*,
39:10 a *r* with a sardius, a topaz,
39:10 and an emerald was the first *r*;
39:11 the second *r*, a turquoise,
39:12 the third *r*, a jacinth,
39:13 the fourth *r*, a beryl,
Lev 24: 6 them in two rows, six in a *r*,
24: 7 pure frankincense on each *r*,
1 Ki 6:36 rows of hewn stone and a *r* of
7: 3 pillars, fifteen to a *r*.
7:12 rows of hewn stones and a *r* of
Ezra 6: 4 of heavy stones and one *r* of
Ezek 46:23 There was a *r* of building

ROWED (2/2) ROWS

Jon 1:13 Nevertheless the men *r* hard to

Jn 6:19 So when they had *r* about three

ROWERS (KJV) See OARSMEN

ROWING (1/1)

Mk 6:48 Then He saw them straining at *r*,

ROWS (17/17) ROWED

Ex 28:17 four *r* of stones: The first
39:10 And they set in it four *r* of
Lev 24: 6 "You shall set them in two *r*,
1 Ki 6:36 the inner court with three *r*
7: 2 with four *r* of cedar pillars,
7: 4 beveled frames in three *r*,
7:12 was enclosed with three *r* of
7:18 and two *r* of pomegranates above
7:20 hundred such pomegranates in *r*
7:24 buds were cast in two *r* when
7:42 for the two networks (two *r* of
2 Chr 4: 3 The oxen were cast in two *r*,
4:13 for the two networks (two *r* of
Ezra 6: 4 with three *r* of heavy stones
Job 41:15 His *r* of scales are his
Isa 28:25 Plant the wheat in *r*,
Ezek 46:23 hearths were made under the *r*

ROYAL (39/35)

Gen 49:20 And he shall yield *r* dainties.
Josh 10: 2 like one of the *r* cities, and
1 Sam 27: 5 servant dwell in the *r* city
2 Sam 12:26 and took the *r* city.
1 Ki 10:13 given her according to the *r*
2 Ki 11: 1 and destroyed all the *r* heirs.
15: 5 son was over the *r* house,
25:25 of the *r* family, came with ten
1 Chr 29:25 bestowed on him such *r* majesty
2 Chr 2: 1 and a *r* house for himself.
2:12 for the LORD and a *r* house
22:10 and destroyed all the *r* heirs
Esth 1: 7 with *r* wine in abundance,
1: 9 for the women in the *r* palace
1:11 wearing her *r* crown, in order
1:19 let a *r* decree go out from him,
1:19 the king give her *r* position
2:16 into his *r* palace, in the tenth
2:17 so he set the *r* crown upon her
5: 1 Esther put on her *r* robes
5: 1 the king sat on his *r* throne
5: 1 royal throne in the *r* house,
6: 8 let a *r* robe be brought which
6: 8 which has a *r* crest placed on
8:10 riding on *r* horses bred from
8:14 couriers who rode on *r* horses
8:15 of the king in *r* apparel
Ps 45:13 The *r* daughter is all glorious
Isa 62: 3 And a *r* diadem In the hand of
Jer 41: 1 of the *r* family and of the
43:10 he will spread his *r* pavilion
Dan 4:29 was walking about the *r* palace
4:30 I have built for a *r* dwelling
6: 7 to establish a *r* statute
Am 7:13 And it is the *r* residence."
Zech 10: 3 And will make them as His *r*
Acts 12:21 arrayed in *r* apparel, sat on
Jas 2: 8 If you really fulfill the *r* law
1 Pe 2: 9 a *r* priesthood, a holy nation,

ROYALTY (3/3)

1 Sam 10:25 to the people the behavior of *r*,
Ezek 16:13 beautiful, and succeeded to *r*.
Dan 11:21 will not give the honor of *r*;

RUBBED (2/2) RUBBING

Ezek 16: 4 you were not *r* with salt nor
29:18 and every shoulder *r* raw;

RUBBING (1/1) RUBBED

Lk 6: 1 *r* them in their hands.

RUBBISH (4/4)

2 Chr 29: 5 and carry out the *r* from the
Neh 4: 2 the stones from the heaps of *r*—
4:10 and there is so much *r* that
Phil 3: 8 all things, and count them as *r*,

RUBIES (8/8)

Job 28:18 the price of wisdom is above *r*.
Prov 3:15 She is more precious than *r*,
8:11 For wisdom is better than *r*,
20:15 is gold and a multitude of *r*,
31:10 For her worth is far above *r*.
Isa 54:12 will make your pinnacles of *r*,
Lam 4: 7 were more ruddy in body than *r*,
Ezek 27:16 fine linen, corals, and *r*.

RUDDER (2/2)

Acts 27:40 meanwhile loosing the *r* ropes;
Jas 3: 4 are turned by a very small *r*

RUDDY (4/4)

1 Sam 16:12 brought him in. Now he was *r*,
17:42 *r* and good-looking.
Song 5:10 My beloved is white and *r*,
Lam 4: 7 They were more *r* in body than

RUDELY (1/1)

1 Cor 13: 5 does not behave *r*,

RUDIMENTS (KJV) See PRINCIPLES

RUE (1/1)

Lk 11:42 For you tithe mint and *r* and

RUFUS (2/2)

Mk 15:21 the father of Alexander and *R*,
Rom 16:13 Greet *R*, chosen in the Lord,

RUGGED (1/1)

Isa 2:21 And into the crags of the *r*

RUHAMAH (KJV) See MERCY (IS SHOWN)

RUIN (20/19) RUINED, RUINOUS, RUINS

Ruth 4: 6 lest I *r* my own inheritance.
2 Ki 3:19 and *r* every good piece of land
2 Chr 28:23 But they were the *r* of him
Ps 89:40 brought his strongholds to *r*.
Prov 5:14 I was on the verge of total *r*,
19:13 A foolish son is the *r* of his
24:22 And who knows the *r* those two
26:28 And a flattering mouth works *r*.
Isa 23:13 palaces, And brought it to *r*.
25: 2 For You have made a city a *r*,
25: 2 a ruin, A fortified city a *r*,
Jer 13: 9 In this manner I will *r* the
Lam 2:13 For your *r* is spread wide as
Ezek 18:30 iniquity will not be your *r*.
27:27 the seas on the day of your *r*.
31:13 On its *r* will remain all the
Hos 10: 2 He will *r* their sacred
Am 5: 9 He rains *r* upon the strong,
Lk 6:49 And the *r* of that house was
2 Tim 2:14 to the *r* of the hearers.

RUINED (16/15) RUIN

Prov 25:10 And your reputation be *r*.
Isa 24:16 But I said, "I am *r*,
24:16 *r*! Woe to me! The treacherous
60:12 nations shall be utterly *r*.
61: 4 And they shall repair the *r*
Jer 13: 7 and there was the sash, *r*.
Ezek 36:35 and *r* cities are now
36:36 have rebuilt the *r* places and
36:38 so shall the *r* cities be filled
Joel 1: 7 And *r* My fig tree;
1:10 mourns; For the grain is *r*,
Nah 2: 2 have emptied them out And *r*
Zech 11: 2 the mighty trees are *r*.
Mt 9:17 and the wineskins are *r*.
Mk 2:22 and the wineskins are *r*.
Lk 5:37 and the wineskins will be *r*.

RUINOUS (2/2)

Job 30:14 Under the *r* storm they roll
Isa 17: 1 And it will be a *r* heap.

RUINS (24/23) RUIN

2 Ki 19:25 cities into heaps of *r*.
Ezra 9: 9 of our God, to rebuild its *r*,
Job 3:14 Who built *r* for themselves,
15:28 Which are destined to become *r*.
30:24 His hand against a heap of *r*,
Isa 3: 6 And let these *r* be under
17:11 harvest will be a heap of *r*
37:26 cities into heaps of *r*.
61: 4 they shall rebuild the old *r*,
Jer 9:11 will make Jerusalem a heap of *r*,
26:18 shall become heaps of *r*,
50:26 Cast her up as heaps of *r*,
Ezek 33:24 they who inhabit those *r* in the
33:27 surely those who are in the *r*
36:10 shall be inhabited and the *r*
36:33 and the *r* shall be rebuilt.
Am 9:11 I will raise up its *r*,
Mic 1: 6 I will make Samaria a heap of *r*
3:12 shall become heaps of *r*,
Hag 1: 4 and this temple to lie in *r*?
1: 9 of My house that is in *r*,
Zech 11: 3 For their glory is in *r*.
11: 3 the pride of the Jordan is in *r*.
Acts 15:16 I will rebuild its *r*,

RULE (61/58) RULED, RULER, RULES, RULING

Gen 1:16 the greater light to *r* the day,
1:16 and the lesser light to *r* the
1:18 and to *r* over the day and over
3:16 And he shall *r* over you."
4: 7 but you should *r* over it."
Lev 25:43 You shall not *r* over him with
25:46 you shall not *r* over one
25:53 and he shall not *r* with rigor
Judg 8:22 *R* over us, both you and your
8:23 I will not *r* over you, nor shall
8:23 nor shall my son *r* over you;
8:23 the LORD shall *r* over you."
13:12 What will be the boy's *r* of
15:11 not know that the Philistines *r*
2 Chr 20: 6 and do You not *r* over all the
21:10 Libnah revolted against his *r*,
36:20 to him and his sons until the *r*
Neh 5:15 even their servants bore *r* over
Ps 89: 9 You *r* the raging of the sea;
110: 2 *R* in the midst of Your
136: 8 The sun to *r* by day, For His
136: 9 The moon and stars to *r* by
Prov 8:16 By me princes *r*,
12:24 hand of the diligent will *r*,
17: 2 A wise servant will *r* over a
19:10 Much less for a servant to *r*
25:28 Whoever has no *r* over his own
Eccl 2:19 Yet he will *r* over all my labor
Isa 3: 4 And babes shall *r* over them.
3:12 And women *r* over them. O My
14: 2 and *r* over their oppressors.
19: 4 And a fierce king will *r* over
28:14 Who *r* this people who are in
32: 1 And princes will *r* with
40:10 And His arm shall *r* for Him;
41: 2 And made him *r* over kings?
44:13 craftsman stretches out his *r*,
52: 5 Those who *r* over them
Jer 5:31 And the priests *r* by their
13:18 For your *r* shall collapse,
Lam 5: 8 Servants *r* over us; There is
Ezek 20:33 I will *r* over you.
29:15 them so that they will not *r*
Dan 2:39 which shall *r* over all the
8:25 deceit to prosper under his *r*;
11: 3 who shall *r* with great
11:39 and he shall cause them to *r*
Joel 2:17 That the nations should *r* over
Zech 6:13 And shall sit and *r* on His
1 Cor 15:24 when He puts an end to all *r*
Gal 6:16 as walk according to this *r*,
Phil 3:16 let us walk by the same *r*,
Col 3:15 And let the peace of God *r* in
1 Tim 3: 5 if a man does not know how to *r*
5:17 Let the elders who *r* well be
Heb 13: 7 Remember those who *r* over you,
13:17 Obey those who *r* over you, and
13:24 Greet all those who *r* over you,
Rev 2:27 He shall *r* them with a rod
12: 5 bore a male Child who was to *r*
19:15 And He Himself will *r* them with

RULED (13/13) RULE

Gen 24: 2 who *r* over all that he had,
41:40 and all my people shall be *r*
Josh 12: 2 who dwelt in Heshbon and *r*
Ruth 1: 1 in the days when the judges *r*,
1 Ki 9:23 who *r* over the people who did
1 Chr 4:22 who *r* in Moab, and
2 Chr 8:10 who *r* over the people.
Ezra 4:20 who have *r* over all the
Ps 106:41 And those who hated them *r*
Isa 14: 6 He who *r* the nations in anger,
63:19 of old, over whom You never *r*,
Ezek 34: 4 force and cruelty you have *r*
Dan 11: 4 to his dominion with which he *r*;

RULER (77/75) RULE, RULER'S, RULERS

Gen 45: 8 and a *r* throughout all the land
Ex 22:28 nor curse a *r* of your people.
Lev 4:22 When a *r* has sinned, and done
Josh 22:14 one *r* each from the chief house
Judg 9:30 the *r* of the city, heard the
1 Sam 25:30 and has appointed you *r* over
2 Sam 5: 2 and be *r* over Israel.'"
6:21 to appoint me *r* over the people
7: 8 to be *r* over My people,
1 Ki 1:35 I have appointed him to be *r*
11:34 because I have made him *r* all
14: 7 and made you *r* over My people
16: 2 out of the dust and made you *r*
1 Chr 5: 2 and from him came a *r*,
11: 2 and be *r* over My people
17: 7 to be *r* over My people Israel.
28: 4 has chosen Judah to be the *r*;
2 Chr 6: 5 did I choose any man to be a *r*
7:18 not fail to have a man as *r*
19:11 the *r* of the house of Judah,
31:13 the king and Azariah the *r* of
Ps 105:20 The *r* of the people let him go
105:21 And *r* of all his possessions,
Prov 6: 7 no captain, Overseer or *r*,
23: 1 you sit down to eat with a *r*,
25:15 By long forbearance a *r* is
28:15 a charging bear Is a wicked *r*
28:16 A *r* who lacks understanding is
29:12 If a *r* pays attention to lies,
Eccl 9:17 Rather than the shout of a *r*
10: 4 If the spirit of the *r* rises
10: 5 an error proceeding from the *r*:
Isa 3: 6 have clothing; You be our *r*,
3: 7 Do not make me a *r* of the
16: 1 Send the lamb to the *r* of the
Jer 51:46 *R* against ruler),
51:46 in the land, Ruler against *r*),
Dan 2:10 or *r* has ever asked such
2:38 and has made you *r* over them
2:48 and he made him *r* over the
5: 7 and he shall be the third *r* in
5:16 and shall be the third *r* in the
5:29 that he should be the third *r*
11:18 But a *r* shall bring the

Mic 5: 2 forth to Me The One to be *R*
Hab 1:14 things that have no *r* over
Zech 10: 4 From him every *r* together.
Mt 2: 6 of you shall come a *R*
9:18 a *r* came and worshiped Him,
9:34 He casts out demons by the *r* of
12:24 the *r* of the demons."
24:45 whom his master made *r* over his
24:47 to you that he will make him *r*
25:21 I will make you *r* over many
25:23 I will make you *r* over many
Mk 3:22 By the *r* of the demons He casts
5:35 some came from the *r* of the
5:36 He said to the *r* of the
5:38 He came to the house of the *r*
Lk 8:41 and he was a *r* of the
8:49 someone came from the *r* of the
11:15 the *r* of the demons."
12:42 whom his master will make *r*
12:44 to you that he will make him *r*
13:14 But the *r* of the synagogue
18:18 Now a certain *r* asked Him,
Jn 3: 1 a *r* of the Jews.
12:31 now the *r* of this world will be
14:30 for the *r* of this world is
16:11 because the *r* of this world is
Acts 7:27 Who made you a *r* and a
7:35 Who made you a *r* and a
7:35 is the one God sent to be a *r*
18: 8 the *r* of the synagogue,
18:17 the *r* of the synagogue, and
23: 5 not speak evil of a *r*
Rev 1: 5 and the *r* over the kings of the

RULER'S (2/2) RULER

Prov 29:26 Many seek the *r* favor,
Mt 9:23 Jesus came into the *r* house,

RULERS (81/73) RULER

Ex 16:22 And all the *r* of the
18:21 such over them to be *r* of
18:21 *r* of hundreds, rulers of
18:21 *r* of fifties, and rulers of
18:21 of fifties, and *r* of tens.
18:25 *r* of thousands, rulers of
18:25 *r* of hundreds, rulers of
18:25 *r* of fifties, and rulers of
18:25 of fifties, and *r* of tens.
34:31 and Aaron and all the *r* of the
35:27 The *r* brought onyx stones, and
Josh 9:15 and the *r* of the congregation
9:18 because the *r* of the
9:18 complained against the *r*.
9:19 Then all the *r* said to all the
9:21 And the *r* said to them, "Let
9:21 as the *r* had promised them."
17: 4 son of Nun, and before the *r*,
22:14 and with him ten *r*,
22:30 Phinehas the priest and the *r*
22:32 Eleazar the priest, and the *r*,
Judg 5: 9 My heart is with the *r* of
5:14 From Machir *r* came down,
18: 7 There were no *r* in the land
2 Ki 10: 1 to the *r* of Jezreel, to the
2 Chr 29:20 gathered the *r* of the city, and
35: 8 *r* of the house of God, gave to
Ezra 9: 2 the hand of the leaders and *r*
Neh 4:19 I said to the nobles, the *r*,
5: 7 I rebuked the nobles and *r*,
5:17 hundred and fifty Jews and *r*,
7: 5 to gather the nobles, the *r*,
12:40 I and the half of the *r* with
13:11 So I contended with the *r*,
Ps 2: 2 And the *r* take counsel
Prov 8:15 And *r* decree justice.
Eccl 7:19 the wise More than ten *r* of
Isa 1:10 You *r* of Sodom; Give ear to
14: 5 wicked, The scepter of the *r*;
22: 3 All your *r* have fled together;
49: 7 To the Servant of *r*:
Jer 2: 8 The *r* also transgressed
12:10 Many *r* have destroyed My
22:22 wind shall eat up all your *r*,
33:26 of his descendants to be *r*
51:23 break in pieces governors and *r*.
51:28 Its governors and all its *r*,
Ezek 19:11 branches for scepters of *r*.
23: 6 in purple, Captains and *r*,
23:12 Assyrians, Captains and *r*,
23:23 young men, Governors and *r*,
Hos 4:18 Her *r* dearly love dishonor.
Mic 3: 1 And you *r* of the house of
3: 9 the house of Jacob And *r* of
Mt 2: 6 the least among the *r* of
20:25 You know that the *r* of the
Mk 5:22 one of the *r* of the synagogue
10:42 that those who are considered *r*
13: 9 You will be brought before *r*
Lk 14: 1 into the house of one of the *r*
21:12 be brought before kings and *r*
23:13 the chief priests, the *r*,
23:35 But even the *r* with them
24:20 priests and our *r* delivered
Jn 7:26 Do the *r* know indeed that this
7:48 Have any of the *r* or the
12:42 Nevertheless even among the *r*
Acts 3:17 ignorance, as did also your *r*.
4: 5 on the next day, that their *r*,
4: 8 *R* of the people and elders of
4:26 And the *r* were gathered
13:15 the *r* of the synagogue sent to
13:27 dwell in Jerusalem, and their *r*,
14: 5 Gentiles and Jews, with their *r*,
17: 6 and some brethren to the *r* of
17: 8 troubled the crowd and the *r*
Rom 13: 3 For *r* are not a terror to good
1 Cor 2: 6 nor of the *r* of this age, who
2: 8 which none of the *r* of this age
Eph 6:12 against the *r* of the darkness
Titus 3: 1 Remind them to be subject to *r*

RULES (16/16) RULE

2 Sam 23: 3 He who *r* over men must be
Ps 22:28 And He *r* over the nations.
59:13 And let them know that God *r*
66: 7 He *r* by His power forever;
103:19 And His kingdom *r* over all.
Prov 16:32 And he who *r* his spirit than
22: 7 The rich *r* over the poor,
29: 2 But when a wicked man *r*,
Eccl 8: 9 is a time in which one man *r*
Dan 4:17 may know That the Most High *r*
4:25 you know that the Most High *r*
4:26 you come to know that Heaven *r*.
4:32 you know that the Most High *r*
5:21 knew that the Most High God *r*
1 Tim 3: 4 one who *r* his own house well,
2 Tim 2: 5 he competes according to the *r*.

RULING (4/4) RULE

2 Sam 23: 3 *R* in the fear of God.
Jer 22:30 And *r* anymore in Judah.'"
Ezek 19:14 strong branch—a scepter for *r*.
1 Tim 3:12 *r* their children and their own

RUMAH (1/1)

2 Ki 23:36 the daughter of Pedaiah of *R*.

RUMBLING (2/2)

Job 37: 2 And the *r* that comes from His
Jer 47: 3 At the *r* of his wheels,

RUMOR (7/4) RUMORS

2 Ki 19: 7 and he shall hear a *r* and
Isa 37: 7 and he shall hear a *r* and
Jer 51:46 And you fear for the *r* that
51:46 be heard in the land (A *r*
51:46 in another year A *r* will
Ezek 7:26 And *r* will be upon rumor.
7:26 And rumor will be upon *r*.

RUMORS (3/3) RUMOR

Neh 6: 6 therefore, according to these *r*,
Mt 24: 6 you will hear of wars and *r* of
Mk 13: 7 when you hear of wars and *r* of

RUMP (KJV) See FLANKS

RUN (73/67) RAN, RUNNING, RUNS

Gen 49:22 His branches *r* over the wall.
1 Sam 8:11 and some will *r* before his
17:17 and *r* to your brothers at the
20: 6 of me that he might *r* over to
20:36 he said to his lad, "Now *r*,
2 Sam 15: 1 and fifty men to *r* before him.
18:19 Let me *r* now and take the news
18:22 please let me also *r* after the
18:22 So Joab said, "Why will you *r*,
18:23 he said, "let me *r*."
18:23 run." So he said to him, "*R*."
22:30 For by You I can *r* against a
1 Ki 1: 5 and fifty men to *r* before him.
17:14 nor shall the jar of oil *r* dry,
17:16 nor did the jar of oil *r* dry,
2 Ki 4:22 that I may *r* to the man of God
4:26 Please *r* now to meet her, and
5:20 I will *r* after him and take
2 Chr 16: 9 For the eyes of the LORD *r* to
Job 1: 5 days of feasting had *r* their
Ps 18:29 For by You I can *r* against a
19: 5 like a strong man to *r* its
58: 7 flow away as waters which *r*
59: 4 They *r* and prepare themselves
78:16 And caused waters to *r* down
119:32 I will *r* the course of Your
119:136 Rivers of water *r* down from my
Prov 1:16 For their feet *r* to evil,
4:12 be hindered, And when you *r*,
18:10 The righteous *r* to it and are
Eccl 1: 7 All the rivers *r* into the sea,
Song 1: 4 We will *r* after you.
Isa 33: 4 He shall *r* upon them.
40:31 They shall *r* and not be weary,
55: 5 know you shall *r* to you,
59: 7 Their feet *r* to evil, And they
Jer 5: 1 *R* to and fro through the streets
9:18 That our eyes may *r* with
12: 5 If you have *r* with the footmen,
13:17 eyes will weep bitterly And *r*
49: 3 with sackcloth! Lament and *r*
49:19 But I will suddenly make him *r*
50:44 I will make them suddenly *r*
51:31 One runner will *r* to meet
Lam 2:18 Let tears *r* down like a river
Ezek 24:16 nor shall your tears *r* down.
32:14 And make their rivers *r* like
Dan 12: 4 many shall *r* to and fro, and
Joel 2: 4 like swift steeds, so they *r*.
2: 7 They *r* like mighty men,
2: 9 They *r* to and fro in the city,
2: 9 They *r* on the wall;
Am 5:24 But let justice *r* down like
6:12 Do horses *r* on rocks?
8:12 They shall *r* to and fro,
Nah 2: 4 They *r* like lightning.
Hab 2: 2 That he may *r* who reads it.
Zech 2: 4 who said to him, "*R*,
Acts 27:17 and fearing lest they should *r*
27:26 we must *r* aground on a certain
27:29 fearing lest we should *r*
27:39 onto which they planned to *r*
1 Cor 9:24 you not know that those who *r*
9:24 those who run in a race all *r*,
9:24 *R* in such a way that you may
9:26 Therefore I *r* thus: not with
Gal 2: 2 lest by any means I might *r*,
2: 2 any means I might run, or had *r*,
Phil 2:16 of Christ that I have not *r* in
2 Th 3: 1 that the word of the Lord may *r*
Heb 12: 1 and let us *r* with endurance the
1 Pe 4: 4 it strange that you do not *r*
Jude 11 have *r* greedily in the error of

RUNNER (2/2)

Job 9:25 my days are swifter than a *r*;
Jer 51:31 One *r* will run to meet another,

RUNNERS (2/2)

2 Chr 30: 6 Then the *r* went throughout all
30:10 So the *r* passed from city to

RUNNING (30/27) RUN

Gen 26:19 and found a well of *r* water
Lev 14: 5 in an earthen vessel over *r*
14: 6 that was killed over the *r*
14:50 in an earthen vessel over *r*
14:51 of the slain bird and in the *r*
14:52 the blood of the bird and the *r*
15:13 and bathe his body in *r* water;
Num 19:17 and *r* water shall be put on
2 Sam 18:24 there was a man, *r* alone.
18:26 the watchman saw another man *r*,
18:26 another man, *r* alone!"
18:27 I think the *r* of the first is
18:27 of the first is like the *r* of
2 Ki 5:21 When Naaman saw him *r* after
2 Chr 23:12 the noise of the people *r* and
Job 15:26 *R* stubbornly against Him
Ps 133: 2 *R* down on the beard,
133: 2 *R* down on the edge of his
Prov 5:15 And *r* water from your own
6:18 Feet that are swift in *r* to
Isa 33: 4 As the *r* to and fro of
Ezek 31: 4 With their rivers *r* around the
47: 2 *r* out on the right side.
Mk 9:15 and *r* to Him, greeted Him.
9:25 saw that the people came *r*
10:17 out on the road, one came *r*,
Lk 6:38 and *r* over will be put into
Acts 21: 1 *r* a straight course we came to
27:16 And *r* under the shelter of an
Rev 9: 9 of chariots with many horses *r*

RUNS (7/7) RUN

Lev 15: 3 whether his body *r* with his
15:25 or if it *r* beyond her usual
Job 16:14 He *r* at me like a warrior.
Ps 23: 5 My cup *r* over.
147:15 His word *r* very swiftly.
Hag 1: 9 while every one of you *r* to his
Rom 9:16 him who wills, nor of him who *r*,

RURAL (1/1)

Deut 3: 5 besides a great many *r* towns.

RUSH (2/2)

Judg 9:33 you shall rise early and *r*
Isa 17:13 The nations will *r* like the

RUSHED (5/4) RUSHES, RUSHING

Judg 9:44 that was with him *r* forward
9:44 and the other two companies *r*
20:37 And the men in ambush quickly *r*
1 Sam 14:32 And the people *r* on the spoil,
Acts 19:29 and *r* into the theater with one

RUSHES (4/4) RUSHED

Job 41:20 a boiling pot and burning *r*.
Isa 19: 6 The reeds and *r* will wither.
35: 7 be grass with reeds and *r*.
Jer 8: 6 As the horse *r* into the

RUSHING (6/4) RUSHED

Isa 17:12 And to the *r* of nations
17:12 of nations That make a *r*
17:12 make a rushing like the *r* of
17:13 nations will rush like the *r*
Jer 47: 3 At the *r* of his chariots,
Acts 2: 2 as of a *r* mighty wind, and it

RUST (2/2)

Mt 6:19 where moth and *r* destroy and
6:20 where neither moth nor *r*

RUTH (13/13)

Ruth 1: 4 and the name of the other *R*.
1:14 but *R* clung to her.
1:16 But *R* said: "Entreat me not
1:22 and *R* the Moabitess her
2: 2 So *R* the Moabitess said to
2: 8 Then Boaz said to *R*,
2:21 *R* the Moabitess said, "He also
2:22 And Naomi said to *R* her
3: 9 So she answered, "I am *R*,
4: 5 you must also buy it from *R*
4:10 *R* the Moabitess, the widow of
4:13 So Boaz took *R* and she became
Mt 1: 5 by Rahab, Boaz begot Obed by *R*,

RUTHLESS (1/1)

Prov 11:16 But *r* men retain riches.

S

SABACHTHANI (2/2)

Mt 27:46 saying, "Eli, Eli, lama *s*?
Mk 15:34 saying, "Eloi, Eloi, lama *s*?

SABAOTH (2/2)

Rom 9:29 Unless the LORD of *S* had
Jas 5: 4 the ears of the Lord of *S*.

SABBATH (132/111) SABBATHS

Ex 16:23 Tomorrow is a *S* rest, a holy
16:23 a holy *S* to the LORD.
16:25 for today is a *S* to the LORD;
16:26 seventh day, which is the *S*,
16:29 the LORD has given you the *S*;
20: 8 Remember the *S* day, to keep it
20:10 but the seventh day is the *S* of
20:11 the LORD blessed the *S* day
31:14 'You shall keep the *S*,
31:15 but the seventh is the *S* of
31:15 does any work on the *S* day,
31:16 of Israel shall keep the *S*,
31:16 to observe the *S* throughout
35: 2 a *S* of rest to the LORD.
35: 3 your dwellings on the *S* day.
Lev 16:31 It is a *s* of solemn rest for
23: 3 but the seventh day is a *S* of
23: 3 it is the *S* of the LORD in
23:11 on the day after the *S* the
23:15 from the day after the *S*,
23:16 to the day after the seventh *S*;
23:32 It shall be to you a *s* of
23:32 you shall celebrate your *s*.
24: 8 Every *S* he shall set it in order
25: 2 then the land shall keep a *s* to
25: 4 year there shall be a *s* of
25: 4 a *s* to the LORD. You shall
25: 6 And the *s* produce of the land
Num 15:32 a man gathering sticks on the *S*
28: 9 And on the *S* day two lambs in
28:10 the burnt offering for every *S*,
Deut 5:12 Observe the *S* day, to keep it
5:14 but the seventh day is the *S* of
5:15 God commanded you to keep the *S*
2 Ki 4:23 neither the New Moon nor the *S*.
11: 5 you who come on duty on the *S*
11: 7 of you who go off duty on the *S*
11: 9 who were to be on duty on the *S*,
11: 9 were going off duty on the *S*,
16:18 Also he removed the *S* pavilion
1 Chr 9:32 the showbread for every *S*.
2 Chr 23: 4 of you entering on the *S*,
23: 8 who were to be on duty on the *S*,
23: 8 were going off duty on the *S*;
36:21 as she lay desolate she kept *S*,
Neh 9:14 made known to them Your holy *S*,
10:31 or any grain to sell on the *S*
10:31 not buy it from them on the *S*,
13:15 treading wine presses on the *S*,
13:15 into Jerusalem on the *S* day.
13:16 and sold them on the *S* to the
13:17 by which you profane the *S* day?
13:18 on Israel by profaning the *S*.
13:19 began to be dark before the *S*,
13:19 not be opened till after the *S*.
13:19 would be brought in on the *S*
13:21 on they came no more on the *S*.
13:22 to sanctify the *S* day.
Ps 92: A Song for the *S* day.
Isa 56: 2 Who keeps from defiling the *S*,
56: 6 who keeps from defiling the *S*,
58:13 turn away your foot from the *S*,
58:13 And call the *S* a delight,
66:23 And from one *S* to another,
Jer 17:21 and bear no burden on the *S*
17:22 out of your houses on the *S*
17:22 but hallow the *S* day, as I
17:24 the gates of this city on the *S*
17:24 but hallow the *S* day, to do no
17:27 not heed Me to hallow the *S*
17:27 the gates of Jerusalem on the *S*
Ezek 46: 1 but on the *S* it shall be
46: 4 offers to the LORD on the *S*
46:12 offerings as he did on the *S*
Am 8: 5 And the *S*, That we may trade
Mt 12: 1 the grainfields on the *S*.
12: 2 is not lawful to do on the *S*!
12: 5 read in the law that on the *S*
12: 5 in the temple profane the *S*,
12: 8 of Man is Lord even of the *S*.
12:10 "Is it lawful to heal on the *S*?
12:11 if it falls into a pit on the *S*,
12:12 is lawful to do good on the *S*.
24:20 not be in winter or on the *S*.
28: 1 Now after the *S*,
Mk 1:21 and immediately on the *S* He
2:23 the grainfields on the *S*;
2:24 do what is not lawful on the *S*?
2:27 The *S* was made for man, and not
2:27 for man, and not man for the *S*.
2:28 of Man is also Lord of the *S*.
3: 2 He would heal him on the *S*,
3: 4 Is it lawful on the *S* to do good
6: 2 And when the *S* had come, He
15:42 that is, the day before the *S*,
16: 1 Now when the *S* was past, Mary
Lk 4:16 into the synagogue on the *S*
6: 1 Now it happened on the second *S*
6: 2 is not lawful to do on the *S*?
6: 5 of Man is also Lord of the *S*.
6: 6 Now it happened on another *S*,
6: 7 whether He would heal on the *S*,
6: 9 Is it lawful on the *S* to do
13:10 one of the synagogues on the *S*.
13:14 Jesus had healed on the *S*;
13:14 and not on the *S* day."
13:15 not each one of you on the *S*
13:16 loosed from this bond on the *S*?
14: 1 Pharisees to eat bread on the *S*,
14: 3 "Is it lawful to heal on the *S*?
14: 5 pull him out on the *S* day?
23:54 and the *S* drew near.
23:56 And they rested on the *S*
Jn 5: 9 And that day was the *S*.
5:10 who was cured, "It is the *S*;
5:16 had done these things on the *S*.
5:18 because He not only broke the *S*,
7:22 you circumcise a man on the *S*.
7:23 receives circumcision on the *S*,
7:23 a man completely well on the *S*?
9:14 Now it was a *S* when Jesus made
9:16 because He does not keep the *S*.
19:31 remain on the cross on the *S*
19:31 on the Sabbath (for that *S* was
Acts 1:12 a *S* day's journey.
13:14 into the synagogue on the *S*
13:27 Prophets which are read every *S*,
13:42 be preached to them the next *S*.
13:44 On the next *S* almost the whole
15:21 read in the synagogues every *S*.
16:13 And on the *S* day we went out of
18: 4 in the synagogue every *S*,

SABBATH-REST (3/2)

Lev 23:24 the month, you shall have a *s*,
23:39 first day there shall be a *s*,
23:39 and on the eighth day a *s*.

SABBATHS (37/35) SABBATH

Ex 31:13 Surely My *S* you shall keep, for
Lev 19: 3 and his father, and keep My *S*:
19:30 You shall keep My *S* and
23:15 seven *S* shall be completed.
23:38 besides the *S* of the LORD,
25: 8 And you shall count seven *s* of
25: 8 and the time of the seven *s* of
26: 2 You shall keep My *S* and
26:34 the land shall enjoy its *s* as
26:34 land shall rest and enjoy its *s*.
26:35 time it did not rest on your *s*
26:43 and will enjoy its *s* while it
1 Chr 23:31 offering to the LORD on the *S*
2 Chr 2: 4 morning and evening, on the *S*,
8:13 commandment of Moses, for the *S*,
31: 3 the burnt offerings for the *S*
36:21 the land had enjoyed her *S*.
Neh 10:33 regular burnt offering of the *S*,
Isa 1:13 The New Moons, the *S*,
56: 4 "To the eunuchs who keep My *S*,
Lam 2: 6 The appointed feasts and *S* to
Ezek 20:12 I also gave them My *S*,
20:13 and they greatly defiled My *S*.
20:16 My statutes, but profaned My *S*;
20:20 'hallow My *S*, and they will
20:21 but they profaned My *S*.
20:24 My statutes, profaned My *S*,
22: 8 holy things and profaned My *S*.
22:26 hidden their eyes from My *S*,
23:38 the same day and profaned My *S*.
44:24 and they shall hallow My *S*.
45:17 feasts, the New Moons, the *S*,
46: 3 before the LORD on the *S* and
Hos 2:11 days, Her New Moons, Her *S*—
Lk 4:31 and was teaching them on the *S*.
Acts 17: 2 and for three *S* reasoned with
Col 2:16 a festival or a new moon or *s*,

SABEANS (4/4)

Job 1:15 when the *S* raided them and took

Isa 45:14 of Cush And of the *S*,
Ezek 23:42 and *S* were brought from the
Joel 3: 8 they will sell them to the *S*,

SABTA (1/1)

1 Chr 1: 9 of Cush were Seba, Havilah, *S*,

SABTAH (1/1)

Gen 10: 7 of Cush were Seba, Havilah, *S*,

SABTECHA (1/1)

1 Chr 1: 9 Havilah, Sabta, Raama, and *S*.

SABTECHAH (1/1)

Gen 10: 7 Havilah, Sabtah, Raamah, and *S*;

SACAR (2/2)

1 Chr 11:35 Ahiam the son of *S* the Hararite,
26: 4 *S* the fourth, Nethanel the

SACHIAH (1/1)

1 Chr 8:10 Jeuz, *S*, and Mirmah.

SACK (12/10) KNAPSACK, SACKS

Gen 42:25 every man's money to his *s*,
42:27 as one of them opened his *s*
42:27 it was, in the mouth of his *s*.
42:28 there it is, in my *s*!"
42:35 bundle of money was in his *s*;
43:21 was in the mouth of his *s*,
44: 1 money in the mouth of his *s*.
44: 2 in the mouth of the *s* of the
44:11 man speedily let down his *s* to
44:11 ground, and each opened his *s*.
44:12 cup was found in Benjamin's *s*.
Lev 11:32 wood or clothing or skin or *s*,

SACKBUT (KJV) See LYRE

SACKCLOTH (47/46)

Gen 37:34 put *s* on his waist, and mourned
2 Sam 3:31 clothes, gird yourselves with *s*,
21:10 the daughter of Aiah took *s*
1 Ki 20:31 let us put *s* around our waists
20:32 So they wore *s* around their
21:27 he tore his clothes and put *s*
21:27 body, and fasted and lay in *s*,
2 Ki 6:30 there underneath he had *s* on
19: 1 clothes, covered himself with *s*,
19: 2 of the priests, covered with *s*,
1 Chr 21:16 and the elders, clothed in *s*,
Neh 9: 1 assembled with fasting, in *s*,
Esth 4: 1 tore his clothes and put on *s*
4: 2 the king's gate clothed with *s*.
4: 3 and many lay in *s* and ashes.
4: 4 clothe Mordecai and take his *s*
Job 16:15 I have sewn *s* over my skin, And
Ps 30:11 You have put off my *s* and
35:13 were sick, My clothing was *s*;
69:11 I also made *s* my garment;
Isa 3:24 of a rich robe, a girding of *s*;
15: 3 will clothe themselves with *s*;
20: 2 and remove the *s* from your
22:12 baldness and for girding with *s*.
32:11 And gird *s* on your waists.
37: 1 clothes, covered himself with *s*,
37: 2 of the priests, covered with *s*,
50: 3 And I make *s* their covering."
58: 5 And to spread out *s* and ashes?
Jer 4: 8 this, clothe yourself with *s*,
6:26 Dress in *s* And roll about in
48:37 be cuts, and on the loins *s*—
49: 3 Gird yourselves with *s*!
Lam 2:10 And gird themselves with *s*.
Ezek 7:18 will also be girded with *s*;
27:31 of you, Gird themselves with *s*,
Dan 9: 3 supplications, with fasting, *s*,
Joel 1: 8 like a virgin girded with *s*
1:13 Come, lie all night in *s*,
Am 8:10 I will bring *s* on every waist,
Jon 3: 5 proclaimed a fast, and put on *s*,
3: 6 covered himself with *s* and sat
3: 8 man and beast be covered with *s*,
Mt 11:21 have repented long ago in *s*
Lk 10:13 sitting in *s* and ashes.
Rev 6:12 and the sun became black as *s*
11: 3 and sixty days, clothed in *s*.

SACKS (10/10) SACK

Gen 42:25 gave a command to fill their *s*
42:35 as they emptied their *s*,
43:12 returned in the mouth of your *s*;
43:18 which was returned in our *s* the
43:21 that we opened our *s*,
43:22 know who put our money in our *s*.
43:23 given you treasure in your *s*;
44: 1 Fill the men's *s* with food, as
44: 8 we found in the mouth of our *s*.
Josh 9: 4 And they took old *s* on their

SACRED (32/31)

Ex 23:24 break down their *s* pillars.
34:13 break their *s* pillars, and cut

Lev 23:36 It is a *s* assembly, and you
26: 1 a carved image nor a *s* pillar
Num 29:35 you shall have a *s* assembly.
Deut 7: 5 break down their *s* pillars,
12: 3 break their *s* pillars, and
16: 8 shall be a *s* assembly
16:15 days you shall keep a *s* feast
16:22 You shall not set up a *s* pillar,
1 Ki 14:23 *s* pillars, and wooden images
2 Ki 3: 2 for he put away the *s* pillar
10:26 And they brought the *s* pillars
10:27 they broke down the *s* pillar
12:18 Judah took all the *s* things
12:18 and his own *s* things, and all
17:10 up for themselves *s* pillars
18: 4 and broke the *s* pillars,
23:14 broke in pieces the *s* pillars
2 Chr 7: 9 day they held a *s* assembly,
14: 3 and broke down the *s* pillars
31: 1 Judah and broke the *s* pillars
Neh 8:18 day there was a *s* assembly,
Isa 1:13 iniquity and the *s* meeting.
Jer 43:13 also break the *s* pillars
Hos 3: 4 without sacrifice or *s* pillar,
10: 1 embellished his *s* pillars.
10: 2 He will ruin their *s* pillars.
Joel 1:14 Call a *s* assembly; Gather the
2:15 Call a *s* assembly;
Am 5:21 not savor your *s* assemblies.
Mic 5:13 And your *s* pillars from your

SACRIFICE (185/175) SACRIFICED, SACRIFICES

Gen 31:54 Then Jacob offered a *s* on the
Ex 3:18 that we may *s* to the LORD our
5: 3 journey into the desert and *s*
5: 8 Let us go and *s* to our God.'
5:17 Let us go and *s* to the LORD.'
8: 8 that they may *s* to the LORD."
8:25 *s* to your God in the land."
8:26 If we *s* the abomination of the
8:27 into the wilderness and *s* to
8:28 that you may *s* to the LORD
8:29 not letting the people go to *s*
10:25 that we may *s* to the LORD our
12:27 It is the Passover *s* of the
13:15 Therefore I *s* to the LORD all
20:24 and you shall *s* on it your
23:18 not offer the blood of My *s*
23:18 nor shall the fat of My *s*
34:15 with their gods and make *s* to
34:15 you and you eat of his *s*,
34:25 not offer the blood of My *s*
34:25 nor shall the *s* of the Feast of
Lev 1: 3 'If his offering is a burnt *s*
1: 9 all on the altar as a burnt *s*,
1:10 or of the goats—as a burnt *s*,
1:13 on the altar; it is a burnt *s*,
1:14 And if the burnt *s* of his
1:17 It is a burnt *s*, an offering
3: 1 When his offering is a *s* of a
3: 3 'Then he shall offer from the *s*
3: 5 on the altar upon the burnt *s*,
3: 6 If his offering as a *s* of a
3: 9 'Then he shall offer from the *s*
4:10 taken from the bull of the *s*
4:26 like the fat of the *s* of the
4:31 as fat is removed from the *s* of
4:35 the lamb is removed from the *s*
7:11 This is the law of the *s* of
7:12 with the *s* of thanksgiving,
7:13 leavened bread with the *s* of
7:15 The flesh of the *s* of his peace
7:16 But if the *s* of his offering is
7:16 same day that he offers his *s*;
7:17 of the flesh of the *s* on the
7:18 if any of the flesh of the *s*
7:20 who eats the flesh of the *s* of
7:21 who eats the flesh of the *s* of
7:29 He who offers the *s* of his peace
7:29 to the LORD from the *s* of his
7:37 and the *s* of the peace
8:21 It was a burnt *s* for a sweet
9: 4 to *s* before the LORD, and a
9:17 besides the burnt *s* of the
17: 8 offers a burnt offering or *s*,
19: 5 And if you offer a *s* of a peace
22:18 who offers his *s* for any of his
22:21 And whoever offers a *s* of a
22:29 And when you offer a *s* of
23:19 Then you shall *s* one kid of the
23:19 lambs of the first year as a *s*
23:37 a *s* and drink offerings,
27:11 which they do not offer as a *s*
Num 6:17 he shall offer the ram as a *s*
6:18 the fire which is under the *s*
7:17 and for the *s* of peace
7:23 and as the *s* of peace offerings:
7:29 and for the *s* of peace
7:35 and as the *s* of peace offerings:
7:41 and as the *s* of peace offerings:
7:47 and as the *s* of peace offerings:
7:53 and as the *s* of peace offerings:
7:59 and as the *s* of peace offerings:
7:65 and as the *s* of peace offerings:
7:71 and as the *s* of peace offerings:
7:77 and as the *s* of peace offerings:
7:83 and as the *s* of peace offerings:
7:88 And all the oxen for the *s* of
15: 3 LORD, a burnt offering or a *s*,
15: 5 the burnt offering or the *s*,
15: 8 or as a *s* to fulfill a vow, or
Deut 15:21 you shall not *s* it to the LORD
16: 2 Therefore you shall *s* the
16: 4 any of the meat which you *s*
16: 5 You may not *s* the Passover
16: 6 there you shall *s* the Passover
17: 1 You shall not *s* to the LORD
18: 3 from those who offer a *s*,
33:10 And a whole burnt *s* on Your
Josh 22:26 for burnt offering nor for *s*,
Judg 6:26 bull and offer a burnt *s* with
16:23 together to offer a great *s* to
1 Sam 1: 3 city yearly to worship and *s*
1:21 to the LORD the yearly *s* and
2:13 that when any man offered a *s*,
2:19 husband to offer the yearly *s*.
2:29 Why do you kick at My *s* and My
3:14 shall not be atoned for by *s*
9:12 because there is a *s* of the
9:13 because he must bless the *s*; and
15:15 to *s* to the LORD your God; and
15:21 to *s* to the LORD your God in
15:22 to obey is better than *s*,
16: 2 I have come to *s* to the LORD.'
16: 3 "Then invite Jesse to the *s*,
16: 5 I have come to *s* to the LORD.
16: 5 and come with me to the *s*.
16: 5 sons, and invited them to the *s*.
20: 6 for there is a yearly *s* there
20:29 for our family has a *s* in the
2 Sam 24:22 here are oxen for burnt *s*,
1 Ki 3: 4 the king went to Gibeon to *s*
8:63 And Solomon offered a *s* of peace
13: 2 and on you he shall *s* the
18:29 the offering of the evening *s*.
18:33 and pour it on the burnt *s* and
18:36 the offering of the evening *s*,
18:38 fell and consumed the burnt *s*,
2 Ki 5:17 either burnt offering or *s* to
10:19 for I have a great *s* for Baal.
16:15 offering, the king's burnt *s*,
16:15 and all the blood of the *s*.
17:35 to them nor serve them nor *s*
17:36 and to Him you shall offer *s*.
2 Chr 2: 6 except to burn *s* before Him?
7: 5 King Solomon offered a *s* of
7:12 for Myself as a house of *s*.
11:16 came to Jerusalem to *s* to the
28:23 I will *s* to them that they may
Ezra 9: 4 astonished until the evening *s*.
9: 5 At the evening *s* I arose from
Ps 20: 3 And accept your burnt *s*.
40: 6 *S* and offering You did not
50: 5 made a covenant with Me by *s*.
51:16 For You do not desire *s*,
54: 6 I will freely *s* to You;
107:22 Let them *s* the sacrifices of
116:17 I will offer to You the *s* of
118:27 Bind the *s* with cords to the
141: 2 of my hands as the evening *s*.
Prov 15: 8 The *s* of the wicked is an
21: 3 acceptable to the LORD than *s*.
21:27 The *s* of the wicked is an
Eccl 5: 1 hear rather than to give the *s*
9: 2 and him who does not *s*.
Isa 19:21 and will make *s* and offering;
34: 6 For the LORD has a *s* in
57: 7 there you went up To offer *s*.
65: 3 Who *s* in gardens, And burn
Jer 33:11 of those who will bring the *s*
33:18 and to *s* continually.'"
46:10 the Lord GOD of hosts has a *s*
Ezek 40:42 the burnt offering and the *s*.
44:11 the burnt offering and the *s*
44:30 and every *s* of any kind from
Dan 9:27 He shall bring an end to *s*
12:11 the time that the daily *s* is
Hos 3: 4 without *s* or sacred pillar,
6: 6 For I desire mercy and not *s*,
8:13 of My offerings they *s* flesh
12:11 Though they *s* bulls in Gilgal,
13: 2 Let the men who *s* kiss the
Am 4: 5 Offer a *s* of thanksgiving with
Jon 1:16 and offered a *s* to the LORD
2: 9 But I will *s* to You With the
Hab 1:16 Therefore they *s* to their net,
Zeph 1: 7 For the LORD has prepared a *s*;
1: 8 In the day of the LORD's *s*,
Mal 1: 8 when you offer the blind as a *s*,
Mt 9:13 'I desire mercy and not *s*.'
12: 7 'I desire mercy and not *s*,'
Mk 9:49 and every *s* will be seasoned
Lk 2:24 and to offer a *s* according to
Acts 14:13 intending to *s* with the
Rom 12: 1 present your bodies a living *s*,
1 Cor 10:20 the things which the Gentiles *s*
10:20 the Gentiles sacrifice they *s*
Eph 5: 2 an offering and a *s* to God for
Phil 2:17 a drink offering on the *s*
4:18 aroma, an acceptable *s*,
Heb 9:26 to put away sin by the *s* of
10: 5 *S* and offering You did not
10: 8 *S* and offering, burnt
10:12 after He had offered one *s* for
10:26 there no longer remains a *s* for
11: 4 to God a more excellent *s* than
13:15 let us continually offer the *s*

SACRIFICED (35/35) SACRIFICE

Ex 24: 5 offered burnt offerings and *s*
32: 8 and worshiped it and *s* to it,
Deut 32:17 They *s* to demons, not to God,
Josh 8:31 and *s* peace offerings.
Judg 2: 5 and they *s* there to the LORD.
1 Sam 2:15 come and say to the man who *s*,
2 Sam 6:13 that he *s* oxen and fatted
1 Ki 1: 9 And Adonijah *s* sheep and oxen
1:19 He has *s* oxen and fattened
1:25 and has *s* oxen and fattened
3: 2 Meanwhile the people *s* at the
3: 3 except that he *s* and burned
11: 8 who burned incense and *s* to
2 Ki 12: 3 the people still *s* and burned
14: 4 and the people still *s* and
15: 4 the people still *s* and burned
15:35 the people still *s* and burned
16: 4 And he *s* and burned incense on
17:32 who *s* for them in the shrines
1 Chr 21:28 the Jebusite, he *s* there.
2 Chr 28: 4 And he *s* and burned incense on
28:23 For he *s* to the gods of Damascus
33:16 *s* peace offerings and thank
33:17 the people still *s* on the high
33:22 for Amon *s* to all the carved
34: 4 the graves of those who had *s*
Ezra 4: 2 and we have *s* to Him since the
Ps 106:37 They even *s* their sons And
106:38 Whom they *s* to the idols of
Ezek 16:20 and these you *s* to them to be
23:37 and even *s* their sons whom they
Hos 11: 2 They *s* to the Baals, And
1 Cor 5: 7 our Passover, was *s* for us.
Rev 2:14 to eat things *s* to idols, and
2:20 immorality and eat things *s* to

SACRIFICES (106/103) SACRIFICE

Gen 46: 1 and offered *s* to the God of his
Ex 10:25 You must also give us *s* and
18:12 a burnt offering and other *s*
22:20 He who *s* to any god, except to
29:28 children of Israel from the *s*
Lev 7:32 a heave offering from the *s* of
7:34 from the *s* of their peace
9:18 the bull and the ram as *s* of
10:13 of the *s* made by fire to the
10:14 which are given from the *s* of
17: 5 of Israel may bring their *s*
17: 7 shall no more offer their *s* to
Num 10:10 burnt offerings and over the *s*
25: 2 invited the people to the *s* of
Deut 12: 6 your burnt offerings, your *s*,
12:11 your burnt offerings, your *s*,
12:27 and the blood of your *s* shall
32:38 Who ate the fat of their *s*,
33:19 There they shall offer *s* of
Josh 13:14 the *s* of the LORD God of
22:27 our burnt offerings, with our *s*,
22:28 for burnt offerings nor for *s*;
22:29 for grain offerings, or for *s*,
1 Sam 6:15 burnt offerings and made *s* the
10: 8 burnt offerings and make *s* of
11:15 There they made *s* of peace
15:22 in burnt offerings and *s*,
2 Sam 15:12 Giloh—while he offered *s*.
1 Ki 8:62 all Israel with him offered *s*
12:27 these people go up to offer *s*
12:32 and offered *s* on the altar.
12:33 and offered *s* on the altar and
22:43 for the people offered *s* and
2 Ki 10:24 So they went in to offer *s* and
1 Chr 6:49 Aaron and his sons offered *s*
29:21 And they made *s* to the LORD
29:21 and *s* in abundance for all
2 Chr 7: 1 the burnt offering and the *s*;
7: 4 and all the people offered *s*
13:11 and every evening burnt *s* and
29:31 and bring *s* and thank offerings
29:31 So the assembly brought in *s*
Ezra 6: 3 the place where they offered *s*;
6:10 that they may offer *s* of sweet
6:17 And they offered *s* at the
Neh 4: 2 Will they offer *s*?
12:43 that day they offered great *s*,
Ps 4: 5 Offer the *s* of righteousness,
27: 6 Therefore I will offer *s* of
50: 8 will not rebuke you for your *s*
51:17 The *s* of God are a broken
51:19 shall be pleased with the *s* of
66:15 I will offer You burnt *s* of fat
106:28 And ate *s* made to the dead.
107:22 Let them sacrifice the *s* of
Eccl 9: 2 To him who *s* and him who does
Isa 1:11 is the multitude of your *s* to
1:13 Bring no more futile *s*;
43:23 have you honored Me with your *s*.
43:24 Me with the fat of your *s*;
56: 7 burnt offerings and their *s*
66: 3 He who *s* a lamb, as if he
Jer 6:20 Nor your *s* sweet to Me."
7:21 your burnt offerings to your *s*
7:22 concerning burnt offerings or *s*.
17:26 bringing burnt offerings and *s*,
17:26 bringing *s* of praise to the
48:35 in Moab The one who offers *s*
Ezek 20:28 there they offered their *s* and
20:40 and the firstfruits of your *s*,
36:38 a flock offered as holy *s*,
40:41 which they slaughtered the *s*.
40:43 and the flesh of the *s* was on
44:30 of any kind from all your *s*,
46:24 of the temple shall boil the *s*
Dan 8:11 and by him the daily *s* were

S

8:12 horn to oppose the daily *s*;
8:13 concerning the daily *s* and
11:31 shall take away the daily *s*,
Hos 4:13 They offer *s* on the
4:14 And offer *s* with a ritual
4:19 be ashamed because of their *s*.
8:13 For the *s* of My offerings they
9: 4 Nor shall their *s* be pleasing
14: 2 For we will offer the *s* of our
Am 4: 4 Bring your *s* every morning,
5:25 Did you offer Me *s* and
Zech 14:21 Everyone who *s* shall come and
Mal 1:14 But *s* to the Lord what is
Mk 12:33 the whole burnt offerings and *s*.
Lk 13: 1 Pilate had mingled with their *s*.
Acts 7:41 offered *s* to the idol, and
7:42 slaughtered animals and *s*
1 Cor 10:18 Are not those who eat of the *s*
Heb 5: 1 he may offer both gifts and *s*
5: 3 to offer *s* for sins.
7:27 high priests, to offer up *s*,
8: 3 to offer both gifts and *s*.
9: 9 time in which both gifts and *s*
9:23 themselves with better *s* than
10: 1 can never with these same *s*,
10: 3 But in those *s* there is a
10: 6 In burnt offerings and *s*
10:11 offering repeatedly the same *s*,
13:16 for with such *s* God is well
1 Pe 2: 5 to offer up spiritual *s*

SACRIFICIAL (3/2)

Ezek 39:17 from all sides to My *s* meal
39:17 A great *s* meal on the
39:19 At My *s* meal Which I am

SACRIFICING (8/8)

Ex 8:26 for we would be *s* the
1 Ki 8: 5 *s* sheep and oxen that could not
12:32 *s* to the calves that he had
2 Chr 5: 6 were *s* sheep and oxen that
Ezek 39:17 sacrificial meal Which I am *s*
39:19 sacrificial meal Which I am *s*
43:18 for *s* burnt offerings on it,
Acts 14:18 restrain the multitudes from *s*

SACRILEGE (KJV) See ADULTERY

SAD (13/12)

Gen 40: 6 them, and saw that they were *s*.
40: 7 Why do you look so *s* today?"
1 Sam 1:18 and her face was no longer *s*.
Neh 2: 1 Now I had never been *s* in his
2: 2 to me, "Why is your face *s*,
2: 3 Why should my face not be *s*,
Job 9:27 I will put off my *s* face and
Eccl 7: 3 For by a *s* countenance the
Ezek 13:22 the heart of the righteous *s*,
13:22 sad, whom I have not made *s*;
Mt 6:16 with a *s* countenance.
Mk 10:22 But he was *s* at this word, and
Lk 24:17 another as you walk and are *s*?

SADDLE (5/5) SADDLED

Gen 31:34 put them in the camel's *s*,
Lev 15: 9 Any *s* on which he who has the
2 Sam 19:26 I will *s* a donkey for myself,
1 Ki 13:13 *S* the donkey for me." So they
13:27 *S* the donkey for me." So they

SADDLECLOTHS (1/1)

Ezek 27:20 Dedan was your merchant in *s*

SADDLED (10/10) SADDLE

Gen 22: 3 early in the morning and *s* his
Num 22:21 *s* his donkey, and went with the
Judg 19:10 him were the two *s* donkeys;
2 Sam 16: 1 him with a couple of *s* donkeys,
17:23 he *s* a donkey, and arose and
1 Ki 2:40 *s* his donkey, and went to
13:13 So they *s* the donkey for him;
13:23 that he *s* the donkey for him,
13:27 for me." So they *s* it.
2 Ki 4:24 Then she *s* a donkey, and said to

SADDUCEES (14/14)

Mt 3: 7 saw many of the Pharisees and *S*
16: 1 Then the Pharisees and *S* came,
16: 6 of the Pharisees and the *S*.
16:11 leaven of the Pharisees and *S*.
16:12 doctrine of the Pharisees and *S*.
22:23 The same day the *S*,
22:34 that He had silenced the *S*,
Mk 12:18 Then some *S*, who say
Lk 20:27 Then some of the *S*,
Acts 4: 1 and the *S* came upon them,
5:17 (which is the sect of the *S*),
23: 6 perceived that one part were *S*
23: 7 between the Pharisees and the *S*;
23: 8 For *S* say that there is no

SADLY (1/1)

Isa 59:11 And moan *s* like doves;

SADOC (KJV) See ZADOK

SAFE (12/12) SAFELY, SAFETY

1 Sam 20: 7 your servant will be *s*.
22:23 but with me you shall be *s*.
2 Sam 18:29 "Is the young man Absalom *s*?
18:32 "Is the young man Absalom *s*?
Job 21: 9 Their houses are *s* from fear,
Ps 119:117 Hold me up, and I shall be *s*,
Prov 18:10 righteous run to it and are *s*.
29:25 trusts in the LORD shall be *s*.
Ezek 34:27 They shall be *s* in their land;
Nah 1:12 LORD: "Though they are *s*,
Lk 15:27 because he has received him *s*
Phil 3: 1 tedious, but for you it is *s*.

SAFEKEEPING (2/2)

Lev 6: 2 what was delivered to him for *s*,
6: 4 what was delivered to him for *s*,

SAFELY (28/28) SAFE

Gen 33:18 Then Jacob came *s* to the city
Lev 26: 5 full, and dwell in your land *s*.
Judg 18: 7 were there, how they dwelt *s*,
1 Sam 24:19 will he let him get away *s*?
1 Ki 4:25 And Judah and Israel dwelt *s*,
2 Chr 19: 1 the king of Judah returned *s*
Ps 78:53 And He led them on *s*,
141:10 own nets, While I escape *s*.
Prov 1:33 listens to me will dwell *s*,
3:23 Then you will walk *s* in your
31:11 The heart of her husband *s*
Isa 5:29 They will carry it away *s*,
41: 3 and passed *s* By the way that
Jer 23: 6 saved, And Israel will dwell *s*;
32:37 I will cause them to dwell *s*.
33:16 And Jerusalem will dwell *s*.
Ezek 28:26 And they will dwell *s* there,
34:25 and they will dwell *s* in the
34:28 but they shall dwell *s*,
38: 8 and now all of them dwell *s*.
38:11 a peaceful people, who dwell *s*,
38:14 when My people Israel dwell *s*,
39:26 when they dwelt *s* in their own
Hos 2:18 earth, To make them lie down *s*.
Zech 14:11 But Jerusalem shall be *s*
Mk 14:44 seize Him and lead Him away *s*.
Acts 23:24 and bring him *s* to Felix the
27:44 it was that they all escaped *s*

SAFETY (18/18) SAFE

Lev 25:18 you will dwell in the land in *s*.
25:19 your fill, and dwell there in *s*.
Deut 12:10 about, so that you dwell in *s*,
33:12 of the LORD shall dwell in *s*
33:28 Then Israel shall dwell in *s*
1 Sam 12:11 every side; and you dwelt in *s*.
20:13 you away, that you may go in *s*.
20:21 there is *s* for you and no
Job 5: 4 His sons are far from *s*,
5:11 those who mourn are lifted to *s*.
11:18 you, and take your rest in *s*.
Ps 4: 8 O LORD, make me dwell in *s*.
12: 5 I will set him in the *s* for
33:17 A horse is a vain hope for *s*;
Prov 11:14 of counselors there is *s*.
24: 6 of counselors there is *s*.
Isa 14:30 the needy will lie down in *s*;
1 Th 5: 3 they say, "Peace and *s*!"

SAFETY'S (1/1)

Prov 3:29 he dwells by you for *s* sake.

SAFFRON (1/1)

Song 4:14 Spikenard and *s*, Calamus and

SAID (4197/3771)

Gen 1: 3 Then God *s*, "Let there be
1: 6 Then God *s*, "Let there be
1: 9 Then God *s*, "Let the waters
1:11 Then God *s*, "Let the earth
1:14 Then God *s*, "Let there be
1:20 Then God *s*, "Let the waters
1:24 Then God *s*, "Let the earth
1:26 Then God *s*, "Let Us make
1:28 and God *s* to them, "Be
1:29 And God *s*, "See, I have given
2:18 And the LORD God *s*, "It is
2:23 And Adam *s*: "This is now
3: 1 And he *s* to the woman, "Has
3: 1 the woman, "Has God indeed *s*,
3: 2 And the woman *s* to the serpent,
3: 3 midst of the garden, God has *s*,
3: 4 Then the serpent *s* to the woman,
3: 9 LORD God called to Adam and *s*
3:10 So he *s*, "I heard Your voice
3:11 And He *s*, "Who told you
3:12 Then the man *s*, "The woman
3:13 And the LORD God *s* to the
3:13 The woman *s*, "The serpent
3:14 So the LORD God *s* to the
3:16 To the woman He *s*: "I will
3:17 Then to Adam He *s*, "Because
3:22 Then the LORD God *s*,
4: 1 conceived and bore Cain, and *s*,
4: 6 So the LORD *s* to Cain, "Why
4: 9 Then the LORD *s* to Cain,
4: 9 He *s*, "I do not know. Am I
4:10 And He *s*, "What have you
4:13 And Cain *s* to the LORD, "My
4:15 And the LORD *s* to him,
4:23 Then Lamech *s* to his wives:
6: 3 And the LORD *s*, "My Spirit
6: 7 So the LORD *s*, "I will
6:13 And God *s* to Noah, "The end of
7: 1 Then the LORD *s* to Noah, "Come
8:21 Then the LORD *s* in His heart,
9: 1 and *s* to them: "Be fruitful
9:12 And God *s*: "This is the
9:17 And God *s* to Noah, "This is
9:25 he *s*: "Cursed be Canaan;
9:26 And he *s*: "Blessed be the
10: 9 the LORD; therefore it is *s*,
11: 3 Then they *s* to one another,
11: 4 And they *s*, "Come, let us
11: 6 And the LORD *s*, "Indeed
12: 1 Now the LORD had *s* to Abram:
12: 7 LORD appeared to Abram and *s*,
12:11 that he *s* to Sarai his wife,
12:18 And Pharaoh called Abram and *s*,
13: 8 So Abram *s* to Lot, "Please let
13:14 And the LORD *s* to Abram, after
14:19 And he blessed him and *s*:
14:21 Now the king of Sodom *s* to
14:22 But Abram *s* to the king of
15: 2 But Abram *s*, "Lord GOD,
15: 3 Then Abram *s*, "Look, You
15: 5 He brought him outside and *s*,
15: 5 And He *s* to him, "So shall
15: 7 Then He *s* to him, "I am the
15: 8 And he *s*, "Lord GOD, how
15: 9 So He *s* to him, "Bring Me a
15:13 Then He *s* to Abram: "Know
16: 2 So Sarai *s* to Abram, "See now,
16: 5 Then Sarai *s* to Abram, "My
16: 6 So Abram *s* to Sarai, "Indeed
16: 8 And He *s*, "Hagar, Sarai's
16: 8 She *s*, "I am fleeing from the
16: 9 The Angel of the LORD *s* to her,
16:10 Then the Angel of the LORD *s* to
16:11 And the Angel of the LORD *s* to
16:13 for she *s*, "Have I also
17: 1 LORD appeared to Abram and *s*
17: 9 And God *s* to Abraham: "As for
17:15 Then God *s* to Abraham, "As for
17:17 and *s* in his heart, "Shall a
17:18 And Abraham *s* to God, "Oh, that
17:19 Then God *s*: "No, Sarah your
17:23 as God had *s* to him.
18: 3 and *s*, "My Lord, if I have
18: 5 They *s*, "Do as you have
18: 5 They said, "Do as you have *s*.
18: 6 into the tent to Sarah and *s*,
18: 9 Then they *s* to him, "Where is
18: 9 So he *s*, "Here, in the tent."
18:10 And He *s*, "I will certainly
18:13 And the LORD *s* to Abraham,
18:15 And He *s*, "No, but you did
18:17 And the LORD *s*, "Shall I
18:20 And the LORD *s*, "Because the
18:23 And Abraham came near and *s*,
18:26 So the LORD *s*, "If I find
18:27 Then Abraham answered and *s*,
18:28 So He *s*, "If I find there
18:29 he spoke to Him yet again and *s*,
18:29 be forty found there?" So He *s*,
18:30 Then he *s*, "Let not the Lord
18:30 So He *s*, "I will not do it
18:31 And he *s*, "Indeed now, I
18:31 So He *s*, "I will not destroy
18:32 Then he *s*, "Let not the Lord
18:32 And He *s*, "I will not destroy
19: 2 And he *s*, "Here now, my
19: 2 go on your way." And they *s*,
19: 5 And they called to Lot and *s* to
19: 7 and *s*, "Please, my brethren,
19: 9 And they *s*, "Stand back!"
19: 9 "Stand back!" Then they *s*,
19:12 Then the men *s* to Lot, "Have
19:14 married his daughters, and *s*,
19:17 brought them outside, that he *s*,
19:18 Then Lot *s* to them, "Please,
19:21 And he *s* to him, "See, I have
19:31 Now the firstborn *s* to the
19:34 next day that the firstborn *s*
20: 2 Now Abraham *s* of Sarah his wife,
20: 3 and *s* to him, "Indeed you are
20: 4 had not come near her; and he *s*,
20: 5 And she, even she herself *s*,
20: 6 And God *s* to him in a dream,
20: 9 Abimelech called Abraham and *s*
20:10 Then Abimelech *s* to Abraham,
20:11 And Abraham *s*, "Because I
20:13 that I *s* to her, 'This is your
20:15 And Abimelech *s*, "See, my
20:16 Then to Sarah he *s*,
21: 1 LORD visited Sarah as He had *s*,
21: 6 And Sarah *s*, "God has made
21: 7 She also *s*, "Who would
21: 7 Who would have *s* to Abraham that
21:10 Therefore she *s* to Abraham,
21:12 But God *s* to Abraham, "Do not
21:12 Whatever Sarah has *s* to you,
21:16 for she *s* to herself, "Let me

21:17 and *s* to her, "What ails you,
21:24 And Abraham *s*, "I will
21:26 And Abimelech *s*, "I do not
21:30 And he *s*, "You will take
22: 1 and *s* to him, "Abraham!"
22: 1 to him, "Abraham!" And he *s*,
22: 2 Then He *s*, "Take now your
22: 5 And Abraham *s* to his young men,
22: 7 to Abraham his father and *s*,
22: 7 said, "My father!" And he *s*,
22: 7 I am, my son." Then he *s*,
22: 8 And Abraham *s*, "My son, God
22:11 called to him from heaven and *s*,
22:11 "Abraham, Abraham!" So he *s*,
22:12 And He *s*, "Do not lay your
22:14 as it is *s* to this day, "In
22:16 and *s*: "By Myself I have
24: 2 So Abraham *s* to the oldest
24: 5 And the servant *s* to him,
24: 6 But Abraham *s* to him, "Beware
24:12 Then he *s*, "O LORD God of my
24:17 servant ran to meet her and *s*,
24:18 So she *s*, "Drink, my lord."
24:19 giving him a drink, she *s*,
24:23 and *s*, "Whose daughter
24:24 So she *s* to him, "I am the
24:25 Moreover she *s* to him, "We have
24:27 And he *s*, "Blessed be the
24:31 And he *s*, "Come in, O blessed
24:33 set before him to eat, but he *s*,
24:33 And he *s*, "Speak on."
24:34 So he *s*, "I am Abraham's
24:39 And I *s* to my master, 'Perhaps
24:40 But he *s* to me, 'The LORD,
24:42 day I came to the well and *s*,
24:45 And I *s* to her, 'Please let me
24:46 down from her shoulder, and *s*,
24:47 "Then I asked her, and *s*,
24:47 daughter are you?' And she *s*,
24:50 and Bethuel answered and *s*,
24:54 arose in the morning, and he *s*,
24:55 her brother and her mother *s*,
24:56 And he *s* to them, "Do not
24:57 So they *s*, "We will call
24:58 Then they called Rebekah and *s*
24:58 go with this man?" And she *s*,
24:60 And they blessed Rebekah and *s*
24:65 for she had *s* to the servant,
24:65 to meet us?" The servant *s*,
25:22 together within her; and she *s*,
25:23 And the LORD *s* to her: "Two
25:30 And Esau *s* to Jacob, "Please
25:31 But Jacob *s*, "Sell me your
25:32 And Esau *s*, "Look, I am about
25:33 Then Jacob *s*, "Swear to me
26: 2 the LORD appeared to him and *s*:
26: 7 asked about his wife. And he *s*,
26: 9 Abimelech called Isaac and *s*,
26: 9 And Isaac *s* to him, "Because
26: 9 said to him, "Because I *s*,
26:10 And Abimelech *s*, "What is
26:16 And Abimelech *s* to Isaac, "Go
26:22 its name Rehoboth, because he *s*,
26:24 to him the same night and *s*,
26:27 And Isaac *s* to them, "Why have
26:28 But they *s*, "We have
26:28 the LORD is with you. So we *s*,
26:32 and *s* to him, "We have found
27: 1 Esau his older son and *s* to
27: 2 Then he *s*, "Behold now,
27:11 And Jacob *s* to Rebekah his
27:13 But his mother *s* to him, "Let
27:18 So he went to his father and *s*,
27:18 said, "My father.' And he *s*,
27:19 Jacob *s* to his father, "I am
27:20 But Isaac *s* to his son, "How
27:20 And he *s*, "Because the LORD
27:21 Then Isaac *s* to Jacob, "Please
27:22 father, and he felt him and *s*,
27:24 Then he *s*, "Are you really
27:24 son Esau?" He *s*, "I am."
27:25 He *s*, "Bring it near to me,
27:26 Then his father Isaac *s* to him,
27:27 clothing, and blessed him and *s*:
27:31 and *s* to his father, "Let my
27:32 And his father Isaac *s* to him,
27:32 So he *s*, "I am your son,
27:33 trembled exceedingly, and *s*,
27:34 and *s* to his father, "Bless
27:35 But he *s*, "Your brother
27:36 And Esau *s*, "Is he not
27:36 away my blessing!" And he *s*,
27:37 Then Isaac answered and *s* to
27:38 And Esau *s* to his father, "Have
27:39 his father answered and *s* to
27:41 and Esau *s* in his heart, "The
27:42 and *s* to him, "Surely your
27:46 And Rebekah *s* to Isaac, "I am
28: 1 and *s* to him: "You shall not
28:13 the LORD stood above it and *s*:
28:16 awoke from his sleep and *s*,
28:17 And he was afraid and *s*,
29: 4 And Jacob *s* to them, "My
29: 4 are you from?" And they *s*,
29: 5 Then he *s* to them, "Do you know
29: 5 the son of Nahor?" And they *s*,
29: 6 So he *s* to them, "Is he well?"
29: 6 "Is he well?" And they *s*,
29: 7 Then he *s*, "Look, it is still
29: 8 But they *s*, "We cannot
29:14 And Laban *s* to him, "Surely you
29:15 Then Laban *s* to Jacob,
29:18 so he *s*, "I will serve you
29:19 And Laban *s*, "It is better
29:21 Then Jacob *s* to Laban, "Give
29:25 And he *s* to Laban, "What is
29:26 And Laban *s*, "It must not
29:32 his name Reuben; for she *s*,
29:33 again and bore a son, and *s*,
29:34 again and bore a son, and *s*,
29:35 again and bore a son, and *s*,
30: 1 and *s* to Jacob, "Give me
30: 2 against Rachel, and he *s*,
30: 3 So she *s*, "Here is my maid
30: 6 Then Rachel *s*, "God has
30: 8 Then Rachel *s*, "With great
30:11 Then Leah *s*, "A troop
30:13 Then Leah *s*, "I am happy,
30:14 Then Rachel *s* to Leah, "Please
30:15 But she *s* to her, "Is it a
30:15 mandrakes also?" And Rachel *s*,
30:16 Leah went out to meet him and *s*,
30:18 Leah *s*, "God has given me
30:20 And Leah *s*, "God has
30:23 conceived and bore a son, and *s*,
30:24 called his name Joseph, and *s*,
30:25 that Jacob *s* to Laban, "Send
30:27 And Laban *s* to him, "Please
30:28 Then he *s*, "Name me your
30:29 So Jacob *s* to him, "You know
30:31 So he *s*, "What shall I give
30:31 shall I give you?" And Jacob *s*,
30:34 And Laban *s*, "Oh, that it
31: 3 Then the LORD *s* to Jacob,
31: 5 and *s* to them, "I see your
31: 8 If he *s* thus: 'The speckled
31: 8 And if he *s* thus: 'The streaked
31:11 dream, saying, 'Jacob.' And I *s*,
31:12 'And He *s*, 'Lift your eyes
31:14 Rachel and Leah answered and *s*
31:16 whatever God has *s* to you, do
31:24 and *s* to him, "Be careful that
31:26 And Laban *s* to Jacob: "What
31:31 Then Jacob answered and *s* to
31:31 "Because I was afraid, for I *s*,
31:35 And she *s* to her father, "Let
31:36 and Jacob answered and *s* to
31:43 And Laban answered and *s* to
31:46 Then Jacob *s* to his brethren,
31:48 And Laban *s*, "This heap is
31:49 also Mizpah, because he *s*,
31:51 Then Laban *s* to Jacob, "Here
32: 2 When Jacob saw them, he *s*,
32: 8 And he *s*, "If Esau comes to
32: 9 Then Jacob *s*, "O God of my
32: 9 the LORD who *s* to me, 'Return
32:12 'For You *s*, 'I will surely
32:16 and *s* to his servants, "Pass
32:20 is behind us.'" For he *s*,
32:26 And He *s*, "Let Me go, for
32:26 for the day breaks." But he *s*,
32:27 So He *s* to him, "What is your
32:27 "What is your name?" He *s*,
32:28 And He *s*, "Your name shall
32:29 Your name, I pray." And He *s*,
33: 5 the women and children, and *s*,
33: 5 So he *s*, "The children
33: 8 Then Esau *s*, "What do you mean
33: 8 company which I met?" And he *s*,
33: 9 But Esau *s*, "I have enough,
33:10 And Jacob *s*, "No, please,
33:12 Then Esau *s*, "Let us take
33:13 But Jacob *s* to him, "My lord
33:15 And Esau *s*, "Now let me
33:15 who are with me." But he *s*,
34:11 Then Shechem *s* to her father and
34:14 And they *s* to them, "We cannot
34:30 Then Jacob *s* to Simeon and Levi,
34:31 But they *s*, "Should he treat
35: 1 Then God *s* to Jacob, "Arise, go
35: 2 And Jacob *s* to his household and
35:10 And God *s* to him, "Your name
35:11 Also God *s* to him: "I am God
35:17 that the midwife *s* to her, "Do
37: 6 So he *s* to them, "Please hear
37: 8 And his brothers *s* to him,
37: 9 told it to his brothers, and *s*,
37:10 his father rebuked him and *s*
37:13 And Israel *s* to Joseph, "Are
37:13 So he *s* to him, "Here I
37:14 Then he *s* to him, "Please go
37:16 So he *s*, "I am seeking my
37:17 And the man *s*, "They have
37:19 Then they *s* to one another,
37:21 him out of their hands, and *s*,
37:22 And Reuben *s* to them, "Shed no
37:26 So Judah *s* to his brothers,
37:30 returned to his brothers and *s*,
37:32 it to their father and *s*,
37:33 And he recognized it and *s*,
37:35 to be comforted, and he *s*,
38: 8 And Judah *s* to Onan, "Go in to
38:11 Then Judah *s* to Tamar his
38:11 For he *s*, "Lest he also die
38:16 turned to her by the way, and *s*,
38:16 So she *s*, "What will you give
38:17 And he *s*, "I will send a
38:17 goat from the flock." So she *s*,
38:18 Then he *s*, "What pledge shall
38:18 So she *s*, "Your signet and
38:21 by the roadside?" And they *s*,
38:22 So he returned to Judah and *s*,
38:22 the men of the place *s* there
38:23 Then Judah *s*, "Let her take
38:24 child by harlotry." So Judah *s*,
38:25 I am with child." And she *s*,
38:26 Judah acknowledged them and *s*,
38:29 out unexpectedly; and she *s*,
39: 7 eyes on Joseph, and she *s*,
39: 8 But he refused and *s* to his
40: 8 And they *s* to him, "We each
40: 8 So Joseph *s* to them, "Do not
40: 9 and *s* to him, "Behold, in my
40:12 And Joseph *s* to him, "This is
40:16 he *s* to Joseph, "I also was
40:18 So Joseph answered and *s*,
41:15 And Pharaoh *s* to Joseph, "I
41:15 But I have heard it *s* of you
41:17 Then Pharaoh *s* to Joseph:
41:25 Then Joseph *s* to Pharaoh, "The
41:38 And Pharaoh *s* to his servants,
41:39 Then Pharaoh *s* to Joseph,
41:41 And Pharaoh *s* to Joseph, "See,
41:44 Pharaoh also *s* to Joseph, "I
41:54 began to come, as Joseph had *s*.
41:55 Then Pharaoh *s* to all the
42: 1 Jacob *s* to his sons, "Why do
42: 2 And he *s*, "Indeed I have
42: 4 with his brothers, for he *s*,
42: 7 Then he *s* to them, "Where do
42: 7 do you come from?" And they *s*,
42: 9 and *s* to them, "You are
42:10 And they *s* to him, "No, my
42:12 But he *s* to them, "No, but you
42:13 And they *s*, "Your servants
42:14 But Joseph *s* to them, "It is
42:18 Then Joseph *s* to them the third
42:21 Then they *s* to one another, "We
42:28 So he *s* to his brothers, "My
42:31 But we *s* to him, 'We are honest
42:33 *s* to us, 'By this I will know
42:36 And Jacob their father *s* to
42:38 But he *s*, "My son shall not
43: 2 that their father *s* to them,
43: 5 for the man *s* to us, 'You shall
43: 6 And Israel *s*, "Why did you
43: 7 But they *s*, "The man asked
43: 8 Then Judah *s* to Israel his
43:11 And their father Israel *s* to
43:16 he *s* to the steward of his
43:18 into Joseph's house; and they *s*,
43:20 and *s*, "O sir, we indeed
43:23 But he *s*, "Peace be with you,
43:27 about their well-being, and *s*,
43:29 his mother's son, and *s*,
43:29 And he *s*, "God be gracious
43:31 he restrained himself, and *s*,
44: 4 Joseph *s* to his steward, "Get
44: 7 And they *s* to him, "Why does my
44:10 And he *s*, "Now also let it
44:15 And Joseph *s* to them, "What
44:16 Then Judah *s*, "What shall we
44:17 But he *s*, "Far be it from me
44:18 Judah came near to him and *s*:
44:20 And we *s* to my lord, 'We have a
44:21 Then you *s* to your servants,
44:22 And we *s* to my lord, 'The lad
44:23 But you *s* to your servants,
44:25 "And our father *s*, 'Go back
44:26 'But we *s*, 'We cannot go
44:27 Then your servant my father *s* to
44:28 one went out from me, and I *s*,
45: 3 Then Joseph *s* to his brothers,
45: 4 And Joseph *s* to his brothers,
45: 4 So they came near. Then he *s*:
45:17 And Pharaoh *s* to Joseph, "Say
45:24 and he *s* to them, "See that
45:27 the words which Joseph had *s*
45:28 Then Israel *s*, "It is enough.
46: 2 the visions of the night, and *s*,
46: 2 "Jacob, Jacob!" And he *s*,
46: 3 So He *s*, "I am God, the
46:30 And Israel *s* to Joseph, "Now
46:31 Then Joseph *s* to his brothers
47: 1 went and told Pharaoh, and *s*,
47: 3 Then Pharaoh *s* to his brothers,
47: 3 And they *s* to Pharaoh, "Your
47: 4 And they *s* to Pharaoh, "We have
47: 8 Pharaoh *s* to Jacob, "How old
47: 9 And Jacob *s* to Pharaoh, "The
47:15 Egyptians came to Joseph and *s*,
47:16 Then Joseph *s*, "Give your
47:18 to him the next year and *s* to
47:23 Then Joseph *s* to the people,
47:25 So they *s*, "You have saved
47:29 he called his son Joseph and *s*
47:30 And he *s*, "I will do as you
47:30 said, "I will do as you have *s*.
47:31 Then he *s*, "Swear to me."
48: 3 Then Jacob *s* to Joseph: "God
48: 4 and *s* to me, 'Behold, I will
48: 8 Israel saw Joseph's sons, and *s*,
48: 9 And Joseph *s* to his father,
48: 9 me in this place." And he *s*,
48:11 And Israel *s* to Joseph, "I had
48:15 And he blessed Joseph, and *s*:
48:18 And Joseph *s* to his father,
48:19 But his father refused and *s*,
48:21 Then Israel *s* to Joseph,
49: 1 And Jacob called his sons and *s*,
49:29 Then he charged them and *s* to
50: 6 And Pharaoh *s*, "Go up and
50:11 threshing floor of Atad, they *s*,
50:15 their father was dead, they *s*,
50:18 before his face, and they *s*,
50:19 Joseph *s* to them, "Do not be

50:24 And Joseph *s* to his brethren,
Ex 1: 9 And he *s* to his people, "Look,
1:16 and he *s*, "When you do the
1:18 called for the midwives and *s*
1:19 And the midwives *s* to Pharaoh,
2: 6 had compassion on him, and *s*,
2: 7 Then his sister *s* to Pharaoh's
2: 8 And Pharaoh's daughter *s* to her,
2: 9 Then Pharaoh's daughter *s* to
2:13 and he *s* to the one who did the
2:14 Then he *s*, "Who made you
2:14 So Moses feared and *s*,
2:18 to Reuel their father, he *s*,
2:19 And they *s*, "An Egyptian
2:20 So he *s* to his daughters, "And
2:22 his name Gershom; for he *s*,
3: 3 Then Moses *s*, "I will now
3: 4 the midst of the bush and *s*,
3: 4 And he *s*, "Here I am."
3: 5 Then He *s*, "Do not draw near
3: 6 Moreover He *s*, "I am the
3: 7 And the LORD *s*:
3:11 But Moses *s* to God, "Who am I
3:12 So He *s*, "I will certainly
3:13 Then Moses *s* to God, "Indeed,
3:14 And God *s* to Moses, "I AM WHO I
3:14 And He *s*, "Thus you shall
3:15 Moreover God *s* to Moses, "Thus
3:17 and I have *s* I will bring you up
4: 1 Then Moses answered and *s*,
4: 2 So the LORD *s* to him, "What
4: 2 your hand?" He *s*, "A rod."
4: 3 And He *s*, "Cast it on the
4: 4 Then the LORD *s* to Moses,
4: 6 Furthermore the LORD *s* to him,
4: 7 And He *s*, "Put your hand
4:10 Then Moses *s* to the LORD,
4:11 So the LORD *s* to him, "Who has
4:13 But he *s*, "O my Lord, please
4:14 kindled against Moses, and He *s*:
4:18 and *s* to him, "Please let me
4:18 And Jethro *s* to Moses, "Go
4:19 And the LORD *s* to Moses in
4:21 And the LORD *s* to Moses, "When
4:25 cast it at Moses' feet, and *s*,
4:26 So He let him go. Then she *s*,
4:27 And the LORD *s* to Aaron, "Go
5: 2 And Pharaoh *s*, "Who is the
5: 3 So they *s*, "The God of the
5: 4 Then the king of Egypt *s* to
5: 5 And Pharaoh *s*, "Look, the
5:17 But he *s*, "You are idle!
5:19 were in trouble after it was *s*,
5:21 And they *s* to them, "Let the
5:22 returned to the LORD and *s*,
6: 1 Then the LORD *s* to Moses, "Now
6: 2 And God spoke to Moses and *s* to
6:26 and Moses to whom the LORD *s*,
6:30 But Moses *s* before the LORD,
7: 1 So the LORD *s* to Moses: "See,
7:13 heed them, as the LORD had *s*.
7:14 So the LORD *s* to Moses:
7:22 heed them, as the LORD had *s*.
8: 8 for Moses and Aaron, and *s*,
8: 9 And Moses *s* to Pharaoh, "Accept
8:10 So he *s*, "Tomorrow." And he
8:10 And he *s*, "Let it be
8:15 heed them, as the LORD had *s*.
8:16 So the LORD *s* to Moses, "Say
8:19 Then the magicians *s* to Pharaoh,
8:19 them, just as the LORD had *s*.
8:20 And the LORD *s* to Moses,
8:25 for Moses and Aaron, and *s*,
8:26 And Moses *s*, "It is not
8:28 And Pharaoh *s*, "I will let
8:29 Then Moses *s*, "Indeed I am
9: 1 Then the LORD *s* to Moses, "Go
9: 8 So the LORD *s* to Moses and
9:13 Then the LORD *s* to Moses,
9:22 Then the LORD *s* to Moses,
9:27 and *s* to them, "I have sinned
9:29 So Moses *s* to him, "As soon as
10: 1 Now the LORD *s* to Moses, "Go
10: 3 Aaron came in to Pharaoh and *s*
10: 7 Then Pharaoh's servants *s* to
10: 8 and he *s* to them, "Go, serve
10: 9 And Moses *s*, "We will go
10:10 Then he *s* to them, "The LORD
10:12 Then the LORD *s* to Moses,
10:16 Moses and Aaron in haste, and *s*,
10:21 Then the LORD *s* to Moses,
10:24 Pharaoh called to Moses and *s*,
10:25 But Moses *s*, "You must also
10:28 Then Pharaoh *s* to him, "Get
10:29 And Moses *s*, "You have spoken
11: 1 And the LORD *s* to Moses, "I
11: 4 Then Moses *s*, "Thus says
11: 9 But the LORD *s* to Moses,
12:21 all the elders of Israel and *s*
12:31 Moses and Aaron by night, and *s*,
12:31 serve the LORD as you have *s*.
12:32 and your herds, as you have *s*,
12:33 For they *s*, "We shall all
12:43 And the LORD *s* to Moses and
13: 3 And Moses *s* to the people:
13:17 that was near; for God *s*,
14: 5 and they *s*, "Why have we
14:11 Then they *s* to Moses, "Because
14:13 And Moses *s* to the people, "Do
14:15 And the LORD *s* to Moses, "Why
14:25 difficulty; and the Egyptians *s*,
14:26 Then the LORD *s* to Moses,
15: 9 The enemy *s*, 'I will pursue,
15:26 and *s*, "If you diligently
16: 3 And the children of Israel *s* to
16: 4 Then the LORD *s* to Moses,
16: 6 Then Moses and Aaron *s* to all
16: 8 Also Moses *s*, "This shall be
16:15 they *s* to one another, "What
16:15 And Moses *s* to them, "This is
16:19 And Moses *s*, "Let no one
16:23 Then he *s* to them, "This is
16:23 is what the LORD has *s*:
16:25 Then Moses *s*, "Eat that
16:28 And the LORD *s* to Moses, "How
16:32 Then Moses *s*, "This is
16:33 And Moses *s* to Aaron, "Take a
17: 2 contended with Moses, and *s*,
17: 2 And Moses *s* to them, "Why do
17: 3 complained against Moses, and *s*,
17: 5 And the LORD *s* to Moses, "Go
17: 9 And Moses *s* to Joshua, "Choose
17:10 So Joshua did as Moses *s* to him,
17:14 Then the LORD *s* to Moses,
17:16 for he *s*, "Because the LORD
18: 3 of one was Gershom (for he *s*,
18: 4 other was Eliezer (for he *s*,
18: 6 Now he had *s* to Moses, "I, your
18:10 And Jethro *s*, "Blessed be
18:14 he did for the people, he *s*,
18:15 And Moses *s* to his
18:17 So Moses' father-in-law *s* to
18:24 and did all that he had *s*.
19: 8 people answered together and *s*,
19: 9 And the LORD *s* to Moses,
19:10 Then the LORD *s* to Moses, "Go
19:15 And he *s* to the people, "Be
19:21 And the LORD *s* to Moses, "Go
19:23 But Moses *s* to the LORD, "The
19:24 Then the LORD *s* to him, "Away!
20:19 Then they *s* to Moses, "You
20:20 And Moses *s* to the people, "Do
20:22 Then the LORD *s* to Moses,
23:13 And in all that I have *s* to you,
24: 1 Now He *s* to Moses, "Come up to
24: 3 answered with one voice and *s*,
24: 3 words which the LORD has *s* we
24: 7 And they *s*, "All that the
24: 7 All that the LORD has *s* we will
24: 8 it on the people, and *s*,
24:12 Then the LORD *s* to Moses,
24:14 And he *s* to the elders, "Wait
30:34 And the LORD *s* to Moses:
32: 1 and *s* to him, "Come, make us
32: 2 And Aaron *s* to them, "Break off
32: 4 Then they *s*, "This is your
32: 5 Aaron made a proclamation and *s*,
32: 7 And the LORD *s* to Moses, "Go,
32: 8 it and sacrificed to it, and *s*,
32: 9 And the LORD *s* to Moses, "I
32:11 with the LORD his God, and *s*:
32:13 and *s* to them, 'I will multiply
32:14 from the harm which He *s* He
32:17 he *s* to Moses, "There is a
32:18 But he *s*: "It is not the
32:21 And Moses *s* to Aaron, "What did
32:22 So Aaron *s*, "Do not let the
32:23 For they *s* to me, 'Make us gods
32:24 And I *s* to them, 'Whoever has
32:26 the entrance of the camp, and *s*,
32:27 And he *s* to them, "Thus says
32:29 Then Moses *s*, "Consecrate
32:30 on the next day that Moses *s*
32:31 returned to the LORD and *s*,
32:33 And the LORD *s* to Moses,
33: 1 Then the LORD *s* to Moses,
33: 5 For the LORD had *s* to Moses,
33:12 Then Moses *s* to the LORD,
33:12 send with me. Yet You have *s*,
33:14 And He *s*, "My Presence will
33:15 Then he *s* to Him, "If Your
33:17 So the LORD *s* to Moses, "I
33:18 And he *s*, "Please, show me
33:19 Then He *s*, "I will make
33:20 But He *s*, "You cannot see
33:21 And the LORD *s*, "Here is
34: 1 And the LORD *s* to Moses, "Cut
34: 9 Then he *s*, "If now I
34:10 And He *s*: "Behold, I make
34:27 Then the LORD *s* to Moses,
35: 1 and *s* to them, "These are the
35:30 And Moses *s* to the children of
Lev 8: 5 And Moses *s* to the congregation,
8:31 And Moses *s* to Aaron and his
9: 2 And he *s* to Aaron, "Take for
9: 6 Then Moses *s*, "This is the
9: 7 And Moses *s* to Aaron, "Go to
10: 3 And Moses *s* to Aaron, "This is
10: 4 and *s* to them, "Come near,
10: 5 out of the camp, as Moses had *s*.
10: 6 And Moses *s* to Aaron, and to
10:19 And Aaron *s* to Moses, "Look,
16: 2 and the LORD *s* to Moses: "Tell
17:12 Therefore I *s* to the children of
17:14 Therefore I *s* to the children
20:24 But I have *s* to you, "You shall
21: 1 And the LORD *s* to Moses,
Num 3:40 Then the LORD *s* to Moses:
7:11 For the LORD *s* to Moses, "They
9: 7 And those men *s* to him, "We
9: 8 And Moses *s* to them, "Stand
10:29 Now Moses *s* to Hobab the son of
10:29 the place of which the LORD *s*,
10:30 And he *s* to him, "I will not
10:31 So Moses *s*, "Please do not
10:35 the ark set out, that Moses *s*:
10:36 And when it rested, he *s*:
11: 4 of Israel also wept again and *s*:
11:11 So Moses *s* to the LORD, "Why
11:16 So the LORD *s* to Moses:
11:21 And Moses *s*, "The people
11:21 men on foot; yet You have *s*,
11:23 And the LORD *s* to Moses, "Has
11:27 man ran and told Moses, and *s*,
11:28 his choice men, answered and *s*,
11:29 Then Moses *s* to him, "Are you
12: 2 So they *s*, "Has the LORD
12: 4 Suddenly the LORD *s* to Moses,
12: 6 Then He *s*, "Hear now My
12:11 So Aaron *s* to Moses, "Oh, my
12:14 Then the LORD *s* to Moses, "If
13:17 and *s* to them, "Go up this
13:27 Then they told him, and *s*:
13:30 the people before Moses, and *s*,
13:31 men who had gone up with him *s*,
14: 2 and the whole congregation *s* to
14: 4 So they *s* to one another, "Let
14:10 And all the congregation *s* to
14:11 Then the LORD *s* to Moses:
14:13 And Moses *s* to the LORD:
14:20 Then the LORD *s*:
14:31 whom you *s* would be victims, I
14:41 And Moses *s*, "Now why do
15:35 Then the LORD *s* to Moses, "The
16: 3 and *s* to them, "You take too
16: 8 Then Moses *s* to Korah, "Hear
16:12 the sons of Eliab, but they *s*,
16:15 and *s* to the LORD, "Do not
16:16 And Moses *s* to Korah,
16:22 they fell on their faces, and *s*,
16:28 And Moses *s*: "By this
16:34 fled at their cry, for they *s*,
16:40 just as the LORD had *s* to him
16:46 So Moses *s* to Aaron, "Take a
17:10 And the LORD *s* to Moses,
18: 1 Then the LORD *s* to Aaron: "You
18:20 Then the LORD *s* to Aaron: "You
18:24 therefore I have *s* to them,
20:10 and he *s* to them, "Hear now,
20:18 Then Edom *s* to him, "You shall
20:19 So the children of Israel *s* to
20:20 Then he *s*, "You shall not
21: 2 made a vow to the LORD, and *s*,
21: 7 the people came to Moses, and *s*,
21: 8 Then the LORD *s* to Moses,
21:14 Therefore it is *s* in the Book of
21:16 is the well where the LORD *s*
21:34 Then the LORD *s* to Moses, "Do
22: 4 So Moab *s* to the elders of
22: 8 And he *s* to them, "Lodge here
22: 9 Then God came to Balaam and *s*,
22:10 So Balaam *s* to God, "Balak the
22:12 And God *s* to Balaam, "You shall
22:13 rose in the morning and *s* to
22:14 rose and went to Balak, and *s*,
22:16 And they came to Balaam and *s* to
22:18 Then Balaam answered and *s* to
22:20 came to Balaam at night and *s*
22:28 and she *s* to Balaam, "What
22:29 And Balaam *s* to the donkey,
22:30 So the donkey *s* to Balaam, "Am
22:30 to you?" And he *s*, "No."
22:32 And the Angel of the LORD *s* to
22:34 And Balaam *s* to the Angel of the
22:35 Then the Angel of the LORD *s* to
22:37 Then Balak *s* to Balaam, "Did I
22:38 And Balaam *s* to Balak, "Look, I
23: 1 Then Balaam *s* to Balak, "Build
23: 3 Then Balaam *s* to Balak, "Stand
23: 4 and he *s* to Him, "I have
23: 5 a word in Balaam's mouth, and *s*,
23: 7 And he took up his oracle and *s*:
23:11 Then Balak *s* to Balaam, "What
23:12 So he answered and *s*,
23:13 Then Balak *s* to him, "Please
23:15 And he *s* to Balak, "Stand here
23:16 put a word in his mouth, and *s*,
23:17 And Balak *s* to him, "What has
23:18 he took up his oracle and *s*:
23:19 Has He *s*, and will He
23:23 It now must be *s* of Jacob And
23:25 Then Balak *s* to Balaam,
23:26 So Balaam answered and *s* to
23:27 Then Balak *s* to Balaam,
23:29 Then Balaam *s* to Balak, "Build
23:30 And Balak did as Balaam had *s*,
24: 3 he took up his oracle and *s*:
24:10 and Balak *s* to Balaam, "I
24:11 I *s* I would greatly honor you,
24:12 So Balaam *s* to Balak, "Did I
24:15 So he took up his oracle and *s*:
24:20 and he took up his oracle and *s*:
24:21 and he took up his oracle and *s*:
24:23 he took up his oracle and *s*:
25: 4 Then the LORD *s* to Moses,
25: 5 So Moses *s* to the judges of
26:65 For the LORD had *s* of them,
27:12 Now the LORD *s* to Moses: "Go
27:18 And the LORD *s* to Moses:
31:15 And Moses *s* to them: "Have you
31:21 Then Eleazar the priest *s* to
31:49 and they *s* to Moses, "Your
32: 5 Therefore they *s*, "If we
32: 6 And Moses *s* to the children of
32:16 they came near to him and *s*:
32:20 Then Moses *s* to them: "If you

32:29 And Moses *s* to them: “If the
32:31 As the LORD has *s* to your
36: 2 And they *s*: “The LORD
Deut 1:14 “And you answered me and *s*,
1:20 And I *s* to you, ‘You have come
1:22 of you came near to me and *s*,
1:27 complained in your tents, and *s*,
1:29 Then I *s* to you, ‘Do not be
1:41 Then you answered and *s* to me,
1:42 And the LORD *s* to me, ‘Tell
2: 9 Then the LORD *s* to me, ‘Do not
2:31 And the LORD *s* to me, ‘See, I
3: 2 And the LORD *s* to me, ‘Do not
3:26 So the LORD *s* to me: ‘Enough
4:10 when the LORD *s* to me, ‘Gather
5: 1 and *s* to them: “Hear, O
5: 5 not go up the mountain. He *s*:
5:24 ‘And you *s*: ‘Surely the
5:28 and the LORD *s* to me: ‘I have
9: 2 and of whom you heard it *s*,
9: 3 as the LORD has *s* to you.
9:12 Then the LORD *s* to me, ‘Arise,
9:25 because the LORD had *s* He
9:26 I prayed to the LORD, and *s*:
10: 1 At that time the LORD *s* to me,
10:11 Then the LORD *s* to me, ‘Arise,
11:25 just as He has *s* to you.
17:16 for the LORD has *s* to you,
18: 2 as He *s* to them.
18:17 And the LORD *s* to me: ‘What
28:68 by the way of which I *s* to you,
29: 2 Moses called all Israel and *s*
31: 2 And he *s* to them: “I am one
31: 2 Also the LORD has *s* to me,
31: 3 you, just as the LORD has *s*.
31: 7 Moses called Joshua and *s* to
31:14 Then the LORD *s* to Moses,
31:16 And the LORD *s* to Moses:
31:23 Joshua the son of Nun, and *s*,
32:20 And He *s*: ‘I will hide
32:26 I would have *s*,
32:46 and He *s* to them: “Set your
33: 2 And he *s*: “The LORD came
33: 7 And this he *s* of Judah:
33: 8 And of Levi he *s*: “Let
33:12 Of Benjamin he *s*: “The
33:13 And of Joseph he *s*:
33:18 And of Zebulun he *s*:
33:20 And of Gad he *s*: “Blessed
33:22 And of Dan he *s*: “Dan is
33:23 And of Naphtali he *s*:
33:24 And of Asher he *s*:
34: 4 Then the LORD *s* to him, “This
Josh 1: 3 as I *s* to Moses.
2: 4 two men and hid them. So she *s*,
2: 9 and *s* to the men: “I know that
2:16 And she *s* to them, “Get to the
2:17 So the men *s* to her: “We will
2:21 Then she *s*, “According to
2:24 And they *s* to Joshua, “Truly
3: 5 And Joshua *s* to the people,
3: 7 And the LORD *s* to Joshua,
3: 9 So Joshua *s* to the children of
3:10 And Joshua *s*, “By this you
4: 5 and Joshua *s* to them: “Cross
5: 2 At that time the LORD *s* to
5: 9 Then the LORD *s* to Joshua,
5:13 And Joshua went to Him and *s* to
5:14 So He *s*, “No, but as
5:14 and *s* to Him, “What does my
5:15 of the LORD’s army *s* to
6: 2 And the LORD *s* to Joshua:
6: 6 of Nun called the priests and *s*
6: 7 And he *s* to the people,
6:16 that Joshua *s* to the people:
6:22 But Joshua had *s* to the two men
7: 3 they returned to Joshua and *s*
7: 7 And Joshua *s*, “Alas, Lord GOD,
7:10 So the LORD *s* to Joshua: “Get
7:19 Now Joshua *s* to Achan, “My son,
7:20 And Achan answered Joshua and *s*,
7:25 And Joshua *s*, “Why have
8: 1 Now the LORD *s* to Joshua: “Do
8:18 Then the LORD *s* to Joshua,
9: 6 and *s* to him and to the men of
9: 7 Then the men of Israel *s* to the
9: 8 But they *s* to Joshua, “We are
9: 8 And Joshua *s* to them, “Who
9: 9 So they *s* to him: “From a very
9:19 Then all the rulers *s* to all the
9:21 And the rulers *s* to them, “Let
9:24 So they answered Joshua and *s*,
10: 8 And the LORD *s* to Joshua, “Do
10:12 and he *s* in the sight of
10:18 So Joshua *s*, “Roll large
10:22 Then Joshua *s*, “Open the
10:24 and *s* to the captains of the
10:25 Then Joshua *s* to them, “Do not
11: 6 But the LORD *s* to Joshua, “Do
11:23 to all that the LORD had *s* to
13: 1 And the LORD *s* to him: “You
13:14 as He *s* to them.
13:33 as He had *s* to them.
14: 6 of Jephunneh the Kenizzite *s*
14: 6 the word which the LORD *s* to
14:10 has kept me alive, as He *s*,
14:12 drive them out as the LORD *s*.
15:16 And Caleb *s*, “He who
15:18 and Caleb *s* to her, “What do
17:16 But the children of Joseph *s*,
18: 3 Then Joshua *s* to the children of
22: 2 and *s* to them: “You have kept
22:21 of Manasseh answered and *s* to
22:26 ‘Therefore we *s*, ‘Let us
22:28 Therefore we *s* that it will be,
22:31 son of Eleazar the priest *s* to
23: 2 and *s* to them: “I am old,
24: 2 And Joshua *s* to all the people,
24:16 So the people answered and *s*:
24:19 But Joshua *s* to the people,
24:21 And the people *s* to Joshua,
24:22 So Joshua *s* to the people, “You
24:22 And they *s*, “We are
24:23 “Now therefore,” he *s*,
24:24 And the people *s* to Joshua,
24:27 And Joshua *s* to all the people,
Judg 1: 2 And the LORD *s*, “Judah shall
1: 3 So Judah *s* to Simeon his
1: 7 And Adoni-Bezek *s*, “Seventy
1:12 Then Caleb *s*, “Whoever
1:14 and Caleb *s* to her, “What do
1:15 So she *s* to him, “Give me a
1:20 Hebron to Caleb, as Moses had *s*.
1:24 they *s* to him, “Please show us
2: 1 up from Gilgal to Bochim, and *s*:
2: 1 swore to your fathers; and I *s*,
2: 3 “Therefore I also *s*,
2:15 calamity, as the LORD had *s*,
2:20 hot against Israel; and He *s*,
3:19 that were at Gilgal, and *s*,
3:19 He *s*, “Keep silence!”
3:20 Then Ehud *s*, “I have a
3:24 So they *s*, “He is probably
3:28 Then he *s* to them, “Follow me,
4: 6 and *s* to him, “Has not the
4: 8 And Barak *s* to her, “If you
4: 9 So she *s*, “I will surely
4:14 Then Deborah *s* to Barak, “Up!
4:18 and *s* to him, “Turn aside, my
4:19 Then he *s* to her, “Please give
4:20 And he *s* to her, “Stand at the
4:22 and *s* to him, “Come, I will
5:23 *s* the angel of the LORD,
6: 8 who *s* to them, “Thus says the
6:10 Also I *s* to you, “I am the
6:12 and *s* to him, “The LORD is
6:13 Gideon *s* to Him, “O my lord, if
6:14 the LORD turned to him and *s*,
6:15 So he *s* to Him, “O my Lord, how
6:16 And the LORD *s* to him, “Surely
6:17 Then he *s* to Him, “If now I
6:18 And He *s*, “I will wait
6:20 The Angel of God *s* to him,
6:22 Angel of the LORD. So Gideon *s*,
6:23 Then the LORD *s* to him, “Peace
6:25 same night that the LORD *s* to
6:27 and did as the LORD had *s* to
6:29 So they *s* to one another, “Who
6:29 had inquired and asked, they *s*,
6:30 Then the men of the city *s* to
6:31 But Joash *s* to all who stood
6:36 So Gideon *s* to God, “If You
6:36 Israel by my hand as You have *s*—
6:37 by my hand, as You have *s*.
6:39 Then Gideon *s* to God, “Do not
7: 2 And the LORD *s* to Gideon,
7: 4 But the LORD *s* to Gideon,
7: 5 And the LORD *s* to Gideon,
7: 7 Then the LORD *s* to Gideon, “By
7: 9 same night that the LORD *s* to
7:13 He *s*, “I have had a dream:
7:14 his companion answered and *s*,
7:15 to the camp of Israel, and *s*,
7:17 And he *s* to them, “Look at me
8: 1 Now the men of Ephraim *s* to him,
8: 2 So he *s* to them, “What have I
8: 3 toward him subsided when he *s*
8: 5 Then he *s* to the men of Succoth,
8: 6 And the leaders of Succoth *s*,
8: 7 So Gideon *s*, “For this cause,
8:15 to the men of Succoth and *s*,
8:18 And he *s* to Zebah and Zalmunna,
8:19 Then he *s*, “They were my
8:20 And he *s* to Jether his
8:21 So Zebah and Zalmunna *s*,
8:22 Then the men of Israel *s* to
8:23 But Gideon *s* to them, “I will
8:24 Then Gideon *s* to them, “I would
9: 3 to follow Abimelech, for they *s*,
9: 7 And he *s* to them: “Listen to
9: 8 And they *s* to the olive tree,
9: 9 But the olive tree *s* to them,
9:10 Then the trees *s* to the fig
9:11 But the fig tree *s* to them,
9:12 Then the trees *s* to the vine,
9:13 But the vine *s* to them,
9:14 Then all the trees *s* to the
9:15 And the bramble *s* to the trees,
9:28 Then Gaal the son of Ebed *s*,
9:29 So he *s* to Abimelech,
9:36 he *s* to Zebul, “Look, people
9:36 But Zebul *s* to him, “You see
9:37 So Gaal spoke again and *s*,
9:38 Then Zebul *s* to him, “Where
9:38 mouth now, with which you *s*,
9:48 then he *s* to the people who
9:54 and *s* to him, “Draw your sword
10:11 So the LORD *s* to the children
10:15 And the children of Israel *s* to
10:18 *s* to one another, “Who is the
11: 2 and *s* to him, “You shall have
11: 6 Then they *s* to Jephthah, “Come
11: 7 So Jephthah *s* to the elders of
11: 8 And the elders of Gilead *s* to
11: 9 So Jephthah *s* to the elders of
11:10 And the elders of Gilead *s* to
11:15 and *s* to him, “Thus says
11:19 and Israel *s* to him, “Please
11:30 made a vow to the LORD, and *s*,
11:35 that he tore his clothes, and *s*,
11:36 So she *s* to him, “My father,
11:37 Then she *s* to her father, “Let
11:38 So he *s*, “Go.” And he
12: 1 and *s* to Jephthah, “Why did
12: 2 And Jephthah *s* to them, “My
12: 4 Ephraim, because they *s*,
12: 5 any Ephraimite who escaped *s*,
12: 5 you an Ephraimite?” If he *s*,
13: 3 appeared to the woman and *s* to
13: 7 And He *s* to me, ‘Behold, you
13: 8 prayed to the LORD, and *s*,
13:10 and *s* to him, “Look, the Man
13:11 he *s* to Him, “Are You the Man
13:11 And He *s*, “I am.”
13:12 Manoah *s*, “Now let Your
13:13 So the Angel of the LORD *s* to
13:13 Of all that I *s* to the woman let
13:15 Then Manoah *s* to the Angel of
13:16 And the Angel of the LORD *s* to
13:17 Then Manoah *s* to the Angel of
13:18 And the Angel of the LORD *s* to
13:22 And Manoah *s* to his wife, “We
13:23 But his wife *s* to him, “If the
14: 3 Then his father and mother *s* to
14: 3 And Samson *s* to his father,
14:12 Then Samson *s* to them, “Let me
14:13 And they *s* to him, “Pose
14:14 So he *s* to them: “Out of the
14:15 on the seventh day that they *s*
14:16 wife wept on him, and *s*,
14:16 And he *s* to her, “Look, I
14:18 So the men of the city *s* to him
14:18 And he *s* to them: “If you
15: 1 And he *s*, “Let me go in
15: 2 Her father *s*, “I really
15: 3 And Samson *s* to them, “This
15: 6 Then the Philistines *s*,
15: 7 Samson *s* to them, “Since you
15:10 And the men of Judah *s*,
15:11 and *s* to Samson, “Do you not
15:11 And he *s* to them, “As they
15:12 But they *s* to him, “We have
15:12 Then Samson *s* to them,
15:16 Then Samson *s*: “With the
15:18 he cried out to the LORD and *s*,
16: 5 came up to her and *s* to her,
16: 6 So Delilah *s* to Samson,
16: 7 And Samson *s* to her, “If they
16: 9 And she *s* to him, “The
16:10 Then Delilah *s* to Samson,
16:11 So he *s* to her, “If they bind
16:12 and *s* to him, “The Philistines
16:13 Delilah *s* to Samson, “Until
16:13 And he *s* to her, “If you
16:14 and *s* to him, “The Philistines
16:15 Then she *s* to him, “How can
16:17 and *s* to her, “No razor has
16:20 And she *s*, “The Philistines
16:20 he awoke from his sleep, and *s*,
16:23 And they *s*: “Our god has
16:24 for they *s*: “Our god has
16:25 hearts were merry, that they *s*,
16:26 Then Samson *s* to the lad who
16:30 Then Samson *s*, “Let me
17: 2 And he *s* to his mother, “The
17: 2 And his mother *s*, “May you
17: 3 to his mother, his mother *s*,
17: 9 And Micah *s* to him, “Where do
17: 9 So he *s* to him, “I am a
17:10 Micah *s* to him, “Dwell with me,
17:13 Then Micah *s*, “Now I know
18: 2 They *s* to them, “Go, search
18: 3 They turned aside and *s* to him,
18: 4 He *s* to them, “Thus and so
18: 5 So they *s* to him, “Please
18: 6 And the priest *s* to them, “Go
18: 8 and their brethren *s* to them,
18: 9 So they *s*, “Arise, let
18:14 of Laish answered and *s* to
18:18 the priest *s* to them, “What
18:19 And they *s* to him, “Be quiet,
18:23 So they turned around and *s* to
18:24 So he *s*, “You have taken
18:25 And the children of Dan *s* to
19: 5 but the young woman’s father *s*
19: 6 the young woman’s father *s* to
19: 8 but the young woman’s father *s*
19: 9 *s* to him, “Look, the day is
19:11 and the servant *s* to his
19:12 But his master *s* to him, “We
19:13 So he *s* to his servant, “Come,
19:17 of the city; and the old man *s*,
19:18 So he *s* to him, “We are
19:20 And the old man *s*,
19:23 went out to them and *s* to them,
19:28 And he *s* to her, “Get up and
19:30 so it was that all who saw it *s*,
20: 3 Then the children of Israel *s*,
20: 4 was murdered, answered and *s*,
20:18 They *s*, “Which of us shall
20:18 The LORD *s*, “Judah first!”
20:23 And the LORD *s*, “Go up
20:28 And the LORD *s*, “Go up,
20:32 And the children of Benjamin *s*,
20:32 But the children of Israel *s*,
20:39 For they *s*, “Surely they

21: 3 and *s*, “O LORD God of
21: 5 The children of Israel *s*,
21: 6 Benjamin their brother, and *s*,
21: 8 And they *s*, “What one is
21:16 elders of the congregation *s*,
21:17 And they *s*, “There must be
21:19 Then they *s*, “In fact,
Ruth 1: 8 And Naomi *s* to her two
1:10 And they *s* to her, “Surely we
1:11 But Naomi *s*, “Turn back,
1:15 And she *s*, “Look, your
1:16 But Ruth *s*: “Entreat me
1:19 and the women *s*, “Is this
1:20 But she *s* to them, “Do not call
2: 2 So Ruth the Moabitess *s* to
2: 2 And she *s* to her, “Go, my
2: 4 and *s* to the reapers, “The
2: 5 Then Boaz *s* to his servant who
2: 6 of the reapers answered and *s*,
2: 7 ‘And she *s*, ‘Please let me
2: 8 Then Boaz *s* to Ruth, “You will
2:10 and *s* to him, “Why have I
2:11 And Boaz answered and *s* to her,
2:13 Then she *s*, “Let me find
2:14 Now Boaz *s* to her at mealtime,
2:19 And her mother-in-law *s* to her,
2:19 with whom she had worked, and *s*,
2:20 Then Naomi *s* to her
2:20 And Naomi *s* to her, “This
2:21 Ruth the Moabitess *s*,
2:21 He also *s* to me, ‘You shall stay
2:22 And Naomi *s* to Ruth her
3: 1 Then Naomi her mother-in-law *s*
3: 5 And she *s* to her, “All that you
3: 9 And he *s*, “Who are you?”
3:10 Then he *s*, “Blessed are you
3:14 Then he *s*, “Do not let
3:15 Also he *s*, “Bring the
3:16 to her mother-in-law, she *s*,
3:17 And she *s*, “These six
3:17 for he *s* to me, ‘Do not go
3:18 Then she *s*, “Sit still,
4: 1 had spoken came by. So Boaz *s*,
4: 2 the elders of the city, and *s*,
4: 3 Then he *s* to the close relative,
4: 4 And he *s*, “I will redeem
4: 5 Then Boaz *s*, “On the day
4: 6 And the close relative *s*,
4: 8 Therefore the close relative *s*
4: 9 And Boaz *s* to the elders and all
4:11 at the gate, and the elders, *s*,
4:14 Then the women *s* to Naomi,
1 Sam 1: 8 Then Elkanah her husband *s* to
1:11 Then she made a vow and *s*,
1:14 So Eli *s* to her, “How long will
1:15 And Hannah answered and *s*,
1:17 Then Eli answered and *s*,
1:18 And she *s*, “Let your
1:22 for she *s* to her husband,
1:23 And Elkanah her husband *s* to
1:26 And she *s*, “O my lord!
2: 1 And Hannah prayed and *s*:
2:16 And if the man *s* to him, “They
2:23 So he *s* to them, “Why do you do
2:27 a man of God came to Eli and *s*
2:30 I *s* indeed that your house and
3: 5 So he ran to Eli and *s*,
3: 5 And he *s*, “I did not call;
3: 6 arose and went to Eli, and *s*,
3: 8 he arose and went to Eli, and *s*,
3: 9 Therefore Eli *s* to Samuel, “Go,
3:11 Then the LORD *s* to Samuel:
3:16 Then Eli called Samuel and *s*,
3:17 And he *s*, “What is the
3:17 me of all the things that He *s*
3:18 And he *s*, “It is the LORD.
4: 3 camp, the elders of Israel *s*,
4: 6 the noise of the shout, they *s*,
4: 7 were afraid, for they *s*,
4: 7 And they *s*, “Woe to us!
4:14 the noise of the outcry, he *s*,
4:16 Then the man *s* to Eli, “I am
4:16 And he *s*, “What happened,
4:17 So the messenger answered and *s*,
4:20 the women who stood by her *s*
4:22 And she *s*, “The glory
5: 7 Ashdod saw how it was, they *s*,
5: 8 lords of the Philistines, and *s*,
5:11 lords of the Philistines, and *s*,
6: 3 So they *s*, “If you send
6: 4 Then they *s*, “What is the
6:20 And the men of Beth Shemesh *s*,
7: 5 And Samuel *s*, “Gather all
7: 6 and *s* there, “We have sinned
7: 8 So the children of Israel *s* to
8: 5 and *s* to him, “Look, you are
8: 6 displeased Samuel when they *s*,
8: 7 And the LORD *s* to Samuel,
8:11 And he *s*, “This will be
8:19 and they *s*, “No, but we
8:22 So the LORD *s* to Samuel, “Heed
8:22 And Samuel *s* to the men of
9: 3 And Kish *s* to his son Saul,
9: 5 Saul *s* to his servant who was
9: 6 And he *s* to him, “Look now,
9: 7 Then Saul *s* to his servant,
9: 8 answered Saul again and *s*,
9:10 Then Saul *s* to his servant,
9:10 said to his servant, “Well *s*;
9:11 and *s* to them, “Is the seer
9:12 And they answered them and *s*,
9:17 the LORD *s* to him, “There he
9:18 to Samuel in the gate, and *s*,
9:19 And Samuel answered Saul and *s*,
9:21 And Saul answered and *s*,
9:23 And Samuel *s* to the cook,
9:23 of which I *s* to you, ‘Set it
9:24 And Samuel *s*, “Here it is,
9:24 since I *s* I invited the
9:27 Samuel *s* to Saul, “Tell the
10: 1 his head, and kissed him and *s*:
10:11 that the people *s* to one
10:12 a man from there answered and *s*,
10:14 Then Saul’s uncle *s* to him and
10:14 “Where did you go?” So he *s*,
10:15 And Saul’s uncle *s*,
10:15 what Samuel *s* to you.”
10:16 So Saul *s* to his uncle, “He
10:16 not tell him what Samuel had *s*.
10:18 and *s* to the children of Israel,
10:19 and you have *s* to Him, ‘No, set
10:24 And Samuel *s* to all the people,
10:24 So all the people shouted and *s*,
10:27 But some rebels *s*,
11: 1 and all the men of Jabesh *s* to
11: 3 Then the elders of Jabesh *s* to
11: 5 and Saul *s*, “What troubles
11: 9 And they *s* to the messengers who
11:10 Therefore the men of Jabesh *s*,
11:12 Then the people *s* to Samuel,
11:12 to Samuel, “Who is he who *s*,
11:13 But Saul *s*, “Not a man
11:14 Then Samuel *s* to the people,
12: 1 Now Samuel *s* to all Israel:
12: 1 your voice in all that you *s*
12: 4 And they *s*, “You have not
12: 5 Then he *s* to them, “The LORD
12: 6 Then Samuel *s* to the people,
12:10 cried out to the LORD, and *s*,
12:12 you *s* to me, ‘No, but a king
12:19 And all the people *s* to Samuel,
12:20 Then Samuel *s* to the people,
13: 4 Now all Israel heard it *s* that
13: 9 So Saul *s*, “Bring a burnt
13:11 And Samuel *s*, “What have
13:11 And Saul *s*, “When I saw
13:12 ‘then I *s*, ‘The Philistines
13:13 And Samuel *s* to Saul, “You have
13:19 Israel, for the Philistines *s*,
14: 1 Jonathan the son of Saul *s* to
14: 6 Then Jonathan *s* to the young
14: 7 So his armorbearer *s* to him,
14: 8 Then Jonathan *s*, “Very well,
14:11 And the Philistines *s*,
14:12 and his armorbearer, and *s*,
14:12 Jonathan *s* to his
14:17 Then Saul *s* to the people who
14:18 And Saul *s* to Ahijah, “Bring
14:19 so Saul *s* to the priest,
14:28 Then one of the people *s*,
14:29 But Jonathan *s*, “My father
14:33 So he *s*, “You have dealt
14:34 And Saul *s*, “Disperse
14:36 Now Saul *s*, “Let us go
14:36 And they *s*, “Do whatever
14:36 Then the priest *s*,
14:38 And Saul *s*, “Come over
14:40 Then he *s* to all Israel, “You
14:40 And the people *s* to Saul,
14:41 Therefore Saul *s* to the LORD
14:42 And Saul *s*, “Cast lots
14:43 Then Saul *s* to Jonathan, “Tell
14:43 And Jonathan told him, and *s*,
14:45 But the people *s* to Saul,
15: 1 Samuel also *s* to Saul, “The
15: 6 Then Saul *s* to the Kenites,
15:13 and Saul *s* to him, “Blessed
15:14 But Samuel *s*, “What then
15:15 And Saul *s*, “They have
15:16 Then Samuel *s* to Saul, “Be
15:16 will tell you what the LORD *s*
15:16 And he *s* to him, “Speak
15:17 So Samuel *s*, “When you
15:18 sent you on a mission, and *s*,
15:20 And Saul *s* to Samuel, “But I
15:22 Then Samuel *s*: “Has the
15:24 Then Saul *s* to Samuel, “I have
15:26 But Samuel *s* to Saul, “I will
15:28 So Samuel *s* to him, “The LORD
15:30 Then he *s*, “I have sinned;
15:32 Then Samuel *s*, “Bring Agag
15:32 And Agag *s*, “Surely the
15:33 But Samuel *s*, “As your
16: 1 Now the LORD *s* to Samuel, “How
16: 2 And Samuel *s*, “How can I
16: 2 And the LORD *s*, “Take a
16: 4 So Samuel did what the LORD *s*,
16: 4 trembled at his coming, and *s*,
16: 5 And he *s*, “Peaceably;
16: 6 that he looked at Eliab and *s*,
16: 7 But the LORD *s* to Samuel, “Do
16: 8 And he *s*, “Neither has the
16: 9 And he *s*, “Neither has the
16:10 And Samuel *s* to Jesse, “The
16:11 And Samuel *s* to Jesse, “Are all
16:11 Then he *s*, “There remains
16:11 And Samuel *s* to Jesse, “Send
16:12 And the LORD *s*, “Arise,
16:15 And Saul’s servants *s* to him,
16:17 So Saul *s* to his servants,
16:18 of the servants answered and *s*,
16:19 sent messengers to Jesse, and *s*,
17: 8 and *s* to them, “Why have you
17:10 And the Philistine *s*,
17:17 Then Jesse *s* to his son David,
17:25 So the men of Israel *s*,
17:28 aroused against David, and he *s*,
17:29 And David *s*, “What have
17:30 from him toward another and *s*
17:32 Then David *s* to Saul, “Let no
17:33 And Saul *s* to David, “You are
17:34 But David *s* to Saul, “Your
17:37 Moreover David *s*, “The LORD,
17:37 And Saul *s* to David, “Go,
17:39 And David *s* to Saul, “I cannot
17:43 So the Philistine *s* to David,
17:44 And the Philistine *s* to David,
17:45 Then David *s* to the Philistine,
17:55 he *s* to Abner, the commander of
17:55 And Abner *s*, “As your
17:56 So the king *s*, “Inquire
17:58 And Saul *s* to him, “Whose son
18: 7 sang as they danced, and *s*:
18: 8 and he *s*, “They have
18:11 Saul cast the spear, for he *s*,
18:17 Then Saul *s* to David, “Here is
18:18 So David *s* to Saul, “Who am I,
18:21 So Saul *s*, “I will give
18:21 Therefore Saul *s* to David a
18:23 And David *s*, “Does it seem
18:25 Then Saul *s*, “Thus you
19: 4 and *s* to him, “Let not the
19:14 messengers to take David, she *s*,
19:17 Then Saul *s* to Michal, “Why
19:17 ‘He *s* to me, ‘Let me go!
19:22 So he asked, and *s*, “Where
19:22 And someone *s*, “Indeed
20: 1 and went and *s* to Jonathan,
20: 2 So Jonathan *s* to him, “By no
20: 3 David took an oath again, and *s*,
20: 3 in your eyes, and he has *s*,
20: 4 So Jonathan *s* to David,
20: 5 And David *s* to Jonathan,
20: 9 But Jonathan *s*, “Far be it
20:10 Then David *s* to Jonathan, “Who
20:11 And Jonathan *s* to David, “Come,
20:12 Then Jonathan *s* to David: “The
20:18 Then Jonathan *s* to David,
20:27 And Saul *s* to Jonathan his son,
20:29 ‘And he *s*, ‘Please let me
20:30 and he *s* to him, “You son of a
20:32 and *s* to him, “Why should he
20:36 Then he *s* to his lad, “Now run,
20:37 cried out after the lad and *s*,
20:40 and *s* to him, “Go, carry them
20:42 Then Jonathan *s* to David, “Go
21: 1 and *s* to him, “Why are you
21: 2 So David *s* to Ahimelech the
21: 2 and *s* to me, ‘Do not let anyone
21: 4 the priest answered David and *s*,
21: 5 and *s* to him, “Truly, women
21: 8 And David *s* to Ahimelech, “Is
21: 9 So the priest *s*, “The sword
21: 9 And David *s*, “There is
21:11 And the servants of Achish *s* to
21:14 Then Achish *s* to his servants,
22: 3 and he *s* to the king of Moab,
22: 5 Now the prophet Gad *s* to David,
22: 7 then Saul *s* to his servants who
22: 9 the servants of Saul, and *s*,
22:12 And Saul *s*, “Hear now,
22:13 Then Saul *s* to him, “Why have
22:14 answered the king and *s*,
22:16 And the king *s*, “You shall
22:17 Then the king *s* to the guards
22:18 And the king *s* to Doeg, “You
22:22 So David *s* to Abiathar, “I knew
23: 2 And the LORD *s* to David,
23: 3 But David’s men *s* to him,
23: 4 the LORD answered him and *s*,
23: 7 So Saul *s*, “God has
23: 9 he *s* to Abiathar the priest,
23:10 Then David *s*, “O LORD
23:11 And the LORD *s*, “He will
23:12 Then David *s*, “Will the
23:12 And the LORD *s*, “They will
23:17 And he *s* to him, “Do not fear,
23:21 And Saul *s*, “Blessed are
24: 4 Then the men of David *s* to him,
24: 4 is the day of which the LORD *s*
24: 6 And he *s* to his men, “The LORD
24: 9 And David *s* to Saul: “Why do
24:10 my eye spared you, and I *s*,
24:16 words to Saul, that Saul *s*,
24:17 Then he *s* to David: “You are
25: 5 and David *s* to the young men,
25:10 David’s servants, and *s*,
25:13 Then David *s* to his men, “Every
25:19 And she *s* to her servants, “Go
25:21 Now David had *s*, “Surely in
25:24 So she fell at his feet and *s*:
25:32 Then David *s* to Abigail:
25:35 and *s* to her, “Go up in peace
25:39 heard that Nabal was dead, he *s*,
25:41 her face to the earth, and *s*,
26: 6 and *s* to Ahimelech the Hittite
26: 6 And Abishai *s*, “I will
26: 8 Then Abishai *s* to David, “God
26: 9 And David *s* to Abishai, “Do not
26:10 David *s* furthermore, “As the
26:14 Then Abner answered and *s*,
26:15 So David *s* to Abner, “Are you
26:17 Saul knew David’s voice, and *s*,
26:17 And David *s*, “It is my
26:18 And he *s*, “Why does my
26:21 Then Saul *s*, “I have

26:22 And David answered and *s*,
26:25 Then Saul *s* to David, "May you
27: 1 And David *s* in his heart, "Now
27: 5 Then David *s* to Achish, "If I
28: 1 And Achish *s* to David, "You
28: 2 And David *s* to Achish, "Surely
28: 2 And Achish *s* to David,
28: 7 Then Saul *s* to his servants,
28: 7 And his servants *s* to him,
28: 8 And he *s*, "Please conduct a
28: 9 Then the woman *s* to him, "Look,
28:11 Then the woman *s*, "Whom
28:11 And he *s*, "Bring up Samuel
28:13 And the king *s* to her, "Do not
28:13 And the woman *s* to Saul, "I
28:14 So he *s* to her, "What is his
28:14 And she *s*, "An old man
28:15 Now Samuel *s* to Saul, "Why
28:16 Then Samuel *s*: "Why then do
28:21 and *s* to him, "Look, your
28:23 But he refused and *s*,
29: 3 princes of the Philistines *s*,
29: 3 And Achish *s* to the princes
29: 4 princes of the Philistines *s*
29: 6 Achish called David and *s* to
29: 8 So David *s* to Achish, "But
29: 9 Then Achish answered and *s* to
29: 9 of the Philistines have *s*,
30: 7 Then David *s* to Abiathar the
30:13 Then David *s* to him, "To whom
30:13 And he *s*, "I am a young
30:15 And David *s* to him, "Can you
30:15 So he *s*, "Swear to me
30:20 those other livestock, and *s*,
30:22 went with David answered and *s*,
30:23 But David *s*, "My brethren,
31: 4 Then Saul *s* to his armorbearer,
2 Sam 1: 3 And David *s* to him, "Where have
1: 3 So he *s* to him, "I have
1: 4 Then David *s* to him, "How did
1: 5 So David *s* to the young man who
1: 6 the young man who told him *s*,
1: 8 And he *s* to me, 'Who are you?'
1: 9 He *s* to me again, 'Please stand
1:13 Then David *s* to the young man
1:14 So David *s* to him, "How was it
1:15 one of the young men and *s*,
1:16 So David *s* to him, "Your blood
2: 1 And the LORD *s* to him, "Go
2: 1 to him, "Go up." David *s*,
2: 1 And He *s*, "To Hebron."
2: 5 and *s* to them, "You are
2:14 Then Abner *s* to Joab, "Let the
2:14 Joab *s*, "Let them arise."
2:20 Abner looked behind him and *s*,
2:21 And Abner *s* to him, "Turn aside
2:22 So Abner *s* again to Asahel,
2:26 Then Abner called to Joab and *s*,
2:27 And Joab *s*, "As God lives,
3: 7 So Ishbosheth *s* to Abner,
3: 8 the words of Ishbosheth, and *s*,
3:13 And David *s*, "Good, I
3:16 So Abner *s* to him, "Go,
3:21 Then Abner *s* to David, "I will
3:24 Joab came to the king and *s*,
3:28 when David heard it, he *s*,
3:31 Then David *s* to Joab and to all
3:33 a lament over Abner and *s*:
3:38 Then the king *s* to his servants,
4: 8 and *s* to the king, "Here is
4: 9 and *s* to them, "As the LORD
5: 2 and the LORD *s* to you, 'You
5: 8 Now David *s* on that day,
5:19 And the LORD *s* to David,
5:20 defeated them there; and he *s*,
5:23 inquired of the LORD, and He *s*,
6: 9 of the LORD that day; and he *s*,
6:20 came out to meet David, and *s*,
6:21 So David *s* to Michal, "It was
7: 2 that the king *s* to Nathan the
7: 3 Then Nathan *s* to the king, "Go,
7:18 sat before the LORD; and he *s*:
7:25 forever and do as You have *s*.
9: 1 Now David *s*, "Is there
9: 2 the king *s* to him, "Are you
9: 2 "Are you Ziba?" And he *s*,
9: 3 Then the king *s*, "Is there
9: 3 And Ziba *s* to the king,
9: 4 So the king *s* to him, "Where
9: 4 And Ziba *s* to the king,
9: 6 David *s*, "Mephibosheth?"
9: 7 So David *s* to him, "Do not
9: 8 Then he bowed himself, and *s*,
9: 9 and *s* to him, "I have given to
9:11 Then Ziba *s* to the king,
9:11 *s* the king, "he shall eat
10: 2 Then David *s*, "I will show
10: 3 of the people of Ammon *s* to
10: 5 greatly ashamed. And the king *s*,
10:11 Then he *s*, "If the Syrians
11: 3 And someone *s*, "Is this not
11: 5 she sent and told David, and *s*,
11: 8 And David *s* to Uriah, "Go down
11:10 David *s* to Uriah, "Did you
11:11 And Uriah *s* to David, "The ark
11:12 Then David *s* to Uriah, "Wait
11:23 And the messenger *s* to David,
11:25 Then David *s* to the messenger,
12: 1 and *s* to him: "There were two
12: 5 and he *s* to Nathan, "As the
12: 7 Then Nathan *s* to David, "You
12:13 So David *s* to Nathan, "I have
12:13 And Nathan *s* to David, "The
12:18 the child was dead. For they *s*,
12:19 Therefore David *s* to his
12:19 And they *s*, "He is dead."
12:21 Then his servants *s* to him,
12:22 And he *s*, "While the child
12:22 I fasted and wept; for I *s*,
12:27 sent messengers to David, and *s*,
13: 4 And he *s* to him, "Why are you,
13: 4 Amnon *s* to him, "I love
13: 5 So Jonadab *s* to him, "Lie down
13: 6 Amnon *s* to the king, "Please
13: 9 he refused to eat. Then Amnon *s*,
13:10 Then Amnon *s* to Tamar, "Bring
13:11 he took hold of her and *s* to
13:15 And Amnon *s* to her, "Arise, be
13:16 So she *s* to him, "No, indeed!
13:17 servant who attended him, and *s*,
13:20 And Absalom her brother *s* to
13:24 Absalom came to the king and *s*,
13:25 But the king *s* to Absalom, "No,
13:26 Then Absalom *s*, "If not,
13:26 And the king *s* to him, "Why
13:32 David's brother, answered and *s*,
13:35 And Jonadab *s* to the king,
13:35 are coming; as your servant *s*,
14: 2 and *s* to her, "Please pretend
14: 4 and prostrated herself, and *s*,
14: 5 Then the king *s* to her, "What
14: 7 your maidservant, and they *s*,
14: 8 Then the king *s* to the woman,
14: 9 And the woman of Tekoa *s* to the
14:10 So the king *s*, "Whoever
14:11 Then she *s*, "Please let
14:11 And he *s*, "As the LORD
14:12 Therefore the woman *s*,
14:12 And he *s*, "Say on."
14:13 So the woman *s*: "Why then
14:15 And your maidservant *s*,
14:17 "Your maidservant *s*,
14:18 Then the king answered and *s* to
14:18 And the woman *s*, "Please, let
14:19 So the king *s*, "Is the
14:19 And the woman answered and *s*,
14:21 And the king *s* to Joab, "All
14:22 And Joab *s*, "Today your
14:24 And the king *s*, "Let him
14:30 So he *s* to his servants, "See,
14:31 and *s* to him, "Why have your
15: 7 forty years that Absalom *s* to
15: 9 And the king *s* to him, "Go in
15:14 So David *s* to all his servants
15:15 And the king's servants *s* to the
15:19 Then the king *s* to Ittai the
15:21 Ittai answered the king and *s*,
15:22 So David *s* to Ittai, "Go, and
15:25 Then the king *s* to Zadok,
15:27 The king also *s* to Zadok the
15:31 And David *s*, "O LORD, I
15:33 David *s* to him, "If you go on
16: 2 And the king *s* to Ziba, "What
16: 2 So Ziba *s*, "The donkeys
16: 3 Then the king *s*, "And where
16: 3 And Ziba *s* to the king,
16: 3 staying in Jerusalem, for he *s*,
16: 4 So the king *s* to Ziba, "Here,
16: 4 And Ziba *s*, "I humbly
16: 7 Also Shimei *s* thus when he
16: 9 Abishai the son of Zeruiah *s*
16:10 But the king *s*, "What have
16:10 because the LORD has *s* to him,
16:11 And David *s* to Abishai and all
16:16 that Hushai *s* to Absalom,
16:17 So Absalom *s* to Hushai, "Is
16:18 And Hushai *s* to Absalom, "No,
16:20 Then Absalom *s* to Ahithophel,
16:21 And Ahithophel *s* to Absalom,
17: 1 Moreover Ahithophel *s* to
17: 5 Then Absalom *s*, "Now call
17: 7 So Hushai *s* to Absalom: "The
17: 8 *s* Hushai, "you know your
17:14 and all the men of Israel *s*,
17:15 Then Hushai *s* to Zadok and
17:20 the woman at the house, they *s*,
17:20 So the woman *s* to them,
17:21 and *s* to David, "Arise and
17:29 For they *s*, "The people
18: 2 And the king *s* to the people,
18: 4 Then the king *s* to them,
18:10 saw it and told Joab, and *s*,
18:11 So Joab *s* to the man who told
18:12 But the man *s* to Joab, "Though
18:14 Then Joab *s*, "I cannot
18:18 For he *s*, "I have no son
18:19 Ahimaaz the son of Zadok *s*,
18:20 And Joab *s* to him, "You shall
18:21 Then Joab *s* to the Cushite,
18:22 And Ahimaaz the son of Zadok *s*
18:22 So Joab *s*, "Why will
18:23 whatever happens," he *s*,
18:23 So he *s* to him, "Run."
18:25 And the king *s*, "If he is
18:26 called to the gatekeeper and *s*,
18:26 And the king *s*, "He also
18:27 So the watchman *s*, "I think
18:27 And the king *s*, "He is a
18:28 And Ahimaaz called out and *s* to
18:28 earth before the king, and *s*,
18:29 The king *s*, "Is the young
18:30 And the king *s*, "Turn aside
18:31 Cushite came, and the Cushite *s*,
18:32 And the king *s* to the Cushite,
18:33 he *s* thus: "O my son
19: 2 For the people heard it *s* that
19: 5 the house to the king, and *s*,
19:19 Then he *s* to the king, "Do not
19:21 son of Zeruiah answered and *s*,
19:22 And David *s*, "What have I
19:23 Therefore the king *s* to Shimei,
19:25 that the king *s* to him, "Why
19:26 For your servant *s*, 'I will
19:29 So the king *s* to him, "Why do
19:29 I have *s*, 'You and Ziba
19:30 Then Mephibosheth *s* to the king,
19:33 And the king *s* to Barzillai,
19:34 But Barzillai *s* to the king,
19:41 and *s* to the king, "Why have
19:43 the men of Judah, and *s*,
20: 1 And he blew a trumpet, and *s*:
20: 4 And the king *s* to Amasa,
20: 6 And David *s* to Abishai, "Now
20: 9 Then Joab *s* to Amasa, "Are you
20:11 men stood near Amasa, and *s*,
20:17 come near to her, the woman *s*,
20:17 Then she *s* to him, "Hear the
20:20 And Joab answered and *s*,
20:21 So the woman *s* to Joab,
21: 3 Therefore David *s* to the
21: 4 And the Gibeonites *s* to him,
21: 4 So he *s*, "Whatever you say,
21: 6 And the king *s*, "I will
22: 2 And he *s*: "The LORD is
23: 3 The God of Israel *s*,
23:15 And David *s* with longing, "Oh,
23:17 And he *s*, "Far be it
24: 2 So the king *s* to Joab the
24: 3 And Joab *s* to the king, "Now
24:10 So David *s* to the LORD, "I
24:13 and he *s* to him, "Shall seven
24:14 And David *s* to Gad, "I am in
24:16 and *s* to the angel who was
24:17 was striking the people, and *s*,
24:18 came that day to David and *s*
24:21 Then Araunah *s*, "Why
24:21 And David *s*, "To buy the
24:22 Now Araunah *s* to David, "Let my
24:23 And Araunah *s* to the king,
24:24 Then the king *s* to Araunah,
1 Ki 1: 2 Therefore his servants *s* to him,
1:16 Then the king *s*, "What is
1:17 Then she *s* to him, "My lord,
1:24 And Nathan *s*, "My lord,
1:24 "My lord, O king, have you *s*,
1:28 Then King David answered and *s*,
1:29 And the king took an oath and *s*,
1:31 paid homage to the king, and *s*,
1:32 And King David *s*, "Call
1:33 The king also *s* to them, "Take
1:36 answered the king and *s*,
1:39 the horn, and all the people *s*,
1:41 the sound of the horn, he *s*,
1:42 And Adonijah *s* to him, "Come
1:43 Then Jonathan answered and *s* to
1:48 Also the king *s* thus, 'Blessed
1:52 Then Solomon *s*, "If he
1:53 and Solomon *s* to him, "Go to
2: 4 and with all their soul,' He *s*,
2:13 So she *s*, "Do you come
2:13 And he *s*, "Peaceably."
2:14 Moreover he *s*, "I have
2:14 to say to you." And she *s*,
2:15 Then he *s*, "You know that
2:16 And she *s* to him, "Say it."
2:17 Then he *s*, "Please speak
2:18 So Bathsheba *s*, "Very well,
2:20 Then she *s*, "I desire
2:20 And the king *s* to her, "Ask
2:21 So she *s*, "Let Abishag
2:22 King Solomon answered and *s* to
2:26 Abiathar the priest the king *s*,
2:30 and *s* to him, "Thus says the
2:30 king, 'Come out!'" And he *s*,
2:30 Thus *s* Joab, and thus he
2:31 Then the king *s* to him, "Do as
2:31 said to him, "Do as he has *s*,
2:36 and *s* to him, "Build yourself
2:38 And Shimei *s* to the king, "The
2:38 As my lord the king has *s*,
2:42 and *s* to him, "Did I not make
2:42 And you *s* to me, 'The word I
2:44 The king *s* moreover to Shimei,
3: 5 in a dream by night; and God *s*,
3: 6 And Solomon *s*: "You have shown
3:11 Then God *s* to him: "Because you
3:17 And one woman *s*, "O my lord,
3:22 Then the other woman *s*,
3:22 And the first woman *s*,
3:23 And the king *s*, "The one
3:24 Then the king *s*, "Bring me
3:25 And the king *s*, "Divide the
3:26 and she *s*, "O my lord,
3:26 But the other *s*, "Let him
3:27 So the king answered and *s*,
5: 7 that he rejoiced greatly and *s*,
8:12 The LORD *s* He would dwell in
8:15 And he *s*: "Blessed be
8:18 But the LORD *s* to my father
8:20 and he *s*: "LORD God of
8:29 toward the place of which You *s*,
9: 3 And the LORD *s* to him: "I have
9:13 So he *s*, "What kind of
10: 6 Then she *s* to the king: "It was
11: 2 of whom the LORD had *s* to the

11:11 Therefore the LORD *s* to
11:21 Hadad *s* to Pharaoh, "Let me
11:22 Then Pharaoh *s* to him, "But
11:31 And he *s* to Jeroboam, "Take for
12: 5 So he *s* to them, "Depart for
12: 6 while he still lived, and he *s*,
12: 9 And he *s* to them, "What advice
12:26 And Jeroboam *s* in his heart,
12:28 and *s* to the people, "It is
13: 2 by the word of the LORD, and *s*,
13: 6 Then the king answered and *s* to
13: 7 Then the king *s* to the man of
13: 8 But the man of God *s* to the
13:12 And their father *s* to them,
13:13 Then he *s* to his sons, "Saddle
13:14 Then he *s* to him, "Are you
13:14 And he *s*, "I am."
13:15 Then he *s* to him, "Come home
13:16 And he *s*, "I cannot
13:18 He *s* to him, "I too am a
13:22 place of which the LORD *s*
13:26 from the way heard it, he *s*,
14: 2 And Jeroboam *s* to his wife,
14: 5 Now the LORD had *s* to Ahijah,
14: 6 she came through the door, he *s*,
16:16 who were encamped heard it *s*,
17: 1 *s* to Ahab, "As the LORD God
17:10 And he called to her and *s*,
17:11 get it, he called to her and *s*,
17:12 So she *s*, "As the LORD
17:13 And Elijah *s* to her, "Do not
17:13 go and do as you have *s*,
17:18 So she *s* to Elijah, "What have
17:19 And he *s* to her, "Give me your
17:20 he cried out to the LORD and *s*,
17:21 cried out to the LORD and *s*,
17:23 And Elijah *s*, "See, your son
17:24 Then the woman *s* to Elijah,
18: 5 And Ahab had *s* to Obadiah, "Go
18: 7 and fell on his face, and *s*,
18: 9 So he *s*, "How have I
18:10 hunt for you; and when they *s*,
18:15 Then Elijah *s*, "As the
18:17 that Ahab *s* to him, "Is that
18:21 came to all the people, and *s*,
18:22 Then Elijah *s* to the people, "I
18:24 all the people answered and *s*,
18:25 Now Elijah *s* to the prophets of
18:27 that Elijah mocked them and *s*,
18:30 Then Elijah *s* to all the
18:33 and laid it on the wood, and *s*,
18:34 Then he *s*, "Do it a second
18:34 and he *s*, "Do it a third
18:36 the prophet came near and *s*,
18:39 and they *s*, "The LORD, He is
18:40 And Elijah *s* to them, "Seize
18:41 Then Elijah *s* to Ahab, "Go up,
18:43 and *s* to his servant, "Go up
18:43 he went up and looked, and *s*,
18:43 And seven times he *s*,
18:44 the seventh time, that he *s*,
18:44 So he *s*, "Go up,
19: 4 prayed that he might die, and *s*,
19: 5 and *s* to him, "Arise and
19: 7 time, and touched him, and *s*,
19: 9 and He *s* to him, "What are you
19:10 So he *s*, "I have been very
19:11 Then He *s*, "Go out, and
19:13 a voice came to him, and *s*,
19:14 And he *s*, "I have been
19:15 Then the LORD *s* to him: "Go,
19:20 and ran after Elijah, and *s*,
19:20 And he *s* to him, "Go back
20: 2 and *s* to him, "Thus says
20: 4 king of Israel answered and *s*,
20: 5 the messengers came back and *s*,
20: 7 the elders of the land, and *s*,
20: 8 elders and all the people *s* to
20: 9 Therefore he *s* to the messengers
20:10 Ben-Hadad sent to him and *s*,
20:11 king of Israel answered and *s*,
20:12 that he *s* to his servants,
20:14 So Ahab *s*, "By whom?"
20:14 said, "By whom?" And he *s*,
20:14 Then he *s*, "Who will set
20:18 So he *s*, "If they have
20:22 to the king of Israel and *s* to
20:23 of the king of Syria *s* to him,
20:28 to the king of Israel, and *s*,
20:28 'Because the Syrians have *s*,
20:31 Then his servants *s* to him,
20:32 to the king of Israel and *s*,
20:32 And he *s*, "Is he still
20:33 grasped at this word and *s*,
20:33 So he *s*, "Go, bring him."
20:34 So Ben-Hadad *s* to him, "The
20:34 Then Ahab *s*, "I will send
20:35 of the sons of the prophets *s*
20:36 Then he *s* to him, "Because you
20:37 And he found another man, and *s*,
20:39 he cried out to the king and *s*,
20:39 and brought a man to me, and *s*,
20:40 Then the king of Israel *s* to
20:42 Then he *s* to him, "Thus says
21: 3 But Naboth *s* to Ahab, "The
21: 4 had spoken to him; for he had *s*,
21: 5 and *s* to him, "Why is your
21: 6 He *s* to her, "Because I spoke
21: 6 and *s* to him, 'Give me your
21: 7 Then Jezebel his wife *s* to him,
21:15 that Jezebel *s* to Ahab,
21:20 So Ahab *s* to Elijah, "Have you
22: 3 And the king of Israel *s* to his
22: 4 So he *s* to Jehoshaphat, "Will
22: 4 Jehoshaphat *s* to the king of
22: 5 Also Jehoshaphat *s* to the king
22: 6 and *s* to them, "Shall I go
22: 6 So they *s*, "Go up, for
22: 7 And Jehoshaphat *s*,
22: 8 So the king of Israel *s* to
22: 8 And Jehoshaphat *s*, "Let not
22: 9 Israel called an officer and *s*,
22:11 of iron for himself; and he *s*,
22:14 And Micaiah *s*, "As the LORD
22:15 and the king *s* to him,
22:16 So the king *s* to him, "How many
22:17 Then he *s*, "I saw all
22:17 And the LORD *s*, 'These
22:18 And the king of Israel *s* to
22:19 Then Micaiah *s*, "Therefore
22:20 "And the LORD *s*, 'Who will
22:21 stood before the LORD, and *s*,
22:22 The LORD *s* to him, 'In what
22:22 to him, 'In what way?' So he *s*,
22:22 And the LORD *s*, 'You shall
22:24 Micaiah on the cheek, and *s*,
22:25 And Micaiah *s*, "Indeed,
22:26 So the king of Israel *s*,
22:28 But Micaiah *s*, "If you
22:28 And he *s*, "Take heed, all
22:30 And the king of Israel *s* to
22:32 saw Jehoshaphat, that they *s*,
22:34 So he *s* to the driver of his
22:49 Then Ahaziah the son of Ahab *s*
2 Ki 1: 2 so he sent messengers and *s* to
1: 3 But the angel of the LORD *s* to
1: 5 he *s* to them, "Why have you
1: 6 So they *s* to him, "A man came
1: 6 and *s* to us, 'Go, return to the
1: 7 Then he *s* to them, "What kind
1: 8 And he *s*, "It is Elijah
1: 9 "Man of God, the king has *s*,
1:10 So Elijah answered and *s* to the
1:11 And he answered and *s* to him:
1:11 of God, thus has the king *s*,
1:12 So Elijah answered and *s* to
1:13 and *s* to him: "Man of God,
1:15 And the angel of the LORD *s* to
1:16 Then he *s* to him, "Thus says
2: 2 Then Elijah *s* to Elisha, "Stay
2: 2 But Elisha *s*, "As the LORD
2: 3 and *s* to him, "Do you know
2: 3 And he *s*, "Yes, I know; keep
2: 4 Then Elijah *s* to him, "Elisha,
2: 4 But he *s*, "As the LORD
2: 5 at Jericho came to Elisha and *s*
2: 6 Then Elijah *s* to him, "Stay
2: 6 But he *s*, "As the LORD
2: 9 that Elijah *s* to Elisha, "Ask!
2: 9 Elisha *s*, "Please let a
2:10 So he *s*, "You have asked
2:14 and struck the water, and *s*,
2:15 from Jericho saw him, they *s*,
2:16 Then they *s* to him, "Look now,
2:16 And he *s*, "You shall not
2:17 him till he was ashamed, he *s*,
2:18 he *s* to them, "Did I not say
2:19 Then the men of the city *s* to
2:20 And he *s*, "Bring me a
2:21 cast in the salt there, and *s*,
2:23 and *s* to him, "Go up, you
3: 7 And he *s*, "I will go up;
3: 8 Then he *s*, "Which way
3:10 And the king of Israel *s*,
3:11 But Jehoshaphat *s*,
3:11 king of Israel answered and *s*,
3:12 And Jehoshaphat *s*,
3:13 Then Elisha *s* to the king of
3:13 But the king of Israel *s* to
3:14 And Elisha *s*, "As the LORD
3:16 And he *s*, "Thus says the
3:23 And they *s*, "This is blood; the
4: 2 So Elisha *s* to her, "What shall
4: 2 And she *s*, "Your
4: 3 Then he *s*, "Go, borrow
4: 6 that she *s* to her son, "Bring
4: 6 And he *s* to her, "There is
4: 7 And he *s*, "Go, sell the oil
4: 9 And she *s* to her husband, "Look
4:12 Then he *s* to Gehazi his servant,
4:13 And he *s* to him, "Say now to
4:14 So he *s*, "What then is
4:15 So he *s*, "Call her."
4:16 Then he *s*, "About this time
4:16 And she *s*, "No, my lord.
4:19 And he *s* to his father, "My
4:19 So he *s* to a servant,
4:22 called to her husband, and *s*,
4:23 So he *s*, "Why are you
4:23 And she *s*, "It is well."
4:24 and *s* to her servant, "Drive,
4:25 that he *s* to his servant
4:27 But the man of God *s*,
4:28 So she *s*, "Did I ask
4:29 Then he *s* to Gehazi, "Get
4:30 And the mother of the child *s*,
4:36 And he called Gehazi and *s*,
4:36 when she came in to him, he *s*,
4:38 and he *s* to his servant, "Put
4:40 stew, that they cried out and *s*,
4:41 So he *s*, "Then bring some
4:41 he put it into the pot, and *s*,
4:42 And he *s*, "Give it to the
4:43 But his servant *s*, "What?
4:43 He *s* again, "Give it to the
5: 3 Then she *s* to her mistress, "If
5: 4 Thus and thus *s* the girl who is
5: 5 Then the king of Syria *s*,
5: 6 to the king of Israel, which *s*,
5: 7 that he tore his clothes and *s*,
5:11 furious, and went away and *s*,
5:11 I *s* to myself, 'He will surely
5:13 near and spoke to him, and *s*,
5:15 and stood before him; and he *s*,
5:16 But he *s*, "As the LORD
5:17 So Naaman *s*, "Then, if not,
5:19 Then he *s* to him, "Go in
5:20 of Elisha the man of God, *s*,
5:21 the chariot to meet him, and *s*,
5:22 And he *s*, "All is well.
5:23 So Naaman *s*, "Please, take
5:25 Elisha *s* to him, "Where did
5:25 And he *s*, "Your servant
5:26 Then he *s* to him, "Did not my
6: 1 And the sons of the prophets *s*
6: 3 Then one *s*, "Please consent
6: 5 and he cried out and *s*,
6: 6 So the man of God *s*,
6: 7 Therefore he *s*, "Pick it
6:11 he called his servants and *s*
6:12 And one of his servants *s*,
6:13 So he *s*, "Go and see
6:15 And his servant *s* to him,
6:17 And Elisha prayed, and *s*,
6:18 prayed to the LORD, and *s*,
6:19 Now Elisha *s* to them, "This
6:20 come to Samaria, that Elisha *s*,
6:21 he *s* to Elisha, "My father,
6:27 And he *s*, "If the LORD
6:28 Then the king *s* to her, "What
6:28 This woman *s* to me, 'Give your
6:29 And I *s* to her on the next day,
6:31 Then he *s*, "God do so
6:32 he *s* to the elders, "Do you
6:33 and then the king *s*,
7: 1 Then Elisha *s*, "Hear the
7: 2 answered the man of God and *s*,
7: 2 And he *s*, "In fact, you
7: 3 and they *s* to one another,
7: 6 so they *s* to one another,
7: 9 Then they *s* to one another,
7:12 king arose in the night and *s*
7:13 of his servants answered and *s*,
7:17 just as the man of God had *s*,
7:19 answered the man of God, and *s*,
7:19 such a thing be?" And he had *s*,
8: 5 and for her land. And Gehazi *s*,
8: 8 And the king *s* to Hazael, "Take
8: 9 and stood before him, and *s*,
8:10 And Elisha *s* to him, "Go, say
8:12 And Hazael *s*, "Why is my
8:13 So Hazael *s*, "But what is
8:14 who *s* to him, "What did Elisha
9: 1 and *s* to him, "Get yourself
9: 5 of the army sitting; and he *s*,
9: 5 Jehu *s*, "For which one
9: 5 And he *s*, "For you,
9: 6 and *s* to him, "Thus says the
9:11 and one *s* to him, "Is all
9:11 And he *s* to them, "You know
9:12 And they *s*, "A lie!
9:12 So he *s*, "Thus and thus
9:15 king of Syria.) And Jehu *s*,
9:17 of Jehu as he came, and *s*,
9:17 And Joram *s*, "Get a
9:18 went to meet him, and *s*,
9:18 And Jehu *s*, "What have
9:19 who came to them, and *s*,
9:21 Then Joram *s*, "Make
9:22 when Joram saw Jehu, that he *s*,
9:23 and *s* to Ahaziah, "Treachery,
9:25 Then Jehu *s* to Bidkar his
9:27 So Jehu pursued him, and *s*,
9:31 Jehu entered at the gate, she *s*,
9:32 looked up at the window, and *s*,
9:33 Then he *s*, "Throw her down."
9:34 Then he *s*, "Go now, see to
9:36 And he *s*, "This is the
10: 4 were exceedingly afraid, and *s*,
10: 8 And he *s*, "Lay them in two
10: 9 and *s* to all the people, "You
10:13 of Ahaziah king of Judah, and *s*,
10:14 And he *s*, "Take them
10:15 and he greeted him and *s* to
10:15 Jehu *s*, "If it is, give me
10:16 Then he *s*, "Come with me,
10:18 and *s* to them, "Ahab served
10:20 And Jehu *s*, "Proclaim a
10:22 And he *s* to the one in charge of
10:23 and *s* to the worshipers of
10:24 men on the outside, and had *s*,
10:25 that Jehu *s* to the guard and to
10:30 And the LORD *s* to Jehu,
11:12 they clapped their hands and *s*,
11:15 and *s* to them, "Take her
11:15 For the priest had *s*,
12: 4 And Jehoash *s* to the priests,
12: 7 and *s* to them, "Why have you
13:14 and wept over his face, and *s*,
13:15 And Elisha *s* to him, "Take a
13:16 Then he *s* to the king of Israel,
13:17 And he *s*, "Open the east
13:17 Then Elisha *s*, "Shoot";
13:17 And he *s*, "The arrow of
13:18 Then he *s*, "Take the
13:18 And he *s* to the king of Israel,

13:19 God was angry with him, and ***s***,
17:12 of which the LORD had ***s*** to
17:23 as He had ***s*** by all His servants
18:19 Then the Rabshakeh ***s*** to them,
18:22 and ***s*** to Judah and Jerusalem,
18:25 The LORD ***s*** to me, 'Go up
18:26 and Joah ***s*** to the Rabshakeh,
18:27 But the Rabshakeh ***s*** to them,
19: 3 And they ***s*** to him, "Thus says
19: 6 And Isaiah ***s*** to them, "Thus you
19:15 prayed before the LORD, and ***s***:
19:23 reproached the Lord, And ***s***:
20: 1 went to him and ***s*** to him,
20: 7 Then Isaiah ***s***, "Take a
20: 8 And Hezekiah ***s*** to Isaiah,
20: 9 Then Isaiah ***s***, "This is
20:14 and ***s*** to him, "What did these
20:14 So Hezekiah ***s***, "They came
20:15 And he ***s***, "What have
20:16 Then Isaiah ***s*** to Hezekiah,
20:19 So Hezekiah ***s*** to Isaiah, "The
20:19 For he ***s***, "Will there
21: 4 LORD, of which the LORD had ***s***,
21: 7 house of which the LORD had ***s***
22: 8 Hilkiah the high priest ***s*** to
22:15 Then she ***s*** to them, "Thus says
23:17 Then he ***s***, "What gravestone
23:18 And he ***s***, "Let him alone;
23:27 And the LORD ***s***, "I will
23:27 and the house of which I ***s***,
24:13 the LORD, as the LORD had ***s***.
25:24 and ***s*** to them, "Do not be
1 Chr 10: 4 Then Saul ***s*** to his armorbearer,
11: 2 and the LORD your God ***s*** to
11: 5 the inhabitants of Jebus ***s*** to
11: 6 Now David ***s***, "Whoever
11:17 And David ***s*** with longing, "Oh,
11:19 And he ***s***, "Far be it from
12:17 and answered and ***s*** to them,
12:18 of the captains, and he ***s***:
13: 2 And David ***s*** to all the assembly
13: 4 Then all the assembly ***s*** that
14:10 And the LORD ***s*** to him, "Go
14:11 Then David ***s***, "God has
14:14 and God ***s*** to him, "You shall
15: 2 Then David ***s***, "No one
15:12 He ***s*** to them, "You are the
16:36 And all the people ***s***,
17: 1 that David ***s*** to Nathan the
17: 2 Then Nathan ***s*** to David, "Do all
17:16 and he ***s***: "Who am I, O LORD
17:23 forever, and do as You have ***s***.
19: 2 Then David ***s***, "I will
19: 3 of the people of Ammon ***s*** to
19: 5 And the king ***s***, "Wait at
19:12 Then he ***s***, "If the Syrians
21: 2 So David ***s*** to Joab and to the
21: 8 So David ***s*** to God, "I have
21:11 So Gad came to David and ***s*** to
21:13 And David ***s*** to Gad, "I am in
21:15 and ***s*** to the angel who was
21:17 And David ***s*** to God, "Was it not
21:22 Then David ***s*** to Ornan, "Grant
21:23 And Ornan ***s*** to David, "Take it
21:24 Then King David ***s*** to Ornan,
22: 1 Then David ***s***, "This is the
22: 5 Now David ***s***, "Solomon my
22: 7 And David ***s*** to Solomon: "My
22:11 as He has ***s*** to you.
23: 5 ***s*** David, "for giving
23:25 For David ***s***, "The LORD God
27:23 because the LORD had ***s*** He
28: 2 David rose to his feet and ***s***,
28: 3 But God ***s*** to me, 'You shall not
28: 6 Now He ***s*** to me, 'It is your son
28:19 ***s*** David, "the LORD made
28:20 And David ***s*** to his son Solomon,
29: 1 Furthermore King David ***s*** to all
29:10 all the assembly; and David ***s***:
29:20 Then David ***s*** to all the
2 Chr 1: 7 and ***s*** to him, "Ask! What shall
1: 8 And Solomon ***s*** to God: "You have
1:11 And God ***s*** to Solomon: "Because
2:12 Hiram also ***s***: Blessed be
6: 1 The LORD ***s*** He would dwell in
6: 4 And he ***s***: "Blessed be the
6: 8 But the LORD ***s*** to my father
6:14 and he ***s***: "LORD God of
6:20 toward the place where You ***s***
7:12 and ***s*** to him: "I have heard
8:11 he had built for her, for he ***s***,
9: 5 Then she ***s*** to the king: "It
10: 5 So he ***s*** to them, "Come back to
10: 9 And he ***s*** to them, "What advice
12: 5 and ***s*** to them, "Thus says the
12: 6 humbled themselves; and they ***s***,
13: 4 the mountains of Ephraim, and ***s***,
14: 7 Therefore he ***s*** to Judah, "Let
14:11 out to the LORD his God, and ***s***,
15: 2 and ***s*** to him: "Hear me, Asa,
16: 7 and ***s*** to him: "Because you
18: 3 So Ahab king of Israel ***s*** to
18: 4 And Jehoshaphat ***s*** to the king
18: 5 and ***s*** to them, "Shall we go to
18: 5 And they ***s***, "Go up, for God
18: 6 But Jehoshaphat ***s***,
18: 7 So the king of Israel ***s*** to
18: 7 And Jehoshaphat ***s***,
18: 8 one of his officers and ***s***,
18:10 of iron for himself; and he ***s***,
18:13 And Micaiah ***s***, "As the
18:14 and the king ***s*** to him,
18:14 And he ***s***, "Go and prosper,
18:15 So the king ***s*** to him, "How many
18:16 Then he ***s***, "I saw all
18:16 And the LORD ***s***, 'These have
18:17 And the king of Israel ***s*** to
18:18 Then Micaiah ***s***, "Therefore
18:19 "And the LORD ***s***, 'Who will
18:20 stood before the LORD, and ***s***,
18:20 The LORD ***s*** to him, 'In what
18:21 'So he ***s***, 'I will go
18:21 And the LORD ***s***, 'You shall
18:23 Micaiah on the cheek, and ***s***,
18:24 And Micaiah ***s***, "Indeed
18:25 Then the king of Israel ***s***,
18:27 Then Micaiah ***s***, "If you
18:27 And he ***s***, "Take heed,
18:29 And the king of Israel ***s*** to
18:31 saw Jehoshaphat, that they ***s***,
18:33 So he ***s*** to the driver of his
19: 2 and ***s*** to King Jehoshaphat,
19: 6 and ***s*** to the judges, "Take heed
20: 6 and ***s***: "O LORD God of
20:15 And he ***s***, "Listen, all you
20:20 out, Jehoshaphat stood and ***s***,
22: 9 buried him, "because," they ***s***,
23: 3 And he ***s*** to them, "Behold, the
23: 3 as the LORD has ***s*** of the sons
23:11 his sons anointed him, and ***s***,
23:13 Athaliah tore her clothes and ***s***,
23:14 and ***s*** to them, "Take her
23:14 For the priest had ***s***,
24: 5 and ***s*** to them, "Go out to the
24: 6 and ***s*** to him, "Why have you
24:20 and ***s*** to them, "Thus says God:
24:22 and as he died, he ***s***,
25: 9 Then Amaziah ***s*** to the man of
25:15 He sent him a prophet who ***s*** to
25:16 that the king ***s*** to him,
25:16 Then the prophet ceased, and ***s***,
26:18 and ***s*** to him, "It is not for
26:23 to the kings, for they ***s***,
28: 9 and ***s*** to them: "Look, because
28:13 and ***s*** to them, "You shall not
29: 5 and ***s*** to them: "Hear me,
29:18 went in to King Hezekiah and ***s***,
29:31 Then Hezekiah answered and ***s***,
31:10 of Zadok, answered him and ***s***,
33: 4 LORD, of which the LORD had ***s***,
33: 7 of which God had ***s*** to David and
34:15 Then Hilkiah answered and ***s*** to
35: 3 Then he ***s*** to the Levites who
35:23 and the king ***s*** to his servants,
Ezra 2:63 And the governor ***s*** to them that
4: 2 and ***s*** to them, "Let us build
4: 3 fathers' houses of Israel ***s***
5:15 And he ***s*** to him, 'Take these
8:28 And I ***s*** to them, "You are holy
9: 6 And I ***s***: "O my God,
10: 2 spoke up and ***s*** to Ezra, "We
10:10 Ezra the priest stood up and ***s***
10:12 all the assembly answered and ***s***
10:12 voice, "Yes! As you have ***s***,
Neh 1: 3 And they ***s*** to me, "The
1: 5 And I ***s***: "I pray, LORD God
2: 2 Therefore the king ***s*** to me,
2: 3 and ***s*** to the king, "May the
2: 4 Then the king ***s*** to me, "What do
2: 5 And I ***s*** to the king, "If it
2: 6 Then the king ***s*** to me (the queen
2: 7 Furthermore I ***s*** to the king,
2:17 Then I ***s*** to them, "You see the
2:18 he had spoken to me. So they ***s***,
2:19 at us and despised us, and ***s***,
2:20 and ***s*** to them, "The God of
4: 2 and the army of Samaria, and ***s***,
4: 3 was beside him, and he ***s***,
4:10 Then Judah ***s***, "The strength
4:11 And our adversaries ***s***,
4:14 and arose and ***s*** to the nobles,
4:19 Then I ***s*** to the nobles, the
4:22 At the same time I also ***s*** to the
5: 2 For there were those who ***s***,
5: 3 There were also some who ***s***,
5: 4 There were also those who ***s***,
5: 7 and ***s*** to them, "Each of you is
5: 8 And I ***s*** to them, "According to
5: 9 Then I ***s***, "What you are
5:12 So they ***s***, "We will restore
5:13 the fold of my garment and ***s***,
5:13 And all the assembly ***s***,
6:10 and he ***s***, "Let us meet
6:11 And I ***s***, "Should such
7: 3 And I ***s*** to them, "Do not let
7:65 And the governor ***s*** to them that
8: 9 who taught the people ***s*** to all
8:10 Then he ***s*** to them, "Go your
9: 5 Shebaniah, and Pethahiah, ***s***:
9:18 calf for themselves, And ***s***,
13:11 with the rulers, and ***s***,
13:17 and ***s*** to them, "What evil
13:21 and ***s*** to them, "Why do you
Esth 1:13 Then the king ***s*** to the wise men
2: 2 servants who attended him ***s***:
3: 3 were within the king's gate ***s***
3: 8 Then Haman ***s*** to King Ahasuerus,
3:11 And the king ***s*** to Haman, "The
5: 3 And the king ***s*** to her, "What do
5: 5 Then the king ***s***, "Bring
5: 5 that he may do as Esther has ***s***.
5: 6 the banquet of wine the king ***s***
5: 7 Then Esther answered and ***s***,
5: 8 I will do as the king has ***s***.
5:12 Moreover Haman ***s***, "Besides,
5:14 Zeresh and all his friends ***s***
6: 3 Then the king ***s***, "What
6: 3 servants who attended him ***s***,
6: 4 So the king ***s***, "Who is
6: 5 The king's servants ***s*** to him,
6: 5 And the king ***s***, "Let him
6:10 Then the king ***s*** to Haman,
6:13 wise men and his wife Zeresh ***s***
7: 2 the king again ***s*** to Esther,
7: 3 Queen Esther answered and ***s***,
7: 5 King Ahasuerus answered and ***s***
7: 6 And Esther ***s***, "The adversary
7: 8 Esther was. Then the king ***s***,
7: 9 ***s*** to the king, "Look!
7: 9 Then the king ***s***, "Hang him
8: 5 and ***s***, "If it pleases the
8: 7 Then King Ahasuerus ***s*** to Queen
9:12 And the king ***s*** to Queen Esther,
9:13 Then Esther ***s***, "If it
Job 1: 5 For Job ***s***, "It may be
1: 7 And the LORD ***s*** to Satan, "From
1: 7 Satan answered the LORD and ***s***,
1: 8 Then the LORD ***s*** to Satan,
1: 9 Satan answered the LORD and ***s***,
1:12 And the LORD ***s*** to Satan,
1:14 a messenger came to Job and ***s***,
1:16 another also came and ***s***,
1:17 another also came and ***s***,
1:18 another also came and ***s***,
1:21 And he ***s***: "Naked I
2: 2 And the LORD ***s*** to Satan, "From
2: 2 Satan answered the LORD and ***s***,
2: 3 Then the LORD ***s*** to Satan,
2: 4 Satan answered the LORD and ***s***,
2: 6 And the LORD ***s*** to Satan,
2: 9 Then his wife ***s*** to him, "Do
2:10 But he ***s*** to her, "You speak as
3: 2 And Job spoke, and ***s***:
3: 3 the night in which it was ***s***,
4: 1 the Temanite answered and ***s***:
6: 1 Then Job answered and ***s***:
8: 1 the Shuhite answered and ***s***:
9: 1 Then Job answered and ***s***:
11: 1 the Naamathite answered and ***s***:
11: 4 For you have ***s***, 'My doctrine
12: 1 Then Job answered and ***s***:
15: 1 the Temanite answered and ***s***:
16: 1 Then Job answered and ***s***:
18: 1 the Shuhite answered and ***s***:
19: 1 Then Job answered and ***s***:
20: 1 the Naamathite answered and ***s***:
21: 1 Then Job answered and ***s***:
22: 1 the Temanite answered and ***s***:
22:17 They ***s*** to God, 'Depart from us!
23: 1 Then Job answered and ***s***:
25: 1 the Shuhite answered and ***s***:
26: 1 But Job answered and ***s***:
27: 1 continued his discourse, and ***s***:
28:28 And to man He ***s***,
29: 1 continued his discourse, and ***s***:
29:18 'Then I ***s***, 'I shall
31:24 Or ***s*** to fine gold, 'You are
31:31 the men of my tent have not ***s***,
32: 6 the Buzite, answered and ***s***:
32: 7 I ***s***, 'Age should speak,
34: 1 Elihu further answered and ***s***:
34: 5 'For Job has ***s***, 'I am
34: 9 For he has ***s***, 'It profits
34:31 For has anyone ***s*** to God, 'I
35: 1 Moreover Elihu answered and ***s***:
36: 1 Elihu also proceeded and ***s***:
36:23 Him His way, Or who has ***s***,
38: 1 Job out of the whirlwind, and ***s***:
38:11 When I ***s***, 'This far
40: 1 the LORD answered Job, and ***s***:
40: 3 Job answered the LORD and ***s***:
40: 6 Job out of the whirlwind, and ***s***:
42: 1 Job answered the LORD and ***s***:
42: 4 You ***s***, 'I will question
42: 7 that the LORD ***s*** to Eliphaz the
Ps 2: 7 The LORD has ***s*** to Me, 'You
10: 6 He has ***s*** in his heart, "I
10:11 He has ***s*** in his heart, "God
10:13 He has ***s*** in his heart, "You
12: 4 Who have ***s***, "With our
14: 1 The fool has ***s*** in his heart,
16: 2 you have ***s*** to the LORD, "You
18: from the hand of Saul. And he ***s***:
27: 8 When You ***s***, "Seek My
27: 8 My heart ***s*** to You, "Your
30: 6 Now in my prosperity I ***s***,
31:22 For I ***s*** in my haste, "I am
32: 5 I ***s***, "I will confess
35:21 mouth wide against me, And ***s***,
38:16 For I ***s***, "Hear me,
39: 1 I ***s***, "I will guard
40: 7 Then I ***s***, "Behold, I come;
41: 4 I ***s***, "LORD, be merciful
52: and ***s*** to him, "David has gone
53: 1 The fool has ***s*** in his heart,
54: when the Ziphites went and ***s***
55: 6 So I ***s***, "Oh, that I
68:22 The Lord ***s***, "I will
73:15 If I had ***s***, "I will
74: 8 They ***s*** in their hearts, "Let
75: 4 I ***s*** to the boastful, 'Do not
77:10 And I ***s***, "This is my
78:19 they spoke against God: They ***s***,
82: 6 I ***s***, "You are gods,
83: 4 They have ***s***, "Come, and
83:12 Who ***s***, "Let us take

S

87: 5 And of Zion it will be *s*,
89: 2 For I have *s*, "Mercy shall
89:19 vision to Your holy one, And *s*:
95:10 with that generation, And *s*,
102:24 I *s*, "O my God, Do not
106:23 Therefore He *s* that He would
110: 1 The LORD *s* to my Lord, "Sit
116:11 I *s* in my haste, "All men
119:57 I have *s* that I would keep
122: 1 I was glad when they *s* to me,
126: 2 Then they *s* among the nations,
137: 7 The day of Jerusalem, Who *s*,
140: 6 I *s* to the LORD: "You are my
142: 5 cried out to You, O LORD: I *s*,
Prov 4: 4 and *s* to me: "Let your heart
7:13 With an impudent face she *s* to
Eccl 1:10 anything of which it may be *s*,
2: 1 I *s* in my heart, "Come now, I
2: 2 I *s* of laughter—"Madness!";
2:15 So I *s* in my heart, "As it
2:15 Then I *s* in my heart,
3:17 I *s* in my heart, "God shall
3:18 I *s* in my heart, "Concerning
7:23 I have proved by wisdom. I *s*,
8:14 I *s* that this also is vanity.
9:16 Then I *s*: "Wisdom is better
Song 2:10 and *s* to me: "Rise up, my
3: 2 I *s*, "And go about
3: 3 I *s*, "Have you seen
7: 8 I *s*, "I will go up
Isa 5: 9 hearing the LORD of hosts *s*,
6: 3 And one cried to another and *s*:
6: 5 So I *s*: "Woe is me,
6: 7 my mouth with it, and *s*:
6: 8 who will go for Us?" Then I *s*,
6: 9 And He *s*, "Go, and tell
6:11 Then I *s*, "Lord, how long?"
7: 3 Then the LORD *s* to Isaiah,
7:12 But Ahaz *s*, "I will not
7:13 Then he *s*, "Hear now,
8: 1 Moreover the LORD *s* to me,
8: 3 Then the LORD *s* to me, "Call
14:13 For you have *s* in your heart:
18: 4 For so the LORD *s* to me, "I
20: 3 Then the LORD *s*,
21: 6 For thus has the Lord *s* to me:
21: 9 Then he answered and *s*,
21:12 The watchman *s*, "The
21:16 For thus the LORD has *s* to me:
22: 4 Therefore I *s*, "Look away
23:12 And He *s*, "You will
24:16 But I *s*, "I am ruined,
25: 9 And it will be *s* in that day:
28:12 To whom He *s*, "This is
28:15 Because you have *s*,
29:13 Therefore the LORD *s*:
30:16 And you *s*, "No, for we
32: 5 Nor the miser *s* to be
36: 4 Then the Rabshakeh *s* to them,
36: 7 and *s* to Judah and Jerusalem,
36:10 The LORD *s* to me, 'Go up
36:11 and Joah *s* to the Rabshakeh,
36:12 But the Rabshakeh *s*,
36:13 a loud voice in Hebrew, and *s*,
37: 3 And they *s* to him, "Thus says
37: 6 And Isaiah *s* to them, "Thus
37:24 reproached the Lord, And *s*,
38: 1 went to him and *s* to him,
38: 3 and *s*, "Remember now,
38:10 *s*, "In the prime of my
38:11 I *s*, "I shall not see
38:21 Now Isaiah had *s*,
38:22 And Hezekiah had *s*,
39: 3 and *s* to him, "What did these
39: 3 So Hezekiah *s*, "They came
39: 4 And he *s*, "What have
39: 5 Then Isaiah *s* to Hezekiah,
39: 8 So Hezekiah *s* to Isaiah, "The
39: 8 For he *s*, "At least there
40: 6 The voice *s*, "Cry out!"
40: 6 said, "Cry out!" And he *s*,
41: 6 And *s* to his brother, "Be of
41: 9 And *s* to you, 'You are My
41:27 The first time I *s* to Zion,
47: 7 And you *s*, 'I shall be
47:10 You have *s*, 'No one sees
47:10 And you have *s* in your heart,
49: 3 And He *s* to me, 'You are My
49: 4 Then I *s*, 'I have labored
49:14 But Zion *s*, "The LORD
51:23 Who have *s* to you, 'Lie down,
63: 8 For He *s*, "Surely they
65: 1 who did not seek Me. I *s*,
66: 5 you out for My name's sake, *s*,
Jer 1: 6 Then *s* I: "Ah, Lord GOD!
1: 7 But the LORD *s* to me: "Do
1: 9 and the LORD *s* to me:
1:11 And I *s*, "I see a branch
1:12 Then the LORD *s* to me, "You
1:13 "What do you see?" And I *s*,
1:14 Then the LORD *s* to me: "Out
2:20 burst your bonds; And you *s*,
2:25 throat from thirst. But you *s*,
3: 6 The LORD *s* also to me in the
3: 7 'And I *s*, after she had
3:11 Then the LORD *s* to me,
3:19 But I *s*: 'How can I
3:19 hosts of nations?' "And I *s*:
4:10 Then I *s*, "Ah, Lord GOD!
4:11 At that time it will be *s* To
5: 4 Therefore I *s*, "Surely
5:12 lied about the LORD, And *s*,
6: 6 thus has the LORD of hosts *s*:
6:16 But they *s*, 'We will not
6:17 But they *s*, 'We will not
9:13 And the LORD *s*, "Because
11: 5 And I answered and *s*,
11: 6 Then the LORD *s* to me,
11: 9 And the LORD *s* to me, "A
12: 4 dwell there, Because they *s*,
13: 1 Thus the LORD *s* to me: "Go and
13: 6 many days that the LORD *s* to
14:11 Then the LORD *s* to me, "Do
14:13 Then I *s*, "Ah, Lord GOD!
14:14 And the LORD *s* to me, "The
15: 1 Then the LORD *s* to me, "Even
15:11 The LORD *s*: "Surely it
16:14 "that it shall no more be *s*,
17:19 Thus the LORD *s* to me: "Go
18:10 the good with which I *s* I
18:12 And they *s*, "That is
18:18 Then they *s*, "Come and
19:14 of the Lord's house and *s* to
20: 3 Then Jeremiah *s* to him, "The
20: 9 Then I *s*, "I will not
21: 3 Then Jeremiah *s* to them, "Thus
22:21 in your prosperity, But you *s*,
23:17 despise Me, 'The LORD has *s*,
23:25 heard what the prophets have *s*
24: 3 Then the LORD *s* to me, "What
24: 3 And I *s*, "Figs, the good figs,
25: 5 'They *s*, 'Repent now
26:16 princes and all the people *s*
28: 6 and the prophet Jeremiah *s*,
28:15 Then the prophet Jeremiah *s* to
29:15 Because you have *s*,
32: 6 And Jeremiah *s*, "The word
32: 8 and *s* to me, 'Please buy my
32:25 And You have *s* to me, O Lord
35: 5 and I *s* to them, "Drink
35: 6 But they *s*, "We will
35:11 up into the land, that we *s*,
35:18 And Jeremiah *s* to the house of
36:15 And they *s* to him, "Sit down
36:16 and *s* to Baruch, "We will
36:19 Then the princes *s* to Baruch,
37:14 Then Jeremiah *s*, "False!
37:17 secretly in his house, and *s*,
37:17 And Jeremiah *s*, "There is."
37:17 said, "There is." Then he *s*,
37:18 Moreover Jeremiah *s* to King
38: 4 Therefore the princes *s* to the
38: 5 Then Zedekiah the king *s*,
38:12 Ebed-Melech the Ethiopian *s* to
38:14 And the king *s* to Jeremiah, "I
38:15 Jeremiah *s* to Zedekiah, "If I
38:17 Then Jeremiah *s* to Zedekiah,
38:19 And Zedekiah the king *s* to
38:20 But Jeremiah *s*, "They shall
38:24 Then Zedekiah *s* to Jeremiah,
38:25 to us now what you have *s* to
38:25 and also what the king *s* to
40: 2 the guard took Jeremiah and *s*
40: 3 it, and has done just as He *s*.
40: 5 yet gone back, Nebuzaradan *s*,
40:14 and *s* to him, "Do you certainly
40:16 Gedaliah the son of Ahikam *s*
41: 6 as he met them that he *s* to
41: 8 were found among them who *s* to
42: 2 and *s* to Jeremiah the prophet,
42: 4 Then Jeremiah the prophet *s* to
42: 5 So they *s* to Jeremiah, "Let the
42: 9 and *s* to them, "Thus says the
42:19 The LORD has *s* concerning you,
44:19 The women also *s*,
44:24 Moreover Jeremiah *s* to all the
45: 3 'You *s*, "Woe is me
46:16 And they *s*, 'Arise! Let us
50: 7 them; And their adversaries *s*,
51:61 And Jeremiah *s* to Seraiah,
Lam 3:18 And I *s*, "My strength
3:54 flowed over my head; I *s*,
3:57 the day I called on You, And *s*,
4:15 Those among the nations *s*,
4:20 in their pits, Of whom we *s*,
Ezek 2: 1 And He *s* to me, "Son of man,
2: 3 And He *s* to me: "Son of man, I
3: 1 Moreover He *s* to me, "Son of
3: 3 And He *s* to me, "Son of man,
3: 4 Then He *s* to me: "Son of man,
3:10 Moreover He *s* to me: "Son of
3:22 and He *s* to me, "Arise, go out
3:24 and spoke with me and *s* to me:
4:13 Then the LORD *s*,
4:14 So I *s*, "Ah, Lord GOD!
4:15 Then He *s* to me, "See, I am
4:16 Moreover He *s* to me, "Son of
6:10 I have not *s* in vain that I
8: 5 Then He *s* to me, "Son of man,
8: 6 Furthermore He *s* to me, "Son of
8: 8 Then He *s* to me, "Son of man,
8: 9 And He *s* to me, "Go in, and see
8:12 Then He *s* to me, "Son of man,
8:13 And He *s* to me, "Turn again,
8:15 Then He *s* to me, "Have you
8:17 And He *s* to me, "Have you seen
9: 4 and the LORD *s* to him, "Go
9: 5 To the others He *s* in my
9: 7 Then He *s* to them, "Defile the
9: 8 on my face and cried out, and *s*,
9: 9 Then He *s* to me, "The iniquity
9:11 his side, reported back and *s*,
10: 2 man clothed with linen, and *s*,
11: 2 And He *s* to me: "Son of man,
11: 5 and *s* to me, "Speak!
11: 5 the LORD: "Thus you have *s*,
11:13 cried with a loud voice, and *s*,
11:15 inhabitants of Jerusalem have *s*,
12: 9 *s* to you, 'What are you doing?'
13:12 will it not be *s* to you, 'Where
16: 6 I *s* to you in your blood,
16: 6 I *s* to you in your blood,
20: 7 Then I *s* to them, 'Each of you,
20: 8 Then I *s*, 'I will pour
20:13 Then I *s* I would pour out My
20:18 But I *s* to their children in
20:21 Then I *s* I would pour out My
20:29 Then I *s* to them, 'What is this
20:49 Then I *s*, "Ah, Lord GOD!
23:36 The LORD also *s* to me: "Son
23:43 Then I *s* concerning her who
24:19 And the people *s* to me, "Will
25: 3 the Lord GOD: "Because you *s*,
26: 2 because Tyre has *s* against
27: 3 GOD: "O Tyre, you have *s*,
29: 3 midst of his rivers, Who has *s*,
29: 9 I am the LORD, because he *s*,
33:21 from Jerusalem came to me and *s*,
35:10 "Because you have *s*,
36: 2 Because the enemy has *s* of you,
36:20 when they *s* of them, 'These are
37: 3 And He *s* to me, "Son of man,
37: 4 Again He *s* to me, "Prophesy to
37: 9 Also He *s* to me, "Prophesy to
37:11 Then He *s* to me, "Son of man,
40: 4 And the man *s* to me, "Son of
40:45 Then he *s* to me, "This chamber
41: 4 and he *s* to me, "This is the
41:22 and he *s* to me, "This is the
42:13 Then he *s* to me, "The north
43: 7 And He *s* to me, "Son of man,
43:18 And He *s* to me, "Son of man,
44: 2 And the LORD *s* to me, "This
44: 5 And the LORD *s* to me, "Son of
46:20 And he *s* to me, "This is the
46:24 And he *s* to me, "These are the
47: 6 He *s* to me, "Son of man, have
47: 8 Then he *s* to me: "This water
Dan 1:10 And the chief of the eunuchs *s*
1:11 So Daniel *s* to the steward whom
1:18 when the king had *s* that they
2: 3 And the king *s* to them, "I have
2: 5 The king answered and *s* to the
2: 7 They answered again and *s*,
2: 8 The king answered and *s*,
2:10 answered the king, and *s*,
2:15 he answered and *s* to Arioch the
2:20 Daniel answered and *s*:
2:24 He went and *s* thus to him: "Do
2:25 and *s* thus to him, "I have
2:26 The king answered and *s* to
2:27 the presence of the king, and *s*,
2:47 The king answered Daniel, and *s*,
3: 9 They spoke and *s* to King
3:16 and Abed-Nego answered and *s* to
3:24 They answered and *s* to the
4:14 He cried aloud and *s* thus:
4:19 him. So the king spoke, and *s*,
4:19 Belteshazzar answered and *s*,
5:13 and *s* to Daniel, "Are you
5:17 and *s* before the king, "Let
6: 5 Then these men *s*,
6: 6 and *s* thus to him: "King
6:12 The king answered and *s*,
6:13 So they answered and *s* before
6:15 and *s* to the king, "Know,
6:21 Then Daniel *s* to the king,
7: 5 And they *s* thus to it: 'Arise,
7:23 Thus he *s*: 'The fourth
8:13 and another holy one *s* to that
8:14 And he *s* to me, "For two
8:16 of the Ulai, who called, and *s*,
8:17 but he *s* to me, "Understand,
8:19 And he *s*, "Look, I am
9: 4 God, and made confession, and *s*,
9:22 me, and talked with me, and *s*,
10:11 And he *s* to me, "O Daniel, man
10:12 Then he *s* to me, "Do not fear,
10:19 And he *s*, "O man greatly
10:19 to me I was strengthened, and *s*,
10:20 Then he *s*, "Do you know
12: 6 And one *s* to the man clothed in
12: 8 I did not understand. Then I *s*,
12: 9 And he *s*, "Go your way,
Hos 1: 2 the LORD *s* to Hosea: "Go,
1: 4 Then the LORD *s* to him:
1: 6 Then God *s* to him: "Call
1: 9 Then God *s*: "Call his
1:10 In the place where it was *s*
1:10 There it shall be *s* to them,
2: 5 For she *s*, 'I will go after
2:12 fig trees, Of which she has *s*,
3: 1 Then the LORD *s* to me, "Go
3: 3 And I *s* to her, "You shall stay
12: 8 And Ephraim *s*, 'Surely I
13:10 And your judges to whom you *s*,
Joel 2:32 As the LORD has *s*,
Am 1: 2 And he *s*: "The LORD roars
7: 2 the grass of the land, that I *s*:
7: 3 not be," *s* the LORD.
7: 5 Then I *s*: "O Lord GOD,
7: 6 *s* the Lord GOD.
7: 8 And the LORD *s* to me, "Amos,
7: 8 And I *s*, "A plumb line."
7: 8 Then the Lord *s*: "Behold, I
7:11 "For thus Amos has *s*:

7:12 Then Amaziah *s* to Amos: "Go,
7:14 and *s* to Amaziah: "I was no
7:15 And the LORD *s* to me, 'Go,
8: 2 And He *s*, "Amos, what
8: 2 So I *s*, "A basket of
8: 2 Then the LORD *s* to me:
9: 1 standing by the altar, and He *s*:
Jon 1: 6 and *s* to him, "What do you
1: 7 And they *s* to one another,
1: 8 Then they *s* to him, "Please
1: 9 So he *s* to them, "I am a
1:10 and *s* to him, "Why have you
1:11 Then they *s* to him, "What shall
1:12 And he *s* to them, "Pick me up
1:14 cried out to the LORD and *s*,
2: 2 And he *s*: "I cried out to
2: 4 Then I *s*, 'I have been
3: 4 Then he cried out and *s*,
3:10 the disaster that He had *s* He
4: 2 he prayed to the LORD, and *s*,
4: 2 was not this what I *s* when I
4: 4 Then the LORD *s*,
4: 8 wished death for himself, and *s*,
4: 9 Then God *s* to Jonah, "Is it
4: 9 And he *s*, "It is right for
4:10 But the LORD *s*, "You have
Mic 3: 1 And I *s*: "Hear now,
7:10 shame will cover her who *s* to
Hab 2: 2 the LORD answered me and *s*:
Zeph 2:15 That *s* in her heart, "I am
3: 7 I *s*, 'Surely you will
3:16 In that day it shall be *s* to
Hag 2:12 Then the priests answered and *s*,
2:13 And Haggai *s*, "If one who
2:13 So the priests answered and *s*,
2:14 Then Haggai answered and *s*,
Zech 1: 6 "So they returned and *s*:
1: 9 Then I *s*, "My lord, what
1: 9 the angel who talked with me *s*
1:10 the myrtle trees answered and *s*,
1:11 among the myrtle trees, and *s*,
1:12 of the LORD answered and *s*,
1:14 the angel who spoke with me *s*
1:19 And I *s* to the angel who talked
1:21 And I *s*, "What are
1:21 So he *s*, "These are the
2: 2 So I *s*, "Where are you
2: 2 And he *s* to me, "To measure
2: 4 who *s* to him, "Run, speak to
3: 2 And the LORD *s* to Satan, "The
3: 4 And to him He *s*, "See, I
3: 5 And I *s*, "Let them put
4: 2 And he *s* to me, "What do you
4: 2 So I *s*, "I am looking, and
4: 5 talked with me answered and *s*
4: 5 And I *s*, "No, my lord."
4: 6 So he answered and *s* to me:
4:11 Then I answered and *s* to him,
4:12 And I further answered and *s* to
4:13 Then he answered me and *s*,
4:13 And I *s*, "No, my lord."
4:14 So he *s*, "These are the
5: 2 And he *s* to me, "What do you
5: 3 Then he *s* to me, "This is the
5: 5 talked with me came out and *s*
5: 6 And he *s*, "It is a basket
5: 6 He also *s*, "This is their
5: 8 then he *s*, "This is
5:10 So I *s* to the angel who talked
5:11 And he *s* to me, "To build a
6: 4 Then I answered and *s* to the
6: 5 And the angel answered and *s* to
6: 7 And He *s*, "Go, walk to and
11: 9 Then I *s*, "I will not
11:12 Then I *s* to them, "If it is
11:13 And the LORD *s* to me, "Throw
11:15 And the LORD *s* to me, "Next,
Mal 1: 4 Even though Edom has *s*,
3: 7 LORD of hosts. "But you *s*,
3:14 You have *s*, 'It is useless
Mt 2: 5 So they *s* to him, "In Bethlehem
2: 8 he sent them to Bethlehem and *s*,
3: 7 he *s* to them, "Brood of
3:15 But Jesus answered and *s* to him,
4: 3 the tempter came to Him, he *s*,
4: 4 But He answered and *s*,
4: 6 and *s* to Him, "If You are the
4: 7 Jesus *s* to him, "It is written
4: 9 And he *s* to Him, "All these
4:10 Then Jesus *s* to him, "Away with
4:19 Then He *s* to them, "Follow Me,
5:21 You have heard that it was *s* to
5:27 You have heard that it was *s* to
5:31 "Furthermore it has been *s*,
5:33 you have heard that it was *s*
5:38 "You have heard that it was *s*,
5:43 "You have heard that it was *s*,
8: 4 And Jesus *s* to him, "See that
8: 7 And Jesus *s* to him, "I will
8: 8 The centurion answered and *s*,
8:10 and *s* to those who followed,
8:13 Then Jesus *s* to the centurion,
8:19 a certain scribe came and *s* to
8:20 And Jesus *s* to him, "Foxes have
8:21 another of His disciples *s* to
8:22 But Jesus *s* to him, "Follow Me,
8:26 But He *s* to them, "Why are you
8:32 And He *s* to them, "Go." So
9: 2 He *s* to the paralytic, "Son,
9: 3 at once some of the scribes *s*
9: 4 knowing their thoughts, *s*,
9: 6 then He *s* to the paralytic,
9: 9 And He *s* to him, "Follow Me."
9:11 they *s* to His disciples, "Why
9:12 He *s* to them, "Those who are
9:15 And Jesus *s* to them, "Can the
9:21 For she *s* to herself, "If only
9:22 and when He saw her He *s*,
9:24 He *s* to them, "Make room, for
9:28 And Jesus *s* to them, "Do you
9:28 They *s* to Him, "Yes, Lord."
9:34 But the Pharisees *s*,
9:37 Then He *s* to His disciples,
11: 3 and *s* to Him, "Are You the
11: 4 Jesus answered and *s* to them,
11:25 that time Jesus answered and *s*,
12: 2 they *s* to Him, "Look, Your
12: 3 But He *s* to them, "Have you not
12:11 Then He *s* to them, "What man is
12:13 Then He *s* to the man, "Stretch
12:23 multitudes were amazed and *s*,
12:24 the Pharisees heard it they *s*,
12:25 and *s* to them: "Every kingdom
12:39 But He answered and *s* to them,
12:47 Then one *s* to Him, "Look, Your
12:48 But He answered and *s* to the one
12:49 hand toward His disciples and *s*,
13:10 And the disciples came and *s* to
13:11 He answered and *s* to them,
13:27 of the owner came and *s* to him,
13:28 He *s* to them, 'An enemy has done
13:28 The servants *s* to him, 'Do you
13:29 'But he *s*, 'No, lest while
13:37 He answered and *s* to them: "He
13:51 Jesus *s* to them, "Have you
13:51 They *s* to Him, "Yes, Lord."
13:52 Then He *s* to them, "Therefore
13:54 that they were astonished and *s*,
13:57 But Jesus *s* to them, "A
14: 2 and *s* to his servants, "This is
14: 4 Because John had *s* to him, "It
14: 8 been prompted by her mother, *s*,
14:16 But Jesus *s* to them, "They do
14:17 And they *s* to Him, "We have
14:18 He *s*, "Bring them here
14:28 And Peter answered Him and *s*,
14:29 So He *s*, "Come." And when
14:31 and *s* to him, "O you of little
15: 3 He answered and *s* to them, "Why
15:10 He *s* to them, "Hear and
15:12 Then His disciples came and *s* to
15:13 But He answered and *s*,
15:15 Then Peter answered and *s* to
15:16 So Jesus *s*, "Are you also
15:24 But He answered and *s*,
15:26 But He answered and *s*,
15:27 And she *s*, "Yes, Lord,
15:28 Then Jesus answered and *s* to
15:32 His disciples to Himself and *s*,
15:33 Then His disciples *s* to Him,
15:34 Jesus *s* to them, "How many
15:34 And they *s*, "Seven, and a
16: 2 He answered and *s* to them,
16: 6 Then Jesus *s* to them, "Take
16: 8 *s* to them, "O you of little
16:14 So they *s*, "Some say
16:15 He *s* to them, "But who do you
16:16 Simon Peter answered and *s*,
16:17 Jesus answered and *s* to him,
16:23 But He turned and *s* to Peter,
16:24 Then Jesus *s* to His disciples,
17: 4 Then Peter answered and *s* to
17: 7 came and touched them and *s*,
17:11 Jesus answered and *s* to them,
17:17 Then Jesus answered and *s*,
17:19 came to Jesus privately and *s*,
17:20 So Jesus *s* to them, "Because of
17:22 Jesus *s* to them, "The Son of
17:24 temple tax came to Peter and *s*,
17:25 He *s*, "Yes." And when
17:26 Peter *s* to Him, "From
17:26 Jesus *s* to him, "Then the
18: 3 and *s*, "Assuredly, I
18:21 Then Peter came to Him and *s*,
18:22 Jesus *s* to him, "I do not say
18:32 *s* to him, 'You wicked servant!
19: 4 And He answered and *s* to them,
19: 5 'and *s*, 'For this reason
19: 7 They *s* to Him, "Why then did
19: 8 He *s* to them, "Moses, because
19:10 His disciples *s* to Him, "If
19:11 But He *s* to them, "All cannot
19:14 But Jesus *s*, "Let the
19:16 one came and *s* to Him, "Good
19:17 So He *s* to him, "Why do you
19:18 He *s* to Him, "Which ones?"
19:18 Jesus *s*, " 'You shall not
19:20 The young man *s* to Him, "All
19:21 Jesus *s* to him, "If you want to
19:23 Then Jesus *s* to His disciples,
19:26 Jesus looked at them and *s* to
19:27 Then Peter answered and *s* to
19:28 So Jesus *s* to them, "Assuredly
20: 4 and *s* to them, 'You also go into
20: 6 and *s* to them, 'Why have you
20: 7 They *s* to him, 'Because no one
20: 7 He *s* to them, 'You also go
20: 8 the owner of the vineyard *s* to
20:13 he answered one of them and *s*,
20:17 aside on the road and *s* to
20:21 And He *s* to her, "What do you
20:21 She *s* to Him, "Grant that
20:22 But Jesus answered and *s*,
20:22 They *s* to Him, "We are
20:23 So He *s* to them, "You will
20:25 called them to Himself and *s*,
20:32 still and called them, and *s*,
20:33 They *s* to Him, "Lord, that our
21:11 So the multitudes *s*,
21:13 And He *s* to them, "It is
21:16 and *s* to Him, "Do You hear what
21:16 And Jesus *s* to them, "Yes.
21:19 and *s* to it, "Let no fruit
21:21 So Jesus answered and *s* to them,
21:23 Him as He was teaching, and *s*,
21:24 But Jesus answered and *s* to
21:27 So they answered Jesus and *s*,
21:27 And He *s* to them, "Neither
21:28 and he came to the first and *s*,
21:29 "He answered and *s*,
21:30 he came to the second and *s*
21:30 And he answered and *s*,
21:31 They *s* to Him, "The first."
21:31 Jesus *s* to them, "Assuredly,
21:38 they *s* among themselves, 'This
21:41 They *s* to Him, "He will destroy
21:42 Jesus *s* to them, "Have you
22: 1 to them again by parables and *s*:
22: 8 Then he *s* to his servants, 'The
22:12 So he *s* to him, 'Friend, how did
22:13 Then the king *s* to the servants,
22:18 their wickedness, and *s*,
22:20 And He *s* to them, "Whose image
22:21 They *s* to Him, "Caesar's."
22:21 And He *s* to them, "Render
22:24 Moses *s* that if a man dies,
22:29 Jesus answered and *s* to them,
22:37 Jesus *s* to him, " 'You shall
22:42 They *s* to Him, "The Son of
22:43 He *s* to them, "How then does
22:44 The LORD *s* to my Lord,
24: 2 And Jesus *s* to them, "Do you
24: 4 And Jesus answered and *s* to
25: 8 And the foolish *s* to the wise,
25:12 "But he answered and *s*,
25:21 His lord *s* to him, 'Well done,
25:22 received two talents came and *s*,
25:23 His lord *s* to him, 'Well done,
25:24 the one talent came and *s*,
25:26 But his lord answered and *s* to
26: 1 that He *s* to His disciples,
26: 5 But they *s*, "Not during
26:10 He *s* to them, "Why do you
26:15 and *s*, "What are you
26:18 And He *s*, "Go into the
26:21 Now as they were eating, He *s*,
26:23 He answered and *s*,
26:25 betraying Him, answered and *s*,
26:25 He *s* to him, "You have said
26:25 You have *s* it."
26:26 gave it to the disciples and *s*,
26:31 Then Jesus *s* to them, "All of
26:33 Peter answered and *s* to Him,
26:34 Jesus *s* to him, "Assuredly, I
26:35 Peter *s* to Him, "Even if I have
26:35 And so *s* all the disciples.
26:36 and *s* to the disciples, "Sit
26:38 Then He *s* to them, "My soul is
26:40 and *s* to Peter, "What? Could
26:45 He came to His disciples and *s*
26:49 he went up to Jesus and *s*,
26:50 But Jesus *s* to him, "Friend,
26:52 But Jesus *s* to him, "Put your
26:55 In that hour Jesus *s* to the
26:61 and *s*, "This fellow said,
26:61 and said, "This fellow *s*,
26:62 the high priest arose and *s* to
26:63 the high priest answered and *s*
26:64 Jesus *s* to him, "It is as
26:64 to him, "It is as you *s*.
26:66 They answered and *s*,
26:71 another girl saw him and *s* to
26:73 who stood by came up and *s* to
26:75 the word of Jesus who had *s* to
27: 4 And they *s*, "What is that
27: 6 took the silver pieces and *s*,
27:11 So Jesus *s* to him, "It is
27:13 Then Pilate *s* to Him, "Do You
27:17 Pilate *s* to them, "Whom do you
27:21 The governor answered and *s* to
27:21 They *s*, "Barabbas!"
27:22 Pilate *s* to them, "What then
27:22 They all *s* to him, "Let Him
27:23 Then the governor *s*,
27:25 all the people answered and *s*,
27:41 with the scribes and elders, *s*,
27:43 for He *s*, 'I am the Son
27:47 there, when they heard that, *s*,
27:49 The rest *s*, "Let Him alone;
27:63 alive, how that deceiver *s*,
27:65 Pilate *s* to them, "You have a
28: 5 But the angel answered and *s* to
28: 6 here; for He is risen, as He *s*.
28:10 Then Jesus *s* to them, "Do not
Mk 1:17 Then Jesus *s* to them, "Follow
1:37 they *s* to Him, "Everyone is
1:38 But He *s* to them, "Let us go
1:41 and *s* to him, "I am willing;
1:44 and *s* to him, "See that you say
2: 5 He *s* to the paralytic, "Son,
2: 8 He *s* to them, "Why do you
2:10 He *s* to the paralytic,
2:14 And He *s* to him, "Follow Me."
2:16 they *s* to His disciples, "How
2:17 He *s* to them, "Those who are
2:18 Then they came and *s* to Him,

2:19 And Jesus *s* to them, “Can the
2:24 And the Pharisees *s* to Him,
2:25 But He *s* to them, “Have you
2:27 And He *s* to them, “The Sabbath
3: 3 And He *s* to the man who had the
3: 4 Then He *s* to them, “Is it
3: 5 He *s* to the man, “Stretch out
3:21 to lay hold of Him, for they *s*,
3:22 who came down from Jerusalem *s*,
3:23 called them to Himself and *s*
3:30 because they *s*, “He has
3:32 and they *s* to Him, “Look, Your
3:34 those who sat about Him, and *s*,
4: 2 and *s* to them in His teaching:
4: 9 And He *s* to them, “He who has
4:11 And He *s* to them, “To you it
4:13 And He *s* to them, “Do you not
4:21 Also He *s* to them, “Is a lamp
4:24 Then He *s* to them, “Take heed
4:26 And He *s*, “The kingdom
4:30 Then He *s*, “To what shall
4:35 He *s* to them, “Let us cross
4:38 And they awoke Him and *s* to
4:39 and *s* to the sea, “Peace, be
4:40 But He *s* to them, “Why are you
4:41 and *s* to one another, “Who can
5: 7 out with a loud voice and *s*,
5: 8 For He *s* to him, “Come out of
5:19 but *s* to him, “Go home to your
5:28 For she *s*, “If only I
5:30 around in the crowd and *s*,
5:31 But His disciples *s* to Him,
5:34 And He *s* to her, “Daughter,
5:35 of the synagogue’s house who *s*,
5:36 He *s* to the ruler of the
5:39 He *s* to them, “Why make this
5:41 and *s* to her, “Talitha,
5:43 and *s* that something should be
6: 4 But Jesus *s* to them, “A prophet
6:10 Also He *s* to them, “In whatever
6:14 had become well known. And he *s*,
6:15 Others *s*, “It is Elijah.”
6:15 “It is Elijah.” And others *s*,
6:16 But when Herod heard, he *s*,
6:18 For John had *s* to Herod, “It is
6:22 the king *s* to the girl, “Ask
6:24 So she went out and *s* to her
6:24 “What shall I ask?” And she *s*,
6:31 And He *s* to them, “Come aside
6:35 His disciples came to Him and *s*,
6:37 But He answered and *s* to them,
6:37 And they *s* to Him, “Shall we
6:38 But He *s* to them, “How many
6:38 And when they found out they *s*,
6:50 He talked with them and *s* to
7: 6 He answered and *s* to them,
7: 9 He *s* to them, “All too well
7:10 ‘For Moses *s*, ‘Honor your
7:14 He *s* to them, “Hear Me,
7:18 So He *s* to them, “Are you thus
7:20 And He *s*, “What comes out
7:27 But Jesus *s* to her, “Let the
7:28 And she answered and *s* to Him,
7:29 Then He *s* to her, “For this
7:34 and *s* to him, “Ephphatha,”
8: 1 His disciples to Him and *s*
8: 5 do you have?” And they *s*,
8: 7 He *s* to set them also before
8:12 deeply in His spirit, and *s*,
8:17 *s* to them, “Why do you reason
8:19 They *s* to Him, “Twelve.”
8:20 And they *s*, “Seven.”
8:21 So He *s* to them, “How is it
8:24 And he looked up and *s*,
8:29 He *s* to them, “But who do you
8:29 Peter answered and *s* to Him,
8:34 He *s* to them, “Whoever desires
9: 1 And He *s* to them, “Assuredly, I
9: 5 Then Peter answered and *s* to
9:17 one of the crowd answered and *s*,
9:19 He answered him and *s*,
9:21 happening to him?” And he *s*,
9:23 Jesus *s* to him, “If you can
9:24 of the child cried out and *s*
9:26 as one dead, so that many *s*,
9:29 So He *s* to them, “This kind can
9:31 He taught His disciples and *s*
9:35 and *s* to them, “If anyone
9:36 His arms, He *s* to them,
9:39 But Jesus *s*, “Do not forbid
10: 3 And He answered and *s* to them,
10: 4 They *s*, “Moses permitted
10: 5 And Jesus answered and *s* to
10:11 So He *s* to them, “Whoever
10:14 He was greatly displeased and *s*
10:18 So Jesus *s* to him, “Why do you
10:20 And he answered and *s* to Him,
10:21 and *s* to him, “One thing you
10:23 Jesus looked around and *s* to
10:24 But Jesus answered again and *s*
10:27 But Jesus looked at them and *s*,
10:29 So Jesus answered and *s*,
10:36 And He *s* to them, “What do you
10:37 They *s* to Him, “Grant us that
10:38 But Jesus *s* to them, “You do
10:39 They *s* to Him, “We are able.”
10:39 So Jesus *s* to them, “You
10:42 called them to Himself and *s*
10:51 So Jesus answered and *s* to him,
10:51 The blind man *s* to Him,
10:52 Then Jesus *s* to him, “Go your
11: 2 and He *s* to them, “Go into the
11: 5 of those who stood there *s* to
11:14 In response Jesus *s* to it, “Let
11:21 *s* to Him, “Rabbi, look!
11:22 So Jesus answered and *s* to them,
11:28 And they *s* to Him, “By what
11:29 But Jesus answered and *s* to
11:33 So they answered and *s* to Jesus,
11:33 And Jesus answered and *s* to
12: 7 But those vinedressers *s* among
12:14 they *s* to Him, “Teacher, we
12:15 *s* to them, “Why do you test
12:16 And He *s* to them, “Whose image
12:16 They *s* to Him, “Caesar’s.”
12:17 And Jesus answered and *s* to
12:24 Jesus answered and *s* to them,
12:32 So the scribe *s* to Him, “Well
12:32 scribe said to Him, “Well *s*,
12:34 He *s* to him, “You are not far
12:35 Then Jesus answered and *s*,
12:36 For David himself *s* by the Holy
12:36 The LORD *s* to my Lord,
12:38 Then He *s* to them in His
12:43 disciples to Himself and *s* to
13: 1 one of His disciples *s* to Him,
13: 2 And Jesus answered and *s* to him,
14: 2 But they *s*, “Not during
14: 4 among themselves, and *s*,
14: 6 But Jesus *s*, “Let her
14:12 His disciples *s* to Him, “Where
14:13 out two of His disciples and *s*
14:16 and found it just as He had *s*
14:18 as they sat and ate, Jesus *s*,
14:19 “Is it I?” And another *s*,
14:20 He answered and *s* to them, “It
14:22 it, and gave it to them and *s*,
14:24 And He *s* to them, “This is My
14:27 Then Jesus *s* to them, “All of
14:29 Peter *s* to Him, “Even if all
14:30 Jesus *s* to him, “Assuredly, I
14:31 not deny You!” And they all *s*
14:32 and He *s* to His disciples,
14:34 Then He *s* to them, “My soul is
14:36 And He *s*, “Abba, Father,
14:37 and *s* to Peter, “Simon, are
14:41 He came the third time and *s*
14:45 he went up to Him and *s* to Him,
14:48 Then Jesus answered and *s* to
14:62 Jesus *s*, “I am. And you
14:63 priest tore his clothes and *s*,
14:67 she looked at him and *s*,
14:70 later those who stood by *s* to
14:72 mind the word that Jesus had *s*
15: 2 He answered and *s* to him,
15:12 Pilate answered and *s* to them
15:14 Then Pilate *s* to them, “Why,
15:31 themselves with the scribes, *s*,
15:35 by, when they heard that, *s*,
15:39 and breathed His last, he *s*,
16: 3 And they *s* among themselves,
16: 6 But he *s* to them, “Do not be
16: 7 see Him, as He *s* to you.”
16: 8 And they *s* nothing to anyone,
16:15 And He *s* to them, “Go into all
Lk 1:13 But the angel *s* to him, “Do not
1:18 And Zacharias *s* to the angel,
1:19 And the angel answered and *s* to
1:28 the angel *s* to her, “Rejoice,
1:30 Then the angel *s* to her, “Do
1:34 Then Mary *s* to the angel, “How
1:35 And the angel answered and *s* to
1:38 Then Mary *s*, “Behold the
1:42 out with a loud voice and *s*,
1:46 And Mary *s*: “My soul
1:60 His mother answered and *s*,
1:61 But they *s* to her, “There is no
2:10 Then the angel *s* to them, “Do
2:15 that the shepherds *s* to one
2:24 according to what is *s* in the
2:28 his arms and blessed God and *s*:
2:34 and *s* to Mary His mother,
2:48 and His mother *s* to Him, “Son,
2:49 And He *s* to them, “Why did you
3: 7 Then he *s* to the multitudes
3:11 He answered and *s* to them, “He
3:12 and *s* to him, “Teacher, what
3:13 And he *s* to them, “Collect no
3:14 So he *s* to them, “Do not
3:22 voice came from heaven which *s*,
4: 3 And the devil *s* to Him, “If You
4: 6 And the devil *s* to Him, “All
4: 8 And Jesus answered and *s* to him,
4: 9 and *s* to Him, “If You are the
4:12 And Jesus answered and *s* to him,
4:12 said to him, “It has been *s*,
4:22 out of His mouth. And they *s*,
4:23 He *s* to them, “You will surely
4:24 Then He *s*, “Assuredly, I
4:43 but He *s* to them, “I must
5: 4 He *s* to Simon, “Launch out
5: 5 But Simon answered and *s* to Him,
5:10 And Jesus *s* to Simon, “Do not
5:20 He *s* to him, “Man, your sins
5:22 He answered and *s* to them,
5:24 He *s* to the man who was
5:27 And He *s* to him, “Follow Me.”
5:31 Jesus answered and *s* to them,
5:33 Then they *s* to Him, “Why do
5:34 And He *s* to them, “Can you make
6: 2 And some of the Pharisees *s* to
6: 3 But Jesus answering them *s*,
6: 5 And He *s* to them, “The Son of
6: 8 and *s* to the man who had the
6: 9 Then Jesus *s* to them, “I will
6:10 He *s* to the man, “Stretch out
6:20 toward His disciples, and *s*:
7: 9 and turned around and *s* to the
7:13 He had compassion on her and *s*
7:14 And He *s*, “Young man, I say
7:20 the men had come to Him, they *s*,
7:22 Jesus answered and *s* to them,
7:31 And the Lord *s*, “To what
7:40 And Jesus answered and *s* to him,
7:40 So he *s*, “Teacher, say
7:43 Simon answered and *s*,
7:43 And He *s* to him, “You have
7:44 He turned to the woman and *s*
7:48 Then He *s* to her, “Your sins
7:50 Then He *s* to the woman, “Your
8: 8 When He had *s* these things He
8:10 And He *s*, “To you it has
8:20 was told Him by some, who *s*,
8:21 But He answered and *s* to them,
8:22 And He *s* to them, “Let us
8:25 But He *s* to them, “Where is
8:28 Him, and with a loud voice *s*,
8:30 “What is your name?” And he *s*,
8:45 And Jesus *s*, “Who touched
8:45 it, Peter and those with him *s*,
8:46 But Jesus *s*, “Somebody
8:48 And He *s* to her, “Daughter, be
8:52 but He *s*, “Do not weep;
9: 3 And He *s* to them, “Take nothing
9: 7 because it was *s* by some that
9: 9 Herod *s*, “John I have
9:12 the twelve came and *s* to Him,
9:13 But He *s* to them, “You give
9:13 And they *s*, “We have no
9:14 Then He *s* to His disciples,
9:19 So they answered and *s*,
9:20 He *s* to them, “But who do you
9:20 Peter answered and *s*,
9:23 Then He *s* to them all, “If
9:33 that Peter *s* to Jesus,
9:33 Elijah”—not knowing what he *s*.
9:41 Then Jesus answered and *s*,
9:43 He *s* to His disciples,
9:48 and *s* to them, “Whoever
9:49 Now John answered and *s*,
9:50 But Jesus *s* to him, “Do not
9:54 and John saw this, they *s*,
9:55 turned and rebuked them, and *s*,
9:57 that someone *s* to Him, “Lord,
9:58 And Jesus *s* to him, “Foxes have
9:59 Then He *s* to another, “Follow
9:59 But he *s*, “Lord, let me
9:60 Jesus *s* to him, “Let the dead
9:61 And another also *s*,
9:62 But Jesus *s* to him, “No one,
10: 2 Then He *s* to them, “The harvest
10:18 And He *s* to them, “I saw Satan
10:21 rejoiced in the Spirit and *s*,
10:23 turned to His disciples and *s*
10:26 He *s* to him, “What is written
10:27 So he answered and *s*,
10:28 And He *s* to him, “You have
10:29 *s* to Jesus, “And who is my
10:30 Then Jesus answered and *s*:
10:35 and *s* to him, ‘Take care of
10:37 And he *s*, “He who showed
10:37 Then Jesus *s* to him, “Go and
10:40 and she approached Him and *s*,
10:41 And Jesus answered and *s* to her,
11: 1 that one of His disciples *s* to
11: 2 So He *s* to them, “When you
11: 5 And He *s* to them, “Which of
11:15 But some of them *s*,
11:17 *s* to them: “Every kingdom
11:27 crowd raised her voice and *s*
11:28 But He *s*, “More than that,
11:39 Then the Lord *s* to him, “Now
11:45 of the lawyers answered and *s*
11:46 And He *s*, “Woe to you
11:49 the wisdom of God also *s*,
11:53 And as He *s* these things to
12:13 Then one from the crowd *s* to
12:14 But He *s* to him, “Man, who made
12:15 And He *s* to them, “Take heed
12:18 ‘So he *s*, ‘I will do this:
12:20 ‘But God *s* to him, ‘Fool!
12:22 Then He *s* to His disciples,
12:41 Then Peter *s* to Him, “Lord, do
12:42 And the Lord *s*, “Who then
12:54 Then He also *s* to the
13: 2 And Jesus answered and *s* to
13: 7 Then he *s* to the keeper of his
13: 8 But he answered and *s* to him,
13:12 He called her to Him and *s* to
13:14 and he *s* to the crowd, “There
13:15 Lord then answered him and *s*,
13:17 And when He *s* these things, all
13:18 Then He *s*, “What is the
13:20 And again He *s*, “To what
13:23 Then one *s* to Him, “Lord, are
13:23 And He *s* to them,
13:32 And He *s* to them, “Go, tell
14:12 Then He also *s* to him who
14:15 he *s* to Him, “Blessed is he
14:16 Then He *s* to him, “A certain
14:18 The first *s* to him, ‘I have
14:19 ‘And another *s*, ‘I have
14:20 “Still another *s*,
14:21 *s* to his servant, ‘Go out
14:22 “And the servant *s*,
14:23 Then the master *s* to the

14:25 And He turned and *s* to them,
15:11 Then He *s*: "A certain man
15:12 And the younger of them *s* to
15:17 when he came to himself, he *s*,
15:21 And the son *s* to him, 'Father, I
15:22 But the father *s* to his
15:27 And he *s* to him, 'Your brother
15:29 So he answered and *s* to his
15:31 And he *s* to him, 'Son, you are
16: 1 He also *s* to His disciples:
16: 2 So he called him and *s* to him,
16: 3 Then the steward *s* within
16: 5 and *s* to the first, 'How much
16: 6 'And he *s*, 'A hundred
16: 6 So he *s* to him, 'Take your
16: 7 Then he *s* to another, 'And how
16: 7 So he *s*, 'A hundred measures
16: 7 And he *s* to him, 'Take your
16:15 And He *s* to them, "You are
16:24 "Then he cried and *s*,
16:25 'But Abraham *s*, 'Son,
16:27 'Then he *s*, 'I beg you
16:29 Abraham *s* to him, 'They have
16:30 'And he *s*, 'No, father
16:31 But he *s* to him, 'If they do not
17: 1 Then He *s* to the disciples, "It
17: 5 And the apostles *s* to the Lord,
17: 6 So the Lord *s*, "If you
17:13 lifted up their voices and *s*,
17:14 He *s* to them, "Go, show
17:17 So Jesus answered and *s*,
17:19 And He *s* to him, "Arise, go
17:20 come, He answered them and *s*,
17:22 Then He *s* to the disciples,
17:37 And they answered and *s* to Him,
17:37 So He *s* to them, "Wherever
18: 4 but afterward he *s* within
18: 6 Then the Lord *s*, "Hear what
18: 6 "Hear what the unjust judge *s*.
18:16 Jesus called them to Him and *s*,
18:19 So Jesus *s* to him, "Why do you
18:21 And he *s*, "All these
18:22 He *s* to him, "You still lack
18:24 he became very sorrowful, He *s*,
18:26 And those who heard it *s*,
18:27 But He *s*, "The things which
18:28 Then Peter *s*, "See, we
18:29 So He *s* to them, "Assuredly, I
18:31 He took the twelve aside and *s*
18:41 He *s*, "Lord, that I
18:42 Then Jesus *s* to him, "Receive
19: 5 and *s* to him, "Zacchaeus, make
19: 8 Then Zacchaeus stood and *s* to
19: 9 And Jesus *s* to him, "Today
19:12 Therefore He *s*: "A certain
19:13 and *s* to them, 'Do business
19:17 And he *s* to him, 'Well done,
19:19 Likewise he *s* to him, 'You also
19:22 And he *s* to him, 'Out of your
19:24 And he *s* to those who stood by,
19:25 But they *s* to him, 'Master, he
19:28 When He had *s* this, He went on
19:32 and found it just as He had *s*
19:33 the owners of it *s* to them,
19:34 And they *s*, "The Lord has
19:40 But He answered and *s* to them,
20: 3 But He answered and *s* to them,
20: 8 And Jesus *s* to them, "Neither
20:13 the owner of the vineyard *s*,
20:16 And when they heard it they *s*,
20:17 Then He looked at them and *s*,
20:23 and *s* to them, "Why do you
20:24 They answered and *s*,
20:25 And He *s* to them, "Render
20:34 And Jesus answered and *s* to
20:39 of the scribes answered and *s*,
20:41 And He *s* to them, "How can
20:42 Now David himself *s* in the Book
20:42 The LORD *s* to my Lord,
20:45 He *s* to His disciples,
21: 3 So He *s*, "Truly I say
21: 5 stones and donations, He *s*,
21: 8 And He *s*: "Take heed
21:10 Then He *s* to them, "Nation will
22: 9 So they *s* to Him, "Where do You
22:10 And He *s* to them, "Behold, when
22:13 and found it just as He had *s*
22:15 Then He *s* to them, "With
22:17 the cup, and gave thanks, and *s*,
22:25 And He *s* to them, "The kings of
22:31 And the Lord *s*, "Simon,
22:33 But he *s* to Him, "Lord, I am
22:34 Then He *s*, "I tell you,
22:35 And He *s* to them, "When I sent
22:35 So they *s*, "Nothing."
22:36 Then He *s* to them, "But now, he
22:38 So they *s*, "Lord, look,
22:38 And He *s* to them, "It is
22:40 He *s* to them, "Pray that you
22:46 Then He *s* to them, "Why do you
22:48 But Jesus *s* to him, "Judas, are
22:49 they *s* to Him, "Lord, shall we
22:51 But Jesus answered and *s*,
22:52 Then Jesus *s* to the chief
22:56 looked intently at him and *s*,
22:58 while another saw him and *s*,
22:58 But Peter *s*, "Man, I am
22:60 But Peter *s*, "Man, I do
22:61 how He had *s* to him, "Before
22:67 But He *s* to them, "If I tell
22:70 Then they all *s*, "Are You
22:70 So He *s* to them, "You
22:71 And they *s*, "What further
23: 3 Jews?" He answered him and *s*,
23: 4 So Pilate *s* to the chief priests
23:14 *s* to them, "You have brought
23:22 Then he *s* to them the third
23:28 But Jesus, turning to them, *s*,
23:34 Then Jesus *s*, "Father,
23:42 Then he *s* to Jesus, "Lord,
23:43 And Jesus *s* to him, "Assuredly,
23:46 out with a loud voice, He *s*,
23:46 Having *s* this, He breathed
24: 5 they *s* to them, "Why do you
24:17 And He *s* to them, "What kind of
24:18 was Cleopas answered and *s* to
24:19 And He *s* to them, "What
24:19 So they *s* to Him, "The
24:23 seen a vision of angels who *s*
24:24 it just as the women had *s*;
24:25 Then He *s* to them, "O foolish
24:32 And they *s* to one another, "Did
24:36 Now as they *s* these things,
24:36 and *s* to them, "Peace to
24:38 And He *s* to them, "Why are you
24:40 When He had *s* this, He showed
24:41 He *s* to them, "Have you any
24:44 Then He *s* to them, "These are
24:46 Then He *s* to them, "Thus it is
Jn 1:15 "This was He of whom I *s*,
1:21 He *s*, "I am not."
1:22 Then they *s* to him, "Who are
1:23 He *s*: "I am 'The voice
1:23 as the prophet Isaiah *s*.
1:29 Jesus coming toward him, and *s*,
1:30 "This is He of whom I *s*,
1:33 me to baptize with water *s* to
1:36 at Jesus as He walked, he *s*,
1:38 *s* to them, "What do you
1:38 They *s* to Him, "Rabbi"
1:39 He *s* to them, "Come and see."
1:41 and *s* to him, "We have found
1:42 when Jesus looked at him, He *s*,
1:43 and He found Philip and *s* to
1:45 Philip found Nathanael and *s* to
1:46 And Nathanael *s* to him, "Can
1:46 Philip *s* to him, "Come and
1:47 and *s* of him, "Behold, an
1:48 Nathanael *s* to Him, "How do You
1:48 Jesus answered and *s* to him,
1:49 Nathanael answered and *s* to Him,
1:50 Jesus answered and *s* to him,
1:50 Because I *s* to you, 'I saw you
1:51 And He *s* to him, "Most
2: 3 the mother of Jesus *s* to Him,
2: 4 Jesus *s* to her, "Woman, what
2: 5 His mother *s* to the servants,
2: 7 Jesus *s* to them, "Fill the
2: 8 And He *s* to them, "Draw some
2:10 And he *s* to him, "Every man at
2:16 And He *s* to those who sold
2:18 So the Jews answered and *s* to
2:19 Jesus answered and *s* to them,
2:20 Then the Jews *s*, "It has
2:22 remembered that He had *s* this
2:22 and the word which Jesus had *s*.
3: 2 came to Jesus by night and *s*
3: 3 Jesus answered and *s* to him,
3: 4 Nicodemus *s* to Him, "How can a
3: 7 Do not marvel that I *s* to you,
3: 9 Nicodemus answered and *s* to Him,
3:10 Jesus answered and *s* to him,
3:26 And they came to John and *s* to
3:27 John answered and *s*,
3:28 bear me witness, that I *s*,
4: 7 Jesus *s* to her, "Give Me a
4: 9 Then the woman of Samaria *s* to
4:10 Jesus answered and *s* to her,
4:11 The woman *s* to Him, "Sir, You
4:13 Jesus answered and *s* to her,
4:15 The woman *s* to Him, "Sir, give
4:16 Jesus *s* to her, "Go, call your
4:17 The woman answered and *s*,
4:17 Jesus *s* to her, "You have
4:17 said to her, "You have well *s*,
4:19 The woman *s* to Him, "Sir, I
4:21 Jesus *s* to her, "Woman, believe
4:25 The woman *s* to Him, "I know
4:26 Jesus *s* to her, "I who speak to
4:27 with a woman; yet no one *s*,
4:28 the city, and *s* to the men,
4:32 But He *s* to them, "I have food
4:33 Therefore the disciples *s* to one
4:34 Jesus *s* to them, "My food is to
4:42 Then they *s* to the woman, "Now
4:42 not because of what you *s*,
4:48 Then Jesus *s* to him, "Unless
4:49 The nobleman *s* to Him, "Sir,
4:50 Jesus *s* to him, "Go your way;
4:52 And they *s* to him, "Yesterday
4:53 the same hour in which Jesus *s*
5: 6 He *s* to him, "Do you want to
5: 8 Jesus *s* to him, "Rise, take up
5:10 The Jews therefore *s* to him who
5:11 He who made me well *s* to me,
5:12 Who is the Man who *s* to you,
5:14 and *s* to him, "See, you have
5:18 but also *s* that God was His
5:19 Then Jesus answered and *s* to
6: 5 He *s* to Philip, "Where shall
6: 6 But this He *s* to test him, for
6: 8 Peter's brother, *s* to Him,
6:10 Then Jesus *s*, "Make the
6:12 He *s* to His disciples, "Gather
6:14 seen the sign that Jesus did, *s*,
6:20 But He *s* to them, "It is I;
6:25 they *s* to Him, "Rabbi, when
6:26 Jesus answered them and *s*,
6:28 Then they *s* to Him, "What shall
6:29 Jesus answered and *s* to them,
6:30 Therefore they *s* to Him, "What
6:32 Then Jesus *s* to them, "Most
6:34 Then they *s* to Him, "Lord, give
6:35 And Jesus *s* to them, "I am the
6:36 But I *s* to you that you have
6:41 about Him, because He *s*,
6:42 And they *s*, "Is not this
6:43 Jesus therefore answered and *s*
6:53 Then Jesus *s* to them, "Most
6:59 These things He *s* in the
6:60 when they heard this, *s*,
6:61 He *s* to them, "Does this
6:65 And He *s*, "Therefore I have
6:65 Therefore I have *s* to you that
6:67 Then Jesus *s* to the twelve, "Do
7: 3 His brothers therefore *s* to Him,
7: 6 Then Jesus *s* to them, "My time
7: 9 When He had *s* these things to
7:11 sought Him at the feast, and *s*,
7:12 Some *s*, "He is good";
7:12 others *s*, "No, on the
7:16 Jesus answered them and *s*,
7:20 The people answered and *s*,
7:21 Jesus answered and *s* to them,
7:25 some of them from Jerusalem *s*,
7:31 people believed in Him, and *s*,
7:33 Then Jesus *s* to them, "I shall
7:35 Then the Jews *s* among
7:36 "What is this thing that He *s*,
7:38 in Me, as the Scripture has *s*,
7:40 when they heard this saying, *s*,
7:41 Others *s*, "This is the
7:41 But some *s*, "Will the
7:42 Has not the Scripture *s* that the
7:45 who *s* to them, "Why have you
7:50 being one of them) *s* to them,
7:52 They answered and *s* to him,
8: 4 they *s* to Him, "Teacher, this
8: 6 This they *s*, testing Him,
8: 7 He raised Himself up and *s* to
8:10 He *s* to her, "Woman, where are
8:11 She *s*, "No one, Lord."
8:11 And Jesus *s* to her, "Neither
8:13 The Pharisees therefore *s* to
8:14 Jesus answered and *s* to them,
8:19 Then they *s* to Him, "Where is
8:21 Then Jesus *s* to them again, "I
8:22 So the Jews *s*, "Will He kill
8:23 And He *s* to them, "You are from
8:24 Therefore I *s* to you that you
8:25 Then they *s* to Him, "Who are
8:25 And Jesus *s* to them, "Just
8:28 Then Jesus *s* to them, "When you
8:31 Then Jesus *s* to those Jews who
8:39 They answered and *s* to Him,
8:39 Jesus *s* to them, "If you
8:41 Then they *s* to Him, "We were
8:42 Jesus *s* to them, "If God were
8:48 Then the Jews answered and *s* to
8:52 Then the Jews *s* to Him, "Now we
8:57 Then the Jews *s* to Him, "You
8:58 Jesus *s* to them, "Most
9: 6 When He had *s* these things, He
9: 7 And He *s* to him, "Go, wash in
9: 8 had seen that he was blind *s*,
9: 9 Some *s*, "This is he."
9: 9 said, "This is he." Others *s*,
9: 9 He *s*, "I am he."
9:10 Therefore they *s* to him, "How
9:11 He answered and *s*, "A Man
9:11 and anointed my eyes and *s* to
9:12 Then they *s* to him, "Where is
9:12 to him, "Where is He?" He *s*,
9:15 He *s* to them, "He put clay on
9:16 some of the Pharisees *s*,
9:16 Others *s*, "How can a man
9:17 They *s* to the blind man again,
9:17 He *s*, "He is a prophet."
9:20 His parents answered them and *s*,
9:22 His parents *s* these things
9:23 Therefore his parents *s*,
9:24 and *s* to him, "Give God the
9:25 He answered and *s*, "Whether
9:26 Then they *s* to him again, "What
9:28 Then they reviled him and *s*,
9:30 The man answered and *s* to them,
9:34 They answered and *s* to him,
9:35 He *s* to him, "Do you believe
9:36 He answered and *s*, "Who is
9:37 And Jesus *s* to him, "You have
9:38 Then he *s*, "Lord, I believe!"
9:39 And Jesus *s*, "For judgment
9:40 and *s* to Him, "Are we blind
9:41 Jesus *s* to them, "If you were
10: 7 Then Jesus *s* to them again,
10:20 And many of them *s*,
10:21 Others *s*, "These are not
10:24 the Jews surrounded Him and *s*
10:26 My sheep, as I *s* to you.
10:34 not written in your law, 'I *s*,
10:36 are blaspheming,' because I *s*,
10:41 Then many came to Him and *s*,
11: 4 When Jesus heard that, He *s*,
11: 7 Then after this He *s* to the
11: 8 The disciples *s* to Him,
11:11 These things He *s*, and after

11:11 and after that He *s* to them,
11:12 Then His disciples *s*,
11:14 Then Jesus *s* to them plainly,
11:16 *s* to his fellow disciples,
11:21 Then Martha *s* to Jesus, "Lord,
11:23 Jesus *s* to her, "Your brother
11:24 Martha *s* to Him, "I know that
11:25 Jesus *s* to her, "I am the
11:27 She *s* to Him, "Yes, Lord, I
11:28 And when she had *s* these
11:34 And He *s*, "Where have
11:34 They *s* to Him, "Lord, come
11:36 Then the Jews *s*, "See how
11:37 And some of them *s*,
11:39 Jesus *s*, "Take away the
11:39 *s* to Him, "Lord, by this time
11:40 Jesus *s* to her, "Did I not say
11:41 Jesus lifted up His eyes and *s*,
11:42 people who are standing by I *s*
11:43 Now when He had *s* these things,
11:44 Jesus *s* to them, "Loose him,
11:47 gathered a council and *s*,
11:49 *s* to them, "You know nothing
12: 4 son, who would betray Him, *s*,
12: 6 This he *s*, not that he
12: 7 But Jesus *s*, "Let her alone;
12:19 The Pharisees therefore *s* among
12:29 who stood by and heard it *s*
12:29 Others *s*, "An angel has
12:30 Jesus answered and *s*,
12:33 This He *s*, signifying by
12:35 Then Jesus *s* to them, "A little
12:39 because Isaiah *s* again:
12:41 These things Isaiah *s* when he
12:44 Then Jesus cried out and *s*,
13: 6 And Peter *s* to Him, "Lord,
13: 7 Jesus answered and *s* to him,
13: 8 Peter *s* to Him, "You shall
13: 9 Simon Peter *s* to Him, "Lord,
13:10 Jesus *s* to him, "He who is
13:11 therefore He *s*, "You are
13:12 He *s* to them, "Do you know
13:21 When Jesus had *s* these things,
13:21 in spirit, and testified and *s*,
13:25 he *s* to Him, "Lord, who is
13:27 Then Jesus *s* to him, "What you
13:28 knew for what reason He *s* this
13:29 that Jesus had *s* to him, "Buy
13:31 when he had gone out, Jesus *s*,
13:33 and as I *s* to the Jews, 'Where
13:36 Simon Peter *s* to Him, "Lord,
13:37 Peter *s* to Him, "Lord, why can
14: 5 Thomas *s* to Him, "Lord, we do
14: 6 Jesus *s* to him, "I am the way,
14: 8 Philip *s* to Him, "Lord, show us
14: 9 Jesus *s* to him, "Have I been
14:22 Judas (not Iscariot) *s* to Him,
14:23 Jesus answered and *s* to him,
14:26 all things that I *s* to you.
14:28 you would rejoice because I *s*,
15:20 Remember the word that I *s* to
16: 6 But because I have *s* these
16:15 Therefore I *s* that He will take
16:17 Then some of His disciples *s*
16:18 They *s* therefore, "What is this
16:19 and He *s* to them, "Are you
16:19 among yourselves about what I *s*,
16:29 His disciples *s* to Him, "See,
17: 1 up His eyes to heaven, and *s*:
18: 4 went forward and *s* to them,
18: 5 Jesus *s* to them, "I am
18: 6 Now when He *s* to them, "I am
18: 7 And they *s*, "Jesus of
18:11 So Jesus *s* to Peter, "Put your
18:17 girl who kept the door *s* to
18:17 are you?" He *s*, "I am
18:20 and in secret I have *s* nothing.
18:21 who have heard Me what I *s* to
18:21 Indeed they know what I *s*."
18:22 And when He had *s* these things,
18:25 Therefore they *s* to him, "You
18:25 He denied it and *s*, "I am
18:26 him whose ear Peter cut off, *s*,
18:29 then went out to them and *s*,
18:30 They answered and *s* to him, "If
18:31 Then Pilate *s* to them, "You
18:31 Therefore the Jews *s* to him,
18:33 and *s* to Him, "Are You the
18:37 Pilate therefore *s* to Him, "Are
18:38 Pilate *s* to Him, "What is
18:38 And when he had *s* this, he
18:38 and *s* to them, "I find no
19: 3 Then they *s*, "Hail, King
19: 4 and *s* to them, "Behold, I am
19: 5 And Pilate *s* to them, "Behold
19: 6 Pilate *s* to them, "You
19: 9 and *s* to Jesus, "Where are You
19:10 Then Pilate *s* to Him, "Are You
19:14 And he *s* to the Jews, "Behold
19:15 Pilate *s* to them, "Shall I
19:21 chief priests of the Jews *s* to
19:21 King of the Jews,' but, 'He *s*,
19:24 They *s* therefore among
19:26 He *s* to His mother, "Woman,
19:27 Then He *s* to the disciple,
19:28 Scripture might be fulfilled, *s*,
19:30 received the sour wine, He *s*,
20: 2 and *s* to them, "They have
20:13 Then they *s* to her, "Woman, why
20:13 She *s* to them, "Because they
20:14 Now when she had *s* this, she
20:15 Jesus *s* to her, "Woman, why are
20:15 *s* to Him, "Sir, if You have
20:16 Jesus *s* to her, "Mary!"
20:16 She turned and *s* to Him,
20:17 Jesus *s* to her, "Do not cling
20:19 and *s* to them, "Peace be with
20:20 When He had *s* this, He showed
20:21 So Jesus *s* to them again,
20:22 And when He had *s* this, He
20:22 and *s* to them, "Receive the
20:25 other disciples therefore *s* to
20:25 So he *s* to them, "Unless I
20:26 and stood in the midst, and *s*,
20:27 Then He *s* to Thomas, "Reach
20:28 And Thomas answered and *s* to
20:29 Jesus *s* to him, "Thomas,
21: 3 Simon Peter *s* to them, "I am
21: 3 They *s* to him, "We are going
21: 5 Then Jesus *s* to them,
21: 6 And He *s* to them, "Cast the net
21: 7 disciple whom Jesus loved *s* to
21:10 Jesus *s* to them, "Bring some of
21:12 Jesus *s* to them, "Come and eat
21:15 Jesus *s* to Simon Peter,
21:15 He *s* to Him, "Yes, Lord; You
21:15 He *s* to him, "Feed My
21:16 He *s* to him again a second time,
21:16 He *s* to Him, "Yes, Lord; You
21:16 He *s* to him, "Tend My
21:17 He *s* to him the third time,
21:17 Peter was grieved because He *s*
21:17 And he *s* to Him, "Lord, You
21:17 Jesus *s* to him, "Feed My
21:19 He *s* to him, "Follow Me."
21:20 His breast at the supper, and *s*,
21:21 *s* to Jesus, "But Lord, what
21:22 Jesus *s* to him, "If I will that
Acts 1: 4 the Father, "which," He *s*,
1: 7 And He *s* to them, "It is not
1:11 who also *s*, "Men of Galilee,
1:15 a hundred and twenty), and *s*,
1:24 And they prayed and *s*,
2:13 Others mocking *s*, "They are
2:14 raised his voice and *s* to them,
2:34 The LORD *s* to my Lord,
2:37 and *s* to Peter and the rest of
2:38 Then Peter *s* to them, "Repent,
3: 4 eyes on him, with John, Peter *s*,
3: 6 Then Peter *s*, "Silver and gold
3:22 For Moses truly *s* to the
4: 8 *s* to them, "Rulers of the
4:19 Peter and John answered and *s*
4:23 chief priests and elders had *s*
4:24 to God with one accord and *s*:
4:25 of Your servant David have *s*:
5: 3 But Peter *s*, "Ananias, why
5: 8 She *s*, "Yes, for so much."
5: 9 Then Peter *s* to her, "How is it
5:19 and brought them out, and *s*,
5:29 other apostles answered and *s*:
5:35 And he *s* to them: "Men of
6: 2 of the disciples and *s*,
6:13 set up false witnesses who *s*,
7: 1 Then the high priest *s*,
7: 2 And he *s*, "Brethren and
7: 3 and *s* to him, 'Get out of
7: 7 *s* God, 'and after that
7:33 Then the LORD *s* to him,
7:37 This is that Moses who *s* to the
7:56 and *s*, "Look! I see the
7:60 And when he had *s* this, he
8:20 But Peter *s* to him, "Your money
8:24 Then Simon answered and *s*,
8:29 Then the Spirit *s* to Philip,
8:30 the prophet Isaiah, and *s*,
8:31 And he *s*, "How can I, unless
8:34 eunuch answered Philip and *s*,
8:36 And the eunuch *s*, "See, here
8:37 Then Philip *s*, "If you
8:37 And he answered and *s*,
9: 5 And he *s*, "Who are You,
9: 5 Then the Lord *s*, "I am
9: 6 he, trembling and astonished, *s*,
9: 6 Then the Lord *s* to him,
9:10 and to him the Lord *s* in a
9:10 And he *s*, "Here I am,
9:11 So the Lord *s* to him, "Arise
9:15 But the Lord *s* to him, "Go, for
9:17 laying his hands on him he *s*,
9:21 who heard were amazed, and *s*,
9:34 And Peter *s* to him, "Aeneas,
9:40 And turning to the body he *s*,
10: 4 him, he was afraid, and *s*,
10: 4 So he *s* to him, "Your
10:14 But Peter *s*, "Not so, Lord!
10:19 the Spirit *s* to him, "Behold,
10:21 to him from Cornelius, and *s*,
10:22 And they *s*, "Cornelius the
10:28 Then he *s* to them, "You know
10:30 So Cornelius *s*, "Four days
10:31 'and *s*, 'Cornelius, your
10:34 Peter opened his mouth and *s*:
11: 8 'But I *s*, 'Not so, Lord!
11:13 who *s* to him, 'Send men to
11:16 the word of the Lord, how He *s*,
12: 8 Then the angel *s* to him, "Gird
12: 8 And he *s* to him, "Put on your
12:11 Peter had come to himself, he *s*,
12:15 But they *s* to her, "You are
12:15 so. So they *s*, "It is his
12:17 And he *s*, "Go, tell these
13: 2 and fasted, the Holy Spirit *s*,
13:10 and *s*, "O full of all deceit
13:16 and motioning with his hand *s*,
13:22 also He gave testimony and *s*,
13:25 was finishing his course, he *s*,
13:46 and Barnabas grew bold and *s*,
14:10 *s* with a loud voice, "Stand up
15: 7 Peter rose up and *s* to them:
15:36 Then after some days Paul *s* to
16:18 turned and *s* to the spirit, "I
16:20 them to the magistrates, and *s*,
16:30 And he brought them out and *s*,
16:31 So they *s*, "Believe on the
16:37 But Paul *s* to them, "They have
17:18 And some *s*, "What does this
17:18 Others *s*, "He seems to be
17:22 midst of the Areopagus and *s*,
17:28 some of your own poets have *s*,
17:32 some mocked, while others *s*,
18: 6 he shook his garments and *s* to
18:14 Gallio *s* to the Jews, "If it
19: 2 he *s* to them, "Did you receive
19: 2 So they *s* to him, "We have
19: 3 And he *s* to them, "Into what
19: 3 So they *s*, "Into John's
19: 4 Then Paul *s*, "John indeed
19:15 the evil spirit answered and *s*,
19:25 of similar occupation, and *s*:
19:35 had quieted the crowd, he *s*:
19:41 And when he had *s* these things,
20:10 on him, and embracing him *s*,
20:18 he *s* to them: "You know, from
20:35 of the Lord Jesus, that He *s*,
20:36 And when he had *s* these things,
21:11 his own hands and feet, and *s*,
21:20 And they *s* to him, "You see,
21:37 he *s* to the commander, "May I
21:39 But Paul *s*, "I am a Jew
22: 2 more silent. Then he *s*:
22: 8 And He *s* to me, 'I am Jesus of
22:10 'So I *s*, 'What shall I do,
22:10 And the Lord *s* to me, 'Arise
22:13 and he stood and *s* to me,
22:14 'Then he *s*, 'The God of
22:19 'So I *s*, 'Lord, they know
22:21 Then He *s* to me, 'Depart, for I
22:22 they raised their voices and *s*,
22:24 and *s* that he should be
22:25 Paul *s* to the centurion who
22:27 Then the commander came and *s* to
22:27 Roman?" He *s*, "Yes."
22:28 And Paul *s*, "But I was born
23: 1 earnestly at the council, *s*,
23: 3 Then Paul *s* to him, "God will
23: 4 And those who stood by *s*,
23: 5 Then Paul *s*, "I did not
23: 7 And when he had *s* this, a
23:11 the Lord stood by him and *s*,
23:14 chief priests and elders, and *s*,
23:17 of the centurions to him and *s*,
23:18 him to the commander and *s*,
23:20 And he *s*, "The Jews have
23:35 he *s*, "I will hear you
24:22 adjourned the proceedings and *s*,
25: 5 "Therefore," he *s*, "let those
25: 9 a favor, answered Paul and *s*,
25:10 So Paul *s*, "I stand at
25:22 Then Agrippa *s* to Festus, "I
25:22 'Tomorrow," he *s*, "you
25:24 And Festus *s*: "King Agrippa
26: 1 Then Agrippa *s* to Paul, "You
26:15 'So I *s*, 'Who are You,
26:15 And He *s*, 'I am Jesus,
26:22 which the prophets and Moses *s*
26:24 Festus *s* with a loud voice,
26:25 But he *s*, "I am not mad,
26:28 Then Agrippa *s* to Paul, "You
26:29 And Paul *s*, "I would to God
26:30 When he had *s* these things, the
26:32 Then Agrippa *s* to Festus, "This
27:21 in the midst of them and *s*,
27:31 Paul *s* to the centurion and the
27:35 And when he had *s* these things,
28: 4 they *s* to one another, "No
28: 6 they changed their minds and *s*
28:17 he *s* to them: "Men and
28:21 Then they *s* to him, "We neither
28:25 they departed after Paul had *s*
28:29 And when he had *s* these words,
Rom 7: 7 unless the law had *s*,
9:12 it was *s* to her, "The older
9:26 the place where it was *s*
9:29 And as Isaiah *s* before:
11:20 Well *s*. Because of unbelief
1 Cor 11:24 thanks, He broke it and *s*,
2 Cor 6:16 of the living God. As God has *s*:
7: 3 for I have *s* before that you
9: 3 in this respect, that, as I *s*,
12: 9 And He *s* to me, "My grace is
Gal 1: 9 As we have *s* before, so now I
2:14 I *s* to Peter before them all,
Titus 1:12 them, a prophet of their own, *s*,
Heb 1:13 of the angels has He ever *s*:
3:10 that generation, And *s*,
3:15 while it is *s*: "Today, if
4: 3 do enter that rest, as He has *s*:
4: 7 a long time, as it has been *s*:
5: 5 but it was He who *s* to Him:
7:21 He with an oath by Him who *s*
8: 5 make the tabernacle. For He *s*,
10: 5 He came into the world, He *s*:
10: 7 Then I *s*, 'Behold, I
10: 9 then He *s*, "Behold, I have
10:15 for after He had *s* before,

10:30 For we know Him who *s*,
11:18 of whom it was *s*,
12:21 was the sight that Moses *s*,
13: 5 He Himself has *s*, "I will
Jas 2:11 For He who *s*, "Do not
2:11 commit adultery," also *s*,
Jude 9 a reviling accusation, but *s*,
Rev 5: 5 But one of the elders *s* to me,
5:14 the four living creatures *s*,
6:11 and it was *s* to them that they
6:16 and *s* to the mountains and
7:14 And I *s* to him, "Sir, you
7:14 So he *s* to me, "These are
10: 8 heaven spoke to me again and *s*,
10: 9 So I went to the angel and *s* to
10: 9 And he *s* to me, "Take and
10:11 And he *s* to me, "You must
17: 7 But the angel *s* to me, "Why
17:15 Then he *s* to me, "The waters
19: 3 Again they *s*, "Alleluia!
19: 9 Then he *s* to me, "Write:
19: 9 of the Lamb!'" And he *s* to
19:10 But he *s* to me, "See that
21: 5 Then He who sat on the throne *s*,
21: 5 And He *s* to me, "Write, for
21: 6 And He *s* to me, "It is done!
22: 6 Then he *s* to me, "These words
22: 9 Then he *s* to me, "See that
22:10 And he *s* to me, "Do not seal

SAIL (14/14)

Ps 104:26 There the ships *s* about;
Isa 33:21 no galley with oars will *s*,
33:23 They could not spread the *s*.
Ezek 27: 7 was what you spread for your *s*;
Acts 13:13 when Paul and his party set *s*
20: 3 him as he was about to *s* to
20:16 For Paul had decided to *s* past
21: 1 departed from them and set *s*,
21: 2 we went aboard and set *s*.
27: 1 it was decided that we should *s*
27: 2 meaning to *s* along the coasts
27:12 the majority advised to set *s*
27:17 they struck *s* and so were
27:24 has granted you all those who *s*

SAILED (19/18)

1 Ki 22:48 for gold; but they never *s*,
Lk 8:23 But as they *s* He fell asleep.
8:26 Then they *s* to the country of
Acts 13: 4 and from there they *s* to
14:26 From there they *s* to Antioch,
15:39 so Barnabas took Mark and *s* to
18:18 leave of the brethren and *s*
18:21 And he *s* from Ephesus.
20: 6 But we *s* away from Philippi
20:13 we went ahead to the ship and *s*
20:15 We *s* from there, and the next
21: 3 *s* to Syria, and landed at Tyre;
27: 4 we *s* under the shelter of
27: 5 And when we had *s* over the sea
27: 7 When we had *s* slowly many days,
27: 7 we *s* under the shelter of
27:13 they *s* close by Crete.
27:21 and not have *s* from Crete and
28:11 After three months we *s* in an

SAILING (4/4)

Acts 16:11 *s* from Troas, we ran a straight
21: 2 And finding a ship *s* over to
27: 6 found an Alexandrian ship *s* to
27: 9 and *s* was now dangerous because

SAILORS (3/3)

Acts 27:27 about midnight the *s* sensed
27:30 And as the *s* were seeking to
Rev 18:17 all who travel by ship, *s*,

SAINT (2/2) SAINTS

Ps 106:16 And Aaron the *s* of the LORD,
Phil 4:21 Greet every *s* in Christ Jesus.

SAINTS (94/92) SAINT

Deut 33: 2 He came with ten thousands of *s*;
33: 3 All His *s* are in Your hand;
1 Sam 2: 9 will guard the feet of His *s*,
2 Chr 6:41 And let Your *s* rejoice in
Job 15:15 If God puts no trust in His *s*,
Ps 16: 3 As for the *s* who are on the
30: 4 You *s* of His, And give thanks
31:23 all you His *s*! For the LORD
34: 9 you His *s*! There is no want
37:28 And does not forsake His *s*;
50: 5 Gather My *s* together to Me,
52: 9 And in the presence of Your *s*
79: 2 The flesh of Your *s* to the
85: 8 To His people and to His *s*;
89: 5 also in the assembly of the *s*.
89: 7 feared in the assembly of the *s*,
97:10 preserves the souls of His *s*;
116:15 LORD Is the death of His *s*.
132: 9 And let Your *s* shout for joy.
132:16 And her *s* shall shout aloud
145:10 And Your *s* shall bless You.
148:14 The praise of all His *s*—
149: 1 His praise in the assembly of *s*.
149: 5 Let the *s* be joyful in glory;
149: 9 honor have all His *s*.
Prov 2: 8 And preserves the way of His *s*.
Dan 7:18 But the *s* of the Most High shall
7:21 was making war against the *s*,
7:22 was made in favor of the *s*
7:22 and the time came for the *s* to
7:25 Shall persecute the *s* of the
7:25 Then the *s* shall be given
7:27 the *s* of the Most High.
Zech 14: 5 And all the *s* with You.
Mt 27:52 and many bodies of the *s* who
Acts 9:13 harm he has done to Your *s* in
9:32 he also came down to the *s* who
9:41 and when he had called the *s*
26:10 and many of the *s* I shut up in
Rom 1: 7 of God, called to be *s*:
8:27 He makes intercession for the *s*
12:13 to the needs of the *s*,
15:25 Jerusalem to minister to the *s*.
15:26 for the poor among the *s* who
15:31 may be acceptable to the *s*,
16: 2 in a manner worthy of the *s*,
16:15 and all the *s* who are with
1 Cor 1: 2 Christ Jesus, called to be *s*,
6: 1 and not before the *s*?
6: 2 Do you not know that the *s* will
14:33 as in all the churches of the *s*.
16: 1 the collection for the *s*,
16:15 to the ministry of the *s*—
2 Cor 1: 1 with all the *s* who are in all
8: 4 of the ministering to the *s*.
9: 1 the ministering to the *s*,
9:12 supplies the needs of the *s*,
13:13 All the *s* greet you.
Eph 1: 1 To the *s* who are in Ephesus,
1:15 and your love for all the *s*,
1:18 of His inheritance in the *s*,
2:19 but fellow citizens with the *s*
3: 8 than the least of all the *s*,
3:18 to comprehend with all the *s*
4:12 for the equipping of the *s* for
5: 3 among you, as is fitting for *s*;
6:18 and supplication for all the *s*—
Phil 1: 1 To all the *s* in Christ Jesus
4:22 All the *s* greet you, but
Col 1: 2 To the *s* and faithful brethren
1: 4 and of your love for all the *s*;
1:12 of the inheritance of the *s* in
1:26 now has been revealed to His *s*.
1 Th 3:13 Jesus Christ with all His *s*.
2 Th 1:10 to be glorified in His *s* and to
Phm 1: 5 Lord Jesus and toward all the *s*,
1: 7 because the hearts of the *s*
Heb 6:10 you have ministered to the *s*,
13:24 rule over you, and all the *s*.
Jude 3 once for all delivered to the *s*.
14 with ten thousands of His *s*,
Rev 5: 8 which are the prayers of the *s*.
8: 3 with the prayers of all the *s*
8: 4 with the prayers of the *s*,
11:18 servants the prophets and the *s*,
13: 7 to him to make war with the *s*
13:10 patience and the faith of the *s*.
14:12 Here is the patience of the *s*;
15: 3 O King of the *s*!
16: 6 they have shed the blood of *s*
17: 6 drunk with the blood of the *s*
18:24 the blood of prophets and *s*,
19: 8 is the righteous acts of the *s*.
20: 9 surrounded the camp of the *s*

SAINTS' (1/1)

1 Tim 5:10 if she has washed the *s* feet,

SAKE (147/135) SAKES

Gen 3:17 is the ground for your *s*;
8:21 curse the ground for man's *s*,
12:13 may be well with me for your *s*,
12:16 He treated Abram well for her *s*.
18:29 I will not do it for the *s* of
18:31 will not destroy it for the *s*
18:32 will not destroy it for the *s*
26:24 for My servant Abraham's *s*.
30:27 LORD has blessed me for your *s*.
39: 5 Egyptian's house for Joseph's *s*;
Ex 18: 8 to the Egyptians for Israel's *s*,
21:26 let him go free for the *s* of
21:27 let him go free for the *s* of
Lev 26:45 But for their *s* I will remember
Num 11:29 him, "Are you zealous for my *s*?
1 Sam 12:22 people, for His great name's *s*,
23:10 to destroy the city for my *s*.
2 Sam 5:12 exalted His kingdom for the *s*
7:21 "For Your word's *s*,
9: 1 him kindness for Jonathan's *s*?
9: 7 for Jonathan your father's *s*,
18: 5 Deal gently for my *s* with the
1 Ki 8:41 far country for Your name's *s*
11:12 for the *s* of your father David;
11:13 tribe to your son for the *s* of
11:13 and for the *s* of Jerusalem
11:32 shall have one tribe for the *s*
11:32 and for the *s* of Jerusalem, the
11:34 the days of his life for the *s*
15: 4 Nevertheless for David's *s* the
2 Ki 8:19 for the *s* of his servant David,
19:34 to save it For My own *s* and
19:34 and for My servant David's *s*.
20: 6 defend this city for My own *s*,
20: 6 and for the *s* of My servant
1 Chr 14: 2 was highly exalted for the *s*
17:19 "O LORD, for Your servant's *s*,
2 Chr 6:32 from a far country for the *s*
Ps 6: 4 save me for Your mercies' *s*!
23: 3 righteousness For His name's *s*.
25: 7 me, For Your goodness' *s*,
25:11 For Your name's *s*,
31: 3 Therefore, for Your name's *s*,
31:16 Save me for Your mercies' *s*.
44:22 Yet for Your *s* we are killed
44:26 redeem us for Your mercies' *s*.
69: 7 Because for Your *s* I have borne
79: 9 For Your name's *s*!
106: 8 He saved them for His name's *s*,
106:45 And for their *s* He remembered
109:21 Deal with me for Your name's *s*;
122: 8 For the *s* of my brethren and
132:10 For Your servant David's *s*,
143:11 for Your name's *s*! For Your
143:11 For Your righteousness' *s*
Prov 3:29 he dwells by you for safety's *s*.
Eccl 8: 2 king's commandment for the *s*
Isa 37:35 to save it For My own *s* and
37:35 and for My servant David's *s*.
42:21 for His righteousness' *s*;
43:14 For your *s* I will send to
43:25 transgressions for My own *s*;
45: 4 For Jacob My servant's *s*,
48: 9 For My name's *s* I will defer My
48:11 For My own *s*, for My own
48:11 for My own *s*, I will do it;
54:15 you shall fall for your *s*.
62: 1 For Zion's *s* I will not hold My
62: 1 And for Jerusalem's *s* I will
63:17 Return for Your servants' *s*,
65: 8 will I do for My servants' *s*,
66: 5 cast you out for My name's *s*,
Jer 14: 7 us, Do it for Your name's *s*;
14:21 abhor us, for Your name's *s*;
15:15 Know that for Your *s* I have
Ezek 20: 9 "But I acted for My name's *s*,
20:14 "But I acted for My name's *s*,
20:22 hand and acted for My name's *s*,
20:44 dealt with you for My name's *s*,
28:17 your wisdom for the *s* of your
36:22 "I do not do this for your *s*,
36:22 but for My holy name's *s*,
36:32 Not for your *s* do I do this,"
Dan 9:17 and for the Lord's *s* cause Your
9:19 Do not delay for Your own *s*,
Mt 5:10 persecuted for righteousness' *s*,
5:11 against you falsely for My *s*.
10:18 governors and kings for My *s*,
10:22 be hated by all for My name's *s*.
10:39 he who loses his life for My *s*
14: 3 put him in prison for the *s*
16:25 loses his life for My *s* will
19:12 for the kingdom of heaven's *s*.
19:29 or lands, for My name's *s*,
24: 9 by all nations for My name's *s*.
24:22 but for the elect's *s* those
Mk 4:17 arises for the word's *s*,
6:17 bound him in prison for the *s*
8:35 loses his life for My *s* and
10:29 for My *s* and the gospel's,
13: 9 rulers and kings for My *s*,
13:13 be hated by all for My name's *s*.
13:20 be saved; but for the elect's *s*,
Lk 6:22 evil, For the Son of Man's *s*.
9:24 loses his life for My *s* will
18:29 for the *s* of the kingdom of
21:12 and rulers for My name's *s*.
21:17 be hated by all for My name's *s*.
Jn 12: 9 not for Jesus' *s* only, but that
12:30 because of Me, but for your *s*.
13:37 lay down my life for Your *s*.
13:38 you lay down your life for My *s*?
14:11 or else believe Me for the *s* of
15:21 will do to you for My name's *s*,
Acts 9:16 he must suffer for My name's *s*.
26: 7 to attain. For this hope's *s*,
Rom 4:23 it was not written for his *s*
8:36 For Your *s* we are killed
11:28 they are enemies for your *s*,
11:28 they are beloved for the *s*
13: 5 but also for conscience' *s*.
14:20 the work of God for the *s* of
1 Cor 4:10 We are fools for Christ's *s*,
9:23 this I do for the gospel's *s*,
10:25 no questions for conscience' *s*;
10:27 no question for conscience' *s*.
10:28 do not eat it for the *s* of
10:28 told you, and for conscience' *s*;
2 Cor 4: 5 your bondservants for Jesus' *s*.
4:11 delivered to death for Jesus' *s*,
7:12 I did not do it for the *s*
7:12 nor for the *s* of him who
12:10 in distresses, for Christ's *s*.
Phil 1:29 but also to suffer for His *s*,
Col 1:24 for the *s* of His body, which is
1 Th 1: 5 we were among you for your *s*.
3: 9 which we rejoice for your *s*
5:13 in love for their work's *s*.
1 Tim 5:23 wine for your stomach's *s* and
2 Tim 2:10 I endure all things for the *s*
Titus 1:11 for the *s* of dishonest gain.
Phm 1: 9 yet for love's *s* I rather
1 Pe 2:13 of man for the Lord's *s*,
3:14 suffer for righteousness' *s*,
1 Jn 2:12 forgiven you for His name's *s*.
3 Jn 7 went forth for His name's *s*,
Rev 2: 3 have labored for My name's *s*

SAKES (18/17) SAKE

Gen 18:26 spare all the place for their *s*.
Deut 1:37 also angry with me for your *s*,
4:21 was angry with me for your *s*,
Judg 21:22 'Be kind to them for our *s*,
Ruth 1:13 me very much for your *s* that
1 Chr 16:21 He rebuked kings for their *s*,
Ps 7: 7 For their *s*, therefore,
105:14 He rebuked kings for their *s*,
Dan 2:30 but for our *s* who make known
Mal 3:11 rebuke the devourer for your *s*,
Jn 11:15 And I am glad for your *s* that I
17:19 And for their *s* I sanctify
1 Cor 4: 6 myself and Apollos for your *s*,
9:10 He say it altogether for our *s*?
9:10 For our *s*, no doubt,
2 Cor 2:10 forgiven that one for your *s*
4:15 For all things are for your *s*,
8: 9 yet for your *s* He became poor,

SALAH (6/5)

Gen 10:24 Arphaxad begot *S*,
10:24 Salah, and *S* begot Eber.
11:12 thirty-five years, and begot *S*.
11:13 After he begot *S*, Arphaxad
11:14 *S* lived thirty years, and begot
11:15 *S* lived four hundred and three

SALAMIS (1/1)

Acts 13: 5 And when they arrived in *S*,

SALATHIEL (KJV) See SHEALTIEL

SALCAH (4/4)

Deut 3:10 as far as *S* and Edrei, cities
Josh 12: 5 over Mount Hermon, over *S*,
13:11 and all Bashan as far as *S*;
1 Chr 5:11 the land of Bashan as far as *S*:

SALCHAH (KJV) See SALCAH

SALE (3/3)

Lev 25:27 him count the years since its *s*,
Deut 18: 8 besides what comes from the *s*
28:68 you shall be offered for *s* to

SALEM (4/4) JERUSALEM

Gen 14:18 Then Melchizedek king of *S*
Ps 76: 2 In *S* also is His tabernacle,
Heb 7: 1 For this Melchizedek, king of *S*,
7: 2 and then also king of *S*,

SALIM (1/1)

Jn 3:23 was baptizing in Aenon near *S*,

SALIVA (3/3)

1 Sam 21:13 and let his *s* fall down on his
Job 7:19 me alone till I swallow my *s*?
Jn 9: 6 ground and made clay with the *s*;

SALLAI (2/2)

Neh 11: 8 and after him Gabbai and *S*,
12:20 of *S*, Kallai; of Amok,

SALLU (3/3)

1 Chr 9: 7 *S* the son of Meshullam, the son
Neh 11: 7 *S* the son of Meshullam, the son
12: 7 *S*, Amok, Hilkiah, and

SALMA (4/3)

1 Chr 2:11 Nahshon begot *S*,
2:11 Salma, and *S* begot Boaz;
2:51 *S* the father of Bethlehem, and
2:54 The sons of *S* were Bethlehem,

SALMAI (1/1)

Neh 7:48 sons of Hagaba, the sons of *S*,

SALMON (5/5)

Ruth 4:20 Nahshon, and Nahshon begot *S*;
4:21 *S* begot Boaz, and Boaz begot
Mt 1: 4 Nahshon, and Nahshon begot *S*.
1: 5 *S* begot Boaz by Rahab, Boaz
Lk 3:32 son of Boaz, the son of *S*,

SALMONE (1/1)

Acts 27: 7 the shelter of Crete off *S*.

SALOME (2/2)

Mk 15:40 the Less and of Joses, and *S*,
16: 1 and *S* bought spices, that they

SALT (42/36)

Gen 14: 3 (that is, the *S* Sea).
19:26 and she became a pillar of *s*.
Lev 2:13 you shall season with *s*;
2:13 you shall not allow the *s* of
2:13 offerings you shall offer *s*.
Num 18:19 it is a covenant of *s* forever
34: 3 to the end of the *S* Sea;
34:12 and it shall end at the *S* Sea.
Deut 3:17 Sea of the Arabah (the *S* Sea),
29:23 whole land is brimstone, *s*,
Josh 3:16 the *S* Sea, failed, and were
12: 3 Sea of the Arabah (the *S* Sea),
15: 2 at the shore of the *S* Sea,
15: 5 The east border was the *S* Sea
15:62 Nibshan, the City of *S*,
18:19 at the north bay at the *S* Sea,
Judg 9:45 the city and sowed it with *s*.
2 Sam 8:13 Syrians in the Valley of *S*.
2 Ki 2:20 new bowl, and put *s* in it."
2:21 and cast in the *s* there, and
14: 7 Edomites in the Valley of *S*,
1 Chr 18:12 Edomites in the Valley of *S*.
2 Chr 13: 5 his sons, by a covenant of *s*?
25:11 he went to the Valley of *S* and
Ezra 6: 9 of the God of heaven, wheat, *s*,
7:22 and *s* without prescribed limit.
Job 6: 6 food be eaten without *s*?
Ps 60: Edomites in the Valley of *S*.
Jer 17: 6 In a *s* land which is not
Ezek 16: 4 you were not rubbed with *s* nor
43:24 the priests shall throw *s* on
47:11 they will be given over to *s*.
Mt 5:13 You are the *s* of the earth;
5:13 but if the *s* loses its flavor,
Mk 9:49 will be seasoned with *s*.
9:50 *S* is good, but if the salt
9:50 but if the *s* loses its flavor,
9:50 Have *s* in yourselves, and have
Lk 14:34 *S* is good; but if the salt has
14:34 but if the *s* has lost its
Col 4: 6 be with grace, seasoned with *s*,
Jas 3:12 Thus no spring yields both *s*

SALTED (1/1)

Ex 30:35 perfumer, *s*, pure, and holy.

SALTPITS (1/1)

Zeph 2: 9 with weeds and *s*, And a

SALU (1/1)

Num 25:14 woman, was Zimri the son of *S*,

SALUTATION (3/3) SALUTE

1 Cor 16:21 The *s* with my own hand—Paul's.
Col 4:18 This *s* by my own hand—Paul.
2 Th 3:17 The *s* of Paul with my own hand,

SALUTATIONS (KJV) See GREETINGS

SALUTE (1/1) SALUTATION

Mk 15:18 and began to *s* Him, "Hail, King

SALUTED (KJV) See GREET, GREETED

SALVATION (162/156) SAVE

Gen 49:18 I have waited for your *s*,
Ex 14:13 and see the *s* of the LORD,
15: 2 song, And He has become my *s*;
Deut 32:15 esteemed the Rock of his *s*.
1 Sam 2: 1 Because I rejoice in Your *s*.
11:13 the LORD has accomplished *s*
2 Sam 22: 3 My shield and the horn of my *s*,
22:36 given me the shield of Your *s*;
22:47 The Rock of my *s*!
22:51 He is the tower of *s* to His
23: 5 For this is all my *s* and all
1 Chr 16:23 the good news of His *s* from
16:35 say, "Save us, O God of our *s*;
2 Chr 6:41 O LORD God, be clothed with *s*,
20:17 stand still and see the *s* of
Job 13:16 He also shall be my *s*,
Ps 3: 8 *S* belongs to the LORD
9:14 I will rejoice in Your *s*.
13: 5 heart shall rejoice in Your *s*.
14: 7 that the *s* of Israel would
18: 2 My shield and the horn of my *s*,
18:35 given me the shield of Your *s*;
18:46 my Rock! Let the God of my *s*
20: 5 We will rejoice in your *s*,
21: 1 And in Your *s* how greatly
21: 5 His glory is great in Your *s*;
24: 5 from the God of his *s*.
25: 5 For You are the God of my *s*;
27: 1 LORD is my light and my *s*;
27: 9 nor forsake me, O God of my *s*.
35: 3 to my soul, "I am your *s*.
35: 9 It shall rejoice in His *s*.
37:39 But the *s* of the righteous is
38:22 help me, O Lord, my *s*!
40:10 Your faithfulness and Your *s*;
40:16 Let such as love Your *s* say
50:23 aright I will show the *s* of
51:12 to me the joy of Your *s*,
51:14 O God, The God of my *s*,
53: 6 that the *s* of Israel would come
62: 1 for God; From Him comes my *s*.
62: 2 He only is my rock and my *s*;
62: 6 He only is my rock and my *s*;
62: 7 In God is my *s* and my glory;
65: 5 will answer us, O God of our *s*,
67: 2 Your *s* among all nations.
68:19 The God of our *s*! Selah
68:20 Our God is the God of *s*;
69:13 Hear me in the truth of Your *s*.
69:29 Let Your *s*, O God, set me up on
70: 4 And let those who love Your *s*
71:15 And Your *s* all the day,
74:12 Working *s* in the midst of the
78:22 And did not trust in His *s*.
79: 9 Help us, O God of our *s*,
85: 4 Restore us, O God of our *s*,
85: 7 LORD, And grant us Your *s*.
85: 9 Surely His *s* is near to those
88: 1 O LORD, God of my *s*,
89:26 My God, and the rock of my *s*.
91:16 satisfy him, And show him My *s*.
95: 1 joyfully to the Rock of our *s*.
96: 2 the good news of His *s* from
98: 2 The LORD has made known His *s*;
98: 3 of the earth have seen the *s*
106: 4 Oh, visit me with Your *s*,
116:13 I will take up the cup of *s*,
118:14 song, And He has become my *s*.
118:15 The voice of rejoicing and *s*
118:21 me, And have become my *s*.
119:41 Your *s* according to Your word.
119:81 My soul faints for Your *s*,
119:123 eyes fail from seeking Your *s*
119:155 *S* is far from the wicked, For
119:166 LORD, I hope for Your *s*,
119:174 I long for Your *s*,
132:16 also clothe her priests with *s*,
140: 7 the Lord, the strength of my *s*,
144:10 The One who gives *s* to kings,
149: 4 will beautify the humble with *s*.
Isa 12: 2 Behold, God is my *s*,
12: 2 He also has become my *s*.'
12: 3 draw water From the wells of *s*.
17:10 forgotten the God of your *s*,
25: 9 be glad and rejoice in His *s*.
26: 1 God will appoint *s* for walls
33: 2 Our *s* also in the time of
33: 6 times, And the strength of *s*;
45: 8 open, let them bring forth *s*,
45:17 LORD With an everlasting *s*;
46:13 My *s* shall not linger. And I
46:13 And I will place *s* in Zion,
49: 6 That You should be My *s* to the
49: 8 And in the day of *s* I have
51: 5 My *s* has gone forth, And My
51: 6 But My *s* will be forever, And
51: 8 And My *s* from generation to
52: 7 good things, Who proclaims *s*,
52:10 of the earth shall see The *s*
56: 1 For My *s* is about to come,
59:11 For *s*, but it is far from us.
59:16 His own arm brought *s* for Him;
59:17 And a helmet of *s* on His head;
60:18 you shall call your walls *S*,
61:10 me with the garments of *s*,
62: 1 And her *s* as a lamp that
62:11 Surely your *s* is coming;
63: 5 My own arm brought *s* for Me;
Jer 3:23 in vain is *s* hoped for from
3:23 in the LORD our God Is the *s*
Lam 3:26 and wait quietly For the *s* of
Jon 2: 9 *S* is of the LORD."
Mic 7: 7 will wait for the God of my *s*;
Hab 3: 8 horses, Your chariots of *s*?
3:13 You went forth for the *s* of
3:13 For *s* with Your Anointed.
3:18 I will joy in the God of my *s*.
Zech 9: 9 He is just and having *s*,
Lk 1:69 And has raised up a horn of *s*
1:77 To give knowledge of *s* to His
2:30 For my eyes have seen Your *s*
3: 6 flesh shall see the *s* of
19: 9 Today *s* has come to this house,
Jn 4:22 for *s* is of the Jews.
Acts 4:12 Nor is there *s* in any other, for
13:26 to you the word of this *s* has
13:47 you should be for *s* to
16:17 who proclaim to us the way of *s*.
28:28 it be known to you that the *s*
Rom 1:16 for it is the power of God to *s*
10:10 mouth confession is made unto *s*.
11:11 *s* has come to the Gentiles.
13:11 for now our *s* is nearer than
2 Cor 1: 6 is for your consolation and *s*,
1: 6 is for your consolation and *s*.
6: 2 And in the day of *s* I
6: 2 behold, now is the day of *s*.
7:10 repentance leading to *s*,
Eph 1:13 of truth, the gospel of your *s*;
6:17 And take the helmet of *s*,
Phil 1:28 of perdition, but to you of *s*,
2:12 work out your own *s* with fear
1 Th 5: 8 and as a helmet the hope of *s*.
5: 9 but to obtain *s* through our
2 Th 2:13 the beginning chose you for *s*
2 Tim 2:10 that they also may obtain the *s*
3:15 are able to make you wise for *s*
Titus 2:11 the grace of God that brings *s*
Heb 1:14 for those who will inherit *s*?
2: 3 if we neglect so great a *s*,
2:10 to make the captain of their *s*
5: 9 became the author of eternal *s*
6: 9 yes, things that accompany *s*,
9:28 time, apart from sin, for *s*.
1 Pe 1: 5 of God through faith for *s*
1: 9 the *s* of your souls.
1:10 Of this *s* the prophets have
2 Pe 3:15 longsuffering of our Lord is *s*—

Jude 3 to you concerning our common *s*,
Rev 7:10 *S* belongs to our God who sits
12:10 voice saying in heaven, "Now *s*,
19: 1 Alleluia! *S* and glory and honor

SALVE (1/1)

Rev 3:18 and anoint your eyes with eye *s*,

SAMARIA (123/115) SAMARITAN

1 Ki 13:32 which are in the cities of *S*,
16:24 And he bought the hill of *S* from
16:24 of the city which he built, *S*,
16:28 his fathers and was buried in *S*.
16:29 Omri reigned over Israel in *S*
16:32 Baal, which he had built in *S*.
18: 2 was a severe famine in *S*.
20: 1 And he went up and besieged *S*,
20:10 if enough dust is left of *S* for
20:17 Men are coming out of *S*!"
20:34 Damascus, as my father did in *S*.
20:43 and displeased, and came to *S*.
21: 1 to the palace of Ahab king of *S*.
21:18 king of Israel, who lives in *S*.
22:10 the entrance of the gate of *S*;
22:37 king died, and was brought to *S*.
22:37 And they buried the king in *S*.
22:38 the chariot at a pool in *S*,
22:51 became king over Israel in *S*
2 Ki 1: 2 lattice of his upper room in *S*,
1: 3 the messengers of the king of *S*,
2:25 and from there he returned to *S*.
3: 1 became king over Israel at *S*
3: 6 So King Jehoram went out of *S*
5: 3 with the prophet who is in *S*!
6:19 But he led them to *S*.
6:20 it was, when they had come to *S*,
6:20 there they were, inside *S*!
6:24 and went up and besieged *S*.
6:25 there was a great famine in *S*;
7: 1 for a shekel, at the gate of *S*.
7:18 this time in the gate of *S*.
10: 1 Now Ahab had seventy sons in *S*.
10: 1 wrote and sent letters to *S*,
10:12 and departed and went to *S*.
10:17 And when he came to *S*,
10:17 all who remained to Ahab in *S*,
10:35 and they buried him in *S*.
10:36 Jehu reigned over Israel in *S*
13: 1 became king over Israel in *S*,
13: 6 wooden image also remained in *S*.
13: 9 and they buried him in *S*.
13:10 became king over Israel in *S*,
13:13 And Joash was buried in *S* with
14:14 and hostages, and returned to *S*.
14:16 and was buried in *S* with the
14:23 of Israel, became king in *S*,
15: 8 reigned over Israel in *S* six
15:13 he reigned a full month in *S*.
15:14 went up from Tirzah, came to *S*,
15:14 Shallum the son of Jabesh in *S*
15:17 and reigned ten years in *S*.
15:23 became king over Israel in *S*,
15:25 against him and killed him in *S*,
15:27 became king over Israel in *S*,
17: 1 Elah became king of Israel in *S*,
17: 5 and went up to *S* and besieged
17: 6 the king of Assyria took *S* and
17:24 placed them in the cities of *S*
17:24 and they took possession of *S*
17:26 and placed in the cities of *S*
17:28 they had carried away from *S*
18: 9 of Assyria came up against *S*
18:10 king of Israel, *S* was taken.
18:34 have they delivered *S* from my
21:13 the measuring line of *S* and
23:18 of the prophet who came from *S*.
23:19 that were in the cities of *S*,
2 Chr 18: 2 went down to visit Ahab in *S*;
18: 9 the entrance of the gate of *S*;
22: 9 caught him (he was hiding in *S*)
25:13 the cities of Judah from *S* to
25:24 and hostages, and returned to *S*.
28: 8 and brought the spoil to *S*.
28: 9 before the army that came to *S*,
28:15 Then they returned to *S*.
Ezra 4:10 and settled in the cities of *S*
4:17 their companions who dwell in *S*,
Neh 4: 2 his brethren and the army of *S*,
Isa 7: 9 The head of Ephraim is *S*,
7: 9 And the head of *S* is
8: 4 of Damascus and the spoil of *S*
9: 9 and the inhabitant of *S*—
10: 9 Is not *S* like Damascus?
10:10 those of Jerusalem and *S*,
10:11 As I have done to *S* and her
36:19 have they delivered *S* from my
Jer 23:13 seen folly in the prophets of *S*:
31: 5 vines on the mountains of *S*;
41: 5 from Shiloh, and from *S*,
Ezek 16:46 "Your elder sister is *S*,
16:51 *S* did not commit half of your
16:53 and the captives of *S* and her
16:55 and *S* and her daughters return
23: 4 *S* is Oholah, and Jerusalem
23:33 The cup of your sister *S*.
Hos 7: 1 And the wickedness of *S*.
8: 5 O *S*! My anger is aroused
8: 6 But the calf of *S* shall be
10: 5 The inhabitants of *S* fear
10: 7 As for *S*, her king is cut
13:16 *S* is held guilty, For she has
Am 3: 9 on the mountains of *S*;
3:12 be taken out Who dwell in *S*—
4: 1 who are on the mountain of *S*,
6: 1 in Zion, And trust in Mount *S*,
8:14 who swear by the sin of *S*,
Ob 19 of Ephraim And the fields of *S*.
Mic 1: 1 which he saw concerning *S* and
1: 5 of Jacob? Is it not *S*?
1: 6 Therefore I will make *S* a heap
Lk 17:11 passed through the midst of *S*
Jn 4: 4 But He needed to go through *S*.
4: 5 So He came to a city of *S* which
4: 7 A woman of *S* came to draw water.
4: 9 Then the woman of *S* said to Him,
Acts 1: 8 and in all Judea and *S*,
8: 1 the regions of Judea and *S*,
8: 5 went down to the city of *S* and
8: 9 and astonished the people of *S*,
8:14 were at Jerusalem heard that *S*
9:31 and *S* had peace and were
15: 3 passed through Phoenicia and *S*,

SAMARITAN (4/4) SAMARIA, SAMARITANS

Lk 10:33 "But a certain *S*,
17:16 Him thanks. And he was a *S*.
Jn 4: 9 a drink from me, a *S* woman?"
8:48 say rightly that You are a *S*

SAMARITANS (7/7) SAMARITAN

2 Ki 17:29 on the high places which the *S*
Mt 10: 5 do not enter a city of the *S*.
Lk 9:52 they entered a village of the *S*,
Jn 4: 9 Jews have no dealings with *S*.
4:39 And many of the *S* of that city
4:40 So when the *S* had come to Him,
Acts 8:25 in many villages of the *S*.

SAME (237/226)

Gen 7:13 On the very *s* day Noah and
15:18 On the *s* day the LORD made a
17:23 foreskins that very *s* day,
17:26 That very *s* day Abraham was
21: 8 a great feast on the *s* day
25:30 Please feed me with that *s* red
26:12 and reaped in the *s* year a
26:24 appeared to him the *s* night
26:32 It came to pass the *s* day that
32:13 lodged there that *s* night,
44: 6 spoke to them these *s* words.
Ex 5: 6 So the *s* day Pharaoh commanded
6:26 These are the *s* Aaron and
6:27 These are the *s* Moses and
12: 6 fourteenth day of the *s* month.
12:17 for on this *s* day I will have
12:19 that *s* person shall be cut off
12:41 on that very *s* day—it came to
12:51 on that very *s* day, that the
19: 1 on the *s* day, they came to the
25:35 first two branches of the *s*,
25:35 second two branches of the *s*,
25:35 third two branches of the *s*,
26: 2 shall have the *s* measurements.
26: 8 all have the *s* measurements.
28: 8 shall be of the *s* workmanship,
36: 9 were all the *s* size.
36:15 curtains were the *s* size.
37:17 flowers were of the *s* piece.
37:21 first two branches of the *s*,
37:21 second two branches of the *s*,
37:21 third two branches of the *s*,
38:15 and the *s* for the other side of
39: 5 it was of the *s* workmanship,
Lev 7:15 shall be eaten the *s* day it is
7:16 it shall be eaten the *s* day
19: 6 It shall be eaten the *s* day you
22:28 her and her young on the *s* day.
22:30 On the *s* day it shall be eaten;
23: 6 fifteenth day of the *s* month
23:14 fresh grain until the *s* day
23:21 shall proclaim on the *s* day
23:28 shall do no work on that *s* day,
23:29 in soul on that *s* day
23:30 does any work on that *s* day,
24:22 You shall have the *s* law for the
Num 4: 8 and cover the *s* with a covering
6:11 sanctify his head that *s* day.
9:13 that *s* person shall be cut off
10:32 the *s* we will do to you."
11:17 upon you and will put the *s*
11:25 and placed the *s* upon the
Deut 9:20 for Aaron also at the *s* time.
22: 3 You shall do the *s* with his
27:11 the people on the *s* day,
31:22 wrote this song the *s* day,
32:48 spoke to Moses that very *s* day,
Josh 5:11 on the very *s* day.
6:15 seven times in the *s* manner.
Judg 6:25 Now it came to pass the *s* night
7: 4 the *s* shall go with you;
7: 4 the *s* shall not go."
7: 9 It happened on the *s* night that
8: 8 and spoke to them in the *s* way.
1 Sam 4:12 the battle line the *s* day,
6: 4 For the *s* plague was on all of
6:15 and made sacrifices the *s* day
6:16 returned to Ekron the *s* day.
17:23 spoke according to the *s* words.
17:30 another and said the *s* thing;
31: 6 men died together that *s* day.
1 Ki 3:17 and I dwell in the *s* house;
6:25 cherubim were of the *s* size
7:35 panels were of the *s* casting.
7:37 All of them were of the *s* mold,
8:64 On the *s* day the king
13: 3 And he gave a sign the *s* day,
13: 9 nor return by the *s* way you
2 Ki 19:29 year what springs from the *s*;
19:33 By the *s* shall he return;
25:17 The second pillar was the *s*,
2 Chr 28:16 At the *s* time King Ahaz sent to
32:12 Has not the *s* Hezekiah taken
32:30 This *s* Hezekiah also stopped the
35:16 LORD was prepared the *s* day,
Ezra 5: 3 At the *s* time Tattenai the
5:16 Then the *s* Sheshbazzar came and
10:23 Kelaiah (the *s* is Kelita),
Neh 4:22 At the *s* time I also said to the
6: 4 answered them in the *s* manner.
12:44 And at the *s* time some were
Job 4: 8 And sow trouble reap the *s*.
24:17 For the morning is the *s* to
31:15 Did not the *s* One fashion us
Ps 102:27 But You are the *s*,
Prov 28:24 The *s* is companion to a
Eccl 2:14 perceived That the *s* event
9:15 remembered that *s* poor man.
Isa 7:20 In the *s* day the Lord will
20: 2 at the *s* time the LORD spoke by
37:30 year what springs from the *s*;
37:34 By the *s* shall he return;
Jer 28: 1 And it happened in the *s* year,
28:17 the prophet died the *s* year in
31: 1 At the *s* time," says the LORD,
39:10 and fields at the *s* time.
41: 9 was the *s* one Asa the king had
52:22 with pomegranates was the *s*.
Ezek 1:16 all four had the *s* likeness.
3:18 that *s* wicked man shall die in
10:16 the *s* wheels also did not turn
10:22 of their faces was the *s* as
14:10 of the prophet shall be the *s*
21:19 shall go from the *s* land.
21:26 Nothing shall remain the *s*.
23:13 Both took the *s* way.
23:38 My sanctuary on the *s* day
23:39 on the *s* day they came into My
38:18 come to pass at the *s* time,
40: 1 on the very *s* day the hand of
40:10 the three were all the *s* size;
40:10 gateposts were of the *s* size
40:21 had the *s* measurements as the
40:22 had the *s* measurements as the
40:24 to these *s* measurements.
40:28 to these *s* measurements.
40:29 to these *s* measurements;
40:32 to these *s* measurements.
40:33 to these *s* measurements;
40:35 to these *s* measurements—
44: 3 and go out the *s* way."
45:11 shall be of the *s* measure,
46: 8 and go out the *s* way.
46:22 corners were the *s* size.
47:10 fish will be of the *s* kinds
48: 8 and in length the *s* as one of
Dan 4:36 At the *s* time my reason
5: 5 In the *s* hour the fingers of a
7:21 and the *s* horn was making war
11:27 speak lies at the *s* table;
Am 2: 7 father go in to the *s* girl,
Zeph 1: 9 In the *s* day I will punish All
Zech 6:10 and go the *s* day and enter the
Mt 5:46 the tax collectors do the *s*?
8:13 was healed that *s* hour.
13: 1 On the *s* day Jesus went out of
20:14 give to this last man the *s*
22:23 The *s* day the Sadducees, who
26:44 saying the *s* words.
27:44 reviled Him with the *s* thing.
Mk 4:24 With the *s* measure you use, it
4:35 On the *s* day, when evening had
10:10 again about the *s* matter.
14:39 and spoke the *s* words.
Lk 2: 8 Now there were in the *s* country
6:33 For even sinners do the *s*.
6:38 For with the *s* measure that you
7:47 the *s* loves little."
10: 7 And remain in the *s* house,
23:40 are under the *s* condemnation?
24:13 were traveling that *s* day
Jn 4:53 that it was at the *s* hour
10: 1 the *s* is a thief and a robber.
20:19 the *s* day at evening, being the
Acts 1:11 This *s* Jesus, who was taken up
11:17 God gave them the *s* gift
14:15 are men with the *s* nature
15:11 be saved in the *s* manner
15:27 also report the *s* things
16:33 And he took them the *s* hour of
18: 3 because he was of the *s* trade,
22:13 And at that *s* hour I looked up
Rom 1:32 not only do the *s* but also
2: 1 judge practice the *s* things.
2: 3 such things, and doing the *s*,
9:21 from the *s* lump to make one
10:12 for the *s* Lord over all is rich
12: 4 do not have the *s* function,
12:16 Be of the *s* mind toward one
13: 3 you will have praise from the *s*.
1 Cor 1:10 that you all speak the *s* thing,

1:10 joined together in the *s* mind
1:10 mind and in the *s* judgment.
7:20 one remain in the *s* calling
9: 8 not the law say the *s* also?
10: 3 all ate the *s* spiritual food,
10: 4 and all drank the *s* spiritual
11: 5 for that is one and the *s* as if
11:23 Lord Jesus on the *s* night
11:25 In the *s* manner He also took
12: 4 gifts, but the *s* Spirit.
12: 5 ministries, but the *s* Lord.
12: 6 but it is the *s* God who works
12: 8 knowledge through the *s* Spirit,
12: 9 faith by the *s* Spirit,
12: 9 of healings by the *s* Spirit,
12:11 But one and the *s* Spirit works
12:25 should have the *s* care
15:39 All flesh is not the *s* flesh,
2 Cor 1: 6 for enduring the *s* sufferings
3:14 For until this day the *s* veil
3:18 transformed into the *s* image
4:13 And since we have the *s* spirit
6:13 Now in return for the *s* (I speak
7: 8 perceive that the *s* epistle
8:16 who puts the *s* earnest care
12:18 not walk in the *s* spirit?
12:18 not walk in the *s* steps?
Eph 3: 6 of the *s* body, and partakers of
6: 8 he will receive the *s* from the
6: 9 do the *s* things to them, giving
Phil 1:30 having the *s* conflict which you
2: 2 having the *s* love, being of
2:18 For the *s* reason you also be
3: 1 For me to write the *s* things to
3:16 let us walk by the *s* rule, let
3:16 let us be of the *s* mind.
4: 2 Syntyche to be of the *s* mind
1 Th 2:14 also suffered the *s* things
1 Tim 3: 6 fall into the *s* condemnation
Heb 1:12 But You are the *s*,
2:14 likewise shared in the *s*,
4:11 according to the *s* example
6:11 one of you show the *s* diligence
10: 1 with these *s* sacrifices,
10:11 repeatedly the *s* sacrifices,
11: 9 with him of the *s* promise;
13: 8 Jesus Christ is the *s*
Jas 3:10 Out of the *s* mouth proceed
3:11 bitter from the *s* opening?
1 Pe 4: 1 also with the *s* mind,
4: 4 run with them in the *s* flood
5: 9 knowing that the *s* sufferings
2 Pe 3: 7 now preserved by the *s* word,
1 Jn 2:27 but as the *s* anointing teaches
Rev 11:13 In the *s* hour there was a great
18: 7 in the *s* measure give her

SAMGAR-NEBO (1/1)

Jer 39: 3 Middle Gate: Nergal-Sharezer, *S*,

SAMLAH (4/4)

Gen 36:36 *S* of Masrekah reigned in his
36:37 And when *S* died, Saul of
1 Chr 1:47 *S* of Masrekah reigned in his
1:48 And when *S* died, Saul of

SAMOS (1/1)

Acts 20:15 following day we arrived at *S*

SAMOTHRACE (1/1)

Acts 16:11 we ran a straight course to *S*,

SAMSON (36/35)

Judg 13:24 a son and called his name *S*;
14: 1 Now *S* went down to Timnah, and
14: 3 And *S* said to his father,
14: 5 So *S* went down to Timnah with
14: 7 and she pleased *S* well.
14:10 And *S* gave a feast there, for
14:12 Then *S* said to them, "Let me
15: 1 it happened that *S* visited his
15: 3 And *S* said to them, "This time
15: 4 Then *S* went and caught three
15: 6 And they answered, "*S*,
15: 7 *S* said to them, "Since you
15:10 "We have come up to arrest *S*,
15:11 the rock of Etam, and said to *S*,
15:12 Then *S* said to them, "Swear
15:16 Then *S* said: "With the
16: 1 Now *S* went to Gaza and saw a
16: 2 '*S* has come here!"
16: 3 And *S* lay low till midnight;
16: 6 So Delilah said to *S*,
16: 7 And *S* said to her, "If they
16: 9 *S*!" But he broke the
16:10 Then Delilah said to *S*,
16:12 are upon you, *S*!" And men
16:13 Delilah said to *S*,
16:14 are upon you, *S*!" But he
16:20 are upon you, *S*!" So he
16:23 has delivered into our hands *S*
16:25 that they said, "Call for *S*,
16:25 So they called for *S* from the
16:26 Then *S* said to the lad who held
16:27 on the roof watching while *S*
16:28 Then *S* called to the LORD,
16:29 And *S* took hold of the two
16:30 Then *S* said, "Let me die with
Heb 11:32 tell of Gideon and Barak and *S*

SAMSON'S (3/3)

Judg 14:15 day that they said to *S* wife,
14:16 Then *S* wife wept on him, and
14:20 And *S* wife was given to his

SAMUEL (143/122) SHEMUEL

1 Sam 1:20 a son, and called his name *S*,
2:18 But *S* ministered before the
2:21 Meanwhile the child *S* grew
2:26 And the child *S* grew in stature,
3: 1 Then the boy *S* ministered to the
3: 3 and while *S* was lying down,
3: 4 that the LORD called *S*.
3: 6 yet again, "*S*!" So Samuel
3: 6 yet again, "Samuel!" So *S* arose
3: 7 (Now *S* did not yet know the
3: 8 And the LORD called *S* again the
3: 9 Therefore Eli said to *S*,
3: 9 So *S* went and lay down in
3:10 *S*! Samuel!" And Samuel
3:10 Samuel! *S*!" And Samuel
3:10 Samuel! Samuel!" And *S*
3:11 Then the LORD said to *S*:
3:15 So *S* lay down until morning,
3:15 And *S* was afraid to tell Eli
3:16 Then Eli called *S* and said,
3:16 Eli called Samuel and said, "*S*,
3:18 Then *S* told him everything, and
3:19 So *S* grew, and the LORD was
3:20 Dan to Beersheba knew that *S*
3:21 LORD revealed Himself to *S* in
4: 1 And the word of *S* came to all
7: 3 Then *S* spoke to all the house of
7: 5 And *S* said, "Gather all Israel
7: 6 And *S* judged the children of
7: 8 children of Israel said to *S*,
7: 9 And *S* took a suckling lamb and
7: 9 Then *S* cried out to the LORD
7:10 Now as *S* was offering up the
7:12 Then *S* took a stone and set it
7:13 Philistines all the days of *S*.
7:15 And *S* judged Israel all the
8: 1 Now it came to pass when *S* was
8: 4 together and came to *S* at
8: 6 But the thing displeased *S* when
8: 6 So *S* prayed to the LORD.
8: 7 And the LORD said to *S*,
8:10 So *S* told all the words of the
8:19 refused to obey the voice of *S*;
8:21 And *S* heard all the words of the
8:22 So the LORD said to *S*,
8:22 And *S* said to the men of
9:14 into the city, there was *S*,
9:15 Now the LORD had told *S* in his
9:17 And when *S* saw Saul, the LORD
9:18 Then Saul drew near to *S* in the
9:19 And *S* answered Saul and said,
9:22 Now *S* took Saul and his servant
9:23 And *S* said to the cook, "Bring
9:24 And *S* said, "Here it is, what
9:24 So Saul ate with *S* that day.
9:25 *S* spoke with Saul on the top
9:26 the dawning of the day that *S*
9:26 of them went outside, he and *S*.
9:27 *S* said to Saul, "Tell the
10: 1 Then *S* took a flask of oil and
10: 9 turned his back to go from *S*,
10:14 to be found, we went to *S*.
10:15 what *S* said to you."
10:16 he did not tell him what *S* had
10:17 Then *S* called the people
10:20 And when *S* had caused all the
10:24 And *S* said to all the people,
10:25 Then *S* explained to the people
10:25 And *S* sent all the people away,
11: 7 not go out with Saul and *S* to
11:12 Then the people said to *S*,
11:14 Then *S* said to the people,
12: 1 Now *S* said to all Israel:
12: 6 Then *S* said to the people,
12:11 Bedan, Jephthah, and *S*,
12:18 So *S* called to the LORD, and
12:18 greatly feared the LORD and *S*.
12:19 And all the people said to *S*,
12:20 Then *S* said to the people, "Do
13: 8 according to the time set by *S*.
13: 8 But *S* did not come to Gilgal;
13:10 that *S* came; and Saul went out
13:11 And *S* said, "What have you
13:13 And *S* said to Saul, "You have
13:15 Then *S* arose and went up from
15: 1 *S* also said to Saul, "The LORD
15:10 the word of the LORD came to *S*,
15:11 And it grieved *S*, and he
15:12 So when *S* rose early in the
15:12 to meet Saul, it was told *S*,
15:13 Then *S* went to Saul, and Saul
15:14 But *S* said, "What then is this
15:16 Then *S* said to Saul, "Be quiet!
15:17 So *S* said, "When you were
15:20 And Saul said to *S*,
15:22 Then *S* said: "Has the LORD
15:24 Then Saul said to *S*,
15:26 But *S* said to Saul, "I will not
15:27 And as *S* turned around to go
15:28 So *S* said to him, "The LORD
15:31 So *S* turned back after Saul, and
15:32 Then *S* said, "Bring Agag king
15:33 But *S* said, "As your sword has
15:33 And *S* hacked Agag in pieces
15:34 Then *S* went to Ramah, and Saul
15:35 And *S* went no more to see Saul
15:35 Nevertheless *S* mourned for
16: 1 Now the LORD said to *S*,
16: 2 And *S* said, "How can I go?
16: 4 So *S* did what the LORD said,
16: 7 But the LORD said to *S*,
16: 8 and made him pass before *S*.
16:10 seven of his sons pass before *S*.
16:10 And *S* said to Jesse, "The
16:11 And *S* said to Jesse, "Are all
16:11 And *S* said to Jesse, "Send
16:13 Then *S* took the horn of oil and
16:13 So *S* arose and went to Ramah.
19:18 and went to *S* at Ramah, and
19:18 And he and *S* went and stayed in
19:20 and *S* standing as leader over
19:22 'Where are *S* and David?"
19:24 and prophesied before *S* in
25: 1 Then *S* died; and the Israelites
28: 3 Now *S* had died, and all Israel
28:11 Bring up *S* for me."
28:12 When the woman saw *S*,
28:14 Saul perceived that it was *S*,
28:15 Now *S* said to Saul, "Why have
28:16 Then *S* said: "Why then do you
28:20 because of the words of *S*.
1 Chr 6:28 The sons of *S* were Joel the
6:33 the son of Joel, the son of *S*,
9:22 David and *S* the seer had
11: 3 to the word of the LORD by *S*.
26:28 And all that *S* the seer, Saul
29:29 are written in the book of *S*
2 Chr 35:18 like that since the days of *S*
Ps 99: 6 And *S* was among those who
Jer 15: 1 Even if Moses and *S* stood
Acts 3:24 from *S* and those who follow, as
13:20 until *S* the prophet.
Heb 11:32 also of David and *S* and the

SANBALLAT (10/10)

Neh 2:10 When *S* the Horonite and Tobiah
2:19 But when *S* the Horonite, Tobiah
4: 1 when *S* heard that we were
4: 7 Now it happened, when *S*,
6: 1 Now it happened when *S*,
6: 2 that *S* and Geshem sent to me,
6: 5 Then *S* sent his servant to me as
6:12 me because Tobiah and *S* had
6:14 My God, remember Tobiah and *S*,
13:28 was a son-in-law of *S* the

SANCTIFICATION (5/5) SANCTIFY

1 Cor 1:30 and righteousness and *s* and
1 Th 4: 3 this is the will of God, your *s*:
4: 4 to possess his own vessel in *s*
2 Th 2:13 you for salvation through *s* by
1 Pe 1: 2 in *s* of the Spirit, for

SANCTIFIED (38/37) SANCTIFY

Gen 2: 3 blessed the seventh day and *s*
Ex 19:14 mountain to the people and *s*
29:43 the tabernacle shall be *s* by
Num 3:13 I *s* to Myself all the firstborn
8:17 in the land of Egypt I *s* them
1 Sam 21: 5 even though it was *s* in the
1 Chr 15:14 the priests and the Levites *s*
2 Chr 5:11 priests who were present had *s*
7:16 For now I have chosen and *s* this
7:20 and this house which I have *s*
29:15 *s* themselves, and went
29:17 Then they *s* the house of the
29:19 we have prepared and *s*;
29:34 until the other priests had *s*
30: 8 which He has *s* forever, and
30:15 and *s* themselves, and brought
30:17 in the assembly who had not *s*
30:24 and a great number of priests *s*
31:18 in their faithfulness they *s*
Isa 13: 3 I have commanded My *s* ones;
Jer 1: 5 Before you were born I *s* you;
Ezek 48:11 of the sons of Zadok, who are *s*,
Jn 10:36 say of Him whom the Father *s*
17:19 that they also may be *s* by the
Acts 20:32 among all those who are *s*.
26:18 among those who are *s* by faith
Rom 15:16 *s* by the Holy Spirit.
1 Cor 1: 2 to those who are *s* in Christ
6:11 you were washed, but you were *s*,
7:14 the unbelieving husband is *s*
7:14 and the unbelieving wife is *s*
1 Tim 4: 5 for it is *s* by the word of God
2 Tim 2:21 *s* and useful for the Master,
Heb 2:11 and those who are being *s* are
10:10 By that will we have been *s*
10:14 forever those who are being *s*.
10:29 the covenant by which he was *s*
Jude 1 *s* by God the Father, and

SANCTIFIES (8/8) SANCTIFY

Ex 31:13 that I am the LORD who *s* you.
Lev 20: 8 I am the LORD who *s* you.
22:32 I am the LORD who *s* you,
Ezek 20:12 know that I am the LORD who *s*
Mt 23:17 the gold or the temple that *s*
23:19 the gift or the altar that *s*

Heb 2:11 For both He who *s* and those who
9:13 *s* for the purifying of the

SANCTIFY (36/34) SANCTIFICATION, SANCTIFIED, SANCTIFIES

Ex 28:41 and *s* them, that they may
29:33 to consecrate and to *s* them;
29:36 and you shall anoint it to *s*
29:37 atonement for the altar and *s*
Lev 21: 8 who *s* you, am holy.
21:15 for I the LORD *s* him.'"
21:23 for I the LORD *s* them.'"
22: 9 I the LORD *s* them.
22:16 for I the LORD *s* them.'"
Num 6:11 and he shall *s* his head that
Deut 15:19 and your flock you shall *s* to
Josh 3: 5 *S* yourselves, for tomorrow the
7:13 *s* the people, and say,
7:13 *S* yourselves for tomorrow,
1 Sam 16: 5 *S* yourselves, and come with me
1 Chr 15:12 *s* yourselves, you and your
23:13 that he should *s* the most holy
2 Chr 29: 5 Now *s* yourselves, sanctify
29: 5 *s* the house of the LORD God of
29:17 Now they began to *s* on the first
30:17 to *s* them to the LORD.
Neh 13:22 to *s* the Sabbath day.
Job 1: 5 that Job would send and *s* them,
Isa 66:17 Those who *s* themselves and
Ezek 36:23 And I will *s* My great name,
37:28 *s* Israel, when My sanctuary is
38:23 I will magnify Myself and *s*
44:19 holy garments they shall not *s*
46:20 out into the outer court to *s*
Joel 2:16 *S* the congregation, Assemble
Jn 17:17 *S* them by Your truth. Your word
17:19 And for their sakes I *s* Myself,
Eph 5:26 that He might *s* and cleanse her
1 Th 5:23 may the God of peace Himself *s*
Heb 13:12 that He might *s* the people with
1 Pe 3:15 But *s* the Lord God in your

SANCTIFYING (1/1)

2 Chr 29:34 Levites were more diligent in *s*

SANCTUARIES (7/7)

Lev 21:23 a defect, lest he profane My *s*;
26:31 cities waste and bring your *s*
1 Ki 6:29 both the inner and outer *s*,
6:30 both the inner and outer *s*.
Jer 51:51 strangers have come into the *s*
Ezek 28:18 You defiled your *s* By the
Am 7: 9 And the *s* of Israel shall be

SANCTUARY (158/153)

Ex 15:17 For Your own dwelling, The *s*,
25: 8 "And let them make Me a *s*,
30:13 to the shekel of the *s* (a
30:24 to the shekel of the *s*,
36: 1 work for the service of the *s*,
36: 3 of the service of making the *s*.
36: 4 doing all the work of the *s*
36: 6 work for the offering of the *s*.
38:24 to the shekel of the *s*.
38:25 to the shekel of the *s*:
38:26 to the shekel of the *s*),
38:27 were cast the sockets of the *s*
Lev 4: 6 in front of the veil of the *s*.
5:15 to the shekel of the *s*,
10: 4 brethren from before the *s* out
12: 4 nor come into the *s* until the
16:33 make atonement for the Holy *S*,
19:30 My Sabbaths and reverence My *s*:
20: 3 to defile My *s* and profane My
21:12 'nor shall he go out of the *s*,
21:12 nor profane the *s* of his God;
26: 2 My Sabbaths and reverence My *s*:
27: 3 to the shekel of the *s*.
27:25 to the shekel of the *s*:
Num 3:28 hundred keeping charge of the *s*.
3:31 the utensils of the *s* with
3:32 those who kept charge of the *s*.
3:38 sons, keeping charge of the *s*,
3:47 currency of the shekel of the *s*,
3:50 to the shekel of the *s*.
4:12 which they minister in the *s*,
4:15 have finished covering the *s*
4:15 all the furnishings of the *s*,
4:16 with the *s* and its
7:13 to the shekel of the *s*,
7:19 to the shekel of the *s*,
7:25 to the shekel of the *s*,
7:31 to the shekel of the *s*,
7:37 to the shekel of the *s*,
7:43 to the shekel of the *s*,
7:49 to the shekel of the *s*,
7:55 to the shekel of the *s*,
7:61 to the shekel of the *s*,
7:67 to the shekel of the *s*,
7:73 to the shekel of the *s*,
7:79 to the shekel of the *s*,
7:85 to the shekel of the *s*,
7:86 to the shekel of the *s*;
8:19 of Israel come near the *s*.
18: 1 the iniquity related to the *s*,
18: 3 near the articles of the *s* and
18: 5 attend to the duties of the *s*
18:16 to the shekel of the *s*,
19:20 because he has defiled the *s* of
Josh 24:26 the oak that was by the *s* of
1 Ki 6: 3 vestibule in front of the *s* of
6: 5 all around the *s* and the inner
6: 5 the sanctuary and the inner *s*.
6:16 built it inside as the inner *s*,
6:17 And in front of it the temple *s*
6:19 And he prepared the inner *s*
6:20 The inner *s* was twenty cubits
6:21 across the front of the inner *s*,
6:22 altar that was by the inner *s*.
6:23 Inside the inner *s* he made two
6:31 the entrance of the inner *s* he
6:33 So for the door of the *s* he also
7:49 left in front of the inner *s*,
8: 6 into the inner *s* of the temple,
8: 8 place, in front of the inner *s*;
1 Chr 9:29 all the implements of the *s*,
22:19 arise and build the *s* of the
24: 5 there were officials of the *s*
28:10 you to build a house for the *s*;
2 Chr 3: 4 that was in front of the *s*
3:16 of chainwork, as in the inner *s*,
4:20 manner in front of the inner *s*,
4:22 As for the entry of the *s*,
5: 7 into the inner *s* of the temple,
5: 9 in front of the inner *s*;
20: 8 and have built You a *s* in it
26:18 Get out of the *s*, for you have
29:21 for the kingdom, for the *s*,
30: 8 to the LORD; and enter His *s*,
30:19 to the purification of the *s*.
36:17 sword in the house of their *s*,
Neh 10:39 where the articles of the *s*
Ps 20: 2 He send you help from the *s*,
28: 2 up my hands toward Your holy *s*.
63: 2 I have looked for You in the *s*,
68:24 of my God, my King, into the *s*.
73:17 Until I went into the *s* of God;
74: 3 has damaged everything in the *s*.
74: 7 They have set fire to Your *s*;
77:13 Your way, O God, is in the *s*;
78:69 And He built His *s* like the
96: 6 and beauty are in His *s*.
102:19 down from the height of His *s*;
114: 2 Judah became His *s*,
134: 2 Lift up your hands in the *s*,
150: 1 the LORD! Praise God in His *s*;
Isa 8:14 He will be as a *s*,
16:12 That he will come to his *s* to
43:28 profane the princes of the *s*;
60:13 To beautify the place of My *s*;
63:18 have trodden down Your *s*.
Jer 17:12 Is the place of our *s*.
Lam 1:10 seen the nations enter her *s*,
2: 7 altar, He has abandoned His *s*;
2:20 and prophet be slain In the *s*
4: 1 The stones of the *s* are
Ezek 5:11 because you have defiled My *s*
8: 6 make Me go far away from My *s*?
9: 6 is the mark; and begin at My *s*.
11:16 yet I shall be a little *s* for
23:38 They have defiled My *s* on the
23:39 same day they came into My *s*
24:21 'Behold, I will profane My *s*,
25: 3 against My *s* when it was
37:26 and I will set My *s* in their
37:28 when My *s* is in their midst
41: 1 Then he brought me into the *s*
41: 4 twenty cubits, beyond the *s*,
41:20 door, and on the wall of the *s*,
41:21 as was the front of the *s*;
41:23 The temple and the *s* had two
43:21 of the temple, outside the *s*.
44: 1 back to the outer gate of the *s*
44: 5 and all who go out from the *s*.
44: 7 to be in My *s* to defile it—My
44: 8 others to keep charge of My *s*
44: 9 in flesh, shall enter My *s*,
44:11 they shall be ministers in My *s*,
44:15 who kept charge of My *s* when
44:16 "They shall enter My *s*,
44:27 the day that he goes to the *s*
44:27 sanctuary to minister in the *s*,
45: 2 be a square plot for the *s*,
45: 3 in it shall be the *s*,
45: 4 priests, the ministers of the *s*,
45: 4 and a holy place for the *s*.
45:18 blemish and cleanse the *s*.
47:12 their water flows from the *s*.
48: 8 with the *s* in the center.
48:10 The *s* of the LORD shall be in
48:21 and the *s* of the temple shall
Dan 8:11 and the place of His *s* was cast
8:13 the giving of both the *s* and
8:14 then the *s* shall be cleansed."
9:17 Your face to shine on Your *s*,
9:26 destroy the city and the *s*.
11:31 and they shall defile the *s*
Am 7:13 For it is the king's *s*,
Zeph 3: 4 priests have polluted the *s*,
Heb 8: 2 a Minister of the *s* and of the
9: 1 service and the earthly *s*.
9: 2 which is called the *s*;
13:11 blood is brought into the *s* by

SAND (31/29) SANDS

Gen 22:17 of the heaven and as the *s*
32:12 make your descendants as the *s*
41:49 as the *s* of the sea, until he
Ex 2:12 Egyptian and hid him in the *s*.
Lev 11:30 the *s* reptile, the sand lizard,
11:30 the *s* lizard, and the
Deut 33:19 of treasures hidden in the *s*.
Josh 11: 4 as many people as the *s* that
Judg 7:12 as the *s* by the seashore in
1 Sam 13: 5 and people as the *s* which is
2 Sam 17:11 like the *s* that is by the sea
1 Ki 4:20 were as numerous as the *s* by
4:29 largeness of heart like the *s*
Job 6: 3 it would be heavier than the *s*
29:18 And multiply my days as the *s*.
Ps 78:27 Feathered fowl like the *s* of
139:18 be more in number than the *s*;
Prov 27: 3 A stone is heavy and *s* is
Isa 10:22 be as the *s* of the sea, A
48:19 also would have been like the *s*,
48:19 your body like the grains of *s*;
Jer 5:22 Who have placed the *s* as the
15: 8 to Me more than the *s* of the
33:22 nor the *s* of the sea measured,
Hos 1:10 of Israel Shall be as the *s*
Hab 1: 9 They gather captives like *s*.
Mt 7:26 who built his house on the *s*:
Rom 9:27 of Israel be as the *s*
Heb 11:12 innumerable as the *s* which is by
Rev 13: 1 Then I stood on the *s* of the
20: 8 whose number is as the *s* of

SANDAL (10/10) SANDALS

Gen 14:23 from a thread to a *s* strap, and
Deut 25: 9 remove his *s* from his foot,
25:10 'The house of him who had his *s*
Josh 5:15 Take your *s* off your foot, for
Ruth 4: 7 one man took off his *s* and gave
4: 8 So he took off his *s*.
Isa 9: 5 For every warrior's *s* from the
Mk 1: 7 whose *s* strap I am not worthy
Lk 3:16 whose *s* strap I am not worthy
Jn 1:27 whose *s* strap I am not worthy

SANDALS (25/25) SANDAL

Ex 3: 5 Take your *s* off your feet, for
12:11 your *s* on your feet, and your
Deut 29: 5 and your *s* have not worn out on
33:25 Your *s* shall be iron and
Josh 9: 5 old and patched *s* on their feet,
9:13 these our garments and our *s*
1 Ki 2: 5 and on his *s* that were on his
2 Chr 28:15 dressed them and gave them *s*,
Song 7: 1 beautiful are your feet in *s*,
Isa 5:27 Nor the strap of their *s* be
20: 2 and take your *s* off your
Ezek 16:10 cloth and gave you *s* of badger
24:17 and put your *s* on your feet;
24:23 be on your heads and your *s* on
Am 2: 6 And the poor for a pair of *s*.
8: 6 And the needy for a pair of *s*—
Mt 3:11 whose *s* I am not worthy to
10:10 journey, nor two tunics, nor *s*,
Mk 6: 9 but to wear *s*, and not to
Lk 10: 4 money bag, knapsack, nor *s*;
15:22 put a ring on his hand and *s*
22:35 money bag, knapsack, and *s*,
Acts 7:33 Take your *s* off your feet,
12: 8 yourself and tie on your *s*";
13:25 the *s* of whose feet I am not

SANDS (1/1)

Acts 27:17 run aground on the Syrtis *S*,

SANG (15/15) SING

Ex 15: 1 and the children of Israel *s*
Num 21:17 Then Israel *s* this song:
Judg 5: 1 and Barak the son of Abinoam *s*
1 Sam 18: 7 So the women *s* as they danced,
29: 5 of whom they *s* to one another
2 Sam 3:33 And the king *s* a lament over
2 Chr 29:28 worshiped, the singers *s*,
29:30 So they *s* praises with
Ezra 3:11 And they *s* responsively,
Neh 12:42 The singers *s* loudly with
Job 38: 7 When the morning stars *s*
Ps 7: which he *s* to the LORD
106:12 They *s* His praise.
Rev 5: 9 And they *s* a new song, saying:
14: 3 They *s* as it were a new song

SANK (9/7) SINK

Ex 15: 5 They *s* to the bottom like a
15:10 They *s* like lead in the mighty
Num 21:18 The well the leaders *s*,
Judg 5:27 At her feet he *s*,
5:27 he lay still; At her feet he *s*,
5:27 he sank, he fell; Where he *s*,
1 Sam 17:49 so that the stone *s* into his
2 Ki 9:24 and he *s* down in his chariot.
Jer 38: 6 So Jeremiah *s* in the mire.

SANSANNAH (1/1)

Josh 15:31 Ziklag, Madmannah, *S*,

SAP (2/2)

Ps 104:16 of the LORD are full of *s*,
Am 3:11 He shall *s* your strength from

SAPH (1/1)
2 Sam 21:18 the Hushathite killed *S*,

SAPHIR (KJV) See SHAPHIR

SAPPHIRA (1/1)
Acts 5: 1 with *S* his wife, sold a

SAPPHIRE (9/9)
Ex 24:10 as it were a paved work of *s*
28:18 row shall be a turquoise, a *s*,
39:11 second row, a turquoise, a *s*,
Job 28:16 Ophir, In precious onyx or *s*.
Lam 4: 7 Like *s* in their appearance.
Ezek 1:26 in appearance like a *s* stone;
10: 1 appeared something like a *s*
28:13 Beryl, onyx, and jasper, *S*,
Rev 21:19 was jasper, the second *s*,

SAPPHIRES (3/3)
Job 28: 6 stones are the source of *s*,
Song 5:14 carved ivory Inlaid with *s*.
Isa 54:11 lay your foundations with *s*.

SARAH (39/33) SARAI
Gen 17:15 but *S* shall be her name.
17:17 shall *S*, who is ninety years
17:19 *S* your wife shall bear you a
17:21 whom *S* shall bear to you at
18: 6 hurried into the tent to *S* and
18: 9 'Where is *S* your wife?"
18:10 *S* your wife shall have a son."
18:10 (*S* was listening in the tent
18:11 Now Abraham and *S* were old, well
18:11 and *S* had passed the age of
18:12 Therefore *S* laughed within
18:13 Why did *S* laugh, saying, 'Shall
18:14 and *S* shall have a son."
18:15 But *S* denied it, saying, "I
20: 2 Now Abraham said of *S* his wife,
20: 2 king of Gerar sent and took *S*.
20:14 and he restored *S* his wife to
20:16 Then to *S* he said, "Behold, I
20:18 house of Abimelech because of *S*,
21: 1 And the LORD visited *S* as He
21: 1 and the LORD did for *S* as He
21: 2 For *S* conceived and bore Abraham
21: 3 whom *S* bore to him—Isaac.
21: 6 And *S* said, "God has made me
21: 7 have said to Abraham that *S*
21: 9 And *S* saw the son of Hagar the
21:12 Whatever *S* has said to you,
23: 1 *S* lived one hundred and
23: 1 the years of the life of *S*.
23: 2 So *S* died in Kirjath Arba
23: 2 and Abraham came to mourn for *S*
23:19 Abraham buried *S* his wife in
24:36 And *S* my master's wife bore a
25:10 was buried, and *S* his wife.
49:31 they buried Abraham and *S* his
Isa 51: 2 And to *S* who bore you;
Rom 9: 9 time I will come and *S*
Heb 11:11 By faith *S* herself also received
1 Pe 3: 6 as *S* obeyed Abraham, calling him

SARAH'S (3/3)
Gen 24:67 her into his mother *S* tent;
25:12 *S* maidservant, bore to Abraham.
Rom 4:19 and the deadness of *S* womb.

SARAI (16/13) SARAH
Gen 11:29 the name of Abram's wife was *S*,
11:30 But *S* was barren; she had no
11:31 and his daughter-in-law *S*,
12: 5 Then Abram took *S* his wife and
12:11 that he said to *S* his wife,
12:17 with great plagues because of *S*,
16: 1 Now *S*, Abram's wife,
16: 2 So *S* said to Abram, "See now,
16: 2 And Abram heeded the voice of *S*.
16: 3 Then *S*, Abram's wife, took
16: 5 Then *S* said to Abram, "My wrong
16: 6 So Abram said to *S*,
16: 6 And when *S* dealt harshly with
16: 8 the presence of my mistress *S*.
17:15 As for *S* your wife, you shall
17:15 you shall not call her name *S*,

SARAI'S (1/1)
Gen 16: 8 *S* maid, where have you come

SARAPH (1/1)
1 Chr 4:22 *S*, who ruled in Moab, and

SARDINE (KJV) See SARDIUS

SARDIS (3/3)
Rev 1:11 to Pergamos, to Thyatira, to *S*,
3: 1 to the angel of the church in *S*
3: 4 have a few names even in *S*

SARDITES (1/1)
Num 26:26 of Sered, the family of the *S*;

SARDIUS (5/5)
Ex 28:17 The first row shall be a *s*,
39:10 rows of stones: a row with a *s*,
Ezek 28:13 was your covering: The *s*,
Rev 4: 3 there was like a jasper and a *s*
21:20 the fifth sardonyx, the sixth *s*,

SARDONYX (1/1)
Rev 21:20 the fifth *s*, the sixth

SAREPTA (KJV) See ZAREPHATH

SARGON (1/1)
Isa 20: 1 when *S* the king of Assyria sent

SARID (2/2)
Josh 19:10 inheritance was as far as *S*.
19:12 Then from *S* it went eastward

SARON (KJV) See SHARON

SARSECHIM (1/1)
Jer 39: 3 Nergal-Sharezer, Samgar-Nebo, *S*,

SARUCH (KJV) See SERUG

SASH (14/13)
Ex 28: 4 woven tunic, a turban, and a *s*.
28:39 and you shall make the *s* of
39:29 and a *s* of fine woven linen with
Lev 8: 7 on him, girded him with the *s*,
16: 4 shall be girded with a linen *s*,
Isa 3:24 Instead of a *s*, a rope;
Jer 13: 1 "Go and get yourself a linen *s*,
13: 2 So I got a *s* according to the
13: 4 Take the *s* that you acquired,
13: 6 and take from there the *s* which
13: 7 and I took the *s* from the place
13: 7 hidden it; and there was the *s*,
13:10 shall be just like this *s* which
13:11 For as the *s* clings to the waist

SASHES (4/4)
Ex 28:40 and you shall make *s* for them.
29: 9 you shall gird them with *s*,
Lev 8:13 on them, girded them with *s*,
Prov 31:24 And supplies *s* for the

SAT (175/165) SIT
Gen 21:16 Then she went and *s* down across
21:16 So she *s* opposite him, and
31:34 camel's saddle, and *s* on them.
37:25 And they *s* down to eat a meal.
38:14 and *s* in an open place which
43:33 And they *s* before him, the
48: 2 strengthened himself and *s* up
Ex 2:15 and he *s* down by a well.
12:29 the firstborn of Pharaoh who *s*
16: 3 when we *s* by the pots of meat
17:12 under him, and he *s* on it.
18:13 that Moses *s* to judge the
32: 6 and the people *s* down to eat
Lev 15: 6 he who has the discharge *s*
15:22 touches anything that she *s* on
Judg 6:11 Angel of the LORD came and *s*
19: 6 So they *s* down, and the two of
19:15 he *s* down in the open square of
20:26 They *s* there before the LORD
Ruth 2:14 So she *s* beside the reapers,
4: 1 Boaz went up to the gate and *s*
4: 1 So he came aside and *s* down.
4: 2 down here." So they *s* down.
1 Sam 19: 9 LORD came upon Saul as he *s*
20:24 the king *s* down to eat the
20:25 Now the king *s* on his seat, as
20:25 and Abner *s* by Saul's side, but
28:23 he arose from the ground and *s*
2 Sam 2:13 So they *s* down, one on one side
7:18 Then King David went in and *s*
19: 8 Then the king arose and *s* in the
1 Ki 2:12 Then Solomon *s* on the throne of
2:19 and *s* down on his throne and
2:19 so she *s* at his right hand.
13:20 as they *s* at the table, that
19: 4 and came and *s* down under a
21:13 came in and *s* before him; and
22:10 *s* each on his throne, at a
2 Ki 4:20 he *s* on her knees till noon,
11:19 Then he *s* on the throne of the
13:13 Then Jeroboam *s* on his throne.
1 Chr 17:16 Then King David went in and *s*
29:23 Then Solomon *s* on the throne of
2 Chr 18: 9 *s* each on his throne; and they
18: 9 and they *s* at a threshing floor
Ezra 9: 3 and *s* down astonished.
9: 4 and I *s* astonished until the
10: 9 and all the people *s* in the
10:16 and they *s* down on the first
Neh 1: 4 that I *s* down and wept, and
8:17 the captivity made booths and *s*
Esth 1: 2 days when King Ahasuerus *s* on
2:19 Mordecai *s* within the king's
2:21 while Mordecai *s* within the
3:15 So the king and Haman *s* down to
5: 1 while the king *s* on his royal
Job 2: 8 to scrape himself while he *s*
2:13 So they *s* down with him on the
29:25 for them, and *s* as chief;
Ps 9: 4 You *s* on the throne judging in
26: 4 I have not *s* with idolatrous
29:10 The LORD *s* enthroned at the
107:10 Those who *s* in darkness and in
137: 1 There we *s* down, yea, we wept
Song 2: 3 I *s* down in his shade with
Isa 21: 8 I have *s* at my post every
Jer 3: 2 By the road you have *s* for
15:17 I *s* alone because of Your
26:10 to the house of the LORD and *s*
32:12 before all the Jews who *s* in
39: 3 king of Babylon came in and *s*
Ezek 3:15 and I *s* where they sat, and
3:15 and I sat where they *s*,
8: 1 as I *s* in my house with the
14: 1 of Israel came to me and *s*
20: 1 the LORD, and *s* before me.
23:41 You *s* on a stately couch, with a
Dan 2:49 but Daniel *s* in the gate of
Jon 3: 6 himself with sackcloth and *s*
4: 5 went out of the city and *s* on
4: 5 he made himself a shelter and *s*
Mt 4:16 The people who *s* in
4:16 And upon those who *s* in
9:10 as Jesus *s* at the table in the
9:10 and sinners came and *s* down
13: 1 went out of the house and *s* by
13: 2 that He got into a boat and *s*;
13:48 and they *s* down and gathered
14: 9 and because of those who *s*
15:29 went up on the mountain and *s*
24: 3 Now as He *s* on the Mount of
26: 7 poured it on His head as He *s*
26:20 He *s* down with the twelve.
26:55 I *s* daily with you, teaching in
26:58 And he went in and *s* with the
26:69 Now Peter *s* outside in the
28: 2 from the door, and *s* on it.
Mk 2:15 collectors and sinners also *s*
3:34 in a circle at those who *s*
4: 1 that He got into a boat and *s*
6:22 pleased Herod and those who *s*
6:26 and because of those who *s*
6:40 So they *s* down in ranks, in
9:35 And He *s* down, called the
10:46 *s* by the road begging.
11: 2 tied, on which no one has *s*.
11: 7 on it, and He *s* on it.
12:41 Now Jesus *s* opposite the
13: 3 Now as He *s* on the Mount of
14: 3 as He *s* at the table, a woman
14:18 Now as they *s* and ate, Jesus
14:54 And he *s* with the servants and
16:14 to the eleven as they *s* at the
16:19 and *s* down at the right hand of
Lk 4:20 it back to the attendant and *s*
5: 3 And He *s* down and taught the
5:29 tax collectors and others who *s*
7:15 So he who was dead *s* up and
7:36 and *s* down to eat.
7:37 when she knew that Jesus *s* at
7:49 And those who *s* at the table
10:39 who also *s* at Jesus' feet and
11:37 So He went in and *s* down to
14:15 Now when one of those who *s* at
18:35 that a certain blind man *s* by
19:30 on which no one has ever *s*.
22:14 He *s* down, and the twelve
22:55 midst of the courtyard and *s*
22:55 Peter *s* among them.
22:56 seeing him as he *s* by the fire,
24:30 as He *s* at the table with them,
Jn 4: 6 *s* thus by the well. It was
6: 3 and there He *s* with His
6:10 So the men *s* down, in number
8: 2 and He *s* down and taught them.
9: 8 Is not this he who *s* and
12: 2 Lazarus was one of those who *s*
12:14 a young donkey, *s* on it;
13:12 and *s* down again, He said to
19:13 he brought Jesus out and *s* down
Acts 2: 3 and one *s* upon each of them.
3:10 they knew that it was he who *s*
6:15 And all who *s* in the council,
9:40 and when she saw Peter she *s*
12:21 *s* on his throne and gave an
13:14 on the Sabbath day and *s* down.
16:13 and we *s* down and spoke to the
20: 9 And in a window *s* a certain
25:17 the next day I *s* on the
26:30 and Bernice and those who *s*
1 Cor 10: 7 The people *s* down to eat
Heb 1: 3 *s* down at the right hand of the
10:12 *s* down at the right hand of
12: 2 and has *s* down at the right
Rev 3:21 as I also overcame and *s* down
4: 2 and One *s* on the throne.
4: 3 And He who *s* there was like a
5: 1 in the right hand of Him who *s*
5: 7 of the right hand of Him who *s*
6: 2 He who *s* on it had a bow;
6: 4 it was granted to the one who *s*
6: 5 and he who *s* on it had a pair
6: 8 And the name of him who *s* on it

9:17 those who *s* on them had
11:16 the twenty-four elders who *s*
14:14 and on the cloud *s* One like
14:15 with a loud voice to Him who *s*
14:16 So He who *s* on the cloud thrust
19: 4 down and worshiped God who *s*
19:11 And He who *s* on him was called
19:19 to make war against Him who *s*
19:21 from the mouth of Him who *s* on
20: 4 and they *s* on them, and
20:11 white throne and Him who *s* on
21: 5 Then He who *s* on the throne

SATAN (54/48) SATAN'S

1 Chr 21: 1 Now *S* stood up against Israel,
Job 1: 6 and *S* also came among them.
1: 7 And the LORD said to *S*,
1: 7 So *S* answered the LORD and
1: 8 Then the LORD said to *S*,
1: 9 So *S* answered the LORD and
1:12 And the LORD said to *S*,
1:12 So *S* went out from the
2: 1 and *S* came also among them to
2: 2 And the LORD said to *S*,
2: 2 So *S* answered the LORD and
2: 3 Then the LORD said to *S*,
2: 4 So *S* answered the LORD and
2: 6 And the LORD said to *S*,
2: 7 So *S* went out from the presence
Zech 3: 1 and *S* standing at his right
3: 2 And the LORD said to *S*,
3: 2 *S*! The LORD who has chosen
Mt 4:10 *S*! For it is written, 'You
12:26 If *S* casts out Satan, he is
12:26 "If Satan casts out *S*,
16:23 *S*! You are an offense to Me,
Mk 1:13 forty days, tempted by *S*,
3:23 How can *S* cast out Satan?
3:23 "How can Satan cast out *S*?
3:26 And if *S* has risen up against
4:15 *S* comes immediately and takes
8:33 'Get behind Me, *S*! For you
Lk 4: 8 'Get behind Me, *S*! For it is
10:18 I saw *S* fall like lightning from
11:18 If *S* also is divided against
13:16 whom *S* has bound—think of
22: 3 Then *S* entered Judas, surnamed
22:31 *S* has asked for you, that he
Jn 13:27 *S* entered him. Then Jesus said
Acts 5: 3 why has *S* filled your heart to
26:18 and from the power of *S* to
Rom 16:20 the God of peace will crush *S*
1 Cor 5: 5 deliver such a one to *S* for the
7: 5 come together again so that *S*
2 Cor 2:11 lest *S* should take advantage of
11:14 And no wonder! For *S* himself
12: 7 a messenger of *S* to buffet me,
1 Th 2:18 but *S* hindered us.
2 Th 2: 9 according to the working of *S*,
1 Tim 1:20 whom I delivered to *S* that they
5:15 already turned aside after *S*.
Rev 2: 9 not, but are a synagogue of *S*.
2:13 among you, where *S* dwells.
2:24 have not known the depths of *S*,
3: 9 those of the synagogue of *S*,
12: 9 of old, called the Devil and *S*,
20: 2 of old, who is the Devil and *S*,
20: 7 *S* will be released from his

SATAN'S (1/1) SATAN

Rev 2:13 where *S* throne is. And you

SATIATE (1/1)

Jer 31:14 I will *s* the soul of the

SATIATED (2/2)

Jer 31:25 For I have *s* the weary soul, and
46:10 It shall be *s* and made drunk

SATISFACTION (1/1)

Prov 19:23 who has it will abide in *s*;

SATISFIED (50/50) SATISFY

Ex 15: 9 My desire shall be *s* on them.
Lev 26:26 and you shall eat and not be *s*.
Deut 14:29 may come and eat and be *s*,
33:23 *s* with favor, And full of the
Ruth 2:14 to her; and she ate and was *s*,
2:18 kept back after she had been *s*.
Job 19:22 And are not *s* with my flesh?
27:14 his offspring shall not be *s*
31:31 is there that has not been *s*
Ps 17:14 They are *s* with children, And
17:15 I shall be *s* when I awake in
22:26 The poor shall eat and be *s*;
36: 8 They are abundantly *s* with the
37:19 days of famine they shall be *s*.
59:15 And howl if they are not *s*.
63: 5 My soul shall be *s* as with
65: 4 We shall be *s* with the
81:16 from the rock I would have *s*
104:13 The earth is *s* with the fruit
105:40 And *s* them with the bread of
Prov 12:11 who tills his land will be *s*
14:14 But a good man will be *s*
18:20 A man's stomach shall be *s* from
20:13 and you will be *s* with bread.
27: 7 A *s* soul loathes the honeycomb,
27:20 So the eyes of man are never *s*.
30:15 three things that are never *s*,
30:16 The earth that is not *s* with
Eccl 1: 8 The eye is not *s* with seeing,
4: 8 Nor is his eye *s* with riches.
5:10 who loves silver will not be *s*
6: 3 but his soul is not *s* with
6: 7 And yet the soul is not *s*.
Isa 9:20 on the left hand And not be *s*;
43:24 Nor have you *s* Me with the fat
44:16 He roasts a roast, and is *s*.
53:11 labor of His soul, and be *s*.
66:11 That you may feed and be *s*
Jer 31:14 And My people shall be *s* with
50:10 All who plunder her shall be *s*,
50:19 His soul shall be *s* on Mount
Lam 5: 6 to be *s* with bread.
Ezek 16:28 with them and still were not *s*.
16:29 and even then you were not *s*.
27:33 You *s* many people;
Joel 2:19 And you will be *s* by them;
2:26 shall eat in plenty and be *s*,
Am 4: 8 water, But they were not *s*;
Mic 6:14 You shall eat, but not be *s*;
Hab 2: 5 is like death, and cannot be *s*,

SATISFIES (2/2) SATISFY

Ps 103: 5 Who *s* your mouth with good
107: 9 For He *s* the longing soul, And

SATISFY (13/13) SATISFIED, SATISFIES

Job 38:27 To *s* the desolate waste, And
38:39 Or *s* the appetite of the young
Ps 90:14 *s* us early with Your mercy,
91:16 With long life I will *s* him,
132:15 I will *s* her poor with bread.
145:16 You open Your hand And *s* the
Prov 5:19 Let her breasts *s* you at all
6:30 a thief If he steals to *s*
Isa 55: 2 your wages for what does not *s*?
58:10 your soul to the hungry And *s*
58:11 And *s* your soul in drought,
Ezek 7:19 They will not *s* their souls,
Mk 8: 4 How can one *s* these people with

SATISFYING (1/1)

Prov 13:25 The righteous eats to the *s* of

SATISFIED (1/1)

Prov 12:14 A man will be *s* with good by

SATRAPS (13/13)

Ezra 8:36 king's orders to the king's *s*
Esth 3:12 Haman commanded—to the king's *s*,
8: 9 commanded, to the Jews, the *s*,
9: 3 of the provinces, the *s*,
Dan 3: 2 word to gather together the *s*,
3: 3 So the *s*, the administrators,
3:27 And the *s*, administrators,
6: 1 one hundred and twenty *s*,
6: 2 that the *s* might give account
6: 3 above the governors and *s*,
6: 4 So the governors and *s* sought to
6: 6 So these governors and *s*
6: 7 the administrators and *s*,

SATURATED (1/1)

Isa 34: 7 And their dust *s* with

SATURATES (1/1)

Job 37:11 Also with moisture He *s* the

SATYRS (KJV) See GOATS

SAUL (394/333) PAUL, SAUL'S

Gen 36:37 *S* of Rehoboth-by-the-River
36:38 When *S* died, Baal-Hanan the son
1 Sam 9: 2 handsome son whose name was *S*.
9: 3 And Kish said to his son *S*,
9: 5 *S* said to his servant who was
9: 7 Then *S* said to his servant,
9: 8 And the servant answered *S* again
9:10 Then *S* said to his servant,
9:15 in his ear the day before *S*
9:17 And when Samuel saw *S*,
9:18 Then *S* drew near to Samuel in
9:19 And Samuel answered *S* and said,
9:21 And *S* answered and said, "Am I
9:22 Now Samuel took *S* and his
9:24 upper part and set it before *S*.
9:24 So *S* ate with Samuel that
9:25 Samuel spoke with *S* on the top
9:26 day that Samuel called to *S* on
9:26 And *S* arose, and both of them
9:27 of the city, Samuel said to *S*,
10:11 Is *S* also among the
10:12 Is *S* also among the prophets?"
10:16 So *S* said to his uncle, "He
10:21 And *S* the son of Kish was
10:26 And *S* also went home to Gibeah;
11: 4 messengers came to Gibeah of *S*
11: 5 Now there was *S*, coming
11: 5 and *S* said, "What troubles
11: 6 the Spirit of God came upon *S*
11: 7 does not go out with *S*
11:11 that *S* put the people in three
11:12 'Shall *S* reign over us?'
11:13 But *S* said, "Not a man shall be
11:15 and there they made *S* king
11:15 and there *S* and all the men of
13: 1 *S* reigned one year; and when he
13: 2 *S* chose for himself three
13: 2 Two thousand were with *S* in
13: 3 Then *S* blew the trumpet
13: 4 Israel heard it said that *S*
13: 4 were called together to *S* at
13: 7 As for *S*, he was still in
13: 9 So *S* said, "Bring a burnt
13:10 and *S* went out to meet him,
13:11 And *S* said, "When I saw that
13:13 And Samuel said to *S*,
13:15 And *S* numbered the people
13:16 *S*, Jonathan his son,
13:22 of the people who were with *S*
13:22 But they were found with *S* and
14: 1 day that Jonathan the son of *S*
14: 2 And *S* was sitting in the
14:16 Now the watchmen of *S* in Gibeah
14:17 Then *S* said to the people who
14:18 And *S* said to Ahijah, "Bring
14:19 while *S* talked to the priest,
14:19 so *S* said to the priest,
14:20 Then *S* and all the people who
14:21 the Israelites who were with *S*
14:24 for *S* had placed the people
14:33 Then they told *S*,
14:34 And *S* said, "Disperse
14:35 Then *S* built an altar to the
14:36 Now *S* said, "Let us go down
14:37 So *S* asked counsel of God,
14:38 And *S* said, "Come over here,
14:40 And the people said to *S*,
14:41 Therefore *S* said to the LORD
14:41 So *S* and Jonathan were taken,
14:42 And *S* said, "Cast lots between
14:43 Then *S* said to Jonathan, "Tell
14:44 And *S* answered, "God do so and
14:45 But the people said to *S*,
14:46 Then *S* returned from pursuing
14:47 So *S* established his
14:49 The sons of *S* were Jonathan,
14:51 Kish was the father of *S*,
14:52 Philistines all the days of *S*.
14:52 And when *S* saw any strong man
15: 1 Samuel also said to *S*,
15: 4 So *S* gathered the people
15: 5 And *S* came to a city of Amalek,
15: 6 Then *S* said to the Kenites,
15: 7 And *S* attacked the Amalekites,
15: 9 But *S* and the people spared Agag
15:11 regret that I have set up *S*
15:12 early in the morning to meet *S*,
15:12 *S* went to Carmel, and indeed, he
15:13 Then Samuel went to *S*,
15:13 and *S* said to him, "Blessed
15:15 And *S* said, "They have brought
15:16 Then Samuel said to *S*,
15:20 And *S* said to Samuel, "But I
15:24 Then *S* said to Samuel, "I have
15:26 But Samuel said to *S*,
15:27 *S* seized the edge of his robe,
15:31 So Samuel turned back after *S*,
15:31 and *S* worshiped the LORD.
15:34 and *S* went up to his house at
15:34 up to his house at Gibeah of *S*.
15:35 Samuel went no more to see *S*
15:35 Samuel mourned for *S*,
15:35 regretted that He had made *S*
16: 1 "How long will you mourn for *S*,
16: 2 If *S* hears it, he will kill
16:14 of the LORD departed from *S*,
16:17 So *S* said to his servants,
16:19 Therefore *S* sent messengers to
16:20 them by his son David to *S*.
16:21 So David came to *S* and stood
16:22 Then *S* sent to Jesse, saying,
16:23 the spirit from God was upon *S*,
16:23 Then *S* would become refreshed
17: 2 And *S* and the men of Israel were
17: 8 and you the servants of *S*?
17:11 When *S* and all Israel heard
17:12 in years, in the days of *S*.
17:13 of Jesse had gone to follow *S*
17:14 And the three oldest followed *S*.
17:15 went and returned from *S* to
17:19 Now *S* and they and all the men
17:31 heard, they reported them to *S*;
17:32 Then David said to *S*,
17:33 And *S* said to David, "You are
17:34 But David said to *S*,
17:37 And *S* said to David, "Go,
17:38 So *S* clothed David with his
17:39 And David said to *S*,
17:55 When *S* saw David going out
17:57 him and brought him before *S*
17:58 And *S* said to him, "Whose son
18: 1 he had finished speaking to *S*,
18: 2 *S* took him that day, and would
18: 5 So David went out wherever *S*
18: 5 And *S* set him over the men of
18: 6 and dancing, to meet King *S*,
18: 7 *S* has slain his thousands, And
18: 8 Then *S* was very angry, and the
18: 9 So *S* eyed David from that day
18:10 spirit from God came upon *S*,
18:11 And *S* cast the spear, for he

S

18:12 Now S was afraid of David,
18:12 him, but had departed from S.
18:13 Therefore S removed him from his
18:15 when S saw that he behaved very
18:17 Then S said to David, "Here is
18:17 For S thought, "Let my hand
18:18 So David said to S,
18:20 loved David. And they told S,
18:21 So S said, "I will give her to
18:21 Therefore S said to David a
18:22 And S commanded his servants,
18:24 And the servants of S told him,
18:25 Then S said, "Thus you shall
18:25 But S thought to make David
18:27 Then S gave him Michal his
18:28 Thus S saw and knew that the
18:29 and S was still more afraid of
18:29 So S became David's enemy
18:30 than all the servants of S,
19: 1 Now S spoke to Jonathan his son
19: 2 My father S seeks to kill you.
19: 4 spoke well of David to S his
19: 6 So S heeded the voice of
19: 6 and S swore, "As the LORD
19: 7 So Jonathan brought David to S,
19: 9 from the LORD came upon S as
19:10 Then S sought to pin David to
19:11 S also sent messengers to
19:14 So when S sent messengers to
19:15 Then S sent the messengers back
19:17 Then S said to Michal, "Why
19:17 And Michal answered S,
19:18 and told him all that S had
19:19 Now it was told S,
19:20 Then S sent messengers to take
19:20 came upon the messengers of S,
19:21 And when S was told, he sent
19:21 Then S sent messengers again
19:24 Is S also among the prophets?"
20:26 Nevertheless S did not say
20:27 And S said to Jonathan his son,
20:28 So Jonathan answered S,
20:32 And Jonathan answered S his
20:33 Then S cast a spear at him to
21: 7 man of the servants of S was
21: 7 the herdsmen who belonged to S.
21:10 and fled that day from before S,
21:11 S has slain his thousands, And
22: 6 When S heard that David and the
22: 6 now S was staying in Gibeah
22: 7 then S said to his servants who
22: 9 was set over the servants of S,
22:12 And S said, "Hear now, son of
22:13 Then S said to him, "Why have
22:21 And Abiathar told David that S
22:22 that he would surely tell S.
23: 7 And S was told that David had
23: 7 So S said, "God has delivered
23: 8 Then S called all the people
23: 9 When David knew that S plotted
23:10 has certainly heard that S
23:11 Will S come down, as Your
23:12 and my men into the hand of S?
23:13 Then it was told S that David
23:14 S sought him every day, but God
23:15 So David saw that S had come out
23:17 for the hand of S my father
23:17 Even my father S knows that."
23:19 the Ziphites came up to S at
23:21 And S said, "Blessed are you
23:24 arose and went to Ziph before S.
23:25 When S and his men went to seek
23:25 And when S heard that, he
23:26 Then S went on one side of the
23:26 made haste to get away from S,
23:26 for S and his men were
23:27 But a messenger came to S,
23:28 Therefore S returned from
24: 1 when S had returned from
24: 2 Then S took three thousand
24: 3 and S went in to attend to his
24: 7 allow them to rise against S.
24: 7 And S got up from the cave and
24: 8 the cave, and called out to S,
24: 8 the king!" And when S looked
24: 9 And David said to S:
24:16 speaking these words to S,
24:16 that S said, "Is this your
24:16 And S lifted up his voice and
24:22 So David swore to S.
24:22 And S went home, but David and
25:44 But S had given Michal his
26: 1 Now the Ziphites came to S at
26: 2 Then S arose and went down to
26: 3 And S encamped in the hill of
26: 3 and he saw that S came after
26: 4 and understood that S had
26: 5 and came to the place where S
26: 5 And David saw the place where S
26: 5 Now S lay within the camp, with
26: 6 Who will go down with me to S in
26: 7 and there S lay sleeping within
26:17 Then S knew David's voice, and
26:21 Then S said, "I have sinned.
26:25 Then S said to David, "May you
26:25 and S returned to his place.
27: 1 perish someday by the hand of S.
27: 1 and S will despair of me, to
27: 4 And it was told S that David had
28: 3 And S had put the mediums and
28: 4 So S gathered all Israel
28: 5 When S saw the army of the
28: 6 And when S inquired of the
28: 7 Then S said to his servants,
28: 8 So S disguised himself and put
28: 9 you know what S has done, how
28:10 And S swore to her by the LORD,
28:12 And the woman spoke to S,
28:12 For you are S!"
28:13 the woman said to S, "I saw
28:14 And S perceived that it was
28:15 Now Samuel said to S,
28:15 And S answered, "I am deeply
28:20 Then immediately S fell full
28:21 And the woman came to S and saw
28:25 So she brought it before S and
29: 3 the servant of S king of
29: 5 S has slain his thousands, And
31: 2 followed hard after S and his
31: 3 battle became fierce against S.
31: 4 Then S said to his armorbearer,
31: 4 Therefore S took a sword and
31: 5 his armorbearer saw that S was
31: 6 So S, his three sons,
31: 7 of Israel had fled and that S
31: 8 that they found S and his three
31:11 the Philistines had done to S,
31:12 and took the body of S and the
2 Sam 1: 1 to pass after the death of S,
1: 4 and S and Jonathan his son are
1: 5 How do you know that S and
1: 6 on Mount Gilboa, there was S,
1:12 and fasted until evening for S
1:17 with this lamentation over S
1:21 shield of S, not anointed
1:22 And the sword of S did not
1:23 S and Jonathan were beloved and
1:24 of Israel, weep over S,
2: 4 were the ones who buried S.
2: 5 kindness to your lord, to S,
2: 7 for your master S is dead, and
2: 8 took Ishbosheth the son of S
2:12 of Ishbosheth the son of S,
2:15 of Ishbosheth the son of S,
3: 1 war between the house of S and
3: 1 and the house of S grew weaker
3: 6 was war between the house of S
3: 6 his hold on the house of S.
3: 7 And S had a concubine, whose
3: 8 show loyalty to the house of S
3:10 the kingdom from the house of S,
4: 4 old when the news about S and
4: 8 the son of S your enemy, who
4: 8 my lord the king this day of S
4:10 S is dead,' thinking to have
5: 2 when S was king over us, you
6:20 And Michal the daughter of S
6:23 Michal the daughter of S had
7:15 from him, as I took it from S,
9: 1 who is left of the house of S,
9: 2 a servant of the house of S
9: 3 still someone of the house of S,
9: 6 son of Jonathan, the son of S,
9: 7 to you all the land of S your
9: 9 son all that belonged to S and
12: 7 you from the hand of S.
16: 5 the family of the house of S,
16: 8 all the blood of the house of S,
19:17 the servant of the house of S,
19:24 Now Mephibosheth the son of S
21: 1 It is because of S and his
21: 2 but S had sought to kill them
21: 4 have no silver or gold from S
21: 6 before the LORD in Gibeah of S,
21: 7 son of Jonathan, the son of S,
21: 7 David and Jonathan the son of S.
21: 8 of Aiah, whom she bore to S;
21: 8 of Michal the daughter of S,
21:11 of Aiah, the concubine of S,
21:12 went and took the bones of S,
21:12 Philistines had struck down S
21:13 So he brought up the bones of S
21:14 They buried the bones of S and
22: 1 enemies, and from the hand of S.
1 Chr 1:48 S of Rehoboth-by-the-River
1:49 When S died, Baal-Hanan the son
5:10 Now in the days of S they made
8:33 Ner begot Kish, Kish begot S,
8:33 and S begot Jonathan,
9:39 Ner begot Kish, Kish begot S,
9:39 and S begot Jonathan,
10: 2 followed hard after S and his
10: 3 battle became fierce against S.
10: 4 Then S said to his armorbearer,
10: 4 Therefore S took a sword and
10: 5 his armorbearer saw that S was
10: 6 So S and his three sons died,
10: 7 that they had fled and that S
10: 8 that they found S and his sons
10:11 the Philistines had done to S,
10:12 arose and took the body of S
10:13 So S died for his
11: 2 even when S was king, you were
12: 1 he was still a fugitive from S
12:19 Philistines to battle against S;
12:19 He may defect to his master S
12:23 to turn over the kingdom of S
12:29 of Benjamin, relatives of S,
12:29 loyal to the house of S);
13: 3 at it since the days of S.
26:28 S the son of Kish, Abner the
Ps 18: enemies and from the hand of S.
52: the Edomite went and told S,
54: Ziphites went and said to to S,
57: of David when he fled from S
59: A Michtam of David when S
Isa 10:29 Gibeah of S has fled.
Acts 7:58 the feet of a young man named S.
8: 1 Now S was consenting to his
8: 3 As for S, he made havoc
9: 1 Then S, still breathing
9: 4 a voice saying to him, "S,
9: 4 voice saying to him, "Saul, S,
9: 8 Then S arose from the ground,
9:11 of Judas for one called S of
9:17 on him he said, "Brother S,
9:19 Then S spent some days with the
9:22 But S increased all the more in
9:24 their plot became known to S.
9:26 And when S had come to
11:25 departed for Tarsus to seek S.
11:30 by the hands of Barnabas and S.
12:25 And Barnabas and S returned
13: 1 with Herod the tetrarch, and S.
13: 2 separate to Me Barnabas and S
13: 7 man called for Barnabas and S
13: 9 Then S, who also is called
13:21 so God gave them S the son of
22: 7 heard a voice saying to me, 'S,
22: 7 a voice saying to me, 'Saul, S,
22:13 and said to me, 'Brother S,
26:14 in the Hebrew language, 'S,
26:14 the Hebrew language, 'Saul, S,

SAUL'S (34/33) SAUL

1 Sam 9: 3 S father, were lost. And Kish
10:14 Then S uncle said to him and
10:15 And S uncle said, "Tell me,
14:50 The name of S wife was Ahinoam
14:50 Abner the son of Ner, S uncle.
16:15 And S servants said to him,
18: 5 in the sight of S servants.
18:10 was a spear in S hand.
18:19 S daughter, should have been
18:20 S daughter, loved David.
18:23 So S servants spoke those words
18:28 S daughter, loved him;
19: 1 S son, delighted greatly in
19:10 slipped away from S presence;
20:25 and Abner sat by S side, but
20:30 Then S anger was aroused against
23:16 S son, arose and went to David
24: 4 cut off a corner of S robe.
24: 5 him because he had cut S robe.
26:12 jug of water by S head,
31: 2 and Malchishua, S sons.
2 Sam 1: 2 that a man came from S camp
2: 8 commander of S army, took
2:10 S son, was forty years old
3:13 S daughter, when you come to
3:14 S son, saying, "Give me my
4: 1 When S son heard that Abner had
4: 2 Now S son had two men who
4: 4 S son, had a son who was lame
6:16 S daughter, looked through a
9: 9 S servant, and said to him, "I
1 Chr 10: 2 and Malchishua, S sons.
12: 2 of Benjamin, S brethren.
15:29 S daughter, looked through a

SAVAGE (1/1)

Acts 20:29 after my departure s wolves

SAVE (160/156) SALVATION, SAVED, SAVES, SAVING

Gen 45: 7 and to s your lives by a great
50:20 to s many people alive.
Ex 1:22 and every daughter you shall s
Deut 20: 4 your enemies, to s you.'
22:27 but there was no one to s
28:29 and no one shall s you.
Josh 10: 6 s us and help us, for all the
22:22 do not s us this day.
Judg 6:14 and you shall s Israel from the
6:15 how can I s Israel? Indeed my
6:31 Would you s him? Let the one
6:36 If You will s Israel by my hand
6:37 I shall know that You will s
7: 7 men who lapped I will s you,
10: 1 Abimelech there arose to s
1 Sam 4: 3 it comes among us it may s us
7: 8 that He may s us from the hand
9:16 that he may s My people from
10:27 'How can this man s us?"
11: 3 if there is no one to s us,
17:47 know that the LORD does not s
19:11 If you do not s your life
23: 2 Philistines, and s Keilah."
27:11 David would s neither man nor
2 Sam 3:18 I will s My people Israel from
22: 3 You s me from violence.
22:28 You will s the humble people;
22:42 but there was none to s;
1 Ki 1:12 that you may s your own life
2 Ki 16: 7 Come up and s me from the hand
19:19 s us from his hand, that all
19:34 to s it For My own sake and
1 Chr 16:35 S us, O God of our salvation;
2 Chr 20: 9 and You will hear and s.
Neh 6:11 would go into the temple to s
Job 20:20 He will not s anything he
22:29 Then He will s the humble
40:14 your own right hand can s you.

Ps 3: 7 *S* me, O my God! For You have
6: 4 *s* me for Your mercies' sake!
7: 1 *S* me from all those who
17: 7 O You who *s* those who trust
18:27 For You will *s* the humble
18:41 out, but there was none to *s*;
20: 9 *S*, LORD! May the King
22:21 *S* Me from the lion's mouth And
28: 9 *S* Your people, And bless Your
31: 2 A fortress of defense to *s* me.
31:16 *S* me for Your mercies' sake.
37:40 And *s* them, Because they
44: 3 Nor did their own arm *s* them;
44: 6 Nor shall my sword *s* me.
54: 1 *S* me, O God, by Your name, And
55:16 And the LORD shall *s* me.
57: 3 shall send from heaven and *s*
59: 2 And *s* me from bloodthirsty
60: 5 *S* with Your right hand, and
69: 1 *S* me, O God! For the waters
69:35 For God will *s* Zion And build
71: 2 Your ear to me, and *s* me.
71: 3 given the commandment to *s* me,
72: 4 He will *s* the children of the
72:13 And will *s* the souls of the
80: 2 And come and *s* us!
86: 2 *S* Your servant who trusts in
86:16 And *s* the son of Your
106:47 *S* us, O LORD our God, And
108: 6 *S* with Your right hand, and
109:26 *s* me according to Your mercy,
109:31 To *s* him from those who
118:25 *S* now, I pray, O LORD
119:94 I am Yours, *s* me; For I have
119:146 *S* me, and I will keep Your
138: 7 And Your right hand will *s* me.
145:19 also will hear their cry and *s*
Prov 20:22 and He will *s* you.
Isa 25: 9 and He will *s* us. This is the
33:22 is our King; He will *s* us);
35: 4 He will come and *s* you."
37:20 *s* us from his hand, that all
37:35 to *s* it For My own sake and
38:20 The LORD was ready to *s* me;
45:20 pray to a god that cannot *s*.
46: 7 yet it cannot answer Nor *s* him
47:13 Stand up and *s* you From what
47:15 No one shall *s* you.
49:25 And I will *s* your children.
59: 1 shortened, That it cannot *s*;
63: 1 in righteousness, mighty to *s*.
Jer 2:27 will say, 'Arise and *s* us.'
2:28 If they can *s* you in the time
11:12 but they will not *s* them at all
14: 9 a mighty one who cannot *s*?
15:20 For I am with you to *s* you
17:14 *S* me, and I shall be saved,
30:10 I will *s* you from afar, And
30:11 says the LORD, 'to *s* you;
31: 7 *s* Your people, The remnant of
42:11 to *s* you and deliver you from
46:27 I will *s* you from afar, And
48: 6 Flee, *s* your lives! And be
51: 6 And every one *s* his life!
Lam 4:17 a nation that could not *s* us.
Ezek 3:18 to *s* his life, that same wicked
13:22 turn from his wicked way to *s*
33: 5 But he who takes warning will *s*
34:22 therefore I will *s* My flock, and
Hos 1: 7 Will *s* them by the LORD their
1: 7 And will not *s* them by bow,
13:10 That he may *s* you in all your
14: 3 Assyria shall not *s* us, We
Mic 6:14 but shall not *s* them;
Hab 1: 2 And You will not *s*.
Zeph 3:17 midst, The Mighty One, will *s*;
3:19 I will *s* the lame, And gather
Zech 8: 7 I will *s* My people from the
8:13 So I will *s* you, and you shall
9:16 The LORD their God will *s* them
10: 6 And I will *s* the house of
12: 7 The LORD will *s* the tents of
Mt 1:21 for He will *s* His people from
8:25 *s* us! We are perishing!"
14:30 out, saying, "Lord, *s* me!"
16:25 For whoever desires to *s* his
18:11 the Son of Man has come to *s*
27:40 it in three days, *s* Yourself!
27:42 others; Himself He cannot *s*.
27:49 us see if Elijah will come to *s*
Mk 3: 4 to *s* life or to kill?"
8:35 For whoever desires to *s* his
8:35 My sake and the gospel's will *s*
15:30 *s* Yourself, and come down from
15:31 others; Himself He cannot *s*.
Lk 6: 9 to *s* life or to destroy?"
9:24 For whoever desires to *s* his
9:24 his life for My sake will *s* it.
9:56 to destroy men's lives but to *s*
17:33 Whoever seeks to *s* his life will
19:10 Man has come to seek and to *s*
23:35 let Him *s* Himself if He is the
23:37 of the Jews, *s* Yourself."
23:39 *s* Yourself and us."
Jn 12:27 *s* Me from this hour'? But for
12:47 to judge the world but to *s*
Acts 27:43 wanting to *s* Paul, kept them
Rom 11:14 who are my flesh and *s* some
1 Cor 1:21 of the message preached to *s*
7:16 whether you will *s* your
7:16 whether you will *s* your wife?
9:22 that I might by all means *s*
1 Tim 1:15 Jesus came into the world to *s*
4:16 for in doing this you will *s*
Heb 5: 7 tears to Him who was able to *s*
7:25 Therefore He is also able to *s*
Jas 1:21 which is able to *s* your souls.
2:14 Can faith *s* him?
4:12 who is able to *s* and to
5:15 And the prayer of faith will *s*
5:20 the error of his way will *s* a
Jude 23 but others *s* with fear, pulling

SAVED (101/101) SAVE

Gen 47:25 You have *s* our lives; let us
Ex 1:17 but *s* the male children alive.
1:18 and *s* the male children
14:30 So the LORD *s* Israel that day
Num 10: 9 and you will be *s* from your
Deut 33:29 a people *s* by the LORD, The
Judg 7: 2 My own hand has *s* me.'
21:14 them the women whom they had *s*
1 Sam 10:19 who Himself *s* you from all your
14:23 So the LORD *s* Israel that day,
23: 5 So David *s* the inhabitants of
2 Sam 19: 5 your servants who today have *s*
19: 9 The king *s* us from the hand of
22: 4 So shall I be *s* from my
2 Ki 14:27 but He *s* them by the hand of
2 Chr 32:22 Thus the LORD *s* Hezekiah and
Neh 9:27 You gave them deliverers who *s*
Job 26: 2 How have you *s* the arm that
Ps 18: 3 So shall I be *s* from my
33:16 No king is *s* by the multitude
34: 6 And *s* him out of all his
44: 7 But You have *s* us from our
80: 3 And we shall be *s*!
80: 7 And we shall be *s*!
80:19 And we shall be *s*!
106: 8 Nevertheless He *s* them for His
106:10 He *s* them from the hand of him
107:13 And He *s* them out of their
107:19 And He *s* them out of their
116: 6 brought low, and He *s* me.
Prov 28:18 walks blamelessly will be *s*,
Isa 30:15 and rest you shall be *s*;
43:12 I have declared and *s*,
45:17 But Israel shall be *s* by the
45:22 "Look to Me, and be *s*,
63: 9 the Angel of His Presence *s*
64: 5 And we need to be *s*.
Jer 4:14 wickedness, That you may be *s*.
8:20 And we are not *s*!"
17:14 Save me, and I shall be *s*,
23: 6 In His days Judah will be *s*,
30: 7 But he shall be *s* out of it.
33:16 In those days Judah will be *s*,
Joel 2:32 name of the LORD Shall be *s*.
Mt 10:22 endures to the end will be *s*.
19:25 saying, "Who then can be *s*?
24:13 endures to the end shall be *s*.
24:22 shortened, no flesh would be *s*;
27:42 He *s* others; Himself He cannot
Mk 10:26 themselves, "Who then can be *s*?
13:13 endures to the end shall be *s*.
13:20 those days, no flesh would be *s*;
15:31 He *s* others; Himself He cannot
16:16 and is baptized will be *s*;
Lk 1:71 That we should be *s* from our
7:50 Your faith has *s* you. Go in
8:12 they should believe and be *s*.
13:23 "Lord, are there few who are *s*?
18:26 it said, "Who then can be *s*?
23:35 He *s* others; let Him save
Jn 3:17 world through Him might be *s*.
5:34 these things that you may be *s*.
10: 9 enters by Me, he will be *s*,
Acts 2:21 of the LORD Shall be *s*.
2:40 Be *s* from this perverse
2:47 daily those who were being *s*.
4:12 among men by which we must be *s*.
11:14 all your household will be *s*.
15: 1 of Moses, you cannot be *s*.
15:11 Jesus Christ we shall be *s* in
16:30 "Sirs, what must I do to be *s*?
16:31 Jesus Christ, and you will be *s*,
27:20 all hope that we would be *s* was
27:31 in the ship, you cannot be *s*.
Rom 5: 9 we shall be *s* from wrath
5:10 we shall be *s* by His life.
8:24 For we were *s* in this hope, but
9:27 The remnant will be *s*.
10: 1 Israel is that they may be *s*.
10: 9 from the dead, you will be *s*.
10:13 of the LORD shall be *s*.
11:26 And so all Israel will be *s*,
1 Cor 1:18 but to us who are being *s* it is
3:15 loss; but he himself will be *s*,
5: 5 that his spirit may be *s* in the
10:33 of many, that they may be *s*.
15: 2 by which also you are *s*,
2 Cor 2:15 among those who are being *s*
Eph 2: 5 (by grace you have been *s*),
2: 8 For by grace you have been *s*
1 Th 2:16 the Gentiles that they may be *s*,
2 Th 2:10 the truth, that they might be *s*.
1 Tim 2: 4 who desires all men to be *s* and
2:15 Nevertheless she will be *s* in
2 Tim 1: 9 who has *s* us and called us with
Titus 3: 5 according to His mercy He *s* us,
1 Pe 3:20 were *s* through water.
4:18 one is scarcely *s*,
2 Pe 2: 5 but *s* Noah, one of eight
Jude 5 having *s* the people out of the
Rev 21:24 the nations of those who are *s*

SAVES (6/6) SAVE

1 Sam 14:39 who *s* Israel, though it be in
Job 5:15 But He *s* the needy from the
Ps 7:10 Who *s* the upright in heart.
20: 6 Now I know that the LORD *s* His
34:18 And *s* such as have a contrite
1 Pe 3:21 is also an antitype which now *s*

SAVING (6/6) SAVE

Gen 19:19 which you have shown me by *s*
1 Sam 14: 6 restrains the LORD from *s* by
Ps 20: 6 His holy heaven With the *s*
28: 8 And He is the *s* refuge of His
Heb 10:39 of those who believe to the *s*
11: 7 prepared an ark for the *s* of

SAVIOR (36/36) SAVIORS

2 Sam 22: 3 My *S*, You save me from
Ps 106:21 They forgot God their *S*,
Isa 19:20 and He will send them a *S* and a
43: 3 The Holy One of Israel, your *S*;
43:11 And besides Me there is no *s*.
45:15 O God of Israel, the *S*!
45:21 besides Me, A just God and a *S*;
49:26 That I, the LORD, am your *S*,
60:16 am your *S* And your Redeemer,
63: 8 So He became their *S*.
Jer 14: 8 his *S* in time of trouble, Why
Hos 13: 4 For there is no *S* besides
Lk 1:47 spirit has rejoiced in God my *S*.
2:11 day in the city of David a *S*,
Jn 4:42 the *S* of the world."
Acts 5:31 right hand to be Prince and *S*,
13:23 God raised up for Israel a *S*—
Eph 5:23 and He is the *S* of the body.
Phil 3:20 we also eagerly wait for the *S*,
1 Tim 1: 1 by the commandment of God our *S*
2: 3 in the sight of God our *S*,
4:10 who is the *S* of all men,
2 Tim 1:10 by the appearing of our *S*
Titus 1: 3 to the commandment of God our *S*;
1: 4 and the Lord Jesus Christ our *S*.
2:10 the doctrine of God our *S* in
2:13 of our great God and *S* Jesus
3: 4 and the love of God our *S*
3: 6 through Jesus Christ our *S*,
2 Pe 1: 1 righteousness of our God and *S*
1:11 kingdom of our Lord and *S*
2:20 the knowledge of the Lord and *S*
3: 2 the apostles of the Lord and *S*,
3:18 and knowledge of our Lord and *S*
1 Jn 4:14 Father has sent the Son as *S*
Jude 25 To God our *S*, Who alone is

SAVIORS (1/1)

Ob 21 Then *s* shall come to Mount Zion

SAVOR (1/1)

Am 5:21 And I do not *s* your sacred

SAVORY (6/6)

Gen 27: 4 And make me *s* food, such as I
27: 7 Bring me game and make *s* food
27: 9 and I will make *s* food from
27:14 and his mother made *s* food,
27:17 Then she gave the *s* food and the
27:31 He also had made *s* food, and

SAVOUR (KJV) See AROMA

SAVOURY (KJV) See SAVORY

SAW (585/571)

Gen 1: 4 And God *s* the light, that it
1:10 And God *s* that it was good.
1:12 And God *s* that it was good.
1:18 And God *s* that it was good.
1:21 And God *s* that it was good.
1:25 And God *s* that it was good.
1:31 Then God *s* everything that He
3: 6 So when the woman *s* that the
6: 2 that the sons of God *s* the
6: 5 Then the LORD *s* that the
9:22 *s* the nakedness of his father,
12:14 that the Egyptians *s* the woman,
12:15 The princes of Pharaoh also *s*
13:10 And Lot lifted his eyes and *s*
16: 4 And when she *s* that she had
16: 5 and when she *s* that she had
18: 2 and when he *s* them, he ran
19: 1 When Lot *s* them, he rose to
19:28 the land of the plain; and he *s*,
21: 9 And Sarah *s* the son of Hagar the
21:19 and she *s* a well of water.
22: 4 Abraham lifted his eyes and *s*
24:30 when he *s* the nose ring, and
24:64 and when she *s* Isaac she
26: 8 looked through a window, and *s*,
28: 6 Esau *s* that Isaac had blessed
28: 8 Also Esau *s* that the daughters
29: 2 and *s* a well in the field; and
29:10 when Jacob *s* Rachel the

29:31 When the LORD *s* that Leah was
30: 1 Now when Rachel *s* that she bore
30: 9 When Leah *s* that she had
31: 2 And Jacob *s* the countenance of
31:10 that I lifted my eyes and *s* in
32: 2 When Jacob *s* them, he said,
32:25 Now when He *s* that He did not
33: 5 And he lifted his eyes and *s* the
34: 2 *s* her, he took her and lay with
37: 4 But when his brothers *s* that
37:18 Now when they *s* him afar off,
38: 2 And Judah *s* there a daughter of
38:14 for she *s* that Shelah was
38:15 When Judah *s* her, he thought she
39: 3 And his master *s* that the LORD
39:13 when she *s* that he had left his
40: 6 and *s* that they were sad.
40:16 When the chief baker *s* that the
41:22 Also I *s* in my dream, and
42: 1 When Jacob *s* that there was
42: 7 Joseph *s* his brothers and
42:21 for we *s* the anguish of his
42:27 he *s* his money; and there it
42:35 when they and their father *s*
43:16 When Joseph *s* Benjamin with
43:29 Then he lifted his eyes and *s*
45:27 and when he *s* the carts which
48: 8 Then Israel *s* Joseph's sons,
48:17 Now when Joseph *s* that his
49:15 He *s* that rest was good, And
50:11 *s* the mourning at the threshing
50:15 When Joseph's brothers *s* that
50:23 Joseph *s* Ephraim's children to
Ex 2: 2 And when she *s* that he was a
2: 5 and when she *s* the ark among
2: 6 she *s* the child, and behold,
2:11 And he *s* an Egyptian beating a
2:12 and when he *s* no one, he killed
3: 4 So when the LORD *s* that he
5:19 of the children of Israel *s*
8:15 But when Pharaoh *s* that there
9:34 And when Pharaoh *s* that the
14:30 and Israel *s* the Egyptians dead
14:31 Thus Israel *s* the great work
16:15 when the children of Israel *s*
18:14 So when Moses' father-in-law *s*
20:18 and when the people *s* it, they
24:10 and they *s* the God of Israel.
24:11 So they *s* God, and they ate and
32: 1 Now when the people *s* that Moses
32: 5 So when Aaron *s* it, he built an
32:19 that he *s* the calf and the
32:25 Now when Moses *s* that the
33:10 All the people *s* the pillar of
34:30 all the children of Israel *s*
34:35 the children of Israel *s* the
Lev 9:24 When all the people *s* it, they
Num 13:28 moreover we *s* the descendants
13:32 and all the people whom we *s* in
13:33 'There we *s* the giants
20:29 Now when all the congregation *s*
22: 2 Now Balak the son of Zippor *s*
22:23 Now the donkey *s* the Angel of
22:25 And when the donkey *s* the Angel
22:27 And when the donkey *s* the Angel
22:31 and he *s* the Angel of the LORD
22:33 The donkey *s* Me and turned aside
24: 1 Now when Balaam *s* that it
24: 2 and *s* Israel encamped according
25: 7 *s* it, he rose from among the
32: 1 and when they *s* the land of
32: 9 to the Valley of Eshcol and *s*
Deut 1:19 wilderness which you *s* on the
1:31 in the wilderness where you *s*
4:12 but *s* no form; you only heard
4:15 for you *s* no form when the
7:19 great trials which your eyes *s*,
29:17 and you *s* their abominations and
32:19 And when the LORD *s* it, He
Josh 7:21 When I *s* among the spoils a
8:14 when the king of Ai *s* it, that
8:20 Ai looked behind them, they *s*,
8:21 when Joshua and all Israel *s*
24: 7 And your eyes *s* what I did in
Judg 1:24 And when the spies *s* a man
9:36 And when Gaal *s* the people, he
9:55 And when the men of Israel *s*
11:35 when he *s* her, that he tore his
12: 3 So when I *s* that you would not
13:20 When Manoah and his wife *s*
14: 1 and *s* a woman in Timnah of the
14:11 when they *s* him, that they
16: 1 Now Samson went to Gaza and *s* a
16:18 When Delilah *s* that he had told
16:24 When the people *s* him, they
18: 7 They *s* the people who were
18:26 And when Micah *s* that they
19: 3 the father of the young woman *s*
19:17 he *s* the traveler in the open
19:30 And so it was that all who *s* it
20:36 So the children of Benjamin *s*
20:41 for they *s* that disaster had
Ruth 1:18 When she *s* that she was
2:18 and her mother-in-law *s* what
1 Sam 5: 7 And when the men of Ashdod *s* how
6:13 they lifted their eyes and *s*
9:17 And when Samuel *s* Saul, the
10:11 all who knew him formerly *s*
10:14 When we *s* that they were
12:12 And when you *s* that Nahash king
13: 6 When the men of Israel *s* that
13:11 When I *s* that the people were
14:52 And when Saul *s* any strong man
17:24 when they *s* the man, fled from
17:42 Philistine looked about and *s*
17:51 And when the Philistines *s* that
17:55 When Saul *s* David going out
18:15 when Saul *s* that he behaved
18:28 Thus Saul *s* and knew that the
19: 5 You *s* it and rejoiced.
19:20 And when they *s* the group of
22: 9 I *s* the son of Jesse going to
23:15 So David *s* that Saul had come
25:23 Now when Abigail *s* David, she
26: 3 and he *s* that Saul came after
26: 5 And David *s* the place where
26:12 and no man *s* it or knew it or
28: 5 When Saul *s* the army of the
28:12 When the woman *s* Samuel, she
28:13 I *s* a spirit ascending out of
28:21 the woman came to Saul and *s*
31: 5 And when his armorbearer *s* that
31: 7 *s* that the men of Israel had
2 Sam 1: 7 he looked behind him, he *s* me
6:16 looked through a window and *s*
10: 6 When the people of Ammon *s* that
10: 9 When Joab *s* that the battle
10:14 When the people of Ammon *s* that
10:15 When the Syrians *s* that they
10:19 were servants to Hadadezer *s*
11: 2 And from the roof he *s* a woman
12:19 When David *s* that his servants
17:18 Nevertheless a lad *s* them, and
17:23 Now when Ahithophel *s* that his
18:10 Now a certain man *s* it and told
18:10 I just *s* Absalom hanging in a
18:11 You just *s* him! And why did you
18:26 Then the watchman *s* another man
18:29 I *s* a great tumult, but I did
20:12 And when the man *s* that all the
20:12 when he *s* that everyone who
24:17 spoke to the LORD when he *s*
24:20 and *s* the king and his servants
1 Ki 3:28 for they *s* that the wisdom of
10: 7 the words until I came and *s*
12:16 Now when all Israel *s* that the
13:25 men passed by and *s* the corpse
16:18 when Zimri *s* that the city was
18:17 when Ahab *s* Elijah, that Ahab
18:39 Now when all the people *s* it,
19: 3 And when he *s* that, he arose
22:17 I *s* all Israel scattered on the
22:19 I *s* the LORD sitting on His
22:32 the captains of the chariots *s*
22:33 the chariots *s* that it was
2 Ki 2:12 And Elisha *s* it, and he cried
2:12 So he *s* him no more.
2:15 who were from Jericho *s* him,
3:22 and the Moabites *s* the water on
3:26 And when the king of Moab *s*
4:25 when the man of God *s* her afar
5:21 When Naaman *s* him running
6:17 eyes of the young man, and he *s*.
6:20 opened their eyes, and they *s*;
6:21 Now when the king of Israel *s*
9:17 and he *s* the company of Jehu as
9:22 when Joram *s* Jehu, that he
9:26 Surely I *s* yesterday the blood
9:27 when Ahaziah king of Judah *s*
11: 1 the mother of Ahaziah *s* that
12:10 whenever they *s* that there
13: 4 for He *s* the oppression of
14:26 For the LORD *s* that the
16:10 and *s* an altar that was at
16:12 the king *s* the altar; and the
23:16 he *s* the tombs that were there
1 Chr 10: 5 And when his armorbearer *s* that
10: 7 who were in the valley *s* that
15:29 looked through a window and *s*
19: 6 When the people of Ammon *s* that
19:10 When Joab *s* that the battle
19:15 When the people of Ammon *s* that
19:16 Now when the Syrians *s* that
19:19 the servants of Hadadezer *s*
21:16 David lifted his eyes and *s*
21:20 Now Ornan turned and *s* the
21:21 and Ornan looked and *s* David.
21:28 when David *s* that the LORD had
2 Chr 7: 3 all the children of Israel *s*
9: 6 their words until I came and *s*
10:16 Now when all Israel *s* that the
12: 7 Now when the LORD *s* that they
15: 9 from Israel when they *s* that
18:16 I *s* all Israel scattered on the
18:18 I *s* the LORD sitting on His
18:31 the captains of the chariots *s*
18:32 the captains of the chariots *s*
22:10 the mother of Ahaziah *s* that
24:11 and when they *s* that there
31: 8 and the leaders came and *s* the
32: 2 And when Hezekiah *s* that
Neh 6:16 and all the nations around us *s*
9: 9 You *s* the affliction of our
13:15 In those days I *s* people in
13:23 In those days I also *s* Jews
Esth 2:15 in the sight of all who *s* her.
3: 5 When Haman *s* that Mordecai did
5: 2 when the king *s* Queen Esther
5: 9 but when Haman *s* Mordecai in
7: 7 for he *s* that evil was
Job 2:13 for they *s* that his grief was
3:16 Like infants who never *s*
20: 9 The eye that *s* him will see
28:27 Then He *s* wisdom and declared
29: 8 The young men *s* me and hid,
29:11 And when the eye *s*, then it
31:21 When I *s* I had help in the
32: 5 When Elihu *s* that there was no
42:16 and *s* his children and
Ps 48: 5 They *s* it, and so they
50:18 When you *s* a thief, you
73: 3 When I *s* the prosperity of the
77:16 The waters *s* You, O God;
77:16 The waters *s* You, they were
95: 9 though they *s* My work.
114: 3 The sea *s* it and fled;
139:16 Your eyes *s* my substance, being
Prov 7: 7 And *s* among the simple, I
24:32 When I *s* it, I considered it
Eccl 2:13 Then I *s* that wisdom excels
2:24 in his labor. This also, I *s*,
3:16 Moreover I *s* under the sun:
4: 4 I *s* that for all toil and every
4: 7 and I *s* vanity under the sun:
4:15 I *s* all the living who walk
8:10 Then I *s* the wicked buried, who
8:17 then I *s* all the work of God,
9:11 I returned and *s* under the sun
Song 6: 9 The daughters *s* her And
Isa 1: 1 which he *s* concerning Judah and
2: 1 that Isaiah the son of Amoz *s*
6: 1 I *s* the Lord sitting on a
10:15 Or shall the *s* exalt itself
13: 1 which Isaiah the son of Amoz *s*.
21: 3 I was dismayed when I *s* it.
21: 7 And he *s* a chariot with a pair
22: 9 You also *s* the damage to the
41: 5 The coastlands *s* it and
57: 8 Where you *s* their nudity.
59:15 Then the LORD *s* it, and it
59:16 He *s* that there was no man,
Jer 3: 7 her treacherous sister Judah *s*
3: 8 Then I *s* that for all the causes
39: 4 Judah and all the men of war *s*
41:13 people who were with Ishmael *s*
44:17 and *s* no trouble.
Lam 1: 7 The adversaries *s* her And
Ezek 1: 1 the heavens were opened and I *s*
1:27 of His waist and upward I *s*,
1:27 of His waist and downward I *s*,
1:28 So when I *s* it, I fell on my
3:23 like the glory which I *s* by the
8: 4 like the vision that I *s* in the
8:10 So I went in and *s*,
10:15 was the living creature I *s*
10:20 is the living creature I *s*
11: 1 among whom I *s* Jaazaniah the
16: 6 when I passed by you and *s* you
16:50 I took them away as I *s* fit.
19: 5 When she *s* that she waited,
20:28 and they *s* all the high hills
23:11 although her sister Oholibah *s*
23:13 Then I *s* that she was defiled;
23:16 As soon as her eyes *s* them,
28:18 In the sight of all who *s* you.
41: 8 I also *s* an elevation all around
43: 3 of the vision which I *s*—
43: 3 like the vision which I *s* when I
43: 3 like the vision which I *s* by
Dan 2:41 Whereas you *s* the feet and toes,
2:41 just as you *s* the iron mixed
2:43 As you *s* iron mixed with ceramic
2:45 Inasmuch as you *s* that the stone
3:27 and they *s* these men on whose
4: 5 I *s* a dream which made me
4:13 I *s* in the visions of my head
4:20 The tree that you *s*,
4:23 And inasmuch as the king *s* a
5: 5 and the king *s* the part of the
7: 2 I *s* in my vision by night, and
7: 7 After this I *s* in the night
8: 2 I *s* in the vision, and it so
8: 2 and I *s* in the vision that I
8: 3 Then I lifted my eyes and *s*,
8: 4 I *s* the ram pushing westward,
8: 7 And I *s* him confronting the ram;
8:20 "The ram which you *s*,
10: 7 alone *s* the vision, for the men
10: 8 I was left alone when I *s* this
Hos 5:13 When Ephraim *s* his sickness,
5:13 And Judah *s* his wound, Then
9:10 I *s* your fathers As the
9:13 Just as I *s* Ephraim like Tyre,
Am 1: 1 which he *s* concerning Israel in
9: 1 I *s* the Lord standing by the
Jon 3:10 Then God *s* their works, that
Mic 1: 1 which he *s* concerning Samaria
Hab 1: 1 which the prophet Habakkuk *s*.
3: 7 I *s* the tents of Cushan in
3:10 The mountains *s* You and
Hag 2: 3 Who is left among you who *s* this
Zech 1: 8 I *s* by night, and behold, a man
5: 1 and *s* there a flying scroll.
Mt 2:10 When they *s* the star, they
2:11 they *s* the young Child with
2:16 when he *s* that he was deceived
3: 7 But when he *s* many of the
3:16 and He *s* the Spirit of God
4:18 *s* two brothers, Simon called
4:21 He *s* two other brothers, James
8:14 He *s* his wife's mother lying
8:18 And when Jesus *s* great
8:34 And when they *s* Him, they
9: 2 When Jesus *s* their faith, He
9: 8 Now when the multitudes *s* it,
9: 9 He *s* a man named Matthew

9:11 And when the Pharisees *s* it,
9:22 and when He *s* her He said, "Be
9:23 and *s* the flute players and the
9:36 But when He *s* the multitudes, He
12: 2 And when the Pharisees *s* it,
12:22 and mute man both spoke and *s*.
14:14 And when Jesus went out He *s* a
14:26 And when the disciples *s* Him
14:30 But when he *s* that the wind was
15:31 multitude marveled when they *s*
17: 8 they *s* no one but Jesus only.
18:31 So when his fellow servants *s*
20: 3 out about the third hour and *s*
21:15 the chief priests and scribes *s*
21:20 And when the disciples *s* it,
21:32 and when you *s* it, you did not
21:38 But when the vinedressers *s* the
22:11 he *s* a man there who did not
26: 8 But when His disciples *s* it,
26:71 another girl *s* him and said to
27:24 When Pilate *s* that he could not
27:54 *s* the earthquake and the things
28:17 When they *s* Him, they worshiped
Mk 1:10 He *s* the heavens parting and
1:16 He *s* Simon and Andrew his
1:19 He *s* James the son of Zebedee,
2: 5 When Jesus *s* their faith, He
2:12 We never *s* anything like
2:14 He *s* Levi the son of Alphaeus
2:16 the scribes and Pharisees *s*
3:11 whenever they *s* Him, fell down
5: 6 When he *s* Jesus from afar, he
5:15 and *s* the one who had been
5:16 And those who *s* it told them how
5:22 And when he *s* Him, he fell at
5:38 and *s* a tumult and those who
6:33 But the multitudes *s* them
6:34 *s* a great multitude and was
6:48 Then He *s* them straining at
6:49 And when they *s* Him walking on
6:50 for they all *s* Him and were
7: 2 Now when they *s* some of His
8:23 He asked him if he *s* anything.
8:25 And he was restored and *s*
9: 8 they *s* no one anymore, but only
9:14 He *s* a great multitude around
9:15 when they *s* Him, all the people
9:20 And when he *s* Him, immediately
9:25 When Jesus *s* that the people
9:38 we *s* someone who does not
10:14 But when Jesus *s* it, He was
11:20 they *s* the fig tree dried up
12:34 Now when Jesus *s* that he
12:41 sat opposite the treasury and *s*
14:67 And when she *s* Peter warming
14:69 And the servant girl *s* him
15:39 *s* that He cried out like this
16: 4 they *s* that the stone had been
16: 5 they *s* a young man clothed in a
Lk 1:12 And when Zacharias *s* him, he
1:29 But when she *s* him, she was
2:48 So when they *s* Him, they were
5: 2 and *s* two boats standing by the
5: 8 When Simon Peter *s* it, he fell
5:12 a man who was full of leprosy *s*
5:20 When He *s* their faith, He said
5:27 these things He went out and *s*
7:13 When the Lord *s* her, He had
7:39 Pharisee who had invited Him *s*
8:28 When he *s* Jesus, he cried out,
8:34 When those who fed them *s* what
8:47 Now when the woman *s* that she
9:32 they *s* His glory and the two
9:49 we *s* someone casting out demons
9:54 His disciples James and John *s*
10:18 I *s* Satan fall like lightning
10:31 And when he *s* him, he passed by
10:33 And when he *s* him, he had
11:38 When the Pharisee *s* it, he
13:12 But when Jesus *s* her, He called
15:20 his father *s* him and had
16:23 he lifted up his eyes and *s*
17:14 So when He *s* them, He said to
17:15 when he *s* that he was healed,
18:15 but when the disciples *s* it,
18:24 And when Jesus *s* that he became
18:43 when they *s* it, gave praise to
19: 5 He looked up and *s* him, and
19: 7 But when they *s* it, they all
19:41 He *s* the city and wept over it,
20:14 But when the vinedressers *s* him,
21: 1 And He looked up and *s* the rich
21: 2 and He *s* also a certain poor
22:49 When those around Him *s* what was
22:58 a little while another *s* him
23: 8 Now when Herod *s* Jesus, he was
23:47 So when the centurion *s* what had
24:12 he *s* the linen cloths lying by
Jn 1:29 The next day John *s* Jesus
1:32 I *s* the Spirit descending from
1:39 They came and *s* where He was
1:47 Jesus *s* Nathanael coming toward
1:48 under the fig tree, I *s* you."
1:50 'I *s* you under the fig tree,'
2:23 in His name when they *s* the
5: 6 When Jesus *s* him lying there,
6: 2 because they *s* His signs which
6:19 they *s* Jesus walking on the sea
6:22 on the other side of the sea *s*
6:24 when the people therefore *s* that
6:26 not because you *s* the signs,
8:10 had raised Himself up and *s* no
8:56 and he *s* it and was glad."
9: 1 He *s* a man who was blind from
11:31 when they *s* that Mary rose up
11:32 and *s* Him, she fell down at His
11:33 when Jesus *s* her weeping, and
12:41 things Isaiah said when he *s*
19: 6 chief priests and officers *s*
19:26 When Jesus therefore *s* His
19:33 when they came to Jesus and *s*
20: 1 and *s* that the stone had been
20: 5 *s* the linen cloths lying
20: 6 and he *s* the linen cloths lying
20: 8 and he *s* and believed.
20:12 And she *s* two angels in white
20:14 she turned around and *s* Jesus
20:20 were glad when they *s* the Lord.
21: 9 they *s* a fire of coals there,
21:20 *s* the disciple whom Jesus loved
Acts 1:11 so come in like manner as you *s*
3: 9 And all the people *s* him walking
3:12 So when Peter *s* it, he
4:13 Now when they *s* the boldness of
6:15 *s* his face as the face of an
7:31 When Moses *s* it, he marveled at
7:55 gazed into heaven and *s* the
8:18 And when Simon *s* that through
8:39 so that the eunuch *s* him no
9: 8 when his eyes were opened he *s*
9:35 who dwelt at Lydda and Sharon *s*
9:40 and when she *s* Peter she sat
10: 3 the ninth hour of the day he *s*
10:11 and *s* heaven opened and an
11: 5 and in a trance I *s* a vision,
11: 6 I *s* four-footed animals of the
12: 3 And because he *s* that it pleased
12:16 they opened the door and *s*
13:12 when he *s* what had been done,
13:36 and *s* corruption;
13:37 but He whom God raised up *s* no
13:45 But when the Jews *s* the
14:11 Now when the people *s* what Paul
16:19 But when her masters *s* that
17:16 provoked within him when he *s*
21:32 And when they *s* the commander
22: 9 who were with me indeed *s* the
22:18 and *s* Him saying to me, 'Make
26:13 along the road I *s* a light from
28: 4 So when the natives *s* the
28: 6 looked for a long time and *s*
28:15 When Paul *s* them, he thanked
Gal 1:19 But I *s* none of the other
2: 7 when they *s* that the gospel for
2:14 But when I *s* that they were not
Phil 1:30 the same conflict which you *s*
4: 9 and received and heard and *s*
Heb 3: 9 And *s* My works forty
11:23 because they *s* he was a
Rev 1: 2 Christ, to all things that he *s*.
1:12 And having turned I *s* seven
1:17 And when I *s* Him, I fell at His
1:20 of the seven stars which you *s*
1:20 seven lampstands which you *s*
4: 4 and on the thrones I *s*
5: 1 And I *s* in the right hand of
5: 2 Then I *s* a strong angel
6: 1 Now I *s* when the Lamb opened one
6: 9 I *s* under the altar the souls
7: 1 After these things I *s* four
7: 2 Then I *s* another angel ascending
8: 2 And I *s* the seven angels who
9: 1 And I *s* a star fallen from
9:17 And thus I *s* the horses in the
10: 1 I *s* still another mighty angel
10: 5 The angel whom I *s* standing on
11:11 great fear fell on those who *s*
11:12 and their enemies *s* them.
12:13 Now when the dragon *s* that he
13: 1 And I *s* a beast rising up out
13: 2 Now the beast which I *s* was like
13: 3 And I *s* one of his heads as if
13:11 Then I *s* another beast coming
14: 6 Then I *s* another angel flying
15: 1 Then I *s* another sign in heaven,
15: 2 And I *s* something like a sea of
16:13 And I *s* three unclean spirits
17: 3 And I *s* a woman sitting on a
17: 6 I *s* the woman, drunk with the
17: 6 And when I *s* her, I marveled
17: 8 The beast that you *s* was, and is
17:12 The ten horns which you *s* are
17:15 to me, "The waters which you *s*,
17:16 And the ten horns which you *s* on
17:18 And the woman whom you *s* is that
18: 1 After these things I *s* another
18:18 and cried out when they *s* the
19:11 Now I *s* heaven opened, and
19:17 Then I *s* an angel standing in
19:19 And I *s* the beast, the kings of
20: 1 Then I *s* an angel coming down
20: 4 And I *s* thrones, and they sat
20: 4 Then I *s* the souls of those
20:11 Then I *s* a great white throne
20:12 And I *s* the dead, small and
21: 1 Now I *s* a new heaven and a new
21: 2 *s* the holy city, New Jerusalem,
21:22 But I *s* no temple in it, for
22: 8 *s* and heard these things.
22: 8 And when I heard and *s*,

SAWN (1/1)

Heb 11:37 they were *s* in two, were

SAWS (4/4)

2 Sam 12:31 and put them to work with *s*
1 Ki 7: 9 cut to size, trimmed with *s*,
1 Chr 20: 3 and put them to work with *s*,
Isa 10:15 exalt itself against him who *s*

SAY (1052/999)

Gen 12:12 see you, that they will *s*,
12:13 Please *s* you are my sister,
12:19 'Why did you *s*, 'She is my
14:23 is yours, lest you should *s*,
20: 5 Did he not *s* to me, 'She is my
20:13 *s* of me, "He is my brother."
24:14 the young woman to whom I *s*,
24:43 and I *s* to her, "Please give
26: 7 for he was afraid to *s*,
26: 9 your wife; so how could you *s*,
32:18 "then you shall *s*,
32:20 'and also *s*, 'Behold, your
34:11 and whatever you *s* to me I will
34:12 give according to what you *s*
37:17 from here, for I heard them *s*,
37:20 into some pit; and we shall *s*,
43: 7 have known that he would *s*,
44: 4 *s* to them, 'Why have you repaid
44: 7 Why does my lord *s* these words?
44:16 'What shall we *s* to my lord?
45: 9 and *s* to him, 'Thus says your
45:17 *S* to your brothers, 'Do this:
46:31 and *s* to him, 'My brothers and
46:34 'that you shall *s*, 'Your
50:17 Thus you shall *s* to Joseph: "I
Ex 3:13 to the children of Israel and *s*
3:13 and they *s* to me, 'What is
3:13 what shall I *s* to them?"
3:14 Thus you shall *s* to the children
3:15 Thus you shall *s* to the children
3:16 and *s* to them, 'The LORD God
3:18 and you shall *s* to him, 'The
4: 1 to my voice; suppose they *s*,
4:12 and teach you what you shall *s*.
4:22 Then you shall *s* to Pharaoh,
4:23 So I *s* to you, let My son go
5:16 and they *s* to us, 'Make brick!'
5:17 idle! Idle! Therefore you *s*,
6: 6 Therefore *s* to the children of
6:29 king of Egypt all that I *s* to
7: 9 then you shall *s* to Aaron,
7:16 And you shall *s* to him, 'The
7:19 *S* to Aaron, 'Take your rod and
8: 1 Go to Pharaoh and *s* to him,
8: 5 *S* to Aaron, 'Stretch out your
8:16 *S* to Aaron, 'Stretch out your
8:20 Then *s* to him, 'Thus says the
9:13 and *s* to him, 'Thus says the
12:26 when your children *s* to you,
12:27 'that you shall *s*, 'It is
13:14 that you shall *s* to him, 'By
14: 3 For Pharaoh will *s* of the
16: 9 *S* to all the congregation of the
19: 3 Thus you shall *s* to the house of
20:22 Thus you shall *s* to the children
32:12 the Egyptians speak, and *s*,
33: 5 *S* to the children of Israel,
33:12 You *s* to me, 'Bring up this
Lev 1: 2 and *s* to them: 'When any one of
15: 2 and *s* to them: 'When any man
17: 2 and *s* to them, 'This is the
17: 8 Also you shall *s* to them:
18: 2 and *s* to them: 'I am the LORD
19: 2 and *s* to them: 'You shall be
20: 2 you shall *s* to the children of
21: 1 and *s* to them: 'None shall
22: 3 *S* to them: 'Whoever of all your
22:18 and *s* to them: 'Whatever man of
23: 2 and *s* to them: 'The feasts of
23:10 and *s* to them: 'When you come
25: 2 and *s* to them: 'When you come
25:20 'And if you *s*, "What shall we
27: 2 and *s* to them: 'When a man
Num 5:12 and *s* to them: 'If any man's
5:19 and *s* to the woman, "If no man
5:21 and he shall *s* to the
5:22 Then the woman shall *s*,
6: 2 and *s* to them: 'When either a
6:23 children of Israel. *S* to them:
8: 2 and *s* to him, 'When you arrange
11:12 that You should *s* to me, 'Carry
11:18 Then you shall *s* to the people,
11:23 you shall see whether what I *s*
14:28 *S* to them, 'As I live,' says the
15: 2 and *s* to them: 'When you have
15:18 and *s* to them: 'When you come
18:26 and *s* to them: 'When you take
18:30 Therefore you shall *s* to them:
21:27 those who speak in proverbs *s*:
22:17 and I will do whatever you *s* to
22:19 what more the LORD will *s* to
22:38 have I any power at all to *s*
25:12 'Therefore *s*, 'Behold, I give
28: 2 and *s* to them, 'My offering, My
28: 3 And you shall *s* to them, 'This
33:51 and *s* to them: 'When you have
34: 2 and *s* to them: 'When you come
35:10 and *s* to them: 'When you cross
Deut 1:39 who you *s* will be victims, who
4: 6 hear all these statutes, and *s*,
5:27 that the LORD our God may *s*,
5:30 Go and *s* to them, "Return to
6:21 then you shall *s* to your son:

S

7:17 If you should *s* in your heart,
8:17 then you *s* in your heart, 'My
9:28 which You brought us should *s*,
12:20 He has promised you, and you *s*,
17:14 it and dwell in it, and *s*,
18:21 And if you *s* in your heart, 'How
20: 3 'And he shall *s* to them, 'Hear,
20: 8 further to the people, and *s*,
21: 7 "Then they shall answer and *s*,
21:20 And they shall *s* to the elders
22:16 young woman's father shall *s*
25: 7 the gate to the elders, and *s*,
25: 9 in his face, and answer and *s*,
26: 3 and *s* to him, 'I declare today
26: 5 And you shall answer and *s*
26:13 then you shall *s* before the
27:14 speak with a loud voice and *s*
27:15 the people shall answer and *s*,
27:16 And all the people shall *s*,
27:17 And all the people shall *s*,
27:18 And all the people shall *s*,
27:19 And all the people shall *s*,
27:20 And all the people shall *s*,
27:21 And all the people shall *s*,
27:22 And all the people shall *s*,
27:23 And all the people shall *s*,
27:24 And all the people shall *s*,
27:25 And all the people shall *s*,
27:26 And all the people shall *s*,
28:67 "In the morning you shall *s*,
28:67 And at evening you shall *s*,
29:22 comes from a far land, would *s*,
29:24 "All nations would *s*:
29:25 "Then people would *s*:
30:12 in heaven, that you should *s*,
30:13 the sea, that you should *s*,
31:17 so that they will *s* in that
32:27 Lest they should *s*,
32:37 He will *s*: 'Where are their
32:40 raise My hand to heaven, And *s*,
33:27 from before you, And will *s*,
Josh 5:14 What does my Lord *s* to His
6:10 until the day I *s* to you,
7: 8 what shall I *s* when Israel
7:13 up, sanctify the people, and *s*,
8: 6 from the city, for they will *s*,
9:11 and *s* to them, "We are your
22:11 of Israel heard someone *s*,
22:27 your descendants may not *s* to
22:28 when they *s* this to us or to
22:28 in time to come, that we may *s*,
Judg 4:20 you shall *s*, 'No.'
7: 4 that of whom I *s* to you, 'This
7: 4 and of whomever I *s* to you,
7:11 you shall hear what they *s*;
7:18 side of the whole camp, and *s*,
9:54 lest men *s* of me, 'A woman
12: 5 the men of Gilead would *s* to
12: 6 then they would *s* to him, "Then
12: 6 they would say to him, "Then *s*,
12: 6 And he would *s*, "Sibboleth,"
16:15 said to him, "How can you *s*,
18:24 How can you *s* to me, 'What ails
21:22 that we will *s* to them, 'Be
Ruth 1:12 If I should *s* I have hope, if
3: 5 All that you *s* to me I will
1 Sam 2:15 servant would come and *s* to
2:20 Elkanah and his wife, and *s*,
2:36 and a morsel of bread, and *s*,
3: 9 He calls you, that you must *s*,
8: 7 the people in all that they *s*
10: 2 and they will *s* to you, 'The
11: 9 Thus you shall *s* to the men of
14: 9 If they *s* thus to us, 'Wait
14:10 But if they *s* thus, 'Come up to
14:34 and *s* to them, 'Bring me here
16: 2 "Take a heifer with you, and *s*,
18:22 with David secretly, and *s*,
18:25 Thus you shall *s* to David: 'The
19:24 they *s*, "Is Saul also among
20: 6 father misses me at all, then *s*,
20:21 If I expressly *s* to him,
20:22 But if I *s* thus to the young
20:26 Nevertheless Saul did not *s*
24: 9 to the words of men who *s*,
25: 6 And thus you shall *s* to him who
27:10 Then Achish would *s*,
27:10 David would *s*, "Against the
2 Sam 5: 8 Therefore they *s*, "The blind
7: 8 thus shall you *s* to My servant
7:20 Now what more can David *s* to
11:21 the wall?'—then you shall *s*,
11:25 Thus you shall *s* to Joab: 'Do
13: 5 *s* to him, 'Please let my sister
13:28 and when I *s* to you, 'Strike
14:12 And he said, "*S* on."
14:32 may send you to the king, to *s*,
15: 2 Absalom would call to him and *s*,
15: 2 And he would *s*, "Your servant
15: 3 Then Absalom would *s* to him,
15: 4 Moreover Absalom would *s*,
15:10 the trumpet, then you shall *s*,
15:34 and *s* to Absalom, 'I will be
16:10 Who then shall *s*, 'Why have
17: 9 that whoever hears it will *s*,
19:10 why do you *s* nothing about
19:13 And *s* to Amasa, 'Are you not my
20:16 Hear! Please *s* to Joab, 'Come
21: 4 So he said, "Whatever you *s*,
24: 1 moved David against them to *s*,
1 Ki 1:13 to King David and *s* to him,
1:25 drinking before him; and they *s*,
1:34 and blow the horn, and *s*,
1:36 God of my lord the king *s* so
2:14 I have something to *s* to
2:14 And she said, "*S* it."
2:16 she said to him, "*S* it."
5: 6 according to whatever you *s*.
9: 8 astonished and will hiss, and *s*,
12:10 thus you shall *s* to them: 'My
14: 5 Thus and thus you shall *s* to
18:11 'And now you *s*, 'Go, tell
18:14 'And now you *s*, 'Go, tell
18:44 *s* to Ahab, 'Prepare your
20: 4 lord, O king, just as you *s*,
22: 8 Let not the king *s* such
22:27 'and *s*, 'Thus says the king:
2 Ki 1: 3 and *s* to them, 'Is it because
1: 6 and *s* to him, "Thus says the
2:18 Did I not *s* to you, 'Do not
4:13 *S* now to her, 'Look, you have
4:26 and *s* to her, 'Is it well
4:28 a son of my lord? Did I not *s*,
7: 4 'If we *s*, 'We will enter
7:13 left in it; or indeed, I *s*,
8:10 *s* to him, 'You shall certainly
8:14 'What did Elisha *s* to you?"
9: 3 and pour it on his head, and *s*,
9:17 him to meet them, and let him *s*,
9:37 so that they shall not *s*,
14:27 And the LORD did not *s* that He
18:19 *S* now to Hezekiah, 'Thus says
18:22 But if you *s* to me, 'We trust in
19: 6 Thus you shall *s* to your master,
20:14 to him, "What did these men *s*,
1 Chr 16:31 And let them *s* among the
16:35 And *s*, "Save us, O God of
17: 7 thus shall you *s* to My servant
17:18 What more can David *s* to You
21:18 of the LORD commanded Gad to *s*
2 Chr 7:21 by it will be astonished and *s*,
10:10 thus you shall *s* to them: 'My
18: 7 Let not the king *s* such
18:26 'and *s*, 'Thus says the
25:19 Indeed you *s* that you have
Ezra 8:17 I told them what they should *s*
9:10 what shall we *s* after this?
Neh 5: 8 and found nothing to *s*.
5:12 we will do as you *s*."
6: 8 No such things as you *s* are
Esth 1:18 of Persia and Media will *s* to
Job 6:22 Did I ever *s*, 'Bring
7: 4 When I lie down, I *s*,
7:13 When I *s*, 'My bed will
9:12 Who can *s* to Him, 'What are
9:22 all one thing; Therefore I *s*,
9:27 If I *s*, 'I will forget my
10: 2 I will *s* to God, 'Do not
17:12 'The light is near,' they *s*,
17:14 If I *s* to corruption, 'You are
19:28 If you should *s*, 'How shall
20: 7 Those who have seen him will *s*,
21:14 Yet they *s* to God, 'Depart from
21:19 They *s*, 'God lays up one's
21:28 For you *s*, 'Where is the
22:13 And you *s*, 'What does God
22:29 they cast you down, and you *s*,
23: 5 understand what He would *s* to
27: 5 be it from me That I should *s*
28:22 Destruction and Death *s*,
32:10 'Therefore I *s*, 'Listen to
32:11 you searched out what to *s*.
32:13 Lest you *s*, 'We have found
33:32 If you have anything to *s*,
34:18 Is it fitting to *s* to a
34:34 Men of understanding *s* to me,
35: 2 Do you *s*, 'My righteousness
35: 3 For you *s*, 'What advantage
35:14 Although you *s* you do not see
37:19 Teach us what we should *s* to
38:35 And *s* to you, 'Here we are!'?
Ps 3: 2 Many are they who *s* of me,
4: 6 There are many who *s*,
11: 1 How can you *s* to my soul,
13: 4 Lest my enemy *s*,
27:14 Wait, I *s*, on the LORD!
31:14 I *s*, "You are my God."
35: 3 *S* to my soul, "I am your
35:10 All my bones shall *s*,
35:25 Let them not *s* in their hearts,
35:25 Let them not *s*, "We have
35:27 And let them *s* continually,
40:15 Who *s* to me, "Aha, aha!"
40:16 such as love Your salvation *s*
41: 8 "An evil disease," they *s*,
42: 3 While they continually *s* to
42: 9 I will *s* to God my Rock, "Why
42:10 While they *s* to me all day
58:11 So that men will *s*,
59: 7 in their lips; For they *s*,
64: 5 They *s*, "Who will see them?"
66: 3 *S* to God, "How awesome are
70: 3 because of their shame, Who *s*,
70: 4 those who love Your salvation *s*
73:11 And they *s*, "How does God
79:10 Why should the nations *s*,
87: 7 the players on instruments *s*,
90: 3 turn man to destruction, And *s*,
91: 2 I will *s* of the LORD, "He
94: 7 Yet they *s*, "The LORD does
94:18 If I *s*, "My foot slips,"
96:10 *S* among the nations, "The
106:48 And let all the people *s*,
107: 2 the redeemed of the LORD *s*
115: 2 Why should the Gentiles *s*,
118: 2 Let Israel now *s*,
118: 3 Let the house of Aaron now *s*,
118: 4 those who fear the LORD now *s*,
122: 8 and companions, I will now *s*,
124: 1 Let Israel now *s*—
129: 1 Let Israel now *s*—
129: 8 let those who pass by them *s*,
139:11 If I *s*, "Surely the
Prov 1:11 If they *s*, "Come with us,
3:28 Do not *s* to your neighbor,
5:12 And *s*: "How I have hated
7: 4 *S* to wisdom, "You are my
20: 9 Who can *s*, "I have made
20:22 Do not *s*, "I will
24:12 If you *s*, "Surely we did
24:29 Do not *s*, "I will do to
25: 7 For it is better that he *s* to
27:21 is valued by what others *s*
30: 9 I be full and deny You, And *s*,
30:15 never satisfied, Four never *s*,
Eccl 5: 6 nor *s* before the messenger of
6: 3 I *s* that a stillborn child is
7:10 Do not *s*, "Why were the
7:21 to heart everything people *s*,
8: 2 I *s*, "Keep the king's
8: 4 And who may *s* to him, "What
12: 1 the years draw near when you *s*,
Isa 2: 3 Many people shall come and *s*,
3:10 *S* to the righteous that it
5:19 That *s*, "Let Him make
7: 4 and *s* to him: 'Take heed, and be
8:12 'Do not *s*, 'A conspiracy,'
8:19 And when they *s* to you, "Seek
9: 9 Who *s* in pride and arrogance of
10:12 Jerusalem, that He will *s*,
12: 1 And in that day you will *s*:
12: 4 And in that day you will *s*:
14: 4 the king of Babylon, and *s*:
14:10 They all shall speak and *s* to
19:11 How do you *s* to Pharaoh, "I
20: 6 of this territory will *s* in
22:15 who is over the house, and *s*:
29:15 They *s*, "Who sees us?"
29:16 For shall the thing made *s* of
29:16 Or shall the thing formed *s* of
30:10 Who *s* to the seers, "Do not
30:22 You will *s* to them, "Get
33:24 And the inhabitant will not *s*,
35: 4 *S* to those who are
36: 4 *S* now to Hezekiah, 'Thus says
36: 5 I *s* you speak of having plans
36: 7 But if you *s* to me, 'We trust in
37: 6 Thus shall you *s* to your master,
38:15 "What shall I *s*?
39: 3 to him, "What did these men *s*,
40: 9 *S* to the cities of Judah,
40:27 Why do you *s*, O Jacob,
41:26 former times, that we may *s*,
42:17 Who *s* to the molded images,
43: 6 I will *s* to the north, 'Give
43: 9 Or let them hear and *s*,
44: 5 will *s*, 'I am the LORD's';
44:19 nor understanding to *s*,
44:20 cannot deliver his soul, Nor *s*,
45: 9 of the earth! Shall the clay *s*
45: 9 Or shall your handiwork *s*,
45:19 I did not *s* to the seed of
45:24 He shall *s*, 'Surely in the
47: 8 Who *s* in your heart, 'I am,
48: 5 it to you, Lest you should *s*,
48: 7 heard them, Lest you should *s*,
48:20 *S*, "The LORD has redeemed
49: 9 That You may *s* to the
49:20 Will *s* again in your ears,
49:21 Then you will *s* in your heart,
51:16 And *s* to Zion, 'You are My
56: 3 Nor let the eunuch *s*, "Here
57:10 Yet you did not *s*, 'There
57:14 And one shall *s*,
58: 3 'Why have we fasted,' they *s*,
58: 9 You shall cry, and He will *s*,
62:11 *S* to the daughter of Zion,
65: 5 Who *s*, 'Keep to yourself,
Jer 1: 7 LORD said to me: "Do not *s*,
2: 6 Neither did they *s*,
2: 8 The priests did not *s*,
2:23 "How can you *s*,
2:27 of their trouble They will *s*,
2:31 Why do My people *s*, 'We are
2:35 Yet you *s*, 'Because I am
2:35 against you, Because you *s*,
3: 1 'They *s*, 'If a man
3:12 words toward the north, and *s*:
3:16 that they will *s* no more, 'The
4: 5 proclaim in Jerusalem, and *s*:
4: 5 Cry, 'Gather together,' And *s*,
5: 2 Though they *s*, 'As the LORD
5:15 can you understand what they *s*.
5:19 "And it will be when you *s*,
5:24 They do not *s* in their heart,
7: 2 proclaim there this word, and *s*,
7:10 is called by My name, and *s*,
7:28 So you shall *s* to them, 'This
8: 4 Moreover you shall *s* to them,
8: 8 How can you *s*, 'We are
10:11 Thus you shall *s* to them: "The
10:19 But I *s*, "Truly this is an
11: 3 and *s* to them, 'Thus says the
13:12 And they will *s* to you, 'Do
13:13 Then you shall *s* to them, 'Thus
13:18 *S* to the king and to the queen

13:21 What will you *s* when He
13:22 And if you *s* in your heart,
14:13 the prophets *s* to them, 'You
14:15 whom I did not send, and who *s*,
14:17 Therefore you shall *s* this word
15: 2 if they *s* to you, 'Where should
16:10 and they *s* to you, 'Why has the
16:11 then you shall *s* to them,
16:19 the ends of the earth and *s*,
17:15 Indeed they *s* to me, "Where
17:20 and *s* to them, 'Hear the word of
19: 3 'and *s*, 'Hear the word of
19:11 and *s* to them, 'Thus says the
20:10 'Report," they *s*,
21: 3 Thus you shall *s* to Zedekiah,
21: 8 Now you shall *s* to this people,
21:11 house of the king of Judah, *s*,
21:13 says the LORD, "Who *s*,
22: 2 'and *s*, 'Hear the word of
22: 8 and everyone will *s* to his
23: 7 "that they shall no longer *s*,
23:17 They continually *s* to those who
23:17 of his own heart, they *s*,
23:31 "who use their tongues and *s*,
23:33 you shall then *s* to them,
23:34 the priest and the people who *s*,
23:35 Thus every one of you shall *s* to
23:37 Thus you shall *s* to the prophet,
23:38 'But since you *s*, 'The oracle
23:38 Because you *s* this word, "The
23:38 sent to you, saying, "Do not *s*,
25:27 Therefore you shall *s* to them,
25:28 then you shall *s* to them, 'Thus
25:30 and *s* to them: 'The LORD
26: 4 And you shall *s* to them, 'Thus
27: 4 And command them to *s* to their
27: 4 thus you shall *s* to your
31: 7 Proclaim, give praise, and *s*,
31:10 in the isles afar off, and *s*,
31:29 In those days they shall *s* no
32: 3 "Why do you prophesy and *s*,
32:36 this city of which you *s*,
32:43 in this land of which you *s*,
33:10 in this place—of which you *s*,
33:11 the voice of those who will *s*:
36:29 And you shall *s* to Jehoiakim
37: 7 Thus you shall *s* to the king of
38:22 and those women shall *s*:
38:25 and they come to you and *s* to
38:26 then you shall *s* to them, 'I
42:13 But if you *s*, 'We will
43: 2 our God has not sent you to *s*,
43:10 and *s* to them, 'Thus says the
45: 4 Thus you shall *s* to him, 'Thus
46:14 *S*, 'Stand fast and prepare
48:14 'How can you *s*, 'We are
48:17 all you who know his name, *S*,
48:19 *S*, 'What has happened?'
50: 2 *S*, 'Babylon is taken, Bel
51:35 The inhabitant of Zion will *s*;
51:35 of Chaldea!" Jerusalem will *s*.
51:62 'then you shall *s*, 'O LORD,
51:64 'Then you shall *s*, 'Thus
Lam 2:12 They *s* to their mothers,
2:16 They *s*, "We have swallowed
Ezek 2: 4 and you shall *s* to them, 'Thus
2: 8 hear what I *s* to you. Do not be
3:18 When I *s* to the wicked, 'You
3:27 and you shall *s* to them, 'Thus
6: 3 'and *s*, 'O mountains of
6:11 and stamp your feet, and *s*,
8:12 For they *s*, 'The LORD does
9: 9 for they *s*, 'The LORD has
11: 3 'who *s*, 'The time is not
11:16 'Therefore *s*, 'Thus says the
11:17 'Therefore *s*, 'Thus says the
12:10 *S* to them, 'Thus says the Lord
12:11 '*S*, 'I am a sign to you.
12:19 And *s* to the people of the land,
12:23 But *s* to them, "The days are
12:25 I will *s* the word and perform
12:28 Therefore *s* to them, 'Thus says
13: 2 and *s* to those who prophesy out
13: 7 You *s*, 'The LORD says,'
13:11 *s* to those who plaster it with
13:15 and I will *s* to you, 'The wall
13:18 'and *s*, 'Thus says the Lord
14: 4 and *s* to them, 'Thus says the
14: 6 Therefore *s* to the house of
14:17 a sword on that land, and *s*,
16: 3 'and *s*, 'Thus says
17: 3 'and *s*, 'Thus says the
17: 9 *S*, 'Thus says the Lord
17:12 *S* now to the rebellious house:
18:19 Yet you *s*, 'Why should the
18:25 Yet you *s*, 'The way of
19: 2 'and *s*: 'What is your
20: 3 and *s* to them, 'Thus says the
20: 5 *S* to them, 'Thus says the Lord
20:27 and *s* to them, 'Thus says the
20:30 Therefore *s* to the house of
20:32 mind shall never be, when you *s*,
20:47 and *s* to the forest of the
20:49 Lord GOD! They *s* of me, 'Does
21: 3 and *s* to the land of Israel,
21: 7 And it shall be when they *s* to
21: 9 "Son of man, prophesy and *s*,
21: 9 say, 'Thus says the LORD!' *S*:
21:28 you, son of man, prophesy and *s*,
21:28 their reproach,' and *s*:
22: 3 'Then *s*, 'Thus says the
22:24 *s* to her: 'You are a land that
24: 3 and *s* to them, 'Thus says the
25: 3 *S* to the Ammonites, 'Hear the
25: 8 GOD: "Because Moab and Seir *s*,
26:17 and *s* to you: "How you have
27: 3 and *s* to Tyre, 'You who are
28: 2 *s* to the prince of Tyre, 'Thus
28: 2 heart is lifted up, And you *s*,
28: 9 Will you still *s* before him who
28:12 and *s* to him, 'Thus says the
28:22 'and *s*, 'Thus says the Lord
29: 3 'Speak, and *s*, 'Thus says the
30: 2 "Son of man, prophesy and *s*,
31: 2 *s* to Pharaoh king of Egypt and
32: 2 and *s* to him: 'You are like a
33: 2 and *s* to them: 'When I bring
33: 8 'When I *s* to the wicked,
33:10 *s* to the house of Israel: 'Thus
33:10 house of Israel: 'Thus you *s*,
33:11 *S* to them: 'As I live,' says
33:12 *s* to the children of your
33:13 When I *s* to the righteous that
33:14 when I *s* to the wicked, 'You
33:17 the children of your people *s*,
33:20 'Yet you *s*, 'The way of the
33:25 Therefore *s* to them, 'Thus says
33:27 *S* thus to them, 'Thus says the
34: 2 prophesy and *s* to them, 'Thus
35: 3 and *s* to it, 'Thus says the Lord
36: 1 the mountains of Israel, and *s*,
36: 3 "therefore prophesy, and *s*,
36: 6 and *s* to the mountains, the
36:13 Because they *s* to you, 'You
36:22 Therefore *s* to the house of
36:35 'So they will *s*, 'This
37: 4 and *s* to them, 'O dry bones,
37: 9 and *s* to the breath, 'Thus says
37:11 They indeed *s*, 'Our bones are
37:12 Therefore prophesy and *s* to
37:19 *s* to them, 'Thus says the Lord
37:21 Then *s* to them, 'Thus says the
38: 3 'and *s*, 'Thus says
38:11 'You will *s*, 'I will go
38:13 all their young lions will *s*
38:14 prophesy and *s* to Gog, 'Thus
39: 1 prophesy against Gog, and *s*,
44: 5 all that I *s* to you concerning
44: 6 Now *s* to the rebellious, to the
Dan 4:35 can restrain His hand Or *s* to
Hos 2: 1 *S* to your brethren, 'My
2: 7 Then she will *s*, 'I will
2:23 Then I will *s* to those who
2:23 And they shall *s*, 'You are
10: 3 For now they *s*, "We have
10: 8 They shall *s* to the mountains,
13: 2 They *s* of them, "Let the men
14: 2 *S* to Him, "Take away all
14: 3 Nor will we *s* anymore to the
14: 8 "Ephraim shall *s*,
Joel 2:17 Let them *s*, "Spare Your
2:17 Why should they *s* among the
2:19 The LORD will answer and *s* to
3:10 Let the weak *s*, 'I am
Am 3: 9 in the land of Egypt, and *s*:
4: 1 Who *s* to your husbands,
5:16 And they shall *s* in all the
6:10 he will *s* to one inside the
6:10 Then someone will *s*, "None."
6:10 say, "None." And he will *s*,
6:13 rejoice over Lo Debar, Who *s*,
7:16 the word of the LORD: You *s*,
8:14 by the sin of Samaria, Who *s*,
9:10 shall die by the sword, Who *s*,
Ob 3 You who *s* in your heart,
Mic 2: 6 you *s* to those who
3:11 they lean on the LORD, and *s*,
4: 2 Many nations shall come and *s*,
4:11 gathered against you, Who *s*,
Nah 3: 7 you Will flee from you, and *s*,
Hab 2: 1 watch to see what He will *s* to
2: 6 riddle against him, and *s*,
Zeph 1:12 Who *s* in their heart, 'The
Zech 1: 3 Therefore *s* to them, 'Thus says
7: 5 *S* to all the people of the land,
11: 5 those who sell them *s*,
12: 5 the governors of Judah shall *s*
13: 3 mother who begot him will *s* to
13: 5 'But he will *s*, 'I am no
13: 6 And one will *s* to him, 'What
13: 9 I will answer them. I will *s*,
13: 9 And each one will *s*,
Mal 1: 2 says the LORD. "Yet you *s*,
1: 5 shall see, And you shall *s*,
1: 6 who despise My name. Yet you *s*,
1: 7 But *s*, 'In what way have
1:12 you profane it, In that you *s*,
1:13 You also *s*, 'Oh, what a
2:14 Yet you *s*, "For what reason?"
2:17 Yet you *s*, "In what way
2:17 In that you *s*, "Everyone
3: 8 you have robbed Me! But you *s*,
3:13 Says the LORD, "Yet you *s*,
Mt 3: 9 and do not think to *s* to
3: 9 For I *s* to you that God is
4:17 Jesus began to preach and to *s*,
5:11 and *s* all kinds of evil against
5:18 I *s* to you, till heaven and
5:20 For I *s* to you, that unless your
5:22 But I *s* to you that whoever is
5:26 I *s* to you, you will by no
5:28 But I *s* to you that whoever
5:32 But I *s* to you that whoever
5:34 But I *s* to you, do not swear at
5:44 But I *s* to you, love your
6: 2 I *s* to you, they have their
6: 5 I *s* to you, they have their
6:16 I *s* to you, they have their
6:25 Therefore I *s* to you, do not
6:29 and yet I *s* to you that even
7: 4 Or how can you *s* to your
7:22 Many will *s* to Me in that day,
8: 9 And I *s* to this one, 'Go,'
8:10 I *s* to you, I have not found
8:11 And I *s* to you that many will
9: 5 "For which is easier, to *s*,
9: 5 sins are forgiven you,' or to *s*,
10:15 I *s* to you, it will be more
10:23 I *s* to you, you will not have
10:42 I *s* to you, he shall by no
11: 7 Jesus began to *s* to the
11: 9 I *s* to you, and more than a
11:11 I *s* to you, among those born of
11:18 eating nor drinking, and they *s*,
11:19 eating and drinking, and they *s*,
11:22 But I *s* to you, it will be more
11:24 But I *s* to you that it shall be
12: 6 Yet I *s* to you that in this
12:31 Therefore I *s* to you, every sin
12:36 But I *s* to you that for every
13:17 I *s* to you that many prophets
13:30 at the time of harvest I will *s*
15: 5 'But you *s*, 'Whoever says
16: 2 "When it is evening you *s*,
16:13 Who do men *s* that I, the Son of
16:14 Some *s* John the Baptist, some
16:15 But who do you *s* that I am?"
16:18 And I also *s* to you that you are
16:28 I *s* to you, there are some
17:10 Why then do the scribes *s* that
17:12 But I *s* to you that Elijah has
17:20 I *s* to you, if you have faith
17:20 you will *s* to this mountain,
18: 3 I *s* to you, unless you are
18:10 for I *s* to you that in heaven
18:13 I *s* to you, he rejoices more
18:18 I *s* to you, whatever you bind
18:19 Again I *s* to you that if two of
18:22 I do not *s* to you, up to seven
19: 9 And I *s* to you, whoever divorces
19:23 I *s* to you that it is hard for
19:24 And again I *s* to you, it is
19:28 Assuredly I *s* to you, that in
21: 3 anything to you, you shall *s*,
21:21 I *s* to you, if you have faith
21:21 but also if you *s* to this
21:25 themselves, saying, "If we *s*,
21:25 He will *s* to us, 'Why then did
21:26 'But if we *s*, 'From men,'
21:31 I *s* to you that tax collectors
21:43 Therefore I *s* to you, the
22:23 who *s* there is no resurrection,
23: 3 for they *s*, and do not
23:16 to you, blind guides, who *s*,
23:30 'and *s*, 'If we had lived
23:36 I *s* to you, all these things
23:39 for I *s* to you, you shall see Me
23:39 shall see Me no more till you *s*,
24: 2 I *s* to you, not one stone
24:26 Therefore if they *s* to you,
24:34 I *s* to you, this generation
24:47 I *s* to you that he will make
25:12 I *s* to you, I do not know you.'
25:34 Then the King will *s* to those on
25:40 the King will answer and *s*
25:40 I *s* to you, inasmuch as you did
25:41 Then He will also *s* to those on
25:45 I *s* to you, inasmuch as you did
26:13 I *s* to you, wherever this
26:18 and *s* to him, 'The Teacher
26:21 I *s* to you, one of you will
26:22 and each of them began to *s* to
26:29 But I *s* to you, I will not drink
26:34 I *s* to you that this night,
26:64 I *s* to you, hereafter you will
27:11 to him, "It is as you *s*.
27:33 called Golgotha, that is to *s*,
27:64 and *s* to the people, 'He has
Mk 1:44 See that you *s* nothing to
2: 9 to *s* to the paralytic, 'Your
2: 9 sins are forgiven you,' or to *s*,
2:11 I *s* to you, arise, take up your
3:28 I *s* to you, all sins will be
5:31 thronging You, and You *s*,
5:41 I *s* to you, arise."
6:11 I *s* to you, it will be more
7:11 'But you *s*, 'If a man says
8:12 I *s* to you, no sign shall be
8:27 Who do men *s* that I am?"
8:28 "John the Baptist; but some *s*,
8:29 But who do you *s* that I am?"
9: 1 I *s* to you that there are some
9: 6 he did not know what to *s*,
9:11 Why do the scribes *s* that Elijah
9:13 But I *s* to you that Elijah has
9:41 I *s* to you, he will by no means
10:15 I *s* to you, whoever does not
10:28 Then Peter began to *s* to Him,
10:29 I *s* to you, there is no one who
10:47 he began to cry out and *s*,
11: 3 *s*, 'The Lord has need of it,'
11:23 I *s* to you, whoever says to
11:24 Therefore I *s* to you, whatever
11:31 themselves, saying, "If we *s*,
11:31 say, 'From heaven,' He will *s*,
11:32 'But if we *s*, 'From

12:18 who *s* there is no resurrection,
12:35 is it that the scribes *s*
12:43 I *s* to you that this poor widow
13: 5 answering them, began to *s*:
13:30 I *s* to you, this generation
13:37 And what I *s* to you, I say to
13:37 I *s* to all: Watch!"
14: 9 I *s* to you, wherever this
14:14 *s* to the master of the house,
14:18 I *s* to you, one of you who eats
14:19 and to *s* to Him one by one,
14:25 I *s* to you, I will no longer
14:30 I *s* to you that today, even
14:58 "We heard Him *s*,
14:65 and to *s* to Him, "Prophesy!"
14:69 and began to *s* to those who
15: 2 to him, "It is as you *s*.
Lk 3: 8 and do not begin to *s* to
3: 8 For I *s* to you that God is
4:21 And He began to *s* to them,
4:23 You will surely *s* this proverb
4:24 I *s* to you, no prophet is
5:23 "Which is easier, to *s*,
5:23 sins are forgiven you,' or to *s*,
5:24 I *s* to you, arise, take up your
6:27 But I *s* to you who hear:
6:42 Or how can you *s* to your
6:46 do not do the things which I *s*?
7: 7 But *s* the word, and my servant
7: 8 And I *s* to one, 'Go,' and he
7: 9 I *s* to you, I have not found
7:14 I *s* to you, arise."
7:26 I *s* to you, and more than a
7:28 For I *s* to you, among those born
7:33 nor drinking wine, and you *s*,
7:34 eating and drinking, and you *s*,
7:40 I have something to *s* to you."
7:40 he said, "Teacher, *s* it."
7:47 Therefore I *s* to you, her sins,
7:49 the table with Him began to *s*
8:45 throng and press You, and You *s*,
9:18 Who do the crowds *s* that I am?"
9:19 but some *s* Elijah; and others
9:19 and others *s* that one of the
9:20 But who do you *s* that I am?"
10: 5 house you enter, first *s*,
10: 9 and *s* to them, 'The kingdom of
10:10 go out into its streets and *s*,
10:12 But I *s* to you that it will be
11: 2 to them, "When you pray, *s*:
11: 5 go to him at midnight and *s* to
11: 7 will answer from within and *s*,
11: 8 I *s* to you, though he will not
11: 9 So I *s* to you, ask, and it will
11:18 Because you *s* I cast out demons
11:29 together, He began to *s*,
11:51 I *s* to you, it shall be
11:54 Him in something He might *s*,
12: 1 He began to *s* to His disciples
12: 4 And I *s* to you, My friends, do
12: 5 I *s* to you, fear Him!
12: 8 Also I *s* to you, whoever
12:11 answer, or what you should *s*.
12:12 very hour what you ought to *s*.
12:19 And I will *s* to my soul, "Soul,
12:22 Therefore I *s* to you, do not
12:27 and yet I *s* to you, even
12:37 I *s* to you that he will gird
12:44 I *s* to you that he will make
12:54 of the west, immediately you *s*,
12:55 see the south wind blow, you *s*,
13:24 I *s* to you, will seek to enter
13:25 and He will answer and *s* to
13:26 "then you will begin to *s*,
13:27 'But He will *s*, 'I tell
13:35 I *s* to you, you shall not see
13:35 the time comes when you *s*,
14: 9 invited you and him come and *s*
14:10 who invited you comes he may *s*
14:17 servant at supper time to *s* to
14:24 For I *s* to you that none of
15: 7 I *s* to you that likewise there
15:10 I *s* to you, there is joy in the
15:18 and will *s* to him, "Father, I
16: 9 And I *s* to you, make friends for
17: 6 you can *s* to this mulberry
17: 7 will *s* to him when he has come
17: 8 But will he not rather *s* to him,
17:10 which you are commanded, *s*,
17:21 'nor will they *s*, 'See here!'
17:23 And they will *s* to you, 'Look
18:17 I *s* to you, whoever does not
18:29 I *s* to you, there is no one who
19:26 For I *s* to you, that to everyone
19:31 thus you shall *s* to him,
20: 5 themselves, saying, "If we *s*,
20: 5 say, 'From heaven,' He will *s*,
20: 6 'But if we *s*, 'From men,'
20:21 we know that You *s* and teach
20:41 How can they *s* that the Christ
21: 3 Truly I *s* to you that this poor
21:32 I *s* to you, this generation
22:11 Then you shall *s* to the master
22:16 for I *s* to you, I will no longer
22:18 for I *s* to you, I will not drink
22:37 For I *s* to you that this which
22:70 You rightly *s* that I am."
23: 3 and said, "It is as you *s*.
23:29 are coming in which they will *s*,
23:30 to *s* to the mountains,
23:43 I *s* to you, today you will be
Jn 1:22 What do you *s* about yourself?"
1:38 (which is to *s*, when
1:51 I *s* to you, hereafter you shall
3: 3 I *s* to you, unless one is born
3: 5 I *s* to you, unless one is born
3:11 I *s* to you, We speak what We
4:20 and you Jews *s* that in
4:35 'Do you not *s*, 'There are
4:35 I *s* to you, lift up your eyes
5:19 I *s* to you, the Son can do
5:24 I *s* to you, he who hears My
5:25 I *s* to you, the hour is coming,
5:34 but I *s* these things that you
6:26 I *s* to you, you seek Me, not
6:32 I *s* to you, Moses did not give
6:47 I *s* to you, he who believes in
6:53 I *s* to you, unless you eat the
7:26 and they *s* nothing to Him.
8: 5 be stoned. But what do You *s*?
8:26 I have many things to *s* and to
8:33 How can you *s*, 'You will
8:34 I *s* to you, whoever commits sin
8:48 Do we not *s* rightly that You are
8:51 I *s* to you, if anyone keeps My
8:52 and You *s*, 'If anyone
8:54 of whom you *s* that He is your
8:55 And if I *s*, 'I do not know
8:58 I *s* to you, before Abraham was,
9:17 What do you *s* about Him because
9:19 who you *s* was born blind?
9:41 but now you *s*, 'We see.'
10: 1 I *s* to you, he who does not
10: 7 I *s* to you, I am the door of
10:36 do you *s* of Him whom the Father
11:40 Did I not *s* to you that if you
11:51 Now this he did not *s* on his own
12:24 I *s* to you, unless a grain of
12:27 is troubled, and what shall I *s*?
12:34 and how can You *s*,
12:49 what I should *s* and what I
13:13 and you *s* well, for so I am.
13:16 I *s* to you, a servant is not
13:20 I *s* to you, he who receives
13:21 I *s* to you, one of you will
13:33 so now I *s* to you.
13:38 I *s* to you, the rooster shall
14: 9 so how can you *s*, 'Show us
14:12 I *s* to you, he who believes in
14:28 You have heard Me *s* to you, 'I
16: 4 And these things I did not *s* to
16:12 I still have many things to *s* to
16:20 I *s* to you that you will weep
16:23 I *s* to you, whatever you ask
16:26 and I do not *s* to you that I
18:37 You *s* rightly that I am a king.
20:16 "Rabboni!" (which is to *s*,
20:17 but go to My brethren and *s* to
21:18 I *s* to you, when you were
21:23 Yet Jesus did not *s* to him that
Acts 4:14 they could *s* nothing against
4:32 neither did anyone *s* that any
5:38 And now I *s* to you, keep away
6:11 they secretly induced men to *s*,
6:14 for we have heard him *s* that
8:34 of whom does the prophet *s*
13:15 for the people, *s* on."
17:18 does this babbler want to *s*?
23: 8 For Sadducees *s* that there is no
23:18 He has something to *s* to you."
24:20 who are here themselves *s* if
28:26 to this people and *s*:
Rom 2:22 You who *s*, "Do not commit
3: 5 of God, what shall we *s*?
3: 8 And why not *s*, "Let us do
3: 8 and as some affirm that we *s*.
4: 1 What then shall we *s* that
4: 3 For what does the Scripture *s*?
4: 9 For we *s* that faith was
6: 1 What shall we *s* then?
7: 7 What shall we *s* then?
8:31 What then shall we *s* to these
9:14 What shall we *s* then?
9:19 You will *s* to me then, "Why
9:20 Will the thing formed *s* to him
9:30 What shall we *s* then?
10: 6 Do not *s* in your heart,
10: 8 But what does it *s*?
10:18 But I *s*, have they not
10:19 But I *s*, did Israel not
11: 1 I *s* then, has God cast away His
11: 4 does the divine response *s* to
11:11 I *s* then, have they stumbled
11:19 You will *s* then, "Branches were
12: 3 For I *s*, through the grace
15: 8 Now I *s* that Jesus Christ has
1 Cor 1:12 Now I *s* this, that each of you
1:15 lest anyone should *s* that I had
6: 5 I *s* this to your shame.
7: 6 But I *s* this as a concession,
7: 8 But I *s* to the unmarried and to
7:12 to the rest I, not the Lord, *s*:
7:29 But this I *s*, brethren, the
7:35 And this I *s* for your own
9: 8 Do I *s* these things as a mere
9: 8 Or does not the law *s* the same
9:10 Or does He *s* it altogether for
10:15 judge for yourselves what I *s*.
10:29 "Conscience," I *s*,
11:22 What shall I *s* to you?
12: 3 and no one can *s* that Jesus is
12:15 If the foot should *s*,
12:16 And if the ear should *s*,
12:21 And the eye cannot *s* to the
14:16 the place of the uninformed *s* '
14:16 does not understand what you *s*?
14:23 will they not *s* that you are
15:12 how do some among you *s* that
15:35 But someone will *s*, "How
15:50 Now this I *s*, brethren, that
2 Cor 7: 3 I do not *s* this to condemn; for
9: 6 But this I *s*: He who sows
10:10 "For his letters," they *s*,
11:16 I *s* again, let no one think me
11:21 I *s* that we were too weak for
Gal 1: 9 so now I *s* again, if anyone
3:16 He does not *s*, "And to
3:17 And this I *s*, that the law,
4: 1 Now I *s* that the heir, as long
4:30 what does the Scripture *s*?
5: 2 *s* to you that if you become
5:16 I *s* then: Walk in the Spirit,
Eph 4:17 This I *s*, therefore, and
Phil 4: 4 Again I will *s*, rejoice!
Col 2: 4 Now this I *s* lest anyone should
4:17 And *s* to Archippus, "Take heed
1 Th 1: 8 so that we do not need to *s*
4:15 For this we *s* to you by the word
5: 3 For when they *s*, "Peace and
1 Tim 1: 7 neither what they *s* nor the
2 Tim 2: 7 Consider what I *s*, and may
Titus 2: 8 having nothing evil to *s* of
Phm 1:21 you will do even more than I *s*.
Heb 1: 5 of the angels did He ever *s*:
5:11 of whom we have much to *s*,
11:14 For those who *s* such things
11:32 And what more shall I *s*?
13: 6 So we may boldly *s*:
Jas 1:13 Let no one *s* when he is tempted,
2: 3 wearing the fine clothes and *s*
2: 3 and *s* to the poor man, "You
2:18 But someone will *s*, "You have
4:13 Come now, you who *s*, "Today
4:15 Instead you ought to *s*,
1 Jn 1: 6 If we *s* that we have fellowship
1: 8 If we *s* that we have no sin, we
1:10 If we *s* that we have not sinned,
5:16 I do not *s* that he should pray
Rev 2: 2 And you have tested those who *s*
2: 9 the blasphemy of those who *s*
2:24 'Now to you I *s*, and to the
2:24 the depths of Satan, as they *s*,
3: 9 who *s* they are Jews and are
3:17 'Because you *s*, 'I am rich,
6: 5 the third living creature *s*,
22:17 And the Spirit and the bride *s*,
22:17 And let him who hears *s*,

SAYING (1430/1396)

Gen 1:22 And God blessed them, *s*,
2:16 LORD God commanded the man, *s*,
3:17 of which I commanded you, *s*,
5:29 And he called his name Noah, *s*,
8:15 Then God spoke to Noah, *s*,
9: 8 and to his sons with him, *s*:
15: 1 came to Abram in a vision, *s*,
15: 4 of the LORD came to him, *s*,
15:18 made a covenant with Abram, *s*:
17: 3 and God talked with him, *s*:
18:12 Sarah laughed within herself, *s*,
18:13 "Why did Sarah laugh, *s*,
18:15 But Sarah denied it, *s*,
19:15 angels urged Lot to hurry, *s*,
21:22 his army, spoke to Abraham, *s*,
22:20 that it was told Abraham, *s*,
23: 3 spoke to the sons of Heth, *s*,
23: 5 answered Abraham, *s* to him,
23: 8 And he spoke with them, *s*,
23:10 at the gate of his city, *s*,
23:13 of the people of the land, *s*,
23:14 Abraham, *s* to him,
24: 7 spoke to me and swore to me, *s*,
24:30 words of his sister Rebekah, *s*,
24:37 my master made me swear, *s*,
26:11 charged all his people, *s*,
26:20 with Isaac's herdsmen, *s*,
27: 6 spoke to Jacob her son, *s*,
27: 6 speak to Esau your brother, *s*,
28: 6 him he gave him a charge, *s*,
28:20 Then Jacob made a vow, *s*,
31: 1 the words of Laban's sons, *s*,
31:11 God spoke to me in a dream, *s*,
31:29 spoke to me last night, *s*,
32: 4 And he commanded them, *s*,
32: 6 messengers returned to Jacob, *s*,
32:17 he commanded the first one, *s*,
32:17 meets you and asks you, *s*,
32:19 all who followed the droves, *s*,
32:29 Then Jacob asked, *s*,
34: 4 spoke to his father Hamor, *s*,
34: 8 But Hamor spoke with them, *s*,
34:20 with the men of their city, *s*:
37:15 field. And the man asked him, *s*,
38:13 And it was told Tamar, *s*,
38:21 asked the men of that place, *s*,
38:24 after, that Judah was told, *s*,
38:25 sent to her father-in-law, *s*,
38:28 and bound it on his hand, *s*,
39:12 caught him by his garment, *s*,
39:14 her house and spoke to them, *s*,
39:17 to him with words like these, *s*,
39:19 which his wife spoke to him, *s*,
40: 7 custody of his lord's house, *s*,
41: 9 butler spoke to Pharaoh, *s*:
41:16 So Joseph answered Pharaoh, *s*,

42:14 “It is as I spoke to you, *s*,
42:22 And Reuben answered them, *s*,
42:22 “Did I not speak to you, *s*,
42:28 *s* to one another, “What is
42:29 that had happened to them, *s*:
42:37 Reuben spoke to his father, *s*,
43: 3 But Judah spoke to him, *s*,
43: 3 “The man solemnly warned us, *s*,
43: 7 ourselves and our family, *s*,
44: 1 the steward of his house, *s*,
44:19 “My lord asked his servants, *s*,
44:32 for the lad to my father, *s*,
45:16 was heard in Pharaoh’s house, *s*,
45:26 And they told him, *s*,
47: 5 Then Pharaoh spoke to Joseph, *s*,
48:20 So he blessed them that day, *s*,
48:20 “By you Israel will bless, *s*,
50: 4 to the household of Pharaoh, *s*,
50: 4 in the hearing of Pharaoh, *s*,
50: 5 ‘My father made me swear, *s*,
50:16 sent messengers to Joseph, *s*,
50:16 father died he commanded, *s*,
50:25 from the children of Israel, *s*,
Ex 1:22 commanded all his people, *s*,
2:10 So she called his name Moses, *s*,
3:16 and of Jacob, appeared to me, *s*,
5: 6 people and their officers, *s*,
5: 8 therefore they cry out, *s*,
5:10 out and spoke to the people, *s*,
5:13 forced them to hurry, *s*,
5:15 and cried out to Pharaoh, *s*,
6:10 the LORD spoke to Moses, *s*,
6:12 Moses spoke before the LORD, *s*,
6:29 the LORD spoke to Moses, *s*,
7: 8 spoke to Moses and Aaron, *s*,
7: 9 “When Pharaoh speaks to you, *s*,
7:16 Hebrews has sent me to you, *s*,
8: 9 Accept the honor of *s* when I
9: 5 LORD appointed a set time, *s*,
11: 8 to me and bow down to me, *s*,
12: 1 Aaron in the land of Egypt, *s*,
12: 3 the congregation of Israel, *s*:
13: 1 the LORD spoke to Moses, *s*,
13: 8 tell your son in that day, *s*,
13:14 son asks you in time to come, *s*,
13:19 of Israel under solemn oath, *s*,
14: 1 Now the LORD spoke to Moses, *s*:
14:12 that we told you in Egypt, *s*,
15: 1 song to the LORD, and spoke, *s*:
15:24 complained against Moses, *s*,
16:11 And the LORD spoke to Moses, *s*,
16:12 of Israel. Speak to them, *s*,
17: 4 Moses cried out to the LORD, *s*,
17: 7 they tempted the LORD, *s*,
19: 3 to him from the mountain, *s*,
19:12 for the people all around, *s*,
19:23 for You warned us, *s*,
20: 1 God spoke all these words, *s*:
25: 1 the LORD spoke to Moses, *s*:
30:11 the LORD spoke to Moses, *s*:
30:17 the LORD spoke to Moses, *s*:
30:22 the LORD spoke to Moses, *s*:
30:31 to the children of Israel, *s*:
31: 1 the LORD spoke to Moses, *s*:
31:12 the LORD spoke to Moses, *s*,
31:13 to the children of Israel, *s*:
33: 1 to Abraham, Isaac, and Jacob, *s*,
35: 4 of the children of Israel, *s*,
35: 4 which the LORD commanded, *s*:
36: 5 and they spoke to Moses, *s*,
36: 6 throughout the camp, *s*,
40: 1 the LORD spoke to Moses, *s*:
Lev 1: 1 the tabernacle of meeting, *s*,
4: 1 Now the LORD spoke to Moses, *s*,
4: 2 to the children of Israel, *s*:
5:14 the LORD spoke to Moses, *s*:
6: 1 And the LORD spoke to Moses, *s*:
6: 8 the LORD spoke to Moses, *s*,
6: 9 “Command Aaron and his sons, *s*,
6:19 the LORD spoke to Moses, *s*,
6:24 the LORD spoke to Moses, *s*,
6:25 to Aaron and to his sons, *s*,
7:22 the LORD spoke to Moses, *s*,
7:23 to the children of Israel, *s*:
7:28 the LORD spoke to Moses, *s*,
7:29 to the children of Israel, *s*:
8: 1 And the LORD spoke to Moses, *s*:
8:31 offerings, as I commanded, *s*,
9: 3 of Israel you shall speak, *s*,
10: 3 is what the LORD spoke, *s*:
10: 8 the LORD spoke to Aaron, *s*:
10:16 of Aaron who were left, *s*,
11: 1 Moses and Aaron, *s* to them,
11: 2 to the children of Israel, *s*,
12: 1 the LORD spoke to Moses, *s*,
12: 2 to the children of Israel, *s*:
13: 1 spoke to Moses and Aaron, *s*:
14: 1 the LORD spoke to Moses, *s*,
14:33 spoke to Moses and Aaron, *s*:
14:35 comes and tells the priest, *s*,
15: 1 spoke to Moses and Aaron, *s*,
17: 1 And the LORD spoke to Moses, *s*,
17: 2 the LORD has commanded, *s*:
18: 1 the LORD spoke to Moses, *s*,
19: 1 And the LORD spoke to Moses, *s*,
20: 1 the LORD spoke to Moses, *s*,
21:16 the LORD spoke to Moses, *s*,
21:17 “Speak to Aaron, *s*:
22: 1 the LORD spoke to Moses, *s*,
22:17 the LORD spoke to Moses, *s*,
22:26 the LORD spoke to Moses, *s*,
23: 1 And the LORD spoke to Moses, *s*,
23: 9 the LORD spoke to Moses, *s*,
23:23 the LORD spoke to Moses, *s*,
23:24 to the children of Israel, *s*:
23:26 the LORD spoke to Moses, *s*:
23:33 the LORD spoke to Moses, *s*,
23:34 to the children of Israel, *s*:
24: 1 the LORD spoke to Moses, *s*:
24:13 the LORD spoke to Moses, *s*,
24:15 to the children of Israel, *s*:
25: 1 to Moses on Mount Sinai, *s*,
27: 1 Now the LORD spoke to Moses, *s*,
Num 1: 1 out of the land of Egypt, *s*:
1:48 LORD had spoken to Moses, *s*:
2: 1 spoke to Moses and Aaron, *s*:
3: 5 the LORD spoke to Moses, *s*:
3:11 the LORD spoke to Moses, *s*:
3:14 in the Wilderness of Sinai, *s*:
3:44 the LORD spoke to Moses, *s*:
4: 1 spoke to Moses and Aaron, *s*:
4:17 spoke to Moses and Aaron, *s*:
4:21 the LORD spoke to Moses, *s*:
5: 1 And the LORD spoke to Moses, *s*:
5: 5 the LORD spoke to Moses, *s*,
5:11 the LORD spoke to Moses, *s*,
6: 1 the LORD spoke to Moses, *s*,
6:22 the LORD spoke to Moses, *s*:
6:23 to Aaron and his sons, *s*,
7: 4 the LORD spoke to Moses, *s*,
8: 1 And the LORD spoke to Moses, *s*:
8: 5 the LORD spoke to Moses, *s*:
8:23 the LORD spoke to Moses, *s*,
9: 1 out of the land of Egypt, *s*:
9: 9 the LORD spoke to Moses, *s*,
9:10 to the children of Israel, *s*:
10: 1 And the LORD spoke to Moses, *s*:
11:13 For they weep all over me, *s*,
11:18 in the hearing of the LORD, *s*,
11:20 and have wept before Him, *s*,
12:13 Moses cried out to the LORD, *s*,
13: 1 And the LORD spoke to Moses, *s*,
13:32 which they had spied out, *s*,
14: 7 of the children of Israel, *s*:
14:15 of Your fame will speak, *s*,
14:17 just as You have spoken, *s*,
14:26 spoke to Moses and Aaron, *s*,
14:40 to the top of the mountain, *s*,
15: 1 And the LORD spoke to Moses, *s*,
15:17 the LORD spoke to Moses, *s*,
15:37 the LORD spoke to Moses, *s*,
16: 5 to Korah and all his company, *s*,
16:20 spoke to Moses and Aaron, *s*,
16:23 So the LORD spoke to Moses, *s*,
16:24 “Speak to the congregation, *s*,
16:26 he spoke to the congregation, *s*,
16:36 the LORD spoke to Moses, *s*:
16:41 against Moses and Aaron, *s*,
16:44 And the LORD spoke to Moses, *s*,
17: 1 And the LORD spoke to Moses, *s*:
17:12 of Israel spoke to Moses, *s*,
18:25 the LORD spoke to Moses, *s*,
19: 1 spoke to Moses and Aaron, *s*,
19: 2 the LORD has commanded, *s*:
20: 3 with Moses and spoke, *s*:
20: 7 the LORD spoke to Moses, *s*,
20:23 border of the land of Edom, *s*:
21:21 Sihon king of the Amorites, *s*,
22: 5 of his people, to call him, *s*:
22:10 of Moab, has sent to me, *s*,
23:26 Balak, “Did I not tell you, *s*,
24:12 whom you sent to me, *s*,
25:10 the LORD spoke to Moses, *s*:
25:16 the LORD spoke to Moses, *s*:
26: 1 the son of Aaron the priest, *s*:
26: 3 across from Jericho, *s*:
26:52 the LORD spoke to Moses, *s*:
27: 2 of the tabernacle of meeting, *s*:
27: 6 the LORD spoke to Moses, *s*:
27: 8 to the children of Israel, *s*:
27:15 Moses spoke to the LORD, *s*:
28: 1 Now the LORD spoke to Moses, *s*,
30: 1 the children of Israel, *s*,
31: 1 And the LORD spoke to Moses, *s*:
31: 3 So Moses spoke to the people, *s*,
31:25 the LORD spoke to Moses, *s*:
32: 2 leaders of the congregation, *s*,
32:10 day, and He swore an oath, *s*,
32:25 of Reuben spoke to Moses, *s*:
32:31 children of Reuben answered, *s*:
33:50 across from Jericho, *s*,
34: 1 the LORD spoke to Moses, *s*,
34:13 the children of Israel, *s*:
34:16 the LORD spoke to Moses, *s*,
35: 1 Jordan across from Jericho, *s*:
35: 9 the LORD spoke to Moses, *s*,
36: 5 to the word of the LORD, *s*:
36: 6 the daughters of Zelophehad, *s*,
Deut 1: 5 began to explain this law, *s*,
1: 6 our God spoke to us in Horeb, *s*:
1: 9 I spoke to you at that time, *s*:
1:16 your judges at that time, *s*,
1:25 they brought back word to us, *s*,
1:28 have discouraged our hearts, *s*,
1:34 was angry, and took an oath, *s*,
1:37 angry with me for your sakes, *s*,
2: 2 “And the LORD spoke to me, *s*:
2: 4 ‘And command the people, *s*,
2:17 “that the LORD spoke to me, *s*:
2:26 Heshbon, with words of peace, *s*,
3:18 I commanded you at that time, *s*:
3:21 Joshua at that time, *s*,
3:23 with the LORD at that time, *s*:
6:20 son asks you in time to come, *s*,
9: 4 has cast them out before you, *s*,
9:13 the LORD spoke to me, *s*,
9:23 sent you from Kadesh Barnea, *s*,
12:30 not inquire after their gods, *s*,
13: 2 of which he spoke to you, *s*,
13: 6 soul, secretly entices you, *s*,
13:12 God gives you to dwell in, *s*,
13:13 inhabitants of their city, *s*,
15: 9 wicked thought in your heart, *s*,
15:11 therefore I command you, *s*,
18:16 in the day of the assembly, *s*,
19: 7 “Therefore I command you, *s*,
20: 5 shall speak to the people, *s*:
22:17 her with shameful conduct, *s*,
27: 1 Israel, commanded the people, *s*:
27: 9 Levites, spoke to all Israel, *s*,
27:11 the people on the same day, *s*,
29:19 blesses himself in his heart, *s*,
31:10 And Moses commanded them, *s*:
31:25 of the covenant of the LORD, *s*:
32:48 to Moses that very same day, *s*:
34: 4 Abraham, Isaac, and Jacob, *s*,
Josh 1: 1 son of Nun, Moses’ assistant, *s*:
1:10 the officers of the people, *s*,
1:11 camp and command the people, *s*,
1:12 of Manasseh Joshua spoke, *s*,
1:13 of the LORD commanded you, *s*,
1:16 So they answered Joshua, *s*,
2: 1 Acacia Grove to spy secretly, *s*,
2: 2 was told the king of Jericho, *s*,
2: 3 of Jericho sent to Rahab, *s*,
3: 3 they commanded the people, *s*,
3: 6 Joshua spoke to the priests, *s*,
3: 8 bear the ark of the covenant, *s*,
4: 1 the LORD spoke to Joshua, *s*:
4: 3 “and command them, *s*,
4: 6 children ask in time to come, *s*,
4:15 the LORD spoke to Joshua, *s*,
4:17 commanded the priests, *s*,
4:21 to the children of Israel, *s*:
4:21 fathers in time to come, *s*,
4:22 shall let your children know, *s*,
6:10 had commanded the people, *s*,
6:26 charged them at that time, *s*,
7: 2 of Bethel, and spoke to them, *s*,
8: 4 And he commanded them, *s*:
9:11 of our country spoke to us, *s*,
9:22 them, and he spoke to them, *s*,
9:22 “Why have you deceived us, *s*,
10: 3 and Debir king of Eglon, *s*,
10: 6 Joshua at the camp at Gilgal, *s*,
10:17 And it was told Joshua, *s*,
14: 9 “So Moses swore on that day, *s*,
17: 4 Nun, and before the rulers, *s*,
17:14 of Joseph spoke to Joshua, *s*,
17:17 Ephraim and Manasseh—*s*,
18: 8 who went to survey the land, *s*,
20: 1 LORD also spoke to Joshua, *s*,
20: 2 to the children of Israel, *s*:
21: 2 Shiloh in the land of Canaan, *s*,
22: 8 and spoke to them, *s*,
22:15 and they spoke with them, *s*,
22:24 it for fear, for a reason, *s*,
22:24 may speak to our descendants, *s*,
Judg 1: 1 of Israel asked the LORD, *s*,
5: 1 of Abinoam sang on that day, *s*:
6:13 our fathers told us about, *s*,
6:32 day he called him Jerubbaal, *s*,
7: 2 glory for itself against Me, *s*,
7: 3 in the hearing of the people, *s*,
7:24 all the mountains of Ephraim, *s*,
8: 9 spoke to the men of Penuel, *s*,
8:15 about whom you ridiculed me, *s*,
9: 1 house of his mother’s father, *s*,
9:31 to Abimelech secretly, *s*,
10:10 cried out to the LORD, *s*,
11:12 king of the people of Ammon, *s*,
11:17 to the king of Edom, *s*,
13: 6 came and told her husband, *s*,
14: 2 told his father and mother, *s*,
15:13 So they spoke to him, *s*,
16: 2 They were quiet all night, *s*,
16:18 the lords of the Philistines, *s*,
16:28 Samson called to the LORD, *s*,
17: 2 even *s* it in my ears—here is
19:22 of the house, the old man, *s*,
20: 8 the people arose as one man, *s*,
20:12 all the tribe of Benjamin, *s*,
20:23 asked counsel of the LORD, *s*,
20:28 *s*, “Shall I yet again go
21: 1 had sworn an oath at Mizpah, *s*,
21: 5 up to the LORD at Mizpah, *s*,
21:10 men, and commanded them, *s*,
21:18 of Israel have sworn an oath, *s*,
21:20 the children of Benjamin, *s*,
Ruth 2:15 Boaz commanded his young men, *s*,
4: 4 I thought to inform you, *s*,
4:17 women gave him a name, *s*,
1 Sam 1:20 and called his name Samuel, *s*,
4:21 she named the child Ichabod, *s*,
5:10 that the Ekronites cried out, *s*,
6: 2 the priests and the diviners, *s*,
6:21 of Kirjath Jearim, *s*,
7: 3 to all the house of Israel, *s*,
7:12 and called its name Ebenezer, *s*,
9:15 ear the day before Saul came, *s*,
9:26 Saul on the top of the house, *s*,
10: 2 and is worrying about you, *s*,
11: 7 by the hands of messengers, *s*,
13: 3 throughout all the land, *s*,
14:24 placed the people under oath, *s*,
14:28 the people with an oath, *s*,

S

14:33 Then they told Saul, *s*,
15:10 of the LORD came to Samuel, *s*,
15:12 Saul, it was told Samuel, *s*,
16:22 Then Saul sent to Jesse, *s*,
17:26 to the men who stood by him, *s*,
17:27 answered him in this manner, *s*,
18: 8 and the *s* displeased him;
18:24 servants of Saul told him, *s*,
19: 2 So Jonathan told David, *s*,
19:11 David's wife, told him, *s*,
19:15 back to see David, *s*,
19:19 Now it was told Saul, *s*,
20:16 with the house of David, *s*,
20:21 there I will send a lad, *s*,
20:42 in the name of the LORD, *s*,
21:11 him to one another in dances, *s*:
23: 1 Then they told David, *s*,
23: 2 David inquired of the LORD, *s*,
23:19 came up to Saul at Gibeah, *s*,
23:27 a messenger came to Saul, *s*,
24: 1 that it was told him, *s*,
24: 8 cave, and called out to Saul, *s*,
25:14 told Abigail, Nabal's wife, *s*,
25:40 at Carmel, they spoke to her *s*,
26: 1 came to Saul at Gibeah, *s*,
26: 6 of Zeruiah, brother of Joab, *s*,
26:14 and to Abner the son of Ner, *s*,
26:19 the inheritance of the LORD, *s*,
27:11 to bring news to Gath, *s*,
27:11 they should inform on us, *s*,
27:12 So Achish believed David, *s*,
28:10 swore to her by the LORD, *s*,
28:12 And the woman spoke to Saul, *s*,
29: 5 to one another in dances, *s*:
30: 8 David inquired of the LORD, *s*,
30:26 of Judah, to his friends, *s*,
2 Sam 1:16 has testified against you, *s*,
2: 1 David inquired of the LORD, *s*,
2: 4 Judah. And they told David, *s*,
3:12 on his behalf to David, *s*,
3:12 *s* also, "Make your covenant
3:14 to Ishbosheth, Saul's son, *s*,
3:17 with the elders of Israel, *s*,
3:18 LORD has spoken of David, *s*,
3:23 him had come, they told Joab, *s*,
3:35 day, David took an oath, *s*,
4:10 "when someone told me, *s*,
5: 1 to David at Hebron and spoke, *s*,
5: 6 the land, who spoke to David, *s*,
5:19 David inquired of the LORD, *s*,
6:12 Now it was told King David, *s*,
7: 4 of the LORD came to Nathan, *s*,
7: 7 to shepherd My people Israel, *s*,
7:26 name be magnified forever, *s*,
7:27 this to Your servant, *s*,
11: 6 Then David sent to Joab, *s*,
11:10 So when they told David, *s*,
11:15 And he wrote in the letter, *s*,
11:19 and charged the messenger, *s*,
13: 7 David sent home to Tamar, *s*,
13:28 had commanded his servants, *s*,
13:30 way, that news came to David, *s*,
14:32 Joab, "Look, I sent to you, *s*,
15: 8 I dwelt at Geshur in Syria, *s*,
15:10 all the tribes of Israel, *s*,
15:13 a messenger came to David, *s*,
15:31 Then someone told David, *s*,
17: 4 And the *s* pleased Absalom and
17: 6 Absalom spoke to him, *s*,
17:16 send quickly and tell David, *s*,
18: 5 Joab, Abishai, and Ittai, *s*,
18:12 you and Abishai and Ittai, *s*,
19: 8 And they told all the people, *s*,
19: 9 all the tribes of Israel, *s*,
19:11 and Abiathar the priests, *s*,
19:11 to the elders of Judah, *s*,
20:18 So she spoke, *s*, "They used
20:18 used to talk in former times, *s*,
21:17 men of David swore to him, *s*,
24:11 prophet Gad, David's seer, *s*,
1 Ki 1: 5 of Haggith exalted himself, *s*,
1: 6 rebuked him at any time by *s*,
1:11 the mother of Solomon, *s*,
1:13 swear to your maidservant, *s*,
1:17 God to your maidservant, *s*,
1:23 So they told the king, *s*,
1:30 by the LORD God of Israel, *s*,
1:47 to bless our lord King David, *s*,
1:51 And it was told Solomon, *s*,
1:51 of the horns of the altar, *s*,
2: 1 he charged Solomon his son, *s*:
2: 4 which He spoke concerning me, *s*,
2: 8 I swore to him by the LORD, *s*,
2:23 Solomon swore by the LORD, *s*,
2:29 Benaiah the son of Jehoiada, *s*,
2:30 back word to the king, *s*,
2:38 to the king, "The *s* is good.
2:39 And they told Shimei, *s*,
2:42 by the LORD, and warn you, *s*,
5: 2 Then Solomon sent to Hiram, *s*:
5: 5 spoke to my father David, *s*,
5: 8 Then Hiram sent to Solomon, *s*:
6:11 of the LORD came to Solomon, *s*:
8:15 His hand has fulfilled it, *s*,
8:25 Your servant David my father, *s*,
8:47 those who took them captive, *s*,
8:55 of Israel with a loud voice, *s*:
9: 5 I promised David your father, *s*,
12: 3 came and spoke to Rehoboam, *s*,
12: 7 And they spoke to him, *s*,
12: 9 people who have spoken to me, *s*,
12:10 up with him spoke to him, *s*,
12:10 who have spoken to you, *s*,
12:12 as the king had directed, *s*,
12:14 the advice of the young men, *s*,
12:16 the people answered the king, *s*:
12:22 to Shemaiah the man of God, *s*,
12:23 to the rest of the people, *s*,
13: 3 he gave a sign the same day, *s*,
13: 4 when King Jeroboam heard the *s*
13: 4 out his hand from the altar, *s*,
13: 9 me by the word of the LORD, *s*,
13:18 me by the word of the LORD, *s*,
13:21 of God who came from Judah, *s*,
13:27 And he spoke to his sons, *s*,
13:30 and they mourned over him, *s*,
13:31 that he spoke to his sons, *s*,
13:32 For the *s* which he cried out by
15:18 Syria, who dwelt in Damascus, *s*,
16: 1 of Hanani, against Baasha, *s*:
17: 2 of the LORD came to him, *s*,
17: 8 of the LORD came to him, *s*,
18: 1 to Elijah, in the third year, *s*,
18:26 from morning even till noon, *s*,
18:31 word of the LORD had come, *s*,
19: 2 sent a messenger to Elijah, *s*,
20: 5 "Thus speaks Ben-Hadad, *s*,
20: 5 'Indeed I have sent to you, *s*,
20:13 Ahab king of Israel, *s*,
20:17 patrol, and they told him, *s*,
21: 2 So Ahab spoke to Naboth, *s*,
21: 9 She wrote in the letters, *s*,
21:10 to bear witness against him, *s*,
21:13 the presence of the people, *s*,
21:14 Then they sent to Jezebel, *s*,
21:17 came to Elijah the Tishbite, *s*,
21:19 "You shall speak to him, *s*,
21:19 And you shall speak to him, *s*,
21:23 Jezebel the LORD also spoke, *s*,
21:28 came to Elijah the Tishbite, *s*,
22:12 the prophets prophesied so, *s*,
22:13 to call Micaiah spoke to him, *s*,
22:31 captains of his chariots, *s*,
22:36 went throughout the army, *s*,
2 Ki 3: 7 to Jehoshaphat king of Judah, *s*,
4: 1 prophets cried out to Elisha, *s*,
4:31 to meet him, and told him, *s*,
5: 4 went in and told his master, *s*,
5: 8 that he sent to the king, *s*,
5:10 sent a messenger to him, *s*,
5:14 according to the *s* of the man
5:22 well. My master has sent me, *s*,
6: 8 consulted with his servants, *s*,
6: 9 sent to the king of Israel, *s*,
6:13 And it was told him, *s*,
6:26 a woman cried out to him, *s*,
7:10 of the city, and told them, *s*,
7:12 hide themselves in the field, *s*,
7:14 direction of the Syrian army, *s*,
7:18 God had spoken to the king, *s*,
8: 1 son he had restored to life, *s*,
8: 2 and did according to the *s* of
8: 4 servant of the man of God, *s*,
8: 6 a certain officer for her, *s*,
8: 7 and it was told him, *s*,
8: 8 inquire of the LORD by him, *s*,
8: 9 of Syria has sent me to you, *s*,
9:12 and thus he spoke to me, *s*,
9:13 and they blew trumpets, *s*,
9:18 So the watchman reported, *s*,
9:20 So the watchman reported, *s*,
9:36 servant Elijah the Tishbite, *s*,
10: 1 who reared Ahab's sons, *s*:
10: 5 the sons, sent to Jehu, *s*,
10: 6 a second letter to them, *s*:
10: 8 messenger came and told him, *s*,
11: 5 Then he commanded them, *s*,
14: 6 in which the LORD commanded, *s*,
14: 8 son of Jehu, king of Israel, *s*,
14: 9 to Amaziah king of Judah, *s*,
14: 9 cedar that was in Lebanon, *s*,
15:12 LORD which He spoke to Jehu, *s*,
16: 7 king of Assyria, *s*, "I am
16:15 commanded Urijah the priest, *s*,
17:13 of His prophets, every seer, *s*,
17:26 spoke to the king of Assyria, *s*,
17:27 king of Assyria commanded, *s*,
17:35 a covenant and charged them, *s*:
18:14 king of Assyria at Lachish, *s*,
18:28 voice in Hebrew, and spoke, *s*,
18:30 make you trust in the LORD, *s*,
18:32 lest he persuade you, *s*,
19: 9 sent messengers to Hezekiah, *s*,
19:10 to Hezekiah king of Judah, *s*:
19:10 whom you trust deceive you, *s*,
19:20 son of Amoz sent to Hezekiah, *s*,
20: 2 and prayed to the LORD, *s*,
20: 4 of the LORD came to him, *s*,
21:10 by His servants the prophets, *s*,
22: 3 to the house of the LORD, *s*:
22: 9 king, bringing the king word, *s*,
22:10 the scribe showed the king, *s*,
22:12 Asaiah a servant of the king, *s*,
23:21 commanded all the people, *s*,
1 Chr 4: 9 mother called his name Jabez, *s*,
4:10 called on the God of Israel *s*,
11: 1 together to David at Hebron, *s*,
12:19 sent him away by agreement, *s*,
13:12 was afraid of God that day, *s*,
14:10 And David inquired of God, *s*,
16:18 *S*, "To you I will give the
16:22 *S*, "Do not touch My
17: 3 word of God came to Nathan, *s*,
17: 6 to shepherd My people, *s*,
17:24 may be magnified forever, *s*,
21: 9 spoke to Gad, David's seer, *s*,
21:10 "Go and tell David, *s*,
22: 8 word of the LORD came to me, *s*,
22:17 to help Solomon his son, *s*,
2 Chr 2: 3 sent to Hiram king of Tyre, *s*:
5:13 and praised the LORD, *s*:
6: 4 His mouth to my father David, *s*,
6:16 Your servant David my father, *s*,
6:37 the land of their captivity, *s*,
7: 3 and praised the LORD, *s*:
7: 6 had made to praise the LORD, *s*,
7:18 with David your father, *s*,
10: 3 came and spoke to Rehoboam, *s*,
10: 6 Solomon while he still lived, *s*,
10: 7 And they spoke to him, *s*,
10: 9 people who have spoken to me, *s*,
10:10 up with him spoke to him, *s*,
10:10 who have spoken to you, *s*,
10:12 as the king had directed, *s*,
10:14 the advice of the young men, *s*,
10:16 the people answered the king, *s*:
11: 2 to Shemaiah the man of God, *s*,
11: 3 Israel in Judah and Benjamin, *s*,
12: 7 the LORD came to Shemaiah, *s*,
16: 2 Syria, who dwelt in Damascus, *s*,
18:11 the prophets prophesied so, *s*,
18:12 to call Micaiah spoke to him, *s*,
18:30 chariots who were with him, *s*,
19: 9 And he commanded them, *s*,
20: 2 came and told Jehoshaphat, *s*,
20: 8 in it for Your name, *s*,
20:21 out before the army and were *s*:
20:37 against Jehoshaphat, *s*,
21:12 him from Elijah the prophet, *s*,
25: 4 where the LORD commanded, *s*,
25: 7 But a man of God came to him, *s*,
25:17 son of Jehu, king of Israel, *s*,
25:18 to Amaziah king of Judah, *s*,
25:18 cedar that was in Lebanon, *s*,
28:23 which had defeated him, *s*,
30:18 But Hezekiah prayed for them, *s*,
32: 4 that ran through the land, *s*,
32: 6 and gave them encouragement, *s*,
32: 9 Judah who were in Jerusalem, *s*,
32:11 die by famine and by thirst, *s*,
32:12 and Jerusalem, *s*, "You shall
32:17 and to speak against Him, *s*,
34:16 king, bringing the king word, *s*,
34:18 the scribe told the king, *s*,
34:20 Asaiah a servant of the king, *s*,
35:21 he sent messengers to him, *s*,
36:22 and also put it in writing, *s*,
Ezra 1: 1 and also put it in writing, *s*,
5:11 they returned us an answer, *s*:
8:22 we had spoken to the king, *s*,
9: 1 done, the leaders came to me, *s*,
9:11 Your servants the prophets, *s*,
Neh 1: 8 commanded Your servant Moses, *s*,
6: 2 and Geshem sent to me, *s*,
6: 3 So I sent messengers to them, *s*,
6: 7 concerning you at Jerusalem, *s*,
6: 8 Then I sent to him, *s*,
6: 9 trying to make us afraid, *s*,
8:11 quieted all the people, *s*,
8:15 cities and in Jerusalem, *s*,
13:25 and made them swear by God, *s*,
Job 4:16 Then I heard a voice *s*:
8:18 Then it will deny him, *s*,
15:23 He wanders about for bread, *s*,
24:15 waits for the twilight, *S*,
33: 8 the sound of your words, *s*,
Ps 2: 2 and against His Anointed, *s*,
22: 7 lip, they shake the head, *s*,
49: 4 I will disclose my dark *s* on
52: 6 And shall laugh at him, *s*,
71:11 *S*, "God has forsaken him;
105:11 *S*, "To you I will give the
105:15 *S*, "Do not touch My
119:82 from searching Your word, *S*,
137: 3 us requested mirth, *S*,
Prov 23:34 lies at the top of the mast, *s*:
Eccl 1:16 I communed with my heart, *s*,
Song 5: 2 He knocks, *s*, "Open for me,
Isa 3: 6 In the house of his father, *s*,
3: 7 In that day he will protest, *s*,
4: 1 shall take hold of one man, *s*,
6: 8 heard the voice of the Lord, *s*:
7: 2 told to the house of David, *s*,
7: 5 plotted evil against you, *s*,
7:10 LORD spoke again to Ahaz, *s*,
8: 5 LORD also spoke to me again, *s*:
8:11 in the way of this people, *s*:
14: 8 the cedars of Lebanon, *S*,
14:16 at you, And consider you, *s*:
14:24 LORD of hosts has sworn, *s*,
16:14 But now the LORD has spoken, *s*,
18: 2 of reed on the waters, *s*,
19:25 LORD of hosts shall bless, *s*,
20: 2 by Isaiah the son of Amoz, *s*,
23: 4 The strength of the sea, *s*,
29:11 to one who is literate, *s*,
29:12 to one who is illiterate, *s*,
30:21 shall hear a word behind you, *s*,
36:15 make you trust in the LORD, *s*,
36:18 lest Hezekiah persuade you, *s*,
37: 9 sent messengers to Hezekiah, *s*,
37:10 to Hezekiah king of Judah, *s*:
37:10 whom you trust deceive you, *s*,
37:15 Hezekiah prayed to the LORD, *s*:
37:21 son of Amoz sent to Hezekiah, *s*,
38: 4 of the LORD came to Isaiah, *s*,

41: 7 him who strikes the anvil, *S*,
41:13 *S* to you, 'Fear not, I will
44:28 *S* to Jerusalem, "You shall be
45:14 make supplication to you, *s*,
46:10 that are not yet done, *S*,
56: 3 himself to the LORD Speak, *s*,
63:11 old, Moses and his people, *s*:
Jer 1: 4 word of the LORD came to me, *s*:
1:11 word of the LORD came to me, *s*,
1:13 came to me the second time, *s*,
2: 1 word of the LORD came to me, *s*,
2: 2 in the hearing of Jerusalem, *s*,
2:27 *S* to a tree, 'You are my
4:10 this people and Jerusalem, *S*,
4:31 She spreads her hands, *s*,
5:20 And proclaim it in Judah, *s*,
6:14 hurt of My people slightly, *S*,
6:17 I set watchmen over you, *s*,
7: 1 to Jeremiah from the LORD, *s*,
7: 4 trust in these lying words, *s*,
7:23 is what I commanded them, *s*,
8: 6 repented of his wickedness, *S*,
8:11 of My people slightly, *S*,
11: 1 to Jeremiah from the LORD, *s*,
11: 4 Egypt, from the iron furnace, *s*,
11: 6 in the streets of Jerusalem, *s*:
11: 7 rising early and exhorting, *s*,
11:19 devised schemes against me, *s*,
11:21 Anathoth who seek your life, *s*,
13: 3 came to me the second time, *s*,
13: 8 word of the LORD came to me, *s*,
16: 1 of the LORD also came to me, *s*,
18: 1 to Jeremiah from the LORD, *s*:
18: 5 word of the LORD came to me, *s*:
18:11 the inhabitants of Jerusalem, *s*,
20:10 watched for my stumbling, *s*,
20:15 brought news to my father, *s*,
21: 1 son of Maaseiah, the priest, *s*,
22:18 shall not lament for him, *S*,
22:18 shall not lament for him, *S*,
23:25 who prophesy lies in My name, *s*,
23:33 or the priest ask you, *s*,
23:38 and I have sent to you, *s*,
24: 4 word of the LORD came to me, *s*,
25: 2 the inhabitants of Jerusalem, *s*:
26: 1 word came from the LORD, *s*,
26: 8 all the people seized him, *s*,
26: 9 in the name of the LORD, *s*,
26:11 princes and all the people, *s*,
26:12 princes and all the people, *s*:
26:17 the assembly of the people, *s*:
26:18 to all the people of Judah, *s*,
27: 1 to Jeremiah from the LORD, *s*,
27: 9 sorcerers, who speak to you, *s*,
27:12 according to all these words, *s*,
27:14 prophets who speak to you, *s*,
27:16 and to all this people, *s*,
27:16 prophets who prophesy to you, *s*,
28: 1 and of all the people, *s*,
28: 2 of hosts, the God of Israel, *s*:
28:11 presence of all the people, *s*,
28:12 neck of the prophet Jeremiah, *s*,
28:13 "Go and tell Hananiah, *s*,
29: 3 king of Babylon, *s*,
29:22 of Judah who are in Babylon, *s*,
29:24 to Shemaiah the Nehelamite, *s*,
29:25 of hosts, the God of Israel, *s*:
29:25 and to all the priests, *s*,
29:28 has sent to us in Babylon, *s*,
29:30 the LORD came to Jeremiah, *s*:
29:31 to all those in captivity, *s*,
30: 1 to Jeremiah from the LORD, *s*,
30: 2 the LORD God of Israel, *s*:
30:17 they called you an outcast *s*:
31: 3 has appeared of old to me, *s*:
31:34 and every man his brother, *s*,
32: 3 of Judah had shut him up, *s*,
32: 6 word of the LORD came to me, *s*,
32: 7 your uncle will come to you, *s*,
32:13 I charged Baruch before them, *s*,
32:16 I prayed to the LORD, *s*:
32:26 the LORD came to Jeremiah, *s*,
33: 1 in the court of the prison, *s*,
33:19 the LORD came to Jeremiah, *s*,
33:23 the LORD came to Jeremiah, *s*,
33:24 these people have spoken, *s*,
34: 1 Jerusalem and all its cities, *s*,
34: 5 for you and lament for you, *s*,
34:12 to Jeremiah from the LORD, *s*,
34:13 out of the house of bondage, *s*,
35: 1 son of Josiah, king of Judah, *s*,
35: 6 our father, commanded us, *s*,
35:12 of the LORD to Jeremiah, *s*,
35:15 up early and sending them, *s*,
36: 1 to Jeremiah from the LORD, *s*,
36: 5 Jeremiah commanded Baruch, *s*,
36:14 the son of Cushi, to Baruch, *s*,
36:17 And they asked Baruch, *s*,
36:27 the LORD came to Jeremiah, *s*:
36:29 have burned this scroll, *s*,
37: 3 to the prophet Jeremiah, *s*,
37: 6 came to the prophet Jeremiah, *s*,
37: 9 'Do not deceive yourselves, *s*,
37:13 seized Jeremiah the prophet, *s*,
37:19 who prophesied to you, *s*,
38: 1 had spoken to all the people, *s*,
38: 8 house and spoke to the king, *s*:
38:10 Ebed-Melech the Ethiopian, *s*,
38:16 swore secretly to Jeremiah, *s*,
39:11 the captain of the guard, *s*,
39:15 in the court of the prison, *s*,
39:16 to Ebed-Melech the Ethiopian, *s*,
40: 9 before them and their men, *s*,
40:15 to Gedaliah in Mizpah, *s*,
42:14 '*s*, 'No, but we will go to
42:20 me to the LORD your God, *s*,
43: 2 *s* to Jeremiah, "You speak
43: 8 to Jeremiah in Tahpanhes, *s*,
44: 1 in the country of Pathros, *s*,
44: 4 early and sending them, *s*,
44:15 Pathros, answered Jeremiah, *s*:
44:20 had given him that answer—*s*:
44:25 of hosts, the God of Israel, *s*:
44:25 fulfilled with your hands, *s*,
44:26 in all the land of Egypt, *s*,
45: 1 son of Josiah, king of Judah, *s*,
49: 4 trusted in her treasures, *s*,
49:34 of Zedekiah king of Judah, *s*,
50: 5 With their faces toward it, *s*,
Ezek 3:16 word of the LORD came to me, *s*,
6: 1 word of the LORD came to me, *s*,
7: 1 word of the LORD came to me, *s*,
9: 1 my hearing with a loud voice, *s*,
10: 6 the man clothed in linen, *s*,
11:14 word of the LORD came to me, *s*,
12: 1 word of the LORD came to me, *s*:
12: 8 word of the LORD came to me, *s*,
12:17 word of the LORD came to me, *s*,
12:21 word of the LORD came to me, *s*,
12:26 word of the LORD came to me, *s*,
12:27 look, the house of Israel is *s*,
13: 1 word of the LORD came to me, *s*,
13: 6 and false divination, *s*,
13:10 they have seduced My people, *s*,
14: 2 word of the LORD came to me, *s*,
14:12 the LORD came again to me, *s*:
15: 1 word of the LORD came to me, *s*:
16: 1 word of the LORD came to me, *s*,
17: 1 word of the LORD came to me, *s*,
17:11 word of the LORD came to me, *s*,
18: 1 the LORD came to me again, *s*,
18: 2 the land of Israel, *s*:
20: 2 word of the LORD came to me, *s*,
20: 5 My hand in an oath to them, *s*,
20:45 word of the LORD came to me, *s*,
21: 1 word of the LORD came to me, *s*,
21: 8 word of the LORD came to me, *s*,
21:18 the LORD came to me again, *s*:
22: 1 word of the LORD came to me, *s*,
22:17 word of the LORD came to me, *s*,
22:23 word of the LORD came to me, *s*,
22:28 and divining lies for them, *s*,
23: 1 the LORD came again to me, *s*:
24: 1 word of the LORD came to me, *s*,
24:15 word of the LORD came to me, *s*,
24:20 word of the LORD came to me, *s*,
25: 1 word of the LORD came to me, *s*,
26: 1 word of the LORD came to me, *s*,
27: 1 the LORD came again to me, *s*,
28: 1 the LORD came to me again, *s*,
28:11 word of the LORD came to me, *s*,
28:20 word of the LORD came to me, *s*,
29: 1 word of the LORD came to me, *s*,
29:17 word of the LORD came to me, *s*,
30: 1 the LORD came to me again, *s*,
30:20 word of the LORD came to me, *s*,
31: 1 word of the LORD came to me, *s*,
32: 1 word of the LORD came to me, *s*,
32:17 word of the LORD came to me, *s*:
33: 1 word of the LORD came to me, *s*,
33:23 word of the LORD came to me, *s*:
33:24 in the land of Israel are *s*,
33:30 everyone *s* to his brother,
34: 1 word of the LORD came to me, *s*,
35: 1 word of the LORD came to me, *s*,
35:12 the mountains of Israel, *s*,
36:16 word of the LORD came to me, *s*:
37:15 word of the LORD came to me, *s*,
37:18 of your people speak to you, *s*,
38: 1 word of the LORD came to me, *s*,
Dan 3:14 *s* to them, "Is it true,
3:24 *s* to his counselors, "Did we
3:26 fiery furnace and spoke, *s*,
3:28 Nebuchadnezzar spoke, *s*,
4: 8 I told the dream before him, *s*:
4:23 coming down from heaven and *s*,
4:30 The king spoke, *s*, "Is not
5: 7 *s* to the wise men of Babylon,
5:10 The queen spoke, *s*, "O king,
6:16 *s* to Daniel, "Your God, whom
6:20 *s* to Daniel, "Daniel, servant
7: 2 Daniel spoke, *s*, "I saw in
10:16 *s* to him who stood before me,
Hos 4:15 Aven, Nor swear an oath, *s*,
Am 2:12 And commanded the prophets *s*,
3: 1 up from the land of Egypt, *s*:
7:10 to Jeroboam king of Israel, *s*,
8: 5 *S*: "When will the New Moon
Ob 1 been sent among the nations, *s*,
Jon 1: 1 to Jonah the son of Amittai, *s*,
3: 1 to Jonah the second time, *s*,
3: 7 of the king and his nobles, *s*,
Mic 2: 4 with a bitter lamentation, *s*:
2:11 spirit And speak a lie, *s*,
Hag 1: 1 Jehozadak, the high priest, *s*,
1: 2 speaks the LORD of hosts, *s*:
1: 3 came by Haggai the prophet, *s*,
1:13 message to the people, *s*,
2: 1 came by Haggai the prophet, *s*:
2: 2 to the remnant of the people, *s*:
2:10 came by Haggai the prophet, *s*,
2:11 priests concerning the law, *s*,
2:20 day of the month, *s*,
2:21 governor of Judah, *s*: 'I will
Zech 1: 1 the son of Iddo the prophet, *s*,
1: 4 the former prophets preached, *s*,
1:14 me said to me, "Proclaim, *s*,
1:17 "Again proclaim, *s*,
2: 4 speak to this young man, *s*:
3: 4 those who stood before Him, *s*,
3: 6 the LORD admonished Joshua, *s*,
4: 4 the angel who talked with me, *s*,
4: 8 word of the LORD came to me, *s*:
6: 8 to me, and spoke to me, *s*,
6: 9 word of the LORD came to me, *s*:
6:12 "Then speak to him, *s*,
6:12 says the LORD of hosts, *s*:
7: 3 of hosts, and the prophets, *s*,
7: 4 LORD of hosts came to me, *s*,
7: 8 the LORD came to Zechariah, *s*,
8: 1 of the LORD of hosts came, *s*,
8:18 LORD of hosts came to me, *s*,
8:21 city shall go to another, *s*,
8:23 the sleeve of a Jewish man, *s*,
Mal 1: 7 By *s*, 'The table of the LORD
Mt 1:20 appeared to him in a dream, *s*,
1:22 the Lord through the prophet, *s*:
2: 2 *s*, "Where is He who has been
2:13 to Joseph in a dream, *s*,
2:15 the Lord through the prophet, *s*,
2:17 by Jeremiah the prophet, *s*:
2:20 *s*, "Arise, take the young
3: 2 and *s*, "Repent, for the
3: 3 of by the prophet Isaiah, *s*:
3:14 John tried to prevent Him, *s*,
3:17 a voice came from heaven, *s*,
4:14 spoken by Isaiah the prophet, *s*:
5: 2 His mouth and taught them, *s*:
6:31 "Therefore do not worry, *s*,
8: 2 leper came and worshiped Him, *s*,
8: 3 His hand and touched him, *s*,
8: 6 *s*, "Lord, my servant is lying
8:17 spoken by Isaiah the prophet, *s*:
8:25 came to Him and awoke Him, *s*,
8:27 So the men marveled, *s*,
8:29 And suddenly they cried out, *s*,
8:31 So the demons begged Him, *s*,
9:14 of John came to Him, *s*,
9:18 ruler came and worshiped Him, *s*,
9:27 followed Him, crying out and *s*,
9:29 Then He touched their eyes, *s*,
9:30 Jesus sternly warned them, *s*,
9:33 And the multitudes marveled, *s*,
10: 5 sent out and commanded them, *s*:
10: 7 "And as you go, preach, *s*,
11:17 'and *s*: 'We played the
12:10 And they asked Him, *s*,
12:17 spoken by Isaiah the prophet, *s*:
12:38 and Pharisees answered, *s*,
13: 3 things to them in parables, *s*:
13:24 parable He put forth to them, *s*:
13:31 parable He put forth to them, *s*:
13:35 was spoken by the prophet, *s*:
13:36 His disciples came to Him, *s*,
14:15 His disciples came to Him, *s*,
14:26 the sea, they were troubled, *s*,
14:27 Jesus spoke to them, *s*,
14:30 to sink he cried out, *s*,
14:33 boat came and worshiped Him, *s*,
15: 1 from Jerusalem came to Jesus, *s*,
15: 4 "For God commanded, *s*,
15: 7 Isaiah prophesy about you, *s*:
15:12 offended when they heard this *s*?
15:22 region and cried out to Him, *s*,
15:23 disciples came and urged Him, *s*,
15:25 she came and worshiped Him, *s*,
16: 7 reasoned among themselves, *s*,
16:13 He asked His disciples, *s*,
16:22 and began to rebuke Him, *s*,
17: 5 voice came out of the cloud, *s*,
17: 9 Jesus commanded them, *s*,
17:10 And His disciples asked Him, *s*,
17:14 Him, kneeling down to Him and *s*,
17:25 house, Jesus anticipated him, *s*,
18: 1 the disciples came to Jesus, *s*,
18:26 fell down before him, *s*,
18:28 and took him by the throat, *s*,
18:29 at his feet and begged him, *s*,
19: 3 and *s* to Him, "Is it lawful
19:11 "All cannot accept this *s*,
19:22 when the young man heard that *s*,
19:25 they were greatly astonished, *s*,
20:12 '*s*, 'These last men have
20:30 was passing by, cried out, *s*,
20:31 they cried out all the more, *s*,
21: 2 *s* to them, "Go into the village
21: 4 was spoken by the prophet, *s*:
21: 9 those who followed cried out, *s*:
21:10 all the city was moved, *s*,
21:15 crying out in the temple and *s*,
21:16 "Do You hear what these are *s*?
21:20 saw it, they marveled, *s*,
21:25 reasoned among themselves, *s*,
21:37 all he sent his son to them, *s*,
22: 4 he sent out other servants, *s*,
22:16 disciples with the Herodians, *s*,
22:24 *s*: "Teacher, Moses said that
22:31 was spoken to you by God, *s*,
22:35 question, testing Him, and *s*,
22:42 *s*, "What do you think
22:43 the Spirit call Him 'Lord,' *s*:
23: 2 *s*: "The scribes and the
24: 3 came to Him privately, *s*,
24: 5 many will come in My name, *s*,
25: 9 "But the wise answered, *s*,
25:11 the other virgins came also, *s*,

S

25:20 brought five other talents, *s*,
25:37 righteous will answer Him, *s*,
25:44 they also will answer Him, *s*,
25:45 "Then He will answer them, *s*,
26: 8 saw it, they were indignant, *s*,
26:17 *s* to Him, "Where do You want
26:27 thanks, and gave it to them, *s*,
26:39 fell on His face, and prayed, *s*,
26:42 He went away and prayed, *s*,
26:44 third time, *s* the same words.
26:48 had given them a sign, *s*,
26:65 high priest tore his clothes, *s*,
26:68 *s*, "Prophesy to us, Christ!
26:69 a servant girl came to him, *s*,
26:70 denied it before them all, *s*,
26:70 "I do not know what you are *s*.
26:74 he began to curse and swear, *s*,
27: 4 *s*, "I have sinned by
27: 9 by Jeremiah the prophet, *s*,
27:11 And the governor asked Him, *s*,
27:19 seat, his wife sent to him, *s*,
27:23 they cried out all the more, *s*,
27:24 hands before the multitude, *s*,
27:29 before Him and mocked Him, *s*,
27:40 and *s*, "You who destroy the
27:46 cried out with a loud voice, *s*,
27:54 they feared greatly, *s*,
27:63 *s*, "Sir, we remember, while
28: 9 behold, Jesus met them, *s*,
28:13 *s*, "Tell them, 'His disciples
28:15 and this *s* is commonly reported
28:18 Jesus came and spoke to them, *s*,
Mk 1: 7 And he preached, *s*, "There
1:15 and *s*, "The time is fulfilled,
1:24 *s*, "Let us alone! What have
1:25 But Jesus rebuked him, *s*,
1:27 questioned among themselves, *s*,
1:40 kneeling down to Him and *s* to
2:12 amazed and glorified God, *s*,
3:11 before Him and cried out, *s*,
3:33 But He answered them, *s*,
5: 9 *s*, "My name is Legion;
5:12 So all the demons begged Him, *s*,
5:23 and begged Him earnestly, *s*,
6: 2 hearing Him were astonished, *s*,
6:25 haste to the king and asked, *s*,
7:29 'For this *s* go your way;
7:37 astonished beyond measure, *s*,
8:15 Then He charged them, *s*,
8:16 reasoned among themselves, *s*,
8:26 sent him away to his house, *s*,
8:27 *s* to them, "Who do men say
8:33 disciples, He rebuked Peter, *s*,
9: 7 voice came out of the cloud, *s*,
9:11 And they asked Him, *s*,
9:25 *s* to it, "Deaf and dumb
9:32 they did not understand this *s*,
9:38 Now John answered Him, *s*,
10:26 *s* among themselves, "Who then
10:35 sons of Zebedee, came to Him, *s*,
10:49 *s* to him, "Be of good cheer.
11: 9 those who followed cried out, *s*:
11:17 *s* to them, "Is it not written,
11:31 reasoned among themselves, *s*,
12: 6 also sent him to them last, *s*,
12:18 to Him; and they asked Him, *s*:
12:26 how God spoke to him, *s*,
13: 6 many will come in My name, *s*,
14:44 had given them a signal, *s*,
14:57 false witness against Him, *s*,
14:60 in the midst and asked Jesus, *s*,
14:61 *s* to Him, "Are You the Christ,
14:68 But he denied it, *s*,
14:68 nor understand what you are *s*.
15: 4 Then Pilate asked Him again, *s*,
15: 9 But Pilate answered them, *s*,
15:29 Him, wagging their heads and *s*,
15:34 cried out with a loud voice, *s*,
15:36 offered it to Him to drink, *s*,
Lk 1:24 she hid herself five months, *s*,
1:29 him, she was troubled at his *s*,
1:63 a writing tablet, and wrote, *s*,
1:66 kept them in their hearts, *s*,
1:67 Holy Spirit, and prophesied, *s*:
2:13 host praising God and *s*:
2:17 they made widely known the *s*
3: 4 words of Isaiah the prophet, *s*:
3:10 So the people asked him, *s*,
3:14 the soldiers asked him, *s*,
3:16 *s* to all, "I indeed baptize
4: 4 But Jesus answered him, *s*,
4:34 *s*, "Let us alone! What have
4:35 But Jesus rebuked him, *s*,
4:36 and spoke among themselves, *s*,
4:41 out of many, crying out and *s*,
5: 8 he fell down at Jesus' knees, *s*,
5:12 his face and implored Him, *s*,
5:13 His hand and touched him, *s*,
5:21 Pharisees began to reason, *s*,
5:26 and were filled with fear, *s*,
5:30 against His disciples, *s*,
7: 4 *s* that the one for whom He
7: 6 *s* to Him, "Lord, do not
7:16 all, and they glorified God, *s*,
7:19 to him, sent them to Jesus, *s*,
7:20 Baptist has sent us to You, *s*,
7:32 and calling to one another, *s*:
7:39 this, he spoke to himself, *s*,
8: 9 His disciples asked Him, *s*,
8:24 came to Him and awoke Him, *s*,
8:25 *s* to one another, "Who can
8:30 Jesus asked him, *s*, "What
8:38 Him. But Jesus sent him away, *s*,
8:49 *s* to him, "Your daughter is
8:50 heard it, He answered him, *s*,
8:54 her by the hand and called, *s*,
9:18 Him, and He asked them, *s*,
9:22 *s*, "The Son of Man must
9:34 While he was *s* this, a cloud
9:35 voice came out of the cloud, *s*,
9:38 from the multitude cried out, *s*,
9:45 they did not understand this *s*,
9:45 afraid to ask Him about this *s*.
10:17 seventy returned with joy, *s*,
10:25 stood up and tested Him, *s*,
11:45 by *s* these things You reproach
12:16 He spoke a parable to them, *s*:
12:17 he thought within himself, *s*,
13:25 and knock at the door, *s*,
13:31 *s* to Him, "Get out and depart
14: 3 to the lawyers and Pharisees, *s*,
14: 5 Then He answered them, *s*,
14: 7 the best places, *s* to them:
14:30 '*s*, 'This man began
15: 2 and scribes complained, *s*,
15: 3 spoke this parable to them, *s*:
15: 6 *s* to them, 'Rejoice with me,
15: 9 and neighbors together, *s*,
17: 4 in a day returns to you, *s*,
18: 2 *s*: "There was in a certain
18: 3 and she came to him, *s*,
18:13 heaven, but beat his breast, *s*,
18:18 a certain ruler asked Him, *s*,
18:34 this *s* was hidden from them,
18:38 And he cried out, *s*,
18:41 *s*, "What do you want Me to
19: 7 saw it, they all complained, *s*,
19:14 sent a delegation after him, *s*,
19:16 "Then came the first, *s*,
19:18 "And the second came, *s*,
19:20 "Then another came, *s*,
19:30 *s*, "Go into the village
19:38 *s*: " 'Blessed is the King
19:42 *s*, "If you had known, even
19:46 *s* to them, "It is written, 'My
20: 2 and spoke to Him, *s*,
20: 5 reasoned among themselves, *s*,
20:14 reasoned among themselves, *s*,
20:21 Then they asked Him, *s*,
20:28 *s*: "Teacher, Moses wrote to
21: 7 So they asked Him, *s*,
21: 8 many will come in My name, *s*,
22: 8 And He sent Peter and John, *s*,
22:19 it, and gave it to them, *s*,
22:20 took the cup after supper, *s*,
22:42 *s*, "Father, if it is Your
22:57 But he denied Him, *s*, "Woman,
22:59 another confidently affirmed, *s*,
22:60 I do not know what you are *s*!"
22:64 on the face and asked Him, *s*,
22:66 led Him into their council, *s*,
23: 2 And they began to accuse Him, *s*,
23: 2 *s* that He Himself is Christ, a
23: 3 Then Pilate asked Him, *s*,
23: 5 they were the more fierce, *s*,
23:18 they all cried out at once, *s*,
23:21 But they shouted, *s*, "Crucify
23:35 the rulers with them sneered, *s*,
23:37 and *s*, "If You are the King
23:39 were hanged blasphemed Him, *s*,
23:40 answering, rebuked him, *s*,
23:47 happened, he glorified God, *s*,
24: 7 '*s*, 'The Son of Man must
24:23 they came *s* that they had also
24:29 But they constrained Him, *s*,
24:34 *s*, "The Lord is risen
Jn 1:15 witness of Him and cried out, *s*,
1:25 they asked him, *s*, "Why then
1:26 John answered them, *s*,
1:32 And John bore witness, *s*,
4:31 His disciples urged Him, *s*,
4:37 For in this the *s* is true: 'One
4:51 met him and told him, *s*,
6:52 quarreled among themselves, *s*,
6:60 this, said, "This is a hard *s*;
7:15 And the Jews marveled, *s*,
7:28 as He taught in the temple, *s*,
7:37 Jesus stood and cried out, *s*,
7:40 crowd, when they heard this *s*,
8:12 Jesus spoke to them again, *s*,
8:25 Just what I have been *s* to you
9: 2 And His disciples asked Him, *s*,
9:19 And they asked them, *s*,
10:33 The Jews answered Him, *s*,
11: 3 the sisters sent to Him, *s*,
11:28 called Mary her sister, *s*,
11:31 and went out, followed her, *s*,
11:32 *s* to Him, "Lord, if You had
12:21 of Galilee, and asked him, *s*,
12:23 But Jesus answered them, *s*,
12:28 a voice came from heaven, *s*,
16:18 We do not know what He is *s*.
18: 9 that the *s* might be fulfilled
18:22 with the palm of his hand, *s*,
18:32 that the *s* of Jesus might be
18:40 Then they all cried again, *s*,
19: 6 saw Him, they cried out, *s*,
19: 8 when Pilate heard that *s*,
19:12 Him, but the Jews cried out, *s*,
19:13 Pilate therefore heard that *s*,
21:23 Then this *s* went out among the
Acts 1: 6 together, they asked Him, *s*,
2: 7 *s* to one another, "Look, are
2:12 *s* to one another, "Whatever
2:40 testified and exhorted them, *s*,
3:25 *s* to Abraham, 'And in your
4:16 *s*, "What shall we do to
5:23 *s*, "Indeed we found the
5:25 So one came and told them, *s*,
5:28 *s*, "Did we not strictly
6: 5 And the *s* pleased the whole
7:26 tried to reconcile them, *s*,
7:27 wrong pushed him away, *s*,
7:29 'Then, at this *s*, Moses
7:32 *s*, 'I am the God of
7:35 Moses whom they rejected, *s*,
7:40 *s* to Aaron, 'Make us gods to
7:59 as he was calling on God and *s*,
8:10 the least to the greatest, *s*,
8:19 *s*, "Give me this power
8:26 of the Lord spoke to Philip, *s*,
9: 4 and heard a voice *s* to him,
10: 3 an angel of God coming in and *s*
10:26 But Peter lifted him up, *s*,
11: 3 *s*, "You went in to
11: 4 in order from the beginning, *s*:
11: 7 And I heard a voice *s* to me,
11:18 and they glorified God, *s*,
12: 7 the side and raised him up, *s*,
13:15 the synagogue sent to them, *s*,
14:11 *s* in the Lycaonian language,
14:15 and *s*, "Men, why are you
14:22 continue in the faith, and *s*,
15: 5 who believed rose up, *s*,
15:13 silent, James answered, *s*,
15:24 words, unsettling your souls, *s*,
16: 9 stood and pleaded with him, *s*,
16:15 baptized, she begged us, *s*,
16:17 Paul and us, and cried out, *s*,
16:28 called with a loud voice, *s*,
16:35 sent the officers, *s*, "Let
16:36 reported these words to Paul, *s*,
17: 3 again from the dead, and *s*,
17: 7 *s* there is another
17:19 brought him to the Areopagus, *s*,
18:13 *s*, "This fellow persuades
18:21 but took leave of them, *s*,
19: 4 *s* to the people that they
19:13 those who had evil spirits, *s*,
19:21 Achaia, to go to Jerusalem, *s*,
19:26 *s* that they are not gods which
19:28 full of wrath and cried out, *s*,
20:23 *s* that chains and tribulations
21:14 not be persuaded, we ceased, *s*,
21:21 *s* that they ought not to
21:40 them in the Hebrew language, *s*,
22: 7 the ground and heard a voice *s*
22:18 and saw Him *s* to me, 'Make haste
22:26 went and told the commander, *s*,
23: 9 party arose and protested, *s*,
23:12 *s* that they would neither eat
23:23 he called for two centurions, *s*,
24: 2 began his accusation, *s*:
25:14 Paul's case before the king, *s*:
26:14 a voice speaking to me and *s*
26:22 *s* no other things than those
26:31 they talked among themselves, *s*,
27:10 *s*, "Men, I perceive that
27:24 '*s*, 'Do not be afraid,
27:33 them all to take food, *s*,
28:26 '*s*, 'Go to this people
Rom 11: 2 with God against Israel, *s*,
13: 9 are all summed up in this *s*,
1 Cor 10:19 What am I *s* then? That an idol
11:25 took the cup after supper, *s*,
15:54 shall be brought to pass the *s*
Gal 3: 8 to Abraham beforehand, *s*,
1 Tim 1:15 This is a faithful *s* and worthy
3: 1 This is a faithful *s*:
4: 9 This is a faithful *s* and worthy
5:13 *s* things which they ought not.
2 Tim 2:11 This is a faithful *s*:
2:18 *s* that the resurrection is
Titus 3: 8 This is a faithful *s*,
Heb 2: 6 testified in a certain place, *s*:
2:12 *s*: "I will declare
4: 7 *s* in David, "Today," after
6:14 *s*, "Surely blessing I
8: 1 point of the things we are *s*:
8:11 and none his brother, *s*,
9:20 *s*, "This is the blood of
10: 8 Previously *s*, "Sacrifice
12:26 but now He has promised, *s*,
2 Pe 3: 4 and *s*, "Where is the
Jude 14 about these men also, *s*,
Rev 1:11 *s*, "I am the Alpha and the
1:17 *s* to me, "Do not be afraid; I
4: 1 a trumpet speaking with me, *s*,
4: 8 do not rest day or night, *s*:
4:10 crowns before the throne, *s*:
5: 9 And they sang a new song, *s*:
5:12 *s* with a loud voice: "Worthy
5:13 all that are in them, I heard *s*:
6: 1 of the four living creatures *s*
6: 3 the second living creature *s*
6: 6 of the four living creatures *s*,
6: 7 of the fourth living creature *s*,
6:10 they cried with a loud voice, *s*,
7: 3 *s*, "Do not harm the
7:10 crying out with a loud voice, *s*,
7:12 *s*: "Amen! Blessing and
7:13 *s* to me, "Who are these
8:13 *s* with a loud voice, "Woe,
9:14 *s* to the sixth angel who had the
10: 4 I heard a voice from heaven *s*
11: 1 And the angel stood, *s*,

11:12 a loud voice from heaven *s* to
11:15 were loud voices in heaven, *s*,
11:17 *s*: "We give You thanks,
12:10 Then I heard a loud voice *s* in
13: 4 and they worshiped the beast, *s*,
14: 7 *s* with a loud voice, "Fear God
14: 8 And another angel followed, *s*,
14: 9 *s* with a loud voice, "If
14:13 I heard a voice from heaven *s*
14:18 him who had the sharp sickle, *s*,
15: 3 and the song of the Lamb, *s*:
16: 1 a loud voice from the temple *s*
16: 5 heard the angel of the waters *s*:
16: 7 heard another from the altar *s*,
16:17 of heaven, from the throne, *s*,
17: 1 *s* to me, "Come, I will show
18: 2 mightily with a loud voice, *s*,
18: 4 another voice from heaven *s*,
18:10 for fear of her torment, *s*,
18:16 'and *s*, 'Alas, alas, that
18:18 saw the smoke of her burning, *s*,
18:19 out, weeping and wailing, and *s*,
18:21 and threw it into the sea, *s*,
19: 1 a great multitude in heaven, *s*,
19: 4 God who sat on the throne, *s*,
19: 5 a voice came from the throne, *s*,
19: 6 sound of mighty thunderings, *s*,
19:17 *s* to all the birds that fly in
21: 3 a loud voice from heaven *s*,
21: 9 to me and talked with me, *s*,

SAYINGS (19/19)

Num 12: 8 plainly, and not in dark *s*;
2 Chr 13:22 and his *s* are written in the
33:19 they are written among the *s*
Ps 49:13 posterity who approve their *s*.
78: 2 I will utter dark *s* of old,
Prov 4:10 Hear, my son, and receive my *s*,
4:20 Incline your ear to my *s*.
Mt 7:24 whoever hears these *s* of Mine,
7:26 everyone who hears these *s*
7:28 when Jesus had ended these *s*,
19: 1 when Jesus had finished these *s*,
26: 1 Jesus had finished all these *s*,
Lk 1:65 and all these *s* were discussed
6:47 and hears My *s* and does them, I
7: 1 when He concluded all His *s* in
9:28 about eight days after these *s*,
Jn 10:19 the Jews because of these *s*.
Acts 14:18 And with these *s* they could
Rev 19: 9 These are the true *s* of God."

SAYS (1075/1022)

Gen 22:16 *s* the LORD, because you have
24:14 that I may drink,' and she *s*,
24:44 and she *s* to me, "Drink, and I
32: 4 'Thus your servant Jacob *s*:
41:55 whatever he *s* to you, do."
45: 9 Thus *s* your son Joseph: "God
46:33 when Pharaoh calls you and *s*,
Ex 4:22 Thus *s* the LORD: "Israel is
5: 1 Thus *s* the LORD God of Israel:
5:10 Thus *s* Pharaoh: 'I will not give
7:17 Thus *s* the LORD: "By this you
8: 1 Thus *s* the LORD: "Let My
8:20 Thus *s* the LORD: "Let My
9: 1 Thus *s* the LORD God of the
9:13 Thus *s* the LORD God of the
10: 3 Thus *s* the LORD God of the
11: 4 Thus *s* the LORD: 'About
21: 5 "But if the servant plainly *s*,
32:27 Thus *s* the LORD God of Israel:
Num 14:28 *s* the LORD, 'just as you have
20:14 Thus *s* your brother Israel: 'You
22:16 Thus *s* Balak the son of Zippor:
24:13 What the LORD *s*, that I
32:27 to battle, just as my lord *s*.
Deut 5:27 the LORD our God *s* to you,
15:16 And if it happens that he *s* to
22:14 brings a bad name on her, and *s*,
25: 8 But if he stands firm and *s*,
33: 9 Who *s* of his father and mother,
Josh 7:13 because thus *s* the LORD God of
22:16 Thus *s* the whole congregation of
24: 2 Thus *s* the LORD God of Israel:
Judg 4:20 and inquires of you, and *s*,
6: 8 Thus *s* the LORD God of Israel:
11:15 Thus *s* Jephthah: 'Israel did not
1 Sam 2:27 Thus *s* the LORD: 'Did I not
2:30 the LORD God of Israel *s*:
2:30 But now the LORD *s*: 'Far be
9: 6 all that he *s* surely comes to
10:18 Thus *s* the LORD God of Israel:
15: 2 Thus *s* the LORD of hosts: 'I
20: 7 If he *s* thus: 'It is well,'
24:13 the proverb of the ancients *s*,
2 Sam 7: 5 Thus *s* the LORD: "Would you
7: 8 Thus *s* the LORD of hosts: "I
11:20 and he *s* to you: 'Why did you
12: 7 Thus *s* the LORD God of
12:11 Thus *s* the LORD: 'Behold, I
14:10 Whoever *s* anything to you,
15:26 But if He *s* thus: 'I have no
17: 5 and let us hear what he *s*
17: 6 Shall we do as he *s*?
23: 1 Thus *s* David the son of Jesse;
23: 1 Thus *s* the man raised up on
24:12 Thus *s* the LORD: "I offer you
1 Ki 2:30 Thus *s* the king, 'Come out!'"
3:23 And the king said, "The one *s*,
3:23 the dead one'; and the other *s*,
11:31 for thus *s* the LORD, the God
12:24 Thus *s* the LORD: "You shall
13: 2 Thus *s* the LORD: 'Behold,
13:21 Thus *s* the LORD: 'Because you
14: 7 Thus *s* the LORD God of Israel:
17:14 For thus *s* the LORD God of
20: 2 to him, "Thus *s* Ben-Hadad:
20:13 Thus *s* the LORD: 'Have you seen
20:14 Thus *s* the LORD: 'By the young
20:28 Thus *s* the LORD: 'Because the
20:32 "Your servant Ben-Hadad *s*,
20:42 Thus *s* the LORD: 'Because you
21:19 Thus *s* the LORD: "Have you
21:19 Thus *s* the LORD: "In the place
22:11 Thus *s* the LORD: 'With these
22:14 whatever the LORD *s* to me,
22:27 Thus *s* the king: "Put this
2 Ki 1: 4 thus *s* the LORD: 'You shall
1: 6 Thus *s* the LORD: 'Is it
1:16 Thus *s* the LORD: 'Because you
2:21 Thus *s* the LORD: 'I have healed
3:16 Thus *s* the LORD: 'Make this
3:17 For thus *s* the LORD: 'You shall
4:43 for thus *s* the LORD: 'They
5:13 when he *s* to you, 'Wash, and be
7: 1 Thus *s* the LORD: 'Tomorrow
9: 3 Thus *s* the LORD: "I have
9: 6 Thus *s* the LORD God of Israel:
9:12 Thus *s* the LORD: "I have
9:18 Thus *s* the king: 'Is it
9:19 Thus *s* the king: 'Is it
9:26 of his sons,' *s* the LORD,
9:26 *s* the LORD. Now therefore,
18:19 Thus *s* the great king, the king
18:29 Thus *s* the king: 'Do not let
18:31 for thus *s* the king of Assyria:
19: 3 Thus *s* Hezekiah: 'This day is a
19: 6 Thus *s* the LORD: "Do not be
19:20 Thus *s* the LORD God of Israel:
19:32 Therefore thus *s* the LORD
19:33 into this city,' *S* the LORD.
20: 1 Thus *s* the LORD: 'Set your
20: 5 Thus *s* the LORD, the God of
20:17 shall be left,' *s* the LORD.
21:12 therefore thus *s* the LORD God
22:15 Thus *s* the LORD God of Israel,
22:16 Thus *s* the LORD: 'Behold, I
22:18 Thus *s* the LORD God of Israel:
22:19 have heard you," *s* the LORD.
1 Chr 17: 4 Thus *s* the LORD: "You shall
17: 7 Thus *s* the LORD of hosts: "I
21:10 Thus *s* the LORD: "I offer you
21:11 Thus *s* the LORD: 'Choose for
2 Chr 11: 4 Thus *s* the LORD: "You shall
12: 5 Thus *s* the LORD: 'You have
18:10 Thus *s* the LORD: 'With these
18:13 LORD lives, whatever my God *s*,
18:26 Thus *s* the king: "Put this
20:15 Thus *s* the LORD to you:
21:12 Thus *s* the LORD God of your
24:20 Thus *s* God: 'Why do you
32:10 Thus *s* Sennacherib king of
34:23 Thus *s* the LORD God of Israel,
34:24 Thus *s* the LORD: 'Behold, I
34:26 Thus *s* the LORD God of Israel:
34:27 have heard you," *s* the LORD.
36:23 Thus *s* Cyrus king of Persia: All
Ezra 1: 2 Thus *s* Cyrus king of Persia: All
Neh 6: 6 among the nations, and Geshem *s*,
Job 28:14 The deep *s*, 'It is not in
28:14 is not in me'; And the sea *s*,
33:24 He is gracious to him, and *s*,
33:27 Then he looks at men and *s*,
35:10 But no one *s*, 'Where is God
37: 6 For He *s* to the snow, 'Fall on
39:25 the blast of the trumpet he *s*,
Ps 12: 5 *s* the LORD; "I will set
29: 9 And in His temple everyone *s*,
50:16 But to the wicked God *s*:
Prov 9: 4 understanding, she *s* to him,
9:16 understanding, she *s* to him,
22:13 The lazy man *s*,
23: 7 Eat and drink!" he *s* to you,
24:24 He who *s* to the wicked, "You
26:13 The lazy man *s*,
26:19 deceives his neighbor, And *s*,
28:24 father or his mother, And *s*,
30:16 And the fire never *s*,
30:20 and wipes her mouth, And *s*,
Eccl 1: 2 *s* the Preacher; "Vanity of
7:27 *s* the Preacher, "Adding
12: 8 *s* the Preacher, "All is
Isa 1:11 *S* the LORD. "I have had
1:18 *S* the LORD, "Though your
1:24 Therefore the Lord *s*,
3:15 *S* the Lord GOD of hosts.
3:16 Moreover the LORD *s*:
7: 7 thus *s* the Lord GOD: "It
10: 8 For he *s*, 'Are not my
10:13 For he *s*: "By the strength
10:24 Therefore thus *s* the Lord GOD
14:22 *s* the LORD of hosts, "And
14:22 and posterity," *s* the LORD.
14:23 *s* the LORD of hosts.
17: 3 *S* the LORD of hosts.
17: 6 *S* the LORD God of Israel.
19: 4 *S* the Lord, the LORD of
22:14 *s* the Lord GOD of hosts.
22:15 Thus *s* the Lord GOD of hosts:
22:25 *s* the LORD of hosts, 'the peg
28:16 Therefore thus *s* the Lord GOD:
29:11 And he *s*, "I cannot, for it
29:12 And he *s*, "I am not
29:22 Therefore thus *s* the LORD, who
30: 1 *s* the LORD, "Who take
30:12 Therefore thus *s* the Holy One
30:15 For thus *s* the Lord GOD, the
31: 9 *S* the LORD, Whose fire is
33:10 *s* the LORD; "Now I will be
36: 4 Thus *s* the great king, the king
36:14 Thus *s* the king: 'Do not let
36:16 for thus *s* the king of Assyria:
37: 3 Thus *s* Hezekiah: 'This day is a
37: 6 Thus *s* the LORD: "Do not be
37:21 Thus *s* the LORD God of Israel,
37:33 Therefore thus *s* the LORD
37:34 this city,' *S* the LORD.
38: 1 Thus *s* the LORD: 'Set your
38: 5 Thus *s* the LORD, the God of
39: 6 shall be left,' *s* the LORD.
40: 1 comfort My people!" *S* your
40:25 be equal?" *s* the Holy One.
41:14 *s* the LORD And your
41:21 *s* the LORD. "Bring forth
41:21 *s* the King of Jacob.
42: 5 Thus *s* God the LORD, Who
42:22 For plunder, and no one *s*,
43: 1 thus *s* the LORD, who created
43:10 *s* the LORD, "And My
43:12 *S* the LORD, "that I am
43:14 Thus *s* the LORD, your
43:16 Thus *s* the LORD, who makes a
44: 2 Thus *s* the LORD who made you
44: 6 Thus *s* the LORD, the King of
44:16 He even warms himself and *s*,
44:17 it, Prays to it and *s*,
44:24 Thus *s* the LORD, your
44:26 Who *s* to Jerusalem, 'You shall
44:27 Who *s* to the deep, 'Be dry!
44:28 Who *s* of Cyrus, 'He is My
45: 1 Thus *s* the LORD to His
45:10 Woe to him who *s* to his
45:11 Thus *s* the LORD, The Holy
45:13 *S* the LORD of hosts.
45:14 Thus *s* the LORD: "The labor
45:18 For thus *s* the LORD, Who
48:17 Thus *s* the LORD, your
48:22 *s* the LORD, "for the
49: 5 "And now the LORD *s*,
49: 6 Indeed He *s*, 'It is too
49: 7 Thus *s* the LORD, The
49: 8 Thus *s* the LORD: "In an
49:18 *s* the LORD, "You shall
49:22 Thus *s* the Lord GOD:
49:25 But thus *s* the LORD: "Even
50: 1 Thus *s* the LORD: "Where is
51:22 Thus *s* your Lord, The LORD
52: 3 For thus *s* the LORD: "You
52: 4 For thus *s* the Lord GOD: "My
52: 5 *s* the LORD, "That My
52: 5 *s* the LORD, "And My name
52: 7 Who *s* to Zion, "Your God
54: 1 married woman," *s* the LORD.
54: 6 were refused," *S* your God.
54: 8 *S* the LORD, your Redeemer.
54:10 *S* the LORD, who has mercy
54:17 is from Me," *S* the LORD.
55: 8 My ways," *s* the LORD.
56: 1 Thus *s* the LORD: "Keep
56: 4 For thus *s* the LORD: "To the
56: 8 the outcasts of Israel, *s*,
56:12 "Come," one *s*,
57:15 For thus *s* the High and Lofty
57:19 *S* the LORD, "And I will
57:21 *S* my God, "for the
59:20 in Jacob," *S* the LORD.
59:21 *s* the LORD, "this is My
59:21 *s* the LORD, "from this time
65: 7 *S* the LORD, "Who have
65: 8 Thus *s* the LORD: "As the
65: 8 in the cluster, And one *s*,
65:13 Therefore thus *s* the Lord GOD:
65:25 holy mountain," *S* the LORD.
66: 1 Thus *s* the LORD: "Heaven is
66: 2 *S* the LORD. "But on this
66: 9 *s* the LORD. "Shall I who
66: 9 the womb?" *s* your God.
66:12 For thus *s* the LORD:
66:17 together," *s* the LORD.
66:20 *s* the LORD, "as the
66:21 and Levites," *s* the LORD.
66:22 *s* the LORD, "So shall your
66:23 before Me," *s* the LORD.
Jer 1: 8 deliver you," *s* the LORD.
1:15 *s* the LORD; "They shall
1:19 *s* the LORD, "to deliver
2: 2 Thus *s* the LORD: "I remember
2: 3 upon them," *s* the LORD.'
2: 5 Thus *s* the LORD: "What
2: 9 *s* the LORD, "And against
2:12 very desolate," *s* the LORD.
2:19 *S* the Lord GOD of hosts.
2:22 *s* the Lord GOD.
2:29 against Me," *s* the LORD.
3: 1 return to Me," *s* the LORD.
3:10 in pretense," *s* the LORD.
3:12 *s* the LORD; 'I will not
3:12 *s* the LORD; 'I will not
3:13 My voice,' *s* the LORD.
3:14 *s* the LORD; "for I am
3:16 *s* the LORD, "that they will
3:20 of Israel," *s* the LORD.
4: 1 *s* the LORD, "Return to Me;

S

4: 3 For thus *s* the LORD to the men
4: 9 *s* the LORD, "That the
4:17 against Me," *s* the LORD.
4:27 For thus *s* the LORD: "The
5: 9 *s* the LORD. "And shall I
5:11 with Me," *s* the LORD.
5:14 Therefore thus *s* the LORD God
5:15 *s* the LORD. "It is a
5:18 *s* the LORD, "I will not
5:22 *s* the LORD. 'Will you not
5:29 *s* the LORD. 'Shall I not
6: 9 Thus *s* the LORD of hosts:
6:12 of the land," *s* the LORD.
6:15 cast down," *s* the LORD.
6:16 Thus *s* the LORD: "Stand in
6:21 Therefore thus *s* the LORD:
6:22 Thus *s* the LORD: "Behold, a
7: 3 Thus *s* the LORD of hosts, the
7:11 have seen it," *s* the LORD.
7:13 *s* the LORD, "and I spoke to
7:19 *s* the LORD. "Do they not
7:20 Therefore thus *s* the Lord GOD:
7:21 Thus *s* the LORD of hosts, the
7:30 *s* the LORD. "They have set
7:32 *s* the LORD, "when it will
8: 1 *s* the LORD, "they shall
8: 3 *s* the LORD of hosts.
8: 4 Thus *s* the LORD: "Will they
8:12 cast down," *s* the LORD.
8:13 *s* the LORD. "No grapes
8:17 bite you," *s* the LORD.
9: 3 know Me," *s* the LORD.
9: 6 know Me," *s* the LORD.
9: 7 Therefore thus *s* the LORD of
9: 9 *s* the LORD. "Shall I not
9:15 therefore thus *s* the LORD of
9:17 Thus *s* the LORD of hosts:
9:22 Thus *s* the LORD: 'Even the
9:23 Thus *s* the LORD: "Let not
9:24 I delight," *s* the LORD.
9:25 *s* the LORD, "that I will
10: 2 Thus *s* the LORD: "Do not
10:18 For thus *s* the LORD:
11: 3 Thus *s* the LORD God of Israel:
11:11 Therefore thus *s* the LORD:
11:21 Therefore thus *s* the LORD
11:22 therefore thus *s* the LORD of
12:14 Thus *s* the LORD: "Against all
12:17 that nation," *s* the LORD.
13: 9 Thus *s* the LORD: 'In this
13:11 *s* the LORD, 'that they may
13:12 Thus *s* the LORD God of Israel:
13:13 Thus *s* the LORD: "Behold, I
13:14 *s* the LORD. "I will not
13:25 *s* the LORD, "Because you
14:10 Thus *s* the LORD to this
14:15 Therefore thus *s* the LORD
15: 2 Thus *s* the LORD: "Such as
15: 3 *s* the LORD: "the sword to
15: 6 *s* the LORD, "You have gone
15: 9 their enemies," *s* the LORD.
15:19 Therefore thus *s* the LORD:
15:20 deliver you," *s* the LORD.
16: 3 For thus *s* the LORD concerning
16: 5 For thus *s* the LORD: "Do not
16: 5 *s* the LORD, "lovingkindness
16: 9 For thus *s* the LORD of hosts,
16:11 *s* the LORD; 'they have walked
16:14 *s* the LORD, "that it shall
16:16 *s* the LORD, "and they shall
17: 5 Thus *s* the LORD: "Cursed
17:21 Thus *s* the LORD: "Take heed to
17:24 *s* the LORD, "to bring no
18: 6 *s* the LORD. "Look, as the
18:11 Thus *s* the LORD: "Behold, I am
18:13 Therefore thus *s* the LORD:
19: 1 Thus *s* the LORD: "Go and get a
19: 3 Thus *s* the LORD of hosts, the
19: 6 *s* the LORD, "that this
19:11 Thus *s* the LORD of hosts:
19:12 *s* the LORD, "and to its
19:15 Thus *s* the LORD of hosts, the
20: 4 For thus *s* the LORD: 'Behold, I
21: 4 Thus *s* the LORD God of Israel:
21: 7 *s* the LORD, "I will deliver
21: 8 Thus *s* the LORD: "Behold, I
21:10 *s* the LORD. "It shall be
21:12 Thus *s* the LORD: "Execute
21:13 *s* the LORD, "Who say, 'Who
21:14 *s* the LORD; "I will kindle
22: 1 Thus *s* the LORD: "Go down to
22: 3 Thus *s* the LORD: "Execute
22: 5 *s* the LORD, "that this
22: 6 For thus *s* the LORD to the
22:11 For thus *s* the LORD concerning
22:14 Who *s*, 'I will build myself
22:16 knowing Me?" *s* the LORD.
22:18 Therefore thus *s* the LORD
22:24 *s* the LORD, "though Coniah
22:30 Thus *s* the LORD: 'Write this
23: 1 My pasture!" *s* the LORD.
23: 2 Therefore thus *s* the LORD God
23: 2 your doings," *s* the LORD.
23: 4 be lacking," *s* the LORD.
23: 5 *s* the LORD, "That I will
23: 7 *s* the LORD, "that they
23:11 wickedness," *s* the LORD.
23:12 punishment," *s* the LORD.
23:15 Therefore thus *s* the LORD of
23:16 Thus *s* the LORD of hosts:
23:23 *s* the LORD, "And not a God
23:24 *s* the LORD; "Do I not fill
23:24 and earth?" *s* the LORD.
23:28 the wheat?" *s* the LORD.
23:29 *s* the LORD, "And like a
23:30 *s* the LORD, "who steal My
23:31 *s* the LORD, "who use their
23:31 their tongues and say, 'He *s*.
23:32 *s* the LORD, "and tell them,
23:32 people at all," *s* the LORD.
23:33 forsake you," *s* the LORD.
23:38 therefore thus *s* the LORD:
24: 5 Thus *s* the LORD, the God of
24: 8 surely thus *s* the LORD—'SO will
25: 7 *s* the LORD, "that you might
25: 8 Therefore thus *s* the LORD of
25: 9 of the north,' *s* the LORD,
25:12 *s* the LORD; 'and I will make
25:15 For thus *s* the LORD God of
25:27 Thus *s* the LORD of hosts, the
25:28 Thus *s* the LORD of hosts: "You
25:29 *s* the LORD of hosts.'
25:31 the sword,' *s* the LORD."
25:32 Thus *s* the LORD of hosts:
26: 2 Thus *s* the LORD: 'Stand in the
26: 4 Thus *s* the LORD: "If you will
26:18 Thus *s* the LORD of hosts:
27: 2 Thus *s* the LORD to me: 'Make
27: 4 Thus *s* the LORD of hosts, the
27: 8 *s* the LORD, 'with the sword,
27:11 *s* the LORD, 'and they shall
27:15 *s* the LORD, "yet they
27:16 Thus *s* the LORD: 'Do not listen
27:19 For thus *s* the LORD of hosts
27:21 thus *s* the LORD of hosts, the
27:22 *s* the LORD. 'Then I will
28: 4 *s* the LORD, 'for I will break
28:11 Thus *s* the LORD: 'Even so I
28:13 Thus *s* the LORD: "You have
28:14 For thus *s* the LORD of hosts,
28:16 Therefore thus *s* the LORD:
29: 4 Thus *s* the LORD of hosts, the
29: 8 For thus *s* the LORD of hosts,
29: 9 not sent them, *s* the LORD.
29:10 For thus *s* the LORD: After
29:11 *s* the LORD, thoughts of peace
29:14 *s* the LORD, and I will bring
29:14 *s* the LORD, and I will bring
29:16 therefore thus *s* the LORD
29:17 thus *s* the LORD of hosts:
29:19 *s* the LORD, which I sent to
29:19 would you heed, *s* the LORD.
29:21 Thus *s* the LORD of hosts, the
29:23 am a witness, *s* the LORD.
29:31 Thus *s* the LORD concerning
29:32 therefore thus *s* the LORD:
29:32 *s* the LORD, because he has
30: 3 *s* the LORD, 'that I will
30: 3 and Judah,' *s* the LORD.
30: 5 For thus *s* the LORD: 'We have
30: 8 *S* the LORD of hosts, 'That
30:10 *s* the LORD, 'Nor be
30:11 *s* the LORD, 'to save you;
30:12 For thus *s* the LORD: 'Your
30:17 *s* the LORD, 'Because they
30:18 Thus *s* the LORD: 'Behold, I
30:21 approach Me?' *s* the LORD.
31: 1 *s* the LORD, "I will be the
31: 2 Thus *s* the LORD: "The
31: 7 For thus *s* the LORD: "Sing
31:14 My goodness, *s* the LORD."
31:15 Thus *s* the LORD: "A voice
31:16 Thus *s* the LORD: "Refrain
31:16 *s* the LORD, And they shall
31:17 *s* the LORD, That your
31:20 mercy on him, *s* the LORD.
31:23 Thus *s* the LORD of hosts, the
31:27 *s* the LORD, that I will sow
31:28 and to plant, *s* the LORD.
31:31 *s* the LORD, when I will make a
31:32 husband to them, *s* the LORD.
31:33 *s* the LORD: I will put My law
31:34 *s* the LORD. For I will forgive
31:35 Thus *s* the LORD, Who gives
31:36 *s* the LORD, Then the seed of
31:37 Thus *s* the LORD: "If heaven
31:37 have done, *s* the LORD.
31:38 *s* the LORD, that the city
32: 3 Thus *s* the LORD: "Behold, I
32: 5 *s* the LORD; "though you
32:14 Thus *s* the LORD of hosts, the
32:15 For thus *s* the LORD of hosts,
32:28 Therefore thus *s* the LORD:
32:30 of their hands," *s* the LORD.
32:36 thus *s* the LORD, the God of
32:42 For thus *s* the LORD: 'Just as
32:44 to return,' *s* the LORD."
33: 2 Thus *s* the LORD who made it,
33: 4 For thus *s* the LORD, the God
33:10 Thus *s* the LORD: 'Again there
33:11 at the first,' *s* the LORD.
33:12 Thus *s* the LORD of hosts: 'In
33:13 counts them,' *s* the LORD.
33:14 *s* the LORD, 'that I will
33:17 For thus *s* the LORD: 'David
33:20 Thus *s* the LORD: 'If you can
33:25 Thus *s* the LORD: 'If My
34: 2 Thus *s* the LORD, the God of
34: 2 Thus *s* the LORD: 'Behold, I
34: 4 Thus *s* the LORD concerning
34: 5 the word, *s* the LORD.'
34:13 Thus *s* the LORD, the God of
34:17 Therefore thus *s* the LORD:
34:17 *s* the LORD—'TO the sword, to
34:22 *s* the LORD, 'and cause them
35:13 Thus *s* the LORD of hosts, the
35:13 My words?" *s* the LORD.
35:17 Therefore thus *s* the LORD God
35:18 Thus *s* the LORD of hosts, the
35:19 therefore thus *s* the LORD of
36:29 Thus *s* the LORD: "You have
36:30 Therefore thus *s* the LORD
37: 7 Thus *s* the LORD, the God of
37: 9 Thus *s* the LORD: 'Do not
38: 2 Thus *s* the LORD: 'He who
38: 3 Thus *s* the LORD: 'This city
38:17 Thus *s* the LORD, the God of
39:12 but do to him just as he *s* to
39:16 Thus *s* the LORD of hosts, the
39:17 *s* the LORD, "and you shall
39:18 in Me," *s* the LORD.'
42: 9 Thus *s* the LORD, the God of
42:11 *s* the LORD, 'for I am with
42:15 Thus *s* the LORD of hosts, the
42:18 For thus *s* the LORD of hosts,
42:20 all that the LORD your God *s*,
43:10 Thus *s* the LORD of hosts, the
44: 2 Thus *s* the LORD of hosts, the
44: 7 thus *s* the LORD, the God of
44:11 Therefore thus *s* the LORD of
44:25 Thus *s* the LORD of hosts, the
44:26 *s* the LORD, 'that My name
44:29 *s* the LORD, 'that I will
44:30 Thus *s* the LORD: 'Behold, I
45: 2 Thus *s* the LORD, the God of
45: 4 Thus *s* the LORD: "Behold, what
45: 5 *s* the LORD. "But I will
46: 5 all around," *s* the LORD.
46: 8 And he *s*, 'I will go up
46:18 *s* the King, Whose name is
46:23 *s* the LORD, "Though it
46:25 of hosts, the God of Israel, *s*:
46:26 days of old," *s* the LORD.
46:28 *s* the LORD, "For I am
47: 2 Thus *s* the LORD: "Behold,
48: 1 Thus *s* the LORD of hosts, the
48:12 *s* the LORD, "That I shall
48:15 *s* the King, Whose name is
48:25 is broken," *s* the LORD.
48:30 *s* the LORD, "But it is
48:35 *s* the LORD, "I will cause
48:38 no pleasure," *s* the LORD.
48:40 For thus *s* the LORD:
48:43 of Moab," *s* the LORD.
48:44 punishment," *s* the LORD.
48:47 *s* the LORD. Thus far is
49: 1 Thus *s* the LORD: "Has
49: 2 *s* the LORD, "That I will
49: 2 inheritance," *s* the LORD.
49: 5 *S* the Lord GOD of hosts,
49: 6 of Ammon," *s* the LORD.
49: 7 Thus *s* the LORD of hosts:
49:12 For thus *s* the LORD: "Behold,
49:13 *s* the LORD, "that Bozrah
49:16 from there," *s* the LORD.
49:18 *s* the LORD, "No one shall
49:26 *s* the LORD of hosts.
49:28 Thus *s* the LORD: "Arise, go
49:30 of Hazor!" *s* the LORD.
49:31 *s* the LORD, "Which has
49:32 all its sides," *s* the LORD.
49:35 Thus *s* the LORD of hosts:
49:37 *s* the LORD; 'And I will send
49:38 the princes,' *s* the LORD.
49:39 of Elam,' *s* the LORD."
50: 4 *s* the LORD, "The children
50:10 be satisfied," *s* the LORD.
50:18 Therefore thus *s* the LORD of
50:20 *s* the LORD, "The iniquity
50:21 *s* the LORD, "And do
50:30 in that day," *s* the LORD.
50:31 haughty one!" *s* the Lord
50:33 Thus *s* the LORD of hosts:
50:35 *s* the LORD, "Against the
50:40 *s* the LORD, "So no one
51: 1 Thus *s* the LORD: "Behold, I
51:24 in your sight," *s* the LORD.
51:25 *s* the LORD. "And I will
51:26 forever," *s* the LORD.
51:33 For thus *s* the LORD of hosts,
51:36 Therefore thus *s* the LORD:
51:39 not awake," *s* the LORD.
51:48 the north," *s* the LORD.
51:52 *s* the LORD, "That I will
51:53 come to her," *s* the LORD.
51:57 *s* the King, Whose name is
51:58 Thus *s* the LORD of hosts:
Lam 3:24 *s* my soul, "Therefore I
Ezek 2: 4 Thus *s* the Lord GOD.'
3:11 Thus *s* the Lord GOD,' whether
3:27 Thus *s* the Lord GOD.' He who
5: 5 Thus *s* the Lord GOD: 'This is
5: 7 Therefore thus *s* the Lord GOD:
5: 8 therefore thus *s* the Lord GOD:
5:11 *s* the Lord GOD, 'surely,
6: 3 Lord GOD!' Thus *s* the Lord
6:11 Thus *s* the Lord GOD: "Pound
7: 2 thus *s* the Lord GOD to the
7: 5 Thus *s* the Lord GOD: 'A
11: 5 Thus *s* the LORD: "Thus you
11: 7 Therefore thus *s* the Lord GOD:
11: 8 upon you," *s* the Lord GOD.
11:16 Thus *s* the Lord GOD: "Although
11:17 Thus *s* the Lord GOD: "I will
11:21 own heads," *s* the Lord GOD.
12:10 Thus *s* the Lord GOD: "This

12:19 Thus *s* the Lord GOD to the
12:22 the land of Israel, which *s*,
12:23 Thus *s* the Lord GOD: "I will
12:25 perform it," *s* the Lord GOD.'
12:28 Thus *s* the Lord GOD: "None of
12:28 be done," *s* the Lord GOD.'
13: 3 Thus *s* the Lord GOD: "Woe to
13: 6 Thus *s* the LORD!' But the LORD
13: 7 You say, 'The LORD *s*,
13: 8 Therefore thus *s* the Lord GOD:
13: 8 against you," *s* the Lord GOD.
13:13 Therefore thus *s* the Lord GOD:
13:16 no peace,'" *s* the Lord GOD.
13:18 Thus *s* the Lord GOD: "Woe to
13:20 Therefore thus *s* the Lord GOD:
14: 4 Thus *s* the Lord GOD: "Everyone
14: 6 Thus *s* the Lord GOD: "Repent,
14:11 their God," *s* the Lord GOD.'
14:14 righteousness," *s* the Lord
14:16 *s* the Lord GOD, "they would
14:18 *s* the Lord GOD, "they would
14:20 *s* the Lord GOD, "they would
14:21 For thus *s* the Lord GOD: "How
14:23 done in it," *s* the Lord GOD.
15: 6 Therefore thus *s* the Lord GOD:
15: 8 *s* the Lord GOD."
16: 3 Thus *s* the Lord GOD to
16: 8 became Mine," *s* the Lord GOD.
16:14 you," *s* the Lord GOD.
16:19 it was," *s* the Lord GOD.
16:23 woe to you!' *s* the Lord GOD—
16:30 is your heart!" *s* the Lord
16:36 Thus *s* the Lord GOD: "Because
16:43 *s* the Lord GOD. "And you
16:48 *s* the Lord GOD, "neither
16:58 abominations," *s* the LORD.
16:59 For thus *s* the Lord GOD: "I
16:63 done," *s* the Lord GOD.'
17: 3 Thus *s* the Lord GOD: "A
17: 9 Thus *s* the Lord GOD: "Will
17:16 *s* the Lord GOD, 'surely in
17:19 Therefore thus *s* the Lord GOD:
17:22 Thus *s* the Lord GOD: "I will
18: 3 *s* the Lord GOD, "you shall
18: 9 surely live!" *S* the Lord
18:23 *s* the Lord GOD, "and not
18:29 "Yet the house of Israel *s*,
18:30 *s* the Lord GOD. "Repent,
18:32 *s* the Lord GOD. "Therefore
20: 3 Thus *s* the Lord GOD: "Have you
20: 3 *s* the Lord GOD, "I will not
20: 5 Thus *s* the Lord GOD: "On the
20:27 Thus *s* the Lord GOD: "In this
20:30 Thus *s* the Lord GOD: "Are you
20:31 *s* the Lord GOD, "I will not
20:33 *s* the Lord GOD, "surely
20:36 with you," *s* the Lord GOD.
20:39 thus *s* the Lord GOD: "Go,
20:40 *s* the Lord GOD, "there all
20:44 Israel," *s* the Lord GOD.'
20:47 of the LORD! Thus *s* the Lord
21: 3 Thus *s* the LORD: "Behold, I
21: 7 to pass,' *s* the Lord GOD."
21: 9 Thus *s* the LORD!' Say: 'A
21:13 no more," *s* the Lord GOD.
21:24 Therefore thus *s* the Lord GOD:
21:26 thus *s* the Lord GOD: "Remove
21:28 Thus *s* the Lord GOD concerning
22: 3 Thus *s* the Lord GOD: "The city
22:12 Me," *s* the Lord GOD.
22:19 Therefore thus *s* the Lord GOD:
22:28 Thus *s* the Lord GOD,' when the
22:31 own heads," *s* the Lord GOD.
23:22 thus *s* the Lord GOD:
23:28 For thus *s* the Lord GOD:
23:32 Thus *s* the Lord GOD: 'You
23:34 have spoken,' *S* the Lord
23:35 Therefore thus *s* the Lord GOD:
23:46 For thus *s* the Lord GOD:
24: 3 Thus *s* the Lord GOD: "Put on
24: 6 Therefore thus *s* the Lord GOD:
24: 9 Therefore thus *s* the Lord GOD:
24:14 *S* the Lord GOD.'"
24:21 Thus *s* the Lord GOD: 'Behold, I
25: 3 Lord GOD! Thus *s* the Lord
25: 6 For thus *s* the Lord GOD:
25: 8 Thus *s* the Lord GOD: "Because
25:12 Thus *s* the Lord GOD: "Because
25:13 therefore thus *s* the Lord GOD:
25:14 vengeance," *s* the Lord GOD.
25:15 Thus *s* the Lord GOD: "Because
25:16 therefore thus *s* the Lord GOD:
26: 3 Therefore thus *s* the Lord GOD:
26: 5 *s* the Lord GOD; 'it shall
26: 7 For thus *s* the Lord GOD:
26:14 have spoken,' *s* the Lord GOD.
26:15 Thus *s* the Lord GOD to Tyre:
26:19 For thus *s* the Lord GOD: 'When
26:21 again,' *s* the Lord GOD."
27: 3 thus *s* the Lord GOD:
28: 2 Thus *s* the Lord GOD:
28: 6 Therefore thus *s* the Lord GOD:
28:10 *s* the Lord GOD.'"
28:12 Thus *s* the Lord GOD: "You
28:22 Thus *s* the Lord GOD:
28:25 Thus *s* the Lord GOD: "When I
29: 3 Thus *s* the Lord GOD:
29: 8 Therefore thus *s* the Lord GOD:
29:13 thus *s* the Lord GOD: "At the
29:19 Therefore thus *s* the Lord GOD:
29:20 for Me,' *s* the Lord GOD.
30: 2 Thus *s* the Lord GOD: "Wail,
30: 6 Thus *s* the LORD: "Those who
30: 6 the sword," *S* the Lord GOD.
30:10 Thus *s* the Lord GOD: "I
30:13 Thus *s* the Lord GOD: "I
30:22 Therefore thus *s* the Lord GOD:
31:10 Therefore thus *s* the Lord GOD:
31:15 Thus *s* the Lord GOD: 'In the
31:18 multitude,' *s* the Lord GOD."
32: 3 Thus *s* the Lord GOD: 'I will
32: 8 your land,' *S* the Lord GOD.
32:11 For thus *s* the Lord GOD: 'The
32:14 like oil,' *S* the Lord GOD.
32:16 multitude,' *S* the Lord
32:31 the sword," *S* the Lord GOD.
32:32 multitude," *S* the Lord GOD.
33:11 *s* the Lord GOD, 'I have no
33:25 Thus *s* the Lord GOD: "You eat
33:27 Thus *s* the Lord GOD: "As I
34: 2 Thus *s* the Lord GOD to the
34: 8 *s* the Lord GOD, "surely
34:10 Thus *s* the Lord GOD: "Behold,
34:11 For thus *s* the Lord GOD:
34:15 lie down," *s* the Lord GOD.
34:17 thus *s* the Lord GOD: "Behold,
34:20 Therefore thus *s* the Lord GOD
34:30 *s* the Lord GOD.'"
34:31 your God," *s* the Lord GOD.
35: 3 Thus *s* the Lord GOD:
35: 6 *s* the Lord GOD, "I will
35:11 *s* the Lord GOD, "I will do
35:14 Thus *s* the Lord GOD: "The
36: 2 Thus *s* the Lord GOD: "Because
36: 3 Thus *s* the Lord GOD: "Because
36: 4 Lord GOD! Thus *s* the Lord
36: 5 therefore thus *s* the Lord GOD:
36: 6 Thus *s* the Lord GOD: "Behold,
36: 7 Therefore thus *s* the Lord GOD:
36:13 Thus *s* the Lord GOD: "Because
36:14 anymore," *s* the Lord GOD.
36:15 *s* the Lord GOD.'"
36:22 Thus *s* the Lord GOD: "I do not
36:23 *s* the Lord GOD, "when I am
36:32 *s* the Lord GOD, "let it be
36:33 Thus *s* the Lord GOD: "On the
36:37 Thus *s* the Lord GOD: "I will
37: 5 Thus *s* the Lord GOD to these
37: 9 Thus *s* the Lord GOD: "Come
37:12 Thus *s* the Lord GOD: "Behold,
37:14 performed it," *s* the LORD.'
37:19 Thus *s* the Lord GOD: "Surely I
37:21 Thus *s* the Lord GOD: "Surely I
38: 3 Thus *s* the Lord GOD: "Behold,
38:10 Thus *s* the Lord GOD: "On that
38:14 Thus *s* the Lord GOD: "On that
38:17 Thus *s* the Lord GOD: "Are you
38:18 *s* the Lord GOD, "that My
38:21 *s* the Lord GOD. "Every
39: 1 Thus *s* the Lord GOD: "Behold,
39: 5 spoken," *s* the Lord GOD.
39: 8 *s* the Lord GOD. "This is
39:10 them," *s* the Lord GOD.
39:13 glorified," *s* the Lord GOD.
39:17 thus *s* the Lord GOD, 'Speak to
39:20 of war," *s* the Lord GOD.
39:25 Therefore thus *s* the Lord GOD:
39:29 of Israel,' *s* the Lord GOD."
43:18 thus *s* the Lord GOD: 'These
43:19 to Me,' *s* the Lord GOD.
43:27 accept you,' *s* the Lord GOD."
44: 6 Thus *s* the Lord GOD: "O house
44: 9 Thus *s* the Lord GOD: "No
44:12 *s* the Lord GOD, "that they
44:15 the blood," *s* the Lord GOD.
44:27 court," *s* the Lord GOD.
45: 9 Thus *s* the Lord GOD: "Enough,
45: 9 My people," *s* the Lord GOD.
45:15 for them," *s* the Lord GOD.
45:18 Thus *s* the Lord GOD: "In the
46: 1 Thus *s* the Lord GOD: "The
46:16 Thus *s* the Lord GOD: "If the
47:13 Thus *s* the Lord GOD: "These
47:23 inheritance," *s* the Lord GOD.
48:29 portions," *s* the Lord GOD.
Hos 2:13 she forgot," *s* the LORD.
2:16 *S* the LORD, "That you
2:21 *s* the LORD; "I will answer
11:11 their houses," *S* the LORD.
Joel 2:12 *s* the LORD, "Turn to Me
Am 1: 3 Thus *s* the LORD: "For three
1: 5 to Kir," *S* the LORD.
1: 6 Thus *s* the LORD: "For three
1: 8 perish," *S* the Lord GOD.
1: 9 Thus *s* the LORD: "For three
1:11 Thus *s* the LORD: "For three
1:13 Thus *s* the LORD: "For three
1:15 together," *S* the LORD.
2: 1 Thus *s* the LORD: "For three
2: 3 with him," *S* the LORD.
2: 4 Thus *s* the LORD: "For three
2: 6 Thus *s* the LORD: "For three
2:11 of Israel?" *S* the LORD.
2:16 that day," *S* the LORD.
3:10 *S* the LORD, 'Who store up
3:11 Therefore thus *s* the Lord GOD:
3:12 Thus *s* the LORD: "As a
3:13 *S* the Lord GOD, the God of
3:15 an end," *S* the LORD.
4: 3 into Harmon," *S* the LORD.
4: 5 of Israel!" *S* the Lord
4: 6 to Me," *S* the LORD.
4: 8 to Me," *S* the LORD.
4: 9 to Me," *S* the LORD.
4:10 to Me," *S* the LORD.
4:11 to Me," *S* the LORD.
5: 3 For thus *s* the Lord GOD:
5: 4 For thus *s* the LORD to the
5:16 *s* this: "There shall be
5:17 through you," *S* the LORD.
5:27 *S* the LORD, whose name is
6: 8 The LORD God of hosts *s*:
6:14 *S* the LORD God of hosts;
7:17 Therefore thus *s* the LORD:
8: 3 *S* the Lord GOD—"MANY dead
8: 9 *s* the Lord GOD, "That I
8:11 *s* the Lord GOD, "That I
9: 7 *s* the LORD. "Did I not
9: 8 of Jacob," *S* the LORD.
9:12 *S* the LORD who does this
9:13 *s* the LORD, "When the
9:15 *S* the LORD your God.
Ob 1 Thus *s* the Lord GOD concerning
4 you down," *s* the LORD.
8 *s* the LORD, "Even destroy
Mic 2: 3 Therefore thus *s* the LORD:
3: 5 Thus *s* the LORD concerning
4: 6 *s* the LORD, "I will
5:10 *s* the LORD, "That I will
6: 1 Hear now what the LORD *s*:
Nah 1:12 Thus *s* the LORD: "Though
2:13 *s* the LORD of hosts, "I
3: 5 *s* the LORD of hosts; "I
Hab 2:19 Woe to him who *s* to wood,
Zeph 1: 2 of the land," *S* the LORD;
1: 3 of the land," *S* the LORD.
1:10 *s* the LORD, "The sound of
2: 9 *S* the LORD of hosts, the
3: 8 *s* the LORD, "Until the day
3:20 your eyes," *S* the LORD.
Hag 1: 2 hosts, saying: 'This people *s*,
1: 5 thus *s* the LORD of hosts:
1: 7 Thus *s* the LORD of hosts:
1: 8 be glorified," *s* the LORD.
1: 9 *s* the LORD of hosts.
1:13 am with you, *s* the LORD."
2: 4 *s* the LORD; 'and be strong,
2: 4 *s* the LORD, 'and work; for I
2: 4 *s* the LORD of hosts.
2: 6 For thus *s* the LORD of hosts:
2: 7 *s* the LORD of hosts.
2: 8 *s* the LORD of hosts.
2: 9 *s* the LORD of hosts. 'And in
2: 9 *s* the LORD of hosts."
2:11 Thus *s* the LORD of hosts: 'Now,
2:14 *s* the LORD, 'and so is every
2:17 turn to Me,' *s* the LORD.
2:23 *s* the LORD of hosts, 'I will
2:23 *s* the LORD, 'and will make
2:23 *s* the LORD of hosts."
Zech 1: 3 Thus *s* the LORD of hosts:
1: 3 *s* the LORD of hosts, "and I
1: 3 *s* the LORD of hosts.
1: 4 Thus *s* the LORD of hosts:
1: 4 heed Me," *s* the LORD.
1:14 Thus *s* the LORD of hosts: "I
1:16 Therefore thus *s* the LORD:
1:16 *s* the LORD of hosts, "And
1:17 Thus *s* the LORD of hosts:
2: 5 *s* the LORD, 'will be a wall
2: 6 *s* the LORD; "for I have
2: 6 of heaven," *s* the LORD.
2: 8 For thus *s* the LORD of hosts:
2:10 in your midst," *s* the LORD.
3: 7 'Thus *s* the LORD of hosts:
3: 9 *S* the LORD of hosts, 'And I
3:10 *s* the LORD of hosts,
4: 6 *S* the LORD of hosts.
5: 4 *s* the LORD of hosts; "It
6:12 Thus *s* the LORD of hosts,
7: 9 Thus *s* the LORD of hosts:
7:13 *s* the LORD of hosts.
8: 2 Thus *s* the LORD of hosts: 'I
8: 3 Thus *s* the LORD: 'I will
8: 4 Thus *s* the LORD of hosts:
8: 6 Thus *s* the LORD of hosts: 'If
8: 6 *S* the LORD of hosts.
8: 7 Thus *s* the LORD of hosts:
8: 9 Thus *s* the LORD of hosts:
8:11 *s* the LORD of hosts.
8:14 For thus *s* the LORD of hosts:
8:14 *S* the LORD of hosts, 'And I
8:17 I hate,' *S* the LORD."
8:19 Thus *s* the LORD of hosts:
8:20 Thus *s* the LORD of hosts:
8:23 Thus *s* the LORD of hosts: 'In
10:12 in His name," *S* the LORD.
11: 4 Thus *s* the LORD my God, "Feed
11: 6 *s* the LORD. "But indeed I
12: 1 Thus *s* the LORD, who stretches
12: 4 *s* the LORD, "I will strike
13: 2 *s* the LORD of hosts, "that
13: 7 *S* the LORD of hosts.
13: 8 *S* the LORD, "That
Mal 1: 2 *s* the LORD. "Yet you say,
1: 2 *S* the LORD. "Yet Jacob I
1: 4 Thus *s* the LORD of hosts:
1: 6 *S* the LORD of hosts To you
1: 8 *S* the LORD of hosts.
1: 9 *S* the LORD of hosts.
1:10 *S* the LORD of hosts, "Nor
1:11 *S* the LORD of hosts.
1:13 *S* the LORD of hosts. "And
1:13 your hand?" *S* the LORD.
1:14 *S* the LORD of hosts, "And
2: 2 *S* the LORD of hosts, "I

S

2: 4 *S* the LORD of hosts.
2: 8 *S* the LORD of hosts.
2:16 For the LORD God of Israel *s*
2:16 *S* the LORD of hosts.
3: 1 *S* the LORD of hosts.
3: 5 *S* the LORD of hosts.
3: 7 *S* the LORD of hosts. "But
3:10 *S* the LORD of hosts, "If
3:11 *S* the LORD of hosts;
3:12 *S* the LORD of hosts.
3:13 *S* the LORD, "Yet you say,
3:17 *s* the LORD of hosts, "On
4: 1 *S* the LORD of hosts,
4: 3 *S* the LORD of hosts.
Mt 5:22 And whoever *s* to his brother,
5:22 But whoever *s*, 'You fool!'
7:21 Not everyone who *s* to Me,
12:44 'Then he *s*, 'I will return
13:14 of Isaiah is fulfilled, which *s*:
15: 5 Whoever *s* to his father or
21: 3 And if anyone *s* anything to you,
24:23 Then if anyone *s* to you, 'Look,
24:48 But if that evil servant *s* in
26:18 and say to him, 'The Teacher *s*,
Mk 7:11 If a man *s* to his father or
11: 3 And if anyone *s* to you, 'Why are
11:23 whoever *s* to this mountain, 'Be
11:23 that those things he *s* will be
11:23 he will have whatever he *s*.
13:21 Then if anyone *s* to you, 'Look,
14:14 of the house, 'The Teacher *s*,
15:28 Scripture was fulfilled which *s*,
Lk 5:39 he *s*, 'The old is better.'
11:24 and finding none, he *s*,
12:45 But if that servant *s* in his
22:11 The Teacher *s* to you, "Where is
Jn 2: 5 Whatever He *s* to you, do it."
4:10 and who it is who *s* to you,
6:42 How is it then that He *s*,
8:22 He kill Himself, because He *s*,
16:17 What is this that He *s* to us, 'A
16:18 "What is this that He *s*,
19:24 might be fulfilled which *s*:
19:37 And again another Scripture *s*,
Acts 2:17 *s* God, That I will pour
2:25 For David *s* concerning Him:
2:34 but he *s* himself: 'The
3:22 whatever He *s* to you.
7:48 with hands, as the prophet *s*:
7:49 *s* the LORD, Or what is
13:35 Therefore He also *s* in another
15:17 *S* the LORD who does all
21:11 Thus *s* the Holy Spirit, 'So
Rom 3:19 we know that whatever the law *s*,
3:19 it *s* to those who are under the
9:15 For He *s* to Moses, "I will
9:17 For the Scripture *s* to Pharaoh,
9:25 As He *s* also in Hosea: "I
10:11 For the Scripture *s*,
10:16 obeyed the gospel. For Isaiah *s*,
10:19 First Moses *s*: "I will
10:20 But Isaiah is very bold and *s*:
10:21 But to Israel he *s*:
11: 2 not know what the Scripture *s*
11: 9 And David *s*: "Let their
12:19 I will repay," *s* the Lord.
14:11 *s* the LORD, Every knee
15:10 And again he *s*: "Rejoice,
15:12 And again, Isaiah *s*:
1 Cor 1:12 I say this, that each of you *s*,
3: 4 when one *s*, "I am of Paul,"
6:16 He *s*, "shall become one
10:28 But if anyone *s* to you, "This
14:21 not hear Me," *s* the Lord.
14:34 submissive, as the law also *s*.
15:27 But when He *s* "all things
2 Cor 6: 2 He *s*: "In an acceptable
6:17 *s* the Lord. Do not touch
6:18 *S* the LORD Almighty."
Eph 4: 8 Therefore He *s*: "When He
5:14 Therefore He *s*: "Awake, you
1 Tim 4: 1 Now the Spirit expressly *s* that
5:18 For the Scripture *s*,
Heb 1: 6 firstborn into the world, He *s*:
1: 7 And of the angels He *s*:
1: 8 But to the Son He *s*:
3: 7 as the Holy Spirit *s*:
5: 6 As He also *s* in another
8: 8 finding fault with them, He *s*:
8: 8 *s* the LORD, when I will
8: 9 them, *s* the LORD.
8:10 *s* the LORD: I will put
8:13 In that He *s*, "A new
10:16 *s* the LORD: I will put
10:30 *s* the Lord. And again, "The
Jas 2:14 if someone *s* he has faith but
2:16 and one of you *s* to them,
2:23 Scripture was fulfilled which *s*,
4: 5 you think that the Scripture *s*
4: 6 more grace. Therefore He *s*:
1 Jn 2: 4 He who *s*, "I know Him,"
2: 6 He who *s* he abides in Him ought
2: 9 He who *s* he is in the light, and
4:20 If someone *s*, "I love God,"
Rev 1: 8 *s* the Lord, "who is and who
2: 1 These things *s* He who holds the
2: 7 let him hear what the Spirit *s*
2: 8 These things *s* the First and
2:11 let him hear what the Spirit *s*
2:12 These things *s* He who has the
2:17 let him hear what the Spirit *s*
2:18 These things *s* the Son of God,
2:29 let him hear what the Spirit *s*
3: 1 These things *s* He who has the
3: 6 let him hear what the Spirit *s*
3: 7 These things *s* He who is holy,
3:13 let him hear what the Spirit *s*
3:14 These things *s* the Amen, the
3:22 let him hear what the Spirit *s*
14:13 *s* the Spirit, "that they may
18: 7 for she *s* in her heart, 'I sit
22:20 who testifies to these things *s*,

SCAB (8/8)

Lev 13: 2 of his body a swelling, a *s*,
13: 6 him clean; it is only a *s*,
13: 7 But if the *s* should at all
13: 8 if the priest sees that the *s*
14:56 for a swelling and a *s* and a
21:20 in his eye, or eczema or *s*,
Deut 28:27 Egypt, with tumors, with the *s*,
Isa 3:17 the Lord will strike with a *s*

SCABBARD (1/1)

Jer 47: 6 Put yourself up into your *s*,

SCABBED (KJV) See SCAB

SCABS (1/1)

Lev 22:22 or have an ulcer or eczema or *s*,

SCAFFOLD (KJV) See PLATFORM

SCALE (12/8)

Lev 13:31 the one who has the *s*
13:32 and indeed if the *s* has not
13:32 and the *s* does not appear
13:33 but the *s* he shall not shave.
13:33 the one who has the *s*
13:34 the priest shall examine the *s*;
13:34 and indeed if the *s* has not
13:35 But if the *s* should at all
13:36 and indeed if the *s* has spread
13:37 But if the *s* appears to be at a
13:37 the *s* has healed. He is clean,
14:54 law for any leprous sore and *s*,

SCALES (27/26)

Lev 11: 9 in the water has fins and *s*,
11:10 that do not have fins and *s*,
11:12 water does not have fins or *s*—
19:36 'You shall have honest *s*,
Deut 14: 9 eat all that have fins and *s*.
14:10 does not have fins and *s* you
Job 6: 2 calamity laid with it on the *s*!
31: 6 Let me be weighed on honest *s*,
41:15 His rows of *s* are his pride,
Ps 62: 9 If they are weighed on the *s*,
Prov 11: 1 Dishonest *s* are an abomination
16:11 Honest weights and *s* are the
20:23 And dishonest *s* are not good.
21:22 A wise man *s* the city of the
Isa 40:12 Weighed the mountains in *s*
40:15 as the small dust on the *s*;
46: 6 bag, And weigh silver on the *s*;
Jer 32:10 and weighed the money on the *s*.
Ezek 5: 1 then take *s* to weigh and divide
29: 4 your rivers to stick to your *s*;
29: 4 rivers will stick to your *s*.
45:10 "You shall have honest *s*,
Hos 12: 7 Deceitful *s* are in his
Am 8: 5 Falsifying the *s* by deceit,
Mic 6:11 pure those with the wicked *s*,
Acts 9:18 from his eyes something like *s*,
Rev 6: 5 who sat on it had a pair of *s*

SCALL (KJV) See SCALE

SCALP (1/1)

Ps 68:21 The hairy *s* of the one who

SCALY (2/2)

Lev 13:30 It is a *s* leprosy of the head
13:31 priest examines the *s* sore,

SCAN (1/1)

Zech 4:10 Which *s* to and fro throughout

SCANT (KJV) See SHORT

SCAPEGOAT (4/3)

Lev 16: 8 and the other lot for the *s*.
16:10 which the lot fell to be the *s*
16:10 and to let it go as the *s* into
16:26 who released the goat as the *s*

SCAR (2/2)

Lev 13:23 it is the *s* of the boil;
13:28 for it is the *s* from the burn.

SCARCELY (8/6)

Gen 27:30 and Jacob had *s* gone out from
Song 3: 4 *S* had I passed by them, When I
Isa 40:24 *S* shall they be planted,
40:24 *S* shall they be sown,
40:24 *S* shall their stock take root
Acts 14:18 they could *s* restrain the
Rom 5: 7 For *s* for a righteous man will
1 Pe 4:18 righteous one is *s* saved,

SCARCITY (1/1)

Deut 8: 9 you will eat bread without *s*,

SCARE (1/1)

Job 7:14 Then You *s* me with dreams And

SCARLET (49/49)

Gen 38:28 midwife took a *s* thread
38:30 came out who had the *s* thread
Ex 25: 4 and *s* thread, fine linen, and
26: 1 and *s* thread; with artistic
26:31 and *s* thread, and fine woven
26:36 and *s* thread, and fine woven
27:16 and *s* thread, and fine woven
28: 5 and *s* thread, and fine linen,
28: 6 and *s* thread, and fine woven
28: 8 and *s* thread, and fine woven
28:15 and *s* thread, and fine woven
28:33 of blue, purple, and *s*,
35: 6 and *s* thread, fine linen, and
35:23 and *s* thread, fine linen, and
35:25 spun, of blue , purple, and *s*,
35:35 and *s* thread, and fine linen,
36: 8 and *s* thread; with artistic
36:35 and *s* thread, and fine woven
36:37 and *s* thread, and fine woven
38:18 and *s* thread, and of fine
38:23 and *s* thread, and of fine
39: 1 and *s* thread they made
39: 2 and *s* thread, and of fine
39: 3 and *s* thread and the fine
39: 5 and *s* thread, and of fine
39: 8 and *s* thread, and of fine
39:24 of blue, purple, and *s*,
39:29 and *s* thread, made by a
Lev 14: 4 and clean birds, cedar wood, *s*,
14: 6 the cedar wood and the *s* and
14:49 house, two birds, cedar wood, *s*,
14:51 cedar wood, the hyssop, the *s*,
14:52 wood, the hyssop, and the *s*.
Num 4: 8 spread over them a *s* cloth,
19: 6 cedar wood and hyssop and *s*,
Josh 2:18 you bind this line of *s* cord in
2:21 And she bound the *s* cord in the
2 Sam 1:24 Saul, Who clothed you in *s*,
Prov 31:21 household is clothed with *s*.
Song 4: 3 lips are like a strand of *s*,
Isa 1:18 "Though your sins are like *s*,
Lam 4: 5 Those who were brought up in *s*
Nah 2: 3 red, The valiant men are in *s*.
Mt 27:28 stripped Him and put a *s* robe
Heb 9:19 *s* wool, and hyssop, and
Rev 17: 3 woman sitting on a *s* beast
17: 4 was arrayed in purple and *s*,
18:12 linen and purple, silk and *s*,
18:16 in fine linen, purple, and *s*,

SCARVES (1/1)

Isa 3:18 The jingling anklets, the *s*,

SCATTER (36/36) SCATTERED, SCATTERS

Gen 49: 7 them in Jacob And *s* them
Ex 9: 8 and let Moses *s* it toward the
Lev 26:33 I will *s* you among the nations
Num 16:37 and *s* the fire some distance
Deut 4:27 And the LORD will *s* you among
28:64 Then the LORD will *s* you among
1 Ki 14:15 and will *s* them beyond the
Neh 1: 8 I will *s* you among the nations;
Ps 59:11 *S* them by Your power, And
68:30 *S* the peoples who delight in
106:27 And to *s* them in the lands.
144: 6 forth lightning and *s* them;
Isa 28:25 black cummin And *s* the cummin,
41:16 the whirlwind shall *s* them;
Jer 9:16 I will *s* them also among the
13:24 Therefore I will *s* them like
18:17 I will *s* them as with an east
23: 1 who destroy and *s* the sheep
49:32 I will *s* to all winds those in
49:36 And *s* them toward all those
Ezek 5: 2 and one-third you shall *s* in
5:10 all of you who remain I will *s*
5:12 and I will *s* another third to
6: 5 and I will *s* your bones all
10: 2 and *s* them over the city."
12:14 I will *s* to every wind all who
12:15 when I *s* them among the nations
20:23 that I would *s* them among the
22:15 I will *s* you among the nations,
29:12 and I will *s* the Egyptians
30:23 I will *s* the Egyptians among the
30:26 I will *s* the Egyptians among the
Dan 4:14 Strip off its leaves and *s* its
Hab 3:14 out like a whirlwind to *s* me;
Zech 1:21 the land of Judah to *s* it."
Mk 4:26 as if a man should *s* seed

SCATTERED (77/75) SCATTER

Gen 11: 4 lest we be *s* abroad over the
11: 8 So the LORD *s* them abroad from
11: 9 and from there the LORD *s* them
Ex 5:12 So the people were *s* abroad
9:10 and Moses *s* them toward
32:20 and he *s* it on the water and
Num 10:35 O LORD! Let Your enemies be *s*,
Deut 30: 3 the LORD your God has *s* you.
1 Sam 11:11 that those who survived were *s*,
13: 8 and the people were *s* from him.
13:11 I saw that the people were *s*
2 Sam 18: 8 For the battle there was *s* over
22:15 He sent out arrows and *s* them;
1 Ki 22:17 I saw all Israel *s* on the
2 Ki 25: 5 All his army was *s* from him.
2 Chr 18:16 I saw all Israel *s* on the
34: 4 and made dust of them and *s* it
Esth 3: 8 There is a certain people *s* and
Job 4:11 the cubs of the lioness are *s*.
18:15 Brimstone is *s* on his
38:24 Or the east wind *s* over the
Ps 18:14 out His arrows and *s* the foe,
44:11 And have *s* us among the
53: 5 For God has *s* the bones of him
68: 1 arise, Let His enemies be *s*;
68:14 When the Almighty *s* kings in
89:10 You have *s* Your enemies with
92: 9 workers of iniquity shall be *s*.
141: 7 Our bones are *s* at the mouth of
Isa 33: 3 up, the nations shall be *s*;
Jer 3:13 And have *s* your charms To
10:21 all their flocks shall be *s*.
23: 2 You have *s* My flock, driven them
30:11 nations where I have *s* you,
31:10 He who *s* Israel will gather him,
40:15 are gathered to you would be *s*,
50:17 Israel is like *s* sheep;
52: 8 All his army was *s* from him.
Lam 4: 1 stones of the sanctuary are *s*
4:16 The face of the LORD *s* them;
Ezek 6: 8 when you are *s* through the
11:16 and although I have *s* them
11:17 countries where you have been *s*,
17:21 those who remain shall be *s* to
20:34 the countries where you are *s*,
20:41 countries where you have been *s*;
28:25 peoples among whom they are *s*,
29:13 peoples among whom they were *s*.
34: 5 So they were *s* because there
34: 5 of the field when they were *s*.
34: 6 My flock was *s* over the whole
34:12 he is among his *s* sheep,
34:12 the places where they were *s*
34:21 and *s* them abroad,
36:19 So I *s* them among the nations,
46:18 that none of My people may be *s*
Joel 3: 2 Whom they have *s* among the
Nah 3:18 Your people are *s* on the
Hab 3: 6 everlasting mountains were *s*,
Zech 1:19 are the horns that have *s*
1:21 These are the horns that *s*
7:14 But I *s* them with a whirlwind
13: 7 And the sheep will be *s*;
Mt 9:36 because they were weary and *s*,
25:24 gathering where you have not *s*
25:26 and gather where I have not *s*
26:31 of the flock will be *s*.
Mk 14:27 And the sheep will be *s*.
Lk 1:51 He has *s* the proud in the
Jn 11:52 the children of God who were *s*
16:32 now come, that you will be *s*,
Acts 5:36 and all who obeyed him were *s*
8: 1 and they were all *s* throughout
8: 4 Therefore those who were *s* went
11:19 Now those who were *s* after the
1 Cor 10: 5 for their bodies were *s* in
Jas 1: 1 the twelve tribes which are *s*

SCATTERING (2/2)

Job 37: 9 And cold from the *s* winds of
Isa 30:30 of a devouring fire, With *s*,

SCATTERS (10/10) SCATTER

Job 36:30 He *s* his light upon it,
37:11 He *s* His bright clouds.
Ps 147:16 He *s* the frost like ashes;
Prov 11:24 There is one who *s*,
20: 8 of judgment *S* all evil
Isa 24: 1 its surface And *s* abroad
Nah 2: 1 He who *s* has come up before
Mt 12:30 not gather with Me *s* abroad.
Lk 11:23 who does not gather with Me *s*.
Jn 10:12 catches the sheep and *s* them.

SCENT (4/4) SCENTED

Job 14: 9 Yet at the *s* of water it will
Song 4:10 And the *s* of your perfumes
Jer 48:11 And his *s* has not changed.
Hos 14: 7 Their *s* shall be like the

SCENTED (2/2) SCENT

Ps 45: 8 All Your garments are *s* with
Song 5:13 Banks of *s* herbs. His lips

SCEPTER (19/15)

Gen 49:10 The *s* shall not depart from
Num 24:17 A *S* shall rise out of Israel,
Esth 4:11 the king holds out the golden *s*,
5: 2 held out to Esther the golden *s*
5: 2 and touched the top of the *s*.
8: 4 the king held out the golden *s*
Ps 45: 6 A *s* of righteousness is the
45: 6 of righteousness is the *s* of
125: 3 For the *s* of wickedness shall
Isa 14: 5 The *s* of the rulers;
Ezek 19:14 branch—a *s* for ruling.'
21:10 It despises the *s* of My Son,
21:13 the sword despises even the *s*?
21:13 The *s* shall be no more,"
Am 1: 5 And the one who holds the *s*
1: 8 And the one who holds the *s*
Zech 10:11 And the *s* of Egypt shall
Heb 1: 8 A *s* of righteousness is
1: 8 of righteousness is the *s*

SCEPTERS (1/1)

Ezek 19:11 She had strong branches for *s*

SCEVA (1/1)

Acts 19:14 Also there were seven sons of *S*,

SCHEDULE (2/2)

1 Chr 24: 3 them according to the *s* of
24:19 This was the *s* of their service

SCHEME (6/6) SCHEMED, SCHEMER, SCHEMES

Esth 8: 3 and the *s* which he had devised
Ps 26:10 whose hands is a sinister *s*,
31:13 They *s* to take away my life.
64: 6 "We have perfected a shrewd *s*.
140: 8 Do not further his wicked *s*,
Mic 7: 3 So they *s* together.

SCHEMED (1/1)

2 Sam 14:13 Why then have you *s* such a thing

SCHEMER (2/2)

Prov 24: 8 to do evil Will be called a *s*.
Isa 32: 7 Also the schemes of the *s* are

SCHEMES (9/9) SCHEME

Num 25:18 they harassed you with their *s*
Job 21:27 And the *s* with which you
Ps 37: 7 of the man who brings wicked *s*
Eccl 7:29 they have sought out many *s*.
Isa 32: 7 Also the *s* of the schemer are
Jer 11:19 know that they had devised *s*
Lam 3:60 All their *s* against me.
3:61 All their *s* against me,
Dan 8:23 Who understands sinister *s*.

SCHISM (1/1)

1 Cor 12:25 that there should be no *s* in the

SCHOLARS (1/1)

Eccl 12:11 and the words of *s* are like

SCHOOL (1/1)

Acts 19: 9 reasoning daily in the *s* of

SCHOOLMASTER (KJV) See TUTOR

SCIENCE (KJV) See KNOWLEDGE

SCOFF (3/3)

Ps 73: 8 They *s* and speak wickedly
Prov 9:12 for yourself, And if you *s*,
Hab 1:10 They *s* at kings, And princes

SCOFFED (1/1)

2 Chr 36:16 and *s* at His prophets, until

SCOFFER (11/11) SCOFFERS

Prov 9: 7 He who corrects a *s* gets shame
9: 8 Do not correct a *s*,
13: 1 But a *s* does not listen to
14: 6 A *s* seeks wisdom and does not
15:12 A *s* does not love one who
17:21 He who begets a *s* does so to
19:25 Strike a *s*, and the simple
21:11 When the *s* is punished, the
21:24 '*S*' is his name; He acts
22:10 Cast out the *s*, and
24: 9 And the *s* is an abomination

SCOFFERS (4/4) SCOFFER

Prov 19:29 Judgments are prepared for *s*,
29: 8 *S* set a city aflame, But wise
Hos 7: 5 stretched out his hand with *s*.
2 Pe 3: 3 that *s* will come in the last

SCOFFING (1/1)

Gen 21: 9 she had borne to Abraham, *s*.

SCORCH (2/2)

Isa 43: 2 Nor shall the flame *s* you.
Rev 16: 8 and power was given to him to *s*

SCORCHED (4/4)

Ezek 20:47 south to the north shall be *s*
Mt 13: 6 when the sun was up they were *s*,
Mk 4: 6 when the sun was up it was *s*,
Rev 16: 9 And men were *s* with great heat,

SCORCHING (1/1)

Deut 28:22 fever, with the sword, with *s*,

SCORN (9/9) SCORNFUL, SCORNS

2 Ki 19:21 despised you, laughed you to *s*;
Job 16:20 My friends *s* me; My eyes pour
34: 7 Who drinks *s* like water,
Ps 44:13 A *s* and a derision to those
79: 4 A *s* and derision to those who
123: 4 exceedingly filled With the *s*
Isa 37:22 despised you, laughed you to *s*;
Jer 48:27 You shake your head in *s*.
Ezek 23:32 You shall be laughed to *s* And

SCORNED (3/3)

Lam 1:11 and consider, For I am *s*.
Ezek 16:31 because you *s* payment.
Hab 1:10 And princes are *s* by them.

SCORNERS (1/1)

Prov 1:22 For *s* delight in their

SCORNFUL (4/4) SCORN

Ps 1: 1 Nor sits in the seat of the *s*;
Prov 3:34 Surely He scorns the *s*,
Isa 28:14 you *s* men, Who rule this
29:20 The *s* one is consumed, And

SCORNFULLY (1/1)

Deut 32:15 And *s* esteemed the Rock of his

SCORNING (1/1)

Prov 1:22 scorners delight in their *s*,

SCORNS (5/5) SCORN

Job 39: 7 He *s* the tumult of the city;
39:18 She *s* the horse and its rider.
Prov 3:34 Surely He *s* the scornful, But
19:28 A disreputable witness *s*
30:17 And *s* obedience to his

SCORPION (2/2) SCORPIONS

Lk 11:12 an egg, will he offer him a *s*?
Rev 9: 5 was like the torment of a *s*

SCORPIONS (5/5) SCORPION

Deut 8:15 were fiery serpents and *s* and
Ezek 2: 6 with you and you dwell among *s*;
Lk 10:19 to trample on serpents and *s*,
Rev 9: 3 as the *s* of the earth have
9:10 They had tails like *s*,

SCOUNDREL (2/2) SCOUNDRELS

1 Sam 25:17 For he is such a *s* that one
25:25 let not my lord regard this *s*

SCOUNDRELS (3/2) SCOUNDREL

1 Ki 21:10 and seat two men, *s*, before
21:13 And two men, *s*, came in and
21:13 and the *s* witnessed against

SCOURED (1/1)

Lev 6:28 it shall be both *s* and rinsed

SCOURGE (11/11) SCOURGED, SCOURGES, SCOURGINGS

Job 5:21 shall be hidden from the *s* of
9:23 If the *s* slays suddenly, He
Isa 10:26 of hosts will stir up a *s* for
28:15 When the overflowing *s* passes
28:18 When the overflowing *s* passes
Mt 10:17 you up to councils and *s* you
20:19 the Gentiles to mock and to *s*
23:34 and some of them you will *s* in
Mk 10:34 and *s* Him, and spit on Him, and
Lk 18:33 They will *s* Him and kill Him.
Acts 22:25 Is it lawful for you to *s* a man

SCOURGED (4/4) SCOURGE

Job 30: 8 They were *s* from the land.
Mt 27:26 and when he had *s* Jesus, he
Mk 15:15 after he had *s* Him, to be
Jn 19: 1 Pilate took Jesus and *s* Him.

SCOURGES (6/6) SCOURGE

Josh 23:13 and *s* on your sides and thorns
1 Ki 12:11 but I will chastise you with *s*!

12:14 but I will chastise you with *s*!
2 Chr 10:11 I will chastise you with *s*!
10:14 I will chastise you with *s*!
Heb 12: 6 And *s* every son whom He

SCOURGETH (KJV) See SCOURGES

SCOURGING (2/2)

Lev 19:20 for this there shall be *s*;
Acts 22:24 he should be examined under *s*,

SCOURGINGS (1/1) SCOURGE

Heb 11:36 had trial of mockings and *s*,

SCRAPE (4/4)

Lev 14:41 and the dust that they *s* off
Num 5:23 and he shall *s* them off into
Job 2: 8 a potsherd with which to *s*
Ezek 26: 4 I will also *s* her dust from

SCRAPED (2/2)

Lev 14:41 shall cause the house to be *s*
14:43 after he has *s* the house, and

SCRAPS (1/1)

Judg 1: 7 toes cut off used to gather *s*

SCRATCHED (1/1)

1 Sam 21:13 *s* on the doors of the gate, and

SCREECH (2/2)

Lev 11:17 the fisher owl, and the *s* owl;
Deut 14:16 the *s* owl, the white owl,

SCREEN (18/18)

Ex 26:36 You shall make a *s* for the door
26:37 And you shall make for the *s*
27:16 the court there shall be a *s*
35:15 and the *s* for the door at the
35:17 and the *s* for the gate of the
36:37 He also made a *s* for the
38:18 The *s* for the gate of the court
39:38 the *s* for the tabernacle door;
39:40 the *s* for the court gate, its
40: 5 and put up the *s* for the door
40: 8 and hang up the *s* at the court
40:28 He hung up the *s* at the door of
40:33 and hung up the *s* of the court
Num 3:25 the *s* for the door of the
3:26 the *s* for the door of the court,
3:31 which they ministered, the *s*,
4:25 the *s* for the door of the
4:26 the *s* for the door of the gate

SCRIBE (51/51) SCRIBE'S, SCRIBES

2 Sam 8:17 the priests; Seraiah was the *s*;
20:25 Sheva was *s*; Zadok and
2 Ki 12:10 that the king's *s* and the high
18:18 the household, Shebna the *s*,
18:37 the household, Shebna the *s*,
19: 2 the household, Shebna the *s*,
22: 3 the king sent Shaphan the *s*,
22: 8 priest said to Shaphan the *s*,
22: 9 So Shaphan the *s* went to the
22:10 Then Shaphan the *s* showed the
22:12 son of Michaiah, Shaphan the *s*,
1 Chr 18:16 the priests; Shavsha was the *s*;
24: 6 And the *s*, Shemaiah the son
27:32 counselor, a wise man, and a *s*;
2 Chr 24:11 that the king's *s* and the high
26:11 as prepared by Jeiel the *s* and
34:15 and said to Shaphan the *s*,
34:18 Then Shaphan the *s* told the
34:20 the son of Micah, Shaphan the *s*,
Ezra 4: 8 commander and Shimshai the *s*
4: 9 the commander, Shimshai the *s*,
4:17 commander, to Shimshai the *s*,
4:23 before Rehum, Shimshai the *s*,
7: 6 and he was a skilled *s* in the
7:11 gave Ezra the priest, the *s*,
7:12 a *s* of the Law of the God of
7:21 the *s* of the Law of the God of
Neh 8: 1 and they told Ezra the *s* to
8: 4 So Ezra the *s* stood on a
8: 9 Ezra the priest and *s*,
8:13 were gathered to Ezra the *s*,
12:26 and of Ezra the priest, the *s*.
12:36 Ezra the *s* went before them.
13:13 the priest and Zadok the *s*,
Isa 33:18 on terror: "Where is the *s*?
36: 3 the household, Shebna the *s*,
36:22 the household, Shebna the *s*,
37: 2 the household, Shebna the *s*,
Jer 8: 8 the false pen of the *s*
36:10 the son of Shaphan the *s*,
36:12 were sitting—Elishama the *s*,
36:20 the chamber of Elishama the *s*,
36:26 to seize Baruch the *s* and
36:32 and gave it to Baruch the *s*,
37:15 in the house of Jonathan the *s*.
37:20 to the house of Jonathan the *s*,
52:25 the principal *s* of the army who
Mt 8:19 Then a certain *s* came and said
13:52 Therefore every *s* instructed
Mk 12:32 So the *s* said to Him, "Well
1 Cor 1:20 is the wise? Where is the *s*?

SCRIBE'S (3/3) SCRIBE

Jer 36:12 into the *s* chamber; and there
36:21 from Elishama the *s* chamber.
36:23 cut it with the *s* knife

SCRIBES (67/67) SCRIBE

1 Ki 4: 3 Ahijah, the sons of Shisha, *s*;
1 Chr 2:55 And the families of the *s* who
2 Chr 34:13 some of the Levites were *s*,
Esth 3:12 Then the king's *s* were called
8: 9 So the king's *s* were called at
Mt 2: 4 all the chief priests and *s* of
5:20 the righteousness of the *s*
7:29 authority, and not as the *s*.
9: 3 And at once some of the *s* said
12:38 Then some of the *s* and
15: 1 Then the *s* and Pharisees who
16:21 elders and chief priests and *s*,
17:10 Why then do the *s* say that
20:18 the chief priests and to the *s*;
21:15 when the chief priests and *s*
23: 2 The *s* and the Pharisees sit in
23:13 *s* and Pharisees, hypocrites!
23:14 *s* and Pharisees, hypocrites!
23:15 *s* and Pharisees, hypocrites!
23:23 *s* and Pharisees, hypocrites!
23:25 *s* and Pharisees, hypocrites!
23:27 *s* and Pharisees, hypocrites!
23:29 *s* and Pharisees, hypocrites!
23:34 you prophets, wise men, and *s*:
26: 3 Then the chief priests, the *s*,
26:57 where the *s* and the elders were
27:41 mocking with the *s* and elders,
Mk 1:22 authority, and not as the *s*.
2: 6 And some of the *s* were sitting
2:16 And when the *s* and Pharisees saw
3:22 And the *s* who came down from
7: 1 the Pharisees and some of the *s*
7: 5 Then the Pharisees and *s* asked
8:31 elders and chief priests and *s*,
9:11 Why do the *s* say that Elijah
9:14 and *s* disputing with them.
9:16 And He asked the *s*,
10:33 the chief priests and to the *s*;
11:18 And the *s* and chief priests
11:27 the chief priests, the *s*,
12:28 Then one of the *s* came, and
12:35 How is it that the *s* say that
12:38 His teaching, "Beware of the *s*,
14: 1 And the chief priests and the *s*
14:43 the chief priests and the *s*
14:53 priests, the elders, and the *s*.
15: 1 with the elders and *s* and the
15:31 among themselves with the *s*,
Lk 5:21 And the *s* and the Pharisees
5:30 And their *s* and the Pharisees
6: 7 So the *s* and Pharisees watched
9:22 elders and chief priests and *s*,
11:44 *s* and Pharisees, hypocrites!
11:53 the *s* and the Pharisees began
15: 2 And the Pharisees and *s*
19:47 But the chief priests, the *s*,
20: 1 the chief priests and the *s*,
20:19 And the chief priests and the *s*
20:39 Then some of the *s* answered and
20:46 "Beware of the *s*,
22: 2 And the chief priests and the *s*
22:66 both chief priests and *s*,
23:10 And the chief priests and *s*
Jn 8: 3 Then the *s* and Pharisees brought
Acts 4: 5 their rulers, elders, and *s*,
6:12 people, the elders, and the *s*;
23: 9 And the *s* of the Pharisees'

SCRIP (KJV) See BAG, POUCH

SCRIPT (5/4)

Ezra 4: 7 was written in Aramaic *s*,
Esth 1:22 to each province in its own *s*,
3:12 province according to its *s*,
8: 9 to every province in its own *s*,
8: 9 and to the Jews in their own *s*

SCRIPTURE (32/32) SCRIPTURES

Dan 10:21 you what is noted in the *S* of
Mk 12:10 "Have you not even read this *S*:
15:28 So the *S* was fulfilled which
Lk 4:21 Today this *S* is fulfilled in
Jn 2:22 and they believed the *S* and the
7:38 as the *S* has said, out of his
7:42 Has not the *S* said that the
10:35 (and the *S* cannot be broken),
13:18 but that the *S* may be
17:12 that the *S* might be fulfilled.
19:24 that the *S* might be fulfilled
19:28 that the *S* might be fulfilled,
19:36 things were done that the *S*
19:37 And again another *S* says,
20: 9 as yet they did not know the *S*,
Acts 1:16 this *S* had to be fulfilled,
8:32 The place in the *S* which he read
8:35 mouth, and beginning at this *S*,
Rom 4: 3 For what does the *S* say?
9:17 For the *S* says to Pharaoh,
10:11 For the *S* says, "Whoever
11: 2 you not know what the *S* says
Gal 3: 8 And the *S*, foreseeing that
3:22 But the *S* has confined all under
4:30 what does the *S* say?
1 Tim 5:18 For the *S* says, "You shall
2 Tim 3:16 All *S* is given by inspiration
Jas 2: 8 royal law according to the *S*,
2:23 And the *S* was fulfilled which
4: 5 Or do you think that the *S* says
1 Pe 2: 6 it is also contained in the *S*,
2 Pe 1:20 that no prophecy of *S* is of any

SCRIPTURES (21/21) SCRIPTURE

Mt 21:42 "Have you never read in the *S*:
22:29 not knowing the *S* nor the power
26:54 How then could the *S* be
26:56 all this was done that the *S*
Mk 12:24 because you do not know the *S*
14:49 But the *S* must be fulfilled."
Lk 24:27 expounded to them in all the *S*
24:32 and while He opened the *S* to
24:45 they might comprehend the *S*.
Jn 5:39 "You search the *S*,
Acts 17: 2 reasoned with them from the *S*,
17:11 and searched the *S* daily to
18:24 man and mighty in the *S*,
18:28 showing from the *S* that Jesus
Rom 1: 2 His prophets in the Holy *S*,
15: 4 patience and comfort of the *S*
16:26 and by the prophetic *S* has been
1 Cor 15: 3 for our sins according to the *S*,
15: 4 third day according to the *S*,
2 Tim 3:15 you have known the Holy *S*,
2 Pe 3:16 do also the rest of the *S*.

SCROLL (35/33)

Ezra 6: 2 a *s* was found, and in it a
Ps 40: 7 In the *s* of the book it is
Isa 8: 1 said to me, "Take a large *s*,
30: 8 a tablet, And note it on a *s*,
34: 4 shall be rolled up like a *s*;
Jer 36: 2 Take a *s* of a book and write on
36: 4 and Baruch wrote on a *s* of a
36: 6 and read from the *s* which you
36:14 Take in your hand the *s* from
36:14 the son of Neriah took the *s*
36:20 but they stored the *s* in the
36:21 king sent Jehudi to bring the *s*,
36:23 until all the *s* was consumed in
36:25 the king not to burn the *s*;
36:27 the king had burned the *s* with
36:28 "Take yet another *s*,
36:28 words that were in the first *s*
36:29 'You have burned this *s*,
36:32 Then Jeremiah took another *s*
Ezek 2: 9 a *s* of a book was in it.
3: 1 eat what you find; eat this *s*,
3: 2 and He caused me to eat that *s*.
3: 3 fill your stomach with this *s*
Zech 5: 1 eyes, and saw there a flying *s*.
5: 2 I answered, "I see a flying *s*.
5: 3 to this side of the *s*;
Rev 5: 1 Him who sat on the throne a *s*
5: 2 Who is worthy to open the *s* and
5: 3 earth was able to open the *s*,
5: 4 worthy to open and read the *s*,
5: 5 has prevailed to open the *s* and
5: 7 Then He came and took the *s* out
5: 8 Now when He had taken the *s*,
5: 9 are worthy to take the *s*,
6:14 Then the sky receded as a *s* when

SCRUPLES (1/1)

Rom 15: 1 ought to bear with the *s* of

SCULPTURED (1/1)

Ps 144:12 *S* in palace style;

SCUM (5/3)

Ezek 24: 6 To the pot whose *s* is in it,
24: 6 And whose *s* is not gone from
24:11 That its *s* may be consumed.
24:12 And her great *s* has not gone
24:12 Let her *s* be in the fire!

SCURVY (KJV) See SCAB

SCYTHIAN (1/1)

Col 3:11 nor uncircumcised, barbarian, *S*,

SEA (390/340) SEAS, SEASHORE

Gen 1:21 So God created great *s* creatures
1:26 dominion over the fish of the *s*,
1:28 dominion over the fish of the *s*,
9: 2 and on all the fish of the *s*.
14: 3 of Siddim (that is, the Salt *S*).
32:12 as the sand of the *s*,
41:49 grain, as the sand of the *s*,
49:13 dwell by the haven of the *s*;
Ex 10:19 and blew them into the Red *S*.
13:18 of the wilderness of the Red *S*.
14: 2 between Migdol and the *s*,
14: 2 shall camp before it by the *s*.
14: 9 overtook them camping by the *s*
14:16 out your hand over the *s* and
14:16 through the midst of the *s*.

14:21 out his hand over the s;
14:21 and the LORD caused the s to
14:21 and made the s into dry land,
14:22 went into the midst of the s
14:23 them into the midst of the s,
14:26 out your hand over the s,
14:27 out his hand over the s;
14:27 the s returned to its full
14:27 Egyptians in the midst of the s.
14:28 of Pharaoh that came into the s
14:29 dry land in the midst of the s,
15: 1 He has thrown into the s!
15: 4 also are drowned in the Red S.
15: 8 congealed in the heart of the s.
15:10 The s covered them; They sank
15:19 and his horsemen into the s,
15:19 back the waters of the s upon
15:19 dry land in the midst of the s.
15:21 He has thrown into the s!"
15:22 brought Israel from the Red S;
20:11 heavens and the earth, the s,
23:31 set your bounds from the Red S to
23:31 from the Red Sea to the s,
Lev 11:16 the s gull, and the hawk after
Num 11:22 Or shall all the fish of the s
11:31 and it brought quail from the s
13:29 the Canaanites dwell by the s
14:25 by the Way of the Red S."
21: 4 Hor by the Way of the Red S,
33: 8 through the midst of the s
33:10 Elim and camped by the Red S.
33:11 They moved from the Red S and
34: 3 to the end of the Salt S;
34: 5 and it shall end at the S.
34: 6 you shall have the Great S for
34: 7 From the Great S you shall mark
34:11 to the eastern side of the S
34:12 and it shall end at the Salt S.
Deut 1:40 by the Way of the Red S.'
2: 1 of the Way of the Red S,
3:17 far as the east side of the S
3:17 Sea of the Arabah (the Salt S),
4:49 of the Jordan as far as the S
11: 4 He made the waters of the Red S
11:24 even to the Western S,
14:15 the s gull, and the hawk after
30:13 "Nor is it beyond the s,
30:13 Who will go over the s for us
34: 2 Judah as far as the Western S,
Josh 1: 4 and to the Great S toward the
2:10 up the water of the Red S for
3:16 that went down into the S of
3:16 Sea of the Arabah, the Salt S,
4:23 LORD your God did to the Red S,
5: 1 Canaanites who were by the s,
9: 1 all the coasts of the Great S
12: 3 Jordan plain from the S of
12: 3 of Chinneroth as far as the S
12: 3 Sea of the Arabah (the Salt S),
13:27 as far as the edge of the S of
15: 2 at the shore of the Salt S,
15: 4 and the border ended at the s.
15: 5 east border was the Salt S as
15: 5 began at the bay of the s at
15:11 and the border ended at the s.
15:12 the coastline of the Great S.
15:46 from Ekron to the s,
15:47 Brook of Egypt and the Great S
16: 3 to Gezer; and it ended at the s.
16: 6 border went out toward the s
16: 8 Kanah, and it ended at the s.
17: 9 and it ended at the s.
17:10 and the s was its border.
18:19 at the north bay at the Salt S,
19:29 and ended at the s by the
23: 4 as far as the Great S westward.
24: 6 and horsemen to the Red S.
24: 7 brought the s upon them, and
Judg 11:16 wilderness as far as the Red S and
2 Sam 17:11 the sand that is by the s for
22:16 Then the channels of the s were
1 Ki 4:20 numerous as the sand by the s
5: 9 down from Lebanon to the s;
5: 9 I will float them in rafts by s
7:23 And he made the S of cast
7:24 cubit, all the way around the S.
7:25 the S was set upon them, and
7:39 He set the S on the right side
7:44 one S, and twelve oxen under
7:44 and twelve oxen under the S;
9:26 Elath on the shore of the Red S,
9:27 fleet, seamen who knew the s,
10:22 king had merchant ships at s
18:43 "Go up now, look toward the s.
18:44 rising out of the s!"
2 Ki 14:25 entrance of Hamath to the S of
16:17 and he took down the S from the
25:13 and the carts and the bronze S
25:16 The two pillars, one S,
1 Chr 16:32 Let the s roar, and all its
18: 8 which Solomon made the bronze S,
2 Chr 2:16 bring it to you in rafts by s
4: 2 Then he made the S of cast
4: 3 cubit, all the way around the S.
4: 4 the S was set upon them, and
4: 6 but the S was for the priests
4:10 He set the S on the right side,
4:15 one S and twelve oxen under it;
8:18 and servants who knew the s.
20: 2 against you from beyond the s,
Ezra 3: 7 logs from Lebanon to the s,
Neh 9: 9 heard their cry by the Red S.
9:11 And You divided the s before
9:11 through the midst of the s on
Esth 10: 1 and on the islands of the s.
Job 6: 3 heavier than the sand of the s—
7:12 Am I a s, or a sea serpent,
7:12 or a s serpent, That You set a
9: 8 treads on the waves of the s;
11: 9 earth And broader than the s.
12: 8 And the fish of the s will
14:11 water disappears from the s,
26:12 He stirs up the s with His
28:14 And the s says, 'It is not
36:30 And covers the depths of the s.
38: 8 Or who shut in the s with
38:16 entered the springs of the s?
41:31 He makes the s like a pot of
Ps 8: 8 And the fish of the s That
18:15 Then the channels of the s were
33: 7 He gathers the waters of the s
46: 2 carried into the midst of the s;
66: 6 He turned the s into dry land;
68:22 back from the depths of the s,
72: 8 have dominion also from s to
72: 8 dominion also from sea to s,
74:13 You divided the s by Your
74:13 You broke the heads of the s
77:19 Your way was in the s,
78:13 He divided the s and caused
78:53 But the s overwhelmed their
80:11 sent out her boughs to the S,
89: 9 You rule the raging of the s;
89:25 I will set his hand over the s,
93: 4 the mighty waves of the s.
95: 5 The s is His, for He made it;
96:11 Let the s roar, and all its
98: 7 Let the s roar, and all its
104:25 This great and wide s,
106: 7 rebelled by the sea—the Red S.
106: 9 He rebuked the Red S also, and
106:22 Awesome things by the Red S.
107:23 Those who go down to the s in
107:25 lifts up the waves of the s.
114: 3 The s saw it and fled;
114: 5 What ails you, O s,
136:13 To Him who divided the Red S in
136:15 and his army in the Red S,
139: 9 in the uttermost parts of the s,
146: 6 made heaven and earth, The s,
148: 7 You great s creatures and all
Prov 8:29 When He assigned to the s its
23:34 lies down in the midst of the s,
30:19 of a ship in the midst of the s,
Eccl 1: 7 All the rivers run into the s,
1: 7 Yet the s is not full;
Isa 5:30 them Like the roaring of the s.
9: 1 her, By the way of the s,
10:22 Israel, be as the sand of the s,
10:26 Oreb; as His rod was on the s,
11: 9 As the waters cover the s.
11:11 Hamath and the islands of the s.
11:15 destroy the tongue of the S of
16: 8 out, They are gone over the s.
18: 2 Which sends ambassadors by s,
19: 5 waters will fail from the s,
21: 1 against the Wilderness of the S.
23: 2 Whom those who cross the s
23: 4 For the s has spoken, The
23: 4 spoken, The strength of the s,
23:11 out His hand over the s,
24:14 shall cry aloud from the s.
24:15 in the coastlands of the s.
27: 1 the reptile that is in the s.
42:10 You who go down to the s,
43:16 who makes a way in the s And a
48:18 like the waves of the s.
50: 2 with My rebuke I dry up the s,
51:10 the One who dried up the s,
51:10 That made the depths of the s
51:15 Who divided the s whose waves
57:20 wicked are like the troubled s,
60: 5 the abundance of the s shall
63:11 brought them up out of the s
Jer 5:22 the sand as the bound of the s,
6:23 Their voice roars like the s;
25:22 which are across the s;
27:19 the pillars, concerning the S,
31:35 by night, Who disturbs the s,
33:22 nor the sand of the s measured,
46:18 And as Carmel by the s,
48:32 plants have gone over the s,
48:32 They reach to the s of Jazer.
49:21 its noise is heard at the Red S.
49:23 There is trouble on the s;
50:42 voice shall roar like the s.
51:36 I will dry up her s and make
51:42 The s has come up over Babylon;
52:17 and the carts and the bronze S
52:20 The two pillars, one S,
Lam 2:13 ruin is spread wide as the s;
Ezek 26: 3 as the s causes its waves to
26: 5 nets in the midst of the s,
26:16 Then all the princes of the s
26:17 city, Who was strong at s,
26:18 the coastlands by the s are
27: 3 at the entrance of the s,
27: 9 All the ships of the s And
27:29 All the pilots of the s Will
27:32 in the midst of the s?
27:33 'When your wares went out by s,
38:20 'so that the fish of the s,
39:11 those who pass by east of the s;
47: 8 the valley, and enters the s.
47: 8 When it reaches the s,
47:10 as the fish of the Great S,
47:15 on the north: from the Great S,
47:17 boundary shall be from the S
47:18 along the eastern side of the s.
47:19 along the brook to the Great S.
47:20 side shall be the Great S,
48:28 along the brook to the Great S.
Dan 7: 2 were stirring up the Great S.
7: 3 great beasts came up from the s,
Hos 1:10 Shall be as the sand of the s,
4: 3 Even the fish of the s will be
Joel 2:20 his face toward the eastern s
2:20 his back toward the western s;
Am 5: 8 calls for the waters of the s
8:12 They shall wander from s to
8:12 shall wander from sea to s,
9: 3 My sight at the bottom of the s,
9: 6 calls for the waters of the s,
Jon 1: 4 sent out a great wind on the s,
1: 4 was a mighty tempest on the s,
1: 5 was in the ship into the s,
1: 9 who made the s and the dry
1:11 shall we do to you that the s
1:11 for the s was growing more
1:12 me up and throw me into the s;
1:12 then the s will become calm for
1:13 for the s continued to grow
1:15 Jonah and threw him into the s,
1:15 and the s ceased from its
Mic 7:12 From s to sea, And mountain
7:12 to the River, From sea to s,
7:19 sins Into the depths of the s.
Nah 1: 4 He rebukes the s and makes it
3: 8 her, Whose rampart was the s,
3: 8 the sea, Whose wall was the s?
Hab 1:14 You make men like fish of the s,
2:14 As the waters cover the s.
3: 8 Was Your wrath against the s,
3:15 You walked through the s with
Zeph 1: 3 the heavens, The fish of the s,
Hag 2: 6 the s and dry land;
Zech 9: 4 will destroy her power in the s,
9:10 from s to sea, And from the
9:10 shall be 'from sea to s,
10:11 He shall pass through the s
10:11 And strike the waves of the s:
14: 8 of them toward the eastern s
14: 8 of them toward the western s;
Mt 4:13 in Capernaum, which is by the s,
4:15 By the way of the s,
4:18 walking by the S of Galilee,
4:18 casting a net into the s;
8:24 a great tempest arose on the s,
8:26 and rebuked the winds and the s,
8:27 that even the winds and the s
8:32 down the steep place into the s,
13: 1 of the house and sat by the s.
13:47 that was cast into the s and
14:24 was now in the middle of the s,
14:25 went to them, walking on the s.
14:26 saw Him walking on the s,
15:29 skirted the S of Galilee, and
17:27 we offend them, go to the s,
18: 6 drowned in the depth of the s.
21:21 removed and be cast into the s,
23:15 For you travel land and s to
Mk 1:16 And as He walked by the S of
1:16 casting a net into the s;
2:13 He went out again by the s;
3: 7 with His disciples to the s.
4: 1 He began to teach by the s.
4: 1 a boat and sat in it on the s;
4: 1 was on the land facing the s.
4:39 the wind, and said to the s,
4:41 that even the wind and the s
5: 1 came to the other side of the s,
5:13 down the steep place into the s,
5:13 the sea, and drowned in the s.
5:21 to Him; and He was by the s.
6:47 boat was in the middle of the s;
6:48 came to them, walking on the s,
6:49 they saw Him walking on the s,
7:31 region of Decapolis to the S
9:42 and he were thrown into the s.
11:23 removed and be cast into the s,
Lk 17: 2 and he were thrown into the s,
17: 6 roots and be planted in the s,
21:25 the s and the waves roaring;
Jn 6: 1 things Jesus went over the S
6: 1 which is the S of Tiberias.
6:16 disciples went down to the s,
6:17 and went over the s toward
6:18 Then the s arose because a great
6:19 saw Jesus walking on the s and
6:22 on the other side of the s saw
6:25 Him on the other side of the s,
21: 1 to the disciples at the S of
21: 7 and plunged into the s.
Acts 4:24 made heaven and earth and the s,
7:36 land of Egypt, and in the Red S,
10: 6 tanner, whose house is by the s.
10:32 of Simon, a tanner, by the s.
14:15 the heaven, the earth, the s,
17:14 sent Paul away, to go to the s;
27: 2 of Adramyttium, we put to s,
27: 4 When we had put to s from there,
27: 5 when we had sailed over the s
27:13 their desire, putting out to s,
27:27 up and down in the Adriatic S,
27:30 let down the skiff into the s,

27:38 threw out the wheat into the *s*.
27:40 anchors and left them in the *s*,
28: 4 though he has escaped the *s*,
Rom 9:27 be as the sand of the *s*,
1 Cor 10: 1 cloud, all passed through the *s*,
10: 2 Moses in the cloud and in the *s*,
2 Cor 11:26 wilderness, in perils in the *s*,
Heb 11:29 they passed through the Red *S* as
Jas 1: 6 doubts is like a wave of the *s*
3: 7 reptile and creature of the *s*,
Jude 13 raging waves of the *s*,
Rev 4: 6 the throne there was a *s* of
5:13 earth and such as are in the *s*,
7: 1 not blow on the earth, on the *s*,
7: 2 to harm the earth and the *s*,
7: 3 "Do not harm the earth, the *s*,
8: 8 with fire was thrown into the *s*,
8: 8 and a third of the *s* became
8: 9 the living creatures in the *s*
10: 2 he set his right foot on the *s*
10: 5 whom I saw standing on the *s*
10: 6 and the *s* and the things that
10: 8 the angel who stands on the *s*
12:12 of the earth and the *s*!
13: 1 I stood on the sand of the *s*.
13: 1 a beast rising up out of the *s*,
14: 7 the *s* and springs of water."
15: 2 And I saw something like a *s* of
15: 2 standing on the *s* of glass,
16: 3 poured out his bowl on the *s*,
16: 3 every living creature in the *s*
18:17 and as many as trade on the *s*,
18:19 all who had ships on the *s*
18:21 and threw it into the *s*,
20: 8 number is as the sand of the *s*.
20:13 The *s* gave up the dead who were
21: 1 Also there was no more *s*.

SEACOAST (6/6)

Deut 1: 7 in the South and on the *s*,
2 Chr 8:17 Ezion Geber and Elath on the *s*,
Ezek 25:16 destroy the remnant of the *s*.
Zeph 2: 5 to the inhabitants of the *s*,
2: 6 The *s* shall be pastures, With
Lk 6:17 and from the *s* of Tyre and

SEAFARING (1/1)

Ezek 26:17 O one inhabited by *s* men,

SEAH (3/3)

2 Ki 7: 1 Tomorrow about this time a *s* of
7:16 So a *s* of fine flour was sold
7:18 and a *s* of fine flour for a

SEAHS (5/5)

1 Sam 25:18 five *s* of roasted grain, one
1 Ki 18:32 large enough to hold two *s* of
2 Ki 7: 1 and two *s* of barley for a
7:16 and two *s* of barley for a
7:18 Two *s* of barley for a shekel,

SEAL (29/28) SEALED, SEALING, SEALS

1 Ki 21: 8 name, sealed them with his *s*,
Neh 9:38 and our priests *s* it."
10: 1 Now those who placed their *s* on
Esth 8: 8 and *s* it with the king's
Job 38:14 on form like clay under a *s*,
41:15 Shut up tightly as with a *s*;
Song 8: 6 Set me as a *s* upon your heart,
8: 6 As a *s* upon your arm;
Isa 8:16 *S* the law among my disciples.
Jer 32:44 sign deeds and *s* them, and
Ezek 28:12 You were the *s* of perfection,
Dan 8:26 Therefore *s* up the vision,
9:24 To *s* up vision and prophecy,
12: 4 and *s* the book until the time
Jn 6:27 God the Father has set His *s*
Rom 4:11 a *s* of the righteousness of the
1 Cor 9: 2 For you are the *s* of my
2 Tim 2:19 of God stands, having this *s*:
Rev 6: 3 When He opened the second *s*,
6: 5 When He opened the third *s*,
6: 7 When He opened the fourth *s*,
6: 9 When He opened the fifth *s*,
6:12 when He opened the sixth *s*,
7: 2 having the *s* of the living God.
8: 1 When He opened the seventh *s*,
9: 4 men who do not have the *s* of
10: 4 *S* up the things which the seven
20: 3 and set a *s* on him, so that he
22:10 Do not *s* the words of the

SEALED (34/24) SEAL

Deut 32:34 *S* up among My treasures?
1 Ki 21: 8 *s* them with his seal, and sent
Esth 3:12 and *s* with the king's signet
8: 8 in the king's name and *s* with
8:10 *s* it with the king's signet
Job 14:17 My transgression is *s* up in a
Song 4:12 spring shut up, A fountain *s*.
Isa 29:11 the words of a book that is *s*,
29:11 says, "I cannot, for it is *s*.
Jer 32:10 And I signed the deed and *s* it,
32:11 both that which was *s*
32:14 this purchase deed which is *s*
Dan 6:17 and the king *s* it with his own
12: 9 the words are closed up and *s*

Rom 15:28 have performed this and have *s*
2 Cor 1:22 who also has *s* us and given us
Eph 1:13 you were *s* with the Holy Spirit
4:30 by whom you were *s* for the day
Rev 5: 1 *s* with seven seals.
7: 3 or the trees till we have *s* the
7: 4 the number of those who were *s*.
7: 4 the children of Israel were *s*:
7: 5 Judah twelve thousand were *s*;
7: 5 Reuben twelve thousand were *s*;
7: 5 of Gad twelve thousand were *s*;
7: 6 Asher twelve thousand were *s*;
7: 6 twelve thousand were *s*;
7: 6 twelve thousand were *s*;
7: 7 Simeon twelve thousand were *s*;
7: 7 of Levi twelve thousand were *s*;
7: 7 twelve thousand were *s*;
7: 8 Zebulun twelve thousand were *s*;
7: 8 Joseph twelve thousand were *s*;
7: 8 twelve thousand were *s*.

SEALING (1/1) SEAL

Mt 27:66 *s* the stone and setting the

SEALS (8/8) SEAL

Job 9: 7 He *s* off the stars;
33:16 And *s* their instruction.
37: 7 He *s* the hand of every man,
Rev 5: 1 the back, sealed with seven *s*.
5: 2 the scroll and to loose its *s*?
5: 5 scroll and to loose its seven *s*.
5: 9 the scroll, And to open its *s*;
6: 1 the Lamb opened one of the *s*;

SEAM (3/3)

Ex 28:27 right at the *s* above the
39:20 right at the *s* above the
Jn 19:23 Now the tunic was without *s*,

SEAMEN (1/1)

1 Ki 9:27 *s* who knew the sea, to work

SEAMS (1/1)

Ezek 27: 9 Were in you to caulk your *s*;

SEANCE (1/1)

1 Sam 28: 8 Please conduct a *s* for me, and

SEARCH (48/46) SEARCHED, SEARCHES, SEARCHING

Num 10:33 to *s* out a resting place for
Deut 1:22 and let them *s* out the land for
1:33 in the way before you to *s* out
13:14 *s* out, and ask diligently.
Josh 2: 2 the children of Israel to *s*
2: 3 for they have come to *s* out all
Judg 18: 2 to spy out the land and *s* it.
18: 2 'Go, *s* the land." So they
1 Sam 23:23 that I will *s* for him
2 Sam 5:17 the Philistines went up to *s*
10: 3 sent his servants to you to *s*
1 Ki 20: 6 and they shall *s* your house and
2 Ki 2:16 Please let them go and *s* for
10:23 *S* and see that no servants of
1 Chr 14: 8 the Philistines went up to *s*
19: 3 servants not come to you to *s*
Ezra 4:15 that a *s* may be made in the book
4:19 and a *s* has been made, and it
5:17 let a *s* be made in the king's
6: 1 and a *s* was made in the
Job 3:21 And *s* for it more than hidden
10: 6 seek for my iniquity And *s*
11: 7 Can you *s* out the deep things of
38:16 Or have you walked in *s* of the
Ps 44:21 Would not God *s* this out?
77: 6 And my spirit makes diligent *s*.
139:23 *S* me, O God, and know my heart
Prov 2: 4 And *s* for her as for hidden
23:30 Those who go in *s* of mixed
25: 2 the glory of kings is to *s*
Eccl 1:13 I set my heart to seek and *s*
7:25 To *s* and seek out wisdom and
Isa 34:16 *S* from the book of the LORD,
Jer 2:34 have not found it by secret *s*,
17:10 *s* the heart, I test the mind,
29:13 when you *s* for Me with all your
Lam 3:40 Let us *s* out and examine our
Ezek 34: 8 nor did My shepherds *s* for My
34:11 Indeed I Myself will *s* for My
39:14 with the help of a *s* party, to
39:14 seven months they will make a *s*.
39:15 The *s* party will pass through
Am 9: 3 From there I will *s* and take
Zeph 1:12 at that time That I will *s*
Mt 2: 8 Go and *s* carefully for the young
Lk 15: 8 and *s* carefully until she finds
Jn 5:39 You *s* the Scriptures, for in
7:52 *S* and look, for no prophet has

SEARCHED (21/21) SEARCH

Gen 31:34 And Laban *s* all about the tent
31:35 And he *s* but did not find the
31:37 Although you have *s* all my
44:12 So he *s*. He began with the
2 Sam 17:20 And when they had *s* and could

2 Ki 2:17 and they *s* for three days but
2 Chr 22: 9 Then he *s* for Ahaziah; and they
Job 5:27 this we have *s* out; It is
28:27 indeed, He *s* it out.
29:16 And I *s* out the case that I
32:11 while you *s* out what to say.
Ps 139: 1 You have *s* me and known me.
Eccl 2: 3 I *s* in my heart how to gratify
Jer 31:37 the foundations of the earth *s*
46:23 LORD, "Though it cannot be *s*,
Ezek 20: 6 Egypt into a land that I had *s*
Ob 6 how Esau shall be *s* out!
Mk 1:36 and those who were with Him *s*
Acts 12:19 But when Herod had *s* for him and
17:11 and *s* the Scriptures daily to
1 Pe 1:10 prophets have inquired and *s*

SEARCHES (8/8) SEARCH

1 Chr 28: 9 for the LORD *s* all hearts and
Job 13: 9 Will it be well when He *s* you
28: 3 And *s* every recess For ore in
39: 8 And he *s* after every green
Prov 28:11 has understanding *s* him out.
Rom 8:27 Now He who *s* the hearts knows
1 Cor 2:10 For the Spirit *s* all things,
Rev 2:23 shall know that I am He who *s*

SEARCHING (5/5) SEARCH, SEARCHINGS

Job 24: 5 to their work, *s* for food.
Ps 119:82 My eyes fail from *s* Your
Prov 20:27 *S* all the inner depths of his
Ezek 34: 6 and no one was seeking or *s*
1 Pe 1:11 *s* what, or what manner of time,

SEARCHINGS (1/1) SEARCHING

Judg 5:16 of Reuben have great *s* of

SEARED (2/2)

Prov 6:28 coals, And his feet not be *s*?
1 Tim 4: 2 having their own conscience *s*

SEAS (26/26) SEA

Gen 1:10 of the waters He called *S*.
1:22 and fill the waters in the *s*,
Lev 11: 9 whether in the *s* or in the
11:10 But all in the *s* or in the
Deut 33:19 of the abundance of the *s*
Neh 9: 6 The *s* and all that is in them,
Ps 8: 8 pass through the paths of the *s*.
24: 2 He has founded it upon the *s*,
65: 5 earth, And of the far-off *s*;
65: 7 who still the noise of the *s*,
69:34 The *s* and everything that
78:27 fowl like the sand of the *s*;
135: 6 In the *s* and in all deep
Isa 17:12 a noise like the roar of the *s*,
Jer 15: 8 Me more than the sand of the *s*;
Ezek 27: 4 are in the midst of the *s*.
27:25 glorious in the midst of the *s*.
27:26 broke you in the midst of the *s*.
27:27 fall into the midst of the *s*
27:34 But you are broken by the *s* in
28: 2 of gods, In the midst of the *s*,
28: 8 slain In the midst of the *s*.
32: 2 are like a monster in the *s*,
Dan 11:45 of his palace between the *s*
Jon 2: 3 deep, Into the heart of the *s*,
Acts 27:41 striking a place where two *s*

SEASHORE (9/9) SEA

Gen 22:17 as the sand which is on the *s*;
Ex 14:30 saw the Egyptians dead on the *s*.
Josh 11: 4 as the sand that is on the *s*
Judg 5:17 Asher continued at the *s*,
7:12 as the sand by the *s* in
1 Sam 13: 5 as the sand which is on the *s*
1 Ki 4:29 of heart like the sand on the *s*.
Jer 47: 7 Ashkelon and against the *s*?
Heb 11:12 as the sand which is by the *s*.

SEASON (31/30) SEASONED, SEASONS

Ex 13:10 keep this ordinance in its *s*
Lev 2:13 your grain offering you shall *s*
26: 4 I will give you rain in its *s*,
Num 13:20 Now the time was the *s* of
Deut 11:14 the rain for your land in its *s*,
28:12 the rain to your land in its *s*,
Ezra 10:13 it is the *s* for heavy rain,
Job 5:26 sheaf of grain ripens in its *s*.
38:32 bring out Mazzaroth in its *s*?
Ps 1: 3 brings forth its fruit in its *s*,
4: 7 More than in the *s* that their
22: 2 not hear; And in the night *s*,
104:27 give them their food in due *s*.
145:15 give them their food in due *s*.
Prov 15:23 And a word spoken in due *s*,
Eccl 3: 1 To everything there is a *s*,
Isa 50: 4 know how to speak A word in *s*
Jer 5:24 former and the latter, in its *s*.
33:20 not be day and night in their *s*,
Ezek 34:26 showers to come down in their *s*;
Dan 7:12 lives were prolonged for a *s*
Hos 2: 9 time And My new wine in its *s*,
9:10 on the fig tree in its first *s*.
Mt 24:45 to give them food in due *s*?

Mk 9:50 its flavor, how will you *s* it?
11:13 for it was not the *s* for figs.
Lk 12:42 their portion of food in due *s*?
13: 1 There were present at that *s*
Gal 6: 9 for in due *s* we shall reap if
2 Tim 4: 2 Be ready in *s* and out of
4: 2 ready in season and out of *s*.

SEASONED (5/4) SEASON

Mt 5:13 its flavor, how shall it be *s*?
Mk 9:49 For everyone will be *s* with
9:49 and every sacrifice will be *s*
Lk 14:34 its flavor, how shall it be *s*?
Col 4: 6 *s* with salt, that you may know

SEASONS (10/10) SEASON

Gen 1:14 and let them be for signs and *s*,
Ps 16: 7 instructs me in the night *s*.
104:19 He appointed the moon for *s*;
Ezek 45:17 and at all the appointed *s* of
Dan 2:21 He changes the times and the *s*;
Mt 21:41 to him the fruits in their *s*.
Acts 1: 7 not for you to know times or *s*
14:17 rain from heaven and fruitful *s*,
Gal 4:10 observe days and months and *s*
1 Th 5: 1 concerning the times and the *s*,

SEAT (62/56) SEATED, SEATS

Ex 25:17 You shall make a mercy *s* of pure
25:18 at the two ends of the mercy *s*.
25:19 one piece with the mercy *s*.
25:20 covering the mercy *s* with their
25:20 shall be toward the mercy *s*.
25:21 You shall put the mercy *s* on top
25:22 with you from above the mercy *s*,
26:34 You shall put the mercy *s* upon
30: 6 before the mercy *s* that is
31: 7 the Testimony and the mercy *s*
35:12 its poles, with the mercy *s*,
37: 6 He also made the mercy *s* of pure
37: 7 at the two ends of the mercy *s*:
37: 8 one piece with the mercy *s*.
37: 9 and covered the mercy *s* with
37: 9 were toward the mercy *s*.
39:35 with its poles, and the mercy *s*;
40:20 and put the mercy *s* on top of
Lev 16: 2 before the mercy *s* which is on
16: 2 in the cloud above the mercy *s*.
16:13 incense may cover the mercy *s*
16:14 with his finger on the mercy *s*
16:14 and before the mercy *s* he shall
16:15 and sprinkle it on the mercy *s*
16:15 seat and before the mercy *s*.
Num 7:89 to him from above the mercy *s*
Judg 3:20 So he arose from his *s*.
1 Sam 1: 9 priest was sitting on the *s* by
4:13 sitting on a *s* by the wayside
4:18 that Eli fell off the *s*
20:18 because your *s* will be empty.
20:25 Now the king sat on his *s*,
20:25 on a *s* by the wall.
1 Ki 10:19 side of the place of the *s*,
21: 9 and *s* Naboth with high honor
21:10 and *s* two men, scoundrels,
2 Ki 25:28 and gave him a more prominent *s*
1 Chr 28:11 and the place of the mercy *s*;
2 Chr 9:18 side of the place of the *s*,
Esth 3: 1 and advanced him and set his *s*
Job 23: 3 That I might come to His *s*!
29: 7 When I took my *s* in the open
Ps 1: 1 Nor sits in the *s* of the
113: 8 That He may *s* him with
Prov 9:14 On a *s* by the highest places
Song 3:10 Its *s* of purple, Its
Jer 52:32 and gave him a more prominent *s*
Ezek 8: 3 where the *s* of the image of
28: 2 I sit in the *s* of gods, In
Am 6: 3 Who cause the *s* of violence to
Mt 23: 2 the Pharisees sit in Moses' *s*.
27:19 was sitting on the judgment *s*,
Jn 19:13 and sat down in the judgment *s*
Acts 18:12 brought him to the judgment *s*,
18:16 drove them from the judgment *s*.
18:17 beat him before the judgment *s*.
25: 6 day, sitting on the judgment *s*,
25:10 stand at Caesar's judgment *s*,
25:17 day I sat on the judgment *s*
Rom 14:10 stand before the judgment *s* of
2 Cor 5:10 appear before the judgment *s*
Heb 9: 5 glory overshadowing the mercy *s*.

SEATED (9/9) SEAT

1 Ki 16:11 as soon as he was *s* on his
21:12 and *s* Naboth with high honor
Job 36: 7 For He has *s* them forever,
Dan 7: 9 And the Ancient of Days was *s*;
7:10 The court was *s*, And the
7:26 'But the court shall be *s*,
Mt 5: 1 and when He was *s* His disciples
Eph 1:20 from the dead and *s* Him at
Heb 8: 1 who is *s* at the right hand of

SEATING (2/2)

1 Ki 10: 5 the *s* of his servants, the
2 Chr 9: 4 the *s* of his servants, the

SEATS (6/6) SEAT

Mt 21:12 of the money changers and the *s*
23: 6 the best *s* in the synagogues,
Mk 11:15 of the money changers and the *s*
12:39 the best *s* in the synagogues,
Lk 11:43 For you love the best *s* in the
20:46 the best *s* in the synagogues,

SEBA (4/4)

Gen 10: 7 The sons of Cush were *S*,
1 Chr 1: 9 The sons of Cush were *S*,
Ps 72:10 The kings of Sheba and *S* Will
Isa 43: 3 Ethiopia and *S* in your place.

SEBAT (KJV) See SHEBAT

SECACAH (1/1)

Josh 15:61 Beth Arabah, Middin, *S*,

SECHU (1/1)

1 Sam 19:22 to the great well that is at *S*.

SECLUSION (1/1)

2 Sam 20: 3 and put them in *s* and supported

SECOND (177/171)

Gen 1: 8 and the morning were the *s* day.
2:13 The name of the *s* river is
4:19 and the name of the *s* was
6:16 shall make it with lower, *s*,
7:11 in the *s* month, the seventeenth
8:14 And in the *s* month, on the
22:15 the LORD called to Abraham a *s*
30: 7 again and bore Jacob a *s* son.
30:12 maid Zilpah bore Jacob a *s* son.
32:19 So he commanded the *s*,
41: 5 He slept and dreamed a *s* time;
41:43 him ride in the *s* chariot
41:52 And the name of the *s* he called
43:10 we would have returned this *s*
Ex 2:13 And when he went out the *s* day,
16: 1 fifteenth day of the *s* month
25:35 a knob under the *s* two
26: 4 other curtain of the *s* set.
26: 5 is on the end of the *s* set,
26:10 of the curtain of the *s* set.
26:20 And for the *s* side of the
28:18 the *s* row shall be a
36:11 other curtain of the *s* set.
36:12 on the end of the *s* set;
36:17 of the curtain of the *s* set.
37:21 a knob under the *s* two
39:11 the *s* row, a turquoise, a
40:17 first month of the *s* year,
Lev 5:10 And he shall offer the *s* as a
8:22 And he brought the *s* ram, the
13:58 shall be washed a *s* time,
Num 1: 1 first day of the *s* month,
1: 1 in the *s* year after they had
1:18 first day of the *s* month;
2:16 they shall be the *s* to break
7:18 On the *s* day Nethanel the son
9: 1 first month of the *s* year
9:11 fourteenth day of the *s* month,
10: 6 sound the advance the *s* time,
10:11 twentieth day of the *s* month,
10:11 in the *s* year, that the cloud
29:17 On the *s* day present twelve
Josh 5: 2 of Israel again the *s* time."
6:14 And the *s* day they marched
10:32 who took it on the *s* day, and
19: 1 The *s* lot came out for Simeon,
Judg 6:25 the *s* bull of seven years old,
6:26 and take the *s* bull and offer a
6:28 and the *s* bull was being
20:24 of Benjamin on the *s* day.
20:25 them from Gibeah on the *s* day,
1 Sam 8: 2 was Joel, and the name of his *s*,
18:21 Saul said to David a *s* time,
20:27 the *s* day of the month, that
20:34 and ate no food the *s* day of
26: 8 not have to strike him a *s*
2 Sam 3: 3 his *s*, Chileab, by Abigail
14:29 he sent again the *s* time,
1 Ki 6: 1 which is the *s* month, that he
9: 2 appeared to Solomon the *s* time,
15:25 king over Israel in the *s* year
18:34 Do it a *s* time," and they did
18:34 and they did it a *s* time;
19: 7 LORD came back the *s* time,
2 Ki 1:17 in the *s* year of Jehoram the
9:19 Then he sent out a *s* horseman
10: 6 Then he wrote a *s* letter to
14: 1 In the *s* year of Joash the son
15:32 In the *s* year of Pekah the son
19:29 And in the *s* year what springs
22:14 Jerusalem in the *S* Quarter.)
23: 4 the priests of the *s* order, and
25:17 The *s* pillar was the same, with
25:18 Zephaniah the *s* priest, and the
1 Chr 2:13 his firstborn, Abinadab the *s*,
3: 1 the *s*, Daniel, by Abigail the
3:15 the *s* Jehoiakim, the third
6:28 the firstborn, and Abijah the *s*.
8: 1 his firstborn, Ashbel the *s*,
8:39 Ulam his firstborn, Jeush the *s*,
12: 9 Ezer the first, Obadiah the *s*,
15:18 their brethren of the *s* rank:
23:11 was the first and Zizah the *s*.
23:19 was the first, Amariah the *s*,
23:20 the first and Jesshiah the *s*.
24: 7 Jehoiarib, the *s* to Jedaiah,
24:23 was the first, Amariah the *s*,
25: 9 the *s* for Gedaliah, him with
26: 2 the firstborn, Jediael the *s*,
26: 4 the firstborn, Jehozabad the *s*,
26:11 Hilkiah the *s*, Tebaliah the
27: 4 Over the division of the *s* month
29:22 David king the *s* time,
2 Chr 3: 2 he began to build on the *s* day
3: 2 second day of the *s* month
27: 5 paid this to him in the *s* and
28: 7 and Elkanah who was *s* to the
30: 2 the Passover in the *s* month.
30:13 Bread in the *s* month.
30:15 fourteenth day of the *s* month.
34:22 Jerusalem in the *S* Quarter.)
35:24 and put him in the *s* chariot
Ezra 3: 8 Now in the *s* month of the
3: 8 second month of the *s* year
4:24 discontinued until the *s* year
Neh 8:13 Now on the *s* day the heads of
11: 9 Judah the son of Senuah was *s*
11:17 the *s* among his brethren;
Esth 2:14 she returned to the *s* house
2:19 gathered together a *s* time,
7: 2 And on the *s* day, at the banquet
9:29 to confirm this *s* letter
10: 3 For Mordecai the Jew was *s* to
Job 42:14 the name of the *s* Keziah, and
Eccl 4:15 They were with the *s* youth who
Isa 11:11 set His hand again the *s* time
37:30 And the *s* year what springs
Jer 1:13 LORD came to me the *s* time,
13: 3 LORD came to me the *s* time,
33: 1 came to Jeremiah a *s* time,
41: 4 on the *s* day after he had
52:22 The *s* pillar, with pomegranates
52:24 Zephaniah the *s* priest, and the
Ezek 10:14 the *s* face the face of a man,
43:22 On the *s* day you shall offer a
Dan 2: 1 Now in the *s* year of
7: 5 suddenly another beast, a *s*,
Jon 3: 1 came to Jonah the *s* time,
Nah 1: 9 will not rise up a *s* time.
Zeph 1:10 A wailing from the *S* Quarter,
Hag 1: 1 In the *s* year of King Darius,
1:15 in the *s* year of King Darius.
2:10 in the *s* year of Darius, the
Zech 1: 1 eighth month of the *s* year
1: 7 in the *s* year of Darius, the
6: 2 with the *s* chariot black
Mal 2:13 And this is the *s* thing you
Mt 21:30 Then he came to the *s* and said
22:26 Likewise the *s* also, and the
22:39 And the *s* is like it: 'You
26:42 a *s* time, He went away and
Mk 12:21 And the *s* took her, and he died;
12:31 'And the *s*, like it, is this:
14:72 A *s* time the rooster crowed.
Lk 6: 1 Now it happened on the *s* Sabbath
12:38 if he should come in the *s*
19:18 And the *s* came, saying, 'Master,
20:30 And the *s* took her as wife, and
Jn 3: 4 Can he enter a *s* time into his
4:54 This again is the *s* sign Jesus
21:16 He said to him again a *s* time,
Acts 7:13 And the *s* time Joseph was made
10:15 spoke to him again the *s* time,
12:10 first and the *s* guard posts,
13:33 also written in the *s* Psalm:
1 Cor 12:28 *s* prophets, third teachers,
15:47 the *s* Man is the Lord from
2 Cor 1:15 you might have a *s* benefit—
13: 2 I were present the *s* time,
Titus 3:10 the first and *s* admonition,
Heb 8: 7 would have been sought for a *s*.
9: 3 and behind the *s* veil, the part
9: 7 But into the *s* part the high
9:28 He will appear a *s* time,
10: 9 that He may establish the *s*.
2 Pe 3: 1 write to you this *s* epistle
Rev 2:11 be hurt by the *s* death."
4: 7 the *s* living creature like a
6: 3 When He opened the *s* seal,
6: 3 I heard the *s* living creature
8: 8 Then the *s* angel sounded:
11:14 The *s* woe is past. Behold, the
16: 3 Then the *s* angel poured out his
20: 6 Over such the *s* death has no
20:14 This is the *s* death.
21: 8 which is the *s* death."
21:19 the *s* sapphire, the third

SECRET (59/56) SECRETLY, SECRETS

Deut 27:15 craftsman, and sets it up in *s*.
29:29 The *s* things belong to the
Judg 3:19 'I have a *s* message for you,
16: 9 So the *s* of his strength was
1 Sam 19: 2 and stay in a *s* place and
Neh 6:10 who was a *s* informer; and he
Ps 10: 8 In the *s* places he murders the
17:12 like a young lion lurking in *s*
18:11 He made darkness His *s* place;
19:12 Cleanse me from *s* faults.
25:14 The *s* of the LORD is with
27: 5 In the *s* place of His

31:20 hide them in the *s* place
64: 2 Hide me from the *s* plots of the
64: 4 That they may shoot in *s* at the
81: 7 I answered you in the *s* place
90: 8 Our *s* sins in the light of
91: 1 He who dwells in the *s* place of
139:15 from You, When I was made in *s*,
Prov 3:32 But His *s* counsel is with the
9:17 And bread eaten in *s* is
21:14 A gift in *s* pacifies anger,
25: 9 And do not disclose the *s* to
Eccl 12:14 Including every *s* thing,
Song 2:14 In the *s* places of the cliff,
Isa 3:17 will uncover their *s* parts."
45: 3 And hidden riches of *s* places,
45:19 I have not spoken in *s*,
48:16 I have not spoken in *s* from
Jer 2:34 I have not found it by *s*
13:17 My soul will weep in *s* for
23:24 Can anyone hide himself in *s*
49:10 I have uncovered his *s* places,
Ezek 7:22 will defile My *s* place;
28: 3 than Daniel! There is no *s*
Dan 2:18 God of heaven concerning this *s*,
2:19 Then the *s* was revealed to
2:22 He reveals deep and *s* things;
2:27 The *s* which the king has
2:30 this *s* has not been revealed to
2:47 since you could reveal this *s*.
4: 9 and no *s* troubles you, explain
Am 3: 7 Unless He reveals His *s* to His
Hab 3:14 like feasting on the poor in *s*.
Mt 6: 4 charitable deed may be in *s*;
6: 4 and your Father who sees in *s*
6: 6 to your Father who is in the *s*
6: 6 and your Father who sees in *s*
6:18 Father who is in the *s* place;
6:18 and your Father who sees in *s*
13:35 will utter things kept *s*
Mk 4:22 nor has anything been kept *s*
Lk 8:17 For nothing is *s* that will not
11:33 puts it in a *s* place or under
Jn 7: 4 For no one does anything in *s*
7:10 not openly, but as it were in *s*.
18:20 and in *s* I have said nothing.
Rom 16:25 of the mystery kept *s* since
Eph 5:12 which are done by them in *s*.

SECRETLY (34/34) SECRET

Gen 31:27 "Why did you flee away *s*,
Deut 13: 6 *s* entices you, saying, 'Let us
27:24 one who attacks his neighbor *s*.
28:57 for she will eat them *s* for
Josh 2: 1 men from Acacia Grove to spy *s*,
Judg 9:31 sent messengers to Abimelech *s*,
1 Sam 18:22 "Communicate with David *s*,
24: 4 And David arose and *s* cut
2 Sam 12:12 'For you did it *s*,
2 Ki 17: 9 the children of Israel *s* did
Job 4:12 Now a word was *s* brought to me,
13:10 If you *s* show partiality.
31:27 my heart has been *s* enticed,
Ps 10: 8 His eyes are *s* fixed on the
10: 9 He lies in wait *s*,
11: 2 That they may shoot *s* at the
31: 4 net which they have *s* laid
31:20 You shall keep them *s* in a
64: 5 They talk of laying snares *s*;
101: 5 Whoever *s* slanders his
142: 3 They have *s* set a snare
Prov 1:11 Let us lurk *s* for the innocent
1:18 They lurk *s* for their own
Jer 37:17 The king asked him *s* in his
38:16 So Zedekiah the king swore *s* to
40:15 the son of Kareah spoke *s* to
Mt 1:19 was minded to put her away *s*.
2: 7 when he had *s* called the wise
Jn 11:28 she went her way and *s* called
19:38 a disciple of Jesus, but *s*,
Acts 6:11 Then they *s* induced men to say,
16:37 And now do they put us out *s*?
Gal 2: 4 false brethren *s* brought in
2 Pe 2: 1 who will *s* bring in destructive

SECRETS (9/9) SECRET

Job 11: 6 That He would show you the *s* of
Ps 44:21 For He knows the *s* of the
Prov 11:13 A talebearer reveals *s*,
20:19 as a talebearer reveals *s*;
Dan 2:28 a God in heaven who reveals *s*,
2:29 and He who reveals *s* has made
2:47 of kings, and a revealer of *s*,
Rom 2:16 day when God will judge the *s*
1 Cor 14:25 And thus the *s* of his heart are

SECT (6/6)

Acts 5:17 were with him (which is the *s*
15: 5 But some of the *s* of the
24: 5 and a ringleader of the *s* of
24:14 to the Way which they call a *s*,
26: 5 according to the strictest *s*
28:22 for concerning this *s*,

SECTION (25/24)

Neh 3:11 Pahath-Moab repaired another *s*,
3:19 repaired another *s* in front of
3:20 carefully repaired the other *s*,
3:21 son of Koz, repaired another *s*,
3:24 of Henadad repaired another *s*,
3:27 the Tekoites repaired another *s*,
3:30 of Zalaph, repaired another *s*.
Ezek 45: 1 a holy *s* of the land; its
45: 4 It shall be a holy *s* of the
45: 6 to the district of the holy *s*;
45: 7 The prince shall have a *s* on
48: 1 there shall be one *s* for
48: 2 one *s* for Asher;
48: 3 one *s* for Naphtali;
48: 4 one *s* for Manasseh;
48: 5 one *s* for Ephraim;
48: 6 one *s* for Reuben;
48: 7 one *s* for Judah;
48:18 the district of the holy *s*,
48:18 to the district of the holy *s*,
48:23 Benjamin shall have one *s*;
48:24 Simeon shall have one *s*;
48:25 Issachar shall have one *s*;
48:26 Zebulun shall have one *s*;
48:27 west, Gad shall have one *s*;

SECUNDUS (1/1)

Acts 20: 4 also Aristarchus and *S* of the

SECURE (17/17) SECURELY

Judg 8:11 the army while the camp felt *s*.
18: 7 of the Sidonians, quiet and *s*.
18:10 you will come to a *s* people and
18:27 Laish, to a people quiet and *s*;
2 Sam 23: 5 Ordered in all things and *s*.
Job 11:18 And you would be *s*,
12: 6 those who provoke God are *s*—
21:23 Being wholly at ease and *s*;
Prov 1:33 dwell safely, And will be *s*,
11:15 one who hates being surety is *s*.
Isa 22:23 him as a peg in a *s* place,
22:25 is fastened in the *s* place
32:18 In *s* dwellings, and in quiet
Mt 27:64 that the tomb be made *s* until
27:65 make it as *s* as you know
27:66 they went and made the tomb *s*,
28:14 will appease him and make you *s*.

SECURED (1/1)

Acts 27:16 we *s* the skiff with difficulty.

SECURELY (10/10) SECURE

Josh 6: 1 Now Jericho was *s* shut up
Judg 15:13 but we will tie you *s* and
16:11 If they bind me *s* with new ropes
Prov 10: 9 walks with integrity walks *s*,
Isa 47: 8 to pleasures, Who dwell *s*,
Jer 49:31 wealthy nation that dwells *s*,
Ezek 28:26 yes, they will dwell *s*,
Zeph 2:15 rejoicing city That dwelt *s*,
Acts 5:23 we found the prison shut *s*,
16:23 the jailer to keep them *s*.

SECURES (1/1)

Isa 44:14 He *s* it for himself among the

SECURITY (4/4)

Ruth 3: 1 shall I not seek *s* for you,
Job 24:23 He gives them *s*,
Ezek 39: 6 and on those who live in *s* in
Acts 17: 9 So when they had taken *s* from

SEDITION (2/2)

Ezra 4:15 and that they have incited *s*
4:19 and rebellion and *s* have been

SEDITIONS (KJV) See DISSENSIONS

SEDUCE (1/1)

Rev 2:20 to teach and *s* My servants to

SEDUCED (5/5) SEDUCTRESS

Num 25:18 their schemes by which they *s*
2 Ki 21: 9 and Manasseh *s* them to do more
2 Chr 33: 9 So Manasseh *s* Judah and the
Prov 7:21 her flattering lips she *s* him.
Ezek 13:10 because they have *s* My people,

SEDUCTIVE (1/1)

Nah 3: 4 of harlotries of the *s* harlot,

SEDUCTRESS (7/7) SEDUCED

Prov 2:16 From the *s* who flatters with
5:20 be embraced in the arms of a *s*?
6:24 the flattering tongue of a *s*.
7: 5 From the *s* who flatters with
20:16 a pledge when it is for a *s*.
23:27 And a *s* is a narrow well.
27:13 when he is surety for a *s*.

SEE (705/662)

Gen 1:29 And God said, "*S*,
2:19 them to Adam to *s* what
8: 8 to *s* if the waters had receded
9:23 and they did not *s* their
11: 5 But the LORD came down to *s* the
12:12 when the Egyptians *s* you, that
13:15 for all the land which you *s* I
16: 2 *S* now, the LORD has restrained
18:21 I will go down now and *s* whether
19: 8 *S* now, I have two daughters who
19:20 *S* now, this city is near
19:21 '*S*, I have favored you
20:15 '*S*, my land is before
21:16 Let me not *s* the death of the
27: 1 were so dim that he could not *s*,
31: 5 I *s* your father's countenance,
31:12 said, 'Lift your eyes now and *s*,
31:43 all that you *s* is mine.
31:50 although no man is with us—*s*,
32:20 and afterward I will *s* his
34: 1 went out to *s* the daughters of
37:14 Please go and *s* if it is well
37:20 We shall *s* what will become of
39:14 saying, "*S*, he has brought in
41:41 to Joseph, "*S*, I have set
42: 9 have come to *s* the nakedness
42:12 but you have come to *s* the
42:16 may be tested to *s* whether
43: 3 You shall not *s* my face unless
43: 5 You shall not *s* my face unless
44:23 you shall *s* my face no more.'
44:26 for we may not *s* the man's face
44:34 lest perhaps I *s* the evil that
45:12 eyes of my brother Benjamin *s*
45:24 *S* that you do not become
45:28 I will go and *s* him before I
48:10 age, so that he could not *s*.
48:11 I had not thought to *s* your
Ex 1:16 and *s* them on the birthstools,
3: 3 I will now turn aside and *s* this
4:18 and *s* whether they are still
4:21 *s* that you do all those wonders
6: 1 Now you shall *s* what I will do
7: 1 to Moses: "*S*, I have made
10: 5 that no one will be able to *s*
10:23 They did not *s* one another; nor
10:28 Take heed to yourself and *s* my
10:28 For in the day you *s* my face
10:29 I will never *s* your face
12:13 And when I *s* the blood, I will
13:17 change their minds when they *s*
14:13 and *s* the salvation of the
14:13 For the Egyptians whom you *s*
14:13 you shall *s* again no more
16: 7 in the morning you shall *s*
16:29 *S*! For the LORD has given you
16:32 that they may *s* the bread with
22: 8 to the judges to *s* whether
23: 5 If you *s* the donkey of one who
25:40 And *s* to it that you make them
31: 2 '*S*, I have called by name
33:12 to the LORD, "*S*, You say
33:20 You cannot *s* My face; for no man
33:20 for no man shall *s* Me, and
33:23 and you shall *s* My back; but My
34:10 among whom you are shall *s*
35:30 '*S*, the LORD has called by name
Lev 10:18 *S*! Its blood was not brought
Num 11:15 and do not let me *s* my
11:23 Now you shall *s* whether what I
13:18 and *s* what the land is like:
14:23 they certainly shall not *s* the
14:23 those who rejected Me *s* it.
22: 5 *S*, they cover the face of
23: 9 from the top of the rocks I *s*
23:13 place from which you may *s*
23:13 you shall *s* only the outer part
23:13 and shall not *s* them all;
24:17 I *s* Him, but not now; I behold
27:12 and *s* the land which I have
32: 8 Kadesh Barnea to *s* the land.
32:11 shall *s* the land of which I
Deut 1: 8 '*S*, I have set the land before
1:35 shall *s* that good land of
1:36 he shall *s* it, and to him and
2:31 to me, '*S*, I have begun
3:25 let me cross over and *s* the
3:28 the land which you will *s*.
4:19 and when you *s* the sun, the
4:28 which neither *s* nor hear nor
12:13 in every place that you *s*;
18:16 nor let me *s* this great fire
20: 1 and *s* horses and chariots and
21:11 and you *s* among the captives a
22: 1 You shall not *s* your brother's
22: 4 You shall not *s* your brother's
23:14 that He may *s* no unclean thing
28:10 peoples of the earth shall *s*
28:34 of the sight which your eyes *s*.
28:67 of the sight which your eyes *s*.
28:68 You shall never *s* it again.' And
29: 4 to perceive and eyes to *s* and
29:22 when they *s* the plagues of that
30:15 *S*, I have set before you
32:20 I will *s* what their end will
32:39 Now *s* that I, even I, am He,
32:52 Yet you shall *s* the land before
34: 4 I have caused you to *s* it
Josh 3: 3 When you *s* the ark of the
6: 2 *S*! I have given Jericho into
8: 1 *S*, I have given into your
8: 8 *S*, I have commanded you."
9:13 we filled were new, and *s*,
23: 4 '*S*, I have divided to you
Judg 9:36 You *s* the shadows of the
9:37 said, "*S*, people are coming
14: 8 he turned aside to *s* the

19: 9 *S*, the day is coming to an
1 Sam 2:32 And you will *s* an enemy in My
3: 2 grow so dim that he could not *s*,
4:15 were so dim that he could not *s*.
6:13 and rejoiced to *s* it.
10:24 Do you *s* him whom the LORD has
12:16 stand and *s* this great thing
12:17 that you may perceive and *s*
14:17 Now call the roll and *s* who has
14:38 and know and *s* what this sin
15:35 And Samuel went no more to *s*
16: 7 For the LORD does not *s* as
17:18 and *s* how your brothers fare,
17:28 for you have come down to *s* the
19:15 messengers back to *s* David,
20:29 please let me get away and *s* my
21:14 you *s* the man is insane.
23:22 and *s* the place where his
23:23 *S* therefore, and take knowledge
24:11 'Moreover, my father, *s*!
24:11 *s* the corner of your robe in my
24:11 know and *s* that there is
24:15 and *s* and plead my case, and
25:19 *s*, I am coming after you."
25:25 did not *s* the young men of my
25:35 *S*, I have heeded your voice
26:16 And now *s* where the king's
28:13 not be afraid. What did you *s*?
2 Sam 3:13 you shall not *s* my face unless
3:13 when you come to *s* my face."
7: 2 *S* now, I dwell in a house of
13: 5 your father comes to *s* you,
13: 5 that I may *s* it and eat it
13: 6 the king came to *s* him,
14:24 but do not let him *s* my face."
14:24 but did not *s* the king's face.
14:28 but did not *s* the king's face.
14:30 servants, "*S*, Joab's field
14:32 let me *s* the king's face; but
15:28 '*S*, I will wait in the
16:11 *S* how my son who came from my
24: 3 the eyes of my lord the king *s*
24:13 Now consider and *s* what answer
1 Ki 1:48 while my eyes *s* it!'"
2: 8 'And *s*, you have with you
3:12 *s*, I have given you a wise
9:12 went from Tyre to *s* the cities
12:16 *s* to your own house, O
14: 4 But Ahijah could not *s*,
15:19 *S*, I have sent you a
17: 9 *S*, I have commanded a
17:12 and *s*, I am gathering a couple
17:23 said, "*S*, your son lives!"
20: 7 and *s* how this man seeks
20:22 and *s* what you should do, for
20:33 watching closely to *s* whether
21:29 *S* how Ahab has humbled himself
22:25 you shall *s* on that day when
2 Ki 2:10 if you *s* me when I am taken
3:14 not look at you, nor *s* you.
3:17 You shall not *s* wind, nor shall
3:17 nor shall you *s* rain; yet that
5: 7 and *s* how he seeks a quarrel
6: 1 *S* now, the place where we dwell
6:13 Go and *s* where he is, that I
6:17 open his eyes that he may *s*.
6:20 of these men, that they may *s*.
6:32 Do you *s* how this son of a
7: 2 you shall *s* it with your eyes,
7:13 so let us send them and *s*.
7:14 Syrian army, saying, "Go and *s*.
7:19 you shall *s* it with your eyes,
8:29 went down to *s* Joram the son of
9:16 had come down to *s* Joram.
9:17 'I *s* a company of men."
9:34 *s* to this accursed woman, and
10:16 and *s* my zeal for the LORD."
10:23 Search and *s* that no servants of
19:16 open Your eyes, O LORD, and *s*;
22:20 and your eyes shall not *s* all
23:17 gravestone is this that I *s*?
1 Chr 17: 1 *S* now, I dwell in a house of
2 Chr 10:16 O Israel! Now *s* to your own
18:24 Indeed you shall *s* on that day
20:17 stand still and *s* the salvation
22: 6 went down to *s* Jehoram the son
24: 5 and *s* that you do it quickly."
29: 8 as you *s* with your eyes.
30: 7 them up to desolation, as you *s*.
34:28 and your eyes shall not *s* all
Ezra 4:14 it was not proper for us to *s*
Neh 2:17 You *s* the distress that we are
4:11 They will neither know nor *s*
Esth 3: 4 to *s* whether Mordecai's words
5:13 so long as I *s* Mordecai the Jew
8: 6 For how can I endure to *s* the
8: 6 Or how can I endure to *s* the
Job 3: 9 And not *s* the dawning of the
6:21 You *s* terror and are afraid.
7: 7 My eye will never again *s*
7: 8 eye of him who sees me will *s*
9:11 I do not *s* Him; If He moves
9:25 flee away, they *s* no good.
10: 4 Or do You *s* as man sees?
10:15 of disgrace; *S* my misery!
13:18 *S* now, I have prepared my
17:15 for my hope, who can *s* it?
19:26 in my flesh I shall *s* God,
19:27 Whom I shall *s* for myself, And
20: 9 The eye that saw him will *s*
20:17 He will not *s* the streams, The
21:20 Let his eyes *s* his destruction,
22:11 darkness so that you cannot *s*;
22:12 And *s* the highest stars, how
22:14 cover Him, so that He cannot *s*,
22:19 The righteous *s* it and are
23: 9 right hand, I cannot *s* Him.
24: 1 who know Him *s* not His days?
24:15 No eye will *s* me'; And he
31: 4 Does He not *s* my ways, And
33:26 He shall *s* His face with joy,
33:28 And his life shall *s* the
34:29 who then can *s* Him, Whether
34:32 Teach me what I do not *s*;
35: 5 Look to the heavens and *s*;
35:14 Although you say you do not *s*
40:16 *S* now, his strength is in his
Ps 10:11 His face; He will never *s*.
14: 2 To *s* if there are any who
16:10 Your Holy One to *s* corruption.
17:15 I will *s* Your face in
22: 7 All those who *s* Me ridicule Me;
27:13 I had believed That I would *s*
31:11 Those who *s* me outside flee
34: 8 taste and *s* that the LORD is
34:12 that he may *s* good?
36: 9 In Your light we *s* light.
37:34 are cut off, you shall *s* it.
40: 3 Many will *s* it and fear, And
41: 6 And if he comes to *s* me, he
49: 9 And not *s* the Pit.
49:19 They shall never *s* light.
52: 6 The righteous also shall *s* and
53: 2 To *s* if there are any who
58: 8 that they may not *s* the sun.
59:10 God shall let me *s* my desire
63: 2 To *s* Your power and Your
64: 5 Who will *s* them?"
64: 8 All who *s* them shall flee
66: 5 Come and *s* the works of God;
69:23 darkened, so that they do not *s*;
69:32 The humble shall *s* this and
74: 9 We do not *s* our signs;
80:14 Look down from heaven and *s*,
86:17 That those who hate me may *s*
89:48 What man can live and not *s*
91: 8 And *s* the reward of the
94: 7 say, "The LORD does not *s*,
94: 9 formed the eye, shall He not *s*?
97: 6 And all the peoples *s* His
106: 5 That I may *s* the benefit of
107:24 They *s* the works of the LORD,
107:42 The righteous *s* it and
112:10 The wicked will *s* it and be
115: 5 they have, but they do not *s*;
118: 7 Therefore I shall *s* my
119:18 that I may *s* Wondrous things
119:74 You will be glad when they *s*
119:158 I *s* the treacherous, and am
128: 5 And may you *s* the good of
128: 6 may you *s* your children's
135:16 they have, but they do not *s*;
139:24 And *s* if there is any wicked
142: 4 Look on my right hand and *s*,
Prov 22:29 Do you *s* a man who excels in
23:33 Your eyes will *s* strange
24:18 Lest the LORD *s* it, and it
26:12 Do you *s* a man wise in his own
29:16 But the righteous will *s* their
29:20 Do you *s* a man hasty in his
Eccl 1:10 be said, "*S*, this is new"?
2: 3 till I might *s* what was good
3:18 that they may *s* that they
3:22 For who can bring him to *s* what
5: 8 If you *s* the oppression of the
5:11 the owners Except to *s* them
7:11 And profitable to those who *s*
8:16 wisdom and to *s* the business
9: 1 hatred by anything they *s*
Song 2:14 Let me *s* your face, Let me
3:11 And *s* King Solomon with the
6:11 to the garden of nuts To *s* the
6:11 To *s* whether the vine had
6:13 What would you *s* in the
7:12 Let us *s* if the vine has
Isa 5:19 That we may *s* it; And let
6:10 Lest they *s* with their eyes,
8:22 and *s* trouble and darkness,
14:16 Those who *s* you will gaze at
18: 3 you *s* it; And when he blows a
26:11 is lifted up, they will not *s*.
26:11 But they will *s* and be ashamed
29:18 the eyes of the blind shall *s*
30:10 say to the seers, "Do not *s*,
30:20 But your eyes shall *s* your
32: 3 The eyes of those who *s* will
33:17 Your eyes will *s* the King in
33:17 They will *s* the land that is
33:19 You will not *s* a fierce people,
33:20 Your eyes will *s* Jerusalem, a
35: 2 They shall *s* the glory of the
37:17 open Your eyes, O LORD, and *s*;
38:11 I shall not *s* YAH, The LORD
40: 5 And all flesh shall *s* it
40:26 And *s* who has created these
41:20 That they may *s* and know, And
41:23 we may be dismayed and *s* it
42:18 look, you blind, that you may *s*.
44: 9 They neither *s* nor know, that
44:18 eyes, so that they cannot *s*,
48: 6 *S* all this. And will you not
49: 7 Kings shall *s* and arise,
49:16 *S*, I have inscribed you on
49:18 up your eyes, look around and *s*;
51:22 '*S*, I have taken out of your
52: 8 For they shall *s* eye to eye
52:10 the ends of the earth shall *s*
52:15 not been told them they shall *s*,
53: 2 And when we *s* Him, There is
53:10 He shall *s* His seed, He shall
53:11 He shall *s* the labor of His
58: 7 When you *s* the naked, that you
60: 4 up your eyes all around, and *s*:
60: 5 Then you shall *s* and become
61: 9 All who *s* them shall
62: 2 The Gentiles shall *s* your
63:15 And *s* from Your habitation,
66: 5 That we may *s* your joy.'
66:14 When you *s* this, your heart
66:18 and they shall come and *s* My
Jer 1:10 *S*, I have this day set you
1:11 "Jeremiah, what do you *s*?
1:11 I *s* a branch of an almond
1:13 time, saying, "What do you *s*?
1:13 I *s* a boiling pot, and it is
2:10 the coasts of Cyprus and *s*,
2:10 And *s* if there has been such
2:19 Know therefore and *s* that it
2:23 *S* your way in the valley;
2:31 *s* the word of the LORD!
3: 2 to the desolate heights and *s*:
4:21 How long will I *s* the standard,
5: 1 *S* now and know; And seek in
5:12 Nor shall we *s* sword or
5:21 Who have eyes and *s* not, And
6:16 "Stand in the ways and *s*,
7:12 and *s* what I did to it because
7:17 Do you not *s* what they do in the
11:20 Let me *s* Your vengeance on
12: 4 He will not *s* our final end."
13:20 Lift up your eyes and *s* Those
14:13 You shall not *s* the sword, nor
17: 6 And shall not *s* when good
20: 4 and your eyes shall *s* it.
20:12 And *s* the mind and heart,
20:12 Let me *s* Your vengeance on
20:18 forth from the womb to *s* labor
22:10 Nor *s* his native country.
22:12 and shall *s* this land no more.
23:24 So I shall not *s* him?" says
24: 3 said to me, "What do you *s*,
29:32 nor shall he *s* the good that I
30: 6 Ask now, and *s*, Whether a
30: 6 So why do I *s* every man with
32: 4 and *s* him eye to eye;
32:24 happened; there You *s* it!
34: 3 your eyes shall *s* the eyes of
40: 4 *S*, all the land is before you;
42: 2 a few of many, as you can *s*),
42:14 land of Egypt where we shall *s*
42:18 and you shall *s* this place no
51:61 you arrive in Babylon and *s* it,
Lam 1:11 '*S*, O LORD, and consider,
1:12 Behold and *s* If there is any
1:20 '*S*, O LORD, that I am in
2:20 *S*, O LORD, and consider!
Ezek 4:15 to me, "*S*, I am giving you
8: 6 do you *s* what they are doing,
8: 6 will *s* greater abominations."
8: 9 and *s* the wicked abominations
8:12 The LORD does not *s* us, the
8:13 and you will *s* greater
8:15 you will *s* greater abominations
9: 9 and the LORD does not *s*!'
12: 2 which has eyes to *s* but does
12: 2 has eyes to see but does not *s*,
12: 6 so that you cannot *s* the
12:12 so that he cannot *s* the ground
12:13 yet he shall not *s* it, though
13:16 and who *s* visions of peace for
14:22 and you will *s* their ways and
14:23 when you *s* their ways and their
16:37 that they may *s* all your
20:48 All flesh shall *s* that I, the
21:29 While they *s* false visions for
30:21 and *s*, it has not been
32:31 Pharaoh will *s* them And be
39:21 all the nations shall *s* My
40: 4 of Israel everything you *s*.
44: 5 *s* with your eyes and hear with
Dan 1:10 For why should he *s* your faces
1:13 and as you *s* fit, so deal with
2: 8 because you *s* that my decision
3:25 I *s* four men loose, walking in
5:23 which do not *s* or hear or know;
9:18 open Your eyes and *s* our
10: 7 men who were with me did not *s*
Joel 2:28 young men shall *s* visions.
Am 3: 9 *S* great tumults in her midst,
6: 2 Go over to Calneh and *s*;
7: 8 to me, "Amos, what do you *s*?
8: 2 He said, "Amos, what do you *s*?
Jon 4: 5 till he might *s* what would
Mic 6: 9 Wisdom shall *s* Your name:
7: 9 I will *s* His righteousness.
7:10 she who is my enemy will *s*,
7:10 My eyes will *s* her; Now she
7:16 The nations shall *s* and be
Hab 1: 3 And cause me to *s* trouble?
2: 1 And watch to *s* what He will
Zeph 3:15 You shall *s* disaster no more.
Hag 2: 3 And how do you *s* it now?
Zech 2: 2 to *s* what is its width and
3: 4 said, "*S*, I have removed
4: 2 he said to me, "What do you *s*?
4:10 For these seven rejoice to *s*

5: 2 he said to me, "What do you *s*?
5: 2 I *s* a flying scroll. Its length
5: 5 and *s* what this is that goes
6: 8 '*S*, those who go toward the
9: 5 Ashkelon shall *s* it and fear;
10: 7 their children shall *s* it and
Mal 1: 5 Your eyes shall *s*,
Mt 5: 8 For they shall *s* God.
5:16 that they may *s* your good works
7: 5 and then you will *s* clearly to
8: 4 *S* that you tell no one; but go
9:30 *S* that no one knows it."
11: 4 the things which you hear and *s*:
11: 5 The blind *s* and the lame walk;
11: 7 go out into the wilderness to *s*?
11: 8 "But what did you go out to *s*?
11: 9 "But what did you go out to *s*?
12:38 we want to *s* a sign from You."
13:13 because seeing they do not *s*,
13:14 And seeing you will *s*
13:15 Lest they should *s* with
13:16 are your eyes for they *s*,
13:17 and righteous men desired to *s*
13:17 men desired to see what you *s*,
13:17 and did not *s* it, and to hear
16:28 not taste death till they *s*
18:10 their angels always *s* the face
19:27 to Him, "*S*, we have left all
22: 4 '*S*, I have prepared my
22:11 king came in to *s* the guests,
23:38 *S*! Your house is left to you
23:39 you shall *s* Me no more till you
24: 2 Do you not *s* all these things?
24: 6 *S* that you are not troubled;
24:15 Therefore when you *s* the
24:25 '*S*, I have told you
24:30 and they will *s* the Son of Man
24:33 when you *s* all these things,
25:37 when did we *s* You hungry and
25:38 When did we *s* You a stranger and
25:39 Or when did we *s* You sick, or in
25:44 when did we *s* You hungry or
26:46 *S*, My betrayer is at hand."
26:58 with the servants to *s* the end.
26:64 hereafter you will *s* the Son of
27: 4 that to us? You *s* to it!"
27:24 just Person. You *s* to it."
27:49 let us *s* if Elijah will come to
28: 1 other Mary came to *s* the tomb.
28: 6 *s* the place where the Lord lay.
28: 7 there you will *s* Him.
28:10 and there they will *s* Me."
Mk 1:44 *S* that you say nothing to
4:12 Seeing they may *s* and not
5:14 And they went out to *s* what it
5:31 You *s* the multitude thronging
5:32 And He looked around to *s* her
6:38 loaves do you have? Go and *s*.
8:18 "Having eyes, do you not *s*?
8:24 I *s* men like trees, walking."
9: 1 not taste death till they *s*
10:28 to Him, "*S*, we have left all
11:13 He went to *s* if perhaps He
12:15 Me a denarius that I may *s* it.
13: 1 *s* what manner of stones and
13: 2 Do you *s* these great buildings?
13:14 So when you *s* the 'abomination
13:23 'But take heed; *s*, I have told
13:26 Then they will *s* the Son of Man
13:29 when you *s* these things
14:42 *S*, My betrayer is at hand."
14:62 And you will *s* the Son of Man
15: 4 *S* how many things they testify
15:32 that we may *s* and believe."
15:36 let us *s* if Elijah will come to
16: 6 *S* the place where they laid
16: 7 there you will *s* Him, as He
Lk 2:15 Bethlehem and *s* this thing
2:26 that he would not *s* death
3: 6 And all flesh shall *s* the
6:42 when you yourself do not *s* the
6:42 and then you will *s* clearly to
7:22 and heard: that the blind *s*,
7:24 go out into the wilderness to *s*?
7:25 "But what did you go out to *s*?
7:26 "But what did you go out to *s*?
7:44 Do you *s* this woman? I entered
8:10 'Seeing they may not *s*,
8:16 that those who enter may *s* the
8:20 desiring to *s* You."
8:35 Then they went out to *s* what had
9: 9 So he sought to *s* Him.
9:27 not taste death till they *s*
10:23 Blessed are the eyes which *s*
10:23 eyes which see the things you *s*;
10:24 and kings have desired to *s*
10:24 have desired to see what you *s*,
11:33 that those who come in may *s*
12:54 Whenever you *s* a cloud rising
12:55 And when you *s* the south wind
13:28 when you *s* Abraham and Isaac
13:35 *S*! Your house is left to you
13:35 you shall not *s* Me until the
14:18 and I must go and *s* it.
14:29 all who *s* it begin to mock
17:21 '*S* here!' or 'See there!'
17:21 *S* there!' For indeed, the
17:22 desire to *s* one of the days
17:22 and you will not *s* it.
18:28 '*S*, we have left all and
19: 3 And he sought to *s* who Jesus
19: 4 up into a sycamore tree to *s*

20:13 respect him when they *s* him.'
21: 6 "These things which you *s*—
21:20 But when you *s* Jerusalem
21:27 Then they will *s* the Son of Man
21:30 you *s* and know for yourselves
21:31 when you *s* these things
23: 8 for a long time to *s* Him,
23: 8 and he hoped to *s* some miracle
24:24 said; but Him they did not *s*.
24:39 it is I Myself. Handle Me and *s*,
24:39 have flesh and bones as you *s*
Jn 1:33 Upon whom you *s* the Spirit
1:39 He said to them, "Come and *s*.
1:46 said to him, "Come and *s*.
1:50 You will *s* greater things than
1:51 hereafter you shall *s* heaven
3: 3 he cannot *s* the kingdom of
3:36 the Son shall not *s* life,
4:29 *s* a Man who told me all things
4:48 Unless you people *s* signs and
5:14 '*S*, you have been made well.
6:30 that we may *s* it and believe
6:62 What then if you should *s* the
7: 3 disciples also may *s* the works
8:51 word he shall never *s* death."
8:56 Abraham rejoiced to *s* My day,
9:15 my eyes, and I washed, and I *s*.
9:19 How then does he now *s*?"
9:25 though I was blind, now I *s*.
9:39 that those who do not *s* may
9:39 that those who do not see may *s*,
9:39 and that those who *s* may be
9:41 no sin; but now you say, 'We *s*.
11:34 said to Him, "Lord, come and *s*.
11:36 *S* how He loved him!"
11:40 believe you would *s* the glory
12: 9 but that they might also *s*
12:19 You *s* that you are accomplishing
12:21 we wish to *s* Jesus."
12:40 Lest they should *s* with
14:19 longer and the world will *s* Me
14:19 no more, but you will *s* Me.
16:10 I go to My Father and you *s* Me
16:16 and you will not *s* Me; and
16:16 and you will *s* Me, because I go
16:17 and you will not *s* Me; and
16:17 and you will *s* Me'; and,
16:19 and you will not *s* Me; and
16:19 and you will *s* Me'?
16:22 but I will *s* you again and your
16:29 '*S*, now You are speaking
18:26 Did I not *s* you in the garden
20:25 Unless I *s* in His hands the
Acts 2:17 young men shall *s* visions,
2:27 Holy One to *s* corruption.
2:31 nor did His flesh *s* corruption.
2:33 out this which you now *s* and
3:16 whom you *s* and know.
7:56 I *s* the heavens opened and
8:23 For I *s* that you are poisoned by
8:36 said, "*S*, here is water.
13:35 allow Your Holy One to *s*
15:36 and *s* how they are doing."
19:21 I must also *s* Rome."
19:26 Moreover you *s* and hear that not
20:22 'And *s*, now I go bound in
20:25 will *s* my face no more.
20:38 that they would *s* his face no
21:20 said to him, "You *s*, brother,
22:11 And since I could not *s* for the
22:14 and *s* the Just One, and hear
25: 5 to *s* if there is any fault in
25:24 you *s* this man about whom the
28:20 to *s* you and speak with you,
28:26 And seeing you will *s*,
28:27 Lest they should *s* with
Rom 1:11 For I long to *s* you, that I may
7:23 But I *s* another law in my
8:25 if we hope for what we do not *s*,
11: 8 that they should not *s*
11:10 so that they do not *s*,
15:21 announced, they shall *s*;
15:24 For I hope to *s* you on my
1 Cor 1:26 For you *s* your calling,
13:12 For now we *s* in a mirror, dimly,
16: 7 For I do not wish to *s* you now
16:10 *s* that he may be with you
2 Cor 8: 7 *s* that you abound in this grace
Gal 1:18 up to Jerusalem to *s* Peter,
6:11 *S* with what large letters I
Eph 3: 9 and to make all *s* what is the
5:15 *S* then that you walk
5:33 and let the wife *s* that she
Phil 1:27 whether I come and *s* you
2:23 as soon as I *s* how it goes with
2:28 that when you *s* him again you
Col 2: 5 rejoicing to *s* your good order
4:16 *s* that it is read also in the
1 Th 2:17 endeavored more eagerly to *s*
3: 6 greatly desiring to *s* us, as we
3: 6 as we also to *s* you—
3:10 exceedingly that we may *s* your
5:15 *S* that no one renders evil for
1 Tim 6:16 whom no man has seen or can *s*,
2 Tim 1: 4 greatly desiring to *s* you, being
Heb 2: 8 But now we do not yet *s* all
2: 9 But we *s* Jesus, who was made a
3:19 So we *s* that they could not
8: 5 *S* that you make all things
10:25 and so much the more as you *s*
11: 5 taken away so that he did not *s*
12:14 without which no one will *s* the

12:25 *S* that you do not refuse Him
13:23 with whom I shall *s* you if he
Jas 2:22 Do you *s* that faith was working
2:24 You *s* then that a man is
3: 5 *S* how great a forest a little
5: 7 *S* how the farmer waits for the
1 Pe 1: 8 Though now you do not *s* Him,
3:10 life And *s* good days,
1 Jn 3: 2 for we shall *s* Him as He is.
3 Jn 14 but I hope to *s* you shortly, and
Rev 1: 7 and every eye will *s* Him, even
1:11 'What you *s*, write in a book
1:12 Then I turned to *s* the voice
3: 8 *S*, I have set before you
3:18 with eye salve, that you may *s*.
6: 1 like thunder, "Come and *s*.
6: 3 creature saying, "Come and *s*.
6: 5 creature say, "Come and *s*.
6: 7 creature saying, "Come and *s*.
9:20 which can neither *s* nor hear
11: 9 and nations will *s* their dead
16:15 naked and they *s* his shame."
17: 8 when they *s* the beast that was,
18: 7 and will not *s* sorrow.'
18: 9 when they *s* the smoke of her
19:10 *S* that you do not do that!
22: 4 They shall *s* His face, and His
22: 9 *S* that you do not do that.

SEED (113/103) SEEDS, SEEDTIME

Gen 1:11 grass, the herb that yields *s*,
1:11 whose *s* is in itself, on the
1:12 the herb that yields *s*
1:12 whose *s* is in itself according
1:29 you every herb that yields *s*
1:29 every tree whose fruit yields *s*;
3:15 And between your *s* and her
3:15 between your seed and her *S*;
4:25 God has appointed another *s*
21:12 for in Isaac your *s* shall be
21:13 because he is your *s*.
22:18 In your *s* all the nations of the
26: 4 and in your *s* all the nations
28:14 and in you and in your *s* all
47:19 servants of Pharaoh; give us *s*,
47:23 here is *s* for you, and you
47:24 as *s* for the field and for your
Ex 16:31 it was like white coriander *s*,
Lev 11:37 falls on any planting *s* which
11:38 'But if water is put on the *s*,
19:19 not sow your field with mixed *s*.
26:16 And you shall sow your *s* in
27:16 shall be according to the *s*
27:16 A homer of barley *s* shall be
27:30 whether of the *s* of the land
Num 6: 4 the grapevine, from *s* to skin.
11: 7 the manna was like coriander *s*,
24: 7 And his *s* shall be in many
Deut 11:10 where you sowed your *s* and
22: 9 with different kinds of *s*,
22: 9 lest the yield of the *s* which
28:38 You shall carry much *s* out to
2 Sam 7:12 I will set up your *s* after you,
1 Ki 18:32 enough to hold two seahs of *s*.
1 Chr 16:13 O *s* of Israel His servant, You
17:11 that I will set up your *s* after
Ezra 9: 2 so that the holy *s* is mixed
Ps 89: 4 Your *s* I will establish forever,
89:29 His *s* also I will make to
89:36 His *s* shall endure forever,
105: 6 O *s* of Abraham His servant,
126: 6 Bearing *s* for sowing, Shall
Eccl 11: 6 In the morning sow your *s*,
Isa 5:10 And a homer of *s* shall yield
6:13 So the holy *s* shall be its
17:11 morning you will make your *s*
30:23 will give the rain for your *s*
45:19 I did not say to the *s* of
53:10 for sin, He shall see His *s*,
55:10 That it may give *s* to the
Jer 2:21 a *s* of highest quality.
30:10 And your *s* from the land of
31:27 the house of Judah with the *s*
31:27 with the seed of man and the *s*
31:36 Then the *s* of Israel shall
31:37 I will also cast off all the *s*
35: 7 shall not build a house, sow *s*,
35: 9 we have vineyard, field, or *s*.
Ezek 17: 5 Then he took some of the *s* of
43:19 who are of the *s* of Zadok, who
Dan 2:43 they will mingle with the *s* of
Joel 1:17 The *s* shrivels under the clods,
Am 9:13 of grapes him who sows *s*;
Hag 2:19 'Is the *s* still in the barn?
Zech 8:12 For the *s* shall be prosperous,
Mt 13: 4 some *s* fell by the wayside;
13:19 This is he who received *s* by
13:20 But he who received the *s* on
13:22 Now he who received *s* among the
13:23 But he who received *s* on the
13:24 is like a man who sowed good *s*
13:27 did you not sow good *s* in your
13:31 of heaven is like a mustard *s*,
13:37 He who sows the good *s* is the
17:20 you have faith as a mustard *s*,
25:24 where you have not scattered *s*.
25:26 where I have not scattered *s*.
Mk 4: 4 that some *s* fell by the
4: 7 And some *s* fell among thorns;
4: 8 But other *s* fell on good ground
4:26 is as if a man should scatter *s*

4:27 and the *s* should sprout and
4:31 It is like a mustard *s* which,
Lk 1:55 To Abraham and to his *s*.
8: 5 "A sower went out to sow his *s*.
8:11 The *s* is the word of God.
13:19 "It is like a mustard *s*,
17: 6 you have faith as a mustard *s*,
Jn 7:42 the Christ comes from the *s* of
Acts 3:25 And in your *s* all the
13:23 "From this man's *s*,
Rom 1: 3 who was born of the *s* of David
4:13 was not to Abraham or to his *s*
4:16 might be sure to all the *s*,
9: 7 because they are the *s* of
9: 7 In Isaac your *s* shall be
9: 8 promise are counted as the *s*.
9:29 Sabaoth had left us a *s*,
11: 1 of the *s* of Abraham, of the
1 Cor 15:38 and to each *s* its own body.
2 Cor 9:10 Now may He who supplies *s* to the
9:10 supply and multiply the *s* you
11:22 Are they the *s* of Abraham?
Gal 3:16 Now to Abraham and his *S* were
3:16 as of one, "And to your *S*,
3:19 till the *S* should come to whom
3:29 then you are Abraham's *s*,
2 Tim 2: 8 of the *s* of David, was raised
Heb 2:16 but He does give aid to the *s*
11:11 received strength to conceive *s*,
11:18 In Isaac your *s* shall be
1 Pe 1:23 not of corruptible *s* but
1 Jn 3: 9 for His *s* remains in him; and

SEEDLINGS (1/1)

Isa 17:10 plants And set out foreign *s*;

SEEDS (5/5) SEED

2 Sam 17:28 beans, lentils and parched *s*,
Mt 13:32 is the least of all the *s*;
13:38 the good *s* are the sons of the
Mk 4:31 is smaller than all the *s* on
Gal 3:16 He does not say, "And to *s*,

SEEDTIME (1/1) SEED

Gen 8:22 *S* and harvest, Cold and heat,

SEEING (55/55)

Gen 15: 2 *s* I go childless, and the heir
Ex 4:11 makes the mute, the deaf, the *s*,
22:10 driven away, no one *s* it,
Num 35:23 it at him without *s* him,
Judg 13:18 *s* it is wonderful?"
19:23 so wickedly! *S* this man
21: 7 *s* we have sworn by the LORD
1 Sam 16: 1 *s* I have rejected him from
17:36 *s* he has defied the armies of
18:23 *s* I am a poor and lightly
24: 6 *s* he is the anointed of the
28:16 *s* the LORD has departed from
1 Ki 11:28 *s* that the young man was
Ps 50:17 *S* you hate instruction And
Prov 20:12 The hearing ear and the *s* eye,
Eccl 1: 8 eye is not satisfied with *s*,
Isa 6: 9 do not understand; Keep on *s*,
33:15 And shuts his eyes from *s*
42:20 *S* many things, but you do not
Jer 47: 7 *S* the LORD has given it a
Ezek 16:30 *s* you do all these things, the
22:28 *s* false visions, and divining
Mt 5: 1 And *s* the multitudes, He went up
13:13 because *s* they do not see, and
13:14 And *s* you will see and
15:31 lame walking, and the blind *s*;
21:19 And *s* a fig tree by the road, He
27: 3 *s* that He had been condemned,
Mk 4:12 *S* they may see and not
11:13 And *s* from afar a fig tree
Lk 8:10 *S* they may not see, And
22:56 *s* him as he sat by the fire,
23:40 *s* you are under the same
23:48 *s* what had been done, beat
Jn 1:38 and *s* them following, said to
6: 5 and *s* a great multitude coming
9: 7 and washed, and came back *s*.
21:21 *s* him, said to Jesus, "But
Acts 3: 3 *s* Peter and John about to go
4:14 And *s* the man who had been
7:24 And *s* one of them suffer wrong,
8: 6 hearing and *s* the miracles
8:13 *s* the miracles and signs which
9: 7 hearing a voice but *s* no one.
12: 9 but thought he was *s* a vision.
13:11 not *s* the sun for a time."
14: 9 *s* that he had faith to be
16:27 and *s* the prison doors open,
21:27 *s* him in the temple, stirred up
24: 2 *S* that through you we enjoy
28:26 And *s* you will see, and
2 Cor 11:18 *S* that many boast according to
Heb 4:14 *S* then that we have a great
11:27 for he endured as *s* Him who is
2 Pe 2: 8 soul from day to day by *s* and

SEEK (243/229) MAKE, SEEKING, SEEKS, SOUGHT

Lev 13:36 the priest need not *s* for
19:31 do not *s* after them, to be
Num 24: 1 to *s* to use sorcery, but he set
Deut 4:29 But from there you will *s* the
4:29 and you will find Him if you *s*
12: 5 But you shall *s* the place where
23: 6 You shall not *s* their peace nor
Judg 4:22 show you the man whom you *s*.
Ruth 3: 1 shall I not *s* security for you,
1 Sam 16:16 to *s* out a man who is a
23:15 had come out to *s* his life.
23:25 and his men went to *s* him,
24: 2 and went to *s* David and his men
25:26 your enemies and those who *s*
25:29 pursue you and *s* your life,
26: 2 to *s* David in the Wilderness of
26:20 of Israel has come out to *s* a
27: 1 to *s* me anymore in any part of
2 Sam 17: 3 except the man whom you *s*,
20:18 They shall surely *s* guidance at
20:19 You *s* to destroy a city and a
1 Ki 2:40 Achish at Gath to *s* his slaves.
11:22 that suddenly you *s* to go to
19:10 and they *s* to take my life."
19:14 and they *s* to take my life."
2 Ki 6:19 bring you to the man whom you *s*.
1 Chr 4:39 to *s* pasture for their flocks.
16:10 hearts of those rejoice who *s*
16:11 *S* the LORD and His strength
16:11 *S* His face evermore!
22:19 and your soul to *s* the LORD
28: 8 be careful to *s* out all the
28: 9 If you *s* Him, He will be found
2 Chr 7:14 and pray and *s* My face, and
11:16 set their heart to *s* the LORD
12:14 his heart to *s* the LORD.
14: 4 He commanded Judah to *s* the
15: 2 If you *s* Him, He will be found
15:12 a covenant to *s* the LORD
15:13 and whoever would not *s* the
16:12 disease he did not *s* the LORD,
17: 3 he did not *s* the Baals,
19: 3 prepared your heart to *s* God."
20: 3 and set himself to *s* the LORD,
20: 4 Judah they came to *s* the LORD.
30:19 prepares his heart to *s* God,
31:21 to *s* his God, he did it with
34: 3 he began to *s* the God of his
Ezra 4: 2 for we *s* your God as you do;
6:21 of the land in order to *s* the
7:10 his heart to *s* the Law of the
8:21 to *s* from Him the right way for
8:22 upon all those for good who *s*
9:12 and never *s* their peace or
Neh 2:10 that a man had come to *s* the
Job 3: 4 May God above not *s* it, Nor
5: 8 I would *s* God, And to God I
7:21 And You will *s* me diligently,
8: 5 If you would earnestly *s* God
10: 6 That You should *s* for my
20:10 His children will *s* the favor
Ps 4: 2 And *s* falsehood? Selah
9:10 have not forsaken those who *s*
10: 4 proud countenance does not *s*
10:15 *S* out his wickedness until
14: 2 who understand, who *s* God.
22:26 Those who *s* Him will praise
24: 6 the generation of those who *s*
24: 6 Who *s* Your face. Selah
27: 4 of the LORD, That will I *s*:
27: 8 *S* My face," My heart said to
27: 8 "Your face, LORD, I will *s*.
34:10 But those who *s* the LORD
34:14 *S* peace and pursue it.
35: 4 Who *s* after my life;
38:12 Those also who *s* my life lay
38:12 Those who *s* my hurt speak of
40:14 to mutual confusion Who *s* to
40:16 Let all those who *s* You rejoice
45:12 the people will *s* your favor.
53: 2 who understand, who *s* God.
63: 1 Early will I *s* You; My soul
63: 9 But those who *s* my life, to
69: 6 Let not those who *s* You be
69:32 And you who *s* God, your hearts
70: 2 confounded Who *s* my life;
70: 4 Let all those who *s* You rejoice
71:13 and dishonor Who *s* my hurt.
71:24 are brought to shame Who *s* my
83:16 That they may *s* Your name, O
104:21 And *s* their food from God.
105: 3 those rejoice who *s* the LORD!
105: 4 *S* the LORD and His strength
105: 4 *S* His face evermore!
109:10 Let them *s* their bread also
119: 2 Who *s* Him with the whole
119:45 For I *s* Your precepts.
119:155 For they do not *s* Your
119:176 *S* Your servant, For I do not
122: 9 I will *s* your good.
Prov 1:28 They will *s* me diligently, but
2: 4 If you *s* her as silver, And
7:15 Diligently to *s* your face,
8:17 And those who *s* me diligently
21: 6 fantasy of those who *s* death.
23:35 that I may *s* another drink?"
25:27 So to *s* one's own glory is
28: 5 But those who *s* the LORD
29:10 But the upright *s* his
29:26 Many *s* the ruler's favor, But
Eccl 1:13 And I set my heart to *s* and
7:25 To search and *s* out wisdom and
Song 3: 2 I will *s* the one I love."
6: 1 That we may *s* him with you?
Isa 1:17 *S* justice, Rebuke the
8:19 *S* those who are mediums and
8:19 should not a people *s* their
8:19 Should they *s* the dead on
9:13 Nor do they *s* the LORD of
10:31 inhabitants of Gebim *s* refuge.
11:10 For the Gentiles shall *s* Him,
26: 9 spirit within me I will *s* You
29:15 Woe to those who *s* deep to
31: 1 of Israel, Nor *s* the LORD!
41:12 You shall *s* them and not find
41:17 The poor and needy *s* water, but
45:19 *S* Me in vain'; I, the LORD,
51: 1 You who *s* the LORD: Look to
55: 6 *S* the LORD while He may be
58: 2 Yet they *s* Me daily, And
65: 1 by those who did not *s* Me.
Jer 2:24 All those who *s* her will not
2:33 beautify your way to *s* love?
4:30 They will *s* your life.
5: 1 And *s* in her open places If
11:21 the men of Anathoth who *s* your
19: 7 and by the hands of those who *s*
19: 9 their enemies and those who *s*
21: 7 into the hand of those who *s*
22:25 into the hand of those who *s*
26:19 LORD and *s* the LORD's favor?
29: 7 And *s* the peace of the city
29:13 And you will *s* Me and find Me,
30:14 They do not *s* you; For I have
34:20 into the hand of those who *s*
34:21 into the hand of those who *s*
38: 4 For this man does not *s* the
38:16 the hand of these men who *s*
44:30 into the hand of those who *s*
45: 5 And do you *s* great things for
45: 5 Do not *s* them; for behold, I
46:26 into the hand of those who *s*
49:37 And before those who *s* their
50: 4 And *s* the LORD their God.
Lam 1:11 They *s* bread; They have given
Ezek 7:25 They will *s* peace, but there
7:26 Then they will *s* a vision from
34:11 search for My sheep and *s* them
34:12 so will I *s* out My sheep and
34:16 I will *s* what was lost and bring
Dan 2:18 that they might *s* mercies from
Hos 2: 7 she will *s* them, but not find
3: 5 shall return and *s* the LORD
5: 6 They shall go to *s* the LORD,
5:15 Then they will *s* My face;
5:15 they will earnestly *s* Me.
7:10 Nor *s* Him for all this.
10:12 For it is time to *s* the
Am 5: 4 of Israel: "*S* Me and live;
5: 5 But do not *s* Bethel, Nor enter
5: 6 *S* the LORD and live, Lest He
5:14 *S* good and not evil, That you
Nah 3: 7 Where shall I *s* comforters
3:11 You also will *s* refuge from
Zeph 2: 3 *S* the LORD, all you meek of
2: 3 *S* righteousness, seek
2: 3 righteousness, *s* humility.
Zech 8:21 And *s* the LORD of hosts.
8:22 nations Shall come to *s* the
11:16 nor *s* the young, nor heal those
12: 9 day that I will *s* to destroy
Mal 2: 7 And people should *s* the law
3: 1 And the Lord, whom you *s*,
Mt 2:13 for Herod will *s* the young
6:32 all these things the Gentiles *s*.
6:33 But *s* first the kingdom of God
7: 7 *s*, and you will find;
18:12 the mountains to *s* the one
28: 5 for I know that you *s* Jesus who
Mk 8:12 Why does this generation *s* a
16: 6 You *s* Jesus of Nazareth, who
Lk 2:49 Why did you *s* Me? Did you not
11: 9 *s*, and you will find;
12:29 And do not *s* what you should eat
12:30 nations of the world *s* after,
12:31 But *s* the kingdom of God, and
13:24 will *s* to enter and will not be
19:10 the Son of Man has come to *s*
24: 5 Why do you *s* the living among
Jn 1:38 said to them, "What do you *s*?
4:27 no one said, "What do You *s*?
5:30 because I do not *s* My own will
5:44 and do not *s* the honor that
6:26 you *s* Me, not because you saw
7:19 Why do you *s* to kill Me?"
7:25 Is this not He whom they *s* to
7:34 You will *s* Me and not find Me,
7:36 You will *s* Me and not find Me,
8:21 and you will *s* Me, and will die
8:37 but you *s* to kill Me, because
8:40 But now you *s* to kill Me, a Man
8:50 And I do not *s* My own glory;
13:33 You will *s* Me; and as I said to
18: 8 if you *s* Me, let these go their
Acts 6: 3 *s* out from among you seven men
10:21 said, "Yes, I am he whom you *s*.
11:25 departed for Tarsus to *s* Saul.
15:17 mankind may *s* the LORD,
17:27 so that they should *s* the Lord,
Rom 2: 7 in doing good *s* for glory,
9:32 Because they did not *s* it
10:20 those who did not *s* Me;
11: 3 and they *s* my life"?
1 Cor 1:22 and Greeks *s* after wisdom;
7:27 Do not *s* to be loosed.
7:27 from a wife? Do not *s* a wife.

10:24 Let no one *s* his own, but each
13: 5 does not *s* its own, is not
14:12 of the church that you *s* to
2 Cor 12:14 for I do not *s* yours, but you.
13: 3 since you *s* a proof of Christ
Gal 1:10 Or do I *s* to please men?
2:17 while we *s* to be justified by
Phil 2:21 For all *s* their own, not the
4:17 Not that I *s* the gift, but I
4:17 but I *s* the fruit that abounds
Col 3: 1 *s* those things which are above,
1 Th 2: 6 Nor did we *s* glory from men,
Heb 11: 6 of those who diligently *s* Him.
11:14 declare plainly that they *s* a
13:14 but we *s* the one to come.
1 Pe 3:11 Let him *s* peace and
Rev 9: 6 In those days men will *s* death

SEEKING (38/38) SEEK

Gen 37:15 him, saying, "What are you *s*?
37:16 I am *s* my brothers. Please tell
Num 16:10 And are you *s* the priesthood
35:23 he was not his enemy or *s* his
Judg 14: 4 that He was *s* an occasion to
18: 1 the tribe of the Danites was *s*
2 Sam 3:17 In time past you were *s* for
Esth 10: 3 *s* the good of his people and
Ps 119:123 My eyes fail from *s* Your
Isa 16: 5 Judging and *s* justice and
Ezek 34: 6 and no one was *s* or searching
Dan 8:15 vision and was *s* the meaning,
Am 8:12 *s* the word of the LORD, But
Mt 12:43 *s* rest, and finds none.
12:46 *s* to speak with Him.
12:47 *s* to speak with You."
13:45 a merchant *s* beautiful pearls,
Mk 3:32 brothers are outside *s* You."
8:11 *s* from Him a sign from heaven,
Lk 2:45 to Jerusalem, *s* Him.
11:24 *s* rest; and finding none, he
11:54 and *s* to catch Him in something
13: 6 and he came *s* fruit on it and
13: 7 for three years I have come *s*
Jn 4:23 for the Father is *s* such to
6:24 to Capernaum, *s* Jesus.
7:20 Who is *s* to kill You?"
18: 4 said to them, "Whom are you *s*?
18: 7 them again, "Whom are you *s*?
20:15 are you weeping? Whom are you *s*?
Acts 10:19 three men are *s* you.
13: 8 *s* to turn the proconsul away
13:11 and he went around *s* someone to
21:31 Now as they were *s* to kill him,
27:30 And as the sailors were *s* to
Rom 10: 3 and *s* to establish their own
1 Cor 10:33 not *s* my own profit, but the
1 Pe 5: 8 *s* whom he may devour.

SEEKS (41/38) SEEK

Deut 22: 2 until your brother *s* it;
1 Sam 19: 2 My father Saul *s* to kill you.
20: 1 that he *s* my life?"
22:23 For he who *s* my life seeks your
22:23 For he who seeks my life *s* your
23:10 certainly heard that Saul *s* to
24: 9 Indeed David *s* your harm'?
2 Sam 16:11 who came from my own body *s* my
1 Ki 20: 7 see how this man *s* trouble,
2 Ki 5: 7 and see how he *s* a quarrel with
Ps 37:32 And *s* to slay him.
Prov 11:27 He who earnestly *s* good finds
11:27 will come to him who *s* evil.
14: 6 A scoffer *s* wisdom and does not
15:14 understanding *s* knowledge,
17: 9 covers a transgression *s* love,
17:11 An evil man *s* only rebellion;
17:19 exalts his gate *s* destruction.
18: 1 isolates himself *s* his own
18:15 ear of the wise *s* knowledge.
31:13 She *s* wool and flax, And
Eccl 7:28 Which my soul still *s* but I
Isa 40:20 He *s* for himself a skillful
Jer 5: 1 Who *s* the truth, And I will
30:17 No one *s* her." '
Lam 3:25 To the soul who *s* Him.
Ezek 34:12 As a shepherd *s* out his flock on
Mic 7: 3 The judge *s* a bribe, And the
Mal 2:15 He *s* godly offspring.
Mt 7: 8 and he who *s* finds, and to him
12:39 adulterous generation *s* after
16: 4 adulterous generation *s* after
Lk 11:10 and he who *s* finds, and to him
11:29 It *s* a sign, and no sign will
17:33 Whoever *s* to save his life will
Jn 7: 4 while he himself *s* to be known
7:18 He who speaks from himself *s* his
7:18 but He who *s* the glory of the
8:50 there is One who *s* and judges.
Rom 3:11 none who *s* after God.
11: 7 has not obtained what it *s*;

SEEM (12/12) SEEMED, SEEMS

Gen 27:12 and I shall *s* to be a deceiver
Deut 15:18 It shall not *s* hard to you when
1 Sam 18:23 Does it *s* to you a light thing
Neh 9:32 let all the trouble *s* small
Job 10: 3 Does it *s* good to You that
Ps 74: 5 They *s* like men who lift up
Isa 5:28 hooves will *s* like flint,
Nah 2: 4 They *s* like torches, They run
1 Cor 12:22 members of the body which *s* to
2 Cor 10: 9 lest I *s* to terrify you by
13: 7 though we may *s* disqualified.
Heb 4: 1 any of you *s* to have come

SEEMED (18/17)

Gen 19:14 But to his sons-in-law he *s* to
29:20 and they *s* only a few days to
2 Sam 3:19 in Hebron all that *s* good
1 Ki 1:40 so that the earth *s* to split
Eccl 9:13 and it *s* great to me:
Jer 18: 4 as it *s* good to the potter to
27: 5 given it to whom it *s* proper
Mt 11:26 for so it *s* good in Your sight.
Lk 1: 3 it *s* good to me also, having had
10:21 for so it *s* good in Your sight.
24:11 And their words *s* to them like
Acts 15:25 it *s* good to us, being assembled
15:28 For it *s* good to the Holy
15:34 it *s* good to Silas to remain
Gal 2: 6 But from those who *s* to be
2: 6 for those who *s* to be
2: 9 who *s* to be pillars, perceived
Heb 12:10 chastened us as *s* best

SEEMLY (KJV) See FITTING

SEEMS (36/34)

Lev 14:35 It *s* to me that there is some
Deut 23:16 where it *s* best to him; you
Josh 9:25 do with us as it *s* good and
24:15 And if it *s* evil to you to serve
Judg 10:15 Do to us whatever *s* best
1 Sam 1:23 Do what *s* best to you; wait
3:18 Let Him do what *s* good to
11:10 do with us whatever *s* good
14:36 Do whatever *s* good to you."
14:40 Do what *s* good to you."
24: 4 you may do to him as it *s* good
2 Sam 15:26 let Him do to me as *s* good to
18: 4 Whatever *s* best to you I will
19:37 and do for him what *s* good to
19:38 will do for him what *s* good
24:22 and offer up whatever *s* good
1 Ki 21: 2 if it *s* good to you, I will
1 Chr 13: 2 If it *s* good to you, and if it
Ezra 5:17 if it *s* good to the king, let
7:18 And whatever *s* good to you and
Esth 3:11 to do with them as *s* good to
8: 5 the thing *s* right to the king
Prov 14:12 There is a way that *s* right
16:25 There is a way that *s* right
18:17 plead his cause *s* right,
Jer 26:14 do with me as *s* good and proper
40: 4 If it *s* good to you to come
40: 4 But if it *s* wrong for you to
40: 4 wherever it *s* good and
40: 5 Or go wherever it *s* convenient
Lk 8:18 even what he *s* to have will be
Acts 17:18 He *s* to be a proclaimer of
25:27 For it *s* to me unreasonable to
1 Cor 3:18 If anyone among you *s* to be
11:16 But if anyone *s* to be
Heb 12:11 Now no chastening *s* to be joyful

SEEN (274/259)

Gen 7: 1 because I have *s* that you are
8: 5 tops of the mountains were *s*.
9:14 that the rainbow shall be *s* in
16:13 Have I also here *s* Him who sees
26:28 We have certainly *s* that the
31:12 for I have *s* all that Laban is
31:42 God has *s* my affliction and the
32:30 For I have *s* God face to face,
33:10 inasmuch as I have *s* your face
33:10 as though I had *s* the face
41:19 ugliness as I have never *s* in
44:28 and I have not *s* him since.
45:13 and of all that you have *s*;
46:30 since I have *s* your face,
Ex 3: 7 I have surely *s* the oppression
3: 9 and I have also *s* the
3:16 visited you and *s* what is
10: 6 your fathers' fathers have *s*,
13: 7 no leavened bread shall be *s*
13: 7 nor shall leaven be *s* among you
16: 8 This shall be *s* when the
19: 4 You have *s* what I did to the
20:22 You have *s* that I have talked
32: 9 I have *s* this people, and indeed
33:23 but My face shall not be *s*.
34: 3 and let no man be *s* throughout
Lev 5: 1 whether he has *s* or known of
13: 7 after he has been *s* by the
13: 7 he shall be *s* by the priest
Num 14:14 are *s* face to face and Your
14:22 all these men who have *s* My
23:21 Nor has He *s* wickedness in
27:13 And when you have *s* it, you also
Deut 1:28 moreover we have *s* the sons of
3:21 Your eyes have *s* all that the
4: 3 Your eyes have *s* what the LORD
4: 9 the things your eyes have *s*,
5:24 We have *s* this day that God
9:13 I have *s* this people, and indeed
10:21 things which your eyes have *s*.
11: 2 not known and who have not *s*
11: 7 but your eyes have *s* every great
16: 4 And no leaven shall be *s* among
21: 7 nor have our eyes *s* it.
29: 2 You have *s* all that the LORD
29: 3 trials which your eyes have *s*,
33: 9 I have not *s* them'; Nor did he
Josh 23: 3 You have *s* all that the LORD
Judg 2: 7 who had *s* all the great works
5: 8 Not a shield or spear was *s*
6:22 For I have *s* the Angel of
9:48 What you have *s* me do, make
13:22 because we have *s* God!"
14: 2 I have *s* a woman in Timnah of
18: 9 For we have *s* the land, and
19:30 such deed has been done or *s*
1 Sam 6:16 of the Philistines had *s* it,
16:18 I have *s* a son of Jesse the
17:25 Have you *s* this man who has come
23:22 and who has *s* him there.
24:10 this day your eyes have *s* that
2 Sam 17:17 for they dared not be *s* coming
18:21 tell the king what you have *s*.
22:11 And He was *s* upon the wings of
22:16 the channels of the sea were *s*,
1 Ki 6:18 there was no stone to be *s*.
8: 8 ends of the poles could be *s*
8: 8 but they could not be *s* from
10: 4 the queen of Sheba had *s* all
10:12 nor has the like been *s* to this
13:12 For his sons had *s* which way
20:13 Have you *s* all this great
2 Ki 20: 5 I have *s* your tears; surely I
20:15 What have they *s* in your
20:15 They have *s* all that is in my
23:24 the abominations that were *s*
1 Chr 29:17 and now with joy I have *s* Your
2 Chr 5: 9 the poles of the ark could be *s*
5: 9 but they could not be *s* from
9: 3 queen of Sheba had *s* the wisdom
9:11 none such as these *s* before
Ezra 3:12 old men who had *s* the first
Esth 9:26 what they had *s* concerning this
Job 4: 8 Even as I have *s*, Those who
5: 3 I have *s* the foolish taking
8:18 saying, 'I have not *s* you.'
10:18 perished and no eye had *s* me!
13: 1 my eye has *s* all this, My ear
15:17 What I have *s* I will declare,
20: 7 Those who have *s* him will say,
27:12 Surely all of you have *s* it;
28: 7 Nor has the falcon's eye *s* it.
31:19 If I have *s* anyone perish for
33:21 out which once were not *s*.
36:25 Everyone has *s* it; Man looks
38:17 Or have you *s* the doors of the
38:22 Or have you *s* the treasury of
Ps 10:14 But You have *s*, for You
18:15 the channels of the sea were *s*,
35:21 Our eyes have *s* it."
35:22 This You have *s*, O LORD;
37:25 Yet I have not *s* the righteous
37:35 I have *s* the wicked in great
48: 8 So we have *s* In the city of
54: 7 And my eye has *s* its desire
55: 9 For I have *s* violence and
68:24 They have *s* Your procession,
90:15 in which we have *s* evil.
92:11 My eye also has *s* my desire
98: 3 the earth have *s* the salvation
119:96 I have *s* the consummation of
Prov 25: 7 prince, Whom your eyes have *s*.
Eccl 1:14 I have *s* all the works that are
3:10 I have *s* the God-given task with
4: 3 Who has not *s* the evil work
5:13 a severe evil which I have *s*
5:18 Here is what I have *s*:
6: 1 There is an evil which I have *s*
6: 5 Though it has not *s* the sun or
6: 6 —but has not *s* goodness.
7:15 I have *s* everything in my days
8: 9 All this I have *s*, and applied
9:13 This wisdom I have also *s* under
10: 5 There is an evil I have *s*
10: 7 I have *s* servants on horses,
Song 3: 3 Have you *s* the one I love?"
Isa 6: 5 For my eyes have *s* the King,
9: 2 darkness Have *s* a great light;
16:12 When it is *s* that Moab is
38: 5 I have *s* your tears; surely I
39: 4 What have they *s* in your
39: 4 They have *s* all that is in my
44:16 I have *s* the fire."
47: 3 Yes, your shame will be *s*;
57:18 I have *s* his ways, and will
58: 3 they say, 'and You have not *s*?
60: 2 And His glory will be *s* upon
64: 4 Nor has the eye *s* any God
66: 8 Who has *s* such things?
66:19 heard My fame nor *s* My glory.
Jer 1:12 You have *s* well, for I am ready
3: 6 Have you *s* what backsliding
7:11 I, even I, have *s* it,"
12: 3 You have *s* me, And You have
13:27 I have *s* your adulteries And
23:13 And I have *s* folly in the
23:14 Also I have *s* a horrible thing
44: 2 You have *s* all the calamity that
46: 5 Why have I *s* them dismayed and
Lam 1: 8 her Because they have *s* her
1:10 For she has *s* the nations
2:14 Your prophets have *s* for you
2:16 found it, we have *s* it!"
3: 1 the man who has *s* affliction

3:59 You have *s* how I am wronged;
3:60 You have *s* all their vengeance,
Ezek 8:12 have you *s* what the elders of
8:15 Have you *s* this, O son of man?
8:17 Have you *s* this, O son of man?
10:22 as the faces which I had *s* by
11:24 And the vision that I had *s*
13: 3 own spirit and have *s* nothing!
13: 7 Have you not *s* a futile vision,
19:11 And was *s* in her height amid
47: 6 of man, have you *s* this?"
Dan 2:26 to me the dream which I have *s*,
4: 9 of my dream that I have *s*,
4:11 And it could be *s* to the ends
4:18 I, King Nebuchadnezzar, have *s*.
4:20 and which could be *s* by all
8: 6 which I had *s* standing beside
8:15 had *s* the vision and was
9:21 whom I had *s* in the vision at
Hos 6:10 I have *s* a horrible thing in
Zech 9: 8 For now I have *s* with My eyes.
9:14 Then the LORD will be *s* over
Mt 2: 2 For we have *s* His star in the
2: 9 the star which they had *s* in
4:16 sat in darkness have *s* a
6: 1 to be *s* by them. Otherwise you
6: 5 that they may be *s* by men.
9:33 It was never *s* like this in
23: 5 their works they do to be *s* by
Mk 9: 9 no one the things they had *s*,
16:11 He was alive and had been *s* by
16:14 not believe those who had *s* Him
Lk 1:22 they perceived that he had *s* a
2:17 Now when they had *s* Him, they
2:20 that they had heard and *s*,
2:26 he had *s* the Lord's Christ.
2:30 For my eyes have *s* Your
5:26 We have *s* strange things
7:22 John the things you have *s* and
8:36 They also who had *s* it told
9:36 any of the things they had *s*.
10:24 and have not *s* it, and to hear
11:44 are like graves which are not *s*,
19:37 all the mighty works they had *s*,
24:23 saying that they had also *s* a
24:37 and supposed they had *s* a
Jn 1:18 No one has *s* God at any time.
1:34 And I have *s* and testified that
3:11 know and testify what We have *s*,
3:21 that his deeds may be clearly *s*,
3:32 And what He has *s* and heard,
4:45 having *s* all the things He did
5:37 at any time, nor *s* His form.
6:14 when they had *s* the sign that
6:36 to you that you have *s* Me
6:46 Not that anyone has *s* the
6:46 He has *s* the Father.
8:38 I speak what I have *s* with My
8:38 and you do what you have *s* with
8:57 and have You *s* Abraham?"
9: 8 who previously had *s* that he
9:37 You have both *s* Him and it is He
11:45 and had *s* the things Jesus did,
14: 7 now on you know Him and have *s*
14: 9 He who has *s* Me has seen the
14: 9 He who has seen Me has *s* the
15:24 but now they have *s* and also
19:35 And he who has *s* has testified,
20:18 that she had *s* the Lord,
20:25 We have *s* the Lord." So he said
20:29 because you have *s* Me, you have
20:29 are those who have not *s* and
Acts 1: 3 being *s* by them during forty
4:20 the things which we have *s* and
7:34 I have surely *s* the
7:44 to the pattern that he had *s*,
9:12 And in a vision he has *s* a man
9:27 to them how he had *s* the Lord
10:17 what this vision which he had *s*
11:13 And he told us how he had *s* an
11:23 When he came and had *s* the grace
13:31 He was *s* for many days by those
16:10 Now after he had *s* the vision,
16:40 and when they had *s* the
21:29 had previously *s* Trophimus
22:15 of what you have *s* and heard.
26:16 of the things which you have *s*
Rom 1:20 attributes are clearly *s*,
8:24 but hope that is *s* is not hope;
1 Cor 2: 9 written: "Eye has not *s*,
9: 1 Have I not *s* Jesus Christ our
15: 5 and that He was *s* by Cephas,
15: 6 After that He was *s* by over five
15: 7 After that He was *s* by James,
15: 8 Then last of all He was *s* by me
2 Cor 4:18 look at the things which are *s*,
4:18 at the things which are not *s*.
4:18 For the things which are *s* are
4:18 but the things which are not *s*
Col 2: 1 as many as have not *s* my face
2:18 those things which he has not *s*,
1 Tim 3:16 *S* by angels, Preached among
6:16 whom no man has *s* or can see,
Heb 11: 1 the evidence of things not *s*.
11: 3 so that the things which are *s*
11: 7 warned of things not yet *s*,
11:13 but having *s* them afar off were
Jas 5:11 of Job and *s* the end intended
1 Pe 1: 8 whom having not *s* you love.
1 Jn 1: 1 which we have *s* with our eyes,
1: 2 was manifested, and we have *s*,
1: 3 that which we have *s* and heard
3: 6 Whoever sins has neither *s* Him
4:12 No one has *s* God at any time.
4:14 And we have *s* and testify that
4:20 love his brother whom he has *s*,
4:20 he love God whom he has not *s*?
3 Jn 11 who does evil has not *s* God.
Rev 1:19 the things which you have *s*,
11:19 the ark of His covenant was *s*

SEER (22/20)

1 Sam 9: 9 let us go to the *s*"; for he
9: 9 prophet was formerly called a *s*.
9:11 to them, "Is the *s* here?"
9:19 Saul and said, "I am the *s*.
2 Sam 15:27 the priest, "Are you not a *s*?
24:11 to the prophet Gad, David's *s*,
2 Ki 17:13 by all of His prophets, every *s*,
1 Chr 9:22 David and Samuel the *s* had
21: 9 LORD spoke to Gad, David's *s*,
25: 5 the sons of Heman the king's *s*
26:28 And all that Samuel the *s*,
29:29 in the book of Samuel the *s*,
29:29 and in the book of Gad the *s*,
2 Chr 9:29 in the visions of Iddo the *s*
12:15 and of Iddo the *s* concerning
16: 7 And at that time Hanani the *s*
16:10 Then Asa was angry with the *s*,
19: 2 Jehu the son of Hanani the *s*
29:25 of David, of Gad the king's *s*,
29:30 of David and of Asaph the *s*.
35:15 and Jeduthun the king's *s*.
Am 7:12 to Amos: "Go, you *s*!

SEER'S (1/1)

1 Sam 9:18 where is the *s* house?"

SEERS (4/4)

2 Chr 33:18 and the words of the *s* who
Isa 29:10 your heads, namely, the *s*.
30:10 Who say to the *s*,
Mic 3: 7 So the *s* shall be ashamed, And

SEES (55/53)

Gen 16:13 I also here seen Him who *s* me?
44:31 when he *s* that the lad is not
Ex 4:14 When he *s* you, he will be glad
12:23 and when He *s* the blood on the
Lev 13: 8 And if the priest *s* that the
13:20 when the priest *s* it, it indeed
20:17 and *s* her nakedness and she
20:17 and she *s* his nakedness,
Num 12: 8 And he *s* the form of the
24: 4 Who *s* the vision of the
24:16 Who *s* the vision of the
Deut 32:36 When He *s* that their power is
1 Sam 16: 7 LORD does not see as man *s*;
2 Ki 2:19 city is pleasant, as my lord *s*;
Job 7: 8 The eye of him who *s* me will
10: 4 Or do You see as man *s*?
11:11 He *s* wickedness also.
28:10 And his eye *s* every precious
28:24 And *s* under the whole
34:21 And He *s* all his steps.
42: 5 But now my eye *s* You.
Ps 33:13 He *s* all the sons of men.
37:13 For He *s* that his day is
49:10 For he *s* wise men die;
58:10 shall rejoice when he *s* the
97: 4 The earth *s* and trembles.
112: 8 Until he *s* his desire upon
Eccl 8:16 even though one *s* no sleep day
Isa 21: 6 Let him declare what he *s*.
28: 4 summer, Which an observer *s*;
29:15 They say, "Who *s* us?" and,
29:23 But when he *s* his children,
47:10 No one *s* me'; Your wisdom and
Lam 3:50 from heaven Looks down and *s*.
Ezek 12:27 The vision that he *s* is for
18:14 he begets a son Who *s* all the
33: 3 when he *s* the sword coming upon
33: 6 But if the watchman *s* the sword
39:15 when anyone *s* a man's bone,
Mt 6: 4 and your Father who *s* in secret
6: 6 and your Father who *s* in secret
6:18 and your Father who *s* in secret
Jn 5:19 but what He *s* the Father do;
6:40 that everyone who *s* the Son and
9:21 but by what means he now *s* we do
10:12 *s* the wolf coming and leaves
11: 9 because he *s* the light of this
12:45 And he who *s* Me sees Him who
12:45 And he who sees Me *s* Him who
14:17 because it neither *s* Him nor
Rom 8:24 one still hope for what he *s*?
1 Cor 8:10 For if anyone *s* you who have
2 Cor 12: 6 think of me above what he *s* me
1 Jn 3:17 and *s* his brother in need, and
5:16 If anyone *s* his brother sinning

SEGUB (3/3)

1 Ki 16:34 and with his youngest son *S* he
1 Chr 2:21 years old; and she bore him *S*.
2:22 *S* begot Jair, who had

SEIR (39/38)

Gen 14: 6 Horites in their mountain of *S*,
32: 3 his brother in the land of *S*,
33:14 until I come to my lord in *S*.
33:16 that day on his way to *S*.
36: 8 So Esau dwelt in Mount *S*.
36: 9 of the Edomites in Mount *S*.
36:20 These were the sons of *S* the
36:21 of the Horites, the sons of *S*,
36:30 their chiefs in the land of *S*.
Num 24:18 *S* also, his enemies, shall be
Deut 1: 2 from Horeb by way of Mount *S*
1:44 and drove you back from *S* to
2: 1 and we skirted Mount *S* for many
2: 4 of Esau, who live in *S*;
2: 5 because I have given Mount *S* to
2: 8 of Esau who dwell in *S*,
2:12 The Horites formerly dwelt in *S*,
2:22 of Esau, who dwelt in *S*,
2:29 of Esau who dwell in *S* and the
33: 2 And dawned on them from *S*;
Josh 11:17 Mount Halak and the ascent to *S*,
12: 7 Mount Halak and the ascent to *S*,
15:10 westward from Baalah to Mount *S*,
24: 4 Esau I gave the mountains of *S*
Judg 5: 4 when You went out from *S*,
1 Chr 1:38 The sons of *S* were Lotan,
4:42 sons of Simeon, went to Mount *S*,
2 Chr 20:10 of Ammon, Moab, and Mount *S*—
20:22 of Ammon, Moab, and Mount *S*,
20:23 the inhabitants of Mount *S* to
20:23 an end of the inhabitants of *S*,
25:11 ten thousand of the people of *S*.
25:14 the gods of the people of *S*,
Isa 21:11 He calls to me out of *S*,
Ezek 25: 8 Because Moab and *S* say, 'Look!
35: 2 set your face against Mount *S*
35: 3 GOD: "Behold, O Mount *S*,
35: 7 Thus I will make Mount *S* most
35:15 shall be desolate, O Mount *S*,

SEIRAH (1/1)

Judg 3:26 stone images and escaped to *S*.

SEIZE (27/27) SEIZED, SEIZES

Josh 8: 7 rise from the ambush and *s* the
Judg 7:24 and *s* from them the watering
1 Ki 18:40 '*S* the prophets of Baal!
Job 3: 6 may darkness *s* it; May it not
24: 2 They *s* flocks violently and
Ps 55:15 Let death *s* them; Let them go
109:11 Let the creditor *s* all that he
Isa 10: 6 To *s* the spoil, to take the
22:17 And will surely *s* you.
Jer 13:21 Will not pangs *s* you, Like a
20: 5 *s* them, and carry them to
36:26 to *s* Baruch the scribe and
Ezek 14: 5 that I may *s* the house of Israel
Dan 11:21 and *s* the kingdom by intrigue.
Mic 2: 2 Also houses, and *s* them.
Hab 1:10 earthen mounds and *s* it.
Zech 14:13 Everyone will *s* the hand of
Mt 21:38 let us kill him and *s* his
26:48 He is the One; *s* Him."
26:55 and you did not *s* Me.
Mk 14:44 *s* Him and lead Him away
14:49 and you did not *s* Me.
Lk 20:20 that they might *s* on His words,
22:53 you did not try to *s* Me.
Jn 10:39 they sought again to *s* Him,
11:57 that they might *s* Him.
Acts 12: 3 he proceeded further to *s* Peter

SEIZED (27/27) SEIZE

Gen 21:25 Abimelech's servants had *s*.
Judg 3:28 *s* the fords of the Jordan
7:24 gathered together and *s* the
12: 5 The Gileadites *s* the fords of
1 Sam 15:27 Saul *s* the edge of his robe,
1 Ki 18:40 So they *s* them; and Elijah
2 Ki 11:16 So they *s* her; and she went by
2 Chr 8: 3 went to Hamath Zobah and *s* it.
23:15 So they *s* her; and she went by
Job 20:19 He has violently *s* a house
Isa 33:14 Fearfulness has *s* the
Jer 26: 8 and all the people *s* him,
37:13 and he *s* Jeremiah the prophet,
37:14 So Irijah *s* Jeremiah and
49:24 And fear has *s* her.
51:41 praise of the whole earth is *s*!
Mic 4: 9 For pangs have *s* you like a
Mt 22: 6 And the rest *s* his servants,
Lk 8:29 For it had often *s* him, and he
8:37 for they were *s* with great
Acts 6:12 *s* him, and brought him to the
16:19 they *s* Paul and Silas and
19:29 having *s* Gaius and Aristarchus,
21:30 *s* Paul, and dragged him out of
23:27 This man was *s* by the Jews and
24: 6 and we *s* him, and wanted to
26:21 For these reasons the Jews *s* me

SEIZES (4/4) SEIZE

Deut 22:28 and he *s* her and lies with her,
25:11 and puts out her hand and *s* him
Mk 9:18 And wherever it *s* him, it throws
Lk 9:39 a spirit *s* him, and he suddenly

SELA (4/4)

Judg 1:36 the Ascent of Akrabbim, from *S*,
2 Ki 14: 7 and took *S* by war, and called

Isa 16: 1 From *S* to the wilderness, To
42:11 Let the inhabitants of *S* sing,

SELAH (74/74)

Ps 3: 2 help for him in God." *S*
3: 4 from His holy hill. *S*
3: 8 upon Your people. *S*
4: 2 And seek falsehood? *S*
4: 4 your bed, and be still. *S*
7: 5 my honor in the dust. *S*
9:16 own hands. Meditation. *S*
9:20 to be but men. *S*
20: 3 your burnt sacrifice. *S*
21: 2 the request of his lips. *S*
24: 6 Who seek Your face. *S*
24:10 He is the King of glory. *S*
32: 4 the drought of summer. *S*
32: 5 the iniquity of my sin. *S*
32: 7 songs of deliverance. *S*
39: 5 best state is but vapor. *S*
39:11 Surely every man is vapor. *S*
44: 8 praise Your name forever. *S*
46: 3 shake with its swelling. *S*
46: 7 God of Jacob is our refuge. *S*
46:11 God of Jacob is our refuge. *S*
47: 4 Jacob whom He loves. *S*
48: 8 will establish it forever. *S*
49:13 who approve their sayings. *S*
49:15 He shall receive me. *S*
50: 6 For God Himself is Judge. *S*
52: 3 speaking righteousness. *S*
52: 5 the land of the living. *S*
54: 3 set God before them. *S*
55: 7 remain in the wilderness. *S*
55:19 who abides from of old. *S* Because
57: 3 would swallow me up. *S* God
57: 6 themselves have fallen. *S*
59: 5 to any wicked transgressors. *S*
59:13 To the ends of the earth. *S*
60: 4 because of the truth. *S*
61: 4 the shelter of Your wings. *S*
62: 4 But they curse inwardly. *S*
62: 8 God is a refuge for us. *S*
66: 4 praises to Your name." *S*
66: 7 rebellious exalt themselves. *S*
66:15 offer bulls with goats. *S*
67: 1 His face to shine upon us. *S*
67: 4 govern the nations on earth. *S*
68: 7 through the wilderness, *S*
68:19 The God of our salvation! *S*
68:32 sing praises to the Lord, *S*
75: 3 I set up its pillars firmly. *S*
76: 3 shield and sword of battle. *S*
76: 9 the oppressed of the earth. *S*
77: 3 my spirit was overwhelmed. *S*
77: 9 shut up His tender mercies? *S*
77:15 sons of Jacob and Joseph. *S*
81: 7 the waters of Meribah. *S*
82: 2 partiality to the wicked? *S*
83: 8 helped the children of Lot. *S*
84: 4 will still be praising You. *S*
84: 8 Give ear, O God of Jacob! *S*
85: 2 have covered all their sin. *S*
87: 3 of you, O city of God! *S*
87: 6 'This one was born there." *S*
88: 7 with all Your waves. *S*
88:10 dead arise and praise You? *S*
89: 4 to all generations.'" *S*
89:37 witness in the sky." *S*
89:45 covered him with shame. *S*
89:48 the power of the grave? *S*
140: 3 is under their lips. *S*
140: 5 They have set traps for me. *S*
140: 8 Lest they be exalted. *S*
143: 6 like a thirsty land. *S*
Hab 3: 3 One from Mount Paran. *S* His
3: 9 sworn over Your arrows. *S* You
3:13 from foundation to neck. *S*

SELDOM (1/1)

Prov 25:17 *S* set foot in your neighbor's

SELECT (6/6)

Gen 41:33 let Pharaoh *s* a discerning and
Ex 18:21 Moreover you shall *s* from all
Num 14: 4 Let us *s* a leader and return to
Judg 20:15 numbered seven hundred *s* men.
20:16 were seven hundred *s* men
20:34 And ten thousand *s* men from all

SELECTED (1/1)

2 Chr 2: 2 Solomon *s* seventy thousand men

SELED (2/1)

1 Chr 2:30 The sons of Nadab were *S* and
2:30 *S* died without children.

SELEUCIA (1/1)

Acts 13: 4 Spirit, they went down to *S*,

SELF (2/2)

Ex 32:13 to whom You swore by Your own *s*,
Phm 1:19 that you owe me even your own *s*

SELF-CONDEMNED (1/1)

Titus 3:11 is warped and sinning, being *s*.

SELF-CONFIDENT (1/1)

Prov 14:16 But a fool rages and is *s*.

SELF-CONTROL (8/7)

Acts 24:25 reasoned about righteousness, *s*,
1 Cor 7: 5 you because of your lack of *s*.
7: 9 but if they cannot exercise *s*,
Gal 5:23 gentleness, *s*. Against such
1 Tim 2:15 love, and holiness, with *s*.
2 Tim 3: 3 slanderers, without *s*,
2 Pe 1: 6 to knowledge *s*, to
1: 6 to *s* perseverance, to

SELF-CONTROLLED (1/1)

Titus 1: 8 sober-minded, just, holy, *s*,

SELF-IMPOSED (1/1)

Col 2:23 of wisdom in *s* religion,

SELF-INDULGENCE (1/1)

Mt 23:25 are full of extortion and *s*.

SELF-SEEKING (3/3)

Rom 2: 8 but to those who are *s* and do
Jas 3:14 if you have bitter envy and *s*
3:16 For where envy and *s* exist,

SELF-SUFFICIENCY (1/1)

Job 20:22 In his *s* he will be in

SELF-WILL (1/1)

Gen 49: 6 And in their *s* they hamstrung

SELF-WILLED (2/2)

Titus 1: 7 as a steward of God, not *s*,
2 Pe 2:10 They are presumptuous, *s*.

SELFISH (4/4)

2 Cor 12:20 *s* ambitions, backbitings,
Gal 5:20 *s* ambitions, dissensions,
Phil 1:16 preach Christ from *s* ambition,
2: 3 be done through *s* ambition

SELFSAME (KJV) See (VERY) SAME, VERY (THING)

SELL (32/31) SELLER, SELLS, SOLD

Gen 25:31 *S* me your birthright as of this
37:27 Come and let us *s* him to the
47:22 therefore they did not *s* their
Ex 21: 8 He shall have no right to *s* her
21:35 then they shall *s* the live ox
Lev 25:14 And if you *s* anything to your
25:15 of years of crops he shall *s*
Deut 2:28 You shall *s* me food for money,
14:21 or you may *s* it to a foreigner;
21:14 but you certainly shall not *s*
Judg 4: 9 for the LORD will *s* Sisera
2 Ki 4: 7 *s* the oil and pay your debt;
Neh 5: 8 will you even *s* your brethren?
10:31 wares or any grain to *s* on the
Ps 44:12 You *s* Your people for next to
Prov 23:23 and do not *s* it, Also wisdom
Ezek 30:12 And *s* the land into the hand
48:14 And they shall not *s* or exchange
Joel 3: 8 I will *s* your sons and your
3: 8 And they will *s* them to the
Am 2: 6 Because they *s* the righteous
8: 5 That we may *s* grain?
8: 6 Even *s* the bad wheat?"
Zech 11: 5 those who *s* them say, 'Blessed
Mt 19:21 *s* what you have and give to the
25: 9 but go rather to those who *s*,
Mk 10:21 *s* whatever you have and give to
Lk 12:33 *S* what you have and give alms;
18:22 *S* all that you have and
22:36 let him *s* his garment and buy
Jas 4:13 spend a year there, buy and *s*,
Rev 13:17 and that no one may buy or *s*

SELLER (4/4) SELL

Isa 24: 2 with the buyer, so with the *s*;
Ezek 7:12 Nor the *s* mourn, For wrath
7:13 For the *s* shall not return to
Acts 16:14 She was a *s* of purple from the

SELLERS (1/1)

Neh 13:20 Now the merchants and *s* of all

SELLING (2/2)

Neh 13:15 the day on which they were *s*
Ps 44:12 And are not enriched by *s*

SELLS (12/12) SELL

Ex 21: 7 And if a man *s* his daughter to
21:16 He who kidnaps a man and *s* him,
22: 1 and slaughters it or *s* it, he
Lev 25:16 for he *s* to you according to
25:29 If a man *s* a house in a walled
25:39 and *s* himself to you, you shall
25:47 and *s* himself to the stranger
Deut 24: 7 and mistreats him or *s* him,
Prov 11:26 on the head of him who *s* it.
31:24 linen garments and *s* them,
Nah 3: 4 Who *s* nations through her
Mt 13:44 joy over it he goes and *s* all

SELVEDGE (2/2)

Ex 26: 4 edge of the curtain on the *s*
36:11 edge of the curtain on the *s*

SEM (KJV) See SHEM

SEMACHIAH (1/1)

1 Chr 26: 7 whose brothers Elihu and *S*

SEMEI (1/1)

Lk 3:26 of Mattathiah, the son of *S*,

SEMEN (5/5)

Lev 15:16 any man has an emission of *s*,
15:17 any leather on which there is *s*,
15:18 and there is an emission of *s*,
15:32 and for him who emits *s* and
22: 4 who has had an emission of *s*,

SENAAH (2/2)

Ezra 2:35 the people of *S*, three
Neh 7:38 the sons of *S*, three

SENATE (KJV) See ELDERS

SEND (231/222) SENDING, SENDS, SENT

Gen 18:16 went with them to *s* them
24: 7 He will *s* His angel before
24:40 will *s* His angel with you and
24:54 *S* me away to my master."
24:56 *s* me away so that I may go to
27:45 then I will *s* and bring you
30:25 *S* me away, that I may go to my
37:13 I will *s* you to them."
38:17 I will *s* a young goat from the
38:17 a pledge till you *s* it?"
42: 4 But Jacob did not *s* Joseph's
42:16 *S* one of you, and let him bring
43: 4 If you *s* our brother with us, we
43: 5 But if you will not *s* him, we
43: 8 *S* the lad with me, and we will
Ex 3:10 and I will *s* you to Pharaoh
4:13 please *s* by the hand of
4:13 of whomever else You may *s*.
7: 2 to Pharaoh to *s* the children
8:21 I will *s* swarms of flies on
9:14 for at this time I will *s* all My
9:19 Therefore *s* now and gather your
12:33 that they might *s* them out of
23:20 I *s* an Angel before you to keep
23:27 I will *s* My fear before you,
23:28 And I will *s* hornets before you,
33: 2 And I will *s* My Angel before
33:12 know whom You will *s* with me.
Lev 16:21 and shall *s* it away into the
26:22 I will also *s* wild beasts among
26:25 I will *s* pestilence among
26:36 I will *s* faintness into their
Num 13: 2 *S* men to spy out the land of
13: 2 of their fathers you shall *s* a
22:37 Did I not earnestly *s* to you,
31: 4 tribes of Israel you shall *s*
Deut 1:22 Let us *s* men before us, and let
7:20 the LORD your God will *s* the
11:15 And I will *s* grass in your
15:13 And when you *s* him away free
15:18 not seem hard to you when you *s*
19:12 the elders of his city shall *s*
28:20 The LORD will *s* on you
28:48 whom the LORD will *s* against
32:24 I will also *s* against them the
Josh 1:16 and wherever you *s* us we will
18: 4 and I will *s* them; they shall
1 Sam 5:11 *S* away the ark of the God of
6: 2 Tell us how we should *s* it to
6: 3 If you *s* away the ark of the God
6: 3 do not *s* it empty; but by all
6: 8 Then *s* it away, and let it go.
9:16 about this time I will *s* you a
9:26 that I may *s* you on your way."
11: 3 that we may *s* messengers to all
12:17 and He will *s* thunder and rain,
16:11 *S* and bring him. For we will not
16:19 *S* me your son David, who is
20:12 and I do not *s* to you and tell
20:13 report it to you and *s* you
20:21 and there I will *s* a lad,
20:31 *s* and bring him to me, for he
21: 2 the business on which I *s* you,
2 Sam 11: 6 '*S* me Uriah the Hittite."
14:29 to *s* him to the king, but he
14:32 so that I may *s* you to the
15:36 and by them you shall *s* me
17:16 *s* quickly and tell David,

1 Ki 8:36 and *s* rain on Your land which
8:44 wherever You *s* them, and when
18: 1 and I will *s* rain on the
18:19 *s* and gather all Israel to me
20: 6 but I will *s* my servants to you
20:34 I will *s* you away with this
2 Ki 2:16 You shall not *s* anyone."
2:17 ashamed, he said, "*S* them!"
4:22 Please *s* me one of the young men
5: 5 and I will *s* a letter to the
6:13 that I may *s* and get him."
7:13 so let us *s* them and see."
9:17 Get a horseman and *s* him to meet
15:37 the LORD began to *s* Rezin
17:27 *S* there one of the priests whom
19: 7 Surely I will *s* a spirit upon
1 Chr 13: 2 let us *s* out to our brethren
2 Chr 2: 7 Therefore *s* me at once a man
2: 8 Also *s* me cedar and cypress and
2:15 let him *s* to his servants.
6:27 and *s* rain on Your land which
6:34 wherever You *s* them, and when
7:13 or *s* pestilence among My
Ezra 5:17 and let the king *s* us his
Neh 2: 5 I ask that you *s* me to Judah,
2: 6 it pleased the king to *s* me;
8:10 and *s* portions to those for
8:12 to *s* portions and rejoice
Job 1: 4 and would *s* and invite their
1: 5 that Job would *s* and sanctify
14:20 countenance and *s* him away.
21:11 They *s* forth their little ones
38:35 Can you *s* out lightnings, that
Ps 20: 2 May He *s* you help from the
43: 3 *s* out Your light and Your
57: 3 He shall *s* from heaven and save
57: 3 Selah God shall *s* forth His
104:30 You *s* forth Your Spirit, they
110: 2 The LORD shall *s* the rod of
118:25 I pray, *s* now prosperity.
Prov 10:26 man to those who *s* him.
22:21 truth To those who *s* to you?
25:13 messenger to those who *s* him,
Isa 6: 8 saying: "Whom shall I *s*,
6: 8 Here am I! *S* me."
10: 6 I will *s* him against an ungodly
10:16 Will *s* leanness among his fat
16: 1 *S* the lamb to the ruler of the
19:20 and He will *s* them a Savior and
32:20 Who *s* out freely the feet of
37: 7 Surely I will *s* a spirit upon
42:19 deaf as My messenger whom I *s*?
43:14 For your sake I will *s* to
66:19 I will *s* to the nations:
Jer 1: 7 go to all to whom I *s* you,
2:10 *S* to Kedar and consider
8:17 I will *s* serpents among you,
9:16 And I will *s* a sword after them
9:17 And *s* for skillful wailing
14:15 in My name, whom I did not *s*,
16:16 I will *s* for many fishermen,"
16:16 and afterward I will *s* for many
23:32 Yet I did not *s* them or command
24:10 And I will *s* the sword, the
25: 9 I will *s* and take all the
25:15 to whom I *s* you, to drink it.
25:16 that I will *s* among them."
25:27 which I will *s* among you."
27: 3 and *s* them to the king of Edom,
29:17 I will *s* on them the sword, the
29:31 *S* to all those in captivity,
42: 6 our God to whom we *s* you,
43:10 I will *s* and bring
48:12 That I shall *s* him wine-workers
49:37 And I will *s* the sword after
51: 2 And I will *s* winnowers to
Lam 4:22 He will no longer *s* you into
Ezek 5:16 When I *s* against them the
5:16 which I will *s* to destroy you,
5:17 So I will *s* against you famine
7: 3 And I will *s* My anger against
14:13 *s* famine on it, and cut off man
14:19 Or if I *s* a pestilence into
14:21 I *s* My four severe judgments
28:23 For I will *s* pestilence upon
39: 6 And I will *s* fire on Magog and
Hos 8:14 But I will *s* fire upon his
Joel 2:19 I will *s* you grain and new wine
Am 1: 4 But I will *s* a fire into the
1: 7 But I will *s* a fire upon the
1:10 But I will *s* a fire upon the
1:12 But I will *s* a fire upon Teman,
2: 2 But I will *s* a fire upon Moab,
2: 5 But I will *s* a fire upon Judah,
5:27 Therefore I will *s* you into
8:11 That I will *s* a famine on the
Zech 5: 4 I will *s* out the curse," says
Mal 2: 2 I will *s* a curse upon you, And
3: 1 I *s* My messenger, And he will
4: 5 I will *s* you Elijah the prophet
Mt 9:38 the harvest to *s* out laborers
10:16 I *s* you out as sheep in the
11:10 I *s* My messenger before
13:41 The Son of Man will *s* out His
14:15 *S* the multitudes away, that
15:23 *S* her away, for she cries out
15:32 And I do not want to *s* them
21: 3 immediately he will *s* them."
23:34 I *s* you prophets, wise men, and
24:31 And He will *s* His angels with a
Mk 1: 2 I *s* My messenger before
3:14 Him and that He might *s* them
5:10 that He would not *s* them out
5:12 *S* us to the swine, that we may
6: 7 and began to *s* them out two by
6:36 *S* them away, that they may go
8: 3 And if I *s* them away hungry to
11: 3 and immediately he will *s* it
13:27 And then He will *s* His angels,
Lk 7:27 I *s* My messenger before
9:12 *S* the multitude away, that they
10: 2 the harvest to *s* out laborers
10: 3 I *s* you out as lambs among
11:49 I will *s* them prophets and
12:49 I came to *s* fire on the earth,
16:24 and *s* Lazarus that he may dip
16:27 that you would *s* him to my
20:13 I will *s* my beloved son.
24:49 I *s* the Promise of My Father
Jn 3:17 For God did not *s* His Son into
13:20 he who receives whomever I *s*
14:26 whom the Father will *s* in My
15:26 whom I shall *s* to you from the
16: 7 I will *s* Him to you.
20:21 has sent Me, I also *s* you."
Acts 3:20 and that He may *s* Jesus Christ,
7:34 I will *s* you to Egypt."
10: 5 Now *s* men to Joppa, and send for
10: 5 and *s* for Simon whose surname
10:32 *S* therefore to Joppa and call
11:13 *S* men to Joppa, and call for
11:29 determined to *s* relief to the
15:22 to *s* chosen men of their own
15:25 to *s* chosen men to you with our
22:21 for I will *s* you far from here
25:21 to be kept till I could *s* him
25:25 I decided to *s* him.
25:27 unreasonable to *s* a prisoner
26:17 to whom I now *s* you,
1 Cor 1:17 For Christ did not *s* me to
16: 3 by your letters I will *s* to
16: 6 that you may *s* me on my
16:11 But *s* him on his journey in
Phil 2:19 the Lord Jesus to *s* Timothy
2:23 Therefore I hope to *s* him at
2:25 it necessary to *s* to you
2 Th 2:11 this reason God will *s* them
Titus 3:12 When I *s* Artemas to you, or
3:13 *S* Zenas the lawyer and Apollos
Jas 3:11 Does a spring *s* forth fresh
3 Jn 6 If you *s* them forward on their
Rev 1:11 write in a book and *s* it to
11:10 and *s* gifts to one another,

SENDING (20/20) SEND

1 Sam 16: 1 I am *s* you to Jesse the
2 Sam 13:16 This evil of *s* me away
2 Ki 1: 6 that you are *s* to inquire of
2 Chr 36:15 rising up early and *s* them,
Esth 9:19 and for *s* presents to one
9:22 of *s* presents to one another
Ps 78:49 By *s* angels of destruction
Isa 27: 8 by *s* it away, You contended
Jer 7:25 rising up early and *s* them.
25: 4 rising early and *s* them, but
26: 5 rising up early and *s* them
29:19 rising up early and *s* them;
35:15 rising up early and *s* them,
44: 4 rising early and *s* them,
Ezek 2: 3 I am *s* you to the children of
2: 4 I am *s* you to them, and you
17:15 rebelled against him by *s* his
Rom 8: 3 God did by *s* His own Son in
Col 4: 8 I am *s* him to you for this very
Phm 1:12 I am *s* him back. You therefore

SENDS (18/18) SEND

Deut 24: 1 and *s* her out of his house,
24: 3 and *s* her out of his house, or
1 Ki 17:14 until the day the LORD *s* rain
2 Ki 5: 7 that this man *s* a man to me to
Job 5:10 And *s* waters on the fields.
12:15 If He *s* them out, they
37: 3 He *s* it forth under the whole
Ps 68:33 He *s* out His voice, a mighty
104:10 He *s* the springs into the
147:15 He *s* out His command to the
147:18 He *s* out His word and melts
Prov 26: 6 He who *s* a message by the hand
Song 1:12 My spikenard *s* forth its
Isa 18: 2 Which *s* ambassadors by sea,
Jer 42: 5 which the LORD your God *s* us
Mt 5:45 and *s* rain on the just and on
12:20 Till He *s* forth justice
Lk 14:32 he *s* a delegation and asks

SENEH (1/1)

1 Sam 14: 4 and the name of the other *S*.

SENIR (4/4) HERMON

Deut 3: 9 and the Amorites call it *S*),
1 Chr 5:23 to Baal Hermon, that is, to *S*,
Song 4: 8 From the top of *S* and Hermon,
Ezek 27: 5 planks of fir trees from *S*;

SENNACHERIB (13/13)

2 Ki 18:13 *S* king of Assyria came up
19:16 and hear the words of *S*,
19:20 you have prayed to Me against *S*
19:36 So *S* king of Assyria departed
2 Chr 32: 1 *S* king of Assyria came and
32: 2 And when Hezekiah saw that *S* had
32: 9 After this *S* king of Assyria
32:10 Thus says *S* king of Assyria: 'In
32:22 of Jerusalem from the hand of *S*
Isa 36: 1 year of King Hezekiah that *S*
37:17 and hear all the words of *S*,
37:21 you have prayed to Me against *S*
37:37 So *S* king of Assyria departed

SENSE (3/3)

Neh 8: 8 Law of God; and they gave the *s*,
Hos 7:11 is like a silly dove, without *s*—
Heb 11:19 received him in a figurative *s*.

SENSED (1/1)

Acts 27:27 about midnight the sailors *s*

SENSELESS (3/3)

Ps 49:10 the fool and the *s* person
92: 6 A *s* man does not know, Nor
94: 8 you *s* among the people;

SENSES (2/2)

2 Tim 2:26 that they may come to their *s*
Heb 5:14 by reason of use have their *s*

SENSIBLY (1/1)

Prov 26:16 seven men who can answer *s*.

SENSITIVE (1/1)

Deut 28:54 The *s* and very refined man among

SENSITIVITY (1/1)

Deut 28:56 of her delicateness and *s*,

SENSUAL (2/2)

Jas 3:15 from above, but is earthly, *s*,
Jude 19 These are *s* persons, who cause

SENT (688/665) SEND

Gen 3:23 therefore the LORD God *s* him
8: 7 Then he *s* out a raven, which
8: 8 He also *s* out from himself a
8:10 and again he *s* the dove out
8:12 days and *s* out the dove,
12:20 and they *s* him away, with his
19:13 and the LORD has *s* us to
19:29 and *s* Lot out of the midst of
20: 2 of Gerar *s* and took Sarah.
21:14 and *s* her away. Then she
24:59 So they *s* away Rebekah their
25: 6 he was still living he *s* them
26:27 since you hate me and have *s* me
26:29 to you but good and have *s* you
26:31 and Isaac *s* them away, and they
27:42 So she *s* and called Jacob her
28: 5 So Isaac *s* Jacob away, and he
28: 6 blessed Jacob and *s* him away
31: 4 So Jacob *s* and called Rachel and
31:27 for I might have *s* you away
31:42 surely now you would have *s* me
32: 3 Then Jacob *s* messengers before
32: 5 and I have *s* to tell my lord,
32:18 It is a present *s* to my lord
32:23 *s* them over the brook, and sent
32:23 and *s* over what he had.
37:14 So he *s* him out of the Valley
37:32 Then they *s* the tunic of many
38:20 And Judah *s* the young goat by
38:23 for I *s* this young goat and you
38:25 she *s* to her father-in-law,
41: 8 and he *s* and called for all the
41:14 Then Pharaoh *s* and called
44: 3 the men were *s* away, they and
45: 5 for God *s* me before you to
45: 7 And God *s* me before you to
45: 8 it was not you who *s* me
45:23 And he *s* to his father these
45:24 So he *s* his brothers away, and
45:27 the carts which Joseph had *s*
46: 5 the carts which Pharaoh had *s*
46:28 Then he *s* Judah before him to
50:16 So they *s* messengers to Joseph,
Ex 2: 5 she *s* her maid to get it.
3:12 sign to you that I have *s* you:
3:13 The God of your fathers has *s* me
3:14 I AM has *s* me to you.'"
3:15 of Jacob, has *s* me to you.
4:28 of the LORD who had *s* him,
5:22 Why is it You have *s* me?
7:16 God of the Hebrews has *s* me
9: 7 Then Pharaoh *s*, and indeed,
9:23 and the LORD *s* thunder and
9:27 And Pharaoh *s* and called for
15: 7 You *s* forth Your wrath;
18: 2 after he had *s* her back,
24: 5 Then he *s* young men of the
Num 13: 3 So Moses *s* them from the
13:16 names of the men whom Moses *s*
13:17 Then Moses *s* them to spy out
13:27 to the land where you *s* us.
14:36 Now the men whom Moses *s* to spy
16:12 And Moses *s* to call Dathan and

S

16:28 know that the LORD has *s* me
16:29 then the LORD has not *s* me.
20:14 Now Moses *s* messengers from
20:16 He heard our voice and *s* the
21: 6 So the LORD *s* fiery serpents
21:21 Then Israel *s* messengers to
21:32 Then Moses *s* to spy out Jazer;
22: 5 Then he *s* messengers to Balaam
22:10 has *s* to me, saying,
22:15 Then Balak again *s* princes,
22:40 and he *s* some to Balaam and to
24:12 to your messengers whom you *s*
31: 6 Then Moses *s* them to the war,
31: 6 he *s* them to the war with
32: 8 fathers did when I *s* them
Deut 2:26 And I *s* messengers from the
9:23 when the LORD *s* you from
34:11 and wonders which the LORD *s*
Josh 2: 1 Now Joshua the son of Nun *s* out
2: 3 So the king of Jericho *s* to
2:21 And she *s* them away, and they
6:17 hid the messengers that we *s*.
6:25 the messengers whom Joshua *s*
7: 2 Now Joshua *s* men from Jericho
7:22 So Joshua *s* messengers, and
8: 3 mighty men of valor and *s* them
8: 9 Joshua therefore *s* them out;
10: 3 king of Jerusalem *s* to Hoham
10: 6 And the men of Gibeon *s* to
11: 1 that he *s* to Jobab king of
14: 7 the servant of the LORD *s* me
14:11 on the day that Moses *s* me;
22: 6 blessed them and *s* them
22: 7 when Joshua *s* them away to
22:13 children of Israel *s* Phinehas
24: 5 Also I *s* Moses and Aaron, and I
24: 9 and *s* and called Balaam the son
24:12 I *s* the hornet before you which
Judg 1:23 So the house of Joseph *s* men to
3:15 children of Israel *s* tribute
3:18 he *s* away the people who had
4: 6 Then she *s* and called for Barak
5:15 so was Barak *S* into the
6: 8 that the LORD *s* a prophet to
6:14 Have I not *s* you?"
6:35 And he *s* messengers throughout
6:35 He also *s* messengers to Asher,
7: 8 And he *s* away all the rest
7:24 Then Gideon *s* messengers
9:23 God *s* a spirit of ill will
9:31 And he *s* messengers to Abimelech
11:12 Now Jephthah *s* messengers to
11:14 So Jephthah again *s* messengers
11:17 Then Israel *s* messengers to the
11:17 And in like manner they *s* to
11:19 Then Israel *s* messengers to
11:28 the words which Jephthah *s* him.
11:38 And he *s* her away for two
13: 8 let the Man of God whom You *s*
16:18 she *s* and called for the lords
18: 2 So the children of Dan *s* five
19:29 and *s* her throughout all the
20: 6 and *s* her throughout all the
20:12 Then the tribes of Israel *s* men
21:10 So the congregation *s* out there
21:13 the whole congregation *s* word
1 Sam 4: 4 So the people *s* to Shiloh, that
5: 8 Therefore they *s* and gathered to
5:10 Therefore they *s* the ark of God
5:11 So they *s* and gathered together
6:21 So they *s* messengers to the
10:25 And Samuel *s* all the people
11: 7 and *s* them throughout all the
12: 8 then the LORD *s* Moses and
12:11 And the LORD *s* Jerubbaal,
12:18 and the LORD *s* thunder and
13: 2 of the people he *s* away,
15: 1 The LORD *s* me to anoint you
15:18 Now the LORD *s* you on a
15:20 on which the LORD *s* me,
16:12 So he *s* and brought him in.
16:19 Therefore Saul *s* messengers to
16:20 and *s* them by his son David to
16:22 Then Saul *s* to Jesse, saying,
17:31 to Saul; and he *s* for him.
18: 5 went out wherever Saul *s* him,
19:11 Saul also *s* messengers to
19:14 So when Saul *s* messengers to
19:15 Then Saul *s* the messengers back
19:17 and *s* my enemy away, so that he
19:20 Then Saul *s* messengers to take
19:21 he *s* other messengers, and they
19:21 Then Saul *s* messengers again
20:22 for the LORD has *s* you away.
22:11 So the king *s* to call Ahimelech
25: 5 David *s* ten young men; and David
25:14 David *s* messengers from the
25:25 young men of my lord whom you *s*.
25:32 who *s* you this day to meet me!
25:39 And David *s* and proposed to
25:40 David *s* us to you, to ask you to
26: 4 David therefore *s* out spies, and
30:26 he *s* some of the spoil to the
31: 9 and *s* word throughout the land
2 Sam 2: 5 So David *s* messengers to the men
3:12 Then Abner *s* messengers on his
3:14 So David *s* messengers to
3:15 And Ishbosheth *s* and took her
3:21 So David *s* Abner away, and he
3:22 for he had *s* him away, and he
3:23 and he *s* him away, and he has
3:24 why is it that you *s* him
3:26 he *s* messengers after Abner,
5:11 king of Tyre *s* messengers
8:10 then Toi *s* Joram his son to King
9: 5 Then King David *s* and brought
10: 2 So David *s* by the hand of his
10: 3 because he has *s* comforters
10: 3 Has David not rather *s* his
10: 4 and *s* them away.
10: 5 he *s* to meet them, because the
10: 6 the people of Ammon *s* and hired
10: 7 he *s* Joab and all the army of
10:16 Then Hadadezer *s* and brought out
11: 1 that David *s* Joab and his
11: 3 So David *s* and inquired about
11: 4 Then David *s* messengers, and
11: 5 so she *s* and told David, and
11: 6 Then David *s* to Joab, saying,
11: 6 And Joab *s* Uriah to David.
11:14 a letter to Joab and *s* it
11:18 Then Joab *s* and told David all
11:22 all that Joab had *s* by him.
11:27 David *s* and brought her to his
12: 1 Then the LORD *s* Nathan to
12:25 and He *s* word by the hand of
12:27 And Joab *s* messengers to David,
13: 7 And David *s* home to Tamar,
14: 2 And Joab *s* to Tekoa and brought
14:29 Therefore Absalom *s* for Joab, to
14:29 And when he *s* again the second
14:32 I *s* to you, saying, 'Come here,
15:10 Then Absalom *s* spies throughout
15:12 Then Absalom *s* for Ahithophel
18: 2 Then David *s* out one third of
18:29 When Joab *s* the king's servant
19:11 So King David *s* to Zadok and
19:14 so that they *s* this word to
22:15 He *s* out arrows and scattered
22:17 He *s* from above, He took me, He
24:13 take back to Him who *s* me."
24:15 So the LORD *s* a plague upon
1 Ki 1:44 The king has *s* with him Zadok
1:53 So King Solomon *s* them to bring
2:25 So King Solomon *s* by the hand of
2:29 Then Solomon *s* Benaiah the
2:36 Then the king *s* and called for
2:42 Then the king *s* and called for
5: 1 Now Hiram king of Tyre *s* his
5: 2 Then Solomon *s* to Hiram, saying:
5: 8 Then Hiram *s* to Solomon, saying:
5: 8 the message which you *s* me,
5:14 And he *s* them to Lebanon, ten
7:13 Now King Solomon *s* and brought
8:66 On the eighth day he *s* the
9:14 Then Hiram *s* the king one
9:27 Then Hiram *s* his servants with
12: 3 that they *s* and called him.
12:18 Then King Rehoboam *s* Adoram,
12:20 they *s* for him and called him
14: 6 For I have been *s* to you
15:18 And King Asa *s* them to
15:19 I have *s* you a present of
15:20 and *s* the captains of his
18:10 my master has not *s* someone
18:20 So Ahab *s* for all the children
19: 2 Then Jezebel *s* a messenger to
20: 2 Then he *s* messengers into the
20: 5 Indeed I have *s* to you, saying,
20: 7 for he *s* to me for my wives, my
20: 9 All that you *s* for to your
20:10 Then Ben-Hadad *s* to him and
20:17 And Ben-Hadad *s* out a patrol,
20:34 treaty with him and *s* him away.
21: 8 and *s* the letters to the elders
21:11 did as Jezebel had *s* to them,
21:11 which she had *s* to them.
21:14 Then they *s* to Jezebel, saying,
2 Ki 1: 2 so he *s* messengers and said to
1: 6 return to the king who *s* you,
1: 9 Then the king *s* to him a
1:11 Then he *s* to him another captain
1:13 he *s* a third captain of fifty
1:16 Because you have *s* messengers to
2: 2 for the LORD has *s* me on to
2: 4 for the LORD has *s* me on to
2: 6 for the LORD has *s* me on to
2:17 Therefore they *s* fifty men,
3: 7 Then he went and *s* to
5: 6 that I have *s* Naaman my servant
5: 8 that he *s* to the king, saying,
5:10 And Elisha *s* a messenger to him,
5:22 My master has *s* me, saying,
6: 9 And the man of God *s* to the king
6:10 the king of Israel *s* someone
6:14 Therefore he *s* horses and
6:23 he *s* them away and they went to
6:32 And the king *s* a man ahead of
6:32 of a murderer has *s* someone
7:14 and the king *s* them in the
8: 9 king of Syria has *s* me to you,
9:19 Then he *s* out a second horseman
10: 1 And Jehu wrote and *s* letters to
10: 5 *s* to Jehu, saying, "We are
10: 7 heads in baskets and *s* them
10:21 Then Jehu *s* throughout all
11: 4 In the seventh year Jehoiada *s*
12:18 and *s* them to Hazael king of
14: 8 Then Amaziah *s* messengers to
14: 9 And Jehoash king of Israel *s* to
14: 9 thistle that was in Lebanon *s*
14:19 but they *s* after him to Lachish
16: 7 So Ahaz *s* messengers to
16: 8 and *s* it as a present to the
16:10 and King Ahaz *s* to Urijah the
16:11 to all that King Ahaz had *s*
17: 4 for he had *s* messengers to So,
17:13 and which I *s* to you by My
17:25 therefore the LORD *s* lions
17:26 therefore He has *s* lions among
18:14 Then Hezekiah king of Judah *s* to
18:17 Then the king of Assyria *s* the
18:27 Has my master *s* me to your
19: 2 Then he *s* Eliakim, who was over
19: 4 the king of Assyria has *s* to
19: 9 So he again *s* messengers to
19:16 which he has *s* to reproach the
19:20 the son of Amoz *s* to Hezekiah,
20:12 *s* letters and a present to
22: 3 that the king *s* Shaphan the
22:15 Tell the man who *s* you to Me,
22:18 who *s* you to inquire of the
23: 1 Now the king *s* them to gather
23:16 And he *s* and took the bones out
24: 2 And the LORD *s* against him
24: 2 He *s* them against Judah to
1 Chr 8: 8 after he had *s* away Hushim and
10: 9 and *s* word throughout the land
12:19 lords of the Philistines *s* him
14: 1 king of Tyre *s* messengers
18:10 he *s* Hadoram his son to King
19: 2 So David *s* messengers to
19: 3 because he has *s* comforters
19: 4 and *s* them away.
19: 5 and he *s* to meet them, because
19: 6 and the people of Ammon *s* a
19: 8 he *s* Joab and all the army of
19:16 they *s* messengers and brought
21:12 take back to Him who *s* me."
21:14 So the LORD *s* a plague upon
21:15 And God *s* an angel to Jerusalem
2 Chr 2: 3 Then Solomon *s* to Hiram king of
2: 3 and *s* him cedars to build
2:11 which he *s* to Solomon: Because
2:13 And now I have *s* a skillful man,
7:10 seventh month he *s* the people
8:18 And Hiram *s* him ships by the
10: 3 Then they *s* for him and called
10:18 Then King Rehoboam *s* Hadoram,
16: 2 and *s* to Ben-Hadad king of
16: 3 I have *s* you silver and gold;
16: 4 and *s* the captains of his
17: 7 his reign he *s* his leaders,
17: 8 And with them he *s* Levites:
24:19 Yet He *s* prophets to them, to
24:23 and *s* all their spoil to the
25:15 and He *s* him a prophet who said
25:17 of Judah asked advice and *s* to
25:18 And Joash king of Israel *s* to
25:18 thistle that was in Lebanon *s*
25:27 but they *s* after him to Lachish
28:16 At the same time King Ahaz *s* to
30: 1 And Hezekiah *s* to all Israel and
32: 9 king of Assyria *s* his servants
32:21 Then the LORD *s* an angel who
32:31 whom they *s* to him to inquire
34: 8 he *s* Shaphan the son of
34:23 Tell the man who *s* you to Me,
34:26 who *s* you to inquire of the
34:29 Then the king *s* and gathered
35:21 But he *s* messengers to him,
36:15 of their fathers *s* warnings
Ezra 4:11 copy of the letter that they *s*
4:14 therefore we have *s* and
4:17 The king *s* an answer: To Rehum
4:18 The letter which you *s* to us has
5: 6 of the letter that Tattenai *s*:
5: 7 They *s* a letter to him, in which
6:13 to what King Darius had *s*.
7:14 And whereas you are being *s* by
8:16 Then I *s* for Eliezer, Ariel,
Neh 2: 9 Now the king had *s* captains of
6: 2 that Sanballat and Geshem *s* to
6: 3 So I *s* messengers to them,
6: 4 But they *s* me this message four
6: 5 Then Sanballat *s* his servant to
6: 8 Then I *s* to him, saying, "No
6:12 that God had not *s* him at all,
6:17 nobles of Judah *s* many letters
6:19 Tobiah *s* letters to frighten
Esth 1:22 Then he *s* letters to all the
3:13 And the letters were *s* by
4: 4 Then she *s* garments to clothe
5:10 and he *s* and called for his
8:10 and *s* letters by couriers on
9:20 these things and *s* letters
9:30 And Mordecai *s* letters to all
Job 22: 9 You have *s* widows away empty,
Ps 18:14 He *s* out His arrows and
18:16 He *s* from above, He took me;
59: of David when Saul *s* men,
68: 9 *s* a plentiful rain, Whereby
77:17 The skies *s* out a sound;
78:25 He *s* them food to the full.
78:45 He *s* swarms of flies among
80:11 She *s* out her boughs to the
105:17 He *s* a man before
105:20 The king *s* and released him,
105:26 He *s* Moses His servant, And
105:28 He *s* darkness, and made it
106:15 But *s* leanness into their
107:20 He *s* His word and healed them,
111: 9 He has *s* redemption to His
135: 9 He *s* signs and wonders into the
Prov 9: 3 She has *s* out her maidens, She

17:11 messenger will be *s* against
Isa 9: 8 The LORD *s* a word against
20: 1 the king of Assyria *s* him,
36: 2 Then the king of Assyria *s* the
36:12 Has my master *s* me to your
37: 2 Then he *s* Eliakim, who was over
37: 4 the king of Assyria has *s* to
37: 9 he *s* messengers to Hezekiah,
37:17 which he has *s* to reproach the
37:21 the son of Amoz *s* to Hezekiah,
39: 1 *s* letters and a present to
48:16 GOD and His Spirit Have *s* Me.
55:11 in the thing for which I *s*
57: 9 You *s* your messengers far off,
61: 1 He has *s* Me to heal the
Jer 7:25 I have even *s* to you all My
14: 3 Their nobles have *s* their lads
14:14 I have not *s* them, commanded
19:14 where the LORD had *s* him to
21: 1 when King Zedekiah *s* to him
23:21 I have not *s* these prophets,
23:38 and I have *s* to you, saying,
24: 5 whom I have *s* out of this place
25: 4 And the LORD has *s* to you all
25:17 to whom the LORD had *s* me:
26: 5 servants the prophets whom I *s*
26:12 The LORD *s* me to prophesy
26:15 for truly the LORD has *s* me to
26:22 Then Jehoiakim the king *s* men to
27:15 for I have not *s* them," says
28: 9 one whom the LORD has truly *s*.
28:15 the LORD has not *s* you, but
29: 1 Jeremiah the prophet *s* from
29: 3 The letter was *s* by the hand
29: 3 whom Zedekiah king of Judah *s*
29: 9 I have not *s* them, says the
29:19 which I *s* to them by My
29:20 whom I have *s* from Jerusalem to
29:25 You have *s* letters in your name
29:28 For he has *s* to us in Babylon,
29:31 and I have not *s* him, and he
35:15 I have also *s* to you all My
36:14 all the princes *s* Jehudi
36:21 So the king *s* Jehudi to bring
37: 3 And Zedekiah the king *s* Jehucal
37: 7 who *s* you to Me to inquire of
37:17 then Zedekiah the king *s* and
38:14 Then Zedekiah the king *s* and
39:13 the guard *s* Nebushasban,
39:14 then they *s* someone to take
40:14 of the Ammonites has *s* Ishmael
42: 9 to whom you *s* me to present
42:20 in your hearts when you *s* me
42:21 or anything which He has *s* you
43: 1 the LORD their God had *s* him
43: 2 LORD our God has not *s* you
44: 4 However I have *s* to you all My
49:14 And an ambassador has been *s*
Lam 1:13 From above He has *s* fire into my
Ezek 3: 5 For you are not *s* to a people
3: 6 had I *s* you to them, they would
13: 6 But the LORD has not *s* them;
20:28 There they also *s* up their
23:16 And *s* messengers to them
23:40 Furthermore you *s* for men to
23:40 to whom a messenger was *s*;
31: 4 And *s* out rivulets to all the
31: 5 As it *s* them out.
39:28 who *s* them into captivity among
Dan 3: 2 And King Nebuchadnezzar *s* word
3:28 who *s* His Angel and delivered
5:24 the fingers of the hand were *s*
6:22 My God *s* His angel and shut the
10:11 for I have now been *s* to you."
Hos 5:13 Assyria And *s* to King Jareb;
Joel 2:25 My great army which I *s* among
Am 4:10 I *s* among you a plague after the
7:10 priest of Bethel *s* to Jeroboam
Ob 1 And a messenger has been *s*
Jon 1: 4 But the LORD *s* out a great
Mic 6: 4 And I *s* before you Moses,
Hag 1:12 LORD their God had *s* him;
Zech 1:10 ones whom the LORD has *s* to
2: 8 He *s* Me after glory, to the
2: 9 the LORD of hosts has *s* Me.
2:11 the LORD of hosts has *s* Me
4: 9 the LORD of hosts has *s* Me
6:15 the LORD of hosts has *s* Me
7: 2 when the people *s* Sherezer,
7:12 which the LORD of hosts had *s*
Mal 2: 4 shall know that I have *s* this
Mt 2: 8 And he *s* them to Bethlehem and
2:16 and he *s* forth and put to death
10: 5 These twelve Jesus *s* out and
10:40 receives Him who *s* Me.
11: 2 he *s* two of his disciples
13:36 Then Jesus *s* the multitude away
14:10 So he *s* and had John beheaded in
14:22 while He *s* the multitudes away.
14:23 And when He had *s* the multitudes
14:35 they *s* out into all that
15:24 I was not *s* except to the lost
15:39 And He *s* away the multitude, got
20: 2 he *s* them into his vineyard.
21: 1 then Jesus *s* two disciples,
21:34 he *s* his servants to the
21:36 Again he *s* other servants, more
21:37 Then last of all he *s* his son to
22: 3 and *s* out his servants to call
22: 4 he *s* out other servants,
22: 7 And he *s* out his armies,
22:16 And they *s* to Him their
23:37 and stones those who are *s* to
27:19 his wife *s* to him, saying,
Mk 1:43 warned him and *s* him away
3:31 and standing outside they *s* to
6:17 For Herod himself had *s* and laid
6:27 Immediately the king *s* an
6:45 while He *s* the multitude away.
6:46 And when He had *s* them away, He
8: 9 And He *s* them away,
8:26 Then He *s* him away to his house,
9:37 not Me but Him who *s* Me."
11: 1 He *s* two of His disciples;
12: 2 Now at vintage-time he *s* a
12: 3 him and beat him and *s* him
12: 4 Again he *s* them another servant,
12: 4 and *s* him away shamefully
12: 5 And again he *s* another, and him
12: 6 he also *s* him to them last,
12:13 Then they *s* to Him some of the
14:13 And He *s* out two of His
Lk 1:19 and was *s* to speak to you and
1:26 month the angel Gabriel was *s*
1:53 And the rich He has *s* away
4:18 He has *s* Me to heal the
4:26 to none of them was Elijah *s*
4:43 for this purpose I have been *s*.
7: 3 he *s* elders of the Jews to Him,
7: 6 the centurion *s* friends to Him,
7:10 And those who were *s*,
7:19 *s* them to Jesus, saying, "Are
7:20 John the Baptist has *s* us to
8:38 But Jesus *s* him away, saying,
9: 2 He *s* them to preach the kingdom
9:48 Me receives Him who *s* Me.
9:52 and *s* messengers before His
10: 1 and *s* them two by two before
10:16 Me rejects Him who *s* Me."
13:34 and stones those who are *s* to
14:17 and *s* his servant at supper time
15:15 and he *s* him into his fields to
19:14 and *s* a delegation after him,
19:29 that He *s* two of His
19:32 So those who were *s* went their
20:10 Now at vintage-time he *s* a
20:10 beat him and *s* him away
20:11 'Again he *s* another servant;
20:11 and *s* him away empty-handed.
20:12 And again he *s* a third; and they
20:20 and *s* spies who pretended to be
22: 8 And He *s* Peter and John, saying,
22:35 When I *s* you without money bag,
23: 7 he *s* Him to Herod, who was also
23:11 and *s* Him back to Pilate.
23:15 for I *s* you back to him;
Jn 1: 6 There was a man *s* from God,
1: 8 but was *s* to bear witness of
1:19 when the Jews *s* priests and
1:22 an answer to those who *s* us?
1:24 Now those who were *s* were from
1:33 but He who *s* me to baptize with
3:28 I have been *s* before Him.'
3:34 For He whom God has *s* speaks the
4:34 do the will of Him who *s* Me,
4:38 I *s* you to reap that for which
5:23 not honor the Father who *s* Him.
5:24 and believes in Him who *s* Me
5:30 will of the Father who *s* Me.
5:33 You have *s* to John, and he has
5:36 that the Father has *s* Me.
5:37 who *s* Me, has testified of Me.
5:38 in you, because whom He *s*,
6:29 you believe in Him whom He *s*.
6:38 but the will of Him who *s* Me.
6:39 will of the Father who *s* Me,
6:40 is the will of Him who *s* Me,
6:44 unless the Father who *s* Me
6:57 As the living Father *s* Me, and I
7:16 is not Mine, but His who *s* Me.
7:18 the glory of the One who *s* Him
7:28 but He who *s* Me is true, whom
7:29 am from Him, and He *s* Me."
7:32 chief priests *s* officers
7:33 and then I go to Him who *s* Me.
8:16 I am with the Father who *s* Me.
8:18 and the Father who *s* Me bears
8:26 but He who *s* Me is true; and I
8:29 'And He who *s* Me is with Me.
8:42 come of Myself, but He *s* Me.
9: 4 work the works of Him who *s* Me
9: 7 (which is translated, *S*).
10:36 Father sanctified and *s* into
11: 3 Therefore the sisters *s* to Him,
11:42 they may believe that You *s* Me.
12:44 not in Me but in Him who *s* Me.
12:45 sees Me sees Him who *s* Me.
12:49 but the Father who *s* Me gave Me
13:16 nor is he who is *s* greater than
13:16 greater than he who *s* him.
13:20 Me receives Him who *s* Me."
14:24 Mine but the Father's who *s* Me.
15:21 they do not know Him who *s* Me.
16: 5 now I go away to Him who *s* Me,
17: 3 Jesus Christ whom You have *s*.
17: 8 have believed that You *s* Me.
17:18 As You *s* Me into the world, I
17:18 I also have *s* them into the
17:21 may believe that You *s* Me.
17:23 may know that You have *s* Me,
17:25 these have known that You *s* Me.
18:24 Then Annas *s* Him bound to
20:21 As the Father has *s* Me,
Acts 3:26 *s* Him to bless you, in turning
5:21 and *s* to the prison to have
7:12 he *s* out our fathers first.
7:14 Then Joseph *s* and called his
7:35 is the one God *s* to be a
8:14 they *s* Peter and John to them,
9:17 has *s* me that you may receive
9:30 him down to Caesarea and *s* him
9:38 they *s* two men to him,
10: 8 he *s* them to Joppa.
10:17 the men who had been *s* from
10:20 for I have *s* them."
10:21 down to the men who had been *s*
10:29 objection as soon as I was *s*
10:29 for what reason have you *s* for
10:33 So I *s* to you immediately, and
10:36 The word which God *s* to the
11:11 having been *s* to me from
11:22 and they *s* out Barnabas to go
11:30 and *s* it to the elders by the
12:11 that the Lord has *s* His angel,
13: 3 they *s* them away.
13: 4 being *s* out by the Holy Spirit,
13:15 of the synagogue *s* to them,
13:26 of this salvation has been *s*.
15: 3 being *s* on their way by the
15:27 We have therefore *s* Judas and
15:30 So when they were *s* off, they
15:33 they were *s* back with greetings
16:35 the magistrates *s* the officers,
16:36 The magistrates have *s* to let
17:10 brethren immediately *s* Paul
17:14 immediately the brethren *s* Paul
19:22 So he *s* into Macedonia two of
19:31 *s* to him pleading that he would
20:17 From Miletus he *s* to Ephesus
23:30 I *s* him immediately to you, and
24:24 he *s* for Paul and heard him
24:26 Therefore he *s* for him more
28:28 salvation of God has been *s* to
Rom 10:15 they preach unless they are *s*?
1 Cor 4:17 For this reason I have *s* Timothy
2 Cor 8:18 And we have *s* with him the
8:22 And we have *s* with them our
9: 3 Yet I have *s* the brethren, lest
12:17 of you by any of those whom I *s*
12:18 and *s* our brother with him.
Gal 4: 4 God *s* forth His Son, born of a
4: 6 God has *s* forth the Spirit of
Eph 6:22 whom I have *s* to you for this
Phil 2:28 Therefore I *s* him the more
4:16 even in Thessalonica you *s* aid
4:18 from Epaphroditus the things *s*
1 Th 3: 2 and *s* Timothy, our brother and
3: 5 I *s* to know your faith, lest by
2 Tim 4:12 And Tychicus I have *s* to
Heb 1:14 ministering spirits *s* forth
Jas 2:25 the messengers and *s* them out
1 Pe 1:12 *s* from heaven—things which
2:14 as to those who are *s* by him
1 Jn 4: 9 that God has *s* His only
4:10 but that He loved us and *s* His
4:14 the Father has *s* the Son
Rev 1: 1 And He *s* and signified it by
5: 6 the seven Spirits of God *s* out
22: 6 God of the holy prophets *s* His
22:16 have *s* My angel to testify to

SENTENCE (8/7)

Deut 17: 9 shall pronounce upon you the *s*
17:10 shall do according to the *s*
17:11 According to the *s* of the law in
17:11 hand or to the left from the *s*
Eccl 8:11 Because the *s* against an evil
Dan 4:17 And the *s* by the word of the
Lk 23:24 So Pilate gave *s* that it should
2 Cor 1: 9 we had the *s* of death in

SENTENCES (KJV) See RIDDLES, SCHEMES

SENUAH (1/1)

Neh 11: 9 and Judah the son of *S* was

SEORIM (1/1)

1 Chr 24: 8 third to Harim, the fourth to *S*,

SEPARATE (25/25) SEPARATED, SEPARATES, SEPARATION

Gen 13: 9 Please *s* from me. If you take
49:26 of the head of him who was *s*
Ex 33:16 So we shall be *s*, Your people
Lev 15:31 Thus you shall *s* the children
22: 2 that they *s* themselves from the
Num 6: 2 to *s* himself to the LORD,
6: 3 he shall *s* himself from wine and
8:14 Thus you shall *s* the Levites
16:21 *S* yourselves from among this
Deut 19: 2 you shall *s* three cities for
19: 7 You shall *s* three cities for
29:21 And the LORD would *s* him from
33:16 of the head of him who was *s*
Josh 16: 9 The *s* cities for the children of
Ezra 10:11 *s* yourselves from the peoples
Ezek 42:20 to *s* the holy areas from the
Mt 13:49 *s* the wicked from among the
19: 6 joined together, let not man *s*.
25:32 and He will *s* them one from
Mk 10: 9 joined together, let not man *s*.

S

Acts 13: 2 Now *s* to Me Barnabas and Saul
Rom 8:35 Who shall *s* us from the love of
8:39 shall be able to *s* us from the
2 Cor 6:17 from among them And be *s*,
Heb 7:26 *s* from sinners, and has become

SEPARATED (33/33) SEPARATE

Gen 10: 5 of the Gentiles were *s* into
13:11 And they *s* from each other.
13:14 after Lot had *s* from him:
25:23 Two peoples shall be *s* from
30:40 Then Jacob *s* the lambs, and made
Lev 20:24 who has *s* you from the peoples.
20:25 which I have *s* from you as
20:26 and have *s* you from the
Num 6: 5 are fulfilled for which he *s*
16: 9 the God of Israel has *s* you
31:42 which Moses *s* from the men who
Deut 10: 8 At that time the LORD *s* the
32: 8 When He *s* the sons of Adam,
Judg 4:11 had *s* himself from the Kenites
1 Ki 8:53 For You *s* them from among all
2 Ki 2:11 and *s* the two of them;
1 Chr 23: 6 Also David *s* them into divisions
25: 1 and the captains of the army *s*
Ezra 6:21 with all who had *s* themselves
8:24 And I *s* twelve of the leaders
9: 1 Levites have not *s* themselves
10: 8 and he himself would be *s* from
Neh 4:19 and we are *s* far from one
9: 2 those of Israelite lineage *s*
10:28 those who had *s* themselves
13: 3 that they *s* all the mixed
Prov 19: 4 But the poor is *s* from his
Isa 56: 3 The LORD has utterly *s* me from
59: 2 But your iniquities have *s* you
Hos 9:10 And *s* themselves to that
Rom 1: 1 *s* to the gospel of God
Gal 1:15 who *s* me from my mother's womb
2:12 he withdrew and *s* himself,

SEPARATES (4/4) SEPARATE

Num 6: 6 All the days that he *s* himself
Prov 16:28 And a whisperer *s* the best of
17: 9 repeats a matter *s* friends.
Ezek 14: 7 who *s* himself from Me and sets

SEPARATING (7/7)

Ezek 41:12 that faced the *s* courtyard
41:13 and the *s* courtyard with the
41:14 including the *s* courtyard, was
41:15 facing the *s* courtyard, with
42: 1 opposite the *s* courtyard,
42:10 opposite the *s* courtyard and
42:13 opposite the *s* courtyard,

SEPARATION (10/8) SEPARATE

Num 6: 4 All the days of his *s* he shall
6: 5 the days of the vow of his *s*
6: 7 because his *s* to God is on his
6: 8 All the days of his *s* he shall
6:12 to the LORD the days of his *s*,
6:12 because his *s* was defiled.
6:13 When the days of his *s* are
6:21 LORD the offering for his *s*,
6:21 according to the law of his *s*.
Eph 2:14 down the middle wall of *s*,

SEPHAR (1/1)

Gen 10:30 from Mesha as you go toward *S*,

SEPHARAD (1/1)

Ob 20 of Jerusalem who are in *S*

SEPHARVAIM (6/6)

2 Ki 17:24 Cuthah, Ava, Hamath, and from *S*,
17:31 and Anammelech, the gods of *S*.
18:34 Where are the gods of *S* and
19:13 and the king of the city of *S*,
Isa 36:19 Where are the gods of *S*?
37:13 and the king of the city of *S*,

SEPHARVITES (1/1)

2 Ki 17:31 and the *S* burned their children

SEPULCHER (2/1)

Isa 22:16 That you have hewn a *s* here,
22:16 As he who hews himself a *s* on

SEPULCHRES (KJV) See (BURIAL) PLACES, TOMBS

SERAH (5/5)

Gen 46:17 Ishuah, Isui, Beriah, and *S*,
Num 26:46 of the daughter of Asher was *S*.
1 Chr 7:30 Beriah, and their sister *S*.

SERAIAH (20/18)

2 Sam 8:17 *S* was the scribe;
2 Ki 25:18 the captain of the guard took *S*
25:23 *S* the son of Tanhumeth the
1 Chr 4:13 of Kenaz were Othniel and *S*.
4:14 *S* begot Joab the father of Ge
4:35 son of Joshibiah, the son of *S*,
6:14 Azariah begot *S*, and Seraiah
6:14 and *S* begot Jehozadak.
Ezra 2: 2 were Jeshua, Nehemiah, *S*,
7: 1 of Persia, Ezra the son of *S*,
Neh 10: 2 *S*, Azariah, Jeremiah,
11:11 *S* the son of Hilkiah, the son of
12: 1 son of Shealtiel, and Jeshua: *S*,
12:12 fathers' houses were: of *S*,
Jer 36:26 *S* the son of Azriel, and
40: 8 *S* the son of Tanhumeth, the
51:59 the prophet commanded *S* the
51:59 And *S* was the quartermaster.
51:61 And Jeremiah said to *S*,
52:24 captain of the guard took *S*

SERAPHIM (2/2) SERAPHIMS

Isa 6: 2 Above it stood *s*;
6: 6 Then one of the *s* flew to me,

SERAPHIMS (KJV) See SERAPHIM

SERED (2/2)

Gen 46:14 The sons of Zebulun were *S*,
Num 26:26 to their families were: of *S*,

SERGIUS (1/1)

Acts 13: 7 *S* Paulus, an intelligent man.

SERIOUS (7/7)

Deut 15:21 blind or has any *s* defect,
28:59 and *s* and prolonged sicknesses.
1 Ki 17:17 And his sickness was so *s* that
2 Chr 21:14 people with a *s* affliction—your
Neh 5: 7 After *s* thought, I rebuked the
Acts 25: 7 and laid many *s* complaints
1 Pe 4: 7 therefore be *s* and watchful in

SERPENT (42/39) SERPENT'S, SERPENTS

Gen 3: 1 Now the *s* was more cunning than
3: 2 And the woman said to the *s*,
3: 4 Then the *s* said to the woman,
3:13 The *s* deceived me, and I ate."
3:14 So the LORD God said to the *s*:
49:17 Dan shall be a *s* by the way, A
Ex 4: 3 the ground, and it became a *s*;
7: 9 Pharaoh, and let it become a *s*.
7:10 his servants, and it became a *s*.
7:15 the rod which was turned to a *s*
Num 21: 8 to Moses, "Make a fiery *s*,
21: 9 So Moses made a bronze *s*,
21: 9 if a *s* had bitten anyone, when
21: 9 when he looked at the bronze *s*,
2 Ki 18: 4 broke in pieces the bronze *s*
Neh 2:13 the Valley Gate to the *S* Well
Job 7:12 Am I a sea, or a sea *s*,
26:13 His hand pierced the fleeing *s*.
Ps 58: 4 is like the poison of a *s*;
91:13 The young lion and the *s* you
140: 3 sharpen their tongues like a *s*;
Prov 23:32 At the last it bites like a *s*,
30:19 The way of a *s* on a rock, The
Eccl 10: 8 a wall will be bitten by a *s*.
10:11 A *s* may bite when it is not
Isa 14:29 will be a fiery flying *s*.
27: 1 punish Leviathan the fleeing *s*,
27: 1 Leviathan that twisted *s*;
30: 6 The viper and fiery flying *s*,
51: 9 apart, And wounded the *s*?
Jer 46:22 Her noise shall go like a *s*,
Am 5:19 on the wall, And a *s* bit him!
9: 3 there I will command the *s*,
Mic 7:17 shall lick the dust like a *s*;
Mt 7:10 a fish, will he give him a *s*?
Lk 11:11 will he give him a *s* instead of
Jn 3:14 And as Moses lifted up the *s* in
2 Cor 11: 3 as the *s* deceived Eve by his
Rev 12: 9 that *s* of old, called the Devil
12:14 from the presence of the *s*.
12:15 So the *s* spewed water out of his
20: 2 that *s* of old, who is the

SERPENT'S (2/2) SERPENT

Isa 14:29 For out of the *s* roots will
65:25 And dust shall be the *s*

SERPENTS (14/14) SERPENT

Ex 7:12 down his rod, and they became *s*.
Num 21: 6 So the LORD sent fiery *s* among
21: 7 LORD that He take away the *s*
Deut 8:15 in which were fiery *s* and
32:24 With the poison of *s* of the
32:33 Their wine is the poison of *s*,
Ps 74:13 broke the heads of the sea *s*
Jer 8:17 I will send *s* among you,
Mt 10:16 Therefore be wise as *s* and
23:33 '*S*, brood of vipers!
Mk 16:18 "they will take up *s*;
Lk 10:19 the authority to trample on *s*
1 Cor 10: 9 and were destroyed by *s*;
Rev 9:19 for their tails are like *s*,

SERUG (6/6)

Gen 11:20 thirty-two years, and begot *S*.
11:21 After he begot *S*, Reu lived
11:22 *S* lived thirty years, and begot
11:23 *S* lived two hundred years, and
1 Chr 1:26 *S*, Nahor, Terah,
Lk 3:35 the son of *S*, the son of

SERVANT (508/462) MAIDSERVANT, SERVANT'S, SERVANTS, SERVE

Gen 9:25 A *s* of servants He shall be
9:26 Shem, And may Canaan be his *s*.
9:27 And may Canaan be his *s*."
18: 3 sight, do not pass on by Your *s*.
18: 5 as you have come to your *s*.
19:19 your *s* has found favor in your
24: 2 So Abraham said to the oldest *s*
24: 5 And the *s* said to him, "Perhaps
24: 9 So the *s* put his hand under the
24:10 Then the *s* took ten of his
24:14 You have appointed for Your *s*
24:17 And the *s* ran to meet her and
24:34 So he said, "I am Abraham's *s*.
24:52 when Abraham's *s* heard their
24:53 Then the *s* brought out jewelry
24:59 and Abraham's *s* and his men.
24:61 So the *s* took Rebekah and
24:65 for she had said to the *s*,
24:65 The *s* said, "It is my
24:66 And the *s* told Isaac all the
26:24 your descendants for My *s*
32: 4 Thus your *s* Jacob says: "I have
32:10 which You have shown Your *s*;
32:18 'They are your *s* Jacob's.
32:20 your *s* Jacob is behind us.'"
33: 5 God has graciously given your *s*.
33:14 lord go on ahead before his *s*.
39:17 The Hebrew *s* whom you brought to
39:19 Your *s* did to me after this
41:12 a *s* of the captain of the
43:28 Your *s* our father is in good
44:18 please let your *s* speak a word
44:18 your anger burn against your *s*;
44:24 when we went up to your *s* my
44:27 Then your *s* my father said to
44:30 when I come to your *s* my
44:31 down the gray hair of your *s*
44:32 For your *s* became surety for the
44:33 please let your *s* remain
Ex 4:10 since You have spoken to Your *s*;
11: 5 the firstborn of the female *s*
12:44 But every man's *s* who is bought
12:45 A sojourner and a hired *s* shall
14:31 believed the LORD and His *s*
20:10 your daughter, nor your male *s*,
20:10 male servant, nor your female *s*,
20:17 neighbor's wife, nor his male *s*,
20:17 male servant, nor his female *s*,
21: 2 "If you buy a Hebrew *s*,
21: 5 But if the *s* plainly says, 'I
21:20 man beats his male or female *s*
21:26 the eye of his male or female *s*,
21:27 tooth of his male or female *s*,
21:32 the ox gores a male or female *s*,
23:12 and the son of your female *s*
33:11 but his *s* Joshua the son of
Lev 22:10 with the priest, or a hired *s*,
25:40 As a hired *s* and a sojourner he
25:50 to the time of a hired *s* for
25:53 be with him as a yearly hired *s*,
Num 11:11 "Why have You afflicted Your *s*?
12: 7 Not so with My *s* Moses;
12: 8 afraid To speak against My *s*
14:24 But My *s* Caleb, because he has a
Deut 3:24 You have begun to show Your *s*
5:14 your daughter, nor your male *s*,
5:14 male servant, nor your female *s*,
5:14 that your male *s* and your
5:14 male servant and your female *s*
5:21 house, his field, his male *s*,
5:21 his male servant, his female *s*,
12:18 your male *s* and your female
12:18 male servant and your female *s*,
15:17 and he shall be your *s* forever.
15:17 Also to your female *s* you shall
15:18 been worth a double hired *s* in
16:11 your male *s* and your female
16:11 male servant and your female *s*,
16:14 your male *s* and your female
16:14 male servant and your female *s*
24:14 shall not oppress a hired *s*
34: 5 So Moses the *s* of the LORD
Josh 1: 1 the death of Moses the *s* of
1: 2 'Moses My *s* is dead.
1: 7 to all the law which Moses My *s*
1:13 the word which Moses the *s* of
1:15 which Moses the LORD's *s* gave
5:14 does my Lord say to His *s*?
8:31 as Moses the *s* of the LORD had
8:33 as Moses the *s* of the LORD had
9:24 LORD your God commanded His *s*
11:12 as Moses the *s* of the LORD had
11:15 LORD had commanded Moses his *s*,
12: 6 These Moses the *s* of the LORD
12: 6 and Moses the *s* of the LORD
13: 8 as Moses the *s* of the LORD had
14: 7 years old when Moses the *s* of
18: 7 which Moses the *s* of the LORD
22: 2 have kept all that Moses the *s*
22: 4 which Moses the *s* of the LORD
22: 5 and the law which Moses the *s*
24:29 the *s* of the LORD, died,

Judg 2: 8 the *s* of the LORD, died when
7:10 to the camp with Purah your *s*,
7:11 he went down with Purah his *s*
9:18 the son of his female *s*,
15:18 by the hand of Your *s*;
19: 3 having his *s* and a couple of
19: 9 and his concubine and his *s*—
19:11 and the *s* said to his master,
19:13 So he said to his *s*,
19:19 for myself, for your female *s*,
19:19 young man who is with your *s*;
Ruth 2: 5 Then Boaz said to his *s* who was
2: 6 So the *s* who was in charge of
1 Sam 2:13 the priest's *s* would come with
2:15 the priest's *s* would come and
3: 9 LORD, for Your *s* hears.'
3:10 'Speak, for Your *s* hears."
9: 5 Saul said to his *s* who was
9: 7 Then Saul said to his *s*,
9: 8 And the *s* answered Saul again
9:10 Then Saul said to his *s*,
9:22 Now Samuel took Saul and his *s*
9:27 Tell the *s* to go on ahead of
10:14 uncle said to him and his *s*,
17:32 your *s* will go and fight with
17:34 Your *s* used to keep his father's
17:36 Your *s* has killed both lion and
17:58 I am the son of your *s* Jesse
19: 4 not the king sin against his *s*,
20: 7 your *s* will be safe. But if he
20: 8 shall deal kindly with your *s*,
20: 8 for you have brought your *s*
22: 8 that my son has stirred up my *s*
22:15 king impute anything to his *s*,
22:15 For your *s* knew nothing of all
23:10 Your *s* has certainly heard that
23:11 down, as Your *s* has heard?
23:11 of Israel, I pray, tell Your *s*.
25:39 and has kept His *s* from evil!
25:41 a *s* to wash the feet of the
26:18 does my lord thus pursue his *s*?
26:19 king hear the words of his *s*:
27: 5 For why should your *s* dwell in
27:12 therefore he will be my *s*
28: 2 Surely you know what your *s* can
29: 3 the *s* of Saul king of Israel,
29: 8 what have you found in your *s*
30:13 *s* of an Amalekite; and my
2 Sam 3:18 By the hand of My *s* David, I
7: 5 Go and tell My *s* David, 'Thus
7: 8 thus shall you say to My *s*
7:20 For You, Lord GOD, know Your *s*.
7:21 to make Your *s* know them.
7:25 have spoken concerning Your *s*
7:26 And let the house of Your *s*
7:27 have revealed this to Your *s*,
7:27 Therefore Your *s* has found it
7:28 this goodness to Your *s*.
7:29 to bless the house of Your *s*,
7:29 let the house of Your *s* be
9: 2 And there was a *s* of the house
9: 6 answered, "Here is your *s*!"
9: 8 and said, "What is your *s*,
9: 9 king called to Ziba, Saul's *s*,
9:11 the king has commanded his *s*,
9:11 so will your *s* do."
11:21 Your *s* Uriah the Hittite is dead
11:24 and your *s* Uriah the Hittite is
13:17 Then he called his *s* who
13:18 And his *s* put her out and
13:24 your *s* has sheepshearers;
13:24 and his servants go with your *s*.
13:35 as your *s* said, so it is."
14:19 For your *s* Joab commanded me,
14:20 this change of affairs your *s*
14:22 Today your *s* knows that I have
14:22 fulfilled the request of his *s*.
15: 2 Your *s* is from such and such a
15: 8 For your *s* took a vow while I
15:21 even there also your *s* will
15:34 to Absalom, 'I will be your *s*,
15:34 as I was your father's *s*
15:34 so I will now also be your *s*,
16: 1 there was Ziba the *s* of
17:17 so a female *s* would come and
18:29 When Joab sent the king's *s* and
18:29 king's servant and me your *s*,
19:17 and Ziba the *s* of the house of
19:19 or remember what wrong your *s*
19:20 'For I, your *s*, know that
19:26 O king, my *s* deceived me.
19:26 For your *s* said, 'I will saddle
19:26 because your *s* is lame.
19:27 And he has slandered your *s* to
19:28 Yet you set your *s* among those
19:35 Can your *s* taste what I eat or
19:35 Why then should your *s* be a
19:36 Your *s* will go a little way
19:37 Please let your *s* turn back
19:37 But here is your *s* Chimham; let
24:10 away the iniquity of Your *s*,
24:21 my lord the king come to his *s*?
1 Ki 1:19 but Solomon your *s* he has not
1:26 he has not invited me—me your *s*—
1:26 nor your *s* Solomon.
1:27 and you have not told your *s*
1:51 that he will not put his *s* to
2:38 so your *s* will do."
3: 6 shown great mercy to Your *s*
3: 7 You have made Your *s* king
3: 8 And Your *s* is in the midst of
3: 9 Therefore give to Your *s* an
8:24 kept what You promised Your *s*
8:25 keep what You promised Your *s*
8:26 which You have spoken to Your *s*
8:28 regard the prayer of Your *s*
8:28 and the prayer which Your *s* is
8:29 hear the prayer which Your *s*
8:30 the supplication of Your *s* and
8:52 to the supplication of Your *s*
8:53 as You spoke by Your *s* Moses,
8:56 which He promised through His *s*
8:59 may maintain the cause of His *s*
8:66 the LORD had done for His *s*
11:11 from you and give it to your *s*.
11:13 your son for the sake of my *s*
11:26 Then Solomon's *s*, Jeroboam
11:32 one tribe for the sake of My *s*
11:34 his life for the sake of My *s*
11:36 that My *s* David may always have
11:38 as My *s* David did, then I will
12: 7 If you will be a *s* to these
14: 8 yet you have not been as My *s*
14:18 which He spoke through His *s*
15:29 which He had spoken by His *s*
16: 9 Now his *s* Zimri, commander of
18: 9 that you are delivering your *s*
18:12 But I your *s* have feared the
18:36 God in Israel and I am Your *s*,
18:43 and said to his *s*, "Go up now,
19: 3 and left his *s* there.
19:21 Elijah, and became his *s*.
20: 9 that you sent for to your *s*
20:32 Your *s* Ben-Hadad says, 'Please
20:39 Your *s* went out into the midst
20:40 While your *s* was busy here and
2 Ki 4: 1 Your *s* my husband is dead, and
4: 1 and you know that your *s* feared
4:12 Then he said to Gehazi his *s*,
4:19 So he said to a *s*, "Carry
4:24 a donkey, and said to her *s*,
4:25 that he said to his *s* Gehazi,
4:38 him; and he said to his *s*,
4:43 But his *s* said, "What? Shall I
5: 6 that I have sent Naaman my *s* to
5:15 please take a gift from your *s*.
5:17 please let your *s* be given two
5:17 for your *s* will no longer offer
5:18 may the LORD pardon your *s*:
5:18 the LORD please pardon your *s*
5:20 the *s* of Elisha the man of God,
5:25 Your *s* did not go anywhere."
6:15 And when the *s* of the man of God
6:15 And his *s* said to him, "Alas,
8: 4 the *s* of the man of God,
8:13 said, "But what is your *s*—
8:19 for the sake of his *s* David, as
9: 4 the *s* of the prophet, went to
9:36 which He spoke by His *s* Elijah
10:10 has done what He spoke by His *s*
14:25 He had spoken through His *s*
16: 7 'I am your *s* and your son.
18:12 and all that Moses the *s* of
19:34 For My own sake and for My *s*
20: 6 and for the sake of My *s*
21: 8 to all the law that My *s* Moses
22:12 and Asaiah a *s* of the king,
25: 8 a *s* of the king of Babylon,
1 Chr 2:34 And Sheshan had an Egyptian *s*
2:35 his daughter to Jarha his *s* as
6:49 to all that Moses the *s* of God
16:13 O seed of Israel His *s*,
17: 4 Go and tell My *s* David, 'Thus
17: 7 thus shall you say to My *s*
17:18 to You for the honor of Your *s*?
17:18 For You know Your *s*.
17:23 have spoken concerning Your *s*
17:24 And let the house of Your *s*
17:25 have revealed to Your *s* that
17:25 Therefore Your *s* has found it
17:26 this goodness to Your *s*.
17:27 to bless the house of Your *s*,
21: 8 away the iniquity of Your *s*,
2 Chr 1: 3 which Moses the *s* of the LORD
6:15 kept what You promised Your *s*
6:16 keep what You promised Your *s*
6:17 which You have spoken to Your *s*
6:19 regard the prayer of Your *s*
6:19 and the prayer which Your *s* is
6:20 hear the prayer which Your *s*
6:21 the supplications of Your *s*
6:42 the mercies of Your *s* David.
13: 6 the *s* of Solomon the son of
24: 6 commandment of Moses the *s* of
24: 9 collection that Moses the *s*
32:16 the LORD God and against His *s*
34:20 and Asaiah a *s* of the king,
Neh 1: 6 may hear the prayer of Your *s*
1: 7 which You commanded Your *s*
1: 8 word that You commanded Your *s*
1:11 to the prayer of Your *s*,
1:11 and let Your *s* prosper this
2: 5 and if your *s* has found favor
4:22 Let each man and his *s* stay at
6: 5 Then Sanballat sent his *s* to me
9:14 By the hand of Moses Your *s*.
10:29 which was given by Moses the *s*
Job 1: 8 Have you considered My *s* Job,
2: 3 Have you considered My *s* Job,
3:19 And the *s* is free from his
7: 2 Like a *s* who earnestly desires
19:16 I call my *s*, but he gives
31:13 cause of my male or female *s*
41: 4 Will you take him as a *s*
42: 7 is right, as My *s* Job has.
42: 8 go to My *s* Job, and offer up
42: 8 and My *s* Job shall pray for
42: 8 is right, as My *s* Job has."
Ps 18: A Psalm of David the *s* of the
19:11 Moreover by them Your *s* is
19:13 Keep back Your *s* also from
27: 9 Do not turn Your *s* away in
31:16 Your face shine upon Your *s*;
35:27 in the prosperity of His *s*.
36: A Psalm of David the *s* of the
69:17 not hide Your face from Your *s*,
78:70 He also chose David His *s*,
86: 2 Save Your *s* who trusts in You!
86: 4 Rejoice the soul of Your *s*,
86:16 Give Your strength to Your *s*,
89: 3 I have sworn to My *s* David:
89:20 I have found My *s* David;
89:39 the covenant of Your *s*;
105: 6 O seed of Abraham His *s*,
105:26 He sent Moses His *s*,
105:42 promise, And Abraham His *s*.
109:28 But let Your *s* rejoice.
116:16 O LORD, truly I am Your *s*;
116:16 I am Your *s*, the son of
119:17 Deal bountifully with Your *s*,
119:23 But Your *s* meditates on Your
119:38 Establish Your word to Your *s*,
119:49 Remember the word to Your *s*,
119:65 have dealt well with Your *s*,
119:76 to Your word to Your *s*.
119:84 many are the days of Your *s*?
119:122 Be surety for Your *s* for good;
119:124 Deal with Your *s* according to
119:125 I am Your *s*; Give me
119:135 Your face shine upon Your *s*,
119:140 Therefore Your *s* loves it.
119:176 like a lost sheep; Seek Your *s*,
132:10 For Your *s* David's sake, Do
136:22 A heritage to Israel His *s*,
143: 2 enter into judgment with Your *s*,
143:12 my soul; For I am Your *s*.
144:10 Who delivers David His *s* From
Prov 11:29 And the fool will be *s* to
12: 9 who is slighted but has a *s*,
14:35 favor is toward a wise *s*,
17: 2 A wise *s* will rule over a son
19:10 Much less for a *s* to rule over
22: 7 And the borrower is *s* to the
29:19 A *s* will not be corrected by
29:21 He who pampers his *s* from
30:10 Do not malign a *s* to his
30:22 For a *s* when he reigns, A fool
Eccl 7:21 Lest you hear your *s* cursing
Isa 20: 3 Just as My *s* Isaiah has walked
22:20 That I will call My *s* Eliakim
24: 2 As with the *s*, so with his
37:35 For My own sake and for My *s*
41: 8 "But you, Israel, are My *s*,
41: 9 said to you, 'You are My *s*,
42: 1 My *S* whom I uphold, My
42:19 Who is blind but My *s*,
42:19 And blind as the LORD's *s*?
43:10 And My *s* whom I have chosen,
44: 1 "Yet hear now, O Jacob My *s*,
44: 2 you: 'Fear not, O Jacob My *s*;
44:21 And Israel, for you are My *s*;
44:21 have formed you, you are My *s*;
44:26 Who confirms the word of His *s*,
48:20 The LORD has redeemed His *s*
49: 3 He said to me, 'You are My *s*,
49: 5 Me from the womb to be His *S*,
49: 6 a thing that You should be My *S*
49: 7 To the *S* of rulers: "Kings
50:10 Who obeys the voice of His *S*?
52:13 My *S* shall deal prudently;
53:11 His knowledge My righteous *S*
Jer 2:14 Is Israel a *s*? Is he a
25: 9 the king of Babylon, My *s*,
27: 6 the king of Babylon, My *s*;
30:10 O My *s* Jacob,' says the LORD,
33:21 also be broken with David My *s*,
33:22 the descendants of David My *s*
33:26 of Jacob and David My *s*,
43:10 the king of Babylon, My *s*,
46:27 O My *s* Jacob, And do not be
46:28 Do not fear, O Jacob My *s*,
Ezek 28:25 own land which I gave to My *s*
34:23 shall feed them—My *s* David.
34:24 and My *s* David a prince among
37:24 David My *s* shall be king over
37:25 that I have given to Jacob My *s*,
37:25 and My *s* David shall be their
Dan 6:20 *s* of the living God, has your
9:11 in the Law of Moses the *s* of
9:17 God, hear the prayer of Your *s*,
10:17 For how can this *s* of my lord
Hag 2:23 will take you, Zerubbabel My *s*,
Zech 3: 8 I am bringing forth My *S* the
Mal 1: 6 And a *s* his master.
4: 4 the Law of Moses, My *s*,
Mt 8: 6 my *s* is lying at home
8: 8 and my *s* will be healed.
8: 9 and he comes; and to my *s*,
8:13 And his *s* was healed that
10:24 nor a *s* above his master.
10:25 and a *s* like his master.
12:18 My *S* whom I have
18:26 The *s* therefore fell down before
18:27 Then the master of that *s* was
18:28 But that *s* went out and found
18:29 So his fellow *s* fell down at his

18:32 You wicked *s*! I forgave you all
18:33 had compassion on your fellow *s*,
20:26 among you, let him be your *s*.
23:11 among you shall be your *s*.
24:45 then is a faithful and wise *s*,
24:46 Blessed is that *s* whom his
24:48 But if that evil *s* says in his
24:50 the master of that *s* will come
25:21 done, good and faithful *s*;
25:23 done, good and faithful *s*;
25:26 to him, 'You wicked and lazy *s*,
25:30 And cast the unprofitable *s* into
26:51 struck the *s* of the high
26:69 And a *s* girl came to him,
Mk 9:35 he shall be last of all and *s*
10:43 great among you shall be your *s*.
12: 2 at vintage-time he sent a *s* to
12: 4 "Again he sent them another *s*,
14:47 his sword and struck the *s* of
14:66 one of the *s* girls of the high
14:69 And the *s* girl saw him again,
Lk 1:54 He has helped His *s* Israel, In
1:69 for us In the house of His *s*
2:29 now You are letting Your *s*
7: 2 And a certain centurion's *s*,
7: 3 with Him to come and heal his *s*.
7: 7 and my *s* will be healed.
7: 8 and to my *s*, 'Do this,' and
7:10 found the *s* well who had been
12:43 Blessed is that *s* whom his
12:45 But if that *s* says in his heart,
12:46 the master of that *s* will come
12:47 And that *s* who knew his master's
14:17 and sent his *s* at supper time to
14:21 So that *s* came and reported
14:21 being angry, said to his *s*,
14:22 And the *s* said, 'Master, it is
14:23 "Then the master said to the *s*,
16:13 'No *s* can serve two masters;
17: 7 having a *s* plowing or tending
17: 9 Does he thank that *s* because he
19:17 to him, 'Well done, good *s*;
19:22 I will judge you, you wicked *s*.
20:10 at vintage-time he sent a *s* to
20:11 "Again he sent another *s*;
22:50 And one of them struck the *s* of
22:56 And a certain *s* girl, seeing him
Jn 12:26 there My *s* will be also.
13:16 a *s* is not greater than his
15:15 for a *s* does not know what his
15:20 A *s* is not greater than his
18:10 and struck the high priest's *s*,
18:17 Then the *s* girl who kept the
Acts 3:13 glorified His *S* Jesus, whom you
3:26 having raised up His *S* Jesus,
4:25 who by the mouth of Your *s* David
4:27 For truly against Your holy *S*
4:30 the name of Your holy *S* Jesus.
Rom 14: 4 are you to judge another's *s*?
15: 8 Jesus Christ has become a *s* to
16: 1 who is a *s* of the church in
1 Cor 9:19 I have made myself a *s* to all,
Col 1: 7 Epaphras, our dear fellow *s*,
4: 7 and fellow *s* in the Lord, will
2 Tim 2:24 And a *s* of the Lord must not
Heb 3: 5 in all His house as a *s*,
Rev 1: 1 it by His angel to His *s* John,
15: 3 the *s* of God, and the song of
19:10 do that! I am your fellow *s*,
22: 9 For I am your fellow *s*,

SERVANT'S (6/6) SERVANT

Gen 19: 2 please turn in to your *s* house
2 Sam 7:19 also spoken of Your *s* house
1 Chr 17:17 also spoken of Your *s* house
17:19 for Your *s* sake, and according
Isa 45: 4 For Jacob My *s* sake, And
Jn 18:10 The *s* name was Malchus.

SERVANTS (464/430) SERVANT, SERVANTS'

Gen 9:25 A servant of *s* He shall be to
12:16 male donkeys, male and female *s*,
14:14 and eighteen trained *s* who
14:15 and he and his *s* attacked them
20: 8 the morning, called all his *s*,
20:14 oxen, and male and female *s*,
20:17 his wife, and his female *s*.
21:25 of water which Abimelech's *s*
24:35 and gold, male and female *s*,
26:14 herds and a great number of *s*.
26:15 the wells which his father's *s*
26:19 Also Isaac's *s* dug in the
26:25 and there Isaac's *s* dug a well.
26:32 the same day that Isaac's *s*
27:37 I have given to him as *s*;
30:43 large flocks, female and male *s*,
32: 5 flocks, and male and female *s*;
32:16 them to the hand of his *s*,
32:16 by itself, and said to his *s*,
32:22 his two wives, his two female *s*,
40:20 he made a feast for all his *s*;
40:20 of the chief baker among his *s*.
41:10 Pharaoh was angry with his *s*,
41:37 and in the eyes of all his *s*.
41:38 And Pharaoh said to his *s*,
42:10 but your *s* have come to buy
42:11 your *s* are not spies."
42:13 Your *s* are twelve brothers, the
44: 7 Far be it from us that your *s*
44: 9 With whomever of your *s* it is
44:16 out the iniquity of your *s*;
44:19 "My lord asked his *s*,
44:21 "Then you said to your *s*,
44:23 "But you said to your *s*,
44:31 So your *s* will bring down the
45:16 So it pleased Pharaoh and his *s*
47: 3 Your *s* are shepherds, both we
47: 4 because your *s* have no pasture
47: 4 please let your *s* dwell in the
47:19 and we and our land will be *s*
47:25 and we will be Pharaoh's *s*.
50: 2 And Joseph commanded his *s* the
50: 7 and with him went up all the *s*
50:17 forgive the trespass of the *s*
50:18 said, "Behold, we are your *s*.
Ex 5:15 you dealing thus with your *s*?
5:16 is no straw given to your *s*,
5:16 'Make brick!' And indeed your *s*
5:21 and in the sight of his *s*,
7:10 before Pharaoh and before his *s*,
7:20 and in the sight of his *s*.
8: 3 bed, into the houses of your *s*,
8: 4 your people, and on all your *s*.
8: 9 intercede for you, for your *s*,
8:11 from your houses, from your *s*,
8:21 of flies on you and your *s*,
8:29 from Pharaoh, from his *s*,
8:31 flies from Pharaoh, from his *s*,
9:14 and on your *s* and on your
9:20 word of the LORD among the *s*
9:20 servants of Pharaoh made his *s*
9:21 word of the LORD left his *s*
9:30 "But as for you and your *s*,
9:34 his heart, he and his *s*.
10: 1 heart and the hearts of his *s*,
10: 6 the houses of all your *s*,
10: 7 Then Pharaoh's *s* said to him,
11: 3 in the sight of Pharaoh's *s* and
11: 8 And all these your *s* shall come
12:30 in the night, he, all his *s*,
14: 5 the heart of Pharaoh and his *s*
32:13 Isaac, and Israel, Your *s*,
Lev 25: 6 for you, your male and female *s*,
25:42 'For they are My *s*,
25:55 the children of Israel are *s*
25:55 they are My *s* whom I brought
Num 22:18 answered and said to the *s* of
22:22 and his two *s* were with him.
31:49 Your *s* have taken a count of the
32: 4 and your *s* have livestock."
32: 5 this land be given to your *s*
32:25 Your *s* will do as my lord
32:27 but your *s* will cross over,
32:31 the LORD has said to your *s*,
Deut 9:27 'Remember Your *s*, Abraham,
12:12 your male and female *s*,
29: 2 to Pharaoh and to all his *s* and
32:36 And have compassion on His *s*,
32:43 will avenge the blood of His *s*,
34:11 Pharaoh, before all his *s*,
Josh 9: 8 to Joshua, "We are your *s*.
9: 9 a very far country your *s*
9:11 say to them, "We are your *s*;
9:24 Because your *s* were clearly told
10: 6 saying, "Do not forsake your *s*;
Judg 3:24 Eglon's *s* came to look, and to
6:27 took ten men from among his *s*
1 Sam 4: 9 that you do not become *s* of the
8:14 groves, and give them to his *s*.
8:15 give it to his officers and *s*.
8:16 "And he will take your male *s*,
8:16 male servants, your female *s*,
8:17 And you will be his *s*.
9: 3 take one of the *s* with you, and
12:19 Pray for your *s* to the LORD
16:15 And Saul's *s* said to him,
16:16 our master now command your *s*,
16:17 So Saul said to his *s*,
16:18 Then one of the *s* answered and
17: 8 and you the *s* of Saul?
17: 9 kill me, then we will be your *s*.
17: 9 then you shall be our *s* and
18: 5 also in the sight of Saul's *s*.
18:22 And Saul commanded his *s*,
18:22 and all his *s* love you.
18:23 So Saul's *s* spoke those words in
18:24 And the *s* of Saul told him,
18:26 So when his *s* told David these
18:30 more wisely than all the *s* of
19: 1 his son and to all his *s*,
21: 7 Now a certain man of the *s* of
21:11 And the *s* of Achish said to him,
21:14 Then Achish said to his *s*,
22: 6 and all his *s* standing about
22: 7 then Saul said to his *s* who
22: 9 who was set over the *s* of Saul,
22:14 And who among all your *s* is as
22:17 But the *s* of the king would
24: 7 So David restrained his *s* with
25: 8 comes to your hand to your *s*
25:10 Then Nabal answered David's *s*,
25:10 There are many *s* nowadays who
25:19 And she said to her *s*,
25:40 When the *s* of David had come to
25:41 to wash the feet of the *s* of
28: 7 Then Saul said to his *s*,
28: 7 And his *s* said to him, "In
28:23 So his *s*, together with the
28:25 it before Saul and his *s*,
29:10 morning with your master's *s*
2 Sam 2:12 and the *s* of Ishbosheth the son
2:13 and the *s* of David, went out
2:15 and twelve from the *s* of David.
2:17 were beaten before the *s* of
2:30 there were missing of David's *s*
2:31 But the *s* of David had struck
3:22 At that moment the *s* of David
3:38 Then the king said to his *s*,
6:20 the eyes of the maids of his *s*,
8: 2 the Moabites became David's *s*,
8: 6 the Syrians became David's *s*,
8: 7 that had belonged to the *s* of
8:14 the Edomites became David's *s*.
9:10 and your sons and your *s*,
9:10 had fifteen sons and twenty *s*.
9:12 in the house of Ziba were *s*
10: 2 sent by the hand of his *s* to
10: 2 And David's *s* came into the
10: 3 David not rather sent his *s*
10: 4 Therefore Hanun took David's *s*,
10:19 all the kings who were *s* to
11: 1 that David sent Joab and his *s*
11: 9 king's house with all the *s* of
11:11 and my lord Joab and the *s* of
11:13 to lie on his bed with the *s*
11:17 some of the people of the *s*
11:24 shot from the wall at your *s*;
11:24 and some of the king's *s* are
12:18 And the *s* of David were afraid
12:19 When David saw that his *s* were
12:19 Therefore David said to his *s*,
12:21 Then his *s* said to him, "What
13:24 let the king and his *s* go with
13:28 Absalom had commanded his *s*,
13:29 So the *s* of Absalom did to Amnon
13:31 and all his *s* stood by with
13:36 Also the king and all his *s*
14:30 So he said to his *s*,
14:30 And Absalom's *s* set the field
14:31 Why have your *s* set my field on
15:14 So David said to all his *s* who
15:15 And the king's *s* said to the
15:15 to the king, "We are your *s*,
15:18 Then all his *s* passed before
16: 6 at David and at all the *s* of
16:11 said to Abishai and all his *s*,
17:20 And when Absalom's *s* came to the
18: 7 overthrown there before the *s*
18: 9 Then Absalom met the *s* of
19: 5 you have disgraced all your *s*
19: 6 regard neither princes nor *s*;
19: 7 out and speak comfort to your *s*.
19:14 you and all your *s*!"
19:17 fifteen sons and his twenty *s*
20: 6 Take your lord's *s* and pursue
21:15 David and his *s* with him went
21:22 David and by the hand of his *s*.
24:20 and saw the king and his *s*
1 Ki 1: 2 Therefore his *s* said to him,
1: 9 the men of Judah, the king's *s*.
1:33 Take with you the *s* of your
1:47 And moreover the king's *s* have
3:15 and made a feast for all his *s*.
5: 1 Hiram king of Tyre sent his *s*
5: 6 and my *s* will be with your
5: 6 my servants will be with your *s*,
5: 6 I will pay you wages for your *s*
5: 9 My *s* shall bring them down from
8:23 covenant and mercy with Your *s*
8:32 and act, and judge Your *s*,
8:36 and forgive the sin of Your *s*,
9:22 they were men of war and his *s*:
9:27 Then Hiram sent his *s* with the
9:27 to work with the *s* of Solomon.
10: 5 his table, the seating of his *s*,
10: 8 men and happy are these your *s*,
10:13 her own country, she and her *s*.
11:17 Edomites of his father's *s*
12: 7 then they will be your *s*
15:18 them into the hand of his *s*.
20: 6 but I will send my *s* to you
20: 6 house and the houses of your *s*.
20:12 post, that he said to his *s*,
20:23 Then the *s* of the king of Syria
20:31 Then his *s* said to him, "Look
22: 3 king of Israel said to his *s*,
22:49 Let my *s* go with your servants
22:49 my servants go with your *s*
2 Ki 1:13 and the life of these fifty *s*
2:16 fifty strong men with your *s*.
3:11 So one of the *s* of the king
5:13 And his *s* came near and spoke to
5:23 handed them to two of his *s*;
5:26 and oxen, male and female *s*?
6: 3 consent to go with your *s*.
6: 8 and he consulted with his *s*,
6:11 and he called his *s* and said to
6:12 And one of his *s* said, "None,
7:12 in the night and said to his *s*,
7:13 And one of his *s* answered and
9: 7 I may avenge the blood of My *s*
9: 7 and the blood of all the *s* of
9:11 Then Jehu came out to the *s* of
9:28 And his *s* carried him in the
10: 5 Jehu, saying, "We are your *s*,
10:19 the prophets of Baal, all his *s*,
10:23 Search and see that no *s* of the
12:20 And his *s* arose and formed a
12:21 the son of Shomer, his *s*,
14: 5 that he executed his *s* who had
17:13 and which I sent to you by My *s*
17:23 as He had said by all His *s* the
18:24 of the least of my master's *s*,

18:26 Please speak to your *s* in
19: 5 So the *s* of King Hezekiah came
19: 6 with which the *s* of the king of
21:10 And the LORD spoke by His *s*
21:23 Then the *s* of Amon conspired
22: 9 Your *s* have gathered the money
23:30 Then his *s* moved his body in a
24: 2 which He had spoken by His *s*
24:10 At that time the *s* of
24:11 as his *s* were besieging it.
24:12 of Judah, his mother, his *s*,
25:24 Do not be afraid of the *s* of the
1 Chr 18: 2 the Moabites became David's *s*,
18: 6 the Syrians became David's *s*,
18: 7 of gold that were on the *s* of
18:13 the Edomites became David's *s*.
19: 2 And David's *s* came to Hanun in
19: 3 Did his *s* not come to you to
19: 4 Therefore Hanun took David's *s*,
19:19 And when the *s* of Hadadezer saw
19:19 with David and became his *s*.
20: 8 David and by the hand of his *s*.
21: 3 are they not all my lord's *s*?
2 Chr 2: 8 for I know that your *s* have
2: 8 and indeed my *s* will be with
2: 8 servants will be with your *s*,
2:10 indeed I will give to your *s*,
2:15 of, let him send to his *s*.
6:14 covenant and mercy with Your *s*
6:23 and act, and judge Your *s*,
6:27 and forgive the sin of Your *s*,
8: 9 make the children of Israel *s*
8:18 him ships by the hand of his *s*,
8:18 and *s* who knew the sea.
8:18 They went with the *s* of Solomon
9: 4 his table, the seating of his *s*,
9: 7 men and happy are these your *s*,
9:10 the *s* of Hiram and the servants
9:10 servants of Hiram and the *s* of
9:12 her own country, she and her *s*.
9:21 went to Tarshish with the *s* of
10: 7 they will be your *s* forever."
12: 8 they will be his *s*,
24:25 his own *s* conspired against him
25: 3 that he executed his *s* who had
32: 9 king of Assyria sent his *s* to
32:16 his *s* spoke against the LORD
33:24 Then his *s* conspired against
34:16 that was committed to your *s*
35:23 and the king said to his *s*,
35:24 His *s* therefore took him out of
36:20 where they became *s* to him and
Ezra 2:55 The sons of Solomon's *s*:
2:58 and the children of Solomon's *s*
2:65 besides their male and female *s*,
4:11 To King Artaxerxes from your *s*,
5:11 We are the *s* of the God of
7:24 or *s* of this house of God.
8:17 that they should bring us *s* for
9:11 which You commanded by Your *s*
Neh 1: 6 the children of Israel Your *s*,
1:10 Now these are Your *s* and Your
1:11 and to the prayer of Your *s* who
2:20 therefore we His *s* will arise
4:16 that half of my *s* worked at
4:23 So neither I, my brethren, my *s*,
5:10 with my brethren and my *s*,
5:15 even their *s* bore rule over the
5:16 All my *s* were gathered there
7:57 The sons of Solomon's *s*:
7:60 and the sons of Solomon's *s*,
7:67 besides their male and female *s*,
9:10 Pharaoh, Against all his *s*,
9:36 'Here we are, *s* today!
9:36 Here we are, *s* in it!
11: 3 and descendants of Solomon's *s*.
13:19 Then I posted some of my *s* at
Esth 1: 3 for all his officials and *s*—
2: 2 Then the king's *s* who attended
2:18 for all his officials and *s*;
3: 2 And all the king's *s* who were
3: 3 Then the king's *s* who were
4:11 All the king's *s* and the people
5:11 him above the officials and *s*
6: 3 And the king's *s* who attended
6: 5 The king's *s* said to him,
Job 1:15 indeed they have killed the *s*
1:16 burned up the sheep and the *s*,
1:17 and killed the *s* with the edge
4:18 If He puts no trust in His *s*,
Ps 34:22 LORD redeems the soul of His *s*,
69:36 the descendants of His *s* shall
79: 2 The dead bodies of Your *s* They
79:10 of the blood of Your *s* which
89:50 Lord, the reproach of Your *s*—
90:13 And have compassion on Your *s*.
90:16 Let Your work appear to Your *s*,
102:14 For Your *s* take pleasure in her
102:28 The children of Your *s* will
105:25 To deal craftily with His *s*.
113: 1 O *s* of the LORD, Praise the
119:91 For all are Your *s*.
123: 2 as the eyes of *s* look to the
134: 1 All you *s* of the LORD, Who
135: 1 O you *s* of the LORD!
135: 9 Upon Pharaoh and all his *s*.
135:14 will have compassion on His *s*.
Prov 29:12 All his *s* become wicked.
Eccl 2: 7 I acquired male and female *s*,
2: 7 and had *s* born in my house.
10: 7 I have seen *s* on horses, While
10: 7 walk on the ground like *s*.

Isa 14: 2 Israel will possess them for *s*
36: 9 of the least of my master's *s*,
36:11 Please speak to your *s* in the
37: 5 So the *s* of King Hezekiah came
37: 6 with which the *s* of the king of
37:24 By your *s* you have reproached
54:17 is the heritage of the *s* of
56: 6 name of the LORD, to be His *s*—
61: 6 They shall call you the *s* of
65: 9 And My *s* shall dwell there.
65:13 My *s* shall eat, But you shall
65:13 My *s* shall drink, But you
65:13 My *s* shall rejoice, But you
65:14 My *s* shall sing for joy of
65:15 And call His *s* by another
66:14 LORD shall be known to His *s*,
Jer 7:25 have even sent to you all My *s*
21: 7 his *s* and the people, and such
22: 2 you and your *s* and your people
22: 4 accompanied by *s* and people,
25: 4 has sent to you all His *s* the
25:19 Pharaoh king of Egypt, his *s*,
26: 5 to heed the words of My *s* the
29:19 which I sent to them by My *s*
35:15 have also sent to you all My *s*
36:24 the king nor any of his *s* who
36:31 and his *s* for their iniquity;
37: 2 But neither he nor his *s* nor the
37:18 against you, against your *s*,
44: 4 I have sent to you all My *s*
46:26 Babylon and the hand of his *s*.
Lam 5: 8 *S* rule over us; There is
Ezek 38:17 spoken in former days by My *s*
46:17 his inheritance to one of his *s*,
Dan 1:12 Please test your *s* for ten days,
1:13 see fit, so deal with your *s*.
2: 4 Tell your *s* the dream, and
2: 7 Let the king tell his *s* the
3:26 *s* of the Most High God, come
3:28 His Angel and delivered His *s*
9: 6 Neither have we heeded Your *s*
9:10 He set before us by His *s* the
Am 3: 7 He reveals His secret to His *s*
Zech 1: 6 Which I commanded My *s* the
2: 9 shall become spoil for their *s*.
Mt 13:27 So the *s* of the owner came and
13:28 The *s* said to him, 'Do you
14: 2 and said to his *s*, "This is
18:23 to settle accounts with his *s*.
18:28 and found one of his fellow *s*
18:31 So when his fellow *s* saw what
21:34 he sent his *s* to the
21:35 the vinedressers took his *s*,
21:36 "Again he sent other *s*,
22: 3 and sent out his *s* to call those
22: 4 "Again, he sent out other *s*,
22: 6 "And the rest seized his *s*,
22: 8 "Then he said to his *s*,
22:10 So those *s* went out into the
22:13 "Then the king said to the *s*,
24:49 begins to beat his fellow *s*,
25:14 who called his own *s* and
25:19 a long time the lord of those *s*
26:58 he went in and sat with the *s*
Mk 1:20 in the boat with the hired *s*,
13:34 and gave authority to his *s*,
14:54 And he sat with the *s* and
Lk 12:37 Blessed are those *s* whom the
12:38 them so, blessed are those *s*.
12:45 to beat the male and female *s*,
15:17 many of my father's hired *s*
15:19 me like one of your hired *s*.
15:22 "But the father said to his *s*,
15:26 So he called one of the *s* and
17:10 say, 'We are unprofitable *s*.
19:13 "So he called ten of his *s*,
19:15 he then commanded these *s*,
Jn 2: 5 His mother said to the *s*,
2: 9 (but the *s* who had drawn
4:51 his *s* met him and told him,
15:15 "No longer do I call you *s*,
18:18 Now the *s* and officers who had
18:26 One of the *s* of the high priest,
18:36 My *s* would fight, so that I
Acts 4:29 and grant to Your *s* that with
10: 7 called two of his household *s*
16:17 These men are the *s* of the Most
1 Cor 4: 1 as *s* of Christ and stewards of
1 Pe 2:18 *S*, be submissive to your
Rev 1: 1 God gave Him to show His *s*—
2:20 to teach and seduce My *s* to
6:11 number of their fellow *s* and
7: 3 till we have sealed the *s* of
10: 7 as He declared to His *s* the
11:18 that You should reward Your *s*
19: 2 on her the blood of His *s*
19: 5 all you His *s* and those who
22: 3 and His *s* shall serve Him.
22: 6 sent His angel to show His *s*

SERVANTS' (4/4) SERVANTS

Gen 46:34 Your *s* occupation has been with
Ex 8:24 into his *s* houses, and into
Isa 63:17 Return for Your *s* sake, The
65: 8 So will I do for My *s* sake,

SERVE (214/201) SERVANT, SERVED, SERVES, SERVICE, SERVING

Gen 15:13 and will *s* them, and they will
15:14 also the nation whom they *s* I
25:23 And the older shall *s* the
27:29 Let peoples *s* you, And nations
27:40 And you shall *s* your brother;
29:15 should you therefore *s* me for
29:18 I will *s* you seven years for
29:27 the service which you will *s*
43:31 and said, "*S* the bread."
Ex 1:13 made the children of Israel *s*
1:14 in which they made them *s* was
3:12 you shall *s* God on this
4:23 let My son go that he may *s* Me.
7:16 that they may *s* Me in the
8: 1 that they may *s* Me.
8:20 that they may *s* Me.
9: 1 that they may *s* Me.
9:13 that they may *s* Me,
10: 3 that they may *s* Me.
10: 7 that they may *s* the LORD their
10: 8 *s* the LORD your God.
10:11 and *s* the LORD, for that is
10:24 *s* the LORD; only let your
10:26 we must take some of them to *s*
10:26 do not know with what we must *s*
12:31 *s* the LORD as you have said.
14:12 Let us alone that we may *s* the
14:12 have been better for us to *s*
20: 5 not bow down to them nor *s*
21: 2 he shall *s* six years;
21: 6 and he shall *s* him forever.
23:24 nor *s* them, nor do according to
23:25 So you shall *s* the LORD your
23:33 For if you *s* their gods, it
Lev 25:39 you shall not compel him to *s*
25:40 and shall *s* you until the Year
Num 3: 6 that they may *s* him.
4:26 these things: so shall they *s*.
4:37 all who might *s* in the
4:41 of all who might *s* in the
16: 9 before the congregation to *s*
18: 2 may be joined with you and *s*
18: 7 the veil; and you shall *s*.
Deut 4:19 driven to worship them and *s*
4:28 And there you will *s* gods, the
5: 9 not bow down to them nor *s*
6:13 fear the LORD your God and *s*
7: 4 to *s* other gods; so the anger
7:16 nor shall you *s* their gods, for
8:19 and *s* them and worship them,
10:12 to *s* the LORD your God with
10:20 you shall *s* Him, and to Him you
11:13 love the LORD your God and *s*
11:16 and you turn aside and *s* other
12:30 How did these nations *s* their
13: 2 and let us *s* them,'
13: 4 and you shall *s* Him and hold
13: 6 Let us go and *s* other gods,'
13:13 Let us go and *s* other gods"
18: 7 then he may *s* in the name of the
19:17 priests and the judges who *s*
20:11 tribute to you, and *s* you.
28:14 to go after other gods to *s*
28:36 and there you shall *s* other
28:47 Because you did not *s* the LORD
28:48 therefore you shall *s* your
28:64 and there you shall *s* other
29:18 to go and *s* the gods of these
30:17 and worship other gods and *s*
31:20 will turn to other gods and *s*
Josh 22: 5 and to *s* Him with all your
23: 7 you shall not *s* them nor bow
24:14 *S* Him in sincerity and in
24:14 and in Egypt. *S* the LORD!
24:15 if it seems evil to you to *s*
24:15 this day whom you will *s*,
24:15 we will *s* the LORD."
24:16 should forsake the LORD to *s*
24:18 We also will *s* the LORD, for
24:19 You cannot *s* the LORD, for He
24:20 you forsake the LORD and *s*
24:21 but we will *s* the LORD!"
24:22 for yourselves, to *s* Him."
24:24 "The LORD our God we will *s*,
Judg 2:19 to *s* them and bow down to them.
9:28 that we should *s* him?
9:28 *S* the men of Hamor the father
9:28 but why should we *s* him?
9:38 that we should *s* him?'
10: 6 the LORD and did not *s* Him.
1 Sam 7: 3 and *s* Him only; and He will
11: 1 and we will *s* you."
12:10 and we will *s* You.'
12:14 If you fear the LORD and *s* Him
12:20 but *s* the LORD with all your
12:24 and *s* Him in truth with all
17: 9 shall be our servants and *s* us.
26:19 saying, 'Go, *s* other gods.'
2 Sam 15: 8 then I will *s* the LORD.'"
16:19 "Furthermore, whom should I *s*?
16:19 Should I not *s* in the
22:44 I have not known shall *s* me.
1 Ki 9: 6 but go and *s* other gods and
12: 4 and we will *s* you."
12: 7 and *s* them, and answer them,
2 Ki 4:41 *S* it to the people, that they
10:18 Jehu will *s* him much.
17:35 nor bow down to them nor *s* them
18: 7 king of Assyria and did not *s*
25:24 Dwell in the land and *s* the
1 Chr 26:12 to *s* in the house of the LORD.
28: 9 and *s* Him with a loyal heart
2 Chr 7:19 and go and *s* other gods, and
8:14 their duties (to praise and *s*

S

10: 4 and we will *s* you.”
23: 6 and those of the Levites who *s*.
29:11 to *s* Him, and that you should
30: 8 and *s* the LORD your God, that
31: 2 and peace offerings, to *s*,
33:16 and commanded Judah to *s* the
34:33 present in Israel diligently *s*
35: 3 Now *s* the LORD your God and
Job 21:15 that we should *s* Him?
36:11 If they obey and *s* Him, They
39: 9 the wild ox be willing to *s*
Ps 2:11 *S* the LORD with fear, And
18:43 I have not known shall *s* me.
22:30 A posterity shall *s* Him.
72:11 All nations shall *s* Him.
97: 7 Let all be put to shame who *s*
100: 2 *S* the LORD with gladness
101: 6 a perfect way, He shall *s* me.
102:22 the kingdoms, to *s* the LORD.
Isa 14: 3 in which you were made to *s*,
19:23 and the Egyptians will *s* with
43:23 I have not caused you to *s*
56: 6 to *s* Him, And to love the name
60:12 and kingdom which will not *s*
Jer 5:19 so you shall *s* aliens in a land
11:10 have gone after other gods to *s*
13:10 and walk after other gods to *s*
16:13 and there you shall *s* other
17: 4 And I will cause you to *s* your
25: 6 not go after other gods to *s*
25:11 and these nations shall *s* the
27: 6 I have also given him to *s* him.
27: 7 So all nations shall *s* him and
27: 7 great kings shall make him *s*
27: 8 and kingdom which will not *s*
27: 9 You shall not *s* the king of
27:11 of the king of Babylon and *s*
27:12 and *s* him and his people, and
27:13 the nation that will not *s* the
27:14 You shall not *s* the king of
27:17 *s* the king of Babylon, and
28:14 that they may *s* Nebuchadnezzar
28:14 and they shall *s* him.
30: 9 But they shall *s* the LORD
35:15 do not go after other gods to *s*
40: 9 Do not be afraid to *s* the
40: 9 Dwell in the land and *s* the
40:10 indeed dwell at Mizpah and *s*
44: 3 went to burn incense and to *s*
Ezek 20:39 *s* every one of you his
20:40 them in the land, shall *s* Me;
Dan 1: 4 who had ability to *s* in the
1: 5 end of that time they might *s*
3:12 They do not *s* your gods or
3:14 that you do not *s* my gods or
3:17 our God whom we *s* is able to
3:18 that we do not *s* your gods, nor
3:28 that they should not *s* nor
6:16 whom you *s* continually, He will
6:20 whom you *s* continually, been
7:14 and languages should *s* Him.
7:27 And all dominions shall *s* and
Zeph 3: 9 To *s* Him with one accord.
Mal 3:14 ‘It is useless to *s* God;
3:18 God And one who does not *s*
Mt 4:10 and Him only you shall *s*.
6:24 No one can *s* two masters;
6:24 You cannot *s* God and mammon.
20:28 not come to be served, but to *s*,
Mk 10:45 not come to be served, but to *s*,
Lk 1:74 Might *s* Him without fear,
4: 8 and Him only you shall *s*.
10:40 that my sister has left me to *s*
12:37 and will come and *s* them.
16:13 No servant can *s* two masters;
16:13 You cannot *s* God and mammon.”
17: 8 and gird yourself and *s* me till
Acts 6: 2 leave the word of God and *s*
7: 7 shall come out and *s* Me
27:23 to whom I belong and whom I *s*,
Rom 1: 9 whom I *s* with my spirit in the
7: 6 so that we should *s* in the
7:25 with the mind I myself *s* the
9:12 The older shall *s* the
16:18 For those who are such do not *s*
1 Cor 7:35 and that you may *s* the Lord
9:13 and those who *s* at the altar
Gal 3:19 purpose then does the law *s*?
5:13 but through love *s* one another.
Col 3:24 for you *s* the Lord Christ.
1 Th 1: 9 turned to God from idols to *s*
1 Tim 3:10 then let them *s* as deacons,
6: 2 but rather *s* them because
2 Tim 1: 3 whom I *s* with a pure
Heb 8: 5 who *s* the copy and shadow of the
9:14 from dead works to *s* the
12:28 by which we may *s* God
13:10 an altar from which those who *s*
Rev 7:15 and *s* Him day and night in His
22: 3 and His servants shall *s* Him.

SERVED (84/83) SERVE

Gen 14: 4 Twelve years they *s*
29:20 So Jacob *s* seven years for
29:25 Was it not for Rachel that I *s*
29:30 And he *s* with Laban still
30:26 my children for whom I have *s*
30:29 You know how I have *s* you and
31: 6 that with all my might I have *s*
31:41 I *s* you fourteen years for your
39: 4 in his sight, and *s* him.
40: 4 with them, and he *s* them;
Deut 12: 2 which you shall dispossess *s*
17: 3 who has gone and *s* other gods
29:26 for they went and *s* other gods
Josh 23:16 and have gone and *s* other gods,
24: 2 and they *s* other gods.
24:14 the gods which your fathers *s*
24:15 the gods which your fathers *s*
24:31 Israel *s* the LORD all the days
Judg 2: 7 So the people *s* the LORD all
2:11 of the LORD, and *s* the Baals;
2:13 They forsook the LORD and *s*
3: 6 and they *s* their gods.
3: 7 and *s* the Baals and Asherahs.
3: 8 and the children of Israel *s*
3:14 So the children of Israel *s*
10: 6 and *s* the Baals and the
10:10 both forsaken our God and *s*
10:13 you have forsaken Me and *s*
10:16 gods from among them and *s* the
1 Sam 7: 4 and *s* the LORD only.
8: 8 they have forsaken Me and *s*
12:10 have forsaken the LORD and *s*
2 Sam 10:19 made peace with Israel and *s*
16:19 As I have *s* in your father’s
1 Ki 1: 4 cared for the king, and *s* him;
4:21 They brought tribute and *s*
9: 9 and worshiped them and *s* them;
16:31 and he went and *s* Baal and
22:53 for he *s* Baal and worshiped him,
2 Ki 4:40 Then they *s* it to the men to
10:18 Ahab *s* Baal a little, Jehu will
17:12 for they *s* idols, of which the
17:16 host of heaven, and *s* Baal.
17:33 yet *s* their own gods—according
17:41 yet *s* their carved images;
21: 3 all the host of heaven and *s*
21:21 and he *s* the idols that his
21:21 the idols that his father had *s*,
1 Chr 6:32 and they *s* in their office
27: 1 *s* the king in every matter of
28: 1 of the divisions who *s* the
2 Chr 7:22 and worshiped them and *s* them;
17:19 These *s* the king, besides those
22: 8 of Ahaziah’s brothers who *s*
24:18 and *s* wooden images and idols;
33: 3 all the host of heaven and *s*
33:22 had made, and *s* them.
Neh 9:35 For they have not *s* You in
Esth 1: 7 And they *s* drinks in golden
1:10 seven eunuchs who *s* in the
Ps 106:36 They *s* their idols, Which
137: 8 who repays you as you have *s*
Eccl 5: 9 even the king is *s* from the
Jer 5:19 as you have forsaken Me and *s*
8: 2 loved and which they have *s*
16:11 after other gods and have *s*
22: 9 and worshiped other gods and *s*
25:14 and great kings shall be *s* by
34:14 and when he has *s* you six
52:12 who *s* the king of Babylon,
Dan 1:19 therefore they *s* before the
Hos 12:12 Israel *s* for a spouse, And
Mt 8:15 And she arose and *s* them.
20:28 Son of Man did not come to be *s*,
Mk 1:31 fever left her. And she *s* them.
10:45 Son of Man did not come to be *s*,
Lk 2:37 but *s* God with fastings and
4:39 And immediately she arose and *s*
Jn 12: 2 made Him a supper; and Martha *s*,
Acts 13:36 after he had *s* his own
Rom 1:25 and worshiped and *s* the
Gal 4: 8 you *s* those which by nature are
Phil 2:22 as a son with his father he *s*
1 Tim 3:13 For those who have *s* well as

SERVES (10/8) SERVE

Deut 15:12 is sold to you and *s* you six
Ps 73: 6 Therefore pride *s* as their
Mal 3:17 spares his own son who *s* him.”
3:18 Between one who *s* God And one
Lk 22:26 and he who governs as he who *s*.
22:27 sits at the table, or he who *s*?
22:27 I am among you as the One who *s*.
Jn 12:26 If anyone *s* Me, let him follow
12:26 If anyone *s* Me, him My Father
Rom 14:18 For he who *s* Christ in these

SERVICE (105/96) SERVE

Gen 29:27 you this one also for the *s*
30:26 for you know my *s* which I have
Ex 1:14 and in all manner of *s* in the
1:14 All their *s* in which they made
12:25 that you shall keep this *s*.
12:26 ‘What do you mean by this *s*?
13: 5 that you shall keep this *s* in
27:19 of the tabernacle for all its *s*,
30:16 and shall appoint it for the *s*
35:21 of meeting, for all its *s*,
35:24 wood for any work of the *s*,
36: 1 do all manner of work for the *s*
36: 3 brought for the work of the *s*
36: 5 more than enough for the *s* of
38:21 for the *s* of the Levites, by
39:40 all the utensils for the *s* of
Num 4: 3 all who enter the *s* to do the
4: 4 This is the *s* of the sons of
4: 9 with which they *s* it.
4:12 take all the utensils of *s*
4:19 appoint each of them to his *s*
4:23 all who enter to perform the *s*,
4:24 This is the *s* of the families
4:26 all the furnishings for their *s*
4:27 sons shall assign all the *s* of
4:27 all their tasks and all their *s*.
4:28 This is the *s* of the families
4:30 everyone who enters the *s* to do
4:31 they must carry as all their *s*
4:32 furnishings and all their *s*;
4:33 This is the *s* of the families
4:33 as all their *s* for the
4:35 everyone who entered the *s* for
4:39 everyone who entered the *s* for
4:43 everyone who entered the *s* for
4:47 who came to do the work of *s*
4:49 each according to his *s* and
7: 5 every man according to his *s*.
7: 7 Gershon, according to their *s*;
7: 8 of Merari, according to their *s*,
7: 9 because theirs was the *s* of
8:15 the Levites shall go in to *s*
8:24 one may enter to perform *s* in
18: 7 to you as a gift for *s*,
Josh 22:27 that we may perform the *s* of
2 Sam 9: 2 he said, “At your *s*!”
1 Ki 10: 5 the *s* of his waiters and their
12: 4 lighten the burdensome *s* of
1 Chr 6:31 David appointed over the *s* of
6:48 appointed to every kind of *s*
9:13 able men for the work of the *s*
9:19 in charge of the work of the *s*,
23:24 who did the work for the *s* of
23:26 any of the articles for its *s*.
23:28 the sons of Aaron in the *s* of
23:28 things and the work of the *s*
24: 3 to the schedule of their *s*.
24:19 was the schedule of their *s*
25: 1 of the army separated for the *s*
25: 1 skilled men performing their *s*
25: 6 for the *s* of the house of God.
26:30 and in the *s* of the king.
28:13 for all the work of the *s* of
28:13 and for all the articles of *s*
28:14 used in every kind of *s*;
28:14 used in every kind of *s*;
28:20 all the work for the *s* of the
28:21 and the Levites for all the *s*
28:21 for every kind of *s*;
2 Chr 8:14 of the priests for their *s*,
9: 4 the *s* of his waiters and their
10: 4 lighten the burdensome *s* of
12: 8 that they may distinguish My *s*
12: 8 My service from the *s* of the
24:12 who did the work of the *s* of
29:35 So the *s* of the house of the
31: 2 each man according to his *s*,
31:16 portion for the work of his *s*,
31:21 work that he began in the *s* of
34:13 who did work in any kind of *s*.
35: 2 and encouraged them for the *s*
35:10 So the *s* was prepared, and the
35:16 So all the *s* of the LORD was
Ezra 6:18 over the *s* of God in Jerusalem,
7:19 are given to you for the *s* of
8:20 had appointed for the *s* of the
Neh 10:32 of a shekel for the *s* of the
11:22 the singers in charge of the *s*
13:30 and the Levites, each to his *s*,
Job 7: 1 there not a time of hard *s*
14:14 All the days of my hard *s* I
Ps 104:14 And vegetation for the *s* of
Jer 22:13 Who uses his neighbor’s *s*
Lk 1:23 as soon as the days of his *s*
Jn 16: 2 will think that he offers God *s*.
Rom 9: 4 the *s* of God, and the
12: 1 which is your reasonable *s*.
15:31 and that my *s* for Jerusalem may
2 Cor 9:12 the administration of this *s*
Eph 6: 7 with goodwill doing *s*,
Phil 2:17 on the sacrifice and *s* of your
2:30 what was lacking in your *s*
Heb 9: 1 had ordinances of divine *s* and
9: 9 make him who performed the *s*
Rev 2:19 “I know your works, love, *s*,

SERVICES (3/3)

2 Chr 7: 6 the priests attended to their *s*;
Neh 13:14 of my God, and for its *s*!
Heb 9: 6 tabernacle, performing the *s*.

SERVILE (KJV) See CUSTOMARY

SERVING (20/20) SERVE

Gen 43:34 but Benjamin’s *s* was five times
Ex 14: 5 we have let Israel go from *s*
38: 8 mirrors of the *s* women
Num 4:24 in *s* and carrying:
Deut 15:18 a double hired servant in *s*
1 Ki 1:15 Abishag the Shunammite was *s*
1 Chr 9:28 in charge of the *s* vessels,
2 Chr 11:14 sons had rejected them from *s*
24:14 articles for *s* and offering,
Eccl 11: 2 Give a *s* to seven, and also to
Ezek 20:32 *s* wood and stone.’
Lk 1: 8 that while he was *s* as priest
10:40 was distracted with much *s*,
15:29 these many years I have been *s*
Acts 20:19 *s* the Lord with all humility,
26: 7 earnestly *s* God night and day,
Rom 12:11 fervent in spirit, *s* the Lord;

Titus 3: 3 s various lusts and pleasures,
1 Pe 5: 2 s as overseers, not by
Jude 12 s only themselves. They are

SERVINGS (1/1)

Gen 43:34 Then he took s to them from

SERVITOR (KJV) See SERVANT

SERVITUDE (1/1)

Lam 1: 3 Under affliction and hard s;

SET (619/596)

Gen 1:17 God s them in the firmament of
4:15 And the LORD s a mark on
6:16 and s the door of the ark in
9:13 I s My rainbow in the cloud, and
17:21 bear to you at this s time
18: 8 and s it before them; and he
19:16 they brought him out and s him
21: 2 at the s time of which God had
21:28 And Abraham s seven ewe lambs of
21:29 ewe lambs which you have s by
24:33 Food was s before him to eat,
28:11 night, because the sun had s.
28:12 a ladder was s up on the
28:18 s it up as a pillar, and poured
28:22 And this stone which I have s as
30:38 he s before the flocks in the
31:17 Then Jacob rose and s his sons
31:37 S it here before my brethren
31:45 So Jacob took a stone and s it
35:14 So Jacob s up a pillar in the
35:20 And Jacob s a pillar on her
41:33 and s him over the land of
41:41 I have s you over all the land
41:43 Bow the knee!" So he s him over
43: 9 him back to you and s him
43:32 So they s him a place by
44:21 that I may s my eyes on him.'
47: 7 in his father Jacob and s him
48:20 And thus he s Ephraim before
Ex 1:11 Therefore they s taskmasters
4:20 wife and his sons and s them
5:14 Pharaoh's taskmasters had s
8:22 And in that day I will s apart
9: 5 the LORD appointed a s time,
13:12 that you shall s apart to the
17: 1 children of Israel s out
19:12 You shall s bounds for the
19:23 S bounds around the mountain and
21: 1 the judgments which you shall s
23:31 And I will s your bounds from
25: 7 and stones to be s in the ephod
25:30 And you shall s the showbread on
26: 4 on the selvedge of one s,
26: 4 other curtain of the second s.
26: 5 is on the end of the second s,
26:10 that is outermost in one s,
26:10 of the curtain of the second s.
26:35 You shall s the table outside
28:11 You shall s them in settings of
28:20 They shall be s in gold
32:22 that they are s on evil.
35: 9 and stones to be s in the ephod
35:27 and the stones to be s in the
36:11 on the selvedge of one s;
36:11 other curtain of the second s.
36:12 on the end of the second s;
36:17 that is outermost in one s,
36:17 of the curtain of the second s.
37: 3 four rings of gold to be s
39: 6 And they s onyx stones,
39:10 And they s in it four rows of
39:37 with its lamps (the lamps s in
40: 2 of the first month you shall s
40: 4 the things that are to be s in
40: 5 You shall also s the altar of
40: 6 Then you shall s the altar of
40: 7 And you shall s the laver
40: 8 You shall s up the court all
40:18 s up its boards, put in its
40:23 and he s the bread in order upon
40:30 He s the laver between the
Lev 15:19 she shall be s apart seven
17:10 I will s My face against that
20: 3 I will s My face against that
20: 5 then I will s My face against
20: 6 I will s My face against that
24: 6 You shall s them in two rows,
24: 8 Every Sabbath he shall s it in
26: 1 nor shall you s up an engraved
26:11 I will s My tabernacle among
26:17 I will s My face against you,
27: 8 and the priest shall s a value
27:12 and the priest shall s a value
27:14 then the priest shall s a value
Num 1:51 the tabernacle is to be s up,
1:51 the Levites shall s it up. The
4:15 when the camp is s to go, then
5:16 and s her before the LORD.
10:12 And the children of Israel s out
10:14 of the children of Judah s out
10:17 and the sons of Merari s out,
10:18 of the camp of Reuben s out
10:21 Then the Kohathites s out,
10:22 children of Ephraim s out
10:25 s out according to their
10:35 whenever the ark s out, that
21: 8 and s it on a pole; and it
24: 1 but he s his face toward the
24:21 And your nest is s in the
27:16 s a man over the congregation,
27:19 s him before Eleazar the priest
27:22 He took Joshua and s him before
Deut 1: 8 I have s the land before you;
1:21 the LORD your God has s the
4: 8 are in all this law which I s
4:41 Then Moses s apart three cities
4:44 this is the law which Moses s
7: 7 The LORD did not s His love on
11:26 I s before you today a blessing
11:32 and judgments which I s before
16:22 You shall not s up a sacred
17:14 I will s a king over me like all
17:15 you shall surely s a king over
17:15 your brethren you shall s as
17:15 you may not s a foreigner over
19:14 which the men of old have s,
21:14 then you shall s her free, but
23:20 you in all to which you s your
24:15 for he is poor and has s his
26: 4 out of your hand and s it
26:10 Then you shall s it before the
26:19 and that He will s you high
27: 2 that you shall s up for
27: 4 on Mount Ebal you shall s up
28: 1 the LORD your God will s you
28: 8 and in all to which you s your
28:20 in all that you s your hand
28:36 king whom you s over you
28:56 who would not venture to s the
30: 1 which I have s before you,
30:15 I have s before you today life
30:19 that I have s before you life
32: 8 He s the boundaries of the
32:22 And s on fire the foundations
32:46 S your hearts on all the words
Josh 3: 1 and they s out from Acacia
3: 3 then you shall s out from your
3:14 when the people s out from
4: 9 Then Joshua s up twelve stones
4:20 Joshua s up in Gilgal.
6:26 he shall s up its gates."
8: 8 that you shall s the city on
8:12 five thousand men and s them
8:13 And when they had s the people,
8:19 and hurried to s the city on
10:18 and s men by it to guard them.
18: 1 and s up the tabernacle of
24:26 and s it up there under the oak
Judg 1: 8 sword and s the city on fire.
6:18 bring out my offering and s it
7: 5 you shall s apart by himself;
7:22 the LORD s every man's sword
8:27 made it into an ephod and s it
9:25 And the men of Shechem s men in
9:49 and s the stronghold on fire
15: 5 When he had s the torches on
18:30 Then the children of Dan s up
18:31 So they s up for themselves
20:29 Then Israel s men in ambush all
20:36 whom they had s against
20:48 They also s fire to all the
1 Sam 2: 8 To s them among princes And
2: 8 And He has s the world upon
5: 2 the temple of Dagon and s it
5: 3 So they took Dagon and s it in
6: 8 the ark of the LORD and s it
6:11 And they s the ark of the LORD
6:18 of Abel on which they s the
7:12 Samuel took a stone and s it
8:12 will s some to plow his
9:23 said to you, 'S it apart.'
9:24 with its upper part and s it
9:24 It was s apart for you.
10:19 'No, s a king over us!'
12:13 the LORD has s a king over
13: 8 according to the time s by
13:21 and to s the points of the
15:11 regret that I have s up
15:12 he s up a monument for himself;
18: 5 And Saul s him over the men of
22: 9 who was s over the servants of
28:22 and let me s a piece of bread
2 Sam 3:10 and s up the throne of David
4: 5 s out and came at about the
6: 3 So they s the ark of God on a
6:17 and s it in its place in the
7:12 I will s up your seed after
10:10 that he might s them in battle
10:17 And the Syrians s themselves in
11:15 S Uriah in the forefront of the
12:20 they s food before him, and he
12:30 And it was s on David's head.
14:30 go and s it on fire."
14:30 And Absalom's servants s the
14:31 Why have your servants s my
15:24 And they s down the ark of God,
18: 1 and s captains of thousands and
18:13 yourself would have s yourself
18:18 his lifetime had taken and s up
19:28 Yet you s your servant among
20: 5 longer than the s time
1 Ki 2:15 and all Israel had s their
2:19 his throne and had a throne s
2:24 who has confirmed me and s me
5: 5 whom I will s on your throne in
6:19 to s the ark of the covenant of
6:27 Then he s the cherubim inside
7:16 to s on the tops of the
7:21 Then he s up the pillars by the
7:21 he s up the pillar on the right
7:21 and he s up the pillar on the
7:25 the Sea was s upon them, and
7:39 He s the Sea on the right side
9: 6 statutes which I have s before
10:25 at a s rate year by year.
12:29 And he s up one in Bethel, and
16:32 Then he s up an altar for Baal
16:34 youngest son Segub he s up
20:14 Who will s the battle in
20:34 and you may s up marketplaces
2 Ki 4: 4 and s aside the full ones."
4:43 Shall I s this before one
4:44 So he s it before them; and
6:22 S food and water before them,
8:11 Then he s his countenance in a
8:12 Their strongholds you will s on
10: 3 s him on his father's throne,
12: 9 and s it beside the altar, on
12:17 then Hazael s his face to go up
17:10 They s up for themselves sacred
20: 1 S your house in order, for you
21: 7 He even s a carved image of
1 Chr 16: 1 and s it in the midst of the
17:11 that I will s up your seed
19:11 and they s themselves in
19:17 and s up in battle array
19:17 So when David had s up in
20: 2 And it was s on David's head.
22:19 Now s your heart and your soul
23:13 and Aaron was s apart, he and
23:31 Moons and on the s feasts,
29: 2 onyx stones, stones to be s,
29: 3 because I have s my affection
2 Chr 2: 4 and on the s feasts of the
3:17 Then he s up the pillars before
4: 4 the Sea was s upon them, and
4: 7 and s them in the temple, five
4:10 He s the Sea on the right side,
6:13 and had s it in the midst of
7:19 My commandments which I have s
9:24 at a s rate year by year.
11:16 such as s their heart to seek
13: 3 Abijah s the battle in order
13:11 they also s the showbread in
14:10 and they s the troops in battle
17: 2 and s garrisons in the land of
19: 5 Then he s judges in the land
20: 3 and s himself to seek the
20:22 the LORD s ambushes against
23:10 Then he s all the people, every
23:14 of hundreds who were s over
23:19 And he s the gatekeepers at the
23:20 and s the king on the throne of
24: 4 after this that Joash s his
24: 8 and s it outside at the gate of
25: 5 and s over them captains of
25:14 s them up to be his gods, and
29:35 of the house of the LORD was s
31: 3 New Moons and the s feasts,
32: 6 Then he s military captains over
33: 7 He even s a carved image, the
33:19 he built high places and s up
35: 2 And he s the priests in their
Ezra 3: 3 they s the altar on its bases;
7:25 s magistrates and judges who
10:16 were s apart by the fathers'
Neh 2: 6 and I s him a time.
2:18 Then they s their hands to
4: 9 and because of them we s a
4:13 and I s the people according to
9:35 large and rich land which You s
9:37 to the kings You have s over
10:33 and the s feasts; for the holy
13:11 and s them in their place.
Esth 2:17 so he s the royal crown upon
3: 1 and advanced him and s his seat
Job 7:12 That You s a guard over me?
7:17 That You should s Your heart
7:20 Why have You s me as Your
13:27 You s a limit for the soles of
14:13 You would appoint me a s time,
16:12 He has s me up for His target,
19: 8 And He has s darkness in my
33: 5 S your words in order before
34:14 If He should s His heart on it,
36:16 And what is s on your table
38:10 And s bars and doors;
38:33 Can you s their dominion over
39: 5 'Who s the wild donkey free?
Ps 2: 2 of the earth s themselves,
2: 6 Yet I have s My King On My holy
3: 6 people Who have s themselves
4: 3 that the LORD has s apart
8: 1 Who have s Your glory above
12: 5 I will s him in the safety for
16: 8 I have s the LORD always
17:11 They have s their eyes,
19: 4 In them He has s a tabernacle
20: 5 name of our God we will s up
21: 3 You s a crown of pure gold
22: S to "The Deer of the Dawn."
27: 5 He shall s me high upon a
31: 8 You have s my feet in a wide
40: 2 And s my feet upon a rock,
41:12 And s me before Your face
45: S to "The Lilies."
50:21 And s them in order before
53: S to "Mahalath."
54: 3 They have not s God before
56: S to "The Silent Dove in

57: S to "Do Not Destroy."
57: 4 the sons of men Who are s on
58: S to "Do Not Destroy."
59: S to "Do Not Destroy."
60: S to "Lily of the Testimony."
62:10 Do not s your heart on
69: S to "The Lilies." A Psalm
69:29 O God, s me up on high.
73: 9 They s their mouth against the
73:18 Surely You s them in slippery
74: 4 They s up their banners for
74: 7 They have s fire to Your
74:17 You have s all the borders of
75: S to "Do Not Destroy."
75: 3 I s up its pillars firmly.
78: 7 That they may s their hope in
78: 8 that did not s its heart
80: S to "The Lilies."
84: 5 Whose heart is s on
86:14 And have not s You before
88: S to "Mahalath Leannoth."
89:25 Also I will s his hand over the
90: 8 You have s our iniquities
91:14 Because he has s his love upon
91:14 I will s him on high, because
101: 3 I will s nothing wicked before
102:13 the s time, has come.
104: 9 You have s a boundary that they
109: 6 S a wicked man over him, And
118: 5 LORD answered me and s me
122: 5 For thrones are s there for
132:11 I will s upon your throne the
140: 5 They have s traps for me.
141: 2 Let my prayer be s before You
141: 3 S a guard, O LORD, over my
142: 3 I walk They have secretly s a
Prov 19:18 And do not s your heart on his
22:25 you learn his ways And s a
22:28 Which your fathers have s.
23: 5 Will you s your eyes on that
25:17 Seldom s foot in your
29: 8 Scoffers s a city aflame, But
Eccl 1:13 And I s my heart to seek and
1:17 And I s my heart to know wisdom
8:11 of the sons of men is fully s
10: 6 Folly is s in great dignity,
12: 9 and sought out and s in order
Song 5:12 with milk, And fitly s.
5:14 rods of gold S with beryl.
5:15 pillars of marble S on bases
7: 2 a heap of wheat S about
8: 6 S me as a seal upon your
Isa 7: 6 and s a king over them, the son
9:11 Therefore the LORD shall s up
11:11 the LORD shall s His hand
11:12 He will s up a banner for the
17:10 pleasant plants And s out
19: 2 I will s Egyptians against
21: 5 S a watchman in the tower,
21: 6 s a watchman, Let him declare
22: 7 horsemen shall s themselves
23:13 They s up its towers, They
23:18 Her gain and her pay will be s
27: 4 Who would s briers and thorns
27:11 The women come and s them on
38: 1 S your house in order, for you
41:19 I will s in the desert the
42:25 It has s him on fire all
44: 7 let him declare it and s it
46: 7 they carry it And s it in its
49:22 And s up My standard for the
50: 7 Therefore I have s My face
57: 7 You have s your bed;
57: 8 and their posts You have s up
62: 6 I have s watchmen on your
66:19 I will s a sign among them; and
Jer 1:10 I have this day s you over the
1:15 and each one s his throne
4: 6 S up the standard toward Zion
5:26 They s a trap; They catch
6: 1 And s up a signal-fire in Beth
6:17 I s watchmen over you, saying,
6:23 As men of war s in array
6:27 I have s you as an assayer
7:12 where I s My name at the first,
7:30 They have s their abominations
9:13 have forsaken My law which I s
10:20 Or s up my curtains.
11:13 of Jerusalem you have s up
21: 8 I s before you the way of life
21:10 For I have s My face against
23: 4 I will s up shepherds over them
24: 1 two baskets of figs s before
24: 6 For I will s My eyes on them for
26: 4 walk in My law which I have s
31:21 S up signposts, Make
31:21 S your heart toward the
31:29 the children's teeth are s on
31:30 his teeth shall be s on edge.
32:20 You have s signs and wonders in
32:29 city shall come and s fire
32:34 But they s their abominations in
34: 9 that every man should s free his
34:10 that everyone should s free
34:11 whom they had s free, and
34:14 years let every man s free
34:16 whom he had s at liberty, at
35: 5 Then I s before the sons of the
38:22 Your close friends have s upon
40:11 and that he had s over them
42:15 If you wholly s your faces to
42:17 all the men who s their faces
43: 3 the son of Neriah has s you
43:10 and will s his throne above
44:10 statutes that I s before you
44:11 I will s My face against you
44:12 Judah who have s their faces
49:38 I will s My throne in Elam,
50: 2 and s up a standard;
50:42 S in array, like a man for the
51:12 S up the standard on the walls
51:12 S up the watchmen, Prepare
51:27 S up a banner in the land,
Lam 1: 4 no one comes to the s feasts.
2: 7 As on the day of a s feast.
3: 6 He has s me in dark places
3:12 He has bent His bow And s me
Ezek 2: 2 and s me on my feet; and I
3:24 the Spirit entered me and s me
4: 2 s camps against it also, and
4: 3 and s it as an iron wall
4: 3 S your face against it, and it
4: 7 Therefore you shall s your face
5: 5 I have s her in the midst of
6: 2 s your face toward the
7:20 He s it in majesty; But they
13:17 s your face against the
14: 3 these men have s up their idols
14: 8 I will s My face against that
15: 7 and I will s My face against
15: 7 when I s My face against them.
16:18 and you s My oil and My incense
16:19 you s it before them as sweet
17: 4 He s it in a city of
17: 5 by abundant waters And s it
17:22 of the high cedar and s it
18: 2 the children's teeth are s on
19: 8 Then the nations s against him
20:46 s your face toward the south;
21: 2 s your face toward Jerusalem,
21:15 I have s the point of the sword
21:16 Thrust right! S your blade!
21:22 to s up battering rams, to call
21:22 to s battering rams against the
22:10 they violate women who are s
23:25 I will s My jealousy against
23:41 on which you had s My incense
24: 3 s it on, And also pour water
24: 7 She s it on top of a rock;
24: 8 I have s her blood on top of a
24:11 Then s the pot empty on the
24:25 and that on which they s their
25: 2 s your face against the
25: 4 and they shall s their
28: 2 Though you s your heart as the
28: 6 Because you have s your heart as
28:21 s your face toward Sidon, and
29: 2 s your face against Pharaoh
30: 8 When I have s a fire in Egypt
30:14 S fire to Zoan, And execute
30:16 And s a fire in Egypt;
31:10 and it s its top among the
31:14 nor s their tops among the
32:23 Her graves are s in the
32:25 They have s her bed in the
35: 2 s your face against Mount Seir
37: 1 and s me down in the midst of
37:26 and I will s My sanctuary in
38: 2 s your face against Gog, of the
39: 9 of Israel will go out and s on
39:14 They will s apart men regularly
39:15 he shall s up a marker by it,
39:21 I will s My glory among the
40: 2 the land of Israel and s me
43: 8 When they s their threshold by
44: 8 but you have s others to keep
45: 1 you shall s apart a district
48: 8 the district which you shall s
48: 9 district that you shall s
48:12 district of land that is s
48:20 You shall s apart the holy
Dan 1:11 the eunuchs had s over Daniel,
2:44 the God of heaven will s up
2:49 and he s Shadrach, Meshach, and
3: 1 He s it up in the plain of
3: 2 King Nebuchadnezzar had s up.
3: 3 King Nebuchadnezzar had s up;
3: 3 that Nebuchadnezzar had s up.
3: 5 King Nebuchadnezzar has s up;
3: 7 King Nebuchadnezzar had s up.
3:12 certain Jews whom you have s
3:12 gold image which you have s up.
3:14 the gold image which I have s
3:18 gold image which you have s up.
5:19 whomever he wished, he s up;
6: 1 It pleased Darius to s over the
6:14 and s his heart on Daniel to
9: 3 Then I s my face toward the
9:10 which He s before us by His
10:12 day that you s your heart
11:17 He shall also s his face to
12:11 abomination of desolation is s
Hos 2: 3 And s her like a dry land,
4: 8 They s their heart on their
8: 1 S the trumpet to your mouth!
8: 4 They s up kings, but not by Me;
11: 8 How can I s you like Zeboiim?
Joel 2: 5 Like a strong people s in
Am 9: 4 I will s My eyes on them for
Ob 4 And though you s your nest
Hab 1: 9 Their faces are s like the
2: 1 stand my watch And s myself
2: 9 That he may s his nest on
Zech 5:11 the basket will be s there on
6:11 and s it on the head of Joshua
8:10 For I s all men, everyone,
9:11 I will s your prisoners free
11:13 that princely price they s on
Mt 4: 5 s Him on the pinnacle of the
5:14 A city that is s on a hill
10:35 s a man against his father,
18: 2 s him in the midst of them,
21: 7 and s Him on them.
21:33 a vineyard and s a hedge
25:33 And He will s the sheep on His
Mk 1:32 At evening, when the sun had s,
4:21 Is it not to be s on a
6:41 disciples to s before them;
8: 6 disciples to s before them;
8: 6 and they s them before the
8: 7 He said to s them also before
9:36 a little child and s him
12: 1 a vineyard and s a hedge
Lk 1: 1 taken in hand to s in order
4: 9 s Him on the pinnacle of the
4:18 To s at liberty those
9:16 to the disciples to s before
9:47 took a little child and s him
9:51 that He steadfastly s His face
9:53 because His face was s for the
10: 8 eat such things as are s before
10:34 and he s him on his own animal,
11: 6 and I have nothing to s before
19:35 and they s Jesus on him.
Jn 2: 6 Now there were s there six
6:27 God the Father has s His seal
8: 3 And when they had s her in the
Acts 4: 7 And when they had s them in the
5:27 they s them before the
6: 6 whom they s before the apostles;
6:13 They also s up false witnesses
7: 5 not even enough to s his foot
7:21 But when he was s out, Pharaoh's
12:21 So on a s day Herod, arrayed in
13:13 Paul and his party s sail
13:47 I have s you as a light
15:16 And I will s it up;
16:34 he s food before them; and he
17: 5 s all the city in an uproar and
21: 1 departed from them and s sail,
21: 2 we went aboard and s sail.
22:30 and brought Paul down and s him
23:24 and provide mounts to s Paul on,
26:32 This man might have been s free
27:12 the majority advised to s sail
Rom 3:25 whom God s forth as a
6:18 And having been s free from sin,
6:22 But now having been s free from
8: 5 to the flesh s their minds on
12:16 Do not s your mind on high
1 Cor 10:27 eat whatever is s before you,
11:34 And the rest I will s in order
12:18 But now God has s the members,
Gal 2:21 I do not s aside the grace of
Phil 3:19 who s their mind on earthly
Col 3: 2 S your mind on things above, not
Titus 1: 5 that you should s in order the
Heb 2: 7 And s him over the works
6:18 of the hope s before us.
12: 1 endurance the race that is s
12: 2 who for the joy that was s
13:23 Timothy has been s free,
Jas 3: 6 The tongue is so s among our
3: 6 and it is s on fire by hell.
Jude 7 are s forth as an example,
Rev 3: 8 I have s before you an open
4: 2 a throne s in heaven, and One
10: 2 And he s his right foot on the
20: 3 and s a seal on him, so that he

SETH (9/9)

Gen 4:25 she bore a son and named him S,
4:26 And as for S, to him also a
5: 3 his image, and named him S.
5: 4 After he begot S,
5: 6 S lived one hundred and five
5: 7 S lived eight hundred and seven
5: 8 So all the days of S were nine
1 Chr 1: 1 Adam, S, Enosh,
Lk 3:38 son of Enos, the son of S,

SETHUR (1/1)

Num 13:13 S the son of Michael;

SETS (17/17)

Deut 23:11 with water; and when the sun s,
27:15 and s it up in secret.'
2 Sam 22:34 And s me on my high places.
Job 5:11 He s on high those who are
34:24 And s others in their place.
Ps 18:33 And s me on my high places.
36: 4 He s himself in a way that
68: 6 God s the solitary in families;
83:14 And as the flame s the
107:41 Yet He s the poor on high, far
Jer 5:26 in wait as one who s snares;
Ezek 14: 4 the house of Israel who s up
14: 7 himself from Me and s up his
Dan 4:17 And s over it the lowest of
Lk 8:16 but s it on a lampstand, that
Jn 2:10 Every man at the beginning s out

Jas 3: 6 and *s* on fire the course of

SETTER (KJV) See PROCLAIMER

SETTING (13/13)

Ex 31: 5 "in cutting jewels for *s*,
35:33 "in cutting jewels for *s*,
Num 7: 1 when Moses had finished *s* up
10:29 We are *s* out for the place of
Deut 11:30 toward the *s* sun, in the land
1 Ki 10: 9 *s* you on the throne of Israel!
15: 4 by *s* up his son after him and
2 Chr 9: 8 *s* you on His throne to be
Isa 45: 6 the rising of the sun to its *s*
Dan 6: 3 the king gave thought to *s* him
Am 7: 8 I am *s* a plumb line In the
Mt 27:66 sealing the stone and *s* the
Lk 4:40 When the sun was *s*,

SETTINGS (11/11)

Ex 28:11 You shall set them in *s* of
28:13 You shall also make *s* of gold,
28:14 the braided chains to the *s*.
28:17 And you shall put *s* of stones in
28:20 They shall be set in gold *s*.
28:25 you shall fasten to the two *s*,
39: 6 enclosed in *s* of gold; they
39:13 They were enclosed in *s* of
39:16 They also made two *s* of gold and
39:18 they fastened in the two *s*,
Prov 25:11 is like apples of gold In *s*

SETTLE (11/11) SETTLED

Deut 29:20 is written in this book would *s*
Job 3: 5 May a cloud *s* on it; May the
Ps 65:10 You *s* its furrows; You make
Isa 14: 1 and *s* them in their own land.
Ezek 32: 4 And cause to *s* on you all the
Zech 9: 6 A mixed race shall *s* in Ashdod,
Mt 18:23 a certain king who wanted to *s*
18:24 And when he had begun to *s*
Lk 12:58 effort along the way to *s* with
21:14 Therefore *s* it in your hearts
1 Pe 5:10 strengthen, and *s* you.

SETTLED (15/15) SETTLE

Num 9:17 in the place where the cloud *s*,
10:12 then the cloud *s* down in the
Deut 21: 5 and every assault shall be *s*.
Judg 9:24 sons of Jerubbaal might be *s*
1 Chr 5: 9 Eastward they *s* as far as the
2 Chr 8: 2 and he *s* the children of Israel
Ezra 4:10 Osnapper took captive and *s* in
Job 29:22 And my speech *s* on them as
Ps 94:17 My soul would soon have *s* in
119:89 Your word is *s* in heaven.
Prov 8:25 Before the mountains were *s*,
Isa 13:20 Nor will it be *s* from
Jer 48:11 He has *s* on his dregs, And
Zeph 1:12 And punish the men Who are *s*
Mt 25:19 of those servants came and *s*

SETTLEMENTS (2/2)

Gen 25:16 by their towns and their *s*,
1 Chr 6:54 places throughout their *s* in

SETTLING (1/1)

Num 22: 5 and are *s* next to me!

SEVEN (433/365) SEVENTH

Gen 5: 7 Seth lived eight hundred and *s*
5:26 Methuselah lived *s* hundred and
5:31 days of Lamech were *s* hundred
7: 2 You shall take with you *s* each
7: 3 also *s* each of birds of the air,
7: 4 For after *s* more days I will
7:10 And it came to pass after *s* days
8:10 waited yet another *s* days,
8:12 So he waited yet another *s* days
11:21 Reu lived two hundred and *s*
21:28 And Abraham set *s* ewe lambs of
21:29 meaning of these *s* ewe
21:30 You will take these *s* ewe lambs
29:18 I will serve you *s* years for
29:20 So Jacob served *s* years for
29:27 me still another *s* years."
29:30 Laban still another *s* years.
31:23 pursued him for *s* days'
33: 3 to the ground *s* times,
41: 2 out of the river *s* cows,
41: 3 *s* other cows came up after them
41: 4 ate up the *s* fine looking
41: 5 and suddenly *s* heads of grain
41: 6 *s* thin heads, blighted by the
41: 7 And the *s* thin heads devoured
41: 7 thin heads devoured the *s* plump
41:18 Suddenly *s* cows came up out of
41:19 *s* other cows came up after
41:20 ugly cows ate up the first *s*,
41:22 and suddenly *s* heads came up on
41:23 *s* heads, withered, thin, and
41:24 devoured the *s* good heads.
41:26 The *s* good cows are seven
41:26 good cows are *s* years,
41:26 and the *s* good heads are seven
41:26 seven good heads are *s* years;
41:27 And the *s* thin and ugly cows
41:27 up after them are *s* years,
41:27 and the *s* empty heads blighted
41:27 by the east wind are *s* years
41:29 Indeed *s* years of great plenty
41:30 but after them *s* years of famine
41:34 in the *s* plentiful years.
41:36 for the land for the *s* years
41:47 Now in the *s* plentiful years the
41:48 up all the food of the *s* years
41:53 Then the *s* years of plenty
41:54 and the *s* years of famine began
46:25 to Jacob: *s* persons in all.
50:10 He observed *s* days of mourning
Ex 2:16 of Midian had *s* daughters.
7:25 And *s* days passed after the
12:15 *S* days you shall eat unleavened
12:19 For *s* days no leaven shall be
13: 6 *S* days you shall eat unleavened
13: 7 bread shall be eaten *s* days.
22:30 be with its mother *s* days;
23:15 eat unleavened bread *s* days,
25:37 You shall make *s* lamps for it,
29:30 shall put them on for *s* days,
29:35 *S* days you shall consecrate
29:37 *S* days you shall make atonement
34:18 *S* days you shall eat unleavened
37:23 And he made its *s* lamps, its
38:24 talents and *s* hundred and
38:25 and one thousand *s* hundred
38:28 one thousand *s* hundred
Lev 4: 6 some of the blood *s* times
4:17 blood and sprinkle it *s* times
8:11 it on the altar *s* times,
8:33 of meeting for *s* days, until
8:33 For *s* days he shall consecrate
8:35 day and night for *s* days,
12: 2 she shall be unclean *s* days;
13: 4 one who has the sore *s* days.
13: 5 isolate him another *s* days.
13:21 shall isolate him *s* days;
13:26 shall isolate him *s* days.
13:31 who has the scale *s* days.
13:33 the scale another *s* days.
13:50 which has the plague *s* days.
13:54 isolate it another *s* days.
14: 7 And he shall sprinkle it *s* times
14: 8 stay outside his tent *s* days.
14:16 oil with his finger *s* times
14:27 is in his left hand *s* times
14:38 and shut up the house *s* days.
14:51 and sprinkle the house *s* times.
15:13 shall count for himself *s* days
15:19 she shall be set apart *s* days;
15:24 he shall be unclean *s* days; and
15:28 shall count for herself *s* days,
16:14 blood with his finger *s* times.
16:19 on it with his finger *s* times,
22:27 it shall be *s* days with its
23: 6 *s* days you must eat unleavened
23: 8 fire to the LORD for *s* days.
23:15 *s* Sabbaths shall be completed.
23:18 offer with the bread *s* lambs
23:34 of Tabernacles for *s* days
23:36 For *s* days you shall offer an
23:39 of the LORD for *s* days;
23:40 the LORD your God for *s* days.
23:41 feast to the LORD for *s* days
23:42 dwell in booths for *s* days.
25: 8 And you shall count *s* sabbaths
25: 8 *s* times seven years; and the
25: 8 seven times *s* years; and the
25: 8 and the time of the *s* sabbaths
26:18 then I will punish you *s* times
26:21 I will bring on you *s* times
26:24 will punish you yet *s* times
26:28 will chastise you *s* times for
Num 1:39 Dan were sixty-two thousand *s*
2:26 at sixty-two thousand *s*
3:22 there were *s* thousand five
4:36 families were two thousand *s*
8: 2 the *s* lamps shall give light in
12:14 would she not be shamed *s* days?
12:14 shut out of the camp *s* days,
12:15 shut out of the camp *s* days,
13:22 (Now Hebron was built *s* years
16:49 plague were fourteen thousand *s*
19: 4 some of its blood *s* times
19:11 shall be unclean *s* days.
19:14 tent shall be unclean *s* days;
19:16 shall be unclean *s* days.
23: 1 Build *s* altars for me here, and
23: 1 here *s* bulls and seven rams."
23: 1 for me here seven bulls and *s*
23: 4 I have prepared the *s* altars,
23:14 and built *s* altars, and offered
23:29 Build for me here *s* altars, and
23:29 here *s* bulls and seven rams."
23:29 for me here seven bulls and *s*
26: 7 were forty-three thousand *s*
26:34 them were fifty-two thousand *s*
26:51 six hundred and one thousand *s*
28:11 and *s* lambs in their first
28:17 shall be eaten for *s* days.
28:19 and *s* lambs in their first
28:21 for each of the *s* lambs;
28:24 made by fire daily for *s* days,
28:27 and *s* lambs in their first
28:29 for each of the *s* lambs;
29: 2 and *s* lambs in their first
29: 4 for each of the *s* lambs;
29: 8 and *s* lambs in their first
29:10 for each of the *s* lambs;
29:12 a feast to the LORD *s* days.
29:32 seventh day present *s* bulls,
29:36 *s* lambs in their first year
31:19 remain outside the camp *s* days;
31:52 was sixteen thousand *s* hundred
Deut 7: 1 *s* nations greater and mightier
15: 1 At the end of every *s* years you
16: 3 *s* days you shall eat unleavened
16: 4 all your territory for *s* days,
16: 9 You shall count *s* weeks for
16: 9 begin to count the *s* weeks from
16:13 Feast of Tabernacles *s* days,
16:15 *S* days you shall keep a sacred
28: 7 and flee before you *s* ways.
28:25 against them and flee *s* ways
31:10 At the end of every *s* years, at
Josh 6: 4 And *s* priests shall bear seven
6: 4 priests shall bear *s* trumpets
6: 4 march around the city *s* times,
6: 6 and let *s* priests bear seven
6: 6 seven priests bear *s* trumpets
6: 8 that the *s* priests bearing the
6: 8 priests bearing the *s* trumpets
6:13 Then *s* priests bearing seven
6:13 priests bearing *s* trumpets
6:15 around the city *s* times
6:15 around the city *s* times.
18: 2 the children of Israel *s* tribes
18: 5 divide it into *s* parts.
18: 6 survey the land in *s* parts
18: 9 the survey in a book in *s* parts
Judg 6: 1 hand of Midian for *s* years,
6:25 the second bull of *s* years old,
8:26 he requested was one thousand *s*
12: 9 He judged Israel *s* years.
14:12 it to me within the *s* days
14:17 had wept on him the *s* days
16: 7 If they bind me with *s* fresh
16: 8 brought up to her *s* fresh
16:13 If you weave the *s* locks of my
16:19 had him shave off the *s* locks
20:15 who numbered *s* hundred select
20:16 this people were *s* hundred
Ruth 4:15 better to you than *s* sons,
1 Sam 2: 5 Even the barren has borne *s*,
6: 1 of the Philistines *s* months.
10: 8 *S* days you shall wait, till I
11: 3 Hold off for *s* days, that we may
13: 8 Then he waited *s* days,
16:10 Thus Jesse made *s* of his sons
31:13 and fasted *s* days.
2 Sam 2:11 house of Judah was *s* years
5: 5 he reigned over Judah *s* years
8: 4 *s* hundred horsemen, and twenty
10:18 and David killed *s* hundred
21: 6 let *s* men of his descendants be
21: 9 all *s* together, and were put
24:13 Shall *s* years of famine come to
1 Ki 2:11 *s* years he reigned in Hebron,
6: 6 and the third was *s* cubits
6:38 So he was *s* years in building
7:17 *s* chains for one capital and
7:17 for one capital and *s* for
8:65 *s* days and seven more
8:65 seven days and *s* more
11: 3 And he had *s* hundred wives,
16:15 had reigned in Tirzah *s* days.
18:43 And *s* times he said, "Go
19:18 Yet I have reserved *s* thousand
20:15 of Israel—*s* thousand.
20:29 opposite each other for *s* days.
2 Ki 3: 9 roundabout route *s* days;
3:26 he took with him *s* hundred men
4:35 then the child sneezed *s* times,
5:10 wash in the Jordan *s* times,
5:14 went down and dipped *s* times
8: 1 upon the land for *s* years."
8: 2 of the Philistines *s* years.
8: 3 at the end of *s* years, that the
11:21 Jehoash was *s* years old when he
24:16 *s* thousand, and craftsmen and
1 Chr 3: 4 There he reigned *s* years and
3:24 and Anani—*s* in all.
5:13 Zia, and Eber—*s* in all.
5:18 had forty-four thousand *s*
9:13 one thousand *s* hundred and
9:25 from time to time for *s* days.
10:12 and fasted *s* days.
12:25 *s* thousand one hundred;
12:27 and with him three thousand *s*
15:26 that they offered *s* bulls and
15:26 offered seven bulls and *s* rams.
18: 4 *s* thousand horsemen, and twenty
19:18 and David killed *s* thousand
26:30 one thousand *s* hundred able
26:32 brethren were two thousand *s*
29: 4 and *s* thousand talents of
29:27 *s* years he reigned in Hebron,
2 Chr 7: 8 Solomon kept the feast *s* days,
7: 9 dedication of the altar *s* days,
7: 9 and the feast *s* days.
13: 9 with a young bull and *s* rams
15:11 LORD at that time *s* hundred
15:11 hundred bulls and *s* thousand
17:11 *s* thousand seven hundred rams
17:11 seven thousand *s* hundred rams
17:11 seven hundred rams and *s*
17:11 rams and seven thousand *s*
24: 1 Joash was *s* years old when he
26:13 an army of three hundred and *s*
29:21 And they brought *s* bulls, seven

S

29:21 *s* rams, seven lambs, and seven
29:21 *s* lambs, and seven male goats
29:21 and *s* male goats for a sin
30:21 of Unleavened Bread *s* days
30:22 throughout the feast *s* days,
30:23 the feast another *s* days,
30:23 they kept it another *s* days
30:24 assembly a thousand bulls and *s*
35:17 of Unleavened Bread for *s* days.
Ezra 2: 5 *s* hundred and seventy-five;
2: 9 *s* hundred and sixty;
2:25 *s* hundred and forty-three;
2:33 *s* hundred and twenty-five;
2:65 of whom there were *s* thousand
2:66 Their horses were *s* hundred and
2:67 their donkeys six thousand *s*
6:22 of Unleavened Bread *s* days
7:14 king and his *s* counselors
Neh 7:14 *s* hundred and sixty;
7:29 *s* hundred and forty-three;
7:37 *s* hundred and twenty-one;
7:67 of whom there were *s* thousand
7:68 Their horses were *s* hundred and
7:69 and donkeys six thousand *s*
8:18 And they kept the feast *s* days;
Esth 1: 5 made a feast lasting *s* days
1:10 *s* eunuchs who served in the
1:14 the *s* princes of Persia and
2: 9 Then *s* choice maidservants were
Job 1: 2 And *s* sons and three daughters
1: 3 his possessions were *s* thousand
2:13 with him on the ground *s* days
2:13 ground seven days and *s* nights,
5:19 in *s* no evil shall touch you.
42: 8 take for yourselves *s* bulls and
42: 8 seven bulls and *s* rams,
42:13 He also had *s* sons and three
Ps 12: 6 of earth, Purified *s* times.
119:164 *S* times a day I praise You,
Prov 6:16 *s* are an abomination to Him:
9: 1 hewn out her *s* pillars;
24:16 righteous man may fall *s* times
26:16 in his own eyes Than *s* men
26:25 For there are *s* abominations
Eccl 11: 2 Give a serving to *s*,
Isa 4: 1 And in that day *s* women shall
11:15 strike it in the *s* streams,
30:26 As the light of *s* days, In
Jer 15: 9 languishes who has borne *s*;
34:14 At the end of *s* years let every
52:25 *s* men of the king's close
52:30 captive of the Jews *s* hundred
Ezek 3:15 astonished among them *s* days.
3:16 to pass at the end of *s* days
39: 9 fires with them for *s* years.
39:12 For *s* months the house of Israel
39:14 At the end of *s* months they
40:22 it was ascended by *s* steps, and
40:26 *S* steps led up to it, and its
41: 3 of the entrance, *s* cubits.
43:25 Every day for *s* days you shall
43:26 *S* days they shall make atonement
44:26 they shall count *s* days for
45:21 a feast of *s* days;
45:23 On the *s* days of the feast he
45:23 *s* bulls and seven rams without
45:23 seven bulls and *s* rams without
45:23 daily for *s* days, and a kid of
45:25 shall do likewise for *s* days,
Dan 3:19 they heat the furnace *s* times
4:16 And let *s* times pass over him.
4:23 till *s* times pass over him';
4:25 and *s* times shall pass over
4:32 and *s* times shall pass over
9:25 There shall be *s* weeks and
Mic 5: 5 against him *S* shepherds
Zech 3: 9 Upon the stone are *s* eyes.
4: 2 and on the stand *s* lamps with
4: 2 seven lamps with *s* pipes
4: 2 seven pipes to the *s* lamps.
4:10 For these *s* rejoice to see
Mt 12:45 takes with him *s* other
15:34 '*S*, and a few little fish."
15:36 And He took the *s* loaves and the
15:37 and they took up *s* large
16:10 Nor the *s* loaves of the four
18:21 forgive him? Up to *s* times?"
18:22 up to *s* times, but up to
18:22 but up to seventy times *s*.
22:25 were with us *s* brothers.
22:28 whose wife of the *s* will she
Mk 8: 5 you have?" And they said, "*S*.
8: 6 And He took the *s* loaves and
8: 8 and they took up *s* large
8:20 when I broke the *s* for the four
8:20 take up?" And they said, "*S*.
12:20 'Now there were *s* brothers.
12:22 So the *s* had her and left no
12:23 For all *s* had her as wife."
16: 9 whom He had cast *s* demons.
Lk 2:36 lived with a husband *s* years
8: 2 out of whom had come *s* demons,
11:26 and takes with him *s* other
17: 4 he sins against you *s* times
17: 4 and *s* times in a day returns to
20:29 'Now there were *s* brothers.
20:31 and in like manner the *s* also;
20:33 For all *s* had her as wife."
24:13 which was *s* miles from
Acts 6: 3 seek out from among you *s* men
13:19 He had destroyed *s* nations
19:14 Also there were *s* sons of Sceva,
20: 6 where we stayed *s* days.
21: 4 we stayed there *s* days.
21: 8 who was one of the *s*,
21:27 Now when the *s* days were almost
28:14 to stay with them *s* days.
Rom 11: 4 for Myself *s* thousand
Heb 11:30 they were encircled for *s* days.
Rev 1: 4 to the *s* churches which are in
1: 4 and from the *s* Spirits who are
1:11 and send it to the *s* churches
1:12 I saw *s* golden lampstands,
1:13 midst of the *s* lampstands
1:16 in His right hand *s* stars,
1:20 The mystery of the *s* stars which
1:20 and the *s* golden lampstands:
1:20 The *s* stars are the angels of
1:20 the angels of the *s* churches,
1:20 and the *s* lampstands which you
1:20 you saw are the *s* churches.
2: 1 says He who holds the *s* stars
2: 1 in the midst of the *s* golden
3: 1 says He who has the *s* Spirits
3: 1 Spirits of God and the *s* stars:
4: 5 *S* lamps of fire were burning
4: 5 which are the *s* Spirits of God.
5: 1 sealed with *s* seals.
5: 5 and to loose its *s* seals."
5: 6 having *s* horns and seven eyes,
5: 6 having seven horns and *s* eyes,
5: 6 which are the *s* Spirits of God
8: 2 And I saw the *s* angels who stand
8: 2 them were given *s* trumpets.
8: 6 So the *s* angels who had the
8: 6 angels who had the *s* trumpets
10: 3 *s* thunders uttered their
10: 4 Now when the *s* thunders uttered
10: 4 things which the *s* thunders
11:13 In the earthquake *s* thousand
12: 3 fiery red dragon having *s* heads
12: 3 and *s* diadems on his heads.
13: 1 having *s* heads and ten horns,
15: 1 *s* angels having the seven last
15: 1 seven angels having the *s* last
15: 6 the temple came the *s* angels
15: 6 angels having the *s* plagues,
15: 7 creatures gave to the *s* angels
15: 7 angels *s* golden bowls full
15: 8 the temple till the *s* plagues
15: 8 seven plagues of the *s* angels
16: 1 temple saying to the *s* angels,
17: 1 Then one of the *s* angels who had
17: 1 angels who had the *s* bowls
17: 3 having *s* heads and ten horns.
17: 7 which has the *s* heads and the
17: 9 The *s* heads are seven mountains
17: 9 The seven heads are *s* mountains
17:10 'There are also *s* kings.
17:11 the eighth, and is of the *s*,
21: 9 Then one of the *s* angels who
21: 9 angels who had the *s* bowls
21: 9 filled with the *s* last plagues

SEVENFOLD (5/5)

Gen 4:15 shall be taken on him *s*.
4:24 If Cain shall be avenged *s*,
Ps 79:12 And return to our neighbors *s*
Prov 6:31 he is found, he must restore *s*;
Isa 30:26 the light of the sun will be *s*,

SEVENTEEN (9/9)

Gen 37: 2 being *s* years old, was feeding
47:28 the land of Egypt *s* years.
1 Ki 14:21 He reigned *s* years in
2 Ki 13: 1 and reigned *s* years.
1 Chr 7:11 there were *s* thousand two
2 Chr 12:13 and he reigned *s* years in
Ezra 2:39 of Harim, one thousand and *s*.
Neh 7:42 of Harim, one thousand and *s*.
Jer 32: 9 *s* shekels of silver.

SEVENTEENTH (6/6)

Gen 7:11 the *s* day of the month, on that
8: 4 the *s* day of the month, on the
1 Ki 22:51 Israel in Samaria in the *s* year
2 Ki 16: 1 In the *s* year of Pekah the son
1 Chr 24:15 the *s* to Hezir, the eighteenth
25:24 the *s* for Joshbekashah, his sons

SEVENTH (116/111) SEVEN

Gen 2: 2 And on the *s* day God ended His
2: 2 and He rested on the *s* day from
2: 3 Then God blessed the *s* day and
8: 4 ark rested in the *s* month,
Ex 12:15 the first day until the *s* day,
12:16 and on the *s* day there shall be
13: 6 and on the *s* day there shall
16:26 but on the *s* day, which is
16:27 people went out on the *s* day
16:29 of his place on the *s* day."
16:30 people rested on the *s* day.
20:10 but the *s* day is the Sabbath of
20:11 and rested the *s* day.
21: 2 and in the *s* he shall go out
23:11 but the *s* year you shall let it
23:12 and on the *s* day you shall
24:16 And on the *s* day He called to
31:15 but the *s* is the Sabbath of
31:17 and on the *s* day He rested and
34:21 but on the *s* day you shall
35: 2 but the *s* day shall be a holy
Lev 13: 5 shall examine him on the *s* day;
13: 6 examine him again on the *s* day;
13:27 shall examine him on the *s* day.
13:32 And on the *s* day the priest
13:34 On the *s* day the priest shall
13:51 the plague on the *s* day.
14: 9 But on the *s* day he shall shave
14:39 shall come again on the *s* day
16:29 In the *s* month, on the tenth
23: 3 but the *s* day is a Sabbath of
23: 8 The *s* day shall be a holy
23:16 the day after the *s* Sabbath;
23:24 In the *s* month, on the first
23:27 tenth day of this *s* month
23:34 day of this *s* month
23:39 fifteenth day of the *s* month,
23:41 celebrate it in the *s* month.
25: 4 but in the *s* year there shall be
25: 9 tenth day of the *s* month;
25:20 What shall we eat in the *s* year,
Num 6: 9 on the *s* day he shall shave it.
7:48 On the *s* day Elishama the son
19:12 third day and on the *s* day;
19:12 third day and on the *s* day,
19:19 third day and on the *s* day;
19:19 and on the *s* day he shall
28:25 And on the *s* day you shall have
29: 1 And in the *s* month, on the first
29: 7 tenth day of this *s* month
29:12 fifteenth day of the *s* month
29:32 On the *s* day present seven
31:19 third day and on the *s* day.
31:24 wash your clothes on the *s* day
Deut 5:14 but the *s* day is the Sabbath of
15: 9 The *s* year, the year of release,
15:12 then in the *s* year you shall
16: 8 and on the *s* day there shall
Josh 6: 4 But the *s* day you shall march
6:15 it came to pass on the *s* day
6:16 And the *s* time it happened, when
19:40 The *s* lot came out for the
Judg 14:15 it came to pass on the *s* day
14:17 And it happened on the *s* day
14:18 city said to him on the *s* day
2 Sam 12:18 Then on the *s* day it came to
1 Ki 8: 2 which is the *s* month.
18:44 came to pass the *s* time,
20:29 So it was that on the *s* day the
2 Ki 11: 4 In the *s* year Jehoiada sent and
12: 1 In the *s* year of Jehu, Jehoash
18: 9 which was the *s* year of Hoshea
25: 8 on the *s* day of the month
25:25 But it happened in the *s* month
1 Chr 2:15 the sixth, and David the *s*.
12:11 Attai the sixth, Eliel the *s*,
24:10 the *s* to Hakkoz, the eighth to
25:14 the *s* for Jesharelah, his sons
26: 3 the sixth, Eliehoenai the *s*.
26: 5 the sixth, Issachar the *s*,
27:10 The *s* captain for the seventh
27:10 captain for the *s* month
2 Chr 5: 3 which was in the *s* month.
7:10 day of the *s* month he sent
23: 1 In the *s* year Jehoiada
31: 7 finished in the *s* month.
Ezra 3: 1 And when the *s* month had come,
3: 6 the first day of the *s* month
7: 7 up to Jerusalem in the *s* year
7: 8 which was in the *s* year of the
Neh 7:73 When the *s* month came, the
8: 2 first day of the *s* month.
8:14 the feast of the *s* month,
10:31 forego the *s* year's produce
Esth 1:10 On the *s* day, when the heart of
2:16 in the *s* year of his reign.
Jer 28:17 same year in the *s* month.
41: 1 came to pass in the *s* month
52:28 in the *s* year, three thousand
Ezek 20: 1 It came to pass in the *s* year,
30:20 on the *s* day of the month,
45:20 so you shall do on the *s* day
45:25 In the *s* month, on the
Hag 2: 1 In the *s* month, on the
Zech 7: 5 in the fifth and *s* months
8:19 the fifth, The fast of the *s*,
Mt 22:26 and the third, even to the *s*.
Jn 4:52 Yesterday at the *s* hour the
Heb 4: 4 certain place of the *s* day
4: 4 God rested on the *s* day
Jude 14 the *s* from Adam, prophesied
Rev 8: 1 When He opened the *s* seal, there
10: 7 the sounding of the *s* angel,
11:15 Then the *s* angel sounded:
16:17 Then the *s* angel poured out his
21:20 the *s* chrysolite, the eighth

SEVENTY (67/66)

Gen 5:12 Cainan lived *s* years, and begot
11:26 Now Terah lived *s* years, and
46:27 Jacob who went to Egypt were *s*.
50: 3 mourned for him *s* days.
Ex 1: 5 of Jacob were *s* persons
15:27 of water and *s* palm trees;
24: 1 and *s* of the elders of Israel,
24: 9 and *s* of the elders of Israel,
38:29 of bronze was *s* talents and
Num 7:13 one silver bowl of *s* shekels,
7:19 one silver bowl of *s* shekels,
7:25 one silver bowl of *s* shekels,

7:31 one silver bowl of *s* shekels,
7:37 one silver bowl of *s* shekels,
7:43 one silver bowl of *s* shekels,
7:49 one silver bowl of *s* shekels,
7:55 one silver bowl of *s* shekels,
7:61 one silver bowl of *s* shekels,
7:67 one silver bowl of *s* shekels,
7:73 one silver bowl of *s* shekels,
7:79 one silver bowl of *s* shekels,
7:85 and each bowl *s* shekels.
11:16 Gather to Me *s* men of the elders
11:24 and he gathered the *s* men of
11:25 the same upon the *s* elders;
33: 9 of water and *s* palm trees;
Deut 10:22 to Egypt with *s* persons,
Judg 1: 7 *S* kings with their thumbs and
8:30 Gideon had *s* sons who were his
9: 2 that all *s* of the sons of
9: 4 So they gave him *s* shekels of
9: 5 the *s* sons of Jerubbaal, on one
9:18 and killed his *s* sons on one
9:24 the crime done to the *s* sons
9:56 by killing his *s* brothers.
12:14 who rode on *s* young donkeys.
1 Sam 6:19 He struck fifty thousand and *s*
2 Sam 24:15 *s* thousand men of the people
1 Ki 5:15 Solomon had *s* thousand who
2 Ki 10: 1 Now Ahab had *s* sons in Samaria.
10: 6 *s* persons, were with the great
10: 7 and slaughtered *s* persons,
1 Chr 21: 5 Judah had four hundred and *s*
21:14 and *s* thousand men of Israel
2 Chr 2: 2 Solomon selected *s* thousand men
2:18 And he made *s* thousand of them
29:32 assembly brought was *s* bulls,
36:21 to fulfill *s* years.
Ezra 8: 7 and with him *s* males;
8:14 and with them *s* males.
Ps 90:10 of our lives are *s* years;
Isa 23:15 will be forgotten *s* years,
23:15 At the end of *s* years it will
23:17 at the end of *s* years, that the
Jer 25:11 the king of Babylon *s* years.
25:12 when *s* years are completed,
29:10 After *s* years are completed at
Ezek 8:11 there stood before them *s* men
41:12 western end was *s* cubits
Dan 9: 2 would accomplish *s* years
9:24 *S* weeks are determined For
Zech 1:12 were angry these *s* years?"
7: 5 months during those *s* years,
Mt 18:22 but up to *s* times seven.
Lk 10: 1 the Lord appointed *s* others
10:17 Then the *s* returned with joy,
Acts 23:23 *s* horsemen, and two hundred

SEVENTY-FIVE (9/9)

Gen 12: 4 And Abram was *s* years old when
25: 7 one hundred and *s* years.
Ex 38:25 thousand seven hundred and *s*
38:28 thousand seven hundred and *s*
Num 31:32 was six hundred and *s* thousand
31:37 the sheep was six hundred and *s*.
Ezra 2: 5 of Arah, seven hundred and *s*;
Esth 9:16 and killed *s* thousand of their
Acts 7:14 relatives to him, *s* people.

SEVENTY-FOUR (4/4)

Num 1:27 of the tribe of Judah were *s*
2: 4 And his army was numbered at *s*
Ezra 2:40 of the sons of Hodaviah, *s*.
Neh 7:43 and of the sons of Hodevah, *s*.

SEVENTY-SEVEN (3/3)

Gen 5:31 were seven hundred and *s* years;
Judg 8:14 Succoth and its elders, *s* men.
Ezra 8:35 *s* lambs, and twelve male goats

SEVENTY-SEVENFOLD (1/1)

Gen 4:24 sevenfold, Then Lamech *s*.

SEVENTY-SIX (2/2)

Num 26:22 *s* thousand five hundred.
Acts 27:37 all we were two hundred and *s*

SEVENTY-THREE (4/4)

Num 3:43 thousand two hundred and *s*.
3:46 of the two hundred and *s* of
Ezra 2:36 of Jeshua, nine hundred and *s*;
Neh 7:39 of Jeshua, nine hundred and *s*;

SEVENTY-TWO (7/7)

Num 31:33 *s* thousand cattle,
31:38 the LORD's tribute was *s*.
Ezra 2: 3 two thousand one hundred and *s*;
2: 4 Shephatiah, three hundred and *s*;
Neh 7: 8 two thousand one hundred and *s*;
7: 9 Shephatiah, three hundred and *s*;
11:19 gates, were one hundred and *s*.

SEVER (1/1)

Isa 2:22 *S* yourselves from such a man,

SEVERAL (1/1)

2 Ki 7:13 let *s* men take five of the

SEVERE (29/29) SEVERELY, SEVERITY

Gen 12:10 for the famine was *s* in the
41:31 for it will be very *s*.
41:56 And the famine became *s* in the
41:57 because the famine was *s* in all
43: 1 Now the famine was *s* in the
47: 4 for the famine is *s* in the
47:13 for the famine was very *s*,
47:20 because the famine was *s* upon
Ex 9: 3 a very *s* pestilence.
10:14 They were very *s*;
Deut 6:22 before our eyes, great and *s*,
28:22 with *s* burning fever, with the
28:35 and on the legs with *s* boils
1 Ki 18: 2 and there was a *s* famine in
2 Ki 25: 3 the famine had become so *s* in
2 Chr 16:12 his feet, and his malady was *s*;
21:19 so he died in *s* pain.
Ps 71:20 shown me great and *s* troubles,
Eccl 5:13 There is a *s* evil which I
5:16 this also is a *s* evil—Just
Isa 27: 1 the LORD with His *s* sword,
Jer 10:19 me for my hurt! My wound is *s*.
14:17 with a very *s* blow.
30:12 incurable, Your wound is *s*.
52: 6 the famine had become so *s* in
Ezek 14:21 I send My four *s* judgments
Nah 3:19 no healing, Your wound is *s*.
Lk 15:14 there arose a *s* famine in that
2 Cor 2: 5 to some extent—not to be too *s*.

SEVERELY (14/14) SEVERE

Judg 10: 9 Israel was *s* distressed.
1 Sam 1: 6 her rival also provoked her *s*,
28:21 saw that he was *s* troubled,
31: 3 and he was *s* wounded by the
2 Chr 24:25 they left him *s* wounded),
35:23 for I am *s* wounded."
Ps 38: 8 I am feeble and *s* broken;
44:19 But You have *s* broken us in the
55: 4 My heart is *s* pained within me,
118:18 The LORD has chastened me *s*,
Isa 64:12 peace, and afflict us very *s*?
Mt 15:22 is *s* demon-possessed."
17:15 is an epileptic and suffers *s*;
Acts 4:17 let us *s* threaten them, that

SEVERITY (2/1) SEVERE

Rom 11:22 consider the goodness and *s* of
11:22 of God: on those who fell, *s*;

SEW (2/2) SEWED, SEWS

Eccl 3: 7 time to tear, And a time to *s*;
Ezek 13:18 Woe to the women who *s* magic

SEWED (1/1) SEW

Gen 3: 7 and they *s* fig leaves together

SEWN (1/1)

Job 16:15 I have *s* sackcloth over my skin,

SEWS (1/1) SEW

Mk 2:21 No one *s* a piece of unshrunk

SEXUAL (19/17) SEXUALLY

Mt 5:32 reason except *s* immorality
19: 9 except for *s* immorality, and
Acts 15:20 from *s* immorality, from
15:29 and from *s* immorality.
21:25 and from *s* immorality."
Rom 1:29 *s* immorality, wickedness,
1 Cor 5: 1 there is *s* immorality
5: 1 and such *s* immorality as is not
6:13 is not for *s* immorality
6:18 Flee *s* immorality. Every sin
6:18 but he who commits *s* immorality
7: 2 because of *s* immorality, let
10: 8 Nor let us commit *s* immorality,
1 Th 4: 3 abstain from *s* immorality;
Jude 7 over to *s* immorality and
Rev 2:14 and to commit *s* immorality.
2:20 servants to commit *s* immorality
2:21 repent of her *s* immorality,
9:21 sorceries or their *s* immorality

SEXUALLY (5/5) SEXUAL

1 Cor 5: 9 with *s* immoral people.
5:10 mean with the *s* immoral
5:11 who is *s* immoral, or covetous,
Rev 21: 8 *s* immoral, sorcerers,
22:15 sorcerers and *s* immoral

SHAALABBIN (1/1)

Josh 19:42 *S*, Aijalon, Jethlah,

SHAALBIM (2/2)

Judg 1:35 Heres, in Aijalon, and in *S*;
1 Ki 4: 9 Ben-Deker, in Makaz, *S*,

SHAALBONITE (2/2)

2 Sam 23:32 Eliahba the *S* (of the sons of
1 Chr 11:33 the Baharumite, Eliahba the *S*,

SHAALIM (1/1)

1 Sam 9: 4 passed through the land of *S*,

SHAAPH (2/2)

1 Chr 2:47 Geshan, Pelet, Ephah, and *S*.
2:49 She also bore *S* the father of

SHAARAIM (2/2)

1 Sam 17:52 fell along the road to *S*,
1 Chr 4:31 Susim, Beth Biri, and at *S*.

SHAASHGAZ (1/1)

Esth 2:14 the women, to the custody of *S*,

SHABBETHAI (3/3)

Ezra 10:15 and Meshullam and *S* the Levite
Neh 8: 7 Sherebiah, Jamin, Akkub, *S*,
11:16 *S* and Jozabad, of the heads of

SHACHIA (KJV) See SACHIAH

SHACKLES (3/2)

Mk 5: 4 he had often been bound with *s*
5: 4 and the *s* broken in pieces;
Lk 8:29 guard, bound with chains and *s*;

SHADE (12/12)

Judg 9:15 come and take shelter in my *s*;
Job 7: 2 who earnestly desires the *s*,
40:22 trees cover him with their *s*;
Ps 121: 5 The LORD is your *s* at your
Song 2: 3 I sat down in his *s* with great
Isa 4: 6 will be a tabernacle for *s* in
25: 4 A *s* from the heat;
Dan 4:12 beasts of the field found *s*
Hos 4:13 Because their *s* is good.
Jon 4: 5 and sat under it in the *s*,
4: 6 that it might be *s* for his head
Mk 4:32 of the air may nest under its *s*.

SHADED (1/1)

Ezek 31: 3 With fine branches that *s* the

SHADOW (60/58) SHADOWS

Gen 19: 8 they have come under the *s* of
2 Ki 20: 9 shall the *s* go forward ten
20:10 It is an easy thing for the *s* to
20:10 but let the *s* go backward ten
20:11 and He brought the *s* ten
1 Chr 29:15 Our days on earth are as a *s*,
Job 3: 5 May darkness and the *s* of death
8: 9 our days on earth are a *s*.
10:21 the land of darkness and the *s*
10:22 As the *s* of death, without any
12:22 And brings the *s* of death to
14: 2 He flees like a *s* and does not
16:16 And on my eyelids is the *s* of
24:17 is the same to them as the *s*
24:17 are in the terrors of the *s*
28: 3 ore in the darkness and the *s*
34:22 There is no darkness nor *s* of
38:17 you seen the doors of the *s* of
Ps 17: 8 Hide me under the *s* of Your
23: 4 through the valley of the *s* of
36: 7 put their trust under the *s* of
39: 6 every man walks about like a *s*;
44:19 And covered us with the *s* of
57: 1 And in the *s* of Your wings I
63: 7 Therefore in the *s* of Your
80:10 hills were covered with its *s*,
91: 1 High Shall abide under the *s*
102:11 My days are like a *s* that
107:10 sat in darkness and in the *s*
107:14 them out of darkness and the *s*
109:23 I am gone like a *s* when it
144: 4 His days are like a passing *s*.
Eccl 6:12 life which he passes like a *s*?
8:13 his days, which are as a *s*,
Isa 9: 2 who dwelt in the land of the *s*
16: 3 Make your *s* like the night in
25: 5 As heat in the *s* of a cloud,
30: 2 And to trust in the *s* of
30: 3 And trust in the *s* of Egypt
32: 2 As the *s* of a great rock in a
34:15 and gather them under her *s*;
38: 8 I will bring the *s* on the
49: 2 In the *s* of His hand He has
51:16 I have covered you with the *s*
Jer 2: 6 a land of drought and the *s* of
13:16 He turns it into the *s* of
48:45 who fled stood under the *s* of
Lam 4:20 Under his *s* We shall live among
Ezek 17:23 in the *s* of its branches they
31: 6 And in its *s* all great nations
31:12 have gone from under its *s* and
Hos 14: 7 Those who dwell under his *s*
Am 5: 8 He turns the *s* of death into
Mt 4:16 sat in the region and *s*
Lk 1:79 who sit in darkness and the *s*

Acts 5:15 that at least the *s* of Peter
Col 2:17 which are a *s* of things to come,
Heb 8: 5 who serve the copy and *s* of the
10: 1 having a *s* of the good things
Jas 1:17 there is no variation or *s* of

SHADOWED (1/1)

Isa 18: 1 Woe to the land *s* with buzzing

SHADOWS (6/6) SHADOW

Judg 9:36 You see the *s* of the mountains
Job 17: 7 And all my members are like *s*.
Song 2:17 the day breaks And the *s* flee
4: 6 the day breaks And the *s* flee
Jer 6: 4 For the *s* of the evening are
Ezek 31:17 its strong arm dwelt in its *s*

SHADRACH (15/14) HANANIAH

Dan 1: 7 Belteshazzar; to Hananiah, *S*;
2:49 the king, and he set *S*,
3:12 of the province of Babylon: *S*,
3:13 gave the command to bring *S*,
3:14 to them, "Is it true, *S*,
3:16 *S*, Meshach, and Abed-Nego
3:19 on his face changed toward *S*,
3:20 who were in his army to bind *S*,
3:22 killed those men who took up *S*,
3:23 And these three men, *S*,
3:26 spoke, saying, "*S*, Meshach,
3:26 Then *S*, Meshach, and Abed-Nego
3:28 "Blessed be the God of *S*,
3:29 amiss against the God of *S*,
3:30 Then the king promoted *S*,

SHAFT (9/9)

Ex 25:31 Its *s*, its branches, its bowls,
37:17 Its *s*, its branches, its bowls,
Num 8: 4 from its *s* to its flowers it
2 Sam 5: 8 up by way of the water *s* and
21:19 the *s* of whose spear was like
23: 7 be armed with iron and the *s*
1 Chr 20: 5 the *s* of whose spear was like
Job 28: 4 He breaks open a *s* away from
Isa 49: 2 Me, And made Me a polished *s*;

SHAFTS (1/1)

Ps 7:13 makes His arrows into fiery *s*.

SHAGEH (1/1)

1 Chr 11:34 Jonathan the son of *S* the

SHAHARAIM (1/1)

1 Chr 8: 8 And *S* had children in the

SHAHAZIMAH (1/1)

Josh 19:22 the border reached to Tabor, *S*,

SHAKE (40/40) SHAKEN, SHAKES, SHOOK

Judg 16:20 and *s* myself free!" But he did
Neh 5:13 So may God *s* out each man from
Job 4:14 Which made all my bones *s*.
15:33 He will *s* off his unripe grape
16: 4 And *s* my head at you;
17: 3 Who is he who will *s* hands
Ps 22: 7 they *s* the head, saying,
46: 3 Though the mountains *s* with
69:23 And make their loins *s*
109:25 they *s* their heads.
Isa 2:19 When He arises to *s* the earth
2:21 When He arises to *s* the earth
10:32 He will *s* his fist at the
11:15 His mighty wind He will *s* His
13:13 Therefore I will *s* the heavens,
33: 9 And Bashan and Carmel *s* off
52: 2 *S* yourself from the dust, arise
64: 1 That the mountains might *s* at
Jer 18:16 be astonished And *s* his head.
23: 9 the prophets; All my bones *s*.
48:27 You *s* your head in scorn.
Lam 2:15 They hiss and *s* their heads
Ezek 26:10 your walls will *s* at the noise
26:15 Will the coastlands not *s* at the
27:28 The common-land will *s* at the
31:16 I made the nations *s* at the
38:20 the face of the earth shall *s*
Joel 3:16 The heavens and earth will *s*;
Am 9: 1 that the thresholds may *s*,
Nah 2:10 heart melts, and the knees *s*;
Zeph 2:15 Shall hiss and *s* his fist.
Hag 2: 6 I will *s* heaven and earth,
2: 7 and I will *s* all nations, and
2:21 I will *s* heaven and earth.
Zech 2: 9 For surely I will *s* My hand
Mt 10:14 *s* off the dust from your feet.
Mk 6:11 *s* off the dust under your feet
Lk 6:48 and could not *s* it, for it was
9: 5 *s* off the very dust from your
Heb 12:26 Yet once more I *s* not only

SHAKEN (32/31) SHAKE

Lev 26:36 the sound of a *s* leaf shall
2 Sam 22: 8 of heaven quaked and were *s*,
1 Ki 14:15 as a reed is *s* in the water.
2 Ki 19:21 Jerusalem Has *s* her head
Neh 5:13 Even thus may he be *s* out and
Job 16:12 and *s* me to pieces; He has set
34:20 The people are *s* and pass
38:13 And the wicked be *s* out of it?
Ps 18: 7 hills also quaked and were *s*,
109:23 I am *s* off like a locust.
112: 6 Surely he will never be *s*;
Prov 6: 1 If you have *s* hands in pledge
Isa 6: 4 the posts of the door were *s*
24:18 foundations of the earth are *s*.
24:19 The earth is *s* exceedingly.
37:22 daughter of Jerusalem Has *s*
Nah 3:12 ripened figs: If they are *s*,
Mt 11: 7 A reed *s* by the wind?
24:29 powers of the heavens will be *s*.
Mk 13:25 powers in the heavens will be *s*.
Lk 6:38 *s* together, and running over
7:24 A reed *s* by the wind?
21:26 the powers of heaven will be *s*.
Acts 2:25 that I may not be *s*.
4:31 were assembled together was *s*;
16:26 of the prison were *s*;
1 Th 3: 3 that no one should be *s* by these
2 Th 2: 2 not to be soon *s* in mind or
Heb 12:27 those things that are being *s*,
12:27 the things which cannot be *s*
12:28 a kingdom which cannot be *s*,
Rev 6:13 its late figs when it is *s* by

SHAKES (7/6) SHAKE

Job 9: 6 He *s* the earth out of its
Ps 29: 8 The voice of the LORD *s* the
29: 8 The LORD *s* the Wilderness of
Prov 17:18 of understanding *s* hands in
22:26 who *s* hands in a pledge,
Jer 49:21 The earth *s* at the noise of
Ezek 21:21 he *s* the arrows, he consults

SHAKING (4/4)

Ps 44:14 A *s* of the head among the
60: 2 Heal its breaches, for it is *s*.
Isa 17: 6 Like the *s* of an olive tree,
24:13 It shall be like the *s* of

SHALIM (KJV) See SHAALIM

SHALISHA (2/2)

1 Sam 9: 4 and through the land of *S*,

SHALL (7231/4686) See APPENDIX

SHALLECHETH (1/1)

1 Chr 26:16 with the *S* Gate on the

SHALLUM (27/26) JEHOAHAZ

2 Ki 15:10 Then *S* the son of Jabesh
15:13 *S* the son of Jabesh became king
15:14 and struck *S* the son of Jabesh
15:15 Now the rest of the acts of *S*,
22:14 the wife of *S* the son of
1 Chr 2:40 Sismai, and Sismai begot *S*;
2:41 *S* begot Jekamiah, and Jekamiah
3:15 Zedekiah, and the fourth *S*.
4:25 *S* his son, Mibsam his son, and
6:12 begot Zadok, and Zadok begot *S*;
6:13 *S* begot Hilkiah, and Hilkiah
7:13 Jahziel, Guni, Jezer, and *S*,
9:17 And the gatekeepers were *S*,
9:17 *S* was the chief.
9:19 *S* the son of Kore, the son of
9:31 the firstborn of *S* the
2 Chr 28:12 Jehizkiah the son of *S*,
34:22 the wife of *S* the son of
Ezra 2:42 the gatekeepers: the sons of *S*,
7: 2 the son of *S*, the son of Zadok,
10:24 and of the gatekeepers: *S*,
10:42 *S*, Amariah, and Joseph;
Neh 3:12 And next to him was *S* the son of
7:45 The gatekeepers: the sons of *S*,
Jer 22:11 says the LORD concerning *S*
32: 7 Hanamel the son of *S* your uncle
35: 4 of Maaseiah the son of *S*,

SHALLUN (1/1)

Neh 3:15 *S* the son of Col-Hozeh, leader

SHALMAI (1/1)

Ezra 2:46 sons of Hagab, the sons of *S*,

SHALMAN (1/1)

Hos 10:14 As *S* plundered Beth Arbel

SHALMANESER (2/2)

2 Ki 17: 3 *S* king of Assyria came up
18: 9 that *S* king of Assyria came up

SHAMA (1/1)

1 Chr 11:44 *S* and Jeiel the sons of Hotham

SHAMARIAH (1/1)

2 Chr 11:19 she bore him children: Jeush, *S*,

SHAMBLES (1/1)

Joel 1:17 clods, Storehouses are in *s*;

SHAME (115/109) SHAMEFUL

Ex 32:25 to their *s* among their
Judg 18: 7 land who might put them to *s*
1 Sam 20:30 the son of Jesse to your own *s*
20:30 to your own shame and to the *s*
2 Sam 13:13 I, where could I take my *s*?
Job 8:22 hate you will be clothed with *s*,
Ps 4: 2 Will you turn my glory to *s*?
14: 6 You *s* the counsel of the poor,
35: 4 Let those be put to *s* and
35:26 Let them be clothed with *s* and
40:15 confounded because of their *s*,
44: 7 And have put to *s* those who
44: 9 cast us off and put us to *s*,
44:15 And the *s* of my face has
53: 5 You have put them to *s*,
69: 7 *S* has covered my face.
69:19 You know my reproach, my *s*,
70: 3 turned back because of their *s*,
71: 1 Let me never be put to *s*.
71:24 For they are brought to *s* Who
83:16 Fill their faces with *s*,
83:17 let them be put to *s* and
89:45 You have covered him with *s*.
97: 7 Let all be put to *s* who serve
109:29 my accusers be clothed with *s*,
119:31 do not put me to *s*!
129: 5 who hate Zion Be put to *s* and
132:18 enemies I will clothe with *s*,
Prov 3:35 But *s* shall be the legacy of
9: 7 who corrects a scoffer gets *s*
10: 5 harvest is a son who causes *s*.
11: 2 When pride comes, then comes *s*;
12: 4 But she who causes *s* is like
12:16 But a prudent man covers *s*.
13: 5 is loathsome and comes to *s*.
13:18 Poverty and *s* will come to
14:35 is against him who causes *s*.
17: 2 rule over a son who causes *s*,
18:13 It is folly and *s* to him.
19:26 mother Is a son who causes *s*
25: 8 your neighbor has put you to *s*?
25:10 he who hears it expose your *s*,
29:15 left to himself brings *s* to
Isa 20: 4 uncovered, to the *s* of Egypt.
22:18 chariots Shall be the *s* of
30: 3 of Pharaoh Shall be your *s*,
30: 5 But a *s* and also a
47: 3 your *s* will be seen;
50: 6 I did not hide My face from *s*
54: 4 for you will not be put to *s*;
54: 4 For you will forget the *s* of
61: 7 Instead of your *s* you shall
Jer 3:24 For *s* has devoured The labor
3:25 We lie down in our *s*,
7:19 to the *s* of their own faces?"
10:14 Every metalsmith is put to *s*
13:26 That your *s* may appear.
17:18 But do not let me be put to *s*;
20:18 days should be consumed with *s*?
23:40 upon you, and a perpetual *s*,
46:12 nations have heard of your *s*,
48:39 has turned her back with *s*!'
51:17 Every metalsmith is put to *s*
51:51 *S* has covered our faces, For
Ezek 7:18 *S* will be on every face,
16:52 bear your own *s* also, because
16:52 also, and bear your own *s*,
16:54 that you may bear your own *s* and
16:63 mouth anymore because of your *s*,
32:24 Now they bear their *s* with
32:25 Yet they bear their *s* With
32:30 gone down with the slain In *s*
32:30 And bear their *s* with those
34:29 nor bear the *s* of the Gentiles
36: 6 because you have borne the *s* of
36: 7 you shall bear their own *s*.
39:26 'after they have borne their *s*,
44:13 but they shall bear their *s* and
Dan 9: 7 but to us *s* of face, as it is
9: 8 to us belongs *s* of face, to
12: 2 Some to *s* and everlasting
Hos 4: 7 will change their glory into *s*.
9:10 themselves to that *s*;
10: 6 Ephraim shall receive *s*,
Joel 2:26 people shall never be put to *s*.
2:27 people shall never be put to *s*.
Ob 10 *S* shall cover you, And you
Mic 1:11 Pass by in naked *s*,
7:10 And *s* will cover her who said
Nah 3: 5 And the kingdoms your *s*,
Hab 2:16 You are filled with *s* instead
2:16 And utter *s* will be on your
Zeph 3: 5 But the unjust knows no *s*.
3:19 land where they were put to *s*.
Zech 10: 5 on horses shall be put to *s*.
Lk 13:17 His adversaries were put to *s*;
14: 9 and then you begin with *s* to
Acts 5:41 counted worthy to suffer *s* for
Rom 9:33 Him will not be put to *s*.
10:11 Him will not be put to *s*.
1 Cor 1:27 of the world to put to *s* the
1:27 of the world to put to *s* the

4:14 do not write these things to *s*
6: 5 I say this to your *s*.
11:22 the church of God and *s* those
15:34 I speak this to your *s*.
2 Cor 4: 2 the hidden things of *s*,
11:21 To our *s*, I say that we were
Phil 3:19 and whose glory is in their *s*—
Heb 6: 6 God, and put Him to an open *s*.
12: 2 the cross, despising the *s*,
1 Pe 2: 6 by no means be put to *s*.
Jude 13 the sea, foaming up their own *s*;
Rev 3:18 that the *s* of your nakedness
16:15 walk naked and they see his *s*.

SHAMED (9/8)

Gen 38:23 them for herself, lest we be *s*;
Num 12:14 would she not be *s* seven days?
Isa 33: 9 Lebanon is *s* and shriveled;
Jer 48: 1 Kirjathaim is *s* and taken;
48: 1 The high stronghold is *s* and
48:20 Moab is *s*, for he is broken
49:23 "Hamath and Arpad are *s*,
50: 2 'Babylon is taken, Bel is *s*.
Zeph 3:11 In that day you shall not be *s*

SHAMEFACED (1/1)

2 Chr 32:21 So he returned *s* to his own

SHAMEFACEDNESS (KJV) See PROPRIETY

SHAMEFUL (8/8) SHAME

Deut 22:14 and charges her with *s* conduct,
22:17 charged her with *s* conduct,
Jer 11:13 altars to that *s* thing,
Hab 2:10 You give *s* counsel to your
Rom 1:27 with men committing what is *s*,
1 Cor 11: 6 But if it is *s* for a woman to
14:35 for it is *s* for women to speak
Eph 5:12 For it is *s* even to speak of

SHAMEFULLY (4/4)

1 Sam 20:34 his father had treated him *s*.
Hos 2: 5 conceived them has behaved *s*.
Mk 12: 4 and sent him away *s* treated.
Lk 20:11 beat him also, treated him *s*,

SHAMELESSLY (1/1)

2 Sam 6:20 the base fellows *s* uncovers

SHAMER (1/1)

1 Chr 6:46 the son of Bani, the son of *S*,

SHAMES (1/1)

Prov 28: 7 But a companion of gluttons *s*

SHAMGAR (2/2)

Judg 3:31 After him was *S* the son of
5: 6 "In the days of *S*,

SHAMHUTH (1/1)

1 Chr 27: 8 for the fifth month was *S* the

SHAMIR (4/4)

Josh 15:48 And in the mountain country: *S*,
Judg 10: 1 and he dwelt in *S* in the
10: 2 and he died and was buried in *S*.
1 Chr 24:24 of the sons of Michah, *S*.

SHAMMA (1/1)

1 Chr 7:37 Bezer, Hod, *S*, Shilshah,

SHAMMAH (8/8)

Gen 36:13 sons of Reuel: Nahath, Zerah, *S*,
36:17 Nahath, Chief Zerah, Chief *S*,
1 Sam 16: 9 Then Jesse made *S* pass by.
17:13 him Abinadab, and the third *S*.
2 Sam 23:11 And after him was *S* the son of
23:25 *S* the Harodite, Elika the
23:33 *S* the Hararite, Ahiam the son of
1 Chr 1:37 of Reuel were Nahath, Zerah, *S*,

SHAMMAI (6/5)

1 Chr 2:28 The sons of Onam were *S* and
2:28 The sons of *S* were Nadab and
2:32 sons of Jada, the brother of *S*,
2:44 of Jorkoam, and Rekem begot *S*.
2:45 And the son of *S* was Maon, and
4:17 Mered's wife bore Miriam, *S*,

SHAMMOTH (1/1)

1 Chr 11:27 *S* the Harorite, Helez the

SHAMMUA (5/5)

Num 13: 4 *S* the son of Zaccur;
2 Sam 5:14 born to him in Jerusalem: *S*,
1 Chr 14: 4 whom he had in Jerusalem: *S*,
Neh 11:17 brethren; and Abda the son of *S*,
12:18 of Bilgah, *S*; of Shemaiah,

SHAMSHERAI (1/1)

1 Chr 8:26 *S*, Sheharіah, Athaliah,

SHAPE (5/5)

1 Ki 6:25 were of the same size and *s*.
7:19 in the hall were in the *s* of
7:22 of the pillars were in the *s*
7:37 mold, one measure, and one *s*.
Rev 9: 7 The *s* of the locusts was like

SHAPED (4/4)

1 Ki 7:26 and its brim was *s* like the
7:31 *s* like a pedestal, one and a
2 Chr 4: 5 and its brim was *s* like the
Acts 17:29 something *s* by art and man's

SHAPHAM (1/1)

1 Chr 5:12 *S* the next, then Jaanai and

SHAPHAN (30/24)

2 Ki 22: 3 that the king sent *S* the
22: 8 the high priest said to *S* the
22: 8 And Hilkiah gave the book to *S*,
22: 9 So *S* the scribe went to the
22:10 Then *S* the scribe showed the
22:10 And *S* read it before the
22:12 the priest, Ahikam the son of *S*,
22:12 *S* the scribe, and Asaiah a
22:14 the priest, Ahikam, Achbor, *S*,
25:22 the son of Ahikam, the son of *S*,
2 Chr 34: 8 he sent *S* the son of Azaliah,
34:15 Hilkiah answered and said to *S*
34:15 And Hilkiah gave the book to *S*.
34:16 So *S* carried the book to the
34:18 Then *S* the scribe told the king,
34:18 And *S* read it before the
34:20 Hilkiah, Ahikam the son of *S*,
34:20 *S* the scribe, and Asaiah a
Jer 26:24 the hand of Ahikam the son of *S*
29: 3 the hand of Elasah the son of *S*,
36:10 of Gemariah the son of *S* the
36:11 son of Gemariah, the son of *S*,
36:12 Achbor, Gemariah the son of *S*,
39:14 the son of Ahikam, the son of *S*,
40: 5 the son of Ahikam, the son of *S*,
40: 9 the son of Ahikam, the son of *S*,
40:11 the son of Ahikam, the son of *S*,
41: 2 the son of Ahikam, the son of *S*,
43: 6 the son of Ahikam, the son of *S*,
Ezek 8:11 stood Jaazaniah the son of *S*.

SHAPHAT (8/8)

Num 13: 5 of Simeon, *S* the son of Hori;
1 Ki 19:16 And Elisha the son of *S* of Abel
19:19 and found Elisha the son of *S*,
2 Ki 3:11 Elisha the son of *S* is here,
6:31 the head of Elisha the son of *S*
1 Chr 3:22 Igal, Bariah, Neariah, and *S*—
5:12 then Jaanai and *S* in Bashan,
27:29 and *S* the son of Adlai was over

SHAPHER (KJV) See SHEPHER

SHAPHIR (1/1)

Mic 1:11 shame, you inhabitant of *S*;

SHARAI (1/1)

Ezra 10:40 Machnadebai, Shashai, *S*,

SHARAIM (1/1)

Josh 15:36 *S*, Adithaim, Gederah, and

SHARAR (1/1)

2 Sam 23:33 Ahiam the son of *S* the

SHARD (1/1)

Isa 30:14 found among its fragments A *s*

SHARDS (1/1)

Ezek 23:34 it, You shall break its *s*,

SHARE (20/19) PART, SHARED, SHARING

Josh 15:13 son of Jephunneh he gave a *s*
17:14 us only one lot and one *s* to
19: 9 Simeon was included in the *s*
19: 9 for the *s* of the children of
1 Sam 30:24 they shall *s* alike."
2 Sam 20: 1 We have no *s* in David, Nor do
1 Ki 12:16 'What *s* have we in David?
2 Chr 10:16 'What *s* have we in David?
Prov 14:10 And a stranger does not *s* its
17: 2 And will *s* an inheritance
Eccl 9: 6 Nevermore will they have a *s*
Isa 58: 7 Is it not to *s* your bread
Hab 1:16 Because by them their *s* is
Gal 6: 6 him who is taught the word *s*
Eph 4:16 by which every part does its *s*,
1 Tim 5:22 nor *s* in other people's sins;
6:18 ready to give, willing to *s*,
2 Tim 1: 8 but *s* with me in the sufferings
Heb 13:16 not forget to do good and to *s*,
Rev 18: 4 lest you *s* in her sins, and

SHARED (5/5) SHARE

Prov 21: 9 Than in a house *s* with a
25:24 Than in a house *s* with a
Phil 4:14 you have done well that you *s*
4:15 no church *s* with me concerning
Heb 2:14 He Himself likewise *s* in the

SHARES (3/3)

Josh 17: 5 Ten *s* fell to Manasseh, besides
2 Sam 19:43 We have ten *s* in the king;
2 Jn 11 for he who greets him *s* in his

SHAREZER (2/2)

2 Ki 19:37 that his sons Adrammelech and *S*
Isa 37:38 that his sons Adrammelech and *S*

SHARING (3/3) SHARE

1 Sam 26:19 driven me out this day from *s*
2 Cor 9:13 and for your liberal *s* with
Phm 1: 6 that the *s* of your faith may

SHARON (7/7)

1 Chr 5:16 in all the common-lands of *S*
27:29 over the herds that fed in *S*,
Song 2: 1 I am the rose of *S*,
Isa 33: 9 *S* is like a wilderness, And
35: 2 The excellence of Carmel and *S*.
65:10 *S* shall be a fold of flocks,
Acts 9:35 So all who dwelt at Lydda and *S*

SHARONITE (1/1)

1 Chr 27:29 And Shitrai the *S* was over the

SHARP (23/21) SHARPER

Ex 4:25 Then Zipporah took a *s* stone and
1 Sam 14: 4 there was a *s* rock on one
14: 4 rock on one side and a *s* rock
2 Sam 2:16 place was called the Field of *S*
Job 41:30 are like *s* potsherds;
Ps 45: 5 Your arrows are *s* in the heart
52: 2 Like a *s* razor, working
57: 4 And their tongue a *s* sword.
120: 4 *S* arrows of the warrior, With
Prov 5: 4 *S* as a two-edged sword.
25:18 a sword, and a *s* arrow.
Isa 5:28 Whose arrows are *s*,
41:15 threshing sledge with *s* teeth;
49: 2 made My mouth like a *s* sword;
Ezek 5: 1 take a *s* sword, take it as a
Acts 15:39 Then the contention became so *s*
Rev 1:16 went a *s* two-edged sword,
2:12 who has the *s* two-edged sword:
14:14 and in His hand a *s* sickle.
14:17 he also having a *s* sickle.
14:18 to him who had the *s* sickle,
14:18 Thrust in your *s* sickle and
19:15 of His mouth goes a *s* sword,

SHARPEN (5/5) SHARPENING, SHARPENS

1 Sam 13:20 the Philistines to *s* each man's
Ps 7:12 He will *s* His sword; He bends
64: 3 Who *s* their tongue like a
140: 3 They *s* their tongues like a
Eccl 10:10 And one does not *s* the edge,

SHARPENED (3/3)

Ezek 21: 9 a sword is *s* And also
21:10 *S* to make a dreadful slaughter,
21:11 be handled; This sword is *s*,

SHARPENING (1/1) SHARPEN

1 Sam 13:21 and the charge for a *s* was a pim

SHARPENS (3/2) SHARPEN

Job 16: 9 My adversary *s* His gaze on me.
Prov 27:17 As iron *s* iron, So a man
27:17 So a man *s* the countenance of

SHARPER (2/2) SHARP

Mic 7: 4 The most upright is *s* than a
Heb 4:12 and *s* than any two-edged sword,

SHARPLY (3/3)

Judg 8: 1 And they reprimanded him *s*.
Mk 14: 5 And they criticized her *s*.
Titus 1:13 Therefore rebuke them *s*,

SHARPNESS (1/1)

2 Cor 13:10 being present I should use *s*,

SHARUHEN (1/1)

Josh 19: 6 Beth Lebaoth, and *S*: thirteen

SHASHAI (1/1)

Ezra 10:40 Machnadebai, *S*, Sharai,

SHASHAK (2/2)
1 Chr 8:14 Ahio, *S*, Jeremoth,
8:25 and Penuel were the sons of *S*.

SHATTER (1/1)
Hos 2:18 and sword of battle I will *s*

SHATTERED (4/4) SHATTERS
Job 16:12 was at ease, but He has *s* me;
Eccl 12: 6 Or the pitcher *s* at the
Isa 8: 9 Be *s*, O you peoples, and
Dan 12: 7 people has been completely *s*,

SHATTERS (1/1) SHATTERED
Dan 2:40 as iron breaks in pieces and *s*

SHAUL (5/5)
Gen 46:10 Ohad, Jachin, Zohar, and *S*,
Ex 6:15 and *S* the son of a Canaanite
Num 26:13 family of the Zarhites; of *S*,
1 Chr 4:24 Jamin, Jarib, Zerah, and *S*,
6:24 Uzziah his son, and *S* his son.

SHAULITES (1/1)
Num 26:13 of Shaul, the family of the *S*.

SHAVE (18/15) SHAVED, SHAVEN
Lev 13:33 he shall *s* himself, but the
13:33 but the scale he shall not *s*.
14: 8 *s* off all his hair, and wash
14: 9 on the seventh day he shall *s*
14: 9 —all his hair he shall *s* off.
19:27 You shall not *s* around the sides
21: 5 nor shall they *s* the edges of
Num 6: 9 then he shall *s* his head on the
6: 9 on the seventh day he shall *s*
6:18 Then the Nazirite shall *s* his
8: 7 and let them *s* all their body,
Deut 14: 1 shall not cut yourselves nor *s*
21:12 and she shall *s* her head and
Judg 16:19 called for a man and had him *s*
Isa 7:20 the same day the Lord will *s*
Ezek 27:31 They will *s* themselves
44:20 They shall neither *s* their heads
Acts 21:24 expenses so that they may *s*

SHAVED (8/8) SHAVE
Gen 41:14 out of the dungeon; and he *s*,
Num 6:19 of the Nazirite after he has *s*
2 Sam 10: 4 *s* off half of their beards, cut
1 Chr 19: 4 *s* them, and cut off their
Job 1:20 and *s* his head; and he fell to
Jer 41: 5 eighty men with their beards *s*
1 Cor 11: 5 the same as if her head were *s*.
11: 6 for a woman to be shorn or *s*,

SHAVEH (1/1)
Gen 14:17 to meet him at the Valley of *S*

SHAVEH KIRIATHAIM (1/1)
Gen 14: 5 the Zuzim in Ham, the Emim in *S*,

SHAVEN (2/2) SHAVE
Judg 16:17 If I am *s*, then my strength
16:22 grow again after it had been *s*.

SHAVSHA (1/1)
1 Chr 18:16 the priests; *S* was the scribe;

SHAWL (1/1)
Ruth 3:15 Bring the *s* that is on you and

SHE (973/719) See APPENDIX

SHEAF (8/7) SHEAVES
Gen 37: 7 my *s* arose and also stood
37: 7 around and bowed down to my *s*.
Lev 23:10 then you shall bring a *s* of the
23:11 He shall wave the *s* before the
23:12 that day, when you wave the *s*,
23:15 the day that you brought the *s*
Deut 24:19 and forget a *s* in the field,
Job 5:26 As a *s* of grain ripens in its

SHEAL (1/1)
Ezra 10:29 Malluch, Adaiah, Jashub, *S*,

SHEALTIEL (13/12)
1 Chr 3:17 were Assir, *S* his son,
Ezra 3: 2 and Zerubbabel the son of *S* and
3: 8 Zerubbabel the son of *S*,
5: 2 So Zerubbabel the son of *S* and
Neh 12: 1 up with Zerubbabel the son of *S*,
Hag 1: 1 to Zerubbabel the son of *S*,
1:12 Then Zerubbabel the son of *S*,
1:14 of Zerubbabel the son of *S*,
2: 2 now to Zerubbabel the son of *S*,
2:23 My servant, the son of *S*,
Mt 1:12 to Babylon, Jeconiah begot *S*,
1:12 and *S* begot Zerubbabel.
Lk 3:27 of Zerubbabel, the son of *S*,

SHEAR (3/3)
Gen 31:19 Now Laban had gone to *s* his
38:13 is going up to Timnah to *s* his
Deut 15:19 nor *s* the firstborn of your

SHEAR-JASHUB (1/1)
Isa 7: 3 you and *S* your son, at the end

SHEARER (1/1) SHEARERS, SHORN
Acts 8:32 as a lamb before its *s*

SHEARERS (3/3) SHEARER
1 Sam 25: 7 I have heard that you have *s*.
25:11 that I have killed for my *s*,
Isa 53: 7 And as a sheep before its *s* is

SHEARIAH (2/2)
1 Chr 8:38 Azrikam, Bocheru, Ishmael, *S*,
9:44 Azrikam, Bocheru, Ishmael, *S*,

SHEARING (2/2)
1 Sam 25: 2 And he was *s* his sheep in
25: 4 the wilderness that Nabal was *s*

SHEATH (8/8)
1 Sam 17:51 sword and drew it out of its *s*
2 Sam 20: 8 a sword fastened in its *s* at
1 Chr 21:27 he returned his sword to its *s*.
Ezek 21: 3 draw My sword out of its *s* and
21: 4 My sword shall go out of its *s*
21: 5 drawn My sword out of its *s*;
21:30 'Return it to its *s*.
Jn 18:11 "Put your sword into the *s*.

SHEAVES (11/10) SHEAF
Gen 37: 7 binding *s* in the field.
37: 7 and indeed your *s* stood all
Ruth 2: 7 after the reapers among the *s*.
2:15 her glean even among the *s*,
Neh 13:15 the Sabbath, and bringing in *s*,
Job 24:10 And they take away the *s* from
Ps 126: 6 Bringing his *s* with him.
129: 7 his hand, Nor he who binds *s*,
Am 2:13 As a cart full of *s* is weighed
Mic 4:12 He will gather them like *s* to
Zech 12: 6 and like a fiery torch in the *s*;

SHEBA (33/33)
Gen 10: 7 and the sons of Raamah were *S*
10:28 Obal, Abimael, *S*,
25: 3 Jokshan begot *S* and Dedan.
Josh 19: 2 their inheritance Beersheba (*S*)
2 Sam 20: 1 whose name was *S* the son of
20: 2 and followed *S* the son of
20: 6 Now *S* the son of Bichri will do
20: 7 out of Jerusalem to pursue *S*
20:10 Abishai his brother pursued *S*
20:13 went on after Joab to pursue *S*
20:14 together and also went after *S*.
20:21 *S* the son of Bichri by name,
20:22 And they cut off the head of *S*
1 Ki 10: 1 Now when the queen of *S* heard of
10: 4 And when the queen of *S* had seen
10:10 of spices as the queen of *S*
10:13 Solomon gave the queen of *S*
1 Chr 1: 9 The sons of Raama were *S* and
1:22 Ebal, Abimael, *S*,
1:32 The sons of Jokshan were *S* and
5:13 house: Michael, Meshullam, *S*,
2 Chr 9: 1 Now when the queen of *S* heard
9: 3 And when the queen of *S* had seen
9: 9 such as those the queen of *S*
9:12 Solomon gave to the queen of *S*
Job 6:19 The travelers of *S* hope for
Ps 72:10 The kings of *S* and Seba Will
72:15 And the gold of *S* will be
Isa 60: 6 All those from *S* shall come;
Jer 6:20 Me Comes frankincense from *S*,
Ezek 27:22 The merchants of *S* and Raamah
27:23 Eden, the merchants of *S*,
38:13 '*S*, Dedan, the merchants of

SHEBAH (1/1)
Gen 26:33 So he called it *S*.

SHEBAM (1/1)
Num 32: 3 Nimrah, Heshbon, Elealeh, *S*,

SHEBANIAH (7/7)
1 Chr 15:24 *S*, Joshaphat, Nethanel, Amasai,
Neh 9: 4 Then Jeshua, Bani, Kadmiel, *S*,
9: 5 Sherebiah, Hodijah, *S*,
10: 4 Hattush, *S*, Malluch,
10:10 Their brethren: *S*, Hodijah,
10:12 Zaccur, Sherebiah, *S*,
12:14 of Melichu, Jonathan; of *S*,

SHEBARIM (1/1)
Josh 7: 5 before the gate as far as *S*,

SHEBAT (1/1)
Zech 1: 7 month, which is the month *S*,

SHEBER (1/1)
1 Chr 2:48 concubine, bore *S* and Tirhanah.

SHEBNA (9/9)
2 Ki 18:18 *S* the scribe, and Joah the son
18:26 Eliakim the son of Hilkiah, *S*,
18:37 *S* the scribe, and Joah the son
19: 2 *S* the scribe, and the elders of
Isa 22:15 proceed to this steward, To *S*,
36: 3 *S* the scribe, and Joah the son
36:11 Then Eliakim, *S*, and Joah
36:22 *S* the scribe, and Joah the son
37: 2 *S* the scribe, and the elders of

SHEBUEL (3/3)
1 Chr 23:16 of Gershon, *S* was the first.
25: 4 Bukkiah, Mattaniah, Uzziel, *S*,
26:24 *S* the son of Gershom, the son of

SHECANIAH (3/3)
1 Chr 24:11 ninth to Jeshua, the tenth to *S*,
2 Chr 31:15 Shemaiah, Amariah, and *S*,
Ezra 8: 3 of the sons of *S*, of the sons

SHECHANIAH (7/7)
1 Chr 3:21 of Obadiah, and the sons of *S*.
3:22 The son of *S* was Shemaiah.
Ezra 8: 5 of the sons of *S*, Ben-Jahaziel,
10: 2 And *S* the son of Jehiel, one of
Neh 3:29 After him Shemaiah the son of *S*,
6:18 he was the son-in-law of *S* the
12: 3 *S*, Rehum, Meremoth,

SHECHEM (66/57) SYCHAR
Gen 12: 6 the land to the place of *S*,
33:18 came safely to the city of *S*,
34: 2 And when *S* the son of Hamor the
34: 4 So *S* spoke to his father Hamor,
34: 6 Then Hamor the father of *S* went
34: 8 The soul of my son *S* longs for
34:11 Then *S* said to her father and
34:13 the sons of Jacob answered *S*
34:18 their words pleased Hamor and *S*,
34:20 And Hamor and *S* his son came to
34:24 of his city heeded Hamor and *S*
34:26 And they killed Hamor and *S* his
35: 4 terebinth tree which was by *S*.
37:12 feed their father's flock in *S*.
37:13 feeding the flock in *S*?
37:14 of Hebron, and he went to *S*.
Num 26:31 of *S*, the family of the
Josh 17: 2 of Asriel, the children of *S*,
17: 7 that lies east of *S*;
20: 7 *S* in the mountains of Ephraim,
21:21 For they gave them *S* with its
24: 1 all the tribes of Israel to *S*
24:25 a statute and an ordinance in *S*.
24:32 out of Egypt, they buried at *S*,
24:32 sons of Hamor the father of *S*
Judg 8:31 And his concubine who was in *S*
9: 1 the son of Jerubbaal went to *S*,
9: 2 the hearing of all the men of *S*:
9: 3 the hearing of all the men of *S*;
9: 6 And all the men of *S* gathered
9: 6 at the pillar that was in *S*.
9: 7 "Listen to me, you men of *S*,
9:18 servant, king over the men of *S*,
9:20 and devour the men of *S* and
9:20 let fire come from the men of *S*
9:23 Abimelech and the men of *S*;
9:23 and the men of *S* dealt
9:24 them, and on the men of *S*,
9:25 And the men of *S* set men in
9:26 his brothers and went over to *S*;
9:26 and the men of *S* put their
9:28 is Abimelech, and who is *S*,
9:28 men of Hamor the father of *S*;
9:31 and his brothers have come to *S*;
9:34 and lay in wait against *S* in
9:39 went out, leading the men of *S*,
9:41 that they would not dwell in *S*.
9:46 all the men of the tower of *S*
9:47 all the men of the tower of *S*
9:49 the people of the tower of *S*
9:57 all the evil of the men of *S*
21:19 that goes up from Bethel to *S*,
1 Ki 12: 1 And Rehoboam went to *S*,
12: 1 for all Israel had gone to *S* to
12:25 Then Jeroboam built *S* in the
1 Chr 6:67 *S* with its common-lands, in the
7:19 sons of Shemida were Ahian, *S*,
7:28 and *S* and its towns, as far as
2 Chr 10: 1 And Rehoboam went to *S*,
10: 1 for all Israel had gone to *S* to
Ps 60: 6 I will divide *S* And measure
108: 7 I will divide *S* And measure
Jer 41: 5 that certain men came from *S*,
Hos 6: 9 priests murder on the way to *S*;
Acts 7:16 they were carried back to *S*

7:16 of Hamor, the father of *S*.

SHECHEM'S (2/2)

Gen 33:19 *S* father, for one hundred
34:26 and took Dinah from *S* house,

SHECHEMITES (1/1)

Num 26:31 Shechem, the family of the *S*;

SHED (44/42) SHEDDING, SHEDS

Gen 9: 6 By man his blood shall be *s*;
37:22 *S* no blood, but cast him into
Lev 17: 4 He has *s* blood; and that man
Num 35:33 for the blood that is *s* on it,
35:33 by the blood of him who *s* it.
Deut 19:10 lest innocent blood be *s* in the
21: 7 Our hands have not *s* this blood,
1 Sam 25:31 either that you have *s* blood
1 Ki 2: 5 And he *s* the blood of war in
2:31 the innocent blood which Joab *s*.
2 Ki 21:16 Moreover Manasseh *s* very much
24: 4 innocent blood that he had *s*;
1 Chr 22: 8 You have *s* much blood and have
22: 8 because you have *s* much blood
28: 3 man of war and have *s* blood.'
Ps 79: 3 Their blood they have *s* like
79:10 servants which has been *s*.
106:38 And *s* innocent blood, The
Prov 1:11 lie in wait to *s* blood;
1:16 they make haste to *s* blood.
6:17 Hands that *s* innocent blood,
Isa 59: 7 haste to *s* innocent blood;
Jer 7: 6 and do not *s* innocent blood in
22: 3 nor *s* innocent blood in this
Lam 4:13 Who *s* in her midst The blood
Ezek 16:38 who break wedlock or *s* blood
22: 4 by the blood which you have *s*,
22: 6 used his power to *s* blood
22:12 they take bribes to *s* blood;
22:27 to *s* blood, to destroy people,
23:45 manner of women who *s* blood,
33:25 toward your idols, and *s* blood.
35: 5 and have *s* the blood of the
36:18 them for the blood they had *s*
Joel 3:19 For they have *s* innocent blood
Mt 23:35 come all the righteous blood *s*
26:28 which is *s* for many for the
Mk 14:24 which is *s* for many.
Lk 11:50 of all the prophets which was *s*
22:20 which is *s* for you.
Acts 22:20 of Your martyr Stephen was *s*,
Rom 3:15 are swift to *s* blood;
Rev 16: 6 For they have *s* the blood of
19: 2 of His servants *s* by her."

SHEDDER (1/1)

Ezek 18:10 a son who is a robber Or a *s*

SHEDDING (2/2) SHED

Jer 22:17 For *s* innocent blood, And
Heb 9:22 and without *s* of blood there is

SHEDEUR (5/5)

Num 1: 5 Reuben, Elizur the son of *S*;
2:10 shall be Elizur the son of *S*.
7:30 fourth day Elizur the son of *S*,
7:35 offering of Elizur the son of *S*.
10:18 army was Elizur the son of *S*.

SHEDS (2/2) SHED

Gen 9: 6 Whoever *s* man's blood, By man
Ezek 22: 3 The city *s* blood in her own

SHEEP (193/182) SHEEPFOLD, SHEEP'S, SHEEPSKINS

Gen 4: 2 Now Abel was a keeper of *s*,
12:16 He had *s*, oxen, male donkeys,
20:14 Then Abimelech took *s*,
21:27 So Abraham took *s* and oxen and
29: 2 there were three flocks of *s*
29: 3 the well's mouth, water the *s*,
29: 6 Rachel is coming with the *s*.
29: 7 Water the *s*, and go and feed
29: 8 then we water the *s*."
29: 9 Rachel came with her father's *s*,
29:10 and the *s* of Laban his mother's
30:32 all the speckled and spotted *s*,
31:19 Laban had gone to shear his *s*,
34:28 They took their *s*,
38:13 up to Timnah to shear his *s*.
Ex 9: 3 on the oxen, and on the *s*—
12: 5 You may take it from the *s* or
20:24 your *s* and your oxen.
22: 1 "If a man steals an ox or a *s*,
22: 1 five oxen for an ox and four *s*
22: 1 an ox and four sheep for a *s*.
22: 4 it is an ox or donkey or *s*,
22: 9 concerns an ox, a donkey, a *s*,
22:10 neighbor a donkey, an ox, a *s*,
22:30 do with your oxen and your *s*.
34:19 livestock, whether ox or *s*.
Lev 1:10 of the *s* or of the goats—as a
7:23 of ox or *s* or goat.
22:19 from the cattle, from the *s*,
22:21 from the cattle or the *s*,
22:27 When a bull or a *s* or a goat is
27:26 whether it is an ox or *s*,
Num 18:17 of a cow, the firstborn of a *s*,
22:40 Then Balak offered oxen and *s*,
27:17 of the LORD may not be like *s*
31:28 cattle, the donkeys, and the *s*;
31:30 cattle, the donkeys, and the *s*,
31:32 and seventy-five thousand *s*,
31:36 thousand five hundred *s*;
31:37 the LORD's tribute of the *s*
31:43 thousand five hundred *s*,
32:24 ones and folds for your *s*,
32:36 cities, and folds for *s*.
Deut 14: 4 you may eat: the ox, the *s*,
14: 5 antelope, and the mountain *s*.
14:26 heart desires: for oxen or *s*,
17: 1 the LORD your God a bull or *s*
18: 3 whether it is bull or *s*:
18: 4 first of the fleece of your *s*,
22: 1 see your brother's ox or his *s*
28:31 your *s* shall be given to your
Josh 6:21 ox and *s* and donkey, with the
7:24 his oxen, his donkeys, his *s*,
Judg 6: 4 neither *s* nor ox nor donkey.
1 Sam 8:17 will take a tenth of your *s*.
14:32 rushed on the spoil, and took *s*,
14:34 man's ox and every man's *s*,
15: 3 and nursing child, ox and *s*,
15: 9 Agag and the best of the *s*,
15:14 is this bleating of the *s* in
15:15 spared the best of the *s* and
15:21 *s* and oxen, the best of the
16:11 and there he is, keeping the *s*.
16:19 son David, who is with the *s*.
17:15 Saul to feed His father's *s* at
17:20 left the *s* with a keeper, and
17:28 whom have you left those few *s*
17:34 used to keep his father's *s*,
22:19 infants, oxen and donkeys and *s*—
25: 2 He had three thousand *s* and a
25: 2 And he was shearing his *s* in
25: 4 that Nabal was shearing his *s*,
25:16 we were with them keeping the *s*.
25:18 five *s* already dressed, five
27: 9 alive, but took away the *s*,
2 Sam 6:13 he sacrificed oxen and fatted *s*.
7: 8 sheepfold, from following the *s*,
17:29 *s* and cheese of the herd, for
24:17 but these *s*, what have they
1 Ki 1: 9 And Adonijah sacrificed *s* and
1:19 oxen and fattened cattle and *s*
1:25 oxen and fattened cattle and *s*
4:23 the pastures, and one hundred *s*,
8: 5 sacrificing *s* and oxen that
8:63 hundred and twenty thousand *s*.
22:17 as *s* that have no shepherd.
2 Ki 5:26 *s* and oxen, male and female
1 Chr 5:21 and fifty thousand of their *s*,
12:40 wine and oil and oxen and *s*
17: 7 sheepfold, from following the *s*,
21:17 but these *s*, what have they
2 Chr 5: 6 were sacrificing *s* and oxen
7: 5 hundred and twenty thousand *s*.
14:15 and carried off *s* and camels in
15:11 bulls and seven thousand *s*
18: 2 and Ahab killed *s* and oxen in
18:16 as *s* that have no shepherd.
29:33 bulls and three thousand *s*.
30:24 bulls and seven thousand *s*,
30:24 bulls and ten thousand *s*;
31: 6 brought the tithe of oxen and *s*;
Neh 3: 1 the priests and built the *S*
3:32 as far as the *S* Gate, the
5:18 was one ox and six choice *s*.
12:39 as far as the *S* Gate; and they
Job 1: 3 were seven thousand *s*,
1:16 heaven and burned up the *s* and
31:20 warmed with the fleece of my *s*;
42:12 for he had fourteen thousand *s*,
Ps 8: 7 All *s* and oxen—Even the beasts
44:11 You have given us up like *s*
44:22 We are accounted as *s* for the
49:14 Like *s* they are laid in the
74: 1 Your anger smoke against the *s*
78:52 His own people go forth like *s*,
79:13 Your people and *s* of Your
95: 7 And the *s* of His hand.
100: 3 We are His people and the *s*
119:176 have gone astray like a lost *s*;
144:13 That our *s* may bring forth
Song 4: 2 are like a flock of shorn *s*
6: 6 teeth are like a flock of *s*
Isa 7:21 alive a young cow and two *s*;
7:25 for oxen And a place for *s* to
13:14 And as a *s* that no man takes
22:13 Slaying oxen and killing *s*,
43:23 You have not brought Me the *s*
53: 6 All we like *s* have gone astray;
53: 7 And as a *s* before its shearers
Jer 12: 3 Pull them out like *s* for the
13:20 given to you, Your beautiful *s*?
23: 1 who destroy and scatter the *s*
50: 6 "My people have been lost *s*.
50:17 "Israel is like scattered *s*;
Ezek 34: 6 My *s* wandered through all the
34:10 them to cease feeding the *s*,
34:11 I Myself will search for My *s*
34:12 day he is among his scattered *s*,
34:12 so will I seek out My *s*
34:17 I shall judge between *s* and
34:17 shall judge between sheep and *s*,
34:20 between the fat and the lean *s*.
34:22 and I will judge between *s* and
34:22 will judge between sheep and *s*.
Hos 12:12 And for a wife he tended *s*.
Joel 1:18 Even the flocks of *s* suffer
Mic 2:12 will put them together like *s*
5: 8 a young lion among flocks of *s*,
Zech 10: 2 people wend their way like *s*;
13: 7 And the *s* will be scattered;
Mt 9:36 like *s* having no shepherd.
10: 6 But go rather to the lost *s* of
10:16 I send you out as *s* in the
12:11 there among you who has one *s*,
12:12 value then is a man than a *s*?
15:24 not sent except to the lost *s*
18:12 If a man has a hundred *s*,
18:13 he rejoices more over that *s*
25:32 as a shepherd divides his *s*
25:33 And He will set the *s* on His
26:31 And the *s* of the flock
Mk 6:34 because they were like *s* not
14:27 And the *s* will be
Lk 15: 4 man of you, having a hundred *s*,
15: 6 for I have found my *s* which was
17: 7 a servant plowing or tending *s*,
Jn 2:14 those who sold oxen and *s* and
2:15 with the *s* and the oxen, and
5: 2 is in Jerusalem by the *S* Gate
10: 2 door is the shepherd of the *s*.
10: 3 and the *s* hear his voice;
10: 3 and he calls his own *s* by name
10: 4 when he brings out his own *s*,
10: 4 and the *s* follow him, for they
10: 7 to you, I am the door of the *s*.
10: 8 but the *s* did not hear them.
10:11 gives His life for the *s*.
10:12 one who does not own the *s*,
10:12 wolf coming and leaves the *s*
10:12 and the wolf catches the *s* and
10:13 and does not care about the *s*.
10:14 and I know My *s*, and am known
10:15 I lay down My life for the *s*.
10:16 And other *s* I have which are not
10:26 because you are not of My *s*,
10:27 My *s* hear My voice, and I know
21:16 He said to him, "Tend My *s*.
21:17 Jesus said to him, "Feed My *s*.
Acts 8:32 He was led as a *s* to the
Rom 8:36 We are accounted as *s*
Heb 13:20 that great Shepherd of the *s*,
1 Pe 2:25 For you were like *s* going
Rev 18:13 flour and wheat, cattle and *s*,

SHEEP'S (1/1) SHEEP

Mt 7:15 who come to you in *s* clothing,

SHEEPBREEDER (2/2)

2 Ki 3: 4 Now Mesha king of Moab was a *s*,
Am 7:14 But I was a *s* And a tender

SHEEPBREEDERS (1/1)

Am 1: 1 who was among the *s* of Tekoa,

SHEEPCOTE (KJV) See SHEEPFOLD

SHEEPFOLD (3/3) SHEEP

2 Sam 7: 8 hosts: "I took you from the *s*,
1 Chr 17: 7 hosts: "I took you from the *s*,
Jn 10: 1 he who does not enter the *s* by

SHEEPFOLDS (6/6)

Num 32:16 We will build *s* here for our
Judg 5:16 Why did you sit among the *s*,
1 Sam 24: 3 So he came to the *s* by the road,
Ps 68:13 you lie down among the *s*,
78:70 And took him from the *s*;
Isa 13:20 will the shepherds make their *s*

SHEEPMASTER (KJV) See SHEEPBREEDER

SHEEPSHEARERS (3/3)

Gen 38:12 and went up to his *s* at Timnah,
2 Sam 13:23 that Absalom had *s* in Baal
13:24 note, your servant has *s*;

SHEEPSKINS (1/1) SHEEP

Heb 11:37 They wandered about in *s* and

SHEERAH (1/1)

1 Chr 7:24 Now his daughter was *S*,

SHEET (2/2)

Acts 10:11 and an object like a great *s*
11: 5 descending like a great *s*,

SHEETS (1/1)

Ex 39: 3 they beat the gold into thin *s*

SHEHARIAH (1/1)

1 Chr 8:26 Shamsherai, *S*, Athaliah,

S

SHEKEL (42/34) SHEKELS

Gen 24:22 nose ring weighing half a *s*,
Ex 30:13 half a *s* according to the
30:13 a shekel according to the *s* of
30:13 (a *s* is twenty gerahs).
30:15 not give less than half a *s*,
30:24 according to the *s* of the
38:24 according to the *s* of the
38:25 according to the *s* of the
38:26 each man (that is, half a *s*,
38:26 according to the *s* of the
Lev 5:15 of silver according to the *s*
27: 3 according to the *s* of the
27:25 shall be according to the *s* of
27:25 twenty gerahs to the *s*.
Num 3:47 them in the currency of the *s*
3:47 the *s* of twenty gerahs.
3:50 according to the *s* of the
7:13 according to the *s* of the
7:19 according to the *s* of the
7:25 according to the *s* of the
7:31 according to the *s* of the
7:37 according to the *s* of the
7:43 according to the *s* of the
7:49 according to the *s* of the
7:55 according to the *s* of the
7:61 according to the *s* of the
7:67 according to the *s* of the
7:73 according to the *s* of the
7:79 according to the *s* of the
7:85 according to the *s* of the
7:86 according to the *s* of the
18:16 according to the *s* of the
1 Sam 9: 8 here at hand one fourth of a *s*
2 Ki 7: 1 flour shall be sold for a *s*,
7: 1 and two seahs of barley for a *s*,
7:16 of fine flour was sold for a *s*,
7:16 and two seahs of barley for a *s*,
7:18 "Two seahs of barley for a *s*,
7:18 a seah of fine flour for a *s*,
Neh 10:32 yearly one-third of a *s* for
Ezek 45:12 The *s* shall be twenty gerahs;
Am 8: 5 the ephah small and the *s*

SHEKELS (104/80) SHEKEL

Gen 23:15 land is worth four hundred *s*
23:16 four hundred *s* of silver,
24:22 for her wrists weighing ten *s*
37:28 the Ishmaelites for twenty *s*
Ex 21:32 give to their master thirty *s*
30:23 five hundred *s* of liquid myrrh,
30:23 (two hundred and fifty *s*),
30:23 two hundred and fifty *s* of
30:24 five hundred *s* of cassia,
38:24 and seven hundred and thirty *s*,
38:25 hundred and seventy-five *s*,
38:28 hundred and seventy-five *s* he
38:29 and two thousand four hundred *s*.
Lev 5:15 with your valuation in *s* of
27: 3 valuation shall be fifty *s* of
27: 4 valuation shall be thirty *s*;
27: 5 for a male shall be twenty *s*,
27: 5 shekels, and for a female ten *s*;
27: 6 for a male shall be five *s* of
27: 6 valuation shall be three *s* of
27: 7 valuation shall be fifteen *s*,
27: 7 shekels, and for a female ten *s*.
27:16 shall be valued at fifty *s*
Num 3:47 you shall take five *s* for each
3:50 three hundred and sixty-five *s*,
7:13 was one hundred and thirty *s*,
7:13 one silver bowl of seventy *s*,
7:14 one gold pan of ten *s*,
7:19 was one hundred and thirty *s*,
7:19 one silver bowl of seventy *s*,
7:20 one gold pan of ten *s*,
7:25 was one hundred and thirty *s*,
7:25 one silver bowl of seventy *s*,
7:26 one gold pan of ten *s*,
7:31 was one hundred and thirty *s*,
7:31 one silver bowl of seventy *s*,
7:32 one gold pan of ten *s*,
7:37 was one hundred and thirty *s*,
7:37 one silver bowl of seventy *s*,
7:38 one gold pan of ten *s*,
7:43 was one hundred and thirty *s*,
7:43 one silver bowl of seventy *s*,
7:44 one gold pan of ten *s*,
7:49 was one hundred and thirty *s*,
7:49 one silver bowl of seventy *s*,
7:50 one gold pan of ten *s*,
7:55 was one hundred and thirty *s*,
7:55 one silver bowl of seventy *s*,
7:56 one gold pan of ten *s*,
7:61 was one hundred and thirty *s*,
7:61 one silver bowl of seventy *s*,
7:62 one gold pan of ten *s*,
7:67 was one hundred and thirty *s*,
7:67 one silver bowl of seventy *s*,
7:68 one gold pan of ten *s*,
7:73 was one hundred and thirty *s*,
7:73 one silver bowl of seventy *s*,
7:74 one gold pan of ten *s*,
7:79 was one hundred and thirty *s*,
7:79 one silver bowl of seventy *s*,
7:80 one gold pan of ten *s*,
7:85 one hundred and thirty *s* and
7:85 and each bowl seventy *s*.
7:85 two thousand four hundred *s*,
7:86 full of incense weighed ten *s*
7:86 one hundred and twenty *s*.
18:16 for five *s* of silver, according
31:52 seven hundred and fifty *s*.
Deut 22:19 shall fine him one hundred *s*
22:29 young woman's father fifty *s*
Josh 7:21 two hundred *s* of silver, and a
7:21 wedge of gold weighing fifty *s*,
Judg 8:26 one thousand seven hundred *s*
9: 4 So they gave him seventy *s* of
17: 2 The eleven hundred *s* of silver
17: 3 returned the eleven hundred *s*
17: 4 his mother took two hundred *s*
17:10 and I will give you ten *s* of
1 Sam 17: 5 the coat was five thousand *s*
17: 7 weighed six hundred *s*;
2 Sam 14:26 of his head at two hundred *s*
18:11 I would have given you ten *s*
18:12 I were to receive a thousand *s*
21:16 spear was three hundred *s*,
24:24 floor and the oxen for fifty *s*
1 Ki 10:16 six hundred *s* of gold went
10:29 from Egypt cost six hundred *s*
2 Ki 5: 5 six thousand *s* of gold, and
6:25 head was sold for eighty *s*
6:25 of dove droppings for five *s*
15:20 from each man fifty *s* of
1 Chr 21:25 David gave Ornan six hundred *s*
2 Chr 1:17 a chariot for six hundred *s*
3: 9 of the nails was fifty *s* of
9:15 six hundred *s* of hammered gold
9:16 three hundred *s* of gold went
Neh 5:15 besides forty *s* of silver.
Isa 7:23 vines Worth a thousand *s* of
Jer 32: 9 seventeen *s* of silver.
Ezek 4:10 by weight, twenty *s* a day;
45:12 twenty gerahs; twenty *s*,
45:12 twenty shekels, twenty-five *s*,
45:12 and fifteen *s* shall be your
Hos 3: 2 her for myself for fifteen *s*

SHELAH (13/12)

Gen 38: 5 a son, and called his name *S*.
38:11 father's house till my son *S*
38:14 for she saw that *S* was grown,
38:26 I did not give her to *S* my son.
46:12 sons of Judah were Er, Onan, *S*,
Num 26:20 to their families were: of *S*,
1 Chr 1:18 Arphaxad begot *S*,
1:18 Shelah, and *S* begot Eber.
1:24 Shem, Arphaxad, *S*,
2: 3 of Judah were Er, Onan, and *S*.
4:21 The sons of *S* the son of Judah
Neh 3:15 the wall of the Pool of *S* by
Lk 3:35 son of Eber, the son of *S*,

SHELANITES (1/1)

Num 26:20 of Shelah, the family of the *S*;

SHELEMIAH (10/10)

1 Chr 26:14 for the East Gate fell to *S*.
Ezra 10:39 *S*, Nathan, Adaiah,
10:41 Azarel, *S*, Shemariah,
Neh 3:30 After him Hananiah the son of *S*,
13:13 over the storehouse *S* the
Jer 36:14 son of Nethaniah, the son of *S*,
36:26 and *S* the son of Abdeel, to
37: 3 king sent Jehucal the son of *S*,
37:13 name was Irijah the son of *S*,
38: 1 of Pashhur, Jucal the son of *S*,

SHELEPH (2/2)

Gen 10:26 Joktan begot Almodad, *S*,
1 Chr 1:20 Joktan begot Almodad, *S*,

SHELESH (1/1)

1 Chr 7:35 Helem were Zophah, Imna, *S*,

SHELOMI (1/1)

Num 34:27 of Asher, Ahihud the son of *S*;

SHELOMITH (9/9)

Lev 24:11 (His mother's name was *S* the
1 Chr 3:19 Hananiah, *S* their sister,
23: 9 The sons of Shimei: *S*, Haziel,
23:18 of Izhar, *S* was the first.
26:25 his son, and *S* his son.
26:26 This *S* and his brethren were
26:28 was under the hand of *S* and his
2 Chr 11:20 him Abijah, Attai, Ziza, and *S*.
Ezra 8:10 the sons of *S*, Ben-Josiphiah,

SHELOMOTH (2/1)

1 Chr 24:22 Of the Izharites, *S*;
24:22 Shelomoth; of the sons of *S*,

SHELTER (13/13)

Judg 9:15 Then come and take *s* in my
Job 18:14 He is uprooted from the *s* of
24: 8 around the rock for want of *s*.
Ps 61: 3 For You have been a *s* for me,
61: 4 I will trust in the *s* of Your
143: 9 my enemies; In You I take *s*.
Isa 4: 6 and for a *s* from storm and
16: 4 Be a *s* to them from the face
Joel 3:16 But the LORD will be a *s* for
Jon 4: 5 There he made himself a *s* and
Acts 27: 4 we sailed under the *s* of
27: 7 we sailed under the *s* of
27:16 And running under the *s* of an

SHELTERED (1/1)

Ps 83: 3 together against Your *s* ones.

SHELTERS (2/2)

Deut 33:12 Who *s* him all the day long;
Zeph 2: 6 With *s* for shepherds and folds

SHELUMIEL (5/5)

Num 1: 6 *S* the son of Zurishaddai;
2:12 of Simeon shall be *S* the son
7:36 On the fifth day *S* the son of
7:41 This was the offering of *S* the
10:19 the children of Simeon was *S*

SHEM (18/17)

Gen 5:32 years old, and Noah begot *S*,
6:10 And Noah begot three sons: *S*,
7:13 day Noah and Noah's sons, *S*,
9:18 who went out of the ark were *S*,
9:23 But *S* and Japheth took a
9:26 be the LORD, The God of *S*,
9:27 may he dwell in the tents of *S*;
10: 1 of the sons of Noah: *S*,
10:21 children were born also to *S*,
10:22 The sons of *S* were Elam,
10:31 These were the sons of *S*,
11:10 This is the genealogy of *S*:
11:10 *S* was one hundred years old,
11:11 *S* lived five hundred years, and
1 Chr 1: 4 Noah, *S*, Ham, and Japheth.
1:17 The sons of *S* were Elam,
1:24 *S*, Arphaxad, Shelah,
Lk 3:36 of Arphaxad, the son of *S*,

SHEMA (6/6)

Josh 15:26 Amam, *S*, Moladah,
1 Chr 2:43 Korah, Tappuah, Rekem, and *S*.
2:44 *S* begot Raham the father of
5: 8 the son of Azaz, the son of *S*,
8:13 Beriah and *S*, who were heads
Neh 8: 4 right hand, stood Mattithiah, *S*,

SHEMAAH (1/1)

1 Chr 12: 3 the sons of *S* the Gibeathite;

SHEMAIAH (41/39) SHIMEI

1 Ki 12:22 But the word of God came to *S*
1 Chr 3:22 The son of Shechaniah was *S*.
3:22 The sons of *S* were Hattush,
4:37 the son of Shimri, the son of *S*—
5: 4 The sons of Joel were *S* his
9:14 *S* the son of Hasshub, the son
9:16 Obadiah the son of *S*,
15: 8 *S* the chief, and two hundred of
15:11 for Uriel, Asaiah, Joel, *S*,
24: 6 *S* the son of Nethanel, one of
26: 4 the sons of Obed-Edom were *S*
26: 6 Also to *S* his son were sons born
26: 7 The sons of *S* were Othni,
2 Chr 11: 2 the word of the LORD came to *S*
12: 5 Then *S* the prophet came to
12: 7 the word of the LORD came to *S*,
12:15 not written in the book of *S*
17: 8 with them he sent Levites: *S*,
29:14 of Jeduthun, *S* and Uzziel.
31:15 were Eden, Miniamin, Jeshua, *S*,
35: 9 his brothers *S* and Nethanel,
Ezra 8:13 these—Eliphelet, Jeiel, and *S*—
8:16 I sent for Eliezer, Ariel, *S*,
10:21 of Harim: Maaseiah, Elijah, *S*,
10:31 Eliezer, Ishijah, Malchijah, *S*,
Neh 3:29 After him *S* the son of
6:10 I came to the house of *S* the
10: 8 Maaziah, Bilgai, and *S*.
11:15 *S* the son of Hasshub, the son
12: 6 *S*, Joiarib, Jedaiah,
12:18 of Bilgah, Shammua; of *S*,
12:34 Judah, Benjamin, *S*,
12:35 son of Jonathan, the son of *S*,
12:36 and his brethren, *S*, Azarel,
12:42 also Maaseiah, *S*, Eleazar,
Jer 26:20 Urijah the son of *S* of Kirjath
29:24 You shall also speak to *S* the
29:31 says the LORD concerning *S*
29:31 Because *S* has prophesied to
29:32 I will punish *S* the Nehelamite
36:12 scribe, Delaiah the son of *S*,

SHEMARIAH (3/3)

1 Chr 12: 5 Eluzai, Jerimoth, Bealiah, *S*,
Ezra 10:32 Benjamin, Malluch, and *S*;
10:41 Azarel, Shelemiah, *S*,

SHEMEBER (1/1)

Gen 14: 2 *S* king of Zeboiim, and the king

SHEMED (1/1)

1 Chr 8:12 were Eber, Misham, and *S*,

SHEMER (3/2)

1 Ki 16:24 the hill of Samaria from *S* for
16:24 Samaria, after the name of *S*,
1 Chr 7:34 The sons of *S* were Ahi, Rohgah,

SHEMIDA (3/3)

Num 26:32 of *S*, the family of the
Josh 17: 2 Hepher, and the children of *S*;
1 Chr 7:19 And the sons of *S* were Ahian,

SHEMIDAITES (1/1)

Num 26:32 Shemida, the family of the *S*;

SHEMINITH (1/1)

1 Chr 15:21 to direct with harps on the *S*;

SHEMIRAMOTH (4/4)

1 Chr 15:18 Zechariah, Ben, Jaaziel, *S*,
15:20 Zechariah, Aziel, *S*,
16: 5 him Zechariah, then Jeiel, *S*,
2 Chr 17: 8 Nethaniah, Zebadiah, Asahel, *S*,

SHEMUEL (2/2)

Num 34:20 *S* the son of Ammihud;
1 Chr 7: 2 Jeriel, Jahmai, Jibsam, and *S*,

SHEN (1/1)

1 Sam 7:12 set it up between Mizpah and *S*,

SHENAZZAR (1/1)

1 Chr 3:18 and Malchiram, Pedaiah, *S*,

SHENIR (KJV) See SENIR

SHEOL (18/18)

2 Sam 22: 6 The sorrows of *S* surrounded me;
Job 11: 8 Deeper than *S*—what can you
17:16 they go down to the gates of *S*?
26: 6 *S* is naked before Him, And
Ps 16:10 You will not leave my soul in *S*,
18: 5 The sorrows of *S* surrounded me;
86:13 my soul from the depths of *S*.
116: 3 And the pangs of *S* laid hold
Prov 1:12 us swallow them alive like *S*,
Isa 5:14 Therefore *S* has enlarged itself
14:11 Your pomp is brought down to *S*,
14:15 you shall be brought down to *S*,
28:15 And with *S* we are in
28:18 And your agreement with *S* will
38:10 I shall go to the gates of *S*;
38:18 For *S* cannot thank You, Death
57: 9 off, And even descended to *S*.
Jon 2: 2 Out of the belly of *S* I cried,

SHEPHAM (2/2)

Num 34:10 border from Hazar Enan to *S*;
34:11 border shall go down from *S* to

SHEPHATIAH (13/13)

2 Sam 3: 4 *S* the son of Abital;
1 Chr 3: 3 the fifth, *S*, by Abital;
9: 8 Michri; Meshullam the son of *S*,
12: 5 and *S* the Haruphite;
27:16 *S* the son of Maachah;
2 Chr 21: 2 Azaryahu, Michael, and *S*;
Ezra 2: 4 the people of *S*, three hundred
2:57 the sons of *S*, the sons of
8: 8 of the sons of *S*,
Neh 7: 9 the sons of *S*, three hundred
7:59 the sons of *S*, the sons of
11: 4 son of Amariah, the son of *S*,
Jer 38: 1 Now *S* the son of Mattan,

SHEPHER (2/2)

Num 33:23 and camped at Mount *S*.
33:24 They moved from Mount *S* and

SHEPHERD (55/52) SHEPHERDS

Gen 46:34 for every *s* is an abomination
49:24 of Jacob (From there is the *S*,
Num 27:17 be like sheep which have no *s*.
2 Sam 5: 2 You shall *s* My people Israel,
7: 7 whom I commanded to *s* My people
1 Ki 22:17 as sheep that have no *s*.
1 Chr 11: 2 You shall *s* My people Israel,
17: 6 whom I commanded to *s* My
2 Chr 18:16 as sheep that have no *s*.
Ps 23: 1 The LORD is my *s*;
28: 9 *S* them also, And bear them up
78:71 To *s* Jacob His people, And
80: 1 O *S* of Israel, You who lead
Eccl 12:11 nails, given by one *S*.
Isa 40:11 will feed His flock like a *s*;
44:28 says of Cyrus, 'He is My *s*,
63:11 up out of the sea With the *s*
Jer 17:16 hurried away from being a *s*
31:10 And keep him as a *s* does his
43:12 as a *s* puts on his garment, and
49:19 And who is that *s* Who will
50:44 And who is that *s* Who will
51:23 I will break in pieces the *s*
Ezek 34: 5 because there was no *s*;
34: 8 field, because there was no *s*,
34:12 As a *s* seeks out his flock on
34:23 I will establish one *s* over
34:23 shall feed them and be their *s*.
37:24 and they shall all have one *s*;
Am 3:12 As a *s* takes from the mouth of a
Mic 7:14 *S* Your people with Your staff,
Zech 10: 2 trouble because there is no *s*.
11:15 the implements of a foolish *s*.
11:16 indeed I will raise up a *s*
11:17 "Woe to the worthless *s*,
13: 7 O sword, against My *S*,
13: 7 'Strike the *S*, And the sheep
Mt 2: 6 come a Ruler Who will *s*
9:36 like sheep having no *s*.
25:32 as a *s* divides his sheep from
26:31 'I will strike the *S*,
Mk 6:34 were like sheep not having a *s*.
14:27 'I will strike the *S*,
Jn 10: 2 enters by the door is the *s* of
10:11 'I am the good *s*. The good
10:11 The good *s* gives His life for
10:12 he who is not the *s*,
10:14 'I am the good *s*; and I know
10:16 will be one flock and one *s*.
Acts 20:28 to *s* the church of God which He
Heb 13:20 that great *S* of the sheep,
1 Pe 2:25 but have now returned to the *S*
5: 2 *S* the flock of God which is
5: 4 and when the Chief *S* appears,
Rev 7:17 the midst of the throne will *s*

SHEPHERD'S (2/2)

1 Sam 17:40 and put them in a *s* bag, in a
Isa 38:12 Taken from me like a *s* tent;

SHEPHERDED (1/1)

Ps 78:72 So he *s* them according to the

SHEPHERDESS (1/1)

Gen 29: 9 father's sheep, for she was a *s*.

SHEPHERDS (43/38) SHEPHERD

Gen 46:32 'And the men are *s*,
47: 3 Pharaoh, "Your servants are *s*,
Ex 2:17 Then the *s* came and drove them
2:19 us from the hand of the *s*,
Num 14:33 And your sons shall be *s* in the
1 Sam 25: 7 Your *s* were with us, and we did
2 Ki 10:12 the way, at Beth Eked of the *S*,
Isa 13:20 Nor will the *s* make their
31: 4 (When a multitude of *s* is
56:11 And they are *s* Who cannot
Jer 3:15 And I will give you *s* according
6: 3 The *s* with their flocks shall
10:21 For the *s* have become
23: 1 Woe to the *s* who destroy and
23: 2 God of Israel against the *s*
23: 4 I will set up *s* over them who
25:34 Wail, *s*, and cry!
25:35 And the *s* will have no way to
25:36 A voice of the cry of the *s*,
33:12 again be a dwelling place of *s*
50: 6 Their *s* have led them astray;
Ezek 34: 2 prophesy against the *s* of
34: 2 says the Lord GOD to the *s*:
34: 2 Woe to the *s* of Israel who feed
34: 2 Should not the *s* feed the
34: 7 Therefore, you *s*, hear the
34: 8 nor did My *s* search for My
34: 8 but the *s* fed themselves and
34: 9 'therefore, O *s*, hear the
34:10 "Behold, I am against the *s*,
34:10 and the *s* shall feed themselves
Am 1: 2 The pastures of the *s* mourn,
Mic 5: 5 raise against him Seven *s* and
Nah 3:18 Your *s* slumber, O king of
Zeph 2: 6 With shelters for *s* and folds
Zech 10: 3 anger is kindled against the *s*,
11: 3 is the sound of wailing *s*!
11: 5 and their *s* do not pity them.
11: 8 I dismissed the three *s* in one
Lk 2: 8 were in the same country *s*
2:15 that the *s* said to one another,
2:18 which were told them by the *s*.
2:20 Then the *s* returned, glorifying

SHEPHERDS' (1/1)

Song 1: 8 goats Beside the *s* tents.

SHEPHI (1/1)

1 Chr 1:40 were Alian, Manahath, Ebal, *S*,

SHEPHO (1/1)

Gen 36:23 Alvan, Manahath, Ebal, *S*,

SHEPHUPHAN (1/1)

1 Chr 8: 5 Gera, *S*, and Huram.

SHERAH (KJV) See SHEERAH

SHERD, SHERDS (KJV) See SHARD, SHARDS

SHEREBIAH (8/8)

Ezra 8:18 the son of Israel, namely *S*,
8:24 of the leaders of the priests—*S*,
Neh 8: 7 Also Jeshua, Bani, *S*,
9: 4 Kadmiel, Shebaniah, Bunni, *S*,
9: 5 Kadmiel, Bani, Hashabniah, *S*,
10:12 Zaccur, *S*, Shebaniah,
12: 8 Jeshua, Binnui, Kadmiel, *S*,
12:24 the Levites were Hashabiah, *S*,

SHERESH (1/1)

1 Chr 7:16 The name of his brother was *S*,

SHEREZER (1/1)

Zech 7: 2 when the people sent *S*,

SHERIFFS (KJV) See TREASURERS

SHESHACH (2/2) BABYLON

Jer 25:26 Also the king of *S* shall drink
51:41 how *S* is taken! Oh, how the

SHESHAI (3/3)

Num 13:22 and came to Hebron; Ahiman, *S*,
Josh 15:14 sons of Anak from there: *S*,
Judg 1:10 And they killed *S*, Ahiman,

SHESHAN (4/3)

1 Chr 2:31 Ishi, the son of Ishi was *S*,
2:34 Now *S* had no sons, only
2:34 And *S* had an Egyptian servant
2:35 *S* gave his daughter to Jarha his

SHESHAN'S (1/1)

1 Chr 2:31 and *S* child was Ahlai.

SHESHBAZZAR (4/4) ZERUBBABEL

Ezra 1: 8 and counted them out to *S* the
1:11 All these *S* took with the
5:14 they were given to one named *S*,
5:16 Then the same *S* came and laid

SHETHAR (1/1)

Esth 1:14 to him being Carshena, *S*,

SHETHAR-BOZNAI (4/4)

Ezra 5: 3 region beyond the River and *S*
5: 6 region beyond the River, and *S*,
6: 6 region beyond the River, and *S*,
6:13 region beyond the River, *S*,

SHEVA (2/2)

2 Sam 20:25 *S* was scribe; Zadok and
1 Chr 2:49 *S* the father of Machbenah and

SHEWBREAD (KJV) See SHOWBREAD

SHIBBOLETH (1/1) SIBBOLETH

Judg 12: 6 to him, "Then say, '*S*'!"

SHIBMAH (1/1)

Num 32:38 names being changed) and *S*;

SHICRON (1/1)

Josh 15:11 the border went around to *S*,

SHIELD (51/50) SHIELDS

Gen 15: 1 I am your *s*, your exceedingly
Deut 33:29 The *s* of your help And the
Judg 5: 8 Not a *s* or spear was seen
1 Sam 17:41 and the man who bore the *s*
2 Sam 1:21 For the *s* of the mighty is
1:21 The *s* of Saul, not anointed
22: 3 My *s* and the horn of my
22:31 He is a *s* to all who trust in
22:36 You have also given me the *s* of
1 Ki 10:16 of gold went into each *s*.
10:17 minas of gold went into each *s*.
2 Ki 19:32 Nor come before it with *s*,
1 Chr 5:18 men able to bear *s* and sword,
12: 8 who could handle *s* and spear,
12:24 of the sons of Judah bearing *s*
12:34 thirty-seven thousand with *s*
2 Chr 9:15 hammered gold went into each *s*.
9:16 of gold went into each *s*.
17:17 men armed with bow and *s*;
25: 5 who could handle spear and *s*.
Job 15:26 With his strong, embossed *s*.
Ps 3: 3 are a *s* for me, My glory and
5:12 will surround him as with a *s*.
18: 2 My *s* and the horn of my
18:30 He is a *s* to all who trust in
18:35 You have also given me the *s* of
28: 7 LORD is my strength and my *s*;
33:20 He is our help and our *s*.
35: 2 Take hold of *s* and buckler,
59:11 bring them down, O Lord our *s*.
76: 3 The *s* and sword of battle.
84: 9 O God, behold our *s*,

84:11 the LORD God is a sun and *s*;
89:18 For our *s* belongs to the
91: 4 His truth shall be your *s*
115: 9 He is their help and their *s*.
115:10 He is their help and their *s*.
115:11 He is their help and their *s*.
119:114 are my hiding place and my *s*;
144: 2 My *s* and the One in whom I
Prov 2: 7 He is a *s* to those who walk
30: 5 He is a *s* to those who put
Isa 21: 5 you princes, Anoint the *s*!
22: 6 And Kir uncovered the *s*.
37:33 Nor come before it with *s*,
Jer 46: 3 "Order the buckler and *s*,
46: 9 the Libyans who handle the *s*,
Ezek 23:24 array against you Buckler, *s*,
27:10 They hung *s* and helmet in you;
38: 5 all of them with *s* and helmet;
Eph 6:16 taking the *s* of faith with

SHIELD-BEARER (1/1)

1 Sam 17: 7 and a *s* went before him.

SHIELDS (26/25) SHIELD

2 Sam 8: 7 And David took the *s* of gold
1 Ki 10:16 made two hundred large *s* of
10:17 He also made three hundred *s*
14:26 also took away all the gold *s*
14:27 King Rehoboam made bronze *s* in
2 Ki 11:10 of hundreds the spears and *s*
1 Chr 18: 7 And David took the *s* of gold
2 Chr 9:15 made two hundred large *s* of
9:16 He also made three hundred *s*
11:12 Also in every city he put *s*
12: 9 He also carried away the gold *s*
12:10 King Rehoboam made bronze *s* in
14: 8 from Judah who carried *s* and
14: 8 thousand men who carried *s* and
23: 9 and the large and small *s*
26:14 them, for the entire army, *s*,
32: 5 and made weapons and *s* in
32:27 stones, for spices, for *s*,
Neh 4:16 half held the spears, the *s*,
Ps 47: 9 For the *s* of the earth belong
Song 4: 4 All *s* of mighty men.
Jer 51:11 arrows bright! Gather the *s*!
Ezek 27:11 They hung their *s* on your
38: 4 company with bucklers and *s*,
39: 9 both the *s* and bucklers, the
Nah 2: 3 The *s* of his mighty men are

SHIFTED (1/1)

1 Sam 14:23 and the battle *s* to Beth Aven.

SHIFTS (1/1)

1 Ki 5:14 ten thousand a month in *s*:

SHIGIONOTH (1/1)

Hab 3: 1 of Habakkuk the prophet, on *S*.

SHIHON (KJV) See SHION

SHIHOR (2/2)

1 Chr 13: 5 from *S* in Egypt to as far as
Isa 23: 3 on great waters the grain of *S*,

SHIHOR LIBNATH (1/1)

Josh 19:26 westward, along the Brook *S*.

SHILHI (2/2)

1 Ki 22:42 was Azubah the daughter of *S*.
2 Chr 20:31 was Azubah the daughter of *S*.

SHILHIM (1/1)

Josh 15:32 Lebaoth, *S*, Ain, and Rimmon:

SHILLEM (2/2)

Gen 46:24 Jahzeel, Guni, Jezer, and *S*.
Num 26:49 family of the Jezerites; of *S*,

SHILLEMITES (1/1)

Num 26:49 of Shillem, the family of the *S*.

SHILOAH (1/1) SILOAM

Isa 8: 6 refused The waters of *S* that

SHILOH (33/31)

Gen 49:10 Until *S* comes; And to Him
Josh 18: 1 Israel assembled together at *S*,
18: 8 you here before the LORD in *S*.
18: 9 came to Joshua at the camp in *S*.
18:10 Joshua cast lots for them in *S*
19:51 as an inheritance by lot in *S*
21: 2 And they spoke to them at *S* in
22: 9 the children of Israel at *S*,
22:12 Israel gathered together at *S*
Judg 18:31 that the house of God was in *S*.
21:12 brought them to the camp at *S*,
21:19 yearly feast of the LORD in *S*,
21:21 just when the daughters of *S*
21:21 himself from the daughters of *S*;
1 Sam 1: 3 to the LORD of hosts in *S*.
1: 9 eating and drinking in *S*.
1:24 to the house of the LORD in *S*.
2:14 So they did in *S* to all the
3:21 the LORD appeared again in *S*.
3:21 Himself to Samuel in *S* by the
4: 3 covenant of the LORD from *S*
4: 4 So the people sent to *S*,
4:12 and came to *S* with his clothes
14: 3 of Eli, the LORD's priest in *S*,
1 Ki 2:27 the house of Eli at *S*.
14: 2 wife of Jeroboam, and go to *S*.
14: 4 did so; she arose and went to *S*,
Ps 78:60 He forsook the tabernacle of *S*,
Jer 7:12 now to My place which was in *S*,
7:14 fathers, as I have done to *S*.
26: 6 I will make this house like *S*,
26: 9 'This house shall be like *S*,
41: 5 men came from Shechem, from *S*,

SHILONI (1/1)

Neh 11: 5 son of Zechariah, the son of *S*.

SHILONITE (5/5)

1 Ki 11:29 that the prophet Ahijah the *S*
12:15 had spoken by Ahijah the *S* to
15:29 by His servant Ahijah the *S*,
2 Chr 9:29 in the prophecy of Ahijah the *S*,
10:15 by the hand of Ahijah the *S* to

SHILONITES (1/1)

1 Chr 9: 5 Of the *S*: Asaiah the firstborn

SHILSHAH (1/1)

1 Chr 7:37 Bezer, Hod, Shamma, *S*,

SHIMEA (6/6)

2 Sam 21:21 Israel, Jonathan the son of *S*,
1 Chr 2:13 the second, *S* the third,
3: 5 born to him in Jerusalem: *S*,
6:30 *S* his son, Haggiah his son, and
6:39 son of Berachiah, the son of *S*,
20: 7 Israel, Jonathan the son of *S*,

SHIMEAH (3/3)

2 Sam 13: 3 name was Jonadab the son of *S*,
13:32 Then Jonadab the son of *S*,
1 Chr 8:32 and Mikloth, who begot *S*.

SHIMEAM (1/1)

1 Chr 9:38 And Mikloth begot *S*.

SHIMEATH (2/2)

2 Ki 12:21 For Jozachar the son of *S* and
2 Chr 24:26 Zabad the son of *S* the

SHIMEATHITES (1/1)

1 Chr 2:55 were the Tirathites, the *S*,

SHIMEI (44/40) SHEMAIAH

Num 3:18 by their families: Libni and *S*.
2 Sam 16: 5 whose name was *S* the son of
16: 7 Also *S* said thus when he cursed:
16:13 *S* went along the hillside
19:16 And *S* the son of Gera, a
19:18 Now *S* the son of Gera fell
19:21 Shall not *S* be put to death for
19:23 Therefore the king said to *S*,
1 Ki 1: 8 Jehoiada, Nathan the prophet, *S*,
2: 8 you have with you *S* the son
2:36 the king sent and called for *S*,
2:38 And *S* said to the king, "The
2:38 So *S* dwelt in Jerusalem many
2:39 that two slaves of *S* ran away
2:39 they told *S*, saying, "Look,
2:40 So *S* arose, saddled his donkey,
2:40 And *S* went and brought his
2:41 And Solomon was told that *S* had
2:42 the king sent and called for *S*,
2:44 The king said moreover to *S*,
4:18 *S* the son of Elah, in Benjamin;
1 Chr 3:19 Pedaiah were Zerubbabel and *S*.
4:26 Zacchur his son, and *S* his son.
4:27 *S* had sixteen sons and six
5: 4 Gog his son, *S* his son,
6:17 sons of Gershon: Libni and *S*.
6:29 *S* his son, Uzzah his son,
6:42 the son of Zimmah, the son of *S*,
8:21 Shimrath were the sons of *S*.
23: 7 the Gershonites: Laadan and *S*.
23: 9 The sons of *S*: Shelomith,
23:10 And the sons of *S*: Jahath,
23:10 These were the four sons of *S*.
25: 3 Gedaliah, Zeri, Jeshaiah, *S*,
25:17 the tenth for *S*, his sons
27:27 And *S* the Ramathite was over
2 Chr 29:14 the sons of Heman, Jehiel and *S*;
31:12 and *S* his brother was the
31:13 the hand of Cononiah and *S* his
Ezra 10:23 Also of the Levites: Jozabad, *S*,
10:33 Jeremai, Manasseh, and *S*;
10:38 Bani, Binnui, *S*,
Esth 2: 5 the son of Jair, the son of *S*,
Zech 12:13 the family of *S* by itself, and

SHIMEON (1/1)

Ezra 10:31 Ishijah, Malchijah, Shemaiah, *S*,

SHIMHI (KJV) See SHIMEI

SHIMI (1/1)

Ex 6:17 of Gershon were Libni and *S*

SHIMITES (1/1)

Num 3:21 and the family of the *S*;

SHIMMA (KJV) See SHIMEA

SHIMON (1/1)

1 Chr 4:20 And the sons of *S* were Amnon,

SHIMRATH (1/1)

1 Chr 8:21 and *S* were the sons of Shimei.

SHIMRI (4/4)

1 Chr 4:37 son of Jedaiah, the son of *S*,
11:45 Jediael the son of *S*,
26:10 *S* the first (for though he was
2 Chr 29:13 of Elizaphan, *S* and Jeiel;

SHIMRITH (1/1)

2 Chr 24:26 and Jehozabad the son of *S* the

SHIMRON (5/5)

Gen 46:13 were Tola, Puvah, Job, and *S*.
Num 26:24 family of the Jashubites; of *S*,
Josh 11: 1 king of Madon, to the king of *S*,
19:15 were Kattath, Nahallal, *S*,
1 Chr 7: 1 were Tola, Puah, Jashub, and *S*—

SHIMRON MERON (1/1)

Josh 12:20 the king of *S*, one; the king

SHIMRONITES (1/1)

Num 26:24 of Shimron, the family of the *S*.

SHIMSHAI (4/4)

Ezra 4: 8 Rehum the commander and *S* the
4: 9 *S* the scribe, and the rest of
4:17 to *S* the scribe, to the rest
4:23 *S* the scribe, and their

SHINAB (1/1)

Gen 14: 2 *S* king of Admah, Shemeber king

SHINAR (7/7)

Gen 10:10 and Calneh, in the land of *S*.
11: 2 found a plain in the land of *S*,
14: 1 the days of Amraphel king of *S*,
14: 9 of nations, Amraphel king of *S*,
Isa 11:11 and Cush, From Elam and *S*,
Dan 1: 2 he carried into the land of *S*
Zech 5:11 a house for it in the land of *S*;

SHINE (29/29) SHINED, SHINES, SHINING, SHONE

Num 6:25 The LORD make His face *s* upon
Job 3: 4 Nor the light *s* upon it.
18: 5 flame of his fire does not *s*.
22:28 So light will *s* on your ways.
25: 5 If even the moon does not *s*,
37:15 the light of His cloud to *s*?
Ps 31:16 Make Your face *s* upon Your
50: 2 God will *s* forth.
67: 1 And cause His face to *s* upon
80: 1 between the cherubim, *s* forth!
80: 3 O God; Cause Your face to *s*,
80: 7 of hosts; Cause Your face to *s*,
80:19 of hosts; Cause Your face to *s*,
94: 1 vengeance belongs, *s* forth!
104:15 man, Oil to make his face *s*,
119:135 Make Your face *s* upon Your
Eccl 8: 1 man's wisdom makes his face *s*,
Isa 13:10 will not cause its light to *s*.
60: 1 Arise, *s*; For your light
Dan 9:17 sake cause Your face to *s* on
12: 3 Those who are wise shall *s*
Mt 5:16 Let your light so *s* before men,
13:43 Then the righteous will *s* forth
2 Cor 4: 4 of God, should *s* on them.
4: 6 God who commanded light to *s*
Phil 2:15 among whom you *s* as lights in
Rev 8:12 A third of the day did not *s*,
18:23 light of a lamp shall not *s* in
21:23 of the sun or of the moon to *s*

SHINED (1/1) SHINE

Isa 9: 2 death, Upon them a light has *s*.

SHINES (6/6) SHINE

Job 31:26 have observed the sun when it *s*,
Ps 139:12 But the night *s* as the day;
Prov 4:18 That *s* ever brighter unto the

Lk 17:24 of one part under heaven *s* to
Jn 1: 5 And the light *s* in the darkness,
2 Pe 1:19 well to heed as a light that *s*

SHINING (13/13) SHINE

2 Sam 23: 4 By clear *s* after rain.'
2 Ki 3:22 and the sun was *s* on the water;
Job 41:32 He leaves a *s* wake behind him;
Prov 4:18 of the just is like the *s* sun,
Isa 4: 5 and smoke by day and the *s* of
Hab 3:11 At the *s* of Your glittering
Mk 9: 3 His clothes became *s*,
Lk 11:36 as when the bright *s* of a lamp
24: 4 stood by them in *s* garments.
Jn 5:35 He was the burning and *s* lamp,
Acts 26:13 *s* around me and those who
1 Jn 2: 8 and the true light is already *s*.
Rev 1:16 was like the sun *s* in its

SHION (1/1)

Josh 19:19 Haphraim, *S*, Anaharath,

SHIP (27/26) SHIPS, SHIPWRECK

Prov 30:19 The way of a *s* in the midst of
Jon 1: 3 and found a *s* going to
1: 4 so that the *s* was about to be
1: 5 the cargo that was in the *s*
1: 5 into the lowest parts of the *s*,
Acts 20:13 Then we went ahead to the *s* and
20:38 they accompanied him to the *s*.
21: 2 And finding a *s* sailing over to
21: 3 for there the *s* was to unload
21: 6 one another, we boarded the *s*,
27: 2 entering a *s* of Adramyttium, we
27: 6 found an Alexandrian *s* sailing
27:10 not only of the cargo and *s*,
27:11 and the owner of the *s* than by
27:15 So when the *s* was caught, and
27:17 used cables to undergird the *s*;
27:18 next day they lightened the *s*.
27:22 among you, but only of the *s*.
27:30 seeking to escape from the *s*,
27:31 these men stay in the *s*,
27:37 seventy-six persons on the *s*.
27:38 they lightened the *s* and threw
27:39 they planned to run the *s* if
27:41 they ran the *s* aground;
27:44 and some on parts of the *s*.
28:11 we sailed in an Alexandrian *s*
Rev 18:17 shipmaster, all who travel by *s*,

SHIP'S (1/1)

Acts 27:19 day we threw the *s* tackle

SHIPHI (1/1)

1 Chr 4:37 Ziza the son of *S*,

SHIPHMITE (1/1)

1 Chr 27:27 and Zabdi the *S* was over the

SHIPHRAH (1/1)

Ex 1:15 of whom the name of one was *S*

SHIPHTAN (1/1)

Num 34:24 of Ephraim, Kemuel the son of *S*;

SHIPMASTER (1/1)

Rev 18:17 Every *s*, all who travel by

SHIPMEN (KJV) See SAILORS, SEAMEN

SHIPPING (KJV) See BOATS

SHIPS (37/33) SHIP

Gen 49:13 shall become a haven for *s*,
Num 24:24 But *s* shall come from the
Deut 28:68 take you back to Egypt in *s*,
Judg 5:17 And why did Dan remain on *s*?
1 Ki 9:26 also built a fleet of *s* at
10:11 the *s* of Hiram, which brought
10:22 For the king had merchant *s* at
10:22 three years the merchant *s*
22:48 Jehoshaphat made merchant *s* to
22:48 for the *s* were wrecked at Ezion
22:49 go with your servants in the *s*.
2 Chr 8:18 And Hiram sent him *s* by the hand
9:21 For the king's *s* went to
9:21 three years the merchant *s*
20:36 himself with him to make *s* to
20:36 and they made the *s* in Ezion
20:37 Then the *s* were wrecked, so
Job 9:26 They pass by like swift *s*,
Ps 48: 7 As when You break the *s* of
104:26 There the *s* sail about;
107:23 who go down to the sea in *s*,
Prov 31:14 She is like the merchant *s*,
Isa 2:16 Upon all the *s* of Tarshish,
23: 1 Wail, you *s* of Tarshish!
23:14 Wail, you *s* of Tarshish!
33:21 Nor majestic *s* pass by
43:14 who rejoice in their *s*.
60: 9 And the *s* of Tarshish will
Ezek 27: 9 All the *s* of the sea And
27:25 The *s* of Tarshish were carriers
27:29 Will come down from their *s*
30: 9 shall go forth from Me in *s*
Dan 11:30 For *s* from Cyprus shall come
11:40 horsemen, and with many *s*;
Jas 3: 4 Look also at *s*: although
Rev 8: 9 and a third of the *s* were
18:19 in which all who had *s* on the

SHIPWRECK (1/1) SHIP, SHIPWRECKED

1 Tim 1:19 the faith have suffered *s*,

SHIPWRECKED (1/1) SHIPWRECK

2 Cor 11:25 was stoned; three times I was *s*;

SHISHA (1/1)

1 Ki 4: 3 and Ahijah, the sons of *S*,

SHISHAK (7/6)

1 Ki 11:40 to *S* king of Egypt, and was in
14:25 year of King Rehoboam that *S*
2 Chr 12: 2 that *S* king of Egypt came up
12: 5 in Jerusalem because of *S*,
12: 5 have left you in the hand of *S*.
12: 7 on Jerusalem by the hand of *S*.
12: 9 So *S* king of Egypt came up

SHITRAI (1/1)

1 Chr 27:29 And *S* the Sharonite was over

SHIVERS (KJV) See PIECES

SHIZA (1/1)

1 Chr 11:42 Adina the son of *S* the Reubenite

SHOA (1/1)

Ezek 23:23 All the Chaldeans, Pekod, *S*,

SHOBAB (4/4)

2 Sam 5:14 to him in Jerusalem: Shammua, *S*,
1 Chr 2:18 these were her sons: Jesher, *S*,
3: 5 to him in Jerusalem: Shimea, *S*,
14: 4 he had in Jerusalem: Shammua, *S*,

SHOBACH (2/2)

2 Sam 10:16 And *S* the commander of
10:18 and struck *S* the commander of

SHOBAI (2/2)

Ezra 2:42 of Hatita, and the sons of *S*,
Neh 7:45 sons of Hatita, the sons of *S*,

SHOBAL (9/9)

Gen 36:20 inhabited the land: Lotan, *S*,
36:23 These were the sons of *S*:
36:29 Horites: Chief Lotan, Chief *S*,
1 Chr 1:38 sons of Seir were Lotan, *S*,
1:40 The sons of *S* were Alian,
2:50 were *S* the father of Kirjath
2:52 And *S* the father of Kirjath
4: 1 Hezron, Carmi, Hur, and *S*.
4: 2 And Reaiah the son of *S* begot

SHOBEK (1/1)

Neh 10:24 Hallohesh, Pilha, *S*,

SHOBI (1/1)

2 Sam 17:27 that *S* the son of Nahash from

SHOCHO, SHOCO (KJV) See SOCHOH

SHOCHOH (KJV) See SOCHOH

SHOCKS (1/1)

Judg 15: 5 and burned up both the *s* and

SHOD (1/1)

Eph 6:15 and having *s* your feet with the

SHOE (2/2)

Ps 60: 8 Over Edom I will cast My *s*;
108: 9 Over Edom I will cast My *s*;

SHOE'S, SHOES (KJV) See SANDAL, SANDALS

SHOELATCHET (KJV) See STRAP

SHOHAM (1/1)

1 Chr 24:27 Merari by Jaaziah were Beno, *S*,

SHOMER (2/2)

2 Ki 12:21 and Jehozabad the son of *S*,
1 Chr 7:32 And Heber begot Japhlet, *S*,

SHONE (12/12) SHINE

Ex 34:29 that the skin of his face *s*
34:30 behold, the skin of his face *s*,
34:35 that the skin of Moses' face *s*,
Deut 33: 2 He *s* forth from Mount Paran,
Job 29: 3 When His lamp *s* upon my head,
Ezek 43: 2 and the earth *s* with His glory.
Mt 17: 2 His face *s* like the sun, and
Lk 2: 9 and the glory of the Lord *s*
Acts 9: 3 and suddenly a light *s* around
12: 7 and a light *s* in the prison;
22: 6 a great light from heaven *s*
2 Cor 4: 6 who has *s* in our hearts to

SHOOK (14/14) SHAKE

1 Sam 4: 5 so loudly that the earth *s*.
2 Sam 22: 8 Then the earth *s* and trembled;
Neh 5:13 Then I *s* out the fold of my
Ps 18: 7 Then the earth *s* and trembled;
68: 8 The earth *s*; The heavens also
77:18 The earth trembled and *s*.
Isa 14:16 earth tremble, Who *s* kingdoms,
23:11 He *s* the kingdoms; The LORD
64: 3 The mountains *s* at Your
Mt 28: 4 And the guards *s* for fear of
Acts 13:51 But they *s* off the dust from
18: 6 he *s* his garments and said to
28: 5 But he *s* off the creature into
Heb 12:26 whose voice then *s* the earth;

SHOOT (19/18) SHOOTS, SHOT

1 Sam 20:20 Then I will *s* three arrows to
20:36 run, find the arrows which I *s*.
2 Sam 11:20 you not know that they would *s*
2 Ki 9:27 *S* him also in the chariot."
13:17 Then Elisha said, "*S*";
19:32 Nor *s* an arrow there, Nor
1 Chr 5:18 to *s* with the bow, and skillful
2 Chr 26:15 to *s* arrows and large stones.
Job 41:19 Sparks of fire *s* out.
Ps 11: 2 That they may *s* secretly at
22: 7 They *s* out the lip, they shake
64: 3 And bend their bows to *s*
64: 4 That they may *s* in secret at
64: 4 Suddenly they *s* at him and do
64: 7 But God shall *s* at them with
144: 6 *S* out Your arrows and destroy
Isa 37:33 Nor *s* an arrow there, Nor
Jer 50:14 *S* at her, spare no arrows,
Ezek 36: 8 you shall *s* forth your branches

SHOOTING (1/1)

1 Chr 12: 2 hurling stones and *s* arrows

SHOOTS (3/3) SHOOT

Job 14: 7 And that its tender *s* will not
Ezek 17: 6 branches, And put forth *s*.
Mk 4:32 and *s* out large branches, so

SHOPHACH (2/2)

1 Chr 19:16 and *S* the commander of
19:18 and killed *S* the commander of

SHOPHAN (1/1)

Num 32:35 Atroth and *S* and Jazer and

SHORE (8/8)

Josh 15: 2 southern border began at the *s*
1 Ki 9:26 which is near Elath on the *s*
Ezek 27:29 their ships and stand on the *s*.
Mt 13: 2 whole multitude stood on the *s*.
13:48 it was full, they drew to *s*;
Jn 21: 4 now come, Jesus stood on the *s*;
Acts 21: 5 And we knelt down on the *s* and
27:40 to the wind and made for *s*.

SHORES (1/1)

Zeph 2:11 Indeed all the *s* of the

SHORN (3/2) SHEARER

Song 4: 2 are like a flock of *s* sheep
1 Cor 11: 6 not covered, let her also be *s*.
11: 6 is shameful for a woman to be *s*

SHORT (18/17) SHORTENED, SHORTLY

Ex 39:28 *s* trousers of fine woven linen,
Lev 22:23 has any limb too long or too *s*
2 Ki 5:19 from him a *s* distance.
Job 20: 5 triumphing of the wicked is *s*,
Ps 89:47 Remember how *s* my time is; For
Isa 28:20 For the bed is too *s* to
Mic 6:10 And the *s* measure that is an
Lk 19: 3 for he was of *s* stature.
Rom 3:23 for all have sinned and fall *s*
9:28 the work and cut it *s* in
9:28 will make a *s* work
1 Cor 1: 7 so that you come *s* in no gift,
7:29 I say, brethren, the time is *s*,
1 Th 2:17 away from you for a *s* time
Heb 4: 1 any of you seem to have come *s*
12:15 carefully lest anyone fall *s*

S

Rev 12:12 he knows that he has a *s* time.
17:10 he must continue a *s* time.

SHORT-EARED (2/2)

Lev 11:16 the *s* owl, the sea gull, and
Deut 14:15 the *s* owl, the sea gull, and

SHORTENED (12/10) SHORT

Num 11:23 "Has the LORD's arm been *s*?
Job 18: 7 steps of his strength are *s*,
Ps 89:45 days of his youth You have *s*;
102:23 in the way; He *s* my days.
Prov 10:27 years of the wicked will be *s*.
Isa 50: 2 Is My hand *s* at all that it
59: 1 the LORD's hand is not *s*,
Ezek 42: 6 the upper level was *s* more
Mt 24:22 "And unless those days were *s*,
24:22 sake those days will be *s*.
Mk 13:20 And unless the Lord had *s* those
13:20 whom He chose, He *s* the days.

SHORTER (1/1)

Ezek 42: 5 Now the upper chambers were *s*,

SHORTLY (13/13) SHORT

Gen 41:32 and God will *s* bring it to
Jer 27:16 house will now *s* be brought
Acts 25: 4 he himself was going there *s*.
Rom 16:20 crush Satan under your feet *s*.
1 Cor 4:19 But I will come to you *s*,
Phil 2:19 Jesus to send Timothy to you *s*,
2:24 that I myself shall also come *s*.
1 Tim 3:14 though I hope to come to you *s*;
Heb 13:23 I shall see you if he comes *s*.
2 Pe 1:14 knowing that *s* I must put off
3 Jn 14 but I hope to see you *s*,
Rev 1: 1 things which must *s* take place.
22: 6 the things which must *s* take

SHORTSIGHTED (1/1)

2 Pe 1: 9 he who lacks these things is *s*,

SHOT (14/14) SHOOT

Gen 40:10 its blossoms *s* forth, and its
49:23 *S* at him and hated him.
Ex 19:13 he shall surely be stoned or *s*
Num 21:30 'But we have *s* at them;
1 Sam 20:20 as though I *s* at a target;
20:36 he *s* an arrow beyond him.
20:37 arrow was which Jonathan had *s*,
2 Sam 11:24 The archers *s* from the wall at
2 Ki 9:24 bow with full strength and *s*
9:27 And they *s* him at the
13:17 said, "Shoot"; and he *s*.
2 Chr 35:23 And the archers *s* King Josiah;
Jer 9: 8 Their tongue is an arrow *s*
Heb 12:20 it shall be stoned or *s*

SHOULD (626/553)

Gen 2:18 It is not good that man *s* be
3:11 I commanded you that you *s* not
4: 7 but you *s* rule over it."
4:15 lest anyone finding him *s* kill
14:23 lest you *s* say, 'I have made
18:25 so that the righteous *s* be as
18:29 Suppose there *s* be forty found
18:30 Suppose thirty *s* be found
18:31 Suppose twenty *s* be found
18:32 Suppose ten *s* be found there?"
20:13 your kindness that you *s* do
27:45 Why *s* I be bereaved also of you
29:15 *s* you therefore serve me for
29:15 what *s* your wages be?"
29:19 than that I *s* give her to
30:38 so that they *s* conceive when
33:13 And if the men *s* drive them
34:31 *S* he treat our sister like a
38: 9 lest he *s* give an heir to his
40:15 *s* put me into the dungeon."
42:38 If any calamity *s* befall him
44: 7 from us that your servants *s* do
44:17 Far be it from me that I *s* do
44:22 for if he *s* leave his father,
47:15 for why *s* we die in your
47:19 Why *s* we die before your eyes,
47:26 that Pharaoh *s* have one-fifth,
Ex 3:11 Who am I that I *s* go to
3:11 and that I *s* bring the children
5: 2 that I *s* obey His voice to let
14:12 Egyptians than that we *s* die
22: 3 He *s* make full restitution;
32:12 Why *s* the Egyptians speak, and
Lev 4:13 anything which *s* not be done,
4:22 which *s* not be done,
10:18 indeed you *s* have eaten it in a
13: 7 But if the scab *s* at all spread
13:22 and if it *s* at all spread over
13:35 But if the scale *s* at all spread
20: 4 if the people of the land *s* in
20:26 that you *s* be Mine.
26:13 that you *s* not be their
27:26 which *s* be the LORD's
Num 9: 4 they *s* keep the Passover.
11:12 that You *s* say to me, 'Carry
14: 3 and children *s* become victims?
15:34 been explained what *s* be done
16:13 that you *s* keep acting like a
16:40 *s* come near to offer incense
20: 4 that we and our animals *s* die
23:19 that He *s* lie, Nor a son of
23:19 that He *s* repent. Has He said,
27: 4 Why *s* the name of our father be
35:28 because he *s* have remained in
Deut 1:18 all the things which you *s* do.
1:22 of the way by which we *s* go
1:33 to show you the way you *s* go,
4: 5 that you *s* act according to
5:25 why *s* we die? For this great
7:17 If you *s* say in your heart,
8: 5 You *s* know in your heart that as
9:28 which You brought us *s* say,
15:10 and your heart *s* not be grieved
25: 3 lest he *s* exceed this and beat
26:18 that you *s* keep all His
30:12 that you *s* say, 'Who will
30:13 that you *s* say, 'Who will go
32:27 adversaries *s* misunderstand,
32:27 Lest they *s* say, "Our hand
Josh 8:29 commanded that they *s* take
8:33 that they *s* bless the people of
11:20 that they *s* come against Israel
22:29 from us that we *s* rebel
24:16 from us that we *s* forsake
Judg 8: 6 that we *s* give bread to your
8:15 that we *s* give bread to your
9: 9 *S* I cease giving my oil, With
9:11 *S* I cease my sweetness and my
9:13 *S* I cease my new wine, Which
9:28 that we *s* serve him?
9:28 but why *s* we serve him?
9:38 that we *s* serve him?'
11:23 *s* you then possess it?
14:16 so *s* I explain it to you?"
18:14 consider what you *s* do."
21: 3 that today there *s* be one tribe
Ruth 1:12 If I *s* say I have hope, if I
1:12 if I *s* have a husband tonight
1:12 tonight and *s* also bear sons,
2:10 that you *s* take notice of me,
3: 4 he will tell you what you *s* do.
1 Sam 2:16 They *s* really burn the fat
6: 2 Tell us how we *s* send it to its
8: 7 that I *s* not reign over them.
9: 6 us the way that we *s* go."
10: 8 and show you what you *s* do."
12:23 far be it from me that I *s* sin
15:21 the things which *s* have been
15:29 a man, that He *s* relent."
17:26 that he *s* defy the armies of
18:18 that I *s* be son-in-law to the
18:19 *s* have been given to David,
19: 1 that they *s* kill David; but
19:17 Let me go! Why *s* I kill you?'"
20: 2 And why *s* my father hide this
20: 5 and I *s* not fail to sit with
20: 8 for why *s* you bring me to your
20:32 Why *s* he be killed? What has he
22:13 that he *s* rise against me, to
24: 6 The LORD forbid that I *s* do
26:11 forbid that I *s* stretch
27: 1 that I *s* speedily escape
27: 5 For why *s* your servant dwell in
27:11 Lest they *s* inform on us,
28:15 reveal to me what I *s* do."
2 Sam 2:22 Why *s* I strike you to the
3:33 *S* Abner die as a fool dies?
9: 8 that you *s* look upon such a
12:23 why *s* I fast? Can I bring him
13:12 for no such thing *s* be done in
13:26 Why *s* he go with you?"
15:20 *S* I make you wander up and down
16: 9 Why *s* this dead dog curse my
16:19 whom *s* I serve? Should I not
16:19 *S* I not serve in the
16:20 counsel as to what we *s* do."
19:19 that the king *s* take it to
19:22 that you *s* be adversaries to me
19:34 that I *s* go up with the king to
19:35 Why then *s* your servant be a
19:36 And why *s* the king repay me
20:20 that I *s* swallow up or destroy!
21: 5 that we *s* be destroyed from
23:17 that I *s* do this! Is this not
24:13 and see what answer I *s* take
1 Ki 1:20 that you *s* tell them who will
1:27 told your servant who *s* sit
2: 1 drew near that he *s* die,
2:15 that I *s* reign. However, the
8:36 way in which they *s* walk;
11:10 that he *s* not go after other
12: 9 How *s* we answer this people who
12:10 Thus you *s* speak to this people
20:22 and see what you *s* do, for in
21: 3 The LORD forbid that I *s* give
2 Ki 6:33 why *s* I wait for the LORD any
8:13 that he *s* do this gross
11:17 that they *s* be the LORD's
13:19 You *s* have struck five or six
14:10 for why *s* you meddle with
17:15 that they *s* not do like them.
17:28 and taught them how they *s* fear
18:35 that the LORD *s* deliver
19:25 That you *s* be For crushing
1 Chr 11:19 that I *s* do this! Shall I drink
21: 3 Why *s* he be a cause of guilt in
21:12 what answer I *s* take back to
21:17 Your people that they *s* be
21:18 to David that David *s* go
23:13 that he *s* sanctify the most
23:32 and that they *s* attend to the
25: 1 who *s* prophesy with harps,
29:14 That we *s* be able to offer so
2 Chr 2: 6 that I *s* build Him a temple,
6:27 way in which they *s* walk;
10: 9 How *s* we answer this people who
10:10 Thus you *s* speak to the people
13: 5 *S* you not know that the LORD
19: 2 *S* you help the wicked and love
20:21 he appointed those who *s* sing
20:21 and who *s* praise the beauty of
23:16 that they *s* be the LORD's
23:19 in any way unclean *s* enter.
25:16 Why *s* you be killed?"
25:19 why *s* you meddle with trouble,
25:19 that you *s* fall—you and Judah
29:11 and that you *s* minister to Him
30: 1 that they *s* come to the house
30: 5 that they *s* come to keep the
32: 4 Why *s* the kings of Assyria come
32:14 that your God *s* be able to
Ezra 2:63 said to them that they *s* not
4:22 Why *s* damage increase to the
7:23 For why *s* there be wrath
8:17 and I told them what they *s* say
8:17 that they *s* bring us servants
9:14 *s* we again break Your
Neh 2: 3 Why *s* my face not be sad,
5: 8 Or *s* they be sold to us?"
5: 9 *S* you not walk in the fear of
6: 3 Why *s* the work cease while I
6:11 '*S* such a man as I flee?
6:13 that I *s* be afraid and act that
7:65 said to them that they *s* not
8:14 children of Israel *s* dwell
8:15 and that they *s* announce and
9:12 the road Which they *s* travel.
9:19 And the way they *s* go.
10:37 for the Levites *s* receive the
11:23 that a certain portion *s* be
13: 1 no Ammonite or Moabite *s* ever
13:22 Levites that they *s* cleanse
13:22 and that they *s* go and guard
13:27 *S* we then hear of your doing all
Esth 1: 8 that they *s* do according to
1:22 that each man *s* be master in
3:14 that they *s* be ready for that
9:21 that they *s* celebrate
9:22 that they *s* make them days of
9:25 against the Jews *s* return on
9:25 and that he and his sons *s* be
9:27 without fail they *s* celebrate
9:28 that these days *s* be
9:28 that these days of Purim *s* not
9:28 memory of them *s* not perish
Job 3:12 the breasts, that I *s* nurse?
6:11 that I *s* hope? And what is my
6:11 that I *s* prolong my life?
6:14 kindness *s* be shown by his
7:17 that You *s* exalt him, That
7:17 That You *s* set Your heart on
7:18 That You *s* visit him every
9:32 And that we *s* go to court
10: 3 good to You that You *s* oppress,
10: 3 That You *s* despise the work of
10: 6 That You *s* seek for my iniquity
11: 2 *S* not the multitude of words be
11: 2 And *s* a man full of talk be
11: 3 *S* your empty talk make men hold
11: 3 *s* no one rebuke you?
15: 2 *S* a wise man answer with empty
15: 3 *S* he reason with unprofitable
19:28 If you *s* say, 'How shall we
21: 4 why *s* I not be impatient?
21:15 that we *s* serve Him? And what
24:18 They *s* be swift on the face of
24:18 Their portion *s* be cursed in
24:20 The womb *s* forget him, The
24:20 The worm *s* feed sweetly on
24:20 He *s* be remembered no more,
24:20 And wickedness *s* be broken
27: 5 Far be it from me That I *s* say
31: 1 Why then *s* I look upon a young
32: 7 Age *s* speak, And multitude of
32: 7 And multitude of years *s* teach
34: 6 *S* I lie concerning my right
34: 9 That he *s* delight in God.'
34:14 If He *s* set His heart on it,
34:14 If He *s* gather to Himself His
34:17 *S* one who hates justice govern
34:23 That he *s* go before God in
34:30 That the hypocrite *s* not reign,
34:33 *S* He repay it according to
37:19 Teach us what we *s* say to Him,
37:20 *S* He be told that I wish to
41:11 Me, that I *s* pay him?
Ps 27: 3 Though war *s* rise against me,
30: 3 that I *s* not go down to the
32: 8 teach you in the way you *s* go;
49: 5 Why *s* I fear in the days of
49: 9 That he *s* continue to live
78: 5 That they *s* make them known to
79:10 Why *s* the nations say, "Where
104: 5 So that it *s* not be moved
115: 2 Why *s* the Gentiles say, "So
130: 3 *s* mark iniquities, O Lord, who
139:18 If I *s* count them, they would
143: 8 know the way in which I *s* walk,
Prov 5:16 *S* your fountains be dispersed
5:20 For why *s* you, my son, be
12:26 The righteous *s* choose his

22: 6 up a child in the way he *s* go,
22:27 Why *s* he take away your bed
25: 7 Than that you *s* be put lower
Eccl 2:24 for a man than that he *s* eat
2:24 and that his soul *s* enjoy good
3:13 and also that every man *s* eat
3:14 that men *s* fear before Him.
3:22 than that a man *s* rejoice
5: 6 Why *s* God be angry at your
7:16 Why *s* you destroy yourself?
7:17 Why *s* you die before your
9:17 *s* be heard Rather than the
Song 1: 7 For why *s* I be as one who
8: 1 If I *s* find you outside,
Isa 1: 5 Why *s* you be stricken again?
8:11 and instructed me that I *s* not
8:19 *s* not a people seek their
8:19 *S* they seek the dead on
36:20 that the LORD *s* deliver
37:26 That you *s* be For crushing
46: 5 that we *s* be alike?
48: 5 Lest you *s* say, 'My idol has
48: 7 Lest you *s* say, 'Of course I
48:11 For how *s* My name be
48:17 leads you by the way you *s* go.
49: 6 small a thing that You *s* be
49: 6 That You *s* be My salvation to
50: 4 That I *s* know how to speak A
51:12 Who are you that you *s* be
51:14 That he *s* not die in the pit,
51:14 And that his bread *s* not fail.
53: 2 is no beauty that we *s* desire
57: 6 *S* I receive comfort in these?
Jer 5:17 your sons and daughters *s* eat.
14: 8 Why *s* You be like a stranger
14: 9 Why *s* You be like a man
15: 2 Where *s* we go?' then you shall
20:18 That my days *s* be consumed
25:29 and *s* you be utterly
26:24 so that they *s* not give him
27:17 *s* this city be laid waste?
29:26 so that there *s* be officers in
29:26 that you *s* put him in prison
32:35 into My mind that they *s* do
33:24 as if they *s* no more be a
34: 9 that every man *s* set free his
34: 9 that no one *s* keep a Jewish
34:10 heard that everyone *s* set free
34:10 that no one *s* keep them in
37:21 commanded that they *s* commit
37:21 and that they *s* give him daily
39:14 that he *s* take him home.
40:15 Why *s* he murder you, so that
42: 3 the way in which we *s* walk
42: 3 walk and the thing we *s* do."
Lam 1:16 who *s* restore my life, Is far
2:20 *S* the women eat their
2:20 *S* the priest and prophet be
3:26 It is good that one *s* hope
3:39 Why *s* a living man complain,
3:44 That prayer *s* not pass
Ezek 3:21 man that the righteous *s* not
13:19 killing people who *s* not die,
13:19 people alive who *s* not live,
14: 3 *S* I let Myself be inquired of
16:16 Such things *s* not happen, nor
18:19 Why *s* the son not bear the guilt
18:23 at all that the wicked *s* die?
18:23 and not that he *s* turn from his
18:31 For why *s* you die, O house of
19: 9 That his voice *s* no longer be
20: 9 that it *s* not be profaned
20:14 that it *s* not be profaned
20:22 that it *s* not be profaned in
21:10 *S* we then make mirth?
22:30 that I *s* not destroy it;
33:11 For why *s* you die, O house
33:25 *S* you then possess the land?
33:26 *S* you then possess the land?"
34: 2 *S* not the shepherds feed the
Dan 1:10 For why *s* he see your faces
1:18 said that they *s* be brought
2:46 commanded that they *s* present
3:28 that they *s* not serve nor
5:15 that they *s* read this writing
5:29 concerning him that he *s* be
6:23 and commanded that they *s* take
7:14 and languages *s* serve Him.
Hos 8: 7 If it *s* produce, Aliens would
13:13 For he *s* not stay long where
Joel 2:17 That the nations *s* rule over
2:17 Why *s* they say among the
Ob 12 But you *s* not have gazed on the
12 Nor *s* you have rejoiced over
12 Nor *s* you have spoken proudly
13 You *s* not have entered the gate
13 you *s* not have gazed on their
14 You *s* not have stood at the
14 Nor *s* you have delivered up
Jon 4:11 And *s* I not pity Nineveh, that
Mic 2:11 If a man *s* walk in a false
Hab 2:18 that its maker *s* carve it, The
2:18 maker of its mold *s* trust
Hag 1: 2 the LORD's house *s* be built."
Zech 7: 3 *S* I weep in the fifth month and
7: 7 *S* you not have obeyed the
Mal 1:13 *S* I accept this from your
2: 7 For the lips of a priest *s* keep
2: 7 And people *s* seek the law
Mt 2:12 dream that they *s* not return
8: 8 I am not worthy that You *s* come
10:19 about how or what you *s* speak.
10:19 in that hour what you *s* speak;
13:15 Lest they *s* see with
13:15 Lest they *s* understand
13:15 So that I *s* heal them.'
16:20 His disciples that they *s* tell
18:13 And if he *s* find it, assuredly,
18:14 of these little ones *s* perish.
18:30 him into prison till he *s* pay
18:33 *S* you not also have had
18:34 to the torturers until he *s* pay
20:31 warned them that they *s* be
25: 9 lest there *s* not be enough for
27:20 the multitudes that they *s* ask
Mk 3: 9 a small boat *s* be kept ready
3: 9 lest they *s* crush Him.
3:12 warned them that they *s* not
4:12 Lest they *s* turn, And
4:22 kept secret but that it *s* come
4:26 is as if a man *s* scatter seed
4:27 and *s* sleep by night and rise by
4:27 and the seed *s* sprout and grow,
5:43 that no one *s* know it,
5:43 and said that something *s* be
6:12 preached that people *s* repent.
7:36 them that they *s* tell no one;
8:30 warned them that they *s* tell
9: 9 them that they *s* tell no one
9:18 that they *s* cast it out, but
12:19 his brother *s* take his wife and
15:11 so that he *s* rather release
15:24 what every man *s* take.
Lk 1:43 the mother of my Lord *s* come
1:71 That we *s* be saved from our
2: 1 the world *s* be registered.
7: 4 that the one for whom He *s* do
7: 6 not worthy that You *s* enter
8:12 lest they *s* believe and be
12: 5 show you whom you *s* fear:
12:11 how or what you *s* answer,
12:11 or what you *s* say.
12:29 And do not seek what you *s* eat
12:29 eat or what you *s* drink,
12:38 And if he *s* come in the second
13:33 that a prophet *s* perish
15:32 It was right that we *s* make
17: 1 that no offenses *s* come,
17: 2 than that he *s* offend one of
18:39 before warned him that he *s* be
19:40 I tell you that if these *s* keep
20:28 his brother *s* take his wife and
22:24 as to which of them *s* be
22:32 that your faith *s* not fail; and
23:24 gave sentence that it *s* be as
24:47 and remission of sins *s* be
Jn 1:31 but that He *s* be revealed to
2:25 no need that anyone *s* testify
3:15 believes in Him *s* not perish
3:16 believes in Him *s* not perish
3:20 lest his deeds *s* be exposed.
5:23 that all *s* honor the Son just as
6:39 of all He has given Me I *s* lose
6:39 but *s* raise it up at the last
6:62 What then if you *s* see the Son
7:23 so that the law of Moses *s* not
8: 5 commanded us that such *s* be
9: 3 but that the works of God *s* be
11:50 for us that one man *s* die for
11:50 the whole nation *s* perish."
11:57 he *s* report it, that they
12:23 the Son of Man *s* be glorified.
12:40 Lest they *s* see with
12:40 Lest they *s* understand
12:40 So that I *s* heal
12:42 lest they *s* be put out of the
12:46 believes in Me *s* not abide
12:49 *s* say and what I should speak.
12:49 what I should say and what I *s*
13: 1 had come that He *s* depart
13:15 that you *s* do as I have done to
13:29 or that he *s* give something
15:16 appointed you that you *s* go
15:16 and that your fruit *s* remain,
16: 1 that you *s* not be made to
16:30 need that anyone *s* question
17: 2 that He *s* give eternal life to
17:15 I do not pray that You *s* take
17:15 but that You *s* keep them from
18:14 expedient that one man *s* die
18:28 lest they *s* be defiled, but
18:36 so that I *s* not be delivered to
18:37 that I *s* bear witness to the
18:39 a custom that I *s* release
19:31 that the bodies *s* not remain on
19:36 Scripture *s* be fulfilled,
Acts 2:24 possible that He *s* be held
5:26 lest they *s* be stoned.
5:40 they commanded that they *s* not
6: 2 desirable that we *s* leave
10:28 shown me that I *s* not call
10:47 that these *s* not be baptized
11:23 of heart they *s* continue
12:19 and commanded that they *s* be
13:28 they asked Pilate that He *s* be
13:46 that the word of God *s* be
13:47 That you *s* be for
14:15 preach to you that you *s* turn
15: 2 certain others of them *s* go
15: 7 by my mouth the Gentiles *s* hear
15:19 Therefore I judge that we *s* not
15:38 insisted that they *s* not take
17:27 so that they *s* seek the Lord, in
18:14 would be reason why I *s* bear
19: 4 people that they *s* believe
21:25 decided that they *s* observe
21:25 except that they *s* keep
21:26 at which time an offering *s* be
22:14 has chosen you that you *s* know
22:24 and said that he *s* be examined
25: 4 Festus answered that Paul *s* be
26: 8 Why *s* it be thought incredible
26:20 that they *s* repent, turn to
27: 1 it was decided that we *s* sail
27:17 and fearing lest they *s* run
27:21 you *s* have listened to me, and
27:29 fearing lest we *s* run aground
27:42 lest any of them *s* swim away
27:43 those who could swim *s* jump
28:27 Lest they *s* see with
28:27 Lest they *s* understand
28:27 So that I *s* heal them."
Rom 2:21 You who preach that a man *s* not
6: 4 even so we also *s* walk in
6: 6 that we *s* no longer be slaves
6:12 that you *s* obey it in its
7: 4 that we *s* bear fruit to God.
7: 6 so that we *s* serve in the
8:26 do not know what we *s* pray
11: 8 Eyes that they *s* not see
11: 8 ears that they *s* not hear,
11:11 stumbled that they *s* fall?
11:25 that you *s* be ignorant of this
11:25 lest you *s* be wise in your own
15:20 lest I *s* build on another man's
1 Cor 1:15 lest anyone *s* say that I had
1:17 lest the cross of Christ *s* be
1:29 that no flesh *s* glory in His
2: 5 that your faith *s* not be in the
4: 3 small thing that I *s* be judged
7:29 even those who have wives *s* be
9:10 that he who plows *s* plow in
9:10 in hope *s* be partaker
9:14 who preach the gospel *s* live
9:15 these things that it *s* be done
9:15 die than that anyone *s* make
9:27 I myself *s* become disqualified.
10: 6 to the intent that we *s* not
12:15 If the foot *s* say, "Because I
12:16 And if the ear *s* say, "Because
12:25 that there *s* be no schism in the
12:25 but that the members *s* have
2 Cor 1: 9 that we *s* not trust in
1:17 that with me there *s* be Yes,
2: 3 I *s* have sorrow over those from
2: 4 not that you *s* be grieved, but
2:11 lest Satan *s* take advantage of
4: 4 image of God, *s* shine on them.
5:15 that those who live *s* live no
8:13 mean that others *s* be eased
8:20 that anyone *s* blame us in this
9: 3 lest our boasting of you *s* be
9: 4 we (not to mention you!) *s* be
10: 8 For even if I *s* boast somewhat
12: 6 lest anyone *s* think of me above
12: 7 And lest I *s* be exalted above
13: 7 not that we *s* appear approved,
13: 7 but that you *s* do what is
13:10 lest being present I *s* use
Gal 2: 9 that we *s* go to the Gentiles
2:10 only that we *s* remember
3: 1 you that you *s* not obey the
3:17 that it *s* make the promise of
3:19 till the Seed *s* come to whom
6:14 But God forbid that I *s* boast
Eph 1: 4 that we *s* be holy and without
1:12 first trusted in Christ *s* be
2: 9 lest anyone *s* boast.
2:10 beforehand that we *s* walk in
3: 6 that the Gentiles *s* be fellow
3: 8 that I *s* preach among the
4:14 that we *s* no longer be children,
4:17 that you *s* no longer walk as
5:27 but that she *s* be holy and
Phil 2:10 of Jesus every knee *s* bow,
2:11 and that every tongue *s* confess
2:27 lest I *s* have sorrow upon
Col 1:19 Him all the fullness *s* dwell,
2: 4 I say lest anyone *s* deceive
1 Th 3: 3 that no one *s* be shaken by these
4: 1 Lord Jesus that you *s* abound
4: 3 that you *s* abstain from sexual
4: 4 that each of you *s* know how to
4: 6 that no one *s* take advantage of
4: 9 have no need that I *s* write
5: 1 you have no need that I *s* write
5: 4 so that this Day *s* overtake you
5:10 we *s* live together with Him.
2 Th 2:11 that they *s* believe the lie,
3: 9 an example of how you *s* follow
Titus 1: 5 that you *s* set in order the
2:12 we *s* live soberly, righteously,
3: 7 His grace we *s* become heirs
3: 8 who have believed in God *s* be
Heb 7:11 that another priest *s* rise
9:23 in the heavens *s* be purified
9:25 not that He *s* offer Himself
11:28 the firstborn *s* touch them.
11:40 that they *s* not be made perfect
12:19 it begged that the word *s* not
Jas 2: 2 For if there *s* come into your
2: 2 and there *s* also come in a poor
1 Pe 2:21 that you *s* follow His steps:
3:14 But even if you *s* suffer for
4: 2 that he no longer *s* live the
2 Pe 3: 9 not willing that any *s* perish

3: 9 perish but that all *s* come
1 Jn 3: 1 that we *s* be called children of
3:11 that we *s* love one another,
3:23 that we *s* believe on the name
5:16 I do not say that he *s* pray
2 Jn 6 you *s* walk in it.
Rev 6: 4 and that people *s* kill one
6:11 said to them that they *s* rest
7: 1 that the wind *s* not blow on the
8: 3 that he *s* offer it with the
9:20 that they *s* not worship demons,
10: 6 that there *s* be delay no
11:18 that they *s* be judged, And
11:18 And that You *s* reward Your
11:18 And *s* destroy those who
12: 6 that they *s* feed her there one
13:15 image of the beast *s* both
19:15 that with it He *s* strike the
20: 3 so that he *s* deceive the

SHOULDER (29/29) SHOULDERS

Gen 21:14 water; and putting it on her *s*,
24:15 out with her pitcher on her *s*.
24:45 out with her pitcher on her *s*;
24:46 her pitcher down from her *s*,
49:15 He bowed his *s* to bear a
Ex 28: 7 It shall have two *s* straps
28:25 and put them on the *s* straps of
28:27 put them on the two *s* straps,
39: 4 They made *s* straps for it to
39:18 and put them on the *s* straps of
39:20 put them on the two *s* straps,
Num 6:19 priest shall take the boiled *s*
Deut 18: 3 shall give to the priest the *s*,
Josh 4: 5 of you take up a stone on his *s*,
Judg 9:48 took it and laid it on his *s*;
Job 31:22 let my arm fall from my *s*,
31:36 I would carry it on my *s*,
Ps 81: 6 I removed his *s* from the burden;
Isa 9: 4 burden And the staff of his *s*,
9: 6 government will be upon His *s*.
10:27 will be taken away from your *s*,
11:14 they shall fly down upon the *s*
22:22 of David I will lay on his *s*;
46: 7 They bear it on the *s*,
Ezek 12: 7 and I bore them on my *s* in
12:12 his belongings on his *s* at
24: 4 piece, The thigh and the *s*.
29:18 and every *s* rubbed raw; yet
34:21 you have pushed with side and *s*,

SHOULDERS (22/21) SHOULDER

Gen 9:23 laid it on both their *s*,
Ex 12:34 up in their clothes on their *s*.
28:12 put the two stones on the *s* of
28:12 before the LORD on his two *s*
39: 7 He put them on the *s* of the
Num 7: 9 which they carried on their *s*.
Deut 33:12 he shall dwell between His *s*.
Judg 16: 3 bar and all, put them on his *s*,
1 Sam 9: 2 From his *s* upward he was
10:23 any of the people from his *s*
17: 6 a bronze javelin between his *s*.
1 Chr 15:15 bore the ark of God on their *s*,
2 Chr 35: 3 longer be a burden on your *s*.
Neh 3: 5 nobles did not put their *s* to
9:29 And they shrugged their *s*,
Isa 14:25 his burden removed from their *s*.
49:22 shall be carried on their *s*;
Ezek 12: 6 you shall bear them on your *s*
29: 7 You broke and tore all their *s*;
Zech 7:11 to heed, shrugged their *s*,
Mt 23: 4 bear, and lay them on men's *s*;
Lk 15: 5 found it, he lays it on his *s*,

SHOUT (48/43) SHOUTED, SHOUTING, SHOUTS

Ex 32:18 is not the noise of the *s*
Num 23:21 And the *s* of a King is among
Josh 6: 5 that all the people shall *s*
6: 5 shall shout with a great *s*;
6:10 You shall not *s* or make any
6:10 I say to you, '*S*!' Then you
6:10 you, 'Shout!' Then you shall *s*.
6:16 '*S*, for the LORD has given
6:20 people shouted with a great *s*,
1 Sam 4: 6 heard the noise of the *s*,
4: 6 the sound of this great *s* in
1 Ki 22:36 a *s* went throughout the army,
2 Chr 13:15 Then the men of Judah gave a *s*;
Ezra 3:11 people shouted with a great *s*,
3:13 not discern the noise of the *s*
3:13 people shouted with a loud *s*,
Job 3: 7 no joyful *s* come into it!
Ps 5:11 Let them ever *s* for joy,
32:11 And *s* for joy, all you
33: 3 Play skillfully with a *s* of
35:27 Let them *s* for joy and be glad,
47: 1 *S* to God with the voice of
47: 5 God has gone up with a *s*,
60: 8 *s* in triumph because of Me."
65:13 They *s* for joy, they also
66: 1 Make a joyful *s* to God, all the
81: 1 Make a joyful *s* to the God of
95: 1 Let us *s* joyfully to the Rock
95: 2 Let us *s* joyfully to Him with
98: 4 *S* joyfully to the LORD, all
98: 6 *S* joyfully before the LORD,
100: 1 Make a joyful *s* to the LORD,
132: 9 And let Your saints *s* for joy.
132:16 And her saints shall *s* aloud
Eccl 9:17 be heard Rather than the *s*
Isa 12: 6 Cry out and *s*, O inhabitant
42:11 Let them *s* from the top of the
42:13 shall cry out, yes, *s* aloud;
44:23 *S*, you lower parts of the
Jer 25:30 He will give a *s*, as those
31: 7 And *s* among the chief of the
50:15 *S* against her all around
51:14 And they shall lift up a *s*
Lam 3: 8 Even when I cry and *s*,
Zeph 3:14 of Zion! *S*, O Israel!
Zech 9: 9 *S*, O daughter of Jerusalem!
Gal 4:27 bear! Break forth and *s*,
1 Th 4:16 descend from heaven with a *s*,

SHOUTED (16/15) SHOUT

Ex 32:17 noise of the people as they *s*,
Lev 9:24 they *s* and fell on their faces.
Josh 6:20 So the people *s* when the
6:20 and the people *s* with a great
1 Sam 4: 5 all Israel *s* so loudly that the
10:24 So all the people *s* and said,
17:52 of Israel and Judah arose and *s*,
2 Chr 13:15 and as the men of Judah *s*,
Ezra 3:11 Then all the people *s* with a
3:12 Yet many *s* aloud for joy,
3:13 for the people *s* with a loud
Job 30: 5 They *s* at them as at a thief.
38: 7 And all the sons of God *s* for
Jer 20: 8 I *s*, "Violence and plunder!"
Lk 23:21 But they *s*, saying, "Crucify
Acts 22:24 that he might know why they *s*

SHOUTING (15/13) SHOUT

Judg 15:14 the Philistines came *s* against
1 Sam 17:20 going out to the fight and *s*
2 Sam 6:15 up the ark of the LORD with *s*
1 Chr 15:28 covenant of the LORD with *s*
2 Chr 15:14 with *s* and trumpets and rams'
Job 39:25 The thunder of captains and *s*.
Isa 16:10 singing, Nor will there be *s*;
16:10 I have made their *s* cease.
Jer 20:16 cry in the morning And the *s*
48:33 *s*—Not joyous shouting!
48:33 Not joyous *s*!
Ezek 21:22 to lift the voice with *s*,
Am 1:14 Amid *s* in the day of battle,
2: 2 With *s* and trumpet sound.
Acts 12:22 And the people kept *s*,

SHOUTS (3/3) SHOUT

Job 39: 7 He does not heed the *s* of the
Ps 78:65 Like a mighty man who *s*
Zech 4: 7 forth the capstone With *s* of

SHOVEL (1/1)

Isa 30:24 has been winnowed with the *s*

SHOVELS (9/9)

Ex 27: 3 and its *s* and its basins and
38: 3 for the altar: the pans, the *s*,
Num 4:14 firepans, the forks, the *s*,
1 Ki 7:40 made the lavers and the *s* and
7:45 the pots, the *s*, and the
2 Ki 25:14 also took away the pots, the *s*,
2 Chr 4:11 Huram made the pots and the *s*
4:16 also the pots, the *s*,
Jer 52:18 also took away the pots, the *s*,

SHOW (163/155) SHOWED, SHOWING, SHOWN, SHOWS

Gen 12: 1 To a land that I will *s* you.
24:12 and *s* kindness to my master
40:14 and please *s* kindness to me;
Ex 7: 9 *S* a miracle for yourselves,'
9:16 that I may *s* My power in you,
10: 1 that I may *s* these signs of
18:20 and *s* them the way in which
23: 3 You shall not *s* partiality to a
25: 9 According to all that I *s* you,
33:13 *s* me now Your way, that I may
33:18 'Please, *s* me Your glory."
Num 16: 5 morning the LORD will *s* who
Deut 1:17 You shall not *s* partiality in
1:33 to *s* you the way you should go,
3:24 You have begun to *s* Your
7: 2 with them nor *s* mercy to
13:17 His anger and *s* you mercy,
16:19 you shall not *s* partiality, nor
28:50 the elderly nor *s* favor to
32: 7 and he will *s* you; Your
Josh 2:12 that you also will *s* kindness
5: 6 swore that He would not *s* them
Judg 1:24 Please *s* us the entrance to the
1:24 and we will *s* you mercy."
4:22 I will *s* you the man whom you
6:17 then *s* me a sign that it is You
8:35 nor did they *s* kindness to the
1 Sam 8: 9 and *s* them the behavior of the
9: 6 perhaps he can *s* us the way
10: 8 till I come to you and *s* you
14: 8 and we will *s* ourselves to
14:12 and we will *s* you something."
16: 3 and I will *s* you what you shall
20:14 And you shall not only *s* me the
2 Sam 2: 6 And now may the LORD *s* kindness
3: 8 Today I *s* loyalty to the house
9: 1 that I may *s* him kindness for
9: 3 to whom I may *s* the kindness of
9: 7 for I will surely *s* you
10: 2 I will *s* kindness to Hanun the
15:25 He will bring me back and *s* me
22:26 You will *s* Yourself merciful;
22:26 will *s* Yourself blameless;
22:27 You will *s* Yourself pure;
22:27 You will *s* Yourself shrewd.
1 Ki 2: 7 But *s* kindness to the sons of
2 Ki 6:11 Will you not *s* me which of us
20:13 that Hezekiah did not *s* them.
1 Chr 19: 2 I will *s* kindness to Hanun the
2 Chr 16: 9 to *s* Himself strong on behalf
Neh 9:19 To *s* them light, And the way
Esth 1:11 in order to *s* her beauty to the
4: 8 that he might *s* it to Esther
Job 10: 2 *S* me why You contend with me.
10:16 And again You *s* Yourself
11: 6 That He would *s* you the secrets
13: 8 Will you *s* partiality for Him?
13:10 If you secretly *s* partiality.
32:21 *s* partiality to anyone;
33:23 To *s* man His uprightness,
36: 2 and I will *s* you That there
Ps 4: 6 Who will *s* us any good?"
16:11 You will *s* me the path of life;
17: 7 *S* Your marvelous lovingkindness
18:25 You will *s* Yourself merciful;
18:25 You will *s* Yourself blameless;
18:26 You will *s* Yourself pure;
18:26 You will *s* Yourself shrewd.
25: 4 *S* me Your ways, O LORD
25:14 And He will *s* them His
50:23 I will *s* the salvation of
51:15 And my mouth shall *s* forth
79:13 We will *s* forth Your praise to
82: 2 And *s* partiality to the
85: 7 *S* us Your mercy, LORD, And
86:17 *S* me a sign for good, That
91:16 And *s* him My salvation."
102:14 And *s* favor to her dust.
109:16 he did not remember to *s* mercy,
Prov 18: 5 not good to *s* partiality
24:23 not good to *s* partiality
28:21 To *s* partiality is not good,
Isa 27:11 who formed them will *s* them
30:30 And *s* the descent of His arm,
39: 2 that Hezekiah did not *s* them.
41:22 Let them bring forth and *s* us
41:22 Let them *s* the former things,
41:23 *S* the things that are to come
43: 9 And *s* us former things?
44: 7 Let them *s* these to them.
46: 8 and *s* yourselves men;
49: 9 in darkness, '*S* yourselves.'
Jer 16:10 when you *s* this people all
16:13 where I will not *s* you favor.'
18:17 I will *s* them the back and not
32:18 You *s* lovingkindness to
33: 3 and *s* you great and mighty
42: 3 that the LORD your God may *s* us
42:12 And I will *s* you mercy, that he
50:42 and shall not *s* mercy.
51:31 To *s* the king of Babylon that
Lam 3:32 Yet He will *s* compassion
4:16 Nor *s* favor to the elders.
Ezek 22: 2 *s* her all her abominations!
33:31 their mouth they *s* much love,
37:18 Will you not *s* us what you mean
38:18 that My fury will *s* in My face.
40: 4 mind on everything I *s* you;
40: 4 here so that I might *s* them
Dan 6:13 does not *s* due regard for you,
11:30 So he shall return and *s* regard
Joel 2:30 And I will *s* wonders in the
Mic 7:15 I will *s* them wonders."
Nah 3: 5 I will *s* the nations your
Hab 1: 3 Why do You *s* me iniquity, And
Zech 1: 9 I will *s* you what they are."
7: 9 *S* mercy and compassion
Mt 8: 4 *s* yourself to the priest, and
16: 1 Him asked that He would *s* them
16:21 that time Jesus began to *s* to
22:19 '*S* Me the tax money."
24: 1 His disciples came up to *s* Him
24:24 will rise and *s* great signs
Mk 1:44 *s* yourself to the priest, and
13:22 prophets will rise and *s* signs
14:15 Then he will *s* you a large upper
Lk 5:14 But go and *s* yourself to the
6:47 I will *s* you whom he is like:
12: 5 But I will *s* you whom you should
17:14 *s* yourselves to the priests."
20:21 and You do not *s* personal
20:24 *S* Me a denarius. Whose image and
22:12 Then he will *s* you a large,
Jn 2:18 What sign do You *s* to us, since
5:20 and He will *s* Him greater works
7: 4 *s* Yourself to the world."
14: 8 *s* us the Father, and it is
14: 9 you say, '*S* us the Father'?
Acts 1:24 *s* which of these two You have
2:19 I will *s* wonders in
7: 3 land that I will *s* you.'
9:16 For I will *s* him how many things
Rom 2:15 who *s* the work of the law
9:17 that I may *s* My power in
9:22 wanting to *s* His wrath and to
14:10 Or why do you *s* contempt for

1 Cor 12:31 And yet I *s* you a more
2 Cor 8:19 and to *s* your ready mind,
8:24 Therefore *s* to them, and before
Eph 2: 7 might *s* the exceeding riches
1 Tim 1:16 Jesus Christ might *s* all
5: 4 let them first learn to *s* piety
Heb 6:11 each one of you *s* the same
6:17 determining to *s* more
Jas 2: 9 but if you *s* partiality, you
2:18 *S* me your faith without your
2:18 and I will *s* you my faith by my
3:13 Let him *s* by good conduct that
Rev 1: 1 which God gave Him to *s* His
4: 1 and I will *s* you things which
17: 1 I will *s* you the judgment of
21: 9 I will *s* you the bride, the
22: 6 angel to *s* His servants

SHOWBREAD (19/18)

Ex 25:30 And you shall set the *s* on the
35:13 all its utensils, and the *s*;
39:36 all its utensils, and the *s*;
Num 4: 7 On the table of *s* they shall
4: 7 and the *s* shall be on it.
1 Sam 21: 6 was no bread there but the *s*
1 Ki 7:48 of gold on which was the *s*;
1 Chr 9:32 in charge of preparing the *s*
23:29 both with the *s* and the fine
28:16 gold for the tables of the *s*,
2 Chr 2: 4 incense, for the continual *s*,
4:19 the tables on which was the *s*;
13:11 they also set the *s* in
29:18 and the table of the *s* with all
Neh 10:33 for the *s*, for the regular
Mt 12: 4 the house of God and ate the *s*
Mk 2:26 the high priest, and ate the *s*,
Lk 6: 4 of God, took and ate the *s*,
Heb 9: 2 lampstand, the table, and the *s*,

SHOWED (48/47) SHOW

Gen 39:21 with Joseph and *s* him mercy,
Ex 15:25 and the LORD *s* him a tree.
Num 13:26 and *s* them the fruit of the
Deut 4:36 on earth He *s* you His great
6:22 and the LORD *s* signs and
34: 1 And the LORD *s* him all the
Judg 1:25 So he *s* them the entrance to the
1 Sam 14:11 So both of them *s* themselves to
15: 6 For you *s* kindness to all the
2 Sam 10: 2 as his father *s* kindness to
1 Ki 16:27 he did, and the might that he *s*,
22:45 the might that he *s*,
2 Ki 6: 6 And he *s* him the place.
11: 4 and *s* them the king's son.
20:13 and *s* them all the house of his
22:10 Then Shaphan the scribe *s* the
1 Chr 19: 2 because his father *s* kindness
Neh 9:10 You *s* signs and wonders against
Esth 1: 4 when he *s* the riches of his
Isa 39: 2 and *s* them the house of his
40:14 And *s* Him the way of
47: 6 You *s* them no mercy; On the
Jer 11:18 for You *s* me their doings.
24: 1 The LORD *s* me, and there were
Ezek 20:11 them My statutes and *s* them
35:11 to the envy which you *s* in
Am 7: 1 Thus the Lord GOD *s* me: Behold,
7: 4 Thus the Lord GOD *s* me:
7: 7 Thus He *s* me: Behold, the Lord
8: 1 Thus the Lord GOD *s* me: Behold,
Zech 1:20 Then the LORD *s* me four
3: 1 Then he *s* me Joshua the high
Mt 4: 8 and *s* Him all the kingdoms of
Lk 4: 5 *s* Him all the kingdoms of the
10:37 'He who *s* mercy on him."
20:37 But even Moses *s* in the burning
24:40 He *s* them His hands and His
Jn 20:20 He *s* them His hands and His
21: 1 Jesus *s* Himself again to
21: 1 and in this way He *s* Himself:
21:14 third time Jesus *s* Himself
Acts 10:40 third day, and *s* Him openly,
11:28 stood up and *s* by the Spirit
28: 2 And the natives *s* us unusual
2 Pe 1:14 as our Lord Jesus Christ *s* me.
Rev 21:10 and *s* me the great city, the
22: 1 And he *s* me a pure river of
22: 8 the feet of the angel who *s* me

SHOWER (1/1)

Lk 12:54 A *s* is coming'; and so it is.

SHOWERS (10/9)

Deut 32: 2 And as *s* on the grass.
Job 24: 8 They are wet with the *s* of the
Ps 65:10 You make it soft with *s*,
72: 6 Like *s* that water the earth.
Jer 3: 3 Therefore the *s* have been
14:22 Or can the heavens give *s*?
Ezek 34:26 and I will cause *s* to come down
34:26 there shall be *s* of blessing.
Mic 5: 7 Like *s* on the grass, That
Zech 10: 1 He will give them *s* of rain,

SHOWING (12/11) SHOW

Gen 26: 8 *s* endearment to Rebekah his
Ex 20: 6 but *s* mercy to thousands, to
Deut 5:10 but *s* mercy to thousands, to
Dan 4:27 and your iniquities by *s* mercy
Acts 9:39 *s* the tunics and garments which
18:28 *s* from the Scriptures that
Gal 6:12 as desire to make a good *s* in
2 Th 2: 4 *s* himself that he is God.
Titus 2: 7 in all things *s* yourself to be
2: 7 in doctrine *s* integrity,
2:10 but *s* all good fidelity, that
3: 2 *s* all humility to all men.

SHOWN (54/54) SHOW

Gen 19:19 your mercy which you have *s* me
24:14 that You have *s* kindness
32:10 all the truth which You have *s*
41:25 God has *s* Pharaoh what He is
41:28 God has *s* Pharaoh what He is
41:39 Inasmuch as God has *s* you all
48:11 God has also *s* me your
Ex 25:40 to the pattern which was *s* you
26:30 to its pattern which you were *s*
27: 8 as it was *s* you on the
Lev 13:19 then it shall be *s* to the
13:49 a leprous plague and shall be *s*
24:12 mind of the LORD might be *s*
Num 8: 4 pattern which the LORD had *s*
Deut 4:35 "To you it was *s*,
5:24 our God has *s* us His glory
Josh 2:12 since I have *s* you kindness,
Judg 13:23 nor would He have *s* us all
Ruth 3:10 you have *s* more kindness
1 Sam 24:18 And you have *s* this day how you
2 Sam 2: 5 for you have *s* this kindness to
1 Ki 3: 6 You have *s* great mercy to Your
2 Ki 8:10 However the LORD has *s* me
8:13 The LORD has *s* me that you
20:15 my treasures that I have not *s*
2 Chr 1: 8 You have *s* great mercy to David
32:25 according to the favor *s* him,
Ezra 9: 8 little while grace has been *s*
Job 6:14 kindness should be *s* by his
Ps 31:21 For He has *s* me His marvelous
60: 3 You have *s* Your people hard
71:20 who have *s* me great and severe
78:11 And His wonders that He had *s*
Eccl 2:19 I toiled and in which I have *s*
Isa 26:10 Let grace be *s* to the wicked,
39: 4 my treasures that I have not *s*
Jer 3:11 Backsliding Israel has *s* herself
38:21 the word that the LORD has *s*
Ezek 11:25 all the things the LORD had *s*
Hos 2: 1 to your sisters, 'Mercy is *s*.
Mic 6: 8 He has *s* you, O man, what is
Mal 2: 9 But have *s* partiality in the
Lk 1:51 He has *s* strength with His arm;
1:58 heard how the Lord had *s* great
Jn 10:32 Many good works I have *s* you
Acts 7:36 after he had *s* wonders and
10:28 But God has *s* me that I should
20:35 I have *s* you in every way, by
Rom 1:19 for God has *s* it to them.
11:31 that through the mercy *s* you
Heb 6:10 labor of love which you have *s*
8: 5 to the pattern *s* you on
Jas 2: 4 have you not *s* partiality among
2:13 mercy to the one who has *s* no

SHOWS (16/16) SHOW

Num 23: 3 and whatever He *s* me I will
Deut 10:17 who *s* no partiality nor takes a
2 Sam 22:51 And *s* mercy to His anointed,
Job 37:24 He *s* no partiality to any who
Ps 18:50 And *s* mercy to His anointed,
19: 1 And the firmament *s* His
37:21 But the righteous *s* mercy and
Prov 27:25 and the tender grass *s* itself,
Eccl 10: 3 And he *s* everyone that he is
Isa 41:26 Surely there is no one who *s*,
Mk 14:70 and your speech *s* it."
Jn 5:20 and *s* Him all things that He
Acts 10:34 that God *s* no partiality.
Rom 9:16 but of God who *s* mercy.
12: 8 he who *s* mercy, with
Gal 2: 6 God *s* personal favoritism to no

SHRANK (2/1)

Gen 32:32 do not eat the muscle that *s*,
32:32 hip in the muscle that *s*.

SHRED (KJV) See SLICED

SHREWD (4/4) SHREWDLY

2 Sam 22:27 You will show Yourself *s*.
Ps 18:26 You will show Yourself *s*.
64: 6 We have perfected a *s* scheme."
Lk 16: 8 sons of this world are more *s*

SHREWDLY (2/2) SHREWD

Ex 1:10 let us deal *s* with them, lest
Lk 16: 8 steward because he had dealt *s*.

SHRIEK (1/1)

Hos 10: 5 And its priests *s* for

SHRINE (3/3) SHRINES

Judg 17: 5 The man Micah had a *s*,
Ezek 16:24 you also built for yourself a *s*,
16:31 You erected your *s* at the head

SHRINES (7/7) SHRINE

1 Ki 12:31 He made *s* on the high places,
13:32 and against all the *s* on the
2 Ki 17:29 and put them in the *s* on the
17:32 sacrificed for them in the *s*
23:19 also took away all the *s* of
Ezek 16:39 they shall throw down your *s*
Acts 19:24 who made silver *s* of Diana,

SHRIVELED (2/2)

Job 16: 8 You have *s* me up, And it is a
Isa 33: 9 Lebanon is shamed and *s*;

SHRIVELS (1/1)

Joel 1:17 The seed *s* under the clods,

SHRUB (1/1)

Jer 17: 6 For he shall be like a *s* in the

SHRUBS (1/1)

Gen 21:15 the boy under one of the *s*.

SHRUGGED (2/2)

Neh 9:29 And they *s* their shoulders,
Zech 7:11 *s* their shoulders, and stopped

SHUA (4/4)

Gen 38: 2 Canaanite whose name was *S*,
38:12 of time the daughter of *S*,
1 Chr 2: 3 to him by the daughter of *S*,
7:32 Hotham, and their sister *S*.

SHUAH (2/2)

Gen 25: 2 Medan, Midian, Ishbak, and *S*.
1 Chr 1:32 Medan, Midian, Ishbak, and *S*.

SHUAL (2/2)

1 Sam 13:17 to Ophrah, to the land of *S*,
1 Chr 7:36 Zophah were Suah, Harnepher, *S*,

SHUBAEL (3/2)

1 Chr 24:20 Levi: of the sons of Amram, *S*;
24:20 Shubael; of the sons of *S*,
25:20 the thirteenth for *S*,

SHUFFLES (1/1)

Prov 6:13 He *s* his feet, He points with

SHUHAH (1/1)

1 Chr 4:11 Chelub the brother of *S* begot

SHUHAM (1/1)

Num 26:42 to their families: of *S*,

SHUHAMITES (2/2)

Num 26:42 of Shuham, the family of the *S*.
26:43 All the families of the *S*,

SHUHITE (5/5)

Job 2:11 the Temanite, Bildad the *S*,
8: 1 Then Bildad the *S* answered and
18: 1 Then Bildad the *S* answered and
25: 1 Then Bildad the *S* answered and
42: 9 the Temanite and Bildad the *S*

SHULAMITE (2/1)

Song 6:13 Return, return, O *S*;
6:13 What would you see in the *S*—

SHUMATHITES (1/1)

1 Chr 2:53 Ithrites, the Puthites, the *S*,

SHUN (1/1) SHUNNED, SHUNS

2 Tim 2:16 But *s* profane and idle

SHUNAMMITE (8/8)

1 Ki 1: 3 Israel, and found Abishag the *S*,
1:15 and Abishag the *S* was serving
2:17 he may give me Abishag the *S*
2:21 Let Abishag the *S* be given to
2:22 why do you ask Abishag the *S*
2 Ki 4:12 Call this *S* woman." When he had
4:25 'Look, the *S* woman!.
4:36 Call this *S* woman." So he

SHUNEM (3/3)

Josh 19:18 and included Chesulloth, *S*,

1 Sam 28: 4 and came and encamped at *S*.
2 Ki 4: 8 one day that Elisha went to *S*,

SHUNI (2/2)

Gen 46:16 of Gad were Ziphion, Haggi, *S*,
Num 26:15 family of the Haggites; of *S*,

SHUNITES (1/1)

Num 26:15 of Shuni, the family of the *S*;

SHUNNED (2/2) SHUN

Job 1: 1 who feared God and *s* evil.
Acts 20:27 For I have not *s* to declare to

SHUNS (2/2) SHUN

Job 1: 8 one who fears God and *s* evil?"
2: 3 one who fears God and *s* evil?

SHUPHAM (1/1)

Num 26:39 of *S*, the family of the

SHUPHAMITES (1/1)

Num 26:39 of Shupham, the family of the *S*;

SHUPPIM (3/3)

1 Chr 7:12 *S* and Huppim were the sons of
7:15 the sister of Huppim and *S*,
26:16 To *S* and Hosah the lot came

SHUR (6/6)

Gen 16: 7 by the spring on the way to *S*.
20: 1 and dwelt between Kadesh and *S*,
25:18 dwelt from Havilah as far as *S*,
Ex 15:22 out into the Wilderness of *S*.
1 Sam 15: 7 from Havilah all the way to *S*,
27: 8 from of old, as you go to *S*,

SHUSHAN (22/20)

Ezra 4: 9 and Erech and Babylon and *S*,
Neh 1: 1 as I was in *S* the citadel,
Esth 1: 2 which was in *S* the citadel,
1: 5 people who were present in *S*
2: 3 beautiful young virgins to *S*
2: 5 In *S* the citadel there was a
2: 8 young women were gathered at *S*
3:15 the decree was proclaimed in *S*
3:15 but the city of *S* was
4: 8 which was given at *S*,
4:16 the Jews who are present in *S*,
8:14 And the decree was issued in *S*
8:15 and the city of *S* rejoiced and
9: 6 And in *S* the citadel the Jews
9:11 of those who were killed in *S*
9:12 five hundred men in *S* the
9:13 to the Jews who are in *S* to
9:14 the decree was issued in *S*,
9:15 And the Jews who were in *S*
9:15 killed three hundred men at *S*;
9:18 But the Jews who were at *S*
Dan 8: 2 I was looking, that I was in *S*,

SHUT (82/80) SHUTS

Gen 7:16 and the LORD *s* him in.
19: 6 *s* the door behind him,
19:10 with them, and *s* the door.
Lev 14:38 and *s* up the house seven days.
14:46 the house at all while it is *s*
Num 12:14 Let her be *s* out of the camp
12:15 So Miriam was *s* out of the camp
Deut 11:17 and He *s* up the heavens so that
15: 7 your heart nor *s* your hand
Josh 2: 5 as the gate was being *s*,
2: 7 had gone out, they *s* the gate.
6: 1 Now Jericho was securely *s* up
Judg 3:23 the porch and *s* the doors
9:51 fled there and *s* themselves in;
1 Sam 6:10 and *s* up their calves at home.
23: 7 for he has *s* himself in by
2 Sam 20: 3 So they were *s* up to the day of
1 Ki 8:35 When the heavens are *s* up and
2 Ki 4: 4 you shall *s* the door behind you
4: 5 So she went from him and *s* the
4:21 *s* the door upon him, and went
4:33 *s* the door behind the two of
6:32 *s* the door, and hold him fast
17: 4 the king of Assyria *s* him up,
2 Chr 6:26 When the heavens are *s* up and
7:13 When I *s* up heaven and there is
28:24 *s* up the doors of the house of
29: 7 They have also *s* up the doors of
Neh 7: 3 let them *s* and bar the doors;
13:19 I commanded the gates to be *s*,
Job 3:10 Because it did not *s* up the
38: 8 Or who *s* in the sea with doors,
41:15 *S* up tightly as with a seal;
Ps 31: 8 And have not *s* me up into the
69:15 And let not the pit *s* its
77: 9 Has He in anger *s* up His
88: 8 I am *s* up, and I cannot get
Eccl 12: 4 When the doors are *s* in the
Song 4:12 A spring *s* up, A fountain
Isa 6:10 And *s* their eyes; Lest they
22:22 shall open, and no one shall *s*;
22:22 one shall shut; And he shall *s*,
24:10 Every house is *s* up, so that
24:22 And will be *s* up in the
26:20 And *s* your doors behind you;
44:18 For He has *s* their eyes, so
45: 1 that the gates will not be *s*:
52:15 Kings shall *s* their mouths at
60:11 They shall not be *s* day or
66: 9 Shall I who cause delivery *s* up
Jer 13:19 of the South shall be *s* up,
20: 9 fire *S* up in my bones;
32: 2 Jeremiah the prophet was *s* up
32: 3 king of Judah had *s* him up,
33: 1 while he was still *s* up in the
39:15 to Jeremiah while he was *s* up
Ezek 3:24 *s* yourself inside your house.
44: 1 toward the east, but it was *s*.
44: 2 to me, "This gate shall be *s*;
44: 2 by it; therefore it shall be *s*.
46: 1 toward the east shall be *s* the
46: 2 but the gate shall not be *s*
46:12 he goes out the gate shall be *s*.
Dan 6:22 My God sent His angel and *s* the
12: 4 *s* up the words, and seal the
Mal 1:10 even among you who would *s* the
Mt 6: 6 and when you have *s* your door,
23:13 For you *s* up the kingdom
25:10 the wedding; and the door was *s*.
Lk 3:20 that he *s* John up in prison.
4:25 when the heaven was *s* up three
11: 7 trouble me; the door is now *s*,
13:25 has risen up and *s* the door,
Jn 20:19 when the doors were *s* where the
20:26 Jesus came, the doors being *s*,
Acts 5:23 Indeed we found the prison *s*
21:30 immediately the doors were *s*.
26:10 and many of the saints I *s* up
Rev 3: 8 and no one can *s* it; for you
11: 6 These have power to *s* heaven, so
20: 3 and *s* him up, and set a seal on
21:25 Its gates shall not be *s* at all

SHUTHALHITES (1/1)

Num 26:35 Shuthelah, the family of the *S*;

SHUTHELAH (4/4)

Num 26:35 to their families: of *S*,
26:36 And these are the sons of *S*:
1 Chr 7:20 The sons of Ephraim were *S*,
7:21 *S* his son, and Ezer and Elead.

SHUTS (8/7) SHUT

Job 5:16 And injustice *s* her mouth.
Prov 17:28 When he *s* his lips, he is
21:13 Whoever *s* his ears to the cry
Isa 33:15 And *s* his eyes from seeing
Lam 3: 8 He *s* out my prayer.
1 Jn 3:17 and *s* up his heart from him,
Rev 3: 7 who opens and no one *s*,
3: 7 and *s* and no one opens":

SHUTTLE (1/1)

Job 7: 6 are swifter than a weaver's *s*,

SIA (1/1)

Neh 7:47 sons of Keros, the sons of *S*,

SIAHA (1/1)

Ezra 2:44 sons of Keros, the sons of *S*,

SIBBECHAI (4/4)

2 Sam 21:18 Then *S* the Hushathite killed
1 Chr 11:29 *S* the Hushathite, Ilai the
20: 4 at which time *S* the Hushathite
27:11 for the eighth month was *S*

SIBBOLETH (1/1) SHIBBOLETH

Judg 12: 6 And he would say, "*S*,

SIBMAH (4/4)

Josh 13:19 Kirjathaim, *S*, Zereth Shahar
Isa 16: 8 languish, And the vine of *S*;
16: 9 I will bewail the vine of *S*,
Jer 48:32 O vine of *S*! I will weep for

SIBRAIM (1/1)

Ezek 47:16 *S* (which is between the border

SICHEM (KJV) See SHECHEM

SICK (78/78) SICKNESS

Gen 48: 1 'Indeed your father is *s*";
Num 22: 3 and Moab was *s* with dread
1 Sam 19:14 David, she said, "He is *s*.
30:13 because three days ago I fell *s*.
2 Sam 13: 2 sister Tamar that he became *s*;
1 Ki 14: 1 the son of Jeroboam became *s*.
14: 5 about her son, for he is *s*.
17:17 who owned the house became *s*.
2 Ki 8: 7 Ben-Hadad king of Syria was *s*;
8:29 in Jezreel, because he was *s*.
13:14 Elisha had become *s* with the
20: 1 In those days Hezekiah was *s* and
20:12 heard that Hezekiah had been *s*.
2 Chr 21:15 and you will become very *s*
22: 6 in Jezreel, because he was *s*.
32:24 In those days Hezekiah was *s*
Neh 2: 2 face sad, since you are not *s*?
Ps 35:13 as for me, when they were *s*,
Prov 13:12 deferred makes the heart *s*,
Isa 1: 5 The whole head is *s*,
10:18 they will be as when a *s* man
33:24 will not say, "I am *s*";
38: 1 In those days Hezekiah was *s* and
38: 9 when he had been *s* and had
39: 1 for he heard that he had been *s*
Jer 14:18 those *s* from famine!
Ezek 34: 4 you healed those who were *s*,
34:16 and strengthen what was *s*;
Dan 8:27 fainted and was *s* for days;
Hos 7: 5 king Princes have made him *s*,
Mic 6:13 I will also make you *s* by
Mal 1: 8 when you offer the lame and *s*,
1:13 the stolen, the lame, and the *s*;
Mt 4:24 brought to Him all *s* people
8:14 saw his wife's mother lying *s*
8:16 word, and healed all who were *s*,
9:12 physician, but those who are *s*.
10: 8 'Heal the *s*, cleanse the
14:14 for them, and healed their *s*.
14:35 brought to Him all who were *s*,
25:36 I was *s* and you visited Me;
25:39 'Or when did we see You *s*,
25:43 *s* and in prison and you did not
25:44 or a stranger or naked or *s* or
Mk 1:30 But Simon's wife's mother lay *s*
1:32 brought to Him all who were *s*
1:34 Then He healed many who were *s*
2:17 physician, but those who are *s*.
6: 5 His hands on a few *s* people
6:13 with oil many who were *s*,
6:55 about on beds those who were *s*
6:56 they laid the *s* in the
16:18 they will lay hands on the *s*,
Lk 4:38 But Simon's wife's mother was *s*
4:40 those who had any that were *s*
5:31 physician, but those who are *s*.
7: 2 was *s* and ready to die.
7:10 the servant well who had been *s*.
9: 2 of God and to heal the *s*.
10: 9 And heal the *s* there, and say to
Jn 4:46 nobleman whose son was *s* at
5: 3 great multitude of *s* people,
5: 7 The *s* man answered Him, "Sir, I
11: 1 Now a certain man was *s*,
11: 2 whose brother Lazarus was *s*.
11: 3 behold, he whom You love is *s*.
11: 6 So, when He heard that he was *s*,
Acts 5:15 so that they brought the *s* out
5:16 bringing *s* people and those who
9:37 in those days that she became *s*
19:12 brought from his body to the *s*,
28: 8 the father of Publius lay *s* of
1 Cor 11:30 reason many are weak and *s*
Phil 2:26 you had heard that he was *s*.
2:27 For indeed he was *s* almost unto
2 Tim 4:20 I have left in Miletus *s*.
Jas 5:14 Is anyone among you *s*?
5:15 prayer of faith will save the *s*,

SICKBED (2/2)

Ps 41: 3 You will sustain him on his *s*.
Rev 2:22 I will cast her into a *s*,

SICKLE (13/12)

Deut 16: 9 time you begin to put the *s*
23:25 but you shall not use a *s* on
1 Sam 13:20 his mattock, his ax, and his *s*;
Jer 50:16 And him who handles the *s* at
Joel 3:13 Put in the *s*, for the harvest
Mk 4:29 immediately he puts in the *s*,
Rev 14:14 and in His hand a sharp *s*.
14:15 Thrust in Your *s* and reap, for
14:16 on the cloud thrust in His *s*
14:17 he also having a sharp *s*.
14:18 cry to him who had the sharp *s*,
14:18 Thrust in your sharp *s* and
14:19 So the angel thrust his *s* into

SICKNESS (17/17) SICK, SICKNESSES

Ex 23:25 And I will take *s* away from the
Lev 20:18 lies with a woman during her *s*
Deut 7:15 will take away from you all *s*,
28:61 Also every *s* and every plague,
1 Ki 8:37 whatever plague or whatever *s*
17:17 And his *s* was so serious that
2 Chr 6:28 whatever plague or whatever *s*
21:15 come out by reason of the *s*,
21:19 came out because of his *s*;
Prov 18:14 of a man will sustain him in *s*,
Eccl 5:17 he has much sorrow and *s* and
Isa 38: 9 and had recovered from his *s*:
Hos 5:13 "When Ephraim saw his *s*,
Mt 4:23 and healing all kinds of *s* and
9:35 and healing every *s* and every
10: 1 and to heal all kinds of *s* and
Jn 11: 4 This *s* is not unto death, but

SICKNESSES (4/4) SICKNESS

Deut	28:59	serious and prolonged *s*.
	29:22	plagues of that land and the *s*
Mt	8:17	And bore our *s*.
Mk	3:15	and to have power to heal *s* and

SIDDIM (3/3)

Gen	14: 3	together in the Valley of *S*
	14: 8	in battle in the Valley of *S*
	14:10	Now the Valley of *S* was full

SIDE (396/310) RIVERSIDE, SIDES

Gen	6:16	the door of the ark in its *s*.
Ex	17:12	his hands, one on one *s*,
	17:12	and the other on the other *s*;
	25:12	two rings shall be on one *s*,
	25:12	and two rings on the other *s*.
	25:32	of the lampstand out of one *s*,
	25:32	lampstand out of the other *s*.
	26:13	And a cubit on one *s* and a cubit
	26:13	side and a cubit on the other *s*,
	26:13	on this *s* and on that side, to
	26:13	on this side and on that *s*,
	26:18	twenty boards for the south *s*.
	26:20	And for the second *s* of the
	26:20	of the tabernacle, the north *s*,
	26:22	For the far *s* of the tabernacle,
	26:26	five for the boards on one *s* of
	26:27	for the boards on the other *s*
	26:27	bars for the boards of the *s*
	26:27	for the far *s* westward.
	26:35	across from the table on the *s*
	26:35	put the table on the north *s*.
	27: 9	For the south *s* there shall
	27: 9	hundred cubits long for one *s*.
	27:11	along the length of the north *s*
	27:12	of the court on the west *s*
	27:13	of the court on the east *s*
	27:14	The hangings on one *s* of the
	27:15	And on the other *s* shall be
	28:26	which is on the inner *s* of the
	32:15	on the one *s* and on the other
	32:26	"Whoever is on the LORD's *s*—
	32:27	man put his sword on his *s*,
	36:23	twenty boards for the south *s*.
	36:25	And for the other *s* of the
	36:25	of the tabernacle, the north *s*,
	36:27	For the west *s* of the tabernacle
	36:31	five for the boards on one *s* of
	36:32	for the boards on the other *s*
	36:32	of the tabernacle on the far *s*
	37: 3	corners: two rings on one *s*,
	37: 3	and two rings on the other *s* of
	37: 8	one cherub at one end on this *s*,
	37: 8	at the other end on that *s*.
	37:18	of the lampstand out of one *s*,
	37:18	lampstand out of the other *s*.
	38: 9	made the court on the south *s*;
	38:11	On the north *s* the hangings
	38:12	And on the west *s* there were
	38:13	For the east *s* the hangings
	38:14	The hangings of one *s* of the
	38:15	and the same for the other *s* of
	38:15	on this *s* and that were
	39:19	which was on the inward *s* of
	40:22	on the north *s* of the
	40:24	on the south *s* of the
Lev	1:11	shall kill it on the north *s*
	1:15	shall be drained out at the *s*
	1:16	beside the altar on the east *s*,
	5: 9	of the sin offering on the *s*
	16:14	the mercy seat on the east *s*;
Num	2: 3	'On the east *s*, toward the
	2:10	On the south *s* shall be the
	2:18	On the west *s* shall be the
	2:25	Dan shall be on the north *s*
	3:29	were to camp on the south *s* of
	3:35	were to camp on the north *s*
	10: 5	camps that lie on the east *s*
	10: 6	camps that lie on the south *s*
	11:31	a day's journey on this *s* and
	11:31	a day's journey on the other *s*,
	21:13	and camped on the other *s* of
	22: 1	in the plains of Moab on the *s*
	22:24	with a wall on this *s* and a
	22:24	this side and a wall on that *s*.
	32:19	with them on the other *s* of
	32:19	fallen to us on this eastern *s*
	32:32	remain with us on this *s* of
	34: 4	shall turn from the southern *s*
	34:11	to Riblah on the east *s* of Ain;
	34:11	and reach to the eastern *s* of
	34:15	their inheritance on this *s* of
	35: 5	outside the city on the east *s*
	35: 5	on the south *s* two thousand
	35: 5	on the west *s* two thousand
	35: 5	and on the north *s* two thousand
	35:14	appoint three cities on this *s*
Deut	1: 1	spoke to all Israel on this *s*
	1: 5	On this *s* of the Jordan in the
	3: 8	Amorites who were on this *s*
	3:17	as far as the east *s* of the
	4:41	apart three cities on this *s*
	4:46	on this *s* of the Jordan, in the
	4:47	who were on this *s* of the
	4:49	all the plain on the east *s* of
	11:30	Are they not on the other *s* of
Josh	1:14	which Moses gave you on this *s*
	1:15	servant gave you on this *s* of
	2:10	who were on the other *s* of
	5: 1	who were on the west *s* of the
	7: 2	on the east *s* of Bethel, and
	7: 7	and dwelt on the other *s* of the
	8: 9	on the west *s* of Ai; but Joshua
	8:11	city and camped on the north *s*
	8:12	on the west *s* of the city.
	8:22	some on this *s* and some on that
	8:22	on this side and some on that *s*.
	8:33	stood on either *s* of the ark
	9: 1	the kings who were on this *s*
	12: 1	they possessed on the other *s*
	12: 7	of Israel conquered on this *s*
	13:27	on the other *s* of the Jordan
	13:32	plains of Moab on the other *s*
	14: 3	the half-tribe on the other *s*
	15: 3	it went out to the southern *s*
	15: 3	ascended on the south *s* of
	15: 7	which is on the south *s* of the
	15:10	passed along to the *s* of Mount
	15:11	the border went out to the *s*
	16: 5	inheritance on the east *s* was
	16: 6	toward the sea on the north *s*
	17: 5	which were on the other *s* of
	17: 9	of Manasseh was on the north *s*
	18:12	Their border on the north *s*
	18:12	the border went up to the *s* of
	18:13	to the *s* of Luz (which is
	18:13	hill that lies on the south *s*
	18:14	extended around the west *s* to
	18:14	This was the west *s*.
	18:15	The south *s* began at the end of
	18:16	to the *s* of the Jebusite city
	18:18	along toward the north *s* of
	18:19	passed along to the north *s* of
	18:20	was its border on the east *s*.
	19:14	went around it on the north *s*
	19:34	Zebulun on the south *s* and
	19:34	side and Asher on the west *s*,
	20: 8	And on the other *s* of the
	22: 4	LORD gave you on the other *s*
	22: 7	among their brethren on this *s*
	22:11	the children of Israel's *s*.
	24: 2	dwelt on the other *s* of the
	24: 3	Abraham from the other *s* of
	24: 8	who dwelt on the other *s* of the
	24:14	fathers served on the other *s*
	24:15	that were on the other *s* of
	24:30	on the north *s* of Mount Gaash.
Judg	2: 3	they shall be thorns in your *s*,
	2: 9	on the north *s* of Mount Gaash.
	7: 1	Midianites was on the north *s*
	7:18	blow the trumpets on every *s*
	7:25	Zeeb to Gideon on the other *s*
	8:34	of all their enemies on every *s*;
	10: 8	who were on the other *s* of
	11:18	came to the east *s* of the land
	11:18	and encamped on the other *s* of
	21:19	on the east *s* of the highway
1 Sam	4:18	off the seat backward by the *s*
	6: 8	offering in a chest by its *s*.
	12:11	hand of your enemies on every *s*;
	14: 1	that is on the other *s*.
	14: 4	was a sharp rock on one *s* and
	14: 4	and a sharp rock on the other *s*.
	14:40	all Israel, "You be on one *s*,
	14:40	and I will be on the other *s*.
	14:47	all his enemies on every *s*,
	17: 3	stood on a mountain on one *s*,
	17: 3	on a mountain on the other *s*,
	20:20	shoot three arrows to the *s*,
	20:21	the arrows are on this *s* of
	20:25	and Abner sat by Saul's *s*,
	23:26	Then Saul went on one *s* of the
	23:26	and his men on the other *s* of
	26:13	David went over to the other *s*,
	31: 7	who were on the other *s* of
	31: 7	who were on the other *s* of
2 Sam	2:13	one on one *s* of the pool and
	2:13	and the other on the other *s*
	2:16	his sword in his opponent's *s*;
	24: 5	on the right *s* of the town
1 Ki	3:20	night and took my son from my *s*,
	4:12	as far as the other *s* of
	4:24	all the region on this *s* of
	4:24	over all the kings on this *s*
	4:24	and he had peace on every *s* all
	5: 3	fought against him on every *s*,
	5: 4	has given me rest on every *s*;
	6: 5	Thus he made *s* chambers all
	6: 8	story was on the right *s* of
	6:10	And he built *s* chambers against
	7:39	put five carts on the right *s*
	7:39	and five on the left *s* of the
	7:39	He set the Sea on the right *s*
	7:49	five on the right *s* and five
	10:19	were armrests on either *s* of
	10:20	one on each *s* of the six steps;
2 Ki	3:22	saw the water on the other *s*
	9:32	and said, "Who is on my *s*?
	11:11	from the right *s* of the temple
	11:11	of the temple to the left *s* of
	12: 9	on the right *s* as one comes
	16:14	and put it on the north *s* of the
1 Chr	4:39	as far as the east *s* of the
	5: 9	of the wilderness this *s* of
	6:78	And on the other *s* of the
	6:78	on the east *s* of the Jordan,
	12:18	O David; We are on your *s*,
	12:37	from the other *s* of the Jordan,
	18:17	chief ministers at the king's *s*.
	22:18	not given you rest on every *s*?
	26:30	of Israel on the west *s* of the
2 Chr	4: 6	and put five on the right *s* and
	4: 7	five on the right *s* and five on
	4: 8	five on the right *s* and five on
	4:10	He set the Sea on the right *s*,
	9:18	were armrests on either *s* of
	9:19	one on each *s* of the six steps;
	11:12	Judah and Benjamin on his *s*.
	14: 7	He has given us rest on every *s*.
	23:10	from the right *s* of the temple
	23:10	of the temple to the left *s* of
	32:22	and guided them on every *s*.
	32:30	water by tunnel to the west *s*
	33:14	City of David on the west *s* of
Neh	4:18	had his sword girded at his *s*
Job	1:10	all that he has on every *s*?
	18:11	frighten him on every *s*,
	18:12	destruction is ready at his *s*.
	19:10	He breaks me down on every *s*,
Ps	12: 8	The wicked prowl on every *s*,
	31:13	of many; Fear is on every *s*;
	65:12	little hills rejoice on every *s*.
	71:21	And comfort me on every *s*.
	91: 7	A thousand may fall at your *s*,
	118: 6	The LORD is on my *s*;
	124: 1	been the LORD who was on our *s*,
	124: 2	been the LORD who was on our *s*,
Eccl	4: 1	On the *s* of their oppressors
Isa	60: 4	shall be nursed at your *s*.
Jer	6:25	the enemy, Fear is on every *s*.
	20:10	Fear on every *s*!" "Report,"
	49:29	Fear is on every *s*!'
Ezek	1:10	face of a lion on the right *s*,
	1:10	the face of an ox on the left *s*,
	1:23	one had two which covered one *s*,
	1:23	two which covered the other *s*
	4: 4	"Lie also on your left *s*,
	4: 6	them, lie again on your right *s*;
	4: 8	you cannot turn from one *s* to
	4: 9	of days that you lie on your *s*,
	9: 2	had a writer's inkhorn at his *s*.
	9: 3	the writer's inkhorn at his *s*;
	9:11	who had the inkhorn at his *s*,
	10: 3	were standing on the south *s*
	11:23	which is on the east *s* of the
	19: 8	from the provinces on every *s*,
	23:22	them against you from every *s*:
	28:23	sword against her on every *s*;
	34:21	you have pushed with *s*
	36: 3	and swallowed you up on every *s*,
	37:21	will gather them from every *s*
	40:10	three gate chambers on one *s*
	40:10	of the same size on this *s* and
	40:10	size on this side and that *s*.
	40:12	one cubit on this *s* and one
	40:12	side and one cubit on that *s*;
	40:12	were six cubits on this *s* and
	40:12	side and six cubits on that *s*.
	40:18	The pavement was by the *s* of the
	40:21	three on this *s* and three on
	40:21	this side and three on that *s*,
	40:26	one on this *s* and one on that
	40:26	on this side and one on that *s*.
	40:34	on its gateposts on this *s* and
	40:34	on this side and on that *s*;
	40:37	on its gateposts on this *s* and
	40:37	on this side and on that *s*,
	40:39	were two tables on this *s* and
	40:39	side and two tables on that *s*,
	40:40	At the outer *s* of the vestibule,
	40:40	and on the other *s* of the
	40:41	Four tables were on this *s* and
	40:41	side and four tables on that *s*,
	40:41	by the *s* of the gateway, eight
	40:44	one facing south at the *s* of
	40:44	other facing north at the *s* of
	40:48	five cubits on this *s* and five
	40:48	side and five cubits on that *s*;
	40:48	was three cubits on this *s* and
	40:48	side and three cubits on that *s*.
	40:49	one on this *s* and another on
	40:49	this side and another on that *s*.
	41: 1	six cubits wide on one *s* and
	41: 1	six cubits wide on the other *s*—
	41: 2	and the *s* walls of the entrance
	41: 2	were five cubits on this *s*
	41: 2	and five cubits on the other *s*;
	41: 5	The width of each *s* chamber all
	41: 5	was four cubits on every *s*.
	41: 6	The *s* chambers were in three
	41: 6	on ledges which were for the *s*
	41: 7	the *s* chambers became wider all
	41: 8	it was the foundation of the *s*
	41: 9	of the outer wall of the *s*
	41: 9	terrace by the place of the *s*
	41:10	around the temple on every *s*.
	41:11	The doors of the *s* chambers
	41:15	its galleries on the one *s* and
	41:15	the one side and on the other *s*,
	41:19	toward a palm tree on one *s*,
	41:19	a palm tree on the other *s*;
	41:26	and palm trees on one *s* and on
	41:26	also on the *s* chambers of the
	42: 9	was the entrance on the east *s*,
	42:16	He measured the east *s* with the
	42:17	He measured the north *s*,
	42:18	He measured the south *s*,
	42:19	He came around to the west *s*
	45: 7	have a section on one *s* and
	45: 7	westward on the west *s* and

45: 7 side and eastward on the east s,
45: 7 the length shall be s by side
45: 7 the length shall be side by s
46:19 which was at the s of the
47: 1 flowing from under the right s
47: 2 running out on the right s.
47: 7 were very many trees on one s
47:12 on this s and that, will grow
47:17 This is the north s.
47:18 On the east s you shall mark out
47:18 and along the eastern s of the
47:18 This is the east s.
47:19 'The south s, toward the
47:19 This is the south s,
47:20 The west s shall be the Great
47:20 This is the west s.
48: 1 Dan from its east to its west s;
48: 2 from the east s to the west,
48: 3 from the east s to the west,
48: 4 from the east s to the west,
48: 5 from the east s to the west,
48: 6 from the east s to the west,
48: 7 from the east s to the west,
48: 8 from the east s to the west,
48: 8 from the east s to the west,
48:16 the north s four thousand five
48:16 the south s four thousand five
48:16 the east s four thousand five
48:16 and the west s four thousand
48:21 on one s and on the other of
48:23 from the east s to the west,
48:24 from the east s to the west,
48:25 from the east s to the west,
48:26 from the east s to the west,
48:27 from the east s to the west,
48:28 border of Gad, on the south s,
48:30 On the north s, measuring
48:32 'on the east s, four thousand
48:33 'on the south s, measuring
48:34 'on the west s, four thousand
Dan 7: 5 It was raised up on one s,
10: 4 as I was by the s of the great
Ob 11 that you stood on the other s—
Jon 4: 5 the city and sat on the east s
Nah 2:10 Much pain is in every s,
Zech 5: 3 according to this s of the
5: 3 according to that s of it."
Mt 8:18 to depart to the other s.
8:28 He had come to the other s,
14:22 go before Him to the other s,
16: 5 had come to the other s,
Mk 4:35 us cross over to the other s.
5: 1 Then they came to the other s of
5:21 again by boat to the other s,
6:45 go before Him to the other s,
8:13 again, departed to the other s.
9:40 is not against us is on our s.
10: 1 region of Judea by the other s
16: 5 robe sitting on the right s;
Lk 1:11 standing on the right s of the
8:22 us cross over to the other s
9:50 is not against us is on our s.
10:31 he passed by on the other s.
10:32 and passed by on the other s.
19:43 you and close you in on every s,
Jn 6:22 were standing on the other s
6:25 they found Him on the other s
19:18 with Him, one on either s,
19:34 of the soldiers pierced His s
20:20 them His hands and His s.
20:25 and put my hand into His s,
20:27 here, and put it into My s.
21: 6 Cast the net on the right s of
Acts 12: 7 and he struck Peter on the s
2 Cor 4: 8 are hard pressed on every s,
7: 5 but we were troubled on every s.
Rev 22: 2 and on either s of the river,

SIDED (1/1)

Acts 14: 4 part s with the Jews, and part

SIDES (33/32) SIDE

Ex 25:14 poles into the rings on the s
25:32 shall come out of its s:
26:13 shall hang over the s of the
27: 7 poles shall be on the two s of
30: 3 its s all around, and its horns
30: 4 under the molding on both its s.
30: 4 shall place them on its two s,
32:15 tablets were written on both s;
37: 5 poles into the rings at the s
37:18 six branches came out of its s:
37:26 its s all around, and its
37:27 by its two corners on both s,
38: 7 poles into the rings on the s
Lev 19:27 shall not shave around the s
Num 33:55 your eyes and thorns in your s,
Josh 23:13 and scourges on your s and
2 Ki 11: 8 surround the king on all s,
2 Chr 23: 7 surround the king on all s,
Ps 48: 2 Is Mount Zion on the s of
141: 6 judges are overthrown by the s
Isa 14:13 On the farthest s of the
66:12 On her s shall you be
Jer 48:28 makes her nest In the s of
49:32 their calamity from all its s,
51:31 his city is taken on all s;
52:23 pomegranates on the s;
Ezek 1: 8 their wings on their four s;
39:17 Gather together from all s to
41:22 and its s were of wood; and he
41:26 on the s of the vestibule—also
42:20 He measured it on the four s;
43:17 and fourteen wide on its four s,
Heb 9: 4 the covenant overlaid on all s

SIDON (35/35) SIDONIANS

Gen 10:15 Canaan begot S his firstborn,
10:19 of the Canaanites was from S
49:13 And his border shall adjoin S.
Josh 11: 8 and chased them to Greater S,
19:28 and Kanah, as far as Greater S.
Judg 1:31 of Acco or the inhabitants of S,
10: 6 gods of Syria, the gods of S,
18:28 because it was far from S,
2 Sam 24: 6 to Dan Jaan and around to S;
1 Ki 17: 9 Zarephath, which belongs to S,
1 Chr 1:13 Canaan begot S, his firstborn,
Ezra 3: 7 and oil to the people of S and
Isa 23: 2 coastland, You merchants of S,
23: 4 Be ashamed, O S; For the sea
23:12 oppressed virgin daughter of S.
Jer 25:22 of Tyre, all the kings of S,
27: 3 king of Tyre, and the king of S,
47: 4 To cut off from Tyre and S
Ezek 27: 8 Inhabitants of S and Arvad were
28:21 of man, set your face toward S,
28:22 I am against you, O S;
Joel 3: 4 to do with Me, O Tyre and S,
Zech 9: 2 on it, And against Tyre and S,
Mt 11:21 you had been done in Tyre and S,
11:22 more tolerable for Tyre and S
15:21 to the region of Tyre and S.
Mk 3: 8 and those from Tyre and S,
7:24 to the region of Tyre and S.
7:31 from the region of Tyre and S,
Lk 4:26 in the region of S,
6:17 from the seacoast of Tyre and S,
10:13 you had been done in Tyre and S,
10:14 more tolerable for Tyre and S
Acts 12:20 with the people of Tyre and S;
27: 3 the next day we landed at S.

SIDONIANS (15/14) SIDON

Deut 3: 9 (the S call Hermon Sirion, and
Josh 13: 4 Mearah that belongs to the S
13: 6 Misrephoth, and all the S—
Judg 3: 3 all the Canaanites, the S,
10:12 Also the S and Amalekites and
18: 7 safely, in the manner of the S,
18: 7 They were far from the S,
1 Ki 5: 6 skill to cut timber like the S.
11: 1 Ammonites, Edomites, S,
11: 5 Ashtoreth the goddess of the S,
11:33 Ashtoreth the goddess of the S,
16:31 of Ethbaal, king of the S;
2 Ki 23:13 the abomination of the S,
1 Chr 22: 4 for the S and those from Tyre
Ezek 32:30 All of them, and all the S,

SIEGE (31/30)

Deut 20:19 cut them down to use in the s,
28:53 in the s and desperate straits
28:55 he has nothing left in the s
28:57 for lack of everything in the s
2 Sam 20:15 and they cast up a s mound
1 Ki 15:27 Nadab and all Israel laid s to
2 Ki 19:32 Nor build a s mound against
25: 1 and they built a s wall against
2 Chr 32: 9 the forces with him laid s
32:10 that you remain under s in
Isa 29: 3 I will lay s against you with
37:33 Nor build a s mound against
Jer 19: 9 flesh of his friend in the s
32:24 'Look, the s mounds! They have
33: 4 down to fortify against the s
37:11 of the Chaldeans left the s
52: 4 and they built a s wall
Ezek 4: 2 Lay s against it, build a siege
4: 2 build a s wall against it, and
4: 3 and you shall lay s against it.
4: 7 set your face toward the s of
4: 8 have ended the days of your s.
5: 2 when the days of the s are
17:17 when they heap up a s mound and
21:22 to heap up a s mound, and to
24: 2 king of Babylon started his s
26: 8 he will heap up a s mound
Dan 11:15 North shall come and build a s
Mic 5: 1 He has laid s against us;
Nah 3:14 Draw your water for the s!
Zech 12: 2 when they lay s against Judah

SIEGEWORKS (2/2)

Deut 20:20 to build s against the city
Isa 29: 3 And I will raise s against

SIEVE (2/2)

Isa 30:28 sift the nations with the s of
Am 9: 9 As grain is sifted in a s;

SIFT (3/3) SIFTED, SIFTS

Isa 30:28 To s the nations with the
Am 9: 9 And will s the house of Israel
Lk 22:31 that he may s you as wheat.

SIFTED (1/1) SIFT

Am 9: 9 As grain is s in a sieve;

SIFTS (1/1) SIFT

Prov 20:26 A wise king s out the wicked,

SIGH (9/8) SIGHED, SIGHING

Ps 90: 9 We finish our years like a s.
Isa 24: 7 All the merry-hearted s.
Lam 1: 4 Her priests s, Her virgins
1:11 All her people s, They seek
1:21 "They have heard that I s,
Ezek 9: 4 the foreheads of the men who s
21: 6 S therefore, son of man, with a
21: 6 and s with bitterness before
24:17 S in silence, make no mourning

SIGHED (2/2) SIGH

Mk 7:34 looking up to heaven, He s,
8:12 But He s deeply in His spirit,

SIGHING (10/10) SIGH

Job 3:24 For my s comes before I eat,
Ps 12: 5 for the s of the needy, Now I
31:10 grief, And my years with s;
38: 9 And my s is not hidden from
Isa 21: 2 O Media! All its s I have made
35:10 And sorrow and s shall flee
51:11 Sorrow and s shall flee away.
Jer 45: 3 I fainted in my s, and I find
Lam 3:56 not hide Your ear From my s,
Ezek 21: 7 they say to you, 'Why are you s?

SIGHS (2/2)

Lam 1: 8 she s and turns away.
1:22 For my s are many, And my

SIGHT (318/304)

Gen 2: 9 grow that is pleasant to the s
18: 3 have now found favor in Your s,
19:19 has found favor in your s,
21:11 very displeasing in Abraham's s
21:12 let it be displeasing in your s
23: 4 I may bury my dead out of my s.
23: 8 that I bury my dead out of my s,
32: 5 that I may find favor in your s.
33: 8 are to find favor in the s of
33:10 have now found favor in your s,
33:15 Let me find favor in the s of
38: 7 was wicked in the s of the
39: 4 So Joseph found favor in his s,
39:21 and He gave him favor in the s
47:18 There is nothing left in the s
47:25 let us find favor in the s of
47:29 if I have found favor in your s,
Ex 3: 3 turn aside and see this great s,
3:21 this people favor in the s of
4:30 Then he did the signs in the s
5:21 made us abhorrent in the s of
5:21 sight of Pharaoh and in the s
7:20 in the s of Pharaoh and in the
7:20 sight of Pharaoh and in the s
9: 8 it toward the heavens in the s
11: 3 gave the people favor in the s
11: 3 in the s of Pharaoh's servants
11: 3 servants and in the s of the
12:36 the people favor in the s of
15:26 and do what is right in His s,
17: 6 And Moses did so in the s of
19:11 down upon Mount Sinai in the s
24:17 The s of the glory of the LORD
33:12 have also found grace in My s.
33:13 if I have found grace in Your s,
33:13 that I may find grace in Your s.
33:16 I have found grace in Your s,
33:17 you have found grace in My s,
34: 9 I have found grace in Your s,
40:38 in the s of all the house of
Lev 10:19 it have been accepted in the s
20:17 they shall be cut off in the s
25:53 with rigor over him in your s.
26:45 of the land of Egypt in the s
Num 11:11 I not found favor in Your s,
11:15 I have found favor in Your s—
13:33 like grasshoppers in our own s,
13:33 and so we were in their s.
19: 5 heifer shall be burned in his s:
20:27 went up to Mount Hor in the s
25: 6 a Midianite woman in the s of
25: 6 sight of Moses and in the s of
27:19 and inaugurate him in their s.
32: 5 we have found favor in your s,
32:13 that had done evil in the s of
33: 3 out with boldness in the s of
Deut 4: 6 your understanding in the s of
4:25 and do evil in the s of the
6:18 is right and good in the s of
9:18 in doing wickedly in the s of
12:25 do what is right in the s of
12:28 is good and right in the s of
17: 2 who has been wicked in the s

21: 9 do what is right in the *s* of
25: 3 brother be humiliated in your *s*.
28:34 be driven mad because of the *s*
28:67 and because of the *s* which your
31: 7 and said to him in the *s* of
31:29 you will do evil in the *s* of
34:12 which Moses performed in the *s*
Josh 3: 7 begin to exalt you in the *s* of
4:14 LORD exalted Joshua in the *s*
10:12 and he said in the *s* of Israel:
23: 5 and drive them out of your *s*.
24:17 did those great signs in our *s*,
Judg 2:11 of Israel did evil in the *s* of
3: 7 of Israel did evil in the *s* of
3:12 Israel again did evil in the *s*
3:12 they had done evil in the *s* of
4: 1 Israel again did evil in the *s*
6: 1 of Israel did evil in the *s* of
6:17 I have found favor in your *s*,
6:21 the LORD departed out of his *s*.
10: 6 Israel again did evil in the *s*
13: 1 of Israel did evil in the *s* of
Ruth 2: 2 of grain after him in whose *s*
2:13 "Let me find favor in your *s*,
1 Sam 1:18 find favor in your *s*.
12:17 which you have done in the *s* of
15:19 and do evil in the *s* of the
16:22 for he has found favor in my *s*.
18: 5 and he was accepted in the *s* of
18: 5 the people and also in the *s*
29: 6 me in the army is good in my *s*.
29: 9 that you are as good in my *s*
2 Sam 6:22 and will be humble in my own *s*.
7:19 was a small thing in Your *s*,
10:12 do what is good in His *s*.
12: 9 the LORD, to do evil in His *s*?
12:11 lie with your wives in the *s*
13: 5 and prepare the food in my *s*,
13: 6 couple of cakes for me in my *s*,
13: 8 it, made cakes in his *s*,
14:22 I have found favor in your *s*,
16: 4 I may find favor in your *s*,
16:22 father's concubines in the *s*
1 Ki 9: 7 My name I will cast out of My *s*.
11: 6 Solomon did evil in the *s* of the
11:19 found great favor in the *s* of
11:38 and do what is right in My *s*,
14:22 Now Judah did evil in the *s* of
15:26 And he did evil in the *s* of the
15:34 He did evil in the *s* of the
16: 7 the evil that he did in the *s*
16:19 in doing evil in the *s* of the
16:30 son of Omri did evil in the *s*
21:20 yourself to do evil in the *s*
21:25 to do wickedness in the *s* of
22:52 He did evil in the *s* of the
2 Ki 1:13 of yours be precious in your *s*.
1:14 life now be precious in your *s*.
3: 2 And he did evil in the *s* of the
3:18 is a simple matter in the *s* of
8:18 and he did evil in the *s* of the
8:27 and did evil in the *s* of the
10: 5 Do what is good in your *s*.
10:30 doing what is right in My *s*,
12: 2 did what was right in the *s*
13: 2 And he did evil in the *s* of the
13:11 And he did evil in the *s* of the
14: 3 did what was right in the *s*
14:24 And he did evil in the *s* of the
15: 3 did what was right in the *s*
15: 9 And he did evil in the *s* of the
15:18 And he did evil in the *s* of the
15:24 And he did evil in the *s* of the
15:28 And he did evil in the *s* of the
15:34 did what was right in the *s*
16: 2 do what was right in the *s*
17: 2 And he did evil in the *s* of the
17:17 themselves to do evil in the *s*
17:18 and removed them from His *s*;
17:20 He had cast them from His *s*.
17:23 removed Israel out of His *s*,
18: 3 did what was right in the *s*
20: 3 done what was good in Your *s*.
21: 2 And he did evil in the *s* of the
21: 6 He did much evil in the *s* of
21:15 they have done evil in My *s*,
21:16 in doing evil in the *s* of the
21:20 And he did evil in the *s* of the
22: 2 did what was right in the *s*
23:27 also remove Judah from My *s*,
23:32 And he did evil in the *s* of the
23:37 And he did evil in the *s* of the
24: 3 to remove them from His *s*
24: 9 And he did evil in the *s* of the
24:19 He also did evil in the *s* of the
1 Chr 2: 3 was wicked in the *s* of the
17:17 was a small thing in Your *s*,
19:13 do what is good in His *s*.
22: 8 much blood on the earth in My *s*.
28: 8 in the *s* of all Israel, the
29:25 Solomon exceedingly in the *s*
2 Chr 7:20 My name I will cast out of My *s*,
20:32 what was right in the *s* of
21: 6 and he did evil in the *s* of the
22: 4 Therefore he did evil in the *s*
24: 2 did what was right in the *s*
25: 2 did what was right in the *s*
26: 4 did what was right in the *s*
27: 2 did what was right in the *s*
28: 1 do what was right in the *s*
29: 2 did what was right in the *s*
32:23 so that he was exalted in the *s*
33: 2 But he did evil in the *s* of the
33: 6 He did much evil in the *s* of
33:22 But he did evil in the *s* of the
34: 2 did what was right in the *s*
36: 5 And he did evil in the *s* of the
36: 9 And he did evil in the *s* of the
36:12 He did evil in the *s* of the
Ezra 9: 9 extended mercy to us in the *s*
Neh 1:11 and grant him mercy in the *s* of
2: 5 has found favor in your *s*,
8: 5 Ezra opened the book in the *s*
Esth 2:15 Esther obtained favor in the *s*
2:17 grace and favor in his *s* more
5: 2 that she found favor in his *s*,
5: 8 I have found favor in the *s*
7: 3 I have found favor in your *s*,
8: 5 if I have found favor in his *s*
Job 15:15 heavens are not pure in His *s*,
18: 3 regarded as stupid in your *s*?
19:15 I am an alien in their *s*.
21: 8 with them in their *s*,
25: 5 the stars are not pure in His *s*,
33:21 His flesh wastes away from *s*,
34:26 as wicked men In the open *s*
41: 9 not be overwhelmed at the *s*
Ps 5: 5 shall not stand in Your *s*;
9:19 the nations be judged in Your *s*.
10: 5 are far above, out of his *s*;
18:24 cleanness of my hands in His *s*.
19:14 heart Be acceptable in Your *s*,
51: 4 And done this evil in Your *s*—
72:14 shall be their blood in His *s*.
78:12 things He did in the *s* of
79:10 among the nations in our *s*
90: 4 For a thousand years in Your *s*
98: 2 He has revealed in the *s* of
116:15 Precious in the *s* of the LORD
143: 2 For in Your *s* no one living is
Prov 1:17 the net is spread In the *s* of
3: 4 and high esteem In the *s* of
4: 3 and the only one in the *s* of
17:24 Wisdom is in the *s* of him who
Eccl 2:26 to a man who is good in His *s*;
6: 9 Better is the *s* of the eyes
11: 9 And in the *s* of your eyes;
Isa 5:21 And prudent in their own *s*!
11: 3 He shall not judge by the *s* of
26:17 So have we been in Your *s*,
38: 3 done what is good in Your *s*.
43: 4 you were precious in My *s*,
Jer 4: 1 your abominations out of My *s*,
7:15 I will cast you out of My *s*,
7:30 of Judah have done evil in My *s*,
15: 1 Cast them out of My *s*,
18:10 if it does evil in My *s* so that
18:23 blot out their sin from Your *s*;
19:10 shall break the flask in the *s*
34:15 and did what was right in My *s*—
43: 9 and hide them in the *s* of the
51:24 have done In Zion in your *s*,
52: 2 He also did evil in the *s* of the
Ezek 4:12 fuel of human waste in their *s*.
5: 8 in your midst in the *s* of the
5:14 in the *s* of all who pass by.
10:19 up from the earth in my *s*.
12: 3 captivity by day in their *s*.
12: 3 to another place in their *s*.
12: 4 out your belongings in their *s*,
12: 4 evening you shall go in their *s*,
12: 5 through the wall in their *s*,
12: 6 In their *s* you shall bear them
12: 7 on my shoulder in their *s*.
16:41 judgments on you in the *s* of
20: 9 in whose *s* I had made Myself
20:14 in whose *s* I had brought them
20:22 not be profaned in the *s* of
20:22 in whose *s* I had brought them
20:43 loathe yourselves in your own *s*
22:16 shall defile yourself in the *s*
28:18 ashes upon the earth In the *s*
28:25 am hallowed in them in the *s*
36:31 loathe yourselves in your own *s*,
36:34 of lying desolate in the *s* of
39:27 I am hallowed in them in the *s*
43:11 Write it down in their *s*,
Hos 2: 2 away her harlotries from her *s*,
2:10 uncover her lewdness in the *s*
6: 2 up, That we may live in His *s*.
Am 9: 3 Though they hide from My *s* at
Jon 2: 4 'I have been cast out of Your *s*;
Mal 2:17 does evil Is good in the *s*
Mt 11:26 for so it seemed good in Your *s*.
20:34 their eyes received *s*,
Mk 10:51 that I may receive my *s*.
10:52 immediately he received his *s*
Lk 1:15 For he will be great in the *s* of
4:18 And recovery of *s* to
7:21 and to many blind He gave *s*.
10:21 for so it seemed good in Your *s*.
15:21 against heaven and in your *s*,
16:15 men is an abomination in the *s*
18:41 "Lord, that I may receive my *s*.
18:42 said to him, "Receive your *s*;
18:43 immediately he received his *s*,
23:48 who came together to that *s*,
24:31 and He vanished from their *s*.
Jn 9:11 and washed, and I received *s*.
9:15 again how he had received his *s*.
9:18 been blind and received his *s*,
9:18 of him who had received his *s*.
Acts 1: 9 received Him out of their *s*.
4:19 Whether it is right in the *s* of
7:31 saw it, he marveled at the *s*;
8:21 heart is not right in the *s* of
9: 9 And he was three days without *s*,
9:12 so that he might receive his *s*.
9:17 me that you may receive your *s*
9:18 and he received his *s* at once;
10:31 alms are remembered in the *s*
19:19 and burned them in the *s* of
22:13 'Brother Saul, receive your *s*.
Rom 2:13 of the law are just in the *s*
3:20 will be justified in His *s*,
12:17 for good things in the *s* of
2 Cor 2:17 we speak in the *s* of God in
4: 2 man's conscience in the *s* of
5: 7 For we walk by faith, not by *s*.
7:12 that our care for you in the *s*
8:21 not only in the *s* of the Lord,
8:21 but also in the *s* of men.
Gal 3:11 justified by the law in the *s*
Col 1:22 and above reproach in His *s*—
1 Th 1: 3 our Lord Jesus Christ in the *s*
1 Tim 2: 3 good and acceptable in the *s*
6:13 I urge you in the *s* of God who
Heb 4:13 no creature hidden from His *s*,
12:21 And so terrifying was the *s*
13:21 what is well pleasing in His *s*,
Jas 4:10 Humble yourselves in the *s* of
1 Pe 3: 4 is very precious in the *s* of
1 Jn 3:22 that are pleasing in His *s*.
Rev 13:13 heaven on the earth in the *s*
13:14 he was granted to do in the *s*

SIGHTED (1/1)

Acts 21: 3 When we had *s* Cyprus, we passed

SIGHTS (1/1)

Lk 21:11 and there will be fearful *s* and

SIGN (92/83) SIGNED, SIGNS

Gen 9:12 This is the *s* of the covenant
9:13 and it shall be for the *s* of
9:17 This is the *s* of the covenant
17:11 and it shall be a *s* of the
Ex 3:12 And this shall be a *s* to you
4: 8 heed the message of the first *s*,
4: 8 the message of the latter *s*.
8:23 Tomorrow this *s* shall be." '
12:13 Now the blood shall be a *s* for
13: 9 It shall be as a *s* to you on
13:16 It shall be as a *s* on your hand
31:13 for it is a *s* between Me and
31:17 It is a *s* between Me and the
Num 16:38 and they shall be a *s* to the
17:10 to be kept as a *s* against the
26:10 fifty men; and they became a *s*.
Deut 6: 8 You shall bind them as a *s* on
11:18 and bind them as a *s* on your
13: 1 and he gives you a *s* or a
13: 2 and the *s* or the wonder comes to
28:46 they shall be upon you for a *s*
Josh 4: 6 that this may be a *s* among you
Judg 6:17 then show me a *s* that it is You
1 Sam 2:34 Now this shall be a *s* to you
14:10 and this will be a *s* to us."
1 Ki 13: 3 And he gave a *s* the same day,
13: 3 This is the *s* which the LORD
13: 5 according to the *s* which the
20:33 closely to see whether any *s*
2 Ki 19:29 This shall be a *s* to you:
20: 8 What is the *s* that the LORD
20: 9 This is the *s* to you from the
2 Chr 32:24 spoke to him and gave him a *s*.
Ps 86:17 Show me a *s* for good, That
Isa 7:11 Ask a *s* for yourself from the
7:14 Lord Himself will give you a *s*:
19:20 And it will be for a *s* and for a
20: 3 barefoot three years for a *s*
37:30 This shall be a *s* to you:
38: 7 And this is the *s* to you from
38:22 What is the *s* that I shall go
55:13 For an everlasting *s* that
66:19 I will set a *s* among them; and
Jer 32:44 *s* deeds and seal them, and
44:29 And this shall be a *s* to you,'
Ezek 4: 3 This will be a *s* to the house
12: 6 for I have made you a *s* to the
12:11 I am a *s* to you. As I have
14: 8 that man and make him a *s* and
20:12 to be a *s* between them and Me,
20:20 and they will be a *s* between Me
21:19 Make a *s*; put it at the head
24:24 Thus Ezekiel is a *s* to you;
24:27 Thus you will be a *s* to them,
Dan 6: 8 establish the decree and *s* the
Zech 3: 8 you, For they are a wondrous *s*;
Mt 12:38 we want to see a *s* from You."
12:39 generation seeks after a *s*,
12:39 and no *s* will be given to it
12:39 be given to it except the *s* of
16: 1 that He would show them a *s*
16: 4 generation seeks after a *s*,
16: 4 and no *s* shall be given to it
16: 4 be given to it except the *s* of
24: 3 And what will be the *s* of
24:30 Then the *s* of the Son of Man
26:48 His betrayer had given them a *s*,

S

Mk 8:11 seeking from Him a *s* from
8:12 does this generation seek a *s*?
8:12 no *s* shall be given to this
13: 4 And what will be the *s* when
Lk 2:12 And this will be the *s* to you:
2:34 and for a *s* which will be
11:16 sought from Him a *s* from
11:29 It seeks a *s*, and no sign will
11:29 and no *s* will be given to it
11:29 be given to it except the *s* of
11:30 For as Jonah became a *s* to the
21: 7 And what *s* will there be
Jn 2:18 What *s* do You show to us, since
4:54 This again is the second *s*
6:14 when they had seen the *s* that
6:30 What *s* will You perform then,
10:41 and said, "John performed no *s*,
12:18 heard that He had done this *s*.
Rom 4:11 And he received the *s* of
1 Cor 1:22 For Jews request a *s*,
14:22 Therefore tongues are for a *s*,
2 Th 3:17 which is a *s* in every epistle;
Rev 12: 1 Now a great *s* appeared in
12: 3 And another *s* appeared in
15: 1 Then I saw another *s* in heaven,

SIGNAL (3/3)

Num 31: 6 the holy articles and the *s*
Judg 20:38 Now the appointed *s* between the
Mk 14:44 His betrayer had given them a *s*,

SIGNAL-FIRE (1/1)

Jer 6: 1 And set up a *s* in Beth

SIGNALED (1/1)

Lk 5: 7 So they *s* to their partners in

SIGNED (6/6) SIGN

Jer 32:10 And I *s* the deed and sealed it,
32:12 of the witnesses who *s* the
Dan 6: 9 Therefore King Darius *s* the
6:10 knew that the writing was *s*,
6:12 Have you not *s* a decree that
6:13 for the decree that you have *s*,

SIGNET (18/17)

Gen 38:18 Your *s* and cord, and your staff
38:25 the *s* and cord, and staff."
41:42 Then Pharaoh took his *s* ring off
Ex 28:11 like the engravings of a *s*,
28:21 like the engravings of a *s*,
28:36 it, like the engraving of a *s*:
39:14 names, engraved like a *s*,
39:30 like the engraving of a *s*:
Num 31:50 armlets and bracelets and *s*
Esth 3:10 So the king took his *s* ring from
3:12 and sealed with the king's *s*
8: 2 So the king took off his *s* ring,
8: 8 and seal it with the king's *s*
8: 8 and sealed with the king's *s*
8:10 sealed it with the king's *s*
Jer 22:24 were the *s* on My right hand,
Dan 6:17 king sealed it with his own *s*
Hag 2:23 and will make you like a *s*

SIGNETS (2/2)

Ex 39: 6 as *s* are engraved, with the
Dan 6:17 own signet ring and with the *s*

SIGNIFICANCE (1/1)

1 Cor 14:10 and none of them is without *s*.

SIGNIFICATION (KJV) See SIGNIFICANCE

SIGNIFIED (1/1) SIGNIFYING

Rev 1: 1 And He sent and *s* it by His

SIGNIFY (1/1)

Ezek 24:19 tell us what these things *s*

SIGNIFYING (3/3) SIGNIFIED

Jn 12:33 *s* by what death He would die.
18:32 *s* by what death He would die.
21:19 *s* by what death he would

SIGNPOSTS (1/1)

Jer 31:21 Set up *s*, Make landmarks;

SIGNS (73/72) MIRACLES, SIGN

Gen 1:14 and let them be for *s* and
Ex 4: 9 do not believe even these two *s*,
4:17 with which you shall do the *s*.
4:28 and all the *s* which He had
4:30 Then he did the *s* in the sight
7: 3 and multiply My *s* and My
10: 1 that I may show these *s* of Mine
10: 2 and My *s* which I have done
Num 14:11 with all the *s* which I have
14:22 have seen My glory and the *s*
Deut 4:34 nation, by trials, by *s*,
6:22 and the LORD showed *s* and
7:19 the *s* and the wonders, the
11: 3 His *s* and His acts which He did
26: 8 with great terror and with *s*
29: 3 your eyes have seen, the *s*,
34:11 in all the *s* and wonders which
Josh 24:17 who did those great *s* in our
1 Sam 10: 7 when these *s* come to you, that
10: 9 and all those *s* came to pass
Neh 9:10 You showed *s* and wonders
Job 21:29 And do you not know their *s*?
Ps 65: 8 parts are afraid of Your *s*;
74: 4 set up their banners for *s*.
74: 9 We do not see our *s*;
78:43 When He worked His *s* in Egypt,
105:27 They performed His *s* among
135: 9 He sent *s* and wonders into the
Isa 8:18 has given me! We are for *s*
44:25 Who frustrates the *s* of the
Jer 10: 2 Do not be dismayed at the *s* of
32:20 You have set *s* and wonders in
32:21 out of the land of Egypt with *s*
Dan 4: 2 it good to declare the *s* and
4: 3 How great are His *s*,
6:27 And He works *s* and wonders In
Mt 16: 3 but you cannot discern the *s*
24:24 will rise and show great *s* and
Mk 13:22 prophets will rise and show *s*
16:17 And these *s* will follow those
16:20 word through the accompanying *s*.
Lk 1:62 So they made *s* to his
21:11 be fearful sights and great *s*
21:25 And there will be *s* in the sun,
Jn 2:11 This beginning of *s* Jesus did in
2:23 in His name when they saw the *s*
3: 2 for no one can do these *s* that
4:48 Unless you people see *s* and
6: 2 because they saw His *s* which He
6:26 Me, not because you saw the *s*,
7:31 will He do more *s* than these
9:16 a man who is a sinner do such *s*?
11:47 For this Man works many *s*.
12:37 although He had done so many *s*
20:30 truly Jesus did many other *s*
Acts 2:19 in heaven above And *s*
2:22 and *s* which God did through Him
2:43 and many wonders and *s* were
4:30 and that *s* and wonders may be
5:12 hands of the apostles many *s*
6: 8 did great wonders and *s* among
7:36 he had shown wonders and *s* in
8:13 seeing the miracles and *s* which
14: 3 granting *s* and wonders to be
Rom 15:19 in mighty *s* and wonders, by the
2 Cor 12:12 Truly the *s* of an apostle were
12:12 in *s* and wonders and mighty
2 Th 2: 9 of Satan, with all power, *s*,
Heb 2: 4 bearing witness both with *s*
Rev 13:13 He performs great *s*,
13:14 dwell on the earth by those *s*
16:14 spirits of demons, performing *s*,
19:20 the false prophet who worked *s*

SIGNS AND WONDERS (19/19)

Deut 6:22 and the LORD showed *s* before
26: 8 with great terror and with *s*.
34:11 in all the *s* which the LORD
Neh 9:10 You showed *s* against Pharaoh,
Ps 135: 9 He sent *s* into the midst of
Isa 8:18 We are for *s* in Israel
Jer 32:20 You have set *s* in the land of
32:21 out of the land of Egypt with *s*,
Dan 4: 2 it good to declare the *s* that
6:27 And He works *s* In heaven and
Mt 24:24 will rise and show great *s* to
Mk 13:22 prophets will rise and show *s*
Jn 4:48 him, "Unless you people see *s*,
Acts 4:30 and that *s* may be done through
5:12 hands of the apostles many *s*
14: 3 granting *s* to be done by their
Rom 15:19 in mighty *s*, by the power of
2 Cor 12:12 in *s* and mighty deeds.
Heb 2: 4 bearing witness both with *s*,

SIHON (37/34)

Num 21:21 Israel sent messengers to *S*
21:23 But *S* would not allow Israel to
21:23 So *S* gathered all his people
21:26 For Heshbon was the city of *S*
21:27 Let the city of *S* be repaired.
21:28 A flame from the city of *S*;
21:29 To *S* king of the Amorites.
21:34 do to him as you did to *S* king
32:33 the kingdom of *S* king of the
Deut 1: 4 after he had killed *S* king of
2:24 I have given into your hand *S*
2:26 the Wilderness of Kedemoth to *S*
2:30 But *S* king of Heshbon would not
2:31 I have begun to give *S* and his
2:32 Then *S* and all his people came
3: 2 do to him as you did to *S* king
3: 6 as we did to *S* king of Heshbon,
4:46 in the land of *S* king of the
29: 7 *S* king of Heshbon and Og king
31: 4 will do to them as He did to *S*
Josh 2:10 *S* and Og, whom you utterly
9:10 to *S* king of Heshbon, and Og
12: 2 One king was *S* king of the
12: 5 of Gilead to the border of *S*
13:10 all the cities of *S* king of the
13:21 plain and all the kingdom of *S*
13:21 who were princes of *S* dwelling
13:27 the rest of the kingdom of *S*
Judg 11:19 Israel sent messengers to *S*
11:20 But *S* did not trust Israel to
11:20 So *S* gathered all his people
11:21 God of Israel delivered *S* and
1 Ki 4:19 in the country of *S* king of
Neh 9:22 possession of the land of *S*,
Ps 135:11 *S* king of the Amorites, Og
136:19 *S* king of the Amorites, For
Jer 48:45 A flame from the midst of *S*,

SIHOR (2/2)

Josh 13: 3 'from *S*, which is east of
Jer 2:18 To drink the waters of *S*?

SIKKUTH (1/1)

Am 5:26 You also carried *S* your king

SILAS (13/13) SILVANUS

Acts 15:22 was also named Barsabas, and *S*,
15:27 have therefore sent Judas and *S*,
15:32 Now Judas and *S*, themselves
15:34 it seemed good to *S* to remain
15:40 but Paul chose *S* and departed,
16:19 they seized Paul and *S* and
16:25 But at midnight Paul and *S* were
16:29 trembling before Paul and *S*.
17: 4 women, joined Paul and *S*.
17:10 immediately sent Paul and *S*
17:14 but both *S* and Timothy remained
17:15 and receiving a command for *S*
18: 5 When *S* and Timothy had come from

SILENCE (24/24) SILENCED, SILENCING, SILENT

Judg 3:19 Keep *s*!" And all who attended
Job 4:16 before my eyes; There was *s*;
29:21 And kept *s* for my counsel.
31:34 So that I kept *s* And did not
Ps 8: 2 That You may *s* the enemy and
31:18 Let the lying lips be put to *s*,
35:22 seen, O LORD; Do not keep *s*.
39: 2 I was mute with *s*,
94:17 would soon have settled in *s*.
115:17 Nor any who go down into *s*.
Eccl 3: 7 time to sew; A time to keep *s*,
Isa 41: 1 Keep *s* before Me, O coastlands,
47: 5 Sit in *s*, and go into
65: 6 before Me: I will not keep *s*,
Jer 8:14 LORD our God has put us to *s*
Lam 2:10 Sit on the ground and keep *s*;
Ezek 24:17 'Sigh in *s*, make no mourning
Am 8: 3 They shall be thrown out in *s*.
Hab 2:20 Let all the earth keep *s*
Acts 21:40 And when there was a great *s*,
1 Tim 2:11 Let a woman learn in *s* with all
2:12 over a man, but to be in *s*.
1 Pe 2:15 by doing good you may put to *s*
Rev 8: 1 there was *s* in heaven for about

SILENCED (3/3) SILENCE

Neh 5: 8 Then they were *s* and found
Lam 3:53 They *s* my life in the pit And
Mt 22:34 that He had *s* the Sadducees,

SILENCING (1/1) SILENT

Jer 51:55 And *s* her loud voice,

SILENT (46/45) SILENCE

Gen 24:21 remained *s* so as to know
1 Sam 2: 9 But the wicked shall be *s* in
2 Ki 2: 3 said, "Yes, I know; keep *s*!"
2: 5 'Yes, I know; keep *s*!"
7: 9 of good news, and we remain *s*.
Esth 4:14 if you remain completely *s*
Job 13: 5 Oh, that you would be *s*,
16: 6 And if I remain *s*, how am I
Ps 22: 2 the night season, and am not *s*.
28: 1 Do not be *s* to me, Lest, if
28: 1 if You are *s* to me, I become
30:12 sing praise to You and not be *s*.
31:17 Let them be *s* in the grave.
32: 3 When I kept *s*, my bones grew
39:12 Do not be *s* at my tears;
50: 3 come, and shall not keep *s*;
50:21 you have done, and I kept *s*;
56: 'The *S* Dove in Distant Lands."
58: 1 righteousness, you *s* ones?
83: 1 Do not keep *s*, O God!
109: 1 Do not keep *s*, O God
Isa 53: 7 sheep before its shearers is *s*,
62: 6 of the LORD, do not keep *s*,
Jer 8:14 And let us be *s* there.
Lam 3:28 Let him sit alone and keep *s*,
Am 5:13 Therefore the prudent keep *s* at
Hab 2:19 To *s* stone, 'Arise!
Zeph 1: 7 Be *s* in the presence of the
Zech 2:13 'Be *s*, all flesh, before the
Mt 26:63 But Jesus kept *s*. And the

Mk 3: 4 or to kill?" But they kept *s*.
9:34 But they kept *s*, for on the
14:61 But He kept *s* and answered
Lk 14: 4 But they kept *s*. And He took
19:40 you that if these should keep *s*,
20:26 at His answer and kept *s*.
Acts 8:32 before its shearer is *s*,
11:18 these things they became *s*;
12:17 to them with his hand to keep *s*,
15:12 Then all the multitude kept *s*
15:13 And after they had become *s*,
18: 9 but speak, and do not keep *s*;
22: 2 they kept all the more *s*.
1 Cor 14:28 let him keep *s* in church, and
14:30 sits by, let the first keep *s*.
14:34 Let your women keep *s* in the

SILENTLY (2/2)

Ps 62: 1 Truly my soul *s* waits for God;
62: 5 wait *s* for God alone, For my

SILK (3/3)

Ezek 16:10 linen and covered you with *s*.
16:13 clothing was of fine linen, *s*,
Rev 18:12 *s* and scarlet, every kind of

SILLA (1/1)

2 Ki 12:20 the Millo, which goes down to *S*.

SILLY (2/2)

Jer 4:22 They are *s* children, And
Hos 7:11 Ephraim also is like a *s* dove,

SILOAH (KJV) See SHELAH

SILOAM (3/3) SHILOAH

Lk 13: 4 on whom the tower in *S* fell
Jn 9: 7 wash in the pool of *S*"
9:11 Go to the pool of *S* and wash.'

SILVANUS (4/4) SILAS

2 Cor 1:19 among you by us—by me, *S*,
1 Th 1: 1 Paul, *S*, and Timothy,
2 Th 1: 1 Paul, *S*, and Timothy,
1 Pe 5:12 By *S*, our faithful brother

SILVER (320/283) SILVERSMITH

Gen 13: 2 very rich in livestock, in *s*,
20:16 brother a thousand pieces of *s*;
23:15 four hundred shekels of *s*.
23:16 and Abraham weighed out the *s*
23:16 Heth, four hundred shekels of *s*,
24:35 *s* and gold, male and female
24:53 brought out jewelry of *s*,
37:28 for twenty shekels of *s*.
44: 2 the *s* cup, in the mouth of the
44: 8 How then could we steal *s* or
45:22 three hundred pieces of *s* and
Ex 3:22 near her house, articles of *s*,
11: 2 articles of *s* and articles of
12:35 the Egyptians articles of *s*,
20:23 gods of *s* or gods of gold you
21:32 master thirty shekels of *s*,
25: 3 shall take from them: gold, *s*,
26:19 shall make forty sockets of *s*
26:21 "and their forty sockets of *s*:
26:25 boards with their sockets of *s*—
26:32 gold, upon four sockets of *s*.
27:10 and their bands shall be *s*.
27:11 pillars and their bands of *s*.
27:17 the court shall have bands of *s*;
27:17 their hooks shall be of *s* and
31: 4 works, to work in gold, in *s*,
35: 5 offering to the LORD: gold, *s*,
35:24 who offered an offering of *s*
35:32 to work in gold and *s* and
36:24 Forty sockets of *s* he made to go
36:26 and their forty sockets of *s*:
36:30 sockets—sixteen sockets of *s*—
36:36 and he cast four sockets of *s*
38:10 pillars and their bands were *s*.
38:11 pillars and their bands were *s*.
38:12 pillars and their bands were *s*.
38:17 pillars and their bands were *s*,
38:17 of their capitals was *s*;
38:17 of the court had bands of *s*.
38:19 of bronze; their hooks were *s*,
38:19 capitals and their bands was *s*.
38:25 And the *s* from those who were
38:27 from the hundred talents of *s*
Lev 5:15 your valuation in shekels of *s*
27: 3 shall be fifty shekels of *s*,
27: 6 male shall be five shekels of *s*,
27: 6 shall be three shekels of *s*;
27:16 valued at fifty shekels of *s*.
Num 7:13 His offering was one *s* platter,
7:13 and one *s* bowl of seventy
7:19 he offered one *s* platter,
7:19 and one *s* bowl of seventy
7:25 His offering was one *s* platter,
7:25 and one *s* bowl of seventy
7:31 His offering was one *s* platter,
7:31 and one *s* bowl of seventy
7:37 His offering was one *s* platter,
7:37 and one *s* bowl of seventy
7:43 His offering was one *s* platter,
7:43 and one *s* bowl of seventy
7:49 His offering was one *s* platter,
7:49 and one *s* bowl of seventy
7:55 His offering was one *s* platter,
7:55 and one *s* bowl of seventy
7:61 His offering was one *s* platter,
7:61 and one *s* bowl of seventy
7:67 His offering was one *s* platter,
7:67 and one *s* bowl of seventy
7:73 His offering was one *s* platter,
7:73 and one *s* bowl of seventy
7:79 His offering was one *s* platter,
7:79 and one *s* bowl of seventy
7:84 twelve *s* platters, twelve
7:84 twelve *s* bowls, and twelve gold
7:85 Each *s* platter weighed one
7:85 All the *s* of the vessels
10: 2 Make two *s* trumpets for
18:16 for five shekels of *s*,
22:18 to give me his house full of *s*
24:13 to give me his house full of *s*
31:22 "Only the gold, the *s*,
Deut 7:25 you shall not covet the *s* or
8:13 and your *s* and your gold are
17:17 nor shall he greatly multiply *s*
22:19 him one hundred shekels of *s*
22:29 father fifty shekels of *s*,
29:17 wood and stone and *s* and gold);
Josh 6:19 But all the *s* and gold, and
6:24 Only the *s* and gold, and the
7:21 two hundred shekels of *s*,
7:21 with the *s* under it."
7:22 with the *s* under it.
7:24 Achan the son of Zerah, the *s*,
22: 8 very much livestock, with *s*,
24:32 for one hundred pieces of *s*,
Judg 5:19 They took no spoils of *s*.
9: 4 gave him seventy shekels of *s*
16: 5 you eleven hundred pieces of *s*.
17: 2 eleven hundred shekels of *s*
17: 2 —here is the *s* with me;
17: 3 eleven hundred shekels of *s*
17: 3 I had wholly dedicated the *s*
17: 4 Thus he returned the *s* to his
17: 4 took two hundred shekels of *s*
17:10 give you ten shekels of *s* per
1 Sam 2:36 down to him for a piece of *s*
9: 8 one fourth of a shekel of *s*.
2 Sam 8:10 brought with him articles of *s*,
8:11 along with the *s* and gold that
18:11 given you ten shekels of *s*
18:12 a thousand shekels of *s* in my
21: 4 We will have no *s* or gold from
24:24 the oxen for fifty shekels of *s*.
1 Ki 7:51 the *s* and the gold and the
10:21 pure gold. Not one was *s*,
10:22 ships came bringing gold, *s*,
10:25 articles of *s* and gold,
10:27 The king made *s* as common in
10:29 cost six hundred shekels of *s*,
15:15 *s* and gold and utensils.
15:18 Then Asa took all the *s* and gold
15:19 I have sent you a present of *s*
16:24 Shemer for two talents of *s*;
20: 3 Your *s* and your gold are mine;
20: 5 shall deliver to me your *s*
20: 7 for my wives, my children, my *s*,
20:39 you shall pay a talent of *s*.
2 Ki 5: 5 took with him ten talents of *s*,
5:22 Please give them a talent of *s*
5:23 and bound two talents of *s* in
6:25 sold for eighty shekels of *s*,
6:25 for five shekels of *s*.
7: 8 and carried from it *s* and gold
12:13 house of the LORD basins of *s*,
12:13 of gold or articles of *s*,
14:14 And he took all the gold and *s*,
15:19 Pul a thousand talents of *s*,
15:20 each man fifty shekels of *s*,
16: 8 And Ahaz took the *s* and gold
18:14 three hundred talents of *s* and
18:15 So Hezekiah gave him all the *s*
20:13 the *s* and gold, the spices and
23:33 of one hundred talents of *s*
23:35 So Jehoiakim gave the *s* and
23:35 he exacted the *s* and gold from
25:15 of solid gold and solid *s*,
1 Chr 18:10 kinds of articles of gold, *s*,
18:11 along with the *s* and gold that
19: 6 sent a thousand talents of *s*
22:14 and one million talents of *s*,
22:16 Of gold and *s* and bronze and
28:14 also *s* for all articles of
28:14 silver for all articles of *s*,
28:15 for the lampstands of *s* by
28:16 and *s* for the tables of silver;
28:16 and silver for the tables of *s*;
28:17 and for the *s* bowls, silver by
28:17 *s* by weight for every bowl;
29: 2 *s* for things of silver,
29: 2 gold, silver for things of *s*,
29: 3 special treasure of gold and *s*:
29: 4 thousand talents of refined *s*,
29: 5 for things of gold and the *s*
29: 5 the silver for things of *s*,
29: 7 gold, ten thousand talents of *s*,
2 Chr 1:15 Also the king made *s* and gold as
1:17 for six hundred shekels of *s*,
2: 7 skillful to work in gold and *s*,
2:14 skilled to work in gold and *s*,
5: 1 the *s* and the gold and all the
9:14 the country brought gold and *s*
9:20 pure gold. Not one was *s*,
9:21 ships came, bringing gold, *s*,
9:24 articles of *s* and gold,
9:27 The king made *s* as common in
15:18 *s* and gold and utensils.
16: 2 Then Asa brought *s* and gold from
16: 3 I have sent you *s* and gold;
17:11 Jehoshaphat presents and *s* as
21: 3 gave them great gifts of *s* and
24:14 and vessels of gold and *s*.
25: 6 for one hundred talents of *s*.
25:24 he took all the gold and *s*,
27: 5 year one hundred talents of *s*,
32:27 made himself treasuries for *s*,
36: 3 of one hundred talents of *s*
Ezra 1: 4 of his place help him with *s*
1: 6 them with articles of *s* and
1: 9 one thousand *s* platters,
1:10 four hundred and ten *s* basins
1:11 All the articles of gold and *s*
2:69 five thousand minas of *s*,
5:14 the gold and *s* articles of the
6: 5 Also let the gold and *s* articles
7:15 you are to carry the *s* and
7:16 and whereas all the *s* and gold
7:18 to do with the rest of the *s*
7:22 up to one hundred talents of *s*,
8:25 and weighed out to them the *s*,
8:26 hundred and fifty talents of *s*,
8:26 *s* articles weighing one
8:28 and the *s* and the gold are a
8:30 and the Levites received the *s*
8:33 Now on the fourth day the *s* and
Neh 5:15 besides forty shekels of *s*.
7:71 and two thousand two hundred *s*
7:72 two thousand *s* minas, and
Esth 1: 6 of fine linen and purple on *s*
1: 6 couches were of gold and *s* on
3: 9 pay ten thousand talents of *s*
Job 3:15 filled their houses with *s*;
22:25 your gold And your precious *s*;
27:16 Though he heaps up *s* like dust,
27:17 the innocent will divide the *s*.
28: 1 "Surely there is a mine for *s*,
28:15 Nor can *s* be weighed for its
42:11 Each one gave him a piece of *s*
Ps 12: 6 Like *s* tried in a furnace of
66:10 You have refined us as *s* is
68:13 wings of a dove covered with *s*,
68:30 himself with pieces of *s*.
105:37 also brought them out with *s*
115: 4 Their idols are *s* and gold,
119:72 of coins of gold and *s*.
135:15 idols of the nations are *s*
Prov 2: 4 If you seek her as *s*,
3:14 better than the profits of *s*,
8:10 my instruction, and not *s*,
8:19 And my revenue than choice *s*.
10:20 of the righteous is choice *s*;
16:16 is to be chosen rather than *s*.
17: 3 The refining pot is for *s* and
22: 1 Loving favor rather than *s* and
25: 4 Take away the dross from *s*,
25:11 of gold In settings of *s*.
26:23 earthenware covered with *s*
27:21 The refining pot is for *s* and
Eccl 2: 8 I also gathered for myself *s* and
5:10 He who loves *s* will not be
5:10 will not be satisfied with *s*;
12: 6 Creator before the *s* cord
Song 1:11 of gold With studs of *s*.
3:10 He made its pillars of *s*,
8: 9 upon her A battlement of *s*;
8:11 for its fruit A thousand *s*
Isa 1:22 Your *s* has become dross, Your
2: 7 Their land is also full of *s*
2:20 will cast away his idols of *s*
7:23 a thousand shekels of *s*,
13:17 them, Who will not regard *s*;
30:22 of your graven images of *s*,
31: 7 throw away his idols of *s* and
39: 2 the *s* and gold, the spices and
40:19 silversmith casts *s* chains.
46: 6 And weigh *s* on the scales;
48:10 have refined you, but not as *s*;
60: 9 Their *s* and their gold with
60:17 Instead of iron I will bring *s*,
Jer 6:30 will call them rejected *s*,
10: 4 They decorate it with *s* and
10: 9 *S* is beaten into plates
32: 9 money—seventeen shekels of *s*.
52:19 gold and whatever was solid *s*,
Ezek 7:19 They will throw their *s* into the
7:19 Their *s* and their gold will
16:13 were adorned with gold and *s*,
16:17 jewelry from My gold and My *s*,
22:18 they have become dross from *s*.
22:20 'As men gather *s*,
22:22 As *s* is melted in the midst of a
27:12 They gave you *s*, iron, tin, and
28: 4 And gathered gold and *s* into
38:13 to carry away *s* and gold, to
Dan 2:32 gold, its chest and arms of *s*,
2:35 the clay, the bronze, the *s*,
2:45 the bronze, the clay, the *s*,
5: 2 command to bring the gold and *s*
5: 4 praised the gods of gold and *s*,
5:23 you have praised the gods of *s*
11: 8 their precious articles of *s*
11:38 he shall honor with gold and *s*,
11:43 the treasures of gold and *s*,

S

Hos 2: 8 And multiplied her *s* and
3: 2 for fifteen shekels of *s*,
8: 4 From their *s* and gold They
9: 6 possess their valuables of *s*;
13: 2 images, Idols of their *s*,
Joel 3: 5 Because you have taken My *s* and
Am 2: 6 they sell the righteous for *s*,
8: 6 That we may buy the poor for *s*,
Nah 2: 9 Take spoil of *s*! Take spoil of
Hab 2:19 it is overlaid with gold and *s*,
Zeph 1:18 Neither their *s* nor their gold
Hag 2: 8 The *s* is Mine, and the gold
Zech 6:11 Take the *s* and gold, make an
9: 3 Heaped up *s* like the dust,
11:12 my wages thirty pieces of *s*.
11:13 I took the thirty pieces of *s*
13: 9 Will refine them as *s* is
14:14 be gathered together: Gold, *s*,
Mal 3: 3 a refiner and a purifier of *s*;
3: 3 And purge them as gold and *s*,
Mt 10: 9 Provide neither gold nor *s* nor
26:15 out to him thirty pieces of *s*.
27: 3 back the thirty pieces of *s* to
27: 5 he threw down the pieces of *s*
27: 6 the chief priests took the *s*
27: 9 the thirty pieces of *s*,
Lk 15: 8 having ten *s* coins, if she
Acts 3: 6 *S* and gold I do not have, but
17:29 Nature is like gold or *s* or
19:19 fifty thousand pieces of *s*.
19:24 who made *s* shrines of Diana,
20:33 I have coveted no one's *s* or
1 Cor 3:12 this foundation with gold, *s*,
2 Tim 2:20 not only vessels of gold and *s*,
Jas 5: 3 Your gold and *s* are corroded,
1 Pe 1:18 like *s* or gold, from your
Rev 9:20 demons, and idols of gold, *s*,
18:12 "merchandise of gold and *s*,

SILVER-HAIRED (1/1)

Prov 16:31 The *s* head is a crown of

SILVERSMITH (4/4) SILVER

Judg 17: 4 silver and gave them to the *s*,
Prov 25: 4 And it will go to the *s* for
Isa 40:19 And the *s* casts silver chains.
Acts 19:24 man named Demetrius, a *s*,

SIMEON (49/44) NIGER

Gen 29:33 And she called his name *S*.
34:25 *S* and Levi, Dinah's brothers,
34:30 Then Jacob said to *S* and Levi,
35:23 Jacob's firstborn, and *S*,
42:24 And he took *S* from them and
42:36 *S* is no more, and you want to
43:23 Then he brought *S* out to
46:10 The sons of *S* were Jemuel,
48: 5 as Reuben and *S*, they shall
49: 5 *S* and Levi are brothers;
Ex 1: 2 Reuben, *S*, Levi, and Judah;
6:15 And the sons of *S* were Jemuel,
6:15 These are the families of *S*.
Num 1: 6 'from *S*, Shelumiel the son of
1:22 From the children of *S*,
1:23 were numbered of the tribe of *S*
2:12 him shall be the tribe of *S*,
2:12 the leader of the children of *S*
7:36 leader of the children of *S*,
10:19 the tribe of the children of *S*
13: 5 from the tribe of *S*,
26:12 The sons of *S* according to
34:20 the tribe of the children of *S*,
Deut 27:12 have crossed over the Jordan: *S*,
Josh 19: 1 The second lot came out for *S*,
19: 1 the tribe of the children of *S*
19: 8 the tribe of the children of *S*
19: 9 of the children of *S* was
19: 9 Therefore the children of *S* had
21: 4 of Judah, from the tribe of *S*,
21: 9 the tribe of the children of *S*
Judg 1: 3 So Judah said to *S* his brother,
1: 3 And *S* went with him.
1:17 Judah went with his brother *S*,
1 Chr 2: 1 the sons of Israel: Reuben, *S*,
4:24 The sons of *S* were Nemuel,
4:42 hundred men of the sons of *S*,
6:65 the tribe of the children of *S*,
12:25 of the sons of *S*, mighty men
2 Chr 15: 9 from Ephraim, Manasseh, and *S*,
34: 6 of Manasseh, Ephraim, and *S*,
Ezek 48:24 *S* shall have one section;
48:25 "by the border of *S*,
48:33 three gates: one gate for *S*,
Lk 2:25 in Jerusalem whose name was *S*,
2:34 Then *S* blessed them, and said to
3:30 the son of *S*, the son of
Acts 13: 1 *S* who was called Niger, Lucius
Rev 7: 7 of the tribe of *S* twelve

SIMEONITES (3/3)

Num 25:14 of a father's house among the *S*.
26:14 are the families of the *S*:
1 Chr 27:16 the son of Zichri; over the *S*,

SIMILAR (12/11)

Num 6: 3 himself from wine and *s* drink;
6: 3 vinegar made from *s* drink;
Deut 14:26 for wine or *s* drink, for
29: 6 you drunk wine or *s* drink,
Judg 13: 4 not to drink wine or *s* drink,
13: 7 Now drink no wine or *s* drink,
13:14 she drink wine or *s* drink,
Ezra 1:10 silver basins of a *s* kind,
Jer 36:32 added to them many *s* words.
Ezek 41:21 their appearance was *s*.
Acts 19:25 the workers of *s* occupation,
Jude 7 around them in a *s* manner

SIMILITUDE (1/1)

Jas 3: 9 who have been made in the *s* of

SIMMER (1/1)

Ezek 24: 5 And let the cuts *s* in it."

SIMON (70/66) BAR-JONAH, CEPHAS, NIGER, PETER

Mt 4:18 *S* called Peter, and Andrew his
10: 2 apostles are these: first, *S*,
10: 4 *S* the Canaanite, and Judas
13:55 His brothers James, Joses, *S*,
16:16 *S* Peter answered and said, "You
16:17 *S* Bar-Jonah, for flesh and
17:25 saying, "What do you think, *S*?
26: 6 in Bethany at the house of *S*
27:32 man of Cyrene, *S* by name.
Mk 1:16 He saw *S* and Andrew his brother
1:29 they entered the house of *S* and
1:36 And *S* and those who were with
3:16 *S*, to whom He gave the name
3:18 Thaddaeus, *S* the Cananite;
6: 3 of James, Joses, Judas, and *S*?
14: 3 in Bethany at the house of *S*
14:37 and said to Peter, "*S*,
15:21 *S* a Cyrenian, the father of
Lk 5: 4 stopped speaking, He said to *S*,
5: 5 But *S* answered and said to Him,
5: 8 When *S* Peter saw it, he fell
5:10 who were partners with *S*.
5:10 And Jesus said to *S*,
6:14 *S*, whom He also named Peter,
6:15 and *S* called the Zealot;
7:40 answered and said to him, "*S*,
7:43 *S* answered and said, "I suppose
7:44 to the woman and said to *S*,
22:31 And the Lord said, "*S*,
22:31 *S*! Indeed, Satan has asked for
23:26 *S* a Cyrenian, who was coming
24:34 and has appeared to *S*!"
Jn 1:40 *S* Peter's brother.
1:41 first found his own brother *S*,
1:42 'You are *S* the son of Jonah.
6: 8 *S* Peter's brother, said to Him,
6:68 But *S* Peter answered Him,
6:71 Judas Iscariot, the son of *S*,
13: 6 Then He came to *S* Peter.
13: 9 *S* Peter said to Him, "Lord, not
13:24 *S* Peter therefore motioned to
13:26 Judas Iscariot, the son of *S*.
13:36 *S* Peter said to Him, "Lord,
18:10 Then *S* Peter, having a sword,
18:15 And *S* Peter followed Jesus, and
18:25 Now *S* Peter stood and warmed
20: 2 Then she ran and came to *S*
20: 6 Then *S* Peter came, following
21: 2 *S* Peter, Thomas called the Twin,
21: 3 *S* Peter said to them, "I am
21: 7 Now when *S* Peter heard that
21:11 *S* Peter went up and dragged the
21:15 Jesus said to *S* Peter, "Simon,
21:15 Jesus said to Simon Peter, "*S*,
21:16 to him again a second time, "*S*,
21:17 said to him the third time, "*S*,
Acts 1:13 the son of Alphaeus and *S*
8: 9 was a certain man called *S*,
8:13 Then *S* himself also believed;
8:18 And when *S* saw that through the
8:24 Then *S* answered and said, "Pray
9:43 many days in Joppa with *S*,
10: 5 and send for *S* whose surname is
10: 6 "He is lodging with *S*,
10:18 they called and asked whether *S*,
10:32 therefore to Joppa and call *S*
10:32 He is lodging in the house of *S*,
11:13 and call for *S* whose surname is
15:14 *S* has declared how God at the
2 Pe 1: 1 *S* Peter, a bondservant and

SIMON'S (7/6)

Mk 1:30 But *S* wife's mother lay sick
Lk 4:38 synagogue and entered *S* house.
4:38 But *S* wife's mother was sick
5: 3 one of the boats, which was *S*,
Jn 12: 4 *S* son, who would betray Him,
13: 2 *S* son, to betray Him,
Acts 10:17 had made inquiry for *S* house,

SIMPLE (21/21) SIMPLICITY

2 Ki 3:18 And this is a *s* matter in the
Job 5: 2 And envy slays a *s* one.
Ps 19: 7 is sure, making wise the *s*;
116: 6 The LORD preserves the *s*;
119:130 gives understanding to the *s*.
Prov 1: 4 To give prudence to the *s*,
1:22 you *s* ones, will you love
1:32 For the turning away of the *s*
7: 7 And saw among the *s*,
8: 5 O you *s* ones, understand
9: 4 "Whoever is *s*,
9:13 woman is clamorous; She is *s*,
9:16 "Whoever is *s*,
14:15 The *s* believes every word,
14:18 The *s* inherit folly, But the
19:25 and the *s* will become wary;
21:11 the *s* is made wise; But when
22: 3 But the *s* pass on and are
27:12 The *s* pass on and are
Rom 16:18 deceive the hearts of the *s*.
16:19 and *s* concerning evil.

SIMPLICITY (4/4) SIMPLE

Prov 1:22 simple ones, will you love *s*?
Acts 2:46 their food with gladness and *s*
2 Cor 1:12 ourselves in the world in *s*
11: 3 may be corrupted from the *s*

SIMRI (KJV) See SHIMRI

SIN (446/393) SINFUL, SINNED, SINNER, SINNING, SINS

Gen 4: 7 *s* lies at the door. And its
18:20 and because their *s* is very
20: 9 me and on my kingdom a great *s*?
31:36 is my trespass? What is my *s*,
39: 9 and *s* against God?"
42:22 'Do not *s* against the boy';
50:17 of your brothers and their *s*;
Ex 10:17 please forgive my *s* only this
16: 1 came to the Wilderness of *S*,
17: 1 from the Wilderness of *S*,
20:20 you, so that you may not *s*.
23:33 lest they make you *s* against
29:14 It is a *s* offering.
29:36 every day as a *s* offering
30:10 the blood of the *s* offering
32:21 you have brought so great a *s*
32:30 "You have committed a great *s*.
32:30 I can make atonement for your *s*.
32:31 people have committed a great *s*,
32:32 if You will forgive their *s*—
32:34 upon them for their *s*.
34: 7 and transgression and *s*,
34: 9 pardon our iniquity and our *s*,
Lev 4: 3 offer to the LORD for his *s*
4: 3 blemish as a *s* offering.
4: 8 the bull as the *s* offering.
4:14 when the *s* which they have
4:14 offer a young bull for the *s*,
4:20 the bull as a *s* offering;
4:21 It is a *s* offering for the
4:23 or if his *s* which he has
4:24 It is a *s* offering.
4:25 the blood of the *s* offering
4:26 for him concerning his *s*,
4:28 or if his *s* which he has
4:28 for his *s* which he has
4:29 the head of the *s* offering,
4:29 and kill the *s* offering at the
4:32 a lamb as his *s* offering,
4:33 the head of the *s* offering,
4:33 and kill it as a *s* offering at
4:34 blood of the *s* offering
4:35 shall make atonement for his *s*
5: 6 to the LORD for his *s* which
5: 6 the goats as a *s* offering.
5: 6 for him concerning his *s*.
5: 7 one as a *s* offering and the
5: 8 which is for the *s* offering
5: 9 blood of the *s* offering
5: 9 It is a *s* offering.
5:10 on his behalf for his *s* which
5:11 fine flour as a *s* offering.
5:11 for it is a *s* offering.
5:12 It is a *s* offering.
5:13 for his *s* that he has committed
6:17 like the *s* offering and the
6:25 the law of the *s* offering:
6:25 the *s* offering shall be killed
6:26 'The priest who offers it for *s*
6:30 But no *s* offering from which
7: 7 is like the *s* offering;
7:37 the *s* offering, the trespass
8: 2 a bull as the *s* offering, two
8:14 the bull for the *s* offering.
8:14 of the bull for the *s* offering,
9: 2 young bull as a *s* offering
9: 3 of the goats as a *s* offering,
9: 7 offer your *s* offering and your
9: 8 the calf of the *s* offering,
9:10 the liver of the *s* offering
9:15 which was the *s* offering for
9:15 killed it and offered it for *s*,
9:22 from offering the *s* offering,
10:16 the goat of the *s* offering,
10:17 you not eaten the *s* offering
10:19 have offered their *s* offering
10:19 I had eaten the *s* offering
12: 6 a turtledove as a *s* offering,
12: 8 the other as a *s* offering.
14:13 where he kills the *s* offering
14:13 for as the *s* offering is the
14:19 shall offer the *s* offering,
14:22 one shall be a *s* offering and
14:31 the one as a *s* offering and
15:15 the one as a *s* offering and
15:30 the one as a *s* offering

	16: 3	young bull as a *s* offering,
	16: 5	the goats as a *s* offering,
	16: 6	the bull as a *s* offering,
	16: 9	and offer it as a *s* offering.
	16:11	the bull of the *s* offering,
	16:11	the bull as the *s* offering
	16:15	the goat of the *s* offering,
	16:25	The fat of the *s* offering he
	16:27	The bull for the *s* offering and
	16:27	the goat for the *s* offering,
	19:17	and not bear *s* because of him.
	19:22	before the LORD for his *s*
	19:22	And the *s* which he has
	20:20	They shall bear their *s*;
	22: 9	lest they bear *s* for it and die
	23:19	the goats as a *s* offering,
	24:15	curses his God shall bear his *s*.
Num	5: 6	a man or woman commits any *s*
	5: 7	then he shall confess the *s*
	6:11	offer one as a *s* offering
	6:14	blemish as a *s* offering,
	6:16	LORD and offer his *s* offering
	7:16	the goats as a *s* offering;
	7:22	the goats as a *s* offering;
	7:28	the goats as a *s* offering;
	7:34	the goats as a *s* offering;
	7:40	the goats as a *s* offering;
	7:46	the goats as a *s* offering;
	7:52	the goats as a *s* offering;
	7:58	the goats as a *s* offering;
	7:64	the goats as a *s* offering;
	7:70	the goats as a *s* offering;
	7:76	the goats as a *s* offering;
	7:82	the goats as a *s* offering;
	7:87	the goats as a *s* offering
	8: 8	young bull as a *s* offering.
	8:12	shall offer one as a *s* offering
	9:13	that man shall bear his *s*.
	12:11	Please do not lay this *s* on
	15:22	If you *s* unintentionally, and
	15:24	of the goats as a *s* offering.
	15:25	and their *s* offering before the
	15:25	LORD, for their unintended *s*.
	15:27	first year as a *s* offering.
	16:22	of all flesh, shall one man *s*,
	18: 9	offering and every *s* offering
	18:22	lest they bear *s* and die.
	18:32	And you shall bear no *s* because
	19: 9	it is for purifying from *s*.
	19:17	burnt for purification from *s*,
	27: 3	Korah, but he died in his own *s*;
	28:15	of the goats as a *s* offering
	28:22	also one goat as a *s* offering,
	29: 5	the goats as a *s* offering,
	29:11	the goats as a *s* offering,
	29:11	besides the *s* offering for
	29:16	the goats as a *s* offering,
	29:19	the goats as a *s* offering,
	29:22	also one goat as a *s* offering,
	29:25	the goats as a *s* offering,
	29:28	also one goat as a *s* offering,
	29:31	also one goat as a *s* offering,
	29:34	also one goat as a *s* offering,
	29:38	also one goat as a *s* offering,
	32:23	and be sure your *s* will find
	33:11	camped in the Wilderness of *S*.
	33:12	from the Wilderness of *S* and
Deut	9:18	because of all your *s* which you
	9:21	"Then I took your *s*,
	9:27	on their wickedness or their *s*,
	15: 9	and it become *s* among you.
	19:15	any iniquity or any *s* that he
	20:18	and you *s* against the LORD
	21:22	If a man has committed a *s*
	22:26	is in the young woman no *s*
	23:21	and it would be *s* to you.
	23:22	it shall not be *s* to you.
	24: 4	and you shall not bring *s* on
	24:15	and it be *s* to you.
	24:16	be put to death for his own *s*.
1 Sam	2:17	Therefore the *s* of the young men
	12:23	be it from me that I should *s*
	14:34	and do not *s* against the LORD
	14:38	and know and see what this *s*
	15:23	For rebellion is as the *s* of
	15:25	therefore, please pardon my *s*,
	19: 4	Let not the king *s* against his
	19: 5	Why then will you *s* against
	20: 1	and what is my *s* before your
2 Sam	12:13	LORD also has put away your *s*;
1 Ki	8:34	and forgive the *s* of Your
	8:35	and turn from their *s* because
	8:36	and forgive the *s* of Your
	8:46	When they *s* against You
	8:46	is no one who does not *s*),
	12:30	Now this thing became a *s*,
	13:34	And this thing was the *s* of the
	14:16	sinned and who made Israel *s*.
	15:26	and in his *s* by which he had
	15:26	by which he had made Israel *s*.
	15:30	by which he had made Israel *s*,
	15:34	and in his *s* by which he had
	15:34	by which he had made Israel *s*.
	16: 2	have made My people Israel *s*,
	16:13	by which they had made Israel *s*,
	16:19	and in his *s* which he had
	16:19	had committed to make Israel *s*.
	16:26	and in his *s* by which he had
	16:26	by which he had made Israel *s*,
	17:18	you come to me to bring my *s*
	21:22	Me to anger, and made Israel *s*.
	22:52	of Nebat, who had made Israel *s*;
2 Ki	3: 3	of Nebat, who had made Israel *s*;
	10:29	of Nebat, who had made Israel *s*,
	10:31	Jeroboam, who had made Israel *s*.
	12:16	money from the *s* offerings
	13: 2	of Nebat, who had made Israel *s*.
	13: 6	Jeroboam, who had made Israel *s*,
	13:11	son of Nebat, who made Israel *s*,
	14: 6	be put to death for his own *s*.
	14:24	of Nebat, who had made Israel *s*.
	15: 9	of Nebat, who had made Israel *s*.
	15:18	of Nebat, who had made Israel *s*.
	15:24	of Nebat, who had made Israel *s*.
	15:28	of Nebat, who had made Israel *s*.
	17:21	and made them commit a great *s*.
	21:11	and has also made Judah *s* with
	21:16	besides his *s* by which he made
	21:16	sin by which he made Judah *s*,
	21:17	*s* that he committed—are
	23:15	son of Nebat, who made Israel *s*,
2 Chr	6:25	from heaven and forgive the *s*
	6:26	and turn from their *s* because
	6:27	and forgive the *s* of Your
	6:36	When they *s* against You
	6:36	is no one who does not *s*),
	7:14	and will forgive their *s* and
	25: 4	person shall die for his own *s*.
	29:21	male goats for a *s* offering
	29:23	goats for the *s* offering
	29:24	on the altar as a *s* offering
	29:24	offering and the *s* offering
	33:19	and all his *s* and trespass, and
Ezra	6:17	and as a *s* offering for all
	8:35	male goats as a *s* offering.
Neh	4: 5	and do not let their *s* be
	6:13	afraid and act that way and *s*,
	10:33	for the *s* offerings to make
	13:26	not Solomon king of Israel *s*
	13:26	women caused even him to *s*.
Job	1:22	In all this Job did not *s* nor
	2:10	In all this Job did not *s*
	10: 6	iniquity And search out my *s*,
	10:14	If I *s*, then You mark me,
	13:23	know my transgression and my *s*.
	14:16	But do not watch over my *s*.
	31:30	have not allowed my mouth to *s*
	34:37	For he adds rebellion to his *s*;
	35: 6	If you *s*, what do you
Ps	4: 4	Be angry, and do not *s*.
	32: 1	Whose *s* is covered.
	32: 5	I acknowledged my *s* to You,
	32: 5	forgave the iniquity of my *s*.
	38: 3	in my bones Because of my *s*.
	38:18	I will be in anguish over my *s*.
	39: 1	Lest I *s* with my tongue;
	40: 6	Burnt offering and *s* offering
	51: 2	And cleanse me from my *s*.
	51: 3	And my *s* is always before me.
	51: 5	And in *s* my mother conceived
	59: 3	my transgression nor for my *s*,
	59:12	For the *s* of their mouth and
	85: 2	You have covered all their *s*.
	109: 7	And let his prayer become *s*.
	109:14	And let not the *s* of his
	119:11	That I might not *s* against
Prov	5:22	is caught in the cords of his *s*.
	10:16	The wages of the wicked to *s*.
	10:19	In the multitude of words *s* is
	14: 9	Fools mock at *s*, But among
	14:34	But *s* is a reproach to any
	20: 9	I am pure from my *s*"?
	21: 4	plowing of the wicked are *s*.
	24: 9	devising of foolishness is *s*,
Eccl	5: 6	mouth cause your flesh to *s*,
	7:20	who does good And does not *s*.
Isa	3: 9	And they declare their *s* as
	5:18	And *s* as if with a cart rope;
	6: 7	And your *s* purged."
	27: 9	the fruit of taking away his *s*:
	30: 1	That they may add *s* to sin;
	30: 1	That they may add sin to *s*;
	31: 7	silver and his idols of gold—*s*,
	53:10	make His soul an offering for *s*,
	53:12	And He bore the *s* of many,
Jer	16:10	Or what is our *s* that we have
	16:18	for their iniquity and their *s*,
	17: 1	The *s* of Judah is written with
	17: 3	And your high places of *s*
	18:23	Nor blot out their *s* from Your
	31:34	and their *s* I will remember no
	32:35	to cause Judah to *s*.
	36: 3	their iniquity and their *s*.
	51: 5	their land was filled with *s*
Lam	4: 6	than the punishment of the *s*
Ezek	3:20	warning, he shall die in his *s*,
	3:21	that the righteous should not *s*,
	3:21	not sin, and he does not *s*,
	18:24	of which he is guilty and the *s*
	30:15	I will pour My fury on *S*,
	30:16	*S* shall have great pain, No
	33:14	if he turns from his *s* and
	40:39	the *s* offering, and the
	42:13	the *s* offering, and the
	43:19	a young bull for a *s* offering
	43:21	the bull of the *s* offering,
	43:22	blemish for a *s* offering;
	43:25	a goat for a *s* offering;
	44:27	he must offer his *s* offering in
	44:29	the *s* offering, and the
	45:17	shall prepare the *s* offering,
	45:19	of the blood of the *s* offering
	45:22	land a bull for a *s* offering.
	45:23	goats daily for a *s* offering.
	45:25	according to the *s* offering,
	46:20	offering and the *s* offering,
Dan	9:20	and confessing my *s* and the sin
	9:20	confessing my sin and the *s* of
Hos	4: 8	They eat up the *s* of My people;
	8:11	has made many altars for *s*,
	10: 8	the *s* of Israel, Shall be
	12: 8	in me no iniquity that is *s*.
	13: 2	Now they *s* more and more, And
	13:12	His *s* is stored up.
Am	8:14	Those who swear by the *s* of
Mic	1:13	(She was the beginning of *s*
	3: 8	And to Israel his *s*.
	6: 7	fruit of my body for the *s* of
Hab	2:10	And *s* against your soul.
Zech	13: 1	for *s* and for uncleanness.
Mt	5:29	your right eye causes you to *s*,
	5:30	your right hand causes you to *s*,
	12:31	every *s* and blasphemy will be
	18: 6	ones who believe in Me to *s*,
	18: 8	hand or foot causes you to *s*,
	18: 9	if your eye causes you to *s*,
	18:21	how often shall my brother *s*
Mk	9:43	"If your hand causes you to *s*,
	9:45	if your foot causes you to *s*,
	9:47	if your eye causes you to *s*,
Jn	1:29	of God who takes away the *s* of
	5:14	*S* no more, lest a worse thing
	8: 7	He who is without *s* among you,
	8:11	go and *s* no more."
	8:21	seek Me, and will die in your *s*.
	8:34	whoever commits *s* is a slave of
	8:34	commits sin is a slave of *s*.
	8:46	"Which of you convicts Me of *s*?
	9:41	were blind, you would have no *s*;
	9:41	Therefore your *s* remains.
	15:22	to them, they would have no *s*,
	15:22	they have no excuse for their *s*.
	15:24	else did, they would have no *s*;
	16: 8	He will convict the world of *s*,
	16: 9	'of *s*, because they do not
	19:11	Me to you has the greater *s*.
Acts	7:60	do not charge them with this *s*.
Rom	3: 9	that they are all under *s*.
	3:20	the law is the knowledge of *s*.
	4: 8	LORD shall not impute *s*.
	5:12	just as through one man *s*
	5:12	the world, and death through *s*,
	5:13	(For until the law *s* was in the
	5:13	but *s* is not imputed when there
	5:20	But where *s* abounded, grace
	5:21	so that as *s* reigned in death,
	6: 1	Shall we continue in *s* that
	6: 2	How shall we who died to *s* live
	6: 6	that the body of *s* might be
	6: 6	should no longer be slaves of *s*.
	6: 7	has died has been freed from *s*.
	6:10	He died to *s* once for all;
	6:11	to be dead indeed to *s*,
	6:12	Therefore do not let *s* reign in
	6:13	of unrighteousness to *s*,
	6:14	For *s* shall not have dominion
	6:15	Shall we *s* because we are not
	6:16	whether of *s* leading to death,
	6:17	though you were slaves of *s*,
	6:18	And having been set free from *s*,
	6:20	For when you were slaves of *s*,
	6:22	now having been set free from *s*,
	6:23	For the wages of *s* is death,
	7: 7	we say then? Is the law *s*?
	7: 7	I would not have known *s* except
	7: 8	But *s*, taking opportunity by
	7: 8	For apart from the law *s* was
	7: 9	*s* revived and I died.
	7:11	For *s*, taking occasion by
	7:13	But *s*, that it might appear
	7:13	But sin, that it might appear *s*,
	7:13	so that *s* through the
	7:14	but I am carnal, sold under *s*.
	7:17	but *s* that dwells in me.
	7:20	but *s* that dwells in me.
	7:23	into captivity to the law of *s*
	7:25	but with the flesh the law of *s*.
	8: 2	made me free from the law of *s*
	8: 3	sinful flesh, on account of *s*:
	8: 3	He condemned *s* in the flesh,
	8:10	the body is dead because of *s*,
	14:23	is not from faith is *s*.
1 Cor	6:18	Every *s* that a man does is
	7:36	what he wishes. He does not *s*;
	8:12	But when you thus *s* against the
	8:12	you *s* against Christ.
	15:34	to righteousness, and do not *s*;
	15:56	The sting of death is *s*,
	15:56	and the strength of *s* is the
2 Cor	5:21	For He made Him who knew no *s*
	5:21	Him who knew no sin to be *s*
	11: 7	Did I commit *s* in humbling
Gal	2:17	therefore a minister of *s*?
	3:22	has confined all under *s*,
Eph	4:26	and do not *s*": do not let
2 Th	2: 3	and the man of *s* is revealed,
Heb	3:13	through the deceitfulness of *s*.
	4:15	as we are, yet without *s*.
	9:26	He has appeared to put away *s*
	9:28	a second time, apart from *s*,
	10: 6	and sacrifices for *s* You
	10: 8	and offerings for *s* You
	10:18	is no longer an offering for *s*.
	10:26	For if we *s* willfully after we
	11:25	the passing pleasures of *s*,
	12: 1	and the *s* which so easily

S

12: 4 bloodshed, striving against *s*.
13:11 by the high priest for *s*,
Jas 1:15 conceived, it gives birth to *s*;
1:15 and *s*, when it is full-grown,
2: 9 show partiality, you commit *s*,
4:17 does not do it, to him it is *s*.
1 Pe 2:22 "Who committed no *s*,
4: 1 in the flesh has ceased from *s*,
2 Pe 2:14 and that cannot cease from *s*,
1 Jn 1: 7 His Son cleanses us from all *s*.
1: 8 If we say that we have no *s*,
2: 1 to you, so that you may not *s*.
3: 4 Whoever commits *s* also commits
3: 4 and *s* is lawlessness.
3: 5 sins, and in Him there is no *s*.
3: 6 abides in Him does not *s*.
3: 9 has been born of God does not *s*,
3: 9 remains in him; and he cannot *s*,
5:16 sees his brother sinning a *s*
5:16 him life for those who commit *s*
5:16 There is *s* leading to death.
5:17 All unrighteousness is *s*,
5:17 and there is *s* not leading to
5:18 is born of God does not *s*;

SINA (KJV) See SINAI

SINAI (39/38) HOREB

Ex 16: 1 which is between Elim and *S*,
19: 1 came to the Wilderness of *S*.
19: 2 come to the Wilderness of *S*,
19:11 will come down upon Mount *S* in
19:18 Now Mount *S* was completely in
19:20 LORD came down upon Mount *S*,
19:23 cannot come up to Mount *S*;
24:16 of the LORD rested on Mount *S*,
31:18 of speaking with him on Mount *S*,
34: 2 up in the morning to Mount *S*,
34: 4 the morning and went up Mount *S*,
34:29 Moses came down from Mount *S*
34:32 had spoken with him on Mount *S*.
Lev 7:38 commanded Moses on Mount *S*,
7:38 LORD in the Wilderness of *S*.
25: 1 LORD spoke to Moses on Mount *S*,
26:46 children of Israel on Mount *S*
27:34 children of Israel on Mount *S*.
Num 1: 1 to Moses in the Wilderness of *S*,
1:19 them in the Wilderness of *S*.
3: 1 spoke with Moses on Mount *S*.
3: 4 LORD in the Wilderness of *S*;
3:14 to Moses in the Wilderness of *S*,
9: 1 to Moses in the Wilderness of *S*,
9: 5 in the Wilderness of *S*;
10:12 out from the Wilderness of *S*
26:64 Israel in the Wilderness of *S*.
28: 6 which was ordained at Mount *S*
33:15 camped in the Wilderness of *S*.
33:16 moved from the Wilderness of *S*
Deut 33: 2 said: "The LORD came from *S*,
Judg 5: 5 This *S*, before the LORD God
Neh 9:13 came down also on Mount *S*,
Ps 68: 8 *S* itself was moved at the
68:17 Lord is among them as in *S*,
Acts 7:30 in the wilderness of Mount *S*.
7:38 who spoke to him on Mount *S*,
Gal 4:24 the one from Mount *S* which
4:25 for this Hagar is Mount *S* in

SINCE (175/174)

Gen 18:13 bear a child, *s* I am old?'
18:18 *s* Abraham shall surely become a
19: 8 *s* this is the reason they have
22:12 *s* you have not withheld your
24:56 *s* the LORD has prospered my
26:27 *s* you hate me and have sent me
26:29 *s* we have not touched you, and
26:29 and *s* we have done nothing to
30:30 the LORD has blessed you *s* my
34:30 and *s* I am few in number, they
44:28 and I have not seen him *s*.
44:30 *s* his life is bound up in the
46:30 *s* I have seen your face,
Ex 4:10 neither before nor *s* You have
5:23 For *s* I came to Pharaoh to speak
9:18 as has not been in Egypt *s* its
9:24 of Egypt *s* it became a nation.
10: 6 *s* the day that they were on the
12:19 *s* whoever eats what is
21: 8 *s* he has dealt deceitfully with
Lev 10:17 *s* it is most holy, and God
25:20 *s* we shall not sow nor gather
25:27 count the years *s* its sale,
Num 22:30 ever *s* I became yours, to
Deut 4:32 *s* the day that God created man
12:12 *s* he has no portion nor
15:16 *s* he prospers with you,
19: 6 *s* he had not hated the victim
34:10 But *s* then there has not arisen
Josh 2:12 *s* I have shown you kindness,
14:10 ever *s* the LORD spoke this
15:19 *s* you have given me land in the
17:14 *s* we are a great people,
17:15 *s* the mountains of Ephraim are
Judg 1:15 *s* you have given me land in the
15: 7 *S* you would do a thing like
17:13 *s* I have a Levite as priest!"
21:16 *s* the women of Benjamin have
Ruth 1:21 *s* the LORD has testified
2:10 *s* I am a foreigner?"
2:11 your mother-in-law *s* the death
1 Sam 8: 8 they have done *s* the day that I
9:24 *s* I said I invited the
20:42 *s* we have both sworn in the
21: 5 three days *s* I came out.
25:26 *s* the LORD has held you back
29: 3 no fault in him *s* he defected
29: 6 found evil in you *s* the day
2 Sam 3:36 *s* whatever the king did pleased
7: 6 dwelt in a house *s* the time
7:11 *s* the time that I commanded
15:20 *s* I go I know not where?
18:22 *s* you have no news ready?"
19:11 *s* the words of all Israel have
1 Ki 8:16 *S* the day that I brought My
2 Ki 10: 2 *s* your master's sons are with
21:15 provoked Me to anger *s* the day
23:22 never been held *s* the days
1 Chr 12:17 *s* there is no wrong in my
13: 3 at it *s* the days of Saul."
17: 5 dwelt in a house *s* the time
17:10 *s* the time that I commanded
2 Chr 2: 6 *s* heaven and the heaven of
6: 5 *S* the day that I brought My
21: 7 and *s* He had promised to give a
29:36 *s* the events took place so
30: 5 *s* they had not done it for a
30:26 for *s* the time of Solomon the
31:10 *S* the people began to bring
35:18 in Israel like that *s* the days
Ezra 4: 2 sacrificed to Him *s* the days
9: 7 *S* the days of our fathers to
9:13 *s* You our God have punished us
Neh 2: 2 *s* you are not sick?
8:17 for *s* the days of Joshua the
Job 14: 5 *S* his days are determined,
19:28 *S* the root of the matter is
20: 4 *S* man was placed on earth,
21:22 *S* He judges those on high?
21:34 *S* falsehood remains in your
24: 1 *S* times are not hidden from the
38:12 morning *s* your days began,
Ps 22: 8 *s* He delights in Him!"
Prov 17:16 *S* he has no heart for it?
20: 3 *S* any fool can start a
Eccl 2:16 *S* all that now is will be
6:11 *S* there are many things that
Isa 7:17 that have not come *s* the day
14: 8 *S* you were cut down, No
16:13 concerning Moab *s* that time.
43: 4 *S* you were precious in My
44: 7 *S* I appointed the ancient
49:21 *S* I have lost my children and
64: 4 For *s* the beginning of the
Jer 7:25 *S* the day that your fathers came
14:22 *S* You have made all these.
15: 7 *S* they do not return from
23:38 But *s* you say, 'The oracle of
42: 2 this remnant (*s* we are left
44:18 But *s* we stopped burning incense
Ezek 17:18 *S* he despised the oath by
35: 6 *s* you have not hated blood,
Dan 2:47 *s* you could reveal this
4:18 *s* all the wise men of my
6:10 as was his custom *s* early days.
12: 1 Such as never was *s* there was
Hos 12: 9 Ever *s* the land of Egypt;
13: 4 Ever *s* the land of Egypt,
Hag 2:16 *s* those days, when one came to
Mt 24:21 not been *s* the beginning
Mk 13:19 not been *s* the beginning
Lk 1:34 *s* I do not know a man?"
1:70 Who have been *s* the world
7:45 to kiss My feet *s* the time
12:17 *s* I have no room to store my
16:16 *S* that time the kingdom of God
24:21 the third day *s* these things
Jn 2:18 *s* You do these things?"
9:32 *S* the world began it has been
Acts 2:15 *s* it is only the third hour of
3:21 prophets *s* the world began.
4:21 *s* they all glorified God for
9:38 And *s* Lydda was near Joppa, and
13:46 but *s* you reject it, and judge
15:24 *S* we have heard that some who
17:24 *s* He is Lord of heaven and
17:25 *s* He gives to all life, breath,
17:29 *s* we are the offspring of God,
19:36 *s* these things cannot be
22:11 And *s* I could not see for the
24:11 twelve days *s* I went up to
26:26 *s* this thing was not done in a
27:34 *s* not a hair will fall from the
Rom 1:20 For *s* the creation of the world
3:30 *s* there is one God who will
4:19 already dead (*s* he was about a
16:25 kept secret *s* the world began
1 Cor 1:21 For *s*, in the wisdom of God,
5: 7 *s* you truly are unleavened.
5:10 *s* then you would need to go out
11: 7 *s* he is the image and glory of
11:17 *s* you come together not for the
14:12 *s* you are zealous for spiritual
14:16 *s* he does not understand what
15:21 For *s* by man came death, by Man
2 Cor 3:12 *s* we have such hope, we use
4: 1 *s* we have this ministry, as we
4:13 And *s* we have the same spirit of
11:19 *s* you yourselves are wise!
13: 3 *s* you seek a proof of Christ
Phil 2:26 *s* he was longing for you all,
Col 1: 4 *s* we heard of your faith in
1: 6 is also among you *s* the day
1: 9 *s* the day we heard it, do not
3: 9 *s* you have put off the old man
2 Th 1: 6 *s* it is a righteous thing with
Heb 4: 1 *s* a promise remains of entering
4: 6 *S* therefore it remains that some
5: 2 *s* he himself is also subject to
5:11 *s* you have become dull of
6: 6 *s* they crucify again for
7:25 *s* He always lives to make
8: 4 *s* there are priests who offer
9:17 *s* it has no power at all while
9:26 suffer often *s* the foundation
12: 1 *s* we are surrounded by so great
12:28 *s* we are receiving a kingdom
13: 3 *s* you yourselves are in the body
1 Pe 1:22 *S* you have purified your souls
4: 1 *s* Christ suffered for us in the
2 Pe 3: 4 For *s* the fathers fell asleep,
3:11 *s* all these things will be
3:17 *s* you know this beforehand,
Rev 16:18 as had not occurred *s* men were
16:21 *s* that plague was exceedingly

SINCERE (4/4) SINCERITY

2 Cor 6: 6 the Holy Spirit, by *s* love,
Phil 1:10 that you may be *s* and without
1 Tim 1: 5 conscience, and from *s* faith,
1 Pe 1:22 through the Spirit in *s* love

SINCERELY (2/2)

Phil 1:16 from selfish ambition, not *s*,
2:20 who will *s* care for your state.

SINCERITY (10/10) SINCERE

Josh 24:14 serve Him in *s* and in truth,
Judg 9:16 you have acted in truth and *s*
9:19 you have acted in truth and *s*
1 Cor 5: 8 the unleavened bread of *s* and
2 Cor 1:12 world in simplicity and godly *s*,
2:17 the word of God; but as of *s*,
8: 8 but I am testing the *s* of your
Eph 6: 5 in *s* of heart, as to Christ;
6:24 love our Lord Jesus Christ in *s*.
Col 3:22 but in *s* of heart, fearing God.

SINEW (1/1)

Isa 48: 4 And your neck was an iron *s*,

SINEWS (4/4)

Job 10:11 me together with bones and *s*?
40:17 The *s* of his thighs are
Ezek 37: 6 I will put *s* on you and bring
37: 8 the *s* and the flesh came upon

SINFUL (10/10) SIN

Gen 13:13 were exceedingly wicked and *s*
Num 32:14 a brood of *s* men, to increase
Isa 1: 4 *s* nation, A people laden with
Am 9: 8 GOD are on the *s* kingdom,
Mk 8:38 adulterous and *s* generation,
Lk 5: 8 for I am a *s* man, O Lord!"
24: 7 into the hands of *s* men,
Rom 7: 5 the *s* passions which were
7:13 might become exceedingly *s*.
8: 3 in the likeness of *s* flesh,

SING (116/99) SANG, SINGERS, SINGING, SINGS, SONG, SUNG

Ex 15: 1 I will *s* to the LORD, For He
15:21 *S* to the LORD, For He has
Num 21:17 O well! All of you *s* to it—
Judg 5: 3 will *s* to the LORD; I will
5: 3 I will *s* praise to the LORD
5:12 *s* a song! Arise, Barak, and
1 Sam 21:11 Did they not *s* of him to one
2 Sam 22:50 And *s* praises to Your name.
1 Chr 16: 9 *S* to Him, sing psalms to Him
16: 9 *s* psalms to Him; Talk of all
16:23 *S* to the LORD, all the earth;
2 Chr 20:21 he appointed those who should *s*
20:22 Now when they began to *s* and to
29:30 commanded the Levites to *s*
Job 21:12 They *s* to the tambourine and
29:13 I caused the widow's heart to *s*
Ps 7:17 And will *s* praise to the name
9: 2 I will *s* praise to Your name,
9:11 *S* praises to the LORD, who
13: 6 I will *s* to the LORD, Because
18:49 And *s* praises to Your name.
21:13 We will *s* and praise Your
27: 6 I will *s*, yes, I will sing
27: 6 I will *s* praises to the LORD.
30: 4 *S* praise to the LORD, You
30:12 the end that my glory may *s*
33: 3 *S* to Him a new song
47: 6 *S* praises to God, sing praises!
47: 6 *s* praises! Sing praises to our
47: 6 sing praises! *S* praises to our
47: 6 to our King, *s* praises!
47: 7 *S* praises with understanding.
51:14 And my tongue shall *s* aloud
57: 7 I will *s* and give praise.
57: 9 I will *s* to You among the
59:16 But I will *s* of Your power;
59:16 I will *s* aloud of Your mercy in
59:17 I will *s* praises; For God is

61: 8 So I will *s* praise to Your name
65:13 shout for joy, they also *s*.
66: 2 *S* out the honor of His name
66: 4 earth shall worship You And *s*
66: 4 They shall *s* praises to Your
67: 4 let the nations be glad and *s*
68: 4 *S* to God, sing praises to His
68: 4 *s* praises to His name;
68:32 *S* to God, you kingdoms of the
68:32 *s* praises to the Lord, Selah
71:22 O my God! To You I will *s* with
71:23 shall greatly rejoice when I *s*
75: 9 I will *s* praises to the God of
81: 1 *S* aloud to God our strength
89: 1 I will *s* of the mercies of the
92: 1 And to *s* praises to Your name,
95: 1 let us *s* to the LORD!
96: 1 *s* to the LORD a new song!
96: 1 to the LORD a new song! *S* to
96: 2 *S* to the LORD, bless His name
98: 1 *s* to the LORD a new song!
98: 4 song, rejoice, and *s* praises.
98: 5 *S* to the LORD with the harp,
101: 1 I will *s* of mercy and justice;
101: 1 O LORD, I will *s* praises.
104:12 They *s* among the branches.
104:33 I will *s* to the LORD as long
104:33 I will *s* praise to my God
105: 2 *S* to Him, sing psalms to Him
105: 2 *s* psalms to Him; Talk of all
108: 1 I will *s* and give praise, even
108: 3 And I will *s* praises to You
135: 3 *S* praises to His name, for it
137: 3 *S* us one of the songs of
137: 4 How shall we *s* the LORD's song
138: 1 Before the gods I will *s*
138: 5 they shall *s* of the ways of the
144: 9 I will *s* a new song to You,
144: 9 a harp of ten strings I will *s*
145: 7 And shall *s* of Your
146: 2 I will *s* praises to my God
147: 1 For it is good to *s* praises
147: 7 *S* to the LORD with
147: 7 *S* praises on the harp to our
149: 1 *S* to the LORD a new song,
149: 3 Let them *s* praises to Him with
149: 5 Let them *s* aloud on their
Isa 5: 1 Now let me *s* to my Well-beloved
12: 5 *S* to the LORD, For He has
23:16 *s* many songs, That you may be
24:14 up their voice, they shall *s*;
26:19 Awake and *s*, you who dwell
27: 2 In that day *s* to her, "A
35: 6 And the tongue of the dumb *s*.
38:20 Therefore we will *s* my songs
42:10 *S* to the LORD a new song,
42:11 Let the inhabitants of Sela *s*,
44:23 *S*, O heavens, for the LORD
49:13 *S*, O heavens! Be joyful,
52: 8 With their voices they shall *s*
52: 9 *s* together, You waste places
54: 1 '*S*, O barren, You who have
65:14 My servants shall *s* for joy of
Jer 20:13 *S* to the LORD! Praise the
31: 7 *S* with gladness for Jacob, And
31:12 they shall come and *s* in the
51:48 all that is in them Shall *s*
Hos 2:15 She shall *s* there, As in the
Am 6: 5 Who *s* idly to the sound of
Zeph 2:14 Their voice shall *s* in the
3:14 *S*, O daughter of Zion!
Zech 2:10 *S* and rejoice, O daughter of
Rom 15: 9 And *s* to Your name."
1 Cor 14:15 I will *s* with the spirit, and I
14:15 and I will also *s* with the
Heb 2:12 of the assembly I will *s*
Jas 5:13 Let him *s* psalms.
Rev 15: 3 They *s* the song of Moses, the

SINGED (1/1)

Dan 3:27 hair of their head was not *s*

SINGER (1/1) SING

1 Chr 6:33 Kohathites were Heman the *s*,

SINGERS (38/37) SINGER

1 Ki 10:12 and stringed instruments for *s*.
1 Chr 9:33 These are the *s*,
15:16 their brethren to be the *s*
15:19 the *s*, Heman, Asaph, and
15:27 Levites who bore the ark, the *s*,
15:27 the music master with the *s*.
2 Chr 5:12 the Levites who were the *s*,
5:13 when the trumpeters and *s* were
9:11 and stringed instruments for *s*;
23:13 also the *s* with musical
29:28 the *s* sang, and the trumpeters
35:15 And the *s*, the sons of Asaph,
Ezra 2:41 The *s*: the sons of Asaph,
2:65 had two hundred men and women *s*.
2:70 some of the people, the *s*,
7: 7 the priests, the Levites, the *s*,
7:24 any of the priests, Levites, *s*,
10:24 Also of the *s*: Eliashib;
Neh 7: 1 when the gatekeepers, the *s*,
7:44 The *s*: the sons of Asaph,
7:67 and forty-five men and women *s*.
7:73 Levites, the gatekeepers, the *s*,
10:28 Levites, the gatekeepers, the *s*,
10:39 and the gatekeepers and the *s*
11:22 the *s* in charge of the service
11:23 portion should be for the *s*,
12:28 And the sons of the *s* gathered
12:29 for the *s* had built themselves
12:42 The *s* sang loudly with
12:45 Both the *s* and the gatekeepers
12:46 there were chiefs of the *s*,
12:47 gave the portions for the *s*
13: 5 be given to the Levites and *s*
13:10 each of the Levites and the *s*
Ps 68:25 The *s* went before, the players
87: 7 Both the *s* and the players on
Eccl 2: 8 I acquired male and female *s*,
Ezek 40:44 were the chambers for the *s*

SINGING (27/25) SING

Ex 32:18 But the sound of *s* I hear."
1 Sam 18: 6 *s* and dancing, to meet King
2 Sam 19:35 hear any longer the voice of *s*
19:35 of singing men and *s* women?
1 Chr 13: 8 with all their might, with *s*,
2 Chr 23:18 with rejoicing and with *s*,
30:21 *s* to the LORD, accompanied by
35:25 And to this day all the *s* men
35:25 singing men and the *s* women
Neh 12:27 both with thanksgivings and *s*,
Ps 100: 2 before His presence with *s*.
126: 2 And our tongue with *s*.
Song 2:12 The time of *s* has come, And
Isa 14: 7 They break forth into *s*.
16:10 vineyards there will be no *s*,
35: 2 rejoice, Even with joy and *s*.
35:10 And come to Zion with *s*,
44:23 the earth; Break forth into *s*,
48:20 With a voice of *s*, Declare,
49:13 O earth! And break out in *s*,
51:11 And come to Zion with *s*,
54: 1 not borne! Break forth into *s*,
55:12 hills Shall break forth into *s*
Zeph 3:17 will rejoice over you with *s*.
Acts 16:25 and Silas were praying and *s*
Eph 5:19 *s* and making melody in your
Col 3:16 *s* with grace in your hearts to

SINGLE (2/2)

2 Chr 28:25 And in every *s* city of Judah he
31:19 in every *s* city, there were

SINGLENESS (1/1)

2 Chr 30:12 was on Judah to give them *s* of

SINGS (2/2)

Prov 25:20 Is one who *s* songs to a heavy
29: 6 But the righteous *s* and

SINGULAR (1/1)

Ezek 7: 5 a *s* disaster; Behold, it has

SINIM (1/1)

Isa 49:12 And these from the land of *S*.

SINISTER (2/2)

Ps 26:10 In whose hands is a *s* scheme,
Dan 8:23 Who understands *s* schemes.

SINITE (2/2)

Gen 10:17 Hivite, the Arkite, and the *S*;
1 Chr 1:15 Hivite, the Arkite, and the *S*;

SINK (6/6) SANK, SUNK

Ps 69: 2 I *s* in deep mire, Where there
69:14 of the mire, And let me not *s*;
Jer 51:64 Thus Babylon shall *s* and not
Mt 14:30 and beginning to *s* he cried
Lk 5: 7 boats, so that they began to *s*.
9:44 Let these words *s* down into your

SINKING (1/1)

Acts 20: 9 who was *s* into a deep sleep.

SINKS (1/1)

Lam 3:20 My soul still remembers And *s*

SINNED (110/106) SIN

Ex 9:27 I have *s* this time. The LORD
9:34 he *s* yet more; and he hardened
10:16 I have *s* against the LORD your
32:33 Whoever has *s* against Me, I will
Lev 4: 3 for his sin which he has *s* a
4:22 'When a ruler has *s*,
5: 5 he shall confess that he has *s*
5:11 then he who *s* shall bring for
6: 4 because he has *s* and is guilty,
Num 6:11 because he *s* in regard to the
12:11 and in which we have *s*.
14:40 has promised, for we have *s*!"
16:38 censers of these men who *s*
21: 7 to Moses, and said, "We have *s*,
22:34 Angel of the LORD, "I have *s*,
32:23 you have *s* against the LORD;
Deut 1:41 We have *s* against the LORD; we
9:16 you had *s* against the LORD
Josh 7:11 'Israel has *s*, and they have
7:20 Indeed I have *s* against the
Judg 10:10 We have *s* against You, because
10:15 We have *s*! Do to us whatever
11:27 Therefore I have not *s* against
1 Sam 7: 6 We have *s* against the LORD."
12:10 the LORD, and said, 'We have *s*,
15:24 Saul said to Samuel, "I have *s*,
15:30 Then he said, "I have *s*;
19: 4 because he has not *s* against
24:11 and I have not *s* against you.
26:21 Then Saul said, "I have *s*.
2 Sam 12:13 I have *s* against the LORD."
19:20 servant, know that I have *s*.
24:10 I have *s* greatly in what I have
24:17 and said, "Surely I have *s*,
1 Ki 8:33 an enemy because they have *s*
8:35 is no rain because they have *s*
8:47 We have *s* and done wrong, we
8:50 forgive Your people who have *s*
14:16 who *s* and who made Israel
15:30 which he had *s* and by which he
16:13 by which they had *s* and by
18: 9 So he said, "How have I *s*,
2 Ki 17: 7 the children of Israel had *s*
1 Chr 21: 8 I have *s* greatly, because I have
21:17 I am the one who has *s* and done
2 Chr 6:24 an enemy because they have *s*
6:26 is no rain because they have *s*
6:37 captivity, saying, 'We have *s*,
6:39 forgive Your people who have *s*
Neh 1: 6 of Israel which we have *s*
1: 6 my father's house and I have *s*.
9:29 But *s* against Your judgments,
Job 1: 5 It may be that my sons have *s*
7:20 Have I *s*? What have I done
8: 4 If your sons have *s* against
24:19 consumes those who have *s*.
33:27 at men and says, 'I have *s*,
35: 3 I have, more than if I had *s*?
Ps 41: 4 for I have *s* against You."
51: 4 You, You only, have I *s*,
78:17 But they *s* even more against
78:32 In spite of this they still *s*,
106: 6 We have *s* with our fathers, We
Isa 42:24 He against whom we have *s*?
43:27 Your first father *s*,
64: 5 are indeed angry, for we have *s*—
Jer 2:35 Because you say, 'I have not *s*.
3:25 For we have *s* against the
8:14 Because we have *s* against the
14: 7 We have *s* against You.
14:20 For we have *s* against You.
33: 8 iniquity by which they have *s*
33: 8 by which they have *s* and by
40: 3 Because you people have *s*
44:23 incense and because you have *s*
50: 7 Because they have *s* against
50:14 For she has *s* against the
Lam 1: 8 Jerusalem has *s* gravely,
5: 7 Our fathers *s* and are no
5:16 Woe to us, for we have *s*!
Ezek 28:16 violence within, And you *s*;
37:23 places in which they have *s*,
45:20 month for everyone who has *s*
Dan 9: 5 we have *s* and committed
9: 8 because we have *s* against You.
9:11 because we have *s* against Him.
9:15 as it is this day—we have *s*,
Hos 4: 7 The more they *s* against Me;
10: 9 you have *s* from the days of
Mic 7: 9 Because I have *s* against Him,
Zeph 1:17 Because they have *s* against
Mt 27: 4 I have *s* by betraying innocent
Lk 15:18 I have *s* against heaven and
15:21 I have *s* against heaven and in
Jn 9: 2 Him, saying, "Rabbi, who *s*,
9: 3 this man nor his parents *s*,
Rom 2:12 For as many as have *s* without
2:12 and as many as have *s* in the
3:23 for all have *s* and fall short of
5:12 to all men, because all *s*—
5:14 even over those who had not *s*
5:16 came through the one who *s*.
1 Cor 7:28 if you do marry, you have not *s*;
7:28 a virgin marries, she has not *s*.
2 Cor 12:21 shall mourn for many who have *s*
13: 2 I write to those who have *s*
Heb 3:17 Was it not with those who *s*,
2 Pe 2: 4 did not spare the angels who *s*,
1 Jn 1:10 If we say that we have not *s*,
3: 8 for the devil has *s* from the

SINNER (21/21) SIN, SINNERS

Prov 11:31 much more the ungodly and the *s*.
13: 6 wickedness overthrows the *s*.
13:22 But the wealth of the *s* is
Eccl 2:26 but to the *s* He gives the work
7:26 But the *s* shall be trapped by
8:12 Though a *s* does evil a hundred
9: 2 As is the good, so is the *s*;
9:18 But one *s* destroys much
Isa 65:20 But the *s* being one hundred
Lk 7:37 a woman in the city who was a *s*,
7:39 is touching Him, for she is a *s*.
15: 7 more joy in heaven over one *s*
15:10 of the angels of God over one *s*
18:13 be merciful to me a *s*!'
19: 7 a guest with a man who is a *s*.
Jn 9:16 How can a man who is a *s* do such

9:24 We know that this Man is a *s*.
9:25 Whether He is a *s* or not I do
Rom 3: 7 am I also still judged as a *s*?
Jas 5:20 him know that he who turns a *s*
1 Pe 4:18 the ungodly and the *s*

SINNERS (46/44) SINNER

1 Sam 15:18 'Go, and utterly destroy the *s*,
Ps 1: 1 Nor stands in the path of *s*,
1: 5 Nor *s* in the congregation of
25: 8 Therefore He teaches *s* in the
26: 9 Do not gather my soul with *s*,
51:13 And *s* shall be converted to
104:35 May *s* be consumed from the
Prov 1:10 if *s* entice you, Do not
13:21 Evil pursues *s*, But to the
23:17 Do not let your heart envy *s*,
Isa 1:28 of transgressors and of *s*
13: 9 And He will destroy its *s* from
33:14 The *s* in Zion are afraid;
Am 9:10 All the *s* of My people shall
Mt 9:10 many tax collectors and *s* came
9:11 eat with tax collectors and *s*?
9:13 to call the righteous, but *s*,
11:19 friend of tax collectors and *s*!
26:45 betrayed into the hands of *s*.
Mk 2:15 that many tax collectors and *s*
2:16 with the tax collectors and *s*,
2:16 with tax collectors and *s*?
2:17 to call the righteous, but *s*,
14:41 betrayed into the hands of *s*.
Lk 5:30 drink with tax collectors and *s*?
5:32 to call the righteous, but *s*,
6:32 For even *s* love those who love
6:33 For even *s* do the same.
6:34 For even *s* lend to sinners to
6:34 For even sinners lend to *s* to
7:34 friend of tax collectors and *s*!
13: 2 these Galileans were worse *s*
13: 4 think that they were worse *s*
15: 1 the tax collectors and the *s*
15: 2 This Man receives *s* and eats
Jn 9:31 know that God does not hear *s*;
Rom 5: 8 in that while we were still *s*,
5:19 disobedience many were made *s*,
Gal 2:15 and not *s* of the Gentiles,
2:17 we ourselves also are found *s*,
1 Tim 1: 9 for the ungodly and for *s*,
1:15 came into the world to save *s*,
Heb 7:26 undefiled, separate from *s*,
12: 3 endured such hostility from *s*
Jas 4: 8 Cleanse your hands, you *s*;
Jude 15 harsh things which ungodly *s*

SINNING (6/6) SIN

Gen 20: 6 For I also withheld you from *s*
1 Sam 14:33 the people are *s* against the
Hos 8:11 become for him altars for *s*.
1 Tim 5:20 Those who are *s* rebuke in the
Titus 3:11 such a person is warped and *s*,
1 Jn 5:16 If anyone sees his brother *s* a

SINS (197/190) SIN

Lev 4: 2 If a person *s* unintentionally
4: 3 'if the anointed priest *s*,
4:13 whole congregation of Israel *s*
4:27 anyone of the common people *s*
5: 1 If a person *s* in hearing the
5:15 and *s* unintentionally in regard
5:17 "If a person *s*,
6: 2 If a person *s* and commits a
6: 3 that a man may do in which he *s*:
16:16 transgressions, for all their *s*;
16:21 concerning all their *s*,
16:30 may be clean from all your *s*
16:34 of Israel, for all their *s*,
26:18 you seven times more for your *s*.
26:21 plagues, according to your *s*.
26:24 you yet seven times for your *s*.
26:28 you seven times for your *s*.
Num 15:27 And if a person *s*
15:28 atonement for the person who *s*
15:28 when he *s* unintentionally
15:29 have one law for him who *s*
16:26 you be consumed in all their *s*.
Josh 24:19 your transgressions nor your *s*.
1 Sam 2:25 If one man *s* against another,
2:25 But if a man *s* against the
12:19 for we have added to all our *s*
1 Ki 8:31 When anyone *s* against his
14:16 Israel up because of the *s* of
14:22 Him to jealousy with their *s*
15: 3 And he walked in all the *s* of
15:30 because of the *s* of Jeroboam,
16: 2 Me to anger with their *s*,
16:13 for all the *s* of Baasha and the
16:13 the sins of Baasha and the *s*
16:19 because of the *s* which he had
16:31 thing for him to walk in the *s*
2 Ki 3: 3 he persisted in the *s* of
10:29 did not turn away from the *s*
10:31 he did not depart from the *s*
13: 2 and followed the *s* of Jeroboam
13: 6 they did not depart from the *s*
13:11 did not depart from all the *s*
14:24 did not depart from all the *s*
15: 9 he did not depart from the *s* of
15:18 depart all his days from the *s*
15:24 he did not depart from the *s* of
15:28 he did not depart from the *s* of
17:22 of Israel walked in all the *s*
24: 3 His sight because of the *s* of
2 Chr 6:22 If anyone *s* against his
28:13 You intend to add to our *s* and
Neh 1: 6 and confess the *s* of the
9: 2 stood and confessed their *s*
9:37 set over us, Because of our *s*;
Job 13:23 many are my iniquities and *s*?
Ps 19:13 also from presumptuous *s*;
25: 7 Do not remember the *s* of my
25:18 my pain, And forgive all my *s*.
51: 9 Hide Your face from my *s*,
69: 5 And my *s* are not hidden from
79: 9 and provide atonement for our *s*,
90: 8 Our secret *s* in the light of
103:10 with us according to our *s*,
Prov 8:36 But he who *s* against me wrongs
10:12 strife, But love covers all *s*.
14:21 He who despises his neighbor *s*;
19: 2 And he *s* who hastens with his
20: 2 provokes him to anger *s*
28:13 He who covers his *s* will not
Isa 1:18 Though your *s* are like scarlet,
38:17 For You have cast all my *s*
40: 2 hand Double for all her *s*.
43:24 have burdened Me with your *s*,
43:25 And I will not remember your *s*.
44:22 And like a cloud, your *s*.
58: 1 And the house of Jacob their *s*.
59: 2 And your *s* have hidden His
59:12 And our *s* testify against us;
Jer 5:25 And your *s* have withheld good
14:10 now, And punish their *s*.
15:13 price, Because of all your *s*,
30:14 Because your *s* have
30:15 Because your *s* have
50:20 And the *s* of Judah, but they
Lam 3:39 man for the punishment of his *s*?
4:13 Because of the *s* of her
4:22 He will uncover your *s*!
Ezek 14:13 when a land *s* against Me by
16:51 did not commit half of your *s*;
16:52 because the *s* which you
18: 4 The soul who *s* shall die.
18:14 a son Who sees all the *s*
18:20 'The soul who *s* shall die.
18:21 man turns from all his *s* which
21:24 that in all your doings your *s*
23:49 shall pay for your idolatrous *s*.
33:10 our transgressions and our *s*
33:12 in the day that he *s*.
33:16 None of his *s* which he has
Dan 4:27 break off your *s* by being
9:16 because for our *s*, and for
9:24 To make an end of *s*,
Hos 8:13 iniquity and punish their *s*.
9: 9 He will punish their *s*.
Am 5:12 And your mighty *s*:
Mic 1: 5 of Jacob And for the *s* of the
6:13 you desolate because of your *s*.
7:19 You will cast all our *s* Into
Mt 1:21 save His people from their *s*.
3: 6 the Jordan, confessing their *s*.
9: 2 your *s* are forgiven you."
9: 5 Your *s* are forgiven you,'
9: 6 power on earth to forgive *s*"—
18:15 Moreover if your brother *s*
26:28 for many for the remission of *s*.
Mk 1: 4 for the remission of *s*.
1: 5 River, confessing their *s*.
2: 5 your *s* are forgiven you."
2: 7 Who can forgive *s* but God
2: 9 Your *s* are forgiven you,'
2:10 power on earth to forgive *s*"—
3:28 all *s* will be forgiven the sons
4:12 And their *s* be forgiven
Lk 1:77 By the remission of their *s*,
3: 3 for the remission of *s*,
5:20 your *s* are forgiven you."
5:21 Who can forgive *s* but God
5:23 Your *s* are forgiven you,' or to
5:24 power on earth to forgive *s*"—
7:47 "Therefore I say to you, her *s*,
7:48 Your *s* are forgiven."
7:49 is this who even forgives *s*?
11: 4 And forgive us our *s*,
17: 3 If your brother *s* against you,
17: 4 And if he *s* against you seven
24:47 repentance and remission of *s* should
Jn 8:24 you that you will die in your *s*;
8:24 am He, you will die in your *s*.
9:34 "You were completely born in *s*,
20:23 If you forgive the *s* of any,
20:23 if you retain the *s* of any,
Acts 2:38 Christ for the remission of *s*;
3:19 that your *s* may be blotted out,
5:31 to Israel and forgiveness of *s*.
10:43 Him will receive remission of *s*."
13:38 to you the forgiveness of *s*;
22:16 baptized, and wash away your *s*,
26:18 may receive forgiveness of *s*
Rom 3:25 God had passed over the *s* that
4: 7 And whose *s* are covered;
11:27 When I take away their *s*.
1 Cor 6:18 who commits sexual immorality *s*
15: 3 that Christ died for our *s*
15:17 you are still in your *s*!
Gal 1: 4 who gave Himself for our *s*,
Eph 1: 7 His blood, the forgiveness of *s*,
2: 1 were dead in trespasses and *s*,
Col 1:14 His blood, the forgiveness of *s*.
2:11 putting off the body of the *s*
1 Th 2:16 up the measure of their *s*;
1 Tim 5:22 nor share in other people's *s*;
5:24 Some men's *s* are clearly
2 Tim 3: 6 women loaded down with *s*,
Heb 1: 3 He had by Himself purged our *s*,
2:17 to make propitiation for the *s*
5: 1 both gifts and sacrifices for *s*.
5: 3 to offer sacrifices for *s*.
7:27 first for His own *s* and then
8:12 and their *s* and their
9: 7 himself and for the people's *s*
9:28 was offered once to bear the *s*
10: 2 had no more consciousness of *s*.
10: 3 there is a reminder of *s*
10: 4 and goats could take away *s*.
10:11 which can never take away *s*.
10:12 had offered one sacrifice for *s*
10:17 Their *s* and their lawless
10:26 remains a sacrifice for *s*,
Jas 5:15 And if he has committed *s*,
5:20 and cover a multitude of *s*.
1 Pe 2:24 who Himself bore our *s* in His
2:24 tree, that we, having died to *s*,
3:18 Christ also suffered once for *s*,
4: 8 cover a multitude of *s*.
2 Pe 1: 9 he was cleansed from his old *s*.
1 Jn 1: 9 If we confess our *s*,
1: 9 and just to forgive us our *s*
2: 1 And if anyone *s*, we have an
2: 2 is the propitiation for our *s*,
2:12 Because your *s* are forgiven
3: 5 manifested to take away our *s*,
3: 6 Whoever *s* has neither seen Him
3: 8 He who *s* is of the devil, for
4:10 be the propitiation for our *s*.
Rev 1: 5 us and washed us from our *s* in
18: 4 people, lest you share in her *s*,
18: 5 For her *s* have reached to

SION (1/1)

Deut 4:48 even to Mount *S* (that is,

SIPHMOTH (1/1)

1 Sam 30:28 in Aroer, those who were in *S*,

SIPPAI (1/1)

1 Chr 20: 4 the Hushathite killed *S*,

SIR (13/13) SIRS

Gen 43:20 and said, "O *s*, we indeed
Mt 13:27 owner came and said to him, '*S*,
21:30 he answered and said, 'I go, *s*,
27:63 saying, "*S*, we remember,
Lk 13: 8 he answered and said to him, '*S*,
Jn 4:11 The woman said to Him, "*S*,
4:15 The woman said to Him, "*S*,
4:19 The woman said to Him, "*S*,
4:49 The nobleman said to Him, "*S*,
5: 7 The sick man answered Him, "*S*,
12:21 and asked him, saying, "*S*,
20:15 the gardener, said to Him, "*S*,
Rev 7:14 And I said to him, "*S*,

SIRAH (1/1)

2 Sam 3:26 him back from the well of *S*.

SIRION (2/2) HERMON

Deut 3: 9 '(the Sidonians call Hermon *S*,
Ps 29: 6 Lebanon and *S* like a young

SIRS (1/1) SIR

Acts 16:30 brought them out and said, "*S*,

SISAMAI (KJV) See SISMAI

SISERA (21/19)

Judg 4: 2 commander of his army was *S*,
4: 7 against you I will deploy *S*,
4: 9 for the LORD will sell *S* into
4:12 And they reported to *S* that
4:13 So *S* gathered together all his
4:14 the LORD has delivered *S* into
4:15 And the LORD routed *S* and all
4:15 and *S* alighted from his
4:16 and all the army of *S* fell by
4:17 *S* had fled away on foot to the
4:18 And Jael went out to meet *S*,
4:22 And then, as Barak pursued *S*,
4:22 into her tent, there lay *S*,
5:20 their courses fought against *S*.
5:26 She pounded *S*, she pierced
5:28 The mother of *S* looked through
5:30 man a girl or two; For *S*,
1 Sam 12: 9 He sold them into the hand of *S*,
Ezra 2:53 sons of Barkos, the sons of *S*,
Neh 7:55 sons of Barkos, the sons of *S*,
Ps 83: 9 as with Midian, As with *S*,

SISMAI (2/1)

1 Chr 2:40 Eleasah begot *S*, and
2:40 and *S* begot Shallum;

SISTER (105/101) SISTER-IN-LAW, SISTERS

Gen 4:22 And the *s* of Tubal-Cain was
12:13 "Please say you are my *s*,
12:19 did you say, 'She is my *s*'?
20: 2 Sarah his wife, "She is my *s*.
20: 5 not say to me, 'She is my *s*'?
20:12 indeed she is truly my *s*.
24:30 he heard the words of his *s*
24:59 they sent away Rebekah their *s*
24:60 'Our *s*, may you become
25:20 the *s* of Laban the Syrian.
26: 7 She is my *s*"; for he was
26: 9 could you say, 'She is my *s*'?
28: 9 the *s* of Nebajoth, to be his
30: 1 children, Rachel envied her *s*,
30: 8 I have wrestled with my *s*,
34:13 he had defiled Dinah their *s*.
34:14 to give our *s* to one who is
34:27 because their *s* had been
34:31 Should he treat our *s* like a
36: 3 daughter, *s* of Nebajoth.
36:22 Lotan's *s* was Timna.
46:17 Beriah, and Serah, their *s*.
Ex 2: 4 And his *s* stood afar off, to
2: 7 Then his *s* said to Pharaoh's
6:20 Jochebed, his father's *s*,
6:23 *s* of Nahshon, as wife; and she
15:20 the *s* of Aaron, took the
Lev 18: 9 'The nakedness of your *s*,
18:11 by your father—she is your *s*—
18:12 nakedness of your father's *s*;
18:13 nakedness of your mother's *s*,
18:18 a woman as a rival to her *s*,
20:17 'If a man takes his *s*,
20:19 nakedness of your mother's *s*
20:19 sister nor of your father's *s*,
21: 3 also his virgin *s* who is near to
Num 6: 7 for his brother or his *s*,
25:18 of a leader of Midian, their *s*,
26:59 Aaron and Moses and their *s*
Deut 27:22 is the one who lies with his *s*,
Judg 15: 2 Is not her younger *s* better
2 Sam 13: 1 the son of David had a lovely *s*,
13: 2 was so distressed over his *s*
13: 4 Tamar, my brother Absalom's *s*.
13: 5 Please let my *s* Tamar come and
13: 6 Please let Tamar my *s* come and
13:11 her, "Come, lie with me, my *s*.
13:20 But now hold your peace, my *s*.
13:22 because he had forced his *s*
13:32 the day that he forced his *s*
17:25 *s* of Zeruiah, Joab's mother.
1 Ki 11:19 that he gave him as wife the *s*
11:19 the *s* of Queen Tahpenes.
11:20 Then the *s* of Tahpenes bore him
2 Ki 11: 2 *s* of Ahaziah, took Joash the
1 Chr 1:39 Lotan's *s* was Timna.
3: 9 concubines, and Tamar their *s*.
3:19 Hananiah, Shelomith their *s*,
4: 3 and the name of their *s* was
4:19 the *s* of Naham, were the
7:15 took as his wife the *s* of
7:18 His *s* Hammoleketh bore Ishhod,
7:30 and their *s* Serah.
7:32 and their *s* Shua.
2 Chr 22:11 the priest (for she was the *s*
Job 17:14 'You are my mother and my *s*,
Prov 7: 4 Say to wisdom, "You are my *s*,
Song 4: 9 have ravished my heart, My *s*,
4:10 How fair is your love, My *s*,
4:12 A garden enclosed Is my *s*,
5: 1 I have come to my garden, my *s*,
5: 2 saying, "Open for me, my *s*,
8: 8 We have a little *s*,
8: 8 What shall we do for our *s* In
Jer 3: 7 And her treacherous *s* Judah saw
3: 8 yet her treacherous *s* Judah did
3:10 for all this her treacherous *s*
22:18 my *s*!' They shall not lament
Ezek 16:45 and you are the *s* of your
16:46 Your elder *s* is Samaria, who
16:46 and your younger *s*, who
16:48 neither your *s* Sodom nor her
16:49 this was the iniquity of your *s*
16:56 For your *s* Sodom was not a
22:11 another in you violates his *s*,
23: 4 the elder and Oholibah her *s*;
23:11 Now although her *s* Oholibah saw
23:18 had alienated Myself from her *s*.
23:31 walked in the way of your *s*;
23:33 The cup of your *s* Samaria.
44:25 for brother or unmarried *s* may
Mt 12:50 in heaven is My brother and *s*
Mk 3:35 of God is My brother and My *s*
Lk 10:39 And she had a *s* called Mary, who
10:40 do You not care that my *s* has
Jn 11: 1 the town of Mary and her *s*
11: 5 Jesus loved Martha and her *s*
11:28 and secretly called Mary her *s*,
11:39 the *s* of him who was dead, said
19:25 His mother, and His mother's *s*,
Rom 16: 1 I commend to you Phoebe our *s*,
16:15 and Julia, Nereus and his *s*,
1 Cor 7:15 a brother or a *s* is not under
Jas 2:15 If a brother or *s* is naked and
2 Jn 13 The children of your elect *s*

SISTER-IN-LAW (2/1) SISTER

Ruth 1:15 your *s* has gone back to her
1:15 her gods; return after your *s*.

SISTER'S (6/6)

Gen 24:30 bracelets on his *s* wrists,
29:13 about Jacob his *s* son,
Lev 20:17 uncovered his *s* nakedness.
Ezek 23:11 than her *s* harlotry.
23:32 You shall drink of your *s* cup,
Acts 23:16 So when Paul's *s* son heard of

SISTERS (19/18) SISTER

Josh 2:13 my mother, my brothers, my *s*,
1 Chr 2:16 Now their *s* were Zeruiah and
Job 1: 4 send and invite their three *s*
42:11 all his brothers, all his *s*,
Ezek 16:45 you are the sister of your *s*,
16:51 and have justified your *s* by
16:52 "You who judged your *s*,
16:52 because you justified your *s*.
16:55 'When your *s*, Sodom and her
16:61 your older and your younger *s*;
Hos 2: 1 'My people,' And to your *s*,
Mt 13:56 'And His *s*, are they not
19:29 left houses or brothers or *s*
Mk 6: 3 And are not His *s* here with
10:29 left house or brothers or *s* or
10:30 houses and brothers and *s* and
Lk 14:26 and children, brothers and *s*,
Jn 11: 3 Therefore the *s* sent to Him,
1 Tim 5: 2 women as mothers, younger as *s*,

SISTRUMS (1/1)

2 Sam 6: 5 on tambourines, on *s*,

SIT (122/119) SAT, SITS, SITTING

Gen 27:19 *s* and eat of my game, that your
Ex 18:14 the people? Why do you alone *s*,
Num 32: 6 brethren go to war while you *s*
Deut 6: 7 shall talk of them when you *s*
11:19 speaking of them when you *s* in
23:13 and when you *s* down outside,
33: 3 They *s* down at Your feet;
Judg 4: 5 And she would *s* under the palm
5:10 Who *s* in judges' attire, And
5:16 Why did you *s* among the
Ruth 3:18 *S* still, my daughter, until you
4: 1 aside, friend, *s* down here."
4: 2 and said, "*S* down here."
1 Sam 9:22 and had them *s* in the place of
16:11 For we will not *s* down till he
20: 5 and I should not fail to *s* with
1 Ki 1:13 and he shall *s* on my throne"?
1:17 and he shall *s* on my throne.'
1:20 should tell them who will *s* on
1:24 and he shall *s* on my throne'?
1:27 told your servant who should *s*
1:30 and he shall *s* on my throne in
1:35 and he shall come and *s* on my
1:48 who has given one to *s* on my
3: 6 You have given him a son to *s*
8:20 and *s* on the throne of Israel,
8:25 shall not fail to have a man *s*
2 Ki 7: 4 And if we *s* here, we die also.
10:30 your sons shall *s* on the throne
15:12 Your sons shall *s* on the throne
18:27 and not to the men who *s* on the
1 Chr 28: 5 has chosen my son Solomon to *s*
2 Chr 6:10 and *s* on the throne of Israel,
6:16 shall not fail to have a man *s*
Ps 26: 5 And will not *s* with the
50:20 You *s* and speak against your
69:12 Those who *s* in the gate speak
110: 1 *S* at My right hand, Till I make
119:23 Princes also *s* and speak
127: 2 To *s* up late, To eat the
132:12 Their sons also shall *s* upon
Prov 23: 1 When you *s* down to eat with a
Eccl 10: 6 While the rich *s* in a lowly
Isa 3:26 she being desolate shall *s* on
14:13 I will also *s* on the mount of
16: 5 And One will *s* on it in truth,
36:12 and not to the men who *s* on the
42: 7 Those who *s* in darkness from
47: 1 'Come down and *s* in the dust,
47: 1 *S* on the ground without a
47: 5 *S* in silence, and go into
47: 8 I shall not *s* as a widow,
47:14 Nor a fire to *s* before!
52: 2 *S* down, O Jerusalem!
65: 4 Who *s* among the graves, And
Jer 8:14 'Why do we *s* still?
13:13 even the kings who *s* on David's
13:18 *S* down, For your rule shall
15:17 I did not *s* in the assembly of
16: 8 into the house of feasting to *s*
22: 2 you who *s* on the throne of
22: 4 kings who *s* on the throne of
33:17 shall never lack a man to *s* on
36:15 *S* down now, and read it in our
36:30 He shall have no one to *s* on the
48:18 And *s* in thirst; For the
Lam 2:10 of the daughter of Zion *S* on
3:28 Let him *s* alone and keep
Ezek 26:16 they will *s* on the ground,
28: 2 I *s* in the seat of gods, In
33:31 they *s* before you as My
44: 3 he may *s* in it to eat bread
Joel 3:12 For there I will *s* to judge
Mic 4: 4 But everyone shall *s* under his
7: 8 When I *s* in darkness, The
Zech 3: 8 You and your companions who *s*
6:13 And shall *s* and rule on His
8: 4 men and old women shall again *s*
Mal 3: 3 He will *s* as a refiner and a
Mt 8:11 and *s* down with Abraham, Isaac,
14:19 commanded the multitudes to *s*
15:35 He commanded the multitude to *s*
19:28 have followed Me will also *s*
20:21 these two sons of mine may *s*,
20:23 but to *s* on My right hand and
22:44 *S* at My right hand, Till
23: 2 scribes and the Pharisees *s* in
25:31 then He will *s* on the throne of
26:36 *S* here while I go and pray over
Mk 6:39 them to make them all *s* down
8: 6 He commanded the multitude to *s*
10:37 Him, "Grant us that we may *s*,
10:40 but to *s* on My right hand and on
12:36 *S* at My right hand, Till
14:32 *S* here while I pray."
Lk 1:79 To give light to those who *s* in
9:14 Make them *s* down in groups of
9:15 and made them all *s* down.
12:37 gird himself and have them *s*
13:29 and *s* down in the kingdom of
14: 8 do not *s* down in the best
14:10 go and *s* down in the lowest
14:10 in the presence of those who *s*
14:28 does not *s* down first and count
14:31 does not *s* down first and
16: 6 and *s* down quickly and write
17: 7 Come at once and *s* down to eat'?
20:42 *S* at My right hand,
22:30 and *s* on thrones judging the
22:69 the Son of Man will *s* on the
Jn 6:10 'Make the people *s* down."
Acts 2:30 would raise up the Christ to *s*
2:34 *S* at My right hand,
8:31 asked Philip to come up and *s*
23: 3 For you *s* to judge me
Eph 2: 6 and made us *s* together in the
Heb 1:13 *S* at My right hand, Till
Jas 2: 3 You *s* here in a good place,"
2: 3 *S* here at my footstool,"
Rev 3:21 who overcomes I will grant to *s*
18: 7 I *s* as queen, and am no widow,
19:18 of horses and of those who *s*

SITE (3/2)

Ezra 5:15 carry them to the temple *s*
5:15 God be rebuilt on its former *s*.
6: 7 this house of God on its *s*.

SITES (1/1)

2 Chr 33:19 and the *s* where he built high

SITH (KJV) See SINCE

SITNAH (1/1)

Gen 26:21 So he called its name *S*.

SITS (36/35) SIT

Ex 11: 5 the firstborn of Pharaoh who *s*
Lev 15: 4 and everything on which he *s*
15: 6 He who *s* on anything on which he
15:20 also everything that she *s* on
15:23 or on anything on which she *s*,
15:26 and whatever she *s* on shall be
Deut 17:18 when he *s* on the throne of his
1 Ki 1:46 Also Solomon *s* on the throne of
Esth 6:10 so for Mordecai the Jew who *s*
Ps 1: 1 Nor *s* in the seat of the
2: 4 He who *s* in the heavens shall
10: 8 He *s* in the lurking places of
29:10 And the LORD *s* as King
47: 8 God *s* on His holy throne.
Prov 9:14 For she *s* at the door of her
20: 8 A king who *s* on the throne of
31:23 When he *s* among the elders of
Isa 28: 6 spirit of justice to him who *s*
40:22 It is He who *s* above the
Jer 29:16 concerning the king who *s* on
Lam 1: 1 How lonely *s* the city That
Mt 19:28 when the Son of Man *s* on the
23:22 throne of God and by Him who *s*
Lk 22:27 he who *s* at the table, or he
22:27 Is it not he who *s* at the
1 Cor 14:30 is revealed to another who *s*
2 Th 2: 4 so that he *s* as God in the
Rev 4: 9 honor and thanks to Him who *s*
4:10 fall down before Him who *s* on
5:13 and power Be to Him who *s* on
6:16 us from the face of Him who *s*
7:10 belongs to our God who *s* on
7:15 And He who *s* on the throne will
17: 1 of the great harlot who *s* on
17: 9 mountains on which the woman *s*.
17:15 you saw, where the harlot *s*,

SITTING (64/63) SIT

Gen 18: 1 as he was *s* in the tent door in
19: 1 and Lot was *s* in the gate of
Deut 22: 6 with the mother *s* on the young
Judg 3:20 (now he was *s* upstairs in his
13: 9 as she was *s* in the field;

S

1 Sam 1: 9 Now Eli the priest was *s* on the
4:13 *s* on a seat by the wayside
14: 2 And Saul was *s* in the outskirts
2 Sam 18:24 Now David was *s* between the two
19: 8 is the king, *s* in the gate."
1 Ki 13:14 and found him *s* under an oak.
22:19 I saw the LORD *s* on His
2 Ki 1: 9 *s* on the top of a hill.
4:38 prophets were *s* before him;
6:32 But Elisha was *s* in his house,
6:32 and the elders were *s* with him.
7: 3 Why are we *s* here until we die?
9: 5 the captains of the army *s*;
2 Chr 18:18 I saw the LORD *s* on His
Neh 2: 6 (the queen also *s* beside him),
Esth 5:13 as I see Mordecai the Jew *s* at
Ps 139: 2 You know my *s* down and my
Isa 6: 1 I saw the Lord *s* on a throne,
Jer 17:25 and princes *s* on the throne
22:30 *S* on the throne of David, And
36:12 there all the princes were *s*—
36:22 Now the king was *s* in the winter
38: 7 When the king was *s* at the Gate
Lam 3:63 Look at their *s* down and their
Ezek 8: 1 elders of Judah *s* before me,
8:14 women were *s* there weeping for
Zech 5: 7 and this is a woman *s* inside
Mt 9: 9 He saw a man named Matthew *s* at
11:16 It is like children *s* in the
20:30 two blind men *s* by the road,
21: 5 and *s* on a donkey, A
26:64 the Son of Man *s* at the right
27:19 While he was *s* on the judgment
27:36 *S* down, they kept watch over Him
27:61 *s* opposite the tomb.
Mk 2: 6 of the scribes were *s* there
2:14 Levi the son of Alphaeus *s* at
3:32 And a multitude was *s* around
5:15 *s* and clothed and in his right
14:62 you will see the Son of Man *s*
16: 5 clothed in a long white robe *s*
Lk 2:46 *s* in the midst of the teachers,
5:17 and teachers of the law *s* by,
5:27 *s* at the tax office.
7:32 They are like children *s* in the
8:35 *s* at the feet of Jesus, clothed
10:13 *s* in sackcloth and ashes.
Jn 6:11 disciples to those *s* down;
11:20 but Mary was *s* in the house.
12:15 *S* on a donkey's colt."
19:29 full of sour wine was *s* there;
20:12 she saw two angels in white *s*,
Acts 2: 2 whole house where they were *s*.
8:28 And *s* in his chariot, he was
14: 8 strength in his feet was *s*,
25: 6 *s* on the judgment seat, he
Col 3: 1 *s* at the right hand of God.
Rev 4: 4 I saw twenty-four elders *s*,
17: 3 And I saw a woman *s* on a

SITUATED (4/4)

Gen 47:11 And Joseph *s* his father and his
Ezek 27: 3 You who are *s* at the entrance of
46:19 and there a place was *s* at
Nah 3: 8 than No Amon That was *s* by

SITUATION (1/1)

2 Ki 2:19 the *s* of this city is

SIVAN (1/1)

Esth 8: 9 month, which is the month of *S*,

SIX (175/167) SIXTH

Gen 7: 6 Noah was *s* hundred years old
7:11 In the *s* hundredth year of
8:13 came to pass in the *s* hundred
30:20 I have borne him *s* sons."
31:41 and *s* years for your flock, and
Ex 12:37 about *s* hundred thousand men on
14: 7 he took *s* hundred choice
16:26 *S* days you shall gather it, but
20: 9 *S* days you shall labor and do
20:11 For in *s* days the LORD made
21: 2 he shall serve *s* years;
23:10 *S* years you shall sow your land
23:12 *S* days you shall do your work,
24:16 the cloud covered it *s* days.
25:32 And *s* branches shall come out of
25:33 and so for the *s* branches that
25:35 according to the *s* branches
26: 9 by themselves and *s* curtains
26:22 you shall make *s* boards.
28:10 *s* of their names on one stone,
28:10 and *s* names on the other stone,
31:15 Work shall be done for *s* days,
31:17 for in *s* days the LORD made
34:21 *S* days you shall work, but on
35: 2 Work shall be done for *s* days,
36:16 by themselves and *s* curtains
36:27 tabernacle he made *s* boards.
37:18 And *s* branches came out of its
37:19 and so for the *s* branches coming
37:21 according to the *s* branches
38:26 for *s* hundred and three
Lev 23: 3 *S* days shall work be done, but
24: 6 *s* in a row, on the pure gold
25: 3 *S* years you shall sow your
25: 3 and *s* years you shall prune
Num 1:25 forty-five thousand *s* hundred
1:27 were seventy-four thousand *s*
1:46 were numbered were *s* hundred
2: 4 at seventy-four thousand *s*
2:15 at forty-five thousand *s*
2:31 and fifty-seven thousand *s*
2:32 the forces were *s* hundred
3:28 eight thousand *s* hundred
3:34 were *s* thousand two hundred.
4:40 were two thousand *s* hundred and
7: 3 *s* covered carts and twelve
11:21 I am among are *s* hundred
26:41 were forty-five thousand *s*
26:51 *s* hundred and one thousand
31:32 was *s* hundred and seventy-five
31:37 of the sheep was *s* hundred
35: 6 you shall appoint *s* cities
35:13 you shall have *s* cities of
35:15 These *s* cities shall be for
Deut 5:13 *S* days you shall labor and do
15:12 to you and serves you *s* years,
15:18 servant in serving you *s* years.
16: 8 *S* days you shall eat unleavened
Josh 6: 3 This you shall do *s* days.
6:14 So they did *s* days.
15:59 *s* cities with their villages;
15:62 *s* cities with their villages.
Judg 3:31 who killed *s* hundred men of the
12: 7 judged Israel *s* years.
18:11 And *s* hundred men of the family
18:16 The *s* hundred men armed with
18:17 of the gate with the *s* hundred
20:47 But *s* hundred men turned and
Ruth 3:15 he measured *s* ephahs of
3:17 These *s* ephahs of barley he
1 Sam 13: 5 and *s* thousand horsemen,
13:15 about *s* hundred men.
14: 2 were about *s* hundred men.
17: 4 whose height was *s* cubits and
17: 7 weighed *s* hundred shekels;
23:13 about *s* hundred, arose and
27: 2 over with the *s* hundred men
30: 9 he and the *s* hundred men who
2 Sam 2:11 was seven years and *s* months.
5: 5 seven years and *s* months,
6:13 of the LORD had gone *s* paces,
15:18 *s* hundred men who had followed
21:20 who had *s* fingers on each hand
21:20 on each hand and *s* toes on
1 Ki 6: 6 the middle was *s* cubits wide,
10:14 Solomon yearly was *s* hundred
10:16 *s* hundred shekels of gold went
10:19 The throne had *s* steps, and the
10:20 on each side of the *s* steps;
10:29 Egypt cost *s* hundred shekels
11:16 (because for *s* months Joab
16:23 *S* years he reigned in Tirzah.
2 Ki 5: 5 *s* thousand shekels of gold,
11: 3 house of the LORD for *s* years,
13:19 have struck five or *s* times;
15: 8 Israel in Samaria *s* months.
1 Chr 3: 4 These *s* were born to him in
3: 4 he reigned seven years and *s*
3:22 and Shaphat—*s* in all.
4:27 sixteen sons and *s* daughters;
7: 2 was twenty-two thousand *s*
8:38 Azel had *s* sons whose names
9: 6 *s* hundred and ninety.
9:44 And Azel had *s* sons whose names
12:24 *s* thousand eight hundred armed
12:26 Levi four thousand *s* hundred;
12:35 twenty-eight thousand *s*
20: 6 *s* on each hand and six on
20: 6 six on each hand and *s* on
21:25 So David gave Ornan *s* hundred
23: 4 *s* thousand were officers and
25: 3 Hashabiah, and Mattithiah, *s*,
26:17 On the east were *s* Levites, on
2 Chr 1:17 chariot for *s* hundred shekels
2: 2 and three thousand *s* hundred to
2:17 and fifty-three thousand *s*
2:18 and three thousand *s* hundred
3: 8 He overlaid it with *s* hundred
9:13 Solomon yearly was *s* hundred
9:15 *s* hundred shekels of hammered
9:18 The throne had *s* steps, with a
9:19 each side of the *s* steps;
22:12 the house of God for *s* years,
26:12 was two thousand *s* hundred.
29:33 things were *s* hundred bulls
35: 8 two thousand *s* hundred from
Ezra 2:10 *s* hundred and forty-two;
2:11 *s* hundred and twenty-three;
2:13 *s* hundred and sixty-six;
2:26 *s* hundred and twenty-one;
2:35 three thousand *s* hundred and
2:60 *s* hundred and fifty-two;
2:67 and their donkeys *s* thousand
8:26 into their hand *s* hundred
Neh 5:18 one ox and *s* choice sheep.
7:10 *s* hundred and fifty-two;
7:15 *s* hundred and forty-eight;
7:16 *s* hundred and twenty-eight;
7:18 *s* hundred and sixty-seven;
7:20 *s* hundred and fifty-five;
7:30 *s* hundred and twenty-one;
7:62 *s* hundred and forty-two;
7:69 and donkeys *s* thousand seven
Esth 2:12 *s* months with oil of myrrh, and
2:12 and *s* months with perfumes and
Job 5:19 deliver you in *s* troubles,
42:12 *s* thousand camels, one thousand
Prov 6:16 These *s* things the LORD
Isa 6: 2 each one had *s* wings: with two
Jer 34:14 he has served you *s* years,
52:30 were four thousand *s* hundred.
Ezek 9: 2 And suddenly *s* men came from the
40: 5 measuring rod *s* cubits long,
40:12 the gate chambers were *s*
40:12 on this side and *s* cubits
41: 1 *s* cubits wide on one side and
41: 1 wide on one side and *s* cubits
41: 3 *s* cubits high; and the width
41: 5 of the temple, *s* cubits.
41: 8 that is, *s* cubits high.
46: 1 be shut the *s* working days;
46: 4 Sabbath day shall be *s* lambs
46: 6 *s* lambs, and a ram; they shall
Dan 3: 1 and its width *s* cubits.
Mt 17: 1 Now after *s* days Jesus took
Mk 9: 2 Now after *s* days Jesus took
Lk 4:25 up three years and *s* months,
13:14 There are *s* days on which men
Jn 2: 6 were set there *s* waterpots
12: 1 *s* days before the Passover,
Acts 11:12 Moreover these *s* brethren
18:11 there a year and *s* months,
Jas 5:17 for three years and *s* months.
Rev 4: 8 each having *s* wings, were full
14:20 for one thousand *s* hundred

SIXSCORE (KJV) See HUNDRED (AND TWENTY)

SIXTEEN (21/21)

Gen 46:18 bore to Jacob: *s* persons.
Ex 26:25 *s* sockets—two sockets under each
36:30 *s* sockets of silver—two sockets
Num 31:40 The persons were *s* thousand, of
31:46 and *s* thousand persons—
31:52 was *s* thousand seven hundred
Josh 15:41 *s* cities with their villages;
19:22 *s* cities with their villages.
2 Ki 13:10 and reigned *s* years.
14:21 who was *s* years old, and made
15: 2 He was *s* years old when he
15:33 and he reigned *s* years in
16: 2 and he reigned *s* years in
1 Chr 4:27 Shimei had *s* sons and six
24: 4 the sons of Eleazar were *s*
2 Chr 13:21 sons and *s* daughters.
26: 1 who was *s* years old, and made
26: 3 Uzziah was *s* years old when he
27: 1 and he reigned *s* years in
27: 8 and he reigned *s* years in
28: 1 and he reigned *s* years in

SIXTEENTH (3/3)

1 Chr 24:14 to Bilgah, the *s* to Immer,
25:23 the *s* for Hananiah, his sons and
2 Chr 29:17 and on the *s* day of the first

SIXTH (42/40) SIX

Gen 1:31 and the morning were the *s* day.
30:19 again and bore Jacob a *s* son.
Ex 16: 5 And it shall be on the *s* day
16:22 on the *s* day, that they
16:29 He gives you on the *s* day
26: 9 double over the *s* curtain
Lev 25:21 on you in the *s* year,
Num 7:42 On the *s* day Eliasaph the son
29:29 On the *s* day present eight
Josh 19:32 The *s* lot came out to the
2 Sam 3: 5 and the *s*, Ithream,
2 Ki 18:10 In the *s* year of Hezekiah, that
1 Chr 2:15 Ozem the *s*, and David
3: 3 Shephatiah, by Abital; the *s*,
12:11 Attai the *s*, Eliel the
24: 9 the *s* to Mijamin,
25:13 the *s* for Bukkiah, his sons and
26: 3 Elam the fifth, Jehohanan the *s*,
26: 5 Ammiel the *s*, Issachar the
27: 9 The *s* captain for the sixth
27: 9 captain for the *s* month
Ezra 6:15 which was in the *s* year of the
Neh 3:30 the *s* son of Zalaph, repaired
Ezek 8: 1 came to pass in the *s* year,
8: 1 in the *s* month, on the fifth
46:14 a *s* of an ephah, and a third of
Hag 1: 1 in the *s* month, on the first
1:15 day of the *s* month, in the
Mt 20: 5 Again he went out about the *s*
27:45 Now from the *s* hour until the
Mk 15:33 Now when the *s* hour had come,
Lk 1:26 Now in the *s* month the angel
1:36 and this is now the *s* month for
23:44 Now it was about the *s* hour,
Jn 4: 6 It was about the *s* hour.
19:14 and about the *s* hour. And he
Acts 10: 9 to pray, about the *s* hour.
Rev 6:12 when He opened the *s* seal,
9:13 Then the *s* angel sounded: And I
9:14 saying to the *s* angel who had
16:12 Then the *s* angel poured out his
21:20 the *s* sardius, the seventh

SIXTY (42/38)

Gen 25:26 Isaac was *s* years old when she
Lev 27: 3 years old up to *s* years old,
27: 7 and if from *s* years old and

Num 7:88 twenty-four bulls, the rams *s*,
7:88 rams sixty, the male goats *s*,
7:88 the lambs in their first year *s*.
26:27 *s* thousand five hundred.
Deut 3: 4 *s* cities, all the region of
Josh 13:30 are in Bashan, *s* cities;
2 Sam 2:31 three hundred and *s* men who
1 Ki 4:13 *s* large cities with walls and
4:22 *s* kors of meal,
6: 2 its length was *s* cubits, its
2 Ki 25:19 and *s* men of the people of the
1 Chr 2:21 when he was *s* years old;
2:23 and its towns—*s* towns.)
5:18 thousand seven hundred and *s*
9:13 thousand seven hundred and *s*.
2 Chr 3: 3 The length was *s* cubits
11:21 wives and *s* concubines, and
11:21 sons and *s* daughters.
12: 3 *s* thousand horsemen, and people
Ezra 2: 9 of Zaccai, seven hundred and *s*;
2:64 thousand three hundred and *s*,
6: 3 its height *s* cubits and its
6: 3 and its width *s* cubits,
8:10 and with him one hundred and *s*
8:13 and with them *s* males;
Neh 7:14 of Zaccai, seven hundred and *s*;
7:66 thousand three hundred and *s*,
Song 3: 7 With *s* valiant men around it,
6: 8 There are *s* queens And eighty
Jer 52:25 and *s* men of the people of the
Ezek 40:14 *s* cubits high, and the court
Dan 3: 1 whose height was *s* cubits and
Mt 13: 8 some a hundredfold, some *s*,
13:23 some a hundredfold, some *s*,
Mk 4: 8 some thirtyfold, some *s*,
4:20 fruit: some thirtyfold, some *s*,
1 Tim 5: 9 Do not let a widow under *s* years
Rev 11: 3 one thousand two hundred and *s*
12: 6 one thousand two hundred and *s*

SIXTY-EIGHT (2/2)

1 Chr 16:38 Obed-Edom with his *s* brethren,
Neh 11: 6 hundred and *s* valiant men.

SIXTY-FIVE (5/5)

Gen 5:15 Mahalalel lived *s* years, and
5:21 Enoch lived *s* years, and begot
5:23 three hundred and *s* years.
Num 3:50 three hundred and *s* shekels,
Isa 7: 8 Within *s* years Ephraim will be

SIXTY-FOUR (2/2)

Num 26:25 *s* thousand three hundred.
26:43 were *s* thousand four hundred.

SIXTY-NINE (1/1)

Gen 5:27 were nine hundred and *s* years;

SIXTY-ONE (3/3)

Num 31:34 *s* thousand donkeys,
31:39 the LORD's tribute was *s*.
Ezra 2:69 work *s* thousand gold drachmas,

SIXTY-SEVEN (3/3)

Neh 7:18 of Adonikam, six hundred and *s*;
7:19 of Bigvai, two thousand and *s*;
7:72 and *s* priestly garments.

SIXTY-SIX (5/5)

Gen 46:26 were *s* persons in all.
Lev 12: 5 of her purification *s* days.
1 Ki 10:14 six hundred and *s* talents of
2 Chr 9:13 six hundred and *s* talents of
Ezra 2:13 of Adonikam, six hundred and *s*;

SIXTY-TWO (8/8)

Gen 5:18 Jared lived one hundred and *s*
5:20 Jared were nine hundred and *s*
Num 1:39 of Dan were *s* thousand
2:26 And his army was numbered at *s*
1 Chr 26: 8 the work: *s* of Obed-Edom.
Dan 5:31 being about *s* years old.
9:25 be seven weeks and *s* weeks;
9:26 And after the *s* weeks Messiah

SIZE (8/7)

Ex 36: 9 curtains were all the same *s*.
36:15 curtains were the same *s*.
1 Ki 6:25 cherubim were of the same *s*
7: 9 of costly stones cut to *s*,
7:11 were costly stones, hewn to *s*,
Ezek 40:10 the three were all the same *s*;
40:10 gateposts were of the same *s*
46:22 four corners were the same *s*.

SIZES (1/1)

1 Chr 23:29 all kinds of measures and *s*;

SKIES (7/7)

2 Sam 22:12 and thick clouds of the *s*.
Job 37:18 Him, have you spread out the *s*,
37:21 when it is bright in the *s*,
Ps 18:11 And thick clouds of the *s*.
77:17 The *s* sent out a sound;
Isa 45: 8 And let the *s* pour down
Jer 51: 9 and is lifted up to the *s*.

SKIFF (3/3)

Acts 27:16 we secured the *s* with
27:30 when they had let down the *s*
27:32 cut away the ropes of the *s*

SKILL (11/11) SKILLED, SKILLFUL

Ex 35:35 He has filled them with *s* to do
1 Ki 5: 6 is none among us who has *s* to
7:14 wisdom and understanding and *s*
2 Chr 2: 7 who has *s* to engrave with the
2: 8 know that your servants have *s*
Ps 137: 5 my right hand forget its *s*!
Eccl 2:21 with wisdom, knowledge, and *s*;
9:11 Nor favor to men of *s*;
Dan 1:17 God gave them knowledge and *s*
9:22 now come forth to give you *s*
Hos 13: 2 silver, according to their *s*;

SKILLED (3/3) SKILL

1 Chr 25: 1 And the number of the *s* men
2 Chr 2:14 *s* to work in gold and silver,
Ezra 7: 6 and he was a *s* scribe in the

SKILLFUL (22/20) GIFTED, SKILL, SKILLFULLY

Gen 25:27 And Esau was a *s* hunter, a man
1 Sam 16:16 to seek out a man who is a *s*
16:18 who is *s* in playing, a mighty
1 Chr 5:18 and *s* in war, who went to war.
15:22 the music, because he was *s*;
22:15 and all types of *s* men for
25: 7 of the LORD, all who were *s*,
2 Chr 2: 7 send me at once a man *s* to
2: 7 has skill to engrave with the *s*
2:13 And now I have sent a *s* man,
2:14 with your *s* men and with the
2:14 skillful men and with the *s*
26:15 invented by *s* men, to be on the
34:12 all of whom were *s* with
Eccl 4: 4 that for all toil and every *s*
Song 7: 1 The work of the hands of a *s*
Isa 3: 3 The counselor and the *s*
40:20 He seeks for himself a *s*
Jer 9:17 And send for *s* wailing women,
10: 9 They are all the work of *s*
Ezek 21:31 of brutal men who are *s* to
Am 5:16 And *s* lamenters to wailing.

SKILLFULLY (6/6) SKILLFUL

Ex 28: 4 a *s* woven tunic, a turban, and
28:39 You shall *s* weave the tunic of
Ps 33: 3 Play *s* with a shout of joy.
58: 5 charmers, Charming ever so *s*.
139:15 And *s* wrought in the lowest
Prov 30:28 The spider *s* grasps with its

SKILLFULNESS (1/1)

Ps 78:72 And guided them by the *s* of

SKIN (75/67) SKINS, SMOOTH-SKINNED

Gen 3:21 the LORD God made tunics of *s*,
21:14 and took bread and a *s* of
21:15 And the water in the *s* was used
21:19 And she went and filled the *s*
Ex 22:27 it is his garment for his *s*.
29:14 with its *s* and its offal, you
34:29 Moses did not know that the *s*
34:30 the *s* of his face shone, and
34:35 that the *s* of Moses' face
Lev 1: 6 And he shall *s* the burnt
7: 8 shall have for himself the *s*
11:32 item of wood or clothing or *s*
13: 2 When a man has on the *s* of his
13: 2 and it becomes on the *s* of his
13: 3 examine the sore on the *s* of
13: 3 to be deeper than the *s* of
13: 4 bright spot is white on the *s*
13: 4 to be deeper than the *s*,
13: 5 sore has not spread on the *s*,
13: 6 sore has not spread on the *s*,
13: 7 should at all spread over the *s*,
13: 8 scab has indeed spread on the *s*,
13:10 if the swelling on the *s* is
13:11 is an old leprosy on the *s*
13:12 breaks out all over the *s*,
13:12 the leprosy covers all the *s*
13:18 body develops a boil in the *s*,
13:20 appears deeper than the *s*,
13:21 it is not deeper than the *s*,
13:22 should at all spread over the *s*,
13:24 body receives a burn on its *s*
13:25 it appears deeper than the *s*,
13:26 it is not deeper than the *s*,
13:27 it has at all spread over the *s*,
13:28 and has not spread on the *s*,
13:30 if it appears deeper than the *s*,
13:31 not appear deeper than the *s*,
13:32 not appear deeper than the *s*,
13:34 scale has not spread over the *s*,
13:34 not appear deeper than the *s*,
13:35 at all spread over the *s* after
13:36 the scale has spread over the *s*,
13:38 has bright spots on the *s* of
13:39 if the bright spots on the *s*
13:39 white spot that grows on the *s*.
13:43 appearance of leprosy on the *s*
Num 6: 4 the grapevine, from seed to *s*.
1 Sam 1:24 and a *s* of wine, and brought
10: 3 and another carrying a *s* of
16:20 a *s* of wine, and a young goat,
2 Sam 16: 1 and a *s* of wine.
2 Chr 29:34 so that they could not *s* all
Job 2: 4 *S* for skin! Yes, all that a man
2: 4 LORD and said, "Skin for *s*!
7: 5 My *s* is cracked and breaks out
10:11 Clothe me with *s* and flesh,
16:15 have sewn sackcloth over my *s*,
18:13 It devours patches of his *s*;
19:20 My bone clings to my *s* and to
19:20 And I have escaped by the *s* of
19:26 And after my *s* is destroyed,
30:30 My *s* grows black and falls from
41: 7 Can you fill his *s* with
Ps 102: 5 My bones cling to my *s*.
Isa 18: 2 a nation tall and smooth of *s*,
18: 7 a people tall and smooth of *s*,
Jer 13:23 the Ethiopian change his *s* or
Lam 3: 4 He has aged my flesh and my *s*,
4: 8 Their *s* clings to their bones,
5:10 Our *s* is hot as an oven,
Ezek 16:10 gave you sandals of badger *s*;
37: 6 cover you with *s* and put breath
37: 8 and the *s* covered them over;
Mic 3: 2 Who strip the *s* from My
3: 3 Flay their *s* from them, Break

SKINNED (1/1) SKIN

2 Chr 35:11 while the Levites *s* the

SKINS (22/16) SKIN

Gen 27:16 And she put the *s* of the kids of
Ex 25: 5 ram *s* dyed red, badger skins,
25: 5 "ram skins dyed red, badger *s*,
26:14 also make a covering of ram *s*
26:14 and a covering of badger *s*
35: 7 ram *s* dyed red, badger skins,
35: 7 'ram skins dyed red, badger *s*,
35:23 red *s* of rams, and badger
35:23 red skins of rams, and badger *s*,
36:19 covering for the tent of ram *s*
36:19 and a covering of badger *s*
39:34 the covering of ram *s* dyed red,
39:34 red, the covering of badger *s*,
Lev 16:27 shall burn in the fire their *s*,
Num 4: 6 on it a covering of badger *s*,
4: 8 with a covering of badger *s*;
4:10 in a covering of badger *s*,
4:11 it with a covering of badger *s*;
4:12 with a covering of badger *s*,
4:14 on it a covering of badger *s*,
4:25 the covering of badger *s* that
1 Sam 25:18 two *s* of wine, five sheep

SKIP (1/1) SKIPPED, SKIPPING

Ps 29: 6 He makes them also *s* like a

SKIPPED (2/2) SKIP

Ps 114: 4 The mountains *s* like rams,
114: 6 that you *s* like rams?

SKIPPING (1/1) SKIP

Song 2: 8 mountains, *S* upon the hills.

SKIRT (1/1) SKIRTED, SKIRTS

Isa 47: 2 your veil, Take off the *s*,

SKIRTED (3/3)

Deut 2: 1 and we *s* Mount Seir for many
2: 3 You have *s* this mountain long
Mt 15:29 *s* the Sea of Galilee, and went

SKIRTS (6/6)

Gen 2:11 it is the one which *s* the
Jer 2:34 Also on your *s* is found The
13:22 of your iniquity Your *s* have
13:26 I will uncover your *s* over
Lam 1: 9 Her uncleanness is in her *s*;
Nah 3: 5 I will lift your *s* over your

SKULL (5/5)

Judg 9:53 head and crushed his *s*.
2 Ki 9:35 no more of her than the *s* and
Mt 27:33 that is to say, Place of a *S*,
Mk 15:22 is translated, Place of a *S*.
Jn 19:17 place called the Place of a *S*,

SKY (9/8)

1 Ki 18:45 in the meantime that the *s*
Ps 89:37 the faithful witness in the *s*.
Am 9: 6 who builds His layers in the *s*,
Mt 16: 2 for the *s* is red';
16: 3 for the *s* is red and
16: 3 to discern the face of the *s*,
Lk 12:56 can discern the face of the *s*
Heb 11:12 many as the stars of the *s* in
Rev 6:14 Then the *s* receded as a scroll

SLABS (1/1)
1 Chr 29: 2 and marble *s* in abundance.

SLACK (3/3) SLACKNESS
Deut 7:10 He will not be *s* with him who
Prov 10: 4 He who has a *s* hand becomes
2 Pe 3: 9 The Lord is not *s* concerning

SLACKEN (1/1)
2 Ki 4:24 do not *s* the pace for me unless

SLACKNESS (1/1) SLACK
2 Pe 3: 9 His promise, as some count *s*,

SLAIN (106/97) SLAY
Gen 34:27 sons of Jacob came upon the *s*,
Lev 14:51 in the blood of the *s* bird
Num 19:16 field touches one who is *s* by
19:18 one who touched a bone, the *s*,
23:24 And drinks the blood of the *s*.
31:19 and whoever has touched any *s*,
Deut 21: 1 "If anyone is found *s*,
21: 2 the distance from the *s* man
21: 3 city nearest to the *s* man
21: 6 city nearest to the *s* man
32:42 With the blood of the *s* and
Josh 11: 6 I will deliver all of them *s*
Judg 15:16 jawbone of a donkey I have *s*
1 Sam 18: 7 Saul has *s* his thousands, And
21:11 Saul has *s* his thousands, And
29: 5 Saul has *s* his thousands, And
31: 1 and fell *s* on Mount Gilboa.
31: 8 Philistines came to strip the *s*,
2 Sam 1:19 The beauty of Israel is *s* on
1:22 From the blood of the *s*,
1:25 of the battle! Jonathan was *s*
1 Ki 11:15 army had gone up to bury the *s*,
2 Ki 11:20 for they had *s* Athaliah with
1 Chr 10: 1 and fell *s* on Mount Gilboa.
10: 8 Philistines came to strip the *s*,
2 Chr 13:17 choice men of Israel fell *s*.
23:21 for they had *s* Athaliah with
Job 39:30 And where the *s* are, there it
Ps 62: 3 You shall be *s*, all of you,
88: 5 Like the *s* who lie in the
89:10 in pieces, as one who is *s*;
Prov 7:26 And all who were *s* by her were
22:13 I shall be *s* in the
Isa 10: 4 they shall fall among the *s*.
14:19 the garment of those who are *s*,
14:20 And *s* your people.
22: 2 Your *s* men are not slain
22: 2 Your slain men are not *s*
26:21 And will no more cover her *s*.
27: 7 Or has He been *s* according to
27: 7 slaughter of those who were *s*
34: 3 Also their *s* shall be thrown
66:16 And the *s* of the LORD shall
Jer 9: 1 weep day and night For the *s*
14:18 those *s* with the sword! And if
18:21 Their young men be *s* By the
25:33 And at that day the *s* of the
41: 9 bodies of the men whom he had *s*,
41: 9 Nethaniah filled it with the *s*.
51: 4 Thus the *s* shall fall in the
51:47 And all her *s* shall fall in
51:49 Babylon has caused the *s* of
51:49 So at Babylon the *s* of all the
Lam 2: 4 He has *s* all who were
2:20 the priest and prophet be *s*
2:21 You have *s* them in the day of
3:43 You have *s* and not pitied.
4: 9 Those *s* by the sword are
Ezek 6: 4 will cast down your *s* men
6: 7 The *s* shall fall in your midst,
6:13 when their *s* are among their
9: 7 and fill the courts with the *s*.
11: 6 You have multiplied your *s* in
11: 6 filled its streets with the *s*.
11: 7 Your *s* whom you have laid in its
16:21 that you have *s* My children and
21:29 the *s* Whose day has come,
23:39 For after they had *s* their
26: 6 are in the fields shall be *s*
28: 8 shall die the death of the *s*
30: 4 When the *s* fall in Egypt, And
30:11 And fill the land with the *s*.
31:17 with those *s* by the sword;
31:18 with those *s* by the sword.
32:20 fall in the midst of those *s*
32:21 *s* by the sword.'
32:22 all around her, All of them *s*,
32:23 her grave, All of them *s*,
32:24 her grave, All of them *s*,
32:25 her bed in the midst of the *s*,
32:25 *s* by the sword; Though their
32:25 was put in the midst of the *s*.
32:26 *s* by the sword, Though they
32:28 And lie with those *s* by the
32:29 Are laid beside those *s* by
32:30 Who have gone down with the *s*
32:30 uncircumcised with those *s* by
32:31 *S* by the sword," Says the
32:32 uncircumcised With those *s*
35: 8 fill its mountains with the *s*;
35: 8 your ravines those who are *s*
37: 9 breath, and breathe on these *s*,
Dan 5:30 king of the Chaldeans, was *s*.
7:11 I watched till the beast was *s*,
11:26 and many shall fall down *s*.
Hos 6: 5 I have *s* them by the words of
Nah 3: 3 There is a multitude of *s*,
Zeph 2:12 You shall be *s* by My sword."
Acts 5:36 He was *s*, and all who obeyed
Heb 11:37 were *s* with the sword.
Rev 5: 6 a Lamb as though it had been *s*,
5: 9 For You were *s*, And have
5:12 Worthy is the Lamb who was *s* To
6: 9 souls of those who had been *s*
13: 8 the Book of Life of the Lamb *s*
18:24 and of all who were *s* on the

SLANDER (4/4) SLANDERED, SLANDERER, SLANDERERS, SLANDEROUSLY, SLANDERS
Ps 31:13 For I hear the *s* of many;
50:20 You *s* your own mother's son.
Prov 10:18 And whoever spreads *s* is a
Ezek 22: 9 In you are men who *s* to cause

SLANDERED (2/2)
2 Sam 19:27 And he has *s* your servant to my
Ezek 36: 3 up by the lips of talkers and *s*

SLANDERER (1/1)
Ps 140:11 Let not a *s* be established in

SLANDERERS (5/5) SLANDER
Jer 6:28 stubborn rebels, walking as *s*.
9: 4 every neighbor will walk with *s*.
1 Tim 3:11 wives must be reverent, not *s*,
2 Tim 3: 3 unloving, unforgiving, *s*,
Titus 2: 3 be reverent in behavior, not *s*,

SLANDEROUSLY (1/1)
Rom 3: 8 as we are *s* reported and as some

SLANDERS (1/1)
Ps 101: 5 Whoever secretly *s* his

SLANG (KJV) See SLUNG

SLAPS (1/1)
Mt 5:39 But whoever *s* you on your right

SLASH (1/1)
Hos 11: 6 And the sword shall *s* in his

SLAUGHTER (60/59) SLAUGHTERED
Gen 43:16 and *s* an animal and make ready;
Deut 12:15 you may *s* and eat meat within
12:21 then you may *s* from your herd
Josh 10:10 killed them with a great *s* at
10:20 them with a very great *s*,
Judg 11:33 Keramim, with a very great *s*.
15: 8 hip and thigh with a great *s*;
1 Sam 4:10 There was a very great *s*,
4:17 and there has been a great *s*
6:19 the people with a great *s*.
14:14 That first *s* which Jonathan and
14:30 not have been a much greater *s*
14:34 *s* them here, and eat; and do
17:57 as David returned from the *s* of
18: 6 David was returning from the *s*
2 Sam 1: 1 David had returned from the *s*
17: 9 There is a *s* among the people
18: 7 and a great *s* of twenty
1 Ki 20:21 the Syrians with a great *s*.
2 Chr 13:17 struck them with a great *s*;
25:14 after Amaziah came from the *s*
28: 5 who defeated him with a great *s*.
30:17 Levites had charge of the *s* of
35: 6 So *s* the Passover offerings,
Esth 9: 5 with *s* and destruction, and did
Ps 44:22 accounted as sheep for the *s*.
Prov 7:22 her, as an ox goes to the *s*,
24:11 back those stumbling to the *s*.
Isa 10:26 up a scourge for him like the *s*
14:21 Prepare *s* for his children
27: 7 been slain according to the *s*
30:25 In the day of the great *s*,
34: 2 has given them over to the *s*.
34: 6 And a great *s* in the land of
53: 7 He was led as a lamb to the *s*,
65:12 you shall all bow down to the *s*;
Jer 7:32 of Hinnom, but the Valley of *S*;
11:19 a docile lamb brought to the *s*;
12: 3 them out like sheep for the *s*,
12: 3 prepare them for the day of *s*.
19: 6 of Hinnom, but the Valley of *S*.
25:34 For the days of your *s* and
48:15 men have gone down to the *s*,
50:27 Let them go down to the *s*.
51:40 them down Like lambs to the *s*,
Ezek 21:10 Sharpened to make a dreadful *s*,
21:15 It is grasped for *s*:
21:22 battering rams, to call for a *s*,
21:28 is drawn, Polished for *s*,
26:15 when *s* is made in the midst of
34: 3 you *s* the fatlings, but you do
Hos 5: 2 are deeply involved in *s*,
Ob 9 of Esau May be cut off by *s*.
Zech 11: 4 my God, "Feed the flock for *s*,
11: 5 whose owners *s* them and feel no
11: 7 So I fed the flock for *s*,
Acts 8:32 led as a sheep to the *s*;
Rom 8:36 as sheep for the *s*.
Heb 7: 1 Abraham returning from the *s*
Jas 5: 5 your hearts as in a day of *s*.

SLAUGHTERED (17/17) SLAUGHTER
Num 11:22 Shall flocks and herds be *s* for
19: 3 and it shall be *s* before him;
Deut 28:31 Your ox shall be *s* before your
1 Sam 1:25 Then they *s* a bull, and brought
14:32 and *s* them on the ground;
14:34 and *s* it there.
1 Ki 19:21 and took a yoke of oxen and *s*
2 Ki 10: 7 they took the king's sons and *s*
2 Chr 30:15 Then they *s* the Passover lambs
35: 1 and they *s* the Passover lambs
35:11 And they *s* the Passover
Ezra 6:20 And they *s* the Passover lambs
Prov 9: 2 She has *s* her meat, She has
Lam 2:21 You have *s* and not pitied.
Ezek 40:41 eight tables on which they *s*
40:42 instruments with which they *s*
Acts 7:42 Did you offer Me *s* animals

SLAUGHTERS (1/1)
Ex 22: 1 and *s* it or sells it, he shall

SLAVE (33/31) SLAVERY, SLAVES
Gen 44:10 whom it is found shall be my *s*,
44:17 cup was found, he shall be my *s*.
44:33 instead of the lad as a *s* to
Ex 21: 7 his daughter to be a female *s*,
Lev 25:39 not compel him to serve as a *s*.
Deut 5:15 And remember that you were a *s*
15:15 remember that you were a *s* in
16:12 remember that you were a *s* in
23:15 give back to his master the *s*
24:18 remember that you were a *s* in
24:22 remember that you were a *s* in
Ps 105:17 was sold as a *s*.
Jer 2:14 Is he a homeborn *s*?
34: 9 set free his male and female *s*—
Lam 1: 1 the provinces Has become a *s*!
Mt 20:27 among you, let him be your *s*—
Mk 10:44 desires to be first shall be *s*
Jn 8:34 whoever commits sin is a *s* of
8:35 And a *s* does not abide in the
Acts 16:16 that a certain *s* girl possessed
1 Cor 7:21 Were you called while a *s*?
7:22 called in the Lord while a *s*
7:22 while free is Christ's *s*.
Gal 3:28 there is neither *s* nor free,
4: 1 does not differ at all from a *s*,
4: 7 you are no longer a *s* but a
Eph 6: 8 whether he is a *s* or free.
Col 3:11 *s* nor free, but Christ is all
Phm 1:16 no longer as a *s* but more than a
1:16 as a slave but more than a *s*—
Rev 6:15 every *s* and every free man, hid
13:16 rich and poor, free and *s*,
19:18 of all people, free and *s*,

SLAVERY (1/1)
Neh 5: 5 have been brought into *s*.

SLAVES (39/32) SLAVE
Gen 43:18 to take us as *s* with our
44: 9 and we also will be my lord's *s*.
44:16 here we are, my lord's *s*,
49:15 And became a band of *s*.
Ex 21: 7 shall not go out as the male *s*
Lev 25:42 they shall not be sold as *s*.
25:44 as for your male and female *s*
25:44 you may buy male and female *s*.
25:46 they shall be your permanent *s*.
26:13 that you should not be their *s*;
Deut 6:21 We were *s* of Pharaoh in Egypt,
28:68 enemies as male and female *s*,
Josh 9:23 you shall be freed from being *s*—
1 Ki 2:39 that two *s* of Shimei ran away
2:39 your *s* are in Gath!"
2:40 to Achish at Gath to seek his *s*.
2:40 Shimei went and brought his *s*
2 Ki 4: 1 to take my two sons to be his *s*.
2 Chr 28:10 to be your male and female *s*;
Ezra 9: 9 'For we were *s*. Yet our
Neh 5: 5 sons and our daughters to be *s*,
Esth 7: 4 been sold as male and female *s*,
Jer 34:10 set free his male and female *s*,
34:11 and made the male and female *s*
34:11 subjection as male and female *s*.
34:16 back his male and female *s*,
34:16 to be your male and female *s*.
Rom 6: 6 that we should no longer be *s*
6:16 whom you present yourselves *s*
6:16 you are that one's *s* whom you
6:17 that though you were *s* of sin,
6:18 you became *s* of righteousness.
6:19 presented your members as *s*
6:19 now present your members as *s*
6:20 For when you were *s* of sin, you
6:22 and having become *s* of God, you
1 Cor 7:23 do not become *s* of men.
12:13 whether *s* or free—and have all
2 Pe 2:19 they themselves are *s* of

SLAY (39/39) SLAIN, SLAYER, SLEW

Gen 18:25 to *s* the righteous with the
20: 4 will You *s* a righteous nation
22:10 hand and took the knife to *s*
Deut 27:25 the one who takes a bribe to *s*
2 Ki 11:15 and *s* with the sword whoever
2 Chr 23:14 and *s* with the sword whoever
Job 13:15 Though He *s* me, yet will I
20:16 The viper's tongue will *s* him.
Ps 34:21 Evil shall *s* the wicked, And
37:14 To *s* those who are of upright
37:32 And seeks to *s* him.
59:11 Do not *s* them, lest my people
94: 6 They *s* the widow and the
109:16 That he might even *s* the
139:19 that You would *s* the wicked,
Prov 1:32 away of the simple will *s* them,
Isa 11: 4 breath of His lips He shall *s*
14:30 And it will *s* your remnant.
27: 1 And He will *s* the reptile that
65:15 For the Lord GOD will *s* you,
Jer 5: 6 a lion from the forest shall *s*
15: 3 the LORD: "the sword to *s*,
18:23 is against me, to *s* me.
20: 4 them captive to Babylon and *s*
29:21 and he shall *s* them before your
33: 5 bodies of men whom I will *s* in
50:27 *S* all her bulls, Let them go
Ezek 9: 6 Utterly *s* old and young men,
23:47 they shall *s* their sons and
26: 8 He will *s* with the sword your
26:11 he will *s* your people by the
40:39 on which to *s* the burnt
44:11 they shall *s* the burnt offering
Hos 2: 3 And *s* her with thirst.
Am 2: 3 And *s* all its princes with
9: 1 I will *s* the last of them with
9: 4 And it shall *s* them. I will
Hab 1:17 And continue to *s* nations
Lk 19:27 and *s* them before me.'"

SLAYER (9/9) SLAY

Josh 20: 3 that the *s* who kills a person
20: 5 they shall not deliver the *s*
20: 6 Then the *s* may return and come
21:13 (a city of refuge for the *s*),
21:21 (a city of refuge for the *s*),
21:27 (a city of refuge for the *s*),
21:32 (a city of refuge for the *s*),
21:38 (a city of refuge for the *s*),
Ezek 21:11 be given into the hand of the *s*.

SLAYING (4/4)

Josh 8:24 Israel had made an end of *s*
10:20 of Israel made an end of *s*
Isa 22:13 *S* oxen and killing sheep,
57: 5 *S* the children in the valleys,

SLAYS (7/5)

Job 5: 2 And envy *s* a simple one.
9:23 If the scourge *s* suddenly, He
Isa 66: 3 bull is as if he *s* a man;
Ezek 21:14 It is the sword that *s*,
21:14 The sword that *s* the great
28: 9 say before him who *s* you,
28: 9 In the hand of him who *s* you.

SLEDGE (2/2)

Isa 28:27 not threshed with a threshing *s*,
41:15 make you into a new threshing *s*

SLEEK (1/1)

Jer 5:28 have grown fat, they are *s*;

SLEEP (73/65) SLEEPER, SLEEPING, SLEEPLESSNESS, SLEEPS, SLEPT

Gen 2:21 the LORD God caused a deep *s*
15:12 a deep *s* fell upon Abram;
28:11 he lay down in that place to *s*.
28:16 Then Jacob awoke from his *s* and
31:40 and my *s* departed from my eyes.
Ex 22:27 What will he *s* in? And it will
Deut 24:13 that he may *s* in his own
Judg 16:14 But he awoke from his *s*,
16:19 Then she lulled him to *s* on her
16:20 So he awoke from his *s*,
1 Sam 26:12 because a deep *s* from the LORD
Esth 6: 1 That night the king could not *s*.
Job 4:13 When deep *s* falls on men,
14:12 Nor be roused from their *s*.
33:15 When deep *s* falls upon men,
Ps 4: 8 both lie down in peace, and *s*;
13: 3 Lest I *s* the sleep of death;
13: 3 Lest I sleep the *s* of death;
44:23 Awake! Why do You *s*,
76: 5 They have sunk into their *s*;
76: 6 horse were cast into a dead *s*.
78:65 Then the Lord awoke as from *s*,
90: 5 a flood; They are like a *s*.
121: 4 Shall neither slumber nor *s*.
127: 2 For so He gives His beloved *s*.
132: 4 I will not give *s* to my eyes
Prov 3:24 you will lie down and your *s*
4:16 For they do not *s* unless they
4:16 And their *s* is taken away
6: 4 Give no *s* to your eyes, Nor
6: 9 When will you rise from your *s*?
6:10 A little *s*, a little
6:10 folding of the hands to *s*—
6:22 When you *s*, they will keep you;
19:15 casts one into a deep *s*,
20:13 Do not love *s*, lest you
24:33 A little *s*, a little
Eccl 5:12 The *s* of a laboring man is
5:12 rich will not permit him to *s*.
8:16 even though one sees no *s* day
Song 5: 2 I *s*, but my heart
Isa 5:27 them, No one will slumber or *s*;
14:18 *s* in glory, Everyone in his
29:10 on you The spirit of deep *s*,
Jer 31:26 and my *s* was sweet to me.
51:39 And *s* a perpetual sleep And
51:39 And sleep a perpetual *s* And
51:57 And they shall *s* a perpetual
51:57 they shall sleep a perpetual *s*
Ezek 34:25 safely in the wilderness and *s*
Dan 2: 1 was so troubled that his *s*
6:18 Also his *s* went from him.
8:18 I was in a deep *s* with my face
10: 9 of his words I was in a deep *s*
12: 2 And many of those who *s* in the
Zech 4: 1 man who is wakened out of his *s*.
Mt 1:24 Joseph, being aroused from *s*,
Mk 4:27 and should *s* by night and rise
Lk 9:32 with him were heavy with *s*;
22:46 He said to them, "Why do you *s*?
Jn 11:13 speaking about taking rest in *s*.
Acts 16:27 awaking from *s* and seeing the
20: 9 who was sinking into a deep *s*.
20: 9 sleep. He was overcome by *s*;
Rom 13:11 is high time to awake out of *s*;
1 Cor 11:30 and sick among you, and many *s*.
15:51 a mystery: We shall not all *s*,
Eph 5:14 He says: "Awake, you who *s*,
1 Th 4:14 bring with Him those who *s* in
5: 6 Therefore let us not *s*,
5: 7 For those who *s*, sleep at
5: 7 *s* at night, and those who get
5:10 us, that whether we wake or *s*,

SLEEPER (1/1) SLEEP

Jon 1: 6 to him, "What do you mean, *s*?

SLEEPERS (1/1)

Song 7: 9 Moving gently the lips of *s*.

SLEEPING (13/12) SLEEP

1 Sam 26: 7 and there Saul lay *s* within the
1 Ki 18:27 or perhaps he is *s* and must be
Isa 56:10 *S*, lying down, loving to
Mt 9:24 for the girl is not dead, but *s*.
26:45 Are you still *s* and resting?
Mk 5:39 The child is not dead, but *s*.
13:36 coming suddenly, he find you *s*.
14:37 Then He came and found them *s*,
14:37 to Peter, "Simon, are you *s*?
14:41 'Are you still *s* and resting?
Lk 8:52 she is not dead, but *s*."
22:45 He found them *s* from sorrow.
Acts 12: 6 him out, that night Peter was *s*,

SLEEPLESSNESS (2/2) SLEEP

2 Cor 6: 5 in tumults, in labors, in *s*,
11:27 in *s* often, in hunger and

SLEEPS (4/4) SLEEP

Prov 10: 5 He who *s* in harvest is a son
Hos 7: 6 Their baker *s* all night;
Jn 11:11 to them, "Our friend Lazarus *s*,
11:12 if he *s* he will get well."

SLEEVE (1/1)

Zech 8:23 the nations shall grasp the *s*

SLEEVES (1/1)

Ezek 13:18 sew magic charms on their *s*

SLEIGHT (KJV) See CRAFTINESS

SLEPT (9/9) SLEEP

Gen 2:21 sleep to fall on Adam, and he *s*;
41: 5 He *s* and dreamed a second time;
2 Sam 11: 9 But Uriah *s* at the door of the
1 Ki 3:20 side, while your maidservant *s*,
19: 5 Then as he lay and *s* under a
Ps 3: 5 I lay down and *s*;
Mt 13:25 'but while men *s*, his enemy
25: 5 they all slumbered and *s*.
28:13 and stole Him away while we *s*.

SLEW (6/6) SLAY

Gen 49: 6 For in their anger they *s* a
Ps 78:31 And *s* the stoutest of them,
78:34 When He *s* them, then they
135:10 defeated many nations And *s*
136:18 And *s* famous kings, For His
Ezek 23:10 And *s* her with the sword;

SLICED (1/1)

2 Ki 4:39 and came and *s* them into the

SLIDDEN (1/1)

Jer 8: 5 Why has this people *s* back,

SLIDE (1/1)

Ps 37:31 None of his steps shall *s*.

SLIGHTED (1/1)

Prov 12: 9 Better is the one who is *s*

SLIGHTLY (2/2)

Jer 6:14 healed the hurt of My people *s*,
8:11 of the daughter of My people *s*,

SLIMEPITS (KJV) See (ASPHALT) PITS

SLING (6/5)

Judg 20:16 every one could *s* a stone at a
1 Sam 17:40 and his *s* was in his hand.
17:50 over the Philistine with a *s*
25:29 of your enemies He shall *s* out,
25:29 as from the pocket of a *s*.
Prov 26: 8 one who binds a stone in a *s*

SLINGERS (1/1)

2 Ki 3:25 However the *s* surrounded and

SLINGS (1/1)

2 Chr 26:14 and *s* to cast stones.

SLINGSTONES (2/2)

Job 41:28 *S* become like stubble to him.
Zech 9:15 shall devour and subdue with *s*.

SLIP (7/7) SLIPPED, SLIPPERY, SLIPS

Deut 32:35 Their foot shall *s* in due
2 Sam 22:37 under me; So my feet did not *s*.
1 Ki 20:42 Because you have let *s* out of
Job 12: 5 ready for those whose feet *s*.
Ps 17: 5 That my footsteps may not *s*.
18:36 under me, So my feet did not *s*.
26: 1 in the LORD; I shall not *s*.

SLIPPED (2/2) SLIP

1 Sam 19:10 but he *s* away from Saul's
Ps 73: 2 My steps had nearly *s*.

SLIPPERY (3/3) SLIP

Ps 35: 6 Let their way be dark and *s*,
73:18 You set them in *s* places;
Jer 23:12 be to them Like *s* ways;

SLIPS (3/3) SLIP

Deut 19: 5 and the head *s* from the handle
Ps 38:16 over me, Lest, when my foot *s*,
94:18 If I say, "My foot *s*,

SLOOPS (1/1)

Isa 2:16 And upon all the beautiful *s*.

SLOPE (2/2)

Num 21:15 And the *s* of the brooks That
Josh 15: 8 of Hinnom to the southern *s* of

SLOPES (6/6)

Deut 3:17 below the *s* of Pisgah.
4:49 below the *s* of Pisgah.
Josh 10:40 lowland and the wilderness *s*,
12: 3 and southward below the *s* of
12: 8 in the Jordan plain, in the *s*,
13:20 the *s* of Pisgah, and Beth

SLOTHFUL (1/1) LAZY

Prov 18: 9 He who is *s* in his work Is a

SLOW (15/13)

Ex 4:10 but I am *s* of speech and slow
4:10 but I am slow of speech and *s*
Neh 9:17 *S* to anger, Abundant in
Ps 103: 8 *S* to anger, and abounding in
145: 8 *S* to anger and great in mercy.
Prov 14:29 He who is *s* to wrath has
15:18 But he who is *s* to anger
16:32 He who is *s* to anger is
19:11 of a man makes him *s* to anger,
Joel 2:13 *S* to anger, and of great
Jon 4: 2 *s* to anger and abundant in
Nah 1: 3 The LORD is *s* to anger and
Lk 24:25 and *s* of heart to believe in
Jas 1:19 *s* to speak, slow to wrath;
1:19 to speak, *s* to wrath;

SLOWLY (2/2)

Gen 33:14 I will lead on *s* at a pace

Acts 27: 7 When we had sailed *s* many days,

SLUGGARD (2/2) LAZY

Prov 6: 6 Go to the ant, you *s*!
6: 9 How long will you slumber, O *s*?

SLUGGISH (1/1)

Heb 6:12 that you do not become *s*,

SLUMBER (11/11) SLUMBERED

Ps 121: 3 He who keeps you will not *s*.
121: 4 keeps Israel Shall neither *s*
132: 4 Or *s* to my eyelids,
Prov 6: 4 Nor *s* to your eyelids.
6: 9 How long will you *s*,
6:10 A little sleep, a little *s*,
24:33 A little sleep, a little *s*,
Isa 5:27 No one will *s* or sleep;
56:10 lying down, loving to *s*.
Nah 3:18 Your shepherds *s*,
2 Pe 2: 3 their destruction does not *s*.

SLUMBERED (1/1) SLUMBER

Mt 25: 5 they all *s* and slept.

SLUMBERING (1/1)

Job 33:15 While *s* on their beds,

SLUNG (1/1)

1 Sam 17:49 and he *s* it and struck the

SMALL (87/87) SMALLER, SMALLEST

Gen 19:11 both *s* and great, so that they
30:15 Is it a *s* matter that you have
Ex 12: 4 And if the household is too *s*
16:14 was a *s* round substance, as
18:22 but every *s* matter they
18:26 but they judged every *s* case
Num 16: 9 Is it a *s* thing to you that
16:13 Is it a *s* thing that you have
26:54 and to a *s* tribe you shall
32:41 went and took its *s* towns,
Deut 1:17 you shall hear the *s* as well as
9:21 it and ground it very *s*,
25:14 measures, a large and a *s*.
1 Sam 5: 9 both *s* and great, and tumors
20: 2 do nothing either great or *s*
30: 2 from *s* to great; they did not
30:19 either *s* or great, sons or
2 Sam 7:19 And yet this was a *s* thing in
17:13 until there is not one *s* stone
1 Ki 2:20 I desire one *s* petition of you;
8:64 before the LORD was too *s* to
17:13 but make me a *s* cake from it
18:44 as *s* as a man's hand, rising
19:12 the fire a still *s* voice.
22:31 Fight with no one *s* or great,
2 Ki 4:10 let us make a *s* upper room on
6: 1 we dwell with you is too *s* for
23: 2 the people, both *s* and great.
25:26 *s* and great, and the captains
1 Chr 17:17 And yet this was a *s* thing in
25: 8 the *s* as well as the great, the
26:13 the *s* as well as the great,
2 Chr 15:13 whether *s* or great, whether man
18:30 Fight with no one *s* or great,
23: 9 and the large and *s* shields
24:24 of the Syrians came with a *s*
31:15 to the great as well as the *s*.
34:30 and all the people, great and *s*.
36:18 the house of God, great and *s*,
Neh 9:32 not let all the trouble seem *s*
Esth 1: 5 the citadel, from great to *s*,
1:20 husbands, both great and *s*.
Job 3:19 The *s* and great are there, And
8: 7 Though your beginning was *s*,
15:11 the consolations of God too *s*
26:14 And how *s* a whisper we hear of
Ps 104:25 Living things both *s* and
115:13 Both *s* and great.
119:141 I am *s* and despised, Yet I
Prov 24:10 adversity, Your strength is *s*.
Isa 1: 9 left to us a very *s* remnant,
7:13 Is it a *s* thing for you to
16:14 the remnant will be very *s*
22:24 all vessels of *s* quantity, from
40:15 And are counted as the *s* dust
41:15 the mountains and beat them *s*,
49: 6 It is too *s* a thing that You
49:19 Will even now be too *s* for the
49:20 The place is too *s* for me;
60:22 And a *s* one a strong nation.
Jer 16: 6 Both the great and the *s* shall
30:19 them, and they shall not be *s*.
44:28 Yet a *s* number who escape the
49:15 I will make you *s* among
Ezek 5: 3 You shall also take a *s* number
16:20 acts of harlotry a *s* matter,
Dan 11:23 up and become strong with a *s*
Am 7: 2 may stand, For he is *s*!"
7: 5 may stand, For he is *s*!"
8: 5 Making the ephah *s* and the
Ob 2 I will make you *s* among the
Zech 4:10 despised the day of *s* things?
Mk 3: 9 His disciples that a *s* boat
8: 7 They also had a few *s* fish;
Jn 6: 9 barley loaves and two *s* fish,
Acts 12:18 there was no *s* stir among the
15: 2 Barnabas had no *s* dissension
19:24 brought no *s* profit to the
26:22 witnessing both to *s* and great,
27:20 and no *s* tempest beat on us,
1 Cor 4: 3 But with me it is a very *s* thing
Jas 3: 4 turned by a very *s* rudder
Rev 11:18 *s* and great, And should
13:16 both *s* and great, rich and
19: 5 both *s* and great!"
19:18 both *s* and great."
20:12 *s* and great, standing before

SMALLER (7/6) SMALL

Num 26:54 you shall give a *s* inheritance.
26:56 between the larger and the *s*.
33:54 and to the *s* you shall give a
33:54 shall give a *s* inheritance;
35: 8 from the *s* you shall give few.
Ezek 43:14 from the *s* ledge to the larger
Mk 4:31 is *s* than all the seeds on

SMALLEST (3/3) SMALL

1 Sam 9:21 of the *s* of the tribes of
Am 9: 9 Yet not the *s* grain shall fall
1 Cor 6: 2 are you unworthy to judge the *s*

SMART (KJV) See SUFFER

SMELL (10/8) SMELLED, SMELLING

Gen 27:27 and he smelled the *s* of his
27:27 the *s* of my son Is like the
27:27 of my son Is like the *s* of a
Ex 30:38 to *s* it, he shall be cut off
Lev 26:31 and I will not *s* the fragrance
Deut 4:28 see nor hear nor eat nor *s*.
Ps 115: 6 they have, but they do not *s*;
Song 2:13 tender grapes Give a good *s*.
Isa 3:24 Instead of a sweet *s* there will
Dan 3:27 and the *s* of fire was not on

SMELLED (2/2) SMELL

Gen 8:21 And the LORD *s* a soothing
27:27 and he *s* the smell of his

SMELLING (1/1) SMELL

1 Cor 12:17 hearing, where would be the *s*?

SMELLS (1/1)

Job 39:25 He *s* the battle from

SMELTED (1/1)

Job 28: 2 And copper is *s* from ore.

SMELTER (1/1)

Jer 6:29 The *s* refines in vain, For

SMILE (3/3)

1 Sam 2: 1 I *s* at my enemies, Because I
Job 9:27 off my sad face and wear a *s*,
10: 3 And *s* on the counsel of the

SMITE (1/1)

Ex 8: 2 I will *s* all your territory

SMITHS (4/4)

2 Ki 24:14 and all the craftsmen and *s*.
24:16 thousand, and craftsmen and *s*,
Jer 24: 1 Judah with the craftsmen and *s*,
29: 2 and the *s* had departed from

SMITTEN (1/1)

Isa 53: 4 *S* by God, and afflicted.

SMOKE (45/39) SMOKING

Gen 19:28 the *s* of the land which went up
19:28 land which went up like the *s*
Ex 19:18 Sinai was completely in *s*,
19:18 Its *s* ascended like the smoke
19:18 Its smoke ascended like the *s*
Josh 8:20 the *s* of the city ascended to
8:21 taken the city and that the *s*
Judg 20:38 would make a great cloud of *s*
20:40 from the city in a column of *s*,
20:40 the whole city going up in *s*
2 Sam 22: 9 *S* went up from His nostrils,
Job 41:20 *S* goes out of his nostrils, As
Ps 18: 8 *S* went up from His nostrils,
37:20 Into *s* they shall vanish away.
68: 2 As *s* is driven away, So drive
74: 1 Why does Your anger *s* against
102: 3 my days are consumed like *s*,
104:32 touches the hills, and they *s*.
119:83 become like a wineskin in *s*,
144: 5 the mountains, and they shall *s*.
Prov 10:26 As vinegar to the teeth and *s*
Song 3: 6 wilderness Like pillars of *s*,
Isa 4: 5 a cloud and *s* by day and the
6: 4 and the house was filled with *s*.
9:18 shall mount up like rising *s*.
14:31 For *s* will come from the
34:10 Its *s* shall ascend forever.
51: 6 heavens will vanish away like *s*,
65: 5 These are *s* in My nostrils,
Hos 13: 3 a threshing floor And like *s*
Joel 2:30 and fire and pillars of *s*.
Nah 2:13 will burn your chariots in *s*,
Acts 2:19 and fire and vapor of *s*.
Rev 8: 4 And the *s* of the incense, with
9: 2 and *s* arose out of the pit like
9: 2 out of the pit like the *s* of a
9: 2 were darkened because of the *s*
9: 3 Then out of the *s* locusts came
9:17 of their mouths came fire, *s*,
9:18 by the fire and the *s* and the
14:11 And the *s* of their torment
15: 8 The temple was filled with *s*
18: 9 when they see the *s* of her
18:18 cried out when they saw the *s*
19: 3 Alleluia! Her *s* rises up forever

SMOKING (5/5) SMOKE

Gen 15:17 there appeared a *s* oven and a
Ex 20:18 the trumpet, and the mountain *s*;
Isa 7: 4 two stubs of *s* firebrands,
42: 3 And *s* flax He will not quench;
Mt 12:20 And *s* flax He will not

SMOOTH (11/11) SMOOTHER, SMOOTHLY, SMOOTH-SKINNED

Gen 27:16 on his hands and on the *s* part
1 Sam 17:40 chose for himself five *s* stones
Ps 27:11 And lead me in a *s* path,
Isa 18: 2 to a nation tall and *s* of
18: 7 From a people tall and *s* of
30:10 Speak to us *s* things, prophesy
40: 4 And the rough places *s*;
57: 6 Among the *s* stones of the
Jer 12: 6 Even though they speak *s* words
Lk 3: 5 And the rough ways *s*;
Rom 16:18 and by *s* words and flattering

SMOOTH-SKINNED (1/1) SKIN, SMOOTH

Gen 27:11 and I am a *s* man.

SMOOTHER (2/2) SMOOTH

Ps 55:21 words of his mouth were *s*
Prov 5: 3 And her mouth is *s* than oil;

SMOOTHLY (2/2) SMOOTH

Prov 23:31 cup, When it swirls around *s*;
Song 7: 9 The wine goes down *s* for

SMOOTHS (1/1)

Isa 41: 7 He who *s* with the hammer

SMYRNA (2/2)

Rev 1:11 are in Asia: to Ephesus, to *S*,
2: 8 to the angel of the church in *S*

SNAIL (1/1)

Ps 58: 8 Let them be like a *s* which

SNAKE (1/1)

Isa 34:15 There the arrow *s* shall make

SNAKES (1/1)

Mic 7:17 crawl from their holes like *s*

SNARE (46/44) SNARED, SNARES

Ex 10: 7 long shall this man be a *s*
23:33 it will surely be a *s* to you."
34:12 lest it be a *s* in your midst.
Deut 7:16 for that will be a *s* to you.
Judg 2: 3 and their gods shall be a *s* to
8:27 It became a *s* to Gideon and to
1 Sam 18:21 that she may be a *s* to him, and
28: 9 Why then do you lay a *s* for my
Job 5: 5 And a *s* snatches their
18: 8 feet, And he walks into a *s*.
18: 9 And a *s* lays hold of him.
40:24 one pierces his nose with a *s*.
41: 1 Or *s* his tongue with a line
Ps 69:22 Let their table become a *s*
91: 3 He shall deliver you from the *s*
106:36 Which became a *s* to them.
119:110 The wicked have laid a *s* for
124: 7 escaped as a bird from the *s*
124: 7 The *s* is broken, and we have
140: 5 The proud have hidden a *s* for
142: 3 They have secretly set a *s*
Prov 7:23 As a bird hastens to the *s*,
18: 7 And his lips are the *s* of his
20:25 It is a *s* for a man to devote
22:25 you learn his ways And set a *s*
29:25 The fear of man brings a *s*,
Eccl 9:12 net, Like birds caught in a *s*,
Isa 8:14 As a trap and a *s* to the
24:17 Fear and the pit and the *s*
24:18 pit Shall be caught in the *s*;

29:21 And lay a *s* for him who
Jer 48:43 Fear and the pit and the *s*
48:44 pit shall be caught in the *s*.
50:23 I have laid a *s* for you;
Lam 3:47 Fear and a *s* have come upon us,
Ezek 12:13 and he shall be caught in My *s*.
17:20 and he shall be taken in My *s*.
Hos 5: 1 Because you have been a *s* to
9: 8 the prophet is a fowler's *s*
Am 3: 5 Will a bird fall into a *s* on
3: 5 Will a *s* spring up from the
Lk 21:35 For it will come as a *s* on all
Rom 11: 9 their table become a *s*
1 Tim 3: 7 he fall into reproach and the *s*
6: 9 fall into temptation and a *s*,
2 Tim 2:26 senses and escape the *s* of

SNARED (8/8) SNARE

Deut 7:25 lest you be *s* by it; for it is
Ps 9:16 The wicked is *s* in the work of
Prov 6: 2 You are *s* by the words of your
29: 6 transgression an evil man is *s*,
Eccl 9:12 So the sons of men are *s* in
Isa 8:15 broken, Be *s* and taken."
28:13 and be broken And *s* and
42:22 All of them are *s* in holes,

SNARES (14/14) SNARE

Josh 23:13 But they shall be *s* and traps
2 Sam 22: 6 The *s* of death confronted me.
Job 22:10 Therefore *s* are all around
Ps 18: 5 The *s* of death confronted me.
38:12 also who seek my life lay *s*
64: 5 They talk of laying *s*
141: 9 Keep me from the *s* they have
Prov 13:14 To turn one away from the *s*
14:27 To turn one away from the *s*
22: 5 Thorns and *s* are in the way
Eccl 7:26 The woman whose heart is *s*
9:14 and built great *s* around it.
Jer 5:26 lie in wait as one who sets *s*;
18:22 And hidden *s* for my feet.

SNATCH (4/4) SNATCHES

Job 24: 9 Some *s* the fatherless from the
Isa 9:20 And he shall *s* on the right
Jn 10:28 neither shall anyone *s* them out
10:29 and no one is able to *s* them

SNATCHES (2/2) SNATCH

Job 5: 5 And a snare *s* their substance.
Mt 13:19 the wicked one comes and *s*

SNEER (1/1)

Mal 1:13 And you *s* at it," Says the

SNEERED (1/1)

Lk 23:35 But even the rulers with them *s*,

SNEERS (1/1)

Ps 10: 5 his enemies, he *s* at them.

SNEEZED (1/1)

2 Ki 4:35 then the child *s* seven times,

SNEEZINGS (1/1)

Job 41:18 His *s* flash forth light, And

SNIFFED (1/1)

Jer 14: 6 They *s* at the wind like

SNIFFS (1/1)

Jer 2:24 That *s* at the wind in her

SNORTING (2/2)

Job 39:20 His majestic *s* strikes terror.
Jer 8:16 The *s* of His horses was heard

SNOUT (1/1)

Prov 11:22 a ring of gold in a swine's *s*,

SNOW (21/21)

Ex 4: 6 his hand was leprous, like *s*.
Num 12:10 leprous, as white as *s*.
2 Ki 5:27 leprous, as white as *s*.
Job 6:16 And into which the *s*
24:19 drought and heat consume the *s*
37: 6 For He says to the *s*,
38:22 you entered the treasury of *s*,
Ps 51: 7 and I shall be whiter than *s*.
68:14 It was white as *s* in Zalmon.
147:16 He gives *s* like wool;
148: 8 Fire and hail, *s* and clouds;
Prov 25:13 Like the cold of *s* in time of
26: 1 As *s* in summer and rain in
31:21 She is not afraid of *s* for her
Isa 1:18 They shall be as white as *s*;
55:10 and the *s* from heaven, And do
Lam 4: 7 Nazirites were brighter than *s*
Dan 7: 9 His garment was white as *s*,
Mt 28: 3 and his clothing as white as *s*.
Mk 9: 3 exceedingly white, like *s*,
Rev 1:14 white like wool, as white as *s*,

SNOW WATER (2/2)

Job 9:30 If I wash myself with *s*,
Jer 18:14 Will a man leave the *s* of

SNOWY (2/2)

2 Sam 23:20 midst of a pit on a *s* day.
1 Chr 11:22 midst of a pit on a *s* day.

SNUFFDISHES (KJV) See WICK-TRIMMERS

SNUFFERS (KJV) See TRIMMERS

SO (1/1) See APPENDIX

2 Ki 17: 4 for he had sent messengers to *S*,

SO-CALLED (1/1)

1 Cor 8: 5 For even if there are *s* gods,

SOAKED (1/1)

Isa 34: 7 Their land shall be *s* with

SOAP (3/3)

Job 9:30 And cleanse my hands with *s*,
Jer 2:22 with lye, and use much *s*,
Mal 3: 2 fire And like launderer's *s*.

SOBER (6/6) SOBERLY, SOBER-MINDED

Deut 29:19 could be included with the *s*.
1 Th 5: 6 do, but let us watch and be *s*.
5: 8 let us who are of the day be *s*,
Titus 2: 2 that the older men be *s*,
1 Pe 1:13 up the loins of your mind, be *s*,
5: 8 Be *s*, be vigilant;

SOBER-MINDED (3/3) SOBER

1 Tim 3: 2 of one wife, temperate, *s*,
Titus 1: 8 a lover of what is good, *s*,
2: 6 exhort the young men to be *s*,

SOBERLY (2/2) SOBER

Rom 12: 3 ought to think, but to think *s*,
Titus 2:12 worldly lusts, we should live *s*,

SOBRIETY (KJV) See MODERATION, SELF-CONTROL

SOCHO (KJV) See SOCHOH

SOCHOH (7/6)

Josh 15:48 country: Shamir, Jattir, *S*,
1 Sam 17: 1 and were gathered together at *S*,
17: 1 they encamped between *S* and
1 Ki 4:10 to him belonged *S* and all the
1 Chr 4:18 of Gedor, Heber the father of *S*,
2 Chr 11: 7 Beth Zur, *S*, Adullam,
28:18 *S* with its villages, Timnah

SOCKET (6/4)

Gen 32:25 He touched the *s* of his hip;
32:25 and the *s* of Jacob's hip was
32:32 shrank, which is on the hip *s*,
32:32 because He touched the *s* of
Ex 38:27 talents, one talent for each *s*.
Job 31:22 Let my arm be torn from the *s*.

SOCKETS (47/38)

Ex 26:19 You shall make forty *s* of silver
26:19 two *s* under each of the boards
26:21 'and their forty *s* of silver:
26:21 two *s* under each of the boards.
26:25 be eight boards with their *s*
26:25 sockets of silver—sixteen *s*—
26:25 two *s* under each board.
26:32 upon four *s* of silver.
26:37 and you shall cast five *s* of
27:10 pillars and their twenty *s*
27:11 pillars and their twenty *s* of
27:12 ten pillars and their ten *s*.
27:14 three pillars and their three *s*.
27:15 three pillars and their three *s*.
27:16 have four pillars and four *s*.
27:17 be of silver and their *s* of
27:18 and its *s* of bronze.
35:11 bars, its pillars, and its *s*;
35:17 the court, its pillars, their *s*,
36:24 Forty *s* of silver he made to go
36:24 two *s* under each of the boards
36:26 and their forty *s* of silver:
36:26 two *s* under each of the boards.
36:30 were eight boards and their *s*—
36:30 sixteen *s* of silver—two sockets
36:30 two *s* under each of the boards.
36:36 and he cast four *s* of silver
36:38 but their five *s* were bronze.
38:10 for them, with twenty bronze *s*.
38:11 and their twenty bronze *s*.
38:12 ten pillars and their ten *s*.
38:14 three pillars and their three *s*,
38:15 three pillars and their three *s*.
38:17 The *s* for the pillars were
38:19 pillars with their four *s* of
38:27 of silver were cast the *s* of
38:27 one hundred *s* from the hundred
38:30 And with it he made the *s* for
38:31 the *s* for the court all around,
39:33 bars, its pillars, and its *s*;
39:40 court, its pillars and its *s*,
40:18 the tabernacle, fastened its *s*,
Num 3:36 its bars, its pillars, its *s*,
3:37 court all around, with their *s*,
4:31 its bars, its pillars, its *s*,
4:32 around the court with their *s*,
Zech 14:12 eyes shall dissolve in their *s*,

SOCOH (1/1)

Josh 15:35 Jarmuth, Adullam, *S*,

SOD, SODDEN (KJV) See BOILED, COOKED

SODA (1/1)

Prov 25:20 And like vinegar on *s*,

SODI (1/1)

Num 13:10 Zebulun, Gaddiel the son of *S*;

SODOM (49/48) SODOMITES

Gen 10:19 then as you go toward *S*,
13:10 (before the LORD destroyed *S*
13:12 his tent even as far as *S*.
13:13 But the men of *S* were
14: 2 made war with Bera king of *S*,
14: 8 And the king of *S*,
14:10 and the kings of *S* and Gomorrah
14:11 they took all the goods of *S*
14:12 brother's son who dwelt in *S*,
14:17 And the king of *S* went out to
14:21 Now the king of *S* said to
14:22 But Abram said to the king of *S*,
18:16 from there and looked toward *S*,
18:20 Because the outcry against *S* and
18:22 from there and went toward *S*,
18:26 If I find in *S* fifty righteous
19: 1 Now the two angels came to *S* in
19: 1 was sitting in the gate of *S*.
19: 4 men of the city, the men of *S*,
19:24 rained brimstone and fire on *S*
19:28 Then he looked toward *S* and
Deut 29:23 like the overthrow of *S* and
32:32 vine is of the vine of *S* And
Isa 1: 9 We would have become like *S*,
1:10 of the LORD, You rulers of *S*;
3: 9 they declare their sin as *S*;
13:19 be as when God overthrew *S* and
Jer 23:14 All of them are like *S* to Me,
49:18 As in the overthrow of *S* and
50:40 As God overthrew *S* and Gomorrah
Lam 4: 6 the punishment of the sin of *S*,
Ezek 16:46 is *S* and her daughters.
16:48 neither your sister *S* nor her
16:49 the iniquity of your sister *S*:
16:53 the captives of *S* and her
16:55 *S* and her daughters, return to
16:56 For your sister *S* was not a
Am 4:11 As God overthrew *S* and
Zeph 2: 9 "Surely Moab shall be like *S*,
Mt 10:15 tolerable for the land of *S*
11:23 done in you had been done in *S*,
11:24 tolerable for the land of *S* in
Mk 6:11 it will be more tolerable for *S*
Lk 10:12 tolerable in that Day for *S*
17:29 the day that Lot went out of *S*
Rom 9:29 would have become like *S*,
2 Pe 2: 6 and turning the cities of *S* and
Jude 7 as *S* and Gomorrah, and the
Rev 11: 8 which spiritually is called *S*

SODOMA (KJV) See SODOM

SODOMITE (KJV) See PERVERTED (ONE)

SODOMITES (2/2) SODOM

1 Cor 6: 9 nor homosexuals, nor *s*,
1 Tim 1:10 for fornicators, for *s*,

SOFT (5/4) SOFTLY

Ps 65:10 You make it *s* with showers,
Prov 15: 1 A *s* answer turns away wrath,
Mt 11: 8 A man clothed in *s* garments?
11: 8 those who wear *s* clothing are
Lk 7:25 A man clothed in *s* garments?

SOFTER (1/1)

Ps 55:21 His words were *s* than oil,

SOFTLY (5/5) SOFT

Judg 4:21 and went *s* to him and drove the

Ruth 3: 7 and she came *s*, uncovered his
Job 41: 3 Will he speak *s* to you?
Isa 8: 6 waters of Shiloah that flow *s*,
Acts 27:13 When the south wind blew *s*,

SOIL (5/5)

2 Chr 26:10 in Carmel, for he loved the *s*.
Job 14:19 as torrents wash away the *s*
Isa 28:24 Does he keep turning his *s* and
Ezek 17: 8 It was planted in good *s* by
26:12 and your *s* in the midst of the

SOJOURN (1/1) SOJOURNED, SOJOURNER, SOJOURNING

Ex 12:40 Now the *s* of the children of

SOJOURNED, SOJOURNETH, SOJOURNING (KJV) See DWELLS, DWELT, STAYED, STAYING

SOJOURNER (8/7) SOJOURN, SOJOURNERS

Ex 12:45 A *s* and a hired servant shall
Lev 25:35 him, like a stranger or a *s*,
25:40 As a hired servant and a *s* he
25:47 Now if a *s* or stranger close to
25:47 himself to the stranger or *s*
Num 35:15 and for the *s* among them, that
Job 31:32 (But no *s* had to lodge in the
Ps 39:12 I am a stranger with You, A *s*,

SOJOURNERS (5/5) SOJOURNER

Lev 25:23 for you are strangers and *s*
2 Sam 4: 3 fled to Gittaim and have been *s*
2 Chr 30:25 the *s* who came from the land of
Jer 35: 7 in the land where you are *s*.
1 Pe 2:11 I beg you as *s* and pilgrims,

SOLACE (KJV) See TAKE (OUR FILL)

SOLD (79/72) SELL

Gen 25:33 and *s* his birthright to Jacob.
31:15 For he has *s* us, and also
37:28 and *s* him to the Ishmaelites
37:36 Now the Midianites had *s* him in
41:56 all the storehouses and *s* to
42: 6 and it was he who *s* to all the
45: 4 whom you *s* into Egypt.
45: 5 with yourselves because you *s*
47:20 every man of the Egyptians *s*
Ex 22: 3 then he shall be *s* for his
Lev 25:23 The land shall not be *s*
25:25 and has *s* some of his
25:25 may redeem what his brother *s*.
25:27 to the man to whom he *s* it,
25:28 then what was *s* shall remain in
25:29 a whole year after it is *s*;
25:33 then the house that was *s* in
25:34 of their cities may not be *s*,
25:42 they shall not be *s* as slaves.
25:48 after he is *s* he may be redeemed
25:50 from the year that he was *s* to
27:20 or if he has *s* the field to
27:27 then it shall be *s* according to
27:28 shall be *s* or redeemed;
Deut 15:12 is *s* to you and serves you six
32:30 Unless their Rock had *s* them,
Judg 2:14 and He *s* them into the hands of
3: 8 and He *s* them into the hand of
4: 2 So the LORD *s* them into the
10: 7 and He *s* them into the hands of
Ruth 4: 3 *s* the piece of land which
1 Sam 12: 9 He *s* them into the hand of
1 Ki 21:20 because you have *s* yourself to
21:25 was no one like Ahab who *s*
2 Ki 6:25 it until a donkey's head was *s*
7: 1 of fine flour shall be *s*
7:16 So a seah of fine flour was *s*
7:18 shall be *s* tomorrow about this
17:17 and *s* themselves to do evil in
Neh 5: 8 our Jewish brethren who were *s*
5: 8 Or should they be *s* to us?"
13:16 and *s* them on the Sabbath to
Esth 7: 4 "For we have been *s*,
7: 4 Had we been *s* as male and
Ps 105:17 who was *s* as a slave.
Isa 50: 1 is it to whom I have *s* you?
50: 1 For your iniquities you have *s*
52: 3 You have *s* yourselves for
Jer 34:14 who has been *s* to him; and when
Ezek 7:13 not return to what has been *s*,
Joel 3: 3 And *s* a girl for wine, that
3: 6 of Jerusalem You have *s* to
3: 7 the place to which you have *s*
Mt 10:29 Are not two sparrows *s* for a
13:46 went and *s* all that he had and
18:25 master commanded that he be *s*,
21:12 out all those who bought and *s*
21:12 and the seats of those who *s*
26: 9 fragrant oil might have been *s*
Mk 11:15 out those who bought and *s* in
11:15 and the seats of those who *s*
14: 5 For it might have been *s* for
Lk 12: 6 Are not five sparrows *s* for two
17:28 they drank, they bought, they *s*,
19:45 out those who bought and *s* in
Jn 2:14 in the temple those who *s* oxen
2:16 And He said to those who *s*
12: 5 was this fragrant oil not *s*
Acts 2:45 and *s* their possessions and
4:34 of lands or houses *s* them,
4:34 of the things that were *s*,
4:37 *s* it, and brought the money
5: 1 his wife, *s* a possession.
5: 4 your own? And after it was *s*,
5: 8 Tell me whether you *s* the land
7: 9 envious, *s* Joseph into Egypt.
Rom 7:14 I am carnal, *s* under sin.
1 Cor 10:25 Eat whatever is *s* in the meat
Heb 12:16 who for one morsel of food *s*

SOLDERING (1/1)

Isa 41: 7 'It is ready for the *s*";

SOLDIER (7/7) SOLDIERS

Jn 19:23 to each *s* a part, and also the
Acts 10: 7 servants and a devout *s* from
28:16 to dwell by himself with the *s*
Phil 2:25 fellow worker, and fellow *s*,
2 Tim 2: 3 endure hardship as a good *s* of
2: 4 him who enlisted him as a *s*.
Phm 1: 2 Apphia, Archippus our fellow *s*,

SOLDIERS (35/34) SOLDIER

Judg 20: 2 four hundred thousand foot *s*
1 Sam 4:10 Israel thirty thousand foot *s*.
15: 4 two hundred thousand foot *s* and
2 Sam 8: 4 and twenty thousand foot *s*.
10: 6 of Zoba, twenty thousand foot *s*;
1 Ki 20:29 one hundred thousand foot *s*
2 Ki 13: 7 and ten thousand foot *s*;
1 Chr 18: 4 and twenty thousand foot *s*.
19:18 and forty thousand foot *s* of
2 Chr 25:13 But as for the *s* of the army
Ezra 8:22 of the king an escort of *s* and
Isa 15: 4 Therefore the armed *s* of Moab
Mt 8: 9 having *s* under me. And I say to
27:27 Then the *s* of the governor took
28:12 a large sum of money to the *s*,
Mk 15:16 Then the *s* led Him away into
Lk 3:14 Likewise the *s* asked him,
7: 8 authority, having *s* under me.
23:36 The *s* also mocked Him, coming
Jn 19: 2 And the *s* twisted a crown of
19:23 Then the *s*, when they had
19:24 Therefore the *s* did these
19:32 Then the *s* came and broke the
19:34 But one of the *s* pierced His
Acts 12: 4 him to four squads of *s* to
12: 6 with two chains between two *s*;
12:18 was no small stir among the *s*
21:32 He immediately took *s* and
21:32 saw the commander and the *s*,
21:35 he had to be carried by the *s*
23:10 commanded the *s* to go down and
23:23 saying, "Prepare two hundred *s*,
23:31 Then the *s*, as they were
27:31 said to the centurion and the *s*,
27:32 Then the *s* cut away the ropes of

SOLDIERS' (1/1)

Acts 27:42 And the *s* plan was to kill the

SOLE (9/9) SOLES

Gen 8: 9 no resting place for the *s* of
Deut 11:24 Every place on which the *s* of
28:35 and from the *s* of your foot to
28:56 would not venture to set the *s*
28:65 nor shall the *s* of your foot
Josh 1: 3 Every place that the *s* of your
2 Sam 14:25 From the *s* of his foot to the
Job 2: 7 with painful boils from the *s*
Isa 1: 6 From the *s* of the foot even to

SOLEMN (11/10) SOLEMNLY

Gen 50:10 great and very *s* lamentation.
Ex 12:42 It is a night of *s* observance
12:42 a *s* observance for all the
13:19 of Israel under *s* oath,
Lev 16:31 It is a sabbath of *s* rest for
23: 3 day is a Sabbath of *s* rest,
23:32 you a sabbath of *s* rest,
25: 4 shall be a sabbath of *s* rest
2 Ki 10:20 Proclaim a *s* assembly for
Ps 81: 3 on our *s* feast day.
Mal 2: 3 The refuse of your *s* feasts;

SOLEMNITIES, SOLEMNITY (KJV) See FEASTS, FESTIVAL

SOLEMNLY (3/3) SOLEMN

Gen 43: 3 The man *s* warned us, saying,
1 Sam 8: 9 you shall *s* forewarn them, and
Acts 28:23 explained and *s* testified

SOLES (11/10) SOLE

Josh 3:13 as soon as the *s* of the feet of
4:18 and the *s* of the priests' feet
1 Ki 5: 3 put his foes under the *s* of
2 Ki 19:24 And with the *s* of my feet I
Job 13:27 You set a limit for the *s* of
Isa 37:25 And with the *s* of my feet I
60:14 shall fall prostrate at the *s*
Ezek 1: 7 and the *s* of their feet were
1: 7 of their feet were like the *s*
43: 7 throne and the place of the *s*
Mal 4: 3 shall be ashes under the *s* of

SOLICITED (1/1)

Ezek 16:34 because no one *s* you to be a

SOLID (9/7)

2 Ki 25:15 the things of *s* gold and solid
25:15 the things of solid gold and *s*
Jer 52:19 whatever was *s* gold and
52:19 and whatever was *s* silver,
Zech 4: 2 is a lampstand of *s* gold
1 Cor 3: 2 milk and not with *s* food;
2 Tim 2:19 Nevertheless the *s* foundation of
Heb 5:12 need milk and not *s* food.
5:14 But *s* food belongs to those who

SOLITARILY (1/1)

Mic 7:14 Who dwell *s* in a woodland,

SOLITARY (2/2)

Ps 68: 6 God sets the *s* in families;
Mk 1:35 out and departed to a *s* place;

SOLOMON (284/256) JEDIDIAH, SOLOMON'S

2 Sam 5:14 Shammua, Shobab, Nathan, *S*,
12:24 a son, and he called his name *S*.
1 Ki 1:10 mighty men, or *S* his brother.
1:11 to Bathsheba the mother of *S*,
1:12 life and the life of your son *S*.
1:13 Assuredly your son *S* shall reign
1:17 Assuredly *S* your son shall reign
1:19 but *S* your servant he has not
1:21 that I and my son *S* will be
1:26 of Jehoiada, nor your servant *S*.
1:30 Assuredly *S* your son shall be
1:33 and have *S* my son ride on my
1:34 Long live King *S*!'
1:37 king, even so may He be with *S*,
1:38 Pelethites went down and had *S*
1:39 the tabernacle and anointed *S*.
1:39 Long live King *S*!"
1:43 Our lord King David has made *S*
1:46 Also *S* sits on the throne of the
1:47 May God make the name of *S*
1:50 Now Adonijah was afraid of *S*;
1:51 And it was told *S*,
1:51 Adonijah is afraid of King *S*;
1:51 Let King *S* swear to me today
1:52 Then *S* said, "If he proves
1:53 So King *S* sent them to bring him
1:53 and fell down before King *S*;
1:53 and *S* said to him, "Go to your
2: 1 and he charged *S* his son,
2:12 Then *S* sat on the throne of his
2:13 to Bathsheba the mother of *S*.
2:17 said, "Please speak to King *S*,
2:19 therefore went to King *S*,
2:22 And King *S* answered and said to
2:23 Then King *S* swore by the LORD,
2:25 So King *S* sent by the hand of
2:27 So *S* removed Abiathar from being
2:29 And King *S* was told, "Joab has
2:29 Then *S* sent Benaiah the son
2:41 And *S* was told that Shimei had
2:45 But King *S* shall be blessed,
2:46 established in the hand of *S*.
3: 1 Now *S* made a treaty with Pharaoh
3: 3 And *S* loved the LORD, walking
3: 4 *S* offered a thousand burnt
3: 5 Gibeon the LORD appeared to *S*
3: 6 And *S* said: "You have shown
3:10 that *S* had asked this thing.
3:15 Then *S* awoke; and indeed it had
4: 1 So King *S* was king over all
4: 7 And *S* had twelve governors over
4:11 had Taphath the daughter of *S*
4:15 Basemath the daughter of *S* as
4:21 So *S* reigned over all kingdoms
4:21 brought tribute and served *S*
4:25 as Beersheba, all the days of *S*.
4:26 *S* had forty thousand stalls of
4:27 provided food for King *S* and
4:29 And God gave *S* wisdom and
4:34 came to hear the wisdom of *S*.
5: 1 of Tyre sent his servants to *S*,
5: 2 Then *S* sent to Hiram, saying:
5: 7 when Hiram heard the words of *S*,
5: 8 Then Hiram sent to *S*,
5:10 Then Hiram gave *S* cedar and
5:11 And *S* gave Hiram twenty thousand
5:11 Thus *S* gave to Hiram year by
5:12 So the LORD gave *S* wisdom, as
5:12 was peace between Hiram and *S*,
5:13 Then King *S* raised up a labor

5:15 *S* had seventy thousand who
6: 2 Now the house which King *S* built
6:11 the word of the LORD came to *S*,
6:14 So *S* built the temple and
6:21 So *S* overlaid the inside of the
7: 1 But *S* took thirteen years to
7: 8 *S* also made a house like this
7:13 Now King *S* sent and brought
7:14 So he came to King *S* and did
7:40 that he was to do for King *S*
7:45 which Huram made for King *S*
7:47 And *S* did not weigh all the
7:48 Thus *S* had all the furnishings
7:51 So all the work that King *S* had
7:51 and *S* brought in the things
8: 1 Now *S* assembled the elders of
8: 1 to King *S* in Jerusalem, that
8: 2 of Israel assembled with King *S*
8: 5 Also King *S*, and all the
8:12 Then *S* spoke: "The LORD said
8:22 Then *S* stood before the altar
8:54 when *S* had finished praying all
8:63 And *S* offered a sacrifice of
8:65 At that time *S* held a feast, and
9: 1 when *S* had finished building
9: 2 that the LORD appeared to *S* the
9:10 when *S* had built the two
9:11 the king of Tyre had supplied *S*
9:11 that King *S* then gave Hiram
9:12 Tyre to see the cities which *S*
9:15 the labor force which King *S*
9:17 And *S* built Gezer, Lower Beth
9:19 all the storage cities that *S*
9:19 and whatever *S* desired to build
9:21 from these *S* raised forced
9:22 But of the children of Israel *S*
9:24 of David to her house which *S*
9:25 Now three times a year *S*
9:26 King *S* also built a fleet of
9:27 to work with the servants of *S*.
9:28 and brought it to King *S*.
10: 1 of Sheba heard of the fame of *S*
10: 2 and when she came to *S*,
10: 3 So *S* answered all her questions;
10: 4 had seen all the wisdom of *S*,
10:10 queen of Sheba gave to King *S*.
10:13 Now King *S* gave the queen of
10:13 besides what *S* had given her
10:14 weight of gold that came to *S*
10:16 And King *S* made two hundred
10:21 as nothing in the days of *S*.
10:23 So King *S* surpassed all the
10:24 earth sought the presence of *S*
10:26 And *S* gathered chariots and
10:28 Also *S* had horses imported from
11: 1 But King *S* loved many foreign
11: 2 *S* clung to these in love.
11: 4 when *S* was old, that his wives
11: 5 For *S* went after Ashtoreth the
11: 6 *S* did evil in the sight of the
11: 7 Then *S* built a high place for
11: 9 the LORD became angry with *S*,
11:11 Therefore the LORD said to *S*,
11:14 up an adversary against *S*,
11:25 of Israel all the days of *S*
11:27 *S* had built the Millo and
11:28 and *S*, seeing that the
11:31 kingdom out of the hand of *S*
11:40 *S* therefore sought to kill
11:40 in Egypt until the death of *S*.
11:41 Now the rest of the acts of *S*,
11:41 in the book of the acts of *S*?
11:42 And the period that *S* reigned in
11:43 Then *S* rested with his fathers,
12: 2 from the presence of King *S*
12: 6 who stood before his father *S*
12:21 to Rehoboam the son of *S*.
12:23 to Rehoboam the son of *S*,
14:21 And Rehoboam the son of *S*
14:26 all the gold shields which *S*
2 Ki 21: 7 had said to David and to *S* his
23:13 which *S* king of Israel had
24:13 the articles of gold which *S*
25:16 which *S* had made for the house
1 Chr 3: 5 Shimea, Shobab, Nathan, and *S*—
6:10 as priest in the temple that *S*
6:32 until *S* had built the house of
14: 4 Shammua, Shobab, Nathan, *S*,
18: 8 with which *S* made the bronze
22: 5 *S* my son is young and
22: 6 Then he called for his son *S*,
22: 7 And David said to *S*:
22: 9 His name shall be *S*, for I
22:17 the leaders of Israel to help *S*
23: 1 he made his son *S* king over
28: 5 sons) He has chosen my son *S*
28: 6 It is your son *S* who shall
28: 9 "As for you, my son *S*,
28:11 Then David gave his son *S* the
28:20 And David said to his son *S*,
29: 1 'My son *S*, whom alone God has
29:19 And give my son *S* a loyal heart
29:22 And they made *S* the son of
29:23 Then *S* sat on the throne of the
29:24 submitted themselves to King *S*.
29:25 So the LORD exalted *S*
29:28 and *S* his son reigned in his
2 Chr 1: 1 Now *S* the son of David was
1: 2 And *S* spoke to all Israel, to
1: 3 Then *S*, and all the assembly
1: 5 *S* and the assembly sought Him
1: 6 And *S* went up there to the
1: 7 that night God appeared to *S*,
1: 8 And *S* said to God: "You have
1:11 And God said to *S*:
1:13 So *S* came to Jerusalem from the
1:14 And *S* gathered chariots and
1:16 And *S* had horses imported from
2: 1 Then *S* determined to build a
2: 2 *S* selected seventy thousand men
2: 3 Then *S* sent to Hiram king of
2:11 in writing, which he sent to *S*:
2:17 Then *S* numbered all the aliens
3: 1 Now *S* began to build the house
3: 3 is the foundation which *S* laid
4:11 that he was to do for King *S*
4:16 of burnished bronze for King *S*
4:18 And *S* had all these articles
4:19 Thus *S* had all the furnishings
5: 1 So all the work that *S* had done
5: 1 and *S* brought in the things
5: 2 Now *S* assembled the elders of
5: 6 Also King *S*, and all the
6: 1 Then *S* spoke: "The LORD said
6:12 Then *S* stood before the altar
6:13 (for *S* had made a bronze
7: 1 When *S* had finished praying,
7: 5 King *S* offered a sacrifice of
7: 7 Furthermore *S* consecrated the
7: 7 the bronze altar which *S* had
7: 8 At that time *S* kept the feast
7:10 for *S*, and for His people
7:11 Thus *S* finished the house of the
7:11 and *S* successfully accomplished
7:12 Then the LORD appeared to *S* by
8: 1 in which *S* had built the house
8: 2 which Hiram had given to *S*,
8: 2 to Solomon, *S* built them;
8: 3 And *S* went to Hamath Zobah and
8: 6 all the storage cities that *S*
8: 6 and all that *S* desired to build
8: 8 from these *S* raised forced
8: 9 But *S* did not make the children
8:10 of the officials of King *S*:
8:11 Now *S* brought the daughter of
8:12 Then *S* offered burnt offerings
8:16 Now all the work of *S* was
8:17 Then *S* went to Ezion Geber and
8:18 went with the servants of *S* to
8:18 there, and brought it to King *S*.
9: 1 of Sheba heard of the fame of *S*,
9: 1 she came to Jerusalem to test *S*
9: 1 and when she came to *S*,
9: 2 So *S* answered all her questions;
9: 2 was nothing so difficult for *S*
9: 3 Sheba had seen the wisdom of *S*,
9: 9 queen of Sheba gave to King *S*.
9:10 of Hiram and the servants of *S*,
9:12 Now King *S* gave to the queen of
9:13 weight of gold that came to *S*
9:14 brought gold and silver to *S*.
9:15 And King *S* made two hundred
9:20 as nothing in the days of *S*.
9:22 So King *S* surpassed all the
9:23 earth sought the presence of *S*
9:25 *S* had four thousand stalls for
9:28 And they brought horses to *S*
9:29 Now the rest of the acts of *S*,
9:30 *S* reigned in Jerusalem over all
9:31 Then *S* rested with his fathers,
10: 2 from the presence of King *S*),
10: 6 who stood before his father *S*
11: 3 to Rehoboam the son of *S*,
11:17 and made Rehoboam the son of *S*
11:17 in the way of David and *S* for
12: 9 away the gold shields which *S*
13: 6 the servant of *S* the son of
13: 7 against Rehoboam the son of *S*,
30:26 for since the time of *S* the son
33: 7 God had said to David and to *S*
35: 3 holy ark in the house which *S*
35: 4 the written instruction of *S*
Neh 12:45 to the command of David and *S*
13:26 Did not *S* king of Israel sin by
Ps 72: A Psalm of *S*.
127: A Song of Ascents. Of *S*.
Prov 1: 1 The proverbs of *S* the son of
10: 1 The Proverbs of *S*:
25: 1 These also are proverbs of *S*
Song 1: 5 Kedar, Like the curtains of *S*.
3: 9 Of the wood of Lebanon *S* the
3:11 And see King *S* with the crown
8:11 *S* had a vineyard at Baal Hamon
8:12 You, O *S*, may have a
Jer 52:20 which King *S* had made for the
Mt 1: 6 David the king begot *S* by her
1: 7 *S* begot Rehoboam,
6:29 yet I say to you that even *S*
12:42 earth to hear the wisdom of *S*;
12:42 and indeed a greater than *S* is
Lk 11:31 earth to hear the wisdom of *S*;
11:31 and indeed a greater than *S* is
12:27 even *S* in all his glory was not
Acts 7:47 But *S* built Him a house.

SOLOMON'S (23/23) SOLOMON

1 Ki 4:22 Now *S* provision for one day was
4:27 all who came to King *S* table.
4:30 Thus *S* wisdom excelled the
5:16 the chiefs of *S* deputies,
5:18 So *S* builders, Hiram's builders,
6: 1 in the fourth year of *S* reign
9: 1 and all *S* desire which he
9:16 to his daughter, *S* wife.)
9:23 who were over *S* work:
10:21 All King *S* drinking vessels
11:26 Then *S* servant, Jeroboam the
1 Chr 3:10 *S* son was Rehoboam
2 Chr 9:20 All King *S* drinking vessels
Ezra 2:55 The sons of *S* servants:
2:58 and the children of *S* servants
Neh 7:57 The sons of *S* servants:
7:60 and the sons of *S* servants,
11: 3 and descendants of *S* servants.)
Song 1: 1 The song of songs, which is *S*.
3: 7 it is *S* couch, With sixty
Jn 10:23 in the temple, in *S* porch.
Acts 3:11 in the porch which is called *S*,
5:12 with one accord in *S* Porch.

SOLVE (1/1) SOLVED, SOLVING

Judg 14:12 If you can correctly *s* and

SOLVED (1/1) SOLVE

Judg 14:18 You would not have *s* my

SOLVING (1/1) SOLVE

Dan 5:12 *s* riddles, and explaining

SOME (405/359)

Gen 14:10 *s* fell there, and the
19:19 lest *s* evil overtake me and I
30:14 Please give me *s* of your son's
30:35 every one that had *s* white in
32:16 and put *s* distance between
33:15 leave with you *s* of the people
37:20 and cast him into *s* pit;
37:20 *S* wild beast has devoured him.'
42: 4 Lest *s* calamity befall him."
43:11 Take *s* of the best fruits of
Ex 10:26 For we must take *s* of them to
12: 7 they shall take *s* of the blood
16:17 *s* more, some less.
16:17 some more, *s* less.
16:20 But *s* of them left part of it
16:27 it happened that *s* of the people
17: 5 take with you *s* of the elders
17: 9 Choose us *s* men and go out,
29:12 You shall take *s* of the blood
29:20 and take *s* of its blood and put
29:21 you shall take *s* of the blood
29:21 and *s* of the anointing oil, and
30:36 And you shall beat *s* of it very
30:36 and put *s* of it before the
Lev 4: 5 anointed priest shall take *s*
4: 6 and sprinkle *s* of the blood
4: 7 priest shall put *s* of the blood
4:16 priest shall bring *s* of the
4:18 And he shall put *s* of the blood
4:25 priest shall take *s* of the blood
4:30 priest shall take *s* of its blood
4:34 priest shall take *s* of the blood
5: 9 shall sprinkle *s* of the blood
8:11 He sprinkled *s* of it on the
8:12 And he poured *s* of the anointing
8:15 and put *s* on the horns of the
8:23 Also he took *s* of its blood
8:24 And Moses put *s* of the blood
8:30 Then Moses took *s* of the
8:30 anointing oil and *s* of the blood
14:14 priest shall take *s* of the blood
14:15 And the priest shall take *s* of
14:16 and shall sprinkle *s* of the oil
14:17 the priest shall put *s* on the
14:25 priest shall take *s* of the blood
14:26 priest shall pour *s* of the oil
14:27 his right finger *s* of the oil
14:28 priest shall put *s* of the oil
14:35 to me that there is *s* plague
16:14 He shall take *s* of the blood of
16:14 he shall sprinkle *s* of the blood
16:18 and shall take *s* of the blood
16:18 of the bull and *s* of the blood
16:19 shall sprinkle *s* of the blood
20: 3 because he has given *s* of his
20: 4 when he gives *s* of his
25:25 has sold *s* of his possession
Num 2: 2 they shall camp *s* distance from
5:17 and take *s* of the dust that is
5:20 have defiled yourself and *s* man
11: 1 and consumed *s* in the
13:20 And bring *s* of the fruit of the
13:23 They also brought *s* of the
16: 2 rose up before Moses with *s* of
16:37 and scatter the fire *s* distance
19: 4 priest shall take *s* of its blood
19: 4 and sprinkle *s* of its blood
19:17 they shall take *s* of them
21: 1 Israel and took *s* of them
22:40 and he sent *s* to Balaam and to
27:20 shall give *s* of your authority
30: 2 bind himself by *s* agreement,
30: 3 herself by *s* agreement
31: 3 Arm *s* of yourselves for war, and
35: 8 Each shall give *s* of its cities
Deut 1:25 They also took *s* of the fruit
23:10 unclean by *s* occurrence in
24: 1 he has found *s* uncleanness in
26: 2 that you shall take *s* of the

S

Josh 7:11 For they have even taken s of
8:22 s on this side and some on that
8:22 some on this side and s on that
9:14 Then the men of Israel took s of
Judg 14: 8 After s time, when he returned
14: 9 He took s of it in his hands and
14: 9 he gave s to them, and they
20:31 down and kill s of the people
Ruth 2:14 satisfied, and kept s back.
1 Sam 8:11 and s will run before his
8:12 will set s to plow his
8:12 and s to make his weapons of
9:11 they met s young women going
10:27 But s rebels said, "How can
13: 7 And s of the Hebrews crossed
21: 2 ordered me on s business,
27: 5 give me a place in s town
30:26 he sent s of the spoil to the
2 Sam 10: 9 he chose s of Israel's best and
11:17 And s of the people of the
11:24 and s of the king's servants
12:18 He may do s harm!"
17: 9 by now he is hidden in s pit,
17: 9 or in s other place.
17: 9 when s of them are overthrown
17:12 will come upon him in s place
1 Ki 7:10 s ten cubits and some eight
7:10 some ten cubits and s eight
14: 3 s cakes, and a jar of honey,
17:13 and afterward make s for
2 Ki 2:16 cast him upon s mountain
2:16 mountain or into s valley."
2:23 s youths came from the city and
4: 8 persuaded him to eat s food.
4: 8 turn in there to eat s food.
4:41 Then bring s flour." And he put
4:43 They shall eat and have s left
4:44 and they ate and had s left
7: 8 and carried s from there
7: 9 s punishment will come upon us.
9:33 and s of her blood spattered
13:15 'Take a bow and s arrows."
13:15 himself a bow and s arrows.
17:25 which killed s of them.
20:18 shall take away s of your sons
25:12 of the guard left s of the poor
1 Chr 4:40 for s Hamites formerly lived
4:42 Now s of them, five hundred men
6:66 Now s of the families of the
9: 3 and s of the children of
9:28 Now s of them were in charge
9:29 S of them were appointed over
9:30 And s of the sons of the
9:32 And s of their brethren of the
12: 8 S Gadites joined David at the
12:16 Then s of the sons of Benjamin
12:19 And s from Manasseh defected
16: 4 he appointed s of the Levites
19: 5 Then s went and told David
19:10 he chose s of Israel's best and
25: 1 the service s of the sons
26:27 S of the spoils won in battles
2 Chr 8: 9 S were men of war, captains of
11:23 and dispersed s of his sons
12: 7 grant them s deliverance.
16:10 And Asa oppressed s of the
17:11 Also s of the Philistines
18: 2 After s years he went down to
19: 8 Jehoshaphat appointed s of the
19: 8 and s of the chief fathers of
20: 2 Then s came and told
28:12 Then s of the heads of the
30:11 Nevertheless s from Asher,
32:21 s of his own offspring struck
34:13 And s of the Levites were
36: 7 also carried off s of the
Ezra 2:68 S of the heads of the fathers'
2:70 s of the people, the singers,
7: 7 S of the children of Israel,
9: 2 have taken s of their daughters
9: 3 and plucked out s of the hair
10:44 and s of them had wives by
Neh 1: 9 though s of you were cast out
5: 3 There were also s who said,
5: 5 and s of our daughters have
7:70 And s of the heads of the
7:71 S of the heads of the fathers'
7:73 s of the people, the Nethinim,
11: 4 Also in Jerusalem dwelt s of
11:25 s of the children of Judah
11:36 S of the Judean divisions of
12:35 and s of the priests' sons with
12:44 And at the same time s were
13:19 Then I posted s of my servants
13:25 struck s of them and pulled out
Job 24: 2 S remove landmarks; They seize
24: 9 S snatch the fatherless from
Ps 20: 7 S trust in chariots, and some
20: 7 in chariots, and s in horses;
Isa 32:10 In a year and s days You will
39: 7 shall take away s of your sons
44:15 For he will take s of it and
66:21 And I will also take s of them
Jer 19: 1 and take s of the elders of
19: 1 people and s of the elders
49: 9 Would they not leave s
52:15 away captive s of the poor
52:16 guard left s of the poor
Ezek 5: 4 Then take s of them again and
6: 8 so that you may have s who
10: 7 and took s of it and put it
14: 1 Now s of the elders of Israel
16:16 You took s of your garments and
17: 5 Then he took s of the seed of
43:20 You shall take s of its blood
45:19 priest shall take s of the blood
46:16 gift of s of his inheritance
46:17 But if he gives a gift of s of
Dan 1: 2 with s of the articles of the
1: 3 to bring s of the children of
1: 3 and s of the king's descendants
1: 3 and s of the nobles,
6: 4 sought to find s charge
8:10 and it cast down s of the host
8:10 and s of the stars to the
11: 6 And at the end of s years they
11:13 come at the end of s years
11:35 And s of those of understanding
12: 2 S to everlasting life, Some
12: 2 S to shame and everlasting
Am 2:11 I raised up s of your sons as
2:11 And s of your young men as
4:11 I overthrew s of you, As God
Ob 5 not have left s gleanings?
Mic 6:14 You may carry s away, but
Mt 9: 3 And at once s of the scribes
12:38 Then s of the scribes and
13: 4 s seed fell by the wayside;
13: 5 S fell on stony places, where
13: 7 And s fell among thorns, and the
13: 8 s a hundredfold, some sixty,
13: 8 s sixty, some thirty.
13: 8 some sixty, s thirty.
13:23 s a hundredfold, some sixty,
13:23 s sixty, some thirty."
13:23 some sixty, s thirty."
13:47 and gathered s of every kind
16:14 S say John the Baptist, some
16:14 s Elijah, and others Jeremiah
16:28 there are s standing here who
23:34 s of them you will kill and
23:34 and s of them you will scourge
25: 8 Give us s of your oil, for our
27:47 S of those who stood there, when
28:11 s of the guard came into the
28:17 but s doubted.
Mk 2: 1 Capernaum after s days,
2: 6 And s of the scribes were
2:26 and also gave s to those who
4: 4 that s seed fell by the
4: 5 S fell on stony ground, where it
4: 7 And s seed fell among thorns;
4: 8 s thirtyfold, some sixty, and
4: 8 s sixty, and some a hundred."
4: 8 and s a hundred."
4:20 s thirtyfold, some sixty, and
4:20 s sixty, and some a hundred."
4:20 and s a hundred."
5:35 s came from the ruler of the
7: 1 Pharisees and s of the scribes
7: 2 they saw s of His disciples
8: 3 for s of them have come from
8:28 but s say, Elijah; and others,
9: 1 I say to you that there are s
11: 5 But s of those who stood there
12: 2 might receive s of the fruit
12: 5 beating s and killing some.
12: 5 beating some and killing s.
12:13 sent to Him s of the Pharisees
12:18 Then s Sadducees, who say
14: 4 But there were s who were
14:57 Then s rose up and bore false
14:65 Then s began to spit on Him, and
15:35 S of those who stood by, when
15:44 He had been dead for s time.
Lk 6: 2 And s of the Pharisees said to
6: 4 and also gave s to those with
8: 5 s fell by the wayside; and it
8: 6 S fell on rock; and as soon as
8: 7 And s fell among thorns, and the
8:20 And it was told Him by s,
9: 7 because it was said by s that
9: 8 and by s that Elijah had
9:19 but s say Elijah; and others
9:27 there are s standing here who
11:15 But s of them said, "He casts
11:49 and s of them they will kill
13: 1 present at that season s who
13:31 On that very day s Pharisees
18: 9 He spoke this parable to s who
19:39 And s of the Pharisees called to
20:10 that they might give him s of
20:27 Then s of the Sadducees, who
20:39 Then s of the scribes answered
21: 5 as s spoke of the temple, how
21:16 and they will put s of you to
23: 8 and he hoped to see s miracle
24:42 broiled fish and s honeycomb.
Jn 2: 8 Draw s out now, and take it to
3:25 arose a dispute between s of
6:64 But there are s of you who do
7:12 S said, "He is good";
7:25 Now s of them from Jerusalem
7:41 But s said, "Will the Christ
7:44 Now s of them wanted to take
9: 9 S said, "This is he."
9:16 Therefore s of the Pharisees
9:40 Then s of the Pharisees who
10: 1 but climbs up s other way, the
11:37 And s of them said, "Could not
11:46 But s of them went away to the
13:29 For s thought, because Judas had
16:17 Then s of His disciples said
21: 6 the boat, and you will find s.
21:10 Bring s of the fish which you
Acts 5:15 passing by might fall on s of
5:36 For s time ago Theudas rose up,
6: 9 Then there arose s from what is
8:34 of himself or of s other man?"
8:36 they came to s water.
9:19 Then Saul spent s days with the
10:23 and s brethren from Joppa
11:20 But s of them were men from
12: 1 out his hand to harass s from
15: 5 But s of the sect of the
15:24 Since we have heard that s who
15:36 Then after s days Paul said to
16:12 in that city for s days.
17: 4 And s of them were persuaded;
17: 5 took s of the evil men from the
17: 6 they dragged Jason and s
17:18 And s said, "What does this
17:20 For you are bringing s strange
17:21 to tell or to hear s new thing.
17:28 as also s of your own poets
17:32 s mocked, while others said,
17:34 s men joined him and believed,
18:23 After he had spent s time
19: 1 And finding s disciples
19: 9 But when s were hardened and did
19:13 Then s of the itinerant Jewish
19:31 Then s of the officials of Asia,
19:32 S therefore cried one thing and
19:32 cried one thing and s another,
21:16 Also s of the disciples from
21:34 And s among the multitude cried
21:34 cried one thing and s another.
21:38 you not the Egyptian who s
23:12 s of the Jews banded together
24:18 in the midst of which s Jews
24:24 And after s days, when Felix
25:13 And after s days King Agrippa
25:19 but had s questions against him
27: 1 they delivered Paul and s other
27:27 were drawing near s land.
27:44 s on boards and some on parts
27:44 some on boards and s on parts
28:24 And s were persuaded by the
28:24 spoken, and s disbelieved.
Rom 1:10 by s means, now at last I may
1:11 to you s spiritual gift,
1:13 that I might have s fruit among
3: 3 For what if s did not believe?
3: 8 reported and as s affirm that
11:14 my flesh and save s of them
11:17 And if s of the branches were
15:15 boldly to you on s points,
1 Cor 4:18 Now s are puffed up, as though I
6:11 And such were s of you.
8: 7 for s, with consciousness
9:22 I might by all means save s.
10: 7 become idolaters as were s of
10: 8 as s of them did, and in one
10: 9 as s of them also tempted, and
10:10 as s of them also complained,
15: 6 but s have fallen asleep.
15:12 how do s among you say that
15:34 for s do not have the knowledge
15:37 perhaps wheat or s other grain.
2 Cor 2: 5 but all of you to s extent—not
3: 1 as s others, epistles of
9: 4 lest if s Macedonians come with
10: 2 I intend to be bold against s,
Gal 1: 7 but there are s who trouble you
Eph 4:11 And He Himself gave s to be
4:11 s prophets, some evangelists,
4:11 s evangelists, and some pastors
4:11 and s pastors and teachers,
Phil 1:15 S indeed preach Christ even from
1:15 and s also from good will:
1 Th 3: 5 lest by s means the tempter had
2 Th 3:11 For we hear that there are s who
1 Tim 1: 3 Ephesus that you may charge s
1: 6 from which s, having strayed,
1:19 which s having rejected,
4: 1 says that in latter times s
5:15 For s have already turned aside
5:24 S men's sins are clearly
5:24 but those of s men follow
5:25 the good works of s are
6:10 for which s have strayed from
6:21 by professing it s have strayed
2 Tim 2:18 they overthrow the faith of s.
2:20 s for honor and some for
2:20 some for honor and s for
Heb 4: 6 therefore it remains that s
10:25 as is the manner of s,
13: 2 for by so doing s have
1 Pe 3: 1 that even if s do not obey the
4:12 as though s strange thing
2 Pe 3: 9 as s count slackness, but is
3:16 in which are s things hard to
2 Jn 4 greatly that I have found s
Jude 22 And on s have compassion, making
Rev 2:10 is about to throw s of you
2:17 who overcomes I will give s of

SOMEBODY (2/2)

Lk 8:46 S touched Me, for I perceived
Acts 5:36 rose up, claiming to be s.

SOMEDAY (1/1)

1 Sam 27: 1 Now I shall perish s by the hand

SOMEHOW (2/2)

1 Cor 8: 9 But beware lest *s* this liberty
2 Cor 11: 3 But I fear, lest *s*,

SOMEONE (36/36)

Deut 13:12 If you hear *s* in one of your
Josh 22:11 the children of Israel heard *s*
1 Sam 19:22 And *s* said, "Indeed they
24:10 and *s* urged me to kill you.
2 Sam 4:10 when *s* told me, saying, 'Look,
9: 3 Is there not still *s* of the
11: 3 And *s* said, "Is this not
15:31 Then *s* told David, saying,
23:15 that *s* would give me a drink of
1 Ki 18:10 where my master has not sent *s*
22:38 Then *s* washed the chariot at a
2 Ki 6:10 the king of Israel sent *s* to
6:32 son of a murderer has sent *s*
1 Chr 11:17 that *s* would give me a drink of
Job 24:17 If *s* recognizes them, They
Ps 69:20 I looked for *s* to take pity,
Prov 4:16 taken away unless they make *s*
Jer 39:14 then they sent *s* to take
Am 6:10 Then *s* will say, "None."
Mk 9:38 we saw *s* who does not follow us
15:36 Then *s* ran and filled a sponge
Lk 8:49 *s* came from the ruler of the
9:49 we saw *s* casting out demons in
9:57 that *s* said to Him, "Lord, I
Jn 18:39 custom that I should release *s*
Acts 8: 9 claiming that he was *s* great,
8:31 unless *s* guides me?" And he
13:11 and he went around seeking *s* to
Rom 5: 7 yet perhaps for a good man *s*
1 Cor 15:35 But *s* will say, "How are the
Heb 3: 4 For every house is built by *s*,
5:12 you need *s* to teach you again
Jas 2:14 if *s* says he has faith but does
2:18 But *s* will say, "You have
5:19 and *s* turns him back,
1 Jn 4:20 If *s* says, "I love God,"

SOMETHING (52/49)

Lev 4:13 and they have done *s* against
4:22 and done *s* unintentionally
4:27 unintentionally by doing *s*
Num 35:20 hurls *s* at him so that he dies,
Judg 14:14 Out of the eater came *s* to eat,
14:14 And out of the strong came *s*
1 Sam 3:11 I will do *s* in Israel at which
14:12 to us, and we will show you *s*.
20:26 *S* has happened to him; he is
1 Ki 2:14 'I have *s* to say to you.'
14: 5 coming to ask you *s* about her
14:13 in him there is found *s* good
2 Ki 5:13 prophet had told you to do *s*
5:20 I will run after him and take *s*
Job 6:22 Bring *s* to me'? Or, 'Offer a
Prov 20:25 for a man to devote rashly *s*
Jer 18: 3 making *s* at the wheel.
38:14 to Jeremiah, "I will ask you *s*.
Ezek 10: 1 there appeared *s* like a
40: 2 on it toward the south was *s*
Mt 5:23 that your brother has *s*
14:16 You give them *s* to eat."
20:20 kneeling down and asking *s* from
Mk 5:43 and said that *s* should be
6:37 'You give them *s* to eat."
6:37 of bread and give them *s* to
11:13 see if perhaps He would find *s*
Lk 7:40 I have *s* to say to you."
8:55 commanded that she be given *s*
9:13 'You give them *s* to eat."
11:54 and seeking to catch Him in *s*
17: 8 Prepare *s* for my supper, and
Jn 8: 6 that they might have *s* of
13:29 or that he should give *s* to
Acts 3: 5 expecting to receive *s* from
9:18 there fell from his eyes *s*
17:29 *s* shaped by art and man's
23:17 for he has *s* to tell him."
23:18 He has *s* to say to you."
25:26 has taken place I may have *s*
Rom 4: 2 he has *s* to boast about, but
1 Cor 14:35 And if they want to learn *s*,
16: 2 week let each one of you lay *s*
Gal 2: 6 from those who seemed to be *s*—
2: 6 those who seemed to be *s*
6: 3 anyone thinks himself to be *s*,
Eph 4:28 that he may have *s* to give him
Heb 8: 3 that this One also have *s* to
11:40 God having provided *s* better for
Rev 8: 8 And *s* like a great mountain
9: 7 On their heads were crowns of *s*
15: 2 And I saw *s* like a sea of glass

SOMETIME (1/1)

1 Sam 20:12 I have sounded out my father *s*

SOMEWHAT (1/1)

2 Cor 10: 8 For even if I should boast *s*

SOMEWHERE (1/1)

Gen 43:30 made haste and sought *s* to

SON (2363/1776) GRANDSON, MAN, SON-IN-LAW, SON'S, SONS

Gen 4:17 city after the name of his *s*—
4:25 and she bore a *s* and named him
4:26 to him also a *s* was born;
5: 3 and begot a *s* in his own
5:28 eighty-two years, and had a *s*.
9:24 and knew what his younger *s* had
11:31 And Terah took his *s* Abram and
11:31 the *s* of Haran, and his
11:31 his *s* Abram's wife, and they
12: 5 wife and Lot his brother's *s*,
14:12 Abram's brother's *s* who dwelt
16:11 child, And you shall bear a *s*.
16:15 So Hagar bore Abram a *s*;
16:15 a son; and Abram named his *s*,
17:16 her and also give you a *s* by
17:19 your wife shall bear you a *s*,
17:23 So Abraham took Ishmael his *s*,
17:25 And Ishmael his *s* was thirteen
17:26 and his *s* Ishmael;
18:10 Sarah your wife shall have a *s*.
18:14 life, and Sarah shall have a *s*.
19:37 The firstborn bore a *s* and
19:38 she also bore a *s* and called
21: 2 conceived and bore Abraham a *s*
21: 3 called the name of his *s* who
21: 4 Then Abraham circumcised his *s*
21: 5 hundred years old when his *s*
21: 7 For I have borne him a *s* in
21: 9 And Sarah saw the *s* of Hagar the
21:10 out this bondwoman and her *s*;
21:10 for the *s* of this bondwoman
21:10 shall not be heir with my *s*,
21:11 sight because of his *s*.
21:13 also make a nation of the *s* of
22: 2 Then He said, "Take now your *s*,
22: 2 your only *s* Isaac, whom you
22: 3 men with him, and Isaac his *s*;
22: 6 and laid it on Isaac his *s*;
22: 7 And he said, "Here I am, my *s*.
22: 8 And Abraham said, "My *s*,
22: 9 and he bound Isaac his *s* and
22:10 took the knife to slay his *s*.
22:12 you have not withheld your *s*,
22:12 withheld your son, your only *s*,
22:13 burnt offering instead of his *s*.
22:16 and have not withheld your *s*,
22:16 withheld your son, your only *s*—
23: 8 and meet with Ephron the *s* of
24: 3 will not take a wife for my *s*
24: 4 and take a wife for my *s*
24: 5 Must I take your *s* back to the
24: 6 that you do not take my *s* back
24: 7 you shall take a wife for my *s*
24: 8 only do not take my *s* back
24:15 *s* of Milcah, the wife of Nahor,
24:24 daughter of Bethuel, Milcah's *s*,
24:36 my master's wife bore a *s* to
24:37 shall not take a wife for my *s*
24:38 and take a wife for my *s*.
24:40 you shall take a wife for my *s*
24:44 has appointed for my master's *s*.
24:47 daughter of Bethuel, Nahor's *s*,
24:48 my master's brother for his *s*.
25: 6 eastward, away from Isaac his *s*,
25: 9 in the field of Ephron the *s* of
25:11 that God blessed his *s* Isaac.
25:12 of Ishmael, Abraham's *s*,
25:19 genealogy of Isaac, Abraham's *s*.
27: 1 he called Esau his older *s* and
27: 1 son and said to him, "My *s*.
27: 5 when Isaac spoke to Esau his *s*.
27: 6 So Rebekah spoke to Jacob her *s*,
27: 8 "Now therefore, my *s*,
27:13 your curse be on me, my *s*;
27:15 choice clothes of her elder *s*
27:15 put them on Jacob her younger *s*.
27:17 into the hand of her *s* Jacob.
27:18 "Here I am. Who are you, my *s*?
27:20 But Isaac said to his *s*,
27:20 have found it so quickly, my *s*?
27:21 near, that I may feel you, my *s*,
27:21 whether you are really my *s*
27:24 Are you really my *s* Esau?"
27:26 near now and kiss me, my *s*.
27:27 the smell of my *s* Is like the
27:32 So he said, "I am your *s*,
27:37 shall I do now for you, my *s*?
27:42 the words of Esau her older *s*
27:42 and called Jacob her younger *s*,
27:43 "Now therefore, my *s*,
28: 5 to Laban the *s* of Bethuel the
28: 9 of Ishmael, Abraham's *s*,
29: 5 Do you know Laban the *s* of
29:12 and that he was Rebekah's *s*.
29:13 about Jacob his sister's *s*,
29:32 So Leah conceived and bore a *s*,
29:33 conceived again and bore a *s*,
29:33 has therefore given me this *s*
29:34 conceived again and bore a *s*,
29:35 conceived again and bore a *s*,
30: 5 conceived and bore Jacob a *s*.
30: 6 heard my voice and given me a *s*.
30: 7 again and bore Jacob a second *s*.
30:10 maid Zilpah bore Jacob a *s*.
30:12 Zilpah bore Jacob a second *s*.
30:17 and bore Jacob a fifth *s*.
30:19 again and bore Jacob a sixth *s*.
30:23 And she conceived and bore a *s*,
30:24 LORD shall add to me another *s*.
34: 2 And when Shechem the *s* of Hamor
34: 8 The soul of my *s* Shechem longs
34:18 Hamor and Shechem, Hamor's *s*.
34:20 And Hamor and Shechem his *s* came
34:24 heeded Hamor and Shechem his *s*;
34:26 killed Hamor and Shechem his *s*
35:17 you will have this *s* also."
36:10 Eliphaz the *s* of Adah the wife
36:10 and Reuel the *s* of Basemath the
36:12 concubine of Eliphaz, Esau's *s*,
36:15 the firstborn *s* of Esau, were
36:17 the sons of Reuel, Esau's *s*:
36:32 Bela the *s* of Beor reigned in
36:33 Jobab the *s* of Zerah of Bozrah
36:35 Hadad the *s* of Bedad, who
36:38 Baal-Hanan the *s* of Achbor
36:39 And when Baal-Hanan the *s* of
37: 3 because he was the *s* of his
37:34 and mourned for his *s* many
37:35 go down into the grave to my *s*
38: 3 So she conceived and bore a *s*,
38: 4 conceived again and bore a *s*,
38: 5 yet again and bore a *s*,
38:11 your father's house till my *s*
38:26 did not give her to Shelah my *s*.
42:38 My *s* shall not go down with you,
43:29 Benjamin, his mother's *s*,
43:29 "God be gracious to you, my *s*.
45: 9 Thus says your *s* Joseph: "God
45:28 Joseph my *s* is still alive.
46:10 the *s* of a Canaanite woman.
46:23 The *s* of Dan was Hushim.
47:29 he called his *s* Joseph and said
48: 2 your *s* Joseph is coming to
48:19 and said, "I know, my *s*,
49: 9 From the prey, my *s*,
50:23 the *s* of Manasseh, were also
Ex 1:16 the birthstools, if it is a *s*,
1:22 Every *s* who is born you shall
2: 2 woman conceived and bore a *s*.
2:10 daughter, and he became her *s*.
2:22 And she bore him a *s*,
4:22 the LORD: "Israel is My *s*,
4:23 let My *s* go that he may serve
4:23 go, indeed I will kill your *s*,
4:25 cut off the foreskin of her *s*
6:15 and Shaul the *s* of a Canaanite
6:25 Eleazar, Aaron's *s*,
10: 2 tell in the hearing of your *s*
10: 2 of your son and your son's *s*
13: 8 And you shall tell your *s* in
13:14 when your *s* asks you in time to
20:10 do no work: you, nor your *s*,
21: 9 he has betrothed her to his *s*,
21:31 Whether it has gored a *s* or
23:12 and the *s* of your female
29:30 That *s* who becomes priest in his
31: 2 called by name Bezalel the *s*
31: 2 the *s* of Hur, of the tribe of
31: 6 with him Aholiab the *s* of
32:29 for every man has opposed his *s*
33:11 but his servant Joshua the *s* of
35:30 called by name Bezalel the *s*
35:30 the *s* of Hur, of the tribe of
35:34 in him and Aholiab the *s* of
38:21 *s* of Aaron the priest.
38:22 Bezalel the *s* of Uri, the son of
38:22 the *s* of Hur, of the tribe of
38:23 with him was Aholiab the *s* of
Lev 12: 6 whether for a *s* or a daughter,
21: 2 his mother, his father, his *s*,
24:10 Now the *s* of an Israelite
24:10 and this Israelite woman's *s*
24:11 And the Israelite woman's *s*
25:49 or his uncle or his uncle's *s*
Num 1: 5 Elizur the *s* of Shedeur;
1: 6 Shelumiel the *s* of Zurishaddai;
1: 7 Nahshon the *s* of Amminadab;
1: 8 Nethanel the *s* of Zuar;
1: 9 Eliab the *s* of Helon;
1:10 Elishama the *s* of Ammihud;
1:10 Gamaliel the *s* of Pedahzur;
1:11 Abidan the *s* of Gideoni;
1:12 Ahiezer the *s* of Ammishaddai;
1:13 Pagiel the *s* of Ocran;
1:14 Eliasaph the *s* of Deuel;
1:15 Ahira the *s* of Enan."
1:20 of Reuben, Israel's oldest *s*,
2: 3 and Nahshon the *s* of Amminadab
2: 5 and Nethanel the *s* of Zuar
2: 7 and Eliab the *s* of Helon shall
2:10 Reuben shall be Elizur the *s*
2:12 shall be Shelumiel the *s* of
2:14 Gad shall be Eliasaph the *s*
2:18 shall be Elishama the *s* of
2:20 shall be Gamaliel the *s* of
2:22 shall be Abidan the *s* of
2:25 of Dan shall be Ahiezer the *s*
2:27 Asher shall be Pagiel the *s*
2:29 shall be Ahira the *s* of Enan.
3:24 was Eliasaph the *s* of Lael.
3:30 was Elizaphan the *s* of Uzziel.
3:32 And Eleazar the *s* of Aaron the
3:35 of Merari was Zuriel the *s* of
4:16 duty of Eleazar the *s* of Aaron
4:28 the authority of Ithamar the *s*
4:33 the authority of Ithamar the *s*
7: 8 the authority of Ithamar the *s*
7:12 first day was Nahshon the *s*
7:17 the offering of Nahshon the *s*
7:18 the second day Nethanel the *s*

S

7:23 the offering of Nethanel the s
7:24 On the third day Eliab the s of
7:29 the offering of Eliab the s of
7:30 the fourth day Elizur the s of
7:35 the offering of Elizur the s
7:36 the fifth day Shelumiel the s
7:41 offering of Shelumiel the s of
7:42 the sixth day Eliasaph the s
7:47 the offering of Eliasaph the s
7:48 the seventh day Elishama the s
7:53 the offering of Elishama the s
7:54 the eighth day Gamaliel the s
7:59 the offering of Gamaliel the s
7:60 On the ninth day Abidan the s
7:65 the offering of Abidan the s
7:66 the tenth day Ahiezer the s of
7:71 the offering of Ahiezer the s
7:72 the eleventh day Pagiel the s
7:77 the offering of Pagiel the s
7:78 the twelfth day Ahira the s of
7:83 the offering of Ahira the s of
10:14 their army was Nahshon the s
10:15 of Issachar was Nethanel the s
10:16 of Zebulun was Eliab the s of
10:18 their army was Elizur the s
10:19 of Simeon was Shelumiel the s
10:20 of Gad was Eliasaph the s of
10:22 their army was Elishama the s
10:23 of Manasseh was Gamaliel the s
10:24 of Benjamin was Abidan the s
10:25 their army was Ahiezer the s
10:26 of Asher was Pagiel the s of
10:27 of Naphtali was Ahira the s
10:29 Now Moses said to Hobab the s
11:28 So Joshua the s of Nun, Moses'
13: 4 Shammua the s of Zaccur;
13: 5 Shaphat the s of Hori;
13: 6 Caleb the s of Jephunneh;
13: 7 Igal the s of Joseph;
13: 8 Hoshea the s of Nun;
13: 9 Palti the s of Raphu;
13:10 Gaddiel the s of Sodi;
13:11 Gaddi the s of Susi;
13:12 Ammiel the s of Gemalli;
13:13 Sethur the s of Michael;
13:14 Nahbi the s of Vophsi;
13:15 Geuel the s of Machi.
13:16 And Moses called Hoshea the s
14: 6 But Joshua the s of Nun and
14: 6 the son of Nun and Caleb the s
14:30 Except for Caleb the s of
14:30 of Jephunneh and Joshua the s
14:38 But Joshua the s of Nun and
14:38 the son of Nun and Caleb the s
16: 1 Now Korah the s of Izhar, the
16: 1 the s of Kohath, the son of
16: 1 the s of Levi, with Dathan and
16: 1 and On the s of Peleth, sons of
16:37 the s of Aaron the priest, to
20:25 "Take Aaron and Eleazar his s,
20:26 and put them on Eleazar his s;
20:28 and put them on Eleazar his s;
22: 2 Now Balak the s of Zippor saw
22: 4 And Balak the s of Zippor
22: 5 messengers to Balaam the s of
22:10 Balak the s of Zippor, king of
22:16 Thus says Balak the s of Zippor:
23:18 Listen to me, s of Zippor!
23:19 Nor a s of man, that He should
24: 3 The utterance of Balaam the s of
24:15 The utterance of Balaam the s of
25: 7 Now when Phinehas the s of
25: 7 the s of Aaron the priest, saw
25:11 Phinehas the s of Eleazar, the
25:11 the s of Aaron the priest, has
25:14 was Zimri the s of Salu, a
26: 1 to Moses and Eleazar the s of
26: 8 And the s of Pallu was Eliab.
26:33 Now Zelophehad the s of Hepher
26:65 except Caleb the s of Jephunneh
26:65 of Jephunneh and Joshua the s
27: 1 daughters of Zelophehad the s
27: 1 the s of Gilead, the son of
27: 1 the s of Machir, the son of
27: 1 the s of Manasseh, from the
27: 1 the families of Manasseh the s
27: 4 his family because he had no s?
27: 8 'If a man dies and has no s,
27:18 Take Joshua the s of Nun with
31: 6 to the war with Phinehas the s
31: 8 Balaam the s of Beor they also
32:12 except Caleb the s of Jephunneh,
32:12 and Joshua the s of Nun, for
32:28 to Joshua the s of Nun, and to
32:33 the tribe of Manasseh the s of
32:39 the children of Machir the s
32:40 gave Gilead to Machir the s of
32:41 Also Jair the s of Manasseh went
34:17 the priest and Joshua the s of
34:19 Caleb the s of Jephunneh;
34:20 Shemuel the s of Ammihud;
34:21 Elidad the s of Chislon;
34:22 Bukki the s of Jogli;
34:23 Hanniel the s of Ephod,
34:24 Kemuel the s of Shiphtan;
34:25 Elizaphan the s of Parnach;
34:26 Paltiel the s of Azzan;
34:27 Ahihud the s of Shelomi;
34:28 Pedahel the s of Ammihud."
36: 1 of the children of Gilead the s
36: 1 the s of Manasseh, of the
36:12 the children of Manasseh the s

Deut 1:31 you, as a man carries his s,
1:36 except Caleb the s of Jephunneh;
1:38 Joshua the s of Nun, who stands
3:14 Jair the s of Manasseh took all
5:14 do no work: you, nor your s,
6: 2 you and your s and your
6:20 When your s asks you in time to
6:21 "then you shall say to your s:
7: 3 give your daughter to their s,
7: 3 take their daughter for your s.
8: 5 that as a man chastens his s,
10: 6 and Eleazar his s ministered as
11: 6 the s of Reuben: how the earth
12:18 you and your s and your
13: 6 the s of your mother, your son
13: 6 your s or your daughter, the
16:11 you and your s and your
16:14 you and your s and your
18:10 you anyone who makes his s or
21:15 and if the firstborn s is of
21:16 firstborn status on the s of
21:16 wife in preference to the s of
21:17 he shall acknowledge the s
21:18 has a stubborn and rebellious s
21:20 This s of ours is stubborn and
23: 4 hired against you Balaam the s
25: 5 one of them dies and has no s,
25: 6 shall be that the firstborn s
28:56 and to her s and her daughter,
31:23 He inaugurated Joshua the s of
32:44 Moses came with Joshua the s
34: 9 Now Joshua the s of Nun was
Josh 1: 1 LORD spoke to Joshua the s of
2: 1 Now Joshua the s of Nun sent out
2:23 and they came to Joshua the s
6: 6 Then Joshua the s of Nun called
7: 1 for Achan the s of Carmi, the
7: 1 the s of Zabdi, the son of
7: 1 the s of Zerah, of the tribe of
7:18 and Achan the s of Carmi, the
7:18 the s of Zabdi, the son of
7:18 the s of Zerah, of the tribe of
7:19 Joshua said to Achan, "My s,
7:24 took Achan the s of Zerah, the
13:22 with the sword Balaam the s of
13:31 the children of Machir the s
14: 1 Joshua the s of Nun, and the
14: 6 And Caleb the s of Jephunneh
14:13 and gave Hebron to Caleb the s
14:14 the inheritance of Caleb the s
15: 6 up to the stone of Bohan the s
15: 8 went up by the Valley of the S
15:13 Now to Caleb the s of Jephunneh
15:17 So Othniel the s of Kenaz, the
17: 2 children of Manasseh the s of
17: 3 But Zelophehad the s of Hepher,
17: 3 the s of Gilead, the son of
17: 3 the s of Machir, the son of
17: 3 the s of Manasseh, had no sons,
17: 4 before Joshua the s of Nun, and
18:16 before the Valley of the S of
18:17 to the stone of Bohan the s of
19:49 among them to Joshua the s of
19:51 Joshua the s of Nun, and the
21: 1 to Joshua the s of Nun, and to
21:12 they gave to Caleb the s of
22:13 of Israel sent Phinehas the s
22:20 Did not Achan the s of Zerah
22:31 Then Phinehas the s of Eleazar
22:32 And Phinehas the s of Eleazar
24: 9 Then Balak the s of Zippor, king
24: 9 sent and called Balaam the s
24:29 these things that Joshua the s
24:33 And Eleazar the s of Aaron died.
24:33 belonging to Phinehas his s,
Judg 1:13 And Othniel the s of Kenaz,
2: 8 Now Joshua the s of Nun, the
3: 9 Othniel the s of Kenaz, Caleb's
3:11 Then Othniel the s of Kenaz
3:15 Ehud the s of Gera, the
3:31 After him was Shamgar the s of
4: 6 and called for Barak the s of
4:12 to Sisera that Barak the s of
5: 1 Then Deborah and Barak the s of
5: 6 s of Anath, In the days of
5:12 away, O s of Abinoam!
6:11 while his s Gideon threshed
6:29 Gideon the s of Joash has done
6:30 to Joash, "Bring out your s,
7:14 but the sword of Gideon the s
8:13 Then Gideon the s of Joash
8:18 each one resembled the s of a
8:22 over us, both you and your s,
8:23 nor shall my s rule over you;
8:29 Then Jerubbaal the s of Joash
8:31 in Shechem also bore him a s,
8:32 Now Gideon the s of Joash died
9: 1 Then Abimelech the s of
9: 5 But Jotham the youngest s of
9:18 the s of his female servant,
9:26 Now Gaal the s of Ebed came
9:28 Then Gaal the s of Ebed said,
9:28 Is he not the s of Jerubbaal,
9:30 heard the words of Gaal the s
9:31 Take note! Gaal the s of Ebed
9:35 When Gaal the s of Ebed went out
9:57 came the curse of Jotham the s
10: 1 to save Israel Tola the s of
10: 1 the s of Dodo, a man of
11: 1 but he was the s of a harlot;
11: 2 for you are the s of another
11:25 any better than Balak the s of

11:34 Besides her he had neither s
12:13 Abdon the s of Hillel the
12:15 Then Abdon the s of Hillel the
13: 3 you shall conceive and bear a s.
13: 5 you shall conceive and bear a s.
13: 7 you shall conceive and bear a s.
13:24 So the woman bore a s and
17: 2 by the LORD, my s!"
17: 3 my hand to the LORD for my s,
18:30 and Jonathan the s of Gershom,
18:30 the s of Manasseh, and his sons
20:28 and Phinehas the s of Eleazar,
20:28 the s of Aaron, stood before it
Ruth 4:13 conception, and she bore a s.
4:17 There is a s born to Naomi."
1 Sam 1: 1 his name was Elkanah the s of
1: 1 the s of Elihu, the son of
1: 1 the s of Tohu, the son of Zuph,
1: 1 the s of Zuph, an Ephraimite.
1:20 Hannah conceived and bore a s,
1:23 woman stayed and nursed her s
3: 6 "I did not call, my s;
3:16 and said, "Samuel, my s!"
4:16 he said, "What happened, my s?
4:20 fear, for you have borne a s.
7: 1 and consecrated Eleazar his s
9: 1 whose name was Kish the s of
9: 1 the s of Zeror, the son of
9: 1 the s of Bechorath, the son of
9: 1 the s of Aphiah, a Benjamite, a
9: 2 he had a choice and handsome s
9: 3 And Kish said to his s Saul,
10: 2 "What shall I do about my s?
10:11 this that has come upon the s
10:21 And Saul the s of Kish was
13:16 Saul, Jonathan his s,
13:22 with Saul and Jonathan his s.
14: 1 one day that Jonathan the s of
14: 3 Ahijah the s of Ahitub,
14: 3 the s of Phinehas, the son of
14: 3 the s of Eli, the LORD's
14:39 though it be in Jonathan my s,
14:40 and my s Jonathan and I will be
14:42 Cast lots between my s Jonathan
14:50 of his army was Abner the s
14:51 the father of Abner was the s
16:18 I have seen a s of Jesse the
16:19 Send me your s David, who is
16:20 and sent them by his s David
17:12 Now David was the s of that
17:17 Then Jesse said to his s David,
17:55 whose s is this youth?"
17:56 Inquire whose s this young man
17:58 Whose s are you, young man?"
17:58 I am the s of your servant
19: 1 Saul spoke to Jonathan his s
19: 1 but Jonathan, Saul's s,
20:27 And Saul said to Jonathan his s,
20:27 Why has the s of Jesse not come
20:30 You s of a perverse, rebellious
20:30 that you have chosen the s of
20:31 For as long as the s of Jesse
22: 7 you Benjamites! Will the s of
22: 8 one who reveals to me that my s
22: 8 has made a covenant with the s
22: 8 me or reveals to me that my s
22: 9 I saw the s of Jesse going to
22: 9 to Ahimelech the s of Ahitub.
22:11 the s of Ahitub, and all his
22:12 'Hear now, s of Ahitub!"
22:13 you and the s of Jesse, in that
22:20 of the sons of Ahimelech the s
23: 6 when Abiathar the s of
23:16 Then Jonathan, Saul's s,
24:16 your voice, my s David?"
25: 8 to your servants and to your s
25:10 and who is the s of Jesse?
25:44 to Palti the s of Laish, who
26: 5 and Abner the s of Ner, the
26: 6 Hittite and to Abishai the s
26:14 the people and to Abner the s
26:17 your voice, my s David?"
26:21 Return, my s David.
26:25 be blessed, my s David!
27: 2 were with him to Achish the s
30: 7 the priest, Ahimelech's s,
2 Sam 1: 4 and Saul and Jonathan his s are
1: 5 that Saul and Jonathan his s
1:12 for Saul and for Jonathan his s,
1:13 I am the s of an alien, an
1:17 Saul and over Jonathan his s,
2: 8 But Abner the s of Ner,
2: 8 took Ishbosheth the s of Saul
2:10 Ishbosheth, Saul's s,
2:12 Now Abner the s of Ner, and the
2:12 servants of Ishbosheth the s
2:13 And Joab the s of Zeruiah, and
2:15 followers of Ishbosheth the s
3: 3 Absalom the s of Maacah, the
3: 4 Adonijah the s of Haggith;
3: 4 Shephatiah the s of Abital;
3:14 to Ishbosheth, Saul's s,
3:15 from Paltiel the s of Laish.
3:23 Abner the s of Ner came to the
3:25 you realize that Abner the s
3:28 of the blood of Abner the s of
3:37 intent to kill Abner the s of
4: 1 When Saul's s heard that Abner
4: 2 Now Saul's s had two men who
4: 4 Jonathan, Saul's s,
4: 4 had a s who was lame in his
4: 8 the s of Saul your enemy, who

7:14 Father, and he shall be My *s*.
8: 3 also defeated Hadadezer the *s*
8:10 then Toi sent Joram his *s* to
8:12 the spoil of Hadadezer the *s*
8:16 Joab the *s* of Zeruiah was over
8:16 Jehoshaphat the *s* of Ahilud
8:17 Zadok the *s* of Ahitub and
8:17 of Ahitub and Ahimelech the *s*
8:18 Benaiah the *s* of Jehoiada was
9: 3 There is still a *s* of Jonathan
9: 4 in the house of Machir the *s*
9: 5 of the house of Machir the *s*
9: 6 Now when Mephibosheth the *s* of
9: 6 the *s* of Saul, had come to
9: 9 have given to your master's *s*
9:10 that your master's *s* may have
9:10 Mephibosheth your master's *s*
9:12 Mephibosheth had a young *s* whose
10: 1 and Hanun his *s* reigned in his
10: 2 show kindness to Hanun the *s*
11:21 Who struck Abimelech the *s* of
11:27 his wife and bore him a *s*.
12:24 So she bore a *s*, and he
13: 1 After this Absalom the *s* of
13: 1 and Amnon the *s* of David loved
13: 3 whose name was Jonadab the *s*
13: 4 "Why are you, the king's *s*,
13:25 said to Absalom, "No, my *s*,
13:32 Then Jonadab the *s* of Shimeah,
13:37 fled and went to Talmai the *s*
13:37 And David mourned for his *s*
14: 1 So Joab the *s* of Zeruiah
14:11 anymore, lest they destroy my *s*.
14:11 not one hair of your *s* shall
14:16 who would destroy me and my *s*
15:27 sons with you, Ahimaaz your *s*,
15:27 and Jonathan the *s* of Abiathar.
15:36 two sons, Ahimaaz, Zadok's *s*,
15:36 and Jonathan, Abiathar's *s*;
16: 3 "And where is your master's *s*?
16: 5 whose name was Shimei the *s* of
16: 8 into the hand of Absalom your *s*.
16: 9 Then Abishai the *s* of Zeruiah
16:11 See how my *s* who came from my
16:19 serve in the presence of his *s*?
17:25 This Amasa was the *s* of a man
17:27 that Shobi the *s* of Nahash from
17:27 Machir the *s* of Ammiel from Lo
18: 2 the hand of Abishai the *s* of
18:12 my hand against the king's *s*.
18:18 I have no *s* to keep my name in
18:19 Then Ahimaaz the *s* of Zadok
18:20 because the king's *s* is dead."
18:22 And Ahimaaz the *s* of Zadok said
18:22 said, "Why will you run, my *s*,
18:27 the running of Ahimaaz the *s*
18:33 O my *s* Absalom—my son, my son
18:33 thus: "O my son Absalom—my *s*,
18:33 my *s* Absalom—if only I had died
18:33 in your place! O Absalom my *s*,
18:33 my son, my *s*!"
19: 2 "The king is grieved for his *s*.
19: 4 O my *s* Absalom! O Absalom, my
19: 4 my son Absalom! O Absalom, my *s*,
19: 4 my son, my *s*!"
19:16 And Shimei the *s* of Gera, a
19:18 Now Shimei the *s* of Gera fell
19:21 But Abishai the *s* of Zeruiah
19:24 Now Mephibosheth the *s* of Saul
20: 1 whose name was Sheba the *s* of
20: 1 do we have inheritance in the *s*
20: 2 and followed Sheba the *s* of
20: 6 Now Sheba the *s* of Bichri will
20: 7 to pursue Sheba the *s* of
20:10 brother pursued Sheba the *s* of
20:13 Joab to pursue Sheba the *s* of
20:21 Sheba the *s* of Bichri by name,
20:22 off the head of Sheba the *s* of
20:23 Benaiah the *s* of Jehoiada was
20:24 Jehoshaphat the *s* of Ahilud
21: 7 king spared Mephibosheth the *s*
21: 7 the *s* of Saul, because of the
21: 7 David and Jonathan the *s* of
21: 8 brought up for Adriel the *s* of
21:12 and the bones of Jonathan his *s*,
21:13 and the bones of Jonathan his *s*
21:14 of Saul and Jonathan his *s* in
21:17 But Abishai the *s* of Zeruiah
21:19 where Elhanan the *s* of
21:21 Jonathan the *s* of Shimea,
23: 1 Thus says David the *s* of
23: 9 after him was Eleazar the *s*
23:11 after him was Shammah the *s*
23:18 the *s* of Zeruiah, was chief of
23:20 Benaiah was the *s* of Jehoiada,
23:20 the *s* of a valiant man from
23:22 These things Benaiah the *s* of
23:24 Elhanan the *s* of Dodo of
23:26 Ira the *s* of Ikkesh the
23:29 Heleb the *s* of Baanah
23:29 Ittai the *s* of Ribai from
23:33 Ahiam the *s* of Sharar the
23:34 Eliphelet the *s* of Ahasbai, the
23:34 the *s* of the Maachathite, Eliam
23:34 Eliam the *s* of Ahithophel the
23:36 Igal the *s* of Nathan of Zobah,
23:37 (armorbearer of Joab the *s* of
1 Ki 1: 5 Then Adonijah the *s* of Haggith
1: 7 he conferred with Joab the *s*
1: 8 Benaiah the *s* of Jehoiada,
1:11 not heard that Adonijah the *s*
1:12 own life and the life of your *s*
1:13 Assuredly your *s* Solomon shall
1:17 Assuredly Solomon your *s* shall
1:21 that I and my *s* Solomon will be
1:26 nor Benaiah the *s* of Jehoiada,
1:30 Assuredly Solomon your *s* shall
1:32 and Benaiah the *s* of
1:33 and have Solomon my *s* ride on
1:36 Benaiah the *s* of Jehoiada
1:38 Benaiah the *s* of Jehoiada, the
1:42 the *s* of Abiathar the priest.
1:44 Benaiah the *s* of Jehoiada, the
2: 1 and he charged Solomon his *s*,
2: 5 you know also what Joab the *s*
2: 5 to Abner the *s* of Ner and Amasa
2: 5 the son of Ner and Amasa the *s*
2: 8 have with you Shimei the *s* of
2:13 Now Adonijah the *s* of Haggith
2:22 and for Joab the *s* of
2:25 by the hand of Benaiah the *s*
2:29 Solomon sent Benaiah the *s* of
2:32 Abner the *s* of Ner, the
2:32 and Amasa the *s* of Jether, the
2:34 So Benaiah the *s* of Jehoiada
2:35 The king put Benaiah the *s* of
2:39 ran away to Achish the *s* of
2:46 king commanded Benaiah the *s*
3: 6 and You have given him a *s* to
3:19 And this woman's *s* died in the
3:20 of the night and took my *s*
3:21 in the morning to nurse my *s*,
3:21 he was not my *s* whom I had
3:22 But the living one is my *s*,
3:22 and the dead one is your *s*.
3:22 But the dead one is your *s*,
3:22 and the living one is my *s*.
3:23 "The one says, 'This is my *s*,
3:23 and your *s* is the dead one';
3:23 No! But your *s* is the dead one,
3:23 and my *s* is the living one.'
3:26 Then the woman whose *s* was
3:26 with compassion for her *s*;
4: 2 Azariah the *s* of Zadok, the
4: 3 Jehoshaphat the *s* of Ahilud,
4: 4 Benaiah the *s* of Jehoiada, over
4: 5 Azariah the *s* of Nathan, over
4: 5 Zabud the *s* of Nathan, a priest
4: 6 and Adoniram the *s* of Abda,
4:12 Baana the *s* of Ahilud, in
4:13 the towns of Jair the *s* of
4:14 Ahinadab the *s* of Iddo, in
4:16 Baanah the *s* of Hushai, in Asher
4:17 Jehoshaphat the *s* of Paruah, in
4:18 Shimei the *s* of Elah, in
4:19 Geber the *s* of Uri, in the land
5: 5 father David, saying, "Your *s*,
5: 7 for He has given David a wise *s*
7:14 He was the *s* of a widow from
8:19 but your *s* who will come from
11:12 it out of the hand of your *s*.
11:13 I will give one tribe to your *s*
11:20 bore him Genubath his *s*,
11:23 Rezon the *s* of Eliadah, who had
11:26 Jeroboam the *s* of Nebat, an
11:36 And to his *s* I will give one
11:43 And Rehoboam his *s* reigned in
12: 2 when Jeroboam the *s* of Nebat
12:15 Shilonite to Jeroboam the *s* of
12:16 have no inheritance in the *s*
12:21 the kingdom to Rehoboam the *s*
12:23 Speak to Rehoboam the *s* of
14: 1 At that time Abijah the *s* of
14: 5 ask you something about her *s*,
14:20 Then Nadab his *s* reigned in his
14:21 And Rehoboam the *s* of Solomon
14:31 Then Abijam his *s* reigned in
15: 1 year of King Jeroboam the *s* of
15: 4 by setting up his *s* after him
15: 8 Then Asa his *s* reigned in his
15:18 sent them to Ben-Hadad the *s*
15:18 the *s* of Hezion, king of Syria,
15:24 Then Jehoshaphat his *s* reigned
15:25 Now Nadab the *s* of Jeroboam
15:27 Then Baasha the *s* of Ahijah, of
15:33 Baasha the *s* of Ahijah became
16: 1 of the LORD came to Jehu the *s*
16: 3 the house of Jeroboam the *s* of
16: 6 Then Elah his *s* reigned in his
16: 7 came by the prophet Jehu the *s*
16: 8 Elah the *s* of Baasha became
16:13 and the sins of Elah his *s*,
16:21 people followed Tibni the *s* of
16:22 who followed Tibni the *s* of
16:26 all the ways of Jeroboam the *s*
16:28 Then Ahab his *s* reigned in his
16:29 Ahab the *s* of Omri became king
16:29 and Ahab the *s* of Omri reigned
16:30 Now Ahab the *s* of Omri did evil
16:31 in the sins of Jeroboam the *s*
16:34 and with his youngest *s* Segub
16:34 spoken through Joshua the *s* of
17:12 prepare it for myself and my *s*,
17:13 some for yourself and your *s*.
17:17 after these things that the *s*
17:18 remembrance, and to kill my *s*?
17:19 said to her, "Give me your *s*.
17:20 whom I lodge, by killing her *s*?
17:23 'See, your *s* lives!"
19:16 you shall anoint Jehu the *s* of
19:16 And Elisha the *s* of Shaphat of
19:19 and found Elisha the *s* of
21:22 the house of Jeroboam the *s* of
21:22 like the house of Baasha the *s*
21:29 In the days of his *s* I will
22: 8 Micaiah the *s* of Imlah, by whom
22: 9 Bring Micaiah the *s* of Imlah
22:11 Now Zedekiah the *s* of Chenaanah
22:24 Now Zedekiah the *s* of Chenaanah
22:26 city and to Joash the king's *s*;
22:40 Then Ahaziah his *s* reigned in
22:41 Jehoshaphat the *s* of Asa had
22:49 Then Ahaziah the *s* of Ahab said
22:50 Then Jehoram his *s* reigned in
22:51 Ahaziah the *s* of Ahab became
22:52 in the way of Jeroboam the *s*
2 Ki 1:17 Because he had no *s*, Jehoram
1:17 second year of Jehoram the *s*
3: 1 Now Jehoram the *s* of Ahab became
3: 3 in the sins of Jeroboam the *s*
3:11 Elisha the *s* of Shaphat is
3:27 Then he took his eldest *s* who
4: 6 full, that she said to her *s*,
4:14 "Actually, she has no *s*,
4:16 next year you shall embrace a *s*.
4:17 and bore a *s* when the appointed
4:28 'Did I ask a *s* of my lord?
4:36 him, he said, "Pick up your *s*.
4:37 then she picked up her *s* and
6:28 woman said to me, 'Give your *s*,
6:28 and we will eat my *s* tomorrow.'
6:29 "So we boiled my *s*,
6:29 on the next day, 'Give your *s*,
6:29 him'; but she has hidden her *s*.
6:31 if the head of Elisha the *s* of
6:32 Do you see how this *s* of a
8: 1 spoke to the woman whose *s* he
8: 5 there was the woman whose *s* he
8: 5 and this is her *s* whom Elisha
8: 9 Your *s* Ben-Hadad king of Syria
8:16 the fifth year of Joram the *s* of
8:16 Jehoram the *s* of Jehoshaphat
8:24 Then Ahaziah his *s* reigned in
8:25 twelfth year of Joram the *s* of
8:25 Ahaziah the *s* of Jehoram, king
8:28 Now he went with Joram the *s* of
8:29 And Ahaziah the *s* of Jehoram,
8:29 went down to see Joram the *s* of
9: 2 look there for Jehu the *s* of
9: 2 the *s* of Nimshi, and go in and
9: 9 the house of Jeroboam the *s* of
9: 9 like the house of Baasha the *s*
9:14 So Jehu the *s* of Jehoshaphat,
9:14 the *s* of Nimshi, conspired
9:20 like the driving of Jehu the *s*
9:29 eleventh year of Joram the *s*
10:15 he met Jehonadab the *s* of
10:23 Then Jehu and Jehonadab the *s* of
10:29 the sins of Jeroboam the *s* of
10:35 Then Jehoahaz his *s* reigned in
11: 1 of Ahaziah saw that her *s* was
11: 2 took Joash the *s* of Ahaziah,
11: 4 and showed them the king's *s*.
11:12 And he brought out the king's *s*,
12:21 For Jozachar the *s* of Shimeath
12:21 of Shimeath and Jehozabad the *s*
12:21 Then Amaziah his *s* reigned in
13: 1 year of Joash the *s* of Ahaziah,
13: 1 Jehoahaz the *s* of Jehu became
13: 2 the sins of Jeroboam the *s* of
13: 3 the hand of Ben-Hadad the *s* of
13: 9 Then Joash his *s* reigned in his
13:10 Jehoash the *s* of Jehoahaz
13:11 all the sins of Jeroboam the *s*
13:24 Then Ben-Hadad his *s* reigned in
13:25 And Jehoash the *s* of Jehoahaz
13:25 the *s* of Hazael, the cities
14: 1 the second year of Joash the *s*
14: 1 Amaziah the *s* of Joash, king of
14: 8 messengers to Jehoash the *s* of
14: 8 the *s* of Jehu, king of Israel,
14: 9 Give your daughter to my *s* as
14:13 the *s* of Jehoash, the son of
14:13 the *s* of Ahaziah, at Beth
14:16 Then Jeroboam his *s* reigned in
14:17 Amaziah the *s* of Joash, king of
14:17 the death of Jehoash the *s* of
14:23 year of Amaziah the *s* of Joash,
14:23 Jeroboam the *s* of Joash, king
14:24 all the sins of Jeroboam the *s*
14:25 His servant Jonah the *s* of
14:27 by the hand of Jeroboam the *s*
14:29 Then Zechariah his *s* reigned in
15: 1 Azariah the *s* of Amaziah, king
15: 5 And Jotham the king's *s* was
15: 7 Then Jotham his *s* reigned in
15: 8 Zechariah the *s* of Jeroboam
15: 9 the sins of Jeroboam the *s* of
15:10 Then Shallum the *s* of Jabesh
15:13 Shallum the *s* of Jabesh became
15:14 For Menahem the *s* of Gadi went
15:14 and struck Shallum the *s* of
15:17 Menahem the *s* of Gadi became
15:18 the sins of Jeroboam the *s* of
15:22 Then Pekahiah his *s* reigned in
15:23 Pekahiah the *s* of Menahem
15:24 the sins of Jeroboam the *s* of
15:25 Then Pekah the *s* of Remaliah, an
15:27 Pekah the *s* of Remaliah became
15:28 the sins of Jeroboam the *s* of
15:30 Then Hoshea the *s* of Elah led a
15:30 conspiracy against Pekah the *s*
15:30 twentieth year of Jotham the *s*
15:32 the second year of Pekah the *s*
15:32 Jotham the *s* of Uzziah, king of
15:37 king of Syria and Pekah the *s*

15:38 Then Ahaz his *s* reigned in his
16: 1 year of Pekah the *s* of
16: 1 Ahaz the *s* of Jotham, king of
16: 3 indeed he made his *s* pass
16: 5 king of Syria and Pekah the *s*
16: 7 "I am your servant and your *s*.
16:20 Then Hezekiah his *s* reigned in
17: 1 Hoshea the *s* of Elah became
17:21 and they made Jeroboam the *s* of
18: 1 the third year of Hoshea the *s*
18: 1 that Hezekiah the *s* of Ahaz,
18: 9 seventh year of Hoshea the *s*
18:18 Eliakim the *s* of Hilkiah, who
18:18 and Joah the *s* of Asaph, the
18:26 Then Eliakim the *s* of Hilkiah,
18:37 Then Eliakim the *s* of Hilkiah,
18:37 and Joah the *s* of Asaph, the
19: 2 the prophet, the *s* of Amoz.
19:20 Then Isaiah the *s* of Amoz sent
19:37 Then Esarhaddon his *s* reigned
20: 1 the *s* of Amoz, went to him and
20:12 time Berodach-Baladan the *s* of
20:21 Then Manasseh his *s* reigned in
21: 6 Also he made his *s* pass through
21: 7 to David and to Solomon his *s*,
21:18 Then his *s* Amon reigned in his
21:24 people of the land made his *s*
21:26 Then Josiah his *s* reigned in
22: 3 the *s* of Azaliah, the son of
22: 3 the *s* of Meshullam, to the
22:12 Ahikam the *s* of Shaphan, Achbor
22:12 Achbor the *s* of Michaiah,
22:14 the wife of Shallum the *s* of
22:14 the *s* of Harhas, keeper of the
23:10 is in the Valley of the *S* of
23:10 that no man might make his *s* or
23:15 place which Jeroboam the *s* of
23:30 of the land took Jehoahaz the *s*
23:34 Necho made Eliakim the *s* of
24: 6 Then Jehoiachin his *s* reigned
25:22 Then he made Gedaliah the *s* of
25:22 the *s* of Shaphan, governor over
25:23 Ishmael the *s* of Nethaniah,
25:23 Johanan the *s* of Careah,
25:23 Seraiah the *s* of Tanhumeth the
25:23 and Jaazaniah the *s* of a
25:25 month that Ishmael the *s* of
25:25 the *s* of Elishama, of the royal
1 Chr 1:41 The *s* of Anah was Dishon.
1:43 Bela the *s* of Beor, and the
1:44 Jobab the *s* of Zerah of Bozrah
1:46 Hadad the *s* of Bedad, who
1:49 Baal-Hanan the *s* of Achbor
2: 7 The *s* of Carmi was Achar, the
2: 8 The *s* of Ethan was Azariah.
2:18 Caleb the *s* of Hezron had
2:31 The *s* of Appaim was Ishi, the
2:31 the *s* of Ishi was Sheshan, and
2:45 And the *s* of Shammai was Maon,
3: 2 Absalom the *s* of Maacah, the
3: 2 Adonijah the *s* of Haggith;
3:10 Solomon's *s* was Rehoboam;
3:10 Abijah was his *s*, Asa his
3:10 Abijah was his son, Asa his *s*,
3:10 Asa his son, Jehoshaphat his *s*,
3:11 Joram his *s*, Ahaziah his
3:11 Joram his son, Ahaziah his *s*,
3:11 Ahaziah his son, Joash his *s*,
3:12 Amaziah his *s*, Azariah his
3:12 Amaziah his son, Azariah his *s*,
3:12 Azariah his son, Jotham his *s*,
3:13 Ahaz his *s*, Hezekiah his
3:13 Ahaz his son, Hezekiah his *s*,
3:13 his son, Manasseh his *s*,
3:14 Amon his *s*, and Josiah his
3:14 Amon his son, and Josiah his *s*.
3:16 Jehoiakim were Jeconiah his *s*
3:16 his son and Zedekiah his *s*.
3:17 were Assir, Shealtiel his *s*,
3:22 The *s* of Shechaniah was
4: 2 And Reaiah the *s* of Shobal begot
4: 8 the families of Aharhel the *s*
4:15 The sons of Caleb the *s* of
4:15 The *s* of Elah was Kenaz.
4:21 The sons of Shelah the *s* of
4:25 Shallum his *s*, Mibsam his
4:25 Shallum his son, Mibsam his *s*,
4:25 his son, and Mishma his *s*.
4:26 of Mishma were Hamuel his *s*,
4:26 Hamuel his son, Zacchur his *s*,
4:26 his son, and Shimei his *s*.
4:34 and Joshah the *s* of Amaziah;
4:35 and Jehu the *s* of Joshibiah,
4:35 the *s* of Seraiah, the son of
4:35 Seraiah, the *s* of Asiel;
4:37 Ziza the *s* of Shiphi, the son of
4:37 the *s* of Allon, the son of
4:37 the *s* of Jedaiah, the son of
4:37 the *s* of Shimri, the son of
4:37 the *s* of Shemaiah—
5: 1 the *s* of Israel, so that the
5: 4 of Joel were Shemaiah his *s*,
5: 4 Shemaiah his son, Gog his *s*,
5: 4 son, Gog his son, Shimei his *s*,
5: 5 Micah his *s*, Reaiah his
5: 5 Micah his son, Reaiah his *s*,
5: 5 son, Reaiah his son, Baal his *s*,
5: 6 and Beerah his *s*,
5: 8 and Bela the *s* of Azaz, the son
5: 8 the *s* of Shema, the son of
5: 8 the *s* of Joel, who dwelt in
5:14 the children of Abihail the *s*
5:14 the *s* of Jaroah, the son of
5:14 the *s* of Gilead, the son of
5:14 the *s* of Michael, the son of
5:14 the *s* of Jeshishai, the son of
5:14 the *s* of Jahdo, the son of Buz;
5:14 son of Jahdo, the *s* of Buz;
5:15 Ahi the *s* of Abdiel, the son of
5:15 the *s* of Guni, was chief of
6:20 Of Gershon were Libni his *s*,
6:20 Libni his son, Jahath his *s*,
6:20 Jahath his son, Zimmah his *s*,
6:21 Joah his *s*, Iddo his son,
6:21 Joah his son, Iddo his *s*,
6:21 son, Iddo his son, Zerah his *s*,
6:21 his son, and Jeatherai his *s*.
6:22 of Kohath were Amminadab his *s*,
6:22 Amminadab his son, Korah his *s*,
6:22 son, Korah his son, Assir his *s*,
6:23 Elkanah his *s*, Ebiasaph his
6:23 Elkanah his son, Ebiasaph his *s*,
6:23 Ebiasaph his son, Assir his *s*,
6:24 Tahath his *s*, Uriel his son,
6:24 Tahath his son, Uriel his *s*,
6:24 Uriel his son, Uzziah his *s*,
6:24 Uzziah his son, and Shaul his *s*.
6:26 of Elkanah were Zophai his *s*,
6:26 Zophai his son, Nahath his *s*,
6:27 Eliab his *s*, Jeroham his
6:27 Eliab his son, Jeroham his *s*,
6:27 his son, and Elkanah his *s*.
6:29 Merari were Mahli, Libni his *s*,
6:29 Libni his son, Shimei his *s*,
6:29 Shimei his son, Uzzah his *s*,
6:30 Shimea his *s*, Haggiah his
6:30 Shimea his son, Haggiah his *s*,
6:30 his son, and Asaiah his *s*.
6:33 the *s* of Joel, the son of
6:33 of Joel, the *s* of Samuel,
6:34 the *s* of Elkanah, the son of
6:34 the *s* of Jeroham, the son of
6:34 the *s* of Eliel, the son of
6:34 of Eliel, the *s* of Toah,
6:35 the *s* of Zuph, the son of
6:35 the *s* of Elkanah, the son of
6:35 the *s* of Mahath, the son of
6:35 of Mahath, the *s* of Amasai,
6:36 the *s* of Elkanah, the son of
6:36 the *s* of Joel, the son of
6:36 the *s* of Azariah, the son of
6:36 the *s* of Zephaniah,
6:37 the *s* of Tahath, the son of
6:37 the *s* of Assir, the son of
6:37 the *s* of Ebiasaph, the son of
6:37 of Ebiasaph, the *s* of Korah,
6:38 the *s* of Izhar, the son of
6:38 the *s* of Kohath, the son of
6:38 the *s* of Levi, the son of
6:38 of Levi, the *s* of Israel.
6:39 was Asaph the *s* of Berachiah,
6:39 Berachiah, the *s* of Shimea,
6:40 the *s* of Michael, the son of
6:40 the *s* of Baaseiah, the son of
6:40 Baaseiah, the *s* of Malchijah,
6:41 the *s* of Ethni, the son of
6:41 the *s* of Zerah, the son of
6:41 of Zerah, the *s* of Adaiah,
6:42 the *s* of Ethan, the son of
6:42 the *s* of Zimmah, the son of
6:42 Zimmah, the *s* of Shimei,
6:43 the *s* of Jahath, the son of
6:43 the *s* of Gershon, the son of
6:43 of Gershon, the *s* of Levi.
6:44 were Ethan the *s* of Kishi, the
6:44 the *s* of Abdi, the son of
6:44 of Abdi, the *s* of Malluch,
6:45 the *s* of Hashabiah, the son of
6:45 the *s* of Amaziah, the son of
6:45 Amaziah, the *s* of Hilkiah,
6:46 the *s* of Amzi, the son of Bani,
6:46 the *s* of Bani, the son of
6:46 of Bani, the *s* of Shamer,
6:47 the *s* of Mahli, the son of
6:47 the *s* of Mushi, the son of
6:47 the *s* of Merari, the son of
6:47 of Merari, the *s* of Levi.
6:50 sons of Aaron: Eleazar his *s*,
6:50 Eleazar his son, Phinehas his *s*,
6:50 Phinehas his son, Abishua his *s*,
6:51 Bukki his *s*, Uzzi his son,
6:51 Bukki his son, Uzzi his *s*,
6:51 Uzzi his son, Zerahiah his *s*,
6:52 Meraioth his *s*, Amariah
6:52 Meraioth his son, Amariah his *s*,
6:52 Amariah his son, Ahitub his *s*,
6:53 Zadok his *s*, and Ahimaaz
6:53 his son, and Ahimaaz his *s*.
6:56 they gave to Caleb the *s* of
7: 3 The *s* of Uzzi was Izrahiah, and
7:10 The *s* of Jediael was Bilhan,
7:12 and Hushim was the *s* of Aher.
7:16 the wife of Machir bore a *s*,
7:17 The *s* of Ulam was Bedan.)
7:17 descendants of Gilead the *s* of
7:17 the *s* of Manasseh.
7:20 were Shuthelah, Bered his *s*,
7:20 Bered his son, Tahath his *s*,
7:20 Tahath his son, Eladah his *s*,
7:20 Eladah his son, Tahath his *s*,
7:21 Zabad his *s*, Shuthelah
7:21 Zabad his son, Shuthelah his *s*,
7:23 she conceived and bore a *s*;
7:25 and Rephah was his *s*,
7:25 as Resheph, and Telah his *s*,
7:25 and Telah his son, Tahan his *s*,
7:26 Laadan his *s*, Ammihud his
7:26 Laadan his son, Ammihud his *s*,
7:26 Ammihud his son, Elishama his *s*,
7:27 Nun his *s*, and Joshua his
7:27 Nun his son, and Joshua his *s*.
7:29 the *s* of Israel.
8:30 And his firstborn *s* was Abdon,
8:34 The *s* of Jonathan was
8:37 Moza begot Binea, Raphah his *s*,
8:37 Raphah his son, Eleasah his *s*,
8:37 his son, and Azel his *s*.
9: 4 Uthai the *s* of Ammihud, the son
9: 4 the *s* of Omri, the son of Imri,
9: 4 the *s* of Imri, the son of Bani,
9: 4 the *s* of Bani, of the
9: 4 of Perez, the *s* of Judah.
9: 7 Sallu the *s* of Meshullam, the
9: 7 the *s* of Hodaviah, the son of
9: 7 the *s* of Hassenuah;
9: 8 Ibneiah the *s* of Jeroham; Elah
9: 8 Elah the *s* of Uzzi, the son of
9: 8 the *s* of Michri; Meshullam the
9: 8 Meshullam the *s* of Shephatiah,
9: 8 the *s* of Reuel, the son of
9: 8 the *s* of Ibnijah;
9:11 Azariah the *s* of Hilkiah, the
9:11 the *s* of Meshullam, the son of
9:11 the *s* of Zadok, the son of
9:11 the *s* of Meraioth, the son of
9:11 the *s* of Ahitub, the officer
9:12 Adaiah the *s* of Jeroham, the son
9:12 the *s* of Pashur, the son of
9:12 the *s* of Malchijah; Maasai the
9:12 Maasai the *s* of Adiel, the son
9:12 the *s* of Jahzerah, the son of
9:12 the *s* of Meshullam, the son of
9:12 the *s* of Meshillemith, the son
9:12 Meshillemith, the *s* of Immer;
9:14 Shemaiah the *s* of Hasshub, the
9:14 the *s* of Azrikam, the son of
9:14 the *s* of Hashabiah, of the sons
9:15 and Mattaniah the *s* of Micah,
9:15 the *s* of Zichri, the son of
9:15 of Zichri, the *s* of Asaph;
9:16 Obadiah the *s* of Shemaiah, the
9:16 the *s* of Galal, the son of
9:16 the *s* of Jeduthun;
9:16 and Berechiah the *s* of Asa, the
9:16 the *s* of Elkanah, who lived in
9:19 Shallum the *s* of Kore, the son
9:19 the *s* of Ebiasaph, the son of
9:19 the *s* of Korah, and his
9:20 And Phinehas the *s* of Eleazar
9:21 Zechariah the *s* of Meshelemiah
9:36 His firstborn *s* was Abdon, then
9:40 The *s* of Jonathan was
9:43 begot Binea, Rephaiah his *s*,
9:43 Rephaiah his son, Eleasah his *s*,
9:43 Eleasah his son, and Azel his *s*.
10:14 kingdom over to David the *s* of
11: 6 And Joab the *s* of Zeruiah
11:11 Jashobeam the *s* of a
11:12 After him was Eleazar the *s* of
11:22 Benaiah was the *s* of Jehoiada,
11:22 the *s* of a valiant man from
11:24 These things Benaiah the *s* of
11:26 Elhanan the *s* of Dodo of
11:28 Ira the *s* of Ikkesh the Tekoite,
11:30 Heled the *s* of Baanah the
11:31 Ithai the *s* of Ribai of Gibeah,
11:34 Jonathan the *s* of Shageh the
11:35 Ahiam the *s* of Sacar the
11:35 Eliphal the *s* of Ur,
11:37 Naarai the *s* of Ezbai,
11:38 Mibhar the *s* of Hagri,
11:39 (the armorbearer of Joab the *s*
11:41 Zabad the *s* of Ahlai,
11:42 Adina the *s* of Shiza the
11:43 Hanan the *s* of Maachah,
11:45 Jediael the *s* of Shimri, and
12: 1 a fugitive from Saul the *s* of
12:18 O *s* of Jesse! Peace, peace to
15:17 Levites appointed Heman the *s*
15:17 Asaph the *s* of Berechiah;
15:17 Ethan the *s* of Kushaiah;
16:38 including Obed-Edom the *s* of
17:13 Father, and he shall be My *s*;
18:10 he sent Hadoram his *s* to King
18:12 Moreover Abishai the *s* of
18:15 Joab the *s* of Zeruiah was over
18:15 Jehoshaphat the *s* of Ahilud
18:16 Zadok the *s* of Ahitub and
18:16 of Ahitub and Abimelech the *s*
18:17 Benaiah the *s* of Jehoiada was
19: 1 and his *s* reigned in his place.
19: 2 show kindness to Hanun the *s*
20: 5 and Elhanan the *s* of Jair
20: 7 Jonathan the *s* of Shimea,
22: 5 Solomon my *s* is young and
22: 6 Then he called for his *s*
22: 7 David said to Solomon: "My *s*,
22: 9 a *s* shall be born to you, who
22:10 My name, and he shall be My *s*,
22:11 'Now, my *s*, may the LORD
22:17 of Israel to help Solomon his *s*,
23: 1 he made his *s* Solomon king over
24: 6 Shemaiah the *s* of Nethanel,
24: 6 Ahimelech the *s* of Abiathar,
24:26 the *s* of Jaaziah, Beno.
24:29 the *s* of Kish, Jerahmeel.

26: 1 Meshelemiah the *s* of Kore, of
26: 6 Also to Shemaiah his *s* were sons
26:14 Then they cast lots for his *s*
26:24 Shebuel the *s* of Gershom, the
26:24 the *s* of Moses, was overseer
26:25 by Eliezer were Rehabiah his *s*,
26:25 his son, Jeshaiah his *s*,
26:25 Jeshaiah his son, Joram his *s*,
26:25 Joram his son, Zichri his *s*,
26:25 his son, and Shelomith his *s*.
26:28 Saul the *s* of Kish, Abner the
26:28 Abner the *s* of Ner, and Joab
26:28 and Joab the *s* of Zeruiah had
27: 2 month was Jashobeam the *s* of
27: 5 the *s* of Jehoiada the priest,
27: 6 division was Ammizabad his *s*.
27: 7 and Zebadiah his *s* after him;
27: 9 the sixth month was Ira the *s*
27:16 Reubenites was Eliezer the *s*
27:16 Shephatiah the *s* of Maachah;
27:17 Hashabiah the *s* of Kemuel;
27:18 Omri the *s* of Michael;
27:19 Ishmaiah the *s* of Obadiah;
27:19 Jerimoth the *s* of Azriel;
27:20 Hoshea the *s* of Azaziah;
27:20 Joel the *s* of Pedaiah;
27:21 Iddo the *s* of Zechariah;
27:21 Jaasiel the *s* of Abner;
27:22 Azarel the *s* of Jeroham.
27:24 Joab the *s* of Zeruiah began a
27:25 And Azmaveth the *s* of Adiel
27:25 and Jehonathan the *s* of Uzziah
27:26 Ezri the *s* of Chelub was over
27:29 and Shaphat the *s* of Adlai was
27:32 and Jehiel the *s* of Hachmoni
27:34 Ahithophel was Jehoiada the *s*
28: 5 many sons) He has chosen my *s*
28: 6 It is your *s* Solomon who shall
28: 6 I have chosen him to be My *s*,
28: 9 my *s* Solomon, know the God of
28:11 Then David gave his *s* Solomon
28:20 And David said to his *s*
29: 1 My *s* Solomon, whom alone God has
29:19 And give my *s* Solomon a loyal
29:22 And they made Solomon the *s* of
29:26 Thus David the *s* of Jesse
29:28 and Solomon his *s* reigned in
2 Chr 1: 1 Now Solomon the *s* of David was
1: 5 altar that Bezalel the *s* of
1: 5 the *s* of Hur, had made, he put
2:12 has given King David a wise *s*,
2:14 (the *s* of a woman of the
6: 9 but your *s* who will come from
9:29 seer concerning Jeroboam the *s*
9:31 And Rehoboam his *s* reigned in
10: 2 when Jeroboam the *s* of Nebat
10:15 Shilonite to Jeroboam the *s* of
10:16 have no inheritance in the *s*
11: 3 Speak to Rehoboam the *s* of
11:17 and made Rehoboam the *s* of
11:18 the daughter of Jerimoth the *s*
11:18 the daughter of Eliah the *s* of
11:22 appointed Abijah the *s* of
12:16 Then Abijah his *s* reigned in
13: 6 Yet Jeroboam the *s* of Nebat, the
13: 6 the servant of Solomon the *s* of
13: 7 against Rehoboam the *s* of
14: 1 Then Asa his *s* reigned in his
15: 1 of God came upon Azariah the *s*
17: 1 Then Jehoshaphat his *s* reigned
17:16 next to him was Amasiah the *s*
18: 7 He is Micaiah the *s* of Imla."
18: 8 Bring Micaiah the *s* of Imla
18:10 Now Zedekiah the *s* of Chenaanah
18:23 Then Zedekiah the *s* of
18:25 city and to Joash the king's *s*;
19: 2 And Jehu the *s* of Hanani the
19:11 and Zebadiah the *s* of Ishmael,
20:14 LORD came upon Jahaziel the *s*
20:14 the *s* of Benaiah, the son of
20:14 the *s* of Jeiel, the son of
20:14 the *s* of Mattaniah, a Levite of
20:34 in the book of Jehu the *s* of
20:37 But Eliezer the *s* of Dodavah of
21: 1 Then Jehoram his *s* reigned in
21:17 so that there was not a *s* left
22: 1 made Ahaziah his youngest *s*
22: 1 So Ahaziah the *s* of Jehoram,
22: 5 and went with Jehoram the *s* of
22: 6 And Azariah the *s* of Jehoram,
22: 6 went down to see Jehoram the *s*
22: 7 Jehoram against Jehu the *s* of
22: 9 he is the *s* of Jehoshaphat, who
22:10 of Ahaziah saw that her *s* was
22:11 took Joash the *s* of Ahaziah,
23: 1 Azariah the *s* of Jeroham,
23: 1 Ishmael the *s* of Jehohanan,
23: 1 Azariah the *s* of Obed, Maaseiah
23: 1 Maaseiah the *s* of Adaiah, and
23: 1 and Elishaphat the *s* of Zichri.
23: 3 the king's *s* shall reign, as
23:11 they brought out the king's *s*,
24:20 God came upon Zechariah the *s*
24:22 done to him, but killed his *s*;
24:26 Zabad the *s* of Shimeath the
24:26 and Jehozabad the *s* of Shimrith
24:27 Then Amaziah his *s* reigned in
25:17 advice and sent to Joash the *s*
25:17 the *s* of Jehu, king of Israel,
25:18 Give your daughter to my *s* as
25:23 the *s* of Joash, the son of
25:23 the *s* of Jehoahaz, at Beth
25:25 Amaziah the *s* of Joash, king of
25:25 after the death of Joash the *s*
26:21 Then Jotham his *s* was over the
26:22 the prophet Isaiah the *s* of
26:23 Then Jotham his *s* reigned in
27: 9 Then Ahaz his *s* reigned in his
28: 3 incense in the Valley of the *S*
28: 6 For Pekah the *s* of Remaliah
28: 7 killed Maaseiah the king's *s*,
28:12 Azariah the *s* of Johanan,
28:12 Berechiah the *s* of
28:12 Jehizkiah the *s* of Shallum, and
28:12 and Amasa the *s* of Hadlai,
28:27 Then Hezekiah his *s* reigned in
29:12 Mahath the *s* of Amasai and Joel
29:12 son of Amasai and Joel the *s*
29:12 Kish the *s* of Abdi and Azariah
29:12 son of Abdi and Azariah the *s*
29:12 Joah the *s* of Zimmah and Eden
29:12 son of Zimmah and Eden the *s*
30:26 the time of Solomon the *s* of
31:14 Kore the *s* of Imnah the Levite,
32:20 the *s* of Amoz, prayed and cried
32:32 the *s* of Amoz, and in the book
32:33 Then Manasseh his *s* reigned in
33: 6 fire in the Valley of the *S* of
33: 7 to David and to Solomon his *s*,
33:20 Then his *s* Amon reigned in his
33:25 people of the land made his *s*
34: 8 he sent Shaphan the *s* of
34: 8 and Joah the *s* of Joahaz the
34:20 Ahikam the *s* of Shaphan, Abdon
34:20 Abdon the *s* of Micah, Shaphan
34:22 the wife of Shallum the *s* of
34:22 the *s* of Hasrah, keeper of the
35: 3 the house which Solomon the *s*
35: 4 instruction of Solomon his *s*.
36: 1 of the land took Jehoahaz the *s*
36: 8 Then Jehoiachin his *s* reigned
Ezra 3: 2 Then Jeshua the *s* of Jozadak and
3: 2 and Zerubbabel the *s* of
3: 8 Zerubbabel the *s* of Shealtiel,
3: 8 Jeshua the *s* of Jozadak, and
5: 1 Haggai and Zechariah the *s* of
5: 2 So Zerubbabel the *s* of Shealtiel
5: 2 of Shealtiel and Jeshua the *s*
6:14 prophet and Zechariah the *s* of
7: 1 Ezra the *s* of Seraiah, the son
7: 1 the *s* of Azariah, the son of
7: 1 the *s* of Hilkiah,
7: 2 the *s* of Shallum, the son of
7: 2 the *s* of Zadok, the son of
7: 2 of Zadok, the *s* of Ahitub,
7: 3 the *s* of Amariah, the son of
7: 3 the *s* of Azariah, the son of
7: 3 the *s* of Meraioth,
7: 4 the *s* of Zerahiah, the son of
7: 4 the *s* of Uzzi, the son of
7: 4 of Uzzi, the *s* of Bukki,
7: 5 the *s* of Abishua, the son of
7: 5 the *s* of Phinehas, the son of
7: 5 the *s* of Eleazar, the son of
7: 5 the *s* of Aaron the chief
8: 4 Eliehoenai the *s* of Zerahiah,
8: 6 Ebed the *s* of Jonathan, and
8: 7 Jeshaiah the *s* of Athaliah, and
8: 8 Zebadiah the *s* of Michael, and
8: 9 Obadiah the *s* of Jehiel, and
8:11 Zechariah the *s* of Bebai, and
8:12 Johanan the *s* of Hakkatan, and
8:18 of the sons of Mahli the *s* of
8:18 the *s* of Israel, namely
8:33 by the hand of Meremoth the *s*
8:33 with him was Eleazar the *s* of
8:33 Jozabad the *s* of Jeshua and
8:33 of Jeshua and Noadiah the *s* of
10: 2 And Shechaniah the *s* of Jehiel,
10: 6 the chamber of Jehohanan the *s*
10:15 Only Jonathan the *s* of Asahel
10:15 of Asahel and Jahaziah the *s*
10:18 of the sons of Jeshua the *s* of
Neh 1: 1 The words of Nehemiah the *s* of
3: 2 And next to them Zaccur the *s*
3: 4 next to them Meremoth the *s* of
3: 4 the *s* of Koz, made repairs.
3: 4 Next to them Meshullam the *s* of
3: 4 the *s* of Meshezabel, made
3: 4 Next to them Zadok the *s* of
3: 6 Moreover Jehoiada the *s* of
3: 6 of Paseah and Meshullam the *s*
3: 8 Next to him Uzziel the *s* of
3: 9 next to them Rephaiah the *s* of
3:10 Next to them Jedaiah the *s* of
3:10 And next to him Hattush the *s*
3:11 Malchijah the *s* of Harim and
3:11 son of Harim and Hashub the *s*
3:12 next to him was Shallum the *s*
3:14 Malchijah the *s* of Rechab,
3:15 Shallun the *s* of Col-Hozeh,
3:16 After him Nehemiah the *s* of
3:17 under Rehum the *s* of Bani,
3:18 under Bavai the *s* of Henadad,
3:19 And next to him Ezer the *s* of
3:20 After him Baruch the *s* of Zabbai
3:21 After him Meremoth the *s* of
3:21 the *s* of Koz, repaired another
3:23 After them Azariah the *s* of
3:23 the *s* of Ananiah, made repairs
3:24 After him Binnui the *s* of
3:25 Palal the *s* of Uzai made
3:25 After him Pedaiah the *s* of
3:29 After them Zadok the *s* of Immer
3:29 After him Shemaiah the *s* of
3:30 After him Hananiah the *s* of
3:30 the sixth *s* of Zalaph, repaired
3:30 After him Meshullam the *s* of
6:10 to the house of Shemaiah the *s*
6:10 the *s* of Mehetabel, who was a
6:18 son-in-law of Shechaniah the *s*
6:18 and his *s* Jehohanan had married
6:18 daughter of Meshullam the *s* of
8:17 since the days of Joshua the *s*
10: 1 the *s* of Hacaliah, and
10: 9 Jeshua the *s* of Azaniah, Binnui
11: 4 Athaiah the *s* of Uzziah, the
11: 4 the *s* of Zechariah, the son of
11: 4 the *s* of Amariah, the son of
11: 4 the *s* of Shephatiah, the son of
11: 4 the *s* of Mahalalel, of the
11: 5 and Maaseiah the *s* of Baruch,
11: 5 the *s* of Col-Hozeh, the son of
11: 5 the *s* of Hazaiah, the son of
11: 5 the *s* of Adaiah, the son of
11: 5 the *s* of Joiarib, the son of
11: 5 the *s* of Zechariah, the son of
11: 5 Zechariah, the *s* of Shiloni.
11: 7 Sallu the *s* of Meshullam, the
11: 7 the *s* of Joed, the son of
11: 7 the *s* of Pedaiah, the son of
11: 7 the *s* of Kolaiah, the son of
11: 7 the *s* of Maaseiah, the son of
11: 7 the *s* of Ithiel, the son of
11: 7 the *s* of Jeshaiah;
11: 9 Joel the *s* of Zichri was their
11: 9 and Judah the *s* of Senuah was
11:10 Jedaiah the *s* of Joiarib, and
11:11 Seraiah the *s* of Hilkiah, the
11:11 the *s* of Meshullam, the son of
11:11 the *s* of Zadok, the son of
11:11 the *s* of Meraioth, the son of
11:11 the *s* of Ahitub, was the
11:12 and Adaiah the *s* of Jeroham,
11:12 the *s* of Pelaliah, the son of
11:12 the *s* of Amzi, the son of
11:12 the *s* of Zechariah, the son of
11:12 the *s* of Pashhur, the son of
11:12 the *s* of Malchijah,
11:13 and Amashai the *s* of Azarel,
11:13 the *s* of Ahzai, the son of
11:13 the *s* of Meshillemoth, the son
11:13 Meshillemoth, the *s* of Immer,
11:14 overseer was Zabdiel the *s* of
11:15 Shemaiah the *s* of Hasshub, the
11:15 the *s* of Azrikam, the son of
11:15 the *s* of Hashabiah, the son of
11:15 Hashabiah, the *s* of Bunni;
11:17 Mattaniah the *s* of Micha, the
11:17 the *s* of Zabdi, the son of
11:17 the *s* of Asaph, the leader who
11:17 and Abda the *s* of Shammua, the
11:17 the *s* of Galal, the son of
11:17 the *s* of Jeduthun.
11:22 at Jerusalem was Uzzi the *s*
11:22 the *s* of Hashabiah, the son of
11:22 the *s* of Mattaniah, the son of
11:22 the *s* of Micha, of the sons of
11:24 Pethahiah the *s* of Meshezabel,
11:24 of the children of Zerah the *s*
12: 1 came up with Zerubbabel the *s*
12:17 the *s* of Minjamin;
12:23 the days of Johanan the *s* of
12:24 and Jeshua the *s* of Kadmiel,
12:26 in the days of Joiakim the *s*
12:26 the *s* of Jozadak, and in the
12:35 Zechariah the *s* of Jonathan, the
12:35 the *s* of Shemaiah, the son of
12:35 the *s* of Mattaniah, the son of
12:35 the *s* of Michaiah, the son of
12:35 the *s* of Zaccur, the son of
12:35 the *s* of Asaph,
12:45 of David and Solomon his *s*.
13:13 next to them was Hanan the *s*
13:13 the *s* of Mattaniah; for they
13:28 the *s* of Eliashib the high
Esth 2: 5 whose name was Mordecai the *s*
2: 5 the *s* of Shimei, the son of
2: 5 the *s* of Kish, a Benjamite.
3: 1 the *s* of Hammedatha the
3:10 the *s* of Hammedatha the
8: 5 the *s* of Hammedatha the
9:10 the ten sons of Haman the *s* of
9:24 the *s* of Hammedatha the
Job 18:19 He has neither *s* nor posterity
25: 6 And a *s* of man, who is a
32: 2 the *s* of Barachel the Buzite,
32: 6 the *s* of Barachel the Buzite,
35: 8 And your righteousness a *s* of
Ps 2: 7 has said to Me, 'You are My *S*,
2:12 Kiss the *S*, lest He be
3: when he fled from Absalom his *s*.
8: 4 And the *s* of man that You
9: the tune of "Death of the *S*.
50:20 slander your own mother's *s*.
72: 1 righteousness to the king's *S*.
72:20 The prayers of David the *s* of
80:17 Upon the *s* of man whom You
86:16 And save the *s* of Your
89:22 Nor the *s* of wickedness
116:16 the *s* of Your maidservant;
144: 3 Or the *s* of man, that You are
146: 3 Nor in a *s* of man, in whom
Prov 1: 1 The proverbs of Solomon the *s*
1: 8 My *s*, hear the instruction
1:10 My *s*, if sinners entice you,

1:15 My *s*, do not walk in the way
2: 1 My *s*, if you receive
3: 1 My *s*, do not forget my law,
3:11 My *s*, do not despise the
3:12 Just as a father the *s* in
3:21 My *s*, let them not depart
4: 3 When I was my father's *s*,
4:10 Hear, my *s*, and receive my
4:20 My *s*, give attention to my
5: 1 My *s*, pay attention to my
5:20 For why should you, my *s*,
6: 1 My *s*, if you become surety
6: 3 So do this, my *s*,
6:20 My *s*, keep your father's
7: 1 My *s*, keep my words,
10: 1 A wise *s* makes a glad father,
10: 1 But a foolish *s* is the grief
10: 5 gathers in summer is a wise *s*;
10: 5 who sleeps in harvest is a *s*
13: 1 A wise *s* heeds his father's
13:24 who spares his rod hates his *s*,
15:20 A wise *s* makes a father glad,
17: 2 servant will rule over a *s* who
17:25 A foolish *s* is a grief to his
19:13 A foolish *s* is the ruin of his
19:18 Chasten your *s* while there is
19:26 away his mother Is a *s* who
19:27 listening to instruction, my *s*,
23:15 My *s*, if your heart is wise,
23:19 Hear, my *s*, and be wise;
23:26 My *s*, give me your heart,
24:13 My *s*, eat honey because it
24:21 My *s*, fear the LORD
27:11 My *s*, be wise, and make my
28: 7 the law is a discerning *s*,
29:17 Correct your *s*, and he
29:21 Will have him as a *s* in the
30: 1 The words of Agur the *s* of
31: 2 What, my *s*? And what,
31: 2 And what, *s* of my womb?
31: 2 And what, *s* of my vows?
Eccl 1: 1 the *s* of David, king in
4: 8 He has neither *s* nor brother.
5:14 When he begets a *s*, there is
10:17 when your king is the *s* of
12:12 And further, my *s*, be
Isa 1: 1 The vision of Isaiah the *s* of
2: 1 The word that Isaiah the *s* of
7: 1 pass in the days of Ahaz the *s*
7: 1 the *s* of Uzziah, king of Judah,
7: 1 king of Syria and Pekah the *s*
7: 3 you and Shear-Jashub your *s*,
7: 4 and the *s* of Remaliah.
7: 5 and the *s* of Remaliah have
7: 6 over them, the *s* of Tabel"—
7: 9 of Samaria is Remaliah's *s*.
7:14 shall conceive and bear a *S*,
8: 2 the priest and Zechariah the *s*
8: 3 and she conceived and bore a *s*.
8: 6 in Rezin and in Remaliah's *s*;
9: 6 Unto us a *S* is given;
13: 1 Babylon which Isaiah the *s* of
14:12 O Lucifer, *s* of the morning!
19:11 I am the *s* of the wise, The
19:11 The *s* of ancient kings?"
20: 2 LORD spoke by Isaiah the *s* of
22:20 call My servant Eliakim the *s*
36: 3 And Eliakim the *s* of Hilkiah,
36: 3 and Joah the *s* of Asaph, the
36:22 Then Eliakim the *s* of Hilkiah,
36:22 and Joah the *s* of Asaph, the
37: 2 prophet, the *s* of Amoz.
37:21 Then Isaiah the *s* of Amoz sent
37:38 Then Esarhaddon his *s* reigned
38: 1 the *s* of Amoz, went to him and
39: 1 time Merodach-Baladan the *s* of
49:15 not have compassion on the *s*
51:12 And of the *s* of a man who
56: 2 And the *s* of man who lays
56: 3 Do not let the *s* of the
Jer 1: 1 The words of Jeremiah the *s* of
1: 2 in the days of Josiah the *s* of
1: 3 in the days of Jehoiakim the *s*
1: 3 year of Zedekiah the *s* of
6:26 mourning as for an only *s*,
7:31 is in the Valley of the *S* of
7:32 or the Valley of the *S* of
15: 4 because of Manasseh the *s* of
19: 2 go out to the Valley of the *S*
19: 6 Tophet or the Valley of the *S*
20: 1 Now Pashhur the *s* of Immer, the
21: 1 sent to him Pashhur the *s* of
21: 1 and Zephaniah the *s* of
22:11 LORD concerning Shallum the *s*
22:18 concerning Jehoiakim the *s* of
22:24 though Coniah the *s* of
24: 1 away captive Jeconiah the *s* of
25: 1 fourth year of Jehoiakim the *s*
25: 3 year of Josiah the *s* of Amon,
26: 1 of the reign of Jehoiakim the *s*
26:20 Urijah the *s* of Shemaiah of
26:22 Elnathan the *s* of Achbor, and
26:24 the hand of Ahikam the *s* of
27: 1 of the reign of Jehoiakim the *s*
27: 7 shall serve him and his *s* and
27: 7 him and his son and his son's *s*,
27:20 away captive Jeconiah the *s* of
28: 1 that Hananiah the *s* of Azur
28: 4 to this place Jeconiah the *s*
29: 3 by the hand of Elasah the *s* of
29: 3 and Gemariah the *s* of Hilkiah,
29:21 concerning Ahab the *s* of
29:21 and Zedekiah the *s* of Maaseiah,
29:25 to Zephaniah the *s* of Maaseiah
31:20 Is Ephraim My dear *s*?
32: 7 Hanamel the *s* of Shallum your
32: 8 Then Hanamel my uncle's *s* came
32: 9 the *s* of my uncle who was in
32:12 purchase deed to Baruch the *s*
32:12 *s* of Mahseiah, in the presence
32:12 of Hanamel my uncle's *s*,
32:16 purchase deed to Baruch the *s*
32:35 are in the Valley of the *S* of
33:21 so that he shall not have a *s*
35: 1 in the days of Jehoiakim the *s*
35: 3 Then I took Jaazaniah the *s* of
35: 3 the *s* of Habazziniah, his
35: 4 of the sons of Hanan the *s* of
35: 4 the chamber of Maaseiah the *s*
35: 6 for Jonadab the *s* of Rechab,
35: 8 the voice of Jonadab the *s* of
35:14 The words of Jonadab the *s* of
35:16 the sons of Jonadab the *s* of
35:19 Jonadab the *s* of Rechab shall
36: 1 fourth year of Jehoiakim the *s*
36: 4 Jeremiah called Baruch the *s*
36: 8 And Baruch the *s* of Neriah did
36: 9 fifth year of Jehoiakim the *s*
36:10 the chamber of Gemariah the *s*
36:11 When Michaiah the *s* of
36:11 the *s* of Shaphan, heard all the
36:12 Delaiah the *s* of Shemaiah,
36:12 Elnathan the *s* of Achbor,
36:12 Gemariah the *s* of Shaphan,
36:12 Zedekiah the *s* of Hananiah, and
36:14 the princes sent Jehudi the *s*
36:14 the *s* of Shelemiah, the son of
36:14 the *s* of Cushi, to Baruch,
36:14 So Baruch the *s* of Neriah
36:26 Jerahmeel the king's *s*,
36:26 Seraiah the *s* of Azriel, and
36:26 and Shelemiah the *s* of Abdeel,
36:32 the *s* of Neriah, who wrote on
37: 1 Now King Zedekiah the *s* of
37: 1 instead of Coniah the *s* of
37: 3 the king sent Jehucal the *s* of
37: 3 and Zephaniah the *s* of
37:13 whose name was Irijah the *s*
37:13 the *s* of Hananiah; and he
38: 1 Now Shephatiah the *s* of Mattan,
38: 1 Gedaliah the *s* of Pashhur,
38: 1 Jucal the *s* of Shelemiah, and
38: 1 and Pashhur the *s* of Malchiah
38: 6 of Malchiah the king's *s*,
39:14 him to Gedaliah the *s* of
39:14 the *s* of Shaphan, that he
40: 5 Go back to Gedaliah the *s* of
40: 5 the *s* of Shaphan, whom the king
40: 6 went to Gedaliah the *s* of
40: 7 had made Gedaliah the *s* of
40: 8 Ishmael the *s* of Nethaniah,
40: 8 Seraiah the *s* of Tanhumeth, the
40: 8 and Jezaniah the *s* of a
40: 9 And Gedaliah the *s* of Ahikam,
40: 9 the *s* of Shaphan, took an oath
40:11 set over them Gedaliah the *s*
40:11 the *s* of Shaphan,
40:13 Moreover Johanan the *s* of
40:14 has sent Ishmael the *s* of
40:14 But Gedaliah the *s* of Ahikam
40:15 Then Johanan the *s* of Kareah
40:15 and I will kill Ishmael the *s*
40:16 But Gedaliah the *s* of Ahikam
40:16 of Ahikam said to Johanan the *s*
41: 1 month that Ishmael the *s* of
41: 1 the *s* of Elishama, of the royal
41: 1 with ten men to Gedaliah the *s*
41: 2 Then Ishmael the *s* of Nethaniah,
41: 2 and struck Gedaliah the *s* of
41: 2 the *s* of Shaphan, with the
41: 6 Now Ishmael the *s* of Nethaniah
41: 6 Come to Gedaliah the *s* of
41: 7 that Ishmael the *s* of Nethaniah
41: 9 Ishmael the *s* of Nethaniah
41:10 committed to Gedaliah the *s* of
41:10 And Ishmael the *s* of Nethaniah
41:11 But when Johanan the *s* of
41:11 the evil that Ishmael the *s* of
41:12 to fight with Ishmael the *s* of
41:13 with Ishmael saw Johanan the *s*
41:14 and went to Johanan the *s* of
41:15 But Ishmael the *s* of Nethaniah
41:16 Then Johanan the *s* of Kareah,
41:16 recovered from Ishmael the *s*
41:16 he had murdered Gedaliah the *s*
41:18 because Ishmael the *s* of
41:18 had murdered Gedaliah the *s* of
42: 1 Johanan the *s* of Kareah,
42: 1 Jezaniah the *s* of Hoshaiah, and
42: 8 Then he called Johanan the *s* of
43: 2 that Azariah the *s* of Hoshaiah,
43: 2 Johanan the *s* of Kareah, and
43: 3 But Baruch the *s* of Neriah has
43: 4 So Johanan the *s* of Kareah, all
43: 5 But Johanan the *s* of Kareah and
43: 6 had left with Gedaliah the *s*
43: 6 the *s* of Shaphan, and Jeremiah
43: 6 the prophet and Baruch the *s*
45: 1 prophet spoke to Baruch the *s*
45: 1 fourth year of Jehoiakim the *s*
46: 2 fourth year of Jehoiakim the *s*
49:18 Nor shall a *s* of man dwell in
49:33 Nor *s* of man dwell in it."
50:40 Nor *s* of man dwell in it.
51:43 Through which no *s* of man
51:59 commanded Seraiah the *s* of
51:59 the *s* of Mahseiah, when he went
Ezek 1: 3 the *s* of Buzi, in the land of
2: 1 *S* of man, stand on your feet,
2: 3 *S* of man, I am sending you to
2: 6 *s* of man, do not be afraid of
2: 8 *s* of man, hear what I say to
3: 1 '*S* of man, eat what you find;
3: 3 *S* of man, feed your belly, and
3: 4 *S* of man, go to the house of
3:10 *S* of man, receive into your
3:17 *S* of man, I have made you a
3:25 O *s* of man, surely they will
4: 1 *s* of man, take a clay tablet
4:16 *S* of man, surely I will cut off
5: 1 *s* of man, take a sharp sword,
6: 2 *S* of man, set your face toward
7: 2 *s* of man, thus says the Lord
8: 5 *S* of man, lift your eyes now
8: 6 *S* of man, do you see what they
8: 8 *S* of man, dig into the wall";
8:11 midst stood Jaazaniah the *s* of
8:12 *S* of man, have you seen what the
8:15 O *s* of man? Turn again, you
8:17 O *s* of man? Is it a trivial
11: 1 whom I saw Jaazaniah the *s* of
11: 1 and Pelatiah the *s* of Benaiah,
11: 2 *S* of man, these are the men who
11: 4 prophesy, O *s* of man!"
11:13 that Pelatiah the *s* of Benaiah
11:15 *S* of man, your brethren, your
12: 2 *S* of man, you dwell in the midst
12: 3 *s* of man, prepare your
12: 9 *S* of man, has not the house of
12:18 *S* of man, eat your bread with
12:22 *S* of man, what is this proverb
12:27 *S* of man, look, the house of
13: 2 *S* of man, prophesy against the
13:17 *s* of man, set your face against
14: 3 *S* of man, these men have set up
14:13 *S* of man, when a land sins
14:20 they would deliver neither *s* nor
15: 2 *S* of man, how is the wood of the
16: 2 *S* of man, cause Jerusalem to
17: 2 *S* of man, pose a riddle, and
18: 4 As well as the soul of the *s*
18:10 If he begets a *s* who is a
18:14 he begets a *s* Who sees all the
18:19 Why should the *s* not bear the
18:19 Because the *s* has done what is
18:20 The *s* shall not bear the guilt
18:20 father bear the guilt of the *s*.
20: 3 *S* of man, speak to the elders of
20: 4 *s* of man, will you judge them?
20:27 *s* of man, speak to the house of
20:46 *S* of man, set your face toward
21: 2 *S* of man, set your face toward
21: 6 *s* of man, with a breaking
21: 9 *S* of man, prophesy and say,
21:10 despises the scepter of My *S*,
21:12 'Cry and wail, *s* of man;
21:14 *s* of man, prophesy, And strike
21:19 And *s* of man, appoint for
21:28 *s* of man, prophesy and say,
22: 2 *s* of man, will you judge, will
22:18 *S* of man, the house of Israel
22:24 *S* of man, say to her: 'You are
23: 2 *S* of man, there were two women,
23:36 *S* of man, will you judge Oholah
24: 2 *S* of man, write down the name of
24:16 *S* of man, behold, I take away
24:25 *s* of man—will it not be in
25: 2 *S* of man, set your face against
26: 2 *S* of man, because Tyre has said
27: 2 *s* of man, take up a lamentation
28: 2 *S* of man, say to the prince of
28:12 *S* of man, take up a lamentation
28:21 *S* of man, set your face toward
29: 2 *S* of man, set your face against
29:18 *S* of man, Nebuchadnezzar king of
30: 2 *S* of man, prophesy and say,
30:21 *S* of man, I have broken the arm
31: 2 *S* of man, say to Pharaoh king of
32: 2 *S* of man, take up a lamentation
32:18 *S* of man, wail over the
33: 2 *S* of man, speak to the children
33: 7 *s* of man: I have made you a
33:10 O *s* of man, say to the house of
33:12 O *s* of man, say to the children
33:24 *S* of man, they who inhabit those
33:30 *s* of man, the children of your
34: 2 *S* of man, prophesy against the
35: 2 *S* of man, set your face against
36: 1 *s* of man, prophesy to the
36:17 *S* of man, when the house of
37: 3 *S* of man, can these bones
37: 9 *s* of man, and say to the
37:11 *S* of man, these bones are the
37:16 *s* of man, take a stick for
38: 2 *S* of man, set your face against
38:14 *s* of man, prophesy and say to
39: 1 *s* of man, prophesy against Gog,
39:17 *s* of man, thus says the Lord
40: 4 *S* of man, look with your eyes
43: 7 *S* of man, this is the place of
43:10 *S* of man, describe the temple
43:18 *S* of man, thus says the Lord
44: 5 *S* of man, mark well, see with
44:25 for *s* or daughter, for brother
47: 6 *S* of man, have you seen this?"
Dan 3:25 of the fourth is like the *S* of

5:22 'But you his *s*, Belshazzar,
7:13 One like the *S* of Man, Coming
8:17 *s* of man, that the vision
9: 1 the first year of Darius the *s*
Hos 1: 1 LORD that came to Hosea the *s*
1: 1 in the days of Jeroboam the *s*
1: 3 she conceived and bore him a *s*.
1: 8 she conceived and bore a *s*.
11: 1 And out of Egypt I called My *s*.
13:13 He is an unwise *s*, For he
Joel 1: 1 LORD that came to Joel the *s*
Am 1: 1 in the days of Jeroboam the *s*
7:14 Nor was I a *s* of a prophet,
8:10 it like mourning for an only *s*,
Jon 1: 1 the LORD came to Jonah the *s*
Mic 6: 5 And what Balaam the *s* of Beor
7: 6 For *s* dishonors father,
Zeph 1: 1 which came to Zephaniah the *s*
1: 1 the *s* of Gedaliah, the son of
1: 1 the *s* of Amariah, the son of
1: 1 the *s* of Hezekiah, in the days
1: 1 in the days of Josiah the *s* of
Hag 1: 1 prophet to Zerubbabel the *s* of
1: 1 and to Joshua the *s* of
1:12 Then Zerubbabel the *s* of
1:12 and Joshua the *s* of Jehozadak,
1:14 the spirit of Zerubbabel the *s*
1:14 and the spirit of Joshua the *s*
2: 2 Speak now to Zerubbabel the *s* of
2: 2 and to Joshua the *s* of
2: 4 *s* of Jehozadak, the high
2:23 the *s* of Shealtiel,' says the
Zech 1: 1 LORD came to Zechariah the *s*
1: 1 the *s* of Iddo the prophet,
1: 7 LORD came to Zechariah the *s*
1: 7 the *s* of Iddo the prophet:
6:10 the house of Josiah the *s* of
6:11 on the head of Joshua the *s* of
6:14 and Hen the *s* of Zephaniah.
12:10 as one mourns for his only *s*,
Mal 1: 6 A *s* honors his father, And a
3:17 As a man spares his own *s* who
Mt 1: 1 the *S* of David, the Son of
1: 1 the *S* of Abraham:
1:20 *s* of David, do not be afraid to
1:21 "And she will bring forth a *S*,
1:23 with child, and bear a *S*,
1:25 brought forth her firstborn *S*.
2:15 of Egypt I called My *S*.
3:17 saying, "This is My beloved *S*,
4: 3 If You are the *S* of God, command
4: 6 If You are the *S* of God, throw
4:21 James the *s* of Zebedee, and
7: 9 if his *s* asks for bread, will
8:20 but the *S* of Man has nowhere to
8:29 You, Jesus, You *S* of God?
9: 2 '*S*, be of good cheer;
9: 6 that you may know that the *S*
9:27 *S* of David, have mercy on us!"
10: 2 James the *s* of Zebedee, and
10: 3 James the *s* of Alphaeus, and
10:23 cities of Israel before the *S*
10:37 And he who loves *s* or daughter
11:19 The *S* of Man came eating and
11:27 and no one knows the *S* except
11:27 know the Father except the *S*,
11:27 and the one to whom the *S*
12: 8 For the *S* of Man is Lord even of
12:23 Could this be the *S* of David?"
12:32 a word against the *S* of Man,
12:40 so will the *S* of Man be three
13:37 good seed is the *S* of Man.
13:41 The *S* of Man will send out His
13:55 "Is this not the carpenter's *s*?
14:33 Truly You are the *S* of God."
15:22 on me, O Lord, *S* of David!
16:13 the *S* of Man, am?"
16:16 the *S* of the living God."
16:27 For the *S* of Man will come in
16:28 death till they see the *S* of
17: 5 saying, "This is My beloved *S*,
17: 9 vision to no one until the *S*
17:12 Likewise the *S* of Man is also
17:15 "Lord, have mercy on my *s*,
17:22 The *S* of Man is about to be
18:11 For the *S* of Man has come to
19:28 when the *S* of Man sits on the
20:18 and the *S* of Man will be
20:28 just as the *S* of Man did not
20:30 on us, O Lord, *S* of David!"
20:31 on us, O Lord, *S* of David!"
21: 9 Hosanna to the *S* of David!
21:15 Hosanna to the *S* of David!"
21:28 '*S*, go, work today in my
21:37 last of all he sent his *s*
21:37 saying, 'They will respect my *s*.
21:38 when the vinedressers saw the *s*,
22: 2 arranged a marriage for his *s*,
22:42 Whose *S* is He?" They said to
22:42 to Him, "The *S* of David."
22:45 Him 'Lord,' how is He his *S*?
23:15 you make him twice as much a *s*
23:35 *s* of Berechiah, whom you
24:27 also will the coming of the *S*
24:30 Then the sign of the *S* of Man
24:30 and they will see the *S* of Man
24:37 also will the coming of the *S*
24:39 also will the coming of the *S*
24:44 for the *S* of Man is coming at
25:13 nor the hour in which the *S* of
25:31 When the *S* of Man comes in His
26: 2 and the *S* of Man will be
26:24 The *S* of Man indeed goes just as
26:24 woe to that man by whom the *S*
26:45 and the *S* of Man is being
26:63 the Christ, the *S* of God!"
26:64 hereafter you will see the *S* of
27:40 If You are the *S* of God,
27:43 I am the *S* of God.'"
27:54 Truly this was the *S* of God!"
28:19 of the Father and of the *S* and
Mk 1: 1 Jesus Christ, the *S* of God.
1:11 heaven, "You are My beloved *S*,
1:19 He saw James the *s* of Zebedee,
2: 5 '*S*, your sins are forgiven
2:10 that you may know that the *S*
2:14 He saw Levi the *s* of Alphaeus
2:28 Therefore the *S* of Man is also
3:11 You are the *S* of God."
3:17 James the *s* of Zebedee and John
3:18 James the *s* of Alphaeus,
5: 7 *S* of the Most High God?
6: 3 the *S* of Mary, and brother of
8:31 began to teach them that the *S*
8:38 of him the *S* of Man also will
9: 7 saying, "This is My beloved *S*.
9: 9 till the *S* of Man had risen
9:12 is it written concerning the *S*
9:17 "Teacher, I brought You my *s*,
9:31 The *S* of Man is being betrayed
10:33 and the *S* of Man will be
10:45 For even the *S* of Man did not
10:46 the *s* of Timaeus, sat by the
10:47 *S* of David, have mercy on me!"
10:48 *S* of David, have mercy on me!"
12: 6 "Therefore still having one *s*,
12: 6 saying, 'They will respect my *s*.
12:35 say that the Christ is the *S*
12:37 'Lord'; how is He then his *S*?
13:26 Then they will see the *S* of Man
13:32 the angels in heaven, nor the *S*,
14:21 The *S* of Man indeed goes just as
14:21 woe to that man by whom the *S*
14:41 the *S* of Man is being betrayed
14:61 the *S* of the Blessed?"
14:62 And you will see the *S* of Man
15:39 Truly this Man was the *S* of
Lk 1:13 Elizabeth will bear you a *s*,
1:31 your womb and bring forth a *S*,
1:32 and will be called the *S* of the
1:35 to be born will be called the *S*
1:36 has also conceived a *s* in her
1:57 and she brought forth a *s*.
2: 7 brought forth her firstborn *S*,
2:48 and His mother said to Him, "*S*,
3: 2 word of God came to John the *s*
3:22 said, "You are My beloved *S*;
3:23 being (as was supposed) the *s* of
3:23 of Joseph, the *s* of Heli,
3:24 the *s* of Matthat, the son of
3:24 the *s* of Levi, the son of
3:24 the *s* of Melchi, the son of
3:24 the *s* of Janna, the son of
3:24 of Janna, the *s* of Joseph,
3:25 the *s* of Mattathiah, the son
3:25 the *s* of Amos, the son of
3:25 the *s* of Nahum, the son of
3:25 the *s* of Esli, the son of
3:25 of Esli, the *s* of Naggai,
3:26 the *s* of Maath, the son of
3:26 the *s* of Mattathiah, the
3:26 the *s* of Semei, the son of
3:26 the *s* of Joseph, the son of
3:26 of Joseph, the *s* of Judah,
3:27 the *s* of Joannas, the son of
3:27 the *s* of Rhesa, the son of
3:27 the *s* of Zerubbabel, the
3:27 the *s* of Shealtiel, the son
3:27 Shealtiel, the *s* of Neri,
3:28 the *s* of Melchi, the son of
3:28 the *s* of Addi, the son of
3:28 the *s* of Cosam, the son of
3:28 the *s* of Elmodam, the son
3:28 of Elmodam, the *s* of Er,
3:29 the *s* of Jose, the son of
3:29 the *s* of Eliezer, the son
3:29 the *s* of Jorim, the son of
3:29 the *s* of Matthat, the son
3:29 of Matthat, the *s* of Levi,
3:30 the *s* of Simeon, the son of
3:30 the *s* of Judah, the son of
3:30 the *s* of Joseph, the son of
3:30 the *s* of Jonan, the son of
3:30 of Jonan, the *s* of Eliakim,
3:31 the *s* of Melea, the son of
3:31 the *s* of Menan, the son of
3:31 the *s* of Mattathah, the son
3:31 the *s* of Nathan, the son of
3:31 of Nathan, the *s* of David,
3:32 the *s* of Jesse, the son of
3:32 the *s* of Obed, the son of
3:32 the *s* of Boaz, the son of
3:32 the *s* of Salmon, the son of
3:32 of Salmon, the *s* of Nahshon,
3:33 the *s* of Amminadab, the son
3:33 the *s* of Ram, the son of
3:33 the *s* of Hezron, the son of
3:33 the *s* of Perez, the son of
3:33 of Perez, the *s* of Judah,
3:34 the *s* of Jacob, the son of
3:34 the *s* of Isaac, the son of
3:34 the *s* of Abraham, the son
3:34 the *s* of Terah, the son of
3:34 of Terah, the *s* of Nahor,
3:35 the *s* of Serug, the son of
3:35 the *s* of Reu, the son of
3:35 the *s* of Peleg, the son of
3:35 the *s* of Eber, the son of
3:35 of Eber, the *s* of Shelah,
3:36 the *s* of Cainan, the son of
3:36 the *s* of Arphaxad, the son
3:36 the *s* of Shem, the son of
3:36 the *s* of Noah, the son of
3:36 of Noah, the *s* of Lamech,
3:37 the *s* of Methuselah, the son
3:37 the *s* of Enoch, the son of
3:37 the *s* of Jared, the son of
3:37 the *s* of Mahalalel, the son
3:37 Mahalalel, the *s* of Cainan,
3:38 the *s* of Enos, the son of
3:38 the *s* of Seth, the son of
3:38 the *s* of Adam, the son of
3:38 of Adam, the *s* of God.
4: 3 If You are the *S* of God, command
4: 9 If You are the *S* of God, throw
4:22 said, "Is this not Joseph's *s*?
4:41 the Christ, the *S* of God!"
5:24 that you may know that the *S*
6: 5 The *S* of Man is also Lord of the
6:15 James the *s* of Alphaeus, and
6:16 Judas the *s* of James, and
6:22 For the *S* of Man's sake.
7:12 the only *s* of his mother;
7:34 The *S* of Man has come eating and
8:28 *S* of the Most High God?
9:22 The *S* of Man must suffer many
9:26 of him the *S* of Man will be
9:35 saying, "This is My beloved *S*.
9:38 I implore You, look on my *s*,
9:41 Bring your *s* here."
9:44 for the *S* of Man is about to be
9:56 For the *S* of Man did not come to
9:58 but the *S* of Man has nowhere to
10: 6 And if a *s* of peace is there,
10:22 and no one knows who the *S* is
10:22 who the Father is except the *S*,
10:22 and the one to whom the *S*
11:11 If a *s* asks for bread from any
11:30 so also the *S* of Man will be to
12: 8 him the *S* of Man also will
12:10 speaks a word against the *S* of
12:40 for the *S* of Man is coming at
12:53 will be divided against *s* and
12:53 be divided against son and *s*
15:13 the younger *s* gathered all
15:19 worthy to be called your *s*.
15:21 And the *s* said to him, 'Father,
15:21 worthy to be called your *s*.
15:24 for this my *s* was dead and is
15:25 Now his older *s* was in the
15:30 But as soon as this *s* of yours
15:31 "And he said to him, '*S*,
16:25 "But Abraham said, '*S*,
17:22 to see one of the days of the *S*
17:24 so also the *S* of Man will be in
17:26 be also in the days of the *S*
17:30 it be in the day when the *S* of
18: 8 when the *S* of Man comes, will
18:31 the prophets concerning the *S*
18:38 *S* of David, have mercy on me!"
18:39 *S* of David, have mercy on me!"
19: 9 because he also is a *s* of
19:10 for the *S* of Man has come to
20:13 I will send my beloved *s*.
20:41 say that the Christ is the *S*
20:44 how is He then his *S*?"
21:27 Then they will see the *S* of Man
21:36 and to stand before the *S* of
22:22 And truly the *S* of Man goes as
22:48 are you betraying the *S* of Man
22:69 Hereafter the *S* of Man will sit
22:70 'Are You then the *S* of God?"
24: 7 The *S* of Man must be delivered
Jn 1:18 any time. The only begotten *S*,
1:34 testified that this is the *S*
1:42 You are Simon the *s* of Jonah.
1:45 Nazareth, the *s* of Joseph."
1:49 You are the *S* of God! You are
1:51 and descending upon the *S* of
3:13 the *S* of Man who is in heaven.
3:14 even so must the *S* of Man be
3:16 He gave His only begotten *S*,
3:17 For God did not send His *S* into
3:18 name of the only begotten *S* of
3:35 "The Father loves the *S*,
3:36 He who believes in the *S* has
3:36 he who does not believe the *S*
4: 5 ground that Jacob gave to his *s*
4:46 was a certain nobleman whose *s*
4:47 Him to come down and heal his *s*,
4:50 your *s* lives." So the man
4:51 saying, "Your *s* lives!"
4:53 Your *s* lives." And he himself
5:19 the *S* can do nothing of
5:19 the *S* also does in like manner.
5:20 "For the Father loves the *S*,
5:21 even so the *S* gives life to
5:22 committed all judgment to the *S*,
5:23 that all should honor the *S* just
5:23 He who does not honor the *S*
5:25 will hear the voice of the *S*
5:26 so He has granted the *S* to have
5:27 because He is the *S* of Man.
6:27 which the *S* of Man will give
6:40 that everyone who sees the *S*
6:42 the *s* of Joseph, whose father

6:53 you eat the flesh of the *S* of
6:62 then if you should see the *S*
6:69 the *S* of the living God."
6:71 the *s* of Simon, for it was he
8:28 When you lift up the *S* of Man,
8:35 but a *s* abides forever.
8:36 Therefore if the *S* makes you
9:19 them, saying, "Is this your *s*,
9:20 "We know that this is our *s*,
9:35 Do you believe in the *S* of
10:36 I am the *S* of God'?
11: 4 that the *S* of God may be
11:27 the *S* of God, who is to come
12: 4 Judas Iscariot, Simon's *s*,
12:23 The hour has come that the *S* of
12:34 The *S* of Man must be lifted up'?
12:34 Who is this *S* of Man?"
13: 2 of Judas Iscariot, Simon's *s*,
13:26 the *s* of Simon.
13:31 Now the *S* of Man is glorified,
14:13 may be glorified in the *S*.
17: 1 Glorify Your *S*, that Your
17: 1 that Your *S* also may glorify
17:12 of them is lost except the *s*
19: 7 because He made Himself the *S*
19:26 'Woman, behold your *s*!"
20:31 the *S* of God, and that
21:15 *s* of Jonah, do you love Me
21:16 *s* of Jonah, do you love Me?"
21:17 *s* of Jonah, do you love Me?"
Acts 1:13 James the *s* of Alphaeus and
1:13 and Judas the *s* of James.
4:36 (which is translated *S* of
7:21 and brought him up as her own *s*.
7:56 the heavens opened and the *S*
8:37 that Jesus Christ is the *S* of
9:20 that He is the *S* of God.
13:10 you *s* of the devil, you enemy
13:21 so God gave them Saul the *s* of
13:22 I have found David the *s* of
13:33 Psalm: 'You are My *S*,
16: 1 the *s* of a certain Jewish
23: 6 Pharisee, the *s* of a Pharisee;
23:16 So when Paul's sister's *s* heard
Rom 1: 3 concerning His *S* Jesus Christ
1: 4 declared to be the *S* of God
1: 9 spirit in the gospel of His *S*,
5:10 God through the death of His *S*,
8: 3 God did by sending His own *S*
8:29 conformed to the image of His *S*,
8:32 He who did not spare His own *S*,
9: 9 and Sarah shall have a *s*.
1 Cor 1: 9 into the fellowship of His *S*,
4:17 is my beloved and faithful *s*
15:28 then the *S* Himself will also be
2 Cor 1:19 For the *S* of God, Jesus Christ,
Gal 1:16 to reveal His *S* in me, that I
2:20 live by faith in the *S* of God,
4: 4 had come, God sent forth His *S*,
4: 6 sent forth the Spirit of His *S*
4: 7 are no longer a slave but a *s*,
4: 7 a slave but a son, and if a *s*,
4:30 the bondwoman and her *s*,
4:30 for the *s* of the
4:30 not be heir with the *s*
Eph 4:13 and of the knowledge of the *S*
Phil 2:22 that as a *s* with his father he
Col 1:13 us into the kingdom of the *S*
1 Th 1:10 and to wait for His *S* from
2 Th 2: 3 the *s* of perdition,
1 Tim 1: 2 a true *s* in the faith: Grace,
1:18 *s* Timothy, according to the
2 Tim 1: 2 To Timothy, a beloved *s*:
2: 1 You therefore, my *s*,
Titus 1: 4 a true *s* in our common faith:
Phm 1:10 I appeal to you for my *s*
Heb 1: 2 days spoken to us by His *S*,
1: 5 ever say: "You are My *S*,
1: 5 He shall be to Me a *S*"?
1: 8 But to the *S* He says:
2: 6 Or the *s* of man that
3: 6 but Christ as a *S* over His own
4:14 Jesus the *S* of God, let us hold
5: 5 to Him: "You are My *S*,
5: 8 though He was a *S*,
6: 6 again for themselves the *S* of
7: 3 but made like the *S* of God,
7:28 appoints the *S* who has been
10:29 worthy who has trampled the *S*
11:17 offered up his only begotten *s*,
11:24 refused to be called the *s* of
12: 5 to you as to sons: "My *s*,
12: 6 And scourges every *s* whom
12: 7 for what *s* is there whom a
Jas 2:21 when he offered Isaac his *s* on
1 Pe 5:13 you; and so does Mark my *s*.
2 Pe 1:17 Glory: "This is My beloved *S*,
2:15 the way of Balaam the *s* of
1 Jn 1: 3 with the Father and with His *S*
1: 7 the blood of Jesus Christ His *S*
2:22 who denies the Father and the *S*.
2:23 Whoever denies the *S* does not
2:23 he who acknowledges the *S* has
2:24 you also will abide in the *S*
3: 8 For this purpose the *S* of God
3:23 believe on the name of His *S*
4: 9 has sent His only begotten *S*
4:10 He loved us and sent His *S* to
4:14 that the Father has sent the *S*
4:15 confesses that Jesus is the *S*
5: 5 believes that Jesus is the *S*
5: 9 which He has testified of His *S*.
5:10 He who believes in the *S* of God
5:10 that God has given of His *S*.
5:11 life, and this life is in His *S*.
5:12 He who has the *S* has life;
5:12 he who does not have the *S* of
5:13 believe in the name of the *S*
5:13 believe in the name of the *S*
5:20 And we know that the *S* of God
5:20 in His *S* Jesus Christ. This is
2 Jn 3 the *S* of the Father, in truth
9 has both the Father and the *S*.
Rev 1:13 lampstands One like the *S* of
2:18 These things says the *S* of God,
14:14 the cloud sat One like the *S*
21: 7 be his God and he shall be My *s*.

SON OF DAVID (27/26)

2 Sam 13: 1 After this Absalom the *s* had a
13: 1 and Amnon the *s* loved her.
1 Chr 29:22 And they made Solomon the *s*
2 Chr 1: 1 Now Solomon the *s* was
11:18 the daughter of Jerimoth the *s*,
13: 6 the servant of Solomon the *s*,
30:26 since the time of Solomon the *s*,
35: 3 the house which Solomon the *s*,
Prov 1: 1 The proverbs of Solomon the *s*,
Eccl 1: 1 words of the Preacher, the *s*,
Mt 1: 1 of Jesus Christ, the *S*,
1:20 in a dream, saying, "Joseph, *s*,
9:27 Him, crying out and saying, "*S*,
12:23 and said, "Could this be the *S*?
15:22 *S*! My daughter is severely
20:30 mercy on us, O Lord, *S*!"
20:31 mercy on us, O Lord, *S*!"
21: 9 Hosanna to the *S*! 'Blessed is
21:15 Hosanna to the *S*!" they were
22:42 They said to Him, "The *S*.
Mk 10:47 to cry out and say, "Jesus, *S*,
10:48 he cried out all the more, "*S*,
12:35 say that the Christ is the *S*?
Lk 3:31 the son of Nathan, the *s*,
18:38 cried out, saying, "Jesus, *S*,
18:39 he cried out all the more, "*S*,
20:41 say that the Christ is the *S*?

SON OF GOD (47/46)

Dan 3:25 of the fourth is like the *S*.
Mt 4: 3 he said, "If You are the *S*,
4: 6 said to Him, "If You are the *S*,
8:29 we to do with You, Jesus, You *S*?
14:33 saying, "Truly You are the *S*.
26:63 You are the Christ, the *S*!"
27:40 save Yourself! If You are the *S*,
27:43 Him; for He said, 'I am the *S*.
27:54 Truly this was the *S*!"
Mk 1: 1 gospel of Jesus Christ, the *S*.
3:11 out, saying, "You are the *S*.
15:39 Truly this Man was the *S*!"
Lk 1:35 to be born will be called the *S*.
3:38 the son of Adam, the *s*.
4: 3 said to Him, "If You are the *S*,
4: 9 said to Him, "If You are the *S*,
4:41 the *S*!" And He, rebuking
22:70 all said, "Are You then the *S*?
Jn 1:34 testified that this is the *S*.
1:49 You are the *S*! You are the King
3:18 the name of the only begotten *S*.
5:25 will hear the voice of the *S*;
9:35 him, "Do you believe in the *S*?
10:36 because I said, 'I am the *S*'?
11: 4 that the *S* may be glorified
11:27 that You are the Christ, the *S*,
19: 7 because He made Himself the *S*.
20:31 that Jesus is the Christ, the *S*,
Acts 8:37 that Jesus Christ is the *S*.
9:20 synagogues, that He is the *S*.
Rom 1: 4 and declared to be the *S* with
2 Cor 1:19 For the *S*, Jesus Christ,
Gal 2:20 flesh I live by faith in the *S*,
Eph 4:13 and of the knowledge of the *S*,
Heb 4:14 the heavens, Jesus the *S*,
6: 6 again for themselves the *S*,
7: 3 of life, but made like the *S*,
10:29 worthy who has trampled the *S*
1 Jn 3: 8 For this purpose the *S* was
4:15 confesses that Jesus is the *S*,
5: 5 believes that Jesus is the *S*?
5:10 He who believes in the *S* has the
5:12 he who does not have the *S* does
5:13 believe in the name of the *S*,
5:13 believe in the name of the *S*.
5:20 And we know that the *S* has come
Rev 2:18 'These things says the *S*,

SON OF MAN (194/190)

Num 23:19 that He should lie, Nor a *s*,
Job 25: 6 who is a maggot, And a *s*,
35: 8 And your righteousness a *s*.
Ps 8: 4 And the *s* that You visit him?
80:17 Upon the *s* whom You made
144: 3 knowledge of him? Or the *s*,
146: 3 trust in princes, Nor in a *s*,
Isa 56: 2 And the *s* who lays hold on
Jer 49:18 Nor shall a *s* dwell in it.
49:33 Nor *s* dwell in it."
50:40 Nor *s* dwell in it.
51:43 Through which no *s* passes.
Ezek 2: 1 And He said to me, "*S*,
2: 3 And He said to me: "*S*,
2: 6 And you, *s*, do not be afraid
2: 8 'But you, *s*, hear what I say
3: 1 Moreover He said to me, "*S*,
3: 3 And He said to me, "*S*,
3: 4 Then He said to me: "*S*,
3:10 Moreover He said to me: "*S*,
3:17 '*S*, I have made you a
3:25 "And you, O *s*,
4: 1 'You also, *s*, take a clay
4:16 Moreover He said to me, "*S*,
5: 1 'And you, *s*, take a sharp
6: 2 '*S*, set your face toward
7: 2 'And you, *s*, thus says the
8: 5 Then He said to me, "*S*,
8: 6 Furthermore He said to me, "*S*,
8: 8 Then He said to me, "*S*,
8:12 Then He said to me, "*S*,
8:15 me, "Have you seen this, O *s*?
8:17 me, "Have you seen this, O *s*?
11: 2 And He said to me: "*S*,
11: 4 against them, prophesy, O *s*!"
11:15 '*S*, your brethren, your
12: 2 '*S*, you dwell in the midst
12: 3 'Therefore, *s*, prepare
12: 9 '*S*, has not the house of
12:18 '*S*, eat your bread with
12:22 '*S*, what is this proverb
12:27 '*S*, look, the house of
13: 2 '*S*, prophesy against the
13:17 Likewise, *s*, set your face
14: 3 '*S*, these men have set up
14:13 '*S*, when a land sins
15: 2 '*S*, how is the wood of the
16: 2 '*S*, cause Jerusalem to know
17: 2 '*S*, pose a riddle,
20: 3 '*S*, speak to the elders of
20: 4 "Will you judge them, *s*,
20:27 Therefore, *s*, speak to the
20:46 '*S*, set your face toward
21: 2 '*S*, set your face toward
21: 6 "Sigh therefore, *s*,
21: 9 '*S*, prophesy and say,
21:12 "Cry and wail, *s*;
21:14 "You therefore, *s*,
21:19 'And *s*, appoint for yourself
21:28 And you, *s*, prophesy and say,
22: 2 'Now, *s*, will you judge,
22:18 '*S*, the house of Israel
22:24 '*S*, say to her:
23: 2 '*S*, there were two women,
23:36 The LORD also said to me: "*S*,
24: 2 '*S*, write down the name
24:16 '*S*, behold, I take away
24:25 And you, *s*—will it not be in
25: 2 '*S*, set your face against
26: 2 '*S*, because Tyre has said
27: 2 'Now, *s*, take up a
28: 2 '*S*, say to the prince of
28:12 '*S*, take up a lamentation
28:21 '*S*, set your face toward
29: 2 '*S*, set your face against
29:18 '*S*, Nebuchadnezzar king of
30: 2 '*S*, prophesy and say,
30:21 '*S*, I have broken the arm
31: 2 '*S*, say to Pharaoh king of
32: 2 '*S*, take up a lamentation
32:18 '*S*, wail over the
33: 2 '*S*, speak to the children
33: 7 *s*: I have made
33:10 "Therefore you, O *s*,
33:12 "Therefore you, O *s*,
33:24 '*S*, they who inhabit those
33:30 "As for you, *s*,
34: 2 '*S*, prophesy against the
35: 2 '*S*, set your face against
36: 1 'And you, *s*, prophesy to
36:17 '*S*, when the house of Israel
37: 3 And He said to me, "*S*,
37: 9 to the breath, prophesy, *s*,
37:11 Then He said to me, "*S*,
37:16 "As for you, *s*,
38: 2 '*S*, set your face against
38:14 Therefore, *s*, prophesy and
39: 1 'And you, *s*, prophesy
39:17 "And as for you, *s*,
40: 4 And the man said to me, "*S*,
43: 7 And He said to me, "*S*,
43:10 *S*, describe the temple to
43:18 And He said to me, "*S*,
44: 5 And the LORD said to me, "*S*,
47: 6 He said to me, "*S*,
Dan 7:13 And behold, One like the *S*,
8:17 he said to me, "Understand, *s*,
Mt 8:20 but the *S* has nowhere to lay
9: 6 that you may know that the *S*
10:23 cities of Israel before the *S*
11:19 The *S* came eating and drinking,
12: 8 For the *S* is Lord even of the
12:32 who speaks a word against the *S*,
12:40 so will the *S* be three days and
13:37 who sows the good seed is the *S*.
13:41 The *S* will send out His angels,
16:13 "Who do men say that I, the *S*,
16:27 For the *S* will come in the glory
16:28 taste death till they see the *S*
17: 9 vision to no one until the *S*
17:12 Likewise the *S* is also about to
17:22 The *S* is about to be betrayed
18:11 For the *S* has come to save that
19:28 when the *S* sits on the throne
20:18 and the *S* will be betrayed to
20:28 just as the *S* did not come to be

24:27 also will the coming of the *S*
24:30 Then the sign of the *S* will
24:30 and they will see the *S* coming
24:37 also will the coming of the *S*
24:39 also will the coming of the *S*
24:44 for the *S* is coming at an hour
25:13 nor the hour in which the *S* is
25:31 When the *S* comes in His glory,
26: 2 and the *S* will be delivered up
26:24 The *S* indeed goes just as it is
26:24 woe to that man by whom the *S*
26:45 and the *S* is being betrayed
26:64 hereafter you will see the *S*
Mk 2:10 that you may know that the *S*
2:28 Therefore the *S* is also Lord of
8:31 began to teach them that the *S*
8:38 of him the *S* also will be
9: 9 till the *S* had risen from the
9:12 is it written concerning the *S*,
9:31 The *S* is being betrayed into the
10:33 and the *S* will be betrayed to
10:45 For even the *S* did not come to
13:26 Then they will see the *S* coming
14:21 The *S* indeed goes just as it is
14:21 woe to that man by whom the *S*
14:41 the *S* is being betrayed into
14:62 And you will see the *S* sitting
Lk 5:24 that you may know that the *S*
6: 5 The *S* is also Lord of the
7:34 The *S* has come eating and
9:22 The *S* must suffer many things,
9:26 of him the *S* will be ashamed
9:44 for the *S* is about to be
9:56 For the *S* did not come to
9:58 but the *S* has nowhere to lay
11:30 so also the *S* will be to this
12: 8 him the *S* also will confess
12:10 who speaks a word against the *S*,
12:40 for the *S* is coming at an hour
17:22 to see one of the days of the *S*,
17:24 so also the *S* will be in His
17:26 be also in the days of the *S*:
17:30 it be in the day when the *S* is
18: 8 when the *S* comes, will He
18:31 the prophets concerning the *S*
19:10 for the *S* has come to seek and
21:27 Then they will see the *S* coming
21:36 pass, and to stand before the *S*.
22:22 And truly the *S* goes as it has
22:48 are you betraying the *S* with a
22:69 Hereafter the *S* will sit on the
24: 7 The *S* must be delivered into the
Jn 1:51 and descending upon the *S*.
3:13 the *S* who is in heaven.
3:14 even so must the *S* be lifted
5:27 also, because He is the *S*.
6:27 which the *S* will give you,
6:53 you eat the flesh of the *S* and
6:62 then if you should see the *S*
8:28 them, "When you lift up the *S*,
12:23 The hour has come that the *S*
12:34 The *S* must be lifted up'? Who is
12:34 be lifted up'? Who is this *S*?
13:31 Now the *S* is glorified, and God
Acts 7:56 the heavens opened and the *S*
Heb 2: 6 Or the *s* that You take
Rev 1:13 lampstands One like the *S*,
14:14 the cloud sat One like the *S*,

SON-IN-LAW (13/13) SON, SONS-IN-LAW

Gen 19:12 "Have you anyone else here? *S*,
Judg 15: 6 the *s* of the Timnite, because
19: 5 woman's father said to his *s*,
1 Sam 18:18 that I should be *s* to the
18:21 You shall be my *s* today."
18:22 therefore, become the king's *s*.
18:23 light thing to be a king's *s*,
18:26 well to become the king's *s*.
18:27 he might become the king's *s*.
22:14 as David, who is the king's *s*,
2 Ki 8:27 for he was the *s* of the house
Neh 6:18 because he was the *s* of
13:28 was a *s* of Sanballat the

SON'S (16/15) SON

Gen 24:51 her be your master's *s* wife,
27:25 and I will eat of my *s* game, so
27:31 arise and eat of his *s* game,
30:14 me some of your *s* mandrakes."
30:15 take away my *s* mandrakes
30:15 tonight for your *s* mandrakes."
30:16 you with my *s* mandrakes."
37:32 whether it is your *s* tunic
37:33 It is my *s* tunic. A wild beast
Ex 10: 2 of your son and your *s* son
Lev 18:10 The nakedness of your *s* daughter
18:15 she is your *s* wife—you shall
18:17 shall you take her *s* daughter
1 Ki 11:35 the kingdom out of his *s* hand
Prov 30: 4 and what is His *S* name,
Jer 27: 7 him and his son and his *s* son,

SONG (80/77) SING, SONGS

Ex 15: 1 children of Israel sang this *s*
15: 2 LORD is my strength and *s*,
Num 21:17 Then Israel sang this *s*:
Deut 31:19 write down this *s* for
31:19 that this *s* may be a witness
31:21 that this *s* will testify
31:22 Therefore Moses wrote this *s*
31:30 of Israel the words of this *s*
32:44 spoke all the words of this *s*
Judg 5:12 sing a *s*! Arise, Barak, and
2 Sam 1:18 the children of Judah the *S*
22: 1 the LORD the words of this *s*,
1 Chr 6:31 over the service of *s* in the
2 Chr 29:27 the *s* of the LORD also began,
Ps 18: the LORD the words of this *s*
28: 7 And with my *s* I will praise
30: A *S* at the dedication of the
33: 3 Sing to Him a new *s*;
40: 3 He has put a new *s* in my
42: 8 And in the night His *s* shall
45: A *S* of Love.
46: A *S* for Alamoth.
48: A *S*. A Psalm of the sons
65: A Psalm of David. A *S*.
66: To the Chief Musician. A *S*.
67: instruments. A Psalm. A *S*.
68: A Psalm of David. A *S*.
69:12 And I am the *s* of the
69:30 praise the name of God with a *s*,
75: A Psalm of Asaph. A *S*.
76: A Psalm of Asaph. A *S*.
77: 6 I call to remembrance my *s* in
81: 2 Raise a *s* and strike the
83: A *S*. A Psalm of Asaph.
87: Psalm of the sons of Korah. A *S*.
88: A *S*. A Psalm of the sons
92: A *S* for the Sabbath day.
96: 1 sing to the LORD a new *s*!
98: 1 sing to the LORD a new *s*!
98: 4 the earth; Break forth in *s*,
108: A *S*. A Psalm of David.
118:14 LORD is my strength and *s*,
120: A *S* of Ascents.
121: A *S* of Ascents.
122: A *S* of Ascents. Of David.
123: A *S* of Ascents.
124: A *S* of Ascents. Of David.
125: A *S* of Ascents.
126: A *S* of Ascents.
127: A *S* of Ascents. Of Solomon.
128: A *S* of Ascents.
129: A *S* of Ascents.
130: A *S* of Ascents.
131: A *S* of Ascents. Of David.
132: A *S* of Ascents.
133: A *S* of Ascents. Of David.
134: A *S* of Ascents.
137: 3 us away captive asked of us a *s*,
137: 4 shall we sing the LORD's *s*
144: 9 I will sing a new *s* to You,
149: 1 Sing to the LORD a new *s*,
Eccl 7: 5 Than for a man to hear the *s*
Song 1: 1 The *s* of songs, which is
Isa 5: 1 me sing to my Well-beloved A *s*
12: 2 LORD, is my strength and *s*;
23:15 happen to Tyre as in the *s* of
24: 9 shall not drink wine with a *s*;
25: 5 The *s* of the terrible ones
26: 1 In that day this *s* will be sung
30:29 You shall have a *s* As in the
42:10 Sing to the LORD a new *s*,
Ezek 33:32 to them as a very lovely *s* of
Rev 5: 9 And they sang a new *s*,
14: 3 They sang as it were a new *s*
14: 3 and no one could learn that *s*
15: 3 They sing the *s* of Moses, the
15: 3 and the *s* of the Lamb, saying:

SONGS (19/19) SONG

Gen 31:27 sent you away with joy and *s*,
1 Ki 4:32 and his *s* were one thousand and
1 Chr 25: 7 who were instructed in the *s*
Neh 12:46 and *s* of praise and
Job 35:10 Who gives *s* in the night,
Ps 32: 7 You shall surround me with *s*
119:54 Your statutes have been my *s*
137: 3 Sing us one of the *s* of Zion!"
Prov 25:20 Is one who sings *s* to a heavy
Song 1: 1 The song of *s*,
Isa 23:16 Make sweet melody, sing many *s*,
24:16 of the earth we have heard *s*:
38:20 Therefore we will sing my *s*
Ezek 26:13 an end to the sound of your *s*,
Am 5:23 from Me the noise of your *s*,
8: 3 And the *s* of the temple Shall
8:10 And all your *s* into
Eph 5:19 and hymns and spiritual *s*,
Col 3:16 and hymns and spiritual *s*,

SONS (1327/1122) SON, SONS'

Gen 5: 4 and he had *s* and daughters.
5: 7 and had *s* and daughters.
5:10 and had *s* and daughters.
5:13 and had *s* and daughters.
5:16 and had *s* and daughters.
5:19 and had *s* and daughters.
5:22 and had *s* and daughters.
5:26 and had *s* and daughters.
5:30 and had *s* and daughters.
6: 2 that the *s* of God saw the
6: 4 when the *s* of God came in to
6:10 And Noah begot three *s*:
6:18 go into the ark—you, your *s*,
7: 7 So Noah, with his *s*,
7:13 very same day Noah and Noah's *s*,
7:13 and the three wives of his *s*
8:16 and your *s* and your sons' wives
8:18 and his *s* and his wife and his
9: 1 So God blessed Noah and his *s*,
9: 8 God spoke to Noah and to his *s*
9:18 Now the *s* of Noah who went out
9:19 These three were the *s* of Noah,
10: 1 is the genealogy of the *s* of
10: 1 And *s* were born to them after
10: 2 The *s* of Japheth were Gomer,
10: 3 The *s* of Gomer were Ashkenaz,
10: 4 The *s* of Javan were Elishah,
10: 6 The *s* of Ham were Cush,
10: 7 The *s* of Cush were Seba,
10: 7 and the *s* of Raamah were Sheba
10:20 These were the *s* of Ham,
10:22 The *s* of Shem were Elam,
10:23 The *s* of Aram were Uz, Hul,
10:25 To Eber were born two *s*:
10:29 All these were the *s* of
10:31 These were the *s* of Shem,
10:32 were the families of the *s* of
11: 5 city and the tower which the *s*
11:11 and begot *s* and daughters.
11:13 and begot *s* and daughters.
11:15 and begot *s* and daughters.
11:17 and begot *s* and daughters.
11:19 and begot *s* and daughters.
11:21 and begot *s* and daughters.
11:23 and begot *s* and daughters.
11:25 and begot *s* and daughters.
19:12 else here? Son-in-law, your *s*,
23: 3 and spoke to the *s* of Heth,
23: 5 And the *s* of Heth answered
23: 7 of the land, the *s* of Heth.
23:10 Now Ephron dwelt among the *s* of
23:10 in the presence of the *s* of
23:11 to you in the presence of the *s*
23:16 named in the hearing of the *s*
23:18 in the presence of the *s* of
23:20 deeded to Abraham by the *s* of
25: 3 And the *s* of Dedan were
25: 4 And the *s* of Midian were Ephah,
25: 6 Abraham gave gifts to the *s* of
25: 9 And his *s* Isaac and Ishmael
25:10 Abraham purchased from the *s*
25:13 these were the names of the *s*
25:16 These were the *s* of Ishmael and
27:29 And let your mother's *s* bow
29:34 I have borne him three *s*.
30:20 because I have borne him six *s*.
30:35 them into the hand of his *s*.
31: 1 heard the words of Laban's *s*,
31:17 Then Jacob rose and set his *s*
31:28 did not allow me to kiss my *s*
31:55 and kissed his *s* and daughters
32:22 servants, and his eleven *s*,
34: 5 Now his *s* were with his
34: 7 And the *s* of Jacob came in from
34:13 But the *s* of Jacob answered
34:25 that two of the *s* of Jacob,
34:27 The *s* of Jacob came upon the
35: 5 and they did not pursue the *s*
35:22 Now the *s* of Jacob were
35:23 the *s* of Leah were Reuben,
35:24 the *s* of Rachel were Joseph and
35:25 the *s* of Bilhah, Rachel's
35:26 and the *s* of Zilpah, Leah's
35:26 These were the *s* of Jacob who
35:29 And his *s* Esau and Jacob buried
36: 5 These were the *s* of Esau who
36: 6 Then Esau took his wives, his *s*,
36:10 were the names of Esau's *s*:
36:11 And the *s* of Eliphaz were Teman,
36:12 These were the *s* of Adah,
36:13 These were the *s* of Reuel:
36:13 These were the *s* of Basemath,
36:14 These were the *s* of Aholibamah,
36:15 were the chiefs of the *s* of
36:15 The *s* of Eliphaz, the firstborn
36:16 They were the *s* of Adah.
36:17 These were the *s* of Reuel,
36:17 These were the *s* of Basemath,
36:18 And these were the *s* of
36:19 These were the *s* of Esau, who
36:20 These were the *s* of Seir the
36:21 the *s* of Seir, in the land of
36:22 And the *s* of Lotan were Hori and
36:23 These were the *s* of Shobal:
36:24 These were the *s* of Zibeon:
36:26 These were the *s* of Dishon:
36:27 These were the *s* of Ezer:
36:28 These were the *s* of Dishan: Uz
37: 2 And the lad was with the *s* of
37: 2 the sons of Bilhah and the *s*
37:35 And all his *s* and all his
41:50 And to Joseph were born two *s*
42: 1 in Egypt, Jacob said to his *s*,
42: 5 And the *s* of Israel went to buy
42:11 "We are all one man's *s*;
42:13 the *s* of one man in the land of
42:32 *s* of our father; one is no
42:37 Kill my two *s* if I do not bring
44:27 know that my wife bore me two *s*;
45:21 Then the *s* of Israel did so;
46: 5 and the *s* of Israel carried
46: 7 His *s* and his sons' sons, his
46: 7 His sons and his sons' *s*, his
46: 8 of Israel, Jacob and his *s*,
46: 9 The *s* of Reuben were Hanoch,
46:10 The *s* of Simeon were Jemuel,
46:11 The *s* of Levi were Gershon,
46:12 The *s* of Judah were Er, Onan,

S

46:12 The *s* of Perez were Hezron and
46:13 The *s* of Issachar were Tola,
46:14 The *s* of Zebulun were Sered,
46:15 These were the *s* of Leah, whom
46:15 his *s* and his daughters, were
46:16 The *s* of Gad were Ziphion,
46:17 The *s* of Asher were Jimnah,
46:17 And the *s* of Beriah were Heber
46:18 These were the *s* of Zilpah,
46:19 The *s* of Rachel, Jacob's wife,
46:21 The *s* of Benjamin were Belah,
46:22 These were the *s* of Rachel, who
46:24 The *s* of Naphtali were Jahzeel,
46:25 These were the *s* of Bilhah,
46:27 And the *s* of Joseph who were
48: 1 and he took with him his two *s*,
48: 5 "And now your two *s*,
48: 8 Then Israel saw Joseph's *s*,
48: 9 to his father, "They are my *s*,
49: 1 And Jacob called his *s* and said,
49: 2 you *s* of Jacob, And listen to
49:32 were purchased from the *s* of
49:33 had finished commanding his *s*,
50:12 So his *s* did for him just as he
50:13 For his *s* carried him to the
Ex 3:22 you shall put them on your *s*
4:20 Moses took his wife and his *s*
6:14 The *s* of Reuben, the firstborn
6:15 And the *s* of Simeon were
6:16 These are the names of the *s* of
6:17 The *s* of Gershon were Libni and
6:18 And the *s* of Kohath were Amram,
6:19 The *s* of Merari were Mahali and
6:21 The *s* of Izhar were Korah,
6:22 And the *s* of Uzziel were
6:24 And the *s* of Korah were Assir,
10: 9 with our *s* and our daughters,
12:24 an ordinance for you and your *s*
13:13 firstborn of man among your *s*
13:15 but all the firstborn of my *s*
18: 3 with her two *s*,
18: 5 came with his *s* and his wife to
18: 6 with your wife and her two *s*
21: 4 and she has borne him *s* or
22:29 The firstborn of your *s* you
27:21 Aaron and his *s* shall tend it
28: 1 and his *s* with him, from among
28: 1 as priest, Aaron and Aaron's *s*:
28: 4 Aaron your brother and his *s*,
28: 9 on them the names of the *s* of
28:11 stones with the names of the *s*
28:12 as memorial stones for the *s*
28:21 shall have the names of the *s*
28:29 shall bear the names of the *s*
28:40 For Aaron's *s* you shall make
28:41 your brother and on his *s* with
28:43 shall be on Aaron and on his *s*
29: 4 And Aaron and his *s* you shall
29: 8 Then you shall bring his *s* and
29: 9 with sashes, Aaron and his *s*,
29: 9 consecrate Aaron and his *s*.
29:10 and Aaron and his *s* shall put
29:15 and Aaron and his *s* shall put
29:19 and Aaron and his *s* shall put
29:20 tip of the right ear of his *s*,
29:21 on his *s* and on the garments of
29:21 and on the garments of his *s*
29:21 and his *s* and his sons'
29:24 Aaron and in the hands of his *s*,
29:27 and of that which is for his *s*.
29:28 of Israel for Aaron and his *s*
29:32 Then Aaron and his *s* shall eat
29:35 you shall do to Aaron and his *s*,
29:44 both Aaron and his *s* to
30:19 for Aaron and his *s* shall wash
30:30 shall anoint Aaron and his *s*,
31:10 and the garments of his *s*,
32: 2 the ears of your wives, your *s*,
32:26 And all the *s* of Levi
32:28 So the *s* of Levi did according
34:16 of his daughters for your *s*,
34:16 with their gods and make your *s*
34:20 All the firstborn of your *s* you
35:19 and the garments of his *s*,
39: 6 with the names of the *s* of
39: 7 as memorial stones for the *s*
39:14 to the names of the *s* of
39:27 fine linen, for Aaron and his *s*,
40:12 shall bring Aaron and his *s* to
40:14 And you shall bring his *s* and
40:31 and his *s* would wash their
Lev 1: 5 and the priests, Aaron's *s*,
1: 7 The *s* of Aaron the priest shall
1: 8 'Then the priests, Aaron's *s*,
1:11 and the priests, Aaron's *s*,
2: 2 'He shall bring it to Aaron's *s*,
2: 3 shall be Aaron's and his *s*'.
2:10 shall be Aaron's and his *s*'.
3: 2 of meeting; and Aaron's *s*,
3: 5 and Aaron's *s* shall burn it on
3: 8 and Aaron's *s* shall sprinkle
3:13 and the *s* of Aaron shall
6: 9 "Command Aaron and his *s*,
6:14 The *s* of Aaron shall offer it
6:16 of it Aaron and his *s* shall
6:20 the offering of Aaron and his *s*,
6:22 'The priest from among his *s*,
6:25 "Speak to Aaron and to his *s*,
7:10 shall belong to all the *s* of
7:31 shall be Aaron's and his *s*'.
7:33 He among the *s* of Aaron, who
7:34 Aaron the priest and to his *s*
7:35 portion for Aaron and his *s*,
8: 2 Take Aaron and his *s* with him,
8: 6 Moses brought Aaron and his *s*
8:13 Then Moses brought Aaron's *s* and
8:14 Then Aaron and his *s* laid their
8:18 And Aaron and his *s* laid their
8:22 Then Aaron and his *s* laid their
8:24 Then he brought Aaron's *s*.
8:30 on his garments, on his *s*,
8:30 and on the garments of his *s*
8:30 Aaron, his garments, his *s*,
8:30 and the garments of his *s* with
8:31 Moses said to Aaron and his *s*,
8:31 Aaron and his *s* shall eat it.'
8:36 So Aaron and his *s* did all the
9: 1 Moses called Aaron and his *s*
9: 9 Then the *s* of Aaron brought the
9:12 and Aaron's *s* presented to him
9:18 And Aaron's *s* presented to him
10: 1 the *s* of Aaron, each took his
10: 4 the *s* of Uzziel the uncle of
10: 6 to Eleazar and Ithamar, his *s*,
10: 9 nor your *s* with you, when you
10:12 his *s* who were left: "Take the
10:14 in a clean place, you, your *s*,
10:16 the *s* of Aaron who were left,
13: 2 the priest or to one of his *s*
16: 1 after the death of the two *s*
17: 2 "Speak to Aaron, to his *s*,
21: 1 the *s* of Aaron, and say to
21:24 told it to Aaron and his *s*,
22: 2 "Speak to Aaron and his *s*,
22:18 "Speak to Aaron and his *s*,
24: 9 it shall be for Aaron and his *s*,
26:29 shall eat the flesh of your *s*,
Num 1:10 'from the *s* of Joseph:
1:32 From the *s* of Joseph, the
3: 2 these are the names of the *s*
3: 3 These are the names of the *s* of
3: 9 the Levites to Aaron and his *s*;
3:10 shall appoint Aaron and his *s*,
3:17 These were the *s* of Levi by
3:18 these are the names of the *s*
3:19 And the *s* of Kohath by their
3:20 And the *s* of Merari by their
3:38 were Moses, Aaron, and his *s*,
3:48 is redeemed, to Aaron and his *s*.
3:51 money to Aaron and his *s*,
4: 2 Take a census of the *s* of Kohath
4: 4 is the service of the *s*
4: 5 Aaron and his *s* shall come, and
4:15 And when Aaron and his *s* have
4:15 then the *s* of Kohath shall come
4:15 of meeting which the *s* of
4:19 Aaron and his *s* shall go in and
4:22 Also take a census of the *s* of
4:27 Aaron and his *s* shall assign all
4:27 all the service of the *s* of
4:28 of the families of the *s* of
4:29 As for the *s* of Merari, you
4:33 of the families of the *s* of
4:34 congregation numbered the *s* of
4:38 who were numbered of the *s* of
4:41 of the families of the *s* of
4:42 of the families of the *s* of
4:45 of the families of the *s* of
6:23 "Speak to Aaron and his *s*,
7: 7 and four oxen he gave to the *s*
7: 8 eight oxen he gave to the *s* of
7: 9 But to the *s* of Kohath he gave
8:13 Levites before Aaron and his *s*,
8:19 as a gift to Aaron and his *s*
8:22 meeting before Aaron and his *s*;
10: 8 The *s* of Aaron, the priests,
10:17 and the *s* of Gershon and the
10:17 the sons of Gershon and the *s*
14:33 And your *s* shall be shepherds in
16: 1 with Dathan and Abiram the *s* of
16: 1 *s* of Reuben, took men;
16: 7 you *s* of Levi!"
16: 8 'Hear now, you *s* of Levi:
16:10 the *s* of Levi, with you?
16:12 to call Dathan and Abiram the *s*
16:27 with their wives, their *s*,
18: 1 You and your *s* and your father's
18: 1 and you and your *s* with you
18: 2 serve you while you and your *s*
18: 7 Therefore you and your *s* with
18: 8 as a portion to you and your *s*,
18: 9 most holy for you and your *s*.
18:11 and your *s* and daughters with
18:19 I have given to you and your *s*
21:29 of Chemosh! He has given his *s*
21:35 So they defeated him, his *s*,
22: 5 the River in the land of the *s*
24:17 And destroy all the *s* of
26: 9 The *s* of Eliab were Nemuel,
26:12 The *s* of Simeon according to
26:15 The *s* of Gad according to their
26:18 are the families of the *s* of
26:19 The *s* of Judah were Er and
26:20 And the *s* of Judah according to
26:21 And the *s* of Perez were: of
26:23 The *s* of Issachar according to
26:26 The *s* of Zebulun according to
26:28 The *s* of Joseph according to
26:29 The *s* of Manasseh: of Machir,
26:30 These are the *s* of Gilead:
26:33 the son of Hepher had no *s*,
26:35 These are the *s* of Ephraim
26:36 And these are the *s* of
26:37 are the families of the *s* of
26:37 These are the *s* of Joseph
26:38 The *s* of Benjamin according to
26:40 And the *s* of Bela were Ard and
26:41 These are the *s* of Benjamin
26:42 These are the *s* of Dan
26:44 The *s* of Asher according to
26:45 Of the *s* of Beriah: of Heber,
26:47 are the families of the *s* of
26:48 The *s* of Naphtali according to
27: 3 in his own sin; and he had no *s*.
34:23 from the *s* of Joseph: a leader
36: 1 of the families of the *s* of
36: 3 are married to any of the *s* of
36: 5 What the tribe of the *s* of
36:11 were married to the *s* of their
Deut 1:28 moreover we have seen the *s* of
2:33 we defeated him, his *s*,
7: 4 For they will turn your *s* away
11: 6 did to Dathan and Abiram the *s*
12:12 you and your *s* and your
12:31 for they burn even their *s* and
18: 5 him and his *s* forever.
21: 5 the *s* of Levi, shall come near,
21:16 his possessions to his *s*,
23:17 or a perverted one of the *s* of
28:32 Your *s* and your daughters shall
28:41 You shall beget *s* and daughters,
28:53 the flesh of your *s* and your
31: 9 the *s* of Levi, who bore the ark
32: 8 When He separated the *s* of
32:19 of the provocation of His *s*
33:24 "Asher is most blessed of *s*;
Josh 5: 2 and circumcise the *s* of Israel
5: 3 and circumcised the *s* of Israel
5: 7 Then Joshua circumcised their *s*
7:24 the wedge of gold, his *s*,
15:14 Caleb drove out the three *s* of
17: 3 the son of Manasseh, had no *s*,
17: 6 an inheritance among his *s*;
17: 6 and the rest of Manasseh's *s*
24:32 Jacob had bought from the *s* of
Judg 1:20 from there the three *s* of Anak.
3: 6 gave their daughters to their *s*;
4: 6 you ten thousand men of the *s*
4: 6 sons of Naphtali and of the *s*
8:19 the *s* of my mother. As the
8:30 Gideon had seventy *s* who were
9: 2 that all seventy of the *s* of
9: 5 the seventy *s* of Jerubbaal, on
9:18 and killed his seventy *s* on one
9:24 crime done to the seventy *s*
10: 4 Now he had thirty *s* who rode on
11: 2 Gilead's wife bore *s*;
11: 2 and when his wife's *s* grew up,
12: 9 He had thirty *s*.
12: 9 from elsewhere for his *s*.
12:14 He had forty *s* and thirty
14:16 have posed a riddle to the *s*
14:17 explained the riddle to the *s*
17: 5 and he consecrated one of his *s*,
17:11 man became like one of his *s*
18:30 and his *s* were priests to the
Ruth 1: 1 he and his wife and his two *s*.
1: 2 and the names of his two *s*
1: 3 and she was left, and her two *s*.
1: 5 so the woman survived her two *s*
1:11 Are there still *s* in my womb,
1:12 tonight and should also bear *s*,
4:15 is better to you than seven *s*,
1 Sam 1: 3 Also the two *s* of Eli, Hophni
1: 4 his wife and to all her *s* and
1: 8 I not better to you than ten *s*?
2:12 Now the *s* of Eli were corrupt;
2:21 she conceived and bore three *s*
2:22 and he heard everything his *s*
2:24 my *s*! For it is not a good
2:29 and honor your *s* more than Me,
2:34 that will come upon your two *s*,
3:13 because his *s* made themselves
4: 4 And the two *s* of Eli, Hophni
4:11 and the two *s* of Eli, Hophni
4:17 the people. Also your two *s*,
8: 1 was old that he made his *s*
8: 3 But his *s* did not walk in his
8: 5 and your *s* do not walk in your
8:11 He will take your *s* and appoint
12: 2 my *s* are with you. I have
14:49 The *s* of Saul were Jonathan,
16: 1 Myself a king among his *s*.
16: 5 he consecrated Jesse and his *s*,
16:10 Thus Jesse made seven of his *s*
17:12 was Jesse, and who had eight *s*.
17:13 The three oldest *s* of Jesse had
17:13 The names of his three *s* who
22:20 Now one of the *s* of Ahimelech
28:19 And tomorrow you and your *s*
30: 3 fire; and their wives, their *s*,
30: 6 every man for his *s* and his
30:19 *s* or daughters, spoil or
31: 2 hard after Saul and his *s*.
31: 2 and Malchishua, Saul's *s*.
31: 6 So Saul, his three *s*,
31: 7 fled and that Saul and his *s*
31: 8 they found Saul and his three *s*
31:12 of Saul and the bodies of his *s*
2 Sam 2:18 Now the three *s* of Zeruiah were
3: 2 *S* were born to David in Hebron
3:39 the *s* of Zeruiah, are too
4: 2 the *s* of Rimmon the Beerothite,
4: 5 Then the *s* of Rimmon the
4: 9 the *s* of Rimmon the Beerothite,
5:13 Also more *s* and daughters were

6: 3 the *s* of Abinadab, drove the
7:10 nor shall the *s* of wickedness
7:14 and with the blows of the *s* of
8:18 and David's *s* were chief
9:10 and your *s* and your servants,
9:10 Now Ziba had fifteen *s* and
9:11 table like one of the king's *s*.
13:23 invited all the king's *s*.
13:27 let Amnon and all the king's *s*
13:29 Then all the king's *s* arose,
13:30 has killed all the king's *s*,
13:32 all the young men, the king's *s*,
13:33 to think that all the king's *s*
13:35 the king's *s* are coming;
13:36 that the king's *s* indeed came,
14: 6 your maidservant had two *s*;
14:27 To Absalom were born three *s*,
15:27 and your two *s* with you,
15:36 there with them their two *s*,
16:10 you *s* of Zeruiah? So let him
19: 5 the lives of your *s* and
19:17 and his fifteen *s* and his
19:22 you *s* of Zeruiah, that you
21: 8 the two *s* of Rizpah the
21: 8 and the five *s* of Michal the
21:16 who was one of the *s* of the
21:18 who was one of the *s* of the
23: 6 But the *s* of rebellion shall
23:32 the Shaalbonite (of the *s* of
1 Ki 1: 9 all his brothers, the king's *s*,
1:19 and has invited all the *s* of
1:25 has invited all the king's *s*,
2: 4 If your *s* take heed to their
2: 7 But show kindness to the *s* of
4: 3 the *s* of Shisha, scribes;
4:31 the *s* of Mahol; and his fame
8:25 only if your *s* take heed to
8:39 know the hearts of all the *s*
9: 6 But if you or your *s* at all
11:20 household among the *s* of
12:31 who were not of the *s* of Levi.
13:11 and his *s* came and told him all
13:12 For his *s* had seen which way
13:13 Then he said to his *s*,
13:27 And he spoke to his *s*,
13:31 him, that he spoke to his *s*,
18:31 number of the tribes of the *s*
20:35 Now a certain man of the *s* of
2 Ki 2: 3 Now the *s* of the prophets who
2: 5 Now the *s* of the prophets who
2: 7 And fifty men of the *s* of the
2:15 Now when the *s* of the prophets
4: 1 woman of the wives of the *s* of
4: 1 is coming to take my two *s* to
4: 4 the door behind you and your *s*;
4: 5 the door behind her and her *s*,
4: 7 and you and your *s* live on the
4:38 Now the *s* of the prophets were
4:38 and boil stew for the *s* of the
5:22 now two young men of the *s* of
6: 1 And the *s* of the prophets said
8:19 give a lamp to him and his *s*
9: 1 prophet called one of the *s* of
9:26 Naboth and the blood of his *s*,
10: 1 Now Ahab had seventy *s* in
10: 1 to those who reared Ahab's *s*,
10: 2 since your master's *s* are with
10: 3 qualified of your master's *s*,
10: 5 and those who reared the *s*,
10: 6 of the men, your master's *s*,
10: 6 time tomorrow. Now the king's *s*,
10: 7 that they took the king's *s* and
10: 8 the heads of the king's *s*.
10:13 have come down to greet the *s*
10:13 the sons of the king and the *s*
10:30 your *s* shall sit on the throne
11: 2 away from among the king's *s*
15:12 Your *s* shall sit on the throne
17:17 And they caused their *s* and
19:37 that his *s* Adrammelech and
20:18 shall take away some of your *s*
25: 7 Then they killed the *s* of
1 Chr 1: 5 The *s* of Japheth were Gomer,
1: 6 The *s* of Gomer were Ashkenaz,
1: 7 The *s* of Javan were Elishah,
1: 8 The *s* of Ham were Cush,
1: 9 The *s* of Cush were Seba,
1: 9 The *s* of Raama were Sheba and
1:17 The *s* of Shem were Elam,
1:19 To Eber were born two *s*:
1:23 All these were the *s* of
1:28 The *s* of Abraham were Isaac and
1:31 These were the *s* of Ishmael.
1:32 Now the *s* born to Keturah,
1:32 The *s* of Jokshan were Sheba
1:33 The *s* of Midian were Ephah,
1:34 The *s* of Isaac were Esau and
1:35 The *s* of Esau were Eliphaz,
1:36 And the *s* of Eliphaz were
1:37 The *s* of Reuel were Nahath,
1:38 The *s* of Seir were Lotan,
1:39 And the *s* of Lotan were Hori
1:40 The *s* of Shobal were Alian,
1:40 The *s* of Zibeon were Ajah and
1:41 The *s* of Dishon were Hamran,
1:42 The *s* of Ezer were Bilhan,
1:42 The *s* of Dishan were Uz and
2: 1 These were the *s* of Israel:
2: 3 The *s* of Judah were Er, Onan,
2: 4 All the *s* of Judah were five.
2: 5 The *s* of Perez were Hezron and
2: 6 The *s* of Zerah were Zimri,

2: 9 Also the *s* of Hezron who were
2:16 And the *s* of Zeruiah were
2:18 Now these were her *s*:
2:23 All these belonged to the *s*
2:25 The *s* of Jerahmeel, the
2:27 The *s* of Ram, the firstborn of
2:28 The *s* of Onam were Shammai and
2:28 The *s* of Shammai were Nadab
2:30 The *s* of Nadab were Seled and
2:32 The *s* of Jada, the brother of
2:33 The *s* of Jonathan were Peleth
2:33 These were the *s* of Jerahmeel.
2:34 Now Sheshan had no *s*,
2:42 and the *s* of Mareshah the
2:43 The *s* of Hebron were Korah,
2:47 And the *s* of Jahdai were Regem,
2:50 The *s* of Hur, the firstborn of
2:54 The *s* of Salma were Bethlehem,
3: 1 Now these were the *s* of David
3: 9 These were all the *s* of David,
3: 9 besides the *s* of the
3:15 The *s* of Josiah were Johanan
3:16 The *s* of Jehoiakim were
3:17 And the *s* of Jeconiah were
3:19 The *s* of Pedaiah were
3:19 The *s* of Zerubbabel were
3:21 The *s* of Hananiah were Pelatiah
3:21 the *s* of Rephaiah, the sons of
3:21 the *s* of Arnan, the sons of
3:21 the *s* of Obadiah, and the sons
3:21 and the *s* of Shechaniah.
3:22 The *s* of Shemaiah were
3:23 The *s* of Neariah were Elioenai,
3:24 The *s* of Elioenai were
4: 1 The *s* of Judah were Perez,
4: 3 These were the *s* of the
4: 4 These were the *s* of Hur, the
4: 6 These were the *s* of Naarah.
4: 7 The *s* of Helah were Zereth,
4:13 The *s* of Kenaz were Othniel
4:13 The *s* of Othniel were Hathath,
4:15 The *s* of Caleb the son of
4:16 The *s* of Jehallelel were Ziph,
4:17 The *s* of Ezrah were Jether,
4:18 And these were the *s* of
4:19 The *s* of Hodiah's wife, the
4:20 And the *s* of Shimon were Amnon,
4:20 And the *s* of Ishi were Zoheth
4:21 The *s* of Shelah the son of Judah
4:24 The *s* of Simeon were Nemuel,
4:26 And the *s* of Mishma were Hamuel
4:27 Shimei had sixteen *s* and six
4:42 five hundred men of the *s* of
4:42 and Uzziel, the *s* of Ishi.
5: 1 Now the *s* of Reuben the
5: 1 birthright was given to the *s*
5: 3 the *s* of Reuben the firstborn of
5: 4 The *s* of Joel were Shemaiah his
5:18 The *s* of Reuben, the Gadites,
6: 1 The *s* of Levi were Gershon,
6: 2 The *s* of Kohath were Amram,
6: 3 And the *s* of Aaron were Nadab,
6:16 The *s* of Levi were Gershon,
6:17 These are the names of the *s* of
6:18 The *s* of Kohath were Amram,
6:19 The *s* of Merari were Mahli and
6:22 The *s* of Kohath were Amminadab
6:25 The *s* of Elkanah were Amasai
6:26 the *s* of Elkanah were Zophai
6:28 The *s* of Samuel were Joel the
6:29 The *s* of Merari were Mahli,
6:33 who ministered with their *s*:
6:33 Of the *s* of the Kohathites
6:44 the *s* of Merari, on the left
6:49 But Aaron and his *s* offered
6:50 Now these are the *s* of Aaron:
6:54 were given by lot to the *s* of
6:57 And to the *s* of Aaron they gave
6:62 And to the *s* of Gershon,
6:63 To the *s* of Merari, throughout
6:66 some of the families of the *s*
6:70 rest of the family of the *s* of
6:71 half-tribe of Manasseh the *s*
7: 1 The *s* of Issachar were Tola,
7: 2 The *s* of Tola were Uzzi,
7: 2 The *s* of Tola were mighty
7: 3 and the *s* of Izrahiah were
7: 4 for they had many wives and *s*.
7: 6 The *s* of Benjamin were Bela,
7: 7 The *s* of Bela were Ezbon, Uzzi,
7: 8 The *s* of Becher were Zemirah,
7: 8 All these are the *s* of Becher.
7:10 and the *s* of Bilhan were
7:11 All these *s* of Jediael were
7:12 Shuppim and Huppim were the *s*
7:13 The *s* of Naphtali were
7:13 and Shallum, the *s* of Bilhah.
7:16 and his *s* were Ulam and Rakem.
7:19 And the *s* of Shemida were Ahian,
7:20 The *s* of Ephraim were
7:30 The *s* of Asher were Imnah,
7:31 The *s* of Beriah were Heber and
7:33 The *s* of Japhlet were Pasach,
7:34 The *s* of Shemer were Ahi,
7:35 And the *s* of his brother Helem
7:36 The *s* of Zophah were Suah,
7:38 The *s* of Jether were Jephunneh,
7:39 The *s* of Ulla were Arah,
8: 3 The *s* of Bela were Addar, Gera,
8: 6 These are the *s* of Ehud, who
8:10 and Mirmah. These were his *s*,
8:12 The *s* of Elpaal were Eber,

8:16 and Joha were the *s* of Beriah.
8:18 and Jobab were the *s* of
8:21 and Shimrath were the *s* of
8:25 and Penuel were the *s* of
8:27 and Zichri were the *s* of
8:35 The *s* of Micah were Pithon,
8:38 Azel had six *s* whose names were
8:38 All these were the *s* of Azel.
8:39 And the *s* of Eshek his brother
8:40 The *s* of Ulam were mighty men of
8:40 They had many *s* and grandsons,
8:40 These were all *s* of Benjamin.
9: 5 Asaiah the firstborn and his *s*.
9: 6 Of the *s* of Zerah: Jeuel, and
9: 7 Of the *s* of Benjamin: Sallu the
9:14 of the *s* of Merari;
9:30 And some of the *s* of the
9:32 of their brethren of the *s* of
9:41 The *s* of Micah were Pithon,
9:44 And Azel had six *s* whose names
9:44 these were the *s* of Azel.
10: 2 hard after Saul and his *s*.
10: 2 and Malchishua, Saul's *s*.
10: 6 So Saul and his three *s* died,
10: 7 fled and that Saul and his *s*
10: 8 that they found Saul and his *s*
10:12 of Saul and the bodies of his *s*;
11:31 of the *s* of Benjamin, Benaiah
11:34 the *s* of Hashem the Gizonite,
11:44 Shama and Jeiel the *s* of Hotham
11:46 Jeribai and Joshaviah the *s* of
12: 3 the *s* of Shemaah the
12: 3 Jeziel and Pelet the *s* of
12: 7 and Joelah and Zebadiah the *s* of
12:14 These were from the *s* of Gad,
12:16 Then some of the *s* of Benjamin
12:24 of the *s* of Judah bearing shield
12:25 of the *s* of Simeon, mighty men
12:26 of the *s* of Levi four thousand
12:29 of the *s* of Benjamin, relatives
12:30 of the *s* of Ephraim twenty
12:32 of the *s* of Issachar who had
14: 3 and David begot more *s* and
15: 5 of the *s* of Kohath, Uriel the
15: 6 of the *s* of Merari, Asaiah the
15: 7 of the *s* of Gershom, Joel the
15: 8 of the *s* of Elizaphan, Shemaiah
15: 9 of the *s* of Hebron, Eliel the
15:10 of the *s* of Uzziel, Amminadab
15:17 the *s* of Merari, Ethan the son
16:42 Now the *s* of Jeduthun were
17: 9 nor shall the *s* of wickedness
17:11 you, who will be of your *s*;
18:17 and David's *s* were chief
20: 4 who was one of the *s* of the
21:20 and his four *s* who were with
23: 6 into divisions among the *s* of
23: 8 The *s* of Laadan: the first
23: 9 The *s* of Shimei: Shelomith,
23:10 And the *s* of Shimei: Jahath,
23:10 These were the four *s* of
23:11 and Beriah did not have many *s*;
23:12 The *s* of Kohath: Amram, Izhar,
23:13 The *s* of Amram: Aaron and Moses;
23:13 he and his *s* forever, that he
23:14 Now the *s* of Moses the man of
23:15 The *s* of Moses were Gershon and
23:16 Of the *s* of Gershon, Shebuel
23:17 And Eliezer had no other *s*,
23:17 but the *s* of Rehabiah were very
23:18 Of the *s* of Izhar, Shelomith
23:19 Of the *s* of Hebron, Jeriah was
23:20 Of the *s* of Uzziel, Michah was
23:21 The *s* of Merari were Mahli and
23:21 The *s* of Mahli were Eleazar
23:22 And Eleazar died, and had no *s*,
23:22 the *s* of Kish, took them as
23:23 The *s* of Mushi were Mahli,
23:24 These were the *s* of Levi by
23:28 their duty was to help the *s*
23:32 and the needs of the *s* of Aaron
24: 1 are the divisions of the *s* of
24: 1 The *s* of Aaron were Nadab,
24: 3 Then David with Zadok of the *s*
24: 3 and Ahimelech of the *s* of
24: 4 more leaders found of the *s* of
24: 4 sons of Eleazar than of the *s*
24: 4 Among the *s* of Eleazar were
24: 4 fathers' houses among the *s* of
24: 5 from the *s* of Eleazar and from
24: 5 sons of Eleazar and from the *s*
24:20 And the rest of the *s* of Levi:
24:20 of the *s* of Amram, Shubael; of
24:20 of the *s* of Shubael, Jehdeiah.
24:21 of the *s* of Rehabiah, the first
24:22 of the *s* of Shelomoth, Jahath.
24:23 Of the *s* of Hebron, Jeriah
24:24 Of the *s* of Uzziel, Michah; of
24:24 of the *s* of Michah, Shamir.
24:25 of the *s* of Isshiah, Zechariah.
24:26 The *s* of Merari were Mahli and
24:27 The *s* of Merari by Jaaziah were
24:28 Of Mahli: Eleazar, who had no *s*.
24:30 Also the *s* of Mushi were Mahli,
24:30 These were the *s* of the
24:31 just as their brothers the *s*
25: 1 for the service some of the *s*
25: 2 Of the *s* of Asaph: Zaccur,
25: 2 the *s* of Asaph were under the
25: 3 the *s* of Jeduthun: Gedaliah,
25: 4 the *s* of Heman: Bukkiah,
25: 5 All these were the *s* of Heman

S

25: 5 For God gave Heman fourteen *s*
25: 9 him with his brethren and *s*,
25:10 his *s* and his brethren, twelve;
25:11 his *s* and his brethren, twelve;
25:12 his *s* and his brethren, twelve;
25:13 his *s* and his brethren, twelve;
25:14 his *s* and his brethren, twelve;
25:15 his *s* and his brethren, twelve;
25:16 his *s* and his brethren, twelve;
25:17 his *s* and his brethren, twelve;
25:18 his *s* and his brethren, twelve;
25:19 his *s* and his brethren, twelve;
25:20 his *s* and his brethren, twelve;
25:21 his *s* and his brethren, twelve;
25:22 his *s* and his brethren, twelve;
25:23 his *s* and his brethren, twelve;
25:24 his *s* and his brethren, twelve;
25:25 his *s* and his brethren, twelve;
25:26 his *s* and his brethren, twelve;
25:27 his *s* and his brethren, twelve;
25:28 his *s* and his brethren, twelve;
25:29 his *s* and his brethren, twelve;
25:30 his *s* and his brethren, twelve;
25:31 his *s* and his brethren, twelve.
26: 1 of the *s* of Asaph.
26: 2 And the *s* of Meshelemiah were
26: 4 Moreover the *s* of Obed-Edom
26: 6 Also to Shemaiah his son were *s*
26: 7 The *s* of Shemaiah were Othni,
26: 8 All these were of the *s* of
26: 8 they and their *s* and their
26: 9 And Meshelemiah had *s* and
26:10 the children of Merari, had *s*:
26:11 all the *s* and brethren of Hosah
26:15 and to his *s* the storehouse.
26:19 of the gatekeepers among the *s*
26:19 sons of Korah and among the *s*
26:21 The *s* of Laadan, the descendants
26:22 The *s* of Jehieli, Zetham and
26:29 Chenaniah and his *s* performed
27:32 Hachmoni was with the king's *s*.
28: 1 of the king and of his *s*,
28: 4 and among the *s* of my father,
28: 5 And of all my *s* (for the LORD
28: 5 the LORD has given me many *s*)
29:24 and also all the *s* of King
2 Chr 5:12 with their *s* and their
6:16 only if your *s* take heed to
6:30 alone know the hearts of the *s*
11:14 for Jeroboam and his *s* had
11:21 and begot twenty-eight *s* and
11:23 and dispersed some of his *s*
13: 5 David forever, to him and his *s*,
13: 8 which is in the hand of the *s*
13: 9 the *s* of Aaron, and the
13:10 to the LORD are the *s* of
13:21 and begot twenty-two *s* and
20:14 a Levite of the *s* of Asaph, in
21: 2 the *s* of Jehoshaphat: Azariah,
21: 2 all these were the *s* of
21: 7 give a lamp to him and to his *s*
21:17 and also his *s* and his wives,
21:17 Jehoahaz, the youngest of his *s*.
22: 1 had killed all the older *s*.
22: 8 the princes of Judah and the *s*
22:11 away from among the king's *s*
23: 3 as the LORD has said of the *s*
23:11 Then Jehoiada and his *s*
24: 3 and he had *s* and daughters.
24: 7 For the *s* of Athaliah, that
24:25 because of the blood of the *s*
24:27 Now concerning his *s*,
26:18 the *s* of Aaron, who are
28: 8 two hundred thousand women, *s*,
29: 9 fallen by the sword; and our *s*,
29:11 'My *s*, do not be negligent
29:12 of the *s* of the Kohathites;
29:12 of the *s* of Merari, Kish the
29:13 of the *s* of Elizaphan, Shimri
29:13 of the *s* of Asaph, Zechariah
29:14 of the *s* of Heman, Jehiel and
29:14 and of the *s* of Jeduthun,
29:21 the *s* of Aaron, to offer them
31:18 their *s* and daughters,
31:19 Also for the *s* of Aaron the
32:33 in the upper tombs of the *s* of
33: 6 Also he caused his *s* to pass
34:12 of the *s* of Merari,
34:12 of the *s* of the Kohathites,
35:14 the *s* of Aaron, were busy in
35:14 the priests, the *s* of Aaron.
35:15 the *s* of Asaph, were in their
36:20 servants to him and his *s*
Ezra 2:36 the *s* of Jedaiah, of the house
2:37 the *s* of Immer, one thousand and
2:38 the *s* of Pashhur, one thousand
2:39 the *s* of Harim, one thousand and
2:40 the *s* of Jeshua and Kadmiel, of
2:40 of the *s* of Hodaviah,
2:41 the *s* of Asaph, one hundred and
2:42 The *s* of the gatekeepers:
2:42 the *s* of Shallum, the sons of
2:42 the *s* of Ater, the sons of
2:42 the *s* of Talmon, the sons of
2:42 the *s* of Akkub, the sons of
2:42 the *s* of Hatita, and the sons
2:42 and the *s* of Shobai, one
2:43 the *s* of Ziha, the sons of
2:43 the *s* of Hasupha, the sons of
2:43 the *s* of Tabbaoth,
2:44 the *s* of Keros, the sons of
2:44 the *s* of Siaha, the sons of
2:44 the *s* of Padon,
2:45 the *s* of Lebanah, the sons of
2:45 the *s* of Hagabah, the sons of
2:45 the *s* of Akkub,
2:46 the *s* of Hagab, the sons of
2:46 the *s* of Shalmai, the sons of
2:46 the *s* of Hanan,
2:47 the *s* of Giddel, the sons of
2:47 the *s* of Gahar, the sons of
2:47 the *s* of Reaiah,
2:48 the *s* of Rezin, the sons of
2:48 the *s* of Nekoda, the sons of
2:48 the *s* of Gazzam,
2:49 the *s* of Uzza, the sons of
2:49 the *s* of Paseah, the sons of
2:49 the *s* of Besai,
2:50 the *s* of Asnah, the sons of
2:50 the *s* of Meunim, the sons of
2:50 the *s* of Nephusim,
2:51 the *s* of Bakbuk, the sons of
2:51 the *s* of Hakupha, the sons of
2:51 the *s* of Harhur,
2:52 the *s* of Bazluth, the sons of
2:52 the *s* of Mehida, the sons of
2:52 the *s* of Harsha,
2:53 the *s* of Barkos, the sons of
2:53 the *s* of Sisera, the sons of
2:53 the *s* of Tamah,
2:54 the *s* of Neziah, and the sons of
2:54 and the *s* of Hatipha.
2:55 The *s* of Solomon's servants:
2:55 the *s* of Sotai, the sons of
2:55 the *s* of Sophereth, the sons of
2:55 the *s* of Peruda,
2:56 the *s* of Jaala, the sons of
2:56 the *s* of Darkon, the sons of
2:56 the *s* of Giddel,
2:57 the *s* of Shephatiah, the sons of
2:57 the *s* of Hattil, the sons of
2:57 the *s* of Pochereth of Zebaim,
2:57 and the *s* of Ami.
2:60 the *s* of Delaiah, the sons of
2:60 the *s* of Tobiah, and the sons
2:60 and the *s* of Nekoda, six
2:61 and of the *s* of the priests:
2:61 the *s* of Habaiah, the sons of
2:61 the *s* of Koz, and the sons of
2:61 and the *s* of Barzillai, who
3: 9 Then Jeshua with his *s* and
3: 9 brothers, Kadmiel with his *s*,
3: 9 and the *s* of Judah, arose as
3: 9 the *s* of Henadad with their
3: 9 sons of Henadad with their *s*
3:10 the *s* of Asaph, with cymbals,
6:10 the life of the king and his *s*.
7:23 the realm of the king and his *s*?
8: 2 of the *s* of Phinehas, Gershom;
8: 2 of the *s* of Ithamar, Daniel;
8: 2 of the *s* of David, Hattush;
8: 3 of the *s* of Shecaniah, of the
8: 3 of the *s* of Parosh, Zechariah;
8: 4 of the *s* of Pahath-Moab,
8: 5 of the *s* of Shechaniah,
8: 6 of the *s* of Adin, Ebed the son
8: 7 of the *s* of Elam, Jeshaiah the
8: 8 of the *s* of Shephatiah, Zebadiah
8: 9 of the *s* of Joab, Obadiah the
8:10 of the *s* of Shelomith,
8:11 of the *s* of Bebai, Zechariah the
8:12 of the *s* of Azgad, Johanan the
8:13 of the last *s* of Adonikam, whose
8:14 also of the *s* of Bigvai, Uthai
8:15 and found none of the *s* of Levi
8:18 of the *s* of Mahli the son of
8:18 with his *s* and brothers,
8:19 and with him Jeshaiah of the *s*
8:19 his brothers and their *s*,
9: 2 for themselves and their *s*,
9:12 daughters as wives for their *s*,
9:12 take their daughters to your *s*;
10: 2 one of the *s* of Elam, spoke up
10:18 And among the *s* of the priests
10:18 following were found of the *s*
10:20 Also of the *s* of Immer: Hanani
10:21 of the *s* of Harim: Maaseiah,
10:22 of the *s* of Pashhur: Elioenai,
10:25 of the *s* of Parosh: Ramiah,
10:26 of the *s* of Elam: Mattaniah,
10:27 of the *s* of Zattu: Elioenai,
10:28 of the *s* of Bebai: Jehohanan,
10:29 of the *s* of Bani: Meshullam,
10:30 of the *s* of Pahath-Moab: Adna,
10:31 of the *s* of Harim: Eliezer,
10:33 of the *s* of Hashum: Mattenai,
10:34 of the *s* of Bani: Maadai, Amram,
10:43 of the *s* of Nebo: Jeiel,
Neh 3: 3 Also the *s* of Hassenaah built
4:14 fight for your brethren, your *s*,
5: 2 those who said, "We, our *s*,
5: 5 and indeed we are forcing our *s*
7: 8 the *s* of Parosh, two thousand
7: 9 the *s* of Shephatiah, three
7:10 the *s* of Arah, six hundred and
7:11 the *s* of Pahath-Moab, of the
7:11 of the *s* of Jeshua and Joab,
7:12 the *s* of Elam, one thousand two
7:13 the *s* of Zattu, eight hundred
7:14 the *s* of Zaccai, seven hundred
7:15 the *s* of Binnui, six hundred and
7:16 the *s* of Bebai, six hundred and
7:17 the *s* of Azgad, two thousand
7:18 the *s* of Adonikam, six hundred
7:19 the *s* of Bigvai, two thousand
7:20 the *s* of Adin, six hundred and
7:21 the *s* of Ater of Hezekiah,
7:22 the *s* of Hashum, three hundred
7:23 the *s* of Bezai, three hundred
7:24 the *s* of Hariph, one hundred and
7:25 the *s* of Gibeon, ninety-five;
7:34 the *s* of the other Elam, one
7:35 the *s* of Harim, three hundred
7:36 the *s* of Jericho, three hundred
7:37 the *s* of Lod, Hadid, and Ono,
7:38 the *s* of Senaah, three thousand
7:39 the *s* of Jedaiah, of the house
7:40 the *s* of Immer, one thousand and
7:41 the *s* of Pashhur, one thousand
7:42 the *s* of Harim, one thousand and
7:43 the *s* of Jeshua, of Kadmiel,
7:43 and of the *s* of Hodevah,
7:44 the *s* of Asaph, one hundred and
7:45 the *s* of Shallum, the sons of
7:45 the *s* of Ater, the sons of
7:45 the *s* of Talmon, the sons of
7:45 the *s* of Akkub, the sons of
7:45 the *s* of Hatita, the sons of
7:45 the *s* of Shobai, one hundred
7:46 the *s* of Ziha, the sons of
7:46 the *s* of Hasupha, the sons of
7:46 the *s* of Tabbaoth,
7:47 the *s* of Keros, the sons of Sia,
7:47 the *s* of Sia, the sons of
7:47 the *s* of Padon,
7:48 the *s* of Lebana, the sons of
7:48 the *s* of Hagaba, the sons of
7:48 the *s* of Salmai,
7:49 the *s* of Hanan, the sons of
7:49 the *s* of Giddel, the sons of
7:49 the *s* of Gahar,
7:50 the *s* of Reaiah, the sons of
7:50 the *s* of Rezin, the sons of
7:50 the *s* of Nekoda,
7:51 the *s* of Gazzam, the sons of
7:51 the *s* of Uzza, the sons of
7:51 the *s* of Paseah,
7:52 the *s* of Besai, the sons of
7:52 the *s* of Meunim, the sons of
7:52 the *s* of Nephishesim,
7:53 the *s* of Bakbuk, the sons of
7:53 the *s* of Hakupha, the sons of
7:53 the *s* of Harhur,
7:54 the *s* of Bazlith, the sons of
7:54 the *s* of Mehida, the sons of
7:54 the *s* of Harsha,
7:55 the *s* of Barkos, the sons of
7:55 the *s* of Sisera, the sons of
7:55 the *s* of Tamah,
7:56 the *s* of Neziah, and the sons of
7:56 and the *s* of Hatipha.
7:57 The *s* of Solomon's servants:
7:57 the *s* of Sotai, the sons of
7:57 the *s* of Sophereth, the sons of
7:57 the *s* of Perida,
7:58 the *s* of Jaala, the sons of
7:58 the *s* of Darkon, the sons of
7:58 the *s* of Giddel,
7:59 the *s* of Shephatiah, the sons of
7:59 the *s* of Hattil, the sons of
7:59 the *s* of Pochereth of Zebaim,
7:59 and the *s* of Amon.
7:60 and the *s* of Solomon's
7:62 the *s* of Delaiah, the sons of
7:62 the *s* of Tobiah, the sons of
7:62 the *s* of Nekoda, six hundred
7:63 the *s* of Habaiah, the sons of
7:63 the *s* of Koz, the sons of
7:63 the *s* of Barzillai, who took a
10: 9 Binnui of the *s* of Henadad,
10:28 of God, their wives, their *s*,
10:30 take their daughters for our *s*;
10:36 to bring the firstborn of our *s*
11: 6 All the *s* of Perez who dwelt at
11: 7 And these are the *s* of
11:22 of the *s* of Asaph, the singers
12:23 The *s* of Levi, the heads of the
12:28 And the *s* of the singers
12:35 and some of the priests' *s* with
13:25 daughters as wives to their *s*,
13:25 their daughters for your *s* or
13:28 And one of the *s* of Joiada,
Esth 9:10 the ten *s* of Haman the son of
9:12 and the ten *s* of Haman.
9:13 and let Haman's ten *s* be hanged
9:14 and they hanged Haman's ten *s*.
9:25 and that he and his *s* should be
Job 1: 2 And seven *s* and three daughters
1: 4 And his *s* would go and feast
1: 5 It may be that my *s* have sinned
1: 6 there was a day when the *s* of
1:13 there was a day when his *s* and
1:18 Your *s* and daughters were
2: 1 there was a day when the *s* of
5: 4 His *s* are far from safety,
8: 4 If your *s* have sinned against
14:21 His *s* come to honor, and he
30: 8 They were *s* of fools,
30: 8 *s* of vile men; They were
38: 7 And all the *s* of God shouted
42:13 He also had seven *s* and three
Ps 4: 2 O you *s* of men, Will you
11: 4 His eyelids test the *s* of men.
12: 1 disappear from among the *s* of
12: 8 is exalted among the *s* of men.
21:10 descendants from among the *s*

31:19 In the presence of the s of
33:13 He sees all the s of men.
42: A Contemplation of the s of
44: A Contemplation of the s of
45: A Contemplation of the s of
45: 2 You are fairer than the s of
45:16 of Your fathers shall be Your s,
46: A Psalm of the s of Korah.
47: A Psalm of the s of Korah.
48: A Psalm of the s of Korah.
49: A Psalm of the s of Korah.
57: 4 I lie among the s of men Who
58: 1 judge uprightly, you s of men?
66: 5 in His doing toward the s of
77:15 The s of Jacob and Joseph.
84: A Psalm of the s of Korah.
85: A Psalm of the s of Korah.
87: A Psalm of the s of Korah.
88: A Psalm of the s of Korah.
89: 6 Who among the s of the mighty
89:30 If his s forsake My law And do
106:37 They even sacrificed their s
106:38 The blood of their s and
132:12 If your s will keep My covenant
132:12 Their s also shall sit upon
137: 7 against the s of Edom The day
144:12 That our s may be as plants
145:12 To make known to the s of men
Prov 8: 4 And my voice is to the s of
8:31 my delight was with the s of
15:11 much more the hearts of the s
Eccl 1:13 task God has given to the s of
2: 3 see what was good for the s
2: 8 the delights of the s of men,
3:10 task with which the s of men
3:18 the condition of the s of men,
3:19 For what happens to the s of men
3:21 Who knows the spirit of the s of
8:11 therefore the heart of the s of
9: 3 Truly the hearts of the s of
9:12 So the s of men are snared in
Song 1: 6 My mother's s were angry with
2: 3 So is my beloved among the s.
Isa 37:38 that his s Adrammelech and
39: 7 take away some of your s who
43: 6 keep them back!' Bring My s
45:11 things to come concerning My s;
49:17 Your s shall make haste;
49:22 They shall bring your s in
51:18 to guide her Among all the s
51:18 by the hand Among all the s
51:20 Your s have fainted, They lie
52:14 And His form more than the s
56: 5 a name Better than that of s
56: 6 Also the s of the foreigner
57: 3 You s of the sorceress,
60: 4 Your s shall come from afar,
60: 9 To bring your s from afar,
60:10 The s of foreigners shall build
60:14 Also the s of those who
61: 5 And the s of the foreigner
62: 5 So shall your s marry you;
62: 8 And the s of the foreigner
Jer 3:24 Their s and their daughters.
5:17 Which your s and daughters
6:21 And the fathers and the s
7:31 to burn their s and their
11:22 their s and their daughters
13:14 even the fathers and the s
14:16 their s nor their daughters—for
16: 2 nor shall you have s or
16: 3 the LORD concerning the s and
19: 5 to burn their s with fire for
19: 9 to eat the flesh of their s
29: 6 Take wives and beget s and
29: 6 and take wives for your s and
29: 6 so that they may bear s and
32:19 open to all the ways of the s
32:35 to cause their s and their
35: 3 his brothers and all his s,
35: 4 into the chamber of the s of
35: 5 Then I set before the s of the
35: 6 drink no wine, you nor your s,
35: 8 our days, we, our wives, our s,
35:14 which he commanded his s,
35:16 Surely the s of Jonadab the son
39: 6 king of Babylon killed the s
40: 8 Johanan and Jonathan the s of
40: 8 the s of Ephai the
48:45 crown of the head of the s of
48:46 For your s have been taken
49: 1 the LORD: "Has Israel no s?
52:10 king of Babylon killed the s
Lam 4: 2 The precious s of Zion,
Ezek 5:10 fathers shall eat their s in
5:10 and s shall eat their fathers;
14:16 they would deliver neither s nor
14:18 they would deliver neither s nor
14:22 both s and daughters;
16:20 Moreover you took your s and
20:31 your gifts and make your s
23: 4 And they bore s and daughters.
23:10 Took away her s and daughters,
23:25 They shall take your s and
23:37 and even sacrificed their s
23:47 they shall slay their s and
24:21 and your s and daughters whom
24:25 their s and their daughters:
40:46 these are the s of Zadok, from
40:46 from the s of Levi, who come
44:15 the s of Zadok, who kept charge
46:16 his inheritance to any of his s,
46:16 sons, it shall belong to his s;
46:17 shall belong to his s;
46:18 an inheritance for his s from
48:11 be for the priests of the s
Dan 1: 6 Now from among those of the s of
5:21 Then he was driven from the s of
10:16 having the likeness of the s
11:10 However his s shall stir up
12: 1 who stands watch over the s
Hos 1:10 You are s of the living God.'
11:10 Then His s shall come
Joel 1:12 has withered away from the s
2:28 Your s and your daughters
3: 8 I will sell your s and your
Am 2:11 I raised up some of your s as
7:17 Your s and daughters shall
Mic 5: 7 for no man Nor wait for the s
Zech 9:13 Ephraim, And raised up your s,
9:13 sons, O Zion, Against your s,
Mal 3: 3 He will purify the s of Levi,
3: 6 not consumed, O s of Jacob.
Mt 5: 9 For they shall be called s of
5:45 that you may be s of your Father
8:12 But the s of the kingdom will be
12:27 by whom do your s cast them
13:38 the good seeds are the s of the
13:38 but the tares are the s of the
17:25 from their s or from
17:26 Then the s are free.
20:20 the mother of Zebedee's s came
20:20 sons came to Him with her s,
20:21 Grant that these two s of mine
21:28 do you think? A man had two s,
23:31 yourselves that you are s of
26:37 with Him Peter and the two s
27:56 and the mother of Zebedee's s.
Mk 3:17 that is, "S of Thunder";
3:28 sins will be forgiven the s of
10:35 the s of Zebedee, came to Him,
Lk 5:10 the s of Zebedee, who were
6:35 and you will be s of the Most
11:19 by whom do your s cast them
15:11 said: "A certain man had two s.
16: 8 For the s of this world are
16: 8 in their generation than the s
20:34 The s of this age marry and are
20:36 equal to the angels and are s
20:36 being s of the resurrection.
Jn 4:12 as well as his s and his
12:36 that you may become s of
21: 2 the s of Zebedee, and two
Acts 2:17 Your s and your daughters
3:25 You are s of the prophets, and
7:16 for a sum of money from the s
7:29 of Midian, where he had two s.
13:26 s of the family of Abraham,
19:14 Also there were seven s of
Rom 8:14 these are s of God.
8:19 for the revealing of the s of
9:26 they shall be called s
2 Cor 6:18 And you shall be My s and
Gal 3: 7 those who are of faith are s
3:26 For you are all s of God
4: 5 might receive the adoption as s.
4: 6 And because you are s,
4:22 written that Abraham had two s:
Eph 1: 5 us to adoption as s by Jesus
2: 2 spirit who now works in the s
3: 5 was not made known to the s of
5: 6 wrath of God comes upon the s
Col 3: 6 of God is coming upon the s of
1 Th 5: 5 You are all s of light and sons
5: 5 are all sons of light and s of
Heb 2:10 in bringing many s to glory,
7: 5 indeed those who are of the s
11:21 blessed each of the s of
12: 5 which speaks to you as to s:
12: 7 God deals with you as with s;
12: 8 you are illegitimate and not s.

SONS-IN-LAW (2/1) SON-IN-LAW

Gen 19:14 Lot went out and spoke to his s,
19:14 this city!" But to his s he

SONS' (14/13) SONS

Gen 6:18 and your s wives with you.
7: 7 and his s wives, went into the
8:16 and your sons and your s wives
8:18 and his wife and his s wives
46: 7 His sons and his s sons, his
46: 7 daughters and his s daughters,
46:26 besides Jacob's s wives, were
Ex 29:21 and his sons and his s garments
29:29 of Aaron shall be his s after
39:41 and his s garments, to minister
Lev 8:27 hands and in his s hands,
10:13 it is your due and your s due,
10:14 are your due and your s due,
10:15 be yours and your s with you,

SOON (65/64)

Gen 18:33 So the LORD went His way as s
26:10 One of the people might s have
27:30 as s as Isaac had finished
44: 3 As s as the morning dawned, the
Ex 2:18 it that you have come so s
9:29 As s as I have gone out of the
32:19 as s as he came near the camp,
Deut 4:26 that you will s utterly perish
Josh 2: 7 And as s as those who pursued
2:11 And as s as we heard these
3:13 as s as the soles of the feet
8:19 they ran as s as he had
8:29 And as s as the sun was down,
Judg 8:33 as s as Gideon was dead, that
9:33 as s as the sun is up in the
1 Sam 9:13 As s as you come into the city,
13:10 as s as he had finished
20:41 As s as the lad had gone, David
29:10 And as s as you are up early in
2 Sam 13:36 as s as he had finished
15:10 As s as you hear the sound of
22:45 As s as they hear, they obey
1 Ki 16:11 as s as he was seated on his
18:12 as s as I am gone from you,
20:36 as s as you depart from me, a
20:36 And as s as he left him, a
2 Ki 10: 2 Now as s as this letter comes to
10:25 as s as he had made an end of
14: 5 as s as the kingdom was
2 Chr 25: 3 as s as the kingdom was
31: 5 As s as the commandment was
Job 32:22 Else my Maker would s take me
Ps 18:44 As s as they hear of me they
37: 2 For they shall s be cut down
58: 3 They go astray as s as they
81:14 I would s subdue their enemies,
90:10 For it is s cut off, and we
94:17 My soul would s have settled
106:13 They s forgot His works;
Isa 66: 8 For as s as Zion was in labor,
Ezek 7: 8 Now upon you I will s pour out
23:16 As s as her eyes saw them,
Mt 21:20 the fig tree wither away so s?
Mk 1:29 Now as s as they had come out
1:42 As s as He had spoken,
5:36 As s as Jesus heard the word
9:39 a miracle in My name can s
11: 2 and as s as you have entered it
14:45 As s as He had come, immediately
Lk 1:23 as s as the days of his service
1:44 as s as the voice of your
8: 6 and as s as it sprang up, it
15:30 But as s as this son of yours
22:66 As s as it was day, the elders
23: 7 And as s as he knew that He
Jn 11:20 as s as she heard that Jesus
11:29 As s as she heard that, she
16:21 but as s as she has given birth
21: 9 as s as they had come to land,
Acts 10:29 I came without objection as s
12:18 as s as it was day, there was
Gal 1: 6 that you are turning away so s
Phil 2:23 as s as I see how it goes with
2 Th 2: 2 not to be s shaken in mind or
Rev 12: 4 to devour her Child as s as it

SOONER (2/2)

Heb 13:19 I may be restored to you the s.
Jas 1:11 For no s has the sun risen with

SOOT (1/1)

Lam 4: 8 appearance is blacker than s;

SOOTHED (1/1)

Isa 1: 6 Or s with ointment.

SOOTHING (1/1)

Gen 8:21 And the LORD smelled a s aroma.

SOOTHSAYER (2/2) SOOTHSAYERS, SOOTHSAYING

Deut 18:10 practices witchcraft, or a s,
Josh 13:22 Balaam the son of Beor, the s,

SOOTHSAYERS (9/9) SOOTHSAYER

Deut 18:14 will dispossess listened to s
Isa 2: 6 They are s like the
Jer 27: 9 diviners, your dreamers, your s,
50:36 A sword is against the s,
Dan 2:27 and the s cannot declare to the
4: 7 and the s came in, and I told
5: 7 the Chaldeans, and the s.
5:11 astrologers, Chaldeans, and s.
Mic 5:12 And you shall have no s.

SOOTHSAYING (4/4) SOOTHSAYER

Lev 19:26 you practice divination or s.
2 Ki 17:17 practiced witchcraft and s,
21: 6 through the fire, practiced s,
2 Chr 33: 6 Son of Hinnom; he practiced s,

SOP (KJV) See DIPPED

SOPATER (1/1)

Acts 20: 4 And S of Berea accompanied him

SOPE (KJV) See SOAP

SOPHERETH (2/2)

Ezra 2:55 sons of Sotai, the sons of S,
Neh 7:57 sons of Sotai, the sons of S,

SORCERER (3/3) SORCERERS, SORCERY

Deut 18:10 who interprets omens, or a *s*,
Acts 13: 6 Paphos, they found a certain *s*,
13: 8 But Elymas the *s* (for so his

SORCERERS (7/7) SORCERER

Ex 7:11 called the wise men and the *s*;
Isa 19: 3 The mediums and the *s*.
Jer 27: 9 your soothsayers, or your *s*,
Dan 2: 2 the astrologers, the *s*,
Mal 3: 5 be a swift witness Against *s*,
Rev 21: 8 murderers, sexually immoral, *s*,
22:15 But outside are dogs and *s* and

SORCERESS (2/2)

Ex 22:18 You shall not permit a *s* to
Isa 57: 3 come here, You sons of the *s*,

SORCERIES (7/6) SORCERY

Isa 47: 9 of the multitude of your *s*,
47:12 And the multitude of your *s*,
Mic 5:12 I will cut off *s* from your
Nah 3: 4 harlot, The mistress of *s*,
3: 4 And families through her *s*.
Acts 8:11 had astonished them with his *s*
Rev 9:21 of their murders or their *s* or

SORCERY (6/6) SORCERER, SORCERIES

Num 23:23 For there is no *s* against
24: 1 other times, to seek to use *s*,
2 Chr 33: 6 used witchcraft and *s*,
Acts 8: 9 who previously practiced *s* in
Gal 5:20 idolatry, *s*, hatred,
Rev 18:23 for by your *s* all the nations

SORE (31/25) SORES

Lev 13: 2 of his body like a leprous *s*,
13: 3 priest shall examine the *s*
13: 3 and if the hair on the *s* has
13: 3 and the *s* appears to be
13: 3 of his body, it is a leprous *s*.
13: 4 the one who has the *s*
13: 5 and indeed if the *s* appears to
13: 5 and the *s* has not spread on
13: 6 and indeed if the *s* has faded,
13: 6 and the *s* has not spread on
13: 9 When the leprous *s* is on a
13:12 of the one who has the *s*,
13:13 him clean who has the *s*.
13:17 and indeed if the *s* has turned
13:17 him clean who has the *s*.
13:20 It is a leprous *s* which has
13:22 him unclean. It is a leprous *s*.
13:25 him unclean. It is a leprous *s*.
13:27 him unclean. It is a leprous *s*.
13:29 If a man or woman has a *s* on
13:30 the priest shall examine the *s*;
13:31 the priest examines the scaly *s*,
13:32 the priest shall examine the *s*;
13:42 bald forehead a reddish-white *s*,
13:43 if the swelling of the *s* is
13:44 his *s* is on his head.
13:45 Now the leper on whom the *s* is,
13:46 All the days he has the *s* he
14:32 for one who had a leprous *s*,
14:54 is the law for any leprous *s*
Rev 16: 2 and a foul and loathsome *s* came

SOREK (1/1)

Judg 16: 4 a woman in the Valley of *S*,

SORELY (KJV) See ALSO, BITTERLY

SORES (6/6) SORE

Ex 9: 9 boils that break out in *s* on
9:10 boils that break out in *s* on
Isa 1: 6 and bruises and putrefying *s*;
Lk 16:20 beggar named Lazarus, full of *s*,
16:21 the dogs came and licked his *s*.
Rev 16:11 of their pains and their *s*,

SORREL (1/1)

Zech 1: 8 behind him were horses: red, *s*,

SORROW (70/66) SORROWFUL, SORROWS

Gen 3:16 will greatly multiply your *s*
42:38 bring down my gray hair with *s*
44:29 bring down my gray hair with *s*
44:31 your servant our father with *s*
Ex 15:14 *S* will take hold of the
Lev 26:16 consume the eyes and cause *s*
2 Chr 21:20 eight years and, to no one's *s*,
Neh 2: 2 This is nothing but *s* of
8:10 is holy to our LORD. Do not *s*,
Esth 9:22 month which was turned from *s*
Job 3:10 Nor hide *s* from my eyes.
17: 7 has also grown dim because of *s*,
41:22 And *s* dances before him.
Ps 13: 2 Having *s* in my heart daily?
35:12 To the *s* of my soul.
38:17 And my *s* is continually
39: 2 And my *s* was stirred up.
90:10 boast is only labor and *s*;
107:39 oppression, affliction and *s*,
116: 3 of me; I found trouble and *s*.
Prov 10:22 And He adds no *s* with it.
14:13 in laughter the heart may *s*,
15:13 But by *s* of the heart the
17:21 a scoffer does so to his *s*,
22: 8 who sows iniquity will reap *s*,
23:29 Who has woe? Who has *s*?
Eccl 1:18 increases knowledge increases *s*.
5:17 And he has much *s* and
7: 3 *S* is better than laughter,
11:10 Therefore remove *s* from your
Isa 5:30 Behold, darkness and *s*;
14: 3 gives you rest from your *s*,
17:11 day of grief and desperate *s*.
29: 2 There shall be heaviness and *s*,
35:10 And *s* and sighing shall flee
51:11 *S* and sighing shall flee away.
65:14 But you shall cry for *s* of
Jer 8:18 I would comfort myself in *s*;
20:18 the womb to see labor and *s*,
30:15 Your *s* is incurable.
31:12 And they shall *s* no more at
31:13 make them rejoice rather than *s*.
45: 3 LORD has added grief to my *s*.
51:29 the land will tremble and *s*;
Lam 1:12 and see If there is any *s*
1:12 there is any sorrow like my *s*,
1:18 all peoples, And behold my *s*;
Ezek 23:33 filled with drunkenness and *s*,
24:17 do not eat man's bread of *s*.
24:22 lips nor eat man's bread of *s*.
Hos 8:10 And they shall *s* a little,
Zeph 3:18 I will gather those who *s* over
Lk 22:45 He found them sleeping from *s*.
Jn 16: 6 *s* has filled your heart.
16:20 but your *s* will be turned into
16:21 has *s* because her hour has
16:22 "Therefore you now have *s*;
Rom 9: 2 that I have great *s* and
2 Cor 2: 1 not come again to you in *s*.
2: 3 I should have *s* over those from
2: 7 be swallowed up with too much *s*.
7: 9 but that your *s* led to
7:10 For godly *s* produces repentance
7:10 but the *s* of the world produces
Phil 2:27 lest I should have *s* upon
2:27 I should have sorrow upon *s*.
1 Th 4:13 lest you *s* as others who have
Rev 18: 7 measure give her torment and *s*;
18: 7 am no widow, and will not see *s*.
21: 4 shall be no more death, nor *s*,

SORROWED (1/1)

2 Cor 7:11 that you *s* in a godly manner:

SORROWFUL (20/19) SORROW

1 Sam 1:15 I am a woman of *s* spirit.
Ps 69:29 But I am poor and *s*;
Eccl 2:23 For all his days are *s*,
Jer 31:25 and I have replenished every *s*
Zech 9: 5 Gaza also shall be very *s*;
Mt 17:23 And they were exceedingly *s*.
19:22 that saying, he went away *s*,
26:22 And they were exceedingly *s*,
26:37 and He began to be *s* and deeply
26:38 "My soul is exceedingly *s*,
Mk 10:22 at this word, and went away *s*,
14:19 And they began to be *s*,
14:34 "My soul is exceedingly *s*,
Lk 18:23 he heard this, he became very *s*,
18:24 Jesus saw that he became very *s*,
Jn 16:20 will rejoice; and you will be *s*,
2 Cor 2: 2 For if I make you *s*,
2: 2 glad but the one who is made *s*
6:10 as *s*, yet always rejoicing;
Phil 2:28 rejoice, and I may be less *s*.

SORROWING (1/1)

Acts 20:38 *s* most of all for the words

SORROWS (16/16) SORROW

Ex 3: 7 taskmasters, for I know their *s*.
2 Sam 22: 6 The *s* of Sheol surrounded me;
Job 21:17 The *s* God distributes in His
Ps 16: 4 Their *s* shall be multiplied who
18: 5 The *s* of Sheol surrounded me;
32:10 Many *s* shall be to the
127: 2 up late, To eat the bread of *s*;
Isa 13: 8 Pangs and *s* will take hold of
53: 3 A Man of *s* and acquainted with
53: 4 our griefs And carried our *s*;
Jer 49:24 Anguish and *s* have taken her
Dan 10:16 because of the vision my *s* have
Hos 13:13 The *s* of a woman in childbirth
Mt 24: 8 these are the beginning of *s*.
Mk 13: 8 These are the beginnings of *s*.
1 Tim 6:10 themselves through with many *s*.

SORRY (10/8)

Gen 6: 6 And the LORD was *s* that He had
6: 7 for I am *s* that I have made
1 Sam 22: 8 is not one of you who is *s*
Isa 51:19 Who will be *s* for
Mt 14: 9 And the king was *s*;
Mk 6:26 And the king was exceedingly *s*;
2 Cor 7: 8 For even if I made you *s* with my
7: 8 the same epistle made you *s*,
7: 9 not that you were made *s*,
7: 9 For you were made *s* in a godly

SORT (10/10)

Gen 6:19 you shall bring two of every *s*
7:14 its kind, every bird of every *s*.
Ezek 8:10 every *s* of creeping thing,
17:23 it will dwell birds of every *s*;
23:42 with men of the common *s*,
39: 4 you to birds of prey of every *s*
39:17 Speak to every *s* of bird and to
1 Cor 3:13 one's work, of what *s* it is.
2 Tim 2:17 and Philetus are of this *s*,
3: 6 For of this *s* are those who

SORTS (1/1)

Deut 22:11 wear a garment of different *s*,

SOSIPATER (1/1)

Rom 16:21 and Lucius, Jason, and *S*,

SOSTHENES (2/2)

Acts 18:17 Then all the Greeks took *S*,
1 Cor 1: 1 and *S* our brother,

SOTAI (2/2)

Ezra 2:55 servants: the sons of *S*,
Neh 7:57 servants: the sons of *S*,

SOTTISH (KJV) See SILLY

SOUGHT (111/107) SEEK

Gen 43:30 haste and *s* somewhere to weep.
Ex 2:15 he *s* to kill Moses. But Moses
4:19 for all the men who *s* your life
4:24 that the LORD met him and *s* to
33: 7 to pass that everyone who *s*
Deut 13:10 because he *s* to entice you away
32:37 The rock in which they *s*
Josh 2:22 The pursuers *s* them all along
1 Sam 10:21 But when they *s* him, he could
13:14 The LORD has *s* for Himself a
14: 4 by which Jonathan *s* to go over
19:10 Then Saul *s* to pin David to the
23:14 Saul *s* him every day, but God
27: 4 so he *s* him no more.
2 Sam 4: 8 who *s* your life; and the LORD
21: 2 but Saul had *s* to kill them in
1 Ki 1: 2 be *s* for our lord the king,
1: 3 So they *s* for a lovely young
10:24 Now all the earth *s* the
11:40 Solomon therefore *s* to kill
1 Chr 26:31 the reign of David they were *s*,
2 Chr 1: 5 Solomon and the assembly *s* Him
9:23 all the kings of the earth *s*
11:23 He also *s* many wives for
14: 7 because we have *s* the LORD our
14: 7 we have *s* Him, and He has
15: 4 and *s* Him, He was found by
15:15 with all their heart and *s* Him
17: 4 but *s* the God of his father,
22: 9 who *s* the LORD with all his
25:15 Why have you *s* the gods of the
25:20 because they *s* the gods of
26: 5 He *s* God in the days of
26: 5 and as long as he *s* the LORD,
Ezra 2:62 These *s* their listing among
Neh 7:64 These *s* their listing among
12:27 of the wall of Jerusalem they *s*
Esth 2: 2 beautiful young virgins be *s*
2:21 became furious and *s* to lay
3: 6 Haman *s* to destroy all the Jews
6: 2 the doorkeepers who had *s* to
9: 2 on those who *s* their harm.
Ps 34: 4 I *s* the LORD, and He heard me,
37:36 Indeed I *s* him, but he could
54: 3 And oppressors have *s* after my
77: 2 day of my trouble I *s* the Lord;
78:34 then they *s* Him; And they
78:34 and *s* earnestly for God.
86:14 of violent men have *s* my life,
119:10 my whole heart I have *s* You;
119:94 For I have *s* Your precepts.
Eccl 7:29 But they have *s* out many
12: 9 he pondered and *s* out and set
12:10 The Preacher *s* to find
Song 3: 1 By night on my bed I *s* the one
3: 1 I *s* him, but I did not find
3: 2 I *s* him, but I did not find
5: 6 I *s* him, but I could not find
Isa 62:12 And you shall be called *S* Out,
65: 1 I was *s* by those who did not
65:10 For My people who have *s* Me.
Jer 8: 2 which they have *s* and which
10:21 And have not *s* the LORD;
26:21 the king *s* to put him to death;
44:30 his enemy who *s* his life.'"
50:20 iniquity of Israel shall be *s*,
Lam 1:19 While they *s* food To restore
Ezek 22:30 So I *s* for a man among them who
26:21 though you are *s* for, you will
34: 4 nor *s* what was lost; but with
Dan 2:13 and they *s* Daniel and his
6: 4 governors and satraps *s* to find

Hos 12: 4 and *s* favor from Him. He found
Ob 6 his hidden treasures shall be *s*
Zeph 1: 6 And have not *s* the LORD,
Mt 2:20 for those who *s* the young
21:46 But when they *s* to lay hands on
26:16 from that time he *s* opportunity
26:59 and all the council *s* false
Mk 11:18 *s* how they might destroy Him;
12:12 And they *s* to lay hands on Him,
14: 1 priests and the scribes *s* how
14:11 So he *s* how he might
14:55 and all the council *s* testimony
Lk 2:44 and *s* Him among their
2:48 Your father and I have *s* You
4:42 And the crowd *s* Him and came to
5:18 whom they *s* to bring in and lay
6:19 And the whole multitude *s* to
9: 9 So he *s* to see Him.
11:16 *s* from Him a sign from heaven.
19: 3 And he *s* to see who Jesus was,
19:47 the leaders of the people *s* to
20:19 hour *s* to lay hands on Him,
22: 2 priests and the scribes *s* how
22: 6 So he promised and *s* opportunity
Jn 5:16 and *s* to kill Him, because He
5:18 Therefore the Jews *s* all the
7: 1 because the Jews *s* to kill Him.
7:11 Then the Jews *s* Him at the
7:30 Therefore they *s* to take Him;
10:39 Therefore they *s* again to seize
11: 8 lately the Jews *s* to stone You,
11:56 Then they *s* Jesus, and spoke
19:12 From then on Pilate *s* to release
Acts 13: 7 and *s* to hear the word of God.
16:10 immediately we *s* to go to
17: 5 and *s* to bring them out to the
2 Tim 1:17 he *s* me out very zealously and
Heb 8: 7 no place would have been *s* for
12:17 though he *s* it diligently with

SOUL (321/302) SOULS

Gen 19:20 and my *s* shall live."
27: 4 that my *s* may bless you before
27:19 that your *s* may bless me."
27:25 so that my *s* may bless you."
27:31 that your *s* may bless me."
34: 3 His *s* was strongly attracted to
34: 8 The *s* of my son Shechem longs
35:18 as her *s* was departing (for she
42:21 for we saw the anguish of his *s*
49: 6 Let not my *s* enter their
Lev 17:11 that makes atonement for the *s*.
23:29 who is not afflicted in *s* on
26:11 and My *s* shall not abhor you.
26:15 or if your *s* abhors My
26:30 and My *s* shall abhor you.
26:43 and because their *s* abhorred
Num 21: 4 and the *s* of the people became
21: 5 and our *s* loathes this
30:13 binding oath to afflict her *s*,
Deut 4:29 your heart and with all your *s*.
6: 5 all your heart, with all your *s*,
10:12 your heart and with all your *s*,
11:13 your heart and with all your *s*,
11:18 in your heart and in your *s*,
13: 3 your heart and with all your *s*.
13: 6 friend who is as your own *s*,
26:16 your heart and with all your *s*.
28:65 failing eyes, and anguish of *s*.
30: 2 your heart and with all your *s*,
30: 6 your heart and with all your *s*,
30:10 your heart and with all your *s*.
Josh 22: 5 your heart and with all your *s*.
Judg 5:21 the torrent of Kishon. O my *s*,
10:16 And His *s* could no longer
16:16 so that his *s* was vexed to
1 Sam 1:10 And she was in bitterness of *s*,
1:15 but have poured out my *s* before
1:26 O my lord! As your *s* lives, my
17:55 As your *s* lives, O king, I do
18: 1 the *s* of Jonathan was knit to
18: 1 of Jonathan was knit to the *s*
18: 1 Jonathan loved him as his own *s*.
18: 3 he loved him as his own *s*.
20: 3 lives and as your *s* lives,
20:17 loved him as he loved his own *s*.
23:20 to all the desire of your *s* to
25:26 lives and as your *s* lives,
30: 6 because the *s* of all the people
2 Sam 5: 8 who are hated by David's *s*),
11:11 and as your *s* lives, I will
1 Ki 2: 4 heart and with all their *s*,
8:48 heart and with all their *s* in
17:21 let this child's *s* come back to
17:22 and the *s* of the child came
2 Ki 2: 2 and as your *s* lives, I will
2: 4 and as your *s* lives, I will
2: 6 and as your *s* lives, I will
4:27 for her *s* is in deep distress,
4:30 and as your *s* lives, I will
23: 3 all his heart and all his *s*,
23:25 all his heart, with all his *s*,
1 Chr 22:19 Now set your heart and your *s* to
2 Chr 6:38 heart and with all their *s* in
15:12 heart and with all their *s*,
15:15 and sought Him with all their *s*;
34:31 all his heart and all his *s*,
Job 3:20 And life to the bitter of *s*,
6: 7 My *s* refuses to touch them;
7:11 in the bitterness of my *s*.
7:15 So that my *s* chooses strangling
10: 1 My *s* loathes my life; I will
10: 1 speak in the bitterness of my *s*.
14:22 And his *s* will mourn over
16: 4 If your *s* were in my soul's
19: 2 long will you torment my *s*,
21:25 dies in the bitterness of his *s*,
23:13 And whatever His *s* desires,
27: 2 who has made my *s* bitter,
30:16 And now my *s* is poured out
30:25 Has not my *s* grieved for the
31:30 asking for a curse on his *s*);
33:18 He keeps back his *s* from the
33:20 And his *s* succulent food.
33:22 his *s* draws near the Pit,
33:28 He will redeem his *s* from going
33:30 To bring back his *s* from the
Ps 6: 3 My *s* also is greatly troubled;
11: 1 How can you say to my *s*,
11: 5 who loves violence His *s* hates.
13: 2 shall I take counsel in my *s*,
16: 2 O my *s*, you have said to
16:10 For You will not leave my *s* in
19: 7 is perfect, converting the *s*;
23: 3 He restores my *s*;
24: 4 Who has not lifted up his *s* to
25: 1 You, O LORD, I lift up my *s*.
25:20 Keep my *s*, and deliver me;
26: 9 Do not gather my *s* with
30: 3 You brought my *s* up from the
31: 7 You have known my *s* in
31: 9 my *s* and my body!
33:19 To deliver their *s* from death,
33:20 Our *s* waits for the LORD;
34: 2 My *s* shall make its boast in
34:22 The LORD redeems the *s* of His
35: 3 who pursue me. Say to my *s*,
35: 9 And my *s* shall be joyful in the
35:12 To the sorrow of my *s*.
41: 4 be merciful to me; Heal my *s*,
42: 1 So pants my *s* for You, O God.
42: 2 My *s* thirsts for God, for the
42: 4 I pour out my *s* within me.
42: 5 Why are you cast down, O my *s*?
42: 6 my *s* is cast down within me;
42:11 Why are you cast down, O my *s*?
43: 5 Why are you cast down, O my *s*?
44:25 For our *s* is bowed down to the
49:15 But God will redeem my *s* from
55:18 He has redeemed my *s* in peace
56:13 For You have delivered my *s*
57: 1 be merciful to me! For my *s*
57: 4 My *s* is among lions; I lie
57: 6 My *s* is bowed down; They have
62: 1 Truly my *s* silently waits for
62: 5 My *s*, wait silently for God
63: 1 My *s* thirsts for You;
63: 5 My *s* shall be satisfied as with
63: 8 My *s* follows close behind You;
66: 9 Who keeps our *s* among the
66:16 what He has done for my *s*.
69:10 I wept and chastened my *s*
69:18 Draw near to my *s*,
71:23 when I sing to You, And my *s*,
77: 2 My *s* refused to be comforted.
78:50 He did not spare their *s* from
84: 2 My *s* longs, yes, even faints
86: 4 Rejoice the *s* of Your servant,
86: 4 to You, O Lord, I lift up my *s*.
86:13 And You have delivered my *s*
88: 3 For my *s* is full of troubles,
88:14 why do You cast off my *s*?
94:17 My *s* would soon have settled
94:19 Your comforts delight my *s*.
103: 1 Bless the LORD, O my *s*;
103: 2 Bless the LORD, O my *s*,
103:22 Bless the LORD, O my *s*!
104: 1 O my *s*! O LORD my God, You
104:35 O my *s*! Praise the LORD!
106:15 But sent leanness into their *s*.
107: 5 Their *s* fainted in them.
107: 9 For He satisfies the longing *s*,
107: 9 And fills the hungry *s* with
107:18 Their *s* abhorred all manner of
107:26 Their *s* melts because of
116: 4 I implore You, deliver my *s*!"
116: 7 Return to your rest, O my *s*,
116: 8 For You have delivered my *s*
119:20 My *s* breaks with longing For
119:25 My *s* clings to the dust;
119:28 My *s* melts from heaviness;
119:81 My *s* faints for Your
119:129 Therefore my *s* keeps them.
119:167 My *s* keeps Your testimonies,
119:175 Let my *s* live, and it shall
120: 2 Deliver my *s*, O LORD,
120: 6 My *s* has dwelt too long With
121: 7 He shall preserve your *s*.
123: 4 Our *s* is exceedingly filled
124: 4 would have gone over our *s*;
124: 5 Would have gone over our *s*.
124: 7 Our *s* has escaped as a bird
130: 5 my *s* waits, And in His word I
130: 6 My *s* waits for the Lord More
131: 2 I have calmed and quieted my *s*,
131: 2 Like a weaned child is my *s*
138: 3 me bold with strength in my *s*.
139:14 And that my *s* knows very
141: 8 Do not leave my *s* destitute.
142: 4 No one cares for my *s*.
142: 7 Bring my *s* out of prison,
143: 3 the enemy has persecuted my *s*;
143: 6 My *s* longs for You like a
143: 8 For I lift up my *s* to You.
143:11 righteousness' sake bring my *s*
143:12 all those who afflict my *s*;
146: 1 Praise the LORD, O my *s*!
Prov 2:10 knowledge is pleasant to your *s*,
3:22 So they will be life to your *s*
6:32 who does so destroys his own *s*.
8:36 against me wrongs his own *s*;
10: 3 the righteous *s* to famish,
11:17 man does good for his own *s*,
11:25 The generous *s* will be made
13: 2 But the *s* of the unfaithful
13: 4 The *s* of a lazy man desires,
13: 4 But the *s* of the diligent
13:19 accomplished is sweet to the *s*,
13:25 eats to the satisfying of his *s*,
15:32 instruction despises his own *s*,
16:17 keeps his way preserves his *s*.
16:24 Sweetness to the *s* and health
18: 7 lips are the snare of his *s*.
19: 2 Also it is not good for a *s*
19: 8 who gets wisdom loves his own *s*;
19:16 the commandment keeps his *s*,
21:10 The *s* of the wicked desires
21:23 mouth and tongue Keeps his *s*
22: 5 He who guards his *s* will be
22:23 And plunder the *s* of those who
22:25 And set a snare for your *s*.
23:14 And deliver his *s* from hell.
24:12 He who keeps your *s*,
24:14 of wisdom be to your *s*;
25:13 For he refreshes the *s* of his
25:25 As cold water to a weary *s*,
27: 7 A satisfied *s* loathes the
27: 7 But to a hungry *s* every bitter
29:17 he will give delight to your *s*.
Eccl 2:24 and that his *s* should enjoy
6: 3 but his *s* is not satisfied with
6: 7 And yet the *s* is not
7:28 Which my *s* still seeks but I
Song 6:12 My *s* had made me As the
Isa 1:14 and your appointed feasts My *s*
3: 9 Woe to their *s*! For they have
10:18 Both *s* and body; And they
19:10 wages will be troubled of *s*.
26: 8 The desire of our *s* is for
26: 9 With my *s* I have desired You in
29: 8 and his *s* is still empty;
29: 8 And his *s* still craves:
38:15 In the bitterness of my *s*.
38:17 have lovingly delivered my *s*
42: 1 My Elect One in whom My *s*
44:20 And he cannot deliver his *s*,
53:10 When You make His *s* an
53:11 shall see the labor of His *s*,
53:12 Because He poured out His *s*
55: 2 And let your *s* delight itself
55: 3 and your *s* shall live; And I
58: 5 day for a man to afflict his *s*?
58:10 If you extend your *s* to the
58:10 And satisfy the afflicted *s*,
58:11 And satisfy your *s* in drought,
61:10 My *s* shall be joyful in my
66: 3 And their *s* delights in their
Jer 4:19 O my *s*, my soul!
4:19 my *s*! I am pained in my very
4:19 Because you have heard, O my *s*,
4:31 for my *s* is weary Because of
6: 8 Lest My *s* depart from you;
12: 7 the dearly beloved of My *s*
13:17 My *s* will weep in secret for
14:19 Has Your *s* loathed Zion?
31:14 I will satiate the *s* of the
31:25 I have satiated the weary *s*,
31:25 replenished every sorrowful *s*.
32:41 all My heart and with all My *s*.
38:17 then your *s* shall live;
38:20 and your *s* shall live.
50:19 His *s* shall be satisfied on
Lam 1:20 My *s* is troubled; My heart is
3:17 You have moved my *s* far from
3:20 My *s* still remembers And sinks
3:24 is my portion," says my *s*,
3:25 To the *s* who seeks Him.
3:51 eyes bring suffering to my *s*
3:58 have pleaded the case for my *s*;
Ezek 3:19 but you have delivered your *s*.
3:21 you will have delivered your *s*.
18: 4 The *s* of the father As well
18: 4 of the father As well as the *s*
18: 4 The *s* who sins shall die.
18:20 'The *s* who sins shall die.
24:21 eyes, the delight of your *s*;
33: 9 but you have delivered your *s*.
Jon 2: 5 surrounded me, even to my *s*;
2: 7 'When my *s* fainted within me,
Mic 6: 7 of my body for the sin of my *s*?
7: 1 fruit which my *s* desires.
Hab 2: 4 His *s* is not upright in him;
2:10 And sin against your *s*.
Zech 11: 8 My *s* loathed them, and their
11: 8 and their *s* also abhorred me.
Mt 10:28 the body but cannot kill the *s*.
10:28 who is able to destroy both *s*
12:18 whom My *s* is well pleased!
16:26 world, and loses his own *s*?
16:26 man give in exchange for his *s*?
22:37 heart, with all your *s*,
26:38 My *s* is exceedingly sorrowful,
Mk 8:36 world, and loses his own *s*?
8:37 man give in exchange for his *s*?
12:30 heart, with all your *s*,

12:33 understanding, with all the *s*,
14:34 My *s* is exceedingly sorrowful,
Lk 1:46 My *s* magnifies the Lord,
2:35 will pierce through your own *s*
10:27 heart, with all your *s*,
12:19 'And I will say to my *s*,
12:19 'And I will say to my soul, "*S*,
12:20 Fool! This night your *s* will be
Jn 12:27 Now My *s* is troubled, and what
Acts 2:27 You will not leave my *s*
2:31 that His *s* was not left in
2:43 Then fear came upon every *s*,
3:23 every *s* who will not hear
4:32 were of one heart and one *s*;
Rom 2: 9 on every *s* of man who does
13: 1 Let every *s* be subject to the
2 Cor 1:23 God as witness against my *s*,
1 Th 5:23 and may your whole spirit, *s*,
Heb 4:12 even to the division of *s* and
6:19 we have as an anchor of the *s*,
10:38 My *s* has no pleasure in
10:39 believe to the saving of the *s*.
Jas 5:20 error of his way will save a *s*
1 Pe 2:11 lusts which war against the *s*,
2 Pe 2: 8 tormented his righteous *s* from
3 Jn 2 just as your *s* prospers.
Rev 18:14 The fruit that your *s* longed for

SOUL'S (1/1)

Job 16: 4 your soul were in my *s* place.

SOULS (44/41) SOUL

Lev 16:29 month, you shall afflict your *s*,
16:31 and you shall afflict your *s*.
17:11 to make atonement for your *s*;
23:27 you shall afflict your *s*,
23:32 and you shall afflict your *s*;
Num 16:38 who sinned against their own *s*,
29: 7 You shall afflict your *s*;
Josh 23:14 your hearts and in all your *s*
Job 24:12 And the *s* of the wounded cry
Ps 49: 8 For the redemption of their *s*
72:13 And will save the *s* of the
97:10 hate evil! He preserves the *s*
Prov 11:30 And he who wins *s* is wise.
14:25 A true witness delivers *s*,
Isa 57:16 And the *s* which I have made.
58: 3 Why have we afflicted our *s*,
Jer 6:16 you will find rest for your *s*.
31:12 Their *s* shall be like a
38:16 lives, who made our very *s*,
Ezek 7:19 They will not satisfy their *s*,
13:18 of every height to hunt *s*!
13:18 Will you hunt the *s* of
13:20 charms by which you hunt *s*
13:20 and let the *s* go, the souls you
13:20 the *s* you hunt like birds.
18: 4 all *s* are Mine; The soul of
Mt 11:29 you will find rest for your *s*.
Lk 21:19 your patience possess your *s*.
Acts 2:41 that day about three thousand *s*
14:22 strengthening the *s* of the
15:24 with words, unsettling your *s*,
2 Cor 12:15 spend and be spent for your *s*;
Heb 12: 3 weary and discouraged in your *s*.
13:17 for they watch out for your *s*,
Jas 1:21 which is able to save your *s*.
1 Pe 1: 9 faith—the salvation of your *s*.
1:22 you have purified your *s* in
2:25 Shepherd and Overseer of your *s*.
3:20 which a few, that is, eight *s*,
4:19 the will of God commit their *s*
2 Pe 2:14 from sin, enticing unstable *s*.
Rev 6: 9 I saw under the altar the *s* of
18:13 and bodies and *s* of men.
20: 4 Then I saw the *s* of those who

SOUND (121/112) SOUNDED, SOUNDING, SOUNDNESS, SOUNDS

Gen 3: 8 And they heard the *s* of the
Ex 19:16 and the *s* of the trumpet was
20:18 the *s* of the trumpet, and the
28:35 and its *s* will be heard when he
32:18 But the *s* of singing I
Lev 25: 9 trumpet of the Jubilee to *s* on
25: 9 you shall make the trumpet to *s*
26:36 the *s* of a shaken leaf shall
Num 10: 5 When you *s* the advance, the
10: 6 When you *s* the advance the
10: 6 they shall *s* the call for them
10: 7 but not *s* the advance.
10: 9 then you shall *s* an alarm with
Deut 1:34 And the LORD heard the *s* of
4:12 You heard the *s* of the words,
Josh 6: 5 and when you hear the *s* of the
6:20 when the people heard the *s* of
1 Sam 4: 6 What does the *s* of this great
4:14 What does the *s* of this tumult
2 Sam 5:24 when you hear the *s* of marching
6:15 with shouting and with the *s*
15:10 As soon as you hear the *s* of the
1 Ki 1:40 seemed to split with their *s*.
1:41 And when Joab heard the *s* of
14: 6 when Ahijah heard the *s* of her
18:41 for there is the *s* of
2 Ki 6:32 Is not the *s* of his master's
7:10 one was there, not a human *s*—
1 Chr 14:15 when you hear a *s* of marching
15:19 were to *s* the cymbals of
15:28 with shouting and with the *s*
16:42 to *s* aloud with trumpets and
2 Chr 5:13 to make one *s* to be heard in
13:12 with sounding trumpets to *s*
Ezra 3:13 and the *s* was heard afar off.
Neh 4:20 Wherever you hear the *s* of the
Job 21:12 And rejoice to the *s* of the
26: 3 And how have you declared *s*
33: 8 And I have heard the *s* of
34:16 listen to the *s* of my words:
Ps 47: 5 The LORD with the *s* of a
77:17 The skies sent out a *s*;
89:15 people who know the joyful *s*!
92: 3 on the harp, With harmonious *s*.
98: 5 With the harp and the *s* of a
98: 6 With trumpets and the *s* of a
102: 5 Because of the *s* of my groaning
150: 3 Praise Him with the *s* of the
Prov 2: 7 He stores up *s* wisdom for the
3:21 Keep *s* wisdom and discretion;
8:14 and *s* wisdom; I am
14:30 A *s* heart is life to the body,
Eccl 12: 4 And the *s* of grinding is low;
12: 4 When one rises up at the *s* of
Isa 14:11 And the *s* of your stringed
30:19 very gracious to you at the *s*
66: 6 The *s* of noise from the city!
Jer 4:19 The *s* of the trumpet,
4:21 And hear the *s* of the
6:17 Listen to the *s* of the trumpet!'
8:16 whole land trembled at the *s*
25:10 the *s* of the millstones and the
42:14 nor hear the *s* of the trumpet,
50:22 A *s* of battle is in the land,
51:54 The *s* of a cry comes from
Ezek 10: 5 And the *s* of the wings of the
23:42 The *s* of a carefree multitude
26:13 I will put an end to the *s* of
26:13 and the *s* of your harps shall
26:15 coastlands not shake at the *s*
27:28 will shake at the *s* of the cry
31:16 the nations shake at the *s* of
33: 4 then whoever hears the *s* of the
33: 5 He heard the *s* of the trumpet,
43: 2 His voice was like the *s* of
Dan 3: 5 at the time you hear the *s* of
3: 7 all the people heard the *s* of
3:10 that everyone who hears the *s*
3:15 at the time you hear the *s* of
7:11 watched then because of the *s*
10: 6 and the *s* of his words like the
10: 9 Yet I heard the *s* of his words;
10: 9 and while I heard the *s* of his
Joel 2: 1 And *s* an alarm in My holy
Am 2: 2 With shouting and trumpet *s*.
6: 5 Who sing idly to the *s* of
Zeph 1:10 The *s* of a mournful cry from the
Zech 11: 3 There is the *s* of wailing
11: 3 There is the *s* of roaring
Mt 6: 2 do not *s* a trumpet before you
24:31 send His angels with a great *s*
Lk 15:27 he has received him safe and *s*,
Jn 3: 8 and you hear the *s* of it, but
Acts 2: 2 And suddenly there came a *s* from
2: 6 And when this *s* occurred, the
Rom 10:18 Their *s* has gone out to
1 Cor 14: 7 or harp, when they make a *s*,
14: 8 trumpet makes an uncertain *s*,
15:52 For the trumpet will *s*,
2 Cor 5:13 or if we are of *s* mind, it is
1 Tim 1:10 thing that is contrary to *s*
2 Tim 1: 7 of power and of love and of a *s*
1:13 Hold fast the pattern of *s*
4: 3 when they will not endure *s*
Titus 1: 9 by *s* doctrine, both to exhort
1:13 that they may be *s* in the
2: 1 things which are proper for *s*
2: 2 *s* in faith, in love, in
2: 8 *s* speech that cannot be
Heb 12:19 and the *s* of a trumpet and the
Rev 1:15 and His voice as the *s* of many
8: 6 prepared themselves to *s*.
8:13 angels who are about to *s*!"
9: 9 and the *s* of their wings was
9: 9 of their wings was like the *s*
10: 7 angel, when he is about to *s*,
14: 2 And I heard the *s* of harpists
18:22 The *s* of harpists, musicians,
18:22 and the *s* of a millstone shall
19: 6 as the *s* of many waters and as
19: 6 of many waters and as the *s* of

SOUNDED (16/16) SOUND

Ex 19:19 when the blast of the trumpet *s*
1 Sam 20:12 is witness! When I have *s*
2 Chr 7: 6 The priests *s* trumpets opposite
13:14 and the priests *s* the trumpets.
29:28 sang, and the trumpeters *s*;
Neh 4:18 And the one who *s* the trumpet
Job 39:24 halt because the trumpet has *s*.
Lk 1:44 as the voice of your greeting *s*
1 Th 1: 8 you the word of the Lord has *s*
Rev 8: 7 The first angel *s*:
8: 8 Then the second angel *s*:
8:10 Then the third angel *s*:
8:12 Then the fourth angel *s*:
9: 1 Then the fifth angel *s*:
9:13 Then the sixth angel *s*:
11:15 Then the seventh angel *s*:

SOUNDING (4/4) SOUND

2 Chr 5:12 priests *s* with trumpets—
13:12 and His priests with *s* trumpets
1 Cor 13: 1 I have become *s* brass or a
Rev 10: 7 the *s* of the seventh angel,

SOUNDINGS (2/1)

Acts 27:28 And they took *s* and found it to
27:28 they took *s* again and found it

SOUNDNESS (4/4) SOUND

Ps 38: 3 There is no *s* in my flesh
38: 7 And there is no *s* in my
Isa 1: 6 There is no *s* in it,
Acts 3:16 has given him this perfect *s*

SOUNDS (3/3) SOUND

Ex 19:13 When the trumpet *s* long, they
Job 15:21 Dreadful *s* are in his ears;
1 Cor 14: 7 make a distinction in the *s*,

SOUR (12/11)

Job 20:14 his food in his stomach turns *s*;
Isa 18: 5 the bud is perfect And the *s*
Jer 31:29 The fathers have eaten *s* grapes,
31:30 man who eats the *s* grapes,
Ezek 18: 2 The fathers have eaten *s* grapes,
Mt 27:34 they gave Him *s* wine mingled
27:48 filled it with *s* wine and put
Mk 15:36 filled a sponge full of *s* wine,
Lk 23:36 coming and offering Him *s* wine,
Jn 19:29 Now a vessel full of *s* wine was
19:29 filled a sponge with *s* wine,
19:30 Jesus had received the *s* wine,

SOURCE (2/2)

2 Ki 2:21 Then he went out to the *s* of the
Job 28: 6 Its stones are the *s* of

SOUTH (138/127) SOUTHWARD

Gen 12: 9 going on still toward the *S*.
13: 1 had, and Lot with him, to the *S*.
13: 3 went on his journey from the *S*
20: 1 journeyed from there to the *S*,
24:62 Roi, for he dwelt in the *S*.
28:14 east, to the north and the *s*;
Ex 26:18 twenty boards for the *s* side.
26:35 of the tabernacle toward the *s*;
27: 9 For the *s* side there shall
36:23 twenty boards for the *s* side.
38: 9 he made the court on the *s*
40:24 on the *s* side of the
Num 2:10 On the *s* side shall be the
3:29 of Kohath were to camp on the *s*
10: 6 the camps that lie on the *s*
13:17 "Go up this way into the *S*,
13:22 And they went up through the *S*
13:29 dwell in the land of the *S*;
21: 1 Canaanite, who dwelt in the *S*,
33:40 who dwelt in the *S* in the land
34: 4 and be on the *s* of Kadesh
35: 5 on the *s* side two thousand
Deut 1: 7 in the *S* and on the seacoast,
3:27 the west, the north, the *s*,
33:23 Possess the west and the *s*.
34: 3 the *S*, and the plain of the
Josh 10:40 the mountain country and the *S*
11: 2 in the plain *s* of Chinneroth,
11:16 the mountain country, all the *S*,
12: 8 in the wilderness, and in the *S*—
13: 4 'from the *s*, all the land of
15: 3 ascended on the *s* side of
15: 7 which is on the *s* side of the
15:19 you have given me land in the *S*,
15:21 the border of Edom in the *S*,
17: 7 and the border went along *s* to
18: 5 in their territory on the *s*,
18:13 the hill that lies on the *s*
18:14 around the west side to the *s*,
18:15 The *s* side began at the end of
18:16 of the Jebusite city on the *s*,
18:19 at the *s* end of the Jordan.
19: 8 as Baalath Beer, Ramah of the *S*.
19:34 it adjoined Zebulun on the *s*
Judg 1: 9 in the mountains, in the *S*,
1:15 you have given me land in the *S*,
1:16 which lies in the *S* near
21:19 and *s* of Lebonah."
1 Sam 20:41 from a place toward the *s*,
23:19 which is on the *s* of Jeshimon?
23:24 in the plain on the *s* of
30: 1 Amalekites had invaded the *S*
30:27 who were in Ramoth of the *S*,
2 Sam 24: 7 Then they went out to *S* Judah
1 Ki 7:25 three looking toward the *s*,
2 Ki 23:13 which were on the *s* of the
1 Chr 9:24 the east, west, north, and *s*.
26:15 to Obed-Edom the *S* Gate, and to
26:17 on the *s* four each day, and for
2 Chr 4: 4 three looking toward the *s*,
28:18 of the lowland and of the *S* of
Job 9: 9 And the chambers of the *s*;
37: 9 From the chamber of the *s*
37:17 He quiets the earth by the *s*
39:26 spread its wings toward the *s*?
Ps 75: 6 from the west nor from the *s*.

78:26 His power He brought in the *s*
89:12 The north and the *s*,
107: 3 From the north and from the *s*.
126: 4 As the streams in the *S*.
Eccl 1: 6 The wind goes toward the *s*,
11: 3 And if a tree falls to the *s*
Song 4:16 O *s*! Blow upon my garden,
Isa 21: 1 As whirlwinds in the *S* pass
30: 6 against the beasts of the *S*.
43: 6 'Give them up!' And to the *s*,
Jer 13:19 The cities of the *S* shall be
17:26 the mountains and from the *S*,
32:44 and in the cities of the *S*;
33:13 lowland, in the cities of the *S*,
Ezek 10: 3 were standing on the *s* side of
16:46 who dwells to the *s* of you, is
20:46 man, set your face toward the *s*;
20:46 preach against the *s* and
20:46 against the forest land, the *S*,
20:47 say to the forest of the *S*,
20:47 and all faces from the *s* to the
21: 4 against all flesh from *s* to
40: 2 on it toward the *s* was
40:24 that he brought me toward the *s*,
40:24 there a gateway was facing *s*;
40:27 on the inner court, facing *s*;
40:27 gateway to gateway toward the *s*,
40:44 one facing *s* at the side of the
40:45 This chamber which faces *s* is
41:11 north and another toward the *s*;
42:12 chambers that were facing *s*,
42:13 The north chambers and the *s*
42:18 He measured the *s* side, five
46: 9 shall go out by way of the *s*
46: 9 whoever enters by way of the *s*
47: 1 *s* of the altar.
47:19 The *s* side, toward the South,
47:19 "The south side, toward the *S*,
47:19 This is the *s* side, toward
47:19 the south side, toward the *S*.
48:10 and on the *s* twenty-five
48:16 the *s* side four thousand five
48:17 to the *s* two hundred and fifty,
48:28 on the *s* side, toward the
48:28 on the south side, toward the *S*,
48:33 on the *s* side, measuring four
Dan 8: 9 exceedingly great toward the *s*,
11: 5 Also the king of the *S* shall
11: 6 daughter of the king of the *S*
11: 9 kingdom of the king of the *S*,
11:11 And the king of the *S* shall be
11:14 up against the king of the *S*.
11:15 and the forces of the *S* shall
11:25 against the king of the *S* with
11:25 And the king of the *S* shall be
11:29 return and go toward the *s*;
11:40 of the end the king of the *S*
Ob 19 The *S* shall possess the
20 possess the cities of the *S*.
Zech 6: 6 dappled are going toward the *s*
7: 7 and the *S* and the Lowland were
9:14 go with whirlwinds from the *s*.
14: 4 And half of it toward the *s*.
14:10 a plain from Geba to Rimmon *s*
Mt 12:42 The queen of the *S* will rise up
Lk 11:31 The queen of the *S* will rise up
12:55 And when you see the *s* wind
13:29 west, from the north and the *s*,
Acts 8:26 Arise and go toward the *s* along
27:13 When the *s* wind blew softly,
28:13 And after one day the *s* wind
Rev 21:13 the north, three gates on the *s*,

SOUTHEAST (2/2)

1 Ki 7:39 side of the house, toward the *s*.
2 Chr 4:10 on the right side, toward the *s*.

SOUTHERN (18/13)

Num 34: 3 Your *s* border shall be from the
34: 3 then your *s* border shall extend
34: 4 shall turn from the *s* side
Josh 15: 1 was the extreme *s* boundary.
15: 2 And their *s* border began at the
15: 3 Then it went out to the *s* side
15: 4 This shall be your *s* border.
15: 8 Son of Hinnom to the *s* slope
18:19 This was the *s* boundary.
1 Sam 27:10 'Against the *s* area of Judah,
27:10 or against the *s* area of the
27:10 or against the *s* area of the
30:14 made an invasion of the *S* area
30:14 and of the *s* area of Caleb;
Ezek 40:28 court through the *s* gateway;
40:28 he measured the *s* gateway
40:44 at the side of the *s* gateway.
47:20 from the *s* boundary until one

SOUTHWARD (10/10) SOUTH

Gen 13:14 where you are—northward, *s*,
Josh 12: 3 and *s* below the slopes of
15: 1 Edom at the Wilderness of Zin *s*
15: 2 Sea, from the bay that faces *s*.
17: 9 *s* to the brook. These cities of
17:10 *S* it was Ephraim's, northward
18:13 of Luz (which is Bethel) *s*;
18:14 that lies before Beth Horon *s*;
1 Sam 14: 5 and the other *s* opposite
Dan 8: 4 westward, northward, and *s*,

SOUTHWEST (1/1)

Acts 27:12 of Crete opening toward the *s*

SOVEREIGNTY (1/1)

1 Sam 14:47 So Saul established his *s* over

SOW (42/41) SOWED, SOWER, SOWING, SOWN, SOWS

Gen 47:23 and you shall *s* the land.
Ex 23:10 Six years you shall *s* your land
Lev 19:19 You shall not *s* your field with
25: 3 Six years you shall *s* your
25: 4 You shall neither *s* your field
25:11 in it you shall neither *s* nor
25:20 since we shall not *s* nor gather
25:22 And you shall *s* in the eighth
26:16 And you shall *s* your seed in
Deut 22: 9 You shall not *s* your vineyard
2 Ki 19:29 Also in the third year *s* and
Job 4: 8 Those who plow iniquity And *s*
31: 8 Then let me *s*,
Ps 107:37 And *s* fields and plant
126: 5 Those who *s* in tears Shall
Eccl 11: 4 observes the wind will not *s*,
11: 6 In the morning *s* your seed,
Isa 28:24 keep plowing all day to *s*?
28:25 Does he not *s* the black cummin
30:23 for your seed With which you *s*
32:20 Blessed are you who *s* beside
37:30 Also in the third year *s* and
Jer 4: 3 And do not *s* among thorns.
31:27 that I will *s* the house of
35: 7 *s* seed, plant a vineyard,
Hos 2:23 Then I will *s* her for Myself in
8: 7 They *s* the wind, And reap the
10:12 *S* for yourselves
Mic 6:15 "You shall *s*,
Zech 10: 9 I will *s* them among the peoples,
Mt 6:26 for they neither *s* nor reap nor
13: 3 "Behold, a sower went out to *s*.
13:27 did you not *s* good seed in your
Mk 4: 3 Behold, a sower went out to *s*.
Lk 8: 5 A sower went out to *s* his seed.
12:24 for they neither *s* nor reap,
19:21 and reap what you did not *s*.
19:22 and reaping what I did not *s*.
1 Cor 15:36 what you *s* is not made alive
15:37 And what you *s*,
15:37 you do not *s* that body that
2 Pe 2:22 his own vomit," and, "a *s*,

SOWED (10/10) SOW

Gen 26:12 Then Isaac *s* in that land,
Deut 11:10 where you *s* your seed and
Judg 9:45 he demolished the city and *s*
Mt 13: 4 'And as he *s*, some seed fell
13:24 of heaven is like a man who *s*
13:25 his enemy came and *s* tares
13:31 which a man took and *s* in his
13:39 The enemy who *s* them is the
Mk 4: 4 "And it happened, as he *s*,
Lk 8: 5 to sow his seed. And as he *s*,

SOWER (8/8) SOW

Isa 55:10 it may give seed to the *s* And
Jer 50:16 Cut off the *s* from Babylon,
Mt 13: 3 a *s* went out to sow.
13:18 hear the parable of the *s*:
Mk 4: 3 a *s* went out to sow.
4:14 The *s* sows the word.
Lk 8: 5 A *s* went out to sow his seed.
2 Cor 9:10 He who supplies seed to the *s*,

SOWING (2/2) SOW

Lev 26: 5 shall last till the time of *s*;
Ps 126: 6 Bearing seed for *s*,

SOWN (31/29) SOW

Ex 23:16 of your labors which you have *s*
Lev 11:37 planting seed which is to be *s*,
Deut 21: 4 which is neither plowed nor *s*,
22: 9 of the seed which you have *s*
29:23 salt, and burning; it is not *s*,
Judg 6: 3 it was, whenever Israel had *s*,
Ps 97:11 Light is *s* for the righteous,
Isa 19: 7 And everything *s* by the River,
40:24 Scarcely shall they be *s*,
61:11 causes the things that are *s*
Jer 2: 2 wilderness, In a land not *s*.
12:13 They have *s* wheat but reaped
Ezek 36: 9 and you shall be tilled and *s*.
Hag 1: 6 You have *s* much, and bring in
Mt 13:19 and snatches away what was *s*
25:24 reaping where you have not *s*,
25:26 that I reap where I have not *s*,
Mk 4:15 the wayside where the word is *s*.
4:15 takes away the word that was *s*
4:16 These likewise are the ones *s* on
4:18 Now these are the ones *s* among
4:20 But these are the ones *s* on good
4:31 when it is *s* on the ground, is
4:32 "but when it is *s*,
1 Cor 9:11 If we have *s* spiritual things
15:42 The body is *s* in corruption,
15:43 It is *s* in dishonor, it is
15:43 It is *s* in weakness, it is
15:44 It is *s* a natural body, it is
2 Cor 9:10 multiply the seed you have *s*
Jas 3:18 fruit of righteousness is *s* in

SOWS (15/13) SOW

Prov 6:14 He *s* discord.
6:19 And one who *s* discord among
11:18 But he who *s* righteousness
16:28 A perverse man *s* strife, And a
22: 8 He who *s* iniquity will reap
Am 9:13 the treader of grapes him who *s*
Mt 13:37 He who *s* the good seed is the
Mk 4:14 The sower *s* the word.
Jn 4:36 that both he who *s* and he who
4:37 One *s* and another reaps.'
2 Cor 9: 6 He who *s* sparingly will also
9: 6 and he who *s* bountifully will
Gal 6: 7 mocked; for whatever a man *s*,
6: 8 For he who *s* to his flesh will
6: 8 but he who *s* to the Spirit will

SPACE (11/11)

Lev 25:30 it is not redeemed within the *s*
Josh 3: 4 Yet there shall be a *s* between
1 Ki 7:36 wherever there was a clear *s* on
Job 26: 7 out the north over empty *s*;
Jer 28:11 of all nations within the *s* of
Ezek 40: 7 the gate chambers was a *s*
40:12 There was a *s* in front of the
41:17 from the *s* above the door, even
41:20 From the floor to the *s* above
42: 5 the galleries took away *s*
45: 2 cubits around it for an open *s*.

SPACIOUS (2/2)

Neh 7: 4 Now the city was large and *s*,
Jer 22:14 a wide house with *s* chambers,

SPAIN (2/2)

Rom 15:24 whenever I journey to *S*,
15:28 I shall go by way of you to *S*.

SPAN (8/6)

Ex 28:16 a *s* shall be its length, and
28:16 and a *s* shall be its width.
39: 9 a *s* was its length and a span
39: 9 a span was its length and a *s*
1 Sam 17: 4 height was six cubits and a *s*.
Isa 38:12 My life *s* is gone, Taken from
40:12 Measured heaven with a *s* And
Ezek 43:13 all around its edge of one *s*.

SPANNED (1/1)

2 Chr 3:13 *s* twenty cubits overall.

SPARE (43/42) SPARED, SPARES, SPARINGLY

Gen 18:24 destroy the place and not *s*
18:26 then I will *s* all the place for
Deut 13: 8 nor shall you *s* him or conceal
29:20 'The LORD would not *s* him;
Josh 2:13 and *s* my father, my mother, my
1 Sam 15: 3 and do not *s* them. But kill
1 Ki 20:31 perhaps he will *s* your life."
Neh 13:22 and *s* me according to the
Job 2: 6 but *s* his life."
6:10 I would exult, He will not *s*;
27:22 against him and does not *s*;
Ps 72:13 He will *s* the poor and needy,
78:50 He did not *s* their soul from
Prov 6:34 Therefore he will not *s* in the
21:26 righteous gives and does not *s*.
Isa 9:19 No man shall *s* his brother.
13:18 Their eye will not *s* children.
30:14 in pieces; He shall not *s*.
54: 2 of your dwellings; Do not *s*;
58: 1 *s* not; Lift up your voice like
Jer 13:14 I will not pity nor *s* nor have
21: 7 He shall not *s* them, or have
50:14 *s* no arrows, For she has
51: 3 Do not *s* her young men;
Ezek 5:11 My eye will not *s*,
7: 4 My eye will not *s* you,
7: 9 'My eye will not *s*,
8:18 My eye will not *s* nor will I
9: 5 and kill; do not let your eye *s*,
9:10 Me also, My eye will neither *s*,
12:16 But I will *s* a few of their men
24:14 not hold back, Nor will I *s*,
Joel 2:17 *S* Your people, O LORD, And do
Mal 3:17 And I will *s* them As a man
Lk 15:17 have bread enough and to *s*,
Rom 8:32 He who did not *s* His own Son,
11:21 For if God did not *s* the natural
11:21 He may not *s* you either.
1 Cor 7:28 but I would *s* you.
2 Cor 1:23 that to *s* you I came no more to
13: 2 if I come again I will not *s*—
2 Pe 2: 4 For if God did not *s* the angels
2: 5 and did not *s* the ancient world,

SPARED (9/9) SPARE

Josh 6:25 And Joshua *s* Rahab the harlot,

S

1 Sam 15: 9 But Saul and the people *s* Agag
15:15 for the people *s* the best of
24:10 But my eye *s* you, and I said,
2 Sam 8: 4 except that he *s* enough of
21: 7 But the king *s* Mephibosheth the
2 Ki 5:20 my master has *s* Naaman this
1 Chr 18: 4 except that he *s* enough of them
Ezek 20:17 Nevertheless My eye *s* them from

SPARES (4/4) SPARE

Job 20:13 Though he *s* it and does not
Prov 13:24 He who *s* his rod hates his son,
17:27 He who has knowledge *s* his
Mal 3:17 I will spare them As a man *s*

SPARING (1/1)

Acts 20:29 not *s* the flock.

SPARINGLY (2/1) SPARE

2 Cor 9: 6 He who sows *s* will also reap
9: 6 sows sparingly will also reap *s*,

SPARK (1/1)

Isa 1:31 And the work of it as a *s*;

SPARKLED (1/1)

Ezek 1: 7 They *s* like the color of

SPARKLES (1/1)

Prov 23:31 When it *s* in the cup,

SPARKS (4/3)

Job 5: 7 As the *s* fly upward.
41:19 *S* of fire shoot out.
Isa 50:11 encircle yourselves with *s*:
50:11 of your fire and in the *s* you

SPARROW (3/3) SPARROWS

Ps 84: 3 Even the *s* has found a home,
102: 7 And am like a *s* alone on the
Prov 26: 2 Like a flitting *s*,

SPARROWS (4/4) SPARROW

Mt 10:29 Are not two *s* sold for a copper
10:31 are of more value than many *s*.
Lk 12: 6 Are not five *s* sold for two
12: 7 are of more value than many *s*.

SPAT (5/5) SPIT

Mt 26:67 Then they *s* in His face and beat
27:30 Then they *s* on Him, and took the
Mk 7:33 and He *s* and touched his
15:19 on the head with a reed and *s*
Jn 9: 6 He *s* on the ground and made

SPATTERED (1/1)

2 Ki 9:33 and some of her blood *s* on the

SPEAK (509/483) SPEAKING, SPEAKS, SPEECH, SPOKE, SPOKEN

Gen 18:27 have taken it upon myself to *s*
18:30 the Lord be angry, and I will *s*:
18:31 have taken it upon myself to *s*
18:32 and I will *s* but once more:
24:33 And he said, "*S* on."
24:50 we cannot *s* to you either bad
27: 6 Indeed I heard your father *s* to
31:24 Be careful that you *s* to Jacob
31:29 Be careful that you *s* to Jacob
32: 4 *S* thus to my lord Esau, 'Thus
32:19 In this manner you shall *s* to
34: 6 Shechem went out to Jacob to *s*
37: 4 they hated him and could not *s*
42:22 Did I not *s* to you, saying, 'Do
44:16 say to my lord? What shall we *s*?
44:18 please let your servant *s* a
50: 4 please *s* in the hearing of
Ex 4:14 I know that he can *s* well.
4:15 Now you shall *s* to him and put
5:23 since I came to Pharaoh to *s*
6:29 *S* to Pharaoh king of Egypt all
7: 2 You shall *s* all that I command
7: 2 And Aaron your brother shall *s*
11: 2 *S* now in the hearing of the
12: 3 *S* to all the congregation of
14: 2 *S* to the children of Israel,
16:12 *S* to them, saying, 'At twilight
19: 6 the words which you shall *s* to
19: 9 the people may hear when I *s*
20:19 You *s* with us, and we will hear;
20:19 but let not God *s* with us, lest
23:22 His voice and do all that I *s*,
25: 2 *S* to the children of Israel,
25:22 and I will *s* with you from
28: 3 So you shall *s* to all who are
29:42 where I will meet you to *s* with
30:31 And you shall *s* to the children
31:13 *S* also to the children of
32:12 "Why should the Egyptians *s*,
34:34 went in before the LORD to *s*
34:34 and he would come out and *s* to
34:35 until he went in to *s* with Him.
Lev 1: 2 '*S* to the children of Israel,
4: 2 *S* to the children of Israel,
6:25 *S* to Aaron and to his sons,
7:23 *S* to the children of Israel,
7:29 *S* to the children of Israel,
9: 3 children of Israel you shall *s*,
11: 2 *S* to the children of Israel,
12: 2 *S* to the children of Israel,
15: 2 *S* to the children of Israel, and
17: 2 *S* to Aaron, to his sons, and to
18: 2 *S* to the children of Israel, and
19: 2 *S* to all the congregation of the
21: 1 *S* to the priests, the sons of
21:17 *S* to Aaron, saying: 'No man of
22: 2 *S* to Aaron and his sons, that
22:18 *S* to Aaron and his sons, and to
23: 2 *S* to the children of Israel, and
23:10 *S* to the children of Israel, and
23:24 *S* to the children of Israel,
23:34 *S* to the children of Israel,
24:15 Then you shall *s* to the children
25: 2 *S* to the children of Israel, and
27: 2 *S* to the children of Israel, and
Num 5: 6 *S* to the children of Israel:
5:12 *S* to the children of Israel, and
6: 2 *S* to the children of Israel, and
6:23 *S* to Aaron and his sons, saying,
7:89 the tabernacle of meeting to *s*
8: 2 *S* to Aaron, and say to him,
9:10 *S* to the children of Israel,
12: 6 I *s* to him in a dream.
12: 8 I *s* with him face to face,
12: 8 then were you not afraid To *s*
14:15 have heard of Your fame will *s*,
15: 2 *S* to the children of Israel, and
15:18 *S* to the children of Israel, and
15:38 *S* to the children of Israel:
16:24 *S* to the congregation, saying,
17: 2 *S* to the children of Israel, and
18:26 *S* thus to the Levites, and say
19: 2 *S* to the children of Israel,
20: 8 *S* to the rock before their
21:27 Therefore those who *s* in
22:20 but only the word which I *s* to
22:35 but only the word that I *s* to
22:35 speak to you, that you shall *s*.
22:38 puts in my mouth, that I must *s*.
23: 5 to Balak, and thus you shall *s*.
23:12 Must I not take heed to *s* what
23:16 to Balak, and thus you shall *s*.
24:12 Did I not also *s* to your
24:13 the LORD says, that I must *s*'?
27: 7 The daughters of Zelophehad *s*
27: 8 And you shall *s* to the children
33:51 *S* to the children of Israel, and
35:10 *S* to the children of Israel, and
Deut 3:26 Enough of that! *S* no more to Me
5: 1 and judgments which I *s* in
5:31 and I will *s* to you all the
11: 2 Know today that I do not *s*
18:18 and He shall *s* to them all that
18:20 the prophet who presumes to *s*
18:20 I have not commanded him to *s*,
20: 2 priest shall approach and *s* to
20: 5 Then the officers shall *s* to the
20: 8 The officers shall *s* further to
25: 8 his city shall call him and *s*
27:14 And the Levites shall *s* with a
31:28 that I may *s* these words in
32: 1 ear, O heavens, and I will *s*;
Josh 4:10 had commanded Joshua to *s* to
20: 2 *S* to the children of Israel,
22:24 to come your descendants may *s*
Judg 5:10 '*S*, you who ride on white
6:39 but let me *s* just once more:
9: 2 Please *s* in the hearing of all
19: 3 to *s* kindly to her and bring
19:30 confer, and *s* up!"
1 Sam 3: 9 you, that you must say, '*S*,
3:10 And Samuel answered, "*S*,
9:21 Why then do you *s* like this to
15:16 And he said to him, "*S* on."
19: 3 and I will *s* with my father
25:17 a scoundrel that one cannot *s*
25:24 please let your maidservant *s*
2 Sam 3:19 Then Abner also went to *s* in
3:27 took him aside in the gate to *s*
13:13 please *s* to the king; for he
14: 3 Go to the king and *s* to him in
14:12 let your maidservant *s* another
14:15 I have come to *s* of this thing
14:15 I will now *s* to the king; it may
14:18 let my lord the king *s*.
17: 6 do as he says? If not, *s* up."
19: 7 go out and *s* comfort to your
19:11 *S* to the elders of Judah,
19:29 Why do you *s* anymore of your
20:16 that I may *s* with you.'"
1 Ki 2:17 Please *s* to King Solomon, for he
2:18 I will *s* for you to the king."
2:19 to *s* to him for Adonijah.
12: 7 and *s* good words to them, then
12:10 Thus you should *s* to this people
12:23 *S* to Rehoboam the son of
21:19 You shall *s* to him, saying,
21:19 And you shall *s* to him,
22:13 and *s* encouragement."
22:14 LORD says to me, that I will *s*.
22:24 from the LORD go from me to *s*
2 Ki 4:13 Do you want me to *s* on your
6:12 of Israel the words that you *s*
18:20 You *s* of having plans and power
18:26 Please *s* to your servants in
18:26 and do not *s* to us in Hebrew in
18:27 to your master and to you to *s*
19:10 Thus you shall *s* to Hezekiah
22:18 in this manner you shall *s* to
2 Chr 10: 7 and *s* good words to them, they
10:10 Thus you should *s* to the people
11: 3 *S* to Rehoboam the son of
18:12 and *s* encouragement."
18:13 my God says, that I will *s*.
18:23 from the LORD go from me to *s*
32:17 and to *s* against Him, saying,
34:26 in this manner you shall *s* to
35:25 men and the singing women *s* of
Neh 13:24 and could not *s* the language of
Esth 1:22 and *s* in the language of his
Job 2:10 You *s* as one of the foolish
7:11 I will *s* in the anguish of my
8: 2 How long will you *s* these
9:35 Then I would *s* and not fear
10: 1 I will *s* in the bitterness of
11: 5 But oh, that God would *s*,
12: 8 Or *s* to the earth, and it will
13: 3 But I would *s* to the Almighty,
13: 7 Will you *s* wickedly for God,
13:13 peace with me, and let me *s*,
13:22 and I will answer; Or let me *s*,
16: 4 I also could *s* as you do,
16: 6 Though I *s*, my grief is not
18: 2 and afterward we will *s*.
19:18 and they *s* against me.
21: 3 Bear with me that I may *s*,
27: 4 My lips will not *s* wickedness,
29:22 After my words they did not *s*
32: 4 Elihu had waited to *s* to Job.
32: 7 I said, 'Age should *s*,
32:16 waited, because they did not *s*,
32:20 I will *s*, that I may find
33:14 For God may *s* in one way, or in
33:31 Hold your peace, and I will *s*.
33:32 anything to say, answer me; *S*,
34:33 Therefore *s* what you know.
36: 2 there are yet words to *s* on
37:20 He be told that I wish to *s*?
37:20 to speak? If a man were to *s*,
41: 3 Will he *s* softly to you?
42: 4 Listen, please, and let me *s*;
Ps 2: 5 Then He shall *s* to them in His
5: 6 You shall destroy those who *s*
12: 2 They *s* idly everyone with his
12: 2 lips and a double heart they *s*.
17:10 With their mouths they *s*
28: 3 Who *s* peace to their
31:18 Which *s* insolent things
35:20 For they do not *s* peace,
35:28 And my tongue shall *s* of Your
38:12 Those who seek my hurt *s* of
40: 5 If I would declare and *s* of
41: 5 My enemies *s* evil of me:
49: 3 My mouth shall *s* wisdom,
50: 7 O My people, and I will *s*,
50:20 You sit and *s* against your
51: 4 may be found just when You *s*,
58: 1 Do you indeed *s* righteousness,
59:12 cursing and lying which they *s*.
63:11 But the mouth of those who *s*
69:12 Those who sit in the gate *s*
71:10 For my enemies *s* against me;
73: 8 They scoff and *s* wickedly
73: 8 They *s* loftily.
73:15 I will *s* thus," Behold, I
75: 5 Do not *s* with a stiff neck.'
77: 4 am so troubled that I cannot *s*.
85: 8 hear what God the LORD will *s*,
85: 8 For He will *s* peace To His
94: 4 and *s* insolent things;
109:20 And to those who *s* evil
115: 5 have mouths, but they do not *s*;
119:23 Princes also sit and *s* against
119:46 I will *s* of Your testimonies
119:172 My tongue shall *s* of Your word,
120: 7 am for peace; But when I *s*,
127: 5 But shall *s* with their enemies
135:16 have mouths, but they do not *s*;
139:20 For they *s* against You
145: 6 Men shall *s* of the might of
145:11 They shall *s* of the glory of
145:21 My mouth shall *s* the praise of
Prov 6:22 they will *s* with you.
8: 6 for I will *s* of excellent
8: 7 For my mouth will *s* truth;
21:28 the man who hears him will *s*
23: 9 Do not *s* in the hearing of a
23:16 will rejoice When your lips *s*
Eccl 3: 7 keep silence, And a time to *s*;
Isa 8:10 *S* the word, but it will not
8:20 the testimony! If they do not *s*
14:10 They all shall *s* and say to
19:18 in the land of Egypt will *s*
28:11 and another tongue He will *s*
29: 4 You shall *s* out of the ground;
30:10 *S* to us smooth things,
32: 4 stammerers will be ready to *s*
32: 6 For the foolish person will *s*
36: 5 I say you *s* of having plans and
36:11 Please *s* to your servants in the
36:11 and do not *s* to us in Hebrew in
36:12 to your master and to you to *s*
37:10 Thus you shall *s* to Hezekiah
40: 2 *S* comfort to Jerusalem, and cry
40:27 do you say, O Jacob, And *s*,
41: 1 them come near, then let them *s*;

45:19 *s* righteousness, I declare
50: 4 That I should know how to *s* A
56: 3 joined himself to the LORD *S*,
59: 4 trust in empty words and *s*
63: 1 I who *s* in righteousness, mighty
Jer 1: 6 Lord GOD! Behold, I cannot *s*,
1: 7 I command you, you shall *s*.
1:17 And *s* to them all that I
4:12 Now I will also *s* judgment
5: 5 will go to the great men and *s*
5:14 Because you *s* this word,
6:10 To whom shall I *s* and give
7:22 For I did not *s* to your fathers,
7:27 Therefore you shall *s* all these
8: 6 But they do not *s* aright.
9: 5 And will not *s* the truth;
9: 5 have taught their tongue to *s*
9:22 *S*, "Thus says the LORD:
10: 5 a palm tree, And they cannot *s*;
11: 2 and *s* to the men of Judah and
12: 6 Even though they *s* smooth
13:12 Therefore you shall *s* to them
18: 7 The instant I *s* concerning a
18: 9 And the instant I *s* concerning a
18:11 *s* to the men of Judah and to
18:20 that I stood before You To *s*
19: 5 which I did not command or *s*,
20: 9 Nor *s* anymore in His name."
22: 1 and there *s* this word,
23:16 They *s* a vision of their own
23:28 let him *s* My word faithfully.
26: 2 and *s* to all the cities of
26: 2 words that I command you to *s*
26: 8 LORD had commanded him to *s*
26:15 LORD has sent me to you to *s*
27: 9 who *s* to you, saying, "You
27:14 words of the prophets who *s* to
28: 7 hear now this word that I *s* in
29:24 You shall also *s* to Shemaiah
32: 4 and shall *s* with him face to
34: 2 Go and *s* to Zedekiah king of
34: 3 he shall *s* with you face to
35: 2 *s* to them, and bring them into
38:20 voice of the LORD which I *s*
39:16 Go and *s* to Ebed-Melech the
40:16 for you *s* falsely concerning
43: 2 You *s* falsely! The LORD our God
48:27 For whenever you *s* of him,
Ezek 2: 1 and I will *s* to you."
2: 7 You shall *s* My words to them,
3: 1 *s* to the house of Israel."
3: 4 go to the house of Israel and *s*
3:10 heart all My words that I *s* to
3:11 and *s* to them and tell them,
3:18 nor *s* to warn the wicked from
3:27 But when I *s* with you, I will
11: 5 *S*! 'Thus says the LORD: "Thus
12:25 "For I am the LORD. I *s*,
12:25 and the word which I *s* will
12:28 but the word which I *s* will be
14: 4 Therefore *s* to them, and say to
14: 9 if the prophet is induced to *s*
17: 2 and *s* a parable to the house of
20: 3 *s* to the elders of Israel, and
20:27 *s* to the house of Israel, and
20:49 Does he not *s* parables?'"
24:21 *S* to the house of Israel, "Thus
24:27 you shall *s* and no longer be
29: 3 '*S*, and say, 'Thus says
29:21 I will open your mouth to *s* in
32:21 among the mighty Shall *s* to
33: 2 *s* to the children of your
33: 8 surely die!' and you do not *s*
33:30 and they *s* to one another,
37:18 the children of your people *s*
39:17 *S* to every sort of bird and to
Dan 2: 9 For you have agreed to *s* lying
7:25 He shall *s* pompous words
10:11 understand the words that I *s*
10:19 and said, "Let my lord *s*,
11:27 and they shall *s* lies at the
11:36 shall *s* blasphemies against the
Hos 1: 2 When the LORD began to *s* by
2:14 And *s* comfort to her.
Mic 2:11 walk in a false spirit And *s*
Hab 2: 3 But at the end it will *s*,
Zeph 3:13 do no unrighteousness And *s*
Hag 2: 2 *S* now to Zerubbabel the son of
2:21 *S* to Zerubbabel, governor of
Zech 2: 4 *s* to this young man, saying:
6:12 Then *s* to him, saying, 'Thus
8:16 *S* each man the truth to his
9:10 He shall *s* peace to the
10: 2 For the idols *s* delusion;
Mt 8: 8 But only *s* a word, and my
10:19 about how or what you should *s*.
10:19 in that hour what you should *s*;
10:20 "for it is not you who *s*,
10:27 *s* in the light; and what you
12:34 *s* good things? For out of the
12:36 for every idle word men may *s*,
12:46 seeking to *s* with Him.
12:47 seeking to *s* with You."
13:10 Why do You *s* to them in
13:13 Therefore I *s* to them in
13:34 without a parable He did not *s*
16:11 understand that I did not *s* to
Mk 1:34 did not allow the demons to *s*,
2: 7 Why does this Man *s* blasphemies
4:34 without a parable He did not *s*
7:37 deaf to hear and the mute to *s*.
9:39 in My name can soon afterward *s*
12: 1 Then He began to *s* to them in
13:11 or premeditate what you will *s*.
13:11 *s* that; for it is not you who
13:11 for it is not you who *s*,
14:71 know this Man of whom you *s*!"
16:17 they will *s* with new tongues;
Lk 1:19 and was sent to *s* to you and
1:20 will be mute and not able to *s*
1:22 he could not *s* to them;
4:41 them, did not allow them to *s*,
6:26 Woe to you when all men *s* well
7:15 was dead sat up and began to *s*.
7:24 He began to *s* to the multitudes
12:41 do You *s* this parable only to
Jn 1:37 The two disciples heard him *s*,
1:40 of the two who heard John *s*,
3:11 We *s* what We know and testify
4:26 I who *s* to you am He."
6:63 The words that I *s* to you are
7:17 it is from God or whether I *s*
8:26 and I *s* to the world those
8:28 I *s* these things.
8:38 I *s* what I have seen with My
9:21 He will *s* for himself."
12:49 should say and what I should *s*.
12:50 Therefore, whatever I *s*,
12:50 the Father has told Me, so I *s*.
13:18 I do not *s* concerning all of
14:10 The words that I *s* to you I do
14:10 that I speak to you I do not *s*
16:13 for He will not *s* on His own
16:13 but whatever He hears He will *s*;
16:25 coming when I will no longer *s*
17:13 and these things I *s* in the
Acts 2: 4 the Holy Spirit and began to *s*
2: 6 because everyone heard them *s*
2: 7 are not all these who *s*
2:29 let me *s* freely to you of the
4:17 that from now on they *s* to no
4:18 and commanded them not to *s* at
4:20 For we cannot but *s* the things
4:29 with all boldness they may *s*
5:20 stand in the temple and *s* to
5:40 that they should not *s* in the
6:11 We have heard him *s* blasphemous
6:13 This man does not cease to *s*
10:32 he will *s* to you.'
10:46 For they heard them *s* with
11:15 "And as I began to *s*,
17:19 new doctrine is of which you *s*?
18: 9 "Do not be afraid, but *s*,
18:26 So he began to *s* boldly in the
21:37 May I *s* to you?" He replied,
21:37 Can you *s* Greek?
21:39 permit me to *s* to the people."
23: 5 You shall not *s* evil of a
24:10 governor had nodded to him to *s*,
26: 1 You are permitted to *s* for
26:25 but *s* the words of truth and
26:26 before whom I also *s* freely,
28:20 to see you and *s* with you,
Rom 3: 5 (I *s* as a man.)
6:19 I *s* in human terms because of
7: 1 brethren (for I *s* to those who
11:13 For I *s* to you Gentiles;
15:18 For I will not dare to *s* of any
1 Cor 1:10 that you all *s* the same thing,
2: 6 we *s* wisdom among those who are
2: 7 But we *s* the wisdom of God in a
2:13 These things we also *s*,
3: 1 could not *s* to you as to
10:15 I *s* as to wise men; judge for
12:30 Do all *s* with tongues? Do all
13: 1 Though I *s* with the tongues of
14: 2 speaks in a tongue does not *s*
14: 6 shall I profit you unless I *s*
14:18 I thank my God I *s* with tongues
14:19 in the church I would rather *s*
14:21 and other lips I will *s*
14:23 and all *s* with tongues, and
14:28 and let him *s* to himself and to
14:29 Let two or three prophets *s*,
14:34 for they are not permitted to *s*;
14:35 it is shameful for women to *s*
14:39 and do not forbid to *s* with
15:34 I *s* this to your shame.
2 Cor 2:17 we *s* in the sight of God in
4:13 we also believe and therefore *s*,
6:13 in return for the same (I *s* as
8: 8 I *s* not by commandment, but I
11:17 What I *s*, I speak not
11:17 I *s* not according to the Lord,
11:21 I *s* foolishly—I am bold also.
11:23 —I *s* as a fool—I am more:
12: 6 for I will *s* the truth. But I
12:19 We *s* before God in Christ.
Gal 3:15 I *s* in the manner of men:
Eph 4:25 Let each one of you *s*
5:12 For it is shameful even to *s* of
5:32 but I *s* concerning Christ and
6:20 that in it I may *s* boldly, as I
6:20 speak boldly, as I ought to *s*.
Phil 1:14 are much more bold to *s* the
4:11 Not that I *s* in regard to need,
Col 4: 3 to *s* the mystery of Christ,
4: 4 it manifest, as I ought to *s*.
1 Th 2: 2 we were bold in our God to *s* to
2: 4 with the gospel, even so we *s*,
2:16 forbidding us to *s* to the
1 Tim 5:14 to the adversary to *s*
Titus 2: 1 *s* the things which are proper
2:15 *S* these things, exhort, and
3: 2 to *s* evil of no one, to be
Heb 2: 5 world to come, of which we *s*,
6: 9 though we *s* in this manner.
7: 9 tithes through Abraham, so to *s*,
9: 5 Of these things we cannot now *s*
Jas 1:19 man be swift to hear, slow to *s*,
2:12 So *s* and so do as those who will
4:11 Do not *s* evil of one another,
1 Pe 2:12 that when they *s* against you as
4:11 let him *s* as the oracles of
2 Pe 2:10 They are not afraid to *s* evil
2:12 *s* evil of the things they do
2:18 For when they *s* great swelling
1 Jn 4: 5 Therefore they *s* as of the
2 Jn 12 but I hope to come to you and *s*
3 Jn 14 and we shall *s* face to face.
Jude 8 and *s* evil of dignitaries.
10 But these *s* evil of whatever
Rev 13:15 of the beast should both *s* and

SPEAKER (1/1)

Acts 14:12 because he was the chief *s*.

SPEAKING (90/89) SPEAK

Gen 18:33 as soon as He had finished *s*
24:15 before he had finished *s*,
24:45 But before I had finished *s* in
29: 9 Now while he was still *s* with
Ex 31:18 when He had made an end of *s*
34:33 And when Moses had finished *s*
Lev 5: 4 *s* thoughtlessly with his lips
Num 7:89 he heard the voice of One *s* to
16:31 as he finished *s* all these
Deut 4:33 ever hear the voice of God *s*
5:26 the voice of the living God *s*
11:19 *s* of them when you sit in your
20: 9 the officers have finished *s*
32:45 Moses finished *s* all these words
Judg 15:17 it was, when he had finished *s*,
Ruth 1:18 she stopped *s* to her.
1 Sam 18: 1 Now when he had finished *s* to
24:16 when David had finished *s* these
2 Sam 13:36 as soon as he had finished *s*,
1 Ki 1:42 While he was still *s*,
Esth 10: 3 the good of his people and *s*
Job 1:16 While he was still *s*,
1:17 While he was still *s*,
1:18 While he was still *s*,
4: 2 who can withhold himself from *s*?
Ps 34:13 And your lips from *s* deceit.
52: 3 Lying rather than *s*
58: 3 as they are born, *s* lies.
Isa 58: 9 and *s* wickedness,
58:13 Nor *s* your own words,
59:13 *S* oppression and revolt,
65:24 And while they are still *s*,
Jer 7:13 to you, rising up early and *s*,
25: 3 to you, rising early and *s*,
26: 7 all the people heard Jeremiah *s*
26: 8 Jeremiah had made an end of *s*
35:14 to you, rising early and *s*,
38: 4 by *s* such words to them.
38:27 So they stopped *s* with him, for
43: 1 when Jeremiah had stopped *s* to
Ezek 1:28 and I heard a voice of One *s*.
43: 6 Then I heard Him *s* to me from
Dan 7: 8 and a mouth *s* pompous words.
7:11 words which the horn was *s*;
8:13 Then I heard a holy one *s*;
8:13 to that certain one who was *s*,
8:18 as he was *s* with me, I was in a
9:20 Now while I was *s*,
9:21 while I was *s* in prayer, the
10:11 While he was *s* this word to
Mt 15:31 when they saw the mute *s*,
17: 5 While he was still *s*,
21:45 they perceived that He was *s* of
26:47 And while He was still *s*,
Mk 5:35 While He was still *s*,
14:43 while He was still *s*,
Lk 5: 4 When He had stopped *s*,
8:49 While He was still *s*,
22:47 And while He was still *s*,
22:60 while he was still *s*,
Jn 2:21 But He was *s* of the temple of
11:13 but they thought that He was *s*
16:29 now You are *s* plainly, and
18:34 Are you *s* for yourself about
19:10 Are You not *s* to me? Do You not
Acts 1: 3 by them during forty days and *s*
2:11 we hear them *s* in our own
10:44 While Peter was still *s* these
13:43 *s* to them, persuaded them to
14: 3 *s* boldly in the Lord, who was
14: 9 This man heard Paul *s*.
20: 9 sleep; and as Paul continued *s*,
20:30 *s* perverse things, to draw away
26:14 I heard a voice *s* to me and
1 Cor 12: 3 known to you that no one *s* by
14: 6 if I come to you *s* with
14: 9 For you will be *s* into the air.
2 Cor 13: 3 you seek a proof of Christ *s*
Eph 4:15 *s* the truth in love, may grow
4:31 and evil *s* be put away from
5:19 *s* to one another in psalms and
1 Tim 2: 7 I am *s* the truth in Christ and
4: 2 *s* lies in hypocrisy, having
1 Pe 2: 1 hypocrisy, envy, and all evil *s*,
3:10 And his lips from *s*
4: 4 *s* evil of you.

2 Pe 2:16 a dumb donkey *s* with a man's
3:16 *s* in them of these things, in
Rev 4: 1 I heard was like a trumpet *s*
13: 5 And he was given a mouth *s* great

SPEAKS (79/72) SPEAK

Gen 45:12 that it is my mouth that *s*
Ex 7: 9 When Pharaoh *s* to you, saying,
33:11 as a man *s* to his friend.
Num 22: 8 as the LORD *s* to me." So the
23:26 saying, 'All that the LORD *s*,
36: 5 tribe of the sons of Joseph *s*
Deut 5:24 have seen this day that God *s*
18:19 which He *s* in My name, I will
18:20 or who *s* in the name of other
18:22 when a prophet *s* in the name of
2 Sam 14:13 For the king *s* this thing as
1 Ki 20: 5 Thus *s* Ben-Hadad, saying,
Job 2:10 as one of the foolish women *s*.
17: 5 He who *s* flattery to his
33: 2 My tongue *s* in my mouth.
34:35 'Job *s* without knowledge,
Ps 12: 3 And the tongue that *s* proud
15: 2 And *s* the truth in his heart;
37:30 The mouth of the righteous *s*
41: 6 he *s* lies; His heart gathers
144: 8 Whose mouth *s* vain words,
144:11 Whose mouth *s* lying words,
Prov 1:21 of the gates in the city She *s*
2:12 From the man who *s* perverse
6:19 A false witness who *s* lies,
12:17 He who *s* truth declares
12:18 There is one who *s* like the
14:25 But a deceitful witness *s*
16:13 And they love him who *s* what
19: 5 And he who *s* lies will not
19: 9 And he who *s* lies shall
26:25 When he *s* kindly, do not
Isa 9:17 And every mouth *s* folly.
32: 7 Even when the needy *s* justice.
33:15 He who walks righteously and *s*
52: 6 that day That I am He who *s*:
Jer 9: 8 It *s* deceit; One speaks
9: 8 One *s* peaceably to his
10: 1 the word which the LORD *s* to
28: 2 'Thus *s* the LORD of hosts,
29:25 Thus *s* the LORD of hosts,
30: 2 Thus *s* the LORD God of Israel,
Lam 3:37 Who is he who *s* and it comes
Ezek 10: 5 voice of Almighty God when He *s*.
Dan 3:29 or language which *s* anything
Am 5:10 And they abhor the one who *s*
Hag 1: 2 Thus *s* the LORD of hosts,
Mt 10:20 Spirit of your Father who *s* in
12:32 Anyone who *s* a word against the
12:32 but whoever *s* against the Holy
12:34 of the heart the mouth *s*.
Lk 5:21 Who is this who *s* blasphemies?
6:45 of the heart his mouth *s*.
12:10 And anyone who *s* a word against
Jn 3:31 of the earth is earthly and *s*
3:34 For He whom God has sent *s* the
7:18 He who *s* from himself seeks his
7:26 But look! He *s* boldly, and they
8:44 When he *s* a lie, he speaks from
8:44 he *s* from his own resources,
19:12 Whoever makes himself a king *s*
Rom 10: 6 the righteousness of faith *s*
1 Cor 14: 2 For he who *s* in a tongue does
14: 2 in the spirit he *s* mysteries.
14: 3 But he who prophesies *s*
14: 4 He who *s* in a tongue edifies
14: 5 is greater than he who *s* with
14:11 be a foreigner to him who *s*,
14:11 and he who *s* will be a
14:13 Therefore let him who *s* in a
14:27 If anyone *s* in a tongue, let
Heb 11: 4 it he being dead still *s*.
12: 5 the exhortation which *s* to you
12:24 the blood of sprinkling that *s*
12:25 you do not refuse Him who *s*.
12:25 if we turn away from Him who *s*
Jas 4:11 He who *s* evil of a brother and
4:11 *s* evil of the law and judges
1 Pe 4:11 If anyone *s*, let him

SPEAR (50/43) SPEARS

Josh 8:18 Stretch out the *s* that is in
8:18 And Joshua stretched out the *s*
8:26 which he stretched out the *s*,
Judg 5: 8 Not a shield or *s* was seen
1 Sam 13:22 there was neither sword nor *s*
17: 7 Now the staff of his *s* was like
17:45 to me with a sword, with a *s*,
17:47 does not save with sword and *s*;
18:10 but there was a *s* in Saul's
18:11 And Saul cast the *s*,
19: 9 he sat in his house with his *s*
19:10 David to the wall with the *s*,
19:10 and he drove the *s* into the
20:33 Then Saul cast a *s* at him to
21: 8 Is there not here on hand a *s* or
22: 6 with his *s* in his hand, and all
26: 7 with his *s* stuck in the ground
26: 8 strike him at once with the *s*,
26:11 take now the *s* and the jug of
26:12 So David took the *s* and the jug
26:16 And now see where the king's *s*
26:22 said, "Here is the king's *s*.
2 Sam 1: 6 was Saul, leaning on his *s*;
2:23 with the blunt end of the *s*,
2:23 so that the *s* came out of his
21:16 the weight of whose bronze *s*
21:19 the shaft of whose *s* was like
23: 7 with iron and the shaft of a *s*,
23:18 He lifted his *s* against three
23:21 The Egyptian had a *s* in his
23:21 wrested the *s* out of the
23:21 and killed him with his own *s*.
1 Chr 11:11 he had lifted up his *s* against
11:20 He had lifted up his *s* against
11:23 hand there was a *s* like a
11:23 wrested the *s* out of the
11:23 and killed him with his own *s*.
12: 8 who could handle shield and *s*,
12:24 of Judah bearing shield and *s*,
12:34 thousand with shield and *s*;
20: 5 the shaft of whose *s* was like
2 Chr 25: 5 who could handle *s* and shield.
Job 39:23 The glittering *s* and javelin.
41:26 it cannot avail; Nor does *s*,
Ps 35: 3 Also draw out the *s*,
46: 9 breaks the bow and cuts the *s*
Jer 6:23 will lay hold on bow and *s*;
Nah 3: 3 bright sword and glittering *s*.
Hab 3:11 shining of Your glittering *s*.
Jn 19:34 pierced His side with a *s*,

SPEARHEAD (1/1)

1 Sam 17: 7 and his iron *s* weighed six

SPEARMEN (1/1)

Acts 23:23 and two hundred *s* to go to

SPEARS (18/18) SPEAR

1 Sam 13:19 the Hebrews make swords or *s*.
2 Sam 18:14 And he took three *s* in his
2 Ki 11:10 the captains of hundreds the *s*
2 Chr 11:12 city he put shields and *s*,
14: 8 Judah who carried shields and *s*,
23: 9 the captains of hundreds the *s*
26:14 for the entire army, shields, *s*,
Neh 4:13 with their swords, their *s*,
4:16 while the other half held the *s*,
4:21 half of the men held the *s*
Job 41: 7 Or his head with fishing *s*?
Ps 57: 4 Whose teeth are *s* and arrows,
Isa 2: 4 And their *s* into pruning
Jer 46: 4 your helmets, Polish the *s*,
Ezek 39: 9 and arrows, the javelins and *s*;
Joel 3:10 And your pruning hooks into *s*;
Mic 4: 3 And their *s* into pruning
Nah 2: 3 And the *s* are brandished.

SPECIAL (10/10)

Ex 19: 5 then you shall be a *s* treasure
Deut 7: 6 a *s* treasure above all the
14: 2 a *s* treasure above all the
26:18 you to be His *s* people,
1 Chr 29: 3 my own *s* treasure of gold and
Ps 135: 4 Israel for His *s* treasure.
Eccl 2: 8 and gold and the *s* treasures
Mk 7: 3 wash their hands in a *s* way,
Titus 2:14 for Himself His own *s* people,
1 Pe 2: 9 His own *s* people, that you may

SPECIES (1/1)

Gen 7: 3 to keep the *s* alive on the face

SPECIFICALLY (1/1)

Lev 13:38 *s* white bright spots,

SPECIFIED (2/2)

Neh 12:44 of the cities the portions *s*
Dan 9: 2 the number of the years *s* by

SPECIFY (1/1)

Acts 25:27 to send a prisoner and not to *s*

SPECK (6/5)

Mt 7: 3 And why do you look at the *s* in
7: 4 Let me remove the *s* from your
7: 5 see clearly to remove the *s*
Lk 6:41 And why do you look at the *s* in
6:42 let me remove the *s* that is in
6:42 see clearly to remove the *s*

SPECKLED (11/8)

Gen 30:32 removing from there all the *s*
30:32 and the spotted and *s* among the
30:33 every one that is not *s* and
30:35 day the male goats that were *s*
30:35 the female goats that were *s*
30:39 brought forth streaked, *s*,
31: 8 'The *s* shall be your wages,'
31: 8 then all the flocks bore *s*.
31:10 the flocks were streaked, *s*,
31:12 on the flocks are streaked, *s*,
Jer 12: 9 heritage is to Me like a *s*

SPECTACLE (4/4)

Nah 3: 6 you vile, And make you a *s*.
1 Cor 4: 9 for we have been made a *s* to
Col 2:15 He made a public *s* of them,
Heb 10:33 partly while you were made a *s*

SPECTACULAR (1/1)

2 Sam 23:21 a *s* man. The Egyptian had a

SPEECH (43/42) SPEAK, SPEECHLESS

Gen 4:23 listen to my *s*! For I have
11: 1 had one language and one *s*.
11: 7 not understand one another's *s*.
Ex 4:10 but I am slow of *s* and slow of
Deut 32: 2 My *s* distill as the dew,
1 Sam 16:18 a man of war, prudent in *s*,
1 Ki 3:10 The *s* pleased the LORD, that
Job 12:20 deprives the trusted ones of *s*,
13:17 Listen carefully to my *s*,
21: 2 "Listen carefully to my *s*,
24:25 And make my *s* worth
29:22 And my *s* settled on them as
33: 1 "But please, Job, hear my *s*,
Ps 17: 6 Your ear to me, and hear my *s*.
19: 2 Day unto day utters *s*,
19: 3 There is no *s* nor language
94: 4 They utter *s*, and speak
Prov 7:21 With her enticing *s* she caused
17: 7 Excellent *s* is not becoming to
Isa 28:23 my voice, Listen and hear my *s*.
29: 4 Your *s* shall be low, out of
29: 4 And your *s* shall whisper out
32: 9 daughters, Give ear to my *s*.
33:19 A people of obscure *s*,
Jer 31:23 They shall again use this *s* in
Ezek 3: 5 to a people of unfamiliar *s*
3: 6 to many people of unfamiliar *s*
Hab 3: 2 I have heard your *s* and was
Mt 26:73 for your *s* betrays you."
Mk 7:32 and had an impediment in his *s*,
14:70 and your *s* shows it."
Jn 8:43 do you not understand My *s*?
16:29 and using no figure of *s*!
Rom 16:18 smooth words and flattering *s*
1 Cor 2: 1 not come with excellence of *s*
2: 4 And my *s* and my preaching were
2 Cor 3:12 we use great boldness of *s*—
7: 4 Great is my boldness of *s*
8: 7 in everything—in faith, in *s*,
10:10 and his *s* contemptible."
11: 6 though I am untrained in *s*,
Col 4: 6 Let your *s* always be with
Titus 2: 8 sound *s* that cannot be

SPEECHES (2/2)

Job 6:26 And the *s* of a desperate one,
15: 3 Or by *s* with which he can do

SPEECHLESS (5/5) SPEECH

Prov 31: 8 Open your mouth for the *s*,
Dan 10:15 toward the ground and became *s*.
Mt 22:12 wedding garment?' And he was *s*.
Lk 1:22 beckoned to them and remained *s*.
Acts 9: 7 who journeyed with him stood *s*,

SPEED (3/3) SPEEDILY

Isa 5:19 Let Him make *s* and hasten His
5:26 Surely they shall come with *s*,
Acts 17:15 to come to him with all *s*,

SPEEDILY (14/14) SPEED

Gen 44:11 Then each man *s* let down his
1 Sam 27: 1 me than that I should *s* escape
2 Sam 17:16 but *s* cross over, lest the king
Ezra 7:26 let judgment be executed *s* on
Ps 31: 2 Your ear to me, Deliver me *s*;
69:17 I am in trouble; Hear me *s*.
79: 8 Your tender mercies come *s* to
102: 2 day that I call, answer me *s*.
143: 7 Answer me *s*, O LORD;
Eccl 8:11 an evil work is not executed *s*,
Isa 58: 8 healing shall spring forth *s*,
Jer 46: 5 They have *s* fled, And did not
Joel 3: 4 Swiftly and *s* I will return
Lk 18: 8 you that He will avenge them *s*.

SPEEDY (1/1)

Zeph 1:18 For He will make *s* riddance

SPELLS (1/1)

Deut 18:11 "or one who conjures *s*,

SPELT (3/3)

Ex 9:32 But the wheat and the *s* were not
Isa 28:25 And the *s* in its place?
Ezek 4: 9 beans, lentils, millet, and *s*;

SPEND (26/25) SPENT

Gen 19: 2 house and *s* the night,
19: 2 but we will *s* the night in
Deut 14:26 And you shall *s* that money for
32:23 I will *s* My arrows on them.
Judg 19: 9 please *s* the night. See, the
19:10 not willing to *s* that night;
19:13 and *s* the night in Gibeah or in
19:15 into his house to *s* the night.
19:20 only do not *s* the night in the

20: 4 to Benjamin, to *s* the night.
2 Sam 17:16 Do not *s* this night in the
Neh 13:21 Why do you *s* the night around
Job 21:13 They *s* their days in wealth,
24: 7 They *s* the night naked, without
36:11 They shall *s* their days in
Isa 55: 2 Why do you *s* money for what
65: 4 And *s* the night in the tombs;
Ezek 6:12 Thus will I *s* My fury upon
7: 8 And *s* My anger upon you;
Lk 10:35 of him; and whatever more you *s*,
Acts 20:16 so that he would not have to *s*
1 Cor 16: 6 or even *s* the winter with you,
2 Cor 12:15 And I will very gladly *s* and be
Titus 3:12 for I have decided to *s* the
Jas 4: 3 that you may *s* it on your
4:13 *s* a year there, buy and sell,

SPENT (23/22) SPEND

Lev 26:20 And your strength shall be *s* in
Deut 1:46 to the days that you *s* there.
Judg 19:11 Jebus, and the day was far *s*;
1 Ki 19: 9 and *s* the night in that place;
Job 7: 6 And are *s* without hope.
Ps 31:10 For my life is *s* with grief,
Isa 49: 4 I have *s* my strength for
Ezek 5:13 'Thus shall My anger be *s*,
5:13 when I have *s* My fury upon
Dan 6:18 palace and *s* the night fasting;
Mk 5:26 She had *s* all that she had and
6:35 When the day was now far *s*,
Lk 8:43 who had *s* all her livelihood on
15:14 But when he had *s* all, there
24:29 evening, and the day is far *s*.
Acts 9:19 Then Saul *s* some days with the
17:21 who were there *s* their time in
18:23 After he had *s* some time there,
26: 4 which was *s* from the beginning
27: 9 Now when much time had been *s*,
Rom 13:12 The night is far *s*,
2 Cor 12:15 very gladly spend and be *s* for
1 Pe 4: 3 For we have *s* enough of our

SPEWED (2/2)

Rev 12:15 So the serpent *s* water out of
12:16 flood which the dragon had *s*

SPHERE (4/3)

2 Cor 10:13 but within the limits of the *s*
10:13 a *s* which especially includes
10:15 enlarged by you in our *s*,
10:16 to boast in another man's *s* of

SPICE (1/1)

Song 5: 1 gathered my myrrh with my *s*;

SPICED (1/1)

Song 8: 2 cause you to drink of *s* wine,

SPICERY (KJV) See SPICES

SPICES (35/32)

Gen 37:25 with their camels, bearing *s*,
43:11 *s* and myrrh, pistachio nuts and
Ex 25: 6 and *s* for the anointing oil and
30:23 take for yourself quality *s*—
30:34 said to Moses: "Take sweet *s*,
30:34 with these sweet *s*;
35: 8 and *s* for the anointing oil and
35:28 and *s* and oil for the light,
37:29 and the pure incense of sweet *s*,
1 Ki 10: 2 with camels that bore *s*,
10:10 *s* in great quantity, and
10:10 again came such abundance of *s*
10:25 and gold, garments, armor, *s*,
2 Ki 20:13 the *s* and precious ointment,
1 Chr 9:29 oil and the incense and the *s*.
9:30 made the ointment of the *s*.
2 Chr 9: 1 retinue, camels that bore *s*,
9: 9 *s* in great abundance, and
9: 9 there never were any *s* such as
9:24 and gold, garments, armor, *s*,
16:14 the bed which was filled with *s*
32:27 for precious stones, for *s*,
Song 4:10 of your perfumes Than all *s*!
4:14 With all the chief *s*—
4:16 That its *s* may flow out.
5:13 cheeks are like a bed of *s*,
6: 2 his garden, To the beds of *s*,
8:14 On the mountains of *s*.
Isa 39: 2 the *s* and precious ointment,
Ezek 24:10 the meat well, Mix in the *s*,
27:22 for your wares the choicest *s*,
Mk 16: 1 of James, and Salome bought *s*,
Lk 23:56 they returned and prepared *s*
24: 1 came to the tomb bringing the *s*
Jn 19:40 in strips of linen with the *s*,

SPIDER (1/1)

Prov 30:28 The *s* skillfully grasps with

SPIDER'S (2/2)

Job 8:14 And whose trust is a *s* web.
Isa 59: 5 eggs and weave the *s* web;

SPIED (8/8) SPY

Num 13:21 So they went up and *s* out the
13:32 of the land which they had *s*
14: 6 were among those who had *s*
14:34 of the days in which you *s* out
Deut 1:24 of Eshcol, and *s* it out.
Josh 6:22 said to the two men who had *s*
7: 2 So the men went up and *s* out
2 Ki 13:21 that suddenly they *s* a band of

SPIES (16/16) SPY

Gen 42: 9 You are *s*! You have come to see
42:11 your servants are not *s*."
42:14 to you, saying, 'You are *s*!'
42:16 surely you are *s*!"
42:30 and took us for *s* of the
42:31 are honest men; we are not *s*.
42:34 shall know that you are not *s*,
Num 13:32 which we have gone as *s* is a
Josh 6:23 the young men who had been *s*
Judg 1:24 And when the *s* saw a man coming
18: 8 Then the *s* came back to their
1 Sam 26: 4 David therefore sent out *s*,
2 Sam 15:10 Then Absalom sent *s* throughout
Job 39:29 From there it *s* out the prey;
Lk 20:20 and sent *s* who pretended to be
Heb 11:31 when she had received the *s*

SPIKENARD (5/5)

Song 1:12 My *s* sends forth its
4:13 Fragrant henna with *s*,
4:14 *S* and saffron, Calamus and
Mk 14: 3 flask of very costly oil of *s*.
Jn 12: 3 a pound of very costly oil of *s*,

SPILLED (4/4)

2 Sam 14:14 die and become like water *s*
Mt 9:17 wineskins break, the wine is *s*,
Mk 2:22 the wineskins, the wine is *s*,
Lk 5:37 burst the wineskins and be *s*,

SPIN (2/2)

Mt 6:28 grow: they neither toil nor *s*;
Lk 12:27 grow: they neither toil nor *s*;

SPINDLE (1/1)

Prov 31:19 And her hand holds the *s*.

SPIRIT (576/523) HOLY, SPIRITS

Gen 1: 2 And the *S* of God was hovering
6: 3 My *S* shall not strive with man
7:22 was the breath of the *s* of
41: 8 that his *s* was troubled,
41:38 a man in whom is the *S* of
45:27 the *s* of Jacob their father
Ex 6: 9 because of anguish of *s* and
28: 3 whom I have filled with the *s*
31: 3 I have filled him with the *S*
35:21 and everyone whose *s* was
35:31 He has filled him with the *S*
Num 5:14 if the *s* of jealousy comes upon
5:14 or if the *s* of jealousy comes
5:30 or when the *s* of jealousy comes
11:17 I will take of the *S* that is
11:25 and took of the *S* that was
11:25 when the *S* rested upon them,
11:26 And the *S* rested upon them.
11:29 that the LORD would put His *S*
14:24 because he has a different *s* in
24: 2 and the *S* of God came upon him.
27:18 you, a man in whom is the *S*,
Deut 2:30 LORD your God hardened his *s*
34: 9 son of Nun was full of the *s*
Josh 5: 1 and there was no *s* in them any
Judg 3:10 The *S* of the LORD came upon
6:34 But the *S* of the LORD came upon
9:23 God sent a *s* of ill will between
11:29 Then the *S* of the LORD came
13:25 And the *S* of the LORD began to
14: 6 And the *S* of the LORD came
14:19 Then the *S* of the LORD came
15:14 Then the *S* of the LORD came
15:19 and his *s* returned, and he
1 Sam 1:15 I am a woman of sorrowful *s*.
10: 6 Then the *S* of the LORD will
10:10 then the *S* of God came upon
11: 6 Then the *S* of God came upon Saul
16:13 and the *S* of the LORD came
16:14 But the *S* of the LORD departed
16:14 and a distressing *s* from the
16:15 a distressing *s* from God is
16:16 his hand when the distressing *s*
16:23 whenever the *s* from God was
16:23 and the distressing *s* would
18:10 next day that the distressing *s*
19: 9 Now the distressing *s* from the
19:20 the *S* of God came upon the
19:23 Then the *S* of God was upon him
28:13 I saw a *s* ascending out of the
2 Sam 23: 2 The *S* of the LORD spoke by me,
1 Ki 10: 5 there was no more *s* in her.
18:12 that the *S* of the LORD will
21: 5 Why is your *s* so sullen that you
22:21 Then a *s* came forward and stood
22:22 'I will go out and be a lying *s*
22:23 The LORD has put a lying *s* in
22:24 Which way did the *s* from the
2 Ki 2: 9 let a double portion of your *s*
2:15 The *s* of Elijah rests on
2:16 lest perhaps the *S* of the LORD
19: 7 Surely I will send a *s* upon him,
1 Chr 5:26 God of Israel stirred up the *s*
12:18 Then the *S* came upon Amasai,
28:12 for all that he had by the *S*,
2 Chr 9: 4 there was no more *s* in her.
15: 1 Now the *S* of God came upon
18:20 Then a *s* came forward and stood
18:21 'I will go out and be a lying *s*
18:22 The LORD has put a lying *s* in
18:23 Which way did the *s* from the
20:14 Then the *S* of the LORD came
21:16 up against Jehoram the *s* of
24:20 Then the *S* of God came upon
36:22 the LORD stirred up the *s* of
Ezra 1: 1 the LORD stirred up the *s* of
Neh 9:20 You also gave Your good *S* to
9:30 against them by Your *S* in Your
Job 4:15 Then a *s* passed before my face;
6: 4 My *s* drinks in their poison;
7:11 speak in the anguish of my *s*;
10:12 Your care has preserved my *s*.
15:13 That you turn your *s* against
17: 1 My *s* is broken, My days are
20: 3 And the *s* of my understanding
26: 4 And whose *s* came from you?
26:13 By His *S* He adorned the
32: 8 But there is a *s* in man,
32:18 The *s* within me compels me.
33: 4 The *S* of God has made me,
34:14 should gather to Himself His *S*
Ps 31: 5 Into Your hand I commit my *s*;
32: 2 And in whose *s* there is no
34:18 saves such as have a contrite *s*.
51:10 And renew a steadfast *s* within
51:11 And do not take Your Holy *S*
51:12 uphold me by Your generous *S*.
51:17 of God are a broken *s*,
76:12 He shall cut off the *s* of
77: 3 and my *s* was overwhelmed. Selah
77: 6 And my *s* makes diligent
78: 8 And whose *s* was not faithful
104:30 You send forth Your *S*,
106:33 they rebelled against His *S*,
139: 7 Where can I go from Your *S*?
142: 3 When my *s* was overwhelmed
143: 4 Therefore my *s* is overwhelmed
143: 7 My *s* fails! Do not hide Your
143:10 Your *S* is good. Lead me in
146: 4 His *s* departs, he returns to
Prov 1:23 Surely I will pour out my *s* on
11:13 But he who is of a faithful *s*
15: 4 perverseness in it breaks the *s*.
15:13 of the heart the *s* is broken.
16:18 And a haughty *s* before a fall.
16:19 Better to be of a humble *s*
16:32 And he who rules his *s* than he
17:22 But a broken *s* dries the
17:27 of understanding is of a calm *s*.
18:14 The *s* of a man will sustain him
18:14 But who can bear a broken *s*?
20:27 The *s* of a man is the lamp of
25:28 has no rule over his own *s*
29:23 But the humble in *s* will
Eccl 3:21 Who knows the *s* of the sons of
3:21 and the *s* of the animal, which
7: 8 The patient in *s* is better
7: 8 is better than the proud in *s*.
7: 9 Do not hasten in your *s* to be
8: 8 No one has power over the *s* to
8: 8 over the spirit to retain the *s*,
10: 4 If the *s* of the ruler rises
12: 7 And the *s* will return to God
Isa 4: 4 by the *s* of judgment and by the
4: 4 of judgment and by the *s* of
11: 2 The *S* of the LORD shall rest
11: 2 The *S* of wisdom and
11: 2 The *S* of counsel and might,
11: 2 The *S* of knowledge and of the
19: 3 The *s* of Egypt will fail in its
19:14 LORD has mingled a perverse *s*
26: 9 by my *s* within me I will seek
28: 6 For a *s* of justice to him who
29:10 has poured out on you The *s*
29:24 These also who erred in *s* will
30: 1 devise plans, but not of My *S*,
31: 3 horses are flesh, and not *s*.
32:15 Until the *S* is poured upon us
34:16 and His *S* has gathered them.
37: 7 Surely I will send a *s* upon him,
38:16 things is the life of my *s*;
40:13 Who has directed the *S* of the
42: 1 soul delights! I have put My *S*
42: 5 And *s* to those who walk on it:
44: 3 I will pour My *S* on your
48:16 now the Lord GOD and His *S*
54: 6 woman forsaken and grieved in *s*,
57:15 has a contrite and humble *s*,
57:15 To revive the *s* of the humble,
57:16 For the *s* would fail before
59:19 The *S* of the LORD will lift
59:21 My *S* who is upon you, and My
61: 1 The *S* of the Lord GOD is upon
61: 3 garment of praise for the *s* of
63:10 rebelled and grieved His Holy *S*;
63:11 is He who put His Holy *S*
63:14 And the *S* of the LORD causes
65:14 And wail for grief of *s*.
66: 2 is poor and of a contrite *s*,

Jer 51:11 The LORD has raised up the *s*
Ezek 1:12 they went wherever the *s* wanted
1:20 Wherever the *s* wanted to go,
1:20 because there the *s* went;
1:20 for the *s* of the living
1:21 for the *s* of the living
2: 2 Then the *S* entered me when He
3:12 Then the *S* lifted me up, and I
3:14 So the *S* lifted me up and took
3:14 bitterness, in the heat of my *s*;
3:24 Then the *S* entered me and set me
8: 3 and the *S* lifted me up between
10:17 for the *s* of the living
11: 1 Then the *S* lifted me up and
11: 5 Then the *S* of the LORD fell
11:19 and I will put a new *s* within
11:24 Then the *S* took me up and
11:24 me in a vision by the *S* of God
13: 3 who follow their own *s* and have
18:31 a new heart and a new *s*.
21: 7 every *s* will faint, and all
36:26 you a new heart and put a new *s*
36:27 I will put My *S* within you and
37: 1 me and brought me out in the *S*
37:14 I will put My *S* in you, and you
39:29 I shall have poured out My *S*
43: 5 The *S* lifted me up and brought
Dan 2: 1 and his *s* was so troubled that
2: 3 and my *s* is anxious to know the
4: 8 in him is the *S* of the Holy
4: 9 because I know that the *S* of
4:18 for the *S* of the Holy God is
5:11 your kingdom in whom is the *S*
5:12 "Inasmuch as an excellent *s*,
5:14 that the *S* of God is in you,
5:20 and his *s* was hardened in
6: 3 because an excellent *s* was in
7:15 was grieved in my *s* within my
Hos 4:12 For the *s* of harlotry has
5: 4 For the *s* of harlotry is in
Joel 2:28 That I will pour out My *S* on
2:29 I will pour out My *S* in those
Mic 2: 7 Is the *S* of the LORD
2:11 a man should walk in a false *s*
3: 8 I am full of power by the *S* of
Hag 1:14 So the LORD stirred up the *s* of
1:14 and the *s* of Joshua the son of
1:14 and the *s* of all the remnant of
2: 5 so My *S* remains among you;
Zech 4: 6 might nor by power, but by My *S*,
6: 8 have given rest to My *S* in the
7:12 of hosts had sent by His *S*
12: 1 and forms the *s* of man within
12:10 inhabitants of Jerusalem the *S*
13: 2 the prophets and the unclean *s*
Mal 2:15 Having a remnant of the *S*?
2:15 Therefore take heed to your *s*,
2:16 take heed to your *s*,
Mt 1:18 found with child of the Holy *S*.
1:20 in her is of the Holy *S*.
3:11 baptize you with the Holy *S*
3:16 and He saw the *S* of God
4: 1 Then Jesus was led up by the *S*
5: 3 "Blessed are the poor in *s*,
10:20 but the *S* of your Father who
12:18 I will put My *S* upon
12:28 if I cast out demons by the *S*
12:31 the blasphemy against the *S*
12:32 speaks against the Holy *S*,
12:43 When an unclean *s* goes out of a
22:43 How then does David in the *S*
26:41 The *s* indeed is willing, but
27:50 voice, and yielded up His *s*.
28:19 of the Son and of the Holy *S*,
Mk 1: 8 baptize you with the Holy *S*.
1:10 the heavens parting and the *S*
1:12 Immediately the *S* drove Him
1:23 synagogue with an unclean *s*.
1:26 And when the unclean *s* had
2: 8 when Jesus perceived in His *s*
3:29 blasphemes against the Holy *S*
3:30 said, "He has an unclean *s*.
5: 2 tombs a man with an unclean *s*,
5: 8 out of the man, unclean *s*!"
7:25 young daughter had an unclean *s*
8:12 But He sighed deeply in His *s*,
9:17 You my son, who has a mute *s*.
9:20 immediately the *s* convulsed
9:25 He rebuked the unclean *s*,
9:25 saying to it, "Deaf and dumb *s*,
9:26 Then the *s* cried out,
12:36 himself said by the Holy *S*:
13:11 you who speak, but the Holy *S*.
14:38 The *s* indeed is willing, but
Lk 1:15 also be filled with the Holy *S*,
1:17 also go before Him in the *s*
1:35 The Holy *S* will come upon you,
1:41 was filled with the Holy *S*.
1:47 And my *s* has rejoiced in God my
1:67 was filled with the Holy *S*,
1:80 grew and became strong in *s*,
2:25 and the Holy *S* was upon him.
2:26 revealed to him by the Holy *S*
2:27 So he came by the *S* into the
2:40 grew and became strong in *s*,
3:16 baptize you with the Holy *S*
3:22 And the Holy *S* descended in
4: 1 being filled with the Holy *S*,
4: 1 the Jordan and was led by the *S*
4:14 returned in the power of the *S*
4:18 The *S* of the LORD is upon
4:33 there was a man who had a *s* of
8:29 He had commanded the unclean *s*
8:55 Then her *s* returned, and she
9:39 a *s* seizes him, and he suddenly
9:42 Jesus rebuked the unclean *s*,
9:55 do not know what manner of *s*
10:21 hour Jesus rejoiced in the *S*
11:13 Father give the Holy *S* to
11:24 When an unclean *s* goes out of a
12:10 blasphemes against the Holy *S*,
12:12 For the Holy *S* will teach you in
13:11 there was a woman who had a *s*
23:46 Your hands I commit My *s*.
24:37 and supposed they had seen a *s*.
24:39 for a *s* does not have flesh and
Jn 1:32 I saw the *S* descending from
1:33 Upon whom you see the *S*
1:33 He who baptizes with the Holy *S*.
3: 5 one is born of water and the *S*,
3: 6 that which is born of the *S* is
3: 6 is born of the Spirit is *s*.
3: 8 everyone who is born of the *S*.
3:34 for God does not give the *S* by
4:23 will worship the Father in *s*
4:24 'God is *S*, and those who
4:24 worship Him must worship in *s*
6:63 'It is the *S* who gives life;
6:63 words that I speak to you are *s*,
7:39 this He spoke concerning the *S*,
7:39 for the Holy *S* was not yet
11:33 He groaned in the *s* and was
13:21 things, He was troubled in *s*,
14:17 the *S* of truth, whom the world
14:26 "But the Helper, the Holy *S*,
15:26 the *S* of truth who proceeds
16:13 the *S* of truth, has come,
19:30 His head, He gave up His *s*.
20:22 to them, "Receive the Holy *S*.
Acts 1: 2 after He through the Holy *S* had
1: 5 be baptized with the Holy *S*
1: 8 receive power when the Holy *S*
1:16 which the Holy *S* spoke before
2: 4 all filled with the Holy *S* and
2: 4 as the *S* gave them utterance.
2:17 I will pour out of My *S*
2:18 I will pour out My *S*
2:33 the promise of the Holy *S*,
2:38 receive the gift of the Holy *S*.
4: 8 Peter, filled with the Holy *S*,
4:31 were all filled with the Holy *S*,
5: 3 heart to lie to the Holy *S* and
5: 9 agreed together to test the *S*
5:32 and so also is the Holy *S*
6: 3 full of the Holy *S* and wisdom,
6: 5 full of faith and the Holy *S*,
6:10 to resist the wisdom and the *S*
7:51 You always resist the Holy *S*;
7:55 he, being full of the Holy *S*,
7:59 "Lord Jesus, receive my *s*.
8:15 they might receive the Holy *S*.
8:17 and they received the Holy *S*.
8:18 the apostles' hands the Holy *S*
8:19 hands may receive the Holy *S*.
8:29 Then the *S* said to Philip, "Go
8:39 the *S* of the Lord caught Philip
9:17 and be filled with the Holy *S*.
9:31 in the comfort of the Holy *S*,
10:19 the *S* said to him, "Behold,
10:38 of Nazareth with the Holy *S*
10:44 the Holy *S* fell upon all those
10:45 because the gift of the Holy *S*
10:47 who have received the Holy *S*
11:12 Then the *S* told me to go with
11:15 the Holy *S* fell upon them, as
11:16 be baptized with the Holy *S*.
11:24 full of the Holy *S* and of
11:28 stood up and showed by the *S*
13: 2 the Holy *S* said, "Now separate
13: 4 being sent out by the Holy *S*,
13: 9 Paul, filled with the Holy *S*,
13:52 with joy and with the Holy *S*.
15: 8 them by giving them the Holy *S*,
15:28 it seemed good to the Holy *S*,
16: 6 were forbidden by the Holy *S*
16: 7 but the *S* did not permit them.
16:16 slave girl possessed with a *s*
16:18 turned and said to the *s*,
17:16 his *s* was provoked within him
18: 5 Paul was compelled by the *S*,
18:25 Lord; and being fervent in *s*,
19: 2 Did you receive the Holy *S* when
19: 2 heard whether there is a Holy *S*.
19: 6 the Holy *S* came upon them, and
19:15 And the evil *s* answered and
19:16 the man in whom the evil *s* was
19:21 Paul purposed in the *S*,
20:22 now I go bound in the *s* to
20:23 except that the Holy *S* testifies
20:28 among which the Holy *S* has made
21: 4 They told Paul through the *S*
21:11 said, "Thus says the Holy *S*,
23: 8 resurrection—and no angel or *s*;
23: 9 but if a *s* or an angel has
28:25 The Holy *S* spoke rightly through
Rom 1: 4 with power according to the *S*
1: 9 whom I serve with my *s* in the
2:29 that of the heart, in the *S*,
5: 5 out in our hearts by the Holy *S*
7: 6 serve in the newness of the *S*
8: 1 flesh, but according to the *S*.
8: 2 For the law of the *S* of life in
8: 4 flesh but according to the *S*.
8: 5 who live according to the *S*,
8: 5 the Spirit, the things of the *S*.
8: 9 not in the flesh but in the *S*,
8: 9 if indeed the *S* of God dwells
8: 9 if anyone does not have the *S*
8:10 but the *S* is life because of
8:11 But if the *S* of Him who raised
8:11 mortal bodies through His *S*
8:13 but if by the *S* you put to
8:14 as many as are led by the *S* of
8:15 For you did not receive the *s* of
8:15 but you received the *S* of
8:16 The *S* Himself bears witness with
8:16 bears witness with our *s* that
8:23 have the firstfruits of the *S*,
8:26 Likewise the *S* also helps in our
8:26 but the *S* Himself makes
8:27 knows what the mind of the *S*
9: 1 me witness in the Holy *S*,
11: 8 God has given them a *s* of
12:11 in diligence, fervent in *s*,
14:17 and peace and joy in the Holy *S*.
15:13 hope by the power of the Holy *S*.
15:16 sanctified by the Holy *S*.
15:19 by the power of the *S* of God,
15:30 and through the love of the *S*,
1 Cor 2: 4 but in demonstration of the *S*
2:10 them to us through His *S*.
2:10 For the *S* searches all things,
2:11 things of a man except the *s*
2:11 the things of God except the *S*
2:12 not the *s* of the world, but the
2:12 but the *S* who is from God, that
2:13 teaches but which the Holy *S*
2:14 receive the things of the *S* of
3:16 temple of God and that the *S*
4:21 or in love and a *s* of
5: 3 absent in body but present in *s*,
5: 4 together, along with my *s*,
5: 5 that his *s* may be saved in the
6:11 of the Lord Jesus and by the *S*
6:17 is joined to the Lord is one *s*
6:19 is the temple of the Holy *S*
6:20 God in your body and in your *s*,
7:34 be holy both in body and in *s*.
7:40 and I think I also have the *S* of
12: 3 that no one speaking by the *S*
12: 3 is Lord except by the Holy *S*.
12: 4 of gifts, but the same *S*.
12: 7 But the manifestation of the *S*
12: 8 word of wisdom through the *S*,
12: 8 of knowledge through the same *S*,
12: 9 to another faith by the same *S*,
12: 9 gifts of healings by the same *S*,
12:11 But one and the same *S* works all
12:13 For by one *S* we were all
12:13 been made to drink into one *S*.
14: 2 in the *s* he speaks mysteries.
14:14 my *s* prays, but my
14:15 I will pray with the *s*,
14:15 I will sing with the *s*,
14:16 if you bless with the *s*,
15:45 Adam became a life-giving *s*.
16:18 For they refreshed my *s* and
2 Cor 1:22 sealed us and given us the *S*
2:13 I had no rest in my *s*,
3: 3 not with ink but by the *S* of
3: 6 not of the letter but of the *S*;
3: 6 but the *S* gives life.
3: 8 how will the ministry of the *S*
3:17 Now the Lord is the *S*;
3:17 and where the *S* of the Lord
3:18 just as by the *S* of the Lord.
4:13 And since we have the same *s* of
5: 5 who also has given us the *S* as
6: 6 by kindness, by the Holy *S*,
7: 1 filthiness of the flesh and *s*,
7:13 because his *s* has been
11: 4 if you receive a different *s*
12:18 Did we not walk in the same *s*?
13:14 and the communion of the Holy *S*
Gal 3: 2 Did you receive the *S* by the
3: 3 Having begun in the *S*,
3: 5 He who supplies the *S* to you
3:14 receive the promise of the *S*
4: 6 God has sent forth the *S* of His
4:29 was born according to the *S*,
5: 5 For we through the *S* eagerly
5:16 I say then: Walk in the *S*,
5:17 the flesh lusts against the *S*,
5:17 and the *S* against the flesh;
5:18 But if you are led by the *S*,
5:22 But the fruit of the *S* is love,
5:25 If we live in the *S*,
5:25 let us also walk in the *S*.
6: 1 restore such a one in a *s* of
6: 8 but he who sows to the *S* will
6: 8 to the Spirit will of the *S*
6:18 Jesus Christ be with your *s*.
Eph 1:13 were sealed with the Holy *S* of
1:17 may give to you the *s* of wisdom
2: 2 the *s* who now works in the sons
2:18 we both have access by one *S*
2:22 dwelling place of God in the *S*.
3: 5 has now been revealed by the *S*
3:16 with might through His *S* in
4: 3 to keep the unity of the *S* in
4: 4 There is one body and one *S*,
4:23 and be renewed in the *s* of your
4:30 And do not grieve the Holy *S* of
5: 9 (for the fruit of the *S* is in
5:18 but be filled with the *S*,
6:17 and the sword of the *S*,

6:18 and supplication in the *S*,
Phil 1:19 prayer and the supply of the *S*
1:27 that you stand fast in one *s*,
2: 1 if any fellowship of the *S*,
3: 3 who worship God in the *S*,
Col 1: 8 to us your love in the *S*.
2: 5 flesh, yet I am with you in *s*,
1 Th 1: 5 and in the Holy *S* and in much
1: 6 with joy of the Holy *S*,
4: 8 has also given us His Holy *S*.
5:19 Do not quench the *S*.
5:23 and may your whole *s*,
2 Th 2: 2 either by *s* or by word or by
2:13 sanctification by the *S* and
1 Tim 3:16 the flesh, Justified in the *S*,
4: 1 Now the *S* expressly says that in
4:12 word, in conduct, in love, in *s*,
2 Tim 1: 7 For God has not given us a *s* of
1:14 keep by the Holy *S* who dwells
4:22 Jesus Christ be with your *s*.
Titus 3: 5 and renewing of the Holy *S*,
Phm 1:25 Jesus Christ be with your *s*.
Heb 2: 4 and gifts of the Holy *S*,
3: 7 as the Holy *S* says: "Today,
4:12 to the division of soul and *s*,
6: 4 become partakers of the Holy *S*,
9: 8 the Holy *S* indicating this, that
9:14 who through the eternal *S*
10:15 But the Holy *S* also witnesses to
10:29 and insulted the *S* of grace?
Jas 2:26 For as the body without the *s* is
4: 5 The *S* who dwells in us yearns
1 Pe 1: 2 in sanctification of the *S*,
1:11 the *S* of Christ who was in them
1:12 the gospel to you by the Holy *S*
1:22 the truth through the *S* in
3: 4 beauty of a gentle and quiet *s*,
3:18 flesh but made alive by the *S*,
4: 6 live according to God in the *s*.
4:14 for the *S* of glory and of God
2 Pe 1:21 they were moved by the Holy *S*.
1 Jn 3:24 by the *S* whom He has given us.
4: 1 Beloved, do not believe every *s*,
4: 2 By this you know the *S* of God:
4: 2 Every *s* that confesses that
4: 3 and every *s* that does not
4: 3 And this is the *s* of the
4: 6 By this we know the *s* of truth
4: 6 the spirit of truth and the *s*
4:13 He has given us of His *S*.
5: 6 And it is the *S* who bears
5: 6 because the *S* is truth.
5: 7 the Word, and the Holy *S*;
5: 8 bear witness on earth: the *S*,
Jude 19 divisions, not having the *S*.
20 faith, praying in the Holy *S*,
Rev 1:10 I was in the *S* on the Lord's
2: 7 let him hear what the *S* says to
2:11 let him hear what the *S* says to
2:17 let him hear what the *S* says to
2:29 let him hear what the *S* says to
3: 6 let him hear what the *S* says to
3:13 let him hear what the *S* says to
3:22 let him hear what the *S* says to
4: 2 Immediately I was in the *S*;
14:13 'Yes," says the *S*,
17: 3 So he carried me away in the *S*
18: 2 a prison for every foul *s*,
19:10 testimony of Jesus is the *s* of
21:10 he carried me away in the *S* to
22:17 And the *S* and the bride say,

SPIRITIST (1/1)

Deut 18:11 spells, or a medium, or a *s*,

SPIRITISTS (5/5)

1 Sam 28: 3 had put the mediums and the *s*
28: 9 cut off the mediums and the *s*
2 Ki 21: 6 and consulted *s* and mediums.
23:24 who consulted mediums and *s*,
2 Chr 33: 6 and consulted mediums and *s*.

SPIRITS (41/41) SPIRIT

Lev 19:31 to mediums and familiar *s*;
20: 6 turns to mediums and familiar *s*,
20:27 a medium, or who has familiar *s*,
Num 16:22 the God of the *s* of all flesh,
27:16 the God of the *s* of all flesh,
Ezra 1: 5 with all whose *s* God had moved,
Ps 104: 4 Who makes His angels *s*,
Prov 16: 2 But the LORD weighs the *s*.
Zech 6: 5 These are four *s* of heaven, who
Mt 8:16 And He cast out the *s* with a
10: 1 gave them power over unclean *s*,
12:45 takes with him seven other *s*
Mk 1:27 He commands even the unclean *s*,
3:11 And the unclean *s*,
5:13 Then the unclean *s* went out and
6: 7 gave them power over unclean *s*.
Lk 4:36 power He commands the unclean *s*,
6:18 were tormented with unclean *s*.
7:21 afflictions, and evil *s*;
8: 2 who had been healed of evil *s*
10:20 that the *s* are subject to you,
11:26 takes with him seven other *s*
Acts 5:16 who were tormented by unclean *s*,
8: 7 For unclean *s*, crying with a
19:12 left them and the evil *s* went
19:13 Jesus over those who had evil *s*,
1 Cor 12:10 to another discerning of *s*,
14:32 And the *s* of the prophets are
1 Tim 4: 1 giving heed to deceiving *s* and
Heb 1: 7 Who makes His angels *s* And
1:14 Are they not all ministering *s*
12: 9 subjection to the Father of *s*
12:23 to the *s* of just men made
1 Pe 3:19 He went and preached to the *s*
1 Jn 4: 1 every spirit, but test the *s*,
Rev 1: 4 and from the seven *S* who are
3: 1 says He who has the seven *S* of
4: 5 which are the seven *S* of God.
5: 6 which are the seven *S* of God
16:13 And I saw three unclean *s* like
16:14 For they are *s* of demons,

SPIRITUAL (28/23) SPIRITUALLY

Hos 9: 7 The *s* man is insane,
Rom 1:11 that I may impart to you some *s*
7:14 For we know that the law is *s*,
15:27 have been partakers of their *s*
1 Cor 2:13 comparing *s* things with
2:13 spiritual things with *s*.
2:15 But he who is *s* judges all
3: 1 could not speak to you as to *s*
9:11 If we have sown *s* things for
10: 3 all ate the same *s* food,
10: 4 and all drank the same *s* drink.
10: 4 For they drank of that *s* Rock
12: 1 Now concerning *s* gifts,
14: 1 and desire *s* gifts, but
14:12 since you are zealous for *s*
14:37 himself to be a prophet or *s*,
15:44 it is raised a *s* body. There is
15:44 and there is a *s* body.
15:46 the *s* is not first, but the
15:46 natural, and afterward the *s*.
Gal 6: 1 you who are *s* restore such a
Eph 1: 3 who has blessed us with every *s*
5:19 in psalms and hymns and *s*
6:12 against *s* hosts of wickedness
Col 1: 9 of His will in all wisdom and *s*
3:16 in psalms and hymns and *s*
1 Pe 2: 5 are being built up a *s* house,
2: 5 to offer up *s* sacrifices

SPIRITUALLY (3/3) SPIRITUAL

Rom 8: 6 but to be *s* minded is life and
1 Cor 2:14 because they are *s* discerned.
Rev 11: 8 of the great city which *s* is

SPIT (9/9) SPAT, SPITS, SPITTING

Num 12:14 If her father had but *s* in her
Deut 25: 9 *s* in his face, and answer and
Job 17: 6 become one in whose face men *s*.
30:10 They do not hesitate to *s* in
Jer 51:34 He has *s* me out.
Mk 8:23 And when He had *s* on his eyes
10:34 and scourge Him, and *s* on Him,
14:65 Then some began to *s* on Him,
Lk 18:32 mocked and insulted and *s* upon.

SPITE (3/3) SPITEFULLY

Ezra 10: 2 there is hope in Israel in *s*
Neh 5:18 Yet in *s* of this I did not
Ps 78:32 In *s* of this they still sinned,

SPITEFUL (3/3)

Prov 17: 4 listens eagerly to a *s* tongue.
Ezek 25:15 took vengeance with a *s* heart,
36: 5 whole-hearted joy and *s* minds,

SPITEFULLY (4/4) SPITE

Mt 5:44 and pray for those who *s* use
22: 6 his servants, treated them *s*,
Lk 6:28 and pray for those who *s* use
1 Th 2: 2 and were *s* treated at Philippi,

SPITS (1/1)

Lev 15: 8 If he who has the discharge *s* on

SPITTING (1/1)

Isa 50: 6 hide My face from shame and *s*.

SPLENDID (1/1)

Rev 18:14 the things which are rich and *s*

SPLENDIDLY (1/1)

Ezek 38: 4 all *s* clothed, a great company

SPLENDOR (13/13)

Esth 1: 4 his glorious kingdom and the *s*
Job 37:22 from the north as golden *s*;
40:10 yourself with majesty and *s*,
Ps 37:20 Like the *s* of the meadows,
145: 5 meditate on the glorious *s* of
Prov 20:29 And the *s* of old men is their
Lam 1: 6 the daughter of Zion All her *s*
Ezek 16:14 it was perfect through My *s*
27:10 They gave *s* to you.
28: 7 your wisdom, And defile your *s*.
28:17 wisdom for the sake of your *s*;
Dan 2:31 whose *s* was excellent, stood
4:36 my honor and *s* returned to me.

SPLINT (1/1)

Ezek 30:21 nor a *s* put on to bind it,

SPLINTERED (1/1)

Ps 105:33 And *s* the trees of their

SPLINTERS (1/1)

Ps 29: 5 the LORD *s* the cedars of

SPLIT (17/17)

Gen 22: 3 and he *s* the wood for the burnt
Lev 1:17 Then he shall *s* it at its wings,
Num 16:31 that the ground *s* apart under
Deut 14: 6 having the hoof *s* into two
Judg 5:26 She *s* and struck through his
15:19 So God *s* the hollow place that
1 Sam 6:14 So they *s* the wood of the cart
1 Ki 1:40 so that the earth seemed to *s*
13: 3 Surely the altar shall *s* apart,
13: 5 The altar also was *s* apart, and
Ps 78:15 He *s* the rocks in the
Isa 24:19 The earth is *s* open,
48:21 He also *s* the rock, and the
Ezek 30:16 No shall be *s* open, And Noph
Mic 1: 4 And the valleys will *s* Like
Zech 14: 4 the Mount of Olives shall be *s*
Mt 27:51 quaked, and the rocks were *s*,

SPLITS (1/1)

Eccl 10: 9 And he who *s* wood may be

SPOIL (57/53) SPOILS

Gen 49:27 at night he shall divide the *s*.
Ex 15: 9 overtake, I will divide the *s*;
Num 31: 9 and took as *s* all their cattle,
31:11 And they took all the *s* and all
31:12 and the *s* to Moses, to Eleazar
31:53 (The men of war had taken *s*,
Deut 2:35 with the *s* of the cities which
3: 7 all the livestock and the *s* of
20:14 that is in the city, all its *s*,
Josh 8: 2 Only its *s* and its cattle you
8:27 Only the livestock and the *s* of
11:14 And all the *s* of these cities
22: 8 Divide the *s* of your enemies
Judg 5:30 not finding and dividing the *s*:
1 Sam 14:30 eaten freely today of the *s* of
14:32 And the people rushed on the *s*,
15:19 Why did you swoop down on the *s*,
30:16 because of all the great *s*
30:19 *s* or anything which they had
30:20 and said, "This is David's *s*.
30:22 not give them any of the *s*
30:26 he sent some of the *s* to the
30:26 is a present for you from the *s*
2 Sam 3:22 from a raid and brought much *s*
8:12 and from the *s* of Hadadezer the
12:30 Also he brought out the *s* of
2 Ki 3:23 therefore, Moab, to the *s*!"
1 Chr 20: 2 Also he brought out the *s* of
2 Chr 14:13 they carried away very much *s*.
14:14 there was exceedingly much *s*
15:11 thousand sheep from the *s* they
20:25 came to take away their *s*,
20:25 were three days gathering the *s*
24:23 and sent all their *s* to the
25:13 in them, and took much *s*.
28: 8 and they also took away much *s*
28: 8 and brought the *s* to Samaria.
28:14 men left the captives and the *s*
28:15 and from the *s* they clothed all
Job 30:22 You *s* my success.
Ps 44:10 those who hate us have taken *s*
68:12 remains at home divides the *s*.
Prov 1:13 shall fill our houses with *s*;
16:19 Than to divide the *s* with the
Song 2:15 The little foxes that *s* the
Isa 8: 4 riches of Damascus and the *s*
9: 3 rejoice when they divide the *s*.
10: 6 him charge, To seize the *s*,
53:12 And He shall divide the *s* with
Ezek 7:21 to the wicked of the earth as *s*;
29:19 her wealth, carry off her *s*,
Dan 11:24 among them the plunder, *s*,
Hos 7: 1 A band of robbers takes *s*
Nah 2: 9 Take *s* of silver! Take spoil
2: 9 Take spoil of silver! Take *s*
Zech 2: 9 and they shall become *s* for
14: 1 And your *s* will be divided in

SPOILER (2/2)

Isa 16: 4 to them from the face of the *s*.
54:16 And I have created the *s* to

SPOILS (5/5) SPOIL

Josh 7:21 When I saw among the *s* a
Judg 5:19 They took no *s* of silver.
1 Chr 26:27 Some of the *s* won in battles
Lk 11:22 he trusted, and divides his *s*.
Heb 7: 4 Abraham gave a tenth of the *s*.

S

SPOKE (554/548) SPEAK

Gen 8:15 Then God *s* to Noah, saying,
9: 8 Then God *s* to Noah and to his
16:13 the name of the LORD who *s* to
18:29 And he *s* to Him yet again and
19:14 So Lot went out and *s* to his
21:22 *s* to Abraham, saying, "God is
22: 7 But Isaac *s* to Abraham his
23: 3 and *s* to the sons of Heth,
23: 8 And he *s* with them, saying, "If
23:13 and he *s* to Ephron in the
24: 7 and who *s* to me and swore to
24:30 Thus the man *s* to me," that he
27: 5 was listening when Isaac *s* to
27: 6 So Rebekah *s* to Jacob her son,
31:11 Then the Angel of God *s* to me in
31:29 but the God of your father *s* to
34: 3 he loved the young woman and *s*
34: 4 So Shechem *s* to his father
34: 8 But Hamor *s* with them, saying,
34:13 and *s* deceitfully, because he
34:20 and *s* with the men of their
35:15 name of the place where God *s*
39:10 as she *s* to Joseph day by day,
39:14 to the men of her house and *s*
39:17 Then she *s* to him with words
39:19 the words which his wife *s* to
41: 9 Then the chief butler *s* to
42: 7 as a stranger to them and *s*
42:14 It is as I *s* to you, saying,
42:23 for he *s* to them through an
42:30 man who is lord of the land *s*
42:37 Then Reuben *s* to his father,
43: 3 But Judah *s* to him, saying,
43:27 well, the old man of whom you *s*?
43:29 younger brother of whom you *s*
44: 6 and he *s* to them these same
46: 2 Then God *s* to Israel in the
47: 5 Then Pharaoh *s* to Joseph,
49:28 this is what their father *s*
50: 4 Joseph *s* to the household of
50:17 And Joseph wept when they *s*
50:21 And he comforted them and *s*
Ex 1:15 Then the king of Egypt *s* to the
4:30 And Aaron *s* all the words which
5:10 their officers went out and *s*
6: 2 And God *s* to Moses and said to
6: 9 So Moses *s* thus to the children
6:10 And the LORD *s* to Moses,
6:12 And Moses *s* before the LORD,
6:13 Then the LORD *s* to Moses and
6:27 These are the ones who *s* to
6:28 on the day the LORD *s* to Moses
6:29 that the LORD *s* to Moses,
7: 7 years old when they *s* to
7: 8 Then the LORD *s* to Moses and
7:19 Then the LORD *s* to Moses,
8: 1 And the LORD *s* to Moses, "Go
8: 5 Then the LORD *s* to Moses,
12: 1 Now the LORD *s* to Moses and
13: 1 Then the LORD *s* to Moses,
14: 1 Now the LORD *s* to Moses,
15: 1 this song to the LORD, and *s*,
16: 9 Then Moses *s* to Aaron, "Say to
16:10 as Aaron *s* to the whole
16:11 And the LORD *s* to Moses,
19:19 louder and louder, Moses *s*,
19:25 went down to the people and *s*
20: 1 And God *s* all these words,
25: 1 Then the LORD *s* to Moses,
30:11 Then the LORD *s* to Moses,
30:17 Then the LORD *s* to Moses,
30:22 Moreover the LORD *s* to Moses,
31: 1 Then the LORD *s* to Moses,
31:12 And the LORD *s* to Moses,
33:11 So the LORD *s* to Moses face to
35: 4 And Moses *s* to all the
36: 5 and they *s* to Moses, saying,
40: 1 Then the LORD *s* to Moses,
Lev 1: 1 and *s* to him from the
4: 1 Now the LORD *s* to Moses,
5:14 Then the LORD *s* to Moses,
6: 1 And the LORD *s* to Moses,
6: 8 Then the LORD *s* to Moses,
6:19 And the LORD *s* to Moses,
6:24 And the LORD *s* to Moses,
7:22 And the LORD *s* to Moses,
7:28 Then the LORD *s* to Moses,
8: 1 And the LORD *s* to Moses,
10: 3 "This is what the LORD *s*,
10: 8 Then the LORD *s* to Aaron,
10:12 And Moses *s* to Aaron, and to
11: 1 Now the LORD *s* to Moses and
12: 1 Then the LORD *s* to Moses,
13: 1 And the LORD *s* to Moses and
14: 1 Then the LORD *s* to Moses,
14:33 And the LORD *s* to Moses and
15: 1 And the LORD *s* to Moses and
16: 1 Now the LORD *s* to Moses after
17: 1 And the LORD *s* to Moses,
18: 1 Then the LORD *s* to Moses,
19: 1 And the LORD *s* to Moses,
20: 1 Then the LORD *s* to Moses,
21:16 And the LORD *s* to Moses,
22: 1 Then the LORD *s* to Moses,
22:17 And the LORD *s* to Moses,
22:26 And the LORD *s* to Moses,
23: 1 And the LORD *s* to Moses,
23: 9 And the LORD *s* to Moses,
23:23 Then the LORD *s* to Moses,
23:26 And the LORD *s* to Moses,
23:33 Then the LORD *s* to Moses,
24: 1 Then the LORD *s* to Moses,
24:13 And the LORD *s* to Moses,
24:23 Then Moses *s* to the children of
25: 1 And the LORD *s* to Moses on
27: 1 Now the LORD *s* to Moses,
Num 1: 1 Now the LORD *s* to Moses in the
2: 1 And the LORD *s* to Moses and
3: 1 and Moses when the LORD *s*
3: 5 And the LORD *s* to Moses,
3:11 Then the LORD *s* to Moses,
3:14 Then the LORD *s* to Moses in
3:44 Then the LORD *s* to Moses,
4: 1 Then the LORD *s* to Moses and
4:17 Then the LORD *s* to Moses and
4:21 Then the LORD *s* to Moses,
5: 1 And the LORD *s* to Moses,
5: 4 as the LORD *s* to Moses, so the
5: 5 Then the LORD *s* to Moses,
5:11 And the LORD *s* to Moses,
6: 1 Then the LORD *s* to Moses,
6:22 And the LORD *s* to Moses,
7: 4 Then the LORD *s* to Moses,
7:89 thus He *s* to him.
8: 1 And the LORD *s* to Moses,
8: 5 Then the LORD *s* to Moses,
8:23 Then the LORD *s* to Moses,
9: 1 Now the LORD *s* to Moses in the
9: 9 Then the LORD *s* to Moses,
10: 1 And the LORD *s* to Moses,
11:25 and *s* to him, and took of the
12: 1 Then Miriam and Aaron *s* against
13: 1 And the LORD *s* to Moses,
14: 7 and they *s* to all the
14:26 And the LORD *s* to Moses and
15: 1 And the LORD *s* to Moses,
15:17 Again the LORD *s* to Moses,
15:37 Again the LORD *s* to Moses,
16: 5 and he *s* to Korah and all his
16:20 And the LORD *s* to Moses and
16:23 So the LORD *s* to Moses, saying,
16:26 And he *s* to the congregation,
16:36 Then the LORD *s* to Moses,
16:44 And the LORD *s* to Moses,
17: 1 And the LORD *s* to Moses,
17: 6 So Moses *s* to the children of
17:12 So the children of Israel *s* to
18: 8 And the LORD *s* to Aaron:
18:25 Then the LORD *s* to Moses,
19: 1 Now the LORD *s* to Moses and
20: 3 contended with Moses and *s*,
20: 7 Then the LORD *s* to Moses,
20:12 Then the LORD *s* to Moses and
20:23 And the LORD *s* to Moses and
21: 5 And the people *s* against God and
22: 7 and they came to Balaam and *s*
25:10 Then the LORD *s* to Moses,
25:16 Then the LORD *s* to Moses,
26: 1 that the LORD *s* to Moses and
26: 3 Moses and Eleazar the priest *s*
26:52 Then the LORD *s* to Moses,
27: 6 And the LORD *s* to Moses,
27:15 Then Moses *s* to the LORD,
28: 1 Now the LORD *s* to Moses,
30: 1 Then Moses *s* to the heads of the
31: 1 And the LORD *s* to Moses,
31: 3 So Moses *s* to the people,
31:25 Now the LORD *s* to Moses,
32: 2 children of Reuben came and *s*
32:25 and the children of Reuben *s*
33:50 Now the LORD *s* to Moses in the
34: 1 Then the LORD *s* to Moses,
34:16 And the LORD *s* to Moses,
35: 1 And the LORD *s* to Moses in the
35: 9 Then the LORD *s* to Moses,
36: 1 came near and *s* before Moses
Deut 1: 1 are the words which Moses *s*
1: 3 that Moses *s* to the children
1: 6 The LORD our God *s* to us in
1: 9 And I *s* to you at that time,
1:43 So I *s* to you; yet you would not
2: 1 as the LORD *s* to me, and we
2: 2 And the LORD *s* to me, saying:
2:17 that the LORD *s* to me, saying:
4:12 And the LORD *s* to you out of
4:15 saw no form when the LORD *s*
4:45 the judgments which Moses *s* to
5:22 These words the LORD *s* to all
5:28 voice of your words when you *s*
9:13 Furthermore the LORD *s* to me,
13: 2 of which he *s* to you, saying,
27: 9 *s* to all Israel, saying, "Take
31: 1 Then Moses went and *s* these
31:30 Then Moses *s* in the hearing of
32:44 Joshua the son of Nun and *s*
32:48 Then the LORD *s* to Moses that
Josh 1: 1 came to pass that the LORD *s*
1:12 the tribe of Manasseh Joshua *s*,
3: 6 Then Joshua *s* to the priests,
4: 1 that the LORD *s* to Joshua,
4:15 Then the LORD *s* to Joshua,
4:21 Then he *s* to the children of
7: 2 and *s* to them, saying, "Go up
9:11 inhabitants of our country *s*
9:22 and he *s* to them, saying, "Why
10:12 Then Joshua *s* to the LORD in
14:10 ever since the LORD *s* this
14:12 mountain of which the LORD *s*
17:14 Then the children of Joseph *s*
17:17 And Joshua *s* to the house of
20: 1 The LORD also *s* to Joshua,
20: 2 of which I *s* to you through
21: 2 And they *s* to them at Shiloh in
22: 8 and *s* to them, saying, "Return
22:15 and they *s* with them, saying,
22:30 and the children of Manasseh *s*,
22:33 they *s* no more of going against
23:14 which the LORD your God *s*
24:27 words of the LORD which He *s*
Judg 2: 4 when the Angel of the LORD *s*
8: 8 up from there to Penuel and *s*
8: 9 So he also *s* to the men of
9: 1 and *s* with them and with all
9: 3 And his mother's brothers *s* all
9:37 So Gaal *s* again and said, "See,
11:11 and Jephthah *s* all his words
13:11 Are You the Man who *s* to this
15:13 So they *s* to him, saying, "No,
19:22 They *s* to the master of the
1 Sam 1:13 Now Hannah *s* in her heart; only
3:17 the word that the LORD *s* to
7: 3 Then Samuel *s* to all the house
9: 9 he *s* thus: "Come, let us go to
9:17 the man of whom I *s* to you.
9:25 Samuel *s* with Saul on the top
17:23 and he *s* according to the same
17:26 Then David *s* to the men who
17:28 oldest brother heard when he *s*
17:31 when the words which David *s*
18:23 So Saul's servants *s* those words
18:24 "In this manner David *s*.
19: 1 Now Saul *s* to Jonathan his son
19: 4 Thus Jonathan *s* well of David
25: 9 they *s* to Nabal according to
25:40 they *s* to her saying, "David
28:12 And the woman *s* to Saul,
28:17 has done for Himself as He *s*
28:21 heeded the words which you *s*
30: 6 for the people *s* of stoning
2 Sam 3:19 And Abner also *s* in the hearing
5: 1 came to David at Hebron and *s*,
5: 6 who *s* to David, saying, "You
7:17 so Nathan *s* to David.
12:18 we *s* to him, and he would not
13:22 And Absalom *s* to his brother
14: 4 And when the woman of Tekoa *s*
17: 6 Absalom *s* to him, saying,
20:18 So she *s*, saying, "They used
21: 2 called the Gibeonites and *s* to
22: 1 Then David *s* to the LORD the
23: 2 The Spirit of the LORD *s* by me,
23: 3 The Rock of Israel *s* to me:
24:17 Then David *s* to the LORD when
1 Ki 1:11 So Nathan *s* to Bathsheba the
2: 4 may fulfill His word which He *s*
2:27 word of the LORD which He *s*
3:22 Thus they *s* before the king.
3:26 woman whose son was living *s*
4:32 He *s* three thousand proverbs,
4:33 Also he *s* of trees, from the
4:33 he *s* also of animals, of birds,
5: 5 as the LORD *s* to my father
6:12 which I *s* to your father David.
8:12 Then Solomon *s*: "The LORD
8:15 who *s* with His mouth to my
8:20 fulfilled His word which He *s*;
8:53 as You *s* by Your servant Moses,
10: 2 she *s* with him about all that
12: 3 assembly of Israel came and *s*
12: 7 And they *s* to him, saying, "If
12:10 who had grown up with him *s* to
12:14 and he *s* to them according to
13:18 and an angel *s* to me by the
13:26 word of the LORD which He *s*
13:27 And he *s* to his sons, saying,
13:31 that he *s* to his sons, saying,
14:18 word of the LORD which He *s*
16:12 which He *s* against Baasha by
17:16 word of the LORD which He *s*
20:28 Then a man of God came and *s* to
21: 2 So Ahab *s* to Naboth, saying,
21: 6 Because I *s* to Naboth the
21:23 Jezebel the LORD also *s*,
22:13 who had gone to call Micaiah *s*
22:20 So one *s* in this manner, and
22:20 and another *s* in that manner.
2 Ki 1: 9 And he *s* to him: "Man of God,
2:22 the word of Elisha which he *s*.
5:13 his servants came near and *s*
7:17 who *s* when the king came down
8: 1 Then Elisha *s* to the woman whose
9:12 Thus and thus he *s* to me,
9:36 which He *s* by His servant
10:10 of the LORD which the LORD *s*
10:10 the LORD has done what He *s*
10:17 word of the LORD which He *s*
15:12 word of the LORD which He *s*
17:26 So they *s* to the king of
18:28 a loud voice in Hebrew, and *s*,
21:10 And the LORD *s* by His servants
22:14 And they *s* with her.
22:19 LORD when you heard what I *s*
25:28 He *s* kindly to him, and gave him
1 Chr 15:16 Then David *s* to the leaders of
17:15 so Nathan *s* to David.
21: 9 And the LORD *s* to Gad, David's
2 Chr 1: 2 And Solomon *s* to all Israel, to
6: 1 Then Solomon *s*: "The LORD
6: 4 with His hands what He *s* with
6:10 fulfilled His word which He *s*,
9: 1 she *s* with him about all that
10: 3 and all Israel came and *s* to
10: 7 And they *s* to him, saying, "If
10:10 who had grown up with him *s* to

10:14 and he *s* to them according to
18:12 who had gone to call Micaiah *s*
18:19 So one *s* in this manner, and
18:19 and another *s* in that manner.
30: 6 and *s* according to the command
32:16 his servants *s* against the
32:19 And they *s* against the God of
32:24 and He *s* to him and gave him a
33:10 And the LORD *s* to Manasseh and
33:18 the words of the seers who *s*
34:22 And they *s* to her to that
36:12 who *s* from the mouth of the
Ezra 5: 3 companions came to them and *s*
5: 9 and *s* thus to them: "Who
10: 2 *s* up and said to Ezra, "We
Neh 4: 2 And he *s* before his brethren and
9:13 And *s* with them from heaven,
13:24 And half of their children *s* the
13:24 but *s* according to the language
Esth 3: 4 when they *s* to him daily and he
4:10 Then Esther *s* to Hathach,
7: 9 who *s* good on the king's
8: 3 Now Esther *s* again to the king,
Job 2:13 and no one *s* a word to him,
3: 2 And Job *s*, and said:
Ps 18: who *s* to the LORD the words of
33: 9 For He *s*, and it was done;
39: 3 Then I *s* with my tongue:
78:19 they *s* against God: They said,
89:19 Then You *s* in a vision to Your
99: 7 He *s* to them in the cloudy
105:31 He *s*, and there came swarms
105:34 He *s*, and locusts came,
106:33 So that he *s* rashly with his
116:10 I believed, therefore I *s*,
Song 2:10 My beloved *s*, and said to me:
5: 6 My heart leaped up when he *s*.
Isa 7:10 Moreover the LORD *s* again to
8: 5 The LORD also *s* to me again,
8:11 For the LORD *s* thus to me with
20: 2 at the same time the LORD *s* by
65:12 you did not answer; When I *s*,
66: 4 When I *s* they did not hear;
Jer 7:13 and I *s* to you, rising up early
20: 8 For when I *s*, I cried out;
22:21 I *s* to you in your prosperity,
25: 2 which Jeremiah the prophet *s* to
26:11 the priests and the prophets *s*
26:12 Then Jeremiah *s* to all the
26:17 of the land rose up and *s* to
26:18 and *s* to all the people of
27:12 I also *s* to Zedekiah king of
27:16 Also I *s* to the priests and to
28: 1 *s* to me in the house of the
28: 5 Then the prophet Jeremiah *s* to
28:11 And Hananiah *s* in the presence
30: 4 are the words that the LORD *s*
31:20 For though I *s* against him,
34: 6 Then Jeremiah the prophet *s* all
36: 2 from the day I *s* to you, from
37: 2 words of the LORD which He *s*
38: 8 out of the king's house and *s*
40:15 Johanan the son of Kareah *s*
43: 2 Kareah, and all the proud men *s*,
44:20 Then Jeremiah *s* to all the
45: 1 that Jeremiah the prophet *s* to
46:13 The word that the LORD *s* to
50: 1 The word that the LORD *s*
51:12 devised and done What He *s*
52:32 And he *s* kindly to him and gave
Ezek 2: 2 Spirit entered me when He *s* to
2: 2 and I heard Him who *s* to me.
3:24 and *s* with me and said to me:
10: 2 Then He *s* to the man clothed
11:25 So I *s* to those in captivity of
24:18 So I *s* to the people in the
Dan 2: 4 Then the Chaldeans *s* to the king
3: 9 They *s* and said to King
3:14 Nebuchadnezzar *s*, saying to
3:19 He *s* and commanded that they
3:24 and he rose in haste and *s*,
3:26 burning fiery furnace and *s*,
3:28 Nebuchadnezzar *s*, saying,
4:19 troubled him. So the king *s*,
4:30 The king *s*, saying, "Is not
5: 7 and the soothsayers. The king *s*,
5:10 the banquet hall. The queen *s*,
5:13 in before the king. The king *s*,
6:12 and *s* concerning the king's
6:16 den of lions. But the king *s*,
6:20 voice to Daniel. The king *s*,
7: 2 Daniel *s*, saying, "I saw in
7:20 had eyes and a mouth which *s*
9: 6 who *s* in Your name to our kings
9:12 which He *s* against us and
10:16 then I opened my mouth and *s*,
10:19 be strong!" So when he *s* to me
Hos 12: 4 And there He *s* to us—
13: 1 When Ephraim *s*, trembling, He
Jon 2:10 So the LORD *s* to the fish, and
Hag 1:13 *s* the LORD's message to the
Zech 1:14 So the angel who *s* with me said
3: 4 Then He answered and *s* to those
4: 4 So I answered and *s* to the angel
6: 8 and *s* to me, saying, "See,
8: 9 Who *s* in the day the
Mal 3:16 those who feared the LORD *s*
Mt 9:18 While He *s* these things to
9:33 demon was cast out, the mute *s*.
12:22 the blind and mute man both *s*
13: 3 Then He *s* many things to them in
13:33 Another parable He *s* to them:
13:34 All these things Jesus *s* to the
14:27 But immediately Jesus *s* to them,
17:13 disciples understood that He *s*
22: 1 And Jesus answered and *s* to them
23: 1 Then Jesus *s* to the multitudes
28:18 And Jesus came and *s* to them,
Mk 4:33 with many such parables He *s*
7:35 and he *s* plainly.
8:32 He *s* this word openly. And Peter
9:18 So I *s* to Your disciples, that
11: 6 And they *s* to them just as Jesus
12:26 how God *s* to him, saying, 'I
14:31 But he *s* more vehemently, "If I
14:39 and *s* the same words.
Lk 1:42 Then she *s* out with a loud voice
1:55 As He *s* to our fathers,
1:64 his tongue loosed, and he *s*,
1:70 As He *s* by the mouth of His
2:38 and *s* of Him to all those who
2:50 the statement which He *s* to
4:36 Then they were all amazed and *s*
5:36 Then He *s* a parable to them:
6:39 And He *s* a parable to them:
7:39 he *s* to himself, saying, "This
8: 4 He *s* by a parable:
9:11 and He received them and *s* to
9:31 who appeared in glory and *s* of
11:14 had gone out, that the mute *s*;
11:27 as He *s* these things, that a
11:37 as He *s*, a certain Pharisee
12:16 Then He *s* a parable to them,
13: 6 He also *s* this parable: "A
14: 3 *s* to the lawyers and Pharisees,
15: 3 So He *s* this parable to them,
18: 1 Then He *s* a parable to them,
18: 9 Also He *s* this parable to some
19:11 He *s* another parable, because
20: 2 and *s* to Him, saying, "Tell us,
21: 5 as some *s* of the temple, how it
21:29 Then He *s* to them a parable:
22:65 things they blasphemously *s*
24: 6 is risen! Remember how He *s* to
24:44 are the words which I *s*
Jn 4:18 in that you *s* truly."
4:50 believed the word that Jesus *s*
6:71 He *s* of Judas Iscariot, the
7:13 no one *s* openly of Him for fear
7:39 But this He *s* concerning the
7:46 No man ever *s* like this Man!"
8:12 Then Jesus *s* to them again,
8:20 These words Jesus *s* in the
8:27 did not understand that He *s*
8:30 As He *s* these words, many
9:29 'We know that God *s* to Moses;
10: 6 the things which He *s* to them.
10:41 but all the things that John *s*
11:13 Jesus *s* of his death, but they
11:56 and *s* among themselves as they
12:36 These things Jesus *s*,
12:38 might be fulfilled, which he *s*:
12:41 when he saw His glory and *s* of
13:22 perplexed about whom He *s*.
13:24 to ask who it was of whom He *s*.
17: 1 Jesus *s* these words, lifted up
18: 9 might be fulfilled which He *s*,
18:16 went out and *s* to her who kept
18:20 'I *s* openly to the world.
18:32 might be fulfilled which He *s*,
21:19 This He *s*, signifying by
Acts 1:16 which the Holy Spirit *s* before
2:31 *s* concerning the resurrection
4: 1 Now as they *s* to the people, the
4:31 and they *s* the word of God with
6:10 and the Spirit by which he *s*.
7: 6 But God *s* in this way: that his
7:38 with the Angel who *s* to him on
8:26 Now an angel of the Lord *s* to
9:29 And he *s* boldly in the name of
10: 7 And when the angel who *s* to him
10:15 And a voice *s* to him again the
11:20 *s* to the Hellenists, preaching
14: 1 and so *s* that a great multitude
16:13 and we sat down and *s* to the
16:32 Then they *s* the word of the Lord
18: 9 Now the Lord *s* to Paul in the
18:25 he *s* and taught accurately the
19: 6 and they *s* with tongues and
19: 8 went into the synagogue and *s*
19: 9 but *s* evil of the Way before
20: 7 *s* to them and continued his
20:38 of all for the words which he *s*,
21:40 he *s* to them in the Hebrew
22: 2 And when they heard that he *s* to
22: 9 hear the voice of Him who *s* to
28:19 But when the Jews *s* against it,
28:25 The Holy Spirit *s* rightly
1 Cor 13:11 I *s* as a child, I understood as
14: 5 I wish you all *s* with tongues,
2 Cor 4:13 believed and therefore I *s*,
7:14 But as we *s* all things to you
Heb 1: 1 times and in various ways *s* in
7:14 of which tribe Moses *s* nothing
12:25 escape who refused Him who *s*
Jas 5:10 who *s* in the name of the Lord,
2 Pe 1:21 but holy men of God *s* as they
Rev 1:12 turned to see the voice that *s*
10: 8 which I heard from heaven *s* to
13:11 had two horns like a lamb and *s*

SPOKEN (286/280) SPEAK

Gen 12: 4 departed as the LORD had *s* to
18:19 bring to Abraham what He has *s*
19:21 this city for which you have *s*.
21: 1 LORD did for Sarah as He had *s*.
21: 2 set time of which God had *s* to
24:51 son's wife, as the LORD has *s*.
28:15 I have done what I have *s* to
41:28 is the thing which I have *s*
44: 2 to the word that Joseph had *s*.
Ex 4:10 before nor since You have *s* to
4:30 words which the LORD had *s* to
9:12 just as the LORD had *s* to
9:35 as the LORD had *s* by Moses.
10:29 You have *s* well. I will never
19: 8 All that the LORD has *s* we will
32:13 all this land that I have *s* of
32:34 the place of which I have *s*
33:17 do this thing that you have *s*;
34:32 all that the LORD had *s* with
Lev 10:11 statutes which the LORD has *s*
Num 1:48 for the LORD had *s* to Moses,
12: 2 Has the LORD indeed *s* only
12: 2 Has He not *s* through us also?"
14:17 be great, just as You have *s*,
14:28 just as you have *s* in My
14:35 I the LORD have *s* this; I will
15:22 which the LORD has *s* to Moses—
21: 7 for we have *s* against the LORD
23: 2 Balak did just as Balaam had *s*,
23:17 to him, "What has the LORD *s*?
23:19 will He not do? Or has He *s*,
Deut 1:21 God of your fathers has *s* to
5:28 this people which they have *s*
5:28 right in all that they have *s*.
6:19 before you, as the LORD has *s*.
9:10 words which the LORD had *s* to
10: 4 which the LORD had *s* to you in
13: 5 because he has *s* in order to
18:17 What they have *s* is good.
18:21 word which the LORD has not *s*?
18:22 thing which the LORD has not *s*;
18:22 the prophet has *s* it
26:19 your God, just as He has *s*.
29:13 just as He has *s* to you,
Josh 4: 8 as the LORD had *s* to Joshua,
4:12 as Moses had *s* to them.
6: 8 when Joshua had *s* to the
21:45 thing which the LORD had *s* to
Ruth 2:13 and have *s* kindly to your
4: 1 relative of whom Boaz had *s*
1 Sam 1:16 my complaint and grief I have *s*
3:12 against Eli all that I have *s*
20:23 matter which you and I have *s*
25:30 to all the good that He has *s*
2 Sam 2:27 God lives, unless you had *s*,
3:18 do it! For the LORD has *s* of
6:22 maidservants of whom you have *s*,
7: 7 have I ever *s* a word to anyone
7:19 and You have also *s* of Your
7:25 the word which You have *s*
7:29 have *s* it, and with Your
14:19 that my lord the king has *s*.
17: 6 Ahithophel has *s* in this manner.
1 Ki 2:23 if Adonijah has not *s* this word
8:24 You have both *s* with Your mouth
8:26 which You have *s* to Your
12: 9 answer this people who have *s*
12:10 to this people who have *s* to
12:15 which the LORD had *s* by Ahijah
13: 3 the sign which the LORD has *s*:
13:11 the words which he had *s* to
14:11 for the LORD has *s*!" '
15:29 of the LORD which He had *s* by
16:34 which He had *s* through Joshua
18:24 and said, "It is well *s*.
21: 4 Naboth the Jezreelite had *s* to
22:28 the LORD has not *s* by me."
22:38 of the LORD which He had *s*.
2 Ki 1:17 of the LORD which Elijah had *s*.
7:18 just as the man of God had *s*
14:25 which He had *s* through His
19:21 the word which the LORD has *s*
20: 9 do the thing which He has *s*:
20:19 of the LORD which you have *s*
24: 2 of the LORD which He had *s* by
1 Chr 17: 6 have I ever *s* a word to any of
17:17 and You have also *s* of Your
17:23 the word which You have *s*
21:19 which he had *s* in the name of
2 Chr 2:15 the wine which my lord has *s*
6:15 You have both *s* with Your mouth
6:17 which You have *s* to Your
10: 9 answer this people who have *s*
10:10 speak to the people who have *s*
10:15 which He had *s* by the hand of
18:27 the LORD has not *s* by me."
Ezra 8:22 because we had *s* to the king,
Neh 2:18 the king's words that he had *s*
Esth 6:10 undone of all that you have *s*.
Job 15:11 And the word *s* gently with
21: 3 may speak, And after I have *s*,
33: 8 Surely you have *s* in my
40: 5 Once I have *s*, but I will not
42: 7 after the LORD had *s* these
42: 7 for you have not *s* of Me what
42: 8 because you have not *s* of Me
Ps 50: 1 Has *s* and called the earth
60: 6 God has *s* in His holiness: "I
62:11 God has *s* once, Twice I have
66:14 uttered And my mouth has *s*
87: 3 Glorious things are *s* of you,
108: 7 God has *s* in His holiness: "I
109: 2 They have *s* against me with a

S

Prov 15:23 And a word *s* in due season,
25:11 A word fitly *s* is like apples
Eccl 9:17 *s* quietly, should be heard
Song 8: 8 In the day when she is *s* for?
Isa 1: 2 O earth! For the LORD has *s*:
1:20 the mouth of the LORD has *s*.
16:13 the word which the LORD has *s*
16:14 But now the LORD has *s*,
21:17 the LORD God of Israel has *s*
22:25 be cut off; for the LORD has *s*.
23: 4 O Sidon; For the sea has *s*,
24: 3 For the LORD has *s* this word.
25: 8 the earth; For the LORD has *s*.
31: 4 For thus the LORD has *s* to me:
37:22 the word which the LORD has *s*
38: 7 do this thing which He has *s*:
38:15 He has both *s* to me, And He
39: 8 of the LORD which you have *s*
40: 5 the mouth of the LORD has *s*.
45:19 I have not *s* in secret, In a
46:11 Indeed I have *s* it; I will
48:15 I, even I, have *s*;
48:16 I have not *s* in secret from
58:14 The mouth of the LORD has *s*.
59: 3 Your lips have *s* lies,
Jer 3: 5 you have *s* and done evil
4:28 be black, Because I have *s*.
9:12 the mouth of the LORD has *s*,
13:15 be proud, For the LORD has *s*.
14:14 nor *s* to them; they prophesy to
18: 8 nation against whom I have *s*
23:21 I have not *s* to them, yet they
23:35 'What has the LORD *s*?'
23:37 'What has the LORD *s*?'
25: 3 and I have *s* to you, rising
26:16 For he has *s* to us in the name
27:13 as the LORD has *s* against the
29:23 and have *s* lying words in My
30: 2 all the words that I have *s* to
32:24 What You have *s* has happened;
33:24 what these people have *s*,
35:14 But although I have *s* to you,
35:17 because I have *s* to them but
36: 2 it all the words that I have *s*
36: 4 of the LORD which He had *s* to
38: 1 the words that Jeremiah had *s*
44:16 for the word that you have *s*
44:25 You and your wives have *s* with
48: 8 destroyed, As the LORD has *s*.
51:62 You have *s* against this place
Ezek 5:13 have *s* it in My zeal, when I
5:15 rebukes. I, the LORD, have *s*.
5:17 I, the LORD, have *s*.'
13: 7 and have you not *s* false
13: 7 LORD says,' but I have not *s*.
13: 8 Because you have *s* nonsense and
17:21 know that I, the LORD, have *s*.
17:24 have *s* and have done it."
21:17 to rest; I, the LORD, have *s*.
21:32 For I the LORD have *s*.
22:14 with you? I, the LORD, have *s*,
22:28 GOD,' when the LORD had not *s*.
23:34 your own breasts; For I have *s*,
24:14 have *s* it; It shall come to
26: 5 midst of the sea, for I have *s*,
26:14 rebuilt, for I the LORD have *s*,
28:10 hand of aliens; For I have *s*,
30:12 aliens. I, the LORD, have *s*.
34:24 I, the LORD, have *s*.
35:12 blasphemies which you have *s*
36: 5 Surely I have *s* in My burning
36: 6 I have *s* in My jealousy and My
36:36 have *s* it, and I will do
37:14 have *s* it and performed it,"
38:17 Are you he of whom I have *s* in
38:19 the fire of My wrath I have *s*:
39: 5 on the open field; for I have *s*,
39: 8 is the day of which I have *s*.
Dan 4:31 Nebuchadnezzar, to you it is *s*:
10:15 When he had *s* such words to me,
Hos 7:13 Yet they have *s* lies against
10: 4 They have *s* words, Swearing
12:10 I have also *s* by the prophets,
Joel 3: 8 far off; For the LORD has *s*.
Am 3: 1 this word that the LORD has *s*
3: 8 The Lord GOD has *s*! Who can
5:14 be with you, As you have *s*.
Ob 12 Nor should you have *s* proudly
18 of Esau," For the LORD has *s*.
Mic 4: 4 of the LORD of hosts has *s*.
6:12 Her inhabitants have *s* lies,
Zech 13: 3 because you have *s* lies in the
Mal 3:13 What have we *s* against You?'
Mt 1:22 might be fulfilled which was *s*
2:15 might be fulfilled which was *s*
2:17 Then was fulfilled what was *s* by
2:23 might be fulfilled which was *s*
3: 3 For this is he who was *s* of by
4:14 might be fulfilled which was *s*
8:17 might be fulfilled which was *s*
12:17 might be fulfilled which was *s*
13:35 might be fulfilled which was *s*
21: 4 might be fulfilled which was *s*
22:31 have you not read what was *s* to
24:15 *s* of by Daniel the prophet,
26:65 He has *s* blasphemy! What further
27: 9 Then was fulfilled what was *s* by
27:35 might be fulfilled which was *s*
Mk 1:42 As soon as He had *s*,
5:36 Jesus heard the word that was *s*,
12:12 for they knew He had *s* the
12:32 You have *s* the truth, for there
13:14 *s* of by Daniel the prophet,
16:19 after the Lord had *s* to them,
Lk 2:33 at those things which were *s*
2:34 and for a sign which will be *s*
12: 3 Therefore whatever you have *s* in
12: 3 and what you have *s* in the ear
18:34 know the things which were *s*.
20:19 for they knew He had *s* this
20:39 You have *s* well."
24:25 all that the prophets have *s*!
Jn 12:29 An angel has *s* to Him."
12:48 the word that I have *s* will
12:49 For I have not *s* on My own
14:25 These things I have *s* to you
15: 3 of the word which I have *s* to
15:11 These things I have *s* to you,
15:22 If I had not come and *s* to them,
16: 1 These things I have *s* to you,
16:25 These things I have *s* to you in
16:33 These things I have *s* to you,
18: 1 When Jesus had *s* these words, He
18:23 If I have *s* evil, bear witness
20:18 and that He had *s* these things
21:19 And when He had *s* this, He said
Acts 1: 9 Now when He had *s* these things,
2:16 But this is what was *s* by the
3:21 which God has *s* by the mouth of
3:24 who follow, as many as have *s*,
8: 6 one accord heeded the things *s*
8:24 of the things which you have *s*
9:27 and that He had *s* to him, and
13:34 He has *s* thus: 'I will
13:40 lest what has been *s* in the
13:45 they opposed the things *s* by
13:46 the word of God should be *s* to
16: 2 He was well *s* of by the brethren
16:14 her heart to heed the things *s*
23: 9 if a spirit or an angel has *s*
27:11 the ship than by the things *s*
28:21 who came reported or *s* any
28:22 we know that it is *s* against
28:24 by the things which were *s*,
Rom 1: 8 that your faith is *s* of
4:18 according to what was *s*,
14:16 do not let your good be *s* of
1 Cor 10:30 why am I evil *s* of for the
14: 9 how will it be known what is *s*?
2 Cor 6:11 O Corinthians! We have *s* openly
Heb 1: 2 has in these last days *s* to us
2: 2 For if the word *s* through angels
2: 3 at the first began to be *s* by
3: 5 those things which would be *s*
4: 4 For He has *s* in a certain place
4: 8 He would not afterward have *s*
7:13 He of whom these things are *s*
9:19 For when Moses had *s* every
12:19 that the word should not be *s*
13: 7 who have *s* the word of God to
2 Pe 3: 2 of the words which were *s*
Jude 15 which ungodly sinners have *s*
17 the words which were *s* before

SPOKES (1/1)

1 Ki 7:33 axle pins, their rims, their *s*,

SPOKESMAN (2/2)

Ex 4:16 So he shall be your *s* to the
Job 33: 6 Truly I am as your *s* before

SPONGE (3/3)

Mt 27:48 one of them ran and took a *s*,
Mk 15:36 Then someone ran and filled a *s*
Jn 19:29 and they filled a *s* with sour

SPOON (KJV) See PAN

SPOONS (4/4)

2 Ki 25:14 shovels, the trimmers, the *s*,
2 Chr 24:14 *s* and vessels of gold and
Jer 52:18 the trimmers, the bowls, the *s*,
52:19 the pots, the lampstands, the *s*,

SPORT (1/1)

Prov 10:23 To do evil is like *s* to a

SPORTING (KJV) See SHOWING (ENDEARMENT)

SPOT (20/20) SPOTS, SPOTTED, UNSPOTTED

Lev 13: 2 swelling, a scab, or a bright *s*,
13: 4 But if the bright *s* is white on
13:10 and there is a *s* of raw flesh
13:19 a white swelling or a bright *s*,
13:23 But if the bright *s* stays in one
13:24 of the burn becomes a bright *s*,
13:25 if the hair of the bright *s*
13:26 no white hairs in the bright *s*,
13:28 But if the bright *s* stays in one
13:39 it is a white *s* that grows on
14:56 and a scab and a bright *s*,
2 Sam 2:23 down there and died on the *s*.
Job 11:15 lift up your face without *s*;
31: 7 Or if any *s* adheres to my
Song 4: 7 And there is no *s* in you.
Eph 5:27 not having *s* or wrinkle or any
1 Tim 6:14 this commandment without *s*,
Heb 9:14 offered Himself without *s* to
1 Pe 1:19 without blemish and without *s*.
2 Pe 3:14 without *s* and blameless;

SPOTS (6/5) SPOT

Lev 13:38 a man or a woman has bright *s*
13:38 specifically white bright *s*,
13:39 and indeed if the bright *s* on
Jer 13:23 his skin or the leopard its *s*?
2 Pe 2:13 They are *s* and blemishes,
Jude 12 These are *s* in your love

SPOTTED (6/4) SPOT

Gen 30:32 there all the speckled and *s*
30:32 and the *s* and speckled among
30:33 one that is not speckled and *s*
30:35 goats that were speckled and *s*,
30:35 goats that were speckled and *s*,
30:39 forth streaked, speckled, and *s*.

SPOUSE (7/7)

Song 4: 8 with me from Lebanon, my *s*,
4: 9 my heart, My sister, my *s*;
4:10 my *s*! How much better than
4:11 Your lips, O my *s*,
4:12 enclosed Is my sister, my *s*,
5: 1 to my garden, my sister, my *s*;
Hos 12:12 Syria; Israel served for a *s*,

SPOUT (1/1)

Am 7:16 And do not *s* against the house

SPRANG (9/9) SPRING

Gen 41: 6 *s* up after them.
41:23 *s* up after them.
Mt 13: 5 and they immediately *s* up
13: 7 and the thorns *s* up and choked
Mk 4: 5 and immediately it *s* up because
4: 8 and yielded a crop that *s* up,
Lk 8: 6 and as soon as it *s* up, it
8: 7 and the thorns *s* up with it and
8: 8 *s* up, and yielded a crop a

SPREAD (106/103) SPREADING, SPREADS

Gen 28:14 you shall *s* abroad to the west
Ex 9:29 I will *s* out my hands to the
9:33 of the city from Pharaoh and *s*
37: 9 The cherubim *s* out their wings
40:19 And he *s* out the tent over the
Lev 13: 5 and the sore has not *s* on the
13: 6 and the sore has not *s* on the
13: 7 if the scab should at all *s*
13: 8 that the scab has indeed *s* on
13:22 and if it should at all *s* over
13:23 in one place, and has not *s*,
13:27 If it has at all *s* over the
13:28 and has not *s* on the skin, but
13:32 indeed if the scale has not *s*,
13:34 indeed if the scale has not *s*
13:35 if the scale should at all *s*
13:36 and indeed if the scale has *s*
13:51 If the plague has *s* in the
13:53 indeed the plague has not *s* in
13:55 though the plague has not *s*,
14:39 indeed if the plague has *s* on
14:44 indeed if the plague has *s* in
14:48 indeed the plague has not *s* in
Num 4: 6 and *s* over that a cloth
4: 7 of showbread they shall *s* a
4: 8 They shall *s* over them a scarlet
4:11 the golden altar they shall *s*
4:13 and *s* a purple cloth over it.
4:14 and they shall *s* on it a
11:32 and they *s* them out for
Deut 22:17 And they shall *s* the cloth
Josh 6:27 and his fame *s* throughout all
Judg 8:25 And they *s* out a garment, and
20:37 the men in ambush *s* out and
1 Sam 30:16 *s* out over all the land, eating
2 Sam 17:19 Then the woman took and *s* a
17:19 and *s* ground grain on it;
21:10 of Aiah took sackcloth and *s*
22:43 And I *s* them out.
1 Ki 6:32 and he *s* gold on the cherubim
8: 7 For the cherubim *s* their two
8:22 and *s* out his hands toward
8:54 on his knees with his hands *s*
2 Ki 8:15 and *s* it over his face so that
19:14 and *s* it before the LORD.
1 Chr 28:18 the gold cherubim that *s* their
2 Chr 5: 8 For the cherubim *s* their wings
6:12 and *s* out his hands
6:13 and *s* out his hands toward
26: 8 His fame *s* as far as the
26:15 So his fame *s* far and wide, for
Ezra 9: 5 I fell on my knees and *s* out my
Esth 9: 4 and his fame *s* throughout all
Job 8:16 And his branches *s* out in his
29:19 My root is *s* out to the
37:18 have you *s* out the skies,
39:26 And *s* its wings toward the
Ps 105:39 He *s* a cloud for a covering,
140: 5 They have *s* a net by the
143: 6 I *s* out my hands to You;
Prov 1:17 in vain the net is *s* In the
7:16 I have *s* my bed with tapestry,

Isa 1:15 When you *s* out your hands,
14:11 The maggot is *s* under you,
19: 8 And they will languish who *s*
25: 7 And the veil that is *s* over
25:11 And He will *s* out His hands in
33:23 They could not *s* the sail.
37:14 and *s* it before the LORD.
42: 5 Who *s* forth the earth and that
58: 5 And to *s* out sackcloth and
Jer 8: 2 They shall *s* them before the sun
43:10 And he will *s* his royal
48:40 And *s* his wings over Moab.
49:22 And *s* His wings over Bozrah;
Lam 1:10 The adversary has *s* his hand
1:13 He has *s* a net for my feet
2:13 For your ruin is *s* wide as
Ezek 1:23 the firmament their wings *s*
2:10 Then He *s* it before me;
12:13 I will also *s* My net over him,
16: 8 so I *s* My wing over you and
17:20 I will *s* My net over him, and he
19: 8 And *s* their net over him;
27: 7 from Egypt was what you *s* for
32: 3 I will therefore *s* My net over
Hos 5: 1 a snare to Mizpah And a net *s*
7:12 I will *s* My net on them;
14: 6 His branches shall *s*;
Joel 2: 2 Like the morning clouds *s*
Zech 1:17 My cities shall again *s* out
2: 6 for I have *s* you abroad like the
Mal 2: 3 rebuke your descendants And *s*
Mt 9:31 they *s* the news about Him in
21: 8 And a very great multitude *s*
21: 8 branches from the trees and *s*
Mk 1:28 And immediately His fame *s*
1:45 and to *s* the matter, so that
11: 8 And many *s* their clothes on the
11: 8 branches from the trees and *s*
Lk 19:36 many *s* their clothes on the
Acts 6: 7 Then the word of God *s*,
13:49 word of the Lord was being *s*
Rom 5:12 and thus death *s* to all men,
2 Cor 4:15 having *s* through the many, may
2 Tim 2:17 And their message will *s* like

SPREADING (8/8) SPREAD

Lev 13:57 it is a *s* plague; you shall
Deut 32:11 *S* out its wings, taking them
Job 36:29 can anyone understand the *s* of
Ps 37:35 And *s* himself like a native
Ezek 17: 6 And it grew and became a *s* vine
26: 5 It shall be a place for *s*
26:14 you shall be a place for *s*
47:10 they will be places for *s*

SPREADS (13/13) SPREAD

1 Ki 8:38 and *s* out his hands toward this
2 Chr 6:29 and *s* out his hands to this
Job 9: 8 He alone *s* out the heavens,
26: 9 And *s* His cloud over it.
41:30 He *s* pointed marks in the
Prov 10:18 And whoever *s* slander is a
29: 5 who flatters his neighbor *S* a
Isa 40:22 And *s* them out like a tent to
44:24 Who *s* abroad the earth by
Jer 4:31 She *s* her hands, saying,
17: 8 Which *s* out its roots by the
Lam 1:17 Zion *s* out her hands, But no
Acts 4:17 But so that it *s* no further

SPRIGS (1/1)

Isa 18: 5 He will both cut off the *s*

SPRING (35/33) SPRANG, SPRINGING, SPRINGS, WATERSPRINGS, WELLSPRING

Gen 16: 7 of the LORD found her by a *s*
16: 7 by the *s* on the way to Shur.
Lev 11:36 Nevertheless a *s* or a cistern,
Num 21:17 *S* up, O well! All of you sing
Josh 18:15 the west and went out to the *s*
2 Sam 11: 1 It happened in the *s* of the
1 Ki 20:22 for in the *s* of the year the
20:26 in the *s* of the year, that
2 Ki 3:19 and stop up every *s* of water,
13:20 Moab invaded the land in the *s*
1 Chr 20: 1 It happened in the *s* of the
2 Chr 24:23 So it happened in the *s* of the
Job 5: 6 Nor does trouble *s* from the
29:23 their mouth wide as for the *s*
38:27 And cause to *s* forth the
Ps 84: 6 of Baca, They make it a *s*;
85:11 Truth shall *s* out of the earth,
92: 7 When the wicked *s* up like
Prov 4:23 For out of it *s* the issues of
25:26 the wicked Is like a murky *s*
Song 4:12 A *s* shut up, A fountain
Isa 42: 9 Before they *s* forth I tell you
43:19 Now it shall *s* forth;
44: 4 They will *s* up among the grass
45: 8 And let righteousness *s* up
58: 8 Your healing shall *s* forth
58:11 And like a *s* of water, whose
61:11 that are sown in it to *s* forth,
61:11 righteousness and praise to *s*
Ezek 17: 9 All of its *s* leaves will
29:21 of the house of Israel to *s*
Hos 13:15 Then his *s* shall become dry,
Am 3: 5 Will a snare *s* up from the
Jas 3:11 Does a *s* send forth fresh water
3:12 Thus no *s* yields both salt

SPRINGING (4/4) SPRING

2 Sam 23: 4 Like the tender grass *s* out
Joel 2:22 For the open pastures are *s*
Jn 4:14 in him a fountain of water *s*
Heb 12:15 any root of bitterness *s* up

SPRINGS (26/22) SPRING

Num 33: 9 At Elim were twelve *s* of water
Deut 8: 7 of water, of fountains and *s*,
Josh 15:19 give me also *s* of water."
15:19 So he gave her the upper *s*
15:19 upper springs and the lower *s*.
Judg 1:15 give me also *s* of water."
1:15 And Caleb gave her the upper *s*
1:15 upper springs and the lower *s*.
1 Ki 4:33 even to the hyssop that *s* out
18: 5 Go into the land to all the *s* of
2 Ki 3:25 and they stopped up all the *s*
19:29 And in the second year what *s*
2 Chr 32: 3 to stop the water from the *s*
32: 4 together who stopped all the *s*
Job 38:16 Have you entered the *s* of the
Ps 87: 7 All my *s* are in you."
104:10 He sends the *s* into the
Isa 35: 7 And the thirsty land *s* of
37:30 And the second year what *s*
41:18 And the dry land *s* of water.
49:10 Even by the *s* of water He will
Jer 51:36 dry up her sea and make her *s*
Hos 10: 4 Thus judgment *s* up like
Rev 8:10 of the rivers and on the *s* of
14: 7 the sea and *s* of water."
16: 4 his bowl on the rivers and *s*

SPRINKLE (29/28) SPRINKLED, SPRINKLING

Ex 29:16 you shall take its blood and *s*
29:20 and *s* the blood all around on
29:21 and *s* it on Aaron and on his
Lev 1: 5 shall bring the blood and *s* the
1:11 shall *s* its blood all around on
3: 2 shall *s* the blood all around on
3: 8 and Aaron's sons shall *s* its
3:13 and the sons of Aaron shall *s*
4: 6 his finger in the blood and *s*
4:17 his finger in the blood and *s*
5: 9 Then he shall *s* some of the
7: 2 And its blood he shall *s* all
14: 7 And he shall *s* it seven times on
14:16 and shall *s* some of the oil
14:27 Then the priest shall *s* with his
14:51 and *s* the house seven times.
16:14 of the blood of the bull and *s*
16:14 the mercy seat he shall *s* some
16:15 and *s* it on the mercy seat and
16:19 Then he shall *s* some of the
17: 6 And the priest shall *s* the blood
Num 8: 7 *S* water of purification on
18:17 You shall *s* their blood on the
19: 4 and *s* some of its blood seven
19:18 *s* it on the tent, on all the
19:19 The clean person shall *s* the
2 Ki 16:15 and *s* on it all the blood of
Isa 52:15 So shall He *s* many nations.
Ezek 36:25 Then I will *s* clean water on

SPRINKLED (23/20) SPRINKLE

Ex 24: 6 and half the blood he *s* on the
24: 8 *s* it on the people, and said,
Lev 6:27 And when its blood is *s* on any
6:27 wash that on which it was *s*,
8:11 He *s* some of it on the altar
8:19 Then he *s* the blood all around
8:24 And Moses *s* the blood all
8:30 and *s* it on Aaron, on his
9:12 which he *s* all around on the
9:18 which he *s* all around on the
Num 19:13 of purification was not *s* on
19:20 of purification has not been *s*
2 Ki 16:13 his drink offering and *s* the
2 Chr 29:22 received the blood and *s* it
29:22 they killed the rams and *s* the
29:22 the lambs and *s* the blood
30:16 the priests *s* the blood
35:11 and the priests *s* the blood
Job 2:12 one tore his robe and *s* dust
Isa 63: 3 Their blood is *s* upon My
Heb 9:19 and *s* both the book itself and
9:21 Then likewise he *s* with blood
10:22 having our hearts *s* from an

SPRINKLES (2/2)

Lev 7:14 belong to the priest who *s* the
Num 19:21 He who *s* the water of

SPRINKLING (5/5) SPRINKLE

Ezek 43:18 and for *s* blood on it.
Heb 9:13 *s* the unclean, sanctifies for
11:28 he kept the Passover and the *s*
12:24 and to the blood of *s* that
1 Pe 1: 2 for obedience and *s* of the

SPRINKLING-BOWLS (1/1)

2 Ki 12:13 basins of silver, trimmers, *s*,

SPROUT (2/2) SPROUTED

Job 14: 7 that it will *s* again, And that
Mk 4:27 and the seed should *s* and grow,

SPROUTED (2/2) SPROUT

Num 17: 8 had *s* and put forth buds,
Mt 13:26 But when the grain had *s* and

SPUE, SPUED (KJV) See VOMIT, VOMITED

SPUN (3/2)

Ex 35:25 who were gifted artisans *s*
35:25 and brought what they had *s*,
35:26 heart stirred with wisdom *s*

SPUNGE (KJV) See SPONGE

SPUR (1/1)

Isa 9:11 And *s* his enemies on,

SPURNED (3/3)

Deut 32:19 He *s* them, Because of the
Lam 2: 6 burning indignation He has *s*
2: 7 The Lord has *s* His altar,

SPY (18/18) SPIED, SPIES, SPYING

Num 13: 2 Send men to *s* out the land of
13:16 of the men whom Moses sent to *s*
13:17 Then Moses sent them to *s* out
14: 7 land we passed through to *s*
14:36 the men whom Moses sent to *s*
14:38 of the men who went to *s* out
21:32 Then Moses sent to *s* out Jazer;
Josh 2: 1 two men from Acacia Grove to *s*
6:25 whom Joshua sent to *s* out
7: 2 Go up and *s* out the country."
14: 7 me from Kadesh Barnea to *s* out
Judg 1:23 house of Joseph sent men to *s*
18: 2 to *s* out the land and search
18:14 the five men who had gone to *s*
18:17 the five men who had gone to *s*
2 Sam 10: 3 to *s* it out, and to overthrow
1 Chr 19: 3 and to overthrow and to *s* out
Gal 2: 4 in (who came in by stealth to *s*

SPYING (1/1) SPY

Num 13:25 And they returned from *s* out the

SQUADS (1/1)

Acts 12: 4 and delivered him to four *s* of

SQUANDERS (1/1)

Prov 21:20 But a foolish man *s* it.

SQUARE (27/26) SQUARES

Gen 19: 2 spend the night in the open *s*.
Ex 27: 1 wide—the altar shall be *s*—
28:16 "It shall be doubled into a *s*:
30: 2 a cubit its width—it shall be *s*—
37:25 its width a cubit—it was *s*—
38: 1 cubits its width—it was *s*—
39: 9 They made the breastplate *s* by
Judg 19:15 he sat down in the open *s* of
19:17 saw the traveler in the open *s*
19:20 spend the night in the open *s*.
1 Ki 7:31 but the panels were *s*,
2 Chr 29: 4 and gathered them in the East *S*,
32: 6 together to him in the open *s*
Ezra 10: 9 the people sat in the open *s*
Neh 8: 1 as one man in the open *s* that
8: 3 he read from it in the open *s*
8:16 and in the open *s* of the Water
8:16 Water Gate and in the open *s*
Esth 4: 6 out to Mordecai in the city *s*
6: 9 on horseback through the city *s*,
6:11 on horseback through the city *s*,
Job 29: 7 I took my seat in the open *s*,
Prov 7:12 outside, at times in the open *s*,
Ezek 41:21 doorposts of the temple were *s*,
43:16 *s* at its four corners;
45: 2 Of this there shall be a *s* plot
Rev 21:16 The city is laid out as a *s*;

SQUARES (2/2) SQUARE

Prov 1:20 raises her voice in the open *s*.
Song 3: 2 In the streets and in the *s* I

SQUEEZED (1/1)

Judg 6:38 next morning and *s* the fleece

STABBED (2/2)

2 Sam 3:27 and there *s* him in the stomach,
4: 6 and they *s* him in the stomach.

STABILITY (1/1)
Isa 33: 6 and knowledge will be the *s* of

STABLE (1/1)
Ezek 25: 5 And I will make Rabbah a *s* for

STABLISH, STABLISHED, STABLISHETH (KJV) See ESTABLISH, ESTABLISHED, ESTABLISHES

STACHYS (1/1)
Rom 16: 9 fellow worker in Christ, and *S*,

STACKED (1/1)
Ex 22: 6 so that *s* grain, standing

STACKS (KJV) See STACKED

STACTE (1/1)
Ex 30:34 *s* and onycha and galbanum,

STAFF (34/33) STAFFS
Gen 32:10 over this Jordan with my *s*,
38:18 and your *s* that is in your
38:25 are—the signet and cord, and *s*.
Ex 12:11 and your *s* in your hand. So you
21:19 walks about outside with his *s*,
Num 22:27 he struck the donkey with his *s*.
Judg 5:14 who bear the recruiter's *s*.
6:21 LORD put out the end of the *s*
1 Sam 17: 7 Now the *s* of his spear was like
17:40 Then he took his *s* in his hand;
2 Sam 3:29 who leans on a *s* or falls by
23:21 so he went down to him with a *s*,
2 Ki 4:29 and take my *s* in your hand,
4:29 but lay my *s* on the face of the
4:31 and laid the *s* on the face of
18:21 You are trusting in the *s* of
1 Chr 11:23 he went down to him with a *s*,
Ps 23: 4 with me; Your rod and Your *s*,
Isa 9: 4 yoke of his burden And the *s*
10: 5 the rod of My anger And the *s*
10:15 Or as if a *s* could lift up,
10:24 with a rod and lift up his *s*
14: 5 The LORD has broken the *s* of
30:32 in every place where the *s* of
36: 6 You are trusting in the *s* of
Jer 48:17 'How the strong *s* is broken,
Ezek 29: 6 Because they have been a *s* of
Hos 4:12 And their *s* informs them.
Mic 7:14 Your people with Your *s*,
Zech 8: 4 Each one with his *s* in his
11:10 And I took my *s*,
11:14 Then I cut in two my other *s*,
Mk 6: 8 for the journey except a *s*—
Heb 11:21 leaning on the top of his *s*.

STAFFS (3/3) STAFF
Zech 11: 7 I took for myself two *s*:
Mt 10:10 two tunics, nor sandals, nor *s*;
Lk 9: 3 neither *s* nor bag nor bread nor

STAG (3/3)
Song 2: 9 is like a gazelle or a young *s*.
2:17 be like a gazelle Or a young *s*
8:14 be like a gazelle Or a young *s*

STAGGER (4/4) STAGGERS
Job 12:25 And He makes them *s* like a
Ps 107:27 and *s* like a drunken man,
Isa 29: 9 but not with wine; They *s*,
Jer 25:16 And they will drink and *s* and go

STAGGERED (1/1)
Lam 5:13 Boys *s* under loads of wood.

STAGGERS (1/1) STAGGER
Isa 19:14 As a drunken man *s* in his

STAINED (1/1)
Isa 63: 3 And I have *s* all My robes.

STAIRS (7/7)
1 Ki 6: 8 They went up by *s* to the middle
Neh 3:15 as far as the *s* that go down
9: 4 and Chenani stood on the *s* of
12:37 they went up the *s* of the City
Ezek 40: 6 and he went up its *s* and
Acts 21:35 When he reached the *s*,
21:40 Paul stood on the *s* and

STAIRWAY (1/1)
Neh 12:37 on the *s* of the wall, beyond

STAKES (2/2)
Isa 33:20 Not one of its *s* will ever be
54: 2 And strengthen your *s*.

STALK (3/3)
Gen 41: 5 heads of grain came up on one *s*,
41:22 seven heads came up on one *s*,
Hos 8: 7 The *s* has no bud; It shall

STALKS (1/1)
Josh 2: 6 and hidden them with the *s* of

STALL (2/2) STALLS
Am 6: 4 calves from the midst of the *s*;
Lk 13:15 his ox or donkey from the *s*,

STALL-FED (1/1)
Mal 4: 2 And grow fat like *s* calves.

STALLIONS (1/1)
Jer 5: 8 were like well-fed lusty *s*;

STALLS (4/4) STALL
1 Ki 4:26 Solomon had forty thousand *s* of
2 Chr 9:25 Solomon had four thousand *s* for
32:28 and *s* for all kinds of
Hab 3:17 And there be no herd in the *s*—

STAMMERERS (1/1)
Isa 32: 4 And the tongue of the *s* will

STAMMERING (2/2)
Isa 28:11 For with *s* lips and another
33:19 Of a *s* tongue that you

STAMP (1/1)
Ezek 6:11 Pound your fists and *s* your

STAMPED (1/1)
Ezek 25: 6 *s* your feet, and rejoiced in

STAMPING (1/1)
Jer 47: 3 At the noise of the *s* hooves of

STANCHED (KJV) See STOPPED

STAND (249/241) STANDING, STANDS, STOOD
Gen 19: 9 *S* back!" Then they said, "This
24:13 here I *s* by the well of water,
24:31 of the LORD! Why do you *s*
24:43 I *s* by the well of water;
Ex 3: 5 for the place where you *s* is
7:15 and you shall *s* by the river's
8:20 early in the morning and *s*
8:21 the ground on which they *s*.
9:11 And the magicians could not *s*
9:13 early in the morning and *s*
14:13 *S* still, and see the salvation
17: 6 I will *s* before you there on
17: 9 Tomorrow I will *s* on the top of
18:14 and all the people *s* before you
18:19 *S* before God for the people, so
33:21 and you shall *s* on the rock.
Lev 18:23 Nor shall any woman *s* before an
19:16 nor shall you take a *s* against
26:37 you shall have no power to *s*
27:14 priest values it, so it shall *s*.
27:17 to your valuation it shall *s*.
Num 1: 5 names of the men who shall *s*
5:18 Then the priest shall *s* the
5:30 then he shall *s* the woman
8:13 And you shall *s* the Levites
9: 8 *S* still, that I may hear what
11:16 that they may *s* there with you.
16: 9 and to *s* before the
22:22 Angel of the LORD took His *s*
22:32 I have come out to *s* against
23: 3 *S* by your burnt offering, and I
23:15 *S* here by your burnt offering
27:21 He shall *s* before Eleazar the
30: 4 then all her vows shall *s*,
30: 4 she has bound herself shall *s*.
30: 5 she has bound herself shall *s*;
30: 7 he hears, then her vows shall *s*,
30: 7 which she bound herself shall *s*.
30: 9 shall *s* against her.
30:11 her, then all her vows shall *s*,
30:11 which she bound herself shall *s*.
30:12 binding her, it shall not *s*;
Deut 5:31 *s* here by Me, and I will speak
7:24 no one shall be able to *s*
9: 2 Who can *s* before the descendants
10: 8 to *s* before the LORD to
11:25 No man shall be able to *s*
18: 5 out of all your tribes to *s* to
18: 7 who *s* there before the LORD.
19:17 men in the controversy shall *s*
24:11 You shall *s* outside, and the man
27:12 These shall *s* on Mount Gerizim
27:13 and these shall *s* on Mount Ebal
29:10 All of you *s* today before the
Josh 1: 5 No man shall be able to *s*
3: 8 you shall *s* in the Jordan.'"
3:13 and they shall *s* as a heap."
5:15 for the place where you *s* is
7:12 children of Israel could not *s*
7:13 you cannot *s* before your
10: 8 not a man of them shall *s*
10:12 *s* still over Gibeon; And Moon,
23: 9 no one has been able to *s*
Judg 2:14 so that they could no longer *s*
4:20 '*S* at the door of the tent,
1 Sam 6:20 Who is able to *s* before this
9:27 But you *s* here awhile, that I
12: 7 *s* still, that I may reason with
12:16 *s* and see this great thing
14: 9 then we will *s* still in our
16:22 Please let David *s* before me,
19: 3 And I will go out and *s* beside
2 Sam 1: 9 Please *s* over me and kill me,
2:25 and took their *s* on top of a
15: 2 Absalom would rise early and *s*
18:30 Turn aside and *s* here." So he
1 Ki 1: 2 and let her *s* before the king,
10: 8 who *s* continually before you
17: 1 Israel lives, before whom I *s*,
18:15 of hosts lives, before whom I *s*,
19:11 and *s* on the mountain before
2 Ki 3:14 of hosts lives, before whom I *s*,
5:11 and *s* and call on the name of
5:16 LORD lives, before whom I *s*,
10: 4 two kings could not *s* up to
10: 4 up to him; how then can we *s*?
23: 3 And all the people took a *s* for
1 Chr 23:30 to *s* every morning to thank and
2 Chr 9: 7 who *s* continually before you
11:13 in all Israel took their *s*
20: 9 we will *s* before this temple and
20:17 *s* still and see the salvation
29:11 the LORD has chosen you to *s*
34:32 Jerusalem and Benjamin take a *s*.
35: 5 And *s* in the holy place
Ezra 9:15 though no one can *s* before You
10:13 and we are not able to *s*
10:14 of our entire assembly *s*;
Neh 7: 3 and while they *s* guard, let
9: 5 *S* up and bless the LORD your
Esth 3: 4 Mordecai's words would *s*;
5: 9 and that he did not *s* or
Job 8:15 on his house, but it does not *s*.
19:25 And He shall *s* at last on the
30:20 I *s* up, and You regard me.
30:28 I *s* up in the assembly and
33: 5 order before me; Take your *s*.
37:14 *S* still and consider the
41:10 Who then is able to *s* against
Ps 1: 5 the ungodly shall not *s* in the
5: 5 The boastful shall not *s* in
10: 1 Why do You *s* afar off, O LORD?
20: 8 But we have risen and *s*
24: 3 Or who may *s* in His holy
30: 7 You have made my mountain *s*
33: 8 the inhabitants of the world *s*
35: 2 And *s* up for my help.
38:11 My loved ones and my friends *s*
38:11 And my relatives *s* afar off.
76: 7 And who may *s* in Your presence
78:13 And He made the waters *s* up
89:28 And My covenant shall *s* firm
94:16 Who will *s* up for me against
109: 6 And let an accuser *s* at his
109:31 For He shall *s* at the right
111: 8 They *s* fast forever and ever,
130: 3 O Lord, who could *s*?
134: 1 Who by night *s* in the house of
135: 2 You who *s* in the house of the
147:17 Who can *s* before His cold?
Prov 8: 2 She takes her *s* on the top of
12: 7 house of the righteous will *s*.
19:21 the LORD's counsel—that will *s*.
22:29 He will *s* before kings;
22:29 He will not *s* before unknown
25: 6 And do not *s* in the place of
27: 4 But who is able to *s* before
Eccl 8: 3 Do not take your *s* for an evil
Isa 7: 7 Lord GOD: "It shall not *s*,
8:10 the word, but it will not *s*,
11:10 Who shall *s* as a banner to the
14:24 I have purposed, so it shall *s*:
21: 8 my Lord! I *s* continually on
27: 9 and incense altars shall not *s*.
28:18 agreement with Sheol will not *s*;
32: 8 And by generosity he shall *s*.
44:11 Let them *s* up; Yet they shall
46:10 Saying, 'My counsel shall *s*,
47:12 *S* now with your enchantments
47:13 the monthly prognosticators *S*
48:13 They *s* up together.
50: 8 Let us *s* together. Who is My
51:17 *S* up, O Jerusalem,
61: 5 Strangers shall *s* and feed your
Jer 6:16 *S* in the ways and see, And ask
7: 2 *S* in the gate of the LORD's
7:10 and then come and *s* before Me
15:19 You shall *s* before Me; If you
17:19 Go and *s* in the gate of the
26: 2 *S* in the court of the LORD's
35:19 shall not lack a man to *s*
44:28 shall know whose words will *s*,
44:29 that My words will surely *s*
46: 4 you horsemen! *S* forth with
46:14 *S* fast and prepare yourselves,
46:15 They did not *s* Because the
46:21 away together. They did not *s*,
48:19 *S* by the way and watch;
51:50 Get away! Do not *s* still!

Ezek 2: 1 *s* on your feet, and I will
13: 5 for the house of Israel to *s*
17:14 keeping his covenant it might *s*.
22:30 and *s* in the gap before Me on
27:29 down from their ships and *s*
44:11 and they shall *s* before them to
44:15 and they shall *s* before Me to
44:24 In controversy they shall *s* as
46: 2 and *s* by the gatepost.
47:10 be that fishermen will *s* by
Dan 2:44 and it shall *s* forever.
7: 4 up from the earth and made to *s*
10:11 and *s* upright, for I have now
11: 6 he nor his authority shall *s*;
11:16 and no one shall *s* against him.
11:16 He shall *s* in the Glorious Land
11:17 but she shall not *s* with him,
11:25 mighty army; but he shall not *s*,
12: 1 At that time Michael shall *s* up,
Am 2:15 He shall not *s* who handles the
7: 2 I pray! Oh, that Jacob may *s*,
7: 5 I pray! Oh, that Jacob may *s*,
Mic 1:11 Its place to *s* is taken away
5: 4 And He shall *s* and feed His
Nah 1: 6 Who can *s* before His
Hab 2: 1 I will *s* my watch And set
Zech 3: 7 to walk Among these who *s*
4: 2 and on the *s* seven lamps with
4:14 who *s* beside the Lord of the
11:16 nor feed those that still *s*.
14: 4 in that day His feet will *s* on
14:12 shall dissolve while they *s* on
Mal 3: 2 And who can *s* when He appears?
Mt 12:25 against itself will not *s*.
12:26 How then will his kingdom *s*?
Mk 3:24 itself, that kingdom cannot *s*.
3:25 itself, that house cannot *s*.
3:26 and is divided, he cannot *s*,
11:25 And whenever you *s* praying, if
Lk 6: 8 Arise and *s* here." And he arose
11:18 himself, how will his kingdom *s*?
13:25 and you begin to *s* outside and
21:36 and to *s* before the Son of
Jn 8:44 and does not *s* in the truth,
Acts 1:11 why do you *s* gazing up into
4:26 of the earth took their *s*,
5:20 *s* in the temple and speak to
7:33 the place where you *s* is
8:38 he commanded the chariot to *s*
10:26 *S* up; I myself am also a man."
14:10 *S* up straight on your feet!"
25:10 I *s* at Caesar's judgment seat,
26: 6 And now I *s* and am judged for
26:16 'But rise and *s* on your feet;
26:22 help from God, to this day I *s*,
Rom 5: 2 into this grace in which we *s*,
9:11 according to election might *s*,
11:20 and you *s* by faith. Do not be
14: 4 Indeed, he will be made to *s*,
14: 4 for God is able to make him *s*.
14:10 For we shall all *s* before the
1 Cor 15: 1 you received and in which you *s*,
15:30 And why do we *s* in jeopardy
16:13 *s* fast in the faith, be brave,
2 Cor 1:24 your joy; for by faith you *s*.
Gal 5: 1 *S* fast therefore in the liberty
Eph 6:11 that you may be able to *s*
6:13 day, and having done all, to *s*.
6:14 *S* therefore, having girded your
Phil 1:27 that you *s* fast in one spirit,
4: 1 so *s* fast in the Lord, beloved.
Col 4:12 that you may *s* perfect and
1 Th 3: 8 if you *s* fast in the Lord.
2 Th 2:15 *s* fast and hold the traditions
Jas 2: 3 You *s* there," or, "Sit here at
1 Pe 5:12 grace of God in which you *s*.
Rev 3:20 I *s* at the door and knock.
6:17 has come, and who is able to *s*?
8: 2 I saw the seven angels who *s*
18:15 will *s* at a distance for fear

STANDARD (18/18)

Num 1:52 own camp, everyone by his own *s*,
2: 2 Israel shall camp by his own *s*,
2: 3 those of the *s* of the forces
2:10 south side shall be the *s* of
2:18 the west side shall be the *s*
2:25 The *s* of the forces with Dan
10:14 The *s* of the camp of the
10:18 And the *s* of the camp of Reuben
10:22 And the *s* of the camp of the
10:25 Then the *s* of the camp of the
Deut 3:11 according to the *s* cubit.
2 Sam 14:26 according to the king's *s*.
Isa 49:22 And set up My *s* for the
59:19 of the LORD will lift up a *s*
Jer 4: 6 Set up the *s* toward Zion.
4:21 How long will I see the *s*,
50: 2 Proclaim, and set up a *s*;
51:12 Set up the *s* on the walls of

STANDARD-BEARER (KJV) See (SICK) MAN

STANDARDS (3/3)

Num 2:17 in his place, by their *s*.
2:31 break camp last, with their *s*.
2:34 so they camped by their *s* and

STANDING (81/77) STAND

Gen 18: 2 three men were *s* by him;
Ex 22: 6 *s* grain, or the field is
26:15 of acacia wood, *s* upright.
33:10 saw the pillar of cloud *s* at
36:20 of acacia wood, *s* upright.
Num 22:23 saw the Angel of the LORD *s*
22:31 he saw the Angel of the LORD *s*
23: 6 *s* by his burnt offering, he and
23:17 *s* by his burnt offering, and
Deut 23:25 you come into your neighbor's *s*
23:25 a sickle on your neighbor's *s*
Judg 15: 5 let the foxes go into the *s*
15: 5 up both the shocks and the *s*
1 Sam 19:20 and Samuel *s* as leader over
22: 6 and all his servants *s* about
1 Ki 8:14 the assembly of Israel was *s*.
13:25 and the lion *s* by the corpse.
13:28 and the donkey and the lion *s*
22:19 and all the host of heaven *s*
2 Ki 11:14 there was the king *s* by a
1 Chr 21:16 saw the angel of the LORD *s*
2 Chr 6: 3 the assembly of Israel was *s*.
18:18 and all the host of heaven *s* on
23:13 there was the king *s* by his
Neh 8: 5 for he was *s* above all the
Esth 5: 2 the king saw Queen Esther *s* in
6: 5 *s* in the court." And the king
7: 9 is *s* at the house of Haman."
Ps 69: 2 Where there is no *s*;
122: 2 Our feet have been *s* Within
Lam 2: 4 *S* like an enemy, He has bent
Ezek 10: 3 Now the cherubim were *s* on the
Dan 8: 3 *s* beside the river, was a ram
8: 6 which I had seen *s* beside the
Am 9: 1 I saw the Lord *s* by the altar,
Zech 3: 1 me Joshua the high priest *s*
3: 1 and Satan *s* at his right hand
3: 3 and was *s* before the Angel.
Mt 6: 5 For they love to pray *s* in the
12:47 mother and Your brothers are *s*
16:28 there are some *s* here who shall
20: 3 the third hour and saw others *s*
20: 6 he went out and found others *s*
20: 6 Why have you been *s* here idle
24:15 *s* in the holy place" (whoever
Mk 3:31 and *s* outside they sent to Him,
9: 1 to you that there are some *s*
13:14 *s* where it ought not" (let the
Lk 1:11 *s* on the right side of the
5: 2 and saw two boats *s* by the lake;
8:20 mother and Your brothers are *s*
9:27 there are some *s* here who shall
18:13 *s* afar off, would not so much
Jn 6:22 when the people who were *s* on
8: 9 and the woman *s* in the midst.
11:42 of the people who are *s* by I
19:26 the disciple whom He loved *s*
20:14 turned around and saw Jesus *s*
Acts 2:14 *s* up with the eleven, raised
4:14 the man who had been healed *s*
5:23 and the guards *s* outside before
5:25 whom you put in prison are *s*
7:55 and Jesus *s* at the right hand
7:56 opened and the Son of Man *s* at
11:13 us how he had seen an angel *s*
22:20 I also was *s* by consenting to
24:21 *s* among them, 'Concerning the
1 Tim 3:13 obtain for themselves a good *s*
Heb 9: 8 first tabernacle was still *s*.
Jas 5: 9 the Judge is *s* at the door!
2 Pe 3: 5 and the earth *s* out of water
Rev 4: 1 a door *s* open in heaven.
7: 1 things I saw four angels *s* at
7: 9 *s* before the throne and before
10: 5 The angel whom I saw *s* on the
11: 4 trees and the two lampstands *s*
14: 1 a Lamb *s* on Mount Zion,
15: 2 *s* on the sea of glass, having
18:10 *s* at a distance for fear of her
19:17 Then I saw an angel *s* in the
20:12 *s* before God, and books were

STANDS (36/35) STAND

Num 14:14 face to face and Your cloud *s*
35:12 may not die until he *s* before
Deut 1:38 who *s* before you, he shall go
17:12 will not heed the priest who *s*
25: 8 But if he *s* firm and says, 'I
29:15 but with him who *s* here with us
Josh 20: 4 and *s* at the entrance of the
20: 6 dwell in that city until he *s*
22:19 where the LORD's tabernacle *s*,
Job 6:29 my righteousness still *s*!
38:14 And *s* out like a garment.
Ps 1: 1 Nor *s* in the path of sinners,
26:12 My foot *s* in an even place;
33:11 The counsel of the LORD *s*
45: 9 At Your right hand *s* the queen
82: 1 God *s* in the congregation of
119:161 But my heart *s* in awe of Your
Eccl 4:15 with the second youth who *s* in
Song 2: 9 he *s* behind our wall; He is
Isa 3:13 The LORD *s* up to plead,
3:13 And *s* to judge the people.
40: 8 But the word of our God *s*
46: 7 set it in its place, and it *s*;
59:14 And righteousness *s* afar off;
Ezek 21:21 For the king of Babylon *s* at the
Dan 12: 1 The great prince who *s* watch
Lk 1:19 who *s* in the presence of God,
Jn 1:26 but there *s* One among you whom
3:29 who *s* and hears him, rejoices
Acts 4:10 by Him this man *s* here before
Rom 14: 4 To his own master he *s* or
1 Cor 7:37 Nevertheless he who *s* steadfast
10:12 let him who thinks he *s* take
2 Tim 2:19 the solid foundation of God *s*,
Heb 10:11 And every priest *s* ministering
Rev 10: 8 in the hand of the angel who *s*

STANDSTILL (1/1)

Lev 13:37 the scale appears to be at a *s*,

STANK (3/3) STINK

Ex 7:21 in the river died, the river *s*,
8:14 in heaps, and the land *s*.
16:20 and it bred worms and *s*.

STAR (15/14) STARS

Num 24:17 A *S* shall come out of Jacob;
Am 5:26 The *s* of your gods, Which you
Mt 2: 2 For we have seen His *s* in the
2: 7 from them what time the *s*
2: 9 the *s* which they had seen in
2:10 When they saw the *s*,
Acts 7:43 And the *s* of your god
1 Cor 15:41 for one *s* differs from
15:41 star differs from another *s*
2 Pe 1:19 the day dawns and the morning *s*
Rev 2:28 I will give him the morning *s*.
8:10 And a great *s* fell from heaven,
8:11 The name of the *s* is Wormwood.
9: 1 And I saw a *s* fallen from
22:16 David, the Bright and Morning *S*.

STARE (2/2)

2 Ki 8:11 he set his countenance in a *s*
Ps 22:17 They look and *s* at Me.

STARGAZERS (1/1)

Isa 47:13 Let now the astrologers, the *s*,

STARS (50/49) STAR

Gen 1:16 He made the *s* also.
15: 5 and count the *s* if you are able
22:17 your descendants as the *s* of
26: 4 descendants multiply as the *s*
37: 9 and the eleven *s* bowed down to
Ex 32:13 your descendants as the *s* of
Deut 1:10 as the *s* of heaven in
4:19 the sun, the moon, and the *s*,
10:22 your God has made you as the *s*
28:62 whereas you were as the *s* of
Judg 5:20 The *s* from their courses
1 Chr 27:23 multiply Israel like the *s* of
Neh 4:21 from daybreak until the *s*
9:23 their children as the *s* of
Job 3: 9 May the *s* of its morning be
9: 7 not rise; He seals off the *s*;
22:12 And see the highest *s*,
25: 5 And the *s* are not pure in His
38: 7 When the morning *s* sang
Ps 8: 3 fingers, The moon and the *s*,
136: 9 The moon and *s* to rule by
147: 4 He counts the number of the *s*;
148: 3 all you *s* of light!
Eccl 12: 2 the light, The moon and the *s*,
Isa 13:10 For the *s* of heaven and their
14:13 exalt my throne above the *s* of
Jer 31:35 of the moon and the *s* for a
Ezek 32: 7 and make its *s* dark; I will
Dan 8:10 of the host and some of the *s*
12: 3 to righteousness Like the *s*
Joel 2:10 And the *s* diminish their
3:15 And the *s* will diminish their
Ob 4 you set your nest among the *s*,
Nah 3:16 your merchants more than the *s*
Mt 24:29 the *s* will fall from heaven,
Mk 13:25 'the *s* of heaven will fall,
Lk 21:25 sun, in the moon, and in the *s*;
Acts 27:20 Now when neither sun nor *s*
1 Cor 15:41 and another glory of the *s*;
Heb 11:12 were born as many as the *s* of
Jude 13 wandering *s* for whom is
Rev 1:16 had in His right hand seven *s*,
1:20 The mystery of the seven *s* which
1:20 The seven *s* are the angels of
2: 1 says He who holds the seven *s*
3: 1 Spirits of God and the seven *s*:
6:13 And the *s* of heaven fell to the
8:12 the moon, and a third of the *s*,
12: 1 her head a garland of twelve *s*.
12: 4 His tail drew a third of the *s*

START (1/1) STARTS

Prov 20: 3 Since any fool can *s* a quarrel.

STARTED (2/2)

Num 10:13 So they *s* out for the first time
Ezek 24: 2 the king of Babylon *s* his siege

STARTING (2/1)

Num 33: 2 Moses wrote down the *s* points

33: 2 according to their *s* points:

STARTLED (2/2)

Ruth 3: 8 at midnight that the man was *s*,
Hab 3: 6 He looked and *s* the nations.

STARTS (1/1) START

Prov 17:14 contention before a quarrel *s*.

STARVED (1/1)

Job 18:12 His strength is *s*,

STARVING (1/1)

Prov 6:30 to satisfy himself when he is *s*.

STATE (16/14)

Ps 39: 5 every man at his best *s* is
136:23 remembered us in our lowly *s*,
144:15 the people who are in such a *s*;
Prov 27:23 Be diligent to know the *s* of
Isa 43:26 *S* your case, that you may be
Ezek 16:55 return to their former *s*,
16:55 return to their former *s*,
16:55 will return to your former *s*.
Mt 12:45 and the last *s* of that man is
Lk 1:48 He has regarded the lowly *s* of
11:26 and the last *s* of that man is
Acts 23:30 commanded his accusers to *s*
1 Cor 7:24 one remain with God in that *s*
Phil 2:19 encouraged when I know your *s*.
2:20 will sincerely care for your *s*.
4:11 I have learned in whatever *s* I

STATELY (2/2)

Prov 30:29 four which are *s* in walk:
Ezek 23:41 You sat on a *s* couch, with a

STATEMENT (2/2)

Lk 2:50 they did not understand the *s*
Acts 24:21 unless it is for this one *s*

STATION (2/2)

Neh 7: 3 one at his watch *s* and another
Zech 6: 5 who go out from their *s* before

STATIONED (7/7)

Judg 16:25 And they *s* him between the
2 Sam 23:12 But he *s* himself in the middle
1 Ki 10:26 whom he *s* in the chariot cities
1 Chr 11:14 But they *s* themselves in the
2 Chr 1:14 whom he *s* in the chariot cities
9:25 thousand horsemen whom he *s* in
29:25 And he *s* the Levites in the

STATURE (16/16)

Num 13:32 saw in it are men of great *s*.
1 Sam 2:26 And the child Samuel grew in *s*,
16: 7 or at the height of his *s*,
2 Sam 21:20 there was a man of great *s*,
1 Chr 20: 6 there was a man of great *s*,
Song 7: 7 This *s* of yours is like a palm
Isa 10:33 Those of high *s* will be hewn
45:14 And of the Sabeans, men of *s*,
Ezek 17: 6 a spreading vine of low *s*;
19:11 She towered in *s* above the
31: 3 the forest, And of high *s*;
Mt 6:27 can add one cubit to his *s*?
Lk 2:52 Jesus increased in wisdom and *s*,
12:25 can add one cubit to his *s*?
19: 3 crowd, for he was of short *s*.
Eph 4:13 to the measure of the *s* of the

STATUS (1/1)

Deut 21:16 he must not bestow firstborn *s*

STATUTE (35/35) STATUTES

Ex 15:25 There He made a *s* and an
27:21 It shall be a *s* forever to
28:43 It shall be a *s* forever to
29: 9 be theirs for a perpetual *s*.
29:28 for Aaron and his sons by a *s*
30:21 And it shall be a *s* forever to
Lev 3:17 shall be a perpetual *s*
6:18 It shall be a *s* forever in
6:22 It is a *s* forever to the
7:34 the children of Israel by a *s*
7:36 by a *s* forever throughout
10: 9 It shall be a *s* forever
10:15 by a *s* forever, as the LORD
16:29 This shall be a *s* forever for
16:31 It is a *s* forever.
16:34 shall be an everlasting *s*
17: 7 This shall be a *s* forever for
23:14 it shall be a *s* forever
23:21 It shall be a *s* forever in
23:31 it shall be a *s* forever
23:41 It shall be a *s* forever in
24: 3 it shall be a *s* forever in
24: 9 made by fire, by a perpetual *s*.
Num 18:23 it shall be a *s* forever,
19:10 It shall be a *s* forever to the
19:21 It shall be a perpetual *s* for
27:11 to the children of Israel a *s*
35:29 these things shall be a *s* of
Josh 24:25 and made for them a *s* and an
1 Sam 30:25 he made it a *s* and an ordinance
1 Chr 16:17 confirmed it to Jacob for a *s*,
Ps 81: 4 For this is a *s* for Israel,
105:10 confirmed it to Jacob for a *s*,
Dan 6: 7 to establish a royal *s* and to
6:15 Persians that no decree or *s*

STATUTES (134/133) STATUTE

Gen 26: 5 charge, My commandments, My *s*,
Ex 15:26 commandments and keep all His *s*,
18:16 and I make known the *s* of God
18:20 you shall teach them the *s*
Lev 10:11 children of Israel all the *s*
18: 5 You shall therefore keep My *s*
18:26 You shall therefore keep My *s*
19:19 'You shall keep My *s*.
19:37 you shall observe all My *s* and
20: 8 'And you shall keep My *s*,
20:22 shall therefore keep all My *s*
20:23 you shall not walk in the *s* of
25:18 So you shall observe My *s* and
26: 3 If you walk in My *s* and keep My
26:15 and if you despise My *s*,
26:43 their soul abhorred My *s*.
26:46 These are the *s* and judgments
Num 30:16 These are the *s* which the
Deut 4: 1 listen to the *s* and the
4: 5 Surely I have taught you *s* and
4: 6 who will hear all these *s*,
4: 8 is there that has such *s*
4:14 me at that time to teach you *s*
4:40 shall therefore keep His *s*
4:45 are the testimonies, the *s*,
5: 1 the *s* and judgments which I
5:31 you all the commandments, the *s*,
6: 1 and these are the *s* and
6: 2 to keep all His *s* and His
6:17 and His *s* which He has
6:20 of the testimonies, the *s*,
6:24 us to observe all these *s*,
7:11 keep the commandment, the *s*,
8:11 and His *s* which I command you
10:13 of the LORD and His *s* which I
11: 1 God, and keep His charge, His *s*,
11:32 be careful to observe all the *s*
12: 1 These are the *s* and judgments
16:12 be careful to observe these *s*.
17:19 words of this law and these *s*,
26:16 you to observe these *s* and
26:17 walk in His ways and keep His *s*,
27:10 His commandments and His *s*
28:15 all His commandments and His *s*
28:45 keep His commandments and His *s*
30:10 keep His commandments and His *s*
30:16 to keep His commandments, His *s*,
2 Sam 22:23 before me; And as for His *s*,
1 Ki 2: 3 walk in His ways, to keep His *s*,
3: 3 walking in the *s* of his father
3:14 to keep My *s* and My
6:12 building, if you walk in My *s*,
8:58 His commandments and His *s* and
8:61 to walk in His *s* and keep His
9: 4 and if you keep My *s* and My
9: 6 keep My commandments and My *s*
11:11 not kept My covenant and My *s*,
11:33 in My eyes and keep My *s* and
11:34 kept My commandments and My *s*.
11:38 to keep My *s* and My
2 Ki 17: 8 and had walked in the *s* of the
17:13 keep My commandments and My *s*,
17:15 And they rejected His *s* and His
17:19 but walked in the *s* of Israel
17:34 nor do they follow their *s* or
17:37 'And the *s*, the ordinances,
23: 3 and His testimonies and His *s*,
1 Chr 22:13 you take care to fulfill the *s*
29:19 and Your testimonies and Your *s*,
2 Chr 7:17 and if you keep My *s* and My
7:19 you turn away and forsake My *s*
19:10 against *s* or ordinances, you
33: 8 to the whole law and the *s* and
34:31 and His testimonies and His *s*
Ezra 7:10 and to teach *s* and ordinances
7:11 and of His *s* to Israel:
Neh 1: 7 kept the commandments, the *s*,
9:13 Good *s* and commandments.
9:14 *s* and laws, By the hand of
10:29 and His ordinances and His *s*:
Ps 18:22 And I did not put away His *s*
19: 8 The *s* of the LORD are right,
50:16 right have you to declare My *s*,
89:31 If they break My *s* And do not
105:45 That they might observe His *s*
119: 5 were directed To keep Your *s*!
119: 8 I will keep Your *s*;
119:12 O LORD! Teach me Your *s*!
119:16 will delight myself in Your *s*;
119:23 servant meditates on Your *s*.
119:26 answered me; Teach me Your *s*.
119:33 me, O LORD, the way of Your *s*,
119:48 And I will meditate on Your *s*.
119:54 Your *s* have been my songs In
119:64 of Your mercy; Teach me Your *s*.
119:68 and do good; Teach me Your *s*.
119:71 That I may learn Your *s*.
119:80 be blameless regarding Your *s*,
119:83 Yet I do not forget Your *s*.
119:112 my heart to perform Your *s*
119:117 And I shall observe Your *s*
119:118 all those who stray from Your *s*,
119:124 And teach me Your *s*.
119:135 servant, And teach me Your *s*.
119:145 O LORD! I will keep Your *s*.
119:155 For they do not seek Your *s*.
119:171 For You teach me Your *s*.
147:19 His *s* and His judgments to
Jer 44:10 not walked in My law or in My *s*
44:23 in His *s* or in His testimonies,
Ezek 5: 6 and against My *s* more than the
5: 6 they have not walked in My *s*.
5: 7 have not walked in My *s* nor
11:12 for you have not walked in My *s*
11:20 that they may walk in My *s* and
18: 9 If he has walked in My *s* And
18:17 judgments And walked in My *s*—
18:19 and has kept all My *s* and
18:21 has committed, keeps all My *s*,
20:11 And I gave them My *s* and showed
20:13 they did not walk in My *s*;
20:16 and did not walk in My *s*,
20:18 Do not walk in the *s* of your
20:19 LORD your God: Walk in My *s*,
20:21 they did not walk in My *s*,
20:24 but had despised My *s*,
20:25 I also gave them up to *s* that
33:15 and walks in the *s* of life
36:27 and cause you to walk in My *s*,
37:24 My judgments and observe My *s*,
44:24 shall keep My laws and My *s* in
Mic 6:16 For the *s* of Omri are kept;
Zech 1: 6 Yet surely My words and My *s*,
Mal 4: 4 With the *s* and judgments.

STAVES (1/1)

Num 21:18 By the lawgiver, with their *s*.

STAY (53/53)

Gen 19: 9 'This one came in to *s* here,
19:17 Do not look behind you nor *s*
22: 5 *S* here with the donkey; the lad
24:55 Let the young woman *s* with us a
27:44 And *s* with him a few days, until
29:19 another man. *S* with me."
30:27 Laban said to him, "Please *s*,
Ex 9:28 and you shall *s* no longer."
Lev 8:35 Therefore you shall *s* at the
14: 8 and shall *s* outside his tent
Num 22:19 you also *s* here tonight, that I
Deut 3:19 have much livestock) shall *s*
Josh 10:19 And do not *s* there yourselves,
Judg 17: 8 city of Bethlehem in Judah to *s*
17: 9 my way to find a place to *s*.
19: 6 Please be content to *s* all
Ruth 2: 8 but *s* close by my young women.
2:21 You shall *s* close by my young
3:13 *S* this night, and in the morning
1 Sam 19: 2 and *s* in a secret place and
22: 5 Do not *s* in the stronghold;
22:23 *S* with me; do not fear. For he
30:21 whom they also had made to *s* at
2 Sam 19: 7 not one will *s* with you this
2 Ki 2: 2 *S* here, please, for the LORD
2: 4 *s* here, please, for the LORD
2: 6 *S* here, please, for the LORD
8: 1 and *s* wherever you can; for the
14:10 and *s* at home; for why should
15:20 and did not *s* there in the
2 Chr 25:19 *S* at home now; why should you
Neh 4:22 each man and his servant *s*
Prov 7:11 Her feet would not *s* at home.
Hos 3: 3 You shall *s* with me many days;
13:13 For he should not *s* long where
Hab 2: 5 And he does not *s* at home.
Mt 2:13 and *s* there until I bring you
10:11 and *s* there till you go out.
26:38 *S* here and watch with Me."
Mk 6:10 *s* there till you depart from
14:34 *S* here and watch."
Lk 9: 4 *s* there, and from there depart.
19: 5 for today I must *s* at your
24:29 And He went in to *s* with
Jn 2:12 and they did not *s* there many
4:40 they urged Him to *s* with them;
Acts 10:48 Then they asked him to *s* a few
16:15 Lord, come to my house and *s*.
18:20 When they asked him to *s* a
27:31 Unless these men *s* in the ship,
28:14 and were invited to *s* with them
1 Cor 16: 7 but I hope to *s* a while with
1 Pe 1:17 throughout the time of your *s*

STAYED (60/59)

Gen 20: 1 and Shur, and *s* in Gerar.
21:34 And Abraham *s* in the land of the
24:54 with him ate and drank and *s*
28:11 came to a certain place and *s*
29:14 And he *s* with him for a
31:54 And they ate bread and *s* all
32: 4 I have dwelt with Laban and *s*
Num 9:18 as long as the cloud *s* above
11:32 And the people *s* up all that
20: 1 and the people *s* in Kadesh;
22: 8 So the princes of Moab *s* with
Deut 3:29 So we *s* in the valley opposite
9: 9 then I *s* on the mountain forty
10:10 I *s* in the mountain forty days
Josh 2:22 and *s* there three days until

5: 8 that they s in their places in
8: 9 and s between Bethel and Ai, on
Judg 5:17 Gilead s beyond the Jordan,
5:17 And s by his inlets.
19: 4 and he s with him three days.
20:47 and they s at the rock of
Ruth 2:23 So she s close by the young
1 Sam 1:23 So the woman s and nursed her
19:18 And he and Samuel went and s in
20:19 And when you have s three days,
23:14 And David s in strongholds in
23:18 And David s in the woods,
23:25 and s in the Wilderness of
25:13 and two hundred s with the
26: 3 But David s in the wilderness,
30: 9 where those s who were left
30:10 for two hundred s behind, who
2 Sam 1: 1 and David had s two days in
17:17 Now Jonathan and Ahimaaz s at En
19:32 king with supplies while he s
1 Ki 17: 5 for he went and s by the Brook
2 Ki 2:18 for he had s in Jericho, he
1 Chr 20: 1 But David s at Jerusalem.
Ezra 8:32 and s there three days.
Isa 26: 3 Whose mind is s on You,
Lk 21:37 but at night He went out and s
Jn 4:40 and He s there two days.
10:40 at first, and there He s.
11: 6 He s two more days in the place
Acts 9:43 So it was that he s many days in
12:19 to Caesarea, and s there.
14: 3 Therefore they s there a long
14:28 So they s there a long time with
15:33 And after they had s there for
18: 3 he s with them and worked;
19:22 but he himself s in Asia for a
20: 3 and s three months. And when the
20: 6 where we s seven days.
20:15 day we arrived at Samos and s
21: 4 we s there seven days.
21: 7 and s with them one day.
21: 8 of the seven, and s with him.
21:10 And as we s many days, a certain
28:12 we s three days.
2 Tim 4:20 Erastus s in Corinth, but

STAYING (14/14)

Judg 16: 9 s with her in the room. And she
16:12 s in the room. But he broke
17: 7 and was s there.
19: 1 there was a certain Levite s
19:16 he was s in Gibeah, whereas the
1 Sam 22: 6 now Saul was s in Gibeah under a
24: 3 (David and his men were s in
2 Sam 16: 3 'Indeed he is s in Jerusalem,
1 Ki 17:19 the upper room where he was s,
Mt 17:22 Now while they were s in
Jn 1:38 Teacher), "where are You s?
1:39 came and saw where He was s,
Acts 1:13 upper room where they were s:
16:12 And we were s in that city for

STAYS (4/4)

Lev 13:23 But if the bright spot s in one
13:28 But if the bright spot s in one
1 Sam 30:24 so shall his part be who s by
Ps 127: 1 The watchman s awake in vain.

STEAD (1/1)

Deut 10: 6 ministered as priest in his s.

STEADFAST (17/16) STEADFASTLY

1 Chr 28: 7 if he is s to observe My
Job 11:15 Yes, you could be s,
Ps 51:10 And renew a s spirit within
57: 7 My heart is s, O God,
57: 7 steadfast, O God, my heart is s;
78:37 For their heart was not s with
108: 1 O God, my heart is s;
112: 7 evil tidings; His heart is s,
Dan 6:26 And s forever; His kingdom
1 Cor 7:37 Nevertheless he who stands s in
15:58 my beloved brethren, be s,
2 Cor 1: 7 And our hope for you is s,
Col 1:23 in the faith, grounded and s,
Heb 2: 2 spoken through angels proved s,
3:14 beginning of our confidence s
6:19 of the soul, both sure and s,
1 Pe 5: 9 s in the faith, knowing that

STEADFASTLY (5/5) STEADFAST

Lk 9:51 that He s set His face to go to
Acts 1:10 And while they looked s toward
2:42 And they continued s in the
6:15 looking s at him, saw his face
Rom 12:12 continuing s in prayer;

STEADFASTNESS (2/2)

Col 2: 5 see your good order and the s
2 Pe 3:17 you also fall from your own s,

STEADILY (2/2)

2 Cor 3: 7 of Israel could not look s at
3:13 of Israel could not look s at

STEADY (1/1)

Ex 17:12 and his hands were s until the

STEAL (21/20) STEALING, STEALS, STOLE

Gen 31:27 and s away from me, and not
31:30 but why did you s my gods?"
44: 8 How then could we s silver or
Ex 20:15 "You shall not s.
Lev 19:11 'You shall not s,
Deut 5:19 'You shall not s.
2 Sam 19: 3 as people who are ashamed s
Prov 30: 9 Or lest I be poor and s,
Jer 7: 9 'Will you s, murder, commit
23:30 who s My words every one from
Mt 6:19 where thieves break in and s;
6:20 thieves do not break in and s.
19:18 'You shall not s,
27:64 disciples come by night and s
Mk 10:19 not murder,' 'Do not s,
Lk 18:20 not murder,' 'Do not s,
Jn 10:10 thief does not come except to s,
Rom 2:21 preach that a man should not s,
2:21 man should not steal, do you s?
13: 9 "You shall not s,
Eph 4:28 Let him who stole s no longer,

STEALING (1/1) STEAL

Hos 4: 2 Killing and s and committing

STEALS (3/3) STEAL

Ex 22: 1 If a man s an ox or a sheep, and
Job 27:20 A tempest s him away in the
Prov 6:30 do not despise a thief If he s

STEALTH (1/1)

Gal 2: 4 brought in (who came in by s

STEDFAST (KJV) See FAITHFUL, STEADFAST

STEEDS (8/8)

Judg 5:22 galloping, galloping of his s.
1 Ki 4:28 place, for the horses and s,
Esth 8:10 royal horses bred from swift s.
Ezek 27:14 for your wares with horses, s,
Joel 2: 4 of horses; And like swift s,
Mic 1:13 the chariot to the swift s
Zech 6: 3 dappled horses—strong s.
6: 7 Then the strong s went out,

STEEL (KJV) See BRONZE

STEEP (5/5)

Ezek 38:20 the s places shall fall,
Mic 1: 4 waters poured down a s place.
Mt 8:32 ran violently down the s place
Mk 5:13 ran violently down the s place
Lk 8:33 ran violently down the s place

STEM (1/1)

Isa 11: 1 come forth a Rod from the s of

STENCH (5/5)

Isa 3:24 a sweet smell there will be a s;
34: 3 Their s shall rise from their
Joel 2:20 His s will come up, And his
Am 4:10 I made the s of your camps
Jn 11:39 by this time there is a s,

STEP (3/3)

1 Sam 20: 3 there is but a s between me
Job 31: 7 If my s has turned from the
Mk 3: 3 withered hand, "S forward."

STEPHANAS (3/3)

1 Cor 1:16 baptized the household of S.
16:15 know the household of S,
16:17 I am glad about the coming of S,

STEPHEN (7/7)

Acts 6: 5 And they chose S, a man full of
6: 8 And S, full of faith and
6: 9 and Asia), disputing with S.
7:59 And they stoned S as he was
8: 2 And devout men carried S to
11:19 persecution that arose over S
22:20 the blood of Your martyr S was

STEPPED (2/2) STEP

Lk 8:27 And when He s out on the land,
Jn 5: 4 then whoever s in first, after

STEPS (45/45) STEP

Ex 20:26 Nor shall you go up by s to My
1 Ki 10:12 And the king made s of the almug
10:19 The throne had six s,
10:20 one on each side of the six s;
2 Ki 9:13 under him on the top of the s;
2 Chr 9:18 The throne had six s,
9:19 one on each side of the six s;
Job 14:16 For now You number my s,
18: 7 The s of his strength are
23:11 My foot has held fast to His s;
29: 6 When my s were bathed with
31: 4 my ways, And count all my s?
31:37 to Him the number of my s;
34:21 of man, And He sees all his s.
Ps 17: 5 Uphold my s in Your paths,
17:11 have now surrounded us in our s;
37:23 The s of a good man are
37:31 None of his s shall slide.
40: 2 a rock, And established my s.
44:18 Nor have our s departed from
56: 6 They hide, they mark my s,
57: 6 have prepared a net for my s;
73: 2 My s had nearly slipped.
119:133 Direct my s by Your word,
140: 4 Who have purposed to make my s
Prov 4:12 your s will not be hindered,
5: 5 Her s lay hold of hell.
14:15 prudent considers well his s.
16: 9 But the LORD directs his s.
20:24 A man's s are of the LORD;
Isa 26: 6 feet of the poor And the s
Jer 10:23 who walks to direct his own s.
Lam 4:18 They tracked our s So that we
Ezek 40:22 it was ascended by seven s,
40:26 Seven s led up to it, and its
40:31 going up to it were eight s.
40:34 going up to it were eight s.
40:37 going up to it were eight s.
40:49 and by the s which led up to it
41: 7 of the temple ascended like s;
43:17 and its s face toward the
Jn 5: 7 another s down before me."
Rom 4:12 but who also walk in the s of
2 Cor 12:18 Did we not walk in the same s?
1 Pe 2:21 that you should follow His s:

STERN (3/3)

Mk 4:38 But He was in the s,
Acts 27:29 dropped four anchors from the s,
27:41 but the s was being broken up

STERNLY (2/2)

Mt 9:30 And Jesus s warned them,
Mk 3:12 But He s warned them that they

STERNNESS (1/1)

Eccl 8: 1 And the s of his face is

STEW (7/7)

Gen 25:29 Now Jacob cooked a s;
25:30 feed me with that same red s,
25:34 Jacob gave Esau bread and s of
2 Ki 4:38 and boil s for the sons of the
4:39 sliced them into the pot of s,
4:40 as they were eating the s,
Hag 2:12 the edge he touches bread or s,

STEWARD (16/16) STEWARDS, STEWARDSHIP

Gen 43:16 he said to the s of his house,
43:19 When they drew near to the s of
44: 1 And he commanded the s of his
44: 4 far off, Joseph said to his s,
1 Ki 16: 9 s of his house in Tirzah.
Isa 22:15 "Go, proceed to this s,
Dan 1:11 So Daniel said to the s whom
1:16 Thus the s took away their
Mt 20: 8 of the vineyard said to his s,
Lk 8: 3 the wife of Chuza, Herod's s,
12:42 is that faithful and wise s,
16: 1 a certain rich man who had a s,
16: 2 for you can no longer be s.
16: 3 Then the s said within himself,
16: 8 master commended the unjust s
Titus 1: 7 as a s of God, not self-willed,

STEWARDS (5/5) STEWARD

1 Chr 28: 1 and the s over all the
1 Cor 4: 1 as servants of Christ and s of
4: 2 Moreover it is required in s
Gal 4: 2 but is under guardians and s
1 Pe 4:10 as good s of the manifold grace

STEWARDSHIP (5/5) STEWARD

Lk 16: 2 Give an account of your s,
16: 3 For my master is taking the s
16: 4 that when I am put out of the s,
1 Cor 9:17 I have been entrusted with a s.
Col 1:25 a minister according to the s

STICK (14/9) STICKS

2 Ki 6: 6 the place. So he cut off a s,
Job 33:21 And his bones s out which
41:17 They s together and cannot be
Isa 28:27 cummin is beaten out with a s,
57: 4 you make a wide mouth And s
Ezek 29: 4 the fish of your rivers to s
29: 4 the fish in your rivers will s
37:16 take a s for yourself and write
37:16 Then take another s and write
37:16 the s of Ephraim, and for all

37:17 another for yourself into one *s*,
37:19 Surely I will take the *s* of
37:19 with the *s* of Judah, and make
37:19 of Judah, and make them one *s*,

STICKS (8/8) STICK

Num 15:32 they found a man gathering *s* on
15:33 those who found him gathering *s*
1 Sam 17:43 dog, that you come to me with *s*?
1 Ki 17:10 a widow was there gathering *s*.
17:12 I am gathering a couple of *s*
Prov 18:24 who *s* closer than a brother.
Ezek 37:20 And the *s* on which you write
Acts 28: 3 had gathered a bundle of *s* and

STIFF (3/3) STIFFENED

Deut 31:27 your rebellion and your *s* neck.
Ps 75: 5 Do not speak with a *s* neck.'
Jer 17:23 ear, but made their neck *s*,

STIFF-NECKED (7/7) STIFFENED, STIFFNECKED

Ex 32: 9 and indeed it is a *s* people!
33: 3 for you are a *s* people."
33: 5 You are a *s* people. I could
34: 9 even though we are a *s* people;
Deut 9: 6 for you are a *s* people.
9:13 and indeed they are a *s* people.
10:16 and be *s* no longer.

STIFFENED (5/5) STIFF, STIFF-NECKED

2 Ki 17:14 but *s* their necks, like the
2 Chr 36:13 but he *s* his neck and hardened
Neh 9:29 *S* their necks, And would not
Jer 7:26 but *s* their neck. They did
19:15 because they have *s* their necks

STIFFHEARTED (KJV) See STUBBORN

STIFFNECKED (2/2)

2 Chr 30: 8 "Now do not be *s*,
Acts 7:51 You *s* and uncircumcised in

STILL (225/216)

Gen 12: 9 going on *s* toward the South.
18:22 but Abraham *s* stood before the
25: 6 and while he was *s* living he
29: 7 it is *s* high day; it is not
29: 9 Now while he was *s* speaking
29:27 which you will serve with me *s*
29:30 And he served with Laban *s*
31:14 Is there *s* any portion or
37: 9 Then he dreamed *s* another dream
43: 6 tell the man whether you had *s*
43: 7 Is your father *s* alive?
43:27 Is he *s* alive?"
43:28 he is *s* alive." And they
44:14 and he was *s* there; and they
45: 3 does my father *s* live?"
45: 6 and there are *s* five years in
45:11 for there are *s* five years of
45:26 Joseph is *s* alive, and he is
45:26 And Jacob's heart stood *s*,
45:28 Joseph my son is *s* alive.
46:30 because you are *s* alive."
Ex 4:18 and see whether they are *s*
9: 2 and *s* hold them,
14:13 "Do not be afraid. Stand *s*,
15:16 of Your arm They will be as *s*
Lev 25:51 If there are *s* many years
Num 9: 8 Moses said to them, "Stand *s*,
9:10 he may *s* keep the LORD's
11:33 But while the meat was *s*
19:13 his uncleanness is *s* on him.
32:14 to increase *s* more the fierce
Deut 5:24 yet he *s* lives.
Josh 3:16 down from upstream stood *s*,
7:26 *s* there to this day. So the
10:12 stand *s* over Gibeon; And Moon,
10:13 So the sun stood *s*,
10:13 So the sun stood *s* in the midst
Judg 3:25 and *s* he had not opened the
5:27 feet he sank, he fell, he lay *s*;
6:24 To this day it is *s* in Ophrah
7: 4 The people are *s* too many;
8: 4 exhausted but *s* in pursuit.
8:20 because he was *s* a youth.
Ruth 1:11 Are there *s* sons in my womb,
3:18 Then she said, "Sit *s*,
1 Sam 12: 7 "Now therefore, stand *s*,
12:25 But if you *s* do wickedly, you
13: 7 he was *s* in Gilgal, and all
14: 9 then we will stand *s* in our
18:29 and Saul was *s* more afraid of
20:14 of the LORD while I *s* live,
26:25 both do great things and also *s*
2 Sam 1: 9 but my life *s* remains in me.'
2:23 fell down and died, stood *s*.
2:28 and all the people stood *s* and
3:35 to eat food while it was *s* day,
9: 1 Is there *s* anyone who is left of
9: 3 Is there not *s* someone of the
9: 3 There is *s* a son of Jonathan
14:32 better for me to be there *s*.
18:14 while he was *s* alive in the
18:30 So he turned aside and stood *s*.
19:28 Therefore what right have I *s*
20:12 saw that all the people stood *s*,
1 Ki 1:14 while you are *s* talking there
1:22 while she was *s* talking with
1:42 While he was *s* speaking, there
11:17 Hadad was *s* a little child.
12: 2 of Nebat heard it (he was *s*
12: 6 his father Solomon while he *s*
19:12 and after the fire a *s* small
20:32 Is he *s* alive? He is my
22: 7 Is there not *s* a prophet of
22: 8 There is *s* one man, Micaiah
2 Ki 6:33 And while he was *s* talking with
12: 3 the people *s* sacrificed and
14: 4 and the people *s* sacrificed and
15: 4 the people *s* sacrificed and
15:35 the people *s* sacrificed and
25: 4 though the Chaldeans were *s*
1 Chr 12: 1 David at Ziklag while he was *s*
2 Chr 10: 6 his father Solomon while he *s*
18: 6 Is there not *s* a prophet of
18: 7 There is *s* one man by whom we
20:17 stand *s* and see the salvation
27: 2 But *s* the people acted
33:17 Nevertheless the people *s*
34: 3 while he was *s* young, he began
Neh 8:11 all the people, saying, "Be *s*,
Esth 6:14 While they were *s* talking with
Job 1:16 While he was *s* speaking,
1:17 While he was *s* speaking,
1:18 While he was *s* speaking,
2: 3 And *s* he holds fast to his
2: 9 Do you *s* hold fast to your
3:13 For now I would have lain *s* and
4:16 It stood *s*, But I could not
6:10 Then I would *s* have comfort;
6:29 my righteousness *s* stands!
20:13 But *s* keeps it in his mouth,
32:16 Because they stood *s* and
37:14 Stand *s* and consider the
Ps 4: 4 heart on your bed, and be *s*.
23: 2 He leads me beside the *s*
46:10 Be *s*, and know that I am
65: 7 You who *s* the noise of the
68:21 hairy scalp of the one who *s*
69: 4 I *s* must restore it.
76: 8 The earth feared and was *s*,
78:30 But while their food was *s* in
78:32 In spite of this they *s* sinned,
83: 1 Your peace, And do not be *s*,
84: 4 They will *s* be praising You.
89: 9 its waves rise, You *s* them.
92:14 They shall *s* bear fruit in old
107:29 storm, So that its waves are *s*.
139:18 I am *s* with You.
141: 5 For *s* my prayer is against
Prov 9: 9 and he will be *s* wiser; Teach
Eccl 4: 2 More than the living who are *s*
7:28 Which my soul *s* seeks but I
12: 9 he *s* taught the people
Isa 5:25 His hand is stretched out *s*.
9:12 His hand is stretched out *s*.
9:17 His hand is stretched out *s*.
9:21 His hand is stretched out *s*.
10: 4 His hand is stretched out *s*.
14: 1 and will *s* choose Israel, and
23: 2 Be *s*, you inhabitants of
28: 4 He eats it up while it is *s* in
29: 8 and his soul is *s* empty; Or as
29: 8 And his soul *s* craves: So the
42:14 I have been *s* and restrained
65:24 And while they are *s* speaking,
Jer 8:14 "Why do we sit *s*?
13:27 O Jerusalem! Will you *s* not be
31:20 I earnestly remember him *s*;
33: 1 while he was *s* shut up in the
42:10 If you will *s* remain in this
47: 6 Rest and be *s*!
51:50 Get away! Do not stand *s*!
Lam 3:20 My soul *s* remembers And sinks
4:17 *S* our eyes failed us,
Ezek 1:24 an army; and when they stood *s*,
7:13 Though he may *s* be alive;
10:17 When the cherubim stood *s*,
10:17 still, the wheels stood *s*,
16:28 the harlot with them and *s*
17:15 Can he break a covenant and *s*
17:18 and in fact gave his hand and *s*
28: 9 Will you *s* say before him who
Dan 4:31 While the word was *s* in the
11:27 for the end will *s* be at the
11:35 because it is *s* for the
Hos 11:12 But Judah *s* walks with God,
Am 4: 7 When there were *s* three
Jon 4: 2 this what I said when I was *s*
Hab 3:11 The sun and moon stood *s* in
Hag 2:19 'Is the seed *s* in the barn?
Zech 11:16 nor feed those that *s* stand.
13: 3 come to pass that if anyone *s*
Mt 12:46 While He was *s* talking to the
15:16 Are you also *s* without
17: 5 While he was *s* speaking, behold,
19:20 What do I *s* lack?"
20:32 So Jesus stood *s* and called
26:45 Are you *s* sleeping and resting?
26:47 And while He was *s* speaking,
27:63 while He was *s* alive, how that
Mk 4:39 be *s*!" And the wind ceased and
5:35 While He was *s* speaking, some
8:17 Is your heart *s* hardened?
10:49 So Jesus stood *s* and commanded
12: 6 Therefore *s* having one son, his
14:41 Are you *s* sleeping and resting?
14:43 while He was *s* speaking, Judas,
15: 5 But Jesus *s* answered nothing,
Lk 7:14 those who carried him stood *s*.
8:49 While He was *s* speaking, someone
9:42 And as he was *s* coming, the
14:20 *S* another said, 'I have married
14:22 and *s* there is room.'
14:32 while the other is *s* a great
15:20 But when he was *s* a great way
18:22 You *s* lack one thing. Sell all
18:40 So Jesus stood *s* and commanded
22:37 this which is written must *s*
22:47 And while He was *s* speaking,
22:60 while he was *s* speaking, the
24: 6 He spoke to you when He was *s*
24:41 But while they *s* did not believe
24:44 I spoke to you while I was *s*
Jn 4:35 There are *s* four months and
16:12 I *s* have many things to say to
20: 1 while it was *s* dark, and saw
Acts 8:38 the chariot to stand *s*.
9: 1 *s* breathing threats and murder
10:44 While Peter was *s* speaking
18:18 So Paul *s* remained a good
Rom 3: 7 why am I also *s* judged as a
4:11 faith which he had while *s*
4:12 father Abraham had while *s*
5: 6 For when we were *s* without
5: 8 in that while we were *s*
8:24 for why does one *s* hope for
9:19 'Why does He *s* find fault?
1 Cor 3: 2 and even now you are *s* not
3: 3 for you are *s* carnal. For where
15:17 you are *s* in your sins!
2 Cor 1:10 in whom we trust that He will *s*
Gal 1:10 For if I *s* pleased men, I would
5:11 if I *s* preach circumcision, why
5:11 why do I *s* suffer persecution?
Phil 1: 9 that your love may abound *s*
2 Th 2: 5 not remember that when I was *s*
Heb 7:10 for he was *s* in the loins of his
9: 8 the first tabernacle was *s*
11: 4 and through it he being dead *s*
11:36 *S* others had trial of mockings
Rev 9:12 *s* two more woes are coming
10: 1 I saw *s* another mighty angel
22:11 is unjust, let him be unjust *s*;
22:11 is filthy, let him be filthy *s*;
22:11 let him be righteous *s*;
22:11 who is holy, let him be holy *s*.

STILLBORN (3/3)

Job 3:16 why was I not hidden like a *s*
Ps 58: 8 Like a *s* child of a woman,
Eccl 6: 3 I say that a *s* child is

STING (2/2)

1 Cor 15:55 Death, where is your *s*?
15:56 The *s* of death is sin, and the

STINGS (2/2)

Prov 23:32 And *s* like a viper.
Rev 9:10 and there were *s* in their

STINK (3/3) STANK

Ex 7:18 shall die, the river shall *s*,
16:24 commanded; and it did not *s*,
Isa 50: 2 Their fish *s* because there

STIR (20/19) STIRRED, STIRRING, STIRS

Job 41:10 so fierce that he would dare *s*
Ps 35:23 *S* up Yourself, and awake to my
78:38 And did not *s* up all His
80: 2 *S* up Your strength, And come
Song 2: 7 Do not *s* up nor awaken love
3: 5 Do not *s* up nor awaken love
8: 4 Do not *s* up nor awaken love
Isa 10:26 And the LORD of hosts will *s* up
13:17 I will *s* up the Medes against
42:13 He shall *s* up His zeal like a
Ezek 23:22 I will *s* up your lovers against
Dan 11: 2 he shall *s* up all against the
11:10 However his sons shall *s* up
11:10 return to his fortress and *s*
11:25 He shall *s* up his power and his
Acts 12:18 there was no small *s* among the
2 Tim 1: 6 Therefore I remind you to *s* up
Heb 10:24 one another in order to *s* up
2 Pe 1:13 to *s* you up by reminding you,
3: 1 (in both of which I *s* up

STIRRED (24/24) STIR

Ex 35:21 everyone came whose heart was *s*,
35:26 And all the women whose heart *s*
36: 2 everyone whose heart was *s*,
1 Sam 22: 8 to me that my son has *s* up my
26:19 If the LORD has *s* you up
1 Ki 21:25 because Jezebel his wife *s* him
1 Chr 5:26 So the God of Israel *s* up the
2 Chr 21:16 Moreover the LORD *s* up against
36:22 the LORD *s* up the spirit of
Ezra 1: 1 the LORD *s* up the spirit of
Ps 39: 2 And my sorrow was *s* up.
Dan 11:25 king of the South shall be *s*
Hos 11: 8 within Me; My sympathy is *s*.

Hag 1:14 So the LORD *s* up the spirit of
Mk 15:11 But the chief priests *s* up the
Jn 5: 4 time into the pool and *s* up
5: 7 the pool when the water is *s*
Acts 6:12 And they *s* up the people, the
13:50 But the Jews *s* up the devout and
14: 2 But the unbelieving Jews *s* up
17:13 they came there also and *s* up
21:27 *s* up the whole crowd and laid
21:38 Egyptian who some time ago *s*
2 Cor 9: 2 and your zeal has *s* up the

STIRRING (3/3) STIR

Dan 7: 2 four winds of heaven were *s* up
Hos 7: 4 He ceases *s* the fire after
Jn 5: 4 after the *s* of the water, was

STIRS (11/11) STIR

Deut 32:11 As an eagle *s* up its nest,
Job 17: 8 And the innocent *s* himself up
26:12 He *s* up the sea with His power,
Prov 10:12 Hatred *s* up strife, But love
15: 1 But a harsh word *s* up anger.
15:18 A wrathful man *s* up strife,
28:25 He who is of a proud heart *s* up
29:22 An angry man *s* up strife,
Isa 14: 9 It *s* up the dead for you,
64: 7 Who *s* himself up to take hold
Lk 23: 5 He *s* up the people, teaching

STOCK (3/3) STOCKS

Isa 3: 1 and from Judah The *s* and the
40:24 Scarcely shall their *s* take
Phil 3: 5 of the *s* of Israel, of the

STOCKS (7/7) STOCK

Job 13:27 You put my feet in the *s*,
33:11 He puts my feet in the *s*,
Prov 7:22 fool to the correction of the *s*,
Jer 20: 2 and put him in the *s* that were
20: 3 brought Jeremiah out of the *s*.
29:26 put him in prison and in the *s*.
Acts 16:24 fastened their feet in the *s*.

STOIC (1/1)

Acts 17:18 Then certain Epicurean and *S*

STOLE (7/7) STEAL, STOLEN

Gen 31:20 And Jacob *s* away, unknown to
2 Sam 15: 6 So Absalom *s* the hearts of the
19: 3 And the people *s* back into the
2 Ki 11: 2 and *s* him away from among the
2 Chr 22:11 and *s* him away from among the
Mt 28:13 disciples came at night and *s*
Eph 4:28 Let him who *s* steal no longer,

STOLEN (18/17) STOLE

Gen 30:33 the lambs, will be considered *s*,
31:19 and Rachel had *s* the household
31:26 that you have *s* away unknown to
31:32 did not know that Rachel had *s*
31:39 whether *s* by day or stolen by
31:39 whether stolen by day or *s* by
40:15 For indeed I was *s* away from the
Ex 22: 7 and it is *s* out of the man's
22:12 it is *s* from him, he shall make
Lev 6: 4 he shall restore what he has *s*,
Josh 7:11 and have both *s* and deceived;
2 Sam 19:41 *s* you away and brought the
21:12 men of Jabesh Gilead who had *s*
Ps 69: 4 Though I have *s* nothing, I
Prov 9:17 *S* water is sweet, And bread
Ezek 33:15 gives back what he has *s*,
Ob 5 Would they not have *s* till they
Mal 1:13 'And you bring the *s*,

STOMACH (20/19) STOMACH'S

Num 5:22 causes the curse go into your *s*,
Deut 18: 3 shoulder, the cheeks, and the *s*.
2 Sam 2:23 Abner struck him in the *s* with
3:27 and there stabbed him in the *s*,
4: 6 and they stabbed him in the *s*.
20:10 he struck him with it in the *s*,
Job 20:14 Yet his food in his *s* turns
20:23 he is about to fill his *s*,
40:16 And his power is in his *s*
Prov 13:25 But the *s* of the wicked shall
18:20 A man's *s* shall be satisfied
Jer 51:34 He has filled his *s* with my
Ezek 3: 3 and fill your *s* with this
Mt 15:17 the mouth goes into the *s* and
Mk 7:19 not enter his heart but his *s*,
Lk 15:16 would gladly have filled his *s*
1 Cor 6:13 Foods for the *s* and the stomach
6:13 for the stomach and the *s* for
Rev 10: 9 and it will make your *s* bitter,
10:10 my *s* became bitter.

STOMACH'S (1/1) STOMACH

1 Tim 5:23 a little wine for your *s* sake

STOMACHS (1/1)

Ezek 7:19 their souls, Nor fill their *s*,

STONE (187/175) STONED, STONE'S, STONES, STONY

Gen 2:12 Bdellium and the onyx *s* are
11: 3 They had brick for *s*,
28:18 and took the *s* that he had put
28:22 And this *s* which I have set as a
29: 2 A large *s* was on the well's
29: 3 and they would roll the *s* from
29: 3 and put the *s* back in its place
29: 8 and they have rolled the *s* from
29:10 went near and rolled the *s*
31:45 So Jacob took a *s* and set it up
35:14 talked with him, a pillar of *s*;
49:24 the *S* of Israel),
Ex 4:25 Then Zipporah took a sharp *s* and
7:19 of wood and pitchers of *s*.
8:26 then will they not *s* us?
15: 5 sank to the bottom like a *s*.
15:16 They will be as still as a *s*,
17: 4 They are almost ready to *s*
17:12 so they took a *s* and put it
20:25 if you make Me an altar of *s*,
20:25 shall not build it of hewn *s*;
21:18 one strikes the other with a *s*
24:10 were a paved work of sapphire *s*,
24:12 I will give you tablets of *s*,
28:10 "six of their names on one *s*,
28:10 and six names on the other *s*,
28:11 the work of an engraver in *s*,
31:18 of the Testimony, tablets of *s*,
34: 1 Cut two tablets of *s* like the
34: 4 So he cut two tablets of *s* like
34: 4 his hand the two tablets of *s*.
Lev 20: 2 The people of the land shall *s*
20:27 they shall *s* them with stones.
24:14 and let all the congregation *s*
24:16 congregation shall certainly *s*
26: 1 shall you set up an engraved *s*
Num 14:10 all the congregation said to *s*
15:35 all the congregation shall *s*
35:17 'And if he strikes him with a *s*
35:23 'or uses a *s*, by which a man
Deut 4:13 wrote them on two tablets of *s*.
4:28 work of men's hands, wood and *s*,
5:22 wrote them on two tablets of *s*
9: 9 to receive the tablets of *s*,
9:10 to me two tablets of *s* written
9:11 gave me the two tablets of *s*,
10: 1 for yourself two tablets of *s*
10: 3 hewed two tablets of *s* like the
13:10 And you shall *s* him with stones
17: 5 and shall *s* to death that man
21:21 all the men of his city shall *s*
22:21 and the men of her city shall *s*
22:24 and you shall *s* them to death
28:36 serve other gods—wood and *s*.
28:64 fathers have known—wood and *s*.
29:17 wood and *s* and silver and gold);
Josh 4: 5 each one of you take up a *s* on
15: 6 the border went up to the *s* of
18:17 and descended to the *s* of Bohan
24:26 of God. And he took a large *s*,
24:27 this *s* shall be a witness to
Judg 3:19 himself turned back from the *s*
3:26 and passed beyond the *s* images
9: 5 sons of Jerubbaal, on one *s*.
9:18 his seventy sons on one *s*,
20:16 every one could sling a *s* at a
1 Sam 6:14 a large *s* was there. So they
6:15 and put them on the large *s*.
6:18 even as far as the large *s* of
6:18 which *s* remains to this day
7:12 Then Samuel took a *s* and set it
14:33 roll a large *s* to me this
17:49 in his bag and took out a *s*;
17:49 so that the *s* sank into his
17:50 Philistine with a sling and a *s*,
20:19 and remain by the *s* Ezel.
25:37 him, and he became like a *s*.
2 Sam 17:13 until there is not one small *s*
20: 8 When they were at the large *s*
1 Ki 1: 9 and fattened cattle by the *s*
5:15 thousand who quarried *s* in
6: 7 was built with *s* finished at
6:18 there was no *s* to be seen.
6:36 with three rows of hewn *s* and
8: 9 ark except the two tablets of *s*
21:10 and *s* him, that he may die.
2 Ki 3:25 and each man threw a *s* on every
12:12 for buying timber and hewn *s*,
19:18 work of men's hands—wood and *s*.
22: 6 and to buy timber and hewn *s* to
1 Chr 22:14 I have prepared timber and *s*
2 Chr 2: 2 eighty thousand to quarry *s* in
2:14 *s* and wood, purple and blue,
34:11 and builders to buy hewn *s* and
Neh 4: 3 he will break down their *s*
9:11 As a *s* into the mighty waters.
Job 38:30 The waters harden like *s*,
41:24 His heart is as hard as *s*,
Ps 91:12 you dash your foot against a *s*.
118:22 The *s* which the builders
Prov 17: 8 A present is a precious *s* in
24:31 Its *s* wall was broken down.
26: 8 Like one who binds a *s* in a
26:27 And he who rolls a *s* will have
27: 3 A *s* is heavy and sand is
Isa 8:14 But a *s* of stumbling and a
28:16 I lay in Zion a *s* for a
28:16 for a foundation, A tried *s*,
37:19 work of men's hands—wood and *s*.
Jer 2:27 are my father,' And to a *s*,
51:26 shall not take from you a *s*
51:26 a stone for a corner Nor a *s*
51:63 that you shall tie a *s* to it
Lam 3: 9 has blocked my ways with hewn *s*;
Ezek 1:26 in appearance like a sapphire *s*;
3: 9 adamant *s*, harder than flint,
10: 1 something like a sapphire *s*,
10: 9 have the color of a beryl *s*.
16:40 and they shall *s* you with
20:32 countries, serving wood and *s*.
23:47 The assembly shall *s* them with
28:13 Every precious *s* was your
36:26 I will take the heart of *s* out
40:42 also four tables of hewn *s* for
Dan 2:34 You watched while a *s* was cut
2:35 And the *s* that struck the image
2:45 as you saw that the *s*
5: 4 bronze and iron, wood and *s*.
5:23 bronze and iron, wood and *s*,
6:17 Then a *s* was brought and laid on
Am 5:11 you have built houses of hewn *s*,
Hab 2:11 For the *s* will cry out from the
2:19 to wood, 'Awake!' To silent *s*,
Hag 2:15 from before *s* was laid upon
2:15 before stone was laid upon *s*
Zech 3: 9 the *s* That I have laid before
3: 9 Upon the *s* are seven eyes.
12: 3 make Jerusalem a very heavy *s*
Mt 4: 6 your foot against a *s*.
7: 9 for bread, will give him a *s*?
21:42 The *s* which the builders
21:44 And whoever falls on this *s* will
24: 2 not one *s* shall be left here
27:60 and he rolled a large *s* against
27:66 sealing the *s* and setting the
28: 2 and came and rolled back the *s*
Mk 12:10 The *s* which the builders
13: 2 Not one *s* shall be left upon
15:46 and rolled a *s* against the door
16: 3 Who will roll away the *s* from
16: 4 they saw that the *s* had been
Lk 4: 3 command this *s* to become
4:11 your foot against a *s*.
11:11 among you, will he give him a *s*?
19:44 will not leave in you one *s*
20: 6 all the people will *s* us, for
20:17 The *s* which the builders
20:18 Whoever falls on that *s* will be
21: 6 will come in which not one *s*
24: 2 But they found the *s* rolled away
Jn 1:42 (which is translated, A *S*).
2: 6 set there six waterpots of *s*,
8: 7 let him throw a *s* at her
10:31 Jews took up stones again to *s*
10:32 which of those works do you *s*
10:33 For a good work we do not *s* You,
11: 8 lately the Jews sought to *s*
11:38 and a *s* lay against it.
11:39 Jesus said, "Take away the *s*.
11:41 Then they took away the *s* from
20: 1 and saw that the *s* had been
Acts 4:11 *s* which was rejected by you
14: 5 to abuse and *s* them,
17:29 is like gold or silver or *s*,
Rom 9:32 stumbled at that stumbling *s*.
9:33 lay in Zion a stumbling *s*
2 Cor 3: 3 not on tablets of *s* but on
1 Pe 2: 4 to Him as to a living *s*,
2: 7 The *s* which the builders
2: 8 A *s* of stumbling And a
Rev 2:17 And I will give him a white *s*,
2:17 and on the *s* a new name written
4: 3 like a jasper and a sardius *s*
9:20 idols of gold, silver, brass, *s*,
18:21 a mighty angel took up a *s*
21:11 was like a most precious *s*,
21:11 precious stone, like a jasper *s*,

STONE'S (1/1) STONE

Lk 22:41 from them about a *s* throw,

STONECUTTERS (3/3)

2 Ki 12:12 and to masons and *s*,
1 Chr 22:15 in abundance: woodsmen and *s*,
2 Chr 2:18 eighty thousand *s* in the

STONED (23/22) STONE

Ex 19:13 but he shall surely be *s* or
21:28 then the ox shall surely be *s*,
21:29 the ox shall be *s* and its owner
21:32 silver, and the ox shall be *s*.
Lev 24:23 and *s* him with stones. So the
Num 15:36 him outside the camp and *s* him
Josh 7:25 So all Israel *s* him with
7:25 them with fire after they had *s*
1 Ki 12:18 but all Israel *s* him with
21:13 him outside the city and *s* him
21:14 Naboth has been *s* and is dead."
21:15 heard that Naboth had been *s*
2 Chr 10:18 but the children of Israel *s*
24:21 the command of the king they *s*
Mt 21:35 killed one, and *s* another.
Jn 8: 5 us that such should be *s*.
Acts 5:26 people, lest they should be *s*.
7:58 cast him out of the city and *s*
7:59 And they *s* Stephen as he was
14:19 they *s* Paul and dragged him

S

2 Cor 11:25 beaten with rods; once I was *s*;
Heb 11:37 They were *s*, they were sawn
12:20 it shall be *s* or shot

STONES (164/147) STONE

Gen 28:11 And he took one of the *s* of
31:46 to his brethren, "Gather *s*.
31:46 And they took *s* and made a
Ex 25: 7 'onyx *s*, and stones to be
25: 7 and *s* to be set in the ephod
28: 9 you shall take two onyx *s*
28:11 you shall engrave the two *s*
28:12 And you shall put the two *s* on
28:12 of the ephod as memorial *s*
28:17 you shall put settings of *s* in
28:17 of stones in it, four rows of *s*:
28:21 And the *s* shall have the names
35: 9 'onyx *s*, and stones to be
35: 9 and *s* to be set in the ephod
35:27 The rulers brought onyx *s*,
35:27 and the *s* to be set in the
39: 6 And they set onyx *s*,
39: 7 of the ephod as memorial *s*
39:10 they set in it four rows of *s*:
39:14 There were twelve *s* according
Lev 14:40 that they take away the *s* in
14:42 Then they shall take other *s* and
14:42 them in the place of those *s*,
14:43 after he has taken away the *s*,
14:45 break down the house, its *s*,
20: 2 the land shall stone him with *s*.
20:27 they shall stone them with *s*.
24:23 cursed, and stoned him with *s*.
Num 14:10 said to stone them with *s*.
15:35 shall stone him with *s* outside
15:36 the camp and stoned him with *s*,
33:52 destroy all their engraved *s*,
Deut 8: 9 a land whose *s* are iron and
13:10 you shall stone him with *s*
17: 5 death that man or woman with *s*.
21:21 shall stone him to death with *s*;
22:21 shall stone her to death with *s*,
22:24 stone them to death with *s*,
27: 2 set up for yourselves large *s*,
27: 4 Ebal you shall set up these *s*,
27: 5 LORD your God, an altar of *s*;
27: 6 You shall build with whole *s* the
27: 8 write very plainly on the *s*
Josh 4: 3 Take for yourselves twelve *s*
4: 6 What do these *s* mean to you?'
4: 7 And these *s* shall be for a
4: 8 and took up twelve *s* from the
4: 9 Then Joshua set up twelve *s* in
4:20 And those twelve *s* which they
4:21 saying, 'What are these *s*?
7:25 So all Israel stoned him with *s*;
7:25 they had stoned them with *s*.
7:26 over him a great heap of *s*,
8:29 raise over it a great heap of *s*
8:31 an altar of whole *s* over which
8:32 he wrote on the *s* a copy of the
10:18 Roll large *s* against the mouth
10:27 and laid large *s* against the
1 Sam 17:40 for himself five smooth *s* from
2 Sam 12:30 talent of gold, with precious *s*.
16: 6 And he threw *s* at David and at
16:13 threw *s* at him and kicked up
18:17 and laid a very large heap of *s*
1 Ki 5:17 them to quarry large *s*,
5:17 quarry large stones, costly *s*,
5:17 costly stones, and hewn *s*,
5:18 and they prepared timber and *s*
7: 9 All these were of costly *s*
7:10 foundation was of costly *s*,
7:10 was of costly stones, large *s*,
7:11 And above were costly *s*,
7:12 with three rows of hewn *s* and
10: 2 very much gold, and precious *s*;
10:10 great quantity, and precious *s*.
10:11 of almug wood and precious *s*
10:27 as common in Jerusalem as *s*,
12:18 all Israel stoned him with *s*,
15:22 And they took away the *s* and
18:31 And Elijah took twelve *s*,
18:32 Then with the *s* he built an
18:38 and the wood and the *s* and the
21:13 the city and stoned him with *s*,
2 Ki 3:19 every good piece of land with *s*.
3:25 But they left the *s* of Kir
16:17 and put it on a pavement of *s*.
1 Chr 12: 2 and the left in hurling *s* and
20: 2 and there were precious *s* in
22: 2 appointed masons to cut hewn *s*
29: 2 for things of wood, onyx *s*,
29: 2 *s* to be set, glistening stones
29: 2 glistening *s* of various colors,
29: 2 colors, all kinds of precious *s*,
29: 8 And whoever had precious *s* gave
2 Chr 1:15 as common in Jerusalem as *s*,
3: 6 the house with precious *s* for
9: 1 in abundance, and precious *s*;
9: 9 great abundance, and precious *s*;
9:10 algum wood and precious *s*.
9:27 as common in Jerusalem as *s*,
10:18 of Israel stoned him with *s*,
16: 6 and they carried away the *s* and
24:21 king they stoned him with *s* in
26:14 bows, and slings to cast *s*.
26:15 to shoot arrows and large *s*.
32:27 for gold, for precious *s*,
Ezra 5: 8 is being built with heavy *s*,
6: 4 with three rows of heavy *s* and
Neh 4: 2 Will they revive the *s* from the
4: 2 *s* that are burned?"
Job 5:23 have a covenant with the *s* of
6:12 my strength the strength of *s*?
8:17 And look for a place in the *s*.
14:19 As water wears away *s*,
22:24 the gold of Ophir among the *s*
28: 6 Its *s* are the source of
Ps 102:14 servants take pleasure in her *s*,
Eccl 3: 5 A time to cast away *s*,
3: 5 And a time to gather *s*;
10: 9 He who quarries *s* may be hurt
Isa 5: 2 dug it up and cleared out its *s*,
9:10 we will rebuild with hewn *s*;
14:19 Who go down to the *s* of the
27: 9 When he makes all the *s* of the
34:11 line of confusion and the *s* of
54:11 I will lay your *s* with colorful
54:12 all your walls of precious *s*.
57: 6 Among the smooth *s* of the
60:17 wood, bronze, And instead of *s*,
62:10 up the highway! Take out the *s*,
Jer 3: 9 and committed adultery with *s*
43: 9 Take large *s* in your hand, and
43:10 set his throne above these *s*
Lam 3:53 my life in the pit And threw *s*
4: 1 changed the fine gold! The *s*
Ezek 16:40 and they shall stone you with *s*
23:47 shall stone them with *s* and
26:12 houses; they will lay your *s*,
27:22 spices, all kinds of precious *s*,
28:14 forth in the midst of fiery *s*.
28:16 From the midst of the fiery *s*.
46:23 was a row of building *s*
46:23 were made under the rows of *s*
Dan 11:38 with precious *s* and pleasant
Mic 1: 6 I will pour down her *s* into
Zech 5: 4 it, with its timber and *s*.
Mt 3: 9 to Abraham from these *s*.
4: 3 command that these *s* become
23:37 who kills the prophets and *s*
Mk 5: 5 out and cutting himself with *s*.
12: 4 and at him they threw *s*,
13: 1 see what manner of *s* and what
Lk 3: 8 to Abraham from these *s*.
13:34 who kills the prophets and *s*
19:40 the *s* would immediately cry
21: 5 it was adorned with beautiful *s*
Jn 8:59 Then they took up *s* to throw at
10:31 Then the Jews took up *s* again
1 Cor 3:12 with gold, silver, precious *s*,
2 Cor 3: 7 written and engraved on *s*,
1 Pe 2: 5 you also, as living *s*,
Rev 17: 4 with gold and precious *s* and
18:12 precious *s* and pearls, fine
18:16 with gold and precious *s* and
21:19 with all kinds of precious *s*:

STONING (1/1)

1 Sam 30: 6 for the people spoke of *s* him,

STONY (5/5) STONE

Ezek 11:19 and take the *s* heart out of
Mt 13: 5 Some fell on *s* places, where
13:20 received the seed on *s* places,
Mk 4: 5 Some fell on *s* ground, where it
4:16 are the ones sown on *s* ground

STOOD (311/300) STAND

Gen 18: 8 and he *s* by them under the tree
18:22 but Abraham still *s* before the
19:27 to the place where he had *s*
23: 3 Then Abraham *s* up from before
23: 7 Then Abraham *s* up and bowed
24:30 And there he *s* by the camels at
28:13 the LORD *s* above it and said:
37: 7 my sheaf arose and also *s*
37: 7 and indeed your sheaves *s* all
41: 1 he *s* by the river.
41: 3 and *s* by the other cows on the
41:17 in my dream I *s* on the bank of
41:46 was thirty years old when he *s*
43:15 and they *s* before Joseph.
45: 1 himself before all those who *s*
45: 1 go out from me!" So no one *s*
45:26 And Jacob's heart *s* still,
Ex 2: 4 And his sister *s* afar off, to
2:17 but Moses *s* up and helped them,
5:20 they met Moses and Aaron who *s*
9:10 ashes from the furnace and *s*
14:19 went from before them and *s*
15: 8 The floods *s* upright like a
18:13 and the people *s* before Moses
19:17 and they *s* at the foot of the
20:18 they trembled and *s* afar off.
20:21 So the people *s* afar off, but
32:26 then Moses *s* in the entrance of
33: 8 and each man *s* at his tent
33: 9 of cloud descended and *s* at
34: 5 descended in the cloud and *s*
Lev 9: 5 congregation drew near and *s*
Num 12: 5 in the pillar of cloud and *s*
16:18 and *s* at the door of the
16:27 and Abiram came out and *s* at
16:48 And he *s* between the dead and
22:24 Then the Angel of the LORD *s* in
22:26 and *s* in a narrow place where
22:34 for I did not know You *s* in the
27: 2 And they *s* before Moses, before
Deut 4:10 concerning the day you *s*
4:11 Then you came near and *s* at the
5: 5 I *s* between the LORD and you at
31:15 and the pillar of cloud *s* above
Josh 3:16 which came down from upstream *s*
3:17 of the covenant of the LORD *s*
4: 3 where the priests' feet *s* firm.
4: 9 bore the ark of the covenant *s*;
4:10 the priests who bore the ark *s*
5:13 a Man *s* opposite him with His
8:33 *s* on either side of the ark
10:13 So the sun *s* still, And the
10:13 So the sun *s* still in the midst
11:13 But as for the cities that *s*
20: 9 the avenger of blood until he *s*
21:44 a man of all their enemies *s*
Judg 6:31 But Joash said to all who *s*
7:21 And every man *s* in his place all
9: 7 he went and *s* on top of Mount
9:35 the son of Ebed went out and *s*
9:44 with him rushed forward and *s*
18:16 *s* by the entrance of the gate.
18:17 The priest *s* at the entrance of
19: 5 and he *s* to depart; but the
19: 7 And when the man *s* to depart,
19: 9 And when the man *s* to depart—he
20:28 *s* before it in those days),
1 Sam 1:26 I am the woman who *s* by you
3:10 Now the LORD came and *s* and
4:20 of her death the women who *s*
6:14 and *s* there; a large stone was
10:23 and when he *s* among the people,
16:21 So David came to Saul and *s*
17: 3 The Philistines *s* on a mountain
17: 3 and Israel *s* on a mountain on
17: 8 Then he *s* and cried out to the
17:26 David spoke to the men who *s*
17:51 Therefore David ran and *s* over
22: 7 Saul said to his servants who *s*
22:17 king said to the guards who *s*
26:13 and *s* on the top of a hill afar
2 Sam 1:10 So I *s* over him and killed him,
2:23 fell down and died, *s* still.
2:28 and all the people *s* still and
13:31 and all his servants *s* by with
18: 4 So the king *s* beside the
18:30 So he turned aside and *s*
20:11 Meanwhile one of Joab's men *s*
20:12 man saw that all the people *s*
20:15 and it *s* by the rampart.
1 Ki 1:28 into the king's presence and *s*
3:15 And he came to Jerusalem and *s*
3:16 and *s* before him.
7:25 It *s* on twelve oxen: three
8:22 Then Solomon *s* before the altar
8:55 Then he *s* and blessed all the
10:19 and two lions *s* beside the
10:20 Twelve lions *s* there, one on
12: 6 consulted the elders who *s*
12: 8 who *s* before him.
13: 1 and Jeroboam *s* by the altar to
13:24 and the donkey *s* by it.
13:24 The lion also *s* by the corpse.
19:13 his mantle and went out and *s*
22:21 a spirit came forward and *s*
2 Ki 2: 7 sons of the prophets went and *s*
2: 7 while the two of them *s* by the
2:13 and went back and *s* by the bank
3:21 and they *s* at the border.
4:12 she *s* before him.
4:15 she *s* in the doorway.
5: 9 and he *s* at the door of
5:15 and came and *s* before him;
5:25 Now he went in and *s* before his
8: 9 and he came and *s* before him,
9:17 Now a watchman *s* on the tower
10: 9 morning, that he went out and *s*,
11:11 Then the escorts *s*,
13:21 he revived and *s* on his feet.
18:17 they went and *s* by the aqueduct
18:28 Then the Rabshakeh *s* and called
23: 3 Then the king *s* by a pillar and
1 Chr 6:39 who *s* at his right hand, was
21: 1 Now Satan *s* up against Israel,
21:15 And the angel of the LORD *s*
2 Chr 3:13 They *s* on their feet, and they
4: 4 It *s* on twelve oxen: three
5:12 *s* at the east end of the altar,
6:12 Then Solomon *s* before the
6:13 and he *s* on it, knelt down on
7: 6 them, while all Israel *s*.
9:18 and two lions *s* beside the
9:19 Twelve lions *s* there, one on
10: 6 consulted the elders who *s*
10: 8 who *s* before him.
13: 4 Then Abijah *s* on Mount
18:20 a spirit came forward and *s*
20: 5 Then Jehoshaphat *s* in the
20:13 *s* before the LORD.
20:19 children of the Korahites *s* up
20:20 Jehoshaphat *s* and said, "Hear
20:23 the people of Ammon and Moab *s*
24:20 who *s* above the people, and
28:12 *s* up against those who came
29:26 The Levites *s* with the
30:16 They *s* in their place according
34:31 Then the king *s* in his place and
35:10 and the priests *s* in their
Ezra 3:10 the priests *s* in their apparel
10:10 Then Ezra the priest *s* up and
Neh 8: 4 So Ezra the scribe *s* on a

8: 4 *s* Mattithiah, Shema, Anaiah,
8: 5 all the people *s* up.
8: 7 and the people *s* in their
9: 2 and they *s* and confessed their
9: 3 And they *s* up in their place and
9: 4 and Chenani *s* on the stairs of
12: 9 *s* across from them in their
12:40 the two thanksgiving choirs *s*
Esth 5: 1 put on her royal robes and *s*
7: 7 but Haman *s* before Queen
8: 4 So Esther arose and *s* before
Job 4:15 The hair on my body *s* up.
4:16 It *s* still, But I could not
29: 8 And the aged arose and *s*;
32:16 Because they *s* still and
Ps 33: 9 He commanded, and it *s* fast.
104: 6 The waters *s* above the
106:23 Had not Moses His chosen one *s*
106:30 Then Phinehas *s* up and
Isa 6: 2 Above it *s* seraphim; each one
36: 2 And he *s* by the aqueduct from
36:13 Then the Rabshakeh *s* and
Jer 14: 6 And the wild donkeys *s* in the
15: 1 Even if Moses and Samuel *s*
18:20 Remember that I *s* before You
19:14 and he *s* in the court of the
23:18 For who has *s* in the counsel
23:22 But if they had *s* in My
28: 5 of all the people who *s* in the
36:21 of all the princes who *s*
44:15 with all the women who *s* by, a
48:45 Those who fled *s* under the
Ezek 1:21 went, these went; when those *s*,
1:21 when those stood, these *s*;
1:24 and when they *s* still, they let
1:25 their heads; whenever they *s*,
3:23 the glory of the LORD *s* there,
8:11 And there *s* before them seventy
8:11 and in their midst *s* Jaazaniah
9: 2 They went in and *s* beside the
10: 6 that he went in and *s* beside
10:17 When the cherubim *s* still,
10:17 the wheels *s* still, and when
10:18 threshold of the temple and *s*
10:19 and they *s* at the door of the
11:23 the midst of the city and *s* on
37:10 and *s* upon their feet, an
40: 3 and he *s* in the gateway.
43: 6 while a man *s* beside me.
Dan 2: 2 So they came and *s* before the
2:31 *s* before you; and its form was
3: 3 and they *s* before the image
7:10 thousand times ten thousand *s*
7:16 near to one of those who *s* by,
8:15 that suddenly there *s* before me
8:17 So he came near where I *s*,
8:18 and *s* me upright.
8:22 horn and the four that *s* up
10:11 this word to me, I *s* trembling.
10:16 saying to him who *s* before me,
11: 1 *s* up to confirm and strengthen
12: 5 and there *s* two others, one on
Hos 10: 9 days of Gibeah; There they *s*.
Am 7: 7 the Lord *s* on a wall made with
Ob 11 In the day that you *s* on the
14 You should not have *s* at the
Hab 3: 6 He *s* and measured the earth;
3:11 The sun and moon *s* still in
Zech 1: 8 and it *s* among the myrtle trees
1:10 And the man who *s* among the
1:11 who *s* among the myrtle trees,
3: 4 and spoke to those who *s*
3: 5 And the Angel of the LORD *s*
Mt 2: 9 till it came and *s* over where
12:46 His mother and brothers *s*
13: 2 and the whole multitude *s* on
20:32 So Jesus *s* still and called
26:73 And a little later those who *s*
27:11 Now Jesus *s* before the
27:47 Some of those who *s* there, when
Mk 10:49 So Jesus *s* still and commanded
11: 5 But some of those who *s* there
14:47 And one of those who *s* by drew
14:60 And the high priest *s* up in the
14:69 began to say to those who *s* by,
14:70 And a little later those who *s*
15:35 Some of those who *s* by, when
15:39 who *s* opposite Him, saw that He
Lk 2: 9 an angel of the Lord *s* before
4:16 and *s* up to read.
4:39 So He *s* over her and rebuked the
5: 1 that He *s* by the Lake of
6: 8 here." And he arose and *s*.
6:17 He came down with them and *s*
7:14 and those who carried him *s*
7:38 and *s* at His feet behind Him
9:32 His glory and the two men who *s*
10:25 a certain lawyer *s* up and
17:12 were lepers, who *s* afar off.
18:11 The Pharisee *s* and prayed thus
18:40 So Jesus *s* still and commanded
19: 8 Then Zacchaeus *s* and said to the
19:24 And he said to those who *s* by,
23:10 the chief priests and scribes *s*
23:35 And the people *s* looking on.
23:49 *s* at a distance, watching these
24: 4 two men *s* by them in shining
24:36 Jesus Himself *s* in the midst of
Jn 1:35 John *s* with two of his
7:37 Jesus *s* and cried out, saying,
11:56 among themselves as they *s* in
12:29 Therefore the people who *s* by
18: 5 also *s* with them.
18:16 But Peter *s* at the door outside.
18:18 who had made a fire of coals *s*
18:18 And Peter *s* with them and
18:22 one of the officers who *s* by
18:25 Now Simon Peter *s* and warmed
19:25 Now there *s* by the cross of
20:11 But Mary *s* outside by the tomb
20:19 Jesus came and *s* in the midst,
20:26 and *s* in the midst, and said,
21: 4 Jesus *s* on the shore; yet the
Acts 1:10 two men *s* by them in white
1:15 And in those days Peter *s* up in
3: 8 *s* and walked and entered the
5:34 Then one in the council *s* up, a
9: 7 men who journeyed with him *s*
9:39 And all the widows *s* by him
10:17 and *s* before the gate.
10:30 a man *s* before me in bright
11:11 three men *s* before the house
11:28 *s* up and showed by the Spirit
12: 7 an angel of the Lord *s* by him,
12:14 in and announced that Peter *s*
13:16 Then Paul *s* up, and motioning
16: 9 A man of Macedonia *s* and
17:22 Then Paul *s* in the midst of the
21:40 Paul *s* on the stairs and
22:13 and he *s* and said to me,
22:25 said to the centurion who *s* by,
23: 2 Ananias commanded those who *s*
23: 4 And those who *s* by said, "Do
23:11 the following night the Lord *s*
24:20 any wrongdoing in me while I *s*
25: 7 had come down from Jerusalem *s*
25:18 When the accusers *s* up, they
26:30 the king *s* up, as well as the
27:21 then Paul *s* in the midst of
27:23 For there *s* by me this night an
2 Tim 4:16 At my first defense no one *s*
4:17 But the Lord *s* with me and
Rev 5: 6 *s* a Lamb as though it had been
7:11 All the angels *s* around the
8: 3 came and *s* at the altar. He was
11: 1 measuring rod. And the angel *s*,
11:11 and they *s* on their feet, and
12: 4 And the dragon *s* before the
13: 1 Then I *s* on the sand of the sea.
18:17 on the sea, *s* at a distance

STOOP (2/2) STOOPED, STOOPING, STOOPS

Isa 46: 2 They *s*, they bow down
Mk 1: 7 strap I am not worthy to *s*

STOOPED (6/6) STOOP

1 Sam 24: 8 David *s* with his face to the
28:14 and he *s* with his face to the
Hos 11: 4 I *s* and fed them.
Jn 8: 6 But Jesus *s* down and wrote on
8: 8 And again He *s* down and wrote on
20:11 and as she wept she *s* down and

STOOPING (2/2) STOOP

Lk 24:12 and *s* down, he saw the linen
Jn 20: 5 *s* down and looking in, saw the

STOOPS (1/1) STOOP

Isa 46: 1 Bel bows down, Nebo *s*;

STOP (9/9)

2 Ki 3:19 and *s* up every spring of water,
2 Chr 32: 3 his leaders and commanders to *s*
Neh 5:10 let us *s* this usury!
Job 38:11 here your proud waves must *s*!'
Ps 35: 3 And *s* those who pursue me.
Prov 17:14 Therefore *s* contention before
20: 3 is honorable for a man to *s*
Ezek 34:10 and *s* dispossessing My
2 Cor 11:10 no one shall *s* me from this

STOPPED (33/33)

Gen 8: 2 windows of heaven were also *s*,
26:15 Now the Philistines had *s* up all
26:18 for the Philistines had *s* them
29:35 Then she *s* bearing.
30: 9 When Leah saw that she had *s*
41:49 until he *s* counting, for it
Lev 15: 3 or his body is *s* up by his
Num 16:48 the living; so the plague was *s*.
16:50 meeting, for the plague had *s*.
25: 8 So the plague was *s* among the
Josh 10:13 stood still, And the moon *s*,
Ruth 1:18 she *s* speaking to her.
2 Sam 15:17 and *s* at the outskirts.
1 Ki 15:21 that he *s* building Ramah, and
2 Ki 3:25 and they *s* up all the springs
13:18 so he struck three times, and *s*.
2 Chr 16: 5 that he *s* building Ramah and
32: 4 people gathered together who *s*
32:30 This same Hezekiah also *s* the
Neh 12:39 and they *s* by the Gate of the
Ps 63:11 those who speak lies shall be *s*.
106:30 And the plague was *s*.
Jer 38:27 So they *s* speaking with him,
43: 1 when Jeremiah had *s* speaking to
44:18 But since we *s* burning incense
Zech 7:11 and *s* their ears so that they
Lk 5: 4 When He had *s* speaking, He said
8:44 immediately her flow of blood *s*.
Acts 7:57 *s* their ears, and ran at him
21:32 they *s* beating Paul.
Rom 3:19 law, that every mouth may be *s*,
Titus 1:11 whose mouths must be *s*,
Heb 11:33 *s* the mouths of lions,

STOPS (4/4)

1 Ki 18:44 and go down before the rain *s*
Ps 58: 4 like the deaf cobra that *s*
107:42 And all iniquity *s* its mouth.
Isa 33:15 Who *s* his ears from hearing of

STORAGE (5/5) STORE

1 Ki 9:19 all the *s* cities that Solomon
2 Chr 8: 4 and all the *s* cities which he
8: 6 also Baalath and all the *s*
16: 4 and all the *s* cities of
17:12 and he built fortresses and *s*

STORE (11/11) STORAGE, STORED, STOREHOUSE, STORES

Gen 41:35 and *s* up grain under the
Num 19: 9 and *s* them outside the camp in
Deut 14:28 produce of that year and *s* it
32:34 Is this not laid up in *s* with
1 Chr 27:28 and Joash was over the *s* of
Job 36:13 the hypocrites in heart *s*
Prov 10:14 Wise people *s* up knowledge,
Isa 3: 1 from Judah The stock and the *s*,
Am 3:10 Who *s* up violence and robbery in
Lk 12:17 since I have no room to *s* my
12:18 and there I will *s* all my crops

STORED (6/6) STORE

2 Ki 5:24 and *s* them away in the house;
Ezra 6: 1 where the treasures were *s* in
Neh 13: 5 where previously they had *s* the
Prov 13:22 the wealth of the sinner is *s*
Jer 36:20 but they *s* the scroll in the
Hos 13:12 His sin is *s* up.

STOREHOUSE (8/8) STORE, STOREHOUSES

1 Chr 26:15 Gate, and to his sons the *s*.
26:17 and for the *s* two by two.
Neh 10:38 our God, to the rooms of the *s*.
12:44 over the rooms of the *s* for
13:12 new wine and the oil to the *s*.
13:13 as treasurers over the *s*.
Mal 3:10 all the tithes into the *s*,
Lk 12:24 which have neither *s* nor barn;

STOREHOUSES (7/7) STOREHOUSE

Gen 41:56 and Joseph opened all the *s* and
Deut 28: 8 the blessing on you in your *s*
1 Chr 27:25 son of Uzziah was over the *s*
2 Chr 32:28 *s* for the harvest of grain,
Ps 33: 7 He lays up the deep in *s*.
Jer 50:26 farthest border; Open her *s*;
Joel 1:17 *S* are in shambles; Barns are

STOREROOMS (4/4)

Neh 10:37 to the *s* of the house of our
10:39 to the *s* where the articles of
12:25 keeping the watch at the *s* of
13: 4 having authority over the *s* of

STORES (2/2) STORE

2 Chr 11:11 and *s* of food, oil, and wine.
Prov 2: 7 He *s* up sound wisdom for the

STORIES (5/5)

Ezek 41: 6 side chambers were in three *s*,
41:16 all around their three *s*
42: 3 against gallery in three *s*.
42: 5 from the lower and middle *s* of
42: 6 For they were in three *s* and

STORING (2/2)

1 Cor 16: 2 *s* up as he may prosper, that
1 Tim 6:19 *s* up for themselves a good

STORK (5/5)

Lev 11:19 'the *s*, the heron after its
Deut 14:18 'the *s*, the heron after its
Ps 104:17 The *s* has her home in the fir
Jer 8: 7 Even the *s* in the heavens Knows
Zech 5: 9 had wings like the wings of a *s*,

STORK'S (1/1)

Job 39:13 and pinions like the kindly *s*?

STORM (15/14) STORMY, WINDSTORM

Job 21:18 And like chaff that a *s*
26:12 He breaks up the *s*.
30:14 Under the ruinous *s* they roll
36:33 also, concerning the rising *s*.
Ps 55: 8 my escape From the windy *s*
83:15 And frighten them with Your *s*.

S

107:29 He calms the *s*,
Prov 1:27 your terror comes like a *s*,
Isa 4: 6 and for a shelter from *s* and
25: 4 A refuge from the *s*,
25: 4 of the terrible ones is as a *s*
28: 2 of hail and a destroying *s*,
29: 6 With *s* and tempest And the
Ezek 38: 9 will ascend, coming like a *s*,
Nah 1: 3 In the whirlwind and in the *s*,

STORMY (4/4) STORM

Ps 107:25 He commands and raises the *s*
148: 8 *S* wind, fulfilling His word;
Ezek 13:11 and a *s* wind shall tear it
13:13 I will cause a *s* wind to break

STORY (7/4)

1 Ki 6: 8 The doorway for the middle *s*
6: 8 up by stairs to the middle *s*,
Ezek 41: 6 thirty chambers in each *s*;
41: 7 As one went up from *s* to story,
41: 7 As one went up from story to *s*,
41: 7 went up from the lowest *s* to
Acts 20: 9 he fell down from the third *s*

STOUT (1/1)

Judg 3:29 all *s* men of valor; not a man

STOUTEST (1/1)

Ps 78:31 And slew the *s* of them,

STOUTHEARTED (2/2)

1 Chr 12:33 *s* men who could keep ranks;
Ps 76: 5 The *s* were plundered;

STOVE (1/1)

Lev 11:35 it is an oven or cooking *s*,

STRAGGLERS (1/1)

Deut 25:18 all the *s* at your rear, when

STRAIGHT (32/32)

Josh 6: 5 people shall go up every man *s*
6:20 every man *s* before him, and
1 Sam 6:12 Then the cows headed *s* for the
Ps 5: 8 Make Your way *s* before my
Prov 4:25 Let your eyes look *s* ahead,
9:15 Who go *s* on their way:
Eccl 1:15 is crooked cannot be made *s*,
7:13 For who can make *s* what He has
Isa 40: 3 Make *s* in the desert
40: 4 crooked places shall be made *s*
42:16 And crooked places *s*.
45: 2 And make the crooked places *s*;
Jer 31: 9 In a *s* way in which they shall
31:39 line shall again extend *s*
Ezek 1: 7 Their legs were *s*,
1: 9 but each one went *s* forward.
1:12 And each one went *s* forward;
1:23 their wings spread out *s*,
10:22 They each went *s* forward.
Am 4: 3 Each one *s* ahead of her,
Mt 3: 3 LORD; Make His paths *s*.
Mk 1: 3 LORD; Make His paths *s*.
Lk 3: 4 LORD; Make His paths *s*.
3: 5 places shall be made *s*
13:13 and immediately she was made *s*,
Jn 1:23 Make *s* the way of the
Acts 9:11 and go to the street called *S*,
13:10 you not cease perverting the *s*
14:10 'Stand up *s* on your feet!"
16:11 we ran a *s* course to
21: 1 running a *s* course we came to
Heb 12:13 and make *s* paths for your feet,

STRAIGHTFORWARD (1/1)

Gal 2:14 when I saw that they were not *s*

STRAIGHTWAY (KJV) See IMMEDIATELY, SURELY

STRAIN (1/1)

Mt 23:24 who *s* out a gnat and swallow a

STRAINING (1/1)

Mk 6:48 Then He saw them *s* at rowing,

STRAITS (4/4)

Deut 28:53 in the siege and desperate *s* in
28:55 in the siege and desperate *s*
28:57 in the siege and desperate *s*
Lam 1: 3 overtake her in dire *s*.

STRAND (2/2)

Judg 16: 9 he broke the bowstrings as a *s*
Song 4: 3 Your lips are like a *s* of

STRANGE (13/12) STRANGER

Ex 30: 9 You shall not offer *s* incense on
2 Ki 19:24 I have dug and drunk *s* water,
Ps 114: 1 of Jacob from a people of *s*
Prov 23:33 Your eyes will see *s* things,
Jer 18:14 waters be forsaken for *s*
Hos 8:12 But they were considered a *s*
Lk 5:26 We have seen *s* things today!"
Acts 17:20 For you are bringing some *s*
Heb 13: 9 about with various and *s*
1 Pe 4: 4 they think it *s* that you do not
4:12 do not think it *s* concerning
4:12 as though some *s* thing happened
Jude 7 immorality and gone after *s*

STRANGER (82/78) FOREIGNER, STRANGE, STRANGERS

Gen 17: 8 the land in which you are a *s*,
28: 4 the land In which you are a *s*,
37: 1 land where his father was a *s*,
42: 7 but he acted as a *s* to them and
Ex 2:22 I have been a *s* in a foreign
12:19 whether he is a *s* or a native
12:48 And when a *s* dwells with you
12:49 the native-born and for the *s*
18: 3 I have been a *s* in a foreign
20:10 nor your *s* who is within your
22:21 shall neither mistreat a *s* nor
23: 9 you shall not oppress a *s*,
23: 9 for you know the heart of a *s*,
23:12 your female servant and the *s*
Lev 16:29 of your own country or a *s* who
17:12 nor shall any *s* who dwells
17:15 of your own country or a *s*,
18:26 any of your own nation or any *s*
19:10 them for the poor and the *s*:
19:33 And if a *s* dwells with you in
19:34 The *s* who dwells among you shall
23:22 them for the poor and for the *s*:
24:16 the *s* as well as him who is
24:22 have the same law for the *s*
25: 6 and the *s* who dwells with you,
25:35 like a *s* or a sojourner, that
25:47 Now if a sojourner or *s* close
25:47 and sells himself to the *s* or
Num 9:14 And if a *s* dwells among you, and
9:14 both for the *s* and the native
15:14 And if a *s* dwells with you, or
15:15 of the assembly and for the *s*
15:15 so shall the *s* be before the
15:16 shall be for you and for the *s*
15:26 children of Israel and the *s*
15:29 of Israel and for the *s* who
15:30 he is native-born or a *s*,
19:10 of Israel and to the *s* who
35:15 children of Israel, for the *s*,
Deut 1:16 a man and his brother or the *s*
5:14 nor your *s* who is within your
10:18 and the widow, and loves the *s*,
10:19 "Therefore love the *s*,
14:29 and the *s* and the fatherless
16:11 the *s* and the fatherless and
16:14 the *s* and the fatherless and
24:17 not pervert justice due the *s*
24:19 get it; it shall be for the *s*,
24:20 it shall be for the *s*,
24:21 it shall be for the *s*,
25: 5 shall not be married to a *s*
26:11 you and the Levite and the *s*
26:12 given it to the Levite, the *s*,
26:13 given them to the Levite, the *s*,
27:19 perverts the justice due the *s*,
29:11 also the *s* who is in your camp,
31:12 and the *s* who is within your
Josh 8:33 the *s* as well as he who was
20: 9 of Israel and for the *s* who
Job 19:15 maidservants, Count me as a *s*;
Ps 39:12 For I am a *s* with You,
69: 8 I have become a *s* to my
94: 6 They slay the widow and the *s*,
119:19 I am a *s* in the earth; Do not
Prov 6: 1 shaken hands in pledge for a *s*,
11:15 He who is surety for a *s* will
14:10 And a *s* does not share its
20:16 of one who is surety for a *s*,
27: 2 and not your own mouth; A *s*,
27:13 of him who is surety for a *s*,
Jer 7: 6 "if you do not oppress the *s*,
14: 8 Why should You be like a *s* in
22: 3 and do no violence to the *s*,
Ezek 22: 7 midst they have oppressed the *s*;
22:29 they wrongfully oppress the *s*.
47:23 that in whatever tribe the *s*
Mt 25:35 I was a *s* and you took Me in;
25:38 When did we see You a *s* and take
25:43 I was a *s* and you did not take
25:44 You hungry or thirsty or a *s*
Lk 24:18 Are You the only *s* in Jerusalem,
Jn 10: 5 will by no means follow a *s*,

STRANGER'S (1/1)

Lev 25:47 or to a member of the *s* family,

STRANGERS (46/45) STRANGER

Gen 15:13 your descendants will be *s* in
31:15 Are we not considered *s* by him?
36: 7 and the land where they were *s*
Ex 6: 4 in which they were *s*.
22:21 for you were *s* in the land of
23: 9 because you were *s* in the land
Lev 17: 8 or of the *s* who dwell among
17:10 or of the *s* who dwell among
17:13 or of the *s* who dwell among
19:34 for you were *s* in the land of
20: 2 or of the *s* who dwell in
22:18 or of the *s* in Israel, who
25:23 for you are *s* and sojourners
25:45 may buy the children of the *s*
Deut 10:19 for you were *s* in the land of
Josh 8:35 and the *s* who were living among
1 Chr 16:19 very few, and *s* in it.
Ps 54: 3 For *s* have risen up against me,
105:12 very few, and *s* in it.
109:11 And let *s* plunder his labor.
146: 9 The LORD watches over the *s*;
Prov 5:17 And not for *s* with you.
Isa 1: 7 *S* devour your land in your
1: 7 desolate, as overthrown by *s*.
5:17 waste places of the fat ones *s*
14: 1 The *s* will be joined with them,
61: 5 *S* shall stand and feed your
Jer 51:51 For *s* have come into the
Ezek 7:21 as plunder Into the hands of *s*,
11: 9 deliver you into the hands of *s*,
14: 7 or of the *s* who dwell in
16:32 who takes *s* instead of her
28: 7 I will bring *s* against you,
47:22 and for the *s* who dwell among
Ob 11 In the day that *s* carried
Mt 17:25 from their sons or from *s*?
17:26 Peter said to Him, "From *s*.
27: 7 potter's field, to bury *s* in.
Jn 10: 5 they do not know the voice of *s*.
Acts 13:17 people when they dwelt as *s* in
Eph 2:12 commonwealth of Israel and *s*
2:19 you are no longer *s* and
1 Tim 5:10 children, if she has lodged *s*,
Heb 11:13 and confessed that they were *s*
13: 2 Do not forget to entertain *s*,
3 Jn 5 do for the brethren and for *s*,

STRANGLED (3/3)

Acts 15:20 immorality, from things *s*,
15:29 from blood, from things *s*,
21:25 from blood, from things *s*,

STRANGLING (1/1)

Job 7:15 So that my soul chooses *s* And

STRAP (5/5) STRAPS

Gen 14:23 from a thread to a sandal *s*,
Isa 5:27 Nor the *s* of their sandals be
Mk 1: 7 whose sandal *s* I am not worthy
Lk 3:16 whose sandal *s* I am not worthy
Jn 1:27 whose sandal *s* I am not worthy

STRAPS (6/6) STRAP

Ex 28: 7 It shall have two shoulder *s*
28:25 and put them on the shoulder *s*
28:27 put them on the two shoulder *s*,
39: 4 They made shoulder *s* for it to
39:18 and put them on the shoulder *s*
39:20 put them on the two shoulder *s*,

STRATA (1/1)

Am 9: 6 And has founded His *s* in the

STRAW (19/18)

Gen 24:25 We have both *s* and feed enough,
24:32 and provided *s* and feed for the
Ex 5: 7 no longer give the people *s* to
5: 7 Let them go and gather *s* for
5:10 Pharaoh: 'I will not give you *s*.
5:11 get yourselves *s* where you can
5:12 to gather stubble instead of *s*.
5:13 quota, as when there was *s*.
5:16 There is no *s* given to your
5:18 for no *s* shall be given you,
Judg 19:19 although we have both *s* and
1 Ki 4:28 They also brought barley and *s*
Job 21:18 They are like *s* before the
41:27 He regards iron as *s*,
41:29 Darts are regarded as *s*;
Isa 11: 7 And the lion shall eat *s* like
25:10 As *s* is trampled down for the
65:25 The lion shall eat *s* like the
1 Cor 3:12 precious stones, wood, hay, *s*,

STRAWED (KJV) See SCATTERED, SPREAD

STRAY (8/8) STRAYED, STRAYING

Ps 119:21 Who *s* from Your commandments.
119:118 You reject all those who *s* from
Prov 7:25 Do not *s* into her paths;
19:27 And you will *s* from the words
Isa 63:17 why have You made us *s* from
Ezek 14:11 of Israel may no longer *s* from
Hos 4:12 harlotry has caused them to *s*,
Mic 3: 5 Who make my people *s*;

STRAYED (6/6) STRAY

Ps 119:110 Yet I have not *s* from Your
Ezek 44:10 who *s* away from Me after their
1 Tim 1: 6 from which some, having *s*,
6:10 for which some have *s* from the
6:21 by professing it some have *s*

2 Tim 2:18 who have *s* concerning the truth,

STRAYING (1/1) STRAY

Mt 18:12 to seek the one that is *s*?

STREAKED (6/5)

Gen 30:39 and the flocks brought forth *s*,
30:40 the flocks face toward the *s*
31: 8 The *s* shall be your wages,' then
31: 8 then all the flocks bore *s*.
31:10 leaped upon the flocks were *s*,
31:12 which leap on the flocks are *s*,

STREAKS (1/1)

Lev 14:37 of the house with ingrained *s*,

STREAM (11/11) STREAMS

Ps 124: 4 The *s* would have gone over our
Isa 30:28 breath is like an overflowing *s*,
30:33 like a *s* of brimstone,
57: 6 the smooth stones of the *s*
66:12 the Gentiles like a flowing *s*.
Jer 15:18 be to me like an unreliable *s*,
51:44 And the nations shall not *s* to
Dan 7:10 A fiery *s* issued And came
Am 5:24 righteousness like a mighty *s*.
Lk 6:48 the *s* beat vehemently against
6:49 against which the *s* beat

STREAMING (1/1)

Jer 31:12 *S* to the goodness of the

STREAMS (17/17) STREAM

Ex 7:19 waters of Egypt, over their *s*,
8: 5 hand with your rod over the *s*,
Job 6:15 Like the *s* of the brooks that
20:17 He will not see the *s*,
28:11 He dams up the *s* from
Ps 46: 4 There is a river whose *s*
78:16 He also brought *s* out of the
78:20 And the *s* overflowed. Can He
78:44 rivers into blood, And their *s*,
126: 4 As the *s* in the South.
Prov 5:16 *S* of water in the streets?
Song 4:15 And *s* from Lebanon.
Isa 11:15 And strike it in the seven *s*,
30:25 every high hill Rivers and *s*
33:21 A place of broad rivers and *s*
34: 9 Its *s* shall be turned into
35: 6 And *s* in the desert.

STREET (21/21) STREETS

Deut 13:16 into the middle of the *s*,
Josh 2:19 doors of your house into the *s*,
2 Sam 21:12 who had stolen them from the *s*
Job 31:32 sojourner had to lodge in the *s*,
Prov 7: 8 Passing along the *s* near her
Isa 42: 2 His voice to be heard in the *s*.
51:23 like the ground, And as the *s*,
59:14 For truth is fallen in the *s*,
Jer 37:21 of bread from the bakers' *s*,
Lam 2:19 hunger at the head of every *s*.
4: 1 At the head of every *s*.
Ezek 16:24 place for yourself in every *s*.
16:31 your high place in every *s*.
Dan 9:25 The *s* shall be built again,
Nah 3:10 pieces At the head of every *s*;
Mk 11: 4 by the door outside on the *s*,
Acts 9:11 Arise and go to the *s* called
12:10 went out and went down one *s*,
Rev 11: 8 bodies will lie in the *s* of
21:21 And the *s* of the city was pure
22: 2 In the middle of its *s*,

STREETS (61/59) STREET

2 Sam 1:20 Proclaim it not in the *s* of
22:43 I trod them like dirt in the *s*,
Ps 18:42 them out like dirt in the *s*.
55:11 deceit do not depart from its *s*.
144:14 there be no outcry in our *s*.
Prov 5:16 Streams of water in the *s*?
22:13 I shall be slain in the *s*!"
26:13 A fierce lion is in the *s*!"
Eccl 12: 4 the doors are shut in the *s*,
12: 5 the mourners go about the *s*.
Song 3: 2 In the *s* and in the squares
Isa 5:25 as refuse in the midst of the *s*.
10: 6 down like the mire of the *s*.
15: 3 In their *s* they will clothe
15: 3 of their houses And in their *s*
24:11 is a cry for wine in the *s*,
51:20 lie at the head of all the *s*,
58:12 The Restorer of *S* to Dwell In.
Jer 5: 1 Run to and fro through the *s* of
7:17 cities of Judah and in the *s*
7:34 cities of Judah and from the *s*
9:21 young men—no longer on the *s*!
11: 6 cities of Judah and in the *s*
11:13 to the number of the *s* of
14:16 shall be cast out in the *s* of
33:10 in the *s* of Jerusalem that are
44: 6 cities of Judah and in the *s*
44: 9 the land of Judah and in the *s*
44:17 cities of Judah and in the *s*
44:21 cities of Judah and in the *s*
48:38 of Moab, And in its *s*;
49:26 young men shall fall in her *s*,
50:30 young men shall fall in the *s*,
51: 4 those thrust through in her *s*.
Lam 2:11 the infants Faint in the *s* of
2:12 like the wounded In the *s* of
2:21 old lie On the ground in the *s*;
4: 5 Are desolate in the *s*;
4: 8 They go unrecognized in the *s*;
4:14 They wandered blind in the *s*;
4:18 that we could not walk in our *s*.
Ezek 7:19 throw their silver into the *s*,
11: 6 and you have filled its *s* with
26:11 he will trample all your *s*;
28:23 upon her, And blood in her *s*;
Am 5:16 shall be wailing in all *s*,
Mic 7:10 down Like mud in the *s*.
Nah 2: 4 The chariots rage in the *s*,
Zeph 3: 6 I have made their *s* desolate,
Zech 8: 4 shall again sit In the *s* of
8: 5 The *s* of the city Shall be
8: 5 and girls Playing in its *s*.
9: 3 gold like the mire of the *s*.
10: 5 enemies In the mire of the *s*
Mt 6: 2 in the synagogues and in the *s*,
6: 5 and on the corners of the *s*,
12:19 hear His voice in the *s*.
Lk 10:10 go out into its *s* and say,
13:26 and You taught in our *s*.
14:21 Go out quickly into the *s* and
Acts 5:15 the sick out into the *s* and

STRENGTH (230/223) STRENGTHEN

Gen 4:12 it shall no longer yield its *s*
49: 3 might and the beginning of my *s*,
49:24 But his bow remained in *s*,
Ex 13: 3 for by *s* of hand the LORD
13:14 By *s* of hand the LORD brought
13:16 for by *s* of hand the LORD
15: 2 The LORD is my *s* and song,
15:13 have guided them in Your *s*
Lev 26:20 And your *s* shall be spent in
Num 23:22 He has *s* like a wild ox.
24: 8 He has *s* like a wild ox;
Deut 6: 5 your soul, and with all your *s*.
21:17 he is the beginning of his *s*;
28:32 and there shall be no *s* in
33:25 so shall your *s* be.
Josh 14:11 just as my *s* was then, so now
14:11 so now is my *s* for war, both
Judg 1:35 yet when the *s* of the house of
5:21 O my soul, march on in *s*!
5:31 When it comes out in full *s*.
8:21 for as a man is, so is his *s*.
16: 5 and find out where his great *s*
16: 6 tell me where your great *s*
16: 9 So the secret of his *s* was not
16:15 not told me where your great *s*
16:17 then my *s* will leave me, and I
16:19 and his *s* left him.
1 Sam 2: 4 who stumbled are girded with *s*.
2: 9 For by *s* no man shall prevail.
2:10 'He will give *s* to His king,
15:29 And also the *S* of Israel will
28:20 And there was no *s* in him, for
28:22 that you may have *s* when you go
30:12 his *s* came back to him; for he
2 Sam 22: 3 The God of my *s*,
22:33 God is my *s* and power,
22:40 For You have armed me with *s*
1 Ki 19: 8 and he went in the *s* of that
2 Ki 9:24 Jehu drew his bow with full *s*
19: 3 but there is no *s* to bring
1 Chr 16:11 Seek the LORD and His *s*;
16:27 *S* and gladness are in His
16:28 Give to the LORD glory and *s*.
26: 8 able men with *s* for the work:
29:12 to make great And to give *s*
2 Chr 6:41 You and the ark of Your *s*.
13:20 So Jeroboam did not recover *s*
Neh 4:10 The *s* of the laborers is
8:10 the joy of the LORD is your *s*.
Job 6:11 What *s* do I have, that I should
6:12 Is my *s* the strength of
6:12 Is my strength the *s* of
9: 4 wise in heart and mighty in *s*.
9:19 If it is a matter of *s*,
12:13 "With Him are wisdom and *s*,
12:16 With Him are *s* and prudence.
18: 7 The steps of his *s* are
18:12 His *s* is starved, And
21:23 One dies in his full *s*,
22: 9 And the *s* of the fatherless
26: 2 saved the arm that has no *s*?
30: 2 what profit is the *s* of their
30:21 With the *s* of Your hand You
36: 5 He is mighty in *s* of
37: 6 and the heavy rain of His *s*.
39:11 you trust him because his *s*
39:19 "Have you given the horse *s*?
39:21 valley, and rejoices in his *s*;
40:16 his *s* is in his hips, And his
41:22 *S* dwells in his neck, And
Ps 8: 2 infants You have ordained *s*,
10:10 the helpless may fall by his *s*.
18: 1 I will love You, O LORD, my *s*.
18: 2 and my deliverer; My God, my *s*,
18:32 It is God who arms me with *s*,
18:39 For You have armed me with *s*
19:14 my *s* and my Redeemer.
20: 6 holy heaven With the saving *s*
21: 1 king shall have joy in Your *s*,
21:13 in Your own *s*! We will sing
22:15 My *s* is dried up like a
22:19 do not be far from Me; O My *S*,
27: 1 The LORD is the *s* of my
28: 7 The LORD is my *s* and my
28: 8 The LORD is their *s*,
29: 1 unto the LORD glory and *s*.
29:11 The LORD will give *s* to His
31: 4 laid for me, For You are my *s*.
31:10 My *s* fails because of my
33:16 man is not delivered by great *s*.
33:17 it deliver any by its great *s*.
37:39 He is their *s* in the time of
38:10 my *s* fails me; As for the
39:13 from me, that I may regain *s*,
43: 2 For You are the God of my *s*;
46: 1 God is our refuge and *s*,
52: 7 man who did not make God his *s*,
54: 1 And vindicate me by Your *s*.
59: 9 wait for You, O You his *S*;
59:17 To You, O my *S*,
62: 7 and my glory; The rock of my *s*,
65: 6 the mountains by His *s*,
68:28 Your God has commanded your *s*;
68:34 Ascribe *s* to God;
68:34 And His *s* is in the clouds.
68:35 of Israel is He who gives *s*
71: 9 Do not forsake me when my *s*
71:16 I will go in the *s* of the Lord
71:18 Until I declare Your *s* to
73: 4 But their *s* is firm.
73:26 But God is the *s* of my heart
74:13 You divided the sea by Your *s*;
77:14 You have declared Your *s* among
78: 4 And His *s* and His wonderful
78:51 The first of their *s* in the
78:61 And delivered His *s* into
80: 2 and Manasseh, Stir up Your *s*,
81: 1 Sing aloud to God our *s*;
84: 5 Blessed is the man whose *s* is
84: 7 They go from *s* to strength;
84: 7 They go from strength to *s*;
86:16 have mercy on me! Give Your *s*
88: 4 I am like a man who has no *s*,
89:17 You are the glory of their *s*,
90:10 And if by reason of *s* they
93: 1 He has girded Himself with *s*.
96: 6 *S* and beauty are in His
96: 7 Give to the LORD glory and *s*.
99: 4 The King's *s* also loves
102:23 He weakened my *s* in the way;
103:20 you His angels, Who excel in *s*,
105: 4 Seek the LORD and His *s*;
105:36 The first of all their *s*.
110: 2 shall send the rod of Your *s*
118:14 The LORD is my *s* and song,
132: 8 You and the ark of Your *s*.
138: 3 And made me bold with *s* in
140: 7 the *s* of my salvation,
147:10 He does not delight in the *s* of
Prov 3: 8 And *s* to your bones.
8:14 I am understanding, I have *s*.
10:29 The way of the LORD is *s* for
14: 4 much increase comes by the *s*
20:29 glory of young men is their *s*,
24: 5 a man of knowledge increases *s*;
24:10 Your *s* is small.
31: 3 Do not give your *s* to women,
31:17 She girds herself with *s*,
31:25 *S* and honor are her clothing
Eccl 9:16 "Wisdom is better than *s*.
10:10 Then he must use more *s*;
10:17 For *s* and not for drunkenness!
Isa 10:13 By the *s* of my hand I have done
12: 2 is my *s* and song; He also has
23: 4 The *s* of the sea, saying, "I
23:10 Tarshish; There is no more *s*.
23:14 ships of Tarshish! For your *s*
25: 4 For You have been a *s* to the
25: 4 A *s* to the needy in his
26: 4 the LORD, is everlasting *s*.
27: 5 Or let him take hold of My *s*,
28: 6 And for *s* to those who turn
30: 2 strengthen themselves in the *s*
30: 3 Therefore the *s* of Pharaoh
30:15 and confidence shall be your *s*.
33: 6 And the *s* of salvation;
37: 3 but there is no *s* to bring
40: 9 Lift up your voice with *s*,
40:26 of His might And the *s* of
40:29 have no might He increases *s*.
40:31 the LORD Shall renew their *s*;
41: 1 let the people renew their *s*!
42:25 fury of His anger And the *s*
44:12 And works it with the *s* of his
44:12 and his *s* fails; He drinks no
45:24 I have righteousness and *s*.
49: 4 I have spent my *s* for nothing
49: 5 And My God shall be My *s*),
51: 9 Awake, awake, put on *s*,
52: 1 Awake, awake! Put on your *s*,
62: 8 hand And by the arm of His *s*:
63: 1 in the greatness of His *s*?
63: 6 And brought down their *s* to
63:15 are Your zeal and Your *s*,
Jer 16:19 my *s* and my fortress, My
17: 5 in man And makes flesh his *s*,
51:53 to fortify the height of her *s*,
Lam 1: 6 That flee without *s* Before
1:14 He made my *s* fail; The Lord
3:18 My *s* and my hope Have perished

S

Ezek 30:15 the *s* of Egypt; I will cut off
30:18 And her arrogant *s* shall cease
33:28 her arrogant *s* shall cease, and
Dan 2:37 given you a kingdom, power, *s*,
2:41 yet the *s* of the iron shall be
10: 8 and no *s* remained in me; for my
10: 8 in me, and I retained no *s*.
10:16 me, and I have retained no *s*.
10:17 no *s* remains in me now, nor is
11: 2 richer than them all; by his *s*,
11:15 troops shall have no *s* to
11:17 his face to enter with the *s*
Hos 7: 9 Aliens have devoured his *s*,
12: 3 And in his *s* he struggled with
Joel 2:22 tree and the vine yield their *s*.
3:16 And the *s* of the children of
Am 3:11 He shall sap your *s* from you,
6:13 for ourselves By our own *s*?
Mic 5: 4 and feed His flock In the *s*
Nah 3: 9 Ethiopia and Egypt were her *s*,
Hab 3:19 The LORD God is my *s*;
Hag 2:22 I will destroy the *s* of the
Zech 12: 5 of Jerusalem are my *s* in the
Mk 12:30 mind, and with all your *s*.
12:33 the soul, and with all the *s*,
Lk 1:51 He has shown *s* with His arm;
10:27 soul, with all your *s*,
Acts 3: 7 feet and ankle bones received *s*.
9:22 increased all the more in *s*,
14: 8 Lystra a certain man without *s*
Rom 5: 6 when we were still without *s*,
1 Cor 15:56 and the *s* of sin is the law.
2 Cor 1: 8 beyond measure, above *s*,
12: 9 for My *s* is made perfect in
Heb 11:11 Sarah herself also received *s*
Rev 1:16 like the sun shining in its *s*.
3: 8 for you have a little *s*,
5:12 And *s* and honor and glory and
12:10 heaven, "Now salvation, and *s*,
14:10 which is poured out full *s* into

STRENGTHEN (37/37) STRENGTH, STRENGTHENED, STRENGTHENING, STRENGTHENS

Deut 3:28 and encourage him and *s* him;
Judg 16:28 I pray! *S* me, I pray, just this
2 Sam 11:25 *S* your attack against the city,
1 Ki 20:22 *s* yourself; take note, and see
2 Ki 15:19 his hand might be with him to *s*
Ezra 6:22 to *s* their hands in the work of
Neh 6: 9 O God, *s* my hands.
Job 16: 5 But I would *s* you with my
Ps 20: 2 And *s* you out of Zion;
27:14 And He shall *s* your heart;
31:24 And He shall *s* your heart,
41: 3 The LORD will *s* him on his bed
68:28 has commanded your strength; *S*,
89:21 Also My arm shall *s* him.
119:28 *S* me according to Your word.
Isa 22:21 him with your robe And *s* him
30: 2 To *s* themselves in the
33:23 They could not *s* their mast,
35: 3 *S* the weak hands, And make
41:10 I will *s* you, Yes, I will
54: 2 And *s* your stakes.
58:11 And *s* your bones; You shall
Jer 23:14 They also *s* the hands of
Ezek 7:13 No one will *s* himself
16:49 neither did she *s* the hand of
30:24 I will *s* the arms of the king of
30:25 Thus I will *s* the arms of the
34:16 bind up the broken and *s* what
Dan 11: 1 stood up to confirm and *s* him.)
Am 2:14 The strong shall not *s* his
Nah 2: 1 the fort! Watch the road! *S*
Zech 10: 6 I will *s* the house of Judah,
10:12 So I will *s* them in the LORD,
Lk 22:32 *s* your brethren."
Heb 12:12 Therefore *s* the hands which
1 Pe 5:10 a while, perfect, establish, *s*,
Rev 3: 2 and *s* the things which remain,

STRENGTHENED (37/36) STRENGTHEN

Gen 48: 2 and Israel *s* himself and sat up
Judg 3:12 So the LORD *s* Eglon king of
7:11 your hands shall be *s* to go
1 Sam 23:16 to David in the woods and *s*
30: 6 But David *s* himself in the
2 Sam 2: 7 therefore, let your hands be *s*,
1 Chr 11:10 who *s* themselves with him in
2 Chr 1: 1 Solomon the son of David was *s*
11:17 So they *s* the kingdom of Judah,
12: 1 the kingdom and had *s* himself,
12:13 Thus Rehoboam *s* himself in
13: 7 and *s* themselves against
17: 1 and *s* himself against Israel.
21: 4 he *s* himself and killed all his
23: 1 In the seventh year Jehoiada *s*
25:11 Then Amaziah *s* himself, and
32: 5 And he *s* himself, built up all
32: 8 And the people were *s* by the
Job 4: 3 And you have *s* weak hands.
4: 4 And you have *s* the feeble
Ps 52: 7 And *s* himself in his
147:13 For He has *s* the bars of your
Prov 8:28 When He *s* the fountains of the
Ezek 13:22 and you have *s* the hands of the
34: 4 "The weak you have not *s*,
Dan 10:18 of a man touched me and *s* me.
10:19 So when he spoke to me I was *s*,
10:19 for you have *s* me."
11: 6 and with him who *s* her in
Hos 7:15 Though I disciplined and *s*
Acts 9:19 he had received food, he was *s*.
15:32 exhorted and *s* the brethren
16: 5 So the churches were *s* in the
Rom 4:20 but was *s* in faith, giving
Eph 3:16 to be *s* with might through His
Col 1:11 *s* with all might, according to
2 Tim 4:17 the Lord stood with me and *s*

STRENGTHENING (5/5) STRENGTHEN

2 Sam 3: 6 that Abner was *s* his hold on
Lk 22:43 to Him from heaven, *s* Him.
Acts 14:22 *s* the souls of the disciples,
15:41 *s* the churches.
18:23 *s* all the disciples.

STRENGTHENS (4/4) STRENGTHEN

Ps 104:15 And bread which *s* man's
Prov 31:17 And *s* her arms.
Eccl 7:19 Wisdom *s* the wise More than
Phil 4:13 things through Christ who *s* me.

STRENUOUSLY (1/1)

Ezek 29:18 caused his army to labor *s*

STRETCH (49/49) STRETCHED, STRETCHES

Ex 3:20 So I will *s* out My hand and
7: 5 when I *s* out My hand on Egypt
7:19 Take your rod and *s* out your
8: 5 *S* out your hand with your rod
8:16 *S* out your rod, and strike the
9:22 *S* out your hand toward heaven,
10:12 *S* out your hand over the land of
10:21 *S* out your hand toward heaven,
14:16 and *s* out your hand over the
14:26 *S* out your hand over the sea,
25:20 And the cherubim shall *s* out
Num 24: 6 Like valleys that *s* out,
Josh 8:18 *S* out the spear that is in your
1 Sam 24: 6 to *s* out my hand against him,
24:10 I will not *s* out my hand against
26: 9 for who can *s* out his hand
26:11 LORD forbid that I should *s*
26:23 but I would not *s* out my hand
2 Ki 21:13 And I will *s* over Jerusalem the
Job 1:11 *s* out Your hand and touch all
2: 5 But *s* out Your hand now, and
11:13 And *s* out your hands toward
30:24 Surely He would not *s* out His
Ps 68:31 Ethiopia will quickly *s* out
104: 2 Who *s* out the heavens like a
138: 7 You will *s* out Your hand
144: 7 *S* out Your hand from above
Isa 28:20 the bed is too short to *s* out
34:11 And He shall *s* out over it
54: 2 And let them *s* out the
Jer 6:12 For I will *s* out My hand
15: 6 Therefore I will *s* out My hand
51:25 And I will *s* out My hand against
Ezek 6:14 So I will *s* out My hand against
14: 9 and I will *s* out My hand
14:13 I will *s* out My hand against
25: 7 I will *s* out My hand against
25:13 I will also *s* out My hand
25:16 I will *s* out My hand against the
35: 3 I will *s* out My hand against
38:12 to *s* out your hand against the
Dan 11:42 He shall *s* out his hand against
Am 6: 4 *S* out on your couches,
Zeph 1: 4 I will *s* out My hand against
2:13 And He will *s* out His hand
Mt 12:13 *S* out your hand." And he
Mk 3: 5 *S* out your hand." And he
Lk 6:10 *S* out your hand." And he did
Jn 21:18 you will *s* out your hands, and

STRETCHED (66/64) STRETCH

Gen 22:10 And Abraham *s* out his hand and
48:14 Then Israel *s* out his right hand
Ex 8: 6 So Aaron *s* out his hand over the
8:17 For Aaron *s* out his hand with
9:15 Now if I had *s* out My hand and
9:23 And Moses *s* out his rod toward
10:13 So Moses *s* out his rod over the
10:22 So Moses *s* out his hand toward
14:21 Then Moses *s* out his hand over
14:27 And Moses *s* out his hand over
15:12 You *s* out Your right hand;
Josh 8:18 And Joshua *s* out the spear
8:19 they ran as soon as he had *s*
8:26 with which he *s* out the spear,
Judg 5:26 She *s* her hand to the tent peg,
1 Sam 14:27 therefore he *s* out the end of
2 Sam 24:16 And when the angel *s* out His
1 Ki 6:21 He *s* gold chains across the
6:27 and they *s* out the wings of the
13: 4 that he *s* out his hand from the
13: 4 which he *s* out toward him,
17:21 And he *s* himself out on the
2 Ki 4:34 and he *s* himself out on the
4:35 and again went up and *s* himself
1 Chr 21:16 in his hand a drawn sword *s*
Job 38: 5 Surely you know! Or who *s* the
Ps 44:20 Or *s* out our hands to a
77: 2 My hand was *s* out in the night
88: 9 I have *s* out my hands to You.
Prov 1:24 I have *s* out my hand and no
Isa 5:25 He has *s* out His hand against
5:25 But His hand is *s* out still.
9:12 But His hand is *s* out still.
9:17 But His hand is *s* out still.
9:21 But His hand is *s* out still.
10: 4 But His hand is *s* out still.
14:26 this is the hand that is *s*
14:27 His hand is *s* out, And who
16: 8 Her branches are *s* out,
23:11 He *s* out His hand over the sea,
42: 5 Who created the heavens and *s*
45:12 *s* out the heavens, And all
48:13 And My right hand has *s* out
51:13 Who *s* out the heavens And
65: 2 I have *s* out My hands all day
Jer 10:12 And has *s* out the heavens at
51:15 And *s* out the heaven by His
Lam 2: 8 He has *s* out a line; He has
Ezek 1:11 Their wings *s* upward; two
1:22 *s* out over their heads.
2: 9 there was a hand *s* out to me;
8: 3 He *s* out the form of a hand, and
10: 7 And the cherub *s* out his hand
16:27 I *s* out My hand against you,
17: 7 And *s* its branches toward him,
Hos 7: 5 He *s* out his hand with
Zech 1:16 a surveyor's line shall be *s*
Mt 12:13 And he *s* it out, and it was
12:49 And He *s* out His hand toward His
14:31 And immediately Jesus *s* out His
26:51 those who were with Jesus *s*
Mk 1:41 *s* out His hand and touched
3: 5 And he *s* it out, and his
Acts 12: 1 that time Herod the king *s* out
26: 1 So Paul *s* out his hand and
Rom 10:21 All day long I have *s* out

STRETCHES (9/9) STRETCH

Job 15:25 For he *s* out his hand against
26: 7 He *s* out the north over empty
Prov 31:19 She *s* out her hands to the
Isa 31: 3 When the LORD *s* out His hand,
40:22 Who *s* out the heavens like a
44:13 The craftsman *s* out his rule,
44:24 Who *s* out the heavens all
Ezek 30:25 of the king of Babylon and he *s*
Zech 12: 1 who *s* out the heavens, lays the

STRETCHING (2/2)

Isa 8: 8 And the *s* out of his wings
Acts 4:30 'by *s* out Your hand to heal,

STRICKEN (13/13)

1 Sam 5:12 the men who did not die were *s*
Ps 102: 4 My heart is *s* and withered like
Isa 1: 5 Why should you be *s* again?
5:25 His hand against them And *s*
16: 7 Surely they are *s*.
24:12 And the gate is *s* with
53: 4 Yet we esteemed Him *s*,
53: 8 of My people He was *s*.
Jer 5: 3 You have *s* them, But they
14:19 Why have You *s* us so that
Lam 4: 9 *S* for lack of the fruits of
Hos 6: 1 but He will heal us; He has *s*,
9:16 Ephraim is *s*, Their root is

STRICTER (1/1)

Jas 3: 1 we shall receive a *s* judgment.

STRICTEST (1/1)

Acts 26: 5 that according to the *s* sect of

STRICTLY (7/7)

Deut 2:27 I will keep *s* to the road, and
1 Sam 14:28 Your father *s* charged the people
Mk 1:43 And He *s* warned him and sent him
5:43 But He commanded them *s* that no
8:30 Then He *s* warned them that they
Lk 9:21 And He *s* warned and commanded
Acts 5:28 Did we not *s* command you not to

STRICTNESS (1/1)

Acts 22: 3 taught according to the *s* of

STRIFE (31/30)

Gen 13: 7 And there was *s* between the
13: 8 Please let there be no *s* between
Num 27:14 during the *s* of the
Ps 31:20 in a pavilion From the *s* of
55: 9 I have seen violence and *s* in
80: 6 You have made us a *s* to our
106:32 Him also at the waters of *s*,
Prov 10:12 Hatred stirs up *s*,
13:10 By pride comes nothing but *s*,
15:18 A wrathful man stirs up *s*,
16:28 A perverse man sows *s*,
17: 1 house full of feasting with *s*.
17:14 The beginning of *s* is like

17:19 who loves transgression loves *s*,
22:10 *s* and reproach will cease.
26:20 no talebearer, *s* ceases.
26:21 a contentious man to kindle *s*.
28:25 is of a proud heart stirs up *s*,
29:22 An angry man stirs up *s*,
30:33 the forcing of wrath produces *s*.
Isa 58: 4 Indeed you fast for *s* and
Jer 15:10 A man of *s* and a man of
Dan 11:10 his sons shall stir up *s*,
11:10 to his fortress and stir up *s*.
Hab 1: 3 are before me; There is *s*,
Rom 1:29 full of envy, murder, *s*,
13:13 not in *s* and envy.
1 Cor 3: 3 For where there are envy, *s*,
Phil 1:15 Christ even from envy and *s*,
1 Tim 6: 4 words, from which come envy, *s*,
2 Tim 2:23 knowing that they generate *s*.

STRIKE (86/81) STRIKES, STRUCK

Ex 3:20 will stretch out My hand and *s*
7:17 I will *s* the waters which are
8:16 and *s* the dust of the land, so
12:12 and will *s* all the firstborn in
12:13 on you to destroy you when I *s*
12:22 and *s* the lintel and the two
12:23 LORD will pass through to *s*
12:23 to come into your houses to *s*
17: 6 and you shall *s* the rock, and
Num 14:12 I will *s* them with the
Deut 13:15 you shall surely *s* the
20:13 you shall *s* every male in it
28:22 The LORD will *s* you with
28:27 The LORD will *s* you with the
28:28 The LORD will *s* you with
28:35 The LORD will *s* you in the
33:11 *S* the loins of those who rise
Judg 20:31 They began to *s* down and kill
20:39 Now Benjamin had begun to *s*
21:10 Go and *s* the inhabitants of
1 Sam 17:46 and I will *s* you and take your
22:17 not lift their hands to *s* the
26: 8 let me *s* him at once with the
26: 8 and I will not have to *s* him
26:10 the LORD shall *s* him, or his
2 Sam 2:22 Why should I *s* you to the
5:24 will go out before you to *s*
13:28 *S* Amnon!' then kill him. Do not
15:14 and *s* the city with the edge of
17: 2 and I will *s* only the king.
18:11 saw him! And why did you not *s*
20:10 and he did not *s* him again.
1 Ki 2:29 saying, "Go, *s* him down."
2:31 and *s* him down and bury him,
14:15 For the LORD will *s* Israel, as
20:35 *S* me, please." And the man
20:35 And the man refused to *s* him.
20:37 *S* me, please." So the man
2 Ki 6:18 *S* this people, I pray, with
9: 7 You shall *s* down the house of
13:17 for you must *s* the Syrians at
13:18 *S* the ground"; so he struck
13:19 But now you will *s* Syria
1 Chr 14:15 has gone out before you to *s*
2 Chr 21:14 the LORD will *s* your people
Job 16:10 They *s* me reproachfully on the
36:32 And commands it to *s*.
Ps 81: 2 Raise a song and *s* the timbrel,
121: 6 The sun shall not *s* you by day,
141: 5 Let the righteous *s* me;
Prov 17:26 Nor to *s* princes for their
19:25 *S* a scoffer, and the simple
Isa 3:17 Therefore the Lord will *s* with
10:24 He shall *s* you with a rod and
11: 4 He shall *s* the earth with the
11:15 And *s* it in the seven streams,
19:22 And the LORD will *s* Egypt,
19:22 He will *s* and heal it; they
49:10 Neither heat nor sun shall *s*
58: 4 And to *s* with the fist of
Jer 21: 6 I will *s* the inhabitants of this
21: 7 and he shall *s* them with the
43:11 he shall *s* the land of Egypt
46:13 of Babylon would come and *s*
49:28 king of Babylon shall *s*.
Ezek 5: 2 you shall take one-third and *s*
21:12 Therefore *s* your thigh.
21:14 And *s* your hands together.
32:15 When I *s* all who dwell in it,
Am 9: 1 *S* the doorposts, that the
Mic 5: 1 They will *s* the judge of
Zech 10:11 And *s* the waves of the sea:
12: 4 I will *s* every horse with
12: 4 and will *s* every horse of the
13: 7 *S* the Shepherd, And the sheep
14:12 with which the LORD will *s*
Mal 4: 6 Lest I come and *s* the earth
Mt 26:31 'I will *s* the Shepherd,
Mk 14:27 'I will *s* the Shepherd,
Lk 22:49 shall we *s* with the sword?"
Jn 18:23 why do you *s* Me?"
Acts 23: 2 those who stood by him to *s*
23: 3 God will *s* you, you whitewashed
Rev 7:16 the sun shall not *s* them, nor
11: 6 and to *s* the earth with all
19:15 that with it He should *s* the

STRIKER (KJV) See VIOLENT

STRIKES (21/21) STRIKE

Ex 21:12 He who *s* a man so that he dies
21:15 And he who *s* his father or his
21:18 and one *s* the other with a
21:26 If a man *s* the eye of his male
Num 35:16 But if he *s* him with an iron
35:17 And if he *s* him with a stone in
35:18 Or if he *s* him with a wooden
35:21 or in enmity he *s* him with his
Deut 19: 5 slips from the handle and *s*
19:11 rises against him and *s* him
Job 34:26 He *s* them as wicked men In
39:20 His majestic snorting *s*
Isa 9:13 do not turn to Him who *s* them,
30:31 As He *s* with the rod.
41: 7 the hammer inspired him who *s*
Lam 3:30 his cheek to the one who *s*
Ezek 7: 9 know that I am the LORD who *s*.
Zech 14:18 plague with which the LORD *s*
Lk 6:29 To him who *s* you on the one
2 Cor 11:20 if one *s* you on the face.
Rev 9: 5 of a scorpion when it *s* a man.

STRIKING (4/4)

Ex 2:13 Why are you *s* your companion?"
2 Sam 24:17 he saw the angel who was *s* the
Mic 6:13 I will also make you sick by *s*
Acts 27:41 But *s* a place where two seas

STRING (2/2)

Ps 11: 2 make ready their arrow on the *s*,
21:12 ready Your arrows on Your *s*

STRINGED (27/27) STRINGS

1 Sam 10: 5 from the high place with a *s*
2 Sam 6: 5 on *s* instruments, on
1 Ki 10:12 also harps and *s* instruments
1 Chr 13: 8 on *s* instruments, on
15:16 *s* instruments, harps, and
15:28 making music with *s* instruments
16: 5 Jeiel with *s* instruments and
25: 1 *s* instruments, and cymbals.
25: 6 *s* instruments, and harps, for
2 Chr 5:12 *s* instruments and harps, and
9:11 also harps and *s* instruments
20:28 with *s* instruments and harps
29:25 with *s* instruments, and with
Neh 12:27 with cymbals and *s* instruments
Ps 4: With *s* instruments. A Psalm of
6: With *s* instruments.
54: With *s* instruments.
55: With *s* instruments.
61: On a *s* instrument. A Psalm of
67: On *s* instruments. A Psalm.
76: On *s* instruments. A Psalm of
150: 4 Praise Him with *s* instruments
Isa 14:11 And the sound of your *s*
38:20 we will sing my songs with *s*
Am 5:23 not hear the melody of your *s*
6: 5 sing idly to the sound of *s*
Hab 3:19 With my *s* instruments.

STRINGS (5/5) STRINGED

1 Chr 15:20 with *s* according to Alamoth;
Ps 33: 2 Him with an instrument of ten *s*.
92: 3 On an instrument of ten *s*,
144: 9 On a harp of ten *s* I will sing
Isa 5:12 The harp and the *s*,

STRIP (9/9) STRIPPED, STRIPS

Num 20:26 and *s* Aaron of his garments and
1 Sam 31: 8 when the Philistines came to *s*
1 Chr 10: 8 when the Philistines came to *s*
Isa 32:11 *S* yourselves, make yourselves
Ezek 16:39 They shall also *s* you of your
23:26 They shall also *s* you of your
Dan 4:14 *S* off its leaves and scatter
Hos 2: 3 Lest I *s* her naked And expose
Mic 3: 2 Who *s* the skin from My people,

STRIPE (2/1) STRIPES

Ex 21:25 wound for wound, *s* for
21:25 wound for wound, stripe for *s*.

STRIPES (11/11) STRIPE

Ps 89:32 And their iniquity with *s*.
Prov 20:30 As do *s* the inner depths of
Isa 53: 5 And by His *s* we are healed.
Lk 12:47 shall be beaten with many *s*.
12:48 committed things deserving of *s*,
Acts 16:23 And when they had laid many *s* on
16:33 the night and washed their *s*.
2 Cor 6: 5 in *s*, in imprisonments,
11:23 in *s* above measure, in prisons
11:24 five times I received forty *s*
1 Pe 2:24 by whose *s* you were healed.

STRIPLING (KJV) See (YOUNG) MAN

STRIPPED (14/14) STRIP

Gen 37:23 that they *s* Joseph of his
Ex 33: 6 So the children of Israel *s*
Num 20:28 Moses *s* Aaron of his garments
1 Sam 19:24 And he also *s* off his clothes
31: 9 And they cut off his head and *s*
2 Ki 18:16 At that time Hezekiah *s* the
1 Chr 10: 9 And they *s* him and took his head
2 Chr 20:25 which they *s* off for
Job 19: 9 He has *s* me of my glory,
22: 6 And *s* the naked of their
Joel 1: 7 He has *s* it bare and thrown
Mic 1: 8 I will go *s* and naked; I will
Mt 27:28 And they *s* Him and put a scarlet
Lk 10:30 who *s* him of his clothing,

STRIPS (3/3) STRIP

Gen 30:37 peeled white *s* in them, and
Ps 29: 9 And *s* the forests bare;
Jn 19:40 and bound it in *s* of linen with

STRIVE (11/11) STRIVES, STRIVING

Gen 6: 3 My Spirit shall not *s* with man
Judg 11:25 Did he ever *s* against Israel?
Ps 35: 1 with those who *s* with me;
103: 9 He will not always *s* with us,
Prov 3:30 Do not *s* with a man without
Isa 41:11 And those who *s* with you shall
45: 9 Maker! Let the potsherd *s*
Lk 13:24 *S* to enter through the narrow
Acts 24:16 I myself always *s* to have a
Rom 15:30 that you *s* together with me in
2 Tim 2:14 them before the Lord not to *s*

STRIVES (1/1) STRIVE

Isa 45: 9 Woe to him who *s* with his

STRIVING (5/5) STRIVE

Prov 20: 3 honorable for a man to stop *s*,
Eccl 2:22 and for the *s* of his heart with
Phil 1:27 with one mind *s* together for
Col 1:29 *s* according to His working
Heb 12: 4 to bloodshed, *s* against sin.

STRIVINGS (3/3)

2 Sam 22:44 also delivered me from the *s*
Ps 18:43 have delivered me from the *s*
Titus 3: 9 and *s* about the law; for they

STROKE (6/6)

Deut 19: 5 and his hand swings a *s* with
Esth 9: 5 all their enemies with the *s*
Isa 14: 6 in wrath with a continual *s*,
30:26 of His people And heals the *s*
Jer 14:17 been broken with a mighty *s*,
Ezek 24:16 desire of your eyes with one *s*;

STROKES (KJV) See BLOWS

STRONG (195/184) STRONGER

Gen 49:14 Issachar is a *s* donkey, Lying
49:24 arms of his hands were made *s*
Ex 6: 1 For with a *s* hand he will let
6: 1 and with a *s* hand he will drive
10:19 And the LORD turned a very *s*
13: 9 for with a *s* hand the LORD has
14:21 the sea to go back by a *s*
Num 13:18 people who dwell in it are *s*
13:28 who dwell in the land are *s*;
20:20 them with many men and with a *s*
Deut 2:36 there was not one city too *s*
11: 8 you today, that you may be *s*,
31: 6 Be *s* and of good courage, do not
31: 7 'Be *s* and of good courage,
31:23 'Be *s* and of good courage;
Josh 1: 6 Be *s* and of good courage, for to
1: 7 Only be *s* and very courageous,
1: 9 Be *s* and of good courage;
1:18 Only be *s* and of good
10:25 be *s* and of good courage,
14:11 As yet I am as *s* this day as
17:13 the children of Israel grew *s*,
17:18 have iron chariots and are *s*.
23: 9 out from before you great and *s*
Judg 1:28 came to pass, when Israel was *s*,
9:51 But there was a *s* tower in the
14:14 And out of the *s* came
18:26 saw that they were too *s* for
1 Sam 4: 9 Be *s* and conduct yourselves like
14:52 And when Saul saw any *s* man or
2 Sam 10:11 If the Syrians are too *s* for me,
10:11 the people of Ammon are too *s*
10:12 and let us be *s* for our people
15:12 And the conspiracy grew *s*,
16:21 all who are with you will be *s*.
22:18 He delivered me from my *s*
22:18 For they were too *s* for me.
1 Ki 2: 2 the way of all the earth; be *s*,
8:42 of Your great name and Your *s*
19:11 and a great and *s* wind tore
2 Ki 2:16 there are fifty *s* men with your
24:16 all who were *s* and fit for
1 Chr 19:12 If the Syrians are too *s* for me,
19:12 the people of Ammon are too *s*
19:13 and let us be *s* for our people
22:13 Be *s* and of good courage;
28:10 a house for the sanctuary; be *s*,
28:20 Be *s* and of good courage, and do
2 Chr 11:12 spears, and made them very *s*,

S

11:17 Rehoboam the son of Solomon s
15: 7 be s and do not let your hands
16: 9 to show Himself s on behalf of
25: 8 be gone! Be s in battle!
26: 8 for he became exceedingly s.
26:15 helped till he became s.
26:16 But when he was s his heart was
32: 7 Be s and courageous; do not be
Ezra 9:12 that you may be s and eat the
Neh 1:10 and by Your s hand.
9:25 And they took s cities and a
Job 8: 2 of your mouth be like a s
9:19 of strength, indeed He is s;
15:26 against Him With his s,
33:19 And with s pain in many of
37:18 S as a cast metal mirror?
39: 4 They grow s with grain;
Ps 18:17 He delivered me from my s
18:17 For they were too s for me.
19: 5 And rejoices like a s man to
22:12 S bulls of Bashan have
24: 8 The LORD s and mighty,
30: 7 have made my mountain stand s;
31:21 His marvelous kindness in a s
35:10 the poor from him who is too s
38:19 are vigorous, and they are s;
60: 9 Who will bring me to the s
61: 3 A s tower from the enemy.
71: 3 Be my s refuge, To which I may
71: 7 But You are my s refuge.
80:15 the branch that You made s
80:17 the son of man whom You made s
89:13 S is Your hand, and high is
108:10 Who will bring me into the s
136:12 With a s hand, and with an
Prov 7:26 who were slain by her were s
10:15 rich man's wealth is his s
14:26 fear of the LORD there is s
18:10 The name of the LORD is a s
18:11 rich man's wealth is his s
18:19 is harder to win than a s
20: 1 S drink is a brawler,
21:14 behind the back, s wrath.
24: 5 A wise man is s,
30:25 The ants are a people not s,
31: 6 Give s drink to him who is
Eccl 9:11 swift, Nor the battle to the s,
12: 3 And the s men bow down;
Song 8: 6 For love is as s as death,
Isa 1:31 The s shall be as tinder,
8: 7 s and mighty—The king of
8:11 spoke thus to me with a s hand,
17: 9 In that day his s cities will
24: 9 S drink is bitter to those who
25: 3 Therefore the s people will
26: 1 We have a s city; God will
27: 1 His severe sword, great and s,
28: 2 the Lord has a mighty and s
28:22 Lest your bonds be made s;
31: 1 because they are very s,
35: 4 are fearful-hearted, "Be s,
40:10 Lord GOD shall come with a s
41:21 Bring forth your s reasons,"
53:12 divide the spoil with the s,
60:22 And a small one a s nation.
Jer 4:12 A wind too s for these will
8:16 sound of the neighing of His s
21: 5 outstretched hand and with a s
32:21 with a s hand and an
47: 3 of the stamping hooves of his s
48:14 We are mighty And s men for
48:17 'How the s staff is broken,
49:19 the dwelling place of the s;
50:34 Their Redeemer is s;
50:44 the dwelling place of the s;
51:12 of Babylon; Make the guard s,
Ezek 3: 8 I have made your face s against
3: 8 and your forehead s against
3:14 but the hand of the LORD was s
7:24 I will cause the pomp of the s
19:11 She had s branches for scepters
19:12 Her s branches were broken and
19:14 So that she has no s branch—a
22:14 or can your hands remain s,
26:11 and your s pillars will fall to
26:17 Who was s at sea, She and her
30:21 to make it s enough to hold a
30:22 both the s one and the one that
31:17 and those who were its s
32:21 The s among the mighty
34:16 will destroy the fat and the s,
Dan 2:40 fourth kingdom shall be as s
2:42 the kingdom shall be partly s
4:11 The tree grew and became s;
4:20 saw, which grew and became s,
4:22 who have grown and become s;
7: 7 and terrible, exceedingly s.
8: 8 great; but when he became s,
10:19 Peace be to you; be s,
10:19 be s!" So when he spoke to me
11: 5 of the South shall become s,
11:23 he shall come up and become s
11:32 who know their God shall be s,
Joel 1: 6 has come up against My land, S,
2: 2 A people come, great and s,
2: 5 Like a s people set in battle
2:11 For s is the One who
3:10 Let the weak say, 'I am s.
Am 2: 9 And he was as s as the oaks;
2:14 The s shall not strengthen his
5: 9 He rains ruin upon the s,
8:13 fair virgins And s young men
Mic 4: 3 And rebuke s nations afar off;
4: 7 And the outcast a s nation;
6: 2 And you s foundations of the
Nah 3:14 and tread the mortar! Make s
Hag 2: 4 'Yet now be s, Zerubbabel,'
2: 4 says the LORD; 'and be s,
2: 4 the high priest; and be s,
Zech 6: 3 dappled horses—s steeds.
6: 7 Then the s steeds went out,
8: 9 hosts: 'Let your hands be s,
8:13 not fear, Let your hands be s.
8:22 many peoples and s nations
Mt 12:29 Or how can one enter a s man's
12:29 unless he first binds the s
Mk 3:27 No one can enter a s man's house
3:27 unless he first binds the s
Lk 1:15 shall drink neither wine nor s
1:80 So the child grew and became s
2:40 the Child grew and became s in
11:21 When a s man, fully armed,
Acts 3:16 His name, has made this man s,
Rom 15: 1 We then who are s ought to bear
1 Cor 4:10 but you are s! You are
16:13 in the faith, be brave, be s.
2 Cor 12:10 For when I am weak, then I am s.
13: 9 when we are weak and you are s.
Eph 6:10 be s in the Lord and in the
2 Th 2:11 reason God will send them s
2 Tim 2: 1 be s in the grace that is in
Heb 6:18 we might have s consolation,
11:34 out of weakness were made s,
1 Jn 2:14 young men, Because you are s,
Rev 5: 2 Then I saw a s angel proclaiming
18: 8 for s is the Lord God who

STRONGER (23/19) STRONG

Gen 25:23 One people shall be s than
30:41 whenever the s livestock
30:42 feebler were Laban's and the s
Num 13:31 for they are s than we."
Judg 4:24 the children of Israel grew s
4:24 of Israel grew stronger and s
14:18 And what is s than a lion?"
2 Sam 1:23 They were s than lions.
3: 1 But David grew s and stronger,
3: 1 But David grew stronger and s,
13:14 and being s than she, he forced
1 Ki 20:23 Therefore they were s than we;
20:23 surely we will be s than they.
20:25 surely we will be s than
Job 17: 9 who has clean hands will be s
17: 9 hands will be stronger and s.
Ps 105:24 And made them s than their
142: 6 For they are s than I.
Jer 20: 7 You are s than I, and have
31:11 him from the hand of one s
Lk 11:22 But when a s than he comes upon
1 Cor 1:25 and the weakness of God is s
10:22 Are we s than He?

STRONGEST (1/1)

Dan 11:39 he shall act against the s

STRONGHOLD (28/27) STRONGHOLDS

Judg 9:46 they entered the s of the
9:49 put them against the s,
9:49 and set the s on fire above
1 Sam 22: 4 time that David was in the s.
22: 5 David, "Do not stay in the s;
24:22 and his men went up to the s.
2 Sam 5: 7 Nevertheless David took the s of
5: 9 Then David dwelt in the s,
5:17 of it and went down to the s.
22: 3 My s and my refuge;
23:14 David was then in the s,
24: 7 and they came to the s of Tyre
1 Chr 11: 5 Nevertheless David took the s
11: 7 Then David dwelt in the s;
11:16 David was then in the s,
12: 8 Gadites joined David at the s
12:16 Judah came to David at the s.
Job 39:28 the crag of the rock and the s.
Ps 18: 2 the horn of my salvation, my s.
Prov 21:22 And brings down the trusted s.
Isa 17:10 mindful of the Rock of your s,
31: 9 He shall cross over to his s
Jer 48: 1 The high s is shamed and
Ezek 24:25 when I take from them their s,
Mic 4: 8 The s of the daughter of Zion,
Nah 1: 7 A s in the day of trouble;
Hab 1:10 by them. They deride every s,
Zech 9:12 Return to the s,

STRONGHOLDS (20/20) STRONGHOLD

Num 13:19 inhabit are like camps or s;
Judg 6: 2 and the s which are in the
1 Sam 23:14 And David stayed in s in the
23:19 David not hiding with us in s
23:29 up from there and dwelt in s
2 Ki 8:12 Their s you will set on fire,
2 Chr 11:11 And he fortified the s,
Ps 89:40 You have brought his s to
Isa 23:11 Canaan To destroy its s.
Jer 48:18 He has destroyed your s.
48:41 And the s are surprised;
51:30 They have remained in their s;
Lam 2: 2 down in His wrath The s of
2: 5 He has destroyed her s,
Ezek 33:27 and those who are in the s and
Dan 11:24 devise his plans against the s,
Mic 5:11 And throw down all your s.
Nah 3:12 All your s are fig trees with
3:14 for the siege! Fortify your s!
2 Cor 10: 4 in God for pulling down s,

STRONGLY (3/3)

Gen 19: 3 But he insisted s;
34: 3 His soul was s attracted to
1 Cor 16:12 I s urged him to come to you

STRUCK (173/163) STRIKE

Gen 19:11 And they s the men who were at
Ex 7:20 So he lifted up the rod and s
7:25 passed after the LORD had s
8:17 out his hand with his rod and s
9:15 had stretched out My hand and s
9:25 And the hail s throughout the
9:25 and the hail s every herb of
9:31 the flax and the barley were s,
9:32 wheat and the spelt were not s,
12:27 of Israel in Egypt when He s
12:29 at midnight that the LORD s
17: 5 hand your rod with which you s
21:19 then he who s him shall be
22: 2 and he is s so that he dies,
Num 3:13 On the day that I s all the
8:17 on the day that I s all the
11:33 and the LORD s the people with
20:11 Moses lifted his hand and s
22:23 So Balaam s the donkey to turn
22:25 so he s her again.
22:27 and he s the donkey with his
22:28 that you have s me these three
22:32 Why have you s your donkey these
24:10 and he s his hands together;
35:21 the one who s him shall surely
Josh 7: 5 And the men of Ai s down about
7: 5 and s them down on the descent;
8:21 they turned back and s down the
8:22 And they s them down, so that
8:24 returned to Ai and s it with
10:10 and s them down as far as
10:26 And afterward Joshua s them and
10:28 and s it and its king with the
10:30 he s it and all the people who
10:32 and s it and all the people who
10:33 and Joshua s him and his
10:35 They took it on that day and s
10:37 And they took it and s it with
10:39 they s them with the edge of
11:10 and s its king with the sword;
11:11 And they s all the people who
11:12 Joshua took and s with the edge
11:14 but they s every man with the
11:17 and s them down and killed
13:21 whom Moses had s with the
19:47 and they s it with the edge of
20: 5 because he s his neighbor
Judg 1: 8 they s it with the edge of the
1:25 and they s the city with the
5:26 She split and s through his
7:13 it came to a tent and s it so
18:27 and they s them with the edge
20:37 men in ambush spread out and s
20:48 and s them down with the edge
1 Sam 4: 8 These are the gods who s the
5: 6 and He ravaged them and s them
5: 9 and He s the men of the city,
6: 9 it is not His hand that s
6:19 Then He s the men of Beth
6:19 He s fifty thousand and seventy
6:19 because the LORD had s the
17:35 I went out after it and s it,
17:35 and s and killed it.
17:49 and he slung it and s the
17:50 and s the Philistine and killed
19: 8 and s them with a mighty blow,
22:18 Doeg the Edomite turned and s
22:19 he s with the edge of the
23: 5 s them with a mighty blow, and
25:38 that the LORD s Nabal, and he
2 Sam 1:15 and execute him!" And he s
2:23 Therefore Abner s him in the
2:31 But the servants of David had s
4: 7 then they s him and killed him,
6: 7 and God s him there for his
10:18 and s Shobach the commander of
11:15 that he may be s down and
11:21 Who s Abimelech the son of
12:15 And the LORD s the child that
14: 6 but the one s the other and
14: 7 Deliver him who s his brother,
18:15 and s and killed him.
20:10 And he s him with it in the
21:12 after the Philistines had s
21:17 and s the Philistine and killed
1 Ki 2:25 and he s him down, and he died.
2:32 because he s down two men more
2:34 son of Jehoiada went up and s
2:46 and he went out and s him down,
16:10 And Zimri went in and s him and
20:37 So the man s him, inflicting
22:24 of Chenaanah went near and s
22:34 and s the king of Israel
2 Ki 2: 8 and s the water; and it was
2:14 and s the water, and said,
2:14 And when he also had s the
3:23 the kings have surely s swords

6:18 And He *s* them with blindness
12:21 *s* him. So he died, and they
13:18 so he *s* three times, and
13:19 You should have *s* five or six
13:19 then you would have *s* Syria
15: 5 Then the LORD *s* the king, so
15:10 and *s* and killed him in front
15:14 and *s* Shallum the son of Jabesh
15:30 and *s* and killed him; so he
19:37 Adrammelech and Sharezer *s* him
25:21 Then the king of Babylon *s* them
25:25 came with ten men and *s* and
1 Chr 13:10 and He *s* him because he put his
21: 7 therefore He *s* Israel.
2 Chr 13:15 it happened that God *s* Jeroboam
13:17 Then Abijah and his people *s*
13:20 and the LORD *s* him, and he
14:12 So the LORD *s* the Ethiopians
18:23 of Chenaanah went near and *s*
18:33 and *s* the king of Israel
21:18 After all this the LORD *s* him
26:20 because the LORD had *s* him.
32:21 some of his own offspring *s* him
Neh 13:25 *s* some of them and pulled out
Job 1:19 across the wilderness and *s*
2: 7 and *s* Job with painful boils
19:21 For the hand of God has *s* me!
Ps 3: 7 O my God! For You have *s* all
69:26 persecute the ones You have *s*,
78:20 He *s* the rock, So that the
78:31 And *s* down the choice men of
105:33 He *s* their vines also, and
136:10 To Him who *s* Egypt in their
136:17 To Him who *s* down great kings,
Prov 7:23 Till an arrow *s* his liver.
23:35 They have *s* me, but I was not
Song 5: 7 They *s* me, they wounded me;
Isa 14: 6 He who *s* the people in wrath
14:29 Because the rod that *s* you is
27: 7 Has He *s* Israel as He struck
27: 7 Has He struck Israel as He *s*
27: 7 as He struck those who *s* him?
37:38 Adrammelech and Sharezer *s* him
50: 6 I gave My back to those who *s*
57:17 I was angry and *s* him;
60:10 For in My wrath I *s* you,
Jer 20: 2 Then Pashhur *s* Jeremiah the
31:19 I *s* myself on the thigh; I was
37:15 and they *s* him and put him in
41: 2 arose and *s* Gedaliah the son of
41: 3 Ishmael also *s* down all the Jews
52:27 Then the king of Babylon *s* them
Dan 2:34 which *s* the image on its feet
2:35 And the stone that *s* the image
Hab 3:13 You *s* the head from the house
Hag 2:17 I *s* you with blight and mildew
Mt 26:51 *s* the servant of the high
26:67 and others *s* Him with the
26:68 Who is the one who *s* You?"
27:30 and took the reed and *s* Him on
Mk 14:47 stood by drew his sword and *s*
14:65 And the officers *s*
15:19 Then they *s* Him on the head with
Lk 22:50 And one of them *s* the servant of
22:64 they *s* Him on the face and
22:64 Who is the one who *s*
Jn 18:10 drew it and *s* the high priest's
18:22 of the officers who stood by *s*
19: 3 King of the Jews!" And they *s*
Acts 7:24 and *s* down the Egyptian.
12: 7 and he *s* Peter on the side and
12:23 an angel of the Lord *s* him,
23: 3 and do you command me to be *s*
27:17 they *s* sail and so were driven.
2 Cor 4: 9 *s* down, but not destroyed—
Rev 8:12 And a third of the sun was *s*,

STRUCTURE (3/3)

Ezek 40: 2 was something like the *s* of a
40: 5 the width of the wall *s*,
41: 7 therefore the width of the *s*

STRUGGLE (2/2)

Judg 12: 2 people and I were in a great *s*
Heb 10:32 you endured a great *s* with

STRUGGLED (4/4)

Gen 25:22 But the children *s* together
32:28 for you have *s* with God and
Hos 12: 3 And in his strength he *s* with
12: 4 he *s* with the Angel and

STRUGGLING (2/2)

Ezek 16: 6 I passed by you and saw you *s*
16:22 *s* in your blood.

STUBBLE (14/14)

Ex 5:12 the land of Egypt to gather *s*
15: 7 It consumed them like *s*.
Job 13:25 And will You pursue dry *s*?
41:28 Slingstones become like *s* to
Isa 5:24 as the fire devours the *s*,
33:11 You shall bring forth *s*;
40:24 will take them away like *s*.
41: 2 As driven *s* to his bow?
47:14 Behold, they shall be as *s*,
Jer 13:24 I will scatter them like *s*
Joel 2: 5 flaming fire that devours the *s*,
Ob 18 the house of Esau shall be *s*;
Nah 1:10 They shall be devoured like *s*
Mal 4: 1 all who do wickedly will be *s*.

STUBBORN (10/9) STUBBORNNESS

Ex 13:15 when Pharaoh was *s* about
Deut 21:18 If a man has a *s* and rebellious
21:20 This son of ours is *s* and
Judg 2:19 own doings nor from their *s*
Ps 78: 8 A *s* and rebellious generation,
81:12 I gave them over to their own *s*
Jer 6:28 They are all *s* rebels, walking
Ezek 2: 4 For they are impudent and *s*
Hos 4:16 For Israel is *s* Like a stubborn
4:16 Israel is stubborn Like a *s*

STUBBORN-HEARTED (1/1)

Isa 46:12 "Listen to Me, you *s*,

STUBBORNLY (1/1)

Job 15:26 Running *s* against Him With his

STUBBORNNESS (2/2) STUBBORN

Deut 9:27 do not look on the *s* of this
1 Sam 15:23 And *s* is as iniquity and

STUBS (1/1)

Isa 7: 4 be fainthearted for these two *s*

STUCK (4/4)

1 Sam 26: 7 with his spear *s* in the ground
2 Sam 23:10 and his hand *s* to the sword.
Job 29:10 And their tongue *s* to the roof
Acts 27:41 and the prow *s* fast and

STUDENT (1/1)

1 Chr 25: 8 great, the teacher with the *s*.

STUDIED (2/2) STUDY

Ps 111: 2 *S* by all who have pleasure in
Jn 7:15 know letters, having never *s*?

STUDIES (1/1)

Prov 15:28 the righteous *s* how to answer,

STUDS (1/1)

Song 1:11 you ornaments of gold With *s*

STUDY (1/1) STUDIED

Eccl 12:12 and much *s* is wearisome to the

STUFF (1/1)

Josh 7:11 also put it among their own *s*.

STUMBLE (48/44) STUMBLED, STUMBLES, STUMBLING

Lev 26:37 They shall *s* over one another,
Ps 64: 8 So He will make them *s* over
119:165 And nothing causes them to *s*.
140: 4 purposed to make my steps *s*.
Prov 3:23 And your foot will not *s*.
4:12 when you run, you will not *s*.
4:19 do not know what makes them *s*.
Isa 5:27 No one will be weary or *s* among
8:15 And many among them shall *s*;
28: 7 they *s* in judgment.
59:10 We *s* at noonday as at
63:13 That they might not *s*?
Jer 13:16 And before your feet *s* On the
18:15 have caused themselves to *s* in
20:11 my persecutors will *s*,
31: 9 way in which they shall not *s*;
46: 6 They will *s* and fall
50:32 The most proud shall *s* and
Ezek 14: 3 that which causes them to *s*
14: 4 him what causes him to *s* into
14: 7 him what causes him to *s* into
21:15 heart may melt and many may *s*.
36:15 you cause your nation to *s*
Dan 11:19 but he shall *s* and fall, and
Hos 4: 5 Therefore you shall *s* in the
4: 5 The prophet also shall *s* with
5: 5 Israel and Ephraim *s* in their
14: 9 But transgressors *s* in them.
Nah 2: 5 They *s* in their walk;
3: 3 They *s* over the corpses—
Mal 2: 8 You have caused many to *s* at
Mt 26:31 All of you will be made to *s*
26:33 Even if all are made to *s*
26:33 You, I will never be made to *s*.
Mk 4:17 word's sake, immediately they *s*.
9:42 ones who believe in Me to *s*,
14:27 All of you will be made to *s*
14:29 "Even if all are made to *s*,
Jn 11: 9 walks in the day, he does not *s*,
16: 1 you should not be made to *s*.
1 Cor 8:13 if food makes my brother *s*,
8:13 meat, lest I make my brother *s*.
2 Cor 11:29 I am not weak? Who is made to *s*,
Jas 2:10 and yet *s* in one point, he is
3: 2 For we all *s* in many things.
3: 2 If anyone does not *s* in word,
1 Pe 2: 8 rock of offense." They *s*,
2 Pe 1:10 these things you will never *s*;

STUMBLED (10/10) STUMBLE

1 Sam 2: 4 And those who *s* are girded
2 Sam 6: 6 took hold of it, for the oxen *s*.
1 Chr 13: 9 to hold the ark, for the oxen *s*.
Ps 27: 2 They *s* and fell.
73: 2 as for me, my feet had almost *s*;
Isa 3: 8 For Jerusalem *s*,
Jer 46:12 For the mighty man has *s*
Hos 14: 1 For you have *s* because of your
Rom 9:32 For they *s* at that stumbling
11:11 have they *s* that they should

STUMBLES (5/5) STUMBLE

Prov 24:17 your heart be glad when he *s*;
Hos 5: 5 Judah also *s* with them.
Mt 13:21 of the word, immediately he *s*.
Jn 11:10 if one walks in the night, he *s*,
Rom 14:21 by which your brother *s* or is

STUMBLING (20/20) STUMBLE

Lev 19:14 nor put a *s* block before the
Job 4: 4 words have upheld him who was *s*,
Prov 24:11 And hold back those *s* to the
Isa 8:14 But a stone of *s* and a rock of
57:14 Take the *s* block out of the
Jer 6:21 I will lay *s* blocks before this
20:10 acquaintances watched for my *s*,
Ezek 3:20 and I lay a *s* block before him,
7:19 Because it became their *s*
Zeph 1: 3 And the *s* blocks along with
Rom 9:32 For they stumbled at that *s*
9:33 I lay in Zion a *s* stone
11: 9 A *s* block and a
14:13 not to put a *s* block or a cause
1 Cor 1:23 to the Jews a *s* block and to
8: 9 liberty of yours become a *s*
1 Pe 2: 8 A stone of *s* And a rock
1 Jn 2:10 and there is no cause for *s* in
Jude 24 who is able to keep you from *s*,
Rev 2:14 who taught Balak to put a *s*

STUMP (6/5)

Job 14: 8 And its *s* may die in the
Isa 6:13 Whose *s* remains when it is
6:13 the holy seed shall be its *s*.
Dan 4:15 Nevertheless leave the *s* and
4:23 but leave its *s* and roots in
4:26 gave the command to leave the *s*

STUPID (3/3)

Job 18: 3 And regarded as *s* in your
Prov 12: 1 he who hates correction is *s*.
30: 2 Surely I am more *s* than any

STUPOR (1/1)

Rom 11: 8 given them a spirit of *s*,

STURDY (1/1)

Ezek 27:24 in *s* woven cords, which were in

STYLE (1/1)

Ps 144:12 Sculptured in palace *s*;

SUAH (1/1)

1 Chr 7:36 The sons of Zophah were *S*,

SUBDUE (9/9) SUBDUED

Gen 1:28 fill the earth and *s* it;
1 Chr 17:10 Also I will *s* all your enemies.
Ps 47: 3 He will *s* the peoples under us,
81:14 I would soon *s* their enemies,
Isa 45: 1 To *s* nations before him
Dan 7:24 And shall *s* three kings.
Mic 7:19 And will *s* our iniquities.
Zech 9:15 They shall devour and *s* with
Phil 3:21 by which He is able even to *s*

SUBDUED (20/20) SUBDUE

Num 32:22 and the land is *s* before the
32:29 and the land is *s* before you,
Deut 20:20 war with you, until it is *s*.
Josh 18: 1 And the land was *s* before them.
Judg 3:30 So Moab was *s* that day under the
4:23 So on that day God *s* Jabin king
8:28 Thus Midian was *s* before the
11:33 Thus the people of Ammon were *s*
1 Sam 7:13 So the Philistines were *s*,
2 Sam 8: 1 attacked the Philistines and *s*
8:11 all the nations which he had *s*—
22:40 You have *s* under me those who
2 Ki 18: 8 He *s* the Philistines, as far as
1 Chr 18: 1 *s* them, and took Gath and its
20: 4 of the giant. And they were *s*.
22:18 and the land is *s* before the
2 Chr 13:18 the children of Israel were *s*
Neh 9:24 You *s* before them the
Ps 18:39 You have *s* under me those who
Heb 11:33 who through faith *s* kingdoms,

S

SUBDUES (3/3)

2 Sam 22:48 And *s* the peoples under me;
Ps 18:47 And *s* the peoples under me;
144: 2 Who *s* my people under me.

SUBJECT (17/16) SUBJECTED, SUBJECTION

Gen 30:33 when the *s* of my wages comes
Mk 3:29 but is *s* to eternal
Lk 2:51 and was *s* to them, but His
10:17 even the demons are *s* to us in
10:20 that the spirits are *s* to you,
Rom 8: 7 for it is not *s* to the law of
13: 1 Let every soul be *s* to the
13: 5 Therefore you must be *s*,
1 Cor 14:32 spirits of the prophets are *s*
15:28 Now when all things are made *s*
15:28 the Son Himself will also be *s*
Eph 5:24 just as the church is *s* to
Col 2:20 do you yourselves to
Titus 3: 1 Remind them to be *s* to rulers
Heb 2:15 were all their lifetime *s* to
5: 2 since he himself is also *s* to
1 Pe 3:22 and powers having been made *s*

SUBJECTED (2/1) SUBJECT

Rom 8:20 For the creation was *s* to
8:20 but because of Him who *s* it in

SUBJECTION (8/7) SUBJECT

Ps 106:42 And they were brought into *s*
Jer 34:11 and brought them into *s* as male
34:16 and brought them back into *s*,
1 Cor 9:27 my body and bring it into *s*,
Heb 2: 5 which we speak, in *s* to angels.
2: 8 have put all things in *s*
2: 8 For in that He put all in *s*
12: 9 not much more readily be in *s*

SUBMISSION (4/4) SUBMIT

Ps 81:15 of the LORD would pretend *s*
Gal 2: 5 to whom we did not yield *s* even
1 Tim 2:11 learn in silence with all *s*.
3: 4 having his children in *s* with

SUBMISSIVE (6/6) SUBMIT

1 Cor 14:34 but they are to be *s*,
Heb 13:17 who rule over you, and be *s*,
1 Pe 2:18 be *s* to your masters with all
3: 1 be *s* to your own husbands,
3: 5 being *s* to their own husbands,
5: 5 all of you be *s* to one

SUBMIT (11/11) SUBMISSION, SUBMISSIVE

Gen 16: 9 and *s* yourself under her
Deut 33:29 Your enemies shall *s* to
2 Sam 22:45 The foreigners *s* to me;
Ps 18:44 The foreigners *s* to me.
66: 3 Your enemies shall *s* themselves
1 Cor 16:16 that you also *s* to such, and to
Eph 5:22 *s* to your own husbands, as to
Col 3:18 *s* to your own husbands, as is
Jas 4: 7 Therefore *s* to God. Resist the
1 Pe 2:13 Therefore *s* yourselves to every
5: 5 *s* yourselves to your elders.

SUBMITS (1/1)

Ps 68:30 Till everyone *s* himself with

SUBMITTED (2/2)

1 Chr 29:24 *s* themselves to King Solomon.
Rom 10: 3 have not *s* to the righteousness

SUBMITTING (1/1)

Eph 5:21 *s* to one another in the fear of

SUBORNED (KJV) See INDUCED

SUBSCRIBE (KJV) See WRITE

SUBSIDE (2/2)

Am 8: 8 Heave and *s* Like the River of
9: 5 And *s* like the River of Egypt.

SUBSIDED (4/4)

Gen 8: 1 the earth, and the waters *s*.
Judg 8: 3 Then their anger toward him *s*
Esth 2: 1 the wrath of King Ahasuerus *s*,
7:10 Then the king's wrath *s*.

SUBSTANCE (12/12)

Ex 16:14 wilderness, was a small round *s*,
Deut 11: 6 and all the *s* that was in
33:11 Bless his *s*, LORD, And accept
1 Chr 28: 1 and the stewards over all the *s*
Job 5: 5 And a snare snatches their *s*.
Ps 139:16 Your eyes saw my *s*,
Prov 6:31 may have to give up all the *s*
Ob 13 Nor laid hands on their *s* In
Mic 4:13 And their *s* to the Lord of the
Lk 8: 3 provided for Him from their *s*.
Col 2:17 but the *s* is of Christ.
Heb 11: 1 Now faith is the *s* of things

SUBSTITUTE (1/1)

Lev 27:10 He shall not *s* it or exchange

SUBTIL (KJV) See CRAFTY, CUNNING

SUBURBS (KJV) See COMMON-LAND, COMMON-LANDS, (COMMON) LAND

SUBVERT (3/3)

Job 8: 3 Does God *s* judgment? Or does
Lam 3:36 Or *s* a man in his cause—The
Titus 1:11 who *s* whole households,

SUCCEED (3/3)

Num 14:41 the LORD? For this will not *s*.
Deut 25: 6 son which she bears will *s* to
Jer 32: 5 you shall not *s*" '?"

SUCCEEDED (2/2)

Ezek 16:13 and *s* to royalty.
Acts 24:27 two years Porcius Festus *s*

SUCCEEDING (1/1)

Lev 21:17 man of your descendants in *s*

SUCCEEDS (2/2)

Prov 30:23 And a maidservant who *s* her
Eccl 2:12 what can the man do who *s*

SUCCESS (5/5)

Gen 24:12 please give me *s* this day, and
Josh 1: 8 and then you will have good *s*.
Job 6:13 And is *s* driven from me?
30:22 ride on it; You spoil my *s*.
Eccl 10:10 But wisdom brings *s*.

SUCCESSFUL (1/1)

Gen 39: 2 and he was a *s* man; and he was

SUCCESSFULLY (2/2)

2 Chr 7:11 and Solomon *s* accomplished all
Mic 7: 3 That they may *s* do evil with

SUCCESSIVE (2/2)

Gen 32:16 distance between *s* droves."
Joel 2: 2 Even for many *s* generations.

SUCCOTH (18/16)

Gen 33:17 And Jacob journeyed to *S*,
33:17 name of the place is called *S*.
Ex 12:37 journeyed from Rameses to *S*,
13:20 they took their journey from *S*
Num 33: 5 from Rameses and camped at *S*.
33: 6 They departed from *S* and camped
Josh 13:27 Beth Haram, Beth Nimrah, *S*,
Judg 8: 5 Then he said to the men of *S*,
8: 6 And the leaders of *S* said,
8: 8 answered him as the men of *S*
8:14 a young man of the men of *S*
8:14 down for him the leaders of *S*
8:15 Then he came to the men of *S* and
8:16 them he taught the men of *S*.
1 Ki 7:46 between *S* and Zaretan.
2 Chr 4:17 between *S* and Zeredah.
Ps 60: 6 measure out the Valley of *S*.
108: 7 measure out the Valley of *S*.

SUCCOTH BENOTH (1/1)

2 Ki 17:30 The men of Babylon made *S*,

SUCCOUR, SUCCOURED, SUCCOURER (KJV) See AID, HELP, HELPED, HELPER

SUCCULENT (1/1)

Job 33:20 And his soul *s* food.

SUCH (220/207)

Gen 18:25 Far be it from You to do *s* a
27: 4 *s* as I love, and bring it to
27: 9 for your father, *s* as he loves.
27:14 *s* as his father loved.
41:19 *s* ugliness as I have never seen
41:38 Can we find *s* a one as this,
44: 7 that your servants should do *s*
44:15 Did you not know that *s* a man
50: 3 for *s* are the days required for
Ex 9:18 *s* as has not been in Egypt
10:14 previously there had been no *s*
10:14 nor shall there be *s* after
11: 6 *s* as was not like it before,
18:21 *s* as fear God, men of truth,
18:21 and place *s* over them to be
34:10 people I will do marvels *s* as
Lev 7:21 *s* as human uncleanness, an
10:19 and *s* things have befallen me!
11:27 Whoever touches any *s* carcass
11:28 Whoever carries any *s* carcass
11:34 in *s* a vessel, any edible food
11:35 on which a part of any *s*
11:36 but whatever touches any *s*
11:37 And if a part of any *s* carcass
11:38 and if a part of any *s*
14:22 *s* as he is able to afford:
14:30 *s* as he can afford—
14:31 '*s* as he is able to afford,
22: 6 person who has touched any *s*
Deut 4: 8 nation is there that has *s*
5:29 that they had *s* a heart in them
12: 4 the LORD your God with *s*
13:11 and not again do *s* wickedness
13:14 true and certain that *s* an
14: 7 *s* as these: the camel, the
17: 4 true and certain that *s* an
18:14 your God has not appointed *s*
19:20 they shall not again commit *s*
22:11 *s* as wool and linen mixed
25:16 For all who do *s* things, all who
Judg 13:23 nor would He have told us *s*
18:23 that you have gathered *s* a
19:24 but to this man do not do *s* a
19:30 No *s* deed has been done or seen
1 Sam 2:23 Why do you do *s* things? For I
4: 7 Woe to us! For *s* a thing has
21: 2 directed my young men to *s*
21: 2 my young men to such and *s* a
25:17 For he is *s* a scoundrel that
2 Sam 9: 8 that you should look upon *s* a
13:12 for no *s* thing should be done
13:18 king's virgin daughters wore *s*
14:13 Why then have you schemed *s* a
15: 2 Your servant is from *s* and such
15: 2 servant is from such and *s* a
19:36 the king repay me with *s* a
1 Ki 1:41 Why is the city in *s* a noisy
7:20 and there were two hundred *s*
10:10 There never again came *s*
10:12 There never again came *s* almug
22: 8 Let not the king say *s* things!"
2 Ki 6: 8 My camp will be in *s* and such
6: 8 camp will be in such and *s* a
7:19 could *s* a thing be?" And he
19:29 You shall eat this year *s* as
21:12 I am bringing *s* calamity upon
23:22 *S* a Passover surely had never
1 Chr 29:25 and bestowed on him *s* royal
2 Chr 1:12 *s* as none of the kings have had
4: 6 *s* things as they offered for
4:18 all these articles made in *s*
9: 9 there never were any spices *s*
9:11 and there were none *s* as
11:16 *s* as set their heart to seek
18: 7 Let not the king say *s* things!"
35:18 the kings of Israel had kept *s*
Ezra 7:25 all *s* as know the laws of your
7:27 who has put *s* a thing as
9:13 and have given us *s*
Neh 6: 8 No *s* things as you say are being
6:11 'Should *s* a man as I flee?
6:11 And who is there *s* as I who
Esth 4:14 come to the kingdom for *s* a
7: 5 presume in his heart to do *s* a
Job 12: 3 who does not know *s* things as
14: 3 do You open Your eyes on *s* a
15:13 And let *s* words go out of
16: 2 I have heard many *s* things;
18:21 Surely *s* are the dwellings of
23:14 And many *s* things are with
35: 8 wickedness affects a man *s* as
Ps 25:10 To *s* as keep His covenant and
27:12 And *s* as breathe out violence.
34:18 And saves *s* as have a contrite
40: 4 nor *s* as turn aside to lies.
40:16 Let *s* as love Your salvation
73: 1 To *s* as are pure in heart.
103:18 To *s* as keep His covenant,
125: 5 As for *s* as turn aside to their
139: 6 *S* knowledge is too wonderful
144:15 are the people who are in *s* a
Prov 28: 4 But *s* as keep the law contend
29: 7 wicked does not understand *s*
Isa 2:22 Sever yourselves from *s* a man,
10:20 And *s* as have escaped of the
20: 6 Surely *s* is our expectation,
37:30 You shall eat this year *s* as
40:20 is too impoverished for *s* a
66: 8 Who has heard *s* a thing?
66: 8 Who has seen *s* things?
Jer 2:10 And see if there has been *s* a
5: 9 shall I not avenge Myself on *s*
5:29 I not avenge Myself on *s*
9: 9 I not avenge Myself on *s*
15: 2 *S* as are for death, to death;
15: 2 And *s* as are for the sword,
15: 2 And *s* as are for the famine,
15: 2 And *s* as are for the
17:27 *s* as not carrying a burden when
18:13 Who has heard *s* things?
19: 3 I will bring *s* a catastrophe on
21: 7 and *s* as are left in this city
38: 4 by speaking *s* words to them.
Ezek 16:16 *S* things should not happen,
17:15 Will he who does *s* things
Dan 2:10 or ruler has ever asked *s*
9:12 for under the whole heaven *s*

10:15 When he had spoken *s* words to
12: 1 *S* as never was since there was
Joel 2: 2 Nor will there ever be any *s*
Zeph 1: 8 And all *s* as are clothed with
Zech 14:15 *S* also shall be the plague
Mal 3:10 pour out for you *s* blessing
Mt 8:10 I have not found *s* great faith,
9: 8 who had given *s* power to men.
15:33 in the wilderness to fill *s* a
19:10 If *s* is the case of the man with
19:14 for of *s* is the kingdom of
24:21 *s* as has not been since the
Mk 4:33 And with many *s* parables He
6: 2 that *s* mighty works are
7: 8 and many other *s* things you
7:13 And many *s* things you do."
9: 3 *s* as no launderer on earth can
10:14 for of *s* is the kingdom of God.
13: 7 for *s* things must happen, but
13:19 *s* as has not been since the
Lk 7: 9 I have not found *s* great faith,
9: 9 who is this of whom I hear *s*
10: 7 eating and drinking *s* things as
10: 8 eat *s* things as are set before
11:41 But rather give alms of *s* things
13: 2 because they suffered *s* things?
18:16 for of *s* is the kingdom of God.
Jn 4:23 for the Father is seeking *s* to
8: 5 commanded us that *s* should be
9:16 can a man who is a sinner do *s*
Acts 15:24 to whom we gave no *s*
16:24 Having received *s* a charge, he
18:15 do not want to be a judge of *s*
21:25 that they should observe no *s*
22:22 Away with *s* a fellow from the
25:18 no accusation against him of *s*
25:20 because I was uncertain of *s*
26:29 both almost and altogether *s*
28:10 they provided *s* things as were
Rom 1:32 that those who practice *s*
2: 2 against those who practice *s*
2: 3 who judge those practicing *s*
16:18 For those who are *s* do not serve
1 Cor 5: 1 and *s* sexual immorality as is
5: 5 deliver *s* a one to Satan for the
5:11 not even to eat with *s* a person.
6:11 And *s* were some of you. But you
7:15 is not under bondage in *s*
7:28 Nevertheless *s* will have
9:24 Run in *s* a way that you may
10:13 has overtaken you except *s* as
11:16 we have no *s* custom, nor do
16:16 that you also submit to *s*,
16:18 Therefore acknowledge *s* men.
2 Cor 2: 6 majority is sufficient for *s*
2: 7 lest perhaps *s* a one be
3: 4 And we have *s* trust through
3:12 since we have *s* hope, we use
10:11 Let *s* a person consider this,
10:11 *s* we will also be in deed
11:13 For *s* are false apostles,
12: 2 *s* a one was caught up to the
12: 3 And I know *s* a man—whether in
12: 5 Of *s* a one I will boast; yet of
12:20 I shall not find you *s* as I
12:20 I shall be found by you *s* as
Gal 5:21 that those who practice *s*
5:23 Against *s* there is no law.
6: 1 who are spiritual restore *s* a
Eph 5:27 spot or wrinkle or any *s* thing,
Phil 2:29 and hold *s* men in esteem;
1 Th 4: 6 Lord is the avenger of all *s*,
2 Th 3:12 Now those who are *s* we command
1 Tim 6: 5 From *s* withdraw yourself.
2 Tim 3: 5 And from *s* people turn away!
Titus 3:11 knowing that *s* a person is
Phm 1: 9 being *s* a one as Paul, the aged,
Heb 4: 7 after *s* a long time, as it
7:26 For *s* a High Priest was fitting
8: 1 We have *s* a High Priest, who is
11:14 For those who say *s* things
12: 3 For consider Him who endured *s*
13: 5 be content with *s* things as
13:16 for with *s* sacrifices God is
Jas 4:13 or tomorrow we will go to *s*
4:13 we will go to such and *s* a
4:16 All *s* boasting is evil.
2 Pe 1:17 Father honor and glory when *s*
3 Jn 8 We therefore ought to receive *s*,
Rev 5:13 and under the earth and *s* as
16:18 *s* a mighty and great earthquake
18:17 For in one hour *s* great riches
20: 6 Over *s* the second death has no

SUCHATHITES (1/1)

1 Chr 2:55 the Shimeathites, and the *S*.

SUCK (2/2)

Job 20:16 He will *s* the poison of cobras;
39:30 Its young ones *s* up blood;

SUCKED, SUCKING (KJV) See NURSE, NURSED, NURSING, SUCKLING

SUCKLING (1/1)

1 Sam 7: 9 And Samuel took a *s* lamb and

SUCKLINGS (KJV) See INFANTS

SUDDEN (3/3) SUDDENLY

Job 22:10 And *s* fear troubles you,
Prov 3:25 Do not be afraid of *s* terror,
1 Th 5: 3 Peace and safety!" then *s*

SUDDENLY (72/71) SUDDEN

Gen 41: 2 *S* there came up out of the river
41: 5 and *s* seven heads of grain came
41:18 *S* seven cows came up out of the
41:22 and *s* seven heads came up on
Num 6: 9 And if anyone dies very *s*
12: 4 *S* the LORD said to Moses,
12:10 *s* Miriam became leprous, as
16:42 and *s* the cloud covered it, and
35:22 if he pushes him *s* without
Deut 7: 4 against you and destroy you *s*.
Josh 10: 9 therefore came upon them *s*,
11: 7 with him came against them *s*
Judg 19:22 *s* certain men of the city,
2 Sam 15:14 lest he overtake us *s* and bring
1 Ki 11:22 that *s* you seek to go to your
18: 7 *s* Elijah met him; and he
19: 5 *s* an angel touched him, and
19:13 *S* a voice came to him, and
20:13 *S* a prophet approached Ahab
2 Ki 2:11 that *s* a chariot of fire
3:20 that *s* water came by way of
13:21 that *s* they spied a band of
2 Chr 29:36 the events took place so *s*.
Job 1:19 and *s* a great wind came from
5: 3 But *s* I cursed his dwelling
9:23 If the scourge slays *s*,
Ps 6:10 turn back and be ashamed *s*.
64: 4 *S* they shoot at him and do not
64: 7 *S* they shall be wounded.
Prov 6:15 his calamity shall come *s*;
6:15 *S* he shall be broken without
24:22 For their calamity will rise *s*,
28:18 perverse in his ways will *s*
29: 1 Will *s* be destroyed, and that
Eccl 9:12 When it falls *s* upon them.
Isa 29: 5 it shall be in an instant, *s*.
30:13 Whose breaking comes *s*,
47:11 shall come upon you *s*,
48: 3 *S* I did them, and they came
Jer 4:20 *S* my tents are plundered,
6:26 For the plunderer will *s* come
15: 8 and terror to fall on them *s*.
18:22 When You bring a troop *s* upon
49:19 But I will *s* make him run away
50:44 But I will make them *s* run
51: 8 Babylon has *s* fallen and been
Ezek 9: 2 And *s* six men came from the
37: 7 and *s* a rattling; and the bones
Dan 7: 5 And *s* another beast, a second,
8: 5 *s* a male goat came from the
8:15 that *s* there stood before me
10:10 *S*, a hand touched me,
10:16 *s*, one having the likeness
Hab 2: 7 not your creditors rise up *s*?
Mal 3: 1 Will *s* come to His temple,
Mt 3:17 And *s* a voice came from heaven,
8:24 And *s* a great tempest arose on
8:29 And *s* they cried out, saying,
8:32 And *s* the whole herd of swine
9:20 And *s*, a woman who had a
17: 5 and *s* a voice came out of the
26:51 And *s*, one of those who were
Mk 9: 8 *S*, when they had looked
13:36 'lest, coming *s*, he find you
Lk 2:13 And *s* there was with the angel a
9:38 *S* a man from the multitude cried
9:39 and he *s* cries out;
Acts 2: 2 And *s* there came a sound from
9: 3 and *s* a light shone around him
16:26 *S* there was a great earthquake,
22: 6 *s* a great light from heaven
28: 6 that he would swell up or *s*

SUE (1/1) SUIT

Mt 5:40 If anyone wants to *s* you and

SUFFER (46/46) SUFFERED, SUFFERING, SUFFERS

Ex 23:26 No one shall *s* miscarriage or be
Job 24:11 winepresses, yet *s* thirst.
Ps 34:10 The young lions lack and *s*
88:15 I *s* Your terrors; I am
Prov 11:15 is surety for a stranger will *s*,
19:15 And an idle person will *s*
19:19 A man of great wrath will *s*
Dan 6: 2 so that the king would *s* no
Joel 1:18 Even the flocks of sheep *s*
Mt 16:21 and *s* many things from the
17:12 Son of Man is also about to *s*
Mk 8:31 them that the Son of Man must *s*
9:12 that He must *s* many things and
Lk 9:22 The Son of Man must *s* many
17:25 But first He must *s* many things
22:15 Passover with you before I *s*;
24:46 necessary for the Christ to *s*
Acts 3:18 that the Christ would *s*,
5:41 they were counted worthy to *s*
7:24 And seeing one of them *s* wrong,
9:16 him how many things he must *s*
17: 3 that the Christ had to *s* and
26:23 "that the Christ would *s*,
Rom 8:17 if indeed we *s* with Him, that
1 Cor 3:15 he will *s* loss; but he himself
12:26 all the members *s* with it;
2 Cor 1: 6 same sufferings which we also *s*.
7: 9 that you might *s* loss from us
Gal 5:11 why do I still *s* persecution?
6:12 only that they may not *s*
Phil 1:29 but also to *s* for His sake,
4:12 both to abound and to *s* need.
1 Th 3: 4 were with you that we would *s*
2 Th 1: 5 of God, for which you also *s*;
1 Tim 4:10 this end we both labor and *s*
2 Tim 1:12 For this reason I also *s* these
2: 9 for which I *s* trouble as an
3:12 godly in Christ Jesus will *s*
Heb 9:26 He then would have had to *s*
11:25 choosing rather to *s* affliction
1 Pe 2:20 But when you do good and *s*,
3:14 But even if you should *s* for
3:17 to *s* for doing good than for
4:15 But let none of you *s* as a
4:19 Therefore let those who *s*
Rev 2:10 things which you are about to *s*.

SUFFERED (21/20) SUFFER

Jer 15:15 that for Your sake I have *s*
Mt 27:19 for I have *s* many things today
Mk 5:26 and had *s* many things from many
Lk 13: 2 because they *s* such things?
24:26 not the Christ to have *s*
Acts 28: 5 creature into the fire and *s*
2 Cor 7:12 nor for the sake of him who *s*
Gal 3: 4 Have you *s* so many things in
Phil 3: 8 for whom I have *s* the loss of
1 Th 2: 2 But even after we had *s* before
2:14 For you also *s* the same things
1 Tim 1:19 concerning the faith have *s*
Heb 2:18 For in that He Himself has *s*,
5: 8 by the things which He *s*.
13:12 *s* outside the gate.
1 Pe 2:21 because Christ also *s* for us,
2:23 not revile in return; when He *s*,
3:18 For Christ also *s* once for
4: 1 since Christ *s* for us in the
4: 1 for he who has *s* in the flesh
5:10 after you have *s* a while,

SUFFERING (7/7) SUFFER, SUFFERINGS

Lam 3:51 My eyes bring *s* to my soul
Acts 1: 3 Himself alive after His *s* by
Heb 2: 9 for the *s* of death crowned with
Jas 5:10 as an example of *s* and
5:13 Is anyone among you *s*?
1 Pe 2:19 endures grief, *s* wrongfully.
Jude 7 *s* the vengeance of eternal

SUFFERINGS (14/14) SUFFERING

Job 9:28 I am afraid of all my *s*;
Rom 8:18 For I consider that the *s* of
2 Cor 1: 5 For as the *s* of Christ abound in
1: 6 for enduring the same *s* which
1: 7 as you are partakers of the *s*,
Phil 3:10 and the fellowship of His *s*,
Col 1:24 I now rejoice in my *s* for you,
2 Tim 1: 8 but share with me in the *s* for
Heb 2:10 salvation perfect through *s*.
10:32 endured a great struggle with *s*:
1 Pe 1:11 He testified beforehand the *s*
4:13 that you partake of Christ's *s*,
5: 1 elder and a witness of the *s*
5: 9 knowing that the same *s* are

SUFFERS (5/5) SUFFER

Mt 11:12 now the kingdom of heaven *s*
17:15 for he is an epileptic and *s*
1 Cor 12:26 And if one member *s*,
13: 4 Love *s* long and is kind;
1 Pe 4:16 Yet if anyone *s* as a

SUFFICE, SUFFICED, SUFFICETH (KJV) See ENOUGH, SATISFIED, SUFFICIENT

SUFFICIENCY (2/2) SUFFICIENT

2 Cor 3: 5 but our *s* is from God,
9: 8 always having all *s* in all

SUFFICIENT (15/14) SUFFICIENCY

Ex 36: 7 for the material they had was *s*
Num 35:30 but one witness is not *s*
Deut 15: 8 to him and willingly lend him *s*
33: 7 Let his hands be *s* for him,
2 Chr 30: 3 because a *s* number of priests
Isa 40:16 And Lebanon is not *s* to burn,
40:16 Nor its beasts *s* for a burnt
Mt 6:34 *S* for the day is its own
Jn 6: 7 worth of bread is not *s* for
14: 8 and it is *s* for us."
2 Cor 2: 6 by the majority is *s* for such
2:16 And who is *s* for these things?
3: 5 Not that we are *s* of ourselves
3: 6 who also made us *s* as ministers
12: 9 My grace is *s* for you, for My

SUFFICIENTLY (1/1)

Isa 23:18 before the LORD, to eat *s*,

SUGGEST (3/3)

Esth 5:14 and in the morning *s* to the
6: 4 of the king's palace to *s* that
Acts 23:15 *s* to the commander that he be

SUGGESTED (1/1)

Esth 6:10 and the horse, as you have *s*,

SUIT (2/2)

Judg 17:10 a *s* of clothes, and your
2 Sam 15: 4 and everyone who has any *s* or

SUITABLE (2/2)

Lev 16:21 by the hand of a *s* man.
Acts 27:12 the harbor was not *s* to winter

SUKKIIM (1/1)

2 Chr 12: 3 the Lubim and the *S* and the

SUKKIMS (KJV) See SUKKIIM

SULFUR (1/1)

Rev 9:17 and *s* yellow; and the heads of

SULLEN (3/3)

1 Ki 20:43 of Israel went to his house *s*
21: 4 So Ahab went into his house *s*
21: 5 Why is your spirit so *s* that you

SUM (9/9)

Gen 25: 7 This is the *s* of the years of
Ex 21:30 there is imposed on him a *s*
2 Sam 24: 9 Then Joab gave the *s* of the
1 Chr 21: 5 Then Joab gave the *s* of the
Esth 4: 7 and the *s* of money that Haman
Ps 139:17 O God! How great is the *s* of
Mt 28:12 they gave a large *s* of money to
Acts 7:16 that Abraham bought for a *s* of
22:28 With a large *s* I obtained this

SUMMED (1/1)

Rom 13: 9 are all *s* up in this saying,

SUMMER (25/25)

Gen 8:22 Cold and heat, Winter and *s*,
2 Sam 16: 1 one hundred *s* fruits, and a
16: 2 the bread and *s* fruit for the
Ps 32: 4 turned into the drought of *s*.
74:17 You have made *s* and winter.
Prov 6: 8 Provides her supplies in the *s*,
10: 5 He who gathers in *s* is a wise
26: 1 As snow in *s* and rain in
30:25 prepare their food in the *s*;
Isa 16: 9 cries have fallen Over your *s*
18: 6 The birds of prey will *s* on
28: 4 the first fruit before the *s*,
Jer 8:20 The *s* is ended, And we are
40:10 gather wine and *s* fruit and
40:12 and gathered wine and *s* fruit
48:32 plunderer has fallen on your *s*
Dan 2:35 became like chaff from the *s*
Am 3:15 winter house along with the *s*
8: 1 a basket of *s* fruit.
8: 2 A basket of *s* fruit." Then the
Mic 7: 1 I am like those who gather *s*
Zech 14: 8 In both *s* and winter it shall
Mt 24:32 you know that *s* is near.
Mk 13:28 you know that *s* is near.
Lk 21:30 and know for yourselves that *s*

SUMMON (2/2)

Acts 10:22 by a holy angel to *s* you to
25: 3 that he would *s* him to

SUMMONED (3/3)

2 Chr 36:10 the year King Nebuchadnezzar *s*
Isa 31: 4 a multitude of shepherds is *s*
Acts 6: 2 Then the twelve *s* the multitude

SUMMONING (1/1)

Mk 15:44 and *s* the centurion, he asked

SUMPTUOUS (1/1)

Hab 1:16 by them their share is *s* And

SUMPTUOUSLY (1/1)

Lk 16:19 and fine linen and fared *s*

SUN (161/153) SUNDIAL

Gen 15:12 Now when the *s* was going down,
15:17 when the *s* went down and it was
19:23 The *s* had risen upon the earth
28:11 because the *s* had set. And he
32:31 as he crossed over Penuel the *s*
37: 9 And this time, the *s*,
Ex 16:21 And when the *s* became hot, it
17:12 until the going down of the *s*.
22: 3 If the *s* has risen on him,
22:26 return it to him before the *s*
Lev 22: 7 And when the *s* goes down he
Num 2: 3 toward the rising of the *s*,
25: 4 before the LORD, out in the *s*,
Deut 4:19 heaven, and when you see the *s*,
4:41 toward the rising of the *s*,
4:47 toward the rising of the *s*,
11:30 Jordan, toward the setting *s*,
16: 6 at the going down of the *s*,
17: 3 either the *s* or moon or any of
23:11 and when the *s* sets, he may
24:13 pledge to him again when the *s*
24:15 and not let the *s* go down on
33:14 the precious fruits of the *s*,
Josh 1: 4 toward the going down of the *s*,
8:29 And as soon as the *s* was down,
10:12 in the sight of Israel: "*S*,
10:13 So the *s* stood still, And the
10:13 So the *s* stood still in the
10:27 time of the going down of the *s*
12: 1 toward the rising of the *s*,
Judg 5:31 who love Him be like the *s*
9:33 as soon as the *s* is up in the
14:18 on the seventh day before the *s*
19:14 and the *s* went down on them
1 Sam 11: 9 by the time the *s* is hot, you
2 Sam 2:24 And the *s* was going down when
3:35 or anything else till the *s*
12:11 wives in the sight of this *s*.
12:12 before all Israel, before the *s*.
23: 4 of the morning when the *s*
1 Ki 22:36 as the *s* was going down, a
2 Ki 3:22 and the *s* was shining on the
23: 5 incense to Baal, to the *s*,
23:11 of Judah had dedicated to the *s*,
23:11 he burned the chariots of the *s*
Neh 7: 3 be opened until the *s* is hot;
Job 8:16 He grows green in the *s*,
9: 7 He commands the *s*,
30:28 mourning, but not in the *s*;
31:26 If I have observed the *s* when
Ps 19: 4 has set a tabernacle for the *s*,
50: 1 From the rising of the *s* to
58: 8 that they may not see the *s*.
72: 5 fear You As long as the *s* and
72:17 shall continue as long as the *s*.
74:16 prepared the light and the *s*.
84:11 For the LORD God is a *s* and
89:36 And his throne as the *s* before
104:19 The *s* knows its going down.
104:22 When the *s* rises, they gather
113: 3 From the rising of the *s* to its
121: 6 The *s* shall not strike you by
136: 8 The *s* to rule by day, For His
148: 3 *s* and moon; Praise Him, all
Prov 4:18 the just is like the shining *s*,
Eccl 1: 3 In which he toils under the *s*?
1: 5 The *s* also rises, and the sun
1: 5 and the *s* goes down,
1: 9 is nothing new under the *s*.
1:14 works that are done under the *s*;
2:11 was no profit under the *s*.
2:17 work that was done under the *s*
2:18 which I had toiled under the *s*,
2:19 shown myself wise under the *s*.
2:20 which I had toiled under the *s*.
2:22 which he has toiled under the *s*?
3:16 Moreover I saw under the *s*:
4: 1 that is done under the *s*:
4: 3 work that is done under the *s*.
4: 7 and I saw vanity under the *s*:
4:15 the living who walk under the *s*;
5:13 which I have seen under the *s*:
5:18 in which he toils under the *s*
6: 1 which I have seen under the *s*,
6: 5 Though it has not seen the *s* or
6:12 happen after him under the *s*?
7:11 to those who see the *s*.
8: 9 work that is done under the *s*:
8:15 has nothing better under the *s*
8:15 which God gives him under the *s*.
8:17 work that is done under the *s*.
9: 3 in all that is done under the *s*:
9: 6 In anything done under the *s*.
9: 9 He has given you under the *s*,
9: 9 which you perform under the *s*.
9:11 I returned and saw under the *s*
9:13 I have also seen under the *s*,
10: 5 an evil I have seen under the *s*,
11: 7 for the eyes to behold the *s*;
12: 2 While the *s* and the light,
Song 1: 6 Because the *s* has tanned me.
6:10 as the moon, Clear as the *s*,
Isa 13:10 The *s* will be darkened in its
24:23 will be disgraced And the *s*
30:26 will be as the light of the *s*,
30:26 And the light of the *s* will be
38: 8 which has gone down with the *s*
38: 8 So the *s* returned ten degrees
41:25 From the rising of the *s* he
45: 6 know from the rising of the *s*
49:10 Neither heat nor *s* shall
59:19 glory from the rising of the *s*;
60:19 The *s* shall no longer be your
60:20 Your *s* shall no longer go down,
Jer 8: 2 shall spread them before the *s*
15: 9 Her *s* has gone down While it
31:35 Who gives the *s* for a light by
Ezek 8:16 and they were worshiping the *s*
32: 7 I will cover the *s* with a
Dan 6:14 till the going down of the *s*
Joel 2:10 The *s* and moon grow dark,
2:31 The *s* shall be turned into
3:15 The *s* and moon will grow dark,
Am 8: 9 That I will make the *s* go down
Jon 4: 8 when the *s* arose, that God
4: 8 and the *s* beat on Jonah's head,
Mic 3: 6 The *s* shall go down on the
Nah 3:17 When the *s* rises they flee
Hab 3:11 The *s* and moon stood still in
Mal 1:11 For from the rising of the *s*,
4: 2 to you who fear My name The *S*
Mt 5:45 for He makes His *s* rise on the
13: 6 But when the *s* was up they were
13:43 will shine forth as the *s* in
17: 2 His face shone like the *s*,
24:29 of those days the *s* will be
Mk 1:32 when the *s* had set, they
4: 6 But when the *s* was up it was
13:24 the *s* will be darkened, and the
16: 2 came to the tomb when the *s*
Lk 4:40 When the *s* was setting, all
21:25 there will be signs in the *s*,
23:45 Then the *s* was darkened, and the
Acts 2:20 The *s* shall be turned
13:11 not seeing the *s* for a time."
26:13 heaven, brighter than the *s*,
27:20 Now when neither *s* nor stars
1 Cor 15:41 There is one glory of the *s*,
Eph 4:26 do not let the *s* go down on
Jas 1:11 For no sooner has the *s* risen
Rev 1:16 His countenance was like the *s*
6:12 and the *s* became black as
7:16 the *s* shall not strike them,
8:12 And a third of the *s* was
9: 2 So the *s* and the air were
10: 1 head, his face was like the *s*,
12: 1 a woman clothed with the *s*,
16: 8 poured out his bowl on the *s*,
19:17 saw an angel standing in the *s*;
21:23 The city had no need of the *s* or
22: 5 need no lamp nor light of the *s*,

SUNDER (KJV) See APART, PIECES, TWO

SUNDIAL (3/2) SUN

2 Ki 20:11 it had gone down on the *s* of
Isa 38: 8 will bring the shadow on the *s*,
38: 8 down with the sun on the *s* of

SUNDRY (KJV) See VARIOUS

SUNG (4/4) SING

Job 36:24 His work, Of which men have *s*.
Isa 26: 1 In that day this song will be *s*
Mt 26:30 And when they had *s* a hymn, they
Mk 14:26 And when they had *s* a hymn, they

SUNK (4/4) SINK

Ps 9:15 The nations have *s* down in the
76: 5 They have *s* into their sleep;
Jer 38:22 Your feet have *s* in the mire,
Lam 2: 9 Her gates have *s* into the

SUNRISE (7/7)

Num 21:11 is east of Moab, toward the *s*.
34:15 Jericho eastward, toward the *s*.
Josh 1:15 side of the Jordan toward the *s*.
13: 5 and all Lebanon, toward the *s*,
19:12 it went eastward toward the *s*
19:27 It turned toward the *s* to Beth
19:34 by the Jordan toward the *s*.

SUNSET (1/1)

2 Chr 18:34 and about the time of *s* he

SUNSHINE (1/1)

Isa 18: 4 Like clear heat in *s*,

SUP (KJV) See SUPPER

SUPERFLUITY (KJV) See MEEKNESS

SUPERFLUOUS (1/1)

2 Cor 9: 1 it is *s* for me to write to you;

SUPERSCRIPTION (KJV) See INSCRIPTION

SUPERVISE (1/1)

2 Chr 34:12 sons of the Kohathites, to *s*.

SUPERVISED (1/1)

1 Ki 5:16 who *s* the people who labored in

SUPH (1/1)

Deut 1: 1 in the plain opposite *S*,

SUPHAH (1/1)
Num 21:14 of the LORD: "Waheb in *S*,

SUPPER (15/15)
Lk 14:12 "When you give a dinner or a *s*,
14:16 A certain man gave a great *s* and
14:17 and sent his servant at *s* time
14:24 were invited shall taste my *s*.
17: 8 'Prepare something for my *s*,
22:20 He also took the cup after *s*,
Jn 12: 2 There they made Him a *s*;
13: 2 And *s* being ended, the devil
13: 4 rose from *s* and laid aside His
21:20 leaned on His breast at the *s*,
1 Cor 11:20 it is not to eat the Lord's *S*.
11:21 each one takes his own *s* ahead
11:25 He also took the cup after *s*,
Rev 19: 9 are called to the marriage *s*
19:17 and gather together for the *s*

SUPPLANT (1/1)
Jer 9: 4 every brother will utterly *s*,

SUPPLANTED (1/1)
Gen 27:36 For he has *s* me these two

SUPPLE (KJV) See CLEANSE

SUPPLICATION (35/33) SUPPLICATIONS
1 Sam 13:12 and I have not made *s* to the
1 Ki 8:28 of Your servant and his *s*,
8:30 And may You hear the *s* of Your
8:33 and pray and make *s* to You in
8:38 whatever *s* is made by anyone,
8:45 heaven their prayer and their *s*,
8:47 and make *s* to You in the land
8:49 place their prayer and their *s*,
8:52 Your eyes may be open to the *s*
8:52 of Your servant and the *s* of
8:54 praying all this prayer and *s*
8:59 with which I have made *s* before
9: 3 heard your prayer and your *s*
2 Chr 6:19 of Your servant and his *s*,
6:24 and pray and make *s* before You
6:29 whatever *s* is made by anyone,
6:35 heaven their prayer and their *s*,
6:37 and make *s* to You in the land
33:13 his entreaty, heard his *s*,
Esth 4: 8 to go in to the king to make *s*
Job 8: 5 seek God And make your *s* to
Ps 6: 9 The LORD has heard my *s*;
30: 8 And to the LORD I made *s*:
55: 1 do not hide Yourself from my *s*.
119:170 Let my *s* come before You;
142: 1 voice to the LORD I make my *s*.
Isa 45:14 They will make *s* to you,
Jer 36: 7 that they will present their *s*
Dan 6:11 Daniel praying and making *s*
9:20 and presenting my *s* before the
Zech 12:10 the Spirit of grace and *s*;
Acts 1:14 with one accord in prayer and *s*,
Eph 6:18 always with all prayer and *s*
6:18 end with all perseverance and *s*
Phil 4: 6 in everything by prayer and *s*,

SUPPLICATIONS (20/20) SUPPLICATION
2 Chr 6:21 And may You hear the *s* of Your
6:39 place their prayer and their *s*,
Job 41: 3 Will he make many *s* to you?
Ps 28: 2 Hear the voice of my *s* When I
28: 6 He has heard the voice of my *s*!
31:22 You heard the voice of my *s*
86: 6 attend to the voice of my *s*.
116: 1 has heard My voice and my *s*.
130: 2 To the voice of my *s*.
140: 6 my God; Hear the voice of my *s*,
143: 1 Give ear to my *s*! In Your
Jer 3:21 Weeping and *s* of the children
31: 9 And with *s* I will lead them.
Dan 9: 3 to make request by prayer and *s*,
9:17 of Your servant, and his *s*,
9:18 for we do not present our *s*
9:23 At the beginning of your *s* the
1 Tim 2: 1 I exhort first of all that *s*,
5: 5 in God and continues in *s* and
Heb 5: 7 He had offered up prayers and *s*,

SUPPLIED (5/5) SUPPLY
1 Ki 9:11 (Hiram the king of Tyre had *s*
Acts 12:20 because their country was *s*
1 Cor 16:17 was lacking on your part they *s*.
2 Cor 11: 9 who came from Macedonia *s*.
2 Pe 1:11 for so an entrance will be *s* to

SUPPLIES (11/11) SUPPLY
1 Sam 17:22 And David left his *s* in the hand
25:13 two hundred stayed with the *s*.
30:24 his part be who stays by the *s*;
2 Sam 19:32 he had provided the king with *s*
Prov 6: 8 Provides her *s* in the summer,
31:24 And *s* sashes for the
2 Cor 9:10 Now may He who *s* seed to the
9:12 of this service not only *s* the
Gal 3: 5 Therefore He who *s* the Spirit to
Eph 4:16 together by what every joint *s*,
1 Pe 4:11 as with the ability which God *s*,

SUPPLY (18/16) SUPPLIED, SUPPLIES
Ex 1:11 And they built for Pharaoh *s*
Lev 26:26 When I have cut off your *s* of
Deut 15:14 you shall *s* him liberally from
1 Sam 17:22 supplies in the hand of the *s*
2 Sam 12:27 have taken the city's water *s*.
1 Ki 4:27 There was no lack in their *s*.
1 Chr 27:27 of the vineyards for the *s* of
Isa 3: 1 The whole *s* of bread and the
3: 1 of bread and the whole *s* of
Ezek 4:16 surely I will cut off the *s* of
5:16 upon you and cut off your *s* of
14:13 I will cut off its *s* of bread,
2 Cor 8:14 time your abundance may *s*
8:14 that their abundance also may *s*
9:10 *s* and multiply the seed you
Phil 1:19 through your prayer and the *s*
2:30 to *s* what was lacking in your
4:19 And my God shall *s* all your need

SUPPLYING (1/1)
Ps 144:13 *S* all kinds of produce;

SUPPORT (13/13) SUPPORTED
Gen 13: 6 Now the land was not able to *s*
36: 7 they were strangers could not *s*
Judg 16:26 me feel the pillars which *s*
2 Sam 22:19 But the LORD was my *s*.
1 Ki 6: 6 so that the *s* beams would
2 Chr 31: 4 in Jerusalem to contribute *s*
Ezra 4:14 Now because we receive *s* from
8:36 So they gave *s* to the people
10:15 the Levite gave them *s*.
Ps 18:18 But the LORD was my *s*.
Song 3:10 Its *s* of gold, Its seat of
Acts 20:35 that you must *s* the weak.
Rom 11:18 remember that you do not *s*

SUPPORTED (4/4) SUPPORT
Ex 17:12 And Aaron and Hur *s* his hands,
Judg 16:29 the two middle pillars which *s*
2 Sam 20: 3 and put them in seclusion and *s*
Ezek 41: 6 around, that they might be *s*,

SUPPORTING (1/1)
Ezek 41: 7 because their *s* ledges in the

SUPPORTS (5/3)
1 Ki 7:30 bronze, and its four feet had *s*.
7:30 Under the laver were *s* of cast
7:34 And there were four *s* at the
7:34 its *s* were part of the cart
Rom 11:18 but the root *s* you.

SUPPOSE (18/17) SUPPOSED, SUPPOSING
Gen 18:24 *S* there were fifty righteous
18:28 *S* there were five less than the
18:29 *S* there should be forty found
18:30 *S* thirty should be found
18:31 *S* twenty should be found
18:32 *S* ten should be found there?"
Ex 4: 1 But *s* they will not believe me
4: 1 *s* they say, 'The LORD has not
2 Sam 13:32 Let not my lord *s* they have
Lk 7:43 I *s* the one whom he forgave
12:51 Do you *s* that I came to give
13: 2 Do you *s* that these Galileans
Jn 21:25 I *s* that even the world itself
Acts 2:15 these are not drunk, as you *s*,
1 Cor 7:26 I *s* therefore that this is good
1 Tim 6: 5 who *s* that godliness is a
Heb 10:29 much worse punishment, do you *s*,
Jas 1: 7 For let not that man *s* that he

SUPPOSED (7/7) SUPPOSE
Mt 20:10 they *s* that they would receive
Mk 6:49 they *s* it was a ghost,
Lk 3:23 being (as was *s*) the son of
24:37 and *s* they had seen a spirit.
Acts 7:25 For he *s* that his brethren would
21:29 whom they *s* that Paul had
25:18 him of such things as I *s*,

SUPPOSING (6/6) SUPPOSE
Lk 2:44 but *s* Him to have been in the
Jn 20:15 *s* Him to be the gardener,
Acts 14:19 *s* him to be dead.
16:27 *s* the prisoners had fled,
27:13 *s* that they had obtained their
Phil 1:16 *s* to add affliction to my

SUPPRESS (1/1)
Rom 1:18 who *s* the truth in

SUPREME (1/1)
1 Pe 2:13 whether to the king as *s*,

SUR (1/1)
2 Ki 11: 6 shall be at the gate of *S*,

SURE (26/26) SURETY
Ex 3:19 But I am *s* that the king of
Num 28:19 Be *s* they are without blemish.
28:31 Be *s* they are without blemish.
29: 8 Be *s* they are without blemish.
32:23 and be *s* your sin will find you
Deut 12:23 Only be *s* that you do not eat
1 Sam 2:35 I will build him a *s* house,
20: 7 be *s* that evil is determined
23:22 "Please go and find out for *s*,
2 Sam 1:10 because I was *s* that he could
Neh 9:38 We make a *s* covenant,
Job 24:22 but no man is *s* of life.
Ps 19: 7 testimony of the LORD is *s*,
93: 5 Your testimonies are very *s*;
111: 7 All His precepts are *s*.
Prov 11:18 righteousness will have a *s*
Isa 28:16 a *s* foundation; Whoever
33:16 His water will be *s*.
55: 3 The *s* mercies of David.
Dan 2:45 and its interpretation is *s*.
Hos 5: 9 Israel I make known what is *s*.
Jn 16:30 Now we are *s* that You know all
Acts 13:34 I will give you the *s*
Rom 4:16 so that the promise might be *s*
Heb 6:19 both *s* and steadfast,
2 Pe 1:10 make your call and election *s*,

SURELY (377/365)
Gen 2:17 that you eat of it you shall *s*
3: 4 You will not *s* die.
4:14 *S* You have driven me out this
9: 5 *S* for your lifeblood I will
18:13 'Shall I *s* bear a child,
18:18 since Abraham shall *s* become a
20: 7 know that you shall *s* die,
20:11 *s* the fear of God is not in
26:11 this man or his wife shall *s*
27:27 and blessed him and said: "*S*,
27:42 *S* your brother Esau comforts
28:16 *S* the LORD is in this place,
28:22 all that You give me I will *s*
29:14 *S* you are my bone and my
29:32 The LORD has *s* looked on my
30:16 for I have *s* hired you with my
31:30 And now you have *s* gone because
31:42 *s* now you would have sent me
32:12 'I will *s* treat you well,
42:16 *s* you are spies!"
43:10 *s* by now we would have returned
44:28 '*S* he is torn to pieces";
46: 4 and I will also *s* bring you up
50:24 but God will *s* visit you,
50:25 'God will *s* visit you,
Ex 2:14 *S* this thing is known!"
3: 7 I have *s* seen the oppression of
3:16 I have *s* visited you and seen
4:25 *S* you are a husband of blood to
11: 1 he will *s* drive you out of here
13:19 God will *s* visit you, and you
18:18 who are with you will *s* wear
19:12 touches the mountain shall *s*
19:13 but he shall *s* be stoned or
21:12 a man so that he dies shall *s*
21:15 father or his mother shall *s*
21:16 shall *s* be put to death.
21:17 father or his mother shall *s*
21:20 he shall *s* be punished.
21:22 he shall *s* be punished
21:28 then the ox shall *s* be stoned,
21:36 he shall *s* pay ox for ox,
22: 6 he who kindled the fire shall *s*
22:14 he shall *s* make it good.
22:16 he shall *s* pay the bride-price
22:19 lies with an animal shall *s* be
22:23 I will *s* hear their cry;
23: 4 you shall *s* bring it back to
23: 5 you shall *s* help him with it.
23:33 it will *s* be a snare to you."
31:13 *S* My Sabbaths you shall keep,
31:14 who profanes it shall *s* be put
31:15 he shall *s* be put to death.
40:15 for their anointing shall *s* be
Lev 13:44 The priest shall *s* pronounce
19:17 You shall *s* rebuke your
20: 2 he shall *s* be put to death.
20: 9 father or his mother shall *s*
20:10 shall *s* be put to death.
20:11 both of them shall *s* be put to
20:12 both of them shall *s* be put to
20:13 They shall *s* be put to death.
20:15 he shall *s* be put to death,
20:16 They shall *s* be put to death.
20:27 shall *s* be put to death;
24:16 the name of the LORD shall *s*
24:17 'Whoever kills any man shall *s*
27:29 but shall *s* be put to death.
Num 14:35 I will *s* do so to all this evil
15:35 The man must *s* be put to death;
17:12 *S* we die, we perish, we all
18:15 firstborn of man you shall *s*
22:33 *s* I would also have killed you
26:65 They shall *s* die in the
27: 7 *s* give them a possession
32:11 *S* none of the men who came up
35:16 the murderer shall *s* be put to

S

35:17 the murderer shall *s* be put to
35:18 the murderer shall *s* be put to
35:21 one who struck him shall *s* be
35:31 but he shall *s* be put to death.
Deut 1:35 *S* not one of these men of this
4: 5 *S* I have taught you statutes and
4: 6 *S* this great nation is a wise
5:24 *S* the LORD our God has shown us
8:19 you this day that you shall *s*
13: 9 'but you shall *s* kill him;
13:15 *s* strike the inhabitants
15:10 'You shall *s* give to him,
16:15 so that you *s* rejoice.
17:15 you shall *s* set a king over you
21:23 but you shall *s* bury him that
22: 4 you shall *s* help him lift them
22: 7 you shall *s* let the mother go,
23:21 for the LORD your God will *s*
30:18 to you today that you shall *s*
31:18 And I will *s* hide My face in
Josh 14: 9 *S* the land where your foot has
Judg 4: 9 I will *s* go with you;
6:16 '*S* I will be with you,
11:31 shall *s* be the LORD's,
13:22 We shall *s* die, because we have
15: 7 I will *s* take revenge on you,
15:13 but we will *s* not kill you."
20:39 *S* they are defeated before us,
21: 5 He shall *s* be put to death."
Ruth 1:10 *S* we will return with you to
1 Sam 9: 6 all that he says *s* comes to
9:13 you will *s* find him before he
10: 8 and *s* I will come down to you
14:39 he shall *s* die." But not a man
14:44 for you shall *s* die,
15:32 *S* the bitterness of death is
16: 6 *S* the LORD's anointed is
16:15 servants said to him, "*S*,
17:25 *S* he has come up to defy
20:26 *s* he is unclean."
20:31 for he shall *s* die."
22:16 'You shall *s* die, Ahimelech,
22:22 that he would *s* tell Saul.
24:20 I know indeed that you shall *s*
25:21 *S* in vain I have protected all
25:34 *s* by morning light no males
28: 2 *S* you know what your servant can
29: 6 David and said to him, "*S*,
30: 8 for you shall *s* overtake them
2 Sam 2:27 *s* then by morning all the
3:25 *S* you realize that Abner the son
9: 7 for I will *s* show you kindness
11:23 *S* the men prevailed against us
12: 5 man who has done this shall *s*
12:14 who is born to you shall *s*
14:14 For we will *s* die and become
15:21 *s* in whatever place my lord the
17: 9 *S* by now he is hidden in some
18: 2 I also will *s* go out with you
20:18 They shall *s* seek guidance at
24:17 *S* I have sinned, and I have done
24:24 but I will *s* buy it from you
1 Ki 2:37 know for certain you shall *s*
2:42 you shall *s* die'? And you said
8:13 I have *s* built You an exalted
11: 2 *S* they will turn away your
11:11 I will *s* tear the kingdom away
13: 3 *S* the altar shall split apart,
13:32 will *s* come to pass."
16: 3 *s* I will take away the posterity
18:15 I will *s* present myself to him
20:23 *s* we will be stronger than
20:25 *s* we will be stronger than
20:36 *s*, as soon as you depart from
22:32 *S* it is the king of Israel!"
2 Ki 1: 4 but you shall *s* die.'
1: 6 but you shall *s* die.'" '"
1:16 but you shall *s* die.'"
3:14 *s* were it not that I regard the
3:23 the kings have *s* struck swords
5:11 'He will *s* come out to me,
6:13 *S* he is in Dothan."
6:33 *S* this calamity is from the
8:14 He told me you would *s*
9:26 *S* I saw yesterday the blood of
18:30 The LORD will *s* deliver us;
19: 7 *S* I will send a spirit upon him,
20: 5 *s* I will heal you. On the third
22:20 '*S*, therefore, I will gather
23:22 Such a Passover *s* had never been
24: 3 *S* at the commandment of the
1 Chr 21:24 but I will *s* buy it for the
2 Chr 6: 2 I have *s* built You an exalted
20:16 They will *s* come up by the
34:28 *S* I will gather you to your
Esth 6:13 prevail against him but will *s*
Job 1:11 and he will *s* curse You to Your
2: 5 and he will *s* curse You to Your
4: 3 *S* you have instructed many,
8: 6 *S* now He would awake for you,
11:15 Then *s* you could lift up your
13:10 He will *s* rebuke you If you
16:19 *S* even now my witness is in
18:21 *S* such are the dwellings of
22:20 *S* our adversaries are cut down,
27:12 *S* all of you have seen it
28: 1 *S* there is a mine for silver,
30:24 *S* He would not stretch out His
31:36 *S* I would carry it on my
32:12 And *s* not one of you convinced
33: 7 *S* no fear of me will terrify
33: 8 *S* you have spoken in my
34:12 *S* God will never do wickedly,
35:13 *S* God will not listen to empty
37:20 *s* he would be swallowed up.
38: 5 *S* you know! Or who stretched
40:20 *S* the mountains yield food for
Ps 23: 6 *S* goodness and mercy shall
32: 6 *S* in a flood of great waters
39: 6 *S* every man walks about like a
39: 6 *S* they busy themselves in
39:11 *S* every man is vapor. Selah
58:11 *S* there is a reward for the
58:11 *S* He is God who judges in the
62: 9 *S* men of low degree are a
73:13 *S* I have cleansed my heart in
73:18 *S* You set them in slippery
75: 8 *S* its dregs shall all the
76:10 *S* the wrath of man shall praise
77:11 *S* I will remember Your wonders
85: 9 *S* His salvation is near to
91: 3 *S* He shall deliver you from the
93: 1 *S* the world is established,
112: 6 *S* he will never be shaken
131: 2 *S* I have calmed and quieted my
132: 3 *S* I will not go into the chamber
139:11 *S* the darkness shall fall on
140:13 *S* the righteous shall give
Prov 1:17 *S*, in vain the net is spread
1:23 *S* I will pour out my spirit on
3:34 *S* He scorns the scornful,
21: 5 plans of the diligent lead *s*
21: 5 who is hasty, *s* to poverty.
22:16 will *s* come to poverty.
23:18 For *s* there is a hereafter,
24:12 '*S* we did not know this,"
Eccl 2: 1 enjoy pleasure"; but *s*,
3:19 one dies, so dies the other. *S*,
4:16 *S* this also is vanity and
7: 7 *S* oppression destroys a wise
7:14 *S* God has appointed the one as
8:12 yet I *s* know that it will be
Isa 5:26 *S* they shall come with speed,
7: 9 *S* you shall not be
14:24 '*S*, as I have thought,
16: 7 *S* they are stricken.
19:11 *S* the princes of Zoan are
20: 6 *S* such is our expectation,
22:14 *S* for this iniquity there will
22:17 And will *s* seize you.
22:18 He will *s* turn violently and
29:16 *S* you have things turned
33: 7 *S* their valiant ones shall cry
36:15 The LORD will *s* deliver us;
37: 7 *S* I will send a spirit upon him,
38: 5 *s* I will add to your days
40: 7 *S* the people are grass.
41:26 *S* there is no one who shows,
41:26 *S* there is no one who
41:26 *S* there is no one who hears
44:11 *S* all his companions would be
45:14 *S* God is in you, And there
45:24 *S* in the LORD I have
48: 8 *S* you did not hear, Surely you
48: 8 *S* you did not know;
48: 8 *S* from long ago your ear was
49: 4 Yet *s* my just reward is with
49:12 *S* these shall come from afar
49:15 *S* they may forget, Yet I will
49:18 You shall *s* clothe yourselves
50: 9 *S* the Lord GOD will help Me
53: 4 *S* He has borne our griefs
54:15 Indeed they shall *s* assemble,
55: 5 *S* you shall call a nation you
60: 9 *S* the coastlands shall wait for
62: 8 *S* I will no longer give your
62:11 *S* your salvation is coming;
63: 8 '*S* they are My people,
Jer 2:35 *S* His anger shall turn from
3:20 *S*, as a wife treacherously
4:10 Lord GOD! *S* You have greatly
5: 2 *S* they swear falsely."
5: 4 *S* these are poor. They are
8:13 I will *s* consume them,"
11:11 I will *s* bring calamity on them
15:11 *S* it will be well with your
15:11 *S* I will cause the enemy to
15:18 Will You *s* be to me like an
16:19 *S* our fathers have inherited
22: 6 Yet I *s* will make you a
22:22 *S* then you will be ashamed and
24: 8 *s* thus says the LORD—'SO will I
26: 8 You will *s* die!
26:15 you will *s* bring innocent blood
31:18 I have *s* heard Ephraim
31:19 *S*, after my turning,
31:20 I will *s* have mercy on him,
32: 4 but shall *s* be delivered into
34: 3 but shall *s* be taken and
35:16 *S* the sons of Jonadab the son of
36:16 We will *s* tell the king of all
37: 9 The Chaldeans will *s* depart from
38: 3 This city shall *s* be given into
38:15 will you not *s* put me to death?
38:17 If you *s* surrender to the king
39:18 'For I will *s* deliver you,
44:25 We will *s* keep our vows that we
44:25 You will *s* keep your vows and
44:29 may know that My words will *s*
46:18 *S* as Tabor is among the
49:12 but you shall *s* drink of it.
49:20 *S* the least of the flock shall
49:20 *S* He shall make their dwelling
50:45 *S* the least of the flock shall
50:45 *S* He will make their dwelling
51:14 '*S* I will fill you with men,
51:56 He will *s* repay.
Lam 2:16 *S* this is the day we have
3: 3 *S* He has turned His hand
Ezek 3: 6 *S*, had I sent you to them,
3:18 You shall *s* die,' and you give
3:21 he shall *s* live because he took
3:25 *s* they will put ropes on you
4: 8 And *s* I will restrain you so
4:16 *s* I will cut off the supply of
5:11 '*s*, because you have defiled
13:12 '*S*, when the wall has fallen,
14:22 *s* they will come out to you,
16:37 '*s*, therefore, I will gather
16:43 *s* I will also recompense your
17:16 *s* in the place where the king
17:19 *s* My oath which he despised,
18: 9 He shall *s* live!" Says the
18:13 He shall *s* die; His blood
18:17 He shall *s* live!
18:19 he shall *s* live.
18:21 he shall *s* live; he shall not
18:28 he shall *s* live; he shall not
20:33 *s* with a mighty hand, with an
23:28 *S* I will deliver you into the
29: 8 *S* I will bring a sword upon you
29:19 *S* I will give the land of Egypt
30:22 *S* I am against Pharaoh king of
31:11 and he shall *s* deal with it;
33: 8 you shall *s* die!' and you do
33:13 the righteous that he shall *s*
33:14 You shall *s* die,' if he turns
33:15 he shall *s* live; he shall not
33:16 he shall *s* live.
33:27 *s* those who are in the ruins
33:33 *s* it will come—then they will
34: 8 *s* because My flock became a
36: 5 *S* I have spoken in My burning
36: 7 My hand in an oath that *s* the
37: 5 *S* I will cause breath to enter
37:19 *S* I will take the stick of
37:21 *S* I will take the children of
38:19 *S* in that day there shall be a
39: 8 *S* it is coming, and it shall be
Hos 6: 9 *S* they commit lewdness.
12: 8 *S* I have become rich, I have
12:11 *S* they are vanity—Though they
Joel 1:12 *S* joy has withered away from
2: 3 *S* nothing shall escape them.
Am 3: 7 *S* the Lord GOD does nothing,
5: 5 For Gilgal shall *s* go into
7:11 And Israel shall *s* be led away
7:17 And Israel shall *s* be led away
8: 7 *S* I will never forget any of
9: 9 For *s* I will command, And will
Mic 2:12 I will *s* assemble all of you,
2:12 I will *s* gather the remnant of
Nah 3:13 *S*, your people in your midst
Hab 2: 3 Because it will *s* come,
Zeph 2: 9 '*S* Moab shall be like Sodom,
3: 7 *S* you will fear Me, You will
Zech 1: 6 Yet *s* My words and My statutes,
2: 9 For *s* I will shake My hand
12: 3 who would heave it away will *s*
Mt 12:28 *s* the kingdom of God has come
26:73 '*S* you also are one of them,
Mk 14:70 *S* you are one of them; for you
Lk 4:23 You will *s* say this proverb to
11:20 *s* the kingdom of God has come
22:59 *S* this fellow also was with
Jn 17: 8 and have known *s* that I came
Acts 7:34 I have *s* seen the
Phil 4:10 though you *s* did care, but you
Heb 6:14 *S* blessing I will bless
Rev 22:20 *S* I am coming quickly." Amen.

SURETY (12/10) SURE

Gen 43: 9 'I myself will be *s* for him;
44:32 For your servant became *s* for
Ps 119:122 Be *s* for Your servant for good;
Prov 6: 1 if you become *s* for your
11:15 He who is *s* for a stranger will
11:15 But one who hates being *s* is
17:18 And becomes *s* for his friend.
20:16 the garment of one who is *s*
22:26 One of those who is *s* for
27:13 the garment of him who is *s*
27:13 it in pledge when he is *s* for
Heb 7:22 much more Jesus has become a *s*

SURFACE (12/12)

Gen 7:18 the ark moved about on the *s*
8:13 and indeed the *s* of the ground
Ex 16:14 on the *s* of the wilderness, was
Num 11:31 about two cubits above the *s*
1 Ki 7:20 by the convex *s* which was next
2 Ki 9:37 shall be as refuse on the *s* of
Job 38:30 And the *s* of the deep is
Prov 24:31 Its *s* was covered with
Isa 24: 1 Distorts its *s* And scatters
25: 7 on this mountain The *s* of the
28:25 When he has leveled its *s*,
Dan 8: 5 across the *s* of the whole

SURFEITING (KJV) See CAROUSING

SURMISINGS (KJV) See SUSPICIONS

SURNAME (7/7) SURNAMED

Mt 10: 3 whose *s* was Thaddaeus;
Acts 10: 5 send for Simon whose *s* is Peter
10:18 whose *s* was Peter, was lodging
10:32 whose *s* is Peter. He is lodging
11:13 call for Simon whose *s* is Peter
12:12 mother of John whose *s* was Mark
12:25 took with them John whose *s*

SURNAMED (2/2) SURNAME

Lk 22: 3 *s* Iscariot, who was numbered
Acts 1:23 who was *s* Justus, and Matthias.

SURPASS (2/2)

Jer 5:28 they *s* the deeds of the wicked;
Ezek 32:19 'Whom do you *s* in beauty?

SURPASSED (2/2)

1 Ki 10:23 So King Solomon *s* all the kings
2 Chr 9:22 So King Solomon *s* all the kings

SURPASSES (1/1) SURPASSING

Phil 4: 7 which *s* all understanding, will

SURPASSING (1/1) SURPASSES

2 Sam 1:26 *S* the love of women.

SURPRISE (5/5)

Judg 3:24 came to look, and to their *s*,
7:13 "I have had a dream: To my *s*,
14: 5 of Timnah. Now to his *s*,
2 Ki 7: 5 to their *s* no one was there.
2 Chr 13:14 to their *s* the battle line was

SURPRISED (1/1)

Jer 48:41 And the strongholds are *s*;

SURPRISINGLY (3/3)

Gen 42:35 that *s* each man's bundle of
1 Sam 14:17 they had called the roll, *s*,
2 Ki 7:10 and *s* no one was there, not a

SURRENDER (6/6)

2 Ki 7: 4 let us *s* to the army of the
15:16 Because they did not *s*,
Jer 38:17 If you surely *s* to the king of
38:18 But if you do not *s* to the king
38:21 "But if you refuse to *s*,
38:23 So they shall *s* all your wives

SURRENDERED (2/2)

Deut 32:30 And the LORD had *s* them?
Jer 38:22 of Judah's house shall be *s*

SURROUND (17/17) SURROUNDED, SURROUNDS

Josh 7: 9 and *s* us, and cut off our name
2 Ki 11: 8 But you shall *s* the king on all
2 Chr 23: 7 And the Levites shall *s* the king
Job 16:13 His archers *s* me. He pierces
40:22 The willows by the brook *s*
Ps 5:12 With favor You will *s* him as
7: 7 of the peoples shall *s* You;
17: 9 From my deadly enemies who *s*
32: 7 You shall *s* me with songs of
32:10 mercy shall *s* him.
97: 2 Clouds and darkness *s* Him;
125: 2 As the mountains *s* Jerusalem,
140: 9 for the head of those who *s* me
142: 7 The righteous shall *s* me,
Lam 2:22 feast day The terrors that *s* me
Hab 1: 4 the wicked *s* the righteous;
Lk 19:43 *s* you and close you in on every

SURROUNDED (35/34) SURROUND

Gen 19: 4 every quarter, *s* the house.
41:48 the food of the fields which *s*
Judg 16: 2 *s* the place and lay in wait
19:22 *s* the house and beat on the
20: 5 and *s* the house at night
20:43 They *s* the Benjamites, chased
2 Sam 18:15 men who bore Joab's armor *s*
22: 5 When the waves of death *s* me,
22: 6 The sorrows of Sheol *s* me;
2 Ki 3:25 However the slingers *s* and
6:14 came by night and *s* the city
8:21 the Edomites who had *s* him and
2 Chr 18:31 of Israel!" Therefore they *s* him
21: 9 the Edomites who had *s* him and
Job 19: 6 And has *s* me with His net.
Ps 17:11 They have now *s* us in our
18: 4 The pangs of death *s* me,
18: 5 The sorrows of Sheol *s* me;
22:12 Many bulls have *s* Me;
22:16 For dogs have *s* Me;
40:12 For innumerable evils have *s*
109: 3 They have also *s* me with words
116: 3 The pains of death *s* me,
118:10 All nations *s* me, But in the
118:11 They *s* me, Yes, they
118:11 they *s* me; But in the name of
118:12 They *s* me like bees; They were
Lam 3: 5 He has besieged me And *s* me
Hos 7: 2 their own deeds have *s* them
Jon 2: 3 And the floods *s* me; All Your
2: 5 The waters *s* me, even to my
Lk 21:20 But when you see Jerusalem *s* by
Jn 10:24 Then the Jews *s* Him and said to
Heb 12: 1 since we are *s* by so great a
Rev 20: 9 of the earth and *s* the camp

SURROUNDING (26/26)

Gen 23:17 within all the *s* borders
Num 32:33 the cities of the *s* country.
34:12 your land with its *s* boundaries
Deut 21: 2 from the slain man to the *s* cities
Josh 21:11 with the common-land *s* it.
21:42 cities had its common-land *s*
1 Sam 14:21 into the camp from the *s* country
1 Ki 4:31 his fame was in all the *s* nations
2 Ki 6:15 *s* the city with horses and
1 Chr 6:55 with its *s* common-lands.
11: 8 from the Millo to the *s* area.
Ezek 43:12 The whole area *s* the
Joel 3:12 sit to judge all the *s* nations
Zech 12: 2 drunkenness to all the *s* peoples
12: 6 they shall devour all the *s*
14:14 And the wealth of all the *s* nations
Mt 14:35 they sent out into all that *s* region
Mk 6:36 they may go into the *s* country
6:55 ran through that whole *s* region,
Lk 4:14 Him went out through all the *s*
4:37 into every place in the *s* region.
7:17 all Judea and all the *s* region.
8:37 the whole multitude of the *s*
9:12 that they may go into the *s* towns
Acts 5:16 a multitude gathered from the *s*
14: 6 and to the *s* region.

SURROUNDS (3/3) SURROUND

Ps 49: 5 the iniquity at my heels *s* me?
89: 8 Your faithfulness also *s* You.
125: 2 So the LORD *s* His people

SURVEY (8/6)

Josh 18: 4 *s* it according to their
18: 6 You shall therefore *s* the land
18: 6 seven parts and bring the *s*
18: 8 charged those who went to *s*
18: 8 *s* it, and come back to me,
18: 9 and wrote the *s* in a book in
Ps 78:55 them an inheritance by *s*,
Am 7:17 land shall be divided by *s*

SURVEYOR'S (2/2)

Jer 31:39 The *s* line shall again extend
Zech 1:16 And a *s* line shall be stretched

SURVIVAL (1/1)

Acts 27:34 for this is for your *s*,

SURVIVE (3/3)

Job 27:15 Those who *s* him shall be buried
Jer 44:14 dwell there shall escape or *s*,
Ezek 7:16 Those who *s* will escape and be

SURVIVED (4/4)

Ruth 1: 5 so the woman *s* her two sons and
1 Sam 11:11 it happened that those who *s*
Neh 1: 2 who had *s* the captivity, and
Jer 31: 2 The people who *s* the sword

SURVIVOR (4/4)

Num 21:35 until there was no *s* left him;
Ezra 9:14 would be no remnant or *s*?
Lam 2:22 There was no refugee or *s*.
Ob 18 And no *s* shall remain of the

SURVIVORS (4/4)

Deut 3: 3 attacked him until he had no *s*
Judg 5:13 Then the *s* came down, the people
21:17 be an inheritance for the *s*
Neh 1: 3 The *s* who are left from the

SUSANCHITES (KJV) See SHUSHAN

SUSANNA (1/1)

Lk 8: 3 Chuza, Herod's steward, and *S*,

SUSI (1/1)

Num 13:11 of Manasseh, Gaddi the son of *S*;

SUSPICIONS (1/1)

1 Tim 6: 4 envy, strife, reviling, evil *s*,

SUSTAIN (4/4) SUSTAINED, SUSTAINS

Ps 41: 3 You will *s* him on his sickbed.
55:22 And He shall *s* you; He shall
Prov 18:14 The spirit of a man will *s* him
Song 2: 5 *S* me with cakes of raisins,

SUSTAINED (6/6) SUSTAIN

Gen 27:37 with grain and wine I have *s*
Neh 9:21 Forty years You *s* them in the
Ps 3: 5 for the LORD *s* me.
89:43 And have not *s* him in the
Isa 59:16 own righteousness, it *s* Him.
63: 5 And My own fury, it *s* Me.

SUSTAINS (1/1) SUSTAIN

Lev 17:14 Its blood *s* its life.

SUSTENANCE (3/3)

Judg 6: 4 and leave no *s* for Israel,
17:10 a suit of clothes, and your *s*.
Acts 7:11 and our fathers found no *s*.

SWADDLED, SWADDLING-BAND (KJV) See BORNE, SWADDLING (BAND), WRAPPED

SWADDLING (4/4)

Job 38: 9 And thick darkness its *s* band;
Ezek 16: 4 salt nor wrapped in *s* cloths.
Lk 2: 7 and wrapped Him in *s* cloths,
2:12 a Babe wrapped in *s* cloths,

SWALLOW (21/21) SWALLOWED

Num 16:34 Lest the earth *s* us up also!"
2 Sam 20:19 Why would you *s* up the
20:20 that I should *s* up or destroy!
Job 7:19 And let me alone till I *s* my
20:18 And will not *s* it down;
Ps 21: 9 The LORD shall *s* them up in
56: 1 for man would *s* me up;
57: 3 reproaches the one who would *s*
69:15 Nor let the deep *s* me up;
84: 3 And the *s* a nest for herself,
Prov 1:12 Let us *s* them alive like Sheol,
26: 2 sparrow, like a flying *s*,
Eccl 10:12 the lips of a fool shall *s* him
Isa 25: 8 He will *s* up death forever,
38:14 Like a crane or a *s*,
Jer 8: 7 and the *s* Observe the time of
Hos 8: 7 Aliens would *s* it up.
Am 8: 4 you who *s* up the needy,
Ob 16 Yes, they shall drink, and *s*,
Jon 1:17 had prepared a great fish to *s*
Mt 23:24 who strain out a gnat and *s* a

SWALLOWED (24/23) SWALLOW

Ex 7:12 But Aaron's rod *s* up their
15:12 The earth *s* them.
Num 16:32 earth opened its mouth and *s*
26:10 earth opened its mouth and *s*
Deut 11: 6 earth opened its mouth and *s*
2 Sam 17:16 people who are with him be *s*
Job 37:20 surely he would be *s* up.
Ps 35:25 We have *s* him up."
106:17 The earth opened up and *s*
124: 3 Then they would have *s* us
Isa 28: 7 They are *s* up by wine,
49:19 And those who *s* you up will be
Jer 51:34 He has *s* me up like a monster;
51:44 out of his mouth what he has *s*;
Lam 2: 2 The Lord has *s* up and has not
2: 5 He has *s* up Israel, He has
2: 5 He has *s* up all her palaces;
2:16 We have *s* her up! Surely this
Ezek 36: 3 they made you desolate and *s*
Hos 8: 8 Israel is *s* up; Now they are
1 Cor 15:54 Death is *s* up in victory."
2 Cor 2: 7 lest perhaps such a one be *s* up
5: 4 that mortality may be *s* up by
Rev 12:16 earth opened its mouth and *s*

SWALLOWS (2/2)

Num 16:30 the earth opens its mouth and *s*
Job 20:15 He *s* down riches And vomits

SWAMPS (1/1)

Ezek 47:11 But its *s* and marshes will not

SWAN (KJV) See (WHITE) OWL

SWARE (KJV) See SWORE

SWARM (1/1)

Judg 14: 8 a *s* of bees and honey were in

SWARMING (5/4)

Joel 1: 4 the *s* locust has eaten;
1: 4 What the *s* locust left,
2:25 that the *s* locust has eaten,
Nah 3:15 like the *s* locusts!
3:17 are like *s* locusts,

SWARMS (10/8)

Ex 8:21 I will send *s* of flies on you
8:21 Egyptians shall be full of *s*

S

8:22 that no *s* of flies shall be
8:24 Thick *s* of flies came into
8:24 was corrupted because of the *s*
8:29 that the *s* of flies may
8:31 He removed the *s* of flies
Ps 78:45 He sent *s* of flies among them,
105:31 and there came *s* of flies,
Am 7: 1 He formed locust *s* at the

SWAY (4/4)

Judg 9: 9 And go to *s* over trees?'
9:11 And go to *s* over trees?'
9:13 And go to *s* over trees?'
1 Jn 5:19 world lies under the *s* of

SWAYED (1/1)

2 Sam 19:14 So he *s* the hearts of all the

SWEAR (48/46) SWEARING, SWEARS, SWORE, SWORN

Gen 21:23 *s* to me by God that you will
21:24 And Abraham said, "I will *s*.
24: 3 and I will make you *s* by the
24:37 "Now my master made me *s*,
25:33 '*S* to me as of this day."
47:31 *S* to me." And he swore to him.
50: 5 'My father made me *s*,
50: 6 your father, as he made you *s*.
Lev 19:12 And you shall not *s* by My name
Josh 2:12 *s* to me by the LORD, since I
2:17 yours which you have made us *s*,
2:20 your oath which you made us *s*.
23: 7 nor cause anyone to *s* by
Judg 15:12 *S* to me that you will not kill
1 Sam 24:21 Therefore *s* now to me by the
30:15 *S* to me by God that you will
2 Sam 19: 7 For I *s* by the LORD, if you do
1 Ki 1:13 *s* to your maidservant, saying,
1:51 Let King Solomon *s* to me today
2:42 Did I not make you *s* by the
22:16 many times shall I make you *s*
2 Chr 18:15 many times shall I make you *s*
36:13 who had made him *s* an oath by
Ezra 10: 5 and all Israel *s* an oath that
Neh 13:25 and made them *s* by God,
Ps 102: 8 Those who deride me *s* an oath
Isa 19:18 the language of Canaan and *s*
48: 1 Who *s* by the name of the
65:16 swears in the earth Shall *s*
Jer 4: 2 And you shall *s*, 'The LORD
5: 2 Surely they *s* falsely."
7: 9 *s* falsely, burn incense to
12:16 to *s* by My name, 'As the LORD
12:16 as they taught My people to *s*
22: 5 I *s* by Myself," says the
Hos 4:15 Nor *s* an oath, saying, 'As
Am 8:14 Those who *s* by the sin of
Zeph 1: 5 Those who worship and *s* oaths
1: 5 But who also *s* by Milcom;
Mt 5:33 'You shall not *s* falsely,
5:34 do not *s* at all: neither by
5:36 Nor shall you *s* by your head,
26:74 Then he began to curse and *s*,
Mk 14:71 Then he began to curse and *s*,
Heb 3:18 And to whom did He *s* that they
6:13 because He could *s* by no one
6:16 For men indeed *s* by the greater,
Jas 5:12 my brethren, do not *s*,

SWEARING (2/2) SWEAR

Hos 4: 2 By *s* and lying, Killing and
10: 4 *S* falsely in making a

SWEARS (18/13) SWEAR

Lev 5: 4 'Or if a person *s*,
6: 3 and *s* falsely—in any one of
Num 30: 2 or *s* an oath to bind himself by
Ps 15: 4 He who *s* to his own hurt and
63:11 Everyone who *s* by Him shall
Prov 29:24 He *s* to tell the truth,
Isa 65:16 And he who *s* in the earth
Zech 5: 4 And the house of the one who *s*
Mt 23:16 Whoever *s* by the temple, it is
23:16 but whoever *s* by the gold of
23:18 Whoever *s* by the altar, it is
23:18 but whoever *s* by the gift that
23:20 Therefore he who *s* by the altar,
23:20 *s* by it and by all things on
23:21 He who *s* by the temple, swears
23:21 *s* by it and by Him who dwells
23:22 And he who *s* by heaven, swears
23:22 *s* by the throne of God and by

SWEAT (3/3)

Gen 3:19 In the *s* of your face you shall
Ezek 44:18 with anything that causes *s*.
Lk 22:44 Then His *s* became like great

SWEEP (3/3) SWEEPS, SWEPT

Isa 14:23 I will *s* it with the broom of
28:17 The hail will *s* away the
Lk 15: 8 *s* the house, and search

SWEEPS (1/1)

Job 27:21 It *s* him out of his place.

SWEET (94/91) SWEETER, SWEETNESS, SWEET-SMELLING

Ex 15:25 the waters were made *s*.
25: 6 anointing oil and for the *s* incense
29:18 it is a *s* aroma, an offering
29:25 as a *s* aroma before the LORD.
29:41 for a *s* aroma, an offering made
30: 7 Aaron shall burn on it *s* incense
30:34 Take *s* spices, stacte and onycha
30:34 frankincense with these *s* spices
31:11 the anointing oil and *s* incense
35: 8 anointing oil and for the *s* incense
35:15 the *s* incense, and the screen
35:28 and for the *s* incense.
37:29 the pure incense of *s* spices
39:38 and the *s* incense; the screen
40:27 and he burned *s* incense on it,
Lev 1: 9 a *s* aroma to the LORD.
1:13 a *s* aroma to the LORD.
1:17 a *s* aroma to the LORD.
2: 2 a *s* aroma to the LORD.
2: 9 a *s* aroma to the LORD.
2:12 be burned on the altar for a *s*
3: 5 a *s* aroma to the LORD.
3:16 offering made by fire for a *s*
4: 7 on the horns of the altar of *s*
4:31 burn it on the altar for a *s*
6:15 burn it on the altar for a *s* aroma
6:21 you shall offer for a *s* aroma
8:21 was a burnt sacrifice for a *s*
8:28 consecration offerings for a *s*
16:12 with his hands full of *s* incense
17: 6 and burn the fat for a *s* aroma
23:13 for a *s* aroma; and its drink
23:18 offering made by fire for a *s*
26:31 the fragrance of your *s* aromas
Num 4:16 the *s* incense, the daily grain
15: 3 to make a *s* aroma to the LORD,
15: 7 of a HIN of wine as a *s* aroma
15:10 a *s* aroma to the LORD.
15:13 a *s* aroma to the LORD.
15:14 a *s* aroma to the LORD, just as
15:24 as a *s* aroma to the LORD,
18:17 offering made by fire for a *s*
28: 2 offerings made by fire as a *s*
28: 6 at Mount Sinai for a *s* aroma,
28: 8 a *s* aroma to the LORD.
28:13 as a burnt offering of *s* aroma,
28:24 as a *s* aroma to the LORD;
28:27 a burnt offering as a *s* aroma
29: 2 offer a burnt offering as a *s*
29: 6 as a *s* aroma, an offering made
29: 8 offering to the LORD as a *s*
29:13 made by fire as a *s* aroma
29:36 an offering made by fire as a *s*
Judg 14:14 of the strong came something *s*.
2 Sam 23: 1 And the *s* psalmist of Israel:
2 Chr 2: 4 to burn before Him *s* incense,
13:11 burnt sacrifices and *s* incense
Ezra 6:10 they may offer sacrifices of *s* aroma
Neh 8:10 eat the fat, drink the *s*,
Job 20:12 Though evil is *s* in his mouth,
21:33 clods of the valley shall be *s*
Ps 55:14 We took *s* counsel together,
66:15 With the *s* aroma of rams;
104:34 May my meditation be *s* to Him;
119:103 How *s* are Your words to my
141: 6 hear my words, for they are *s*.
Prov 3:24 down and your sleep will be *s*.
9:17 "Stolen water is *s*,
13:19 A desire accomplished is *s* to
20:17 Bread gained by deceit is *s* to
24:13 the honeycomb which is *s* to
27: 7 soul every bitter thing is *s*.
Eccl 5:12 sleep of a laboring man is *s*,
11: 7 Truly the light is *s*,
Song 2: 3 And his fruit was *s* to my
2:14 For your voice is *s*,
5:16 His mouth is most *s*,
Isa 3:24 Instead of a *s* smell there will
5:20 Who put bitter for *s*,
5:20 for sweet, and *s* for bitter!
23:16 Make *s* melody, sing many
43:24 You have bought Me no *s* cane
49:26 their own blood as with *s* wine
Jer 6:20 And *s* cane from a far country?
6:20 Nor your sacrifices *s* to
31:26 and my sleep was *s* to me.
Ezek 6:13 wherever they offered *s* incense
16:19 set it before them as *s* incense
20:28 they also sent up their *s* aroma
20:41 I will accept you as a *s* aroma
Am 9:13 mountains shall drip with *s* wine
Mic 6:15 And make *s* wine, but not
Rev 10: 9 but it will be as *s* as honey in
10:10 and it was as *s* as honey in my

SWEET-SMELLING (4/3) SWEET

Ex 30:23 half as much *s* cinnamon (two
30:23 and fifty shekels of *s* cane,
Eph 5: 2 a sacrifice to God for a *s* aroma
Phil 4:18 a *s* aroma, an acceptable

SWEETER (3/3) SWEET

Judg 14:18 What is *s* than honey? And what
Ps 19:10 *S* also than honey and the
119:103 *S* than honey to my mouth!

SWEETLY (1/1)

Job 24:20 The worm should feed *s* on

SWEETNESS (5/5) SWEET

Judg 9:11 Should I cease my *s* and my good
Prov 16:21 And *s* of the lips increases
16:24 *S* to the soul and health to
27: 9 And the *s* of a man's friend
Ezek 3: 3 was in my mouth like honey in *s*.

SWELL (9/9) SWELLING

Num 5:21 your thigh rot and your belly *s*;
5:22 and make your belly *s* and
5:27 bitter, and her belly will *s*,
Deut 8: 4 nor did your foot *s* these forty
Neh 9:21 And their feet did not *s*.
Isa 60: 5 And your heart shall *s* with
Am 8: 8 All of it shall *s* like the
9: 5 All of it shall *s* like the
Acts 28: 6 were expecting that he would *s*

SWELLING (10/9) SWELL

Lev 13: 2 has on the skin of his body a *s*,
13:10 and indeed if the *s* on the
13:10 a spot of raw flesh in the *s*,
13:19 the boil there comes a white *s*
13:28 it is a *s* from the burn.
13:43 and indeed if the *s* of the
14:56 for a *s* and a scab and a bright
Ps 46: 3 the mountains shake with its *s*.
2 Pe 2:18 For when they speak great *s*
Jude 16 and they mouth great *s* words,

SWEPT (8/8) SWEEP

Judg 5:21 The torrent of Kishon *s* them
1 Sam 12:25 you shall be *s* away, both you
Job 22:16 Whose foundations were *s* away
Jer 46:15 are your valiant men *s* away
Dan 11:22 of a flood they shall be *s* away
11:26 his army shall be *s* away,
Mt 12:44 he comes, he finds it empty, *s*,
Lk 11:25 he finds it *s* and put in

SWIFT (22/21) SWIFTER

Deut 28:49 as *s* as the eagle flies,
1 Chr 12: 8 and were as *s* as gazelles on
Esth 8:10 royal horses bred from *s* steeds.
Job 9:26 They pass by like *s* ships,
24:18 They should be *s* on the face
Prov 6:18 Feet that are *s* in running to
Eccl 9:11 race is not to the *s*,
Isa 18: 2 *s* messengers, to a nation tall
19: 1 the LORD rides on a *s* cloud,
30:16 ride on *s* horses"—Therefore
30:16 who pursue you shall be *s*!
Jer 2:23 You are a *s* dromedary
8: 7 And the turtledove, the *s*,
46: 6 'Do not let the *s* flee away,
Joel 2: 4 And like *s* steeds, so they
Am 2:14 flight shall perish from the *s*,
2:15 The *s* of foot shall not
Mic 1:13 Harness the chariot to the *s* steeds
Mal 3: 5 I will be a *s* witness Against
Rom 3:15 Their feet are *s* to shed
Jas 1:19 let every man be *s* to hear,
2 Pe 2: 1 bring on themselves *s* destruction.

SWIFTER (6/6) SWIFT

2 Sam 1:23 They were *s* than eagles,
Job 7: 6 My days are *s* than a weaver's
9:25 Now my days are *s* than a runner;
Jer 4:13 His horses are *s* than eagles.
Lam 4:19 Our pursuers were *s* Than the
Hab 1: 8 Their horses also are *s* than

SWIFTLY (5/5)

Ps 147:15 His word runs very *s*.
Isa 5:26 they shall come with speed, *s*.
Dan 9:21 being caused to fly *s*,
Joel 3: 4 *S* and speedily I will return
2 Th 3: 1 the word of the Lord may run *s*

SWIM (5/5)

Ps 6: 6 All night I make my bed *s*;
Isa 25:11 As a swimmer reaches out to *s*,
Ezek 47: 5 deep, water in which one must *s*,
Acts 27:42 lest any of them should *s* away
27:43 that those who could *s* should

SWIMMER (1/1)

Isa 25:11 hands in their midst As a *s*

SWINE (16/15) SWINE'S

Lev 11: 7 'and the *s*, though it divides
Deut 14: 8 Also the *s* is unclean for you,
Mt 7: 6 nor cast your pearls before *s*,
8:30 them there was a herd of many *s*
8:31 to go away into the herd of *s*.
8:32 they went into the herd of *s*.
8:32 suddenly the whole herd of *s*
Mk 5:11 Now a large herd of *s* was
5:12 saying, "Send us to the *s*,
5:13 went out and entered the *s*

5:14 So those who fed the *s* fled,
5:16 and about the *s*.
Lk 8:32 Now a herd of many *s* was feeding
8:33 of the man and entered the *s*,
15:15 him into his fields to feed *s*.
15:16 with the pods that the *s* ate,

SWINE'S (4/4) SWINE

Prov 11:22 a ring of gold in a *s* snout,
Isa 65: 4 Who eat *s* flesh, And the
66: 3 as if he offers *s* blood;
66:17 Eating *s* flesh and the

SWING (1/1)

Job 28: 4 They *s* to and fro.

SWINGS (1/1)

Deut 19: 5 and his hand *s* a stroke with

SWIRL (1/1)

Job 37:12 And they *s* about, being turned

SWIRLS (1/1)

Prov 23:31 When it *s* around smoothly;

SWOLLEN (1/1)

Ps 124: 5 Then the *s* waters Would have

SWOON (1/1)

Lam 2:12 As they *s* like the wounded

SWOONED (KJV) See SWOON

SWOOP (1/1)

1 Sam 15:19 Why did you *s* down on the

SWOOPING (1/1)

Job 9:26 Like an eagle *s* on its prey.

SWORD (422/382) SWORDS

Gen 3:24 and a flaming *s* which turned
27:40 By your *s* you shall live,
31:26 like captives taken with the *s*?
34:25 each took his *s* and came boldly
34:26 his son with the edge of the *s*,
48:22 hand of the Amorite with my *s*
Ex 5: 3 with pestilence or with the *s*.
5:21 to put a *s* in their hand to
15: 9 on them. I will draw my *s*,
17:13 people with the edge of the *s*.
18: 4 and delivered me from the *s* of
22:24 and I will kill you with the *s*;
32:27 Let every man put his *s* on his
Lev 26: 6 and the *s* will not go through
26: 7 and they shall fall by the *s*
26: 8 enemies shall fall by the *s*
26:25 And I will bring a *s* against you
26:33 the nations and draw out a *s*
26:36 flee as though fleeing from a *s*,
26:37 another, as it were before a *s*,
Num 14: 3 to this land to fall by the *s*,
14:43 and you shall fall by the *s*;
19:16 one who is slain by a *s* or who
20:18 come out against you with the *s*.
21:24 him with the edge of the *s*,
22:23 in the way with His drawn *s* in
22:29 I wish there were a *s* in my
22:31 in the way with His drawn *s* in
31: 8 they also killed with the *s*.
Deut 13:15 city with the edge of the *s*—
13:15 with the edge of the *s*.
20:13 in it with the edge of the *s*.
28:22 burning fever, with the *s*,
32:25 The *s* shall destroy outside;
32:41 If I whet My glittering *s*,
32:42 And My *s* shall devour flesh,
33:29 shield of your help And the *s*
Josh 5:13 stood opposite him with His *s*
6:21 donkey, with the edge of the *s*.
8:24 had fallen by the edge of the *s*
8:24 it with the edge of the *s*.
10:11 of Israel killed with the *s*.
10:28 its king with the edge of the *s*.
10:30 in it with the edge of the *s*.
10:32 in it with the edge of the *s*,
10:35 it with the edge of the *s*;
10:37 it with the edge of the *s*—
10:39 them with the edge of the *s*
11:10 and struck its king with the *s*;
11:11 in it with the edge of the *s*,
11:12 struck with the edge of the *s*.
11:14 man with the edge of the *s*
13:22 Israel also killed with the *s*
19:47 it with the edge of the *s*,
24:12 but not with your *s* or with
Judg 1: 8 it with the edge of the *s* and
1:25 the city with the edge of the *s*;
4:15 army with the edge of the *s*
4:16 fell by the edge of the *s*;
7:14 is nothing else but the *s* of
7:18 The *s* of the LORD and of
7:20 The *s* of the LORD and of
7:22 the LORD set every man's *s*
8:10 thousand men who drew the *s*
8:20 the youth would not draw his *s*;
9:54 Draw your *s* and kill me, lest
18:27 them with the edge of the *s*
20: 2 foot soldiers who drew the *s*.
20:15 thousand men who drew the *s*,
20:17 thousand men who drew the *s*;
20:25 of Israel; all these drew the *s*.
20:35 all these drew the *s*.
20:37 city with the edge of the *s*.
20:46 thousand men who drew the *s*;
20:48 down with the edge of the *s*—
21:10 Gilead with the edge of the *s*,
1 Sam 13:22 that there was neither *s* nor
14:20 and indeed every man's *s* was
15: 8 people with the edge of the *s*.
15:33 As your *s* has made women
17:39 David fastened his *s* to his
17:45 "You come to me with a *s*,
17:47 the LORD does not save with *s*
17:50 But there was no *s* in the
17:51 took his *s* and drew it out of
18: 4 even to his *s* and his bow and
21: 8 not here on hand a spear or a *s*?
21: 8 For I have brought neither my *s*
21: 9 The *s* of Goliath the Philistine,
22:10 and gave him the *s* of Goliath
22:13 have given him bread and a *s*,
22:19 struck with the edge of the *s*,
22:19 sheep—with the edge of the *s*.
25:13 'Every man gird on his *s*."
25:13 So every man girded on his *s*,
25:13 and David also girded on his *s*.
31: 4 his armorbearer, "Draw your *s*,
31: 4 Therefore Saul took a *s* and
31: 5 was dead, he also fell on his *s*,
2 Sam 1:12 they had fallen by the *s*.
1:22 And the *s* of Saul did not
2:16 by the head and thrust his *s*
2:26 'Shall the *s* devour forever?
3:29 on a staff or falls by the *s*,
11:25 for the *s* devours one as well
12: 9 Uriah the Hittite with the *s*;
12: 9 and have killed him with the *s*
12:10 the *s* shall never depart from
15:14 the city with the edge of the *s*.
18: 8 more people that day than the *s*
20: 8 on it was a belt with a *s*
20:10 But Amasa did not notice the *s*
21:16 who was bearing a new *s*,
23:10 and his hand stuck to the *s*.
24: 9 valiant men who drew the *s*,
1 Ki 1:51 his servant to death with the *s*.
2: 8 not put you to death with the *s*.
2:32 he, and killed them with the *s*—
3:24 the king said, "Bring me a *s*.
3:24 So they brought a *s* before
19: 1 all the prophets with the *s*.
19:10 killed Your prophets with the *s*.
19:14 killed Your prophets with the *s*.
19:17 be that whoever escapes the *s*
19:17 and whoever escapes the *s* of
2 Ki 6:22 have taken captive with your *s*
8:12 men you will kill with the *s*;
10:25 them with the edge of the *s*;
11:15 and slay with the *s* whoever
11:20 had slain Athaliah with the *s*
19: 7 cause him to fall by the *s* in
19:37 struck him down with the *s*;
1 Chr 5:18 men able to bear shield and *s*,
10: 4 his armorbearer, "Draw your *s*,
10: 4 Therefore Saul took a *s* and
10: 5 he also fell on his *s* and died.
21: 5 thousand men who drew the *s*,
21: 5 thousand men who drew the *s*.
21:12 by your foes with the *s* of
21:12 or else for three days the *s* of
21:16 having in his hand a drawn *s*
21:27 and he returned his *s* to its
21:30 for he was afraid of the *s* of
2 Chr 20: 9 'If disaster comes upon us—*s*,
21: 4 all his brothers with the *s*,
23:14 and slay with the *s* whoever
23:21 had slain Athaliah with the *s*.
29: 9 fathers have fallen by the *s*;
32:21 struck him down with the *s*
36:17 their young men with the *s* in
36:20 those who escaped from the *s*
Ezra 9: 7 to the *s*, to captivity,
Neh 4:18 one of the builders had his *s*
Esth 9: 5 with the stroke of the *s*,
Job 1:15 servants with the edge of the *s*;
1:17 servants with the edge of the *s*;
5:15 He saves the needy from the *s*,
5:20 in war from the power of the *s*.
15:22 For a *s* is waiting for him.
19:29 Be afraid of the *s* for
19:29 brings the punishment of the *s*,
27:14 multiplied, it is for the *s*;
33:18 life from perishing by the *s*.
36:12 They shall perish by the *s*,
39:22 does he turn back from the *s*.
40:19 made him can bring near His *s*.
41:26 Though the *s* reaches him,
Ps 7:12 He will sharpen His *s*;
17:13 from the wicked with Your *s*,
22:20 Deliver Me from the *s*,
37:14 The wicked have drawn the *s*
37:15 Their *s* shall enter their own
44: 3 of the land by their own *s*,
44: 6 Nor shall my *s* save me.
45: 3 Gird Your *s* upon Your thigh,
57: 4 And their tongue a sharp *s*.
63:10 They shall fall by the *s*;
64: 3 sharpen their tongue like a *s*,
76: 3 The shield and *s* of battle.
78:62 gave His people over to the *s*,
78:64 Their priests fell by the *s*,
89:43 turned back the edge of his *s*,
144:10 His servant From the deadly *s*.
149: 6 And a two-edged *s* in their
Prov 5: 4 Sharp as a two-edged *s*.
12:18 like the piercings of a *s*,
25:18 club, a *s*, and a sharp arrow.
Song 3: 8 Every man has his *s* on his
Isa 1:20 shall be devoured by the *s*";
2: 4 Nation shall not lift up *s*
3:25 Your men shall fall by the *s*,
13:15 is captured will fall by the *s*.
14:19 Thrust through with a *s*,
21:15 the swords, from the drawn *s*,
22: 2 men are not slain with the *s*,
27: 1 day the LORD with His severe *s*,
31: 8 Assyria shall fall by a *s*
31: 8 And a *s* not of mankind shall
31: 8 But he shall flee from the *s*,
34: 5 For My *s* shall be bathed in
34: 6 The *s* of the LORD is filled
37: 7 cause him to fall by the *s* in
37:38 struck him down with the *s*;
41: 2 them as the dust to his *s*,
49: 2 made My mouth like a sharp *s*;
51:19 and destruction, famine and *s*—
65:12 I will number you for the *s*,
66:16 For by fire and by His *s* The
Jer 2:30 Your *s* has devoured your
4:10 Whereas the *s* reaches to the
5:12 Nor shall we see *s* or famine.
5:17 In which you trust, with the *s*.
6:25 Because of the *s* of the enemy,
9:16 And I will send a *s* after them
11:22 young men shall die by the *s*,
12:12 For the *s* of the LORD shall
14:12 I will consume them by the *s*,
14:13 them, 'You shall not see the *s*,
14:15 *S* and famine shall not be in
14:15 By *s* and famine those prophets
14:16 because of the famine and the *s*;
14:18 those slain with the *s*! And if
15: 2 And such as are for the *s*,
15: 2 as are for the sword, to the *s*;
15: 3 the *s* to slay, the dogs to drag,
15: 9 of them I will deliver to the *s*
16: 4 shall be consumed by the *s* and
18:21 By the force of the *s*;
18:21 young men be slain By the *s*
19: 7 cause them to fall by the *s*
20: 4 and they shall fall by the *s* of
20: 4 and slay them with the *s*.
21: 7 from the pestilence and the *s*
21: 7 them with the edge of the *s*.
21: 9 in this city shall die by the *s*,
24:10 'And I will send the *s*,
25:16 and go mad because of the *s*
25:27 because of the *s* which I will
25:29 for I will call for a *s* on all
25:31 those who are wicked to the *s*,
26:23 who killed him with the *s* and
27: 8 says the LORD, 'with the *s*,
27:13 you and your people, by the *s*,
29:17 I will send on them the *s*,
29:18 I will pursue them with the *s*,
31: 2 The people who survived the *s*
32:24 because of the *s* and famine and
32:36 of the king of Babylon by the *s*,
33: 4 the siege mounds and the *s*:
34: 4 'You shall not die by the *s*.
34:17 you,' says the LORD—'to the *s*,
38: 2 in this city shall die by the *s*,
39:18 and you shall not fall by the *s*;
41: 2 the son of Shaphan, with the *s*,
42:16 then it shall be that the *s*
42:17 They shall die by the *s*,
42:22 that you shall die by the *s*,
43:11 and to the *s* those appointed
43:11 those appointed for the *s*.
44:12 They shall be consumed by the *s*
44:12 by the *s* and by famine;
44:13 punished Jerusalem, by the *s*,
44:18 and have been consumed by the *s*
44:27 shall be consumed by the *s* and
44:28 a small number who escape the *s*
46:10 The *s* shall devour; It shall
46:14 For the *s* devours all around
46:16 From the oppressing *s*.'
47: 6 O you *s* of the LORD, How long
48: 2 O Madmen! The *s* shall pursue
48:10 is he who keeps back his *s*
49:37 And I will send the *s* after them
50:16 For fear of the oppressing *s*
50:35 A *s* is against the
50:36 A *s* is against the
50:36 A *s* is against her mighty
50:37 A *s* is against their horses,
50:37 A *s* is against her treasures,
51:50 You who have escaped the *s*,
Lam 1:20 Outside the *s* bereaves,
2:21 young men Have fallen by the *s*;
4: 9 Those slain by the *s* are
5: 9 Because of the *s* in the
Ezek 5: 1 you, son of man, take a sharp *s*,
5: 2 strike around it with the *s*,
5: 2 I will draw out a *s* after them.
5:12 one-third shall fall by the *s*

S

5:12 and I will draw out a *s* after
5:17 and I will bring the *s* against
6: 3 will bring a *s* against you,
6: 8 may have some who escape the *s*
6:11 For they shall fall by the *s*,
6:12 who is near shall fall by the *s*,
7:15 The *s* is outside, And the
7:15 in the field Will die by the *s*;
11: 8 "You have feared the *s*;
11: 8 and I will bring a *s* upon
11:10 "You shall fall by the *s*.
12:14 and I will draw out the *s* after
12:16 a few of their men from the *s*,
14:17 Or if I bring a *s* on that
14:17 sword on that land, and say, '*S*,
14:21 the *s* and famine and wild beasts
17:21 his troops shall fall by the *s*,
21: 3 and I will draw My *s* out of its
21: 4 therefore My *s* shall go out of
21: 5 have drawn My *s* out of its
21: 9 says the LORD!' Say: 'A *s*,
21: 9 a *s* is sharpened And also
21:11 This *s* is sharpened, and it is
21:12 Terrors including the *s* will
21:13 And what if the *s* despises
21:14 The third time let the *s* do
21:14 It is the *s* that slays,
21:14 The *s* that slays the great
21:15 I have set the point of the *s*
21:19 yourself two ways for the *s* of
21:20 Appoint a road for the *s* to go
21:28 reproach,' and say: 'A *s*,
21:28 a *s* is drawn, Polished for
23:10 And slew her with the *s*;
23:25 remnant shall fall by the *s*;
24:21 left behind shall fall by the *s*.
25:13 Dedan shall fall by the *s*.
26: 6 fields shall be slain by the *s*.
26: 8 He will slay with the *s* your
26:11 will slay your people by the *s*,
28:23 judged in her midst By the *s*
29: 8 Surely I will bring a *s* upon you
30: 4 The *s* shall come upon Egypt,
30: 5 shall fall with them by the *s*.
30: 6 within her shall fall by the *s*,
30:17 Pi Beseth shall fall by the *s*,
30:21 it strong enough to hold a *s*.
30:22 and I will make the *s* fall out
30:24 king of Babylon and put My *s*
30:25 when I put My *s* into the hand
31:17 it, with those slain by the *s*;
31:18 with those slain by the *s*.
32:10 of you when I brandish My *s*
32:11 The *s* of the king of Babylon
32:20 midst of those slain by the *s*;
32:20 She is delivered to the *s*,
32:21 uncircumcised, slain by the *s*.
32:22 of them slain, fallen by the *s*.
32:23 of them slain, fallen by the *s*,
32:24 of them slain, fallen by the *s*,
32:25 uncircumcised, slain by the *s*;
32:26 uncircumcised, slain by the *s*,
32:28 lie with those slain by the *s*.
32:29 beside those slain by the *s*;
32:30 with those slain by the *s*,
32:31 all his army, Slain by the *s*,
32:32 With those slain by the *s*,
33: 2 When I bring the *s* upon a land,
33: 3 when he sees the *s* coming upon
33: 4 if the *s* comes and takes him
33: 6 'But if the watchman sees the *s*
33: 6 and the *s* comes and takes any
33:26 "You rely on your *s*,
33:27 the ruins shall fall by the *s*,
35: 5 of Israel by the power of the *s*
35: 8 those who are slain by the *s*
38: 8 those brought back from the *s*
38:21 I will call for a *s* against Gog
38:21 Every man's *s* will be against
39:23 and they all fell by the *s*.
Dan 11:33 days they shall fall by *s* and
Hos 1: 7 Nor by *s* or battle, By horses
2:18 Bow and *s* of battle I will
7:16 princes shall fall by the *s*
11: 6 And the *s* shall slash in his
13:16 They shall fall by the *s*,
Am 1:11 pursued his brother with the *s*,
4:10 young men I killed with a *s*,
7: 9 I will rise with the *s* against
7:11 'Jeroboam shall die by the *s*,
7:17 daughters shall fall by the *s*;
9: 1 the last of them with the *s*.
9: 4 there I will command the *s*,
9:10 of My people shall die by the *s*,
Mic 4: 3 Nation shall not lift up *s*
5: 6 They shall waste with the *s* the
6:14 I will give over to the *s*.
Nah 2:13 and the *s* shall devour your
3: 3 Horsemen charge with bright *s*
3:15 The *s* will cut you off;
Zeph 2:12 You shall be slain by My *s*.
Hag 2:22 Every one by the *s* of his
Zech 9:13 And made you like the *s* of a
11:17 Who leaves the flock! A *s*
13: 7 Awake, O *s*, against My
Mt 10:34 not come to bring peace but a *s*.
26:51 out his hand and drew his *s*,
26:52 Put your *s* in its place, for all
26:52 for all who take the *s* will
26:52 the sword will perish by the *s*.
Mk 14:47 those who stood by drew his *s*
Lk 2:35 a *s* will pierce through your
21:24 will fall by the edge of the *s*,
22:36 a knapsack; and he who has no *s*,
22:49 shall we strike with the *s*?
Jn 18:10 Then Simon Peter, having a *s*,
18:11 Put your *s* into the sheath.
Acts 12: 2 the brother of John with the *s*.
16:27 drew his *s* and was about to
Rom 8:35 or nakedness, or peril, or *s*?
13: 4 for he does not bear the *s* in
Eph 6:17 and the *s* of the Spirit, which
Heb 4:12 sharper than any two-edged *s*,
11:34 fire, escaped the edge of the *s*,
11:37 tempted, were slain with the *s*.
Rev 1:16 mouth went a sharp two-edged *s*,
2:12 who has the sharp two-edged *s*:
2:16 fight against them with the *s*
6: 4 was given to him a great *s*.
6: 8 of the earth, to kill with *s*,
13:10 he who kills with the *s* must be
13:10 sword must be killed with the *s*.
13:14 beast who was wounded by the *s*
19:15 out of His mouth goes a sharp *s*,
19:21 the rest were killed with the *s*

SWORDS (27/27) SWORD

1 Sam 13:19 Lest the Hebrews make *s* or
2 Sam 2:16 was called the Field of Sharp *S*,
2 Ki 3:23 the kings have surely struck *s*
3:26 seven hundred men who drew *s*,
Neh 4:13 to their families, with their *s*,
Ps 55:21 Yet they were drawn *s*.
59: 7 *S* are in their lips;
Prov 30:14 whose teeth are like *s*,
Song 3: 8 They all hold *s*,
Isa 2: 4 They shall beat their *s* into
21:15 For they fled from the *s*,
Ezek 16:40 thrust you through with their *s*.
21:16 *S* at the ready! Thrust right!
23:47 and execute them with their *s*;
28: 7 And they shall draw their *s*
30:11 They shall draw their *s*
32:12 By the *s* of the mighty warriors,
32:27 They have laid their *s* under
38: 4 shields, all of them handling *s*.
Joel 3:10 Beat your plowshares into *s*
Mic 4: 3 They shall beat their *s* into
Mt 26:47 with a great multitude with *s*
26:55 with *s* and clubs to take Me?
Mk 14:43 with a great multitude with *s*
14:48 with *s* and clubs to take Me?
Lk 22:38 "Lord, look, here are two *s*.
22:52 with *s* and clubs?

SWORE (76/76) SWEAR

Gen 21:31 because the two of them *s* an
24: 7 and who spoke to me and *s* to
24: 9 and *s* to him concerning this
25:33 So he *s* to him, and sold his
26: 3 perform the oath which I *s* to
26:31 early in the morning and *s* an
31:53 And Jacob *s* by the Fear of
47:31 And he *s* to him. So Israel
50:24 land to the land of which He *s*
Ex 6: 8 you into the land which I *s* to
13: 5 which He *s* to your fathers to
13:11 as He *s* to you and your
32:13 to whom You *s* by Your own self,
33: 1 to the land of which I *s* to
Num 11:12 to the land which You *s* to
14:16 people to the land which He *s*
14:23 not see the land of which I *s*
14:30 means enter the land which I *s*
32:10 and He *s* an oath, saying,
32:11 see the land of which I *s* to
Deut 1: 8 the land which the LORD *s* to
1:35 that good land of which I *s* to
4:21 and *s* that I would not cross
4:31 of your fathers which He *s* to
6:10 into the land of which He *s* to
6:18 good land of which the LORD *s*
6:23 give us the land of which He *s*
7: 8 would keep the oath which He *s*
7:12 and the mercy which He *s* to
7:13 in the land of which He *s* to
8: 1 the land of which the LORD *s*
8:18 His covenant which He *s* to
9: 5 the word which the LORD *s* to
10:11 and possess the land which I *s*
11: 9 in the land which the LORD *s*
11:21 the land of which the LORD *s*
13:17 just as He *s* to your fathers,
19: 8 as He *s* to your fathers,
26: 3 the country which the LORD *s*
26:15 just as You *s* to our fathers,
28:11 the land of which the LORD *s*
30:20 in the land which the LORD *s*
31:20 of which I *s* to their fathers,
31:21 them to the land of which I *s*
31:23 into the land of which I *s* to
34: 4 is the land of which I *s*
Josh 1: 6 inheritance the land which I *s*
5: 6 to whom the LORD *s* that He
6:22 as you *s* to her."
9:15 rulers of the congregation *s*
9:20 because of the oath which we *s*
14: 9 So Moses *s* on that day, saying,
Judg 2: 1 you to the land of which I *s*
1 Sam 19: 6 voice of Jonathan, and Saul *s*,
24:22 So David *s* to Saul. And Saul
28:10 And Saul *s* to her by the LORD,
2 Sam 19:23 And the king *s* to him.
21:17 Then the men of David *s* to him,
1 Ki 1:17 you *s* by the LORD your God to
1:30 just as I *s* to you by the LORD
2: 8 and I *s* to him by the LORD,
2:23 Then King Solomon *s* by the
Ezra 10: 5 So they *s* an oath.
Ps 89:49 Which You *s* to David in Your
95:11 So I *s* in My wrath,
132: 2 How he *s* to the LORD,
Jer 32:22 of which You *s* to their fathers
38:16 So Zedekiah the king *s* secretly
Ezek 16: 8 I *s* an oath to you and entered
Dan 12: 7 and *s* by Him who lives forever,
Mk 6:23 He also *s* to her, "Whatever you
Lk 1:73 The oath which He *s* to our
Heb 3:11 So I *s* in My wrath,
4: 3 'So I *s* in My wrath,
6:13 He *s* by Himself,
Rev 10: 6 and *s* by Him who lives forever

SWORN (47/46) SWEAR

Gen 22:16 and said: "By Myself I have *s*,
Ex 17:16 said, "Because the LORD has *s*:
Lev 6: 5 all that about which he has *s*
Deut 2:14 just as the LORD had *s* to
28: 9 just as He has *s* to you, if you
29:13 and just as He has *s* to your
31: 7 the land which the LORD has *s*
Josh 5: 6 the land which the LORD had *s*
9:18 of the congregation had *s* to
9:19 We have *s* to them by the LORD
21:43 all the land of which He had *s*
21:44 according to all that He had *s*
Judg 2:15 and as the LORD had *s* to them.
21: 1 Now the men of Israel had *s* an
21: 7 seeing we have *s* by the LORD
21:18 the children of Israel have *s*
1 Sam 3:14 And therefore I have *s* to the
20:42 since we have both *s* in the
2 Sam 3: 9 do for David as the LORD has *s*
21: 2 the children of Israel had *s*
2 Chr 15:15 for they had *s* with all their
Neh 9:15 the land Which You had *s* to
Ps 24: 4 Nor *s* deceitfully.
89: 3 I have *s* to My servant David:
89:35 Once I have *s* by My holiness;
110: 4 The LORD has *s* And will not
119:106 I have *s* and confirmed That I
132:11 The LORD has *s* in truth to
Isa 14:24 The LORD of hosts has *s*,
45:23 I have *s* by Myself; The word
54: 9 For as I have *s* That the
54: 9 So have I *s* That I would not
62: 8 The LORD has *s* by His right
Jer 5: 7 have forsaken Me And *s* by
11: 5 the oath which I have *s* to
44:26 I have *s* by My great name,'
49:13 For I have *s* by Myself," says
51:14 The LORD of hosts has *s* by
Ezek 21:23 eyes of those who have *s* oaths
Am 4: 2 The Lord GOD has *s* by His
6: 8 The Lord GOD has *s* by Himself
8: 7 The LORD has *s* by the pride
Mic 7:20 Which You have *s* to our
Hab 3: 9 Oaths were *s* over Your
Acts 2:30 that God had *s* with an oath
7:17 drew near which God had *s* to
Heb 7:21 The LORD has *s* And will

SYCAMINE (KJV) See MULBERRY

SYCAMORE (4/4)

1 Chr 27:28 over the olive trees and the *s*
Ps 78:47 And their *s* trees with frost.
Am 7:14 And a tender of *s* fruit.
Lk 19: 4 ahead and climbed up into a *s*

SYCAMORES (4/4)

1 Ki 10:27 trees as abundant as the *s*
2 Chr 1:15 cedars as abundant as the *s*
9:27 trees as abundant as the *s*
Isa 9:10 The *s* are cut down, But we

SYCHAR (1/1) SHECHEM

Jn 4: 5 of Samaria which is called *S*,

SYCHEM (KJV) See SHECHEM

SYCOMORE (KJV) See SYCAMORE, SYCAMORES

SYENE (2/2)

Ezek 29:10 and desolate, from Migdol to *S*,
30: 6 From Migdol to *S* Those

SYMBOL (1/1) SYMBOLIC

1 Cor 11:10 the woman ought to have a *s*

SYMBOLIC (2/2) SYMBOL

Gal 4:24 which things are *s*.
Heb 9: 9 It was *s* for the present time

SYMBOLS (1/1)
Hos 12:10 I have given *s* through the

SYMPATHIZE (1/1)
Heb 4:15 have a High Priest who cannot *s*

SYMPATHY (1/1)
Hos 11: 8 My *s* is stirred.

SYMPHONY (4/4)
Dan 3: 5 in *s* with all kinds of music,
3: 7 in *s* with all kinds of music,
3:10 in *s* with all kinds of music,
3:15 in *s* with all kinds of music,

SYNAGOGUE (41/41) SYNAGOGUES
Mt 12: 9 there, He went into their *s*.
13:54 He taught them in their *s*,
Mk 1:21 on the Sabbath He entered the *s*
1:23 Now there was a man in their *s*
1:29 as they had come out of the *s*,
3: 1 And He entered the *s* again,
5:22 one of the rulers of the *s*
5:36 He said to the ruler of the *s*,
5:38 the house of the ruler of the *s*,
6: 2 He began to teach in the *s*.
Lk 4:16 He went into the *s* on the
4:20 eyes of all who were in the *s*
4:28 So all those in the *s*,
4:33 Now in the *s* there was a man who
4:38 Now He arose from the *s* and
6: 6 that He entered the *s* and
7: 5 nation, and has built us a *s*.
8:41 and he was a ruler of the *s*.
13:14 But the ruler of the *s* answered
Jn 6:59 These things He said in the *s* as
9:22 he would be put out of the *s*.
12:42 they should be put out of the *s*;
Acts 6: 9 some from what is called the *S*
13:14 and went into the *s* on the
13:15 the rulers of the *s* sent to
13:42 when the Jews went out of the *s*,
14: 1 they went together to the *s* of
17: 1 where there was a *s* of the
17:10 they went into the *s* of the
17:17 Therefore he reasoned in the *s*
18: 4 And he reasoned in the *s* every
18: 7 house was next door to the *s*.
18: 8 Crispus, the ruler of the *s*,
18:17 Sosthenes, the ruler of the *s*,
18:19 but he himself entered the *s*
18:26 began to speak boldly in the *s*.
19: 8 And he went into the *s* and spoke
22:19 they know that in every *s* I
26:11 punished them often in every *s*
Rev 2: 9 but are a *s* of Satan.
3: 9 I will make those of the *s* of

SYNAGOGUE'S (2/2)
Mk 5:35 from the ruler of the *s* house
Lk 8:49 from the ruler of the *s* house,

SYNAGOGUES (24/24) SYNAGOGUE
Mt 4:23 Galilee, teaching in their *s*,
6: 2 as the hypocrites do in the *s*
6: 5 love to pray standing in the *s*
9:35 villages, teaching in their *s*,
10:17 and scourge you in their *s*.
23: 6 feasts, the best seats in the *s*,
23:34 you will scourge in your *s* and
Mk 1:39 And He was preaching in their *s*
12:39 "the best seats in the *s*,
13: 9 and you will be beaten in the *s*.
Lk 4:15 And He taught in their *s*,
4:44 And He was preaching in the *s* of
11:43 love the best seats in the *s*
12:11 when they bring you to the *s*
13:10 He was teaching in one of the *s*
20:46 the best seats in the *s*,
21:12 delivering you up to the *s* and
Jn 16: 2 will put you out of the *s*;
18:20 I always taught in *s* and in the
Acts 9: 2 letters from him to the *s* of
9:20 he preached the Christ in the *s*,
13: 5 the word of God in the *s* of
15:21 being read in the *s* every
24:12 either in the *s* or in the city.

SYNTYCHE (1/1)
Phil 4: 2 implore Euodia and I implore *S*

SYRACUSE (1/1)
Acts 28:12 And landing at *S*,

SYRIA (74/70) ARAM, SYRIAN
Judg 10: 6 the Ashtoreths, the gods of *S*,
2 Sam 8: 6 Then David put garrisons in *S* of
8:12 from *S*, from Moab, from the
15: 8 while I dwelt at Geshur in *S*,
1 Ki 10:29 the Hittites and the kings of *S*.
11:25 Israel, and reigned over *S*.
15:18 the son of Hezion, king of *S*,
19:15 anoint Hazael as king over *S*.
20: 1 Now Ben-Hadad the king of *S*
20:20 and Ben-Hadad the king of *S*
20:22 of the year the king of *S* will
20:23 the servants of the king of *S*
22: 1 passed without war between *S*
22: 3 of the hand of the king of *S*?
22:31 Now the king of *S* had commanded
2 Ki 5: 1 of the army of the king of *S*,
5: 1 LORD had given victory to *S*.
5: 5 Then the king of *S* said, "Go
6: 8 Now the king of *S* was making
6:11 the heart of the king of *S* was
6:24 this that Ben-Hadad king of *S*
8: 7 and Ben-Hadad king of *S* was
8: 9 Your son Ben-Hadad king of *S* has
8:13 you will become king over *S*.
8:28 to war against Hazael king of *S*
8:29 fought against Hazael king of *S*.
9:14 against Hazael king of *S*.
9:15 he fought with Hazael king of *S*.
12:17 Hazael king of *S* went up and
12:18 sent them to Hazael king of *S*.
13: 3 the hand of Hazael king of *S*,
13: 4 because the king of *S* oppressed
13: 7 for the king of *S* had destroyed
13:17 the arrow of deliverance from *S*;
13:19 then you would have struck *S*
13:19 But now you will strike *S* only
13:22 And Hazael king of *S* oppressed
13:24 Now Hazael king of *S* died.
15:37 began to send Rezin king of *S*
16: 5 Then Rezin king of *S* and Pekah
16: 6 At that time Rezin king of *S*
16: 6 of Syria captured Elath for *S*,
16: 7 from the hand of the king of *S*
1 Chr 2:23 (Geshur and *S* took from them the
18: 6 Then David put garrisons in *S*
2 Chr 1:17 the Hittites and the kings of *S*.
16: 2 and sent to Ben-Hadad king of *S*,
16: 7 have relied on the king of *S*,
16: 7 the army of the king of *S* has
18:30 Now the king of *S* had commanded
20: 2 you from beyond the sea, from *S*;
22: 5 to war against Hazael king of *S*
22: 6 fought against Hazael king of *S*.
24:23 of the year that the army of *S*
28: 5 into the hand of the king of *S*.
28:23 the gods of the kings of *S*
Ps 60: against Mesopotamia and *S* of
Isa 7: 1 that Rezin king of *S* and Pekah
7: 4 the fierce anger of Rezin and *S*,
7: 5 'Because *S*, Ephraim, and the
7: 8 For the head of *S* is Damascus,
17: 3 And the remnant of *S*;
Ezek 16:57 reproach of the daughters of *S*
27:16 *S* was your merchant because of
Hos 12:12 Jacob fled to the country of *S*;
Am 1: 5 The people of *S* shall go
Mt 4:24 His fame went throughout all *S*;
Lk 2: 2 while Quirinius was governing *S*.
Acts 15:23 of the Gentiles in Antioch, *S*,
15:41 And he went through *S* and
18:18 the brethren and sailed for *S*,
20: 3 as he was about to sail to *S*,
21: 3 it on the left, sailed to *S*,
Gal 1:21 I went into the regions of *S*

SYRIA'S (1/1)
Isa 7: 2 *S* forces are deployed in

SYRIA-DAMASCUS (KJV) See DAMASCUS

SYRIA-MAACHAH (KJV) See MAACHAH

SYRIACK (KJV) See ARAMAIC

SYRIAN (14/13) SYRIA, SYRIANS, SYRO-PHOENICIAN
Gen 25:20 the daughter of Bethuel the *S*
25:20 Aram, the sister of Laban the *S*.
28: 5 Laban the son of Bethuel the *S*,
31:20 unknown to Laban the *S*,
31:24 God had come to Laban the *S* in
Deut 26: 5 your God: 'My father was a *S*,
2 Ki 5:20 master has spared Naaman this *S*,
6:23 So the bands of *S* raiders came
7: 5 to the outskirts of the *S* camp
7:10 'We went to the *S* camp,
7:14 in the direction of the *S* army
1 Chr 7:14 his *S* concubine bore him Machir
19: 6 from *S* Maachah, and from Zobah.
Lk 4:27 cleansed except Naaman the *S*.

SYRIANS (60/54) SYRIAN
2 Sam 8: 5 When the *S* of Damascus came to
8: 5 twenty-two thousand of the *S*.
8: 6 and the *S* became David's
8:13 killing eighteen thousand *S* in
10: 6 of Ammon sent and hired the *S*
10: 6 of Beth Rehob and the *S* of
10: 8 And the *S* of Zoba, Beth Rehob,
10: 9 in battle array against the *S*.
10:11 If the *S* are too strong for me,
10:13 for the battle against the *S*,
10:14 people of Ammon saw that the *S*
10:15 When the *S* saw that they had
10:16 sent and brought out the *S* who
10:17 And the *S* set themselves in
10:18 Then the *S* fled before Israel;
10:18 thousand horsemen of the *S*,
10:19 So the *S* were afraid to help
1 Ki 20:20 so the *S* fled, and Israel
20:21 and killed the *S* with a great
20:26 that Ben-Hadad mustered the *S*
20:27 while the *S* filled the
20:28 Because the *S* have said, "The
20:29 foot soldiers of the *S* in one
22:11 these you shall gore the *S*
22:35 up in his chariot, facing the *S*,
2 Ki 5: 2 And the *S* had gone out on raids,
6: 9 for the *S* are coming down
6:18 So when the *S* came down to
7: 4 surrender to the army of the *S*.
7: 5 to go to the camp of the *S*.
7: 6 had caused the army of the *S*
7:12 me now tell you what the *S*
7:15 and weapons which the *S* had
7:16 plundered the tents of the *S*.
8:28 and the *S* wounded Joram.
8:29 from the wounds which the *S*
9:15 from the wounds which the *S*
13: 5 from under the hand of the *S*;
13:17 for you must strike the *S* at
24: 2 bands of Chaldeans, bands of *S*,
1 Chr 18: 5 When the *S* of Damascus came to
18: 5 twenty-two thousand of the *S*.
18: 6 and the *S* became David's
19:10 in battle array against the *S*.
19:12 If the *S* are too strong for me,
19:14 for the battle against the *S*,
19:15 people of Ammon saw that the *S*
19:16 Now when the *S* saw that they
19:16 messengers and brought the *S*
19:17 in battle array against the *S*,
19:18 Then the *S* fled before Israel;
19:18 thousand foot soldiers of the *S*,
19:19 So the *S* were not willing to
2 Chr 18:10 these you shall gore the *S*
18:34 up in his chariot facing the *S*
22: 5 and the *S* wounded Joram.
24:24 For the army of the *S* came with
Isa 9:12 *S* before and the Philistines
Jer 35:11 for fear of the army of the *S*.
Am 9: 7 And the *S* from Kir?

SYROPHENICIAN (KJV) See SYRO-PHOENICIAN

SYRO-PHOENICIAN (1/1) SYRIAN
Mk 7:26 a *S* by birth, and she kept

SYRTIS (1/1)
Acts 27:17 run aground on the *S* Sands

T

TAANACH (6/6)
Josh 12:21 the king of *T*, one; the king
17:11 the inhabitants of *T* and its
Judg 1:27 or *T* and its villages, or the
5:19 kings of Canaan fought In *T*,
1 Ki 4:12 Baana the son of Ahilud, in *T*,
1 Chr 7:29 *T* and its towns, Megiddo and

TAANATH SHILOH (1/1)
Josh 16: 6 went around eastward to *T*,

TABBAOTH (2/2)
Ezra 2:43 sons of Hasupha, the sons of *T*,
Neh 7:46 sons of Hasupha, the sons of *T*,

TABBATH (1/1)
Judg 7:22 border of Abel Meholah, by *T*.

TABEL (2/2)
Ezra 4: 7 also, Bishlam, Mithredath, *T*,
Isa 7: 6 king over them, the son of *T*'—

TABERAH (2/2)
Num 11: 3 called the name of the place *T*,
Deut 9:22 Also at *T* and Massah and

TABERING (KJV) See BEATING

TABERNACLE (320/286) TABERNACLES
Ex 25: 9 the pattern of the *t* and the
26: 1 Moreover you shall make the *t*
26: 6 clasps, so that it may be one *t*.
26: 7 to be a tent over the *t*.
26:12 hang over the back of the *t*.
26:13 hang over the sides of the *t*,
26:15 And for the *t* you shall make
26:17 for all the boards of the *t*.
26:18 shall make the boards for the *t*,
26:20 for the second side of the *t*,
26:22 "For the far side of the *t*,

T

26:23 the two back corners of the *t*.
26:26 the boards on one side of the *t*,
26:27 on the other side of the *t*,
26:27 the boards of the side of the *t*,
26:30 And you shall raise up the *t*
26:35 the table on the side of the *t*
26:36 a screen for the door of the *t*,
27: 9 also make the court of the *t*.
27:19 All the utensils of the *t* for
27:21 In the *t* of meeting, outside the
28:43 sons when they come into the *t*
29: 4 bring to the door of the *t* of
29:10 the bull brought before the *t*
29:11 by the door of the *t* of
29:30 when he enters the *t* of meeting
29:32 by the door of the *t* of
29:42 at the door of the *t* of
29:43 and the *t* shall be sanctified
29:44 So I will consecrate the *t* of
30:16 it for the service of the *t* of
30:18 You shall put it between the *t*
30:20 When they go into the *t* of
30:26 it you shall anoint the *t*
30:36 before the Testimony in the *t*
31: 7 the *t* of meeting, the ark of the
31: 7 and all the furniture of the *t*—
33: 7 and called it the *t* of meeting.
33: 7 the LORD went out to the *t* of
33: 8 Moses went out to the *t*,
33: 8 until he had gone into the *t*.
33: 9 when Moses entered the *t*,
33: 9 and stood at the door of the *t*,
33:10 of cloud standing at the *t*
33:11 did not depart from the *t*.
35:11 'the *t*, its tent, its covering,
35:15 door at the entrance of the *t*;
35:18 'the pegs of the *t*,
35:21 offering for the work of the *t*
36: 8 among them who worked on the *t*
36:13 clasps, that it might be one *t*.
36:14 hair for the tent over the *t*;
36:20 For the *t* he made boards of
36:22 for all the boards of the *t*.
36:23 And he made boards for the *t*,
36:25 And for the other side of the *t*,
36:27 For the west side of the *t* he
36:28 the two back corners of the *t*.
36:31 the boards on one side of the *t*,
36:32 on the other side of the *t*,
36:32 bars for the boards of the *t*
36:37 also made a screen for the *t*
38: 8 assembled at the door of the *t*
38:20 All the pegs of the *t*,
38:21 This is the inventory of the *t*,
38:21 the *t* of the Testimony, which
38:30 sockets for the door of the *t*
38:31 all the pegs for the *t*,
39:32 Thus all the work of the *t* of
39:33 And they brought the *t* to Moses,
39:38 the screen for the *t* door;
39:40 for the service of the *t*,
40: 2 month you shall set up the *t*
40: 5 screen for the door of the *t*.
40: 6 before the door of the *t* of
40: 7 set the laver between the *t* of
40: 9 and anoint the *t* and all that
40:12 his sons to the door of the *t*
40:17 that the *t* was raised up.
40:18 So Moses raised up the *t*,
40:19 spread out the tent over the *t*
40:21 he brought the ark into the *t*,
40:22 He put the table in the *t* of
40:22 on the north side of the *t*,
40:24 He put the lampstand in the *t* of
40:24 on the south side of the *t*;
40:26 He put the gold altar in the *t*
40:28 screen at the door of the *t*.
40:29 before the door of the *t* of
40:30 He set the laver between the *t*
40:32 Whenever they went into the *t* of
40:33 up the court all around the *t*
40:34 Then the cloud covered the *t* of
40:34 glory of the LORD filled the *t*.
40:35 was not able to enter the *t* of
40:35 glory of the LORD filled the *t*.
40:36 was taken up from above the *t*,
40:38 of the LORD was above the *t*
Lev 1: 1 and spoke to him from the *t* of
1: 3 free will at the door of the *t*
1: 5 that is by the door of the *t*
3: 2 kill it at the door of the *t*
3: 8 and kill it before the *t* of
3:13 head and kill it before the *t*
4: 4 the bull to the door of the *t*
4: 5 blood and bring it to the *t* of
4: 7 which is in the *t* of meeting;
4: 7 which is at the door of the *t*
4:14 and bring it before the *t* of
4:16 of the bull's blood to the *t*
4:18 which is in the *t* of meeting;
4:18 which is at the door of the *t*
6:16 in the court of the *t* of
6:26 in the court of the *t* of
6:30 blood is brought into the *t* of
8: 3 together at the door of the *t*
8: 4 together at the door of the *t*
8:10 and anointed the *t* and all that
8:31 flesh at the door of the *t* of
8:33 go outside the door of the *t*
8:35 stay at the door of the *t* of
9: 5 Moses commanded before the *t*
9:23 and Aaron went into the *t* of
10: 7 go out from the door of the *t*
10: 9 when you go into the *t* of
12: 6 to the door of the *t* of
14:11 at the door of the *t* of
14:23 to the door of the *t* of
15:14 to the door of the *t* of
15:29 to the door of the *t* of
15:31 when they defile My *t* that is
16: 7 LORD at the door of the *t* of
16:16 and so he shall do for the *t* of
16:17 shall be no man in the *t*
16:20 *t* of meeting, and the altar,
16:23 Aaron shall come into the *t* of
16:33 shall make atonement for the *t*
17: 4 bring it to the door of the *t*
17: 4 to the LORD before the *t* of
17: 5 the LORD at the door of the *t*
17: 6 LORD at the door of the *t* of
17: 9 bring it to the door of the *t*
19:21 to the door of the *t* of
24: 3 in the *t* of meeting, Aaron
26:11 I will set My *t* among you,
Num 1: 1 in the *t* of meeting, on the
1:50 appoint the Levites over the *t*
1:50 they shall carry the *t* and all
1:50 to it and camp around the *t*.
1:51 And when the *t* is to go forward,
1:51 and when the *t* is to be set up,
1:53 shall camp around the *t* of the
1:53 shall keep charge of the *t* of
2: 2 camp some distance from the *t*
2:17 And the *t* of meeting shall move
3: 7 congregation before the *t* of
3: 7 to do the work of the *t*.
3: 8 to all the furnishings of the *t*
3: 8 Israel, to do the work of the *t*.
3:23 were to camp behind the *t*
3:25 children of Gershon in the *t*
3:25 of meeting included the *t*,
3:25 screen for the door of the *t*
3:26 court which are around the *t*
3:29 camp on the south side of the *t*.
3:35 camp on the north side of the *t*.
3:36 included the boards of the *t*,
3:38 who were to camp before the *t*
3:38 before the *t* of meeting, were
4: 3 to do the work in the *t* of
4: 4 of the sons of Kohath in the *t*
4:15 These are the things in the *t*
4:16 the oversight of all the *t*,
4:23 to do the work in the *t* of
4:25 carry the curtains of the *t*
4:25 of the tabernacle and the *t* of
4:25 screen for the door of the *t*
4:26 court which are around the *t*
4:28 of the sons of Gershon in the *t*
4:30 to do the work of the *t* of
4:31 as all their service for the *t*
4:31 of meeting: the boards of the *t*,
4:33 as all their service for the *t*
4:35 the service for work in the *t*
4:37 all who might serve in the *t* of
4:39 the service for work in the *t*
4:41 of all who might serve in the *t*
4:43 the service for work in the *t*
4:47 of bearing burdens in the *t* of
5:17 that is on the floor of the *t*
6:10 to the door of the *t* of
6:13 be brought to the door of the *t*
6:18 head at the door of the *t* of
7: 1 had finished setting up the *t*,
7: 3 presented them before the *t*.
7: 5 in doing the work of the *t* of
7:89 when Moses went into the *t* of
8: 9 bring the Levites before the *t*
8:15 shall go in to service the *t*
8:19 children of Israel in the *t* of
8:22 in to do their work in the *t*
8:24 service in the work of the *t*
8:26 with their brethren in the *t*
9:15 Now on the day that the *t* was
9:15 the cloud covered the *t*,
9:15 morning it was above the *t*
9:17 was taken up from above the *t*,
9:18 as the cloud stayed above the *t*
9:19 many days above the *t*,
9:20 when the cloud was above the *t*
9:22 the cloud remained above the *t*,
10: 3 you at the door of the *t* of
10:11 was taken up from above the *t*
10:17 Then the *t* was taken down;
10:17 Merari set out, carrying the *t*.
10:21 (The *t* would be prepared for
11:16 bring them to the *t* of meeting,
11:24 and placed them around the *t*.
11:26 who had not gone out to the *t*;
12: 4 to the *t* of meeting!" So the
12: 5 and stood in the door of the *t*,
12:10 cloud departed from above the *t*,
14:10 of the LORD appeared in the *t*
16: 9 to do the work of the *t* of the
16:18 and stood at the door of the *t*
16:19 them at the door of the *t* of
16:42 that they turned toward the *t*
16:43 and Aaron came before the *t* of
16:50 to Moses at the door of the *t*
17: 4 you shall place them in the *t*
17: 7 rods before the LORD in the *t*
17: 8 day that Moses went into the *t*
17:13 Whoever even comes near the *t* of
18: 2 are with you before the *t* of
18: 3 and all the needs of the *t*;
18: 4 attend to the needs of the *t*
18: 4 for all the work of the *t*;
18: 6 to do the work of the *t* of
18:21 the work of the *t* of meeting.
18:22 shall not come near the *t* of
18:23 perform the work of the *t* of
18:31 reward for your work in the *t*
19: 4 directly in front of the *t* of
19:13 defiles the *t* of the LORD.
20: 6 assembly to the door of the *t*
25: 6 weeping at the door of the *t*
27: 2 by the doorway of the *t* of
31:30 who keep charge of the *t* of
31:47 who kept charge of the *t* of the
31:54 and brought it into the *t* of
Deut 31:14 present yourselves in the *t* of
31:14 presented themselves in the *t*
31:15 the LORD appeared at the *t* in
31:15 stood above the door of the *t*.
Josh 18: 1 and set up the *t* of meeting
19:51 at the door of the *t* of
22:19 where the LORD's *t* stands,
22:29 our God which is before His *t*.
1 Sam 1: 9 seat by the doorpost of the *t*
2:22 assembled at the door of the *t*
3: 3 lamp of God went out in the *t*
2 Sam 6:17 its place in the midst of the *t*
7: 6 about in a tent and in a *t*.
1 Ki 1:39 took a horn of oil from the *t*
2:28 So Joab fled to the *t* of the
2:29 Joab has fled to the *t* of the
2:30 So Benaiah went to the *t* of the
8: 4 the *t* of meeting, and all the
8: 4 furnishings that were in the *t*.
1 Chr 6:32 the dwelling place of the *t* of
6:48 every kind of service of the *t*
9:19 service, gatekeepers of the *t*.
9:21 keeper of the door of the *t* of
9:23 the LORD, the house of the *t*,
16: 1 set it in the midst of the *t*
16:39 before the *t* of the LORD at
17: 5 and from one *t* to another.
21:29 For the *t* of the LORD and the
23:26 shall no longer carry the *t*,
23:32 attend to the needs of the *t*
2 Chr 1: 3 for the *t* of meeting with God
1: 5 he put before the *t* of the
1: 6 which was at the *t* of meeting,
1:13 from before the *t* of meeting,
5: 5 the *t* of meeting, and all the
5: 5 furnishings that were in the *t*.
24: 6 for the *t* of witness?"
Ps 15: 1 LORD, who may abide in Your *t*?
19: 4 In them He has set a *t* for the
27: 5 In the secret place of His *t*
27: 6 sacrifices of joy in His *t*;
43: 3 Your holy hill And to Your *t*.
46: 4 The holy place of the *t* of
61: 4 I will abide in Your *t* forever;
76: 2 In Salem also is His *t*,
78:60 So that He forsook the *t* of
84: 1 How lovely is Your *t*,
132: 7 Let us go into His *t*;
Isa 4: 6 And there will be a *t* for shade
16: 5 in the *t* of David, Judging and
33:20 A *t* that will not be taken
Lam 2: 6 He has done violence to His *t*,
Ezek 37:27 My *t* also shall be with them;
41: 1 other side—the width of the *t*.
Am 9:11 day I will raise up The *t* of
Acts 7:43 You also took up the *t*
7:44 Our fathers had the *t* of
15:16 And will rebuild the *t*
Heb 8: 2 the sanctuary and of the true *t*
8: 5 when he was about to make the *t*.
9: 2 For a *t* was prepared: the first
9: 3 the part of the *t* which is
9: 6 into the first part of the *t*,
9: 8 manifest while the first *t* was
9:11 the greater and more perfect *t*
9:21 with blood both the *t* and all
13:10 which those who serve the *t*
Rev 13: 6 to blaspheme His name, His *t*,
15: 5 the temple of the *t* of the
21: 3 the *t* of God is with men,

TABERNACLES (13/13) TABERNACLE

Lev 23:34 shall be the Feast of *T* for
Deut 16:13 shall observe the Feast of *T*
16:16 of Weeks, and at the Feast of *T*;
31:10 of release, at the Feast of *T*,
2 Chr 8:13 of Weeks, and the Feast of *T*.
Ezra 3: 4 They also kept the Feast of *T*,
Zech 14:16 and to keep the Feast of *T*.
14:18 come up to keep the Feast of *T*.
14:19 come up to keep the Feast of *T*.
Mt 17: 4 wish, let us make here three *t*:
Mk 9: 5 and let us make three *t*:
Lk 9:33 and let us make three *t*:
Jn 7: 2 Now the Jews' Feast of *T* was at

TABITHA (2/2) DORCAS

Acts 9:36 was a certain disciple named *T*,
9:40 to the body he said, "*T*,

TABLE (79/75) TABLES

Ex 25:23 You shall also make a *t* of
25:27 for the poles to bear the *t*.
25:28 that the *t* may be carried with

25:30 set the showbread on the *t*
26:35 You shall set the *t* outside the
26:35 lampstand across from the *t* on
26:35 and you shall put the *t* on the
30:27 'the *t* and all its utensils,
31: 8 the *t* and its utensils, the pure
35:13 the *t* and its poles, all its
37:10 He made the *t* of acacia wood;
37:14 for the poles to bear the *t*.
37:15 of acacia wood to bear the *t*,
37:16 utensils which were on the *t*:
39:36 the *t*, all its utensils,
40: 4 You shall bring in the *t* and
40:22 He put the *t* in the tabernacle
40:24 of meeting, across from the *t*,
Lev 24: 6 on the pure gold *t* before the
Num 3:31 duty included the ark, the *t*,
4: 7 On the *t* of showbread they shall
Judg 1: 7 to gather scraps under my *t*;
1 Sam 20:29 he has not come to the king's *t*.
20:34 So Jonathan arose from the *t* in
2 Sam 9: 7 and you shall eat bread at my *t*
9:10 son shall eat bread at my *t*
9:11 he shall eat at my *t* like one of
9:13 ate continually at the king's *t*.
19:28 those who eat at your own *t*.
1 Ki 2: 7 among those who eat at your *t*,
4:27 who came to King Solomon's *t*.
7:48 and the *t* of gold on which was
10: 5 the food on his *t*,
13:20 happened, as they sat at the *t*,
18:19 Asherah, who eat at Jezebel's *t*.
2 Ki 4:10 and a *t* and a chair and a
1 Chr 28:16 of the showbread, for each *t*,
2 Chr 9: 4 the food on his *t*,
13:11 in order on the pure gold *t*,
29:18 and the *t* of the showbread with
Neh 5:17 And at my *t* were one hundred
Job 36:16 And what is set on your *t*
Ps 23: 5 You prepare a *t* before me in
69:22 Let their *t* become a snare
78:19 Can God prepare a *t* in the
128: 3 olive plants All around your *t*.
Prov 9: 2 She has also furnished her *t*.
Song 1:12 While the king is at his *t*,
Isa 21: 5 Prepare the *t*, Set a watchman
65:11 Who prepare a *t* for Gad,
Ezek 23:41 with a *t* prepared before it,
39:20 You shall be filled at My *t*
41:22 This is the *t* that is before
44:16 and they shall come near My *t*
Dan 11:27 shall speak lies at the same *t*;
Mal 1: 7 The *t* of the LORD is
1:12 The *t* of the LORD is defiled;
Mt 9:10 as Jesus sat at the *t* in the
15:27 fall from their masters' *t*.
26: 7 His head as He sat at the *t*.
Mk 7:28 the little dogs under the *t*
14: 3 the leper, as He sat at the *t*,
16:14 the eleven as they sat at the *t*;
Lk 7:37 knew that Jesus sat at the *t*
7:49 And those who sat at the *t* with
14:10 of those who sit at the *t* with
14:15 one of those who sat at the *t*
16:21 fell from the rich man's *t*.
22:21 betrayer is with Me on the *t*.
22:27 greater, he who sits at the *t*,
22:27 Is it not he who sits at the *t*?
22:30 you may eat and drink at My *t*
24:30 as He sat at the *t* with them,
Jn 12: 2 one of those who sat at the *t*
13:28 But no one at the *t* knew for
Rom 11: 9 Let their *t* become a snare
1 Cor 10:21 cannot partake of the Lord's *t*
10:21 the Lord's table and of the *t*
Heb 9: 2 which was the lampstand, the *t*,

TABLES (18/13) TABLE

1 Chr 28:16 he gave gold for the *t* of
28:16 and silver for the *t* of silver;
2 Chr 4: 8 He also made ten *t*,
4:19 the altar of gold and the *t* on
Isa 28: 8 For all *t* are full of vomit
Ezek 40:39 of the gateway were two *t* on
40:39 tables on this side and two *t*
40:40 northern gateway, were two *t*;
40:40 of the gateway were two *t*.
40:41 Four *t* were on this side and
40:41 were on this side and four *t*
40:41 eight *t* on which they
40:42 There were also four *t* of hewn
40:43 of the sacrifices was on the *t*.
Mt 21:12 and overturned the *t* of the
Mk 11:15 and overturned the *t* of the
Jn 2:15 money and overturned the *t*.
Acts 6: 2 the word of God and serve *t*.

TABLET (6/6) TABLETS

Prov 3: 3 Write them on the *t* of your
7: 3 Write them on the *t* of your
Isa 30: 8 go, write it before them on a *t*,
Jer 17: 1 it is engraved On the *t* of
Ezek 4: 1 take a clay *t* and lay it before
Lk 1:63 And he asked for a writing *t*,

TABLETS (37/26) TABLET

Ex 24:12 and I will give you *t* of stone,
31:18 He gave Moses two *t* of the
31:18 *t* of stone, written with the
32:15 and the two *t* of the Testimony
32:15 The *t* were written on both
32:16 Now the *t* were the work of God,
32:16 of God engraved on the *t*.
32:19 and he cast the *t* out of his
34: 1 Cut two *t* of stone like the
34: 1 and I will write on these *t*
34: 1 words that were on the first *t*
34: 4 So he cut two *t* of stone like
34: 4 he took in his hand the two *t*
34:28 And He wrote on the *t* the words
34:29 Mount Sinai (and the two *t* of
Deut 4:13 and He wrote them on two *t* of
5:22 And He wrote them on two *t* of
9: 9 the mountain to receive the *t*
9: 9 the *t* of the covenant which the
9:10 LORD delivered to me two *t* of
9:11 the LORD gave me the two *t* of
9:11 the *t* of the covenant.
9:15 and the two *t* of the covenant
9:17 Then I took the two *t* and threw
10: 1 Hew for yourself two *t* of stone
10: 2 And I will write on the *t* the
10: 2 words that were on the first *t*,
10: 3 hewed two *t* of stone like the
10: 3 having the two *t* in my hand.
10: 4 And He wrote on the *t* according
10: 5 and put the *t* in the ark which
1 Ki 8: 9 in the ark except the two *t* of
2 Chr 5:10 was in the ark except the two *t*
Hab 2: 2 vision And make it plain on *t*,
2 Cor 3: 3 not on *t* of stone but on
3: 3 on tablets of stone but on *t*
Heb 9: 4 and the *t* of the covenant;

TABOR (12/12)

Josh 19:22 And the border reached to *T*,
Judg 4: 6 and deploy troops at Mount *T*;
4:12 Abinoam had gone up to Mount *T*.
4:14 So Barak went down from Mount *T*
8:18 they whom you killed at *T*?
1 Sam 10: 3 come to the terebinth tree of *T*.
1 Chr 6:77 with its common-lands and *T*
Ps 89:12 *T* and Hermon rejoice in Your
Jer 46:18 Surely as *T* is among the
Hos 5: 1 Mizpah And a net spread on *T*.

TABRET, TABRETS (KJV) See BYWORD, TAMBOURINES, TIMBREL, TIMBRELS

TABRIMMON (1/1)

1 Ki 15:18 them to Ben-Hadad the son of *T*,

TACHES (KJV) See CLASPS

TACHMONITE (1/1)

2 Sam 23: 8 had: Josheb-Basshebeth the *T*,

TACKLE (2/2)

Isa 33:23 Your *t* is loosed, They could
Acts 27:19 day we threw the ship's *t*

TADMOR (2/2)

1 Ki 9:18 and *T* in the wilderness, in the
2 Chr 8: 4 He also built *T* in the

TAHAN (2/2)

Num 26:35 family of the Bachrites; of *T*,
1 Chr 7:25 Telah his son, *T* his son,

TAHANITES (1/1)

Num 26:35 of Tahan, the family of the *T*.

TAHAPANES (KJV) See TAHPANHES

TAHATH (6/5)

Num 33:26 from Makheloth and camped at *T*.
33:27 They departed from *T* and camped
1 Chr 6:24 *T* his son, Uriel his son, Uzziah
6:37 the son of *T*, the son of Assir,
7:20 *T* his son, Eladah his son,
7:20 Eladah his son, *T* his son,

TAHPANHES (6/6)

Jer 2:16 Also the people of Noph and *T*
43: 7 And they went as far as *T*.
43: 8 the LORD came to Jeremiah in *T*,
43: 9 to Pharaoh's house in *T*,
44: 1 who dwell at Migdol, at *T*,
46:14 Proclaim in Noph and in *T*;

TAHPENES (3/2)

1 Ki 11:19 that is, the sister of Queen *T*.
11:20 Then the sister of *T* bore him
11:20 whom *T* weaned in Pharaoh's

TAHREA (1/1)

1 Chr 9:41 Micah were Pithon, Melech, *T*,

TAHTIM HODSHI (1/1)

2 Sam 24: 6 to Gilead and to the land of *T*;

TAIL (15/14) TAILS

Ex 4: 4 hand and take it by the *t*"
29:22 the fat of the ram, the fat *t*,
Lev 3: 9 its fat and the whole fat *t*
7: 3 The fat *t* and the fat that
8:25 he took the fat and the fat *t*,
9:19 bull and the ram—the fatty *t*,
Deut 28:13 make you the head and not the *t*;
28:44 head, and you shall be the *t*.
Judg 15: 4 turned the foxes *t* to tail,
15: 4 turned the foxes tail to *t*,
Job 40:17 He moves his *t* like a cedar;
Isa 9:14 LORD will cut off head and *t*
9:15 who teaches lies, he is the *t*.
19:15 for Egypt, Which the head or *t*,
Rev 12: 4 His *t* drew a third of the stars

TAILS (5/3) TAIL

Judg 15: 4 a torch between each pair of *t*.
Rev 9:10 They had *t* like scorpions, and
9:10 there were stings in their *t*.
9:19 in their mouth and in their *t*;
9:19 for their *t* are like serpents,

TAKE (894/848) TAKEN, TAKES, TAKING, TOOK

Gen 3:22 lest he put out his hand and *t*
6:21 And you shall *t* for yourself of
7: 2 You shall *t* with you seven each
12:19 *t* her and go your way."
13: 9 If you *t* the left, then I
14:21 and *t* the goods for yourself."
14:23 that I will *t* nothing, from a
14:23 and that I will not *t* anything
14:24 let them *t* their portion."
19:12 *t* them out of this place!
19:15 *t* your wife and your two
21:30 You will *t* these seven ewe
22: 2 *T* now your son, your only son
23:13 *t* it from me and I will bury
24: 3 that you will not *t* a wife for
24: 4 and *t* a wife for my son
24: 5 Must I *t* your son back to the
24: 6 Beware that you do not *t* my son
24: 7 and you shall *t* a wife for my
24: 8 only do not *t* my son back
24:37 You shall not *t* a wife for my
24:38 and *t* a wife for my son.'
24:40 and you shall *t* a wife for my
24:48 led me in the way of truth to *t*
24:51 *t* her and go, and let her be
27: 3 please *t* your weapons, your
27:10 Then you shall *t* it to your
28: 1 You shall not *t* a wife from the
28: 2 and *t* yourself a wife from
28: 6 him away to Padan Aram to *t*
28: 6 You shall not *t* a wife from the
30:15 Would you *t* away my son's
31:31 Perhaps you would *t* your
31:32 what I have of yours and *t* it
31:50 or if you *t* other wives
33:11 *t* my blessing that is brought
33:12 Let us *t* our journey; let us go,
34: 9 and *t* our daughters to
34:16 and we will *t* your daughters to
34:17 then we will *t* our daughter and
34:21 Let us *t* their daughters to us
38:23 Let her *t* them for herself,
42:33 *t* food for the famine of your
42:36 and you want to *t* Benjamin.
43:11 *T* some of the best fruits of
43:12 *T* double money in your hand, and
43:12 and *t* back in your hand the
43:13 *T* your brother also, and arise,
43:16 '*T* these men to my home,
43:18 to *t* us as slaves with our
44:29 But if you *t* this one also from
45:19 *T* carts out of the land of
Ex 2: 9 *T* this child away and nurse him
3: 5 *T* your sandals off your feet,
4: 4 Reach out your hand and *t* it by
4: 9 that you shall *t* water from the
4: 9 And the water which you *t* from
4:17 And you shall *t* this rod in your
5: 4 why do you *t* the people from
6: 7 I will *t* you as My people, and I
7: 9 *T* your rod and cast it before
7:15 to a serpent you shall *t* in
7:19 *T* your rod and stretch out your
8: 8 the LORD that He may *t* away
9: 8 *T* for yourselves handfuls of
10:17 that He may *t* away from me this
10:26 For we must *t* some of them to
10:28 Get away from me! *T* heed to
12: 3 of this month every man shall *t*
12: 4 neighbor next to his house *t*
12: 5 You may *t* it from the sheep or
12: 7 And they shall *t* some of the
12:21 Pick out and *t* lambs for
12:22 And you shall *t* a bunch of
12:32 Also *t* your flocks and your
13:22 He did not *t* away the pillar of
15:14 Sorrow will *t* hold of the
15:15 Trembling will *t* hold of them;
16:16 let every man *t* for those who

T

16:33 *T* a pot and put an omer of manna
17: 5 and *t* with you some of the
17: 5 Also *t* in your hand your rod
19:12 *T* heed to yourselves that you
20: 7 You shall not *t* the name of the
21:14 you shall *t* him from My altar,
22:26 If you ever *t* your neighbor's
23: 8 And you shall *t* no bribe, for a
23:25 And I will *t* sickness away from
25: 2 with his heart you shall *t* My
25: 3 the offering which you shall *t*
28: 1 'Now *t* Aaron your brother,
28: 5 They shall *t* the gold, blue,
28: 9 Then you shall *t* two onyx stones
29: 1 *T* one young bull and two rams
29: 5 Then you shall *t* the garments,
29: 7 And you shall *t* the anointing
29:12 You shall *t* some of the blood
29:13 And you shall *t* all the fat that
29:15 You shall also *t* one ram,
29:16 and you shall *t* its blood and
29:19 You shall also *t* the other ram,
29:20 and *t* some of its blood and put
29:21 And you shall *t* some of the
29:22 Also you shall *t* the fat of the
29:26 Then you shall *t* the breast of
29:31 And you shall *t* the ram of the
30:12 When you *t* the census of the
30:16 And you shall *t* the atonement
30:23 Also *t* for yourself quality
30:34 *T* sweet spices, stacte and
33: 5 *t* off your ornaments, that I
33:23 'Then I will *t* away My hand,
34: 9 and *t* us as Your inheritance."
34:12 *T* heed to yourself, lest you
34:16 and you *t* of his daughters for
34:34 he would *t* the veil off until
35: 5 *T* from among you an offering to
40: 9 And you shall *t* the anointing
Lev 2: 2 one of whom shall *t* from it his
2: 9 Then the priest shall *t* from the
4: 5 the anointed priest shall *t*
4: 8 He shall *t* from it all the fat
4:19 He shall *t* all the fat from it
4:25 The priest shall *t* some of the
4:30 Then the priest shall *t* some of
4:34 The priest shall *t* some of the
5:12 and the priest shall *t* his
6:10 and *t* up the ashes of the burnt
6:11 Then he shall *t* off his
6:15 He shall *t* from it his handful
8: 2 *T* Aaron and his sons with him,
9: 2 *T* for yourself a young bull as a
9: 3 *T* a kid of the goats as a sin
10:12 *T* the grain offering that
14: 4 the priest shall command to *t*
14: 6 he shall *t* it, the cedar wood
14:10 on the eighth day he shall *t*
14:12 And the priest shall *t* one male
14:14 The priest shall *t* some of the
14:15 And the priest shall *t* some of
14:21 then he shall *t* one male lamb
14:24 And the priest shall *t* the lamb
14:25 and the priest shall *t* some of
14:40 shall command that they *t* away
14:42 Then they shall *t* other stones
14:42 and he shall *t* other mortar and
14:49 'And he shall *t*, to cleanse
14:51 and he shall *t* the cedar wood,
15:14 On the eighth day he shall *t* for
15:29 on the eighth day she shall *t*
16: 5 And he shall *t* from the
16: 7 He shall *t* the two goats and
16:12 Then he shall *t* a censer full of
16:14 He shall *t* some of the blood of
16:18 and shall *t* some of the blood
16:23 shall *t* off the linen garments
18:17 nor shall you *t* her son's
18:18 Nor shall you *t* a woman as a
19:16 nor shall you *t* a stand against
19:18 'You shall not *t* vengeance,
21: 7 They shall not *t* a wife who is
21: 7 nor shall they *t* a woman
21:13 And he shall *t* a wife in her
21:14 but he shall *t* a virgin of his
23:40 And you shall *t* for yourselves
24: 5 And you shall *t* fine flour and
24:14 *T* outside the camp him who has
25:36 *T* no usury or interest from him
25:46 And you may *t* them as an
Num 1: 2 *T* a census of all the
1:49 nor *t* a census of them among
1:51 the Levites shall *t* it down;
3:40 and *t* the number of their
3:41 And you shall *t* the Levites for
3:45 *T* the Levites instead of all the
3:47 you shall *t* five shekels for
3:47 you shall *t* them in the
4: 2 *T* a census of the sons of Kohath
4: 5 and they shall *t* down the
4: 9 And they shall *t* a blue cloth
4:12 Then they shall *t* all the
4:13 Also they shall *t* away the ashes
4:22 Also *t* a census of the sons of
5:17 The priest shall *t* holy water in
5:17 and *t* some of the dust that is
5:25 Then the priest shall *t* the
5:26 and the priest shall *t* a handful
6: 2 consecrates an offering to *t*
6:18 and shall *t* the hair from his
6:19 And the priest shall *t* the
8: 6 *T* the Levites from among the
8: 8 Then let them *t* a young bull
8: 8 and you shall *t* another young
11:17 I will *t* of the Spirit that is
13:30 Let us go up at once and *t*
16: 3 You *t* too much upon
16: 6 *T* censers, Korah and all your
16: 7 You *t* too much upon
16:17 Let each *t* his censer and put
16:46 *T* a censer and put fire in it
16:46 and *t* it quickly to the
18:26 When you *t* from the children of
19: 3 that he may *t* it outside the
19: 4 'and Eleazar the priest shall *t*
19: 6 And the priest shall *t* cedar
19:17 an unclean person they shall *t*
19:18 A clean person shall *t* hyssop
20: 8 *T* the rod; you and your brother
20:25 '*T* Aaron and Eleazar his son,
21: 7 pray to the LORD that He *t*
23:12 Must I not *t* heed to speak what
23:27 I will *t* you to another place;
25: 4 *T* all the leaders of the people
26: 2 *T* a census of all the
26: 4 *T* a census of the people
27:18 *T* Joshua the son of Nun with
31: 2 *T* vengeance on the Midianites
31: 3 go against the Midianites to *t*
31:29 *t* it from their half, and give
31:30 of Israel's half you shall *t*
32: 5 Do not *t* us over the Jordan."
32:23 then *t* note, you have sinned
34:18 And you shall *t* one leader of
35:31 Moreover you shall *t* no ransom
35:32 And you shall *t* no ransom for
Deut 1: 7 Turn and *t* your journey, and go
1:40 turn and *t* your journey into
2:24 *t* your journey, and cross over
3: 4 not a city which we did not *t*
4: 2 nor *t* from it, that you may
4: 9 Only *t* heed to yourself,
4:15 *T* careful heed to yourselves,
4:19 And *t* heed, lest you lift your
4:23 *T* heed to yourselves, lest you
4:34 did God ever try to go and *t*
5:11 You shall not *t* the name of the
6:13 and shall *t* oaths in His name.
7: 3 nor *t* their daughter for your
7:15 And the LORD will *t* away from
7:25 nor *t* it for yourselves, lest
10:20 and *t* oaths in His name.
11:16 *T* heed to yourselves, lest your
12: 6 There you shall *t* your burnt
12:13 *T* heed to yourself that you do
12:19 *T* heed to yourself that you do
12:26 you shall *t* and go to the place
12:30 *t* heed to yourself that you are
12:32 you shall not add to it nor *t*
14:25 *t* the money in your hand,
15:17 then you shall *t* an awl and
16:19 nor *t* a bribe, for a bribe
20:19 making war against it to *t* it,
21: 3 to the slain man will *t* a
21:10 and you *t* them captive,
21:11 and desire her and would *t* her
21:19 father and his mother shall *t*
22: 6 you shall not *t* the mother with
22: 7 and *t* the young for yourself,
22:15 of the young woman shall *t* and
22:18 the elders of that city shall *t*
22:30 A man shall not *t* his father's
24: 4 who divorced her must not *t*
24: 6 No man shall *t* the lower or the
24: 8 *T* heed in an outbreak of
24:17 nor *t* a widow's garment as a
25: 5 *t* her as his wife, and perform
25: 7 if the man does not want to *t*
25: 8 I do not want to *t* her,'
26: 2 that you shall *t* some of the
26: 4 Then the priest shall *t* the
27: 9 *T* heed and listen, O Israel:
28:68 And the LORD will *t* you back to
31:26 *T* this Book of the Law, and put
Josh 3: 6 *T* up the ark of the covenant and
3:12 *t* for yourselves twelve men
4: 2 *T* for yourselves twelve men from
4: 3 *T* for yourselves twelve stones
4: 5 and each one of you *t* up a
5:15 '*T* your sandal off your foot,
6: 6 *T* up the ark of the covenant,
6:18 you become accursed when you *t*
7:13 your enemies until you *t* away
8: 1 *t* all the people of war with
8: 2 and its cattle you shall *t* as
8:29 commanded that they should *t*
9:11 *T* provisions with you for the
20: 4 they shall *t* him into the city
22: 5 But *t* careful heed to do the
22:19 and *t* possession among us;
23:11 Therefore *t* careful heed to
Judg 4: 6 *t* with you ten thousand men of
6:20 *T* the meat and the unleavened
6:25 '*T* your father's young bull,
6:26 and *t* the second bull and offer
9:15 Then come and *t* shelter in
9:31 *T* note! Gaal the son of Ebed and
11: 9 If you *t* me back home to fight
11:15 Israel did not *t* away the land
12: 6 Then they would *t* him and kill
14:15 you invited us in order to *t*
15: 2 Please, *t* her instead."
15: 7 I will surely *t* revenge on you,
16:28 that I may with one blow *t*
19:15 for no one would *t* them into
19:18 there is no one who will *t* me
20:10 We will *t* ten men out of every
21:22 because we did not *t* a wife for
Ruth 2:10 that you should *t* notice of me,
3: 9 *T* your maidservant under your
1 Sam 1:22 then I will *t* him, that he may
2:14 and the priest would *t* for
2:15 for he will not *t* boiled meat
2:16 then you may *t* as much as
2:16 I will *t* it by force."
6: 7 *t* two milk cows which have
6: 7 and *t* their calves home, away
6: 8 Then *t* the ark of the LORD and
6:21 come down and *t* it up with
8:11 He will *t* your sons and appoint
8:13 He will *t* your daughters to be
8:14 And he will *t* the best of your
8:15 He will *t* a tenth of your grain
8:16 And he will *t* your male
8:17 He will *t* a tenth of your sheep.
9: 3 *t* one of the servants with you,
12:13 And *t* note, the LORD has set a
16: 2 *T* a heifer with you, and say, 'I
16:23 that David would *t* a harp and
17:17 *T* now for your brothers an ephah
17:46 and I will strike you and *t*
18:25 to *t* vengeance on the king's
19:14 when Saul sent messengers to *t*
19:19 *T* note, David is at Naioth in
19:20 Then Saul sent messengers to *t*
21: 9 If you will *t* that, take it.
21: 9 *t* it. For there is no other
23:23 and *t* knowledge of all the
23:26 David and his men to *t* them.
24: 1 *T* note! David is in the
24:11 Yet you hunt my life to *t* it.
25:11 Shall I then *t* my bread and my
25:39 to *t* her as his wife.
26:11 *t* now the spear and the jug of
30:15 Can you *t* me down to this
30:15 and I will *t* you down to this
2 Sam 2:21 on one of the young men and *t*
12: 4 who refused to *t* from his own
12:11 and I will *t* your wives before
12:28 encamp against the city and *t*
12:28 lest I *t* the city and it be
13:13 where could I *t* my shame?
13:20 do not *t* this thing to heart."
13:33 let not my lord the king *t* the
14:14 Yet God does not *t* away a life;
15: 5 he would put out his hand and *t*
15:20 and *t* your brethren back.
16: 9 let me go over and *t* off his
18:19 Let me run now and *t* the news to
18:20 You shall not *t* the news this
18:20 for you shall *t* the news
18:20 But today you shall *t* no news,
19:19 that the king should *t* it to
19:30 let him *t* it all, inasmuch as
20: 6 *T* your lord's servants and
24:10 *t* away the iniquity of Your
24:13 and see what answer I should *t*
24:22 Let my lord the king *t* and offer
1 Ki 1:33 *T* with you the servants of your
1:33 and *t* him down to Gihon.
2: 4 If your sons *t* heed to their
2:31 that you may *t* away from me and
5: 9 then you can *t* them away.
8:25 only if your sons *t* heed to
8:31 and is forced to *t* an oath,
8:46 and they *t* them captive to the
11:31 '*T* for yourself ten pieces,
11:34 However I will not *t* the whole
11:35 But I will *t* the kingdom out of
11:37 So I will *t* you, and you shall
14: 3 Also *t* with you ten loaves,
14:10 I will *t* away the remnant of
16: 3 surely I will *t* away the
19: 4 *t* my life, for I am no better
19:10 and they seek to *t* my life."
19:14 and they seek to *t* my life."
20: 6 put it in their hands and *t*
20:18 *t* them alive; and if they have
20:18 out for war, *t* them alive."
20:22 *t* note, and see what you should
20:41 And he hastened to *t* the bandage
21:10 Then *t* him out, and stone
21:15 *t* possession of the vineyard of
21:16 Ahab got up and went down to *t*
21:18 where he has gone down to *t*
21:21 I will *t* away your posterity,
22: 3 but we hesitate to *t* it out of
22:26 *T* Micaiah, and return him to
22:28 *T* heed, all you people!"
22:34 Turn around and *t* me out of the
2 Ki 2: 1 when the LORD was about to *t*
2: 3 you know that the LORD will *t*
2: 5 you know that the LORD will *t*
4: 1 the creditor is coming to *t* my
4:29 and *t* my staff in your hand,
5:15 please *t* a gift from your
5:16 And he urged him to *t* it,
5:20 I will run after him and *t*
5:23 *t* two talents." And he urged
6: 2 and let every man *t* a beam from
6:32 murderer has sent someone to *t*
7:13 let several men *t* five of the
8: 8 *T* a present in your hand, and go
9: 1 *t* this flask of oil in your
9: 2 and *t* him to an inner room.
9: 3 'Then *t* the flask of oil,

9:13 Then each man hastened to *t* his
9:26 *t* and throw him on the plot
10: 6 *t* the heads of the men,
10:14 *T* them alive!" So they took
11:15 '*T* her outside under guard,
12: 5 let the priests *t* it
12: 7 do not *t* more money from your
13:15 *T* a bow and some arrows." So he
13:18 *T* the arrows"; so he took
18:32 until I come and *t* you away to a
19:30 house of Judah Shall again *t*
20: 7 *T* a lump of figs." So they took
20:18 And they shall *t* away some of
1 Chr 7:21 because they came down to *t*
17:13 and I will not *t* My mercy away
21: 8 *t* away the iniquity of Your
21:12 what answer I should *t* back to
21:23 *T* it to yourself, and let my
21:24 for I will not *t* what is yours
22:13 if you *t* care to fulfill the
27:23 But David did not *t* the number
2 Chr 6:16 only if your sons *t* heed to
6:22 and is forced to *t* an oath,
6:36 and they *t* them captive to a
12:11 then they would *t* them back
18:25 *T* Micaiah, and return him to
18:27 *T* heed, all you people!"
18:33 Turn around and *t* me out of the
19: 6 *T* heed to what you are doing,
19: 7 *t* care and do it, for there
19:11 And *t* notice: Amariah the chief
20:25 and his people came to *t* away
23:14 '*T* her outside under guard,
32:18 that they might *t* the city.
34:32 in Jerusalem and Benjamin *t* a
35:23 *T* me away, for I am severely
Ezra 4:22 *T* heed now that you do not fail
5:15 *T* these articles; go, carry them
9:12 nor *t* their daughters to your
Neh 10:30 nor *t* their daughters for our
13:25 nor *t* their daughters for your
Esth 2:13 whatever she desired to *t* with
4: 4 to clothe Mordecai and *t* his
6:10 *t* the robe and the horse, as
Job 7:21 And *t* away my iniquity?
9:34 Let Him *t* His rod away from me,
10:20 that I may *t* a little comfort,
11:18 and *t* your rest in safety.
13:14 Why do I *t* my flesh in my
23: 6 No! But He would *t* note of
23:10 But He knows the way that I *t*;
24: 3 They *t* the widow's ox as a
24: 9 And *t* a pledge from the poor.
24:10 And they *t* away the sheaves
30:16 The days of affliction *t* hold
30:17 And my gnawing pains *t* no
32:22 Else my Maker would soon *t* me
33: 5 order before me; *T* your stand.
36:17 Judgment and justice *t* hold
36:18 beware lest He *t* you away with
36:21 *T* heed, do not turn to
38:13 That it might *t* hold of the
38:20 That you may *t* it to its
41: 4 Will you *t* him as a servant
42: 8 *t* for yourselves seven bulls
Ps 2: 2 And the rulers *t* counsel
13: 2 How long shall I *t* counsel in
15: 3 Nor does he *t* up a reproach
15: 5 Nor does he *t* a bribe against
16: 4 Nor *t* up their names on my
27:10 Then the LORD will *t* care of
28: 3 Do not *t* me away with the
31:13 While they *t* counsel together
31:13 They scheme to *t* away my life.
35: 2 *T* hold of shield and buckler,
50: 9 I will not *t* a bull from your
50:16 Or *t* My covenant in your
51:11 And do not *t* Your Holy Spirit
52: 5 He shall *t* you away, and pluck
58: 9 He shall *t* them away as with a
69:20 I looked for someone to *t*
69:24 And let Your wrathful anger *t*
71:10 who lie in wait for my life *t*
71:11 Pursue and *t* him, for there
74:11 *T* it out of Your bosom and
80: 9 And caused it to *t* deep root,
83:12 'Let us *t* for ourselves
89:33 I will not utterly *t* from him,
91: 4 under His wings you shall *t*
102:14 For Your servants *t* pleasure in
102:24 Do not *t* me away in the midst
104:29 You *t* away their breath, they
109: 8 And let another *t* his office.
116:13 I will *t* up the cup of
119:43 And *t* not the word of truth
139: 9 If I *t* the wings of the
139:20 Your enemies *t* Your name in
141: 8 In You I *t* refuge; Do not
143: 9 In You I *t* shelter.
144: 2 and the One in whom I *t*
144: 3 that You *t* knowledge of him?
Prov 3:18 a tree of life to those who *t*
4:13 *T* firm hold of instruction, do
6:27 Can a man *t* fire to his bosom,
7:18 let us *t* our fill of love until
20:16 *T* the garment of one who is
22:27 Why should he *t* away your bed
25: 4 *T* away the dross from silver,
25: 5 *T* away the wicked from before
27:13 *T* the garment of him who is
Eccl 5:15 And he shall *t* nothing from
7: 2 And the living will *t* it to
7:21 Also do not *t* to heart
8: 3 Do not *t* your stand for an evil
Song 7: 8 I will *t* hold of its
Isa 1:24 And *t* vengeance on My enemies.
1:25 And *t* away all your alloy.
3:18 In that day the Lord will *t*
4: 1 in that day seven women shall *t*
4: 1 To *t* away our reproach."
5: 5 I will *t* away its hedge,
5:23 And *t* away justice from the
7: 4 *T* heed, and be quiet; do not
8: 1 *T* a large scroll, and write on
8: 2 And I will *t* for Myself faithful
8:10 *T* counsel together, but it will
10: 2 And to *t* what is right from
10: 6 to *t* the prey, And to tread
13: 8 Pangs and sorrows will *t* hold
14: 2 Then people will *t* them and
14: 2 they will *t* them captive whose
14: 4 that you will *t* up this proverb
14:32 the poor of His people shall *t*
16: 3 *T* counsel, execute judgment;
18: 4 I will *t* My rest, And I will
18: 5 with pruning hooks And *t* away
20: 2 and *t* your sandals off your
23:16 *T* a harp, go about the city,
25: 8 of His people He will *t* away
27: 5 Or let him *t* hold of My
27: 6 who come He shall cause to *t*
28:19 often as it goes out it will *t*
30: 1 Who *t* counsel, but not of Me,
30:14 its fragments A shard to *t*
30:14 Or to *t* water from the
33:23 The lame *t* the prey.
36:17 until I come and *t* you away to a
37:31 house of Judah Shall again *t*
38:21 'Let them *t* a lump of figs,
39: 7 And they shall *t* away some of
40:14 With whom did He *t* counsel,
40:24 Scarcely shall their stock *t*
40:24 And the whirlwind will *t* them
42:25 Yet he did not *t* it to heart.
44:15 For he will *t* some of it and
45:21 let them *t* counsel together.
45:23 Every tongue shall *t* an oath.
47: 2 *T* the millstones and grind meal
47: 2 *T* off the skirt, Uncover the
47: 3 I will *t* vengeance, And I
47: 7 So that you did not *t* these
49: 1 And *t* heed, you peoples from
57:13 A breath will *t* them. But he
57:14 *T* the stumbling block out of
58: 2 They *t* delight in approaching
58: 3 and You *t* no notice?' "In
58: 9 If you *t* away the yoke from your
62:10 Build up the highway! *T* out
64: 7 Who stirs himself up to *t* hold
66:21 And I will also *t* some of them
Jer 2:18 And now why *t* the road to
2:18 Or why *t* the road to Assyria,
3:14 I will *t* you, one from a city
4: 4 And *t* away the foreskins of
4: 6 *T* refuge! Do not delay! For I
5:10 *T* away her branches, For they
7:29 and *t* up a lamentation on the
9: 4 Everyone *t* heed to his neighbor,
9:10 I will *t* up a weeping and
9:18 Let them make haste And *t* up a
13: 4 *T* the sash that you acquired,
13: 6 and *t* from there the sash which
15:15 And *t* vengeance for me on my
15:15 do not *t* me away. Know that
15:19 If you *t* out the precious from
16: 2 'You shall not *t* a wife,
17:21 *T* heed to yourselves, and bear
18:22 For they have dug a pit to *t*
19: 1 and *t* some of the elders of
20:10 And we will *t* our revenge on
25: 9 I will send and *t* all the
25:10 Moreover I will *t* from them the
25:15 *T* this wine cup of fury from My
25:28 if they refuse to *t* the cup
27:20 king of Babylon did not *t*,
29: 6 *T* wives and beget sons and
29: 6 and *t* wives for your sons and
32: 3 and he shall *t* it;
32:14 *T* these deeds, both this
32:24 have come to the city to *t* it;
32:25 and *t* witnesses"!—yet the city
32:28 and he shall *t* it.
32:44 and *t* witnesses, in the land of
33:26 so that I will not *t* any of
34:22 will fight against it and *t* it
36: 2 *T* a scroll of a book and write
36:14 *T* in your hand the scroll from
36:28 *T* yet another scroll, and write
37: 8 and *t* it and burn it with
38: 3 which shall *t* it.'"
38:10 *T* from here thirty men with you,
39:12 *T* him and look after him, and do
39:14 then they sent someone to *t*
39:14 that he should *t* him home. So
43: 9 *T* large stones in your hand, and
44:12 And I will *t* the remnant of
46:11 'Go up to Gilead and *t* balm,
49: 2 Then Israel shall *t* possession
49:29 and their flocks they shall *t*
49:29 They shall *t* for themselves
50:15 *T* vengeance on her.
51: 8 Wail for her! *T* balm for her
51:26 They shall not *t* from you a
51:36 I will plead your case and *t*
Ezek 4: 1 *t* a clay tablet and lay it
4: 3 Moreover *t* for yourself an iron
4: 9 Also *t* for yourself wheat,
5: 1 *t* a sharp sword, take it as a
5: 1 *t* it as a barber's razor,
5: 1 then *t* scales to weigh and
5: 2 then you shall *t* one-third and
5: 3 You shall also *t* a small number
5: 4 Then *t* some of them again and
10: 6 *T* fire from among the wheels,
11:18 and they will *t* away all its
11:19 and *t* the stony heart out of
16:39 *t* your beautiful jewelry,
17:22 I will *t* also one of the
19: 1 Moreover *t* up a lamentation for
21:26 and *t* off the crown; Nothing
22:12 In you they *t* bribes to shed
22:12 you *t* usury and increase; you
23:25 They shall *t* your sons and
23:26 you of your clothes And *t*
23:29 *t* away all you have worked for,
24: 5 *T* the choice of the flock
24: 8 it may raise up fury and *t*
24:16 I *t* away from you the desire of
24:25 it not be in the day when I *t*
26:16 and *t* off their embroidered
26:17 And they will *t* up a lamentation
27: 2 *t* up a lamentation for Tyre,
27:32 wailing for you They will *t*
28:12 *t* up a lamentation for the king
29:19 he shall *t* away her wealth,
30: 4 And they *t* away her wealth,
32: 2 *t* up a lamentation for Pharaoh
33: 2 and the people of the land *t* a
33: 4 of the trumpet and does not *t*
33: 5 but did not *t* warning; his
36:12 they shall *t* possession of you,
36:24 For I will *t* you from among the
36:26 I will *t* the heart of stone out
37:16 *t* a stick for yourself and
37:16 Then *t* another stick and write
37:19 Surely I will *t* the stick of
37:21 Surely I will *t* the children of
38:12 to *t* plunder and to take booty,
38:12 to take plunder and to *t* booty,
38:13 Have you come to *t* plunder? Have
38:13 you gathered your army to *t*
38:13 to *t* away livestock and goods,
38:13 to *t* great plunder?"'
39:10 They will not *t* wood from the
43:20 You shall *t* some of its blood
43:21 Then you shall also *t* the bull
44:19 they shall *t* off their garments
44:22 They shall not *t* as wife a widow
44:22 but *t* virgins of the
45:18 you shall *t* a young bull
45:19 The priest shall *t* some of the
46:18 the prince shall not *t* any of
Dan 2:24 *t* me before the king, and I
6:23 commanded that they should *t*
7:26 And they shall *t* away his
11:15 and *t* a fortified city; and the
11:18 and shall *t* many. But a ruler
11:31 then they shall *t* away the
Hos 1: 2 *t* yourself a wife of harlotry
1: 6 But I will utterly *t* them
2: 9 I will return and *t*
2: 9 And will *t* back My wool and My
2:17 For I will *t* from her mouth the
5: 1 O priests! *T* heed, O house of
5:14 I will *t* them away, and no
11: 4 I was to them as those who *t*
14: 2 *T* words with you, And return
14: 2 *T* away all iniquity; Receive
Am 4: 2 come upon you When He will *t*
5: 1 Hear this word which I *t* up
5:11 you tread down the poor And *t*
5:23 *T* away from Me the noise of
6:10 picks up the bodies to *t* them
9: 2 From there my hand shall *t*
9: 3 there I will search and *t* them;
Jon 4: 3 please *t* my life from me, for
Mic 2: 2 They covet fields and *t* them
2: 4 In that day one shall *t* up a
Nah 1: 2 The LORD will *t* vengeance on
2: 9 *T* spoil of silver! Take spoil
2: 9 Take spoil of silver! *T* spoil
Hab 1:15 They *t* up all of them with a
2: 6 Will not all these *t* up a
Zeph 3:11 For then I will *t* away from
Hag 1: 8 that I may *t* pleasure in it and
2:23 I will *t* you, Zerubbabel My
Zech 2:12 And the LORD will *t* possession
3: 4 *T* away the filthy garments from
6:11 *T* the silver and gold, make an
9: 7 I will *t* away the blood from
11:15 *t* for yourself the implements
14:21 who sacrifices shall come and *t*
Mal 2: 2 And if you will not *t* it to
2: 2 Because you do not *t* it to
2: 3 And one will *t* you away with
2:15 Therefore *t* heed to your
2:16 Therefore *t* heed to your spirit,
Mt 1:20 do not be afraid to *t* to you
2:13 *t* the young Child and His
2:20 *t* the young Child and His
5:40 anyone wants to sue you and *t*
6: 1 *T* heed that you do not do your
9: 6 *t* up your bed, and go to your
10:38 And he who does not *t* his cross
11:12 and the violent *t* it by force.
11:29 *T* My yoke upon you and learn

15:26 It is not good to *t* the
16: 5 they had forgotten to *t* bread.
16: 6 *T* heed and beware of the leaven
16:24 and *t* up his cross, and follow
17:25 do the kings of the earth *t*
17:27 and *t* the fish that comes up
17:27 *t* that and give it to them for
18:10 *T* heed that you do not despise
18:16 *t* with you one or two more,
20:14 *T* what is yours and go your
22:13 *t* him away, and cast him into
24: 4 *T* heed that no one deceives you.
24:17 the housetop not go down to *t*
24:34 away till all these things *t*
25:28 Therefore *t* the talent from him,
25:38 did we see You a stranger and *t*
25:43 a stranger and you did not *t*
26: 4 and plotted to *t* Jesus by
26:26 '*T*, eat; this is My body."
26:52 for all who *t* the sword will
26:55 with swords and clubs to *t* Me?
Mk 2: 9 *t* up your bed and walk'?
2:11 *t* up your bed, and go to your
4:24 *T* heed what you hear. With the
6: 8 He commanded them to *t* nothing
7:27 for it is not good to *t* the
8:14 disciples had forgotten to *t*
8:15 *T* heed, beware of the leaven of
8:19 full of fragments did you *t* up?
8:20 full of fragments did you *t* up?
8:34 and *t* up his cross, and follow
10:21 *t* up the cross, and follow
12:19 his brother should *t* his wife
13: 5 *T* heed that no one deceives you.
13:15 nor enter to *t* anything out of
13:23 But *t* heed; see, I have told you
13:30 away till all these things *t*
13:33 *T* heed, watch and pray; for you
14: 1 sought how they might *t* Him by
14:22 '*T*, eat; this is My body."
14:36 *T* this cup away from Me;
14:48 with swords and clubs to *t* Me?
15:23 but He did not *t* it.
15:24 what every man should *t*.
15:36 us see if Elijah will come to *t*
16:18 they will *t* up serpents; and if
Lk 1:20 until the day these things *t*
1:25 to *t* away my reproach among
5:24 *t* up your bed, and go to your
8:18 Therefore *t* heed how you hear.
9: 3 *T* nothing for the journey,
9:23 and *t* up his cross daily,
10:35 *T* care of him; and whatever more
11:35 Therefore *t* heed that the light
12:15 *T* heed and beware of
12:19 *t* your ease; eat, drink, and
14: 9 then you begin with shame to *t*
16: 6 *T* your bill, and sit down
16: 7 *T* your bill, and write eighty.'
17: 3 *T* heed to yourselves. If your
17:31 let him not come down to *t* them
19:24 *T* the mina from him, and give
20:28 his brother should *t* his wife
21: 7 these things are about to *t*
21: 8 *T* heed that you not be deceived.
21:32 pass away till all things *t*
21:34 But *t* heed to yourselves, lest
22:17 *T* this and divide it among
22:36 let him *t* it, and likewise a
22:42 *t* this cup away from Me;
Jn 2: 8 and *t* it to the master of the
2:16 *T* these things away! Do not make
5: 8 *t* up your bed and walk."
5:11 *T* up your bed and walk.'"
5:12 *T* up your bed and walk'?"
6:15 they were about to come and *t*
7:30 Therefore they sought to *t* Him;
7:32 priests sent officers to *t* Him.
7:44 Now some of them wanted to *t*
10:17 I lay down My life that I may *t*
10:18 and I have power to *t* it again.
11:39 '*T* away the stone." Martha,
11:48 and the Romans will come and *t*
12: 6 and he used to *t* what was put
16:14 for He will *t* of what is Mine
16:15 I said that He will *t* of Mine
16:22 and your joy no one will *t* from
17:15 do not pray that You should *t*
18:31 You *t* Him and judge Him
19: 6 You *t* Him and crucify Him, for
19:38 asked Pilate that he might *t*
20:15 and I will *t* Him away."
Acts 1:20 Let another *t* his office.'
1:25 to *t* part in this ministry and
5:35 *t* heed to yourselves what you
7:33 *T* your sandals off your
15:14 visited the Gentiles to *t* out
15:37 Barnabas was determined to *t*
15:38 that they should not *t* with
20:13 there intending to *t* Paul on
20:28 Therefore *t* heed to yourselves
21:24 *T* them and be purified with
22:26 *T* care what you do, for this man
23:10 the soldiers to go down and *t*
23:17 *T* this young man to the
27:22 And now I urge you to *t* heart,
27:25 Therefore *t* heart, men, for I
27:33 Paul implored them all to *t*
27:34 Therefore I urge you to *t*
Rom 11:27 When I *t* away their
1 Cor 3:10 But let each one *t* heed how he
6:15 Shall I then *t* the members of
9: 5 Do we have no right to *t* along a
10:12 let him who thinks he stands *t*
11:24 '*T*, eat; this is My body
2 Cor 2:11 lest Satan should *t* advantage of
12:10 Therefore I *t* pleasure in
12:17 Did I *t* advantage of you by any
12:18 Did Titus *t* advantage of you?
Eph 6:13 Therefore *t* up the whole armor
6:17 And *t* the helmet of salvation,
Col 4:17 *T* heed to the ministry which you
1 Th 4: 6 that no one should *t* advantage
1 Tim 3: 5 how will he *t* care of the
4:16 *T* heed to yourself and to the
Heb 2: 6 son of man that You *t*
10: 4 of bulls and goats could *t*
10:11 which can never *t* away sins.
Jas 5:10 *t* the prophets, who spoke in
1 Pe 2:20 you *t* it patiently? But when
2:20 if you *t* it patiently, this is
1 Jn 3: 5 that He was manifested to *t*
Rev 1: 1 things which must shortly *t*
1:19 and the things which will *t*
3:11 that no one may *t* your crown.
4: 1 show you things which must *t*
5: 9 You are worthy to *t* the scroll,
6: 4 to the one who sat on it to *t*
10: 8 *t* the little book which is open
10: 9 *T* and eat it; and it will make
22: 6 the things which must shortly *t*
22:17 let him *t* the water of life
22:19 God shall *t* away his part from

TAKEN (286/274) TAKE

Gen 2:22 rib which the LORD God had *t*
2:23 Because she was *t* out of
3:19 For out of it you were *t*;
3:23 the ground from which he was *t*.
4:15 vengeance shall be *t* on him
12:15 And the woman was *t* to
12:19 I might have *t* her as my wife.
14:14 heard that his brother was *t*
18:27 am but dust and ashes have *t*
18:31 I have *t* it upon myself to
20: 3 of the woman whom you have *t*,
27:35 came with deceit and has *t*
27:36 he has *t* away my blessing!"
30:15 a small matter that you have *t*
30:23 God has *t* away my reproach."
31: 1 Jacob has *t* away all that was
31: 9 So God has *t* away the livestock
31:16 these riches which God has *t*
31:26 my daughters like captives *t*
31:34 Now Rachel had *t* the household
39: 1 Now Joseph had been *t* down to
39: 1 from the Ishmaelites who had *t*
Ex 14:11 have you *t* us away to die in
25:15 they shall not be *t* from it.
40:36 Whenever the cloud was *t* up from
40:37 But if the cloud was not *t* up,
40:37 till the day that it was *t* up.
Lev 4:10 as it was *t* from the bull of the
7:34 of the heave offering I have *t*
14:43 after he has *t* away the stones,
24: 8 being *t* from the children of
Num 3:12 I Myself have *t* the Levites
8:16 I have *t* them for Myself
8:18 I have *t* the Levites instead of
9:17 Whenever the cloud was *t* up from
9:21 when the cloud was *t* up in the
9:21 whenever the cloud was *t* up,
9:22 but when it was *t* up, they
10:11 that the cloud was *t* up from
10:17 Then the tabernacle was *t* down;
16:15 I have not *t* one donkey from
18: 6 I Myself have *t* your brethren
21:26 and had *t* all his land from his
31:26 up the plunder that was *t*—
31:32 which the men of war had *t*,
31:49 Your servants have *t* a count of
31:53 (The men of war had *t* spoil,
36: 3 their inheritance will be *t*
36: 3 so it will be *t* from the lot of
36: 4 so their inheritance will be *t*
Deut 4:20 But the LORD has *t* you and
24: 5 When a man has *t* a new wife, he
24: 5 to his wife whom he has *t*.
28:31 donkey shall be violently *t*
Josh 1:15 and they also have *t* possession
7:11 For they have even *t* some of
7:15 it shall be that he who is *t*
7:16 and the tribe of Judah was *t*.
7:17 man by man, and Zabdi was *t*.
7:18 of the tribe of Judah, was *t*.
8: 8 when you have *t* the city, that
8:21 saw that the ambush had *t* the
10: 1 heard how Joshua had *t* Ai and
Judg 14: 9 did not tell them that he had *t*
15: 6 because he has *t* his wife and
17: 2 shekels of silver that were *t*
18:24 You have *t* away my gods which I
1 Sam 7:14 which the Philistines had *t*
12: 3 His anointed: Whose ox have I *t*,
12: 3 taken, or whose donkey have I *t*,
12: 4 nor have you *t* anything from
14:24 before I have *t* vengeance on my
14:41 So Saul and Jonathan were *t*,
14:42 and me." So Jonathan was *t*.
21: 6 the showbread which had been *t*
21: 6 on the day when it was *t* away.
30: 2 and had *t* captive the women and
30: 3 and their daughters had been *t*
30: 5 had been *t* captive.
30:16 great spoil which they had *t*
30:19 or anything which they had *t*
2 Sam 12: 9 you have *t* his wife to be
12:10 and have *t* the wife of Uriah
12:27 and I have *t* the city's water
18:18 Absalom in his lifetime had *t*
23: 6 Because they cannot be *t* with
1 Ki 1:51 he has *t* hold of the horns of
7: 8 whom he had *t* as wife.
9:16 king of Egypt had gone up and *t*
16:18 Zimri saw that the city was *t*,
18: 4 that Obadiah had *t* one hundred
21:19 Have you murdered and also *t*
22:43 the high places were not *t*
2 Ki 2: 9 before I am *t* away from you?"
2:10 if you see me when I am *t*
2:16 the Spirit of the LORD has *t*
4:20 When he had *t* him and brought
6:22 you kill those whom you have *t*
12: 3 But the high places were not *t*
13:25 the cities which he had *t* out
14: 4 the high places were not *t*
18:10 king of Israel, Samaria was *t*.
18:22 and whose altars Hezekiah has *t*
24: 7 for the king of Babylon had *t*
1 Chr 22:14 Indeed I have *t* much trouble to
24: 6 one father's house *t* for
2 Chr 15: 8 from the cities which he had *t*
17: 2 which Asa his father had *t*.
20:33 the high places were not *t*
28:11 whom you have *t* captive from
28:18 and had *t* Beth Shemesh,
32:12 Has not the same Hezekiah *t* away
Ezra 1: 7 which Nebuchadnezzar had *t* from
5:14 which Nebuchadnezzar had *t* from
6: 5 be restored and *t* back to the
9: 2 For they have *t* some of their
10: 2 and have *t* pagan wives from the
10:10 have transgressed and have *t*
10:14 those in our cities who have *t*
10:17 all the men who had *t* pagan
10:18 sons of the priests who had *t*
10:44 All these had *t* pagan wives, and
Esth 2: 8 that Esther also was *t* to the
2:15 who had *t* her as his daughter,
2:16 So Esther was *t* to King
8: 2 which he had *t* from Haman,
Job 1:21 and the LORD has *t* away;
16:12 He also has *t* me by my neck,
19: 9 And *t* the crown from my head.
22: 6 For you have *t* pledges from
24:24 They are *t* out of the way like
27: 2 who has *t* away my justice,
28: 2 Iron is *t* from the earth,
34: 5 But God has *t* away my justice;
34:20 The mighty are *t* away without
35:15 Nor *t* much notice of folly,
Ps 44:10 And those who hate us have *t*
59:12 Let them even be *t* in their
83: 3 They have *t* crafty counsel
85: 3 You have *t* away all Your wrath;
119:53 Indignation has *t* hold of me
119:111 Your testimonies I have *t* as a
Prov 4:16 And their sleep is *t* away
6: 2 You are *t* by the words of your
7:20 He has *t* a bag of money with
Eccl 3:14 And nothing *t* from it.
9:12 Like fish *t* in a cruel net,
Song 5: 3 I have *t* off my robe; How can
Isa 6: 6 a live coal which he had *t*
6: 7 Your iniquity is *t* away,
8: 4 the spoil of Samaria will be *t*
8:15 and be broken, Be snared and *t*.
10:27 That his burden will be *t* away
10:29 They have *t* up lodging at
16:10 Gladness is *t* away, And joy
21: 3 Pangs have *t* hold of me, like
23: 8 Who has *t* this counsel against
33:20 tabernacle that will not be *t*
36: 7 and whose altars Hezekiah has *t*
38:12 *T* from me like a shepherd's
41: 9 You whom I have *t* from the
49:24 Shall the prey be *t* from the
49:25 of the mighty shall be *t* away,
51:22 I have *t* out of your hand The
52: 5 That My people are *t* away for
53: 8 He was *t* from prison and from
57: 1 Merciful men are *t* away,
57: 1 That the righteous is *t* away
57:11 Nor *t* it to your heart?
64: 6 Have *t* us away.
Jer 6:11 even the husband shall be *t*
6:24 Anguish has *t* hold of us,
8: 9 They are dismayed and *t*.
8:21 Astonishment has *t* hold of me.
12: 2 they have *t* root; They grow,
13:17 the LORD's flock has been *t*
16: 5 for I have *t* away My peace from
29:22 of them a curse shall be *t* up
34: 3 but shall surely be *t* and
38:23 but shall be *t* by the hand of
38:28 the day that Jerusalem was *t*.
38:28 was there when Jerusalem was *t*.
40: 1 when he had *t* him bound in
40:10 in your cities that you have *t*.
48: 1 Kirjathaim is shamed and *t*;
48: 7 treasures, You also shall be *t*.
48:33 Joy and gladness are *t* From
48:41 Kerioth is *t*, And the
48:46 For your sons have been *t*
49:20 of the LORD that He has *t*

49:24 Anguish and sorrows have *t* her
49:30 king of Babylon has *t* counsel
50: 2 conceal it—Say, 'Babylon is *t*,
50:43 Anguish has *t* hold of him,
50:45 of the LORD that He has *t*
51:31 of Babylon that his city is *t*
51:41 how Sheshach is *t*! Oh, how the
51:56 And her mighty men are *t*.
Ezek 15: 3 Is wood *t* from it to make any
16:17 You have also *t* your beautiful
17:20 and he shall be *t* in My snare.
18: 8 he has not exacted usury Nor *t*
18:13 If he has exacted usury Or *t*
21:23 remembrance, that they may be *t*.
21:24 you shall be *t* in hand.
22:25 they have *t* treasure and
33: 6 he is *t* away in his iniquity;
36: 3 and you are *t* up by the lips of
Dan 5: 2 his father Nebuchadnezzar had *t*
5: 3 gold vessels that had been *t*
6:23 So Daniel was *t* up out of the
7:12 they had their dominion *t* away,
8:11 the daily sacrifices were *t*
11:12 When he has *t* away the
12:11 the daily sacrifice is *t* away,
Hos 4: 3 the fish of the sea will be *t*
Joel 3: 5 Because you have *t* My silver
Am 2: 8 by every altar on clothes *t* in
3:12 the children of Israel be *t*
6:13 Have we not *t* Karnaim for
Mic 1:11 Its place to stand is *t* away
2: 9 their children You have *t*
Zeph 3:15 The LORD has *t* away your
Zech 14: 2 Jerusalem; The city shall be *t*,
Mt 9:15 when the bridegroom will be *t*
13:12 even what he has will be *t* away
16: 7 It is because we have *t* no
21:43 the kingdom of God will be *t*
24:40 one will be *t* and the other
24:41 one will be *t* and the other
25:29 even what he has will be *t*
27:59 When Joseph had *t* the body, he
Mk 2:20 when the bridegroom will be *t*
4:25 even what he has will be *t* away
6:41 And when He had *t* the five
9:36 And when He had *t* him in His
Lk 1: 1 Inasmuch as many have *t* in hand
5: 9 catch of fish which they had *t*;
5:35 when the bridegroom will be *t*
5:36 and also the piece that was *t*
8:18 what he seems to have will be *t*
9:17 the leftover fragments were *t*
10:42 which will not be *t* away from
11:52 to you lawyers! For you have *t*
17:34 the one will be *t* and the other
17:35 the one will be *t* and the other
17:36 the one will be *t* and the other
19: 8 and if I have *t* anything from
19:26 even what he has will be *t* away
Jn 2:20 It has *t* forty-six years to
13:12 *t* His garments, and sat down
19:31 and that they might be *t* away.
20: 1 saw that the stone had been *t*
20: 2 They have *t* away the Lord out of
20:13 Because they have *t* away my
Acts 1: 2 the day in which He was *t* up,
1: 9 He was *t* up, and a cloud
1:11 who was *t* up from you into
1:22 John to that day when He was *t*
2:23 you have *t* by lawless hands,
8:33 His justice was *t* away,
8:33 For His life is *t* from
10:16 And the object was *t* up into
17: 9 So when they had *t* security from
18:18 for he had *t* a vow.
20: 9 from the third story and was *t*
21: 6 When we had *t* our leave of one
21:23 We have four men who have *t* a
21:34 he commanded him to be *t* into
25:26 after the examination has *t*
27:17 When they had *t* it on board,
Rom 9: 6 not that the word of God has *t*
1 Cor 5: 2 has done this deed might be *t*
2 Cor 3:14 because the veil is *t* away in
3:16 the veil is *t* away.
Col 2:14 And He has *t* it out of the way,
1 Th 2:17 having been *t* away from you for
2 Th 2: 7 will do so until He is *t*
1 Tim 5: 9 under sixty years old be *t*
2 Tim 2:26 having been *t* captive by him to
Heb 5: 1 For every high priest *t* from
11: 5 By faith Enoch was *t* away so
11: 5 because God had *t* him";
11: 5 for before he was *t* he had this
Rev 5: 8 Now when He had *t* the scroll,
11:17 Because You have *t* Your great

TAKES (75/73) TAKE

Gen 27:46 if Jacob *t* a wife of the
Ex 20: 7 not hold him guiltless who *t*
21:10 If he *t* another wife, he shall
Lev 20:17 If a man *t* his sister, his
20:21 If a man *t* his brother's wife,
Num 6:21 according to the vow which he *t*,
30: 6 If indeed she *t* a husband,
Deut 5:11 not hold him guiltless who *t*
10:17 who shows no partiality nor *t*
22:13 If any man *t* a wife, and goes
24: 1 When a man *t* a wife and marries
24: 6 for he *t* one's living in
27:25 Cursed is the one who *t* a bribe
32:41 And My hand *t* hold on
Josh 7:14 the tribe which the LORD *t*
7:14 the family which the LORD *t*
7:14 the household which the LORD *t*
15:16 attacks Kirjath Sepher and *t*
Judg 1:12 attacks Kirjath Sepher and *t*
11:24 So whatever the LORD our God *t*
1 Sam 17:26 who kills this Philistine and *t*
1 Ki 8:31 and comes and *t* an oath before
14:10 as one *t* away refuse until it
20:11 boast like the one who *t* it
2 Chr 6:22 and comes and *t* an oath before
Job 9:12 If He *t* away, who can hinder
12:20 And *t* away the discernment of
12:24 He *t* away the understanding of
18: 9 The net *t* him by the heel,
21: 6 And trembling *t* hold of my
27: 8 If God *t* away his life?
38:14 It *t* on form like clay under a
40:24 Though he *t* it in his eyes,
Ps 5: 4 For You are not a God who *t*
137: 9 Happy the one who *t* and dashes
147:10 He *t* no pleasure in the legs
147:11 The LORD *t* pleasure in those
149: 4 For the LORD *t* pleasure in His
Prov 1:19 It *t* away the life of its
8: 2 She *t* her stand on the top of
16:32 rules his spirit than he who *t*
25:20 Like one who *t* away a garment
26:17 his own Is like one who *t* a
Eccl 2:23 even in the night his heart *t*
9: 2 He who *t* an oath as he who
Isa 3: 1 *T* away from Jerusalem and from
3: 6 When a man *t* hold of his
13:14 And as a sheep that no man *t*
44:14 And *t* the cypress and the oak;
51:18 Nor is there any who *t* her
57: 1 And no man *t* it to heart;
59: 8 Whoever *t* that way shall not
Jer 12:11 Because no one *t* it to heart.
Ezek 16:32 who *t* strangers instead of her
33: 4 if the sword comes and *t* him
33: 5 But he who *t* warning will save
33: 6 and the sword comes and *t* any
Hos 7: 1 A band of robbers *t* spoil
Am 3:12 As a shepherd *t* from the mouth
Mal 1:14 And *t* a vow, But sacrifices
Mt 12:45 Then he goes and *t* with him
Mk 4:15 Satan comes immediately and *t*
Lk 6:29 And from him who *t* away your
6:30 And from him who *t* away your
8:12 then the devil comes and *t* away
11:22 he *t* from him all his armor in
11:26 Then he goes and *t* with him
Jn 1:29 Behold! The Lamb of God who *t*
10:18 No one *t* it from Me, but I lay
15: 2 that does not bear fruit He *t*
1 Cor 11:21 each one *t* his own supper ahead
2 Cor 11:20 if one *t* from you, if one
Heb 5: 4 And no man *t* this honor to
10: 9 He *t* away the first that He
Rev 22:19 and if anyone *t* away from the

TAKING (24/24) TAKE

Deut 32:11 *t* them up, Carrying them on
Judg 4: 9 you in the journey you are *t*,
2 Chr 19: 7 nor *t* of bribes."
Job 5: 3 I have seen the foolish *t* root,
5: 5 *T* it even from the thorns,
Ps 119: 9 By *t* heed according to Your
Isa 27: 9 this is all the fruit of *t*
Jer 50:46 At the noise of the *t* of
Ezek 25:12 against the house of Judah by *t*
Hos 11: 3 *T* them by their arms;
Am 5:12 Afflicting the just and *t*
Mk 15:43 coming and *t* courage, went in
Lk 4: 5 *t* Him up on a high mountain,
16: 3 For my master is *t* the
Jn 11:13 that He was speaking about *t*
Rom 7: 8 *t* opportunity by the
7:11 *t* occasion by the commandment,
2 Cor 2:13 but *t* my leave of them,
11: 8 *t* wages from them to minister
Eph 6:16 *t* the shield of faith with
Phil 2: 7 *t* the form of a bondservant,
Col 2:18 *t* delight in false humility
2 Th 1: 8 in flaming fire *t* vengeance on
3 Jn 7 *t* nothing from the Gentiles.

TALE (KJV) See COUNT, QUOTA

TALEBEARER (6/6)

Lev 19:16 'You shall not go about as a *t*
Prov 11:13 A *t* reveals secrets, But he
18: 8 The words of a *t* are like
20:19 He who goes about as a *t*
26:20 And where there is no *t*,
26:22 The words of a *t* are like

TALENT (13/13) TALENTS

Ex 25:39 It shall be made of a *t* of pure
37:24 Of a *t* of pure gold he made it,
38:27 one *t* for each socket.
2 Sam 12:30 Its weight was a *t* of gold,
1 Ki 20:39 or else you shall pay a *t* of
2 Ki 5:22 Please give them a *t* of silver
23:33 talents of silver and a *t* of
1 Chr 20: 2 and found it to weigh a *t* of
2 Chr 36: 3 talents of silver and a *t* of
Mt 25:24 he who had received the one *t*
25:25 and went and hid your *t* in the
25:28 Therefore take the *t* from him,
Rev 16:21 about the weight of a *t*.

TALENTS (51/35) TALENT

Ex 38:24 was twenty-nine *t* and seven
38:25 was one hundred *t* and one
38:27 And from the hundred *t* of silver
38:27 sockets from the hundred *t*,
38:29 of bronze was seventy *t* and
1 Ki 9:14 king one hundred and twenty *t*
9:28 four hundred and twenty *t* of
10:10 king one hundred and twenty *t*
10:14 six hundred and sixty-six *t* of
16:24 Samaria from Shemer for two *t*
2 Ki 5: 5 and took with him ten *t* of
5:23 said, "Please, take two *t*.
5:23 and bound two *t* of silver in
15:19 Menahem gave Pul a thousand *t*
18:14 king of Judah three hundred *t*
18:14 talents of silver and thirty *t*
23:33 a tribute of one hundred *t* of
1 Chr 19: 6 of Ammon sent a thousand *t* of
22:14 LORD one hundred thousand *t*
22:14 of gold and one million *t* of
29: 4 'three thousand *t* of gold,
29: 4 and seven thousand *t* of refined
29: 7 house of God five thousand *t*
29: 7 ten thousand *t* of silver,
29: 7 eighteen thousand *t* of bronze,
29: 7 and one hundred thousand *t* of
2 Chr 3: 8 overlaid it with six hundred *t*
8:18 four hundred and fifty *t* of
9: 9 king one hundred and twenty *t*
9:13 six hundred and sixty-six *t* of
25: 6 from Israel for one hundred *t*
25: 9 we do about the hundred *t*
27: 5 him in that year one hundred *t*
36: 3 a tribute of one hundred *t* of
Ezra 7:22 up to one hundred *t* of silver,
8:26 hand six hundred and fifty *t*
8:26 weighing one hundred *t*,
8:26 one hundred *t* of gold,
Esth 3: 9 and I will pay ten thousand *t*
Mt 18:24 him who owed him ten thousand *t*.
25:15 "And to one he gave five *t*,
25:16 he who had received the five *t*
25:16 them, and made another five *t*.
25:20 So he who had received five *t*
25:20 came and brought five other *t*,
25:20 you delivered to me five *t*;
25:20 I have gained five more *t*
25:22 also who had received two *t*
25:22 you delivered to me two *t*;
25:22 I have gained two more *t*
25:28 give it to him who has ten *t*.

TALES (1/1)

Lk 24:11 seemed to them like idle *t*,

TALITHA (1/1)

Mk 5:41 the hand, and said to her, "*T*,

TALK (25/25)

Num 11:17 Then I will come down and *t* with
Deut 6: 7 and shall *t* of them when you
Judg 6:17 me a sign that it is You who *t*
1 Sam 2: 3 '*T* no more so very proudly;
2 Sam 20:18 They used to *t* in former times,
1 Chr 16: 9 *T* of all His wondrous works!
Job 11: 2 And should a man full of *t* be
11: 3 Should your empty *t* make men
13: 7 And *t* deceitfully for Him?
15: 3 he reason with unprofitable *t*,
35:13 God will not listen to empty *t*,
Ps 64: 5 They *t* of laying snares
69:26 And *t* of the grief of those
71:24 My tongue also shall *t* of Your
77:12 And *t* of Your deeds.
105: 2 *T* of all His wondrous works!
145:11 And *t* of Your power,
Prov 24: 2 And their lips *t* of
Eccl 10:13 And the end of his *t* is
Jer 12: 1 Yet let me *t* with You about
Ezek 3:22 and there I shall *t* with you."
Dan 10:17 can this servant of my lord *t*
Mt 22:15 might entangle Him in His *t*.
Jn 14:30 I will no longer *t* much with
1 Tim 1: 6 have turned aside to idle *t*,

TALKED (41/41)

Gen 4: 8 Now Cain *t* with Abel his
17: 3 and God *t* with him, saying:
35:13 him in the place where He *t*
35:14 pillar in the place where He *t*
42:24 and *t* with them. And he took
43:19 they *t* with him at the door of
45:15 and after that his brothers *t*
Ex 20:22 You have seen that I have *t* with
33: 9 and the LORD *t* with Moses.
34:29 of his face shone while he *t*
34:31 and Moses *t* with them.
Deut 5: 4 The LORD *t* with you face to
Judg 14: 7 Then he went down and *t* with the
1 Sam 14:19 while Saul *t* to the priest,
17:23 Then as he *t* with them, there
2 Ki 2:11 as they continued on and *t*,

T

8: 4 Then the king *t* with Gehazi, the
2 Chr 25:16 as he *t* with him, that the
Jer 38:25 the princes hear that I have *t*
Dan 9:22 and *t* with me, and said, "O
Zech 1: 9 So the angel who *t* with me
1:13 LORD answered the angel who *t*
1:19 And I said to the angel who *t*
2: 3 And there was the angel who *t*
4: 1 Now the angel who *t* with me came
4: 4 and spoke to the angel who *t*
4: 5 Then the angel who *t* with me
5: 5 Then the angel who *t* with me
5:10 So I said to the angel who *t*
6: 4 and said to the angel who *t*
Mk 6:50 But immediately He *t* with them
Lk 9:30 two men *t* with Him, who were
24:14 And they *t* together of all these
24:32 burn within us while He *t* with
Jn 4:27 and they marveled that He *t*
Acts 10:27 And as he *t* with him, he went in
20:11 and *t* a long while, even till
26:31 they *t* among themselves,
Rev 17: 1 had the seven bowls came and *t*
21: 9 last plagues came to me and *t*
21:15 And he who *t* with me had a gold

TALKERS (2/2)

Ezek 36: 3 are taken up by the lips of *t*
Titus 1:10 both idle *t* and deceivers,

TALKING (13/13)

Gen 17:22 Then He finished *t* with him, and
1 Ki 1:14 while you are still *t* there
1:22 while she was still *t* with the
2 Ki 6:33 And while he was still *t* with
Esth 6:14 While they were still *t* with
Job 29: 9 The princes refrained from *t*,
Ezek 33:30 children of your people are *t*
Mt 12:46 While He was still *t* to the
17: 3 appeared to them, *t* with Him.
Mk 9: 4 and they were *t* with Jesus.
Jn 4:27 Why are You *t* with her?"
9:37 seen Him and it is He who is *t*
Eph 5: 4 filthiness, nor foolish *t*,

TALKS (1/1)

Ps 37:30 And his tongue *t* of justice.

TALL (8/8) TALLER

Deut 2:10 as great and numerous and *t* as
2:21 as great and numerous and *t* as
9: 2 "a people great and *t*,
2 Ki 19:23 I will cut down its *t* cedars
1 Chr 11:23 of GREAT height, five cubits *t*.
Isa 18: 2 to a nation *t* and smooth of
18: 7 of hosts From a people *t* and
37:24 I will cut down its *t* cedars

TALLER (3/3) TALL

Deut 1:28 The people are greater and *t*
1 Sam 9: 2 his shoulders upward he was *t*
10:23 he was *t* than any of the people

TALMAI (6/6)

Num 13:22 Hebron; Ahiman, Sheshai, and *T*,
Josh 15:14 there: Sheshai, Ahiman, and *T*,
Judg 1:10 killed Sheshai, Ahiman, and *T*.
2 Sam 3: 3 of Maacah, the daughter of *T*,
13:37 But Absalom fled and went to *T*
1 Chr 3: 2 of Maacah, the daughter of *T*,

TALMON (5/5)

1 Chr 9:17 were Shallum, Akkub, *T*,
Ezra 2:42 the sons of Ater, the sons of *T*,
Neh 7:45 the sons of Ater, the sons of *T*,
11:19 the gatekeepers, Akkub, *T*,
12:25 Obadiah, Meshullam, *T*,

TAMAH (2/2)

Ezra 2:53 sons of Sisera, the sons of *T*,
Neh 7:55 sons of Sisera, the sons of *T*,

TAMAR (28/26)

Gen 38: 6 firstborn, and her name was *T*.
38:11 Then Judah said to *T* his
38:11 And *T* went and dwelt in her
38:13 And it was told *T*,
38:24 *T* your daughter-in-law has
Ruth 4:12 whom *T* bore to Judah, because
2 Sam 13: 1 sister, whose name was *T*;
13: 2 so distressed over his sister *T*
13: 4 Amnon said to him, "I love *T*,
13: 5 Please let my sister *T* come and
13: 6 Please let *T* my sister come and
13: 7 And David sent home to *T*,
13: 8 So *T* went to her brother Amnon's
13:10 Then Amnon said to *T*,
13:10 And *T* took the cakes which
13:19 Then *T* put ashes on her head,
13:20 So *T* remained desolate in her
13:22 he had forced his sister *T*.
13:32 day that he forced his sister *T*.
14:27 one daughter whose name was *T*.
1 Chr 2: 4 And *T*, his daughter-in-law,
3: 9 and *T* their sister.
Ezek 47:19 shall be from *T* to the waters
48:28 the border shall be from *T* to
Mt 1: 3 begot Perez and Zerah by *T*,

TAMARISK (4/4)

Gen 21:33 Then Abraham planted a *t* tree
1 Sam 22: 6 was staying in Gibeah under a *t*
31:13 and buried them under the *t*
1 Chr 10:12 buried their bones under the *t*

TAMBOURINE (4/4)

1 Sam 10: 5 with a stringed instrument, a *t*,
Job 21:12 They sing to the *t* and harp,
Isa 5:12 The *t* and flute, And wine are
24: 8 The mirth of the *t* ceases,

TAMBOURINES (5/5)

1 Sam 18: 6 to meet King Saul, with *t*,
2 Sam 6: 5 on stringed instruments, on *t*,
1 Chr 13: 8 on stringed instruments, on *t*,
Isa 30:32 It will be with *t* and harps;
Jer 31: 4 again be adorned with your *t*,

TAME (2/2)

Mk 5: 4 neither could anyone *t* him.
Jas 3: 8 But no man can *t* the tongue.

TAMED (2/1)

Jas 3: 7 is *t* and has been tamed by
3: 7 is tamed and has been *t* by

TAMMUZ (1/1)

Ezek 8:14 sitting there weeping for *T*.

TANACH (1/1)

Josh 21:25 *T* with its common-land and Gath

TANGLED (1/1)

Nah 1:10 For while *t* like thorns,

TANHUMETH (2/2)

2 Ki 25:23 Seraiah the son of *T* the
Jer 40: 8 of Kareah, Seraiah the son of *T*,

TANNED (1/1)

Song 1: 6 Because the sun has *t* me.

TANNER (3/3)

Acts 9:43 days in Joppa with Simon, a *t*.
10: 6 "He is lodging with Simon, a *t*,
10:32 in the house of Simon, a *t*,

TAPESTRY (3/3)

Ex 35:35 and the designer and the *t*
Prov 7:16 I have spread my bed with *t*,
31:22 She makes *t* for herself;

TAPHATH (1/1)

1 Ki 4:11 he had *T* the daughter of

TAPPUAH (8/7)

Josh 12:17 the king of *T*, one;
15:34 Zanoah, En Gannim, *T*,
16: 8 The border went out from *T*
17: 8 Manasseh had the land of *T*,
17: 8 but *T* on the border of Manasseh
1 Chr 2:43 sons of Hebron were Korah, *T*,

TARAH (KJV) See TERAH

TARALAH (1/1)

Josh 18:27 Rekem, Irpeel, *T*,

TARE (KJV) See CONVULSED, TORE

TAREA (1/1)

1 Chr 8:35 Micah were Pithon, Melech, *T*,

TARES (8/8)

Mt 13:25 his enemy came and sowed *t*
13:26 then the *t* also appeared.
13:27 How then does it have *t*?'
13:29 lest while you gather up the *t*
13:30 First gather together the *t* and
13:36 to us the parable of the *t* of
13:38 but the *t* are the sons of the
13:40 Therefore as the *t* are gathered

TARGET (4/4)

1 Sam 20:20 as though I shot at a *t*;
Job 7:20 Why have You set me as Your *t*,
16:12 He has set me up for His *t*,
Lam 3:12 His bow And set me up as a *t*

TARPELITES (1/1)

Ezra 4: 9 the Apharsathchites, the *T*,

TARRIED, TARRIEST, TARRIETH, TARRYING (KJV) See CONTINUED, DELAY, DELAYED, REMAINS, STAYED, TARRY, WAITED

TARRIES (2/2) TARRY

Judg 5:28 Why *t* the clatter of his
Hab 2: 3 it will not lie. Though it *t*,

TARRY (7/7) TARRIES

Gen 45: 9 come down to me, do not *t*.
Jer 14: 8 traveler who turns aside to *t*
Mic 5: 7 That *t* for no man Nor wait
Hab 2: 3 surely come, It will not *t*.
Lk 24:49 but *t* in the city of Jerusalem
1 Cor 16: 8 But I will *t* in Ephesus until
Heb 10:37 will come and will not *t*.

TARSHISH (22/20) THARSHISH

Gen 10: 4 sons of Javan were Elishah, *T*,
2 Chr 9:21 For the king's ships went to *T*
20:36 him to make ships to go to *T*,
20:37 they were not able to go to *T*.
Esth 1:14 Carshena, Shethar, Admatha, *T*,
Ps 48: 7 when You break the ships of *T*
72:10 The kings of *T* and of the isles
Isa 2:16 Upon all the ships of *T*,
23: 1 you ships of *T*! For it is laid
23: 6 Cross over to *T*;
23:10 the River, O daughter of *T*;
23:14 you ships of *T*! For your
60: 9 And the ships of *T* will come
66:19 to *T* and Pul and Lud, who draw
Jer 10: 9 plates; It is brought from *T*,
Ezek 27:12 *T* was your merchant because of
27:25 The ships of *T* were carriers of
38:13 Dedan, the merchants of *T*,
Jon 1: 3 But Jonah arose to flee to *T*
1: 3 and found a ship going to *T*;
1: 3 to go with them to *T* from the
4: 2 I fled previously to *T*;

TARSHISHAH (1/1)

1 Chr 1: 7 sons of Javan were Elishah, *T*,

TARSUS (5/5)

Acts 9:11 Judas for one called Saul of *T*,
9:30 Caesarea and sent him out to *T*.
11:25 Then Barnabas departed for *T* to
21:39 Paul said, "I am a Jew from *T*,
22: 3 born in *T* of Cilicia,

TARTAK (1/1)

2 Ki 17:31 the Avites made Nibhaz and *T*;

TARTAN (2/2)

2 Ki 18:17 the king of Assyria sent the *T*,
Isa 20: 1 In the year that *T* came to

TASK (6/6)

Ex 5:14 have you not fulfilled your *t*
Num 4:19 them to his service and his *t*.
4:49 service and according to his *t*;
Neh 13:13 and their *t* was to distribute
Eccl 1:13 this burdensome *t* God has given
3:10 I have seen the God-given *t* with

TASKMASTERS (6/6) MASTERS

Ex 1:11 Therefore they set *t* over them
3: 7 their cry because of their *t*,
5: 6 day Pharaoh commanded the *t* of
5:10 And the *t* of the people and
5:13 And the *t* forced them to hurry,
5:14 whom Pharaoh's *t* had set over

TASKS (2/1)

Num 4:27 all their *t* and all their
4:27 appoint to them all their *t* as

TASSEL (1/1)

Num 15:39 "And you shall have the *t*,

TASSELS (3/2)

Num 15:38 Tell them to make *t* on the
15:38 to put a blue thread in the *t*
Deut 22:12 You shall make *t* on the four

TASTE (21/20) TASTED

Ex 16:31 and the *t* of it was like
Num 11: 8 and its *t* was like the taste of
11: 8 taste was like the *t* of pastry
2 Sam 3:35 if I *t* bread or anything else
19:35 Can your servant *t* what I eat
Job 6: 6 Or is there any *t* in the

6:30 Cannot my *t* discern the
12:11 ear test words And the mouth *t*
Ps 34: 8 *t* and see that the LORD is
119:103 sweet are Your words to my *t*,
Prov 24:13 which is sweet to your *t*;
Song 2: 3 his fruit was sweet to my *t*.
Jer 48:11 Therefore his *t* remained in
Jon 3: 7 *t* anything; do not let them
Mt 16:28 standing here who shall not *t*
Mk 9: 1 standing here who will not *t*
Lk 9:27 standing here who shall not *t*
14:24 men who were invited shall *t*
Jn 8:52 keeps My word he shall never *t*
Col 2:21 "Do not touch, do not *t*,
Heb 2: 9 might *t* death for everyone.

TASTED (9/9) TASTE

1 Sam 14:24 So none of the people *t* food.
14:29 has brightened because I *t* a
14:43 I only *t* a little honey with the
Dan 5: 2 While he *t* the wine, Belshazzar
Mt 27:34 But when He had *t* it, He would
Jn 2: 9 the master of the feast had *t*
Heb 6: 4 and have *t* the heavenly gift,
6: 5 and have *t* the good word of God
1 Pe 2: 3 if indeed you have *t* that the

TASTES (1/1)

Job 34: 3 tests words As the palate *t*

TASTY (2/2)

Prov 18: 8 of a talebearer are like *t*
26:22 of a talebearer are like *t*

TATTENAI (4/4)

Ezra 5: 3 At the same time *T* the governor
5: 6 is a copy of the letter that *T*
6: 6 Now therefore, *T*,
6:13 *T*, governor of the region

TATTLERS (KJV) See GOSSIPS

TATTOO (1/1)

Lev 19:28 nor *t* any marks on you: I am

TAUGHT (74/72) TEACH

Deut 4: 5 Surely I have *t* you statutes and
31:22 and *t* it to the children of
Judg 3: 2 children of Israel might be *t*
8:16 and with them he *t* the men of
2 Ki 17:28 and *t* them how they should fear
2 Chr 17: 9 So they *t* in Judah, and had the
17: 9 all the cities of Judah and *t*
30:22 to all the Levites who *t* the
35: 3 he said to the Levites who *t*
Neh 8: 9 and the Levites who *t* the
Ps 71:17 You have *t* me from my youth;
119:102 For You Yourself have *t* me.
Prov 4: 4 He also *t* me, and said to me:
4:11 I have *t* you in the way of
31: 1 utterance which his mother *t*
Eccl 12: 9 he still *t* the people
Isa 29:13 And their fear toward Me is *t*
40:13 Or as His counselor has *t*
40:14 And *t* Him in the path of
40:14 Who *t* Him knowledge,
54:13 your children shall be *t* by
Jer 2:33 Therefore you have also *t* The
9: 5 They have *t* their tongue to
9:14 which their fathers *t* them,"
12:16 as they *t* My people to swear
13:21 For you have *t* them To be
28:16 because you have *t* rebellion
29:32 because he has *t* rebellion
32:33 though I *t* them, rising up
Ezek 23:48 that all women may be *t* not to
Hos 11: 3 'I *t* Ephraim to walk,
Zech 13: 5 for a man *t* me to keep cattle
Mt 5: 2 Then He opened His mouth and *t*
7:29 for He *t* them as one having
13:54 He *t* them in their synagogue,
Mk 1:21 He entered the synagogue and *t*.
1:22 for He *t* them as one having
2:13 came to Him, and He *t* them.
4: 2 Then He *t* them many things by
6:30 had done and what they had *t*.
9:31 For He *t* His disciples and said
10: 1 He *t* them again.
11:17 Then He *t*, saying to them,
12:35 while He *t* in the temple, "How
Lk 4:15 And He *t* in their synagogues,
5: 3 And He sat down and *t* the
6: 6 He entered the synagogue and *t*.
11: 1 as John also *t* his disciples."
13:26 and You *t* in our streets.'
20: 1 as He *t* the people in the
Jn 6:45 And they shall all be *t* by
6:59 said in the synagogue as He *t*
7:14 went up into the temple and *t*.
7:28 as He *t* in the temple, saying,
8: 2 and He sat down and *t* them.
8:20 as He *t* in the temple;
8:28 but as My Father *t* Me, I speak
18:20 I always *t* in synagogues and in
Acts 4: 2 greatly disturbed that they *t*
5:21 early in the morning and *t*.
11:26 with the church and *t* a great
15: 1 came down from Judea and *t* the
18:25 he spoke and *t* accurately the
20:20 and *t* you publicly and from
22: 3 *t* according to the strictness
Gal 1:12 nor was I *t* it, but it came
6: 6 Let him who is *t* the word share
Eph 4:21 have heard Him and have been *t*
Col 2: 7 the faith, as you have been *t*,
1 Th 4: 9 for you yourselves are *t* by God
2 Th 2:15 the traditions which you were *t*,
Titus 1: 9 faithful word as he has been *t*,
1 Jn 2:27 and just as it has *t* you,
Rev 2:14 who *t* Balak to put a stumbling

TAUNT (2/2)

Jer 24: 9 a *t* and a curse, in all places
Ezek 5:15 'So it shall be a reproach, a *t*,

TAUNTING (4/4)

Hab 2: 6 And a *t* riddle against him,

TAUNTING SONG (3/3)

Job 30: 9 "And now I am their *t*;
Lam 3:14 Their *t* all the day.
3:63 their rising up; I am their *t*.

TAUNTS (1/1)

Ezek 36:15 Nor will I let you hear the *t* of

TAX (33/30) TAXES

Ezra 4:13 completed, they will not pay *t*,
4:20 region beyond the River; and *t*,
7:24 shall not be lawful to impose *t*,
Neh 5: 4 money for the king's *t* on our
Mt 5:46 Do not even the *t* collectors do
5:47 Do not even the *t* collectors do
9: 9 named Matthew sitting at the *t*
9:10 many *t* collectors and sinners
9:11 does your Teacher eat with *t*
10: 3 Thomas and Matthew the *t*
11:19 a friend of *t* collectors and
17:24 who received the temple *t*
17:24 Teacher not pay the temple *t*?
18:17 to you like a heathen and a *t*
21:31 I say to you that *t* collectors
21:32 but *t* collectors and harlots
22:19 Show Me the *t* money." So they
Mk 2:14 of Alphaeus sitting at the *t*
2:15 that many *t* collectors and
2:16 saw Him eating with the *t*
2:16 that He eats and drinks with *t*
Lk 3:12 Then *t* collectors also came to
5:27 things He went out and saw a *t*
5:27 sitting at the *t* office.
5:29 there were a great number of *t*
5:30 do You eat and drink with *t*
7:29 even the *t* collectors justified
7:34 a friend of *t* collectors and
15: 1 Then all the *t* collectors and
18:10 a Pharisee and the other a *t*
18:11 or even as this *t* collector.
18:13 And the *t* collector, standing
19: 2 Zacchaeus who was a chief *t*

TAXED (1/1)

2 Ki 23:35 but he *t* the land to give money

TAXES (12/11) TAX

1 Sam 17:25 house exemption from *t* in
Ezra 6: 8 at the king's expense from *t*
Dan 11:20 in his place one who imposes *t*
Am 5:11 down the poor And take grain *t*
Mt 17:25 of the earth take customs or *t*,
22:17 Is it lawful to pay *t* to
Mk 12:14 Is it lawful to pay *t* to
Lk 20:22 Is it lawful for us to pay *t* to
23: 2 and forbidding to pay *t* to
Rom 13: 6 because of this you also pay *t*,
13: 7 *t* to whom taxes are due,
13: 7 taxes to whom *t* are due,

TAXING (KJV) See CENSUS

TEACH (106/104) TAUGHT, TEACHER, TEACHES, TEACHING

Ex 4:12 I will be with your mouth and *t*
4:15 and I will *t* you what you shall
18:20 And you shall *t* them the
24:12 that you may *t* them."
35:34 in his heart the ability to *t*,
Lev 10:11 and that you may *t* the children
14:57 to *t* when it is unclean and
Deut 4: 1 and the judgments which I *t*
4: 9 And *t* them to your children and
4:10 and that they may *t* their
4:14 commanded me at that time to *t*
5:31 the judgments which you shall *t*
6: 1 your God has commanded to *t*
6: 7 You shall *t* them diligently to
11:19 You shall *t* them to your
20:18 lest they *t* you to do according
24: 8 shall *t* you; just as I
31:19 and *t* it to the children of
33:10 They shall *t* Jacob Your
Judg 13: 8 sent come to us again and *t* us
1 Sam 12:23 but I will *t* you the good and
2 Sam 1:18 and he told them to *t* the
1 Ki 8:36 that You may *t* them the good
2 Ki 17:27 and let him *t* them the rituals
2 Chr 6:27 that You may *t* them the good
17: 7 to *t* in the cities of Judah.
Ezra 7:10 and to *t* statutes and
7:25 and *t* those who do not know
Job 6:24 *T* me, and I will hold my
8:10 Will they not *t* you and tell
12: 7 and they will *t* you;
12: 8 and it will *t* you;
21:22 Can anyone *t* God knowledge,
27:11 I will *t* you about the hand of
32: 7 multitude of years should *t*
33:33 and I will *t* you wisdom."
34:32 *T* me what I do not see
37:19 *T* us what we should say to Him,
Ps 25: 4 *T* me Your paths.
25: 5 Lead me in Your truth and *t* me,
25:12 Him shall He *t* in the way He
27:11 *T* me Your way, O LORD, And
32: 8 I will instruct you and *t* you
34:11 I will *t* you the fear of the
45: 4 And Your right hand shall *t*
51:13 Then I will *t* transgressors
86:11 *T* me Your way, O LORD
90:12 So *t* us to number our days,
94:12 And *t* out of Your law,
105:22 And *t* his elders wisdom.
119:12 O LORD! *T* me Your statutes!
119:26 *T* me Your statutes.
119:33 *T* me, O LORD, the way of Your
119:64 *T* me Your statutes.
119:66 *T* me good judgment and
119:68 *T* me Your statutes.
119:108 And *t* me Your judgments.
119:124 And *t* me Your statutes.
119:135 And *t* me Your statutes.
119:171 For You *t* me Your statutes.
132:12 My testimony which I shall *t*
143:10 *T* me to do Your will, For You
Prov 9: 9 *T* a just man, and he will
Isa 2: 3 He will *t* us His ways, And we
28: 9 Whom will he *t* knowledge?
Jer 9:20 *T* your daughters wailing,
31:34 No more shall every man *t* his
Ezek 44:23 And they shall *t* My people the
Dan 1: 4 and whom they might *t* the
Mic 3:11 Her priests *t* for pay,
4: 2 He will *t* us His ways,
Hab 2:19 Arise! It shall *t*!' Behold, it
Mt 11: 1 He departed from there to *t*
22:16 and *t* the way of God in truth;
Mk 4: 1 And again He began to *t* by the
6: 2 He began to *t* in the synagogue.
6:34 So He began to *t* them many
8:31 And He began to *t* them that the
12:14 but *t* the way of God in truth.
Lk 11: 1 *t* us to pray, as John also
12:12 For the Holy Spirit will *t* you
20:21 we know that You say and *t*
20:21 but *t* the way of God in truth:
Jn 7:35 among the Greeks and *t* the
14:26 He will *t* you all things,
Acts 1: 1 Jesus began both to do and *t*,
4:18 them not to speak at all nor *t*
5:28 strictly command you not to *t*
16:21 and they *t* customs which are not
21:21 informed about you that you *t*
Rom 2:21 who *t* another, do you not teach
2:21 do you not *t* yourself? You who
1 Cor 4:17 as I *t* everywhere in every
11:14 Does not even nature itself *t*
14:19 that I may *t* others also,
1 Tim 1: 3 may charge some that they *t* no
2:12 I do not permit a woman to *t*
3: 2 behavior, hospitable, able to *t*;
4:11 These things command and *t*.
6: 2 *T* and exhort these things.
2 Tim 2: 2 men who will be able to *t*
2:24 but be gentle to all, able to *t*,
Heb 5:12 you need someone to *t* you
8:11 None of them shall *t* his
1 Jn 2:27 you do not need that anyone *t*
Rev 2:20 to *t* and seduce My servants to

TEACHER (55/54) TEACH, TEACHERS

1 Chr 25: 8 the *t* with the student.
Hab 2:18 a *t* of lies, That the maker of
Mt 8:19 came and said to Him, "*T*,
9:11 Why does your *T* eat with tax
10:24 disciple is not above his *t*,
10:25 disciple that he be like his *t*,
12:38 Pharisees answered, saying, "*T*,
17:24 Does your *T* not pay the temple
19:16 came and said to Him, "Good *T*,
22:16 with the Herodians, saying, "*T*,
22:24 saying: "*T*, Moses said that
22:36 '*T*, which is the great
23: 8 'Rabbi'; for One is your *T*,
23:10 teachers; for One is your *T*,
26:18 The *T* says, "My time is at
Mk 4:38 awoke Him and said to Him, "*T*,
5:35 Why trouble the *T* any
9:17 crowd answered and said, "*T*,
9:38 John answered Him, saying, "*T*,
10:17 Him, and asked Him, "Good *T*,
10:20 answered and said to Him, "*T*,
10:35 came to Him, saying, "*T*,

T

12:14 had come, they said to Him, "*T*,
12:19 '*T*, Moses wrote to us
12:32 said to Him, "Well said, *T*.
13: 1 His disciples said to Him, "*T*,
14:14 The *T* says, "Where is the guest
Lk 3:12 baptized, and said to him, "*T*,
6:40 "A disciple is not above his *t*,
6:40 trained will be like his *t*.
7:40 say to you." So he said, "*T*,
8:49 is dead. Do not trouble the *T*.
9:38 cried out, saying, "*T*,
10:25 up and tested Him, saying, "*T*,
11:45 answered and said to Him, "*T*,
12:13 from the crowd said to Him, "*T*,
18:18 asked Him, saying, "Good *T*,
19:39 to Him from the crowd, "*T*,
20:21 they asked Him, saying, "*T*,
20:28 saying: "*T*, Moses wrote to us
20:39 scribes answered and said, "*T*,
21: 7 So they asked Him, saying, "*T*,
22:11 The *T* says to you, "Where is
Jn 1:38 is to say, when translated, *T*),
3: 2 we know that You are a *t* come
3:10 Are you the *t* of Israel, and do
8: 4 they said to Him, "*T*,
11:28 The *T* has come and is calling
13:13 You call me *T* and Lord, and you
13:14 "If I then, your Lord and *T*,
20:16 (which is to say, *T*).
Acts 5:34 a *t* of the law held in respect
Rom 2:20 a *t* of babes, having the form
1 Tim 2: 7 a *t* of the Gentiles in faith and
2 Tim 1:11 and a *t* of the Gentiles.

TEACHERS (17/16) TEACHER

Ps 119:99 understanding than all my *t*,
Prov 5:13 not obeyed the voice of my *t*,
Isa 30:20 Yet your *t* will not be moved
30:20 But your eyes shall see your *t*.
Mt 23:10 "And do not be called *t*;
Lk 2:46 sitting in the midst of the *t*,
5:17 there were Pharisees and *t* of
Acts 13: 1 were certain prophets and *t*:
1 Cor 12:28 second prophets, third *t*,
12:29 Are all prophets? Are all *t*?
Eph 4:11 and some pastors and *t*,
1 Tim 1: 7 desiring to be *t* of the law,
2 Tim 4: 3 will heap up for themselves *t*;
Titus 2: 3 *t* of good things—
Heb 5:12 by this time you ought to be *t*,
Jas 3: 1 let not many of you become *t*,
2 Pe 2: 1 even as there will be false *t*

TEACHES (21/19) TEACH

2 Sam 22:35 He *t* my hands to make war,
Job 15: 5 For your iniquity *t* your mouth,
35:11 Who *t* us more than the beasts
36:22 Who *t* like Him?
Ps 18:34 He *t* my hands to make war,
25: 8 Therefore He *t* sinners in the
25: 9 And the humble He *t* His way.
94:10 He who *t* man knowledge?
Prov 16:23 The heart of the wise *t* his
Isa 9:15 The prophet who *t* lies, he is
28:26 His God *t* him.
48:17 Who *t* you to profit, Who
Mt 5:19 and *t* men so, shall be called
5:19 but whoever does and *t* them,
Acts 21:28 help! This is the man who *t* all
Rom 12: 7 in our ministering; he who *t*,
1 Cor 2:13 in words which man's wisdom *t*
2:13 but which the Holy Spirit *t*,
Gal 6: 6 all good things with him who *t*.
1 Tim 6: 3 If anyone *t* otherwise and does
1 Jn 2:27 but as the same anointing *t* you

TEACHING (42/42) TEACH

Deut 32: 2 Let my *t* drop as the rain,
2 Chr 15: 3 without a *t* priest, and without
Ps 60: A Michtam of David. For *t*.
Jer 32:33 rising up early and *t* them,
Mt 4:23 *t* in their synagogues,
7:28 people were astonished at His *t*,
9:35 *t* in their synagogues,
15: 9 *T* as doctrines the
21:23 confronted Him as He was *t*,
22:33 they were astonished at His *t*.
26:55 *t* in the temple, and you did
28:20 *t* them to observe all things
Mk 1:22 they were astonished at His *t*,
4: 2 and said to them in His *t*:
6: 6 the villages in a circuit, *t*.
7: 7 *T* as doctrines the
11:18 people were astonished at His *t*.
12:38 Then He said to them in His *t*,
14:49 daily with you in the temple *t*,
Lk 4:31 and was *t* them on the Sabbaths.
4:32 they were astonished at His *t*,
5:17 on a certain day, as He was *t*,
13:10 Now He was *t* in one of the
13:22 the cities and villages, *t*,
19:47 And He was *t* daily in the
21:37 And in the daytime He was *t* in
23: 5 *t* throughout all Judea,
Jn 9:34 and are you *t* us?" And they
Acts 5:25 standing in the temple and *t*
5:42 they did not cease *t* and
13:12 being astonished at the *t* of
15:35 *t* and preaching the word of the
18:11 *t* the word of God among them.
28:31 the kingdom of God and *t* the
Rom 12: 7 he who teaches, in *t*;
1 Cor 14: 6 by prophesying, or by *t*?
14:26 of you has a psalm, has a *t*,
Col 1:28 warning every man and *t* every
3:16 *t* and admonishing one another
2 Tim 4: 2 with all longsuffering and *t*.
Titus 1:11 *t* things which they ought not,
2:12 *t* us that, denying ungodliness

TEAR (35/34) TEARS, TORE, TORN

Ex 28:32 of mail, so that it does not *t*.
39:23 opening, so that it would not *t*.
Lev 10: 6 not uncover your heads nor *t*
13:56 then he shall *t* it out of the
21:10 not uncover his head nor *t* his
Judg 2: 2 you shall *t* down their altars.'
6:25 and *t* down the altar of Baal
8: 7 then I will *t* your flesh with
8: 9 I will *t* down this tower!"
2 Sam 3:31 *T* your clothes, gird yourselves
1 Ki 11:11 I will surely *t* the kingdom
11:12 I will *t* it out of the hand of
11:13 However I will not *t* away the
11:31 I will *t* the kingdom out of the
Job 18: 4 You who *t* yourself in anger,
Ps 7: 2 Lest they *t* me like a lion,
17:12 As a lion is eager to *t* his
50:22 Lest I *t* you in pieces,
Eccl 3: 7 A time to *t*, And a time to sew;
Jer 36:24 nor did they *t* their garments,
Ezek 13:11 and a stormy wind shall *t* it
13:20 I will *t* them from your arms,
13:21 I will also *t* off your veils and
23:34 And *t* at your own breasts;
Hos 5:14 will *t* them and go away;
13: 8 I will *t* open their rib cage,
13: 8 The wild beast shall *t* them.
Zech 11:16 eat the flesh of the fat and *t*
Mt 7: 6 and turn and *t* you in pieces.
9:16 and the *t* is made worse.
Mk 2:21 and the *t* is made worse.
Lk 5:36 otherwise the new makes a *t*,
Jn 19:24 Let us not *t* it, but cast lots
Rev 7:17 And God will wipe away every *t*
21: 4 God will wipe away every *t*

TEARING (2/2)

Ezek 22:25 midst is like a roaring lion *t*
22:27 in her midst are like wolves *t*

TEARS (37/36) TEAR

Deut 33:20 And *t* the arm and the crown of
2 Ki 20: 5 your prayer, I have seen your *t*;
Esth 8: 3 and implored him with *t* to
Job 16: 9 He *t* me in His wrath,
16:20 My eyes pour out *t* to God.
Ps 6: 6 I drench my couch with my *t*.
39:12 cry; Do not be silent at my *t*;
42: 3 My *t* have been my food day and
56: 8 Put my *t* into Your bottle;
80: 5 fed them with the bread of *t*,
80: 5 And given them *t* to drink in
116: 8 from death, My eyes from *t*,
126: 5 Those who sow in *t* Shall reap
Eccl 4: 1 And look! The *t* of the
Isa 16: 9 I will drench you with my *t*,
25: 8 the Lord GOD will wipe away *t*
38: 5 your prayer, I have seen your *t*;
Jer 9: 1 And my eyes a fountain of *t*,
9:18 That our eyes may run with *t*,
13:17 bitterly And run down with *t*,
14:17 Let my eyes flow with *t* night
31:16 weeping, And your eyes from *t*;
Lam 1: 2 Her *t* are on her cheeks;
2:11 My eyes fail with *t*,
2:18 Let *t* run down like a river
Ezek 24:16 nor shall your *t* run down.
Mic 5: 8 Both treads down and *t* in
Mal 2:13 the altar of the LORD with *t*,
Mk 9:24 child cried out and said with *t*,
Lk 7:38 to wash His feet with her *t*,
7:44 has washed My feet with her *t*
Acts 20:19 with many *t* and trials which
20:31 everyone night and day with *t*.
2 Cor 2: 4 I wrote to you, with many *t*,
2 Tim 1: 4 you, being mindful of your *t*,
Heb 5: 7 with vehement cries and *t* to
12:17 he sought it diligently with *t*.

TEATS (KJV) See BOSOM, BREASTS

TEBAH (1/1)

Gen 22:24 name was Reumah, also bore *T*,

TEBALIAH (1/1)

1 Chr 26:11 *T* the third, Zechariah the

TEBETH (1/1)

Esth 2:16 month, which is the month of *T*,

TEDIOUS (2/2)

Acts 24: 4 not to be *t* to you any further,
Phil 3: 1 same things to you is not *t*,

TEEMING (1/1)

Ps 104:25 In which are innumerable *t*

TEETH (45/43) TOOTH

Gen 49:12 And his *t* whiter than milk.
Num 11:33 meat was still between their *t*,
Deut 32:24 also send against them the *t*
Job 4:10 And the *t* of the young lions
13:14 Why do I take my flesh in my *t*,
16: 9 He gnashes at me with His *t*;
19:20 escaped by the skin of my *t*.
29:17 plucked the victim from his *t*.
41:14 With his terrible *t* all
Ps 3: 7 You have broken the *t* of the
35:16 gnashed at me with their *t*.
37:12 And gnashes at him with his *t*.
57: 4 Whose *t* are spears and
58: 6 Break their *t* in their mouth,
112:10 He will gnash his *t* and melt
124: 6 given us as prey to their *t*.
Prov 10:26 As vinegar to the *t* and smoke
30:14 is a generation whose *t* are
Song 4: 2 Your *t* are like a flock of
6: 6 Your *t* are like a flock of
Isa 41:15 threshing sledge with sharp *t*;
Jer 31:29 And the children's *t* are set
31:30 his *t* shall be set on edge.
Lam 2:16 They hiss and gnash their *t*.
3:16 He has also broken my *t* with
Ezek 18: 2 And the children's *t* are set
Dan 7: 5 ribs in its mouth between its *t*.
7: 7 strong. It had huge iron *t*;
7:19 with its *t* of iron and its
Joel 1: 6 His *t* are the teeth of a
1: 6 His teeth are the *t* of a
Am 4: 6 I gave you cleanness of *t* in
Mic 3: 5 While they chew with their *t*,
Zech 9: 7 abominations from between his *t*.
Mt 8:12 be weeping and gnashing of *t*.
13:42 be wailing and gnashing of *t*.
13:50 be wailing and gnashing of *t*.
22:13 be weeping and gnashing of *t*.
24:51 be weeping and gnashing of *t*.
25:30 be weeping and gnashing of *t*.
Mk 9:18 at the mouth, gnashes his *t*,
Lk 13:28 be weeping and gnashing of *t*,
Acts 7:54 gnashed at him with their *t*.
Rev 9: 8 and their *t* were like lions'
9: 8 their teeth were like lions' *t*.

TEHAPHNEHES (1/1)

Ezek 30:18 At *T* the day shall also be

TEHINNAH (1/1)

1 Chr 4:12 and *T* the father of Ir-Nahash.

TEIL (KJV) See TEREBINTH

TEKEL (2/2)

Dan 5:25 that was written: MENE, MENE, *T*,
5:27 *T*: You have been weighed

TEKOA (9/9)

2 Sam 14: 2 And Joab sent to *T* and brought
14: 4 And when the woman of *T* spoke
14: 9 And the woman of *T* said to the
1 Chr 2:24 bore him Ashhur the father of *T*.
4: 5 And Ashhur the father of *T* had
2 Chr 11: 6 And he built Bethlehem, Etam, *T*,
20:20 out into the Wilderness of *T*;
Jer 6: 1 Blow the trumpet in *T*,
Am 1: 1 among the sheepbreeders of *T*,

TEKOITE (3/3)

2 Sam 23:26 Ira the son of Ikkesh the *T*,
1 Chr 11:28 Ira the son of Ikkesh the *T*,
27: 9 Ira the son of Ikkesh the *T*;

TEKOITES (2/2)

Neh 3: 5 Next to them the *T* made repairs;
3:27 After them the *T* repaired

TEL (5/3)

Ezek 3:15 I came to the captives at *T*

TEL ABIB (1/1)

Ezek 3:15 I came to the captives at *T*,

TEL HARSHA (2/2)

Ezra 2:59 who came up from Tel Melah, *T*,
Neh 7:61 who came up from Tel Melah, *T*,

TEL MELAH (2/2)

Ezra 2:59 the ones who came up from *T*,
Neh 7:61 the ones who came up from *T*,

TELAH (1/1)

1 Chr 7:25 and *T* his son, Tahan his son,

TELAIM (1/1)

1 Sam 15: 4 together and numbered them in ***T***,

TELASSAR (2/2)

2 Ki 19:12 people of Eden who were in ***T***?
Isa 37:12 people of Eden who were in ***T***?

TELEM (2/2)

Josh 15:24 Ziph, ***T***, Bealoth,
Ezra 10:24 of the gatekeepers: Shallum, ***T***,

TELL (263/256)

Gen 12:18 Why did you not ***t*** me that she
21:26 you did not ***t*** me, nor had I
22: 2 mountains of which I shall ***t***
24:23 ***T*** me, please, is there room in
24:49 ***t*** me. And if not, tell me, that
24:49 ***t*** me, that I may turn to the
26: 2 in the land of which I shall ***t***
29:15 ***T*** me, what should your wages
31:20 in that he did not ***t*** him that
31:27 and not ***t*** me; for I might have
32: 5 and I have sent to ***t*** my lord,
32:29 '***T*** me Your name, I pray."
37:16 Please ***t*** me where they are
40: 8 ***T*** them to me, please."
43: 6 so wrongfully with me as to ***t***
45:13 So you shall ***t*** my father of all
46:31 'I will go up and ***t*** Pharaoh,
49: 1 that I may ***t*** you what shall
Ex 6:11 ***t*** Pharaoh king of Egypt to let
9: 1 Go in to Pharaoh and ***t*** him,
10: 2 and that you may ***t*** in the
13: 8 And you shall ***t*** your son in that
14:15 ***T*** the children of Israel to go
19: 3 and ***t*** the children of Israel:
Lev 5: 1 if he does not ***t*** it, he bears
16: 2 ***T*** Aaron your brother not to come
Num 14:14 and they will ***t*** it to the
15:38 ***T*** them to make tassels on the
16:37 ***T*** Eleazar, the son of Aaron the
23: 3 whatever He shows me I will ***t***
23:26 Did I not ***t*** you, saying, 'All
Deut 1:42 ***T*** them, "Do not go up nor
5:27 and ***t*** us all that the LORD our
17:11 to the judgment which they ***t***
32: 7 and they will ***t*** you:
Josh 2:14 if none of you ***t*** this business
2:20 And if you ***t*** this business of
7:19 and ***t*** me now what you have
Judg 13: 6 and He did not ***t*** me His name.
14: 6 But he did not ***t*** his father or
14: 9 But he did not ***t*** them that he
16: 6 Please ***t*** me where your great
16:10 please ***t*** me what you may be
16:13 ***T*** me what you may be bound
20: 3 ***T*** us, how did this wicked deed
Ruth 3: 4 and he will ***t*** you what you
4: 4 then ***t*** me, that I may know;
1 Sam 3:15 And Samuel was afraid to ***t*** Eli
6: 2 ***T*** us how we should send it to
9: 8 man of God, to ***t*** us our way."
9:18 Please ***t*** me, where is the
9:19 I will let you go and will ***t***
9:27 ***T*** the servant to go on ahead of
10:15 ***T*** me, please, what Samuel said
10:16 he did not ***t*** him what Samuel
14: 1 But he did not ***t*** his father.
14:43 ***T*** me what you have done." And
15:16 Be quiet! And I will ***t*** you what
19: 3 I observe, I will ***t*** you."
20: 9 then would I not ***t*** you?"
20:10 Who will ***t*** me, or what if your
20:12 and I do not send to you and ***t***
22:17 when he fled and did not ***t*** it
22:22 that he would surely ***t*** Saul. I
23:11 ***t*** Your servant." And the LORD
25: 8 and they will ***t*** you. Therefore
25:19 But she did not ***t*** her husband
2 Sam 1: 4 Please ***t*** me." And he answered,
1:20 ***T*** it not in Gath, Proclaim
2:26 will it be then until you ***t***
7: 5 Go and ***t*** My servant David, 'Thus
12:18 of David were afraid to ***t*** him
12:18 How can we ***t*** him that the child
12:22 Who can ***t*** whether the LORD
13: 4 Will you not ***t*** me?" Amnon said
15:35 you shall ***t*** to Zadok and
17:16 send quickly and ***t*** David,
17:17 servant would come and ***t*** them,
17:17 and they would go and ***t*** King
18:21 ***t*** the king what you have
24:12 Go and ***t*** David, 'Thus says the
1 Ki 1:20 that you should ***t*** them who will
14: 3 he will ***t*** you what will become
14: 7 ***t*** Jeroboam, 'Thus says the
18: 8 ***t*** your master, 'Elijah is
18:11 ***t*** your master, "Elijah is
18:12 so when I go and ***t*** Ahab, and he
18:14 ***t*** your master, "Elijah is
20: 9 ***T*** my lord the king, 'All that
20:11 ***T*** him, 'Let not the one who
22:16 I make you swear that you ***t*** me
22:18 Did I not ***t*** you he would not
2 Ki 4: 2 ***T*** me, what do you have in the
4:24 the pace for me unless I ***t*** you.
7: 9 let us go and ***t*** the king's
7:12 Let me now ***t*** you what the
8: 4 ***T*** me, please, all the great
9:12 A lie! ***T*** us now." So he said,
9:15 from the city to go and ***t*** it
10: 5 we will do all you ***t*** us; but we
20: 5 Return and ***t*** Hezekiah the leader
22:15 ***T*** the man who sent you to Me,
1 Chr 17: 4 Go and ***t*** My servant David, 'Thus
17:10 Furthermore I ***t*** you that the
21:10 Go and ***t*** David, saying, 'Thus
2 Chr 18:15 I make you swear that you ***t*** me
18:17 Did I not ***t*** you he would not
34:23 ***T*** the man who sent you to Me,
Job 1:15 and I alone have escaped to ***t***
1:16 and I alone have escaped to ***t***
1:17 and I alone have escaped to ***t***
1:19 and I alone have escaped to ***t***
8:10 Will they not teach you and ***t***
12: 7 and they will ***t*** you;
15:17 I will ***t*** you, hear me; What I
38: 4 ***T*** Me, if you have
38:18 ***T*** Me, if you know all this.
Ps 9: 1 I will ***t*** of all Your marvelous
9:14 That I may ***t*** of all Your praise
26: 7 And ***t*** of all Your wondrous
48:13 That you may ***t*** it to the
50:12 I would not ***t*** you; For the
71:15 My mouth shall ***t*** of Your
Prov 29:24 He swears to ***t*** the truth, but
Eccl 6:12 Who can ***t*** a man what will
8: 7 So who can ***t*** him when it will
10:14 Who can ***t*** him what will be
10:20 And a bird in flight may ***t*** the
Song 1: 7 ***T*** me, O you whom I love,
5: 8 That you ***t*** him I am lovesick!
Isa 5: 5 please let Me ***t*** you what I will
6: 9 and ***t*** this people: 'Keep on
19:12 Let them ***t*** you now, And let
38: 5 Go and ***t*** Hezekiah, 'Thus says
42: 9 Before they spring forth I ***t***
45:21 ***T*** and bring forth your case
58: 1 ***T*** My people their
Jer 15: 2 then you shall ***t*** them, 'Thus
19: 2 there the words that I will ***t***
23:28 let him ***t*** a dream; And he who
23:32 and ***t*** them, and cause My people
28:13 Go and ***t*** Hananiah, saying, 'Thus
34: 2 to Zedekiah king of Judah and ***t***
35:13 Go and ***t*** the men of Judah and
36:16 We will surely ***t*** the king of all
36:17 ***T*** us now, how did you write all
48:20 Wail and cry! ***T*** it in Arnon,
Ezek 3:11 and speak to them and ***t*** them,
12:23 ***T*** them therefore, 'Thus says the
17:12 ***T*** them, 'Indeed the king of
24:19 Will you not ***t*** us what these
Dan 2: 2 and the Chaldeans to ***t*** the king
2: 4 live forever! ***T*** your servants
2: 6 if you ***t*** the dream and its
2: 6 Therefore ***t*** me the dream and
2: 7 Let the king ***t*** his servants the
2: 9 Therefore ***t*** me the dream, and I
2:10 is not a man on earth who can ***t***
2:11 there is no other who can ***t*** it
2:16 that he might ***t*** the king the
2:24 and I will ***t*** the king the
2:36 Now we will ***t*** the
9:23 and I have come to ***t*** you, for
10:21 But I will ***t*** you what is noted
11: 2 And now I will ***t*** you the truth:
Joel 1: 3 ***T*** your children about it,
1: 3 Let your children ***t*** their
Jon 1: 8 Please ***t*** us! For whose cause is
3: 2 to it the message that I ***t*** you.
3: 9 Who can ***t*** if God will turn and
Mic 1:10 ***T*** it not in Gath, Weep not at
Zech 10: 2 And ***t*** false dreams;
Mt 5:39 But I ***t*** you not to resist an
8: 4 See that you ***t*** no one; but go
10:27 Whatever I ***t*** you in the dark,
11: 4 Go and ***t*** John the things which
16:12 understood that He did not ***t***
16:20 disciples that they should ***t***
17: 9 ***T*** the vision to no one until the
18:15 go and ***t*** him his fault between
18:17 ***t*** it to the church. But if he
21: 5 ***T*** the daughter of Zion,
21:24 which if you ***t*** Me, I likewise
21:24 I likewise will ***t*** you by what
21:27 Neither will I ***t*** you by what
22: 4 ***T*** those who are invited, "See,
22:17 ***T*** us, therefore, what do You
23: 3 Therefore whatever they ***t*** you to
24: 3 ***T*** us, when will these things be?
26:63 ***T*** us if You are the Christ,
28: 7 And go quickly and ***t*** His
28: 9 And as they went to ***t*** His
28:10 Go and ***t*** My brethren to go to
28:13 ***T*** them, 'His disciples came at
Mk 5:19 and ***t*** them what great things
7:36 them that they should ***t*** no one;
8:26 nor ***t*** anyone in the town."
8:30 warned them that they should ***t***
9: 9 them that they should ***t*** no one
10:32 aside again and began to ***t***
11:29 and I will ***t*** you by what
11:33 Neither will I ***t*** you by what
13: 4 ***T*** us, when will these things be?
16: 7 ***t*** His disciples—and Peter—that
Lk 4:25 But I ***t*** you truly, many widows
5:14 And He charged him to ***t*** no one,
7:22 Go and ***t*** John the things you
7:42 ***T*** Me, therefore, which of them
8:39 and ***t*** what great things God has
8:56 but He charged them to ***t*** no one
9:21 warned and commanded them to ***t***
9:27 But I ***t*** you truly, there are
10:24 for I ***t*** you that many prophets
10:40 Therefore ***t*** her to help me."
12:13 ***t*** my brother to divide the
12:51 I ***t*** you, not at all, but rather
12:59 I ***t*** you, you shall not depart
13: 3 I ***t*** you, no; but unless you
13: 5 I ***t*** you, no; but unless you
13:27 I ***t*** you I do not know you, where
13:32 ***t*** that fox, 'Behold, I cast out
17:34 I ***t*** you, in that night there
18: 8 I ***t*** you that He will avenge them
18:14 I ***t*** you, this man went down to
19:40 I ***t*** you that if these should
20: 2 ***T*** us, by what authority are You
20: 8 Neither will I ***t*** you by what
20: 9 Then He began to ***t*** the people
22:34 I ***t*** you, Peter, the rooster
22:67 ***t*** us." But He said to them,
22:67 If I ***t*** you, you will by no means
Jn 3: 8 but cannot ***t*** where it comes
3:12 how will you believe if I ***t*** you
4:25 He will ***t*** us all things."
8:45 But because I ***t*** the truth, you
8:46 And if I ***t*** the truth, why do
10:24 the Christ, ***t*** us plainly."
13:19 Now I ***t*** you before it comes,
16: 7 Nevertheless I ***t*** you the truth.
16:13 and He will ***t*** you things to
16:25 but I will ***t*** you plainly about
18:34 or did others ***t*** you this
20:15 ***t*** me where You have laid Him,
Acts 5: 8 ***T*** me whether you sold the land
10: 6 He will ***t*** you what you must
11:14 who will ***t*** you words by which
12:17 ***t*** these things to James and to
17:21 in nothing else but either to ***t***
21:23 'Therefore do what we ***t*** you:
22:27 '***T*** me, are you a Roman?"
23:17 for he has something to ***t***
23:19 What is it that you have to ***t***
23:22 ***T*** no one that you have revealed
Rom 9: 1 I ***t*** the truth in Christ, I am
1 Cor 15:51 I ***t*** you a mystery: We shall not
Gal 4:16 become your enemy because I ***t***
4:21 ***T*** me, you who desire to be
5:21 of which I ***t*** you beforehand,
Phil 1:22 what I shall choose I cannot ***t***.
3:18 and now ***t*** you even weeping,
Col 4: 7 will ***t*** you all the news about
Heb 11:32 the time would fail me to ***t*** of
Rev 17: 7 I will ***t*** you the mystery of the

TELLING (10/10)

Judg 7:13 there was a man ***t*** a dream to
7:15 when Gideon heard the ***t*** of the
1 Sam 20: 2 great or small without first ***t***
2 Sam 11:19 When you have finished ***t*** the
2 Ki 8: 5 as he was ***t*** the king how he had
Ps 78: 4 ***T*** to the generation to come
Dan 7: 1 the dream, ***t*** the main facts.
Jn 19:35 and he knows that he is ***t*** the
Acts 19:18 believed came confessing and ***t***
Rev 13:14 ***t*** those who dwell on the earth

TELLS (8/8)

Lev 14:35 who owns the house comes and ***t***
2 Sam 7:11 Also the LORD ***t*** you that He
2 Ki 6:12 ***t*** the king of Israel the words
Job 36: 9 Then He ***t*** them their work and
Ps 41: 6 When he goes out, he ***t*** it.
101: 7 He who ***t*** lies shall not
Jer 23:27 their dreams which everyone ***t***
Dan 5: 7 and ***t*** me its interpretation,

TEMA (5/5)

Gen 25:15 Hadar, ***T***, Jetur, Naphish,
1 Chr 1:30 Mishma, Dumah, Massa, Hadad, ***T***,
Job 6:19 The caravans of ***T*** look,
Isa 21:14 O inhabitants of the land of ***T***,
Jer 25:23 Dedan, ***T***, Buz, and all who

TEMAN (11/11) TEMANITE

Gen 36:11 And the sons of Eliphaz were ***T***,
36:15 son of Esau, were Chief ***T***,
36:42 Chief Kenaz, Chief ***T***,
1 Chr 1:36 And the sons of Eliphaz were ***T***,
1:53 Chief Kenaz, Chief ***T***,
Jer 49: 7 "Is wisdom no more in ***T***?
49:20 against the inhabitants of ***T***:
Ezek 25:13 it, and make it desolate from ***T***;
Am 1:12 But I will send a fire upon ***T***,
Ob 9 Then your mighty men, O ***T***,
Hab 3: 3 God came from ***T***,

TEMANITE (6/6) TEMAN

Job 2:11 his own place—Eliphaz the ***T***,
4: 1 Then Eliphaz the ***T*** answered and
15: 1 Then Eliphaz the ***T*** answered and
22: 1 Then Eliphaz the ***T*** answered and
42: 7 the LORD said to Eliphaz the ***T***,
42: 9 So Eliphaz the ***T*** and Bildad the

T

TEMANITES (2/2)

Gen 36:34 Husham of the land of the *T*
1 Chr 1:45 Husham of the land of the *T*

TEMENI (1/1)

1 Chr 4: 6 bore him Ahuzzam, Hepher, *T*,

TEMPERANCE (KJV) See SELF-CONTROL

TEMPERATE (4/4)

1 Cor 9:25 competes for the prize is *t*
1 Tim 3: 2 the husband of one wife, *t*,
3:11 be reverent, not slanderers, *t*,
Titus 2: 2 older men be sober, reverent, *t*,

TEMPERED (KJV) See ANOINTED, COMPOSED, SALTED

TEMPEST (16/16) TEMPESTUOUS

Job 9:17 For He crushes me with a *t*,
27:20 A *t* steals him away in the
Ps 55: 8 From the windy storm and *t*.
83:15 So pursue them with Your *t*,
Isa 28: 2 Like a *t* of hail and a
29: 6 With storm and *t* And the
30:30 fire, With scattering, *t*,
32: 2 wind, And a cover from the *t*,
54:11 afflicted one, Tossed with *t*,
Am 1:14 And a *t* in the day of the
Jon 1: 4 and there was a mighty *t* on the
1:12 For I know that this great *t*
Mt 8:24 And suddenly a great *t* arose on
Acts 27:20 and no small *t* beat on us, all
Heb 12:18 to blackness and darkness and *t*,
2 Pe 2:17 water, clouds carried by a *t*,

TEMPEST-TOSSED (1/1)

Acts 27:18 because we were exceedingly *t*,

TEMPESTUOUS (4/4) TEMPEST

Ps 50: 3 And it shall be very *t* all
Jon 1:11 the sea was growing more *t*.
1:13 sea continued to grow more *t*
Acts 27:14 a *t* head wind arose,

TEMPLE (371/326) TEMPLES, THRESHOLD

Judg 4:21 and drove the peg into his *t*,
4:22 dead with the peg in his *t*.
5:26 split and struck through his *t*.
9: 4 shekels of silver from the *t*
9:46 the stronghold of the *t* of the
16:26 the pillars which support the *t*,
16:27 Now the *t* was full of men and
16:29 pillars which supported the *t*,
16:30 and the *t* fell on the lords and
1 Sam 5: 2 they brought it into the *t* of
31: 9 to proclaim it in the *t* of
31:10 they put his armor in the *t* of
2 Sam 22: 7 He heard my voice from His *t*,
1 Ki 5:17 to lay the foundation of the *t*.
5:18 and stones to build the *t*.
6: 5 Against the wall of the *t* he
6: 5 against the walls of the *t*,
6: 6 around the outside of the *t*,
6: 6 into the walls of the *t*.
6: 7 And the *t*, when it was being
6: 7 iron tool was heard in the *t*
6: 8 was on the right side of the *t*.
6: 9 So he built the *t* and finished
6: 9 and he paneled the *t* with beams
6:10 chambers against the entire *t*,
6:10 they were attached to the *t*
6:12 Concerning this *t* which you are
6:14 So Solomon built the *t* and
6:15 the inside walls of the *t* with
6:15 from the floor of the *t* to the
6:15 he covered the floor of the *t*
6:16 room at the rear of the *t*,
6:17 And in front of it the *t*
6:18 The inside of the *t* was cedar,
6:19 inner sanctuary inside the *t*,
6:21 overlaid the inside of the *t*
6:22 The whole *t* he overlaid with
6:22 until he had finished all the *t*;
6:29 carved all the walls of the *t*
6:30 And the floor of the *t* he
7:12 and the vestibule of the *t*.
7:21 by the vestibule of the *t*;
7:50 doors of the main hall of the *t*.
8: 6 the inner sanctuary of the *t*,
8:17 of my father David to build a *t*
8:18 was in your heart to build a *t*
8:19 you shall not build the *t*,
8:19 he shall build the *t* for My
8:20 and I have built a *t* for the
8:27 How much less this *t* which I
8:29 eyes may be open toward this *t*
8:31 before Your altar in this *t*,
8:33 supplication to You in this *t*,
8:38 out his hands toward this *t*:
8:42 comes and prays toward this *t*,
8:43 that they may know that this *t*
8:44 which You have chosen and the *t*
8:48 which You have chosen and the *t*
9:25 the LORD. So he finished the *t*.
16:32 up an altar for Baal in the *t*
2 Ki 5:18 when my master goes into the *t*
5:18 and I bow down in the *t* of
5:18 when I bow down in the *t* of
10:21 So they came into the *t* of
10:21 and the *t* of Baal was full from
10:23 son of Rechab went into the *t*
10:25 into the inner room of the *t*
10:26 sacred pillars out of the *t*
10:27 and tore down the *t* of Baal and
11:10 that were in the *t* of the
11:11 from the right side of the *t* to
11:11 to the left side of the *t*,
11:13 came to the people in the *t*
11:18 of the land went to the *t* of
12: 5 repair the damages of the *t*,
12: 6 repaired the damages of the *t*.
12: 7 repaired the damages of the *t*?
12: 7 repairing the damages of the *t*.
12: 8 nor repair the damages of the *t*.
12:12 was paid out to repair the *t*.
16:14 LORD, from the front of the *t*—
16:18 which they had built in the *t*,
18:16 gold from the doors of the *t*
19:37 as he was worshiping in the *t*
23: 4 to bring out of the *t* of the
24:13 of Israel had made in the *t* of
1 Chr 6:10 ministered as priest in the *t*
10: 9 proclaim the news in the *t*
10:10 they put his armor in the *t* of
10:10 and fastened his head in the *t*
29: 1 because the *t* is not for man
29:19 and to build the *t* for which I
2 Chr 2: 1 determined to build a *t* for
2: 4 I am building a *t* for the name
2: 5 And the *t* which I build will
2: 6 who is able to build Him a *t*,
2: 6 that I should build Him a *t*,
2: 9 for the *t* which I am about to
2:12 who will build a *t* for the
3:15 he made in front of the *t* two
3:17 set up the pillars before the *t*,
4: 7 design, and set them in the *t*,
4: 8 and placed them in the *t*,
4:22 doors of the main hall of the *t*,
5: 7 the inner sanctuary of the *t*,
6: 7 of my father David to build a *t*
6: 8 was in your heart to build a *t*
6: 9 you shall not build the *t*,
6: 9 he shall build the *t* for My
6:10 and I have built the *t* for the
6:18 How much less this *t* which I
6:20 eyes may be open toward this *t*
6:22 before Your altar in this *t*,
6:24 before You in this *t*,
6:29 spreads out his hands to this *t*:
6:32 they come and pray in this *t*;
6:33 that they may know that this *t*
6:34 which You have chosen and the *t*
6:38 and toward the *t* which I have
7: 1 glory of the LORD filled the *t*.
7: 3 the glory of the LORD on the *t*,
20: 9 we will stand before this *t* and
20: 9 (for Your name is in this *t*),
23: 9 that were in the *t* of God.
23:10 from the right side of the *t* to
23:10 to the left side of the *t*,
23:10 along by the altar and by the *t*,
23:12 came to the people in the *t*
23:17 all the people went to the *t*
26:16 his God by entering the *t* of
27: 2 he did not enter the *t* of the
29:16 that they found in the *t* of
32:21 when he had gone into the *t* of
34: 8 had purged the land and the *t*,
35:20 when Josiah had prepared the *t*,
36: 7 and put them in his *t* at
Ezra 1: 7 Jerusalem and put in the *t* of
3: 6 the foundation of the *t* of the
3:10 laid the foundation of the *t*
3:12 men who had seen the first *t*,
3:12 when the foundation of this *t*
4: 1 captivity were building the *t*
5: 3 commanded you to build this *t*
5: 8 to the *t* of the great God,
5: 9 commanded you to build this *t*
5:11 and we are rebuilding the *t*
5:12 who destroyed this *t* and
5:14 had taken from the *t* that was
5:14 and carried into the *t* of
5:14 King Cyrus took from the *t* of
5:15 carry them to the *t* site that
6: 5 Nebuchadnezzar took from the *t*
6: 5 and taken back to the *t* which
6:15 Now the *t* was finished on the
Neh 2: 8 which pertains to the *t*,
6:10 the house of God, within the *t*,
6:10 let us close the doors of the *t*,
6:11 as I who would go into the *t*
Ps 5: 7 will worship toward Your holy *t*.
11: 4 The LORD is in His holy *t*,
18: 6 He heard my voice from His *t*,
27: 4 LORD, And to inquire in His *t*.
29: 9 And in His *t* everyone says,
48: 9 In the midst of Your *t*.
65: 4 of Your house, Of Your holy *t*.
68:29 Because of Your *t* at Jerusalem,
79: 1 Your holy *t* they have defiled;
138: 2 will worship toward Your holy *t*,
Isa 6: 1 train of His robe filled the *t*.
15: 2 He has gone up to the *t* and
44:28 shall be built," And to the *t*,
64:11 Our holy and beautiful *t*,
66: 6 the city! A voice from the *t*!
Jer 7: 4 The *t* of the LORD, the temple
7: 4 the *t* of the LORD, the temple
7: 4 the *t* of the LORD are these.'
24: 1 of figs set before the *t* of
26:18 And the mountain of the *t*
50:28 God, The vengeance of His *t*.
51:11 LORD, The vengeance for His *t*.
Ezek 8:16 at the door of the *t* of the
8:16 with their backs toward the *t*
9: 3 been, to the threshold of the *t*.
9: 6 elders who were before the *t*.
9: 7 He said to them, "Defile the *t*,
10: 3 on the south side of the *t*
10: 4 over the threshold of the *t*;
10:18 from the threshold of the *t*
40: 5 all around the outside of the *t*.
40:45 who have charge of the *t*.
40:47 altar was in front of the *t*.
40:48 me to the vestibule of the *t*
41: 5 he measured the wall of the *t*,
41: 5 side chamber all around the *t*
41: 6 fastened to the wall of the *t*.
41: 7 ledges in the wall of the *t*
41: 8 an elevation all around the *t*;
41: 9 of the side chambers of the *t*.
41:10 twenty cubits all around the *t*
41:13 So he measured the *t*,
41:14 of the eastern face of the *t*,
41:15 as well as the inner *t* and the
41:19 it was made throughout the *t*
41:21 The doorposts of the *t* were
41:23 The *t* and the sanctuary had two
41:25 carved on the doors of the *t*
41:26 on the side chambers of the *t*
42: 8 whereas that facing the *t* was
42:15 finished measuring the inner *t*,
43: 4 of the LORD came into the *t*
43: 5 glory of the LORD filled the *t*.
43: 6 Him speaking to me from the *t*,
43:10 describe the *t* to the house of
43:11 to them the design of the *t*
43:12 "This is the law of the *t*:
43:12 this is the law of the *t*.
43:21 in the appointed place of the *t*,
44: 4 gate to the front of the *t*;
44:14 make them keep charge of the *t*,
45: 5 Levites, the ministers of the *t*;
45:19 it on the doorposts of the *t*,
45:20 shall make atonement for the *t*.
46:24 where the ministers of the *t*
47: 1 me back to the door of the *t*;
47: 1 under the threshold of the *t*
47: 1 for the front of the *t* faced
47: 1 under the right side of the *t*,
48:21 and the sanctuary of the *t*
Dan 5: 2 had taken from the *t* which
5: 3 that had been taken from the *t*
Am 8: 3 And the songs of the *t* Shall
Jon 2: 4 look again toward Your holy *t*.
2: 7 up to You, Into Your holy *t*.
Mic 1: 2 The Lord from His holy *t*.
3:12 And the mountain of the *t*
Hab 2:20 But the LORD is in His holy *t*.
Hag 1: 4 and this *t* to lie in ruins?"
1: 8 and bring wood and build the *t*,
2: 3 left among you who saw this *t*
2: 7 and I will fill this *t* with
2: 9 The glory of this latter *t* shall
2:15 was laid upon stone in the *t*
2:18 the foundation of the LORD's *t*
Zech 4: 9 laid the foundation of this *t*;
6:12 And He shall build the *t* of
6:13 He shall build the *t* of the
6:14 be for a memorial in the *t* of
6:15 shall come and build the *t* of
8: 9 That the *t* might be built.
Mal 3: 1 Will suddenly come to His *t*,
Mt 4: 5 Him on the pinnacle of the *t*,
12: 5 Sabbath the priests in the *t*
12: 6 is One greater than the *t*.
17:24 those who received the *t* tax
17:24 your Teacher not pay the *t*
21:12 Then Jesus went into the *t* of
21:12 who bought and sold in the *t*,
21:14 the lame came to Him in the *t*,
21:15 children crying out in the *t*
21:23 Now when He came into the *t*,
23:16 say, 'Whoever swears by the *t*,
23:16 swears by the gold of the *t*,
23:17 the gold or the *t* that
23:21 "He who swears by the *t*,
23:35 you murdered between the *t* and
24: 1 out and departed from the *t*,
24: 1 show Him the buildings of the *t*.
26:55 with you, teaching in the *t*,
26:61 I am able to destroy the *t* of
27: 5 the pieces of silver in the *t*
27:40 You who destroy the *t* and build
27:51 the veil of the *t* was torn in
Mk 11:11 into Jerusalem and into the *t*.
11:15 Then Jesus went into the *t* and
11:15 who bought and sold in the *t*,
11:16 to carry wares through the *t*.
11:27 And as He was walking in the *t*,
12:35 said, while He taught in the *t*,
13: 1 Then as He went out of the *t*,
13: 3 Mount of Olives opposite the *t*,
14:49 I was daily with you in the *t*

14:58 I will destroy this ***t*** made with
15:29 Aha! You who destroy the ***t*** and
15:38 Then the veil of the ***t*** was torn
Lk 1: 9 when he went into the ***t*** of the
1:21 he lingered so long in the ***t***.
1:22 he had seen a vision in the ***t***,
2:27 came by the Spirit into the ***t***.
2:37 who did not depart from the ***t***,
2:46 days they found Him in the ***t***,
4: 9 Him on the pinnacle of the ***t***,
11:51 between the altar and the ***t***.
18:10 Two men went up to the ***t*** to
19:45 Then He went into the ***t*** and
19:47 He was teaching daily in the ***t***.
20: 1 He taught the people in the ***t***
21: 5 Then, as some spoke of the ***t***,
21:37 He was teaching in the ***t***,
21:38 people came to Him in the ***t*** to
22:52 priests, captains of the ***t***,
22:53 I was with you daily in the ***t***,
23:45 and the veil of the ***t*** was torn
24:53 and were continually in the ***t***
Jn 2:14 And He found in the ***t*** those who
2:15 He drove them all out of the ***t***,
2:19 said to them, "Destroy this ***t***,
2:20 forty-six years to build this ***t***,
2:21 But He was speaking of the ***t*** of
5:14 Jesus found him in the ***t***,
7:14 feast Jesus went up into the ***t***
7:28 out, as He taught in the ***t***,
8: 2 He came again into the ***t***,
8:20 treasury, as He taught in the ***t***;
8:59 Himself and went out of the ***t***,
10:23 And Jesus walked in the ***t***,
11:56 as they stood in the ***t***,
18:20 in synagogues and in the ***t***,
Acts 2:46 daily with one accord in the ***t***,
3: 1 John went up together to the ***t***
3: 2 laid daily at the gate of the ***t***
3: 2 from those who entered the ***t***;
3: 3 and John about to go into the ***t***,
3: 8 and walked and entered the ***t***
3:10 at the Beautiful Gate of the ***t***;
4: 1 priests, the captain of the ***t***,
5:20 stand in the ***t*** and speak to the
5:21 they entered the ***t*** early in the
5:24 priest, the captain of the ***t***,
5:25 in prison are standing in the ***t***
5:42 And daily in the ***t***,
14:13 whose ***t*** was in front of their
19:27 but also the ***t*** of the great
19:35 the city of the Ephesians is ***t***
21:26 entered the ***t*** to announce the
21:27 from Asia, seeing him in the ***t***,
21:28 also brought Greeks into the ***t***
21:29 Paul had brought into the ***t***.
21:30 and dragged him out of the ***t***;
22:17 and was praying in the ***t***,
24: 6 even tried to profane the ***t***,
24:12 they neither found me in the ***t***
24:18 Asia found me purified in the ***t***,
25: 8 of the Jews, nor against the ***t***,
26:21 the Jews seized me in the ***t***
1 Cor 3:16 not know that you are the ***t*** of
3:17 If anyone defiles the ***t*** of God,
3:17 For the ***t*** of God is holy, which
3:17 which ***t*** you are.
6:19 know that your body is the ***t***
8:10 knowledge eating in an idol's ***t***,
9:13 eat of the things of the ***t***,
2 Cor 6:16 And what agreement has the ***t*** of
6:16 For you are the ***t*** of the living
Eph 2:21 grows into a holy ***t*** in the
2 Th 2: 4 so that he sits as God in the ***t***
Rev 3:12 make him a pillar in the ***t*** of
7:15 Him day and night in His ***t***.
11: 1 Rise and measure the ***t*** of God,
11: 2 court which is outside the ***t***,
11:19 Then the ***t*** of God was opened in
11:19 His covenant was seen in His ***t***.
14:15 another angel came out of the ***t***,
14:17 angel came out of the ***t*** which
15: 5 the ***t*** of the tabernacle of the
15: 6 And out of the ***t*** came the seven
15: 8 The ***t*** was filled with smoke from
15: 8 no one was able to enter the ***t***
16: 1 I heard a loud voice from the ***t***
16:17 a loud voice came out of the ***t***
21:22 But I saw no ***t*** in it, for the
21:22 Almighty and the Lamb are its ***t***.

TEMPLES (8/8) TEMPLE

Song 4: 3 Your ***t*** behind your veil
6: 7 of pomegranate Are your ***t***
Hos 8:14 his Maker, And has built ***t***;
Joel 3: 5 And have carried into your ***t***
Acts 7:48 Most High does not dwell in ***t***
17:24 does not dwell in ***t*** made with
19:37 who are neither robbers of ***t***
Rom 2:22 who abhor idols, do you rob ***t***?

TEMPORAL (KJV) See TEMPORARY

TEMPORARY (1/1)

2 Cor 4:18 things which are seen are ***t***,

TEMPT (8/8) TEMPTATION, TEMPTED, TEMPTER

Ex 17: 2 Why do you ***t*** the LORD?"
Deut 6:16 You shall not ***t*** the LORD your
Mal 3:15 They even ***t*** God and go free.'
Mt 4: 7 You shall not ***t*** the LORD
Lk 4:12 You shall not ***t*** the LORD
1 Cor 7: 5 again so that Satan does not ***t***
10: 9 nor let us ***t*** Christ, as some of
Jas 1:13 nor does He Himself ***t*** anyone.

TEMPTATION (12/11) TEMPT

Mt 6:13 And do not lead us into ***t***,
26:41 and pray, lest you enter into ***t***.
Mk 14:38 and pray, lest you enter into ***t***.
Lk 4:13 the devil had ended every ***t***,
8:13 for a while and in time of ***t***
11: 4 And do not lead us into ***t***,
22:40 that you may not enter into ***t***.
22:46 and pray, lest you enter into ***t***.
1 Cor 10:13 No ***t*** has overtaken you except
10:13 but with the ***t*** will also make
1 Tim 6: 9 desire to be rich fall into ***t***
Jas 1:12 is the man who endures ***t***;

TEMPTATIONS (1/1)

2 Pe 2: 9 to deliver the godly out of ***t***

TEMPTED (18/15) TEMPT

Ex 17: 7 and because they ***t*** the LORD,
Deut 6:16 the LORD your God as you ***t***
Ps 78:41 again and again they ***t*** God,
Mt 4: 1 into the wilderness to be ***t*** by
Mk 1:13 ***t*** by Satan, and was with the
Lk 4: 2 being ***t*** for forty days by the
1 Cor 10: 9 Christ, as some of them also ***t***,
10:13 who will not allow you to be ***t***
Gal 6: 1 yourself lest you also be ***t***.
1 Th 3: 5 by some means the tempter had ***t***
Heb 2:18 Himself has suffered, being ***t***,
2:18 is able to aid those who are ***t***.
4:15 but was in all points ***t*** as we
11:37 they were sawn in two, were ***t***,
Jas 1:13 Let no one say when he is ***t***,
1:13 I am ***t*** by God"; for God cannot
1:13 for God cannot be ***t*** by evil,
1:14 But each one is ***t*** when he is

TEMPTER (2/2) TEMPT

Mt 4: 3 Now when the ***t*** came to Him, he
1 Th 3: 5 lest by some means the ***t*** had

TEN (226/200) TENS, TENTH

Gen 5:14 Cainan were nine hundred and ***t***
16: 3 after Abram had dwelt ***t*** years
18:32 Suppose ***t*** should be found
18:32 destroy it for the sake of ***t***.
24:10 Then the servant took ***t*** of his
24:22 for her wrists weighing ***t*** shekels
24:55 us a few days, at least ***t***;
24:60 mother of thousands of ***t***
31: 7 changed my wages ***t*** times
31:41 and you have changed my wages ***t***
32:15 forty cows and ***t*** bulls, twenty
32:15 twenty female donkeys and ***t*** foals
42: 3 So Joseph's ***t*** brothers went down
45:23 ***t*** donkeys loaded with the good
45:23 and ***t*** female donkeys loaded
50:22 Joseph lived one hundred and ***t***
50:26 being one hundred and ***t*** years
Ex 26: 1 the tabernacle with ***t*** curtains
26:16 ***T*** cubits shall be the length
27:12 with their ***t*** pillars and their
27:12 ten pillars and their ***t*** sockets
34:28 the ***T*** Commandments.
36: 8 the tabernacle made ***t*** curtains
36:21 length of each board was ***t*** cubits
38:12 with ***t*** pillars and their ten
38:12 with ten pillars and their ***t*** sockets
Lev 26: 8 shall put ***t*** thousand to flight
26:26 ***t*** women shall bake your bread
27: 5 and for a female ***t*** shekels;
27: 7 and for a female ***t*** shekels.
Num 7:14 one gold pan of ***t*** shekels, full
7:20 one gold pan of ***t*** shekels, full
7:26 one gold pan of ***t*** shekels, full
7:32 one gold pan of ***t*** shekels, full
7:38 one gold pan of ***t*** shekels, full
7:44 one gold pan of ***t*** shekels, full
7:50 one gold pan of ***t*** shekels, full
7:56 one gold pan of ***t*** shekels, full
7:62 one gold pan of ***t*** shekels, full
7:68 one gold pan of ***t*** shekels, full
7:74 one gold pan of ***t*** shekels, full
7:80 one gold pan of ***t*** shekels, full
7:86 full of incense weighed ***t*** shekels
11:19 nor ***t*** days, nor twenty days,
11:32 gathered least gathered ***t*** homers
14:22 put Me to the test now these ***t***
29:23 On the fourth day present ***t*** bulls
Deut 4:13 the ***T*** Commandments; and He
10: 4 the ***T*** Commandments, which the
32:30 And two put ***t*** thousand to
33: 2 And He came with ***t*** thousands
33:17 They are the ***t*** thousands of
Josh 15:57 ***t*** cities with their villages;
17: 5 ***T*** shares fell to Manasseh,
21: 5 children of Kohath had ***t*** cities
21:26 All the ***t*** cities with their
22:14 and with him ***t*** rulers, one ruler
24:29 being one hundred and ***t*** years
Judg 1: 4 and they killed ***t*** thousand men
2: 8 he was one hundred and ***t***
3:29 they killed about ***t*** thousand
4: 6 take with you ***t*** thousand men of
4:10 he went up with ***t*** thousand men
4:14 Mount Tabor with ***t*** thousand men
6:27 So Gideon took ***t*** men from among
7: 3 and ***t*** thousand remained.
12:11 He judged Israel ***t*** years.
17:10 and I will give you ***t*** shekels
20:10 We will take ***t*** men out of every
20:10 and a thousand out of every ***t***
20:34 And ***t*** thousand select men from
Ruth 1: 4 they dwelt there about ***t*** years
4: 2 And he took ***t*** men of the elders
1 Sam 1: 8 not better to you than ***t*** sons?
15: 4 foot soldiers and ***t*** thousand men
17:17 dried grain and these ***t*** loaves
17:18 And carry these ***t*** cheeses to the
18: 7 And David his ***t*** thousands."
18: 8 They have ascribed to David ***t***
21:11 And David his ***t*** thousands'?"
25: 5 David sent ***t*** young men; and
25:38 after about ***t*** days, that the
29: 5 And David his ***t*** thousands'?"
2 Sam 15:16 But the king left ***t*** women,
18: 3 But you are worth ***t*** thousand
18:11 I would have given you ***t*** shekels
18:15 And ***t*** young men who bore Joab's
19:43 We have ***t*** shares in the king;
20: 3 And the king took the ***t*** women,
1 Ki 4:23 ***t*** fatted oxen, twenty oxen from
5:14 ***t*** thousand a month in shifts:
6: 3 of the vestible extended ***t*** cubits
6:23 each ***t*** cubits high.
6:24 ***t*** cubits from the tip of one
6:25 the other cherub was ***t*** cubits
6:26 height of one cherub was ***t*** cubits
7:10 some ***t*** cubits and some eight
7:23 ***t*** cubits from one brim to the
7:24 ***t*** to a cubit, all the way
7:27 He also made ***t*** carts of bronze;
7:37 Thus he made the ***t*** carts. All of
7:38 Then he made ***t*** lavers of
7:38 On each of the ***t*** carts was a
7:43 the ***t*** carts, and ten lavers on
7:43 and ***t*** lavers on the carts;
11:31 Take for yourself ***t*** pieces, for
11:31 Solomon and will give ***t*** tribes
11:35 give it to you—***t*** tribes.
14: 3 Also take with you ***t*** loaves,
2 Ki 5: 5 and took with him ***t*** talents
5: 5 and ***t*** changes of clothing.
13: 7 ***t*** chariots, and ten thousand
13: 7 and ***t*** thousand foot soldiers;
14: 7 He killed ***t*** thousand Edomites in
15:17 and reigned ***t*** years in
20: 9 shall the shadow go forward ***t***
20: 9 ten degrees or go backward ***t***
20:10 shadow to go down ***t*** degrees
20:10 shadow go backward ***t*** degrees
20:11 He brought the shadow ***t*** degrees
24:14 ***t*** thousand captives, and all
25:25 came with ***t*** men and struck and
1 Chr 6:61 they gave by lot ***t*** cities
29: 7 God five thousand talents and ***t***
29: 7 ***t*** thousand talents of silver,
2 Chr 4: 1 and ***t*** cubits its height.
4: 2 ***t*** cubits from one brim to the
4: 3 ***t*** to a cubit, all the way
4: 6 He also made ***t*** lavers, and put
4: 7 And he made ***t*** lampstands of gold
4: 8 He also made ***t*** tables,
14: 1 the land was quiet for ***t*** years
25:11 the Valley of Salt and killed ***t***
25:12 of Judah took captive ***t***
27: 5 ***t*** thousand kors of wheat,
27: 5 and ***t*** thousand of barley.
30:24 a thousand bulls and ***t*** thousand
36: 9 Jerusalem three months and ***t*** days
Ezra 1:10 four hundred and ***t*** silver
8:12 him one hundred and ***t*** males
8:24 and ***t*** of their brethren with
Neh 4:12 that they told us ***t*** times,
5:18 and once every ***t*** days an
11: 1 lots to bring one out of ***t*** to
Esth 3: 9 and I will pay ***t*** thousand
9:10 the ***t*** sons of Haman the son of
9:12 and the ***t*** sons of Haman.
9:13 and let Haman's ***t*** sons be
9:14 and they hanged Haman's ***t*** sons.
Job 19: 3 These ***t*** times you have
Ps 3: 6 I will not be afraid of ***t***
33: 2 with an instrument of ***t*** strings
91: 7 And ***t*** thousand at your right
92: 3 On an instrument of ***t*** strings,
144: 9 On a harp of ***t*** strings I will
144:13 And ***t*** thousands in our fields
Eccl 7:19 the wise More than ***t*** rulers
Song 5:10 Chief among ***t*** thousand.
Isa 5:10 For ***t*** acres of vineyard shall
38: 8 ***t*** degrees backward." So the
38: 8 So the sun returned ***t*** degrees
Jer 41: 1 came with ***t*** men to Gedaliah the
41: 2 and the ***t*** men who were with
41: 8 But ***t*** men were found among them
42: 7 And it happened after ***t*** days
Ezek 40:11 ***t*** cubits; and the length of
41: 2 the entryway was ***t*** cubits,
42: 4 was a walk ***t*** cubits wide, at a
45: 1 and the width ***t*** thousand.
45: 3 long and ***t*** thousand wide

45: 5 long and *t* thousand wide
45:14 A kor is a homer or *t* baths,
45:14 for *t* baths are a homer.
48: 9 length and *t* thousand in
48:10 on the west *t* thousand in
48:10 on the east *t* thousand in
48:13 cubits in length and *t*
48:13 thousand and its width *t*
48:18 shall be *t* thousand cubits
48:18 *t* thousand to the west
Dan 1:12 test your servants for *t* days,
1:14 and tested them *t* days.
1:15 And at the end of *t* days their
1:20 he found them *t* times better
7: 7 and it had *t* horns.
7:10 *T* thousand times ten thousand
7:10 Ten thousand times *t* thousand
7:20 and the *t* horns that were on
7:24 The *t* horns are ten kings
7:24 The ten horns are *t* kings
Am 5: 3 Shall have *t* left to
6: 9 that if *t* men remain in one
Mic 6: 7 *T* thousand rivers of oil?
Hag 2:16 ephahs, there were but *t*;
Zech 5: 2 twenty cubits and its width *t*
8:23 In those days *t* men from every
Mt 18:24 who owed him *t* thousand talents.
20:24 And when the *t* heard it, they
25: 1 shall be likened to *t* virgins
25:28 give it to him who has *t* talents
Mk 10:41 And when the *t* heard it, they
Lk 14:31 he is able with *t* thousand
15: 8 having *t* silver coins, if she
17:12 there met Him *t* men who were
17:17 'Were there not *t* cleansed?
19:13 So he called *t* of his servants,
19:13 delivered to them *t* minas,
19:16 your mina has earned *t* minas.'
19:17 have authority over *t* cities.'
19:24 give it to him who has *t* talents
19:25 he has *t* minas.')
Acts 25: 6 among them more than *t* days,
1 Cor 4:15 you might have *t* thousand
14:19 than *t* thousand words in a
Jude 14 the Lord comes with *t* thousands
Rev 2:10 you will have tribulation *t* days
5:11 and the number of them was *t*
5:11 them was ten thousand times *t*
12: 3 having seven heads and *t* horns,
13: 1 having seven heads and *t* horns,
13: 1 and on his horns *t* crowns,
17: 3 having seven heads and *t* horns.
17: 7 the seven heads and the *t* horns
17:12 The *t* horns which you saw are
17:12 horns which you saw are *t* kings
17:16 And the *t* horns which you saw on

TEND (5/5) TENDER

Gen 2:15 him in the garden of Eden to *t*
Ex 27:21 Aaron and his sons shall *t* it
Deut 28:39 shall plant vineyards and *t*
Song 8:12 And those who *t* its fruit two
Jn 21:16 said to him, "*T* My sheep."

TENDED (3/3)

Ex 21:29 But if the ox *t* to thrust with
21:36 if it was known that the ox *t*
Hos 12:12 And for a wife he *t* sheep.

TENDER (33/33) TEND, TENDERHEARTED

Gen 18: 7 took a *t* and good calf,
Deut 28:56 The *t* and delicate woman among
32: 2 As raindrops on the *t* herb,
2 Sam 23: 4 Like the *t* grass springing
2 Ki 22:19 "because your heart was *t*,
2 Chr 34:27 "because your heart was *t*,
Job 14: 7 And that its *t* shoots will not
38:27 the growth of *t* grass
Ps 25: 6 Your *t* mercies and Your
40:11 Do not withhold Your *t* mercies
51: 1 multitude of Your *t* mercies
69:16 multitude of Your *t* mercies
77: 9 in anger shut up His *t* mercies
79: 8 Let Your *t* mercies come
103: 4 lovingkindness and *t* mercies
119:77 Let Your *t* mercies come to me,
119:156 Great are Your *t* mercies, O
145: 9 And His *t* mercies are over
Prov 4: 3 *T* and the only one in the
12:10 But the *t* mercies of the
27:25 and the *t* grass shows itself,
Song 2:13 And the vines with the *t* grapes
2:15 For our vines have *t* grapes.
Isa 47: 1 you shall no more be called *T*
53: 2 grow up before Him as a *t* plant
Ezek 17:22 of its young twigs a *t* one
Dan 4:15 In the *t* grass of the field.
4:23 iron and bronze in the *t* grass
Am 7:14 I was a sheepbreeder And a *t*
Mt 24:32 its branch has already become *t*
Mk 13:28 its branch has already become *t*,
Lk 1:78 Through the *t* mercy of our God,
Col 3:12 put on *t* mercies, kindness,

TENDERHEARTED (2/2) TENDER

Eph 4:32 And be kind to one another, *t*,
1 Pe 3: 8 love as brothers, be *t*,

TENDING (2/2) KEPT

Ex 3: 1 Now Moses was *t* the flock of
Lk 17: 7 having a servant plowing or *t*

TENDS (2/2)

Ex 30: 7 when he *t* the lamps, he shall
1 Cor 9: 7 Or who *t* a flock and does not

TENONS (4/4)

Ex 26:17 Two *t* shall be in each board
26:19 of the boards for its two *t*.
36:22 Each board had two *t* for binding
36:24 of the boards for its two *t*.

TENOR (1/1)

Ex 34:27 for according to the *t* of these

TENS (4/4) TEN

Ex 18:21 of fifties, and rulers of *t*.
18:25 of fifties, and rulers of *t*.
Deut 1:15 of fifties, leaders of *t*,
Dan 11:12 and he will cast down *t* of

TENT (112/101) TENTMAKERS, TENTS

Gen 9:21 and became uncovered in his *t*.
12: 8 and he pitched his *t* with
13: 3 to the place where his *t* had
13:12 of the plain and pitched his *t*
13:18 Then Abram moved his *t*,
18: 1 as he was sitting in the *t* door
18: 2 he ran from the *t* door to meet
18: 6 So Abraham hurried into the *t* to
18: 9 So he said, "Here, in the *t*.
18:10 (Sarah was listening in the *t*
24:67 her into his mother Sarah's *t*;
26:17 from there and pitched his *t*
26:25 and he pitched his *t* there; and
31:25 Now Jacob had pitched his *t* in
31:33 And Laban went into Jacob's *t*,
31:33 Jacob's tent, into Leah's *t*,
31:33 Then he went out of Leah's *t*
31:33 tent and entered Rachel's *t*.
31:34 Laban searched all about the *t*
33:18 and he pitched his *t* before the
33:19 where he had pitched his *t*,
35:21 journeyed and pitched his *t*
Ex 16:16 for those who are in his *t*.
18: 7 and they went into the *t*.
26: 7 to be a *t* over the tabernacle.
26: 9 at the forefront of the *t*.
26:11 and couple the *t* together, that
26:12 of the curtains of the *t*,
26:13 length of the curtains of the *t*,
26:14 of ram skins dyed red for the *t*,
33: 7 Moses took his *t* and pitched it
33: 8 and each man stood at his *t*
33:10 each man in his *t* door.
35:11 'the tabernacle, its *t*,
36:14 of goats' hair for the *t* over
36:18 bronze clasps to couple the *t*
36:19 he made a covering for the *t*
39:32 of the tabernacle of the *t* of
39:33 the *t* and all its furnishings:
39:40 for the *t* of meeting;
40: 2 set up the tabernacle of the *t*
40: 6 of the tabernacle of the *t* of
40:19 And he spread out the *t* over the
40:19 and put the covering of the *t*
40:29 of the tabernacle of the *t* of
Lev 14: 8 and shall stay outside his *t*
Num 3:25 the *t* with its covering,
9:15 the *t* of the Testimony;
11:10 everyone at the door of his *t*;
19:14 the law when a man dies in a *t*:
19:14 All who come into the *t* and all
19:14 tent and all who are in the *t*
19:18 water, sprinkle it on the *t*,
25: 8 the man of Israel into the *t*
Josh 7:21 the earth in the midst of my *t*,
7:22 and they ran to the *t*;
7:22 there it was, hidden in his *t*,
7:23 them from the midst of the *t*,
7:24 his donkeys, his sheep, his *t*,
Judg 4:11 the Kenites and pitched his *t*
4:17 had fled away on foot to the *t*
4:18 aside with her into the *t*,
4:20 "Stand at the door of the *t*,
4:21 took a *t* peg and took a hammer
4:22 And when he went into her *t*,
5:26 stretched her hand to the *t*
7: 8 of Israel, every man to his *t*,
7:13 it came to a *t* and struck it so
7:13 and the *t* collapsed."
20: 8 "None of us will go to his *t*,
1 Sam 4:10 and every man fled to his *t*.
13: 2 sent away, every man to his *t*.
17:54 but he put his armor in his *t*.
2 Sam 7: 2 the ark of God dwells inside *t*
7: 6 but have moved about in a *t* and
16:22 So they pitched a *t* for Absalom
18:17 Israel fled, everyone to his *t*.
19: 8 of Israel had fled to his *t*.
20:22 the city, every man to his *t*.
2 Ki 7: 8 they went into one *t* and ate
7: 8 came back and entered another *t*,
14:12 and every man fled to his *t*.
1 Chr 15: 1 and pitched a *t* for it.
17: 1 of the LORD is under *t*
17: 5 but have gone from *t* to tent,
17: 5 but have gone from tent to *t*,
2 Chr 1: 4 for he had pitched a *t* for it
25:22 and every man fled to his *t*.
Job 5:24 You shall know that your *t* is
18: 6 The light is dark in his *t*,
18:14 from the shelter of his *t*,
18:15 They dwell in his *t* who are
19:12 They encamp all around my *t*.
20:26 with him who is left in his *t*.
21:28 prince? And where is the *t*,
29: 4 counsel of God was over my *t*;
31:31 If the men of my *t* have not
Ps 78:60 The *t* He had placed among men,
78:67 Moreover He rejected the *t* of
Prov 14:11 But the *t* of the upright will
Isa 38:12 from me like a shepherd's *t*;
40:22 And spreads them out like a *t*
54: 2 "Enlarge the place of your *t*,
Jer 10:20 My *t* is plundered, And all my
10:20 is no one to pitch my *t*
37:10 rise up, every man in his *t*,
Lam 2: 4 On the *t* of the daughter of
Zech 10: 4 From him the *t* peg, From him
2 Cor 5: 1 if our earthly house, this *t*,
5: 4 For we who are in this *t* groan,
2 Pe 1:13 as long as I am in this *t*,
1:14 shortly I must put off my *t*,

TENTH (45/39) TEN

Gen 8: 5 continually until the *t* month.
8: 5 In the *t* month, on the first
28:22 give me I will surely give a *t*
Ex 12: 3 On the *t* day of this month
Lev 16:29 on the *t* day of the month, you
23:27 Also the *t* day of this seventh
25: 9 Jubilee to sound on the *t* day
27:32 the *t* one shall be holy to the
Num 7:66 On the *t* day Ahiezer the son of
18:26 a *t* of the tithe.
29: 7 On the *t* day of this seventh
Deut 23: 2 even to the *t* generation none
23: 3 even to the *t* generation none
Josh 4:19 from the Jordan on the *t* day
1 Sam 8:15 He will take a *t* of your grain
8:17 He will take a *t* of your sheep.
2 Ki 25: 1 in the *t* month, on the tenth
25: 1 on the *t* day of the month,
1 Chr 12:13 Jeremiah the *t*, and Machbanai
24:11 the *t* to Shecaniah,
25:17 the *t* for Shimei, his sons and
27:13 The *t* captain for the tenth
27:13 tenth captain for the *t* month
Ezra 10:16 on the first day of the *t* month
Neh 10:38 shall bring up a *t* of the tithes
Esth 2:16 in the *t* month, which is the
Isa 6:13 But yet a *t* will be in it,
Jer 32: 1 from the LORD in the *t* year
39: 1 in the *t* month, Nebuchadnezzar
52: 4 in the *t* month, on the tenth
52: 4 on the *t* day of the month,
52:12 on the *t* day of the month
Ezek 20: 1 on the *t* day of the month,
24: 1 in the *t* month, on the tenth
24: 1 on the *t* day of the month,
29: 1 In the *t* year, in the tenth
29: 1 in the *t* month, on the twelfth
33:21 in the *t* month, on the fifth
40: 1 on the *t* day of the month,
Zech 8:19 seventh, And the fast of the *t*,
Jn 1:39 (now it was about the *t* hour).
Heb 7: 2 also Abraham gave a *t* part
7: 4 Abraham gave a *t* of the spoils
Rev 11:13 and a *t* of the city fell.
21:20 the *t* chrysoprase, the eleventh

TENTMAKERS (1/1) TENT

Acts 18: 3 for by occupation they were *t*.

TENTS (69/66) TENT

Gen 4:20 father of those who dwell in *t*
9:27 And may he dwell in the *t* of
13: 5 had flocks and herds and *t*.
25:27 was a mild man, dwelling in *t*.
31:33 tent, and into the two maids' *t*,
Num 1:52 of Israel shall pitch their *t*,
9:17 of Israel would pitch their *t*.
16:24 Get away from the *t* of Korah,
16:26 Depart now from the *t* of these
16:27 got away from around the *t* of
16:27 stood at the door of their *t*,
24: 5 "How lovely are your *t*,
Deut 1:27 "and you complained in your *t*,
1:33 a place for you to pitch your *t*,
5:30 say to them, "Return to your *t*.
11: 6 up, their households, their *t*,
16: 7 you shall turn and go to your *t*.
33:18 And Issachar in your *t*!
Josh 22: 4 return and go to your *t* and to
22: 6 away, and they went to their *t*.
22: 7 sent them away to their *t*,
22: 8 with much riches to your *t*,
Judg 5:24 is she among women in *t*.
6: 5 their livestock and their *t*,
8:11 road of those who dwell in *t*
1 Sam 17:53 and they plundered their *t*.
2 Sam 11:11 and Judah are dwelling in *t*,
20: 1 of Jesse; Every man to his *t*,

1 Ki 8:66 and went to their *t* joyful and
12:16 in the son of Jesse. To your *t*,
12:16 So Israel departed to their *t*.
2 Ki 7: 7 left the camp intact—their *t*,
7:10 and the *t* intact."
7:16 went out and plundered the *t*
8:21 and the troops fled to their *t*.
13: 5 of Israel dwelt in their *t* as
1 Chr 4:41 and they attacked their *t* and
5:10 and they dwelt in their *t*
2 Chr 7:10 sent the people away to their *t*,
10:16 of Jesse. Every man to your *t*,
10:16 all Israel departed to their *t*.
Job 11:14 let wickedness dwell in your *t*;
12: 6 The *t* of robbers prosper,
15:34 And fire will consume the *t* of
22:23 remove iniquity far from your *t*.
Ps 69:25 Let no one live in their *t*.
78:51 of their strength in the *t* of
78:55 of Israel dwell in their *t*.
83: 6 The *t* of Edom and the
84:10 of my God Than dwell in the *t*
106:25 But complained in their *t*,
118:15 and salvation Is in the *t* of
120: 5 That I dwell among the *t* of
Song 1: 5 Like the *t* of Kedar, Like the
1: 8 goats Beside the shepherds' *t*.
Isa 13:20 Nor will the Arabian pitch *t*
Jer 4:20 Suddenly my *t* are plundered,
6: 3 They shall pitch their *t*
30:18 back the captivity of Jacob's *t*,
35: 7 your days you shall dwell in *t*,
35:10 "But we have dwelt in *t*,
49:29 Their *t* and their flocks they
Dan 11:45 And he shall plant the *t* of his
Hos 9: 6 Thorns shall be in their *t*.
12: 9 will again make you dwell in *t*,
Hab 3: 7 I saw the *t* of Cushan in
Zech 12: 7 The LORD will save the *t* of
Mal 2:12 the LORD cut off from the *t*
Heb 11: 9 dwelling in *t* with Isaac and

TERAH (14/12)

Gen 11:24 twenty-nine years, and begot *T*.
11:25 After he begot *T*,
11:26 Now *T* lived seventy years, and
11:27 This is the genealogy of *T*:
11:27 *T* begot Abram, Nahor,
11:28 Haran died before his father *T*
11:31 And *T* took his son Abram and
11:32 So the days of *T* were two
11:32 and *T* died in Haran.
Num 33:27 from Tahath and camped at *T*.
33:28 They moved from *T* and camped at
Josh 24: 2 'Your fathers, including *T*,
1 Chr 1:26 Serug, Nahor, *T*,
Lk 3:34 son of Abraham, the son of *T*,

TERAPHIM (1/1)

Hos 3: 4 pillar, without ephod or *t*.

TEREBINTH (21/20)

Gen 12: 6 as far as the *t* tree of Moreh.
13:18 and went and dwelt by the *t*
14:13 for he dwelt by the *t* trees of
18: 1 LORD appeared to him by the *t*
35: 4 and Jacob hid them under the *t*
35: 8 below Bethel under the *t* tree.
Deut 11:30 beside the *t* trees of Moreh?
Josh 19:33 the territory from the *t* tree
Judg 4:11 and pitched his tent near the *t*
6:11 LORD came and sat under the *t*
6:19 them out to Him under the *t*
9: 6 Abimelech king beside the *t*
9:37 is coming from the Diviners' *T*
1 Sam 10: 3 from there and come to the *t*
2 Sam 18: 9 the thick boughs of a great *t*
18: 9 and his head caught in the *t*;
18:10 just saw Absalom hanging in a *t*
18:14 alive in the midst of the *t*
Isa 1:29 they shall be ashamed of the *t*
1:30 For you shall be as a *t* whose
6:13 As a *t* tree or as an oak,

TEREBINTHS (1/1)

Hos 4:13 Under oaks, poplars, and *t*,

TERESH (2/2)

Esth 2:21 king's eunuchs, Bigthan and *T*,
6: 2 had told of Bigthana and *T*,

TERMED (2/1)

Isa 62: 4 You shall no longer be *t*
62: 4 shall your land any more be *t*

TERMS (2/2)

Job 34:33 repay it according to your *t*,
Rom 6:19 I speak in human *t* because of

TERRACE (5/4)

Ezek 17: 7 From the garden *t* where it had
17:10 It will wither in the garden *t*
41: 9 and so also the remaining *t* by
41:11 side chambers opened on the *t*,
41:11 and the width of the *t* was

TERRESTRIAL (2/1)

1 Cor 15:40 also celestial bodies and *t*
15:40 and the glory of the *t* is

TERRIBLE (23/23) TERROR

Deut 1:19 that great and *t* wilderness
7:15 with none of the *t* diseases
8:15 that great and *t* wilderness
Job 41:14 With his *t* teeth all around?
Isa 13:11 low the haughtiness of the *t*.
18: 2 To a people *t* from their
18: 7 And from a people *t* from their
21: 1 from the desert, from a *t* land.
25: 3 The city of the *t* nations will
25: 4 For the blast of the *t* ones
25: 5 The song of the *t* ones will be
29: 5 the multitude of the *t* ones
29:20 For the *t* one is brought to
49:25 And the prey of the *t* be
Jer 15:21 you from the grip of the *t*.
Ezek 5:16 send against them the *t* arrows
28: 7 The most *t* of the nations;
30:11 the most *t* of the nations,
31:12 the most *t* of the nations, have
32:12 all of them the most *t* of the
Dan 7: 7 a fourth beast, dreadful and *t*,
Joel 2:11 the LORD is great and very *t*;
Hab 1: 7 They are *t* and dreadful;

TERRIFIED (11/11)

Deut 1:29 I said to you, 'Do not be *t*,
7:21 'You shall not be *t* of them;
20: 3 and do not tremble or be *t*
Esth 7: 6 wicked Haman!" So Haman was *t*
Job 21: 6 Even when I remember I am *t*,
23:15 Therefore I am *t* at His
Ps 90: 7 And by Your wrath we are *t*.
Jer 51:32 fire, And the men of war are *t*.
Lk 21: 9 and commotions, do not be *t*;
24:37 But they were *t* and frightened,
Phil 1:28 and not in any way *t* by your

TERRIFIES (2/2)

Deut 28:67 because of the fear which *t*
Job 23:16 And the Almighty *t* me;

TERRIFY (6/6)

Job 3: 5 the blackness of the day *t* it.
7:14 scare me with dreams And *t* me
9:34 And do not let dread of Him *t*
33: 7 Surely no fear of me will *t*
Zech 1:21 the craftsmen are coming to *t*
2 Cor 10: 9 lest I seem to *t* you by letters.

TERRIFYING (1/1)

Heb 12:21 And so *t* was the sight that

TERRITORIES (4/4)

2 Sam 21: 5 from remaining in any of the *t*
2 Chr 11:13 And from all their *t* the
11:23 his sons throughout all the *t*
Jer 15:13 your sins, Throughout your *t*.

TERRITORY (71/66)

Ex 8: 2 I will smite all your *t* with
10: 4 will bring locusts into your *t*.
10:14 Egypt and rested on all the *t*
10:19 not one locust in all the *t* of
Num 20:17 we have passed through your *t*.
20:21 Israel passage through his *t*;
21:22 we have passed through your *t*.
21:23 Israel to pass through his *t*.
22:36 Arnon, the boundary of the *t*.
Deut 2: 4 about to pass through the *t*
11:24 Western Sea, shall be your *t*.
16: 4 be seen among you in all your *t*
19: 3 divide into three parts the *t*
19: 8 LORD your God enlarges your *t*,
28:40 trees throughout all your *t*,
Josh 1: 4 of the sun, shall be your *t*.
12: 4 Og king of Bashan and his *t*,
13: 2 all the *t* of the Philistines
13:16 Their *t* was from Aroer, which
13:25 Their *t* was Jazer, and all the
13:30 Their *t* was from Mahanaim,
17: 7 And the *t* of Manasseh was from
17:10 Manasseh's *t* was adjoining
18: 5 Judah shall remain in their *t*
18: 5 Joseph shall remain in their *t*
18:11 and the *t* of their lot came out
19:18 And their *t* went to Jezreel,
19:25 And their *t* included Helkath,
19:33 enclosing the *t* from the
19:41 And the *t* of their inheritance
Judg 1: 3 up with me to my allotted *t*,
1: 3 go with you to your allotted *t*.
1:18 Also Judah took Gaza with its *t*,
1:18 territory, Ashkelon with its *t*,
1:18 territory, and Ekron with its *t*.
11:20 Israel to pass through his *t*.
11:22 took possession of all the *t*
18: 2 of their family from their *t*,
19:29 sent her throughout all the *t*
20: 6 sent her throughout all the *t*
1 Sam 5: 6 tumors, both Ashdod and its *t*.
6: 9 goes up the road to its own *t*,
7:13 not come anymore into the *t* of
7:14 and Israel recovered its *t* from
10: 2 men by Rachel's tomb in the *t*
11: 3 send messengers to all the *t*
11: 7 them throughout all the *t* of
30:14 in the *t* which belongs to
2 Sam 8: 3 as he went to recover his *t* at
1 Ki 1: 3 woman throughout all the *t* of
2 Ki 10:32 conquered them in all the *t* of
14:25 He restored the *t* of Israel from
15:16 all who were there, and its *t*.
18: 8 as far as Gaza and its *t*,
1 Chr 4:10 me indeed, and enlarge my *t*,
6:54 their settlements in their *t*,
6:66 were given cities as their *t*
21:12 throughout all the *t* of Israel.
Job 38:20 That you may take it to its *t*,
Ps 105:31 And lice in all their *t*.
105:33 splintered the trees of their *t*.
Isa 20: 6 And the inhabitant of this *t*
56:11 his own gain, From his own *t*.
Ezek 25: 9 I will clear the *t* of Moab of
33: 2 land take a man from their *t*
45: 1 be holy throughout its *t* all
Am 1:13 they might enlarge their *t*.
6: 2 Or is their *t* greater than
6: 2 territory greater than your *t*?
7: 4 great deep and devoured the *t*.
Mal 1: 4 They shall be called the *T* of

TERROR (39/39) TERRIBLE, TERRORS

Gen 35: 5 and the *t* of God was upon the
Lev 26:16 I will even appoint *t* over you,
Deut 26: 8 with great *t* and with signs and
32:25 There shall be *t* within
34:12 power and all the great *t*
Josh 2: 9 that the *t* of you has fallen on
Job 6:21 You see *t* and are afraid.
31:23 destruction from God is a *t*
39:20 majestic snorting strikes *t*.
Ps 91: 5 shall not be afraid of the *t*
Prov 1:26 I will mock when your *t* comes,
1:27 When your *t* comes like a storm,
3:25 Do not be afraid of sudden *t*,
Isa 2:10 From the *t* of the LORD
2:19 From the *t* of the LORD
2:21 From the *t* of the LORD
10:33 Will lop off the bough with *t*;
19:17 the land of Judah will be a *t*
28:19 It will be a *t* just to
33:18 Your heart will meditate on *t*:
54:14 you shall not fear; And from *t*,
Jer 15: 8 I will cause anguish and *t* to
17:17 Do not be a *t* to me; You are
20: 4 I will make you a *t* to yourself
32:21 and with great *t*;
Ezek 26:17 Who caused their *t* to be on
26:21 'I will make you a *t*,
32:23 Who caused *t* in the land of
32:24 Who caused their *t* in the land
32:25 Though their *t* was caused In
32:26 Though they caused their *t* in
32:27 Because of the *t* of the mighty
32:30 the slain In shame at the *t*
32:32 For I have caused My *t* in the
Dan 10: 7 but a great *t* fell upon them,
Hos 11: 9 And I will not come with *t*.
Rom 13: 3 For rulers are not a *t* to good
2 Cor 5:11 the *t* of the Lord, we persuade
1 Pe 3: 6 and are not afraid with any *t*.

TERRORS (15/15) TERROR

Deut 4:34 arm, and by great *t*,
Job 6: 4 The *t* of God are arrayed
18:11 *T* frighten him on every side,
18:14 parade him before the king of *t*.
20:25 *T* come upon him;
24:17 They are in the *t* of the
27:20 *T* overtake him like a flood
30:15 *T* are turned upon me
Ps 55: 4 And the *t* of death have fallen
73:19 are utterly consumed with *t*.
88:15 my youth; I suffer Your *t*;
88:16 Your *t* have cut me off.
Eccl 12: 5 And of *t* in the way; When the
Lam 2:22 as to a feast day The *t* that
Ezek 21:12 *T* including the sword will be

TERTIUS (1/1)

Rom 16:22 I, *T*, who wrote this epistle,

TERTULLUS (2/2)

Acts 24: 1 and a certain orator named *T*.
24: 2 *T* began his accusation, saying:

TEST (37/37) TESTED, TESTING, TESTS

Ex 16: 4 that I may *t* them, whether they
20:20 for God has come to *t* you,
Num 14:22 and have put Me to the *t* now
Deut 8: 2 to humble you and *t* you, to
8:16 humble you and that He might *t*
Judg 2:22 so that through them I may *t*
3: 1 that He might *t* Israel by them,
3: 4 that He might *t* Israel by
6:39 speak just once more: Let me *t*,
7: 4 and I will *t* them for you
1 Ki 10: 1 she came to *t* him with hard

T

1 Chr 29:17 that You *t* the heart and have
2 Chr 9: 1 she came to Jerusalem to *t*
32:31 in order to *t* him, that He
Job 7:18 And *t* him every moment?
12:11 Does not the ear *t* words
Ps 11: 4 His eyelids *t* the sons of men.
Eccl 2: 1 I will *t* you with mirth;
Isa 7:12 nor will I *t* the LORD!"
Jer 6:27 That you may know and *t* their
17:10 I *t* the mind, Even to give
20:12 You who *t* the righteous,
Dan 1:12 Please *t* your servants for ten
Zech 13: 9 And *t* them as gold is tested.
Mt 22:18 'Why do you *t* Me,
Mk 12:15 Why do you *t* Me? Bring Me a
Lk 14:19 and I am going to *t* them. I ask
20:23 Why do you *t* Me?
Jn 6: 6 But this He said to *t* him,
Acts 5: 9 you have agreed together to *t*
15:10 why do you *t* God by putting a
1 Cor 3:13 and the fire will *t* each one's
2 Cor 2: 9 that I might put you to the *t*,
13: 5 *T* yourselves. Do you not know
1 Th 5:21 *T* all things; hold fast what is
1 Jn 4: 1 but *t* the spirits, whether they
Rev 3:10 to *t* those who dwell on the

TESTAMENT (3/3) TESTATOR

2 Cor 3:14 in the reading of the Old *T*,
Heb 9:16 For where there is a *t*,
9:17 For a *t* is in force after men

TESTATOR (2/2) TESTAMENT

Heb 9:16 necessity be the death of the *t*.
9:17 has no power at all while the *t*

TESTED (27/26) PROVED, TEST

Gen 22: 1 after these things that God *t*
42:15 this manner you shall be *t*:
42:16 that your words may be *t* to see
Ex 15:25 And there He *t* them,
Deut 33: 8 Whom You *t* at Massah,
1 Sam 17:39 for he had not *t* them. And
17:39 for I have not *t* them."
Job 23:10 When He has *t* me, I shall
Ps 17: 3 You have *t* my heart; You have
66:10 have *t* us; You have refined us
78:18 And they *t* God in their heart
78:56 Yet they *t* and provoked the
81: 7 I *t* you at the waters of
95: 9 When your fathers *t* Me;
105:19 The word of the LORD *t* him.
106:14 And *t* God in the desert.
Isa 48:10 I have *t* you in the furnace of
Jer 12: 3 And You have *t* my heart toward
Dan 1:14 and *t* them ten days.
Zech 13: 9 And test them as gold is *t*.
Lk 10:25 a certain lawyer stood up and *t*
1 Tim 3:10 But let these also first be *t*;
Heb 3: 9 Where your fathers *t* Me,
11:17 faith Abraham, when he was *t*,
1 Pe 1: 7 though it is *t* by fire, may be
Rev 2: 2 And you have *t* those who say
2:10 into prison, that you may be *t*,

TESTIFIED (29/29) TESTIFY

Deut 19:18 who has *t* falsely against his
Ruth 1:21 since the LORD has *t* against
2 Sam 1:16 for your own mouth has *t*
2 Ki 17:13 Yet the LORD *t* against Israel
17:15 His testimonies which He had *t*
2 Chr 24:19 and they *t* against them, but
Neh 9:26 who *t* against them To turn
9:29 And *t* against them, That You
9:30 And *t* against them by Your
9:34 With which You *t* against them.
Jn 1:34 And I have seen and *t* that this
3:26 the Jordan, to whom you have *t*—
4:39 of the word of the woman who *t*,
4:44 For Jesus Himself *t* that a
5:37 has *t* of Me. You have neither
13:21 and *t* and said, "Most
19:35 And he who has seen has *t*,
Acts 2:40 with many other words he *t* and
8:25 So when they had *t* and preached
18: 5 and *t* to the Jews that Jesus
23:11 for as you have *t* for Me in
28:23 he explained and solemnly *t* of
1 Cor 15:15 because we have *t* of God that
1 Th 4: 6 as we also forewarned you and *t*.
1 Tim 2: 6 to be *t* in due time,
Heb 2: 6 But one *t* in a certain place,
1 Pe 1:11 them was indicating when He *t*
1 Jn 5: 9 witness of God which He has *t*
3 Jn 3 when brethren came and *t* of

TESTIFIES (7/7) TESTIFY

Hos 5: 5 The pride of Israel *t* to his
7:10 And the pride of Israel *t* to
Jn 3:32 has seen and heard, that He *t*;
21:24 This is the disciple who *t* of
Acts 20:23 except that the Holy Spirit *t* in
Heb 7:17 He *t*: "You are a priest
Rev 22:20 He who *t* to these things says,

TESTIFY (30/30) TESTIFIED, TESTIFIES, TESTIFYING

Ex 23: 2 nor shall you *t* in a dispute so
Deut 8:19 I *t* against you this day that
19:16 rises against any man to *t*
31:21 that this song will *t* against
32:46 on all the words which I *t*
Job 15: 6 your own lips *t* against you.
Ps 50: 7 and I will *t* against you;
Isa 59:12 And our sins *t* against us;
Jer 14: 7 though our iniquities *t* against
Am 3:13 Hear and *t* against the house of
Mic 6: 3 I wearied you? *T* against Me.
Mt 26:62 What is it these men *t*
27:13 not hear how many things they *t*
Mk 14:60 What is it these men *t*
15: 4 See how many things they *t*
Lk 16:28 that he may *t* to them, lest
Jn 2:25 no need that anyone should *t*
3:11 We speak what We know and *t*
5:39 and these are they which *t* of
7: 7 but it hates Me because I *t* of
15:26 He will *t* of Me.
Acts 10:42 and to *t* that it is He who was
20:24 to *t* to the gospel of the grace
20:26 Therefore I *t* to you this day
26: 5 if they were willing to *t*,
Gal 5: 3 And I *t* again to every man who
Eph 4:17 and *t* in the Lord, that you
1 Jn 4:14 And we have seen and *t* that the
Rev 22:16 have sent My angel to *t* to you
22:18 For I *t* to everyone who hears

TESTIFYING (3/3) TESTIFY

Acts 20:21 *t* to Jews, and also to Greeks,
Heb 11: 4 God *t* of his gifts; and through
1 Pe 5:12 exhorting and *t* that this is

TESTIMONIES (37/37) TESTIMONY

Deut 4:45 These are the *t*,
6:17 of the LORD your God, His *t*,
6:20 is the meaning of the *t*,
1 Ki 2: 3 His judgments, and His *t*,
2 Ki 17:15 and His *t* which He had
23: 3 His commandments and His *t* and
1 Chr 29:19 Your commandments and Your *t*
2 Chr 34:31 His commandments and His *t* and
Neh 9:34 Your commandments and Your *t*,
Ps 25:10 as keep His covenant and His *t*.
78:56 God, And did not keep His *t*,
93: 5 Your *t* are very sure; Holiness
99: 7 They kept His *t* and the
119: 2 are those who keep His *t*,
119:14 rejoiced in the way of Your *t*,
119:22 For I have kept Your *t*.
119:24 Your *t* also are my delight
119:31 I cling to Your *t*;
119:36 Incline my heart to Your *t*,
119:46 I will speak of Your *t* also
119:59 And turned my feet to Your *t*.
119:79 to me, Those who know Your *t*.
119:95 But I will consider Your *t*.
119:99 For Your *t* are my meditation.
119:111 Your *t* I have taken as a
119:119 dross; Therefore I love Your *t*.
119:125 That I may know Your *t*.
119:129 Your *t* are wonderful;
119:138 Your *t*, which You have
119:144 The righteousness of Your *t* is
119:146 and I will keep Your *t*.
119:152 Concerning Your *t*,
119:157 Yet I do not turn from Your *t*.
119:167 My soul keeps Your *t*,
119:168 keep Your precepts and Your *t*,
Jer 44:23 in His statutes or in His *t*,
Mk 14:56 but their *t* did not agree.

TESTIMONY (96/90) TESTIMONIES

Ex 16:34 Aaron laid it up before the *T*,
25:16 shall put into the ark the *T*
25:21 in the ark you shall put the *T*
25:22 which are on the ark of the *T*,
26:33 shall bring the ark of the *T*
26:34 seat upon the ark of the *T* in
27:21 the veil which is before the *T*,
30: 6 is before the ark of the *T*,
30: 6 mercy seat that is over the *T*,
30:26 of meeting and the ark of the *T*;
30:36 put some of it before the *T* in
31: 7 the ark of the *T* and the mercy
31:18 gave Moses two tablets of the *T*,
32:15 and the two tablets of the *T*
34:29 (and the two tablets of the *T*
38:21 the tabernacle of the *T*,
39:35 the ark of the *T* with its poles,
40: 3 put in it the ark of the *T*,
40: 5 incense before the ark of the *T*,
40:20 He took the *T* and put it into
40:21 off the ark of the *T*,
Lev 16:13 mercy seat that is on the *T*,
24: 3 "Outside the veil of the *T*,
Num 1:50 over the tabernacle of the *T*,
1:53 around the tabernacle of the *T*,
1:53 of the tabernacle of the *T*.
4: 5 veil and cover the ark of the *T*
7:89 that was on the ark of the *T*,
9:15 tabernacle, the tent of the *T*;
10:11 above the tabernacle of the *T*.
17: 4 of meeting before the *T*,
17:10 Aaron's rod back before the *T*,
35:30 shall be put to death on the *t*
35:30 witness is not sufficient *t*
Deut 17: 6 shall be put to death on the *t*
17: 6 not be put to death on the *t*
Josh 4:16 who bear the ark of the *T* to
2 Ki 11:12 on him, and gave him the *T*;
2 Chr 23:11 crown on him, gave him the *T*,
Ps 19: 7 The *t* of the LORD is sure,
60: Set to "Lily of the *T*.
78: 5 For He established a *t* in
80: A *T* of Asaph. A Psalm.
81: 5 established in Joseph as a *t*,
119:88 So that I may keep the *t* of
122: 4 To the *T* of Israel, To give
132:12 will keep My covenant And My *t*
Isa 8:16 Bind up the *t*,
8:20 To the law and to the *t*! If they
Mt 8: 4 as a *t* to them."
10:18 as a *t* to them and to the
26:59 all the council sought false *t*
Mk 1:44 as a *t* to them."
6:11 the dust under your feet as a *t*
13: 9 for a *t* to them.
14:55 and all the council sought *t*
14:59 But not even then did their *t*
Lk 5:14 as a *t* to them, just as Moses
9: 5 very dust from your feet as a *t*
21:13 for you as an occasion for *t*.
22:71 'What further *t* do we need?
Jn 1:19 Now this is the *t* of John,
3:32 and no one receives His *t*.
3:33 He who has received His *t* has
5:34 Yet I do not receive *t* from man,
8:17 written in your law that the *t*
19:35 and his *t* is true; and he knows
21:24 and we know that his *t* is true.
Acts 13:22 to whom also He gave *t* and
22:12 having a good *t* with all the
22:18 they will not receive your *t*
1 Cor 1: 6 even as the *t* of Christ was
2: 1 wisdom declaring to you the *t*
2 Cor 1:12 the *t* of our conscience that we
2 Th 1:10 because our *t* among you was
1 Tim 3: 7 Moreover he must have a good *t*
2 Tim 1: 8 do not be ashamed of the *t* of
Titus 1:13 This *t* is true. Therefore rebuke
Heb 3: 5 for a *t* of those things which
10:28 dies without mercy on the *t* of
11: 2 the elders obtained a good *t*.
11: 5 he was taken he had this *t*,
11:39 having obtained a good *t*
1 Jn 5:10 he has not believed the *t* that
5:11 And this is the *t*:
3 Jn 12 Demetrius has a good *t* from
12 and you know that our *t* is
Rev 1: 2 and to the *t* of Jesus Christ,
1: 9 the word of God and for the *t*
6: 9 the word of God and for the *t*
11: 7 When they finish their *t*,
12:11 Lamb and by the word of their *t*,
12:17 of God and have the *t* of Jesus
15: 5 of the tabernacle of the *t* in
19:10 of your brethren who have the *t*
19:10 Worship God! For the *t* of Jesus

TESTING (12/12) TEST

Deut 13: 3 for the LORD your God is *t* you
Jer 11:20 *T* the mind and the heart,
Ezek 21:13 "Because it is a *t*,
Mt 16: 1 and *t* Him asked that He would
19: 3 *t* Him, and saying to Him, "Is
22:35 *t* Him, and saying,
Mk 8:11 a sign from heaven, *t* Him.
10: 2 divorce his wife?" *t* Him.
Lk 11:16 *t* Him, sought from Him a sign
Jn 8: 6 *t* Him, that they might have
2 Cor 8: 8 but I am *t* the sincerity of
Jas 1: 3 knowing that the *t* of your faith

TESTS (6/6) TEST

Job 34: 3 For the ear *t* words As the
Ps 7: 9 For the righteous God *t* the
11: 5 The LORD *t* the righteous,
Prov 17: 3 But the LORD *t* the hearts.
Eccl 3:18 God *t* them, that they may see
1 Th 2: 4 but God who *t* our hearts.

TETRARCH (7/5)

Mt 14: 1 At that time Herod the *t* heard
Lk 3: 1 Herod being *t* of Galilee, his
3: 1 his brother Philip *t* of Iturea
3: 1 and Lysanias *t* of Abilene,
3:19 But Herod the *t*,
9: 7 Now Herod the *t* heard of all
Acts 13: 1 brought up with Herod the *t*,

THADDAEUS (2/2) JUDAS

Mt 10: 3 Lebbaeus, whose surname was *T*;
Mk 3:18 James the son of Alphaeus, *T*,

THAHASH (1/1)

Gen 22:24 also bore Tebah, Gaham, *T*,

THAMAR (KJV) See TAMAR

THAN (515/458) See APPENDIX

THANK (25/24) PRAISE, THANKFUL, THANKS

1 Chr 16: 4 the LORD, to commemorate, to *t*,
16: 7 his brethren, to *t* the LORD:
23:30 to stand every morning to *t* and
29:13 We *t* You And praise Your
2 Chr 29:31 and bring sacrifices and *t*
29:31 brought in sacrifices and *t*
33:16 peace offerings and *t*
Isa 38:18 For Sheol cannot *t* You,
Dan 2:23 I *t* You and praise You, O God
Mt 11:25 I *t* You, Father, Lord of heaven
Lk 10:21 I *t* You, Father, Lord of heaven
17: 9 Does he *t* that servant because
18:11 I *t* You that I am not like
Jn 11:41 I *t* You that You have heard Me.
Rom 1: 8 I *t* my God through Jesus Christ
7:25 I *t* God—through Jesus Christ our
1 Cor 1: 4 I *t* my God always concerning
1:14 I *t* God that I baptized none of
14:18 I *t* my God I speak with tongues
Phil 1: 3 I *t* my God upon every
1 Th 2:13 For this reason we also *t* God
2 Th 1: 3 We are bound to *t* God always
1 Tim 1:12 And I *t* Christ Jesus our Lord
2 Tim 1: 3 I *t* God, whom I serve with a
Phm 1: 4 I *t* my God, making mention of

THANKED (3/3)

2 Sam 14:22 and *t* the king. And Joab said,
Acts 28:15 he *t* God and took courage.
Rom 6:17 But God be *t* that though you

THANKFUL (3/3) THANK, UNTHANKFUL

Ps 100: 4 Be *t* to Him, and bless His
Rom 1:21 glorify Him as God, nor were *t*,
Col 3:15 called in one body; and be *t*.

THANKFULNESS (1/1)

Acts 24: 3 most noble Felix, with all *t*.

THANKING (1/1)

2 Chr 5:13 to be heard in praising and *t*

THANKS (75/72) THANK, THANKSGIVING

2 Sam 22:50 Therefore I will give *t* to You,
1 Chr 16: 8 give *t* to the LORD! Call upon
16:34 give *t* to the LORD, for He
16:35 To give *t* to Your holy name,
16:41 to give *t* to the LORD, because
25: 3 with a harp to give *t* and to
2 Chr 31: 2 offerings, to serve, to give *t*,
Ezra 3:11 praising and giving *t* to the
Neh 12:24 them, to praise and give *t*,
Ps 6: 5 the grave who will give You *t*?
18:49 Therefore I will give *t* to You,
30: 4 And give *t* at the remembrance
30:12 I will give *t* to You forever.
35:18 I will give You *t* in the great
75: 1 We give *t* to You, O God, we
75: 1 we give *t*! For Your wondrous
79:13 Will give You *t* forever;
92: 1 It is good to give *t* to the
97:12 And give *t* at the remembrance
105: 1 give *t* to the LORD! Call upon
106: 1 give *t* to the LORD, for He
106:47 To give *t* to Your holy name,
107: 1 give *t* to the LORD, for He
107: 8 that men would give *t* to the
107:15 that men would give *t* to the
107:21 that men would give *t* to the
107:31 that men would give *t* to the
118: 1 give *t* to the LORD, for He
118:29 give *t* to the LORD, for He
119:62 midnight I will rise to give *t*
122: 4 To give *t* to the name of the
136: 1 give *t* to the LORD, for He
136: 2 give *t* to the God of gods!
136: 3 give *t* to the Lord of lords!
136:26 give *t* to the God of heaven!
140:13 the righteous shall give *t* to
Dan 6:10 and prayed and gave *t* before
Mt 15:36 loaves and the fish and gave *t*,
26:27 He took the cup, and gave *t*,
Mk 8: 6 the seven loaves and gave *t*,
14:23 and when He had given *t* He gave
Lk 2:38 in that instant she gave *t* to
17:16 face at His feet, giving Him *t*.
22:17 He took the cup, and gave *t*,
22:19 gave *t* and broke it, and gave
Jn 6:11 and when He had given *t* He
6:23 after the Lord had given *t*—
Acts 27:35 he took bread and gave *t* to God
Rom 14: 6 to the Lord, for he gives God *t*;
14: 6 does not eat, and gives God *t*.
16: 4 life, to whom not only I give *t*,
1 Cor 10:30 But if I partake with *t*,
10:30 the food over which I give *t*?
11:24 and when He had given *t*,
14:16 "Amen" at your giving of *t*,
14:17 For you indeed give *t* well,
15:57 But *t* be to God, who gives us
2 Cor 1:11 that *t* may be given by many
2:14 Now *t* be to God who always
8:16 But *t* be to God who puts the
9:15 *T* be to God for His
Eph 1:16 do not cease to give *t* for you,
5: 4 fitting, but rather giving of *t*.
5:20 giving *t* always for all things
Col 1: 3 We give *t* to the God and Father
1:12 giving *t* to the Father who has
3:17 giving *t* to God the Father
1 Th 1: 2 We give *t* to God always for you
3: 9 For what *t* can we render to God
5:18 in everything give *t*;
2 Th 2:13 But we are bound to give *t* to
1 Tim 2: 1 and giving of *t* be made for
Heb 13:15 giving *t* to His name.
Rev 4: 9 give glory and honor and *t* to
11:17 saying: "We give You *t*,

THANKSGIVING (32/31) THANKS

Lev 7:12 'If he offers it for a *t*,
7:12 offer, with the sacrifice of *t*,
7:13 bread with the sacrifice of *t*
7:15 of his peace offering for *t*
22:29 you offer a sacrifice of *t* to
Neh 11:17 the leader who began the *t*
12: 8 and Mattaniah who led the *t*
12:31 and appointed two large *t*
12:38 The other *t* choir went the
12:40 So the two *t* choirs stood in the
12:46 and songs of praise and *t* to
Ps 26: 7 proclaim with the voice of *t*,
50:14 Offer to God *t*,
69:30 And will magnify Him with *t*.
95: 2 come before His presence with *t*;
100: A Psalm of *T*.
100: 4 Enter into His gates with *t*,
107:22 sacrifice the sacrifices of *t*,
116:17 offer to You the sacrifice of *t*,
147: 7 Sing to the LORD with *t*;
Isa 51: 3 *T* and the voice of melody.
Jer 30:19 out of them shall proceed *t*
Am 4: 5 Offer a sacrifice of *t* with
Jon 2: 9 to You With the voice of *t*;
2 Cor 4:15 may cause *t* to abound to the
9:11 which causes *t* through us to
Phil 4: 6 prayer and supplication, with *t*,
Col 2: 7 taught, abounding in it with *t*.
4: 2 being vigilant in it with *t*;
1 Tim 4: 3 created to be received with *t*
4: 4 if it is received with *t*;
Rev 7:12 *T* and honor and power and

THANKSGIVINGS (2/2)

Neh 12:27 both with *t* and singing, with
2 Cor 9:12 is abounding through many *t* to

THANKWORTHY (KJV) See COMMENDABLE

THARA (KJV) See TERAH

THARSHISH (1/1)

1 Chr 7:10 Ehud, Chenaanah, Zethan, *T*,

THAT (7380/6205) See APPENDIX

THE (61782/23845) See APPENDIX

THE-LORD-IS-MY-BANNER (1/1) LORD

Ex 17:15 an altar and called its name, *T*;

THE-LORD-IS-PEACE (1/1)

Judg 6:24 to the LORD, and called it *T*.

THE-LORD-WILL-PROVIDE (1/1) LORD

Gen 22:14 called the name of the place, *T*;

THEATER (2/2)

Acts 19:29 and rushed into the *t* with one
19:31 he would not venture into the *t*.

THEBEZ (3/2)

Judg 9:50 Then Abimelech went to *T*,
9:50 and he encamped against *T* and
2 Sam 11:21 the wall, so that he died in *T*?

THEFT (2/2)

Ex 22: 3 then he shall be sold for his *t*.
22: 4 If the *t* is certainly found

THEFTS (3/3)

Mt 15:19 adulteries, fornications, *t*,
Mk 7:22 '*t*, covetousness, wickedness,
Rev 9:21 sexual immorality or their *t*.

THEIR (3904/2783) See APPENDIX

THEIRS (20/20) See APPENDIX

THELASAR (KJV) See TELASSAR

THEM (5537/4286)

Gen 1:14 and let *t* be for signs and
1:15 and let *t* be for lights in the
1:17 God set *t* in the firmament of
1:22 And God blessed *t*,
1:26 let *t* have dominion over the
1:27 male and female He created *t*.
1:28 Then God blessed *t*,
1:28 blessed them, and God said to *t*,
2: 1 earth, and all the host of *t*,
2:19 and brought *t* to Adam to see
2:19 to see what he would call *t*.
3: 7 Then the eyes of both of *t* were
3:21 tunics of skin, and clothed *t*.
5: 2 He created *t* male and female,
5: 2 and blessed *t* and called them
5: 2 and blessed them and called *t*
6: 1 and daughters were born to *t*,
6: 4 and they bore children to *t*.
6: 7 I am sorry that I have made *t*.
6:13 filled with violence through *t*;
6:13 I will destroy *t* with the
6:19 to keep *t* alive with you;
6:20 will come to you to keep *t*
6:21 shall be food for you and for *t*.
7:13 three wives of his sons with *t*,
9: 1 and his sons, and said to *t*:
10: 1 And sons were born to *t* after
11: 3 let us make bricks and bake *t*
11: 6 to do will be withheld from *t*.
11: 8 So the LORD scattered *t* abroad
11: 9 there the LORD scattered *t*
11:31 and they went out with *t* from
13: 6 land was not able to support *t*,
14:15 He divided his forces against *t*
14:15 he and his servants attacked *t*
14:15 attacked them and pursued *t* as
14:24 let *t* take their portion."
15: 5 if you are able to number *t*.
15:10 all these to Him and cut *t* in
15:11 Abram drove *t* away.
15:13 not theirs, and will serve *t*,
15:13 and they will afflict *t* four
18: 2 by him; and when he saw *t*,
18: 2 from the tent door to meet *t*,
18: 8 prepared, and set it before *t*;
18: 8 and he stood by *t* under the
18:16 and Abraham went with *t* to send
18:16 went with them to send *t* on
19: 1 gate of Sodom. When Lot saw *t*,
19: 1 saw them, he rose to meet *t*,
19: 3 Then he made *t* a feast,
19: 5 Bring *t* out to us that we may
19: 5 out to us that we may know *t*
19: 6 So Lot went out to *t* through the
19: 8 let me bring *t* out to you,
19: 8 and you may do to *t* as you
19: 9 deal worse with you than with *t*.
19:10 Lot into the house with *t*,
19:12 take *t* out of this place!
19:13 because the outcry against *t*
19:17 when they had brought *t*
19:18 Then Lot said to *t*,
20:14 and gave *t* to Abraham; and he
21:27 took sheep and oxen and gave *t*
21:27 and the two of *t* made a
21:31 because the two of *t* swore an
22: 6 and the two of *t* went together.
22: 8 So the two of *t* went
23: 8 And he spoke with *t*,
24:53 and gave *t* to Rebekah. He also
24:56 And he said to *t*,
24:60 The gates of those who hate *t*.
25: 6 he was still living he sent *t*
25:26 sixty years old when she bore *t*.
26:15 and they had filled *t* with
26:18 the Philistines had stopped *t*
26:18 He called *t* by the names which
26:18 which his father had called *t*.
26:27 And Isaac said to *t*,
26:30 So he made *t* a feast, and they
26:31 and Isaac sent *t* away, and they
27: 9 I will make savory food from *t*
27:13 get *t* for me."
27:14 And he went and got *t* and
27:14 and got them and brought *t*
27:15 and put *t* on Jacob her younger
29: 4 And Jacob said to *t*,
29: 5 Then he said to *t*,
29: 6 So he said to *t*,
29: 7 the sheep, and go and feed *t*.
29: 9 he was still speaking with *t*,
30:14 and brought *t* to his mother
30:35 and gave *t* into the hand of
30:37 trees, peeled white strips in *t*,
30:40 by themselves and did not put *t*
30:42 he did not put *t* in;
31: 5 and said to *t*, "I see your
31: 9 of your father and given *t* to
31:32 know that Rachel had stolen *t*.
31:33 tents, but he did not find *t*.
31:34 put *t* in the camel's saddle,
31:34 camel's saddle, and sat on *t*.
31:34 the tent but did not find *t*.

31:55 and daughters and blessed **t**.
32: 2 When Jacob saw **t**,
32: 4 And he commanded **t**,
32:16 Then he delivered **t** to the hand
32:23 He took **t**, sent them over
32:23 sent **t** over the brook, and sent
33: 3 Then he crossed over before **t**
33:13 And if the men should drive **t**
34: 8 But Hamor spoke with **t**,
34:14 And they said to **t**,
34:21 Therefore let **t** dwell in the
34:21 the land is large enough for **t**.
34:21 and let us give **t** our
34:23 ours? Only let us consent to **t**,
35: 4 and Jacob hid **t** under the
35: 5 cities that were all around **t**,
36: 7 were too great for **t** to dwell
36: 7 strangers could not support **t**
37: 2 brought a bad report of **t** to
37: 6 So he said to **t**,
37:13 Come, I will send you to **t**.
37:17 for I heard **t** say, 'Let us go
37:17 after his brothers and found **t**
37:18 off, even before he came near **t**,
37:22 And Reuben said to **t**,
37:25 on their way to carry **t** down
38:18 Then he gave **t** to her, and
38:23 Let her take **t** for herself,
38:26 So Judah acknowledged **t** and
39:14 men of her house and spoke to **t**,
40: 3 So he put **t** in custody in the
40: 4 the guard charged Joseph with **t**,
40: 4 with them, and he served **t**;
40: 5 prison, had a dream, both of **t**,
40: 6 And Joseph came in to **t** in the
40: 6 in the morning and looked at **t**,
40: 8 of it." So Joseph said to **t**,
40: 8 Tell **t** to me, please."
40:11 I took the grapes and pressed **t**
40:17 and the birds ate **t** out of the
40:22 as Joseph had interpreted to **t**.
41: 3 other cows came up after **t** out
41: 6 east wind, sprang up after **t**.
41: 8 And Pharaoh told **t** his dreams,
41: 8 no one who could interpret **t**
41:19 other cows came up after **t**,
41:21 When they had eaten **t** up, no one
41:21 known that they had eaten **t**,
41:23 east wind, sprang up after **t**.
41:27 ugly cows which came up after **t**
41:30 but after **t** seven years of
41:35 And let **t** gather all the food of
41:35 and let **t** keep food in the
41:48 the fields which surrounded **t**.
42: 7 his brothers and recognized **t**,
42: 7 but he acted as a stranger to **t**
42: 7 to them and spoke roughly to **t**.
42: 7 to them. Then he said to **t**,
42: 9 which he had dreamed about **t**,
42: 9 about them, and said to **t**,
42:12 But he said to **t**,
42:14 But Joseph said to **t**,
42:17 So he put **t** all together in
42:18 Then Joseph said to **t** the third
42:22 And Reuben answered **t**,
42:23 know that Joseph understood **t**,
42:23 for he spoke to **t** through an
42:24 he turned himself away from **t**
42:24 Then he returned to **t** again,
42:24 them again, and talked with **t**.
42:24 And he took Simeon from **t** and
42:25 and to give **t** provisions for
42:25 the journey. Thus he did for **t**.
42:27 But as one of **t** opened his
42:28 Then their hearts failed **t**
42:29 him all that had happened to **t**,
42:36 Jacob their father said to **t**,
43: 2 that their father said to **t**,
43:11 their father Israel said to **t**,
43:16 When Joseph saw Benjamin with **t**,
43:23 Then he brought Simeon out to **t**.
43:24 into Joseph's house and gave **t**
43:27 Then he asked **t** about their
43:32 and **t** by themselves, and the
43:34 Then he took servings to **t** from
44: 4 men; and when you overtake **t**,
44: 4 you overtake them, say to **t**,
44: 6 So he overtook **t**,
44: 6 and he spoke to **t** these same
44:15 And Joseph said to **t**,
45:15 his brothers and wept over **t**,
45:21 and Joseph gave **t** carts,
45:21 and he gave **t** provisions for
45:22 He gave to all of **t**,
45:24 they departed; and he said to **t**,
45:26 because he did not believe **t**.
45:27 which Joseph had said to **t**,
47: 2 his brothers and presented **t**
47: 6 let **t** dwell in the land of
47: 6 know any competent men among **t**,
47: 6 then make **t** chief herdsmen over
47:11 and gave **t** a possession in the
47:17 and Joseph gave **t** bread in
47:17 Thus he fed **t** with bread in
47:20 the famine was severe upon **t**.
47:21 he moved **t** into the cities,
47:22 had rations allotted to **t**
47:22 rations which Pharaoh gave **t**;
48: 6 whom you beget after **t** shall
48: 9 Please bring **t** to me, and I will
48: 9 them to me, and I will bless **t**.
48:10 Then Joseph brought **t** near him,
48:10 and he kissed **t** and embraced
48:10 he kissed them and embraced **t**.
48:12 So Joseph brought **t** from beside
48:13 And Joseph took **t** both, Ephraim
48:13 and brought **t** near him.
48:16 Let my name be named upon **t**,
48:16 And let **t** grow into a
48:20 So he blessed **t** that day,
49: 7 it is cruel! I will divide **t**
49: 7 them in Jacob And scatter **t**
49:28 what their father spoke to **t**.
49:28 spoke to them. And he blessed **t**;
49:29 Then he charged **t** and said to
49:29 he charged them and said to **t**:
50:12 him just as he had commanded **t**.
50:19 Joseph said to **t**,
50:21 And he comforted **t** and spoke
50:21 them and spoke kindly to **t**.
Ex 1: 7 and the land was filled with **t**.
1:10 let us deal shrewdly with **t**,
1:11 they set taskmasters over **t** to
1:11 over them to afflict **t** with
1:12 But the more they afflicted **t**,
1:14 service in which they made **t**
1:16 and see **t** on the birthstools,
1:17 the king of Egypt commanded **t**,
1:18 for the midwives and said to **t**,
1:19 before the midwives come to **t**.
1:21 He provided households for **t**.
2:17 the shepherds came and drove **t**
2:17 but Moses stood up and helped **t**,
2:25 Israel, and God acknowledged **t**.
3: 8 I have come down to deliver **t**
3: 8 and to bring **t** up from that
3: 9 which the Egyptians oppress **t**.
3:13 children of Israel and say to **t**,
3:13 what shall I say to **t**?"
3:16 Israel together, and say to **t**,
3:22 and you shall put **t** on your
4:20 wife and his sons and set **t** on
5: 4 the king of Egypt said to **t**,
5: 5 and you make **t** rest from their
5: 7 Let **t** go and gather straw for
5: 8 And you shall lay on **t** the quota
5: 9 and let **t** not regard false
5:13 And the taskmasters forced **t** to
5:14 taskmasters had set over **t**,
5:20 Aaron who stood there to meet **t**.
5:21 And they said to **t**,
6: 1 a strong hand he will let **t** go,
6: 1 a strong hand he will drive **t**
6: 3 name LORD I was not known to **t**.
6: 4 established My covenant with **t**,
6: 4 to give **t** the land of Canaan,
6:13 and gave **t** a command for the
7: 5 children of Israel from among **t**.
7: 6 just as the LORD commanded **t**,
7:13 hard, and he did not heed **t**,
7:22 hard, and he did not heed **t**,
8: 2 But if you refuse to let **t** go,
8:14 They gathered **t** together in
8:15 his heart and did not heed **t**,
8:19 hard, and he did not heed **t**,
9: 2 For if you refuse to let **t** go,
9: 2 let them go, and still hold **t**,
9:10 and Moses scattered **t** toward
9:12 Pharaoh; and he did not heed **t**,
9:17 in that you will not let **t** go.
9:27 Moses and Aaron, and said to **t**,
10: 2 signs which I have done among **t**,
10: 8 to Pharaoh, and he said to **t**,
10:10 Then he said to **t**,
10:14 nor shall there be such after **t**.
10:19 the locusts away and blew **t**
10:26 For we must take some of **t** to
10:27 and he would not let **t** go.
12:16 of work shall be done on **t**;
12:21 elders of Israel and said to **t**,
12:33 that they might send **t** out of
12:36 so that they granted **t** what
12:38 mixed multitude went up with **t**
12:42 to the LORD for bringing **t**
13:17 that God did not lead **t** by way
13:21 And the LORD went before **t** by
13:21 in a pillar of fire to give **t**
14: 3 the wilderness has closed **t**
14: 4 heart, so that he will pursue **t**;
14: 7 captains over every one of **t**.
14: 9 So the Egyptians pursued **t**,
14: 9 and overtook **t** camping by the
14:10 the Egyptians marched after **t**.
14:17 and they shall follow **t**.
14:19 Israel, moved and went behind **t**;
14:19 of cloud went from before **t**
14:19 before them and stood behind **t**.
14:22 the waters were a wall to **t**
14:23 pursued and went after **t** into
14:25 so that they drove **t** with
14:25 for the LORD fights for **t**
14:28 that came into the sea after **t**.
14:28 Not so much as one of **t**
14:29 the waters were a wall to **t**
15: 5 The depths have covered **t**;
15: 7 It consumed **t** like stubble.
15: 9 desire shall be satisfied on **t**.
15: 9 sword, My hand shall destroy **t**.
15:10 Your wind, The sea covered **t**;
15:12 hand; The earth swallowed **t**.
15:13 You have guided **t** in Your
15:15 Trembling will take hold of **t**;
15:16 Fear and dread will fall on **t**;
15:17 You will bring **t** in and plant
15:17 will bring them in and plant **t**
15:19 the waters of the sea upon **t**.
15:21 And Miriam answered **t**:
15:25 statute and an ordinance for **t**.
15:25 for them. And there He tested **t**,
16: 3 children of Israel said to **t**,
16: 4 every day, that I may test **t**,
16:12 children of Israel. Speak to **t**,
16:15 it was. And Moses said to **t**,
16:20 But some of **t** left part of it
16:20 And Moses was angry with **t**.
16:23 Then he said to **t**,
17: 2 drink." And Moses said to **t**,
18: 8 hardship that had come upon **t**
18: 8 how the LORD had delivered **t**.
18:11 proudly, He was above **t**.
18:20 And you shall teach **t** the
18:20 and show **t** the way in which
18:21 and place such over **t** to be
18:22 And let **t** judge the people at
18:25 and made **t** heads over the
19: 7 and laid before **t** all these
19:10 to the people and consecrate **t**
19:10 and let **t** wash their clothes.
19:11 And let **t** be ready for the third
19:21 and many of **t** perish.
19:22 the LORD break out against **t**.
19:24 lest He break out against **t**.
19:25 to the people and spoke to **t**.
20: 5 you shall not bow down to **t** nor
20: 5 bow down to them nor serve **t**.
20:11 the sea, and all that is in **t**,
21: 1 which you shall set before **t**:
22:11 of the LORD shall be between **t**
22:23 If you afflict **t** in any way,
23:23 and I will cut **t** off.
23:24 down to their gods, nor serve **t**,
23:24 you shall utterly overthrow **t**
23:29 I will not drive **t** out from
23:30 by little I will drive **t** out
23:31 and you shall drive **t** out
23:32 shall make no covenant with **t**,
24:12 written, that you may teach **t**.
24:14 a difficulty, let him go to **t**.
25: 3 which you shall take from **t**:
25: 8 And let **t** make Me a sanctuary,
25: 8 that I may dwell among **t**.
25:12 and put **t** in its four corners;
25:13 and overlay **t** with gold.
25:14 the ark may be carried by **t**.
25:18 hammered work you shall make **t**
25:28 and overlay **t** with gold, that
25:28 the table may be carried with **t**.
25:29 You shall make **t** of pure gold.
25:40 see to it that you make **t**
26: 1 of cherubim you shall weave **t**.
26:24 Thus it shall be for both of **t**.
26:37 and overlay **t** with gold; their
26:37 five sockets of bronze for **t**.
27: 6 and overlay **t** with bronze.
28: 9 onyx stones and engrave on **t**
28:11 You shall set **t** in settings of
28:25 and put **t** on the shoulder
28:26 and put **t** on the two ends of
28:27 and put **t** on the two shoulder
28:33 and bells of gold between **t** all
28:40 and you shall make sashes for **t**.
28:40 And you shall make hats for **t**,
28:41 So you shall put **t** on Aaron your
28:41 with him. You shall anoint **t**,
28:41 shall anoint them, consecrate **t**,
28:41 consecrate them, and sanctify **t**,
28:42 And you shall make for **t** linen
29: 1 this is what you shall do to **t**
29: 1 shall do to them to hallow **t**
29: 2 with oil (you shall make **t** of
29: 3 You shall put **t** in one basket
29: 3 them in one basket and bring **t**
29: 4 and you shall wash **t** with
29: 8 his sons and put tunics on **t**.
29: 9 And you shall gird **t** with
29: 9 his sons, and put the hats on **t**.
29:13 and the fat that is on **t**,
29:13 and burn **t** on the altar.
29:17 and put **t** with its pieces and
29:22 two kidneys and the fat on **t**,
29:24 and you shall wave **t** as a wave
29:25 You shall receive **t** back from
29:25 from their hands and burn **t**
29:29 to be anointed in **t** and to be
29:29 them and to be consecrated in **t**.
29:30 in his place shall put **t** on
29:33 consecrate and to sanctify **t**;
29:33 an outsider shall not eat **t**,
29:35 days you shall consecrate **t**.
29:46 who brought **t** up out of the
29:46 Egypt, that I may dwell among **t**.
30: 4 You shall place **t** on its two
30: 5 and overlay **t** with gold.
30:12 to the LORD, when you number **t**,
30:12 there may be no plague among **t**
30:12 among them when you number **t**.
30:21 shall be a statute forever to **t**—
30:29 "You shall consecrate **t**,
30:29 whatever touches **t** must be
30:30 and his sons, and consecrate **t**,
32: 2 And Aaron said to **t**,
32: 2 and bring **t** to me."
32: 3 and brought **t** to Aaron.
32: 8 of the way which I commanded **t**.
32:10 My wrath may burn hot against **t**
32:10 them and I may consume **t**.

32:12 He brought *t* out to harm them,
32:12 'He brought them out to harm *t*,
32:12 to kill *t* in the mountains, and
32:12 and to consume *t* from the face
32:13 by Your own self, and said to *t*,
32:19 out of his hands and broke *t*
32:21 brought so great a sin upon *t*?
32:24 "And I said to *t*,
32:24 let *t* break it off.' So they
32:25 (for Aaron had not restrained *t*,
32:27 And he said to *t*,
32:34 I will visit punishment upon *t*
34:15 and one of *t* invites you and
34:31 Then Moses called to *t*,
34:31 to him; and Moses talked with *t*.
34:32 and he gave *t* as commandments
34:33 had finished speaking with *t*,
35: 1 Israel together, and said to *t*,
35:23 and badger skins, brought *t*.
35:35 He has filled *t* with skill to do
36: 8 all the gifted artisans among *t*
36: 8 designs of cherubim they made *t*.
36:29 Thus he made both of *t* for the
36:36 and overlaid *t* with gold, with
36:36 four sockets of silver for *t*.
37: 4 and overlaid *t* with gold.
37: 7 he made *t* of one piece at the
37:15 and overlaid *t* with gold.
37:28 and overlaid *t* with gold.
38: 6 and overlaid *t* with bronze.
38:10 were twenty pillars for *t*,
38:28 capitals, and made bands for *t*.
39: 7 He put *t* on the shoulders of the
39:18 and put *t* on the shoulder
39:19 two rings of gold and put *t*
39:20 other gold rings and put *t* on
39:43 done it. And Moses blessed *t*.
40:12 of meeting and wash *t* with
40:14 bring his sons and clothe *t*
40:15 "You shall anoint *t*,
Lev 1: 2 of Israel, and say to *t*:
1:12 and the priest shall lay *t* in
2:12 you shall offer *t* to the LORD,
3: 4 and the fat that is on *t* by
3:10 and the fat that is on *t* by
3:11 and the priest shall burn *t* on
3:15 and the fat that is on *t* by
3:16 and the priest shall burn *t* on
4: 2 to be done, and does any of *t*,
4: 9 and the fat that is on *t* by
4:10 and the priest shall burn *t* on
4:20 shall make atonement for *t*,
4:20 and it shall be forgiven *t*.
5: 8 And he shall bring *t* to the
6:10 and he shall put *t* beside the
6:18 Everyone who touches *t* must be
7: 4 and the fat that is on *t* by
7: 5 and the priest shall burn *t* on
7: 7 there is one law for *t* both:
7:34 and I have given *t* to Aaron the
7:35 day when Moses presented *t* to
7:36 this to be given to *t* by the
7:36 on the day that He anointed *t*,
8: 6 and his sons and washed *t* with
8:10 was in it, and consecrated *t*.
8:11 and its base, to consecrate *t*.
8:13 sons and put tunics on *t*,
8:13 girded *t* with sashes, and put
8:13 with sashes, and put hats on *t*,
8:16 and Moses burned *t* on the
8:26 and put *t* on the fat and on
8:27 and waved *t* as a wave offering
8:28 Then Moses took *t* from their
8:28 from their hands and burned *t*
9: 2 and offer *t* before the LORD.
9: 7 and make atonement for *t*,
9:13 and he burned *t* on the altar.
9:14 and burned *t* with the burnt
9:22 toward the people, blessed *t*,
10: 1 which He had not commanded *t*.
10: 2 from the LORD and devoured *t*,
10: 4 uncle of Aaron, and said to *t*,
10: 5 So they went near and carried *t*
10:11 the LORD has spoken to *t* by
10:17 to make atonement for *t* before
11: 1 to Moses and Aaron, saying to *t*,
11:24 the carcass of any of *t* shall
11:25 part of the carcass of any of *t*
11:31 Whoever touches *t* when they are
11:32 Anything on which any of *t*
11:33 vessel into which any of *t*
11:43 make yourselves unclean with *t*,
11:43 them, lest you be defiled by *t*.
14: 6 and dip *t* and the living bird
14:12 and wave *t* as a wave offering
14:23 He shall bring *t* to the priest
14:24 and the priest shall wave *t* as
14:40 and they shall cast *t* into an
14:42 take other stones and put *t*
14:45 and he shall carry *t* outside
14:51 and dip *t* in the blood of the
15: 2 of Israel, and say to *t*:
15:14 and give *t* to the priest.
15:15 'Then the priest shall offer *t*,
15:29 and bring *t* to the priest, to
15:31 My tabernacle that is among *t*.
16: 4 in water, and put *t* on.
16: 7 the two goats and present *t*
16:16 meeting which remains among *t*
16:21 putting *t* on the head of the
16:23 and shall leave *t* there.
16:28 Then he who burns *t* shall wash
17: 2 of Israel, and say to *t*,
17: 5 that they may bring *t* to the
17: 5 and offer *t* as peace offerings
17: 7 be a statute forever for *t*
17: 8 "Also you shall say to *t*:
17:16 But if he does not wash *t* or
18: 2 of Israel, and say to *t*:
18: 4 My ordinances, to walk in *t*:
18: 5 a man does, he shall live by *t*:
18:29 the persons who commit *t* shall
18:30 do not defile yourselves by *t*:
19: 2 of Israel, and say to *t*:
19:10 you shall leave *t* for the poor
19:31 spirits; do not seek after *t*,
19:31 after them, to be defiled by *t*:
19:37 all My judgments, and perform *t*:
20: 6 to prostitute himself with *t*,
20: 8 keep My statutes, and perform *t*:
20:11 both of *t* shall surely be put
20:11 Their blood shall be upon *t*.
20:12 both of *t* shall surely be put
20:12 Their blood shall be upon *t*.
20:13 both of *t* have committed an
20:13 Their blood shall be upon *t*.
20:16 death. Their blood is upon *t*.
20:18 Both of *t* shall be cut off from
20:22 all My judgments, and perform *t*,
20:23 things, and therefore I abhor *t*.
20:27 they shall stone *t* with stones.
20:27 Their blood shall be upon *t*.
21: 1 the sons of Aaron, and say to *t*:
21:23 for I the LORD sanctify *t*.
22: 3 'Say to *t*: 'Whoever of all
22: 9 it: I the LORD sanctify *t*.
22:16 or allow *t* to bear the guilt of
22:16 for I the LORD sanctify *t*.
22:18 of Israel, and say to *t*:
22:22 make an offering by fire of *t*
22:24 you make any offering of *t*
22:25 their corruption is in *t*,
22:25 in them, and defects are in *t*.
22:31 My commandments, and perform *t*:
23: 2 of Israel, and say to *t*:
23:10 of Israel, and say to *t*:
23:20 The priest shall wave *t* with the
23:22 You shall leave *t* for the poor
23:43 in booths when I brought *t* out
24: 6 'You shall set *t* in two rows,
24:12 the LORD might be shown to *t*.
25: 2 of Israel, and say to *t*:
25:18 My judgments, and perform *t*;
25:31 which have no wall around *t*
25:44 from *t* you may buy male and
25:46 And you may take *t* as an
25:46 to inherit *t* as a possession;
25:51 according to *t* he shall repay
26: 3 My commandments, and perform *t*,
26:36 of a shaken leaf shall cause *t*
26:39 iniquities, which are with *t*,
26:41 also have walked contrary to *t*
26:41 to them and have brought *t*
26:43 also shall be left empty by *t*,
26:43 it lies desolate without *t*;
26:44 I will not cast *t* away,
26:44 them away, nor shall I abhor *t*,
26:44 to utterly destroy *t* and break
26:44 and break My covenant with *t*;
27: 2 of Israel, and say to *t*:
Num 1: 3 You and Aaron shall number *t* by
1:19 so he numbered *t* in the
1:47 were not numbered among *t* by
1:49 nor take a census of *t* among
3: 6 and present *t* before Aaron the
3:16 So Moses numbered *t* according to
3:26 to all the work relating to *t*.
3:31 and all the work relating to *t*.
3:36 all the work relating to *t*,
3:43 of those who were numbered of *t*,
3:47 you shall take *t* in the
3:48 which the excess number of *t*
4: 8 They shall spread over *t* a
4:12 put *t* in a blue cloth, cover
4:12 cover *t* with a covering of
4:12 and put *t* on a carrying beam.
4:15 Kohath shall come to carry *t*;
4:19 "but do this in regard to *t*,
4:19 go in and appoint each of *t* to
4:23 years old, you shall number *t*,
4:27 And you shall appoint to *t* all
4:29 you shall number *t* by their
4:30 years old, you shall number *t*,
5: 3 you shall put *t* outside the
5: 4 and put *t* outside the camp;
5:12 of Israel, and say to *t*:
5:23 and he shall scrape *t* off into
6: 2 of Israel, and say to *t*:
6:16 'Then the priest shall bring *t*
6:19 and put *t* upon the hands of
6:20 and the priest shall wave *t* as a
6:23 children of Israel. Say to *t*:
6:27 of Israel, and I will bless *t*.
7: 1 so he anointed *t* and
7: 1 anointed them and consecrated *t*.
7: 3 and they presented *t* before the
7: 5 "Accept these from *t*,
7: 5 and you shall give *t* to the
7: 6 and gave *t* to the Levites.
7:13 both of *t* full of fine flour
7:19 both of *t* full of fine flour
7:25 both of *t* full of fine flour
7:31 both of *t* full of fine flour
7:37 both of *t* full of fine flour
7:43 both of *t* full of fine flour
7:49 both of *t* full of fine flour
7:55 both of *t* full of fine flour
7:61 both of *t* full of fine flour
7:67 both of *t* full of fine flour
7:73 both of *t* full of fine flour
7:79 both of *t* full of fine flour
8: 6 of Israel and cleanse *t*
8: 7 Thus you shall do to *t* to
8: 7 shall do to them to cleanse *t*:
8: 7 water of purification on *t*,
8: 7 and let *t* shave all their body,
8: 7 and let *t* wash their clothes,
8: 8 Then let *t* take a young bull
8:13 and then offer *t* like a wave
8:15 So you shall cleanse *t* and
8:15 shall cleanse them and offer *t*,
8:16 I have taken *t* for Myself
8:17 land of Egypt I sanctified *t*
8:20 the children of Israel did to *t*.
8:21 clothes; then Aaron presented *t*,
8:21 and Aaron made atonement for *t*
8:21 atonement for them to cleanse *t*.
8:22 the Levites, so they did to *t*.
9: 8 And Moses said to *t*,
10: 2 you shall make *t* of hammered
10: 2 you shall use *t* for calling the
10: 3 "When they blow both of *t*,
10: 6 shall sound the call for *t* to
10:33 of the LORD went before *t* for
10:33 out a resting place for *t*.
10:34 of the LORD was above *t* by
11: 1 of the LORD burned among *t*,
11: 3 of the LORD had burned among *t*.
11: 4 multitude who were among *t*
11:12 all these people? Did I beget *t*,
11:12 Carry *t* in your bosom, as a
11:16 the people and officers over *t*;
11:16 bring *t* to the tabernacle of
11:17 and will put the same upon *t*;
11:21 I will give *t* meat, that they
11:22 and herds be slaughtered for *t*,
11:22 them, to provide enough for *t*?
11:22 sea be gathered together for *t*,
11:22 them, to provide enough for *t*?
11:24 of the people and placed *t*
11:25 when the Spirit rested upon *t*,
11:26 And the Spirit rested upon *t*.
11:28 'Moses my lord, forbid *t*!"
11:29 would put His Spirit upon *t*!"
11:31 quail from the sea and left *t*
11:32 and they spread *t* out for
12: 9 the LORD was aroused against *t*,
13: 2 man, every one a leader among *t*.
13: 3 So Moses sent *t* from the
13: 3 all of *t* men who were heads of
13:17 Then Moses sent *t* to spy out
13:17 land of Canaan, and said to *t*,
13:23 carried it between two of *t* on
13:26 they brought back word to *t* and
13:26 and showed *t* the fruit of the
14: 2 whole congregation said to *t*,
14: 9 protection has departed from *t*,
14: 9 is with us. Do not fear *t*.
14:10 congregation said to stone *t*
14:11 which I have performed among *t*?
14:12 I will strike *t* with the
14:12 the pestilence and disinherit *t*,
14:13 these people up from among *t*,
14:14 and Your cloud stands above *t*,
14:14 and You go before *t* in a pillar
14:16 land which He swore to give *t*,
14:16 therefore He killed *t* in the
14:28 'Say to *t*, 'As I live,'
14:45 came down and attacked *t*,
14:45 and drove *t* back as far as
15: 2 of Israel, and say to *t*:
15:18 of Israel, and say to *t*:
15:25 and it shall be forgiven *t*,
15:26 the stranger who dwells among *t*,
15:29 the stranger who dwells among *t*.
15:38 Tell *t* to make tassels on the
15:39 of the LORD and do *t*,
16: 3 Moses and Aaron, and said to *t*,
16: 3 is holy, every one of *t*,
16: 3 them, and the LORD is among *t*.
16: 7 put fire in *t* and put incense in
16: 7 in them and put incense in *t*
16: 9 the congregation to serve *t*;
16:15 not taken one donkey from *t*,
16:15 them, nor have I hurt one of *t*.
16:19 all the congregation against *t*
16:21 that I may consume *t* in a
16:28 for I have not done *t* of my
16:30 opens its mouth and swallows *t*
16:30 up with all that belongs to *t*,
16:31 the ground split apart under *t*,
16:32 its mouth and swallowed *t* up,
16:33 So they and all those with *t*
16:33 pit; the earth closed over *t*,
16:34 all Israel who were around *t*
16:38 let *t* be made into hammered
16:38 Because they presented *t* before
16:45 that I may consume *t* in a
16:46 and make atonement for *t*;
17: 2 and get from *t* a rod from each
17: 4 Then you shall place *t* in the
18: 8 I have given *t* as a portion to
18:11 I have given *t* to you,
18:12 I have given *t* to you.
18:20 you have any portion among *t*;
18:24 therefore I have said to *t*,

18:26 to the Levites, and say to *t*:
18:26 which I have given you from *t*
18:29 LORD, from all the best of *t*,
18:29 them, the consecrated part of *t*.
18:30 "Therefore you shall say to *t*:
19: 6 and cast *t* into the midst of
19: 9 and store *t* outside the camp
19:10 the stranger who dwells among *t*.
19:17 water shall be put on *t* in a
19:21 be a perpetual statute for *t*.
20: 6 of the LORD appeared to *t*.
20: 8 you shall bring water for *t*
20:10 the rock; and he said to *t*,
20:12 the land which I have given *t*.
20:13 and He was hallowed among *t*.
20:20 So Edom came out against *t*
20:25 and bring *t* up to Mount Hor;
20:26 of his garments and put *t* on
20:28 of his garments and put *t* on
21: 1 Israel and took some of *t*
21: 3 and they utterly destroyed *t*
21:16 and I will give *t* water."
21:30 "But we have shot at *t*;
21:33 of Bashan went out against *t*,
22: 6 I shall be able to defeat *t*
22: 6 to defeat them and drive *t* out
22: 8 And he said to *t*,
22:11 curse *t* for me; perhaps I shall
22:11 I shall be able to overpower *t*
22:11 to overpower them and drive *t*
22:12 "You shall not go with *t*;
22:20 call you, rise and go with *t*;
23:11 you have blessed *t*
23:13 place from which you may see *t*;
23:13 see only the outer part of *t*,
23:13 and shall not see *t* all; curse
23:13 curse *t* for me from there."
23:21 the shout of a King is among *t*.
23:22 God brings *t* out of Egypt;
23:25 Neither curse *t* at all, nor
23:25 nor bless *t* at all!"
23:27 God that you may curse *t* for
24: 8 their bones And pierce *t*
24:10 you have bountifully blessed *t*
25: 8 the tent and thrust both of *t*
25:11 zealous with My zeal among *t*,
25:17 the Midianites, and attack *t*;
26: 3 the priest spoke with *t* in the
26: 7 those who were numbered of *t*
26:10 its mouth and swallowed *t* up
26:18 to those who were numbered of *t*:
26:22 to those who were numbered of *t*:
26:25 to those who were numbered of *t*:
26:27 to those who were numbered of *t*:
26:34 those who were numbered of *t*
26:37 to those who were numbered of *t*:
26:41 those who were numbered of *t*
26:43 to those who were numbered of *t*,
26:47 to those who were numbered of *t*:
26:50 those who were numbered of *t*
26:54 to those who were numbered of *t*.
26:62 those who were numbered of *t*
26:62 was no inheritance given to *t*
26:65 For the LORD had said of *t*,
26:65 there was not left a man of *t*,
27: 7 you shall surely give *t* a
27: 7 of their father to pass to *t*.
27:17 who may go out before *t* and go
27:17 before them and go in before *t*,
27:17 who may lead *t* out and bring
27:17 may lead them out and bring *t*
28: 2 of Israel, and say to *t*,
28: 3 "And you shall say to *t*,
28:31 You shall present *t* with their
30:12 if her husband truly made *t*
30:12 void on the day he heard *t*,
30:12 her husband has made *t* void,
30:14 that bind her; he confirms *t*,
30:14 her on the day that he heard *t*.
30:15 But if he does make *t* void after
30:15 them void after he has heard *t*,
31: 3 and let *t* go against the
31: 6 Then Moses sent *t* to the war,
31: 6 he sent *t* to the war with
31:13 went to meet *t* outside the
31:15 And Moses said to *t*:
31:30 and give *t* to the Levites who
31:47 and gave *t* to the Levites, who
31:51 priest received the gold from *t*,
32: 7 which the LORD has given *t*?
32: 8 your fathers did when I sent *t*
32: 9 which the LORD had given *t*.
32:13 and He made *t* wander in the
32:15 He will once again leave *t* in
32:17 Israel until we have brought *t*
32:19 we will not inherit with *t*
32:20 Then Moses said to *t*:
32:28 gave command concerning *t* to
32:29 And Moses said to *t*:
32:29 then you shall give *t* the land
32:41 and called *t* Havoth Jair.
33: 4 the LORD had killed among *t*.
33:51 of Israel, and say to *t*:
33:56 to you as I thought to do to *t*.
34: 2 of Israel, and say to *t*:
35: 5 This shall belong to *t* as
35:10 of Israel, and say to *t*:
35:15 and for the sojourner among *t*,
36: 6 Let *t* marry whom they think
Deut 1: 3 given him as commandments to *t*,
1: 8 to give to *t* and their
1: 8 and their descendants after *t*.
1:13 and I will make *t* heads over
1:15 and made *t* heads over you,
1:22 and let *t* search out the land
1:29 be terrified, or afraid of *t*.
1:39 to *t* I will give it, and they
1:42 the LORD said to me, 'Tell *t*,
2: 5 "Do not meddle with *t*,
2: 6 You shall buy food from *t* with
2: 6 you shall also buy water from *t*
2: 9 nor contend with *t* in battle,
2:11 but the Moabites call *t* Emim.
2:12 of Esau dispossessed *t* and
2:12 them and destroyed *t* from
2:12 destroyed them from before *t*,
2:12 which the LORD gave *t*.
2:14 as the LORD had sworn to *t*.
2:15 hand of the LORD was against *t*,
2:15 to destroy *t* from the midst of
2:19 do not harass *t* or meddle with
2:19 harass them or meddle with *t*,
2:20 But the Ammonites call *t*
2:21 But the LORD destroyed *t*
2:21 LORD destroyed them before *t*,
2:21 and they dispossessed *t* and
2:22 the Horites from before *t*.
2:22 They dispossessed *t* and dwelt
2:23 destroyed *t* and dwelt in their
3: 4 which we did not take from *t*:
3: 6 "And we utterly destroyed *t*,
3:20 the LORD your God is giving *t*
3:22 'You must not fear *t*,
3:28 and he shall cause *t* to inherit
4: 5 should act according to *t* in
4: 6 be careful to observe *t*;
4: 9 And teach *t* to your children
4:10 and I will let *t* hear My words,
4:13 and He wrote *t* on two tablets
4:14 that you might observe *t* in the
4:19 you feel driven to worship *t*
4:19 to worship them and serve *t*,
4:31 fathers which He swore to *t*.
4:37 chose their descendants after *t*;
5: 1 all Israel, and said to *t*:
5: 1 that you may learn *t* and be
5: 1 and be careful to observe *t*.
5: 9 you shall not bow down to *t* nor
5: 9 bow down to them nor serve *t*.
5:22 And He wrote *t* on two tablets
5:22 tablets of stone and gave *t* to
5:29 that they had such a heart in *t*
5:29 that it might be well with *t*
5:30 'Go and say to *t*,
5:31 which you shall teach *t*,
5:31 that they may observe *t* in the
5:31 in the land which I am giving *t*
6: 1 that you may observe *t* in the
6: 7 You shall teach *t* diligently to
6: 7 and shall talk of *t* when you
6: 8 You shall bind *t* as a sign on
6: 9 You shall write *t* on the
7: 2 the LORD your God delivers *t*
7: 2 you shall conquer *t* and
7: 2 them and utterly destroy *t*.
7: 2 shall make no covenant with *t*
7: 2 with them nor show mercy to *t*.
7: 3 shall you make marriages with *t*.
7: 5 thus you shall deal with *t*:
7:10 Him to their face, to destroy *t*.
7:11 command you today, to observe *t*.
7:12 judgments, and keep and do *t*,
7:15 but will lay *t* on all those
7:16 eye shall have no pity on *t*;
7:17 than I; how can I dispossess *t*?
7:18 "you shall not be afraid of *t*,
7:20 will send the hornet among *t*
7:21 shall not be terrified of *t*;
7:22 will be unable to destroy *t* at
7:23 LORD your God will deliver *t*
7:23 and will inflict defeat upon *t*
7:24 you until you have destroyed *t*.
7:25 silver or gold that is on *t*,
8:12 houses and dwell in *t*;
8:19 and serve *t* and worship them, I
8:19 and serve them and worship *t*,
9: 3 He will destroy *t* and bring
9: 3 will destroy them and bring *t*
9: 3 so you shall drive *t* out and
9: 3 drive them out and destroy *t*
9: 4 the LORD your God has cast *t*
9: 4 that the LORD is driving *t*
9: 5 the LORD your God drives *t*
9:10 and on *t* were all the words
9:12 the way which I commanded *t*;
9:14 that I may destroy *t* and blot
9:17 the two tablets and threw *t*
9:17 out of my two hands and broke *t*
9:28 LORD was not able to bring *t*
9:28 to the land which He promised *t*,
9:28 them, and because He hated *t*,
9:28 He has brought *t* out to kill
9:28 has brought them out to kill *t*
10: 2 and you shall put *t* in the
10: 4 and the LORD gave *t* to me.
10:11 to their fathers to give *t*.
10:15 only in your fathers, to love *t*;
10:15 chose their descendants after *t*,
11: 4 of the Red Sea overflow *t* as
11: 4 how the LORD has destroyed *t*
11: 6 its mouth and swallowed *t* up,
11: 9 to *t* and their descendants, 'a
11:16 serve other gods and worship *t*,
11:18 and bind *t* as a sign on your
11:19 You shall teach *t* to your
11:19 speaking of *t* when you sit in
11:20 And you shall write *t* on the
11:21 swore to your fathers to give *t*,
12:18 But you must eat *t* before the
12:22 are eaten, so you may eat *t*;
12:22 and the clean alike may eat *t*.
12:29 and you displace *t* and dwell in
12:30 are not ensnared to follow *t*,
13: 2 not known—'and let us serve *t*,
17: 3 other gods and worshiped *t*,
17: 9 those days, and inquire of *t*;
18: 2 inheritance, as He said to *t*.
18:12 the LORD your God drives *t*
18:18 I will raise up for *t* a Prophet
18:18 and He shall speak to *t* all
19: 1 and you dispossess *t* and dwell
19: 9 all these commandments and do *t*,
20: 1 than you, do not be afraid of *t*;
20: 3 "And he shall say to *t*,
20: 3 or be terrified because of *t*;
20:17 you shall utterly destroy *t*:
20:19 by wielding an ax against *t*;
20:19 them; if you can eat of *t*,
20:19 do not cut *t* down to use in the
21: 5 LORD your God has chosen *t* to
21:10 the LORD your God delivers *t*
21:10 and you take *t* captive,
21:18 chastened him, will not heed *t*,
22: 1 and hide yourself from *t*;
22: 1 you shall certainly bring *t*
22: 4 road, and hide yourself from *t*;
22: 4 shall surely help him lift *t*
22:19 shekels of silver and give *t*
22:22 then both of *t* shall die—the
22:24 then you shall bring *t* both out
22:24 and you shall stone *t* to death
23: 8 the third generation born to *t*
24: 8 you; just as I commanded *t*,
25: 1 that the judges may judge *t*,
25: 5 and one of *t* dies and has no
26:13 and also have given *t* to the
26:13 nor have I forgotten *t*.
26:16 shall be careful to observe *t*
27: 2 and whitewash *t* with lime.
27: 3 You shall write on *t* all the
27: 4 and you shall whitewash *t* with
27: 5 not use an iron tool on *t*.
28:13 and are careful to observe *t*.
28:14 go after other gods to serve *t*.
28:25 shall go out one way against *t*
28:25 and flee seven ways before *t*;
28:26 and no one shall frighten *t*
28:31 shall have no one to rescue *t*.
28:32 and fail with longing for *t*
28:39 plant vineyards and tend *t*,
28:39 for the worms shall eat *t*.
28:55 that he will not give any of *t*
28:57 for she will eat *t* secretly for
29: 1 covenant which He made with *t*
29: 2 called all Israel and said to *t*:
29: 7 to battle, and we conquered *t*.
29: 9 of this covenant, and do *t*,
29:17 their idols which were among *t*—
29:25 which He made with *t* when He
29:25 with them when He brought *t*
29:26 other gods and worshiped *t*,
29:26 and that He had not given to *t*.
29:28 And the LORD uprooted *t* from
29:28 and cast *t* into another land,
30: 1 and you call *t* to mind among
30:17 worship other gods and serve *t*,
30:20 Isaac, and Jacob, to give *t*.
31: 2 And he said to *t*:
31: 3 you, and you shall dispossess *t*.
31: 4 And the LORD will do to *t* as He
31: 4 their land, when He destroyed *t*.
31: 5 The LORD will give *t* over to
31: 5 that you may do to *t* according
31: 6 do not fear nor be afraid of *t*;
31: 7 to their fathers to give *t*,
31: 7 and you shall cause *t* to
31:10 And Moses commanded *t*,
31:16 where they go to be among *t*,
31:16 which I have made with *t*.
31:17 shall be aroused against *t* in
31:17 that day, and I will forsake *t*,
31:17 and I will hide My face from *t*,
31:17 and troubles shall befall *t*,
31:20 When I have brought *t* to the
31:20 turn to other gods and serve *t*;
31:21 and troubles have come upon *t*,
31:21 song will testify against *t* as
31:21 even before I have brought *t* to
31:21 of which I swore to give *t*.
31:23 the land of which I swore to *t*,
31:28 and earth to witness against *t*.
32:11 taking *t* up, Carrying them on
32:11 Carrying *t* on its wings,
32:19 LORD saw it, He spurned *t*,
32:20 'I will hide My face from *t*,
32:21 But I will provoke *t* to
32:21 I will move *t* to anger by a
32:23 'I will heap disasters on *t*;
32:23 I will spend My arrows on *t*.
32:24 I will also send against *t* the
32:26 I will dash *t* in pieces, I will
32:26 I will make the memory of *t* to
32:28 there any understanding in *t*.
32:30 Unless their Rock had sold *t*,
32:30 the LORD had surrendered *t*?
32:35 things to come hasten upon *t*.

32:38 Let **t** rise and help you,
32:46 and He said to **t**:
33: 2 And dawned on **t** from Seir; He
33: 2 hand Came a fiery law for **t**.
33: 9 mother, 'I have not seen **t**';
33:17 Together with **t** He shall push
Josh 1: 2 the land which I am giving to **t**—
1: 6 to their fathers to give **t**.
1:14 mighty men of valor, and help **t**,
1:15 the LORD your God is giving **t**.
2: 4 took the two men and hid **t**.
2: 5 pursue **t** quickly, for you may
2: 5 quickly, for you may overtake **t**.
2: 6 (But she had brought **t** up to the
2: 6 up to the roof and hidden **t**
2: 7 Then the men pursued **t** by the
2: 7 as soon as those who pursued **t**
2: 8 she came up to **t** on the roof,
2:15 Then she let **t** down by a rope
2:16 And she said to **t**,
2:21 And she sent **t** away, and they
2:22 The pursuers sought **t** all
2:22 the way, but did not find **t**.
2:23 him all that had befallen **t**.
4: 3 "and command **t**,
4: 3 You shall carry **t** over with you
4: 3 them over with you and leave **t**
4: 5 and Joshua said to **t**:
4: 7 Then you shall answer **t** that the
4: 8 and carried **t** over with them to
4: 8 and carried them over with **t** to
4: 8 and laid **t** down there.
4:12 as Moses had spoken to **t**.
5: 1 and there was no spirit in **t**
5: 4 reason why Joshua circumcised **t**:
5: 6 swore that He would not show **t**
6: 6 the priests and said to **t**,
6: 8 of the LORD followed **t**.
6:13 And the armed men went before **t**.
6:23 all her relatives and left **t**
6:26 Then Joshua charged **t** at that
7: 2 side of Bethel, and spoke to **t**,
7: 5 for they chased **t** from before
7: 5 and struck **t** down on the
7:11 My covenant which I commanded **t**.
7:21 I coveted **t** and took them. And
7:21 I coveted them and took **t**.
7:23 And they took **t** from the midst
7:23 brought **t** to Joshua and to all
7:23 and laid **t** out before the
7:24 and they brought **t** to the
7:25 and they burned **t** with fire
7:25 fire after they had stoned **t**
8: 3 mighty men of valor and sent **t**
8: 4 And he commanded **t**,
8: 5 that we shall flee before **t**.
8: 6 after us till we have drawn **t**
8: 6 Therefore we will flee before **t**.
8: 9 Joshua therefore sent **t** out;
8:11 Now a valley lay between **t** and
8:12 five thousand men and set **t** in
8:15 as if they were beaten before **t**,
8:16 called together to pursue **t**.
8:20 the men of Ai looked behind **t**,
8:22 came out of the city against **t**;
8:22 And they struck **t** down, so that
8:22 so that they let none of **t**
8:24 wilderness where they pursued **t**,
8:33 well as he who was born among **t**.
8:33 Half of **t** were in front of
8:33 of Mount Gerizim and half of **t**
8:35 who were living among **t**.
9: 8 And Joshua said to **t**,
9:11 the journey, and go to meet **t**,
9:11 go to meet them, and say to **t**,
9:15 So Joshua made peace with **t**,
9:15 and made a covenant with **t** to
9:15 a covenant with them to let **t**
9:15 of the congregation swore to **t**.
9:16 they had made a covenant with **t**,
9:16 neighbors who dwelt near **t**.
9:18 of Israel did not attack **t**,
9:18 congregation had sworn to **t** by
9:19 We have sworn to **t** by the LORD
9:19 therefore, we may not touch **t**.
9:20 "This we will do to **t**:
9:20 We will let **t** live, lest wrath
9:20 of the oath which we swore to **t**.
9:21 And the rulers said to **t**,
9:21 Let **t** live, but let them be
9:21 but let **t** be woodcutters and
9:21 as the rulers had promised **t**.
9:22 Then Joshua called for **t**,
9:22 for them, and he spoke to **t**,
9:26 So he did to **t**, and delivered
9:26 and delivered **t** out of the hand
9:26 so that they did not kill **t**.
9:27 And that day Joshua made **t**
10: 1 with Israel and were among **t**,
10: 8 said to Joshua, "Do not fear **t**,
10: 8 for I have delivered **t** into
10: 8 not a man of **t** shall stand
10: 9 Joshua therefore came upon **t**
10:10 So the LORD routed **t** before
10:10 killed **t** with a great slaughter
10:10 chased **t** along the road that
10:10 and struck **t** down as far as
10:11 hailstones from heaven on **t** as
10:18 and set men by it to guard **t**.
10:19 Do not allow **t** to enter their
10:19 LORD your God has delivered **t**
10:20 made an end of slaying **t** with
10:25 Then Joshua said to **t**,
10:26 And afterward Joshua struck **t**
10:26 Joshua struck them and killed **t**,
10:26 and hanged **t** on five trees; and
10:27 and they took **t** down from the
10:27 cast **t** into the cave where they
10:28 sword. He utterly destroyed **t**—
10:39 they struck **t** with the edge of
10:41 And Joshua conquered **t** from
11: 4 and all their armies with **t**,
11: 6 "Do not be afraid because of **t**,
11: 6 time I will deliver all of **t**
11: 7 of war with him came against **t**
11: 7 of Merom, and they attacked **t**.
11: 8 And the LORD delivered **t** into
11: 8 who defeated **t** and chased them
11: 8 who defeated them and chased **t**
11: 8 they attacked **t** until they left
11: 8 them until they left none of **t**
11: 9 So Joshua did to **t** as the LORD
11:11 sword, utterly destroying **t**.
11:12 He utterly destroyed **t**,
11:13 mounds, Israel burned none of **t**,
11:14 until they had destroyed **t**,
11:17 and struck **t** down and killed
11:17 struck them down and killed **t**.
11:20 that He might utterly destroy **t**,
11:20 but that He might destroy **t**,
11:21 Joshua utterly destroyed **t** with
13: 6 **t** I will drive out from before
13: 8 which Moses had given **t**,
13: 8 of the LORD had given **t**:
13:14 inheritance, as He said to **t**.
13:22 those who were killed by **t**.
13:33 as He had said to **t**.
14: 1 as an inheritance to **t**.
14: 3 given no inheritance among **t**.
14:12 and I shall be able to drive **t**
15:63 of Judah could not drive **t** out;
17: 4 he gave **t** an inheritance among
17:13 but did not utterly drive **t**
17:15 So Joshua answered **t**,
18: 1 the land was subdued before **t**.
18: 4 each tribe, and I will send **t**;
18: 7 the servant of the LORD gave **t**.
18:10 Then Joshua cast lots for **t** in
19: 9 of Judah was too much for **t**.
19:49 gave an inheritance among **t** to
20: 4 him into the city as one of **t**,
20: 4 that he may dwell among **t**.
20: 9 the stranger who dwelt among **t**,
21: 2 And they spoke to **t** at Shiloh in
21:11 And they gave **t** Kirjath Arba
21:21 For they gave **t** Shechem with its
21:44 The LORD gave **t** rest all
21:44 their enemies stood against **t**;
22: 2 and said to **t**: "You have kept
22: 4 your brethren, as He promised **t**;
22: 6 So Joshua blessed **t** and sent
22: 6 Joshua blessed them and sent **t**
22: 7 when Joshua sent **t** away to
22: 7 to their tents, he blessed **t**,
22: 8 and spoke to **t**, saying, "Return
22:12 Shiloh to go to war against **t**.
22:15 Gilead, and they spoke with **t**,
22:30 of Manasseh spoke, it pleased **t**.
22:32 and brought back word to **t**.
22:33 no more of going against **t** in
23: 2 their officers, and said to **t**:
23: 5 the LORD your God will expel **t**
23: 5 from before you and drive **t**
23: 7 cause anyone to swear by **t**;
23: 7 you shall not serve **t** nor bow
23: 7 serve them nor bow down to **t**,
23:12 you—and make marriages with **t**,
23:12 and go in to **t** and they to you,
23:14 not one word of **t** has failed.
23:16 other gods, and bowed down to **t**,
24: 5 according to what I did among **t**.
24: 7 brought the sea upon **t**,
24: 7 sea upon them, and covered **t**.
24: 8 But I gave **t** into your hand,
24: 8 and I destroyed **t** from before
24:11 But I delivered **t** into your
24:12 before you which drove **t** out
24:13 not build, and you dwell in **t**;
24:25 and made for **t** a statute and an
Judg 1: 1 Canaanites to fight against **t**?
1:22 and the LORD was with **t**.
1:25 So he showed **t** the entrance to
1:28 but did not completely drive **t**
1:29 dwelt in Gezer among **t**.
1:30 so the Canaanites dwelt among **t**,
1:32 for they did not drive **t** out.
1:33 were put under tribute to **t**.
1:34 for they would not allow **t** to
2: 3 I will not drive **t** out before
2:10 generation arose after **t** who
2:12 who had brought **t** out of the
2:12 people who were all around **t**,
2:12 them, and they bowed down to **t**;
2:14 So He delivered **t** into the
2:14 of plunderers who despoiled **t**;
2:14 and He sold **t** into the hands of
2:15 of the LORD was against **t** for
2:15 and as the LORD had sworn to **t**.
2:16 up judges who delivered **t** out
2:16 hand of those who plundered **t**.
2:17 other gods, and bowed down to **t**.
2:18 LORD raised up judges for **t**,
2:18 with the judge and delivered **t**
2:18 of those who oppressed **t** and
2:18 oppressed them and harassed **t**.
2:19 to serve **t** and bow down to
2:19 to serve them and bow down to **t**.
2:21 no longer drive out before **t**
2:22 so that through **t** I may test
2:22 to walk in **t** as their fathers
2:22 them as their fathers kept **t**,
2:23 without driving **t** out
2:23 nor did He deliver **t** into the
3: 1 that He might test Israel by **t**,
3: 4 He might test Israel by **t**,
3: 8 and He sold **t** into the hand of
3: 9 of Israel, who delivered **t**:
3:15 raised up a deliverer for **t**:
3:23 room behind him and locked **t**.
3:25 they took the key and opened **t**.
3:27 the mountains; and he led **t**.
3:28 Then he said to **t**,
4: 2 So the LORD sold **t** into the
5:21 The torrent of Kishon swept **t**
6: 1 So the LORD delivered **t** into
6: 3 East would come up against **t**.
6: 4 they would encamp against **t**
6: 8 of Israel, who said to **t**,
6: 9 and drove **t** out before you and
6:19 and he brought **t** out to Him
6:19 terebinth tree and presented **t**.
6:20 unleavened bread and lay **t** on
6:35 and they came up to meet **t**.
7: 1 was on the north side of **t** by
7: 4 bring **t** down to the water, and
7: 4 and I will test **t** for you
7:17 And he said to **t**,
7:24 and seize from **t** the watering
8: 2 So he said to **t**,
8: 8 there to Penuel and spoke to **t**
8:10 Karkor, and their armies with **t**,
8:12 and Zalmunna fled, he pursued **t**;
8:16 and with **t** he taught the men of
8:19 if you had let **t** live, I would
8:20 kill **t**!" But the youth would
8:23 But Gideon said to **t**,
8:24 Then Gideon said to **t**,
8:25 "We will gladly give **t**.
8:34 who had delivered **t** from the
9: 1 and spoke with **t** and with all
9: 7 and cried out. And he said to **t**:
9: 8 forth to anoint a king over **t**.
9: 9 But the olive tree said to **t**,
9:11 But the fig tree said to **t**,
9:13 But the vine said to **t**,
9:24 their brother, who killed **t**,
9:25 they robbed all who passed by **t**
9:27 their vineyards and trod **t**,
9:33 you may then do to **t** as you
9:38 and fight with **t** now."
9:43 divided **t** into three companies,
9:43 and he rose against **t** and
9:43 against them and attacked **t**.
9:44 in the fields and killed **t**.
9:49 put **t** against the stronghold,
9:49 the stronghold on fire above **t**,
9:57 and on **t** came the curse of
10: 7 and He sold **t** into the hands of
10:14 let **t** deliver you in your time
10:16 the foreign gods from among **t**
11: 9 and the LORD delivers **t** to me,
11:11 him head and commander over **t**;
11:21 of Israel, and they defeated **t**.
11:25 Did he ever fight against **t**?
11:26 why did you not recover **t**
11:32 of Ammon to fight against **t**,
11:32 and the LORD delivered **t** into
11:33 And he defeated **t** from Aroer as
12: 2 And Jephthah said to **t**,
12: 3 and the LORD delivered **t** into
13: 1 and the LORD delivered **t** into
14: 9 and mother, he gave some to **t**,
14: 9 But he did not tell **t** that he
14:12 Then Samson said to **t**,
14:14 So he said to **t**:
14:18 a lion?" And he said to **t**:
15: 3 And Samson said to **t**,
15: 3 the Philistines if I harm **t**!"
15: 7 Samson said to **t**,
15: 8 So he attacked **t** hip and thigh
15:11 done to us?" And he said to **t**,
15:11 did to me, so I have done to **t**.
15:12 Then Samson said to **t**,
16: 3 pulled **t** up, bar and all,
16: 3 put **t** on his shoulders,
16: 3 and carried **t** to the top of the
16: 8 dried, and she bound him with **t**.
16:12 new ropes and bound him with **t**,
16:12 But he broke **t** off his arms
16:25 prison, and he performed for **t**.
16:26 temple, so that I can lean on **t**.
16:29 and he braced himself against **t**,
17: 4 shekels of silver and gave **t**
18: 1 of Israel had not fallen to **t**.
18: 2 and search it. They said to **t**,
18: 4 He said to **t**, "Thus and so
18: 6 And the priest said to **t**,
18: 7 in the land who might put **t**
18: 8 and their brethren said to **t**,
18: 9 "Arise, let us go up against **t**.
18:18 image, the priest said to **t**,
18:21 and the goods in front of **t**.
18:27 and they struck **t** with the edge
19: 6 and the two of **t** ate and drank
19: 8 and both of **t** ate.
19:14 and the sun went down on **t** near

T

19:15 for no one would take **t** into
19:23 went out to **t** and said to them,
19:23 went out to them and said to **t**,
19:24 let me bring **t** out now. Humble
19:24 me bring them out now. Humble **t**,
19:24 and do with **t** as you please;
19:25 and brought her out to **t**.
20:13 that we may put **t** to death and
20:20 array to fight against **t** at
20:25 And Benjamin went out against **t**
20:28 for tomorrow I will deliver **t**
20:32 Let us flee and draw **t** away from
20:34 know that disaster was upon **t**.
20:40 the Benjamites looked behind **t**,
20:41 that disaster had come upon **t**.
20:42 but the battle overtook **t**,
20:43 the Benjamites, chased **t**,
20:43 and easily trampled **t** down as
20:45 cut down five thousand of **t** on
20:45 Then they pursued **t**
20:45 and killed two thousand of **t**.
20:48 and struck **t** down with the edge
21: 7 LORD that we will not give **t**
21:10 valiant men, and commanded **t**,
21:12 and they brought **t** to the camp
21:13 and announced peace to **t**.
21:14 and they gave **t** the women whom
21:14 they had not found enough for **t**.
21:18 we cannot give **t** wives from our
21:22 complain, that we will say to **t**,
21:22 Be kind to **t** for our sakes,
21:22 not take a wife for any of **t**
21:22 you have given the women to **t**
21:23 the cities and dwelt in **t**.
Ruth 1: 6 visited His people by giving **t**
1: 9 husband." Then she kissed **t**,
1:13 would you wait for **t** till they
1:19 Now the two of **t** went until
1:19 city was excited because of **t**;
1:20 But she said to **t**,
2: 9 which they reap, and go after **t**.
1 Sam 2: 8 To set **t** among princes And
2: 8 them among princes And make **t**
2: 8 He has set the world upon **t**.
2:10 He will thunder against **t**.
2:23 So he said to **t**,
2:25 the LORD desired to kill **t**.
2:34 day they shall die, both of **t**.
3:13 and he did not restrain **t**.
5: 6 and He ravaged **t** and struck
5: 6 He ravaged them and struck **t**
5: 9 and tumors broke out on **t**.
6: 6 He did mighty things among **t**,
6: 7 their calves home, away from **t**.
6:10 two milk cows and hitched **t** to
6:12 of the Philistines went after **t**
6:15 and put **t** on the large stone.
7:10 and so confused **t** that they
7:11 and drove **t** back as far as
8: 7 that I should not reign over **t**.
8: 8 since the day that I brought **t**
8: 9 you shall solemnly forewarn **t**,
8: 9 and show **t** the behavior of the
8: 9 the king who will reign over **t**.
8:11 take your sons and appoint **t**
8:14 and give **t** to his servants.
8:16 and put **t** to his work.
8:21 and he repeated **t** in the
8:22 and make **t** a king." And Samuel
9: 4 but they did not find **t**.
9: 4 but they did not find **t**.
9:11 to draw water, and said to **t**,
9:12 And they answered **t** and said,
9:14 coming out toward **t** on his way
9:20 do not be anxious about **t**,
9:22 and his servant and brought **t**
9:22 and had **t** sit in the place of
9:26 and both of **t** went outside, he
10: 5 a flute, and a harp before **t**;
10: 6 and you will prophesy with **t**
10:10 and he prophesied among **t**.
11: 2 Nahash the Ammonite answered **t**,
11: 7 took a yoke of oxen and cut **t**
11: 7 and sent **t** throughout all the
11: 8 When he numbered **t** in Bezek, the
11:11 so that no two of **t** were left
11:12 that we may put **t** to death."
12: 5 Then he said to **t**,
12: 8 out of Egypt and made **t** dwell
12: 9 He sold **t** into the hand of
12: 9 Moab; and they fought against **t**.
13:16 and the people present with **t**
14: 8 and we will show ourselves to **t**.
14: 9 in our place and not go up to **t**.
14:10 For the LORD has delivered **t**
14:11 So both of **t** showed themselves
14:12 for the LORD has delivered **t**
14:13 his armorbearer killed **t**.
14:21 who went up with **t** into the
14:22 also followed hard after **t** in
14:32 and slaughtered **t** on the
14:32 and the people ate **t** with the
14:34 among the people, and say to **t**,
14:34 slaughter **t** here, and eat; and
14:36 and plunder **t** until the morning
14:36 and let us not leave a man of **t**.
14:37 Will You deliver **t** into the
14:47 he turned, he harassed **t**.
14:48 hands of those who plundered **t**.
15: 3 they have, and do not spare **t**.
15: 4 people together and numbered **t**
15: 6 lest I destroy you with **t**.
15: 9 unwilling to utterly destroy **t**.
15:15 They have brought **t** from the
15:18 and fight against **t** until they
16: 5 and invited **t** to the sacrifice.
16:20 and sent **t** by his son David to
17: 3 side, with a valley between **t**.
17: 8 armies of Israel, and said to **t**,
17:18 fare, and bring back news of **t**.
17:23 Then as he talked with **t**,
17:23 same words. So David heard **t**.
17:31 they reported **t** to Saul; and
17:36 will be like one of **t**,
17:39 walk, for he had not tested **t**.
17:39 these, for I have not tested **t**.
17:39 So David took **t** off.
17:40 and put **t** in a shepherd's bag,
18:16 went out and came in before **t**.
18:27 and they gave **t** in full count
19: 8 and struck **t** with a mighty
19:20 standing as leader over **t**,
20:11 So both of **t** went out into
20:21 get **t** and come'—then, as the
20:40 carry **t** to the city."
21:13 changed his behavior before **t**,
22: 2 So he became captain over **t**.
22: 4 So he brought **t** before the king
23: 5 struck **t** with a mighty blow,
23:18 So the two of **t** made a covenant
23:26 David and his men to take **t**.
24: 7 and did not allow **t** to rise
25: 7 with us, and we did not hurt **t**,
25: 7 there anything missing from **t**
25:14 our master; and he reviled **t**.
25:15 as long as we accompanied **t**,
25:16 all the time we were with **t**
25:18 and loaded **t** on donkeys.
25:20 down toward her, and she met **t**.
25:43 and so both of **t** were his
26:12 from the LORD had fallen on **t**.
26:13 great distance being between **t**.
27: 5 let **t** give me a place in some
30: 2 but carried **t** away and went
30: 8 this troop? Shall I overtake **t**?
30: 8 you shall surely overtake **t**
30:17 Then David attacked **t** from
30:17 Not a man of **t** escaped, except
30:19 which they had taken from **t**;
30:21 near the people, he greeted **t**.
30:22 we will not give **t** any of the
30:22 that they may lead **t** away and
31: 7 Philistines came and dwelt in **t**.
31:12 came to Jabesh and burned **t**
31:13 took their bones and buried **t**
2 Sam 1:10 and have brought **t** here to my
1:11 of his own clothes and tore **t**,
1:18 and he told **t** to teach the
2: 5 of Jabesh Gilead, and said to **t**,
2: 7 has anointed me king over **t**.
2:13 went out and met **t** by the pool
2:14 Let **t** arise."
3:22 and brought much spoil with **t**.
3:36 note of it, and it pleased **t**,
4: 9 the Beerothite, and said to **t**,
4:12 young men, and they executed **t**,
4:12 and hanged **t** by the pool in
5: 2 led Israel out and brought **t**
5: 3 David made a covenant with **t**
5:19 Will You deliver **t** into my
5:20 and David defeated **t** there; and
5:21 and David and his men carried **t**
5:23 go up; circle around behind **t**,
5:23 and come upon **t** in front of the
6:22 by **t** I will be held in honor."
7:10 people Israel, and will plant **t**,
7:10 sons of wickedness oppress **t**
7:21 to make Your servant know **t**.
8: 1 the Philistines and subdued **t**.
8: 2 Forcing **t** down to the ground,
8: 2 he measured **t** off with a line.
8: 4 that he spared enough of **t**
8: 7 and brought **t** to Jerusalem.
10: 4 and sent **t** away.
10: 5 told David, he sent to meet **t**,
10: 9 of Israel's best and put **t** in
10:10 that he might set **t** in battle
10:16 Hadadezer's army went before **t**.
10:19 peace with Israel and served **t**.
11:23 then we drove **t** back as far as
12:11 before your eyes and give **t**
12:17 not, nor did he eat food with **t**.
12:31 and put **t** to work with saws
12:31 and made **t** cross over to the
13: 9 she took the pan and placed **t**
13:10 and brought **t** to Amnon her
13:11 Now when she had brought **t** to
13:30 and not one of **t** is left!"
14: 6 there was no one to part **t**,
15:36 they have there with **t** their
15:36 and by **t** you shall send me
16: 1 and on **t** two hundred loaves of
17: 9 when some of **t** are overthrown
17:17 servant would come and tell **t**,
17:18 Nevertheless a lad saw **t**,
17:18 But both of **t** went away quickly
17:20 So the woman said to **t**,
17:20 searched and could not find **t**,
17:22 By morning light not one of **t**
18: 1 and captains of hundreds over **t**.
18: 4 Then the king said to **t**,
18:14 spears in his hand and thrust **t**
20: 3 and put **t** in seclusion and
20: 3 in seclusion and supported **t**,
20: 3 them, but did not go in to **t**.
20: 8 in Gibeon, Amasa came before **t**.
21: 2 the Gibeonites and spoke to **t**.
21: 2 had sworn protection to **t**,
21: 2 but Saul had sought to kill **t**
21: 6 and we will hang **t** before the
21: 6 the king said, "I will give **t**.
21: 7 oath that was between **t**,
21: 9 and he delivered **t** into the
21: 9 and they hanged **t** on the hill
21:10 the late rains poured on **t**
21:10 birds of the air to rest on **t**
21:12 Jabesh Gilead who had stolen **t**
21:12 the Philistines had hung **t** up,
22:15 sent out arrows and scattered **t**;
22:15 bolts, and He vanquished **t**.
22:23 I did not depart from **t**.
22:28 that You may bring **t** down.
22:38 my enemies and destroyed **t**;
22:39 And I have destroyed **t** and
22:39 destroyed them and wounded **t**,
22:42 LORD, but He did not answer **t**.
22:43 Then I beat **t** as fine as the
22:43 I trod **t** like dirt in the
22:43 And I spread **t** out.
23: 7 But the man who touches **t**
23:18 three hundred men, killed **t**,
24: 1 and He moved David against **t** to
24:12 choose one of **t** for yourself,
1 Ki 1:20 that you should tell **t** who will
1:33 The king also said to **t**,
1:53 So King Solomon sent **t** to bring
2: 7 and let **t** be among those who
2:32 and killed **t** with the
5: 9 My servants shall bring **t** down
5: 9 I will float **t** in rafts by sea
5: 9 and will have **t** broken apart
5: 9 then you can take **t** away.
5:12 and the two of **t** made a treaty
5:14 And he sent **t** to Lebanon, ten
5:17 And the king commanded **t** to
5:18 and the Gebalites quarried **t**;
6:12 My commandments, and walk in **t**,
6:32 and he carved on **t** figures of
6:32 and overlaid **t** with gold;
6:35 trees, and open flowers on **t**,
6:35 and overlaid **t** with gold
7: 6 and in front of **t** was a
7: 6 and a canopy was in front of **t**.
7:25 east; the Sea was set upon **t**,
7:37 All of **t** were of the same mold,
7:46 plain of Jordan the king had **t**
7:51 He put **t** in the treasuries of
8: 4 and the Levites brought **t** up.
8:21 when He brought **t** out of the
8:34 and bring **t** back to the land
8:35 their sin because You afflict **t**,
8:36 that You may teach **t** the good
8:37 when their enemy besieges **t** in
8:44 enemy, wherever You send **t**,
8:46 and You become angry with **t** and
8:46 angry with them and deliver **t**
8:46 and they take **t** captive to the
8:47 in the land of those who took **t**
8:48 land of their enemies who led **t**
8:50 and grant **t** compassion before
8:50 before those who took **t**
8:50 they may have compassion on **t**
8:52 to listen to **t** whenever they
8:53 For You separated **t** from among
9: 6 serve other gods and worship **t**,
9: 7 the land which I have given **t**;
9: 9 and worshiped **t** and served
9: 9 and worshiped them and served **t**;
9: 9 brought all this calamity on **t**.
9:13 And he called **t** the land of
9:21 were left in the land after **t**,
9:25 and he burned incense with **t**
10:17 The king put **t** in the House of
10:28 the king's merchants bought **t**
10:29 they exported **t** to all the
11: 2 shall not intermarry with **t**,
11:18 and they took men with **t** from
12: 5 So he said to **t**,
12: 7 these people today, and serve **t**,
12: 7 and serve them, and answer **t**,
12: 7 and speak good words to **t**,
12: 9 And he said to **t**,
12:10 on us'—thus you shall say to **t**:
12:14 and he spoke to **t** according to
12:16 the king did not listen to **t**,
13:12 And their father said to **t**,
14:15 and will scatter **t** beyond the
14:27 and committed **t** to the hands
14:28 the LORD, the guards carried **t**,
14:28 then brought **t** back into the
15:18 and delivered **t** into the hand
15:18 And King Asa sent **t** to
15:22 and with **t** King Asa built Geba
16: 7 and because he killed **t**.
18: 4 hundred prophets and hidden **t**,
18: 4 and had fed **t** with bread and
18: 6 divided the land between **t** to
18:13 and fed **t** with bread and water?
18:23 Therefore let **t** give us two
18:23 and let **t** choose one bull for
18:26 took the bull which was given **t**,
18:27 that Elijah mocked **t** and said,
18:28 until the blood gushed out on **t**.
18:40 And Elijah said to **t**,
18:40 of Baal! Do not let one of **t**
18:40 them escape!" So they seized **t**;

18:40 and Elijah brought **t** down to
18:40 the Brook Kishon and executed **t**
19: 2 life as the life of one of **t**
19:21 yoke of oxen and slaughtered **t**
20:15 and after **t** he mustered all the
20:18 take **t** alive; and if they have
20:18 out for war, take **t** alive."
20:19 with the army which followed **t**.
20:20 fled, and Israel pursued **t**;
20:23 but if we fight against **t** in
20:25 Then we will fight against **t** in
20:27 and they went against **t**.
20:27 of Israel encamped before **t**
21: 8 sealed **t** with his seal, and
21:11 did as Jezebel had sent to **t**.
21:11 letters which she had sent to **t**.
22: 6 four hundred men, and said to **t**,
22:10 prophets prophesied before **t**.
22:13 be like the word of one of **t**,
22:43 He did not turn aside from **t**,
2 Ki 1: 2 sent messengers and said to **t**,
1: 3 king of Samaria, and say to **t**,
1: 5 returned to him, he said to **t**,
1: 7 Then he said to **t**,
1:12 Elijah answered and said to **t**,
2: 6 leave you!" So the two of **t**
2: 7 went and stood facing **t** at a
2: 7 while the two of **t** stood by the
2: 8 so that the two of **t** crossed
2:11 and separated the two of **t**;
2:12 of his own clothes and tore **t**
2:16 Please let **t** go and search for
2:17 Send **t**!" Therefore they sent
2:18 stayed in Jericho, he said to **t**,
2:24 turned around and looked at **t**,
2:24 and pronounced a curse on **t** in
3: 3 sin; he did not depart from **t**.
3: 9 for the animals that followed **t**.
3:10 kings together to deliver **t**
3:13 kings together to deliver **t**
3:21 had come up to fight against **t**,
3:24 so that they fled before **t**;
4:31 Now Gehazi went on ahead of **t**,
4:33 the door behind the two of **t**,
4:39 and came and sliced **t** into the
4:44 So he set it before **t**;
5:12 Could I not wash in **t** and be
5:22 Please give **t** a talent of
5:23 and handed **t** to two of his
5:23 and they carried **t** on ahead of
5:24 he took **t** from their hand, and
5:24 and stored **t** away in the
6: 4 So he went with **t**.
6:11 his servants and said to **t**,
6:16 more than those who are with **t**.
6:18 And He struck **t** with
6:19 Now Elisha said to **t**,
6:19 But he led **t** to Samaria.
6:21 when the king of Israel saw **t**,
6:21 "My father, shall I kill **t**?
6:21 I kill them? Shall I kill **t**?
6:22 "You shall not kill **t**.
6:22 Set food and water before **t**,
6:23 he prepared a great feast for **t**;
6:23 he sent **t** away and they went to
6:33 he was still talking with **t**,
7: 8 clothing, and went and hid **t**;
7:10 of the city, and told **t**,
7:12 we shall catch **t** alive, and get
7:13 so let us send **t** and see."
7:14 and the king sent **t** in the
7:15 And they went after **t** to the
9:11 come to you?" And he said to **t**,
9:17 horseman and send him to meet **t**,
9:18 "The messenger went to **t**,
9:19 a second horseman who came to **t**,
9:20 He went up to **t** and is not
10: 6 he wrote a second letter to **t**,
10: 6 the city, who were rearing **t**.
10: 7 was, when the letter came to **t**,
10: 7 heads in baskets and sent **t**
10: 8 Lay **t** in two heaps at the
10:14 Take **t** alive!" So they took
10:14 them alive!" So they took **t**
10:14 and killed **t** at the well of
10:14 men; and he left none of **t**.
10:17 till he had destroyed **t**,
10:18 people together, and said to **t**,
10:22 he brought out vestments for **t**.
10:25 captains, "Go in and kill **t**;
10:25 come out!" And they killed **t**
10:25 and the officers threw **t** out,
10:26 the temple of Baal and burned **t**.
10:32 and Hazael conquered **t** in all
11: 4 and brought **t** into the house of
11: 4 And he made a covenant with **t**
11: 4 them and took an oath from **t**
11: 4 and showed **t** the king's son.
11: 5 Then he commanded **t**,
11: 9 Each of **t** took his men who were
11:15 of the army, and said to **t**,
12: 5 and let **t** repair the damages of
12: 7 other priests, and said to **t**,
12:18 and sent **t** to Hazael king of
13: 2 sin. He did not depart from **t**.
13: 3 and He delivered **t** into the
13: 4 the king of Syria oppressed **t**.
13: 6 Israel sin, but walked in **t**;
13: 7 king of Syria had destroyed **t**
13: 7 had destroyed them and made **t**
13:11 Israel sin, but walked in **t**.
13:17 till you have destroyed **t**.
13:18 the arrows"; so he took **t**.
13:23 But the LORD was gracious to **t**,
13:23 to them, had compassion on **t**,
13:23 on them, and regarded **t**,
13:23 and would not yet destroy **t** or
13:23 not yet destroy them or cast **t**
14:27 but He saved **t** by the hand of
15:29 and he carried **t** captive to
16:17 and removed the lavers from **t**;
17: 6 and placed **t** in Halah and by
17: 7 who had brought **t** up out of the
17:11 LORD had carried away before **t**;
17:12 which the LORD had said to **t**,
17:15 He had testified against **t**;
17:15 nations who were all around **t**,
17:15 whom the LORD had charged **t**
17:15 that they should not do like **t**.
17:18 and removed **t** from His sight;
17:20 of Israel, afflicted **t**,
17:20 and delivered **t** into the hand
17:20 until He had cast **t** from His
17:21 and made **t** commit a great sin.
17:22 they did not depart from **t**,
17:24 and placed **t** in the cities of
17:25 the LORD sent lions among **t**,
17:25 which killed some of **t**.
17:26 He has sent lions among **t**,
17:26 they are killing **t** because they
17:27 and let him teach **t** the rituals
17:28 and taught **t** how they should
17:29 and put **t** in the shrines on
17:32 who sacrificed for **t** in the
17:35 made a covenant and charged **t**,
17:35 nor bow down to **t** nor serve
17:35 bow down to them nor serve **t**
17:35 serve them nor sacrifice to **t**;
18:11 and put **t** in Halah and by the
18:12 would neither hear nor do **t**.
18:13 cities of Judah and took **t**.
18:18 the recorder, came out to **t**.
18:19 Then the Rabshakeh said to **t**,
18:23 your part to put riders on **t**!
18:27 But the Rabshakeh said to **t**,
19: 3 is no strength to bring **t**
19: 6 And Isaiah said to **t**,
19:11 lands by utterly destroying **t**;
19:18 Therefore they destroyed **t**.
19:29 and eat the fruit of **t**.
20:13 And Hezekiah was attentive to **t**,
20:13 and showed **t** all the house of
20:13 that Hezekiah did not show **t**.
20:15 that I have not shown **t**.
21: 3 the host of heaven and served **t**.
21: 8 to all that I have commanded **t**,
21: 8 My servant Moses commanded **t**.
21: 9 and Manasseh seduced **t** to do
21:14 of My inheritance and deliver **t**
21:21 had served, and worshiped **t**.
22: 5 And let **t** deliver it into the
22: 5 let **t** give it to those who are
22: 7 be no accounting made with **t**
22:15 Then she said to **t**,
23: 1 Now the king sent **t** to gather
23: 4 and he burned **t** outside
23:16 out of the tombs and burned **t**
23:19 and he did to **t** according to
23:20 and burned men's bones on **t**;
24: 2 He sent **t** against Judah to
24: 3 to remove **t** from His sight
24:20 that He finally cast **t** out from
25:20 took these and brought **t** to the
25:21 the king of Babylon struck **t**
25:21 Babylon struck them and put **t**
25:24 Gedaliah took an oath before **t**
25:24 and their men, and said to **t**,
1 Chr 2: 6 five of **t** in all.
2:23 (Geshur and Syria took from **t**
4:41 there, and utterly destroyed **t**,
4:42 Now some of **t**,
5:11 of Gad dwelt next to **t** in the
5:20 And they were helped against **t**,
5:20 hand, and all who were with **t**,
5:25 whom God had destroyed before **t**.
5:26 He took **t** to Halah, Habor,
6:55 They gave **t** Hebron in the land
6:67 And they gave **t** one of the
7: 3 All five of **t** were chief men.
7: 4 And with **t**, by their
7:21 born in that land killed **t**
8: 6 and who forced **t** to move to
8: 7 and Gera who forced **t** to move.
9:20 had been the officer over **t** in
9:22 the seer had appointed **t** to
9:25 villages had to come with **t**
9:28 Now some of **t** were in charge
9:28 for they brought **t** in and took
9:28 brought them in and took **t** out
9:29 Some of **t** were appointed over
10: 7 Philistines came and dwelt in **t**.
10:12 and they brought **t** to Jabesh,
11: 2 led Israel out and brought **t**
11: 3 David made a covenant with **t**
11:20 three hundred men, killed **t**,
12:17 And David went out to meet **t**,
12:17 and answered and said to **t**,
12:18 you." So David received **t**,
12:18 and made **t** captains of the
12:19 Saul; but they did not help **t**,
12:29 then the greatest part of **t**
12:34 and with **t** thirty-seven
12:39 brethren had prepared for **t**.
12:40 those who were near to **t**,
13: 2 and with **t** to the priests and
14: 8 of it and went out against **t**.
14:10 Will You deliver **t** into my
14:10 for I will deliver **t** into your
14:11 and David defeated **t** there.
14:14 "You shall not go up after **t**;
14:14 up after them; circle around **t**,
14:14 and come upon **t** in front of the
15: 2 for the LORD has chosen **t** to
15:12 He said to **t**, "You are the
15:18 and with **t** their brethren of the
16:21 He permitted no man to do **t**
16:31 And let **t** say among the
16:41 and with **t** Heman and Jeduthun
16:42 and with **t** Heman and Jeduthun,
17: 9 people Israel, and will plant **t**,
17: 9 sons of wickedness oppress **t**
18: 1 the Philistines, subdued **t**,
18: 4 that he spared enough of **t** for
18: 7 and brought **t** to Jerusalem.
19: 4 took David's servants, shaved **t**,
19: 4 and sent **t** away.
19: 5 the men; and he sent to meet **t**,
19:10 of Israel's best and put **t** in
19:16 Hadadezer's army went before **t**.
19:17 over the Jordan and came upon **t**,
19:17 up in battle array against **t**.
20: 3 and put **t** to work with saws,
21: 2 and bring the number of **t** to me
21: 6 count Levi and Benjamin among **t**,
21:10 choose one of **t** for yourself,
22:14 also, and you may add to **t**.
23: 6 Also David separated **t** into
23:22 took **t** as wives.
23:31 to the ordinance governing **t**,
24: 3 divided **t** according to the
24: 6 wrote **t** down before the king,
25: 7 So the number of **t**,
26:31 and there were found among **t**
29: 8 had precious stones gave **t**
2 Chr 1:16 the king's merchants bought **t**
1:17 they exported **t** to all the
2: 2 six hundred to oversee **t**.
2:11 He has made you king over **t**.
2:17 David his father had numbered **t**;
2:18 he made seventy thousand of **t**
3:10 and overlaid **t** with gold.
3:15 was on the top of each of **t**
3:16 and put **t** on top of the
3:16 and put **t** on the wreaths of
4: 4 east; the Sea was set upon **t**,
4: 6 five on the left, to wash in **t**;
4: 6 offering they would wash in **t**,
4: 7 and set **t** in the temple,
4: 8 and placed **t** in the temple,
4:17 plain of Jordan the king had **t**
5: 1 And he put **t** in the treasuries
5: 5 and the Levites brought **t** up.
5:12 and with **t** one hundred and
6:25 and bring **t** back to the land
6:25 to the land which You gave to **t**
6:26 their sin because You afflict **t**,
6:27 that You may teach **t** the good
6:28 when their enemies besiege **t** in
6:34 enemies, wherever You send **t**,
6:36 and You become angry with **t** and
6:36 angry with them and deliver **t**
6:36 and they take **t** captive to a
7: 6 sounded trumpets opposite **t**,
7:19 serve other gods, and worship **t**,
7:20 then I will uproot **t** from My
7:20 My land which I have given **t**;
7:22 who brought **t** out of the land
7:22 and worshiped **t** and served
7:22 and worshiped them and served **t**;
7:22 brought all this calamity on **t**.
8: 2 to Solomon, Solomon built **t**;
8: 8 were left in the land after **t**,
9: 8 to establish **t** forever,
9: 8 He made you king over **t**,
9:16 The king put **t** in the House of
10: 5 So he said to **t**,
10: 7 to these people, and please **t**,
10: 7 and speak good words to **t**,
10: 9 And he said to **t**,
10:10 on us'—thus you shall say to **t**:
10:13 Then the king answered **t**
10:14 and he spoke to **t** according to
10:16 the king did not listen to **t**,
11:11 and put captains in **t**,
11:12 and made **t** very strong,
11:14 and his sons had rejected **t**
11:23 and he gave **t** provisions in
11:23 also sought many wives for **t**.
12: 5 of Shishak, and said to **t**,
12: 7 therefore I will not destroy **t**,
12: 7 but I will grant **t** some
12:10 and committed **t** to the hands
12:11 the guard would go and bring **t**
12:11 then they would take **t** back
13: 7 and could not withstand **t**.
13:13 an ambush to go around behind **t**;
13:13 and the ambush was behind **t**.
13:16 and God delivered **t** into their
13:17 Abijah and his people struck **t**
14: 7 cities and make walls around **t**,
14: 9 Ethiopian came out against **t**
14:13 who were with him pursued **t**
14:14 fear of the LORD came upon **t**;
14:14 was exceedingly much spoil in **t**.
15: 4 sought Him, He was found by **t**.
15: 6 for God troubled **t** with every

T

15: 9 and those who dwelt with *t* from
15:15 soul; and He was found by *t*,
15:15 and the LORD gave *t* rest all
16: 6 and with *t* he built Geba and
16: 8 He delivered *t* into your hand.
17: 8 And with *t* he sent Levites:
17: 8 and with *t* Elishama and
17: 9 of the Law of the LORD with *t*;
18: 5 four hundred men, and said to *t*,
18: 9 prophets prophesied before *t*.
18:12 be like the word of one of *t*,
18:31 and God diverted *t* from him.
19: 4 and brought *t* back to the LORD
19: 9 And he commanded *t*,
19:10 or ordinances, you shall warn *t*,
20: 1 and others with *t* besides the
20:10 but they turned from *t* and did
20:10 from them and did not destroy *t*—
20:12 our God, will You not judge *t*?
20:16 'Tomorrow go down against *t*.
20:16 and you will find *t* at the end
20:17 tomorrow go out against *t*,
20:23 to utterly kill and destroy *t*.
20:25 they found among *t* an abundance
20:27 with Jehoshaphat in front of *t*,
20:27 for the LORD had made *t*
21: 3 Their father gave *t* great gifts
22: 8 Ahaziah, that he killed *t*.
22:12 And he was hidden with *t* in the
23: 3 house of God. And he said to *t*,
23:14 over the army, and said to *t*,
24: 5 and the Levites, and said to *t*,
24:10 and put *t* into the chest until
24:13 and the work was completed by *t*;
24:17 And the king listened to *t*.
24:19 Yet He sent prophets to *t*,
24:19 to bring *t* back to the LORD;
24:19 and they testified against *t*,
24:20 above the people, and said to *t*,
25: 5 Judah together and set over *t*
25: 5 and he numbered *t* from twenty
25: 5 and found *t* to be three hundred
25:12 brought *t* to the top of the
25:12 and cast *t* down from the top of
25:13 killed three thousand in *t*,
25:14 set *t* up to be his gods, and
25:14 and bowed down before *t* and
25:14 them and burned incense to *t*.
25:20 that He might give *t* into the
26: 9 the wall; then he fortified *t*.
26:14 Then Uzziah prepared for *t*,
27: 5 of the Ammonites and defeated *t*.
28: 5 away a great multitude of *t* as
28: 5 and brought *t* to Damascus.
28: 8 took away much spoil from *t*,
28: 9 came to Samaria, and said to *t*:
28: 9 He has delivered *t* into your
28: 9 but you have killed *t* in a rage
28:13 and said to *t*,
28:15 all who were naked among *t*,
28:15 dressed *t* and gave them
28:15 dressed them and gave *t*
28:15 gave *t* food and drink, and
28:15 food and drink, and anointed *t*;
28:15 So they brought *t* to their
28:23 of the kings of Syria help *t*,
28:23 I will sacrifice to *t* that they
29: 3 of the LORD and repaired *t*.
29: 4 and gathered *t* in the East
29: 5 and said to *t*: "Hear me,
29: 8 and He has given *t* up to
29:21 to offer *t* on the altar of the
29:23 and they laid their hands on *t*.
29:24 And the priests killed *t*;
29:27 Then Hezekiah commanded *t* to
29:34 brethren the Levites helped *t*
30: 7 so that He gave *t* up to
30: 9 compassion by those who lead *t*
30:10 but they laughed at *t* and
30:10 laughed at them and mocked *t*.
30:12 of God was on Judah to give *t*
30:14 the incense altars and cast *t*
30:17 to sanctify *t* to the LORD.
30:18 But Hezekiah prayed for *t*,
31: 1 they had utterly destroyed *t*
31: 7 month they began laying *t* in
31:11 Now Hezekiah commanded *t* to
31:11 the LORD, and they prepared *t*.
31:12 the Levite had charge of *t*,
31:18 the whole company of *t*—
32: 1 thinking to win *t* over to
32: 6 gathered *t* together to him in
32: 6 and gave *t* encouragement,
32:18 to frighten *t* and trouble them,
32:18 to frighten them and trouble *t*,
32:22 and guided *t* on every side.
32:26 the LORD did not come upon *t*
33: 3 the host of heaven and served *t*.
33: 8 do all that I have commanded *t*,
33:11 the LORD brought upon *t* the
33:15 and he cast *t* out of the city.
33:22 Manasseh had made, and served *t*.
34: 4 altars which were above *t* he
34: 4 and made dust of *t* and
34: 4 those who had sacrificed to *t*.
34:23 Then she answered *t*,
35: 2 their duties and encouraged *t*
35: 6 and prepare *t* for your
35:12 that they might give *t* to the
35:13 and divided *t* quickly among
35:15 Levites prepared portions for *t*.
36: 7 and put *t* in his temple at
36:15 fathers sent warnings to *t* by
36:15 rising up early and sending *t*,
36:17 He brought against *t* the king
36:17 He gave *t* all into his hand.

Ezra 1: 6 all those who were around *t*
1: 6 were around them encouraged *t*
1: 8 Cyrus king of Persia brought *t*
1: 8 and counted *t* out to
1: 9 This is the number of *t*:
2:63 And the governor said to *t* that
3: 3 Though fear had come upon *t*
4: 2 fathers' houses, and said to *t*,
4: 3 houses of Israel said to *t*,
4: 4 They troubled *t* in building,
4: 5 and hired counselors against *t*
4:20 and custom were paid to *t*.
4:23 and by force of arms made *t*
5: 1 God of Israel, who was over *t*.
5: 2 prophets of God were with *t*,
5: 2 God were with them, helping *t*.
5: 3 and their companions came to *t*
5: 3 to them and spoke thus to *t*:
5: 4 we told *t* the names of the men
5: 5 so that they could not make *t*
5: 9 elders, and spoke thus to *t*:
5:10 We also asked *t* their names to
5:10 the men who were chief among *t*.
5:12 He gave *t* into the hand of
5:15 carry *t* to the temple site
6: 5 and deposit *t* in the house of
6: 9 let it be given *t* day by day
6:20 all of *t* were ritually clean.
6:22 for the LORD made *t* joyful,
6:22 of the king of Assyria toward *t*,
7:17 and offer *t* on the altar of the
7:25 teach those who do not know *t*.
8:13 and with *t* sixty males;
8:14 and with *t* seventy males.
8:15 Now I gathered *t* by the river
8:17 And I gave *t* a command for Iddo
8:17 and I told *t* what they should
8:20 All of *t* were designated by
8:24 ten of their brethren with *t*—
8:25 and weighed out to *t* the silver,
8:28 And I said to *t*,
8:29 Watch and keep *t* until you
8:29 keep them until you weigh *t*
8:30 to bring *t* to Jerusalem to the
8:33 with *t* were the Levites,
10: 3 those who have been born to *t*,
10:10 priest stood up and said to *t*,
10:15 Shabbethai the Levite gave *t*
10:16 each of *t* by name; and they sat
10:44 and some of *t* had wives by

Neh 1: 2 and I asked *t* concerning the
1: 9 keep My commandments and do *t*,
1: 9 yet I will gather *t* from
1: 9 and bring *t* to the place which
2: 8 And the king granted *t* to me
2: 9 and gave *t* the king's letters.
2:17 Then I said to *t*,
2:18 And I told *t* of the hand of my
2:20 So I answered *t*,
2:20 I answered them, and said to *t*,
3: 2 And next to *t* Zaccur the son of
3: 4 And next to *t* Meremoth the son
3: 4 Next to *t* Meshullam the son of
3: 4 Next to *t* Zadok the son of
3: 5 Next to *t* the Tekoites made
3: 7 And next to *t* Melatiah the
3: 9 And next to *t* Rephaiah the son
3:10 Next to *t* Jedaiah the son of
3:23 After *t* Azariah the son of
3:27 After *t* the Tekoites repaired
3:29 After *t* Zadok the son of Immer
4: 4 and give *t* as plunder to a land
4: 8 and all of *t* conspired together
4: 9 and because of *t* we set a watch
4: 9 them we set a watch against *t*
4:11 into their midst and kill *t*
4:12 when the Jews who dwelt near *t*
4:14 people, "Do not be afraid of *t*.
4:23 except that everyone took *t*
5: 5 not in our power to redeem *t*,
5: 7 and rulers, and said to *t*,
5: 7 a great assembly against *t*.
5: 8 And I said to *t*,
5:10 am lending *t* money and grain.
5:11 "Restore now to *t*,
5:11 that you have charged *t*."
5:12 and will require nothing from *t*;
5:12 and required an oath from *t*
5:15 and took from *t* bread and wine,
6: 3 So I sent messengers to *t*,
6: 4 and I answered *t* in the same
6: 8 but you invent *t* in your own
6:17 letters of Tobiah came to *t*.
7: 3 And I said to *t*,
7: 3 let *t* shut and bar the doors;
7:65 And the governor said to *t* that
8: 8 and helped *t* to understand the
8:10 Then he said to *t*,
8:12 words that were declared to *t*.
8:16 people went out and brought *t*
9: 6 The seas and all that is in *t*,
9: 6 And You preserve *t* all.
9:10 they acted proudly against *t*.
9:11 You divided the sea before *t*,
9:12 Moreover You led *t* by day with
9:12 To give *t* light on the road
9:13 And spoke with *t* from heaven,
9:13 And gave *t* just ordinances and
9:14 You made known to *t* Your holy
9:14 And commanded *t* precepts,
9:15 You gave *t* bread from heaven
9:15 And brought *t* water out of the
9:15 And told *t* to go in to possess
9:15 Which You had sworn to give *t*.
9:17 wonders That You did among *t*.
9:17 And did not forsake *t*.
9:19 mercies You did not forsake *t*
9:19 cloud did not depart from *t* by
9:19 To lead *t* on the road;
9:19 To show *t* light, And the way
9:20 Your good Spirit to instruct *t*,
9:20 And gave *t* water for their
9:21 Forty years You sustained *t* in
9:22 Moreover You gave *t* kingdoms and
9:22 And divided *t* into districts.
9:23 And brought *t* into the land
9:24 You subdued before *t* the
9:24 And gave *t* into their hands,
9:24 That they might do with *t* as
9:26 who testified against *t* To
9:26 against them To turn *t* to
9:27 Therefore You delivered *t* into
9:27 their enemies, Who oppressed *t*;
9:27 abundant mercies You gave *t*
9:27 them deliverers who saved *t*
9:28 Therefore You left *t* in the
9:28 that they had dominion over *t*;
9:28 And many times You delivered *t*
9:29 And testified against *t*,
9:29 That You might bring *t* back to
9:29 a man does, he shall live by *t*.
9:30 years You had patience with *t*,
9:30 And testified against *t* by
9:30 Therefore You gave *t* into the
9:31 You did not utterly consume *t*
9:31 consume them nor forsake *t*;
9:34 which You testified against *t*.
9:35 good things that You gave *t*,
9:35 land which You set before *t*;
10:31 we would not buy it from *t* on
11:23 the king's command concerning *t*
12: 9 stood across from *t* in their
12:24 their brothers across from *t*,
12:27 to bring *t* to Jerusalem to
12:32 After *t* went Hoshaiah and half
12:36 Ezra the scribe went before *t*.
12:37 Fountain Gate, in front of *t*,
12:38 and I was behind *t* with half
12:43 for God had made *t* rejoice with
12:44 to gather into *t* from the
12:47 and the Levites consecrated *t*
13: 2 but hired Balaam against *t* to
13: 2 Balaam against them to curse *t*.
13: 9 Then I commanded *t* to cleanse
13: 9 and I brought back into *t* the
13:10 Levites had not been given *t*;
13:11 And I gathered *t* together and
13:11 them together and set *t* in
13:13 and next to *t* was Hanan the
13:15 And I warned *t* about the day
13:16 and sold *t* on the Sabbath to
13:17 nobles of Judah, and said to *t*,
13:21 Then I warned *t*,
13:21 I warned them, and said to *t*,
13:25 So I contended with *t* and cursed
13:25 with them and cursed *t*,
13:25 struck some of *t* and pulled out
13:25 and made *t* swear by God,
13:29 Remember *t*, O my God,
13:30 Thus I cleansed *t* of everything

Esth 2: 3 beauty preparations be given *t*.
3: 4 and he would not listen to *t*,
3: 4 for Mordecai had told *t* that
3: 8 fitting for the king to let *t*
3:11 to do with *t* as seems good to
4: 4 but he would not accept *t*.
4:13 And Mordecai told *t* to answer
4:15 Then Esther told *t* to reply to
5: 8 which I will prepare for *t*,
5:11 Then Haman told *t* of his great
8:11 province that would assault *t*,
8:17 fear of the Jews fell upon *t*.
9: 1 Jews had hoped to overpower *t*,
9: 1 overpowered those who hated *t*.
9: 2 And no one could withstand *t*,
9: 2 because fear of *t* fell upon all
9: 3 fear of Mordecai fell upon *t*.
9: 5 pleased with those who hated *t*.
9:21 to establish among *t* that they
9:22 turned from sorrow to joy for *t*,
9:22 that they should make *t* days of
9:23 as Mordecai had written to *t*,
9:24 the Jews to annihilate *t*,
9:24 to consume *t* and destroy them;
9:24 to consume them and destroy *t*;
9:26 and what had happened to *t*,
9:27 and all who would join *t*,
9:28 and that the memory of *t*
9:31 Esther had prescribed for *t*,

Job 1: 4 sisters to eat and drink with *t*.
1: 5 Job would send and sanctify *t*,
1: 5 according to the number of *t*
1: 6 and Satan also came among *t*.
1:14 the donkeys feeding beside *t*,
1:15 when the Sabeans raided *t* and
1:15 raided them and took *t* away—
1:16 the servants, and consumed *t*;
1:17 raided the camels and took *t*
2: 1 and Satan came also among *t* to
5:13 cunning comes quickly upon *t*.

6: 7 My soul refuses to touch ***t***;
6:19 travelers of Sheba hope for ***t***.
8: 4 He has cast ***t*** away for their
9: 5 not know When He overturns ***t***
12:15 If He sends ***t*** out, they
12:23 nations great, and destroys ***t***;
12:23 enlarges nations, and guides ***t***.
12:24 And makes ***t*** wander in a
12:25 And He makes ***t*** stagger like a
15:19 And no alien passed among ***t***:
17: 4 You will not exalt ***t***.
20:15 down riches And vomits ***t*** up
20:15 God casts ***t*** out of his belly.
21: 8 are established with ***t*** in
21: 9 is the rod of God upon ***t***.
21:17 their destruction come upon ***t***,
21:26 in the dust, And worms cover ***t***.
22:17 What can the Almighty do to ***t***?
22:19 And the innocent laugh at ***t***:
24: 2 violently and feed on ***t***;
24: 5 wilderness yields food for ***t***
24:12 Yet God does not charge ***t***
24:17 the morning is the same to ***t***
24:17 If someone recognizes ***t***,
24:23 He gives ***t*** security, and they
26: 5 waters and those inhabiting ***t***.
29:22 And my speech settled on ***t*** as
29:24 If I mocked at ***t***,
29:25 I chose the way for ***t***,
30: 5 They shouted at ***t*** as at a
31:15 who made me in the womb make ***t***?
32:15 answer no more; Words escape ***t***.
34:25 He overthrows ***t*** in the night,
34:26 He strikes ***t*** as wicked men
36: 7 For He has seated ***t*** forever,
36: 9 Then He tells ***t*** their work and
36:13 cry for help when He binds ***t***.
37: 4 And He does not restrain ***t***
37:12 may do whatever He commands ***t***
37:15 you know when God dispatches ***t***,
37:21 wind has passed and cleared ***t***.
39: 4 depart and do not return to ***t***.
39:14 And warms ***t*** in the dust;
39:15 forgets that a foot may crush ***t***,
39:15 that a wild beast may break ***t***.
40:13 Hide ***t*** in the dust together,
41:16 That no air can come between ***t***;
42: 9 did as the LORD commanded ***t***;
42:15 and their father gave ***t*** an
Ps 2: 4 The LORD shall hold ***t*** in
2: 5 Then He shall speak to ***t*** in His
2: 5 And distress ***t*** in His deep
2: 9 You shall break ***t*** with a rod of
2: 9 You shall dash ***t*** to pieces
5:10 Pronounce ***t*** guilty, O God!
5:10 O God! Let ***t*** fall by their own
5:10 Cast ***t*** out in the multitude of
5:11 Let ***t*** ever shout for joy,
5:11 for joy, because You defend ***t***;
6:10 Let ***t*** turn back and be
9:12 avenges blood, He remembers ***t***;
9:20 Put ***t*** in fear, O LORD, That
10: 2 Let ***t*** be caught in the plots
10: 5 all his enemies, he sneers at ***t***.
12: 7 You shall keep ***t***,
12: 7 You shall preserve ***t*** from this
17: 7 those who rise up against ***t***.
18:14 abundance, and He vanquished ***t***.
18:37 my enemies and overtaken ***t***;
18:38 I have wounded ***t***,
18:41 LORD, but He did not answer ***t***.
18:42 Then I beat ***t*** as fine as the
18:42 I cast ***t*** out like dirt in the
19: 4 In ***t*** He has set a tabernacle
19:11 Moreover by ***t*** Your servant is
19:11 And in keeping ***t*** there is
19:13 Let ***t*** not have dominion over
21: 9 You shall make ***t*** as a fiery
21: 9 The LORD shall swallow ***t*** up
21: 9 And the fire shall devour ***t***.
21:12 Therefore You will make ***t*** turn
22: 4 trusted, and You delivered ***t***.
22:18 divide My garments among ***t***,
25:14 And He will show ***t*** His
28: 4 Give ***t*** according to their
28: 4 Give ***t*** according to the work
28: 4 Render to ***t*** what they deserve.
28: 5 He shall destroy ***t*** And not
28: 5 destroy them And not build ***t***
28: 9 Shepherd ***t*** also, And bear
28: 9 And bear ***t*** up forever.
29: 6 He makes ***t*** also skip like a
31:17 Let ***t*** be silent in the grave.
31:20 You shall hide ***t*** in the secret
31:20 You shall keep ***t*** secretly in a
33: 6 And all the host of ***t*** by the
33:19 And to keep ***t*** alive in famine.
34: 7 who fear Him, And delivers ***t***.
34:16 cut off the remembrance of ***t***
34:17 And delivers ***t*** out of all
34:19 the LORD delivers him out of ***t***
34:20 Not one of ***t*** is broken.
35: 5 Let ***t*** be like chaff before the
35: 5 the angel of the LORD chase ***t***.
35: 6 the angel of the LORD pursue ***t***.
35:19 Let ***t*** not rejoice over me who
35:19 Nor let ***t*** wink with the eye
35:24 And let ***t*** not rejoice over me.
35:25 Let ***t*** not say in their hearts,
35:25 so we would have it!" Let ***t***
35:26 Let ***t*** be ashamed and brought to
35:26 Let ***t*** be clothed with shame
35:27 Let ***t*** shout for joy and be
35:27 And let ***t*** say continually,
36: 8 And You give ***t*** drink from the
37:40 And the LORD shall help ***t*** and
37:40 shall help them and deliver ***t***;
37:40 He shall deliver ***t*** from the
37:40 from the wicked, And save ***t***,
39: 6 does not know who will gather ***t***.
40: 5 would declare and speak of ***t***,
40:14 Let ***t*** be ashamed and brought to
40:14 Let ***t*** be driven backward and
40:15 Let ***t*** be confounded because of
41:10 me up, That I may repay ***t***.
42: 4 I went with ***t*** to the house of
43: 3 light and Your truth! Let ***t***
43: 3 Let ***t*** bring me to Your holy
44: 2 But ***t*** You planted;
44: 2 the peoples, and cast ***t*** out.
44: 3 Nor did their own arm save ***t***;
44: 3 Because You favored ***t***.
44:12 are not enriched by selling ***t***.
48: 6 Fear took hold of ***t*** there,
49: 7 None of ***t*** can by any means
49:14 grave; Death shall feed on ***t***;
49:14 shall have dominion over ***t*** in
50:21 And set ***t*** in order before
53: 3 Every one of ***t*** has turned
53: 5 You have put ***t*** to shame,
53: 5 Because God has despised ***t***.
54: 3 They have not set God before ***t***.
54: 5 Cut ***t*** off in Your truth.
55:15 Let death seize ***t***;
55:15 Let ***t*** go down alive into hell,
55:15 in their dwellings and among ***t***.
55:19 God will hear, and afflict ***t***,
55:23 shall bring ***t*** down to the pit
58: 7 Let ***t*** flow away as waters
58: 8 Let ***t*** be like a snail which
58: 9 He shall take ***t*** away as with a
59: 8 You, O LORD, shall laugh at ***t***;
59:11 Do not slay ***t***,
59:11 Scatter ***t*** by Your power,
59:11 And bring ***t*** down, O Lord our
59:12 Let ***t*** even be taken in their
59:13 Consume ***t*** in wrath, consume
59:13 them in wrath, consume ***t***,
59:13 And let ***t*** know that God rules
62:10 Do not set your heart on ***t***.
64: 5 They say, "Who will see ***t***?
64: 7 But God shall shoot at ***t*** with
64: 8 So He will make ***t*** stumble over
64: 8 All who see ***t*** shall flee away.
65: 3 will provide atonement for ***t***.
68: 2 So drive ***t*** away; As wax
68: 3 Let ***t*** rejoice before God;
68: 3 let ***t*** rejoice exceedingly.
68:17 The Lord is among ***t*** as in
68:22 I will bring ***t*** back from the
68:23 That your foot may crush ***t*** in
68:25 Among ***t*** were the maidens
69:11 I became a byword to ***t***.
69:22 table become a snare before ***t***,
69:24 out Your indignation upon ***t***,
69:24 wrathful anger take hold of ***t***.
69:27 And let ***t*** not come into Your
69:28 Let ***t*** be blotted out of the
69:34 and everything that moves in ***t***.
70: 2 Let ***t*** be ashamed and confounded
70: 2 Let ***t*** be turned back and
70: 3 Let ***t*** be turned back because of
71:13 Let ***t*** be confounded and
71:13 Let ***t*** be covered with
73: 6 Violence covers ***t*** like a
73:10 of a full cup are drained by ***t***.
73:18 Surely You set ***t*** in slippery
73:18 You cast ***t*** down to
74: 8 Let us destroy ***t*** altogether."
74:11 of Your bosom and destroy ***t***.
76:11 the LORD your God, and pay ***t***;
78: 4 We will not hide ***t*** from their
78: 5 That they should make ***t*** known
78: 6 to come might know ***t***,
78: 6 they may arise and declare ***t***
78:11 His wonders that He had shown ***t***.
78:13 divided the sea and caused ***t***
78:14 In the daytime also He led ***t***
78:15 And gave ***t*** drink in abundance
78:24 Had rained down manna on ***t*** to
78:24 And given ***t*** of the bread of
78:25 He sent ***t*** food to the full.
78:27 He also rained meat on ***t*** like
78:28 And He let ***t*** fall in the midst
78:29 For He gave ***t*** their own
78:31 wrath of God came against ***t***,
78:31 And slew the stoutest of ***t***,
78:34 When He slew ***t***,
78:38 And did not destroy ***t***.
78:42 The day when He redeemed ***t***
78:45 sent swarms of flies among ***t***,
78:45 among them, which devoured ***t***,
78:45 And frogs, which destroyed ***t***.
78:49 He cast on ***t*** the fierceness of
78:49 angels of destruction among ***t***.
78:52 And guided ***t*** in the wilderness
78:53 And He led ***t*** on safely, so that
78:54 And He brought ***t*** to His holy
78:55 drove out the nations before ***t***,
78:55 Allotted ***t*** an inheritance by
78:66 He put ***t*** to a perpetual
78:72 So he shepherded ***t*** according to
78:72 And guided ***t*** by the
79: 3 there was no one to bury ***t***.
80: 5 You have fed ***t*** with the bread
80: 5 And given ***t*** tears to drink in
81:12 So I gave ***t*** over to their own
81:16 He would have fed ***t*** also with
82: 4 Free ***t*** from the hand of the
83: 4 and let us cut ***t*** off from
83: 8 Assyria also has joined with ***t***;
83: 9 Deal with ***t*** as with Midian,
83:13 make ***t*** like the whirling dust,
83:15 So pursue ***t*** with Your tempest,
83:15 And frighten ***t*** with Your
83:17 Let ***t*** be confounded and
83:17 let ***t*** be put to shame and
85: 8 But let ***t*** not turn back to
86:14 And have not set You before ***t***.
88: 8 made me an abomination to ***t***;
89: 9 its waves rise, You still ***t***.
89:11 fullness, You have founded ***t***.
89:12 the south, You have created ***t***;
90: 5 You carry ***t*** away like a flood;
94:23 He has brought on ***t*** their own
94:23 And shall cut ***t*** off in their
94:23 The LORD our God shall cut ***t***
97:10 He delivers ***t*** out of the hand
99: 3 Let ***t*** praise Your great and
99: 6 the LORD, and He answered ***t***.
99: 7 He spoke to ***t*** in the cloudy
99: 7 and the ordinance He gave ***t***.
99: 8 You answered ***t***,
99: 8 were to ***t*** God-Who-Forgives,
102:26 Like a cloak You will change ***t***,
103:18 His commandments to do ***t***.
104: 8 place which You founded for ***t***.
104:12 By ***t*** the birds of the heavens
104:24 In wisdom You have made ***t*** all.
104:27 That You may give ***t*** their
104:28 What You give ***t*** they gather
105:14 He permitted no one to do ***t***
105:17 He sent a man before ***t***—
105:24 And made ***t*** stronger than their
105:27 performed His signs among ***t***,
105:32 He gave ***t*** hail for rain,
105:37 He also brought ***t*** out with
105:38 For the fear of ***t*** had fallen
105:38 fear of them had fallen upon ***t***.
105:40 And satisfied ***t*** with the bread
105:44 He gave ***t*** the lands of the
106: 8 Nevertheless He saved ***t*** for His
106: 9 So He led ***t*** through the
106:10 He saved ***t*** from the hand of him
106:10 the hand of him who hated ***t***,
106:10 And redeemed ***t*** from the hand
106:11 There was not one of ***t*** left.
106:15 And He gave ***t*** their request,
106:23 He said that He would destroy ***t***,
106:23 His wrath, lest He destroy ***t***.
106:26 hand in an oath against ***t***,
106:26 To overthrow ***t*** in the
106:27 And to scatter ***t*** in the lands.
106:29 the plague broke out among ***t***.
106:32 ill with Moses on account of ***t***;
106:34 whom the LORD had commanded ***t***,
106:36 Which became a snare to ***t***.
106:41 And He gave ***t*** into the hand of
106:41 And those who hated ***t*** ruled
106:41 who hated them ruled over ***t***.
106:42 Their enemies also oppressed ***t***,
106:43 Many times He delivered ***t***;
106:46 He also made ***t*** to be pitied
106:46 By all those who carried ***t***
107: 5 Their soul fainted in ***t***.
107: 6 And He delivered ***t*** out of
107: 7 And He led ***t*** forth by the right
107:13 And He saved ***t*** out of their
107:14 He brought ***t*** out of darkness
107:19 And He saved ***t*** out of their
107:20 He sent His word and healed ***t***,
107:20 And delivered ***t*** from their
107:22 Let ***t*** sacrifice the sacrifices
107:28 And He brings ***t*** out of their
107:30 So He guides ***t*** to their
107:32 Let ***t*** exalt Him also in the
107:38 He also blesses ***t***,
107:40 And causes ***t*** to wander in the
109:10 Let ***t*** seek their bread also
109:15 Let ***t*** be continually before the
109:15 He may cut off the memory of ***t***
109:25 have become a reproach to ***t***;
109:28 Let ***t*** curse, but You bless;
109:28 let ***t*** be ashamed, But let Your
109:29 And let ***t*** cover themselves
111: 2 by all who have pleasure in ***t***.
111: 6 In giving ***t*** the heritage of
115: 8 Those who make ***t*** are like them;
115: 8 Those who make them are like ***t***;
115: 8 is everyone who trusts in ***t***.
118:10 of the LORD I will destroy ***t***.
118:11 of the LORD I will destroy ***t***.
118:12 of the LORD I will destroy ***t***.
118:19 I will go through ***t***,
119:93 For by ***t*** You have given me
119:129 Therefore my soul keeps ***t***.
119:152 of old that You have founded ***t***
119:165 And nothing causes ***t*** to
119:167 And I love ***t*** exceedingly.
125: 5 The LORD shall lead ***t*** away
126: 2 has done great things for ***t***.
127: 5 who has his quiver full of ***t***;
129: 6 Let ***t*** be as the grass on the
129: 8 let those who pass by ***t*** say,
132:12 testimony which I shall teach ***t***,
135:18 Those who make ***t*** are like them;

135:18 Those who make them are like *t*;
135:18 is everyone who trusts in *t*.
136:11 brought out Israel from among *t*,
139:16 as yet there were none of *t*.
139:17 How great is the sum of *t*!
139:18 If I should count *t*,
139:21 Do I not hate *t*,
139:22 I hate *t* with perfect hatred;
139:22 I count *t* my enemies.
140: 9 the evil of their lips cover *t*;
140:10 Let burning coals fall upon *t*;
140:10 Let *t* be cast into the fire,
144: 6 forth lightning and scatter *t*;
144: 6 out Your arrows and destroy *t*.
145:15 And You give *t* their food in
145:19 will hear their cry and save *t*.
146: 6 The sea, and all that is in *t*;
147: 4 He calls *t* all by name.
147:18 sends out His word and melts *t*;
147:20 they have not known *t*.
148: 5 Let *t* praise the name of the
148: 6 He also established *t* forever
148:13 Let *t* praise the name of the
149: 3 Let *t* praise His name with the
149: 3 Let *t* sing praises to Him with
149: 5 Let *t* sing aloud on their
149: 9 To execute on *t* the written
Prov 1:12 Let us swallow *t* alive like
1:15 do not walk in the way with *t*,
1:32 away of the simple will slay *t*,
1:32 of fools will destroy *t*;
3: 3 Bind *t* around your neck,
3: 3 Write *t* on the tablet of your
3:21 let *t* not depart from your
4:19 They do not know what makes *t*
4:21 Do not let *t* depart from your
4:21 Keep *t* in the midst of your
4:22 are life to those who find *t*,
5: 6 unstable; You do not know *t*.
5:17 Let *t* be only your own,
6:21 Bind *t* continually upon your
6:21 Tie *t* around your neck.
7: 3 Bind *t* on your fingers;
7: 3 Write *t* on the tablet of your
8: 8 crooked or perverse is in *t*.
11: 3 of the upright will guide *t*,
11: 3 the unfaithful will destroy *t*.
11: 6 of the upright will deliver *t*,
12: 6 of the upright will deliver *t*.
12:26 the way of the wicked leads *t*
14: 3 of the wise will preserve *t*.
17:15 Both of *t* alike are an
19: 7 far from him! He may pursue *t*
20:12 The LORD has made *t* both.
20:26 the threshing wheel over *t*.
21: 7 of the wicked will destroy *t*,
22: 2 The LORD is the maker of *t*
22: 5 his soul will be far from *t*.
22:18 a pleasant thing if you keep *t*
22:18 Let *t* all be fixed upon your
22:23 the soul of those who plunder *t*.
24: 1 men, Nor desire to be with *t*;
24:25 good blessing will come upon *t*.
27: 3 is heavier than both of *t*.
28: 4 as keep the law contend with *t*.
28:13 confesses and forsakes *t* will
29:11 But a wise man holds *t* back.
31:24 linen garments and sells *t*,
31:29 But you excel *t* all."
Eccl 2: 5 all kinds of fruit trees in *t*.
2:10 desired I did not keep from *t*.
2:14 the same event happens to *t*
3:12 that nothing is better for *t*
3:18 of the sons of men, God tests *t*,
3:19 to animals; one thing befalls *t*:
5: 8 and higher officials are over *t*.
5:11 They increase who eat *t*;
5:11 the owners Except to see *t*
7:18 he who fears God will escape *t*
8:11 sons of men is fully set in *t*
9: 1 anything they see before *t*.
9: 5 For the memory of *t* is
9:11 time and chance happen to *t*
9:12 When it falls suddenly upon *t*.
10: 9 stones may be hurt by *t*,
10:15 The labor of fools wearies *t*,
11: 8 many years And rejoices in *t*
12: 1 I have no pleasure in *t*":
Song 3: 4 Scarcely had I passed by *t*,
4: 2 And none is barren among *t*.
5: 3 my feet; How can I defile *t*?
6: 6 And none is barren among *t*.
Isa 1:14 Me, I am weary of bearing *t*.
1:23 of the widow come before *t*.
1:31 And no one shall quench *t*.
2: 9 Therefore do not forgive *t*.
3: 4 And babes shall rule over *t*.
3: 9 countenance witnesses against *t*,
3:10 it shall be well with *t*,
3:12 And women rule over *t*.
5:11 till wine inflames *t*!
5:25 out His hand against *t* And
5:25 against them And stricken *t*,
5:26 And will whistle to *t* from the
5:27 be weary or stumble among *t*,
5:30 day they will roar against *t*
7: 6 and set a king over *t*,
7:19 and all of *t* will rest In the
8: 7 the Lord brings up over *t* The
8:15 And many among *t* shall stumble;
8:20 there is no light in *t*.
9: 2 Upon *t* a light has shined.
9:10 But we will replace *t* with
9:13 not turn to Him who strikes *t*,
9:16 of this people cause *t* to err,
9:16 And those who are led by *t*
10: 6 And to tread *t* down like the
10:19 That a child may write *t*.
10:20 depend on him who defeated *t*,
10:22 A remnant of *t* will return;
11: 6 a little child shall lead *t*.
11:14 people of Ammon shall obey *t*.
13: 2 Raise your voice to *t*;
13: 8 sorrows will take hold of *t*;
13:17 stir up the Medes against *t*,
14: 1 and settle *t* in their own land.
14: 1 strangers will be joined with *t*,
14: 2 Then people will take *t* and
14: 2 will take them and bring *t* to
14: 2 house of Israel will possess *t*
14: 2 they will take *t* captive whose
14:18 kings of the nations, All of *t*,
14:20 You will not be joined with *t*
14:22 I will rise up against *t*,
14:25 yoke shall be removed from *t*,
16: 4 Be a shelter to *t* from the
17: 2 and no one will make *t* afraid.
17:13 But God will rebuke *t* and
18: 6 birds of prey will summer on *t*,
18: 6 of the earth will winter on *t*.
19: 4 a fierce king will rule over *t*,
19:12 Let *t* tell you now, And let
19:12 And let *t* know what the LORD
19:20 and He will send *t* a Savior and
19:20 One, and He will deliver *t*.
19:22 and He will be entreated by *t*
19:22 be entreated by them and heal *t*.
23: 1 of Cyprus it is revealed to *t*.
26:11 of Your enemies shall devour *t*.
26:14 have punished and destroyed *t*,
26:16 Your chastening was upon *t*.
27: 4 battle? I would go through *t*,
27: 4 I would burn *t* together.
27:11 The women come and set *t* on
27:11 Therefore He who made *t* will
27:11 them will not have mercy on *t*,
27:11 And He who formed *t* will show
27:11 He who formed them will show *t*
28: 2 Who will bring *t* down to the
28:13 the word of the LORD was to *t*,
30: 5 people who could not benefit *t*,
30: 8 write it before *t* on a tablet,
30:12 and perversity, And rely on *t*,
30:22 You will throw *t* away as an
30:22 You will say to *t*,
30:28 Causing *t* to err.
33: 4 locusts, He shall run upon *t*.
34: 2 He has utterly destroyed *t*,
34: 2 He has given *t* over to the
34: 7 oxen shall come down with *t*,
34:15 and gather *t* under her shadow;
34:16 and His Spirit has gathered *t*.
34:17 He has cast the lot for *t*,
34:17 His hand has divided it among *t*
35: 1 wasteland shall be glad for *t*,
36: 1 cities of Judah and took *t*.
36: 4 Then the Rabshakeh said to *t*,
36: 8 your part to put riders on *t*!
37: 3 is no strength to bring *t*
37: 6 And Isaiah said to *t*,
37:11 lands by utterly destroying *t*;
37:19 Therefore they have destroyed *t*.
37:30 and eat the fruit of *t*.
38:21 Let *t* take a lump of figs, and
39: 2 And Hezekiah was pleased with *t*,
39: 2 and showed *t* the house of his
39: 2 that Hezekiah did not show *t*.
39: 4 that I have not shown *t*.
40:11 And carry *t* in His bosom,
40:22 And spreads *t* out like a tent
40:24 When He will also blow on *t*,
40:24 And the whirlwind will take *t*
40:26 He calls *t* all by name,
41: 1 renew their strength! Let *t*
41: 1 then let *t* speak; Let us come
41: 2 Who gave *t* as the dust to
41: 3 Who pursued *t*, and passed
41:12 You shall seek *t* and not find
41:12 shall seek them and not find *t*—
41:15 the mountains and beat *t*
41:16 You shall winnow *t*,
41:16 the wind shall carry *t* away,
41:16 the whirlwind shall scatter *t*;
41:17 I, the LORD, will hear *t*;
41:17 of Israel, will not forsake *t*.
41:22 Let *t* bring forth and show us
41:22 Let *t* show the former things,
41:22 That we may consider *t*,
41:22 And know the latter end of *t*;
41:28 was no man; I looked among *t*,
41:28 Who, when I asked of *t*,
42: 5 the heavens and stretched *t*
42: 9 spring forth I tell you of *t*.
42:10 and you inhabitants of *t*!
42:11 Let *t* shout from the top of
42:12 Let *t* give glory to the LORD,
42:16 I will lead *t* in paths they
42:16 make darkness light before *t*,
42:16 These things I will do for *t*,
42:16 do for them, And not forsake *t*.
42:22 All of *t* are snared in holes,
43: 6 Give *t* up!' And to the south,
43: 6 Do not keep *t* back!' Bring My
43: 9 Who among *t* can declare this,
43: 9 Let *t* bring out their
43: 9 Or let *t* hear and say, "It
43:14 And bring *t* all down as
44: 7 Let *t* show these to them.
44: 7 come, Let them show these to *t*.
44: 9 all of *t* are useless, And
44:11 Let *t* all be gathered
44:11 Let *t* stand up; Yet they
45: 8 let *t* bring forth salvation,
45:16 And also disgraced, all of *t*;
45:21 let *t* take counsel together.
47: 6 And given *t* into your hand.
47: 6 You showed *t* no mercy; On the
47: 7 remember the latter end of *t*.
47:14 stubble, The fire shall burn *t*;
48: 3 and I caused *t* to hear it.
48: 3 to hear it. Suddenly I did *t*,
48: 5 should say, 'My idol has done *t*,
48: 5 molded image Have commanded *t*.
48: 6 things, and you did not know *t*.
48: 7 this day you have not heard *t*,
48: 7 should say, 'Of course I knew *t*.
48:13 the heavens; When I call to *t*,
48:14 and hear! Who among *t* has
48:21 did not thirst When He led *t*
48:21 to flow from the rock for *t*;
49: 8 To cause *t* to inherit the
49:10 heat nor sun shall strike *t*;
49:10 For He who has mercy on *t* will
49:10 has mercy on them will lead *t*,
49:10 of water He will guide *t*.
49:18 clothe yourselves with *t* all
49:18 And bind *t* on you as a bride
50: 9 The moth will eat *t* up.
51: 8 For the moth will eat *t* up like
51: 8 And the worm will eat *t* like
52: 4 Then the Assyrian oppressed *t*
52: 5 Those who rule over *t* Make
52: 5 who rule over them Make *t*
52:15 For what had not been told *t*
54: 2 And let *t* stretch out the
56: 5 Even to *t* I will give in My
56: 5 I will give *t* an everlasting
56: 7 Even *t* I will bring to My holy
56: 7 And make *t* joyful in My house
57: 6 are your lot! Even to *t* you
57: 8 than Me, And have gone up to *t*;
57: 8 And made a covenant with *t*;
57:13 But the wind will carry *t* all
57:13 away, A breath will take *t*.
59:12 for our iniquities, we know *t*:
59:21 "this is My covenant with *t*:
60: 9 silver and their gold with *t*,
61: 3 To give *t* beauty for ashes,
61: 8 And will make with *t* an
61: 9 All who see *t* shall
61: 9 see them shall acknowledge *t*,
62:12 And they shall call *t* The Holy
63: 3 For I have trodden *t* in My
63: 3 And trampled *t* in My fury;
63: 6 Made *t* drunk in My fury, And
63: 7 Which He has bestowed on *t*
63: 9 Angel of His Presence saved *t*;
63: 9 and in His pity He redeemed *t*;
63: 9 And He bore *t* and carried them
63: 9 And He bore them and carried *t*
63:10 He turned Himself against *t* as
63:10 And He fought against *t*.
63:11 Where is He who brought *t* up
63:11 put His Holy Spirit within *t*,
63:12 Who led *t* by the right hand of
63:12 Dividing the water before *t*
63:13 Who led *t* through the deep,
65: 8 That I may not destroy *t* all.
65:21 build houses and inhabit *t*;
65:23 And their offspring with *t*.
66: 4 And bring their fears on *t*;
66:19 "I will set a sign among *t*;
66:19 and those among *t* who escape I
66:21 I will also take some of *t*
Jer 1:16 utter My judgments Against *t*
1:17 And speak to *t* all that I
1:17 Lest I dismay you before *t*.
2: 3 Disaster will come upon *t*,
2:25 and after *t* I will go.'
2:28 Let *t* arise, If they can save
2:37 And you will not prosper by *t*.
3: 2 By the road you have sat for *t*
4:12 also speak judgment against *t*.
5: 3 the truth? You have stricken *t*,
5: 3 grieved; You have consumed *t*,
5: 5 to the great men and speak to *t*,
5: 6 from the forest shall slay *t*,
5: 6 of the deserts shall destroy *t*;
5: 7 When I had fed *t* to the full,
5: 9 Shall I not punish *t* for these
5:13 For the word is not in *t*.
5:13 Thus shall it be done to *t*.
5:14 wood, And it shall devour *t*.
5:19 then you shall answer *t*,
5:29 Shall I not punish *t* for these
6:10 of the LORD is a reproach to *t*;
6:13 Because from the least of *t* even
6:13 them even to the greatest of *t*,
6:15 At the time I punish *t*,
6:18 congregation, what is among *t*.
6:21 sons together shall fall on *t*.
6:30 People will call *t* rejected
6:30 the LORD has rejected *t*.
7:16 lift up a cry or prayer for *t*,
7:22 or command *t* in the day that I
7:22 in the day that I brought *t*

7:23 this is what I commanded *t*,
7:25 rising up early and sending *t*.
7:27 speak all these words to *t*,
7:27 You shall also call to *t*,
7:28 "So you shall say to *t*,
7:33 And no one will frighten *t*
8: 2 They shall spread *t* before the
8: 3 places where I have driven *t*,
8: 4 "Moreover you shall say to *t*,
8:10 to those who will inherit *t*;
8:13 "I will surely consume *t*,
8:13 the things I have given *t*
8:13 them shall pass away from *t*.
9: 2 And go from *t*! For they are
9: 7 I will refine *t* and try them;
9: 7 I will refine them and try *t*;
9: 9 Shall I not punish *t* for these
9:13 My law which I set before *t*,
9:14 which their fathers taught *t*,
9:15 Israel: "Behold, I will feed *t*,
9:15 and give *t* water of gall to
9:16 I will scatter *t* also among the
9:16 And I will send a sword after *t*
9:16 them until I have consumed *t*.
9:18 Let *t* make haste And take up a
9:22 And no one shall gather *t*.
10: 2 the Gentiles are dismayed at *t*.
10: 5 Do not be afraid of *t*,
10:11 Thus you shall say to *t*:
10:14 And there is no breath in *t*.
10:16 Portion of Jacob is not like *t*,
10:18 the land, And will distress *t*,
11: 3 'and say to *t*, 'Thus says
11: 4 fathers in the day I brought *t*
11: 5 to your fathers, to give *t* '
11: 6 words of this covenant and do *t*.
11: 7 fathers in the day I brought *t*
11: 8 therefore I will bring upon *t*
11: 8 which I commanded *t* to do, but
11:10 after other gods to serve *t*;
11:11 will surely bring calamity on *t*
11:11 to Me, I will not listen to *t*.
11:12 but they will not save *t* at all
11:14 lift up a cry or prayer for *t*;
11:14 for I will not hear *t* in the
11:20 Let me see Your vengeance on *t*,
11:22 hosts: 'Behold, I will punish *t*.
11:23 there shall be no remnant of *t*,
12: 2 You have planted *t*,
12: 3 Pull *t* out like sheep for the
12: 3 And prepare *t* for the day of
12: 6 after you. Do not believe *t*,
12: 9 Bring *t* to devour!
12:14 I will pluck *t* out of their
12:14 the house of Judah from among *t*.
12:15 after I have plucked *t* out,
12:15 and have compassion on *t* and
12:15 compassion on them and bring *t*
13:10 after other gods to serve *t*
13:10 to serve them and worship *t*,
13:12 you shall speak to *t* this word:
13:13 "Then you shall say to *t*,
13:14 And I will dash *t* one against
13:14 have mercy, but will destroy *t*.
13:19 And no one shall open *t*;
13:21 For you have taught *t* To be
13:24 Therefore I will scatter *t* like
14:10 the LORD does not accept *t*;
14:12 offering, I will not accept *t*.
14:12 But I will consume *t* by the
14:13 Behold, the prophets say to *t*,
14:14 in My name. I have not sent *t*,
14:14 have not sent them, commanded *t*,
14:14 commanded them, nor spoken to *t*;
14:16 they will have no one to bury *t*—
14:16 *t* nor their wives, their sons
14:16 will pour their wickedness on *t*.
14:17 you shall say this word to *t*:
14:17 And let *t* not cease; For the
15: 1 Cast *t* out of My sight, and
15: 1 and let *t* go forth.
15: 2 we go?' then you shall tell *t*,
15: 3 And I will appoint over *t* four
15: 4 I will hand *t* over to trouble,
15: 7 And I will winnow *t* with a
15: 7 I will bereave *t* of children;
15: 8 seas; I will bring against *t*,
15: 8 anguish and terror to fall on *t*
15: 9 And the remnant of *t* I will
15:10 Every one of *t* curses me.
15:16 words were found, and I ate *t*,
15:19 Let *t* return to you, But you
15:19 But you must not return to *t*.
16: 3 their mothers who bore *t* and
16: 3 and their fathers who begot *t*
16: 5 nor go to lament or bemoan *t*;
16: 6 neither shall men lament for *t*,
16: 6 nor make themselves bald for *t*.
16: 7 break bread in mourning for *t*,
16: 7 to comfort *t* for the dead; nor
16: 7 nor shall men give *t* the cup
16: 8 house of feasting to sit with *t*,
16:11 "then you shall say to *t*,
16:11 other gods and have served *t*
16:11 served them and worshiped *t*,
16:15 the lands where He had driven *t*.
16:15 For I will bring *t* back into
16:16 LORD, "and they shall fish *t*;
16:16 and they shall hunt *t* from
16:21 I will this once cause *t* to
16:21 I will cause *t* to know
17:18 Let *t* be ashamed who persecute
17:18 Let *t* be dismayed, But do not
17:18 Bring on *t* the day of doom,
17:18 And destroy *t* with double
17:20 'and say to *t*, 'Hear the word
18:17 I will scatter *t* as with an
18:17 I will show *t* the back and not
18:20 before You To speak good for *t*,
18:20 To turn away Your wrath from *t*.
18:22 bring a troop suddenly upon *t*;
18:23 But let *t* be overthrown before
18:23 Deal thus with *t* In the time
19: 7 and I will cause *t* to fall by
19: 9 And I will cause *t* to eat the
19: 9 seek their lives shall drive *t*
19:11 'and say to *t*, 'Thus says the
19:11 and they shall bury *t* in
20: 4 and he shall carry *t* captive to
20: 4 captive to Babylon and slay *t*
20: 5 enemies, who will plunder *t*,
20: 5 who will plunder them, seize *t*,
20: 5 and carry *t* to Babylon.
20:12 Let me see Your vengeance on *t*;
21: 3 Then Jeremiah said to *t*,
21: 4 and I will assemble *t* in the
21: 7 and he shall strike *t* with the
21: 7 the sword. He shall not spare *t*,
22: 7 your choice cedars And cast *t*
22: 9 other gods and served *t*.
23: 2 driven *t* away, and not attended
23: 2 away, and not attended to *t*.
23: 3 countries where I have driven *t*,
23: 3 and bring *t* back to their
23: 4 will set up shepherds over *t*
23: 4 over them who will feed *t*;
23: 8 countries where I had driven *t*.
23:12 their way shall be to *t* Like
23:12 be driven on And fall in *t*;
23:12 For I will bring disaster on *t*,
23:14 All of *t* are like Sodom to Me,
23:15 I will feed *t* with wormwood,
23:15 And make *t* drink the water of
23:21 I have not spoken to *t*,
23:22 Then they would have turned *t*
23:32 says the LORD, "and tell *t*,
23:32 Yet I did not send *t* or command
23:32 did not send them or command *t*;
23:33 LORD?' you shall then say to *t*,
24: 1 and had brought *t* to Babylon.
24: 6 For I will set My eyes on *t* for
24: 6 and I will bring *t* back to this
24: 6 I will build *t* and not pull
24: 6 will build them and not pull *t*
24: 6 and I will plant *t* and not
24: 6 plant them and not pluck *t* up.
24: 7 Then I will give *t* a heart to
24: 9 I will deliver *t* to trouble into
24: 9 places where I shall drive *t*.
24:10 and the pestilence among *t*,
24:10 from the land that I gave to *t*
25: 4 rising early and sending *t*,
25: 6 go after other gods to serve *t*
25: 6 to serve them and worship *t*,
25: 9 and will bring *t* against this
25: 9 and will utterly destroy *t*,
25: 9 and make *t* an astonishment, a
25:10 Moreover I will take from *t* the
25:14 kings shall be served by *t*
25:14 and I will repay *t* according to
25:16 sword that I will send among *t*.
25:18 to make *t* a desolation,
25:26 of Sheshach shall drink after *t*.
25:27 "Therefore you shall say to *t*,
25:28 drink, then you shall say to *t*,
25:30 Therefore prophesy against *t*
25:30 all these words, and say to *t*:
26: 2 I command you to speak to *t*.
26: 3 which I purpose to bring on *t*
26: 4 "And you shall say to *t*,
26: 5 rising up early and sending *t*
26:19 He had pronounced against *t*.
27: 2 and put *t* on your neck,
27: 3 and send *t* to the king of Edom,
27: 4 And command *t* to say to their
27: 7 kings shall make him serve *t*.
27: 8 until I have consumed *t* by his
27:11 I will let *t* remain in their
27:15 "for I have not sent *t*,
27:17 'Do not listen to *t*;
27:18 the word of the LORD is with *t*,
27:18 let *t* now make intercession to
27:22 be until the day that I visit *t*,
27:22 Then I will bring *t* up and
27:22 bring them up and restore *t* to
29: 5 Build houses and dwell in *t*;
29: 9 in My name; I have not sent *t*,
29:17 I will send on *t* the sword, the
29:17 and will make *t* like rotten
29:18 And I will pursue *t* with the
29:18 and I will deliver *t* to trouble
29:18 nations where I have driven *t*,
29:19 which I sent to *t* by My
29:19 rising up early and sending *t*;
29:21 I will deliver *t* into the hand
29:21 and he shall slay *t* before your
29:22 And because of *t* a curse shall
29:23 which I have not commanded *t*.
29:28 build houses and dwell in *t*,
30: 3 And I will cause *t* to return to
30: 8 shall no more enslave *t*.
30: 9 Whom I will raise up for *t*.
30:16 adversaries, every one of *t*,
30:19 Then out of *t* shall proceed
30:19 make merry; I will multiply *t*,
30:19 I will also glorify *t*,
30:20 I will punish all who oppress *t*.
30:21 nobles shall be from among *t*,
31: 5 shall plant and eat *t* as
31: 8 I will bring *t* from the north
31: 8 And gather *t* from the ends of
31: 8 Among *t* the blind and the
31: 9 supplications I will lead *t*.
31: 9 I will cause *t* to walk by the
31:13 to joy, Will comfort *t*,
31:13 And make *t* rejoice rather than
31:28 that as I have watched over *t*
31:28 so I will watch over *t* to build
31:32 in the day that I took *t* by
31:32 them by the hand to lead *t* out
31:32 though I was a husband to *t*,
31:34 from the least of *t* to the
31:34 of them to the greatest of *t*,
32:13 I charged Baruch before *t*,
32:14 and put *t* in an earthen vessel,
32:18 bosom of their children after *t*—
32:22 You have given *t* this land, of
32:22 to their fathers to give *t*—
32:23 of all that You commanded *t* to
32:23 this calamity to come upon *t*.
32:33 not the face; though I taught *t*,
32:33 rising up early and teaching *t*,
32:35 which I did not command *t*,
32:37 I will gather *t* out of all
32:37 where I have driven *t* in My
32:37 I will bring *t* back to this
32:37 and I will cause *t* to dwell
32:39 then I will give *t* one heart and
32:39 for the good of *t* and their
32:39 them and their children after *t*.
32:40 an everlasting covenant with *t*,
32:40 will not turn away from doing *t*
32:41 I will rejoice over *t* to do
32:41 will rejoice over them to do *t*
32:41 and I will assuredly plant *t* in
32:42 so I will bring on *t* all the
32:42 the good that I have promised *t*.
32:44 money, sign deeds and seal *t*,
33: 6 I will heal *t* and reveal to
33: 6 will heal them and reveal to *t*
33: 8 I will cleanse *t* from all their
33: 9 all the good that I do to *t*;
33:13 the hands of him who counts *t*,
33:24 He has also cast *t* off"? Thus
33:24 no more be a nation before *t*.
33:26 and will have mercy on *t*.
34: 8 to proclaim liberty to *t*:
34:10 that no one should keep *t* in
34:10 they obeyed and let *t* go.
34:11 and brought *t* into subjection
34:13 in the day that I brought *t*
34:16 and brought *t* back into
34:20 I will give *t* into the hand of
34:22 and cause *t* to return to this
35: 2 of the Rechabites, speak to *t*,
35: 2 and bring *t* into the house of
35: 2 and give *t* wine to drink."
35: 4 and I brought *t* into the house
35: 5 wine, and cups; and I said to *t*,
35:15 rising up early and sending *t*,
35:15 go after other gods to serve *t*;
35:16 father, which he commanded *t*,
35:17 I have pronounced against *t*;
35:17 because I have spoken to *t* but
35:17 and I have called to *t* but they
36: 3 which I purpose to bring upon *t*,
36: 6 And you shall also read *t* in
36:13 Then Michaiah declared to *t* all
36:14 in his hand and came to *t*.
36:18 So Baruch answered *t*,
36:18 and I wrote *t* with ink in the
36:25 but he would not listen to *t*.
36:26 prophet, but the LORD hid *t*.
36:31 iniquity; and I will bring on *t*,
36:31 I have pronounced against *t*;
36:32 there were added to *t* many
37: 5 Jerusalem heard news of *t*,
37:10 only wounded men among *t*,
38: 4 by speaking such words to *t*.
38:11 and let *t* down by ropes into
38:26 "then you shall say to *t*,
38:27 And he told *t* according to all
39: 4 and all the men of war saw *t*,
39: 5 But the Chaldean army pursued *t*
39:10 and gave *t* vineyards and fields
40: 9 took an oath before *t* and their
40:10 put *t* in your vessels,
40:11 and that he had set over *t*
40:14 son of Ahikam did not believe *t*.
41: 5 to bring *t* to the house of the
41: 6 went out from Mizpah to meet *t*,
41: 6 and it happened as he met *t*
41: 6 he met them that he said to *t*,
41: 7 the son of Nethaniah killed *t*
41: 7 killed them and cast *t* into
41: 8 But ten men were found among *t*
41: 8 he desisted and did not kill *t*
41:10 the son of Nethaniah carried *t*
41:18 for they were afraid of *t*,
42: 4 Jeremiah the prophet said to *t*,
42: 9 and said to *t*, "Thus says
42:17 And none of *t* shall remain or
42:17 that I will bring upon *t*.
43: 1 their God had sent him to *t*,
43: 9 and hide *t* in the sight of the
43:10 'and say to *t*, 'Thus says

43:10 his royal pavilion over ***t***.
43:12 and he shall burn ***t*** and carry
43:12 he shall burn them and carry ***t***
44: 2 and no one dwells in ***t***,
44: 4 rising early and sending ***t***,
44:21 did not the LORD remember ***t***,
44:27 I will watch over ***t*** for
44:27 until there is an end to ***t***.
45: 5 for yourself? Do not seek ***t***;
46: 5 Why have I seen ***t*** dismayed and
46:15 Because the LORD drove ***t***
46:21 their calamity had come upon ***t***,
46:26 And I will deliver ***t*** into the
48: 9 Without any to dwell in ***t***.
49:11 I will preserve ***t*** alive;
49:20 of the flock shall draw ***t*** out;
49:20 dwelling places desolate with ***t***.
49:29 And they shall cry out to ***t***,
49:36 And scatter ***t*** toward all those
49:37 I will bring disaster upon ***t***,
49:37 I will send the sword after ***t***
49:37 Until I have consumed ***t***.
50: 6 Their shepherds have led ***t***
50: 6 They have turned ***t*** away on
50: 7 All who found ***t*** have devoured
50: 7 who found them have devoured ***t***;
50:21 Waste and utterly destroy ***t***,
50:27 Let ***t*** go down to the
50:27 Woe to ***t***! For their day has
50:29 Let none of ***t*** escape. Repay
50:33 All who took ***t*** captive have
50:33 took them captive have held ***t***
50:33 They have refused to let ***t*** go.
50:43 has heard the report about ***t***,
50:44 But I will make ***t*** suddenly run
50:45 of the flock shall draw ***t*** out;
50:45 dwelling place desolate with ***t***.
51:17 And there is no breath in ***t***.
51:19 Portion of Jacob is not like ***t***,
51:39 I will make ***t*** drunk,
51:40 I will bring ***t*** down Like lambs
51:48 the earth and all that is in ***t***
52: 3 till He finally cast ***t*** out from
52:26 guard took these and brought ***t***
52:27 the king of Babylon struck ***t***
52:27 Babylon struck them and put ***t***
Lam 1:13 my bones, And it overpowered ***t***;
1:17 become an unclean thing among ***t***.
1:22 And do to ***t*** as You have done
2: 2 He has brought ***t*** down to the
2:21 You have slain ***t*** in the day
3:64 Repay ***t***, O LORD,
3:65 Give ***t*** a veiled heart;
3:65 Your curse be upon ***t***!
3:66 Pursue and destroy ***t*** From
4: 4 But no one breaks it for ***t***.
4:10 They became food for ***t*** In the
4:15 They cried out to ***t***,
4:16 face of the LORD scattered ***t***;
4:16 He no longer regards ***t***.
Ezek 1:18 all around the four of ***t***.
1:19 the wheels went beside ***t***;
1:20 were lifted together with ***t***,
1:21 were lifted up together with ***t***,
2: 4 children. I am sending you to ***t***,
2: 4 to them, and you shall say to ***t***,
2: 5 'As for ***t***, whether they hear
2: 5 that a prophet has been among ***t***.
2: 6 do not be afraid of ***t*** nor be
2: 7 "You shall speak My words to ***t***,
3: 4 and speak with My words to ***t***.
3: 6 Surely, had I sent you to ***t***,
3: 9 forehead; do not be afraid of ***t***,
3:11 and speak to ***t*** and tell them,
3:11 and speak to them and tell ***t***,
3:13 noise of the wheels beside ***t***,
3:15 there astonished among ***t*** seven
3:17 and give ***t*** warning from Me:
3:25 on you and bind you with ***t***,
3:25 that you cannot go out among ***t***.
3:26 mute and not be one to rebuke ***t***,
3:27 mouth, and you shall say to ***t***,
4: 6 "And when you have completed ***t***,
4: 9 put ***t*** into one vessel, and make
4: 9 and make bread of ***t*** for
4:13 Gentiles, where I will drive ***t***.
5: 2 I will draw out a sword after ***t***.
5: 3 also take a small number of ***t***
5: 3 number of them and bind ***t*** in
5: 4 Then take some of ***t*** again and
5: 4 some of them again and throw ***t***
5: 4 and burn ***t*** in the fire. From
5:12 I will draw out a sword after ***t***.
5:13 cause My fury to rest upon ***t***,
5:13 I have spent My fury upon ***t***.
5:16 When I send against ***t*** the
6: 2 and prophesy against ***t***,
6:10 bring this calamity upon ***t***.
6:12 will I spend My fury upon ***t***.
6:14 stretch out My hand against ***t***
7:11 None of ***t*** shall remain,
7:11 of their multitude, None of ***t***;
7:11 shall there be wailing for ***t***.
7:16 All of ***t*** mourning, Each for
7:18 sackcloth; Horror will cover ***t***;
7:19 will not be able to deliver ***t***
7:20 have made it Like refuse to ***t***.
7:22 I will turn My face from ***t***,
7:27 I will do to ***t*** according to
7:27 they deserve I will judge ***t***;
8:11 And there stood before ***t*** seventy
8:18 a loud voice, I will not hear ***t***.
9: 2 One man among ***t*** was clothed
9: 7 Then He said to ***t***,
9: 8 that while they were killing ***t***,
10: 2 and scatter ***t*** over the city."
10:16 the wheels went beside ***t***;
10:16 also did not turn from beside ***t***.
10:17 the living creature was in ***t***.
10:19 the wheels were beside ***t***;
10:19 the God of Israel was above ***t***.
11: 4 "Therefore prophesy against ***t***,
11:16 Although I have cast ***t*** far off
11:16 and although I have scattered ***t***
11:16 be a little sanctuary for ***t*** in
11:19 Then I will give ***t*** one heart,
11:19 will put a new spirit within ***t***,
11:19 and give ***t*** a heart of flesh,
11:20 and keep My judgments and do ***t***;
11:22 with the wheels beside ***t***,
11:22 God of Israel was high above ***t***.
12: 6 their sight you shall bear ***t***
12: 6 your shoulders and carry ***t***
12: 7 I brought ***t*** out at twilight,
12: 7 and I bore ***t*** on my shoulder
12:10 'Say to ***t***, 'Thus says the
12:10 house of Israel who are among ***t***.
12:11 so shall it be done to ***t***;
12:12 the prince who is among ***t***
12:12 through the wall to carry ***t***
12:14 will draw out the sword after ***t***.
12:15 when I scatter ***t*** among the
12:15 the nations and disperse ***t***
12:23 Tell ***t*** therefore, 'Thus says the
12:23 in Israel." But say to ***t***,
12:28 "Therefore say to ***t***,
13: 6 But the LORD has not sent ***t***;
13:17 own heart; prophesy against ***t***,
13:20 I will tear ***t*** from your arms,
14: 3 and put before ***t*** that which
14: 3 them that which causes ***t*** to
14: 3 be inquired of at all by ***t***?
14: 4 "Therefore speak to ***t***,
14: 4 speak to them, and say to ***t***,
15: 7 I will set My face against ***t***.
15: 7 another fire shall devour ***t***.
15: 7 when I set My face against ***t***.
16:16 and played the harlot on ***t***.
16:17 and played the harlot with ***t***.
16:18 garments and covered ***t***,
16:18 My oil and My incense before ***t***.
16:19 you set it before ***t*** as sweet
16:20 and these you sacrificed to ***t***
16:21 My children and offered ***t*** up
16:21 and offered them up to ***t*** by
16:21 them up to them by causing ***t***
16:28 you played the harlot with ***t***
16:33 and hired ***t*** to come to you from
16:36 children which you gave to ***t***,
16:37 I will gather ***t*** from all around
16:37 uncover your nakedness to ***t***,
16:50 therefore I took ***t*** away as I
16:53 of your captivity among ***t***,
16:54 you did when you comforted ***t***.
16:61 for I will give ***t*** to you for
17:12 these things mean?' Tell ***t***,
17:12 and led ***t*** with him to Babylon.
18:19 all My statutes and observed ***t***,
18:24 because of ***t*** he shall die.
19:12 withered; The fire consumed ***t***.
20: 3 elders of Israel, and say to ***t***,
20: 4 "Will you judge ***t***,
20: 4 son of man, will you judge ***t***?
20: 4 Then make known to ***t*** the
20: 5 Say to ***t***, 'Thus says the
20: 5 and made Myself known to ***t*** in
20: 5 raised My hand in an oath to ***t***,
20: 6 raised My hand in an oath to ***t***,
20: 6 to bring ***t*** out of the land of
20: 6 that I had searched out for ***t***,
20: 7 "Then I said to ***t***,
20: 8 I will pour out My fury on ***t*** and
20: 8 and fulfill My anger against ***t***
20: 9 I had made Myself known to ***t***,
20: 9 to bring ***t*** out of the land of
20:10 Therefore I made ***t*** go out of
20:10 the land of Egypt and brought ***t***
20:11 And I gave ***t*** My statutes and
20:11 them My statutes and showed ***t***
20:11 a man does, he shall live by ***t***.
20:12 Moreover I also gave ***t*** My
20:12 to be a sign between ***t*** and Me,
20:12 am the LORD who sanctifies ***t***.
20:13 a man does, he shall live by ***t***';
20:13 I would pour out My fury on ***t***
20:13 in the wilderness, to consume ***t***.
20:14 in whose sight I had brought ***t***
20:15 raised My hand in an oath to ***t***
20:15 that I would not bring ***t*** into
20:15 the land which I had given ***t***,
20:17 Nevertheless My eye spared ***t***
20:17 I did not make an end of ***t*** in
20:19 keep My judgments, and do ***t***;
20:21 a man does, he shall live by ***t***';
20:21 I would pour out My fury on ***t***
20:21 and fulfill My anger against ***t***
20:22 in whose sight I had brought ***t***
20:23 that I would scatter ***t*** among
20:23 the Gentiles and disperse ***t***
20:25 Therefore I also gave ***t*** up to
20:26 and I pronounced ***t*** unclean
20:26 that I might make ***t*** desolate
20:27 house of Israel, and say to ***t***,
20:28 When I brought ***t*** into the land
20:28 My hand in an oath to give ***t***,
20:29 "Then I said to ***t***,
20:38 I will bring ***t*** out of the
20:40 all of ***t*** in the land, shall
20:40 serve Me; there I will accept ***t***,
21:19 both of ***t*** shall go from the
21:23 And it will be to ***t*** like a false
21:23 who have sworn oaths with ***t***;
22:26 so that I am profaned among ***t***.
22:28 Her prophets plastered ***t*** with
22:28 and divining lies for ***t***,
22:30 So I sought for a man among ***t***
22:31 poured out My indignation on ***t***;
22:31 I have consumed ***t*** with the fire
23: 6 All of ***t*** desirable young men,
23: 7 committed her harlotry with ***t***,
23: 7 All of ***t*** choice men of
23:12 All of ***t*** desirable young men.
23:15 All of ***t*** looking like
23:16 As soon as her eyes saw ***t***,
23:16 She lusted for ***t*** And sent
23:16 And sent messengers to ***t*** in
23:17 So she was defiled by ***t***,
23:17 and alienated herself from ***t***.
23:22 And I will bring ***t*** against you
23:23 Koa, All the Assyrians with ***t***,
23:23 All of ***t*** desirable young men,
23:23 All of ***t*** riding on horses.
23:24 'I will delegate judgment to ***t***,
23:27 will not lift your eyes to ***t***,
23:36 Then declare to ***t*** their
23:37 passing ***t*** through the fire,
23:37 the fire, to devour ***t***.
23:40 And you washed yourself for ***t***,
23:43 with her now, and she with ***t***?
23:45 righteous men will judge ***t***
23:46 'Bring up an assembly against ***t***,
23:46 give ***t*** up to trouble and
23:47 The assembly shall stone ***t*** with
23:47 them with stones and execute ***t***
24: 3 rebellious house, and say to ***t***,
24:20 Then I answered ***t***,
24:25 in the day when I take from ***t***
24:27 Thus you will be a sign to ***t***,
25: 2 and prophesy against ***t***.
25:12 by avenging itself on ***t***,
25:17 execute great vengeance on ***t***
25:17 when I lay My vengeance upon ***t***.
28:24 among all who are around ***t***,
28:24 are around them, who despise ***t***.
28:25 and am hallowed in ***t*** in the
28:26 on all those around ***t*** who
28:26 those around them who despise ***t***.
29:12 the nations and disperse ***t***
29:14 captives of Egypt and cause ***t***
29:15 for I will diminish ***t*** so that
29:16 but will remind ***t*** of their
29:16 when they turned to follow ***t***.
30: 5 shall fall with ***t*** by the
30: 9 great anguish shall come upon ***t***,
30:23 and disperse ***t*** throughout the
30:26 the nations and disperse ***t***
31: 5 As it sent ***t*** out.
31:14 be high enough to reach up to ***t***.
32:10 I brandish My sword before ***t***;
32:12 all of ***t*** the most terrible of
32:13 The foot of man shall muddy ***t***
32:13 the hooves of animals muddy ***t***.
32:18 And cast ***t*** down to the depths
32:22 All of ***t*** slain, fallen by the
32:23 All of ***t*** slain, fallen by the
32:24 All of ***t*** slain, fallen by the
32:25 All of ***t*** uncircumcised, slain
32:26 All of ***t*** uncircumcised, slain
32:30 princes of the north, All of ***t***,
32:31 Pharaoh will see ***t*** And be
33: 2 of your people, and say to ***t***:
33: 6 takes any person from among ***t***,
33: 7 a word from My mouth and warn ***t***
33:10 upon us, and we pine away in ***t***,
33:11 'Say to ***t***: 'As I live,'
33:25 "Therefore say to ***t***,
33:27 "Say thus to ***t***,
33:31 but they do not do ***t***;
33:32 Indeed you are to ***t*** as a very
33:32 but they do not do ***t***.
33:33 that a prophet has been among ***t***.
34: 2 Israel, prophesy and say to ***t***,
34: 4 and cruelty you have ruled ***t***.
34: 6 seeking or searching for ***t***.
34:10 I will cause ***t*** to cease feeding
34:10 may no longer be food for ***t***.
34:11 search for My sheep and seek ***t***
34:12 seek out My sheep and deliver ***t***
34:13 And I will bring ***t*** out from the
34:13 from the peoples and gather ***t***
34:13 and will bring ***t*** to their own
34:13 I will feed ***t*** on the mountains
34:14 I will feed ***t*** in good pasture,
34:15 and I will make ***t*** lie down,"
34:16 and feed ***t*** in judgment."
34:20 thus says the Lord GOD to ***t***:
34:21 and scattered ***t*** abroad,
34:23 establish one shepherd over ***t***,
34:23 over them, and he shall feed ***t***—
34:23 He shall feed ***t*** and be their
34:24 servant David a prince among ***t***;
34:25 make a covenant of peace with ***t***,
34:26 I will make ***t*** and the places all
34:27 of their yoke and delivered ***t***
34:27 hand of those who enslaved ***t***.
34:28 beasts of the land devour ***t***;

34:28 and no one shall make *t*
34:29 I will raise up for *t* a garden
34:30 the LORD their God, am with *t*,
35:10 be mine, and we will possess *t*,
35:11 showed in your hatred against *t*;
35:11 will make Myself known among *t*
35:13 against Me; I have heard *t*.
36:12 no more shall you bereave *t* of
36:18 I poured out My fury on *t* for
36:19 So I scattered *t* among the
36:19 I judged *t* according to their
36:20 holy name—when they said of *t*,
36:27 keep My judgments and do *t*.
36:37 inquire of Me to do this for *t*:
37: 2 Then He caused me to pass by *t*
37: 4 to these bones, and say to *t*,
37: 8 and the flesh came upon *t*,
37: 8 and the skin covered *t* over;
37: 8 but there was no breath in *t*.
37:10 me, and breath came into *t*,
37:12 prophesy and say to *t*,
37:17 Then join *t* one to another for
37:19 'say to *t*, 'Thus says the Lord
37:19 and I will join *t* with it, with
37:19 and make *t* one stick, and they
37:21 "Then say to *t*,
37:21 and will gather *t* from every
37:21 from every side and bring *t*
37:22 and I will make *t* one nation in
37:22 one king shall be king over *t*
37:23 but I will deliver *t* from all
37:23 have sinned, and will cleanse *t*.
37:24 servant shall be king over *t*,
37:24 observe My statutes, and do *t*.
37:26 make a covenant of peace with *t*,
37:26 an everlasting covenant with *t*;
37:26 I will establish *t* and multiply
37:26 establish them and multiply *t*,
37:27 tabernacle also shall be with *t*;
38: 4 all of *t* handling swords.
38: 5 Ethiopia, and Libya are with *t*,
38: 5 all of *t* with shield and
38: 7 about you; and be a guard for *t*.
38: 8 and now all of *t* dwell safely.
38:11 all of *t* dwelling without
38:15 all of *t* riding on horses,
38:17 I would bring you against *t*?
39: 7 and I will not let *t* profane
39: 9 and they will make fires with *t*
39:10 plunder those who plundered *t*,
39:10 pillage those who pillaged *t*,
39:12 of Israel will be burying *t*,
39:18 All of *t* fatlings of Bashan.
39:21 My hand which I have laid on *t*.
39:23 therefore I hid My face from *t*.
39:23 I gave *t* into the hand of their
39:24 I have dealt with *t*,
39:24 them, and hidden My face from *t*.
39:26 own land and no one made *t*
39:27 When I have brought *t* back from
39:27 the peoples and gathered *t* out
39:27 and I am hallowed in *t* in the
39:28 who sent *t* into captivity among
39:28 but also brought *t* back to
39:28 and left none of *t* captive any
39:29 I will not hide My face from *t*
40: 4 here so that I might show *t*
40:26 its archway was in front of *t*;
42: 5 took away space from *t* more
42: 9 as one goes into *t* from the
42:11 was a walk in front of *t* also,
42:12 facing south, as one enters *t*,
42:14 "When the priests enter *t*,
43: 8 with a wall between *t* and Me,
43: 8 therefore I have consumed *t* in
43: 9 Now let *t* put their harlotry and
43:10 and let *t* measure the pattern.
43:11 make known to *t* the design of
43:11 its ordinances, and perform *t*.
43:24 When you offer *t* before the
43:24 priests shall throw salt on *t*,
43:24 and they will offer *t* up as a
44:11 and they shall stand before *t*
44:11 before them to minister to *t*.
44:12 Because they ministered to *t*
44:12 My hand in an oath against *t*,
44:14 Nevertheless I will make *t* keep
44:17 no wool shall come upon *t* while
44:19 leave *t* in the holy chambers,
44:23 and cause *t* to discern between
44:28 You shall give *t* no possession
45:15 to make atonement for *t*,
46:18 inheritance by evicting *t* from
46:20 so that they do not bring *t*
46:23 stones all around in *t*,
46:23 all around the four of *t*;
48:12 is set apart shall be to *t* a
Dan 1: 5 And the king appointed for *t* a
1: 5 three years of training for *t*,
1: 7 To *t* the chief of the eunuchs
1:12 and let *t* give us vegetables to
1:14 So he consented with *t* in this
1:14 and tested *t* ten days.
1:16 and gave *t* vegetables.
1:17 God gave *t* knowledge and skill
1:18 chief of the eunuchs brought *t*
1:19 Then the king interviewed *t*,
1:19 and among *t* all none was found
1:20 about which the king examined *t*,
1:20 he found *t* ten times better
2: 3 And the king said to *t*,
2:13 and his companions, to kill *t*.
2:34 and broke *t* in pieces.
2:35 the wind carried *t* away so that
2:35 away so that no trace of *t* was
2:38 He has given *t* into your hand,
2:38 and has made you ruler over *t*
3:14 spoke, saying to *t*,
3:20 and cast *t* into the burning
3:27 the smell of fire was not on *t*.
4: 7 and I told *t* the dream;
5: 2 concubines might drink from *t*.
5: 3 and his concubines drank from *t*.
5:23 have drunk wine from *t*.
6: 2 satraps might give account to *t*,
6:24 and they cast *t* into the den
6:24 them into the den of lions—*t*,
6:24 and the lions overpowered *t*,
7: 8 a little one, coming up among *t*,
7:21 and prevailing against *t*,
7:24 And another shall rise after *t*;
8: 9 And out of one of *t* came a
8:10 to the ground, and trampled *t*.
9: 7 to which You have driven *t*,
10: 7 but a great terror fell upon *t*,
11: 2 shall be far richer than *t*
11: 7 and deal with *t* and prevail.
11:18 bring the reproach against *t*
11:24 he shall disperse among *t* the
11:34 but many shall join with *t* by
11:35 shall fall, to refine *t*,
11:35 fall, to refine them, purify *t*,
11:35 and make *t* white, until the
11:37 he shall exalt himself above *t*
11:39 and he shall cause *t* to rule
11:40 the countries, overwhelm *t*,
Hos 1: 6 But I will utterly take *t*
1: 7 Will save *t* by the LORD their
1: 7 And will not save *t* by bow,
1:10 place where it was said to *t*,
1:10 There it shall be said to *t*,
2: 5 She who conceived *t* has
2: 7 her lovers, But not overtake *t*;
2: 7 Yes, she will seek *t*,
2: 7 will seek them, but not find *t*.
2:12 So I will make *t* a forest,
2:12 beasts of the field shall eat *t*.
2:18 I will make a covenant for *t*
2:18 To make *t* lie down safely.
4: 9 So I will punish *t* for their
4: 9 And reward *t* for their deeds.
4:12 And their staff informs *t*.
4:12 of harlotry has caused *t* to
4:16 Now the LORD will let *t*
5: 2 Though I rebuke *t* all.
5: 5 Judah also stumbles with *t*.
5: 6 has withdrawn Himself from *t*.
5: 7 Now a New Moon shall devour *t*
5:10 I will pour out my wrath on *t*
5:14 will tear *t* and go away;
5:14 I will take *t* away, and no
6: 5 Therefore I have hewn *t* by the
6: 5 I have slain *t* by the words of
7: 2 own deeds have surrounded *t*;
7: 7 None among *t* calls upon Me.
7:12 go, I will spread My net on *t*;
7:12 I will bring *t* down like birds
7:12 I will chastise *t* According
7:13 Woe to *t*, for they have
7:13 fled from Me! Destruction to *t*,
7:13 Though I redeemed *t*,
8: 4 but I did not acknowledge *t*.
8: 5 My anger is aroused against *t*—
8:10 nations, Now I will gather *t*;
8:13 the LORD does not accept *t*.
9: 2 the winepress Shall not feed *t*,
9: 4 be like bread of mourners to *t*;
9: 6 Egypt shall gather *t* up;
9: 6 them up; Memphis shall bury *t*.
9:12 Yet I will bereave *t* to the
9:12 woe to *t* when I depart from
9:12 to them when I depart from *t*!
9:14 Give *t*, O LORD—WHAT
9:14 Give *t* a miscarrying womb
9:15 in Gilgal, For there I hated *t*.
9:15 of their deeds I will drive *t*
9:15 I will love *t* no more.
9:17 My God will cast *t* away,
10: 9 of iniquity Did not overtake *t*.
10:10 is My desire, I will chasten *t*.
10:10 shall be gathered against *t*
10:10 against them When I bind *t*
11: 2 As they called *t*,
11: 2 So they went from *t*;
11: 3 Taking *t* by their arms;
11: 3 did not know that I healed *t*.
11: 4 I drew *t* with gentle cords,
11: 4 And I was to *t* as those who
11: 4 I stooped and fed *t*.
11: 6 his districts, And consume *t*,
11:11 And I will let *t* dwell in
13: 2 of craftsmen. They say of *t*,
13: 7 So I will be to *t* like a lion;
13: 8 I will meet *t* like a bear
13: 8 And there I will devour *t* like
13: 8 The wild beast shall tear *t*.
13:14 I will ransom *t* from the power
13:14 I will redeem *t* from death.
14: 4 I will love *t* freely, For My
14: 9 is prudent? Let him know *t*.
14: 9 right; The righteous walk in *t*,
14: 9 But transgressors stumble in *t*.
Joel 2: 2 there ever be any such after *t*,
2: 3 A fire devours before *t*,
2: 3 And behind *t* a flame burns;
2: 3 the Garden of Eden before *t*,
2: 3 And behind *t* a desolate
2: 3 Surely nothing shall escape *t*.
2: 6 Before *t* the people writhe in
2:10 The earth quakes before *t*,
2:17 Let *t* say, "Spare Your
2:17 the nations should rule over *t*.
2:19 And you will be satisfied by *t*;
3: 2 And bring *t* down to the Valley
3: 2 will enter into judgment with *t*
3: 6 That you may remove *t* far from
3: 7 I will raise *t* Out of the
3: 7 place to which you have sold *t*,
3: 8 And they will sell *t* to the
3: 9 draw near, Let *t* come up.
3:21 For I will acquit *t* of the guilt
Am 1: 6 whole captivity To deliver *t*
2: 4 Their lies lead *t* astray,
2: 9 destroyed the Amorite before *t*,
4: 9 trees, The locust devoured *t*;
5: 8 waters of the sea And pours *t*
5:11 Yet you shall not dwell in *t*;
5:11 you shall not drink wine from *t*.
5:22 I will not accept *t*,
6:10 picks up the bodies to take *t*
7: 8 I will not pass by *t* anymore.
8: 2 I will not pass by *t* anymore.
9: 1 And break *t* on the heads of
9: 1 break them on the heads of *t*
9: 1 I will slay the last of *t* with
9: 1 He who flees from *t* shall not
9: 1 And he who escapes from *t*
9: 2 there my hand shall take *t*;
9: 2 From there I will bring *t*
9: 3 there I will search and take *t*;
9: 3 serpent, and it shall bite *t*;
9: 4 the sword, And it shall slay *t*.
9: 4 I will set My eyes on *t* for
9: 6 And pours *t* out on the face of
9:14 the waste cities and inhabit *t*;
9:14 vineyards and drink wine from *t*;
9:14 gardens and eat fruit from *t*.
9:15 I will plant *t* in their land,
9:15 From the land I have given *t*,
Ob 11 you were as one of *t*.
14 To cut off those among *t* who
14 delivered up those among *t* who
18 They shall kindle *t* and devour
18 shall kindle them and devour *t*
Jon 1: 3 to go with *t* to Tarshish from
1: 9 So he said to *t*,
1:10 LORD, because he had told *t*.
1:12 And he said to *t*,
1:13 grow more tempestuous against *t*.
3: 5 the greatest to the least of *t*.
3: 7 do not let *t* eat, or drink
3:10 had said He would bring upon *t*,
Mic 2: 2 They covet fields and take *t*
2: 2 Also houses, and seize *t*.
2:12 I will put *t* together like
2:13 open will come up before *t*;
2:13 Their king will pass before *t*,
3: 3 people, Flay their skin from *t*,
3: 3 And chop *t* in pieces Like
3: 4 LORD, But He will not hear *t*;
3: 4 will even hide His face from *t*
3: 6 the day shall be dark for *t*.
4: 4 And no one shall make *t*
4: 7 the LORD will reign over *t* in
4:12 For He will gather *t* like
5: 3 Therefore He shall give *t* up,
6:14 but shall not save *t*;
7: 4 The best of *t* is like a brier;
7:14 Let *t* feed in Bashan and
7:15 I will show *t* wonders."
Nah 2: 2 the emptiers have emptied *t*
2:11 And no one made *t* afraid?
3:18 And no one gathers *t*.
Hab 1:10 And princes are scorned by *t*.
1:12 You have appointed *t* for
1:12 You have marked *t* for
1:14 that have no ruler over *t*?
1:15 They take up all of *t* with a
1:15 They catch *t* in their net,
1:15 And gather *t* in their dragnet.
1:16 Because by *t* their share is
2:17 of beasts which made *t* afraid,
3:16 He will invade *t* with his
Zeph 1:13 houses, but not inhabit *t*;
1:18 Shall be able to deliver *t*
2: 7 their God will intervene for *t*,
2: 9 of My people shall plunder *t*,
2: 9 of My people shall possess *t*.
2:11 LORD will be awesome to *t*,
3: 8 To pour on *t* My indignation,
3:13 And no one shall make *t*
3:19 I will appoint *t* for praise
Hag 2:22 And those who ride in *t*;
Zech 1: 3 "Therefore say to *t*,
1:21 are coming to terrify *t*,
2: 9 I will shake My hand against *t*,
3: 5 Let *t* put a clean turban on his
6: 6 the white are going after *t*,
6:13 of peace shall be between *t*
7:14 But I scattered *t* with a
7:14 land became desolate after *t*,
8: 8 I will bring *t* back, And they
9: 8 an oppressor pass through *t*,
9:14 the LORD will be seen over *t*,
9:15 LORD of hosts will defend *t*;
9:16 LORD their God will save *t* in

10: 1 He will give *t* showers of
10: 3 And will make *t* as His royal
10: 5 because the LORD is with *t*,
10: 6 I will bring *t* back, Because
10: 6 Because I have mercy on *t*.
10: 6 be as though I had not cast *t*
10: 6 their God, And I will hear *t*.
10: 8 I will whistle for *t* and gather
10: 8 whistle for them and gather *t*,
10: 8 them, For I will redeem *t*;
10: 9 I will sow *t* among the peoples,
10:10 I will also bring *t* back from
10:10 And gather *t* from Assyria.
10:10 I will bring *t* into the land
10:10 no more room is found for *t*.
10:12 So I will strengthen *t* in the
11: 5 whose owners slaughter *t* and
11: 5 those who sell *t* say, 'Blessed
11: 5 their shepherds do not pity *t*.
11: 6 and I will not deliver *t* from
11: 8 in one month. My soul loathed *t*,
11:12 Then I said to *t*,
11:13 pieces of silver and threw *t*
12: 8 the one who is feeble among *t*
12: 8 the Angel of the LORD before *t*.
13: 9 Will refine *t* as silver is
13: 9 And test *t* as gold is tested.
13: 9 My name, And I will answer *t*.
14: 8 Half of *t* toward the eastern
14: 8 the eastern sea And half of *t*
14:13 from the LORD will be among *t*.
14:17 on *t* there will be no rain.
14:21 shall come and take *t* and cook
14:21 and take them and cook in *t*.
Mal 2: 2 I have cursed *t* already,
2: 5 And I gave *t* to him that he
2:15 But did He not make *t* one,
2:17 LORD, And He delights in *t*,
3: 3 And purge *t* as gold and
3: 7 And have not kept *t*.
3:16 the LORD listened and heard *t*;
3:17 On the day that I make *t* My
3:17 And I will spare *t* As a man
4: 1 which is coming shall burn *t*
4: 1 That will leave *t* neither root
Mt 2: 4 he inquired of *t* where the
2: 7 determined from *t* what time the
2: 8 And he sent *t* to Bethlehem and
2: 9 seen in the East went before *t*,
3: 7 to his baptism, he said to *t*,
4:19 Then He said to *t*,
4:21 mending their nets. He called *t*,
4:24 and paralytics; and He healed *t*.
5: 2 opened His mouth and taught *t*,
5:19 but whoever does and teaches *t*,
6: 1 before men, to be seen by *t*.
6: 8 "Therefore do not be like *t*.
6:26 your heavenly Father feeds *t*.
7: 6 lest they trample *t* under their
7:12 men to do to you, do also to *t*,
7:16 You will know *t* by their fruits.
7:20 by their fruits you will know *t*.
7:23 "And then I will declare to *t*,
7:24 sayings of Mine, and does *t*,
7:26 of Mine, and does not do *t*,
7:29 for He taught *t* as one having
8: 4 commanded, as a testimony to *t*.
8:15 And she arose and served *t*.
8:26 But He said to *t*,
8:30 Now a good way off from *t* there
8:32 And He said to *t*,
8:33 Then those who kept *t* fled; and
9:12 Jesus heard that, He said to *t*,
9:15 And Jesus said to *t*,
9:15 as the bridegroom is with *t*?
9:15 will be taken away from *t*,
9:18 He spoke these things to *t*,
9:24 He said to *t*, "Make room, for
9:28 to Him. And Jesus said to *t*,
9:30 And Jesus sternly warned *t*,
9:36 was moved with compassion for *t*,
10: 1 He gave *t* power over unclean
10: 1 to cast *t* out, and to heal all
10: 5 Jesus sent out and commanded *t*,
10:18 as a testimony to *t* and to the
10:21 up against parents and cause *t*
10:26 "Therefore do not fear *t*.
10:29 And not one of *t* falls to the
11: 4 Jesus answered and said to *t*,
11: 5 have the gospel preached to *t*.
11:25 prudent and have revealed *t* to
12: 3 But He said to *t*,
12:11 Then He said to *t*,
12:15 and He healed *t* all.
12:16 Yet He warned *t* not to make Him
12:25 their thoughts, and said to *t*:
12:27 by whom do your sons cast *t*
12:39 But He answered and said to *t*,
13: 3 Then He spoke many things to *t*
13: 4 the birds came and devoured *t*.
13: 7 thorns sprang up and choked *t*.
13:10 Why do You speak to *t* in
13:11 He answered and said to *t*,
13:11 but to *t* it has not been given.
13:13 Therefore I speak to *t* in
13:14 And in *t* the prophecy of Isaiah
13:15 So that I should heal *t*.
13:24 parable He put forth to *t*,
13:28 'He said to *t*, 'An enemy
13:28 us then to go and gather *t* up?
13:29 also uproot the wheat with *t*.
13:30 together the tares and bind *t*
13:30 bind them in bundles to burn *t*,
13:31 parable He put forth to *t*,
13:33 Another parable He spoke to *t*:
13:34 a parable He did not speak to *t*,
13:37 He answered and said to *t*:
13:39 The enemy who sowed *t* is the
13:42 and will cast *t* into the furnace
13:50 and cast *t* into the furnace of
13:51 Jesus said to *t*,
13:52 Then He said to *t*,
13:54 He taught *t* in their synagogue,
13:57 But Jesus said to *t*,
14: 6 of Herodias danced before *t*
14:14 was moved with compassion for *t*,
14:16 But Jesus said to *t*,
14:16 You give *t* something to eat."
14:18 Bring *t* here to Me."
14:25 of the night Jesus went to *t*,
14:27 immediately Jesus spoke to *t*,
15: 3 He answered and said to *t*,
15:10 to Himself, He said to *t*,
15:14 Let *t* alone. They are blind
15:30 having with *t* the lame, blind,
15:30 and they laid *t* down at Jesus'
15:30 at Jesus' feet, and He healed *t*.
15:32 And I do not want to send *t*
15:34 Jesus said to *t*,
15:36 broke *t* and gave them to His
15:36 broke them and gave *t* to His
16: 1 Him asked that He would show *t*
16: 2 He answered and said to *t*,
16: 4 And He left *t* and departed.
16: 6 Then Jesus said to *t*,
16: 8 being aware of it, said to *t*,
16:12 that He did not tell *t* to
16:15 He said to *t*, "But who do you
17: 1 led *t* up on a high mountain by
17: 2 He was transfigured before *t*.
17: 3 Moses and Elijah appeared to *t*,
17: 5 a bright cloud overshadowed *t*;
17: 7 But Jesus came and touched *t* and
17: 9 the mountain, Jesus commanded *t*,
17:11 Jesus answered and said to *t*,
17:13 understood that He spoke to *t*
17:20 So Jesus said to *t*,
17:22 in Galilee, Jesus said to *t*,
17:27 lest we offend *t*,
17:27 take that and give it to *t* for
18: 2 set him in the midst of *t*,
18:12 and one of *t* goes astray,
18:17 "And if he refuses to hear *t*,
18:19 it will be done for *t* by My
18:20 I am there in the midst of *t*.
19: 2 and He healed *t* there.
19: 4 And He answered and said to *t*,
19: 4 not read that He who made *t*
19: 4 made *t* male and female,'
19: 8 said to *t*, "Moses, because
19:11 But He said to *t*,
19:13 He might put His hands on *t*
19:13 but the disciples rebuked *t*.
19:14 come to Me, and do not forbid *t*;
19:15 And He laid His hands on *t* and
19:26 But Jesus looked at *t* and said
19:26 looked at them and said to *t*,
19:28 So Jesus said to *t*,
20: 2 he sent *t* into his vineyard.
20: 4 "and said to *t*,
20: 6 standing idle, and said to *t*,
20: 7 no one hired us.' He said to *t*,
20: 8 Call the laborers and give *t*
20:12 and you made *t* equal to us who
20:13 But he answered one of *t* and
20:17 aside on the road and said to *t*,
20:23 So He said to *t*,
20:25 But Jesus called *t* to Himself
20:25 of the Gentiles lord it over *t*,
20:25 great exercise authority over *t*.
20:31 Then the multitude warned *t* that
20:32 Jesus stood still and called *t*,
21: 2 saying to *t*, "Go into the
21: 2 Loose *t* and bring them to Me.
21: 2 Loose them and bring *t* to Me.
21: 3 say, 'The Lord has need of *t*,
21: 3 and immediately he will send *t*.
21: 6 and did as Jesus commanded *t*.
21: 7 colt, laid their clothes on *t*,
21: 7 on them, and set Him on *t*.
21: 8 from the trees and spread *t*
21:13 And He said to *t*,
21:14 in the temple, and He healed *t*.
21:16 saying?" And Jesus said to *t*,
21:17 Then He left *t* and went out of
21:21 So Jesus answered and said to *t*,
21:24 Jesus answered and said to *t*,
21:27 do not know." And He said to *t*,
21:31 "The first." Jesus said to *t*,
21:36 and they did likewise to *t*.
21:37 of all he sent his son to *t*,
21:42 Jesus said to *t*,
21:45 that He was speaking of *t*.
22: 1 Jesus answered and spoke to *t*
22: 6 treated *t* spitefully, and
22: 6 them spitefully, and killed *t*.
22:20 And He said to *t*,
22:21 "Caesar's." And He said to *t*,
22:29 Jesus answered and said to *t*,
22:35 Then one of *t*, a lawyer,
22:41 together, Jesus asked *t*,
22:43 He said to *t*, "How then does
23: 4 and lay *t* on men's shoulders;
23: 4 themselves will not move *t*
23:26 that the outside of *t* may be
23:30 not have been partakers with *t*
23:34 some of *t* you will kill and
23:34 and some of *t* you will scourge
24: 2 And Jesus said to *t*,
24: 4 Jesus answered and said to *t*:
24:39 the flood came and took *t* all
24:45 to give *t* food in due season?
25: 2 'Now five of *t* were wise,
25: 3 lamps and took no oil with *t*,
25:14 and delivered his goods to *t*.
25:16 talents went and traded with *t*,
25:19 and settled accounts with *t*.
25:20 five more talents besides *t*.
25:22 two more talents besides *t*.
25:32 and He will separate *t* one from
25:40 King will answer and say to *t*,
25:45 "Then He will answer *t*,
26:10 was aware of it, He said to *t*,
26:19 did as Jesus had directed *t*;
26:22 and each of *t* began to say to
26:27 gave thanks, and gave it to *t*,
26:31 Then Jesus said to *t*,
26:36 Then Jesus came with *t* to a
26:38 Then He said to *t*,
26:40 to the disciples and found *t*
26:43 And He came and found *t* asleep
26:44 So He left *t*, went away
26:45 to His disciples and said to *t*,
26:48 Now His betrayer had given *t* a
26:70 But he denied it before *t* all,
26:73 "Surely you also are one of *t*,
27: 6 It is not lawful to put *t* into
27: 7 together and bought with *t* the
27:10 and gave *t* for the potter's
27:17 together, Pilate said to *t*,
27:21 governor answered and said to *t*,
27:22 Pilate said to *t*,
27:26 Then he released Barabbas to *t*;
27:35 My garments among *t*,
27:48 Immediately one of *t* ran and
27:65 Pilate said to *t*,
28: 9 disciples, behold, Jesus met *t*,
28:10 Then Jesus said to *t*,
28:13 saying, "Tell *t*,
28:16 which Jesus had appointed for *t*.
28:18 And Jesus came and spoke to *t*,
28:19 baptizing *t* in the name of the
28:20 teaching *t* to observe all things
Mk 1:17 Then Jesus said to *t*,
1:20 And immediately He called *t*,
1:22 for He taught *t* as one having
1:31 left her. And she served *t*.
1:38 But He said to *t*,
1:44 commanded, as a testimony to *t*.
2: 2 no longer room to receive *t*,
2: 2 And He preached the word to *t*.
2: 8 within themselves, He said to *t*,
2:12 went out in the presence of *t*
2:13 came to Him, and He taught *t*.
2:17 Jesus heard it, He said to *t*,
2:19 And Jesus said to *t*,
2:19 while the bridegroom is with *t*?
2:19 they have the bridegroom with *t*
2:20 will be taken away from *t*,
2:25 But He said to *t*,
2:27 And He said to *t*,
3: 4 Then He said to *t*,
3: 5 when He had looked around at *t*
3:12 But He sternly warned *t* that
3:14 Him and that He might send *t*
3:23 So He called *t* to Himself and
3:23 them to Himself and said to *t*
3:33 But He answered *t*,
4: 2 Then He taught *t* many things by
4: 2 and said to *t* in His teaching:
4: 9 And He said to *t*,
4:11 And He said to *t*,
4:12 their sins be forgiven *t*.
4:13 And He said to *t*,
4:21 Also He said to *t*,
4:24 Then He said to *t*,
4:33 He spoke the word to *t* as they
4:34 a parable He did not speak to *t*.
4:35 evening had come, He said to *t*,
4:40 But He said to *t*,
5:10 that He would not send *t* out
5:12 the swine, that we may enter *t*.
5:13 And at once Jesus gave *t*
5:16 And those who saw it told *t* how
5:19 and tell *t* what great things
5:39 When He came in, He said to *t*,
5:40 But when He had put *t* all
5:43 But He commanded *t* strictly that
6: 4 But Jesus said to *t*,
6: 5 a few sick people and healed *t*.
6: 7 and began to send *t* out two by
6: 7 and gave *t* power over unclean
6: 8 He commanded *t* to take nothing
6:10 Also He said to *t*,
6:11 feet as a testimony against *t*.
6:13 who were sick, and healed *t*.
6:31 And He said to *t*,
6:33 But the multitudes saw *t*
6:33 They arrived before *t* and came
6:34 was moved with compassion for *t*,
6:34 So He began to teach *t* many
6:36 Send *t* away, that they may go
6:37 But He answered and said to *t*,
6:37 You give *t* something to eat."
6:37 worth of bread and give *t*
6:38 But He said to *t*,

6:39 Then He commanded ***t*** to make them
6:39 He commanded them to make ***t***
6:41 and gave ***t*** to His disciples to
6:41 His disciples to set before ***t***;
6:41 two fish He divided among ***t***
6:46 And when He had sent ***t*** away, He
6:48 Then He saw ***t*** straining at
6:48 for the wind was against ***t***.
6:48 watch of the night He came to ***t***,
6:48 and would have passed ***t*** by.
6:50 immediately He talked with ***t***
6:50 talked with them and said to ***t***,
6:51 He went up into the boat to ***t***,
7: 6 He answered and said to ***t***,
7: 9 He said to ***t***, "All too well
7:14 to Himself, He said to ***t***,
7:18 So He said to ***t***,
7:36 Then He commanded ***t*** that they
7:36 but the more He commanded ***t***,
8: 1 to Him and said to ***t***,
8: 3 And if I send ***t*** away hungry to
8: 3 for some of ***t*** have come from
8: 5 He asked ***t***, "How many loaves
8: 6 broke ***t*** and gave them to His
8: 6 broke them and gave ***t*** to His
8: 6 His disciples to set before ***t***;
8: 6 and they set ***t*** before the
8: 7 fish; and having blessed ***t***,
8: 7 He said to set ***t*** also before
8: 7 said to set them also before ***t***.
8: 9 And He sent ***t*** away,
8:13 And He left ***t***, and getting
8:14 have more than one loaf with ***t***
8:15 Then He charged ***t***,
8:17 being aware of it, said to ***t***,
8:21 So He said to ***t***,
8:27 His disciples, saying to ***t***,
8:29 He said to ***t***, "But who do you
8:30 Then He strictly warned ***t*** that
8:31 And He began to teach ***t*** that
8:34 disciples also, He said to ***t***,
9: 1 And He said to ***t***,
9: 2 and led ***t*** up on a high mountain
9: 2 He was transfigured before ***t***.
9: 3 launderer on earth can whiten ***t***.
9: 4 And Elijah appeared to ***t*** with
9: 7 a cloud came and overshadowed ***t***;
9: 9 He commanded ***t*** that they should
9:12 Then He answered and told ***t***,
9:14 saw a great multitude around ***t***,
9:14 and scribes disputing with ***t***.
9:16 are you discussing with ***t***?
9:29 So He said to ***t***,
9:31 His disciples and said to ***t***,
9:33 He was in the house He asked ***t***,
9:35 the twelve, and said to ***t***,
9:36 and set him in the midst of ***t***.
9:36 him in His arms, He said to ***t***,
10: 1 He taught ***t*** again.
10: 3 And He answered and said to ***t***,
10: 5 Jesus answered and said to ***t***,
10: 6 made ***t*** male and female.'
10:11 So He said to ***t***,
10:13 to Him, that He might touch ***t***;
10:13 rebuked those who brought ***t***.
10:14 displeased and said to ***t***,
10:14 come to Me, and do not forbid ***t***;
10:16 And He took ***t*** up in His arms,
10:16 His arms, put His hands on ***t***,
10:16 hands on them, and blessed ***t***.
10:24 answered again and said to ***t***,
10:27 But Jesus looked at ***t*** and said,
10:32 and Jesus was going before ***t***;
10:32 again and began to tell ***t*** the
10:36 And He said to ***t***,
10:38 But Jesus said to ***t***,
10:39 are able." So Jesus said to ***t***,
10:42 But Jesus called ***t*** to Himself
10:42 them to Himself and said to ***t***,
10:42 the Gentiles lord it over ***t***,
10:42 ones exercise authority over ***t***.
11: 2 and He said to ***t***,
11: 5 those who stood there said to ***t***,
11: 6 And they spoke to ***t*** just as
11: 6 So they let ***t*** go.
11: 8 from the trees and spread ***t***
11:17 Then He taught, saying to ***t***,
11:22 So Jesus answered and said to ***t***,
11:24 believe that you receive ***t***,
11:24 them, and you will have ***t***.
11:29 Jesus answered and said to ***t***,
11:33 Jesus answered and said to ***t***,
12: 1 Then He began to speak to ***t*** in
12: 4 Again he sent ***t*** another servant,
12: 6 he also sent him to ***t*** last,
12:12 spoken the parable against ***t***.
12:15 their hypocrisy, said to ***t***,
12:16 brought it. And He said to ***t***,
12:17 Jesus answered and said to ***t***,
12:24 Jesus answered and said to ***t***,
12:28 and having heard ***t*** reasoning
12:28 that He had answered ***t*** well,
12:38 Then He said to ***t*** in His
12:43 to Himself and said to ***t***,
13: 5 And Jesus, answering ***t***,
13: 9 My sake, for a testimony to ***t***.
13:12 up against parents and cause ***t***
14: 7 whenever you wish you may do ***t***
14:10 priests to betray Him to ***t***.
14:13 of His disciples and said to ***t***,
14:16 it just as He had said to ***t***;
14:20 He answered and said to ***t***,
14:22 and gave it to ***t*** and said,
14:23 given thanks He gave it to ***t***,
14:24 And He said to ***t***,
14:27 Then Jesus said to ***t***,
14:34 Then He said to ***t***,
14:37 Then He came and found ***t***
14:40 He found ***t*** asleep again,
14:41 the third time and said to ***t***,
14:44 Now His betrayer had given ***t*** a
14:48 Jesus answered and said to ***t***,
14:52 the linen cloth and fled from ***t***
14:69 stood by, "This is one of ***t***.
14:70 "Surely you are one of ***t***;
15: 6 to releasing one prisoner to ***t***,
15: 8 as he had always done for ***t***.
15: 9 But Pilate answered ***t***,
15:11 rather release Barabbas to ***t***.
15:12 Pilate answered and said to ***t***
15:14 Then Pilate said to ***t***,
15:15 released Barabbas to ***t***;
15:24 casting lots for ***t*** to determine
16: 6 But he said to ***t***,
16:12 in another form to two of ***t*** as
16:13 but they did not believe ***t***
16:15 And He said to ***t***,
16:18 it will by no means hurt ***t***;
16:19 after the Lord had spoken to ***t***,
16:20 the Lord working with ***t*** and
Lk 1: 2 of the word delivered ***t*** to us,
1:22 out, he could not speak to ***t***;
1:22 for he beckoned to ***t*** and
1:65 came on all who dwelt around ***t***;
1:66 And all those who heard ***t*** kept
1:66 those who heard them kept ***t***
2: 7 there was no room for ***t*** in the
2: 9 of the Lord stood before ***t***,
2: 9 of the Lord shone around ***t***,
2:10 Then the angel said to ***t***,
2:15 the angels had gone away from ***t***
2:17 the saying which was told ***t***
2:18 those things which were told ***t***
2:19 these things and pondered ***t***
2:20 and seen, as it was told ***t***.
2:34 Then Simeon blessed ***t***,
2:46 both listening to ***t*** and asking
2:46 listening to them and asking ***t***
2:49 And He said to ***t***,
2:50 statement which He spoke to ***t***.
2:51 Then He went down with ***t*** and
2:51 Nazareth, and was subject to ***t***,
3:11 He answered and said to ***t***,
3:13 And he said to ***t***,
3:14 shall we do?" So he said to ***t***,
4:21 And He began to say to ***t***,
4:23 He said to ***t***, "You will surely
4:26 but to none of ***t*** was Elijah sent
4:27 and none of ***t*** was cleansed
4:30 passing through the midst of ***t***,
4:31 and was teaching ***t*** on the
4:39 she arose and served ***t***.
4:40 various diseases brought ***t*** to
4:40 His hands on every one of ***t***
4:40 every one of them and healed ***t***.
4:41 of God!" And He, rebuking ***t***,
4:41 did not allow ***t*** to speak, for
4:42 to keep Him from leaving ***t***;
4:43 but He said to ***t***,
5: 2 the fishermen had gone from ***t***
5: 7 other boat to come and help ***t***.
5:14 cleansing, as a testimony to ***t***,
5:17 the Lord was present to heal ***t***.
5:22 He answered and said to ***t***,
5:25 Immediately he rose up before ***t***,
5:29 and others who sat down with ***t***.
5:31 Jesus answered and said to ***t***,
5:34 And He said to ***t***,
5:34 while the bridegroom is with ***t***?
5:35 will be taken away from ***t***;
5:36 Then He spoke a parable to ***t***:
6: 1 the heads of grain and ate ***t***,
6: 1 rubbing ***t*** in their hands.
6: 2 some of the Pharisees said to ***t***,
6: 3 But Jesus answering ***t*** said,
6: 5 And He said to ***t***,
6: 9 Then Jesus said to ***t***,
6:10 when He had looked around at ***t***
6:13 and from ***t*** He chose twelve whom
6:17 And He came down with ***t*** and
6:19 out from Him and healed ***t*** all.
6:30 away your goods do not ask ***t***
6:31 you also do to ***t*** likewise.
6:32 sinners love those who love ***t***.
6:39 And He spoke a parable to ***t***:
6:47 and hears My sayings and does ***t***,
7: 6 Then Jesus went with ***t***.
7:19 sent ***t*** to Jesus, saying, "Are
7:22 Jesus answered and said to ***t***,
7:22 have the gospel preached to ***t***.
7:38 and wiped ***t*** with the hair of
7:38 His feet and anointed ***t*** with
7:42 he freely forgave ***t*** both.
7:42 which of ***t*** will love him
7:44 with her tears and wiped ***t***
8:21 But He answered and said to ***t***,
8:22 His disciples. And He said to ***t***,
8:25 But He said to ***t***,
8:31 that He would not command ***t*** to
8:32 Him that He would permit ***t*** to
8:32 He would permit them to enter ***t***.
8:32 enter them. And He permitted ***t***.
8:34 When those who fed ***t*** saw what
8:36 also who had seen it told ***t***
8:37 asked Him to depart from ***t***,
8:54 But He put ***t*** all outside,
8:56 but He charged ***t*** to tell no one
9: 1 disciples together and gave ***t***
9: 2 He sent ***t*** to preach the kingdom
9: 3 And He said to ***t***,
9: 5 feet as a testimony against ***t***.
9:10 Then He took ***t*** and went aside
9:11 and He received ***t*** and spoke to
9:11 He received them and spoke to ***t***
9:13 But He said to ***t***,
9:13 You give ***t*** something to eat."
9:14 Make ***t*** sit down in groups of
9:15 and made ***t*** all sit down.
9:16 heaven, He blessed and broke ***t***,
9:16 and gave ***t*** to the disciples to
9:17 fragments were taken up by ***t***.
9:18 joined Him, and He asked ***t***,
9:20 He said to ***t***, "But who do you
9:21 warned and commanded ***t*** to tell
9:23 Then He said to ***t*** all, "If
9:34 a cloud came and overshadowed ***t***;
9:45 and it was hidden from ***t*** so
9:46 Then a dispute arose among ***t*** as
9:46 among them as to which of ***t***
9:48 and said to ***t***, "Whoever
9:54 down from heaven and consume ***t***,
9:55 But He turned and rebuked ***t***,
9:56 men's lives but to save ***t***.
9:61 but let me first go and bid ***t***
10: 1 and sent ***t*** two by two before
10: 2 Then He said to ***t***,
10: 9 the sick there, and say to ***t***,
10:18 And He said to ***t***,
10:21 and prudent and revealed ***t*** to
10:35 gave ***t*** to the innkeeper,
11: 2 So He said to ***t***,
11: 5 And He said to ***t***,
11:15 But some of ***t*** said, "He casts
11:17 their thoughts, said to ***t***:
11:19 by whom do your sons cast ***t***
11:31 this generation and condemn ***t***,
11:44 and the men who walk over ***t***
11:44 over them are not aware of ***t***.
11:47 and your fathers killed ***t***.
11:48 for they indeed killed ***t***,
11:49 I will send ***t*** prophets and
11:49 and some of ***t*** they will kill
11:53 as He said these things to ***t***,
12: 6 And not one of ***t*** is forgotten
12:15 And He said to ***t***,
12:16 Then He spoke a parable to ***t***,
12:24 nor barn; and God feeds ***t***.
12:37 he will gird himself and have ***t***
12:37 eat, and will come and serve ***t***.
12:38 and find ***t*** so, blessed are
12:42 to give ***t*** their portion of
13: 2 Jesus answered and said to ***t***,
13: 4 in Siloam fell and killed ***t***,
13:14 come and be healed on ***t***,
13:23 are saved?" And He said to ***t***,
13:32 And He said to ***t***,
14: 5 Then He answered ***t***,
14: 7 the best places, saying to ***t***:
14:19 and I am going to test ***t***.
14:23 and compel ***t*** to come in, that
14:25 And He turned and said to ***t***,
15: 2 sinners and eats with ***t***.
15: 3 So He spoke this parable to ***t***,
15: 4 sheep, if he loses one of ***t***,
15: 6 and neighbors, saying to ***t***,
15:12 And the younger of ***t*** said to
15:12 So he divided to ***t*** his
16:15 And He said to ***t***,
16:28 that he may testify to ***t***,
16:29 let ***t*** hear them.'
16:29 the prophets; let them hear ***t***.
16:30 but if one goes to ***t*** from the
17:14 So when He saw ***t***,
17:14 when He saw them, He said to ***t***,
17:15 And one of ***t***, when he saw
17:20 He answered ***t*** and said, "The
17:23 there!' Do not go after ***t*** or
17:23 not go after them or follow ***t***.
17:27 the flood came and destroyed ***t***
17:29 from heaven and destroyed ***t***
17:31 let him not come down to take ***t***
17:37 Lord?" So He said to ***t***,
18: 1 Then He spoke a parable to ***t***,
18: 7 though He bears long with ***t***?
18: 8 tell you that He will avenge ***t***
18:15 to Him that He might touch ***t***;
18:15 saw it, they rebuked ***t***.
18:16 But Jesus called ***t*** to Him and
18:16 come to Me, and do not forbid ***t***;
18:29 So He said to ***t***,
18:31 the twelve aside and said to ***t***,
18:34 this saying was hidden from ***t***,
19:13 delivered to ***t*** ten minas,
19:13 them ten minas, and said to ***t***,
19:27 did not want me to reign over ***t***,
19:27 and slay ***t*** before me.'"
19:32 it just as He had said to ***t***.
19:33 the owners of it said to ***t***,
19:40 But He answered and said to ***t***,
19:46 saying to ***t***, "It is written,
20: 3 But He answered and said to ***t***,
20: 8 And Jesus said to ***t***,
20:15 owner of the vineyard do to ***t***?
20:17 Then He looked at ***t*** and said,
20:19 spoken this parable against ***t***.
20:23 their craftiness, and said to ***t***,

20:25 And He said to ***t***,
20:34 Jesus answered and said to ***t***,
20:41 And He said to ***t***,
21: 8 Therefore do not go after ***t***.
21:10 Then He said to ***t***,
21:26 men's hearts failing ***t*** from fear
21:29 Then He spoke to ***t*** a parable:
22: 4 how he might betray Him to ***t***.
22: 6 opportunity to betray Him to ***t***
22:10 And He said to ***t***,
22:13 it just as He had said to ***t***,
22:15 Then He said to ***t***,
22:19 broke it, and gave it to ***t***,
22:23 which of ***t*** it was who would do
22:24 was also a dispute among ***t***,
22:24 as to which of ***t*** should be
22:25 And He said to ***t***,
22:25 exercise lordship over ***t***,
22:25 who exercise authority over ***t***
22:35 And He said to ***t***,
22:36 Then He said to ***t***,
22:38 two swords." And He said to ***t***,
22:40 came to the place, He said to ***t***,
22:41 And He was withdrawn from ***t***
22:45 He found ***t*** sleeping from
22:46 Then He said to ***t***,
22:47 went before ***t*** and drew near to
22:50 And one of ***t*** struck the servant
22:55 together, Peter sat among ***t***.
22:58 and said, "You also are of ***t***.
22:67 tell us." But He said to ***t***,
22:70 Son of God?" So He said to ***t***,
23: 1 Then the whole multitude of ***t***
23:14 said to ***t***, "You have brought
23:17 for him to release one to ***t*** at
23:20 Jesus, again called out to ***t***.
23:22 Then he said to ***t*** the third
23:25 And he released to ***t*** the one
23:28 But Jesus, turning to ***t***,
23:34 Jesus said, "Father, forgive ***t***,
23:35 But even the rulers with ***t***
24: 1 certain other women with ***t***,
24: 4 two men stood by ***t*** in shining
24: 5 to the earth, they said to ***t***,
24:10 and the other women with ***t***,
24:11 And their words seemed to ***t*** like
24:11 and they did not believe ***t***.
24:13 two of ***t*** were traveling that
24:15 drew near and went with ***t***.
24:17 And He said to ***t***,
24:19 And He said to ***t***,
24:25 Then He said to ***t***,
24:27 He expounded to ***t*** in all the
24:29 And He went in to stay with ***t***.
24:30 as He sat at the table with ***t***,
24:30 and broke it, and gave it to ***t***.
24:33 and those who were with ***t***
24:35 and how He was known to ***t*** in
24:36 Himself stood in the midst of ***t***,
24:36 midst of them, and said to ***t***,
24:38 And He said to ***t***,
24:40 He showed ***t*** His hands and His
24:41 and marveled, He said to ***t***,
24:44 Then He said to ***t***,
24:46 Then He said to ***t***,
24:50 And He led ***t*** out as far as
24:50 up His hands and blessed ***t***.
24:51 to pass, while He blessed ***t***,
24:51 that He was parted from ***t*** and
Jn 1:12 to ***t*** He gave the right to
1:26 John answered ***t***,
1:38 and seeing ***t*** following, said to
1:38 them following, said to ***t***,
1:39 He said to ***t***, "Come and see."
2: 7 Jesus said to ***t***,
2: 7 And they filled ***t*** up to the
2: 8 And He said to ***t***,
2:15 He drove ***t*** all out of the
2:19 Jesus answered and said to ***t***,
2:22 that He had said this to ***t***;
2:24 did not commit Himself to ***t***,
3:22 and there He remained with ***t***
4:32 But He said to ***t***,
4:34 Jesus said to ***t***,
4:40 they urged Him to stay with ***t***;
4:52 Then he inquired of ***t*** the hour
5:11 He answered ***t***, "He who made
5:17 But Jesus answered ***t***,
5:19 Jesus answered and said to ***t***,
5:21 the dead and gives life to ***t***,
5:39 for in ***t*** you think you have
6: 7 bread is not sufficient for ***t***,
6: 7 that every one of ***t*** may have a
6:11 given thanks He distributed ***t***
6:13 Therefore they gathered ***t*** up,
6:17 and Jesus had not come to ***t***.
6:20 But He said to ***t***,
6:26 Jesus answered ***t*** and said,
6:29 Jesus answered and said to ***t***,
6:31 He gave ***t*** bread from heaven
6:32 Then Jesus said to ***t***,
6:35 And Jesus said to ***t***,
6:43 answered and said to ***t***,
6:53 Then Jesus said to ***t***,
6:61 about this, He said to ***t***,
6:70 Jesus answered ***t***,
7: 6 Then Jesus said to ***t***,
7: 9 He had said these things to ***t***,
7:16 Jesus answered ***t*** and said, "My
7:21 Jesus answered and said to ***t***,
7:25 Now some of ***t*** from Jerusalem
7:33 Then Jesus said to ***t***,
7:44 Now some of ***t*** wanted to take
7:45 and Pharisees, who said to ***t***,
7:47 Then the Pharisees answered ***t***,
7:50 being one of ***t***) said to them,
7:50 being one of them) said to ***t***,
8: 2 and He sat down and taught ***t***.
8: 7 raised Himself up and said to ***t***,
8:12 Then Jesus spoke to ***t*** again,
8:14 Jesus answered and said to ***t***,
8:21 Then Jesus said to ***t*** again, "I
8:23 And He said to ***t***,
8:25 are You?" And Jesus said to ***t***,
8:27 understand that He spoke to ***t***
8:28 Then Jesus said to ***t***,
8:34 Jesus answered ***t***,
8:39 our father." Jesus said to ***t***,
8:42 Jesus said to ***t***,
8:58 Jesus said to ***t***,
8:59 going through the midst of ***t***,
9:15 his sight. He said to ***t***,
9:16 there was a division among ***t***.
9:19 And they asked ***t***,
9:20 His parents answered ***t*** and said,
9:27 He answered ***t***, "I told you
9:30 The man answered and said to ***t***,
9:41 Jesus said to ***t***,
10: 3 own sheep by name and leads ***t***
10: 4 his own sheep, he goes before ***t***;
10: 6 the things which He spoke to ***t***.
10: 7 Then Jesus said to ***t*** again,
10: 8 but the sheep did not hear ***t***.
10:12 the sheep and scatters ***t***.
10:16 ***t*** also I must bring, and they
10:20 And many of ***t*** said, "He has a
10:25 Jesus answered ***t***,
10:27 hear My voice, and I know ***t***,
10:28 'And I give ***t*** eternal life,
10:28 neither shall anyone snatch ***t***
10:29 who has given ***t*** to Me, is
10:29 and no one is able to snatch ***t***
10:32 Jesus answered ***t***,
10:34 Jesus answered ***t***,
10:35 If He called ***t*** gods, to whom the
11:11 and after that He said to ***t***,
11:14 Then Jesus said to ***t*** plainly,
11:19 to comfort ***t*** concerning their
11:37 And some of ***t*** said, "Could not
11:44 with a cloth. Jesus said to ***t***,
11:46 But some of ***t*** went away to the
11:46 to the Pharisees and told ***t***
11:49 And one of ***t***, Caiaphas,
11:49 priest that year, said to ***t***,
12:23 But Jesus answered ***t***,
12:35 Then Jesus said to ***t***,
12:36 departed, and was hidden from ***t***.
12:37 had done so many signs before ***t***,
12:40 So that I should heal ***t***.
13: 1 He loved ***t*** to the end.
13: 5 and to wipe ***t*** with the towel
13:12 sat down again, He said to ***t***,
13:17 blessed are you if you do ***t***.
14:21 has My commandments and keeps ***t***,
15: 6 and they gather ***t*** and throw
15: 6 they gather them and throw ***t***
15:22 I had not come and spoken to ***t***,
15:24 If I had not done among ***t*** the
16: 4 remember that I told you of ***t***.
16:12 but you cannot bear ***t*** now.
16:19 to ask Him, and He said to ***t***,
16:31 Jesus answered ***t***,
17: 6 You gave ***t*** to Me, and they have
17: 8 For I have given to ***t*** the words
17: 8 and they have received ***t***,
17: 9 'I pray for ***t***. I do not pray
17:10 Mine, and I am glorified in ***t***.
17:12 While I was with ***t*** in the world,
17:12 I kept ***t*** in Your name.
17:12 and none of ***t*** is lost except
17:14 'I have given ***t*** Your word;
17:14 and the world has hated ***t***
17:15 not pray that You should take ***t***
17:15 but that You should keep ***t*** from
17:17 Sanctify ***t*** by Your truth. Your
17:18 I also have sent ***t*** into the
17:22 You gave Me I have given ***t***,
17:23 'I in ***t***, and You in Me;
17:23 and have loved ***t*** as You have
17:26 And I have declared to ***t*** Your
17:26 which You loved Me may be in ***t***,
17:26 Me may be in them, and I in ***t***.
18: 4 went forward and said to ***t***,
18: 5 of Nazareth." Jesus said to ***t***,
18: 5 betrayed Him, also stood with ***t***.
18: 6 Now when He said to ***t***,
18: 7 Then He asked ***t*** again, "Whom
18:18 And Peter stood with ***t*** and
18:21 have heard Me what I said to ***t***.
18:29 Pilate then went out to ***t*** and
18:31 Then Pilate said to ***t***,
18:38 to the Jews, and said to ***t***,
19: 4 went out again, and said to ***t***,
19: 5 And Pilate said to ***t***,
19: 6 Him!" Pilate said to ***t***,
19:15 Crucify Him!" Pilate said to ***t***,
19:16 Then he delivered Him to ***t*** to be
19:24 My garments among ***t***,
20: 2 whom Jesus loved, and said to ***t***,
20:13 you weeping?" She said to ***t***,
20:17 go to My brethren and say to ***t***,
20:19 in the midst, and said to ***t***,
20:20 He showed ***t*** His hands and His
20:21 So Jesus said to ***t*** again,
20:22 said this, He breathed on ***t***,
20:22 on them, and said to ***t***,
20:23 of any, they are forgiven ***t***;
20:24 was not with ***t*** when Jesus came.
20:25 the Lord." So he said to ***t***,
20:26 again inside, and Thomas with ***t***.
21: 3 Simon Peter said to ***t***,
21: 5 Then Jesus said to ***t***,
21: 6 And He said to ***t***,
21:10 Jesus said to ***t***,
21:12 Jesus said to ***t***,
21:13 took the bread and gave it to ***t***,
Acts 1: 3 being seen by ***t*** during forty
1: 4 assembled together with ***t***,
1: 4 He commanded ***t*** not to depart
1: 7 And He said to ***t***,
1:10 two men stood by ***t*** in white
2: 3 Then there appeared to ***t*** divided
2: 3 and one sat upon each of ***t***.
2: 4 as the Spirit gave ***t*** utterance.
2: 6 because everyone heard ***t*** speak
2:11 we hear ***t*** speaking in our own
2:14 raised his voice and said to ***t***,
2:38 Then Peter said to ***t***,
2:40 he testified and exhorted ***t***,
2:41 souls were added to ***t***.
2:45 and divided ***t*** among all,
3: 5 So he gave ***t*** his attention,
3: 5 to receive something from ***t***.
3: 8 and entered the temple with ***t***—
3:11 the people ran together to ***t***
4: 1 and the Sadducees came upon ***t***,
4: 3 And they laid hands on ***t***,
4: 3 and put ***t*** in custody until the
4: 7 And when they had set ***t*** in the
4: 8 with the Holy Spirit, said to ***t***,
4:14 had been healed standing with ***t***,
4:15 But when they had commanded ***t*** to
4:16 has been done through ***t*** is
4:17 let us severely threaten ***t***,
4:18 And they called ***t*** and commanded
4:18 called them and commanded ***t***
4:19 and John answered and said to ***t***,
4:21 they had further threatened ***t***,
4:21 they let ***t*** go, finding no way
4:21 finding no way of punishing ***t***,
4:23 and elders had said to ***t***.
4:24 the sea, and all that is in ***t***,
4:33 And great grace was upon ***t*** all.
4:34 Nor was there anyone among ***t*** who
4:34 of lands or houses sold ***t***,
4:35 and laid ***t*** at the apostles'
5:13 none of the rest dared join ***t***,
5:13 but the people esteemed ***t***
5:15 into the streets and laid ***t***
5:15 by might fall on some of ***t***.
5:18 on the apostles and put ***t*** in
5:19 the prison doors and brought ***t***
5:21 sent to the prison to have ***t***
5:22 came and did not find ***t*** in the
5:23 the doors; but when we opened ***t***,
5:25 So one came and told ***t***,
5:26 with the officers and brought ***t***
5:27 And when they had brought ***t***,
5:27 they set ***t*** before the council.
5:27 And the high priest asked ***t***,
5:33 furious and plotted to kill ***t***.
5:34 and commanded ***t*** to put the
5:35 And he said to ***t***:
5:38 away from these men and let ***t***
5:40 for the apostles and beaten ***t***,
5:40 name of Jesus, and let ***t*** go.
6: 6 prayed, they laid hands on ***t***.
7: 6 and that they would bring ***t***
7: 6 into bondage and oppress ***t***
7:19 making ***t*** expose their babies,
7:24 And seeing one of ***t*** suffer
7:25 that God would deliver ***t*** by
7:26 day he appeared to two of ***t*** as
7:26 and tried to reconcile ***t***,
7:34 come down to deliver ***t***.
7:36 He brought ***t*** out, after he had
7:42 Then God turned and gave ***t*** up to
7:60 do not charge ***t*** with this
8: 3 committing ***t*** to prison.
8: 5 and preached Christ to ***t***.
8:11 him because he had astonished ***t***
8:14 they sent Peter and John to ***t***,
8:15 prayed for ***t*** that they might
8:16 He had fallen upon none of ***t***.
8:17 Then they laid hands on ***t***,
8:18 he offered ***t*** money,
9: 2 he might bring ***t*** bound to
9:21 so that he might bring ***t*** bound
9:27 And he declared to ***t*** how he had
9:28 So he was with ***t*** at Jerusalem,
9:38 not to delay in coming to ***t***.
9:39 Peter arose and went with ***t***.
9:39 had made while she was with ***t***.
9:40 But Peter put ***t*** all out, and
10: 8 all these things to ***t***,
10: 8 he sent ***t*** to Joppa.
10:20 go down and go with ***t***,
10:20 nothing; for I have sent ***t***.
10:23 Then he invited ***t*** in and lodged
10:23 invited them in and lodged ***t***.
10:23 next day Peter went away with ***t***,
10:24 Now Cornelius was waiting for ***t***,
10:28 Then he said to ***t***,
10:46 For they heard ***t*** speak with
10:48 And he commanded ***t*** to be
11: 3 men and ate with ***t***!"

11: 4 But Peter explained it to **t** in
11:12 the Spirit told me to go with **t**,
11:15 the Holy Spirit fell upon **t**,
11:17 If therefore God gave **t** the same
11:20 But some of **t** were men from
11:21 the hand of the Lord was with **t**,
11:23 and encouraged **t** all that with
11:28 Then one of **t**, named Agabus,
12:10 which opened to **t** of its own
12:17 But motioning to **t** with his hand
12:17 he declared to **t** how the Lord
12:21 throne and gave an oration to **t**.
12:25 and they also took with **t** John
13: 2 work to which I have called **t**.
13: 3 and prayed, and laid hands on **t**,
13: 3 they sent **t** away.
13: 8 name is translated) withstood **t**,
13:13 and John, departing from **t**,
13:15 of the synagogue sent to **t**,
13:17 an uplifted arm He brought **t**
13:19 He distributed their land to **t**
13:20 After that He gave **t** judges for
13:21 so God gave **t** Saul the son of
13:22 He raised up for **t** David as
13:27 have fulfilled **t** in condemning
13:42 words might be preached to **t**
13:43 Barnabas, who, speaking to **t**,
13:43 persuaded **t** to continue in the
13:50 and expelled **t** from their
13:51 dust from their feet against **t**,
14: 5 rulers, to abuse and stone **t**,
14:15 and all things that are in **t**,
14:18 from sacrificing to **t**.
14:22 exhorting **t** to continue in the
14:23 they commended **t** to the Lord in
14:27 all that God had done with **t**,
15: 2 dissension and dispute with **t**,
15: 2 and certain others of **t** should
15: 4 things that God had done with **t**.
15: 5 is necessary to circumcise **t**,
15: 5 and to command **t** to keep the
15: 7 Peter rose up and said to **t**:
15: 8 acknowledged **t** by giving them
15: 8 acknowledged them by giving **t**
15: 9 no distinction between us and **t**,
15:12 God had worked through **t** among
15:14 the Gentiles to take out of **t**
15:20 but that we write to **t** to
15:23 They wrote this letter by **t**:
15:37 was determined to take with **t**
15:38 they should not take with **t**
15:38 one who had departed from **t** in
15:38 and had not gone with **t** to the
16: 4 they delivered to **t** the decrees
16: 7 but the Spirit did not permit **t**.
16:10 us to preach the gospel to **t**.
16:19 Paul and Silas and dragged **t**
16:20 And they brought **t** to the
16:22 rose up together against **t**;
16:22 their clothes and commanded **t**
16:23 they had laid many stripes on **t**,
16:23 they threw **t** into prison,
16:23 the jailer to keep **t** securely.
16:24 he put **t** into the inner prison
16:25 prisoners were listening to **t**.
16:30 And he brought **t** out and said,
16:33 And he took **t** the same hour of
16:34 Now when he had brought **t** into
16:34 his house, he set food before **t**;
16:37 But Paul said to **t**,
16:37 No indeed! Let **t** come
16:39 they came and pleaded with **t**
16:39 with them and brought **t** out,
16:39 and asked **t** to depart from the
16:40 they encouraged **t** and departed.
17: 2 as his custom was, went in to **t**,
17: 2 three Sabbaths reasoned with **t**
17: 4 And some of **t** were persuaded;
17: 5 and sought to bring **t** out to
17: 6 But when they did not find **t**,
17: 7 "Jason has harbored **t**,
17: 9 and the rest, they let **t** go.
17:12 Therefore many of **t** believed,
17:16 Now while Paul waited for **t** at
17:18 because he preached to **t**
17:33 So Paul departed from among **t**.
17:34 among **t** Dionysius the
17:34 Damaris, and others with **t**.
18: 2 from Rome); and he came to **t**.
18: 3 he stayed with **t** and worked;
18: 6 his garments and said to **t**,
18:11 the word of God among **t**.
18:16 And he drove **t** from the judgment
18:19 and left **t** there; but he
18:20 to stay a longer time with **t**,
18:21 but took leave of **t**,
19: 2 he said to **t**, "Did you
19: 3 And he said to **t**,
19: 6 when Paul had laid hands on **t**,
19: 6 the Holy Spirit came upon **t**,
19: 9 he departed from **t** and withdrew
19:12 and the diseases left **t** and the
19:12 the evil spirits went out of **t**.
19:16 the evil spirit was leaped on **t**,
19:16 leaped on them, overpowered **t**,
19:16 them, and prevailed against **t**,
19:17 and fear fell on **t** all, and the
19:19 books together and burned **t**
19:19 they counted up the value of **t**,
19:25 He called **t** together with the
19:32 and most of **t** did not know why
19:38 Let **t** bring charges against one

20: 1 to himself, embraced **t**,
20: 2 that region and encouraged **t**
20: 6 and in five days joined **t** at
20: 7 spoke to **t** and continued his
20:18 had come to him, he said to **t**:
20:36 he knelt down and prayed with **t**
21: 1 when we had departed from **t**
21: 7 and stayed with **t** one day.
21:16 with us and brought with **t** a
21:19 When he had greeted **t**,
21:24 Take **t** and be purified with
21:24 them and be purified with **t**,
21:26 having been purified with **t**,
21:26 be made for each one of **t**.
21:32 centurions, and ran down to **t**.
21:40 he spoke to **t** in the Hebrew
22: 2 they heard that he spoke to **t**
22:30 Paul down and set him before **t**.
23:10 might be pulled to pieces by **t**,
23:10 take him by force from among **t**,
23:21 "But do not yield to **t**,
23:21 for more than forty of **t** lie in
23:27 and was about to be killed by **t**.
24:21 I cried out, standing among **t**,
25: 6 when he had remained among **t**
25:11 no one can deliver me to **t**.
25:16 To **t** I answered, 'It is not the
26:10 I cast my vote against **t**.
26:11 And I punished **t** often in every
26:11 synagogue and compelled **t** to
26:11 exceedingly enraged against **t**,
26:11 I persecuted **t** even to foreign
26:18 in order to turn **t** from
26:30 and those who sat with **t**;
27: 9 already over, Paul advised **t**,
27:21 Paul stood in the midst of **t**
27:33 Paul implored **t** all to take
27:35 to God in the presence of **t**
27:40 let go the anchors and left **t**
27:42 lest any of **t** should swim away
27:43 kept **t** from their purpose,
28: 3 a bundle of sticks and laid **t**
28:14 and were invited to stay with **t**
28:15 and Three Inns. When Paul saw **t**,
28:17 had come together, he said to **t**:
28:23 persuading **t** concerning Jesus
28:27 So that I should heal **t**.
Rom 1:19 known of God is manifest in **t**,
1:19 for God has shown it to **t**.
1:24 Therefore God also gave **t** up to
1:26 For this reason God gave **t** up to
1:28 God gave **t** over to a debased
1:32 approve of those who practice **t**.
2:15 accusing or else excusing **t**)
3: 2 way! Chiefly because to **t** were
4:11 might be imputed to **t** also,
9:25 I will call **t** My people,
9:26 where it was said to **t**,
10: 2 For I bear **t** witness that they
10: 5 things shall live by **t**.
11: 8 God has given **t** a spirit
11: 9 and a recompense to **t**.
11:11 to provoke **t** to jealousy,
11:14 my flesh and save some of **t**.
11:17 tree, were grafted in among **t**,
11:17 and with **t** became a partaker of
11:23 for God is able to graft **t** in
11:27 is My covenant with **t**,
11:32 For God has committed **t** all to
12: 6 given to us, let us use **t**:
15:27 It pleased **t** indeed, and they
15:27 duty is also to minister to **t**
15:28 this and have sealed to **t** this
16:14 and the brethren who are with **t**.
16:15 all the saints who are with **t**.
16:17 which you learned, and avoid **t**.
1 Cor 2:10 But God has revealed **t** to us
2:14 to him; nor can he know **t**,
6:13 God will destroy both it and **t**.
6:15 members of Christ and make **t**
7: 8 It is good for **t** if they remain
7: 9 let **t** marry. For it is better
7:36 does not sin; let **t** marry.
10: 4 spiritual Rock that followed **t**,
10: 5 But with most of **t** God was not
10: 7 idolaters as were some of **t**.
10: 8 as some of **t** did, and in one
10: 9 as some of **t** also tempted,
10:10 as some of **t** also complained,
10:11 all these things happened to **t**
11: 2 just as I delivered **t** to you.
12:18 set the members, each one of **t**,
14:10 and none of **t** is without
14:35 let **t** ask their own husbands at
2 Cor 2:13 but taking my leave of **t**,
4: 4 image of God, should shine on **t**.
5:15 but for Him who died for **t** and
5:19 imputing their trespasses to **t**,
6:16 I will dwell in **t** And
6:16 in them And walk among **t**.
6:17 'Come out from among **t** And
8:22 And we have sent with **t** our
8:24 Therefore show to **t**,
9:13 your liberal sharing with **t**
11: 8 taking wages from **t** to
Gal 2: 2 and communicated to **t** that
2:14 I said to Peter before **t** all,
3:10 book of the law, to do **t**.
3:12 the man who does **t** shall
3:12 does them shall live by **t**.
4:15 out your own eyes and given **t**
4:17 that you may be zealous for **t**.

6:16 peace and mercy be upon **t**,
Eph 2:10 that we should walk in **t**.
2:16 and that He might reconcile **t**
4:18 of the ignorance that is in **t**,
5: 7 do not be partakers with **t**.
5:11 darkness, but rather expose **t**.
5:12 things which are done by **t** in
6: 4 but bring **t** up in the training
6: 9 do the same things to **t**,
Phil 1:28 which is to **t** a proof of
3: 8 and count **t** as rubbish, that I
Col 1:27 To **t** God willed to make known
2:15 He made a public spectacle of **t**,
2:15 triumphing over **t** in it.
3: 7 once walked when you lived in **t**.
3:19 and do not be bitter toward **t**.
1 Th 2:16 but wrath has come upon **t** to
4:17 be caught up together with **t**
5: 3 sudden destruction comes upon **t**,
5:13 and to esteem **t** very highly in
2 Th 2:11 for this reason God will send **t**
1 Tim 1:18 that by **t** you may wage the good
3:10 then let **t** serve as deacons,
4:15 give yourself entirely to **t**,
4:16 to the doctrine. Continue in **t**,
5: 4 let **t** first learn to show piety
5:16 let **t** relieve them, and do not
5:16 has widows, let them relieve **t**,
5:24 preceding **t** to judgment, but
6: 2 let **t** not despise them because
6: 2 let them not despise **t** because
6: 2 but rather serve **t** because
6:18 Let **t** do good, that they be
2 Tim 2:14 Remind **t** of these things,
2:14 charging **t** before the Lord not
2:25 if God perhaps will grant **t**
3:11 And out of **t** all the Lord
3:14 from whom you have learned **t**,
4:16 May it not be charged against **t**.
Titus 1:12 One of **t**, a prophet
1:13 Therefore rebuke **t** sharply,
3: 1 Remind **t** to be subject to rulers
Heb 1:12 a cloak You will fold **t**
2:11 He is not ashamed to call **t**
4: 2 preached to us as well as to **t**;
4: 2 they heard did not profit **t**,
4: 8 For if Joshua had given **t** rest,
6: 6 to renew **t** again to repentance,
6:16 for confirmation is for **t** an
7: 6 is not derived from **t** received
7: 8 but there he receives **t**,
7:25 to make intercession for **t**.
8: 8 Because finding fault with **t**,
8: 9 in the day when I took **t**
8: 9 by the hand to lead **t**
8: 9 and I disregarded **t**,
8:10 in their mind and write **t**
8:11 None of **t** shall teach his
8:11 from the least of **t** to
8:11 them to the greatest of **t**.
10: 8 nor had pleasure in **t**"
10:16 that I will make with **t**
10:16 minds I will write **t**,
11:13 but having seen **t** afar off were
11:13 them afar off were assured of **t**,
11:13 embraced **t** and confessed that
11:16 He has prepared a city for **t**.
11:28 the firstborn should touch **t**.
12: 9 and we paid **t** respect. Shall
12:10 us as seemed best to **t**,
12:19 word should not be spoken to **t**
13: 3 prisoners as if chained with **t**—
13: 9 who have been occupied with **t**.
13:17 Let **t** do so with joy and not
Jas 2:16 and one of you says to **t**,
2:16 but you do not give **t** the
2:25 the messengers and sent **t** out
5:11 Indeed we count **t** blessed who
5:14 and let **t** pray over him,
1 Pe 1:11 Spirit of Christ who was in **t**
1:12 To **t** it was revealed that, not
3: 7 dwell with **t** with
4: 4 that you do not run with **t** in
2 Pe 2: 1 denying the Lord who bought **t**,
2: 4 but cast **t** down to hell and
2: 4 down to hell and delivered **t**
2: 6 condemned **t** to destruction,
2: 6 making **t** an example to those
2: 8 righteous man, dwelling among **t**,
2:11 a reviling accusation against **t**
2:19 While they promise **t** liberty,
2:20 they are again entangled in **t**
2:20 the latter end is worse for **t**
2:21 it would have been better for **t**
2:21 holy commandment delivered to **t**.
2:22 But it has happened to **t**
3:16 speaking in **t** of these things,
1 Jn 2:19 that none of **t** were of us.
4: 4 children, and have overcome **t**,
4: 5 world, and the world hears **t**.
3 Jn 6 If you send **t** forward on their
9 to have the preeminence among **t**,
10 putting **t** out of the church.
Jude 7 and the cities around **t** in a
11 Woe to **t**! For they have gone in
15 all who are ungodly among **t** of
23 pulling **t** out of the fire,
Rev 2: 2 and have found **t** liars;
2:16 and will fight against **t** with
2:27 He shall rule **t** with a rod
3: 9 indeed I will make **t** come and
5:11 and the number of **t** was ten

5:13 the sea, and all that are in ***t***,
6: 8 And power was given to ***t*** over a
6:11 robe was given to each of ***t***;
6:11 and it was said to ***t*** that they
7:14 washed their robes and made ***t***
7:15 the throne will dwell among ***t***.
7:16 the sun shall not strike ***t***,
7:17 of the throne will shepherd ***t***
7:17 will shepherd them and lead ***t***
8: 2 and to ***t*** were given seven
8:12 so that a third of ***t*** were
9: 3 And to ***t*** was given power,
9: 5 not given authority to kill ***t***,
9: 5 but to torment ***t*** for five
9: 6 and death will flee from ***t***.
9:11 And they had as king over ***t*** the
9:16 I heard the number of ***t***.
9:17 those who sat on ***t*** had
9:19 and with ***t*** they do harm.
10: 4 uttered, and do not write ***t***.
11: 5 And if anyone wants to harm ***t***,
11: 5 And if anyone wants to harm ***t***,
11: 6 power over waters to turn ***t*** to
11: 7 pit will make war against ***t***,
11: 7 overcome ***t***, and kill them.
11: 7 them, overcome them, and kill ***t***.
11:10 the earth will rejoice over ***t***,
11:11 of life from God entered ***t***,
11:11 fear fell on those who saw ***t***.
11:12 voice from heaven saying to ***t***,
11:12 cloud, and their enemies saw ***t***.
12: 4 stars of heaven and threw ***t*** to
12: 8 nor was a place found for ***t*** in
12:10 who accused ***t*** before our God
12:12 and you who dwell in ***t***! Woe to
13: 7 the saints and to overcome ***t***.
14: 9 Then a third angel followed ***t***,
14:13 and their works follow ***t***.
15: 1 for in ***t*** the wrath of God is
16: 6 And You have given ***t*** blood to
16:14 to gather ***t*** to the battle of
16:16 And they gathered ***t*** together to
17:14 and the Lamb will overcome ***t***,
18:14 and you shall find ***t*** no more at
19:15 And He Himself will rule ***t*** with
19:18 and of those who sit on ***t***,
20: 4 saw thrones, and they sat on ***t***,
20: 4 and judgment was committed to ***t***.
20: 8 to gather ***t*** together to battle,
20: 9 out of heaven and devoured ***t***.
20:10 The devil, who deceived ***t***,
20:11 there was found no place for ***t***.
20:13 up the dead who were in ***t***.
21: 3 and He will dwell with ***t***,
21: 3 God Himself will be with ***t*** and
21:12 gates, and names written on ***t***,
21:14 and on ***t*** were the names of the
22: 5 for the Lord God gives ***t*** light.

THEME (1/1)

Ps 45: 1 is overflowing with a good ***t***;

THEMSELVES (316/295) See APPENDIX

THEN (3990/3913) See APPENDIX

THEOPHILUS (2/2)

Lk 1: 3 account, most excellent ***T***,
Acts 1: 1 The former account I made, O ***T***,

THERE (2223/2002) See APPENDIX

THEREAFTER (3/3)

Lev 22:27 and from the eighth day and ***t***
2 Chr 32:23 in the sight of all nations ***t***.
Ezek 43:27 be, on the eighth day and ***t***,

THEREBY (5/5)

Lev 15:32 emits semen and is unclean ***t***,
22: 9 they bear sin for it and die ***t***,
Job 22:21 ***T*** good will come to you.
Eph 2:16 ***t*** putting to death the enmity.
1 Pe 2: 2 the word, that you may grow ***t***,

THEREFORE (1356/1340) See APPENDIX

THEREIN (2/2) See APPENDIX

Ps 24: 1 world and those who dwell ***t***.
Jer 50: 3 And no one shall dwell ***t***.

THESE (1285/1210) See APPENDIX

THESSALONIANS (3/3)

Acts 20: 4 and Secundus of the ***T***,
1 Th 1: 1 To the church of the ***T*** in God
2 Th 1: 1 To the church of the ***T*** in God

THESSALONICA (6/6)

Acts 17: 1 and Apollonia, they came to ***T***,
17:11 fair-minded than those in ***T***,
17:13 But when the Jews from ***T*** learned
27: 2 Aristarchus, a Macedonian of ***T***,
Phil 4:16 For even in ***T*** you sent aid once
2 Tim 4:10 world, and has departed for ***T***—

THEUDAS (1/1)

Acts 5:36 For some time ago ***T*** rose up,

THEY (6961/5169) See APPENDIX

THICK (32/32) THICKER

Ex 8:24 ***T*** swarms of flies came into
10:22 and there was ***t*** darkness in all
19: 9 I come to you in the ***t*** cloud,
19:16 and a ***t*** cloud on the mountain;
20:21 Moses drew near the ***t*** darkness
Deut 4:11 cloud, and ***t*** darkness.
5:22 and the ***t*** darkness, with a loud
32:15 You grew fat, you grew ***t***,
2 Sam 18: 9 mule went under the ***t*** boughs
22:12 Dark waters and ***t*** clouds of
1 Ki 7:26 It was a handbreadth ***t***;
2 Ki 8:15 that he took a ***t*** cloth
2 Chr 4: 5 It was a handbreadth ***t***;
Job 22:14 ***T*** clouds cover Him, so that He
26: 8 the water in His ***t*** clouds
37:11 He saturates the ***t*** clouds
38: 9 And ***t*** darkness its swaddling
Ps 18:11 dark waters And ***t*** clouds
18:12 His ***t*** clouds passed with
74: 5 lift up Axes among the ***t*** trees.
Isa 44:22 like a ***t*** cloud, your
Ezek 6:13 and under every ***t*** oak, wherever
8:11 and a ***t*** cloud of incense went
19:11 in stature above the ***t*** branches
20:28 the high hills and all the ***t*** trees
31: 3 its top was among the ***t*** boughs
31:10 and it set its top among the ***t***
31:14 nor set their tops among the ***t***
41:12 the building was five cubits ***t***
Joel 2: 2 A day of clouds and ***t*** darkness
Zeph 1:15 A day of clouds and ***t*** darkness
Zech 11: 2 For the ***t*** forest has come

THICKER (2/2) THICK

1 Ki 12:10 My little finger shall be ***t***
2 Chr 10:10 My little finger shall be ***t***

THICKET (2/2) THICKETS

Gen 22:13 him was a ram caught in a ***t***
Jer 4: 7 lion has come up from his ***t***,

THICKETS (4/4) THICKET

1 Sam 13: 6 the people hid in caves, in ***t***,
Isa 9:18 And kindle in the ***t*** of the
10:34 He will cut down the ***t*** of the
Jer 4:29 They shall go into ***t*** and climb

THICKLY (1/1)

Lk 11:29 the crowds were ***t*** gathered

THICKNESS (3/3)

Jer 52:21 and its ***t*** was four fingers;
Ezek 41: 9 The ***t*** of the outer wall of the
42:10 there were chambers in the ***t***

THIEF (25/25) THIEVES

Ex 22: 2 If the ***t*** is found breaking in,
22: 7 if the ***t*** is found, he shall pay
22: 8 If the ***t*** is not found, then the
Job 24:14 in the night he is like a ***t***.
30: 5 shouted at them as at a ***t***.
Ps 50:18 When you saw a ***t***,
Prov 6:30 People do not despise a ***t*** If
29:24 Whoever is a partner with a ***t***
Jer 2:26 As the ***t*** is ashamed when he is
Hos 7: 1 A ***t*** comes in; A band of
Joel 2: 9 enter at the windows like a ***t***.
Zech 5: 3 Every ***t*** shall be expelled,'
5: 4 shall enter the house of the ***t***
Mt 24:43 house had known what hour the ***t***
Lk 12:33 where no ***t*** approaches nor moth
12:39 house had known what hour the ***t***
Jn 10: 1 the same is a ***t*** and a robber.
10:10 The ***t*** does not come except to
12: 6 poor, but because he was a ***t***,
1 Th 5: 2 of the Lord so comes as a ***t*** in
5: 4 Day should overtake you as a ***t***.
1 Pe 4:15 you suffer as a murderer, a ***t***,
2 Pe 3:10 of the Lord will come as a ***t***
Rev 3: 3 I will come upon you as a ***t***,
16:15 "Behold, I am coming as a ***t***.

THIEVES (14/14) THIEF

Isa 1:23 And companions of ***t***;
Jer 7:11 become a den of ***t*** in your eyes?
48:27 Was he found among ***t***?
49: 9 If ***t*** by night, Would they not
Ob 5 If ***t*** had come to you,
Mt 6:19 and rust destroy and where ***t***
6:20 nor rust destroys and where ***t***
21:13 you have made it a 'den of ***t***.
Mk 11:17 you have made it a 'den of ***t***.
Lk 10:30 to Jericho, and fell among ***t***,
10:36 to him who fell among the ***t***?
19:46 you have made it a 'den of ***t***.
Jn 10: 8 who ever came before Me are ***t***
1 Cor 6:10 nor ***t***, nor covetous,

THIGH (29/29) THIGHS

Gen 24: 2 put your hand under my ***t***,
24: 9 put his hand under the ***t*** of
47:29 please put your hand under my ***t***,
Ex 29:22 the right ***t*** (for it is a ram
29:27 and the ***t*** of the heave offering
Lev 7:32 Also the right ***t*** you shall give
7:33 shall have the right ***t*** for his
7:34 of the wave offering and the ***t***
8:25 and their fat, and the right ***t***;
8:26 on the fat and on the right ***t***;
9:21 but the breasts and the right ***t***
10:14 of the wave offering and the ***t***
10:15 The ***t*** of the heave offering and
Num 5:21 when the LORD makes your ***t*** rot
5:22 your belly swell and your ***t***
5:27 her ***t*** will rot, and the woman
6:20 of the wave offering and the ***t***
18:18 the wave breast and the right ***t***
Judg 3:16 his clothes on his right ***t***.
3:21 the dagger from his right ***t***,
15: 8 So he attacked them hip and ***t***
1 Sam 9:24 So the cook took up the ***t*** with
Ps 45: 3 Gird Your sword upon Your ***t***,
Song 3: 8 man has his sword on his ***t***
Isa 47: 2 off the skirt, Uncover the ***t***,
Jer 31:19 I struck myself on the ***t***;
Ezek 21:12 Therefore strike your ***t***.
24: 4 The ***t*** and the shoulder.
Rev 19:16 has on His robe and on His ***t***

THIGHS (4/4) THIGH

Ex 28:42 reach from the waist to the ***t***.
Job 40:17 The sinews of his ***t*** are
Song 7: 1 The curves of your ***t*** are
Dan 2:32 its belly and ***t*** of bronze,

THIMNATHAH (KJV) See TIMNAH

THIN (7/7)

Gen 41: 6 seven ***t*** heads, blighted by the
41: 7 And the seven ***t*** heads devoured
41:23 seven heads, withered, ***t***,
41:24 And the ***t*** heads devoured the
41:27 And the seven ***t*** and ugly cows
Ex 39: 3 And they beat the gold into ***t***
Lev 13:30 and there is in it ***t*** yellow

THING (302/290)

Gen 1:21 creatures and every living ***t***
1:24 cattle and creeping ***t*** and beast
1:26 and over every creeping ***t*** that
1:28 and over every living ***t*** that
6: 7 creeping ***t*** and birds of the
6:19 And of every living ***t*** of all
6:20 and of every creeping ***t*** of the
7:14 every creeping ***t*** that creeps on
7:21 and beasts and every creeping ***t***
7:23 creeping ***t*** and bird of the air.
8: 1 Noah, and every living ***t***,
8:17 out with you every living ***t*** of
8:17 and cattle and every creeping ***t***
8:19 Every animal, every creeping ***t***,
8:21 I again destroy every living ***t***
9: 3 Every moving ***t*** that lives shall
18:25 be it from You to do such a ***t***
19:21 favored you concerning this ***t***
20:10 view, that you have done this ***t***?
21:26 do not know who has done this ***t***;
22:16 because you have done this ***t***,
24:50 'The ***t*** comes from the LORD;
30:31 If you will do this ***t*** for me,
34: 7 he had done a disgraceful ***t*** in
34: 7 a ***t*** which ought not to be done.
34:14 to them, "We cannot do this ***t***,
34:19 man did not delay to do the ***t***,
38:10 And the ***t*** which he did
41:28 This is the ***t*** which I have
41:32 to Pharaoh twice because the ***t***
44: 7 servants should do such a ***t***.
Ex 1:18 "Why have you done this ***t***,
2:14 Surely this ***t*** is known!"
9: 5 the LORD will do this ***t*** in
9: 6 So the LORD did this ***t*** on the
12:24 And you shall observe this ***t*** as
16:16 This is the ***t*** which the LORD
16:32 This is the ***t*** which the LORD
18:11 for in the very ***t*** in which they
18:14 What is this ***t*** that you are
18:17 The ***t*** that you do is not good.
18:18 For this ***t*** is too much for
18:23 "If you do this ***t***,
22: 9 or for any kind of lost ***t***
33:17 I will also do this ***t*** that you
34:10 For it is an awesome ***t*** that I
35: 4 This is the ***t*** which the LORD
Lev 4:13 and the ***t*** is hidden from the
5: 2 a person touches any unclean ***t***,
5: 5 that he has sinned in that ***t***;
5:16 done in regard to the holy ***t***,
6: 4 or the ***t*** which he has extorted,
6: 4 or the lost ***t*** which he found,
7:19 that touches any unclean ***t***
7:21 who touches any unclean ***t***,
7:21 or any abominable unclean ***t***,
9: 6 This is the ***t*** which the LORD
11:10 in the water or any living ***t***
11:41 And every creeping ***t*** that

11:43 abominable with any creeping *t*
11:44 yourselves with any creeping *t*
12: 4 shall not touch any hallowed *t*,
13:54 command that they wash the *t*
17: 2 This is the *t* which the LORD
20:17 nakedness, it is a wicked *t*.
20:21 it is an unclean *t*.
20:25 or by any kind of living *t* that
22: 5 whoever touches any creeping *t*
22: 6 who has touched any such *t*
22:10 shall not eat the holy *t*.
Num 4:15 they shall not touch any holy *t*,
16: 9 Is it a small *t* to you that
16:13 Is it a small *t* that you have
16:30 if the LORD creates a new *t*,
18:14 Every devoted *t* in Israel shall
30: 1 This is the *t* which the LORD
32:20 to them: "If you do this *t*,
Deut 1:14 The *t* which you have told us to
4:32 whether any great *t* like this
7:26 for it is an accursed *t*.
14: 3 shall not eat any detestable *t*.
14:19 Also every creeping *t* that flies
15:10 because for this *t* the LORD
15:15 therefore I command you this *t*
17: 5 who has committed that wicked *t*,
18:22 if the *t* does not happen or
18:22 that is the *t* which the LORD
22: 3 with any lost *t* of your
22:20 'But if the *t* is true,
22:21 she has done a disgraceful *t*
23: 9 yourself from every wicked *t*.
23:14 that He may see no unclean *t*
24:18 I command you to do this *t*.
24:22 I command you to do this *t*.
26:11 shall rejoice in every good *t*
32:47 For it is not a futile *t* for
Josh 7:13 There is an accursed *t* in your
7:13 you take away the accursed *t*
7:15 is taken with the accursed *t*
7:15 he has done a disgraceful *t* in
9:24 of you, and have done this *t*.
21:45 Not a word failed of any good *t*
22:20 a trespass in the accursed *t*,
22:33 So the *t* pleased the children of
23:14 all your souls that not one *t*
Judg 6:29 another, "Who has done this *t*?
6:29 son of Joash has done this *t*.
11:37 Let this *t* be done for me: let
13:19 And He did a wondrous *t* while
15: 7 Since you would do a *t* like
19:24 man do not do such a vile *t*!"
20: 9 but now this is the *t* which we
21:11 And this is the *t* that you
1 Sam 4: 7 Woe to us! For such a *t* has
8: 6 But the *t* displeased Samuel
12:16 stand and see this great *t*
17:30 another and said the same *t*;
18:20 and the *t* pleased him.
18:23 it seem to you a light *t* to
20: 2 should my father hide this *t*
24: 6 forbid that I should do this *t*
26:16 This *t* that you have done is
28:10 shall come upon you for this *t*.
28:18 the LORD has done this *t* to
2 Sam 2: 6 because you have done this *t*.
3:13 But one *t* I require of you: you
7:19 And yet this was a small *t* in
11:11 I will not do this *t*."
11:25 Do not let this *t* displease you,
11:27 But the *t* that David had done
12: 6 because he did this *t* and
12:12 but I will do this *t* before all
13:12 for no such *t* should be done in
13:12 Do not do this disgraceful *t*!
13:20 do not take this *t* to heart."
13:33 my lord the king take the *t* to
14:13 then have you schemed such a *t*
14:13 For the king speaks this *t* as
14:15 I have come to speak of this *t*
14:20 servant Joab has done this *t*;
14:21 right, I have granted this *t*.
17:19 and the *t* was not known.
24: 3 my lord the king desire this *t*?
1 Ki 1:27 Has this *t* been done by my lord
3:10 that Solomon had asked this *t*.
3:11 "Because you have asked this *t*,
11:10 commanded him concerning this *t*,
12:24 for this *t* is from Me." '"
12:30 Now this *t* became a sin, for the
13:34 And this *t* was the sin of the
16:31 though it had been a trivial *t*
20: 9 but this *t* I cannot do.'
20:24 'So do this *t*: Dismiss the
2 Ki 2:10 said, "You have asked a hard *t*.
5:18 Yet in this *t* may the LORD
5:18 pardon your servant in this *t*.
6:11 was greatly troubled by this *t*;
7: 2 could this *t* be?" And he said,
7:19 could such a *t* be?" And he had
8: 9 of every good *t* of Damascus,
8:13 that he should do this gross *t*?
17:12 'You shall not do this *t*."
20: 9 that the LORD will do the *t*
20:10 It is an easy *t* for the shadow
1 Chr 2: 7 transgressed in the accursed *t*.
13: 4 for the *t* was right in the eyes
17:17 And yet this was a small *t* in
21: 3 does my lord require this *t*?
21: 7 God was displeased with this *t*;
21: 8 because I have done this *t*;
26:28 dedicated, every dedicated *t*,
2 Chr 11: 4 for this *t* is from Me." '"
Ezra 7:27 who has put such a *t* as this
9: 3 So when I heard this *t*,
Neh 2:19 What is this *t* that you are
13:17 What evil *t* is this that you
Esth 2: 4 This *t* pleased the king,
5:14 And the *t* pleased Haman;
7: 5 in his heart to do such a *t*?
8: 5 favor in his sight and the *t*
Job 3:25 For the *t* I greatly feared has
6: 8 God would grant me the *t* that
9:22 It is all one *t*;
12:10 is the life of every living *t*,
12:14 If He breaks a *t* down,
13:28 "Man decays like a rotten *t*,
14: 4 Who can bring a clean *t* out of
22:28 You will also declare a *t*,
28:10 his eye sees every precious *t*.
39: 8 he searches after every green *t*.
41:34 He beholds every high *t*;
Ps 2: 1 And the people plot a vain *t*?
27: 4 One *t* I have desired of the
34:10 shall not lack any good *t*.
84:11 No good *t* will He withhold
141: 4 incline my heart to any evil *t*,
145:16 the desire of every living *t*.
Prov 4: 7 Wisdom is the principal *t*;
18:22 finds a wife finds a good *t*,
22:18 For it is a pleasant *t* if you
27: 7 to a hungry soul every bitter *t*
Eccl 3:19 one *t* befalls them: as one
7: 8 The end of a *t* is better than
7:27 Adding one *t* to the other to
8: 1 knows the interpretation of a *t*?
8: 3 take your stand for an evil *t*,
9: 3 that one *t* happens to all.
12:14 Including every secret *t*,
Isa 7:13 of David! Is it a small *t*
17:13 Like a rolling *t* before the
29:16 For shall the *t* made say of
29:16 Or shall the *t* formed say of
30:22 throw them away as an unclean *t*;
38: 7 that the LORD will do this *t*
40:15 up the isles as a very little *t*.
41:12 as nothing, As a nonexistent *t*.
43:19 Behold, I will do a new *t*,
49: 6 It is too small a *t* that You
52:11 there, Touch no unclean *t*;
55:11 it shall prosper in the *t*
64: 6 we are all like an unclean *t*,
66: 8 Who has heard such a *t*?
Jer 2:10 if there has been such a *t*.
2:19 it is an evil and bitter *t*
5:30 astonishing and horrible *t*
11:13 up altars to that shameful *t*,
14:14 divination, a worthless *t*,
18:13 has done a very horrible *t*.
22: 4 "For if you indeed do this *t*,
23:14 Also I have seen a horrible *t*
31:22 the LORD has created a new *t*
33:14 I will perform that good *t*
40: 3 therefore this *t* has come upon
40:16 "You shall not do this *t*,
42: 3 which we should walk and the *t*
44: 4 do not do this abominable *t*
Lam 1:17 has become an unclean *t* among
Ezek 8:10 there—every sort of creeping *t*,
8:17 Is it a trivial *t* to the house
28:16 I cast you as a profane *t* Out
44:29 every dedicated *t* in Israel
47: 9 shall be that every living *t*
48:12 set apart shall be to them a *t*
Dan 2:11 It is a difficult *t* that the
5:15 the interpretation of the *t*.
6:12 The *t* is true, according to the
Hos 6:10 I have seen a horrible *t* in the
8:12 were considered a strange *t*.
9:10 an abomination like the *t* they
Am 9:12 Says the LORD who does this *t*.
Mal 2:13 And this is the second *t* you
Mt 19:16 what good *t* shall I do that I
21:24 "I also will ask you one *t*,
27:44 Him reviled Him with the same *t*.
Mk 5:32 to see her who had done this *t*.
10:21 One *t* you lack: Go your way,
Lk 2:15 go to Bethlehem and see this *t*
6: 9 to them, "I will ask you one *t*:
10:42 But one *t* is needed, and Mary
18:22 to him, "You still lack one *t*.
20: 3 "I also will ask you one *t*,
22:23 them it was who would do this *t*.
Jn 5:14 lest a worse *t* come upon you."
7:36 What is this *t* that He said,
9:25 One *t* I know: that though I was
9:30 "Why, this is a marvelous *t*,
Acts 5: 4 Why have you conceived this *t*
17:21 to tell or to hear some new *t*.
19:32 Some therefore cried one *t* and
21:25 they should observe no such *t*,
21:34 the multitude cried one *t* and
26:26 since this *t* was not done in a
Rom 8:39 depth, nor any other created *t*,
9:20 Will the *t* formed say to him
1 Cor 13: 6 continually to this very *t*.
1:10 that you all speak the same *t*,
4: 3 with me it is a very small *t*
8: 7 until now eat it as a *t*
9:11 is it a great *t* if we reap
2 Cor 2: 3 And I wrote this very *t* to you,
5: 5 has prepared us for this very *t*
7:11 For observe this very *t*,
10: 5 down arguments and every high *t*
11:15 Therefore it is no great *t* if
12: 8 Concerning this *t* I pleaded with
Gal 2:10 the very *t* which I also was
4:18 good to be zealous in a good *t*
Eph 5:27 spot or wrinkle or any such *t*,
Phil 1: 6 being confident of this very *t*,
3:13 but one *t* I do, forgetting
2 Th 1: 6 since it is a righteous *t* with
1 Tim 1:10 and if there is any other *t*
2 Tim 1:14 That good *t* which was committed
Phm 1: 6 acknowledgment of every good *t*
Heb 10:29 he was sanctified a common *t*,
10:31 It is a fearful *t* to fall into
Jas 3:16 confusion and every evil *t* are
1 Pe 4:12 as though some strange *t*
2 Pe 3: 8 do not forget this one *t*,
1 Jn 2: 8 which *t* is true in Him and in
Rev 2:15 Nicolaitans, which *t* I hate.
9: 4 of the earth, or any green *t*,

THINGS (1100/964)

Gen 7: 4 face of the earth all living *t*
7:23 So He destroyed all living *t*
9: 3 for you. I have given you all *t*,
15: 1 After these *t* the word of the
20: 8 and told all these *t* in their
22: 1 it came to pass after these *t*
22:20 it came to pass after these *t*
24: 1 had blessed Abraham in all *t*.
24:28 her mother's household these *t*.
24:53 He also gave precious *t* to her
24:66 servant told Isaac all the *t*
29:13 So he told Laban all these *t*.
31:37 you have searched all my *t*,
31:37 what part of your household *t*
39: 7 it came to pass after these *t*
40: 1 It came to pass after these *t*
42:36 All these *t* are against me."
45:23 he sent to his father these *t*:
45:23 donkeys loaded with the good *t*
48: 1 it came to pass after these *t*
Ex 10: 2 your son's son the mighty *t* I
28:38 bear the iniquity of the holy *t*
29:33 They shall eat those *t* with
40: 4 in the table and arrange the *t*
Lev 2: 8 that is made of these *t* to the
5: 2 carcass of unclean creeping *t*,
5:15 in regard to the holy *t* of the
5:17 and commits any of these *t*
6: 3 in any one of these *t* that a man
6: 7 for any one of these *t* that he
8:36 and his sons did all the *t*
10:19 and such *t* have befallen me!
11:29 to you among the creeping *t*
11:42 many feet among all creeping *t*
14:11 to be made clean, and those *t*,
15:10 He who carries any of those *t*
15:27 Whoever touches those *t* shall be
18:24 yourselves with any of these *t*;
20:23 for they commit all these *t*,
22: 2 themselves from the holy *t* of
22: 3 who goes near the holy *t* which
26:23 And if by these *t* you are not
Num 1:50 and over all *t* that belong to
4: 4 relating to the most holy *t*:
4:15 These are the *t* in the
4:19 they approach the most holy *t*:
4:20 go in to watch while the holy *t*
4:26 all that is made for these *t*:
5: 9 offering of all the holy *t* of
5:10 And every man's holy *t* shall be
7: 9 was the service of the holy *t*,
10:21 set out, carrying the holy *t*.
10:29 the LORD has promised good *t*
15:13 native-born shall do these *t*
18: 9 be yours of the most holy *t*
18:16 redeemed of the devoted *t* you
18:19 heave offerings of the holy *t*,
35:29 And these *t* shall be a statute
Deut 1:18 you at that time all the *t*
4: 9 lest you forget the *t* your eyes
4:30 and all these *t* come upon you
6:11 "houses full of all good *t*,
10:21 you these great and awesome *t*
12: 4 LORD your God with such *t*.
12:26 Only the holy *t* which you have,
13:17 So none of the accursed *t* shall
18:12 For all who do these *t* are an
25:16 "For all who do such *t*,
29:29 The secret *t* belong to the
29:29 but those *t* which are
30: 1 when all these *t* come upon you,
32:35 And the *t* to come hasten upon
33:13 With the precious *t* of heaven,
33:15 With the best *t* of the ancient
33:15 With the precious *t* of the
33:16 With the precious *t* of the
Josh 1:17 as we heeded Moses in all *t*,
2:11 as soon as we heard these *t*,
6:18 abstain from the accursed *t*,
6:18 when you take of the accursed *t*,
7: 1 regarding the accursed *t*.
7: 1 Judah, took of the accursed *t*;
7:11 taken some of the accursed *t*,
11: 1 king of Hazor heard these *t*,
23:14 has failed of all the good *t*
23:15 that as all the good *t* have
23:15 bring upon you all harmful *t*,
24:29 it came to pass after these *t*
Judg 13:23 He have shown us all these *t*,
13:23 would He have told us such *t*

T

18:27 So they took the *t* Micah had
1 Sam 2:23 to them, "Why do you do such *t*?
3:17 anything from me of all the *t*
6: 6 When He did mighty *t* among
12:21 you would go after empty *t*
12:24 for consider what great *t* He
15:21 the best of the *t* which should
17:20 and took the *t* and went as
19: 7 Jonathan told him all these *t*.
25:37 his wife had told him these *t*,
26:25 You shall both do great *t* and
2 Sam 7:21 You have done all these great *t*,
11:18 sent and told David all the *t*
13:21 King David heard of all these *t*,
23: 5 Ordered in all *t* and secure.
23:17 These *t* were done by the three
23:22 These *t* Benaiah the son of
24:12 LORD: "I offer you three *t*;
1 Ki 4:33 of birds, of creeping *t*,
7:51 and Solomon brought in the *t*
15:15 the house of the LORD the *t*
15:15 and the *t* which he himself had
17:17 Now it happened after these *t*
18:36 that I have done all these *t*
21: 1 it came to pass after these *t*
22: 8 Let not the king say such *t*!"
2 Ki 8: 4 all the great *t* Elisha has
12:18 of Judah took all the sacred *t*
12:18 dedicated, and his own sacred *t*,
17: 9 against the LORD their God *t*
17:11 and they did wicked *t* to
23:17 Judah and proclaimed these *t*
25:15 the *t* of solid gold and solid
1 Chr 9:31 the trusted office over the *t*
11:19 These *t* were done by the three
11:24 These *t* Benaiah the son of
17:19 making known all these great *t*.
21:10 LORD: "I offer you three *t*;
23:13 should sanctify the most holy *t*,
23:28 in the purifying of all holy *t*
26:20 treasuries of the dedicated *t*.
26:26 treasuries of the dedicated *t*
28:12 treasuries for the dedicated *t*;
28:14 gave gold by weight for *t* of
29: 2 gold for *t* to be made of
29: 2 silver for *t* of silver,
29: 2 bronze for *t* of bronze, iron
29: 2 iron for *t* of iron, wood for
29: 2 wood for *t* of wood, onyx
29: 5 the gold for *t* of gold and the
29: 5 of gold and the silver for *t*
29:14 For all *t* come from You,
29:17 willingly offered all these *t*;
29:19 statutes, to do all these *t*,
2 Chr 4: 6 such *t* as they offered for the
5: 1 and Solomon brought in the *t*
12:12 and *t* also went well in Judah.
13: 9 rams may be a priest of *t*
15:18 into the house of God the *t*
18: 7 Let not the king say such *t*!"
19: 3 Nevertheless good *t* are found in
21: 3 silver and gold and precious *t*,
24: 7 presented all the dedicated *t*
29:33 The consecrated *t* were six
31: 6 also the tithe of holy *t* which
31:12 the tithes, and the dedicated *t*;
31:14 the LORD and the most holy *t*.
Ezra 1: 6 livestock, and with precious *t*,
2:63 not eat of the most holy *t*
7: 1 Now after these *t*,
9: 1 When these *t* were done,
Neh 6: 8 No such *t* as you say are being
6:16 nations around us saw these *t*,
7:65 not eat of the most holy *t*
9:35 Or in the many good *t* that
10:33 the set feasts; for the holy *t*,
12:47 They also consecrated holy *t*
13:26 king of Israel sin by these *t*?
Esth 2: 1 After these *t*, when the wrath
3: 1 After these *t* King Ahasuerus
9:20 And Mordecai wrote these *t* and
Job 5: 9 Who does great *t*,
5: 9 Marvelous *t* without number.
8: 2 long will you speak these *t*,
8: 8 And consider the *t* discovered
9:10 He does great *t* past finding
10:13 And these *t* You have hidden in
11: 7 Can you search out the deep *t* of
12: 3 who does not know such *t* as
12:22 He uncovers deep *t* out of
13:20 Only two *t* do not do to me,
13:26 For You write bitter *t* against
15:31 Let him not trust in futile *t*,
16: 2 "I have heard many such *t*;
22:18 their houses with good *t*;
23:14 And many such *t* are with
33:29 God works all these *t*,
37: 5 He does great *t* which we
42: 3 *T* too wonderful for me,
Ps 8: 6 You have put all *t* under his
12: 3 the tongue that speaks proud *t*,
15: 5 He who does these *t* shall
17: 2 Let Your eyes look on the *t*
31:18 Which speak insolent *t* proudly
35:11 They ask me *t* that I do not
42: 4 When I remember these *t*,
45: 4 hand shall teach You awesome *t*.
50:21 These *t* you have done,
57: 2 To God who performs all *t*
60: 3 have shown Your people hard *t*;
71:19 You who have done great *t*;
72:18 Who only does wondrous *t*!

78:12 Marvelous *t* He did in the sight
86:10 are great, and do wondrous *t*;
87: 3 Glorious *t* are spoken of you,
94: 4 speech, and speak insolent *t*;
98: 1 For He has done marvelous *t*;
103: 5 your mouth with good *t*,
104:25 are innumerable teeming *t*,
104:25 Living *t* both small and great.
106:21 Who had done great *t* in Egypt,
106:22 Awesome *t* by the Red Sea.
107:43 is wise will observe these *t*,
113: 6 Himself to behold The *t*
119:18 that I may see Wondrous *t* from
119:37 from looking at worthless *t*,
119:128 precepts concerning all *t* I
126: 2 The LORD has done great *t* for
126: 3 The LORD has done great *t* for
131: 1 Nor with *t* too profound for
140: 2 Who plan evil *t* in their
148:10 Creeping *t* and flying fowl;
Prov 2:12 the man who speaks perverse *t*,
3:15 And all the *t* you may desire
6:16 These six *t* the LORD hates,
8: 6 for I will speak of excellent *t*,
8: 6 of my lips will come right *t*;
8:11 And all the *t* one may desire
16:30 his eye to devise perverse *t*;
22:20 not written to you excellent *t*
23:16 When your lips speak right *t*.
23:33 Your eyes will see strange *t*,
23:33 heart will utter perverse *t*.
24:23 These *t* also belong to the
30: 7 Two *t* I request of You
30:15 and Give! There are three *t*
30:18 There are three *t* which are
30:21 For three *t* the earth is
30:24 There are four *t* which are
30:29 There are three *t* which are
Eccl 1: 8 All *t* are full of labor;
1:11 is no remembrance of former *t*,
1:11 there be any remembrance of *t*
6:11 Since there are many *t* that
7:25 wisdom and the reason of *t*,
9: 2 All *t* come alike to all:
Isa 12: 5 For He has done excellent *t*;
25: 1 For You have done wonderful *t*;
25: 6 Of fat *t* full of marrow,
29:16 Surely you have *t* turned
30:10 "Do not prophesy to us right *t*;
30:10 things; Speak to us smooth *t*,
32: 8 generous man devises generous *t*,
34: 1 The world and all *t* that come
38:16 by these *t* men live; And in
38:16 And in all these *t* is the
40:26 see who has created these *t*,
41:22 Let them show the former *t*,
41:22 Or declare to us *t* to come.
41:23 Show the *t* that are to come
42: 9 the former *t* have come to pass,
42: 9 And new *t* I declare; Before
42:16 These *t* I will do for them,
42:20 Seeing many *t*, but you do not
43: 9 And show us former *t*?
43:18 "Do not remember the former *t*,
43:18 Nor consider the *t* of old.
44: 7 And the *t* that are coming and
44: 9 And their precious *t* shall not
44:24 am the LORD, who makes all *t*
45: 7 I, the LORD, do all these *t*.
45:11 Ask Me of *t* to come concerning
45:19 I declare *t* that are right.
46: 9 Remember the former *t* of old,
46:10 And from ancient times *t* that
47: 7 that you did not take these *t*
47: 9 But these two *t* shall come to
48: 3 I have declared the former *t*
48: 6 I have made you hear new *t*
48: 6 from this time, Even hidden *t*,
48:14 them has declared these *t*?
51:19 These two *t* have come to you;
52: 7 brings glad tidings of good *t*,
61:11 As the garden causes the *t*
64: 3 When You did awesome *t* for
64:11 And all our pleasant *t* are
64:12 Yourself because of these *t*,
65: 4 And the broth of abominable *t*
66: 2 For all those *t* My hand has
66: 2 And all those *t* exist,"
66: 8 a thing? Who has seen such *t*?
Jer 2: 8 And walked after *t* that do
2:34 But plainly on all these *t*.
3: 5 you have spoken and done evil *t*,
3: 7 after she had done all these *t*,
4:18 doings Have procured these *t*
5: 9 I not punish them for these *t*?
5:19 LORD our God do all these *t*
5:25 have turned these *t* away,
5:29 I not punish them for these *t*?
8:13 And the *t* I have given them
9: 9 I not punish them for these *t*?
10:16 For He is the Maker of all *t*,
13:22 Why have these *t* come upon me?"
16:19 and unprofitable *t*.
17: 9 is deceitful above all *t*,
18:13 Gentiles, Who has heard such *t*?
20: 1 Jeremiah prophesied these *t*.
20: 5 produce, and all its precious *t*;
21:14 And it shall devour all *t*
26:10 princes of Judah heard these *t*,
29:23 they have done disgraceful *t*
30:15 I have done these *t* to you.
33: 3 and show you great and mighty *t*,

45: 5 And do you seek great *t* for
51:19 For He is the Maker of all *t*;
Lam 1: 7 remembers all her pleasant *t*
1:10 hand Over all her pleasant *t*;
1:16 For these *t* I weep; My eye, my
5:17 Because of these *t* our eyes
Ezek 5:11 with all your detestable *t* and
7:20 Their detestable *t*;
11: 5 for I know the *t* that come into
11:18 take away all its detestable *t*
11:21 desire for their detestable *t*
11:25 in captivity of all the *t* the
16: 5 to do any of these *t* for you,
16:16 Such *t* should not happen, nor
16:30 "seeing you do all these *t*,
16:43 agitated Me with all these *t*,
17:12 Do you not know what these *t*
17:15 Will he who does such *t*
17:18 hand and still did all these *t*,
18:10 Who does any of these *t*
20:40 together with all your holy *t*.
22: 8 You have despised My holy *t* and
22:25 taken treasure and precious *t*;
22:26 My law and profaned My holy *t*;
23:30 I will do these *t* to you
24:19 you not tell us what these *t*
37:23 nor with their detestable *t*,
38:20 all creeping *t* that creep on
44: 8 not kept charge of My holy *t*,
44:13 nor come near any of My holy *t*,
Dan 2:10 or ruler has ever asked such *t*
2:22 He reveals deep and secret *t*;
7:16 the interpretation of these *t*:
11:38 precious stones and pleasant *t*.
11:43 and over all the precious *t* of
12: 7 all these *t* shall be finished.
12: 8 shall be the end of these *t*?
Hos 2:18 And with the creeping *t* of
8:12 written for him the great *t* of
9: 3 And shall eat unclean *t* in
14: 9 Let him understand these *t*.
Joel 2:20 he has done monstrous *t*.
2:21 the LORD has done marvelous *t*!
Hab 1:14 Like creeping *t* that have no
Zech 4:10 has despised the day of small *t*?
8:16 These are the *t* you shall do:
8:17 For all these are *t* that I
Mt 1:20 while he thought about these *t*,
4: 9 All these *t* I will give You if
6: 8 For your Father knows the *t* you
6:32 For after all these *t* the
6:32 knows that you need all these *t*.
6:33 and all these *t* shall be added
6:34 will worry about its own *t*.
7:11 who is in heaven give good *t*
9:18 While He spoke these *t* to them,
11: 4 Go and tell John the *t* which you
11:25 that You have hidden these *t*
11:27 All *t* have been delivered to Me
12:34 you, being evil, speak good *t*?
12:35 his heart brings forth good *t*,
12:35 treasure brings forth evil *t*.
13: 3 Then He spoke many *t* to them in
13:34 All these *t* Jesus spoke to the
13:35 I will utter *t* kept
13:41 out of His kingdom all *t* that
13:51 you understood all these *t*?
13:52 brings out of his treasure *t*
13:56 did this Man get all these *t*?
15:18 But those *t* which proceed out of
15:20 These are the *t* which defile a
16:21 and suffer many *t* from the
16:23 you are not mindful of the *t*
16:23 but the *t* of men."
17:11 first and will restore all *t*.
19:20 All these *t* I have kept from my
19:26 but with God all *t* are
20:15 to do what I wish with my own *t*?
21:15 and scribes saw the wonderful *t*
21:22 And whatever *t* you ask in
21:23 authority are You doing these *t*?
21:24 by what authority I do these *t*:
21:27 by what authority I do these *t*.
22: 4 and all *t* are ready. Come to
22:21 therefore to Caesar the *t* that
22:21 and to God the *t* that are
23:20 swears by it and by all *t* on
23:36 all these *t* will come upon this
24: 2 "Do you not see all these *t*?
24: 3 when will these *t* be? And what
24: 6 for all these *t* must come to
24:33 also, when you see all these *t*,
24:34 pass away till all these *t*
25:21 you were faithful over a few *t*,
25:21 will make you ruler over many *t*.
25:23 have been faithful over a few *t*,
25:23 will make you ruler over many *t*.
27:13 Do You not hear how many *t* they
27:19 for I have suffered many *t*
27:54 saw the earthquake and the *t*
28:11 to the chief priests all the *t*
28:20 them to observe all *t*
Mk 1:44 for your cleansing those *t*
2: 8 do you reason about these *t* in
3: 8 when they heard how many *t* He
4: 2 Then He taught them many *t* by
4:11 all *t* come in parables,
4:19 and the desires for other *t*
4:34 He explained all *t* to His
5:19 and tell them what great *t* the
5:26 and had suffered many *t* from
6: 2 did this Man get these *t*?

6:20 he heard him, he did many ***t***,
6:30 to Jesus and told Him all ***t***,
6:34 He began to teach them many ***t***.
7: 4 And there are many other ***t***
7: 8 and many other such ***t*** you do."
7:13 And many such ***t*** you do."
7:15 but the ***t*** which come out of
7:15 those are the ***t*** that defile a
7:23 All these evil ***t*** come from
7:37 He has done all ***t*** well. He makes
8:31 Son of Man must suffer many ***t***,
8:33 you are not mindful of the ***t***
8:33 but the ***t*** of men."
9: 9 they should tell no one the ***t***
9:12 coming first and restores all ***t***.
9:12 that He must suffer many ***t*** and
9:23 all ***t*** are possible to him who
10:20 all these ***t*** I have kept from my
10:27 for with God all ***t*** are
10:32 and began to tell them the ***t***
11:11 He had looked around at all ***t***,
11:23 but believes that those ***t*** he
11:24 whatever ***t*** you ask when you
11:28 authority are You doing these ***t***?
11:28 this authority to do these ***t***?
11:29 by what authority I do these ***t***:
11:33 by what authority I do these ***t***.
12:17 Render to Caesar the ***t*** that are
12:17 and to God the ***t*** that are
13: 4 when will these ***t*** be? And what
13: 4 be the sign when all these ***t***
13: 7 for such ***t*** must happen, but
13:23 I have told you all ***t***
13:29 when you see these ***t*** happening,
13:30 pass away till all these ***t***
14:36 all ***t*** are possible for You.
15: 3 priests accused Him of many ***t***,
15: 4 See how many ***t*** they testify
Lk 1: 1 in order a narrative of those ***t***
1: 3 perfect understanding of all ***t***
1: 4 know the certainty of those ***t***
1:20 to speak until the day these ***t***
1:45 be a fulfillment of those ***t***
1:49 who is mighty has done great ***t***
1:53 filled the hungry with good ***t***,
2:18 heard it marveled at those ***t***
2:19 But Mary kept all these ***t*** and
2:20 and praising God for all the ***t***
2:33 His mother marveled at those ***t***
2:39 when they had performed all ***t***
2:51 His mother kept all these ***t*** in
4:28 when they heard these ***t***,
5:26 We have seen strange ***t*** today!"
5:27 After these ***t*** He went out and
6:46 and do not do the ***t*** which I
7: 9 When Jesus heard these ***t***,
7:18 to him concerning all these ***t***.
7:22 Go and tell John the ***t*** you have
8: 8 When He had said these ***t*** He
8:39 and tell what great ***t*** God has
8:39 the whole city what great ***t***
9: 9 is this of whom I hear such ***t***?
9:22 Son of Man must suffer many ***t***,
9:36 one in those days any of the ***t***
9:43 everyone marveled at all the ***t***
10: 1 After these ***t*** the Lord appointed
10: 7 eating and drinking such ***t*** as
10: 8 eat such ***t*** as are set before
10:21 that You have hidden these ***t***
10:22 All ***t*** have been delivered to Me
10:23 are the eyes which see the ***t***
10:41 and troubled about many ***t***.
11:27 happened, as He spoke these ***t***,
11:41 rather give alms of such ***t***
11:41 then indeed all ***t*** are clean to
11:45 by saying these ***t*** You reproach
11:53 And as He said these ***t*** to them,
11:53 cross-examine Him about many ***t***,
12:15 in the abundance of the ***t*** he
12:20 then whose will those ***t*** be
12:30 For all these ***t*** the nations of
12:30 knows that you need these ***t***.
12:31 and all these ***t*** shall be added
12:48 yet committed ***t*** deserving of
13: 2 because they suffered such ***t***?
13:17 And when He said these ***t***,
13:17 for all the glorious ***t*** that
14: 6 answer Him regarding these ***t***.
14:15 table with Him heard these ***t***,
14:17 for all ***t*** are now ready.'
14:21 came and reported these ***t*** to
15:26 and asked what these ***t*** meant.
16:14 money, also heard all these ***t***,
16:25 you received your good ***t***,
16:25 and likewise Lazarus evil ***t***;
17: 9 servant because he did the ***t***
17:10 when you have done all those ***t***
17:25 first He must suffer many ***t***
18:21 All these ***t*** I have kept from my
18:22 So when Jesus heard these ***t***,
18:27 The ***t*** which are impossible with
18:31 and all ***t*** that are written by
18:34 they understood none of these ***t***;
18:34 and they did not know the ***t***
19:11 Now as they heard these ***t***,
19:42 the ***t*** that make for your
20: 2 authority are You doing these ***t***?
20: 8 by what authority I do these ***t***.
20:25 therefore to Caesar the ***t*** that
20:25 and to God the ***t*** that are
21: 6 These ***t*** which you see—the days
21: 7 but when will these ***t*** be?
21: 7 will there be when these ***t***
21: 9 for these ***t*** must come to pass
21:12 "But before all these ***t***,
21:22 that all ***t*** which are written
21:26 and the expectation of those ***t***
21:28 Now when these ***t*** begin to
21:31 when you see these ***t*** happening,
21:32 no means pass away till all ***t***
21:36 worthy to escape all these ***t***
22:37 For the ***t*** concerning Me have
22:65 And many other ***t*** they
23: 8 because he had heard many ***t***
23:14 in this Man concerning those ***t***
23:31 For if they do these ***t*** in the
23:49 at a distance, watching these ***t***.
24: 9 the tomb and told all these ***t***
24:10 who told these ***t*** to the
24:14 talked together of all these ***t***
24:18 and have You not known the ***t***
24:19 And He said to them, "What ***t***?
24:19 The ***t*** concerning Jesus of
24:21 is the third day since these ***t***
24:26 to have suffered these ***t*** and
24:27 in all the Scriptures the ***t***
24:35 And they told about the ***t*** that
24:36 Now as they said these ***t***,
24:44 that all ***t*** must be fulfilled
24:48 you are witnesses of these ***t***.
Jn 1: 3 All ***t*** were made through Him, and
1:28 These ***t*** were done in Bethabara
1:50 You will see greater ***t*** than
2:16 Take these ***t*** away! Do not make
2:18 since You do these ***t***?"
3: 9 How can these ***t*** be?"
3:10 and do not know these ***t***?
3:12 If I have told you earthly ***t*** and
3:12 if I tell you heavenly ***t***?
3:22 After these ***t*** Jesus and His
3:35 and has given all ***t*** into His
4:25 He comes, He will tell us all ***t***.
4:29 see a Man who told me all ***t***
4:45 having seen all the ***t*** He did in
5:16 because He had done these ***t*** on
5:20 and shows Him all ***t*** that He
5:34 but I say these ***t*** that you may
6: 1 After these ***t*** Jesus went over
6:59 These ***t*** He said in the synagogue
7: 1 After these ***t*** Jesus walked in
7: 4 known openly. If You do these ***t***,
7: 9 When He had said these ***t*** to
7:32 the crowd murmuring these ***t***
8:26 I have many ***t*** to say and to
8:26 I speak to the world those ***t***
8:28 taught Me, I speak these ***t***.
8:29 for I always do those ***t*** that
9: 6 When He had said these ***t***,
9:22 His parents said these ***t***
10: 6 they did not understand the ***t***
10:41 but all the ***t*** that John spoke
11:11 These ***t*** He said, and after that
11:28 And when she had said these ***t***,
11:43 Now when He had said these ***t***,
11:45 and had seen the ***t*** Jesus did,
11:46 Pharisees and told them the ***t***
12:16 did not understand these ***t*** at
12:16 they remembered that these ***t***
12:16 that they had done these ***t*** to
12:36 These ***t*** Jesus spoke,
12:41 These ***t*** Isaiah said when he saw
13: 3 that the Father had given all ***t***
13:17 "If you know these ***t***,
13:21 When Jesus had said these ***t***,
13:29 Buy those ***t*** we need for the
14:25 These ***t*** I have spoken to you
14:26 He will teach you all ***t***,
14:26 to your remembrance all ***t*** that
15:11 These ***t*** I have spoken to you,
15:15 for all ***t*** that I heard from My
15:17 These ***t*** I command you, that you
15:21 But all these ***t*** they will do to
16: 1 These ***t*** I have spoken to you,
16: 3 And these ***t*** they will do to you
16: 4 But these ***t*** I have told you,
16: 4 And these ***t*** I did not say to
16: 6 because I have said these ***t*** to
16:12 I still have many ***t*** to say to
16:13 and He will tell you ***t*** to come.
16:15 All ***t*** that the Father has are
16:25 These ***t*** I have spoken to you in
16:30 we are sure that You know all ***t***,
16:33 These ***t*** I have spoken to you,
17: 7 they have known that all ***t***
17:13 and these ***t*** I speak in the
18: 4 knowing all ***t*** that would come
18:22 And when He had said these ***t***,
19:24 the soldiers did these ***t***.
19:28 knowing that all ***t*** were now
19:36 For these ***t*** were done that the
20:18 that He had spoken these ***t*** to
21: 1 After these ***t*** Jesus showed
21:17 to Him, "Lord, You know all ***t***;
21:24 who testifies of these ***t***,
21:24 these things, and wrote these ***t***;
21:25 And there are also many other ***t***
Acts 1: 3 days and speaking of the ***t***
1: 9 Now when He had spoken these ***t***,
2:44 and had all ***t*** in common,
3:18 But those ***t*** which God foretold
3:21 times of restoration of all ***t***,
3:22 you shall hear in all ***t***,
4:20 For we cannot but speak the ***t***
4:25 the people plot vain ***t***?
4:32 anyone say that any of the ***t***
4:32 but they had all ***t*** in common.
4:34 brought the proceeds of the ***t***
5: 5 all those who heard these ***t***.
5:11 and upon all who heard these ***t***.
5:24 the chief priests heard these ***t***,
5:32 we are His witnesses to these ***t***,
7: 1 Are these ***t*** so?"
7:50 hand not made all these ***t***?
7:54 When they heard these ***t*** they
8: 6 with one accord heeded the ***t***
8:12 Philip as he preached the ***t***
8:24 that none of the ***t*** which you
9:16 I will show him how many ***t***
10: 8 he had explained all these ***t***
10:12 earth, wild beasts, creeping ***t***,
10:33 to hear all the ***t*** commanded you
10:39 And we are witnesses of all ***t***
11: 6 earth, wild beasts, creeping ***t***,
11:18 When they heard these ***t*** they
11:22 Then news of these ***t*** came to the
12:17 tell these ***t*** to James and to
13:39 is justified from all ***t*** from
13:45 they opposed the ***t*** spoken by
14:15 why are you doing these ***t***?
14:15 turn from these useless ***t*** to
14:15 and all ***t*** that are in them,
15: 4 and they reported all ***t*** that
15:17 who does all these ***t***.
15:20 write to them to abstain from ***t***
15:20 from ***t*** strangled, and from
15:27 will also report the same ***t*** by
15:28 burden than these necessary ***t***:
15:29 that you abstain from ***t*** offered
15:29 from ***t*** strangled, and from
16:14 opened her heart to heed the ***t***
17: 8 city when they heard these ***t***.
17:11 to find out whether these ***t***
17:20 are bringing some strange ***t*** to
17:20 we want to know what these ***t***
17:22 I perceive that in all ***t*** you
17:25 to all life, breath, and all ***t***.
18: 1 After these ***t*** Paul departed from
18:17 took no notice of these ***t***.
18:25 and taught accurately the ***t*** of
19: 8 persuading concerning the ***t*** of
19:21 When these ***t*** were accomplished,
19:36 since these ***t*** cannot be denied,
19:41 And when he had said these ***t***,
20:22 not knowing the ***t*** that will
20:24 But none of these ***t*** move me; nor
20:30 rise up, speaking perverse ***t***,
20:36 And when he had said these ***t***,
21:12 Now when we heard these ***t***,
21:19 he told in detail those ***t*** which
21:24 that all may know that those ***t***
21:25 should keep themselves from ***t***
21:25 from ***t*** strangled, and from
22:10 there you will be told all ***t***
23:22 that you have revealed these ***t***
24: 8 you may ascertain all these ***t***
24: 9 maintaining that these ***t*** were
24:13 Nor can they prove the ***t*** of
24:14 believing all ***t*** which are
24:22 But when Felix heard these ***t***,
25: 9 before me concerning these ***t***?
25:11 if there is nothing in these ***t***
25:18 against him of such ***t*** as I
26: 2 you concerning all the ***t*** of
26: 9 myself thought I must do many ***t***
26:16 and a witness both of the ***t***
26:16 you have seen and of the ***t***
26:22 saying no other ***t*** than those
26:26 speak freely, knows these ***t***;
26:26 convinced that none of these ***t***
26:30 When he had said these ***t***,
27:11 owner of the ship than by the ***t***
27:35 And when he had said these ***t***,
28:10 they provided such ***t*** as were
28:24 some were persuaded by the ***t***
28:31 of God and teaching the ***t***
Rom 1:20 being understood by the ***t*** that
1:23 animals and creeping ***t***.
1:28 to do those ***t*** which are not
1:30 boasters, inventors of evil ***t***,
1:32 that those who practice such ***t***
2: 1 who judge practice the same ***t***.
2: 2 those who practice such ***t***.
2: 3 judge those practicing such ***t***,
2:14 by nature do the ***t*** in the law,
2:18 and approve the ***t*** that are
4:17 to the dead and calls those ***t***
6:21 did you have then in the ***t*** of
6:21 For the end of those ***t*** is
8: 5 flesh set their minds on the ***t***
8: 5 the ***t*** of the Spirit.
8:28 And we know that all ***t*** work
8:31 then shall we say to these ***t***?
8:32 Him also freely give us all ***t***?
8:37 Yet in all these ***t*** we are more
8:38 nor ***t*** present nor things to
8:38 nor things present nor ***t*** to
10: 5 The man who does those ***t***
10:15 glad tidings of good ***t***!"
11:36 Him and to Him are all ***t***,
12:16 Do not set your mind on high ***t***,
12:17 Have regard for good ***t*** in the
14: 1 not to disputes over doubtful ***t***.
14: 2 one believes he may eat all ***t***,
14:18 he who serves Christ in these ***t***
14:19 Therefore let us pursue the ***t***
14:19 make for peace and the ***t*** by

14:20 All *t* indeed are pure,
15: 4 For whatever *t* were written
15:17 glory in Christ Jesus in the *t*
15:18 dare to speak of any of those *t*
15:27 partakers of their spiritual *t*,
15:27 minister to them in material *t*.
1 Cor 1:27 God has chosen the foolish *t*
1:27 and God has chosen the weak *t*
1:27 the world to put to shame the *t*
1:28 and the base *t* of the world and
1:28 things of the world and the *t*
1:28 and the *t* which are not,
1:28 to bring to nothing the *t* that
2: 9 the heart of man The *t*
2:10 For the Spirit searches all *t*,
2:10 the deep *t* of God.
2:11 For what man knows the *t* of a
2:11 Even so no one knows the *t* of
2:12 that we might know the *t* that
2:13 These *t* we also speak,
2:13 comparing spiritual *t* with
2:14 man does not receive the *t* of
2:15 who is spiritual judges all *t*,
3:21 For all *t* are yours:
3:22 or *t* present or things to
3:22 or things present or *t* to
4: 5 bring to light the hidden *t* of
4: 6 Now these *t*, brethren, I have
4:13 the offscouring of all *t* until
4:14 I do not write these *t* to shame
6: 3 *t* that pertain to this life?
6: 4 you have judgments concerning *t*
6: 8 and you do these *t* to your
6:12 All *t* are lawful for me,
6:12 but all *t* are not helpful.
6:12 All *t* are lawful for me, but I
7: 1 Now concerning the *t* of which
7:32 is unmarried cares for the *t*
7:33 is married cares about the *t*
7:34 woman cares about the *t* of the
7:34 is married cares about the *t*
8: 1 Now concerning *t* offered to
8: 4 concerning the eating of *t*
8: 6 the Father, of whom are all *t*,
8: 6 Christ, through whom are all *t*,
8:10 be emboldened to eat those *t*
9: 8 Do I say these *t* as a mere man?
9:11 If we have sown spiritual *t* for
9:11 if we reap your material *t*?
9:12 but endure all *t* lest we hinder
9:13 those who minister the holy *t*
9:13 holy things eat of the *t* of
9:15 But I have used none of these *t*,
9:15 nor have I written these *t* that
9:22 I have become all *t* to all
9:25 prize is temperate in all *t*.
10: 6 Now these *t* became our examples,
10: 6 we should not lust after evil *t*
10:11 Now all these *t* happened to them
10:20 that the *t* which the Gentiles
10:23 All *t* are lawful for me,
10:23 but not all *t* are helpful;
10:23 all *t* are lawful for me,
10:23 but not all *t* edify.
10:33 also please all men in all *t*,
11: 2 that you remember me in all *t*
11:12 but all *t* are from God.
12:11 same Spirit works all these *t*,
13: 7 all *t*, believes all things,
13: 7 all things, believes all *t*,
13: 7 all things, hopes all *t*,
13: 7 hopes all things, endures all *t*.
13:11 a man, I put away childish *t*.
14: 7 Even *t* without life, whether
14:26 Let all *t* be done for
14:37 let him acknowledge that the *t*
14:40 Let all *t* be done decently and
15:27 He has put all *t* under His
15:27 'all *t* are put under Him,"
15:27 evident that He who put all *t*
15:28 Now when all *t* are made subject
15:28 be subject to Him who put all *t*
2 Cor 1:13 we are not writing any other *t*
1:17 Or the *t* I plan, do I plan
2: 9 you are obedient in all *t*.
2:16 who is sufficient for these *t*?
4: 2 we have renounced the hidden *t*
4:15 For all *t* are for your sakes,
4:18 while we do not look at the *t*
4:18 but at the *t* which are not
4:18 For the *t* which are seen are
4:18 but the *t* which are not seen
5:10 that each one may receive the *t*
5:17 old *t* have passed away; behold,
5:17 all *t* have become new.
5:18 Now all *t* are of God, who has
6: 4 But in all *t* we commend
6:10 and yet possessing all *t*.
7:11 what vindication! In all *t*
7:14 But as we spoke all *t* to you in
8:21 providing honorable *t*,
8:22 often proved diligent in many *t*,
9: 8 all sufficiency in all *t*,
10: 7 Do you look at *t* according to
10:15 not boasting of *t* beyond
11: 6 manifested among you in all *t*.
11:12 just as we are in the *t* of
11:28 besides the other *t*,
11:30 I will boast in the *t* which
12:19 in Christ. But we do all *t*,
13:10 Therefore I write these *t* being
Gal 1:20 (Now concerning the *t* which I

2:18 For if I build again those *t*
3: 4 Have you suffered so many *t* in
3:10 not continue in all *t*
4:24 which *t* are symbolic. For these
5:17 so that you do not do the *t*
5:21 that those who practice such *t*
6: 6 the word share in all good *t*
Eph 1:10 gather together in one all *t*
1:11 purpose of Him who works all *t*
1:22 And He put all *t* under His
1:22 Him to be head over all *t*
3: 9 hidden in God who created all *t*
4:10 that He might fill all *t*.
4:15 may grow up in all *t* into Him
5: 6 for because of these *t* the
5:12 even to speak of those *t* which
5:13 But all *t* that are exposed are
5:20 giving thanks always for all *t*
6: 9 do the same *t* to them, giving
6:21 will make all *t* known to you;
Phil 1:10 that you may approve the *t* that
1:12 that the *t* which happened to
2:14 Do all *t* without complaining and
2:21 not the *t* which are of Christ
3: 1 For me to write the same *t* to
3: 7 But what *t* were gain to me,
3: 8 Yet indeed I also count all *t*
3: 8 have suffered the loss of all *t*,
3:13 forgetting those *t* which are
3:13 and reaching forward to those *t*
3:19 set their mind on earthly *t*.
3:21 He is able even to subdue all *t*
4: 8 whatever *t* are true, whatever
4: 8 whatever *t* are noble,
4: 8 whatever *t* are just,
4: 8 whatever *t* are pure,
4: 8 whatever *t* are lovely,
4: 8 whatever *t* are of good report,
4: 8 —meditate on these *t*.
4: 9 The *t* which you learned and
4:12 Everywhere and in all *t* I have
4:13 I can do all *t* through Christ
4:18 from Epaphroditus the *t* sent
Col 1:16 For by Him all *t* were created
1:16 All *t* were created through Him
1:17 And He is before all *t*,
1:17 and in Him all *t* consist.
1:18 that in all *t* He may have the
1:20 and by Him to reconcile all *t* to
1:20 whether *t* on earth or things in
1:20 whether things on earth or *t* in
2:17 which are a shadow of *t* to come,
2:18 intruding into those *t* which he
2:22 which all concern *t* which perish
2:23 These *t* indeed have an
3: 1 seek those *t* which are above,
3: 2 Set your mind on *t* above, not on
3: 2 not on *t* on the earth.
3: 6 Because of these *t* the wrath of
3:14 But above all these *t* put on
3:20 obey your parents in all *t*,
3:22 obey in all *t* your masters
4: 9 will make known to you all *t*
1 Th 2:14 you also suffered the same *t*
5:21 Test all *t*; hold fast what is
2 Th 2: 5 with you I told you these *t*?
3: 4 that you do and will do the *t*
1 Tim 1: 7 what they say nor the *t* which
3:11 temperate, faithful in all *t*.
3:14 These *t* I write to you, though
4: 6 the brethren in these *t*,
4: 8 is profitable for all *t*,
4:11 These *t* command and teach.
4:15 Meditate on these *t*;
5: 7 And these *t* command, that they
5:13 saying *t* which they ought not.
5:21 angels that you observe these *t*
6: 2 Teach and exhort these *t*.
6:11 flee these *t* and pursue
6:13 of God who gives life to all *t*,
6:17 who gives us richly all *t* to
2 Tim 1:12 reason I also suffer these *t*;
2: 2 And the *t* that you have heard
2: 7 give you understanding in all *t*.
2:10 Therefore I endure all *t* for the
2:14 Remind them of these *t*,
3:14 But you must continue in the *t*
4: 5 But you be watchful in all *t*,
Titus 1: 5 you should set in order the *t*
1:11 teaching *t* which they ought
1:15 To the pure all *t* are pure,
2: 1 speak the *t* which are proper
2: 3 much wine, teachers of good *t*—
2: 7 in all *t* showing yourself to
2: 9 to be well pleasing in all *t*,
2:10 of God our Savior in all *t*.
2:15 Speak these *t*, exhort,
3: 8 and these *t* I want you to
3: 8 These *t* are good and profitable
Heb 1: 2 He has appointed heir of all *t*,
1: 3 and upholding all *t* by the word
2: 1 the more earnest heed to the *t*
2: 8 You have put all *t* in
2: 8 But now we do not yet see all *t*
2:10 for whom are all *t* and by whom
2:10 things and by whom are all *t*,
2:17 in all *t* He had to be made like
2:17 and faithful High Priest in *t*
3: 4 but He who built all *t* is God.
3: 5 for a testimony of those *t*
4:13 but all *t* are naked and open
5: 1 men is appointed for men in *t*

5: 8 He learned obedience by the *t*
6: 9 we are confident of better *t*
6: 9 *t* that accompany salvation,
6:18 that by two immutable *t*,
7:13 For He of whom these *t* are
8: 1 is the main point of the *t* we
8: 5 and shadow of the heavenly *t*,
8: 5 See that you make all *t*
9: 5 Of these *t* we cannot now speak
9: 6 Now when these *t* had been thus
9:11 as High Priest of the good *t*
9:22 to the law almost all *t* are
9:23 that the copies of the *t* in
9:23 but the heavenly *t* themselves
10: 1 having a shadow of the good *t*
10: 1 not the very image of the *t*,
11: 1 Now faith is the substance of *t*
11: 1 the evidence of *t* not seen.
11: 3 so that the *t* which are seen
11: 3 are seen were not made of *t*
11: 7 being divinely warned of *t* not
11:14 For those who say such *t* declare
11:20 Jacob and Esau concerning *t* to
12:24 that speaks better *t* than
12:27 the removal of those *t* that
12:27 as of *t* that are made, that the
12:27 that the *t* which cannot be
13: 5 be content with such *t* as you
13:18 in all *t* desiring to live
Jas 2:16 but you do not give them the *t*
3: 2 For we all stumble in many *t*.
3: 5 member and boasts great *t*.
3:10 these *t* ought not to be so.
1 Pe 1:12 us they were ministering the *t*
1:12 *t* which angels desire to look
1:18 not redeemed with corruptible *t*,
4: 7 But the end of all *t* is at
4: 8 And above all *t* have fervent
4:11 that in all *t* God may be
2 Pe 1: 3 power has given to us all *t*
1: 8 For if these *t* are yours and
1: 9 For he who lacks these *t* is
1:10 for if you do these *t* you will
1:12 to remind you always of these *t*,
1:15 have a reminder of these *t*
2:12 speak evil of the *t* they do not
3: 4 all *t* continue as they were
3:11 since all these *t* will be
3:14 looking forward to these *t*,
3:16 speaking in them of these *t*,
3:16 in which are some *t* hard to
1 Jn 1: 4 And these *t* we write to you that
2: 1 these *t* I write to you, so that
2:15 not love the world or the *t* in
2:20 Holy One, and you know all *t*.
2:26 These *t* I have written to you
2:27 teaches you concerning all *t*,
3:20 than our heart, and knows all *t*.
3:22 His commandments and do those *t*
5:13 These *t* I have written to you
2 Jn 8 that we do not lose those *t* we
12 Having many *t* to write to you,
3 Jn 2 that you may prosper in all *t*
13 I had many *t* to write, but I do
Jude 10 in these *t* they corrupt
15 and of all the harsh *t* which
Rev 1: 1 *t* which must shortly take place.
1: 2 to all *t* that he saw.
1: 3 and keep those *t* which are
1:19 Write the *t* which you have seen,
1:19 and the *t* which are, and the
1:19 and the *t* which will take place
2: 1 These *t* says He who holds the
2: 8 These *t* says the First and the
2:10 Do not fear any of those *t* which
2:12 These *t* says He who has the
2:14 But I have a few *t* against you,
2:14 to eat *t* sacrificed to idols,
2:18 These *t* says the Son of God,
2:20 Nevertheless I have a few *t*
2:20 sexual immorality and eat *t*
3: 1 These *t* says He who has the
3: 2 and strengthen the *t* which
3: 7 These *t* says He who is holy,
3:14 These *t* says the Amen,
4: 1 After these *t* I looked, and
4: 1 and I will show you *t* which
4:11 power; For You created all *t*,
7: 1 After these *t* I saw four angels
7: 9 After these *t* I looked, and
9:12 woes are coming after these *t*.
10: 4 Seal up the *t* which the seven
10: 6 who created heaven and the *t*
10: 6 the earth and the *t* that are in
10: 6 and the sea and the *t* that are
13: 5 given a mouth speaking great *t*
15: 5 After these *t* I looked,
16: 5 You have judged these *t*.
18: 1 After these *t* I saw another
18:14 and all the *t* which are rich
18:15 "The merchants of these *t*,
19: 1 After these *t* I heard a loud
20: 3 But after these *t* he must be
20:12 by the *t* which were written in
21: 4 for the former *t* have passed
21: 5 I make all *t* new." And He said
21: 7 overcomes shall inherit all *t*,
22: 6 to show His servants the *t*
22: 8 I, John, saw and heard these *t*.
22: 8 the angel who showed me these *t*.
22:16 to testify to you these *t* in
22:18 If anyone adds to these *t*,

22:19 and from the ***t*** which are
22:20 He who testifies to these ***t***

THINK (59/57) THINKS, THOUGHT

Num 36: 6 Let them marry whom they ***t*** best,
Deut 9: 4 Do not ***t*** in your heart, after
2 Sam 10: 3 Do you ***t*** that David really
13:33 to ***t*** that all the king's sons
18:27 I ***t*** the running of the first is
1 Chr 19: 3 Do you ***t*** that David really
2 Chr 13: 8 And now you ***t*** to withstand the
Esth 4:13 Do not ***t*** in your heart that you
Job 35: 2 Do you ***t*** this is right? Do you
41:32 One would ***t*** the deep had
Isa 10: 7 Nor does his heart ***t*** so;
Jer 29:11 I know the thoughts that I ***t***
Zech 8:17 Let none of you ***t*** evil in your
Mt 3: 9 and do not ***t*** to say to
5:17 Do not ***t*** that I came to destroy
6: 7 For they ***t*** that they will be
9: 4 Why do you ***t*** evil in your
10:34 Do not ***t*** that I came to bring
17:25 him, saying, "What do you ***t***,
18:12 "What do you ***t***?
21:28 "But what do you ***t***?
22:17 therefore, what do You ***t***?
22:42 What do you ***t*** about the Christ?
26:53 Or do you ***t*** that I cannot now
26:66 "What do you ***t***?
Mk 14:64 the blasphemy! What do you ***t***?
Lk 7: 7 Therefore I did not even ***t***
10:36 which of these three do you ***t***
13: 4 do you ***t*** that they were worse
13:16 ***t*** of it—for eighteen years, be
17: 9 commanded him? I ***t*** not.
Jn 5:39 for in them you ***t*** you have
5:45 Do not ***t*** that I shall accuse you
11:56 in the temple, "What do you ***t***—
16: 2 that whoever kills you will ***t***
Acts 13:25 Who do you ***t*** I am? I am not He.
17:29 we ought not to ***t*** that the
26: 2 I ***t*** myself happy, King Agrippa,
28:22 to hear from you what you ***t***;
Rom 2: 3 And do you ***t*** this, O man,
12: 3 not to ***t*** of himself more
12: 3 more highly than he ought to ***t***,
12: 3 but to ***t*** soberly, as God has
1 Cor 4: 6 you may learn in us not to ***t***
4: 9 For I ***t*** that God has displayed
7:40 and I ***t*** I also have the Spirit
12:23 of the body which we ***t*** to be
2 Cor 3: 5 sufficient of ourselves to ***t***
10: 2 who ***t*** of us as if we walked
11:16 let no one ***t*** me a fool.
12: 6 lest anyone should ***t*** of me
12:19 do you ***t*** that we excuse
Eph 3:20 above all that we ask or ***t***,
Phil 1: 7 just as it is right for me to ***t***
3:15 and if in anything you ***t***
Jas 4: 5 Or do you ***t*** that the Scripture
1 Pe 4: 4 they ***t*** it strange that you do
4:12 do not ***t*** it strange concerning
2 Pe 1:13 I ***t*** it is right, as long as I

THINKING (3/3)

2 Sam 4:10 ***t*** to have brought good news, I
5: 6 the lame will repel you," ***t***,
2 Chr 32: 1 ***t*** to win them over to himself.

THINKS (10/10) THINK

Ps 40:17 Yet the LORD ***t*** upon me.
Prov 23: 7 For as he ***t*** in his heart, so
1 Cor 7:36 But if any man ***t*** he is behaving
8: 2 And if anyone ***t*** that he knows
10:12 Therefore let him who ***t*** he
13: 5 is not provoked, ***t*** no evil;
14:37 If anyone ***t*** himself to be a
Gal 6: 3 For if anyone ***t*** himself to be
Phil 3: 4 If anyone else ***t*** he may have
Jas 1:26 If anyone among you ***t*** he is

THINNER (1/1)

2 Sam 13: 4 becoming ***t*** day

THIRD (169/152) THREE

Gen 1:13 and the morning were the ***t*** day.
2:14 The name of the ***t*** river is
6:16 lower, second, and ***t*** decks.
22: 4 Then on the ***t*** day Abraham lifted
31:22 And Laban was told on the ***t*** day
32:19 he commanded the second, the ***t***,
34:25 came to pass on the ***t*** day,
40:20 came to pass on the ***t*** day,
42:18 Joseph said to them the ***t*** day,
50:23 children to the ***t*** generation
Ex 19: 1 In the ***t*** month after the
19:11 let them be ready for the ***t*** day
19:11 For on the ***t*** day the LORD will
19:15 Be ready for the ***t*** day; do not
19:16 it came to pass on the ***t*** day
20: 5 on the children to the ***t*** and
25:35 and a knob under the ***t*** two
28:19 the ***t*** row, a jacinth, an agate,
34: 7 children's children to the ***t***
37:21 and a knob under the ***t*** two
39:12 the ***t*** row, a jacinth, an agate,
Lev 7:17 of the sacrifice on the ***t*** day
7:18 is eaten at all on the ***t*** day,
19: 6 if any remains until the ***t*** day
19: 7 if it is eaten at all on the ***t*** day
Num 2:24 they shall be the ***t*** to break
7:24 On the ***t*** day Eliab the son of
14:18 on the children to the ***t*** and
19:12 with the water on the ***t*** day
19:12 not purify himself on the ***t*** day
19:19 the unclean on the ***t*** day
29:20 On the ***t*** day present eleven
31:19 and your captives on the ***t*** day
Deut 5: 9 upon the children to the ***t*** and
14:28 At the end of every ***t*** year you
23: 8 The children of the ***t*** generation
26:12 of your increase in the ***t*** year—
Josh 9:17 to their cities on the ***t*** day
19:10 The ***t*** lot came out for the
Judg 20:30 Benjamin on the ***t*** day
1 Sam 3: 8 called Samuel again the ***t*** time.
17:13 and the ***t*** Shammah.
19:21 messengers again the ***t*** time
20: 5 in the field until the ***t*** day
20:12 or the ***t*** day, and indeed
30: 1 on the ***t*** day, that the
2 Sam 1: 2 on the ***t*** day, behold, it
3: 3 of Nabal the Carmelite; the ***t***,
18: 2 Then David sent out one ***t*** of the
18: 2 one ***t*** under the hand of Abishai
18: 2 and one ***t*** under the hand of
1 Ki 3:18 the ***t*** day after I had given
6: 6 and the ***t*** was seven cubits
6: 8 and from the middle to the ***t***.
12:12 came to Rehoboam the ***t*** day,
12:12 Come back to me the ***t*** day."
15:28 Baasha killed him in the ***t*** year
15:33 In the ***t*** year of Asa king of
18: 1 in the ***t*** year, saying, "Go,
18:34 Do it a ***t*** time," and they did
18:34 and they did it a ***t*** time.
22: 2 in the ***t*** year, that Jehoshaphat
2 Ki 1:13 he sent a ***t*** captain of fifty
1:13 And the ***t*** captain of fifty went
18: 1 came to pass in the ***t*** year
19:29 Also in the ***t*** year sow and
20: 5 On the ***t*** day you shall go up to
20: 8 house of the LORD the ***t*** day
1 Chr 2:13 the second, Shimea the ***t***,
3: 2 the ***t***, Absalom the son of
3:15 the ***t*** Zedekiah, and the fourth
8: 1 Ashbel the second, Aharah the ***t***,
8:39 the second, and Eliphelet the ***t***.
12: 9 Obadiah the second, Eliab the ***t***,
23:19 the second, Jahaziel the ***t***,
24: 8 the ***t*** to Harim, the fourth to
24:23 the second, Jahaziel the ***t***,
25:10 the ***t*** for Zaccur, his sons and
26: 2 the second, Zebadiah the ***t***,
26: 4 the second, Joah the ***t***,
26:11 the second, Tebaliah the ***t***,
27: 5 The ***t*** captain of the army for
27: 5 of the army for the ***t*** month
2 Chr 10:12 came to Rehoboam on the ***t*** day,
10:12 Come back to me the ***t*** day."
15:10 at Jerusalem in the ***t*** month,
17: 7 Also in the ***t*** year of his reign
27: 5 him in the second and ***t*** years
31: 7 In the ***t*** month they began
Ezra 6:15 temple was finished on the ***t*** day
Esth 1: 3 that in the ***t*** year of his reign
5: 1 Now it happened on the ***t*** day
8: 9 in the ***t*** month, which is the
Job 42:14 and the name of the ***t***
Isa 37:30 Also in the ***t*** year sow and
Jer 38:14 brought to him at the ***t*** entrance
Ezek 5:12 and I will scatter another ***t*** to
10:14 the ***t*** the face of a lion,
21:14 The ***t*** time let the sword do
31: 1 in the ***t*** month, on the first
46:14 and a ***t*** of a hin of oil to
Dan 1: 1 In the ***t*** year of the reign of
2:39 a ***t*** kingdom of bronze, which
5: 7 and he shall be the ***t*** ruler in
5:16 and shall be the ***t*** ruler in the
5:29 that he should be the ***t*** ruler
8: 1 In the ***t*** year of the reign of
10: 1 In the ***t*** year of Cyrus king of
Hos 6: 2 On the ***t*** day He will raise us
Zech 6: 3 with the ***t*** chariot white horses,
13: 8 But one- ***t*** shall be left in
Mt 16:21 and be raised the ***t*** day.
17:23 and the ***t*** day He will be raised
20: 3 And he went out about the ***t*** hour
20:19 And the ***t*** day He will rise
22:26 the second also, and the ***t***,
26:44 and prayed the ***t*** time, saying
27:64 be made secure until the ***t*** day,
Mk 9:31 He will rise the ***t*** day."
10:34 And the ***t*** day He will rise
12:21 And the ***t*** likewise.
14:41 Then He came the ***t*** time and said
15:25 Now it was the ***t*** hour, and they
Lk 9:22 and be raised the ***t*** day."
12:38 or come in the ***t*** watch, and
13:32 and the ***t*** day I shall be
18:33 And the ***t*** day He will rise
20:12 "And again he sent a ***t***;
20:31 Then the ***t*** took her, and in like
23:22 Then he said to them the ***t*** time,
24: 7 and the ***t*** day rise again.'"
24:21 today is the ***t*** day since these
24:46 to rise from the dead the ***t*** day
Jn 2: 1 On the ***t*** day there was a wedding
21:14 This is now the ***t*** time Jesus
21:17 He said to him the ***t*** time,
21:17 He said to him the ***t*** time,
Acts 2:15 since it is only the ***t*** hour of
10:40 Him God raised up on the ***t*** day,
20: 9 he fell down from the ***t*** story
23:23 to go to Caesarea at the ***t*** hour
27:19 On the ***t*** day we threw the
1 Cor 12:28 ***t*** teachers, after that
15: 4 that He rose again the ***t*** day
2 Cor 12: 2 caught up to the ***t*** heaven
12:14 Now for the ***t*** time I am ready
13: 1 This will be the ***t*** time I am
Rev 4: 7 the ***t*** living creature had a
6: 5 When He opened the ***t*** seal, I
6: 5 I heard the ***t*** living creature
8: 7 And a ***t*** of the trees were
8: 8 and a ***t*** of the sea became
8: 9 And a ***t*** of the living creatures
8: 9 and a ***t*** of the ships were
8:10 Then the ***t*** angel sounded: And a
8:10 and it fell on a ***t*** of the
8:11 A ***t*** of the waters became
8:12 And a ***t*** of the sun was struck,
8:12 a ***t*** of the moon, and a third of
8:12 and a ***t*** of the stars, so that a
8:12 so that a ***t*** of them were
8:12 A ***t*** of the day did not shine,
9:15 were released to kill a ***t*** of
9:18 By these three plagues a ***t*** of
11:14 the ***t*** woe is coming quickly.
12: 4 His tail drew a ***t*** of the stars
14: 9 Then a ***t*** angel followed them,
16: 4 Then the ***t*** angel poured out his
21:19 the ***t*** chalcedony, the fourth

THIRST (29/29) THIRSTS, THIRSTY

Ex 17: 3 and our livestock with ***t***?
Deut 28:48 against you, in hunger, in ***t***,
Judg 15:18 and now shall I die of ***t*** and
2 Chr 32:11 over to die by famine and by ***t***,
Neh 9:15 out of the rock for their ***t***,
9:20 gave them water for their ***t***.
Job 24:11 tread winepresses, yet suffer ***t***.
Ps 69:21 And for my ***t*** they gave me
104:11 wild donkeys quench their ***t***.
Isa 5:13 their multitude dried up with ***t***.
41:17 Their tongues fail for ***t***.
48:21 And they did not ***t*** When He led
49:10 shall neither hunger nor ***t***,
50: 2 is no water, And die of ***t***.
Jer 2:25 and your throat from ***t***.
48:18 from your glory, And sit in ***t***;
Lam 4: 4 To the roof of its mouth for ***t***;
Hos 2: 3 dry land, And slay her with ***t***.
Am 8:11 Nor a ***t*** for water, But of
8:13 young men Shall faint from ***t***.
Mt 5: 6 are those who hunger and ***t***
Jn 4:13 drinks of this water will ***t***
4:14 I shall give him will never ***t***.
4:15 me this water, that I may not ***t***,
6:35 believes in Me shall never ***t***.
19:28 be fulfilled, said, "I ***t***!"
1 Cor 4:11 hour we both hunger and ***t***,
2 Cor 11:27 often, in hunger and ***t***,
Rev 7:16 neither hunger anymore nor ***t***

THIRSTED (1/1)

Ex 17: 3 And the people ***t*** there for

THIRSTS (6/6) THIRST, THIRSTY

Ps 42: 2 My soul ***t*** for God,
63: 1 My soul ***t*** for You; My flesh
Isa 55: 1 "Ho! Everyone who ***t***,
Jn 7:37 saying, "If anyone ***t***,
Rev 21: 6 of life freely to him who ***t***.
22:17 Come!" And let him who ***t*** come.

THIRSTY (21/21) THIRST

Deut 8:15 serpents and scorpions and ***t***
Judg 4:19 water to drink, for I am ***t***.
15:18 Then he became very ***t***;
Ruth 2: 9 touch you? And when you are ***t***,
2 Sam 17:29 are hungry and weary and ***t*** in
Ps 63: 1 longs for You In a dry and ***t***
107: 5 Hungry and ***t***, Their soul
143: 6 soul longs for You like a ***t***
Prov 25:21 bread to eat; And if he is ***t***,
Isa 21:14 Bring water to him who is ***t***;
29: 8 Or as when a ***t*** man dreams,
32: 6 will cause the drink of the ***t***
35: 7 And the ***t*** land springs of
44: 3 will pour water on him who is ***t***,
65:13 drink, But you shall be ***t***;
Ezek 19:13 In a dry and ***t*** land.
Mt 25:35 I was ***t*** and you gave Me drink;
25:37 or ***t*** and give You drink?
25:42 I was ***t*** and you gave Me no
25:44 did we see You hungry or ***t*** or
Rom 12:20 feed him; If he is ***t***,

THIRTEEN (13/13)

Gen 17:25 And Ishmael his son was ***t*** years
Num 29:13 ***t*** young bulls, two rams,
29:14 an ephah for each of the ***t*** bulls
Josh 19: 6 ***t*** cities and their villages;
21: 4 had ***t*** cities by lot from the
21: 6 children of Gershon had ***t*** cities
21:19 were ***t*** cities with their

21:33 to their families were *t* cities
1 Ki 7: 1 But Solomon took *t* years to
1 Chr 6:60 among their families were *t*.
6:62 they gave *t* cities from the
26:11 and brethren of Hosah were *t*.
Ezek 40:11 length of the gate, *t* cubits.

THIRTEENTH (11/11)

Gen 14: 4 and in the *t* year they
1 Chr 24:13 the *t* to Huppah, the fourteenth
25:20 the *t* for Shubael, his sons and
Esth 3:12 scribes were called on the *t* day
3:13 on the *t* day of the twelfth
8:12 on the *t* day of the twelfth
9: 1 on the *t* day, the time came
9:17 This was on the *t* day of the
9:18 assembled together on the *t* day
Jer 1: 2 in the *t* year of his reign.
25: 3 From the *t* year of Josiah the

THIRTIETH (1/1) THIRTY

Ezek 1: 1 Now it came to pass in the *t*

THIRTY (113/104) THIRTIETH

Gen 5: 3 lived one hundred and *t* years,
5: 5 were nine hundred and *t* years;
5:16 eight hundred and *t* years,
6:15 and its height *t* cubits.
11:14 Salah lived *t* years, and begot
11:17 four hundred and *t* years,
11:18 Peleg lived *t* years, and begot
11:22 Serug lived *t* years, and begot
18:30 Suppose *t* should be found
18:30 not do it if I find *t* there."
32:15 *t* milk camels with their colts,
41:46 Joseph was *t* years old when he
47: 9 are one hundred and *t* years;
Ex 12:40 was four hundred and *t* years.
12:41 the four hundred and *t* years—on
21:32 give to their master *t* shekels
26: 8 curtain shall be *t* cubits,
36:15 of each curtain was *t* cubits,
38:24 seven hundred and *t* shekels,
Lev 27: 4 valuation shall be *t* shekels;
Num 4: 3 'from *t* years old and above,
4:23 'From *t* years old and above,
4:30 'From *t* years old and above,
4:35 from *t* years old and above,
4:39 from *t* years old and above,
4:40 two thousand six hundred and *t*.
4:43 from *t* years old and above,
4:47 from *t* years old and above,
7:13 of which was one hundred and *t*
7:19 of which was one hundred and *t*
7:25 of which was one hundred and *t*
7:31 of which was one hundred and *t*
7:37 of which was one hundred and *t*
7:43 of which was one hundred and *t*
7:49 of which was one hundred and *t*
7:55 of which was one hundred and *t*
7:61 of which was one hundred and *t*
7:67 of which was one hundred and *t*
7:73 of which was one hundred and *t*
7:79 of which was one hundred and *t*
7:85 one hundred and *t* shekels
20:29 mourned for Aaron *t* days.
26: 7 thousand seven hundred and *t*.
26:51 thousand seven hundred and *t*.
31:39 The donkeys were *t* thousand
31:45 *t* thousand five hundred donkeys,
Deut 34: 8 in the plains of Moab *t* days.
Josh 8: 3 and Joshua chose *t* thousand
Judg 10: 4 Now he had *t* sons who rode on
10: 4 sons who rode on *t* donkeys;
10: 4 they also had *t* towns, which
12: 9 He had *t* sons. And he gave away
12: 9 And he gave away *t* daughters in
12: 9 and brought in *t* daughters from
12:14 forty sons and *t* grandsons
14:11 that they brought *t* companions
14:12 then I will give you *t* linen
14:12 linen garments and *t* changes
14:13 then you shall give me *t* linen
14:13 linen garments and *t* changes
14:19 to Ashkelon and killed *t* of
20:31 about *t* men of Israel.
20:39 to strike and kill about *t* of
1 Sam 4:10 fell of Israel *t* thousand
9:22 there were about *t* persons.
11: 8 the men of Judah *t* thousand.
13: 5 *t* thousand chariots and six
2 Sam 5: 4 David was *t* years old when he
6: 1 men of Israel, *t* thousand.
23:13 Then three of the *t* chief men
23:23 He was more honored than the *t*,
23:24 of Joab was one of the *t*;
1 Ki 4:22 for one day was *t* kors of
5:13 the labor force was *t* thousand
6: 2 and its height *t* cubits.
7: 2 and its height *t* cubits,
7: 6 and its width *t* cubits; and in
7:23 and a line of *t* cubits measured
2 Ki 18:14 hundred talents of silver and *t*
1 Chr 11:15 Now three of the *t* chief men
11:25 he was more honored than the *t*,
11:42 chief of the Reubenites) and *t*
12: 4 a mighty man among the *t*,
12: 4 the thirty, and over the *t*;
15: 7 and one hundred and *t* of his
23: 3 were numbered from the age of *t*
27: 6 who was mighty among the *t*,
27: 6 the thirty, and was over the *t*;
2 Chr 4: 2 and a line of *t* cubits measured
24:15 he was one hundred and *t*
35: 7 to the number of *t* thousand,
Ezra 1: 9 *t* gold platters, one thousand
1:10 *t* gold basins, four hundred and
2:35 thousand six hundred and *t*.
Neh 7:38 thousand nine hundred and *t*.
7:70 and five hundred and *t* priestly
Esth 4:11 go in to the king these *t* days
Jer 38:10 Take from here *t* men with you,
Ezek 40:17 *t* chambers faced the pavement.
41: 6 *t* chambers in each story;
46:22 forty cubits long and *t* wide;
Dan 6: 7 any god or man for *t* days
6:12 any god or man within *t* days,
Zech 11:12 for my wages *t* pieces of silver
11:13 So I took the *t* pieces of
Mt 13: 8 hundredfold, some sixty, some *t*.
13:23 hundredfold, some sixty, some *t*.
26:15 counted out to him *t* pieces
27: 3 and brought back the *t* pieces
27: 9 And they took the *t* pieces
Lk 3:23 ministry at about *t* years
Jn 2: 6 containing twenty or *t* gallons
Gal 3:17 which was four hundred and *t*

THIRTY-EIGHT (4/4)

Deut 2:14 the Valley of the Zered was *t*
1 Chr 23: 3 of individual males was *t*
Neh 7:45 of Shobai, one hundred and *t*.
Jn 5: 5 there who had an infirmity *t*

THIRTY-EIGHTH (2/2)

1 Ki 16:29 In the *t* year of Asa king of
2 Ki 15: 8 In the *t* year of Azariah king

THIRTY-FIFTH (1/1)

2 Chr 15:19 there was no war until the *t*

THIRTY-FIRST (1/1)

1 Ki 16:23 In the *t* year of Asa king of

THIRTY-FIVE (9/9)

Gen 11:12 Arphaxad lived *t* years, and
Num 1:37 the tribe of Benjamin were *t*
2:23 And his army was numbered at *t*
1 Ki 22:42 Jehoshaphat was *t* years old
2 Chr 3:15 of the temple two pillars *t* cubits
20:31 He was *t* years old when he
Ezra 2:67 their camels four hundred and *t*,
Neh 7:69 camels four hundred and *t*,
Dan 12:12 thousand three hundred and *t*

THIRTY-FOUR (2/2)

Gen 11:16 Eber lived *t* years, and begot
1 Chr 7: 7 twenty-two thousand and *t*

THIRTY-NINE (1/1)

Ezra 2:42 one hundred and *t* in all.

THIRTY-NINTH (3/3)

2 Ki 15:13 became king in the *t* year
15:17 In the *t* year of Azariah king
2 Chr 16:12 And in the *t* year of his reign,

THIRTY-ONE (3/3)

Josh 12:24 of Tirzah, one—all the kings, *t*.
2 Ki 22: 1 and he reigned *t* years in
2 Chr 34: 1 and he reigned *t* years in

THIRTY-SECOND (2/2)

Neh 5:14 twentieth year until the *t* year
13: 6 for in the *t* year of Artaxerxes

THIRTY-SEVEN (9/9)

Gen 25:17 one hundred and *t* years; and he
Ex 6:16 of Levi were one hundred and *t*.
6:20 Amram were one hundred and *t*.
Num 31:36 in number three hundred and *t*
31:43 was three hundred and *t*
2 Sam 23:39 Uriah the Hittite: *t* in all.
1 Chr 12:34 and with them *t* thousand with
Ezra 2:65 thousand three hundred and *t*;
Neh 7:67 thousand three hundred and *t*;

THIRTY-SEVENTH (3/3)

2 Ki 13:10 In the *t* year of Joash king of
25:27 it came to pass in the *t* year
Jer 52:31 it came to pass in the *t* year

THIRTY-SIX (6/6)

Num 31:38 The cattle were *t* thousand, of
31:44 *t* thousand cattle,
Josh 7: 5 men of Ai struck down about *t*
1 Chr 7: 4 were *t* thousand troops ready
Ezra 2:66 were seven hundred and *t*,
Neh 7:68 horses were seven hundred and *t*,

THIRTY-SIXTH (1/1)

2 Chr 16: 1 In the *t* year of the reign of

THIRTY-THREE (7/7)

Gen 46:15 sons and his daughters, were *t*.
Ex 6:18 Kohath were one hundred and *t*.
Lev 12: 4 blood of her purification *t*
2 Sam 5: 5 Jerusalem he reigned *t* years
1 Ki 2:11 Jerusalem he reigned *t* years
1 Chr 3: 4 Jerusalem he reigned *t* years
29:27 and *t* years he reigned in

THIRTY-TWO (15/15)

Gen 11:20 Reu lived *t* years, and begot
Num 1:35 the tribe of Manasseh were *t*
2:21 And his army was numbered at *t*
26:37 *t* thousand five hundred.
31:35 and *t* thousand persons in all,
31:40 the LORD's tribute was *t* persons
1 Ki 20: 1 *t* kings were with him,
20:15 there were two hundred and *t*;
20:16 Meanwhile Ben-Hadad and the *t*
22:31 of Syria had commanded the *t*
2 Ki 8:17 He was *t* years old when he
1 Chr 19: 7 for themselves *t* thousand chariots
2 Chr 21: 5 Jehoram was *t* years old when he
21:20 He was *t* years old when he
Jer 52:29 Jerusalem eight hundred and *t*

THIRTYFOLD (2/2)

Mk 4: 8 increased and produced: some *t*,
4:20 it, and bear fruit: some *t*,

THIS (2814/2598) See APPENDIX

THISTLE (5/3)

2 Ki 14: 9 The *t* that was in Lebanon sent
14: 9 passed by and trampled the *t*.
2 Chr 25:18 The *t* that was in Lebanon sent
25:18 passed by and trampled the *t*.
Hos 10: 8 The thorn and *t* shall grow on

THISTLES (3/3)

Gen 3:18 Both thorns and *t* it shall
Job 31:40 Then let *t* grow instead of
Mt 7:16 from thornbushes or figs from *t*?

THOMAS (12/12)

Mt 10: 3 *T* and Matthew the tax
Mk 3:18 Philip, Bartholomew, Matthew, *T*,
Lk 6:15 Matthew and *T*; James
Jn 11:16 Then *T*, who is called the Twin,
14: 5 *T* said to Him, "Lord, we do not
20:24 Now *T*, called the Twin,
20:26 and *T* with them. Jesus came,
20:27 Then He said to *T*,
20:28 And *T* answered and said to Him,
20:29 Jesus said to him, "*T*,
21: 2 *T* called the Twin, Nathanael of
Acts 1:13 John, and Andrew; Philip and *T*;

THONGS (1/1)

Acts 22:25 And as they bound him with *t*,

THORN (6/6) THORNBUSHES, THORNS

Prov 26: 9 Like a *t* that goes into the
Isa 55:13 Instead of the *t* shall come up
Ezek 28:24 a pricking brier or a painful *t*
Hos 10: 8 The *t* and thistle shall grow
Mic 7: 4 upright is sharper than a *t*
2 Cor 12: 7 a *t* in the flesh was given to

THORNBUSHES (1/1) THORN

Mt 7:16 Do men gather grapes from *t* or

THORNS (48/45) THORN

Gen 3:18 Both *t* and thistles it shall
Ex 22: 6 breaks out and catches in *t*,
Num 33:55 irritants in your eyes and *t*
Josh 23:13 scourges on your sides and *t*
Judg 2: 3 but they shall be *t* in your
8: 7 tear your flesh with the *t* of
8:16 and *t* of the wilderness and
2 Sam 23: 6 rebellion shall all be as *t*
Job 5: 5 Taking it even from the *t*,
Ps 58: 9 pots can feel the burning *t*,
118:12 were quenched like a fire of *t*;
Prov 15:19 lazy man is like a hedge of *t*,
22: 5 *T* and snares are in the way
24:31 it was, all overgrown with *t*;
Eccl 7: 6 For like the crackling of *t*
Song 2: 2 Like a lily among *t*,
Isa 5: 6 shall come up briers and *t*.
7:19 And on all *t* and in all
7:23 It will be for briers and *t*.
7:24 land will become briers and *t*.
7:25 there for fear of briers and *t*;
9:18 shall devour the briers and *t*,
10:17 It will burn and devour His *t*
27: 4 Who would set briers and *t*
32:13 of my people will come up *t*
33:12 Like *t* cut up they shall be

34:13 And *t* shall come up in its
Jer 4: 3 ground, And do not sow among *t*.
12:13 have sown wheat but reaped *t*;
Ezek 2: 6 though briers and *t* are with
Hos 2: 6 will hedge up your way with *t*,
9: 6 *T* shall be in their tents.
Nah 1:10 For while tangled like *t*,
Mt 13: 7 "And some fell among *t*,
13: 7 and the *t* sprang up and choked
13:22 who received seed among the *t*
27:29 they had twisted a crown of *t*,
Mk 4: 7 "And some seed fell among *t*;
4: 7 and the *t* grew up and choked
4:18 these are the ones sown among *t*;
15:17 and they twisted a crown of *t*,
Lk 6:44 men do not gather figs from *t*,
8: 7 "And some fell among *t*,
8: 7 and the *t* sprang up with it and
8:14 the ones that fell among *t*
Jn 19: 2 soldiers twisted a crown of *t*
19: 5 wearing the crown of *t* and the
Heb 6: 8 but if it bears *t* and briars,

THOROUGHLY (15/14)

Gen 11: 3 us make bricks and bake them *t*.
Ex 21:19 provide for him to be *t* healed
Judg 15: 2 really thought that you *t* hated
2 Ki 11:18 They *t* broke in pieces its
Ps 51: 2 Wash me *t* from my iniquity,
Isa 1:25 And *t* purge away your dross,
Jer 6: 9 They shall *t* glean as a vine the
7: 5 For if you *t* amend your ways and
7: 5 if you *t* execute judgment
50:34 He will *t* plead their case,
Ezek 16: 9 I *t* washed off your blood, and
Mt 3:12 and He will *t* clean out His
Lk 3:17 and He will *t* clean out His
2 Cor 11: 6 But we have been *t* manifested
2 Tim 3:17 *t* equipped for every good work.

THOSE (1508/1349) See APPENDIX

THOUGH (260/234)

Gen 33:10 as I have seen your face as *t*
40:10 it was as *t* it budded,
Ex 34: 9 even *t* we are a stiff-necked
Lev 5:17 *t* he does not know it, yet he
11: 7 *t* it divides the hoof,
13:55 *t* the plague has not spread,
26:36 they shall flee as *t* fleeing
Num 18:27 shall be reckoned to you as *t*
22:18 *T* Balak were to give me his
Deut 19: 6 *t* he was not deserving of
29:19 even *t* I follow the dictates of
29:19 as *t* the drunkard could be
32:52 *t* you shall not go there,
Josh 17:18 *t* they have iron chariots and
22:28 *t* not for burnt offerings nor
Judg 13:16 *T* you detain Me, I will not eat
14: 6 *t* he had nothing in his hand.
21:22 for it is not as *t* you have
Ruth 2: 7 *t* she rested a little in the
2:13 *t* I am not like one of your
1 Sam 14:39 *t* it be in Jonathan my son,
20:20 as *t* I shot at a target;
21: 5 even *t* it was sanctified in the
2 Sam 3:39 am weak today, *t* anointed king;
4: 6 as *t* to get wheat, and they
18:12 *T* I were to receive a thousand
1 Ki 2:28 *t* he had not defected to
2:32 *t* my father David did not know
16:31 as *t* it had been a trivial
2 Ki 4:39 *t* they did not know what they
25: 4 even *t* the Chaldeans were
1 Chr 26:10 Shimri the first (for *t* he was
2 Chr 30:19 *t* he is not cleansed
Ezra 3: 3 *T* fear had come upon them
9:15 *t* no one can stand before You
Neh 1: 9 *t* some of you were cast out to
6: 1 (*t* at that time I had not hung
Job 6:10 *T* in anguish, I would exult,
6:14 Even *t* he forsakes the fear of
8: 7 *T* your beginning was small,
9:15 For *t* I were righteous, I could
9:20 *T* I were righteous, my own
9:20 *T* I were blameless, it would
10:19 I would have been as *t* I had
11:17 *T* you were dark, you would be
13:15 *T* He slay me, yet will I trust
14: 8 *T* its root may grow old in the
15:27 *T* he has covered his face with
16: 6 *T* I speak, my grief is not
20: 6 *T* his haughtiness mounts up to
20:12 *T* evil is sweet in his mouth,
20:13 *T* he spares it and does not
22: 2 *T* he who is wise may be
27: 8 *T* he may gain much, If God
27:16 *T* he heaps up silver like dust,
34: 6 is incurable, *t* I am without
39:16 *t* they were not hers;
40:23 *t* the Jordan gushes into his
40:24 *T* he takes it in his eyes,
41:26 *T* the sword reaches him,
Ps 23: 4 *t* I walk through the valley of
27: 3 *T* an army may encamp against
27: 3 *T* war should rise against me,
35:14 I paced about as *t* he were my
37:24 *T* he fall, he shall not be
46: 2 Even *t* the earth be removed,
46: 2 And *t* the mountains be carried
46: 3 *T* its waters roar and be
46: 3 *T* the mountains shake with
49:12 *t* in honor, does not remain;
49:18 *T* while he lives he blesses
68:13 *T* you lie down among the
69: 4 *T* I have stolen nothing,
95: 9 *t* they saw My work.
99: 8 *T* You took vengeance on their
138: 6 *T* the LORD is on high,
138: 7 *T* I walk in the midst of
Prov 6:35 Nor will he be appeased *t* you
11:21 *T* they join forces, the
16: 5 *T* they join forces, none
26:26 *T* his hatred is covered by
27:22 *T* you grind a fool in a mortar
28: 6 in his ways, *t* he be rich.
29:19 For *t* he understands, he will
Eccl 4:12 *T* one may be overpowered by
6: 5 *T* it has not seen the sun or
8: 6 *T* the misery of man increases
8:12 *T* a sinner does evil a hundred
8:16 even *t* one sees no sleep day or
8:17 For *t* a man labors to discover
8:17 *t* a wise man attempts to know
Isa 1:15 Even *t* you make many prayers,
1:18 *T* your sins are like scarlet,
1:18 *T* they are red like crimson,
10:22 For *t* your people, O Israel, be
12: 1 *T* You were angry with me,
30:20 And *t* the Lord gives you The
32:19 *T* hail comes down on the
33: 1 *t* you have not been
33: 1 *t* they have not dealt
41:25 come against princes as *t*
45: 4 *t* you have not known Me.
45: 5 *t* you have not known Me,
46: 7 *T* one cries out to it, yet it
63:16 *T* Abraham was ignorant of us,
Jer 2:22 For *t* you wash yourself with
4:30 *T* you clothe yourself with
4:30 *T* you adorn yourself with
4:30 *T* you enlarge your eyes with
5: 2 *T* they say, 'As the LORD
5:22 And *t* its waves toss to and
5:22 *T* they roar, yet they cannot
11:11 and *t* they cry out to Me, I
12: 6 Even *t* they speak smooth words
14: 7 *t* our iniquities testify
22:24 *t* Coniah the son of Jehoiakim,
30:11 *T* I make a full end of all
31:20 For *t* I spoke against him,
31:32 *t* I was a husband to them, says
32: 5 *t* you fight with the Chaldeans,
32:33 *t* I taught them, rising up
37:10 For *t* you had defeated the whole
46:23 *T* it cannot be searched,
49:16 *T* you make your nest as high
51: 5 *T* their land was filled with
51:53 *T* Babylon were to mount up to
51:53 And *t* she were to fortify the
51:55 *T* her waves roar like great
52: 7 even *t* the Chaldeans were near
Lam 3:32 *T* He causes grief, Yet He will
Ezek 2: 6 *t* briers and thorns are with
2: 6 *t* they are a rebellious house.
3: 9 *t* they are a rebellious
7:13 *T* he may still be alive;
8:18 and *t* they cry in My ears with
12: 3 *t* they are a rebellious house.
12: 4 as *t* going into captivity;
12: 7 as *t* going into captivity.
12:13 *t* he shall die there.
14:16 even *t* these three men were in
14:18 even *t* these three men were in
14:20 even *t* Noah, Daniel, and Job
23: 5 played the harlot even *t* she
26:21 *t* you are sought for, you will
28: 2 *T* you set your heart as the
32:25 *T* their terror was caused In
32:26 *T* they caused their terror in
Dan 9: 9 *t* we have rebelled against Him.
9:14 *t* we have not obeyed His voice.
Hos 4:15 *T* you, Israel, play the harlot,
5: 2 *T* I rebuke them all.
7:13 *T* I redeemed them, Yet they
7:15 *T* I disciplined and
8:10 *t* they have hired among the
9:12 *T* they bring up their children,
11: 7 *T* they call to the Most High,
12:11 *T* Gilead has idols
12:11 *T* they sacrifice bulls in
13:15 *T* he is fruitful among his
Joel 2: 8 *T* they lunge between the
Am 5:11 *T* you have built houses of
5:19 It will be as *t* a man fled
5:19 a bear met him! Or as *t* he
5:22 *T* you offer Me burnt offerings
9: 2 '*T* they dig into hell,
9: 2 *T* they climb up to heaven,
9: 3 And *t* they hide themselves on
9: 3 *T* they hide from My sight at
9: 4 *T* they go into captivity before
Ob 4 *T* you ascend as high as the
4 And *t* you set your nest among
16 And they shall be as *t* they
Mic 5: 2 *T* you are little among the
Nah 1:12 *T* they are safe, and likewise
1:12 *T* I have afflicted you, I
2: 8 *T* Nineveh of old was like a
Hab 1: 5 *t* it were told you.
2: 3 *T* it tarries, wait for it;
3:17 *T* the fig tree may not
3:17 *T* the labor of the olive may
3:17 *T* the flock may be cut off
Zech 9: 2 *t* they are very wise.
10: 6 They shall be as *t* I had not
12: 3 *t* all nations of the earth are
Mal 1: 4 Even *t* Edom has said, "We
Mt 26:60 Even *t* many false witnesses
Lk 11: 8 *t* he will not rise and give to
16:31 will they be persuaded *t* one
18: 4 *T* I do not fear God nor regard
18: 7 *t* He bears long with them?
Jn 4: 2 (*t* Jesus Himself did not
8: 6 as *t* He did not hear.
9:25 that *t* I was blind, now I
10:38 *t* you do not believe Me,
11:25 *t* he may die, he shall live.
Acts 3:12 as *t* by our own power or
13:28 And *t* they found no cause for
13:41 *T* one were to declare it
17:25 as *t* He needed anything, since
17:27 *t* He is not far from each one
18:25 *t* he knew only the baptism of
23:15 as *t* you were going to make
23:20 as *t* they were going to inquire
28: 4 *t* he has escaped the sea, yet
28:17 *t* I have done nothing against
Rom 4:11 *t* they are uncircumcised,
4:17 things which do not exist as *t*
6:17 But God be thanked that *t* you
7: 3 *t* she has married another man.
9:27 *T* the number of the
1 Cor 4:15 For *t* you might have ten
4:18 as *t* I were not coming to you.
5: 3 have already judged (as *t* I
7:29 who have wives should be as *t*
7:30 those who weep as *t* they did not
7:30 those who rejoice as *t* they did
7:30 those who buy as *t* they did not
9:19 For *t* I am free from all men,
10:17 *t* many, are one bread and one
13: 1 *T* I speak with the tongues of
13: 2 And *t* I have the gift of
13: 2 and *t* I have all faith, so that
13: 3 And *t* I bestow all my goods to
13: 3 and *t* I give my body to be
2 Cor 4:16 Even *t* our outward man is
5:16 Even *t* we have known Christ
5:20 as *t* God were pleading through
7: 8 *t* I did regret it.
7: 8 *t* only for a while.
8: 9 that *t* He was rich, yet for
10: 3 For *t* we walk in the flesh, we
10:14 overextending ourselves (as *t*
11: 6 Even *t* I am untrained in
12: 6 For *t* I might desire to boast, I
12:11 *t* I am nothing.
12:15 *t* the more abundantly I love
13: 4 For *t* He was crucified in
13: 7 *t* we may seem disqualified.
Gal 3:15 *T* it is only a man's
4: 1 *t* he is master of all,
Phil 3: 4 *t* I also might have confidence
4:10 *t* you surely did care, but you
Col 2: 5 For *t* I am absent in the flesh,
2:20 as *t* living in the world,
2 Th 2: 2 as *t* the day of Christ had
1 Tim 3:14 *t* I hope to come to you
Phm 1: 8 *t* I might be very bold in
Heb 5: 8 *t* He was a Son, yet He learned
5:12 For *t* by this time you ought to
6: 9 *t* we speak in this manner.
7: 5 *t* they have come from the loins
12:17 *t* he sought it diligently with
1 Pe 1: 6 *t* now for a little while,
1: 7 *t* it is tested by fire,
1: 8 *T* now you do not see Him, yet
4:12 as *t* some strange thing
2 Pe 1:12 *t* you know and are established
2 Jn 5 not as *t* I wrote a new
Jude 5 *t* you once knew this, that the
Rev 5: 6 stood a Lamb as *t* it had been

THOUGHT (51/51) THINK, THOUGHTS

Gen 20:11 And Abraham said, "Because I *t*,
26: 7 is my wife," because he *t*,
38:15 he *t* she was a harlot, because
48:11 I had not *t* to see your face;
Num 33:56 that I will do to you as I *t*
Deut 15: 9 lest there be a wicked *t* in
19:19 you shall do to him as he *t* to
Judg 15: 2 I really *t* that you thoroughly
Ruth 4: 4 And I *t* to inform you, saying,
1 Sam 1:13 Therefore Eli *t* she was drunk.
18:17 For Saul *t*, "Let my hand not
18:25 " But Saul *t* to make David
20:26 say anything that day, for he *t*,
2 Sam 4:10 the one who *t* I would give him
19:18 and to do what he *t* good.
21:16 *t* he could kill David.
Neh 5: 7 After serious *t*, I rebuked
6: 2 But they *t* to do me harm.
Esth 6: 6 Now Haman *t* in his heart,
Job 12: 5 A lamp is despised in the *t* of
Ps 48: 9 We have *t*, O God, on Your
49:11 Their inner *t* is that their
50:21 You *t* that I was altogether
64: 6 Both the inward *t* and the
73:16 When I *t* how to understand
119:59 I *t* about my ways, And turned
139: 2 You understand my *t* afar off.
Eccl 10:20 curse the king, even in your *t*;

T

Isa 14:24 saying, "Surely, as I have **t**,
Jer 18: 8 of the disaster that I **t** to
Dan 4: 2 I **t** it good to declare the signs
6: 3 and the king gave **t** to setting
Am 4:13 declares to man what his **t** is,
Mt 1:20 But while he **t** about these
Mk 14:72 And when he **t** about it, he
Lk 9:47 perceiving the **t** of their
12:17 And he **t** within himself, saying,
19:11 Jerusalem and because they **t**
Jn 11:13 but they **t** that He was speaking
13:29 For some **t**, because Judas had
Acts 8:20 because you **t** that the gift of
8:22 and pray God if perhaps the **t**
10:19 While Peter **t** about the vision,
12: 9 but **t** he was seeing a vision.
26: 8 Why should it be **t** incredible by
26: 9 I myself **t** I must do many
1 Cor 13:11 I **t** as a child; but when I
2 Cor 9: 5 Therefore I **t** it necessary to
10: 5 bringing every **t** into captivity
1 Th 3: 1 we **t** it good to be left in
Heb 10:29 will he be **t** worthy who has

THOUGHTLESSLY (1/1)

Lev 5: 4 speaking **t** with his lips to do

THOUGHTS (52/48) THOUGHT

Gen 6: 5 that every intent of the **t** of
1 Chr 28: 9 all the intent of the **t**.
29:18 forever in the intent of the **t**
Job 4:13 In disquieting **t** from the
17:11 Even the **t** of my heart.
20: 2 Therefore my anxious **t** make me
21:27 "Look, I know your **t**,
Ps 10: 4 God; God is in none of his **t**.
40: 5 And Your **t** toward us Cannot
56: 5 All their **t** are against me
92: 5 Your **t** are very deep.
94:11 The LORD knows the **t** of man,
139:17 How precious also are Your **t** to
Prov 12: 5 The **t** of the righteous are
15:26 The **t** of the wicked are an
16: 3 And your **t** will be
Isa 55: 7 And the unrighteous man his **t**;
55: 8 For My **t** are not your
55: 8 My thoughts are not your **t**,
55: 9 And My **t** than your thoughts.
55: 9 And My thoughts than your **t**.
59: 7 Their **t** are thoughts of
59: 7 Their thoughts are **t** of
65: 2 According to their own **t**;
66:18 I know their works and their **t**.
Jer 4:14 How long shall your evil **t**
6:19 people—The fruit of their **t**,
23:20 executed and performed the **t**
29:11 For I know the **t** that I think
29:11 **t** of peace and not of evil, to
Ezek 38:10 it shall come to pass that **t**
Dan 2:29 **t** came to your mind while on
2:30 and that you may know the **t** of
4: 5 and the **t** on my bed and the
4:19 and his **t** troubled him.
5: 6 and his **t** troubled him, so that
5:10 Do not let your **t** trouble
7:28 my **t** greatly troubled me,
Mic 4:12 But they do not know the **t** of
Mt 9: 4 But Jesus, knowing their **t**,
12:25 But Jesus knew their **t**,
15:19 out of the heart proceed evil **t**,
Mk 7:21 heart of men, proceed evil **t**,
Lk 2:35 that the **t** of many hearts may
5:22 when Jesus perceived their **t**,
6: 8 But He knew their **t**,
11:17 But He, knowing their **t**,
Rom 1:21 but became futile in their **t**,
2:15 and between themselves their **t**
1 Cor 3:20 The LORD knows the **t** of
Heb 4:12 and is a discerner of the **t** and
Jas 2: 4 and become judges with evil **t**?

THOUSAND (498/394) THOUSANDS

Gen 20:16 I have given your brother a **t**
Ex 12:37 about six hundred **t** men on
32:28 And about three **t** men of the
38:25 one hundred talents and one **t**
38:26 for six hundred and three **t**,
38:28 Then from the one **t** seven
38:29 was seventy talents and two **t**
Lev 26: 8 hundred of you shall put ten **t**
Num 1:21 of Reuben were forty-six **t**
1:23 of Simeon were fifty-nine **t**
1:25 of Gad were forty-five **t** six
1:27 of Judah were seventy-four **t**
1:29 of Issachar were fifty-four **t**
1:31 of Zebulun were fifty-seven **t**
1:33 tribe of Ephraim were forty **t**
1:35 of Manasseh were thirty-two **t**
1:37 of Benjamin were thirty-five **t**
1:39 tribe of Dan were sixty-two **t**
1:41 of Asher were forty-one **t**
1:43 of Naphtali were fifty-three **t**
1:46 were six hundred and three **t**
2: 4 was numbered at seventy-four **t**
2: 6 was numbered at fifty-four **t**
2: 8 was numbered at fifty-seven **t**
2: 9 one hundred and eighty-six **t**
2:11 was numbered at forty-six **t**
2:13 was numbered at fifty-nine **t**
2:15 was numbered at forty-five **t**
2:16 one hundred and fifty-one **t**
2:19 army was numbered at forty **t**
2:21 was numbered at thirty-two **t**
2:23 was numbered at thirty-five **t**
2:24 one hundred and eight **t** one
2:26 was numbered at sixty-two **t**
2:28 was numbered at forty-one **t**
2:30 was numbered at fifty-three **t**
2:31 one hundred and fifty-seven **t**
2:32 were six hundred and three **t**
3:22 numbered there were seven **t**
3:28 there were eight **t** six
3:34 were six **t** two hundred.
3:39 and above, were twenty-two **t**.
3:43 were twenty-two **t** two hundred
3:50 one **t** three hundred and
4:36 by their families were two **t**
4:40 were two **t** six hundred and
4:44 by their families were three **t**
4:48 who were numbered were eight **t**
7:85 of the vessels weighed two **t**
11:21 I am among are six hundred **t**
16:49 in the plague were fourteen **t**
25: 9 the plague were twenty-four **t**.
26: 7 of them were forty-three **t**
26:14 twenty-two **t** two hundred.
26:18 forty **t** five hundred.
26:22 seventy-six **t** five hundred.
26:25 sixty-four **t** three hundred.
26:27 sixty **t** five hundred.
26:34 of them were fifty-two **t**
26:37 thirty-two **t** five hundred.
26:41 of them were forty-five **t** six
26:43 were sixty-four **t** four
26:47 fifty-three **t** four hundred.
26:50 of them were forty-five **t**
26:51 six hundred and one **t** seven
26:62 of them were twenty-three **t**,
31: 4 A **t** from each tribe of all the
31: 5 the divisions of Israel one **t**
31: 5 twelve **t** armed for war.
31: 6 one **t** from each tribe; he sent
31:32 six hundred and seventy-five **t**
31:33 seventy-two **t** cattle,
31:34 sixty-one **t** donkeys,
31:35 and thirty-two **t** persons in all,
31:36 hundred and thirty-seven **t**
31:38 The cattle were thirty-six **t**,
31:39 The donkeys were thirty **t** five
31:40 The persons were sixteen **t**,
31:43 hundred and thirty-seven **t**
31:44 thirty-six **t** cattle,
31:45 thirty **t** five hundred donkeys,
31:46 and sixteen **t** persons—
31:52 was sixteen **t** seven hundred and
35: 4 wall of the city outward a **t**
35: 5 the city on the east side two **t**
35: 5 on the south side two **t** cubits,
35: 5 on the west side two **t** cubits,
35: 5 and on the north side two **t**
Deut 1:11 of your fathers make you a **t**
7: 9 covenant and mercy for a **t**
32:30 How could one chase a **t**,
32:30 And two put ten **t** to flight,
Josh 3: 4 about two **t** cubits by measure.
4:13 About forty **t** prepared for war
7: 3 but let about two or three **t**
7: 4 So about three **t** men went up
8: 3 and Joshua chose thirty **t**
8:12 So he took about five **t** men and
8:25 men and women, were twelve **t**—
23:10 man of you shall chase a **t**,
Judg 1: 4 and they killed ten **t** men at
3:29 time they killed about ten **t**
4: 6 take with you ten **t** men of the
4:10 he went up with ten **t** men under
4:14 from Mount Tabor with ten **t**
5: 8 or spear was seen among forty **t**
7: 3 " And twenty-two **t** of the
7: 3 and ten **t** remained.
8:10 with them, about fifteen **t**,
8:10 for one hundred and twenty **t**
8:26 that he requested was one **t**
9:49 about a **t** men and women.
12: 6 fell at that time forty-two **t**
15:11 Then three **t** men of Judah went
15:15 and killed a **t** men with it.
15:16 of a donkey I have slain a **t**
16:27 about three **t** men and women on
20: 2 four hundred **t** foot soldiers
20:10 a hundred out of every **t**,
20:10 and a **t** out of every ten
20:10 a thousand out of every ten **t**,
20:15 Benjamin numbered twenty-six **t**
20:17 Israel numbered four hundred **t**
20:21 to the ground twenty-two **t** men
20:25 down to the ground eighteen **t**
20:34 And ten **t** select men from all
20:35 that day twenty-five **t** one
20:44 And eighteen **t** men of Benjamin
20:45 and they cut down five **t** of
20:45 and killed two **t** of them.
20:46 that day were twenty-five **t**
21:10 sent out there twelve **t** of
1 Sam 4: 2 who killed about four **t** men of
4:10 there fell of Israel thirty **t**
6:19 He struck fifty **t** and seventy
11: 8 of Israel were three hundred **t**,
11: 8 and the men of Judah thirty **t**.
13: 2 Saul chose for himself three **t**
13: 2 Two **t** were with Saul in
13: 2 and a **t** were with Jonathan in
13: 5 thirty **t** chariots and six
13: 5 thousand chariots and six **t**
15: 4 two hundred **t** foot soldiers and
15: 4 foot soldiers and ten **t** men of
17: 5 weight of the coat was five **t**
17:18 to the captain of their **t**,
18:13 made him his captain over a **t**;
24: 2 Then Saul took three **t** chosen
25: 2 He had three **t** sheep and a
25: 2 three thousand sheep and a **t**
26: 2 having three **t** chosen men of
2 Sam 6: 1 choice men of Israel, thirty **t**.
8: 4 David took from him one **t**
8: 4 and twenty **t** foot soldiers.
8: 5 David killed twenty-two **t** of
8:13 from killing eighteen **t**
10: 6 twenty **t** foot soldiers;
10: 6 from the king of Maacah one **t**
10: 6 and from Ish-Tob twelve **t** men.
10:18 hundred charioteers and forty **t**
17: 1 Now let me choose twelve **t** men,
18: 3 But you are worth ten **t** of us
18: 7 a great slaughter of twenty **t**
18:12 Though I were to receive a **t**
19:17 There were a **t** men of Benjamin
24: 9 were in Israel eight hundred **t**
24: 9 of Judah were five hundred **t**
24:15 Dan to Beersheba seventy **t** men
1 Ki 3: 4 Solomon offered a **t** burnt
4:26 Solomon had forty **t** stalls of
4:26 and twelve **t** horsemen.
4:32 He spoke three **t** proverbs,
4:32 and his songs were one **t** and
5:11 And Solomon gave Hiram twenty **t**
5:13 the labor force was thirty **t**
5:14 ten **t** a month in shifts:
5:15 Solomon had seventy **t** who
5:15 and eighty **t** who quarried
5:16 besides three **t** three hundred
7:26 It contained two **t** baths.
8:63 twenty-two **t** bulls and one
8:63 and one hundred and twenty **t**
10:26 he had one **t** four hundred
10:26 hundred chariots and twelve **t**
12:21 one hundred and eighty **t** chosen
19:18 Yet I have reserved seven **t** in
20:15 the children of Israel—seven **t**.
20:29 of Israel killed one hundred **t**
20:30 a wall fell on twenty-seven **t**
2 Ki 3: 4 king of Israel one hundred **t**
3: 4 and the wool of one hundred **t**
5: 5 six **t** shekels of gold, and ten
13: 7 and ten **t** foot soldiers; for
14: 7 He killed ten **t** Edomites in the
15:19 and Menahem gave Pul a **t**
18:23 and I will give you two **t**
19:35 one hundred and eighty-five **t**;
24:14 ten **t** captives, and all the
24:16 All the valiant men, seven **t**,
24:16 and craftsmen and smiths, one **t**,
1 Chr 5:18 of Manasseh had forty-four **t**
5:21 —fifty **t** of their camels,
5:21 two hundred and fifty **t** of
5:21 and two **t** of their donkeys—also
5:21 also one hundred **t** of their men;
7: 2 of David was twenty-two **t** six
7: 4 were thirty-six **t** troops ready
7: 5 eighty-seven **t** in all.
7: 7 twenty-two **t** and thirty-four
7: 9 twenty **t** two hundred mighty men
7:11 there were seventeen **t** two
7:40 their number was twenty-six **t**.
9:13 one **t** seven hundred and sixty.
12:14 and the greatest was over a **t**.
12:24 six **t** eight hundred armed for
12:25 seven **t** one hundred;
12:26 of the sons of Levi four **t** six
12:27 and with him three **t** seven
12:29 relatives of Saul, three **t**
12:30 of the sons of Ephraim twenty **t**
12:31 of Manasseh eighteen **t**,
12:33 of Zebulun there were fifty **t**
12:34 of Naphtali one **t** captains, and
12:34 and with them thirty-seven **t**
12:35 twenty-eight **t** six hundred;
12:36 keep battle formation, forty **t**;
12:37 one hundred and twenty **t** armed
16:15 for a **t** generations,
18: 4 David took from him one **t**
18: 4 seven **t** horsemen, and twenty
18: 4 and twenty **t** foot soldiers.
18: 5 David killed twenty-two **t** of
18:12 of Zeruiah killed eighteen **t**
19: 6 the people of Ammon sent a **t**
19: 7 for themselves thirty-two **t**
19:18 and David killed seven **t**
19:18 charioteers and forty **t** foot
21: 5 had one million one hundred **t**
21: 5 four hundred and seventy **t** men
21:14 and seventy **t** men of Israel
22:14 of the LORD one hundred **t**
23: 3 males was thirty-eight **t**.
23: 4 twenty-four **t** were to look
23: 4 six **t** were officers and
23: 5 four **t** were gatekeepers,
23: 5 and four **t** praised the LORD
26:30 one **t** seven hundred able men,
26:32 And his brethren were two **t**
27: 1 division having twenty-four **t**.
27: 2 division were twenty-four **t**;
27: 4 division were twenty-four **t**.

27: 5 division were twenty-four *t*.
27: 7 division were twenty-four *t*.
27: 8 his division were twenty-four *t*.
27: 9 division were twenty-four *t*.
27:10 division were twenty-four *t*.
27:11 division were twenty-four *t*.
27:12 division were twenty-four *t*.
27:13 division were twenty-four *t*.
27:14 division were twenty-four *t*.
27:15 division were twenty-four *t*.
29: 4 'three *t* talents of gold,
29: 4 and seven *t* talents of refined
29: 7 work of the house of God five *t*
29: 7 five thousand talents and ten *t*
29: 7 ten *t* talents of silver,
29: 7 eighteen *t* talents of bronze,
29: 7 and one hundred *t* talents of
29:21 a *t* bulls, a thousand rams,
29:21 a *t* rams, a thousand lambs,
29:21 a *t* lambs, with their drink
2 Chr 1: 6 and offered a *t* burnt offerings
1:14 he had one *t* four hundred
1:14 hundred chariots and twelve *t*
2: 2 Solomon selected seventy *t* men
2: 2 eighty *t* to quarry stone in
2: 2 and three *t* six hundred to
2:10 twenty *t* kors of ground wheat,
2:10 twenty *t* kors of barley,
2:10 twenty *t* baths of wine,
2:10 and twenty *t* baths of oil.
2:17 one hundred and fifty-three *t*
2:18 And he made seventy *t* of them
2:18 eighty *t* stonecutters in the
2:18 and three *t* six hundred
4: 5 It contained three *t* baths.
7: 5 a sacrifice of twenty-two *t*
7: 5 and one hundred and twenty *t*
9:25 Solomon had four *t* stalls for
9:25 and twelve *t* horsemen whom he
11: 1 one hundred and eighty *t*
12: 3 sixty *t* horsemen, and people
13: 3 four hundred *t* choice men.
13: 3 him with eight hundred *t*
13:17 so five hundred *t* choice men of
14: 8 had an army of three hundred *t*
14: 8 two hundred and eighty *t* men
15:11 seven hundred bulls and seven *t*
17:11 seven *t* seven hundred rams and
17:11 seven hundred rams and seven *t*
17:14 and with him three hundred *t*
17:15 him two hundred and eighty *t*;
17:16 and with him two hundred *t*
17:17 and with him two hundred *t* men
17:18 him one hundred and eighty *t*
25: 5 them to be three hundred *t*
25: 6 He also hired one hundred *t*
25:11 of Salt and killed ten *t* of
25:12 of Judah took captive ten *t*
25:13 killed three *t* in them,
26:12 mighty men of valor was two *t*
26:13 of three hundred and seven *t*
27: 5 ten *t* kors of wheat, and ten
27: 5 and ten *t* of barley. The people
28: 6 one hundred and twenty *t* in
28: 8 of their brethren two hundred *t*
29:33 six hundred bulls and three *t*
30:24 Judah gave to the assembly a *t*
30:24 a thousand bulls and seven *t*
30:24 gave to the assembly a *t* bulls
30:24 a thousand bulls and ten *t*
35: 7 to the number of thirty *t*,
35: 7 as well as three *t* cattle;
35: 8 the Passover offerings two *t*
35: 9 for Passover offerings five *t*
Ezra 1: 9 one *t* silver platters,
1:10 and one *t* other articles.
1:11 of gold and silver were five *t*
2: 3 two *t* one hundred and
2: 6 two *t* eight hundred and twelve;
2: 7 one *t* two hundred and
2:12 one *t* two hundred and
2:14 two *t* and fifty-six;
2:31 one *t* two hundred and
2:35 three *t* six hundred and thirty.
2:37 one *t* and fifty-two;
2:38 one *t* two hundred and
2:39 one *t* and seventeen.
2:64 together was forty-two *t*
2:65 of whom there were seven *t*
2:67 and their donkeys six *t* seven
2:69 for the work sixty-one *t* gold
2:69 five *t* minas of silver, and one
8:27 twenty gold basins worth a *t*
Neh 3:13 and repaired a *t* cubits of the
7: 8 two *t* one hundred and
7:11 two *t* eight hundred and
7:12 one *t* two hundred and
7:17 two *t* three hundred and
7:19 two *t* and sixty-seven;
7:34 one *t* two hundred and
7:38 three *t* nine hundred and
7:40 one *t* and fifty-two;
7:41 one *t* two hundred and
7:42 one *t* and seventeen.
7:66 whole assembly was forty-two *t*
7:67 of whom there were seven *t*
7:69 and donkeys six *t* seven
7:70 gave to the treasury one *t*
7:71 treasury of the work twenty *t*
7:71 and two *t* two hundred silver
7:72 the people gave was twenty *t*
7:72 two *t* silver minas,
Esth 3: 9 and I will pay ten *t* talents of
9:16 and killed seventy-five *t* of
Job 1: 3 his possessions were seven *t*
1: 3 three *t* camels, five hundred
9: 3 answer Him one time out of a *t*.
33:23 him, A mediator, one among a *t*,
42:12 for he had fourteen *t* sheep,
42:12 six *t* camels, one thousand yoke
42:12 one *t* yoke of oxen, and one
42:12 and one *t* female donkeys.
Ps 50:10 And the cattle on a *t* hills.
60: returned and killed twelve *t*
68:17 chariots of God are twenty *t*,
84:10 Your courts is better than a *t*.
90: 4 For a *t* years in Your sight
91: 7 A *t* may fall at your side,
91: 7 And ten *t* at your right hand;
105: 8 for a *t* generations,
Eccl 6: 6 even if he lives a *t* years
7:28 One man among a *t* I have
Song 4: 4 On which hang a *t* bucklers,
5:10 and ruddy, Chief among ten *t*.
8:11 was to bring for its fruit A *t*
8:12 You, O Solomon, may have a *t*,
Isa 7:23 wherever there could be a *t*
7:23 be a thousand vines Worth a *t*
30:17 One *t* shall flee at the
36: 8 and I will give you two *t*
37:36 one hundred and eighty-five *t*;
60:22 A little one shall become a *t*,
Jer 52:28 three *t* and twenty-three Jews;
52:30 All the persons were four *t*
Ezek 45: 1 length shall be twenty-five *t*
45: 1 cubits, and the width ten *t*.
45: 3 twenty-five *t* cubits long and
45: 3 cubits long and ten *t* wide;
45: 5 An area twenty-five *t* cubits
45: 5 cubits long and ten *t* wide
45: 6 of the city an area five *t*
45: 6 cubits wide and twenty-five *t*
47: 3 he measured one *t* cubits,
47: 4 Again he measured one *t* and
47: 4 Again he measured one *t* and
47: 5 Again he measured one *t*,
48: 8 twenty-five *t* cubits in width,
48: 9 LORD shall be twenty-five *t*
48: 9 cubits in length and ten *t* in
48:10 on the north twenty-five *t*
48:10 on the west ten *t* in width,
48:10 on the east ten *t* in width,
48:10 and on the south twenty-five *t*
48:13 have an area twenty-five *t*
48:13 cubits in length and ten *t* in
48:13 shall be twenty-five *t* and
48:13 thousand and its width ten *t*.
48:15 The five *t* cubits in width
48:15 the edge of the twenty-five *t*,
48:16 the north side four *t* five
48:16 the south side four *t* five
48:16 the east side four *t* five
48:16 and the west side four *t* five
48:18 shall be ten *t* cubits to the
48:18 cubits to the east and ten *t*
48:20 shall be twenty-five *t*
48:20 cubits by twenty-five *t*
48:21 next to the twenty-five *t*
48:21 next to the twenty-five *t* as
48:30 measuring four *t* five hundred
48:32 four *t* five hundred cubits,
48:33 measuring four *t* five hundred
48:34 four *t* five hundred cubits
48:35 around shall be eighteen *t*
Dan 5: 1 made a great feast for a *t* of
5: 1 wine in the presence of the *t*.
7:10 A *t* thousands ministered to
7:10 Ten *t* times ten thousand stood
7:10 Ten thousand times ten *t* stood
8:14 For two *t* three hundred days;
12:11 there shall be one *t* two
12:12 and comes to the one *t* three
Am 5: 3 The city that goes out by a *t*
Jon 4:11 than one hundred and twenty *t*
Mic 6: 7 Ten *t* rivers of oil?
Mt 14:21 who had eaten were about five *t*
15:38 Now those who ate were four *t*
16: 9 the five loaves of the five *t*
16:10 the seven loaves of the four *t*
18:24 to him who owed him ten *t*
Mk 5:13 swine (there were about two *t*);
6:44 the loaves were about five *t*
8: 9 who had eaten were about four *t*.
8:19 the five loaves for the five *t*,
8:20 broke the seven for the four *t*,
Lk 9:14 For there were about five *t* men.
14:31 whether he is able with ten *t*
14:31 comes against him with twenty *t*?
Jn 6:10 down, in number about five *t*.
Acts 2:41 and that day about three *t*
4: 4 the men came to be about five *t*.
19:19 and it totaled fifty *t* pieces
21:38 a rebellion and led the four *t*
Rom 11: 4 for Myself seven *t* men
1 Cor 4:15 For though you might have ten *t*
10: 8 and in one day twenty-three *t*
14:19 than ten *t* words in a tongue.
2 Pe 3: 8 the Lord one day is as a *t*
3: 8 and a *t* years as one day.
Rev 5:11 the number of them was ten *t*
5:11 was ten thousand times ten *t*,
7: 4 One hundred and forty-four *t*
7: 5 the tribe of Judah twelve *t*
7: 5 the tribe of Reuben twelve *t*
7: 5 of the tribe of Gad twelve *t*
7: 6 of the tribe of Asher twelve *t*
7: 6 the tribe of Naphtali twelve *t*
7: 6 the tribe of Manasseh twelve *t*
7: 7 the tribe of Simeon twelve *t*
7: 7 of the tribe of Levi twelve *t*
7: 7 the tribe of Issachar twelve *t*
7: 8 the tribe of Zebulun twelve *t*
7: 8 the tribe of Joseph twelve *t*
7: 8 the tribe of Benjamin twelve *t*
11: 3 and they will prophesy one *t*
11:13 In the earthquake seven *t*
12: 6 should feed her there one *t*
14: 1 one hundred and forty-four *t*,
14: 3 the hundred and forty-four *t*
14:20 for one *t* six hundred furlongs.
20: 2 and bound him for a *t* years;
20: 3 the nations no more till the *t*
20: 4 and reigned with Christ for a *t*
20: 5 did not live again until the *t*
20: 6 and shall reign with Him a *t*
20: 7 Now when the *t* years have
21:16 the reed: twelve *t* furlongs.

THOUSANDS (54/44) THOUSAND

Gen 24:60 become The mother of *t* of
24:60 mother of thousands of ten *t*;
Ex 18:21 over them to be rulers of *t*,
18:25 over the people: rulers of *t*,
20: 6 but showing mercy to *t*,
34: 7 "keeping mercy for *t*,
Num 10:36 To the many *t* of Israel."
31:14 with the captains over *t* and
31:48 the officers who were over *t*
31:48 the captains of *t* and captains
31:52 from the captains of *t* and
31:54 the gold from the captains of *t*
Deut 1:15 heads over you, leaders of *t*,
5:10 but showing mercy to *t*,
33: 2 And He came with ten *t* of
33:17 They are the ten *t* of
33:17 And they are the *t* of
1 Sam 8:12 appoint captains over his *t*
18: 7 said: "Saul has slain his *t*,
18: 7 thousands, And David his ten *t*.
18: 8 have ascribed to David ten *t*,
18: 8 me they have ascribed only *t*.
21:11 saying: 'Saul has slain his *t*,
21:11 And David his ten *t*'?
22: 7 make you all captains of *t* and
29: 2 in review by hundreds and by *t*,
29: 5 saying: 'Saul has slain his *t*,
29: 5 And David his ten *t*'?
2 Sam 18: 1 and set captains of *t* and
18: 4 went out by hundreds and by *t*.
1 Chr 12:20 captains of the *t* who were
13: 1 with the captains of *t* and
15:25 and the captains over *t* went to
26:26 the captains over *t* and
27: 1 the captains of *t* and hundreds
28: 1 the captains over *t* and
29: 6 the captains of *t* and of
2 Chr 1: 2 to the captains of *t* and of
17:14 Of Judah, the captains of *t*:
25: 5 and set over them captains of *t*
Ps 3: 6 I will not be afraid of ten *t*
68:17 Even *t* of thousands;
68:17 thousand, Even thousands of *t*;
119:72 mouth is better to me Than *t*
144:13 our sheep may bring forth *t*
144:13 forth thousands And ten *t* in
Jer 32:18 'You show lovingkindness to *t*,
Dan 7:10 A thousand *t* ministered to
11:12 and he will cast down tens of *t*,
Mic 5: 2 you are little among the *t* of
6: 7 the LORD be pleased with *t* of
Jude 14 the Lord comes with ten *t* of
Rev 5:11 and *t* of thousands,
5:11 thousand, and thousands of *t*,

THREAD (29/29)

Gen 14:23 from a *t* to a sandal strap,
38:28 the midwife took a scarlet *t*
38:30 out who had the scarlet *t* on
Ex 25: 4 "blue, purple, and scarlet *t*,
26: 1 blue, purple, and scarlet *t*;
26:31 of blue, purple, and scarlet *t*,
26:36 blue, purple, and scarlet *t*,
27:16 blue, purple, and scarlet *t*,
28: 5 blue, purple, and scarlet *t*,
28: 6 blue, purple, and scarlet *t*,
28: 8 blue, purple, and scarlet *t*,
28:15 blue, purple, and scarlet *t*,
28:39 the tunic of fine linen *t*,
35: 6 'blue, purple, and scarlet *t*,
35:23 blue, purple, and scarlet *t*,
35:35 in blue, purple, and scarlet *t*,
36: 8 of blue, purple, and scarlet *t*;
36:35 of blue, purple, and scarlet *t*,
36:37 of blue, purple, and scarlet *t*,
38:18 of blue, purple, and scarlet *t*,
38:23 of blue, purple, and scarlet *t*,
39: 1 and scarlet *t* they made
39: 2 blue, purple, and scarlet *t*,
39: 3 and scarlet *t* and the fine
39: 5 blue, purple, and scarlet *t*,
39: 8 blue, purple, and scarlet *t*,
39:29 blue, purple, and scarlet *t*,
Num 15:38 and to put a blue *t* in the
Judg 16:12 them off his arms like a *t*.

T

THREADS (1/1)

Ex 39: 3 thin sheets and cut it into *t*,

THREAT (3/2)

Job 41:29 He laughs at the *t* of
Isa 30:17 thousand shall flee at the *t*
30:17 At the *t* of five you shall

THREATEN (2/2)

Acts 4:17 let us severely *t* them,
1 Pe 2:23 when He suffered, He did not *t*,

THREATENED (1/1)

Acts 4:21 So when they had further *t* them,

THREATENING (2/2) THREATS

Mt 16: 3 today, for the sky is red and *t*.
Eph 6: 9 things to them, giving up *t*,

THREATS (6/6) THREATENING

Isa 8:12 Nor be afraid of their *t*,
Zeph 2: 8 And made arrogant *t* against
2:10 reproached and made arrogant *t*
Acts 4:29 "Now, Lord, look on their *t*,
9: 1 still breathing *t* and murder
1 Pe 3:14 not be afraid of their *t*,

THREE (444/390) THIRD, THREE-AND-A-HALF, THREE-DAY, THREE-PRONGED, THREE-YEAR-OLD

Gen 5:22 Enoch walked with God *t* hundred
5:23 So all the days of Enoch were *t*
6:10 And Noah begot *t* sons: Shem,
6:15 length of the ark shall be *t*
7:13 and Noah's wife and the *t* wives
9:19 These *t* were the sons of Noah,
9:28 Noah lived after the flood *t*
11:13 lived four hundred and *t* years,
11:15 Salah lived four hundred and *t*
14:14 he armed his *t* hundred and
18: 2 *t* men were standing by him;
18: 6 make ready *t* measures of fine
29: 2 there were *t* flocks of sheep
29:34 because I have borne him *t*
30:36 Then he put *t* days' journey
38:24 about *t* months after, that
40:10 and in the vine were *t*
40:12 The *t* branches are three days.
40:12 The three branches are *t* days.
40:13 Now within *t* days Pharaoh will
40:16 and there were *t* white baskets
40:18 The *t* baskets are three days.
40:18 The three baskets are *t* days.
40:19 Within *t* days Pharaoh will lift
42:17 them all together in prison *t*
45:22 but to Benjamin he gave *t*
Ex 2: 2 she hid him *t* months.
3:18 let us go *t* days' journey into
5: 3 let us go *t* days' journey into
8:27 We will go *t* days' journey into
10:22 in all the land of Egypt *t*
10:23 rise from his place for *t* days.
15:22 And they went *t* days in the
21:11 And if he does not do these *t*
23:14 *T* times you shall keep a feast
23:17 *T* times in the year all your
25:32 *t* branches of the lampstand out
25:32 and *t* branches of the lampstand
25:33 *T* bowls shall be made like
25:33 and *t* bowls made like almond
27: 1 and its height shall be *t*
27:14 with their *t* pillars and their
27:14 their three pillars and their *t*
27:15 with their *t* pillars and their
27:15 their three pillars and their *t*
32:28 And about *t* thousand men of the
34:23 *T* times in the year all your men
34:24 before the LORD your God *t*
37:18 *t* branches of the lampstand out
37:18 and *t* branches of the lampstand
37:19 There were *t* bowls made like
37:19 and *t* bowls made like almond
38: 1 and its height was *t* cubits.
38:14 with their *t* pillars and their
38:14 their three pillars and their *t*
38:15 with their *t* pillars and their
38:15 their three pillars and their *t*
38:26 for six hundred and *t* thousand,
Lev 19:23 *T* years it shall be as
25:21 forth produce enough for *t*
27: 6 your valuation shall be *t*
Num 1:23 were fifty-nine thousand *t*
1:46 numbered were six hundred and *t*
2:13 at fifty-nine thousand *t*
2:32 forces were six hundred and *t*
3:50 one thousand *t* hundred and
4:44 by their families were *t*
10:33 of the LORD on a journey of *t*
10:33 went before them for the *t*
12: 4 and Miriam, "Come out, you *t*,
12: 4 meeting!" So the *t* came out.
22:28 that you have struck me these *t*
22:32 you struck your donkey these *t*
22:33 turned aside from Me these *t*
24:10 blessed them these *t* times!
26:25 sixty-four thousand *t* hundred.
31:36 was in number *t* hundred and
31:43 to the congregation was *t*
33: 8 went *t* days' journey in the
35:14 You shall appoint *t* cities on
35:14 and *t* cities you shall appoint
Deut 4:41 Then Moses set apart *t* cities
16:16 *T* times a year all your males
17: 6 on the testimony of two or *t*
19: 2 you shall separate *t* cities for
19: 3 and divide into *t* parts the
19: 7 You shall separate *t* cities for
19: 9 then you shall add *t* more
19: 9 for yourself besides these *t*,
19:15 by the mouth of two or *t*
Josh 1:11 for within *t* days you will
2:16 Hide there *t* days, until the
2:22 and stayed there *t* days until
3: 2 after *t* days, that the officers
7: 3 but let about two or *t* thousand
7: 4 So about *t* thousand men went up
9:16 it happened at the end of *t*
15:14 Caleb drove out the *t* sons of
17:11 and its towns—*t* hilly regions.
18: 4 Pick out from among you *t* men
21:32 its common-land: *t* cities.
Judg 1:20 he expelled from there the *t*
7: 6 their mouth, was *t* hundred men;
7: 7 By the *t* hundred men who lapped
7: 8 and retained those *t* hundred
7:16 Then he divided the *t* hundred
7:16 the three hundred men into *t*
7:20 Then the *t* companies blew the
7:22 When the *t* hundred blew the
8: 4 he and the *t* hundred men who
9:22 had reigned over Israel *t*
9:43 divided them into *t* companies,
11:26 for *t* hundred years, why did
14:14 Now for *t* days they could not
15: 4 Then Samson went and caught *t*
15:11 Then *t* thousand men of Judah
16:15 You have mocked me these *t*
16:27 about *t* thousand men and women
19: 4 and he stayed with him *t* days.
1 Sam 1:24 with *t* bulls, one ephah of
2:21 that she conceived and bore *t*
9:20 your donkeys that were lost *t*
10: 3 There *t* men going up to God at
10: 3 one carrying *t* young goats,
10: 3 another carrying *t* loaves of
11: 8 the children of Israel were *t*
11:11 that Saul put the people in *t*
13: 2 Saul chose for himself *t*
13:17 camp of the Philistines in *t*
17:13 The *t* oldest sons of Jesse had
17:13 The names of his *t* sons who
17:14 And the *t* oldest followed Saul.
20:19 And when you have stayed *t*
20:20 Then I will shoot *t* arrows to
20:41 and bowed down *t* times.
21: 5 been kept from us about *t*
24: 2 Then Saul took *t* thousand chosen
25: 2 He had *t* thousand sheep and a
26: 2 having *t* thousand chosen men of
30:12 no bread nor drunk water for *t*
30:12 water for three days and *t*
30:13 because *t* days ago I fell sick.
31: 6 his *t* sons, his armorbearer,
31: 8 that they found Saul and his *t*
2 Sam 2:18 Now the *t* sons of Zeruiah were
2:31 *t* hundred and sixty men who
6:11 of Obed-Edom the Gittite *t*
13:38 and was there *t* years.
14:27 To Absalom were born *t* sons, and
18:14 And he took *t* spears in his
20: 4 men of Judah for me within *t*
21: 1 in the days of David for *t*
21:16 of whose bronze spear was *t*
23: 9 one of the *t* mighty men with
23:13 Then *t* of the thirty chief men
23:16 So the *t* mighty men broke
23:17 These things were done by the *t*
23:18 was chief of another *t*.
23:18 He lifted his spear against *t*
23:18 and won a name among these *t*.
23:19 he not the most honored of *t*?
23:19 did not attain to the first *t*.
23:22 and won a name among *t* mighty
23:23 did not attain to the first *t*.
24:12 I offer you *t* things; choose
24:13 Or shall you flee *t* months
24:13 Or shall there be *t* days'
1 Ki 2:39 it happened at the end of *t*
4:32 He spoke *t* thousand proverbs,
5:16 besides *t* thousand three hundred
5:16 besides three thousand *t* hundred
6:36 he built the inner court with *t*
7: 4 with beveled frames in *t*
7: 4 was opposite window in *t*
7: 5 was opposite window in *t*
7:12 court was enclosed with *t*
7:25 *t* looking toward the north,
7:25 *t* looking toward the west,
7:25 *t* looking toward the south,
7:25 and *t* looking toward the east;
7:27 and *t* cubits its height.
9:25 Now *t* times a year Solomon
10:17 He also made *t* hundred shields
10:17 *t* minas of gold went into each
10:22 Once every *t* years the merchant
11: 3 and *t* hundred concubines;
12: 5 Depart for *t* days, then come
15: 2 He reigned *t* years in Jerusalem.
17:21 himself out on the child *t*
22: 1 Now *t* years passed without war
2 Ki 2:17 and they searched for *t* days
3:10 the LORD has called these *t*
3:13 the LORD has called these *t*
9:32 So two or *t* eunuchs looked
13:18 so he struck *t* times,
13:19 you will strike Syria only *t*
13:25 *T* times Joash defeated him and
17: 5 Samaria and besieged it for *t*
18:10 And at the end of *t* years they
18:14 Hezekiah king of Judah *t*
23:31 and he reigned *t* months in
24: 1 became his vassal for *t* years.
24: 8 and he reigned in Jerusalem *t*
25:17 The height of the capital was *t*
25:18 and the *t* doorkeepers.
1 Chr 2: 3 These *t* were born to him by
2:16 Abishai, Joab, and Asahel—*t*.
3:23 Azrikam—*t* in all.
7: 6 Jediael—*t* in all.
10: 6 So Saul and his *t* sons died,
11:11 lifted up his spear against *t*
11:12 who was one of the *t* mighty
11:15 Now *t* of the thirty chief men
11:18 So the *t* broke through the camp
11:19 These things were done by the *t*
11:20 of Joab was chief of another *t*.
11:20 lifted up his spear against *t*
11:20 and won a name among these *t*.
11:21 Of the *t* he was more honored
11:21 did not attain to the first *t*.
11:24 and won a name among *t* mighty
11:25 did not attain to the first *t*.
12:27 and with him *t* thousand seven
12:29 *t* thousand (until then the
12:39 they were there with David *t*
13:14 of Obed-Edom in his house *t*
21:10 I offer you *t* things; choose
21:12 either *t* years of famine, or
21:12 or *t* months to be defeated by
21:12 or else for *t* days the sword of
23: 8 and Joel—*t* in all.
23: 9 and Haran—*t* in all.
23:23 Jeremoth—*t* in all.
25: 5 gave Heman fourteen sons and *t*
29: 4 *t* thousand talents of gold, of
2 Chr 2: 2 and *t* thousand six hundred to
2:18 and *t* thousand six hundred
4: 4 *t* looking toward the north,
4: 4 *t* looking toward the west,
4: 4 *t* looking toward the south,
4: 4 and *t* looking toward the east;
4: 5 It contained *t* thousand baths.
6:13 and *t* cubits high, and had set
8:13 and the *t* appointed yearly
9:16 He also made *t* hundred shields
9:16 *t* hundred shekels of gold went
9:21 Once every *t* years the merchant
10: 5 Come back to me after *t* days."
11:17 the son of Solomon strong for *t*
11:17 way of David and Solomon for *t*
13: 2 He reigned *t* years in Jerusalem.
14: 8 And Asa had an army of *t* hundred
14: 9 an army of a million men and *t*
17:14 and with him *t* hundred thousand
20:25 and they were *t* days gathering
25: 5 and found them to be *t* hundred
25:13 killed *t* thousand in them,
26:13 authority was an army of *t*
29:33 were six hundred bulls and *t*
31:16 Besides those males from *t* years
35: 7 as well as *t* thousand cattle;
35: 8 and *t* hundred cattle.
36: 2 and he reigned *t* months in
36: 9 and he reigned in Jerusalem *t*
Ezra 2: 4 *t* hundred and seventy-two;
2:17 *t* hundred and twenty-three;
2:32 *t* hundred and twenty;
2:34 *t* hundred and forty-five;
2:35 *t* thousand six hundred and
2:58 of Solomon's servants were *t*
2:64 was forty-two thousand *t*
2:65 there were seven thousand *t*
6: 4 with *t* rows of heavy stones and
8: 5 and with him *t* hundred males;
8:15 and we camped there *t* days. And
8:32 and stayed there *t* days.
10: 8 would not come within *t* days,
10: 9 gathered at Jerusalem within *t*
Neh 2:11 to Jerusalem and was there *t*
7: 9 *t* hundred and seventy-two;
7:17 two thousand *t* hundred and
7:22 *t* hundred and twenty-eight;
7:23 *t* hundred and twenty-four;
7:35 *t* hundred and twenty;
7:36 *t* hundred and forty-five;
7:38 *t* thousand nine hundred and
7:60 were *t* hundred and ninety-two.
7:66 was forty-two thousand *t*
7:67 there were seven thousand *t*
Esth 4:16 neither eat nor drink for *t*
9:15 the month of Adar and killed *t*
Job 1: 2 And seven sons and *t* daughters
1: 3 *t* thousand camels, five hundred
1: 4 would send and invite their *t*
1:17 The Chaldeans formed *t* bands,
2:11 Now when Job's *t* friends heard
32: 1 So these *t* men ceased answering
32: 3 Also against his *t* friends his
32: 5 answer in the mouth of these *t*

33:29 *t* times with a man,
42:13 He also had seven sons and *t*
Prov 30:15 There are *t* things that are never
30:18 There are *t* things which are
30:21 For *t* things the earth is
30:29 There are *t* things which are
Isa 16:14 Within *t* years, as the years of
17: 6 Two or *t* olives at the top of
19:24 day Israel will be one of *t*
20: 3 has walked naked and barefoot *t*
Jer 36:23 when Jehudi had read *t* or four
52:24 and the *t* doorkeepers.
52:28 *t* thousand and twenty-three
Ezek 4: 5 *t* hundred and ninety days;
4: 9 *t* hundred and ninety days,
14:14 Even if these *t* men, Noah,
14:16 even though these *t* men were
14:18 even though these *t* men were
40:10 In the eastern gateway were *t*
40:10 chambers on one side and *t* on
40:10 the *t* were all the same size;
40:21 *t* on this side and three on
40:21 three on this side and *t* on
40:48 the width of the gateway was *t*
40:48 three cubits on this side and *t*
41: 6 The side chambers were in *t*
41:16 galleries all around their *t*
41:22 *t* cubits high, and its length
42: 3 gallery against gallery in *t*
42: 6 For they were in *t* stories and
48:31 the *t* gates northward: one gate
48:32 *t* gates: one gate for Joseph,
48:33 *t* gates: one gate for Simeon,
48:34 hundred cubits with their *t*
Dan 1: 5 and *t* years of training for
3:23 And these *t* men, Shadrach,
3:24 Did we not cast *t* men bound into
6: 2 *t* governors, of whom Daniel
6:10 he knelt down on his knees *t*
6:13 but makes his petition *t* times
7: 5 and had *t* ribs in its mouth
7: 8 before whom *t* of the first
7:20 before which *t* fell, namely,
7:24 And shall subdue *t* kings.
8:14 For two thousand *t* hundred days;
10: 2 was mourning *t* full weeks.
10: 3 till *t* whole weeks were
11: 2 *t* more kings will arise in
12:12 and comes to the one thousand *t*
Am 1: 3 For *t* transgressions of
1: 6 For *t* transgressions of Gaza,
1: 9 For *t* transgressions of Tyre,
1:11 For *t* transgressions of Edom,
1:13 For *t* transgressions of the
2: 1 For *t* transgressions of Moab,
2: 4 For *t* transgressions of Judah,
2: 6 For *t* transgressions of Israel,
4: 4 Your tithes every *t* days.
4: 7 When there were still *t*
4: 8 So two or *t* cities wandered to
Jon 1:17 was in the belly of the fish *t*
1:17 of the fish three days and *t*
Zech 11: 8 I dismissed the *t* shepherds in
Mt 12:40 For as Jonah was *t* days and
12:40 as Jonah was three days and *t*
12:40 so will the Son of Man be *t*
12:40 Son of Man be three days and *t*
13:33 which a woman took and hid in *t*
15:32 have now continued with Me *t*
17: 4 let us make here *t* tabernacles:
18:16 the mouth of two or *t*
18:20 For where two or *t* are gathered
26:34 you will deny Me *t* times."
26:61 of God and to build it in *t*
26:75 you will deny Me *t* times."
27:40 the temple and build it in *t*
27:63 After *t* days I will rise.'
Mk 8: 2 have now continued with Me *t*
8:31 and after *t* days rise again.
9: 5 and let us make *t* tabernacles:
14: 5 have been sold for more than *t*
14:30 you will deny Me *t* times."
14:58 and within *t* days I will build
14:72 you will deny Me *t* times."
15:29 the temple and build it in *t*
Lk 1:56 Mary remained with her about *t*
2:46 Now so it was that after *t* days
4:25 when the heaven was shut up *t*
9:33 and let us make *t* tabernacles:
10:36 So which of these *t* do you think
11: 5 lend me *t* loaves;
12:52 *t* against two, and two against
12:52 against two, and two against *t*.
13: 7 for *t* years I have come seeking
13:21 which a woman took and hid in *t*
22:34 this day before you will deny *t*
22:61 you will deny Me *t* times."
Jn 2:19 and in *t* days I will raise it
2:20 and will You raise it up in *t*
6:19 So when they had rowed about *t*
12: 5 fragrant oil not sold for *t*
13:38 crow till you have denied Me *t*
Acts 2:41 and that day about *t* thousand
5: 7 Now it was about *t* hours later
7:20 up in his father's house for *t*
9: 9 And he was *t* days without sight,
10:16 This was done *t* times.
10:19 *t* men are seeking you.
11:10 'Now this was done *t* times,
11:11 *t* men stood before the house
17: 2 and for *t* Sabbaths reasoned
19: 8 and spoke boldly for *t* months,
20: 3 and stayed *t* months.
20:31 and remember that for *t* years I
25: 1 after *t* days he went up from
28: 7 us courteously for *t* days.
28:11 After *t* months we sailed in an
28:12 we stayed *t* days.
28:15 us as far as Appii Forum and *T*
28:17 And it came to pass after *t*
1 Cor 13:13 faith, hope, love, these *t*;
14:27 there be two or at the most *t*,
14:29 Let two or *t* prophets speak, and
2 Cor 11:25 *T* times I was beaten with rods;
11:25 *t* times I was shipwrecked;
12: 8 thing I pleaded with the Lord *t*
13: 1 the mouth of two or *t*
Gal 1:18 Then after *t* years I went up to
1 Tim 5:19 an elder except from two or *t*
Heb 10:28 on the testimony of two or *t*
11:23 was hidden *t* months by his
Jas 5:17 did not rain on the land for *t*
1 Jn 5: 7 For there are *t* that bear
5: 7 and these *t* are one.
5: 8 And there are *t* that bear
5: 8 and these *t* agree as one.
Rev 6: 6 and *t* quarts of barley for a
8:13 blasts of the trumpet of the *t*
9:18 By these *t* plagues a third of
16:13 And I saw *t* unclean spirits like
16:19 great city was divided into *t*
21:13 *t* gates on the east, three gates
21:13 *t* gates on the north, three
21:13 *t* gates on the south, and three
21:13 and *t* gates on the west.

THREE-AND-A-HALF (2/2)

Rev 11: 9 will see their dead bodies *t*
11:11 Now after the *t* days the breath

THREE-DAY (1/1) THREE

Jon 3: 3 a *t* journey in extent.

THREE-PRONGED (1/1) THREE

1 Sam 2:13 come with a *t* fleshhook

THREE-TENTHS (8/8)

Lev 14:10 *t* of an ephah of fine flour
Num 15: 9 bull a grain offering of *t* of
28:12 *t* of an ephah of fine flour
28:20 *t* of an ephah you shall
28:28 *t* of an ephah for each bull,
29: 3 *t* of an ephah for the bull,
29: 9 *t* of an ephah for the bull,
29:14 *t* of an ephah for each of

THREE-YEAR-OLD (5/3) THREE

Gen 15: 9 'Bring Me a *t* heifer,
15: 9 a *t* female goat, a
15: 9 a *t* ram, a turtledove, and a
Isa 15: 5 to Zoar, Like a *t* heifer.
Jer 48:34 Like a *t* heifer;

THREEFOLD (1/1)

Eccl 4:12 And a *t* cord is not quickly

THREESCORE (KJV) See SEVENTY

THRESH (6/6)

Isa 27:12 day That the LORD will *t*,
28:28 Therefore he does not *t* it
41:15 You shall *t* the mountains and
Jer 51:33 floor When it is time to *t*
Hos 10:11 heifer That loves to *t* grain;
Mic 4:13 'Arise and *t*, O daughter of

THRESHED (3/3) THRESHES, THRESHING

Judg 6:11 while his son Gideon *t* wheat in
Isa 28:27 For the black cummin is not *t*
Am 1: 3 Because they have *t* Gilead

THRESHES (1/1) THRESHED

1 Cor 9:10 and he who *t* in hope should be

THRESHING (48/48) THRESHED

Lev 26: 5 Your *t* shall last till the time
1 Sam 23: 1 and they are robbing the *t*
2 Sam 24:22 and *t* implements and the yokes
2 Ki 13: 7 made them like the dust at *t*.
1 Chr 21:20 but Ornan continued *t* wheat.
21:23 the *t* implements for wood,
Prov 20:26 And brings the *t* wheel over
Isa 21:10 my *t* and the grain of my floor!
28:27 is not threshed with a *t* sledge
41:15 make you into a new *t* sledge
Jer 50:11 fat like a heifer *t* grain
Dan 2:35 like chaff from the summer *t*
Joel 2:24 The *t* floors shall be full of

THRESHING FLOOR (35/35)

Gen 50:10 Then they came to the *t* of Atad,
50:11 saw the mourning at the *t* of
Num 15:20 as a heave offering of the *t*,
18:27 it were the grain of the *t*
18:30 as the produce of the *t* and as
Deut 15:14 from your flock, from your *t*,
16:13 you have gathered from your *t*
Judg 6:37 put a fleece of wool on the *t*;
Ruth 3: 2 barley tonight at the *t*.
3: 3 garment and go down to the *t*;
3: 6 So she went down to the *t* and
3:14 that the woman came to the *t*.
2 Sam 6: 6 when they came to Nachon's *t*,
24:16 of the LORD was by the *t* of
24:18 an altar to the LORD on the *t*
24:21 To buy the *t* from you, to build
24:24 So David bought the *t* and the
1 Ki 22:10 at a *t* at the entrance of the
2 Ki 6:27 From the *t* or from the
1 Chr 13: 9 when they came to Chidon's *t*,
21:15 of the LORD stood by the *t* of
21:18 an altar to the LORD on the *t*
21:21 And he went out from the *t*,
21:22 "Grant me the place of this *t*,
21:28 had answered him on the *t* of
2 Chr 3: 1 David had prepared on the *t* of
18: 9 and they sat at a *t* at the
Job 39:12 grain, And gather it to your *t*?
Jer 51:33 of Babylon is like a *t* When
Hos 9: 1 made love for hire on every *t*.
9: 2 The *t* and the winepress Shall
13: 3 Like chaff blown off from a *t*
Mic 4:12 them like sheaves to the *t*.
Mt 3:12 will thoroughly clean out His *t*,
Lk 3:17 will thoroughly clean out His *t*,

THRESHOLD (17/15)

Judg 19:27 house with her hands on the *t*.
1 Sam 5: 4 hands were broken off on the *t*;
5: 5 Dagon's house tread on the *t*
1 Ki 14:17 When she came to the *t* of the
Ezek 9: 3 to the *t* of the temple.
10: 4 and paused over the *t* of the
10:18 the LORD departed from the *t*
40: 6 its stairs and measured the *t*
40: 6 and the other *t* was one rod
40: 7 and the *t* of the gateway by the
41:16 three stories opposite the *t*
43: 8 When they set their *t* by My
43: 8 set their threshold by My *t*,
46: 2 He shall worship at the *t* of
47: 1 flowing from under the *t* of the
Zeph 1: 9 All those who leap over the *t*,
2:14 Desolation shall be at the *t*;

THRESHOLDS (1/1)

Am 9: 1 that the *t* may shake,

THREW (41/41) THROW

Ex 7:12 For every man *t* down his rod,
Deut 9:17 I took the two tablets and *t*
9:21 and I *t* its dust into the brook
Judg 8:25 and each man *t* into it the
15:17 that he *t* the jawbone from his
2 Sam 16: 6 And he *t* stones at David and at
16:13 *t* stones at him and kicked up
20:12 the highway to the field and *t*
20:22 and *t* it out to Joab.
1 Ki 19:19 Elijah passed by him and *t* his
2 Ki 3:25 and each man *t* a stone on every
6: 6 and *t* it in there; and he made
9:33 So they *t* her down, and some
10:25 the guards and the officers *t*
23: 6 and *t* its ashes on the graves
23:12 and *t* their dust into the Brook
2 Chr 31: 1 and *t* down the high places and
Neh 9:11 And their persecutors You *t*
13: 8 therefore I *t* all the household
Lam 3:53 my life in the pit And *t*
Jon 1: 5 and *t* the cargo that was in
1:15 So they picked up Jonah and *t*
Zech 5: 8 and *t* the lead cover over its
11:13 thirty pieces of silver and *t*
Mt 13:48 but *t* the bad away.
18:30 but went and *t* him into prison
27: 5 Then he *t* down the pieces of
Mk 11: 7 the colt to Jesus and *t* their
12: 4 and at him they *t* stones,
12:42 Then one poor widow came and *t*
Lk 9:42 the demon *t* him down and
19:35 And they *t* their own clothes on
Acts 16:23 they *t* them into prison,
22:23 tore off their clothes and *t*
27:19 On the third day we *t* the
27:38 they lightened the ship and *t*
Rev 8: 5 and *t* it to the earth.
12: 4 of the stars of heaven and *t*
14:19 and *t* it into the great
18:19 They *t* dust on their heads and
18:21 like a great millstone and *t*

THRICE (KJV) See THREE

THRIVE (5/5)

Ezek 16: 7 I made you *t* like a plant in the
17: 9 the Lord GOD: "Will it *t*?
17:10 it is planted, Will it *t*?
Dan 8:24 And shall prosper and *t*;
Zech 9:17 shall make the young men *t*,

T

THROAT (7/7)

Ps 5: 9 Their *t* is an open tomb;
69: 3 My *t* is dry; My eyes fail
115: 7 do they mutter through their *t*.
Prov 23: 2 And put a knife to your *t* If
Jer 2:25 and your *t* from thirst.
Mt 18:28 on him and took him by the *t*,
Rom 3:13 Their *t* is an open tomb;

THRONE (175/159) THRONES

Gen 41:40 only in regard to the *t* will I
Ex 11: 5 of Pharaoh who sits on his *t*,
12:29 of Pharaoh who sat on his *t* to
Deut 17:18 when he sits on the *t* of his
1 Sam 2: 8 And make them inherit the *t*
2 Sam 3:10 and set up the *t* of David over
7:13 and I will establish the *t* of
7:16 Your *t* shall be established
14: 9 and the king and his *t* be
1 Ki 1:13 and he shall sit on my *t*"?
1:17 me, and he shall sit on my *t*.
1:20 them who will sit on the *t* of
1:24 me, and he shall sit on my *t*'?
1:27 who should sit on the *t* of my
1:30 and he shall sit on my *t* in my
1:35 he shall come and sit on my *t*,
1:37 and make his *t* greater than the
1:37 his throne greater than the *t*
1:46 Also Solomon sits on the *t* of
1:47 and may He make his *t* greater
1:47 his throne greater than your *t*.
1:48 has given one to sit on my *t*
2: 4 shall not lack a man on the *t*
2:12 Then Solomon sat on the *t* of his
2:19 and sat down on his *t* and had a
2:19 down on his throne and had a *t*
2:24 me and set me on the *t* of
2:33 upon his house and his *t*,
2:45 and the *t* of David shall be
3: 6 given him a son to sit on his *t*,
5: 5 whom I will set on your *t* in
7: 7 Then he made a hall for the *t*,
8:20 and sit on the *t* of Israel, as
8:25 a man sit before Me on the *t*
9: 5 then I will establish the *t* of
9: 5 fail to have a man on the *t* of
10: 9 setting you on the *t* of Israel!
10:18 the king made a great *t* of
10:19 The *t* had six steps, and the top
10:19 and the top of the *t* was round
16:11 soon as he was seated on his *t*,
22:10 their robes, sat each on his *t*,
22:19 saw the LORD sitting on His *t*,
2 Ki 10: 3 set him on his father's *t*,
10:30 your sons shall sit on the *t* of
11:19 Then he sat on the *t* of the
13:13 Then Jeroboam sat on his *t*.
15:12 Your sons shall sit on the *t* of
1 Chr 17:12 and I will establish his *t*
17:14 and his *t* shall be established
22:10 and I will establish the *t* of
28: 5 my son Solomon to sit on the *t*
29:23 Then Solomon sat on the *t* of the
2 Chr 6:10 and sit on the *t* of Israel,
6:16 a man sit before Me on the *t*
7:18 then I will establish the *t* of
9: 8 setting you on His *t* to be
9:17 the king made a great *t* of
9:18 The *t* had six steps, with a
9:18 which were fastened to the *t*;
18: 9 their robes, sat each on his *t*;
18:18 saw the LORD sitting on His *t*,
23:20 and set the king on the *t* of
Esth 1: 2 King Ahasuerus sat on the *t* of
5: 1 the king sat on his royal *t* in
Job 26: 9 He covers the face of His *t*,
36: 7 But they are on the *t* with
Ps 9: 4 You sat on the *t* judging in
9: 7 He has prepared His *t* for
11: 4 The LORD's *t* is in heaven;
45: 6 Your *t*, O God, is forever
47: 8 God sits on His holy *t*.
89: 4 And build up your *t* to all
89:14 are the foundation of Your *t*;
89:29 And his *t* as the days of
89:36 And his *t* as the sun before
89:44 And cast his *t* down to the
93: 2 Your *t* is established from of
94:20 Shall the *t* of iniquity,
97: 2 are the foundation of His *t*.
103:19 LORD has established His *t* in
132:11 I will set upon your *t* the fruit
132:12 sons also shall sit upon your *t*
Prov 16:12 For a *t* is established by
20: 8 A king who sits on the *t* of
20:28 lovingkindness he upholds his *t*.
25: 5 And his *t* will be established
29:14 His *t* will be established
Isa 6: 1 I saw the Lord sitting on a *t*,
9: 7 Upon the *t* of David and over
14:13 I will exalt my *t* above the
16: 5 In mercy the *t* will be
22:23 he will become a glorious *t* to
47: 1 Sit on the ground without a *t*,
66: 1 the LORD: "Heaven is My *t*,
Jer 1:15 come and each one set his *t*
3:17 shall be called The *T* of the
13:13 the kings who sit on David's *t*,
14:21 Do not disgrace the *t* of Your
17:12 A glorious high *t* from the
17:25 and princes sitting on the *t*
22: 2 you who sit on the *t* of David,
22: 4 kings who sit on the *t* of
22:30 Sitting on the *t* of David,
29:16 the king who sits on the *t* of
33:17 lack a man to sit on the *t* of
33:21 have a son to reign on his *t*,
36:30 have no one to sit on the *t* of
43:10 and will set his *t* above these
49:38 I will set My *t* in Elam,
Lam 5:19 Your *t* from generation to
Ezek 1:26 heads was the likeness of a *t*,
1:26 on the likeness of the *t* was a
10: 1 of the likeness of a *t*.
43: 7 this is the place of My *t* and
Dan 5:20 was deposed from his kingly *t*,
7: 9 His *t* was a fiery flame,
Jon 3: 6 and he arose from his *t* and
Hag 2:22 I will overthrow the *t* of
Zech 6:13 shall sit and rule on His *t*;
6:13 He shall be a priest on His *t*,
Mt 5:34 by heaven, for it is God's *t*;
19:28 the Son of Man sits on the *t*
23:22 swears by the *t* of God and by
25:31 then He will sit on the *t* of
Lk 1:32 Lord God will give Him the *t*
Acts 2:30 up the Christ to sit on his *t*,
7:49 'Heaven is My *t*,
12:21 sat on his *t* and gave an
Heb 1: 8 the Son He says: "Your *t*,
4:16 therefore come boldly to the *t*
8: 1 at the right hand of the *t* of
12: 2 at the right hand of the *t* of
Rev 1: 4 Spirits who are before His *t*,
2:13 where Satan's *t* is.
3:21 grant to sit with Me on My *t*,
3:21 down with My Father on His *t*.
4: 2 a *t* set in heaven, and One sat
4: 2 heaven, and One sat on the *t*.
4: 3 was a rainbow around the *t*,
4: 4 Around the *t* were twenty-four
4: 5 And from the *t* proceeded
4: 5 fire were burning before the *t*,
4: 6 Before the *t* there was a sea
4: 6 And in the midst of the *t*,
4: 6 of the throne, and around the *t*,
4: 9 thanks to Him who sits on the *t*,
4:10 before Him who sits on the *t*
4:10 cast their crowns before the *t*,
5: 1 hand of Him who sat on the *t*
5: 6 in the midst of the *t* and of
5: 7 hand of Him who sat on the *t*.
5:11 of many angels around the *t*,
5:13 Be to Him who sits on the *t*,
6:16 face of Him who sits on the *t*
7: 9 standing before the *t* and
7:10 to our God who sits on the *t*,
7:11 the angels stood around the *t*
7:11 on their faces before the *t*
7:15 they are before the *t* of God,
7:15 And He who sits on the *t* will
7:17 who is in the midst of the *t*
8: 3 altar which was before the *t*.
12: 5 was caught up to God and His *t*.
13: 2 gave him his power, his *t*,
14: 3 it were a new song before the *t*,
14: 5 are without fault before the *t*
16:10 poured out his bowl on the *t*
16:17 temple of heaven, from the *t*,
19: 4 worshiped God who sat on the *t*,
19: 5 Then a voice came from the *t*,
20:11 Then I saw a great white *t* and
21: 5 Then He who sat on the *t* said,
22: 1 proceeding from the *t* of God
22: 3 but the *t* of God and of the

THRONES (13/11) THRONE

Ps 122: 5 For *t* are set there for
122: 5 The *t* of the house of David.
Isa 14: 9 It has raised up from their *t*
Ezek 26:16 sea will come down from their *t*,
Dan 7: 9 I watched till *t* were put in
Mt 19:28 Me will also sit on twelve *t*,
Lk 1:52 down the mighty from their *t*,
22:30 and sit on *t* judging the twelve
Col 1:16 whether *t* or dominions or
Rev 4: 4 the throne were twenty-four *t*,
4: 4 and on the *t* I saw twenty-four
11:16 who sat before God on their *t*
20: 4 And I saw *t*, and they sat on

THRONG (3/3)

Ps 55:14 to the house of God in the *t*.
Jer 31: 8 A great *t* shall return there.
Lk 8:45 the multitudes *t* and press You,

THRONGED (3/3)

Dan 6: 6 these governors and satraps *t*
Mk 5:24 multitude followed Him and *t*
Lk 8:42 the multitudes *t* Him.

THRONGING (1/1)

Mk 5:31 'You see the multitude *t* You,

THROUGH (525/472) See APPENDIX

THROUGHOUT (159/156)

Gen 17: 9 your descendants after you *t*
41:29 of great plenty will come *t*
41:46 and went *t* all the land of
45: 8 and a ruler *t* all the land of
Ex 5:12 people were scattered abroad *t*
7:19 And there shall be blood *t* all
7:21 So there was blood *t* all the
8:16 so that it may become lice *t*
8:17 dust of the land became lice *t*
9: 9 out in sores on man and beast *t*
9:22 *t* the land of Egypt."
9:25 And the hail struck *t* the whole
10:15 or on the plants of the field *t*
11: 6 there shall be a great cry *t*
12:14 it as a feast to the LORD *t*
12:17 you shall observe this day *t*
12:42 all the children of Israel *t*
27:18 cubits, the width fifty *t*,
29:42 a continual burnt offering *t*
30: 8 incense before the LORD *t*
30:10 shall make atonement upon it *t*
30:21 to him and his descendants *t*
30:31 be a holy anointing oil to Me *t*
31:13 is a sign between Me and you *t*
31:16 to observe the Sabbath *t* their
32:27 out from entrance to entrance *t*
34: 3 and let no man be seen *t* all
35: 3 You shall kindle no fire *t* your
36: 6 caused it to be proclaimed *t*
40:15 be an everlasting priesthood *t*
40:38 *t* all their journeys.
Lev 3:17 be a perpetual statute *t* your
7:36 by a statute forever *t* their
10: 9 shall be a statute forever *t*
17: 7 be a statute forever for them *t*
22: 3 of all your descendants *t* your
23:14 shall be a statute forever *t*
23:21 in all your dwellings *t* your
23:31 shall be a statute forever *t*
25: 9 make the trumpet to sound *t*
25:10 and proclaim liberty *t* all the
25:30 *t* his generations. It shall not
Num 10: 8 you as an ordinance forever *t*
11:10 heard the people weeping *t*
15:14 or whoever is among you *t* your
15:15 an ordinance forever *t* your
15:21 to the LORD a heave offering *t*
15:23 gave commandment and onward *t*
15:38 the corners of their garments *t*
18:23 *t* your generations, that among
28:14 offering for each month *t* the
35:29 a statute of judgment to you *t*
Deut 28:40 You shall have olive trees *t* all
28:52 come down *t* all your land;
28:52 you at all your gates *t* all
Josh 6:27 and his fame spread *t* all the
24: 3 led him *t* all the land of
Judg 6:35 And he sent messengers *t* all
7:22 sword against his companion *t*
7:24 Then Gideon sent messengers *t*
19:29 and sent her *t* all the
20: 6 and sent her *t* all the
20:10 ten men out of every hundred *t*
1 Sam 5:11 was a deadly destruction *t* all
11: 7 and sent them *t* all the
13: 3 Then Saul blew the trumpet *t*
13:19 was no blacksmith to be found *t*
23:23 that I will search for him *t*
25:28 and evil is not found in you *t*
31: 9 and sent word *t* the land of
2 Sam 8:14 *t* all Edom he put garrisons,
15:10 Then Absalom sent spies *t* all
19: 9 the people were in a dispute *t*
24: 2 Now go *t* all the tribes of
1 Ki 1: 3 for a lovely young woman *t* all
15:22 King Asa made a proclamation *t*
22:36 a shout went *t* the army,
2 Ki 10:21 Then Jehu sent *t* all Israel;
17: 5 the king of Assyria went *t* all
1 Chr 5:10 and they dwelt in their tents *t*
6:54 are their dwelling places *t*
6:62 of Gershon, *t* their families,
6:63 of Merari, *t* their families,
9:34 of the Levites were heads *t*
10: 9 and sent word *t* the land of
12:30 famous men *t* their father's
21: 4 Joab departed and went *t* all
21:12 of the LORD destroying *t* all
22: 5 famous and glorious *t* all
27: 1 and went out month by month *t*
2 Chr 11:23 dispersed some of his sons *t*
16: 9 of the LORD run to and fro *t*
17: 9 they went *t* all the cities of
17:19 put in the fortified cities *t*
19: 5 he set judges in the land *t*
20: 3 and proclaimed a fast *t* all
23: 2 And they went *t* Judah and
24: 9 And they made a proclamation *t*
25: 5 *t* all Judah and Benjamin;
30: 5 to make a proclamation *t* all
30: 6 Then the runners went *t* all
30:22 and they ate *t* the feast seven
31:20 Thus Hezekiah did *t* all Judah,
34: 7 down all the incense altars *t*
36:22 that he made a proclamation *t*
Ezra 1: 1 that he made a proclamation *t*
10: 7 they issued a proclamation *t*
Esth 1:20 he will make is proclaimed *t*
3: 6 all the Jews who were *t* the
9: 2 together in their cities *t* all

9: 4 and his fame spread t all the
9:28 be remembered and kept t
Ps 72: 5 T all generations.
81: 5 When He went t the land of
102:24 Your years are t all
135:13 O LORD, t all generations.
145:13 And Your dominion endures t
Jer 15:13 T your territories.
51:52 And t all her land the wounded
Lam 3: 3 me Time and time again t the
Ezek 12:15 the nations and disperse them t
20:23 Gentiles and disperse them t
22:15 disperse you t the countries,
29:12 the nations and disperse them t
30:23 and disperse them t the
30:26 the nations and disperse them t
36:19 and they were dispersed t the
38:21 call for a sword against Gog t
41:19 thus it was made t the temple
45: 1 It shall be holy t its
Jon 3: 7 be proclaimed and published t
Zech 1:10 has sent to walk to and fro t
1:11 We have walked to and fro t the
4:10 Which scan to and fro t the
5: 6 This is their resemblance t the
6: 7 they might walk to and fro t
6: 7 walk to and fro t the earth."
6: 7 So they walked to and fro t
Mt 4:24 Then His fame went t all Syria;
Mk 1:28 immediately His fame spread t
1:39 in their synagogues t all
Lk 1:65 these sayings were discussed t
4:25 and there was a great famine t
7:17 this report about Him went t
8:39 went his way and proclaimed t
23: 5 teaching t all Judea, beginning
Acts 8: 1 and they were all scattered t
9:31 Then the churches t all Judea,
9:42 And it became known t all Joppa,
10:37 which was proclaimed t all
11:28 going to be a great famine t
13:49 of the Lord was being spread t
15:21 For Moses has had t many
19:26 but t almost all Asia,
24: 5 among all the Jews t the world,
26:20 and t all the region of Judea,
Rom 1: 8 that your faith is spoken of t
2 Cor 8:18 praise is in the gospel t all
1 Pe 1:17 conduct yourselves t the time

THROW (37/37) THREW, THROWN, THROWS

Ex 22:31 you shall t it to the dogs.
2 Sam 20:15 Joab battered the wall to t it
2 Ki 9:25 and t him into the tract of
9:26 take and t him on the plot of
9:33 Then he said, "T her down."
2 Chr 20:11 rewarding us by coming to t us
Eccl 3: 6 And a time to t away;
Isa 22:17 the LORD will t you away
30:22 You will t them away as an
31: 7 in that day every man shall t
Jer 1:10 To destroy and to t down,
10:18 I will t out at this time The
31:28 to t down, to destroy, and to
51:63 shall tie a stone to it and t
Lam 2:10 They t dust on their heads
Ezek 5: 4 take some of them again and t
7:19 They will t their silver into
16:39 and they shall t down your
20: 7 t away the abominations which
28: 8 They shall t you down into the
43:24 the priests shall t salt on
Jon 1:12 Pick me up and t me into the
Mic 5:11 the cities of your land And t
Zech 11:13 T it to the potter"—that
Mal 1: 4 may build, but I will t down;
Mt 4: 6 Son of God, t Yourself down.
15:26 the children's bread and t it
Mk 7:27 the children's bread and t it
Lk 4: 9 t Yourself down from here.
4:29 that they might t Him down over
12:58 and the officer t you into
14:35 but men t it out. He who has
22:41 from them about a stone's t,
Jn 8: 7 let him t a stone at her
8:59 Then they took up stones to t at
15: 6 and they gather them and t
Rev 2:10 the devil is about to t some

THROWING (2/2)

Num 35:23 t it at him without seeing
Mk 10:50 And t aside his garment, he rose

THROWN (41/41) THROW

Ex 15: 1 horse and its rider He has t
15:21 He has t into the sea!"
2 Sam 20:21 his head will be t to you over
1 Ki 13:24 And his corpse was t on the
13:25 passed by and saw the corpse t
13:28 he went and found his corpse t
2 Ki 7:15 which the Syrians had t away
Isa 16: 2 shall be as a wandering bird t
34: 3 Also their slain shall be t
Jer 31:40 It shall not be plucked up or t
50:15 Her walls are t down;
Lam 2: 2 He has t down in His wrath
2:17 He has t down and has not
Ezek 15: 4 it is t into the fire for fuel;
16: 5 but you were t out into the
38:20 The mountains shall be t down,
Joel 1: 7 He has stripped it bare and t
Am 8: 3 They shall be t out in
Nah 1: 6 And the rocks are t down by
Mt 3:10 good fruit is cut down and t
5:13 good for nothing but to be t
5:25 and you be t into prison.
6:30 and tomorrow is t into the
7:19 good fruit is cut down and t
24: 2 that shall not be t down."
Mk 9:22 And often he has t him both into
9:42 and he were t into the sea.
13: 2 that shall not be t down."
14:51 having a linen cloth t around
Lk 3: 9 good fruit is cut down and t
4:35 And when the demon had t him
12:28 in the field and tomorrow is t
17: 2 and he were t into the sea,
21: 6 another that shall not be t
23:19 who had been t into prison for a
23:25 and murder had been t into
Jn 3:24 For John had not yet been t into
Acts 16:37 and have t us into prison.
Rev 8: 7 and they were t to the earth.
8: 8 burning with fire was t into
18:21 great city Babylon shall be t

THROWS (3/3) THROW

Num 35:22 or t anything at him without
Prov 26:18 Like a madman who t firebrands,
Mk 9:18 it seizes him, it t him down;

THRUST (31/29)

Ex 21:29 But if the ox tended to t with
21:36 known that the ox tended to t
Num 25: 8 of Israel into the tent and t
Deut 15:17 you shall take an awl and t
33:27 He will t out the enemy from
Judg 3:21 and t it into his belly.
9:54 " So his young man t him
1 Sam 2:14 Then he would t it into the
31: 4 and t me through with it,
31: 4 uncircumcised men come and t
2 Sam 2:16 his opponent by the head and t
18:14 three spears in his hand and t
23: 6 shall all be as thorns t
1 Chr 10: 4 and t me through with it,
2 Chr 26:20 so they t him out of that
Isa 13:15 who is found will be t through,
14:19 T through with a sword,
Jer 51: 4 And those t through in her
Lam 1:14 And t upon my neck.
Ezek 16:40 stone you with stones and t
21:16 Swords at the ready! T right!
21:16 your blade! T left—Wherever
Hab 3:14 You t through with his own
Zech 5: 8 he t her down into the basket,
13: 3 mother who begot him shall t
Lk 4:29 and rose up and t Him out of the
13:28 and yourselves t out.
Rev 14:15 T in Your sickle and reap, for
14:16 So He who sat on the cloud t in
14:18 T in your sharp sickle and
14:19 So the angel t his sickle into

THUMB (6/6) THUMBS

Ex 29:20 on the t of their right hand
Lev 8:23 on the t of his right hand, and
14:14 on the t of his right hand, and
14:17 on the t of his right hand, and
14:25 on the t of his right hand, and
14:28 on the t of the right hand, and

THUMBS (3/3) THUMB

Lev 8:24 on the t of their right hands,
Judg 1: 6 caught him and cut off his t
1: 7 Seventy kings with their t and

THUMMIM (5/5) URIM

Ex 28:30 of judgment the Urim and the T,
Lev 8: 8 and he put the Urim and the T
Deut 33: 8 Let Your T and Your Urim be
Ezra 2:63 consult with the Urim and T.
Neh 7:65 consult with the Urim and T.

THUNDER (22/22) THUNDERED, THUNDERS

Ex 9:23 and the LORD sent t and hail,
9:29 the t will cease, and there
9:33 then the t and the hail ceased,
9:34 and the t had ceased, he sinned
1 Sam 2:10 From heaven He will t against
7:10 LORD thundered with a loud t
12:17 and He will send t and rain,
12:18 and the LORD sent t and rain
Job 26:14 But the t of His power who
36:29 The t from His canopy?
36:33 His t declares it, The cattle
37: 2 Hear attentively the t of His
39:19 you clothed his neck with t?
39:25 The t of captains and
40: 9 Or can you t with a voice like
Ps 77:18 The voice of Your t was in the
81: 7 you in the secret place of t;
104: 7 At the voice of Your t they
Isa 29: 6 by the LORD of hosts With t
Mk 3:17 that is, "Sons of T";
Rev 6: 1 saying with a voice like t,
14: 2 and like the voice of loud t.

THUNDERBOLT (2/2)

Job 28:26 the rain, And a path for the t,
38:25 water, Or a path for the t,

THUNDERED (4/4) THUNDER

1 Sam 7:10 But the LORD t with a loud
2 Sam 22:14 'The LORD t from heaven,
Ps 18:13 The LORD t from heaven,
Jn 12:29 heard it said that it had t.

THUNDERING (1/1)

Ex 9:28 there may be no more mighty t

THUNDERINGS (7/7)

Ex 19:16 that there were t and
20:18 all the people witnessed the t,
Rev 4: 5 throne proceeded lightnings, t,
8: 5 And there were noises, t,
11:19 were lightnings, noises, t,
16:18 And there were noises and t and
19: 6 and as the sound of mighty t,

THUNDEROUS (2/2)

Ezek 3:12 and I heard behind me a great t
3:13 and a great t noise.

THUNDERS (6/5) THUNDER

Job 37: 4 He t with His majestic voice,
37: 5 God t marvelously with His
Ps 29: 3 the waters; The God of glory t;
Rev 10: 3 seven t uttered their voices.
10: 4 Now when the seven t uttered
10: 4 up the things which the seven t

THUS (766/738) See APPENDIX

THYATIRA (4/4)

Acts 16:14 of purple from the city of T,
Rev 1:11 to Smyrna, to Pergamos, to T,
2:18 to the angel of the church in T
2:24 you I say, and to the rest in T,

THYINE (KJV) See CITRON

TIBERIAS (3/3)

Jn 6: 1 which is the Sea of T.
6:23 other boats came from T,
21: 1 the disciples at the Sea of T,

TIBERIUS (1/1) CAESAR

Lk 3: 1 year of the reign of T Caesar,

TIBHATH (1/1)

1 Chr 18: 8 Also from T and from Chun,

TIBNI (3/2)

1 Ki 16:21 half of the people followed T
16:22 over the people who followed T
16:22 So T died and Omri reigned.

TIDAL (2/2)

Gen 14: 1 and T king of nations,
14: 9 T king of nations, Amraphel

TIDINGS (12/11) NEWS

Ps 112: 7 will not be afraid of evil t;
Isa 40: 9 O Zion, You who bring good t,
40: 9 You who bring good t,
41:27 Jerusalem one who brings good t.
52: 7 Who brings glad t of good
61: 1 anointed Me To preach good t
Nah 1:15 feet of him who brings good t,
Lk 1:19 you and bring you these glad t.
2:10 I bring you good t of great joy
8: 1 and bringing the glad t of the
Acts 13:32 "And we declare to you glad t—
Rom 10:15 Who bring glad t of good

TIE (4/4) TIED

Judg 15:13 but we will t you securely and
Prov 6:21 T them around your neck.
Jer 51:63 that you shall t a stone to it
Acts 12: 8 Gird yourself and t on your

TIED (7/7) TIE

Ex 39:31 And they t to it a blue cord,
Lev 8: 7 and with it t the ephod on
2 Ki 7:10 sound—only horses and donkeys t,
Mt 21: 2 you will find a donkey t,
Mk 11: 2 it you will find a colt t,
11: 4 and found the colt t by the
Lk 19:30 enter you will find a colt t,

TIERS (2/2)

1 Ki 7: 4 opposite window in three *t*.
7: 5 opposite window in three *t*.

TIES (2/2)

Judg 18: 7 and they had no *t* with anyone.
18:28 and they had no *t* with anyone.

TIGHTLY (3/3)

Judg 16:14 So she wove it *t* with the
Job 40:17 The sinews of his thighs are *t*
41:15 Shut up *t* as with a seal;

TIGLATH-PILESER (6/6)

2 Ki 15:29 *T* king of Assyria came and took
16: 7 So Ahaz sent messengers to *T*
16:10 Ahaz went to Damascus to meet *T*
1 Chr 5: 6 whom *T* king of Assyria carried
5:26 *T* king of Assyria. He carried
2 Chr 28:20 Also *T* king of Assyria came to

TIGRIS (1/1)

Dan 10: 4 great river, that is, the *T*,

TIKVAH (2/2)

2 Ki 22:14 wife of Shallum the son of *T*,
Ezra 10:15 and Jahaziah the son of *T*

TILING (1/1)

Lk 5:19 with his bed through the *t*

TILL (150/145)

Gen 2: 5 and there was no man to *t* the
3:19 face you shall eat bread *T*
3:23 out of the garden of Eden to *t*
4:12 When you *t* the ground, it shall
38:11 widow in your father's house *t*
38:17 Will you give me a pledge *t* you
46:34 from our youth even *t* now,
Ex 15:16 *T* Your people pass over, O
15:16 *T* the people pass over
16:19 Let no one leave any of it *t*
16:24 So they laid it up *t* morning, as
40:37 then they did not journey *t* the
Lev 26: 5 Your threshing shall last *t* the
26: 5 and the vintage shall last *t*
27:18 to the years that remain *t* the
Num 12:15 the people did not journey *t*
Josh 5: 6 *t* all the people who were men
5: 8 in their places in the camp *t*
8: 6 they will come out after us *t*
10:13 *T* the people had revenge Upon
10:20 slaughter, *t* they had finished,
Judg 3:25 So they waited *t* they were
16: 3 And Samson lay low *t* midnight;
19:26 master was, *t* it was light.
21: 2 and remained there before God *t*
Ruth 1:13 would you wait for them *t* they
1 Sam 10: 8 *t* I come to you and show you
16:11 For we will not sit down *t* he
22: 3 *t* I know what God will do for
2 Sam 3:35 taste bread or anything else *t*
22:38 did I turn back again *t* they
24:15 upon Israel from the morning *t*
1 Ki 18:26 of Baal from morning even *t*
2 Ki 2:17 But when they urged him *t* he was
4:20 he sat on her knees *t* noon, and
10:17 *t* he had destroyed them,
13:17 strike the Syrians at Aphek *t*
13:19 you would have struck Syria *t*
21:16 *t* he had filled Jerusalem from
2 Chr 26:15 he was marvelously helped *t* he
36:16 *t* there was no remedy.
Ezra 2:63 eat of the most holy things *t*
5: 5 could not make them cease *t* a
Neh 2: 7 permit me to pass through *t* I
4:11 *t* we come into their midst and
7:65 eat of the most holy things *t*
13:19 that they must not be opened *t*
Job 4:20 broken in pieces from morning *t*
7: 4 I have had my fill of tossing *t*
7:19 And let me alone *t* I swallow
14: 6 *T* like a hired man he finishes
14:12 *T* the heavens are no more,
14:14 *T* my change comes.
18: 2 How long *t* you put an end to
27: 5 *T* I die I will not put away my
Ps 18:37 did I turn back again *t* they
68:30 *T* everyone submits himself
110: 1 *T* I make Your enemies Your
Prov 7:23 *T* an arrow struck his liver
Eccl 2: 3 *t* I might see what was good
Isa 5: 8 *T* there is no place Where
5:11 *t* wine inflames them!
29:17 not yet a very little while *T*
30:17 *T* you are left as a pole on
42: 4 *T* He has established justice
62: 7 And give Him no rest *t* He
62: 7 till He establishes And *t* He
Jer 19:11 shall bury them in Tophet *t*
24:10 *t* they are consumed from the
27:11 and they shall *t* it and dwell in
52: 3 *t* He finally cast them out from
52:11 and put him in prison *t* the day
Lam 3:50 *T* the LORD from heaven Looks
Ezek 4: 8 from one side to another *t* you
4:14 defiled myself from my youth *t*
24:13 *T* I have caused My fury to
28:15 *T* iniquity was found in you.
39:15 *t* the buriers have buried it in
39:19 You shall eat fat *t* you are
39:19 And drink blood *t* you are
Dan 2: 9 and corrupt words before me *t*
4:23 *t* seven times pass over him';
4:25 *t* you know that the Most High
4:33 wet with the dew of heaven *t*
5:21 *t* he knew that the Most High
6:14 and he labored *t* the going down
7: 4 I watched *t* its wings were
7: 9 I watched *t* thrones were put in
7:11 I watched *t* the beast was
9:26 And *t* the end of the war
10: 3 *t* three whole weeks were
11:36 and shall prosper *t* the wrath
12: 9 are closed up and sealed *t*
12:13 go your way *t* the end;
Hos 5:15 return again to My place *T*
10:12 *T* He comes and rains
Ob 5 Would they not have stolen *t*
Jon 4: 5 *t* he might see what would
Zeph 3: 3 wolves That leave not a bone *t*
Mt 1:25 and did not know her *t* she had
2: 9 *t* it came and stood over where
5:18 *t* heaven and earth pass away,
5:18 by no means pass from the law *t*
5:26 by no means get out of there *t*
10:11 and stay there *t* you go out.
12:20 *T* He sends forth justice
13:33 in three measures of meal *t* it
16:28 who shall not taste death *t*
18:30 and threw him into prison *t* he
22:44 *T* I make Your enemies
23:39 you shall see Me no more *t* you
24:34 will by no means pass away *t*
Mk 6:10 stay there *t* you depart from
9: 1 here who will not taste death *t*
9: 9 *t* the Son of Man had risen from
12:36 *T* I make Your enemies
13:30 will by no means pass away *t*
Lk 1:80 and was in the deserts *t* the
9:27 who shall not taste death *t*
12:50 and how distressed I am *t* it is
12:59 shall not depart from there *t*
13:21 in three measures of meal *t* it
17: 8 gird yourself and serve me *t* I
19:13 Do business *t* I come.'
20:43 *T* I make Your enemies
21:32 will by no means pass away *t*
Jn 13:38 the rooster shall not crow *t*
21:22 If I will that he remain *t* I
21:23 If I will that he remain *t* I
Acts 2:35 *T* I make Your enemies
7:18 *t* another king arose who did not
8:40 he preached in all the cities *t*
20:11 even *t* daybreak, he departed.
21: 5 *t* we were out of the city.
23:12 would neither eat nor drink *t*
23:21 will neither eat nor drink *t*
25:21 I commanded him to be kept *t* I
28:23 from morning *t* evening.
1 Cor 11:26 proclaim the Lord's death *t* He
15:25 For He must reign *t* He has put
Gal 3:19 *t* the Seed should come to whom
Eph 4:13 *t* we all come to the unity of
Phil 1:10 sincere and without offense *t*
1 Tim 4:13 *T* I come, give attention to
Heb 1:13 *T* I make Your enemies
10:13 from that time waiting *t* His
Rev 2:25 But hold fast what you have *t* I
7: 3 or the trees *t* we have sealed
15: 8 was able to enter the temple *t*
20: 3 deceive the nations no more *t*

TILLAGE (KJV) See FARMING, GROUND, TILLING

TILLED (2/2)

Ezek 36: 9 and you shall be *t* and sown.
36:34 The desolate land shall be *t*

TILLER (1/1)

Gen 4: 2 but Cain was a *t* of the ground.

TILLEST, TILLETH (KJV) See TILL, TILLS

TILLING (1/1)

1 Chr 27:26 did the work of the field for *t*

TILLS (2/2)

Prov 12:11 He who *t* his land will be
28:19 He who *t* his land will have

TILON (1/1)

1 Chr 4:20 Amnon, Rinnah, Ben-Hanan, and *T*.

TIMAEUS (1/1) BARTIMAEUS

Mk 10:46 blind Bartimaeus, the son of *T*,

TIMBER (19/19)

Lev 14:45 the house, its stones, its *t*,
Deut 19: 5 with his neighbor to cut *t*,
1 Ki 5: 6 us who has skill to cut *t* like
5:18 and they prepared *t* and stones
15:22 took away the stones and *t* of
2 Ki 12:12 and for buying *t* and hewn
22: 6 and to buy *t* and hewn stone to
1 Chr 22:14 I have prepared *t* and stone
2 Chr 2: 8 servants have skill to cut *t*
2: 9 to prepare *t* for me in
2:10 the woodsmen who cut *t*,
16: 6 carried away the stones and *t*
34:11 to buy hewn stone and *t* for
Ezra 5: 8 and *t* is being laid in the
6: 4 stones and one row of new *t*.
6:11 let a *t* be pulled from his
Neh 2: 8 that he must give me *t* to make
Ezek 26:12 will lay your stones, your *t*,
Zech 5: 4 with its *t* and stones."

TIMBERS (1/1)

Hab 2:11 And the beam from the *t* will

TIMBREL (5/5) TIMBRELS

Gen 31:27 with *t* and harp?
Ex 15:20 took the *t* in her hand;
Ps 81: 2 Raise a song and strike the *t*,
149: 3 sing praises to Him with the *t*
150: 4 Praise Him with the *t* and

TIMBRELS (4/4) TIMBREL

Ex 15:20 went out after her with *t* and
Judg 11:34 coming out to meet him with *t*
Ps 68:25 were the maidens playing *t*.
Ezek 28:13 The workmanship of your *t* and

TIME (609/551) TIMES

Gen 4: 2 this *t* his brother Abel.
4: 3 And in the process of *t* it came
17:21 bear to you at this set *t* next
18:10 to you according to the *t* of
18:14 At the appointed *t* I will
18:14 according to the *t* of life,
21: 2 at the set *t* of which God had
21:22 And it came to pass at that *t*
22:15 called to Abraham a second *t*
24:11 by a well of water at evening *t*,
24:11 the *t* when women go out to draw
26: 8 when he had been there a long *t*,
29: 7 it is not *t* for the cattle to
29:34 Now this *t* my husband will
30:33 will answer for me in *t* to
31:10 at the *t* when the flocks
37: 9 And this *t*, the sun, the moon,
38: 1 It came to pass at that *t* that
38:12 Now in the process of *t* the
38:27 at the *t* for giving birth,
39: 5 from the *t* that he had made
39:11 But it happened about this *t*,
41: 5 He slept and dreamed a second *t*;
43:10 have returned this second *t*.
43:18 in our sacks the first *t*,
43:20 we indeed came down the first *t*
47:29 When the *t* drew near that Israel
Ex 2:23 it happened in the process of *t*
8:32 hardened his heart at this *t*
9: 5 the LORD appointed a set *t*,
9:14 for at this *t* I will send all My
9:18 tomorrow about this *t* I will
9:27 to them, "I have sinned this *t*.
13:14 when your son asks you in *t* to
21:19 only pay for the loss of his *t*,
21:36 the ox tended to thrust in *t*
23:15 at the *t* appointed in the month
34:18 in the appointed *t* of the month
34:21 in plowing *t* and in harvest you
Lev 13:58 it shall be washed a second *t*,
15:25 other than at the *t* of her
15:25 if it runs beyond her usual *t*
16: 2 not to come at just any *t*
25: 8 and the *t* of the seven sabbaths
25:32 the Levites may redeem at any *t*.
25:50 shall be according to the *t*
26: 5 shall last till the *t* of
26: 5 vintage shall last till the *t*
26:35 for the *t* it did not rest on
Num 9: 2 the Passover at its appointed *t*.
9: 3 keep it at its appointed *t*.
9: 7 of the LORD at its appointed *t*
9:13 of the LORD at its appointed *t*;
10: 6 sound the advance the second *t*,
10:13 started out for the first *t*
13:20 Now the *t* was the season of
20:15 and we dwelt in Egypt a long *t*,
22: 4 king of the Moabites at that *t*.
28: 2 to Me at their appointed *t*.
35:26 But if the manslayer at any *t*
Deut 1: 9 "And I spoke to you at that *t*,
1:16 commanded your judges at that *t*,
1:18 And I commanded you at that *t*
2:14 And the *t* we took to come from
2:34 took all his cities at that *t*,
3: 4 took all his cities at that *t*;
3: 8 And at that *t* we took the land
3:12 which we possessed at that *t*,
3:18 I commanded you at that *t*,

3:21 I commanded Joshua at that ***t***,
3:23 with the LORD at that ***t***,
4:14 LORD commanded me at that ***t***
4:40 God is giving you for all ***t***.
4:42 without having hated him in ***t***
5: 5 the LORD and you at that ***t***,
6:20 When your son asks you in ***t*** to
9:19 LORD listened to me at that ***t***
9:20 for Aaron also at the same ***t***.
10: 1 At that ***t*** the LORD said to me,
10: 8 At that ***t*** the LORD separated
10:10 "As at the first ***t***,
10:10 LORD also heard me at that ***t***,
16: 6 at the ***t*** you came out of Egypt.
16: 9 the seven weeks from the ***t***
19: 4 not having hated him in ***t*** past—
19: 6 had not hated the victim in ***t***
20:19 you besiege a city for a long ***t***,
31:10 at the appointed ***t*** in the year
32:35 foot shall slip in due ***t***;
Josh 3:15 its banks during the whole ***t***
4: 6 when your children ask in ***t*** to
4:21 ask their fathers in ***t*** to come,
5: 2 At that ***t*** the LORD said to
5: 2 of Israel again the second ***t***.
6:16 And the seventh ***t*** it happened,
6:26 Joshua charged them at that ***t***,
10:27 So it was at the ***t*** of the going
10:42 their land Joshua took at one ***t***,
11: 6 for tomorrow about this ***t*** I
11:10 Joshua turned back at that ***t***
11:18 Joshua made war a long ***t*** with
11:21 And at that ***t*** Joshua came and
22:24 In ***t*** to come your descendants
22:27 say to our descendants in ***t*** to
22:28 us or to our generations in ***t***
23: 1 a long ***t*** after the LORD had
24: 7 in the wilderness a long ***t***.
Judg 3:29 And at that ***t*** they killed about
4: 4 was judging Israel at that ***t***.
10:14 let them deliver you in your ***t***
11: 4 It came to pass after a ***t*** that
11:26 not recover them within that ***t***?
12: 6 There fell at that ***t*** forty-two
13:23 things as these at this ***t***.
14: 4 For at that ***t*** the Philistines
14: 8 After some ***t***, when he returned
15: 1 in the ***t*** of wheat harvest,
15: 3 This ***t*** I shall be blameless
18:31 all the ***t*** that the house of God
20:15 And from their cities at that ***t***
21:14 So Benjamin came back at that ***t***,
21:22 the women to them at this ***t***,
21:24 departed from there at that ***t***,
1 Sam 1: 4 And whenever the ***t*** came for
1:20 to pass in the process of ***t***
3: 2 And it came to pass at that ***t***,
3: 8 called Samuel again the third ***t***.
4:20 And about the ***t*** of her death the
7: 2 in Kirjath Jearim a long ***t***;
9:13 for about this ***t*** you will find
9:16 Tomorrow about this ***t*** I will
9:24 for until this ***t*** it has been
11: 9 by the ***t*** the sun is hot,
13: 8 according to the ***t*** set by
14:18 (for at that ***t*** the ark of God
14:21 the Philistines before that ***t***,
18:19 But it happened at the ***t*** when
18:21 Saul said to David a second ***t***,
19:21 messengers again the third ***t***,
20:35 out into the field at the ***t***
22: 4 they dwelt with him all the ***t***
25:16 all the ***t*** we were with them
26: 8 to strike him a second ***t***!"
27: 7 Now the ***t*** that David dwelt in
27:11 was his behavior all the ***t*** he
2 Sam 2:11 And the ***t*** that David was king in
3:17 In ***t*** past you were seeking for
5: 2 in ***t*** past, when Saul was king
7: 6 dwelt in a house since the ***t***
7:11 since the ***t*** that I commanded
11: 1 at the ***t*** when kings go out to
14: 2 who has been mourning a long ***t***
14:29 when he sent again the second ***t***,
17: 7 given is not good at this ***t***.
20: 5 delayed longer than the set ***t***
23: 8 eight hundred men at one ***t***.
23:13 men went down at harvest ***t*** and
24:15 morning till the appointed ***t***.
1 Ki 1: 6 had not rebuked him at any ***t***
2:26 not put you to death at this ***t***,
2:26 you were afflicted every ***t*** my
8:65 At that ***t*** Solomon held a feast,
9: 2 to Solomon the second ***t***,
11:29 Now it happened at that ***t***,
14: 1 At that ***t*** Abijah the son of
15:23 But in the ***t*** of his old age he
18:29 they prophesied until the ***t*** of
18:34 he said, "Do it a second ***t***,
18:34 and they did it a second ***t***;
18:34 and he said, "Do it a third ***t***,
18:34 and they did it a third ***t***.
18:36 at the ***t*** of the offering of
18:44 it came to pass the seventh ***t***,
19: 2 them by tomorrow about this ***t***.
19: 7 LORD came back the second ***t***,
20: 6 to you tomorrow about this ***t***,
20: 9 to your servant the first ***t*** I
2 Ki 3: 6 went out of Samaria at that ***t***
4:16 About this ***t*** next year you shall
4:17 a son when the appointed ***t*** had
5:26 Is it ***t*** to receive money and
7: 1 Tomorrow about this ***t*** a seah of
7:18 be sold tomorrow about this ***t***
8:22 And Libnah revolted at that ***t***.
10: 6 come to me at Jezreel by this ***t***
16: 6 At that ***t*** Rezin king of Syria
18:16 At that ***t*** Hezekiah stripped the
20:12 At that ***t*** Berodach-Baladan the
24:10 At that ***t*** the servants of
1 Chr 9:20 been the officer over them in ***t***
9:25 had to come with them from ***t***
9:25 come with them from time to ***t***
11: 2 in ***t*** past, even when Saul was
11:11 killed by him at one ***t***.
12:22 For at that ***t*** they came to
15:13 did not do it the first ***t***,
17: 5 dwelt in a house since the ***t***
17:10 since the ***t*** that I commanded
20: 1 at the ***t*** kings go out to
20: 4 at which ***t*** Sibbechai the
21:28 At that ***t***, when David saw
21:29 were at that ***t*** at the high
29:22 son of David king the second ***t***,
2 Chr 7: 8 At that ***t*** Solomon kept the
13:18 Israel were subdued at that ***t***;
15: 3 For a long ***t*** Israel has been
15:11 offered to the LORD at that ***t***
16: 7 And at that ***t*** Hanani the seer
16:10 some of the people at that ***t***.
18:34 and about the ***t*** of sunset he
21:10 At that ***t*** Libnah revolted
21:19 it happened in the course of ***t***,
24:11 So it was, at that ***t***,
25:27 After the ***t*** that Amaziah turned
28:16 At the same ***t*** King Ahaz sent to
28:22 Now in the ***t*** of his distress
30: 3 not keep it at the regular ***t***,
30: 5 had not done it for a long ***t***
30:26 for since the ***t*** of Solomon the
35:17 kept the Passover at that ***t***,
Ezra 5: 3 At the same ***t*** Tattenai the
5:16 but from that ***t*** even until now
8:34 was written down at that ***t***.
Neh 2: 6 to send me; and I set him a ***t***.
4:16 from that ***t*** on, that half of
4:22 At the same ***t*** I also said to the
5:14 from the ***t*** that I was appointed
6: 1 left in it (though at that ***t*** I
6: 5 to me as before, the fifth ***t***,
9:27 And in the ***t*** of their trouble,
12:44 And at the same ***t*** some were
13:21 From that ***t*** on they came no
Esth 2:19 gathered together a second ***t***,
4:14 completely silent at this ***t***,
4:14 to the kingdom for such a ***t***
8: 9 scribes were called at that ***t***,
9: 1 the ***t*** came for the king's
9:27 according to the prescribed ***t***,
9:31 of Purim at their appointed ***t***,
Job 7: 1 Is there not a ***t*** of hard
9: 3 He could not answer Him one ***t***
14:13 You would appoint me a set ***t***,
15:32 be accomplished before his ***t***,
22:16 were cut down before their ***t***,
38:23 I have reserved for the ***t*** of
39: 1 Do you know the ***t*** when the wild
39: 2 Or do you know the ***t*** when they
Ps 21: 9 them as a fiery oven in the ***t***
27: 5 For in the ***t*** of trouble He
32: 6 shall pray to You In a ***t*** when
37:19 not be ashamed in the evil ***t***,
37:39 is their strength in the ***t*** of
41: 1 LORD will deliver him in ***t*** of
69:13 O LORD, in the acceptable ***t***;
71: 9 Do not cast me off in the ***t*** of
75: 2 "When I choose the proper ***t***,
78:38 many a ***t*** He turned His anger
81: 3 Blow the trumpet at the ***t*** of
89:47 Remember how short my ***t*** is;
102:13 For the ***t*** to favor her, Yes,
102:13 to favor her, Yes, the set ***t***,
105:19 Until the ***t*** that his word came
113: 2 name of the LORD From this ***t***
115:18 bless the LORD From this ***t***
119:126 It is ***t*** for You to act, O
121: 8 and your coming in From this ***t***
125: 2 His people From this ***t*** forth
129: 1 Many a ***t*** they have afflicted me
129: 2 Many a ***t*** they have afflicted me
131: 3 hope in the LORD From this ***t***
Prov 25:13 Like the cold of snow in ***t*** of
25:19 in an unfaithful man in ***t*** of
31:25 She shall rejoice in ***t*** to
Eccl 3: 1 A ***t*** for every purpose under
3: 2 A ***t*** to be born, And a time to
3: 2 And a ***t*** to die; A time to
3: 2 A ***t*** to plant, And a time to
3: 2 And a ***t*** to pluck what is
3: 3 A ***t*** to kill, And a time to
3: 3 And a ***t*** to heal; A time to
3: 3 A ***t*** to break down, And a time
3: 3 And a ***t*** to build up;
3: 4 A ***t*** to weep, And a time to
3: 4 And a ***t*** to laugh; A time to
3: 4 A ***t*** to mourn, And a time to
3: 4 And a ***t*** to dance;
3: 5 A ***t*** to cast away stones, And a
3: 5 And a ***t*** to gather stones;
3: 5 A ***t*** to embrace, And a time to
3: 5 And a ***t*** to refrain from
3: 6 A ***t*** to gain, And a time to
3: 6 And a ***t*** to lose; A time to
3: 6 A ***t*** to keep, And a time to
3: 6 And a ***t*** to throw away;
3: 7 A ***t*** to tear, And a time to
3: 7 And a ***t*** to sew; A time to
3: 7 A ***t*** to keep silence, And a
3: 7 And a ***t*** to speak;
3: 8 A ***t*** to love, And a time to
3: 8 And a ***t*** to hate; A time of
3: 8 A ***t*** of war, And a time of
3: 8 And a ***t*** of peace.
3:11 everything beautiful in its ***t***.
3:17 For there is a ***t*** there for
7:17 should you die before your ***t***?
8: 5 man's heart discerns both ***t***
8: 6 for every matter there is a ***t***
8: 9 There is a ***t*** in which one man
9:11 But ***t*** and chance happen to
9:12 man also does not know his ***t***:
9:12 of men are snared in an evil ***t***,
10:17 princes feast at the proper ***t***—
Song 2:12 The ***t*** of singing has come,
Isa 9: 7 and justice From that ***t***
11:11 set His hand again the second ***t***
13:22 Her ***t*** is near to come,
16:13 concerning Moab since that ***t***.
18: 7 In that ***t*** a present will be
20: 2 at the same ***t*** the LORD spoke by
26:17 When she draws near the ***t*** of
30: 8 That it may be for ***t*** to come,
33: 2 Our salvation also in the ***t*** of
39: 1 At that ***t*** Merodach-Baladan the
41:27 The first ***t*** I said to Zion,
42:14 have held My peace a long ***t***,
42:23 will listen and hear for the ***t***
44: 8 I not told you from that ***t***,
45:21 declared this from ancient ***t***?
45:21 Who has told it from that ***t***?
48: 6 you hear new things from this ***t***,
48:16 From the ***t*** that it was,
49: 8 In an acceptable ***t*** I have heard
59:21 from this ***t*** and forevermore."
60:22 LORD, will hasten it in its ***t***.
66: 9 Shall I bring to the ***t*** of
Jer 1:13 LORD came to me the second ***t***,
2:24 In her ***t*** of mating, who can
2:27 But in the ***t*** of their trouble
2:28 If they can save you in the ***t***
3: 4 Will you not from this ***t*** cry to
3:17 At that ***t*** Jerusalem shall be
4:11 At that ***t*** it will be said To
6:15 At the ***t*** I punish them, They
8: 1 'At that ***t***,' says the LORD,
8: 7 and the swallow Observe the ***t***
8:12 In the ***t*** of their punishment
8:15 And for a ***t*** of health,
10:15 In the ***t*** of their punishment
10:18 I will throw out at this ***t*** The
11:12 not save them at all in the ***t***
11:14 I will not hear them in the ***t***
13: 3 LORD came to me the second ***t***,
14: 8 his Savior in ***t*** of trouble,
14:19 And for the ***t*** of healing,
15:11 to intercede with you In the ***t***
15:11 time of adversity and in the ***t***
18:23 thus with them In the ***t*** of
27: 7 until the ***t*** of his land comes;
30: 7 And it is the ***t*** of Jacob's
31: 1 the same ***t***," says the LORD,
33: 1 came to Jeremiah a second ***t***,
33:15 In those days and at that ***t*** I
39:10 and fields at the same ***t***.
46:17 has passed by the appointed ***t***!
46:21 The ***t*** of their punishment.
49: 8 The ***t*** that I will punish him.
50: 4 "In those days and in that ***t***,
50:16 handles the sickle at harvest ***t***.
50:20 In those days and in that ***t***,
50:27 the ***t*** of their punishment.
50:31 The ***t*** that I will punish you.
51: 6 For this is the ***t*** of the
51:18 In the ***t*** of their punishment
51:33 floor When it is ***t*** to
51:33 Yet a little while And the ***t***
Lam 3: 3 turned His hand against me ***T***
3: 3 His hand against me Time and ***t***
5:20 forsake us for so long a ***t***?
Ezek 4:10 from ***t*** to time you shall eat
4:10 from time to ***t*** you shall eat
4:11 from ***t*** to time you shall drink.
4:11 from time to ***t*** you shall drink.
7: 7 The ***t*** has come, A day of
7:12 The ***t*** has come, The day draws
11: 3 The ***t*** is not near to build
16: 8 indeed your ***t*** was the time of
16: 8 indeed your time was the ***t*** of
16:57 It was like the ***t*** of the
21:14 The third ***t*** let the sword do
22: 3 that her ***t*** may come;
30: 3 the ***t*** of the Gentiles.
35: 5 power of the sword at the ***t*** of
38:18 will come to pass at the same ***t***,
Dan 1: 5 so that at the end of that ***t***
2: 8 certain that you would gain ***t***,
2: 9 words before me till the ***t*** has
2:16 asked the king to give him ***t***,
3: 5 that at the ***t*** you hear the
3: 7 So at that ***t***, when all the
3: 8 Therefore at that ***t*** certain
3:15 Now if you are ready at the ***t***
4:19 was astonished for a ***t***,
4:34 And at the end of the ***t*** I,
4:36 At the same ***t*** my reason
7:12 prolonged for a season and a ***t***.

T

7:22 and the *t* came for the saints
7:25 be given into his hand For a *t*
7:25 a time and times and half a *t*.
8: 1 that appeared to me the first *t*.
8:17 the vision refers to the *t* of
8:19 shall happen in the latter *t*
8:19 for at the appointed *t* the end
8:23 And in the latter *t* of their
9:21 reached me about the *t* of the
10: 1 but the appointed *t* was long;
11:24 strongholds, but only for a *t*.
11:27 still be at the appointed *t*.
11:29 At the appointed *t* he shall
11:35 until the *t* of the end;
11:35 is still for the appointed *t*.
11:40 At the *t* of the end the king of
12: 1 At that *t* Michael shall stand
12: 1 And there shall be a *t* of
12: 1 was a nation, Even to that *t*.
12: 1 And at that *t* your people
12: 4 and seal the book until the *t*
12: 7 that it shall be for a *t*,
12: 7 a time, times, and half a *t*;
12: 9 up and sealed till the *t* of
12:11 And from the *t* that the daily
Hos 2: 9 take away My grain in its *t*
10:12 For it is *t* to seek the
Joel 3: 1 in those days and at that *t*,
Am 5:13 prudent keep silent at that *t*,
5:13 time, For it is an evil *t*.
Jon 3: 1 came to Jonah the second *t*,
Mic 2: 3 For this is an evil *t*.
3: 4 His face from them at that *t*,
5: 3 Until the *t* that she who is
Nah 1: 9 will not rise up a second *t*.
Hab 2: 3 is yet for an appointed *t*;
Zeph 1:12 it shall come to pass at that *t*
3:19 at that *t* I will deal with all
3:20 At that *t* I will bring you
3:20 Even at the *t* I gather you;
Hag 1: 2 The *t* has not come, the time
1: 2 the *t* that the LORD's house
1: 4 Is it *t* for you yourselves to
Zech 10: 1 the LORD for rain In the *t*
14: 7 But at evening *t* it shall
Mt 1:11 and his brothers about the *t*
2: 7 determined from them what *t* the
2:16 according to the *t* which he had
4:17 From that *t* Jesus began to
8:29 here to torment us before the *t*?
11:25 At that *t* Jesus answered and
12: 1 At that *t* Jesus went through the
13:30 and at the *t* of harvest I will
14: 1 At that *t* Herod the tetrarch
16:21 From that *t* Jesus began to show
18: 1 At that *t* the disciples came to
24:21 of the world until this *t*,
25:19 After a long *t* the lord of those
26:16 So from that *t* he sought
26:18 My *t* is at hand; I will keep the
26:42 Again, a second *t*, He went away
26:44 again, and prayed the third *t*,
27:16 And at that *t* they had a
Mk 1:15 'The *t* is fulfilled,
4:17 and so endure only for a *t*.
6:31 and they did not even have *t* to
10:30 a hundredfold now in this *t*—
13:19 which God created until this *t*,
13:33 for you do not know when the *t*
14:41 Then He came the third *t* and
14:72 A second *t* the rooster crowed.
15:44 if He had been dead for some *t*.
Lk 1:20 be fulfilled in their own *t*.
1:57 Now Elizabeth's full *t* came for
4: 5 of the world in a moment of *t*.
4:13 from Him until an opportune *t*.
4:27 lepers were in Israel in the *t*
7:45 to kiss My feet since the *t* I
8:13 believe for a while and in *t*
8:27 who had demons for a long *t*.
9:51 when the *t* had come for Him to
12:56 it you do not discern this *t*?
13:35 shall not see Me until the *t*
14:17 sent his servant at supper *t*
15:29 your commandment at any *t*;
16:16 Since that *t* the kingdom of God
18:30 times more in this present *t*,
19:44 because you did not know the *t*
20: 9 into a far country for a long *t*.
21: 8 The *t* has drawn near.' Therefore
23: 7 was also in Jerusalem at that *t*.
23: 8 he had desired for a long *t*
23:22 he said to them the third *t*,
Jn 1:18 No one has seen God at any *t*.
3: 4 Can he enter a second *t* into
5: 4 angel went down at a certain *t*
5: 6 in that condition a long *t*,
5:35 and you were willing for a *t* to
5:37 heard His voice at any *t*,
6:66 From that *t* many of His
7: 6 'My *t* has not yet come,
7: 6 but your *t* is always ready.
7: 8 for My *t* has not yet fully
11:39 by this *t* there is a stench,
16: 2 the *t* is coming that whoever
16: 4 that when the *t* comes, you may
16:25 but the *t* is coming when I will
21:14 This is now the third *t* Jesus
21:16 He said to him again a second *t*,
21:17 He said to him the third *t*,
21:17 He said to him the third *t*,
Acts 1: 6 will You at this *t* restore the
1:21 have accompanied us all the *t*
5:36 For some *t* ago Theudas rose up,
7:13 And the second *t* Joseph was
7:17 But when the *t* of the promise
7:20 'At this *t* Moses was born,
8: 1 At that *t* a great persecution
8:11 with his sorceries for a long *t*.
10:15 to him again the second *t*,
11: 8 common or unclean has at any *t*
12: 1 Now about that *t* Herod the king
13:11 not seeing the sun for a *t*.
13:18 Now for a *t* of about forty years
14: 3 they stayed there a long *t*,
14:28 So they stayed there a long *t*
15:33 they had stayed there for a *t*,
17:21 who were there spent their *t*
18:20 asked him to stay a longer *t*
18:23 After he had spent some *t*
19:22 himself stayed in Asia for a *t*.
19:23 And about that *t* there arose a
20:16 he would not have to spend *t*
21:26 at which *t* an offering should
21:38 you not the Egyptian who some *t*
24:25 when I have a convenient *t* I
27: 9 Now when much *t* had been spent,
28: 6 they had looked for a long *t*
Rom 3:26 to demonstrate at the present *t*
5: 6 in due *t* Christ died for the
8:18 sufferings of this present *t*
9: 9 At this *t* I will come and
11: 5 at this present *t* there is a
13:11 And do this, knowing the *t*,
13:11 that now it is high *t* to
1 Cor 4: 5 judge nothing before the *t*,
7: 5 except with consent for a *t*,
7:29 the *t* is short, so that from
15: 8 as by one born out of due *t*.
16:12 unwilling to come at this *t*;
16:12 come when he has a convenient *t*.
2 Cor 6: 2 In an acceptable *t* I have
6: 2 Behold, now is the accepted *t*;
8:14 that now at this *t* your
9: 5 to go to you ahead of *t*,
12:14 Now for the third *t* I am ready
13: 1 This will be the third *t* I am
13: 2 if I were present the second *t*,
Gal 4: 2 and stewards until the *t*
4: 4 But when the fullness of the *t*
5:21 just as I also told you in *t*
Eph 2:12 that at that *t* you were without
5:16 redeeming the *t*, because the
Col 4: 5 are outside, redeeming the *t*.
1 Th 2: 5 For neither at any *t* did we use
2:17 away from you for a short *t* in
2:18 *t* and again—but Satan hindered
2 Th 2: 6 he may be revealed in his own *t*.
1 Tim 2: 6 all, to be testified in due *t*,
6:15 He will manifest in His own *t*,
6:19 a good foundation for the *t* to
2 Tim 1: 9 to us in Christ Jesus before *t*
4: 3 For the *t* will come when they
4: 6 and the *t* of my departure is at
Titus 1: 2 promised before *t* began,
1: 3 but has in due *t* manifested His
Heb 1: 1 and in various ways spoke in *t*
4: 7 "Today," after such a long *t*,
4:16 and find grace to help in *t* of
5:12 For though by this *t* you ought
9: 9 symbolic for the present *t* in
9:10 ordinances imposed until the *t*
9:28 Him He will appear a second *t*,
10:13 from that *t* waiting till His
11:32 For the *t* would fail me to tell
Jas 4:14 that appears for a little *t*
1 Pe 1: 5 to be revealed in the last *t*.
1:11 what, or what manner of *t*,
1:17 yourselves throughout the *t* of
4: 2 should live the rest of his *t*
4:17 For the *t* has come for
5: 6 that He may exalt you in due *t*,
2 Pe 2: 3 for a long *t* their judgment has
1 Jn 4:12 No one has seen God at any *t*.
Jude 18 would be mockers in the last *t*
Rev 1: 3 for the *t* is near.
2:21 And I gave her *t* to repent of
11:18 And the *t* of the dead,
12:12 he knows that he has a short *t*.
12:14 where she is nourished for a *t*
12:14 a time and times and half a *t*,
14:15 for the *t* has come for You to
17:10 he must continue a short *t*.
22:10 for the *t* is at hand.

TIMES (159/152) TIME

Gen 27:36 has supplanted me these two *t*.
31: 7 me and changed my wages ten *t*,
31:41 you have changed my wages ten *t*.
33: 3 himself to the ground seven *t*,
43:34 Benjamin's serving was five *t*
Ex 18:22 them judge the people at all *t*.
18:26 they judged the people at all *t*;
21:29 to thrust with its horn in *t*
23:14 Three *t* you shall keep a feast
23:17 Three *t* in the year all your
34:23 Three *t* in the year all your men
34:24 the LORD your God three *t* in
Lev 4: 6 some of the blood seven *t*
4:17 blood and sprinkle it seven *t*
8:11 some of it on the altar seven *t*,
14: 7 he shall sprinkle it seven *t*
14:16 the oil with his finger seven *t*
14:27 is in his left hand seven *t*
14:51 and sprinkle the house seven *t*.
16:14 blood with his finger seven *t*.
16:19 on it with his finger seven *t*,
23: 4 proclaim at their appointed *t*.
25: 8 seven *t* seven years;
26:18 then I will punish you seven *t*
26:21 I will bring on you seven *t*
26:24 I will punish you yet seven *t*
26:28 will chastise you seven *t* for
Num 14:22 Me to the test now these ten *t*,
19: 4 some of its blood seven *t*
22:28 have struck me these three *t*?
22:32 your donkey these three *t*?
22:33 aside from Me these three *t*.
24: 1 he did not go as at other *t*,
24:10 blessed them these three *t*!
Deut 1:11 fathers make you a thousand *t*
2:10 (The Emim had dwelt there in *t*
16:16 Three *t* a year all your males
Josh 6: 4 march around the city seven *t*,
6:15 around the city seven *t* in the
6:15 marched around the city seven *t*.
24: 2 side of the River in old *t*;
Judg 16:15 have mocked me these three *t*,
16:20 go out as before, at other *t*,
20:30 Gibeah as at the other *t*.
20:31 the people, as at the other *t*,
Ruth 4: 7 was the custom in former *t*
1 Sam 3:10 stood and called as at other *t*,
18:10 with his hand, as at other *t*;
19: 7 he was in his presence as in *t*
20:25 sat on his seat, as at other *t*,
20:41 ground, and bowed down three *t*.
2 Sam 20:18 "They used to talk in former *t*,
24: 3 add to the people a hundred *t*
1 Ki 9:25 Now three *t* a year Solomon
17:21 out on the child three *t*,
18:43 And seven *t* he said, "Go
22:16 How many *t* shall I make you
2 Ki 4:35 then the child sneezed seven *t*,
5:10 and wash in the Jordan seven *t*,
5:14 he went down and dipped seven *t*
13:18 ground"; so he struck three *t*,
13:19 have struck five or six *t*;
13:19 will strike Syria only three *t*.
13:25 Three *t* Joash defeated him and
19:25 From ancient *t* that I formed
1 Chr 12:32 who had understanding of the *t*,
21: 3 make His people a hundred *t*
2 Chr 15: 5 And in those *t* there was no
18:15 How many *t* shall I make you
Ezra 4:15 within the city in former *t*,
4:19 that this city in former *t* has
10:14 pagan wives come at appointed *t*,
Neh 4:12 that they told us ten *t*,
6: 4 sent me this message four *t*,
9:28 And many *t* You delivered them
10:34 at the appointed *t* year by
13:31 the firstfruits at appointed *t*.
Esth 1:13 wise men who understood the *t*
Job 19: 3 These ten *t* you have reproached
24: 1 Since *t* are not hidden from the
33:29 three *t* with a man,
Ps 9: 9 A refuge in *t* of trouble.
10: 1 Why do You hide in *t* of
12: 6 of earth, Purified seven *t*.
31:15 My *t* are in Your hand;
34: 1 will bless the LORD at all *t*;
62: 8 Trust in Him at all *t*,
77: 5 The years of ancient *t*.
106: 3 does righteousness at all *t*!
106:43 Many *t* He delivered them;
119:20 For Your judgments at all *t*.
119:164 Seven *t* a day I praise You,
Prov 5:19 breasts satisfy you at all *t*;
7:12 At *t* she was outside,
7:12 at *t* in the open square,
17:17 A friend loves at all *t*,
24:16 man may fall seven *t* And
Eccl 1:10 has already been in ancient *t*
7:22 For many *t*, also, your own
8:12 a sinner does evil a hundred *t*,
Isa 14:31 be alone in his appointed *t*.
33: 6 will be the stability of your *t*,
37:26 From ancient *t* that I formed
41:26 And former *t*, that we may say,
46:10 And from ancient *t* things
Jer 8: 7 heavens Knows her appointed *t*;
Ezek 12:27 and he prophesies of *t* far
36:11 you inhabited as in former *t*,
Dan 1:20 he found them ten *t* better than
2:21 And He changes the *t* and the
3:19 they heat the furnace seven *t*
4:16 And let seven *t* pass over him.
4:23 till seven *t* pass over him';
4:25 and seven *t* shall pass over
4:32 and seven *t* shall pass over
6:10 down on his knees three *t* that
6:13 but makes his petition three *t*
7:10 Ten thousand *t* ten thousand
7:25 And shall intend to change *t*
7:25 his hand For a time and *t* and
9:25 Even in troublesome *t*.
11: 6 strengthened her in those *t*.
11:14 Now in those *t* many shall rise
12: 7 it shall be for a time, *t*,
Mt 16: 3 discern the signs of the *t*.
18:21 I forgive him? Up to seven *t*?
18:22 not say to you, up to seven *t*,
18:22 but up to seventy *t* seven.
26:34 crows, you will deny Me three *t*.

26:75 crows, you will deny Me three *t*.
Mk 14:30 twice, you will deny Me three *t*.
14:72 twice, you will deny Me three *t*.
Lk 17: 4 if he sins against you seven *t*
17: 4 and seven *t* in a day returns to
18:30 who shall not receive many *t*
21:24 by Gentiles until the *t* of the
22:34 before you will deny three *t*
22:61 crows, you will deny Me three *t*.
Jn 13:38 till you have denied Me three *t*.
Acts 1: 7 It is not for you to know *t* or
3:19 so that *t* of refreshing may
3:21 must receive until the *t* of
10:16 This was done three *t*.
11:10 "Now this was done three *t*,
17:26 their preappointed *t* and the
17:30 these *t* of ignorance God
2 Cor 11:24 From the Jews five *t* I received
11:25 Three *t* I was beaten with rods;
11:25 three *t* I was shipwrecked; a
12: 8 I pleaded with the Lord three *t*
Eph 1:10 of the fullness of the *t* He
1 Th 5: 1 But concerning the *t* and the
1 Tim 4: 1 says that in latter *t* some
2 Tim 3: 1 in the last days perilous *t*
Heb 1: 1 who at various *t* and in various
1 Pe 1:20 was manifest in these last *t*
3: 5 For in this manner, in former *t*,
Rev 5:11 of them was ten thousand *t* ten
12:14 is nourished for a time and *t*

TIMNA (4/4)

Gen 36:12 Now *T* was the concubine of
36:22 Hemam. Lotan's sister was *T*.
1 Chr 1:36 Gatam, and Kenaz; and by *T*,
1:39 Homam; Lotan's sister was *T*.

TIMNAH (14/12)

Gen 36:40 places, by their names: Chief *T*,
38:12 up to his sheepshearers at *T*,
38:13 father-in-law is going up to *T*
38:14 which was on the way to *T*;
Josh 15:10 Shemesh, and passed on to *T*.
15:57 Kain, Gibeah, and *T*:
19:43 Elon, *T*, Ekron,
Judg 14: 1 Now Samson went down to *T*,
14: 1 and saw a woman in *T* of the
14: 2 I have seen a woman in *T* of the
14: 5 So Samson went down to *T* with
14: 5 and came to the vineyards of *T*.
1 Chr 1:51 the chiefs of Edom were Chief *T*,
2 Chr 28:18 *T* with its villages, and Gimzo

TIMNATH HERES (1/1)

Judg 2: 9 border of his inheritance at *T*,

TIMNATH SERAH (2/2)

Josh 19:50 *T* in the mountains of Ephraim;
24:30 border of his inheritance at *T*,

TIMNITE (1/1)

Judg 15: 6 the son-in-law of the *T*,

TIMON (1/1)

Acts 6: 5 Philip, Prochorus, Nicanor, *T*,

TIMOTHEUS (KJV) See TIMOTHY

TIMOTHY (24/24)

Acts 16: 1 disciple was there, named *T*,
17:14 but both Silas and *T* remained
17:15 a command for Silas and *T* to
18: 5 When Silas and *T* had come from
19:22 *T* and Erastus, but he himself
20: 4 and Gaius of Derbe, and *T*,
Rom 16:21 *T*, my fellow worker,
1 Cor 4:17 For this reason I have sent *T* to
16:10 Now if *T* comes, see that he may
2 Cor 1: 1 and *T* our brother,
1:19 by us—by me, Silvanus, and *T*—
Phil 1: 1 Paul and *T*, bondservants
2:19 in the Lord Jesus to send *T* to
Col 1: 1 and *T* our brother,
1 Th 1: 1 Paul, Silvanus, and *T*,
3: 2 and sent *T*, our brother and
3: 6 But now that *T* has come to us
2 Th 1: 1 Paul, Silvanus, and *T*,
1 Tim 1: 2 To *T*, a true son in the faith:
1:18 charge I commit to you, son *T*,
6:20 O *T*! Guard what was committed
2 Tim 1: 2 To *T*, a beloved son:
Phm 1: 1 and *T* our brother,
Heb 13:23 Know that our brother *T* has

TIN (4/4)

Num 31:22 the bronze, the iron, the *t*,
Ezek 22:18 to Me; they are all bronze, *t*,
22:20 and *t* into the midst of a
27:12 They gave you silver, iron, *t*,

TINDER (1/1)

Isa 1:31 The strong shall be as *t*,

TINGLE (3/3)

1 Sam 3:11 of everyone who hears it will *t*.
2 Ki 21:12 of it, both his ears will *t*.
Jer 19: 3 hears of it, his ears will *t*.

TINKLING (KJV) See CLANGING, JINGLING

TIP (11/9)

Ex 29:20 its blood and put it on the *t*
29:20 ear of Aaron and on the *t* of
Lev 8:23 its blood and put it on the *t*
14:14 priest shall put it on the *t*
14:17 shall put some on the *t* of
14:25 offering and put it on the *t*
14:28 that is in his hand on the *t*
1 Ki 6:24 ten cubits from the *t* of one
6:24 the tip of one wing to the *t*
Jer 48:12 him wine-workers Who will *t*
Lk 16:24 Lazarus that he may dip the *t*

TIPHSAH (2/2)

1 Ki 4:24 this side of the River from *T*
2 Ki 15:16 from Tirzah, Menahem attacked *T*,

TIPS (1/1)

Lev 8:24 some of the blood on the *t* of

TIRAS (2/2)

Gen 10: 2 Javan, Tubal, Meshech, and *T*.
1 Chr 1: 5 Javan, Tubal, Meshech, and *T*.

TIRATHITES (1/1)

1 Chr 2:55 who dwelt at Jabez were the *T*,

TIRED (1/1)

Deut 25:18 when you were *t* and weary;

TIRES (KJV) See CRESCENTS, TURBAN

TIRHAKAH (2/2)

2 Ki 19: 9 And the king heard concerning *T*
Isa 37: 9 And the king heard concerning *T*

TIRHANAH (1/1)

1 Chr 2:48 concubine, bore Sheber and *T*.

TIRIA (1/1)

1 Chr 4:16 were Ziph, Ziphah, *T*,

TIRSHATHA (KJV) See GOVERNOR

TIRZAH (18/17)

Num 26:33 Noah, Hoglah, Milcah, and *T*.
27: 1 Noah, Hoglah, Milcah, and *T*.
36:11 for Mahlah, *T*, Hoglah,
Josh 12:24 the king of *T*, one—all
17: 3 Noah, Hoglah, Milcah, and *T*.
1 Ki 14:17 and departed, and came to *T*.
15:21 Ramah, and remained in *T*.
15:33 king over all Israel in *T*,
16: 6 his fathers and was buried in *T*.
16: 8 and reigned two years in *T*.
16: 9 against him as he was in *T*
16: 9 steward of his house in *T*.
16:15 Zimri had reigned in *T* seven
16:17 Gibbethon, and they besieged *T*.
16:23 Six years he reigned in *T*.
2 Ki 15:14 the son of Gadi went up from *T*,
15:16 Then from *T*, Menahem
Song 6: 4 you are as beautiful as *T*,

TISHBITE (6/6)

1 Ki 17: 1 And Elijah the *T*,
21:17 the LORD came to Elijah the *T*,
21:28 the LORD came to Elijah the *T*,
2 Ki 1: 3 the LORD said to Elijah the *T*,
1: 8 he said, "It is Elijah the *T*."
9:36 by His servant Elijah the *T*,

TITHE (17/16) TITHES

Gen 14:20 And he gave him a *t* of all.
Lev 27:30 And all the *t* of the land,
27:32 And concerning the *t* of the herd
Num 18:26 to the LORD, a tenth of the *t*.
Deut 12:17 eat within your gates the *t* of
14:22 You shall truly *t* all the
14:23 the *t* of your grain and your
14:24 are not able to carry the *t*,
14:28 year you shall bring out the *t*
26:12 laying aside all the *t* of your
26:13 I have removed the holy *t* from
2 Chr 31: 5 brought in abundantly the *t* of
31: 6 brought the *t* of oxen and
31: 6 also the *t* of holy things which
Neh 13:12 Then all Judah brought the *t* of
Mt 23:23 hypocrites! For you pay *t* of
Lk 11:42 woe to you Pharisees! For you *t*

TITHES (23/20) TITHE

Lev 27:31 at all to redeem any of his *t*,
Num 18:21 the children of Levi all the *t*
18:24 For the *t* of the children of
18:26 the children of Israel the *t*
18:28 to the LORD from all your *t*
Deut 12: 6 your sacrifices, your *t*,
12:11 your *t*, the heave offerings
2 Chr 31:12 brought in the offerings, the *t*,
Neh 10:37 and to bring the *t* of our land
10:37 Levites should receive the *t*
10:38 when the Levites receive *t*;
10:38 bring up a tenth of the *t* to
12:44 the firstfruits, and the *t*,
13: 5 the *t* of grain, the new wine
Am 4: 4 Your *t* every three days.
Mal 3: 8 In *t* and offerings.
3:10 Bring all the *t* into the
Lk 18:12 I give *t* of all that I
Heb 7: 5 have a commandment to receive *t*
7: 6 derived from them received *t*
7: 8 Here mortal men receive *t*,
7: 9 Even Levi, who receives *t*,
7: 9 paid *t* through Abraham,

TITHING (1/1)

Deut 26:12 in the third year—the year of *t*—

TITLE (2/2)

Jn 19:19 Now Pilate wrote a *t* and put it
19:20 many of the Jews read this *t*,

TITTLE (2/2)

Mt 5:18 one jot or one *t* will by no
Lk 16:17 to pass away than for one *t* of

TITUS (13/12)

2 Cor 2:13 because I did not find *T* my
7: 6 comforted us by the coming of *T*,
7:13 more for the joy of *T*,
7:14 even so our boasting to *T* was
8: 6 So we urged *T*, that as he had
8:16 for you into the heart of *T*.
8:23 If anyone inquires about *T*,
12:18 I urged *T*, and sent our brother
12:18 Did *T* take advantage of you?
Gal 2: 1 and also took *T* with me.
2: 3 Yet not even *T* who was with me,
2 Tim 4:10 *T* for Dalmatia.
Titus 1: 4 To *T*, a true son in our

TIZITE (1/1)

1 Chr 11:45 and Joha his brother, the *T*,

TO (20825/13908) See APPENDIX

TOAH (1/1)

1 Chr 6:34 the son of Eliel, the son of *T*,

TOB (2/2)

Judg 11: 3 and dwelt in the land of *T*;
11: 5 get Jephthah from the land of *T*.

TOBADONIJAH (1/1)

2 Chr 17: 8 Adonijah, Tobijah, and *T*—

TOBIAH (15/14)

Ezra 2:60 sons of Delaiah, the sons of *T*,
Neh 2:10 Sanballat the Horonite and *T*
2:19 *T* the Ammonite official,
4: 3 Now *T* the Ammonite was beside
4: 7 it happened, when Sanballat, *T*,
6: 1 it happened when Sanballat, *T*,
6:12 prophecy against me because *T*
6:14 remember *T* and Sanballat,
6:17 of Judah sent many letters to *T*,
6:17 and the letters of *T* came to
6:19 *T* sent letters to frighten me.
7:62 sons of Delaiah, the sons of *T*,
13: 4 of our God, was allied with *T*.
13: 7 that Eliashib had done for *T*,
13: 8 all the household goods of *T*

TOBIJAH (3/3)

2 Chr 17: 8 Jehonathan, Adonijah, *T*,
Zech 6:10 the captives—from Heldai, *T*,
6:14 of the LORD for Helem, *T*,

TOCHEN (1/1)

1 Chr 4:32 were Etam, Ain, Rimmon, *T*,

TODAY (161/147)

Gen 21:26 nor had I heard of it until *t*.
30:32 pass through all your flock *t*,
40: 7 "Why do you look so sad *t*?
42:13 youngest is with our father *t*,
Ex 2:18 that you have come so soon *t*?
5:14 brick both yesterday and *t*,
14:13 He will accomplish for you *t*.
14:13 the Egyptians whom you see *t*,
16:23 Bake what you will bake *t*,

16:25 Then Moses said, "Eat that *t*,
16:25 for *t* is a Sabbath to the
16:25 *t* you will not find it in the
19:10 people and consecrate them *t*
32:29 Consecrate yourselves *t* to the
Lev 9: 4 for *t* the LORD will appear to
10:19 I had eaten the sin offering *t*,
Deut 1:10 you, and here you are *t*,
1:39 who *t* have no knowledge of good
4: 4 the LORD your God are alive *t*,
4:40 which I command you *t*,
5: 1 which I speak in your hearing *t*,
5: 3 with us, those who are here *t*,
6: 6 words which I command you *t*
7:11 judgments which I command you *t*,
8: 1 which I command you *t* you must
8:11 statutes which I command you *t*,
9: 1 are to cross over the Jordan *t*,
9: 3 Therefore understand *t* that the
10:13 statutes which I command you *t*
11: 2 Know *t* that I do not speak
11: 8 which I command you *t*, that you
11:13 which I command you *t*,
11:26 I set before you *t* a blessing
11:27 your God which I command you *t*;
11:28 the way which I command you *t*,
11:32 which I set before you *t*.
12: 8 all do as we are doing here *t*—
13:18 which I command you *t*,
15: 5 which I command you *t*.
15:15 I command you this thing *t*.
19: 9 do them, which I command you *t*,
20: 3 *T* you are on the verge of
26: 3 I declare *t* to the LORD your
26:17 *T* you have proclaimed the LORD
26:18 Also *t* the LORD has proclaimed
27: 1 which I command you *t*.
27: 4 stones, which I command you *t*,
27:10 statutes which I command you *t*.
28: 1 which I command you *t*,
28:13 your God, which I command you *t*,
28:15 statutes which I command you *t*,
29:10 All of you stand *t* before the
29:12 LORD your God makes with you *t*,
29:13 that He may establish you *t* as a
29:15 him who stands here with us *t*
29:15 who is not here with us *t*
29:18 whose heart turns away *t* from
30: 2 to all that I command you *t*,
30: 8 which I command you *t*.
30:11 which I command you *t* is not
30:15 I have set before you *t* life
30:16 in that I command you *t* to love
30:18 I announce to you *t* that you
30:19 heaven and earth as witnesses *t*
31: 2 hundred and twenty years old *t*.
31:21 inclination of their behavior *t*,
31:27 If *t*, while I am yet alive with
32:46 which I testify among you *t*,
Josh 22:18 if you rebel *t* against the
Judg 21: 3 that *t* there should be one
21: 6 tribe is cut off from Israel *t*.
Ruth 2:19 her, "Where have you gleaned *t*?
2:19 name with whom I worked *t* is
1 Sam 4: 3 has the LORD defeated us *t*
4:16 And I fled *t* from the battle
9:12 for *t* he came to this city,
9:12 is a sacrifice of the people *t*
9:19 for you shall eat with me *t*;
10: 2 you have departed from me *t*,
10:19 But you have *t* rejected your
11:13 for *t* the LORD has
12:17 Is *t* not the wheat harvest?
14:30 the people had eaten freely *t*
14:38 and see what this sin was *t*.
15:28 kingdom of Israel from you *t*,
18:21 "You shall be my son-in-law *t*.
20:27 to eat, either yesterday or *t*?
24:10 that the LORD delivered you *t*
26:23 delivered you into my hand *t*,
27:10 "Where have you made a raid *t*?
2 Sam 3: 8 *T* I show loyalty to the house
3: 8 and you charge me *t* with a
3:39 "And I am weak *t*,
6:20 was the king of Israel *t*,
6:20 uncovering himself *t* in the
11:12 Wait here *t* also, and tomorrow I
14:22 *T* your servant knows that I have
15:20 wander up and down with us *t*,
16: 3 *T* the house of Israel will
18:20 But *t* you shall take no news,
19: 5 *T* you have disgraced all your
19: 5 all your servants who *t* have
19: 6 For you have declared *t* that
19: 6 for *t* I perceive that if
19: 6 lived and all of us had died *t*,
19:20 the first to come *t* of all the
19:22 should be adversaries to me *t*?
19:22 any man be put to death *t* in
19:22 For do I not know that *t* I am
19:35 'I am *t* eighty years old.
1 Ki 1:25 "For he has gone down *t*,
1:51 'Let King Solomon swear to me *t*
2:24 shall be put to death *t*!"
8:28 servant is praying before You *t*:
12: 7 be a servant to these people *t*,
18:15 surely present myself to him *t*.
20:13 deliver it into your hand *t*,
22: 5 for the word of the LORD *t*.
2 Ki 2: 3 from over you *t*?" And he said,
2: 5 your master from over you *t*?
4:23 "Why are you going to him *t*?
6:28 your son, that we may eat him *t*,
6:31 son of Shaphat remains on him *t*.
2 Chr 18: 4 for the word of the LORD *t*.
Neh 9:36 'Here we are, servants *t*!
Esth 5: 4 let the king and Haman come *t*
Job 23: 2 Even *t* my complaint is bitter;
Ps 2: 7 *T* I have begotten You.
95: 7 *T*, if you will hear His voice:
Prov 7:14 *T* I have paid my vows.
22:19 I have instructed you *t*, even
Isa 56:12 Tomorrow will be as *t*,
Zech 9:12 Even *t* I declare That I will
Mt 6:30 which *t* is, and tomorrow is
16: 3 'It will be foul weather *t*,
21:28 work *t* in my vineyard.'
27:19 I have suffered many things *t*
Mk 14:30 I say to you that *t*,
Lk 4:21 *T* this Scripture is fulfilled in
5:26 We have seen strange things *t*!"
12:28 which *t* is in the field and
13:32 out demons and perform cures *t*
13:33 "Nevertheless I must journey *t*,
19: 5 for *t* I must stay at your
19: 9 *T* salvation has come to this
23:43 *t* you will be with Me in
24:21 *t* is the third day since these
Acts 13:33 *T* I have begotten You.'
22: 3 toward God as you all are *t*.
26: 2 because *t* I shall answer for
26:29 but also all who hear me *t*,
27:33 *T* is the fourteenth day you have
Heb 1: 5 *T* I have begotten You"?
3: 7 as the Holy Spirit says: "*T*,
3:13 daily, while it is called "*T*,
3:15 while it is said: "*T*,
4: 7 day, saying in David, "*T*,
4: 7 as it has been said: "*T*,
5: 5 *T* I have begotten You."
13: 8 is the same yesterday, *t*,
Jas 4:13 *T* or tomorrow we will go to such

TODAY'S (2/2)

Esth 9:13 tomorrow according to *t* decree,
Acts 19:40 called in question for *t* uproar,

TOE (6/6)

Ex 29:20 right hand and on the big *t* of
Lev 8:23 and on the big *t* of his right
14:14 and on the big *t* of his right
14:17 and on the big *t* of his right
14:25 and on the big *t* of his right
14:28 and on the big *t* of his right

TOES (7/7)

Lev 8:24 and on the big *t* of their right
Judg 1: 6 cut off his thumbs and big *t*.
1: 7 with their thumbs and big *t*
2 Sam 21:20 fingers on each hand and six *t*
1 Chr 20: 6 with twenty-four fingers and *t*,
Dan 2:41 you saw the feet and *t*,
2:42 And as the *t* of the feet were

TOGARMAH (4/4)

Gen 10: 3 were Ashkenaz, Riphath, and *T*.
1 Chr 1: 6 were Ashkenaz, Diphath, and *T*.
Ezek 27:14 Those from the house of *T* traded
38: 6 the house of *T* from the far

TOGETHER (432/418)

Gen 1: 9 the heavens be gathered *t* into
1:10 and the gathering *t* of the
3: 7 and they sewed fig leaves *t* and
13: 6 that they might dwell *t*,
13: 6 that they could not dwell *t*.
14: 3 All these joined *t* in the Valley
14: 8 Zoar) went out and joined *t* in
22: 6 and the two of them went *t*.
22: 8 So the two of them went *t*.
22:19 and they rose and went *t* to
25:22 But the children struggled *t*
29: 7 for the cattle to be gathered *t*.
29: 8 all the flocks are gathered *t*,
29:22 And Laban gathered *t* all the men
34:30 they will gather themselves *t*
36: 7 too great for them to dwell *t*,
42:17 So he put them all *t* in prison
49: 1 his sons and said, "Gather *t*,
49: 2 Gather *t* and hear, you sons of
Ex 3:16 gather the elders of Israel *t*,
4:29 and Aaron went and gathered *t*
8:14 They gathered them *t* in heaps,
15: 8 The waters were gathered *t*;
19: 8 Then all the people answered *t*
26: 6 and couple the curtains *t* with
26:11 loops, and couple the tent *t*,
26:24 They shall be coupled *t* at the
26:24 and they shall be coupled *t* at
28: 7 and so it shall be joined *t*.
32: 1 the people gathered *t* to Aaron,
32:26 of Levi gathered themselves *t*
35: 1 of the children of Israel *t*,
36:18 clasps to couple the tent *t*,
36:29 at the bottom and coupled *t* at
39: 4 straps for it to couple it *t*;
39: 4 it was coupled *t* at its two
Lev 8: 3 gather all the congregation *t*
8: 4 congregation was gathered *t* at
26:25 when you are gathered *t* within
Num 1:18 all the congregation *t* on the
6:20 *t* with the breast of the wave
8: 9 and you shall gather *t* the
10: 7 assembly is to be gathered *t*,
11:22 fish of the sea be gathered *t*
14:35 who are gathered *t* against Me.
16: 3 They gathered *t* against Moses
16:11 your company are gathered *t*
20: 2 so they gathered *t* against
20: 8 Aaron gather the congregation *t*.
20:10 Aaron gathered the assembly *t*
21:16 to Moses, "Gather the people *t*,
21:23 gathered all his people *t* and
24:10 and he struck his hands *t*;
26:10 mouth and swallowed them up *t*
27: 3 company of those who gathered *t*
Deut 22:10 plow with an ox and a donkey *t*.
22:11 as wool and linen mixed *t*.
25: 5 "If brothers dwell *t*,
25:11 "If two men fight *t*,
31:12 "Gather the people *t*,
33: 5 All the tribes of Israel *t*.
33:17 *T* with them He shall push the
Josh 8:16 who were in Ai were called *t*
9: 2 that they gathered *t* to fight
10: 5 gathered *t* and went up,
10: 6 the mountains have gathered *t*
11: 5 when all these kings had met *t*,
11: 5 they came and camped *t* at the
18: 1 children of Israel assembled *t*
22:12 children of Israel gathered *t*
Judg 4:13 So Sisera gathered *t* all his
6:33 people of the East, gathered *t*;
6:38 and squeezed the fleece *t*,
7:23 the men of Israel gathered *t*
7:24 the men of Ephraim gathered *t*
9: 6 the men of Shechem gathered *t*,
9:47 of Shechem were gathered *t*.
10:17 the people of Ammon gathered *t*
10:17 children of Israel assembled *t*
11: 3 and worthless men banded *t* with
11:20 Sihon gathered all his people *t*,
12: 1 the men of Ephraim gathered *t*,
12: 4 Now Jephthah gathered *t* all the
16:23 of the Philistines gathered *t*
18:22 near Micah's house gathered *t*
19: 6 the two of them ate and drank *t*.
20: 1 the congregation gathered *t* as
20:11 united *t* as one man.
20:14 of Benjamin gathered *t* from
1 Sam 5:11 So they sent and gathered *t* all
7: 6 So they gathered *t* at Mizpah,
7: 7 of Israel had gathered *t* at
8: 4 the elders of Israel gathered *t*
10:17 Samuel called the people *t* to
11:11 that no two of them were left *t*.
13: 4 And the people were called *t* to
13: 5 the Philistines gathered *t* to
13:11 the Philistines gathered *t* at
15: 4 So Saul gathered the people *t*
17: 1 gathered their armies *t* to
17: 1 and were gathered *t* at Sochoh,
17: 2 men of Israel were gathered *t*,
17:10 me a man, that we may fight *t*.
20:41 one another; and they wept *t*,
23: 8 Saul called all the people *t*
25: 1 and the Israelites gathered *t*
28: 1 gathered their armies *t* for
28: 4 Then the Philistines gathered *t*,
28: 4 So Saul gathered all Israel *t*,
28:23 *t* with the woman, urged him;
29: 1 the Philistines gathered *t* all
31: 6 and all his men died *t* that
2 Sam 2:16 so they fell down *t*.
2:25 of Benjamin gathered *t* behind
2:30 had gathered all the people *t*,
10:15 by Israel, they gathered *t*.
12: 3 and it grew up *t* with him and
12:28 the rest of the people *t* and
12:29 gathered all the people *t* and
14:16 would destroy me and my son *t*
20:14 So they were gathered *t* and
21: 9 So they fell, all seven *t*.
23:11 The Philistines had gathered *t*
1 Ki 3:18 we were *t*; no one was with
5:12 the two of them made a treaty *t*.
18:20 and gathered the prophets *t* on
20: 1 Syria gathered all his forces *t*;
22: 6 Israel gathered the prophets *t*,
2 Ki 3:10 has called these three kings *t*
3:13 called these three kings *t* to
9:25 when you and I were riding *t*
10:18 Jehu gathered all the people *t*,
1 Chr 10: 6 died, and all his house died *t*.
11: 1 Then all Israel came *t* to David
13: 2 that they may gather *t* to us;
13: 5 So David gathered all Israel *t*,
15: 3 David gathered all Israel *t* at
16:35 Gather us *t*, and deliver us
19: 7 the people of Ammon gathered *t*
23: 2 And he gathered *t* all the
2 Chr 12: 5 who were gathered *t* in
15:10 So they gathered *t* at Jerusalem
18: 5 Israel gathered the prophets *t*,
20: 4 So Judah gathered *t* to ask help
25: 5 Amaziah gathered Judah *t* and
30: 3 nor had the people gathered *t*
32: 4 Thus many people gathered *t* who
32: 6 gathered them *t* to him in the
Ezra 2:64 The whole assembly *t* was
3: 1 the people gathered *t* as one
6:21 from the captivity ate *t* with

10:14 ***t*** with the elders and judges of
Neh 4: 6 the entire wall was joined ***t***
4: 8 and all of them conspired ***t*** to
6: 2 let us meet ***t*** among the
6: 7 therefore, and let us consult ***t***.
6:10 Let us meet ***t*** in the house of
8: 1 Now all the people gathered ***t*** as
12:28 sons of the singers gathered ***t***
13:11 And I gathered them ***t*** and set
Esth 2:19 When virgins were gathered ***t*** a
8:11 in every city to gather ***t*** and
9: 2 The Jews gathered ***t*** in their
9:15 who were in Shushan gathered ***t***
9:16 the king's provinces gathered ***t***
9:18 were at Shushan assembled ***t***
Job 2:11 they had made an appointment ***t***
3:18 There the prisoners rest ***t***;
9:32 that we should go to court ***t***.
10:11 And knit me ***t*** with bones and
16:10 They gather ***t*** against me.
17:16 Shall we have rest ***t*** in the
19:12 His troops come ***t*** And build up
31:38 And its furrows weep ***t***;
34:15 All flesh would perish ***t***,
38: 7 When the morning stars sang ***t***,
38:38 And the clods cling ***t***?
40:13 Hide them in the dust ***t***,
41:17 They stick ***t*** and cannot be
41:23 folds of his flesh are joined ***t***;
Ps 2: 2 And the rulers take counsel ***t***,
14: 3 They have ***t*** become corrupt;
31:13 While they take counsel ***t***
33: 7 the waters of the sea ***t*** as a
34: 3 And let us exalt His name ***t***.
35:15 they rejoiced And gathered ***t***;
37:38 shall be destroyed ***t***;
41: 7 All who hate me whisper ***t***
47: 9 of the people have gathered ***t***,
48: 4 assembled, They passed by ***t***.
49: 2 low and high, Rich and poor ***t***.
50: 5 'Gather My saints ***t*** to Me,
53: 3 They have ***t*** become corrupt;
55:14 We took sweet counsel ***t***,
56: 6 They gather ***t***, They hide,
71:10 wait for my life take counsel ***t***,
83: 3 And consulted ***t*** against Your
83: 5 For they have consulted ***t*** with
85:10 Mercy and truth have met ***t***;
94:21 They gather ***t*** against the life
98: 8 Let the hills be joyful ***t***
102:22 the peoples are gathered ***t***,
104:22 they gather ***t*** And lie down in
122: 3 As a city that is compact ***t***,
133: 1 For brethren to dwell ***t*** in
140: 2 They continually gather ***t*** for
147: 2 He gathers ***t*** the outcasts of
Eccl 4: 6 ***t*** with toil and grasping for
4:11 Again, if two lie down ***t***,
Isa 1:18 and let us reason ***t***,"
1:28 and of sinners shall be ***t***,
1:31 as a spark; Both will burn ***t***,
8:10 Take counsel ***t***,
9:21 ***T*** they shall be against
11: 6 young lion and the fatling ***t***;
11: 7 young ones shall lie down ***t***;
11:12 And gather ***t*** the dispersed of
11:14 ***T*** they shall plunder the
13: 4 kingdoms of nations gathered ***t***!
18: 6 They will be left ***t*** for the
22: 3 All your rulers have fled ***t***;
22: 3 are found in you are bound ***t***;
22: 9 And you gathered ***t*** the waters
24:22 They will be gathered ***t***,
25:11 will bring down their pride ***T***
26:19 ***T*** with my dead body they
27: 4 I would burn them ***t***.
31: 3 They all will perish ***t***.
40: 5 And all flesh shall see it ***t***;
41: 1 Let us come near ***t*** for
41:19 the pine And the box tree ***t***,
41:20 And consider and understand ***t***,
41:23 may be dismayed and see it ***t***.
43: 9 all the nations be gathered ***t***,
43:17 (They shall lie down ***t***,
43:26 Let us contend ***t***;
44:11 Let them all be gathered ***t***,
44:11 They shall be ashamed ***t***.
45: 8 let righteousness spring up ***t***.
45:16 They shall go in confusion ***t***,
45:20 and come; Draw near ***t***,
45:21 Yes, let them take counsel ***t***.
46: 2 They stoop, they bow down ***t***;
48:13 call to them, They stand up ***t***.
49:18 All these gather ***t*** and come
50: 8 Let us stand ***t***.
52: 8 their voices they shall sing ***t***;
52: 9 Break forth into joy, sing ***t***,
60: 4 They all gather ***t***,
60: 7 of Kedar shall be gathered ***t***
60:13 the pine, and the box tree ***t***,
62: 9 Those who have brought it ***t***
65: 7 iniquities of your fathers ***t***,
65:25 wolf and the lamb shall feed ***t***,
66:17 the mouse, Shall be consumed ***t***,
Jer 3:18 and they shall come ***t*** out of
4: 5 in the land; Cry, 'Gather ***t***,
6:11 on the assembly of young men ***t***;
6:12 to others, Fields and wives ***t***;
6:21 And the fathers and the sons ***t***
13:14 even the fathers and the sons ***t***,
31: 8 one who labors with child, ***t***;
31:13 the young men and the old, ***t***;
31:24 itself, and in all its cities ***t***,
41: 1 And there they ate bread ***t*** in
46:12 They both have fallen ***t***.
46:21 They have fled away ***t***.
48: 7 His priests and his princes ***t***.
49: 3 his priests and his princes ***t***.
49:14 to the nations: "Gather ***t***,
50: 4 and the children of Judah ***t***;
50:29 Call ***t*** the archers against
51:27 Call the kingdoms ***t*** against
51:38 They shall roar ***t*** like lions,
Lam 1:14 They were woven ***t*** by His
2: 8 to lament; They languished ***t***.
Ezek 1:20 and the wheels were lifted ***t***
1:21 the wheels were lifted up ***t***
20:40 ***t*** with all your holy things.
21:14 And strike your hands ***t***.
21:17 "I also will beat My fists ***t***,
25:10 ***t*** with the Ammonites, that the
31:16 when I cast it down to hell ***t***
37: 7 rattling; and the bones came ***t***,
39:17 Gather ***t*** from all sides to My
45:24 ***t*** with a hin of oil for each
Dan 2:35 and the gold were crushed ***t***,
3: 2 sent word to gather ***t*** the
3: 3 of the provinces gathered ***t***
3:27 king's counselors gathered ***t***,
6: 7 have consulted ***t*** to establish a
Hos 1:11 of Israel Shall be gathered ***t***,
7:14 They assemble ***t*** for grain and
Joel 3:11 And gather ***t*** all around.
Am 1:15 He and his princes ***t***,
3: 3 Can two walk ***t***,
Mic 2:12 I will put them ***t*** like sheep
7: 3 evil desire; So they scheme ***t***.
Zeph 2: 1 Gather yourselves ***t***,
2: 1 together, yes, gather ***t***,
Zech 10: 4 From him every ruler ***t***.
10: 9 ***t*** with their children,
14:14 nations Shall be gathered ***t***:
Mt 1:18 to Joseph, before they came ***t***,
2: 4 and scribes of the people ***t***,
13: 2 multitudes were gathered ***t*** to
13:30 Let both grow ***t*** until the
13:30 First gather ***t*** the tares and
18:20 two or three are gathered ***t*** in
19: 6 Therefore what God has joined ***t***,
22:10 the highways and gathered ***t***
22:34 the Sadducees, they gathered ***t***.
22:41 the Pharisees were gathered ***t***,
23:37 to gather your children ***t***,
24:28 the eagles will be gathered ***t***.
24:31 and they will gather ***t*** His
27: 7 And they consulted ***t*** and bought
27:17 when they had gathered ***t***,
27:62 and Pharisees gathered ***t*** to
28:12 with the elders and consulted ***t***,
Mk 1:33 the whole city was gathered ***t***
2: 2 Immediately many gathered ***t***,
2:15 and sinners also sat ***t*** with
3:20 Then the multitude came ***t***
6:33 arrived before them and came ***t***
7: 1 and some of the scribes came ***t***
9:25 that the people came running ***t***,
10: 9 what God has joined ***t***,
12:28 having heard them reasoning ***t***,
13:27 and gather ***t*** His elect from the
15:16 and they called ***t*** the whole
Lk 5:15 and great multitudes came ***t*** to
6:38 measure, pressed down, shaken ***t***,
9: 1 called His twelve disciples ***t***
11:29 crowds were thickly gathered ***t***,
12: 1 of people had gathered ***t***,
13:34 to gather your children ***t***,
15: 6 he calls ***t*** his friends and
15: 9 her friends and neighbors ***t***,
15:13 the younger son gathered all ***t***,
17:35 "Two women will be grinding ***t***:
17:37 the eagles will be gathered ***t***.
20: 1 ***t*** with the elders, confronted
22:55 of the courtyard and sat down ***t***,
22:66 ***t*** and led Him into their
23:13 when he had called ***t*** the chief
23:48 And the whole crowd who came ***t***
24:14 And they talked ***t*** of all these
24:33 who were with them gathered ***t***,
Jn 4:36 and he who reaps may rejoice ***t***.
11:52 also that He would gather ***t*** in
17: 5 glorify Me ***t*** with Yourself,
20: 4 So they both ran ***t***,
20: 7 but folded ***t*** in a place by
21: 2 others of His disciples were ***t***.
Acts 1: 4 And being assembled ***t*** with
1: 6 Therefore, when they had come ***t***,
2: 6 occurred, the multitude came ***t***,
2:44 Now all who believed were ***t***,
3: 1 Now Peter and John went up ***t*** to
3:11 all the people ran ***t*** to them in
4: 6 were gathered ***t*** at Jerusalem.
4:26 the rulers were gathered ***t***
4:27 of Israel, were gathered ***t***
4:31 where they were assembled ***t***
5: 9 is it that you have agreed ***t***
5:21 came and called the council ***t***,
10:24 and had called ***t*** his relatives
10:27 and found many who had come ***t***.
12:12 where many were gathered ***t***
13:44 almost the whole city came ***t***
14: 1 in Iconium that they went ***t*** to
14:27 come and gathered the church ***t***,
15: 6 the apostles and elders came ***t***
15:30 had gathered the multitude ***t***,
16:22 Then the multitude rose up ***t***
19:19 magic brought their books ***t***
19:25 He called them ***t*** with the
19:32 not know why they had come ***t***.
20: 7 when the disciples came ***t*** to
20: 8 room where they were gathered ***t***.
21:30 the people ran ***t***, seized Paul,
23:12 some of the Jews banded ***t*** and
23:15 ***t*** with the council, suggest to
25:17 when they had come ***t***,
28:17 the leaders of the Jews ***t***.
28:17 So when they had come ***t***,
Rom 1:12 that I may be encouraged ***t*** with
3:12 They have ***t*** become
6: 5 For if we have been united ***t*** in
8:17 that we may also be glorified ***t***.
8:22 and labors with birth pangs ***t***
8:28 we know that all things work ***t***
15:30 that you strive ***t*** with me in
15:32 and may be refreshed ***t*** with
1 Cor 1:10 you be perfectly joined ***t*** in
5: 4 Christ, when you are gathered ***t***,
7: 5 and come ***t*** again so that Satan
11:17 since you come ***t*** not for the
11:18 when you come ***t*** as a church,
11:20 Therefore when you come ***t*** in one
11:33 when you come ***t*** to eat, wait
11:34 lest you come ***t*** for judgment.
14:23 if the whole church comes ***t*** in
14:26 Whenever you come ***t***, each of
2 Cor 1:11 you also helping ***t*** in prayer for
6: 1 as workers ***t*** with Him also
6:14 Do not be unequally yoked ***t*** with
7: 3 to die ***t*** and to live ***t***.
7: 3 to die together and to live ***t***.
Eph 1:10 of the times He might gather ***t***
2: 5 made us alive ***t*** with Christ (by
2: 6 and raised us up ***t***,
2: 6 and made us sit ***t*** in the
2:21 whole building, being joined ***t***,
2:22 you also are being built ***t*** for
4:16 joined and knit ***t*** by what every
Phil 1:27 with one mind striving ***t*** for
Col 2: 2 being knit ***t*** in love,
2:13 He has made alive ***t*** with Him,
2:19 nourished and knit ***t*** by joints
1 Th 4:17 remain shall be caught up ***t***
5:10 we should live ***t*** with Him.
2 Th 2: 1 Christ and our gathering ***t*** to
Heb 10:25 the assembling of ourselves ***t***,
Jas 2:22 see that faith was working ***t***
1 Pe 3: 7 and as being heirs ***t*** of the
5:13 elect ***t*** with you, greets you;
Rev 16:16 And they gathered them ***t*** to the
19:17 Come and gather ***t*** for the supper
19:19 gathered ***t*** to make war against
20: 8 to gather them ***t*** to battle,

TOHU (1/1)

1 Sam 1: 1 the son of Elihu, the son of ***T***,

TOI (3/2)

2 Sam 8: 9 When ***T*** king of Hamath heard
8:10 then ***T*** sent Joram his son to
8:10 had been at war with ***T***);

TOIL (11/11) TOILED, TOILS

Gen 3:17 In ***t*** you shall eat of it All
5:29 concerning our work and the ***t***
41:51 God has made me forget all my ***t***
Eccl 4: 4 I saw that for all ***t*** and every
4: 6 together with ***t*** and grasping
4: 8 For whom do I ***t*** and deprive
Mt 6:28 they neither ***t*** nor spin;
Lk 12:27 they neither ***t*** nor spin;
2 Cor 11:27 in weariness and ***t***,
1 Th 2: 9 brethren, our labor and ***t***;
2 Th 3: 8 but worked with labor and ***t***

TOILED (6/6) TOIL

Eccl 2:11 on the labor in which I had ***t***;
2:18 all my labor in which I had ***t***
2:19 over all my labor in which I ***t***
2:20 all the labor in which I had ***t***
2:22 his heart with which he has ***t***
Lk 5: 5 we have ***t*** all night and caught

TOILS (2/2) TOIL

Eccl 1: 3 all his labor In which he ***t***
5:18 of all his labor in which he ***t***

TOKEN (1/1)

Josh 2:12 house, and give me a true ***t***,

TOKHATH (1/1)

2 Chr 34:22 wife of Shallum the son of ***T***,

TOLA (6/5)

Gen 46:13 The sons of Issachar were ***T***,
Num 26:23 to their families were: of ***T***,
Judg 10: 1 there arose to save Israel ***T***
1 Chr 7: 1 The sons of Issachar were ***T***,
7: 2 The sons of ***T*** were Uzzi,
7: 2 The sons of ***T*** were mighty

TOLAD (1/1)

1 Chr 4:29 Bilhah, Ezem, *T*,

TOLAITES (1/1)

Num 26:23 of Tola, the family of the *T*;

TOLD (286/280)

Gen 3:11 Who *t* you that you were naked?
9:22 and *t* his two brothers outside.
14:13 one who had escaped came and *t*
20: 8 and *t* all these things in their
22: 3 place of which God had *t* him.
22: 9 place of which God had *t* him.
22:20 things that it was *t* Abraham,
24:28 So the young woman ran and *t* her
24:33 I will not eat until I have *t*
24:66 And the servant *t* Isaac all the
26:32 Isaac's servants came and *t*
27:19 I have done just as you *t* me;
27:42 of Esau her older son were *t*
29:12 And Jacob *t* Rachel that he was
29:12 So she ran and *t* her father.
29:13 So he *t* Laban all these things.
31:22 And Laban was *t* on the third
37: 5 and he *t* it to his brothers;
37: 9 still another dream and *t* it
37:10 So he *t* it to his father and
38:13 And it was *t* Tamar, saying,
38:24 months after, that Judah was *t*,
40: 9 Then the chief butler *t* his
41: 8 And Pharaoh *t* them his dreams,
41:12 And we *t* him, and he
41:24 So I *t* this to the magicians,
42:29 in the land of Canaan and *t*
43: 7 And we *t* him according to
44:24 that we *t* him the words of my
45:26 And they *t* him, saying, "Joseph
45:27 But when they *t* him all the
47: 1 Then Joseph went and *t* Pharaoh,
48: 1 these things that Joseph was *t*,
48: 2 Jacob was *t*, "Look, your son
Ex 4:28 So Moses *t* Aaron all the words
5: 1 Moses and Aaron went in and *t*
14: 5 Now it was *t* the king of Egypt
14:12 this not the word that we *t*
16:22 of the congregation came and *t*
18: 8 And Moses *t* his father-in-law
19: 9 So Moses *t* the words of the
24: 3 So Moses came and *t* the people
Lev 21:24 And Moses *t* it to Aaron and his
Num 9: 4 So Moses *t* the children of
11:24 So Moses went out and *t* the
11:27 And a young man ran and *t* Moses,
13:27 Then they *t* him, and said: "We
14:39 Then Moses *t* these words to all
29:40 So Moses *t* the children of
Deut 1:14 The thing which you have *t* us
17: 4 and it is *t* you, and you hear
Josh 2: 2 And it was *t* the king of
2:23 and *t* him all that had befallen
9:24 your servants were clearly *t*
10:17 And it was *t* Joshua, saying,
11: 9 did to them as the LORD had *t*
Judg 6:13 miracles which our fathers *t*
9: 7 Now when they *t* Jotham, he went
9:25 and it was *t* Abimelech.
9:42 and they *t* Abimelech.
9:47 And it was *t* Abimelech that all
13: 6 So the woman came and *t* her
13:10 the woman ran in haste and *t*
13:23 nor would He have *t* us such
14: 2 So he went up and *t* his father
14:17 on the seventh day that he *t*
16: 2 When the Gazites were *t*,
16:10 you have mocked me and *t* me
16:13 now you have mocked me and *t*
16:15 and have not *t* me where your
16:17 that he *t* her all his heart,
16:18 Delilah saw that he had *t* her
16:18 for he has *t* me all his
Ruth 2:19 So she *t* her mother-in-law
3:16 Then she *t* her all that the
1 Sam 3:13 For I have *t* him that I will
3:18 Then Samuel *t* him everything,
4:13 man came into the city and *t*
4:14 And the man came quickly and *t*
8:10 So Samuel *t* all the words of
9:15 Now the LORD had *t* Samuel in
10:16 He *t* us plainly that the donkeys
11: 4 came to Gibeah of Saul and *t*
11: 5 And they *t* him the words of
14:33 Then they *t* Saul, saying,
14:43 And Jonathan *t* him, and said,
15:12 it was *t* Samuel, saying, "Saul
18:20 And they *t* Saul, and the thing
18:24 And the servants of Saul *t* him,
18:26 So when his servants *t* David
19: 2 So Jonathan *t* David, saying,
19: 7 and Jonathan *t* him all these
19:11 *t* him, saying, "If you do not
19:18 and *t* him all that Saul had
19:19 Now it was *t* Saul, saying,
19:21 And when Saul was *t*,
22:21 And Abiathar *t* David that Saul
23: 1 Then they *t* David, saying,
23: 7 And Saul was *t* that David had
23:13 Then it was *t* Saul that David
23:22 For I am *t* he is very crafty.
23:25 they *t* David. Therefore he went
24: 1 that it was *t* him, saying,
25:12 and they came and *t* him all
25:14 Now one of the young men *t*
25:36 therefore she *t* him nothing,
25:37 and his wife had *t* him these
27: 4 And it was *t* Saul that David had
2 Sam 1: 5 said to the young man who *t*
1: 6 Then the young man who *t* him
1:13 said to the young man who *t*
1:18 and he *t* them to teach the
2: 4 And they *t* David, saying, "The
3:23 they *t* Joab, saying, "Abner
4:10 when someone *t* me, saying,
6:12 Now it was *t* King David,
10: 5 When they *t* David, he sent to
10:17 When it was *t* David, he gathered
11: 5 so she sent and *t* David,
11:10 So when they *t* David, saying,
11:18 Then Joab sent and *t* David all
11:22 and came and *t* David all that
14:33 So Joab went to the king and *t*
15:31 Then someone *t* David, saying,
17:18 a lad saw them, and *t* Absalom.
17:21 out of the well and went and *t*
18:10 Now a certain man saw it and *t*
18:11 Joab said to the man who *t* him,
18:25 the watchman cried out and *t*
19: 1 And Joab was *t*, "Behold, the
19: 8 And they *t* all the people,
21:11 And David was *t* what Rizpah the
24:13 So Gad came to David and *t* him;
1 Ki 1:23 So they *t* the king, saying,
1:27 and you have not *t* your servant
1:51 And it was *t* Solomon, saying,
2:29 And King Solomon was *t*,
2:39 And they *t* Shimei, saying,
2:41 And Solomon was *t* that Shimei
10: 7 and indeed the half was not *t*
13:11 and his sons came and *t* him all
13:11 they also *t* their father the
13:17 For I have been *t* by the word of
13:25 Then they went and *t* it in the
14: 2 who *t* me that I would be
18:16 went to meet Ahab, and *t* him;
19: 1 And Ahab *t* Jezebel all that
20:17 and they *t* him, saying, "Men
2 Ki 1: 7 came up to meet you and *t* you
4: 7 Then she came and *t* the man of
4:17 of which Elisha had *t* her.
4:27 and has not *t* me."
4:31 and *t* him, saying, "The child
5: 4 And Naaman went in and *t* his
5:13 if the prophet had *t* you to
6:10 of which the man of God had *t*
6:13 And it was *t* him, saying,
7:10 and *t* them, saying, "We went
7:11 and they *t* it to the king's
7:15 the messengers returned and *t*
8: 6 asked the woman, she *t* him.
8: 7 and it was *t* him, saying, "The
8:14 He *t* me you would surely
9:36 Therefore they came back and *t*
10: 8 Then a messenger came and *t* him,
18:37 and *t* him the words of the
23:17 So the men of the city *t* him,
1 Chr 19: 5 Then some went and *t* David
19:17 When it was *t* David, he gathered
2 Chr 9: 6 of your wisdom was not *t* me.
20: 2 Then some came and *t*
34:18 Then Shaphan the scribe *t* the
Ezra 5: 4 we *t* them the names of the men
8:17 and I *t* them what they should
Neh 2:12 I *t* no one what my God had put
2:16 I had not yet *t* the Jews,
2:18 And I *t* them of the hand of my
4:12 that they *t* us ten times,
8: 1 and they *t* Ezra the scribe to
9:15 And *t* them to go in to possess
9:23 into the land Which You had *t*
Esth 2:22 who *t* Queen Esther, and Esther
3: 4 that they *t* it to Haman, to
3: 4 for Mordecai had *t* them that
3: 6 for they had *t* him of the
4: 4 maids and eunuchs came and *t*
4: 7 And Mordecai *t* him all that had
4: 9 So Hathach returned and *t* Esther
4:12 So they *t* Mordecai Esther's
4:13 And Mordecai *t* them to answer
4:15 Then Esther *t* them to reply to
5:11 Then Haman *t* them of his great
6: 2 written that Mordecai had *t* of
6:13 When Haman *t* his wife Zeresh and
8: 1 for Esther had *t* how he was
Job 15:18 What wise men have *t*,
37:20 Should He be *t* that I wish to
Ps 44: 1 Our fathers have *t* us,
52: Doeg the Edomite went and *t*
78: 3 And our fathers have *t* us.
Isa 7: 2 And it was *t* to the house of
36:22 and *t* him the words of the
40:21 Has it not been *t* you from the
44: 8 Have I not *t* you from that
45:21 Who has *t* it from that time?
52:15 For what had not been *t* them
Jer 36:20 and *t* all the words in the
38:27 And he *t* them according to all
Dan 4: 7 and I *t* them the dream;
4: 8 and I *t* the dream before him,
7:16 So he *t* me and made known to me
8:26 and mornings Which was *t* is
Jon 1:10 because he had *t* them.
Hab 1: 5 though it were *t* you.
Mt 8:33 went away into the city and *t*
12:48 and said to the one who *t* Him,
14:12 and went and *t* Jesus.
18:31 and came and *t* their master all
24:25 I have *t* you beforehand.
26:13 woman has done will also be *t*
28: 7 Behold, I have *t* you."
Mk 1:30 and they *t* Him about her at
3: 9 So He *t* His disciples that a
5:14 and they *t* it in the city and
5:16 And those who saw it *t* them how
5:33 and fell down before Him and *t*
6:30 gathered to Jesus and *t* Him
9:12 Then He answered and *t* them,
13:23 I have *t* you all things
14: 9 woman has done will also be *t*
16:10 She went and *t* those who had
16:13 And they went and *t* it to the
Lk 1:45 of those things which were *t*
2:17 known the saying which was *t*
2:18 at those things which were *t*
2:20 as it was *t* them.
8:20 And it was *t* Him by some, who
8:34 they fled and *t* it in the city
8:36 They also who had seen it *t*
9:10 *t* Him all that they had done.
9:36 and *t* no one in those days any
13: 1 at that season some who *t* Him
14: 7 So He *t* a parable to those who
18:37 So they *t* him that Jesus of
24: 9 returned from the tomb and *t*
24:10 who *t* these things to the
24:35 And they *t* about the things
Jn 3:12 If I have *t* you earthly things
4:29 see a Man who *t* me all things
4:39 He *t* me all that I ever did."
4:51 his servants met him and *t*
5:15 The man departed and *t* the Jews
8:40 a Man who has *t* you the truth
9:27 I *t* you already, and you did not
10:25 I *t* you, and you do not believe.
11:46 away to the Pharisees and *t*
12:22 Philip came and *t* Andrew,
12:22 and in turn Andrew and Philip *t*
12:50 just as the Father has *t* Me, so
14: 2 I would have *t* you. I go to
14:29 And now I have *t* you before it
16: 4 But these things I have *t* you,
16: 4 you may remember that I *t* you
18: 8 I have *t* you that I am He.
20:18 Mary Magdalene came and *t* the
Acts 5:25 So one came and *t* them, saying,
9: 6 and you will be *t* what you must
11:12 Then the Spirit *t* me to go with
11:13 And he *t* us how he had seen an
16:38 And the officers *t* these words
21: 4 They *t* Paul through the Spirit
21:19 he *t* in detail those things
22:10 and there you will be *t* all
22:26 he went and *t* the commander,
23:16 and entered the barracks and *t*
23:30 And when it was *t* me that the
24:23 and *t* him not to forbid any of
27:25 it will be just as it was *t* me.
1 Cor 10:28 for the sake of the one who *t*
2 Cor 7: 7 when he *t* us of your earnest
13: 2 I have *t* you before,
Gal 5:21 just as I also *t* you in time
Phil 3:18 of whom I have *t* you often,
1 Th 3: 4 we *t* you before when we were
2 Th 2: 5 I was still with you I *t* you
Jude 18 how they *t* you that there would

TOLERABLE (6/6)

Mt 10:15 it will be more *t* for the land
11:22 it will be more *t* for Tyre and
11:24 to you that it shall be more *t*
Mk 6:11 it will be more *t* for Sodom and
Lk 10:12 to you that it will be more *t*
10:14 But it will be more *t* for Tyre

TOLL (KJV) See TAX

TOMB (61/57) TOMBS

Judg 8:32 and was buried in the *t* of
16:31 Zorah and Eshtaol in the *t* of
1 Sam 10: 2 find two men by Rachel's *t* in
2 Sam 2:32 buried him in his father's *t*,
4:12 and buried it in the *t* of
17:23 he was buried in his father's *t*.
21:14 in the *t* of Kish his father.
1 Ki 13:22 corpse shall not come to the *t*
13:30 he laid the corpse in his own *t*;
13:31 then bury me in the *t* where the
2 Ki 9:28 and buried him in his *t* with
13:21 and they put the man in the *t*
21:26 And he was buried in his *t* in
23:17 It is the *t* of the man of God
23:30 and buried him in his own *t*.
2 Chr 16:14 They buried him in his own *t*,
Job 21:32 And a vigil kept over the *t*.
Ps 5: 9 Their throat is an open *t*;
Isa 22:16 Who carves a *t* for himself in
Jer 5:16 quiver is like an open *t*;
Mt 27:60 and laid it in his new *t* which
27:60 stone against the door of the *t*,
27:61 Mary, sitting opposite the *t*.
27:64 Therefore command that the *t* be
27:66 So they went and made the *t*
28: 1 other Mary came to see the *t*.

28: 8 went out quickly from the t
Mk 6:29 his corpse and laid it in a t.
15:46 And he laid Him in a t which
15:46 stone against the door of the t.
16: 2 they came to the t when the sun
16: 3 stone from the door of the t
16: 5 And entering the t,
16: 8 out quickly and fled from the t,
Lk 23:53 and laid it in a t that was
23:55 and they observed the t and how
24: 1 came to the t bringing the
24: 2 stone rolled away from the t.
24: 9 Then they returned from the t
24:12 Peter arose and ran to the t;
24:22 who arrived at the t early,
24:24 were with us went to the t
Jn 11:17 he had already been in the t
11:31 She is going to the t to weep
11:38 in Himself, came to the t.
12:17 He called Lazarus out of his t
19:41 and in the garden a new t in
19:42 for the t was nearby.
20: 1 Mary Magdalene went to the t
20: 1 had been taken away from the t.
20: 2 away the Lord out of the t,
20: 3 and were going to the t.
20: 4 outran Peter and came to the t
20: 6 him, and went into the t;
20: 8 who came to the t first,
20:11 Mary stood outside by the t
20:11 down and looked into the t.
Acts 2:29 and his t is with us to this
7:16 to Shechem and laid in the t
13:29 the tree and laid Him in a t.
Rom 3:13 throat is an open t;

TOMBS (20/19) TOMB

2 Ki 23:16 he saw the t that were there
23:16 and took the bones out of the t
2 Chr 21:20 but not in the t of the kings.
24:25 they did not bury him in the t
28:27 did not bring him into the t
32:33 they buried him in the upper t
35:24 was buried in one of the t
Neh 2: 3 the place of my fathers' t,
2: 5 to the city of my fathers' t,
3:16 the place in front of the t
Isa 65: 4 And spend the night in the t;
Mt 8:28 men, coming out of the t,
23:27 For you are like whitewashed t
23:29 Because you build the t of the
Mk 5: 2 there met Him out of the t a
5: 3 had his dwelling among the t;
5: 5 in the mountains and in the t,
Lk 8:27 he live in a house but in the t.
11:47 For you build the t of
11:48 and you build their t.

TOMORROW (58/57)

Ex 8:10 So he said, "T."
8:23 T this sign shall be." '"
8:29 swarms of flies may depart t
9: 5 T the LORD will do this thing
9:18 t about this time I will cause
10: 4 t I will bring locusts into
16:23 T is a Sabbath rest, a holy
17: 9 T I will stand on the top of
19:10 and consecrate them today and t,
32: 5 T is a feast to the LORD."
Num 11:18 'Consecrate yourselves for t,
14:25 t turn and move out into the
16: 5 T morning the LORD will show
16: 7 in them before the LORD t,
16:16 And Moses said to Korah, "T,
Josh 3: 5 for t the LORD will do wonders
7:13 say, 'Sanctify yourselves for t,
11: 6 for t about this time I will
22:18 that t He will be angry with
Judg 19: 9 T go your way early, so that
20:28 for t I will deliver them into
1 Sam 9:16 T about this time I will send
9:19 and t I will let you go and
11: 9 to the men of Jabesh Gilead: 'T,
11:10 'T we will come out to you,
19:11 t you will be killed."
20: 5 'Indeed t is the New Moon,
20:12 out my father sometime t,
20:18 T is the New Moon; and you will
28:19 And t you and your sons will
2 Sam 11:12 and t I will let you depart."
1 Ki 19: 2 as the life of one of them by t
20: 6 will send my servants to you t
2 Ki 6:28 today, and we will eat my son t.
7: 1 T about this time a seah of fine
7:18 shall be sold t about this
10: 6 to me at Jezreel by this time t.
2 Chr 20:16 T go down against them
20:17 t go out against them,
Esth 5: 8 and t I will do as the king has
5:12 and t I am again invited by
9:13 are in Shushan to do again t
Prov 3:28 And t I will give it,"
27: 1 Do not boast about t,
Isa 22:13 eat and drink, for t we die!"
56:12 T will be as today, And much
Mt 6:30 and t is thrown into the oven,
6:34 do not worry about t,
6:34 for t will worry about its own
Lk 12:28 today is in the field and t is
13:32 and perform cures today and t,
13:33 I must journey today, t,
Acts 23:15 he be brought down to you t,
23:20 Paul down to the council t,
25:22 to hear the man myself." "T,
1 Cor 15:32 for t we die!"
Jas 4:13 Today or t we will go to such
4:14 not know what will happen t.

TONE (1/1)

Gal 4:20 with you now and to change my t;

TONGS (2/2)

Isa 6: 6 which he had taken with the t
44:12 The blacksmith with the t works

TONGUE (114/113) TONGUES

Ex 4:10 slow of speech and slow of t.
11: 7 Israel shall a dog move its t,
Josh 10:21 No one moved his t against any
Judg 7: 5 laps from the water with his t,
2 Sam 23: 2 And His word was on my t.
Esth 7: 4 I would have held my t,
Job 5:21 from the scourge of the t,
6:24 and I will hold my t;
6:30 Is there injustice on my t?
13:19 If now I hold my t,
15: 5 And you choose the t of the
20:12 And he hides it under his t,
20:16 The viper's t will slay him.
27: 4 Nor my t utter deceit.
29:10 And their t stuck to the roof
33: 2 My t speaks in my mouth.
41: 1 Or snare his t with a line
Ps 5: 9 They flatter with their t.
10: 7 Under his t is trouble and
12: 3 And the t that speaks proud
12: 4 'With our t we will prevail;
15: 3 does not backbite with his t,
22:15 And My t clings to My jaws;
34:13 Keep your t from evil,
35:28 And my t shall speak of Your
37:30 And his t talks of justice.
39: 1 Lest I sin with my t;
39: 3 Then I spoke with my t:
45: 1 My t is the pen of a ready
50:19 And your t frames deceit.
51:14 And my t shall sing aloud of
52: 2 Your t devises destruction,
52: 4 You deceitful t.
57: 4 And their t a sharp sword.
64: 3 Who sharpen their t like a
64: 8 them stumble over their own t;
66:17 And He was extolled with my t.
71:24 My t also shall talk of Your
73: 9 And their t walks through the
78:36 they lied to Him with their t;
109: 2 against me with a lying t.
119:172 My t shall speak of Your word,
120: 2 lips And from a deceitful t.
120: 3 be done to you, You false t?
126: 2 And our t with singing.
137: 6 Let my t cling to the roof of
139: 4 there is not a word on my t,
Prov 6:17 A proud look, A lying t,
6:24 From the flattering t of a
10:20 The t of the righteous is
10:31 But the perverse t will be cut
12:18 But the t of the wise
12:19 But a lying t is but for a
15: 2 The t of the wise uses
15: 4 A wholesome t is a tree of
16: 1 But the answer of the t is
17: 4 listens eagerly to a spiteful t.
17:20 And he who has a perverse t
18:21 life are in the power of the t,
21: 6 treasures by a lying t Is
21:23 guards his mouth and t Keeps
25:15 And a gentle t breaks a bone.
25:23 And a backbiting t an angry
26:28 A lying t hates those who
28:23 he who flatters with the t.
31:26 And on her t is the law of
Song 4:11 and milk are under your t;
Isa 3: 8 Because their t and their
11:15 will utterly destroy the t of
28:11 stammering lips and another t
30:27 And His t like a devouring
32: 4 And the t of the stammerers
33:19 Of a stammering t that you
35: 6 And the t of the dumb sing.
45:23 Every t shall take an oath.
50: 4 The t of the learned, That I
54:17 And every t which rises
57: 4 mouth And stick out the t?
59: 3 Your t has muttered
Jer 9: 5 They have taught their t to
9: 8 Their t is an arrow shot out;
18:18 let us attack him with the t,
Lam 4: 4 The t of the infant clings To
Ezek 3:26 I will make your t cling to the
Hos 7:16 For the cursings of their t.
Am 6:10 Hold your t! For we dare not
Mic 6:12 And their t is deceitful in
Hab 1:13 And hold Your t when the
Zeph 3:13 Nor shall a deceitful t be
Mk 7:33 and He spat and touched his t.
7:35 and the impediment of his t was
Lk 1:64 was opened and his t loosed,
16:24 finger in water and cool my t;
Acts 2:26 and my t was glad;
Rom 14:11 And every t shall confess
1 Cor 14: 2 For he who speaks in a t does
14: 4 He who speaks in a t edifies
14: 9 unless you utter by the t words
14:13 let him who speaks in a t pray
14:14 For if I pray in a t,
14:19 than ten thousand words in a t.
14:26 psalm, has a teaching, has a t,
14:27 If anyone speaks in a t,
Phil 2:11 and that every t should confess
Jas 1:26 and does not bridle his t but
3: 5 Even so the t is a little member
3: 6 And the t is a fire, a world of
3: 6 The t is so set among our
3: 8 But no man can tame the t.
1 Pe 3:10 Let him refrain his t
1 Jn 3:18 let us not love in word or in t,
Rev 5: 9 Out of every tribe and t and
13: 7 given him over every tribe, t,
14: 6 earth—to every nation, tribe, t,

TONGUES (35/33) TONGUE

Ps 31:20 From the strife of t.
55: 9 O Lord, and divide their t,
68:23 And the t of your dogs may
140: 3 They sharpen their t like a
Isa 41:17 Their t fail for thirst.
66:18 I will gather all nations and t;
Jer 9: 3 bow they have bent their t
23:31 who use their t and say, 'He
Zech 14:12 And their t shall dissolve in
Mk 16:17 they will speak with new t;
Acts 2: 3 appeared to them divided t,
2: 4 and began to speak with other t,
2:11 them speaking in our own t the
10:46 they heard them speak with t
19: 6 and they spoke with t and
Rom 3:13 With their t they have
1 Cor 12:10 another different kinds of t,
12:10 another the interpretation of t.
12:28 administrations, varieties of t.
12:30 Do all speak with t?
13: 1 Though I speak with the t of men
13: 8 whether there are t, they
14: 5 I wish you all spoke with t,
14: 5 than he who speaks with t,
14: 6 I come to you speaking with t,
14:18 I thank my God I speak with t
14:21 With men of other t and
14:22 Therefore t are for a sign,
14:23 one place, and all speak with t,
14:39 do not forbid to speak with t.
Rev 7: 9 nations, tribes, peoples, and t,
10:11 about many peoples, nations, t,
11: 9 from the peoples, tribes, t,
16:10 and they gnawed their t because
17:15 multitudes, nations, and t.

TONIGHT (11/11)

Gen 19: 5 are the men who came to you t?
19:34 let us make him drink wine t
30:15 he will lie with you t for
Num 22: 8 he said to them, "Lodge here t,
22:19 please, you also stay here t,
Josh 2: 2 men have come here t from the
4: 3 lodging place where you lodge t.
Ruth 1:12 if I should have a husband t
3: 2 he is winnowing barley t at the
1 Sam 19:11 you do not save your life t,
2 Sam 17: 1 I will arise and pursue David t.

TOO (78/74) See APPENDIX

TOOK (747/727) TAKE

Gen 2:15 Then the LORD God t the man
2:21 and He t one of his ribs,
3: 6 she t of its fruit and ate.
4:19 Then Lamech t for himself two
5:24 he was not, for God t him.
6: 2 and they t wives for themselves
8: 9 So he put out his hand and t
8:20 and t of every clean animal and
9:23 But Shem and Japheth t a
11:29 Then Abram and Nahor t wives:
11:31 And Terah t his son Abram and
12: 5 Then Abram t Sarai his wife and
14:11 Then they t all the goods of
14:12 They also t Lot, Abram's
16: 3 t Hagar her maid, the Egyptian,
17:23 So Abraham t Ishmael his son,
18: 7 t a tender and good calf, gave
18: 8 So he t butter and milk and the
19:16 the men t hold of his hand,
20: 2 king of Gerar sent and t Sarah.
20:14 Then Abimelech t sheep, oxen,
21:14 and t bread and a skin of
21:21 and his mother t a wife for him
21:27 So Abraham t sheep and oxen and
22: 3 and t two of his young men with
22: 6 So Abraham t the wood of the
22: 6 and he t the fire in his hand,
22:10 stretched out his hand and t
22:13 So Abraham went and t the ram,
24: 7 who t me from my father's house
24:10 Then the servant t ten of his
24:22 that the man t a golden nose
24:61 So the servant t Rebekah and
24:65 So she t a veil and covered

T

24:67 and he *t* Rebekah and she became
25: 1 Abraham again *t* a wife,
25:20 was forty years old when he *t*
25:26 and his hand *t* hold of Esau's
26:34 he *t* as wives Judith the
27:15 Then Rebekah *t* the choice
27:36 He *t* away my birthright,
28: 9 So Esau went to Ishmael and *t*
28:11 And he *t* one of the stones of
28:18 and *t* the stone that he had put
29:23 that he *t* Leah his daughter and
30: 9 she *t* Zilpah her maid and gave
30:37 Now Jacob *t* for himself rods of
31:23 Then he *t* his brethren with him
31:45 So Jacob *t* a stone and set it up
31:46 And they *t* stones and made a
32:13 and *t* what came to his hand as
32:22 And he arose that night and *t*
32:23 He *t* them, sent them over the
33:11 he urged him, and he *t* it.
34: 2 he *t* her and lay with her,
34:25 each *t* his sword and came
34:26 and *t* Dinah from Shechem's
34:28 They *t* their sheep, their oxen,
34:29 ones and their wives they *t*
36: 2 Esau *t* his wives from the
36: 6 Then Esau *t* his wives, his sons,
37:24 Then they *t* him and cast him
37:28 And they *t* Joseph to Egypt.
37:31 So they *t* Joseph's tunic, killed
38: 6 Then Judah *t* a wife for Er his
38:14 So she *t* off her widow's
38:28 and the midwife *t* a scarlet
39:20 Then Joseph's master *t* him and
40:11 and I *t* the grapes and pressed
41:42 Then Pharaoh *t* his signet ring
42:24 And he *t* Simeon from them and
42:30 and *t* us for spies of the
43:15 So the men *t* that present and
43:15 and they *t* double money in
43:34 Then he *t* servings to them from
46: 1 So Israel *t* his journey with all
46: 6 So they *t* their livestock and
47: 2 And he *t* five men from among his
48: 1 and he *t* with him his two sons,
48:13 And Joseph *t* them both, Ephraim
48:17 so he *t* hold of his father's
48:22 which I *t* from the hand of the
50:25 Then Joseph *t* an oath from the
Ex 2: 1 of the house of Levi went and *t*
2: 3 she *t* an ark of bulrushes for
2: 9 So the woman *t* the child and
4: 6 and when he *t* it out, behold,
4:20 Then Moses *t* his wife and his
4:20 And Moses *t* the rod of God in
4:25 Then Zipporah *t* a sharp stone
6:20 Now Amram *t* for himself
6:23 Aaron *t* to himself Elisheba,
6:25 *t* for himself one of the
9:10 Then they *t* ashes from the
10:19 which *t* the locusts away and
12:34 So the people *t* their dough
13:19 And Moses *t* the bones of Joseph
13:20 So they *t* their journey from
14: 6 his chariot and *t* his people
14: 7 he *t* six hundred choice
14:25 And He *t* off their chariot
15:20 *t* the timbrel in her hand;
17:12 so they *t* a stone and put it
18: 2 *t* Zipporah, Moses' wife, after
18:12 *t* a burnt offering and other
24: 6 And Moses *t* half the blood and
24: 7 Then he *t* the Book of the
24: 8 And Moses *t* the blood, sprinkled
32:20 Then he *t* the calf which they
33: 7 Moses *t* his tent and pitched it
34: 4 and he *t* in his hand the two
40:20 He *t* the Testimony and put it
Lev 8:10 Also Moses *t* the anointing oil,
8:15 Then he *t* the blood, and put
8:16 Then he *t* all the fat that was
8:23 Also he *t* some of its blood
8:25 Then he *t* the fat and the fat
8:26 LORD he *t* one unleavened cake,
8:28 Then Moses *t* them from their
8:29 And Moses *t* the breast and waved
8:30 Then Moses *t* some of the
9:15 and *t* the goat, which was the
9:17 *t* a handful of it, and burned
10: 1 each *t* his censer and put fire
24:23 and they *t* outside the camp him
Num 1:17 Then Moses and Aaron *t* these
3:49 So Moses *t* the redemption money
3:50 of Israel he *t* the money,
7: 6 So Moses *t* the carts and the
11:25 and *t* of the Spirit that was
16: 1 sons of Reuben, *t* men;
16:18 So every man *t* his censer,
16:39 So Eleazar the priest *t* the
16:47 Then Aaron *t* it as Moses
17: 9 and each man *t* his rod.
20: 9 So Moses *t* the rod from before
21: 1 and *t* some of them prisoners.
21:24 and *t* possession of his land
21:25 So Israel *t* all these cities,
21:32 and they *t* its villages and
21:35 and they *t* possession of his
22:22 and the Angel of the LORD *t*
22:41 that Balak *t* Balaam and brought
23: 7 And he *t* up his oracle and said:
23:11 I *t* you to curse my enemies,
23:18 Then he *t* up his oracle and
23:28 So Balak *t* Balaam to the top of
24: 3 Then he *t* up his oracle and
24:15 So he *t* up his oracle and said:
24:20 and he *t* up his oracle and
24:21 and he *t* up his oracle and
24:23 Then he *t* up his oracle and
25: 7 among the congregation and *t* a
27:22 He *t* Joshua and set him before
30: 8 make void her vow which she *t*
31: 9 And the children of Israel *t* the
31: 9 and *t* as spoil all their
31:11 And they *t* all the spoil and all
31:27 between those who *t* part in the
31:47 of Israel's half Moses *t* one
32:39 went to Gilead and *t* it,
32:41 went and *t* its small towns,
32:42 Then Nobah went and *t* Kenath and
Deut 1:15 So I *t* the heads of your tribes,
1:23 so I *t* twelve of your men,
1:25 They also *t* some of the fruit
1:34 and *t* an oath, saying,
2:14 And the time we *t* to come from
2:34 We *t* all his cities at that
2:35 We *t* only the livestock as
2:35 spoil of the cities which we *t*.
3: 4 And we *t* all his cities at that
3: 7 the spoil of the cities we *t*
3: 8 And at that time we *t* the land
3:14 Jair the son of Manasseh *t* all
4:47 And they *t* possession of his
9:17 Then I *t* the two tablets and
9:21 Then I *t* your sin, the calf
22:14 I *t* this woman, and when I came
24: 3 latter husband dies who *t* her
29: 8 We *t* their land and gave it as
Josh 2: 4 Then the woman *t* the two men and
3: 6 So they *t* up the ark of the
4: 8 and *t* up twelve stones from the
4:20 twelve stones which they *t* out
6:12 and the priests *t* up the ark of
6:20 and they *t* the city.
7: 1 *t* of the accursed things;
7:17 and he *t* the family of the
7:21 I coveted them and *t* them.
7:23 And they *t* them from the midst
7:24 *t* Achan the son of Zerah, the
8:12 So he *t* about five thousand men
8:19 they entered the city and *t* it,
8:23 But the king of Ai they *t* alive,
8:27 spoil of that city Israel *t* as
9: 4 And they *t* old sacks on their
9:12 This bread of ours we *t* hot for
9:14 Then the men of Israel *t* some of
10:27 and they *t* them down from the
10:28 On that day Joshua *t* Makkedah,
10:32 who *t* it on the second day,
10:35 They *t* it on that day and struck
10:37 And they *t* it and struck it with
10:39 And he *t* it and its king and all
10:42 kings and their land Joshua *t*
11:10 back at that time and *t* Hazor,
11:12 Joshua *t* and struck with the
11:14 the children of Israel *t* as
11:16 Thus Joshua *t* all this land:
11:19 All the others they *t* in
11:23 So Joshua *t* the whole land,
15:17 the brother of Caleb, *t* it;
16: 4 *t* their inheritance.
19:47 fight against Leshem and *t* it;
19:47 *t* possession of it, and dwelt
21:43 and they *t* possession of it and
24: 3 Then I *t* your father Abraham
24:26 And he *t* a large stone, and set
Judg 1: 8 against Jerusalem and *t* it;
1:13 *t* it; so he gave him his
1:18 Also Judah *t* Gaza with its
3: 6 And they *t* their daughters to be
3:13 and *t* possession of the City of
3:21 *t* the dagger from his right
3:25 Therefore they *t* the key and
4:21 *t* a tent peg and took a hammer
4:21 took a tent peg and *t* a hammer
5:19 They *t* no spoils of silver.
6:27 So Gideon *t* ten men from among
7: 8 So the people *t* provisions and
8:12 and he *t* the two kings of
8:16 And he *t* the elders of the city,
8:21 and *t* the crescent ornaments
9:43 So he *t* his people, divided them
9:45 he *t* the city and killed the
9:48 And Abimelech *t* an ax in his
9:48 and *t* it and laid it on his
9:50 against Thebez and *t* it.
11:13 Because Israel *t* away my land
11:22 They *t* possession of all the
12: 3 I *t* my life in my hands and
13:19 So Manoah *t* the young goat with
14: 9 He *t* some of it in his hands and
14:19 *t* their apparel, and gave the
15: 4 and he *t* torches, turned the
15:15 reached out his hand and *t* it,
16: 3 *t* hold of the doors of the gate
16:12 Therefore Delilah *t* new ropes
16:21 Then the Philistines *t* him and
16:29 And Samson *t* hold of the two
16:31 household came down and *t* him,
17: 2 the silver with me; I *t* it."
17: 4 Then his mother *t* two hundred
18:17 they *t* the carved image,
18:18 house and *t* the carved image,
18:20 and he *t* the ephod,
18:20 and *t* his place among the
18:27 So they *t* the things Micah
19: 1 He *t* for himself a concubine
19:25 So the man *t* his concubine and
19:29 he entered his house he *t* a
20: 6 So I *t* hold of my concubine, cut
21:23 they *t* enough wives for their
Ruth 1: 4 Now they *t* wives of the women of
2:18 Then she *t* it up and went into
2:19 Blessed be the one who *t* notice
4: 2 And he *t* ten men of the elders
4: 7 one man *t* off his sandal and
4: 8 So he *t* off his sandal.
4:13 So Boaz *t* Ruth and she became
4:16 Then Naomi *t* the child and laid
1 Sam 1:24 she *t* him up with her,
5: 1 Then the Philistines *t* the ark
5: 2 When the Philistines *t* the ark
5: 3 So they *t* Dagon and set it in
6:10 they *t* two milk cows and
6:15 The Levites *t* down the ark of
7: 1 and *t* the ark of the LORD,
7: 9 And Samuel *t* a suckling lamb
7:12 Then Samuel *t* a stone and set
8: 3 *t* bribes, and perverted
9:22 Now Samuel *t* Saul and his
9:24 So the cook *t* up the thigh with
10: 1 Then Samuel *t* a flask of oil and
11: 7 So he *t* a yoke of oxen and cut
14:32 and *t* sheep, oxen, and calves,
14:52 he *t* him for himself.
15: 8 He also *t* Agag king of the
15:21 But the people *t* of the plunder,
16:13 Then Samuel *t* the horn of oil
16:20 And Jesse *t* a donkey loaded
17:20 and *t* the things and went as
17:34 a lion or a bear came and *t* a
17:39 So David *t* them off.
17:40 Then he *t* his staff in his
17:49 in his bag and *t* out a stone;
17:51 *t* his sword and drew it out of
17:54 And David *t* the head of the
17:57 Abner *t* him and brought him
18: 2 Saul *t* him that day, and would
18: 4 And Jonathan *t* off the robe that
19: 5 For he *t* his life in his hands
19:13 And Michal *t* an image and laid
20: 3 Then David *t* an oath again,
21:12 Now David *t* these words to
23: 5 and *t* away their livestock.
24: 2 Then Saul *t* three thousand
25:18 Then Abigail made haste and *t*
25:43 David also *t* Ahinoam of Jezreel,
26:12 So David *t* the spear and the jug
27: 9 but *t* away the sheep, the oxen,
28:24 And she *t* flour and kneaded
30:20 Then David *t* all the flocks and
31: 4 Therefore Saul *t* a sword and
31:12 and *t* the body of Saul and the
31:13 Then they *t* their bones and
2 Sam 1:10 And I *t* the crown that was on
1:11 Therefore David *t* hold of his
2: 8 *t* Ishbosheth the son of Saul
2:25 and *t* their stand on top of a
2:32 Then they *t* up Asahel and buried
3:15 And Ishbosheth sent and *t* her
3:27 Joab *t* him aside in the gate to
3:35 David *t* an oath, saying, "God
3:36 Now all the people *t* note of
4: 4 and his nurse *t* him up and
4: 7 beheaded him and *t* his head,
4:12 But they *t* the head of
5: 7 Nevertheless David *t* the
5:13 And David *t* more concubines and
6: 6 ark of God and *t* hold of it,
6:10 but David *t* it aside into the
7: 8 'I *t* you from the sheepfold,
7:15 as I *t* it from Saul,
8: 1 And David *t* Metheg Ammah from
8: 4 David *t* from him one thousand
8: 7 And David *t* the shields of gold
8: 8 King David *t* a large amount of
10: 4 Therefore Hanun *t* David's
11: 4 and *t* her; and she came to him,
12: 4 but he *t* the poor man's lamb
12:26 and *t* the royal city.
12:29 fought against it, and *t* it.
12:30 Then he *t* their king's crown
13: 8 Then she *t* flour and kneaded
13: 9 And she *t* the pan and placed
13:10 And Tamar *t* the cakes which
13:11 he *t* hold of her and said to
15: 8 For your servant *t* a vow while I
17:19 Then the woman *t* and spread a
18: 7 twenty thousand *t* place there
18:14 And he *t* three spears in his
18:17 And they *t* Absalom and cast him
20: 3 And the king *t* the ten women,
20: 9 And Joab *t* Amasa by the beard
21: 8 So the king *t* Armoni and
21:10 daughter of Aiah *t* sackcloth
21:12 Then David went and *t* the bones
22:17 He *t* me, He drew me out of
23:16 and *t* it and brought it to
1 Ki 1:29 And the king *t* an oath and said,
1:38 and *t* him to Gihon.
1:39 Then Zadok the priest *t* a horn
1:50 and went and *t* hold of the
2:28 and *t* hold of the horns of the
3:20 of the night and *t* my son
4:15 he also *t* Basemath the daughter
7: 1 But Solomon *t* thirteen years to
8: 3 and the priests *t* up the ark.

8:47 You in the land of those who *t*
8:50 compassion before those who *t*
11:18 and they *t* men with them from
11:30 Then Ahijah *t* hold of the new
13:29 And the prophet *t* up the corpse
14:26 And he *t* away the treasures of
14:26 he *t* away everything. He also
14:26 He also *t* away all the gold
15:18 Then Asa *t* all the silver and
15:22 And they *t* away the stones and
16:31 that he *t* as wife Jezebel the
17:19 So he *t* him out of her arms
17:23 And Elijah *t* the child and
18:10 he *t* an oath from the kingdom
18:26 So they *t* the bull which was
18:31 And Elijah *t* twelve stones,
19:21 and *t* a yoke of oxen and
20:34 The cities which my father *t*
21:13 they *t* him outside the city
2 Ki 2: 8 Now Elijah *t* his mantle, rolled
2:12 And he *t* hold of his own
2:13 He also *t* up the mantle of
2:14 Then he *t* the mantle of Elijah
3:26 he *t* with him seven hundred men
3:27 Then he *t* his eldest son who
5: 5 So he departed and *t* with him
5:24 he *t* them from their hand,
6: 7 he reached out his hand and *t*
7:14 Therefore they *t* two chariots
8: 9 to meet him and *t* a present
8:15 on the next day that he *t* a
10: 7 that they *t* the king's sons and
10:14 Take them alive!" So they *t*
10:15 and he *t* him up to him into the
10:31 But Jehu *t* no heed to walk in
11: 2 *t* Joash the son of Ahaziah,
11: 4 a covenant with them and *t* an
11: 9 Each of them *t* his men who were
11:19 Then he *t* the captains of
12: 9 Then Jehoiada the priest *t* a
12:17 fought against Gath, and *t* it;
12:18 And Jehoash king of Judah *t* all
13:15 So he *t* himself a bow and
13:18 the arrows"; so he *t* them.
14: 7 and *t* Sela by war, and called
14:14 And he *t* all the gold and
14:21 the people of Judah *t* Azariah,
15:29 king of Assyria came and *t*
16: 8 And Ahaz *t* the silver and gold
16: 9 up against Damascus and *t* it,
16:17 and he *t* down the Sea from the
17: 6 the king of Assyria *t* Samaria
17:24 and they *t* possession of
18:10 end of three years they *t* it.
18:13 cities of Judah and *t* them.
20: 7 So they *t* and laid it on the
23: 3 And all the people *t* a stand
23:16 And he sent and *t* the bones out
23:19 Now Josiah also *t* away all the
23:30 And the people of the land *t*
23:34 And Pharaoh *t* Jehoahaz and
24:12 of his reign, *t* him prisoner.
25: 6 So they *t* the king and brought
25: 7 and *t* him to Babylon.
25:14 They also *t* away the pots,
25:15 the captain of the guard *t*
25:18 And the captain of the guard *t*
25:19 He also *t* out of the city an
25:20 *t* these and brought them to the
25:24 And Gedaliah *t* an oath before
1 Chr 2:19 Caleb *t* Ephrath as his wife,
2:23 (Geshur and Syria *t* from them
4:18 of Pharaoh, whom Mered *t*.
5:21 Then they *t* away their
5:26 He *t* them to Halah, Habor,
7:15 Machir *t* as his wife the
9:28 brought them in and *t* them out
10: 4 Therefore Saul *t* a sword and
10: 9 And they stripped him and *t* his
10:12 all the valiant men arose and *t*
11: 5 David *t* the stronghold of Zion
11:18 and *t* it and brought it to
13:13 but *t* it aside into the house
14: 3 Then David *t* more wives in
17: 7 'I *t* you from the sheepfold,
17:13 as I *t* it from him who was
18: 1 and *t* Gath and its towns from
18: 4 David *t* from him one thousand
18: 7 And David *t* the shields of gold
19: 4 Therefore Hanun *t* David's
20: 2 Then David *t* their king's crown
23:22 *t* them as wives.
2 Chr 5: 4 and the Levites *t* up the ark.
11:13 in all Israel *t* their stand
11:18 Then Rehoboam *t* for himself as
11:20 After her he *t* Maacah the
11:21 for he *t* eighteen wives and
12: 4 And he *t* the fortified cities of
12: 9 and *t* away the treasures of the
12: 9 he *t* everything. He also
13:19 pursued Jeroboam and *t* cities
15: 8 he *t* courage, and removed the
15:14 Then they *t* an oath before the
16: 6 Then King Asa *t* all Judah, and
17: 6 And his heart *t* delight in the
22:11 *t* Joash the son of Ahaziah, and
23: 8 And each man *t* his men who were
23:20 Then he *t* the captains of
24: 3 And Jehoiada *t* two wives for
24:11 and *t* it and returned it to its
25:12 children of Judah *t* captive
25:13 and *t* much spoil.
25:24 And he *t* all the gold and
26: 1 Now all the people of Judah *t*
28: 8 and they also *t* away much spoil
28:15 by name rose up and *t* the
28:21 For Ahaz *t* part of the
29:16 And the Levites *t* it out and
29:36 since the events *t* place so
30:14 They arose and *t* away the altars
30:14 and they *t* away all the incense
33:11 who *t* Manasseh with hooks,
33:15 He *t* away the foreign gods and
35:24 His servants therefore *t* him out
36: 1 Then the people of the land *t*
36: 4 And Necho *t* Jehoahaz his
36:10 summoned him and *t* him to
36:18 all these he *t* to Babylon.
Ezra 1:11 All these Sheshbazzar *t* with
2:61 who *t* a wife of the daughters
4:10 and noble Osnapper *t* captive
5:14 those King Cyrus *t* from the
6: 5 which Nebuchadnezzar *t* from the
Neh 2: 1 that I *t* the wine and gave it
4:23 the guard who followed me *t* off
4:23 except that everyone *t* them
5:15 and *t* from them bread and wine,
7:63 who *t* a wife of the daughters
9:22 So they *t* possession of the
9:25 And they *t* strong cities and a
Esth 2: 7 Mordecai *t* her as his own
3:10 So the king *t* his signet ring
6:11 So Haman *t* the robe and the
8: 2 So the king *t* off his signet
Job 1:15 the Sabeans raided them and *t*
1:17 raided the camels and *t* them
2: 8 And he *t* for himself a potsherd
29: 7 When I *t* my seat in the open
Ps 18:16 He *t* me; He drew me out of
22: 9 But You are He who *t* Me out of
48: 6 Fear *t* hold of them there,
55:14 We *t* sweet counsel together,
71: 6 You are He who *t* me out of my
78:70 And *t* him from the sheepfolds;
99: 8 Though You *t* vengeance on
Prov 7: 8 And he *t* the path to her house
12:27 man does not roast what he *t*
Song 5: 7 The keepers of the walls *T* my
Isa 20: 1 fought against Ashdod and *t* it,
36: 1 cities of Judah and *t* them.
Jer 13: 7 and I *t* the sash from the place
25:17 Then I *t* the cup from the
28: 3 king of Babylon *t* away from
28:10 Then Hananiah the prophet *t* the
31:32 in the day that I *t* them
32:10 *t* witnesses, and weighed the
32:11 'So I *t* the purchase deed,
32:23 they came in and *t* possession
35: 3 Then I *t* Jaazaniah the son of
36:14 the son of Neriah *t* the scroll
36:21 and he *t* it from Elishama the
36:32 Then Jeremiah *t* another scroll
37:17 Zedekiah the king sent and *t*
38: 6 So they *t* Jeremiah and cast him
38:11 So Ebed-Melech *t* the men with
38:11 and *t* from there old clothes
40: 2 captain of the guard *t* Jeremiah
40: 9 *t* an oath before them and their
41:12 they *t* all the men and went to
41:16 *t* from Mizpah all the rest of
43: 5 captains of the forces *t* all
50:33 All who *t* them captive have
52: 9 So they *t* the king and brought
52:11 *t* him to Babylon, and put him
52:18 They also *t* away the pots,
52:19 captain of the guard *t* away.
52:24 captain of the guard *t* Seraiah
52:25 He also *t* out of the city an
52:26 captain of the guard *t* these
Ezek 3:14 lifted me up and *t* me away,
3:21 live because he *t* warning;
8: 3 and *t* me by a lock of my hair;
10: 7 and *t* some of it and put it
10: 7 who *t* it and went out.
11:24 Then the Spirit *t* me up and
16:16 You *t* some of your garments and
16:18 You *t* your embroidered garments
16:20 Moreover you *t* your sons and
16:37 with whom you *t* pleasure,
16:50 therefore I *t* them away as I
17: 3 Came to Lebanon And *t* from
17: 5 Then he *t* some of the seed of
17:12 went to Jerusalem and *t* its
17:13 And he *t* the king's offspring,
17:13 He also *t* away the mighty of
19: 5 She *t* another of her cubs and
23:10 *T* away her sons and daughters,
23:13 Both *t* the same way.
25:15 vengefully and *t* vengeance
27: 5 They *t* a cedar from Lebanon to
29: 7 When they *t* hold of you with
40: 1 and He *t* me there.
40: 2 In the visions of God He *t* me
40: 3 He *t* me there, and behold,
42: 5 because the galleries *t* away
Dan 1:16 Thus the steward *t* away their
3:22 fire killed those men who *t* up
5:20 and they *t* his glory from him.
Hos 1: 3 So he went and *t* Gomer the
12: 3 He *t* his brother by the heel in
13:11 And *t* him away in My wrath.
Am 1: 6 Because they *t* captive the
7:15 Then the LORD *t* me as I
Jon 1:16 to the LORD and *t* vows.
Zech 11: 7 I *t* for myself two staffs:
11:10 And I *t* my staff, Beauty, and
11:13 So I *t* the thirty pieces of
Mt 1:24 Lord commanded him and *t* to him
2:14 he *t* the young Child and His
2:21 *t* the young Child and His
4: 5 Then the devil *t* Him up into the
4: 8 the devil *t* Him up on an
8:17 He Himself *t* our infirmities
9:25 He went in and *t* her by the
13:31 which a man *t* and sowed in his
13:33 which a woman *t* and hid in
14:12 his disciples came and *t* away
14:19 And He *t* the five loaves and
14:20 and they *t* up twelve baskets
15:36 And He *t* the seven loaves and
15:37 and they *t* up seven large
16: 9 and how many baskets you *t* up?
16:10 many large baskets you *t* up?
16:22 Then Peter *t* Him aside and began
17: 1 after six days Jesus *t* Peter,
18:28 he laid hands on him and *t* him
20:17 *t* the twelve disciples aside on
21:35 And the vinedressers *t* his
21:39 So they *t* him and cast him out
21:46 because they *t* Him for a
24:39 until the flood came and *t* them
25: 1 ten virgins who *t* their lamps
25: 3 Those who were foolish *t* their
25: 3 took their lamps and *t* no oil
25: 4 but the wise *t* oil in their
25:35 I was a stranger and you *t* Me
26:26 Jesus *t* bread, blessed and
26:27 Then He *t* the cup, and gave
26:37 And He *t* with Him Peter and the
26:50 laid hands on Jesus and *t* Him.
27: 6 But the chief priests *t* the
27: 9 And they *t* the thirty
27:24 he *t* water and washed his
27:27 the soldiers of the governor *t*
27:30 and *t* the reed and struck Him
27:31 they *t* the robe off Him,
27:48 one of them ran and *t* a sponge,
28:15 So they *t* the money and did as
Mk 1:31 So He came and *t* her by the hand
2:12 *t* up the bed, and went out in
4:36 they *t* Him along in the boat as
5:40 He *t* the father and the mother
5:41 Then He *t* the child by the hand,
6:29 they came and *t* away his corpse
6:43 And they *t* up twelve baskets
7:33 And He *t* him aside from the
8: 6 And He *t* the seven loaves and
8: 8 and they *t* up seven large
8:23 So He *t* the blind man by the
8:32 And Peter *t* Him aside and began
9: 2 after six days Jesus *t* Peter,
9:27 But Jesus *t* him by the hand and
9:36 Then He *t* a little child and set
10:16 And He *t* them up in His arms,
10:32 Then He *t* the twelve aside
12: 3 And they *t* him and beat him and
12: 8 So they *t* him and killed him
12:20 The first *t* a wife; and dying,
12:21 And the second *t* her, and he
14:22 Jesus *t* bread, blessed and
14:23 Then He *t* the cup, and when He
14:33 And He *t* Peter, James, and John
14:46 their hands on Him and *t* Him.
15:20 they *t* the purple off Him,
15:46 *t* Him down, and wrapped Him in
Lk 2: 2 This census first *t* place while
2:28 he *t* Him up in his arms and
5:25 *t* up what he had been lying on,
6: 4 *t* and ate the showbread,
8:54 *t* her by the hand and called,
9:10 Then He *t* them and went aside
9:16 Then He *t* the five loaves and
9:28 that He *t* Peter, John, and
9:47 *t* a little child and set him by
10:34 and *t* care of him.
10:35 he *t* out two denarii, gave
13:19 which a man *t* and put in his
13:21 which a woman *t* and hid in
14: 4 And He *t* him and healed him,
18:31 Then He *t* the twelve aside and
20:29 And the first *t* a wife,
20:30 And the second *t* her as wife,
20:31 'Then the third *t* her,
22:17 Then He *t* the cup, and gave
22:19 And He *t* bread, gave thanks and
22:20 Likewise He also *t* the cup
23:53 Then he *t* it down, wrapped it in
24:30 that He *t* bread, blessed and
24:43 And He *t* it and ate in their
Jn 2: 8 And they *t* it.
5: 9 *t* up his bed, and walked.
6:11 And Jesus *t* the loaves, and when
8:59 Then they *t* up stones to throw
10:31 Then the Jews *t* up stones again
11:41 Then they *t* away the stone from
12: 3 Then Mary *t* a pound of very
12:13 *t* branches of palm trees and
13: 4 *t* a towel and girded Himself.
19: 1 So then Pilate *t* Jesus and
19:16 So they *t* Jesus and led Him
19:23 *t* His garments and made four
19:27 that hour that disciple *t* her
19:38 So he came and *t* the body of
19:40 Then they *t* the body of Jesus,
21:13 Jesus then came and *t* the bread
Acts 3: 7 And he *t* him by the right hand

T

4:26 The kings of the earth *t*
7:21 Pharaoh's daughter *t* him away
7:43 You also *t* up the
9:25 Then the disciples *t* him by
9:27 But Barnabas *t* him and brought
12:25 and they also *t* with them John
13:29 they *t* Him down from the tree
15:39 And so Barnabas *t* Mark and
16: 3 And he *t* him and circumcised
16:33 And he *t* them the same hour of
17: 5 *t* some of the evil men from the
17:19 And they *t* him and brought him
18:17 Then all the Greeks *t* Sosthenes,
18:17 But Gallio *t* no notice of these
18:18 Then he *t* leave of the brethren
18:21 but *t* leave of them, saying, "I
18:26 they *t* him aside and explained
19:13 itinerant Jewish exorcists *t*
20:14 we *t* him on board and came to
21:11 he *t* Paul's belt, bound his
21:26 Then Paul *t* the men, and the
21:32 He immediately *t* soldiers and
21:33 commander came near and *t* him,
23:18 So he *t* him and brought him to
23:19 Then the commander *t* him by the
23:31 *t* Paul and brought him by
24: 7 with great violence *t* him out
27:28 And they *t* soundings and found
27:28 they *t* soundings again and
27:35 he *t* bread and gave thanks to
27:36 and also *t* food themselves.
28:15 he thanked God and *t* courage.
1 Cor 11:23 in which He was betrayed *t*
11:25 same manner He also *t* the cup
Gal 2: 1 and also *t* Titus with me.
Heb 8: 9 in the day when I *t* them
9:19 he *t* the blood of calves and
Rev 5: 7 Then He came and *t* the scroll
8: 5 Then the angel *t* the censer,
10:10 Then I *t* the little book out of
18:21 Then a mighty angel *t* up a

TOOL (5/5)

Ex 20:25 for if you use your *t* on it,
32: 4 it with an engraving *t*,
Deut 27: 5 you shall not use an iron *t* on
Josh 8:31 no man has wielded an iron *t*.
1 Ki 6: 7 or chisel or any iron *t* was

TOOTH (11/6) TEETH

Ex 21:24 *t* for tooth, hand for hand,
21:24 "eye for eye, tooth for *t*,
21:27 And if he knocks out the *t* of
21:27 go free for the sake of his *t*.
Lev 24:20 *t* for tooth; as he has caused
24:20 eye for eye, tooth for *t*;
Deut 19:21 *t* for tooth, hand for hand,
19:21 life, eye for eye, tooth for *t*,
Prov 25:19 of trouble Is like a bad *t*
Mt 5:38 eye for an eye and a *t*
5:38 eye and a tooth for a *t*.

TOP (82/76) TOPS

Gen 11: 4 and a tower whose *t* is in the
28:12 and its *t* reached to heaven;
28:18 and poured oil on *t* of it.
Ex 17: 9 Tomorrow I will stand on the *t*
17:10 and Hur went up to the *t* of the
19:20 on the *t* of the mountain.
19:20 LORD called Moses to the *t* of
24:17 like a consuming fire on the *t*
25:21 shall put the mercy seat on *t*
26:24 be coupled together at the *t*
30: 3 "And you shall overlay its *t*,
34: 2 yourself to Me there on the *t*
36:29 and coupled together at the *t*
37:26 it with pure gold: its *t*,
40:19 the covering of the tent on *t*
40:20 and put the mercy seat on *t* of
Num 14:40 morning and went up to the *t*
20:28 and Aaron died there on the *t*
21:20 to the *t* of Pisgah which looks
23: 9 For from the *t* of the rocks I
23:14 to the *t* of Pisgah, and built
23:28 So Balak took Balaam to the *t* of
Deut 3:27 'Go up to the *t* of Pisgah,
28:35 the sole of your foot to the *t*
34: 1 to the *t* of Pisgah, which is
Josh 15: 8 The border went up to the *t* of
15: 9 border went around from the *t*
Judg 6:26 to the LORD your God on *t* of
9: 7 he went and stood on *t* of Mount
9:51 then they went up to the *t* of
16: 3 and carried them to the *t* of
1 Sam 9:25 spoke with Saul on the *t* of
9:26 Samuel called to Saul on the *t*
26:13 and stood on the *t* of a hill
2 Sam 2:25 and took their stand on *t* of a
15:32 when David had come to the *t*
16: 1 David was a little past the *t*
16:22 a tent for Absalom on the *t* of
1 Ki 7:17 the capitals which were on *t*
7:18 the capitals that were on *t*;
7:19 The capitals which were on *t* of
7:29 the frames was a pedestal on *t*.
7:31 inside the crown at the *t* was
7:35 On the *t* of the cart, at the
7:35 And on the *t* of the cart,
7:41 capitals that were on *t* of
7:41 capitals which were on *t* of
7:42 capitals that were on *t* of
10:19 and the *t* of the throne was
18:42 And Elijah went up to the *t* of
2 Ki 1: 9 sitting on the *t* of a hill.
9:13 and put it under him on the *t*
2 Chr 3:15 the capital that was on the *t*
3:16 and put them on *t* of the
4:12 capitals that were on *t* of
4:12 capitals which were on *t* of
25:12 brought them to the *t* of the
25:12 and cast them down from the *t*
Esth 5: 2 went near and touched the *t* of
Ps 72:16 On the *t* of the mountains;
Prov 8: 2 She takes her stand on the *t* of
23:34 Or like one who lies at the *t*
Song 4: 8 Look from the *t* of Amana,
4: 8 From the *t* of Senir and
Isa 2: 2 on the *t* of the mountains,
17: 6 Two or three olives at the *t*
30:17 you are left as a pole on *t* of
42:11 Let them shout from the *t* of
Ezek 24: 7 She set it on *t* of a rock;
24: 8 I have set her blood on *t* of a
26: 4 and make her like the *t* of a
26:14 I will make you like the *t* of a
31: 3 And its *t* was among the thick
31:10 and it set its *t* among the
Am 1: 2 And the *t* of Carmel
9: 3 they hide themselves on *t* of
Mic 4: 1 on the *t* of the mountains,
Zech 4: 2 of solid gold with a bowl on *t*
Mt 27:51 torn in two from *t* to bottom;
Mk 15:38 torn in two from *t* to bottom.
Jn 19:23 woven from the *t* in one piece.
Heb 11:21 leaning on the *t* of his staff.

TOPAZ (5/5)

Ex 28:17 row shall be a sardius, a *t*,
39:10 a row with a sardius, a *t*,
Job 28:19 The *t* of Ethiopia cannot equal
Ezek 28:13 your covering: The sardius, *t*,
Rev 21:20 the eighth beryl, the ninth *t*,

TOPHEL (1/1)

Deut 1: 1 opposite Suph, between Paran, *T*,

TOPHET (9/8) TOPHETH

Isa 30:33 For *T* was established of old,
Jer 7:31 have built the high places of *T*,
7:32 it will no more be called *T*,
7:32 for they will bury in *T* until
19: 6 shall no more be called *T* or
19:11 and they shall bury them in *T*
19:12 and make this city like *T*.
19:13 be defiled like the place of *T*,
19:14 Then Jeremiah came from *T*,

TOPHETH (1/1) TOPHET

2 Ki 23:10 And he defiled *T*,

TOPMOST (2/2)

Ezek 17: 4 He cropped off its *t* young twig
17:22 I will crop off from the *t* of

TOPPLE (1/1)

Jer 10: 4 So that it will not *t*.

TOPS (9/9) TOP

Gen 8: 5 the *t* of the mountains were
Judg 9:25 him on the *t* of the mountains,
9:36 are coming down from the *t* of
2 Sam 5:24 in the *t* of the mulberry trees,
1 Ki 7:16 to set on the *t* of the pillars.
7:22 The *t* of the pillars were in the
1 Chr 14:15 in the *t* of the mulberry trees,
Isa 15: 3 On the *t* of their houses
Ezek 31:14 nor set their *t* among the thick

TORCH (4/4) TORCHES

Gen 15:17 a smoking oven and a burning *t*
Judg 15: 4 and put a *t* between each pair
Zech 12: 6 and like a fiery *t* in the
Rev 8:10 from heaven, burning like a *t*,

TORCHES (9/9) TORCH

Judg 7:16 and *t* inside the pitchers.
7:20 they held the *t* in their left
15: 4 hundred foxes; and he took *t*,
15: 5 When he had set the *t* on fire,
Ezek 1:13 like the appearance of *t* going
Dan 10: 6 his eyes like *t* of fire,
Nah 2: 3 chariots come with flaming *t*
2: 4 broad roads; They seem like *t*,
Jn 18: 3 came there with lanterns, *t*,

TORE (45/45) TEAR

Gen 37:29 and he *t* his clothes.
37:34 Then Jacob *t* his clothes,
44:13 Then they *t* their clothes,
Num 14: 6 *t* their clothes;
Josh 7: 6 Then Joshua *t* his clothes,
Judg 8:17 Then he *t* down the tower of
11:35 that he *t* his clothes,
14: 6 and he *t* the lion apart as one
1 Sam 15:27 the edge of his robe, and it *t*.
2 Sam 1:11 hold of his own clothes and *t*
13:19 and *t* her robe of many colors
13:31 So the king arose and *t* his
1 Ki 11:30 and *t* it into twelve pieces.
14: 8 and *t* the kingdom away from the
19:11 and a great and strong wind *t*
21:27 that he *t* his clothes and put
2 Ki 2:12 hold of his own clothes and *t*
5: 7 that he *t* his clothes and said,
6:30 that he *t* his clothes; and as
10:27 and *t* down the temple of Baal
11:14 So Athaliah *t* her clothes and
11:18 temple of Baal, and *t* it down.
17:21 For He *t* Israel from the house
19: 1 that he *t* his clothes, covered
22:11 that he *t* his clothes.
22:19 and you *t* your clothes and wept
23: 7 Then he *t* down the ritual
2 Chr 23:13 So Athaliah *t* her clothes and
23:17 of Baal, and *t* it down.
34:19 that he *t* his clothes.
34:27 and you *t* your clothes and wept
Ezra 9: 3 I *t* my garment and my robe,
Esth 4: 1 he *t* his clothes and put on
Job 1:20 *t* his robe, and shaved his
2:12 and each one *t* his robe and
Ps 35:15 They *t* at me and did not
Isa 37: 1 that he *t* his clothes, covered
Ezek 29: 7 You broke and *t* all their
Am 1:11 His anger *t* perpetually,
Nah 2:12 The lion *t* in pieces enough for
Mt 26:65 Then the high priest *t* his
Mk 14:63 Then the high priest *t* his
Acts 14:14 they *t* their clothes and ran in
16:22 and the magistrates *t* off their
22:23 as they cried out and *t* off

TORMENT (15/13) TORMENTED

Judg 16:19 Then she began to *t* him,
Job 19: 2 How long will you *t* my soul,
Isa 50:11 You shall lie down in *t*.
Mt 8:29 Have You come here to *t* us
Mk 5: 7 You by God that You do not *t*
Lk 8:28 I beg You, do not *t* me!"
16:28 also come to this place of *t*.
1 Jn 4:18 because fear involves *t*.
Rev 9: 5 but to *t* them for five months.
9: 5 Their *t* was like the torment
9: 5 Their torment was like the *t*
14:11 And the smoke of their *t* ascends
18: 7 in the same measure give her *t*
18:10 at a distance for fear of her *t*,
18:15 at a distance for fear of her *t*,

TORMENTED (10/10) TORMENT

Mt 8: 6 at home paralyzed, dreadfully *t*.
Lk 6:18 as well as those who were *t* with
16:24 for I am *t* in this flame.'
16:25 he is comforted and you are *t*.
Acts 5:16 people and those who were *t* by
Heb 11:37 being destitute, afflicted, *t*—
2 Pe 2: 8 *t* his righteous soul from day
Rev 11:10 because these two prophets *t*
14:10 He shall be *t* with fire and
20:10 And they will be *t* day and

TORMENTS (2/2)

Mt 4:24 with various diseases and *t*,
Lk 16:23 And being in *t* in Hades, he

TORN (44/42) TEAR

Gen 31:39 That which was *t* by beasts I
37:33 Without doubt Joseph is *t* to
44:28 'Surely he is *t* to pieces";
Ex 22:13 If it is *t* to pieces by a
22:13 shall not make good what was *t*.
22:31 you shall not eat meat *t* by
Lev 7:24 and the fat of what is *t* by
13:45 his clothes shall be *t* and his
17:15 died naturally or what was *t*
22: 8 dies naturally or is *t* by
22:24 or crushed, or *t* or cut;
Josh 9: 4 old wineskins *t* and mended,
9:13 were new, and see, they are *t*;
Judg 6:28 the altar of Baal, *t* down;
6:30 because he has *t* down the altar
6:31 because his altar has been *t*
6:32 because he has *t* down his
14: 6 lion apart as one would have *t*
1 Sam 4:12 to Shiloh with his clothes *t*
15:28 The LORD has *t* the kingdom of
28:17 For the LORD has *t* the kingdom
2 Sam 1: 2 Saul's camp with his clothes *t*
13:31 stood by with their clothes *t*.
15:32 to meet him with his robe *t*
1 Ki 13:26 which has *t* him and killed him,
13:28 had not eaten the corpse nor *t*
19:10 *t* down Your altars, and killed
19:14 covenant, *t* down Your altars,
2 Ki 5: 8 that the king of Israel had *t*
5: 8 Why have you *t* your clothes?
18:37 Hezekiah with their clothes *t*,
Ezra 9: 5 and having *t* my garment and my
Job 31:22 Let my arm be *t* from the
Isa 36:22 Hezekiah with their clothes *t*,
Jer 5: 6 goes out from there shall be *t*

41: 5 shaved and their clothes *t*,
Lam 3:11 has turned aside my ways and *t*
Ezek 4:14 what died of itself or was *t*
44:31 that died naturally or was *t*
Hos 6: 1 For He has *t*, but He will heal
Mt 27:51 the veil of the temple was *t* in
Mk 15:38 the veil of the temple was *t*
Lk 23:45 the veil of the temple was *t*
Rom 11: 3 Your prophets and *t* down

TORRENT (4/2)

Judg 5:21 The *t* of Kishon swept them
5:21 them away, That ancient *t*,
5:21 the *t* of Kishon. O my soul,
Prov 27: 4 Wrath is cruel and anger a *t*,

TORRENTS (1/1)

Job 14:19 And as *t* wash away the soil

TORSO (1/1)

1 Sam 5: 4 only Dagon's *t* was left of it.

TORTOISE (KJV) See LIZARD

TORTURED (1/1) TORTURERS

Heb 11:35 others were *t*, not accepting

TORTURERS (1/1) TORTURED

Mt 18:34 and delivered him to the *t*

TOSS (2/2)

Isa 22:18 surely turn violently and *t*
Jer 5:22 And though its waves *t* to and

TOSSED (4/4)

Isa 54:11 *T* with tempest, and not
Mt 14:24 *t* by the waves, for the wind
Eph 4:14 *t* to and fro and carried about
Jas 1: 6 a wave of the sea driven and *t*

TOSSING (1/1)

Job 7: 4 had my fill of *t* till dawn.

TOTAL (3/3)

2 Chr 26:12 The *t* number of chief officers
Job 20:26 *T* darkness is reserved for his
Prov 5:14 I was on the verge of *t* ruin,

TOTALED (1/1)

Acts 19:19 and it *t* fifty thousand

TOTALLY (1/1)

Zech 11:17 eye shall be *t* blinded."

TOTTER (4/4)

Isa 19: 1 The idols of Egypt will *t* at
24:20 And shall *t* like a hut;
40:20 a carved image that will not *t*.
41: 7 That it might not *t*.

TOTTERING (1/1)

Ps 62: 3 a leaning wall and a *t* fence.

TOU (2/2)

1 Chr 18: 9 Now when *T* king of Hamath heard
18:10 had been at war with *T*);

TOUCH (39/39) TOUCHED, TOUCHES, TOUCHING

Gen 3: 3 nor shall you *t* it, lest you
20: 6 therefore I did not let you *t*
Ex 19:12 go up to the mountain or *t* its
19:13 Not a hand shall *t* him, but he
Lev 11: 8 their carcasses you shall not *t*.
12: 4 She shall not *t* any hallowed
Num 4:15 but they shall not *t* any holy
16:26 *T* nothing of theirs,
Deut 14: 8 or *t* their dead carcasses.
Josh 9:19 we may not *t* them.
Ruth 2: 9 the young men not to *t* you?
2 Sam 14:10 and he shall not *t* you
18:12 Beware lest anyone *t* the young
1 Chr 16:22 'Do not *t* My anointed ones,
Job 1:11 stretch out Your hand and *t* all
2: 5 and *t* his bone and his flesh,
5:19 in seven no evil shall *t* you.
6: 7 My soul refuses to *t* them;
Ps 105:15 'Do not *t* My anointed ones,
144: 5 *T* the mountains, and they
Isa 52:11 *T* no unclean thing;
Jer 12:14 neighbors who *t* the inheritance
Lam 4:14 So that no one would *t* their
4:15 go away, Do not *t* us!"
Mt 9:21 If only I may *t* His garment, I
14:36 Him that they might only *t* the
Mk 3:10 pressed about Him to *t* Him.
5:28 'If only I may *t* His clothes,
6:56 Him that they might just *t* the
8:22 and begged Him to *t* him.
10:13 that He might *t* them;
Lk 6:19 multitude sought to *t* Him,
11:46 and you yourselves do not *t* the
18:15 to Him that He might *t* them;
1 Cor 7: 1 is good for a man not to *t* a
2 Cor 6:17 Do not *t* what is
Col 2:21 'Do not *t*, do not taste,
Heb 11:28 the firstborn should *t* them.
1 Jn 5:18 and the wicked one does not *t*

TOUCHED (48/44) TOUCH

Gen 26:29 since we have not *t* you,
32:25 He *t* the socket of his hip;
32:32 because He *t* the socket of
Lev 22: 6 the person who has *t* any such
Num 19:18 or on the one who *t* a bone,
31:19 and whoever has *t* any slain,
Josh 4:18 soles of the priests' feet *t*
Judg 6:21 and *t* the meat and the
1 Sam 10:26 whose hearts God had *t*.
1 Ki 6:27 wing of the one *t* one wall,
6:27 other cherub *t* the other wall.
6:27 And their wings *t* each other in
19: 5 suddenly an angel *t* him,
19: 7 and *t* him, and said, "Arise
2 Ki 13:21 the man was let down and *t* the
Esth 5: 2 Then Esther went near and *t* the
Isa 6: 7 And he *t* my mouth with it,
6: 7 this has *t* your lips;
Jer 1: 9 LORD put forth His hand and *t*
Ezek 1: 9 Their wings *t* one another.
1:11 two wings of each one *t* one
3:13 of the living creatures that *t*
Dan 8:18 but he *t* me, and stood me
10:10 a hand *t* me, which made me
10:16 of the sons of men *t* my lips;
10:18 the likeness of a man *t* me
Mt 8: 3 Jesus put out His hand and *t*
8:15 So He *t* her hand, and the fever
9:20 years came from behind and *t*
9:29 Then He *t* their eyes, saying,
14:36 And as many as *t* it were made
17: 7 But Jesus came and *t* them and
20:34 So Jesus had compassion and *t*
Mk 1:41 stretched out His hand and *t*
5:27 behind Him in the crowd and *t*
5:30 Who *t* My clothes?"
5:31 and You say, 'Who *t* Me?'
6:56 And as many as *t* Him were made
7:33 and He spat and *t* his tongue.
Lk 5:13 He put out His hand and *t* him,
7:14 Then He came and *t* the open
8:44 came from behind and *t* the
8:45 Who *t* Me?" When all denied it,
8:45 and You say, 'Who *t* Me?'
8:46 Somebody *t* Me, for I perceived
8:47 the reason she had *t* Him
22:51 And He *t* his ear and healed
Heb 12:18 to the mountain that may be *t*

TOUCHES (46/44) TOUCH

Gen 26:11 He who *t* this man or his wife
Ex 19:12 Whoever *t* the mountain shall
29:37 Whatever *t* the altar must be
30:29 whatever *t* them must be holy.
Lev 5: 2 Or if a person *t* any unclean
5: 3 Or if he *t* human uncleanness—
6:18 Everyone who *t* them must be
6:27 Everyone who *t* its flesh must be
7:19 The flesh that *t* any unclean
7:21 Moreover the person who *t* any
11:24 whoever *t* the carcass of any of
11:26 Everyone who *t* it shall be
11:27 Whoever *t* any such carcass
11:31 Whoever *t* them when they are
11:36 but whatever *t* any such carcass
11:39 he who *t* its carcass shall be
15: 5 And whoever *t* his bed shall wash
15: 7 And he who *t* the body of him who
15:10 Whoever *t* anything that was
15:11 the one who has the discharge *t*,
15:12 that he who has the discharge *t*
15:19 and whoever *t* her shall be
15:21 Whoever *t* her bed shall wash his
15:22 And whoever *t* anything that she
15:23 when he *t* it, he shall be
15:27 Whoever *t* those things shall be
22: 4 And whoever *t* anything made
22: 5 or whoever *t* any creeping thing
Num 19:11 He who *t* the dead body of
19:13 Whoever *t* the body of anyone who
19:16 Whoever in the open field *t* one
19:21 and he who *t* the water of
19:22 'Whatever the unclean person *t*
19:22 and the person who *t* it shall
Judg 16: 9 of yarn breaks when it *t* fire.
2 Sam 23: 7 But the man who *t* them Must
Job 4: 5 It *t* you, and you are
Ps 104:32 He *t* the hills, and they
Prov 6:29 Whoever *t* her shall not be
Ezek 17:10 wither when the east wind *t* it?
Am 9: 5 He who *t* the earth and it
Hag 2:12 and with the edge he *t* bread or
2:13 because of a dead body *t* any
Zech 2: 8 for he who *t* you touches the
2: 8 for he who touches you *t* the
Heb 12:20 if so much as a beast *t*

TOUCHING (6/4) TOUCH

2 Chr 3:11 *t* the wall of the room,
3:11 *t* the wing of the other cherub;
3:12 *t* the wall of the room,
3:12 *t* the wing of the other cherub.
Dan 8: 5 without *t* the ground;
Lk 7:39 woman this is who is *t* Him,

TOW (KJV) See TINDER, WICK, YARN

TOWARD (313/275)

Gen 2:14 it is the one which goes *t* the
10:19 from Sidon as you go *t* Gerar,
10:19 then as you go *t* Sodom,
10:30 from Mesha as you go *t* Sephar,
12: 9 going on still *t* the South.
13:10 land of Egypt as you go *t* Zoar.
15: 5 Look now *t* heaven, and count the
18:16 from there and looked *t* Sodom,
18:22 from there and went *t* Sodom,
19: 1 with his face *t* the ground.
19:28 Then he looked *t* Sodom and
19:28 and *t* all the land of the
24:27 His mercy and His truth *t* my
25:18 of Egypt as you go *t* Assyria.)
28:10 Beersheba and went *t* Haran.
30:40 and made the flocks face *t* the
31: 2 it was not favorable *t* him
31: 5 that it is not favorable *t* me
31:21 and headed *t* the mountains of
48:13 hand *t* Israel's left hand,
48:13 hand *t* Israel's right hand,
Ex 9: 8 and let Moses scatter it *t* the
9:10 Moses scattered them *t* heaven.
9:22 Stretch out your hand *t* heaven,
9:23 stretched out his rod *t* heaven;
10:21 Stretch out your hand *t* heaven,
10:22 out his hand *t* heaven,
16:10 that they looked *t* the
25:20 shall be *t* the mercy seat.
26:35 of the tabernacle *t* the south;
28:27 underneath the ephod *t* its
34: 8 haste and bowed his head *t* the
37: 9 cherubim were *t* the mercy seat.
39:20 underneath the ephod *t* its
Lev 9:22 lifted his hand *t* the people,
Num 2: 3 *t* the rising of the sun,
5:12 and behaves unfaithfully *t* him,
5:27 and behaved unfaithfully *t* her
8: 3 the lamps to face *t* the front
12:10 Then Aaron turned *t* Miriam,
16:42 that they turned *t* the
21:11 east of Moab, *t* the sunrise.
24: 1 but he set his face *t* the
34: 8 of the border shall be *t* Zedad;
34:15 eastward, *t* the sunrise."
Deut 3:27 and lift your eyes *t* the west,
4:41 *t* the rising of the sun,
4:47 *t* the rising of the sun,
11:30 *t* the setting sun, in the land
28:54 will be hostile *t* his brother,
28:54 *t* the wife of his bosom,
28:54 and *t* the rest of his children
Josh 1: 4 and to the Great Sea *t* the
1:15 of the Jordan *t* the sunrise."
8:18 that is in your hand *t* Ai,
8:18 was in his hand *t* the city.
9: 1 the Great Sea *t* Lebanon—the
12: 1 Jordan *t* the rising of the sun,
13: 5 *t* the sunrise, from Baal Gad
15: 4 From there it passed *t* Azmon
15: 7 Then the border went up *t* Debir
15: 7 it turned northward *t* Gilgal,
15: 7 The border continued *t* the
15:21 *t* the border of Edom in the
16: 6 And the border went out *t* the
18:13 went over from there *t* Luz,
18:17 and extended *t* Geliloth,
18:18 Then it passed along *t* the north
19:11 Their border went *t* the west and
19:12 it went eastward *t* the sunrise
19:12 and went out *t* Daberath,
19:13 *t* Eth Kazin, and extended to
19:27 It turned *t* the sunrise to Beth
19:34 went out from there *t* Hukkok;
19:34 by the Jordan *t* the sunrise.
Judg 7:22 *t* Zererah, as far as the border
8: 3 Then their anger *t* him
11:29 of Gilead he advanced *t* the
11:32 So Jephthah advanced *t* the
12: 1 crossed over *t* Zaphon, and said
13:20 as the flame went up *t* heaven
19: 9 day is now drawing *t* evening;
19:18 from Bethlehem in Judah *t* the
20:43 the front of Gibeah *t* the east.
20:45 Then they turned and fled *t* the
20:47 and fled *t* the wilderness
1 Sam 5: 7 for His hand is harsh *t* us and
9:14 coming out *t* them on his way up
13:18 the Valley of Zeboim *t* the
17:30 he turned from him *t* another
17:48 hastened and ran *t* the army
19: 4 have been very good *t* you.
20:12 indeed there is good *t* David,
20:41 David arose from a place *t* the
25:20 coming down *t* her, and she met
2 Sam 15: 6 Absalom acted *t* all Israel
15:23 people crossed over *t* the way
24: 5 ravine of Gad, and *t* Jazer.

24:20 and his servants coming *t* him.
1 Ki 7:25 three looking *t* the north,
7:25 three looking *t* the west, three
7:25 three looking *t* the south,
7:25 and three looking *t* the east;
7:39 *t* the southeast.
8:22 spread out his hands *t* heaven;
8:29 eyes may be open *t* this temple
8:29 *t* the place of which You said,
8:29 servant makes *t* this place.
8:30 when they pray *t* this place.
8:35 when they pray *t* this place and
8:38 out his hands *t* this temple:
8:42 when he comes and prays *t* this
8:44 pray to the LORD *t* the city
8:48 and pray to You *t* their land
13: 4 which he stretched out *t* him,
14:13 is found something good *t* the
18:43 'Go up now, look *t* the sea."
2 Ki 10:15 as my heart is *t* your heart?"
20: 2 Then he turned his face *t* the
1 Chr 29:18 and fix their heart *t* You.
2 Chr 4: 4 three looking *t* the north,
4: 4 three looking *t* the west,
4: 4 three looking *t* the south,
4: 4 and three looking *t* the east;
4:10 *t* the southeast.
6:13 spread out his hands *t* heaven);
6:20 eyes may be open *t* this temple
6:20 *t* the place where You said
6:20 servant prays *t* this place.
6:21 when they pray *t* this place.
6:26 when they pray *t* this place and
6:34 they pray to You *t* this city
6:38 and pray *t* their land which You
6:38 and *t* the temple which I have
20:24 they looked *t* the multitude;
24:16 both *t* God and His house.
Ezra 3:11 endures forever *t* Israel."
6:22 of the king of Assyria *t* them,
Neh 3:26 of the Water Gate *t* the east,
12:31 on the wall *t* the Refuse Gate.
Esth 1:13 was the king's manner *t* all
8: 4 the golden scepter *t* Esther.
Job 2:12 dust on his head *t* heaven.
10:17 increase Your indignation *t* me;
11:13 stretch out your hands *t* Him;
39:26 And spread its wings *t* the
Ps 5: 7 worship *t* Your holy temple.
21:12 on Your string *t* their faces.
25:15 My eyes are ever *t* the LORD,
28: 2 When I lift up my hands *t* Your
40: 5 And Your thoughts *t* us Cannot
66: 5 in His doing *t* the sons
85: 4 And cause Your anger *t* us to
86:13 For great is Your mercy *t* me,
103:11 So great is His mercy *t* those
106: 4 You have *t* Your people;
116:12 For all His benefits *t* me?
117: 2 kindness is great *t* us,
119:132 As Your custom is *t* those who
138: 2 I will worship *t* Your holy
Prov 14:35 The king's favor is *t* a wise
23: 5 away like an eagle *t* heaven.
24:11 those who are drawn *t* death,
Eccl 1: 6 The wind goes *t* the south,
Song 7: 4 Which looks *t* Damascus.
7:10 And his desire is *t* me.
Isa 3: 5 will be insolent *t* the elder,
3: 5 And the base *t* the
11:14 of the Philistines *t* the west;
29:13 And their fear *t* Me is taught
38: 2 Hezekiah turned his face *t* the
63: 7 And the great goodness *t* the
63:15 heart and Your mercies *t* me?
Jer 3:12 these words *t* the north,
4: 6 Set up the standard *t* Zion.
4:11 wilderness *T* the daughter of
12: 3 You have tested my heart *t* You.
15: 1 be favorable *t* this people.
29:10 and perform My good word *t* you,
29:11 thoughts that I think *t* you,
31:21 Set your heart *t* the highway,
31:39 then it shall turn *t* Goath.
31:40 of the Horse Gate *t* the east,
46: 6 stumble and fall *T* the north,
49:36 And scatter them *t* all those
50: 5 With their faces *t* it,
Lam 2:19 Lift your hands *t* Him For the
Ezek 1:17 they went *t* any one of four
1:23 out straight, one *t* another.
4: 7 you shall set your face *t* the
6: 2 set your face *t* the mountains
6:14 than the wilderness *t* Diblah,
8: 5 lift your eyes now *t* the
8: 5 So I lifted my eyes *t* the
8:16 men with their backs *t* the
8:16 and their faces *t* the east,
8:16 worshiping the sun *t* the east.
10:11 they went *t* any of their four
16:42 lay to rest My fury *t* you,
17: 6 Its branches turned *t* him,
17: 7 this vine bent its roots *t* him,
17: 7 stretched its branches *t* him,
20:46 set your face *t* the south;
21: 2 set your face *t* Jerusalem,
28:21 set your face *t* Sidon,
33:25 you lift up your eyes *t* your
40: 2 on it *t* the south was
40:19 one hundred cubits *t* the east
40:24 After that he brought me *t* the
40:27 from gateway to gateway *t* the
41:11 one door *t* the north and
41:11 north and another *t* the south;
41:19 of a man was *t* a palm tree
41:19 of a young lion *t* a palm tree
42: 1 by the way *t* the north;
42: 1 the building *t* the north.
42: 4 *t* the inside, was a walk ten
42: 7 *t* the outer court; its length
42: 8 The length of the chambers *t* the
42:10 of the wall of the court *t* the
42:11 the chambers which were *t* the
42:12 in front of the wall *t* the
42:15 the gateway that faces *t* the
43: 1 the gate that faces *t* the east.
43: 4 gate which faces *t* the east.
43:17 and its steps face *t* the
44: 1 which faces *t* the east,
46: 1 court that faces *t* the east
46:12 the gate that faces *t* the east
46:19 priests which face *t* the north;
47: 1 of the temple *t* the east,
47: 8 This water flows *t* the eastern
47:19 *t* the South, shall be from
47:19 the south side, *t* the South.
48:28 *t* the South, the border shall
Dan 3:19 on his face changed *t* Shadrach,
6:10 his windows open *t* Jerusalem,
8: 8 ones came up *t* the four winds
8: 9 exceedingly great *t* the south,
8: 9 *t* the east, and toward the
8: 9 and *t* the Glorious Land.
9: 3 Then I set my face *t* the Lord
10:15 I turned my face *t* the ground
11: 4 be broken up and divided *t* the
11:19 turn his face *t* the fortress
11:29 return and go *t* the south;
Hos 3: 3 will I be *t* you."
5: 4 do not direct their deeds *T*
Joel 2:20 With his face *t* the eastern
2:20 his back *t* the western sea;
Jon 2: 4 Yet I will look again *t* Your
Zech 6: 6 and the dappled are going *t* the
6: 8 those who go *t* the north
14: 4 mountain shall move *t* the north
14: 4 And half of it *t* the south.
14: 8 Half of them *t* the eastern sea
14: 8 And half of them *t* the
Mt 12:49 He stretched out His hand *t* His
Lk 2:14 goodwill *t* men!"
6:20 He lifted up His eyes *t* His
12:21 and is not rich *t* God."
13:22 and journeying *t* Jerusalem.
24:29 for it is *t* evening,
Jn 1:29 John saw Jesus coming *t* him,
1:47 saw Nathanael coming *t* Him,
6: 5 a great multitude coming *t* Him,
6:17 went over the sea *t* Capernaum.
Acts 1:10 looked steadfastly *t* heaven
8:26 Arise and go *t* the south along
20:21 repentance *t* God and faith
20:21 toward God and faith *t* our
22: 3 and was zealous *t* God as you
24:16 without offense *t* God and men.
27:12 a harbor of Crete opening *t* the
28:14 And so we went *t* Rome.
Rom 5: 8 demonstrates His own love *t* us,
11:22 but *t* you, goodness, if you
12:16 Be of the same mind *t* one
15: 5 be like-minded *t* one another,
1 Cor 7:36 is behaving improperly *t* his
9:21 (not being without law *t* God,
9:21 but under law *t* Christ),
15:10 and His grace *t* me was not in
2 Cor 1:12 and more abundantly *t* you.
3: 4 trust through Christ *t* God.
7: 4 my boldness of speech *t* you,
9: 8 to make all grace abound *t* you,
10: 1 but being absent am bold *t* you.
13: 3 who is not weak *t* you,
13: 4 Him by the power of God *t* you.
Gal 2: 8 worked effectively in me *t* the
Eph 1: 8 which He made to abound *t* us in
1:19 greatness of His power *t* us
2: 7 His grace in His kindness *t* us
Phil 2:30 lacking in your service *t* me.
3:14 I press *t* the goal for the prize
Col 3:19 and do not be bitter *t* them.
4: 5 Walk in wisdom *t* those who are
1 Th 1: 8 Your faith *t* God has gone out,
4:10 and indeed you do so *t* all the
4:12 may walk properly *t* those who
2 Th 1: 3 you all abounds *t* each other,
1 Tim 4: 7 exercise yourself *t* godliness.
Titus 3: 4 love of God our Savior *t* man
Phm 1: 5 and faith which you have *t* the
1: 5 Jesus and *t* all the saints,
Heb 6: 1 dead works and of faith *t* God,
6:10 you have shown *t* His name,
1 Pe 2:19 if because of conscience *t* God
3:21 of a good conscience *t* God),
2 Pe 3: 9 but is longsuffering *t* us,
1 Jn 3:21 we have confidence *t* God.
4: 9 of God was manifested *t* us,

TOWEL (2/2)

Jn 13: 4 took a *t* and girded Himself.
13: 5 and to wipe them with the *t*

TOWER (40/35) TOWERS

Gen 11: 4 and a *t* whose top is in the
11: 5 down to see the city and the *t*
35:21 pitched his tent beyond the *t*
Judg 8: 9 I will tear down this *t*!"
8:17 Then he tore down the *t* of
9:46 Now when all the men of the *t*
9:47 that all the men of the *t* of
9:49 so that all the people of the *t*
9:51 But there was a strong *t* in the
9:51 went up to the top of the *t*.
9:52 Abimelech came as far as the *t*
9:52 he drew near the door of the *t*
2 Sam 22:51 He is the *t* of salvation to
2 Ki 9:17 Now a watchman stood on the *t*
Neh 3: 1 They built as far as the *T* of
3: 1 then as far as the *T* of
3:11 as well as the *T* of the Ovens.
3:25 and on the *t* which projects
3:26 east, and on the projecting *t*.
3:27 next to the great projecting *t*,
12:38 going past the *T* of the Ovens
12:39 the *T* of Hananel, the Tower of
12:39 the *T* of the Hundred, as far as
Ps 61: 3 A strong *t* from the enemy.
144: 2 My high *t* and my deliverer,
Prov 18:10 of the LORD is a strong *t*;
Song 4: 4 Your neck is like the *t* of
7: 4 Your neck is like an ivory *t*,
7: 4 Your nose is like the *t* of
Isa 2:15 Upon every high *t*,
5: 2 He built a *t* in its midst,
21: 5 Set a watchman in the *t*,
Jer 31:38 built for the LORD from the *T*
Mic 4: 8 O *t* of the flock,
Zech 9: 3 For Tyre built herself a *t*,
14:10 and from the *T* of Hananeel to
Mt 21:33 a winepress in it and built a *t*.
Mk 12: 1 for the wine vat and built a *t*.
Lk 13: 4 those eighteen on whom the *t*
14:28 of you, intending to build a *t*,

TOWERED (1/1)

Ezek 19:11 She *t* in stature above the

TOWERS (16/16) TOWER

2 Chr 14: 7 make walls around them, and *t*,
26: 9 And Uzziah built *t* in Jerusalem
26:10 Also he built *t* in the desert.
26:15 to be on the *t* and the corners,
27: 4 he built fortresses and *t*.
32: 5 broken, raised it up to the *t*,
Ps 48:12 go all around her. Count her *t*;
Song 8:10 And my breasts like *t*;
Isa 23:13 They set up its *t*,
30:25 When the *t* fall.
32:14 The forts and *t* will become
33:18 Where is he who counts the *t*?
Ezek 26: 4 of Tyre and break down her *t*;
26: 9 axes he will break down your *t*.
27:11 men of Gammad were in your *t*;
Zeph 1:16 And against the high *t*.

TOWN (15/14) TOWNS

Josh 13: 9 and the *t* that is in the midst
Ruth 3:11 for all the people of my *t* know
1 Sam 16: 4 And the elders of the *t*
23: 7 shut himself in by entering a *t*
27: 5 them give me a place in some *t*
2 Sam 24: 5 on the right side of the *t*
Hab 2:12 Woe to him who builds a *t* with
Mt 10:11 Now whatever city or *t* you
Mk 8:23 hand and led him out of the *t*.
8:26 saying, "Neither go into the *t*,
8:26 nor tell anyone in the *t*."
Lk 5:17 who had come out of every *t* of
Jn 7:42 seed of David and from the *t*
11: 1 the *t* of Mary and her sister
11:30 had not yet come into the *t*,

TOWNCLERK (KJV) See CLERK

TOWNS (36/22) TOWN

Gen 25:16 by their *t* and their
Num 32:41 went and took its small *t*,
Deut 3: 5 besides a great many rural *t*.
Josh 13:30 and all the *t* of Jair which are
15:45 with its *t* and villages;
15:47 Ashdod with its *t* and villages,
15:47 Gaza with its *t* and villages—as
17:11 had Beth Shean and its *t*,
17:11 and its towns, Ibleam and its *t*,
17:11 inhabitants of Dor and its *t*,
17:11 inhabitants of En Dor and its *t*,
17:11 of Taanach and its *t*,
17:11 of Megiddo and its *t*—
17:16 are of Beth Shean and its *t*
Judg 10: 4 they also had thirty *t*,
1 Ki 4:13 to him belonged the *t* of Jair
1 Chr 2:23 and Syria took from them the *t*
2:23 of Jair, with Kenath and its *t*—
2:23 Kenath and its towns—sixty *t*.
7:28 places were Bethel and its *t*:
7:28 to the west Gezer and its *t*,
7:28 towns, and Shechem and its *t*,
7:28 as far as Ayyah and its *t*;
7:29 were Beth Shean and its *t*,
7:29 its towns, Taanach and its *t*,
7:29 its towns, Megiddo and its *t*,
7:29 and its towns, Dor and its *t*.

8:12 built Ono and Lod with its *t*;
18: 1 and took Gath and its *t* from
Esth 9:19 who dwelt in the unwalled *t*
Jer 19:15 on this city and on all her *t*
Zech 2: 4 shall be inhabited as *t*
Mk 1:38 "Let us go into the next *t*,
8:27 disciples went out to the *t* of
Lk 9: 6 departed and went through the *t*,
9:12 may go into the surrounding *t*

TRACE (2/2)

Dan 2:35 them away so that no *t* of them
Zeph 1: 4 I will cut off every *t* of Baal

TRACHONITIS (1/1)

Lk 3: 1 of Iturea and the region of *T*,

TRACKED (1/1)

Lam 4:18 They *t* our steps So that we

TRACT (1/1)

2 Ki 9:25 and throw him into the *t* of

TRADE (10/10) TRADED, TRADERS, TRADING

Gen 34:10 Dwell and *t* in it, and acquire
34:21 them dwell in the land and *t*
42:34 and you may *t* in the land.'"
Ezek 17: 4 And carried it to a land of *t*;
28: 5 By your great wisdom in *t* you
Am 8: 5 That we may *t* wheat?
Acts 18: 3 because he was of the same *t*,
19:25 have our prosperity by this *t*.
19:27 So not only is this *t* of ours in
Rev 18:17 and as many as *t* on the sea,

TRADED (5/5) TRADE

Ezek 27:14 of Togarmah *t* for your wares
27:17 They *t* for your merchandise
27:21 They *t* with you in lambs, rams,
27:22 They *t* for your wares the
Mt 25:16 talents went and *t* with them,

TRADER (1/1)

Ezek 16:29 as far as the land of the *t*,

TRADERS (7/7) TRADE

Gen 37:28 Then Midianite *t* passed by;
1 Ki 10:15 merchants, from the income of *t*,
2 Chr 9:14 the traveling merchants and *t*
Isa 23: 8 Whose *t* are the honorable of
Ezek 27:13 Tubal, and Meshech were your *t*.
27:15 "The men of Dedan were your *t*;
27:17 the land of Israel were your *t*.

TRADING (3/3) TRADE

Ezek 28:16 By the abundance of your *t* You
28:18 By the iniquity of your *t*;
Lk 19:15 much every man had gained by *t*.

TRADITION (11/11) TRADITIONS

Mt 15: 2 disciples transgress the *t* of
15: 3 of God because of your *t*?
15: 6 of God of no effect by your *t*.
Mk 7: 3 holding the *t* of the elders.
7: 5 not walk according to the *t* of
7: 8 you hold the *t* of men—the
7: 9 God, that you may keep your *t*.
7:13 God of no effect through your *t*
Col 2: 8 according to the *t* of men,
2 Th 3: 6 and not according to the *t*
1 Pe 1:18 aimless conduct received by *t*

TRADITIONS (3/3) TRADITION

1 Cor 11: 2 me in all things and keep the *t*
Gal 1:14 exceedingly zealous for the *t*
2 Th 2:15 stand fast and hold the *t* which

TRAFFICK, TRAFFICKERS (KJV)

See INCOME, TRADE, TRADING

TRAGEDY (2/2)

1 Ki 17:20 have You also brought *t* on the
1 Chr 7:23 because *t* had come upon his

TRAIN (2/2) TRAINED, TRAINING

Prov 22: 6 *T* up a child in the way he
Isa 6: 1 and the *t* of His robe filled

TRAINED (6/6) TRAIN

Gen 14:14 three hundred and eighteen *t*
1 Chr 12: 8 men *t* for battle, who could
Hos 10:11 Ephraim is a *t* heifer That
Lk 6:40 but everyone who is perfectly *t*
Heb 12:11 to those who have been *t* by it.
2 Pe 2:14 They have a heart *t* in

TRAINING (2/2) TRAIN

Dan 1: 5 and three years of *t* for them,
Eph 6: 4 but bring them up in the *t* and

TRAINS (1/1)

Ps 144: 1 Who *t* my hands for war,

TRAITOR (1/1) TRAITORS

Lk 6:16 Iscariot who also became a *t*.

TRAITORS (1/1) TRAITOR

2 Tim 3: 4 *t*, headstrong, haughty,

TRAMP (1/1)

Gen 49:19 a troop shall *t* upon him,

TRAMPLE (9/9) TRAMPLED

Ps 7: 5 let him *t* my life to the earth,
44: 5 Through Your name we will *t*
91:13 and the serpent you shall *t*
Isa 1:12 To *t* My courts?
Ezek 26:11 hooves of his horses he will *t*
Dan 7:23 *T* it and break it in pieces.
Mal 4: 3 You shall *t* the wicked,
Mt 7: 6 lest they *t* them under their
Lk 10:19 I give you the authority to *t*

TRAMPLED (28/26) TRAMPLE

Judg 20:43 and easily *t* them down as far
2 Ki 7:17 But the people *t* him in the
7:20 for the people *t* him in the
9:33 and he *t* her underfoot.
14: 9 in Lebanon passed by and *t* the
2 Chr 25:18 passed by and *t* the thistle.
Isa 5: 5 and it shall be *t* down.
25:10 And Moab shall be *t* down under
25:10 As straw is *t* down for the
28: 3 Will be *t* underfoot;
28:18 Then you will be *t* down by it.
63: 3 And *t* them in My fury;
Lam 1:15 The Lord has *t* underfoot all my
1:15 The Lord *t* as in a winepress
Ezek 34:19 they eat what you have *t* with
Dan 7:19 and *t* the residue with its
8: 7 him down to the ground and *t*
8:10 to the ground, and *t* them.
8:13 sanctuary and the host to be *t*
Hos 4:14 do not understand will be *t*.
Mic 7:10 Now she will be *t* down Like
Hab 3:12 You *t* the nations in anger.
Mt 5:13 but to be thrown out and *t*
Lk 8: 5 and it was *t* down, and the
12: 1 so that they *t* one another,
21:24 And Jerusalem will be *t* by
Heb 10:29 he be thought worthy who has *t*
Rev 14:20 And the winepress was *t* outside

TRAMPLING (1/1)

Dan 7: 7 and *t* the residue with its

TRANCE (3/3)

Acts 10:10 he fell into a *t*
11: 5 and in a *t* I saw a vision,
22:17 that I was in a *t*

TRANSFER (1/1)

2 Sam 3:10 to *t* the kingdom from the house

TRANSFERRED (1/1)

1 Cor 4: 6 I have figuratively *t* to myself

TRANSFIGURED (2/2)

Mt 17: 2 and He was *t* before them.
Mk 9: 2 and He was *t* before them.

TRANSFORM (2/2) TRANSFORMED, TRANSFORMING, TRANSFORMS

2 Cor 11:15 thing if his ministers also *t*
Phil 3:21 who will *t* our lowly body that

TRANSFORMED (2/2) TRANSFORM

Rom 12: 2 but be *t* by the renewing of
2 Cor 3:18 are being *t* into the same image

TRANSFORMING (1/1) TRANSFORM

2 Cor 11:13 *t* themselves into apostles of

TRANSFORMS (1/1) TRANSFORM

2 Cor 11:14 Satan himself *t* himself into

TRANSGRESS (14/14) TRANSGRESSED, TRANSGRESSION, TRANSGRESSOR

Num 14:41 Now why do you *t* the command of
1 Sam 2:24 You make the LORD's people *t*.
2 Chr 24:20 Why do you *t* the commandments of
Esth 3: 3 Why do you *t* the king's
Ps 17: 3 that my mouth shall not *t*.
Prov 8:29 So that the waters would not *t*
16:10 His mouth must not *t* in
28:21 a piece of bread a man will *t*.
Jer 2:20 And you said, 'I will not *t*,
Ezek 20:38 and those who *t* against Me;
Am 4: 4 "Come to Bethel and *t*,
Zeph 3:11 of your deeds In which you *t*
Mt 15: 2 Why do Your disciples *t* the
15: 3 Why do you also *t* the

TRANSGRESSED (29/29) TRANSGRESS

Deut 26:13 I have not *t* Your commandments,
Josh 7:11 and they have also *t* My
7:15 because he has *t* the covenant
23:16 When you have *t* the covenant of
Judg 2:20 Because this nation has *t* My
1 Sam 15:24 for I have *t* the commandment of
1 Ki 8:50 which they have *t* against You;
2 Ki 18:12 but *t* His covenant and all
1 Chr 2: 7 who *t* in the accursed thing.
2 Chr 12: 2 because they had *t* against the
26:16 for he *t* against the LORD his
36:14 of the priests and the people *t*
Ezra 10:10 You have *t* and have taken pagan
10:13 are many of us who have *t* in
Isa 24: 5 Because they have *t* the laws,
43:27 And your mediators have *t*
66:24 corpses of the men Who have *t*
Jer 2: 8 The rulers also *t* against Me;
2:29 You all have *t* against Me,"
3:13 That you have *t* against the
33: 8 sinned and by which they have *t*
34:18 I will give the men who have *t*
Lam 3:42 We have *t* and rebelled;
Ezek 2: 3 they and their fathers have *t*
Dan 9:11 all Israel has *t* Your law,
Hos 6: 7 But like men they *t* the
7:13 Because they have *t* against
8: 1 Because they have *t* My
Lk 15:29 I never *t* your commandment at

TRANSGRESSES (3/3)

Hab 1:11 his mind changes, and he *t*;
2: 5 because he *t* by wine, He is
2 Jn 9 Whoever *t* and does not abide in

TRANSGRESSING (3/3)

Deut 17: 2 in *t* His covenant,
Neh 13:27 *t* against our God by marrying
Isa 59:13 In *t* and lying against the

TRANSGRESSION (44/43) TRANSGRESS, TRANSGRESSIONS

Ex 34: 7 forgiving iniquity and *t* and
Num 14:18 mercy, forgiving iniquity and *t*;
2 Chr 29:19 reign had cast aside in his *t*
Ezra 9: 4 because of the *t* of those who
Job 7:21 then do You not pardon my *t*,
8: 4 has cast them away for their *t*.
13:23 Make me know my *t* and my sin.
14:17 My *t* is sealed up in a bag,
33: 9 'I am pure, without *t*;
34: 6 though I am without *t*.
Ps 19:13 I shall be innocent of great *t*.
32: 1 Blessed is he whose *t* is
36: 1 my heart concerning the *t* of
59: 3 Not for my *t* nor for my sin,
89:32 Then I will punish their *t* with
107:17 Fools, because of their *t*,
Prov 12:13 wicked is ensnared by the *t* of
17: 9 He who covers a *t* seeks love,
17:19 He who loves *t* loves strife,
19:11 his glory is to overlook a *t*.
28: 2 Because of the *t* of a land,
28:24 And says, "It is no *t*,
29: 6 By *t* an evil man is snared,
29:16 *t* increases; But the righteous
29:22 And a furious man abounds in *t*.
Isa 24:20 Its *t* shall be heavy upon it,
57: 4 Are you not children of *t*,
58: 1 Tell My people their *t*,
59:20 And to those who turn from *t*
Ezek 33:12 deliver him in the day of his *t*;
Dan 8:12 Because of *t*, an army was
8:13 daily sacrifices and the *t* of
9:24 holy city, To finish the *t*,
Am 4: 4 At Gilgal multiply *t*;
Mic 1: 5 All this is for the *t* of Jacob
1: 5 What is the *t* of Jacob?
3: 8 To declare to Jacob his *t* And
6: 7 I give my firstborn for my *t*,
7:18 And passing over the *t* of the
Acts 1:25 from which Judas by *t* fell,
Rom 4:15 there is no law there is no *t*.
5:14 to the likeness of the *t* of
1 Tim 2:14 being deceived, fell into *t*.
Heb 2: 2 and every *t* and disobedience

TRANSGRESSIONS (50/49) TRANSGRESSION

Ex 23:21 for He will not pardon your *t*;
Lev 16:16 Israel, and because of their *t*,

T

16:21 of Israel, and all their *t*,
Josh 24:19 He will not forgive your *t* nor
1 Ki 8:50 and all their *t* which they have
Job 31:33 If I have covered my *t* as Adam,
35: 6 if your *t* are multiplied,
36: 9 them their work and their *t*—
Ps 5:10 out in the multitude of their *t*,
25: 7 the sins of my youth, nor my *t*;
32: 5 I will confess my *t* to the
39: 8 Deliver me from all my *t*;
51: 1 tender mercies, Blot out my *t*.
51: 3 For I acknowledge my *t*,
65: 3 As for our *t*, You will
103:12 So far has He removed our *t*
Isa 43:25 am He who blots out your *t* for
44:22 out, like a thick cloud, your *t*,
50: 1 And for your *t* your mother has
53: 5 But He was wounded for our *t*,
53: 8 For the *t* of My people He was
59:12 For our *t* are multiplied before
59:12 For our *t* are with us,
Jer 5: 6 Because their *t* are many;
Lam 1: 5 of the multitude of her *t*.
1:14 The yoke of my *t* was bound;
1:22 have done to me For all my *t*;
Ezek 14:11 anymore with all their *t*,
18:22 None of the *t* which he has
18:28 and turns away from all the *t*
18:30 and turn from all your *t*,
18:31 Cast away from you all the *t*
21:24 in that your *t* are uncovered,
33:10 If our *t* and our sins lie upon
37:23 things, nor with any of their *t*;
39:24 and according to their *t* I
Hos 10:10 I bind them for their two *t*.
Am 1: 3 For three *t* of Damascus, and for
1: 6 For three *t* of Gaza, and for
1: 9 For three *t* of Tyre, and for
1:11 For three *t* of Edom, and for
1:13 For three *t* of the people of
2: 1 For three *t* of Moab, and for
2: 4 For three *t* of Judah, and for
2: 6 For three *t* of Israel, and for
3:14 day I punish Israel for their *t*,
5:12 For I know your manifold *t* And
Mic 1:13 For the *t* of Israel were found
Gal 3:19 It was added because of *t*,
Heb 9:15 for the redemption of the *t*

TRANSGRESSOR (5/5) TRANSGRESS, TRANSGRESSORS

Prov 26:10 the fool his hire and the *t*
Isa 48: 8 And were called a *t* from the
Rom 2:27 are a *t* of the law?
Gal 2:18 I destroyed, I make myself a *t*.
Jas 2:11 you have become a *t* of the law.

TRANSGRESSORS (12/11) TRANSGRESSOR

Ps 37:38 But the *t* shall be destroyed
51:13 Then I will teach *t* Your ways,
59: 5 not be merciful to any wicked *t*.
Isa 1:28 The destruction of *t* and of
46: 8 Recall to mind, O you *t*.
53:12 And He was numbered with the *t*,
53:12 made intercession for the *t*.
Dan 8:23 When the *t* have reached their
Hos 14: 9 But *t* stumble in them.
Mk 15:28 was numbered with the *t*.
Lk 22:37 was numbered with the *t*.
Jas 2: 9 are convicted by the law as *t*.

TRANSLATE (KJV) See TRANSFER

TRANSLATED (13/13) TAKEN, TRANSLATION

Ezra 4: 7 and *t* into the Aramaic
Mt 1:23 name Immanuel," which is *t*,
Mk 5:41 "Talitha, cumi," which is *t*,
15:22 the place Golgotha, which is *t*,
15:34 lama sabachthani?" which is *t*,
Jn 1:38 (which is to say, when *t*,
1:41 found the Messiah" (which is *t*,
1:42 be called Cephas" (which is *t*,
9: 7 pool of Siloam" (which is *t*,
Acts 4:36 by the apostles (which is *t*
9:36 which is *t* Dorcas. This woman
13: 8 sorcerer (for so his name is *t*)
Heb 7: 2 part of all, first being *t* '

TRANSLATION (KJV) See TAKEN

TRANSPARENT (1/1)

Rev 21:21 was pure gold, like *t* glass.

TRAP (7/7) TRAPS

Job 18:10 And a *t* for him in the road.
Ps 69:22 And their well-being a *t*.
Isa 8:14 As a *t* and a snare to the
Jer 5:26 who sets snares; They set a *t*;
Am 3: 5 where there is no *t* for it?
Ob 7 eat your bread shall lay a *t*
Rom 11: 9 become a snare and a *t*,

TRAPPED (4/4)

Eccl 7:26 But the sinner shall be *t* by
Jer 50:24 You have indeed been *t*,
Ezek 19: 4 He was *t* in their pit,
19: 8 He was *t* in their pit.

TRAPS (3/3) TRAP

Josh 23:13 But they shall be snares and *t*
Ps 140: 5 They have set *t* for me. Selah
141: 9 And from the *t* of the workers

TRAVAIL, TRAVAILED, TRAVAILEST, TRAVAILETH (KJV) See BIRTH, BRINGS (FORTH), HARDSHIP, LABOR, LABORS, TASK, TOIL

TRAVEL (8/8) TRAVELER, TRAVELING

1 Ki 2:42 on the day you go out and *t*
Neh 9:12 the road Which they should *t*.
Job 21:29 you not asked those who *t* the
Prov 4:15 do not *t* on it; Turn away from
Mt 23:15 For you *t* land and sea
Acts 19:29 Paul's *t* companions.
2 Cor 8:19 chosen by the churches to *t*
Rev 18:17 all who *t* by ship, sailors, and

TRAVELED (2/2)

1 Sam 31:12 all the valiant men arose and *t*
Acts 11:19 that arose over Stephen *t* as

TRAVELER (4/4) TRAVEL

Judg 19:17 he saw the *t* in the open square
2 Sam 12: 4 And a *t* came to the rich man,
Job 31:32 have opened my doors to the *t*);
Jer 14: 8 And like a *t* who turns aside

TRAVELERS (4/4)

Judg 5: 6 And the *t* walked along the
Job 6:19 The *t* of Sheba hope for them.
Jer 9: 2 A lodging place for *t*;
Ezek 39:11 the sea; and it will obstruct *t*,

TRAVELING (7/7) TRAVEL

1 Ki 10:15 besides that from the *t*
2 Chr 9:14 besides what the *t* merchants
Isa 21:13 O you *t* companies of
33: 8 The *t* man ceases. He has
63: 1 *T* in the greatness of His
Mt 25:14 of heaven is like a man *t*
Lk 24:13 two of them were *t* that same

TRAVERSE (1/1)

Prov 8:20 I *t* the way of righteousness,

TRAVERSING (1/1)

Ezek 27:19 *t* back and forth. Wrought iron,

TRAYS (3/3)

Ex 25:38 its wick-trimmers and their *t*
37:23 and its *t* of pure gold.
Num 4: 9 lamps, its wick-trimmers, its *t*,

TREACHEROUS (11/10) TREACHEROUSLY

Ps 119:158 I see the *t*, and am disgusted,
Isa 21: 2 The *t* dealer deals
24:16 Woe to me! The *t* dealers
24:16 the *t* dealers have dealt very
Jer 3: 7 And her *t* sister Judah saw it.
3: 8 yet her *t* sister Judah did not
3:10 yet for all this her *t* sister
3:11 herself more righteous than *t*
9: 2 An assembly of *t* men.
Hos 7:16 They are like a *t* bow. Their
Zeph 3: 4 *t* people; Her priests have

TREACHEROUSLY (26/21) TREACHEROUS

Judg 9:23 and the men of Shechem dealt *t*
1 Sam 14:33 So he said, "You have dealt *t*;
Ps 25: 3 those be ashamed who deal *t*
Isa 21: 2 The treacherous dealer deals *t*,
24:16 dealers have dealt *t*,
24:16 dealers have dealt very *t*.
33: 1 And you who deal *t*,
33: 1 though they have not dealt *t*
33: 1 you make an end of dealing *t*,
33: 1 They will deal *t* with you.
48: 8 knew that you would deal very *t*,
Jer 3:20 as a wife *t* departs from her
3:20 So have you dealt *t* with Me,
5:11 of Judah Have dealt very *t*
12: 1 are those happy who deal so *t*?
12: 6 Even they have dealt *t* with
Lam 1: 2 All her friends have dealt *t*
Hos 5: 7 They have dealt *t* with the
6: 7 There they dealt *t* with Me.
Hab 1:13 do You look on those who deal *t*,
Mal 2:10 Why do we deal *t* with one
2:11 Judah has dealt *t*,
2:14 With whom you have dealt *t*;
2:15 And let none deal *t* with the
2:16 That you do not deal *t*."
Acts 7:19 This man dealt *t* with our

TREACHERY (5/5)

Ex 21:14 his neighbor, to kill him by *t*,
Josh 22:16 What *t* is this that you have
22:22 or if in *t* against the LORD,
22:31 you have not committed this *t*
2 Ki 9:23 fled, and said to Ahaziah, "*T*,

TREAD (22/22) TREADER, TREADS

Deut 11:25 upon all the land where you *t*,
33:29 And you shall *t* down their
Josh 1: 3 sole of your foot will *t* upon
1 Sam 5: 5 come into Dagon's house *t* on
Job 24:11 And *t* winepresses, yet suffer
40:12 *T* down the wicked in their
Ps 60:12 it is He who shall *t* down
91:13 You shall *t* upon the lion and
108:13 it is He who shall *t* down
Isa 10: 6 And to *t* them down like the
14:25 And on My mountains *t* him
16:10 No treaders will *t* out wine in
26: 6 The foot shall *t* it down—The
Jer 25:30 as those who *t* the grapes,
48:33 No one will *t* with joyous
Ezek 34:18 that you must *t* down with your
Am 5:11 because you *t* down the poor
Mic 1: 3 He will come down And *t* on
6:15 You shall *t* the olives,
Nah 3:14 Go into the clay and *t* the
Zech 10: 5 Who *t* down their enemies In
Rev 11: 2 And they will *t* the holy city

TREADER (1/1) TREAD

Am 9:13 And the *t* of grapes him who

TREADERS (1/1)

Isa 16:10 No *t* will tread out wine in

TREADING (4/4)

Neh 13:15 people in Judah *t* wine presses
Isa 18: 2 A nation powerful and *t* down,
18: 7 powerful and *t* down, Whose
22: 5 a day of trouble and *t* down

TREADS (12/12) TREAD

Deut 11:24 which the sole of your foot *t*
25: 4 ox while it *t* out the grain.
Job 9: 8 And *t* on the waves of the sea;
Isa 41:25 As the potter *t* clay.
63: 2 one who *t* in the winepress?
Am 4:13 Who *t* the high places of the
Mic 5: 5 And when he *t* in our palaces,
5: 6 And when he *t* within our
5: 8 Both *t* down and tears in
1 Cor 9: 9 an ox while it *t* out
1 Tim 5:18 it *t* out the grain,"
Rev 19:15 He Himself *t* the winepress of

TREASON (6/4)

1 Ki 16:20 Zimri, and the *t* he committed,
2 Ki 11:14 and cried out, "*T*!
11:14 cried out, "Treason! *T*!"
2 Chr 23:13 and said, "*T*! Treason!"
23:13 clothes and said, "Treason! *T*!"
Ezek 17:20 and try him there for the *t*

TREASURE (34/32) TREASURES, TREASURING, TREASURY

Gen 43:23 of your father has given you *t*
Ex 19: 5 then you shall be a special *t*
Deut 7: 6 a special *t* above all the
14: 2 a special *t* above all the
28:12 will open to you His good *t*,
1 Chr 29: 3 my own special *t* of gold and
Ezra 5:17 search be made in the king's *t*
Ps 17:14 You fill with Your hidden *t*.
119:162 As one who finds great *t*.
135: 4 Israel for His special *t*.
Prov 2: 1 And *t* my commands within you,
7: 1 And *t* my commands within you.
15: 6 the righteous there is much *t*,
15:16 Than great *t* with trouble.
21:20 There is desirable *t*,
Isa 33: 6 fear of the LORD is His *t*.
Ezek 22:25 they have taken *t* and precious
Dan 1: 2 the articles into the *t* house
Nah 2: 9 There is no end of *t*,
Mt 6:21 For where your *t* is, there your
12:35 A good man out of the good *t* of
12:35 an evil man out of the evil *t*
13:44 the kingdom of heaven is like *t*
13:52 who brings out of his *t*
19:21 and you will have *t* in heaven;
Mk 10:21 have *t* in heaven; and come,
Lk 6:45 A good man out of the good *t* of
6:45 an evil man out of the evil *t*
12:21 So is he who lays up *t* for
12:33 a *t* in the heavens that does
12:34 For where your *t* is, there your
18:22 and you will have *t* in heaven;
2 Cor 4: 7 But we have this *t* in earthen
Jas 5: 3 You have heaped up *t* in the

TREASURED (2/2)

Job 23:12 I have *t* the words of His
Isa 23:18 it will not be *t* nor laid up,

TREASURER (2/2)

Ezra 1: 8 by the hand of Mithredath the *t*,
Rom 16:23 the *t* of the city, greets you,

TREASURERS (4/4)

Ezra 7:21 issue a decree to all the *t* who
Neh 13:13 And I appointed as *t* over the
Dan 3: 2 the counselors, the *t*,
3: 3 counselors, the *t*, the judges,

TREASURES (44/38) TREASURE

Deut 32:34 Sealed up among My *t*?
33:19 of the seas And of *t* hidden
1 Ki 14:26 And he took away the *t* of the
14:26 house of the LORD and the *t*
2 Ki 20:13 them all the house of his *t*—
20:13 that was found among his *t*.
20:15 there is nothing among my *t*
24:13 out from there all the *t* of
24:13 house of the LORD and the *t*
2 Chr 12: 9 and took away the *t* of the
12: 9 house of the LORD and the *t*
25:24 the *t* of the king's house,
28:21 For Ahaz took part of the *t*
36:18 the *t* of the house of the
36:18 and the *t* of the king and of
Ezra 6: 1 where the *t* were stored in
Job 3:21 for it more than hidden *t*;
20:26 darkness is reserved for his *t*.
Prov 2: 4 search for her as for hidden *t*;
10: 2 *T* of wickedness profit nothing,
21: 6 Getting *t* by a lying tongue
Eccl 2: 8 and gold and the special *t* of
Isa 2: 7 And there is no end to their *t*;
30: 6 And their *t* on the humps of
39: 2 showed them the house of his *t*—
39: 2 that was found among his *t*.
39: 4 there is nothing among my *t*
45: 3 I will give you the *t* of
Jer 15:13 Your wealth and your *t* I will
17: 3 plunder your wealth, all your *t*,
20: 5 all the *t* of the kings of Judah
41: 8 for we have *t* of wheat, barley,
48: 7 in your works and your *t*,
49: 4 Who trusted in her *t*,
50:37 A sword is against her *t*,
51:13 by many waters, Abundant in *t*,
Dan 11:43 shall have power over the *t*
Ob 6 How his hidden *t* shall
Mic 6:10 Are there yet the *t* of
Mt 2:11 when they had opened their *t*,
6:19 not lay up for yourselves *t* on
6:20 but lay up for yourselves *t* in
Col 2: 3 in whom are hidden all the *t* of
Heb 11:26 greater riches than the *t* in

TREASURIES (29/26) TREASURY

1 Ki 7:51 He put them in the *t* of the
15:18 gold that was left in the *t*
15:18 house of the LORD and the *t*
2 Ki 12:18 all the gold found in the *t* of
14:14 of the LORD and in the *t* of
16: 8 and in the *t* of the king's
18:15 of the LORD and in the *t* of
1 Chr 9:26 charge over the chambers and *t*
26:20 Ahijah was over the *t* of the
26:20 house of God and over the *t* of
26:22 were over the *t* of the house
26:24 Moses, was overseer of the *t*.
26:26 brethren were over all the *t*
27:25 of Adiel was over the king's *t*;
28:11 vestibule, its houses, its *t*,
28:12 of the *t* of the house of God,
28:12 and of the *t* for the dedicated
2 Chr 5: 1 And he put them in the *t* of
8:15 any matter or concerning the *t*.
16: 2 silver and gold from the *t* of
32:27 And he made himself *t* for
Esth 3: 9 to bring it into the king's *t*.
4: 7 to pay into the king's *t* to
Ps 135: 7 brings the wind out of His *t*.
Prov 8:21 That I may fill their *t*.
Isa 10:13 And have robbed their *t*;
Jer 10:13 brings the wind out of His *t*.
51:16 brings the wind out of His *t*.
Ezek 28: 4 gold and silver into your *t*;

TREASURING (1/1) TREASURE

Rom 2: 5 impenitent heart you are *t* up

TREASURY (20/18) TREASURE, TREASURIES

Josh 6:19 they shall come into the *t* of
6:24 they put into the *t* of the
1 Chr 29: 8 stones gave them to the *t* of
Ezra 2:69 they gave to the *t* for the work
4:13 and the king's *t* will be
6: 4 be paid from the king's *t*.
7:20 pay for it from the king's *t*.
Neh 7:70 The governor gave to the *t* one
7:71 fathers' houses gave to the *t*
Job 38:22 Have you entered the *t* of snow,
38:22 Or have you seen the *t* of
Jer 38:11 house of the king under the *t*,
Hos 13:15 He shall plunder the *t* of
Mt 27: 6 lawful to put them into the *t*,
Mk 12:41 Now Jesus sat opposite the *t*
12:41 the people put money into the *t*.
12:43 those who have given to the *t*;
Lk 21: 1 putting their gifts into the *t*,
Jn 8:20 words Jesus spoke in the *t*,
Acts 8:27 who had charge of all her *t*,

TREAT (6/6) TREATED

Gen 32:12 'I will surely *t* you well,
34:31 Should he *t* our sister like a
Num 10:29 and we will *t* you well;
11:15 'If You *t* me like this, please
Deut 21:14 you shall not *t* her brutally,
Zech 8:11 But now I will not *t* the

TREATED (12/12) TREAT

Gen 12:16 He *t* Abram well for her sake.
1 Sam 20:34 because his father had *t* him
2 Chr 30: 9 will be *t* with compassion
Ps 119:78 For they *t* me wrongfully with
Mt 22: 6 *t* them spitefully, and killed
Mk 9:12 things and be *t* with contempt?
12: 4 and sent him away shamefully *t*.
Lk 20:11 *t* him shamefully, and sent
23:11 *t* Him with contempt and mocked
Acts 27: 3 And Julius *t* Paul kindly and
1 Th 2: 2 before and were spitefully *t*
Heb 10:33 of those who were so *t*;

TREATISE (KJV) See ACCOUNT

TREATS (2/2)

Deut 27:16 Cursed is the one who *t* his
Job 39:16 She *t* her young harshly,

TREATY (8/5)

1 Ki 3: 1 Now Solomon made a *t* with
5:12 and the two of them made a *t*
15:19 Let there be a *t* between you
15:19 Come and break your *t* with
20:34 will send you away with this *t*.
20:34 So he made a *t* with him and
2 Chr 16: 3 Let there be a *t* between you
16: 3 break your *t* with Baasha king

TREE (202/172) TREES

Gen 1:11 and the fruit *t* that yields
1:12 and the *t* that yields fruit,
1:29 and every *t* whose fruit yields
2: 9 the LORD God made every *t*
2: 9 The *t* of life was also in the
2: 9 and the *t* of the knowledge of
2:16 Of every *t* of the garden you may
2:17 but of the *t* of the knowledge of
3: 1 You shall not eat of every *t* of
3: 3 but of the fruit of the *t* which
3: 6 when the woman saw that the *t*
3: 6 and a *t* desirable to make one
3:11 Have you eaten from the *t* of
3:12 she gave me of the *t*,
3:17 and have eaten from the *t* of
3:22 hand and take also of the *t* of
3:24 to guard the way to the *t* of
12: 6 as far as the terebinth *t* of
18: 4 and rest yourselves under the *t*.
18: 8 he stood by them under the *t*
21:33 Abraham planted a tamarisk *t*
35: 4 hid them under the terebinth *t*
35: 8 Bethel under the terebinth *t*.
40:19 from you and hang you on a *t*;
Ex 9:25 of the field and broke every *t*
10: 5 and they shall eat every *t*
15:25 and the LORD showed him a *t*.
Lev 27:30 land or of the fruit of the *t*,
Deut 12: 2 hills and under every green *t*.
16:21 not plant for yourself any *t*,
19: 5 with the ax to cut down the *t*,
20:19 for the *t* of the field is
21:22 death, and you hang him on a *t*,
21:23 not remain overnight on the *t*,
22: 6 in any *t* or on the ground,
Josh 8:29 the king of Ai he hanged on a *t*
8:29 take his corpse down from the *t*,
19:33 territory from the terebinth *t*
Judg 4: 5 she would sit under the palm *t*
4:11 his tent near the terebinth *t*
6:11 and sat under the terebinth *t*
6:19 to Him under the terebinth *t*
9: 6 king beside the terebinth *t* at
9: 8 And they said to the olive *t*,
9: 9 But the olive *t* said to them,
9:10 the trees said to the fig *t*,
9:11 But the fig *t* said to them,
9:37 from the Diviners' Terebinth *T*.
1 Sam 10: 3 and come to the terebinth *t* of
14: 2 of Gibeah under a pomegranate *t*
22: 6 in Gibeah under a tamarisk *t*
31:13 them under the tamarisk *t* at
2 Sam 18: 9 boughs of a great terebinth *t*,
18:10 hanging in a terebinth *t*!"
18:14 in the midst of the terebinth *t*.
1 Ki 4:25 under his vine and his fig *t*,
4:33 from the cedar *t* of Lebanon
14:23 hill and under every green *t*.
19: 4 and sat down under a broom *t*.
19: 5 lay and slept under a broom *t*,
2 Ki 3:19 and shall cut down every good *t*,
6: 5 But as one was cutting down a *t*,
16: 4 and under every green *t*.
17:10 hill and under every green *t*.
18:31 every one from his own fig *t*,
1 Chr 10:12 bones under the tamarisk *t* at
2 Chr 28: 4 hills, and under every green *t*.
Job 14: 7 "For there is hope for a *t*,
15:33 off his blossom like an olive *t*.
19:10 hope He has uprooted like a *t*.
24:20 should be broken like a *t*.
30: 4 And broom *t* roots for their
Ps 1: 3 He shall be like a *t* Planted
37:35 himself like a native green *t*.
52: 8 I am like a green olive *t* in
92:12 shall flourish like a palm *t*,
120: 4 With coals of the broom *t*!
Prov 3:18 She is a *t* of life to those
11:30 of the righteous is a *t* of
13:12 it is a *t* of life.
15: 4 A wholesome tongue is a *t* of
27:18 Whoever keeps the fig *t* will
Eccl 11: 3 And if a *t* falls to the south
11: 3 In the place where the *t*
12: 5 When the almond *t* blossoms,
Song 2: 3 Like an apple *t* among the trees
2:13 The fig *t* puts forth her green
7: 7 of yours is like a palm *t*,
7: 8 "I will go up to the palm *t*,
8: 5 awakened you under the apple *t*.
Isa 6:13 As a terebinth *t* or as an oak,
17: 6 Like the shaking of an olive *t*,
24:13 like the shaking of an olive *t*,
34: 4 as fruit falling from a fig *t*.
36:16 every one from his own fig *t*,
40:20 a contribution Chooses a *t*
41:19 the cedar and the acacia *t*,
41:19 The myrtle and the oil *t*;
41:19 set in the desert the cypress *t*
41:19 and the pine And the box *t*
44:23 and every *t* in it! For the
55:13 shall come up the cypress *t*,
55:13 shall come up the myrtle *t*;
56: 3 say, "Here I am, a dry *t*.
57: 5 with gods under every green *t*,
60:13 and the box *t* together,
65:22 For as the days of a *t*,
Jer 1:11 "I see a branch of an almond *t*.
2:20 hill and under every green *t*
2:27 Saying to a *t*, 'You are my
3: 6 and under every green *t*,
3:13 deities under every green *t*,
8:13 Nor figs on the fig *t*,
10: 3 For one cuts a *t* from the
10: 5 are upright, like a palm *t*,
11:16 your name, Green Olive *T*,
11:19 Let us destroy the *t* with its
17: 8 For he shall be like a *t*
Ezek 6:13 under every green *t*,
17: 5 And set it like a willow *t*.
17:24 have brought down the high *t*
17:24 high tree and exalted the low *t*,
17:24 dried up the green *t* and made
17:24 green tree and made the dry *t*
20:47 it shall devour every green *t*
20:47 green tree and every dry *t* in
31: 8 No *t* in the garden of God was
31:14 that no *t* which drinks water
41:18 a palm *t* between cherub and
41:19 of a man was toward a palm *t*
41:19 of a young lion toward a palm *t*
Dan 4:10 A *t* in the midst of the earth,
4:11 The *t* grew and became strong;
4:14 Chop down the *t* and cut off its
4:20 The *t* that you saw, which grew
4:23 Chop down the *t* and destroy it,
4:26 the stump and roots of the *t*,
Hos 9:10 the firstfruits on the fig *t*
14: 6 beauty shall be like an olive *t*,
14: 8 I am like a green cypress *t*;
Joel 1: 7 My vine, And ruined My fig *t*;
1:12 And the fig *t* has withered;
1:12 withered; The pomegranate *t*,
1:12 The palm *t* also, And the
1:12 tree also, And the apple *t*—
2:22 And the *t* bears its fruit;
2:22 The fig *t* and the vine yield
Mic 4: 4 his vine and under his fig *t*,
Hab 3:17 Though the fig *t* may not
Hag 2:19 As yet the vine, the fig *t*,
2:19 and the olive *t* have not
Zech 3:10 his vine and under his fig *t*.
Mt 3:10 Therefore every *t* which does
7:17 every good *t* bears good fruit,
7:17 but a bad *t* bears bad fruit.
7:18 A good *t* cannot bear bad fruit,
7:18 nor can a bad *t* bear good
7:19 Every *t* that does not bear good
12:33 Either make the *t* good and its
12:33 or else make the *t* bad and its
12:33 for a *t* is known by its fruit.
13:32 than the herbs and becomes a *t*,
21:19 And seeing a fig *t* by the road,
21:19 Immediately the fig *t*
21:20 How did the fig *t* wither away so
21:21 do what was done to the fig *t*,
24:32 this parable from the fig *t*:
Mk 11:13 And seeing from afar a fig *t*
11:20 they saw the fig *t* dried up

T

11:21 The fig *t* which You
13:28 this parable from the fig *t*:
Lk 3: 9 Therefore every *t* which does
6:43 For a good *t* does not bear bad
6:43 nor does a bad *t* bear good
6:44 For every *t* is known by its own
13: 6 A certain man had a fig *t*
13: 7 seeking fruit on this fig *t*
13:19 it grew and became a large *t*,
17: 6 you can say to this mulberry *t*,
19: 4 climbed up into a sycamore *t*
21:29 a parable: "Look at the fig *t*,
Jn 1:48 when you were under the fig *t*,
1:50 'I saw you under the fig *t*,'
Acts 5:30 you murdered by hanging on a *t*.
10:39 they killed by hanging on a *t*.
13:29 they took Him down from the *t*
Rom 11:17 and you, being a wild olive *t*,
11:17 root and fatness of the olive *t*,
11:24 you were cut out of the olive *t*
11:24 into a cultivated olive *t*,
11:24 grafted into their own olive *t*?
Gal 3:13 who hangs on a *t*"),
Jas 3:12 Can a fig *t*, my brethren,
1 Pe 2:24 sins in His own body on the *t*,
Rev 2: 7 I will give to eat from the *t*
6:13 as a fig *t* drops its late figs
7: 1 earth, on the sea, or on any *t*.
9: 4 or any green thing, or any *t*,
22: 2 was the *t* of life, which bore
22: 2 each *t* yielding its fruit
22: 2 The leaves of the *t* were for
22:14 may have the right to the *t* of

TREES (146/134) TREE

Gen 3: 2 We may eat the fruit of the *t* of
3: 8 of the LORD God among the *t*
13:18 and dwelt by the terebinth *t*
14:13 he dwelt by the terebinth *t* of
18: 1 to him by the terebinth *t* of
23:17 and all the *t* that were in the
30:37 of the almond and chestnut *t*,
Ex 10:15 land and all the fruit of the *t*
10:15 nothing green on the *t* or on
15:27 of water and seventy palm *t*;
Lev 19:23 and have planted all kinds of *t*
23:40 day the fruit of beautiful *t*,
23:40 trees, branches of palm *t*,
23:40 trees, the boughs of leafy *t*,
26: 4 and the *t* of the field shall
26:20 nor shall the *t* of the land
Num 33: 9 of water and seventy palm *t*;
Deut 6:11 vineyards and olive *t* which you
8: 8 of vines and fig *t* and
11:30 beside the terebinth *t* of
20:19 you shall not destroy its *t* by
20:20 Only the *t* which you know are
20:20 which you know are not *t* for
24:20 "When you beat your olive *t*,
28:40 You shall have olive *t*
28:42 shall consume all your *t* and
34: 3 of Jericho, the city of palm *t*,
Josh 10:26 them, and hanged them on five *t*;
10:26 and they were hanging on the *t*
10:27 they took them down from the *t*,
Judg 9: 8 The *t* once went forth to anoint
9: 9 And go to sway over *t*?'
9:10 Then the *t* said to the fig tree,
9:11 And go to sway over *t*?'
9:12 Then the *t* said to the vine,
9:13 and men, And go to sway over *t*?
9:14 Then all the *t* said to the
9:15 And the bramble said to the *t*,
9:48 and cut down a bough from the *t*,
2 Sam 5:11 to David, and cedar *t*,
5:23 them in front of the mulberry *t*.
5:24 in the tops of the mulberry *t*,
1 Ki 4:33 Also he spoke of *t*,
6:29 figures of cherubim, palm *t*,
6:32 figures of cherubim, palm *t*,
6:32 the cherubim and on the palm *t*.
6:35 Then he carved cherubim, palm *t*,
7:36 cherubim, lions, and palm *t*,
10:27 and he made cedar *t* as abundant
2 Ki 3:25 and cut down all the good *t*.
6: 4 to the Jordan, they cut down *t*.
19:23 And its choice cypress *t*;
1 Chr 14: 1 to David, and cedar *t*,
14:14 them in front of the mulberry *t*.
14:15 in the tops of the mulberry *t*,
16:33 Then the *t* of the woods shall
22: 4 and cedar *t* in abundance;
27:28 Gederite was over the olive *t*
27:28 olive trees and the sycamore *t*
2 Chr 3: 5 and he carved palm *t* and
9:27 and he made cedar *t* as abundant
28:15 at Jericho, the city of palm *t*.
Neh 8:15 branches, branches of oil *t*,
8:15 and branches of leafy *t*,
9:25 And fruit *t* in abundance.
10:35 of all fruit of all *t*,
10:37 the fruit from all kinds of *t*,
Job 40:21 He lies under the lotus *t*,
40:22 The lotus *t* cover him with
Ps 74: 5 lift up Axes among the thick *t*.
78:47 And their sycamore *t* with
96:12 Then all the *t* of the woods
104:16 The *t* of the LORD are full of
104:17 stork has her home in the fir *t*.
105:33 vines also, and their fig *t*,
105:33 And splintered the *t* of their
148: 9 Fruitful *t* and all cedars;
Eccl 2: 5 I planted all kinds of fruit *t*
2: 6 which to water the growing *t*
Song 2: 3 an apple tree among the *t* of
4:14 With all *t* of frankincense,
Isa 1:29 be ashamed of the terebinth *t*
7: 2 his people were moved as the *t*
10:19 Then the rest of the *t* of his
14: 8 Indeed the cypress *t* rejoice
37:24 And its choice cypress *t*;
44:14 it for himself among the *t* of
55:12 And all the *t* of the field
61: 3 That they may be called *t* of
Jer 3: 9 adultery with stones and *t*.
5:17 up your vines and your fig *t*;
6: 6 of hosts said: "Cut down *t*,
7:20 on the *t* of the field and on
17: 2 wooden images By the green *t*
Ezek 15: 2 branch which is among the *t* of
15: 6 wood of the vine among the *t*
17:24 And all the *t* of the field shall
20:28 high hills and all the thick *t*,
27: 5 made all your planks of fir *t*
31: 4 sent out rivulets to all the *t*
31: 5 was exalted above all the *t* of
31: 8 The fir *t* were not like its
31: 8 And the chestnut *t* were not
31: 9 So that all the *t* of Eden
31:14 So that no *t* by the waters may
31:15 and all the *t* of the field
31:16 and all the *t* of Eden,
31:18 To which of the *t* in Eden will
31:18 be brought down with the *t* of
34:27 Then the *t* of the field shall
36:30 multiply the fruit of your *t*
40:16 on each gatepost were palm *t*.
40:22 archways, and also its palm *t*,
40:26 and it had palm *t* on its
40:31 palm *t* were on its gateposts,
40:34 and palm *t* were on its
40:37 palm *t* were on its gateposts
41:18 made with cherubim and palm *t*,
41:20 cherubim and palm *t* were
41:25 Cherubim and palm *t* were carved
41:26 window frames and palm *t* on
47: 7 were very many *t* on one side
47:12 will grow all kinds of *t* used
Hos 2:12 destroy her vines and her fig *t*,
Joel 1:12 All the *t* of the field are
1:19 a flame has burned all the *t*
Am 4: 9 Your vineyards, Your fig *t*,
4: 9 fig trees, And your olive *t*,
Nah 3:12 your strongholds are fig *t*
Zech 1: 8 it stood among the myrtle *t* in
1:10 who stood among the myrtle *t*
1:11 who stood among the myrtle *t*,
4: 3 Two olive *t* are by it, one at
4:11 "What are these two olive *t*—
11: 2 Because the mighty *t* are
Mt 3:10 ax is laid to the root of the *t*.
21: 8 cut down branches from the *t*
Mk 8:24 up and said, "I see men like *t*,
11: 8 down leafy branches from the *t*
Lk 3: 9 ax is laid to the root of the *t*.
21:29 at the fig tree, and all the *t*.
Jn 12:13 took branches of palm *t* and went
Jude 12 late autumn *t* without fruit,
Rev 7: 3 or the *t* till we have sealed
8: 7 And a third of the *t* were
11: 4 These are the two olive *t* and

TREMBLE (31/31) TREMBLED, TREMBLES, TREMBLING

Deut 2:25 and shall *t* and be in anguish
20: 3 and do not *t* or be terrified
1 Chr 16:30 *T* before Him, all the earth
Ezra 10: 3 of my master and of those who *t*
Esth 5: 9 and that he did not stand or *t*
Job 9: 6 its place, And its pillars *t*;
26: 5 'The dead *t*, Those under the
26:11 The pillars of heaven *t*,
Ps 60: 2 You have made the earth *t*;
96: 9 *T* before Him, all the earth.
99: 1 Let the peoples *t*! He dwells
114: 7 *T*, O earth, at the presence
Eccl 12: 3 when the keepers of the house *t*,
Isa 14:16 the man who made the earth *t*,
32:11 *T*, you women who are at ease;
64: 2 That the nations may *t* at
66: 5 You who *t* at His word:
Jer 5:22 Will you not *t* at My presence,
10:10 At His wrath the earth will *t*,
33: 9 they shall fear and *t* for all
51:29 And the land will *t* and sorrow;
Ezek 7:27 of the common people will *t*.
26:16 *t* every moment, and be
26:18 Now the coastlands *t* on the day
32:10 and they shall *t* every moment,
Dan 6:26 of my kingdom men must *t* and
10:10 which made me *t* on my knees and
Joel 2: 1 the inhabitants of the land *t*;
2:10 before them, The heavens *t*;
Am 8: 8 Shall the land not *t* for this,
Jas 2:19 demons believe—and *t*!

TREMBLED (23/22) TREMBLE

Gen 27:33 Then Isaac *t* exceedingly,
Ex 19:16 people who were in the camp *t*.
20:18 they *t* and stood afar off.
Judg 5: 4 The earth *t* and the heavens
1 Sam 4:13 for his heart *t* for the ark of
14:15 garrison and the raiders also *t*;
16: 4 And the elders of the town *t* at
28: 5 and his heart *t* greatly.
2 Sam 22: 8 "Then the earth shook and *t*;
Ezra 9: 4 Then everyone who *t* at the words
Ps 18: 7 Then the earth shook and *t*;
77:16 were afraid; The depths also *t*.
77:18 The earth *t* and shook.
Isa 5:25 stricken them, And the hills *t*.
Jer 4:24 mountains, and indeed they *t*,
8:16 The whole land *t* at the sound
Dan 5:19 and languages *t* and feared
Hab 3: 7 of the land of Midian *t*.
3:10 The mountains saw You and *t*;
3:16 When I heard, my body *t*;
3:16 And I *t* in myself, That I
Mk 16: 8 for they *t* and were amazed.
Acts 7:32 And Moses *t* and dared not

TREMBLES (6/6) TREMBLE

Job 37: 1 "At this also my heart *t*,
Ps 97: 4 The earth sees and *t*.
104:32 looks on the earth, and it *t*;
119:120 My flesh *t* for fear of You,
Isa 66: 2 And who *t* at My word.
Jer 50:46 taking of Babylon The earth *t*,

TREMBLING (28/27) TREMBLE

Ex 15:15 *T* will take hold of them;
Deut 28:65 LORD will give you a *t* heart,
1 Sam 13: 7 all the people followed him *t*.
14:15 And there was *t* in the camp,
14:15 so that it was a very great *t*.
Ezra 10: 9 *t* because of this matter and
Job 4:14 Fear came upon me, and *t*,
21: 6 And *t* takes hold of my flesh.
Ps 2:11 with fear, And rejoice with *t*.
55: 5 Fearfulness and *t* have come
Isa 51:17 drunk the dregs of the cup of *t*,
51:22 out of your hand The cup of *t*,
Jer 30: 5 'We have heard a voice of *t*,
Ezek 12:18 and drink your water with *t* and
26:16 will clothe themselves with *t*;
Dan 10:11 this word to me, I stood *t*.
Hos 11:10 Then His sons shall come *t*
11:11 They shall come *t* like a bird
13: 1 When Ephraim spoke, *t*,
Mk 5:33 But the woman, fearing and *t*,
Lk 8:47 she was not hidden, she came *t*;
Acts 9: 6 *t* and astonished, said, "Lord,
16:29 and fell down *t* before Paul and
1 Cor 2: 3 in fear, and in much *t*.
2 Cor 7:15 how with fear and *t* you
Eph 6: 5 to the flesh, with fear and *t*,
Phil 2:12 own salvation with fear and *t*;
Heb 12:21 am exceedingly afraid and *t*.

TRENCH (3/3)

1 Ki 18:32 and he made a *t* around the
18:35 and he also filled the *t* with
18:38 up the water that was in the *t*.

TRESPASS (57/51) TRESPASSED, TRESPASSES

Gen 31:36 said to Laban: "What is my *t*?
50:17 please forgive the *t* of your
50:17 forgive the *t* of the servants
Ex 22: 9 "For any kind of *t*,
Lev 5: 6 and he shall bring his *t*
5: 7 for his *t* which he has
5:15 "If a person commits a *t*,
5:15 bring to the LORD as his *t*
5:15 as a *t* offering.
5:16 for him with the ram of the *t*
5:18 valuation, as a *t* offering.
5:19 'It is a *t* offering;
6: 2 a person sins and commits a *t*
6: 5 on the day of his *t* offering.
6: 6 And he shall bring his *t*
6: 6 as a *t* offering, to the priest.
6:17 like the sin offering and the *t*
7: 1 this is the law of the *t*
7: 2 offering they shall kill the *t*
7: 5 It is a *t* offering.
7: 7 The *t* offering is like the sin
7:37 offering, the *t* offering,
14:12 male lamb and offer it as a *t*
14:13 so is the *t* offering.
14:14 some of the blood of the *t*
14:17 on the blood of the *t* offering.
14:21 take one male lamb as a *t*
14:24 shall take the lamb of the *t*
14:25 he shall kill the lamb of the *t*
14:25 some of the blood of the *t*
14:28 the place of the blood of the *t*
19:21 And he shall bring his *t*
19:21 a ram as a *t* offering.
19:22 for him with the ram of the *t*
22:16 them to bear the guilt of *t*
Num 5: 7 make restitution for his *t* in
6:12 lamb in its first year as a *t*
18: 9 every sin offering and every *t*
31:16 to *t* against the LORD in the
Josh 7: 1 of Israel committed a *t*
22:20 the son of Zerah commit a *t* in
1 Sam 6: 3 return it to Him with a *t*
6: 4 What is the *t* offering which we

6: 8 are returning to Him as a *t*
6:17 Philistines returned as a *t*
25:28 Please forgive the *t* of your
2 Ki 12:16 The money from the *t* offerings
2 Chr 19:10 lest they *t* against the LORD
24:18 Jerusalem because of their *t*.
33:19 entreaty, and all his sin and *t*,
Ezra 9: 2 has been foremost in this *t*.
10:19 a ram of the flock as their *t*
Ezek 40:39 and the *t* offering.
42:13 and the *t* offering—for the
44:29 and the *t* offering;
46:20 the priests shall boil the *t*
Gal 6: 1 if a man is overtaken in any *t*,

TRESPASSED (7/7) TRESPASS

Lev 5:19 he has certainly *t* against the
Deut 32:51 because you *t* against Me among
2 Chr 26:18 for you have *t*! You shall
29: 6 For our fathers have *t* and done
30: 7 who *t* against the LORD God of
33:23 but Amon *t* more and more.
Ezra 10: 2 'We have *t* against our God,

TRESPASSES (14/12) TRESPASS

Lev 6: 7 he may have done in which he *t*.
Ps 68:21 one who still goes on in His *t*.
Mt 6:14 if you forgive men their *t*,
6:15 you do not forgive men their *t*,
6:15 will your Father forgive your *t*.
18:35 not forgive his brother his *t*.
Mk 11:25 may also forgive you your *t*.
11:26 Father in heaven forgive your *t*.
2 Cor 5:19 not imputing their *t* to them,
Eph 2: 1 who were dead in *t* and sins,
2: 5 even when we were dead in *t*,
Col 2:13 being dead in your *t* and the
2:13 Him, having forgiven you all *t*,
Jas 5:16 Confess your *t* to one another,

TRESSES (1/1)

Song 7: 5 is held captive by your *t*.

TRIAL (7/7) TRIALS

Ps 95: 8 As in the day of *t* in the
2 Cor 8: 2 that in a great *t* of affliction
Gal 4:14 And my *t* which was in my flesh
Heb 3: 8 In the day of *t* in the
11:36 Still others had *t* of mockings
1 Pe 4:12 strange concerning the fiery *t*
Rev 3:10 keep you from the hour of *t*

TRIALS (7/7) TRIAL

Deut 4:34 midst of another nation, by *t*,
7:19 the great *t* which your eyes saw,
29: 3 the great *t* which your eyes have
Lk 22:28 have continued with Me in My *t*.
Acts 20:19 with many tears and *t* which
Jas 1: 2 when you fall into various *t*,
1 Pe 1: 6 have been grieved by various *t*,

TRIBAL (2/2)

Ezek 45: 7 side by side with one of the *t*
48:21 adjacent to the *t* portions;

TRIBE (236/200) TRIBES

Ex 31: 2 of the *t* of Judah.
31: 6 of the *t* of Dan; and I have put
35:30 of the *t* of Judah;
35:34 of the *t* of Dan.
38:22 of the *t* of Judah, made all
38:23 of the *t* of Dan, an engraver
Lev 24:11 of the *t* of Dan.)
Num 1: 4 shall be a man from every *t*,
1:21 numbered of the *t* of Reuben
1:23 numbered of the *t* of Simeon
1:25 numbered of the *t* of Gad
1:27 numbered of the *t* of Judah
1:29 numbered of the *t* of Issachar
1:31 numbered of the *t* of Zebulun
1:33 numbered of the *t* of Ephraim
1:35 numbered of the *t* of Manasseh
1:37 numbered of the *t* of Benjamin
1:39 numbered of the *t* of Dan
1:41 numbered of the *t* of Asher
1:43 numbered of the *t* of Naphtali
1:47 among them by their fathers' *t*;
1:49 Only the *t* of Levi you shall not
2: 5 next to him shall be the *t*
2: 7 Then comes the *t* of Zebulun,
2:12 next to him shall be the *t*
2:14 'Then comes the *t* of Gad,
2:20 Next to him comes the *t* of
2:22 Then comes the *t* of Benjamin,
2:27 next to him shall be the *t*
2:29 Then comes the *t* of Naphtali,
3: 6 'Bring the *t* of Levi near,
4:18 Do not cut off the *t* of the
7:12 from the *t* of Judah.
10:15 Over the army of the *t* of the
10:16 And over the army of the *t* of
10:19 Over the army of the *t* of the
10:20 And over the army of the *t* of
10:23 Over the army of the *t* of the
10:24 And over the army of the *t* of
10:26 Over the army of the *t* of the
10:27 And over the army of the *t* of
13: 2 from each *t* of their fathers
13: 4 from the *t* of Reuben, Shammua
13: 5 from the *t* of Simeon, Shaphat
13: 6 from the *t* of Judah, Caleb the
13: 7 from the *t* of Issachar, Igal the
13: 8 from the *t* of Ephraim, Hoshea
13: 9 from the *t* of Benjamin, Palti
13:10 from the *t* of Zebulun, Gaddiel
13:11 from the *t* of Joseph, that is,
13:11 from the *t* of Manasseh, Gaddi
13:12 from the *t* of Dan, Ammiel the
13:13 from the *t* of Asher, Sethur the
13:14 from the *t* of Naphtali, Nahbi
13:15 from the *t* of Gad, Geuel the son
18: 2 you your brethren of the *t* of
18: 2 the *t* of your father,
26:54 To a large *t* you shall give a
26:54 and to a small *t* you shall
31: 4 A thousand from each *t* of all
31: 5 one thousand from each *t*,
31: 6 war, one thousand from each *t*;
32:33 and to half the *t* of Manasseh
34:14 For the *t* of the children of
34:14 and the *t* of the children of
34:18 take one leader of every *t* to
34:19 from the *t* of Judah, Caleb the
34:20 from the *t* of the children of
34:21 from the *t* of Benjamin, Elidad
34:22 a leader from the *t* of the
34:23 a leader from the *t* of the
34:24 and a leader from the *t* of the
34:25 a leader from the *t* of the
34:26 a leader from the *t* of the
34:27 a leader from the *t* of the
34:28 and a leader from the *t* of the
35: 8 from the larger *t* you shall
36: 3 to the inheritance of the *t*
36: 4 to the inheritance of the *t*
36: 4 from the inheritance of the *t*
36: 5 What the *t* of the sons of Joseph
36: 6 the family of their father's *t*.
36: 7 shall not change hands from *t*
36: 7 change hands from tribe to *t*,
36: 7 keep the inheritance of the *t*
36: 8 an inheritance in any *t* of the
36: 8 of the family of her father's *t*,
36: 9 shall change hands from one *t*
36: 9 but every *t* of the children of
36:12 inheritance remained in the *t*
Deut 1:23 your men, one man from each *t*.
3:13 I gave to half the *t* of
10: 8 time the LORD separated the *t*
18: 1 all the *t* of Levi—shall have no
29: 8 and to half the *t* of Manasseh.
29:18 you man or woman or family or *t*,
Josh 1:12 and half the *t* of Manasseh
3:12 of Israel, one man from every *t*.
4: 2 people, one man from every *t*,
4: 4 of Israel, one man from every *t*;
4:12 and half the *t* of Manasseh
7: 1 of the *t* of Judah, took of the
7:14 And it shall be that the *t*
7:16 and the *t* of Judah was taken.
7:18 of the *t* of Judah, was taken.
12: 6 and half the *t* of Manasseh.
13: 7 the nine tribes and half the *t*
13: 8 With the other half *t* the
13:14 Only to the *t* of Levi he had
13:15 And Moses had given to the *t* of
13:24 an inheritance to the *t* of
13:29 an inheritance to half the *t*
13:29 it was for half the *t* of the
13:33 But to the *t* of Levi Moses had
15: 1 So this was the lot of the *t* of
15:20 was the inheritance of the *t*
15:21 cities at the limits of the *t*
16: 8 was the inheritance of the *t*
17: 1 There was also a lot for the *t*
18: 4 among you three men for each *t*,
18: 7 and half the *t* of Manasseh have
18:11 Now the lot of the *t* of the
18:21 Now the cities of the *t* of the
19: 1 for the *t* of the children of
19: 8 was the inheritance of the *t*
19:23 was the inheritance of the *t*
19:24 fifth lot came out for the *t*
19:31 was the inheritance of the *t*
19:39 was the inheritance of the *t*
19:40 seventh lot came out for the *t*
19:48 is the inheritance of the *t*
20: 8 from the *t* of Reuben, Ramoth in
20: 8 from the *t* of Gad, and Golan in
20: 8 from the *t* of Manasseh.
21: 4 cities by lot from the *t* of
21: 4 from the *t* of Simeon, and from
21: 4 and from the *t* of Benjamin.
21: 5 lot from the families of the *t*
21: 5 from the *t* of Dan, and from the
21: 6 lot from the families of the *t*
21: 6 from the *t* of Asher, from the
21: 6 from the *t* of Naphtali,
21: 7 had twelve cities from the *t*
21: 7 from the *t* of Gad, and from the
21: 7 and from the *t* of Zebulun.
21: 9 So they gave from the *t* of the
21: 9 of Judah and from the *t* of the
21:17 and from the *t* of Benjamin,
21:20 cities of their lot from the *t*
21:23 and from the *t* of Dan, Eltekeh
21:28 and from the *t* of Issachar,
21:30 and from the *t* of Asher, Mishal
21:32 and from the *t* of Naphtali,
21:34 from the *t* of Zebulun, Jokneam
21:36 and from the *t* of Reuben, Bezer
21:38 and from the *t* of Gad, Ramoth in
22: 1 and half the *t* of Manasseh,
22: 7 Now to half the *t* of Manasseh
22: 9 and half the *t* of Manasseh
22:10 and half the *t* of Manasseh
22:11 and half the *t* of Manasseh have
22:13 and to half the *t* of Manasseh,
22:14 the chief house of every *t* of
22:15 and to half the *t* of Manasseh,
22:21 and half the *t* of Manasseh
Judg 18: 1 And in those days the *t* of the
18:19 or that you be a priest to a *t*
18:30 his sons were priests to the *t*
20:12 sent men through all the *t* of
21: 3 today there should be one *t*
21: 6 One *t* is cut off from Israel
21:17 that a *t* may not be destroyed
21:24 every man to his *t* and family;
1 Sam 9:21 of all the families of the *t*
10:20 the *t* of Benjamin was chosen.
10:21 When he had caused the *t* of
2 Sam 15: 2 is from such and such a *t* of
1 Ki 7:14 the son of a widow from the *t*
8:16 have chosen no city from any *t*
11:13 I will give one *t* to your son
11:32 (but he shall have one *t* for the
11:36 to his son I will give one *t*,
12:20 but the *t* of Judah only.
12:21 the house of Judah with the *t*
2 Ki 17:18 there was none left but the *t*
1 Chr 5:18 and half the *t* of Manasseh had
6:60 And from the *t* of Benjamin: Geba
6:61 rest of the family of the *t* of
6:61 lot ten cities from half the *t*
6:62 thirteen cities from the *t* of
6:62 from the *t* of Asher, from the
6:62 from the *t* of Naphtali,
6:62 and from the *t* of Manasseh in
6:63 gave twelve cities from the *t*
6:63 from the *t* of Gad, and from the
6:63 and from the *t* of Zebulun.
6:65 they gave by lot from the *t* of
6:65 from the *t* of the children of
6:65 and from the *t* of the children
6:66 as their territory from the *t*
6:72 And from the *t* of Issachar:
6:74 And from the *t* of Asher: Mashal
6:76 And from the *t* of Naphtali:
6:77 From the *t* of Zebulun the rest
6:78 they were given from the *t*
6:80 And from the *t* of Gad: Ramoth in
23:14 of God were reckoned to the *t*
2 Chr 6: 5 have chosen no city from any *t*
Ps 74: 2 The *t* of Your inheritance,
78:67 And did not choose the *t* of
78:68 But chose the *t* of Judah,
Jer 10:16 And Israel is the *t* of His
51:19 And Israel is the *t* of His
Ezek 47:23 it shall be that in whatever *t*
Lk 2:36 of the *t* of Asher. She was of a
Acts 13:21 a man of the *t* of Benjamin,
Rom 11: 1 of the *t* of Benjamin.
Phil 3: 5 of the *t* of Benjamin, a Hebrew
Heb 7:13 are spoken belongs to another *t*,
7:14 of which *t* Moses spoke nothing
Rev 5: 5 the Lion of the *t* of Judah,
5: 9 by Your blood Out of every *t*
7: 5 of the *t* of Judah twelve
7: 5 of the *t* of Reuben twelve
7: 5 of the *t* of Gad twelve
7: 6 of the *t* of Asher twelve
7: 6 of the *t* of Naphtali twelve
7: 6 of the *t* of Manasseh twelve
7: 7 of the *t* of Simeon twelve
7: 7 of the *t* of Levi twelve
7: 7 of the *t* of Issachar twelve
7: 8 of the *t* of Zebulun twelve
7: 8 of the *t* of Joseph twelve
7: 8 of the *t* of Benjamin twelve
13: 7 was given him over every *t*,
14: 6 on the earth—to every nation, *t*,

TRIBES (109/107) TRIBE

Gen 49:16 his people As one of the *t* of
49:28 All these are the twelve *t* of
Ex 24: 4 according to the twelve *t* of
28:21 be according to the twelve *t*.
39:14 name according to the twelve *t*.
Num 1:16 leaders of their fathers' *t*,
7: 2 who were the leaders of the *t*
24: 2 encamped according to their *t*;
26:55 to the names of the *t* of their
30: 1 spoke to the heads of the *t*
31: 4 from each tribe of all the *t*
32:28 to the chief fathers of the *t*
33:54 inherit according to the *t* of
34:13 to give to the nine *t* and to
34:15 The two *t* and the half-tribe
36: 3 of the sons of the other *t* of
Deut 1:13 men from among your *t*,
1:15 "So I took the heads of your *t*,
1:15 tens, and officers for your *t*.
5:23 all the heads of your *t* and
12: 5 God chooses, out of all your *t*,
12:14 LORD chooses, in one of your *t*,
16:18 gives you, according to your *t*,
18: 5 chosen him out of all your *t*
29:10 your leaders and your *t* and

29:21 separate him from all the *t* of
31:28 to me all the elders of your *t*,
33: 5 All the *t* of Israel together.
Josh 3:12 twelve men from the *t* of
4: 5 to the number of the *t* of the
4: 8 to the number of the *t* of the
7:14 be brought according to your *t*.
7:16 and brought Israel by their *t*,
11:23 to their divisions by their *t*.
12: 7 which Joshua gave to the *t* of
13: 7 as an inheritance to the nine *t*
14: 1 heads of the fathers of the *t*
14: 2 for the nine *t* and the
14: 3 the inheritance of the two *t*
14: 4 children of Joseph were two *t*:
18: 2 the children of Israel seven *t*
19:51 heads of the fathers of the *t*
21: 1 the fathers' houses of the *t*
21:16 nine cities from those two *t*;
23: 4 to be an inheritance for your *t*,
24: 1 Then Joshua gathered all the *t*
Judg 18: 1 their inheritance among the *t*
20: 2 all the *t* of Israel, presented
20:10 hundred throughout all the *t*
20:12 Then the *t* of Israel sent men
21: 5 is there among all the *t*
21: 8 one is there from the *t*
21:15 LORD had made a void in the *t*
1 Sam 2:28 choose him out of all the *t* of
9:21 of the smallest of the *t* of
10:19 before the LORD by your *t* and
10:20 Samuel had caused all the *t* of
15:17 were you not head of the *t* of
2 Sam 5: 1 Then all the *t* of Israel came to
7: 7 a word to anyone from the *t* of
15:10 spies throughout all the *t* of
19: 9 a dispute throughout all the *t*
20:14 And he went through all the *t*
24: 2 Now go throughout all the *t* of
1 Ki 8: 1 and all the heads of the *t*,
11:31 of Solomon and will give ten *t*
11:32 I have chosen out of all the *t*
11:35 hand and give it to you—ten *t*.
14:21 had chosen out of all the *t* of
18:31 to the number of the *t* of the
2 Ki 21: 7 I have chosen out of all the *t*
1 Chr 27:16 over the *t* of Israel:
27:22 were the leaders of the *t* of
28: 1 the officers of the *t* and the
29: 6 leaders of the *t* of Israel,
2 Chr 5: 2 and all the heads of the *t*,
11:16 those from all the *t* of Israel,
12:13 had chosen out of all the *t* of
33: 7 I have chosen out of all the *t*
Ezra 6:17 to the number of the *t* of
Ps 78:55 And made the *t* of Israel dwell
105:37 was none feeble among His *t*.
122: 4 Where the *t* go up, The tribes
122: 4 The *t* of the LORD, To the
Isa 19:13 who are the mainstay of its *t*.
49: 6 My Servant To raise up the *t*
63:17 The *t* of Your inheritance.
Ezek 37:19 and the *t* of Israel,
45: 8 of Israel, according to their *t*.
47:13 inheritance among the twelve *t*
47:21 yourselves according to the *t*
47:22 with you among the *t* of Israel.
48: 1 these are the names of the *t*:
48:19 from all the *t* of Israel,
48:23 "As for the rest of the *t*,
48:29 as an inheritance among the *t*
48:31 shall be named after the *t*
Hos 5: 9 Among the *t* of Israel I make
Zech 9: 1 the eyes of men And all the *t*
Mt 19:28 judging the twelve *t* of Israel.
24:30 and then all the *t* of the earth
Lk 22:30 on thrones judging the twelve *t*
Acts 26: 7 "To this promise our twelve *t*,
Jas 1: 1 To the twelve *t* which are
Rev 1: 7 And all the *t* of the earth will
7: 4 thousand of all the *t* of the
7: 9 could number, of all nations, *t*,
11: 9 Then those from the peoples, *t*,
21:12 the names of the twelve *t* of

TRIBULATION (22/22) TRIBULATIONS

1 Sam 26:24 let Him deliver me out of all *t*.
Mt 13:21 For when *t* or persecution
24: 9 they will deliver you up to *t*
24:21 then there will be great *t*,
24:29 Immediately after the *t* of
Mk 4:17 when *t* or persecution arises
13:19 in those days there will be *t*,
13:24 in those days, after that *t*,
Jn 16:33 In the world you will have *t*;
Rom 2: 9 *t* and anguish, on every soul of
5: 3 knowing that *t* produces
8:35 the love of Christ? Shall *t*,
12:12 rejoicing in hope, patient in *t*,
2 Cor 1: 4 who comforts us in all our *t*,
7: 4 exceedingly joyful in all our *t*.
1 Th 3: 4 with you that we would suffer *t*,
2 Th 1: 6 thing with God to repay with *t*
Rev 1: 9 brother and companion in the *t*
2: 9 "I know your works, *t*,
2:10 and you will have *t* ten days.
2:22 adultery with her into great *t*,
7:14 who come out of the great *t*,

TRIBULATIONS (8/8) TRIBULATION

1 Sam 10:19 all your adversities and your *t*;
Acts 14:22 We must through many *t* enter the
20:23 saying that chains and *t* await
Rom 5: 3 but we also glory in *t*,
2 Cor 6: 4 of God: in much patience, in *t*,
Eph 3:13 you do not lose heart at my *t*
2 Th 1: 4 in all your persecutions and *t*
Heb 10:33 both by reproaches and *t*,

TRIBUTARIES, TRIBUTARY (KJV)

See SLAVE, TRIBUTE

TRIBUTE (31/30)

Num 31:28 And levy a *t* for the LORD on
31:37 and the LORD's *t* of the sheep
31:38 of which the LORD's *t* was
31:39 of which the LORD's *t* was
31:40 of which the LORD's *t* was
31:41 So Moses gave the *t* which was
Deut 16:10 the LORD your God with the *t*
20:11 in it shall be placed under *t*
Judg 1:28 they put the Canaanites under *t*,
1:30 and were put under *t*.
1:33 Beth Anath were put under *t* to
1:35 greater, they were put under *t*.
3:15 the children of Israel sent *t*
3:17 So he brought the *t* to Eglon
3:18 had finished presenting the *t*,
3:18 people who had carried the *t*.
2 Sam 8: 2 servants, and brought *t*.
8: 6 servants, and brought *t*.
1 Ki 4:21 They brought *t* and served
2 Ki 17: 3 and paid him *t* money.
17: 4 and brought no *t* to the king of
23:33 and he imposed on the land a *t*
1 Chr 18: 2 servants, and brought *t*.
18: 6 servants, and brought *t*.
2 Chr 17:11 presents and silver as *t*;
26: 8 Also the Ammonites brought *t* to
36: 3 and he imposed on the land a *t*
Ezra 4:13 they will not pay tax, *t*,
4:20 beyond the River; and tax, *t*,
7:24 not be lawful to impose tax, *t*,
Esth 10: 1 And King Ahasuerus imposed *t* on

TRICKERY (4/4)

Isa 25:11 Together with the *t* of
Mt 26: 4 and plotted to take Jesus by *t*
Mk 14: 1 how they might take Him by *t*
Eph 4:14 by the *t* of men, in the cunning

TRICKLETH (KJV) See FLOW

TRICKLING (1/1)

Job 28:11 He dams up the streams from *t*;

TRIED (18/18) TRY

1 Sam 17:39 his sword to his armor and *t*
Ezra 4: 4 Then the people of the land *t* to
Esth 8: 7 on the gallows because he *t*
Job 34:36 that Job were *t* to the utmost,
Ps 12: 6 Like silver *t* in a furnace of
17: 3 You have *t* me and have found
95: 9 They *t* Me, though they saw My
Isa 28:16 A *t* stone, a precious
Mt 3:14 And John *t* to prevent Him,
Lk 4:42 and *t* to keep Him from leaving
Acts 7:26 and *t* to reconcile them,
9:26 he *t* to join the disciples;
16: 7 they *t* to go into Bithynia,
24: 6 He even *t* to profane the temple,
26:21 seized me in the temple and *t*
Gal 1:13 of God beyond measure and *t*
1:23 the faith which he once *t* to
Heb 3: 9 *t* Me, And saw My works

TRIFLES (2/2)

Prov 18: 8 a talebearer are like tasty *t*,
26:22 like tasty *t*, And they go down

TRIM (1/1)

Deut 21:12 she shall shave her head and *t*

TRIMMED (4/4)

2 Sam 19:24 nor *t* his mustache, nor washed
1 Ki 7: 9 *t* with saws, inside and out,
Ezek 44:20 shall keep their hair well *t*.
Mt 25: 7 all those virgins arose and *t*

TRIMMERS (5/5)

1 Ki 7:50 the basins, the *t*,
2 Ki 12:13 the LORD basins of silver, *t*,
25:14 the pots, the shovels, the *t*,
2 Chr 4:22 the *t*, the bowls, the ladles,
Jer 52:18 the pots, the shovels, the *t*,

TRIUMPH (12/12) TRIUMPHED, TRIUMPHING, TRIUMPHS

Gen 49:19 But he shall *t* at last.
2 Sam 1:20 of the uncircumcised *t*.
1 Chr 16:35 To *t* in Your praise."
Ps 25: 2 Let not my enemies *t* over me.
41:11 Because my enemy does not *t*
47: 1 to God with the voice of *t*!
60: 8 shout in *t* because of Me."
92: 4 I will *t* in the works of Your
94: 3 How long will the wicked *t*?
106:47 To *t* in Your praise.
108: 9 Over Philistia I will *t*."
2 Cor 2:14 to God who always leads us in *t*

TRIUMPHED (2/2) TRIUMPH

Ex 15: 1 For He has *t* gloriously!
15:21 LORD, For He has *t* gloriously!

TRIUMPHING (2/2) TRIUMPH

Job 20: 5 That the *t* of the wicked is
Col 2:15 *t* over them in it.

TRIUMPHS (1/1) TRIUMPH

Jas 2:13 Mercy *t* over judgment.

TRIVIAL (2/2)

1 Ki 16:31 as though it had been a *t* thing
Ezek 8:17 Is it a *t* thing to the house of

TROAS (6/6)

Acts 16: 8 by Mysia, they came down to *T*.
16:11 Therefore, sailing from *T*,
20: 5 going ahead, waited for us at *T*.
20: 6 in five days joined them at *T*,
2 Cor 2:12 when I came to *T* to preach
2 Tim 4:13 that I left with Carpus at *T*

TROD (3/3)

Judg 9:27 from their vineyards and *t*
2 Sam 22:43 I *t* them like dirt in the
Job 22:15 Which wicked men have *t*,

TRODDEN (8/7)

Josh 14: 9 the land where your foot has *t*
Job 28: 8 The proud lions have not *t* it,
Isa 14:19 Like a corpse *t* underfoot.
63: 3 I have *t* the winepress alone,
63: 3 For I have *t* them in My anger,
63: 6 I have *t* down the peoples in My
63:18 Our adversaries have *t* down
Jer 12:10 They have *t* My portion

TRODE (KJV) See TRAMPLED, TROD

TROGYLLIUM (1/1)

Acts 20:15 at Samos and stayed at *T*.

TROOP (12/11)

Gen 30:11 Then Leah said, "A *t* comes!"
49:19 a *t* shall tramp upon him,
1 Sam 30: 8 saying, "Shall I pursue this *t*?
30:15 you take me down to this *t*?
30:15 I will take you down to this *t*.
30:23 delivered into our hand the *t*
2 Sam 22:30 by You I can run against a *t*;
23:11 had gathered together into a *t*
23:13 And the *t* of Philistines
1 Chr 12:18 and made them captains of the *t*.
Ps 18:29 by You I can run against a *t*,
Jer 18:22 When You bring a *t* suddenly

TROOPS (26/24)

Judg 4: 6 Go and deploy *t* at Mount Tabor;
2 Sam 3:23 When Joab and all the *t* that
4: 2 men who were captains of *t*.
2 Ki 8:21 and the *t* fled to their tents.
1 Chr 7: 4 were thirty-six thousand *t*
2 Chr 14:10 and they set the *t* in battle
17: 2 And he placed *t* in all the
25: 9 which I have given to the *t* of
25:10 So Amaziah discharged the *t* that
Job 19:12 His *t* come together And build
Prov 30:31 And a king whose *t* are with
Jer 5: 7 And assembled themselves by *t*
Ezek 12:14 him to help him, and all his *t*;
17:21 his fugitives with all his *t*
38: 6 "Gomer and all its *t*;
38: 6 the far north and all its *t*—
38: 9 you and all your *t* and many
38:22 will rain down on him, on his *t*,
39: 4 you and all your *t* and the
Dan 11:15 Even his choice *t* shall have
Mic 5: 1 Now gather yourself in *t*,
5: 1 in troops, O daughter of *t*;
Hab 3:16 He will invade them with his *t*.
Jn 18: 3 received a detachment of *t*,
18:12 Then the detachment of *t* and
Acts 23:27 Coming with the *t* I rescued

TROPHIMUS (3/3)

Acts 20: 4 and Tychicus and *T* of Asia.
21:29 they had previously seen *T* the
2 Tim 4:20 but *T* I have left in Miletus

TROUBLE (143/143) TROUBLED, TROUBLER, TROUBLES, TROUBLESOME, TROUBLING

Ex 5:19 saw that they were in ***t***
5:22 why have You brought ***t*** on this
Josh 6:18 of Israel a curse, and ***t*** it.
7:25 The LORD will ***t*** you this
Judg 11:35 You are among those who ***t*** me!
1 Ki 11:25 days of Solomon (besides the ***t***
20: 7 and see how this man seeks ***t***,
2 Ki 14:10 why should you meddle with ***t***
19: 3 'This day is a day of ***t***,
1 Chr 22:14 Indeed I have taken much ***t*** to
2 Chr 15: 4 but when in their ***t*** they turned
25:19 why should you meddle with ***t***,
29: 8 and He has given them up to ***t***,
32:18 to frighten them and ***t*** them,
Neh 9:27 And in the time of their ***t***,
9:32 Do not let all the ***t*** seem
Job 3:26 no rest, for ***t*** comes."
4: 8 who plow iniquity And sow ***t***
5: 6 Nor does ***t*** spring from the
5: 7 Yet man is born to ***t***,
14: 1 Is of few days and full of ***t***.
15:24 ***T*** and anguish make him afraid
15:35 They conceive ***t*** and bring forth
27: 9 Will God hear his cry When ***t***
30:25 I not wept for him who was in ***t***?
34:29 who then can make ***t***?
38:23 have reserved for the time of ***t***,
Ps 3: 1 how they have increased who ***t***
7:14 he conceives ***t*** and brings forth
7:16 His ***t*** shall return upon his own
9: 9 A refuge in times of ***t***.
9:13 O LORD! Consider my ***t*** from
10: 1 Why do You hide in times of ***t***?
10: 7 Under his tongue is ***t*** and
10:14 for You observe ***t*** and grief,
13: 4 Lest those who ***t*** me rejoice
20: 1 answer you in the day of ***t***;
22:11 For ***t*** is near; For there
27: 5 For in the time of ***t*** He shall
31: 7 For You have considered my ***t***;
31: 9 on me, O LORD, for I am in ***t***;
32: 7 You shall preserve me from ***t***;
37:39 their strength in the time of ***t***.
41: 1 will deliver him in time of ***t***.
46: 1 A very present help in ***t***.
50:15 Call upon Me in the day of ***t***;
54: 7 has delivered me out of all ***t***;
55: 3 For they bring down ***t*** upon me,
55:10 Iniquity and ***t*** are also in
59:16 And refuge in the day of my ***t***.
60:11 Give us help from ***t***,
66:14 has spoken when I was in ***t***.
69:17 Your servant, For I am in ***t***;
73: 5 They are not in ***t*** as other
77: 2 In the day of my ***t*** I sought the
78:49 Wrath, indignation, and ***t***,
81: 7 You called in ***t***,
86: 7 In the day of my ***t*** I will call
91:15 I will be with him in ***t***;
102: 2 face from me in the day of my ***t***;
107: 6 out to the LORD in their ***t***,
107:13 out to the LORD in their ***t***,
107:19 out to the LORD in their ***t***,
107:26 Their soul melts because of ***t***.
107:28 cry out to the LORD in their ***t***,
108:12 Give us help from ***t***,
116: 3 I found ***t*** and sorrow.
119:143 ***T*** and anguish have overtaken
138: 7 I walk in the midst of ***t***,
142: 2 I declare before Him my ***t***.
143:11 sake bring my soul out of ***t***.
Prov 3:25 Nor of ***t*** from the wicked when
10:10 He who winks with the eye causes ***t***;
11: 8 righteous is delivered from ***t***,
11:27 But ***t*** will come to him who
12:13 righteous will come through ***t***.
12:21 No grave ***t*** will overtake the
13:17 wicked messenger falls into ***t***,
15: 6 the revenue of the wicked is ***t***.
15:16 Than great treasure with ***t***.
25:19 an unfaithful man in time of ***t***
Isa 1:14 They are a ***t*** to Me,
7: 6 us go up against Judah and ***t***
8:22 and see ***t*** and darkness, gloom
17:14 Then behold, at eventide, ***t***!
22: 5 For it is a day of ***t*** and
26:16 in ***t*** they have visited You,
30: 6 Through a land of ***t*** and
33: 2 salvation also in the time of ***t***.
37: 3 This day is a day of ***t*** and
46: 7 Nor save him out of his ***t***.
47:11 And ***t*** shall fall upon you;
65:23 Nor bring forth children for ***t***;
Jer 2:27 But in the time of their ***t***
2:28 save you in the time of your ***t***;
8:15 and there was ***t***!
11:12 at all in the time of their ***t***.
11:14 out to Me because of their ***t***.
14: 8 Israel, his Savior in time of ***t***,
14:19 of healing, and there was ***t***.
15: 4 "I will hand them over to ***t***,
24: 9 I will deliver them to ***t*** into
29:18 and I will deliver them to ***t***
30: 7 it is the time of Jacob's ***t***,
34:17 And I will deliver you to ***t***
44:17 were well-off, and saw no ***t***.
49:23 There is ***t*** on the sea;
Lam 1:21 my enemies have heard of my ***t***;
Ezek 7: 7 A day of ***t*** is near, And not
23:46 give them up to ***t*** and plunder.
32: 9 I will also ***t*** the hearts of many
Dan 4:19 dream or its interpretation ***t***
5:10 Do not let your thoughts ***t*** you,
11:44 the east and the north shall ***t***
12: 1 And there shall be a time of ***t***,
Jon 1: 7 may know for whose cause this ***t***
1: 8 For whose cause is this ***t*** upon
Nah 1: 7 A stronghold in the day of ***t***;
Hab 1: 3 And cause me to see ***t***?
3:16 I might rest in the day of ***t***.
Zeph 1:15 A day of ***t*** and distress,
Zech 10: 2 They are in ***t*** because there
Mt 6:34 for the day is its own ***t***.
26:10 Why do you ***t*** the woman? For she
Mk 5:35 Why ***t*** the Teacher any
14: 6 Why do you ***t*** her? She has done
Lk 7: 6 do not ***t*** Yourself, for I am not
8:49 Do not ***t*** the Teacher."
11: 7 Do not ***t*** me; the door is now
Acts 7:11 Now a famine and great ***t*** came
15:19 I judge that we should not ***t***
16:20 exceedingly ***t*** our city;
20:10 Do not ***t*** yourselves, for his
1 Cor 7:28 Nevertheless such will have ***t***
2 Cor 1: 4 comfort those who are in any ***t***,
1: 8 of our ***t*** which came to us in
Gal 1: 7 but there are some who ***t*** you
5:12 I could wish that those who ***t***
6:17 From now on let no one ***t*** me,
2 Th 1: 6 with tribulation those who ***t***
2 Tim 2: 9 for which I suffer ***t*** as an
Heb 12:15 bitterness springing up cause ***t***,
Jas 1:27 orphans and widows in their ***t***,

TROUBLED (62/62) TROUBLE

Gen 34:30 You have ***t*** me by making me
41: 8 morning that his spirit was ***t***,
45:24 See that you do not become ***t***
Ex 14:24 and He ***t*** the army of the
Josh 7:25 Why have you ***t*** us? The LORD
1 Sam 14:29 'My father has ***t*** the land.
16:14 spirit from the LORD ***t*** him.
24: 5 afterward that David's heart ***t***
28:21 and saw that he was severely ***t***,
2 Sam 4: 1 and all Israel was ***t***.
1 Ki 18:18 I have not ***t*** Israel, but you and
2 Ki 6:11 king of Syria was greatly ***t*** by
2 Chr 15: 6 for God ***t*** them with every
Ezra 4: 4 They ***t*** them in building,
Job 4: 5 It touches you, and you are ***t***.
Ps 6: 2 heal me, for my bones are ***t***.
6: 3 My soul also is greatly ***t***;
6:10 be ashamed and greatly ***t***;
30: 7 hid Your face, and I was ***t***.
38: 6 I am ***t***, I am bowed down
46: 3 its waters roar and be ***t***,
48: 5 so they marveled; They were ***t***,
77: 3 I remembered God, and was ***t***;
77: 4 I am so ***t*** that I cannot speak.
104:29 You hide Your face, they are ***t***;
Isa 8:12 of their threats, nor be ***t***.
19:10 who make wages will be ***t*** of
32:10 and some days You will be ***t***,
32:11 Be ***t***, you complacent ones;
57:20 the wicked are like the ***t*** sea,
Lam 1:20 am in distress; My soul is ***t***;
2:11 fail with tears, My heart is ***t***;
Ezek 26:18 coastlands by the sea are ***t*** at
27:35 their countenance will be ***t***.
Dan 2: 1 and his spirit was so ***t*** that
4: 5 and the visions of my head ***t***
4:19 and his thoughts ***t*** him.
5: 6 and his thoughts ***t*** him, so that
5: 9 King Belshazzar was greatly ***t***,
7:15 and the visions of my head ***t***
7:28 my thoughts greatly ***t*** me,
Mt 2: 3 the king heard this, he was ***t***,
14:26 walking on the sea, they were ***t***,
24: 6 of wars. See that you are not ***t***;
Mk 6:50 for they all saw Him and were ***t***.
13: 7 and rumors of wars, do not be ***t***;
14:33 and He began to be ***t*** and deeply
Lk 1:12 Zacharias saw him, he was ***t***,
1:29 she was ***t*** at his saying,
10:41 you are worried and ***t*** about
24:38 said to them, "Why are you ***t***?
Jn 11:33 groaned in the spirit and was ***t***.
12:27 "Now My soul is ***t***,
13:21 He was ***t*** in spirit,
14: 1 "Let not your heart be ***t***;
14:27 to you. Let not your heart be ***t***,
Acts 15:24 who went out from us have ***t***
17: 8 And they ***t*** the crowd and the
2 Cor 7: 5 but we were ***t*** on every side.
2 Th 1: 7 and to give you who are ***t*** rest
2: 2 to be soon shaken in mind or ***t***,
1 Pe 3:14 their threats, nor be ***t***.

TROUBLEMAKING (1/1)

Prov 24: 2 And their lips talk of ***t***.

TROUBLER (2/2) TROUBLE

1 Ki 18:17 O ***t*** of Israel?"
1 Chr 2: 7 the ***t*** of Israel,

TROUBLES (22/22) TROUBLE

Deut 31:17 And many evils and ***t*** shall
31:21 when many evils and ***t*** have come
1 Sam 11: 5 What ***t*** the people, that they
2 Sam 14: 5 What ***t*** you?" And she answered,
Job 5:19 He shall deliver you in six ***t***,
22:10 And sudden fear ***t*** you,
Ps 25:17 The ***t*** of my heart have
25:22 Out of all their ***t***!
34: 6 And saved him out of all his ***t***.
34:17 them out of all their ***t***.
71:20 shown me great and severe ***t***,
88: 3 For my soul is full of ***t***,
Prov 11:17 But he who is cruel ***t*** his
11:29 He who ***t*** his own house will
15:27 He who is greedy for gain ***t*** his
21:23 tongue Keeps his soul from ***t***.
Isa 65:16 Because the former ***t*** are
Dan 4: 9 and no secret ***t*** you, explain to
Mk 13: 8 and there will be famines and ***t***.
Lk 18: 5 yet because this widow ***t*** me I
Acts 7:10 delivered him out of all his ***t***,
Gal 5:10 but he who ***t*** you shall bear his

TROUBLESOME (2/2) TROUBLE

Deut 28:25 and you shall become ***t*** to all
Dan 9:25 Even in ***t*** times.

TROUBLING (4/4) TROUBLE

1 Sam 16:15 spirit from God is ***t*** you.
2 Ki 6:28 What is ***t*** you?" And she
Job 3:17 There the wicked cease from ***t***,
Ezek 32: 2 ***T*** the waters with your feet,

TROUGH (2/2)

Gen 24:20 emptied her pitcher into the ***t***,
Prov 14: 4 the ***t*** is clean; But much

TROUGHS (2/2)

Gen 30:38 in the watering ***t*** where the
Ex 2:16 and they filled the ***t*** to water

TROUSERS (6/6)

Ex 28:42 shall make for them linen ***t*** to
39:28 short ***t*** of fine woven linen,
Lev 6:10 and his linen ***t*** he shall put on
16: 4 linen tunic and the linen ***t*** on
Ezek 44:18 on their heads and linen ***t*** on
Dan 3:21 bound in their coats, their ***t***,

TRUCEBREAKERS (KJV) See DESPISERS (OF GOOD)

TRUDGING (1/1)

Deut 2: 7 He knows your ***t*** through this

TRUE (80/77) TRULY, TRUTH

Deut 13:14 And if it is indeed ***t*** and
17: 4 indeed ***t*** and certain that
21:16 the ***t*** firstborn.
22:20 "But if the thing is ***t***,
Josh 2:12 and give me a ***t*** token,
Ruth 3:12 Now it is ***t*** that I am a close
2 Sam 7:28 are God, and Your words are ***t***,
1 Ki 8:26 of Israel, let Your word come ***t***,
10: 6 It was a ***t*** report which I heard
2 Chr 6:17 of Israel, let Your word come ***t***,
9: 5 It was a ***t*** report which I
15: 3 has been without the ***t*** God,
31:20 what was good and right and ***t***
Neh 9:13 just ordinances and ***t*** laws
Job 5:27 we have searched out; It is ***t***.
Ps 19: 9 judgments of the LORD are ***t***
Prov 14:25 A ***t*** witness delivers souls,
Jer 10:10 But the LORD is the ***t*** God;
42: 5 Let the LORD be a ***t*** and
Ezek 18: 8 And executed ***t*** judgment
Dan 3:14 saying to them, "Is it ***t***,
3:24 and said to the king, "***T***,
6:12 and said, "The thing is ***t***,
8:26 Which was told is ***t***;
10: 1 The message was ***t***,
Zech 7: 9 Execute ***t*** justice, Show mercy
Mt 22:16 we know that You are ***t***,
Mk 12:14 You are ***t***, and care about
Lk 16:11 to your trust the ***t*** riches?
Jn 1: 9 That was the ***t*** Light which gives
3:33 has certified that God is ***t***.
4:23 when the ***t*** worshipers will
4:37 "For in this the saying is ***t***:
5:31 of Myself, My witness is not ***t***.
5:32 which He witnesses of Me is ***t***.
6:32 but My Father gives you the ***t***
7:18 of the One who sent Him is ***t***,
7:28 Myself, but He who sent Me is ***t***,
8:13 Yourself; Your witness is not ***t***.
8:14 of Myself, My witness is ***t***,
8:16 if I do judge, My judgment is ***t***;
8:17 the testimony of two men is ***t***.
8:26 but He who sent Me is ***t***;
10:41 spoke about this Man were ***t***.
15: 1 I am the ***t*** vine, and My Father
17: 3 the only ***t*** God, and Jesus
19:35 and his testimony is ***t***;
21:24 we know that his testimony is ***t***.

T

Rom 3: 4 let God be *t* but every man a
2 Cor 6: 8 as deceivers, and yet *t*;
7:14 boasting to Titus was found *t*.
Eph 4:24 in *t* righteousness and
Phil 4: 3 *t* companion, help these women
4: 8 brethren, whatever things are *t*,
1 Th 1: 9 to serve the living and *t* God,
1 Tim 1: 2 a *t* son in the faith: Grace,
Titus 1: 4 a *t* son in our common faith:
1:13 This testimony is *t*.
Heb 8: 2 of the sanctuary and of the *t*
9:24 which are copies of the *t*,
10:22 let us draw near with a *t* heart
1 Pe 5:12 that this is the *t* grace
2 Pe 2:22 according to the *t* proverb:
1 Jn 2: 8 which thing is *t* in Him and in
2: 8 and the *t* light is already
2:27 concerning all things, and is *t*,
5:20 that we may know Him who is *t*;
5:20 and we are in Him who is *t*,
5:20 This is the *t* God and eternal
3 Jn 12 know that our testimony is *t*.
Rev 3: 7 He who is holy, He who is *t*,
3:14 the Faithful and *T* Witness,
6:10 "How long, O Lord, holy and *t*,
15: 3 God Almighty! Just and *t* are
16: 7 *t* and righteous are Your
19: 2 For *t* and righteous are His
19: 9 These are the *t* sayings of
19:11 him was called Faithful and *T*,
21: 5 for these words are *t* and
22: 6 words are faithful and *t*.

TRULY (59/58) TRUE

Gen 20:12 But indeed she is *t* my sister.
24:49 if you will deal kindly and *t*
42:21 We are *t* guilty concerning our
47:29 and deal kindly and *t* with me.
48:19 but *t* his younger brother shall
Num 13:27 It *t* flows with milk and honey,
14:21 'but *t*, as I live,
30:12 But if her husband *t* made them
Deut 14:22 You shall *t* tithe all the
Josh 2:14 that we will deal kindly and *t*
2:24 *T* the LORD has delivered all
1 Sam 20: 3 But *t*, as the LORD lives
21: 5 priest, and said to him, "*T*,
2 Ki 19:17 '*T*, LORD, the kings of
Job 9: 2 *T* I know it is so, But how
33: 6 *T* I am as your spokesman
36: 4 For *t* my words are not false;
Ps 62: 1 *T* my soul silently waits for
73: 1 *T* God is good to Israel,
116:16 *t* I am Your servant; I am
Eccl 7:29 *T*, this only I have found:
9: 3 *T* the hearts of the sons of men
11: 7 *T* the light is sweet, And it
Isa 5: 9 the LORD of hosts said, "*T*,
37:18 '*T*, LORD, the kings
45:15 *T* You are God, who hide
Jer 3:23 *T*, in vain is salvation hoped
3:23 *T*, in the LORD our God Is
10:19 '*T* this is an infirmity,
26:15 for *t* the LORD has sent me to
28: 9 one whom the LORD has *t* sent."
Dan 2:47 *T* your God is the God of gods,
Mic 3: 8 But *t* I am full of power by
Mt 9:37 'The harvest *t* is plentiful,
14:33 *T* You are the Son of God."
27:54 *T* this was the Son of God!"
Mk 15:39 *T* this Man was the Son of God!"
Lk 4:25 "But I tell you *t*,
9:27 "But I tell you *t*,
10: 2 The harvest *t* is great, but the
12:44 '*T*, I say to you that he will
21: 3 *T* I say to you that this poor
22:22 And *t* the Son of Man goes as it
Jn 4:18 in that you spoke *t*."
6:14 This is *t* the Prophet who is to
7:26 know indeed that this is *t* the
7:40 *T* this is the Prophet."
20:30 And *t* Jesus did many other
Acts 1: 5 for John *t* baptized with water,
3:22 For Moses *t* said to the fathers,
4:27 For *t* against Your holy Servant
17:30 '*T*, these times of ignorance
1 Cor 5: 7 since you *t* are unleavened.
14:25 report that God is *t* among you.
2 Cor 12:12 *T* the signs of an apostle were
Gal 3:21 *t* righteousness would have been
Heb 11:15 And *t* if they had called to mind
1 Jn 1: 3 and *t* our fellowship is with
2: 5 *t* the love of God is perfected

TRUMP (KJV) See TRUMPET

TRUMPET (60/58) TRUMPETS

Ex 19:13 When the *t* sounds long,
19:16 and the sound of the *t* was very
19:19 And when the blast of the *t*
20:18 the sound of the *t*,
Lev 25: 9 Then you shall cause the *t* of
25: 9 Atonement you shall make the *t*
Josh 6: 5 you hear the sound of the *t*,
6:20 people heard the sound of the *t*,
Judg 3:27 that he blew the *t* in the
6:34 upon Gideon; then he blew the *t*,
7:16 and he put a *t* into every man's
7:18 "When I blow the *t*,
1 Sam 13: 3 Then Saul blew the *t* throughout
2 Sam 2:28 So Joab blew a *t*;
6:15 and with the sound of the *t*.
15:10 as you hear the sound of the *t*,
18:16 So Joab blew the *t*,
20: 1 And he blew a *t*, and said:
20:22 out to Joab. Then he blew a *t*,
Neh 4:18 And the one who sounded the *t*
4:20 you hear the sound of the *t*,
Job 39:24 he come to a halt because the *t*
39:25 At the blast of the *t* he
Ps 47: 5 LORD with the sound of a *t*.
81: 3 Blow the *t* at the time of the
150: 3 Him with the sound of the *t*;
Isa 18: 3 see it; And when he blows a *t*,
27:13 The great *t* will be blown;
58: 1 Lift up your voice like a *t*;
Jer 4: 5 'Blow the *t* in the land;
4:19 O my soul, The sound of the *t*,
4:21 And hear the sound of the *t*?
6: 1 Blow the *t* in Tekoa,
6:17 Listen to the sound of the *t*!'
42:14 nor hear the sound of the *t*,
51:27 Blow the *t* among the nations!
Ezek 7:14 They have blown the *t* and made
33: 3 if he blows the *t* and warns the
33: 4 hears the sound of the *t* and
33: 5 'He heard the sound of the *t*,
33: 6 coming and does not blow the *t*,
Hos 5: 8 The *t* in Ramah! Cry aloud at
8: 1 'Set the *t* to your mouth!
Joel 2: 1 Blow the *t* in Zion, And sound
2:15 Blow the *t* in Zion,
Am 2: 2 With shouting and *t* sound.
3: 6 If a *t* is blown in a city,
Zeph 1:16 A day of *t* and alarm Against
Zech 9:14 The Lord GOD will blow the *t*,
Mt 6: 2 do not sound a *t* before you as
24:31 with a great sound of a *t*,
1 Cor 14: 8 For if the *t* makes an uncertain
15:52 of an eye, at the last *t*.
15:52 For the *t* will sound, and the
1 Th 4:16 and with the *t* of God. And the
Heb 12:19 and the sound of a *t* and the
Rev 1:10 me a loud voice, as of a *t*,
4: 1 which I heard was like a *t*
8:13 the remaining blasts of the *t*
9:14 the sixth angel who had the *t*,

TRUMPETERS (5/5)

2 Ki 11:14 and the leaders and the *t* were
2 Chr 5:13 when the *t* and singers were as
23:13 and the leaders and the *t* were
29:28 and the *t* sounded; all this
Rev 18:22 and *t* shall not be heard in you

TRUMPETS (49/43) TRUMPET

Lev 23:24 a memorial of blowing of *t*,
Num 10: 2 Make two silver *t* for yourself;
10: 8 the priests, shall blow the *t*;
10: 9 shall sound an alarm with the *t*,
10:10 you shall blow the *t* over your
29: 1 it is a day of blowing the *t*.
31: 6 holy articles and the signal *t*
Josh 6: 4 priests shall bear seven *t* of
6: 4 the priests shall blow the *t*.
6: 6 let seven priests bear seven *t*
6: 8 priests bearing the seven *t* of
6: 8 LORD advanced and blew the *t*,
6: 9 the priests who blew the *t*,
6: 9 continued blowing the *t*.
6:13 seven priests bearing seven *t*
6:13 continually and blew with the *t*.
6:13 continued blowing the *t*.
6:16 when the priests blew the *t*,
6:20 when the priests blew the *t*.
Judg 7: 8 took provisions and their *t* in
7:18 then you also blow the *t* on
7:19 and they blew the *t* and broke
7:20 the three companies blew the *t*
7:20 in their left hands and the *t*
7:22 the three hundred blew the *t*,
2 Ki 9:13 of the steps; and they blew *t*,
11:14 were rejoicing and blowing *t*.
12:13 trimmers, sprinkling-bowls, *t*,
1 Chr 13: 8 on cymbals, and with *t*.
15:24 were to blow the *t* before the
15:28 with *t* and with cymbals, making
16: 6 priests regularly blew the *t*
16:42 to sound aloud with *t* and
2 Chr 5:12 twenty priests sounding with *t*—
5:13 up their voice with the *t* and
7: 6 The priests sounded *t* opposite
13:12 His priests with sounding *t* to
13:14 and the priests sounded the *t*.
15:14 with shouting and *t* and rams'
20:28 instruments and harps and *t*,
23:13 were rejoicing and blowing *t*,
29:26 and the priests with the *t*.
29:27 with the *t* and with the
Ezra 3:10 stood in their apparel with *t*,
Neh 12:35 of the priests' sons with *t*—
12:41 and Hananiah, with *t*;
Ps 98: 6 With *t* and the sound of a horn;
Rev 8: 2 and to them were given seven *t*.
8: 6 angels who had the seven *t*

TRUST (125/125) TRUSTED, TRUSTING, TRUSTS

Deut 28:52 fortified walls, in which you *t*,
Judg 11:20 But Sihon did not *t* Israel to
2 Sam 22: 3 my strength, in whom I will *t*;
22:31 He is a shield to all who *t*
2 Ki 18:19 is this in which you *t*?
18:20 And in whom do you *t*,
18:21 king of Egypt to all who *t* in
18:22 'We *t* in the LORD our God,'
18:24 and put your *t* in Egypt for
18:30 nor let Hezekiah make you *t* in
19:10 not let your God in whom you *t*
1 Chr 5:20 because they put their *t* in
2 Chr 32:10 of Assyria: 'In what do you *t*,
Job 4:18 If He puts no *t* in His
8:14 And whose *t* is a spider's
13:15 yet will I *t* Him. Even so, I
15:15 If God puts no *t* in His
15:31 Let him not *t* in futile
39:11 Will you *t* him because his
39:12 Will you *t* him to bring home
Ps 2:12 are all those who put their *t*
4: 5 And put your *t* in the LORD.
5:11 those rejoice who put their *t*
7: 1 LORD my God, in You I put my *t*;
9:10 Your name will put their *t* in
11: 1 In the LORD I put my *t*;
16: 1 O God, for in You I put my *t*.
17: 7 O You who save those who *t* in
18: 2 my strength, in whom I will *t*;
18:30 He is a shield to all who *t*
20: 7 Some *t* in chariots, and some
22: 9 You made Me *t* while on My
25: 2 I *t* in You; Let me not be
25:20 for I put my *t* in You.
31: 1 In You, O LORD, I put my *t*;
31: 6 But I *t* in the LORD.
31:14 I *t* in You, O LORD; I say,
31:19 have prepared for those who *t*
34:22 And none of those who *t* in Him
36: 7 the children of men put their *t*
37: 3 *T* in the LORD, and do good
37: 5 *T* also in Him, And He shall
37:40 Because they *t* in Him.
40: 3 And will *t* in the LORD.
40: 4 man who makes the LORD his *t*,
44: 6 For I will not *t* in my bow,
49: 6 Those who *t* in their wealth
52: 8 I *t* in the mercy of God
55:23 But I will *t* in You.
56: 3 I will *t* in You.
56: 4 In God I have put my *t*;
56:11 In God I have put my *t*;
61: 4 I will *t* in the shelter of
62: 8 *T* in Him at all times,
62:10 Do not *t* in oppression, Nor
64:10 in the LORD, and *t* in Him.
71: 1 In You, O LORD, I put my *t*;
71: 5 You are my *t* from my youth.
73:28 I have put my *t* in the Lord
78:22 And did not *t* in His
91: 2 My God, in Him I will *t*.
115: 9 O Israel, *t* in the LORD;
115:10 house of Aaron, *t* in the LORD;
115:11 fear the LORD, *t* in the LORD;
118: 8 It is better to *t* in the
118: 9 better to *t* in the LORD
119:42 For I *t* in Your word.
125: 1 Those who *t* in the LORD
143: 8 the morning, For in You do I *t*;
146: 3 Do not put your *t* in princes,
Prov 3: 5 *T* in the LORD with all your
22:19 So that your *t* may be in the
30: 5 to those who put their *t* in
Isa 12: 2 I will *t* and not be afraid;
26: 4 *T* in the LORD forever, For in
30: 2 And to *t* in the shadow of
30: 3 And *t* in the shadow of Egypt
30:12 And *t* in oppression and
31: 1 Who *t* in chariots because
36: 4 is this in which you *t*?
36: 5 Now in whom do you *t*,
36: 6 king of Egypt to all who *t* in
36: 7 We *t* in the LORD our God,' is
36: 9 and put your *t* in Egypt for
36:15 nor let Hezekiah make you *t* in
37:10 not let your God in whom you *t*
42:17 Who *t* in carved images,
50:10 Let him *t* in the name of the
51: 5 And on My arm they will *t*.
57:13 But he who puts his *t* in Me
59: 4 They *t* in empty words and
Jer 5:17 cities, In which you *t*,
7: 4 Do not *t* in these lying words,
7: 8 you *t* in lying words that
7:14 by My name, in which you *t*,
9: 4 And do not *t* any brother;
28:15 but you make this people *t* in a
29:31 and he has caused you to *t* in a
39:18 because you have put your *t* in
46:25 Pharaoh and those who *t* in him.
49:11 And let your widows *t* in
Am 6: 1 And *t* in Mount Samaria,
Mic 2: 8 the garment From those who *t*
7: 5 Do not *t* in a friend; Do not
Nah 1: 7 And He knows those who *t* in
Hab 2:18 the maker of its mold should *t*
Zeph 3:12 And they shall *t* in the name
Mt 12:21 His name Gentiles will *t*.
Mk 10:24 how hard it is for those who *t*
Lk 16:11 who will commit to your *t* the
Jn 5:45 you—Moses, in whom you *t*.
2 Cor 1: 9 that we should not *t* in
1:10 in whom we *t* that He will still

1:13 Now I ***t*** you will understand,
3: 4 And we have such ***t*** through
5:11 and I also ***t*** are well known in
13: 6 But I ***t*** that you will know that
Phil 2:19 But I ***t*** in the Lord Jesus to
2:24 But I ***t*** in the Lord that I
1 Tim 1:11 God which was committed to my ***t***.
4:10 because we ***t*** in the living God,
6:17 nor to ***t*** in uncertain riches
6:20 what was committed to your ***t***,
Phm 1:22 for I ***t*** that through your
Heb 2:13 I will put My ***t*** in Him."

TRUSTED (32/31) TRUST

2 Ki 18: 5 He ***t*** in the LORD God of Israel,
1 Chr 9:22 had appointed them to their ***t***
9:26 For in this ***t*** office were four
9:31 had the ***t*** office over the
Job 12:20 He deprives the ***t*** ones of
Ps 13: 5 But I have ***t*** in Your mercy;
22: 4 Our fathers ***t*** in You;
22: 4 fathers trusted in You; They ***t***,
22: 5 They ***t*** in You, and were not
22: 8 He ***t*** in the LORD, let Him
26: 1 I have also ***t*** in the LORD;
28: 7 My heart ***t*** in Him, and I am
33:21 Because we have ***t*** in His holy
41: 9 own familiar friend in whom I ***t***,
52: 7 But ***t*** in the abundance of his
Prov 21:22 And brings down the ***t***
Isa 47:10 For you have ***t*** in your
Jer 2:37 the LORD has rejected your ***t***
12: 5 of peace, In which you ***t***,
13:25 you have forgotten Me And ***t***
48: 7 For because you have ***t*** in your
49: 4 Who ***t*** in her treasures,
Ezek 16:15 But you ***t*** in your own beauty,
Dan 3:28 delivered His servants who ***t***
Hos 10:13 Because you ***t*** in your own way,
Zeph 3: 2 She has not ***t*** in the LORD,
Mt 27:43 He ***t*** in God; let Him deliver Him
Lk 11:22 him all his armor in which he ***t***,
18: 9 this parable to some who ***t*** in
Eph 1:12 that we who first ***t*** in Christ
1:13 In Him you also ***t***,
1 Pe 3: 5 the holy women who ***t*** in God

TRUSTING (3/3) TRUST

2 Ki 18:21 Now look! You are ***t*** in the staff
Ps 112: 7 ***t*** in the LORD.
Isa 36: 6 Look! You are ***t*** in the staff of

TRUSTS (19/19) TRUST

Ps 21: 7 For the king ***t*** in the LORD,
32:10 But he who ***t*** in the LORD,
34: 8 Blessed is the man who ***t*** in
57: 1 For my soul ***t*** in You;
84:12 Blessed is the man who ***t*** in
86: 2 Save Your servant who ***t*** in
115: 8 So is everyone who ***t*** in
135:18 is everyone who ***t*** in them.
Prov 11:28 He who ***t*** in his riches will
16:20 And whoever ***t*** in the LORD,
28:25 But he who ***t*** in the LORD will
28:26 He who ***t*** in his own heart is a
29:25 But whoever ***t*** in the LORD
31:11 heart of her husband safely ***t***
Isa 26: 3 Because he ***t*** in You.
Jer 17: 5 Cursed is the man who ***t*** in man
17: 7 Blessed is the man who ***t*** in the
Ezek 33:13 but he ***t*** in his own
1 Tim 5: 5 ***t*** in God and continues in

TRUSTWORTHY (1/1)

1 Cor 7:25 Lord in His mercy has made ***t***.

TRUTH (223/210) TRUE

Gen 24:27 forsaken His mercy and His ***t***
24:48 who had led me in the way of ***t***
32:10 the mercies and of all the ***t***
42:16 to see whether there is any ***t***
Ex 18:21 men, such as fear God, men of ***t***,
34: 6 and abounding in goodness and ***t***,
Deut 32: 4 A God of ***t*** and without
Josh 24:14 serve Him in sincerity and in ***t***,
Judg 9:15 If in ***t*** you anoint me as king
9:16 if you have acted in ***t*** and
9:19 if then you have acted in ***t*** and
1 Sam 12:24 and serve Him in ***t*** with all
2 Sam 2: 6 the LORD show kindness and ***t***
15:20 Mercy and ***t*** be with you."
1 Ki 2: 4 to walk before Me in ***t*** with all
3: 6 he walked before You in ***t***,
17:24 LORD in your mouth is the ***t***.
22:16 you tell me nothing but the ***t***
2 Ki 20: 3 I have walked before You in ***t***
20:19 Will there not be peace and ***t*** at
2 Chr 18:15 you tell me nothing but the ***t***
Esth 9:30 with words of peace and ***t***,
Ps 15: 2 And speaks the ***t*** in his heart;
25: 5 Lead me in Your ***t*** and teach me,
25:10 of the LORD are mercy and ***t***,
26: 3 And I have walked in Your ***t***.
30: 9 Will it declare Your ***t***?
31: 5 redeemed me, O LORD God of ***t***.
33: 4 all His work is done in ***t***.
40:10 Your lovingkindness and Your ***t***
40:11 Your lovingkindness and Your ***t***
43: 3 send out Your light and Your ***t***!
45: 4 ride prosperously because of ***t***,
51: 6 You desire ***t*** in the inward
54: 5 Cut them off in Your ***t***.
57: 3 send forth His mercy and His ***t***.
57:10 And Your ***t*** unto the clouds.
60: 4 be displayed because of the ***t***.
61: 7 Oh, prepare mercy and ***t***,
69:13 Hear me in the ***t*** of Your
85:10 Mercy and ***t*** have met together;
85:11 ***T*** shall spring out of the
86:11 O LORD; I will walk in Your ***t***;
86:15 and abundant in mercy and ***t***.
89:14 Mercy and ***t*** go before Your
89:49 You swore to David in Your ***t***?
91: 4 His ***t*** shall be your shield
96:13 And the peoples with His ***t***.
100: 5 And His ***t*** endures to all
108: 4 And Your ***t*** reaches to the
111: 8 And are done in ***t*** and
115: 1 Your mercy, Because of Your ***t***.
117: 2 And the ***t*** of the LORD
119:30 I have chosen the way of ***t***;
119:43 And take not the word of ***t***
119:142 And Your law is ***t***.
119:151 all Your commandments are ***t***.
119:160 entirety of Your word is ***t***,
132:11 The LORD has sworn in ***t*** to
138: 2 Your lovingkindness and Your ***t***;
145:18 To all who call upon Him in ***t***.
146: 6 Who keeps ***t*** forever,
Prov 3: 3 Let not mercy and ***t*** forsake
8: 7 For my mouth will speak ***t***;
12:17 He who speaks ***t*** declares
14:22 But mercy and ***t*** belong to
16: 6 In mercy and ***t*** Atonement is
20:28 Mercy and ***t*** preserve the king,
22:21 the certainty of the words of ***t***,
22:21 you may answer words of ***t*** To
23:23 Buy the ***t***, and do not sell it,
29:14 king who judges the poor with ***t***,
29:24 He swears to tell the ***t***,
Eccl 12:10 written was upright—words of ***t***.
Isa 10:20 the Holy One of Israel, in ***t***.
16: 5 And One will sit on it in ***t***,
25: 1 of old are faithfulness and ***t***.
26: 2 nation which keeps the ***t*** may
38: 3 I have walked before You in ***t***
38:18 the pit cannot hope for Your ***t***.
38:19 father shall make known Your ***t***
39: 8 there will be peace and ***t*** in
42: 3 will bring forth justice for ***t***.
43: 9 them hear and say, "It is ***t***.
48: 1 But not in ***t*** or in
59: 4 Nor does any plead for ***t***.
59:14 For ***t*** is fallen in the street,
59:15 So ***t*** fails, And he who
61: 8 I will direct their work in ***t***,
65:16 bless himself in the God of ***t***;
65:16 Shall swear by the God of ***t***;
Jer 4: 2 swear, 'The LORD lives,' In ***t***,
5: 1 Who seeks the ***t***,
5: 3 are not Your eyes on the ***t***?
7:28 ***T*** has perished and has been cut
9: 3 are not valiant for the ***t*** on
9: 5 And will not speak the ***t***;
33: 6 the abundance of peace and ***t***.
Dan 4:37 all of whose works are ***t***,
7:16 and asked him the ***t*** of all
7:19 Then I wished to know the ***t***
8:12 and he cast ***t*** down to the
9:13 and understand Your ***t***.
10:21 is noted in the Scripture of ***T***.
11: 2 "And now I will tell you the ***t***:
Hos 4: 1 'There is no ***t*** or mercy
Mic 7:20 You will give ***t*** to Jacob
Zech 8: 3 shall be called the City of ***T***,
8: 8 In ***t*** and righteousness.'
8:16 Speak each man the ***t*** to his
8:16 judgment in your gates for ***t***,
8:19 Therefore love ***t*** and peace.'
Mal 2: 6 The law of ***t*** was in his mouth,
Mt 22:16 and teach the way of God in ***t***;
Mk 5:33 Him and told Him the whole ***t***.
12:14 but teach the way of God in ***t***.
12:32 You have spoken the ***t***,
Lk 20:21 but teach the way of God in ***t***:
Jn 1:14 the Father, full of grace and ***t***.
1:17 but grace and ***t*** came through
3:21 But he who does the ***t*** comes to
4:23 the Father in spirit and ***t***;
4:24 must worship in spirit and ***t***.
5:33 he has borne witness to the ***t***.
8:32 "And you shall know the ***t***,
8:32 and the ***t*** shall make you
8:40 a Man who has told you the ***t***
8:44 and does not stand in the ***t***,
8:44 because there is no ***t*** in him.
8:45 "But because I tell the ***t***,
8:46 Me of sin? And if I tell the ***t***,
14: 6 to him, "I am the way, the ***t***,
14:17 "the Spirit of ***t***,
15:26 the Spirit of ***t*** who proceeds
16: 7 "Nevertheless I tell you the ***t***.
16:13 when He, the Spirit of ***t***,
16:13 He will guide you into all ***t***;
17:17 "Sanctify them by Your ***t***.
17:17 by Your truth. Your word is ***t***.
17:19 also may be sanctified by the ***t***.
18:37 I should bear witness to the ***t***.
18:37 Everyone who is of the ***t*** hears
18:38 Pilate said to Him, "What is ***t***?
19:35 knows that he is telling the ***t***,
Acts 10:34 In ***t*** I perceive that God shows
21:34 he could not ascertain the ***t***
26:25 but speak the words of ***t*** and
Rom 1:18 who suppress the ***t*** in
1:25 who exchanged the ***t*** of God for
2: 2 of God is according to ***t***
2: 8 and do not obey the ***t***,
2:20 the form of knowledge and ***t*** in
3: 7 For if the ***t*** of God has
9: 1 I tell the ***t*** in Christ, I am not
15: 8 to the circumcision for the ***t***
1 Cor 5: 8 bread of sincerity and ***t***.
13: 6 but rejoices in the ***t***;
2 Cor 4: 2 but by manifestation of the ***t***
6: 7 by the word of ***t***,
7:14 we spoke all things to you in ***t***,
11:10 As the ***t*** of Christ is in me,
12: 6 a fool; for I will speak the ***t***.
13: 8 we can do nothing against the ***t***,
13: 8 the truth, but for the ***t***.
Gal 2: 5 that the ***t*** of the gospel might
2:14 straightforward about the ***t*** of
3: 1 that you should not obey the ***t***,
4:16 enemy because I tell you the ***t***?
5: 7 hindered you from obeying the ***t***?
Eph 1:13 after you heard the word of ***t***,
4:15 speaking the ***t*** in love,
4:21 as the ***t*** is in Jesus:
4:25 each one of you speak ***t***
5: 9 goodness, righteousness, and ***t***),
6:14 having girded your waist with ***t***,
Phil 1:18 whether in pretense or in ***t***,
Col 1: 5 before in the word of the ***t*** of
1: 6 and knew the grace of God in ***t***;
1 Th 2:13 word of men, but as it is in ***t***,
2 Th 2:10 not receive the love of the ***t***,
2:12 who did not believe the ***t*** but
2:13 the Spirit and belief in the ***t***,
1 Tim 2: 4 come to the knowledge of the ***t***.
2: 7 I am speaking the ***t*** in Christ
2: 7 of the Gentiles in faith and ***t***.
3:15 the pillar and ground of the ***t***.
4: 3 who believe and know the ***t***.
6: 5 minds and destitute of the ***t***,
2 Tim 2:15 rightly dividing the word of ***t***.
2:18 have strayed concerning the ***t***,
2:25 so that they may know the ***t***,
3: 7 come to the knowledge of the ***t***.
3: 8 so do these also resist the ***t***:
4: 4 their ears away from the ***t***,
Titus 1: 1 and the acknowledgment of the ***t***
1:14 of men who turn from the ***t***.
Heb 10:26 received the knowledge of the ***t***,
Jas 1:18 us forth by the word of ***t***,
3:14 not boast and lie against the ***t***.
5:19 among you wanders from the ***t***,
1 Pe 1:22 your souls in obeying the ***t***
2 Pe 1:12 established in the present ***t***.
2: 2 because of whom the way of ***t***
1 Jn 1: 6 lie and do not practice the ***t***.
1: 8 and the ***t*** is not in us.
2: 4 and the ***t*** is not in him.
2:21 because you do not know the ***t***,
2:21 and that no lie is of the ***t***.
3:18 in tongue, but in deed and in ***t***.
3:19 we know that we are of the ***t***,
4: 6 By this we know the spirit of ***t***
5: 6 because the Spirit is ***t***.
2 Jn 1 her children, whom I love in ***t***,
1 all those who have known the ***t***,
2 because of the ***t*** which abides in
3 of the Father, in ***t*** and love.
4 of your children walking in ***t***,
3 Jn 1 beloved Gaius, whom I love in ***t***:
3 came and testified of the ***t***
3 just as you walk in the ***t***.
4 hear that my children walk in ***t***.
8 become fellow workers for the ***t***.
12 and from the ***t*** itself. And we

TRUTHFUL (1/1)

Prov 12:19 The ***t*** lip shall be established

TRUTHFULLY (1/1)

Prov 12:22 But those who deal ***t*** are His

TRY (10/10) PROVE, TRIED, TRYING

Deut 4:34 Or did God ever ***t*** to go and
Ps 26: 2 ***T*** my mind and my heart.
139:23 ***T*** me, and know my anxieties;
Jer 9: 7 I will refine them and ***t*** them;
23:27 who ***t*** to make My people forget
Ezek 17:20 bring him to Babylon and ***t*** him
Mal 3:10 And ***t*** Me now in this,"
Lk 22:53 you did not ***t*** to seize Me.
1 Pe 4:12 the fiery trial which is to ***t***
1 Jn 2:26 to you concerning those who ***t***

TRYING (2/2) TRY

Gen 19:11 so that they became weary ***t*** to
Neh 6: 9 For they all were ***t*** to make

TRYPHENA (1/1)

Rom 16:12 Greet ***T*** and Tryphosa, who have

TRYPHOSA (1/1)

Rom 16:12 Greet Tryphena and *T*,

TUBAL (8/8)

Gen 10: 2 Gomer, Magog, Madai, Javan, *T*,
1 Chr 1: 5 Gomer, Magog, Madai, Javan, *T*,
Isa 66:19 and *T* and Javan, to the
Ezek 27:13 'Javan, *T*, and Meshech
32:26 There are Meshech and *T* and
38: 2 prince of Rosh, Meshech, and *T*,
38: 3 prince of Rosh, Meshech, and *T*.
39: 1 prince of Rosh, Meshech, and *T*;

TUBAL-CAIN (2/1)

Gen 4:22 as for Zillah, she also bore *T*,
4:22 And the sister of *T* was

TUMBLED (1/1)

Judg 7:13 a loaf of barley bread *t* into

TUMORS (8/8)

Deut 28:27 with the boils of Egypt, with *t*,
1 Sam 5: 6 them and struck them with *t*,
5: 9 and *t* broke out on them.
5:12 die were stricken with the *t*,
6: 4 Five golden *t* and five golden
6: 5 you shall make images of your *t*
6:11 rats and the images of their *t*.
6:17 These are the golden *t* which

TUMULT (20/20)

Num 24:17 And destroy all the sons of *t*.
1 Sam 4:14 does the sound of this *t*
2 Sam 18:29 your servant, I saw a great *t*,
2 Ki 19:28 your rage against Me and your *t*
Job 39: 7 He scorns the *t* of the city;
Ps 65: 7 And the *t* of the peoples.
74:23 The *t* of those who rise up
83: 2 behold, Your enemies make a *t*;
Isa 33: 3 At the noise of the *t* the
37:29 your rage against Me and your *t*
Jer 11:16 With the noise of a great *t*
48:45 of the head of the sons of *t*.
Ezek 1:24 a *t* like the noise of an army;
22: 5 you as infamous and full of *t*.
Hos 10:14 Therefore *t* shall arise among
Am 2: 2 Moab shall die with *t*,
Mt 27:24 but rather that a *t* was
Mk 5:38 and saw a *t* and those who wept
Acts 21:34 the truth because of the *t*,
24:18 neither with a mob nor with *t*.

TUMULTS (3/3)

Am 3: 9 See great *t* in her midst,
2 Cor 6: 5 stripes, in imprisonments, in *t*,
12:20 whisperings, conceits, *t*;

TUMULTUOUS (2/2)

Isa 13: 4 A *t* noise of the kingdoms
22: 2 A *t* city, a joyous city?

TUNE (1/1)

Ps 9: To the *t* of "Death of the

TUNIC (17/13) TUNICS

Gen 37: 3 Also he made him a *t* of many
37:23 they stripped Joseph of his *t*,
37:23 the *t* of many colors that was
37:31 So they took Joseph's *t*,
37:31 and dipped the *t* in the blood.
37:32 Then they sent the *t* of many
37:32 whether it is your son's *t* or
37:33 and said, "It is my son's *t*.
Ex 28: 4 a robe, a skillfully woven *t*,
28:39 shall skillfully weave the *t*
29: 5 put the *t* on Aaron, and the
Lev 8: 7 And he put the *t* on him,
16: 4 He shall put the holy linen *t*
Mt 5:40 to sue you and take away your *t*,
Lk 6:29 do not withhold your *t* either.
Jn 19:23 soldier a part, and also the *t*.
19:23 Now the *t* was without seam,

TUNICS (12/12) TUNIC

Gen 3:21 his wife the LORD God made *t*
Ex 28:40 Aaron's sons you shall make *t*,
29: 8 shall bring his sons and put *t*
39:27 They made *t*, artistically
40:14 his sons and clothe them with *t*.
Lev 8:13 brought Aaron's sons and put *t*
10: 5 and carried them by their *t*
Mt 10:10 for your journey, nor two *t*,
Mk 6: 9 and not to put on two *t*.
Lk 3:11 to them, "He who has two *t*,
9: 3 and do not have two *t* apiece.
Acts 9:39 showing the *t* and garments

TUNNEL (2/2)

2 Ki 20:20 and how he made a pool and a *t*
2 Chr 32:30 and brought the water by *t* to

TURBAN (16/12)

Ex 28: 4 a skillfully woven tunic, a *t*,
28:37 cord, that it may be on the *t*;
28:37 shall be on the front of the *t*.
28:39 you shall make the *t* of fine
29: 6 You shall put the *t* on his head,
29: 6 and put the holy crown on the *t*.
39:28 a *t* of fine linen, exquisite
39:31 to fasten it above on the *t*,
Lev 8: 9 And he put the *t* on his head.
8: 9 Also on the *t*, on its front,
16: 4 and with the linen *t* he shall
Job 29:14 was like a robe and a *t*.
Ezek 21:26 'Remove the *t*, and take off
24:17 bind your *t* on your head,
Zech 3: 5 Let them put a clean *t* on his
3: 5 So they put a clean *t* on his

TURBANS (5/5)

Isa 3:23 The fine linen, the *t*,
Ezek 23:15 Flowing *t* on their heads,
24:23 Your *t* shall be on your heads
44:18 They shall have linen *t* on their
Dan 3:21 coats, their trousers, their *t*,

TURMOIL (4/4)

2 Chr 15: 5 but great *t* was on all the
Job 20: 2 Because of the *t* within me.
30:27 My heart is in *t* and cannot
Ps 38: 8 I groan because of the *t* of my

TURN (288/277) TURNED, TURNING, TURNS, UNTURNED

Gen 19: 2 please *t* in to your servant's
24:49 that I may *t* to the right hand
Ex 3: 3 I will now *t* aside and see this
14: 2 that they *t* and camp before Pi
23: 2 in a dispute so as to *t* aside
23:27 will make all your enemies *t*
32:12 *T* from Your fierce wrath,
Lev 19: 4 Do not *t* to idols, nor make for
Num 14:25 tomorrow *t* and move out into
20:17 we will not *t* aside to the
21:22 We will not *t* aside into fields
22:23 Balaam struck the donkey to *t*
22:26 where there was no way to *t*
22:34 I will *t* back."
25: 4 anger of the LORD may *t* away
32:15 For if you *t* away from following
34: 4 your border shall *t* from the
34: 5 the border shall *t* from Azmon to
Deut 1: 7 '*T* and take your journey,
1:40 *t* and take your journey into
2: 3 long enough; *t* northward.
2:27 and I will *t* neither to the
4:30 when you *t* to the LORD your
5:32 you shall not *t* aside to the
7: 4 For they will *t* your sons away
11:16 and you *t* aside and serve other
11:28 but *t* aside from the way which
13: 5 has spoken in order to *t* you
13:17 that the LORD may *t* from the
16: 7 the morning you shall *t* and go
17:11 you shall not *t* aside to the
17:17 lest his heart *t* away;
17:20 that he may not *t* aside from
23:13 you shall dig with it and *t* and
23:14 and *t* away from you.
28:14 So you shall not *t* aside from
30:10 and if you *t* to the LORD your
31:20 then they will *t* to other gods
31:29 and *t* aside from the way which
Josh 1: 7 do not *t* from it to the right
22:16 to *t* away this day from
22:18 but that you must *t* away this
22:23 built ourselves an altar to *t*
22:29 and *t* from following the LORD
23: 6 lest you *t* aside from it to the
24:20 then He will *t* and do you harm
Judg 4:18 *T* aside, my lord, turn aside to
4:18 *t* aside to me; do not fear."
7: 3 let him *t* and depart at once
19:11 and let us *t* aside into this
19:12 We will not *t* aside here into a
20: 8 nor will any *t* back to his
20:39 the men of Israel would *t* in
Ruth 1:11 *T* back, my daughters; why will
1:12 *T* back, my daughters, go—for I
1:16 Or to *t* back from following
3:18 how the matter will *t* out;
1 Sam 6:12 and did not *t* aside to the
12:20 yet do not *t* aside from
12:21 And do not *t* aside; for then
22:17 *T* and kill the priests of the
22:18 'You *t* and kill the priests!"
2 Sam 1:22 of Jonathan did not *t* back,
2:19 and in going he did not *t* to
2:21 *T* aside to your right hand or to
2:21 But Asahel would not *t* aside
2:22 '*T* aside from following me.
2:23 he refused to *t* aside.
14:19 no one can *t* to the right hand
15:31 *t* the counsel of Ahithophel
18:30 '*T* aside and stand here.'
19:37 Please let your servant *t* back
22:38 Neither did I *t* back again
1 Ki 2: 3 that you do and wherever you *t*;
8:33 and when they *t* back to You and
8:35 and *t* from their sin because
9: 6 you or your sons at all *t* from
11: 2 Surely they will *t* away your
12:15 for the *t* of events was from
12:27 of this people will *t* back
13:33 event Jeroboam did not *t* from
17: 3 away from here and *t* eastward,
22:34 *T* around and take me out of the
22:43 He did not *t* aside from them,
2 Ki 4: 8 he would *t* in there to eat some
4:10 he can *t* in there."
9:18 *T* around and follow me." So
9:19 *T* around and follow me."
10:29 However Jehu did not *t* away
17:13 *T* from your evil ways, and keep
18:14 *t* away from me; whatever you
19:28 And I will *t* you back By the
22: 2 he did not *t* aside to the right
23:26 the LORD did not *t* from the
1 Chr 12:23 to David at Hebron to *t* over
2 Chr 6:26 and *t* from their sin because
6:42 do not *t* away the face of Your
7:14 and *t* from their wicked ways,
7:19 But if you *t* away and forsake
10:15 for the *t* of events was from
18:33 *T* around and take me out of the
20:32 and did not *t* aside from it,
29:10 His fierce wrath may *t* away
30: 8 of His wrath may *t* away from
30: 9 and will not *t* His face from
34: 2 he did not *t* aside to the
35:22 Josiah would not *t* his face
36:10 At the *t* of the year King
Neh 4: 4 *t* their reproach on their own
4:12 "From whatever place you *t*,
9:26 them To *t* them to Yourself;
9:35 Nor did they *t* from their
Esth 2:12 Each young woman's *t* came to go
2:15 Now when the *t* came for Esther
Job 5: 1 of the holy ones will you *t*?
6:18 The paths of their way *t* aside,
10: 9 And will You *t* me into dust
15:13 That you *t* your spirit against
24:18 that no one would *t* into
33:17 In order to *t* man from his
36:10 And commands that they *t* from
36:21 do not *t* to iniquity, For you
39:22 Nor does he *t* back from the
Ps 4: 2 Will you *t* my glory to
6:10 Let them *t* back and be
7:12 If he does not *t* back, He will
9: 3 When my enemies *t* back,
18:37 Neither did I *t* back again
21:12 You will make them *t* their
22:27 Shall remember and *t* to
25:16 *T* Yourself to me, and have
27: 9 Do not *t* Your servant away in
40: 4 nor such as *t* aside to lies.
44:10 You make us *t* back from the
56: 9 Then my enemies will *t* back;
69:16 *T* to me according to the
80:18 Then we will not *t* back from
81:14 And *t* My hand against their
85: 8 But let them not *t* back to
86:16 *t* to me, and have mercy on me!
90: 3 You *t* man to destruction,
106:23 To *t* away His wrath, lest He
119:37 *T* away my eyes from looking at
119:39 *T* away my reproach which I
119:51 Yet I do not *t* aside from
119:79 Let those who fear You *t* to me,
119:157 Yet I do not *t* from Your
125: 5 As for such as *t* aside to their
132:10 Do not *t* away the face of Your
132:11 He will not *t* from it:
Prov 1:23 *T* at my rebuke
4: 5 nor *t* away from the words of my
4:15 *T* away from it and pass on.
4:27 Do not *t* to the right or the
7:25 Do not let your heart *t* aside
9: 4 is simple, let him *t* in here!"
9:16 let him *t* in here"; And as
13:14 To *t* one away from the snares
14:27 fountain of life, To *t* one
15:24 That he may *t* away from hell
24:18 And He *t* away His wrath from
29: 8 But wise men *t* away wrath.
30:30 And does not *t* away from
Song 2:17 And the shadows flee away, *T*,
6: 5 *T* your eyes away from me,
Isa 1:25 I will *t* My hand against you,
9:13 For the people do not *t* to Him
13:14 Every man will *t* to his own
14:27 And who will *t* it back?"
19: 6 The rivers will *t* foul;
22:18 He will surely *t* violently and
28: 6 strength to those who *t* back
29:21 And *t* aside the just by empty
30:11 *T* aside from the path,
30:21 Whenever you *t* to the right
30:21 whenever you *t* to the left.
37:29 And I will *t* you back By the
50: 5 Nor did I *t* away.
58:13 If you *t* away your foot from
59:20 And to those who *t* from
Jer 2:24 who can *t* her away? All those
2:35 Surely His anger shall *t* from
3:19 And not *t* away from Me.'
4:28 Nor will I *t* back from it.
8: 4 Will one *t* away and not
15: 5 Or who will *t* aside to ask how
18:20 To *t* away Your wrath from

21: 4 I will t back the weapons of
23:20 of the LORD will not t back
26: 3 will listen and t from his evil
31:13 For I will t their mourning to
31:21 T back, O virgin of Israel,
31:21 T back to these your cities.
31:39 then it shall t toward Goath.
32:40 that I will not t away from
35:15 T now everyone from his evil
36: 3 that everyone may t from his
36: 7 and everyone will t from his
44: 5 or incline their ear to t from
49: 8 t back, dwell in the depths,
50:16 sword Everyone shall t to his
Lam 3:35 To t aside the justice due a
3:40 And t back to the LORD;
5:21 T us back to You, O LORD,
Ezek 1: 9 The creatures did not t when
1:12 and they did not t when they
1:17 they did not t aside when they
3:19 and he does not t from his
4: 8 you so that you cannot t from
7:13 And it shall not t back;
7:22 I will t My face from them,
8: 6 Now t again, you will see
8:13 T again, and you will see
8:15 T again, you will see greater
10:11 they did not t aside when they
10:11 They did not t aside when they
10:16 the same wheels also did not t
13:22 so that he does not t from his
14: 6 t away from your idols, and
14: 6 and t your faces away from all
18:23 and not that he should t from
18:30 and t from all your
18:32 Therefore t and live!"
33: 9 you warn the wicked to t from
33: 9 and he does not t from his way,
33:11 but that the wicked t from his
33:11 T, turn from your evil ways!
33:11 t from your evil ways! For why
36: 9 and I will t to you, and you
38: 4 I will t you around, put hooks
39: 2 and I will t you around and lead
Dan 9:13 that we might t from our
11:18 After this he shall t his face
11:18 he shall t back on him.
11:19 Then he shall t his face toward
12: 3 And those who t many to
Joel 2:12 T to Me with all your heart,
2:14 Who knows if He will t and
Am 1: 3 I will not t away its
1: 6 not t away its punishment,
1: 8 I will t My hand against
1: 9 I will not t away its
1:11 I will not t away its
1:13 I will not t away its
2: 1 I will not t away its
2: 4 I will not t away its
2: 6 I will not t away its
5: 7 You who t justice to wormwood,
8:10 I will t your feasts into
Jon 3: 8 let every one t from his evil
3: 9 Who can tell if God will t and
3: 9 and t away from His fierce
Hag 2:17 yet you did not t to Me,' says
Zech 1: 4 T now from your evil ways and
13: 7 Then I will t My hand against
Mal 3: 5 And against those who t away
4: 6 And he will t The hearts of
Mt 5:39 t the other to him also.
5:42 borrow from you do not t away.
7: 6 and t and tear you in pieces.
13:15 with their hearts and t,
Mk 4:12 Lest they should t,
Lk 1:16 And he will t many of the
1:17 to t the hearts of the
17:31 let him not t back.
21:13 But it will t out for you as an
Jn 12:22 and in t Andrew and Philip told
12:40 with their hearts and t,
Acts 7:45 having received it in t,
13: 8 seeking to t the proconsul away
13:46 we t to the Gentiles.
14:15 to you that you should t from
26:18 in order to t them from
26:20 t to God, and do works
28:27 with their hearts and t,
Rom 11:26 And He will t away
1 Cor 14:27 at the most three, each in t,
Gal 4: 9 how is it that you t again
Phil 1:19 For I know that this will t out
2 Tim 3: 5 And from such people t away!
4: 4 and they will t their ears away
Titus 1:14 commandments of men who t from
Heb 12:25 we not escape if we t away
Jas 3: 3 and we t their whole body.
1 Pe 3:11 Let him t away from evil
2 Pe 2:21 to t from the holy commandment
Jude 4 who t the grace of our God into
Rev 11: 6 power over waters to t them

TURNCOAT (1/1)

Mic 2: 4 To a t He has divided our

TURNED (259/253) TURN

Gen 3:24 and a flaming sword which t
9:23 Their faces were t away,
14: 7 Then they t back and came to En
18:22 Then the men t away from there
19: 3 so they t in to him and entered
38:16 Then he t to her by the way,
42:24 And he t himself away from them
Ex 3: 4 So when the LORD saw that he t
7:15 and the rod which was t to a
7:17 and they shall be t to blood.
7:20 that were in the river were t
7:23 And Pharaoh t and went into his
10: 6 " And he t and went out from
10:19 And the LORD t a very strong
14: 5 Pharaoh and his servants was t
32: 8 They have t aside quickly out of
32:15 And Moses t and went down from
Lev 13: 3 if the hair on the sore has t
13: 4 and its hair has not t white,
13:10 and it has t the hair white,
13:13 It has all t white. He is
13:17 and indeed if the sore has t
13:20 and its hair has t white,
13:25 hair of the bright spot has t
Num 12:10 Then Aaron t toward Miriam,
14:43 because you have t away from
16:42 that they t toward the
20:21 so Israel t away from him.
21:33 And they t and went up by the
22:23 and the donkey t aside out of
22:33 The donkey saw Me and t aside
22:33 If she had not t aside from Me,
25:11 has t back My wrath from the
33: 7 They moved from Etham and t back
Deut 2: 1 Then we t and journeyed into the
2: 8 we t and passed by way of the
3: 1 Then we t and went up the road
9:12 they have quickly t aside from
9:15 So I t and came down from the
9:16 You had t aside quickly from
10: 5 Then I t and came down from the
23: 5 but the LORD your God t the
31:18 in that they have t to other
Josh 7:12 but t their backs before
7:26 So the LORD t from the
8:20 had fled to the wilderness t
8:21 they t back and struck down the
11:10 Joshua t back at that time and
15: 7 and it t northward toward
15:10 Then the border t westward from
19:27 It t toward the sunrise to Beth
19:29 And the border t to Ramah and to
19:29 then the border t to Hosah,
Judg 2:17 They t quickly from the way in
3:19 But he himself t back from the
4:18 And when he had t aside with
6:14 Then the LORD t to him and
11: 8 That is why we have t again to
14: 8 he t aside to see the carcass
15: 4 t the foxes tail
18: 3 They t aside and said to him,
18:15 So they t aside there, and came
18:21 Then they t and departed,
18:23 So they t around and said to
18:26 he t and went back to his
19:15 They t aside there to go in to
20:41 And when the men of Israel t
20:42 Therefore they t their backs
20:45 Then they t and fled toward the
20:47 But six hundred men t and fled
20:48 And the men of Israel t back
Ruth 3: 8 was startled, and t himself;
1 Sam 8: 3 they t aside after dishonest
10: 6 prophesy with them and be t
10: 9 when he had t his back to go
13:17 One company t to the road to
13:18 another company t to the road
13:18 and another company t to the
14:47 Wherever he t, he harassed
15:11 for he has t back from
15:27 And as Samuel t around to go
15:31 So Samuel t back after Saul,
17:30 Then he t from him toward
22:18 So Doeg the Edomite t and
25:12 So David's young men t on their
2 Sam 18:30 So he t aside and stood
19: 2 So the victory that day was t
1 Ki 2:15 the kingdom has been t over,
8:14 Then the king t around and
10:13 So she t and went to her own
11: 3 and his wives t away his heart.
11: 4 that his wives t his heart
11: 9 because his heart had t from
12:24 and t back, according to the
15: 5 and had not t aside from
18:37 and that You have t their
19:21 So Elisha t back from him,
21: 4 and t away his face, and would
22:32 Therefore they t aside to fight
22:33 that they t back from pursuing
2 Ki 2:24 So he t around and looked at
4:11 and he t in to the upper room
5:12 So he t and went away in a
5:26 go with you when the man t
9:23 Then Joram t around and fled,
15:20 So the king of Assyria t back,
20: 2 Then he t his face toward the
23:16 As Josiah t, he saw the tombs
23:25 who t to the LORD with all his
24: 1 Then he t and rebelled against
1 Chr 10:14 and t the kingdom over to David
21:20 Now Ornan t and saw the angel;
2 Chr 6: 3 Then the king t around and
9:12 So she t and went to her own
11: 4 and t back from attacking
12:12 the wrath of the LORD t from
15: 4 when in their trouble they t
18:32 that they t back from pursuing
20:10 but they t from them and did
25:27 After the time that Amaziah t
29: 6 have t their faces away from
29: 6 and t their backs on Him.
Ezra 6:22 and t the heart of the king of
10:14 fierce wrath of our God is t
Neh 2:15 then I t back and entered by
13: 2 our God t the curse into a
Esth 9:22 as the month which was t from
Job 16:11 And t me over to the hands of
19:19 And those whom I love have t
23:11 I have kept His way and not t
28: 5 But underneath it is t up as
30:15 Terrors are t upon me;
30:31 My harp is t to mourning,
31: 7 If my step has t from the way,
34:27 Because they t back from Him,
37:12 being t by His guidance,
Ps 9:17 The wicked shall be t into
14: 3 They have all t aside,
30:11 You have t for me my mourning
32: 4 My vitality was t into the
35: 4 Let those be t back and
44:18 Our heart has not t back,
53: 3 Every one of them has t aside;
66: 6 He t the sea into dry land;
66:20 Who has not t away my prayer,
70: 2 Let them be t back and
70: 3 Let them be t back because of
78: 9 T back in the day of battle.
78:38 many a time He t His anger
78:44 T their rivers into blood,
78:57 But t back and acted
78:57 They were t aside like a
85: 3 You have t from the fierceness
89:43 You have also t back the edge
105:25 He t their heart to hate His
105:29 He t their waters into blood,
114: 3 Jordan t back.
114: 5 that you t back?
114: 8 Who t the rock into a pool of
119:59 And t my feet to Your
129: 5 Zion Be put to shame and t
Eccl 2:12 Then I t myself to consider
2:20 Therefore I t my heart and
Song 5: 6 But my beloved had t away and
6: 1 Where has your beloved t
Isa 1: 4 They have t away backward.
5:25 this His anger is not t away,
9:12 this His anger is not t away,
9:17 this His anger is not t away,
9:21 this His anger is not t away,
10: 4 this His anger is not t away,
12: 1 Your anger is t away, and You
21: 4 night for which I longed He t
29:16 Surely you have things t
29:17 Till Lebanon shall be t into
34: 9 Its streams shall be t into
38: 2 Then Hezekiah t his face toward
42:17 They shall be t back,
44:20 A deceived heart has t him
53: 6 have gone astray; We have t,
59:14 Justice is t back,
60: 5 of the sea shall be t to you,
63:10 So He t Himself against them
Jer 2:21 How then have you t before Me
2:27 For they have t their back
3:10 sister Judah has not t to Me
4: 8 anger of the LORD Has not t
5:25 Your iniquities have t these
6:12 And their houses shall be t
8: 6 Everyone t to his own course,
11:10 They have t back to the
23:22 Then they would have t them
30: 6 And all faces t pale?
32:33 And they have t to Me the back,
34:15 Then you recently t and did what
34:16 Then you t around and profaned
38:22 And they have t away
41:14 away captive from Mizpah t
46: 5 I seen them dismayed and t
46:21 For they also are t back,
48:39 How Moab has t her back
50: 6 They have t them away on the
Lam 1:13 a net for my feet And t me
3: 3 Surely He has t His hand
3:11 He has t aside my ways and torn
5: 2 Our inheritance has been t over
5:15 Our dance has t into mourning.
Ezek 17: 6 Its branches t toward him,
26: 2 now she is t over to me;
28:18 And I t you to ashes upon the
29:16 of their iniquity when they t
Dan 9:16 Your anger and Your fury be t
10: 8 for my vigor was t to frailty
10:15 I t my face toward the ground
Hos 14: 4 For My anger has t away from
Joel 2:31 The sun shall be t into
Am 6:12 Yet you have t justice into
Jon 3:10 that they t from their evil
Hab 2:16 LORD's right hand will be t
Zeph 1: 6 Those who have t back from
Zech 5: 1 Then I t and raised my eyes,
6: 1 Then I t and raised my eyes and
14:10 All the land shall be t into
Mal 2: 6 And t many away from iniquity.
Mt 2:22 he t aside into the region of
9:22 But Jesus t around, and when He
16:23 But He t and said to Peter,
Mk 5:30 t around in the crowd and said,

8:33 But when He had *t* around and
Lk 7: 9 and *t* around and said to the
7:44 Then He *t* to the woman and said
9:55 But He *t* and rebuked them,
10:23 Then He *t* to His disciples and
14:25 And He *t* and said to them,
22:61 And the Lord *t* and looked at
Jn 1:38 Then Jesus *t*, and seeing them
16:20 but your sorrow will be *t* into
20:14 she *t* around and saw Jesus
20:16 She *t* and said to Him,
Acts 2:20 The sun shall be *t* into
7:39 And in their hearts they *t* back
7:42 Then God *t* and gave them up to
9:35 Lydda and Sharon saw him and *t*
11:21 a great number believed and *t*
16:18 *t* and said to the spirit,
17: 6 These who have *t* the world
19:26 this Paul has persuaded and *t*
Rom 3:12 They have all *t* aside;
Phil 1:12 to me have actually *t* out for
1 Th 1: 9 and how you *t* to God from idols
1 Tim 1: 6 have *t* aside to idle talk,
5:15 For some have already *t* aside
2 Tim 1:15 that all those in Asia have *t*
4: 4 and be *t* aside to fables.
Heb 11:34 *t* to flight the armies of the
Jas 3: 4 they are *t* by a very small
4: 9 your laughter be *t* to mourning
Rev 1:12 Then I *t* to see the voice that
1:12 And having *t* I saw seven golden

TURNING (14/14) TURN

2 Ki 21:13 wiping it and *t* it upside
2 Chr 36:13 hardened his heart against *t*
Prov 1:32 For the *t* away of the simple
Isa 28:24 Does he keep *t* his soil and
Jer 31:19 Surely, after my *t*,
Hos 5: 4 direct their deeds Toward *t*
Lk 23:28 *t* to them, said, "Daughters of
Jn 21:20 *t* around, saw the disciple whom
Acts 3:26 in *t* away every one of you
9:40 And *t* to the body he said,
15:19 among the Gentiles who are *t*
Gal 1: 6 I marvel that you are *t* away so
Jas 1:17 is no variation or shadow of *t*.
2 Pe 2: 6 and *t* the cities of Sodom and

TURNS (40/40) TURN

Gen 27:44 until your brother's fury *t*
27:45 until your brother's anger *t*
Lev 13:16 if the raw flesh changes and *t*
20: 6 And the person who *t* to mediums
Deut 29:18 whose heart *t* away today from
30:17 But if your heart *t* away so that
Josh 7: 8 what shall I say when Israel *t*
Job 20:14 his food in his stomach *t* sour;
23: 9 When He *t* to the right hand,
Ps 107:33 He *t* rivers into a wilderness,
107:35 He *t* a wilderness into pools of
146: 9 But the way of the wicked He *t*
Prov 15: 1 A soft answer *t* away wrath,
17: 8 Wherever he *t*, he
21: 1 He *t* it wherever He wishes.
26:14 As a door *t* on its hinges,
28: 9 One who *t* away his ear from
Eccl 1: 6 And *t* around to the north;
Isa 44:25 Who *t* wise men backward,
Jer 13:16 He *t* it into the shadow of
14: 8 And like a traveler who *t*
18: 8 against whom I have spoken *t*
23:14 So that no one *t* back from his
49:24 She *t* to flee, And fear has
Lam 1: 8 she sighs and *t* away.
Ezek 3:20 when a righteous man *t* from
18:21 But if a wicked man *t* from all
18:24 But when a righteous man *t* away
18:26 When a righteous man *t* away
18:27 when a wicked man *t* away from
18:28 Because he considers and *t* away
33:12 of it in the day that he *t*
33:14 if he *t* from his sin and does
33:18 When the righteous *t* from his
33:19 But when the wicked *t* from his
Am 5: 8 He *t* the shadow of death into
Nah 2: 8 But no one *t* back.
2 Cor 3:16 Nevertheless when one *t* to the
Jas 5:19 and someone *t* him back,
5:20 let him know that he who *t* a

TURQUOISE (4/4)

Ex 28:18 "the second row shall be a *t*,
39:11 the second row, a *t*,
Esth 1: 6 pavement of alabaster, *t*,
Ezek 28:13 onyx, and jasper, Sapphire, *t*,

TURTLEDOVE (5/5) TURTLEDOVES

Gen 15: 9 goat, a three-year-old ram, a *t*,
Lev 12: 6 and a young pigeon or a *t* as a
Ps 74:19 not deliver the life of Your *t*
Song 2:12 And the voice of the *t* Is
Jer 8: 7 And the *t*, the swift,

TURTLEDOVES (10/10) TURTLEDOVE

Lev 1:14 shall bring his offering of *t*
5: 7 two *t* or two young pigeons:
5:11 he is not able to bring two *t*
12: 8 then she may bring two *t* or two
14:22 and two *t* or two young pigeons,
14:30 he shall offer one of the *t* or
15:14 he shall take for himself two *t*
15:29 shall take for herself two *t*
Num 6:10 day he shall bring two *t* or
Lk 2:24 A pair of *t* or two young

TUSKS (1/1)

Ezek 27:15 They brought you ivory *t* and

TUTOR (2/2)

Gal 3:24 Therefore the law was our *t* to
3:25 we are no longer under a *t*.

TUTORS (KJV) See GUARDIANS

TWAIN (KJV) See BOTH, TWO

TWELFTH (23/20)

Num 7:78 On the *t* day Ahira the son of
1 Ki 19:19 and he was with the *t*.
2 Ki 8:25 In the *t* year of Joram the son
17: 1 In the *t* year of Ahaz king of
25:27 in the *t* month, on the
1 Chr 24:12 the *t* to Jakim,
25:19 the *t* for Hashabiah, his sons
27:15 The *t* captain for the twelfth
27:15 captain for the *t* month
2 Chr 34: 3 and in the *t* year he began to
Ezra 8:31 river of Ahava on the *t* day
Esth 3: 7 in the *t* year of King
3: 7 until it fell on the *t*
3:13 thirteenth day of the *t* month
8:12 thirteenth day of the *t* month
9: 1 Now in the *t* month, that is,
Jer 52:31 in the *t* month, on the
Ezek 29: 1 on the *t* day of the month,
32: 1 came to pass in the *t* year,
32: 1 in the *t* month, on the first
32:17 to pass also in the *t* year,
33:21 came to pass in the *t* year
Rev 21:20 and the *t* amethyst.

TWELVE (187/163)

Gen 5: 8 of Seth were nine hundred and *t*
14: 4 *T* years they served
17:20 He shall beget *t* princes,
25:16 *t* princes according to their
35:22 Now the sons of Jacob were *t*:
42:13 Your servants are *t* brothers,
42:32 We are *t* brothers, sons of our
49:28 All these are the *t* tribes of
Ex 15:27 where there were *t* wells of
24: 4 and *t* pillars according to the
24: 4 according to the *t* tribes
28:21 *t* according to their names,
28:21 be according to the *t* tribes
39:14 There were *t* stones according
39:14 name according to the *t* tribes
Lev 24: 5 take fine flour and bake *t* cakes
Num 1:44 *t* men, each one representing
7: 3 six covered carts and *t* oxen,
7:84 *t* silver platters, twelve
7:84 *t* silver bowls, and twelve gold
7:84 and *t* gold pans.
7:86 The *t* gold pans full of incense
7:87 for the burnt offering were *t*
7:87 twelve young bulls, the rams *t*,
7:87 lambs in their first year *t*,
7:87 the goats as a sin offering *t*.
17: 2 their fathers' houses—*t* rods.
17: 6 *t* rods; and the rod of Aaron
29:17 second day present *t* young bulls
31: 5 *t* thousand armed for war.
33: 9 At Elim were *t* springs of
Deut 1:23 so I took *t* of your men,
Josh 3:12 take for yourselves *t* men from
4: 2 Take for yourselves *t* men from
4: 3 Take for yourselves *t* stones
4: 4 Then Joshua called the *t* men
4: 8 and took up *t* stones from the
4: 9 Then Joshua set up *t* stones in
4:20 And those *t* stones which they
8:25 were *t* thousand—all the people
18:24 *t* cities with their villages;
19:15 *t* cities with their villages.
21: 7 to their families had *t* cities
21:40 were by their lot *t* cities.
Judg 19:29 and divided her into *t* pieces,
21:10 congregation sent out there *t*
2 Sam 2:15 *t* from Benjamin, followers of
2:15 and *t* from the servants of
10: 6 and from Ish-Tob *t* thousand
17: 1 Now let me choose *t* thousand
1 Ki 4: 7 And Solomon had *t* governors
4:26 and *t* thousand horsemen.
7:15 and a line of *t* cubits measured
7:25 It stood on *t* oxen:
7:44 and *t* oxen under the Sea;
10:20 *T* lions stood there, one on each
10:26 chariots and *t* thousand horsemen
11:30 and tore it into *t* pieces.
16:23 and reigned *t* years.
18:31 And Elijah took *t* stones,
19:19 who was plowing with *t* yoke
2 Ki 3: 1 of Judah, and reigned *t* years.
21: 1 Manasseh was *t* years old when
1 Chr 6:63 they gave *t* cities from the
9:22 were two hundred and *t*.
15:10 and one hundred and *t* of his
25: 9 with his brethren and sons, *t*;
25:10 his sons and his brethren, *t*;
25:11 his sons and his brethren, *t*;
25:12 his sons and his brethren, *t*;
25:13 his sons and his brethren, *t*;
25:14 his sons and his brethren, *t*;
25:15 his sons and his brethren, *t*;
25:16 his sons and his brethren, *t*;
25:17 his sons and his brethren, *t*;
25:18 his sons and his brethren, *t*;
25:19 his sons and his brethren, *t*;
25:20 his sons and his brethren, *t*;
25:21 his sons and his brethren, *t*;
25:22 his sons and his brethren, *t*;
25:23 his sons and his brethren, *t*;
25:24 his sons and his brethren, *t*;
25:25 his sons and his brethren, *t*;
25:26 his sons and his brethren, *t*;
25:27 his sons and his brethren, *t*;
25:28 his sons and his brethren, *t*;
25:29 his sons and his brethren, *t*;
25:30 his sons and his brethren, *t*;
25:31 his sons and his brethren, *t*.
2 Chr 1:14 chariots and *t* thousand horsemen
4: 4 It stood on *t* oxen:
4:15 one Sea and *t* oxen under it;
9:19 *T* lions stood there, one on each
9:25 and *t* thousand horsemen whom he
12: 3 with *t* hundred chariots, sixty
33: 1 Manasseh was *t* years old when
Ezra 2: 6 thousand eight hundred and *t*;
2:18 of Jorah, one hundred and *t*;
6:17 for all Israel *t* male goats,
8:24 And I separated *t* of the
8:35 *t* bulls for all Israel,
8:35 and *t* male goats as a sin
Neh 5:14 *t* years, neither I nor my
7:24 of Hariph, one hundred and *t*;
Esth 2:12 she had completed *t* months'
Ps 60: and Joab returned and killed *t*
Jer 52:20 the *t* bronze bulls which were
52:21 a measuring line of *t* cubits
Ezek 43:16 The altar hearth is *t* cubits
43:16 *t* wide, square at its four
47:13 inheritance among the *t* tribes
Dan 4:29 At the end of the *t* months he
Mt 9:20 a flow of blood for *t* years
10: 1 He had called His *t* disciples
10: 2 Now the names of the *t* apostles
10: 5 These *t* Jesus sent out and
11: 1 finished commanding His *t* disciples
14:20 and they took up *t* baskets full
19:28 will also sit on *t* thrones
19:28 judging the *t* tribes of Israel.
20:17 took the *t* disciples aside on
26:14 Then one of the *t*,
26:20 He sat down with the *t*.
26:47 behold, Judas, one of the *t*,
26:53 with more than *t* legions
Mk 3:14 Then He appointed *t*,
4:10 those around Him with the *t*
5:25 had a flow of blood for *t* years
5:42 for she was *t* years of age.
6: 7 And He called the *t* to
6:43 And they took up *t* baskets full
8:19 They said to Him, "*T*."
9:35 And He sat down, called the *t*,
10:32 Then He took the *t* aside again
11:11 went out to Bethany with the *t*.
14:10 Judas Iscariot, one of the *t*,
14:17 the evening He came with the *t*.
14:20 to them, "It is one of the *t*,
14:43 speaking, Judas, one of the *t*,
Lk 2:42 And when He was *t* years old,
6:13 and from them He chose *t* whom
8: 1 And the *t* were with Him,
8:42 he had an only daughter about *t*
8:43 a flow of blood for *t* years
9: 1 Then He called His *t* disciples
9:12 the *t* came and said to Him,
9:17 and *t* baskets of the leftover
18:31 Then He took the *t* aside and
22: 3 who was numbered among the *t*.
22:14 and the *t* apostles with Him.
22:30 thrones judging the *t* tribes
22:47 was called Judas, one of the *t*,
Jn 6:13 and filled *t* baskets with the
6:67 Then Jesus said to the *t*,
6:70 "Did I not choose you, the *t*,
6:71 betray Him, being one of the *t*.
11: 9 Are there not *t* hours in the
20:24 called the Twin, one of the *t*,
Acts 6: 2 Then the *t* summoned the
7: 8 Jacob begot the *t* patriarchs
19: 7 Now the men were about *t* in all.
24:11 that it is no more than *t* days
26: 7 To this promise our *t* tribes,
1 Cor 15: 5 seen by Cephas, then by the *t*.
Jas 1: 1 To the *t* tribes which are
Rev 7: 5 of the tribe of Judah *t*
7: 5 of the tribe of Reuben *t*
7: 5 of the tribe of Gad *t* thousand
7: 6 of the tribe of Asher *t*
7: 6 of the tribe of Naphtali *t*
7: 6 of the tribe of Manasseh *t*
7: 7 of the tribe of Simeon *t*
7: 7 of the tribe of Levi *t*
7: 7 of the tribe of Issachar *t*
7: 8 of the tribe of Zebulun *t*
7: 8 of the tribe of Joseph *t*

7: 8 of the tribe of Benjamin ***t***
12: 1 her head a garland of ***t*** stars
21:12 great and high wall with ***t*** gates
21:12 and ***t*** angels at the gates,
21:12 are the names of the ***t*** tribes
21:14 the city had ***t*** foundations,
21:14 were the names of the ***t*** apostles
21:16 ***t*** thousand furlongs.
21:21 The ***t*** gates were twelve pearls:
21:21 The twelve gates were ***t*** pearls:
22: 2 which bore ***t*** fruits, each tree

TWENTIETH (9/9)

Num 10:11 it came to pass on the ***t*** day
1 Ki 15: 9 In the ***t*** year of Jeroboam king
2 Ki 15:30 in his place in the ***t*** year
1 Chr 24:16 the ***t*** to Jehezekel,
25:27 the ***t*** for Eliathah, his sons and
Ezra 10: 9 on the ***t*** of the month; and all
Neh 1: 1 in the ***t*** year, as I was in
2: 1 in the ***t*** year of King
5:14 from the ***t*** year until the

TWENTY (148/129)

Gen 6: 3 days shall be one hundred and ***t***
18:31 Suppose ***t*** should be found
18:31 destroy it for the sake of ***t***.
31:38 These ***t*** years I have been with
31:41 been in your house ***t*** years
32:14 female goats and ***t*** male goats,
32:14 two hundred ewes and ***t*** rams,
32:15 ***t*** female donkeys and ten foals.
37:28 Ishmaelites for ***t*** shekels
Ex 26:18 ***t*** boards for the south side.
26:19 of silver under the ***t*** boards
26:20 there shall be ***t*** boards
27:10 And its ***t*** pillars and their
27:10 pillars and their ***t*** sockets
27:11 with its ***t*** pillars and their
27:11 pillars and their ***t*** sockets
27:16 shall be a screen ***t*** cubits
30:13 (a shekel is ***t*** gerahs).
30:14 from ***t*** years old and above,
36:23 ***t*** boards for the south side.
36:24 to go under the ***t*** boards;
36:25 he made ***t*** boards
38:10 There were ***t*** pillars for them,
38:10 with ***t*** bronze sockets.
38:11 with ***t*** pillars and their twenty
38:11 with twenty pillars and their ***t***
38:18 The length was ***t*** cubits,
38:26 in the numbering from ***t*** years
Lev 27: 3 valuation is of a male from ***t***
27: 5 five years old up to ***t*** years
27: 5 for a male shall be ***t*** shekels,
27:25 ***t*** gerahs to the shekel.
Num 1: 3 from ***t*** years old and above—all
1:18 from ***t*** years old and above,
1:20 from ***t*** years old and above,
1:22 from ***t*** years old and above,
1:24 from ***t*** years old and above,
1:26 from ***t*** years old and above,
1:28 from ***t*** years old and above,
1:30 from ***t*** years old and above,
1:32 from ***t*** years old and above,
1:34 from ***t*** years old and above,
1:36 from ***t*** years old and above,
1:38 from ***t*** years old and above,
1:40 from ***t*** years old and above,
1:42 from ***t*** years old and above,
1:45 from ***t*** years old and above,
3:47 the shekel of ***t*** gerahs.
7:86 pans weighed one hundred and ***t***
11:19 nor ten days, nor ***t*** days,
14:29 from ***t*** years old and above.
18:16 which is ***t*** GERAHS.
26: 2 from ***t*** years old and above,
26: 4 of the people from ***t*** years
32:11 from ***t*** years old and above,
Deut 31: 2 I am one hundred and ***t*** years
34: 7 Moses was one hundred and ***t***
Judg 4: 3 and for ***t*** years he harshly
8:10 for one hundred and ***t*** thousand
11:33 ***t*** cities—and to Abel Keramim,
15:20 And he judged Israel ***t*** years in
16:31 He had judged Israel ***t*** years.
1 Sam 7: 2 it was there ***t*** years. And all
14:14 made was about ***t*** men within
2 Sam 3:20 So Abner and ***t*** men with him came
8: 4 and ***t*** thousand foot soldiers.
9:10 had fifteen sons and ***t*** servants.
10: 6 ***t*** thousand foot soldiers;
18: 7 slaughter of ***t*** thousand
19:17 fifteen sons and his ***t*** servants
24: 8 end of nine months and ***t*** days.
1 Ki 4:23 ***t*** oxen from the pastures,
5:11 gave Hiram ***t*** thousand kors
5:11 and ***t*** kors of pressed oil.
6: 2 was sixty cubits, its width ***t***,
6: 3 sanctuary of the house was ***t***
6:20 The inner sanctuary was ***t***
6:20 ***t*** cubits wide, and twenty
6:20 and ***t*** cubits high. He overlaid
8:63 one hundred and ***t*** thousand sheep.
9:10 happened at the end of ***t*** years
9:11 Solomon then gave Hiram ***t*** cities
9:14 sent the king one hundred and ***t***
9:28 and acquired four hundred and ***t***
10:10 gave the king one hundred and ***t***
2 Ki 4:42 ***t*** loaves of barley bread,
15:27 and reigned ***t*** years.
16: 2 Ahaz was ***t*** years old when he
1 Chr 7: 9 ***t*** thousand two hundred mighty
12:30 of the sons of Ephraim ***t***
12:37 one hundred and ***t*** thousand
15: 5 and one hundred and ***t*** of his
15: 6 and two hundred and ***t*** of his
18: 4 and ***t*** thousand foot soldiers.
23:24 from the age of ***t*** years and
23:27 Levites were numbered from ***t***
27:23 the number of those ***t*** years
2 Chr 2:10 ***t*** thousand kors of ground
2:10 ***t*** thousand kors of barley,
2:10 ***t*** thousand baths of wine,
2:10 and ***t*** thousand baths of oil.
3: 3 former measure) and the width ***t***
3: 4 the sanctuary was ***t*** cubits
3: 4 height was one hundred and ***t***.
3: 8 ***t*** cubits, and its width twenty
3: 8 and its width ***t*** cubits.
3:11 of the cherubim were ***t*** cubits
3:13 cherubim spanned ***t*** cubits
4: 1 ***t*** cubits was its length, twenty
4: 1 ***t*** cubits its width, and ten
5:12 and with them one hundred and ***t***
7: 5 one hundred and ***t*** thousand sheep.
8: 1 pass at the end of ***t*** years
9: 9 gave the king one hundred and ***t***
25: 5 numbered them from ***t*** years
28: 1 Ahaz was ***t*** years old when he
28: 6 killed one hundred and ***t***
31:17 and to the Levites from ***t*** years
Ezra 2:32 of Harim, three hundred and ***t***;
2:67 thousand seven hundred and ***t***.
3: 8 the Levites from ***t*** years old
8:19 brothers and their sons, ***t*** men;
8:20 two hundred and ***t*** Nethinim.
8:27 ***t*** gold basins worth a thousand
Neh 7:35 of Harim, three hundred and ***t***;
7:69 thousand seven hundred and ***t***.
7:71 work ***t*** thousand gold drachmas.
7:72 rest of the people gave was ***t***
Ps 68:17 The chariots of God are ***t***
Ezek 4:10 ***t*** shekels a day; from time to
40:49 of the vestibule was ***t*** cubits
41: 2 and its width, ***t*** cubits.
41: 4 ***t*** cubits; and the width, twenty
41: 4 ***t*** cubits, beyond the sanctuary;
41:10 chambers was a width of ***t*** cubits
42: 3 the inner court of ***t*** cubits,
45: 5 they shall have ***t*** chambers as a
45:12 The shekel shall be ***t*** gerahs;
45:12 ***t*** shekels, twenty-five shekels,
Dan 6: 1 the kingdom one hundred and ***t***
Jon 4:11 are more than one hundred and ***t***
Hag 2:16 came to a heap of ***t*** ephahs,
2:16 the press, there were but ***t***.
Zech 5: 2 Its length is ***t*** cubits and its
Lk 14:31 against him with ***t*** thousand?
Jn 2: 6 containing ***t*** or thirty gallons
Acts 1:15 was about a hundred and ***t***),
27:28 and found it to be ***t*** fathoms;

TWENTY-CUBIT (1/1)

1 Ki 6:16 Then he built the ***t*** room at the

TWENTY-EIGHT (13/13)

Ex 26: 2 each curtain shall be ***t*** cubits,
36: 9 each curtain was ***t*** cubits,
2 Ki 10:36 Israel in Samaria was ***t*** years.
1 Chr 12:35 ***t*** thousand six hundred;
2 Chr 11:21 and begot ***t*** sons and sixty
Ezra 2:23 of Anathoth, one hundred and ***t***;
2:41 of Asaph, one hundred and ***t***.
8:11 and with him ***t*** males;
Neh 7:16 of Bebai, six hundred and ***t***;
7:22 of Hashum, three hundred and ***t***;
7:27 of Anathoth, one hundred and ***t***;
11: 8 and Sallai, nine hundred and ***t***.
11:14 valor, were one hundred and ***t***.

TWENTY-FIFTH (3/3)

Neh 6:15 wall was finished on the ***t*** day
Jer 52:31 on the ***t*** day of the month,
Ezek 40: 1 In the ***t*** year of our captivity,

TWENTY-FIRST (4/4)

Ex 12:18 until the ***t*** day of the month at
1 Chr 24:17 the ***t*** to Jachin,
25:28 the ***t*** for Hothir, his sons and
Hag 2: 1 on the ***t*** of the month, the word

TWENTY-FIVE (40/36)

Num 8:24 From ***t*** years old and above one
Judg 20:35 of Israel destroyed that day ***t***
20:46 of Benjamin that day were ***t***
1 Ki 22:42 and he reigned ***t*** years in
2 Ki 14: 2 He was ***t*** years old when he
15:33 He was ***t*** years old when he
18: 2 He was ***t*** years old when he
23:36 Jehoiakim was ***t*** years old when
2 Chr 20:31 and he reigned ***t*** years in
25: 1 Amaziah was ***t*** years old when
27: 1 Jotham was ***t*** years old when he
27: 8 He was ***t*** years old when he
29: 1 became king when he was ***t***
36: 5 Jehoiakim was ***t*** years old when
Ezra 2:33 and Ono, seven hundred and ***t***;
Ezek 8:16 were about ***t*** men with their
11: 1 door of the gate were ***t*** men
40:13 the width was ***t*** cubits,
40:21 and its width ***t*** cubits.
40:25 and its width ***t*** cubits.
40:29 was fifty cubits long and ***t***
40:30 ***t*** cubits long and five cubits
40:33 long and ***t*** cubits wide.
40:36 cubits and its width ***t*** cubits.
45: 1 length shall be ***t*** thousand
45: 3 ***t*** thousand cubits long and ten
45: 5 An area ***t*** thousand cubits
45: 6 cubits wide and ***t*** thousand long,
45:12 ***t*** shekels, and fifteen shekels
48: 8 ***t*** thousand cubits in width,
48: 9 shall be ***t*** thousand cubits
48:10 on the north ***t*** thousand cubits
48:10 and on the south ***t*** thousand in
48:13 have an area ***t*** thousand cubits
48:13 length shall be ***t*** thousand
48:15 the edge of the ***t*** thousand,
48:20 entire district shall be ***t***
48:20 thousand cubits by ***t*** thousand
48:21 next to the ***t*** thousand cubits
48:21 and westward next to the ***t***

TWENTY-FOUR (27/26)

Num 7:88 offerings were ***t*** bulls,
25: 9 who died in the plague were ***t***
2 Sam 21:20 toes on each foot, ***t*** in number;
1 Ki 15:33 and reigned ***t*** years.
1 Chr 20: 6 with ***t*** fingers and toes,
23: 4 ***t*** thousand were to look after
27: 1 each division having ***t*** thousand.
27: 2 in his division were ***t*** thousand;
27: 4 in his division were ***t*** thousand.
27: 5 in his division were ***t*** thousand.
27: 7 in his division were ***t*** thousand.
27: 8 in his division were ***t*** thousand.
27: 9 in his division were ***t*** thousand.
27:10 in his division were ***t*** thousand.
27:11 in his division were ***t*** thousand.
27:12 in his division were ***t*** thousand.
27:13 in his division were ***t*** thousand.
27:14 in his division were ***t*** thousand.
27:15 in his division were ***t*** thousand.
Neh 7:23 of Bezai, three hundred and ***t***;
Rev 4: 4 Around the throne were ***t*** thrones
4: 4 on the thrones I saw ***t*** elders
4:10 the ***t*** elders fall down before
5: 8 four living creatures and the ***t***
5:14 Amen!" And the ***t*** elders fell
11:16 And the ***t*** elders who sat before
19: 4 And the ***t*** elders and the four

TWENTY-FOURTH (9/9)

1 Chr 24:18 the ***t*** to Maaziah,
25:31 the ***t*** for Romamti-Ezer, his sons
Neh 9: 1 Now on the ***t*** day of this month
Dan 10: 4 Now on the ***t*** day of the first
Hag 1:15 on the ***t*** day of the sixth month,
2:10 On the ***t*** day of the ninth
2:18 from the ***t*** day of the ninth
2:20 came to Haggai on the ***t*** day
Zech 1: 7 On the ***t*** day of the eleventh

TWENTY-NINE (8/8)

Gen 11:24 Nahor lived ***t*** years, and begot
Ex 38:24 was ***t*** talents and seven hundred
Josh 15:32 all the cities are ***t***,
2 Ki 14: 2 and he reigned ***t*** years in
18: 2 and he reigned ***t*** years in
2 Chr 25: 1 and he reigned ***t*** years in
29: 1 and he reigned ***t*** years in
Ezra 1: 9 silver platters, ***t*** knives,

TWENTY-ONE (7/7)

2 Ki 24:18 Zedekiah was ***t*** years old when
2 Chr 36:11 Zedekiah was ***t*** years old when
Ezra 2:26 and Geba, six hundred and ***t***;
Neh 7:30 and Geba, six hundred and ***t***;
7:37 and Ono, seven hundred and ***t***;
Jer 52: 1 Zedekiah was ***t*** years old when
Dan 10:13 of Persia withstood me ***t*** days;

TWENTY-SECOND (2/2)

1 Chr 24:17 the ***t*** to Gamul,
25:29 the ***t*** for Giddalti, his sons and

TWENTY-SEVEN (5/5)

Gen 23: 1 Sarah lived one hundred and ***t***
1 Ki 20:30 then a wall fell on ***t*** thousand
Esth 1: 1 reigned over one hundred and ***t***
8: 9 one hundred and ***t*** provinces in
9:30 the one hundred and ***t*** provinces

TWENTY-SEVENTH (6/6)

Gen 8:14 on the ***t*** day of the month,
1 Ki 16:10 and killed him in the ***t*** year
16:15 In the ***t*** year of Asa king of
2 Ki 15: 1 In the ***t*** year of Jeroboam king
25:27 on the ***t*** day of the month,
Ezek 29:17 came to pass in the ***t*** year

TWENTY-SIX (2/2)
Judg 20:15 children of Benjamin numbered *t*
1 Chr 7:40 their number was *t* thousand.

TWENTY-SIXTH (1/1)
1 Ki 16: 8 In the *t* year of Asa king of

TWENTY-THIRD (8/8)
2 Ki 12: 6 by the *t* year of King Jehoash,
13: 1 In the *t* year of Joash the son
1 Chr 24:18 the *t* to Delaiah,
25:30 the *t* for Mahazioth, his sons
2 Chr 7:10 On the *t* day of the seventh
Esth 8: 9 month of Sivan, on the *t* day;
Jer 25: 3 this is the *t* year in which
52:30 in the *t* year of Nebuchadnezzar,

TWENTY-THREE (14/14)
Num 26:62 were numbered of them were *t*
33:39 Aaron was one hundred and *t*
Judg 10: 2 He judged Israel *t* years; and he
2 Ki 23:31 Jehoahaz was *t* years old when
1 Chr 2:22 who had *t* cities in the land of
2 Chr 36: 2 Jehoahaz was *t* years old when
Ezra 2:11 of Bebai, six hundred and *t*;
2:17 of Bezai, three hundred and *t*;
2:19 of Hashum, two hundred and *t*;
2:21 of Bethlehem, one hundred and *t*;
2:28 and Ai, two hundred and *t*;
Neh 7:32 and Ai, one hundred and *t*;
Jer 52:28 three thousand and *t* Jews;
1 Cor 10: 8 and in one day *t* thousand fell;

TWENTY-TWO (25/25)
Num 3:39 were *t* thousand.
3:43 were *t* thousand two hundred and
26:14 *t* thousand two hundred.
Josh 19:30 *t* cities with their villages.
Judg 7: 3 And *t* thousand of the
10: 3 and he judged Israel *t* years.
20:21 to the ground *t* thousand men
2 Sam 8: 5 David killed *t* thousand of the
1 Ki 8:63 *t* thousand bulls and one
14:20 Jeroboam reigned was *t* years
16:29 over Israel in Samaria *t* years.
2 Ki 8:26 Ahaziah was *t* years old when he
21:19 Amon was *t* years old when he
1 Chr 7: 2 in the days of David was *t*
7: 7 *t* thousand and thirty-four
12:28 father's house *t* captains;
18: 5 David killed *t* thousand of the
2 Chr 7: 5 sacrifice of *t* thousand bulls
13:21 and begot *t* sons and sixteen
33:21 Amon was *t* years old when he
Ezra 2:12 one thousand two hundred and *t*;
2:27 of Michmas, one hundred and *t*;
Neh 7:17 thousand three hundred and *t*;
7:31 of Michmas, one hundred and *t*;
11:12 house were eight hundred and *t*;

TWICE (18/18)
Gen 41:32 dream was repeated to Pharaoh *t*
Ex 16: 5 and it shall be *t* as much as
16:22 that they gathered *t* as much
Num 20:11 his hand and struck the rock *t*
1 Sam 18:11 David escaped his presence *t*.
1 Ki 11: 9 who had appeared to him *t*,
2 Ki 6:10 not just once or *t*.
Neh 13:20 outside Jerusalem once or *t*.
Job 33:29 God works all these things, *T*,
40: 5 Yes, *t*, but I will proceed no
42:10 Indeed the LORD gave Job *t* as
Ps 62:11 *T* I have heard this: That
Eccl 6: 6 if he lives a thousand years *t*—
Mt 23:15 you make him *t* as much a son of
Mk 14:30 before the rooster crows *t*,
14:72 "Before the rooster crows *t*,
Lk 18:12 I fast *t* a week; I give tithes
Jude 12 *t* dead, pulled up by the roots;

TWIG (2/2)
Ezek 17: 4 off its topmost young *t* And
Hos 10: 7 her king is cut off Like a *t*

TWIGS (1/1)
Ezek 17:22 the topmost of its young *t* a

TWILIGHT (21/21)
Ex 12: 6 of Israel shall kill it at *t*.
16:12 At *t* you shall eat meat, and in
29:39 other lamb you shall offer at *t*.
29:41 other lamb you shall offer at *t*;
30: 8 Aaron lights the lamps at *t*,
Lev 23: 5 day of the first month at *t*
Num 9: 3 day of this month, at *t*,
9: 5 day of the first month, at *t*,
9:11 day of the second month, at *t*,
Deut 16: 4 sacrifice the first day at *t*
16: 6 sacrifice the Passover at *t*,
Josh 5:10 day of the month at *t* on the
1 Sam 30:17 Then David attacked them from *t*
2 Ki 7: 5 And they rose at *t* to go to the
7: 7 they arose and fled at *t*,
Job 24:15 the adulterer waits for the *t*,
Prov 7: 9 In the *t*, in the evening,
Isa 59:10 We stumble at noonday as at *t*;
Ezek 12: 6 and carry them out at *t*;
12: 7 I brought them out at *t*,
12:12 on his shoulder at *t* and go

TWIN (4/4)
Jn 11:16 Thomas, who is called the *T*,
20:24 Now Thomas, called the *T*,
21: 2 Peter, Thomas called the *T*,
Acts 28:11 ship whose figurehead was the *T*

TWINED (KJV) See WOVEN

TWINKLING (1/1)
1 Cor 15:52 in the *t* of an eye, at the last

TWINS (6/6)
Gen 25:24 indeed there were *t* in her
38:27 *t* were in her womb.
Song 4: 2 Every one of which bears *t*,
4: 5 *T* of a gazelle, Which feed
6: 6 the washing; Every one bears *t*,
7: 3 *T* of a gazelle.

TWIST (2/2) TWISTED, TWISTS
Ps 56: 5 All day they *t* my words;
2 Pe 3:16 and unstable people *t* to

TWISTED (4/4) TWIST
Isa 27: 1 Leviathan that *t* serpent;
Mt 27:29 When they had *t* a crown of
Mk 15:17 and they *t* a crown of thorns,
Jn 19: 2 And the soldiers *t* a crown of

TWISTS (2/2) TWIST
Deut 16:19 the eyes of the wise and *t* the
Prov 19: 3 The foolishness of a man *t* his

TWO (759/647) TWO-EDGED
Gen 1:16 Then God made *t* great lights:
4:19 took for himself *t* wives:
6:19 you shall bring *t* of every
6:20 *t* of every kind will come to
7: 2 *t* each of animals that are
7: 9 *t* by two they went into the ark
7: 9 two by *t* they went into the ark
7:15 *t* by two, of all flesh in which
7:15 into the ark to Noah, two by *t*,
9:22 and told his *t* brothers
10:25 To Eber were born *t* sons:
11:10 and begot Arphaxad *t* years
11:19 Peleg lived *t* hundred and nine
11:21 Reu lived *t* hundred and seven
11:23 Serug lived *t* hundred years,
11:32 days of Terah were *t* hundred
15:10 these to Him and cut them in *t*,
15:10 he did not cut the birds in *t*.
19: 1 Now the *t* angels came to Sodom
19: 8 I have *t* daughters who have not
19:15 your wife and your *t* daughters
19:16 the hands of his *t* daughters,
19:30 and his *t* daughters were with
19:30 And he and his *t* daughters
21:27 and the *t* of them made a
21:31 because the *t* of them swore an
22: 3 and took *t* of his young men
22: 6 and the *t* of them went
22: 8 So the *t* of them went
24:22 and *t* bracelets for her wrists
25:23 *T* nations are in your womb,
25:23 *T* peoples shall be separated
27: 9 me from there *t* choice kids
27:36 supplanted me these *t* times.
29:16 Now Laban had *t* daughters:
31:33 and into the *t* maids' tents,
31:41 years for your *t* daughters,
32: 7 into *t* companies.
32:10 now I have become *t* companies.
32:14 *t* hundred female goats and
32:14 *t* hundred ewes and twenty rams,
32:22 night and took his *t* wives,
32:22 his *t* female servants, and his
33: 1 and the *t* maidservants.
34:25 that *t* of the sons of Jacob,
40: 2 was angry with his *t* officers,
41: 1 at the end of *t* full years,
41:50 And to Joseph were born *t* sons
42:37 Kill my *t* sons if I do not bring
44:27 that my wife bore me *t* sons;
45: 6 For these *t* years the famine
46:27 him in Egypt were *t* persons.
48: 1 he took with him his *t* sons,
48: 5 And now your *t* sons, Ephraim and
49:14 Lying down between *t* burdens;
Ex 2:13 *t* Hebrew men were fighting,
4: 9 do not believe even these *t*
12: 7 and put it on the *t* doorposts
12:22 the lintel and the *t* doorposts
12:23 lintel and on the *t* doorposts,
16:22 *t* omers for each one. And all
16:29 on the sixth day bread for *t*
18: 3 with her *t* sons, of whom the
18: 6 with your wife and her *t* sons
21:21 if he remains alive a day or *t*,
25:10 *t* and a half cubits shall be
25:12 *t* rings shall be on one side,
25:12 and *t* rings on the other side.
25:17 *t* and a half cubits shall be
25:18 And you shall make *t* cherubim of
25:18 shall make them at the *t* ends
25:19 the cherubim at the *t* ends
25:22 from between the *t* cherubim
25:23 *t* cubits shall be its length,
25:35 be a knob under the first *t*
25:35 a knob under the second *t*
25:35 and a knob under the third *t*
26:17 *T* tenons shall be in each
26:19 *t* sockets under each of
26:19 of the boards for its *t* tenons.
26:21 *t* sockets under each of the
26:23 And you shall also make *t* boards
26:23 boards for the *t* back corners
26:24 shall be for the *t* corners.
26:25 *t* sockets under each board.
27: 7 poles shall be on the *t* sides
28: 7 It shall have *t* shoulder straps
28: 7 straps joined at its *t* edges,
28: 9 Then you shall take *t* onyx
28:11 you shall engrave the *t* stones
28:12 the *t* stones on the shoulders
28:12 names before the LORD on his *t*
28:14 and you shall make *t* chains of
28:23 And you shall make *t* rings of
28:23 the *t* rings on the two ends
28:23 and put the two rings on the *t*
28:24 Then you shall put the *t* braided
28:24 chains of gold in the *t* rings
28:25 the other *t* ends of the two
28:25 other two ends of the *t* braided
28:25 fasten to the *t* settings,
28:26 You shall make *t* rings of gold,
28:26 and put them on the *t* ends of
28:27 And *t* other rings of gold you
28:27 and put them on the *t* shoulder
29: 1 Take one young bull and *t* rams
29: 3 with the bull and the *t* rams.
29:13 and the *t* kidneys and the fat
29:22 the *t* kidneys and the fat on
29:38 *t* lambs of the first year,
30: 2 and *t* cubits shall be its
30: 4 *T* gold rings you shall make for
30: 4 place them on its *t* sides,
30:23 cinnamon (*t* hundred
30:23 *t* hundred and fifty shekels of
31:18 He gave Moses *t* tablets of the
32:15 and the *t* tablets of the
34: 1 Cut *t* tablets of stone like the
34: 4 So he cut *t* tablets of stone
34: 4 took in his hand the *t* tablets
34:29 Mount Sinai (and the *t* tablets
36:22 Each board had *t* tenons for
36:24 *t* sockets under each of the
36:24 the boards for its *t* tenons.
36:26 *t* sockets under each of the
36:28 He also made *t* boards for the
36:28 made two boards for the *t* back
36:29 of them for the *t* corners.
36:30 *t* sockets under each of the
37: 1 *t* and a half cubits was its
37: 3 *t* rings on one side, and two
37: 3 and *t* rings on the other side
37: 6 *t* and a half cubits was its
37: 7 He made *t* cherubim of beaten
37: 7 of one piece at the *t* ends
37: 8 the cherubim at the *t* ends
37:10 *t* cubits was its length,
37:21 was a knob under the first *t*
37:21 a knob under the second *t*
37:21 and a knob under the third *t*
37:25 and *t* cubits was its height.
37:27 He made *t* rings of gold for it
37:27 by its *t* corners on both sides,
38:29 seventy talents and *t* thousand
39: 4 together at its *t* edges.
39:16 They also made *t* settings of
39:16 settings of gold and *t* gold
39:16 and put the *t* rings on the two
39:16 the two rings on the *t* ends
39:17 And they put the *t* braided
39:17 chains of gold in the *t* rings
39:18 The *t* ends of the two braided
39:18 The two ends of the *t* braided
39:18 fastened in the *t* settings,
39:19 And they made *t* rings of gold
39:19 and put them on the *t* ends
39:20 They made *t* other gold rings
39:20 and put them on the *t* shoulder
Lev 3: 4 the *t* kidneys and the fat that
3:10 the *t* kidneys and the fat that
3:15 the *t* kidneys and the fat that
4: 9 the *t* kidneys and the fat that
5: 7 *t* turtledoves or two young
5: 7 two turtledoves or *t* young
5:11 if he is not able to bring *t*
5:11 two turtledoves or *t* young
7: 4 the *t* kidneys and the fat that
8: 2 *t* rams, and a basket of
8:16 and the *t* kidneys with their
8:25 the *t* kidneys and their fat,
12: 5 she shall be unclean *t* weeks,
12: 8 she may bring *t* turtledoves
12: 8 two turtledoves or *t* young
14: 4 who is to be cleansed *t* living
14:10 day he shall take *t* male
14:22 and *t* turtledoves or two young
14:22 and two turtledoves or *t* young
14:49 *t* birds, cedar wood, scarlet,

15:14 take for himself *t* turtledoves
15:14 two turtledoves or *t* young
15:29 she shall take for herself *t*
15:29 two turtledoves or *t* young
16: 1 Moses after the death of the *t*
16: 5 the children of Israel *t* kids
16: 7 He shall take the *t* goats and
16: 8 Aaron shall cast lots for the *t*
23:17 from your dwellings *t* wave
23:18 one young bull, and *t* rams.
23:19 and *t* male lambs of the first
23:20 with the *t* lambs. They shall be
24: 6 You shall set them in *t* rows,
Num 1:35 were thirty-two thousand *t*
2:21 at thirty-two thousand *t*
3:34 were six thousand *t* hundred.
3:43 were twenty-two thousand *t*
3:46 for the redemption of the *t*
4:36 their families were *t* thousand
4:40 were *t* thousand six hundred and
4:44 families were three thousand *t*
6:10 the eighth day he shall bring *t*
6:10 two turtledoves or *t* young
7: 3 a cart for every *t* of the
7: 7 *T* carts and four oxen he gave to
7:17 *t* oxen, five rams, five male
7:23 *t* oxen, five rams, five male
7:29 *t* oxen, five rams, five male
7:35 *t* oxen, five rams, five male
7:41 *t* oxen, five rams, five male
7:47 *t* oxen, five rams, five male
7:53 *t* oxen, five rams, five male
7:59 *t* oxen, five rams, five male
7:65 *t* oxen, five rams, five male
7:71 *t* oxen, five rams, five male
7:77 *t* oxen, five rams, five male
7:83 *t* oxen, five rams, five male
7:85 vessels weighed *t* thousand
7:89 from between the *t* cherubim;
9:22 Whether it was *t* days,
10: 2 Make *t* silver trumpets for
11:19 nor *t* days, nor five days,
11:26 But *t* men had remained in the
11:31 and about *t* cubits above the
13:23 they carried it between *t* of
16: 2 *t* hundred and fifty leaders of
16:17 *t* hundred and fifty censers;
16:35 the LORD and consumed the *t*
22:22 and his *t* servants were with
26:10 the fire devoured *t* hundred
26:14 twenty-two thousand *t* hundred.
28: 3 *t* male lambs in their first
28: 9 And on the Sabbath day *t* lambs
28:11 *t* young bulls, one ram,
28:19 *t* young bulls, one ram,
28:27 *t* young bulls, one ram,
29:13 *t* rams, and fourteen lambs in
29:14 two-tenths for each of the *t*
29:17 *t* rams, fourteen lambs in their
29:20 *t* rams, fourteen lambs in their
29:23 *t* rams, and fourteen lambs in
29:26 *t* rams, and fourteen lambs in
29:29 *t* rams, and fourteen lambs in
29:32 *t* rams, and fourteen lambs in
31:27 the plunder into *t* parts,
34:15 The *t* tribes and the half-tribe
35: 5 on the east side *t* thousand
35: 5 on the south side *t* thousand
35: 5 on the west side *t* thousand
35: 5 and on the north side *t*
Deut 3: 8 from the hand of the *t* kings
3:21 your God has done to these *t*
4:13 and He wrote them on *t* tablets
4:47 *t* kings of the Amorites,
5:22 And He wrote them on *t* tablets
9:10 delivered to me *t* tablets
9:11 that the LORD gave me the *t*
9:15 and the *t* tablets of the
9:15 covenant were in my *t* hands.
9:17 Then I took the *t* tablets and
9:17 threw them out of my *t* hands
10: 1 Hew for yourself *t* tablets of
10: 3 hewed *t* tablets of stone like
10: 3 having the *t* tablets in my
14: 6 the hoof split into *t* parts,
17: 6 to death on the testimony of *t*
19:15 by the mouth of *t* or three
21:15 If a man has *t* wives, one loved
25:11 If *t* men fight together,
32:30 And *t* put ten thousand to
Josh 2: 1 the son of Nun sent out *t* men
2: 4 Then the woman took the *t* men
2:10 and what you did to the *t* kings
2:23 So the *t* men returned,
3: 4 about *t* thousand cubits by
6:22 But Joshua had said to the *t*
7: 3 but let about *t* or three
7:21 *t* hundred shekels of silver,
9:10 and all that He did to the *t*
14: 3 inheritance of the *t* tribes
14: 4 the children of Joseph were *t*
15:60 *t* cities with their villages.
21:16 cities from those *t* tribes;
21:25 its common-land: *t* cities.
21:27 with its common-land: *t* cities;
24:12 also the *t* kings of the
Judg 5:30 To every man a girl or *t*;
5:30 *T* pieces of dyed embroidery
7:25 And they captured *t* princes of
8:12 and he took the *t* kings of
9:44 and the other *t* companies
11:37 let me alone for *t* months,
11:38 he sent her away for *t* months;
11:39 was so at the end of *t* months
15:13 And they bound him with *t* new
16: 3 the city and the *t* gateposts,
16:28 Philistines for my *t* eyes!"
16:29 And Samson took hold of the *t*
17: 4 Then his mother took *t* hundred
19: 6 and the *t* of them ate and drank
19:10 With him were the *t* saddled
20:45 and killed *t* thousand of them.
Ruth 1: 1 he and his wife and his *t* sons.
1: 2 and the names of his *t* sons
1: 3 and her *t* sons.
1: 5 woman survived her *t* sons
1: 7 and her *t* daughters-in-law with
1: 8 to her *t* daughters-in-law,
1:19 Now the *t* of them went until
4:11 the *t* who built the house of
1 Sam 1: 2 And he had *t* wives: the name of
1: 3 Also the *t* sons of Eli,
2:21 three sons and *t* daughters.
2:34 will come upon your *t* sons,
4: 4 And the *t* sons of Eli, Hophni
4:11 and the *t* sons of Eli,
4:17 Also your *t* sons, Hophni and
6: 7 take *t* milk cows which have
6:10 they took *t* milk cows and
10: 2 you will find *t* men by Rachel's
10: 4 you and give you *t* loaves
11:11 so that no *t* of them were left
13: 1 and when he had reigned *t* years
13: 2 *T* thousand were with Saul in
14:49 the names of his *t* daughters
15: 4 *t* hundred thousand foot
18:27 and killed *t* hundred men of the
23:18 So the *t* of them made a covenant
25:13 and *t* hundred stayed with the
25:18 made haste and took *t* hundred
25:18 *t* skins of wine, five sheep
25:18 and *t* hundred cakes of figs,
27: 3 and David with his *t* wives,
28: 8 and *t* men with him; and they
30: 5 And David's *t* wives, Ahinoam the
30:10 for *t* hundred stayed behind,
30:12 a cake of figs and *t* clusters
30:18 and David rescued his *t* wives.
30:21 Now David came to the *t* hundred
2 Sam 1: 1 and David had stayed *t* days in
2: 2 and his *t* wives also, Ahinoam
2:10 and he reigned *t* years.
4: 2 Now Saul's son had *t* men who
8: 2 With *t* lines he measured off
12: 1 There were *t* men in one city,
13:23 after *t* full years,
14: 6 Now your maidservant had *t* sons;
14: 6 and the *t* fought with each
14:26 hair of his head at *t* hundred
14:28 And Absalom dwelt *t* full years
15:11 And with Absalom went *t* hundred
15:27 and your *t* sons with you,
15:36 there with them their *t* sons,
16: 1 and on them *t* hundred loaves
18:24 David was sitting between the *t*
21: 8 the *t* sons of Rizpah the
23:20 He had killed *t* lion-like
1 Ki 2: 5 he did to the *t* commanders
2:32 because he struck down *t* men
2:39 that *t* slaves of Shimei ran
3:16 Now *t* women who were harlots
3:18 except the *t* of us in the
3:25 "Divide the living child in *t*,
5:12 and the *t* of them made a treaty
5:14 in Lebanon and *t* months
6:23 sanctuary he made *t* cherubim
6:32 The *t* doors were of olive
6:34 And the *t* doors were of
6:34 *t* panels comprised one folding
6:34 and *t* panels comprised the
7:15 And he cast *t* pillars of
7:16 Then he made *t* capitals of cast
7:18 and *t* rows of pomegranates
7:20 The capitals on the *t* pillars
7:20 and there were *t* hundred such
7:24 buds were cast in *t* rows when
7:26 It contained *t* thousand baths.
7:41 the *t* pillars, the two
7:41 the *t* bowl-shaped capitals
7:41 on top of the *t* pillars;
7:41 the *t* networks covering the
7:41 covering the *t* bowl-shaped
7:42 hundred pomegranates for the *t*
7:42 for the two networks (*t* rows
7:42 to cover the *t* bowl-shaped
8: 7 cherubim spread their *t* wings
8: 9 the ark except the *t* tablets
9:10 had built the *t* houses,
10:16 And King Solomon made *t* hundred
10:19 and *t* lions stood beside the
11:29 and the *t* were alone in the
12:28 made *t* calves of gold, and said
15:25 reigned over Israel *t* years.
16: 8 and reigned *t* years in
16:21 were divided into *t* parts:
16:24 from Shemer for *t* talents
18:21 you falter between *t* opinions?
18:23 let them give us *t* bulls;
18:32 large enough to hold *t* seahs
20:15 and there were *t* hundred and
20:27 before them like *t* little
21:10 and seat *t* men, scoundrels,
21:13 And *t* men, scoundrels, came in
22:51 and reigned *t* years over
2 Ki 1:14 and burned up the first *t*
2: 6 So the *t* of them went on.
2: 7 while the *t* of them stood by
2: 8 so that the *t* of them crossed
2:11 and separated the *t* of them;
2:12 and tore them into *t* pieces.
2:24 And *t* female bears came out of
4: 1 is coming to take my *t* sons to
4:33 shut the door behind the *t* of
5:17 servant be given *t* mule-loads
5:22 just now *t* young men of the
5:22 talent of silver and *t* changes
5:23 'Please, take *t* talents."
5:23 and bound *t* talents of silver
5:23 talents of silver in *t* bags,
5:23 with *t* changes of garments,
5:23 and handed them to *t* of his
7: 1 and *t* seahs of barley for a
7:14 Therefore they took *t* chariots
7:16 and *t* seahs of barley for a
7:18 *T* seahs of barley for a shekel,
9:32 So *t* or three eunuchs looked
10: 4 *t* kings could not stand up to
10: 8 Lay them in *t* heaps at the
11: 7 The *t* contingents of you who go
15:23 and reigned *t* years.
17:16 a molded image and *t* calves,
18:23 and I will give you *t* thousand
21: 5 host of heaven in the *t* courts
21:19 and he reigned *t* years in
23:12 had made in the *t* courts
25: 4 of the gate between *t* walls,
25:16 The *t* pillars, one Sea, and the
1 Chr 1:19 To Eber were born *t* sons:
4: 5 father of Tekoa had *t* wives,
5:21 *t* hundred and fifty thousand of
5:21 and *t* thousand of their
7: 9 twenty thousand *t* hundred
7:11 were seventeen thousand *t*
9:22 chosen as gatekeepers were *t*
11:21 more honored than the other *t*
11:22 He had killed *t* lion-like
12:32 their chiefs were *t* hundred;
15: 6 and *t* hundred and twenty of his
15: 8 and *t* hundred of his brethren;
25: 7 was *t* hundred and
26:17 and for the storehouse *t* by
26:17 and for the storehouse two by *t*.
26:18 four on the highway and *t* at
26:32 brethren were *t* thousand
2 Chr 3:10 Holy Place he made *t* cherubim,
3:15 front of the temple *t* pillars
4: 3 The oxen were cast in *t* rows,
4:12 the *t* pillars and the
4:12 that were on top of the *t*
4:12 the *t* networks covering the two
4:12 covering the *t* bowl-shaped
4:13 hundred pomegranates for the *t*
4:13 for the two networks (*t* rows
4:13 to cover the *t* bowl-shaped
5:10 the ark except the *t* tablets
8:10 *t* hundred and fifty, who ruled
9:15 And King Solomon made *t* hundred
9:18 and *t* lions stood beside the
14: 8 and from Benjamin *t* hundred and
17:15 and with him *t* hundred and
17:16 and with him *t* hundred thousand
17:17 and with him *t* hundred thousand
21:19 after the end of *t* years,
24: 3 And Jehoiada took *t* wives for
26:12 men of valor was *t* thousand
28: 8 captive of their brethren *t*
29:32 and *t* hundred lambs; all these
33: 5 host of heaven in the *t* courts
33:21 and he reigned *t* years in
35: 8 Passover offerings *t* thousand
Ezra 2: 3 *t* thousand one hundred and
2: 6 *t* thousand eight hundred and
2: 7 one thousand *t* hundred and
2:12 one thousand *t* hundred and
2:14 *t* thousand and fifty-six;
2:19 *t* hundred and twenty-three;
2:28 *t* hundred and twenty-three;
2:31 one thousand *t* hundred and
2:38 one thousand *t* hundred and
2:65 and they had *t* hundred men and
2:66 their mules *t* hundred and
6:17 *t* hundred rams, four hundred
8: 4 and with him *t* hundred males;
8: 9 and with him *t* hundred and
8:20 *t* hundred and twenty Nethinim.
8:27 and *t* vessels of fine polished
10:13 is this the work of one or *t*
Neh 7: 8 *t* thousand one hundred and
7:11 *t* thousand eight hundred and
7:12 one thousand *t* hundred and
7:17 *t* thousand three hundred and
7:19 *t* thousand and sixty-seven;
7:34 one thousand *t* hundred and
7:41 one thousand *t* hundred and
7:67 and they had *t* hundred and
7:68 their mules *t* hundred and
7:71 and *t* thousand two hundred
7:71 and two thousand *t* hundred
7:72 *t* thousand silver minas,
11:13 were *t* hundred and forty-two;
11:18 the holy city were *t* hundred
12:31 and appointed *t* large
12:40 So the *t* thanksgiving choirs
Esth 2:21 *t* of the king's eunuchs,
6: 2 *t* of the king's eunuchs,
9:27 they should celebrate these *t*

Job	13:20	Only *t* things do not do to me,
	42: 7	you and your *t* friends,
Ps	46: 9	the bow and cuts the spear in *t*;
	107:16	And cut the bars of iron in *t*.
	136:13	who divided the Red Sea in *t*,
Prov	24:22	who knows the ruin those *t* can
	30: 7	*T* things I request of You
	30:15	The leech has *t* daughters—Give
Eccl	4: 9	*T* are better than one,
	4:11	if *t* lie down together, they
	4:12	*t* can withstand him.
Song	4: 5	Your *t* breasts are like two
	4: 5	two breasts are like *t* fawns,
	6:13	the dance of the *t* camps?
	7: 3	Your *t* breasts are like two
	7: 3	two breasts are like *t* fawns,
	8:12	who tend its fruit *t* hundred.
Isa	6: 2	with *t* he covered his face,
	6: 2	with *t* he covered his feet,
	6: 2	and with *t* he flew.
	7: 4	or be fainthearted for these *t*
	7:21	alive a young cow and *t* sheep;
	17: 6	*T* or three olives at the top
	22:11	a reservoir between the *t* walls
	36: 8	and I will give you *t* thousand
	47: 9	But these *t* things shall come
	51:19	These *t* things have come to
Jer	2:13	have committed *t* evils:
	3:14	one from a city and *t* from a
	24: 1	and there were *t* baskets of
	28: 3	Within *t* full years I will bring
	28:11	within the space of *t* full
	33:24	The *t* families which the LORD
	34:18	when they cut the calf in *t* and
	39: 4	the gate between the *t* walls.
	52: 7	the gate between the *t* walls,
	52:20	The *t* pillars, one Sea,
Ezek	1:11	*t* wings of each one touched
	1:11	and *t* covered their bodies.
	1:23	Each one had *t* which covered
	1:23	and each one had *t* which
	21:19	appoint for yourself *t* ways for
	21:21	at the fork of the *t* roads,
	23: 2	there were *t* women,
	35:10	These *t* nations and these two
	35:10	nations and these *t* countries
	37:22	they shall no longer be *t*
	37:22	be divided into *t* kingdoms
	40: 9	and the gateposts, *t* cubits.
	40:39	of the gateway were *t* tables
	40:39	on this side and *t* tables
	40:40	gateway, were *t* tables;
	40:40	of the gateway were *t* tables.
	41: 3	*t* cubits; and the entrance, six
	41:18	Each cherub had *t* faces,
	41:22	and its length *t* cubits.
	41:23	temple and the sanctuary had *t*
	41:24	The doors had *t* panels apiece,
	41:24	*t* folding panels: two panels
	41:24	*t* panels for one door and two
	41:24	for one door and *t* panels
	43:14	to the lower ledge, *t* cubits;
	45:15	from a flock of *t* hundred,
	47:13	shall have *t* portions.
	48:17	to the north *t* hundred and
	48:17	to the south *t* hundred and
	48:17	to the east *t* hundred and
	48:17	and to the west *t* hundred and
Dan	7: 4	and made to stand on *t* feet
	8: 3	was a ram which had *t* horns,
	8: 3	and the *t* horns were high; but
	8: 6	to the ram that had *t* horns,
	8: 7	and broke his *t* horns.
	8:14	For *t* thousand three hundred
	8:20	having the *t* horns—they are
	12: 5	and there stood *t* others,
	12:11	shall be one thousand *t*
Hos	6: 2	After *t* days He will revive us;
	10:10	for their *t* transgressions.
Am	1: 1	*t* years before the earthquake.
	3: 3	Can *t* walk together,
	3:12	*T* legs or a piece of an ear,
	4: 8	So *t* or three cities wandered
Zech	4: 3	'*T* olive trees are by it,
	4:11	What are these *t* olive trees—at
	4:12	What are these *t* olive
	4:12	the receptacles of the *t* gold
	4:14	These are the *t* anointed ones,
	5: 9	and there were *t* women,
	6: 1	from between *t* mountains,
	11: 7	I took for myself *t* staffs:
	11:10	staff, Beauty, and cut it in *t*,
	11:14	Then I cut in *t* my other staff,
	14: 4	of Olives shall be split in *t*,
Mt	2:16	from *t* years old and under,
	4:18	saw *t* brothers, Simon called
	4:21	He saw *t* other brothers, James
	5:41	to go one mile, go with him *t*.
	6:24	No one can serve *t* masters;
	8:28	there met Him *t* demon-possessed
	9:27	*t* blind men followed Him,
	10:10	nor *t* tunics, nor sandals,
	10:29	Are not *t* sparrows sold for a
	11: 2	he sent *t* of his disciples
	14:17	only five loaves and *t* fish."
	14:19	the five loaves and the *t* fish,
	18: 8	rather than having *t* hands or
	18: 8	having two hands or *t* feet,
	18: 9	rather than having *t* eyes,
	18:16	take with you one or *t* more,
	18:16	by the mouth of *t* or three
	18:19	Again I say to you that if *t* of
	18:20	For where *t* or three are
	19: 5	and the *t* shall become
	19: 6	they are no longer *t* but one
	20:21	Grant that these *t* sons of mine
	20:24	greatly displeased with the *t*
	20:30	*t* blind men sitting by the
	21: 1	then Jesus sent *t* disciples,
	21:28	A man had *t* sons, and he came
	21:31	Which of the *t* did the will of
	22:40	On these *t* commandments hang all
	24:40	Then *t* men will be in the
	24:41	*T* women will be grinding at
	24:51	and will cut him in *t* and
	25:15	gave five talents, to another *t*,
	25:17	he who had received *t* gained
	25:17	received two gained *t* more
	25:22	who had received *t* talents
	25:22	you delivered to me *t* talents;
	25:22	I have gained *t* more talents
	26: 2	You know that after *t* days is
	26:37	with Him Peter and the *t* sons
	26:60	But at last *t* false witnesses
	27:21	Which of the *t* do you want me to
	27:38	Then *t* robbers were crucified
	27:51	of the temple was torn in *t*
Mk	5:13	the swine (there were about *t*
	6: 7	to send them out *t* by
	6: 7	to send them out two by *t*,
	6: 9	and not to put on *t* tunics.
	6:37	Shall we go and buy *t* hundred
	6:38	said, "Five, and *t* fish."
	6:41	the five loaves and the *t* fish,
	6:41	and the *t* fish He divided among
	9:43	rather than having *t* hands,
	9:45	rather than having *t* feet,
	9:47	rather than having *t* eyes,
	10: 8	and the *t* shall become one
	10: 8	so then they are no longer *t*,
	11: 1	He sent *t* of His disciples;
	12:42	came and threw in *t* mites,
	14: 1	After *t* days it was the Passover
	14:13	And He sent out *t* of His
	15:27	With Him they also crucified *t*
	15:38	of the temple was torn in *t*
	16:12	in another form to *t* of them
Lk	2:24	pair of turtledoves or *t*
	3:11	He who has *t* tunics, let him
	5: 2	and saw *t* boats standing by the
	7:19	calling *t* of his disciples to
	7:41	creditor who had *t* debtors.
	9: 3	and do not have *t* tunics
	9:13	than five loaves and *t* fish,
	9:16	five loaves and the *t* fish,
	9:30	*t* men talked with Him, who were
	9:32	saw His glory and the *t* men
	10: 1	and sent them *t* by two before
	10: 1	and sent them two by *t* before
	10:35	departed, he took out *t* denarii,
	12: 6	sparrows sold for *t* copper
	12:46	and will cut him in *t* and
	12:52	be divided: three against *t*,
	12:52	and *t* against three.
	15:11	A certain man had *t* sons.
	16:13	No servant can serve *t* masters;
	17:34	night there will be *t* men
	17:35	*T* women will be grinding
	17:36	'*T* men will be in the field:
	18:10	*T* men went up to the temple to
	19:29	that He sent *t* of His
	21: 2	poor widow putting in *t* mites.
	22:38	here are *t* swords."
	23:32	There were also *t* others,
	23:45	of the temple was torn in *t*.
	24: 4	*t* men stood by them in shining
	24:13	*t* of them were traveling that
Jn	1:35	John stood with *t* of his
	1:37	The *t* disciples heard him speak,
	1:40	One of the *t* who heard John
	4:40	and He stayed there *t* days.
	4:43	Now after the *t* days He
	6: 7	*T* hundred denarii worth of bread
	6: 9	barley loaves and *t* small
	8:17	that the testimony of *t* men
	11: 6	He stayed *t* more days in the
	11:18	about *t* miles away.
	19:18	and *t* others with Him,
	20:12	And she saw *t* angels in white
	21: 2	and *t* others of His disciples
	21: 8	but about *t* hundred cubits),
Acts	1:10	*t* men stood by them in white
	1:23	And they proposed *t*:
	1:24	show which of these *t* You have
	7:26	day he appeared to *t* of them
	7:29	where he had *t* sons.
	9:38	they sent *t* men to him,
	10: 7	Cornelius called *t* of his
	12: 6	bound with *t* chains between two
	12: 6	two chains between *t* soldiers;
	19:10	And this continued for *t* years,
	19:22	So he sent into Macedonia *t* of
	19:34	cried out for about *t* hours,
	21:33	him to be bound with *t* chains;
	23:23	And he called for *t* centurions,
	23:23	Prepare *t* hundred soldiers,
	23:23	and *t* hundred spearmen to go to
	24:27	But after *t* years Porcius Festus
	27:37	And in all we were *t* hundred and
	27:41	striking a place where *t* seas
	28:30	Then Paul dwelt *t* whole years in
1 Cor	6:16	*t*," He says, "shall become
	14:27	let there be *t* or at the
	14:29	Let *t* or three prophets speak,
2 Cor	13: 1	By the mouth of *t* or three
Gal	4:22	that Abraham had *t* sons:
	4:24	For these are the *t* covenants:
Eph	2:15	Himself one new man from the *t*,
	5:31	and the *t* shall become
Phil	1:23	I am hard pressed between the *t*,
1 Tim	5:19	an elder except from *t* or
Heb	6:18	that by *t* immutable things, in
	10:28	mercy on the testimony of *t* or
	11:37	stoned, they were sawn in *t*,
Rev	9:12	still *t* more woes are coming
	9:16	of the horsemen was *t* hundred
	11: 3	give power to my *t* witnesses,
	11: 3	will prophesy one thousand *t*
	11: 4	These are the *t* olive trees and
	11: 4	trees and the *t* lampstands
	11:10	because these *t* prophets
	12: 6	feed her there one thousand *t*
	12:14	But the woman was given *t* wings
	13:11	and he had *t* horns like a lamb
	19:20	These *t* were cast alive into

TWO-EDGED (5/5) TWO

Ps	149: 6	And a *t* sword in their hand,
Prov	5: 4	Sharp as a *t* sword.
Heb	4:12	and sharper than any *t* sword,
Rev	1:16	mouth went a sharp *t* sword,
	2:12	He who has the sharp *t* sword:

TWO-TENTHS (11/11)

Lev	23:13	offering shall be *t* of an ephah
	23:17	two wave loaves of *t* of an
	24: 5	*T* of an ephah shall be in
Num	15: 6	offering *t* of an ephah of fine
	28: 9	and *t* of an ephah of fine
	28:12	*t* of an ephah of fine flour
	28:20	and *t* for a ram;
	28:28	*t* for the one ram,
	29: 3	for the bull, *t* for the ram,
	29: 9	*t* for the one ram,
	29:14	*t* for each of the two rams,

TWO-THIRDS (1/1)

Zech	13: 8	That *t* in it shall be cut off

TYCHICUS (5/5)

Acts	20: 4	and *T* and Trophimus of Asia.
Eph	6:21	affairs and how I am doing, *T*,
Col	4: 7	*T*, a beloved brother,
2 Tim	4:12	And *T* I have sent to Ephesus.
Titus	3:12	I send Artemas to you, or *T*,

TYPE (1/1)

Rom	5:14	who is a *t* of Him who was to

TYPES (1/1)

1 Chr	22:15	and all *t* of skillful men for

TYRANNUS (1/1)

Acts	19: 9	daily in the school of *T*.

TYRE (59/56)

Josh	19:29	and to the fortified city of *T*;
2 Sam	5:11	Then Hiram king of *T* sent
	24: 7	came to the stronghold of *T*
1 Ki	5: 1	Now Hiram king of *T* sent his
	7:13	sent and brought Huram from *T*.
	7:14	and his father was a man of *T*,
	9:11	(Hiram the king of *T* had
	9:12	Then Hiram went from *T* to see
1 Chr	14: 1	Now Hiram king of *T* sent
	22: 4	the Sidonians and those from *T*
2 Chr	2: 3	Solomon sent to Hiram king of *T*,
	2:11	Then Hiram king of *T* answered
	2:14	and his father was a man of *T*),
Ezra	3: 7	to the people of Sidon and *T*
Neh	13:16	Men of *T* dwelt there also,
Ps	45:12	And the daughter of *T* will
	83: 7	with the inhabitants of *T*;
	87: 4	Behold, O Philistia and *T*,
Isa	23: 1	The burden against *T*.
	23: 5	be in agony at the report of *T*.
	23: 8	taken this counsel against *T*,
	23:15	come to pass in that day that *T*
	23:15	years it will happen to *T* as
	23:17	that the LORD will visit *T*.
Jer	25:22	all the kings of *T*,
	27: 3	of the Ammonites, the king of *T*,
	47: 4	To cut off from *T* and Sidon
Ezek	26: 2	because *T* has said against
	26: 3	'Behold, I am against you, O *T*,
	26: 4	shall destroy the walls of *T*
	26: 7	I will bring against *T* from the
	26:15	"Thus says the Lord GOD to *T*:
	27: 2	take up a lamentation for *T*,
	27: 3	'and say to *T*, 'You who are
	27: 3	says the Lord GOD: "O *T*,
	27: 8	Your wise men, O *T*,
	27:32	'What city is like *T*,
	28: 2	say to the prince of *T*,
	28:12	a lamentation for the king of *T*,
	29:18	to labor strenuously against *T*;
	29:18	his army received wages from *T*,
Hos	9:13	Just as I saw Ephraim like *T*,
Joel	3: 4	O *T* and Sidon, and all the

Am 1: 9 three transgressions of **T**,
1:10 send a fire upon the wall of **T**,
Zech 9: 2 And against **T** and Sidon,
9: 3 For **T** built herself a tower,
Mt 11:21 done in you had been done in **T**
11:22 it will be more tolerable for **T**
15:21 and departed to the region of **T**
Mk 3: 8 and those from **T** and Sidon,
7:24 and went to the region of **T**
7:31 departing from the region of **T**
Lk 6:17 and from the seacoast of **T** and
10:13 done in you had been done in **T**
10:14 it will be more tolerable for **T**
Acts 12:20 angry with the people of **T** and
21: 3 to Syria, and landed at **T**;
21: 7 had finished our voyage from **T**,

TYRUS (KJV) See TYRE

U

UCAL (1/1)

Prov 30: 1 to Ithiel—to Ithiel and **U**:

UEL (1/1)

Ezra 10:34 sons of Bani: Maadai, Amram, **U**,

UGLINESS (1/1)

Gen 41:19 such **u** as I have never seen in

UGLY (6/6)

Gen 41: 3 **u** and gaunt, and stood by the
41: 4 And the **u** and gaunt cows ate up
41:19 poor and very **u** and gaunt,
41:20 And the gaunt and **u** cows ate up
41:21 for they were just as **u** as at
41:27 And the seven thin and **u** cows

ULAI (2/2)

Dan 8: 2 that I was by the River **U**.
8:16 between the banks of the **U**,

ULAM (4/4)

1 Chr 7:16 and his sons were **U** and Rakem.
7:17 The son of **U** was Bedan.)
8:39 of Eshek his brother were **U**
8:40 The sons of **U** were mighty men of

ULCER (1/1)

Lev 22:22 or have an **u** or eczema or

ULLA (1/1)

1 Chr 7:39 The sons of **U** were Arah,

UMMAH (1/1)

Josh 19:30 Also **U**, Aphek, and Rehob

UNABLE (2/2)

Deut 7:22 you will be **u** to destroy them
Lk 19:48 and were **u** to do anything;

UNADVISEDLY (KJV) See RASHLY

UNAFRAID (1/1)

Rom 13: 3 Do you want to be **u** of the

UNAPPROACHABLE (1/1)

1 Tim 6:16 dwelling in **u** light, whom no

UNAWARE (5/5)

Lev 5: 2 and he is **u** of it, he also
5: 3 and he is **u** of it— when he
5: 4 and he is **u** of it—when he
Rom 1:13 Now I do not want you to be **u**,
1 Cor 10: 1 I do not want you to be **u** that

UNAWARES (KJV) See ACCIDENTALLY, SECRETLY, UNEXPECTEDLY, UNWITTINGLY

UNBELIEF (12/12) BELIEF, UNBELIEVING

Mt 13:58 works there because of their **u**.
17:20 to them, "Because of your **u**;
Mk 6: 6 He marveled because of their **u**.
9:24 'Lord, I believe; help my **u**!"
16:14 and He rebuked their **u** and
Rom 3: 3 Will their **u** make the
4:20 at the promise of God through **u**,
11:20 Because of **u** they were broken
11:23 if they do not continue in **u**,
1 Tim 1:13 I did it ignorantly in **u**.
Heb 3:12 any of you an evil heart of **u**
3:19 could not enter in because of **u**.

UNBELIEVER (4/4) BELIEVER, UNBELIEVERS

1 Cor 7:15 But if the **u** departs, let him
14:24 and an **u** or an uninformed
2 Cor 6:15 part has a believer with an **u**?
1 Tim 5: 8 faith and is worse than an **u**.

UNBELIEVERS (6/5) UNBELIEVER

Lk 12:46 him his portion with the **u**.
1 Cor 6: 6 and that before **u**!
14:22 to those who believe but to **u**;
14:22 but prophesying is not for **u**
14:23 who are uninformed or **u**,
2 Cor 6:14 unequally yoked together with **u**.

UNBELIEVING (6/5) UNBELIEF

Jn 20:27 it into My side. Do not be **u**,
Acts 14: 2 But the **u** Jews stirred up the
1 Cor 7:14 For the **u** husband is sanctified
7:14 and the **u** wife is sanctified by
Titus 1:15 to those who are defiled and **u**
Rev 21: 8 "But the cowardly, **u**,

UNBLAMEABLE (KJV) See BLAMELESS

UNCERTAIN (3/3) CERTAIN, UNCERTAINTY

Acts 25:20 And because I was **u** of such
1 Cor 14: 8 the trumpet makes an **u** sound,
1 Tim 6:17 nor to trust in **u** riches but in

UNCERTAINTY (1/1) UNCERTAIN

1 Cor 9:26 I run thus: not with **u**.

UNCHANGEABLE (1/1) CHANGE

Heb 7:24 has an **u** priesthood.

UNCIRCUMCISED (54/47) CIRCUMCISE, UNCIRCUMCISION

Gen 17:14 And the **u** male child, who is not
34:14 give our sister to one who is **u**,
Ex 6:12 for I am of **u** lips?"
6:30 I am of **u** lips, and how shall
12:48 For no **u** person shall eat it.
Lev 19:23 shall count their fruit as **u**.
19:23 Three years it shall be as **u** to
26:41 if their **u** hearts are humbled,
Josh 5: 7 in their place; for they were **u**,
Judg 14: 3 go and get a wife from the **u**
15:18 and fall into the hand of the **u**?
1 Sam 14: 6 over to the garrison of these **u**;
17:26 For who is this **u** Philistine,
17:36 and this **u** Philistine will be
31: 4 lest these **u** men come and
2 Sam 1:20 Lest the daughters of the **u**
1 Chr 10: 4 lest these **u** men come and abuse
Isa 52: 1 For the **u** and the unclean
Jer 6:10 Indeed their ear is **u**,
9:25 are circumcised with the **u**—
9:26 For all these nations are **u**,
9:26 all the house of Israel are **u**
Ezek 28:10 shall die the death of the **u**
31:18 shall lie in the midst of the **u**,
32:19 Go down, be placed with the **u**.
32:21 gone down, They lie with the **u**,
32:24 Who have gone down **u** to the
32:25 all around it, All of them **u**,
32:26 around it, All of them **u**,
32:27 Who are fallen of the **u**,
32:28 be broken in the midst of the **u**,
32:29 They shall lie with the **u**,
32:30 They lie **u** with those slain
32:32 be placed in the midst of the **u**
44: 7 **u** in heart and uncircumcised in
44: 7 uncircumcised in heart and **u** in
44: 9 **u** in heart or uncircumcised in
44: 9 uncircumcised in heart or **u** in
Hab 2:16 And be exposed as **u**!
Acts 7:51 You stiffnecked and **u** in heart
11: 3 You went in to **u** men and ate
Rom 2:26 if an **u** man keeps the righteous
2:27 And will not the physically **u**,
3:30 circumcised by faith and the **u**
4: 9 only, or upon the **u** also?
4:10 While he was circumcised, or **u**?
4:10 while circumcised, but while **u**.
4:11 which he had while still **u**,
4:11 who believe, though they are **u**,
4:12 Abraham had while still **u**.
1 Cor 7:18 Let him not become **u**.
7:18 Was anyone called while **u**?
Gal 2: 7 saw that the gospel for the **u**
Col 3:11 nor Jew, circumcised nor **u**,

UNCIRCUMCISION (7/7) UNCIRCUMCISED

Rom 2:25 your circumcision has become **u**.
2:26 will not his **u** be counted as
1 Cor 7:19 Circumcision is nothing and **u** is
Gal 5: 6 neither circumcision nor **u**
6:15 neither circumcision nor **u**
Eph 2:11 who are called **U** by what is
Col 2:13 in your trespasses and the **u**

UNCLE (11/11)

Lev 10: 4 the sons of Uzziel the **u** of
25:49 or his **u** or his uncle's son may
1 Sam 10:14 Then Saul's **u** said to him and
10:15 And Saul's **u** said, "Tell me,
10:16 So Saul said to his **u**,
14:50 Abner the son of Ner, Saul's **u**.
2 Ki 24:17 made Mattaniah, Jehoiachin's **u**,
1 Chr 27:32 Also Jehonathan, David's **u**,
Esth 2:15 the daughter of Abihail the **u**
Jer 32: 7 the son of Shallum your **u** will
32: 9 the son of my **u** who was in

UNCLE'S (6/5)

Lev 20:20 If a man lies with his **u** wife,
20:20 uncovered his **u** nakedness.
25:49 or his uncle or his **u** son may
Esth 2: 7 Esther, his **u** daughter,
Jer 32: 8 Then Hanamel my **u** son came to me
32:12 presence of Hanamel my **u** son,

UNCLEAN (208/167) CLEAN, UNCLEANNESS

Gen 7: 2 two each of animals that are **u**,
7: 8 of animals that are **u**,
Lev 5: 2 a person touches any **u** thing,
5: 2 is the carcass of an **u** beast,
5: 2 or the carcass of **u** livestock,
5: 2 or the carcass of **u** creeping
5: 2 he also shall be **u** and guilty.
7:19 flesh that touches any **u** thing
7:20 to the LORD, while he is **u**,
7:21 who touches any **u** thing,
7:21 an **u** animal, or any abominable
7:21 or any abominable **u** thing,
10:10 and between **u** and clean,
11: 4 cloven hooves, is **u** to you;
11: 5 cloven hooves, is **u** to you;
11: 6 hooves, is **u** to you;
11: 7 not chew the cud, is **u** to you.
11: 8 They are **u** to you.
11:24 'By these you shall become **u**;
11:24 of any of them shall be **u**
11:25 shall wash his clothes and be **u**
11:26 not chew the cud, is **u** to you.
11:26 who touches it shall be **u**.
11:27 those are **u** to you.
11:27 any such carcass shall be **u**
11:28 shall wash his clothes and be **u**
11:28 It is **u** to you.
11:29 These also shall be **u** to you
11:31 These are **u** to you among all
11:31 when they are dead shall be **u**
11:32 when they are dead shall be **u**,
11:32 And it shall be **u** until
11:33 whatever is in it shall be **u**:
11:34 which water falls becomes **u**,
11:34 may be drunk from it becomes **u**.
11:35 such carcass falls shall be **u**;
11:35 for they are **u**, and shall be
11:35 and shall be **u** to you.
11:36 any such carcass becomes **u**.
11:38 it becomes **u** to you.
11:39 touches its carcass shall be **u**
11:40 shall wash his clothes and be **u**
11:40 shall wash his clothes and be **u**
11:43 nor shall you make yourselves **u**
11:47 to distinguish between the **u** and
12: 2 then she shall be **u** seven days;
12: 2 impurity she shall be **u**.
12: 5 then she shall be **u** two weeks,
13: 3 and pronounce him **u**.
13: 8 priest shall pronounce him **u**.
13:11 priest shall pronounce him **u**,
13:11 not isolate him, for he is **u**.
13:14 appears on him, he shall be **u**.
13:15 flesh and pronounce him to be **u**;
13:15 for the raw flesh is **u**.
13:20 priest shall pronounce him **u**.
13:22 priest shall pronounce him **u**.
13:25 priest shall pronounce him **u**.
13:27 priest shall pronounce him **u**.
13:30 priest shall pronounce him **u**.
13:36 seek for yellow hair. He is **u**.
13:44 "he is a leprous man. He is **u**.
13:44 shall surely pronounce him **u**;
13:45 and cry, '**U**!
13:45 cry, 'Unclean! **U**!'
13:46 "He shall be **u**.
13:46 he has the sore he shall be **u**.
13:46 he shall be unclean. He is **u**,
13:51 is an active leprosy. It is **u**.
13:55 plague has not spread, it is **u**,
13:59 it clean or to pronounce it **u**.
14:36 in the house may not be made **u**;
14:40 they shall cast them into an **u**
14:41 off they shall pour out in an **u**
14:44 leprosy in the house. It is **u**.
14:45 the city to an **u** place.
14:46 while it is shut up shall be **u**
14:57 to teach when it is **u** and when
15: 2 his body, his discharge is **u**.
15: 4 Every bed is **u** on which he who
15: 4 on which he sits shall be **u**.
15: 5 and be **u** until evening.
15: 6 and be **u** until evening.
15: 7 and be **u** until evening.

15: 8 and be *u* until evening.
15: 9 the discharge rides shall be *u*.
15:10 that was under him shall be *u*
15:10 and be *u* until evening.
15:11 and be *u* until evening.
15:16 and be *u* until evening.
15:17 and be *u* until evening.
15:18 and be *u* until evening.
15:19 whoever touches her shall be *u*
15:20 during her impurity shall be *u*;
15:20 that she sits on shall be *u*.
15:21 and be *u* until evening.
15:22 and be *u* until evening.
15:23 he shall be *u* until evening.
15:24 he shall be *u* seven days;
15:24 bed on which he lies shall be *u*.
15:25 all the days of her *u* discharge
15:25 She shall be *u*.
15:26 whatever she sits on shall be *u*,
15:27 touches those things shall be *u*;
15:27 and be *u* until evening.
15:32 him who emits semen and is *u*
15:33 him who lies with her who is *u*.
17:15 and be *u* until evening. Then he
20:21 it is an *u* thing. He has
20:25 between clean animals and *u*,
20:25 between *u* birds and clean,
20:25 I have separated from you as *u*.
22: 4 touches anything made *u* by a
22: 5 by which he would be made *u*,
22: 5 by whom he would become *u*,
22: 6 any such thing shall be *u*
27:11 If it is an *u* animal which
27:27 'And if it is an *u* animal,
Num 6: 7 He shall not make himself *u* even
9:10 of you or your posterity is *u*
18:15 and the firstborn of *u* animals
19: 7 the priest shall be *u* until
19: 8 and shall be *u* until evening.
19:10 and be *u* until evening.
19:11 dead body of anyone shall be *u*
19:13 shall be *u*, because the water
19:14 who are in the tent shall be *u*
19:15 no cover fastened on it, is *u*.
19:16 shall be *u* seven days.
19:17 And for an *u* person they shall
19:19 person shall sprinkle the *u*
19:20 But the man who is *u* and does
19:20 been sprinkled on him; he is *u*.
19:21 of purification shall be *u*
19:22 Whatever the *u* person touches
19:22 person touches shall be *u*;
19:22 who touches it shall be *u*
Deut 12:15 the *u* and the clean may eat of
12:22 the *u* and the clean alike may
14: 7 they are *u* for you.
14: 8 Also the swine is *u* for you,
14:10 it is *u* for you.
14:19 creeping thing that flies is *u*
15:22 the *u* and the clean person
23:10 man among you who becomes *u* by
23:14 that He may see no *u* thing
26:14 I removed any of it for an *u*
Josh 22:19 land of your possession is *u*,
Judg 13: 4 and not to eat anything *u*.
13: 7 drink, nor eat anything *u*,
13:14 drink, nor eat anything *u*.
1 Sam 20:26 has happened to him; he is *u*,
20:26 he is unclean, surely he is *u*.
2 Chr 23:19 no one who was in any way *u*
Ezra 9:11 to possess is an *u* land,
Job 14: 4 a clean thing out of an *u*?
Eccl 9: 2 the good, the clean, and the *u*;
Isa 6: 5 Because I am a man of *u* lips,
6: 5 midst of a people of *u* lips;
30:22 will throw them away as an *u*
35: 8 The *u* shall not pass over it,
52: 1 the uncircumcised and the *u*
52:11 Touch no *u* thing; Go out
64: 6 But we are all like an *u*
Lam 1:17 Jerusalem has become an *u*
4:15 *u*! Go away, go away, Do not
Ezek 20:26 and I pronounced them *u* because
22:26 the difference between the *u*
44:23 them to discern between the *u*
Hos 9: 3 And shall eat *u* things in
Hag 2:13 If one who is *u* because of a
2:13 any of these, will it be *u*?
2:13 and said, "It shall be *u*.
2:14 and what they offer there is *u*.
Zech 13: 2 cause the prophets and the *u*
Mt 10: 1 He gave them power over *u*
12:43 When an *u* spirit goes out of a
Mk 1:23 in their synagogue with an *u*
1:26 And when the *u* spirit had
1:27 He commands even the *u* spirits,
3:11 And the *u* spirits, whenever they
3:30 He has an *u* spirit."
5: 2 tombs a man with an *u* spirit,
5: 8 out of the man, *u* spirit!"
5:13 Then the *u* spirits went out and
6: 7 them power over *u* spirits.
7:25 young daughter had an *u* spirit
9:25 He rebuked the *u* spirit, saying
Lk 4:33 a man who had a spirit of an *u*
4:36 He commands the *u* spirits,
6:18 were tormented with *u* spirits.
8:29 He had commanded the *u* spirit
9:42 Jesus rebuked the *u* spirit,
11:24 When an *u* spirit goes out of a
Acts 5:16 were tormented by *u* spirits,
8: 7 For *u* spirits, crying with a
10:14 eaten anything common or *u*.
10:28 not call any man common or *u*.
11: 8 Lord! For nothing common or *u*
Rom 14:14 that there is nothing *u* of
14:14 who considers anything to be *u*,
14:14 to be unclean, to him it is *u*.
1 Cor 7:14 your children would be *u*,
2 Cor 6:17 Do not touch what is *u*,
Eph 5: 5 *u* person, nor covetous man,
Heb 9:13 of a heifer, sprinkling the *u*,
Rev 16:13 And I saw three *u* spirits like
18: 2 and a cage for every *u* and

UNCLEANNESS (34/30) UNCLEAN

Lev 5: 3 'Or if he touches human *u*—
5: 3 whatever *u* with which a man may
7:21 thing, such as human *u*,
14:19 is to be cleansed from his *u*.
15: 3 And this shall be his *u* in
15: 3 by his discharge, it is his *u*.
15:26 as the *u* of her impurity.
15:30 for the discharge of her *u*.
15:31 children of Israel from their *u*,
15:31 lest they die in their *u* when
16:16 because of the *u* of the
16:16 them in the midst of their *u*.
16:19 and consecrate it from the *u* of
22: 3 while he has *u* upon him,
22: 5 whatever his *u* may be—
Num 5:19 you have not gone astray to *u*
19:13 his *u* is still on him.
Deut 24: 1 because he has found some *u* in
Ezra 9:11 with the *u* of the peoples of
Lam 1: 9 Her *u* is in her skirts;
Ezek 36:17 to Me their way was like the *u*
39:24 According to their *u* and
Zech 13: 1 of Jerusalem, for sin and for *u*.
Mt 23:27 of dead men's bones and all *u*.
Rom 1:24 God also gave them up to *u*,
6:19 your members as slaves of *u*,
2 Cor 12:21 and have not repented of the *u*,
Gal 5:19 are: adultery, fornication, *u*,
Eph 4:19 to work all *u* with greediness.
5: 3 But fornication and all *u* or
Col 3: 5 on the earth: fornication, *u*,
1 Th 2: 3 did not come from error or *u*,
4: 7 For God did not call us to *u*,
2 Pe 2:10 to the flesh in the lust of *u*

UNCLEANNESSES (1/1)

Ezek 36:29 deliver you from all your *u*.

UNCLOTHED (1/1) CLOTHE

2 Cor 5: 4 not because we want to be *u*,

UNCOMELY (KJV) See IMPROPERLY, UNPRESENTABLE

UNCONDEMNED (2/2) CONDEMN

Acts 16:37 *u* Romans, and have thrown us
22:25 a man who is a Roman, and *u*?

UNCORRUPTIBLE (KJV) See INCORRUPTIBLE

UNCOVER (32/28) COVER, UNCOVERED

Lev 10: 6 Do not *u* your heads nor tear
18: 6 to *u* his nakedness: I am the
18: 7 of your mother you shall not *u*.
18: 7 you shall not *u* her nakedness.
18: 8 father's wife you shall not *u*;
18: 9 their nakedness you shall not *u*.
18:10 their nakedness you shall not *u*;
18:11 you shall not *u* her nakedness.
18:12 You shall not *u* the nakedness of
18:13 You shall not *u* the nakedness of
18:14 You shall not *u* the nakedness of
18:15 You shall not *u* the nakedness of
18:15 you shall not *u* her nakedness.
18:16 You shall not *u* the nakedness of
18:17 You shall not *u* the nakedness of
18:17 to *u* her nakedness. They are
18:18 to *u* her nakedness while the
18:19 not approach a woman to *u* her
20:19 You shall not *u* the nakedness of
20:19 for that would *u* his near of
21:10 shall not *u* his head nor tear
Num 5:18 *u* the woman's head, and put the
Deut 22:30 nor *u* his father's bed.
Ruth 3: 4 *u* his feet, and lie down;
Isa 3:17 And the LORD will *u* their
47: 2 *U* the thigh, Pass through the
Jer 13:26 Therefore I will *u* your skirts
Lam 4:22 He will *u* your sins!
Ezek 16:37 around against you and will *u*
22:10 In you men *u* their fathers'
Hos 2:10 Now I will *u* her lewdness in
Mic 1: 6 And I will *u* her foundations.

UNCOVERED (30/30) UNCOVER

Gen 9:21 and became *u* in his tent.
Lev 20:11 with his father's wife has *u*
20:17 He has *u* his sister's
20:18 and she has *u* the flow of her
20:20 he has *u* his uncle's nakedness.
20:21 He has *u* his brother's
Deut 27:20 because he has *u* his father's
Ruth 3: 7 *u* his feet, and lay down.
2 Sam 22:16 foundations of the world were *u*,
2 Ki 17: 4 And the king of Assyria *u* a
Ps 18:15 of the world were *u* At Your
Isa 20: 4 barefoot, with their buttocks *u*,
22: 6 And Kir *u* the shield.
47: 3 Your nakedness shall be *u*,
57: 8 For you have *u* yourself to
Jer 13:22 Your skirts have been *u*,
49:10 I have *u* his secret places,
Lam 2:14 They have not *u* your iniquity,
Ezek 4: 7 your arm shall be *u*,
13:14 that its foundation will be *u*;
16:36 out and your nakedness *u* in
16:57 "before your wickedness was *u*.
21:24 that your transgressions are *u*,
23:10 They *u* her nakedness,
23:18 revealed her harlotry and *u*
23:29 of your harlotry shall be *u*,
Hos 7: 1 the iniquity of Ephraim was *u*,
Mk 2: 4 they *u* the roof where He was.
1 Cor 11: 5 or prophesies with her head *u*
11:13 to pray to God with her head *u*?

UNCOVERING (1/1)

2 Sam 6:20 *u* himself today in the eyes of

UNCOVERS (3/3)

Lev 20:18 during her sickness and *u* her
2 Sam 6:20 the base fellows shamelessly *u*
Job 12:22 He *u* deep things out of

UNCTION (KJV) See ANOINTING

UNDEFILED (5/5) DEFILE

Ps 119: 1 Blessed are the *u* in the way,
Heb 7:26 who is holy, harmless, *u*,
13: 4 among all, and the bed *u*;
Jas 1:27 Pure and *u* religion before God
1 Pe 1: 4 incorruptible and *u* and that

UNDER (372/338)

Gen 1: 7 the waters which were *u* the
1: 9 Let the waters *u* the heavens be
6:17 to destroy from *u* heaven all
7:19 and all the high hills *u* the
16: 9 and submit yourself *u* her
18: 4 and rest yourselves *u* the tree.
18: 8 and he stood by them *u* the tree
19: 8 reason they have come *u* the
21:15 and she placed the boy *u* one of
24: 2 put your hand *u* my thigh,
24: 9 the servant put his hand *u* the
35: 4 and Jacob hid them *u* the
35: 8 was buried below Bethel *u* the
39: 4 all that he had he put *u* his
39:23 anything that was *u* Joseph's
41:35 and store up grain *u* the
47:29 please put your hand *u* my
Ex 6: 6 I will bring you out from *u* the
6: 7 who brings you out from *u* the
13:19 children of Israel *u* solemn
17:12 took a stone and put it *u* him,
17:14 of Amalek from *u* heaven."
18:10 delivered the people from *u* the
20: 4 or that is in the water *u* the
21:20 so that he dies *u* his hand,
23: 5 one who hates you lying *u* its
24:10 And there was *u* His feet as
25:35 there shall be a knob *u* the
25:35 a knob *u* the second two
25:35 and a knob *u* the third two
26:19 forty sockets of silver *u* the
26:19 two sockets *u* each of the
26:21 two sockets *u* each of the
26:25 two sockets *u* each board.
27: 5 You shall put it *u* the rim of
30: 4 *u* the molding on both its
36:24 of silver he made to go *u* the
36:24 two sockets *u* each of the
36:26 two sockets *u* each of the
36:30 two sockets *u* each of the
37:21 There was a knob *u* the first
37:21 a knob *u* the second two
37:21 and a knob *u* the third two
37:27 two rings of gold for it *u* its
38: 4 *u* its rim, midway from the
Lev 15:10 anything that was *u* him shall
27:29 No person *u* the ban, who may
27:32 of whatever passes *u* the rod,
Num 4:28 their duties shall be *u* the
4:33 *u* the authority of Ithamar the
5:19 priest shall put her *u* oath,
5:19 to uncleanness while *u* your
5:20 have gone astray while *u* your
5:21 shall put the woman *u* the oath
5:29 while *u* her husband's
6:18 it on the fire which is *u* the
7: 8 *u* the authority of Ithamar the
15:34 They put him *u* guard, because it
16:31 the ground split apart *u* them,
22:27 she lay down *u* Balaam;
31:49 the men of war who are *u* our
33: 1 of Egypt by their armies *u* the
Deut 2:25 of you upon the nations *u* the
4:19 given to all the peoples *u* the
5: 8 or that is in the water *u* the

7:24 their name from **u** heaven;
9:14 out their name from **u** heaven;
12: 2 and on the hills and **u** every
20:11 it shall be placed **u** tribute
25:19 of Amalek from **u** heaven.
28:23 and the earth which is **u** you
29:20 out his name from **u** heaven.
30: 4 the farthest parts **u** heaven,
Josh 7:21 with the silver **u** it."
7:22 with the silver **u** it.
24:26 and set it up there **u** the oak
Judg 1: 7 used to gather scraps **u** my
1:28 put the Canaanites **u** tribute,
1:30 and were put **u** tribute.
1:33 Beth Anath were put **u** tribute
1:35 they were put **u** tribute.
3:16 and fastened it **u** his clothes
3:30 was subdued that day **u** the
4: 5 And she would sit **u** the palm
4:10 up with ten thousand men **u** his
5:15 Sent into the valley **u** his
6:11 the LORD came and sat **u** the
6:19 brought them out to Him **u** the
9:29 If only this people were **u** my
Ruth 2:12 **u** whose wings you have come for
3: 9 Take your maidservant **u** your
1 Sam 14: 2 in the outskirts of Gibeah **u** a
14:24 had placed the people **u** oath,
22: 6 Saul was staying in Gibeah **u** a
25:20 that she went down **u** cover of
31:13 bones and buried them **u** the
2 Sam 10:10 of the people he put **u** the
18: 2 one third of the people **u** the
18: 2 one third **u** the hand of Abishai
18: 2 and one third **u** the hand of
18: 9 The mule went **u** the thick
18: 9 And the mule which was **u** him
20:26 was a chief minister **u** David.
22:10 With darkness **u** His
22:37 You enlarged my path **u** me;
22:39 They have fallen **u** my feet.
22:40 You have subdued **u** me those
22:48 And subdues the peoples **u** me;
1 Ki 4:25 each man **u** his vine and his fig
5: 3 the LORD put his foes **u** the
7:30 *U* the laver were supports of
7:32 *U* the panels were the four
7:44 and twelve oxen **u** the Sea;
8: 6 **u** the wings of the cherubim.
13:14 and found him sitting **u** an oak.
14:23 on every high hill and **u** every
18:23 but put no fire **u** it; and I
18:23 but put no fire **u** it.
18:25 but put no fire **u** it."
19: 4 and came and sat down **u** a broom
19: 5 Then as he lay and slept **u** a
2 Ki 9:13 his garment and put it **u** him
11:15 'Take her outside **u** guard,
13: 5 so that they escaped from **u** the
14:27 name of Israel from **u** heaven;
15:19 strengthen the kingdom **u** his
16: 4 and **u** every green tree.
16:17 bronze oxen that were **u** it,
17: 7 from **u** the hand of Pharaoh king
17:10 on every high hill and **u** every
1 Chr 10:12 and buried their bones **u** the
17: 1 of the LORD is **u** tent
19:11 of the people he put **u** the
25: 2 the sons of Asaph were **u** the
25: 3 **u** the direction of their father
25: 6 All these were **u** the direction
25: 6 and Heman were **u** the authority
26:28 was **u** the hand of Shelomith and
27:23 of those twenty years old and **u**,
2 Chr 4: 3 And **u** it was the likeness of
4:15 one Sea and twelve oxen **u** it;
5: 7 **u** the wings of the cherubim.
14: 5 kingdom was quiet **u** him.
23:14 'Take her outside **u** guard,
26:11 **u** the hand of Hananiah, one of
26:13 And **u** their authority was an
28: 4 and **u** every green tree.
31:13 Benaiah were overseers **u** the
31:15 And **u** him were Eden, Miniamin,
32:10 that you remain **u** siege in
Ezra 5:16 now it has been **u** construction,
Neh 2:14 room for the animal **u** me
3:17 **u** Rehum the son of Bani,
3:18 **u** Bavai the son of Henadad,
8:17 made booths and sat **u** the
Esth 2: 3 **u** the custody of Hegai the
2: 8 **u** the custody of Hegai,
Job 20:12 And he hides it **u** his tongue,
26: 5 Those **u** the waters and those
26: 8 the clouds are not broken **u** it.
28:24 And sees **u** the whole heavens,
30: 7 *U* the nettles they nestled.
30:14 *U* the ruinous storm they roll
37: 3 He sends it forth **u** the whole
38:14 takes on form like clay **u** a
40:21 He lies **u** the lotus trees,
41:11 Everything **u** heaven is Mine.
Ps 8: 6 You have put all things **u** his
10: 7 *U* his tongue is trouble and
17: 8 Hide me **u** the shadow of Your
18: 9 With darkness **u** His feet.
18:36 You enlarged my path **u** me,
18:38 They have fallen **u** my feet.
18:39 You have subdued **u** me those
18:47 And subdues the peoples **u** me;
36: 7 of men put their trust **u** the
45: 5 The peoples fall **u** You.
47: 3 subdue the peoples **u** us,
47: 3 And the nations **u** our feet.
91: 1 Shall abide **u** the shadow
91: 4 And **u** His wings you shall take
106:42 into subjection **u** their
140: 3 The poison of asps is **u** their
144: 2 Who subdues my people **u** me.
Prov 22:27 take away your bed from **u** you?
Eccl 1: 3 In which he toils **u** the sun?
1: 9 there is nothing new **u** the
1:13 all that is done **u** heaven;
1:14 the works that are done **u** the
2: 3 the sons of men to do **u** heaven
2:11 There was no profit **u** the
2:17 the work that was done **u** the
2:18 in which I had toiled **u** the
2:19 I have shown myself wise **u** the
2:20 in which I had toiled **u** the
2:22 with which he has toiled **u** the
3: 1 for every purpose **u** heaven:
3:16 Moreover I saw **u** the sun:
4: 1 oppression that is done **u** the
4: 3 evil work that is done **u** the
4: 7 and I saw vanity **u** the sun:
4:15 all the living who walk **u** the
5:13 evil which I have seen **u** the
5:18 labor in which he toils **u** the
6: 1 an evil which I have seen **u** the
6:12 will happen after him **u** the
7: 6 the crackling of thorns **u** a
8: 9 work that is done **u** the
8:15 a man has nothing better **u** the
8:15 life which God gives him **u** the
8:17 the work that is done **u** the
9: 3 evil in all that is done **u** the
9: 6 In anything done **u** the sun.
9: 9 which He has given you **u** the
9: 9 labor which you perform **u** the
9:11 I returned and saw **u** the sun
9:13 wisdom I have also seen **u** the
10: 5 is an evil I have seen **u** the
Song 2: 6 His left hand is **u** my head,
4:11 Honey and milk are **u** your
8: 3 His left hand is **u** my head,
8: 5 I awakened you **u** the apple
Isa 3: 6 let these ruins be **u** your
10:16 And **u** his glory He will
14:11 The maggot is spread **u** you,
24: 5 The earth is also defiled **u** its
25:10 shall be trampled down **u** Him,
28:15 And **u** falsehood we have hidden
34:15 and gather them **u** her shadow;
57: 5 yourselves with gods **u** every
57: 5 *U* the clefts of the rocks?
Jer 2:20 on every high hill and **u** every
3: 6 every high mountain and **u** every
3:13 To alien deities **u** every green
10:11 the earth and from **u** these
27: 8 not put its neck **u** the yoke
27:11 that bring their necks **u** the
27:12 Bring your necks **u** the yoke of
33:13 shall again pass **u** the hands
34: 1 the kingdoms of the earth **u** his
38:11 of the king **u** the treasury,
38:12 old clothes and rags **u** your
38:12 your armpits, **u** the ropes."
48:45 Those who fled stood **u** the
52:20 bronze bulls which were **u** it,
Lam 1: 3 *U* affliction and hard
3:34 To crush **u** one's feet All the
3:66 and destroy them From **u** the
4:20 *U* his shadow We shall live
5:13 Boys staggered **u** loads of
Ezek 1: 8 The hands of a man were **u** their
1:23 And **u** the firmament their wings
6:13 **u** every green tree, and under
6:13 and **u** every thick oak,
10: 2 among the wheels, **u** the cherub,
10: 8 form of a man's hand **u** their
10:20 living creature I saw **u** the God
10:21 hands of a man was **u** their
17: 6 But its roots were **u** it.
17:13 and put him **u** oath. He also
17:23 *U* it will dwell birds of every
20:37 I will make you pass **u** the rod,
24: 5 Also pile fuel bones **u** it,
31: 6 *U* its branches all the beasts
31:12 the earth have gone from **u** its
32:27 have laid their swords **u** their
46:23 hearths were made **u** the rows
47: 1 flowing from **u** the threshold of
47: 1 water was flowing from **u** the
Dan 4:12 of the field found shade **u** it,
4:14 the beasts get out from **u** it,
4:21 **u** which the beasts of the field
7:27 of the kingdoms **u** the whole
8:13 host to be trampled **u** foot?"
8:25 cause deceit to prosper **u** his
9:12 for **u** the whole heaven such has
Hos 4:13 *U* oaks, poplars, and
14: 7 Those who dwell **u** his shadow
Joel 1:17 The seed shrivels **u** the clods,
Jon 4: 5 himself a shelter and sat **u** it
Mic 1: 4 The mountains will melt **u** Him,
4: 4 But everyone shall sit **u** his
4: 4 sit under his vine and **u** his
Zech 3:10 invite his neighbor *U* his
3:10 Under his vine and **u** his
Mal 4: 3 For they shall be ashes **u** the
Mt 2:16 from two years old and **u**,
5:15 a lamp and put it **u** a basket,
7: 6 lest they trample them **u** their
8: 8 You should come **u** my roof.
8: 9 For I also am a man **u** authority,
8: 9 having soldiers **u** me. And I say
23:37 her chicks **u** her wings,
26:63 I put You **u** oath by the living
Mk 4:21 put **u** a basket or under a bed?
4:21 to be put under a basket or **u**
4:32 birds of the air may nest **u** its
6:11 shake off the dust **u** your feet
7:28 yet even the little dogs **u** the
Lk 7: 6 You should enter **u** my roof.
7: 8 am a man placed **u** authority,
7: 8 having soldiers **u** me. And I say
8:16 a vessel or puts it **u** a bed,
8:29 and he was kept **u** guard, bound
11:33 it in a secret place or **u** a
13:34 gathers her brood **u** her wings,
17:24 out of one part **u** heaven
17:24 the other part **u** heaven,
23:40 seeing you are **u** the same
Jn 1:48 when you were **u** the fig tree,
1:50 'I saw you **u** the fig tree,'
Acts 2: 5 from every nation **u** heaven.
4:12 is no other name **u** heaven
8:27 of great authority **u** Candace
22:24 should be examined **u** scourging,
23:12 and bound themselves **u** an oath,
23:14 We have bound ourselves **u** a
27: 4 we sailed **u** the shelter of
27: 7 we sailed **u** the shelter of
27:16 And running **u** the shelter of
27:30 **u** pretense of putting out
Rom 3: 9 that they are all **u** sin.
3:13 of asps is **u** their
3:19 it says to those who are **u** the
6:14 for you are not **u** law but under
6:14 are not under law but **u** grace.
6:15 sin because we are not **u** law
6:15 not under law but **u** grace?
7:14 I am carnal, sold **u** sin.
16:20 peace will crush Satan **u** your
1 Cor 6:12 but I will not be brought **u** the
7:15 or a sister is not **u** bondage
9:20 to those who are **u** the law,
9:20 as **u** the law, that I might win
9:20 win those who are **u** the law;
9:21 but **u** law toward Christ),
10: 1 our fathers were **u** the cloud,
15:25 has put all enemies **u** His feet.
15:27 all things **u** His feet."
15:27 'all things are put **u** Him,"
15:27 that He who put all things **u**
15:28 Him who put all things **u** Him,
2 Cor 11:32 **u** Aretas the king, was guarding
Gal 3:10 of the law are **u** the
3:22 has confined all **u** sin,
3:23 we were kept **u** guard by the
3:25 we are no longer **u** a tutor.
4: 2 but is **u** guardians and stewards
4: 3 were in bondage **u** the elements
4: 4 born **u** the law,
4: 5 to redeem those who were **u** the
4:21 you who desire to be **u** the law,
5:18 you are not **u** the law.
Eph 1:22 And He put all things **u** His
Phil 2:10 and of those **u** the earth,
Col 1:23 to every creature **u** heaven,
1 Tim 5: 9 Do not let a widow **u** sixty years
6: 1 bondservants as are **u** the yoke
Heb 2: 8 things in subjection **u** his
2: 8 He put all in subjection **u** him,
2: 8 that is not put **u** him.
2: 8 yet see all things put **u** him.
7:11 Levitical priesthood (for **u** it
9:15 of the transgressions **u** the
1 Pe 5: 6 humble yourselves **u** the mighty
2 Pe 2: 9 the unjust **u** punishment
1 Jn 5:19 whole world lies **u** the sway
Jude 6 chains **u** darkness for
Rev 5: 3 or on the earth or **u** the earth
5:13 on the earth and **u** the earth
6: 9 I saw **u** the altar the souls of
12: 1 with the moon **u** her feet,

UNDERFOOT (10/10)

2 Ki 9:33 and he trampled her **u**.
Ps 91:13 the serpent you shall trample **u**.
Isa 14:19 Like a corpse trodden **u**.
14:25 on My mountains tread him **u**.
28: 3 of Ephraim, Will be trampled **u**;
Jer 12:10 They have trodden My portion **u**;
Lam 1:15 The Lord has trampled **u** all my
Mt 5:13 to be thrown out and trampled **u**
Heb 10:29 has trampled the Son of God **u**,
Rev 11: 2 they will tread the holy city **u**

UNDERGIRD (1/1)

Acts 27:17 they used cables to **u** the ship;

UNDERGIRDING (KJV) See UNDERGIRD

UNDERGROUND (1/1)

Ezek 31: 4 *U* waters gave it height,

UNDERMINE (1/1)

Job 6:27 And you **u** your friend.

UNDERNEATH (5/5)

Ex 28:27 *u* the ephod toward its front,
39:20 *u* the ephod toward its front,
Deut 33:27 And *u* are the everlasting
2 Ki 6:30 and there *u* he had sackcloth
Job 28: 5 But *u* it is turned up as by

UNDERSETTERS (KJV) See SUPPORTS

UNDERSIDES (1/1)

Job 41:30 His *u* are like sharp

UNDERSTAND (121/116) UNDERSTANDING, UNDERSTANDS, UNDERSTOOD

Gen 11: 7 that they may not *u* one
41:15 it said of you that you can *u*
Num 16:30 then you will *u* that these men
Deut 9: 3 Therefore *u* today that the LORD
9: 6 Therefore *u* that the LORD your
28:49 whose language you will not *u*,
2 Ki 18:26 for we *u* it; and do not speak
1 Chr 28:19 the LORD made me *u* in writing,
Neh 8: 3 and women and those who could *u*;
8: 7 helped the people to *u* the Law;
8: 8 and helped them to *u* the
8:13 in order to *u* the words of the
Job 6:24 Cause me to *u* wherein I have
15: 9 What do you *u* that is not in
23: 5 And *u* what He would say to me.
26:14 thunder of His power who can *u*?
32: 9 Nor do the aged always *u*
36:29 can anyone *u* the spreading of
42: 3 I have uttered what I did not *u*,
Ps 14: 2 To see if there are any who *u*,
19:12 Who can *u* his errors?
49:20 is in honor, yet does not *u*,
53: 2 To see if there are any who *u*,
73:16 When I thought how to *u* this,
81: 5 I heard a language I did not *u*.
82: 5 do not know, nor do they *u*;
92: 6 Nor does a fool *u* this.
94: 7 Nor does the God of Jacob *u*.
94: 8 *U*, you senseless among the
106: 7 Our fathers in Egypt did not *u*
107:43 And they will *u* the
119:27 Make me *u* the way of Your
119:100 I *u* more than the ancients,
139: 2 You *u* my thought afar off.
Prov 1: 6 To *u* a proverb and an enigma,
2: 5 Then you will *u* the fear of the
2: 9 Then you will *u* righteousness
8: 5 *u* prudence, And you fools, be
14: 8 wisdom of the prudent is to *u*
20:24 How then can a man *u* his own
28: 5 Evil men do not *u* justice,
28: 5 those who seek the LORD *u* all.
29: 7 But the wicked does not *u*
30:18 Yes, four which I do not *u*:
Isa 6: 9 on hearing, but do not *u*;
6:10 And *u* with their heart,
28: 9 And whom will he make to *u* the
28:19 It will be a terror just to *u*
32: 4 the heart of the rash will *u*
33:19 tongue that you cannot *u*.
36:11 for we *u* it; and do not speak
41:20 And consider and *u* together,
43:10 And *u* that I am He.
44:18 They do not know nor *u*;
44:18 hearts, so that they cannot *u*.
56:11 are shepherds Who cannot *u*;
Jer 5:15 Nor can you *u* what they say.
9:12 Who is the wise man who may *u*
23:20 In the latter days you will *u*
Ezek 3: 6 whose words you cannot *u*.
Dan 1: 4 knowledge and quick to *u*,
8:16 make this man *u* the vision."
8:17 '*U*, son of man, that the vision
9:13 turn from our iniquities and *u*
9:22 forth to give you skill to *u*.
9:23 and *u* the vision:
9:25 "Know therefore and *u*,
10:11 *u* the words that I speak to
10:12 that you set your heart to *u*,
10:14 Now I have come to make you *u*
11:33 And those of the people who *u*
12: 8 Although I heard, I did not *u*.
12:10 and none of the wicked shall *u*,
12:10 but the wise shall *u*.
Hos 4:14 people who do not *u* will be
14: 9 Let him *u* these things.
Mic 4:12 Nor do they *u* His counsel;
Mt 13:13 they do not hear, nor do they *u*.
13:14 will hear and shall not *u*,
13:15 Lest they should *u* with
13:19 and does not *u* it, then the
15:10 He said to them, "Hear and *u*:
15:17 Do you not yet *u* that whatever
16: 9 "Do you not yet *u*,
16:11 How is it you do not *u* that I
24:15 (whoever reads, let him *u*),
Mk 4:12 they may hear and not *u*;
4:13 'Do you not *u* this parable?
4:13 How then will you *u* all the
7:14 "Hear Me, everyone, and *u*:
8:17 Do you not yet perceive nor *u*?
8:21 "How is it you do not *u*?
9:32 But they did not *u* this saying,
13:14 ought not" (let the reader *u*),
14:68 I neither know nor *u* what you
Lk 2:50 But they did not *u* the statement
8:10 hearing they may not *u*.
9:45 But they did not *u* this saying,
Jn 6:60 a hard saying; who can *u* it?"
8:27 They did not *u* that He spoke to
8:43 Why do you not *u* My speech?
10: 6 but they did not *u* the things
12:16 His disciples did not *u* these
12:40 Lest they should *u* with
13: 7 What I am doing you do not *u*
Acts 7:25 by his hand, but they did not *u*.
8:30 Do you *u* what you are reading?"
28:26 hear, and shall not *u*;
28:27 Lest they should *u* with
Rom 7:15 For what I am doing, I do not *u*.
15:21 have not heard shall *u*.
1 Cor 13: 2 and *u* all mysteries and all
14: 9 by the tongue words easy to *u*,
14:16 since he does not *u* what you
2 Cor 1:13 to you than what you read or *u*.
1:13 Now I trust you will *u*,
Eph 3: 4 you may *u* my knowledge in the
5:17 but *u* what the will of the Lord
Heb 11: 3 By faith we *u* that the worlds
2 Pe 2:12 of the things they do not *u*,
3:16 which are some things hard to *u*,

UNDERSTANDING (155/151) UNDERSTAND

Ex 31: 3 Spirit of God, in wisdom, in *u*,
35:31 Spirit of God, in wisdom and *u*,
36: 1 the LORD has put wisdom and *u*,
Deut 1:13 'Choose wise, *u*,
4: 6 is your wisdom and your *u* in
4: 6 great nation is a wise and *u*
32:28 Nor is there any *u* in them.
1 Sam 25: 3 And she was a woman of good *u*
1 Ki 3: 9 give to Your servant an *u*
3:11 but have asked for yourself *u*
3:12 I have given you a wise and *u*
4:29 wisdom and exceedingly great *u*,
7:14 he was filled with wisdom and *u*
1 Chr 12:32 the sons of Issachar who had *u*
22:12 the LORD give you wisdom and *u*,
2 Chr 2:12 endowed with prudence and *u*,
2:13 a skillful man, endowed with *u*,
26: 5 who had *u* in the visions of
Ezra 8:16 Joiarib and Elnathan, men of *u*.
8:18 they brought us a man of *u*,
Neh 8: 2 and all who could hear with *u*
10:28 who had knowledge and *u*—
Job 12: 3 But I have *u* as well as you;
12:12 And with length of days, *u*.
12:13 He has counsel and *u*.
12:24 He takes away the *u* of the
17: 4 have hidden their heart from *u*;
18: 2 Gain *u*, and afterward we will
20: 3 And the spirit of my *u* causes
26:12 And by His *u* He breaks up the
28:12 And where is the place of *u*?
28:20 And where is the place of *u*?
28:28 And to depart from evil is *u*.
32: 8 of the Almighty gives him *u*.
34:10 listen to me, you men of *u*:
34:16 "If you have *u*,
34:34 Men of *u* say to me, Wise men
36: 5 is mighty in strength of *u*.
38: 4 Tell Me, if you have *u*.
38:36 Or who has given *u* to the
39:17 And did not endow her with *u*.
Ps 32: 9 the mule, Which have no *u*,
47: 7 the earth; Sing praises with *u*.
49: 3 of my heart shall give *u*.
111:10 A good *u* have all those who do
119:34 Give me *u*, and I shall keep
119:73 Give me *u*, that I may learn
119:99 I have more *u* than all my
119:104 Through Your precepts I get *u*;
119:125 I am Your servant; Give me *u*,
119:130 It gives *u* to the simple.
119:144 Give me *u*, and I shall live.
119:169 Give me *u* according to Your
147: 5 His *u* is infinite.
Prov 1: 2 To perceive the words of *u*,
1: 5 And a man of *u* will attain
2: 2 And apply your heart to *u*;
2: 3 And lift up your voice for *u*,
2: 6 His mouth come knowledge and *u*;
2:11 *U* will keep you,
3: 5 And lean not on your own *u*;
3:13 And the man who gains *u*;
3:19 By *u* He established the
4: 1 And give attention to know *u*;
4: 5 Get wisdom! Get *u*! Do not
4: 7 And in all your getting, get *u*.
5: 1 Lend your ear to my *u*,
6:32 adultery with a woman lacks *u*;
7: 4 And call *u* your nearest
7: 7 A young man devoid of *u*,
8: 1 And *u* lift up her voice?
8: 5 be of an *u* heart.
8:14 and sound wisdom; I am *u*,
9: 4 As for him who lacks *u*,
9: 6 And go in the way of *u*.
9:10 knowledge of the Holy One is *u*.
9:16 And as for him who lacks *u*,
10:13 on the lips of him who has *u*,
10:13 back of him who is devoid of *u*.
10:23 But a man of *u* has wisdom.
11:12 But a man of *u* holds his
12:11 frivolity is devoid of *u*.
13:15 Good *u* gains favor, But the
14:29 is slow to wrath has great *u*,
14:33 in the heart of him who has *u*,
15:14 The heart of him who has *u*
15:21 But a man of *u* walks
15:32 But he who heeds rebuke gets *u*.
16:16 than gold! And to get *u* is to
16:22 *U* is a wellspring of life to
17:18 A man devoid of *u* shakes hands
17:24 in the sight of him who has *u*,
17:27 And a man of *u* is of a calm
18: 2 A fool has no delight in *u*,
19: 8 He who keeps *u* will find good.
19:25 Rebuke one who has *u*,
20: 5 But a man of *u* will draw it
21:16 who wanders from the way of *u*
21:30 There is no wisdom or *u* Or
23: 4 be rich; Because of your own *u*,
23:23 wisdom and instruction and *u*.
24: 3 And by *u* it is established;
24:30 vineyard of the man devoid of *u*;
28: 2 But by a man of *u* and
28:11 But the poor who has *u*
28:16 A ruler who lacks *u* is a great
30: 2 And do not have the *u* of a
Eccl 9:11 Nor riches to men of *u*,
Isa 11: 2 The Spirit of wisdom and *u*,
27:11 For it is a people of no *u*;
29:14 And the *u* of their prudent
29:16 He has no *u*"?
29:24 erred in spirit will come to *u*,
40:14 And showed Him the way of *u*?
40:28 His *u* is unsearchable.
44:19 is there knowledge nor *u* to
Jer 3:15 feed you with knowledge and *u*.
4:22 And they have no *u*.
5:21 O foolish people, Without *u*,
51:15 out the heaven by His *u*.
Ezek 28: 4 With your wisdom and your *u*
Dan 1:17 and Daniel had *u* in all visions
1:20 in all matters of wisdom and *u*
2:21 knowledge to those who have *u*.
4:34 and my *u* returned to me;
5:11 light and *u* and wisdom,
5:12 excellent spirit, knowledge, *u*,
5:14 and that light and *u* and
10: 1 and had *u* of the vision.
11:35 And some of those of *u* shall
Ob 8 And *u* from the mountains of
Mt 15:16 "Are you also still without *u*?
Mk 7:18 'Are you thus without *u* also?
12:33 all the heart, with all the *u*,
Lk 1: 3 having had perfect *u* of all
2:47 Him were astonished at His *u*
24:45 And He opened their *u*,
1 Cor 1:19 bring to nothing the *u*
14:14 but my *u* is unfruitful.
14:15 and I will also pray with the *u*.
14:15 and I will also sing with the *u*.
14:19 speak five words with my *u*,
14:20 do not be children in *u*;
14:20 but in *u* be mature.
Eph 1:18 the eyes of your *u* being
4:18 having their *u* darkened,
Phil 4: 7 of God, which surpasses all *u*,
Col 1: 9 in all wisdom and spiritual *u*;
2: 2 of the full assurance of *u*,
1 Tim 1: 7 *u* neither what they say nor the
2 Tim 2: 7 and may the Lord give you *u* in
Jas 3:13 Who is wise and *u* among you?
1 Pe 3: 7 dwell with them with *u*,
1 Jn 5:20 has come and has given us an *u*,
Rev 13:18 Let him who has *u* calculate the

UNDERSTANDS (10/10) UNDERSTAND

1 Chr 28: 9 searches all hearts and *u* all
Job 28:23 God *u* its way, And He knows
Prov 8: 9 are all plain to him who *u*,
14: 6 knowledge is easy to him who *u*.
29:19 by mere words; For though he *u*,
Jer 9:24 That he *u* and knows Me,
Dan 8:23 Who *u* sinister schemes.
Mt 13:23 is he who hears the word and *u*
Rom 3:11 There is none who *u*;
1 Cor 14: 2 for no one *u* him; however, in

UNDERSTOOD (24/24) UNDERSTAND

Gen 42:23 they did not know that Joseph *u*
Deut 32:29 that they *u* this, That they
1 Sam 4: 6 Then they *u* that the ark of
26: 4 and *u* that Saul had indeed
2 Sam 3:37 all the people and all Israel *u*
Neh 8:12 because they *u* the words that
Esth 1:13 said to the wise men who *u* the
Job 13: 1 My ear has heard and *u* it.
Ps 73:17 Then I *u* their end.
Eccl 1:16 My heart has *u* great wisdom and
Isa 40:21 Have you not *u* from the
Dan 8:27 but no one *u* it.
9: 2 *u* by the books the number of
10: 1 and he *u* the message, and had
Mt 13:51 Have you *u* all these things?"
16:12 Then they *u* that He did not tell
17:13 Then the disciples *u* that He
Mk 6:52 For they had not *u* about the
Lk 18:34 But they *u* none of these things;

Acts 7:25 that his brethren would have ***u***
23:34 And when he ***u*** that he was
Rom 1:20 being ***u*** by the things that are
1 Cor 13:11 I ***u*** as a child, I thought as a
2 Cor 1:14 (as also you have ***u*** us in part),

UNDERTAKE (1/1)
Isa 38:14 I am oppressed; ***U*** for me!

UNDESIRABLE (1/1) DESIRE
Zeph 2: 1 gather together, O ***u*** nation,

UNDIGNIFIED (1/1)
2 Sam 6:22 And I will be even more ***u*** than

UNDISCERNING (1/1) DISCERN
Rom 1:31 ***u***, untrustworthy,

UNDO (1/1)
Isa 58: 6 To ***u*** the heavy burdens,

UNDONE (5/5)
Josh 11:15 He left nothing ***u*** of all that
Esth 6:10 Leave nothing ***u*** of all that you
Isa 6: 5 for I am ***u***! Because I am a
Mt 23:23 without leaving the others ***u***.
Lk 11:42 without leaving the others ***u***.

UNDRESSED (KJV) See UNTENDED

UNDULY (1/1)
Eccl 5:20 For he will not dwell ***u*** on the

UNEDUCATED (1/1)
Acts 4:13 and perceived that they were ***u***

UNEQUALLY (1/1) EQUAL
2 Cor 6:14 Do not be ***u*** yoked together with

UNEXPECTEDLY (3/3) EXPECT
Gen 38:29 that his brother came out ***u***;
Ps 35: 8 destruction come upon him ***u***,
Lk 21:34 and that Day come on you ***u***.

UNFAITHFUL (16/16) FAITHFUL, UNFAITHFULLY, UNFAITHFULNESS
Lev 26:40 in which they were ***u*** to Me,
1 Chr 5:25 And they were ***u*** to the God of
2 Chr 28:19 and had been continually ***u*** to
28:22 Ahaz became increasingly ***u*** to
Neh 1: 8 Moses, saying, 'If you are ***u***,
Prov 2:22 And the ***u*** will be uprooted
11: 3 But the perversity of the ***u***
11: 6 But the ***u*** will be caught by
13: 2 But the soul of the ***u*** feeds on
13:15 But the way of the ***u*** is hard.
21:18 And the ***u*** for the upright.
23:28 And increases the ***u*** among men.
25:19 Confidence in an ***u*** man in time
Ezek 20:27 by being ***u*** to Me.
39:23 because they were ***u*** to Me,
39:26 in which they were ***u*** to Me,

UNFAITHFULLY (3/3) UNFAITHFUL
Num 5:12 wife goes astray and behaves ***u***
5:27 defiled herself and behaved ***u***
Ps 78:57 But turned back and acted ***u***

UNFAITHFULNESS (9/9) UNFAITHFUL
Lev 26:40 with their ***u*** in which they were
Num 5: 6 any sin that men commit in ***u***
1 Chr 9: 1 to Babylon because of their ***u***.
10:13 So Saul died for his ***u*** which he
Ezek 14:13 sins against Me by persistent ***u***,
15: 8 they have persisted in ***u***,
18:24 because of the ***u*** of which he is
39:26 and all their ***u*** in which they
Dan 9: 7 because of the ***u*** which they

UNFAMILIAR (2/2) FAMILIAR
Ezek 3: 5 sent to a people of ***u*** speech
3: 6 not to many people of ***u*** speech

UNFANNED (1/1) FAN
Job 20:26 An ***u*** fire will consume him;

UNFEIGNED (KJV) See SINCERE

UNFORGIVING (2/2) FORGIVE
Rom 1:31 untrustworthy, unloving, ***u***,
2 Tim 3: 3 unloving, ***u***, slanderers,

UNFORMED (1/1) FORM
Ps 139:16 saw my substance, being yet ***u***.

UNFRUITFUL (6/6) FRUITFUL
Mt 13:22 the word, and he becomes ***u***.
Mk 4:19 the word, and it becomes ***u***.
1 Cor 14:14 but my understanding is ***u***.
Eph 5:11 have no fellowship with the ***u***
Titus 3:14 that they may not be ***u***.
2 Pe 1: 8 will be neither barren nor ***u***

UNGIRDED (KJV) See UNLOADED

UNGODLINESS (7/7) UNGODLY
2 Sam 22: 5 The floods of ***u*** made me
Ps 18: 4 And the floods of ***u*** made me
Isa 32: 6 work iniquity: To practice ***u***,
Rom 1:18 from heaven against all ***u*** and
11:26 And He will turn away ***u***
2 Tim 2:16 they will increase to more ***u***.
Titus 2:12 denying ***u*** and worldly lusts,

UNGODLY (25/22) GODLY, UNGODLINESS
Job 16:11 God has delivered me to the ***u***,
Ps 1: 1 not in the counsel of the ***u***,
1: 4 The ***u*** are not so, But are
1: 5 Therefore the ***u*** shall not stand
1: 6 But the way of the ***u*** shall
3: 7 have broken the teeth of the ***u***.
35:16 With ***u*** mockers at feasts
43: 1 plead my cause against an ***u***
73:12 Behold, these are the ***u***,
Prov 11:31 How much more the ***u*** and the
16:27 An ***u*** man digs up evil, And it
Isa 10: 6 I will send him against an ***u***
Rom 4: 5 on Him who justifies the ***u***,
5: 6 due time Christ died for the ***u***.
1 Tim 1: 9 for the ***u*** and for sinners,
1 Pe 4:18 Where will the ***u*** and the
2 Pe 2: 5 the flood on the world of the ***u***;
2: 6 who afterward would live ***u***;
3: 7 of judgment and perdition of ***u***
Jude 4 ***u*** men, who turn the grace of
15 to convict all who are ***u*** among
15 among them of all their ***u***
15 they have committed in an ***u***
15 of all the harsh things which ***u***
18 walk according to their own ***u***

UNHEARD (1/1) HEAR
Jn 9:32 the world began it has been ***u***

UNHOLY (5/5) HOLY
Lev 10:10 distinguish between holy and ***u***,
Ezek 22:26 between the holy and ***u***,
44:23 between the holy and the ***u***,
1 Tim 1: 9 for the ***u*** and profane,
2 Tim 3: 2 to parents, unthankful, ***u***,

UNICORN, UNICORNS (KJV) See OX, OXEN

UNINFORMED (3/3)
1 Cor 14:16 who occupies the place of the ***u***
14:23 come in those who are ***u*** or
14:24 and an unbeliever or an ***u***

UNINHABITED (3/3) INHABIT
Lev 16:22 all their iniquities to an ***u***
Ezek 29:11 and it shall be ***u*** forty years.
35: 9 and your cities shall be ***u***;

UNINTENDED (1/1) INTEND, UNINTENTIONALLY
Num 15:25 for their ***u*** sin.

UNINTENTIONAL (1/1)
Num 15:25 be forgiven them, for it was ***u***;

UNINTENTIONALLY (18/17) UNINTENDED
Lev 4: 2 If a person sins ***u*** against any
4:13 congregation of Israel sins ***u***,
4:22 and done something ***u*** against
4:27 of the common people sins ***u*** by
5:15 and sins ***u*** in regard to the
22:14 a man eats the holy offering ***u***,
Num 15:22 'If you sin ***u***,
15:24 if it is ***u*** committed,
15:26 all the people did it ***u***.
15:27 'And if a person sins ***u***,
15:28 for the person who sins ***u***,
15:28 when he sins ***u*** before the
15:29 have one law for him who sins ***u***,
Deut 4:42 who kills his neighbor ***u***,
19: 4 Whoever kills his neighbor ***u***,
Josh 20: 3 a person accidentally or ***u***
20: 5 he struck his neighbor ***u***,
Ezek 45:20 for everyone who has sinned ***u***

UNIQUE (1/1)
Job 23:13 "But He is ***u***,

UNIT (1/1)
2 Sam 2:25 behind Abner and became a ***u***,

UNITE (1/1) UNITED, UNITY
Ps 86:11 ***U*** my heart to fear Your name.

UNITED (4/4) UNITE
Gen 49: 6 Let not my honor be ***u*** to their
Judg 20:11 ***u*** together as one man.
1 Chr 12:17 my heart will be ***u*** with you;
Rom 6: 5 For if we have been ***u*** together

UNITY (4/4) UNITE
Job 10: 8 fashioned me, An intricate ***u***;
Ps 133: 1 to dwell together in ***u***!
Eph 4: 3 endeavoring to keep the ***u*** of the
4:13 till we all come to the ***u*** of the

UNJUST (17/15) JUST
Ps 43: 1 me from the deceitful and ***u***
Prov 11: 7 And the hope of the ***u***
29:27 An ***u*** man is an abomination to
Zeph 3: 5 But the ***u*** knows no shame.
Mt 5:45 rain on the just and on the ***u***.
Lk 16: 8 So the master commended the ***u***
16:10 and he who is ***u*** in what is
16:10 unjust in what is least is ***u***
18: 6 Hear what the ***u*** judge said.
18:11 like other men—extortioners, ***u***,
Acts 24:15 both of the just and the ***u***.
Rom 3: 5 Is God ***u*** who inflicts wrath?
Heb 6:10 For God is not ***u*** to forget your
1 Pe 3:18 for sins, the just for the ***u***,
2 Pe 2: 9 and to reserve the ***u*** under
Rev 22:11 'He who is ***u***, let him be
22:11 let him be ***u*** still; he who is

UNJUSTLY (2/2)
Ps 82: 2 How long will you judge ***u***,
Isa 26:10 of uprightness he will deal ***u***,

UNKNOWN (6/6) KNOW
Gen 31:20 ***u*** to Laban the Syrian, in that
31:26 that you have stolen away ***u*** to
Prov 22:29 He will not stand before ***u***
Acts 17:23 inscription: TO THE ***U*** GOD.
2 Cor 6: 9 as ***u***, and yet well known;
Gal 1:22 And I was ***u*** by face to the

UNLADE (KJV) See UNLOAD

UNLAWFUL (1/1) LAWFUL
Acts 10:28 You know how ***u*** it is for a

UNLEARNED (KJV) See IGNORANT, UNEDUCATED, UNINFORMED, UNTAUGHT

UNLEAVENED (61/50) LEAVEN
Gen 19: 3 and baked ***u*** bread, and they
Ex 12: 8 with ***u*** bread and with bitter
12:15 days you shall eat ***u*** bread.
12:17 the Feast of ***U*** Bread,
12:18 you shall eat ***u*** bread,
12:20 you shall eat ***u*** bread.'
12:39 And they baked ***u*** cakes of the
13: 6 days you shall eat ***u*** bread,
13: 7 ***U*** bread shall be eaten seven
23:15 keep the Feast of ***U*** Bread
23:15 Bread (you shall eat ***u*** bread
29: 2 and ***u*** bread, unleavened cakes
29: 2 ***u*** cakes mixed with oil,
29: 2 and ***u*** wafers anointed with oil
29:23 from the basket of the ***u*** bread
34:18 The Feast of ***U*** Bread you shall
34:18 days you shall eat ***u*** bread,
Lev 2: 4 it shall be ***u*** cakes of fine
2: 4 or ***u*** wafers anointed with oil.
2: 5 shall be of fine flour, ***u***,
6:16 with ***u*** bread it shall be eaten
7:12 ***u*** cakes mixed with oil,
7:12 ***u*** wafers anointed with oil,
8: 2 and a basket of ***u*** bread;
8:26 and from the basket of ***u*** bread
8:26 the LORD he took one ***u*** cake,
23: 6 month is the Feast of ***U*** Bread
23: 6 days you must eat ***u*** bread.
Num 6:15 a basket of ***u*** bread, cakes of
6:15 ***u*** wafers anointed with oil,
6:17 with the basket of ***u*** bread;
6:19 one ***u*** cake from the basket,
6:19 and one ***u*** wafer, and put them
9:11 They shall eat it with ***u*** bread
28:17 ***u*** bread shall be eaten for
Deut 16: 3 days you shall eat ***u*** bread
16: 8 Six days you shall eat ***u*** bread,
16:16 at the Feast of ***U*** Bread, at the
Josh 5:11 ***u*** bread and parched grain, on
Judg 6:19 and ***u*** bread from an ephah of
6:20 Take the meat and the ***u*** bread
6:21 the meat and the ***u*** bread;
6:21 the meat and the ***u*** bread.
1 Sam 28:24 and baked ***u*** bread from it.

U

2 Ki 23: 9 but they ate *u* bread among
1 Chr 23:29 with the *u* cakes and what is
2 Chr 8:13 the Feast of *U* Bread, the Feast
30:13 to keep the Feast of *U* Bread
30:21 kept the Feast of *U* Bread
35:17 and the Feast of *U* Bread for
Ezra 6:22 kept the Feast of *U* Bread
Ezek 45:21 *u* bread shall be eaten.
Mt 26:17 Feast of the *U* Bread
Mk 14: 1 and the Feast of *U* Bread.
14:12 the first day of *U* Bread,
Lk 22: 1 Now the Feast of *U* Bread drew
22: 7 Then came the Day of *U* Bread,
Acts 12: 3 during the Days of *U* Bread.
20: 6 after the Days of *U* Bread,
1 Cor 5: 7 new lump, since you truly are *u*.
5: 8 but with the *u* bread of

UNLESS (73/69)

Gen 31:42 *U* the God of my father, the God
32:26 I will not let You go *u* You
42:15 not leave this place *u* your
43: 3 You shall not see my face *u* your
43: 5 You shall not see my face *u* your
44:23 *U* your youngest brother comes
44:26 not see the man's face *u* our
Lev 22: 6 eat the holy offerings *u* he
Deut 32:30 *U* their Rock had sold them,
Josh 2:18 '*u*, when we come into the land,
2:18 and *u* you bring your father,
7:12 *u* you destroy the accursed from
1 Sam 25:34 *u* you had hastened and come to
2 Sam 2:27 *u* you had spoken, surely then
3:13 you shall not see my face *u* you
2 Ki 4:24 slacken the pace for me *u* I
Esth 2:14 to the king again *u* the king
Ps 27:13 *u* I had believed That I would
94:17 *U* the LORD had been my help,
119:92 *U* Your law had been my
127: 1 *U* the LORD builds the house,
127: 1 *U* the LORD guards the city,
Prov 4:16 For they do not sleep *u* they
4:16 sleep is taken away *u* they
Isa 1: 9 *U* the LORD of hosts Had left
Lam 5:22 *U* You have utterly rejected us,
Dan 6: 5 against this Daniel *u* we
Am 3: 3 *u* they are agreed?
3: 7 *U* He reveals His secret to His
Mt 5:20 that *u* your righteousness
12:29 *u* he first binds the strong
18: 3 *u* you are converted and become
24:22 And *u* those days were shortened,
26:42 cannot pass away from Me *u* I
Mk 3:27 *u* he first binds the strong
7: 3 the Jews do not eat *u* they
7: 4 they do not eat *u* they wash.
13:20 And *u* the Lord had shortened
Lk 9:13 *u* we go and buy food for all
13: 3 but *u* you repent you will all
13: 5 but *u* you repent you will all
Jn 3: 2 signs that You do *u* God
3: 3 *u* one is born again, he cannot
3: 5 *u* one is born of water and the
3:27 A man can receive nothing *u* it
4:48 *U* you people see signs and
6:44 No one can come to Me *u* the
6:53 *u* you eat the flesh of the Son
6:65 one can come to Me *u* it has
12:24 *u* a grain of wheat falls into
15: 4 *u* it abides in the vine,
15: 4 *u* you abide in Me.
19:11 at all against Me *u* it had
20:25 *U* I see in His hands the print
Acts 8:31 *u* someone guides me?" And he
15: 1 *U* you are circumcised according
24:21 *u* it is for this one statement
27:31 *U* these men stay in the ship,
Rom 7: 7 known covetousness *u* the law
9:29 *U* the LORD of Sabaoth had
10:15 And how shall they preach *u* they
1 Cor 14: 5 *u* indeed he interprets,
14: 6 what shall I profit you *u* I
14: 7 *u* they make a distinction in
14: 9 *u* you utter by the tongue words
15: 2 *u* you believed in vain.
15:36 you sow is not made alive *u* it
2 Cor 13: 5 *u* indeed you are disqualified.
2 Th 2: 3 not come *u* the falling
1 Tim 5: 9 and not *u* she has been the
2 Tim 2: 5 he is not crowned *u* he competes
Rev 2: 5 from its place—*u* you repent.
2:22 *u* they repent of their deeds.

UNLIFTED (1/1) LIFT

2 Cor 3:14 day the same veil remains *u* in

UNLIKE (1/1)

2 Cor 3:13 *u* Moses, who put a veil over

UNLOAD (1/1) LOAD

Acts 21: 3 for there the ship was to *u* her

UNLOADED (1/1)

Gen 24:32 And he *u* the camels,

UNLOOSE (KJV) See LOOSE

UNLOVED (7/5) LOVE, UNLOVING

Gen 29:31 the LORD saw that Leah was *u*,
29:33 LORD has heard that I am *u*,
Deut 21:15 one loved and the other *u*,
21:15 both the loved and the *u*,
21:15 son is of her who is *u*,
21:16 preference to the son of the *u*,
21:17 acknowledge the son of the *u*

UNLOVING (2/2) UNLOVED

Rom 1:31 undiscerning, untrustworthy, *u*,
2 Tim 3: 3 *u*, unforgiving, slanderers,

UNMARRIED (5/5) MARRY

Ezek 44:25 for brother or *u* sister may
1 Cor 7: 8 But I say to the *u* and to the
7:11 let her remain *u* or be
7:32 He who is *u* cares for the
7:34 The *u* woman cares about the

UNMERCIFUL (1/1) MERCIFUL

Rom 1:31 unloving, unforgiving, *u*;

UNMINDFUL (1/1) MIND

Deut 32:18 Rock who begot you, you are *u*,

UNMOVEABLE (KJV) See IMMOVABLE

UNNI (3/3)

1 Chr 15:18 Jaaziel, Shemiramoth, Jehiel, *U*,
15:20 Aziel, Shemiramoth, Jehiel, *U*,
Neh 12: 9 Also Bakbukiah and *U*,

UNNOTICED (1/1) NOTICE

Jude 4 For certain men have crept in *u*,

UNPERFECT (KJV) See UNFORMED

UNPREPARED (1/1)

2 Cor 9: 4 come with me and find you *u*,

UNPRESENTABLE (1/1) PRESENT

1 Cor 12:23 and our *u* parts have greater

UNPROFITABLE (8/8) PROFITABLE

Job 15: 3 Should he reason with *u* talk,
Jer 16:19 Worthlessness and *u* things."
Mt 25:30 And cast the *u* servant into the
Lk 17:10 We are *u* servants. We have done
Rom 3:12 have together become *u*;
Titus 3: 9 for they are *u* and useless.
Phm 1:11 who once was *u* to you, but now
Heb 13:17 for that would be *u* for you.

UNPROFITABLENESS (1/1)

Heb 7:18 because of its weakness and *u*,

UNPUNISHED (12/10) PUNISH

Prov 11:21 the wicked will not go *u*;
16: 5 join forces, none will go *u*.
17: 5 glad at calamity will not go *u*.
19: 5 A false witness will not go *u*,
19: 9 A false witness will not go *u*,
28:20 to be rich will not go *u*.
Jer 25:29 and should you be utterly *u*?
25:29 unpunished? You shall not be *u*,
30:11 not let you go altogether *u*.
46:28 I will not leave you wholly *u*.
49:12 one who will altogether go *u*?
49:12 unpunished? You shall not go *u*,

UNQUENCHABLE (2/2) QUENCH

Mt 3:12 burn up the chaff with *u* fire.
Lk 3:17 chaff He will burn with *u* fire.

UNREASONABLE (2/2)

Acts 25:27 For it seems to me *u* to send a
2 Th 3: 2 we may be delivered from *u* and

UNREBUKEABLE (KJV) See BLAMELESS

UNRECOGNIZED (1/1)

Lam 4: 8 They go *u* in the streets;

UNRELIABLE (1/1)

Jer 15:18 You surely be to me like an *u*

UNREPROVEABLE (KJV) See (ABOVE) REPROACH

UNRESTRAINED (1/1)

Ex 32:25 saw that the people were *u*

UNRIGHTEOUS (10/10) RIGHTEOUS, UNRIGHTEOUSNESS

Ex 23: 1 hand with the wicked to be an *u*
Job 27: 7 rises up against me like the *u*.
Ps 71: 4 Out of the hand of the *u* and
Isa 10: 1 Woe to those who decree *u*
55: 7 And the *u* man his thoughts;
Lk 16: 9 friends for yourselves by *u*
16:11 have not been faithful in the *u*
1 Cor 6: 1 another, go to law before the *u*,
6: 9 Do you not know that the *u* will
2 Th 2:10 and with all *u* deception among

UNRIGHTEOUSLY (1/1)

Deut 25:16 such things, all who behave *u*,

UNRIGHTEOUSNESS (18/17) UNRIGHTEOUS

Ps 92:15 and there is no *u* in Him.
Jer 22:13 him who builds his house by *u*
Zeph 3: 5 in her midst, He will do no *u*.
3:13 of Israel shall do no *u* And
Jn 7:18 and no *u* is in Him.
Rom 1:18 against all ungodliness and *u*
1:18 who suppress the truth in *u*,
1:29 being filled with all *u*,
2: 8 not obey the truth, but obey *u*—
3: 5 But if our *u* demonstrates the
6:13 members as instruments of *u*
9:14 Is there *u* with God?
2 Th 2:12 the truth but had pleasure in *u*.
Heb 8:12 be merciful to their *u*,
2 Pe 2:13 will receive the wages of *u*,
2:15 Beor, who loved the wages of *u*;
1 Jn 1: 9 and to cleanse us from all *u*.
5:17 All *u* is sin, and there is sin

UNRIPE (1/1)

Job 15:33 He will shake off his *u* grape

UNRULY (2/2)

1 Th 5:14 brethren, warn those who are *u*,
Jas 3: 8 It is an *u* evil,

UNSATIABLE (KJV) See INSATIABLE

UNSATISFIED (1/1)

Isa 32: 6 To keep the hungry *u*,

UNSAVORY (1/1)

Job 6:30 Cannot my taste discern the *u*?

UNSAVOURY (KJV) See FLAVORLESS, SHREWD

UNSEARCHABLE (6/6)

Job 5: 9 Who does great things, and *u*,
Ps 145: 3 And His greatness is *u*.
Prov 25: 3 So the heart of kings is *u*.
Isa 40:28 His understanding is *u*.
Rom 11:33 How *u* are His judgments
Eph 3: 8 preach among the Gentiles the *u*

UNSEEMLY (KJV) See RUDELY, SHAMEFUL

UNSETTLING (1/1)

Acts 15:24 *u* your souls, saying, "You

UNSHOD (1/1)

Jer 2:25 your foot from being *u*,

UNSHRUNK (2/2)

Mt 9:16 No one puts a piece of *u* cloth
Mk 2:21 No one sews a piece of *u* cloth

UNSKILFUL (KJV) See UNSKILLED

UNSKILLED (1/1)

Heb 5:13 partakes only of milk is *u*

UNSPEAKABLE (KJV) See INDESCRIBABLE, INEXPRESSIBLE

UNSPOTTED (1/1) SPOT

Jas 1:27 and to keep oneself *u* from the

UNSTABLE (6/6)

Gen 49: 4 *U* as water, you shall not
Ps 82: 5 foundations of the earth are *u*.
Prov 5: 6 path of life—Her ways are *u*;
Jas 1: 8 *u* in all his ways.
2 Pe 2:14 enticing *u* souls. They have a

3:16 which untaught and *u* people

UNSTOPPED (1/1)

Isa 35: 5 the ears of the deaf shall be *u*.

UNTAKEN (KJV) See UNLIFTED

UNTAUGHT (1/1)

2 Pe 3:16 which *u* and unstable people

UNTEMPERED (5/5)

Ezek 13:10 they plaster it with *u* mortar—
13:11 who plaster it with *u* mortar,
13:14 you have plastered with *u* mortar,
13:15 have plastered it with *u* mortar,
22:28 plastered them with *u* mortar,

UNTENDED (2/2)

Lev 25: 5 gather the grapes of your *u* vine,
25:11 gather the grapes of your *u* vine,

UNTHANKFUL (2/2) THANKFUL

Lk 6:35 For He is kind to the *u* and
2 Tim 3: 2 disobedient to parents, *u*,

UNTIL (441/422)

Gen 8: 5 waters decreased continually *u*
8: 7 which kept going to and fro *u*
19:22 For I cannot do anything *u* you
21:26 nor had I heard of it *u*
24:19 *u* they have finished
24:33 I will not eat *u* I have told
26:13 and continued prospering *u* he
27:44 *u* your brother's fury turns
27:45 *u* your brother's anger turns
28:15 for I will not leave you *u* I
29: 8 We cannot *u* all the flocks are
32: 4 with Laban and stayed there *u*
32:24 and a Man wrestled with him *u*
33: 3 *u* he came near to his brother.
33:14 *u* I come to my lord in Seir."
34: 5 so Jacob held his peace *u* they
39:16 she kept his garment with her *u*
41:49 *u* he stopped counting,
49:10 *U* Shiloh comes; And to Him
Ex 7:16 *u* now you would not hear!
9:18 in Egypt since its founding *u*
10:26 what we must serve the LORD *u*
12: 6 Now you shall keep it *u* the
12:10 shall let none of it remain *u*
12:10 and what remains of it *u*
12:15 bread from the first day *u* the
12:18 *u* the twenty-first day of the
12:22 out of the door of his house *u*
16:20 some of them left part of it *u*
16:23 to be kept *u* morning.'"
16:35 *u* they came to an inhabited
16:35 they ate manna *u* they came to
17:12 and his hands were steady *u* the
18:13 before Moses from morning *u*
18:14 stand before you from morning *u*
23:18 fat of My sacrifice remain *u*
23:30 *u* you have increased,
24:14 Wait here for us *u* we come back
27:21 shall tend it from evening *u*
29:34 remains *u* the morning,
33: 8 tent door and watched Moses *u*
34:25 Feast of the Passover be left *u*
34:34 he would take the veil off *u* he
34:35 *u* he went in to speak with Him.
Lev 6: 9 upon the altar all night *u*
7:15 He shall not leave any of it *u*
8:33 *u* the days of your consecration
11:24 any of them shall be unclean *u*
11:25 his clothes and be unclean *u*
11:27 such carcass shall be unclean *u*
11:28 his clothes and be unclean *u*
11:31 are dead shall be unclean *u*
11:32 And it shall be unclean *u*
11:39 its carcass shall be unclean *u*
11:40 his clothes and be unclean *u*
11:40 his clothes and be unclean *u*
12: 4 nor come into the sanctuary *u*
14:46 is shut up shall be unclean *u*
15: 5 and be unclean *u* evening.
15: 6 and be unclean *u* evening.
15: 7 and be unclean *u* evening.
15: 8 and be unclean *u* evening.
15:10 under him shall be unclean *u*
15:10 and be unclean *u* evening.
15:11 and be unclean *u* evening.
15:16 and be unclean *u* evening.
15:17 and be unclean *u* evening.
15:18 and be unclean *u* evening.
15:19 touches her shall be unclean *u*
15:21 and be unclean *u* evening.
15:22 and be unclean *u* evening.
15:23 he shall be unclean *u* evening.
15:27 and be unclean *u* evening.
16:17 *u* he comes out, that he may
17:15 and be unclean *u* evening.
19: 6 And if any remains *u* the third
19:13 not remain with you all night *u*
22: 4 not eat the holy offerings *u*
22: 6 such thing shall be unclean *u*
22:30 you shall leave none of it *u*
23:14 grain nor fresh grain *u* the
24: 3 in charge of it from evening *u*
25:22 and eat old produce *u* the ninth
25:22 *u* its produce comes in,
25:28 the hand of him who bought it *u*
25:40 and shall serve you *u* the Year
25:50 year that he was sold to him *u*
25:52 there remain but a few years *u*
Num 6: 5 *u* the days are fulfilled for
9:12 They shall leave none of it *u*
9:15 from evening *u* morning it was
9:21 remained only from evening *u*
11:20 *u* it comes out of your nostrils
14:19 from Egypt even *u* now."
14:33 *u* your carcasses are consumed
19: 7 the priest shall be unclean *u*
19: 8 and shall be unclean *u* evening.
19:10 and be unclean *u* evening.
19:21 shall be unclean *u* evening.
19:22 touches it shall be unclean *u*
20:17 right hand or to the left *u* we
21:22 go by the King's Highway *u* we
21:35 *u* there was no survivor left
23:24 It shall not lie down *u* it
24:20 But shall be last *u* he
24:22 How long *u* Asshur carries you
24:24 *u* he perishes."
32:13 *u* all the generation that had
32:17 the children of Israel *u* we
32:18 will not return to our homes *u*
32:21 the Jordan before the LORD *u*
35:12 the manslayer may not die *u* he
35:25 and he shall remain there *u* the
35:28 in his city of refuge *u* the
Deut 1:31 in all the way that you went *u*
2:14 to come from Kadesh Barnea *u*
2:14 *u* all the generation of the men
2:15 from the midst of the camp *u*
2:29 *u* I cross the Jordan to the
3: 3 and we attacked him *u* he had no
3:20 *u* the LORD has given rest to
7:20 send the hornet among them *u*
7:23 will inflict defeat upon them *u*
7:24 be able to stand against you *u*
9: 7 from the land of Egypt *u* you
9:21 *u* it was as fine as dust;
11: 5 did for you in the wilderness *u*
13:10 shall stone him with stones *u*
16: 4 at twilight remain overnight *u*
20:20 *u* it is subdued.
22: 2 and it shall remain with you *u*
28:20 *u* you are destroyed and until
28:20 until you are destroyed and *u*
28:21 make the plague cling to you *u*
28:22 they shall pursue you *u* you
28:24 it shall come down on you *u*
28:45 *u* you are destroyed,
28:48 a yoke of iron on your neck *u*
28:51 *u* you are destroyed;
28:51 *u* they have destroyed you.
28:52 you at all your gates *u* your
28:61 the LORD bring upon you *u* you
31:30 the words of this song *u* they
Josh 1:15 *u* the LORD has given your
2:16 *u* the pursuers have returned.
2:22 and stayed there three days *u*
3:17 *u* all the people had crossed
4:10 in the midst of the Jordan *u*
4:23 of the Jordan before you *u* you
4:23 which He dried up before us *u*
5: 1 the children of Israel *u* we
6:10 *u* the day I say to you,
7: 6 before the ark of the LORD *u*
7:13 stand before your enemies *u*
8:24 by the edge of the sword *u*
8:26 *u* he had utterly destroyed all
8:29 of Ai he hanged on a tree *u*
10:26 were hanging on the trees *u*
10:27 which remain *u* this very day.
10:33 *u* he left him none remaining.
11: 8 they attacked them *u* they left
11:14 with the edge of the sword *u*
13:13 dwell among the Israelites *u*
17:14 as the LORD has blessed us *u*
20: 6 he shall dwell in that city *u*
20: 6 and *u* the death of the one who
20: 9 hand of the avenger of blood *u*
22:17 which we are not cleansed *u*
23:13 *u* you perish from this good
23:15 *u* He has destroyed you from
Judg 4:24 *u* they had destroyed Jabin king
5: 7 *U* I, Deborah, arose, Arose a
6:18 *u* I come to You and bring out
6:18 I will wait *u* you come back."
16:13 *U* now you have mocked me and
18: 1 for *u* that day their
18:30 priests to the tribe of Dan *u*
19: 8 So they delayed *u* afternoon;
19:25 her and abused her all night *u*
19:30 up from the land of Egypt *u*
20:23 up and wept before the LORD *u*
20:26 the LORD and fasted that day *u*
Ruth 1:19 Now the two of them went *u* they
2: 7 has continued from morning *u*
2:17 So she gleaned in the field *u*
2:21 stay close by my young men *u*
2:23 to glean *u* the end of barley
3: 3 yourself known to the man *u* he
3:13 as the LORD lives! Lie down *u*
3:14 So she lay at his feet *u*
3:18 *u* you know how the matter will
3:18 for the man will not rest *u* he
1 Sam 1:16 and grief I have spoken *u* now.
1:22 Not *u* the child is weaned;
1:23 wait *u* you have weaned him.
1:23 stayed and nursed her son *u*
3:15 So Samuel lay down *u* morning,
9:13 For the people will not eat *u*
9:24 for *u* this time it has been
11:11 and killed Ammonites *u* the heat
14: 9 Wait *u* we come to you,' then we
14:24 the man who eats any food *u*
14:36 and plunder them *u* the morning
15:18 and fight against them *u* they
15:35 went no more to see Saul *u* the
19: 2 please be on your guard *u*
19:23 he went on and prophesied *u* he
20: 5 that I may hide in the field *u*
25:36 little or much, *u* morning
30: 4 *u* they had no more power to
30:17 attacked them from twilight *u*
2 Sam 1:12 mourned and wept and fasted *u*
2:26 How long will it be then *u* you
4: 3 have been sojourners there *u*
10: 5 Wait at Jericho *u* your beards
15:24 and Abiathar went up *u* all the
15:28 the plains of the wilderness *u*
17:13 *u* there is not one small stone
19: 7 befallen you from your youth *u*
19:24 the day the king departed *u*
21:10 the beginning of harvest *u* the
23:10 and attacked the Philistines *u*
1 Ki 3: 1 her to the City of David *u* he
3: 2 for the name of the LORD *u*
5: 3 *u* the LORD put his foes
6:22 *u* he had finished all the
10: 7 I did not believe the words *u*
11:16 *u* he had cut down every male in
11:40 and was in Egypt *u* the death of
14:10 as one takes away refuse *u* it
15:29 *u* he had destroyed him,
17:14 *u* the day the LORD sends rain
18:28 *u* the blood gushed out on them.
18:29 they prophesied *u* the time of
22:11 you shall gore the Syrians *u*
22:27 *u* I come in peace." '"
2 Ki 6:25 and indeed they besieged it *u*
7: 3 Why are we sitting here *u* we
7: 9 If we wait *u* morning light,
8: 6 day that she left the land *u*
8:11 his countenance in a stare *u*
10: 8 at the entrance of the gate *u*
10:11 *u* he left him none remaining.
15: 5 so that he was a leper *u* the
17:20 *u* He had cast them from His
17:23 *u* the LORD removed Israel out
18: 4 for *u* those days the children
18:32 *u* I come and take you away to a
20:17 your fathers have accumulated *u*
25: 2 So the city was besieged *u* the
1 Chr 4:31 These were their cities *u* the
5:22 And they dwelt in their place *u*
6:32 *u* Solomon had built the house
9:18 *U* then they had been
12:22 *u* it was a great army,
12:29 three thousand (*u* then the
19: 5 Wait at Jericho *u* your beards
28:20 *u* you have finished all the
2 Chr 8:16 of the house of the LORD *u* it
9: 6 I did not believe their words *u*
15:19 And there was no war *u* the
18:10 you shall gore the Syrians *u*
18:26 and water of affliction *u* I
18:34 chariot facing the Syrians *u*
20:26 The Valley of Berachah *u* this
21:15 *u* your intestines come out by
24:10 and put them into the chest *u*
26:21 King Uzziah was a leper *u* the
29:28 all this continued *u* the
29:34 the Levites helped them *u* the
29:34 until the work was ended and *u*
31: 1 *u* they had utterly destroyed
35:14 burnt offerings and fat *u*
36:16 *u* the wrath of the LORD arose
36:20 servants to him and his sons *u*
36:21 *u* the land had enjoyed her
Ezra 4: 5 even *u* the reign of Darius king
4:21 this city may not be built *u*
4:24 and it was discontinued *u* the
5:16 but from that time even *u* now
8:29 Watch and keep them *u* you weigh
9: 4 and I sat astonished *u* the
9:14 You not be angry with us *u* You
10:14 *u* the fierce wrath of our God
Neh 4:21 the spears from daybreak *u* the
5:14 from the twentieth year *u* the
7: 3 gates of Jerusalem be opened *u*
8: 3 the Water Gate from morning *u*
8:17 days of Joshua the son of Nun *u*
8:18 from the first day *u* the last
9:32 days of the kings of Assyria *u*
12:23 of the fathers' houses *u* the
Esth 3: 7 *u* it fell on the twelfth
Job 14:13 That You would conceal me *u*
Ps 10:15 Seek out his wickedness *u* You
57: 1 *U* these calamities have
71:18 *U* I declare Your strength to
72: 7 *U* the moon is no more.
73:17 *U* I went into the sanctuary of
94:13 *U* the pit is dug for the
104:23 to his work And to his labor *u*
105:19 *U* the time that his word came
112: 8 *U* he sees his desire upon
123: 2 *U* He has mercy on us.

132: 5 *U* I find a place for the LORD,
Prov 7:18 let us take our fill of love *u*
18:17 *U* his neighbor comes and
Song 2: 7 not stir up nor awaken love *U*
2:17 *U* the day breaks And the
3: 4 *U* I had brought him to the
3: 5 not stir up nor awaken love *U*
4: 6 *U* the day breaks And the
8: 4 not stir up nor awaken love *U*
Isa 5:11 Who continue *u* night,
6:11 *U* the cities are laid waste and
26:20 *U* the indignation is past.
32:15 *U* the Spirit is poured upon us
36:17 *u* I come and take you away to a
38:12 From day *u* night You make an
38:13 I have considered *u*
38:13 From day *u* night You make an
39: 6 your fathers have accumulated *u*
62: 1 *U* her righteousness goes forth
Jer 1: 3 *u* the end of the eleventh year
1: 3 *u* the carrying away of
7:25 came out of the land of Egypt *u*
7:32 for they will bury in Tophet *u*
9:16 will send a sword after them *u*
11: 7 *u* this day, rising early and
23:20 LORD will not turn back *U* He
27: 7 *u* the time of his land comes;
27: 8 *u* I have consumed them by his
27:22 and there they shall be *u* the
30:24 of the LORD will not return *u*
30:24 And *u* He has performed the
32: 5 and there he shall be *u* I visit
36:23 *u* all the scroll was consumed
37:21 *u* all the bread in the city was
38:28 in the court of the prison *u*
44:27 *u* there is an end to them.
47: 6 How long *u* you are quiet?
49: 9 Would they not destroy *u* they
49:37 send the sword after them *U* I
52: 5 So the city was besieged *u* the
52:34 a portion for each day *u* the
Ezek 21:27 *U* He comes whose right it is,
46: 2 the gate shall not be shut *u*
46:17 it shall be his *u* the year of
47:20 from the southern boundary *u*
Dan 1:21 Thus Daniel continued *u* the
4:32 *u* you know that the Most High
7:22 '*u* the Ancient of Days came,
9:25 restore and build Jerusalem *U*
9:27 Even *u* the consummation,
11:35 *u* the time of the end;
12: 4 and seal the book *u* the time of
Hos 7: 4 *U* it is leavened.
8: 5 How long *u* they attain to
Mic 5: 3 *U* the time that she who is in
7: 9 *U* He pleads my case And
Zeph 3: 8 *U* the day I rise up for plunder;
Zech 10:10 *U* no more room is found for
Mt 1:17 from David *u* the captivity in
1:17 the captivity in Babylon *u* the
2:13 and stay there *u* I bring you
2:15 and was there *u* the death of
11:12 the days of John the Baptist *u*
11:13 and the law prophesied *u* John.
11:23 it would have remained *u* this
13:30 Let both grow together *u* the
17: 9 Tell the vision to no one *u* the
18:34 him to the torturers *u* he
24:21 the beginning of the world *u*
24:38 *u* the day that Noah entered the
24:39 and did not know *u* the flood
26:29 of the vine from now on *u* that
27:45 Now from the sixth hour *u* the
27:64 that the tomb be made secure *u*
28:15 reported among the Jews *u* this
Mk 13:19 creation which God created *u*
14:25 of the fruit of the vine *u*
15:33 darkness over the whole land *u*
Lk 1:20 be mute and not able to speak *u*
4:13 he departed from Him *u* an
13: 8 *u* I dig around it and fertilize
13:35 you shall not see Me *u* the
15: 4 after the one which is lost *u*
15: 8 and search carefully *u* she
16:16 law and the prophets were *u*
17:27 *u* the day that Noah entered the
21:24 will be trampled by Gentiles *u*
22:16 I will no longer eat of it *u* it
22:18 of the fruit of the vine *u* the
23:44 darkness over all the earth *u*
24:49 in the city of Jerusalem *u* you
Jn 2:10 You have kept the good wine *u*
5:17 My Father has been working *u*
9:18 *u* they called the parents of
16:24 *U* now you have asked nothing in
Acts 1: 2 *u* the day in which He was taken
3:21 whom heaven must receive *u* the
4: 3 and put them in custody *u* the
7:45 the face of our fathers *u* the
10:30 Four days ago I was fasting *u*
13:20 *u* Samuel the prophet.
20: 7 and continued his message *u*
22:22 And they listened to him *u* this
23: 1 good conscience before God *u*
23:14 that we will eat nothing *u* we
Rom 1:13 come to you (but was hindered *u*
5:13 (For *u* the law sin was in the
8:22 with birth pangs together *u*
11:25 part has happened to Israel *u*
1 Cor 3: 2 for *u* now you were not able to
4: 5 *u* the Lord comes, who will both
4:13 the offscouring of all things *u*
8: 7 *u* now eat it as a thing
16: 8 But I will tarry in Ephesus *u*
2 Cor 3:14 For *u* this day the same veil
Gal 4: 2 under guardians and stewards *u*
4:19 whom I labor in birth again *u*
Eph 1:14 guarantee of our inheritance *u*
Phil 1: 5 the gospel from the first day *u*
1: 6 in you will complete it *u* the
1 Th 4:15 we who are alive and remain *u*
2 Th 2: 7 now restrains will do so *u*
1 Tim 6:14 blameless *u* our Lord Jesus
2 Tim 1:12 what I have committed to Him *u*
Heb 6:11 to the full assurance of hope *u*
9:10 fleshly ordinances imposed *u*
Jas 5: 7 *u* the coming of the Lord.
5: 7 waiting patiently for it *u* it
2 Pe 1:19 *u* the day dawns and the morning
3: 7 are reserved for fire *u* the day
1 Jn 2: 9 is in darkness *u* now.
Rev 2:10 Be faithful *u* death, and I will
2:26 and keeps My works *u* the end,
6:10 *u* You judge and avenge our
6:11 *u* both the number of their
17:17 *u* the words of God are
20: 5 the dead did not live again *u*

UNTIMELY (KJV) See LATE, STILLBORN

UNTO (23/17) See APPENDIX

UNTOWARD (KJV) See PERVERSE

UNTRAINED (3/3)

Jer 31:18 Like an *u* bull; Restore me,
Acts 4:13 they were uneducated and *u* men,
2 Cor 11: 6 Even though I am *u* in speech,

UNTRUE (1/1)

Ps 73:15 I would have been *u* to the

UNTRUSTWORTHY (1/1)

Rom 1:31 undiscerning, *u*,

UNTURNED (1/1) TURN

Hos 7: 8 Ephraim is a cake *u*.

UNUSUAL (3/3)

Isa 28:21 to pass His act, His *u* act.
Acts 19:11 Now God worked *u* miracles by
28: 2 the natives showed us *u* kindness

UNVEILED (1/1) VEIL

2 Cor 3:18 with *u* face, beholding as in a

UNWALLED (2/2)

Esth 9:19 who dwelt in the *u* towns
Ezek 38:11 up against a land of *u* villages

UNWASHED (3/3) WASH

Mt 15:20 but to eat with *u* hands does
Mk 7: 2 with *u* hands, they found fault.
7: 5 but eat bread with *u* hands?"

UNWILLING (2/2)

1 Sam 15: 9 and were *u* to utterly destroy
1 Cor 16:12 but he was quite *u* to come at

UNWISE (4/4) WISE

Deut 32: 6 O foolish and *u* people?
Hos 13:13 He is an *u* son, For he
Rom 1:14 both to wise and to *u*.
Eph 5:17 Therefore do not be *u*,

UNWITTINGLY (1/1)

Heb 13: 2 for by so doing some have *u*

UNWORTHY (4/4) WORTHY

Acts 13:46 and judge yourselves *u* of
1 Cor 6: 2 are you *u* to judge the smallest
11:27 this cup of the Lord in an *u*
11:29 he who eats and drinks in an *u*

UP (1937/1783) See APPENDIX

UPBRAID, UPBRAIDED, UPBRAIDETH (KJV) See REBUKE, REBUKED, REPROACH, RIDICULED

UPHARSIN (1/1) PERES

Dan 5:25 written: MENE, MENE, TEKEL, *U*.

UPHAZ (2/2)

Jer 10: 9 from Tarshish, And gold from *U*,
Dan 10: 5 was girded with gold of *U*!

UPHELD (4/4)

Job 4: 4 Your words have *u* him who was
Ps 71: 6 By You I have been *u* from
Isa 46: 3 Who have been *u* by Me from
Zeph 2: 3 Who have *u* His justice.

UPHOLD (11/11) UPHOLDING, UPHOLDS

Job 8:20 Nor will He *u* the evildoers.
Ps 17: 5 *U* my steps in Your paths,
41:12 You *u* me in my integrity,
51:12 And *u* me by Your generous
54: 4 The Lord is with those who *u*
119:116 *U* me according to Your word,
Isa 41:10 I will *u* you with My righteous
42: 1 "Behold! My Servant whom I *u*,
63: 5 That there was no one to *u*;
Ezek 30: 6 Those who *u* Egypt shall fall,
1 Th 5:14 *u* the weak, be patient with

UPHOLDING (1/1) UPHOLD

Heb 1: 3 and *u* all things by the word of

UPHOLDS (6/6) UPHOLD

Ps 37:17 But the LORD *u* the righteous.
37:24 For the LORD *u* him with His
63: 8 Your right hand *u* me.
145:14 The LORD *u* all who fall,
Prov 20:28 And by lovingkindness he *u* his
Dan 10:21 (No one *u* me against these,

UPLIFTED (1/1) LIFT

Acts 13:17 and with an *u* arm He brought

UPON (627/574) See APPENDIX

UPPER (44/44)

Deut 24: 6 the lower or the *u* millstone
Josh 15:19 So he gave her the *u* springs
16: 5 was Ataroth Addar as far as *U*
Judg 1:15 Caleb gave her the *u* springs
3:23 shut the doors of the *u* room
3:24 the doors of the *u* room were
3:25 not opened the doors of the *u*
9:53 woman dropped an *u* millstone
1 Sam 9:24 up the thigh with its *u* part
1 Ki 17:19 carried him to the *u* room
17:23 brought him down from the *u* room
2 Ki 1: 2 the lattice of his *u* room
4:10 let us make a small *u* room on
4:11 and he turned in to the *u* room
15:35 He built the *U* Gate of the
18:17 by the aqueduct from the *u* pool
23:12 the *u* chamber of Ahaz, which
1 Chr 7:24 who built Lower and *U* Beth
28:11 its *u* chambers, its inner
2 Chr 3: 9 and he overlaid the *u* area with
8: 5 He built *U* Beth Horon and Lower
23:20 and they went through the *U* Gate
27: 3 He built the *U* Gate of the house
32:30 the water outlet of *U* Gihon
32:33 they buried him in the *u* tombs
Neh 3:25 projects from the king's *u* house
3:31 and as far as the *u* room at the
3:32 And between the *u* room at the
Ps 104: 3 lays the beams of His *u* chambers
104:13 the hills from His *u* chambers
Isa 7: 3 end of the aqueduct from the *u*
36: 2 aqueduct from the *u* pool
Jer 36:10 in the *u* court at the entry of
Ezek 9: 2 from the direction of the *u* gate
42: 5 Now the *u* chambers were
42: 6 therefore the *u* level was
Dan 6:10 And in his *u* room, with his
Mk 14:15 he will show you a large *u* room
Lk 22:12 furnished *u* room; there make
Acts 1:13 they went up into the *u* room
9:37 they laid her in an *u* room.
9:39 they brought him to the *u* room
19: 1 passed through the *u* regions
20: 8 were many lamps in the *u* room

UPPERMOST (3/3)

Gen 40:17 In the *u* basket were all kinds
Isa 17: 6 olives at the top of the *u*
17: 9 as a forsaken bough And an *u*

UPRAISED (1/1)

Job 38:15 And the *u* arm is broken.

UPRIGHT (66/66) UPRIGHTLY, UPRIGHTNESS

Gen 37: 7 my sheaf arose and also stood *u*;
Ex 15: 8 The floods stood *u* like a
26:15 of acacia wood, standing *u*.
36:20 of acacia wood, standing *u*.
Lev 26:13 your yoke and made you walk *u*.
Deut 32: 4 Righteous and *u* is He.
1 Sam 29: 6 LORD lives, you have been *u*,
Job 1: 1 that man was blameless and *u*,
1: 8 a blameless and *u* man, one who
2: 3 a blameless and *u* man, one who
4: 7 Or where were the *u* ever cut
8: 6 If you were pure and *u*,
17: 8 *U* men are astonished at this,

23: 7 There the ***u*** could reason with
33: 3 My words come from my ***u*** heart;
Ps 7:10 Who saves the ***u*** in heart.
11: 2 may shoot secretly at the ***u*** in
11: 7 His countenance beholds the ***u***.
17: 2 look on the things that are ***u***.
20: 8 But we have risen and stand ***u***.
25: 8 Good and ***u*** is the LORD;
32:11 all you ***u*** in heart!
33: 1 For praise from the ***u*** is
36:10 Your righteousness to the ***u*** in
37:14 To slay those who are of ***u***
37:18 LORD knows the days of the ***u***,
37:37 man, and observe the ***u***;
49:14 The ***u*** shall have dominion over
64:10 And all the ***u*** in heart shall
92:15 To declare that the LORD is ***u***;
94:15 And all the ***u*** in heart will
97:11 And gladness for the ***u*** in
111: 1 In the assembly of the ***u*** and
112: 2 The generation of the ***u*** will
112: 4 Unto the ***u*** there arises light
119:137 And ***u*** are Your judgments.
125: 4 And to those who are ***u*** in
140:13 The ***u*** shall dwell in Your
Prov 2: 7 up sound wisdom for the ***u***;
2:21 For the ***u*** will dwell in the
3:32 secret counsel is with the ***u***.
10:29 LORD is strength for the ***u***,
11: 3 The integrity of the ***u*** will
11: 6 The righteousness of the ***u*** will
11:11 By the blessing of the ***u*** the
12: 6 But the mouth of the ***u*** will
14: 9 But among the ***u*** there is
14:11 But the tent of the ***u*** will
15: 8 But the prayer of the ***u*** is
15:19 But the way of the ***u*** is a
16:17 The highway of the ***u*** is to
21:18 And the unfaithful for the ***u***.
21:29 his face, But as for the ***u***,
28:10 Whoever causes the ***u*** to go
29:10 But the ***u*** seek his well-being.
29:27 And he who is ***u*** in the way
Eccl 7:29 found: That God made man ***u***,
12:10 and what was written was ***u***—
Isa 26: 7 just is uprightness; O Most ***U***,
Jer 10: 5 They are ***u***, like a palm tree,
Dan 8:18 he touched me, and stood me ***u***.
10:11 I speak to you, and stand ***u***,
11:17 and ***u*** ones with him;
Mic 7: 2 And there is no one ***u*** among
7: 4 The most ***u*** is sharper than a
Hab 2: 4 His soul is not ***u*** in him;

UPRIGHTLY (9/9) UPRIGHT

Ps 15: 2 He who walks ***u***,
58: 1 silent ones? Do you judge ***u***,
75: 2 proper time, I will judge ***u***.
84:11 withhold From those who walk ***u***.
Prov 2: 7 a shield to those who walk ***u***;
15:21 a man of understanding walks ***u***.
Isa 33:15 walks righteously and speaks ***u***,
Am 5:10 they abhor the one who speaks ***u***.
Mic 2: 7 do good To him who walks ***u***?

UPRIGHTNESS (17/16) UPRIGHT

Deut 9: 5 of your righteousness or the ***u***
1 Ki 3: 6 and in ***u*** of heart with You;
9: 4 in integrity of heart and in ***u***,
1 Chr 29:17 heart and have pleasure in ***u***.
29:17 in the ***u*** of my heart I have
Job 33:23 a thousand, To show man His ***u***,
Ps 9: 8 judgment for the peoples in ***u***.
25:21 Let integrity and ***u*** preserve
111: 8 And are done in truth and ***u***.
119: 7 I will praise You with ***u*** of
143:10 Lead me in the land of ***u***.
Prov 2:13 those who leave the paths of ***u***
14: 2 He who walks in his ***u*** fears the
17:26 to strike princes for their ***u***.
Isa 26: 7 The way of the just is ***u***;
26:10 In the land of ***u*** he will deal
57: 2 Each one walking in his ***u***.

UPROAR (8/8)

1 Ki 1:41 is the city in such a noisy ***u***?
1:45 so that the city is in an ***u***.
Mt 26: 5 lest there be an ***u*** among the
Mk 14: 2 lest there be an ***u*** of the
Acts 17: 5 set all the city in an ***u*** and
19:40 in question for today's ***u***,
20: 1 After the ***u*** had ceased, Paul
21:31 that all Jerusalem was in an ***u***.

UPROOT (4/4) UPROOTED

1 Ki 14:15 He will ***u*** Israel from this good
2 Chr 7:20 then I will ***u*** them from My land
Ps 52: 5 And ***u*** you from the land of the
Mt 13:29 gather up the tares you also ***u***

UPROOTED (7/7) UPROOT

Deut 29:28 And the LORD ***u*** them from their
Job 18:14 He is ***u*** from the shelter of his
19:10 My hope He has ***u*** like a tree.
Prov 2:22 And the unfaithful will be ***u***
Dan 11: 4 for his kingdom shall be ***u***,
Zeph 2: 4 And Ekron shall be ***u***.
Mt 15:13 has not planted will be ***u***.

UPROOTS (1/1)

Ps 80:13 The boar out of the woods ***u*** it,

UPSIDE (3/3)

2 Ki 21:13 wiping it and turning it ***u***
Ps 146: 9 way of the wicked He turns ***u***
Acts 17: 6 who have turned the world ***u***

UPSTAIRS (1/1)

Judg 3:20 to him (now he was sitting ***u***

UPSTREAM (2/2)

Josh 3:13 waters that come down from ***u***,
3:16 waters which came down from ***u***

UPWARD (16/16)

Gen 7:20 prevailed fifteen cubits ***u***,
Judg 1:36 of Akrabbim, from Sela, and ***u***.
1 Sam 9: 2 From his shoulders ***u*** he was
10:23 the people from his shoulders ***u***.
2 Ki 19:30 downward, And bear fruit ***u***.
Job 5: 7 trouble, As the sparks fly ***u***.
Prov 15:24 The way of life winds ***u*** for
Eccl 3:21 the sons of men, which goes ***u***,
Isa 8:21 king and their God, and look ***u***.
37:31 downward, And bear fruit ***u***.
38:14 My eyes fail from looking ***u***.
Ezek 1:11 Their wings stretched ***u***;
1:27 appearance of His waist and ***u***
8: 2 fire; and from His waist and ***u***,
43:15 with four horns extending ***u***
Phil 3:14 the goal for the prize of the ***u***

UR (7/7)

Gen 11:28 in ***U*** of the Chaldeans.
11:31 they went out with them from ***U***
15: 7 who brought you out of ***U*** of the
1 Chr 11:35 Hararite, Eliphal the son of ***U***,
Neh 9: 7 And brought him out of ***U*** of

URBANE (KJV) See URBANUS

URBANUS (1/1)

Rom 16: 9 Greet ***U***, our fellow worker

URGE (15/15) URGED, URGENT

2 Ki 18:23 I ***u*** you, give a pledge to my
Isa 36: 8 I ***u*** you, give a pledge to my
Acts 27:22 And now I ***u*** you to take heart,
27:34 Therefore I ***u*** you to take
Rom 16:17 Now I ***u*** you, brethren, note
1 Cor 4:16 Therefore I ***u*** you, imitate me.
16:15 I ***u*** you, brethren—you know the
2 Cor 2: 8 Therefore I ***u*** you to reaffirm
Gal 4:12 I ***u*** you to become like me,
Phil 4: 3 And I ***u*** you also,
1 Th 4: 1 we ***u*** and exhort in the Lord
4:10 But we ***u*** you, brethren,
5:12 And we ***u*** you, brethren,
1 Tim 6:13 I ***u*** you in the sight of God who
Heb 13:19 But I especially ***u*** you to do

URGED (19/19) URGE

Gen 19:15 the angels ***u*** Lot to hurry,
33:11 So he ***u*** him, and he took it.
Ex 12:33 And the Egyptians ***u*** the people,
Judg 1:14 that she ***u*** him to ask her
19: 7 his father-in-law ***u*** him;
1 Sam 24:10 and someone ***u*** me to kill you.
28:23 ***u*** him; and he heeded their
2 Sam 13:25 Then he ***u*** him, but he would
13:27 But Absalom ***u*** him; so he let
2 Ki 2:17 But when they ***u*** him till he was
5:16 And he ***u*** him to take it,
5:23 And he ***u*** him, and bound two
Mt 15:23 And His disciples came and ***u***
Jn 4:31 In the meantime His disciples ***u***
4:40 they ***u*** Him to stay with them;
1 Cor 16:12 I strongly ***u*** him to come to you
2 Cor 8: 6 So we ***u*** Titus, that as he had
12:18 I ***u*** Titus, and sent our brother
1 Tim 1: 3 As I ***u*** you when I went into

URGENCY (1/1)

2 Cor 8: 4 imploring us with much ***u*** that we

URGENT (3/3) URGE

Dan 2:15 the decree from the king so ***u***?
3:22 the king's command was ***u***,
Titus 3:14 to meet ***u*** needs, that they may

URI (8/7)

Ex 31: 2 by name Bezalel the son of ***U***,
35:30 by name Bezalel the son of ***U***,
38:22 Bezalel the son of ***U***,
1 Ki 4:19 Geber the son of ***U***,
1 Chr 2:20 And Hur begot ***U***,
2:20 and ***U*** begot Bezalel.
2 Chr 1: 5 altar that Bezalel the son of ***U***,
Ezra 10:24 Shallum, Telem, and ***U***.

URIAH (28/23)

2 Sam 11: 3 the wife of ***U*** the Hittite?"
11: 6 'Send me ***U*** the Hittite."
11: 6 And Joab sent ***U*** to David.
11: 7 When ***U*** had come to him, David
11: 8 And David said to ***U***,
11: 8 So ***U*** departed from the king's
11: 9 But ***U*** slept at the door of the
11:10 ***U*** did not go down to his
11:10 to his house," David said to ***U***,
11:11 And ***U*** said to David, "The ark
11:12 Then David said to ***U***,
11:12 So ***U*** remained in Jerusalem
11:14 and sent it by the hand of ***U***.
11:15 Set ***U*** in the forefront of the
11:16 that he assigned ***U*** to a place
11:17 and ***U*** the Hittite died also.
11:21 Your servant ***U*** the Hittite is
11:24 and your servant ***U*** the Hittite
11:26 When the wife of ***U*** heard that
11:26 the wife of Uriah heard that ***U***
12: 9 You have killed ***U*** the Hittite
12:10 and have taken the wife of ***U***
23:39 and ***U*** the Hittite: thirty-seven
1 Ki 15: 5 except in the matter of ***U*** the
1 Chr 11:41 ***U*** the Hittite, Zabad the son of
Ezra 8:33 hand of Meremoth the son of ***U***
Isa 8: 2 ***U*** the priest and Zechariah the
Mt 1: 6 who had been the wife of ***U***.

URIAH'S (1/1)

2 Sam 12:15 struck the child that ***U*** wife

URIAS (KJV) See URIAH

URIEL (4/4)

1 Chr 6:24 ***U*** his son, Uzziah his son, and
15: 5 ***U*** the chief, and one hundred
15:11 and for the Levites: for ***U***,
2 Chr 13: 2 Michaiah the daughter of ***U*** of

URIJAH (11/10)

2 Ki 16:10 and King Ahaz sent to ***U*** the
16:11 Then ***U*** the priest built an altar
16:11 So ***U*** the priest made it before
16:15 Then King Ahaz commanded ***U*** the
16:16 Thus did ***U*** the priest,
Neh 3: 4 to them Meremoth the son of ***U***,
3:21 After him Meremoth the son of ***U***,
8: 4 Mattithiah, Shema, Anaiah, ***U***,
Jer 26:20 ***U*** the son of Shemaiah of
26:21 but when ***U*** heard it, he was
26:23 And they brought ***U*** from Egypt

URIM (7/7) THUMMIM

Ex 28:30 breastplate of judgment the ***U***
Lev 8: 8 and he put the ***U*** and the
Num 27:21 him by the judgment of the ***U***.
Deut 33: 8 Let Your Thummim and Your ***U*** be
1 Sam 28: 6 either by dreams or by ***U*** or by
Ezra 2:63 could consult with the ***U*** and
Neh 7:65 could consult with the ***U*** and

US (1447/1095) See APPENDIX

USE (39/39)

Ex 20:25 for if you ***u*** your tool on it,
Num 10: 2 you shall ***u*** them for calling
24: 1 to seek to ***u*** sorcery,
Deut 20:19 do not cut them down to ***u*** in
23:25 but you shall not ***u*** a sickle on
26:14 any of it for an unclean ***u***,
27: 5 you shall not ***u*** an iron tool
1 Chr 28:15 according to the ***u*** of each
Ps 76: 5 mighty men have found the ***u*** of
Eccl 10:10 Then he must ***u*** more strength;
Jer 2:22 and ***u*** much soap, Yet your
23:31 who ***u*** their tongues and say, 'He
31:23 They shall again ***u*** this speech
46:11 In vain you will ***u*** many
Ezek 12:23 and they shall no more ***u*** it as
16:44 who quotes proverbs will ***u***
18: 2 What do you mean when you ***u*** this
18: 3 you shall no longer ***u*** this
21:21 to ***u*** divination: he shakes the
48:15 shall be for general ***u*** by the
Mt 5:44 for those who spitefully ***u*** you
6: 7 do not ***u*** vain repetitions as
7: 2 and with the measure you ***u***,
Mk 4:24 With the same measure you ***u***,
Lk 6:28 for those who spitefully ***u*** you.
6:38 the same measure that you ***u***,
13: 7 why does it ***u*** up the ground?'
Rom 1:26 women exchanged the natural ***u***
1:27 leaving the natural ***u*** of the
12: 6 given to us, let us ***u*** them:
12: 7 let us ***u*** it in our
1 Cor 7:21 can be made free, rather ***u*** it.
7:31 and those who ***u*** this world as
2 Cor 3:12 we ***u*** great boldness of speech—
13:10 lest being present I should ***u***
Gal 5:13 only do not ***u*** liberty as an
1 Th 2: 5 neither at any time did we ***u***
1 Tim 5:23 but ***u*** a little wine for your
Heb 5:14 those who by reason of ***u*** have

USED (30/29)
Gen 21:15 the water in the skin was *u* up,
Ex 38:24 All the gold that was *u* in all
Lev 7:24 may be *u* in any other way;
Num 7: 5 that they may be *u* in doing the
Judg 1: 7 thumbs and big toes cut off *u*
14:10 for young men *u* to do so.
16:11 ropes that have never been *u*,
1 Sam 2:19 Moreover his mother *u* to make
17:34 Your servant *u* to keep his
2 Sam 20:18 They *u* to talk in former times,
1 Ki 15:22 which Baasha had *u* for
17:14 bin of flour shall not be *u* up,
17:16 The bin of flour was not *u* up,
2 Ki 21: 6 *u* witchcraft, and consulted
1 Chr 28:14 for all articles *u* in every
28:14 for all articles *u* in every
2 Chr 16: 6 which Baasha had *u* for
33: 6 *u* witchcraft and sorcery,
Ps 42: 4 For I *u* to go with the
Song 8: 2 She who *u* to instruct me.
Isa 9: 5 Will be *u* for burning and
Jer 2:24 A wild donkey *u* to the
Ezek 22: 6 each one has *u* his power to
22:29 The people of the land have *u*
47:12 grow all kinds of trees *u*
Jn 10: 6 Jesus *u* this illustration,
12: 6 and he *u* to take what was put
Acts 27:17 they *u* cables to undergird the
1 Cor 9:12 Nevertheless we have not *u* this
9:15 But I have *u* none of these

USEFUL (5/5)
Ezek 15: 4 Is it *u* for any work?
15: 5 How much less will it be *u* for
2 Tim 2:21 sanctified and *u* for the
4:11 for he is *u* to me for ministry.
Heb 6: 7 and bears herbs *u* for those by

USELESS (10/10)
Ps 31: 6 hated those who regard *u* idols;
60:11 For the help of man is *u*.
108:12 For the help of man is *u*.
Isa 40:23 makes the judges of the earth *u*.
44: 9 an image, all of them are *u*,
Mal 3:14 'It is *u* to serve God;
Acts 14:15 should turn from these *u* things
1 Tim 6: 5 *u* wranglings of men of corrupt
Titus 3: 9 for they are unprofitable and *u*.
Jas 1:26 this one's religion is *u*.

USES (6/6)
Gen 49:21 He *u* beautiful words.
Num 35:23 or *u* a stone, by which a man
Prov 15: 2 The tongue of the wise *u*
18:23 The poor man *u* entreaties,
Jer 22:13 Who *u* his neighbor's service
1 Tim 1: 8 that the law is good if one *u*

USING (7/7)
Ex 28:28 *u* a blue cord, so that it is
1 Ki 19:21 *u* the oxen's equipment,
1 Chr 12: 2 *u* both the right hand and the
Ezek 4:12 and bake it *u* fuel of human
Jn 16:29 and *u* no figure of speech!
Col 2:22 things which perish with the *u*—
1 Pe 2:16 yet not *u* liberty as a cloak

USUAL (2/2)
Lev 14:32 who cannot afford the *u*
15:25 or if it runs beyond her *u*

USUALLY (1/1)
Dan 3:19 times more than it was *u* heated.

USURER (KJV) See MONEYLENDER

USURP [AUTHORITY] (KJV) See (HAVE) AUTHORITY

USURY (10/10)
Lev 25:36 Take no *u* or interest from him;
25:37 not lend him your money for *u*,
Neh 5: 7 Each of you is exacting *u* from
5:10 let us stop this *u*!
Ps 15: 5 does not put out his money at *u*,
Prov 28: 8 increases his possessions by *u*
Ezek 18: 8 If he has not exacted *u* Nor
18:13 If he has exacted *u* Or taken
18:17 the poor And not received *u*
22:12 you take *u* and increase;

UTENSILS (34/31)
Ex 25:39 of pure gold, with all these *u*.
27: 3 you shall make all its *u* of
27:19 All the *u* of the tabernacle for
30:27 "the table and all its *u*,
30:27 the lampstand and its *u*,
30:28 burnt offering with all its *u*,
31: 8 "the table and its *u*,
31: 8 gold lampstand with all its *u*,
31: 9 burnt offering with all its *u*,
35:13 table and its poles, all its *u*,
35:14 lampstand for the light, its *u*,
35:16 grating, its poles, all its *u*,
37:16 He made of pure gold the *u* which
37:24 gold he made it, with all its *u*.
38: 3 He made all the *u* for the altar:
38: 3 all its *u* he made of bronze.
38:30 and all the *u* for the altar,
39:36 the table, all its *u*,
39:37 lamps set in order), all its *u*,
39:39 its poles, and all its *u*;
39:40 all the *u* for the service of
40: 9 shall hallow it and all its *u*,
40:10 burnt offering and all its *u*,
Lev 8:11 the altar and all its *u*,
Num 3:31 the *u* of the sanctuary with
3:36 its pillars, its sockets, its *u*,
4:10 shall put it with all its *u* in
4:12 they shall take all the *u*
4:14 and all the *u* of the altar—and
7: 1 and the altar and all its *u*;
1 Ki 15:15 silver and gold and *u*.
2 Ki 25:14 and all the bronze *u* with which
2 Chr 15:18 silver and gold and *u*.
Jer 52:18 and all the bronze *u* with which

UTHAI (2/2)
1 Chr 9: 4 *U* the son of Ammihud, the son of
Ezra 8:14 *U* and Zabbud, and with them

UTMOST (3/3) UTTERMOST
Gen 49:26 Up to the *u* bound of the
Job 34:36 that Job were tried to the *u*,
2 Tim 4:21 Do your *u* to come before winter.

UTTER (28/28) UTTERANCE, UTTERED, UTTERS
1 Ki 20:42 a man whom I appointed to *u*
Job 8:10 And *u* words from their heart?
27: 4 Nor my tongue *u* deceit.
33: 3 My lips *u* pure knowledge.
Ps 78: 2 I will *u* dark sayings of old,
94: 4 They *u* speech, and speak
106: 2 Who can *u* the mighty acts of
119:171 My lips shall *u* praise,
145: 7 They shall *u* the memory of Your
Prov 14: 5 But a false witness will *u*
23:33 And your heart will *u* perverse
Eccl 5: 2 And let not your heart *u*
Isa 32: 6 To *u* error against the LORD,
48:20 *U* it to the end of the earth;
Jer 1:16 I will *u* My judgments Against
25:30 And *u* His voice from His holy
Ezek 24: 3 And *u* a parable to the
Joel 3:16 And *u* His voice from
Mic 2:10 with *u* destruction.
Nah 1: 8 flood He will make an *u* end
1: 9 He will make an *u* end of it.
Hab 2:16 And *u* shame will be on your
Zech 14:11 And no longer shall there be *u*
Mt 13:35 I will *u* things kept
Mk 3:28 whatever blasphemies they may *u*;
1 Cor 6: 7 it is already an *u* failure for
14: 9 unless you *u* by the tongue
2 Cor 12: 4 it is not lawful for a man to *u*.

UTTERANCE (13/11) UTTER
Lev 5: 1 a person sins in hearing the *u*
Num 24: 3 The *u* of Balaam the son of Beor,
24: 3 The *u* of the man whose eyes
24: 4 The *u* of him who hears the
24:15 The *u* of Balaam the son of Beor,
24:15 And the *u* of the man whose
24:16 The *u* of him who hears the
30: 6 by her vows or by a rash *u*
Prov 30: 1 Agur the son of Jakeh, his *u*.
31: 1 the *u* which his mother taught
Acts 2: 4 as the Spirit gave them *u*.
1 Cor 1: 5 in everything by Him in all *u*
Eph 6:19 that *u* may be given to me,

UTTERED (14/13) UTTER
Num 30: 8 which she took and what she *u*
2 Sam 22:14 And the Most High *u* His voice.
Job 26: 4 To whom have you *u* words?
42: 3 Therefore I have *u* what I did
Ps 18:13 And the Most High *u* His voice,
46: 6 He *u* His voice, the earth
66:14 Which my lips have *u* And my
Jer 48:34 and to Jahaz They have *u*
51:55 the noise of their voice is *u*,
Hab 3:10 The deep *u* its voice,
Rom 8:26 groanings which cannot be *u*.
Rev 10: 3 seven thunders *u* their voices.
10: 4 Now when the seven thunders *u*
10: 4 which the seven thunders *u*,

UTTERING (1/1)
Isa 59:13 Conceiving and *u* from the

UTTERLY (91/87)
Ex 17:14 that I will *u* blot out the
22:17 If her father *u* refuses to give
22:20 he shall be *u* destroyed.
23:24 but you shall *u* overthrow them
Lev 26:44 to *u* destroy them and break My
Num 17:13 Shall we all *u* die?"
21: 2 then I will *u* destroy their
21: 3 and they *u* destroyed them and
Deut 2:34 and we *u* destroyed the men,
3: 6 'And we *u* destroyed them,
3: 6 *u* destroying the men, women,
4:26 that you will soon *u* perish
4:26 but will be *u* destroyed.
7: 2 conquer them and *u* destroy
7:26 You shall *u* detest it and
7:26 utterly detest it and *u* abhor
12: 2 You shall *u* destroy all the
13:15 *u* destroying it, all that is in
20:17 but you shall *u* destroy them:
31:29 death you will become *u* corrupt,
Josh 2:10 whom you *u* destroyed.
6:21 And they *u* destroyed all that
8:26 until he had *u* destroyed all
10: 1 had taken Ai and had *u* destroyed
10:28 He *u* destroyed them—all the
10:35 who were in it he *u* destroyed
10:37 but *u* destroyed it and all the
10:39 edge of the sword and *u* destroyed
10:40 but *u* destroyed all that
11:11 *u* destroying them. There was
11:12 He *u* destroyed them, as Moses
11:20 that He might *u* destroy them,
11:21 Joshua *u* destroyed them with
17:13 but did not *u* drive them out.
Judg 1:17 and *u* destroyed it. So the name
21:11 You shall *u* destroy every male,
1 Sam 15: 3 and *u* destroy all that they
15: 8 and *u* destroyed all the people
15: 9 and were unwilling to *u* destroy
15: 9 that they *u* destroyed.
15:15 the rest we have *u* destroyed
15:18 and *u* destroy the sinners,
15:20 I have *u* destroyed the
15:21 which should have been *u* destroyed
27:12 has made his people Israel *u* abhor
2 Sam 23: 7 And they shall be *u* burned
2 Ki 19:11 to all lands by *u* destroying
1 Chr 4:41 and *u* destroyed them, as it is
2 Chr 20:23 of Mount Seir to *u* kill and
31: 1 until they had *u* destroyed them
32:14 that my fathers *u* destroyed
Neh 9:31 mercy You did not *u* consume
Ps 37:24 he shall not be *u* cast down;
73:19 They are *u* consumed with
89:33 lovingkindness I will not *u* take
119: 8 do not forsake me *u*!
119:43 take not the word of truth *u*
Song 8: 7 It would be *u* despised.
Isa 2:18 the idols He shall *u* abolish.
6:11 The land is *u* desolate,
11:15 The LORD will *u* destroy the
24: 3 entirely emptied and *u* plundered,
34: 2 He has *u* destroyed them,
37:11 to all lands by *u* destroying
40:30 And the young men shall *u* fall,
56: 3 The LORD has *u* separated me
60:12 those nations shall be *u* ruined.
Jer 9: 4 every brother will *u* supplant
12:17 I will *u* pluck up and destroy
14:19 Have You *u* rejected Judah?
23:39 will *u* forget you and forsake
25: 9 and will *u* destroy them,
25:29 and should you be *u* unpunished?
50:21 Waste and *u* destroy them,"
50:26 of ruins, And destroy her *u*;
51: 3 *U* destroy all her army.
51:58 Babylon shall be *u* broken,
Lam 5:22 Unless You have *u* rejected us,
Ezek 9: 6 *U* slay old and young men,
17:10 Will it not *u* wither when the
29:10 make the land of Egypt *u* waste
Hos 1: 6 But I will *u* take them away.
10:15 of Israel Shall be cut off *u*.
Am 9: 8 Yet I will not *u* destroy the
Mic 2: 4 'We are *u* destroyed!
Nah 1:15 He is *u* cut off.
Hab 1: 5 Be *u* astounded! For I will
Zeph 1: 2 I will *u* consume everything
Acts 3:23 Prophet shall be *u* destroyed
2 Pe 2:12 and will *u* perish in their own
Rev 18: 8 And she will be *u* burned with

UTTERMOST (KJV) See EDGE, END, ENDS, EXTREME, FARTHEST, LAST, LIMITS, OUTER, OUTSKIRTS

UTTERMOST (3/3) UTMOST
Ps 139: 9 And dwell in the *u* parts of
1 Th 2:16 has come upon them to the *u*.
Heb 7:25 is also able to save to the *u*

UTTERS (5/5) UTTER
Ps 19: 2 Day unto day *u* speech,
Jer 10:13 When He *u* His voice,
51:16 When He *u* His voice—There
Am 1: 2 And *u* His voice from
Mic 7: 3 And the great man *u* his evil

UZ (7/7)
Gen 10:23 The sons of Aram were *U*,
36:28 sons of Dishan: *U* and Aran.
1 Chr 1:17 Asshur, Arphaxad, Lud, Aram, *U*,
1:42 The sons of Dishan were *U* and
Job 1: 1 was a man in the land of *U*,

Jer 25:20 all the kings of the land of *U*,
Lam 4:21 who dwell in the land of *U*!

UZAI (1/1)

Neh 3:25 Palal the son of *U* made

UZAL (2/2)

Gen 10:27 Hadoram, *U*, Diklah,
1 Chr 1:21 Hadoram, *U*, Diklah,

UZZA (10/9)

2 Ki 21:18 own house, in the garden of *U*.
21:26 in his tomb in the garden of *U*.
1 Chr 8: 7 He begot *U* and Ahihud.
13: 7 and *U* and Ahio drove the cart.
13: 9 *U* put out his hand to hold the
13:10 the LORD was aroused against *U*,
13:11 the LORD's outbreak against *U*;
13:11 that place is called Perez *U*
Ezra 2:49 the sons of *U*, the sons of
Neh 7:51 sons of Gazzam, the sons of *U*,

UZZAH (6/5)

2 Sam 6: 3 and *U* and Ahio, the sons of
6: 6 *U* put out his hand to the ark
6: 7 the LORD was aroused against *U*,
6: 8 the LORD's outbreak against *U*;
1 Chr 6:29 Shimei his son, *U* his son,

UZZEN SHEERAH (1/1)

1 Chr 7:24 and Upper Beth Horon and *U*;

UZZI (11/11)

1 Chr 6: 5 begot Bukki, and Bukki begot *U*;
6: 6 *U* begot Zerahiah, and Zerahiah
6:51 *U* his son, Zerahiah his son,
7: 2 The sons of Tola were *U*,
7: 3 The son of *U* was Izrahiah,
7: 7 The sons of Bela were Ezbon, *U*,
9: 8 of Jeroham; Elah the son of *U*,
Ezra 7: 4 son of Zerahiah, the son of *U*,
Neh 11:22 the Levites at Jerusalem was *U*
12:19 Mattenai; of Jedaiah, *U*;
12:42 Maaseiah, Shemaiah, Eleazar, *U*,

UZZIA (1/1)

1 Chr 11:44 *U* the Ashterathite, Shama and

UZZIAH (29/28)

2 Ki 15:13 in the thirty-ninth year of *U*
15:30 year of Jotham the son of *U*.
15:32 of Israel, Jotham the son of *U*,
15:34 to all that his father *U* had
1 Chr 6:24 *U* his son, and Shaul his son.
27:25 and Jehonathan the son of *U* was
2 Chr 26: 1 all the people of Judah took *U*,
26: 3 *U* was sixteen years old when he
26: 8 Ammonites brought tribute to *U*.
26: 9 And *U* built towers in Jerusalem
26:11 Moreover *U* had an army of
26:14 Then *U* prepared for them,
26:18 And they withstood King *U*,
26:18 It is not for you, *U*,
26:19 Then *U* became furious;
26:21 King *U* was a leper until the day
26:22 Now the rest of the acts of *U*,
26:23 So *U* rested with his fathers,
27: 2 to all that his father *U* had
Ezra 10:21 Elijah, Shemaiah, Jehiel, and *U*;
Neh 11: 4 Athaiah the son of *U*,
Isa 1: 1 and Jerusalem in the days of *U*,
6: 1 In the year that King *U* died,
7: 1 the son of Jotham, the son of *U*,
Hos 1: 1 son of Beeri, in the days of *U*,
Am 1: 1 Israel in the days of *U* king
Zech 14: 5 earthquake In the days of *U*
Mt 1: 8 begot Joram, and Joram begot *U*.
1: 9 *U* begot Jotham, Jotham begot

UZZIEL (16/16)

Ex 6:18 Amram, Izhar, Hebron, and *U*.
6:22 And the sons of *U* were Mishael,
Lev 10: 4 the sons of *U* the uncle of
Num 3:19 Amram, Izehar, Hebron, and *U*.
3:30 was Elizaphan the son of *U*.
1 Chr 4:42 Neariah, Rephaiah, and *U*,
6: 2 Amram, Izhar, Hebron, and *U*.
6:18 Amram, Izhar, Hebron, and *U*.
7: 7 of Bela were Ezbon, Uzzi, *U*,
15:10 of the sons of *U*,
23:12 Amram, Izhar, Hebron, and *U*—
23:20 Of the sons of *U*,
24:24 Of the sons of *U*,
25: 4 of Heman: Bukkiah, Mattaniah, *U*,
2 Chr 29:14 of Jeduthun, Shemaiah and *U*.
Neh 3: 8 Next to him *U* the son of

UZZIELITES (2/2)

Num 3:27 and the family of the *U*;
1 Chr 26:23 the Hebronites, and the *U*:

V

VAGABOND (2/2)

Gen 4:12 A fugitive and a *v* you shall be
4:14 I shall be a fugitive and a *v*

VAGABONDS (1/1)

Ps 109:10 his children continually be *v*,

VAIL, VAILS (KJV) See VEIL, VEILS

VAIN (59/53) EMPTY, USELESS

Ex 20: 7 name of the LORD your God in *v*,
20: 7 who takes His name in *v*.
Lev 26:16 you shall sow your seed in *v*,
26:20 strength shall be spent in *v*;
Deut 5:11 name of the LORD your God in *v*,
5:11 who takes His name in *v*.
1 Sam 25:21 Surely in *v* I have protected all
Job 9:29 Why then do I labor in *v*?
35:16 Job opens his mouth in *v*;
39:16 Her labor is in *v*,
Ps 2: 1 And the people plot a *v* thing?
33:17 A horse is a *v* hope for
39: 6 they busy themselves in *v*;
73:13 I have cleansed my heart in *v*,
127: 1 They labor in *v* who build it;
127: 1 The watchman stays awake in *v*.
127: 2 It is *v* for you to rise up
139:20 enemies take Your name in *v*.
144: 8 Whose mouth speaks *v* words,
Prov 1:17 in *v* the net is spread In the
Eccl 6:12 all the days of his *v* life
9: 9 you love all the days of your *v*
Isa 30: 7 the Egyptians shall help in *v*
45:18 Who did not create it in *v*,
45:19 seed of Jacob, 'Seek Me in *v*';
49: 4 I said, 'I have labored in *v*,
49: 4 strength for nothing and in *v*;
65:23 They shall not labor in *v*,
Jer 2:30 In *v* I have chastened your
3:23 in *v* is salvation hoped for
4:30 In *v* you will make yourself
6:29 fire; The smelter refines in *v*,
46:11 In *v* you will use many
50: 9 None shall return in *v*.
51:58 The people will labor in *v*,
Ezek 6:10 I have not said in *v* that I
Hab 2:13 nations weary themselves in *v*?
Zech 10: 2 dreams; They comfort in *v*.
Mal 1:10 kindle fire on My altar in *v*?
Mt 6: 7 do not use *v* repetitions as the
15: 9 And in *v* they worship Me,
Mk 7: 7 And in *v* they worship Me,
Acts 4:25 And the people plot *v*
Rom 13: 4 he does not bear the sword in *v*;
1 Cor 15: 2 to you—unless you believed in *v*.
15:10 grace toward me was not in *v*;
15:58 that your labor is not in *v* in
2 Cor 6: 1 receive the grace of God in *v*.
9: 3 boasting of you should be in *v*
Gal 2: 2 I might run, or had run, in *v*.
2:21 the law, then Christ died in *v*.
3: 4 suffered so many things in *v*—
3: 4 in vain—if indeed it was in *v*?
4:11 I have labored for you in *v*.
Phil 2:16 that I have not run in *v* or
2:16 not run in vain or labored in *v*.
1 Th 2: 1 our coming to you was not in *v*.
3: 5 and our labor might be in *v*.
Jas 4: 5 that the Scripture says in *v*,

VAINLY (3/3)

Ps 62:10 Nor *v* hope in robbery;
Lam 4:17 Watching *v* for our help;
Col 2:18 *v* puffed up by his fleshly

VAJEZATHA (1/1)

Esth 9: 9 Arisai, Aridai, and *V*—

VALE (KJV) See LOWLAND, VALLEY

VALIANT (31/29) VALIANTLY

Judg 21:10 thousand of their most *v* men,
1 Sam 10:26 and *v* men went with him,
14:52 any strong man or any *v* man,
18:17 Only be *v* for me, and fight the
31:12 all the *v* men arose and traveled
2 Sam 2: 7 hands be strengthened, and be *v*;
11:16 where he knew there were *v* men.
13:28 Be courageous and *v*."
17:10 "And even he who is *v*,
17:10 who are with him are *v* men.
23:20 the son of a *v* man from
24: 9 eight hundred thousand *v* men
2 Ki 24:16 All the *v* men, seven thousand,
1 Chr 5:18 seven hundred and sixty *v* men,
10:12 all the *v* men arose and took the
11:22 the son of a *v* man from
12:28 a *v* warrior, and from his
28: 1 the *v* men, and all the mighty
2 Chr 13: 3 with an army of *v* warriors,
26:17 priests of the LORD—*v* men.
28: 6 all *v* men, because they had
Neh 11: 6 hundred and sixty-eight *v* men.
Song 3: 7 With sixty *v* men around it,
3: 7 Of the *v* of Israel.
Isa 5:22 Woe to men *v* for mixing
10:13 the inhabitants like a *v* man.
33: 7 Surely their *v* ones shall cry
Jer 9: 3 They are not *v* for the truth
46:15 Why are your *v* men swept away?
Nah 2: 3 The *v* men are in scarlet.
Heb 11:34 became *v* in battle,

VALIANTLY (5/5) VALIANT

Num 24:18 While Israel does *v*.
Ps 60:12 Through God we will do *v*,
108:13 Through God we will do *v*,
118:15 right hand of the LORD does *v*.
118:16 right hand of the LORD does *v*.

VALLEY (145/129) VALLEYS

Gen 14: 3 together in the *V* of Siddim
14: 8 together in battle in the *V* of Siddim
14:10 Now the *V* of Siddim was full
14:17 out to meet him at the *V* Shaveh
14:17 Shaveh (that is, the King's *V*),
26:17 his tent in the *V* of Gerar,
26:19 Isaac's servants dug in the *v*,
37:14 sent him out of the *V* of Hebron,
Num 13:23 came to the *V* of Eschol,
13:24 The place was called the *V* of
14:25 the Canaanites dwell in the *v*;
21:12 and camped in the *V* of Zered,
21:20 in the *v* that is in the
32: 9 when they went up to the *V* of Eschol
Deut 1:24 and came to the *V* of Eshcol,
2:13 Now rise and cross over the *V* of
2:13 crossed over the *V* of the Zered
2:14 we crossed over the *V* of the Zered
3:29 So we stayed in the *v* opposite
4:46 in the *v* opposite Beth Peor,
21: 4 bring the heifer down to a *v*
21: 4 heifer's neck there in the *v*.
21: 6 whose neck was broken in the *v*.
34: 3 the plain of the *V* of Jericho
34: 6 And He buried him in a *v* in the
Josh 7:24 brought them to the *V* of Achor
7:26 has been called the *V* of Achor
8:11 Now a *v* lay between them and
8:13 night into the midst of the *v*.
10:12 in the *V* of Aijalon."
11: 8 and to the *V* of Mizpah
11:17 as Baal Gad in the *V* of Lebanon
12: 7 Baal Gad in the *V* of Lebanon
13:19 Shahar on the mountain of the *v*,
13:27 and in the *v* Beth Haram, Beth
15: 7 Debir from the *V* of Achor
15: 7 is on the south side of the *v*.
15: 8 up by the *V* of the Son of Hinnom
15: 8 before the *V* of Hinnom
15: 8 the end of the *V* of Rephaim
17:16 who dwell in the land of the *v*
17:16 who are of the *V* of Jezreel
18:16 the *V* of the Son of Hinnom
18:16 in the *V* of the Rephaim
18:16 descended to the *V* of Hinnom,
19:14 in the *V* of Jiphthah El.
19:27 to Zebulun and to the *V* of
Judg 1:34 them to come down to the *v*;
5:15 so was Barak Sent into the *v*
6:33 encamped in the *V* of Jezreel.
7: 1 by the hill of Moreh in the *v*.
7: 8 Midian was below him in the *v*.
7:12 were lying in the *v* as numerous
16: 4 he loved a woman in the *V* of Sorek
18:28 It was in the *v* that belongs to
1 Sam 6:13 their wheat harvest in the *v*;
13:18 that overlooks the *V* of Zeboim
15: 5 and lay in wait in the *v*.
17: 2 they encamped in the *V* of Elah,
17: 3 with a *v* between them.
17:19 Israel were in the *V* of Elah,
17:52 as far as the entrance of the *v*
21: 9 you killed in the *V* of Elah,
31: 7 on the other side of the *v*,
2 Sam 5:18 themselves in the *V* of Rephaim
5:22 deployed themselves in the *V*
8:13 Syrians in the *V* of Salt.
18:18 which is in the King's *V*.
23:13 encamped in the *V* of Rephaim
2 Ki 2:16 some mountain or into some *v*.
3:16 Make this *v* full of ditches.'
3:17 yet that *v* shall be filled with
14: 7 Edomites in the *V* of Salt, and
23:10 which is in the *V* of the Son
1 Chr 4:39 far as the east side of the *v*,
10: 7 of Israel who were in the *v*
11:15 encamped in the *V* of Rephaim
14: 9 and made a raid on the *V* of Rephaim
14:13 once again made a raid on the *v*.
18:12 Edomites in the *V* of Salt
2 Chr 14:10 in battle array in the *V* of Zephathah
20:26 assembled in the *V* of Berachah,
20:26 place was called The *V* of Berachah
25:11 he went to the *V* of Salt and
26: 9 at the *V* Gate, and at the
28: 3 incense in the *V* of the Son of Hinnom
33: 6 the fire in the *V* of the Son of Hinnom
33:14 west side of Gihon, in the *v*,
35:22 came to fight in the *V* of Megiddo.
Neh 2:13 out by night through the *V* Gate
2:15 I went up in the night by the *v*,
2:15 back and entered by the *V* Gate,

3:13 of Zanoah repaired the *V* Gate.
11:30 Beersheba to the *V* of Hinnom
11:35 and the *V* of Craftsmen.
Job 21:33 The clods of the *v* shall be
39:21 He paws in the *v*,
Ps 23: 4 though I walk through the *v* of
60: Edomites in the *V* of Salt
60: 6 measure out the *V* of Succoth
84: 6 As they pass through the *V* of Baca
108: 7 measure out the *V* of Succoth
Prov 30:17 The ravens of the *v* will pick
Song 6:11 To see the verdure of the *v*,
Isa 17: 5 heads of grain In the *V* of Rephaim
22: 1 The burden against the *V* of Vision
22: 5 In the *V* of Vision—
28: 4 at the head of the verdant *v*,
28:21 be angry as in the *V* of Gibeon
40: 4 Every *v* shall be exalted
63:14 a beast goes down into the *v*,
65:10 And the *V* of Achor a place for
Jer 2:23 See your way in the *v*;
7:31 which is in the *V* of the Son
7:32 or the *V* of the Son of Hinnom,
7:32 but the *V* of Slaughter;
19: 2 And go out to the *V* of the Son
19: 6 Tophet or the *V* of the Son of Hinnom
19: 6 but the *V* of Slaughter.
21:13 O inhabitant of the *v*,
31:40 And the whole *v* of the dead
32:35 in the *V* of the Son of Hinnom
47: 5 With the remnant of their *v*.
48: 8 The *v* also shall perish,
49: 4 in the valleys, Your flowing *v*,
Ezek 37: 1 me down in the midst of the *v*;
37: 2 were very many in the open *v*;
39:11 the *v* of those who pass by east
39:11 call it the *V* of Hamon Gog
39:15 have buried it in the *V* of Hamon Gog
47: 8 region, goes down into the *v*,
Hos 1: 5 of Israel in the *V* of Jezreel
2:15 And the *V* of Achor as a door
Joel 3: 2 down to the *V* of Jehoshaphat
3:12 up to the *V* of Jehoshaphat
3:14 multitudes in the *v* of
3:14 is near in the *v* of decision
3:18 And water the *V* of Acacias
Am 1: 5 inhabitant from the *V* of Aven
6:14 To the *V* of the Arabah
Mic 1: 6 pour down her stones into the *v*,
Zech 14: 4 Making a very large *v*;
14: 5 flee through My mountain *v*,
14: 5 For the mountain *v* shall reach
Lk 3: 5 Every *v* shall be filled

VALLEYS (27/27) VALLEY

Num 24: 6 Like *v* that stretch out,
Deut 8: 7 that flow out of *v* and hills;
11:11 is a land of hills and *v*,
1 Ki 20:28 but He is not God of the *v*,
1 Chr 12:15 to flight all those in the *v*,
27:29 the herds that were in the *v*.
Job 30: 6 to live in the clefts of the *v*,
39:10 Or will he plow the *v* behind
Ps 65:13 The *v* also are covered with
104: 8 They went down into the *v*,
104:10 sends the springs into the *v*,
Song 2: 1 Sharon, And the lily of the *v*.
Isa 7:19 will rest In the desolate *v*
22: 7 to pass that your choicest *v*
28: 1 at the head of the verdant *v*,
41:18 fountains in the midst of the *v*;
57: 5 Slaying the children in the *v*,
Jer 49: 4 Why do you boast in the *v*,
Ezek 6: 3 to the ravines, and to the *v*:
7:16 mountains Like doves of the *v*,
31:12 the mountains and in all the *v*;
32: 5 And fill the *v* with your
34:13 in the *v* and in all the
35: 8 on your hills and in your *v* and
36: 4 the hills, the rivers, the *v*,
36: 6 hills, the rivers, and the *v*,
Mic 1: 4 And the *v* will split Like wax

VALOR (39/39)

Deut 3:18 All you men of *v* shall cross
Josh 1:14 armed, all your mighty men of *v*,
6: 2 king, and the mighty men of *v*.
8: 3 thousand mighty men of *v* and
10: 7 and all the mighty men of *v*.
Judg 3:29 men of Moab, all stout men of *v*;
6:12 you mighty man of *v*!"
11: 1 Gileadite was a mighty man of *v*,
18: 2 men of *v* from Zorah and
20:44 all these were men of *v*.
20:46 all these were men of *v*.
1 Sam 16:18 in playing, a mighty man of *v*,
1 Ki 11:28 Jeroboam was a mighty man of *v*;
2 Ki 5: 1 He was also a mighty man of *v*,
24:14 and all the mighty men of *v*,
1 Chr 5:24 They were mighty men of *v*,
7: 2 of Tola were mighty men of *v*
7: 5 Issachar were mighty men of *v*,
7: 7 and thirty-four mighty men of *v*.
7: 9 two hundred mighty men of *v*.
7:11 two hundred mighty men of *v*
7:40 choice men, mighty men of *v*,
8:40 of Ulam were mighty men of *v*—
12: 8 the wilderness, mighty men of *v*,
12:21 they were all mighty men of *v*,
12:25 mighty men of *v* fit for war,
12:30 eight hundred, mighty men of *v*,
28: 1 and all the mighty men of *v*.
2 Chr 13: 3 choice men, mighty men of *v*.
14: 8 all these were mighty men of *v*.
17:13 the men of war, mighty men of *v*,
17:14 thousand mighty men of *v*;
17:16 thousand mighty men of *v*.
17:17 Eliada a mighty man of *v*,
25: 6 thousand mighty men of *v* from
26:12 of the mighty men of *v* was
32:21 cut down every mighty man of *v*,
Neh 11:14 their brethren, mighty men of *v*,
Dan 3:20 certain mighty men of *v* who

VALOUR (KJV) See VALOR

VALUABLE (1/1)

Lam 4: 2 *V* as fine gold, How they are

VALUABLES (3/3)

2 Chr 20:25 among them an abundance of *v*
Lam 1:11 They have given their *v* for
Hos 9: 6 Nettles shall possess their *v*

VALUATION (23/19)

Lev 5:15 with your *v* in shekels of
5:18 from the flock, with your *v*,
6: 6 from the flock, with your *v*,
27: 2 the LORD, according to your *v*,
27: 3 if your *v* is of a male from
27: 3 then your *v* shall be fifty
27: 4 then your *v* shall be thirty
27: 5 then your *v* for a male shall be
27: 6 then your *v* for a male shall be
27: 6 and for a female your *v* shall
27: 7 then your *v* shall be fifteen
27: 8 if he is too poor to pay your *v*,
27:13 he must add one-fifth to your *v*.
27:15 of the money of your *v* to it,
27:16 then your *v* shall be according
27:17 according to your *v* it shall
27:18 shall be deducted from your *v*.
27:19 of the money of your *v* to it,
27:23 to him the worth of your *v*,
27:23 and he shall give your *v* on
27:27 redeem it according to your *v*,
27:27 be sold according to your *v*.
Num 18:16 month old, according to your *v*,

VALUATIONS (1/1)

Lev 27:25 And all your *v* shall be

VALUE (15/13) FULL, VALUED

Lev 6: 5 He shall restore its full *v*,
27: 8 and the priest shall set a *v*
27: 8 the priest shall *v* him.
27:12 and the priest shall set a *v* for
27:12 *v* it, so it shall be.
27:14 then the priest shall set a *v*
Job 28:13 Man does not know its *v*,
Mt 6:26 Are you not of more *v* than
10:31 you are of more *v* than many
12:12 Of how much more *v* then is a man
27: 9 the *v* of Him who was
Lk 12: 7 you are of more *v* than many
12:24 Of how much more *v* are you than
Acts 19:19 And they counted up the *v* of
Col 2:23 but are of no *v* against the

VALUED (6/5) VALUE

Lev 27:16 of barley seed shall be *v*
1 Sam 26:24 as your life was *v* much this
26:24 so let my life be *v* much in the
Job 28:16 It cannot be *v* in the gold of
28:19 Nor can it be *v* in pure gold.
Prov 27:21 And a man is *v* by what

VALUES (1/1)

Lev 27:14 as the priest *v* it, so it shall

VANIAH (1/1)

Ezra 10:36 *V*, Meremoth, Eliashib,

VANISH (6/5) VANISHED, VANISHES

Job 6:17 they *v* from their place.
Ps 37:20 of the meadows, shall *v*.
37:20 Into smoke they shall *v* away.
Isa 51: 6 For the heavens will *v* away
1 Cor 13: 8 it will *v* away.
Heb 8:13 and growing old is ready to *v*

VANISHED (2/2) VANISH

Jer 49: 7 Has their wisdom *v*?
Lk 24:31 and He *v* from their sight.

VANISHES (3/3) VANISH

Job 6:16 And into which the snow *v*.
7: 9 As the cloud disappears and *v*
Jas 4:14 for a little time and then *v*

VANITIES (3/2) VANITY

Eccl 1: 2 "Vanity of *v*,
1: 2 the Preacher; "Vanity of *v*,
12: 8 "Vanity of *v*,

VANITY (35/31) VANITIES

Eccl 1: 2 *V* of vanities," says the
1: 2 *V* of vanities, all is vanity."
1: 2 of vanities, all is *v*.
1:14 all is *v* and grasping for the
2: 1 but surely, this also was *v*.
2:11 And indeed all was *v* and
2:15 in my heart, "This also is *v*.
2:17 for all is *v* and grasping for
2:19 under the sun. This also is *v*.
2:21 This also is *v* and a great
2:23 takes no rest. This also is *v*.
2:26 This also is *v* and grasping
3:19 over animals, for all is *v*.
4: 4 This also is *v* and grasping
4: 7 and I saw *v* under the sun:
4: 8 This also is *v* and a grave
4:16 Surely this also is *v* and
5: 7 many words there is also *v*.
5:10 with increase. This also is *v*.
6: 2 consumes it. This is *v*,
6: 4 for it comes in *v* and departs in
6: 9 This also is *v* and grasping
6:11 are many things that increase *v*,
7: 6 of the fool. This also is *v*.
7:15 seen everything in my days of *v*:
8:10 had so done. This also is *v*.
8:14 There is a *v* which occurs on
8:14 I said that this also is *v*.
9: 9 the sun, all your days of *v*;
11: 8 All that is coming is *v*.
11:10 For childhood and youth are *v*.
12: 8 *V* of vanities," says the
12: 8 says the Preacher, "All is *v*.
Isa 5:18 draw iniquity with cords of *v*,
Hos 12:11 has idols—Surely they are *v*—

VANQUISH (1/1)

Job 32:13 God will *v* him, not man.

VANQUISHED (2/2)

2 Sam 22:15 Lightning bolts, and He *v* them.
Ps 18:14 in abundance, and He *v* them.

VAPOR (6/5)

Ps 39: 5 man at his best state is but *v*.
39:11 Surely every man is *v*.
62: 9 men of low degree are a *v*,
62: 9 are altogether lighter than *v*.
Acts 2:19 Blood and fire and *v* of
Jas 4:14 It is even a *v* that appears for

VAPORS (3/3)

Ps 135: 7 He causes the *v* to ascend from
Jer 10:13 And He causes the *v* to ascend
51:16 He causes the *v* to ascend from

VAPOUR (KJV) See RAIN, STORM, VAPOR

VARIABLENESS (KJV) See VARIATION

VARIANCE (KJV) See AGAINST, CONTENTIONS

VARIATION (1/1) VARIETIES

Jas 1:17 with whom there is no *v* or

VARIETIES (1/1) VARIATION, VARIOUS

1 Cor 12:28 administrations, *v* of tongues.

VARIOUS (18/17) VARIETIES

1 Chr 29: 2 glistening stones of *v* colors,
2 Chr 16:14 with spices and *v* ingredients
Ezek 17: 3 Full of feathers of *v* colors,
Mt 4:24 were afflicted with *v* diseases
24: 7 and earthquakes in *v* places.
Mk 1:34 who were sick with *v* diseases,
13: 8 will be earthquakes in *v* places,
Lk 4:40 that were sick with *v* diseases
21:11 great earthquakes in *v* places,
2 Tim 3: 6 led away by *v* lusts,
Titus 3: 3 serving *v* lusts and pleasures,
Heb 1: 1 who at *v* times and in various
1: 1 various times and in *v* ways
2: 4 with *v* miracles, and gifts of
9:10 *v* washings, and fleshly
13: 9 with *v* and strange doctrines.
Jas 1: 2 when you fall into *v* trials,
1 Pe 1: 6 have been grieved by *v* trials,

VASHNI (KJV) See JOEL

VASHTI (10/10)

Esth 1: 9 Queen *V* also made a feast for
1:11 to bring Queen *V* before the
1:12 But Queen *V* refused to come at
1:15 "What shall we do to Queen *V*,
1:16 Queen *V* has not only wronged the

1:17 Ahasuerus commanded Queen *V* to
1:19 that *V* shall come no more
2: 1 subsided, he remembered *V*,
2: 4 the king be queen instead of *V*.
2:17 and made her queen instead of *V*.

VASSAL (2/2)

2 Ki 17: 3 and Hoshea became his *v*,
24: 1 and Jehoiakim became his *v* for

VAST (1/1)

Prov 16: 8 Than *v* revenues without

VAT (2/2)

Hag 2:16 when one came to the wine *v* to
Mk 12: 1 dug a place for the wine *v*

VATS (3/3)

Prov 3:10 And your *v* will overflow with
Joel 2:24 And the *v* shall overflow with
3:13 The *v* overflow—For their

VAUNT, VAUNTETH (KJV) See CLAIM (GLORY), PARADE

VEGETABLE (2/2)

Deut 11:10 it by foot, as a *v* garden;
1 Ki 21: 2 that I may have it for a *v*

VEGETABLES (3/3)

Dan 1:12 and let them give us *v* to eat
1:16 were to drink, and gave them *v*.
Rom 14: 2 but he who is weak eats only *v*.

VEGETATION (3/3)

Ps 104:14 And *v* for the service of man,
105:35 And ate up all the *v* in their
Isa 42:15 And dry up all their *v*;

VEHEMENT (4/4) VEHEMENTLY

Song 8: 6 A most *v* flame.
Jon 4: 8 that God prepared a *v* east
2 Cor 7:11 what *v* desire, what zeal,
Heb 5: 7 with *v* cries and tears to Him

VEHEMENTLY (5/5) VEHEMENT

Mk 14:31 But he spoke more *v*,
Lk 6:48 the stream beat *v* against that
6:49 against which the stream beat *v*;
11:53 began to assail Him *v*,
23:10 priests and scribes stood and *v*

VEIL (48/45) UNVEILED, VEILED

Gen 24:65 So she took a *v* and covered
38:14 covered herself with a *v* and
38:19 and laid aside her *v* and put on
Ex 26:31 You shall make a *v* woven of
26:33 And you shall hang the *v* from
26:33 in there, behind the *v*.
26:33 The *v* shall be a divider for
26:35 set the table outside the *v*,
27:21 outside the *v* which is before
30: 6 you shall put it before the *v*
34:33 he put a *v* on his face.
34:34 he would take the *v* off until
34:35 then Moses would put the *v* on
35:12 and the *v* of the covering;
36:35 And he made a *v* of blue,
38:27 and the bases of the *v*:
39:34 and the *v* of the covering;
40: 3 off the ark with the *v*.
40:21 hung up the *v* of the covering,
40:22 the tabernacle, outside the *v*;
40:26 of meeting in front of the *v*;
Lev 4: 6 in front of the *v* of the
4:17 the LORD, in front of the *v*.
16: 2 the Holy Place inside the *v*,
16:12 and bring it inside the *v*.
16:15 bring its blood inside the *v*,
21:23 he shall not go near the *v* or
24: 3 Outside the *v* of the Testimony,
Num 4: 5 shall take down the covering *v*
18: 7 at the altar and behind the *v*;
2 Chr 3:14 And he made the *v* of blue,
Song 4: 1 have dove's eyes behind your *v*.
4: 3 Your temples behind your *v*
5: 7 of the walls Took my *v* away
6: 7 your temples behind your *v*.
Isa 25: 7 And the *v* that is spread over
47: 2 and grind meal. Remove your *v*,
Mt 27:51 the *v* of the temple was torn in
Mk 15:38 Then the *v* of the temple was
Lk 23:45 and the *v* of the temple was
2 Cor 3:13 who put a *v* over his face so
3:14 For until this day the same *v*
3:14 because the *v* is taken away in
3:15 a *v* lies on their heart.
3:16 the *v* is taken away.
Heb 6:19 the Presence behind the *v*,
9: 3 and behind the second *v*,
10:20 for us, through the *v*,

VEILED (3/2) VEIL

Lam 3:65 Give them a *v* heart;
2 Cor 4: 3 But even if our gospel is *v*,
4: 3 it is *v* to those who are

VEILS (4/4)

Song 1: 7 why should I be as one who *v*
Isa 3:19 the bracelets, and the *v*;
Ezek 13:18 on their sleeves and make *v*
13:21 I will also tear off your *v* and

VEIN (KJV) See MINE

VENGEANCE (51/45)

Gen 4:15 *v* shall be taken on him
Lev 19:18 'You shall not take *v*,
26:25 you that will execute the *v* of
Num 31: 2 Take *v* on the Midianites for the
31: 3 the Midianites to take *v* for
Deut 32:35 *V* is Mine, and recompense
32:41 I will render *v* to My enemies,
32:43 And render *v* to His
Judg 16:28 I may with one blow take *v* on
1 Sam 14:24 before I have taken *v* on my
18:25 to take *v* on the king's
Ps 58:10 rejoice when he sees the *v*;
94: 1 to whom *v* belongs—O God,
94: 1 to whom *v* belongs, shine forth!
99: 8 Though You took *v* on their
149: 7 To execute *v* on the nations,
Prov 6:34 will not spare in the day of *v*.
Isa 1:24 And take *v* on My enemies.
34: 8 is the day of the LORD's *v*,
35: 4 your God will come with *v*,
47: 3 will be seen; I will take *v*,
59:17 He put on the garments of *v*
61: 2 And the day of *v* of our God;
63: 4 For the day of *v* is in My
Jer 11:20 Let me see Your *v* on them,
15:15 And take *v* for me on my
20:12 Let me see Your *v* on them;
46:10 Lord GOD of hosts, A day of *v*,
50:15 For it is the *v* of the LORD.
50:15 Take *v* on her. As she has
50:28 Declares in Zion the *v* of the
50:28 The *v* of His temple.
51: 6 is the time of the LORD's *v*;
51:11 Because it is the *v* of the
51:11 The *v* for His temple.
51:36 plead your case and take *v* for
Lam 3:60 You have seen all their *v*,
Ezek 24: 8 it may raise up fury and take *v*,
25:12 the house of Judah by taking *v*,
25:14 I will lay My *v* on Edom by the
25:14 and they shall know My *v*,"
25:15 dealt vengefully and took *v*
25:17 I will execute great *v* on them
25:17 when I lay My *v* upon them." '
Mic 5:15 And I will execute *v* in anger
Nah 1: 2 The LORD will take *v* on His
Lk 21:22 "For these are the days of *v*,
Rom 12:19 *V* is Mine, I will repay,"
2 Th 1: 8 in flaming fire taking *v* on
Heb 10:30 *V* is Mine, I will repay,"
Jude 7 suffering the *v* of eternal

VENGEFULLY (1/1)

Ezek 25:15 the Philistines dealt *v* and

VENISON (KJV) See GAME

VENOM (2/2)

Deut 32:33 And the cruel *v* of cobras.
Job 20:14 It becomes cobra *v* within him.

VENT (1/1)

Job 32:19 is like wine that has no *v*;

VENTS (1/1)

Prov 29:11 A fool *v* all his feelings,

VENTURE (2/2)

Deut 28:56 who would not *v* to set the sole
Acts 19:31 pleading that he would not *v*

VERDANT (2/2)

Isa 28: 1 Which is at the head of the *v*
28: 4 is at the head of the *v* valley,

VERDURE (1/1)

Song 6:11 garden of nuts To see the *v*

VERGE (3/3)

Deut 20: 2 when you are on the *v* of
20: 3 Today you are on the *v* of
Prov 5:14 I was on the *v* of total ruin,

VERIFIED (1/1)

Gen 42:20 so your words will be *v*,

VERILY (KJV) See ASSUREDLY, CERTAINLY, SURELY, TRULY

VERITY (1/1)

Ps 111: 7 The works of His hands are *v*

VERMILION (2/2)

Jer 22:14 cedar And painting it with *v*.
Ezek 23:14 of Chaldeans portrayed in *v*,

VERY (290/280) See APPENDIX

VESSEL (38/34) VESSELS

Lev 6:28 But the earthen *v* in which it is
11:33 Any earthen *v* into which any of
11:34 'in such a *v*, any edible food
14: 5 be killed in an earthen *v* over
14:50 of the birds in an earthen *v*
15:12 The *v* of earth that he who has
15:12 and every *v* of wood shall be
Num 5:17 take holy water in an earthen *v*,
19:15 'and every open *v*,
19:17 shall be put on them in a *v*.
1 Sam 21: 5 it was sanctified in the *v*.
2 Ki 4: 6 her son, "Bring me another *v*.
4: 6 There is not another *v*."
Esth 1: 7 each *v* being different from the
Ps 2: 9 to pieces like a potter's *v*.
31:12 I am like a broken *v*.
Isa 30:14 the breaking of the potter's *v*,
66:20 bring an offering in a clean *v*
Jer 18: 4 And the *v* that he made of clay
18: 4 he made it again into another *v*,
19:11 as one breaks a potter's *v*,
22:28 A *v* in which is no pleasure?
25:34 shall fall like a precious *v*.
32:14 and put them in an earthen *v*,
48:11 has not been emptied from *v* to
48:11 been emptied from vessel to *v*,
48:38 I have broken Moab like a *v* in
51:34 He has made me an empty *v*,
Ezek 4: 9 put them into one *v*,
15: 3 a peg from it to hang any *v* on?
Hos 8: 8 among the Gentiles Like a *v*
Lk 8:16 covers it with a *v* or puts it
Jn 19:29 Now a *v* full of sour wine was
Acts 9:15 for he is a chosen *v* of Mine to
Rom 9:21 the same lump to make one *v*
1 Th 4: 4 know how to possess his own *v*
2 Tim 2:21 he will be a *v* for honor,
1 Pe 3: 7 to the wife, as to the weaker *v*,

VESSELS (50/47) PITCHERS, VESSEL

Gen 43:11 fruits of the land in your *v*
Num 4: 9 its trays, and all its oil *v*,
7:85 All the silver of the *v*
19:18 it on the tent, on all the *v*,
Josh 6:19 and *v* of bronze and iron, are
6:24 and the *v* of bronze and iron,
Ruth 2: 9 go to the *v* and drink from what
1 Sam 9: 7 For the bread in our *v* is all
21: 5 And the *v* of the young men are
2 Sam 17:28 earthen *v* and wheat, barley and
1 Ki 10:21 All King Solomon's drinking *v*
10:21 and all the *v* of the House of
2 Ki 4: 3 borrow *v* from everywhere,
4: 3 from all your neighbors—empty *v*;
4: 4 then pour it into all those *v*,
4: 5 who brought the *v* to her;
4: 6 when the *v* were full, that she
1 Chr 9:28 were in charge of the serving *v*,
2 Chr 9:20 All King Solomon's drinking *v*
9:20 and all the *v* of the House of
24:14 spoons and *v* of gold and
Ezra 8:27 and two *v* of fine polished
Esth 1: 7 they served drinks in golden *v*,
Isa 18: 2 Even in *v* of reed on the
22:24 all *v* of small quantity,
52:11 You who bear the *v* of the
65: 4 things is in their *v*;
Jer 14: 3 They returned with their *v*
27:16 the *v* of the LORD's house will
27:18 that the *v* which are left in
27:19 the remainder of the *v* that
27:21 concerning the *v* that remain in
28: 3 back to this place all the *v*
28: 6 to bring back the *v* of the
40:10 and oil, put them in your *v*,
48:12 tip him over And empty his *v*
49:29 All their *v* and their camels;
Ezek 27:13 bartered human lives and *v* of
Dan 5: 2 to bring the gold and silver *v*
5: 3 Then they brought the gold *v*
5:23 They have brought the *v* of His
Mt 13:48 and gathered the good into *v*,
25: 4 the wise took oil in their *v*
Mk 7: 4 of cups, pitchers, copper *v*,
Rom 9:22 with much longsuffering the *v*
9:23 riches of His glory on the *v*
2 Cor 4: 7 have this treasure in earthen *v*,
2 Tim 2:20 house there are not only *v* of
Heb 9:21 the tabernacle and all the *v*
Rev 2:27 like the potter's *v*'—

VESTIBLE (1/1)

1 Ki 6: 3 and the width of the *v*

VESTIBULE (25/22)

1 Ki 6: 3 The *v* in front of the sanctuary
7:12 house of the LORD and the *v*
7:21 he set up the pillars by the *v*
1 Chr 28:11 son Solomon the plans for the *v*,
2 Chr 3: 4 And the *v* that was in front of
8:12 which he had built before the *v*,
15: 8 LORD that was before the *v*
29: 7 also shut up the doors of the *v*,
29:17 of the month they came to the *v*
Ezek 40: 7 of the gateway by the *v* of the
40: 8 He also measured the *v* of the
40: 9 Then he measured the *v* of the
40: 9 The *v* of the gate was on the
40:15 gate to the front of the *v* of
40:39 In the *v* of the gateway were
40:40 At the outer side of the *v*,
40:40 and on the other side of the *v*
40:48 Then he brought me to the *v* of
40:48 measured the doorposts of the *v*,
40:49 The length of the *v* was twenty
41:25 was on the front of the *v*
41:26 other, on the sides of the *v*—
44: 3 he shall enter by way of the *v*
46: 2 shall enter by way of the *v* of
46: 8 he shall go in by way of the *v*

VESTIBULES (1/1)

Ezek 40:16 around, and likewise in the *v*.

VESTMENTS (2/1)

2 Ki 10:22 Bring out *v* for all the
10:22 So he brought out *v* for them.

VESTRY (KJV) See WARDROBE

VESTURE (KJV) See CLOTHING, GARMENTS

VEX, VEXATION (KJV) See CONFUSION, GRASPING, HARASS, MISTREAT, RIVAL, STRIVING, TROUBLED

VEXED (2/2)

Judg 16:16 so that his soul was *v* to
Ps 73:21 And I was *v* in my mind.

VIAL, VIALS (KJV) See BOWL, BOWLS, FLASK

VICE (1/1)

1 Pe 2:16 using liberty as a cloak for *v*,

VICTIM (4/4)

Deut 19: 6 since he had not hated the *v* in
Job 29:17 And plucked the *v* from his
Prov 23:28 also lies in wait as for a *v*,
Nah 3: 1 Its *v* never departs.

VICTIMS (4/4)

Num 14: 3 and children should become *v*?
14:31 ones, whom you said would be *v*,
Deut 1:39 children, who you say will be *v*,
2 Ki 21:14 and they shall become *v* of

VICTORIES (1/1) VICTORY

Ps 44: 4 Command *v* for Jacob.

VICTORY (14/14) VICTORIES

Ex 32:18 not the noise of the shout of *v*,
2 Sam 19: 2 So the *v* that day was turned
23:10 LORD brought about a great *v*
23:12 LORD brought about a great *v*.
2 Ki 5: 1 by him the LORD had given *v*
1 Chr 11:14 LORD brought about a great *v*.
29:11 The *v* and the majesty;
Ps 98: 1 holy arm have gained Him the *v*.
Mt 12:20 sends forth justice to *v*;
1 Cor 15:54 is swallowed up in *v*.
15:55 O Hades, where is your *v*?
15:57 who gives us the *v* through our
1 Jn 5: 4 And this is the *v* that has
Rev 15: 2 and those who have the *v* over

VICTUAL, VICTUALS (KJV) See FOOD, PROVISIONS, RATIONS, SUSTENANCE

VIEW (3/3)

Gen 20:10 "What did you have in *v*,
Deut 32:49 *v* the land of Canaan, which I
Josh 2: 1 *v* the land, especially

VIEWED (3/3)

Neh 2:13 and *v* the walls of Jerusalem
2:15 and *v* the wall; then I turned
Ps 102:19 From heaven the LORD *v* the

VIGIL (1/1)

Job 21:32 And a *v* kept over the tomb.

VIGILANT (2/2)

Col 4: 2 being *v* in it with
1 Pe 5: 8 Be sober, be *v*;

VIGOR (4/4)

Deut 34: 7 were not dim nor his natural *v*
Job 20:11 are full of his youthful *v*,
30: 2 Their *v* has perished.
Dan 10: 8 for my *v* was turned to frailty

VIGOROUS (1/1)

Ps 38:19 But my enemies are *v*,

VIGOROUSLY (1/1)

Acts 18:28 for he *v* refuted the Jews

VILE (11/11)

Judg 19:24 man do not do such a *v* thing.
1 Sam 3:13 his sons made themselves *v*,
Job 30: 8 Yes, sons of *v* men;
40: 4 "Behold, I am *v*;
Ps 15: 4 In whose eyes a *v* person is
Jer 15:19 out the precious from the *v*,
Lam 1: 8 Therefore she has become *v*.
Dan 11:21 place shall arise a *v* person
Nah 1:14 dig your grave, For you are *v*.
3: 6 filth upon you, Make you *v*,
Rom 1:26 God gave them up to *v* passions

VILENESS (2/2)

Judg 20:10 they may repay all the *v* that
Ps 12: 8 When *v* is exalted among the

VILLAGE (11/11) VILLAGES

Judg 5: 7 *V* life ceased, it ceased in
Mt 21: 2 'Go into the *v* opposite you,
Mk 11: 2 'Go into the *v* opposite you;
Lk 8: 1 went through every city and *v*,
9:52 they entered a *v* of the
9:56 And they went to another *v*.
10:38 that He entered a certain *v*;
17:12 Then as He entered a certain *v*,
19:30 Go into the *v* opposite you,
24:13 traveling that same day to a *v*
24:28 Then they drew near to the *v*

VILLAGERS (1/1)

Judg 5:11 The righteous acts for His *v*

VILLAGES (87/73)

Lev 25:31 However the houses of *v* which
Num 21:25 in Heshbon and in all its *v*.
21:32 and they took its *v* and drove
32:42 went and took Kenath and its *v*,
Deut 2:23 who dwelt in *v* as far as
Josh 13:23 the cities and their *v*.
13:28 the cities and their *v*.
15:32 are twenty-nine, with their *v*.
15:36 fourteen cities with their *v*;
15:41 sixteen cities with their *v*;
15:44 nine cities with their *v*;
15:45 Ekron, with its towns and *v*;
15:46 lay near Ashdod, with their *v*;
15:47 Ashdod with its towns and *v*,
15:47 Gaza with its towns and *v*—
15:51 eleven cities with their *v*;
15:54 Zior: nine cities with their *v*;
15:57 Timnah: ten cities with their *v*;
15:59 six cities with their *v*;
15:60 Rabbah: two cities with their *v*.
15:62 Gedi: six cities with their *v*.
16: 9 all the cities with their *v*.
18:24 twelve cities with their *v*;
18:28 fourteen cities with their *v*.
19: 6 thirteen cities and their *v*;
19: 7 Ashan: four cities and their *v*;
19: 8 and all the *v* that were all
19:15 twelve cities with their *v*.
19:16 these cities with their *v*.
19:22 sixteen cities with their *v*.
19:23 the cities and their *v*.
19:30 twenty-two cities with their *v*.
19:31 these cities with their *v*.
19:38 nineteen cities with their *v*.
19:39 the cities and their *v*.
19:48 these cities with their *v*.
21:12 fields of the city and its *v*
Judg 1:27 of Beth Shean and its *v*,
1:27 villages, or Taanach and its *v*,
1:27 inhabitants of Dor and its *v*,
1:27 inhabitants of Ibleam and its *v*,
1:27 of Megiddo and its *v*;
11:26 dwelt in Heshbon and its *v*,
11:26 villages, in Aroer and its *v*,
1 Sam 6:18 fortified cities and country *v*,
1 Chr 4:32 And their *v* were Etam, Ain,
4:33 and all the *v* that were around
5:16 Gilead, in Bashan and in its *v*,
6:56 fields of the city and its *v*
9:16 who lived in the *v* of the
9:22 by their genealogy, in their *v*.
9:25 And their brethren in their *v*
27:25 field, in the cities, in the *v*,
2 Chr 13:19 Bethel with its *v*,
13:19 villages, Jeshanah with its *v*,
13:19 and Ephrain with its *v*.
28:18 Gederoth, Sochoh with its *v*,
28:18 its villages, Timnah with its *v*,
28:18 villages, and Gimzo with its *v*;
Neh 6: 2 us meet together among the *v*
11:25 And as for the *v* with their
11:25 dwelt in Kirjath Arba and its *v*,
11:25 its villages, Dibon and its *v*,
11:25 villages, Jekabzeel and its *v*;
11:27 Shual, and Beersheba and its *v*;
11:28 in Ziklag and Meconah and its *v*;
11:30 Zanoah, Adullam, and their *v*;
11:30 its fields; in Azekah and its *v*.
11:31 Aija, and Bethel, and their *v*;
12:28 from the *v* of the
12:29 singers had built themselves *v*
Esth 9:19 Therefore the Jews of the *v* who
Ps 10: 8 in the lurking places of the *v*;
Song 7:11 Let us lodge in the *v*.
Isa 42:11 The *v* that Kedar inhabits.
Jer 49: 2 And her *v* shall be burned with
Ezek 26: 6 Also her daughter *v* which are
26: 8 the sword your daughter *v* in
38:11 up against a land of unwalled *v*;
Hab 3:14 own arrows The head of his *v*.
Mt 9:35 went about all the cities and *v*,
14:15 that they may go into the *v* and
Mk 6: 6 Then He went about the *v* in a
6:36 the surrounding country and *v*
6:56 Wherever He entered into *v*,
Lk 13:22 went through the cities and *v*,
Acts 8:25 preaching the gospel in many *v*

VINDICATE (4/4) VINDICATED, VINDICATES

Ps 26: 1 *V* me, O LORD, For I have
35:24 *V* me, O LORD my God, according
43: 1 *V* me, O God, And plead my
54: 1 And *v* me by Your strength.

VINDICATED (2/2) VINDICATE

Job 11: 2 should a man full of talk be *v*?
13:18 case, I know that I shall be *v*.

VINDICATES (1/1) VINDICATE

Gen 20:16 indeed this *v* you before all

VINDICATION (3/3)

Ps 17: 2 Let my *v* come from Your
35:23 up Yourself, and awake to my *v*,
2 Cor 7:11 what *v*! In all things you

VINE (60/55) GRAPEVINE, VINEDRESSER, VINES, VINEYARD

Gen 40: 9 in my dream a *v* was before me,
40:10 and in the *v* were three
49:11 Binding his donkey to the *v*,
49:11 donkey's colt to the choice *v*,
Lev 25: 5 the grapes of your untended *v*,
25:11 the grapes of your untended *v*.
Deut 32:32 For their *v* is of the vine of
32:32 For their vine is of the *v* of
Judg 9:12 "Then the trees said to the *v*,
9:13 But the *v* said to them,
13:14 anything that comes from the *v*,
1 Ki 4:25 each man under his *v* and his
2 Ki 4:39 herbs, and found a wild *v*,
18:31 one of you eat from his own *v*
Job 15:33 off his unripe grape like a *v*,
Ps 80: 8 You have brought a *v* out of
80:14 And visit this *v*
128: 3 shall be like a fruitful *v*
Song 6:11 To see whether the *v* had
7: 8 be like clusters of the *v*,
7:12 Let us see if the *v* has
Isa 5: 2 planted it with the choicest *v*.
16: 8 And the *v* of Sibmah;
16: 9 Therefore I will bewail the *v*
24: 7 the *v* languishes, All the
32:12 fields, for the fruitful *v*.
34: 4 As the leaf falls from the *v*,
36:16 one of you eat from his own *v*
Jer 2:21 I had planted you a noble *v*,
2:21 degenerate plant of an alien *v*?
6: 9 shall thoroughly glean as a *v*
8:13 grapes shall be on the *v*,
48:32 O *v* of Sibmah! I will weep for
Ezek 15: 2 how is the wood of the *v*
15: 2 the *v* branch which is among the
15: 6 Like the wood of the *v* among the
17: 6 grew and became a spreading *v*
17: 6 So it became a *v*,
17: 7 this *v* bent its roots toward
17: 8 And become a majestic *v*.
19:10 Your mother was like a *v* in
Hos 10: 1 Israel empties his *v*;
14: 7 like grain, And grow like a *v*.
Joel 1: 7 He has laid waste My *v*,
1:12 The *v* has dried up, And the
2:22 The fig tree and the *v* yield
Mic 4: 4 everyone shall sit under his *v*
Nah 2: 2 them out And ruined their *v*

Hag 2:19 As yet the *v*, the fig tree,
Zech 3:10 his neighbor Under his *v* and
8:12 The *v* shall give its fruit,
Mal 3:11 Nor shall the *v* fail to bear
Mt 26:29 drink of this fruit of the *v*
Mk 14:25 drink of the fruit of the *v*
Lk 22:18 not drink of the fruit of the *v*
Jn 15: 1 "I am the true *v*,
15: 4 unless it abides in the *v*,
15: 5 'I am the *v*, you are the
Rev 14:18 gather the clusters of the *v*
14:19 the earth and gathered the *v*

VINEDRESSER (1/1) VINE, VINEDRESSERS

Jn 15: 1 vine, and My Father is the *v*.

VINEDRESSERS (21/19) VINEDRESSER

2 Ki 25:12 of the poor of the land as *v*
2 Chr 26:10 he also had farmers and *v* in
Isa 61: 5 be your plowmen and your *v*.
Jer 52:16 of the poor of the land as *v*
Joel 1:11 you farmers, Wail, you *v*,
Mt 21:33 And he leased it to *v* and went
21:34 he sent his servants to the *v*,
21:35 And the *v* took his servants,
21:38 But when the *v* saw the son, they
21:40 what will he do to those *v*?
21:41 lease his vineyard to other *v*
Mk 12: 1 And he leased it to *v* and went
12: 2 he sent a servant to the *v*,
12: 2 of the vineyard from the *v*.
12: 7 But those *v* said among
12: 9 He will come and destroy the *v*,
Lk 20: 9 a vineyard, leased it to *v*,
20:10 he sent a servant to the *v*,
20:10 But the *v* beat him and sent
20:14 But when the *v* saw him, they
20:16 will come and destroy those *v*

VINEGAR (6/5)

Num 6: 3 he shall drink neither *v* made
6: 3 vinegar made from wine nor *v*
Ruth 2:14 your piece of bread in the *v*.
Ps 69:21 for my thirst they gave me *v*
Prov 10:26 As *v* to the teeth and smoke to
25:20 And like *v* on soda, Is one

VINES (12/11) VINE

Num 20: 5 a place of grain or figs or *v*
Deut 8: 8 of *v* and fig trees and
Ps 78:47 He destroyed their *v* with hail,
105:33 He struck their *v* also,
Song 2:13 And the *v* with the tender
2:15 little foxes that spoil the *v*,
2:15 For our *v* have tender grapes.
Isa 7:23 there could be a thousand *v*
Jer 5:17 They shall eat up your *v* and
31: 5 You shall yet plant *v* on the
Hos 2:12 And I will destroy her *v* and her
Hab 3:17 blossom, Nor fruit be on the *v*;

VINEYARD (70/60) VINE, VINEYARDS

Gen 9:20 a farmer, and he planted a *v*.
Ex 22: 5 If a man causes a field or *v* to
22: 5 field and the best of his own *v*.
23:11 you shall do with your *v* and
Lev 19:10 'And you shall not glean your *v*,
19:10 gather every grape of your *v*;
25: 3 years you shall prune your *v*,
25: 4 sow your field nor prune your *v*.
Deut 20: 6 is there who has planted a *v*
22: 9 You shall not sow your *v* with
22: 9 sown and the fruit of your *v*
23:24 you come into your neighbor's *v*,
24:21 you gather the grapes of your *v*,
28:30 in it; you shall plant a *v*,
1 Ki 21: 1 Naboth the Jezreelite had a *v*
21: 2 saying, "Give me your *v*,
21: 2 and for it I will give you a *v*
21: 6 'Give me your *v* for money;
21: 6 I will give you another *v* for
21: 6 'I will not give you my *v*.
21: 7 I will give you the *v* of Naboth
21:15 take possession of the *v* of
21:16 to take possession of the *v* of
21:18 in the *v* of Naboth, where he
Job 24: 6 the field And glean in the *v*
Ps 80:15 And the *v* which Your right hand
Prov 24:30 And by the *v* of the man devoid
31:16 her profits she plants a *v*.
Song 1: 6 But my own *v* I have not kept.
8:11 Solomon had a *v* at Baal Hamon;
8:11 He leased the *v* to keepers;
8:12 My own *v* is before me.
Isa 1: 8 Zion is left as a booth in a *v*,
3:14 "For you have eaten up the *v*;
5: 1 of my Beloved regarding His *v*:
5: 1 My Well-beloved has a *v* On a
5: 3 please, between Me and My *v*.
5: 4 could have been done to My *v*
5: 5 tell you what I will do to My *v*:
5: 7 For the *v* of the LORD of hosts
5:10 For ten acres of *v* shall yield
27: 2 A *v* of red wine!
Jer 12:10 rulers have destroyed My *v*,
35: 7 a house, sow seed, plant a *v*,
35: 9 to dwell in; nor do we have *v*,
Mic 1: 6 field, Places for planting a *v*;
Mt 20: 1 to hire laborers for his *v*.
20: 2 a day, he sent them into his *v*.
20: 4 them, 'You also go into the *v*,
20: 7 them, 'You also go into the *v*,
20: 8 the owner of the *v* said to his
21:28 'Son, go, work today in my *v*.
21:33 landowner who planted a *v* and
21:39 him and cast him out of the *v*
21:40 when the owner of the *v* comes,
21:41 and lease his *v* to other
Mk 12: 1 A man planted a *v* and set a
12: 2 some of the fruit of the *v*
12: 8 him and cast him out of the *v*.
12: 9 what will the owner of the *v*
12: 9 and give the *v* to others.
Lk 13: 6 had a fig tree planted in his *v*,
13: 7 he said to the keeper of his *v*,
20: 9 "A certain man planted a *v*,
20:10 him some of the fruit of the *v*.
20:13 Then the owner of the *v* said,
20:15 So they cast him out of the *v*
20:15 what will the owner of the *v*
20:16 vinedressers and give the *v* to
1 Cor 9: 7 Who plants a *v* and does not eat

VINEYARDS (43/42) VINEYARD

Num 16:14 us inheritance of fields and *v*.
20:17 not pass through fields or *v*,
21:22 not turn aside into fields or *v*;
22:24 in a narrow path between the *v*,
Deut 6:11 *v* and olive trees which you did
28:39 You shall plant *v* and tend
Josh 24:13 you eat of the *v* and olive
Judg 9:27 gathered grapes from their *v*
14: 5 and came to the *v* of Timnah.
15: 5 as well as the *v* and olive
21:20 "Go, lie in wait in the *v*,
21:21 then come out from the *v*,
1 Sam 8:14 the best of your fields, your *v*,
22: 7 every one of you fields and *v*,
2 Ki 5:26 clothing, olive groves and *v*,
18:32 new wine, a land of bread and *v*,
19:29 Plant *v* and eat the fruit of
1 Chr 27:27 the Ramathite was over the *v*,
27:27 was over the produce of the *v*
Neh 5: 3 have mortgaged our lands and *v*
5: 4 king's tax on our lands and *v*.
5: 5 other men have our lands and *v*.
5:11 this day, their lands, their *v*,
9:25 Cisterns already dug, *v*,
Job 24:18 turn into the way of their *v*.
Ps 107:37 And sow fields and plant *v*,
Eccl 2: 4 houses, and planted myself *v*.
Song 1: 6 made me the keeper of the *v*,
1:14 of henna blooms In the *v* of
7:12 Let us get up early to the *v*;
Isa 16:10 In the *v* there will be no
36:17 new wine, a land of bread and *v*.
37:30 Plant *v* and eat the fruit of
65:21 They shall plant *v* and eat
Jer 32:15 Houses and fields and *v* shall be
39:10 and gave them *v* and fields at
Ezek 28:26 build houses, and plant *v*;
Hos 2:15 I will give her her *v* from
Am 4: 9 your gardens increased, Your *v*,
5:11 You have planted pleasant *v*,
5:17 In all *v* there shall be
9:14 They shall plant *v* and drink
Zeph 1:13 They shall plant *v*,

VINTAGE (8/7)

Lev 26: 5 shall last till the time of *v*,
26: 5 and the *v* shall last till the
Judg 8: 2 of Ephraim better than the *v*
1 Sam 8:15 tenth of your grain and your *v*,
Isa 24:13 gleaning of grapes when the *v*
32:10 For the *v* will fail,
Jer 48:32 on your summer fruit and your *v*.
Mic 7: 1 Like those who glean *v* grapes;

VINTAGE-TIME (3/3)

Mt 21:34 Now when *v* drew near, he sent
Mk 12: 2 Now at *v* he sent a servant to
Lk 20:10 Now at *v* he sent a servant to

VIOLATE (1/1)

Ezek 22:10 in you they *v* women who are set

VIOLATED (2/2)

Gen 34: 2 lay with her, and *v* her.
Ezek 22:26 Her priests have *v* My law and

VIOLATES (1/1)

Ezek 22:11 and another in you *v* his

VIOLENCE (60/59) VIOLENT

Gen 6:11 and the earth was filled with *v*.
6:13 for the earth is filled with *v*
2 Sam 22: 3 My Savior, You save me from *v*.
Job 16:17 Although no *v* is in my hands,
Ps 11: 5 wicked and the one who loves *v*
27:12 And such as breathe out *v*.
55: 9 For I have seen *v* and strife
58: 2 You weigh out the *v* of your
72:14 life from oppression and *v*;
73: 6 *V* covers them like a garment.
Prov 4:17 And drink the wine of *v*.
10: 6 But *v* covers the mouth of the
10:11 But *v* covers the mouth of the
13: 2 of the unfaithful feeds on *v*.
21: 7 The *v* of the wicked will
24: 2 For their heart devises *v*,
26: 6 his own feet and drinks *v*.
Isa 53: 9 Because He had done no *v*,
59: 6 And the act of *v* is in their
60:18 *V* shall no longer be heard in
Jer 6: 7 *V* and plundering are heard in
20: 8 *V* and plunder!" Because the
22: 3 Do no wrong and do no *v* to the
22:17 practicing oppression and *v*.
51:35 Let the *v* done to me and my
51:46 And *v* in the land,
Lam 2: 6 He has done *v* to His
Ezek 7:11 *V* has risen up into a rod of
7:23 And the city is full of *v*.
8:17 have filled the land with *v*;
12:19 because of the *v* of all those
18: 7 Has robbed no one by *v*,
18:12 poor and needy, Robbed by *v*,
18:16 Nor robbed by *v*,
18:18 Robbed his brother by *v*,
28:16 You became filled with *v*
45: 9 O princes of Israel! Remove *v*
Joel 3:19 Because of *v* against the
Am 3:10 Who store up *v* and robbery in
6: 3 Who cause the seat of *v* to
Ob 10 For *v* against your brother
Jon 3: 8 his evil way and from the *v*
Mic 2: 2 fields and take them by *v*,
6:12 For her rich men are full of *v*,
Hab 1: 2 *V*!" And You will not save.
1: 3 For plundering and *v* are
1: 9 "They all come for *v*;
2: 8 of men's blood And the *v* of
2:17 For the *v* done to Lebanon
2:17 of men's blood And the *v* of
Zeph 1: 9 their masters' houses with *v*
3: 4 They have done *v* to the law.
Mal 2:16 it covers one's garment with *v*,
Mt 11:12 the kingdom of heaven suffers *v*,
Acts 5:26 and brought them without *v*,
21:35 the soldiers because of the *v*
24: 7 came by and with great *v* took
27:41 was being broken up by the *v*
Heb 11:34 quenched the *v* of fire, escaped
Rev 18:21 Thus with *v* the great city

VIOLENT (16/16) VIOLENCE, VIOLENTLY

2 Sam 22:49 have delivered me from the *v*
Ps 7:16 And his *v* dealing shall come
18:48 have delivered me from the *v*
86:14 And a mob of *v* men have
140: 1 Preserve me from *v* men,
140: 4 Preserve me from *v* men, Who
140:11 Let evil hunt the *v* man to
Prov 16:29 A *v* man entices his neighbor,
Eccl 5: 8 and the *v* perversion of justice
Jer 23:19 A *v* whirlwind! It will fall
Dan 11:14 *v* men of your people shall
Mt 11:12 and the *v* take it by force.
Acts 14: 5 And when a *v* attempt was made by
Rom 1:30 backbiters, haters of God, *v*,
1 Tim 3: 3 not given to wine, not *v*,
Titus 1: 7 not given to wine, not *v*,

VIOLENTLY (12/12) VIOLENT

Deut 28:31 your donkey shall be *v* taken
Job 20:19 He has *v* seized a house which
24: 2 They seize flocks *v* and feed
Ps 118:13 You pushed me *v*,
Isa 22:17 the LORD will throw you away *v*,
22:18 He will surely turn *v* and toss
24:19 The earth is *v* broken,
Jer 23:19 It will fall *v* on the head of
30:23 *v* on the head of the wicked.
Mt 8:32 the whole herd of swine ran *v*
Mk 5:13 and the herd ran *v* down the
Lk 8:33 herd ran *v* down the steep

VIOLS (KJV) See (STRINGED) INSTRUMENTS

VIPER (6/6) VIPER'S, VIPERS

Gen 49:17 A *v* by the path, That bites
Prov 23:32 a serpent, And stings like a *v*.
Isa 14:29 roots will come forth a *v*,
30: 6 The *v* and fiery flying
59: 5 from that which is crushed a *v*
Acts 28: 3 a *v* came out because of the

VIPER'S (2/2) VIPER

Job 20:16 The *v* tongue will slay him.
Isa 11: 8 put his hand in the *v* den.

VIPERS (5/5) VIPER

Jer 8:17 *V* which cannot be charmed,
Mt 3: 7 Brood of *v*! Who warned you to
12:34 Brood of *v*! How can you, being
23:33 brood of *v*! How can you escape
Lk 3: 7 Brood of *v*! Who warned you to

VIPERS' (1/1)

Isa	59: 5	They hatch *v* eggs and weave the

VIRGIN (44/44) VIRGINITY, VIRGIN'S

Gen	24:16	very beautiful to behold, a *v*;
	24:43	come to pass that when the *v*
Ex	22:16	If a man entices a *v* who is not
Lev	21: 3	also his *v* sister who is near to
	21:14	but he shall take a *v* of his
Deut	22:14	to her I found she was not a *v*,
	22:17	your daughter was not a *v*,
	22:19	has brought a bad name on a *v*
	22:23	a young woman who is a *v*
	22:28	a young woman who is a *v*,
	32:25	within For the young man and *v*,
Judg	19:24	here is my *v* daughter and
2 Sam	13: 2	became sick; for she was a *v*.
	13:18	for the king's *v* daughters wore
1 Ki	1: 2	'Let a young woman, a *v*,
2 Ki	19:21	spoken concerning him: 'The *v*,
2 Chr	36:17	no compassion on young man or *v*,
Prov	30:19	And the way of a man with a *v*.
Isa	7:14	the *v* shall conceive and bear a
	23:12	O you oppressed *v* daughter of
	37:22	'The *v*, the daughter of Zion,
	47: 1	O *v* daughter of Babylon; Sit
	62: 5	as a young man marries a *v*,
Jer	2:32	Can a *v* forget her ornaments,
	14:17	For the *v* daughter of my
	18:13	The *v* of Israel has done a
	31: 4	O *v* of Israel! You shall
	31:13	Then shall the *v* rejoice in the
	31:21	O *v* of Israel, Turn back to
	46:11	to Gilead and take balm, O *v*,
Lam	1:15	as in a winepress The *v*
	2:13	O *v* daughter of Zion?
Ezek	23: 3	Their *v* bosom was there
	23: 8	Pressed her *v* bosom,
Joel	1: 8	Lament like a *v* girded with
Am	5: 2	The *v* of Israel has fallen;
Mt	1:23	the *v* shall be with
Lk	1:27	to a *v* betrothed to a man whose
Acts	21: 9	Now this man had four *v*
1 Cor	7:28	and if a *v* marries, she has not
	7:34	between a wife and a *v*.
	7:36	improperly toward his *v*,
	7:37	heart that he will keep his *v*,
2 Cor	11: 2	present you as a chaste *v* to

VIRGIN'S (1/1) VIRGIN

Lk	1:27	The *v* name was Mary.

VIRGINITY (7/7) VIRGIN

Lev	21:13	he shall take a wife in her *v*.
Deut	22:15	of the young woman's *v* to the
	22:17	evidences of my daughter's *v*.
	22:20	and evidences of *v* are not
Judg	11:37	the mountains and bewail my *v*,
	11:38	and bewailed her *v* on the
Lk	2:36	husband seven years from her *v*;

VIRGINS (21/21) VIRGIN

Ex	22:17	to the bride-price of *v*.
Judg	21:12	Gilead four hundred young *v*
Esth	2: 2	Let beautiful young *v* be sought
	2: 3	all the beautiful young *v* to
	2:17	his sight more than all the *v*;
	2:19	When *v* were gathered together a
Ps	45:14	The *v*, her companions who
Song	1: 3	Therefore the *v* love you.
	6: 8	And *v* without number.
Isa	23: 4	young men, Nor bring up *v*.
Lam	1: 4	Her *v* are afflicted, And she
	1:18	My *v* and my young men Have
	2:10	The *v* of Jerusalem Bow their
	2:21	My *v* and my young men Have
Ezek	44:22	but take *v* of the descendants
Am	8:13	In that day the fair *v* And
Mt	25: 1	shall be likened to ten *v* who
	25: 7	Then all those *v* arose and
	25:11	Afterward the other *v* came also,
1 Cor	7:25	Now concerning *v*:
Rev	14: 4	with women, for they are *v*.

VIRTUE (4/3) VIRTUOUS

Phil	4: 8	if there is any *v* and if
2 Pe	1: 3	who called us by glory and *v*,
	1: 5	diligence, add to your faith *v*,
	1: 5	to *v* knowledge,

VIRTUOUS (2/2) VIRTUE

Ruth	3:11	know that you are a *v* woman.
Prov	31:10	Who can find a *v* wife?

VISAGE (1/1) VISION

Isa	52:14	So His *v* was marred more than

VISIBLE (2/2) VISION

Col	1:16	*v* and invisible, whether
Heb	11: 3	not made of things which are *v*.

VISION (77/71) VISAGE, VISIBLE, VISIONS

Gen	15: 1	the LORD came to Abram in a *v*,
Num	12: 6	make Myself known to him in a *v*;
	24: 4	Who sees the *v* of the
	24:16	Who sees the *v* of the
1 Sam	3:15	was afraid to tell Eli the *v*.
2 Sam	7:17	and according to all this *v*,
1 Chr	17:15	and according to all this *v*,
2 Chr	32:32	they are written in the *v* of
Job	20: 8	he will be chased away like a *v*
	33:15	in a *v* of the night, When deep
Ps	89:19	Then You spoke in a *v* to Your
Isa	1: 1	The *v* of Isaiah the son of
	21: 2	A distressing *v* is declared to
	22: 1	burden against the Valley of *V*.
	22: 5	of hosts In the Valley of *V*—
	28: 7	They err in *v*,
	29: 7	be as a dream of a night *v*.
	29:11	The whole *v* has become to you
Jer	14:14	they prophesy to you a false *v*,
	23:16	They speak a *v* of their own
Lam	2: 9	And her prophets find no *v*
Ezek	7:13	For the *v* concerns the whole
	7:26	Then they will seek a *v* from a
	8: 4	like the *v* that I saw in the
	11:24	me up and brought me in a *v* by
	11:24	And the *v* that I had seen went
	12:22	and every *v* fails'?
	12:23	and the fulfillment of every *v*.
	12:24	shall there be any false *v* or
	12:27	The *v* that he sees is for many
	13: 7	"Have you not seen a futile *v*,
	43: 3	like the appearance of the *v*
	43: 3	like the *v* which I saw when I
	43: 3	The visions were like the *v*
Dan	2:19	revealed to Daniel in a night *v*.
	7: 2	'I saw in my *v* by night,
	8: 1	reign of King Belshazzar a *v*
	8: 2	I saw in the *v*,
	8: 2	and I saw in the *v* that I was
	8:13	How long will the *v* be,
	8:15	had seen the *v* and was seeking
	8:16	make this man understand the *v*.
	8:17	that the *v* refers to the time
	8:26	And the *v* of the evenings and
	8:26	Therefore seal up the *v*,
	8:27	I was astonished by the *v*,
	9:21	whom I had seen in the *v* at the
	9:23	and understand the *v*:
	9:24	To seal up *v* and prophecy,
	10: 1	and had understanding of the *v*.
	10: 7	And I, Daniel, alone saw the *v*,
	10: 7	were with me did not see the *v*;
	10: 8	alone when I saw this great *v*,
	10:14	for the *v* refers to many days
	10:16	because of the *v* my sorrows
	11:14	in fulfillment of the *v*,
Ob	1	The *v* of Obadiah. Thus says
Mic	3: 6	you shall have night without *v*,
Nah	1: 1	The book of the *v* of Nahum the
Hab	2: 2	Write the *v* And make it plain
	2: 3	For the *v* is yet for an
Zech	13: 4	will be ashamed of his *v* when
Mt	17: 9	Tell the *v* to no one until the
Lk	1:22	perceived that he had seen a *v*
	24:23	that they had also seen a *v* of
Acts	9:10	and to him the Lord said in a *v*,
	9:12	And in a *v* he has seen a man
	10: 3	the day he saw clearly in a *v*
	10:17	within himself what this *v*
	10:19	While Peter thought about the *v*,
	11: 5	and in a trance I saw a *v*,
	12: 9	but thought he was seeing a *v*.
	16: 9	And a *v* appeared to Paul in the
	16:10	Now after he had seen the *v*,
	18: 9	to Paul in the night by a *v*,
	26:19	disobedient to the heavenly *v*,
Rev	9:17	thus I saw the horses in the *v*:

VISIONS (27/27) VISION

Gen	46: 2	God spoke to Israel in the *v*
2 Chr	9:29	and in the *v* of Iddo the seer
	26: 5	who had understanding in the *v*
Job	4:13	thoughts from the *v* of the
	7:14	dreams And terrify me with *v*,
Lam	2:14	for you False and deceptive *v*;
Ezek	1: 1	were opened and I saw *v* of God.
	8: 3	and brought me in *v* of God to
	13:16	and who see *v* of peace for her
	21:29	While they see false *v* for you,
	22:28	mortar, seeing false *v*,
	40: 2	In the *v* of God He took me into
	43: 3	The *v* were like the vision
Dan	1:17	had understanding in all *v* and
	2:28	and the *v* of your head upon
	4: 5	thoughts on my bed and the *v*
	4: 9	explain to me the *v* of my dream
	4:10	These were the *v* of my head
	4:13	I saw in the *v* of my head
	7: 1	Daniel had a dream and *v* of his
	7: 7	this I saw in the night *v*,
	7:13	was watching in the night *v*,
	7:15	and the *v* of my head troubled
Hos	12:10	And have multiplied *v*;
Joel	2:28	Your young men shall see *v*.
Acts	2:17	young men shall see *v*,
2 Cor	12: 1	I will come to *v* and

VISIT (27/26) VISITATION, VISITED, VISITING

Gen	50:24	but God will surely *v* you,
	50:25	God will surely *v* you, and you
Ex	13:19	God will surely *v* you, and you
	32:34	in the day when I *v* for
	32:34	I will *v* punishment upon them
Lev	18:25	therefore I *v* the punishment of
1 Ki	22: 2	king of Judah went down to *v*
2 Chr	18: 2	some years he went down to *v*
Job	5:24	You shall *v* your dwelling and
	7:18	That You should *v* him every
Ps	8: 4	And the son of man that You *v*
	65: 9	You *v* the earth and water it,
	80:14	And *v* this vine
	106: 4	*v* me with Your salvation,
Isa	23:17	that the LORD will *v* Tyre.
Jer	3:16	nor shall they *v* it, nor shall
	15:15	Remember me and *v* me,
	27:22	be until the day that I *v* them,
	29:10	I will *v* you and perform My
	32: 5	and there he shall be until I *v*
Am	3:14	I will also *v* destruction on
Zech	10: 3	For the LORD of hosts will *v*
Mt	25:43	in prison and you did not *v* Me.
Acts	7:23	it came into his heart to *v* his
	15:36	Let us now go back and *v* our
	24:23	his friends to provide for or *v*
Jas	1:27	to *v* orphans and widows in

VISITATION (2/2) VISIT

Lk	19:44	did not know the time of your *v*.
1 Pe	2:12	glorify God in the day of *v*.

VISITED (17/17) VISIT

Gen	21: 1	And the LORD *v* Sarah as He had
	38: 1	and *v* a certain Adullamite
Ex	3:16	I have surely *v* you and seen
	4:31	heard that the LORD had *v* the
Num	16:29	or if they are *v* by the common
Judg	15: 1	it happened that Samson *v* his
Ruth	1: 6	of Moab that the LORD had *v*
1 Sam	2:21	And the LORD *v* Hannah, so that
Ps	17: 3	You have *v* me in the night;
Prov	19:23	He will not be *v* with evil.
Isa	26:16	in trouble they have *v* You,
Ezek	38: 8	"After many days you will be *v*.
Mt	25:36	I was sick and you *v* Me;
Lk	1:68	For He has *v* and redeemed His
	1:78	Dayspring from on high has *v*
	7:16	God has *v* His people."
Acts	15:14	how God at the first *v* the

VISITING (4/4) VISIT

Ex	20: 5	*v* the iniquity of the fathers
	34: 7	*v* the iniquity of the fathers
Num	14:18	*v* the iniquity of the fathers
Deut	5: 9	*v* the iniquity of the fathers

VISITOR (1/1)

Gen	23: 4	I am a foreigner and a *v* among

VISITORS (1/1)

Acts	2:10	*v* from Rome, both Jews and

VITALITY (1/1)

Ps	32: 4	My *v* was turned into the

VOCATION (KJV) See CALLING

VOICE (458/422) SOUND, VOICES

Gen	3:10	I heard Your *v* in the garden,
	3:17	Because you have heeded the *v* of
	4:10	The *v* of your brother's blood
	4:23	"Adah and Zillah, hear my *v*;
	16: 2	And Abram heeded the *v* of
	21:12	said to you, listen to her *v*;
	21:16	and lifted her *v* and wept.
	21:17	And God heard the *v* of the lad.
	21:17	for God has heard the *v* of the
	22:18	because you have obeyed My *v*.
	26: 5	because Abraham obeyed My *v* and
	27: 8	obey my *v* according to what I
	27:13	on me, my son; only obey my *v*,
	27:22	The *v* is Jacob's voice, but the
	27:22	said, "The voice is Jacob's *v*,
	27:38	And Esau lifted up his *v* and
	27:43	therefore, my son, obey my *v*:
	29:11	and lifted up his *v* and wept.
	30: 6	and He has also heard my *v* and
	39:14	and I cried out with a loud *v*.
	39:15	he heard that I lifted my *v*
	39:18	as I lifted my *v* and cried out,
Ex	3:18	"Then they will heed your *v*;
	4: 1	believe me or listen to my *v*;
	4: 9	two signs, or listen to your *v*,
	5: 2	that I should obey His *v* to let
	15:26	If you diligently heed the *v* of
	18:19	"Listen now to my *v*;
	18:24	So Moses heeded the *v* of his
	19: 5	if you will indeed obey My *v*
	19:19	and God answered him by *v*.
	23:21	"Beware of Him and obey His *v*;
	23:22	But if you indeed obey His *v* and
	24: 3	the people answered with one *v*

Num 7:89 he heard the ***v*** of One speaking
14:22 and have not heeded My ***v***,
20:16 He heard our ***v*** and sent the
21: 3 the LORD listened to the ***v*** of
Deut 1:45 would not listen to your ***v*** nor
4:12 no form; you only heard a ***v***.
4:30 LORD your God and obey His ***v***
4:33 any people ever hear the ***v***
4:36 of heaven He let you hear His ***v***,
5:22 thick darkness, with a loud ***v***;
5:23 when you heard the ***v*** from the
5:24 and we have heard His ***v*** from
5:25 if we hear the ***v*** of the LORD
5:26 all flesh who has heard the ***v***
5:28 Then the LORD heard the ***v*** of
5:28 I have heard the ***v*** of the words
8:20 would not be obedient to the ***v***
9:23 not believe Him nor obey His ***v***.
13: 4 His commandments and obey His ***v***,
13:18 you have listened to the ***v*** of
15: 5 if you carefully obey the ***v*** of
18:16 Let me not hear again the ***v*** of
21:18 son who will not obey the ***v*** of
21:18 voice of his father or the ***v***
21:20 he will not obey our ***v***;
26: 7 and the LORD heard our ***v*** and
26:14 I have obeyed the ***v*** of the
26:17 and that you will obey His ***v***.
27:10 you shall obey the ***v***
27:14 shall speak with a loud ***v*** and
28: 1 if you diligently obey the ***v*** of
28: 2 because you obey the ***v*** of the
28:15 if you do not obey the ***v*** of the
28:45 because you did not obey the ***v***
28:62 you would not obey the ***v*** of
30: 2 LORD your God and obey His ***v***,
30: 8 And you will again obey the ***v*** of
30:10 if you obey the ***v*** of the LORD
30:20 God, that you may obey His ***v***,
33: 7 'Hear, LORD, the ***v*** of Judah,
Josh 5: 6 they did not obey the ***v*** of the
6:10 or make any noise with your ***v***,
10:14 that the LORD heeded the ***v*** of
22: 2 and have obeyed my ***v*** in all
24:24 and His ***v*** we will obey!"
Judg 2: 2 But you have not obeyed My ***v***.
2:20 and has not heeded My ***v***,
6:10 But you have not obeyed My ***v***.
9: 7 and lifted his ***v*** and cried out.
13: 9 And God listened to the ***v*** of
18: 3 they recognized the ***v*** of the
18:25 Do not let your ***v*** be heard among
20:13 would not listen to the ***v*** of
1 Sam 1:13 but her ***v*** was not heard.
2:25 they did not heed the ***v*** of
8: 7 Heed the ***v*** of the people in all
8: 9 "Now therefore, heed their ***v***.
8:19 people refused to obey the ***v***
8:22 said to Samuel, "Heed their ***v***,
12: 1 Indeed I have heeded your ***v*** in
12:14 and serve Him and obey His ***v***,
12:15 if you do not obey the ***v*** of the
15: 1 heed the ***v*** of the words of the
15:19 then did you not obey the ***v*** of
15:20 But I have obeyed the ***v*** of the
15:22 As in obeying the ***v*** of the
15:24 the people and obeyed their ***v***.
19: 6 So Saul heeded the ***v*** of
24:16 Saul said, "Is this your ***v***,
24:16 And Saul lifted up his ***v*** and
25:35 I have heeded your ***v*** and
26:17 Then Saul knew David's ***v***,
26:17 and said, "Is that your ***v***,
26:17 And David said, "It is my ***v***,
28:12 she cried out with a loud ***v***.
28:18 you did not obey the ***v***
28:21 maidservant has obeyed your ***v***,
28:22 heed also the ***v*** of your
28:23 and he heeded their ***v***.
2 Sam 3:32 and the king lifted up his ***v***
12:18 and he would not heed our ***v***.
13:14 he would not heed her ***v***;
13:36 and they lifted up their ***v*** and
15:23 the country wept with a loud ***v***,
19: 4 king cried out with a loud ***v***,
19:35 Can I hear any longer the ***v*** of
22: 7 He heard my ***v*** from His temple,
22:14 the Most High uttered His ***v***.
1 Ki 8:55 of Israel with a loud ***v***,
17:22 Then the LORD heard the ***v*** of
18:26 But there was no ***v***;
18:29 sacrifice. But there was no ***v***;
19:12 after the fire a still small ***v***.
19:13 Suddenly a ***v*** came to him,
20:25 And he listened to their ***v***
20:36 you have not obeyed the ***v*** of
2 Ki 4:31 but there was neither ***v*** nor
10: 6 are for me and will obey my ***v***,
18:12 they did not obey the ***v*** of the
18:28 and called out with a loud ***v***,
19:22 whom have you raised your ***v***,
1 Chr 15:16 by raising the ***v*** with
2 Chr 5:13 and when they lifted up their ***v***
15:14 before the LORD with a loud ***v***,
30:27 and their ***v*** was heard;
32:18 they called out with a loud ***v***
Ezra 3:12 wept with a loud ***v*** when the
10:12 answered and said with a loud ***v***,
Neh 9: 4 and cried out with a loud ***v*** to
Job 3:18 They do not hear the ***v*** of the
4:10 The ***v*** of the fierce lion,
4:16 Then I heard a ***v*** saying:
9:16 that He was listening to my ***v***.
29:10 The ***v*** of nobles was hushed,
30:31 And my flute to the ***v*** of those
37: 2 the thunder of His ***v***,
37: 4 After it a ***v*** roars;
37: 4 thunders with His majestic ***v***,
37: 4 not restrain them when His ***v***
37: 5 thunders marvelously with His ***v***;
38:34 Can you lift up your ***v*** to the
40: 9 Or can you thunder with a ***v***
Ps 3: 4 I cried to the LORD with my ***v***,
5: 2 Give heed to the ***v*** of my cry,
5: 3 My ***v*** You shall hear in the
6: 8 For the LORD has heard the ***v***
18: 6 He heard my ***v*** from His temple,
18:13 the Most High uttered His ***v***,
19: 3 nor language Where their ***v***
26: 7 I may proclaim with the ***v*** of
27: 7 when I cry with my ***v***! Have
28: 2 Hear the ***v*** of my supplications
28: 6 Because He has heard the ***v*** of
29: 3 The ***v*** of the LORD is over the
29: 4 The ***v*** of the LORD is
29: 4 The ***v*** of the LORD is full of
29: 5 The ***v*** of the LORD breaks the
29: 7 The ***v*** of the LORD divides the
29: 8 The ***v*** of the LORD shakes the
29: 9 The ***v*** of the LORD makes the
31:22 Nevertheless You heard the ***v***
42: 4 With the ***v*** of joy and praise,
44:16 Because of the ***v*** of him who
46: 6 He uttered His ***v***,
47: 1 Shout to God with the ***v*** of
55: 3 Because of the ***v*** of the enemy,
55:17 And He shall hear my ***v***.
58: 5 Which will not heed the ***v*** of
64: 1 Hear my ***v***, O God, in my
66: 8 And make the ***v*** of His praise
66:19 He has attended to the ***v*** of my
68:33 Indeed, He sends out His ***v***,
68:33 sends out His voice, a mighty ***v***.
74:23 Do not forget the ***v*** of Your
77: 1 I cried out to God with my ***v***—
77: 1 with my voice—To God with my ***v***;
77:18 The ***v*** of Your thunder was in
81:11 My people would not heed My ***v***,
86: 6 And attend to the ***v*** of my
93: 3 floods have lifted up their ***v***;
95: 7 Today, if you will hear His ***v***:
103:20 Heeding the ***v*** of His word.
104: 7 At the ***v*** of Your thunder they
106:25 And did not heed the ***v*** of the
116: 1 because He has heard My ***v*** and
118:15 The ***v*** of rejoicing and
119:149 Hear my ***v*** according to Your
130: 2 hear my ***v***! Let Your ears be
130: 2 ears be attentive To the ***v*** of
140: 6 Hear the ***v*** of my
141: 1 haste to me! Give ear to my ***v***
142: 1 cry out to the LORD with my ***v***;
142: 1 With my ***v*** to the LORD I make
Prov 1:20 She raises her ***v*** in the open
2: 3 And lift up your ***v*** for
5:13 I have not obeyed the ***v*** of my
8: 1 understanding lift up her ***v***?
8: 4 And my ***v*** is to the sons of
27:14 his friend with a loud ***v***,
Eccl 5: 3 And a fool's ***v*** is known by
10:20 of the air may carry your ***v***,
Song 2: 8 The ***v*** of my beloved!
2:12 And the ***v*** of the turtledove
2:14 your face, Let me hear your ***v***;
2:14 For your ***v*** is sweet,
5: 2 It is the ***v*** of my beloved!
8:13 companions listen for your ***v***—
Isa 6: 4 the door were shaken by the ***v***
6: 8 Also I heard the ***v*** of the Lord,
10:30 Lift up your ***v***,
13: 2 Raise your ***v*** to them;
15: 4 Their ***v*** shall be heard as far
24:14 They shall lift up their ***v***,
28:23 Give ear and hear my ***v***,
29: 4 Your ***v*** shall be like a
30:30 will cause His glorious ***v*** to
30:31 For through the ***v*** of the LORD
31: 4 will not be afraid of their ***v***
32: 9 who are at ease, Hear my ***v***;
36:13 and called out with a loud ***v***
37:23 whom have you raised your ***v***,
40: 3 The ***v*** of one crying in the
40: 6 The ***v*** said, "Cry out!"
40: 9 Lift up your ***v*** with strength,
42: 2 not cry out, nor raise His ***v***,
42: 2 Nor cause His ***v*** to be heard in
42:11 its cities lift up their ***v***,
48:20 With a ***v*** of singing,
50:10 Who obeys the ***v*** of His
51: 3 Thanksgiving and the ***v*** of
58: 1 Lift up your ***v*** like a trumpet;
58: 4 To make your ***v*** heard on high.
65:19 The ***v*** of weeping shall no
65:19 Nor the ***v*** of crying.
66: 6 A ***v*** from the temple!
66: 6 The ***v*** of the LORD, Who fully
Jer 3:13 And you have not obeyed My ***v***,
3:21 A ***v*** was heard on the desolate
3:25 And have not obeyed the ***v*** of
4:15 For a ***v*** declares from Dan And
4:16 far country And raise their ***v***
4:31 For I have heard a ***v*** as of a
4:31 The ***v*** of the daughter of Zion
6:23 Their ***v*** roars like the sea;
7:23 them, saying, 'Obey My ***v***,
7:28 that does not obey the ***v*** of
7:34 the streets of Jerusalem the ***v***
7:34 the voice of mirth and the ***v***
7:34 the ***v*** of the bridegroom and the
7:34 of the bridegroom and the ***v*** of
8:19 Listen! The ***v***, The cry of
9:10 Nor can men hear the ***v*** of the
9:13 and have not obeyed My ***v***,
9:19 For a ***v*** of wailing is heard
10:13 When He utters His ***v***,
11: 4 furnace, saying, 'Obey My ***v***,
11: 7 exhorting, saying, "Obey My ***v***.
16: 9 the ***v*** of mirth and the voice of
16: 9 the voice of mirth and the ***v*** of
16: 9 the ***v*** of the bridegroom and the
16: 9 of the bridegroom and the ***v*** of
18:10 so that it does not obey My ***v***,
18:19 And listen to the ***v*** of those
22:20 And lift up your ***v*** in Bashan;
22:21 That you did not obey My ***v***.
25:10 I will take from them the ***v*** of
25:10 the voice of mirth and the ***v***
25:10 the ***v*** of the bridegroom and the
25:10 of the bridegroom and the ***v*** of
25:30 And utter His ***v*** from His holy
25:36 A ***v*** of the cry of the
26:13 and obey the ***v*** of the LORD
30: 5 We have heard a ***v*** of trembling,
30:19 thanksgiving And the ***v*** of
31:15 A ***v*** was heard in Ramah,
31:16 Refrain your ***v*** from weeping,
32:23 they have not obeyed Your ***v*** or
33:11 the ***v*** of joy and the voice of
33:11 the voice of joy and the ***v*** of
33:11 the ***v*** of the bridegroom and the
33:11 of the bridegroom and the ***v*** of
33:11 the ***v*** of those who will say:
35: 8 Thus we have obeyed the ***v*** of
38:20 obey the ***v*** of the LORD which I
40: 3 the LORD, and not obeyed His ***v***,
42: 6 we will obey the ***v*** of the LORD
42: 6 with us when we obey the ***v*** of
42:13 disobeying the ***v*** of the LORD
42:21 but you have not obeyed the ***v***
43: 4 people would not obey the ***v*** of
43: 7 for they did not obey the ***v*** of
44:23 and have not obeyed the ***v*** of
48: 3 A ***v*** of crying shall be from
48:34 They have uttered their ***v***,
50:28 The ***v*** of those who flee and
50:42 Their ***v*** shall roar like the
51:16 When He utters His ***v***—
51:55 And silencing her loud ***v***,
51:55 And the noise of their ***v*** is
Lam 3:56 You have heard my ***v***:
Ezek 1:24 like the ***v*** of the Almighty, a
1:25 A ***v*** came from above the
1:28 and I heard a ***v*** of One
3:12 behind me a great thunderous ***v***:
8:18 cry in My ears with a loud ***v***,
9: 1 out in my hearing with a loud ***v***,
10: 5 like the ***v*** of Almighty God when
11:13 my face and cried with a loud ***v***,
19: 9 That his ***v*** should no longer be
21:22 to lift the ***v*** with shouting,
27:30 They will make their ***v*** heard
33:32 of one who has a pleasant ***v***
43: 2 His ***v*** was like the sound of
Dan 4:31 a ***v*** fell from heaven: "King
6:20 he cried out with a lamenting ***v***
8:16 And I heard a man's ***v*** between
9:10 We have not obeyed the ***v*** of the
9:11 so as not to obey Your ***v***;
9:14 though we have not obeyed His ***v***.
10: 6 sound of his words like the ***v***
Joel 2:11 The LORD gives ***v*** before His
3:16 And utter His ***v*** from
Am 1: 2 And utters His ***v*** from
Jon 2: 2 I cried, And You heard my ***v***.
2: 9 sacrifice to You With the ***v***
Mic 6: 1 And let the hills hear your ***v***.
6: 9 The LORD's ***v*** cries to the
Nah 2: 7 shall lead her as with the ***v***
2:13 and the ***v*** of your messengers
Hab 3:10 The deep uttered its ***v***,
3:16 My lips quivered at the ***v***;
Zeph 2:14 Their ***v*** shall sing in the
3: 2 She has not obeyed His ***v***,
Hag 1:12 obeyed the ***v*** of the LORD their
Zech 6:15 if you diligently obey the ***v***
Mt 2:18 A ***v*** was heard in Ramah,
3: 3 The ***v*** of one crying in the
3:17 And suddenly a ***v*** came from
12:19 will anyone hear His ***v***
17: 5 and suddenly a ***v*** came out of
27:46 Jesus cried out with a loud ***v***,
27:50 cried out again with a loud ***v***,
Mk 1: 3 The ***v*** of one crying in the
1:11 Then a ***v*** came from heaven, "You
1:26 him and cried out with a loud ***v***,
5: 7 And he cried out with a loud ***v***
9: 7 and a ***v*** came out of the cloud,
15:34 Jesus cried out with a loud ***v***,
15:37 Jesus cried out with a loud ***v***,
Lk 1:42 she spoke out with a loud ***v***
1:44 as soon as the ***v*** of your
3: 4 The ***v*** of one crying in the
3:22 and a ***v*** came from heaven which
4:33 And he cried out with a loud ***v***,
8:28 and with a loud ***v*** said, "What
9:35 And a ***v*** came out of the cloud,

9:36 When the **v** had ceased, Jesus was
11:27 from the crowd raised her **v**
17:15 and with a loud **v** glorified
19:37 and praise God with a loud **v**
23:46 had cried out with a loud **v**,
Jn 1:23 The **v** of one crying in the
3:29 because of the bridegroom's **v**.
5:25 when the dead will hear the **v**
5:28 in the graves will hear His **v**
5:37 You have neither heard His **v** at
10: 3 and the sheep hear his **v**;
10: 4 follow him, for they know his **v**.
10: 5 for they do not know the **v** of
10:16 and they will hear My **v**;
10:27 "My sheep hear My **v**,
11:43 He cried with a loud **v**,
12:28 Then a **v** came from heaven,
12:30 This **v** did not come because of
18:37 who is of the truth hears My **v**.
Acts 2:14 raised his **v** and said to them,
4:24 they raised their **v** to God with
7:31 the **v** of the Lord came to him,
7:57 they cried out with a loud **v**,
7:60 and cried out with a loud **v**,
8: 7 spirits, crying with a loud **v**,
9: 4 and heard a **v** saying to him,
9: 7 hearing a **v** but seeing no one.
10:13 And a **v** came to him, "Rise,
10:15 And a **v** spoke to him again the
11: 7 And I heard a **v** saying to me,
11: 9 But the **v** answered me again from
12:14 When she recognized Peter's **v**,
12:22 The **v** of a god and not of a
14:10 said with a loud **v**,
16:28 But Paul called with a loud **v**,
19:34 all with one **v** cried out for
22: 7 to the ground and heard a **v**
22: 9 but they did not hear the **v** of
22:14 and hear the **v** of His mouth.
26:14 I heard a **v** speaking to me and
26:24 Festus said with a loud **v**,
1 Th 4:16 with the **v** of an archangel,
Heb 3: 7 if you will hear His **v**,
3:15 if you will hear His **v**,
4: 7 if you will hear His **v**,
12:19 sound of a trumpet and the **v**
12:26 whose **v** then shook the earth;
2 Pe 1:17 honor and glory when such a **v**
1:18 And we heard this **v** which came
2:16 donkey speaking with a man's **v**
Rev 1:10 and I heard behind me a loud **v**,
1:12 Then I turned to see the **v** that
1:15 and His **v** as the sound of many
3:20 If anyone hears My **v** and opens
4: 1 And the first **v** which I heard
5: 2 angel proclaiming with a loud **v**,
5:11 and I heard the **v** of many
5:12 saying with a loud **v**:
6: 1 creatures saying with a **v** like
6: 6 And I heard a **v** in the midst of
6: 7 I heard the **v** of the fourth
6:10 And they cried with a loud **v**,
7: 2 And he cried with a loud **v** to
7:10 and crying out with a loud **v**,
8:13 of heaven, saying with a loud **v**,
9:13 And I heard a **v** from the four
10: 3 and cried with a loud **v**,
10: 4 but I heard a **v** from heaven
10: 8 Then the **v** which I heard from
11:12 And they heard a loud **v** from
12:10 Then I heard a loud **v** saying in
14: 2 And I heard a **v** from heaven,
14: 2 like the **v** of many waters,
14: 2 and like the **v** of loud thunder.
14: 7 saying with a loud **v**,
14: 9 them, saying with a loud **v**,
14:13 Then I heard a **v** from heaven
14:15 crying with a loud **v** to Him who
16: 1 Then I heard a loud **v** from the
16:17 and a loud **v** came out of the
18: 2 he cried mightily with a loud **v**,
18: 4 And I heard another **v** from
18:23 and the **v** of bridegroom and
19: 1 these things I heard a loud **v**
19: 5 Then a **v** came from the throne,
19: 6 the **v** of a great multitude, as
19:17 and he cried with a loud **v**,
21: 3 And I heard a loud **v** from heaven

VOICES (21/19) VOICE

Num 14: 1 congregation lifted up their **v**
Judg 2: 4 the people lifted up their **v**
21: 2 They lifted up their **v** and wept
Ruth 1: 9 and they lifted up their **v** and
1:14 Then they lifted up their **v** and
1 Sam 11: 4 the people lifted up their **v**
30: 4 with him lifted up their **v** and
2 Chr 20:19 the LORD God of Israel with **v**
Job 2:12 they lifted their **v** and wept;
Isa 52: 8 watchmen shall lift up their **v**,
52: 8 With their **v** they shall sing
Lk 17:13 And they lifted up their **v** and
23:23 demanding with loud **v** that He
23:23 And the **v** of these men and of
Acts 13:27 nor even the **v** of the Prophets
14:11 had done, they raised their **v**,
22:22 and then they raised their **v**
Rev 4: 5 lightnings, thunderings, and **v**.
10: 3 seven thunders uttered their **v**.
10: 4 seven thunders uttered their **v**,
11:15 And there were loud **v** in

VOID (15/14)

Gen 1: 2 earth was without form, and **v**;
Num 30: 8 he shall make **v** her vow which
30:12 her husband truly made them **v**
30:12 her husband has made them **v**,
30:13 or her husband may make it **v**.
30:15 But if he does make them **v** after
Deut 32:28 For they are a nation **v** of
Judg 21:15 because the LORD had made a **v**
Ps 119:126 have regarded Your law as **v**.
Isa 55:11 It shall not return to Me **v**,
Jer 4:23 it was without form, and **v**;
19: 7 And I will make **v** the counsel of
Rom 3:31 Do we then make **v** the law
4:14 faith is made **v** and the promise
1 Cor 9:15 should make my boasting **v**.

VOLUME (2/2)

Lev 19:35 of length, weight, or **v**.
Heb 10: 7 In the **v** of the book it

VOLUNTARILY (1/1)

Deut 23:23 for you **v** vowed to the LORD

VOLUNTARY (4/3)

Lev 7:16 is a vow or a **v** offering,
Ezek 46:12 prince makes a **v** burnt offering
46:12 offering or **v** peace offering
Phm 1:14 compulsion, as it were, but **v**.

VOLUNTEER (1/1)

Ezra 7:13 who **v** to go up to Jerusalem,

VOLUNTEERS (1/1)

Ps 110: 3 Your people shall be **v** In

VOMIT (11/11) VOMITED

Lev 18:28 lest the land **v** you out also
20:22 you to dwell may not **v** you out.
Prov 23: 8 you will **v** up, And waste your
25:16 you be filled with it and **v**.
26:11 As a dog returns to his own **v**,
Isa 19:14 a drunken man staggers in his **v**.
28: 8 For all tables are full of **v**
Jer 25:27 'Drink, be drunk, and **v**!
48:26 Moab shall wallow in his **v**,
2 Pe 2:22 dog returns to his own **v**,
Rev 3:16 I will **v** you out of My mouth.

VOMITED (2/2) VOMIT

Lev 18:28 as it **v** out the nations that
Jon 2:10 and it **v** Jonah onto dry land.

VOMITS (2/2)

Lev 18:25 and the land **v** out its
Job 20:15 He swallows down riches And **v**

VOPHSI (1/1)

Num 13:14 of Naphtali, Nahbi the son of **V**;

VOTE (1/1)

Acts 26:10 I cast my **v** against them.

VOW (36/35) VOWED, VOWS

Gen 28:20 Then Jacob made a **v**,
31:13 pillar and where you made a **v**
Lev 7:16 of his offering is a **v** or a
22:21 to the LORD, to fulfill his **v**,
22:23 but for a **v** it shall not be
27: 2 When a man consecrates by a **v**
Num 6: 2 an offering to take the **v** of a
6: 5 All the days of the **v** of his
6:21 according to the **v** which he
15: 3 to fulfill a **v** or as a freewill
15: 8 as a sacrifice to fulfill a **v**,
21: 2 So Israel made a **v** to the LORD,
30: 2 If a man makes a **v** to the LORD,
30: 3 Or if a woman makes a **v** to the
30: 4 and her father hears her **v** and
30: 8 he shall make void her **v** which
30: 9 Also any **v** of a widow or a
30:13 Every **v** and every binding oath
Deut 12:11 choice offerings which you **v**
12:17 of your offerings which you **v**,
23:21 When you make a **v** to the LORD
Judg 11:30 And Jephthah made a **v** to the
11:39 and he carried out his **v** with
1 Sam 1:11 Then she made a **v** and said, "O
1:21 the yearly sacrifice and his **v**.
20:17 again caused David to **v**,
2 Sam 15: 7 me go to Hebron and pay the **v**
15: 8 For your servant took a **v** while
Ps 65: 1 And to You the **v** shall be
Eccl 5: 4 When you make a **v** to God,
5: 5 Better not to **v** than to vow and
5: 5 Better not to vow than to **v** and
Isa 19:21 they will make a **v** to the LORD
Mal 1:14 flock a male, And takes a **v**,
Acts 18:18 for he had taken a **v**.
21:23 four men who have taken a **v**.

VOWED (11/11) VOW

Lev 27: 8 to the ability of him who **v**,
Num 29:39 feasts (besides your **v**
30:10 If she **v** in her husband's
Deut 12: 6 your **v** offerings, your freewill
12:26 and your **v** offerings,
23:18 of the LORD your God for any **v**
23:23 for you voluntarily **v** to the
Judg 11:39 his vow with her which he had **v**.
Ps 132: 2 And **v** to the Mighty One of
Eccl 5: 4 Pay what you have **v**—
Jon 2: 9 I will pay what I have **v**.

VOWING (1/1)

Deut 23:22 "But if you abstain from **v**,

VOWS (28/26) MAKES, VOW

Lev 22:18 his sacrifice for any of his **v**
23:38 your gifts, besides all your **v**,
Num 6:21 the law of the Nazirite who **v**
30: 4 then all her **v** shall stand,
30: 5 then none of her **v** nor her
30: 6 while bound by her **v** or by a
30: 7 then her **v** shall stand, and her
30:11 then all her **v** shall stand, and
30:12 from her lips concerning her **v**
30:14 then he confirms all her **v** or
Job 22:27 And you will pay your **v**.
Ps 22:25 I will pay My **v** before those
50:14 And pay your **v** to the Most
56:12 **V** made to You are binding
61: 5 You, O God, have heard my **v**;
61: 8 That I may daily perform my **v**.
66:13 I will pay You my **v**,
76:11 Make **v** to the LORD your God,
116:14 I will pay my **v** to the LORD
116:18 I will pay my **v** to the LORD
Prov 7:14 Today I have paid my **v**.
20:25 afterward to reconsider his **v**.
31: 2 And what, son of my **v**?
Jer 44:25 We will surely keep our **v** that
44:25 You will surely keep your **v**
44:25 your vows and perform your **v**!'
Jon 1:16 to the LORD and took **v**.
Nah 1:15 Perform your **v**.

VOYAGE (2/2)

Acts 21: 7 And when we had finished our **v**
27:10 I perceive that this **v** will end

VULTURE (5/5)

Lev 11:13 abomination: the eagle, the **v**,
11:18 the jackdaw, and the carrion **v**;
Deut 14:12 shall not eat: the eagle, the **v**,
14:17 "the jackdaw, the carrion **v**,
Jer 12: 9 is to Me like a speckled **v**;

VULTURES (2/2)

Gen 15:11 And when the **v** came down on the
Jer 12: 9 The **v** all around are against

W

WAFER (3/3)

Ex 29:23 and one **w** from the basket of
Lev 8:26 anointed with oil, and one **w**,
Num 6:19 basket, and one unleavened **w**,

WAFERS (5/5)

Ex 16:31 and the taste of it was like **w**
29: 2 and unleavened **w** anointed with
Lev 2: 4 or unleavened **w** anointed with
7:12 unleavened **w** anointed with oil,
Num 6:15 unleavened **w** anointed with oil,

WAGE (4/4) WAGES

Prov 20:18 By wise counsel **w** war.
24: 6 For by wise counsel you will **w**
Mal 3: 5 Against those who exploit **w**
1 Tim 1:18 that by them you may **w** the good

WAGES (40/37) WAGE

Gen 29:15 what should your **w** be?"
30:18 said, "God has given me my **w**,
30:28 Then he said, "Name me your **w**,
30:32 goats; and these shall be my **w**.
30:33 when the subject of my **w** comes
31: 7 deceived me and changed my **w**
31: 8 'The speckled shall be your **w**,
31: 8 'The streaked shall be your **w**,
31:41 and you have changed my **w** ten
Ex 2: 9 and I will give you your **w**."
Lev 19:13 The **w** of him who is hired shall
Deut 23:18 You shall not bring the **w** of a
24:15 day you shall give him his **w**,
1 Ki 5: 6 and I will pay you **w** for your
Job 7: 2 man who eagerly looks for his **w**,
Prov 10:16 The **w** of the wicked to sin.
26:10 and the transgressor his **w**.
Isa 19:10 All who make **w** will be

55: 2 And your **w** for what does not
Jer 22:13 neighbor's service without **w**
Ezek 29:18 he nor his army received **w**
29:19 and that will be the **w** for his
Hos 2:12 These are my **w** that my lovers
Hag 1: 6 And he who earns **w**,
1: 6 Earns **w** to put into a bag
Zech 8:10 these days There were no **w**
11:12 agreeable to you, give me my **w**;
11:12 So they weighed out for my **w**
Mt 20: 8 laborers and give them their **w**,
Lk 3:14 and be content with your **w**.
10: 7 the laborer is worthy of his **w**.
Jn 4:36 "And he who reaps receives **w**,
Acts 1:18 purchased a field with the **w**
Rom 4: 4 the **w** are not counted as grace
6:23 For the **w** of sin is death, but
2 Cor 11: 8 taking **w** from them to
1 Tim 5:18 laborer is worthy of his **w**.
Jas 5: 4 Indeed the **w** of the laborers who
2 Pe 2:13 and will receive the **w** of
2:15 who loved the **w** of

WAGGING (2/2)

Mt 27:39 blasphemed Him, **w** their heads
Mk 15:29 **w** their heads and saying,

WAGON (KJV) See CART

WAGONS (2/2)

Ezek 23:24 against you With chariots, **w**,
26:10 noise of the horsemen, the **w**,

WAHEB (1/1)

Num 21:14 **W** in Suphah, The brooks of the

WAIFS (1/1)

Lam 5: 3 We have become orphans and **w**,

WAIL (31/28)

Isa 13: 6 **W**, for the day of the LORD
14:31 **W**, O gate! Cry, O city!
15: 2 Moab will **w** over Nebo and over
15: 3 their streets Everyone will **w**,
16: 7 Therefore Moab shall **w** for
16: 7 for Moab; Everyone shall **w**.
23: 1 The burden against Tyre. **W**,
23: 6 **W**, you inhabitants of the
23:14 **W**, you ships of Tarshish!
52: 5 who rule over them Make them **w**,
65:14 And **w** for grief of spirit.
Jer 4: 8 with sackcloth, Lament and **w**.
25:34 **W**, shepherds, and cry!
47: 2 inhabitants of the land shall **w**.
48:20 **W** and cry! Tell it in Arnon,
48:31 Therefore I will **w** for Moab,
48:36 Therefore My heart shall **w** like
48:36 like flutes My heart shall **w**
48:39 "They shall **w**:
49: 3 '**W**, O Heshbon, for Ai is
51: 8 **W** for her! Take balm for her
Ezek 21:12 'Cry and **w**, son of man;
30: 2 'Thus says the Lord GOD: "**W**,
32:18 **w** over the multitude of Egypt,
Joel 1: 5 you drunkards, and weep; And **w**,
1:11 Be ashamed, you farmers, **W**,
1:13 and lament, you priests; **W**,
Mic 1: 8 Therefore I will **w** and howl,
Zeph 1:11 **W**, you inhabitants of
Zech 11: 2 **W**, O cypress, for the cedar
11: 2 **W**, O oaks of Bashan,

WAILED (2/2)

Hos 7:14 with their heart When they **w**
Mk 5:38 tumult and those who wept and **w**

WAILING (24/22)

Esth 4: 3 with fasting, weeping, and **w**;
Isa 15: 8 Its **w** to Eglaim And its
15: 8 wailing to Eglaim And its **w**
Jer 9:10 I will take up a weeping and **w**
9:17 And send for skillful **w** women,
9:18 make haste And take up a **w**
9:19 For a voice of **w** is heard from
9:20 Teach your daughters **w**,
25:36 And a **w** of the leaders to the
Ezek 7:11 Nor shall there be **w** for
27:31 of heart and bitter **w**.
27:32 In their **w** for you They will
Am 5:16 There shall be **w** in all
5:16 And skillful lamenters to **w**.
5:17 vineyards there shall be **w**,
8: 3 of the temple Shall be **w** in
Mic 1: 8 I will make a **w** like the
Zeph 1:10 A **w** from the Second Quarter,
Zech 11: 3 There is the sound of **w**
Mt 9:23 players and the noisy crowd **w**,
13:42 There will be **w** and gnashing of
13:50 There will be **w** and gnashing of
Rev 18:15 of her torment, weeping and **w**,
18:19 and cried out, weeping and **w**,

WAIST (26/24)

Gen 37:34 put sackcloth on his **w**,
Ex 12:11 eat it: with a belt on your **w**,
28:42 they shall reach from the **w** to
1 Ki 2: 5 his belt that was around his **w**,
12:10 be thicker than my father's **w**!
2 Ki 1: 8 a leather belt around his **w**.
2 Chr 10:10 be thicker than my father's **w**!
Job 12:18 And binds their **w** with a belt.
15:27 And made his **w** heavy with
Song 7: 2 Your **w** is a heap of wheat
Isa 11: 5 faithfulness the belt of His **w**.
Jer 13: 1 sash, and put it around your **w**,
13: 2 LORD, and put it around my **w**.
13: 4 which is around your **w**,
13:11 as the sash clings to the **w** of
Ezek 1:27 from the appearance of His **w**
1:27 from the appearance of His **w**
8: 2 from the appearance of His **w** and
8: 2 and from His **w** and upward,
47: 4 the water came up to my **w**.
Dan 10: 5 whose **w** was girded with gold
Am 8:10 will bring sackcloth on every **w**,
Mt 3: 4 a leather belt around his **w**;
Mk 1: 6 a leather belt around his **w**,
Lk 12:35 Let your **w** be girded and your
Eph 6:14 having girded your **w** with

WAISTS (4/4)

1 Ki 20:31 us put sackcloth around our **w**
20:32 wore sackcloth around their **w**
Isa 32:11 And gird sackcloth on your **w**.
Ezek 23:15 with belts around their **w**,

WAIT (94/91) WAITED, WAITING, WAITS

Ex 12:39 out of Egypt and could not **w**,
21:13 if he did not lie in **w**,
24:14 **W** here for us until we come back
Num 35:20 of hatred or, while lying in **w**,
35:22 at him without lying in **w**,
Deut 19:11 lies in **w** for him, rises
Judg 6:18 I will **w** until you come back."
9:32 and lie in **w** in the field.
9:34 and lay in **w** against Shechem in
9:35 with him rose from lying in **w**.
9:43 and lay in **w** in the field.
16: 2 the place and lay in **w** for
16: 9 Now men were lying in **w**,
16:12 And men were lying in **w**,
21:20 lie in **w** in the vineyards,
Ruth 1:13 would you **w** for them till they
1 Sam 1:23 **w** until you have weaned him.
10: 8 Seven days you shall **w**,
14: 9 **W** until we come to you,' then we
15: 5 and lay in **w** in the valley.
22: 8 servant against me, to lie in **w**,
22:13 rise against me, to lie in **w**,
2 Sam 10: 5 **W** at Jericho until your beards
11:12 **W** here today also, and tomorrow
15:28 I will **w** in the plains of the
2 Ki 6:33 why should I **w** for the LORD
7: 9 If we **w** until morning light,
1 Chr 19: 5 **W** at Jericho until your beards
Job 14:14 of my hard service I will **w**,
17:13 If I **w** for the grave as my
35:14 and you must **w** for Him.
38:40 lurk in their lairs to lie in **w**?
Ps 10: 9 He lies in **w** secretly, as a
10: 9 He lies in **w** to catch the
25: 5 On You I **w** all the day.
25:21 For I **w** for You.
27:14 **W** on the LORD
27:14 **W**, I say, on the LORD!
37: 7 and **w** patiently for Him;
37: 9 But those who **w** on the LORD,
37:34 **W** on the LORD, And keep His
39: 7 what do I **w** for? My hope is
52: 9 of Your saints I will **w** on
56: 6 When they lie in **w** for my
59: 3 they lie in **w** for my life;
59: 9 I will **w** for You, O You his
62: 5 **w** silently for God alone,
69: 3 My eyes fail while I **w** for my
69: 6 Let not those who **w** for You, O
71:10 And those who lie in **w** for my
104:27 These all **w** for You, That You
106:13 They did not **w** for His
119:95 The wicked **w** for me to destroy
130: 5 I **w** for the LORD, my soul
Prov 1:11 Let us lie in **w** to shed
1:18 But they lie in **w** for their
12: 6 'Lie in **w** for blood,"
20:22 **W** for the LORD, and He will
23:28 She also lies in **w** as for a
24:15 Do not lie in **w**,
Isa 8:17 And I will **w** on the LORD,
30:18 Therefore the LORD will **w**,
30:18 Blessed are all those who **w**
40:31 But those who **w** on the LORD
42: 4 And the coastlands shall **w** for
49:23 shall not be ashamed who **w** for
51: 5 The coastlands will **w** upon Me,
60: 9 Surely the coastlands shall **w**
Jer 5:26 They lie in **w** as one who sets
9: 8 But in his heart he lies in **w**.
14:22 Therefore we will **w** for You,
Lam 3:10 been to me a bear lying in **w**,
3:25 LORD is good to those who **w**
3:26 that one should hope and **w**
4:19 on the mountains And lay in **w**
Hos 6: 9 As bands of robbers lie in **w**
7: 6 While they lie in **w**;
12: 6 And **w** on your God continually.
Mic 5: 7 That tarry for no man Nor **w**
7: 2 They all lie in **w** for blood;
7: 7 I will **w** for the God of my
Hab 2: 3 **w** for it; Because it will
Zeph 3: 8 Therefore **w** for Me," says the
Lk 11:54 lying in **w** for Him, and seeking
12:36 yourselves be like men who **w**
Acts 1: 4 but to **w** for the Promise of the
23:21 than forty of them lie in **w**
23:30 told me that the Jews lay in **w**
Rom 8:25 we eagerly **w** for it with
1 Cor 11:33 **w** for one another.
Gal 5: 5 we through the Spirit eagerly **w**
Phil 3:20 from which we also eagerly **w**
1 Th 1:10 and to **w** for His Son from
Heb 9:28 To those who eagerly **w** for Him

WAITED (28/27) WAIT

Gen 8:10 And he **w** yet another seven days,
8:12 So he **w** yet another seven days
49:18 I have **w** for your salvation, O
Judg 3:25 So they **w** till they were
1 Sam 13: 8 Then he **w** seven days,
25: 9 in the name of David, and **w**.
1 Ki 20:38 the prophet departed and **w** for
2 Ki 5: 2 She **w** on Naaman's wife.
Job 29:21 "Men listened to me and **w**,
29:23 They **w** for me as for the rain,
30:26 And when I **w** for light,
32: 4 Elihu had **w** to speak to Job.
32:11 Indeed I **w** for your words,
32:16 And I have **w**, because they
Ps 40: 1 I **w** patiently for the LORD;
Isa 25: 9 We have **w** for Him, and He will
25: 9 We have **w** for Him; We will be
26: 8 we have **w** for You; The desire
33: 2 We have **w** for You.
Lam 2:16 this is the day we have **w** for;
Ezek 19: 5 'When she saw that she **w**,
Lk 1:21 And the people **w** for Zacharias,
Acts 10: 7 soldier from among those who **w**
17:16 Now while Paul **w** for them at
20: 5 **w** for us at Troas.
27:33 the fourteenth day you have **w**
Heb 11:10 for he **w** for the city which has
1 Pe 3:20 the Divine longsuffering **w** in

WAITERS (2/2)

1 Ki 10: 5 the service of his **w** and their
2 Chr 9: 4 of his **w** and their apparel,

WAITING (15/15) WAIT

Job 15:22 For a sword is **w** for him.
Prov 8:34 **W** at the posts of my doors.
Mk 15:43 who was himself **w** for the
Lk 2:25 **w** for the Consolation of
8:40 for they were all **w** for Him.
23:51 who himself was also **w** for the
Jn 5: 3 **w** for the moving of the water.
Acts 10:24 Now Cornelius was **w** for them,
22:16 'And now why are you **w**?
23:21 **w** for the promise from you."
Rom 8:23 eagerly **w** for the adoption,
1 Cor 1: 7 eagerly **w** for the revelation of
16:11 for I am **w** for him with the
Heb 10:13 from that time **w** till His
Jas 5: 7 **w** patiently for it until it

WAITS (11/11) WAIT

Job 24:15 The eye of the adulterer **w** for
Ps 25: 3 let no one who **w** on You be
33:20 Our soul **w** for the LORD;
62: 1 Truly my soul silently **w** for
130: 5 wait for the LORD, my soul **w**,
130: 6 My soul **w** for the Lord More
Prov 27:18 So he who **w** on his master will
Isa 64: 4 Who acts for the one who **w** for
Dan 12:12 "Blessed is he who **w**,
Rom 8:19 of the creation eagerly **w** for
Jas 5: 7 See how the farmer **w** for the

WAKE (4/4)

Job 41:32 He leaves a shining **w** behind
Joel 3: 9 **W** up the mighty men,
Jn 11:11 but I go that I may **w** him up."
1 Th 5:10 that whether we **w** or sleep,

WAKENED (3/2)

Joel 3:12 "Let the nations be **w**,
Zech 4: 1 talked with me came back and **w**
4: 1 as a man who is **w** out of his

WALK (230/220) WALKED, WALKING, WALKS

Gen 13:17 **w** in the land through its
17: 1 **w** before Me and be blameless.
24:40 'The LORD, before whom I **w**,
Ex 16: 4 whether they will **w** in My law
18:20 the way in which they must **w**
Lev 18: 3 nor shall you **w** in their
18: 4 My ordinances, to **w** in them:
20:23 And you shall not **w** in the
26: 3 If you **w** in My statutes and
26:12 I will **w** among you and be your
26:13 of your yoke and made you **w**
26:21 if you **w** contrary to Me,

26:23 but *w* contrary to Me,
26:24 then I also will *w* contrary to
26:27 but *w* contrary to Me,
26:28 then I also will *w* contrary to
Deut 5:33 You shall *w* in all the ways
6: 7 when you *w* by the way,
8: 6 to *w* in His ways and to fear
10:12 to *w* in all His ways and to
11:19 when you *w* by the way, when you
11:22 to *w* in all His ways, and to
13: 4 You shall *w* after the LORD your
13: 5 your God commanded you to *w*.
19: 9 the LORD your God and to *w*
26:17 and that you will *w* in His ways
28: 9 of the LORD your God and *w* in
30:16 to *w* in His ways, and to keep
Josh 18: 8 *w* through the land, survey it,
22: 5 to *w* in all His ways, to keep
Judg 2:22 to *w* in them as their fathers
5:10 And who *w* along the road.
1 Sam 2:30 house of your father would *w*
2:35 and he shall *w* before My
8: 3 But his sons did not *w* in his
8: 5 and your sons do not *w* in your
17:39 to his armor and tried to *w*,
17:39 'I cannot *w* with these,
1 Ki 2: 3 to *w* in His ways, to keep His
2: 4 to *w* before Me in truth with
3:14 So if you *w* in My ways, to keep
6:12 if you *w* in My statutes,
6:12 and *w* in them, then I will
8:23 mercy with Your servants who *w*
8:25 that they *w* before Me as you
8:36 good way in which they should *w*;
8:58 to *w* in all His ways, and to
8:61 to *w* in His statutes and keep
9: 4 Now if you *w* before Me as your
11:38 *w* in My ways, and do what is
16:31 a trivial thing for him to *w*
2 Ki 10:31 But Jehu took no heed to *w* in
21:22 and did not *w* in the way of the
2 Chr 6:14 mercy with Your servants who *w*
6:16 that they *w* in My law as you
6:27 good way in which they should *w*;
6:31 to *w* in Your ways as long as
7:17 if you *w* before Me as your
Neh 5: 9 Should you not *w* in the fear of
10:29 into a curse and an oath to *w*
Ps 23: 4 though I *w* through the valley
26:11 I will *w* in my integrity;
48:12 *W* about Zion, And go all
56:13 That I may *w* before God
78:10 They refused to *w* in His law,
81:12 To *w* in their own counsels.
81:13 That Israel would *w* in My
82: 5 They *w* about in darkness;
84:11 He withhold From those who *w*
86:11 I will *w* in Your truth;
89:15 They *w*, O LORD, in the light
89:30 forsake My law And do not *w*
101: 2 I will *w* within my house with
115: 7 they have, but they do not *w*;
116: 9 I will *w* before the LORD
119: 1 Who *w* in the law of the LORD!
119: 3 They *w* in His ways.
119:35 Make me *w* in the path of Your
119:45 And I will *w* at liberty,
138: 7 Though I *w* in the midst of
142: 3 In the way in which I *w* They
143: 8 the way in which I should *w*,
Prov 1:15 do not *w* in the way with them,
2: 7 is a shield to those who *w*
2:13 the paths of uprightness To *w*
2:20 So you may *w* in the way of
3:23 Then you will *w* safely in your
4:12 When you *w*, your steps will not
4:14 And do not *w* in the way of
6:28 Can one *w* on hot coals,
30:29 four which are stately in *w*:
Eccl 4:15 I saw all the living who *w*
5: 1 *W* prudently when you go to the
6: 8 Who knows how to *w* before the
10: 7 While princes *w* on the ground
11: 9 *W* in the ways of your heart,
Isa 2: 3 And we shall *w* in His paths."
2: 5 come and let us *w* In the light
3:16 And *w* with outstretched necks
8:11 me that I should not *w* in the
30: 2 Who *w* to go down to Egypt,
30:21 *w* in it," Whenever you turn
35: 9 But the redeemed shall *w*
38:15 I shall *w* carefully all my
40:31 They shall *w* and not faint.
42: 5 And spirit to those who *w* on
42:24 For they would not *w* in His
43: 2 When you *w* through the fire,
45:14 They shall *w* behind you,
50:11 *W* in the light of your fire
51:23 that we may *w* over you.'
51:23 for those who *w* over."
59: 9 but we *w* in blackness!
65: 2 Who *w* in a way that is not
Jer 3:18 days the house of Judah shall *w*
6:16 And *w* in it; Then you will
6:16 We will not *w* in it.'
6:25 Nor *w* by the way.
7: 6 or *w* after other gods to your
7: 9 and *w* after other gods whom you
7:23 And *w* in all the ways that I
9: 4 And every neighbor will *w* with
13:10 and *w* after other gods to serve
18:12 So we will *w* according to our
18:15 To *w* in pathways and not on a
23:14 They commit adultery and *w* in
26: 4 to *w* in My law which I have set
31: 9 I will cause them to *w* by the
42: 3 us the way in which we should *w*
Lam 3: 2 He has led me and made me *w*
4:18 steps So that we could not *w*
Ezek 11:20 that they may *w* in My statutes
16:47 You did not *w* in their ways nor
20:13 they did not *w* in My statutes;
20:16 My judgments and did not *w* in
20:18 Do not *w* in the statutes of your
20:19 *W* in My statutes,
20:21 they did not *w* in My statutes,
36:12 I will cause men to *w* on you,
36:27 within you and cause you to *w*
37:24 they shall also *w* in My
42: 4 was a *w* ten cubits wide,
42:11 There was a *w* in front of them
42:12 was a door in front of the *w*,
Dan 4:37 And those who *w* in pride He is
9:10 to *w* in His laws, which He set
Hos 11: 3 "I taught Ephraim to *w*,
11:10 They shall *w* after the LORD.
14: 9 The righteous *w* in them,
Am 3: 3 Can two *w* together, unless they
Jon 3: 4 the city on the first day's *w*.
Mic 2: 3 Nor shall you *w* haughtily,
2:11 If a man should *w* in a false
4: 2 And we shall *w* in His paths."
4: 5 For all people *w* each in the
4: 5 But we will *w* in the name of
6: 8 And to *w* humbly with your God?
6:16 And you *w* in their counsels,
Nah 2: 5 They stumble in their *w*;
Hab 3:19 And He will make me *w* on my
Zeph 1:17 And they shall *w* like blind
Zech 1:10 whom the LORD has sent to *w*
3: 7 'If you will *w* in My ways,
3: 7 I will give you places to *w*
6: 7 that they might *w* to and fro
6: 7 *w* to and fro throughout the
10:12 And they shall *w* up and down
Mt 9: 5 you,' or to say, 'Arise and *w*'?
11: 5 blind see and the lame *w*;
Mk 2: 9 'Arise, take up your bed and *w*'?
7: 5 Why do Your disciples not *w*
Lk 5:23 or to say, 'Rise up and *w*'?
7:22 the blind see, the lame *w*,
11:44 and the men who *w* over them
24:17 have with one another as you *w*
Jn 5: 8 "Rise, take up your bed and *w*."
5:11 to me, 'Take up your bed and *w*.'
5:12 you, 'Take up your bed and *w*'?
7: 1 for He did not want to *w* in
8:12 He who follows Me shall not *w*
12:35 *W* while you have the light,
Acts 3: 6 of Nazareth, rise up and *w*."
3:12 we had made this man *w*?
14:16 allowed all nations to *w* in
21:21 their children nor to *w*
21:24 but that you yourself also *w*
Rom 4:12 but who also *w* in the steps of
6: 4 even so we also should *w* in
8: 1 who do not *w* according to the
8: 4 be fulfilled in us who do not *w*
13:13 Let us *w* properly, as in the
1 Cor 7:17 called each one, so let him *w*.
2 Cor 5: 7 For we *w* by faith, not by sight.
6:16 will dwell in them And *w*
10: 3 For though we *w* in the flesh,
12:18 Did we not *w* in the same
12:18 Did we not *w* in the same
Gal 5:16 *W* in the Spirit, and you shall
5:25 let us also *w* in the Spirit.
6:16 And as many as *w* according to
Eph 2:10 beforehand that we should *w* in
4: 1 beseech you to *w* worthy of the
4:17 that you should no longer *w* as
4:17 as the rest of the Gentiles *w*,
5: 2 And *w* in love, as Christ also
5: 8 *W* as children of light
5:15 See then that you *w*
Phil 3:16 let us *w* by the same rule,
3:17 and note those who so *w*,
3:18 For many *w*, of whom I have told
Col 1:10 that you may *w* worthy of the
2: 6 Jesus the Lord, so *w* in Him,
4: 5 *W* in wisdom toward those who
1 Th 2:12 that you would *w* worthy of God
4: 1 from us how you ought to *w* and
4:12 that you may *w* properly toward
2 Th 3:11 hear that there are some who *w*
2 Pe 2:10 and especially those who *w*
1 Jn 1: 6 and *w* in darkness, we lie and
1: 7 But if we *w* in the light as He
2: 6 in Him ought himself also to *w*
2 Jn 6 that we *w* according to His
6 you should *w* in it.
3 Jn 3 just as you *w* in the truth.
4 to hear that my children *w* in
Jude 18 in the last time who would *w*
Rev 3: 4 and they shall *w* with Me in
9:20 can neither see nor hear nor *w*.
16:15 lest he *w* naked and they see
21:24 of those who are saved shall *w*

WALKED (103/102) FOLLOWED, WALK

Gen 5:22 Enoch *w* with God three hundred
5:24 And Enoch *w* with God; and he
6: 9 Noah *w* with God.
48:15 my fathers Abraham and Isaac *w*,
Ex 2: 5 And her maidens *w* along the
14:29 the children of Israel had *w*
Lev 26:40 and that they also have *w*
26:41 and that I also have *w* contrary
Deut 1:36 giving the land on which he *w*,
Josh 5: 6 For the children of Israel *w*
Judg 2:17 way in which their fathers *w*,
5: 6 And the travelers *w* along the
11:16 they *w* through the wilderness
1 Sam 12: 2 I have *w* before you from my
2 Sam 11: 2 David arose from his bed and *w*
1 Ki 3: 6 because he *w* before You in
3:14 as your father David *w*,
8:25 walk before Me as you have *w*
9: 4 Me as your father David *w*,
11:33 and have not *w* in My ways to do
15: 3 And he *w* in all the sins of his
15:26 and *w* in the way of his father,
15:34 and *w* in the way of Jeroboam,
16: 2 and you have *w* in the way of
16:26 For he *w* in all the ways of
22:43 And he *w* in all the ways of his
22:52 and *w* in the way of his father
2 Ki 4:35 He returned and *w* back and forth
8:18 And he *w* in the way of the kings
8:27 And he *w* in the way of the house
13: 6 but *w* in them; and the wooden
13:11 sin, but *w* in them.
16: 3 But he *w* in the way of the kings
17: 8 and had *w* in the statutes of the
17:19 but *w* in the statutes of Israel
17:22 For the children of Israel *w* in
20: 3 how I have *w* before You in
21:21 So he *w* in all the ways that his
21:21 the ways that his father had *w*;
22: 2 and *w* in all the ways of his
2 Chr 6:16 walk in My law as you have *w*
7:17 Me as your father David *w*,
11:17 because they *w* in the way of
17: 3 because he *w* in the former ways
17: 4 and *w* in His commandments and
20:32 And he *w* in the way of his
21: 6 And he *w* in the way of the kings
21:12 Because you have not *w* in the
21:13 but have *w* in the way of the
22: 3 He also *w* in the ways of the
28: 2 For he *w* in the ways of the
34: 2 and *w* in the ways of his father
Job 29: 3 And when by His light I *w*
31: 5 'If I have *w* with falsehood,
31: 7 Or my heart *w* after my eyes,
38:16 Or have you *w* in search of the
Ps 26: 1 For I have *w* in my integrity.
26: 3 And I have *w* in Your truth.
55:14 And *w* to the house of God in
Isa 9: 2 The people who *w* in darkness
20: 3 as My servant Isaiah has *w*
38: 3 how I have *w* before You in
Jer 2: 8 And *w* after things that do
8: 2 and after which they have *w*,
9:13 nor *w* according to it,
9:14 but they have *w* according to the
16:11 they have *w* after other gods and
32:23 not obeyed Your voice or *w* in
44:10 they have not *w* in My law or in
44:23 the voice of the LORD or *w* in
Ezek 5: 6 and they have not *w* in My
5: 7 have not *w* in My statutes nor
11:12 for you have not *w* in My
18: 9 If he has *w* in My statutes
18:17 executed My judgments And *w*
23:31 You have *w* in the way of your
28:14 You *w* back and forth in the
Hos 5:11 Because he willingly *w* by
Nah 2:11 young lions, Where the lion *w*,
Hab 3:15 You *w* through the sea with Your
Zech 1:11 We have *w* to and fro throughout
6: 7 So they *w* to and fro
Mal 2: 6 He *w* with Me in peace and
3:14 And that we have *w* as mourners
Mt 14:29 he *w* on the water to go to
Mk 1:16 And as He *w* by the Sea of
5:42 the girl arose and *w*,
16:12 form to two of them as they *w*
Jn 1:36 And looking at Jesus as He *w*,
5: 9 well, took up his bed, and *w*.
6:66 His disciples went back and *w*
7: 1 After these things Jesus *w* in
10:23 And Jesus *w* in the temple,
11:54 Therefore Jesus no longer *w*
21:18 you girded yourself and *w* where
Acts 3: 8 stood and *w* and entered the
14: 8 mother's womb, who had never *w*.
14:10 feet!" And he leaped and *w*.
2 Cor 10: 2 who think of us as if we *w*
Eph 2: 2 in which you once *w* according to
Col 3: 7 in which you yourselves once *w*
1 Pe 4: 3 when we *w* in lewdness, lusts,
1 Jn 2: 6 also to walk just as He *w*.

WALKING (32/32) WALK

Gen 3: 8 the sound of the LORD God *w*
24:65 Who is this man *w* in the field
1 Sam 12: 2 the king, *w* before you;
1 Ki 3: 3 *w* in the statutes of his father
16:19 in *w* in the way of Jeroboam,
Job 1: 7 and from *w* back and forth on
2: 2 and from *w* back and forth on
Isa 3:16 *W* and mincing as they go,
20: 2 *w* naked and barefoot.

57: 2 Each one **w** in his
Jer 6:28 **w** as slanderers. They are
Lam 5:18 With foxes **w** about on it.
Dan 3:25 **w** in the midst of the fire;
4:29 of the twelve months he was **w**
Mt 4:18 **w** by the Sea of Galilee,
14:25 went to them, **w** on the sea.
14:26 when the disciples saw Him **w**
15:31 maimed made whole, the lame **w**,
Mk 6:48 **w** on the sea, and would have
6:49 And when they saw Him **w** on the
8:24 said, "I see men like trees, **w**.
11:27 And as He was **w** in the temple,
Lk 1: 6 **w** in all the commandments and
Jn 6:19 they saw Jesus **w** on the sea and
Acts 3: 8 entered the temple with them—**w**,
3: 9 And all the people saw him **w** and
9:31 And **w** in the fear of the Lord
Rom 14:15 you are no longer **w** in love.
2 Cor 4: 2 not **w** in craftiness nor
2 Pe 3: 3 **w** according to their own lusts,
2 Jn 4 found some of your children **w**
Jude 16 **w** according to their own lusts;

WALKS (41/40) WALK

Ex 21:19 if he rises again and **w** about
Deut 23:14 For the LORD your God **w** in the
Job 18: 8 And he **w** into a snare.
22:14 And He **w** above the circle of
34: 8 And **w** with wicked men?
Ps 1: 1 Blessed is the man Who **w** not
15: 2 He who **w** uprightly, And works
39: 6 Surely every man **w** about like a
73: 9 And their tongue **w** through the
91: 6 of the pestilence that **w** in
101: 6 He who **w** in a perfect way,
104: 3 Who **w** on the wings of the
128: 1 Who **w** in His ways.
Prov 6:12 **W** with a perverse mouth;
10: 9 He who **w** with integrity walks
10: 9 He who walks with integrity **w**
13:20 He who **w** with wise men will be
14: 2 He who **w** in his uprightness
15:21 But a man of understanding **w**
19: 1 Better is the poor who **w** in
20: 7 The righteous man **w** in his
28: 6 Better is the poor who **w** in
28:18 Whoever **w** blamelessly will be
28:26 But whoever **w** wisely will be
Eccl 2:14 But the fool **w** in darkness.
10: 3 Even when a fool **w** along the
Isa 33:15 He who **w** righteously and speaks
35: 8 Whoever **w** the road, although a
50:10 Who **w** in darkness And has no
Jer 10:23 It is not in man who **w** to
23:17 And to everyone who **w**
Ezek 33:15 and **w** in the statutes of life
Hos 11:12 But Judah still **w** with God,
Mic 2: 7 My words do good To him who **w**
Jn 11: 9 If anyone **w** in the day, he does
11:10 But if one **w** in the night, he
12:35 he who **w** in darkness does not
2 Th 3: 6 from every brother who **w**
1 Pe 5: 8 your adversary the devil **w**
1 Jn 2:11 brother is in darkness and **w**
Rev 2: 1 who **w** in the midst of the seven

WALKWAYS (1/1)

2 Chr 9:11 And the king made **w** of the

WALL (179/163) WALLS

Gen 49:22 His branches run over the **w**.
Ex 14:22 and the waters were a **w** to
14:29 and the waters were a **w** to
Lev 14:37 appear to be deep in the **w**,
25:31 of villages which have no **w**
Num 22:24 with a **w** on this side and a
22:24 a wall on this side and a **w** on
22:25 pushed herself against the **w**
22:25 Balaam's foot against the **w**;
35: 4 shall extend from the **w** of
Josh 2:15 her house was on the city **w**;
2:15 she dwelt on the **w**.
6: 5 then the **w** of the city will
6:20 that the **w** fell down flat.
1 Sam 18:11 'I will pin David to the **w**!"
19:10 sought to pin David to the **w**
19:10 he drove the spear into the **w**.
20:25 other times, on a seat by the **w**.
25:16 They were a **w** to us both by
31:10 fastened his body to the **w** of
31:12 bodies of his sons from the **w**
2 Sam 11:20 they would shoot from the **w**?
11:21 a millstone on him from the **w**,
11:21 Why did you go near the **w**?
11:24 The archers shot from the **w** at
18:24 roof over the gate, to the **w**,
20:15 were with Joab battered the **w**
20:21 be thrown to you over the **w**.
22:30 By my God I can leap over a **w**.
1 Ki 3: 1 and the **w** all around Jerusalem.
4:33 that springs out of the **w**;
6: 5 Against the **w** of the temple he
6:27 wing of the one touched one **w**,
6:27 cherub touched the other **w**.
6:31 were one-fifth of the **w**.
6:33 wood, one-fourth of the **w**.
9:15 the **w** of Jerusalem, Hazor,
20:30 then a **w** fell on twenty-seven
21:23 shall eat Jezebel by the **w** of
2 Ki 3:27 as a burnt offering upon the **w**;
4:10 a small upper room on the **w**;
6:26 Israel was passing by on the **w**,
6:30 and as he passed by on the **w**,
9:33 of her blood spattered on the **w**
14:13 and broke down the **w** of
18:26 of the people who are on the **w**.
18:27 not to the men who sit on the **w**,
20: 2 he turned his face toward the **w**,
25: 1 and they built a siege **w**
25: 4 Then the city **w** was broken
2 Chr 3:11 touching the **w** of the room,
3:12 touching the **w** of the room, and
25:23 and broke down the **w** of
26: 6 and broke down the **w** of Gath,
26: 6 the **w** of Jabneh, and the wall
26: 6 and the **w** of Ashdod;
26: 9 at the corner buttress of the **w**;
27: 3 he built extensively on the **w**
32: 5 built up all the **w** that was
32: 5 and built another **w** outside;
32:18 of Jerusalem who were on the **w**,
33:14 After this he built a **w** outside
36:19 broke down the **w** of Jerusalem,
Ezra 5: 3 this temple and finish this **w**?
9: 9 and to give us a **w** in Judah and
Neh 1: 3 The **w** of Jerusalem is also
2: 8 to the temple, for the city **w**,
2:15 by the valley, and viewed the **w**;
2:17 Come and let us build the **w** of
3: 8 Jerusalem as far as the Broad **W**.
3:13 a thousand cubits of the **w** as
3:15 and repaired the **w** of the Pool
3:27 and as far as the **w** of Ophel.
4: 1 that we were rebuilding the **w**,
4: 3 will break down their stone **w**.
4: 6 So we built the **w**,
4: 6 and the entire **w** was joined
4:10 we are not able to build the **w**.
4:13 behind the lower parts of the **w**,
4:15 all of us returned to the **w**,
4:17 Those who built on the **w**,
4:19 far from one another on the **w**.
5:16 continued the work on this **w**,
6: 1 heard that I had rebuilt the **w**,
6: 6 you are rebuilding the **w**,
6:15 So the **w** was finished on the
7: 1 when the **w** was built and I had
12:27 at the dedication of the **w** of
12:30 people, the gates, and the **w**.
12:31 leaders of Judah up on the **w**,
12:31 went to the right hand on the **w**
12:37 David, on the stairway of the **w**,
12:38 half of the people on the **w**,
12:38 the Ovens as far as the Broad **W**,
13:21 spend the night around the **w**?
Ps 18:29 By my God I can leap over a **w**.
62: 3 Like a leaning **w** and a
Prov 18:11 And like a high **w** in his own
24:31 Its stone **w** was broken down.
Eccl 10: 8 And whoever breaks through a **w**
Song 2: 9 Behold, he stands behind our **w**;
8: 9 If she is a **w**,
8:10 I am a **w**, And my breasts
Isa 2:15 And upon every fortified **w**;
5: 5 And break down its **w**,
7: 6 and let us make a gap in its **w**
22:10 broke down To fortify the **w**.
25: 4 is as a storm against the **w**.
30:13 A bulge in a high **w**,
36:11 of the people who are on the **w**.
36:12 not to the men who sit on the **w**,
38: 2 turned his face toward the **w**,
59:10 We grope for the **w** like the
Jer 15:20 people a fortified bronze **w**;
49:27 I will kindle a fire in the **w** of
51:44 the **w** of Babylon shall fall.
52: 4 and they built a siege **w**
52: 7 Then the city **w** was broken
Lam 2: 8 has purposed to destroy The **w**
2: 8 He has caused the rampart and **w**
2:18 O **w** of the daughter of Zion,
Ezek 4: 2 build a siege **w** against it, and
4: 3 and set it as an iron **w**
8: 7 there was a hole in the **w**.
8: 8 dig into the **w**"; and when I
8: 8 and when I dug into the **w**,
12: 5 Dig through the **w** in their
12: 7 at evening I dug through the **w**
12:12 They shall dig through the **w** to
13: 5 up into the gaps to build a **w**
13:10 is no peace—and one builds a **w**,
13:12 when the **w** has fallen, will it
13:14 So I will break down the **w** you
13:15 I accomplish My wrath on the **w**
13:15 The **w** is no more, nor those
17:17 up a siege mound and build a **w**
21:22 siege mound, and to build a **w**.
22:30 among them who would make a **w**,
23:14 at men portrayed on the **w**,
26: 8 build a **w** against you, and
38:20 and every **w** shall fall to the
40: 5 Now there was a **w** all around the
40: 5 he measured the width of the **w**
41: 5 he measured the **w** of the
41: 6 but not fastened to the **w** of
41: 7 supporting ledges in the **w** of
41: 9 The thickness of the outer **w** of
41:10 And between it and the **w**
41:12 the **w** of the building was five
41:17 and on every **w** all around,
41:20 and on the **w** of the sanctuary.
42: 7 And a **w** which was outside ran
42:10 in the thickness of the **w** of
42:12 way directly in front of the **w**
42:20 it had a **w** all around,
43: 8 with a **w** between them and Me,
Dan 5: 5 on the plaster of the **w** of the
9:25 shall be built again, and the **w**,
Hos 2: 6 And **w** her in, So that she
Joel 2: 7 They climb the **w** like men of
2: 9 in the city, They run on the **w**;
Am 1: 7 I will send a fire upon the **w**
1:10 I will send a fire upon the **w**
1:14 I will kindle a fire in the **w**
5:19 Leaned his hand on the **w**,
7: 7 the Lord stood on a **w** made
Nah 3: 8 Whose **w** was the sea?
Hab 2:11 stone will cry out from the **w**,
Zech 2: 5 will be a **w** of fire all around
Acts 9:25 let him down through the **w** in
23: 3 you whitewashed **w**! For you sit
2 Cor 11:33 through a window in the **w**,
Eph 2:14 has broken down the middle **w**
Rev 21:12 Also she had a great and high **w**
21:14 Now the **w** of the city had twelve
21:15 the city, its gates, and its **w**.
21:17 Then he measured its **w**:
21:18 The construction of its **w** was
21:19 The foundations of the **w** of the

WALLED (2/2)

Lev 25:29 If a man sells a house in a **w**
25:30 then the house in the **w** city

WALLOW (1/1)

Jer 48:26 Moab shall **w** in his vomit,

WALLOWED (2/2) WALLOWING

2 Sam 20:12 But Amasa **w** in his blood in the
Mk 9:20 and he fell on the ground and **w**,

WALLOWING (1/1) WALLOWED

2 Pe 2:22 to her **w** in the mire."

WALLS (69/67) WALL

Lev 14:37 if the plague is on the **w** of
14:39 the plague has spread on the **w**
Deut 3: 5 were fortified with high **w**,
28:52 until your high and fortified **w**,
1 Ki 4:13 sixty large cities with **w** and
6: 5 against the **w** of the temple,
6: 6 not be fastened into the **w** of
6:15 And he built the inside **w** of the
6:29 Then he carved all the **w** of the
2 Ki 25: 4 way of the gate between two **w**,
25:10 of the guard broke down the **w**
1 Chr 29: 4 to overlay the **w** of the houses;
2 Chr 3: 7 its **w** and doors—with gold;
3: 7 and he carved cherubim on the **w**.
8: 5 Horon, fortified cities with **w**,
14: 7 build these cities and make **w**
Ezra 4:12 and are finishing its **w** and
4:13 if this city is built and the **w**
4:16 this city is rebuilt and its **w**
5: 8 timber is being laid in the **w**;
5: 9 temple and to finish these **w**?
Neh 2:13 and viewed the **w** of Jerusalem
4: 7 Ashdodites heard that the **w** of
Job 24:11 press out oil within their **w**,
Ps 51:18 Build the **w** of Jerusalem.
55:10 they go around it on its **w**;
122: 7 Peace be within your **w**,
Prov 25:28 a city broken down, without **w**.
Song 5: 7 The keepers of the **w** Took my
Isa 22: 5 Breaking down the **w** And of
22:11 a reservoir between the two **w**
25:12 of the high fort of your **w** He
26: 1 will appoint salvation for **w**
49:16 Your **w** are continually before
54:12 And all your **w** of precious
56: 5 in My house And within My **w** a
60:10 shall build up your **w**,
60:18 But you shall call your **w**
62: 6 I have set watchmen on your **w**,
Jer 1:15 Against all its **w** all around,
1:18 And bronze **w** against the whole
5:10 Go up on her **w** and destroy,
21: 4 who besiege you outside the **w**;
39: 4 by the gate between the two **w**.
39: 8 and broke down the **w** of
49: 3 and run to and fro by the **w**;
50:15 Her **w** are thrown down;
51:12 Set up the standard on the **w** of
51:58 The broad **w** of Babylon shall be
52: 7 of the gate between the two **w**,
52:14 the guard broke down all the **w**
Lam 2: 7 He has given up the **w** of her
Ezek 8:10 portrayed all around on the **w**.
26: 4 And they shall destroy the **w** of
26: 9 battering rams against your **w**,
26:10 your **w** will shake at the noise
26:12 they will break down your **w** and
27:11 with your army were on your **w**
27:11 hung their shields on your **w**
33:30 talking about you beside the **w**
38:11 all of them dwelling without **w**,
41: 2 and the side **w** of the entrance
41:13 with the building and its **w**

W

41:25 as they were carved on the *w*.
Am 4: 3 will go out through broken *w*,
Mic 7:11 In the day when your *w* are to
Nah 2: 5 They make haste to her *w*,
Zech 2: 4 inhabited as towns without *w*,
Heb 11:30 By faith the *w* of Jericho fell

WANDER (16/16) WANDERED, WANDERING, WANDERS

Gen 20:13 when God caused me to *w* from my
Num 32:13 and He made them *w* in the
Deut 27:18 one who makes the blind to *w*
Judg 11:37 that I may go and *w* on the
2 Sam 15:20 Should I make you *w* up and down
2 Ki 21: 8 not make the feet of Israel *w*
Job 12:24 And makes them *w* in a pathless
38:41 And *w* about for lack of food?
Ps 55: 7 I would *w* far off, And remain
59:15 They *w* up and down for food,
107:40 And causes them to *w* in the
119:10 let me not *w* from Your
Isa 47:15 They shall *w* each one to his
Jer 14:10 "Thus they have loved to *w*;
49: 5 no one will gather those who *w*
Am 8:12 They shall *w* from sea to sea,

WANDERED (10/10) WANDER

Gen 21:14 Then she departed and *w* in the
Josh 14:10 word to Moses while Israel *w*
Ps 107: 4 They *w* in the wilderness in a
Isa 16: 8 have reached to Jazer And *w*
Lam 4:14 They *w* blind in the streets;
4:15 When they fled and *w*,
Ezek 34: 6 My sheep *w* through all the
Am 4: 8 So two or three cities *w* to
Heb 11:37 They *w* about in sheepskins and
11:38 They *w* in deserts and

WANDERERS (1/1)

Hos 9:17 And they shall be *w* among the

WANDERING (6/6) WANDER, WANDERINGS

Gen 37:15 there he was, *w* in the field.
Eccl 6: 9 the eyes than the *w* of desire.
Isa 16: 2 For it shall be as a *w* bird
49:21 and *w* to and fro? And who has
1 Tim 5:13 *w* about from house to house,
Jude 13 *w* stars for whom is reserved

WANDERINGS (1/1)

Ps 56: 8 You number my *w*;

WANDERS (5/4) WANDER

Job 15:23 He *w* about for bread, saying,
Prov 21:16 A man who *w* from the way of
27: 8 Like a bird that *w* from its
27: 8 from its nest Is a man who *w*
Jas 5:19 if anyone among you *w* from the

WANE (1/1)

Isa 17: 4 the glory of Jacob will *w*,

WANT (71/70) NEED, WANTED, WANTING, WANTS

Gen 42:36 and you *w* to take Benjamin.
Lev 27:20 But if he does not *w* to redeem
Deut 25: 7 But if the man does not *w* to
25: 8 I do not *w* to take her,'
Ruth 3:13 But if he does not *w* to perform
2 Ki 4:13 Do you *w* me to speak on your
Job 24: 8 huddle around the rock for *w*
30: 3 They are gaunt from *w* and
Ps 23: 1 is my shepherd; I shall not *w*.
34: 9 His saints! There is no *w*
Prov 13:25 of the wicked shall be in *w*.
Mt 7:12 whatever you *w* men to do to
12:38 we *w* to see a sign from You."
13:28 Do you *w* us then to go and
15:32 And I do not *w* to send them
19:17 But if you *w* to enter into
19:21 If you *w* to be perfect, go, sell
20:32 What do you *w* Me to do for
26:17 Where do You *w* us to prepare for
27:17 Whom do you *w* me to release to
27:21 Which of the two do you *w* me to
Mk 6:22 girl, "Ask me whatever you *w*,
6:25 I *w* you to give me at once the
6:26 he did not *w* to refuse her.
9:30 and He did not *w* anyone to know
10:35 we *w* You to do for us whatever
10:36 What do you *w* Me to do for
10:51 What do you *w* Me to do for
14:12 Where do You *w* us to go and
15: 9 Do you *w* me to release to you
15:12 What then do you *w* me to do
Lk 6:31 And just as you *w* men to do to
9:54 do You *w* us to command fire to
15:14 and he began to be in *w*.
16:26 so that those who *w* to pass
18:41 What do you *w* Me to do for
19:27 who did not *w* me to reign over
22: 9 Where do You *w* us to prepare?"
Jn 5: 6 Do you *w* to be made well?"
6:67 Do you also *w* to go away?"
7: 1 for He did not *w* to walk in
8:44 desires of your father you *w*
9:27 Why do you *w* to hear it again?
9:27 Do you also *w* to become His
18:39 Do you therefore *w* me to
Acts 7:28 Do you *w* to kill me as
9: 6 what do You *w* me to do?"
17:18 What does this babbler *w* to
17:20 Therefore we *w* to know what
18:15 for I do not *w* to be a judge of
Rom 1:13 Now I do not *w* you to be
13: 3 Do you *w* to be unafraid of the
16:19 but I *w* you to be wise in what
1 Cor 4:21 What do you *w*? Shall I come
7:32 But I *w* you to be without care.
10: 1 I do not *w* you to be unaware
10:20 and I do not *w* you to have
11: 3 But I *w* you to know that the
12: 1 I do not *w* you to be ignorant:
14:35 And if they *w* to learn
2 Cor 1: 8 For we do not *w* you to be
5: 4 not because we *w* to be
Gal 1: 7 are some who trouble you and *w*
3: 2 This only I *w* to learn from you:
4:17 they *w* to exclude you,
Phil 1:12 But I *w* you to know, brethren,
Col 2: 1 For I *w* you to know what a great
1 Th 4:13 But I do not *w* you to be
Titus 3: 8 and these things I *w* you to
Jas 2:20 But do you *w* to know, O foolish
Jude 5 But I *w* to remind you, though

WANTED (24/24) WANT

1 Ki 9: 1 Solomon's desire which he *w* to
Ezek 1:12 went wherever the spirit *w* to
1:20 Wherever the spirit *w* to go,
Mt 14: 5 And although he *w* to put him to
18:23 is like a certain king who *w*
23:37 How often I *w* to gather your
Mk 3:13 to Him those He Himself *w*.
6:19 held it against him and *w* to
7:24 And He entered a house and *w* no
Lk 13:34 How often I *w* to gather
Jn 1:43 The following day Jesus *w* to go
6:11 of the fish, as much as they *w*.
7:44 Now some of them *w* to take Him,
Acts 10:10 he became very hungry and *w* to
16: 3 Paul *w* to have him go on with
19:30 And when Paul *w* to go in to the
19:33 and *w* to make his defense to
22:30 because he *w* to know for
23:28 And when I *w* to know the reason
24: 6 and *w* to judge him according to
28:18 *w* to let me go, because there
1 Th 2:18 Therefore we *w* to come to
Phm 1:14 But without your consent I *w* to
Heb 12:17 when he *w* to inherit the

WANTING (8/8) WANT

Dan 5:27 in the balances, and found *w*;
Mt 1:19 and not *w* to make her a public
Mk 15:15 *w* to gratify the crowd,
Lk 10:29 *w* to justify himself, said to
Acts 24:27 *w* to do the Jews a favor, left
25: 9 *w* to do the Jews a favor,
27:43 *w* to save Paul, kept them from
Rom 9:22 *w* to show His wrath and to

WANTON (2/2)

Isa 3:16 with outstretched necks And *w*
1 Tim 5:11 when they have begun to grow *w*

WANTS (14/13) WANT

Ex 12:48 dwells with you and *w* to
Lev 27:13 But if he *w* at all to redeem
27:15 If he who dedicated it *w* to
27:31 If a man *w* at all to redeem any
Ezek 46: 5 as much as he *w* to give,
46: 7 as much as he *w* to give for the
46:11 as much as he *w* to give for the
Mt 5:40 If anyone *w* to sue you and take
5:42 and from him who *w* to borrow
Lk 13:31 for Herod *w* to kill You."
Jn 7:17 'If anyone *w* to do His will,
Jas 4: 4 Whoever therefore *w* to be a
Rev 11: 5 And if anyone *w* to harm them,
11: 5 And if anyone *w* to harm them,

WAR (232/227) WARFARE, WARRING, WARS

Gen 14: 2 that they made *w* with Bera king
Ex 1:10 it happen, in the event of *w*,
13:17 their minds when they see *w*,
15: 3 The LORD is a man of *w*;
17:16 the LORD will have *w* with
32:17 There is a noise of *w* in the
Num 1: 3 who are able to go to *w*
1:20 all who were able to go to *w*:
1:22 all who were able to go to *w*:
1:24 all who were able to go to *w*:
1:26 all who were able to go to *w*:
1:28 all who were able to go to *w*:
1:30 all who were able to go to *w*:
1:32 all who were able to go to *w*:
1:34 all who were able to go to *w*:
1:36 all who were able to go to *w*:
1:38 all who were able to go to *w*:
1:40 all who were able to go to *w*:
1:42 all who were able to go to *w*:
1:45 who were able to go to *w*
10: 9 When you go to *w* in your land
26: 2 all who are able to go to *w* in
31: 3 "Arm some of yourselves for *w*,
31: 4 Israel you shall send to the *w*.
31: 5 twelve thousand armed for *w*.
31: 6 Then Moses sent them to the *w*,
31: 6 he sent them to the *w* with
31:21 the priest said to the men of *w*
31:27 those who took part in the *w*,
31:28 for the LORD on the men of *w*
31:32 which the men of *w* had taken,
31:36 for those who had gone out to *w*,
31:49 taken a count of the men of *w*
31:53 (The men of *w* had taken spoil,
32: 6 Shall your brethren go to *w*
32:20 before the LORD for the *w*,
32:27 over, every man armed for *w*,
Deut 1:41 had girded on his weapons of *w*,
2:14 the generation of the men of *w*
2:16 when all the men of *w* had
4:34 by signs, by wonders, by *w*,
20:12 but makes *w* against you,
20:19 while making *w* against it to
20:20 against the city that makes *w*
21:10 When you go out to *w* against
24: 5 he shall not go out to *w* or be
Josh 4:13 forty thousand prepared for *w*
5: 4 were males, all the men of *w*,
5: 6 the people who were men of *w*,
6: 3 the city, all you men of *w*;
8: 1 take all the people of *w* with
8: 3 arose, and all the people of *w*,
8:11 And all the people of *w* who
10: 5 camped before Gibeon and made *w*
10: 7 he and all the people of *w* with
10:24 to the captains of the men of *w*
11: 7 Joshua and all the people of *w*
11:18 Joshua made *w* a long time with
11:23 Then the land rested from *w*.
14:11 so now is my strength for *w*,
14:15 Then the land had rest from *w*.
17: 1 because he was a man of *w*;
22:12 together at Shiloh to go to *w*
24: 9 arose to make *w* against Israel,
Judg 3: 2 might be taught to know *w*,
3:10 He went out to *w*, and the LORD
5: 8 Then there was *w* in the
11: 4 that the people of Ammon made *w*
11: 5 when the people of Ammon made *w*
18:11 armed with weapons of *w*.
18:16 armed with their weapons of *w*,
18:17 were armed with weapons of *w*.
20:17 all of these were men of *w*.
21:22 a wife for any of them in the *w*;
1 Sam 8:12 some to make his weapons of *w*
14:52 Now there was fierce *w* with the
16:18 mighty man of valor, a man of *w*,
17:33 and he a man of *w* from his
18: 5 Saul set him over the men of *w*,
18:30 the Philistines went out to *w*.
19: 8 And there was *w* again;
23: 8 all the people together for *w*,
28: 1 their armies together for *w*,
28:15 for the Philistines make *w*
2 Sam 1:27 And the weapons of *w*
3: 1 Now there was a long *w* between
3: 6 while there was *w* between the
8:10 (for Hadadezer had been at *w*
11: 7 and how the *w* prospered.
11:18 all the things concerning the *w*,
11:19 telling the matters of the *w*
17: 8 and your father is a man of *w*,
21:15 When the Philistines were at *w*
21:19 Again there was *w* at Gob with
21:20 Yet again there was *w* at Gath,
22:35 He teaches my hands to make *w*,
1 Ki 2: 5 And he shed the blood of *w* in
2: 5 and put the blood of *w* on his
9:22 because they were men of *w* and
14:19 how he made *w* and how he
14:30 And there was *w* between
15: 6 And there was *w* between
15: 7 And there was *w* between Abijam
15:16 Now there was *w* between Asa and
15:32 And there was *w* between Asa and
20: 1 and made *w* against it.
20:18 and if they have come out for *w*,
22: 1 three years passed without *w*
22:15 shall we go to *w* against Ramoth
22:45 he showed, and how he made *w*
2 Ki 6: 8 the king of Syria was making *w*
8:28 with Joram the son of Ahab to *w*
13:25 of Jehoahaz his father by *w*.
14: 7 of Salt, and took Sela by *w*,
14:28 he did—his might, how he made *w*,
16: 5 came up to Jerusalem to make *w*;
18:20 having plans and power for *w*;
19: 9 he has come out to make *w* with
24:16 were strong and fit for *w*,
25: 4 and all the men of *w* fled at
25:19 who had charge of the men of *w*,
1 Chr 5:10 in the days of Saul they made *w*
5:18 with the bow, and skillful in *w*,
5:18 skillful in war, who went to *w*.
5:19 They made *w* with the Hagrites,
5:22 because the *w* was God's.
7: 4 thousand troops ready for *w*;

7:11 of valor fit to go out for **w**
12: 1 mighty men, helpers in the **w**,
12:23 that were equipped for **w**,
12:24 eight hundred armed for **w**;
12:25 mighty men of valor fit for **w**,
12:33 expert in **w** with all weapons of
12:33 in war with all weapons of **w**,
12:36 those who could go out to **w**,
12:37 with every kind of weapon of **w**.
12:38 All these men of **w**,
18:10 (for Hadadezer had been at **w**
20: 4 it happened afterward that **w**
20: 5 Again there was **w** with the
20: 6 Yet again there was **w** at Gath,
28: 3 you have been a man of **w** and
2 Chr 8: 9 Some were men of **w**,
13: 2 And there was **w** between Abijah
14: 6 he had no **w** in those years,
15:19 And there was no **w** until the
17:10 so that they did not make **w**
17:13 of Judah; and the men of **w**,
17:18 eighty thousand prepared for **w**.
18: 3 we will be with you in the **w**.
18: 5 Shall we go to **w** against Ramoth
18:14 shall we go to **w** against Ramoth
22: 5 son of Ahab king of Israel to **w**
25: 5 choice men, able to go to **w**,
26: 6 Now he went out and made **w**
26:11 fighting men who went out to **w**
26:13 that made **w** with mighty power,
28:12 those who came from the **w**,
32: 2 that his purpose was to make **w**
35:21 the house with which I have **w**;
Job 5:20 And in **w** from the power of the
10:17 Changes and **w** are ever with
38:23 For the day of battle and **w**?
Ps 18:34 He teaches my hands to make **w**,
27: 3 Though **w** should rise against
55:21 But **w** was in his heart;
68:30 the peoples who delight in **w**.
120: 7 when I speak, they are for **w**.
140: 2 gather together for **w**.
144: 1 Who trains my hands for **w**,
Prov 20:18 By wise counsel wage **w**.
24: 6 you will wage your own **w**,
Eccl 3: 8 a time to hate; A time of **w**,
8: 8 is no release from that **w**,
9:18 is better than weapons of **w**;
Song 3: 8 swords, Being expert in **w**.
Isa 2: 4 Neither shall they learn **w**
3: 2 mighty man and the man of **w**,
3:25 And your mighty in the **w**.
7: 1 went up to Jerusalem to make **w**
21:15 and from the distress of **w**.
36: 5 of having plans and power for **w**;
37: 9 He has come out to make **w** with
41:12 Those who **w** against you Shall
42:13 up His zeal like a man of **w**.
Jer 4:19 of the trumpet, The alarm of **w**.
6: 4 'Prepare **w** against her;
6:23 As men of **w** set in array
21: 2 king of Babylon makes **w**
21: 4 will turn back the weapons of **w**
28: 8 of **w** and disaster and
38: 4 the hands of the men of **w** who
39: 4 of Judah and all the men of **w**
41: 3 were found there, the men of **w**.
41:16 the mighty men of **w** and the
42:14 Egypt where we shall see no **w**,
48:14 And strong men for the **w**'?
49: 2 to be heard an alarm of **w** In
49:26 And all the men of **w** shall be
50:30 And all her men of **w** shall be
51:20 My battle-ax and weapons of **w**:
51:32 And the men of **w** are
52: 7 and all the men of **w** fled and
52:25 who had charge of the men of **w**,
Ezek 17:17 company do anything in the **w**,
27:10 Were in your army as men of **w**;
27:27 All your men of **w** who are in
32:27 to hell with their weapons of **w**;
39:20 And with all the men of **w**,"
Dan 7:21 and the same horn was making **w**
9:26 And till the end of the **w**
Joel 2: 7 climb the wall like men of **w**;
3: 9 Prepare for **w**! Wake up the
3: 9 Let all the men of **w** draw
Mic 2: 8 Like men returned from **w**.
3: 5 But who prepare **w** against him
4: 3 Neither shall they learn **w** any
Lk 14:31 going to make **w** against another
23:11 Then Herod, with his men of **w**,
1 Cor 9: 7 Who ever goes to **w** at his own
2 Cor 10: 3 we do not **w** according to the
Jas 4: 1 desires for pleasure that **w**
4: 2 cannot obtain. You fight and **w**.
1 Pe 2:11 from fleshly lusts which **w**
Rev 11: 7 the bottomless pit will make **w**
12: 7 And **w** broke out in heaven:
12:17 and he went to make **w** with the
13: 4 Who is able to make **w** with
13: 7 It was granted to him to make **w**
17:14 These will make **w** with the Lamb,
19:11 He judges and makes **w**.
19:19 gathered together to make **w**

WAR-HORSES (1/1) HORSE

Ezek 23:24 With chariots, wagons, and **w**,

WARDROBE (3/3)

2 Ki 10:22 to the one in charge of the **w**,
22:14 son of Harhas, keeper of the **w**.
2 Chr 34:22 son of Hasrah, keeper of the **w**.

WARES (10/10)

Neh 10:31 peoples of the land brought **w**
13:20 and sellers of all kinds of **w**
Jer 10:17 Gather up your **w** from the
Ezek 27:14 of Togarmah traded for your **w**
27:16 They gave you for your **w**
27:19 "Dan and Javan paid for your **w**,
27:22 They traded for your **w** the
27:27 "Your riches, **w**,
27:33 When your **w** went out by sea,
Mk 11:16 not allow anyone to carry **w**

WARFARE (4/4) WAR

Isa 40: 2 That her **w** is ended,
2 Cor 10: 4 For the weapons of our **w** are
1 Tim 1:18 by them you may wage the good **w**,
2 Tim 2: 4 No one engaged in **w** entangles

WARM (9/8) WARMED, WARMING

1 Ki 1: 1 but he could not get **w**.
1: 2 that our lord the king may be **w**.
2 Ki 4:34 the flesh of the child became **w**.
Job 6:17 When it is **w**, they cease to
Eccl 4:11 down together, they will keep **w**;
4:11 But how can one be **w** alone?
Isa 44:15 he will take some of it and **w**
44:16 and says, "Ah! I am **w**,
Hag 1: 6 yourselves, but no one is **w**;

WARMED (7/6) WARM

Job 31:20 And if he was not **w** with the
Isa 47:14 shall not be a coal to be **w**
Mk 14:54 he sat with the servants and **w**
Jn 18:18 and they **w** themselves.
18:18 And Peter stood with them and **w**
18:25 Now Simon Peter stood and **w**
Jas 2:16 be **w** and filled," but you do

WARMING (1/1) WARM

Mk 14:67 And when she saw Peter **w**

WARMS (2/2)

Job 39:14 And **w** them in the dust;
Isa 44:16 He even **w** himself and says,

WARN (12/12) WARNED, WARNING

Ex 19:21 Go down and **w** the people, lest
1 Ki 2:42 and **w** you, saying, 'Know for
2 Chr 19:10 you shall **w** them, lest they
Ezek 3:18 nor speak to **w** the wicked from
3:19 if you **w** the wicked, and he
3:21 Nevertheless if you **w** the
33: 7 hear a word from My mouth and **w**
33: 8 and you do not speak to **w** the
33: 9 Nevertheless if you **w** the wicked
Acts 20:31 years I did not cease to **w**
1 Cor 4:14 but as my beloved children I **w**
1 Th 5:14 **w** those who are unruly, comfort

WARNED (21/21) WARN

Gen 43: 3 The man solemnly **w** us, saying,
Ex 19:23 for You **w** us, saying, 'Set
2 Ki 6:10 Thus he **w** him, and he was
Neh 13:15 And I **w** them about the day on
13:21 Then I **w** them, and said to them,
Ps 19:11 by them Your servant is **w**,
Ezek 33: 6 and the people are not **w**,
Mt 2:12 being divinely **w** in a dream
2:22 And being **w** by God in a dream,
3: 7 Brood of vipers! Who **w** you to
9:30 And Jesus sternly **w** them,
12:16 Yet He **w** them not to make Him
20:31 Then the multitude **w** them that
Mk 1:43 And He strictly **w** him and sent
3:12 But He sternly **w** them that they
8:30 Then He strictly **w** them that
10:48 Then many **w** him to be quiet;
Lk 3: 7 Brood of vipers! Who **w** you to
9:21 And He strictly **w** and commanded
18:39 Then those who went before **w** him
Heb 11: 7 being divinely **w** of things not

WARNING (9/8) WARN

Jer 6:10 whom shall I speak and give **w**,
Ezek 3:17 and give them **w** from Me:
3:18 die,' and you give him no **w**,
3:20 because you did not give him **w**,
3:21 surely live because he took **w**;
33: 4 the trumpet and does not take **w**,
33: 5 the trumpet, but did not take **w**;
33: 5 But he who takes **w** will save
Col 1:28 **w** every man and teaching every

WARNINGS (1/1)

2 Chr 36:15 God of their fathers sent **w**

WARNS (1/1)

Ezek 33: 3 if he blows the trumpet and **w**

WARP (9/9)

Lev 13:48 whether it is in the **w** or woof
13:49 whether in the **w** or in the
13:51 either in the **w** or in the woof,
13:52 whether **w** or woof, in wool or
13:53 either in the **w** or in the woof,
13:56 whether out of the **w** or out of
13:57 either in the **w** or in the woof,
13:58 either **w** or woof, or whatever
13:59 either in the **w** or woof, or in

WARPED (2/2)

Isa 47:10 and your knowledge have **w** you;
Titus 3:11 that such a person is **w** and

WARRED (1/1)

Num 31: 7 And they **w** against the

WARRING (3/3) WAR

2 Ki 19: 8 and found the king of Assyria **w**
Isa 37: 8 and found the king of Assyria **w**
Rom 7:23 **w** against the law of my mind,

WARRIOR (5/5)

1 Chr 12:28 Zadok, a young man, a valiant **w**,
Job 16:14 He runs at me like a **w**.
Ps 120: 4 Sharp arrows of the **w**,
127: 4 Like arrows in the hand of a **w**,
Jer 50: 9 be like those of an expert **w**;

WARRIOR'S (1/1)

Isa 9: 5 For every **w** sandal from the

WARRIORS (5/5)

1 Ki 12:21 thousand chosen men who were **w**,
1 Chr 11:26 Also the mighty **w** were Asahel
2 Chr 11: 1 thousand chosen men who were **w**,
13: 3 order with an army of valiant **w**,
Ezek 32:12 'By the swords of the mighty **w**,

WARS (14/12) WAR

Num 21:14 it is said in the Book of the ***W***
Judg 3: 1 who had not known any of the **w**
1 Ki 5: 3 LORD his God because of the **w**
1 Chr 22: 8 blood and have made great **w**;
2 Chr 12:15 And there were **w** between
16: 9 from now on you shall have **w**.
27: 7 and all his **w** and his ways,
Ps 46: 9 He makes **w** cease to the end of
Mt 24: 6 And you will hear of **w** and
24: 6 hear of wars and rumors of **w**.
Mk 13: 7 But when you hear of **w** and
13: 7 hear of wars and rumors of **w**,
Lk 21: 9 But when you hear of **w** and
Jas 4: 1 Where do **w** and fights come from

WARY (1/1)

Prov 19:25 and the simple will become **w**;

WAS (4346/3555) See APPENDIX

WASH (85/78) UNWASHED, WASHED, WASHING, WASHPOT

Gen 18: 4 and **w** your feet, and rest
19: 2 and **w** your feet; then you may
24:32 and water to **w** his feet and the
Ex 19:10 and let them **w** their clothes.
29: 4 and you shall **w** them with
29:17 **w** its entrails and its legs,
30:19 Aaron and his sons shall **w**
30:20 they shall **w** with water, lest
30:21 So they shall **w** their hands and
40:12 the tabernacle of meeting and **w**
40:31 and his sons would **w** their
Lev 1: 9 but he shall **w** its entrails and
1:13 but he shall **w** the entrails and
6:27 you shall **w** that on which it
11:25 carcass of any of them shall **w**
11:28 any such carcass shall **w** his
11:40 who eats of its carcass shall **w**
11:40 who carries its carcass shall **w**
13: 6 and he shall **w** his clothes and
13:34 He shall **w** his clothes and be
13:54 shall command that they **w** the
13:58 'And if you **w** the garment,
14: 8 who is to be cleansed shall **w**
14: 8 and **w** himself in water, that he
14: 9 He shall **w** his clothes and wash
14: 9 He shall wash his clothes and **w**
14:47 lies down in the house shall **w**
14:47 who eats in the house shall **w**
15: 5 touches his bed shall **w** his
15: 6 has the discharge sat shall **w**
15: 7 who has the discharge shall **w**
15: 8 then he shall **w** his clothes and
15:10 any of those things shall **w**
15:11 he shall **w** his clothes and
15:13 **w** his clothes, and bathe his
15:16 then he shall **w** all his body in

	15:21	touches her bed shall **w** his
	15:22	that she sat on shall **w** his
	15:27	he shall **w** his clothes and
	16: 4	Therefore he shall **w** his body
	16:24	And he shall **w** his body with
	16:26	goat as the scapegoat shall **w**
	16:28	he who burns them shall **w**
	17:15	he shall both **w** his clothes and
	17:16	But if he does not **w** them or
Num	8: 7	and let them **w** their clothes,
	19: 7	Then the priest shall **w** his
	19: 8	the one who burns it shall **w**
	19:10	the ashes of the heifer shall **w**
	19:19	**w** his clothes, and bathe in
	19:21	water of purification shall **w**
	31:24	And you shall **w** your clothes on
Deut	21: 6	to the slain man shall **w**
	23:11	that he shall **w** with water;
Ruth	3: 3	Therefore **w** yourself and anoint
1 Sam	25:41	a servant to **w** the feet of the
2 Sam	11: 8	Go down to your house and **w** your
2 Ki	5:10	Go and **w** in the Jordan seven
	5:12	Could I not **w** in them and be
	5:13	then, when he says to you, '**W**,
2 Chr	4: 6	on the left, to **w** in them;
	4: 6	burnt offering they would **w** in
	4: 6	Sea was for the priests to **w**
Job	9:30	If I **w** myself with snow water,
	14:19	And as torrents **w** away the
Ps	26: 6	I will **w** my hands in innocence;
	51: 2	**W** me thoroughly from my
	51: 7	**W** me, and I shall be whiter
	58:10	He shall **w** his feet in the
Isa	1:16	**W** yourselves, make yourselves
Jer	2:22	For though you **w** yourself with
	4:14	**w** your heart from wickedness,
Mt	6:17	anoint your head and **w** your
	15: 2	For they do not **w** their hands
Mk	7: 3	Jews do not eat unless they **w**
	7: 4	they do not eat unless they **w**.
Lk	7:38	and she began to **w** His feet
Jn	9: 7	**w** in the pool of Siloam"
	9:11	'Go to the pool of Siloam and **w**.'
	13: 5	into a basin and began to **w**
	13: 8	You shall never **w** my feet!"
	13: 8	If I do not **w** you, you have no
	13:10	who is bathed needs only to **w**
	13:14	you also ought to **w** one
Acts	22:16	and **w** away your sins, calling

WASHED (42/41) WASH

Gen	43:24	and they **w** their feet;
	43:31	Then he **w** his face and came out;
	49:11	He **w** his garments in wine,
Ex	19:14	and they **w** their clothes.
	40:32	came near the altar, they **w**,
Lev	8: 6	Aaron and his sons and **w** them
	8:21	Then he **w** the entrails and the
	9:14	And he **w** the entrails and the
	13:55	the plague after it has been **w**;
	13:58	then it shall be **w** a second
	15:17	it shall be **w** with water,
Num	8:21	purified themselves and **w**
Judg	19:21	And they **w** their feet, and ate
2 Sam	12:20	**w** and anointed himself,
	19:24	nor **w** his clothes, from the day
1 Ki	22:38	Then someone **w** the chariot at a
Ps	73:13	And **w** my hands in innocence.
Prov	30:12	Yet is not **w** from its
Song	5: 3	I have **w** my feet; How can I
	5:12	**W** with milk, And fitly set.
Isa	4: 4	When the Lord has **w** away the
Ezek	16: 4	nor were you **w** in water to
	16: 9	Then I **w** you in water; yes, I
	16: 9	I thoroughly **w** off your blood,
	23:40	And you **w** yourself for them,
	40:38	where they **w** the burnt
Mt	27:24	he took water and **w** his hands
Lk	7:44	but she has **w** My feet with her
	11:38	that He had not first **w** before
Jn	9: 7	So he went and **w**,
	9:11	So I went and **w**,
	9:15	put clay on my eyes, and I **w**,
	13:12	So when He had **w** their feet,
	13:14	have **w** your feet, you also
Acts	9:37	When they had **w** her, they laid
	16:33	same hour of the night and **w**
1 Cor	6:11	But you were **w**, but you were
1 Tim	5:10	if she has **w** the saints' feet,
Heb	10:22	conscience and our bodies **w**
2 Pe	2:22	and, "a sow, having **w**,
Rev	1: 5	To Him who loved us and **w** us
	7:14	and **w** their robes and made them

WASHES (1/1)

Lev	22: 6	the holy offerings unless he **w**

WASHING (12/12) WASH

Ex	30:18	its base also of bronze, for **w**.
	40:30	and put water there for **w**;
Lev	13:56	the plague has faded after **w**
Neh	4:23	everyone took them off for **w**.
Song	4: 2	Which have come up from the **w**,
	6: 6	Which have come up from the **w**;
Mk	7: 4	like the **w** of cups, pitchers,
	7: 8	—the **w** of pitchers and cups,
Lk	5: 2	had gone from them and were **w**
Jn	13: 6	are You **w** my feet?"
Eph	5:26	and cleanse her with the **w** of
Titus	3: 5	through the **w** of regeneration

WASHINGS (1/1)

Heb	9:10	foods and drinks, various **w**,

WASHPOT (2/2) POT, WASH

Ps	60: 8	Moab is My **w**; Over Edom
	108: 9	Moab is My **w**; Over Edom

WASTE (67/64) WASTED, WASTES, WASTING

Lev	26:31	I will lay your cities **w** and
	26:33	be desolate and your cities **w**.
	26:39	of you who are left shall **w**
	26:39	they shall **w** away.
Num	21:30	Then we laid **w** as far as
2 Ki	18:27	will eat and drink their own **w**
	19:17	kings of Assyria have laid **w**
Neh	2: 3	of my fathers' tombs, lies **w**,
	2:17	are in, how Jerusalem lies **w**,
Job	30: 3	the wilderness, desolate and **w**,
	38:27	To satisfy the desolate **w**,
Ps	31:10	And my bones **w** away.
	79: 7	And laid **w** his dwelling place.
	91: 6	of the destruction that lays **w**
Prov	13:23	for lack of justice there is **w**.
	23: 8	And **w** your pleasant words.
Isa	5: 6	I will lay it **w**;
	5:17	And in the **w** places of the fat
	6:11	Until the cities are laid **w** and
	15: 1	the night Ar of Moab is laid **w**
	15: 1	the night Kir of Moab is laid **w**
	23: 1	of Tarshish! For it is laid **w**,
	23:14	For your strength is laid **w**.
	24: 1	the earth empty and makes it **w**,
	33: 8	The highways lie **w**,
	34:10	to generation it shall lie **w**;
	36:12	will eat and drink their own **w**
	37:18	kings of Assyria have laid **w**
	42:15	I will lay **w** the mountains and
	44:26	And I will raise up her **w**
	49:17	and those who laid you **w**
	49:19	For your **w** and desolate places,
	51: 3	He will comfort all her **w**
	52: 9	You **w** places of Jerusalem!
	58:12	you Shall build the old **w**
	64:11	our pleasant things are laid **w**.
Jer	2:15	They made his land **w**;
	4: 7	Your cities will be laid **w**,
	27:17	Why should this city be laid **w**?
	46:19	For Noph shall be **w** and
	49:13	a desolation, a reproach, a **w**,
	50:21	**W** and utterly destroy them,"
Ezek	4:12	bake it using fuel of human **w**
	4:15	you cow dung instead of human **w**,
	4:17	and **w** away because of their
	5:14	Moreover I will make you a **w** and
	6: 6	the cities shall be laid **w**,
	6: 6	that your altars may be laid **w**
	12:20	are inhabited shall be laid **w**,
	19: 7	And laid **w** their cities;
	26: 2	shall be filled; she is laid **w**.
	29: 9	shall become desolate and **w**;
	29:10	the land of Egypt utterly **w**
	29:12	the cities that are laid **w**,
	30: 7	of the cities that are laid **w**.
	30:12	wicked; I will make the land **w**,
	35: 4	I shall lay your cities **w**,
	38:12	out your hand against the **w**
Hos	4: 3	who dwells there will **w** away
Joel	1: 7	He has laid **w** My vine,
Am	7: 9	of Israel shall be laid **w**.
	9:14	They shall build the **w** cities
Mic	5: 6	They shall **w** with the sword the
Nah	2:10	empty, desolate, and **w**!
	3: 7	'Nineveh is laid **w**!
Mal	1: 3	And laid **w** his mountains and
Mt	26: 8	indignant, saying, "Why this **w**?

WASTED (7/7) WASTE

Deut	32:24	They shall be **w** with hunger,
Isa	19: 5	And the river will be **w** and
Jer	44: 6	and they are **w** and desolate,
Ezek	36:35	the garden of Eden; and the **w**,
Joel	1:10	The field is **w**,
Mk	14: 4	"Why was this fragrant oil **w**?
Lk	15:13	and there **w** his possessions

WASTELAND (4/4)

Num	21:20	which looks down on the **w**.
	23:28	of Peor, that overlooks the **w**.
Deut	32:10	in a desert land And in the **w**,
Isa	35: 1	The wilderness and the **w** shall

WASTES (8/8) WASTE

Job	33:21	His flesh **w** away from sight,
Ps	6: 7	My eye **w** away because of grief;
	31: 9	My eye **w** away with grief,
	88: 9	My eye **w** away because of
Prov	29: 3	But a companion of harlots **w**
Isa	10:18	will be as when a sick man **w**
Jer	49:13	its cities shall be perpetual **w**.
Ezek	36: 4	the valleys, the desolate **w**,

WASTING (4/4) WASTE

Lev	26:16	**w** disease and fever which shall
Isa	59: 7	**W** and destruction are in
	60:18	Neither **w** nor destruction
Lk	16: 1	to him that this man was **w** his

WATCH (65/61) WATCHED, WATCHER, WATCHES, WATCHFUL, WATCHING, WATCHMAN

Gen	31:49	May the LORD **w** between you and
Ex	14:24	came to pass, in the morning **w**,
Num	4:20	But they shall not go in to **w**
Deut	2: 4	Therefore **w** yourselves
Judg	7:17	"Look at me and do likewise; **w**,
	7:19	the beginning of the middle **w**,
	7:19	just as they had posted the **w**;
	21:21	**w**; and just when the daughters
1 Sam	6: 9	'And **w**: if it goes up the road
	11:11	of the camp in the morning **w**,
	19:11	to David's house to **w** him and
2 Sam	13:28	**W** now, when Amnon's heart is
	13:34	the young man who was keeping **w**
	20:21	So the woman said to Joab, "**W**,
2 Ki	11: 5	the Sabbath shall be keeping **w**
	11: 6	You shall keep the **w** of the
	11: 7	on the Sabbath shall keep the **w**
2 Chr	23: 4	shall be keeping **w** over the
	23: 6	the people shall keep the **w** of
Ezra	8:29	**W** and keep them until you weigh
Neh	4: 9	and because of them we set a **w**
	7: 3	one at his **w** station and
	12:25	gatekeepers keeping the **w** at
Job	13:27	And **w** closely all my paths.
	14:16	But do not **w** over my sin.
Ps	90: 4	And like a **w** in the night.
	130: 6	the Lord More than those who **w**
	130: 6	more than those who **w** for the
	141: 3	Keep **w** over the door of my
Prov	15: 3	Keeping **w** on the evil and the
Isa	29:20	And all who **w** for iniquity are
Jer	5: 6	A leopard will **w** over their
	31:28	so I will **w** over them to build
	44:27	I will **w** over them for
	48:19	Aroer, Stand by the way and **w**;
Dan	12: 1	The great prince who stands **w**
Nah	2: 1	Man the fort! **W** the road!
Hab	1: 5	among the nations and **w**—
	2: 1	I will stand my **w** And set
	2: 1	And **w** to see what He will say
Mt	14:25	Now in the fourth **w** of the night
	24:42	**W** therefore, for you do not know
	25:13	**W** therefore, for you know
	26:38	Stay here and **w** with Me."
	26:40	Could you not **w** with Me one
	26:41	**W** and pray, lest you enter into
	27:36	they kept **w** over Him there.
Mk	6:48	Now about the fourth **w** of the
	13: 9	'But **w** out for yourselves,
	13:33	**w** and pray; for you do not know
	13:34	commanded the doorkeeper to **w**.
	13:35	**W** therefore, for you do not know
	13:37	I say to all: **W**!"
	14:34	even to death. Stay here and **w**.
	14:37	Could you not **w** one hour?
	14:38	**W** and pray, lest you enter into
Lk	2: 8	keeping **w** over their flock by
	12:38	he should come in the second **w**,
	12:38	watch, or come in the third **w**,
	21:36	**W** therefore, and pray always
Acts	20:31	'Therefore **w**, and remember
1 Cor	16:13	**W**, stand fast in the faith,
1 Th	5: 6	but let us **w** and be sober.
Heb	13:17	for they **w** out for your souls,
Rev	3: 3	Therefore if you will not **w**,

WATCHED (21/20) WATCH

Ex	33: 8	stood at his tent door and **w**
1 Sam	1:12	that Eli **w** her mouth.
Job	29: 2	As in the days when God **w**
Ps	59:	and they **w** the the house in
Jer	20:10	All my acquaintances **w** for
	31:28	that as I have **w** over them to
Lam	4:17	In our watching we **w** For a
Ezek	10: 2	And he went in as I **w**.
Dan	2:34	You **w** while a stone was cut out
	7: 4	I **w** till its wings were plucked
	7: 9	I **w** till thrones were put in
	7:11	I **w** then because of the sound of
	7:11	I **w** till the beast was slain,
Mt	24:43	he would have **w** and not allowed
Mk	3: 2	So they **w** Him closely, whether
Lk	6: 7	So the scribes and Pharisees **w**
	12:39	he would have **w** and not allowed
	14: 1	that they **w** Him closely.
	20:20	So they **w** Him, and sent spies
Acts	1: 9	these things, while they **w**,
	9:24	And they **w** the gates day and

WATCHER (3/3) WATCH, WATCHERS

Job	7:20	O **w** of men? Why have You set
Dan	4:13	on my bed, and there was a **w**,
	4:23	inasmuch as the king saw a **w**,

WATCHERS (2/2) WATCHER

Jer	4:16	That **w** come from a far
Dan	4:17	is by the decree of the **w**,

WATCHES (9/9) WATCH

Job	33:11	He **w** all my paths.'

Ps 37:32 The wicked **w** the righteous,
63: 6 meditate on You in the night **w**.
119:148 are awake through the night **w**,
146: 9 The LORD **w** over the strangers;
Prov 31:27 She **w** over the ways of her
Eccl 5: 8 for high official **w** over high
Lam 2:19 At the beginning of the **w**;
Rev 16:15 Blessed is he who **w**,

WATCHFUL (5/5) WATCH

2 Ki 6:10 and he was **w** there,
Eph 6:18 being **w** to this end with all
2 Tim 4: 5 But you be **w** in all things,
1 Pe 4: 7 therefore be serious and **w** in
Rev 3: 2 'Be **w**, and strengthen

WATCHING (12/11) WATCH

Judg 16:27 men and women on the roof **w**
1 Sam 4:13 on a seat by the wayside **w**,
1 Ki 20:33 Now the men were **w** closely to
Prov 8:34 **W** daily at my gates, Waiting
Lam 4:17 **W** vainly for our help;
4:17 In our **w** we watched For a
Dan 2:31 "You, O king, were **w**;
7:13 I was **w** in the night visions,
7:21 'I was **w**; and the same horn
Zech 11:11 who were **w** me, knew that it
Lk 12:37 when he comes, will find **w**.
23:49 **w** these things.

WATCHMAN (23/20) WATCH, WATCHMEN

2 Sam 18:24 And the **w** went up to the roof
18:25 Then the **w** cried out and told
18:26 Then the **w** saw another man
18:26 and the **w** called to the
18:27 So the **w** said, "I think the
2 Ki 9:17 Now a **w** stood on the tower in
9:18 So the **w** reported, saying,
9:20 So the **w** reported, saying, "He
1 Chr 26:16 **w** opposite watchman.
26:16 highway—watchman opposite **w**.
Job 27:18 Like a booth which a **w** makes.
Ps 127: 1 The **w** stays awake in vain.
Isa 21: 5 Set a **w** in the tower, Eat and
21: 6 Lord said to me: "Go, set a **w**,
21:11 calls to me out of Seir, "**W**,
21:11 what of the night? **W**,
21:12 The **w** said, "The morning
Ezek 3:17 I have made you a **w** for the
33: 2 territory and make him their **w**,
33: 6 But if the **w** sees the sword
33: 7 I have made you a **w** for the
Hos 9: 8 The **w** of Ephraim is with my
Mic 7: 4 The day of your **w** and your

WATCHMAN'S (1/1)

Ezek 33: 6 blood I will require at the **w**

WATCHMEN (9/9) WATCHMAN

1 Sam 14:16 Now the **w** of Saul in Gibeah of
Song 3: 3 The **w** who go about the city
5: 7 The **w** who went about the city
Isa 52: 8 Your **w** shall lift up their
56:10 His **w** are blind, They are all
62: 6 I have set **w** on your walls, O
Jer 6:17 I set **w** over you, saying,
31: 6 shall be a day When the **w**
51:12 the guard strong, Set up the **w**,

WATCHTOWER (3/3)

2 Ki 17: 9 from **w** to fortified city.
18: 8 from **w** to fortified city.
Isa 21: 8 I stand continually on the **w**

WATER (460/416) WATERED, WATERFALLS, WATERING, WATERPOT, WATERS

Gen 2:10 a river went out of Eden to **w**
16: 7 found her by a spring of **w** in
18: 4 Please let a little **w** be
21:14 and took bread and a skin of **w**;
21:15 And the **w** in the skin was used
21:19 eyes, and she saw a well of **w**.
21:19 went and filled the skin with **w**,
21:25 because of a well of **w** which
24:11 the city by a well of **w** at
24:11 when women go out to draw **w**.
24:13 here I stand by the well of **w**,
24:13 city are coming out to draw **w**.
24:17 let me drink a little **w**
24:19 I will draw **w** for your camels
24:20 ran back to the well to draw **w**,
24:32 and **w** to wash his feet and the
24:43 I stand by the well of **w**;
24:43 the virgin comes out to draw **w**,
24:43 Please give me a little **w** from
24:45 down to the well and drew **w**.
26:18 Isaac dug again the wells of **w**
26:19 and found a well of running **w**
26:20 The **w** is ours." So he called
26:32 said to him, "We have found **w**.
29: 3 **w** the sheep, and put the stone
29: 7 **W** the sheep, and go and feed
29: 8 then we **w** the sheep."
36:24 was the Anah who found the **w**
37:24 there was no **w** in it.
43:24 Joseph's house and gave them **w**,
49: 4 Unstable as **w**,
Ex 2:10 I drew him out of the **w**.
2:16 And they came and drew **w**,
2:16 they filled the troughs to **w**
2:19 and he also drew enough **w** for
4: 9 that you shall take **w** from the
4: 9 And the **w** which you take from
7:15 when he goes out to the **w**,
7:18 will loathe to drink the **w** of
7:19 and over all their pools of **w**,
7:21 could not drink the **w** of the
7:24 dug all around the river for **w**
7:24 they could not drink the **w** of
8:20 as he comes out to the **w**.
12: 9 raw, nor boiled at all with **w**,
15:22 the wilderness and found no **w**.
15:27 there were twelve wells of **w**
17: 1 but there was no **w** for the
17: 2 Moses, and said, "Give us **w**,
17: 3 the people thirsted there for **w**,
17: 6 and **w** will come out of it,
20: 4 or that is in the **w** under the
23:25 bless your bread and your **w**.
29: 4 and you shall wash them with **w**.
30:18 And you shall put **w** in it,
30:19 hands and their feet in **w** from
30:20 LORD, they shall wash with **w**,
32:20 and he scattered it on the **w**
34:28 neither ate bread nor drank **w**.
40: 7 and put **w** in it.
40:12 of meeting and wash them with **w**.
40:30 and put **w** there for washing;
40:31 hands and their feet with **w**
Lev 1: 9 entrails and its legs with **w**.
1:13 entrails and the legs with **w**.
6:28 be both scoured and rinsed in **w**.
8: 6 his sons and washed them with **w**.
8:21 the entrails and the legs in **w**.
11: 9 eat of all that are in the **w**:
11: 9 whatever in the **w** has fins and
11:10 all that move in the **w** or any
11:10 living thing which is in the **w**,
11:12 Whatever in the **w** does not have
11:32 is done, it must be put in **w**.
11:34 any edible food upon which **w**
11:36 which there is plenty of **w**,
11:38 'But if **w** is put on the seed,
14: 5 earthen vessel over running **w**.
14: 6 was killed over the running **w**.
14: 8 his hair, and wash himself in **w**,
14: 9 clothes and wash his body in **w**,
14:50 earthen vessel over running **w**;
14:51 slain bird and in the running **w**,
14:52 of the bird and the running **w**
15: 5 wash his clothes and bathe in **w**,
15: 6 wash his clothes and bathe in **w**,
15: 7 wash his clothes and bathe in **w**,
15: 8 wash his clothes and bathe in **w**,
15:10 wash his clothes and bathe in **w**,
15:11 has not rinsed his hands in **w**,
15:11 wash his clothes and bathe in **w**,
15:12 of wood shall be rinsed in **w**.
15:13 and bathe his body in running **w**;
15:16 he shall wash all his body in **w**,
15:17 it shall be washed with **w**,
15:18 of semen, they shall bathe in **w**,
15:21 wash his clothes and bathe in **w**,
15:22 wash his clothes and bathe in **w**,
15:27 wash his clothes and bathe in **w**,
16: 4 he shall wash his body in **w**,
16:24 he shall wash his body with **w**
16:26 clothes and bathe his body in **w**,
16:28 clothes and bathe his body in **w**,
17:15 wash his clothes and bathe in **w**,
22: 6 he washes his body with **w**.
Num 5:17 The priest shall take holy **w** in
5:17 and put it into the **w**.
5:18 have in his hand the bitter **w**
5:19 be free from this bitter **w** that
5:22 and may this **w** that causes the
5:23 them off into the bitter **w**.
5:24 the woman drink the bitter **w**
5:24 and the **w** that brings the curse
5:26 make the woman drink the **w**.
5:27 he has made her drink the **w**,
5:27 that the **w** that brings a curse
8: 7 Sprinkle **w** of purification on
19: 7 clothes, he shall bathe in **w**,
19: 8 it shall wash his clothes in **w**,
19: 8 clothes in water, bathe in **w**,
19: 9 children of Israel for the **w**;
19:12 purify himself with the **w** on
19:13 because the **w** of purification
19:17 and running **w** shall be put on
19:18 hyssop and dip it in the **w**,
19:19 his clothes, and bathe in **w**;
19:20 The **w** of purification has not
19:21 He who sprinkles the **w** of
19:21 and he who touches the **w** of
20: 2 Now there was no **w** for the
20: 5 nor is there any **w** to drink."
20: 8 and it will yield its **w**;
20: 8 thus you shall bring **w** for them
20:10 you rebels! Must we bring **w** for
20:11 and **w** came out abundantly, and
20:13 This was the **w** of Meribah,
20:17 nor will we drink **w** from wells;
20:19 livestock drink any of your **w**,
20:24 against My word at the **w** of
21: 5 For there is no food and no **w**,
21:16 and I will give them **w**.
21:22 we will not drink **w** from wells.
24: 7 He shall pour **w** from his
31:23 it shall be purified with the **w**
31:23 fire you shall put through **w**.
33: 9 Elim were twelve springs of **w**
33:14 where there was no **w** for the
Deut 2: 6 and you shall also buy **w** from
2:28 and give me **w** for money, that I
4:18 of any fish that is in the **w**
5: 8 or that is in the **w** under the
8: 7 land, a land of brooks of **w**,
8:15 land where there was no **w**;
8:15 who brought **w** for you out of
9: 9 I neither ate bread nor drank **w**.
9:18 I neither ate bread nor drank **w**,
10: 7 a land of rivers of **w**.
11:11 which drinks **w** from the rain of
12:16 pour it on the earth like **w**.
12:24 pour it on the earth like **w**.
15:23 pour it on the ground like **w**.
21: 4 down to a valley with flowing **w**,
23: 4 not meet you with bread and **w**
23:11 that he shall wash with **w**;
29:11 to the one who draws your **w**—
Josh 2:10 how the LORD dried up the **w**
3: 8 have come to the edge of the **w**
3:15 ark dipped in the edge of the **w**
7: 5 people melted and became like **w**.
9:21 let them be woodcutters and **w**
9:23 woodcutters and **w** carriers for
9:27 made them woodcutters and **w**
15: 9 hill to the fountain of the **w**
15:19 give me also springs of **w**.
Judg 1:15 give me also springs of **w**.
4:19 Please give me a little **w** to
5: 4 The clouds also poured **w**;
5:25 He asked for **w**,
6:38 of the fleece, a bowlful of **w**.
7: 4 bring them down to the **w**,
7: 5 the people down to the **w**.
7: 5 Everyone who laps from the **w**
7: 6 down on their knees to drink **w**.
15:19 and **w** came out, and he drank;
1 Sam 7: 6 together at Mizpah, drew **w**,
9:11 young women going out to draw **w**,
25:11 I then take my bread and my **w**
26:11 now the spear and the jug of **w**
26:12 the spear and the jug of **w** by
26:16 and the jug of **w** that was by
30:11 and they let him drink **w**.
30:12 had eaten no bread nor drunk **w**
2 Sam 5: 8 climbs up by way of the **w**
5:20 like a breakthrough of **w**."
12:27 and I have taken the city's **w**
14:14 surely die and become like **w**
17:20 They have gone over the **w**
17:21 Arise and cross over the **w**
23:15 would give me a drink of the **w**
23:16 drew **w** from the well of
1 Ki 13: 8 would I eat bread nor drink **w**
13: 9 not eat bread, nor drink **w**,
13:16 can I eat bread nor drink **w**
13:17 shall not eat bread nor drink **w**
13:18 he may eat bread and drink **w**.
13:19 bread in his house, and drank **w**.
13:22 and drank **w** in the place of
13:22 "Eat no bread and drink no **w**,
14:15 as a reed is shaken in the **w**.
17:10 Please bring me a little **w** in a
18: 4 had fed them with bread and **w**.
18: 5 land to all the springs of **w**
18:13 and fed them with bread and **w**?
18:33 "Fill four waterpots with **w**,
18:35 So the **w** ran all around the
18:35 also filled the trench with **w**.
18:38 and it licked up the **w** that
19: 6 baked on coals, and a jar of **w**.
22:27 with bread of affliction and **w**
2 Ki 2: 8 rolled it up, and struck the **w**;
2:14 from him, and struck the **w**,
2:14 when he also had struck the **w**,
2:19 but the **w** is bad, and the
2:21 went out to the source of the **w**,
2:21 LORD: 'I have healed this **w**;
2:22 So the **w** remains healed to this
3: 9 and there was no **w** for the
3:11 who poured **w** on the hands of
3:17 valley shall be filled with **w**,
3:19 and stop up every spring of **w**,
3:20 that suddenly **w** came by way of
3:20 and the land was filled with **w**.
3:22 the sun was shining on the **w**;
3:22 and the Moabites saw the **w** on
3:25 up all the springs of **w** and
6: 5 iron ax head fell into the **w**;
6:22 Set food and **w** before them,
8:15 thick cloth and dipped it in **w**,
19:24 I have dug and drunk strange **w**,
20:20 pool and a tunnel and brought **w**
1 Chr 11:17 would give me a drink of **w**
11:18 drew **w** from the well of
14:11 hand like a breakthrough of **w**.
2 Chr 18:26 with bread of affliction and **w**
32: 3 and commanders to stop the **w**
32: 4 of Assyria come and find much **w**?
32:30 Hezekiah also stopped the **w**
32:30 and brought the **w** by tunnel to
Ezra 10: 6 he ate no bread and drank no **w**,
Neh 3:26 the place in front of the **W**
8: 1 that was in front of the **W**
8: 3 that was in front of the **W**

8:16 and in the open square of the *W*
9:15 And brought them *w* out of the
9:20 And gave them *w* for their
12:37 as far as the *W* Gate eastward.
13: 2 of Israel with bread and *w*,
Job 3:24 my groanings pour out like *w*.
8:11 the reeds flourish without *w*?
14: 9 Yet at the scent of *w* it will
14:11 As *w* disappears from the sea,
14:19 As *w* wears away stones,
15:16 Who drinks iniquity like *w*!
22: 7 have not given the weary *w* to
22:11 And an abundance of *w* covers
26: 8 He binds up the *w* in His thick
34: 7 Job, Who drinks scorn like *w*,
36:27 For He draws up drops of *w*,
38:25 channel for the overflowing *w*,
38:34 That an abundance of *w* may
Ps 1: 3 Planted by the rivers of *w*,
22:14 I am poured out like *w*,
42: 1 As the deer pants for the *w*
63: 1 land Where there is no *w*.
65: 9 You visit the earth and *w* it,
65: 9 The river of God is full of *w*;
65:10 You *w* its ridges abundantly,
66:12 went through fire and through *w*;
72: 6 Like showers that *w* the
77:17 The clouds poured out *w*;
79: 3 blood they have shed like *w*
88:17 around me all day long like *w*;
105:41 and *w* gushed out; It ran in
107:35 a wilderness into pools of *w*,
109:18 let it enter his body like *w*,
114: 8 the rock into a pool of *w*,
119:136 Rivers of *w* run down from my
Prov 5:15 Drink *w* from your own cistern,
5:15 And running *w* from your own
5:16 Streams of *w* in the streets?
8:24 no fountains abounding with *w*.
9:17 Stolen *w* is sweet, And bread
17:14 of strife is like releasing *w*;
20: 5 heart of man is like deep *w*,
21: 1 LORD, Like the rivers of *w*;
25:21 give him *w* to drink;
25:25 As cold *w* to a weary soul,
27:19 As in *w* face reflects face,
30:16 that is not satisfied with *w*—
Eccl 2: 6 I made myself *w* pools from which
2: 6 water pools from which to *w*
Isa 1:22 dross, Your wine mixed with *w*.
1:30 And as a garden that has no *w*.
3: 1 bread and the whole supply of *w*;
12: 3 with joy you will draw *w* From
14:23 And marshes of muddy *w*;
21:14 Bring *w* to him who is thirsty;
22:11 the two walls For the *w* of
27: 3 I *w* it every moment;
30:14 Or to take *w* from the
30:20 bread of adversity and the *w*
32: 2 As rivers of *w* in a dry place,
33:16 His *w* will be sure.
35: 7 the thirsty land springs of *w*;
37:25 I have dug and drunk *w*,
41:17 "The poor and needy seek *w*,
41:18 make the wilderness a pool of *w*,
41:18 And the dry land springs of *w*.
44: 3 For I will pour *w* on him who is
44:12 He drinks no *w* and is faint.
49:10 Even by the springs of *w* He
50: 2 stink because there is no *w*,
55:10 But *w* the earth, And make it
58:11 And like a spring of *w*,
63:12 Dividing the *w* before them
64: 2 As fire causes *w* to boil—To
Jer 2:13 cisterns that can hold no *w*.
6: 7 As a fountain wells up with *w*,
8:14 us to silence And given us *w*
9:15 and give them *w* of gall to
9:18 And our eyelids gush with *w*.
13: 1 but do not put it in *w*."
14: 3 have sent their lads for *w*;
14: 3 to the cisterns and found no *w*.
23:15 And make them drink the *w* of
38: 6 in the dungeon there was no *w*,
Lam 1:16 my eye overflows with *w*;
2:19 Pour out your heart like *w*
3:48 eyes overflow with rivers of *w*
5: 4 We pay for the *w* we drink,
Ezek 4:11 You shall also drink *w* by
4:16 and shall drink *w* by measure
4:17 they may lack bread and *w*,
7:17 knee will be as weak as *w*.
12:18 and drink your *w* with trembling
12:19 and drink their *w* with dread,
16: 4 nor were you washed in *w* to
16: 9 "Then I washed you in *w*;
17: 7 That he might *w* it.
21: 7 all knees will be weak as *w*.
24: 3 And also pour *w* into it.
26:12 your soil in the midst of the *w*.
31: 5 because of the abundance of *w*,
31:14 that no tree which drinks *w* may
31:16 of Lebanon, all that drink *w*,
32: 6 I will also *w* the land with the
36:25 Then I will sprinkle clean *w* on
47: 1 and there was *w*, flowing
47: 1 the *w* was flowing from under
47: 2 faces east; and there was *w*,
47: 3 the *w* came up to my ankles.
47: 4 the *w* came up to my knees.
47: 4 the *w* came up to my waist.
47: 5 for the *w* was too deep, water
47: 5 *w* in which one must swim,
47: 8 This *w* flows toward the eastern
47:12 because their *w* flows from the
Dan 1:12 us vegetables to eat and *w* to
Hos 2: 5 Who give me my bread and my *w*,
5:10 out my wrath on them like *w*.
10: 7 cut off Like a twig on the *w*.
Joel 1:20 For the *w* brooks are dried up,
3:18 Judah shall be flooded with *w*;
3:18 the house of the LORD And *w*
Am 4: 8 to another city to drink *w*,
5:24 let justice run down like *w*,
8:11 of bread, Nor a thirst for *w*,
Jon 3: 7 do not let them eat, or drink *w*.
Nah 2: 8 of old was like a pool of *w*,
3:14 Draw your *w* for the siege!
Hab 3:10 The overflowing of the *w*
Mt 3:11 I indeed baptize you with *w* unto
3:16 came up immediately from the *w*;
8:32 the sea, and perished in the *w*.
10:42 ones only a cup of cold *w* in
14:28 me to come to You on the *w*.
14:29 he walked on the *w* to go to
17:15 the fire and often into the *w*.
27:24 he took *w* and washed his hands
Mk 1: 8 "I indeed baptized you with *w*,
1:10 coming up from the *w*,
9:22 into the fire and into the *w*
9:41 whoever gives you a cup of *w*
14:13 you carrying a pitcher of *w*;
Lk 3:16 "I indeed baptize you with *w*;
7:44 you gave Me no *w* for My feet,
8:23 and they were filling with *w*,
8:24 wind and the raging of the *w*.
8:25 commands even the winds and *w*,
13:15 and lead it away to *w* it?
16:24 dip the tip of his finger in *w*
22:10 you carrying a pitcher of *w*;
Jn 1:26 saying, "I baptize with *w*,
1:31 I came baptizing with *w*.
1:33 who sent me to baptize with *w*
2: 7 "Fill the waterpots with *w*.
2: 9 of the feast had tasted the *w*
2: 9 servants who had drawn the *w*
3: 5 unless one is born of *w* and the
3:23 because there was much *w* there.
4: 7 woman of Samaria came to draw *w*.
4:10 would have given you living *w*.
4:11 then do You get that living *w*?
4:13 Whoever drinks of this *w* will
4:14 but whoever drinks of the *w* that
4:14 But the *w* that I shall give him
4:14 become in him a fountain of *w*
4:15 to Him, "Sir, give me this *w*,
4:46 where He had made the *w* wine.
5: 3 waiting for the moving of the *w*.
5: 4 the pool and stirred up the *w*;
5: 4 after the stirring of the *w*,
5: 7 me into the pool when the *w* is
7:38 will flow rivers of living *w*.
13: 5 He poured *w* into a basin and
19:34 and immediately blood and *w*
Acts 1: 5 John truly baptized with *w*,
8:36 the road, they came to some *w*.
8:36 eunuch said, "See, here is *w*.
8:38 the eunuch went down into the *w*,
8:39 when they came up out of the *w*,
10:47 "Can anyone forbid *w*,
11:16 'John indeed baptized with *w*,
Eph 5:26 her with the washing of *w* by
1 Tim 5:23 No longer drink only *w*,
Heb 9:19 of calves and goats, with *w*,
10:22 our bodies washed with pure *w*.
Jas 3:11 a spring send forth fresh *w*
3:12 no spring yields both salt *w*
1 Pe 3:20 souls, were saved through *w*.
2 Pe 2:17 These are wells without *w*,
3: 5 and the earth standing out of *w*
3: 5 out of water and in the *w*,
3: 6 perished, being flooded with *w*.
1 Jn 5: 6 This is He who came by *w* and
5: 6 Christ; not only by *w*, but by
5: 6 but by *w* and blood.
5: 8 on earth: the Spirit, the *w*,
Jude 12 They are clouds without *w*,
Rev 8:10 rivers and on the springs of *w*.
8:11 and many men died from the *w*,
12:15 So the serpent spewed *w* out of
14: 7 earth, the sea and springs of *w*.
16: 4 on the rivers and springs of *w*,
16:12 and its *w* was dried up, so that
21: 6 give of the fountain of the *w*
22: 1 he showed me a pure river of *w*
22:17 let him take the *w* of life

WATERCOURSES (1/1)

Isa 44: 4 grass Like willows by the *w*.

WATERED (10/10) WATER

Gen 2: 6 went up from the earth and *w*
13:10 that it was well *w* everywhere
29: 2 for out of that well they *w* the
29:10 and *w* the flock of Laban his
Ex 2:17 and *w* their flock.
2:19 drew enough water for us and *w*
Deut 11:10 you sowed your seed and *w* it
Prov 11:25 he who waters will also be *w*
Isa 58:11 You shall be like a *w* garden,
1 Cor 3: 6 I planted, Apollos *w*,

WATERFALLS (1/1) WATER

Ps 42: 7 deep at the noise of Your *w*;

WATERFLOOD (KJV) See FLOODWATER

WATERING (4/3) WATER

Gen 30:38 in the *w* troughs where the
Judg 5:11 among the *w* places,
7:24 seize from them the *w* places
7:24 together and seized the *w*

WATERLESS (1/1)

Zech 9:11 your prisoners free from the *w*

WATERPOT (1/1) POT, WATER, WATERPOTS

Jn 4:28 The woman then left her *w*,

WATERPOTS (3/3) WATERPOT

1 Ki 18:33 Fill four *w* with water, and pour
Jn 2: 6 Now there were set there six *w*
2: 7 Fill the *w* with water." And

WATERS (229/209) FLOODWATERS, WATER

Gen 1: 2 hovering over the face of the *w*.
1: 6 firmament in the midst of the *w*,
1: 6 and let it divide the *w* from
1: 6 it divide the waters from the *w*.
1: 7 and divided the *w* which were
1: 7 under the firmament from the *w*
1: 9 Let the *w* under the heavens be
1:10 gathering together of the *w* He
1:20 Let the *w* abound with an
1:21 with which the *w* abounded,
1:22 and fill the *w* in the seas,
7: 7 into the ark because of the *w*
7:10 after seven days that the *w* of
7:17 The *w* increased and lifted up
7:18 The *w* prevailed and greatly
7:18 about on the surface of the *w*.
7:19 And the *w* prevailed exceedingly
7:20 The *w* prevailed fifteen cubits
7:24 And the *w* prevailed on the earth
8: 1 and the *w* subsided.
8: 3 And the *w* receded continually
8: 3 hundred and fifty days the *w*
8: 5 And the *w* decreased continually
8: 7 going to and fro until the *w*
8: 8 to see if the *w* had receded
8: 9 for the *w* were on the face of
8:11 and Noah knew that the *w* had
8:13 that the *w* were dried up from
9:11 all flesh be cut off by the *w*
9:15 the *w* shall never again become
Ex 7:17 I will strike the *w* which are
7:19 out your hand over the *w* of
7:20 up the rod and struck the *w*
7:20 And all the *w* that were in the
8: 6 out his hand over the *w* of
14:21 and the *w* were divided.
14:22 and the *w* were a wall to them
14:26 that the *w* may come back upon
14:28 Then the *w* returned and covered
14:29 and the *w* were a wall to them
15: 8 blast of Your nostrils The *w*
15:10 sank like lead in the mighty *w*.
15:19 the LORD brought back the *w*
15:23 they could not drink the *w* of
15:25 When he cast it into the *w*,
15:25 the *w* were made sweet.
15:27 so they camped there by the *w*.
Lev 11:46 creature that moves in the *w*,
Num 24: 6 Like cedars beside the *w*.
24: 7 his seed shall be in many *w*.
27:14 command to hallow Me at the *w*
27:14 (These are the *w* of Meribah,
Deut 11: 4 how He made the *w* of the Red
14: 9 eat of all that are in the *w*:
32:51 children of Israel at the *w* of
33: 8 whom You contended at the *w* of
Josh 3:13 shall rest in the *w* of the
3:13 that the *w* of the Jordan shall
3:13 the *w* that come down from
3:16 that the *w* which came down from
3:16 So the *w* that went down into
4: 7 shall answer them that the *w*
4: 7 the *w* of the Jordan were cut
4:18 that the *w* of the Jordan
4:23 LORD your God dried up the *w*
5: 1 the LORD had dried up the *w*
11: 5 and camped together at the *w*
11: 7 against them suddenly by the *w*
15: 7 border continued toward the *w*
16: 1 to the *w* of Jericho on the
18:15 out to the spring of the *w* of
Judg 5:19 by the *w* of Megiddo;
2 Sam 22:12 Dark *w* and thick clouds of
22:17 He drew me out of many *w*.
2 Ki 5:12 better than all the *w* of
18:31 every one of you drink the *w*
Neh 9:11 As a stone into the mighty *w*.
Job 5:10 And sends *w* on the fields.
11:16 And remember it as *w* that
12:15 If He withholds the *w*,

24:18 be swift on the face of the ***w***,
24:19 and heat consume the snow ***w***,
26: 5 Those under the ***w*** and those
26:10 horizon on the face of the ***w***,
28:25 And apportion the ***w*** by
29:19 root is spread out to the ***w***,
37:10 And the broad ***w*** are frozen.
38:30 The ***w*** harden like stone,
Ps 18:11 canopy around Him was dark ***w***
18:16 He drew me out of many ***w***.
23: 2 He leads me beside the still ***w***.
24: 2 And established it upon the ***w***.
29: 3 of the LORD is over the ***w***;
29: 3 The LORD is over many ***w***.
32: 6 Surely in a flood of great ***w***
33: 7 He gathers the ***w*** of the sea
46: 3 Though its ***w*** roar and be
58: 7 Let them flow away as ***w*** which
69: 1 O God! For the ***w*** have come up
69: 2 I have come into deep ***w***,
69:14 hate me, And out of the deep ***w***.
73:10 And ***w*** of a full cup are
74:13 of the sea serpents in the ***w***.
77:16 The ***w*** saw You, O God;
77:16 The ***w*** saw You, they were
77:19 sea, Your path in the great ***w***,
78:13 And He made the ***w*** stand up
78:16 And caused ***w*** to run down like
78:20 So that the ***w*** gushed out,
81: 7 I tested you at the ***w*** of
93: 4 Than the noise of many ***w***,
104: 3 of His upper chambers in the ***w***,
104: 6 The ***w*** stood above the
104:13 He ***w*** the hills from His upper
105:29 He turned their ***w*** into blood,
106:11 The ***w*** covered their enemies;
106:32 angered Him also at the ***w*** of
107:23 Who do business on great ***w***,
114: 8 The flint into a fountain of ***w***.
124: 4 Then the ***w*** would have
124: 5 Then the swollen ***w*** Would have
136: 6 laid out the earth above the ***w***,
144: 7 and deliver me out of great ***w***,
147:18 and the ***w*** flow.
148: 4 And you ***w*** above the heavens!
Prov 8:29 So that the ***w*** would not
11:25 And he who ***w*** will also be
18: 4 of a man's mouth are deep ***w***;
30: 4 Who has bound the ***w*** in a
Eccl 11: 1 Cast your bread upon the ***w***,
Song 4:15 of gardens, A well of living ***w***,
5:12 like doves By the rivers of ***w***,
8: 7 Many ***w*** cannot quench love,
Isa 8: 6 as these people refused The ***w***
8: 7 brings up over them The ***w*** of
11: 9 of the LORD As the ***w*** cover
15: 6 For the ***w*** of Nimrim will be
15: 9 For the ***w*** of Dimon will be full
17:12 like the rushing of mighty ***w***!
17:13 rush like the rushing of many ***w***;
18: 2 in vessels of reed on the ***w***,
19: 5 The ***w*** will fail from the sea,
19: 8 who spread nets on the ***w***.
22: 9 you gathered together the ***w*** of
23: 3 And on great ***w*** the grain of
28: 2 Like a flood of mighty ***w***
28:17 And the ***w*** will overflow the
30:25 hill Rivers and streams of ***w***,
32:20 are you who sow beside all ***w***,
35: 6 For ***w*** shall burst forth in the
36:16 every one of you drink the ***w***
40:12 Who has measured the ***w*** in the
43: 2 When you pass through the ***w***,
43:16 a path through the mighty ***w***,
43:20 Because I give ***w*** in the
48:21 He caused the ***w*** to flow from
48:21 and the ***w*** gushed out.
51:10 The ***w*** of the great deep;
54: 9 For this is like the ***w*** of Noah
54: 9 as I have sworn That the ***w*** of
55: 1 who thirsts, Come to the ***w***;
57:20 Whose ***w*** cast up mire and dirt.
58:11 whose ***w*** do not fail.
Jer 2:13 Me, the fountain of living ***w***,
2:18 To drink the ***w*** of Sihor?
2:18 To drink the ***w*** of the River?
9: 1 Oh, that my head were ***w***,
10:13 There is a multitude of ***w*** in
15:18 As ***w*** that fail?
17: 8 be like a tree planted by the ***w***,
17:13 The fountain of living ***w***.
18:14 Will the cold flowing ***w*** be
18:14 be forsaken for strange ***w***?
31: 9 them to walk by the rivers of ***w***,
46: 7 Whose ***w*** move like the rivers?
46: 8 And its ***w*** move like the
47: 2 ***w*** rise out of the north,
48:34 For the ***w*** of Nimrim also shall
50:38 A drought is against her ***w***,
51:13 O you who dwell by many ***w***,
51:16 There is a multitude of ***w*** in
51:55 her waves roar like great ***w***,
Lam 3:54 The ***w*** flowed over my head;
Ezek 1:24 wings, like the noise of many ***w***,
17: 5 He placed it by abundant ***w***
17: 8 planted in good soil by many ***w***,
19:10 bloodline, Planted by the ***w***,
19:10 of branches Because of many ***w***.
26:19 and great ***w*** cover you,
27:26 oarsmen brought you into many ***w***,
27:34 the seas in the depths of the ***w***;
31: 4 The ***w*** made it grow;
31: 4 Underground ***w*** gave it height,
31: 7 its roots reached to abundant ***w***.
31:14 So that no trees by the ***w*** may
31:15 and the great ***w*** were held back.
32: 2 Troubling the ***w*** with your
32:13 From beside its great ***w***;
32:14 Then I will make their ***w*** clear,
34:18 to have drunk of the clear ***w***,
43: 2 was like the sound of many ***w***;
47: 3 and he brought me through the ***w***;
47: 4 and brought me through the ***w***;
47: 8 its ***w*** are healed.
47: 9 because these ***w*** go there;
47:19 shall be from Tamar to the ***w***
48:28 shall be from Tamar to the ***w***
Dan 12: 6 who was above the ***w*** of the
12: 7 who was above the ***w*** of the
Am 5: 8 He calls for the ***w*** of the sea
9: 6 Who calls for the ***w*** of the
Jon 2: 5 The ***w*** surrounded me,
Mic 1: 4 Like ***w*** poured down a steep
Nah 3: 8 That had the ***w*** around her,
Hab 2:14 As the ***w*** cover the sea.
3:15 Through the heap of great ***w***.
Zech 14: 8 day it shall be That living ***w***
1 Cor 3: 7 is anything, nor he who ***w***,
3: 8 Now he who plants and he who ***w***
2 Cor 11:26 journeys often, in perils of ***w***,
Rev 1:15 voice as the sound of many ***w***;
7:17 them to living fountains of ***w***.
8:11 A third of the ***w*** became
11: 6 and they have power over ***w*** to
14: 2 like the voice of many ***w***,
16: 5 And I heard the angel of the ***w***
17: 1 great harlot who sits on many ***w***,
17:15 The ***w*** which you saw, where the
19: 6 as the sound of many ***w*** and as

WATERSPOUTS (KJV) See WATERFALLS

WATERSPRINGS (2/2)

Ps 107:33 And the ***w*** into dry ground;
107:35 of water, And dry land into ***w***.

WAVE (39/30) WAVED, WAVES

Ex 29:24 and you shall ***w*** them as a wave
29:24 and you shall wave them as a ***w***
29:26 of Aaron's consecration and ***w***
29:26 and wave it as a ***w*** offering
29:27 consecrate the breast of the ***w***
Lev 7:30 the breast may be waved as a ***w***
7:34 For the breast of the ***w*** offering
8:27 and waved them as a ***w*** offering
8:29 the breast and waved it as a ***w***
9:21 right thigh Aaron waved as a ***w***
10:14 The breast of the ***w*** offering and
10:15 and the breast of the ***w***
10:15 to offer as a ***w*** offering
14:12 and ***w*** them as a wave offering
14:12 and wave them as a ***w*** offering
14:24 and the priest shall ***w*** them as
14:24 priest shall wave them as a ***w***
23:11 He shall ***w*** the sheaf before the
23:11 the Sabbath the priest shall ***w***
23:12 when you ***w*** the sheaf,
23:15 you brought the sheaf of the ***w***
23:17 bring from your dwellings two ***w***
23:20 The priest shall ***w*** them with the
23:20 of the firstfruits as a ***w***
Num 5:25 shall ***w*** the offering before the
6:20 and the priest shall ***w*** them as a
6:20 priest shall wave them as a ***w***
6:20 with the breast of the ***w***
8:11 like a ***w*** offering from the
8:13 and then offer them like a ***w***
8:15 like a ***w*** offering.
8:21 like a ***w*** offering before the
18:11 with all the ***w*** offerings of the
18:18 just as the ***w*** breast and the
2 Ki 5:11 and ***w*** his hand over the place,
Job 39:13 The wings of the ostrich ***w***
Ps 72:16 Its fruit shall ***w*** like
Isa 13: 2 ***W*** your hand, that they may
Jas 1: 6 for he who doubts is like a ***w***

WAVED (6/6) WAVE

Ex 29:27 of the wave offering which is ***w***,
Lev 7:30 that the breast may be ***w*** as a
8:27 and ***w*** them as a wave offering
8:29 Moses took the breast and ***w*** it
9:21 and the right thigh Aaron ***w***
14:21 as a trespass offering to be ***w***,

WAVER (1/1)

Rom 4:20 He did not ***w*** at the promise of

WAVERED (1/1)

Isa 21: 4 My heart ***w***, fearfulness

WAVERING (1/1)

Heb 10:23 of our hope without ***w***,

WAVES (27/27) WAVE

2 Sam 22: 5 When the ***w*** of death surrounded
Job 9: 8 And treads on the ***w*** of the
38:11 And here your proud ***w*** must
Ps 42: 7 All Your ***w*** and billows have
65: 7 the seas, The noise of their ***w***,
88: 7 afflicted me with all Your ***w***.
89: 9 When its ***w*** rise, You still
93: 3 The floods lift up their ***w***.
93: 4 Than the mighty ***w*** of the sea.
107:25 Which lifts up the ***w*** of the
107:29 So that its ***w*** are still.
Isa 19:16 which He ***w*** over it.
48:18 your righteousness like the ***w***
51:15 Who divided the sea whose ***w***
Jer 5:22 And though its ***w*** toss to and
31:35 And its ***w*** roar (The LORD of
51:42 with the multitude of its ***w***.
51:55 Though her ***w*** roar like great
Ezek 26: 3 as the sea causes its ***w*** to come
Jon 2: 3 All Your billows and Your ***w***
Zech 10:11 And strike the ***w*** of the sea:
Mt 8:24 the boat was covered with the ***w***.
14:24 of the sea, tossed by the ***w***,
Mk 4:37 and the ***w*** beat into the boat,
Lk 21:25 the sea and the ***w*** roaring;
Acts 27:41 up by the violence of the ***w***.
Jude 13 raging ***w*** of the sea, foaming up

WAVING (1/1)

Isa 19:16 and fear because of the ***w*** of

WAVY (1/1)

Song 5:11 finest gold; His locks are ***w***,

WAX (4/4)

Ps 22:14 My heart is like ***w***;
68: 2 As ***w*** melts before the fire,
97: 5 The mountains melt like ***w*** at
Mic 1: 4 the valleys will split Like ***w***

WAY (557/516) WAYS, WAYSIDE

Gen 3:24 sword which turned every ***w***,
3:24 to guard the ***w*** to the tree of
6:12 flesh had corrupted their ***w*** on
12:19 wife; take her and go your ***w***.
14:11 provisions, and went their ***w***.
16: 7 by the spring on the ***w*** to Shur.
18:16 with them to send them on the ***w***.
18:19 that they keep the ***w*** of the
18:33 So the LORD went His ***w*** as soon
19: 2 may rise early and go on your ***w***.
24:27 As for me, being on the ***w***,
24:40 with you and prosper your ***w***;
24:42 if You will now prosper the ***w***
24:48 who had led me in the ***w*** of
24:56 the LORD has prospered my ***w***;
24:62 Now Isaac came from the ***w*** of
25:34 drank, arose, and went his ***w***.
28:20 and keep me in this ***w*** that I am
32: 1 So Jacob went on his ***w***,
33:16 returned that day on his ***w*** to
35: 3 and has been with me in the ***w***
35:19 died and was buried on the ***w***
37:25 on their ***w*** to carry them down
38:14 open place which was on the ***w***
38:16 Then he turned to her by the ***w***,
42:38 should befall him along the ***w***
45:24 not become troubled along the ***w***.
46:28 to point out before him the ***w***
48: 7 in the land of Canaan on the ***w***,
48: 7 I buried her there on the ***w*** to
49:17 shall be a serpent by the ***w***,
Ex 2:12 So he looked this ***w*** and that
2:12 he looked this way and that ***w***,
4:24 And it came to pass on the ***w***,
13:17 God did not lead them by ***w*** of
13:18 led the people around by ***w*** of
13:21 a pillar of cloud to lead the ***w***,
18: 8 had come upon them on the ***w***,
18:20 and show them the ***w*** in which
18:27 and he went his ***w*** to his own
22:23 "If you afflict them in any ***w***,
23:20 you to keep you in the ***w*** and
32: 8 aside quickly out of the ***w***
33: 3 lest I consume you on the ***w***,
33:13 Your sight, show me now Your ***w***,
Lev 7:24 may be used in any other ***w***;
20: 4 of the land should in any ***w***
Num 6:23 This is the ***w*** you shall bless
13:17 Go up this ***w*** into the South,
14:25 into the wilderness by the ***W***
21: 4 from Mount Hor by the ***W*** of the
21: 4 very discouraged on the ***w***.
21:33 turned and went up by the ***w*** to
22:22 LORD took His stand in the ***w***
22:23 of the LORD standing in the ***w***
22:23 turned aside out of the ***w*** and
22:26 place where there was no ***w*** to
22:31 of the LORD standing in the ***w***
22:32 because your ***w*** is perverse
22:34 did not know You stood in the ***w***
24:25 Balak also went his ***w***.
Deut 1: 2 days' journey from Horeb by ***w***
1:19 which you saw on the ***w*** to the
1:22 bring back word to us of the ***w***
1:31 in all the ***w*** that you went
1:33 who went in the ***w*** before you to
1:33 to show you the ***w*** you should
1:40 into the wilderness by the ***W***
2: 1 into the wilderness of the ***W***

2: 8 we turned and passed by ***w*** of
6: 7 when you walk by the ***w***,
8: 2 your God led you all the ***w***
9:12 turned aside from the ***w*** which
9:16 aside quickly from the ***w*** which
11:19 house, when you walk by the ***w***,
11:28 but turn aside from the ***w*** which
12:31 the LORD your God in that ***w***;
13: 5 to entice you from the ***w*** in
17:16 You shall not return that ***w***
19: 6 because the ***w*** is long, and kill
22: 6 to be before you along the ***w***,
24: 9 your God did to Miriam on the ***w***
25:17 Amalek did to you on the ***w*** as
25:18 how he met you on the ***w*** and
28: 7 come out against you one ***w*** and
28:25 you shall go out one ***w*** against
28:68 by the ***w*** of which I said to
31:29 and turn aside from the ***w*** which
Josh 1: 8 For then you will make your ***w***
2:16 Afterward you may go your ***w***.
2:22 sought them all along the ***w***,
3: 4 that you may know the ***w*** by
3: 4 for you have not passed this ***w***
5: 4 died in the wilderness on the ***w***,
5: 5 on the ***w*** as they came out of
5: 7 not been circumcised on the ***w***.
8:15 and fled by the ***w*** of the
8:20 had no power to flee this ***w*** or
8:20 to flee this way or that ***w***,
23:14 this day I am going the ***w*** of
24:17 and preserved us in all the ***w***
Judg 2:17 They turned quickly from the ***w***
2:19 nor from their stubborn ***w***.
8: 8 and spoke to them in the same ***w***.
9:25 who passed by them along that ***w***;
17: 9 and I am on my ***w*** to find a
18: 6 LORD be with you on your ***w***.
18:22 When they were a good ***w*** from
18:26 children of Dan went their ***w***.
19: 5 bread, and afterward go your ***w***.
19: 9 Tomorrow go your ***w*** early,
19:14 they passed by and went their ***w***;
19:27 house and went out to go his ***w***,
Ruth 1: 7 and they went on the ***w*** to
1 Sam 1:18 So the woman went her ***w*** and
9: 6 perhaps he can show us the ***w***
9: 8 man of God, to tell us our ***w***.
9:14 out toward them on his ***w*** up to
9:26 that I may send you on your ***w***.
12:23 you the good and the right ***w***.
15: 2 how he ambushed him on the ***w***
15: 7 from Havilah all the ***w*** to Shur,
20:22 are beyond you'—go your ***w***,
24: 7 the cave and went on his ***w***.
26:25 So David went on his ***w***,
28:22 strength when you go on your ***w***.
30: 2 them away and went their ***w***.
2 Sam 4: 6 all the ***w*** into the house,
5: 8 Whoever climbs up by ***w*** of the
13:30 pass, while they were on the ***w***,
15: 2 early and stand beside the ***w***
15:23 crossed over toward the ***w*** of
18:23 Then Ahimaaz ran by ***w*** of the
19:36 servant will go a little ***w***
22:31 His ***w*** is perfect; The word of
22:33 And He makes my ***w*** perfect.
1 Ki 1:49 arose, and each one went his ***w***.
2: 2 'I go the ***w*** of all the earth;
2: 4 your sons take heed to their ***w***,
7:24 all the ***w*** around the Sea.
8:25 your sons take heed to their ***w***,
8:32 bringing his ***w*** on his head,
8:36 You may teach them the good ***w***
11:29 the Shilonite met him on the ***w***;
13: 9 nor return by the same ***w*** you
13:10 So he went another ***w*** and did not
13:10 and did not return by the ***w*** he
13:12 'Which ***w*** did he go?"
13:12 For his sons had seen which ***w***
13:17 nor return by going the ***w*** you
13:26 had brought him back from the ***w***
13:33 did not turn from his evil ***w***,
15:26 and walked in the ***w*** of his
15:34 and walked in the ***w*** of
16: 2 and you have walked in the ***w*** of
16:19 in walking in the ***w*** of
18: 6 Ahab went one ***w*** by himself,
18: 6 and Obadiah went another ***w*** by
18: 7 Now as Obadiah was on his ***w***,
19:15 return on your ***w*** to the
22:22 LORD said to him, 'In what ***w***?
22:24 Which ***w*** did the spirit from the
22:52 and walked in the ***w*** of his
22:52 way of his father and in the ***w***
22:52 way of his mother and in the ***w***
2 Ki 2: 8 and it was divided this ***w*** and
2:14 it was divided this ***w*** and that;
3: 8 'Which ***w*** shall we go up?"
3: 8 By ***w*** of the Wilderness of
3:20 that suddenly water came by ***w***
4:29 in your hand, and be on your ***w***.
6:19 to them, "This is not the ***w***,
8:18 And he walked in the ***w*** of the
8:27 And he walked in the ***w*** of the
10:12 and went to Samaria. On the ***w***,
11:16 and she went by ***w*** of the
11:19 and went by ***w*** of the gate of
16: 3 But he walked in the ***w*** of the
19:28 I will turn you back By the ***w***
19:33 By the ***w*** that he came, By the
21:22 and did not walk in the ***w*** of
25: 4 men of war fled at night by ***w***
25: 4 And the king went by ***w*** of the
2 Chr 4: 3 all the ***w*** around the Sea.
6:16 your sons take heed to their ***w***,
6:23 on the wicked by bringing his ***w***
6:27 You may teach them the good ***w***
11:17 because they walked in the ***w*** of
18:20 LORD said to him, 'In what ***w***?
18:23 Which ***w*** did the spirit from the
20:32 And he walked in the ***w*** of his
21: 6 And he walked in the ***w*** of the
21:13 but have walked in the ***w*** of the
23:15 and she went by ***w*** of the
23:19 that no one who was in any ***w***
32:13 of those lands in any ***w*** able
Ezra 8:21 to seek from Him the right ***w***
Neh 6:13 be afraid and act that ***w*** and
8:10 he said to them, "Go your ***w***,
8:12 all the people went their ***w*** to
9:19 And the ***w*** they should go.
12:38 choir went the opposite ***w***,
Esth 4:17 So Mordecai went his ***w*** and did
Job 3:23 light given to a man whose ***w***
6:18 The paths of their ***w*** turn
8:19 this is the joy of His ***w***,
16:22 I shall go the ***w*** of no return.
17: 9 righteous will hold to his ***w***,
19: 8 He has fenced up my ***w***,
21:31 Who condemns his ***w*** to his face?
22:15 Will you keep to the old ***w***
23:10 But He knows the ***w*** that I take;
23:11 I have kept His ***w*** and not
24:18 no one would turn into the ***w***
24:24 They are taken out of the ***w***
28:23 God understands its ***w***,
29:25 I chose the ***w*** for them, and sat
31: 7 my step has turned from the ***w***,
33:14 For God may speak in one ***w***,
34:11 a reward according to his ***w***.
36:23 Who has assigned Him His ***w***,
38:19 Where is the ***w*** to the
38:24 By what ***w*** is light diffused,
Ps 1: 6 For the LORD knows the ***w*** of
1: 6 But the ***w*** of the ungodly shall
2:12 And you perish in the ***w***,
5: 8 Make Your ***w*** straight before my
18:30 His ***w*** is perfect; The word of
18:32 And makes my ***w*** perfect.
25: 8 He teaches sinners in the ***w***.
25: 9 the humble He teaches His ***w***.
25:12 Him shall He teach in the ***w*** He
27:11 Teach me Your ***w***,
32: 8 you and teach you in the ***w*** you
35: 6 Let their ***w*** be dark and
36: 4 He sets himself in a ***w*** that
37: 5 Commit your ***w*** to the LORD,
37: 7 of him who prospers in his ***w***,
37:23 And He delights in his ***w***.
37:34 on the LORD, And keep His ***w***,
44:18 our steps departed from Your ***w***;
49:13 This is the ***w*** of those who are
67: 2 That Your ***w*** may be known on
77:13 Your ***w***, O God, is in the
77:19 Your ***w*** was in the sea, Your
80:12 So that all who pass by the ***w***
86:11 Teach me Your ***w***,
89:41 All who pass by the ***w*** plunder
101: 2 behave wisely in a perfect ***w***.
101: 6 He who walks in a perfect ***w***,
102:23 weakened my strength in the ***w***;
107: 4 the wilderness in a desolate ***w***;
107: 7 led them forth by the right ***w***,
107:40 where there is no ***w***;
119: 1 are the undefiled in the ***w***,
119: 9 can a young man cleanse his ***w***?
119:14 I have rejoiced in the ***w*** of
119:27 Make me understand the ***w*** of
119:29 Remove from me the ***w*** of lying,
119:30 I have chosen the ***w*** of truth;
119:33 the ***w*** of Your statutes,
119:37 And revive me in Your ***w***.
119:101 my feet from every evil ***w***,
119:104 Therefore I hate every false ***w***.
119:128 I hate every false ***w***.
139:24 if there is any wicked ***w*** in
139:24 And lead me in the ***w***
142: 3 In the ***w*** in which I walk They
143: 8 Cause me to know the ***w*** in
146: 9 But the ***w*** of the wicked He
Prov 1:15 do not walk in the ***w*** with them,
1:31 eat the fruit of their own ***w***,
2: 8 And preserves the ***w*** of His
2:12 To deliver you from the ***w*** of
2:20 So you may walk in the ***w*** of
3:23 you will walk safely in your ***w***,
4:11 I have taught you in the ***w*** of
4:14 And do not walk in the ***w*** of
4:19 The ***w*** of the wicked is like
5: 8 Remove your ***w*** far from her,
6:23 of instruction are the ***w*** of
7:27 Her house is the ***w*** to hell,
8: 2 of the high hill, Beside the ***w***,
8:13 and arrogance and the evil ***w***
8:20 I traverse the ***w*** of
8:22 me at the beginning of His ***w***,
9: 6 And go in the ***w*** of
9:15 Who go straight on their ***w***:
10:17 instruction is in the ***w*** of
10:29 The ***w*** of the LORD is strength
11: 5 the blameless will direct his ***w***
12:15 The ***w*** of a fool is right in
12:26 For the ***w*** of the wicked leads
12:28 In the ***w*** of righteousness is
13: 6 guards him whose ***w*** is
13:15 But the ***w*** of the unfaithful
14: 8 prudent is to understand his ***w***,
14:12 There is a ***w*** that seems right
14:12 But its end is the ***w*** of
15: 9 The ***w*** of the wicked is an
15:10 is for him who forsakes the ***w***,
15:19 The ***w*** of the lazy man is like
15:19 But the ***w*** of the upright is a
15:24 The ***w*** of life winds upward for
16: 9 A man's heart plans his ***w***,
16:17 He who keeps his ***w*** preserves
16:25 There is a ***w*** that seems right
16:25 But its end is the ***w*** of
16:29 And leads him in a ***w*** that is
16:31 If it is found in the ***w*** of
19: 3 of a man twists his ***w***,
20:14 But when he has gone his ***w***,
20:24 can a man understand his own ***w***?
21: 2 Every ***w*** of a man is right in
21: 8 The ***w*** of a guilty man is
21:16 A man who wanders from the ***w*** of
21:29 upright, he establishes his ***w***.
22: 5 and snares are in the ***w*** of
22: 6 Train up a child in the ***w*** he
23:19 And guide your heart in the ***w***.
28:10 to go astray in an evil ***w***,
29:27 he who is upright in the ***w***
30:19 The ***w*** of an eagle in the air,
30:19 The ***w*** of a serpent on a rock,
30:19 The ***w*** of a ship in the midst
30:19 And the ***w*** of a man with a
30:20 This is the ***w*** of an
Eccl 10: 3 when a fool walks along the ***w***,
11: 5 you do not know what is the ***w***
12: 5 And of terrors in the ***w***;
Song 4: 6 I will go my ***w*** to the mountain
Isa 3:12 And destroy the ***w*** of your
8:11 I should not walk in the ***w*** of
9: 1 By the ***w*** of the sea, beyond
15: 5 For in the ***w*** of Horonaim
26: 7 The ***w*** of the just is
26: 8 in the ***w*** of Your judgments,
28: 7 drink are out of the ***w***;
28: 7 They are out of the ***w*** through
30:11 Get out of the ***w***,
30:21 you, saying, "This is the ***w***,
37:29 I will turn you back By the ***w***
37:34 By the ***w*** that he came, By the
40: 3 Prepare the ***w*** of the LORD;
40:14 And showed Him the ***w*** of
40:27 My ***w*** is hidden from the LORD,
41: 3 and passed safely By the ***w***
42:16 I will bring the blind by a ***w***
43:16 who makes a ***w*** in the sea And a
48:15 and his ***w*** will prosper.
48:17 Who leads you by the ***w*** you
53: 6 turned, every one, to his own ***w***;
55: 7 Let the wicked forsake his ***w***,
56:11 They all look to their own ***w***,
57:10 wearied in the length of your ***w***;
57:14 Heap it up! Prepare the ***w***,
57:14 stumbling block out of the ***w***
57:17 he went on backsliding in the ***w***
59: 8 The ***w*** of peace they have not
59: 8 Whoever takes that ***w*** shall not
62:10 the gates! Prepare the ***w*** for
65: 2 Who walk in a ***w*** that is not
Jer 2:17 God When He led you in the ***w***?
2:23 See your ***w*** in the valley;
2:33 Why do you beautify your ***w*** to
2:36 about so much to change your ***w***?
3:21 they have perverted their ***w***;
4: 7 of nations is on his ***w***.
5: 4 For they do not know the ***w*** of
5: 5 For they have known the ***w*** of
6:16 where the good ***w*** is, And walk
6:25 the field, Nor walk by the ***w***.
6:27 you may know and test their ***w***.
10: 2 Do not learn the ***w*** of the
10:23 I know the ***w*** of man is not in
12: 1 Why does the ***w*** of the wicked
18:11 now every one from his evil ***w***,
21: 8 I set before you the ***w*** of life
21: 8 you the way of life and the ***w***
23:12 Therefore their ***w*** shall be to
23:22 turned them from their evil ***w***
25: 5 now everyone of his evil ***w*** and
25:35 the shepherds will have no ***w***
26: 3 listen and turn from his evil ***w***,
28:11 the prophet Jeremiah went his ***w***.
31: 9 In a straight ***w*** in which they
31:21 The ***w*** in which you went.
32:39 give them one heart and one ***w***,
35:15 now everyone from his evil ***w***,
36: 3 may turn from his evil ***w***,
36: 7 will turn from his evil ***w***.
39: 4 by ***w*** of the king's garden,
39: 4 And he went out by ***w*** of the
41:17 as they went on their ***w*** to
42: 3 your God may show us the ***w*** in
48:19 Stand by the ***w*** and watch;
50: 5 They shall ask the ***w*** to Zion,
52: 7 out of the city at night by ***w***
52: 7 And they went by ***w*** of the
Ezek 3:18 the wicked from his wicked ***w***,
3:19 nor from his wicked ***w***,
7:27 do to them according to their ***w***,
13:22 not turn from his wicked ***w*** to
18:25 The ***w*** of the Lord is not fair.'
18:25 is it not My ***w*** which is fair,

18:29 The ***w*** of the Lord is not fair.'
23:13 Both took the same ***w***.
23:31 You have walked in the ***w*** of your
33: 8 to warn the wicked from his ***w***,
33: 9 the wicked to turn from his ***w***,
33: 9 and he does not turn from his ***w***,
33:11 the wicked turn from his ***w*** and
33:17 The ***w*** of the LORD is not fair.'
33:17 But it is their ***w*** which is not
33:20 The ***w*** of the LORD is not fair.'
36:17 to Me their ***w*** was like the
41: 7 story to the highest by ***w*** of
42: 1 by the ***w*** toward the north;
42:12 the ***w*** directly in front of the
43: 2 God of Israel came from the ***w***
43: 4 came into the temple by ***w*** of
44: 3 he shall enter by ***w*** of the
44: 3 gateway, and go out the same ***w***.
44: 4 Also He brought me by ***w*** of the
46: 2 The prince shall enter by ***w*** of
46: 8 he shall go in by ***w*** of the
46: 8 gateway, and go out the same ***w***.
46: 9 whoever enters by ***w*** of the
46: 9 to worship shall go out by ***w***
46: 9 and whoever enters by ***w*** of the
46: 9 south gate shall go out by ***w***
46: 9 He shall not return by ***w*** of the
47: 2 He brought me out by ***w*** of the
48:35 All the ***w*** around shall be
Dan 12: 9 And he said, "Go your ***w***,
12:13 go your ***w*** till the end;
Hos 2: 6 I will hedge up your ***w*** with
6: 9 of priests murder on the ***w*** to
10:13 you trusted in your own ***w***,
Am 2: 7 And pervert the ***w*** of the
8:14 As the ***w*** of Beersheba lives!'
Jon 3: 8 every one turn from his evil ***w***
3:10 they turned from their evil ***w***;
Nah 1: 3 The LORD has His ***w*** In the
Zech 10: 2 the people wend their ***w*** like
Mal 1: 2 In what ***w*** have You loved us?'
1: 6 In what ***w*** have we despised Your
1: 7 In what ***w*** have we defiled You?'
2: 8 you have departed from the ***w***;
2:17 In what ***w*** have we wearied
3: 1 And he will prepare the ***w***
3: 7 In what ***w*** shall we return?'
3: 8 In what ***w*** have we robbed You?'
Mt 2:12 for their own country another ***w***.
3: 3 Prepare the ***w*** of the LORD;
4:15 By the ***w*** of the sea,
5:24 before the altar, and go your ***w***.
5:25 while you are on the ***w*** with
7:13 the gate and broad is the ***w***
7:14 gate and difficult is the ***w***
8: 4 you tell no one; but go your ***w***,
8:13 to the centurion, "Go your ***w***;
8:28 that no one could pass that ***w***.
8:30 Now a good ***w*** off from them there
10: 5 Do not go into the ***w*** of the
11:10 Who will prepare Your ***w***
13:25 among the wheat and went his ***w***.
15:32 lest they faint on the ***w***.
20:14 what is yours and go your ***w***.
21:32 For John came to you in the ***w*** of
22:16 and teach the ***w*** of God in
22:22 and left Him and went their ***w***.
27:65 "You have a guard; go your ***w***,
Mk 1: 2 Who will prepare Your ***w***
1: 3 Prepare the ***w*** of the LORD;
1:44 to anyone; but go your ***w***,
7: 3 their hands in a special ***w***,
7:29 "For this saying go your ***w***;
8: 3 they will faint on the ***w***;
10:21 "One thing you lack: Go your ***w***,
10:52 Jesus said to him, "Go your ***w***;
11: 4 So they went their ***w***,
12:14 but teach the ***w*** of God in
Lk 1:79 To guide our feet into the ***w***
3: 4 Prepare the ***w*** of the LORD;
4:30 midst of them, He went His ***w***.
7:27 Who will prepare Your ***w***
8:39 And he went his ***w*** and
10: 3 'Go your ***w***; behold, I send you
12:58 make every effort along the ***w***
13:11 was bent over and could in no ***w***
14:32 the other is still a great ***w***
15:20 But when he was still a great ***w***
17:19 said to him, "Arise, go your ***w***.
19: 4 He was going to pass that ***w***.
19:32 who were sent went their ***w*** and
20:21 but teach the ***w*** of God in
22: 4 So he went his ***w*** and conferred
Jn 1:23 Make straight the ***w*** of the
4:28 went her ***w*** into the city,
4:50 Jesus said to him, "Go your ***w***;
4:50 spoke to him, and he went his ***w***.
10: 1 but climbs up some other ***w***,
11:28 she went her ***w*** and secretly
14: 4 and the ***w*** you know."
14: 5 and how can we know the ***w***?
14: 6 Jesus said to him, "I am the ***w***,
18: 8 seek Me, let these go their ***w***,
21: 1 and in this ***w*** He showed
Acts 4:21 finding no ***w*** of punishing them,
7: 6 "But God spoke in this ***w***:
8:39 and he went on his ***w*** rejoicing.
9: 2 he found any who were of the ***W***,
9:17 And Ananias went his ***w*** and
15: 3 being sent on their ***w*** by the
16:17 who proclaim to us the ***w*** of
18:25 had been instructed in the ***w***
18:26 and explained to him the ***w*** of
19: 9 but spoke evil of the ***W*** before
19:23 a great commotion about the ***W***.
20:35 "I have shown you in every ***w***,
21: 5 we departed and went on our ***w***;
22: 4 I persecuted this ***W*** to the
24:14 that according to the ***W*** which
24:22 accurate knowledge of the ***W***,
Rom 1:10 now at last I may find a ***w*** in
3: 2 Much in every ***w***! Chiefly because
3:17 And the ***w*** of peace they
10: 6 of faith speaks in this ***w***,
14:13 to fall in our brother's ***w***.
15:24 and to be helped on my ***w*** there
15:28 I shall go by ***w*** of you to
1 Cor 9:24 Run in such a ***w*** that you may
10:13 will also make the ***w*** of escape,
12:31 I show you a more excellent ***w***.
16: 7 wish to see you now on the ***w***;
2 Cor 1:16 to pass by ***w*** of you to
1:16 and be helped by you on my ***w*** to
Phil 1:18 Only that in every ***w***,
1:28 and not in any ***w*** terrified by
Col 2:14 He has taken it out of the ***w***,
1 Th 3:11 direct our ***w*** to you.
2 Th 2: 7 until He is taken out of the ***w***.
3:16 you peace always in every ***w***.
Heb 4: 4 of the seventh day in this ***w***:
9: 8 that the ***w*** into the Holiest of
10:20 by a new and living ***w*** which He
Jas 2:25 and sent them out another ***w***?
5:20 sinner from the error of his ***w***
2 Pe 2: 2 because of whom the ***w*** of truth
2:15 They have forsaken the right ***w***
2:15 following the ***w*** of Balaam the
2:21 them not to have known the ***w***
3: 1 I stir up your pure minds by ***w***
Jude 11 For they have gone in the ***w*** of
15 have committed in an ungodly ***w***,
Rev 16:12 so that the ***w*** of the kings from

WAYFARING (1/1)

2 Sam 12: 4 herd to prepare one for the ***w***

WAYMARKS (KJV) See LANDMARKS

WAYS (196/188) WAY

Deut 5:33 You shall walk in all the ***w***
8: 6 to walk in His ***w*** and to fear
10:12 to walk in all His ***w*** and to
11:22 your God, to walk in all His ***w***,
19: 9 God and to walk always in His ***w***,
26:17 and that you will walk in His ***w***
28: 7 way and flee before you seven ***w***.
28: 9 your God and walk in His ***w***.
28:25 against them and flee seven ***w***
28:29 you shall not prosper in your ***w***;
30:16 your God, to walk in His ***w***,
32: 4 For all His ***w*** are justice,
Josh 22: 5 your God, to walk in all His ***w***,
Judg 2:22 whether they will keep the ***w*** of
1 Sam 8: 3 his sons did not walk in his ***w***;
8: 5 your sons do not walk in your ***w***.
18:14 behaved wisely in all his ***w***,
2 Sam 22:22 For I have kept the ***w*** of the
1 Ki 2: 3 your God: to walk in His ***w***,
3:14 "So if you walk in My ***w***,
8:39 everyone according to all his ***w***,
8:58 Himself, to walk in all His ***w***,
11:33 and have not walked in My ***w*** to
11:38 I command you, walk in My ***w***,
16:26 For he walked in all the ***w*** of
22:43 And he walked in all the ***w*** of
2 Ki 17:13 saying, "Turn from your evil ***w***,
21:21 So he walked in all the ***w*** that
22: 2 and walked in all the ***w*** of his
2 Chr 6:30 everyone according to all his ***w***,
6:31 to walk in Your ***w*** as long as
7:14 and turn from their wicked ***w***,
13:22 of the acts of Abijah, his ***w***,
17: 3 he walked in the former ***w*** of
17: 6 heart took delight in the ***w*** of
21:12 you have not walked in the ***w*** of
21:12 or in the ***w*** of Asa king of
22: 3 He also walked in the ***w*** of the
27: 6 because he prepared his ***w***
27: 7 and all his wars and his ***w***,
28: 2 For he walked in the ***w*** of the
28:26 rest of his acts and all his ***w***,
34: 2 and walked in the ***w*** of his
Job 4: 6 And the integrity of your ***w***
13:15 I will defend my own ***w*** before
21:14 desire the knowledge of Your ***w***.
22: 3 to Him that you make your ***w***
22:28 So light will shine on your ***w***.
24:13 They do not know its ***w*** Nor
24:23 Yet His eyes are on their ***w***.
26:14 are the mere edges of His ***w***,
30:12 they raise against me their ***w***
31: 4 Does He not see my ***w***,
34:21 For His eyes are on the ***w*** of
34:27 would not consider any of His ***w***,
40:19 He is the first of the ***w*** of
Ps 10: 5 His ***w*** are always prospering;
18:21 For I have kept the ***w*** of the
25: 4 Show me Your ***w***,
39: 1 I said, "I will guard my ***w***,
51:13 will teach transgressors Your ***w***,
81:13 Israel would walk in My ***w***!
91:11 To keep you in all your ***w***.
95:10 And they do not know My ***w***.
103: 7 He made known His ***w*** to Moses,
119: 3 iniquity; They walk in His ***w***.
119: 5 that my ***w*** were directed To
119:15 And contemplate Your ***w***.
119:26 I have declared my ***w***,
119:59 I thought about my ***w***,
119:168 For all my ***w*** are before You.
125: 5 turn aside to their crooked ***w***,
128: 1 the LORD, Who walks in His ***w***.
138: 5 they shall sing of the ***w*** of the
139: 3 are acquainted with all my ***w***.
145:17 is righteous in all His ***w***,
Prov 1:19 So are the ***w*** of everyone who
2:13 uprightness To walk in the ***w***
2:15 Whose ***w*** are crooked, And who
3: 6 In all your ***w*** acknowledge Him,
3:17 Her ***w*** are ways of
3:17 Her ways are ***w*** of
3:31 And choose none of his ***w***;
4:26 And let all your ***w*** be
5: 6 Her ***w*** are unstable; You do not
5:21 For the ***w*** of man are before
6: 6 Consider her ***w*** and be wise,
7:25 your heart turn aside to her ***w***,
8:32 are those who keep my ***w***.
10: 9 But he who perverts his ***w*** will
11:20 But the blameless in their ***w***
14: 2 he who is perverse in his ***w***
14:14 will be filled with his own ***w***,
16: 2 All the ***w*** of a man are pure in
16: 7 When a man's ***w*** please the
17:23 the back To pervert the ***w*** of
19:16 he who is careless of his ***w***
22:25 Lest you learn his ***w*** And set a
23:26 And let your eyes observe my ***w***.
28: 6 Than one perverse in his ***w***,
28:18 who is perverse in his ***w***
31: 3 Nor your ***w*** to that which
31:27 She watches over the ***w*** of her
Eccl 11: 9 Walk in the ***w*** of your heart,
Isa 2: 3 He will teach us His ***w***,
2: 6 they are filled with eastern ***w***;
42:24 they would not walk in His ***w***,
45:13 And I will direct all his ***w***;
55: 8 Nor are your ***w*** My ways,"
55: 8 Nor are your ways My ***w***,
55: 9 So are My ***w*** higher than your
55: 9 are My ways higher than your ***w***,
57:18 I have seen his ***w***,
58: 2 And delight to know My ***w***,
58:13 honor Him, not doing your own ***w***,
59: 8 is no justice in their ***w***;
63:17 You made us stray from Your ***w***,
64: 5 Who remembers You in Your ***w***.
64: 5 In these ***w*** we continue;
66: 3 as they have chosen their own ***w***,
Jer 2:23 breaking loose in her ***w***,
2:33 taught The wicked women your ***w***.
4:18 Your ***w*** and your doings Have
6:16 Stand in the ***w*** and see, And ask
7: 3 Amend your ***w*** and your doings,
7: 5 if you thoroughly amend your ***w***
7:23 And walk in all the ***w*** that I
12:16 will learn carefully the ***w*** of
15: 7 they do not return from their ***w***.
16:17 My eyes are on all their ***w***;
17:10 every man according to his ***w***,
18:11 and make your ***w*** and your doings
18:15 to stumble in their ***w***,
23:12 be to them Like slippery ***w***;
26:13 amend your ***w*** and your doings,
32:19 eyes are open to all the ***w*** of
32:19 everyone according to his ***w***
Lam 3: 9 He has blocked my ***w*** with hewn
3:11 He has turned aside my ***w*** and
3:40 us search out and examine our ***w***,
Ezek 7: 3 judge you according to your ***w***,
7: 4 But I will repay your ***w***,
7: 8 judge you according to your ***w***,
7: 9 repay you according to your ***w***,
14:22 and you will see their ***w*** and
14:23 when you see their ***w*** and their
16:47 You did not walk in their ***w*** nor
16:47 corrupt than they in all your ***w***.
16:61 Then you will remember your ***w***
18:23 that he should turn from his ***w***
18:25 and your ***w*** which are not fair?
18:29 is it not My ***w*** which are fair,
18:29 and your ***w*** which are not fair?
18:30 every one according to his ***w***,
20:43 you shall remember your ***w*** and
20:44 not according to your wicked ***w***
21:19 appoint for yourself two ***w*** for
24:14 According to your ***w*** And
28:15 You were perfect in your ***w***
33:11 turn from your evil ***w***!
33:20 of you according to his own ***w***.
36:17 they defiled it by their own ***w***
36:19 them according to their ***w*** and
36:31 you will remember your evil ***w***
36:32 and confounded for your own ***w***,
Dan 4:37 and His ***w*** justice.
5:23 in His hand and owns all your ***w***,
Hos 4: 9 I will punish them for their ***w***,
9: 8 a fowler's snare in all his ***w***—
12: 2 punish Jacob according to his ***w***;
14: 9 For the ***w*** of the LORD are
Mic 4: 2 He will teach us His ***w***,
Hab 3: 6 His ***w*** are everlasting.
Hag 1: 5 Consider your ***w***!
1: 7 Consider your ***w***!

Zech 1: 4 Turn now from your evil *w* and
1: 6 According to our *w* and
3: 7 'If you will walk in My *w*,
Mal 2: 9 you have not kept My *w* But
Mt 22: 5 light of it and went their *w*,
Lk 1:76 of the Lord to prepare His *w*,
3: 5 straight And the rough *w*
Acts 2:28 made known to me the *w*
13:10 perverting the straight *w* of
13:18 years He put up with their *w*
14:16 nations to walk in their own *w*.
28:10 They also honored us in many *w*;
Rom 3:16 and misery are in their *w*;
11:33 are His judgments and His *w*
1 Cor 4:17 who will remind you of my *w* in
2 Tim 1:18 you know very well how many *w*
Heb 1: 1 various times and in various *w*
3:10 they have not known My *w*.
Jas 1: 8 man, unstable in all his *w*.
2 Pe 2: 2 will follow their destructive *w*,
Rev 15: 3 Just and true are Your *w*,

WAYSIDE (9/9) WAY

1 Sam 4:13 sitting on a seat by the *w*
Ps 110: 7 drink of the brook by the *w*;
140: 5 have spread a net by the *w*;
Mt 13: 4 sowed, some seed fell by the *w*;
13:19 he who received seed by the *w*.
Mk 4: 4 that some seed fell by the *w*;
4:15 these are the ones by the *w*
Lk 8: 5 as he sowed, some fell by the *w*;
8:12 Those by the *w* are the ones who

WE (1826/1311) See APPENDIX

WEAK (52/49) WEAKER, WEAKNESS

Gen 33:13 knows that the children are *w*,
Num 13:18 dwell in it are strong or *w*,
Judg 16: 7 dried, then I shall become *w*,
16:11 used, then I shall become *w*,
16:17 leave me, and I shall become *w*,
2 Sam 3:39 And I am *w* today, though
17: 2 him while he is weary and *w*,
2 Chr 15: 7 and do not let your hands be *w*,
36:17 or virgin, on the aged or the *w*;
Job 4: 3 And you have strengthened *w*
23:16 For God made my heart *w*,
Ps 6: 2 on me, O LORD, for I am *w*;
109:24 My knees are *w* through fasting,
Isa 14:10 Have you also become as *w* as we?
35: 3 Strengthen the *w* hands,
40:29 He gives power to the *w*,
Ezek 7:17 And every knee will be as *w*
21: 7 and all knees will be *w* as
34: 4 The *w* you have not strengthened,
34:21 butted all the *w* ones with your
Joel 3:10 Let the *w* say, 'I am strong.'
Zeph 3:16 Zion, let not your hands be *w*.
Mt 26:41 willing, but the flesh is *w*.
Mk 14:38 willing, but the flesh is *w*.
Acts 20:35 that you must support the *w*.
Rom 4:19 And not being *w* in faith, he did
8: 3 could not do in that it was *w*
14: 1 Receive one who is *w* in the
14: 2 but he who is *w* eats only
14:21 or is offended or is made *w*.
15: 1 bear with the scruples of the *w*,
1 Cor 1:27 and God has chosen the *w* things
4:10 We are *w*, but you are strong!
8: 7 and their conscience, being *w*,
8: 9 block to those who are *w*.
8:10 the conscience of him who is *w*
8:11 of your knowledge shall the *w*
8:12 and wound their *w* conscience,
9:22 to the *w* I became as weak,
9:22 to the weak I became as *w*,
9:22 as weak, that I might win the *w*.
11:30 For this reason many are *w* and
2 Cor 10:10 but his bodily presence is *w*,
11:21 I say that we were too *w* for
11:29 Who is *w*, and I am not
11:29 Who is weak, and I am not *w*?
12:10 For when I am *w*, then I am
13: 3 who is not *w* toward you, but
13: 4 For we also are *w* in Him, but
13: 9 For we are glad when we are *w*
Gal 4: 9 that you turn again to the *w*
1 Th 5:14 the fainthearted, uphold the *w*,

WEAKENED (3/3)

Neh 6: 9 Their hands will be *w* in the
Ps 102:23 He *w* my strength in the way;
Isa 14:12 You who *w* the nations!

WEAKENS (1/1)

Jer 38: 4 for thus he *w* the hands of the

WEAKER (4/3) WEAK

2 Sam 3: 1 and the house of Saul grew *w*
3: 1 house of Saul grew weaker and *w*.
1 Cor 12:22 of the body which seem to be *w*
1 Pe 3: 7 as to the *w* vessel,

WEAKEST (1/1)

Judg 6:15 Indeed my clan is the *w* in

WEAKNESS (10/10) WEAK, WEAKNESSES

Rom 6:19 human terms because of the *w*
1 Cor 1:25 and the *w* of God is stronger
2: 3 I was with you in *w*,
15:43 in glory. It is sown in *w*,
2 Cor 12: 9 strength is made perfect in *w*.
13: 4 though He was crucified in *w*,
Heb 5: 2 he himself is also subject to *w*.
7:18 commandment because of its *w*
7:28 as high priests men who have *w*,
11:34 out of *w* were made strong,

WEAKNESSES (2/2) WEAKNESS

Rom 8:26 the Spirit also helps in our *w*.
Heb 4:15 cannot sympathize with our *w*,

WEALTH (37/37)

Gen 31: 1 he has acquired all this *w*.
34:29 and all their *w*.
Deut 8:17 my hand have gained me this *w*.
8:18 He who gives you power to get *w*,
Ruth 2: 1 husband, a man of great *w*,
2 Chr 1:11 you have not asked riches or *w*
1:12 I will give you riches and *w*
Job 6:22 a bribe for me from your *w*'?
15:29 Nor will his *w* continue,
20:10 his hands will restore his *w*.
21:13 They spend their days in *w*,
31:25 I have rejoiced because my *w*
Ps 49: 6 Those who trust in their *w* And
49:10 And leave their *w* to others.
112: 3 *W* and riches will be in his
Prov 5:10 aliens be filled with your *w*,
8:21 those who love me to inherit *w*,
10:15 The rich man's *w* is his strong
13:11 *W* gained by dishonesty will
13:22 But the *w* of the sinner is
18:11 The rich man's *w* is his strong
19: 4 *W* makes many friends, But the
29: 3 of harlots wastes his *w*.
Eccl 5:19 whom God has given riches and *w*,
6: 2 God has given riches and *w* and
Song 8: 7 would give for love All the *w*
Isa 60: 5 The *w* of the Gentiles shall
60:11 men may bring to you the *w* of
Jer 15:13 Your *w* and your treasures I
17: 3 I will give as plunder your *w*,
20: 5 I will deliver all the *w* of
Ezek 29:19 he shall take away her *w*,
30: 4 And they take away her *w*,
Hos 12: 8 I have found *w* for myself;
Nah 2: 9 Or *w* of every desirable prize.
Zech 14:14 And the *w* of all the
Rev 18:19 the sea became rich by her *w*!

WEALTHY (3/3)

2 Ki 15:20 Israel, from all the very *w*,
Jer 49:31 go up to the *w* nation that
Rev 3:17 say, 'I am rich, have become *w*,

WEANED (12/9)

Gen 21: 8 So the child grew and was *w*.
21: 8 the same day that Isaac was *w*.
1 Sam 1:22 "Not until the child is *w*;
1:23 wait until you have *w* him.
1:23 nursed her son until she had *w*
1:24 Now when she had *w* him, she
1 Ki 11:20 whom Tahpenes *w* in Pharaoh's
Ps 131: 2 Like a *w* child with his
131: 2 Like a *w* child is my soul
Isa 11: 8 And the *w* child shall put his
28: 9 Those just *w* from milk?
Hos 1: 8 Now when she had *w* Lo-Ruhamah,

WEAPON (7/7) WEAPONS

Num 35:18 him with a wooden hand *w*,
1 Chr 12:37 battle with every kind of *w*
2 Chr 23:10 every man with his *w* in his
Neh 4:17 and with the other held a *w*.
Job 20:24 He will flee from the iron *w*;
Isa 54:17 No *w* formed against you shall
Ezek 9: 1 each with a deadly *w* in his

WEAPONS (28/28) WEAPON

Gen 27: 3 therefore, please take your *w*,
Deut 1:41 of you had girded on his *w* of
Judg 18:11 armed with *w* of war.
18:16 hundred men armed with their *w*
18:17 men who were armed with *w* of
1 Sam 8:12 and some to make his *w* of war
20:40 Then Jonathan gave his *w* to his
21: 8 neither my sword nor my *w* with
2 Sam 1:27 And the *w* of war perished!"
2 Ki 7:15 was full of garments and *w*
10: 2 a fortified city also, and *w*,
11: 8 every man with his *w* in his
11:11 every man with his *w* in his
1 Chr 12:33 expert in war with all *w* of
2 Chr 23: 7 every man with his *w* in his
32: 5 and made *w* and shields in
Eccl 9:18 Wisdom is better than *w* of
Isa 13: 5 The LORD and His *w* of
Jer 21: 4 I will turn back the *w* of war
22: 7 Everyone with his *w*;
50:25 And has brought out the *w* of
51:20 You are My battle-ax and *w* of
Ezek 32:27 gone down to hell with their *w*
39: 9 and set on fire and burn the *w*,
39:10 they will make fires with the *w*;
Joel 2: 8 they lunge between the *w*,
Jn 18: 3 with lanterns, torches, and *w*.
2 Cor 10: 4 For the *w* of our warfare are

WEAR (15/15) WEARING, WORE, WORN

Ex 18:18 who are with you will surely *w*
Lev 21:10 and who is consecrated to *w*
Deut 8: 4 Your garments did not *w* out on
22: 5 A woman shall not *w* anything
22:11 You shall not *w* a garment of
1 Sam 2:28 and to *w* an ephod before Me?
Neh 9:21 Their clothes did not *w* out
Job 9:27 will put off my sad face and *w*
27:17 but the just will *w* it,
Isa 4: 1 will eat our own food and *w*
Zech 13: 4 they will not *w* a robe of
Mt 6:31 we drink?' or 'What shall we *w*?
11: 8 those who *w* soft clothing are
Mk 6: 9 but to *w* sandals, and not to put
Lk 9:12 When the day began to *w* away,

WEARIED (10/8) WEARY

Isa 43:23 Nor *w* you with incense.
43:24 You have *w* Me with your
47:13 You are *w* in the multitude of
57:10 You are *w* in the length of your
Jer 12: 5 and they have *w* you,
12: 5 they *w* you, Then how will
Mic 6: 3 And how have I *w* you?
Mal 2:17 You have *w* the LORD with your
2:17 In what way have we *w* Him?"
Jn 4: 6 being *w* from His journey,

WEARIES (2/2)

Prov 26:15 It *w* him to bring it back to
Eccl 10:15 The labor of fools *w* them,

WEARINESS (2/2) WEARY

Mal 1:13 what a *w*!' And you sneer at
2 Cor 11:27 in *w* and toil, in sleeplessness

WEARING (8/8) WEAR

1 Sam 2:18 *w* a linen ephod.
14: 3 was *w* an ephod. But the people
2 Sam 6:14 and David was *w* a linen ephod.
2 Ki 1: 8 A hairy man *w* a leather belt
Esth 1:11 *w* her royal crown, in order to
Jn 19: 5 *w* the crown of thorns and the
Jas 2: 3 you pay attention to the one *w*
1 Pe 3: 3 *w* gold, or putting on fine

WEARISOME (2/2) WEARY

Job 7: 3 And *w* nights have been
Eccl 12:12 and much study is *w* to the

WEARS (1/1)

Job 14:19 As water *w* away stones,

WEARY (53/52) WEARIED, WEARINESS, WEARISOME

Gen 19:11 so that they became *w* trying
25:29 from the field, and he was *w*.
25:30 same red stew, for I am *w*.
27:46 I am *w* of my life because of the
Deut 25:18 when you were tired and *w*;
Josh 7: 3 Do not *w* all the people there,
Judg 4:21 for he was fast asleep and *w*.
8:15 we should give bread to your *w*
1 Sam 30:10 who were so *w* that they could
30:21 hundred men who had been so *w*
2 Sam 16:14 who were with him became *w*;
17: 2 come upon him while he is *w*
17:29 The people are hungry and *w* and
23:10 until his hand was *w*,
Job 3:17 And there the *w* are at rest.
4: 2 with you, will you become *w*?
4: 5 comes upon you, and you are *w*;
22: 7 You have not given the *w* water
Ps 6: 6 I am *w* with my groaning;
68: 9 inheritance, When it was *w*.
69: 3 I am *w* with my crying;
Prov 25:17 Lest he become *w* of you and
25:25 As cold water to a *w* soul,
Isa 1:14 I am *w* of bearing them.
5:27 No one will be *w* or stumble
7:13 it a small thing for you to *w*
7:13 but will you *w* my God also?
16:12 it is seen that Moab is *w* on
28:12 which You may cause the *w* to
32: 2 shadow of a great rock in a *w*
40:28 earth, Neither faints nor is *w*.
40:30 the youths shall faint and be *w*,
40:31 They shall run and not be *w*,
43:22 And you have been *w* of Me, O
46: 1 A burden to the *w* beast.
50: 4 in season to him who is *w*.
Jer 2:24 those who seek her will not *w*
4:31 for my soul is *w* Because of
6:11 I am *w* of holding it in. "I
9: 5 They *w* themselves to commit
15: 6 I am *w* of relenting!

20: 9 I was **w** of holding it back,
31:25 For I have satiated the **w** soul,
51:58 the fire; And they shall be **w**.
51:64 And they shall be **w**.'
Ezek 24:12 She has grown **w** with lies,
Hab 2:13 And nations **w** themselves in
Mt 9:36 because they were **w** and
Lk 18: 5 by her continual coming she **w**
Gal 6: 9 And let us not grow **w** while
2 Th 3:13 do not grow **w** in doing good.
Heb 12: 3 lest you become **w** and
Rev 2: 3 sake and have not become **w**.

WEATHER (4/4)

Prov 25:20 takes away a garment in cold **w**,
Mt 16: 2 you say, 'It will be fair **w**,
16: 3 It will be foul **w** today,
Lk 12:55 you say, 'There will be hot **w**';

WEAVE (5/5) WEAVER'S, WOVE, WOVEN

Ex 26: 1 of cherubim you shall **w** them.
28:39 You shall skillfully **w** the
Judg 16:13 If you **w** the seven locks of my
Isa 19: 9 in fine flax And those who **w**
59: 5 They hatch vipers' eggs and **w**

WEAVER (7/7)

Ex 26:36 fine woven linen, made by a **w**.
27:16 fine woven linen, made by a **w**.
35:35 and fine linen, and of the **w**—
36:37 fine woven linen, made by a **w**,
38:23 a **w** of blue, purple, and
39:29 scarlet thread, made by a **w**,
Isa 38:12 have cut off my life like a **w**.

WEAVER'S (5/5) WEAVE

1 Sam 17: 7 spear was like a **w** beam
2 Sam 21:19 spear was like a **w** beam
1 Chr 11:23 was a spear like a **w** beam
20: 5 of whose spear was like a **w** beam
Job 7: 6 swifter than a **w** shuttle,

WEB (4/4)

Judg 16:13 locks of my head into the **w** of
16:14 out the batten and the **w** from
Job 8:14 whose trust is a spider's **w**.
Isa 59: 5 eggs and weave the spider's **w**;

WEBS (1/1)

Isa 59: 6 Their **w** will not become

WEDDING (13/13)

Song 3:11 him On the day of his **w**,
Mt 22: 3 those who were invited to the **w**;
22: 4 are ready. Come to the **w**.
22: 8 The **w** is ready, but those who
22: 9 as you find, invite to the **w**.
22:10 And the **w** hall was filled with
22:11 there who did not have on a **w**
22:12 you come in here without a **w**
25:10 ready went in with him to the **w**;
Lk 12:36 when he will return from the **w**,
14: 8 are invited by anyone to a **w**
Jn 2: 1 On the third day there was a **w**
2: 2 disciples were invited to the **w**.

WEDGE (3/3)

Josh 7:21 and a **w** of gold weighing fifty
7:24 the garment, the **w** of gold,
Isa 13:12 A man more than the golden **w**

WEDLOCK (1/1)

Ezek 16:38 judge you as women who break **w**

WEEDS (3/3)

Job 31:40 And **w** instead of barley."
Jon 2: 5 **W** were wrapped around my head.
Zeph 2: 9 Overrun with **w** and saltpits,

WEEK (13/12) WEEKS

Gen 29:27 "Fulfill her **w**,
29:28 did so and fulfilled her **w**.
Dan 9:27 a covenant with many for one **w**;
9:27 But in the middle of the **w** He
Mt 28: 1 as the first day of the **w**
Mk 16: 2 on the first day of the **w**,
16: 9 on the first day of the **w**,
Lk 18:12 'I fast twice a **w**;
24: 1 Now on the first day of the **w**,
Jn 20: 1 Now on the first day of the **w**
20:19 being the first day of the **w**,
Acts 20: 7 Now on the first day of the **w**,
1 Cor 16: 2 On the first day of the **w** let

WEEKS (15/13) WEEK

Ex 34:22 shall observe the Feast of **W**,
Lev 12: 5 then she shall be unclean two **w**,
Num 28:26 the LORD at your Feast of **W**,
Deut 16: 9 You shall count seven **w** for
16: 9 begin to count the seven **w** from
16:10 you shall keep the Feast of **W**
16:16 Bread, at the Feast of **W**,
2 Chr 8:13 Bread, the Feast of **W**,
Jer 5:24 for us the appointed **w** of the
Dan 9:24 Seventy **w** are determined
9:25 There shall be seven **w** and
9:25 be seven weeks and sixty-two **w**;
9:26 And after the sixty-two **w**
10: 2 was mourning three full **w**.
10: 3 till three whole **w** were

WEEP (49/44) WEEPING, WEPT

Gen 23: 2 to mourn for Sarah and to **w**
43:30 and sought somewhere to **w**.
Num 11:13 For they **w** all over me, saying,
1 Sam 1: 8 to her, "Hannah, why do you **w**?
11: 5 the people, that they **w**?
30: 4 they had no more power to **w**.
2 Sam 1:24 daughters of Israel, **w** over
Neh 8: 9 your God; do not mourn nor **w**.
Job 27:15 And their widows shall not **w**,
30:31 to the voice of those who **w**.
31:38 And its furrows **w** together;
Eccl 3: 4 A time to **w**, And a time to
Isa 15: 2 To the high places to **w**.
22: 4 I will **w** bitterly;
30:19 You shall **w** no more.
33: 7 ambassadors of peace shall **w**
Jer 9: 1 That I might **w** day and night
13:17 My soul will **w** in secret for
13:17 My eyes will **w** bitterly And
22:10 **W** not for the dead, nor bemoan
22:10 **W** bitterly for him who goes
48:32 O vine of Sibmah! I will **w** for
Lam 1:16 "For these things I **w**;
Ezek 24:16 you shall neither mourn nor **w**,
24:23 you shall neither mourn nor **w**,
27:31 And **w** for you With bitterness
Joel 1: 5 Awake, you drunkards, and **w**;
2:17 **W** between the porch and the
Mic 1:10 **W** not at all; In Beth Aphrah
Zech 7: 3 Should I **w** in the fifth month
Mk 5:39 "Why make this commotion and **w**?
Lk 6:21 Blessed are you who **w** now,
6:25 For you shall mourn and **w**.
7:13 her and said to her, "Do not **w**.
7:32 to you, And you did not **w**.
8:52 but He said, "Do not **w**;
23:28 do not **w** for Me, but weep for
23:28 but **w** for yourselves and for
Jn 11:31 She is going to the tomb to **w**
16:20 I say to you that you will **w**
Rom 12:15 and **w** with those who weep.
12:15 and weep with those who **w**.
1 Cor 7:30 those who **w** as though they did
7:30 weep as though they did not **w**,
Jas 4: 9 Lament and mourn and **w**!
5: 1 **w** and howl for your miseries
Rev 5: 5 elders said to me, "Do not **w**.
18: 9 luxuriously with her will **w**
18:11 merchants of the earth will **w**

WEEPING (51/48) WEEP

Num 11:10 Then Moses heard the people **w**
25: 6 who were **w** at the door of the
Deut 34: 8 So the days of **w** and mourning
2 Sam 3:16 **w** behind her. So Abner said to
15:30 **w** as they went up.
19: 1 the king is **w** and mourning for
2 Ki 8:12 Hazael said, "Why is my lord **w**?
Ezra 3:13 of joy from the noise of the **w**
10: 1 and while he was confessing, **w**,
Esth 4: 3 among the Jews, with fasting, **w**,
Job 16:16 My face is flushed from **w**,
Ps 6: 8 has heard the voice of my **w**.
30: 5 **W** may endure for a night,
102: 9 And mingled my drink with **w**,
126: 6 who continually goes forth **w**,
Isa 15: 3 Everyone will wail, **w** bitterly.
15: 5 Luhith They will go up with **w**;
16: 9 With the **w** of Jazer;
22:12 GOD of hosts Called for **w**
65:19 The voice of **w** shall no longer
Jer 3:21 **W** and supplications of the
9:10 I will take up a **w** and wailing
31: 9 They shall come with **w**,
31:15 Lamentation and bitter **w**,
31:15 Rachel **w** for her children,
31:16 "Refrain your voice from **w**,
41: 6 **w** as he went along; and it
48: 5 they ascend with continual **w**;
48:32 I will weep for you with the **w**
50: 4 With continual **w** they shall
Ezek 8:14 women were sitting there **w** for
Joel 2:12 heart, With fasting, with **w**,
Mal 2:13 With **w** and crying; So He does
Mt 2:18 in Ramah, Lamentation, **w**,
2:18 Rachel **w** for her
8:12 There will be **w** and gnashing of
22:13 there will be **w** and gnashing of
24:51 There shall be **w** and gnashing
25:30 There will be **w** and gnashing of
Lk 7:38 stood at His feet behind Him **w**;
13:28 There will be **w** and gnashing of
Jn 11:33 Therefore, when Jesus saw her **w**,
11:33 the Jews who came with her **w**,
20:11 stood outside by the tomb **w**,
20:13 to her, "Woman, why are you **w**?
20:15 to her, "Woman, why are you **w**?
Acts 9:39 all the widows stood by him **w**,
21:13 What do you mean by **w** and
Phil 3:18 often, and now tell you even **w**,
Rev 18:15 of her torment, **w** and wailing,
18:19 **w** and wailing, and saying,

WEEPS (1/1)

Lam 1: 2 She **w** bitterly in the night,

WEIGH (7/7) WEIGHED, WEIGHS, WEIGHT

1 Ki 7:47 And Solomon did not **w** all the
1 Chr 20: 2 and found it to **w** a talent of
Ezra 8:29 and keep them until you **w**
Ps 58: 2 You **w** out the violence of your
Isa 26: 7 You **w** the path of the just.
46: 6 And **w** silver on the scales;
Ezek 5: 1 then take scales to **w** and

WEIGHED (23/20) WEIGH

Gen 23:16 and Abraham **w** out the silver
Num 7:85 Each silver platter **w** one
7:85 the silver of the vessels **w**
7:86 gold pans full of incense **w**
7:86 all the gold of the pans **w** one
1 Sam 2: 3 And by Him actions are **w**.
17: 7 and his iron spearhead **w** six
2 Sam 14:26 he **w** the hair of his head at
Ezra 8:25 and **w** out to them the silver,
8:26 I **w** into their hand six hundred
8:33 gold and the articles were **w**
Job 6: 2 that my grief were fully **w**,
28:15 Nor can silver be **w** for its
31: 6 Let me be **w** on honest scales,
Ps 62: 9 If they are **w** on the scales,
Isa 40:12 **W** the mountains in scales
Jer 32: 9 and **w** out to him the
32:10 and **w** the money on the scales.
Dan 5:27 You have been **w** in the
Am 2:13 I am **w** down by you, As a cart
2:13 As a cart full of sheaves is **w**
Zech 11:12 So they **w** out for my wages
Lk 21:34 lest your hearts be **w** down with

WEIGHING (4/3)

Gen 24:22 man took a golden nose ring **w**
24:22 two bracelets for her wrists **w**
Josh 7:21 and a wedge of gold **w** fifty
Ezra 8:26 silver articles **w** one hundred

WEIGHS (4/4) WEIGH

Prov 16: 2 But the LORD **w** the spirits.
21: 2 But the LORD **w** the hearts.
24:12 Does not He who **w** the hearts
Isa 33:18 Where is he who **w**?

WEIGHT (45/40) WEIGH, WEIGHTIER, WEIGHTS

Gen 43:21 his sack, our money in full **w**;
Lev 19:35 in measurement of length, **w**,
26:26 bring back your bread by **w**,
Num 7:13 the **w** of which was one hundred
7:19 the **w** of which was one hundred
7:25 the **w** of which was one hundred
7:31 the **w** of which was one hundred
7:37 the **w** of which was one hundred
7:43 the **w** of which was one hundred
7:49 the **w** of which was one hundred
7:55 the **w** of which was one hundred
7:61 the **w** of which was one hundred
7:67 the **w** of which was one hundred
7:73 the **w** of which was one hundred
7:79 the **w** of which was one hundred
Deut 25:15 shall have a perfect and just **w**,
Judg 8:26 Now the **w** of the gold earrings
1 Sam 17: 5 and the **w** of the coat was five
2 Sam 12:30 Its **w** was a talent of gold,
21:16 the **w** of whose bronze spear
1 Ki 7:47 the **w** of the bronze was not
10:14 The **w** of gold that came to
1 Chr 21:25 hundred shekels of gold by **w**
28:14 He gave gold by **w** for things
28:14 for all articles of silver by **w**,
28:15 the **w** for the lampstands of
28:15 by **w** for each lampstand and its
28:15 the lampstands of silver by **w**,
28:16 And by **w** he gave gold for the
28:17 he gave gold by **w** for every
28:17 silver by **w** for every bowl;
28:18 and refined gold by **w** for the
2 Chr 3: 9 The **w** of the nails was fifty
4:18 great abundance that the **w** of
9:13 The **w** of gold that came to
Ezra 8:30 the gold and the articles by **w**,
8:34 with the number and **w** of
8:34 All the **w** was written down at
Job 28:25 To establish a **w** for the wind,
Prov 11: 1 But a just **w** is His delight.
Ezek 4:10 which you eat shall be by **w**,
4:16 they shall eat bread by **w** and
2 Cor 4:17 more exceeding and eternal **w**
Heb 12: 1 let us lay aside every **w**,
Rev 16:21 each hailstone about the **w** of

WEIGHTIER (1/1) WEIGHT

Mt 23:23 and have neglected the **w**

WEIGHTS (7/6) WEIGHT

Lev 19:36 have honest scales, honest **w**,
Deut 25:13 have in your bag differing **w**,
Prov 16:11 Honest **w** and scales are the
16:11 All the **w** in the bag are His
20:10 Diverse **w** and diverse
20:23 Diverse **w** are an abomination
Mic 6:11 with the bag of deceitful **w**?

WEIGHTY (2/2)

Prov 27: 3 stone is heavy and sand is **w**,
2 Cor 10:10 are **w** and powerful, but his

WELCOME (2/2) WELCOMED

Acts 28: 2 a fire and made us all **w**,
Col 4:10 if he comes to you, **w** him),

WELCOMED (3/3) WELCOME

Lk 8:40 that the multitude **w** Him,
10:38 a certain woman named Martha **w**
1 Th 2:13 you **w** it not as the word of

WELFARE (2/2)

Esth 2:11 to learn of Esther's **w** and what
Jer 38: 4 this man does not seek the **w**

WELL (267/255) WELLS, WELLSPRING

Gen 4: 7 'If you do **w**, will you
4: 7 And if you do not do **w**,
12:13 that it may be **w** with me for
12:16 He treated Abram **w** for her sake.
13:10 that it was **w** watered
14:16 as **w** as the women and the
16:14 Therefore the **w** was called Beer
21:19 and she saw a **w** of water.
21:25 Abimelech because of a **w** of
21:30 witness that I have dug this **w**.
24:11 down outside the city by a **w**
24:13 here I stand by the **w** of
24:16 And she went down to the **w**,
24:20 ran back to the **w** to draw
24:29 ran out to the man by the **w**.
24:30 he stood by the camels at the **w**.
24:42 And this day I came to the **w**
24:43 I stand by the **w** of water;
24:45 and she went down to the **w** and
25:22 and she said, "If all is **w**,
26:19 and found a **w** of running water
26:20 So he called the name of the **w**
26:21 Then they dug another **w**,
26:22 from there and dug another **w**,
26:25 there Isaac's servants dug a **w**.
26:32 came and told him about the **w**
29: 2 and saw a **w** in the field;
29: 2 for out of that **w** they watered
29: 6 So he said to them, "Is he **w**?
29: 6 And they said, "He is **w**.
32: 9 and I will deal **w** with you':
32:12 'I will surely treat you **w**,
37:14 Please go and see if it is **w**
37:14 well with your brothers and **w**
40:14 But remember me when it is **w**
43:27 and said, "Is your father **w**,
45:16 Pharaoh and his servants **w**.
49:22 bough, A fruitful bough by a **w**;
50: 8 as **w** as all the house of Joseph,
Ex 1:20 Therefore God dealt **w** with the
2:15 Midian; and he sat down by a **w**.
4:14 I know that he can speak **w**.
10:29 Moses said, "You have spoken **w**.
Lev 24:16 the stranger as **w** as him who is
Num 10:29 us, and we will treat you **w**;
11:18 For it was **w** with us in
13:30 for we are **w** able to overcome
16:16 —you and they, as **w** as Aaron.
21:16 which is the **w** where the LORD
21:17 O **w**! All of you sing to it—
21:18 The **w** the leaders sank, Dug by
Deut 1:17 you shall hear the small as **w**
1:23 "The plan pleased me **w**;
4:40 that it may go **w** with you and
5:14 female servant may rest as **w**
5:16 and that it may be **w** with you
5:29 that it might be **w** with them
5:33 live and that it may be **w**
6: 3 that it may be **w** with you,
6:18 that it may be **w** with you,
7:18 but you shall remember **w** what
12:25 that it may go **w** with you and
12:28 that it may go **w** with you and
19:13 that it may go **w** with you.
22: 7 that it may be **w** with you and
29:15 as **w** as with him who is not
Josh 8:33 the stranger as **w** as he who was
Judg 7: 1 and encamped beside the **w** of
9:16 and if you have dealt **w** with
14: 3 for me, for she pleases me **w**.
14: 7 and she pleased Samson **w**.
15: 5 as **w** as the vineyards and
20: 1 as **w** as from the land of
Ruth 3: 1 that it may be **w** with you?
1 Sam 9:10 '**W** said; come, let us go."
14: 8 Then Jonathan said, "Very **w**,
16:16 is upon you, and you shall be **w**.
16:17 me now a man who can play **w**,
16:23 would become refreshed and **w**,
18:26 it pleased David **w** to become
19: 4 Thus Jonathan spoke **w** of David
19:22 and came to the great **w** that
20: 7 "If he says thus: 'It is **w**,
24:18 this day how you have dealt **w**
25:31 But when the LORD has dealt **w**
2 Sam 3:26 brought him back from the **w** of
11:25 for the sword devours one as **w**
17:18 who had a **w** in his court;
17:21 that they came up out of the **w**
18:28 All is **w**!" Then he bowed down
19: 6 it would have pleased you **w**.
23:15 a drink of the water from the **w**
23:16 drew water from the **w** of
1 Ki 2:18 So Bathsheba said, "Very **w**,
8:18 you did **w** that it was in your
11: 1 as **w** as the daughter of
18:24 It is **w** spoken."
2 Ki 4:23 And she said, "It is **w**.
4:26 Is it **w** with you? Is it well
4:26 Is it **w** with your husband?
4:26 Is it **w** with the child?'"
4:26 And she answered, "It is **w**.
5:21 meet him, and said, "Is all **w**?
5:22 And he said, "All is **w**.
9:11 one said to him, "Is all **w**?
10:14 and killed them at the **w** of
10:30 Because you have done **w** in doing
25:24 and it shall be **w** with you."
25:25 as **w** as the Chaldeans who were
1 Chr 7:25 as **w** as Resheph, and Telah
11:17 me a drink of water from the **w**
11:18 drew water from the **w** of
25: 8 the small as **w** as the great,
26:13 the small as **w** as the great,
2 Chr 6: 8 you did **w** in that it was in
12:12 and things also went **w** in
31:15 to the great as **w** as the small.
35: 7 as **w** as three thousand cattle;
Neh 2:13 Valley Gate to the Serpent **W**
3:11 as **w** as the Tower of the Ovens.
Esth 9:18 as **w** as on the fourteenth;
Job 12: 3 But I have understanding as **w**
13: 9 Will it be **w** when He searches
Ps 41:11 By this I know that You are **w**
48:13 Mark **w** her bulwarks;
49:18 will praise you when you do **w**
78:29 So they ate and were **w** filled,
119:65 You have dealt **w** with Your
128: 2 and it shall be **w** with you.
139:14 And that my soul knows very **w**.
Prov 5:15 running water from your own **w**.
10:11 mouth of the righteous is a **w**
11:10 When it goes **w** with the
13: 2 A man shall eat **w** by the fruit
14:15 But the prudent considers **w**
23:27 a seductress is a narrow **w**.
24:32 I saw it, I considered it **w**;
25:26 a murky spring and a polluted **w**.
31:29 "Many daughters have done **w**,
Eccl 7:14 God has appointed the one as **w**
8:12 I surely know that it will be **w**
8:13 But it will not be **w** with the
12: 6 Or the wheel broken at the **w**.
Song 4:15 A **w** of living waters,
Isa 3:10 that it shall be **w** with
42:21 The LORD is **w** pleased for His
Jer 1:12 said to me, "You have seen **w**,
7:23 that it may be **w** with you.'
15:11 Surely it will be **w** with your
22:15 Then it was **w** with him.
22:16 Then it was **w**.
38:20 So it shall be **w** with you,
40: 9 and it shall be **w** with you.
42: 6 that it may be **w** with us when
Ezek 18: 4 The soul of the father As **w**
24: 5 bones under it, Make it boil **w**,
24:10 the fire; Cook the meat **w**,
33:32 a pleasant voice and can play **w**
35:15 as **w** as all of Edom—all of it!
41:15 as **w** as the inner temple and
41:17 as **w** as outside, and on every
44: 5 to me, "Son of man, mark **w**,
44: 5 Mark **w** who may enter the house
44:20 they shall keep their hair **w**
46: 5 as **w** as a hin of oil with every
Dan 11: 5 as **w** as one of his princes;
Mt 3:17 in whom I am **w** pleased."
9:12 Those who are **w** have no need of
9:21 His garment, I shall be made **w**.
9:22 your faith has made you **w**.
9:22 And the woman was made **w** from
12:18 in whom My soul is **w**
14:36 it were made perfectly **w**.
15: 7 **W** did Isaiah prophesy about
17: 5 in whom I am **w** pleased.
25:21 **W** done, good and faithful
25:23 **W** done, good and faithful
Mk 1:11 in whom I am **w** pleased."
2:17 Those who are **w** have no need of
5:28 His clothes, I shall be made **w**.
5:34 your faith has made you **w**.
6:56 many as touched Him were made **w**.
7: 6 **W** did Isaiah prophesy of you
7: 9 All too **w** you reject the
7:37 "He has done all things **w**.
10:52 way; your faith has made you **w**.
12:28 that He had answered them **w**,
12:32 '**W** said, Teacher.
Lk 3:22 in You I am **w** pleased."
5:31 Those who are **w** have no need of
6:18 as **w** as those who were tormented
6:26 to you when all men speak **w** of
7:10 found the servant **w** who had
8:48 your faith has made you **w**.
8:50 believe, and she will be made **w**.
13: 9 'And if it bears fruit, **w**.
17:19 Your faith has made you **w**."
18:42 your faith has made you **w**.
19:17 '**W** done, good servant;
20:39 "Teacher, You have spoken **w**.
Jn 2:10 and when the guests have **w**
4: 6 Now Jacob's **w** was there.
4: 6 His journey, sat thus by the **w**.
4:11 and the **w** is deep.
4:12 father Jacob, who gave us the **w**,
4:12 as **w** as his sons and his
4:17 You have **w** said, 'I have no
5: 4 was made **w** of whatever disease
5: 6 him, "Do you want to be made **w**?
5: 9 immediately the man was made **w**,
5:11 He who made me **w** said to me,
5:14 "See, you have been made **w**.
5:15 it was Jesus who had made him **w**.
7:23 I made a man completely **w** on
11:12 if he sleeps he will get **w**.
13:13 Teacher and Lord, and you say **w**,
18:23 **w**, why do you strike Me?"
Acts 4: 6 as **w** as Annas the high priest,
4: 9 what means he has been made **w**,
7:20 and was **w** pleasing to God;
10:33 and you have done **w** to come.
15:29 from these, you will do **w**.
16: 2 He was **w** spoken of by the
17:12 prominent women as **w** as men.
25:10 as you very **w** know.
26:17 as **w** as from the Gentiles,
26:30 as **w** as the governor and
Rom 11:20 **W** said. Because of unbelief
1 Cor 7:37 he will keep his virgin, does **w**.
7:38 gives her in marriage does **w**,
10: 5 with most of them God was not **w**
14:17 For you indeed give thanks **w**,
2 Cor 5: 8 **w** pleased rather to be absent
5: 9 to be **w** pleasing to Him.
8: 6 complete this grace in you as **w**.
11: 4 you may **w** put up with it!
Gal 5: 7 You ran **w**. Who hindered
Eph 6: 3 that it may be **w** with you
Phil 4:14 Nevertheless you have done **w**
4:18 **w** pleasing to God.
Col 3:20 for this is **w** pleasing to the
1 Th 2: 8 we were **w** pleased to impart to
1 Tim 3: 4 one who rules his own house **w**,
3:12 children and their own houses **w**.
3:13 For those who have served **w** as
5:10 **w** reported for good works:
5:17 Let the elders who rule **w** be
2 Tim 1:18 and you know very **w** how many
4:21 as **w** as Pudens, Linus, Claudia,
Titus 2: 9 to be **w** pleasing in all
Heb 4: 2 gospel was preached to us as **w**
13:16 with such sacrifices God is **w**
13:21 working in you what is **w**
Jas 2: 8 as yourself," you do **w**;
2:19 that there is one God. You do **w**.
2 Pe 1:17 in whom I am **w** pleased."
1:19 which you do **w** to heed as a
3 Jn 6 worthy of God, you will do **w**,

WELL ADVANCED (4/4)

Gen 18:11 **w** in age; and Sarah had passed
24: 1 **w** in age; and the LORD had
Lk 1: 7 and they were both **w** in years.
1:18 and my wife is **w** in years."

WELL KNOWN (4/3)

Mk 6:14 Him, for His name had become **w**.
2 Cor 5:11 but we are **w** to God, and I also
5:11 and I also trust are **w** in your
6: 9 as unknown, and yet **w**;

WELL RECEIVED (1/1)

Esth 10: 3 was great among the Jews and **w**

WELL-ADVISED (1/1) ADVISE

Prov 13:10 But with the **w** is wisdom.

WELL-BEING (8/8)

Gen 43:27 he asked them about their **w**,
Ex 18: 7 asked each other about their **w**,
Neh 2:10 a man had come to seek the **w**
Job 20:21 Therefore his **w** will not last.
Ps 69:22 And their **w** a trap.
Prov 29:10 But the upright seek his **w**.
Lam 3:38 the Most High That woe and **w**
1 Cor 10:24 but each one the other's **w**.

WELL-BELOVED (2/1) BELOVED

Isa 5: 1 Now let me sing to my **W** A song
5: 1 My **W** has a vineyard On a very

WELL-DRIVEN (1/1) DRIVE

Eccl 12:11 words of scholars are like **w**

WELL-FED (1/1) FEED

Jer 5: 8 They were like **w** lusty

WELL-LADEN (1/1)
Ps 144:14 That our oxen may be *w*;

WELL-OFF (1/1)
Jer 44:17 we had plenty of food, were *w*,

WELL-ORDERED (1/1)
2 Chr 8:16 all the work of Solomon was *w*

WELL-REFINED (1/1)
Isa 25: 6 Of *w* wines on the lees.

WELL-SET (1/1)
Isa 3:24 Instead of *w* hair, baldness;

WELL-WATERED (1/1)
Jer 31:12 souls shall be like a *w* garden,

WELL'S (6/5)
Gen 29: 2 stone was on the *w* mouth.
29: 3 roll the stone from the *w* mouth
29: 3 in its place on the *w* mouth.
29: 8 the stone from the *w* mouth;
29:10 the stone from the *w* mouth,
2 Sam 17:19 a covering over the *w* mouth,

WELLPLEASING (KJV) See (WELL) PLEASING

WELLS (12/11) WELL, WELLSPRING
Gen 26:15 had stopped up all the *w* which
26:18 And Isaac dug again the *w* of
Ex 15:27 where there were twelve *w* of
Num 20:17 nor will we drink water from *w*;
21:22 we will not drink water from *w*.
Deut 6:11 hewn-out *w* which you did not
10: 6 of Israel journeyed from the *w*
2 Chr 26:10 He dug many *w*, for he had much
Isa 12: 3 will draw water From the *w* of
Jer 6: 7 As a fountain *w* up with water,
6: 7 So she *w* up with her
2 Pe 2:17 These are *w* without water,

WELLSPRING (2/2) SPRING, WELL, WELLS
Prov 16:22 Understanding is a *w* of life
18: 4 The *w* of wisdom is a flowing

WELLSPRINGS (1/1)
Isa 48: 1 have come forth from the *w* of

WEN (KJV) See ULCER

WENCH (KJV) See (FEMALE) SERVANT

WEND (1/1)
Zech 10: 2 Therefore the people *w* their

WENT (1406/1295)
Gen 2: 6 but a mist *w* up from the earth
2:10 Now a river *w* out of Eden to
4:16 Then Cain *w* out from the
7: 7 *w* into the ark because of the
7: 9 two by two they *w* into the ark
7:15 And they *w* into the ark to Noah,
7:16 *w* in as God had commanded him;
8:18 So Noah *w* out, and his sons and
8:19 *w* out of the ark.
9:18 Now the sons of Noah who *w* out
9:23 and *w* backward and covered the
10:11 From that land he *w* to Assyria
11:31 and they *w* out with them from
12: 4 and Lot *w* with him. And Abram
12:10 and Abram *w* down to Egypt to
13: 1 Then Abram *w* up from Egypt, he
13: 3 And he *w* on his journey from the
13: 5 who *w* with Abram, had flocks
13:18 and *w* and dwelt by the
14: 8 Zoar) *w* out and joined together
14:11 and *w* their way.
14:14 and *w* in pursuit as far as Dan.
14:17 And the king of Sodom *w* out to
14:24 the portion of the men who *w*
15:17 when the sun *w* down and it was
16: 4 So he *w* in to Hagar, and she
17:22 and God *w* up from Abraham.
18:16 and Abraham *w* with them to send
18:22 turned away from there and *w*
18:33 So the LORD *w* His way as soon
19: 6 So Lot *w* out to them through the
19:14 So Lot *w* out and spoke to his
19:27 And Abraham *w* early in the
19:28 the smoke of the land which *w*
19:30 Then Lot *w* up out of Zoar and
19:33 And the firstborn *w* in and lay
21:16 Then she *w* and sat down across
21:19 And she *w* and filled the skin
22: 3 and arose and *w* to the place of
22: 6 and the two of them *w* together.
22: 8 So the two of them *w*
22:13 So Abraham *w* and took the ram,
22:19 and they rose and *w* together to
23:18 before all who *w* in at the gate
24:10 And he arose and *w* to
24:16 And she *w* down to the well,
24:30 that he *w* to the man.
24:45 and she *w* down to the well and
24:63 And Isaac *w* out to meditate in
25:22 So she *w* to inquire of the
25:34 drank, arose, and *w* his way.
26: 1 And Isaac *w* to Abimelech king
26:23 Then he *w* up from there to
27: 5 And Esau *w* to the field to hunt
27:14 And he *w* and got them and
27:18 So he *w* to his father and said,
27:22 So Jacob *w* near to Isaac his
28: 5 and he *w* to Padan Aram,
28: 9 So Esau *w* to Ishmael and took
28:10 Now Jacob *w* out from Beersheba
28:10 went out from Beersheba and *w*
29: 1 So Jacob *w* on his journey and
29:10 that Jacob *w* near and rolled
29:23 and he *w* in to her.
29:30 Then Jacob also *w* in to Rachel,
30: 4 and Jacob *w* in to her.
30:14 Now Reuben *w* in the days of
30:16 Leah *w* out to meet him and
31:33 And Laban *w* into Jacob's tent,
31:33 Then he *w* out of Leah's tent
32: 1 So Jacob *w* on his way,
32:21 So the present *w* on over before
34: 1 *w* out to see the daughters of
34: 6 Hamor the father of Shechem *w*
34:24 And all who *w* out of the gate of
34:24 all who *w* out of the gate of
34:26 Shechem's house, and *w* out.
35:13 Then God *w* up from him in the
35:22 that Reuben *w* and lay with
36: 6 and *w* to a country away from
37:12 Then his brothers *w* to feed
37:14 and he *w* to Shechem.
37:17 " So Joseph *w* after his
38: 2 and he married her and *w* in to
38: 9 when he *w* in to his brother's
38:11 And Tamar *w* and dwelt in her
38:12 and *w* up to his sheepshearers
38:18 and *w* in to her, and she
38:19 So she arose and *w* away,
39:11 when Joseph *w* into the house to
39:15 and fled and *w* outside."
41:45 So Joseph *w* out over all the
41:46 And Joseph *w* out from the
41:46 and *w* throughout all the land
42: 3 So Joseph's ten brothers *w* down
42: 5 And the sons of Israel *w* to buy
42:29 Then they *w* to Jacob their
43:15 and arose and *w* down to Egypt;
43:30 And he *w* into his chamber and
44:24 when we *w* up to your servant my
44:28 'and the one *w* out from me,
45:25 Then they *w* up out of Egypt,
46: 6 and *w* to Egypt, Jacob and all
46: 8 who *w* to Egypt: Reuben was
46:26 All the persons who *w* with
46:27 of the house of Jacob who *w* to
46:29 made ready his chariot and *w*
47: 1 Then Joseph *w* and told Pharaoh,
47:10 and *w* out from before Pharaoh.
49: 4 Because you *w* up to your
49: 4 He *w* up to my couch.
50: 7 So Joseph *w* up to bury his
50: 7 and with him *w* up all the
50: 9 And there *w* up with him both
50:14 and his brothers and all who *w*
50:18 Then his brothers also *w* and
Ex 2: 1 a man of the house of Levi *w*
2: 8 So the maiden *w* and called
2:11 that he *w* out to his brethren
2:13 And when he *w* out the second
4:18 So Moses *w* and returned to
4:27 So he *w* and met him on the
4:29 Then Moses and Aaron *w* and
5: 1 Afterward Moses and Aaron *w* in
5:10 the people and their officers *w*
7:10 So Moses and Aaron *w* in to
7:23 And Pharaoh turned and *w* into
8:12 Then Moses and Aaron *w* out from
8:30 So Moses *w* out from Pharaoh and
9:33 So Moses *w* out of the city from
10: 6 " And he turned and *w* out
10:14 And the locusts *w* up over all
10:18 So he *w* out from Pharaoh and
11: 8 Then he *w* out from Pharaoh in
12:28 Then the children of Israel *w*
12:38 A mixed multitude *w* up with them
12:41 all the armies of the LORD *w*
13: 3 this day in which you *w* out of
13:18 And the children of Israel *w* up
13:21 And the LORD *w* before them by
14: 8 and the children of Israel *w*
14:19 who *w* before the camp of
14:19 moved and *w* behind them;
14:19 and the pillar of cloud *w* from
14:22 So the children of Israel *w* into
14:23 And the Egyptians pursued and *w*
15:19 For the horses of Pharaoh *w* with
15:19 But the children of Israel *w* on
15:20 and all the women *w* out after
15:22 then they *w* out into the
15:22 And they *w* three days in the
16:27 that some of the people *w*
17:10 and Hur *w* up to the top of the
18: 7 So Moses *w* out to meet his
18: 7 and they *w* into the tent.
18:27 and he *w* his way to his own
19: 3 And Moses *w* up to God,
19:14 So Moses *w* down from the
19:20 and Moses *w* up.
19:25 So Moses *w* down to the people
24: 9 Then Moses *w* up, also Aaron,
24:13 and Moses *w* up to the mountain
24:15 Then Moses *w* up into the
24:18 So Moses *w* into the midst of the
24:18 the midst of the cloud and *w*
32:15 And Moses turned and *w* down
33: 7 who sought the LORD *w* out to
33: 8 whenever Moses *w* out to the
34: 4 early in the morning and *w* up
34:34 But whenever Moses *w* in before
34:35 until he *w* in to speak with
40:32 Whenever they *w* into the
Lev 9: 8 Aaron therefore *w* to the altar
9:23 And Moses and Aaron *w* into the
10: 2 So fire *w* out from the LORD and
10: 5 So they *w* near and carried them
16:23 which he put on when he *w* into
24:10 *w* out among the children of
Num 7:89 Now when Moses *w* into the
8:22 After that the Levites *w* in to
10:33 of the covenant of the LORD *w*
10:34 above them by day when they *w*
11: 8 The people *w* about and gathered
11:24 So Moses *w* out and told the
11:31 Now a wind *w* out from the
12: 5 And they both *w* forward.
13:21 So they *w* up and spied out the
13:22 And they *w* up through the South
13:27 We *w* to the land where you sent
14:24 bring into the land where he *w*,
14:38 of the men who *w* to spy out the
14:40 early in the morning and *w* up
16:25 Then Moses rose and *w* to Dathan
16:33 they and all those with them *w*
17: 8 on the next day that Moses *w*
20: 6 So Moses and Aaron *w* from the
20:15 how our fathers *w* down to Egypt,
20:27 and they *w* up to Mount Hor in
21:16 From there they *w* to Beer,
21:18 from the wilderness they *w*
21:23 all his people together and *w*
21:28 'For fire *w* out from Heshbon,
21:33 And they turned and *w* up by the
21:33 So Og king of Bashan *w* out
22:14 the princes of Moab rose and *w*
22:21 and *w* with the princes of Moab.
22:22 anger was aroused because he *w*,
22:23 aside out of the way and *w*
22:26 Then the Angel of the LORD *w*
22:35 So Balaam *w* with the princes
22:36 he *w* out to meet him at the
22:39 So Balaam *w* with Balak,
23: 3 So he *w* to a desolate height.
24:25 Balak also *w* his way.
25: 8 and he *w* after the man of Israel
31:13 *w* to meet them outside the
31:27 who *w* out to battle,
31:28 LORD on the men of war who *w*
32: 9 For when they *w* up to the Valley
32:39 of Machir the son of Manasseh *w*
32:41 Jair the son of Manasseh *w* and
32:42 Then Nobah *w* and took Kenath and
33: 1 who *w* out of the land of Egypt
33: 3 the children of Israel *w* out
33: 8 *w* three days' journey in the
33:23 They *w* from Kehelathah and
33:29 They *w* from Mithkah and camped
33:33 They *w* from Hor Hagidgad and
33:38 Then Aaron the priest *w* up to
Deut 1:19 and *w* through all that great
1:24 And they departed and *w* up into
1:31 in all the way that you *w* until
1:33 who *w* in the way before you to
1:43 and presumptuously *w* up into
3: 1 Then we turned and *w* up the road
9: 9 When I *w* up into the mountain to
10: 3 and *w* up the mountain,
10:22 Your fathers *w* down to Egypt
26: 5 and he *w* down to Egypt and
29:26 for they *w* and served other gods
31: 1 Then Moses *w* and spoke these
31:14 So Moses and Joshua *w* and
34: 1 Then Moses *w* up from the plains
Josh 2: 1 they *w*, and came to the house
2: 5 that the men *w* out. Where the
2: 5 Where the men *w* I do not know;
2:22 They departed and *w* to the
3: 2 that the officers *w* through the
3: 6 the ark of the covenant and *w*
3:16 So the waters that *w* down into
5:13 And Joshua *w* to Him and said to
6: 1 none *w* out, and none came in.
6: 9 The armed men *w* before the
6:13 before the ark of the LORD *w*
6:13 And the armed men *w* before
6:20 Then the people *w* up into the
6:23 young men who had been spies *w*
7: 2 So the men *w* up and spied out
7: 4 So about three thousand men *w* up
8: 9 and they *w* to lie in ambush,
8:10 and *w* up, he and the elders of
8:11 of war who were with him *w* up
8:13 Joshua *w* that night into the
8:14 hurried and rose early and *w*
9: 4 and *w* and pretended to be
9: 6 And they *w* to Joshua,

10: 5 gathered together and ***w*** up,
10:24 of the men of war who ***w*** with
10:36 So Joshua ***w*** up from Eglon,
11: 4 So they ***w*** out, they and all
14: 8 my brethren who ***w***
15: 3 Then it ***w*** out to the southern
15: 3 ***w*** up to Adar, and went around
15: 3 and ***w*** around to Karkaa.
15: 4 it passed toward Azmon and ***w***
15: 6 The border ***w*** up to Beth Hoglah
15: 6 and the border ***w*** up to the
15: 7 Then the border ***w*** up toward
15: 8 And the border ***w*** up by the
15: 8 The border ***w*** up to the top of
15: 9 Then the border ***w*** around from
15: 9 And the border ***w*** around to
15:10 ***w*** down to Beth Shemesh,
15:11 And the border ***w*** out to the side
15:11 Then the border ***w*** around to
15:15 Then he ***w*** up from there to the
16: 2 then ***w*** out from Bethel to Luz,
16: 3 and ***w*** down westward to the
16: 6 And the border ***w*** out toward the
16: 6 then the border ***w*** around
16: 7 Then it ***w*** down from Janohah to
16: 8 The border ***w*** out from Tappuah
17: 7 and the border ***w*** along south to
18: 8 and Joshua charged those who ***w***
18: 9 So the men ***w***, passed through
18:12 and the border ***w*** up to the side
18:12 and ***w*** up through the mountains
18:13 The border ***w*** over from there
18:15 extended on the west and ***w*** out
18:17 And it ***w*** around from the north,
18:17 ***w*** out to En Shemesh,
18:18 and ***w*** down to Arabah.
19:11 Their border ***w*** toward the west
19:11 ***w*** to Dabbasheth, and extended
19:12 Then from Sarid it ***w*** eastward
19:12 and ***w*** out toward Daberath,
19:14 Then the border ***w*** around it on
19:18 And their territory ***w*** to
19:34 and ***w*** out from there toward
19:47 border of the children of Dan ***w***
19:47 because the children of Dan ***w***
22: 6 and they ***w*** to their tents.
24: 4 but Jacob and his children ***w***
24:11 Then you ***w*** over the Jordan and
24:17 us in all the way that we ***w***
Judg 1: 3 And Simeon ***w*** with him.
1: 4 Then Judah ***w*** up, and the LORD
1: 9 the children of Judah ***w*** down
1:10 Then Judah ***w*** against the
1:11 From there they ***w*** against the
1:16 ***w*** up from the City of Palms
1:16 and they ***w*** and dwelt among the
1:17 And Judah ***w*** with his brother
1:22 the house of Joseph also ***w*** up
1:26 And the man ***w*** to the land of the
2: 6 the children of Israel ***w*** each
2:15 Wherever they ***w*** out, the hand of
3:10 He ***w*** out to war, and the LORD
3:13 ***w*** and defeated Israel, and took
3:19 And all who attended him ***w*** out
3:22 Even the hilt ***w*** in after the
3:23 Then Ehud ***w*** out through the
3:27 and the children of Israel ***w***
3:28 So they ***w*** down after him,
4: 9 Then Deborah arose and ***w*** with
4:10 he ***w*** up with ten thousand men
4:10 and Deborah ***w*** up with him.
4:14 So Barak ***w*** down from Mount
4:18 And Jael ***w*** out to meet Sisera,
4:21 and ***w*** softly to him and drove
4:21 and it ***w*** down into the ground;
4:22 And when he ***w*** into her tent,
5: 4 when You ***w*** out from Seir,
6:19 So Gideon ***w*** in and prepared a
7:11 Then he ***w*** down with Purah his
8: 1 us by not calling us when you ***w***
8: 8 Then he ***w*** up from there to
8:11 Then Gideon ***w*** up by the road of
8:29 Jerubbaal the son of Joash ***w***
9: 1 the son of Jerubbaal ***w*** to
9: 5 Then he ***w*** to his father's house
9: 6 and they ***w*** and made Abimelech
9: 7 he ***w*** and stood on top of Mount
9: 8 The trees once ***w*** forth to anoint
9:21 and he ***w*** to Beer and dwelt
9:26 came with his brothers and ***w***
9:27 So they ***w*** out into the fields,
9:27 And they ***w*** into the house of
9:35 When Gaal the son of Ebed ***w*** out
9:39 So Gaal ***w*** out, leading the men
9:42 the next day that the people ***w***
9:48 Then Abimelech ***w*** up to Mount
9:50 Then Abimelech ***w*** to Thebez,
9:51 then they ***w*** up to the top of
11: 3 together with Jephthah and ***w***
11: 5 that the elders of Gilead ***w*** to
11:11 Then Jephthah ***w*** with the elders
11:18 And they ***w*** along through the
11:38 and she ***w*** with her friends,
11:40 the daughters of Israel ***w*** four
13:20 it happened as the flame ***w*** up
14: 1 Now Samson ***w*** down to Timnah,
14: 2 So he ***w*** up and told his father
14: 5 So Samson ***w*** down to Timnah with
14: 7 Then he ***w*** down and talked with
14: 9 some of it in his hands and ***w***
14:10 So his father ***w*** down to the
14:18 seventh day before the sun ***w***
14:19 and he ***w*** down to Ashkelon and
14:19 and he ***w*** back up to his
15: 4 Then Samson ***w*** and caught three
15: 8 then he ***w*** down and dwelt in the
15: 9 Now the Philistines ***w*** up,
15:11 three thousand men of Judah ***w***
16: 1 Now Samson ***w*** to Gaza and saw a
16: 1 and ***w*** in to her.
17:10 So the Levite ***w*** in.
18: 2 So they ***w*** to the mountains of
18: 7 the five men departed and ***w*** to
18:11 of the family of the Danites ***w***
18:12 Then they ***w*** up and encamped in
18:17 had gone to spy out the land ***w***
18:18 When these ***w*** into Micah's house
18:26 Then the children of Dan ***w*** their
18:26 he turned and ***w*** back to his
18:27 and ***w*** to Laish, to a people
19: 2 and ***w*** away from him to her
19: 3 Then her husband arose and ***w***
19:14 And they passed by and ***w*** their
19:14 and the sun ***w*** down on them near
19:15 And when he ***w*** in, he sat down
19:18 I ***w*** to Bethlehem in Judah;
19:23 ***w*** out to them and said to them,
19:27 the doors of the house and ***w***
19:28 and the man got up and ***w*** to his
20: 4 My concubine and I ***w*** into
20:18 children of Israel arose and ***w***
20:20 And the men of Israel ***w*** out to
20:23 Then the children of Israel ***w*** up
20:25 And Benjamin ***w*** out against them
20:26 ***w*** up and came to the house of
20:30 And the children of Israel ***w*** up
20:31 So the children of Benjamin ***w***
21:23 Then they ***w*** and returned to
21:24 they ***w*** out from there,
Ruth 1: 1 ***w*** to dwell in the country of
1: 2 And they ***w*** to the country of
1: 7 Therefore she ***w*** out from the
1: 7 and they ***w*** on the way to return
1:19 Now the two of them ***w*** until
1:21 I ***w*** out full, and the LORD has
2: 3 and ***w*** and gleaned in the field
2:18 Then she took it up and ***w*** into
3: 6 So she ***w*** down to the threshing
3: 7 he ***w*** to lie down at the end of
3:15 Then she ***w*** into the city.
4: 1 Now Boaz ***w*** up to the gate and
4:13 and when he ***w*** in to her,
1 Sam 1: 3 This man ***w*** up from his city
1: 7 when she ***w*** up to the house of
1:18 So the woman ***w*** her way and
1:21 Elkanah and all his house ***w*** up
2:11 Then Elkanah ***w*** to his house at
3: 3 and before the lamp of God ***w*** out
3: 5 And he ***w*** and lay down.
3: 6 So Samuel arose and ***w*** to Eli,
3: 8 Then he arose and ***w*** to Eli,
3: 9 " So Samuel ***w*** and lay down in
4: 1 Now Israel ***w*** out to battle
5:12 and the cry of the city ***w*** up to
6:12 and ***w*** along the highway,
6:12 the highway, lowing as they ***w***,
6:12 the lords of the Philistines ***w***
7: 7 the lords of the Philistines ***w***
7:11 And the men of Israel ***w*** out of
7:16 He ***w*** from year to year on a
9: 9 when a man ***w*** to inquire of God,
9:10 So they ***w*** to the city where
9:11 As they ***w*** up the hill to the
9:14 So they ***w*** up to the city.
9:26 and both of them ***w*** outside,
9:27 ahead of us." And he ***w*** on.
10: 2 The donkeys which you ***w*** to look
10:13 he ***w*** to the high place.
10:14 we ***w*** to Samuel."
10:26 And Saul also ***w*** home to Gibeah;
10:26 and valiant men ***w*** with him,
11:15 So all the people ***w*** to Gilgal,
13:10 and Saul ***w*** out to meet him,
13:15 Then Samuel arose and ***w*** up from
13:23 garrison of the Philistines ***w***
14:16 and they ***w*** here and there.
14:20 and they ***w*** to the battle;
14:21 who ***w*** up with them into the
14:46 and the Philistines ***w*** to their
15:12 Saul ***w*** to Carmel, and indeed, he
15:13 Then Samuel ***w*** to Saul, and Saul
15:34 Then Samuel ***w*** to Ramah,
15:34 and Saul ***w*** up to his house at
15:35 And Samuel ***w*** no more to see Saul
16: 4 and ***w*** to Bethlehem.
16:13 So Samuel arose and ***w*** to Ramah.
17: 4 And a champion ***w*** out from the
17: 7 and a shield-bearer ***w*** before
17:13 names of his three sons who ***w***
17:15 But David occasionally ***w*** and
17:20 and took the things and ***w*** as
17:35 I ***w*** out after it and struck it,
17:41 the man who bore the shield ***w***
18: 5 So David ***w*** out wherever Saul
18:13 and he ***w*** out and came in before
18:16 because he ***w*** out and came in
18:27 therefore David arose and ***w***,
18:30 princes of the Philistines ***w***
18:30 whenever they ***w*** out,
19: 8 and David ***w*** out and fought with
19:12 And he ***w*** and fled and escaped.
19:18 and ***w*** to Samuel at Ramah,
19:18 And he and Samuel ***w*** and stayed
19:22 Then he also ***w*** to Ramah,
19:23 So he ***w*** there to Naioth in
19:23 and he ***w*** on and prophesied
20: 1 and ***w*** and said to Jonathan,
20:11 So both of them ***w*** out into
20:35 that Jonathan ***w*** out into the
20:42 and Jonathan ***w*** into the city.
21:10 and ***w*** to Achish the king of
22: 1 they ***w*** down there to him.
22: 3 Then David ***w*** from there to
22: 5 So David departed and ***w*** into
23: 5 And David and his men ***w*** to
23: 6 that he ***w*** down with an ephod
23:13 and departed from Keilah and ***w***
23:16 arose and ***w*** to David in the
23:18 and Jonathan ***w*** to his own
23:24 So they arose and ***w*** to Ziph
23:25 When Saul and his men ***w*** to seek
23:25 Therefore he ***w*** down to the
23:26 Then Saul ***w*** on one side of the
23:28 and ***w*** against the Philistines;
23:29 Then David ***w*** up from there and
24: 2 and ***w*** to seek David and his men
24: 3 and Saul ***w*** in to attend to his
24: 7 got up from the cave and ***w*** on
24: 8 ***w*** out of the cave, and called
24:22 And Saul ***w*** home, but David and
24:22 but David and his men ***w*** up to
25: 1 And David arose and ***w*** down to
25:12 men turned on their heels and ***w***
25:13 And about four hundred men ***w***
25:20 that she ***w*** down under cover of
25:36 Now Abigail ***w*** to Nabal,
26: 2 Then Saul arose and ***w*** down to
26:13 Now David ***w*** over to the other
26:25 So David ***w*** on his way,
27: 2 Then David arose and ***w*** over with
27: 8 And David and his men ***w*** up and
28: 8 put on other clothes, and he ***w***,
28:25 Then they rose and ***w*** away that
29:11 And the Philistines ***w*** up to
30: 2 but carried them away and ***w***
30: 9 So David ***w***, he and the six
30:21 So they ***w*** out to meet David and
30:22 worthless men of those who ***w***
2 Sam 2: 2 So David ***w*** up there, and his two
2:12 ***w*** out from Mahanaim to Gibeon.
2:13 ***w*** out and met them by the pool
2:15 So they arose and ***w*** over by
2:29 Then Abner and his men ***w*** on all
2:29 and ***w*** through all Bithron;
2:32 And Joab and his men ***w*** all
3:16 Then her husband ***w*** along with
3:19 Then Abner also ***w*** to speak in
3:21 and he ***w*** in peace.
5: 6 And the king and his men ***w*** to
5:10 So David ***w*** on and became great,
5:17 all the Philistines ***w*** up to
5:17 And David heard of it and ***w***
5:18 The Philistines also ***w*** and
5:20 So David ***w*** to Baal Perazim,
5:22 Then the Philistines ***w*** up once
6: 2 And David arose and ***w*** with all
6: 4 and Ahio ***w*** before the ark.
6:12 So David ***w*** and brought up the
7:18 Then King David ***w*** in and sat
7:23 nation on the earth whom God ***w***
8: 3 as he ***w*** to recover his
8: 6 preserved David wherever he ***w***.
8:14 preserved David wherever he ***w***.
10:14 from the people of Ammon and ***w***
10:16 of Hadadezer's army ***w*** before
11:13 And at evening he ***w*** out to lie
11:22 So the messenger ***w***,
12:16 and David fasted and ***w*** in and
12:17 of his house arose and ***w*** to
12:20 and he ***w*** into the house of the
12:20 Then he ***w*** to his own house;
12:24 and ***w*** in to her and lay with
12:29 all the people together and ***w***
13: 8 So Tamar ***w*** to her brother
13: 9 And they all ***w*** out from him.
13:19 laid her hand on her head and ***w***
13:37 But Absalom fled and ***w*** to Talmai
13:38 So Absalom fled and ***w*** to Geshur,
14:23 So Joab arose and ***w*** to Geshur,
14:33 So Joab ***w*** to the king and told
15: 9 So he arose and ***w*** to Hebron.
15:11 And with Absalom ***w*** two hundred
15:11 and they ***w*** along innocently and
15:16 Then the king ***w*** out with all his
15:17 And the king ***w*** out with all the
15:24 and Abiathar ***w*** up until all the
15:30 So David ***w*** up by the Ascent of
15:30 and wept as he ***w*** up; and he had
15:30 he had his head covered and ***w***
15:30 him covered their heads and ***w***
15:30 weeping as they ***w*** up.
15:37 friend, ***w*** into the city.
16:13 And as David and his men ***w*** along
16:13 Shimei ***w*** along the hillside
16:13 opposite him and cursed as he ***w***,
16:22 and Absalom ***w*** in to his
17:18 But both of them ***w*** away quickly
17:18 and they ***w*** down into it.
17:21 came up out of the well and ***w***
17:23 and arose and ***w*** home to his
17:24 Then David ***w*** to Mahanaim.
18: 4 and all the people ***w*** out by
18: 6 So the people ***w*** out into the
18: 9 The mule ***w*** under the thick
18: 9 mule which was under him ***w*** on.
18:24 And the watchman ***w*** up to the

18:33 and **w** up to the chamber over
18:33 the gate, and wept. And as he **w**,
19:17 and they **w** over the Jordan
19:18 Then a ferryboat **w** across to
19:31 came down from Rogelim and **w**
19:39 Then all the people **w** over the
19:40 Now the king **w** on to Gilgal,
19:40 and Chimham **w** on with him. And
20: 5 So Amasa **w** to assemble the men
20: 7 mighty men, **w** out after him.
20: 7 And they **w** out of Jerusalem to
20:13 all the people **w** on after Joab
20:14 And he **w** through all the tribes
20:14 gathered together and also **w**
20:22 Then the woman in her wisdom **w**
21:12 Then David **w** and took the bones
21:15 and his servants with him **w**
22: 9 Smoke **w** up from His nostrils,
23:13 of the thirty chief men **w** down
23:17 the blood of the men who **w** in
23:21 so he **w** down to him with a
24: 4 and the captains of the army **w**
24: 7 Then they **w** out to South Judah
24:19 **w** up as the LORD commanded.
24:20 So Araunah **w** out and bowed
1 Ki 1:15 So Bathsheba **w** into the chamber
1:38 and the Pelethites **w** down and
1:40 And all the people **w** up after
1:49 and each one **w** his way.
1:50 and **w** and took hold of the
2: 8 curse in the day when I **w** to
2:19 Bathsheba therefore **w** to King
2:30 So Benaiah **w** to the tabernacle
2:34 Benaiah the son of Jehoiada **w**
2:40 and **w** to Achish at Gath to seek
2:40 And Shimei **w** and brought his
2:46 and he **w** out and struck him
3: 4 Now the king **w** to Gibeon to
6: 8 They **w** up by stairs to the
8:66 and **w** to their tents joyful and
9:12 Then Hiram **w** from Tyre to see
9:28 And they **w** to Ophir,
10: 5 and his entryway by which he **w**
10:13 So she turned and **w** to her own
10:16 six hundred shekels of gold **w**
10:17 three minas of gold **w** into each
11: 5 For Solomon **w** after Ashtoreth
11:24 And they **w** to Damascus and
11:29 when Jeroboam **w** out of
12: 1 And Rehoboam **w** to Shechem,
12:25 Also he **w** out from there and
12:30 for the people **w** to worship
13: 1 a man of God **w** from Judah to
13:10 So he **w** another way and did not
13:12 which way the man of God **w** who
13:14 and **w** after the man of God,
13:19 So he **w** back with him, and ate
13:25 Then they **w** and told it in the
13:28 Then he **w** and found his corpse
14: 4 she arose and **w** to Shiloh,
16:10 And Zimri **w** in and struck him
16:17 Omri and all Israel with him **w**
16:18 that he **w** into the citadel of
16:31 and he **w** and served Baal and
17: 5 So he **w** and did according to the
17: 5 for he **w** and stayed by the
17:10 So he arose and **w** to Zarephath.
17:15 So she **w** away and did according
18: 2 So Elijah **w** to present himself
18: 6 Ahab **w** one way by himself,
18: 6 and Obadiah **w** another way by
18:16 So Obadiah **w** to meet Ahab,
18:16 and Ahab **w** to meet Elijah.
18:42 So Ahab **w** up to eat and drink.
18:42 And Elijah **w** up to the top of
18:43 So he **w** up and looked,
18:45 So Ahab rode away and **w** to
19: 3 and **w** to Beersheba,
19: 4 But he himself **w** a day's
19: 8 and he **w** in the strength of
19: 9 And there he **w** into a cave,
19:13 his face in his mantle and **w**
20: 1 And he **w** up and besieged
20:16 So they **w** out at noon.
20:17 leaders of the provinces **w** out
20:19 leaders of the provinces **w** out
20:21 Then the king of Israel **w** out
20:26 mustered the Syrians and **w** up
20:27 and they **w** against them.
20:30 And Ben-Hadad fled and **w** into
20:39 Your servant **w** out into the
20:43 So the king of Israel **w** to his
21: 4 So Ahab **w** into his house sullen
21:16 that Ahab got up and **w** down to
21:27 and **w** about mourning.
22: 2 the king of Judah **w** down to
22:24 the son of Chenaanah **w** near
22:29 the king of Judah **w** up to
22:30 Israel disguised himself and **w**
22:36 a shout **w** throughout the army,
2 Ki 1: 9 So he **w** up to him; and there he
1:13 the third captain of fifty **w**
1:15 So he arose and **w** down with
2: 1 that Elijah **w** with Elisha from
2: 2 So they **w** down to Bethel.
2: 6 So the two of them **w** on.
2: 7 of the sons of the prophets **w**
2:11 and Elijah **w** up by a whirlwind
2:13 and **w** back and stood by the
2:21 Then he **w** out to the source of
2:23 Then he **w** up from there to
2:25 Then he **w** from there to Mount

3: 6 So King Jehoram **w** out of
3: 7 Then he **w** and sent to
3: 9 So the king of Israel **w** with the
3:12 and the king of Edom **w** down to
4: 5 So she **w** from him and shut the
4: 8 happened one day that Elisha **w**
4:18 it happened one day that he **w**
4:21 And she **w** up and laid him on the
4:21 the door upon him, and **w** out.
4:25 and **w** to the man of God at
4:31 Now Gehazi **w** on ahead of them,
4:31 Therefore he **w** back to meet
4:33 He **w** in therefore, shut the door
4:34 And he **w** up and lay on the
4:35 and again **w** up and stretched
4:37 So she **w** in, fell at his feet,
4:37 she picked up her son and **w**
4:39 So one **w** out into the field to
5: 4 And Naaman **w** in and told his
5: 9 Then Naaman **w** with his horses
5:11 and **w** away and said, "Indeed,
5:12 So he turned and **w** away in a
5:14 So he **w** down and dipped seven
5:25 Now he **w** in and stood before his
5:27 And he **w** out from his
6: 4 So he **w** with them. And when they
6:15 man of God arose early and **w**
6:23 he sent them away and they **w** to
6:24 and **w** up and besieged Samaria.
7: 8 they **w** into one tent and ate
7: 8 and **w** and hid them; then they
7: 8 and **w** and hid it.
7:10 So they **w** and called to the
7:10 'We **w** to the Syrian camp,
7:15 And they **w** after them to the
7:16 Then the people **w** out and
8: 2 and she **w** with her household
8: 3 and she **w** to make an appeal to
8: 7 Then Elisha **w** to Damascus,
8: 9 So Hazael **w** to meet him and took
8:21 So Joram **w** to Zair, and all his
8:28 Now he **w** with Joram the son of
8:29 Then King Joram **w** back to
8:29 **w** down to see Joram the son of
9: 4 **w** to Ramoth Gilead.
9: 6 Then he arose and **w** into the
9:16 So Jehu rode in a chariot and **w**
9:18 So the horseman **w** to meet him,
9:18 'The messenger **w** to them,
9:20 He **w** up to them and is not
9:21 and Ahaziah king of Judah **w**
9:21 and they **w** out to meet Jehu,
9:35 So they **w** to bury her,
10: 9 that he **w** out and stood,
10:12 he arose and departed and **w** to
10:23 Jehonadab the son of Rechab **w**
10:24 So they **w** in to offer sacrifices
10:25 and **w** into the inner room of
11:16 and she **w** by way of the horses'
11:18 all the people of the land **w**
11:19 and **w** by way of the gate of the
12:17 Hazael king of Syria **w** up and
12:18 Then he **w** away from Jerusalem.
14:11 Jehoash king of Israel **w** out;
14:13 and he **w** to Jerusalem,
15:14 For Menahem the son of Gadi **w** up
16: 6 Then the Edomites **w** to Elath,
16: 9 for the king of Assyria **w** up
16:10 Now King Ahaz **w** to Damascus to
17: 5 Now the king of Assyria **w**
17: 5 and **w** up to Samaria and
17:15 and **w** after the nations who
18: 7 him; he prospered wherever he **w**.
18:17 And they **w** up and came to
18:17 they **w** and stood by the
19: 1 and **w** into the house of the
19:14 and Hezekiah **w** up to the house
19:35 that the angel of the LORD **w**
19:36 king of Assyria departed and **w**
20: 1 **w** to him and said to him,
20:14 Then Isaiah the prophet **w** to
22: 9 So Shaphan the scribe **w** to the
22:14 and Asaiah **w** to Huldah the
23: 2 The king **w** up to the house of
23:29 Pharaoh Necho king of Egypt **w**
23:29 and King Josiah **w** against him.
23:34 Pharaoh took Jehoahaz and **w**
24:12 and his officers **w** out to the
25: 4 And the king **w** by way of the
25:26 arose and **w** to Egypt;
1 Chr 2:21 Now afterward Hezron **w** in to
4:39 So they **w** to the entrance of
4:42 **w** to Mount Seir, having as
5:18 skillful in war, who **w** to war.
6:15 Jehozadak **w** into captivity
7:23 And when he **w** in to his wife,
11: 4 And David and all Israel **w** to
11: 6 And Joab the son of Zeruiah **w**
11: 9 Then David **w** on and became
11:15 of the thirty chief men **w** down
11:23 and he **w** down to him with a
12:17 And David **w** out to meet them,
12:20 When he **w** to Ziklag,
12:33 were fifty thousand who **w** out
13: 6 And David and all Israel **w** up to
14: 8 all the Philistines **w** up to
14: 8 And David heard of it and **w**
14: 9 Then the Philistines **w** and made
14:11 So they **w** up to Baal Perazim,
14:17 Then the fame of David **w** out
15:25 the captains over thousands **w**
16:20 When they **w** from one nation to

17:16 Then King David **w** in and sat
17:21 nation on the earth whom God **w**
18: 3 as he **w** to establish his power
18: 6 preserved David wherever he **w**.
18:13 preserved David wherever he **w**.
19: 5 Then some **w** and told David
19:15 So Joab **w** to Jerusalem.
19:16 of Hadadezer's army **w** before
21: 4 Therefore Joab departed and **w**
21:19 So David **w** up at the word of
21:21 And he **w** out from the threshing
27: 1 divisions came in and **w** out
2 Chr 1: 3 **w** to the high place that was
1: 6 And Solomon **w** up there to the
8: 3 And Solomon **w** to Hamath Zobah
8:17 Then Solomon **w** to Ezion Geber
8:18 They **w** with the servants of
9: 4 and his entryway by which he **w**
9:12 So she turned and **w** to her own
9:15 shekels of hammered gold **w**
9:16 hundred shekels of gold **w**
9:21 For the king's ships **w** to
10: 1 And Rehoboam **w** to Shechem,
12:12 and things also **w** well in
14:10 So Asa **w** out against him,
15: 2 And he **w** out to meet Asa,
15: 5 was no peace to the one who **w**
17: 9 they **w** throughout all the
18: 2 After some years he **w** down to
18:23 the son of Chenaanah **w** near
18:28 the king of Judah **w** up to
18:29 and they **w** into battle.
19: 2 the son of Hanani the seer **w**
19: 4 and he **w** out again among the
20:20 early in the morning and **w** out
20:20 and as they **w** out, Jehoshaphat
20:21 as they **w** out before the army
21: 9 So Jehoram **w** out with his
22: 5 and **w** with Jehoram the son of
22: 6 **w** down to see Jehoram the son
22: 7 he **w** out with Jehoram against
23: 2 And they **w** throughout Judah and
23:15 and she **w** by way of the
23:17 And all the people **w** to the
23:20 and they **w** through the Upper
25:11 he **w** to the Valley of Salt and
25:21 So Joash king of Israel **w** out;
26: 6 Now he **w** out and made war
26:11 an army of fighting men who **w**
26:17 So Azariah the priest **w** in after
28: 9 and he **w** out before the army
29:15 and **w** according to the
29:16 Then the priests **w** into the
29:18 Then they **w** in to King Hezekiah
29:20 and **w** up to the house of the
30: 6 Then the runners **w** throughout
31: 1 all Israel who were present **w**
34:22 the king had appointed **w** to
34:30 The king **w** up to the house of
35:20 and Josiah **w** out against him.
Ezra 4:23 they **w** up in haste to Jerusalem
5: 8 be known to the king that we **w**
8: 1 the genealogy of those who **w**
10: 6 and **w** into the chamber of
Neh 2: 9 Then I **w** to the governors in
2:13 And I **w** out by night through the
2:14 Then I **w** on to the Fountain Gate
2:15 So I **w** up in the night by the
8:12 And all the people **w** their way
8:16 Then the people **w** out and
9:11 So that they **w** through the
9:24 So the people **w** in
12:31 One **w** to the right hand on the
12:32 After them **w** Hoshaiah and half
12:36 Ezra the scribe **w** before them.
12:37 they **w** up the stairs of the
12:38 other thanksgiving choir **w** the
Esth 2:13 each young woman **w** to the
2:14 In the evening she **w**,
3:15 The couriers **w** out, hastened by
4: 1 and **w** out into the midst of the
4: 2 He **w** as far as the front of the
4: 6 So Hathach **w** out to Mordecai in
4:17 So Mordecai **w** his way and did
5: 2 Then Esther **w** near and touched
5: 5 So the king and Haman **w** to
5: 9 So Haman **w** out that day joyful
5:10 Haman restrained himself and **w**
6:12 Afterward Mordecai **w** back to
7: 1 So the king and Haman **w** to dine
7: 7 the banquet of wine and **w**
8:14 who rode on royal horses **w** out,
8:15 So Mordecai **w** out from the
Job 1:12 So Satan **w** out from the
2: 7 So Satan **w** out from the
29: 7 When I **w** out to the gate by the
42: 9 and Zophar the Naamathite **w**
Ps 18: 8 Smoke **w** up from His nostrils,
42: 4 I **w** with them to the house of
51: when Nathan the prophet **w** to
52: David when Doeg the Edomite **w**
54: of David when the Ziphites **w**
66: 6 They **w** through the river on
66:12 We **w** through fire and through
68: 7 when You **w** out before Your
68:25 The singers **w** before,
73:17 Until I **w** into the sanctuary of
81: 5 When He **w** throughout the land
104: 8 They **w** up over the mountains;
104: 8 They **w** down into the valleys,
105:13 When they **w** from one nation to
106:32 So that it **w** ill with Moses on

114: 1 When Israel **w** out of Egypt,
119:67 Before I was afflicted I **w**
Prov 7:22 Immediately he **w** after her,
24:30 I **w** by the field of the lazy
Song 5: 7 The watchmen who **w** about the
6:11 I **w** down to the garden of nuts
Isa 7: 1 **w** up to Jerusalem to make war
8: 3 Then I **w** to the prophetess,
37: 1 and **w** into the house of the
37:14 and Hezekiah **w** up to the house
37:36 Then the angel of the LORD **w**
37:37 king of Assyria departed and **w**
38: 1 **w** to him and said to him,
39: 3 Then Isaiah the prophet **w** to
48: 3 They **w** forth from My mouth,
52: 4 My people **w** down at first Into
57: 7 EVEN there you **w** up To offer
57: 9 You **w** to the king with
57:17 And he **w** on backsliding in the
60:15 So that no one **w** through you,
Jer 2: 2 When you **w** after Me in the
3: 8 but **w** and played the harlot
7:24 and **w** backward and not forward.
13: 5 So I **w** and hid it by the
13: 7 Then I **w** to the Euphrates and
14: 3 They **w** to the cisterns and
18: 3 Then I **w** down to the potter's
22:11 who **w** from this place:
26:21 and **w** to Egypt.
26:22 and other men who **w** with him
28: 4 the captives of Judah who **w** to
28:11 ' And the prophet Jeremiah **w**
31: 2 when I **w** to give him rest."
31:21 The way in which you **w**.
36:12 he then **w** down to the king's
36:20 And they **w** to the king,
37:12 that Jeremiah **w** out of Jerusalem
38: 8 Ebed-Melech **w** out of the king's
38:11 took the men with him and **w**
39: 4 that they fled and **w** out of the
39: 4 And he **w** out by way of the
40: 6 Then Jeremiah **w** to Gedaliah the
41: 6 Ishmael the son of Nethaniah **w**
41: 6 weeping as he **w** along;
41:12 they took all the men and **w** to
41:14 and **w** to Johanan the son of
41:15 Johanan with eight men and **w**
41:17 as they **w** on their way to
43: 7 So they **w** to the land of Egypt,
43: 7 And they **w** as far as Tahpanhes.
44: 3 in that they **w** to burn incense
51:59 when he **w** with Zedekiah the
52: 7 all the men of war fled and **w**
52: 7 And they **w** by way of the plain.
Ezek 1: 9 did not turn when they **w**,
1: 9 but each one **w** straight
1:12 And each one **w** straight forward;
1:12 they **w** wherever the spirit
1:12 they did not turn when they **w**.
1:13 and out of the fire **w**
1:17 they **w** toward any one of four
1:17 did not turn aside when they **w**.
1:19 When the living creatures **w**,
1:19 the wheels **w** beside them;
1:20 the spirit wanted to go, they **w**,
1:20 because there the spirit **w**;
1:21 When those **w**, these went;
1:21 When those went, these **w**;
1:24 When they **w**, I heard the noise
3:14 and I **w** in bitterness,
3:23 So I arose and **w** out into the
8:10 So I **w** in and saw,
8:11 and a thick cloud of incense **w**
9: 2 They **w** in and stood beside the
9: 7 Go out!" And they **w** out and
10: 2 And he **w** in as I watched.
10: 3 of the temple when the man **w**
10: 4 Then the glory of the LORD **w** up
10: 6 that he **w** in and stood beside
10: 7 who took it and **w** out.
10:11 When they **w**, they went toward
10:11 they **w** toward any of their
10:11 did not turn aside when they **w**,
10:11 did not turn aside when they **w**.
10:16 When the cherubim **w**,
10:16 the wheels **w** beside them;
10:19 When they **w** out, the wheels
10:22 They each **w** straight forward.
11:23 And the glory of the LORD **w** up
11:24 the vision that I had seen **w**
16:14 Your fame **w** out among the
17:12 Indeed the king of Babylon **w** to
20:16 for their heart **w** after their
23:44 Yet they **w** in to her, as men go
23:44 thus they **w** in to Oholah and
25: 3 the house of Judah when they **w**
27:33 When your wares **w** out by sea,
31:15 In the day when it **w** down to
31:17 They also **w** down to hell with
36:20 to the nations, wherever they **w**,
36:21 the nations wherever they **w**.
36:22 the nations wherever you **w**.
39:23 know that the house of Israel **w**
40: 6 Then he **w** to the gateway which
40: 6 and he **w** up its stairs and
41: 3 Also he **w** inside and measured
41: 7 As one **w** up from story to story,
41: 7 structure increased as one **w**
44:10 And the Levites who **w** far from
44:10 when Israel **w** astray,
44:15 when the children of Israel **w**
47: 3 And when the man **w** out to the
48:11 when the children of Israel **w**
48:11 as the Levites **w** astray.
Dan 2:13 So the decree **w** out,
2:16 So Daniel **w** in and asked the
2:17 Then Daniel **w** to his house,
2:24 Therefore Daniel **w** to Arioch,
2:24 He **w** and said thus to him: "Do
3:26 Then Nebuchadnezzar **w** near the
6:10 writing was signed, he **w** home.
6:12 And they **w** before the king,
6:18 Now the king **w** to his palace
6:18 Also his sleep **w** from him.
6:19 early in the morning and **w** in
8:27 afterward I arose and **w** about
9:23 supplications the command **w**
Hos 1: 3 So he **w** and took Gomer the
2:13 And **w** after her lovers;
5:13 Then Ephraim **w** to Assyria
9:10 But they **w** to Baal Peor,
11: 2 So they **w** from them; They
Am 5:19 Or as though he **w** into the
Jon 1: 3 He **w** down to Joppa, and found a
1: 3 and **w** down into it, to go with
2: 6 I **w** down to the moorings of the
2: 7 And my prayer **w** up to You,
3: 3 So Jonah arose and **w** to Nineveh,
4: 5 So Jonah **w** out of the city and
Nah 3:10 She **w** into captivity;
Hab 3: 5 Before Him **w** pestilence,
3:11 the light of Your arrows they **w**,
3:13 You **w** forth for the salvation
Zech 6: 7 Then the strong steeds **w** out,
8:10 from the enemy for whoever **w**
Mt 2: 9 they had seen in the East **w**
3: 5 the region around the Jordan **w**
4:23 And Jesus **w** about all Galilee,
4:24 Then His fame **w** throughout all
5: 1 He **w** up on a mountain,
8:32 they **w** into the herd of swine.
8:33 and they **w** away into the city
9:25 He **w** in and took her by the
9:26 And the report of this **w** out
9:32 As they **w** out, behold, they
9:35 Then Jesus **w** about all the
12: 1 At that time Jesus **w** through the
12: 9 He **w** into their synagogue.
12:14 Then the Pharisees **w** out and
13: 1 On the same day Jesus **w** out of
13: 3 a sower **w** out to sow.
13:25 tares among the wheat and **w**
13:36 sent the multitude away and **w**
13:46 **w** and sold all that he had and
14:12 and **w** and told Jesus.
14:14 And when Jesus **w** out He saw a
14:23 He **w** up on the mountain by
14:25 watch of the night Jesus **w** to
15:21 Then Jesus **w** out from there and
15:29 and **w** up on the mountain and
18:28 But that servant **w** out and found
18:30 but **w** and threw him into prison
19:22 he **w** away sorrowful, for he had
20: 1 is like a landowner who **w** out
20: 3 And he **w** out about the third
20: 4 I will give you.' So they **w**.
20: 5 Again he **w** out about the sixth
20: 6 about the eleventh hour he **w**
20:29 Now as they **w** out of Jericho, a
21: 6 So the disciples **w** and did as
21: 9 Then the multitudes who **w** before
21:12 Then Jesus **w** into the temple of
21:17 Then He left them and **w** out of
21:29 afterward he regretted it and **w**.
21:33 it to vinedressers and **w** into
22: 5 they made light of it and **w**
22:10 So those servants **w** out into the
22:15 Then the Pharisees **w** and
22:22 and left Him and **w** their way.
24: 1 Then Jesus **w** out and departed
25: 1 who took their lamps and **w** out
25:10 'And while they **w** to buy,
25:10 and those who were ready **w** in
25:15 and immediately he **w** on a
25:16 had received the five talents **w**
25:18 But he who had received one **w**
25:25 and **w** and hid your talent in
26:14 **w** to the chief priests
26:30 they **w** out to the Mount of
26:39 He **w** a little farther and fell
26:42 He **w** away and prayed, saying,
26:44 **w** away again, and prayed the
26:49 Immediately he **w** up to Jesus and
26:58 And he **w** in and sat with the
26:75 So he **w** out and wept
27: 5 and **w** and hanged himself.
27:53 they **w** into the holy city and
27:58 This man **w** to Pilate and asked
27:66 So they **w** and made the tomb
28: 8 So they **w** out quickly from the
28: 9 And as they **w** to tell His
28:16 Then the eleven disciples **w**
Mk 1: 5 **w** out to him and were all
1:20 and **w** after Him.
1:21 Then they **w** into Capernaum,
1:35 He **w** out and departed to a
1:45 he **w** out and began to proclaim
2:12 and **w** out in the presence of
2:13 Then He **w** out again by the sea;
2:23 Now it happened that He **w**
2:23 and as they **w** His disciples
2:26 how he **w** into the house of God
3: 6 Then the Pharisees **w** out and
3:13 And He **w** up on the mountain and
3:19 And they **w** into a house.
3:21 they **w** out to lay hold of Him,
4: 3 a sower **w** out to sow.
5:13 Then the unclean spirits **w** out
5:14 And they **w** out to see what it
5:24 So Jesus **w** with him,
6: 1 Then He **w** out from there and
6: 6 Then He **w** about the villages in
6:12 So they **w** out and preached that
6:24 So she **w** out and said to her
6:27 And he **w** and beheaded him in
6:51 Then He **w** up into the boat to
7:24 From there He arose and **w** to
8:27 Now Jesus and His disciples **w**
10:22 and **w** away sorrowful, for he
10:46 As He **w** out of Jericho with His
11: 4 So they **w** their way, and found
11: 9 Then those who **w** before and
11:11 And Jesus **w** into Jerusalem and
11:11 He **w** out to Bethany with the
11:13 He **w** to see if perhaps He would
11:15 Then Jesus **w** into the temple
11:19 He **w** out of the city.
12: 1 it to vinedressers and **w** into
12:12 So they left Him and **w** away.
13: 1 Then as He **w** out of the temple,
14:10 **w** to the chief priests to
14:16 So His disciples **w** out, and came
14:26 they **w** out to the Mount of
14:35 He **w** a little farther, and fell
14:39 Again He **w** away and prayed,
14:45 immediately he **w** up to Him and
14:68 And he **w** out on the porch,
15:43 **w** in to Pilate and asked for
16: 8 So they **w** out quickly and fled
16:10 She **w** and told those who had
16:12 of them as they walked and **w**
16:13 And they **w** and told it to the
16:20 And they **w** out and preached
Lk 1: 9 fell to burn incense when he **w**
1:39 Mary arose in those days and **w**
2: 1 in those days that a decree **w**
2: 3 So all **w** to be registered,
2: 4 Joseph also **w** up from Galilee,
2:41 His parents **w** to Jerusalem
2:42 they **w** up to Jerusalem
2:44 they **w** a day's journey,
2:51 Then He **w** down with them and
3: 3 And he **w** into all the region
4:14 and news of Him **w** out through
4:16 He **w** into the synagogue on the
4:30 midst of them, He **w** His way.
4:31 Then He **w** down to Capernaum, a
4:37 And the report about Him **w** out
4:42 He departed and **w** into a
5:15 the report **w** around concerning
5:19 they **w** up on the housetop and
5:27 After these things He **w** out and
6: 1 after the first that He **w**
6: 4 how he **w** into the house of God,
6:12 to pass in those days that He **w**
6:19 for power **w** out from Him and
7: 6 Then Jesus **w** with them.
7:11 that He **w** into a city called
7:11 and many of His disciples **w**
7:17 And this report about Him **w**
7:36 And He **w** to the Pharisee's
8: 1 that He **w** through every city
8: 5 A sower **w** out to sow his seed.
8:33 Then the demons **w** out of the man
8:35 Then they **w** out to see what had
8:39 And he **w** his way and
8:42 But as He **w**, the multitudes
9: 6 So they departed and **w** through
9:10 Then He took them and **w** aside
9:28 and James and **w** up on the
9:52 And as they **w**, they entered
9:56 And they **w** to another
10:30 A certain man **w** down from
10:34 So he **w** to him and bandaged his
10:38 Now it happened as they **w** that
11:37 So He **w** in and sat down to eat.
13:22 And He **w** through the cities and
14: 1 as He **w** into the house of one
14:25 Now great multitudes **w** with
15:15 Then he **w** and joined himself to
17:11 Now it happened as He **w** to
17:14 And so it was that as they **w**,
17:29 but on the day that Lot **w** out of
18:10 Two men **w** up to the temple to
18:14 this man **w** down to his house
18:39 Then those who **w** before warned
19:12 A certain nobleman **w** into a far
19:28 He **w** on ahead, going up to
19:32 So those who were sent **w** their
19:36 And as He **w**, many spread their
19:45 Then He **w** into the temple and
20: 9 and **w** into a far country for a
21:37 but at night He **w** out and
22: 4 So he **w** his way and conferred
22:13 So they **w** and found it just as
22:39 He **w** to the Mount of Olives,
22:47 **w** before them and drew near to
22:62 So Peter **w** out and wept
23:52 This man **w** to Pilate and asked
24: 3 Then they **w** in and did not find
24:15 Jesus Himself drew near and **w**
24:24 of those who were with us **w**
24:29 And He **w** in to stay with
Jn 2:12 After this He **w** down to
2:13 and Jesus **w** up to Jerusalem.
4:28 **w** her way into the city,

4:30 Then they *w* out of the city and
4:43 He departed from there and *w*
4:47 he *w* to Him and implored Him to
4:50 and he *w* his way.
5: 1 and Jesus *w* up to Jerusalem.
5: 4 For an angel *w* down at a certain
6: 1 After these things Jesus *w* over
6: 3 And Jesus *w* up on the mountain,
6:16 His disciples *w* down to the
6:17 and *w* over the sea toward
6:66 time many of His disciples *w*
7:10 then He also *w* up to the feast,
7:14 middle of the feast Jesus *w* up
7:53 And everyone *w* to his own
8: 1 But Jesus *w* to the Mount of
8: 9 *w* out one by one, beginning
8:59 but Jesus hid Himself and *w* out
9: 7 So he *w* and washed, and came
9:11 So I *w* and washed, and I
10:40 And He *w* away again beyond the
11:20 *w* and met Him, but Mary was
11:28 she *w* her way and secretly
11:31 Mary rose up quickly and *w* out,
11:46 But some of them *w* away to the
11:54 but *w* from there into the
11:55 and many *w* from the country up
12:11 of him many of the Jews *w* away
12:13 branches of palm trees and *w*
13:30 he then *w* out immediately.
18: 1 He *w* out with His disciples
18: 4 *w* forward and said to them,
18:15 and *w* with Jesus into the
18:16 *w* out and spoke to her who kept
18:29 Pilate then *w* out to them and
18:38 he *w* out again to the Jews,
19: 4 Pilate then *w* out again,
19: 9 and *w* again into the Praetorium,
19:17 *w* out to a place called the
20: 1 of the week Mary Magdalene *w*
20: 3 Peter therefore *w* out,
20: 6 and *w* into the tomb; and he saw
20: 8 *w* in also; and he saw and
20:10 Then the disciples *w* away again
21: 3 They *w* out and immediately
21:11 Simon Peter *w* up and dragged the
21:23 Then this saying *w* out among the
Acts 1:10 toward heaven as He *w* up,
1:13 they *w* up into the upper room
1:21 the time that the Lord Jesus *w*
3: 1 Now Peter and John *w* up together
4:23 they *w* to their own companions
5:26 Then the captain *w* with the
7:15 'So Jacob *w* down to Egypt;
8: 4 those who were scattered *w*
8: 5 Then Philip *w* down to the city
8:27 So he arose and *w*.
8:36 Now as they *w* down the road,
8:38 both Philip and the eunuch *w*
8:39 and he *w* on his way rejoicing.
9: 1 *w* to the high priest
9:17 And Ananias *w* his way and
9:32 as Peter *w* through all parts
9:39 Then Peter arose and *w* with
10: 9 as they *w* on their journey and
10: 9 Peter *w* up on the housetop to
10:21 Then Peter *w* down to the men who
10:23 On the next day Peter *w* away
10:27 he *w* in and found many who had
10:38 who *w* about doing good and
11: 3 You *w* in to uncircumcised men
12: 9 So he *w* out and followed him,
12:10 and they *w* out and went down
12:10 and they went out and *w* down
12:17 And he departed and *w* to
12:19 And he *w* down from Judea to
13: 4 they *w* down to Seleucia,
13:11 and he *w* around seeking someone
13:14 and *w* into the synagogue on the
13:42 So when the Jews *w* out of the
14: 1 happened in Iconium that they *w*
14:20 he rose up and *w* into the city.
14:25 they *w* down to Attalia.
15:24 we have heard that some who *w*
15:41 And he *w* through Syria and
16: 4 And as they *w* through the
16:13 And on the Sabbath day we *w* out
16:16 as we *w* to prayer,
16:40 So they *w* out of the prison and
17: 2 *w* in to them, and for three
17:10 they *w* into the synagogue of
18: 1 departed from Athens and *w* to
18:22 he *w* down to Antioch.
18:23 he departed and *w* over the
19: 8 And he *w* into the synagogue and
19:12 them and the evil spirits *w*
20:10 But Paul *w* down, fell on him,
20:13 Then we *w* ahead to the ship and
21: 2 we *w* aboard and set sail.
21: 5 we departed and *w* on our way;
21:15 those days we packed and *w* up
21:16 the disciples from Caesarea *w*
21:18 On the following day Paul *w* in
22: 5 and *w* to Damascus to bring in
22:26 he *w* and told the commander,
23:16 he *w* and entered the barracks
23:19 *w* aside and asked privately,
24:11 than twelve days since I *w* up
25: 1 after three days he *w* up from
25: 6 he *w* down to Caesarea.
28: 8 Paul *w* in to him and prayed,
28:14 And so we *w* toward Rome.
2 Cor 8:17 he *w* to you of his own accord.
Gal 1:17 but I *w* to Arabia, and returned
1:18 Then after three years I *w* up
1:21 Afterward I *w* into the regions
2: 1 Then after fourteen years I *w* up
2: 2 And I *w* up by revelation,
1 Tim 1: 3 As I urged you when I *w* into
Heb 9: 6 the priests always *w* into the
9: 7 second part the high priest *w*
11: 8 And he *w* out, not knowing where
1 Pe 3:19 by whom also He *w* and preached
1 Jn 2:19 They *w* out from us, but they
2:19 but they *w* out that they
3 Jn 7 because they *w* forth for His
Rev 1:16 out of His mouth *w* a sharp
6: 2 and he *w* out conquering and to
6: 4 *w* out. And it was granted to
10: 9 So I *w* to the angel and said to
12:17 and he *w* to make war with the
16: 2 So the first *w* and poured out
20: 9 They *w* up on the breadth of the

WEPT (72/69) WEEP

Gen 21:16 and lifted her voice and *w*.
27:38 Esau lifted up his voice and *w*.
29:11 and lifted up his voice and *w*.
33: 4 neck and kissed him, and they *w*.
37:35 Thus his father *w* for him.
42:24 himself away from them and *w*.
43:30 he went into his chamber and *w*
45: 2 And he *w* aloud,
45:14 brother Benjamin's neck and *w*,
45:14 and Benjamin *w* on his neck.
45:15 kissed all his brothers and *w*
46:29 and fell on his neck and *w* on
50: 1 and *w* over him, and kissed him.
50:17 And Joseph *w* when they spoke
Ex 2: 6 child, and behold, the baby *w*.
Num 11: 4 the children of Israel also *w*
11:18 for you have *w* in the hearing
11:20 and have *w* before Him, saying,
14: 1 and the people *w* that night.
Deut 1:45 Then you returned and *w* before
34: 8 And the children of Israel *w* for
Judg 2: 4 lifted up their voices and *w*.
14:16 Then Samson's wife *w* on him,
14:17 Now she had *w* on him the seven
20:23 of Israel went up and *w* before
20:26 came to the house of God and *w*.
21: 2 lifted up their voices and *w*.
Ruth 1: 9 lifted up their voices and *w*.
1:14 lifted up their voices and *w*
1 Sam 1: 7 therefore she *w* and did not
1:10 and prayed to the LORD and *w*
11: 4 lifted up their voices and *w*.
20:41 and they *w* together, but David
24:16 Saul lifted up his voice and *w*.
30: 4 lifted up their voices and *w*,
2 Sam 1:12 And they mourned and *w* and
3:32 king lifted up his voice and *w*
3:32 of Abner, and all the people *w*.
3:34 Then all the people *w* over him
12:21 You fasted and *w* for the child
12:22 child was alive, I fasted and *w*;
13:36 lifted up their voice and *w*.
13:36 the king and all his servants *w*
15:23 And all the country *w* with a
15:30 and *w* as he went up; and he had
18:33 chamber over the gate, and *w*.
2 Ki 8:11 ashamed; and the man of God *w*.
13:14 and *w* over his face, and said,
20: 3 And Hezekiah *w* bitterly.
22:19 and you tore your clothes and *w*
2 Chr 34:27 and you tore your clothes and *w*
Ezra 3:12 *w* with a loud voice when the
10: 1 for the people *w* very bitterly.
Neh 1: 4 that I sat down and *w*,
8: 9 weep." For all the people *w*,
Job 2:12 they lifted their voices and *w*;
30:25 Have I not *w* for him who was in
Ps 69:10 When I *w* and chastened my
137: 1 we *w* When we remembered Zion.
Isa 38: 3 And Hezekiah *w* bitterly.
Hos 12: 4 He *w*, and sought favor from
Mt 26:75 So he went out and *w*
Mk 5:38 saw a tumult and those who *w*
14:72 when he thought about it, he *w*.
16:10 with Him, as they mourned and *w*.
Lk 8:52 Now all *w* and mourned for her;
19:41 He saw the city and *w* over it,
22:62 So Peter went out and *w*
Jn 11:35 Jesus *w*.
20:11 and as she *w* she stooped down
Acts 20:37 Then they all *w* freely, and fell
Rev 5: 4 So I *w* much, because no one was

WERE (2813/2362) See APPENDIX

WEST (75/71) WESTERN

Gen 12: 8 his tent with Bethel on the *w*
28:14 shall spread abroad to the *w*
Ex 10:19 turned a very strong *w* wind,
27:12 width of the court on the *w* side
36:27 For the *w* side of the tabernacle
38:12 And on the *w* side there were
Num 2:18 On the *w* side shall be the
35: 5 on the *w* side two thousand
Deut 3:27 and lift your eyes toward the *w*,
33:23 Possess the *w* and the
Josh 5: 1 the Amorites who were on the *w*
8: 9 on the *w* side of Ai; but Joshua
8:12 on the *w* side of the city.
8:13 and its rear guard on the *w* of
11: 2 in the heights of Dor on the *w*,
11: 3 in the east and in the *w*,
12: 7 side of the Jordan, on the *w*,
15:12 The *w* border was the coastline
18:14 extended around the *w* side
18:14 This was the *w* side.
18:15 the border extended on the *w*
19:11 Their border went toward the *w*
19:34 side and Asher on the *w* side
Judg 18:12 *w* of Kirjath Jearim.)
1 Ki 7:25 three looking toward the *w*,
1 Chr 7:28 to the *w* Gezer and its towns,
9:24 four directions: the east, *w*,
12:15 to the east and to the *w*.
26:16 came out for the *W* Gate
26:18 As for the Parbar on the *w*,
26:30 of Israel on the *w* side
2 Chr 4: 4 three looking toward the *w*,
32:30 water by tunnel to the *w* side
33:14 City of David on the *w* side
Job 18:20 Those in the *w* are astonished
Ps 75: 6 from the east Nor from the *w*
103:12 far as the east is from the *w*,
107: 3 From the east and from the *w*,
Isa 11:14 of the Philistines toward the *w*;
43: 5 And gather you from the *w*;
49:12 Those from the north and the *w*,
59:19 name of the LORD from the *w*,
Ezek 42:19 He came around to the *w* side
45: 7 westward on the *w* side
45: 7 from the *w* border to the east
47:20 The *w* side shall be the Great
47:20 This is the *w* side.
48: 1 for Dan from its east to its *w*
48: 2 from the east side to the *w*,
48: 3 from the east side to the *w*,
48: 4 from the east side to the *w*,
48: 5 from the east side to the *w*,
48: 6 from the east side to the *w*,
48: 7 from the east side to the *w*,
48: 8 from the east side to the *w*,
48: 8 from the east side to the *w*,
48:10 on the *w* ten thousand in width,
48:16 and the *w* side four thousand
48:17 and to the *w* two hundred and
48:18 east and ten thousand to the *w*.
48:23 from the east side to the *w*,
48:24 from the east side to the *w*,
48:25 from the east side to the *w*,
48:26 from the east side to the *w*,
48:27 from the east side to the *w*,
48:34 on the *w* side, four thousand
Dan 8: 5 a male goat came from the *w*,
Hos 11:10 shall come trembling from the *w*;
Zech 8: 7 And from the land of the *w*;
14: 4 split in two, From east to *w*,
Mt 8:11 many will come from east and *w*,
24:27 the east and flashes to the *w*,
Lk 12:54 see a cloud rising out of the *w*,
13:29 come from the east and the *w*,
Rev 21:13 south, and three gates on the *w*.

WESTERN (9/8) WEST

Num 34: 6 As for the *w* border, you shall
34: 6 this shall be your *w* border.
Deut 11:24 even to the *W* Sea, shall be
34: 2 of Judah as far as the *W* Sea
Ezek 41:12 courtyard at its *w* end
46:19 situated at their extreme *w* end
48:21 thousand as far as the *w* border
Joel 2:20 And his back toward the *w* sea;
Zech 14: 8 half of them toward the *w* sea

WESTWARD (17/17) WEST

Gen 13:14 southward, eastward, and *w*;
Ex 26:22 far side of the tabernacle, *w*,
26:27 tabernacle, for the far side *w*.
36:32 tabernacle on the far side *w*.
Num 3:23 to camp behind the tabernacle *w*.
Josh 15: 8 before the Valley of Hinnom *w*,
15:10 Then the border turned *w* from
16: 3 and went down *w* to the boundary
16: 8 border went out from Tappuah *w*
18:12 went up through the mountains *w*;
19:26 it reached to Mount Carmel *w*,
19:34 Heleph the border extended *w*
22: 7 on this side of the Jordan, *w*.
23: 4 off, as far as the Great Sea *w*.
Ezek 45: 7 extending *w* on the west side
48:21 and *w* next to the twenty-five
Dan 8: 4 I saw the ram pushing *w*,

WET (6/6)

Job 24: 8 They are *w* with the showers of
Dan 4:15 Let it be *w* with the dew of
4:23 let it be *w* with the dew of
4:25 They shall *w* you with the dew
4:33 his body was *w* with the dew of
5:21 and his body was *w* with the dew

WHALE, WHALE'S, WHALES

(KJV) See (SEA) CREATURE, FISH, MONSTER, (SEA) SERPENT

W

WHAT (1331/1193)

Gen 2:19 brought them to Adam to see *w*
3:13 '*W* is this you have done?"
4:10 *W* have you done? The voice of
9:24 and knew *w* his younger son had
11: 6 and this is *w* they begin to do;
12:18 *W* is this you have done to me?
14:24 except only *w* the young men have
15: 2 *w* will You give me, seeing I go
18:17 Shall I hide from Abraham *w* I am
18:19 LORD may bring to Abraham *w*
19:25 and *w* grew on the ground.
20: 9 '*W* have you done to us?
20:10 *W* did you have in view, that you
21:17 *W* ails you, Hagar? Fear not, for
21:29 *W* is the meaning of these
23:15 *W* is that between you and me?
25:32 so *w* is this birthright to
26:10 *W* is this you have done to us?
27: 8 obey my voice according to *w* I
27:37 *W* shall I do now for you,
27:45 and he forgets *w* you have done
27:46 *w* good will my life be to me?"
28:15 leave you until I have done *w*
29:15 *w* should your wages be?"
29:25 *W* is this you have done to me?
30:30 For *w* you had before I came
30:31 *W* shall I give you?" And Jacob
31: 1 and from *w* was our father's he
31:26 *W* have you done, that you have
31:32 identify *w* I have of yours and
31:36 *W* is my trespass? What is my
31:36 *W* is my sin, that you have so
31:37 *w* part of your household things
31:43 But *w* can I do this day to
32:13 and took *w* came to his hand as
32:23 and sent over *w* he had.
32:27 *W* is your name?" He said,
33: 8 *W* do you mean by all this
33: 9 keep *w* you have for yourself."
33:15 *W* need is there? Let me find
34:12 and I will give according to *w*
34:28 *w* was in the city and what
34:28 what was in the city and *w*
37:10 *W* is this dream that you have
37:15 *W* are you seeking?"
37:20 We shall see *w* will become of
37:26 *W* profit is there if we kill
38:16 *W* will you give me, that you may
38:18 '*W* pledge shall I give you?"
39: 6 and he did not know *w* he had
39: 8 my master does not know *w* is
41:25 God has shown Pharaoh *w* He is
41:28 Pharaoh *w* He is about to do.
42:28 *W* is this that God has done to
44:15 *W* deed is this you have done?
44:16 '*W* shall we say to my lord?
44:16 *W* shall we speak? Or how shall
46:33 *W* is your occupation?'
47: 3 '*W* is your occupation?"
49: 1 that I may tell you *w* shall
49:28 and this is *w* their father
Ex 2: 4 to know *w* would be done to him.
3:13 *W* is His name?' what shall I
3:13 *w* shall I say to them?"
3:16 surely visited you and seen *w*
4: 2 '*W* is that in your hand?"
4:12 your mouth and teach you *w* you
4:15 and I will teach you *w* you
6: 1 Now you shall see *w* I will do to
10: 5 shall eat the residue of *w* is
10:11 for that is *w* you desired."
10:26 and even we do not know with *w*
12:10 and *w* remains of it until
12:19 since whoever eats *w* is
12:26 *W* do you mean by this service?'
12:36 so that they granted them *w*
13: 8 This is done because of *w* the
13:14 *W* is this?' that you shall say
15:24 *W* shall we drink?"
15:26 of the LORD your God and do *w*
16: 5 day that they shall prepare *w*
16: 7 But *w* are we, that you
16: 8 And *w* are we? Your complaints
16:15 *W* is it?" For they did not know
16:15 For they did not know *w* it
16:23 This is *w* the LORD has said:
16:23 Bake *w* you will bake today,
16:23 and boil *w* you will boil;
17: 4 *W* shall I do with this people?
18:14 *W* is this thing that you are
19: 4 You have seen *w* I did to the
22:13 and he shall not make good *w*
22:27 *W* will he sleep in? And it will
23:11 and *w* they leave, the beasts of
26:13 of *w* remains of the length of
29: 1 And this is *w* you shall do to
29:38 Now this is *w* you shall offer
30:13 This is *w* everyone among those
32: 1 we do not know *w* has become of
32:21 *W* did this people do to you that
32:23 we do not know *w* has become of
32:35 the people because of *w* they
33: 5 that I may know *w* to do to
34:11 Observe *w* I command you this
35:25 and brought *w* they had spun,
Lev 2:10 And *w* is left of the grain
6: 2 lying to his neighbor about *w*
6: 3 or if he has found *w* was lost
6: 4 that he shall restore *w* he has
6: 4 or *w* was delivered to him for
7:24 and the fat of *w* is torn by
8: 5 This is *w* the LORD commanded
8:32 *W* remains of the flesh and of
9: 5 So they brought *w* Moses
9:19 *w* covers the entrails and the
10: 3 This is *w* the LORD spoke,
17:15 And every person who eats *w*
17:15 eats what died naturally or *w*
22: 2 not profane My holy name by *w*
22:24 shall not offer to the LORD *w*
25: 5 *W* grows of its own accord of
25:11 shall neither sow nor reap *w*
25:20 *W* shall we eat in the seventh
25:25 then he may redeem *w* his
25:28 then *w* was sold shall remain in
Num 4:31 And this is *w* they must carry
8:24 This is *w* pertains to the
9: 8 that I may hear *w* the LORD
11:23 Now you shall see whether *w* I
13:18 and see *w* the land is like:
15:34 it had not been explained *w*
16:11 And *w* is Aaron that you
22:19 that I may know *w* more the
22:28 *W* have I done to you, that you
23:11 '*W* have you done to me?
23:12 I not take heed to speak *w* the
23:17 *W* has the LORD spoken?"
23:23 *w* God has done!'
24:13 *W* the LORD says, that I must
24:14 I will advise you *w* this people
27: 7 of Zelophehad speak *w* is
30: 8 her vow which she took and *w*
31:50 *w* every man found of ornaments
32:24 and do *w* has proceeded out of
36: 5 *W* the tribe of the sons of
36: 6 This is *w* the LORD commands
Deut 3:24 for *w* god is there in heaven
4: 3 Your eyes have seen *w* the LORD
4: 7 For *w* great nation is there
4: 8 And *w* great nation is there
6:18 And you shall do *w* is right
6:20 *W* is the meaning of the
7:18 but you shall remember well *w*
8: 2 to know *w* was in your heart,
10:12 *w* does the LORD your God
11: 4 *w* He did to the army of Egypt,
11: 5 *w* He did for you in the
11: 6 and *w* He did to Dathan and
12:25 when you do *w* is right in the
12:28 when you do *w* is good and
13:18 to do *w* is right in the eyes
15: 3 shall give up your claim to *w*
15:14 From *w* the LORD has blessed
16:20 You shall follow *w* is altogether
18: 8 besides *w* comes from the sale
18:17 *W* they have spoken is good.
20: 5 *W* man is there who has built a
20: 6 Also *w* man is there who has
20: 7 And *w* man is there who is
20: 8 *W* man is there who is
21: 9 from among you when you do *w*
23:23 vowed to the LORD your God *w*
24: 9 Remember *w* the LORD your God
25:17 Remember *w* Amalek did to you on
29:24 *W* does the heat of this great
32:20 I will see *w* their end will
32:21 provoked Me to jealousy by *w*
Josh 2:10 and *w* you did to the two kings
4: 6 *W* do these stones mean to you?'
4:21 *W* are these stones?'
5:14 *W* does my Lord say to His
7: 8 *w* shall I say when Israel turns
7: 9 Then *w* will You do for Your
7:19 and tell me now *w* you have
7:20 and this is *w* I have done:
9: 3 inhabitants of Gibeon heard *w*
15:18 *W* do you wish?"
22:16 *W* treachery is this that you
22:24 *W* have you to do with the LORD
24: 5 according to *w* I did among
24: 7 And your eyes saw *w* I did in
Judg 1:14 *W* do you wish?"
7:11 and you shall hear *w* they say;
8: 2 *W* have I done now in comparison
8: 3 And *w* was I able to do in
8:18 *W* kind of men were they whom
9:48 *W* you have seen me do, make
11:12 '*W* do you have against me,
11:36 do to me according to *w* has
13: 8 to us again and teach us *w* we
13:12 Your words come to pass! *W*
13:17 *W* is Your name, that when Your
14: 6 his father or his mother *w* he
14:15 invited us in order to take *w*
14:18 '*W* is sweeter than honey?
14:18 And *w* is stronger than a
15:11 *W* is this you have done to
16: 5 and by *w* means we may
16: 6 and with *w* you may be bound to
16:10 please tell me *w* you may be
16:13 Tell me *w* you may be bound
17: 6 everyone did *w* was right in
18: 3 *W* are you doing in this place?
18: 3 *W* do you have here?"
18: 8 *W* is your report?"
18:14 consider *w* you should do."
18:18 *W* are you doing?"
18:23 *W* ails you, that you have
18:24 Now *w* more do I have? How can
18:24 you say to me, '*W* ails you?'
20:12 *W* is this wickedness that has
21: 7 *W* shall we do for wives for
21: 8 *W* one is there from the tribes
21:16 *W* shall we do for wives for
21:25 everyone did *w* was right in
Ruth 2: 9 to the vessels and drink from *w*
2:17 and beat out *w* she had gleaned,
2:18 and her mother-in-law saw *w* she
2:18 brought out and gave to her *w*
3: 4 and he will tell you *w* you
1 Sam 1:23 Do *w* seems best to you; wait
2:35 who shall do according to *w*
3:17 *W* is the word that the LORD
3:18 Let Him do *w* seems good to
4: 6 *W* does the sound of this great
4:14 *W* does the sound of this tumult
4:16 *W* happened, my son?"
5: 8 *W* shall we do with the ark of
6: 2 *W* shall we do with the ark of
6: 4 *W* is the trespass offering
9: 7 *w* shall we bring the man? For
9: 7 *W* do we have?"
9:24 *w* was kept back. It was set
10: 2 *W* shall I do about my son?" '
10: 8 I come to you and show you *w*
10:11 *W* is this that has come upon
10:15 *w* Samuel said to you."
10:16 he did not tell him *w* Samuel
11: 5 *W* troubles the people, that
12:24 for consider *w* great things He
13:11 *W* have you done?" And Saul
13:14 because you have not kept *w* the
14:38 and know and see *w* this sin was
14:40 Do *w* seems good to you."
14:43 "Tell me *w* you have done."
15: 2 I will punish Amalek for *w* he
15:14 *W* then is this bleating of the
15:16 And I will tell you *w* the
16: 3 and I will show you *w* you shall
16: 4 So Samuel did *w* the LORD said,
17:26 *W* shall be done for the man who
17:29 *W* have I done now? Is there
18: 8 Now *w* more can he have but the
18:18 and *w* is my life or my
19: 3 Then *w* I observe, I will tell
20: 1 *W* have I done? What is my
20: 1 *W* is my iniquity, and what is
20: 1 and *w* is my sin before your
20:10 or *w* if your father answers
20:32 *W* has he done?"
21: 2 or *w* I have commanded you.'
21: 3 *w* have you on hand?
22: 3 till I know *w* God will do for
24:19 reward you with good for *w* you
25:17 know and consider *w* you will
25:35 David received from her hand *w*
26:18 For *w* have I done, or what evil
26:18 or *w* evil is in my hand?
28: 2 Surely you know *w* your servant
28: 9 you know *w* Saul has done,
28:13 *W* did you see?" And the woman
28:14 *W* is his form?" And she said,
28:15 that you may reveal to me *w* I
29: 3 *W* are these Hebrews doing
29: 4 For with *w* could he reconcile
29: 8 But *w* have I done? And to this
29: 8 And to this day *w* have you
30:23 you shall not do so with *w* the
31:11 of Jabesh Gilead heard *w* the
2 Sam 3:24 *W* have you done? Look, Abner
7:18 And *w* is my house, that You
7:20 Now *w* more can David say to You?
9: 8 *W* is your servant, that you
10:12 And may the LORD do *w* is
12:21 *W* is this that you have done?
14: 5 *W* troubles you?" And she
15: 2 '*W* city are you from?"
16: 2 *W* do you mean to do with
16:10 '*W* have I to do with you,
16:20 Give counsel as to *w* we should
17: 5 and let us hear *w* he says
18:21 tell the king *w* you have
18:29 but I did not know *w* it was
19:18 and to do *w* he thought good.
19:19 or remember *w* wrong your
19:22 *W* have I to do with you, you
19:27 Therefore do *w* is good in
19:28 Therefore *w* right have I still
19:35 Can your servant taste *w* I eat
19:35 servant taste what I eat or *w*
19:37 and do for him *w* seems good to
19:38 and I will do for him *w* seems
21: 3 '*W* shall I do for you?
21: 3 And with *w* shall I make
21:11 And David was told *w* Rizpah the
24:10 I have sinned greatly in *w* I
24:13 Now consider and see *w* answer I
24:17 *w* have they done?
1 Ki 1:16 *W* is your wish?"
2: 5 Moreover you know also *w* Joab
2: 5 and *w* he did to the two
2: 9 you are a wise man and know *w*
3: 5 Ask! *W* shall I give you?"
3:13 And I have also given you *w* you
8:24 You have kept *w* You promised
8:25 now keep *w* You promised Your
9:13 *W* kind of cities are these
10:13 besides *w* Solomon had given her
11:10 but he did not keep *w* the LORD
11:22 But *w* have you lacked with me,
11:27 And this is *w* caused him to
11:33 not walked in My ways to do *w*
11:38 and do *w* is right in My
12: 9 '*W* advice do you give?

12:16 '**W** share have we in David?
14: 3 he will tell you **w** will become
14: 8 to do only **w** was right in My
14:14 this is the day. **W**? Even now!
15: 5 because David did **w** was right
15:11 Asa did **w** was right in the
16: 5 **w** he did, and his might, are
17:18 **W** have I to do with you, O man
18:13 it not reported to my lord **w** I
19: 9 **W** are you doing here, Elijah?"
19:13 **W** are you doing here, Elijah?"
19:20 for **w** have I done to you?"
20:22 and see **w** you should do, for in
22:22 LORD said to him, 'In **w** way?'
22:43 doing **w** was right in the eyes
2 Ki 1: 7 **W** kind of man was it who came
2: 9 Ask! **W** may I do for you, before
3:13 '**W** have I to do with you?
4: 2 **W** shall I do for you? Tell me,
4: 2 **w** do you have in the house?"
4:13 **W** can I do for you?
4:14 **W** then is to be done for her?"
4:39 though they did not know **w**
4:43 But his servant said, "**W**?
5:20 not receiving from his hands **w**
6:15 my master! **W** shall we do?"
6:28 **W** is troubling you?" And she
7:12 Let me now tell you **w** the
8:13 But **w** is your servant—a dog,
8:14 '**W** did Elisha say to you?"
9:18 **W** have you to do with peace?
9:19 **W** have you to do with peace?
9:22 **W** peace, as long as the
10: 5 Do **w** is good in your sight."
10:10 for the LORD has done **w** He
10:30 you have done well in doing **w**
11: 5 This is **w** you shall do:
12: 2 Jehoash did **w** was right in the
14: 3 And he did **w** was right in the
14: 6 according to **w** is written in
14:28 **w** had belonged to Judah—are
15: 3 And he did **w** was right in the
15:34 And he did **w** was right in the
16: 2 and he did not do **w** was right
18: 3 And he did **w** was right in the
18:19 **W** confidence is this in which
19:11 Look! You have heard **w** the kings
19:29 And in the second year **w**
20: 3 and have done **w** was good in
20: 8 **W** is the sign that the LORD
20:14 **W** did these men say, and from
20:15 **W** have they seen in your
20:17 and **w** your fathers have
22: 2 And he did **w** was right in the
22:19 the LORD when you heard **w** I
23:17 **W** gravestone is this that I
1 Chr 4:10 So God granted him **w** he
12:32 to know **w** Israel ought to do,
17:16 And **w** is my house, that You
17:18 **W** more can David say to You for
19:13 And may the LORD do **w** is
21:12 Now consider **w** answer I should
21:17 these sheep, **w** have they done?
21:23 and let my lord the king do **w**
21:24 for I will not take **w** is yours
23:29 the unleavened cakes and **w**
23:29 with **w** is mixed and with all
2 Chr 1: 7 Ask! **W** shall I give you?"
6: 4 fulfilled with His hands **w** He
6:15 You have kept **w** You promised
6:16 now keep **w** You promised Your
9:14 besides **w** the traveling
10: 9 **W** advice do you give? How should
10:16 '**W** share have we in David?
14: 2 Asa did **w** was good and right
18:20 LORD said to him, 'In **w** way?'
19: 6 Take heed to **w** you are doing,
20:12 nor do we know **w** to do, but our
20:32 doing **w** was right in the
23: 4 This is **w** you shall do:
24: 2 Joash did **w** was right in the
25: 2 And he did **w** was right in the
25: 9 But **w** shall we do about the
26: 4 And he did **w** was right in the
27: 2 And he did **w** was right in the
28: 1 and he did not do **w** was right
29: 2 And he did **w** was right in the
30:18 ate the Passover contrary to **w**
31:10 and **w** is left is this great
31:20 and he did **w** was good and
32:10 In **w** do you trust, that you
32:13 Do you not know **w** I and my
34: 2 And he did **w** was right in the
35:21 **W** have I to do with you, king of
35:26 according to **w** was written in
36: 8 and **w** was found against him,
Ezra 6: 8 I issue a decree as to **w** you
6:13 diligently did according to **w**
8:17 and I told them **w** they should
9:10 **w** shall we say after this? For
Neh 2: 4 **W** do you request?" So I prayed
2:12 I told no one **w** my God had put
2:16 not know where I had gone or **w**
2:19 **W** is this thing that you are
4: 2 **W** are these feeble Jews doing?
5: 9 **W** you are doing is not good.
13:17 **W** evil thing is this that you
Esth 1:15 **W** shall we do to Queen Vashti,
2: 1 **w** she had done, and what had
2: 1 and **w** had been decreed against
2:11 of Esther's welfare and **w** was
2:15 she requested nothing but **w**
4: 5 to learn **w** and why this was.
5: 3 **W** do you wish, Queen Esther?
5: 3 **W** is your request? It shall be
5: 6 **W** is your petition? It shall be
5: 6 **W** is your request, up to half
6: 3 **W** honor or dignity has been
6: 6 **W** shall be done for the man whom
7: 2 **W** is your petition, Queen
7: 2 And **w** is your request, up to
9: 5 and did **w** they pleased with
9:12 **W** have they done in the rest of
9:12 Now **w** is your petition?
9:12 Or **w** is your further request?
9:26 **w** they had seen concerning this
9:26 and **w** had happened to them,
Job 3:25 And **w** I dreaded has happened
6:11 **W** strength do I have, that I
6:11 And **w** is my end, that I
6:25 But **w** does your arguing prove?
7:17 **W** is man, that You should exalt
7:20 **W** have I done to You, O
9:12 **W** are You doing?'
11: 8 **w** can you do? Deeper than
11: 8 **w** can you know?
12: 6 In **w** God provides by His hand.
13: 2 **W** you know, I also know
13:13 Then let come on me **w** may!
15: 9 **W** do you know that we do not
15: 9 **W** do you understand that is
15:12 And **w** do your eyes wink at,
15:14 **W** is man, that he could be
15:17 **W** I have seen I will declare,
15:18 **W** wise men have told,
16: 3 Or **w** provokes you that you
21:15 And **w** profit do we have if we
21:21 For **w** does he care about his
21:31 And who repays him for **w** he
22:13 **W** does God know? Can He judge
22:17 Depart from us! **W** can the
23: 5 And understand **w** He would say
23:14 For He performs **w** is
27: 8 For **w** is the hope of the
27:11 **W** is with the Almighty I will
28:11 **W** is hidden he brings forth
30: 2 **w** profit is the strength of
31: 2 For **w** is the allotment of God
31:14 **W** then shall I do when God
32:11 while you searched out **w** to
33:27 and perverted **w** was right,
34: 4 Let us know among ourselves **w**
34: 7 **W** man is like Job,
34:32 Teach me **w** I do not see;
34:33 Therefore speak **w** you know.
35: 3 **W** advantage will it be to You?
35: 3 **W** profit shall I have,
35: 6 **w** do you accomplish against
35: 6 **w** do you do to Him?
35: 7 **w** do you give Him?
35: 7 Or **w** does He receive from your
36:16 And **w** is set on your table
37:19 Teach us **w** we should say to Him,
38: 6 To **w** were its foundations
38:24 By **w** way is light diffused,
40: 4 **W** shall I answer You?
42: 3 Therefore I have uttered **w** I
42: 7 you have not spoken of Me **w**
42: 8 you have not spoken of Me **w**
Ps 8: 4 **W** is man that You are mindful
11: 3 **W** can the righteous do?
28: 4 Render to them **w** they deserve.
30: 9 **W** profit is there in my blood,
38:20 because I follow **w** is good.
39: 4 And **w** is the measure of my
39: 7 **w** do I wait for? My hope is
50:16 **W** right have you to declare My
56: 4 **W** can flesh do to me?
56:11 **W** can man do to me?
66:16 And I will declare **w** He has
68:28 **w** You have done for us.
85: 8 I will hear **w** God the LORD
85:12 the LORD will give **w** is
89:47 For **w** futility have You
89:48 **W** man can live and not see
104:28 **W** You give them they gather
114: 5 **W** ails you, O sea, that you
116:12 **W** shall I render to the LORD
118: 6 **W** can man do to me?
120: 3 **W** shall be given to you,
120: 3 Or **w** shall be done to you,
144: 3 **w** is man, that You take
Prov 4:19 They do not know **w** makes them
10:32 lips of the righteous know **w**
10:32 the mouth of the wicked **w** is
12:27 lazy man does not roast **w** he
14:33 But **w** is in the heart of
16:13 they love him who speaks **w**
19:17 And He will pay back **w** he has
19:22 **W** is desired in a man is
20:11 Whether **w** he does is pure and
23: 1 Consider carefully **w** is
25: 8 For **w** will you do in the end,
27: 1 For you do not know **w** a day
27:21 And a man is valued by **w**
30: 4 **W** is His name, and what is
30: 4 and **w** is His Son's name,
31: 2
31: 2 What, my son? And **w**,
31: 2 what, son of my womb? And **w**,
Eccl 1: 3 **W** profit has a man from all his
1: 9 That which has been is **w** will
1: 9 That which is done is **w** will
1:15 **W** is crooked cannot be made
1:15 And **w** is lacking cannot be
2: 2 **W** does it accomplish?"
2: 3 till I might see **w** was good
2:12 For **w** can the man do who
2:12 Only **w** he has already done.
2:22 For **w** has man for all his labor,
3: 2 And a time to pluck **w** is
3: 9 **W** profit has the worker from
3:15 And **w** is to be has already
3:15 an account of **w** is past.
3:19 For **w** happens to the sons of men
3:22 bring him to see **w** will happen
5: 4 Pay **w** you have vowed—
5:11 So **w** profit have the owners
5:16 And **w** profit has he who has
5:18 Here is **w** I have seen: It is
6: 8 For **w** more has the wise man
6: 8 **W** does the poor man have,
6:12 For who knows **w** is good for man
6:12 Who can tell a man **w** will
7:13 For who can make straight **w** He
7:27 Here is **w** I have found," says
8: 4 **W** are you doing?"
8: 7 For he does not know **w** will
10:14 No man knows **w** is to be;
10:14 Who can tell him **w** will be
11: 2 For you do not know **w** evil
11: 5 As you do not know **w** is the
12:10 and **w** was written was
Song 5: 9 **W** is your beloved More than
5: 9 **W** is your beloved More than
6:13 **W** would you see in the
8: 8 **W** shall we do for our sister
Isa 1:11 To **w** purpose is the multitude
2:22 For of **w** account is he?
3:15 **W** do you mean by crushing My
5: 4 **W** more could have been done to
5: 5 please let Me tell you **w** I will
10: 2 And to take **w** is right from
10: 3 **W** will you do in the day of
14:32 **W** will they answer the
15: 7 And **w** they have laid up,
17: 8 He will not respect **w** his
19:12 And let them know **w** the LORD
21: 6 Let him declare **w** he sees."
21:11 **w** of the night?" Watchman,
21:11 Watchman, **w** of the night?"
22: 1 **Wt** ails you now, that you have
22:16 **W** have you here, and whom have
33:13 **w** I have done; And you who
36: 4 **W** confidence is this in which
37:11 You have heard **w** the kings
37:30 And the second year **w** springs
38: 3 and have done **w** is good in
38:15 **W** shall I say? He has both
38:22 **W** is the sign that I shall go
39: 3 **W** did these men say, and from
39: 4 **W** have they seen in your
39: 6 and **w** your fathers have
40: 6 **W** shall I cry?" "All flesh
40:18 Or **w** likeness will you compare
41:22 and show us **w** will happen;
41:22 **w** they were, That we may
45: 9 **W** are you making?' Or shall
45:10 **W** are you begetting?' Or to the
45:10 **W** have you brought forth?'"
47:13 save you From **w** shall come
52: 5 **w** have I here," says the
52:15 For **w** had not been told them
52:15 And **w** they had not heard they
55: 2 Why do you spend money for **w**
55: 2 And your wages for **w** does not
55: 2 and eat **w** is good, And let
55:11 But it shall accomplish **w** I
56: 4 And choose **w** pleases Me,
65:18 rejoice forever in **w** I create;
Jer 1:11 **w** do you see?" And I said, "I
1:13 **W** do you see?" And I said, "I
2: 5 **W** injustice have your fathers
2:11 Glory For **w** does not profit.
2:23 Know **w** you have done:
3: 6 Have you seen **w** backsliding
4:30 **W** will you do? Though you
5:15 Nor can you understand **w** they
5:31 But **w** will you do in the end?
6:18 **w** is among them.
6:20 For **w** purpose to Me Comes
7:12 and see **w** I did to it because
7:17 Do you not see **w** they do in the
7:23 But this is **w** I commanded them,
8: 6 **W** have I done?' Everyone turned
8: 9 So **w** wisdom do they have?
11:15 **W** has My beloved to do in My
13:21 **W** will you say when He punishes
15: 4 for **w** he did in Jerusalem.
16:10 Or **w** is our iniquity?
16:10 Or **w** is our sin that we have
17:16 You know **w** came out of my
23:25 I have heard **w** the prophets have
23:28 **W** is the chaff to the
23:33 **W** is the oracle of the LORD?'
23:33 then say to them, '**W** oracle?'
23:35 **W** has the LORD answered?' and,
23:35 **W** has the LORD spoken?'
23:37 **W** has the LORD answered you?'
23:37 **W** has the LORD spoken?'
24: 3 '**W** do you see, Jeremiah?"
32:24 **W** You have spoken has happened;
33:24 Have you not considered **w** these
34:15 turned and did **w** was right
37:18 **W** offense have I committed
38:25 Declare to us now **w** you have

38:25 and also **w** the king said to
45: 4 **w** I have built I will break
45: 4 and **w** I have planted I will
48:19 Say, '**W** has happened?'
51:12 devised and done **W** He spoke
51:44 his mouth **w** he has swallowed;
Lam 2:13 To **w** shall I liken you,
2:13 **W** shall I compare with you,
2:17 The LORD has done **w** He
5: 1 **w** has come upon us; Look, and
Ezek 2: 8 hear **w** I say to you.
2: 8 open your mouth and eat **w** I
3: 1 eat **w** you find; eat this
4:14 I have never eaten **w** died of
5: 9 And I will do among you **w** I have
7:13 not return to **w** has been sold,
7:27 And according to **w** they
8: 6 do you see **w** they are doing,
8:12 have you seen **w** the elders of
12: 9 said to you, '**W** are you doing?'
12:22 **w** is this proverb that you
14: 4 and puts before him **w** causes
14: 7 puts before him **w** causes him
17:12 Do you not know **w** these things
18: 2 **W** do you mean when you use this
18: 5 is just And does **w** is lawful
18:18 And did **w** is not good among
18:19 Because the son has done **w** is
18:21 and does **w** is lawful and right,
18:27 and does **w** is lawful and right,
19: 2 **W** is your mother? A lioness:
20:29 **W** is this high place to which
20:32 **W** you have in your mind shall
21:13 And **w** if the sword despises
24:19 Will you not tell us **w** these
25:12 Because of **w** Edom did against
27: 7 linen from Egypt was **w** you
27: 7 coasts of Elishah was **w** covered
27:32 **W** city is like Tyre,
33:14 his sin and does **w** is lawful
33:15 gives back **w** he has stolen, and
33:16 he has done **w** is lawful and
33:19 wickedness and does **w** is lawful
33:30 Please come and hear **w** the word
34: 4 nor brought back **w** was driven
34: 4 nor sought **w** was lost; but with
34:16 I will seek **w** was lost and bring
34:16 bring back **w** was driven away,
34:16 and strengthen **w** was sick;
34:19 they eat **w** you have trampled
34:19 and they drink **w** you have
36:36 and planted **w** was desolate.
37:18 Will you not show us **w** you mean
48:22 are in the midst of **w** belongs
Dan 2:22 He knows **w** is in the
2:23 have now made known to me **w** we
2:28 King Nebuchadnezzar **w** will be
2:29 about **w** would come to pass
2:29 has made known to you **w** will
2:45 known to the king **w** will come
4:35 **W** have You done?"
8:19 known to you **w** shall happen
9:12 never been done as **w** has been
10:14 come to make you understand **w**
10:21 But I will tell you **w** is noted
11:24 and he shall do **w** his fathers
11:36 for **w** has been determined shall
12: 8 **w** shall be the end of these
Hos 5: 9 of Israel I make known **w** is
6: 4 **w** shall I do to you? O Judah,
6: 4 **w** shall I do to you? For your
7:12 chastise them According to **w**
9: 5 **W** will you do in the appointed
9:14 **W** will You give? Give them a
10: 3 **w** would he do for us?"
14: 8 **W** have I to do anymore with
Joel 1: 4 **W** the chewing locust left, the
1: 4 **W** the swarming locust left,
1: 4 And **w** the crawling locust
3: 4 **w** have you to do with Me,
Am 4:13 Who declares to man **w** his
5:18 For **w** good is the
7: 8 **w** do you see?" And I said, "A
8: 2 **w** do you see?" So I said, "A
Jon 1: 6 '**W** do you mean, sleeper?
1: 8 **W** is your occupation?
1: 8 **W** is your country? And of what
1: 8 And of **w** people are you?"
1:11 **W** shall we do to you that the
2: 9 I will pay **w** I have vowed.
4: 2 was not this **w** I said when I
4: 5 till he might see **w** would
Mic 1: 5 **W** is the transgression of
1: 5 And **w** are the high places of
6: 1 Hear now **w** the LORD says:
6: 3 **w** have I done to you?
6: 5 remember now **W** Balak king of
6: 5 And **w** Balaam the son of Beor
6: 6 With **w** shall I come before the
6: 8 **w** is good; And what does the
6: 8 And **w** does the LORD require
6:14 And **w** you do rescue I will
Nah 1: 9 **W** do you conspire against the
Hab 2: 1 And watch to see **w** He will say
2: 1 And **w** I will answer when I am
2: 6 Woe to him who increases **W** is
2:18 **W** profit is the image, that its
Hag 2:14 and **w** they offer there is
Zech 1: 9 **w** are these?" So the angel
1: 9 I will show you **w** they are."
1:19 **W** are these?" So he answered
1:21 '**W** are these coming to do?"
2: 2 to see **w** is its width and what
2: 2 width and **w** is its length."
4: 2 **W** do you see?" So I said, "I
4: 4 **W** are these, my lord?"
4: 5 Do you not know **w** these are?"
4:11 **W** are these two olive trees—at
4:12 **W** are these two olive branches
4:13 Do you not know **w** these are?"
5: 2 **W** do you see?" So I answered,
5: 5 and see **w** this is that goes
5: 6 **W** is it?" And he said, "It
6: 4 **W** are these, my lord?"
11: 9 Let **w** is dying die, and what is
11: 9 and **w** is perishing perish.
13: 6 **W** are these wounds between your
Mal 1: 2 In **w** way have You loved us?'
1: 6 In **w** way have we despised Your
1: 7 In **w** way have we defiled You?'
1:13 'Oh, **w** a weariness!'
1:14 sacrifices to the Lord **w** is
2:14 For **w** reason?" Because the
2:17 In **w** way have we wearied Him?"
3: 7 In **w** way shall we return?'
3: 8 In **w** way have we robbed You?'
3:13 **W** have we spoken against You?'
3:14 **W** profit is it that we have
Mt 2: 7 determined from them **w** time the
2:17 Then was fulfilled **w** was spoken
5:46 **w** reward have you? Do not even
5:47 **w** do you do more than others?
6: 3 left hand know **w** your right
6:25 **w** you will eat or what you will
6:25 what you will eat or **w** you will
6:25 **w** you will put on. Is not life
6:31 **W** shall we eat?' or 'What shall
6:31 **W** shall we drink?' or 'What
6:31 **W** shall we wear?'
7: 2 For with **w** judgment you judge,
7: 6 Do not give **w** is holy to the
7: 9 Or **w** man is there among you who,
8:29 **W** have we to do with You, Jesus,
8:33 including **w** had happened to
9:13 But go and learn **w** this means:
10:19 do not worry about how or **w** you
10:19 be given to you in that hour **w**
10:27 and **w** you hear in the ear,
11: 7 **W** did you go out into the
11: 8 'But **w** did you go out to see?
11: 9 'But **w** did you go out to see?
11:16 But to **w** shall I liken this
12: 2 Your disciples are doing **w** is
12: 3 Have you not read **w** David did
12: 7 But if you had known **w** this
12:11 **W** man is there among you who has
13:12 even **w** he has will be taken
13:17 men desired to see **w** you see,
13:17 and to hear **w** you hear, and did
13:19 and snatches away **w** was sown
15:11 Not **w** goes into the mouth
15:11 but **w** comes out of the mouth,
16:26 For **w** profit is it to a man if
16:26 Or **w** will a man give in
17:25 '**W** do you think, Simon?
18:12 **W** do you think? If a man has a
18:28 Pay me **w** you owe!'
18:31 servants saw **w** had been done,
19: 6 Therefore **w** God has joined
19:16 **w** good thing shall I do that I
19:20 **W** do I still lack?"
19:21 sell **w** you have and give to the
19:27 Therefore **w** shall we have?"
20:14 Take **w** is yours and go your
20:15 it not lawful for me to do **w** I
20:21 **W** do you wish?" She said to
20:22 'You do not know **w** you ask.
20:32 **W** do you want Me to do for
21:16 Do You hear **w** these are
21:21 you will not only do **w** was done
21:23 By **w** authority are You doing
21:24 will tell you by **w** authority
21:27 I tell you by **w** authority
21:28 But **w** do you think? A man had
21:40 **w** will he do to those
22:17 **w** do You think? Is it lawful to
22:31 have you not read **w** was spoken
22:42 **W** do you think about the Christ?
24: 3 And **w** will be the sign of
24:42 for you do not know **w** hour your
24:43 of the house had known **w** hour
25:25 there you have **w** is yours.'
25:29 even **w** he has will be taken
26:13 **w** this woman has done will also
26:15 **W** are you willing to give me if
26:40 Peter, "**W**? Could you not watch
26:62 **W** is it these men testify
26:65 **W** further need do we have
26:66 **W** do you think?" They answered
26:70 I do not know **w** you are
27: 4 **W** is that to us? You see to
27: 9 Then was fulfilled **w** was spoken
27:22 **W** then shall I do with Jesus who
27:23 **w** evil has He done?"
Mk 1:24 Let us alone! **W** have we to do
1:27 **W** is this? What new doctrine is
1:27 **W** new doctrine is this?
2:24 why do they do **w** is not lawful
2:25 Have you never read **w** David did
4:24 'Take heed **w** you hear.
4:25 even **w** he has will be taken
4:30 To **w** shall we liken the kingdom
4:30 Or with **w** parable shall we
5: 7 **W** have I to do with You, Jesus,
5: 9 **W** is your name?" And he
5:14 And they went out to see **w** it
5:19 and tell them **w** great things
5:33 knowing **w** had happened to her,
6: 2 And **w** wisdom is this which is
6:24 **W** shall I ask?" And she said,
6:30 both **w** they had done and what
6:30 had done and **w** they had taught.
7:20 **W** comes out of a man, that
8:36 For **w** will it profit a man if he
8:37 Or **w** will a man give in exchange
9: 6 because he did not know **w** to
9:10 questioning **w** the rising from
9:16 **W** are you discussing with
9:33 **W** was it you disputed among
10: 3 **W** did Moses command you?"
10: 9 Therefore **w** God has joined
10:17 **w** shall I do that I may inherit
10:36 **W** do you want Me to do for
10:38 'You do not know **w** you ask.
10:51 **W** do you want Me to do for
11: 5 **W** are you doing, loosing the
11:28 By **w** authority are You doing
11:29 tell you by **w** authority
11:33 I tell you by **w** authority
12: 9 Therefore **w** will the owner of
13: 1 see **w** manner of stones and what
13: 1 of stones and **w** buildings
13: 4 And **w** will be the sign when
13:11 or premeditate **w** you will
13:37 And **w** I say to you, I say to
14: 8 'She has done **w** she could.
14: 9 **w** this woman has done will also
14:36 not **w** I will, but what You
14:36 I will, but **w** You will."
14:40 and they did not know **w** to
14:60 **W** is it these men testify
14:63 **W** further need do we have of
14:64 blasphemy! **W** do you think?"
14:68 understand **w** you are saying."
15:12 **W** then do you want me to do
15:14 **w** evil has He done?"
15:24 to determine **w** every man
Lk 1:29 and considered **w** manner of
1:62 **w** he would have him called.
1:66 **W** kind of child will this be?"
2:24 a sacrifice according to **w** is
3:10 **W** shall we do then?"
3:12 'Teacher, **w** shall we do?"
3:13 Collect no more than **w** is
3:14 And **w** shall we do?" So he said
4:34 Let us alone! **W** have we to do
4:36 **W** a word this is! For with
5:25 took up **w** he had been lying on,
6: 2 Why are you doing **w** is not
6: 3 **w** David did when he was hungry,
6:11 discussed with one another **w**
6:32 **w** credit is that to you?
6:33 **w** credit is that to you?
6:34 **w** credit is that to you?
7:24 **W** did you go out into the
7:25 'But **w** did you go out to see?
7:26 'But **w** did you go out to see?
7:31 To **w** then shall I liken the men
7:31 and **w** are they like?
7:39 would know who and **w** manner of
8: 9 **W** does this parable mean?"
8:18 even **w** he seems to have will be
8:28 **W** have I to do with You, Jesus,
8:30 **W** is your name?" And he said,
8:34 When those who fed them saw **w**
8:35 Then they went out to see **w** had
8:36 seen it told them by **w** means
8:39 and tell **w** great things God has
8:39 whole city **w** great things
8:56 charged them to tell no one **w**
9:25 For **w** profit is it to a man if
9:33 not knowing **w** he said.
9:55 You do not know **w** manner of
10:24 have desired to see **w** you see,
10:24 and to hear **w** you hear, and
10:25 **w** shall I do to inherit eternal
10:26 '**W** is written in the law?
10:26 **W** is your reading of it?"
12: 3 and **w** you have spoken in the
12:11 do not worry about how or **w** you
12:11 or **w** you should say.
12:12 very hour **w** you ought to say."
12:17 **W** shall I do, since I have no
12:22 **w** you will eat; nor about the
12:22 **w** you will put on.
12:29 And do not seek **w** you should eat
12:29 seek what you should eat or **w**
12:33 Sell **w** you have and give alms;
12:39 of the house had known **w** hour
12:57 do you not judge **w** is right?
13:18 **W** is the kingdom of God like?
13:18 And to **w** shall I compare it?
13:20 To **w** shall I liken the kingdom
14:31 Or **w** king, going to make war
15: 4 **W** man of you, having a hundred
15: 8 Or **w** woman, having ten silver
15:26 asked **w** these things meant.
16: 2 '**W** is this I hear about you?
16: 3 **W** shall I do? For my master is
16: 4 I have resolved **w** to do, that
16:10 He who is faithful in **w** is
16:10 and he who is unjust in **w** is
16:12 have not been faithful in **w** is
16:12 who will give you **w** is your
16:15 For **w** is highly esteemed among
17:10 We have done **w** was our duty to

18: 6 Hear **w** the unjust judge said.
18:18 **w** shall I do to inherit eternal
18:36 he asked **w** it meant.
18:41 **W** do you want Me to do for
19:21 You collect **w** you did not
19:21 and reap **w** you did not sow.'
19:22 collecting **w** I did not deposit
19:22 and reaping **w** I did not sow.
19:26 even **w** he has will be taken
20: 2 by **w** authority are You doing
20: 8 I tell you by **w** authority
20:13 **W** shall I do? I will send my
20:15 Therefore **w** will the owner of
20:17 **W** then is this that is written:
21: 7 And **w** sign will there be
21:14 on **w** you will answer;
22:49 When those around Him saw **w** was
22:60 I do not know **w** you are
22:71 **W** further testimony do we need?
23:22 **w** evil has He done? I have
23:31 **w** will be done in the dry?"
23:34 for they do not know **w** they
23:47 So when the centurion saw **w** had
23:48 seeing **w** had been done, beat
24:12 marveling to himself at **w** had
24:17 **W** kind of conversation is this
24:19 **W** things?" So they said to Him,
Jn 1:21 '**W** then? Are you Elijah?"
1:22 **W** do you say about yourself?"
1:38 **W** do you seek?" They said to
2: 4 **w** does your concern have to do
2:18 **W** sign do You show to us, since
2:25 for He knew **w** was in man.
3:11 We speak **w** We know and testify
3:11 what We know and testify **w** We
3:32 And **w** He has seen and heard,
4:22 You worship **w** you do not know;
4:22 we know **w** we worship, for
4:27 **W** do You seek?" or, "Why are
4:42 not because of **w** you said, for
5:19 but **w** He sees the Father do;
6: 6 for He Himself knew **w** He would
6: 9 but **w** are they among so many?"
6:28 **W** shall we do, that we may work
6:30 **W** sign will You perform then,
6:30 **W** work will You do?
6:62 **W** then if you should see the
7:36 **W** is this thing that He said,
7:51 it hears him and knows **w** he is
8: 5 But **w** do You say?"
8:25 Just **w** I have been saying to you
8:38 I speak **w** I have seen with My
8:38 and you do **w** you have seen with
9:17 **W** do you say about Him because
9:21 but by **w** means he now sees we do
9:26 **W** did He do to you? How did He
11:47 **W** shall we do? For this Man
11:56 **W** do you think—that He will not
12: 6 and he used to take **w** was put
12:27 and **w** shall I say? 'Father,
12:33 signifying by **w** death He would
12:49 **w** I should say and what I
12:49 what I should say and **w** I
13: 7 **W** I am doing you do not
13:12 Do you know **w** I have done to
13:27 **W** you do, do quickly."
13:28 at the table knew for **w** reason
15: 7 you will ask **w** you desire, and
15:15 for a servant does not know **w**
16:14 for He will take of **w** is Mine
16:17 '**W** is this that He says to us,
16:18 '**W** is this that He says,
16:18 We do not know **w** He is
16:19 among yourselves about **w** I
18:21 who have heard Me **w** I said
18:21 Indeed they know **w** I said."
18:29 **W** accusation do you bring
18:32 signifying by **w** death He would
18:35 **W** have You done?"
18:38 **W** is truth?" And when he had
19:22 **W** I have written, I have
21:19 signifying by **w** death he would
21:21 **w** about this man?"
21:22 **w** is that to you? You follow
21:23 **w** is that to you?"
Acts 2:16 But this is **w** was spoken by the
2:37 brethren, **w** shall we do?"
3: 6 but **w** I do have I give you: In
3:10 amazement at **w** had happened
4: 7 By **w** power or by what name have
4: 7 By what power or by **w** name have
4: 9 by **w** means he has been made
4:16 '**W** shall we do to these men?
4:21 glorified God for **w** had been
5: 7 not knowing **w** had happened.
5:24 they wondered **w** the outcome
5:35 take heed to yourselves **w** you
6: 9 Then there arose some from **w** is
7:40 we do not know **w** has
7:49 **W** house will you build
7:49 Or **w** is the place of My
8:30 Do you understand **w** you are
8:36 **W** hinders me from being
9: 6 **w** do You want me to do?"
9: 6 and you will be told **w** you must
10: 1 a centurion of **w** was called the
10: 4 **W** is it, lord?" So he said to
10: 6 He will tell you **w** you must
10:15 **W** God has cleansed you must not
10:17 wondered within himself **w** this
10:21 For **w** reason have you come?"
10:29 for **w** reason have you sent for
11: 9 **W** God has cleansed you must not
12: 9 and did not know that **w** was
12:18 among the soldiers about **w** had
13:12 when he saw **w** had been done,
13:40 lest **w** has been spoken in the
14:11 Now when the people saw **w** Paul
16:30 **w** must I do to be saved?"
17:18 **W** does this babbler want to
17:19 May we know **w** this new doctrine
17:20 to know **w** these things mean."
19: 3 Into **w** then were you baptized?"
19:35 **w** man is there who does not
20:18 in **w** manner I always lived
21:13 **W** do you mean by weeping and
21:22 **W** then? The assembly must
21:23 Therefore do **w** we tell you: We
21:33 who he was and **w** he had done.
22:10 **W** shall I do, Lord?' And the
22:15 be His witness to all men of **w**
22:26 Take care **w** you do, for this man
23:19 **W** is it that you have to tell
23:34 he asked **w** province he was
28:22 we desire to hear from you **w**
Rom 1:19 because **w** may be known of God is
1:26 the natural use for **w** is
1:27 men with men committing **w** is
2:10 peace to everyone who works **w**
3: 1 **W** advantage then has the Jew, or
3: 1 or **w** is the profit of
3: 3 For **w** if some did not believe?
3: 5 **w** shall we say? Is God unjust
3: 9 **W** then? Are we better than
3:27 By **w** law? Of works? No, but by
4: 1 **W** then shall we say that Abraham
4: 3 For **w** does the Scripture say?
4:18 according to **w** was spoken,
4:21 convinced that **w** He had
6: 1 **W** shall we say then? Shall we
6:15 **W** then? Shall we sin because
6:21 **W** fruit did you have then in the
7: 6 having died to **w** we were held
7: 7 **W** shall we say then
7:13 Has then **w** is good become death
7:13 death in me through **w** is good,
7:15 For **w** I am doing, I do not
7:15 For **w** I will to do, that I do
7:15 but **w** I hate, that I do.
7:16 I do **w** I will not to do, I
7:18 but how to perform **w** is good I
7:20 Now if I do **w** I will not to
8: 3 For **w** the law could not do in
8:24 why does one still hope for **w**
8:25 But if we hope for **w** we do not
8:26 For we do not know **w** we should
8:27 who searches the hearts knows **w**
8:31 **W** then shall we say to these
9:14 **W** shall we say then
9:22 **W** if God, wanting to show His
9:30 **W** shall we say then
10: 8 But **w** does it say? "The word
11: 2 Or do you not know **w** the
11: 4 But **w** does the divine response
11: 7 **W** then? Israel has not obtained
11: 7 Israel has not obtained **w** it
11:15 **w** will their acceptance be
12: 2 that you may prove **w** is that
12: 9 Abhor **w** is evil. Cling to what
12: 9 Cling to **w** is good.
13: 3 Do **w** is good, and you will have
14:22 does not condemn himself in **w**
16:19 to be wise in **w** is good,
1 Cor 2:11 For **w** man knows the things of a
3:13 one's work, of **w** sort it is.
4: 6 in us not to think beyond **w** is
4: 7 And **w** do you have that you did
4:21 **W** do you want? Shall I come to
5:12 For **w** have I to do with
7:19 the commandments of God is **w**
7:35 but for **w** is proper, and that
7:36 let him do **w** he wishes.
9:18 **W** is my reward then? That when I
10:13 you to be tempted beyond **w** you
10:15 judge for yourselves **w** I say.
10:19 **W** am I saying then? That an idol
10:19 or **w** is offered to idols is
11:22 **W**! Do you not have houses to eat
11:22 **W** shall I say to you? Shall I
14: 6 **w** shall I profit you unless I
14: 7 how will it be known **w** is piped
14: 9 how will it be known **w** is
14:15 **W** is the conclusion then?
14:16 does not understand **w** you say?
15:10 But by the grace of God I am **w**
15:29 **w** will they do who are baptized
15:32 **w** advantage is it to me? If
15:35 And with **w** body do they come?"
15:36 **w** you sow is not made alive
15:37 And **w** you sow, you do not sow
16:17 for **w** was lacking on your part
2 Cor 1:13 any other things to you than **w**
3:10 For even **w** was made glorious had
3:11 For if **w** is passing away was
3:11 **w** remains is much more
3:13 look steadily at the end of **w**
4:13 according to **w** is written, "I
5:10 according to **w** he has done,
6:14 For **w** fellowship has
6:14 And **w** communion has light with
6:15 And **w** accord has Christ with
6:15 Or **w** part has a believer with
6:16 And **w** agreement has the temple
6:17 Do not touch **w** is
7:11 **W** diligence it produced in you,
7:11 **w** clearing of yourselves,
7:11 **w** indignation, what fear,
7:11 **w** fear, what vehement desire,
7:11 **w** vehement desire, what zeal,
7:11 **w** zeal, what vindication! In
7:11 **w** vindication! In all things
8:10 not only to be doing **w** you
8:11 may be a completion out of **w**
8:12 it is accepted according to **w**
8:12 and not according to **w** he does
10:11 that **w** we are in word by
11: 9 for **w** I lacked the brethren who
11:12 But **w** I do, I will also continue
11:17 **W** I speak, I speak not according
11:28 **w** comes upon me daily: my deep
12: 6 should think of me above **w** he
12:13 For **w** is it in which you were
13: 7 but that you should do **w** is
Gal 1: 8 any other gospel to you than **w**
1: 9 any other gospel to you than **w**
3:19 **W** purpose then does the law
4:15 **W** then was the blessing you
4:30 Nevertheless **w** does the
6:11 See with **w** large letters I have
Eph 1:18 that you may know **w** is the hope
1:18 **w** are the riches of the glory
1:19 and **w** is the exceeding
2:11 are called Uncircumcision by **w**
3: 9 and to make all see **w** is the
3:18 with all the saints **w** is the
4: 9 **w** does it mean but that He also
4:16 joined and knit together by **w**
4:28 working with his hands **w** is
4:29 but **w** is good for necessary
5:10 finding out **w** is acceptable to
5:17 but understand **w** the will of
Phil 1:18 **W** then? Only that in every way,
1:22 yet **w** I shall choose I cannot
2:30 to supply **w** was lacking in your
3: 7 But **w** things were gain to me,
Col 1:24 and fill up in my flesh **w** is
1:27 God willed to make known **w** are
2: 1 For I want you to know **w** a great
3:25 wrong will be repaid for **w** he
4: 1 give your bondservants **w** is
1 Th 1: 5 as you know **w** kind of men we
1: 9 declare concerning us **w** manner
2:19 For **w** is our hope, or joy, or
3: 9 For **w** thanks can we render to
3:10 see your face and perfect **w** is
4: 2 for you know **w** commandments we
5:15 but always pursue **w** is good
5:21 hold fast **w** is good.
2 Th 2: 6 And now you know **w** is
1 Tim 1: 7 understanding neither **w** they
6:20 Guard **w** was committed to your
6:20 and contradictions of **w** is
2 Tim 1:12 that He is able to keep **w** I
2: 7 Consider **w** I say, and may the
3:11 —**w** persecutions I endured.
Titus 1: 8 a lover of **w** is good,
Phm 1: 8 in Christ to command you **w** is
Heb 2: 6 **W** is man that You are
7:11 **w** further need was there that
8:13 Now **w** is becoming obsolete and
11:32 And **w** more shall I say? For the
12: 7 for **w** son is there whom a
12:13 so that **w** is lame may not be
12:20 (For they could not endure **w** was
13: 6 **W** can man do to me?"
13:21 working in you **w** is well
Jas 1:24 and immediately forgets **w** kind
1:25 will be blessed in **w** he does.
2:14 **W** does it profit, my
2:16 **w** does it profit?
4:14 whereas you do not know **w** will
4:14 For **w** is your life? It is even
1 Pe 1:11 searching **w**, or what manner
1:11 or **w** manner of time, the Spirit
2:20 For **w** credit is it if, when
3:13 followers of **w** is good?
4:17 **w** will be the end of those who
2 Pe 3:11 **w** manner of persons ought you
1 Jn 2:24 If **w** you heard from the
3: 1 Behold **w** manner of love the
3: 2 it has not yet been revealed **w**
3 Jn 11 do not imitate **w** is evil, but
11 but **w** is good. He who does good
Rev 1:11 **W** you see, write in a book and
2: 7 let him hear **w** the Spirit says
2:11 let him hear **w** the Spirit says
2:17 let him hear **w** the Spirit says
2:25 But hold fast **w** you have till I
2:29 let him hear **w** the Spirit says
3: 3 and you will not know **w** hour I
3: 6 let him hear **w** the Spirit says
3:11 Hold fast **w** you have, that
3:13 let him hear **w** the Spirit says
3:22 let him hear **w** the Spirit says
18:18 **W** is like this great city?'

WHATEVER (194/177)

Gen 2:19 And **w** Adam called each living
8:19 and **w** creeps on the earth,
21:12 **W** Sarah has said to you, listen
31:16 **w** God has said to you, do it."
34:11 and **w** you say to me I will
39:22 **w** they did there, it was his
39:23 and **w** he did, the LORD made
41:55 **w** he says to you, do."

Ex 13: 2 ***w*** opens the womb among the
21:30 ***w*** is imposed on him.
29:37 ***W*** touches the altar must be
30:29 ***w*** touches them must be holy.
34:34 to the children of Israel ***w*** he
Lev 5: 3 ***w*** uncleanness with which a man
5: 4 ***w*** it is that a man may
11: 3 ***w*** divides the hoof, having
11: 9 ***w*** in the water has fins and
11:12 ***W*** in the water does not have
11:27 And ***w*** goes on its paws, among
11:32 ***w*** item it is, in which any
11:33 and ***w*** is in it shall be
11:36 but ***w*** touches any such carcass
11:42 ***W*** crawls on its belly, whatever
11:42 ***w*** goes on all fours, or
11:42 or ***w*** has many feet among all
13:58 or ***w*** is made of leather, if the
15:26 and ***w*** she sits on shall be
17: 3 ***W*** man of the house of Israel who
17: 8 ***W*** man of the house of Israel, or
17:10 And ***w*** man of the house of
17:13 ***W*** man of the children of Israel,
22: 4 ***W*** man of the descendants of
22: 5 ***w*** his uncleanness may be—
22: 8 ***W*** dies naturally or is torn by
22:18 ***W*** man of the house of Israel, or
22:20 ***W*** has a defect, you shall not
27:32 of ***w*** passes under the rod, the
Num 5:10 ***w*** any man gives the priest
6:21 ***w*** else his hand is able to
10:32 that ***w*** good the LORD will do to
18:13 ***W*** first ripe fruit is in their
19:22 ***W*** the unclean person touches
22:17 and I will do ***w*** you say to me.
23: 3 and ***w*** He shows me I will tell
30:12 then ***w*** proceeded from her lips
30:14 husband makes no response ***w*** to
33:54 inheritance shall be ***w*** falls
Deut 4: 7 for ***w*** reason we may call upon
12: 8 every man doing ***w*** is right in
12:15 ***w*** your heart desires, according
12:32 ***W*** I command you, be careful to
14:10 And ***w*** does not have fins and
14:26 shall spend that money for ***w***
14:26 for ***w*** your heart desires; you
15: 8 for his need, ***w*** he needs.
Judg 10:15 Do to us ***w*** seems best to You;
11:24 Will you not possess ***w*** Chemosh
11:24 So ***w*** the LORD our God takes
11:31 then it will be that ***w*** comes out
1 Sam 11:10 and you may do with us ***w*** seems
14:36 'Do ***w*** seems good to you."
20: 4 ***W*** you yourself desire, I will do
21: 3 or ***w*** can be found."
25: 8 Please give ***w*** comes to your
2 Sam 3:36 since ***w*** the king did pleased
15:15 ready to do ***w*** my lord the
15:21 surely in ***w*** place my lord the
15:35 it will be that ***w*** you hear
18: 4 ***W*** seems best to you I will do."
18:22 But ***w*** happens, please let me
18:23 But ***w*** happens," he said,
19:38 Now ***w*** you request of me, I will
21: 4 ***W*** you say, I will do for you."
24:22 the king take and offer up ***w***
1 Ki 5: 6 according to ***w*** you say.
8:37 ***w*** plague or whatever sickness
8:37 whatever plague or ***w*** sickness
8:38 ***w*** prayer, whatever supplication
8:38 ***w*** supplication is made by
9:19 and ***w*** Solomon desired to build
10:13 ***w*** she asked, besides what
20: 6 that ***w*** is pleasant in your
22:14 ***w*** the LORD says to me, that I
2 Ki 18:14 ***w*** you impose on me I will
2 Chr 6:28 ***w*** plague or whatever sickness
6:28 whatever plague or ***w*** sickness
6:29 ***w*** prayer, whatever supplication
6:29 ***w*** supplication is made by
9:12 ***w*** she asked, much more than
18:13 ***w*** my God says, that I will
19:10 ***W*** case comes to you from your
Ezra 6: 9 And ***w*** they need—young bulls,
7:18 And ***w*** seems good to you and your
7:20 And ***w*** more may be needed for the
7:21 that ***w*** Ezra the priest, the
7:23 ***W*** is commanded by the God of
Neh 4: 3 ***W*** they build, if even a fox goes
4:12 From ***w*** place you turn, they
Esth 2:13 and she was given ***w*** she desired
8: 8 for ***w*** is written in the king's
Job 23:13 And ***w*** His soul desires, that
37:12 That they may do ***w*** He commands
Ps 1: 3 And ***w*** he does shall prosper.
115: 3 He does ***w*** He pleases.
135: 6 ***W*** the LORD pleases He does,
Eccl 2:10 ***W*** my eyes desired I did not
3:14 know that ***w*** God does,
6:10 ***W*** one is, he has been named
8: 3 for he does ***w*** pleases him."
9:10 ***W*** your hand finds to do, do it
Jer 1: 7 And ***w*** I command you, you shall
42: 4 that ***w*** the LORD answers you,
44:17 But we will certainly do ***w*** has
52:19 ***w*** was solid gold and whatever
52:19 and ***w*** was solid silver,
Ezek 47:23 And it shall be that in ***w*** tribe
Dan 6:23 and no injury ***w*** was found on
Hag 1:11 on ***w*** the ground brings forth,
Mt 5:37 For ***w*** is more than these is
7:12 ***w*** you want men to do to you, do
10:11 Now ***w*** city or town you enter,
10:27 ***W*** I tell you in the dark, speak
14: 7 with an oath to give her ***w*** she
15: 5 ***W*** profit you might have received
15:17 that ***w*** enters the mouth goes
16:19 and ***w*** you bind on earth will be
16:19 and ***w*** you loose on earth will
17:12 but did to him ***w*** they wished.
18:18 ***w*** you bind on earth will be
18:18 and ***w*** you loose on earth will
20: 4 and ***w*** is right I will give
20: 7 and ***w*** is right you will
21:22 And ***w*** things you ask in prayer,
23: 3 Therefore ***w*** they tell you to
Mk 3:28 and ***w*** blasphemies they may
6:10 In ***w*** place you enter a house,
6:22 Ask me ***w*** you want, and I will
6:23 ***W*** you ask me, I will give you,
7:11 ***W*** profit you might have received
7:18 ***w*** enters a man from outside
9:13 and they did to him ***w*** they
10:21 sell ***w*** you have and give to the
10:35 we want You to do for us ***w*** we
11:23 he will have ***w*** he says.
11:24 ***w*** things you ask when you pray,
13:11 But ***w*** is given you in that
Lk 4:23 heal yourself! ***W*** we have heard
9: 4 ***W*** house you enter, stay there,
10: 5 But ***w*** house you enter, first
10: 8 ***W*** city you enter, and they
10:10 But ***w*** city you enter, and they
10:35 and ***w*** more you spend, when I
12: 3 Therefore ***w*** you have spoken in
Jn 2: 5 ***W*** He says to you, do it."
5: 4 was made well of ***w*** disease he
5:19 for ***w*** He does, the Son also
11:22 But even now I know that ***w*** You
12:50 ***w*** I speak, just as the Father
14:13 And ***w*** you ask in My name, that I
15:14 are My friends if you do ***w***
15:16 that ***w*** you ask the Father in My
16:13 but ***w*** He hears He will speak;
16:23 ***w*** you ask the Father in My name
Acts 2:12 ***W*** could this mean?"
3:22 ***w*** He says to you.
4:28 to do ***w*** Your hand and Your
Rom 2: 1 for in ***w*** you judge another you
3:19 Now we know that ***w*** the law says,
14:23 for ***w*** is not from faith is
15: 4 For ***w*** things were written before
16: 2 and assist her in ***w*** business
1 Cor 10:25 Eat ***w*** is sold in the meat
10:27 eat ***w*** is set before you, asking
10:31 or ***w*** you do, do all to the
2 Cor 11:21 But in ***w*** anyone is bold—I
Gal 2: 6 ***w*** they were, it makes no
6: 7 for ***w*** a man sows, that he will
Eph 5:13 for ***w*** makes manifest is light.
6: 8 knowing that ***w*** good anyone does,
Phil 4: 8 ***w*** things are true, whatever
4: 8 ***w*** things are noble, whatever
4: 8 ***w*** things are just, whatever
4: 8 ***w*** things are pure, whatever
4: 8 ***w*** things are lovely, whatever
4: 8 ***w*** things are of good report,
4:11 for I have learned in ***w*** state I
Col 3:17 And ***w*** you do in word or deed,
3:23 And ***w*** you do, do it heartily, as
1 Jn 3:22 And ***w*** we ask we receive from
5: 4 For ***w*** is born of God overcomes
5:15 ***w*** we ask, we know that we have
3 Jn 5 you do faithfully ***w*** you do for
Jude 10 But these speak evil of ***w*** they
10 and ***w*** they know naturally, like

WHEAT (49/49)

Gen 30:14 Reuben went in the days of ***w***
Ex 9:32 But the ***w*** and the spelt were not
29: 2 oil (you shall make them of ***w***
34:22 of the firstfruits of ***w***
Deut 8: 8 a land of ***w*** and barley, of vines
32:14 and goats, With the choicest ***w***;
Judg 6:11 his son Gideon threshed ***w*** in
15: 1 in the time of ***w*** harvest, it
Ruth 2:23 the end of barley harvest and ***w***
1 Sam 6:13 Shemesh were reaping their ***w***
12:17 Is today not the ***w*** harvest?
2 Sam 4: 6 the house, as though to get ***w***,
17:28 basins, earthen vessels and ***w***,
1 Ki 5:11 twenty thousand kors of ***w*** as
1 Chr 21:20 but Ornan continued threshing ***w***.
21:23 and the ***w*** for the grain
2 Chr 2:10 thousand kors of ground ***w***,
2:15 Now therefore, the ***w***,
27: 5 silver, ten thousand kors of ***w***,
Ezra 6: 9 of the God of heaven, ***w***,
7:22 silver, one hundred kors of ***w***,
Job 31:40 let thistles grow instead of ***w***,
Ps 81:16 them also with the finest of ***w***;
147:14 fills you with the finest ***w***.
Song 7: 2 Your waist is a heap of ***w***
Isa 28:25 Plant the ***w*** in rows, The
Jer 12:13 They have sown ***w*** but reaped
23:28 What is the chaff to the ***w***?
31:12 For ***w*** and new wine and oil,
41: 8 us, for we have treasures of ***w***,
Ezek 4: 9 "Also take for yourself ***w***,
27:17 traded for your merchandise ***w***
45:13 of an ephah from a homer of ***w***,
Joel 1:11 For the ***w*** and the barley;
2:24 floors shall be full of ***w***,
Am 8: 5 Sabbath, That we may trade ***w***?
8: 6 of sandals—Even sell the bad ***w***?
Mt 3:12 and gather His ***w*** into the barn;
13:25 and sowed tares among the ***w***
13:29 the tares you also uproot the ***w***
13:30 but gather the ***w*** into my
Lk 3:17 and gather the ***w*** into His barn;
16: 7 said, 'A hundred measures of ***w***.
22:31 you, that he may sift you as ***w***.
Jn 12:24 unless a grain of ***w*** falls into
Acts 27:38 the ship and threw out the ***w***
1 Cor 15:37 perhaps ***w*** or some other grain.
Rev 6: 6 A quart of ***w*** for a denarius, and
18:13 wine and oil, fine flour and ***w***,

WHEEL (13/10) WHEELS

1 Ki 7:32 The height of a ***w*** was one and
7:33 the workmanship of a chariot ***w***;
Prov 20:26 And brings the threshing ***w***
Eccl 12: 6 Or the ***w*** broken at the well.
Jer 18: 3 was, making something at the ***w***.
Ezek 1:15 a ***w*** was on the earth beside
1:16 a ***w*** in the middle of a wheel.
1:16 a wheel in the middle of a ***w***.
10: 9 one ***w*** by one cherub and another
10: 9 by one cherub and another ***w*** by
10:10 a ***w*** in the middle of a wheel.
10:10 a wheel in the middle of a ***w***.
10:13 were called in my hearing, "***W***.

WHEELS (29/22) WHEEL

Ex 14:25 And He took off their chariot ***w***,
1 Ki 7:30 Every cart had four bronze ***w*** and
7:32 the panels were the four ***w***,
7:32 and the axles of the ***w*** were
7:33 The workmanship of the ***w*** was
Isa 5:28 And their ***w*** like a whirlwind.
Jer 47: 3 At the rumbling of his ***w***,
Ezek 1:16 The appearance of the ***w*** and
1:19 the ***w*** went beside them;
1:19 the ***w*** were lifted up.
1:20 and the ***w*** were lifted together
1:20 living creatures was in the ***w***.
1:21 the ***w*** were lifted up together
1:21 living creatures was in the ***w***.
3:13 and the noise of the ***w*** beside
10: 2 and said, "Go in among the ***w***,
10: 6 "Take fire from among the ***w***,
10: 6 went in and stood beside the ***w***.
10: 9 there were four ***w*** by the
10: 9 the ***w*** appeared to have the
10:12 and the ***w*** that the four had,
10:13 As for the ***w***, they were called
10:16 the ***w*** went beside them; and
10:16 the same ***w*** also did not turn
10:17 the ***w*** stood still, and when
10:19 the ***w*** were beside them;
11:22 with the ***w*** beside them, and the
Dan 7: 9 Its ***w*** a burning fire;
Nah 3: 2 And the noise of rattling ***w***,

WHELP (2/2)

Gen 49: 9 Judah is a lion's ***w***;
Deut 33:22 he said: "Dan is a lion's ***w***;

WHELPS (1/1)

Jer 51:38 They shall growl like lions' ***w***.

WHEN (2863/2675) See APPENDIX

WHENCE (1/1)

Ps 121: 1 From ***w*** comes my help?

WHENEVER (35/34)

Gen 30:41 ***w*** the stronger livestock
Ex 33: 8 ***w*** Moses went out to the
34:34 But ***w*** Moses went in before the
34:35 And ***w*** the children of Israel saw
40:32 ***W*** they went into the tabernacle
40:36 ***W*** the cloud was taken up from
Num 9:17 ***W*** the cloud was taken up from
9:21 ***w*** the cloud was taken up, they
10:35 ***w*** the ark set out, that Moses
Judg 6: 3 ***w*** Israel had sown, Midianites
1 Sam 1: 4 And ***w*** the time came for Elkanah
16:23 ***w*** the spirit from God was upon
18:30 ***w*** they went out, that David
27: 9 ***W*** David attacked the land, he
2 Sam 15: 2 ***w*** anyone who had a lawsuit came
15: 5 ***w*** anyone came near to bow down
1 Ki 8:52 to listen to them ***w*** they call
14:28 And ***w*** the king entered the house
2 Ki 4:10 ***w*** he comes to us, he can turn
12:10 ***w*** they saw that there was
2 Chr 7: 6 ***w*** David offered praise by
12:11 And ***w*** the king entered the house
Ps 56: 3 ***W*** I am afraid, I will trust in
Isa 30:21 ***W*** you turn to the right hand
30:21 Or ***w*** you turn to the left.
Jer 48:27 For ***w*** you speak of him,
Ezek 1:25 ***w*** they stood, they let down
44:17 ***w*** they enter the gates of the
Mk 3:11 ***w*** they saw Him, fell down
11:25 And ***w*** you stand praying, if you
14: 7 and ***w*** you wish you may do them
Lk 12:54 ***W*** you see a cloud rising out of

Rom 15:24 ***w*** I journey to Spain, I shall
1 Cor 14:26 ***W*** you come together, each of
Rev 4: 9 ***W*** the living creatures give

WHERE (546/497)

Gen 2:11 ***w*** there is gold.
3: 9 said to him, "***W*** are you?"
4: 9 '***W*** is Abel your brother?"
13: 3 to the place ***w*** his tent had
13:14 the place ***w*** you are—northward,
16: 8 ***w*** have you come from, and where
16: 8 and ***w*** are you going?"
18: 9 '***W*** is Sarah your wife?"
19: 5 ***W*** are the men who came to you
19:27 to the place ***w*** he had stood
20:15 dwell ***w*** it pleases you."
21:17 the voice of the lad ***w*** he is.
22: 7 but ***w*** is the lamb for a burnt
27:33 ***W*** is the one who hunted game
29: 4 ***w*** are you from?" And they
30:38 in the watering troughs ***w*** the
31:13 ***w*** you anointed the pillar and
31:13 and ***w*** you made a vow to Me.
32:17 and ***w*** are you going? Whose are
33:19 ***w*** he had pitched his tent, from
35:13 up from him in the place ***w*** He
35:14 in the place ***w*** He talked
35:15 name of the place ***w*** God spoke
35:27 ***w*** Abraham and Isaac had dwelt.
36: 7 and the land ***w*** they were
37: 1 in the land ***w*** his father was
37:16 Please tell me ***w*** they are
37:30 and I, ***w*** shall I go?"
38:21 ***W*** is the harlot who was openly
39:20 a place ***w*** the king's prisoners
40: 3 the place ***w*** Joseph was
42: 7 ***W*** do you come from?" And they
Ex 2:20 And ***w*** is he? Why is it that
3: 5 for the place ***w*** you stand is
5:11 get yourselves straw ***w*** you can
9:26 ***w*** the children of Israel were,
12: 7 on the lintel of the houses ***w***
12:13 a sign for you on the houses ***w***
12:30 for there was not a house ***w***
15:27 ***w*** there were twelve wells of
18: 5 ***w*** he was encamped at the
20:21 the thick darkness ***w*** God was.
20:24 In every place ***w*** I record My
21:13 a place ***w*** he may flee.
29:42 ***w*** I will meet you to speak with
30: 6 ***w*** I will meet with you.
30:36 ***w*** I will meet with you.
34:12 of the land ***w*** you are going,
Lev 4:12 ***w*** the ashes are poured out, and
4:12 ***w*** the ashes are poured out it
4:24 and kill it at the place ***w*** they
4:33 at the place ***w*** they kill the
6:25 In the place ***w*** the burnt
7: 2 In the place ***w*** they kill the
14:13 in the place ***w*** he kills the
18: 3 ***w*** you dwelt, you shall not do;
18: 3 ***w*** I am bringing you, you shall
20:22 that the land ***w*** I am bringing
Num 9:17 and in the place ***w*** the cloud
11:13 ***W*** am I to get meat to give to
13:27 We went to the land ***w*** you sent
14:24 I will bring into the land ***w*** he
17: 4 ***w*** I meet with you.
21:16 which is the well ***w*** the LORD
22:26 a narrow place ***w*** there was
31:10 all the cities ***w*** they dwelt,
33:14 ***w*** there was no water for the
33:55 shall harass you in the land ***w***
35:25 him to the city of refuge ***w*** he
35:26 limits of the city of refuge ***w***
35:33 shall not pollute the land ***w***
Deut 1:28 '***W*** can we go up? Our brethren
1:31 and in the wilderness ***w*** you saw
4:27 among the nations ***w*** the LORD
8:15 land ***w*** there was no water;
10: 6 ***w*** Aaron died, and where he was
10: 6 and ***w*** he was buried; and
11:10 ***w*** you sowed your seed and
11:25 of you upon all the land ***w*** you
12: 2 destroy all the places ***w*** the
12: 5 you shall seek the place ***w***
12:11 the place ***w*** the LORD your God
12:21 If the place ***w*** the LORD your
14:23 in the place ***w*** He chooses to
14:24 or if the place ***w*** the LORD
16: 2 in the place ***w*** the LORD
16: 6 but at the place ***w*** the LORD
16:11 at the place ***w*** the LORD your
18: 6 from ***w*** he dwells among all
23:12 ***w*** you may go out;
23:16 ***w*** it seems best to him;
26: 2 go to the place ***w*** the LORD
28:37 among all nations ***w*** the LORD
30: 1 all the nations ***w*** the LORD
30: 3 again from all the nations ***w***
31:16 ***w*** they go to be among them,
32:37 ***W*** are their gods, The rock in
Josh 2: 4 but I did not know ***w*** they were
2: 5 ***W*** the men went I do not know;
4: 3 from the place ***w*** the priests'
4: 3 lodging place ***w*** you lodge
4: 8 to the place ***w*** they lodged,
4: 9 in the place ***w*** the feet of the
5:15 for the place ***w*** you stand is
8:24 in the wilderness ***w*** they
9: 8 and ***w*** do you come from?"
10:27 cast them into the cave ***w*** they
14: 9 Surely the land ***w*** your foot has
22:19 ***w*** the LORD's tabernacle
22:33 to destroy the land ***w*** the
Judg 5:27 ***W*** he sank, there he fell dead.
6:13 And ***w*** are all His miracles
9:38 ***W*** indeed is your mouth now,
13: 6 but I did not ask Him ***w*** He was
16: 5 and find out ***w*** his great
16: 6 Please tell me ***w*** your great
16:15 and have not told me ***w*** your
17: 9 ***W*** do you come from?" So he said
18:10 a place ***w*** there is no lack of
19:17 ***W*** are you going, and where do
19:17 and ***w*** do you come from?"
19:26 house ***w*** her master was,
20:22 at the place ***w*** they had put
Ruth 1: 7 out from the place ***w*** she was,
1:17 ***W*** you die, I will die,
2:19 '***W*** have you gleaned today?
2:19 And ***w*** did you work? Blessed be
3: 4 notice the place ***w*** he lies;
1 Sam 3: 3 ***w*** the ark of God was,
9:10 ***w*** the man of God was.
9:18 ***w*** is the seer's house?"
10: 5 come to the hill of God ***w*** the
10:14 '***W*** did you go?" So he said,
14:11 holes ***w*** they have hidden."
19: 3 my father in the field ***w*** you
19:22 '***W*** are Samuel and David?"
20:19 and come to the place ***w*** you
20:37 to the place ***w*** the arrow was
23:22 and see the place ***w*** his hideout
23:23 of all the lurking places ***w*** he
24: 3 ***w*** there was a cave; and Saul
25:11 not know ***w*** they are from?"
26: 5 the place ***w*** Saul had encamped.
26: 5 And David saw the place ***w*** Saul
26:16 And now see ***w*** the king's spear
27:10 ***W*** have you made a raid today?"
30: 9 ***w*** those stayed who were left
30:13 and ***w*** are you from?"
30:31 and to all the places ***w*** David
2 Sam 1: 3 '***W*** have you come from?"
1:13 ***W*** are you from?" And he
2: 1 ***W*** shall I go up?" And He said,
2:23 to the place ***w*** Asahel fell
9: 4 ***W*** is he?" And Ziba said to the
11:16 he assigned Uriah to a place ***w***
13:13 ***w*** could I take my shame?
15:20 today, since I go I know not ***w***?
15:32 ***w*** he worshiped God—there was
16: 3 And ***w*** is your master's son?"
17:12 place ***w*** he may be found,
17:20 ***W*** are Ahimaaz and Jonathan?"
21:12 ***w*** the Philistines had hung them
21:19 ***w*** Elhanan the son of
21:20 ***w*** there was a man of great
23:11 together into a troop ***w*** there
1 Ki 7: 7 ***w*** he might judge; and it was
7: 8 And the house ***w*** he dwelt had
8:47 land ***w*** they were carried
13:25 and told it in the city ***w*** the
13:31 then bury me in the tomb ***w*** the
17:19 him to the upper room ***w*** he was
18:10 is no nation or kingdom ***w*** my
21:18 ***w*** he has gone down to take
21:19 In the place ***w*** dogs licked the
2 Ki 2:14 ***W*** is the LORD God of Elijah?"
4: 8 ***w*** there was a notable woman,
5:25 '***W*** did you go, Gehazi?"
6: 1 the place ***w*** we dwell with you
6: 2 let us make there a place ***w*** we
6: 6 ***W*** did it fall?" And he showed
6:13 Go and see ***w*** he is, that I may
6:27 ***w*** can I find help for you?
17:29 in the cities ***w*** they dwelt.
18:34 ***W*** are the gods of Hamath and
18:34 ***W*** are the gods of Sepharvaim
19:13 ***W*** is the king of Hamath, the
20:14 and from ***w*** did they come to
23: 7 ***w*** the women wove hangings for
23: 8 and defiled the high places ***w***
1 Chr 11: 4 ***w*** the Jebusites were, the
13: 6 ***w*** His name is proclaimed.
20: 6 ***w*** there was a man of great
2 Chr 3: 1 ***w*** the LORD had appeared to
6:20 toward the place ***w*** You said
6:37 land ***w*** they were carried
6:38 ***w*** they have been carried
10: 2 ***w*** he had fled from the presence
25: 4 ***w*** the LORD commanded, saying,
33:19 and the sites ***w*** he built high
36:20 ***w*** they became servants to him
Ezra 1: 4 in any place ***w*** he dwells,
6: 1 ***w*** the treasures were stored in
6: 3 the place ***w*** they offered
Neh 2:16 the officials did not know ***w*** I
10:39 to the storerooms ***w*** the
10:39 ***w*** the priests who minister and
13: 5 ***w*** previously they had stored
Esth 4: 3 And in every province ***w*** the
7: 5 and ***w*** is he, who would dare
7: 8 had fallen across the couch ***w***
Job 1: 7 From ***w*** do you come?" So Satan
2: 2 From ***w*** do you come?" So Satan
4: 7 Or ***w*** were the upright ever
10:22 ***W*** even the light is like
14:10 his last And ***w*** is he?
15:23 ***W*** is it?' He knows that a day
17:15 ***W*** then is my hope
20: 7 seen him will say, '***W*** is he?'
21:28 ***W*** is the house of the prince?
21:28 And ***w*** is the tent, The
23: 3 that I knew ***w*** I might find Him,
28: 1 And a place ***w*** gold is
28:12 But ***w*** can wisdom be found?
28:12 And ***w*** is the place of
28:20 From ***w*** then does wisdom come?
28:20 And ***w*** is the place of
34:22 nor shadow of death ***W*** the
35:10 ***W*** is God my Maker, Who gives
36:16 Into a broad place ***w*** there
38: 4 ***W*** were you when I laid the
38:19 ***W*** is the way to the dwelling
38:19 And darkness, ***w*** is its place,
38:26 to rain on a land ***w*** there is
39:30 And ***w*** the slain are, there it
Ps 19: 3 nor language ***W*** their voice
26: 8 And the place ***w*** Your glory
42: 3 say to me, "***W*** is your God?"
42:10 day long, "***W*** is your God?"
53: 5 they are in great fear ***W*** no
63: 1 land ***W*** there is no water.
69: 2 ***W*** there is no standing;
69: 2 ***W*** the floods overflow me.
74: 2 This Mount Zion ***w*** You have
79:10 ***W*** is their God?" Let there be
81: 5 ***W*** I heard a language I did
84: 3 ***W*** she may lay her young—Even
89:49 Lord, ***w*** are Your former
104:17 ***W*** the birds make their nests
107:40 wilderness ***w*** there is no
115: 2 So ***w*** is their God?"
122: 4 ***W*** the tribes go up, The tribes
139: 7 ***W*** can I go from Your Spirit
139: 7 Or ***w*** can I flee from Your
Prov 8: 2 the way, ***w*** the paths meet.
11:14 ***W*** there is no counsel, the
14: 4 ***W*** no oxen are, the trough is
15:17 is a dinner of herbs ***w*** love
26:20 ***W*** there is no wood, the fire
26:20 And ***w*** there is no
29:18 ***W*** there is no revelation, the
Eccl 1: 5 And hastens to the place ***w*** it
8: 4 ***W*** the word of a king is,
8:10 in the city ***w*** they had so done.
9:10 or wisdom in the grave ***w*** you
11: 3 In the place ***w*** the tree falls,
Song 1: 7 ***W*** you feed your flock,
1: 7 ***W*** you make it rest at noon.
6: 1 ***W*** has your beloved gone,
6: 1 ***W*** has your beloved turned
Isa 5: 8 no place ***W*** they may dwell
10: 3 And ***w*** will you leave your
19:12 ***W*** are they? Where are your
19:12 ***W*** are your wise men?
29: 1 the city ***w*** David dwelt!
30:32 And in every place ***w*** the staff
33:18 ***W*** is the scribe? Where is he
33:18 ***W*** is he who weighs?
33:18 ***W*** is he who counts the
35: 7 ***w*** each lay, There shall be
36:19 ***W*** are the gods of Hamath and
36:19 ***W*** are the gods of Sepharvaim?
37:13 ***W*** is the king of Hamath, the
39: 3 and from ***w*** did they come to
47:11 You shall not know from ***w*** it
49:20 Give me a place ***w*** I may
49:21 But these, ***w*** were they?"
50: 1 ***W*** is the certificate of your
51:13 And ***w*** is the fury of the
57: 8 ***W*** you saw their nudity.
63:11 ***W*** is He who brought them up out
63:11 ***W*** is He who put His Holy
63:15 ***W*** are Your zeal and Your
64:11 ***W*** our fathers praised You,
66: 1 ***W*** is the house that you will
66: 1 And ***w*** is the place of My
Jer 2: 6 ***W*** is the LORD, Who brought us
2: 6 that no one crossed And ***w*** no
2: 8 ***W*** is the LORD?' And those who
2:28 But ***w*** are your gods that you
3: 2 ***W*** have you not lain with
6:16 ***w*** the good way is, And walk
7:12 ***w*** I set My name at the first,
8: 3 places ***w*** I have driven them,"
13: 7 took the sash from the place ***w***
13:20 ***W*** is the flock that was
15: 2 ***W*** should we go?' then you shall
16:13 ***w*** I will not show you favor.'
16:15 lands ***w*** He had driven them.'
17:15 ***W*** is the word of the LORD?
19:14 ***w*** the LORD had sent him to
22:12 he shall die in the place ***w***
22:26 into another country ***w*** you were
23: 3 flock out of all countries ***w*** I
23: 8 and from all the countries ***w*** I
24: 9 in all places ***w*** I shall drive
29: 7 seek the peace of the city ***w*** I
29:14 and from all the places ***w*** I
29:18 among all the nations ***w*** I have
30:11 a full end of all nations ***w*** I
32:37 them out of all countries ***w*** I
35: 7 live many days in the land ***w***
36:19 and let no one know ***w*** you
37:19 ***W*** now are your prophets who
38: 9 die from hunger in the place ***w***
39: 5 ***w*** he pronounced judgment on
40:12 returned out of all places ***w***
42:14 of Egypt ***w*** we shall see no war,
42:22 the place ***w*** you desire to go
43: 5 from all nations ***w*** they had
44: 8 ***w*** you have gone

49:36 *w* the outcasts of Elam will
51:43 A land *w* no one dwells,
Lam 2:12 '*W* is grain and wine?"
Ezek 3:15 and I sat *w* they sat, and
4:13 *w* I will drive them."
6: 9 Me among the nations *w* they
8: 3 *w* the seat of the image of
9: 3 *w* it had been, to the threshold
11:16 countries *w* they have gone."
11:17 you from the countries *w* you
13:12 *W* is the mortar with which you
17: 7 From the garden terrace *w* it
17:10 the garden terrace *w* it grew."
17:16 surely in the place *w* the king
20:34 you out of the countries *w* you
20:38 them out of the country *w* they
20:41 you out of the countries *w* you
21:30 will judge you In the place *w*
31: 4 running around the place *w* it
34:12 all the places *w* they were
37:25 *w* your fathers dwelt; and they
40:38 *w* they washed the burnt
42:13 are the holy chambers *w* the
43: 7 *w* I will dwell in the midst of
46:20 This is the place *w* the priests
46:20 and *w* they shall bake the
46:24 These are the kitchens *w* the
Dan 8:17 So he came near *w* I stood, and
Hos 1:10 the place *w* it was said
13:10 *W* is any other, That he
13:13 stay long *w* children are born.
Joel 2:17 *W* is their God?'"
Am 3: 5 *w* there is no trap for it?
4: 7 And *w* it did not rain the part
Jon 1: 8 And *w* do you come from? What is
Mic 7:10 '*W* is the LORD your God?"
Nah 2:11 *W* is the dwelling of the
2:11 *W* the lion walked, the lioness
3: 7 *W* shall I seek comforters for
3:17 And the place *w* they are is
Zeph 3:19 and fame In every land *w* they
Zech 1: 5 *w* are they? And the prophets,
2: 2 *W* are you going?" And he said
5:10 *W* are they carrying the
Mal 1: 6 *W* is My honor? And if I am
1: 6 *W* is My reverence? Says the
2:17 *W* is the God of justice?"
Mt 2: 2 *W* is He who has been born King
2: 4 he inquired of them *w* the
2: 9 till it came and stood over *w*
6:19 *w* moth and rust destroy and
6:19 rust destroy and *w* thieves
6:20 *w* neither moth nor rust
6:20 rust destroys and *w* thieves
6:21 For *w* your treasure is, there
13: 5 *w* they did not have much earth;
13:54 *W* did this Man get this wisdom
13:56 *W* then did this Man get all
15:33 *W* could we get enough bread in
18:20 For *w* two or three are gathered
21:25 *w* was it from? From heaven or
25:24 reaping *w* you have not sown,
25:24 and gathering *w* you have not
25:26 you knew that I reap *w* I have
25:26 and gather *w* I have not
26:17 *W* do You want us to prepare for
26:57 *w* the scribes and the elders
28: 6 see the place *w* the Lord lay.
Mk 2: 4 they uncovered the roof *w* He
4: 5 *w* it did not have much earth;
4:15 wayside *w* the word is sown.
5:40 and entered *w* the child was
6: 2 *W* did this Man get these
9:44 '*w* 'Their worm does not
9:46 '*w* 'Their worm does not
9:48 '*w* 'Their worm does not
13:14 standing *w* it ought not" (let
14:12 *W* do You want us to go and
14:14 *W* is the guest room in which I
15:47 mother of Joses observed *w* He
16: 6 See the place *w* they laid Him.
Lk 4:16 *w* He had been brought up.
4:17 He found the place *w* it was
8:25 *W* is your faith?" And they were
10: 1 into every city and place *w* He
10:33 came *w* he was. And when he saw
12:33 *w* no thief approaches nor moth
12:34 For *w* your treasure is, there
13:25 know you, *w* you are from,'
13:27 *w* you are from. Depart from Me,
17:17 But *w* are the nine?
17:37 and said to Him, "*W*, Lord?"
19:30 *w* as you enter you will find a
20: 7 that they did not know *w* it
22: 9 *W* do You want us to prepare?"
22:11 *W* is the guest room where I may
22:11 Where is the guest room *w* I may
23:53 *w* no one had ever lain before.
24:28 village *w* they were going,
Jn 1:28 *w* John was baptizing.
1:38 *w* are You staying?"
1:39 They came and saw *w* He was
2: 9 and did not know *w* it came from
3: 8 The wind blows *w* it wishes, and
3: 8 but cannot tell *w* it comes from
3: 8 it comes from and *w* it goes.
4:11 *W* then do You get that living
4:20 place *w* one ought to worship."
4:46 again to Cana of Galilee *w* He
6: 5 *W* shall we buy bread, that these
6:21 the boat was at the land *w*
6:23 near the place *w* they ate bread
6:62 see the Son of Man ascend *w* He
7:11 and said, "*W* is He?"
7:27 we know *w* this Man is from;
7:27 no one knows *w* He is from."
7:28 and you know *w* I am from; and I
7:34 and *w* I am you cannot come."
7:35 *W* does He intend to go that we
7:36 and *w* I am you cannot come'?"
7:42 Bethlehem, *w* David was?"
8:10 *w* are those accusers of yours?
8:14 for I know *w* I came from and
8:14 I came from and *w* I am going;
8:14 but you do not know *w* I come
8:14 know where I come from and *w* I
8:19 *W* is Your Father?" Jesus
8:21 *W* I go you cannot come."
8:22 *W* I go you cannot come'?"
9:12 *W* is He?" He said, "I do not
9:29 we do not know *w* He is from."
9:30 that you do not know *w* He is
10:40 the Jordan to the place *w* John
11: 6 two more days in the place *w*
11:30 but was in the place *w* Martha
11:32 when Mary came *w* Jesus was, and
11:34 *W* have you laid him?" They said
11:41 the stone from the place *w*
11:57 that if anyone knew *w* He was,
12: 1 *w* Lazarus was who had been
12:26 and *w* I am, there My servant
12:35 in darkness does not know *w* he
13:33 *W* I am going, you cannot come,'
13:36 *w* are You going?" Jesus
13:36 *W* I am going you cannot follow
14: 3 that *w* I am, there you may be
14: 4 And *w* I go you know, and the way
14: 5 we do not know *w* You are going,
16: 5 asks Me, '*W* are You going?'
17:24 You gave Me may be with Me *w* I
18: 1 *w* there was a garden, which He
18:20 *w* the Jews always meet, and in
19: 9 *W* are You from?" But Jesus gave
19:18 *w* they crucified Him, and two
19:20 for the place *w* Jesus was
19:41 Now in the place *w* He was
20: 2 and we do not know *w* they have
20:12 *w* the body of Jesus had lain.
20:13 and I do not know *w* they have
20:15 tell me *w* You have laid Him,
20:19 when the doors were shut *w* the
21:18 and walked *w* you wished;
21:18 carry you *w* you do not wish."
Acts 1:13 went up into the upper room *w*
2: 2 and it filled the whole house *w*
4:31 the place *w* they were assembled
7:29 *w* he had two sons.
7:33 for the place *w* you stand
11:11 men stood before the house *w* I
12:12 *w* many were gathered together
14:26 *w* they had been commended to
15:36 every city *w* we have preached
16:13 *w* prayer was customarily made;
17: 1 *w* there was a synagogue of the
20: 6 *w* we stayed seven days.
20: 8 many lamps in the upper room *w*
25:10 *w* I ought to be judged.
27:41 But striking a place *w* two seas
28:14 *w* we found brethren, and were
Rom 3:27 *W* is boasting then
4:15 for *w* there is no law there
5:20 But *w* sin abounded, grace
9:26 the place *w* it was said
15:20 not *w* Christ was named, lest I
1 Cor 1:20 *W* is the wise? Where is the
1:20 *W* is the scribe? Where is the
1:20 *W* is the disputer of this age?
3: 3 For *w* there are envy, strife,
12:17 *w* would be the hearing?
12:17 *w* would be the smelling?
12:19 *w* would the body be?
15:55 *w* is your sting?
15:55 *w* is your victory?"
2 Cor 3:17 and *w* the Spirit of the Lord
Col 3: 1 *w* Christ is, sitting at the
3:11 *w* there is neither Greek nor
Heb 3: 9 *W* your fathers tested Me,
6:20 *w* the forerunner has entered for
9:16 For *w* there is a testament,
10:18 Now *w* there is remission of
11: 8 not knowing *w* he was going.
Jas 3:16 For *w* envy and self-seeking
4: 1 *W* do wars and fights come from
1 Pe 4:18 *W* will the ungodly and
2 Pe 3: 4 *W* is the promise of His coming?
1 Jn 2:11 and does not know *w* he is
Rev 2: 5 Remember therefore from *w* you
2:13 and *w* you dwell, where Satan's
2:13 *w* Satan's throne is.
2:13 among you, *w* Satan dwells.
7:13 and *w* did they come from?"
11: 8 *w* also our Lord was crucified.
12: 6 *w* she has a place prepared by
12:14 *w* she is nourished for a time
17:15 *w* the harlot sits, are peoples,
20:10 lake of fire and brimstone *w*

WHEREAS (17/17)

Deut 28:62 *w* you were as the stars of
Judg 19:16 *w* the men of the place were
1 Sam 24:17 *w* I have rewarded you with
1 Ki 8:18 *W* it was in your heart to build
12:11 *w* my father put a heavy yoke on
2 Chr 6: 8 *W* it was in your heart to build
10:11 *w* my father put a heavy yoke on
Ezra 7:14 And *w* you are being sent by the
7:15 and *w* you are to carry the
7:16 and *w* all the silver and gold
Isa 60:15 *W* you have been forsaken and
Jer 4:10 *W* the sword reaches to the
Ezek 42: 8 *w* that facing the temple was
Dan 2:41 *W* you saw the feet and toes,
Heb 11:29 *w* the Egyptians, attempting
Jas 4:14 *w* you do not know what will
2 Pe 2:11 *w* angels, who are greater in

WHEREBY (1/1)

Ps 68: 9 *W* You confirmed Your

WHEREIN (1/1)

Job 6:24 Cause me to understand *w* I

WHEREUPON (1/1)

Judg 20:39 *w* the men of Israel would turn

WHEREVER (64/62)

Gen 20:13 *w* we go, say of me, "He is my
28:15 will keep you *w* you go,
Lev 13:12 *w* the priest looks,
Deut 2:37 or *w* the LORD our God had
Josh 1: 7 that you may prosper *w* you go.
1: 9 God is with you *w* you go."
1:16 and *w* you send us we will go.
Judg 2:15 *W* they went out, the hand of the
17: 8 stay *w* he could find a place.
Ruth 1:16 For *w* you go, I will go;
1:16 And *w* you lodge, I will lodge;
1 Sam 14:47 *W* he turned, he harassed them.
18: 5 So David went out *w* Saul sent
23:13 from Keilah and went *w* they
2 Sam 7: 7 *W* I have moved about with all
7: 9 And I have been with you *w* you
8: 6 The LORD preserved David *w* he
8:14 the LORD preserved David *w* he
1 Ki 2: 3 in all that you do and *w* you
7:36 *w* there was a clear space on
8:44 *w* You send them, and when they
2 Ki 8: 1 and stay *w* you can; for the
12: 5 *w* any dilapidation is found."
18: 7 he prospered *w* he went.
1 Chr 17: 6 *W* I have moved about with all
17: 8 And I have been with you *w* you
18: 6 So the LORD preserved David *w*
18:13 the LORD preserved David *w* he
2 Chr 6:34 *w* You send them, and when they
Neh 4:20 *W* you hear the sound of the
Esth 8:17 *w* the king's command and decree
Prov 17: 8 *W* he turns, he prospers.
21: 1 He turns it *w* He wishes.
Isa 7:23 That *w* there could be a
20: 6 *w* we flee for help to be
Jer 40: 4 *w* it seems good and convenient
40: 5 Or go *w* it seems convenient for
45: 5 in all places, *w* you go."
Ezek 1:12 they went *w* the spirit wanted
1:20 *W* the spirit wanted to go, they
6:13 *w* they offered sweet incense to
12:16 among the Gentiles *w* they go.
21:16 *W* your edge is ordered!
36:20 *w* they went, they profaned My
36:21 the nations *w* they went.
36:22 the nations *w* you went.
37:21 *w* they have gone, and will
47: 9 *w* the rivers go, will live.
47: 9 and everything will live *w* the
Dan 2:38 and *w* the children of men dwell,
Hos 7:12 *W* they go, I will spread My net
Mt 8:19 I will follow You *w* You go."
24:28 For *w* the carcass is, there the
26:13 *w* this gospel is preached in
Mk 6:55 beds those who were sick to *w*
6:56 *W* He entered into villages,
9:18 And *w* it seizes him, it throws
14: 9 *w* this gospel is preached in
14:14 *W* he goes in, say to the master
Lk 9:57 I will follow You *w* You go."
17:37 *W* the body is, there the eagles
1 Cor 16: 6 on my journey, *w* I go.
Jas 3: 4 by a very small rudder *w* the
Rev 14: 4 who follow the Lamb *w* He goes.

WHET (1/1)

Deut 32:41 If I *w* My glittering sword,

WHETHER (143/130)

Gen 18:21 and see *w* they have done
24:21 silent so as to know *w* the
27:21 *w* you are really my son Esau
31:39 *w* stolen by day or stolen by
37:32 Do you know *w* it is your son's
42:16 to see *w* there is any truth
43: 6 tell the man *w* you had
Ex 4:18 and see *w* they are still
12:19 *w* he is a stranger or a
16: 4 *w* they will walk in My law or
19:13 *w* man or beast, he shall not
21:31 *W* it has gored a son or gored a
22: 4 *w* it is an ox or donkey or
22: 8 to the judges to see *w* he
22: 9 *w* it concerns an ox, a

34:19 livestock, *w* ox or sheep.
Lev 3: 1 *w* male or female, he shall
3: 6 *w* male or female, he shall
5: 1 *w* he has seen or known of the
5: 2 *w* it is the carcass of an
7:10 *w* mixed with oil, or dry,
7:26 *w* of bird or beast.
11: 9 *w* in the seas or in the
11:32 *w* it is any item of wood or
11:35 *w* it is an oven or cooking
12: 6 *w* for a son or a daughter, she
13:47 *w* it is a woolen garment or
13:48 *w* it is in the warp or woof of
13:48 *w* in leather or in anything
13:49 *w* in the warp or in the woof,
13:52 *w* warp or woof, in wool or in
13:55 *w* the damage is outside or
13:56 *w* out of the warp or out of the
15: 3 *w* his body runs with his
16:29 *w* a native of your own country
17:15 *w* he is a native of your own
18: 9 *w* born at home or elsewhere,
22:28 *W* it is a cow or ewe, do not
27:12 *w* it is good or bad; as you,
27:14 *w* it is good or bad; as the
27:26 *w* it is an ox or sheep, it
27:30 *w* of the seed of the land or
27:33 He shall not inquire *w* it is
Num 9:21 *w* by day or by night, whenever
9:22 *W* it was two days, a month,
11:23 Now you shall see *w* what I say
13:18 *w* the people who dwell in it
13:19 *w* the land they dwell in is
13:19 *w* the cities they inhabit are
13:20 *w* the land is rich or poor; and
13:20 and *w* there are forests there
15:30 *w* he is native-born or a
18:15 *w* man or beast, shall be yours;
Deut 4:32 *w* any great thing like this
8: 2 *w* you would keep His
13: 3 God is testing you to know *w*
18: 3 *w* it is bull or sheep: they
24:14 *w* one of your brethren or one
Josh 24:15 *w* the gods which your fathers
Judg 2:22 *w* they will keep the ways of
3: 4 to know *w* they would obey the
18: 5 that we may know *w* the journey
Ruth 3:10 young men, *w* poor or rich.
2 Sam 12:22 Who can tell *w* the LORD will
15:21 *w* in death or life, even there
1 Ki 20:33 to see *w* any sign of mercy
2 Ki 1: 2 *w* I shall recover from this
14:26 and *w* bond or free, there was
2 Chr 14:11 *w* with many or with those who
15:13 *w* small or great, whether man
15:13 or great, *w* man or woman.
19:10 *w* of bloodshed or offenses
Ezra 2:59 *w* they were of Israel:
5:17 *w* it is so that a decree was
7:26 *w* it be death, or banishment,
Neh 7:61 *w* they were of Israel:
Esth 3: 4 to see *w* Mordecai's words would
4:14 Yet who knows *w* you have come
Job 34:29 *W* it is against a nation or
37:13 *W* for correction, Or for His
Prov 20:11 *W* what he does is pure and
29: 9 *W* the fool rages or laughs,
Eccl 2:19 And who knows *w* he will be wise
5:12 *W* he eats little or much;
11: 6 Or *w* both alike will be
12:14 thing, *W* good or evil.
Song 6:11 To see *w* the vine had budded
7:12 *W* the grape blossoms are
Jer 30: 6 *W* a man is ever in labor with
42: 6 *W* it is pleasing or
Ezek 2: 5 *w* they hear or whether they
2: 5 whether they hear or *w* they
2: 7 *w* they hear or whether they
2: 7 whether they hear or *w* they
3:11 *w* they hear, or whether they
3:11 or *w* they refuse."
Mk 3: 2 *w* He would heal him on the
Lk 3:15 *w* he was the Christ or not,
6: 7 *w* He would heal on the Sabbath,
14:28 *w* he has enough to finish it—
14:31 and consider *w* he is able
Jn 7:17 *w* it is from God or whether I
7:17 whether it is from God or *w* I
9:25 *W* He is a sinner or not I do
Acts 4:19 *W* it is right in the sight of
5: 8 Tell me *w* you sold the land for
9: 2 *w* men or women, he might bring
10:18 called and asked *w* Simon,
17:11 daily to find out *w* these
19: 2 *w* there is a Holy Spirit."
25:20 I asked *w* he was willing to go
Rom 6:16 *w* of sin leading to death, or
14: 8 *w* we live or die, we are the
1 Cor 1:16 I do not know *w* I baptized any
3:22 *w* Paul or Apollos or Cephas, or
7:16 *w* you will save your husband?
7:16 *w* you will save your wife?
8: 5 *w* in heaven or on earth
10:31 *w* you eat or drink, or whatever
12:13 *w* Jews or Greeks, whether slaves
12:13 *w* slaves or free—and have all
13: 8 But *w* there are prophecies,
13: 8 *w* there are tongues, they
13: 8 *w* there is knowledge, it will
14: 7 *w* flute or harp, when they make
15:11 *w* it was I or they, so we
2 Cor 2: 9 *w* you are obedient in all
5: 9 *w* present or absent, to be well
5:10 he has done, *w* good or bad.
12: 2 *w* in the body I do not know, or
12: 2 or *w* out of the body I do not
12: 3 *w* in the body or out of the body
13: 5 Examine yourselves as to *w* you
Eph 6: 8 *w* he is a slave or free.
Phil 1:18 *w* in pretense or in truth,
1:20 *w* by life or by death.
1:27 so that *w* I come and see you or
Col 1:16 *w* thrones or dominions or
1:20 *w* things on earth or things in
1 Th 5:10 that *w* we wake or sleep, we
2 Th 2:15 *w* by word or our epistle.
1 Pe 2:13 *w* to the king as supreme,
1 Jn 4: 1 *w* they are of God; because many

WHICH (2908/2594) See APPENDIX

WHICHEVER (1/1)

Zech 14:17 And it shall be that *w* of the

WHILE (319/303)

Gen 8:22 *W* the earth remains, Seedtime
19:16 And *w* he lingered, the men took
25: 6 and *w* he was still living he
29: 9 Now *w* he was still speaking
40: 4 so they were in custody for a *w*.
45: 1 *w* Joseph made himself known
46:29 and wept on his neck a good *w*.
Ex 14:27 *w* the Egyptians were fleeing
33:22 *w* My glory passes by, that I
33:22 will cover you with My hand *w*
34:29 the skin of his face shone *w*
Lev 7:20 *w* he is unclean, that person
14:46 goes into the house at all *w*
18:18 to uncover her nakedness *w* the
22: 3 *w* he has uncleanness upon him,
26:43 and will enjoy its sabbaths *w*
Num 4:20 shall not go in to watch *w* the
5:19 gone astray to uncleanness *w*
5:20 if you have gone astray *w*
5:29 *w* under her husband's
11:33 But *w* the meat was still
15:32 Now *w* the children of Israel
18: 2 with you and serve you *w* you
23:15 burnt offering *w* I meet
24:18 *W* Israel does valiantly.
30: 3 by some agreement *w* in her
30: 6 *w* bound by her vows or by a
32: 6 your brethren go to war *w* you
35:20 *w* lying in wait, hurls
35:23 *w* he was not his enemy or
Deut 5:23 *w* the mountain was burning with
19: 6 *w* his anger is hot, pursue the
20:19 *w* making war against it to take
25: 4 You shall not muzzle an ox *w* it
31:27 *w* I am yet alive with you, you
Josh 6: 9 *w* the priests continued
6:13 *w* the priests continued
10:20 *w* Joshua and the children of
14:10 spoke this word to Moses *w*
Judg 3:26 But Ehud had escaped *w* they
6:11 *w* his son Gideon threshed wheat
8:11 and he attacked the army *w* the
11:26 *W* Israel dwelt in Heshbon and
13:19 a wondrous thing *w* Manoah
14:17 wept on him the seven days *w*
15: 1 After a *w*, in the time of
16:27 women on the roof watching *w*
18: 3 *W* they were at the house of
1 Sam 2:13 fleshhook in his hand *w* the
3: 2 *w* Eli was lying down in his
3: 3 and *w* Samuel was lying down,
14:19 *w* Saul talked to the priest,
20:14 of the LORD *w* I still live,
25: 7 missing from them all the *w*
2 Sam 3: 6 *w* there was war between the
3:35 to persuade David to eat food *w*
7:19 servant's house for a great *w*
11:16 *w* Joab besieged the city, that
12:18 *w* the child was alive, we spoke
12:21 and wept for the child *w* he
12:22 *W* the child was alive, I fasted
13:30 *w* they were on the way, that
15: 8 For your servant took a vow *w* I
15:12 —*w* he offered sacrifices.
17: 2 I will come upon him *w* he is
18:14 *w* he was still alive in the
19:32 the king with supplies *w* he
19:33 provide for you *w* you are
24:13 *w* they pursue you? Or shall
1 Ki 1:14 *w* you are still talking there
1:22 *w* she was still talking with
1:42 *W* he was still speaking, there
1:48 *w* my eyes see it!'"
3:17 and I gave birth *w* she was in
3:20 *w* your maidservant slept, and
6: 7 temple *w* it was being built.
8:14 *w* all the assembly of Israel
12: 6 before his father Solomon *w* he
15:27 *w* Nadab and all Israel laid
17: 7 And it happened after a *w* that
18: 4 *w* Jezebel massacred the
20:27 *w* the Syrians filled the
20:40 *W* your servant was busy here and
22:38 blood *w* the harlots bathed,
2 Ki 2: 7 *w* the two of them stood by the
5:20 *w* not receiving from his hands
6:33 And *w* he was still talking with
11: 3 *w* Athaliah reigned over the
1 Chr 12: 1 to David at Ziklag *w* he was
17:17 servant's house for a great *w*
2 Chr 6: 3 *w* all the assembly of Israel
7: 6 *w* all Israel stood.
10: 6 before his father Solomon *w* he
14: 7 *w* the land is yet before us,
15: 2 The LORD is with you *w* you
22:12 *w* Athaliah reigned over the
26:19 And *w* he was angry with the
34: 3 *w* he was still young, he began
35:11 *w* the Levites skinned the
Ezra 9: 8 And now for a little *w* grace has
10: 1 Now *w* Ezra was praying, and
10: 1 and *w* he was confessing,
Neh 4:16 *w* the other half held the
6: 3 Why should the work cease *w* I
7: 3 and *w* they stand guard, let
8: 6 Amen!" *w* lifting up their
Esth 2:21 *w* Mordecai sat within the
5: 1 *w* the king sat on his royal
6:14 *W* they were still talking with
7: 8 he also assault the queen *w* I
Job 1:16 *W* he was still speaking,
1:17 *W* he was still speaking,
1:18 *W* he was still speaking,
2: 8 to scrape himself *w* he sat
7: 8 *W* your eyes are upon me,
8:12 *W* it is yet green and not cut
20:23 And will rain it on him *w* he
24:24 are exalted for a little *w*,
32:11 *w* you searched out what to say.
33:15 *W* slumbering on their beds,
Ps 7: 2 *w* there is none to deliver.
22: 9 You made Me trust *w* on My
31:13 *W* they take counsel together
37:10 For yet a little *w* and the
39: 1 *W* the wicked are before me."
39: 3 *W* I was musing, the fire
42: 3 *W* they continually say to me,
42:10 *W* they say to me all day long,
49:18 Though *w* he lives he blesses
63: 4 Thus I will bless You *w* I live;
69: 3 My eyes fail *w* I wait for my
78:30 But *w* their food was still in
104:33 will sing praise to my God *w* I
141:10 *W* I escape safely.
146: 2 *W* I live I will praise the
146: 2 will sing praises to my God *w*
Prov 8:26 *W* as yet He had not made the
19:18 Chasten your son *w* there is
31:15 She also rises *w* it is yet
Eccl 2: 3 *w* guiding my heart with wisdom,
9: 3 in their hearts *w* they live,
10: 6 *W* the rich sit in a lowly
10: 7 *W* princes walk on the ground
12: 2 *W* the sun and the light,
Song 1:12 *W* the king is at his table,
Isa 10:25 For yet a very little *w* and the
28: 4 He eats it up *w* it is still in
29:17 it not yet a very little *w*
55: 6 Seek the LORD *w* He may be
55: 6 Call upon Him *w* He is near.
57: 1 *W* no one considers That the
63:18 possessed it but a little *w*;
65:24 And *w* they are still speaking,
Jer 13:16 And *w* you are looking for
15: 9 Her sun has gone down *W* it
17: 2 *W* their children remember
33: 1 *w* he was still shut up in the
39:15 to Jeremiah *w* he was shut up
40: 5 Now *w* Jeremiah had not yet gone
51:33 Yet a little *w* And the time
Lam 1:19 *W* they sought food To restore
Ezek 9: 8 that *w* they were killing them,
11:13 *w* I was prophesying, that
21:29 *W* they see false visions for
21:29 *W* they divine a lie to you,
43: 6 *w* a man stood beside me.
44:17 no wool shall come upon them *w*
Dan 2:29 came to your mind *w* on your
2:34 You watched *w* a stone was cut
4:10 the visions of my head *w* on
4:13 in the visions of my head *w* on
4:31 *W* the word was still in the
5: 2 *W* he tasted the wine, Belshazzar
7: 1 and visions of his head *w* on
8: 2 and it so happened *w* I was
9:20 Now *w* I was speaking, praying,
9:21 *w* I was speaking in prayer,
10: 9 and *w* I heard the sound of his
10:11 *W* he was speaking this word
11:28 *W* returning to his land with
Hos 1: 4 For in a little *w* I will
7: 6 *W* they lie in wait; Their
Mic 3: 5 Peace" *W* they chew with their
Nah 1:10 For *w* tangled like thorns,
1:10 And *w* drunken like drunkards,
Hag 1: 9 *w* every one of you runs to his
2: 6 'Once more (it is a little *w*)
Zech 14:12 shall dissolve *w* they stand
Mal 1: 9 *W* this is being done by your
Mt 1:20 But *w* he thought about these
5:25 *w* you are on the way with him,
9:18 *W* He spoke these things to
12:46 *W* He was still talking to the
13:21 but endures only for a *w*.
13:25 but *w* men slept, his enemy came
13:29 lest *w* you gather up the tares
14:22 *w* He sent the multitudes away.
17: 5 *W* he was still speaking, behold,
17:22 Now *w* they were staying in

22:41 **W** the Pharisees were gathered
25: 5 But **w** the bridegroom was
25:10 And **w** they went to buy, the
26:36 Sit here **w** I go and pray over
26:47 And **w** He was still speaking,
27:12 And **w** He was being accused by
27:19 **W** he was sitting on the judgment
27:63 **w** He was still alive, how that
28:11 Now **w** they were going, behold,
28:13 at night and stole Him away **w**
Mk 1:35 having risen a long **w** before
2:19 of the bridegroom fast **w** the
5:35 **W** He was still speaking, some
6:31 a deserted place and rest a **w**.
6:45 **w** He sent the multitude away.
12:35 **w** He taught in the temple,
14:32 Sit here **w** I pray."
14:43 **w** He was still speaking, Judas,
Lk 1: 8 that **w** he was serving as priest
2: 2 This census first took place **w**
2: 6 that **w** they were there, the
3: 2 **w** Annas and Caiaphas were high
3:21 and **w** He prayed, the heaven was
5:34 of the bridegroom fast **w** the
8:13 who believe for a **w** and in time
8:49 **W** He was still speaking, someone
9:34 **W** he was saying this, a cloud
9:43 But **w** everyone marveled at all
11:29 And **w** the crowds were thickly
14:32 **w** the other is still a great
18: 4 "And he would not for a **w**;
22:47 And **w** He was still speaking,
22:58 And after a little **w** another saw
22:60 **w** he was still speaking, the
24:15 **w** they conversed and reasoned,
24:32 not our heart burn within us **w**
24:32 and **w** He opened the Scriptures
24:41 But **w** they still did not believe
24:44 words which I spoke to you **w** I
24:51 **w** He blessed them, that He was
Jn 5: 7 but **w** I am coming, another
7: 4 does anything in secret **w** he
7:33 shall be with you a little **w**
9: 4 Him who sent Me **w** it is day;
12:35 A little **w** longer the light is
12:35 Walk **w** you have the light, lest
12:36 **W** you have the light, believe in
13:33 I shall be with you a little **w**
14:19 A little **w** longer and the world
14:25 things I have spoken to you **w**
16:16 A little **w**, and you will not
16:16 see Me; and again a little **w**,
16:17 that He says to us, 'A little **w**,
16:17 see Me; and again a little **w**,
16:18 this that He says, 'A little **w**'?
16:19 about what I said, 'A little **w**,
16:19 see Me; and again a little **w**,
17:12 **W** I was with them in the world,
20: 1 **w** it was still dark, and saw
Acts 1: 9 **w** they watched, He was taken
1:10 And **w** they looked steadfastly
5: 4 **W** it remained, was it not your
5:34 apostles outside for a little **w**.
9:39 which Dorcas had made **w** she
10:10 but **w** they made ready, he fell
10:17 Now **w** Peter wondered within
10:19 **W** Peter thought about the
10:44 **W** Peter was still speaking
15: 7 you know that a good **w** ago God
17:16 Now **w** Paul waited for them at
17:32 **w** others said, "We will hear
18:18 Paul still remained a good **w**.
19: 1 **w** Apollos was at Corinth, that
20:11 and eaten, and talked a long **w**,
24:20 found any wrongdoing in me **w** I
25: 3 **w** they lay in ambush along the
25: 8 **w** he answered for himself,
26:12 **W** thus occupied, as I journeyed
Rom 4:10 **W** he was circumcised, or
4:10 Not **w** circumcised, but while
4:10 but **w** uncircumcised.
4:11 of the faith which he had **w**
4:12 our father Abraham had **w**
5: 8 in that **w** we were still
7: 3 **w** her husband lives, she
15:24 may enjoy your company for a **w**.
1 Cor 7:18 Was anyone called **w** circumcised?
7:18 Was anyone called **w**
7:21 Were you called **w** a slave?
7:22 who is called in the Lord **w** a
7:22 he who is called **w** free
9: 9 shall not muzzle an ox **w**
16: 7 but I hope to stay a **w** with
2 Cor 4:18 **w** we do not look at the things
5: 6 knowing that **w** we are at home
7: 8 you sorry, though only for a **w**.
9:11 **w** you are enriched in
9:13 **w**, through the proof of this
Gal 2:17 **w** we seek to be justified by
6: 9 And let us not grow weary **w**
1 Tim 5: 6 pleasure is dead **w** she lives.
5:18 shall not muzzle an ox **w**
Phm 1:10 whom I have begotten **w** in my
1:15 For perhaps he departed for a **w**
Heb 3:13 **w** it is called "Today," lest
3:15 **w** it is said: "Today, if
9: 8 was not yet made manifest **w** the
9:17 it has no power at all **w** the
10:33 partly **w** you were made a
10:33 and partly **w** you became
10:37 "For yet a little **w**,
1 Pe 1: 6 though now for a little **w**,
3:20 **w** the ark was being prepared,
5:10 after you have suffered a **w**,
2 Pe 2:13 in their own deceptions **w** they
2:19 **W** they promise them liberty,
Jude 3 **w** I was very diligent to write
12 **w** they feast with you without
Rev 6:11 they should rest a little **w**
20: 3 must be released for a little **w**.

WHIP (3/3) WHIPS

Prov 26: 3 A **w** for the horse, A bridle
Nah 3: 2 The noise of a **w** And the noise
Jn 2:15 When He had made a **w** of cords,

WHIPS (4/4) WHIP

1 Ki 12:11 my father chastised you with **w**,
12:14 my father chastised you with **w**,
2 Chr 10:11 my father chastised you with **w**,
10:14 my father chastised you with **w**,

WHIRLING (3/3)

2 Sam 6:16 saw King David leaping and **w**
1 Chr 15:29 a window and saw King David **w**
Ps 83:13 make them like the **w** dust,

WHIRLS (1/1)

Eccl 1: 6 The wind **w** about continually,

WHIRLWIND (27/25)

2 Ki 2: 1 up Elijah into heaven by a **w**,
2:11 and Elijah went up by a **w** into
Job 37: 9 of the south comes the **w**,
38: 1 LORD answered Job out of the **w**,
40: 6 LORD answered Job out of the **w**,
Ps 58: 9 take them away as with a **w**,
77:18 of Your thunder was in the **w**;
Prov 1:27 your destruction comes like a **w**,
10:25 When the **w** passes by, the
Isa 5:28 And their wheels like a **w**.
17:13 a rolling thing before the **w**.
40:24 And the **w** will take them away
41:16 And the **w** shall scatter them;
66:15 with His chariots, like a **w**,
Jer 4:13 And his chariots like a **w**.
23:19 a **w** of the LORD has gone forth
23:19 A violent **w**! It will fall
25:32 And a great **w** shall be raised
30:23 the **w** of the LORD Goes forth
30:23 with fury, A continuing **w**;
Ezek 1: 4 a **w** was coming out of the
Dan 11:40 shall come against him like a **w**,
Hos 8: 7 sow the wind, And reap the **w**.
Am 1:14 a tempest in the day of the **w**.
Nah 1: 3 LORD has His way In the **w**
Hab 3:14 They came out like a **w** to
Zech 7:14 But I scattered them with a **w**

WHIRLWINDS (2/2)

Isa 21: 1 As **w** in the South pass through,
Zech 9:14 And go with **w** from the south.

WHISPER (5/5) WHISPERING

Job 4:12 And my ear received a **w** of it.
26:14 And how small a **w** we hear of
Ps 41: 7 All who hate me **w** together
Isa 8:19 who **w** and mutter," should not
29: 4 And your speech shall **w** out of

WHISPERER (1/1)

Prov 16:28 And a **w** separates the best of

WHISPERERS (1/1)

Rom 1:29 evil-mindedness; they are **w**,

WHISPERING (2/2) WHISPER

2 Sam 12:19 saw that his servants were **w**,
Lam 3:62 lips of my enemies And their **w**

WHISPERINGS (1/1)

2 Cor 12:20 ambitions, backbitings, **w**,

WHISTLE (3/3)

Isa 5:26 And will **w** to them from the
7:18 day That the LORD will **w**
Zech 10: 8 I will **w** for them and gather

WHIT (KJV) See (NOT AT) ALL, COMPLETELY, EVERYTHING

WHITE (71/64) WHITEN, WHITER, WHITEWASHED

Gen 30:35 every one that had some **w** in
30:37 peeled **w** strips in them, and
30:37 and exposed the **w** which was in
40:16 and there were three **w** baskets
Ex 16:31 And it was like **w** coriander
Lev 11:18 the **w** owl, the jackdaw, and the
13: 3 hair on the sore has turned **w**,
13: 4 But if the bright spot is **w** on
13: 4 and its hair has not turned **w**,
13:10 the swelling on the skin is **w**,
13:10 and it has turned the hair **w**,
13:13 It has all turned **w**.
13:16 raw flesh changes and turns **w**
13:17 if the sore has turned **w**,
13:19 boil there comes a **w** swelling
13:20 skin, and its hair has turned **w**,
13:21 indeed there are no **w** hairs
13:24 bright spot, reddish-white or **w**,
13:25 of the bright spot has turned **w**,
13:26 indeed there are no **w** hairs
13:38 specifically **w** bright spots,
13:39 skin of the body are dull **w**,
13:39 it is a **w** spot that grows on
Num 12:10 became leprous, as **w** as snow.
Deut 14:16 the screech owl, the **w** owl,
Judg 5:10 you who ride on **w** donkeys,
2 Ki 5:27 leprous, as **w** as snow.
2 Chr 5:12 clothed in **w** linen, having
Esth 1: 6 There were **w** and blue linen
1: 6 and **w** and black marble.
8:15 in royal apparel of blue and **w**,
Job 6: 6 taste in the **w** of an egg?
41:32 think the deep had **w** hair.
Ps 68:14 It was **w** as snow in Zalmon.
Eccl 9: 8 Let your garments always be **w**,
Song 5:10 My beloved is **w** and ruddy,
Isa 1:18 They shall be as **w** as snow;
Ezek 27:18 of Helbon and with **w** wool.
Dan 7: 9 His garment was **w** as snow,
11:35 purify them, and make them **w**,
12:10 shall be purified, made **w**,
Joel 1: 7 Its branches are made **w**.
Zech 1: 8 horses: red, sorrel, and **w**.
6: 3 with the third chariot **w** horses,
6: 6 the **w** are going after them, and
Mt 5:36 you cannot make one hair **w** or
17: 2 and His clothes became as **w** as
28: 3 and his clothing as **w** as snow.
Mk 9: 3 became shining, exceedingly **w**,
16: 5 man clothed in a long **w** robe
Lk 9:29 and His robe became **w** and
Jn 4:35 for they are already **w** for
20:12 And she saw two angels in **w**
Acts 1:10 stood by them in **w** apparel,
Rev 1:14 His head and hair were **w** like
1:14 as **w** as snow, and His eyes like
2:17 And I will give him a **w** stone,
3: 4 they shall walk with Me in **w**,
3: 5 shall be clothed in **w** garments,
3:18 and **w** garments, that you may be
4: 4 clothed in **w** robes; and they
6: 2 a **w** horse. He who sat on it had
6:11 Then a **w** robe was given to each
7: 9 clothed with **w** robes, with palm
7:13 these arrayed in **w** robes,
7:14 their robes and made them **w** in
14:14 a **w** cloud, and on the cloud sat
19:11 a **w** horse. And He who sat on
19:14 **w** and clean, followed Him on
19:14 followed Him on **w** horses.
20:11 Then I saw a great **w** throne and

WHITEN (1/1) WHITE

Mk 9: 3 as no launderer on earth can **w**

WHITER (3/3) WHITE

Gen 49:12 And his teeth **w** than milk.
Ps 51: 7 and I shall be **w** than snow.
Lam 4: 7 than snow And **w** than milk;

WHITEWASH (2/2)

Deut 27: 2 and **w** them with lime.
27: 4 and you shall **w** them with lime.

WHITEWASHED (2/2) WHITE

Mt 23:27 For you are like **w** tombs
Acts 23: 3 you **w** wall! For you sit to

WHITHER (KJV) See WHERE

WHITHERSOEVER (KJV) See WHEREVER

WHO (6045/4885) See APPENDIX

WHOEVER (255/225)

Gen 4:15 **w** kills Cain, vengeance shall
9: 6 **W** sheds man's blood, By man his
Ex 12:15 For **w** eats leavened bread from
12:19 since **w** eats what is leavened,
19:12 **W** touches the mountain shall
22:19 **W** lies with an animal shall
30:33 **W** compounds any like it, or
30:33 or **w** puts any of it on an
30:38 **W** makes any like it, to smell
31:14 for **w** does any work on it,
31:15 **W** does any work on the Sabbath
32:24 **W** has any gold, let them break
32:26 **W** is on the LORD's side—come
32:33 **W** has sinned against Me, I will
35: 2 **W** does any work on it shall be
35: 5 **W** is of a willing heart, let
Lev 7:25 For **w** eats the fat of the animal
7:27 **W** eats any blood, that person
11:24 **w** touches the carcass of any of
11:25 **w** carries part of the carcass of

	11:27	***W*** touches any such carcass
	11:28	***W*** carries any such carcass
	11:31	***W*** touches them when they are
	15: 5	And ***w*** touches his bed shall wash
	15:10	***W*** touches anything that was
	15:19	and ***w*** touches her shall be
	15:21	***W*** touches her bed shall wash his
	15:22	And ***w*** touches anything that she
	15:27	***W*** touches those things shall be
	17:14	***W*** eats it shall be cut off.'
	18:29	For ***w*** commits any of these
	19:20	***W*** lies carnally with a woman who
	20: 2	***W*** of the children of Israel, or
	22: 3	***W*** of all your descendants
	22: 4	And ***w*** touches anything made
	22: 5	or ***w*** touches any creeping thing
	22:21	And ***w*** offers a sacrifice of a
	24:15	***W*** curses his God shall bear his
	24:16	And ***w*** blasphemes the name of the
	24:17	***W*** kills any man shall surely be
	24:18	***W*** kills an animal shall make it
	24:21	And ***w*** kills an animal shall
	24:21	but ***w*** kills a man shall be put
Num	5: 2	and ***w*** becomes defiled by a
	15:14	or ***w*** is among you throughout
	17:13	***W*** even comes near the tabernacle
	19:13	***W*** touches the body of anyone who
	19:16	***W*** in the open field touches one
	31:19	***w*** has killed any person, and
	31:19	and ***w*** has touched any slain,
	35:30	***W*** kills a person, the murderer
Deut	17: 6	***W*** is deserving of death shall be
	18:19	And it shall be that ***w*** will not
	19: 4	***W*** kills his neighbor
Josh	1:18	***W*** rebels against your command
	2:19	So it shall be that ***w*** goes
	2:19	And ***w*** is with you in the house,
	20: 9	that ***w*** killed a person
Judg	1:12	***W*** attacks Kirjath Sepher and
	7: 3	***W*** is fearful and afraid, let
	20:42	and ***w*** came out of the cities
1 Sam	11: 7	***W*** does not go out with Saul and
2 Sam	5: 8	***W*** climbs up by way of the water
	14:10	***W*** says anything to you, bring
	17: 9	that ***w*** hears it will say,
	20:11	***W*** favors Joab and whoever is
	20:11	Whoever favors Joab and ***w*** is
1 Ki	13:33	***w*** wished, he consecrated him,
	14:11	The dogs shall eat ***w*** belongs to
	14:11	of the air shall eat ***w*** dies
	16: 4	The dogs shall eat ***w*** belongs to
	16: 4	of the air shall eat ***w*** dies
	19:17	It shall be that ***w*** escapes the
	19:17	and ***w*** escapes the sword of
	21:24	The dogs shall eat ***w*** belongs to
	21:24	of the air shall eat ***w*** dies
2 Ki	10:19	***W*** is missing shall not live."
	10:24	***w*** lets him escape, it
	11: 8	and ***w*** comes within range, let
	11:15	and slay with the sword ***w***
	21:12	that ***w*** hears of it, both his
1 Chr	11: 6	***W*** attacks the Jebusites first
	29: 8	And ***w*** had precious stones gave
2 Chr	13: 9	so that ***w*** comes to consecrate
	15:13	and ***w*** would not seek the LORD
	23: 7	and ***w*** comes into the house, let
	23:14	and slay with the sword ***w***
Ezra	1: 4	And ***w*** is left in any place where
	6:11	that ***w*** alters this edict,
	7:26	***W*** will not observe the law of
	10: 8	and that ***w*** would not come within
Ps	50:23	***W*** offers praise glorifies Me
	101: 5	***W*** secretly slanders his
	107:43	***W*** is wise will observe these
Prov	1:33	But ***w*** listens to me will dwell
	6:29	***W*** touches her shall not be
	6:32	***W*** commits adultery with a woman
	8:35	For ***w*** finds me finds life,
	9: 4	***W*** is simple, let him turn in
	9:16	***W*** is simple, let him turn in
	10:18	***W*** hides hatred has lying
	10:18	And ***w*** spreads slander is a
	12: 1	***W*** loves instruction loves
	16:20	And ***w*** trusts in the LORD,
	17:13	***W*** rewards evil for good, Evil
	20: 1	And ***w*** is led astray by it is
	20: 2	***W*** provokes him to anger sins
	20:20	***W*** curses his father or his
	21:13	***W*** shuts his ears to the cry of
	21:23	***W*** guards his mouth and tongue
	25:14	***W*** falsely boasts of giving
	25:28	***W*** has no rule over his own
	26:27	***W*** digs a pit will fall into it,
	27:16	***W*** restrains her restrains the
	27:18	***W*** keeps the fig tree will eat
	28: 7	***W*** keeps the law is a
	28:10	***W*** causes the upright to go
	28:13	But ***w*** confesses and forsakes
	28:18	***W*** walks blamelessly will be
	28:24	***W*** robs his father or his
	28:26	But ***w*** walks wisely will be
	29: 3	***W*** loves wisdom makes his father
	29:24	***W*** is a partner with a thief
	29:25	But ***w*** trusts in the LORD
Eccl	10: 8	And ***w*** breaks through a wall
Isa	28:16	***W*** believes will not act
	35: 8	***W*** walks the road, although a
	40:20	***W*** is too impoverished for
	54:15	***W*** assembles against you shall
	59: 8	***W*** takes that way shall not
Jer	19: 3	that ***w*** hears of it, his ears
Ezek	7:15	***W*** is in the field Will die
	7:15	And ***w*** is in the city, Famine
	33: 4	then ***w*** hears the sound of the
	46: 9	***w*** enters by way of the north
	46: 9	and ***w*** enters by way of the
Dan	3: 6	and ***w*** does not fall down and
	3:11	and ***w*** does not fall down and
	5: 7	***W*** reads this writing, and tells
	6: 7	that ***w*** petitions any god or man
Joel	2:32	That ***w*** calls on the name of
Zech	8:10	no peace from the enemy for ***w***
Mt	5:19	***W*** therefore breaks one of the
	5:19	but ***w*** does and teaches them,
	5:21	and ***w*** murders will be in danger
	5:22	But I say to you that ***w*** is angry
	5:22	And ***w*** says to his brother,
	5:22	But ***w*** says, 'You fool!' shall
	5:28	But I say to you that ***w*** looks at
	5:31	***W*** divorces his wife, let him
	5:32	But I say to you that ***w*** divorces
	5:32	and ***w*** marries a woman who is
	5:39	But ***w*** slaps you on your right
	5:41	And ***w*** compels you to go one
	7:24	Therefore ***w*** hears these sayings
	10:14	And ***w*** will not receive you nor
	10:32	Therefore ***w*** confesses Me before
	10:33	But ***w*** denies Me before men, him
	10:42	And ***w*** gives one of these little
	12:32	but ***w*** speaks against the Holy
	12:50	For ***w*** does the will of My Father
	13:12	For ***w*** has, to him more will be
	13:12	but ***w*** does not have, even what
	15: 5	***W*** says to his father or mother,
	16:25	For ***w*** desires to save his life
	16:25	but ***w*** loses his life for My
	18: 4	Therefore ***w*** humbles himself as
	18: 5	***W*** receives one little child like
	18: 6	But ***w*** causes one of these
	19: 9	***w*** divorces his wife, except for
	19: 9	and ***w*** marries her who is
	20:26	but ***w*** desires to become great
	20:27	And ***w*** desires to be first among
	21:44	And ***w*** falls on this stone will
	23:12	And ***w*** exalts himself will be
	23:16	***W*** swears by the temple, it is
	23:16	but ***w*** swears by the gold of the
	23:18	***W*** swears by the altar, it is
	23:18	but ***w*** swears by the gift that
	24:15	in the holy place" (***w*** reads,
Mk	3:35	For ***w*** does the will of God is My
	4:25	For ***w*** has, to him more will be
	4:25	but ***w*** does not have, even what
	6:11	And ***w*** will not receive you nor
	8:34	***W*** desires to come after Me, let
	8:35	For ***w*** desires to save his life
	8:35	but ***w*** loses his life for My
	8:38	For ***w*** is ashamed of Me and My
	9:37	***W*** receives one of these little
	9:37	and ***w*** receives Me, receives not
	9:41	For ***w*** gives you a cup of water
	9:42	But ***w*** causes one of these
	10:11	***W*** divorces his wife and marries
	10:15	***w*** does not receive the kingdom
	10:43	but ***w*** desires to become great
	10:44	And ***w*** of you desires to be first
	11:23	***w*** says to this mountain, 'Be
Lk	6:47	***W*** comes to Me, and hears My
	8:18	For ***w*** has, to him more will be
	8:18	and ***w*** does not have, even what
	9: 5	And ***w*** will not receive you, when
	9:24	For ***w*** desires to save his life
	9:24	but ***w*** loses his life for My
	9:26	For ***w*** is ashamed of Me and My
	9:48	***W*** receives this little child in
	9:48	and ***w*** receives Me receives Him
	12: 8	***w*** confesses Me before men, him
	14:11	For ***w*** exalts himself will be
	14:27	And ***w*** does not bear his cross
	14:33	***w*** of you does not forsake all
	16:18	***W*** divorces his wife and marries
	16:18	and ***w*** marries her who is
	17:33	***W*** seeks to save his life will
	17:33	and ***w*** loses his life will
	18:17	***w*** does not receive the kingdom
	20:18	***W*** falls on that stone will be
Jn	3:15	that ***w*** believes in Him should
	3:16	that ***w*** believes in Him should
	4:13	***W*** drinks of this water will
	4:14	but ***w*** drinks of the water that I
	5: 4	then ***w*** stepped in first, after
	6:54	***W*** eats My flesh and drinks My
	8:34	***w*** commits sin is a slave of
	11:26	And ***w*** lives and believes in Me
	12:46	that ***w*** believes in Me should
	16: 2	the time is coming that ***w*** kills
	19:12	***W*** makes himself a king speaks
Acts	2:21	***w*** calls on the name
	10:35	But in every nation ***w*** fears Him
	10:43	***w*** believes in Him will receive
Rom	2: 1	***w*** you are who judge, for in
	9:33	And ***w*** believes on Him
	10:11	***W*** believes on Him will not
	10:13	***w*** calls on the name of the
	13: 2	Therefore ***w*** resists the
1 Cor	11:27	Therefore ***w*** eats this bread or
Gal	5:10	bear his judgment, ***w*** he is.
Jas	2:10	For ***w*** shall keep the whole law,
	4: 4	***W*** therefore wants to be a
1 Jn	2: 5	But ***w*** keeps His word, truly the
	2:23	***W*** denies the Son does not have
	3: 4	***W*** commits sin also commits
	3: 6	***W*** abides in Him does not sin.
	3: 6	***W*** sins has neither seen Him nor
	3: 9	***W*** has been born of God does not
	3:10	***W*** does not practice
	3:15	***W*** hates his brother is a
	3:17	But ***w*** has this world's goods,
	4:15	***W*** confesses that Jesus is the
	5: 1	***W*** believes that Jesus is the
	5:18	We know that ***w*** is born of God
2 Jn	9	***W*** transgresses and does not
Rev	14:11	and ***w*** receives the mark of his
	22:15	and ***w*** loves and practices a
	22:17	***W*** desires, let him take the

WHOLE (237/232) WHOLE-HEARTED, WHOLLY

Gen	2: 6	watered the ***w*** face of the
	2:11	one which skirts the ***w*** land
	2:13	which goes around the ***w*** land
	7:19	hills under the ***w*** heaven
	8: 9	the face of the ***w*** earth.
	9:19	and from these the ***w*** earth was
	11: 1	Now the ***w*** earth had one language
	11: 4	over the face of the ***w*** earth."
	13: 9	Is not the ***w*** land before you?
Ex	9:25	struck throughout the ***w*** land
	10:15	the face of the ***w*** earth,
	12: 6	Then the ***w*** assembly of the
	16: 2	Then the ***w*** congregation of the
	16: 3	to kill this ***w*** assembly with
	16:10	to the ***w*** congregation
	19:18	and the ***w*** mountain quaked
	29:18	And you shall burn the ***w*** ram on
Lev	3: 9	its fat and the ***w*** fat tail
	4:12	the ***w*** bull he shall carry
	4:13	Now if the ***w*** congregation of
	8:21	And Moses burned the ***w*** ram on
	10: 6	the ***w*** house of Israel, bewail
	25:29	redeem it within a ***w*** year
Num	3: 7	needs of the ***w*** congregation
	8: 9	together the ***w*** congregation
	11: 6	but now our ***w*** being is dried
	11:20	but for a ***w*** month, until it
	11:21	may eat for a ***w*** month.'
	14: 2	and the ***w*** congregation said to
	15:24	that the ***w*** congregation shall
	15:25	for the ***w*** congregation of the
	15:26	forgiven the ***w*** congregation
	20: 1	the ***w*** congregation, came into
	20:22	the ***w*** congregation, journeyed
Deut	2:25	nations under the ***w*** heaven,
	4:19	peoples under the ***w*** heaven
	27: 6	You shall build with ***w*** stones
	29:23	The ***w*** land is brimstone, salt,
	33:10	And a ***w*** burnt sacrifice on
Josh	3:15	banks during the ***w*** time
	8:31	an altar of ***w*** stones over which
	10:13	to go down for about a ***w*** day.
	11:23	So Joshua took the ***w*** land,
	18: 1	Now the ***w*** congregation of the
	22:12	the ***w*** congregation of the
	22:16	Thus says the ***w*** congregation of
	22:18	angry with the ***w*** congregation
Judg	7:14	Midian and the ***w*** camp."
	7:18	on every side of the ***w*** camp,
	7:21	and the ***w*** army ran and cried
	7:22	throughout the ***w*** camp;
	8:12	and routed the ***w*** army.
	19: 2	and was there four ***w*** months.
	20:37	and struck the ***w*** city with
	20:40	and there was the ***w*** city going
	21:13	Then the ***w*** congregation sent
1 Sam	7: 9	as a ***w*** burnt offering to
2 Sam	3:19	good to Israel and the ***w*** house
	6:19	among the ***w*** multitude of
	14: 7	And now the ***w*** family has risen
	18: 8	face of the ***w*** countryside,
1 Ki	6:22	The ***w*** temple he overlaid with
	8:14	and blessed the ***w*** assembly
	11:13	not tear away the ***w*** kingdom;
	11:34	not take the ***w*** kingdom
	12: 3	Jeroboam and the ***w*** assembly
2 Ki	9: 8	For the ***w*** house of Ahab shall
2 Chr	6: 3	and blessed the ***w*** assembly
	16: 9	and fro throughout the ***w*** earth,
	30:23	Then the ***w*** assembly agreed to
	30:25	The ***w*** assembly of Judah
	31:18	the ***w*** company of them—for in
	33: 8	according to the ***w*** law and the
Ezra	2:64	The ***w*** assembly together was
Neh	7:66	Altogether the ***w*** assembly was
	8:17	So the ***w*** assembly of those who
Esth	3: 6	throughout the ***w*** kingdom
Job	5:18	wounds, but His hands make ***w***.
	28:24	And sees under the ***w*** heavens,
	34:13	Him over the ***w*** world?
	37: 3	forth under the ***w*** heaven,
	37:12	the face of the ***w*** earth.
Ps	9: 1	with my ***w*** heart; I will tell
	48: 2	The joy of the ***w*** earth, Is
	51:19	offering and ***w*** burnt offering;
	72:19	And let the ***w*** earth be
	97: 5	of the Lord of the ***w*** earth.
	111: 1	the LORD with my ***w*** heart,
	119: 2	Who seek Him with the ***w*** heart!
	119:10	With my ***w*** heart I have sought
	119:34	observe it with my ***w*** heart.
	119:58	Your favor with my ***w*** heart;
	119:69	precepts with my ***w*** heart.
	119:145	I cry out with my ***w*** heart;
	138: 1	praise You with my ***w*** heart;
Prov	1:12	them alive like Sheol, And ***w***,
Eccl	12:13	the conclusion of the ***w*** matter:

Isa 1: 5 The *w* head is sick, And the
1: 5 And the *w* heart faints.
3: 1 The *w* supply of bread and the
3: 1 and the *w* supply of water;
6: 3 The *w* earth is full of His
13: 5 To destroy the *w* land.
14: 7 The *w* earth is at rest and
14:26 purposed against the *w* earth,
28:22 even upon the *w* earth.
29:11 The *w* vision has become to you
54: 5 the God of the *w* earth.
Jer 1:18 against the *w* land—Against
3:10 turned to Me with her *w* heart,
4:20 For the *w* land is plundered.
4:27 The *w* land shall be desolate;
4:29 The *w* city shall flee from the
7:15 the *w* posterity of Ephraim.
8:16 The *w* land trembled at the
12:11 The *w* land is made desolate,
13:11 so I have caused the *w* house of
13:11 and the *w* house of Judah
15:10 contention to the *w* earth!
19:11 which cannot be made *w* again;
24: 7 to Me with their *w* heart.
25:11 And this *w* land shall be a
31:40 And the *w* valley of the dead
35: 3 and the *w* house of the
37:10 you had defeated the *w* army
45: 4 pluck up, that is, this *w* land.
50:23 How the hammer of the *w* earth
51:41 how the praise of the *w* earth
51:47 Her *w* land shall be ashamed,
Lam 2:15 The joy of the *w* earth'?"
Ezek 7:12 is on their *w* multitude.
7:13 concerns the *w* multitude,
10:12 And their *w* body, with their
15: 5 "Indeed, when it was *w*,
32: 4 the beasts of the *w* earth.
34: 6 scattered over the *w* face of
35:14 The *w* earth will rejoice when I
37:11 these bones are the *w* house of
39:25 and have mercy on the *w* house
43:11 they may keep its *w* design
43:12 The *w* area surrounding the
45: 6 it shall belong to the *w* house
Dan 2:35 and filled the *w* earth.
2:48 ruler over the *w* province
6: 1 to be over the *w* kingdom;
6: 3 setting him over the *w* realm.
7:23 And shall devour the *w* earth,
7:27 kingdoms under the *w* heaven,
8: 5 the surface of the *w* earth,
9:12 for under the *w* heaven such has
10: 3 till three *w* weeks were
11:17 the strength of his *w* kingdom,
Am 1: 6 took captive the *w* captivity
1: 9 delivered up the *w* captivity
3: 1 against the *w* family which I
Mic 4:13 to the Lord of the *w* earth."
Zeph 1:18 But the *w* land shall be
Zech 4:10 throughout the *w* earth."
4:14 the Lord of the *w* earth."
5: 3 goes out over the face of the *w*
Mal 3: 9 Even this *w* nation.
Mt 5:29 than for your *w* body to be cast
5:30 than for your *w* body to be cast
6:22 your *w* body will be full of
6:23 your *w* body will be full of
8:32 And suddenly the *w* herd of
8:34 the *w* city came out to meet
12:13 and it was restored as *w* as the
13: 2 and the *w* multitude stood on
15:31 speaking, the maimed made *w*,
16:26 if he gains the *w* world,
26:13 is preached in the *w* world,
27:27 and gathered the *w* garrison
Mk 1:33 And the *w* city was gathered
3: 5 and his hand was restored as *w*
4: 1 and the *w* multitude was on the
5:33 and told Him the *w* truth.
6:55 ran through that *w* surrounding
8:36 a man if he gains the *w* world,
12:33 is more than all the *w* burnt
12:44 her *w* livelihood."
14: 9 is preached in the *w* world,
15: 1 scribes and the *w* council;
15:16 together the *w* garrison.
15:33 was darkness over the *w* land
Lk 1:10 And the *w* multitude of the
6:10 and his hand was restored as *w*
6:19 And the *w* multitude sought to
8:37 Then the *w* multitude of the
8:39 throughout the *w* city what
9:25 if he gains the *w* world,
11:34 your *w* body also is full of
11:36 If then your *w* body is full of
11:36 the *w* body will be full of
19:37 the *w* multitude of the
21:35 on the face of the *w* earth.
23: 1 Then the *w* multitude of them
23:48 And the *w* crowd who came
Jn 4:53 and his *w* household.
11:50 and not that the *w* nation
Acts 2: 2 and it filled the *w* house where
4:10 man stands here before you *w*.
6: 5 pleased the *w* multitude.
11:26 So it was that for a *w* year
13:44 Sabbath almost the *w* city
15:22 with the *w* church, to send
19:29 So the *w* city was filled with
20:27 declare to you the *w* counsel
21:27 stirred up the *w* crowd and laid
25:24 man about whom the *w* assembly
28:30 Then Paul dwelt two *w* years in
Rom 1: 8 of throughout the *w* world.
8:22 For we know that the *w* creation
16:23 the host of the *w* church,
1 Cor 5: 6 leaven leavens the *w* lump?
12:17 If the *w* body were an eye,
12:17 If the *w* were hearing, where
14:23 Therefore if the *w* church comes
Gal 5: 3 a debtor to keep the *w* law.
5: 9 leaven leavens the *w* lump.
Eph 2:21 in whom the *w* building, being
3:15 from whom the *w* family in heaven
4:16 from whom the *w* body, joined and
6:11 Put on the *w* armor of God, that
6:13 Therefore take up the *w* armor of
Phil 1:13 evident to the *w* palace guard,
1 Th 5:23 and may your *w* spirit, soul,
Titus 1:11 who subvert *w* households,
Jas 2:10 shall keep the *w* law,
3: 2 able also to bridle the *w* body.
3: 3 and we turn their *w* body.
3: 6 that it defiles the *w* body,
1 Jn 2: 2 but also for the *w* world.
5:19 and the *w* world lies under
Rev 3:10 come upon the *w* world,
12: 9 who deceives the *w* world;
16:14 the earth and of the *w* world,

WHOLE-HEARTED (1/1) HEART, WHOLE

Ezek 36: 5 with *w* joy and spiteful minds,

WHOLESOME (2/2)

Prov 15: 4 A *w* tongue is a tree of life,
1 Tim 6: 3 does not consent to *w* words,

WHOLLY (17/17) WHOLE

Lev 6:22 It shall be *w* burned.
6:23 priest shall be *w* burned.
19: 9 you shall not *w* reap the
23:22 you shall not *w* reap the
Num 8:16 For they are *w* given to Me from
32:11 they have not *w* followed Me,
32:12 for they have *w* followed the
Deut 1:36 because he *w* followed the
Josh 14: 8 but I *w* followed the LORD my
14: 9 because you have *w* followed the
14:14 because he *w* followed the LORD
Judg 17: 3 I had *w* dedicated the silver
Job 21:23 Being *w* at ease and secure;
Jer 13:19 It shall be *w* carried away
42:15 If you *w* set your faces to enter
46:28 leave you *w* unpunished."
50:13 But she shall be *w* desolate.

WHOM (761/710) See APPENDIX

WHOMEVER (26/22)

Gen 19:12 and *w* you have in the city—take
31:32 With *w* you find your gods, do
44: 9 With *w* of your servants it is
Ex 4:13 please send by the hand of *w*
22: 9 and *w* the judges condemn shall
Lev 6: 5 and give it to *w* it belongs,
15:11 And *w* the one who has the
Judg 7: 4 and of *w* I say to you, 'This
Dan 4:17 Gives it to *w* He will,
4:25 and gives it to *w* He chooses.
4:32 and gives it to *w* He chooses."
5:19 *W* he wished, he executed;
5:19 *w* he wished, he kept alive;
5:19 *w* he wished, he set up; and
5:19 and *w* he wished, he put down.
5:21 and appoints over it *w* He
Mt 21:44 but on *w* it falls, it will
26:48 *W* I kiss, He is the One; seize
Mk 14:44 *W* I kiss, He is the One; seize
15: 6 to them, *w* they requested.
Lk 4: 6 and I give it to *w* I wish.
20:18 but on *w* it falls, it will
Jn 13:20 he who receives *w* I send
Rom 9:15 I will have mercy on *w* I
9:15 will have compassion on *w*
1 Cor 16: 3 *w* you approve by your letters

WHOMSOEVER (KJV) See WHOM, WHOMEVER

WHORE, WHORE'S, WHORES (KJV) See HARLOT, HARLOT'S, HARLOTRY

WHOREDOM (KJV) See HARLOTRY

WHOREMONGER, WHOREMONGERS (KJV) See FORNICATOR, FORNICATORS

WHOSE (295/267) See APPENDIX

WHOSO, WHOSOEVER (KJV) See WHOEVER

WHY (430/401)

Gen 4: 6 *W* are you angry? And why has
4: 6 And *w* has your countenance
12:18 *W* did you not tell me that she
12:19 *W* did you say, 'She is my
18:13 *W* did Sarah laugh, saying,
24:31 *W* do you stand outside?
25:22 *w* am I like this?"
26:27 *W* have you come to me, since you
27:45 *W* should I be bereaved also of
29:25 *W* then have you deceived me?"
31:27 *W* did you flee away secretly,
31:30 but *w* did you steal my gods?"
32:29 *W* is it that you ask about My
40: 7 *W* do you look so sad today?"
42: 1 *W* do you look at one another?"
43: 6 *W* did you deal so wrongfully
44: 4 *W* have you repaid evil for good?
44: 7 *W* does my lord say these words?
47:15 for *w* should we die in your
47:19 *W* should we die before your
Ex 1:18 *W* have you done this thing, and
2:13 *W* are you striking your
2:20 *W* is it that you have left
3: 3 *w* the bush does not burn."
5: 4 *w* do you take the people from
5:14 *W* have you not fulfilled your
5:15 *W* are you dealing thus with your
5:22 *w* have You brought trouble on
5:22 *W* is it You have sent me?
14: 5 *W* have we done this, that we
14:11 *W* have you so dealt with us, to
14:15 *W* do you cry to Me? Tell the
17: 2 '*W* do you contend with me?
17: 2 *W* do you tempt the LORD?"
17: 3 *W* is it you have brought us up
18:14 *W* do you alone sit, and all the
32:11 *w* does Your wrath burn hot
32:12 *W* should the Egyptians speak,
Lev 10:17 *W* have you not eaten the sin
Num 9: 7 *W* are we kept from presenting
11:11 *W* have You afflicted Your
11:11 And *w* have I not found favor in
11:20 *W* did we ever come up out of
12: 8 *W* then were you not afraid
14: 3 *W* has the LORD brought us to
14:41 Now *w* do you transgress the
16: 3 *W* then do you exalt yourselves
20: 4 *W* have you brought up the
20: 5 And *w* have you made us come up
21: 5 *W* have you brought us up out of
22:32 *W* have you struck your donkey
22:37 *W* did you not come to me?
27: 4 *W* should the name of our father
32: 7 Now *w* will you discourage the
Deut 5:25 *w* should we die? For this great
29:24 *W* has the LORD done so to this
Josh 5: 4 And this is the reason *w* Joshua
7: 7 *w* have You brought this people
7:10 Get up! *W* do you lie thus on
7:25 '*W* have you troubled us?
9:22 *W* have you deceived us, saying,
17:14 *W* have you given us only one
Judg 2: 2 *W* have you done this?
5:16 *W* did you sit among the
5:17 And *w* did Dan remain on ships?
5:28 *W* is his chariot so long in
5:28 *W* tarries the clatter of his
6:13 *w* then has all this happened to
8: 1 *W* have you done this to us by
9:28 but *w* should we serve him?
11: 7 *W* have you come to me now when
11: 8 That is *w* we have turned again
11:26 *w* did you not recover them
12: 1 *W* did you cross over to fight
12: 3 *W* then have you come up to me
13:18 *W* do you ask My name, seeing it
15:10 *W* have you come up against us?"
21: 3 *w* has this come to pass in
Ruth 1:11 *w* will you go with me?
1:21 *W* do you call me Naomi, since
2:10 *W* have I found favor in your
1 Sam 1: 8 *w* do you weep? Why do you not
1: 8 *W* do you not eat? And why is
1: 8 And *w* is your heart grieved?
2:23 '*W* do you do such things?
2:29 *W* do you kick at My sacrifice
4: 3 *W* has the LORD defeated us
6: 3 and it will be known to you *w*
6: 6 *W* then do you harden your hearts
9:21 *W* then do you speak like this
15:19 *W* then did you not obey the
15:19 *W* did you swoop down on the
17: 8 *W* have you come out to line up
17:28 '*W* did you come down here?
19: 5 *W* then will you sin against
19:17 *W* have you deceived me like
19:17 Let me go! *W* should I kill you?'
20: 2 And *w* should my father hide
20: 8 for *w* should you bring me to
20:27 *W* has the son of Jesse not come
20:32 '*W* should he be killed?
21: 1 *W* are you alone, and no one is
21:14 *W* have you brought him to me?
22:13 *W* have you conspired against me,
24: 9 *W* do you listen to the words of
26:15 *W* then have you not guarded
26:18 *W* does my lord thus pursue his
27: 5 For *w* should your servant dwell
28: 9 *W* then do you lay a snare for
28:12 '*W* have you deceived me?

28:15 **W** have you disturbed me by
28:16 **W** then do you ask me, seeing the
2 Sam 2:22 **W** should I strike you to the
3: 7 **W** have you gone in to my
3:24 **w** is it that you sent him
7: 7 **W** have you not built Me a house
11:10 **W** did you not go down to your
11:20 **W** did you approach so near to
11:21 **W** did you go near the
12: 9 **W** have you despised the
12:23 **w** should I fast? Can I bring
13: 4 **W** are you, the king's son,
13:26 **W** should he go with you?"
14:13 **W** then have you schemed such a
14:31 **W** have your servants set my
14:32 '**W** have I come from Geshur?
15:19 **W** are you also going with us?
16: 9 **W** should this dead dog curse my
16:10 **W** have you done so?'"
16:17 **W** did you not go with your
18:11 You just saw him! And **w** did you
18:22 **W** will you run, my son, since
19:10 **w** do you say nothing about
19:11 **W** are you the last to bring the
19:12 **W** then are you the last to
19:25 **W** did you not go with me,
19:29 **W** do you speak anymore of your
19:35 **W** then should your servant be a
19:36 And **w** should the king repay me
19:41 **W** have our brethren, the men of
19:42 **W** then are you angry over this
19:43 **W** then do you despise us—were
20:19 **W** would you swallow up the
24: 3 But **w** does my lord the king
24:21 **W** has my lord the king come to
1 Ki 1: 6 '**W** have you done so?"
1:13 **W** then has Adonijah become
1:41 **W** is the city in such a noisy
2:22 Now **w** do you ask Abishag the
2:43 **W** then have you not kept the
9: 8 **W** has the LORD done thus to
14: 6 **W** do you pretend to be
21: 5 **W** is your spirit so sullen that
2 Ki 1: 5 **W** have you come back?"
4:23 **W** are you going to him today?
5: 8 **W** have you torn your clothes?
6:33 **w** should I wait for the LORD
7: 3 **W** are we sitting here until we
8:12 '**W** is my lord weeping?"
9:11 **W** did this madman come to
12: 7 **W** have you not repaired the
14:10 for **w** should you meddle with
1 Chr 17: 6 **W** have you not built Me a house
21: 3 **W** then does my lord require
21: 3 **W** should he be a cause of guilt
2 Chr 7:21 **W** has the LORD done thus to
24: 6 **W** have you not required the
24:20 **W** do you transgress the
25:15 **W** have you sought the gods of
25:16 **W** should you be killed?"
25:19 **w** should you meddle with
32: 4 **W** should the kings of Assyria
Ezra 4:22 **W** should damage increase to the
7:23 For **w** should there be wrath
Neh 2: 2 **W** is your face sad, since you
2: 3 **W** should my face not be sad,
6: 3 **W** should the work cease while I
13:11 **W** is the house of God
13:21 **W** do you spend the night around
Esth 3: 3 **W** do you transgress the king's
4: 5 to learn what and **w** this was.
Job 3:11 '**W** did I not die at birth?
3:11 **W** did I not perish when I
3:12 **W** did the knees receive me
3:12 Or **w** the breasts, that I
3:16 Or **w** was I not hidden like a
3:20 **W** is light given to him who is
3:23 **W** is light given to a man
7:20 **W** have You set me as Your
7:21 **W** then do You not pardon my
9:29 **W** then do I labor in vain?
10: 2 Show me **w** You contend with me.
10:18 **W** then have You brought me out
13:14 **W** do I take my flesh in my
13:24 **W** do You hide Your face,
15:12 **W** does your heart carry you
18: 3 **W** are we counted as beasts,
19:22 **W** do you persecute me as God
21: 4 **w** should I not be impatient?
21: 7 **W** do the wicked live and
24: 1 **W** do those who know Him see
27:12 **W** then do you behave with
31: 1 **W** then should I look upon a
33:13 **W** do you contend with Him
37:17 **W** are your garments hot, When
Ps 2: 1 **W** do the nations rage, And the
10: 1 **W** do You stand afar off, O
10: 1 **W** do You hide in times of
10:13 **W** do the wicked renounce God
22: 1 **w** have You forsaken Me?
22: 1 **W** are You so far from
42: 5 **W** are you cast down, O my soul
42: 5 And **w** are you disquieted
42: 9 '**W** have You forgotten me?
42: 9 **W** do I go mourning because of
42:11 **W** are you cast down, O my soul
42:11 And **w** are you disquieted
43: 2 **W** do You cast me off?
43: 2 **W** do I go mourning because of
43: 5 **W** are you cast down, O my soul
43: 5 And **w** are you disquieted
44:23 Awake! **W** do You sleep, O Lord?
44:24 **W** do You hide Your face,
49: 5 **W** should I fear in the days of
52: 1 **W** do you boast in evil, O
68:16 **W** do you fume with envy, you
74: 1 **w** have You cast us off
74: 1 **W** does Your anger smoke
74:11 **W** do You withdraw Your hand,
79:10 **W** should the nations say,
80:12 **W** have You broken down her
88:14 **w** do You cast off my soul?
88:14 **W** do You hide Your face from
115: 2 **W** should the Gentiles say,
Prov 5:20 For **w** should you, my son, be
17:16 **W** is there in the hand of a
22:27 **W** should he take away your bed
Eccl 2:15 And **w** was I then more wise?"
5: 6 **W** should God be angry at your
7:10 **W** were the former days better
7:16 **W** should you destroy yourself?
7:17 **W** should you die before your
Song 1: 7 For **w** should I be as one who
Isa 1: 5 **W** should you be stricken
5: 4 **W** then, when I expected it to
40:27 **W** do you say, O Jacob, And
50: 2 **W**, when I came, was there
50: 2 **W**, when I called, was there
55: 2 **W** do you spend money for what
58: 3 **W** have we fasted,' they say,
58: 3 **W** have we afflicted our
63: 2 **W** is Your apparel red, And
63:17 **w** have You made us stray from
Jer 2:14 **W** is he plundered?
2:18 And now **w** take the road to
2:18 Or **w** take the road to Assyria,
2:29 **W** will you plead with Me?
2:31 **W** do My people say, 'We are
2:33 **W** do you beautify your way to
2:36 **W** do you gad about so much to
5:19 **W** does the LORD our God do all
8: 5 **W** has this people slidden back,
8:14 **W** do we sit still? Assemble
8:19 **W** have they provoked Me to anger
8:22 **W** then is there no recovery
9:12 **W** does the land perish and
12: 1 **W** does the way of the wicked
12: 1 **W** are those happy who deal so
13:22 **W** have these things come upon
14: 8 **W** should You be like a
14: 9 **W** should You be like a man
14:19 **W** have You stricken us so that
15:18 **W** is my pain perpetual And my
16:10 **W** has the LORD pronounced all
20:18 **W** did I come forth from the
22: 8 **W** has the LORD done so to this
22:28 **W** are they cast out, he and
26: 9 **W** have you prophesied in the
27:13 **W** will you die, you and your
27:17 **W** should this city be laid
29:27 **w** have you not reproved
30: 6 So **w** do I see every man with
30:15 **W** do you cry about your
32: 3 **W** do you prophesy and say, 'Thus
36:29 **W** have you written in it that
40:15 **W** should he murder you, so that
44: 7 **W** do you commit this great evil
46: 5 **W** have I seen them dismayed
46:15 **W** are your valiant men swept
49: 1 **W** then does Milcom inherit
49: 4 **W** do you boast in the valleys,
49:25 **W** is the city of praise not
Lam 3:39 **W** should a living man complain,
5:20 **W** do You forget us forever,
Ezek 18:19 **W** should the son not bear the
18:31 For **w** should you die, O house
21: 7 **W** are you sighing?' that you
33:11 For **w** should you die, O house
Dan 1:10 For **w** should he see your faces
2:15 **W** is the decree from the king so
10:20 Do you know **w** I have come to
Joel 2:17 **W** should they say among the
Jon 1:10 **W** have you done this?" For the
Mic 4: 9 Now **w** do you cry aloud?
Hab 1: 3 **W** do You show me iniquity,
1:13 **W** do You look on those who
1:14 **W** do You make men like fish of
Hag 1: 9 it home, I blew it away. **W**?
Mal 2:10 **W** do we deal treacherously
2:15 And **w** one? He seeks godly
Mt 6:28 So **w** do you worry about
7: 3 And **w** do you look at the speck
8:26 **W** are you fearful, O you of
9: 4 **W** do you think evil in your
9:11 **W** does your Teacher eat with tax
9:14 **W** do we and the Pharisees fast
13:10 **W** do You speak to them in
14:31 faith, **w** did you doubt?"
15: 2 **W** do Your disciples transgress
15: 3 **W** do you also transgress the
16: 8 **w** do you reason among
17:10 **W** then do the scribes say that
17:19 **W** could we not cast it out?"
19: 7 **W** then did Moses command to give
19:17 '**W** do you call Me good?
20: 6 **W** have you been standing here
21:25 **W** then did you not believe him?'
22:18 **W** do you test Me, you
26: 8 saying, "**W** this waste?
26:10 '**W** do you trouble the woman?
26:50 **w** have you come?" Then they
27:23 Then the governor said, "**W**,
27:46 **w** have You forsaken Me?"
Mk 2: 7 **W** does this Man speak
2: 8 **W** do you reason about these
2:18 **W** do the disciples of John and
2:24 **w** do they do what is not lawful
4:40 **W** are you so fearful? How is
5:35 **W** trouble the Teacher any
5:39 **W** make this commotion and weep?
7: 5 **W** do Your disciples not walk
8:12 **W** does this generation seek a
8:17 **W** do you reason because you have
9:11 **W** do the scribes say that Elijah
9:28 **W** could we not cast it out?"
10:18 **W** do you call Me good? No one
11: 3 **W** are you doing this?' say, 'The
11:31 **W** then did you not believe him?'
12:15 **W** do you test Me? Bring Me a
14: 4 **W** was this fragrant oil wasted?
14: 6 **W** do you trouble her? She has
15:14 Then Pilate said to them, "**W**,
15:34 **w** have You forsaken Me?"
Lk 1:43 But **w** is this granted to me,
2:48 **w** have You done this to us?
2:49 **W** did you seek Me? Did you not
5:22 **W** are you reasoning in your
5:30 **W** do You eat and drink with tax
5:33 **W** do the disciples of John fast
6: 2 **W** are you doing what is not
6:41 And **w** do you look at the speck
6:46 But **w** do you call Me 'Lord,
12:26 **w** are you anxious for the rest?
12:57 Yes, and **w**, even of
13: 7 **w** does it use up the ground?'
18:19 '**W** do you call Me good?
19:23 **W** then did you not put my money
19:31 '**W** are you loosing it?'
19:33 **W** are you loosing the colt?"
20: 5 **W** then did you not believe him?'
20:23 to them, "**W** do you test Me?
22:46 **W** do you sleep? Rise and pray,
23:22 to them the third time, "**W**,
24: 5 **W** do you seek the living among
24:38 **W** are you troubled? And why do
24:38 And **w** do doubts arise in your
Jn 1:25 **W** then do you baptize if you are
4:27 **W** are You talking with her?"
7:19 **W** do you seek to kill Me?"
7:45 **W** have you not brought Him?"
8:43 **W** do you not understand My
8:46 **w** do you not believe Me?
9:27 **W** do you want to hear it
9:30 '**W**, this is a marvelous thing,
10:20 **W** do you listen to Him?"
12: 5 **W** was this fragrant oil not sold
13:37 **w** can I not follow You now?
18:21 **W** do you ask Me? Ask those who
18:23 **w** do you strike Me?"
20:13 **w** are you weeping?" She said
20:15 **w** are you weeping? Whom are you
Acts 1:11 **w** do you stand gazing up into
3:12 **w** do you marvel at this?
3:12 Or **w** look so intently at us, as
4:25 **W** did the nations rage,
5: 3 **w** has Satan filled your heart
5: 4 **W** have you conceived this thing
7:26 **w** do you wrong one another?'
9: 4 **w** are you persecuting Me?"
14:15 **w** are you doing these things?
15:10 **w** do you test God by putting a
18:14 there would be reason **w** I
19:32 and most of them did not know **w**
22: 7 **w** are you persecuting Me?'
22:16 'And now **w** are you waiting?
22:24 so that he might know **w** they
22:30 he wanted to know for certain **w**
26: 8 **W** should it be thought
26:14 **w** are you persecuting Me?
Rom 3: 7 **w** am I also still judged as a
3: 8 And **w** not say, "Let us do
8:24 for **w** does one still hope for
9:19 '**W** does He still find fault?
9:20 **W** have you made me like this?"
9:32 **W**? Because they did not seek
14:10 But **w** do you judge your brother?
14:10 Or **w** do you show contempt for
1 Cor 4: 7 **w** do you boast as if you had
6: 7 **W** do you not rather accept
6: 7 **W** do you not rather let
10:29 For **w** is my liberty judged by
10:30 **w** am I evil spoken of for the
15:29 **W** then are they baptized for
15:30 And **w** do we stand in jeopardy
2 Cor 11:11 **W**? Because I do not love
Gal 2:14 **w** do you compel Gentiles to
5:11 **w** do I still suffer
Col 2:20 **w**, as though living in the
1 Jn 3:12 And **w** did he murder him?
Rev 17: 7 **W** did you marvel? I will tell

WICK (1/1)

Isa 43:17 they are quenched like a **w**:

WICK-TRIMMERS (5/5)

Ex 25:38 And its **w** and their trays shall
37:23 he made its seven lamps, its **w**,
Num 4: 9 light, with its lamps, its **w**,
1 Ki 7:49 and the lamps and the **w** of
2 Chr 4:21 and the lamps and the **w** of

WICKED (342/324) EVIL, WICKEDLY, WICKEDNESS

Gen 13:13 of Sodom were exceedingly ***w***
18:23 the righteous with the ***w***?
18:25 slay the righteous with the ***w***,
18:25 righteous should be as the ***w***;
38: 7 was ***w*** in the sight of the
Ex 9:27 and my people and I are ***w***.
23: 1 Do not put your hand with the ***w***
23: 7 For I will not justify the ***w***.
Lev 20:17 it is a ***w*** thing. And they
Num 16:26 the tents of these ***w*** men!
Deut 15: 9 Beware lest there be a ***w*** thought
17: 2 a man or a woman who has been ***w***
17: 5 who has committed that ***w*** thing,
23: 9 yourself from every ***w*** thing.
25: 1 the righteous and condemn the ***w***,
25: 2 if the ***w*** man deserves to be
Judg 20: 3 how did this ***w*** deed happen?"
1 Sam 1:16 your maidservant a ***w*** woman,
2: 9 But the ***w*** shall be silent in
24:13 'Wickedness proceeds from the ***w***.
30:22 Then all the ***w*** and worthless men
2 Sam 3:34 As a man falls before ***w*** men,
4:11 when ***w*** men have killed a
1 Ki 8:32 Your servants, condemning the ***w***,
2 Ki 17:11 and they did ***w*** things to
1 Chr 2: 3 was ***w*** in the sight of the
2 Chr 6:23 bringing retribution on the ***w***
7:14 and turn from their ***w*** ways,
19: 2 Should you help the ***w*** and love
24: 7 that ***w*** woman, had broken into
Neh 9:35 they turn from their ***w*** works.
Esth 7: 6 and enemy is this ***w*** Haman!"
9:25 by letter that this ***w*** plot
Job 3:17 There the ***w*** cease from
8:22 the dwelling place of the ***w***
9:22 the blameless and the ***w***.
9:24 is given into the hand of the ***w***.
10: 3 smile on the counsel of the ***w***?
10: 7 You know that I am not ***w***,
10:15 If I am ***w***, woe to me;
11:20 But the eyes of the ***w*** will
15:20 The ***w*** man writhes with pain all
16:11 me over to the hands of the ***w***.
18: 5 The light of the ***w*** indeed goes
18:21 are the dwellings of the ***w***,
20: 5 That the triumphing of the ***w*** is
20:29 portion from God for a ***w*** man,
21: 7 Why do the ***w*** live and become
21:16 The counsel of the ***w*** is far
21:17 often is the lamp of the ***w*** put
21:28 The dwelling place of the ***w***?
21:30 For the ***w*** are reserved for the
22:15 way Which ***w*** men have trod,
22:18 But the counsel of the ***w*** is
24: 6 glean in the vineyard of the ***w***.
27: 7 "May my enemy be like the ***w***,
27:13 This is the portion of a ***w*** man
29:17 I broke the fangs of the ***w***,
31: 3 it not destruction for the ***w***,
34: 8 And walks with ***w*** men?
34:18 And to nobles, 'You are ***w***'?
34:26 He strikes them as ***w*** men
34:36 are like those of ***w*** men!
36: 6 not preserve the life of the ***w***,
36:17 with the judgment due the ***w***;
38:13 And the ***w*** be shaken out of it?
38:15 From the ***w*** their light is
40:12 Tread down the ***w*** in their
Ps 7: 9 let the wickedness of the ***w***
7:11 And God is angry with the ***w***
7:14 the ***w*** brings forth iniquity;
9: 5 You have destroyed the ***w***;
9:16 The ***w*** is snared in the work of
9:17 The ***w*** shall be turned into
10: 2 The ***w*** in his pride persecutes
10: 3 For the ***w*** boasts of his heart's
10: 4 The ***w*** in his proud countenance
10:13 Why do the ***w*** renounce God?
10:15 Break the arm of the ***w*** and the
11: 2 For look! The ***w*** bend their
11: 5 But the ***w*** and the one who
11: 6 Upon the ***w*** He will rain coals;
12: 8 The ***w*** prowl on every side,
17: 9 From the ***w*** who oppress me,
17:13 Deliver my life from the ***w***
22:16 The congregation of the ***w*** has
26: 5 And will not sit with the ***w***.
27: 2 When the ***w*** came against me
28: 3 Do not take me away with the ***w***
31:17 Let the ***w*** be ashamed; Let
32:10 sorrows shall be to the ***w***;
34:21 Evil shall slay the ***w***,
36: 1 the transgression of the ***w***:
36:11 And let not the hand of the ***w***
37: 7 brings ***w*** schemes to pass.
37:10 yet a little while and the ***w***
37:12 The ***w*** plots against the just,
37:14 The ***w*** have drawn the sword
37:16 than the riches of many ***w***.
37:17 For the arms of the ***w*** shall be
37:20 But the ***w*** shall perish;
37:21 The ***w*** borrows and does not
37:28 But the descendants of the ***w***
37:32 The ***w*** watches the righteous,
37:34 When the ***w*** are cut off, you
37:35 I have seen the ***w*** in great
37:38 The future of the ***w*** shall be
37:40 shall deliver them from the ***w***,
39: 1 While the ***w*** are before me."
50:16 But to the ***w*** God says: "What
55: 3 of the oppression of the ***w***;
58: 3 The ***w*** are estranged from the
58:10 his feet in the blood of the ***w***,
59: 5 to any ***w*** transgressors.
64: 2 from the secret plots of the ***w***,
68: 2 So let the ***w*** perish at the
71: 4 God, out of the hand of the ***w***,
73: 3 I saw the prosperity of the ***w***.
75: 4 deal boastfully,' And to the ***w***,
75: 8 its dregs shall all the ***w*** of
75:10 All the horns of the ***w*** I will
82: 2 And show partiality to the ***w***?
82: 4 them from the hand of the ***w***.
91: 8 And see the reward of the ***w***.
92: 7 When the ***w*** spring up like
92:11 ears hear my desire on the ***w***
94: 3 LORD, how long will the ***w***,
94: 3 How long will the ***w*** triumph?
94:13 Until the pit is dug for the ***w***.
97:10 them out of the hand of the ***w***.
101: 3 I will set nothing ***w*** before my
101: 8 I will destroy all the ***w*** of
104:35 And the ***w*** be no more.
106:18 The flame burned up the ***w***.
109: 2 For the mouth of the ***w*** and the
109: 6 Set a ***w*** man over him, And let
112:10 The ***w*** will see it and be
112:10 The desire of the ***w*** shall
119:53 hold of me Because of the ***w***,
119:61 The cords of the ***w*** have bound
119:95 The ***w*** wait for me to destroy
119:110 The ***w*** have laid a snare for me,
119:119 You put away all the ***w*** of the
119:155 Salvation is far from the ***w***,
129: 4 in pieces the cords of the ***w***.
139:19 Oh, that You would slay the ***w***,
139:24 see if there is any ***w*** way
140: 4 LORD, from the hands of the ***w***;
140: 8 O LORD, the desires of the ***w***;
140: 8 Do not further his ***w*** scheme,
141: 4 To practice ***w*** works With men
141: 5 is against the deeds of the ***w***.
141:10 Let the ***w*** fall into their own
145:20 But all the ***w*** He will destroy.
146: 9 But the way of the ***w*** He turns
147: 6 He casts the ***w*** down to the
Prov 2:14 in the perversity of the ***w***;
2:22 But the ***w*** will be cut off from
3:25 Nor of trouble from the ***w*** when
3:33 LORD is on the house of the ***w***,
4:14 not enter the path of the ***w***,
4:19 The way of the ***w*** is like
5:22 own iniquities entrap the ***w***
6:12 a ***w*** man, Walks with a perverse
6:18 A heart that devises ***w*** plans,
9: 7 And he who rebukes a ***w*** man
10: 3 casts away the desire of the ***w***.
10: 6 covers the mouth of the ***w***.
10: 7 But the name of the ***w*** will
10:11 covers the mouth of the ***w***.
10:16 The wages of the ***w*** to sin.
10:20 The heart of the ***w*** is worth
10:24 The fear of the ***w*** will come
10:25 the ***w*** is no more, But the
10:27 But the years of the ***w*** will be
10:28 But the expectation of the ***w***
10:30 But the ***w*** will not inhabit the
10:32 But the mouth of the ***w*** what
11: 5 But the ***w*** will fall by his own
11: 7 When a ***w*** man dies, his
11: 8 And it comes to the ***w*** instead.
11:10 And when the ***w*** perish, there
11:11 by the mouth of the ***w***.
11:18 The ***w*** man does deceptive work,
11:21 the ***w*** will not go unpunished;
11:23 But the expectation of the ***w***
12: 2 But a man of ***w*** intentions He
12: 5 But the counsels of the ***w***
12: 6 The words of the ***w*** are, "Lie
12: 7 The ***w*** are overthrown and are
12:10 the tender mercies of the ***w***
12:12 The ***w*** covet the catch of evil
12:13 The ***w*** is ensnared by the
12:21 But the ***w*** shall be filled with
12:26 For the way of the ***w*** leads
13: 5 But a ***w*** man is loathsome and
13: 9 But the lamp of the ***w*** will be
13:17 A ***w*** messenger falls into
13:25 But the stomach of the ***w*** shall
14:11 The house of the ***w*** will be
14:17 And a man of ***w*** intentions is
14:19 And the ***w*** at the gates of the
14:32 The ***w*** is banished in his
15: 6 But in the revenue of the ***w*** is
15: 8 The sacrifice of the ***w*** is an
15: 9 The way of the ***w*** is an
15:26 The thoughts of the ***w*** are an
15:28 But the mouth of the ***w*** pours
15:29 The LORD is far from the ***w***,
16: 4 even the ***w*** for the day of doom.
17:15 He who justifies the ***w***,
17:23 A ***w*** man accepts a bribe behind
18: 3 When the ***w*** comes, contempt
18: 5 to show partiality to the ***w***,
19:28 And the mouth of the ***w*** devours
20:26 A wise king sifts out the ***w***,
21: 4 And the plowing of the ***w*** are
21: 7 The violence of the ***w*** will
21:10 The soul of the ***w*** desires evil;
21:12 considers the house of the ***w***,
21:12 Overthrowing the ***w*** for their
21:18 The ***w*** shall be a ransom for
21:27 The sacrifice of the ***w*** is an
21:27 he brings it with ***w*** intent!
21:29 A ***w*** man hardens his face,
24:15 O ***w*** man, against the dwelling
24:16 But the ***w*** shall fall by
24:19 Nor be envious of the ***w***;
24:20 The lamp of the ***w*** will be put
24:24 He who says to the ***w***,
24:25 But those who rebuke the ***w***
25: 5 Take away the ***w*** from before the
25:26 man who falters before the ***w***
26:23 Fervent lips with a ***w*** heart
28: 1 The ***w*** flee when no one pursues,
28: 4 forsake the law praise the ***w***,
28:12 But when the ***w*** arise, men hide
28:15 charging bear Is a ***w*** ruler
28:28 When the ***w*** arise, men hide
29: 2 But when a ***w*** man rules, the
29: 7 But the ***w*** does not understand
29:12 All his servants become ***w***.
29:16 When the ***w*** are multiplied,
29:27 way is an abomination to the ***w***.
Eccl 3:17 judge the righteous and the ***w***,
7:15 And there is a ***w*** man who
7:17 Do not be overly ***w***,
8:10 Then I saw the ***w*** buried, who
8:13 it will not be well with the ***w***;
8:14 according to the work of the ***w***;
8:14 there are ***w*** men to whom it
9: 2 to the righteous and the ***w***;
Isa 3:11 Woe to the ***w***! It shall be
5:23 Who justify the ***w*** for a bribe,
11: 4 of His lips He shall slay the ***w***.
13:11 And the ***w*** for their iniquity;
14: 5 has broken the staff of the ***w***,
26:10 Let grace be shown to the ***w***,
32: 7 He devises ***w*** plans To destroy
48:22 says the LORD, "for the ***w***.
53: 9 they made His grave with the ***w***—
55: 7 Let the ***w*** forsake his way,
57:20 But the ***w*** are like the
57:21 Says my God, "for the ***w***.
Jer 2:33 you have also taught The ***w***
5:26 My people are found ***w*** men;
5:28 they surpass the deeds of the ***w***;
6:29 For the ***w*** are not drawn off.
12: 1 Why does the way of the ***w***
15:21 you from the hand of the ***w***,
17: 9 all things, And desperately ***w***;
23:19 violently on the head of the ***w***.
25:31 will give those who are ***w*** to
30:23 violently on the head of the ***w***.
Ezek 3:18 "When I say to the ***w***,
3:18 nor speak to warn the ***w*** from
3:18 the wicked from his ***w*** way,
3:18 that same ***w*** man shall die in
3:19 "Yet, if you warn the ***w***,
3:19 nor from his ***w*** way, he shall
7:21 And to the ***w*** of the earth as
8: 9 and see the ***w*** abominations
11: 2 iniquity and give ***w*** counsel
13:22 strengthened the hands of the ***w***,
13:22 does not turn from his ***w*** way
18:20 and the wickedness of the ***w***
18:21 But if a ***w*** man turns from all
18:23 any pleasure at all that the ***w***
18:24 all the abominations that the ***w***
18:27 when a ***w*** man turns away from
20:44 not according to your ***w*** ways
21: 3 cut off both righteous and ***w***
21: 4 cut off both righteous and ***w***
21:25 ***w*** prince of Israel, whose day
21:29 bring you on the necks of the ***w***,
30:12 the land into the hand of the ***w***;
33: 8 "When I say to the ***w***,
33: 8 O ***w*** man, you shall surely die!'
33: 8 you do not speak to warn the ***w***
33: 8 that ***w*** man shall die in his
33: 9 if you warn the ***w*** to turn from
33:11 pleasure in the death of the ***w***,
33:11 but that the ***w*** turn from his
33:12 as for the wickedness of the ***w***,
33:14 "Again, when I say to the ***w***,
33:15 if the ***w*** restores the pledge,
33:19 But when the ***w*** turns from his
Dan 12:10 but the ***w*** shall do wickedly;
12:10 and none of the ***w*** shall
Mic 6:10 In the house of the ***w***,
6:11 I count pure those with the ***w***
Nah 1: 3 will not at all acquit the ***w***.
1:11 the LORD, A ***w*** counselor.
1:15 For the ***w*** one shall no more
Hab 1: 4 For the ***w*** surround the
1:13 hold Your tongue when the ***w***
3:13 head from the house of the ***w***,
Zeph 1: 3 blocks along with the ***w***.
Mal 3:18 the righteous and the ***w***,
4: 3 You shall trample the ***w***,
Mt 12:45 him seven other spirits more ***w***
12:45 be with this ***w*** generation."
13:19 then the ***w*** one comes and
13:38 the tares are the sons of the ***w***
13:49 separate the ***w*** from among the
16: 4 A ***w*** and adulterous generation
18:32 You ***w*** servant! I forgave you all
21:41 He will destroy those ***w*** men
25:26 You ***w*** and lazy servant, you knew
Lk 11:26 him seven other spirits more ***w***
19:22 you ***w*** servant. You knew that I
Acts 18:14 of wrongdoing or ***w*** crimes,

Eph 6:16 all the fiery darts of the ***w***
Col 1:21 in your mind by ***w*** works,
2 Th 3: 2 from unreasonable and ***w*** men;
2 Pe 2: 7 by the filthy conduct of the ***w***
3:17 away with the error of the ***w***;
1 Jn 2:13 you have overcome the ***w*** one.
2:14 And you have overcome the ***w***
3:12 not as Cain who was of the ***w***
5:18 and the ***w*** one does not touch
5:19 under the sway of the ***w***

WICKEDLY (21/21) WICKED

Gen 19: 7 my brethren, do not do so ***w***!
Deut 9:18 which you committed in doing ***w***
Judg 19:23 do not act so ***w***! Seeing this
1 Sam 12:25 "But if you still do ***w***,
2 Sam 22:22 And have not ***w*** departed from my
24:17 have sinned, and I have done ***w***;
2 Ki 21:11 (he has acted more ***w*** than all
2 Chr 20:35 of Israel, who acted very ***w***.
22: 3 his mother advised him to do ***w***.
Neh 9:33 faithfully, But we have done ***w***.
Job 13: 7 Will you speak ***w*** for God, And
34:12 Surely God will never do ***w***,
Ps 18:21 And have not ***w*** departed from
73: 8 They scoff and speak ***w***
106: 6 iniquity, We have done ***w***.
139:20 For they speak against You ***w***;
Dan 9: 5 we have done ***w*** and rebelled,
9:15 have sinned, we have done ***w***!
11:32 Those who do ***w*** against the
12:10 but the wicked shall do ***w***;
Mal 4: 1 all who do ***w*** will be stubble.

WICKEDNESS (128/121) WICKED

Gen 6: 5 Then the LORD saw that the ***w***
39: 9 How then can I do this great ***w***,
Lev 18:17 near of kin to her. It is ***w***.
19:29 and the land become full of ***w***.
20:14 woman and her mother, it is ***w***.
20:14 that there may be no ***w*** among
Num 23:21 Nor has He seen ***w*** in Israel.
Deut 9: 4 but it is because of the ***w*** of
9: 5 but because of the ***w*** of these
9:27 or on their ***w*** or their sin,
13:11 and not again do such ***w*** as this
28:20 because of the ***w*** of your doings
Judg 9:56 Thus God repaid the ***w*** of
20:12 What is this ***w*** that has
1 Sam 12:17 perceive and see that your ***w***
12:20 You have done all this ***w***;
24:13 '***W*** proceeds from the wicked.'
25:39 the LORD has returned the ***w***
2 Sam 3:39 the evildoer according to his ***w***.
7:10 nor shall the sons of ***w*** oppress
1 Ki 1:52 but if ***w*** is found in him, he
2:44 all the ***w*** that you did to my
2:44 the LORD will return your ***w***
8:47 wrong, we have committed ***w***';
21:25 Ahab who sold himself to do ***w***
1 Chr 17: 9 nor shall the sons of ***w*** oppress
2 Chr 6:37 wrong, and have committed ***w***';
Job 11:11 He sees ***w*** also. Will He not
11:14 And would not let ***w*** dwell in
22: 5 Is not your ***w*** great, And your
24:20 And ***w*** should be broken like a
27: 4 My lips will not speak ***w***,
31:11 For that would be ***w***;
34:10 Far be it from God to do ***w***,
35: 8 Your ***w*** affects a man such as
Ps 5: 4 a God who takes pleasure in ***w***,
7: 9 let the ***w*** of the wicked come to
10:15 Seek out his ***w*** until You find
28: 4 And according to the ***w*** of
36: 3 The words of his mouth are ***w***
36: 4 He devises ***w*** on his bed;
45: 7 love righteousness and hate ***w***;
52: 7 strengthened himself in his ***w***.
55:15 For ***w*** is in their dwellings
58: 2 No, in heart you work ***w***;
84:10 Than dwell in the tents of ***w***.
89:22 Nor the son of ***w*** afflict him.
94:23 cut them off in their own ***w***;
101: 4 from me; I will not know ***w***.
107:34 For the ***w*** of those who dwell
119:150 draw near who follow after ***w***;
125: 3 For the scepter of ***w*** shall not
Prov 4:17 For they eat the bread of ***w***,
8: 7 ***W*** is an abomination to my
10: 2 Treasures of ***w*** profit nothing,
11: 5 wicked will fall by his own ***w***.
12: 3 A man is not established by ***w***,
13: 6 But ***w*** overthrows the sinner.
14:32 wicked is banished in his ***w***,
16:12 for kings to commit ***w***,
21:12 the wicked for their ***w***.
26:26 His ***w*** will be revealed before
30:20 And says, "I have done no ***w***.
Eccl 3:16 ***W*** was there; And in the
7:15 who prolongs life in his ***w***.
7:25 To know the ***w*** of folly,
8: 8 And ***w*** will not deliver those
Isa 9:18 For ***w*** burns as the fire;
47:10 you have trusted in your ***w***;
58: 4 to strike with the fist of ***w***.
58: 6 To loose the bonds of ***w***,
58: 9 of the finger, and speaking ***w***,
Jer 1:16 them concerning all their ***w***,
2:19 Your own ***w*** will correct you,
3: 2 your harlotries and your ***w***.
4:14 wash your heart from ***w***,
4:18 for you. This is your ***w***,
6: 7 So she wells up with her ***w***.
7:12 I did to it because of the ***w***
8: 6 No man repented of his ***w***,
12: 4 For the ***w*** of those who dwell
14:16 for I will pour their ***w*** on
14:20 our ***w*** And the iniquity of our
22:22 and humiliated For all your ***w***.
23:11 My house I have found their ***w***,
23:14 no one turns back from his ***w***.
33: 5 all for whose ***w*** I have hidden
44: 3 because of their ***w*** which they
44: 5 their ear to turn from their ***w***,
44: 9 Have you forgotten the ***w*** of your
44: 9 the ***w*** of the kings of Judah,
44: 9 the ***w*** of their wives, your own
44: 9 of their wives, your own ***w***,
44: 9 and the ***w*** of your wives, which
Lam 1:22 Let all their ***w*** come before You,
Ezek 3:19 and he does not turn from his ***w***,
5: 6 My judgments by doing ***w*** more
7:11 has risen up into a rod of ***w***;
16:23 it was so, after all your ***w***—
16:57 'before your ***w*** was uncovered.
18:20 and the ***w*** of the wicked shall
18:27 man turns away from the ***w***
31:11 I have driven it out for its ***w***.
33:12 as for the ***w*** of the wicked, he
33:12 day that he turns from his ***w***;
33:19 the wicked turns from his ***w***
Hos 7: 1 And the ***w*** of Samaria.
7: 2 That I remember all their ***w***;
7: 3 make a king glad with their ***w***,
9:15 'All their ***w*** is in Gilgal,
10:13 You have plowed ***w***;
10:15 Because of your great ***w***.
Joel 3:13 For their ***w*** is great."
Jon 1: 2 for their ***w*** has come up before
Mic 6:10 there yet the treasures of ***w***
Nah 3:19 For upon whom has not your ***w***
Hab 1:13 evil, And cannot look on ***w***.
Zech 5: 8 This is ***W***!" And he thrust her
Mal 1: 4 be called the Territory of ***W***,
3:15 For those who do ***w*** are raised
Mt 22:18 But Jesus perceived their ***w***,
Mk 7:22 "thefts, covetousness, ***w***,
Lk 11:39 part is full of greed and ***w***.
Acts 8:22 therefore of this your ***w***,
Rom 1:29 sexual immorality, ***w***,
1 Cor 5: 8 with the leaven of malice and ***w***,
Eph 6:12 against spiritual hosts of ***w***
Jas 1:21 filthiness and overflow of ***w***,

WIDE (47/43) WIDELY, WIDER, WIDTH

Ex 27: 1 cubits long and five cubits ***w***—
Num 24: 4 falls down, with eyes ***w*** open:
24:16 falls down, with eyes ***w*** open:
Deut 15: 8 you shall open your hand ***w***
15:11 You shall open your hand ***w*** to
1 Ki 6: 6 chamber was five cubits ***w***,
6: 6 the middle was six cubits ***w***,
6: 6 the third was seven cubits ***w***;
6:20 cubits long, twenty cubits ***w***,
2 Chr 6:13 five cubits long, five cubits ***w***,
26:15 So his fame spread far and ***w***,
Job 29:23 And they opened their mouth ***w***
Ps 31: 8 set my feet in a ***w*** place.
35:21 They also opened their mouth ***w***
81:10 of Egypt; Open your mouth ***w***,
104:25 This great and ***w*** sea, In which
Prov 13: 3 But he who opens ***w*** his lips
Isa 57: 4 whom do you make a ***w*** mouth
Jer 22:14 I will build myself a ***w*** house
Lam 2:13 For your ruin is spread ***w*** as
Ezek 23:32 The deep and ***w*** one; You shall
40: 6 gateway, which was one rod ***w***,
40: 6 other threshold was one rod ***w***.
40: 7 was one rod long and one rod ***w***;
40:29 long and twenty-five cubits ***w***.
40:30 cubits long and five cubits ***w***.
40:33 long and twenty-five cubits ***w***.
40:42 long, one cubit and a half ***w***,
40:43 were hooks, a handbreadth ***w***,
40:47 long and one hundred cubits ***w***,
41: 1 six cubits ***w*** on one side and
41: 1 on one side and six cubits ***w***
41:12 end was seventy cubits ***w***;
42: 4 was a walk ten cubits ***w***,
42:11 they were as long and as ***w*** as
42:20 cubits long and five hundred ***w***,
43:13 one cubit high and one cubit ***w***,
43:16 twelve cubits long, twelve ***w***,
43:17 cubits long and fourteen ***w*** on
45: 3 cubits long and ten thousand ***w***;
45: 5 long and ten thousand ***w*** shall
45: 6 area five thousand cubits ***w***
46:22 forty cubits long and thirty ***w***;
Mic 7:11 the decree shall go far and ***w***.
Nah 3:13 The gates of your land are ***w***
Mt 7:13 for ***w*** is the gate and broad
2 Cor 6:11 our heart is ***w*** open.

WIDELY (2/2)

Mk 7:36 the more ***w*** they proclaimed it.
Lk 2:17 they made ***w*** known the saying

WIDENESS (KJV) See WIDTH

WIDER (1/1)

Ezek 41: 7 the side chambers became ***w*** all

WIDESPREAD (1/1)

1 Sam 3: 1 there was no ***w*** revelation.

WIDOW (56/56) WIDOWHOOD, WIDOW'S, WIDOWS

Gen 38:11 Remain a ***w*** in your father's
Ex 22:22 You shall not afflict any ***w*** or
Lev 21:14 A ***w*** or a divorced woman or a
22:13 if the priest's daughter is a ***w***
Num 30: 9 Also any vow of a ***w*** or a
Deut 10:18 for the fatherless and the ***w***,
14:29 and the fatherless and the ***w***
16:11 and the fatherless and the ***w***
16:14 and the fatherless and the ***w***,
24:19 the fatherless, and the ***w***,
24:20 the fatherless, and the ***w***.
24:21 the fatherless, and the ***w***.
25: 5 the ***w*** of the dead man shall not
26:12 the fatherless, and the ***w***,
26:13 the fatherless, and the ***w***,
27:19 stranger, the fatherless, and ***w***.
Ruth 4:10 the ***w*** of Mahlon, I have
1 Sam 27: 3 the Carmelitess, Nabal's ***w***.
30: 5 and Abigail the ***w*** of Nabal the
2 Sam 2: 2 and Abigail the ***w*** of Nabal the
3: 3 by Abigail the ***w*** of Nabal the
14: 5 answered, "Indeed I am a ***w***,
1 Ki 7:14 He was the son of a ***w*** from the
11:26 mother's name was Zeruah, a ***w***,
17: 9 I have commanded a ***w*** there to
17:10 indeed a ***w*** was there gathering
17:20 also brought tragedy on the ***w***
Job 24:21 And does no good for the ***w***.
31:16 Or caused the eyes of the ***w*** to
31:18 mother's womb I guided the ***w***)
Ps 94: 6 They slay the ***w*** and the
109: 9 fatherless, And his wife a ***w***.
146: 9 relieves the fatherless and ***w***;
Prov 15:25 establish the boundary of the ***w***.
Isa 1:17 fatherless, Plead for the ***w***.
1:23 Nor does the cause of the ***w***
47: 8 me; I shall not sit as a ***w***,
Jer 7: 6 the fatherless, and the ***w***,
22: 3 the fatherless, or the ***w***,
Lam 1: 1 How like a ***w*** is she,
Ezek 22: 7 the fatherless and the ***w***.
44:22 shall not take as wife a ***w*** or
Zech 7:10 Do not oppress the ***w*** or the
Mk 12:42 Then one poor ***w*** came and threw
12:43 I say to you that this poor ***w***
Lk 2:37 and this woman was a ***w*** of about
4:26 Sidon, to a woman who was a ***w***.
7:12 of his mother; and she was a ***w***.
18: 3 Now there was a ***w*** in that city;
18: 5 yet because this ***w*** troubles me I
21: 2 He saw also a certain poor ***w***
21: 3 I say to you that this poor ***w***
1 Tim 5: 4 But if any ***w*** has children or
5: 5 Now she who is really a ***w***,
5: 9 Do not let a ***w*** under sixty years
Rev 18: 7 'I sit as queen, and am no ***w***,

WIDOW'S (4/4) WIDOW

Gen 38:14 So she took off her ***w*** garments,
Deut 24:17 nor take a ***w*** garment as a
Job 24: 3 They take the ***w*** ox as a
29:13 And I caused the ***w*** heart to

WIDOWHOOD (4/4) WIDOW

Gen 38:19 put on the garments of her ***w***.
2 Sam 20: 3 day of their death, living in ***w***.
Isa 47: 9 The loss of children, and ***w***.
54: 4 the reproach of your ***w*** anymore.

WIDOWS (26/24) WIDOW, WIDOWS'

Ex 22:24 sword; your wives shall be ***w***,
Job 22: 9 You have sent ***w*** away empty,
27:15 And their ***w*** shall not weep,
Ps 68: 5 the fatherless, a defender of ***w***,
78:64 And their ***w*** made no
Isa 9:17 mercy on their fatherless and ***w***;
10: 2 That ***w*** may be their prey,
Jer 15: 8 Their ***w*** will be increased to Me
18:21 Let their wives become ***w*** And
49:11 And let your ***w*** trust in Me."
Lam 5: 3 Our mothers are like ***w***.
Ezek 22:25 they have made many ***w*** in her
44:22 of Israel, or ***w*** of priests.
Mal 3: 5 who exploit wage earners and ***w***
Lk 4:25 many ***w*** were in Israel in the
Acts 6: 1 because their ***w*** were neglected
9:39 And all the ***w*** stood by him
9:41 he had called the saints and ***w***,
1 Cor 7: 8 to the unmarried and to the ***w***:
1 Tim 5: 3 Honor ***w*** who are really widows.
5: 3 Honor widows who are really ***w***.
5:11 But refuse the younger ***w***;
5:14 I desire that the younger ***w***
5:16 believing man or woman has ***w***,
5:16 relieve those who are really ***w***.
Jas 1:27 to visit orphans and ***w*** in their

WIDOWS' (3/3) WIDOWS

Mt 23:14 For you devour **w** houses, and
Mk 12:40 who devour **w** houses, and for a
Lk 20:47 who devour **w** houses, and for a

WIDTH (71/65) WIDE

Gen 6:15 its **w** fifty cubits, and its
13:17 through its length and its **w**,
Ex 25:10 a cubit and a half its **w**,
25:17 and a cubit and a half its **w**.
25:23 be its length, a cubit its **w**,
26: 2 and the **w** of each curtain four
26: 8 and the **w** of each curtain four
26:16 and a half shall be the **w** of
27:12 And along the **w** of the court on
27:13 The **w** of the court on the east
27:18 the **w** fifty throughout, and the
28:16 and a span shall be its **w**.
30: 2 its length and a cubit its **w**—
36: 9 and the **w** of each curtain four
36:15 and the **w** of each curtain four
36:21 and the **w** of each board a cubit
37: 1 a cubit and a half its **w**,
37: 6 and a cubit and a half its **w**.
37:10 was its length, a cubit its **w**,
37:25 length was a cubit and its **w**
38: 1 length and five cubits its **w**—
38:18 and the height along its **w** was
39: 9 its length and a span its **w**
Deut 3:11 length and four cubits its **w**,
1 Ki 6: 2 its **w** twenty, and its height
6: 3 cubits long across the **w** of
6: 3 and the **w** of the vestible
7: 2 its **w** fifty cubits, and its
7: 6 and its **w** thirty cubits; and in
7:27 of each cart, four cubits its **w**,
2 Chr 3: 3 the former measure) and the **w**
3: 4 cubits long across the **w** of
3: 8 length was according to the **w**
3: 8 and its **w** twenty cubits.
4: 1 its length, twenty cubits its **w**,
Ezra 6: 3 height sixty cubits and its **w**
Ezek 40: 5 and he measured the **w** of the
40:11 He measured the **w** of the
40:13 the **w** was twenty-five cubits,
40:19 Then he measured the **w** from the
40:20 measured its length and its **w**.
40:21 was fifty cubits and its **w**
40:25 was fifty cubits and its **w**
40:36 was fifty cubits and its **w**
40:48 and the **w** of the gateway was
40:49 and the **w** eleven cubits; and by
41: 1 the **w** of the tabernacle.
41: 2 The **w** of the entryway was ten
41: 2 length, forty cubits, and its **w**,
41: 3 and the **w** of the entrance,
41: 4 twenty cubits; and the **w**,
41: 5 The **w** of each side chamber all
41: 7 therefore the **w** of the
41:10 the wall chambers was a **w** of
41:11 and the **w** of the terrace was
41:14 also the **w** of the eastern face
42: 2 (the **w** was fifty cubits),
43:14 the **w** of the ledge, one cubit;
43:14 and the **w** of the ledge, one
45: 1 and the **w** ten thousand.
48: 8 thousand cubits in **w**,
48: 9 in length and ten thousand in **w**.
48:10 on the west ten thousand in **w**,
48:10 on the east ten thousand in **w**,
48:13 in length and ten thousand in **w**;
48:13 twenty-five thousand and its **w**
48:15 five thousand cubits in **w**
Dan 3: 1 was sixty cubits and its **w**
Zech 2: 2 to see what is its **w** and what
5: 2 is twenty cubits and its **w**
Eph 3:18 all the saints what is the **w**

WIELD (1/1)

Isa 10:15 As if a rod could **w** itself

WIELDED (1/1)

Josh 8:31 stones over which no man has **w**

WIELDING (1/1)

Deut 20:19 destroy its trees by **w** an ax

WIFE (389/357) WIFE'S, WIVES

Gen 2:24 mother and be joined to his **w**,
2:25 both naked, the man and his **w**,
3: 8 and Adam and his **w** hid
3:17 have heeded the voice of your **w**,
3:21 Also for Adam and his **w** the
4: 1 Now Adam knew Eve his **w**,
4:17 And Cain knew his **w**,
4:25 And Adam knew his **w** again,
6:18 the ark—you, your sons, your **w**,
7: 7 So Noah, with his sons, his **w**,
7:13 and Noah's **w** and the three
8:16 out of the ark, you and your **w**,
8:18 and his sons and his **w** and his
11:29 the name of Abram's **w** was
11:29 and the name of Nahor's **w**,
11:31 Sarai, his son Abram's **w**,
12: 5 Then Abram took Sarai his **w** and
12:11 that he said to Sarai his **w**,
12:12 they will say, 'This is his **w**';
12:17 because of Sarai, Abram's **w**.
12:18 tell me that she was your **w**?
12:19 I might have taken her as my **w**.
12:19 Now therefore, here is your **w**;
12:20 with his **w** and all that he had.
13: 1 he and his **w** and all that he
16: 1 Now Sarai, Abram's **w**,
16: 3 Then Sarai, Abram's **w**,
16: 3 her husband Abram to be his **w**,
17:15 Abraham, "As for Sarai your **w**,
17:19 Sarah your **w** shall bear you a
18: 9 him, "Where is Sarah your **w**?
18:10 Sarah your **w** shall have a
19:15 take your **w** and your two
19:26 But his **w** looked back behind
20: 2 Now Abraham said of Sarah his **w**,
20: 3 taken, for she is a man's **w**.
20: 7 therefore, restore the man's **w**;
20:11 will kill me on account of my **w**.
20:12 my mother; and she became my **w**.
20:14 and he restored Sarah his **w** to
20:17 and God healed Abimelech, his **w**,
20:18 because of Sarah, Abraham's **w**.
21:21 and his mother took a **w** for him
23:19 Abraham buried Sarah his **w** in
24: 3 that you will not take a **w** for
24: 4 and take a **w** for my son
24: 7 and you shall take a **w** for my
24:15 the **w** of Nahor, Abraham's
24:36 And Sarah my master's **w** bore a
24:37 You shall not take a **w** for my
24:38 and take a **w** for my son.'
24:40 and you shall take a **w** for my
24:51 her be your master's son's **w**,
24:67 Rebekah and she became his **w**,
25: 1 Abraham again took a **w**,
25:10 was buried, and Sarah his **w**.
25:20 old when he took Rebekah as **w**,
25:21 with the LORD for his **w**,
25:21 and Rebekah his **w** conceived.
26: 7 of the place asked about his **w**.
26: 7 afraid to say, "She is my **w**,
26: 8 endearment to Rebekah his **w**.
26: 9 obviously she is your **w**;
26:10 soon have lain with your **w**,
26:11 who touches this man or his **w**
27:46 if Jacob takes a **w** of the
28: 1 You shall not take a **w** from the
28: 2 and take yourself a **w** from
28: 6 Padan Aram to take himself a **w**
28: 6 You shall not take a **w** from the
28: 9 to be his **w** in addition to the
29:21 said to Laban, "Give me my **w**,
29:28 him his daughter Rachel as **w**
30: 4 gave him Bilhah her maid as **w**,
30: 9 maid and gave her to Jacob as **w**.
34: 4 me this young woman as a **w**.
34: 8 Please give her to him as a **w**.
34:12 give me the young woman as a **w**.
36:10 the son of Adah the **w** of Esau,
36:10 the son of Basemath the **w** of
36:12 the sons of Adah, Esau's **w**.
36:13 the sons of Basemath, Esau's **w**.
36:14 sons of Aholibamah, Esau's **w**,
36:17 the sons of Basemath, Esau's **w**.
36:18 sons of Aholibamah, Esau's **w**:
36:18 from Aholibamah, Esau's **w**,
38: 6 Then Judah took a **w** for Er his
38: 8 Go in to your brother's **w** and
38: 9 he went in to his brother's **w**,
38:12 the daughter of Shua, Judah's **w**,
38:14 she was not given to him as a **w**.
39: 7 things that his master's **w**
39: 8 and said to his master's **w**,
39: 9 but you, because you are his **w**.
39:19 the words which his **w** spoke
41:45 And he gave him as a **w** Asenath,
44:27 You know that my **w** bore me two
46:19 The sons of Rachel, Jacob's **w**,
49:31 buried Abraham and Sarah his **w**,
49:31 buried Isaac and Rebekah his **w**,
Ex 2: 1 of Levi went and took as **w** a
4:20 Then Moses took his **w** and his
6:20 his father's sister, as **w**;
6:23 sister of Nahshon, as **w**;
6:25 of the daughters of Putiel as **w**;
18: 2 took Zipporah, Moses' **w**,
18: 5 came with his sons and his **w** to
18: 6 am coming to you with your **w**
20:17 not covet your neighbor's **w**,
21: 3 then his **w** shall go out with
21: 4 his master has given him a **w**,
21: 4 the **w** and her children shall be
21: 5 says, 'I love my master, my **w**,
21:10 "If he takes another **w**,
22:16 for her to be his **w**.
Lev 18: 8 nakedness of your father's **w**
18:14 You shall not approach his **w**;
18:15 is your son's **w**—you shall
18:16 nakedness of your brother's **w**;
18:20 carnally with your neighbor's **w**,
20:10 adultery with another man's **w**,
20:10 adultery with his neighbor's **w**,
20:11 who lies with his father's **w**
20:20 a man lies with his uncle's **w**,
20:21 'If a man takes his brother's **w**,
21: 7 They shall not take a **w** who is
21:13 And he shall take a **w** in her
21:14 a virgin of his own people as **w**.
Num 5:12 If any man's **w** goes astray and
5:14 and he becomes jealous of his **w**,
5:14 and he becomes jealous of his **w**,
5:15 'then the man shall bring his **w**
5:29 the law of jealousy, when a **w**,
5:30 and he becomes jealous of his **w**;
26:59 The name of Amram's **w** was
30:16 Moses, between a man and his **w**,
36: 8 of Israel shall be the **w** of
Deut 5:21 not covet your neighbor's **w**;
13: 6 the **w** of your bosom, or your
21:11 and would take her for your **w**,
21:13 and she shall be your **w**.
21:16 on the son of the loved **w** in
21:17 the son of the unloved **w** as
22:13 "If any man takes a **w**,
22:16 my daughter to this man as **w**,
22:19 And she shall be his **w**;
22:24 he humbled his neighbor's **w**;
22:29 and she shall be his **w** because
22:30 shall not take his father's **w**,
24: 1 When a man takes a **w** and marries
24: 2 and becomes another man's **w**,
24: 3 dies who took her as his **w**,
24: 4 not take her back to be his **w**
24: 5 "When a man has taken a new **w**,
24: 5 and bring happiness to his **w**
25: 5 go in to her, take her as his **w**,
25: 7 want to take his brother's **w**,
25: 7 then let his brother's **w** go up
25: 9 then his brother's **w** shall come
25:11 and the **w** of one draws near to
27:20 who lies with his father's **w**,
28:30 "You shall betroth a **w**,
28:54 toward the **w** of his bosom, and
Josh 15:16 give Achsah my daughter as **w**.
15:17 him Achsah his daughter as **w**.
Judg 1:12 give my daughter Achsah as **w**.
1:13 him his daughter Achsah as **w**.
4: 4 the **w** of Lapidoth, was judging
4:17 the **w** of Heber the Kenite; for
4:21 Then Jael, Heber's **w**,
5:24 The **w** of Heber the Kenite;
11: 2 Gilead's **w** bore sons; and when
13: 2 and his **w** was barren and had
13:11 Manoah arose and followed his **w**.
13:19 while Manoah and his **w** looked
13:20 When Manoah and his **w** saw
13:21 no more to Manoah and his **w**,
13:22 And Manoah said to his **w**,
13:23 But his **w** said to him, "If the
14: 2 get her for me as a **w**.
14: 3 that you must go and get a **w**
14:15 that they said to Samson's **w**,
14:16 Then Samson's **w** wept on him,
14:20 And Samson's **w** was given to his
15: 1 that Samson visited his **w** with
15: 1 he said, "Let me go in to my **w**,
15: 6 because he has taken his **w** and
21: 1 his daughter to Benjamin as a **w**.
21:18 be the one who gives a **w** to
21:21 and every man catch a **w** for
21:22 because we did not take a **w** for
Ruth 1: 1 he and his **w** and his two sons.
1: 2 the name of his **w** was Naomi,
4: 5 the **w** of the dead, to
4:10 Mahlon, I have acquired as my **w**,
4:13 took Ruth and she became his **w**;
1 Sam 1: 4 portions to Peninnah his **w** and
1:19 And Elkanah knew Hannah his **w**,
2:20 would bless Elkanah and his **w**,
4:19 daughter-in-law, Phinehas' **w**,
14:50 The name of Saul's **w** was
18:17 I will give her to you as a **w**.
18:19 Adriel the Meholathite as a **w**.
18:27 him Michal his daughter as a **w**.
19:11 And Michal, David's **w**,
25: 3 and the name of his **w** Abigail.
25:14 men told Abigail, Nabal's **w**,
25:37 and his **w** had told him these
25:39 Abigail, to take her as his **w**.
25:40 you, to ask you to become his **w**.
25:42 of David, and became his **w**.
25:44 Michal his daughter, David's **w**,
30:22 except for every man's **w** and
2 Sam 3: 5 by David's **w** Eglah. These were
3:14 Give me my **w** Michal, whom I
11: 3 the **w** of Uriah the Hittite?"
11:11 and drink, and to lie with my **w**?
11:26 When the **w** of Uriah heard that
11:27 and she became his **w** and bore
12: 9 you have taken his **w** to be
12: 9 taken his wife to be your **w**,
12:10 and have taken the **w** of Uriah
12:10 Uriah the Hittite to be your **w**.
12:15 the child that Uriah's **w** bore
12:24 David comforted Bathsheba his **w**,
1 Ki 2:17 me Abishag the Shunammite as **w**.
2:21 to Adonijah your brother as **w**.
4:11 the daughter of Solomon as **w**;
4:15 the daughter of Solomon as **w**;
7: 8 whom he had taken as **w**.
9:16 to his daughter, Solomon's **w**.
11:19 so that he gave him as **w** the
11:19 as wife the sister of his own **w**,
14: 2 And Jeroboam said to his **w**,
14: 2 may not recognize you as the **w**
14: 4 And Jeroboam's **w** did so;
14: 5 Here is the **w** of Jeroboam,
14: 6 **w** of Jeroboam. Why do you
14:17 Then Jeroboam's **w** arose and
16:31 that he took as **w** Jezebel the
21: 5 But Jezebel his **w** came to him,
21: 7 Then Jezebel his **w** said to him,
21:25 because Jezebel his **w** stirred

2 Ki 5: 2 She waited on Naaman's **w**.
8:18 the daughter of Ahab was his **w**;
14: 9 your daughter to my son as **w**';
22:14 the **w** of Shallum the son of
1 Chr 2:18 had children by Azubah, his **w**,
2:19 Caleb took Ephrath as his **w**,
2:24 Hezron's **w** Abijah bore him
2:26 Jerahmeel had another **w**,
2:29 And the name of the **w** of Abishur
2:35 to Jarha his servant as **w**,
3: 3 Ithream, by his **w** Eglah.
4:17 And Mered's **w** bore Miriam,
4:18 (His **w** Jehudijah bore Jered the
4:19 The sons of Hodiah's **w**,
7:15 Machir took as his **w** the
7:16 (Maachah the **w** of Machir bore a
7:23 And when he went in to his **w**,
8: 9 By Hodesh his **w** he begot Jobab,
2 Chr 8:11 My **w** shall not dwell in the
11:18 Rehoboam took for himself as **w**
21: 6 had the daughter of Ahab as a **w**;
22:11 the **w** of Jehoiada the priest
25:18 your daughter to my son as **w**';
34:22 the **w** of Shallum the son of
Ezra 2:61 who took a **w** of the daughters
Neh 7:63 who took a **w** of the daughters
Esth 5:10 for his friends and his **w**
5:14 Then his **w** Zeresh and all his
6:13 When Haman told his **w** Zeresh and
6:13 his wise men and his **w** Zeresh
Job 2: 9 Then his **w** said to him, "Do
19:17 My breath is offensive to my **w**,
31:10 Then let my **w** grind for
Ps 109: 9 And his **w** a widow.
128: 3 Your **w** shall be like a
Prov 5:18 And rejoice with the **w** of your
6:29 who goes in to his neighbor's **w**;
12: 4 An excellent **w** is the crown of
18:22 He who finds a **w** finds a good
19:13 And the contentions of a **w**
19:14 But a prudent **w** is from the
31:10 Who can find a virtuous **w**?
Eccl 9: 9 Live joyfully with the **w** whom
Isa 54: 6 Like a youthful **w** when you
Jer 3: 1 say, 'If a man divorces his **w**,
3:20 as a **w** treacherously departs
5: 8 neighed after his neighbor's **w**.
6:11 shall be taken with the **w**,
16: 2 "You shall not take a **w**,
Ezek 16:32 "You are an adulterous **w**,
18: 6 Nor defiled his neighbor's **w**,
18:11 Or defiled his neighbor's **w**;
18:15 Nor defiled his neighbor's **w**;
22:11 with his neighbor's **w**;
24:18 and at evening my **w** died;
44:22 They shall not take as **w** a widow
Hos 1: 2 take yourself a **w** of harlotry
2: 2 For she is not My **w**,
12:12 And for a **w** he tended sheep.
Am 7:17 Your **w** shall be a harlot in the
Mal 2:14 witness Between you and the **w**
2:14 is your companion And your **w**
2:15 deal treacherously with the **w**
Mt 1: 6 by her who had been the **w**
1:20 to take to you Mary your **w**,
1:24 him and took to him his **w**,
5:31 said, 'Whoever divorces his **w**,
5:32 you that whoever divorces his **w**
14: 3 his brother Philip's **w**.
18:25 with his **w** and children and all
19: 3 for a man to divorce his **w** for
19: 5 and be joined to his **w**,
19: 9 to you, whoever divorces his **w**,
19:10 the case of the man with his **w**,
19:29 or father or mother or **w** or
22:24 his brother shall marry his **w**
22:25 left his **w** to his brother.
22:28 whose **w** of the seven will she
27:19 his **w** sent to him, saying,
Mk 6:17 his brother Philip's **w**;
6:18 you to have your brother's **w**.
10: 2 for a man to divorce his **w**?
10: 7 and be joined to his **w**,
10:11 Whoever divorces his **w** and
10:29 or father or mother or **w** or
12:19 and leaves his **w** behind,
12:19 his brother should take his **w**
12:20 The first took a **w**;
12:23 whose **w** will she be?
12:23 For all seven had her as **w**."
Lk 1: 5 His **w** was of the daughters of
1:13 and your **w** Elizabeth will bear
1:18 and my **w** is well advanced in
1:24 Now after those days his **w**
2: 5 with Mary, his betrothed **w**,
3:19 his brother Philip's **w**,
8: 3 and Joanna the **w** of Chuza,
14:20 said, 'I have married a **w**,
14:26 **w** and children, brothers and
16:18 Whoever divorces his **w** and
17:32 "Remember Lot's **w**.
18:29 or parents or brothers or **w** or
20:28 man's brother dies, having a **w**,
20:28 his brother should take his **w**
20:29 And the first took a **w**,
20:30 "And the second took her as **w**,
20:33 whose **w** does she become?
20:33 For all seven had her as **w**.
Jn 19:25 Mary the **w** of Clopas, and Mary
Acts 5: 1 Ananias, with Sapphira his **w**,
5: 2 his **w** also being aware of it,
5: 7 three hours later when his **w**
18: 2 come from Italy with his **w**
24:24 when Felix came with his **w**
1 Cor 5: 1 that a man has his father's **w**!
7: 2 let each man have his own **w**,
7: 3 Let the husband render to his **w**
7: 3 and likewise also the **w** to her
7: 4 The **w** does not have authority
7: 4 his own body, but the **w** does.
7:10 A **w** is not to depart from her
7:11 is not to divorce his **w**.
7:12 If any brother has a **w** who does
7:14 husband is sanctified by the **w**,
7:14 and the unbelieving **w** is
7:16 For how do you know, O **w**,
7:16 whether you will save your **w**?
7:27 Are you bound to a **w**?
7:27 Are you loosed from a **w**?
7:27 from a wife? Do not seek a **w**.
7:33 world—how he may please his **w**.
7:34 is a difference between a **w**
7:39 A **w** is bound by law as long as
9: 5 to take along a believing **w**,
Eph 5:23 the husband is head of the **w**,
5:28 he who loves his **w** loves
5:31 and be joined to his **w**,
5:33 in particular so love his own **w**
5:33 and let the **w** see that she
1 Tim 3: 2 blameless, the husband of one **w**,
3:12 be the husbands of one **w**,
5: 9 unless she has been the **w** of
Titus 1: 6 blameless, the husband of one **w**,
1 Pe 3: 7 giving honor to the **w**,
Rev 19: 7 and His **w** has made herself
21: 9 you the bride, the Lamb's **w**.

WIFE'S (11/11) WIFE

Gen 3:20 And Adam called his **w** name Eve,
19:16 his **w** hand, and the hands of
36:39 His **w** name was Mehetabel,
Lev 18:11 of your father's **w** daughter,
Judg 11: 2 and when his **w** sons grew up,
1 Chr 1:50 His **w** name was Mehetabel the
8:29 whose **w** name was Maacah, dwelt
9:35 whose **w** name was Maacah, dwelt
Mt 8:14 He saw his **w** mother lying sick
Mk 1:30 But Simon's **w** mother lay sick
Lk 4:38 But Simon's **w** mother was sick

WILD (59/56)

Gen 16:12 He shall be a **w** man; His hand
37:20 Some **w** beast has devoured him.'
37:33 A **w** beast has devoured him.
Lev 7:24 what is torn by **w** beasts,
26:22 I will also send **w** beasts among
Num 23:22 He has strength like a **w** ox.
24: 8 He has strength like a **w** ox;
Deut 14: 5 the **w** goat, the mountain goat,
33:17 like the horns of the **w** ox;
1 Sam 17:46 of the air and the **w** beasts
24: 2 on the Rocks of the **W** Goats.
2 Sam 2:18 fleet of foot as a **w** gazelle.
2 Ki 4:39 and found a **w** vine,
4:39 from it a lapful of **w** gourds,
14: 9 and a **w** beast that was in
2 Chr 25:18 and a **w** beast that was in
Job 6: 5 Does the **w** donkey bray when it
11:12 When a **w** donkey's colt is born
24: 5 like **w** donkeys in the desert,
39: 1 the **w** mountain goats bear
39: 5 'Who set the **w** donkey free?
39: 9 Will the **w** ox be willing to
39:10 Can you bind the **w** ox in the
39:15 Or that a **w** beast may break
Ps 22:21 the horns of the **w** oxen!
29: 6 and Sirion like a young **w** ox.
50:11 And the **w** beasts of the field
74:19 turtledove to the **w** beast!
80:13 And the **w** beast of the field
92:10 You have exalted like a **w** ox;
104:11 The **w** donkeys quench their
104:18 hills are for the **w** goats;
Isa 5: 2 But it brought forth **w** grapes.
5: 4 Did it bring forth **w** grapes?
13:21 But **w** beasts of the desert will
13:21 And **w** goats will caper there.
23:13 founded it for **w** beasts
32:14 A joy of **w** donkeys, a pasture
34: 7 The **w** oxen shall come down with
34:14 The **w** beasts of the desert
34:14 And the **w** goat shall bleat to
Jer 2:24 A **w** donkey used to the
14: 6 And the **w** donkeys stood in the
50:39 Therefore the **w** desert beasts
Ezek 5:17 you famine and **w** beasts,
14:15 If I cause **w** beasts to pass
14:21 sword and famine and **w** beasts
34:25 and cause **w** beasts to cease
44:31 or was torn by **w** beasts.
Dan 5:21 was with the **w** donkeys.
Hos 8: 9 Like a **w** donkey alone by
13: 8 The **w** beast shall tear them.
Mt 3: 4 food was locusts and **w** honey.
Mk 1: 6 and he ate locusts and **w** honey.
1:13 and was with the **w** beasts;
Acts 10:12 **w** beasts, creeping things,
11: 6 **w** beasts, creeping things,
Rom 11:17 being a **w** olive tree, were
11:24 of the olive tree which is **w**

WILDERNESS (306/293)

Gen 14: 6 as El Paran, which is by the **w**.
16: 7 by a spring of water in the **w**,
21:14 departed and wandered in the **W**
21:20 and he grew and dwelt in the **w**,
21:21 He dwelt in the **W** of Paran;
36:24 who found the water in the **w**
37:22 this pit which is in the **w**,
Ex 3:18 three days' journey into the **w**,
4:27 Go into the **w** to meet Moses."
5: 1 may hold a feast to Me in the **w**.
7:16 they may serve Me in the **w**";
8:27 three days' journey into the **w**
8:28 to the LORD your God in the **w**;
13:18 people around by way of the **w**
13:20 in Etham at the edge of the **w**.
14: 3 the **w** has closed them in.'
14:11 taken us away to die in the **w**?
14:12 that we should die in the **w**.
15:22 then they went out into the **W**
15:22 they went three days in the **w**
16: 1 of Israel came to the **W** of Sin,
16: 2 Moses and Aaron in the **w**.
16: 3 brought us out into this **w** to
16:10 that they looked toward the **w**,
16:14 there, on the surface of the **w**,
16:32 with which I fed you in the **w**,
17: 1 on their journey from the **W** of
18: 5 and his wife to Moses in the **w**,
19: 1 they came to the **W** of Sinai.
19: 2 had come to the **W** of Sinai,
19: 2 of Sinai, and camped in the **w**.
Lev 7:38 to the LORD in the **W** of Sinai.
16:10 go as the scapegoat into the **w**.
16:21 shall send it away into the **w**
16:22 shall release the goat in the **w**.
Num 1: 1 LORD spoke to Moses in the **W**
1:19 so he numbered them in the **W** of
3: 4 fire before the LORD in the **W**
3:14 LORD spoke to Moses in the **W**
9: 1 LORD spoke to Moses in the **W**
9: 5 in the **W** of Sinai; according to
10:12 of Israel set out from the **W**
10:12 cloud settled down in the **W** of
10:31 how we are to camp in the **w**,
12:16 Hazeroth and camped in the **W**
13: 3 So Moses sent them from the **W** of
13:21 spied out the land from the **W**
13:26 children of Israel in the **W** of
14: 2 if only we had died in this **w**!
14:16 He killed them in the **w**.
14:22 I did in Egypt and in the **w**,
14:25 turn and move out into the **w**
14:29 against Me shall fall in this **w**,
14:32 carcasses shall fall in this **w**.
14:33 shall be shepherds in the **w**
14:33 carcasses are consumed in the **w**.
14:35 In this **w** they shall be
15:32 of Israel were in the **w**,
16:13 and honey, to kill us in the **w**,
20: 1 came into the **W** of Zin in the
20: 4 of the LORD into this **w**,
21: 5 up out of Egypt to die in the **w**?
21:11 in the **w** which is east of
21:13 which is in the **w** that extends
21:18 And from the **w** they went to
21:23 out against Israel in the **w**,
24: 1 he set his face toward the **w**.
26:64 children of Israel in the **W** of
26:65 shall surely die in the **w**.
27: 3 "Our father died in the **w**;
27:14 For in the **W** of Zin, during the
27:14 at Kadesh in the **W** of Zin.)
32:13 He made them wander in the **w**
32:15 once again leave them in the **w**,
33: 6 which is on the edge of the **w**.
33: 8 the midst of the sea into the **w**,
33: 8 three days' journey in the **W**
33:11 Red Sea and camped in the **W** of
33:12 They journeyed from the **W** of Sin
33:15 Rephidim and camped in the **W**
33:16 They moved from the **W** of Sinai
33:36 Geber and camped in the **W** of
34: 3 border shall be from the **W** of
Deut 1: 1 side of the Jordan in the **w**,
1:19 all that great and terrible **w**
1:31 and in the **w** where you saw how
1:40 take your journey into the **w**
2: 1 and journeyed into the **w** of
2: 7 trudging through this great **w**.
2: 8 and passed by way of the **W** of
2:26 I sent messengers from the **W**
4:43 Bezer in the **w** on the plateau
8: 2 way these forty years in the **w**,
8:15 that great and terrible **w**,
8:16 who fed you in the **w** with manna,
9: 7 your God to wrath in the **w**.
9:28 them out to kill them in the **w**.
11: 5 what He did for you in the **w**
11:24 from the **w** and Lebanon, from
29: 5 led you forty years in the **w**.
32:10 in the wasteland, a howling **w**;
32:51 in the **W** of Zin, because you
Josh 1: 4 From the **w** and this Lebanon as
5: 4 had died in the **w** on the way,
5: 5 all the people born in the **w**,
5: 6 walked forty years in the **w**,
8:15 and fled by the way of the **w**.
8:20 people who had fled to the **w**
8:24 in the **w** where they pursued
10:40 South and the lowland and the **w**

12: 8 plain, in the slopes, in the **w**,
14:10 while Israel wandered in the **w**;
15: 1 The border of Edom at the **W** of
15:61 In the **w**: Beth Arabah,
16: 1 to the **w** that goes up from
18:12 it ended at the **W** of Beth Aven.
20: 8 they assigned Bezer in the **w** on
24: 7 Then you dwelt in the **w** a long
Judg 1:16 children of Judah into the **W**
8: 7 flesh with the thorns of the **w**
8:16 and thorns of the **w** and briers,
11:16 they walked through the **w** as
11:18 they went along through the **w**
11:22 to the Jabbok and from the **w**
20:42 in the direction of the **w**;
20:45 turned and fled toward the **w**
20:47 turned and fled toward the **w**
1 Sam 4: 8 with all the plagues in the **w**.
13:18 Valley of Zeboim toward the **w**.
17:28 left those few sheep in the **w**?
23:14 stayed in strongholds in the **w**,
23:14 in the mountains in the **W** of
23:15 And David was in the **W** of Ziph
23:24 and his men were in the **W** of
23:25 and stayed in the **W** of Maon.
23:25 he pursued David in the **W** of
24: 1 Take note! David is in the **W** of
25: 1 arose and went down to the **W**
25: 4 When David heard in the **w** that
25:14 sent messengers from the **w** to
25:21 that this fellow has in the **w**,
26: 2 arose and went down to the **W**
26: 2 to seek David in the **W** of Ziph.
26: 3 But David stayed in the **w**,
26: 3 Saul came after him into the **w**.
2 Sam 2:24 Giah by the road to the **W** of
15:23 over toward the way of the **w**.
15:28 wait in the plains of the **w**
16: 2 those who are faint in the **w**
17:16 night in the plains of the **w**,
17:29 and weary and thirsty in the **w**.
1 Ki 2:34 in his own house in the **w**.
9:18 Baalath, and Tadmor in the **w**,
19: 4 went a day's journey into the **w**,
19:15 return on your way to the **W** of
2 Ki 3: 8 By way of the **W** of Edom."
1 Chr 5: 9 as far as the entrance of the **w**
6:78 Bezer in the **w** with its
12: 8 at the stronghold in the **w**,
21:29 which Moses had made in the **w**,
2 Chr 1: 3 of the LORD had made in the **w**.
8: 4 He also built Tadmor in the **w**,
20:16 end of the brook before the **W**
20:20 and went out into the **W** of
20:24 to a place overlooking the **w**,
24: 9 imposed on Israel in the **w**.
Neh 9:19 did not forsake them in the **w**.
9:21 You sustained them in the **w**,
Job 1:19 wind came from across the **w**
12:24 them wander in a pathless **w**.
24: 5 The **w** yields food for them
30: 3 Fleeing late to the **w**,
38:26 A **w** in which there is no
39: 6 Whose home I have made the **w**,
Ps 29: 8 voice of the LORD shakes the **w**;
29: 8 The LORD shakes the **W** of
55: 7 far off, And remain in the **w**.
63: of David when he was in the **w**
65:12 drop on the pastures of the **w**,
68: 7 When You marched through the **w**,
72: 9 Those who dwell in the **w** will
74:14 to the people inhabiting the **w**.
78:15 He split the rocks in the **w**,
78:17 against the Most High in the **w**.
78:19 God prepare a table in the **w**?
78:40 they provoked Him in the **w**,
78:52 And guided them in the **w** like
95: 8 in the day of trial in the **w**,
102: 6 I am like a pelican of the **w**;
106: 9 the depths, As through the **w**.
106:14 lusted exceedingly in the **w**,
106:26 To overthrow them in the **w**,
107: 4 They wandered in the **w** in a
107:33 He turns rivers into a **w**,
107:35 He turns a **w** into pools of
107:40 causes them to wander in the **w**
136:16 led His people through the **w**,
Prov 21:19 Better to dwell in the **w**,
Song 3: 6 is this coming out of the **w**
8: 5 is this coming up from the **w**,
Isa 14:17 Who made the world as a **w** And
16: 1 the land, From Sela to the **w**,
16: 8 And wandered through the **w**.
21: 1 The burden against the **W** of the
27:10 forsaken and left like a **w**;
32:15 And the **w** becomes a fruitful
32:16 justice will dwell in the **w**,
33: 9 Sharon is like a **w**,
35: 1 The **w** and the wasteland shall
35: 6 shall burst forth in the **w**,
40: 3 voice of one crying in the **w**:
41:18 I will make the **w** a pool of
41:19 I will plant in the **w** the cedar
42:11 Let the **w** and its cities lift
43:19 will even make a road in the **w**
43:20 I give waters in the **w** And
50: 2 the sea, I make the rivers a **w**;
51: 3 He will make her **w** like Eden,
63:13 the deep, As a horse in the **w**,
64:10 Your holy cities are a **w**,
64:10 are a wilderness, Zion is a **w**,
Jer 2: 2 you went after Me in the **w**,
2: 6 Who led us through the **w**,
2:24 A wild donkey used to the **w**,
2:31 of the LORD! Have I been a **w**
3: 2 Like an Arabian in the **w**;
4:11 heights blows in the **w**
4:26 the fruitful land was a **w**,
9: 2 that I had in the **w** A lodging
9:10 the dwelling places of the **w** a
9:12 perish and burn up like a **w**,
9:26 corners, who dwell in the **w**.
12:10 pleasant portion a desolate **w**.
12:12 the desolate heights in the **w**,
13:24 away by the wind of the **w**.
17: 6 the parched places in the **w**,
22: 6 I surely will make you a **w**,
23:10 The pleasant places of the **w**
31: 2 the sword Found grace in the **w**—
48: 6 be like the juniper in the **w**.
50:12 of the nations shall be a **w**,
51:43 desolation, A dry land and a **w**,
Lam 4: 3 Like ostriches in the **w**.
4:19 lay in wait for us in the **w**.
5: 9 Because of the sword in the **w**.
Ezek 6:14 more desolate than the **w** toward
19:13 now she is planted in the **w**,
20:10 and brought them into the **w**.
20:13 rebelled against Me in the **w**;
20:13 out My fury on them in the **w**,
20:15 in an oath to them in the **w**,
20:17 make an end of them in the **w**.
20:18 said to their children in the **w**,
20:21 My anger against them in the **w**.
20:23 in an oath to those in the **w**,
20:35 I will bring you into the **w** of
20:36 with your fathers in the **w** of
23:42 were brought from the **w** with
29: 5 I will leave you in the **w**,
34:25 will dwell safely in the **w** and
Hos 2: 3 And make her like a **w**,
2:14 Will bring her into the **w**,
9:10 Like grapes in the **w**;
13: 5 I knew you in the **w**,
13:15 LORD shall come up from the **w**.
Joel 2: 3 And behind them a desolate **w**;
3:19 And Edom a desolate **w**,
Am 2:10 you forty years through the **w**,
5:25 and offerings In the **w** forty
Zeph 2:13 a desolation, As dry as the **w**.
Mal 1: 3 For the jackals of the **w**.
Mt 3: 1 came preaching in the **w** of
3: 3 of one crying in the **w**:
4: 1 up by the Spirit into the **w** to
11: 7 did you go out into the **w**
15:33 we get enough bread in the **w**
Mk 1: 3 of one crying in the **w**:
1: 4 John came baptizing in the **w** and
1:12 the Spirit drove Him into the **w**.
1:13 And He was there in the **w** forty
8: 4 people with bread here in the **w**?
Lk 3: 2 the son of Zacharias in the **w**.
3: 4 of one crying in the **w**:
4: 1 led by the Spirit into the **w**,
5:16 often withdrew into the **w** and
7:24 did you go out into the **w**
8:29 driven by the demon into the **w**.
15: 4 leave the ninety-nine in the **w**,
Jn 1:23 of one crying in the **w**:
3:14 lifted up the serpent in the **w**,
6:49 fathers ate the manna in the **w**,
11:54 into the country near the **w**,
Acts 7:30 in the **w** of Mount Sinai.
7:36 and in the **w** forty years.
7:38 in the congregation in the **w**
7:42 forty years in the **w**,
7:44 tabernacle of witness in the **w**,
13:18 put up with their ways in the **w**.
21:38 assassins out into the **w**?
1 Cor 10: 5 bodies were scattered in the **w**.
2 Cor 11:26 the city, in perils in the **w**,
Heb 3: 8 day of trial in the **w**,
3:17 whose corpses fell in the **w**?
Rev 12: 6 Then the woman fled into the **w**,
12:14 that she might fly into the **w**
17: 3 away in the Spirit into the **w**.

WILES (1/1)

Eph 6:11 be able to stand against the **w**

WILL (105/98) See APPENDIX

Gen 23:13 If you **w** give it, please hear
24:42 if You **w** now prosper the way in
24:49 Now if you **w** deal kindly and
30:31 If you **w** do this thing for me,
43: 4 we **w** go down and buy you food.
43: 5 But if you **w** not send him, we
45: 6 five years in which there **w**
Lev 1: 3 offer it of his own free **w** at
19: 5 offer it of your own free **w**.
22:29 offer it of your own free **w**.
Num 16:28 not done them of my own **w**.
24:13 to do good or bad of my own **w**.
Deut 25: 7 he **w** not perform the duty of my
Judg 6:36 If You **w** save Israel by my hand
9:38 you despised? Go out, if you **w**,
1 Sam 23:11 He **w** come down."
23:12 They **w** deliver you."
2 Ki 3: 7 I **w** go up; I am as you are,
6: 3 And he answered, 'I **w** go.'
Ezra 4:16 the result will be that you **w**
7:18 do it according to the **w** of
10:11 of your fathers, and do His **w**;
Ps 27:12 Do not deliver me to the **w** of
40: 8 I delight to do Your **w**,
41: 2 him to the **w** of his enemies.
143:10 Teach me to do Your **w**,
Isa 8: 8 stretching out of his wings **w**
9: 7 and peace There **w** be no
47:12 Perhaps you **w** prevail.
Jer 18:12 and we **w** every one obey the
Ezek 16:27 the **w** of those who hate you,
Dan 11:16 shall do according to his own **w**,
Mt 6:10 Your **w** be done On earth as
7:21 but he who does the **w** of My
10:29 apart from your Father's **w**.
12:50 For whoever does the **w** of My
21:29 I **w** not,' but afterward he
21:31 two did the **w** of his father?'
26:39 Nevertheless, not as I **w**,
26:39 not as I will, but as You **w**.
26:42 Your **w** be done.'
Mk 3:35 For whoever does the **w** of God is
14:36 nevertheless, not what I **w**,
14:36 what I will, but what You **w**.
Lk 12:47 servant who knew his master's **w**,
12:47 or do according to his **w**,
22:42 "Father, if it is Your **w**,
22:42 from Me; nevertheless not My **w**,
23:25 he delivered Jesus to their **w**.
Jn 1:13 nor of the **w** of the flesh,
1:13 nor of the **w** of man, but of
4:34 My food is to do the **w** of Him
5:30 because I do not seek My own **w**
5:30 own will but the **w** of the Father
6:38 from heaven, not to do My own **w**,
6:38 but the **w** of Him who sent Me.
6:39 This is the **w** of the Father who
6:40 And this is the **w** of Him who
7:17 "If anyone wants to do His **w**,
9:31 worshiper of God and does His **w**,
21:22 If I **w** that he remain till I
21:23 If I **w** that he remain till I
Acts 13:36 own generation by the **w** of God,
21:14 The **w** of the Lord be done.'
22:14 you that you should know His **w**,
Rom 1:10 may find a way in the **w** of God
2:18 and know His **w**,
7:18 for to **w** is present with me,
9:19 For who has resisted His **w**?
12: 2 and acceptable and perfect **w**
15:32 to you with joy by the **w** of God,
1 Cor 1: 1 Christ through the **w** of God,
7:37 but has power over his own **w**,
9:17 a reward; but if against my **w**,
2 Cor 1: 1 Jesus Christ by the **w** of God,
8: 5 then to us by the **w** of God.
Gal 1: 4 according to the **w** of our God
Eph 1: 1 Jesus Christ by the **w** of God,
1: 5 to the good pleasure of His **w**,
1: 9 to us the mystery of His **w**,
1:11 to the counsel of His **w**,
5:17 what the **w** of the Lord is.
6: 6 doing the **w** of God from the
Phil 2:13 God who works in you both to **w**
Col 1: 1 Jesus Christ by the **w** of God,
1: 9 with the knowledge of His **w** in
4:12 complete in all the **w** of God.
1 Th 4: 3 For this is the **w** of God,
5:18 for this is the **w** of God in
2 Tim 1: 1 Jesus Christ by the **w** of God,
2:26 captive by him to do his **w**.
Heb 1:14 to minister for those who **w**
2: 4 Spirit, according to His own **w**?
10: 7 of Me—To do Your **w**,
10: 9 I have come to do Your **w**,
10:36 you have done the **w** of God,
13:21 in every good work to do His **w**,
1 Pe 2:15 For this is the **w** of God,
3:17 if it is the **w** of God,
4: 2 but for the **w** of God.
4:19 who suffer according to the **w**
2 Pe 1:21 prophecy never came by the **w**
1 Jn 2:17 but he who does the **w** of God
5:14 ask anything according to His **w**,
Rev 4:11 And by Your **w** they exist and

WILLED (1/1)

Col 1:27 To them God **w** to make known what

WILLFULLY (2/2) WILL

Heb 10:26 For if we sin **w** after we have
2 Pe 3: 5 For this they **w** forget: that by

WILLING (41/41) WILL, WILLINGLY

Gen 24: 5 the woman will not be **w** to
24: 8 And if the woman is not **w** to
Ex 35: 5 Whoever is of a **w** heart, let
35:21 and everyone whose spirit was **w**,
35:22 as many as had a **w** heart,
35:29 and women whose hearts were **w**
Lev 26:21 and are not **w** to obey Me, I
Judg 19:10 the man was not **w** to spend that
1 Chr 19:19 So the Syrians were not **w** to
28: 9 loyal heart and with a **w** mind;
28:21 and every **w** craftsman will be
29: 5 Who then is **w** to consecrate
2 Chr 29:31 many as were of a **w** heart
Job 39: 9 Will the wild ox be **w** to serve

Isa 1:19 If you are ***w*** and obedient,
Mt 8: 2 saying, "Lord, if You are ***w***,
8: 3 touched him, saying, "I am ***w***;
11:14 And if you are ***w*** to receive it,
22: 3 and they were not ***w*** to come.
23:37 but you were not ***w***!
26:15 What are you ***w*** to give me if I
26:41 The spirit indeed is ***w***,
Mk 1:40 saying to Him, "If You are ***w***,
1:41 him, and said to him, "I am ***w***;
14:38 The spirit indeed is ***w***,
Lk 5:12 saying, "Lord, if You are ***w***,
5:13 touched him, saying, "I am ***w***;
13:34 but you were not ***w***!
Jn 5:35 and you were ***w*** for a time to
5:40 But you are not ***w*** to come to Me
Acts 18:21 will return again to you, God ***w***.
25: 9 Are you ***w*** to go up to Jerusalem
25:20 I asked whether he was ***w*** to go
26: 5 if they were ***w*** to testify, that
1 Cor 7:12 and she is ***w*** to live with him,
7:13 if he is ***w*** to live with her,
2 Cor 8: 3 ability, they were freely ***w***,
8:12 For if there is first a ***w*** mind,
1 Tim 6:18 ready to give, ***w*** to share,
Jas 3:17 ***w*** to yield, full of mercy and
2 Pe 3: 9 not ***w*** that any should perish

WILLINGLY (22/20) WILLING

Ex 25: 2 From everyone who gives it ***w***
Deut 15: 8 hand wide to him and ***w*** lend
Judg 5: 2 When the people ***w*** offer
5: 9 Who offered themselves ***w*** with
1 Chr 29: 6 over the king's work, offered ***w***.
29: 9 for they had offered ***w***,
29: 9 loyal heart they had offered ***w***
29:14 we should be able to offer so ***w***
29:17 of my heart I have ***w*** offered
29:17 are present here to offer ***w*** to
2 Chr 17:16 who ***w*** offered himself to the
35: 8 And his leaders gave ***w*** to the
Ezra 1: 6 all that was ***w*** offered.
3: 5 of everyone who ***w*** offered
Neh 11: 2 all the men who ***w*** offered
Prov 31:13 And ***w*** works with her hands.
Lam 3:33 For He does not afflict ***w***,
Hos 5:11 Because he ***w*** walked by human
Jn 6:21 Then they ***w*** received Him into
Rom 8:20 subjected to futility, not ***w***,
1 Cor 9:17 For if I do this ***w***,
1 Pe 5: 2 not by compulsion but ***w***,

WILLINGNESS (1/1)

2 Cor 9: 2 for I know your ***w***,

WILLOW (1/1)

Ezek 17: 5 waters And set it like a ***w***

WILLOWS (5/5)

Lev 23:40 and ***w*** of the brook; and you
Job 40:22 The ***w*** by the brook surround
Ps 137: 2 We hung our harps Upon the ***w***
Isa 15: 7 away to the Brook of the ***W***.
44: 4 up among the grass Like ***w*** by

WILLS (9/8) WILL

Mt 11:27 the one to whom the Son ***w*** to
Lk 10:22 the one to whom the Son ***w*** to
Rom 7:21 the one who ***w*** to do good.
9:16 then it is not of him who ***w***,
9:18 He has mercy on whom He ***w***,
9:18 and whom He ***w*** He hardens.
1 Cor 4:19 to you shortly, if the Lord ***w***,
12:11 each one individually as He ***w***.
Jas 4:15 ought to say, "If the Lord ***w***,

WILTED (1/1)

Ezek 31:15 all the trees of the field ***w***

WILTS (1/1)

Nah 1: 4 And the flower of Lebanon ***w***.

WIN (8/7) WINS

2 Chr 32: 1 thinking to ***w*** them over to
Prov 18:19 offended is harder to ***w***
Mt 23:15 you travel land and sea to ***w***
1 Cor 9:19 that I might ***w*** the more;
9:20 that I might ***w*** Jews; to those
9:20 that I might ***w*** those who are
9:21 that I might ***w*** those who are
9:22 that I might ***w*** the weak. I have

WIND (131/122) WINDS, WINDSTORM

Gen 8: 1 And God made a ***w*** to pass over
41: 6 heads, blighted by the east ***w***,
41:23 and blighted by the east ***w***,
41:27 heads blighted by the east ***w***
Ex 10:13 the LORD brought an east ***w*** on
10:13 the east ***w*** brought the locusts.
10:19 turned a very strong west ***w***,
14:21 to go back by a strong east ***w***
15:10 You blew with Your ***w***,
Num 11:31 Now a ***w*** went out from the
2 Sam 22:11 seen upon the wings of the ***w***.
1 Ki 18:45 became black with clouds and ***w***,
19:11 and a great and strong ***w*** tore
19:11 the LORD was not in the ***w***;
19:11 and after the ***w*** an earthquake,
2 Ki 3:17 the LORD: 'You shall not see ***w***,
Job 1:19 and suddenly a great ***w*** came from
6:26 desperate one, which are as ***w***?
8: 2 your mouth be like a strong ***w***?
15: 2 fill himself with the east ***w***?
16: 3 Shall words of ***w*** have an end?
21:18 are like straw before the ***w***,
27:21 The east ***w*** carries him away,
28:25 establish a weight for the ***w***,
30:15 They pursue my honor as the ***w***,
30:22 You lift me up to the ***w*** and
37:17 the earth by the south ***w***?
37:21 When the ***w*** has passed and
38:24 Or the east ***w*** scattered over
Ps 1: 4 are like the chaff which the ***w***
11: 6 and brimstone and a burning ***w***
18:10 flew upon the wings of the ***w***.
18:42 fine as the dust before the ***w***;
35: 5 them be like chaff before the ***w***,
48: 7 of Tarshish With an east ***w***.
78:26 He caused an east ***w*** to blow in
78:26 power He brought in the south ***w***.
83:13 Like the chaff before the ***w***!
103:16 For the ***w*** passes over it,
104: 3 walks on the wings of the ***w***,
107:25 and raises the stormy ***w***,
135: 7 He brings the ***w*** out of His
147:18 He causes His ***w*** to blow,
148: 8 snow and clouds; Stormy ***w***,
Prov 11:29 own house will inherit the ***w***,
25:14 giving Is like clouds and ***w***
25:23 The north ***w*** brings forth rain,
27:16 restrains her restrains the ***w***,
30: 4 Who has gathered the ***w*** in His
Eccl 1: 6 The ***w*** goes toward the south,
1: 6 The ***w*** whirls about
1:14 vanity and grasping for the ***w***.
1:17 this also is grasping for the ***w***.
2:11 vanity and grasping for the ***w***.
2:17 vanity and grasping for the ***w***.
2:26 vanity and grasping for the ***w***.
4: 4 vanity and grasping for the ***w***.
4: 6 toil and grasping for the ***w***.
4:16 vanity and grasping for the ***w***.
5:16 he who has labored for the ***w***?
6: 9 vanity and grasping for the ***w***.
11: 4 He who observes the ***w*** will not
11: 5 know what is the way of the ***w***,
Song 4:16 Awake, O north ***w***,
Isa 7: 2 the woods are moved with the ***w***.
11:15 With His mighty ***w*** He will
17:13 of the mountains before the ***w***,
26:18 as it were, brought forth ***w***;
27: 8 He removes it by His rough ***w***
27: 8 In the day of the east ***w***.
32: 2 be as a hiding place from the ***w***,
41:16 the ***w*** shall carry them away,
41:29 Their molded images are ***w*** and
57:13 But the ***w*** will carry them all
64: 6 And our iniquities, like the ***w***,
Jer 2:24 That sniffs at the ***w*** in her
4:11 A dry ***w*** of the desolate heights
4:12 A ***w*** too strong for these will
5:13 And the prophets become ***w***,
10:13 He brings the ***w*** out of His
13:24 That passes away by the ***w*** of
14: 6 They sniffed at the ***w*** like
18:17 scatter them as with an east ***w***
22:22 The ***w*** shall eat up all your
51: 1 in Leb Kamai, A destroying ***w***.
51:16 He brings the ***w*** out of His
Ezek 5: 2 you shall scatter in the ***w***:
12:14 I will scatter to every ***w*** all
13:11 and a stormy ***w*** shall tear it
13:13 I will cause a stormy ***w*** to break
17:10 utterly wither when the east ***w***
17:21 shall be scattered to every ***w***;
19:12 And the east ***w*** dried her
27:26 But the east ***w*** broke you in
Dan 2:35 the ***w*** carried them away so that
Hos 4:19 The ***w*** has wrapped her up in its
8: 7 "They sow the ***w***,
12: 1 "Ephraim feeds on the ***w***,
12: 1 And pursues the east ***w***;
13:15 An east ***w*** shall come;
13:15 The ***w*** of the LORD shall come
Am 4:13 mountains, And creates the ***w***,
Jon 1: 4 the LORD sent out a great ***w***
4: 8 God prepared a vehement east ***w***;
Hab 1: 9 faces are set like the east ***w***.
Zech 5: 9 coming with the ***w*** in their
Mt 11: 7 A reed shaken by the ***w***?
14:24 for the ***w*** was contrary.
14:30 But when he saw that the ***w*** was
14:32 into the boat, the ***w*** ceased.
Mk 4:39 Then He arose and rebuked the ***w***,
4:39 be still!" And the ***w*** ceased
4:41 that even the ***w*** and the sea
6:48 for the ***w*** was against them.
6:51 and the ***w*** ceased. And they were
Lk 7:24 A reed shaken by the ***w***?
8:24 He arose and rebuked the ***w*** and
12:55 And when you see the south ***w***
Jn 3: 8 'The ***w*** blows where it wishes,
6:18 the sea arose because a great ***w***
Acts 2: 2 as of a rushing mighty ***w***,
27: 7 the ***w*** not permitting us to
27:13 When the south ***w*** blew softly,
27:14 a tempestuous head ***w*** arose,
27:15 and could not head into the ***w***,
27:40 hoisted the mainsail to the ***w***
28:13 And after one day the south ***w***
Eph 4:14 and carried about with every ***w***
Jas 1: 6 sea driven and tossed by the ***w***.
Rev 6:13 when it is shaken by a mighty ***w***.
7: 1 that the ***w*** should not blow on

WINDOW (23/21) WINDOWS

Gen 6:16 You shall make a ***w*** for the ark,
8: 6 that Noah opened the ***w*** of the
26: 8 Philistines looked through a ***w***,
Josh 2:15 down by a rope through the ***w***,
2:18 line of scarlet cord in the ***w***
2:21 bound the scarlet cord in the ***w***.
Judg 5:28 of Sisera looked through the ***w***,
1 Sam 19:12 let David down through a ***w***.
2 Sam 6:16 looked through a ***w*** and saw King
1 Ki 7: 4 and ***w*** was opposite window in
7: 4 and window was opposite ***w*** in
7: 5 and ***w*** was opposite window in
7: 5 and window was opposite ***w*** in
2 Ki 9:30 head, and looked through a ***w***.
9:32 And he looked up at the ***w***,
13:17 Open the east ***w***"; and he opened
1 Chr 15:29 looked through a ***w*** and saw King
Prov 7: 6 For at the ***w*** of my house I
Ezek 40:16 There were beveled ***w*** frames
41:16 doorposts and the beveled ***w***
41:26 There were beveled ***w*** frames
Acts 20: 9 And in a ***w*** sat a certain young
2 Cor 11:33 down in a basket through a ***w***

WINDOWS (24/22) WINDOW

Gen 7:11 and the ***w*** of heaven were
8: 2 of the deep and the ***w*** of
1 Ki 6: 4 And he made for the house ***w*** with
7: 4 There were ***w*** with beveled
2 Ki 7: 2 if the LORD would make ***w*** in
7:19 if the LORD would make ***w*** in
Eccl 12: 3 those that look through the ***w***
Song 2: 9 He is looking through the ***w***,
Isa 24:18 For the ***w*** from on high are
Jer 9:21 death has come through our ***w***,
22:14 And cut out ***w*** for it,
Ezek 40:16 There were ***w*** all around on
40:22 Its ***w*** and those of its archways,
40:25 There were ***w*** in it and in its
40:25 all around like those ***w***;
40:29 there were ***w*** in it and in its
40:33 and there were ***w*** in it and in
40:36 It had ***w*** all around; its length
41:16 wood from the ground to the ***w***—
41:16 the ***w*** were covered—
Dan 6:10 with his ***w*** open toward
Joel 2: 9 They enter at the ***w*** like a
Zeph 2:14 voice shall sing in the ***w***;
Mal 3:10 I will not open for you the ***w***

WINDS (23/22) WIND

Job 37: 9 cold from the scattering ***w*** of
Prov 15:24 The way of life ***w*** upward for
Jer 49:32 I will scatter to all ***w*** those
49:36 Elam I will bring the four ***w***
49:36 scatter them toward all those ***w***;
Ezek 5:10 I will scatter to all the ***w***.
5:12 another third to all the ***w***,
37: 9 GOD: "Come from the four ***w***,
Dan 7: 2 the four ***w*** of heaven were
8: 8 ones came up toward the four ***w***
11: 4 and divided toward the four ***w***
Zech 2: 6 you abroad like the four ***w*** of
Mt 7:25 and the ***w*** blew and beat on that
7:27 and the ***w*** blew and beat on that
8:26 He arose and rebuked the ***w*** and
8:27 that even the ***w*** and the sea
24:31 His elect from the four ***w***,
Mk 13:27 His elect from the four ***w***,
Lk 8:25 For He commands even the ***w*** and
Acts 27: 4 because the ***w*** were contrary.
Jas 3: 4 and are driven by fierce ***w***,
Jude 12 water, carried about by the ***w***;
Rev 7: 1 holding the four ***w*** of the

WINDSTORM (2/2) STORM, WIND

Mk 4:37 And a great ***w*** arose, and the
Lk 8:23 And a ***w*** came down on the lake,

WINDY (1/1)

Ps 55: 8 my escape From the ***w*** storm

WINE (235/214) WINEBIBBER, WINEPRESS, WINESKINS

Gen 9:21 Then he drank of the ***w*** and was
9:24 So Noah awoke from his ***w***,
14:18 Salem brought out bread and ***w***;
19:32 let us make our father drink ***w***,
19:33 they made their father drink ***w***
19:34 let us make him drink ***w*** tonight
19:35 they made their father drink ***w***
27:25 he ate; and he brought him ***w***,
27:28 And plenty of grain and ***w***.
27:37 with grain and ***w*** I have
49:11 He washed his garments in ***w***,
49:12 His eyes are darker than ***w***,
Ex 29:40 and one-fourth of a hin of ***w***

Lev 10: 9 Do not drink **w** or intoxicating
23:13 drink offering shall be of **w**,
Num 6: 3 shall separate himself from **w**
6: 3 neither vinegar made from **w**
6:20 that the Nazirite may drink **w**.
15: 5 and one-fourth of a HIN of **w** as
15: 7 offer one-third of a HIN of **w**
15:10 drink offering half a hin of **w**
18:12 all the best of the new **w** and
28:14 shall be half a hin of **w** for a
Deut 7:13 your grain and your new **w** and
11:14 in your grain, your new **w**,
12:17 of your grain or your new **w** or
14:23 of your grain and your new **w**
14:26 for **w** or similar drink,
18: 4 of your grain and your new **w**
28:39 shall neither drink of the **w**
28:51 not leave you grain or new **w**
29: 6 nor have you drunk **w** or
32:14 wheat; And you drank **w**,
32:33 Their **w** is the poison of
32:38 And drank the **w** of their
33:28 In a land of grain and new **w**;
Judg 9:13 'Should I cease my new **w**,
13: 4 be careful not to drink **w** or
13: 7 Now drink no **w** or similar
13:14 nor may she drink **w** or similar
19:19 and bread and **w** for myself,
1 Sam 1:14 Put your **w** away from you!"
1:15 I have drunk neither **w** nor
1:24 ephah of flour, and a skin of **w**,
10: 3 another carrying a skin of **w**.
16:20 with bread, a skin of **w**,
25:18 of bread, two skins of **w**,
25:37 when the **w** had gone from Nabal,
2 Sam 13:28 Amnon's heart is merry with **w**,
16: 1 summer fruits, and a skin of **w**.
16: 2 and the **w** for those who are
2 Ki 18:32 land, a land of grain and new **w**,
1 Chr 9:29 over the fine flour and the **w**
12:40 **w** and oil and oxen and sheep
27:27 vineyards for the supply of **w**.
2 Chr 2:10 twenty thousand baths of **w**,
2:15 and the **w** which my lord has
11:11 and stores of food, oil, and **w**.
31: 5 the firstfruits of grain and **w**,
32:28 for the harvest of grain, **w**,
Ezra 6: 9 God of heaven, wheat, salt, **w**,
7:22 wheat, one hundred baths of **w**,
Neh 2: 1 when **w** was before him, that I
2: 1 that I took the **w** and gave it
5:11 the new **w** and the oil, that you
5:15 and took from them bread and **w**,
5:18 an abundance of all kinds of **w**.
10:37 the new **w** and oil, to the
10:39 of the new **w** and the oil, to
13: 5 the new **w** and oil, which were
13:12 of the grain and the new **w** and
13:15 saw people in Judah treading **w**
13:15 and loading donkeys with **w**,
Esth 1: 7 with royal **w** in abundance,
1:10 of the king was merry with **w**,
5: 6 At the banquet of **w** the king
7: 2 second day, at the banquet of **w**,
7: 7 his wrath from the banquet of **w**
7: 8 the place of the banquet of **w**,
Job 1:13 were eating and drinking **w** in
1:18 were eating and drinking **w** in
32:19 Indeed my belly is like **w**
Ps 4: 7 season that their grain and **w**
60: 3 You have made us drink the **w**
75: 8 And the **w** is red; It is fully
78:65 man who shouts because of **w**.
104:15 And **w** that makes glad the
Prov 3:10 vats will overflow with new **w**.
4:17 And drink the **w** of violence.
9: 2 her meat, She has mixed her **w**,
9: 5 my bread And drink of the **w** I
20: 1 **W** is a mocker, Strong drink
21:17 He who loves **w** and oil will
23:30 Those who linger long at the **w**,
23:30 who go in search of mixed **w**.
23:31 Do not look on the **w** when it is
31: 4 is not for kings to drink **w**,
31: 6 And **w** to those who are bitter
Eccl 2: 3 how to gratify my flesh with **w**,
9: 7 And drink your **w** with a merry
10:19 And **w** makes merry; But money
Song 1: 2 your love is better than **w**.
1: 4 remember your love more than **w**.
4:10 How much better than **w** is
5: 1 I have drunk my **w** with my
7: 9 of your mouth like the best **w**.
7: 9 The **w** goes down smoothly
8: 2 cause you to drink of spiced **w**,
Isa 1:22 Your **w** mixed with water.
5:11 till **w** inflames them!
5:12 And **w** are in their feasts;
5:22 to men mighty at drinking **w**,
16:10 No treaders will tread out **w**
22:13 Eating meat and drinking **w**:
24: 7 The new **w** fails, the vine
24: 9 They shall not drink **w** with a
24:11 There is a cry for **w** in the
27: 2 A vineyard of red **w**!
28: 1 those who are overcome with **w**!
28: 7 they also have erred through **w**,
28: 7 They are swallowed up by **w**,
29: 9 They are drunk, but not with **w**;
36:17 land, a land of grain and new **w**,
49:26 their own blood as with sweet **w**.
51:21 And drunk but not with **w**.
55: 1 buy **w** and milk Without money
56:12 one says, "I will bring **w**,
62: 8 shall not drink your new **w**,
65: 8 As the new **w** is found in the
Jer 13:12 bottle shall be filled with **w**.
13:12 bottle will be filled with **w**?
23: 9 And like a man whom **w** has
25:15 Take this **w** cup of fury from My
31:12 For wheat and new **w** and oil,
35: 2 and give them **w** to drink."
35: 5 the Rechabites bowls full of **w**,
35: 5 and I said to them, "Drink **w**.
35: 6 they said, "We will drink no **w**,
35: 6 saying, 'You shall drink no **w**,
35: 8 to drink no **w** all our days, we,
35:14 his sons, not to drink **w**,
40:10 gather **w** and summer fruit and
40:12 and gathered **w** and summer fruit
48:33 I have caused **w** to fail from
51: 7 The nations drank her **w**;
Lam 2:12 "Where is grain and **w**?
Ezek 27:18 with the **w** of Helbon and with
44:21 No priest shall drink **w** when he
Dan 1: 5 king's delicacies and of the **w**
1: 8 nor with the **w** which he drank;
1:16 of delicacies and the **w** that
5: 1 and drank **w** in the presence of
5: 2 While he tasted the **w**,
5: 4 They drank **w**, and praised the
5:23 have drunk **w** from them.
10: 3 no meat or **w** came into my
Hos 2: 8 That I gave her grain, new **w**,
2: 9 in its time And My new **w** in
2:22 answer With grain, With new **w**,
4:11 Harlotry, **w**, and new wine
4:11 and new **w** enslave the heart.
7: 5 made him sick, inflamed with **w**;
7:14 together for grain and new **w**,
9: 2 And the new **w** shall fail in
9: 4 They shall not offer **w**
14: 7 scent shall be like the **w** of
Joel 1: 5 wail, all you drinkers of **w**,
1: 5 of wine, Because of the new **w**,
1:10 The new **w** is dried up,
2:19 I will send you grain and new **w**
2:24 vats shall overflow with new **w**
3: 3 harlot, And sold a girl for **w**,
3:18 mountains shall drip with new **w**,
Am 2: 8 And drink the **w** of the
2:12 But you gave the Nazirites **w** to
4: 1 to your husbands, "Bring **w**,
5:11 But you shall not drink **w** from
6: 6 Who drink **w** from bowls,
9:13 shall drip with sweet **w**,
9:14 plant vineyards and drink **w**
Mic 2:11 I will prophesy to you of **w** and
6:15 with oil; And make sweet **w**,
6:15 sweet wine, but not drink **w**.
Hab 2: 5 because he transgresses by **w**,
Zeph 1:13 but not drink their **w**.
Hag 1:11 on the grain and the new **w** and
2:12 **w** or oil, or any food, will it
2:16 when one came to the **w** vat to
Zech 9:15 drink and roar as if with **w**;
9:17 And new **w** the young women.
10: 7 shall rejoice as if with **w**.
Mt 9:17 Nor do they put new **w** into old
9:17 the **w** is spilled, and the
9:17 But they put new **w** into new
27:34 they gave Him sour **w** mingled
27:48 filled it with sour **w** and put
Mk 2:22 And no one puts new **w** into old
2:22 or else the new **w** bursts the
2:22 the **w** is spilled, and the
2:22 But new **w** must be put into new
12: 1 dug a place for the **w** vat
15:23 Then they gave Him **w** mingled
15:36 filled a sponge full of sour **w**,
Lk 1:15 and shall drink neither **w** nor
5:37 And no one puts new **w** into old
5:37 or else the new **w** will burst
5:38 But new **w** must be put into new
5:39 no one, having drunk old **w**,
7:33 eating bread nor drinking **w**,
10:34 wounds, pouring on oil and **w**;
23:36 coming and offering Him sour **w**,
Jn 2: 3 And when they ran out of **w**,
2: 3 said to Him, "They have no **w**.
2: 9 the water that was made **w**,
2:10 beginning sets out the good **w**,
2:10 You have kept the good **w** until
4:46 where He had made the water **w**.
19:29 Now a vessel full of sour **w** was
19:29 filled a sponge with sour **w**,
19:30 Jesus had received the sour **w**,
Acts 2:13 said, "They are full of new **w**.
Rom 14:21 to eat meat nor drink **w** nor
Eph 5:18 And do not be drunk with **w**,
1 Tim 3: 3 not given to **w**, not violent,
3: 8 not given to much **w**,
5:23 but use a little **w** for your
Titus 1: 7 quick-tempered, not given to **w**,
2: 3 slanderers, not given to much **w**,
Rev 6: 6 do not harm the oil and the **w**.
14: 8 all nations drink of the **w** of
14:10 shall also drink of the **w** of
16:19 to give her the cup of the **w** of
17: 2 were made drunk with the **w** of
18: 3 nations have drunk of the **w** of
18:13 **w** and oil, fine flour and

WINE-WORKERS (1/1)

Jer 48:12 That I shall send him **w** Who

WINEBIBBER (2/2) WINE

Mt 11:19 say, 'Look, a glutton and a **w**,
Lk 7:34 say, 'Look, a glutton and a **w**,

WINEBIBBERS (1/1)

Prov 23:20 Do not mix with **w**,

WINEFAT (KJV) See (WINE) VAT, WINEPRESS

WINEPRESS (18/17) WINE

Num 18:27 and as the fullness of the **w**.
18:30 and as the produce of the **w**.
Deut 15:14 floor, and from your **w**.
16:13 threshing floor and from your **w**.
Judg 6:11 Gideon threshed wheat in the **w**,
7:25 and Zeeb they killed at the **w**
2 Ki 6:27 threshing floor or from the **w**?
Isa 5: 2 And also made a **w** in it;
63: 2 like one who treads in the **w**?
63: 3 I have trodden the **w** alone,
Lam 1:15 The Lord trampled as in a **w**
Hos 9: 2 The threshing floor and the **w**
Joel 3:13 For the **w** is full, The vats
Mt 21:33 dug a **w** in it and built a
Rev 14:19 and threw it into the great **w**
14:20 And the **w** was trampled outside
14:20 and blood came out of the **w**,
19:15 He Himself treads the **w** of the

WINEPRESSES (3/3)

Job 24:11 their walls, And tread **w**,
Jer 48:33 caused wine to fail from the **w**;
Zech 14:10 of Hananeel to the king's **w**.

WINES (2/1)

Isa 25: 6 A feast of **w** on the lees,
25: 6 Of well-refined **w** on the lees.

WINESKIN (1/1)

Ps 119:83 For I have become like a **w** in

WINESKINS (15/7) WINE

Josh 9: 4 old **w** torn and mended,
9:13 And these **w** which we filled
Job 32:19 is ready to burst like new **w**.
Mt 9:17 do they put new wine into old **w**,
9:17 or else the **w** break, the wine
9:17 and the **w** are ruined. But they
9:17 they put new wine into new **w**,
Mk 2:22 no one puts new wine into old **w**;
2:22 else the new wine bursts the **w**,
2:22 and the **w** are ruined.
2:22 new wine must be put into new **w**.
Lk 5:37 no one puts new wine into old **w**;
5:37 the new wine will burst the **w**
5:37 and the **w** will be ruined.
5:38 new wine must be put into new **w**,

WING (15/8) WINGED, WINGS

Ruth 3: 9 your maidservant under your **w**,
1 Ki 6:24 One **w** of the cherub was five
6:24 and the other **w** of the cherub
6:24 cubits from the tip of one **w**
6:27 of the cherubim so that the **w**
6:27 and the **w** of the other cherub
2 Chr 3:11 one **w** of the one cherub
3:11 and the other **w** was five
3:11 touching the **w** of the other
3:12 one **w** of the other cherub was
3:12 and the other **w** also was five
3:12 touching the **w** of the other
Isa 10:14 was no one who moved his **w**,
Ezek 16: 8 so I spread My **w** over you and
Dan 9:27 And on the **w** of abominations

WINGED (2/2) WING

Gen 1:21 and every **w** bird according to
Deut 4:17 or the likeness of any **w** bird

WINGS (75/63) WING

Ex 19: 4 how I bore you on eagles' **w**
25:20 shall stretch out their **w**
25:20 the mercy seat with their **w**,
37: 9 cherubim spread out their **w**
37: 9 the mercy seat with their **w**.
Lev 1:17 he shall split it at its **w**,
Deut 32:11 its young, Spreading out its **w**,
32:11 Carrying them on its **w**,
Ruth 2:12 under whose **w** you have come for
2 Sam 22:11 And He was seen upon the **w** of
1 Ki 6:27 and they stretched out the **w** of
6:27 And their **w** touched each other
8: 6 under the **w** of the cherubim.
8: 7 cherubim spread their two **w**
1 Chr 28:18 cherubim that spread their **w**
2 Chr 3:11 The **w** of the cherubim were
3:13 The **w** of these cherubim spanned
5: 7 under the **w** of the cherubim.

5: 8 the cherubim spread their *w*
Job 39:13 The *w* of the ostrich wave
39:13 But are her *w* and pinions
39:26 And spread its *w* toward the
Ps 17: 8 me under the shadow of Your *w*,
18:10 He flew upon the *w* of the
36: 7 under the shadow of Your *w*.
55: 6 that I had *w* like a dove!
57: 1 And in the shadow of Your *w* I
61: 4 trust in the shelter of Your *w*.
63: 7 in the shadow of Your *w* I will
68:13 You will be like the *w* of a
91: 4 And under His *w* you shall take
104: 3 Who walks on the *w* of the
139: 9 If I take the *w* of the
Prov 23: 5 certainly make themselves *w*;
Isa 6: 2 seraphim; each one had six *w*:
8: 8 the stretching out of his *w*
18: 1 land shadowed with buzzing *w*,
40:31 They shall mount up with *w*
Jer 48: 9 Give *w* to Moab, That she may
48:40 And spread his *w* over Moab.
49:22 And spread His *w* over Bozrah;
Ezek 1: 6 faces, and each one had four *w*.
1: 8 of a man were under their *w*
1: 8 of the four had faces and *w*.
1: 9 Their *w* touched one another.
1:11 Their *w* stretched upward;
1:11 two *w* of each one touched one
1:23 And under the firmament their *w*
1:24 I heard the noise of their *w*,
1:24 still, they let down their *w*.
1:25 stood, they let down their *w*.
3:13 also heard the noise of the *w*
10: 5 And the sound of the *w* of the
10: 8 of a man's hand under their *w*.
10:12 back, their hands, their *w*,
10:16 the cherubim lifted their *w* to
10:19 And the cherubim lifted their *w*
10:21 four faces and each one four *w*,
10:21 of a man was under their *w*.
11:22 the cherubim lifted up their *w*,
17: 3 A great eagle with large *w* and
17: 7 great eagle with large *w* and
Dan 7: 4 like a lion, and had eagle's *w*.
7: 4 I watched till its *w* were
7: 6 which had on its back four *w* of
Hos 4:19 has wrapped her up in its *w*,
Zech 5: 9 coming with the wind in their *w*;
5: 9 for they had *w* like the wings
5: 9 for they had wings like the *w*
Mal 4: 2 With healing in His *w*;
Mt 23:37 gathers her chicks under her *w*,
Lk 13:34 gathers her brood under her *w*,
Rev 4: 8 creatures, each having six *w*,
9: 9 and the sound of their *w* was
12:14 But the woman was given two *w* of

WINK (2/2)

Job 15:12 And what do your eyes *w* at,
Ps 35:19 Nor let them *w* with the eye

WINKS (3/3)

Prov 6:13 He *w* with his eyes,
10:10 He who *w* with the eye causes
16:30 He *w* his eye to devise perverse

WINNOW (3/3)

Isa 41:16 You shall *w* them, the wind
Jer 15: 7 And I will *w* them with a
51: 2 Who shall *w* her and empty her

WINNOWED (1/1)

Isa 30:24 Which has been *w* with the

WINNOWERS (1/1)

Jer 51: 2 And I will send *w* to Babylon,

WINNOWING (4/4)

Ruth 3: 2 he is *w* barley tonight at the
Jer 15: 7 winnow them with a *w* fan
Mt 3:12 'His *w* fan is in His hand,
Lk 3:17 'His *w* fan is in His hand,

WINS (1/1) WIN

Prov 11:30 And he who *w* souls is wise.

WINTER (16/15)

Gen 8:22 *W* and summer, And day and
Ps 74:17 You have made summer and *w*.
Prov 20: 4 man will not plow because of *w*;
Song 2:11 the *w* is past, The rain is
Isa 18: 6 the beasts of the earth will *w*
Jer 36:22 was sitting in the *w* house
Am 3:15 I will destroy the *w* house
Zech 14: 8 In both summer and *w* it shall
Mt 24:20 your flight may not be in *w* or
Mk 13:18 your flight may not be in *w*.
Jn 10:22 in Jerusalem, and it was *w*.
Acts 27:12 harbor was not suitable to *w*
27:12 northwest, and *w* there.
1 Cor 16: 6 or even spend the *w* with you,
2 Tim 4:21 Do your utmost to come before *w*.
Titus 3:12 I have decided to spend the *w*

WINTERED (1/1)

Acts 28:11 which had *w* at the island.

WIPE (7/7) WIPED, WIPES

2 Ki 21:13 I will *w* Jerusalem as one
Neh 13:14 and do not *w* out my good deeds
Isa 25: 8 And the Lord GOD will *w* away
Lk 10:11 which clings to us we *w* off
Jn 13: 5 and to *w* them with the towel
Rev 7:17 And God will *w* away every tear
21: 4 And God will *w* away every tear

WIPED (6/6) WIPE

Prov 6:33 And his reproach will not be *w*
Lk 7:38 and *w* them with the hair of
7:44 feet with her tears and *w* them
Jn 11: 2 fragrant oil and *w* His feet
12: 3 and *w* His feet with her hair.
Col 2:14 having *w* out the handwriting of

WIPES (2/2) WIPE

2 Ki 21:13 Jerusalem as one *w* a
Prov 30:20 She eats and *w* her mouth,

WIPING (1/1)

2 Ki 21:13 *w* it and turning it upside

WIRES (KJV) See THREADS

WISDOM (227/215) WISE

Ex 28: 3 filled with the spirit of *w*,
31: 3 with the Spirit of God, in *w*,
31: 6 and I have put *w* in the hearts
35:26 whose heart stirred with *w*
35:31 in *w* and understanding,
36: 1 in whom the LORD has put *w*
36: 2 whose heart the LORD had put *w*,
Deut 4: 6 for this is your *w* and your
34: 9 Nun was full of the spirit of *w*,
2 Sam 14:20 according to the *w* of the angel
20:22 Then the woman in her *w* went to
1 Ki 2: 6 do according to your *w*,
3:28 for they saw that the *w* of God
4:29 And God gave Solomon *w* and
4:30 Thus Solomon's *w* excelled the
4:30 wisdom excelled the *w* of all
4:30 men of the East and all the *w*
4:34 earth who had heard of his *w*,
4:34 came to hear the *w* of Solomon.
5:12 So the LORD gave Solomon *w*,
7:14 he was filled with *w* and
10: 4 of Sheba had seen all the *w* of
10: 6 about your words and your *w*.
10: 7 Your *w* and prosperity exceed
10: 8 before you and hear your *w*!
10:23 of the earth in riches and *w*.
10:24 of Solomon to hear his *w*,
11:41 all that he did, and his *w*,
1 Chr 22:12 Only may the LORD give you *w*
2 Chr 1:10 Now give me *w* and knowledge,
1:11 but have asked *w* and knowledge
1:12 *w* and knowledge are granted to
9: 3 queen of Sheba had seen the *w*
9: 5 about your words and your *w*.
9: 6 of the greatness of your *w* was
9: 7 before you and hear your *w*!
9:22 of the earth in riches and *w*.
9:23 of Solomon to hear his *w*,
Ezra 7:25 according to your God-given *w*,
Job 4:21 They die, even without *w*.'
11: 6 show you the secrets of *w*!
12: 2 And *w* will die with you!
12:12 *W* is with aged men, And with
12:13 With Him are *w* and strength,
13: 5 And it would be your *w*!
15: 8 Do you limit *w* to yourself?
26: 3 counseled one who has no *w*?
28:12 But where can *w* be found?
28:18 For the price of *w* is above
28:20 From where then does *w* come?
28:27 Then He saw *w* and declared it;
28:28 fear of the Lord, that is *w*,
32: 7 of years should teach *w*.
32:13 you say, 'We have found *w*';
33:33 peace, and I will teach you *w*.
34:35 His words are without *w*.
38:36 Who has put *w* in the mind?
38:37 Who can number the clouds by *w*?
39:17 Because God deprived her of *w*,
39:26 "Does the hawk fly by your *w*,
Ps 37:30 mouth of the righteous speaks *w*,
49: 3 My mouth shall speak *w*,
51: 6 You will make me to know *w*.
90:12 That we may gain a heart of *w*.
104:24 In *w* You have made them all.
105:22 And teach his elders *w*.
111:10 LORD is the beginning of *w*;
136: 5 To Him who by *w* made the
Prov 1: 2 know *w* and instruction,
1: 3 receive the instruction of *w*,
1: 7 But fools despise *w* and
1:20 *W* calls aloud outside;
2: 2 that you incline your ear to *w*,
2: 6 For the LORD gives *w*;
2: 7 He stores up sound *w* for the
2:10 When *w* enters your heart,
3:13 is the man who finds *w*,
3:19 The LORD by *w* founded the
3:21 Keep sound *w* and discretion;
4: 5 Get *w*! Get understanding!
4: 7 *W* is the principal thing
4: 7 Therefore get *w*.
4:11 have taught you in the way of *w*;
5: 1 My son, pay attention to my *w*;
7: 4 to *w*, "You are my sister,"
8: 1 Does not *w* cry out, And
8:11 For *w* is better than rubies,
8:12 I, *w*, dwell with prudence,
8:14 Counsel is mine, and sound *w*;
9: 1 *W* has built her house, She has
9:10 LORD is the beginning of *w*,
10:13 *W* is found on the lips of him
10:21 But fools die for lack of *w*.
10:23 a man of understanding has *w*.
10:31 of the righteous brings forth *w*,
11: 2 But with the humble is *w*.
11:12 He who is devoid of *w* despises
12: 8 be commended according to his *w*,
13:10 with the well-advised is *w*.
14: 6 A scoffer seeks *w* and does not
14: 8 The *w* of the prudent is to
14:33 *W* rests in the heart of him who
15:33 LORD is the instruction of *w*,
16:16 How much better to get *w* than
17:16 a fool the purchase price of *w*,
17:24 *W* is in the sight of him who
18: 4 The wellspring of *w* is a
19: 8 He who gets *w* loves his own
21:30 There is no *w* or
23: 9 For he will despise the *w* of
23:23 Also *w* and instruction and
24: 3 Through *w* a house is built,
24: 7 *W* is too lofty for a fool
24:14 So shall the knowledge of *w*
29: 3 Whoever loves *w* makes his
29:15 The rod and rebuke give *w*,
30: 3 I neither learned *w* Nor have
31:26 She opens her mouth with *w*,
Eccl 1:13 to seek and search out by *w*
1:16 and have gained more *w* than all
1:16 My heart has understood great *w*
1:17 And I set my heart to know *w* and
1:18 For in much *w* is much grief,
2: 3 while guiding my heart with *w*,
2: 9 Also my *w* remained with me.
2:12 I turned myself to consider *w*
2:13 Then I saw that *w* excels folly
2:21 is a man whose labor is with *w*,
2:26 For God gives *w* and knowledge
7:11 *W* is good with an inheritance,
7:12 For *w* is a defense as money
7:12 of knowledge is that *w* gives
7:19 *W* strengthens the wise More
7:23 All this I have proved by *w*.
7:25 To search and seek out *w* and
8: 1 A man's *w* makes his face
8:16 I applied my heart to know *w*
9:10 or device or knowledge or *w* in
9:13 This *w* I have also seen under
9:15 and he by his *w* delivered the
9:16 *W* is better than strength.
9:16 Nevertheless the poor man's *w*
9:18 *W* is better than weapons of
10: 1 folly to one respected for *w*
10: 3 along the way, He lacks *w*,
10:10 But *w* brings success.
Isa 10:13 I have done it, And by my *w*,
11: 2 The Spirit of *w* and
29:14 For the *w* of their wise men
33: 6 *W* and knowledge will be the
47:10 Your *w* and your knowledge have
Jer 8: 9 So what *w* do they have?
9:23 the wise man glory in his *w*,
10:12 established the world by His *w*,
49: 7 Is *w* no more in Teman?
49: 7 Has their *w* vanished?
51:15 established the world by His *w*,
Ezek 28: 4 With your *w* and your
28: 5 By your great *w* in trade you
28: 7 against the beauty of your *w*,
28:12 Full of *w* and perfect in
28:17 You corrupted your *w* for the
Dan 1: 4 good-looking, gifted in all *w*,
1:17 skill in all literature and *w*;
1:20 And in all matters of *w* and
2:14 Then with counsel and *w* Daniel
2:20 For *w* and might are His.
2:21 He gives *w* to the wise
2:23 You have given me *w* and might,
2:30 to me because I have more *w*
5:11 light and understanding and *w*,
5:11 like the *w* of the gods,
5:14 understanding and excellent *w*
Mic 6: 9 *W* shall see Your name: "Hear
Mt 11:19 But *w* is justified by her
12:42 of the earth to hear the *w* of
13:54 did this Man get this *w*
Mk 6: 2 And what *w* is this which is
Lk 1:17 and the disobedient to the *w*
2:40 strong in spirit, filled with *w*;
2:52 And Jesus increased in *w* and
7:35 But *w* is justified by all her
11:31 of the earth to hear the *w* of
11:49 Therefore the *w* of God also
21:15 I will give you a mouth and *w*
Acts 6: 3 full of the Holy Spirit and *w*,
6:10 were not able to resist the *w*
7:10 and gave him favor and *w* in the

7:22 Moses was learned in all the **w**
Rom 11:33 of the riches both of the **w**
1 Cor 1:17 not with **w** of words, lest the
1:19 I will destroy the **w** of
1:20 Has not God made foolish the **w**
1:21 in the **w** of God, the world
1:21 the world through **w** did not
1:22 a sign, and Greeks seek after **w**;
1:24 the power of God and the **w** of
1:30 who became for us **w** from
2: 1 excellence of speech or of **w**
2: 4 persuasive words of human **w**,
2: 5 faith should not be in the **w**
2: 6 we speak **w** among those who are
2: 6 yet not the **w** of this age,
2: 7 But we speak the **w** of God in a
2: 7 the hidden **w** which God
2:13 not in words which man's **w**
3:19 For the **w** of this world is
12: 8 to one is given the word of **w**
2 Cor 1:12 not with fleshly **w** but by the
Eph 1: 8 to abound toward us in all **w**
1:17 may give to you the spirit of **w**
3:10 intent that now the manifold **w**
Col 1: 9 knowledge of His will in all **w**
1:28 and teaching every man in all **w**,
2: 3 hidden all the treasures of **w**
2:23 indeed have an appearance of **w**
3:16 dwell in you richly in all **w**,
4: 5 Walk in **w** toward those who are
Jas 1: 5 If any of you lacks **w**,
3:13 are done in the meekness of **w**.
3:15 This **w** does not descend from
3:17 But the **w** that is from above is
2 Pe 3:15 according to the **w** given to
Rev 5:12 receive power and riches and **w**,
7:12 Blessing and glory and **w**,
13:18 Here is **w**. Let him who has
17: 9 "Here is the mind which has **w**:

WISE (207/197) UNWISE, WISDOM, WISELY, WISER

Gen 3: 6 a tree desirable to make one **w**,
41: 8 of Egypt and all its **w** men.
41:33 select a discerning and **w** man,
41:39 is no one as discerning and **w**
Ex 7:11 Pharaoh also called the **w** men
Deut 1:13 'Choose **w**, understanding, and
1:15 **w** and knowledgeable men, and
4: 6 this great nation is a **w** and
16:19 bribe blinds the eyes of the **w**
32:29 Oh, that they were **w**,
2 Sam 14: 2 brought from there a **w** woman,
14:20 this thing; but my lord is **w**,
20:16 Then a **w** woman cried out from
1 Ki 2: 9 for you are a **w** man and know
3:12 I have given you a **w** and
5: 7 for He has given David a **w** son
1 Chr 26:14 a **w** counselor, and his lot came
27:32 a **w** man, and a scribe;
2 Chr 2:12 has given King David a **w** son,
Esth 1:13 Then the king said to the **w** men
6:13 his **w** men and his wife Zeresh
Job 5:13 He catches the **w** in their own
9: 4 God is **w** in heart and mighty
11:12 an empty-headed man will be **w**,
15: 2 Should a **w** man answer with empty
15:18 What **w** men have told,
17:10 I shall not find one **w** man
22: 2 Though he who is **w** may be
32: 9 Great men are not always **w**,
34: 2 you **w** men; Give ear to me,
34:34 **W** men who listen to me:
37:24 partiality to any who are **w**
Ps 2:10 Now therefore, be **w**,
19: 7 making **w** the simple;
36: 3 He has ceased to be **w** and to
49:10 For he sees **w** men die;
94: 8 you fools, when will you be **w**?
107:43 Whoever is **w** will observe
Prov 1: 5 A **w** man will hear and increase
1: 5 will attain **w** counsel,
1: 6 The words of the **w** and their
3: 7 Do not be **w** in your own eyes;
3:35 The **w** shall inherit glory,
6: 6 Consider her ways and be **w**,
8:33 Hear instruction and be **w**,
9: 8 Rebuke a **w** man, and he will
9: 9 Give instruction to a **w** man,
9:12 If you are **w**, you are wise
9:12 you are **w** for yourself,
10: 1 A **w** son makes a glad father,
10: 5 gathers in summer is a **w** son;
10: 8 The **w** in heart will receive
10:14 **W** people store up knowledge,
10:19 he who restrains his lips is **w**.
11:29 will be servant to the **w** of
11:30 And he who wins souls is **w**.
12:15 But he who heeds counsel is **w**.
12:18 But the tongue of the **w**
13: 1 A **w** son heeds his father's
13:14 The law of the **w** is a fountain
13:20 He who walks with **w** men will
13:20 walks with wise men will be **w**,
14: 1 The **w** woman builds her house,
14: 3 But the lips of the **w** will
14:16 A **w** man fears and departs from
14:24 The crown of the **w** is their
14:35 favor is toward a **w** servant,
15: 2 The tongue of the **w** uses
15: 7 The lips of the **w** disperse
15:12 Nor will he go to the **w**.
15:20 A **w** son makes a father glad,
15:24 of life winds upward for the **w**,
15:31 of life Will abide among the **w**.
16:14 But a **w** man will appease it.
16:21 The **w** in heart will be called
16:23 The heart of the **w** teaches his
17: 2 A **w** servant will rule over a
17:10 is more effective for a **w** man
17:28 Even a fool is counted **w** when
18: 1 against all **w** judgment.
18:15 And the ear of the **w** seeks
19:20 That you may be **w** in your
20: 1 is led astray by it is not **w**.
20:18 By **w** counsel wage war.
20:26 A **w** king sifts out the wicked,
21:11 punished, the simple is made **w**;
21:11 But when the **w** is instructed,
21:20 oil in the dwelling of the **w**,
21:22 A **w** man scales the city of the
22:17 ear and hear the words of the **w**,
23:15 My son, if your heart is **w**,
23:19 Hear, my son, and be **w**;
23:24 And he who begets a **w** child
24: 5 A **w** man is strong, Yes, a man
24: 6 For by **w** counsel you will wage
24:23 things also belong to the **w**:
25:12 of fine gold Is a **w** rebuker
26: 5 Lest he be **w** in his own eyes.
26:12 Do you see a man **w** in his own
27:11 My son, be **w**, and make my
28:11 The rich man is **w** in his own
29: 8 But **w** men turn away wrath.
29: 9 If a **w** man contends with a
29:11 But a **w** man holds them back.
30:24 But they are exceedingly **w**:
Eccl 2:14 The **w** man's eyes are in his
2:15 And why was I then more **w**?"
2:16 no more remembrance of the **w**
2:16 And how does a **w** man die?
2:19 who knows whether he will be **w**
2:19 in which I have shown myself **w**
4:13 Better a poor and **w** youth
6: 8 For what more has the **w** man
7: 4 The heart of the **w** is in the
7: 5 to hear the rebuke of the **w**
7: 7 oppression destroys a **w** man's
7:16 righteous, Nor be overly **w**:
7:19 Wisdom strengthens the **w** More
7:23 I will be **w**"; But it was far
8: 1 Who is like a **w** man?
8: 5 And a **w** man's heart discerns
8:17 though a **w** man attempts to
9: 1 that the righteous and the **w**
9:11 the strong, Nor bread to the **w**,
9:15 was found in it a poor **w** man,
9:17 Words of the **w**,
10: 2 A **w** man's heart is at his
10:12 The words of a **w** man's mouth
12: 9 because the Preacher was **w**,
12:11 The words of the **w** are like
Isa 5:21 Woe to those who are **w** in
19:11 Pharaoh's **w** counselors give
19:11 "I am the son of the **w**,
19:12 Where are your **w** men?
29:14 For the wisdom of their **w** men
31: 2 Yet He also is **w** and will
44:25 Who turns **w** men backward,
Jer 4:22 They are **w** to do evil,
8: 8 "How can you say, 'We are **w**,
8: 9 The **w** men are ashamed,
9:12 Who is the **w** man who may
9:23 Let not the **w** man glory in his
10: 7 For among all the **w** men of
18:18 priest, nor counsel from the **w**,
50:35 her princes and her **w** men.
51:57 drunk Her princes and **w** men,
Ezek 27: 8 Your **w** men, O Tyre, were in
27: 9 Elders of Gebal and its **w** men
Dan 2:12 to destroy all the **w** men
2:13 they began killing the **w** men;
2:14 had gone out to kill the **w** men
2:18 with the rest of the **w** men
2:21 He gives wisdom to the **w** And
2:24 appointed to destroy the **w** men
2:24 Do not destroy the **w** men of
2:27 the **w** men, the astrologers,
2:48 over all the **w** men of Babylon.
4: 6 to bring in all the **w** men
4:18 since all the **w** men of my
5: 7 saying to the **w** men of
5: 8 Now all the king's **w** men came,
5:15 Now the **w** men, the astrologers,
12: 3 Those who are **w** shall shine
12:10 but the **w** shall understand.
Hos 14: 9 Who is **w**? Let him
Ob 8 Even destroy the **w** men from
Zech 9: 2 Sidon, though they are very **w**.
Mt 2: 1 **w** men from the East came to
2: 7 secretly called the **w** men,
2:16 he was deceived by the **w** men,
2:16 determined from the **w** men.
7:24 I will liken him to a **w** man who
10:16 Therefore be **w** as serpents and
11:25 these things from the **w** and
23:34 **w** men, and scribes: some of
24:45 Who then is a faithful and **w**
25: 2 "Now five of them were **w**,
25: 4 but the **w** took oil in their
25: 8 "And the foolish said to the **w**,
25: 9 But the **w** answered, saying,
Lk 10:21 these things from the **w** and
12:42 then is that faithful and **w**
Rom 1:14 both to **w** and to unwise.
1:22 Professing to be **w**,
11:25 lest you should be **w** in your
12:16 Do not be **w** in your own
16:19 but I want you to be **w** in what
16:27 to God, alone **w**, be glory
1 Cor 1:19 the wisdom of the **w**,
1:20 Where is the **w**? Where is the
1:26 that not many **w** according to
1:27 the world to put to shame the **w**,
3:10 as a **w** master builder I have
3:18 anyone among you seems to be **w**
3:18 a fool that he may become **w**.
3:19 He catches the **w** in their
3:20 the thoughts of the **w**,
4:10 but you are **w** in Christ!
6: 5 that there is not a **w** man among
10:15 I speak as to **w** men; judge for
2 Cor 10:12 among themselves, are not **w**.
11:19 since you yourselves are **w**!
Eph 5:15 not as fools but as **w**,
1 Tim 1:17 to God who alone is **w**,
2 Tim 3:15 which are able to make you **w**
Jas 3:13 Who is **w** and understanding
Jude 25 God our Savior, Who alone is **w**,

WISELY (12/12) SHREWDLY, WISE

1 Sam 18: 5 Saul sent him, and behaved **w**.
18:14 And David behaved **w** in all his
18:15 Saul saw that he behaved very **w**,
18:30 that David behaved more **w** than
2 Chr 11:23 He dealt **w**, and dispersed
Ps 64: 9 For they shall **w** consider His
101: 2 I will behave **w** in a perfect
Prov 16:20 He who heeds the word **w** will
21:12 The righteous God **w** considers
28:26 But whoever walks **w** will be
Eccl 7:10 For you do not inquire **w**
Mk 12:34 Jesus saw that he answered **w**,

WISER (7/7) WISE

1 Ki 4:31 For he was **w** than all men—than
Job 35:11 And makes us **w** than the birds
Ps 119:98 make me **w** than my enemies;
Prov 9: 9 man, and he will be still **w**;
26:16 The lazy man is **w** in his own
Ezek 28: 3 you are **w** than Daniel!
1 Cor 1:25 the foolishness of God is **w**

WISEST (1/1)

Judg 5:29 Her **w** ladies answered her,

WISH (32/31) WISHED, WISHES

Gen 19: 8 and you may do to them as you **w**;
23: 8 If it is your **w** that I bury my
Num 22:29 I **w** there were a sword in my
Josh 15:18 said to her, "What do you **w**?
Judg 1:14 said to her, "What do you **w**?
1 Ki 1:16 the king said, "What is your **w**?
Esth 5: 3 said to her, "What do you **w**,
Job 37:20 Should He be told that I **w** to
Ps 40:14 and brought to dishonor Who **w**
73: 7 have more than heart could **w**.
Mt 17: 4 for us to be here; if You **w**,
20:14 I **w** to give to this last man
20:15 lawful for me to do what I **w**
20:21 He said to her, "What do you **w**?
Mk 14: 7 and whenever you **w** you may do
Lk 4: 6 and I give it to whomever I **w**.
12:49 and how I **w** it were already
Jn 12:21 we **w** to see Jesus."
21:18 carry you where you do not **w**.
Rom 9: 3 For I could **w** that I myself were
1 Cor 4: 8 and indeed I could **w** you did
7: 7 For I **w** that all men were even
14: 5 I **w** you all spoke with tongues,
16: 7 For I do not **w** to see you now on
2 Cor 12:20 shall not find you such as I **w**,
12:20 by you such as you do not **w**;
Gal 5:12 I could **w** that those who trouble
5:17 do not do the things that you **w**.
2 Jn 12 I did not **w** to do so with
3 Jn 10 and forbids those who **w** to,
13 but I do not **w** to write to you
Rev 3:15 I could **w** you were cold or hot.

WISHED (14/11) WISH

1 Ki 13:33 for the high places; whoever **w**,
Neh 9:24 might do with them as they **w**.
Job 9: 3 If one **w** to contend with Him,
Dan 5:19 Whomever he **w**, he executed;
5:19 whomever he **w**, he kept alive;
5:19 whomever he **w**, he set up;
5:19 and whomever he **w**, he put down.
7:19 Then I **w** to know the truth about
Jon 4: 8 Then he **w** death for himself,
Mt 17:12 but did to him whatever they **w**.
27:15 one prisoner whom they **w**.
Mk 9:13 they did to him whatever they **w**,
Jn 21:18 yourself and walked where you **w**;
Phm 1:13 whom I **w** to keep with me,

WISHES (5/5) WISH

Lev 27:19 who dedicates the field ever **w**
Prov 21: 1 He turns it wherever He **w**.
Jn 3: 8 "The wind blows where it **w**,

1 Cor 7:36 must be, let him do what he w.
7:39 to be married to whom she w,

WISHING (1/1)

Lk 23:20 w to release Jesus, again

WIST (KJV) See KNOW

WIT (KJV) See KNOW, (MAKE) KNOWN

WITCH (KJV) See SORCERESS

WITCHCRAFT (6/6)

Deut 18:10 fire, or one who practices w,
1 Sam 15:23 rebellion is as the sin of w,
2 Ki 9:22 your mother Jezebel and her w
17:17 practiced w and soothsaying,
21: 6 practiced soothsaying, used w,
2 Chr 33: 6 used w and sorcery, and

WITH (6200/5081) See APPENDIX

WITH ALL YOUR HEART (20/20)

Deut 4:29 find Him if you seek Him w
6: 5 shall love the LORD your God w,
10:12 to serve the LORD your God w
11:13 LORD your God and serve Him w
13: 3 you love the LORD your God w
26:16 be careful to observe them w
30: 2 w and with all your soul,
30: 6 to love the LORD your God w
30:10 turn to the LORD your God w
Josh 22: 5 and to serve Him w and with all
1 Sam 12:20 LORD, but serve the LORD w.
12:24 LORD, and serve Him in truth w;
Prov 3: 5 Trust in the LORD w,
Jer 29:13 Me, when you search for Me w.
Joel 2:12 says the LORD, "Turn to Me w,
Zeph 3:14 Be glad and rejoice w,
Mt 22:37 love the LORD your God w,
Mk 12:30 love the LORD your God w,
Lk 10:27 love the LORD your God w,
Acts 8:37 Philip said, "If you believe w,

WITHDRAW (10/10) WITHDRAWN, WITHDREW

1 Sam 14:19 the priest, "W your hand."
1 Ki 15:19 so that he will w from me."
2 Chr 16: 3 so that he will w from me."
Job 9:13 God will not w His anger,
13:21 W Your hand far from me,
36: 7 He does not w His eyes from the
Ps 74:11 Why do You w Your hand,
Isa 60:20 Nor shall your moon w itself;
2 Th 3: 6 that you w from every brother
1 Tim 6: 5 From such w yourself.

WITHDRAWN (11/11) WITHDRAW

2 Sam 17:13 if he has w into a city, then
24:21 that the plague may be w from
24:25 and the plague was w from
1 Chr 21:22 that the plague may be w from
2 Chr 24:25 And when they had w from him
Lam 2: 8 He has not w His hand from
Ezek 18: 8 But has w his hand from
18:17 Who has w his hand from the
Hos 5: 6 He has w Himself from them.
Lk 22:41 And He was w from them about a
Jn 5:13 who it was, for Jesus had w,

WITHDREW (9/9) WITHDRAW

2 Sam 20:22 and they w from the city, every
2 Chr 32:31 God w from him, in order to
Ezek 20:22 Nevertheless I w My hand and
Mt 12:15 He w from there. And great
Mk 3: 7 But Jesus w with His disciples
Lk 5:16 So He Himself often w into the
Acts 19: 9 he departed from them and w the
22:29 who were about to examine him w
Gal 2:12 he w and separated himself,

WITHER (15/13) WITHERED, WITHERS

Ps 1: 3 Whose leaf also shall not w;
37: 2 And w as the green herb.
102:11 And I w away like grass.
Isa 19: 6 The reeds and rushes will w.
19: 7 sown by the River, Will w,
40:24 blow on them, And they will w,
Jer 12: 4 And the herbs of every field w?
Ezek 17: 9 its fruit, And leave it to w?
17: 9 of its spring leaves will w,
17:10 Will it not utterly w when the
17:10 It will w in the garden
47:12 their leaves will not w,
Nah 1: 4 Bashan and Carmel w,
Zech 11:17 His arm shall completely w,
Mt 21:20 How did the fig tree w away so

WITHERED (23/21) WITHER

Gen 41:23 "Then behold, seven heads, w,
1 Ki 13: 4 he stretched out toward him, w,
Ps 102: 4 My heart is stricken and w like
Isa 15: 6 For the green grass has w
27:11 When its boughs are w,
Ezek 19:12 branches were broken and w;
Joel 1:12 And the fig tree has w;
1:12 the trees of the field are w;
1:12 Surely joy has w away from the
1:17 For the grain has w.
Am 4: 7 it did not rain the part w.
Jon 4: 7 so damaged the plant that it w.
Mt 12:10 there was a man who had a w
13: 6 they had no root they w away.
21:19 Immediately the fig tree w
Mk 3: 1 man was there who had a w hand.
3: 3 to the man who had the w hand,
4: 6 and because it had no root it w
11:21 fig tree which You cursed has w
Lk 6: 6 there whose right hand was w.
6: 8 the man who had the w hand,
8: 6 it w away because it lacked
Jn 15: 6 cast out as a branch and is w;

WITHERS (9/9) WITHER

Job 8:12 It w before any other plant.
18:16 And his branch w above.
Ps 90: 6 evening it is cut down and w.
129: 6 Which w before it grows up,
Isa 40: 7 The grass w, the flower fades,
40: 8 The grass w, the flower fades,
Am 1: 2 And the top of Carmel w."
Jas 1:11 with a burning heat than it w
1 Pe 1:24 the grass. The grass w,

WITHHELD (15/14) WITHHOLD

Gen 11: 6 they propose to do will be w
20: 6 For I also w you from sinning
22:12 since you have not w your son,
22:16 and have not w your son,
30: 2 who has w from you the fruit of
Job 22: 7 And you have w bread from the
38:15 the wicked their light is w,
42: 2 no purpose of Yours can be w
Ps 21: 2 And have not w the request of
Jer 3: 3 the showers have been w,
5:25 And your sins have w good from
Ezek 18:16 Nor w a pledge, Nor robbed by
Joel 1:13 and the drink offering Are w
Am 4: 7 'I also w rain from you,
4: 7 I w rain from another city.

WITHHOLD (13/13) WITHHELD

Gen 23: 6 None of us will w from you his
2 Sam 13:13 for he will not w me from
Neh 9:20 And did not w Your manna from
Job 4: 2 But who can w himself from
Ps 40:11 Do not w Your tender mercies
84:11 No good thing will He w From
Prov 3:27 Do not w good from those to
23:13 Do not w correction from a
Eccl 2:10 I did not w my heart from any
11: 6 And in the evening do not w
Jer 2:25 W your foot from being unshod,
Hag 1:10 the heavens above you w the
Lk 6:29 do not w your tunic either.

WITHHOLDS (4/4)

Job 12:15 If He w the waters, they dry
Prov 11:24 And there is one who w more
11:26 people will curse him who w
Hag 1:10 and the earth w its fruit.

WITHIN (159/155)

Gen 18:12 Therefore Sarah laughed w
18:24 there were fifty righteous w
18:26 in Sodom fifty righteous w the
23:17 which were w all the
25:22 children struggled together w
40:13 Now w three days Pharaoh will
40:19 W three days Pharaoh will lift
Ex 20:10 nor your stranger who is w
Lev 25:29 then he may redeem it w a whole
25:29 w a full year he may redeem
25:30 But if it is not redeemed w the
26:25 you are gathered together w
Num 32:33 the land with its cities w the
36: 6 but they may marry only w the
Deut 5:14 nor your stranger who is w
12:12 and the Levite who is w your
12:15 may slaughter and eat meat w
12:17 You may not eat w your gates the
12:18 and the Levite who is w your
12:21 and you may eat w your gates as
14:21 give it to the alien who is w
14:27 forsake the Levite who is w
14:28 of that year and store it up w
14:29 and the widow who are w your
15: 7 w any of the gates in your land
15:22 'You may eat it w your gates;
16: 5 not sacrifice the Passover w
16:11 the Levite who is w your
16:14 who are w your gates.
17: 2 w any of your gates which the
17: 8 matters of controversy w your
23:16 in the place which he chooses w
24:14 aliens who is in your land w
26:12 so that they may eat w your
31:12 and the stranger who is w your
32:25 There shall be terror w
Josh 1:11 for w three days you will cross
19: 1 And their inheritance was w the
19: 9 had their inheritance w the
21:41 All the cities of the Levites w
24:30 And they buried him w the border
Judg 2: 9 And they buried him w the border
11:26 why did you not recover them w
14:12 solve and explain it to me w
1 Sam 13:11 not come w the days appointed,
14:14 twenty men w about half an acre
25:36 And Nabal's heart was merry w
25:37 that his heart died w him,
26: 5 Now Saul lay w the camp,
26: 7 Saul lay sleeping w the camp,
2 Sam 20: 4 Judah for me w three days,
2 Ki 11: 8 and whoever comes w range, let
1 Chr 5:16 the common-lands of Sharon w
Ezra 4:15 they have incited sedition w
10: 8 would not come w three days,
10: 9 gathered at Jerusalem w three
Neh 6:10 w the temple, and let us close
Esth 1:12 and his anger burned w him.
2:19 Mordecai sat w the king's gate.
2:21 while Mordecai sat w the king's
3: 2 who were w the king's gate
3: 3 who were w the king's gate
6:10 Jew who sits w the king's gate!
Job 6: 4 arrows of the Almighty are w
6:13 Is my help not w me?
19:27 How my heart yearns w me!
20: 2 Because of the turmoil w me.
20:14 It becomes cobra venom w him.
24:11 They press out oil w their
29:20 My glory is fresh w me,
32:18 The spirit w me compels me.
Ps 4: 4 Meditate w your heart on your
7: 8 according to my integrity w me.
22:14 It has melted w Me.
36: 1 An oracle w my heart concerning
39: 3 My heart was hot w me; While I
40: 8 And Your law is w my heart."
40:10 hidden Your righteousness w my
42: 4 I pour out my soul w me.
42: 5 And why are you disquieted w
42: 6 my soul is cast down w me;
42:11 And why are you disquieted w
43: 5 And why are you disquieted w
45:13 daughter is all glorious w
51:10 renew a steadfast spirit w me.
55: 4 My heart is severely pained w
77: 6 I meditate w my heart, And my
94:19 multitude of my anxieties w me,
101: 2 I will walk w my house with a
101: 7 works deceit shall not dwell w
103: 1 And all that is w me, bless
109:22 And my heart is wounded w me.
122: 2 been standing W your gates,
122: 7 Peace be w your walls,
122: 7 Prosperity w your palaces."
122: 8 now say, "Peace be w you."
131: 2 a weaned child is my soul w
142: 3 my spirit was overwhelmed w me,
143: 4 my spirit is overwhelmed w me;
143: 4 My heart w me is distressed.
147:13 He has blessed your children w
Prov 2: 1 treasure my commands w you,
7: 1 And treasure my commands w
22:18 thing if you keep them w you;
26:24 And lays up deceit w himself;
Isa 7: 8 W sixty-five years Ephraim
16:14 W three years, as the years of a
21:16 W a year, according to the year
26: 9 by my spirit w me I will seek
56: 5 in My house And w My walls
60:18 wasting nor destruction w your
63:11 He who put His Holy Spirit w
Jer 4:14 your evil thoughts lodge w you?
17: 3 your high places of sin w all
23: 9 My heart w me is broken
28: 3 W two full years I will bring
28:11 neck of all nations w the space
47: 2 The city and those who dwell w;
Lam 1:20 My heart is overturned w me,
3:20 remembers And sinks w me.
Ezek 1: 5 Also from w it came the
1:27 of fire all around w it;
7:15 the pestilence and famine w.
9: 4 abominations that are done w
11:19 and I will put a new spirit w
12:24 or flattering divination w the
22: 3 and she makes idols w herself
28:16 became filled with violence w,
30: 6 Migdol to Syene Those w her
36:26 heart and put a new spirit w
36:27 I will put My Spirit w you and
44:17 them while they minister w the
44:17 the inner court or w the house.
Dan 6:12 who petitions any god or man w
7:15 was grieved in my spirit w my
11:20 but w a few days he shall be
Hos 11: 8 My heart churns w Me;
Am 3: 9 And the oppressed w her.
Jon 2: 7 'When my soul fainted w me,
Mic 5: 6 our land And when he treads w
Zech 12: 1 and forms the spirit of man w
Mt 9: 3 the scribes said w themselves,
Mk 2: 8 reasoned thus w themselves,
7:21 'For from w, out of the
7:23 these evil things come from w
14:58 and w three days I will build
Lk 11: 7 and he will answer from w and
12:17 And he thought w himself,
16: 3 Then the steward said w himself,
17:21 the kingdom of God is w you."
18: 4 afterward he said w himself,

19:44 and your children ***w*** you, to the
24:32 Did not our heart burn ***w*** us
Acts 10:17 while Peter wondered ***w*** himself
17:16 his spirit was provoked ***w*** him
Rom 8:23 even we ourselves groan ***w***
2 Cor 2: 1 But I determined this ***w*** myself,
10:13 but ***w*** the limits of the sphere
Rev 4: 8 were full of eyes around and ***w***.

WITHOUT (302/267)

Gen 1: 2 The earth was ***w*** form, and void;
37:33 ***W*** doubt Joseph is torn to
41:44 and ***w*** your consent no man may
Ex 12: 5 'Your lamb shall be ***w*** blemish,
21:11 go out free, ***w*** paying money.
29: 1 bull and two rams ***w*** blemish,
Lev 1: 3 let him offer a male ***w*** blemish;
1:10 shall bring a male ***w*** blemish.
3: 1 he shall offer it ***w*** blemish
3: 6 he shall offer it ***w*** blemish.
4: 3 sinned a young bull ***w*** blemish
4:23 a male ***w*** blemish.
4:28 a female ***w*** blemish, for his sin
4:32 bring a female ***w*** blemish.
5:15 offering a ram ***w*** blemish
5:18 the priest a ram ***w*** blemish
6: 6 a ram ***w*** blemish from the flock,
9: 2 ***w*** blemish, and offer them
9: 3 ***w*** blemish, as a burnt offering,
10:12 and eat it ***w*** leaven beside the
14:10 take two male lambs ***w*** blemish,
14:10 of the first year ***w*** blemish,
22:19 own free will a male ***w*** blemish
23:12 ***w*** blemish, as a burnt offering
23:18 ***w*** blemish, one young bull, and
26:43 while it lies desolate ***w*** them;
Num 6:14 in its first year ***w*** blemish
6:14 in its first year ***w*** blemish
6:14 one ram ***w*** blemish as a peace
15:24 ***w*** the knowledge of the
19: 2 you a red heifer ***w*** blemish,
28: 3 their first year ***w*** blemish,
28: 9 ***w*** blemish, and two-tenths of
28:11 their first year, ***w*** blemish;
28:19 Be sure they are ***w*** blemish.
28:31 'Be sure they are ***w*** blemish.
29: 2 their first year, ***w*** blemish.
29: 8 Be sure they are ***w*** blemish.
29:13 They shall be ***w*** blemish.
29:17 their first year ***w*** blemish,
29:20 their first year ***w*** blemish,
29:23 their first year, ***w*** blemish,
29:26 their first year ***w*** blemish,
29:29 their first year ***w*** blemish,
29:32 their first year ***w*** blemish,
29:36 their first year ***w*** blemish,
35:22 him suddenly ***w*** enmity,
35:22 anything at him ***w*** lying in
35:23 throwing it at him ***w*** seeing
Deut 4:42 ***w*** having hated him in time
8: 9 will eat bread ***w*** scarcity,
32: 4 truth and ***w*** injustice;
Josh 3:10 and that He will ***w*** fail drive
Judg 2:23 ***w*** driving them out immediately;
6: 5 their camels were ***w*** number;
7:12 camels were ***w*** number,
Ruth 4:14 has not left you this day ***w*** a
1 Sam 19: 5 to kill David ***w*** a cause?"
20: 2 either great or small ***w*** first
25:31 you have shed blood ***w*** cause,
30: 8 overtake them and ***w*** fail
2 Sam 23: 4 A morning ***w*** clouds, Like the
1 Ki 22: 1 Now three years passed ***w*** war
2 Ki 18:25 Have I now come up ***w*** the LORD
1 Chr 2:30 Seled died ***w*** children.
2:32 Jether died ***w*** children.
29:15 as a shadow, And ***w*** hope.
2 Chr 5:11 ***w*** keeping to their divisions),
12: 3 and people ***w*** number who came
15: 3 has been ***w*** the true God,
15: 3 ***w*** a teaching priest, and
15: 3 teaching priest, and ***w*** law;
Ezra 6: 9 given them day by day ***w*** fail,
7:22 and salt ***w*** prescribed limit.
Esth 9:27 that ***w*** fail they should
Job 2: 3 to destroy him ***w*** cause."
4:21 They die, even ***w*** wisdom.'
5: 9 Marvelous things ***w*** number.
6: 6 food be eaten ***w*** salt?
7: 6 And are spent ***w*** hope.
8:11 papyrus grow up ***w*** a marsh?
8:11 reeds flourish ***w*** water?
9:10 Yes, wonders ***w*** number.
9:17 multiplies my wounds ***w*** cause.
10:22 ***w*** any order, Where even the
11:15 lift up your face ***w*** spot;
12:25 They grope in the dark ***w*** light,
21:10 Their bull breeds ***w*** failure;
21:10 cow calves ***w*** miscarriage.
22: 5 And your iniquity ***w*** end?
24: 7 ***w*** clothing, And have no
24:10 ***w*** clothing; And they take away
26: 2 helped him who is ***w*** power?
31:19 Or any poor man ***w*** covering;
31:39 eaten its fruit ***w*** money,
33: 9 'I am pure, ***w*** transgression;
34: 6 I am ***w*** transgression.'
34:20 The mighty are taken away ***w*** a
34:24 pieces mighty men ***w*** inquiry,
34:35 'Job speaks ***w*** knowledge,
34:35 His words are ***w*** wisdom.'
35:16 multiplies words ***w*** knowledge."
36:12 shall die ***w*** knowledge.
38: 2 counsel By words ***w*** knowledge?
39:16 labor is in vain, ***w*** concern,
41:33 Which is made ***w*** fear.
42: 3 hides counsel ***w*** knowledge?'
Ps 7: 4 plundered my enemy ***w*** cause,
25: 3 who deal treacherously ***w*** cause.
35: 7 For ***w*** cause they have hidden
35: 7 Which they have dug ***w*** cause
35:19 eye who hate me ***w*** a cause.
69: 4 Those who hate me ***w*** a cause
77: 2 out in the night ***w*** ceasing;
105:34 Young locusts ***w*** number,
109: 3 fought against me ***w*** a cause.
119:161 persecute me ***w*** a cause,
Prov 1:11 for the innocent ***w*** cause;
1:33 be secure, ***w*** fear of evil."
3:30 strive with a man ***w*** cause,
6:15 he shall be broken ***w*** remedy.
15:22 ***W*** counsel, plans go awry,
16: 8 Than vast revenues ***w*** justice.
19: 2 a soul to be ***w*** knowledge,
23:29 Who has wounds ***w*** cause?
24:28 against your neighbor ***w*** cause,
25:14 clouds and wind ***w*** rain.
25:28 city broken down, ***w*** walls.
26: 2 So a curse ***w*** cause shall not
29: 1 and that ***w*** remedy.
Eccl 4: 8 is one alone, ***w*** companion:
Song 6: 8 And virgins ***w*** number.
Isa 5: 9 beautiful ones, ***w*** inhabitant.
6:11 laid waste and ***w*** inhabitant,
6:11 The houses are ***w*** a man,
10: 4 ***W*** Me they shall bow down among
36:10 Have I now come up ***w*** the LORD
47: 1 Sit on the ground ***w*** a throne,
52: 3 shall be redeemed ***w*** money."
52: 4 oppressed them ***w*** cause.
55: 1 buy wine and milk ***W*** money and
55: 1 Without money and ***w*** price.
Jer 2:15 are burned, ***w*** inhabitant.
2:32 forgotten Me days ***w*** number.
4: 7 be laid waste, ***W*** inhabitant.
4:23 and indeed it was ***w*** form,
5:21 people, ***W*** understanding,
9:11 desolate, ***w*** an inhabitant."
10:14 is dull-hearted, ***w*** knowledge;
15:13 give as plunder ***w*** price,
22:13 his neighbor's service ***w*** wages
26: 9 desolate, ***w*** an inhabitant'?"
32:43 is desolate, ***w*** man or beast;
33:10 ***w*** man and without beast"—in
33:10 without man and ***w*** beast"—in
33:10 ***w*** man and without inhabitant
33:10 without man and ***w*** inhabitant
33:10 inhabitant and ***w*** beast,
33:12 ***w*** man and without beast, and in
33:12 without man and ***w*** beast, and in
34:22 a desolation ***w*** inhabitant.'
44:19 ***w*** our husbands' permission?"
44:22 and ***w*** an inhabitant, as it is
46:19 and desolate, ***w*** inhabitant.
48: 9 ***W*** any to dwell in them.
51:17 is dull-hearted, ***w*** knowledge;
51:29 a desolation ***w*** inhabitant.
51:37 a hissing, ***W*** an inhabitant.
Lam 1: 6 That flee ***w*** strength Before
3:49 do not cease, ***W*** interruption,
3:52 My enemies ***w*** cause Hunted me
Ezek 14:23 I have done nothing ***w*** cause
33:15 of life ***w*** committing iniquity,
38:11 all of them dwelling ***w*** walls,
43:22 kid of the goats ***w*** blemish
43:23 offer a young bull ***w*** blemish,
43:23 from the flock ***w*** blemish.
43:25 the flock, both ***w*** blemish.
45:18 take a young bull ***w*** blemish
45:23 and seven rams ***w*** blemish,
46: 4 be six lambs ***w*** blemish,
46: 4 and a ram ***w*** blemish;
46: 6 be a young bull ***w*** blemish,
46: 6 they shall be ***w*** blemish.
46:13 of the first year ***w*** blemish;
Dan 2:34 stone was cut out ***w*** hands,
2:45 out of the mountain ***w*** hands,
8: 5 ***w*** touching the ground; and the
8:25 be broken ***w*** human means.
Hos 3: 4 shall abide many days ***w*** king
3: 4 ***w*** sacrifice or sacred pillar,
3: 4 ***w*** ephod or teraphim.
7:11 ***w*** sense—They call to Egypt,
Joel 1: 6 Strong, and ***w*** number;
Mic 3: 6 you shall have night ***w*** vision,
3: 6 have darkness ***w*** divination;
Hab 1:17 to slay nations ***w*** pity?
Zech 2: 4 be inhabited as towns ***w*** walls,
Mt 5:22 is angry with his brother ***w*** a
13:34 and ***w*** a parable He did not
13:57 A prophet is not ***w*** honor except
15:16 also still ***w*** understanding?
22:12 how did you come in here ***w*** a
23:23 ***w*** leaving the others undone.
Mk 4:34 But ***w*** a parable He did not speak
6: 4 A prophet is not ***w*** honor except
7:18 Are you thus ***w*** understanding
14:58 build another made ***w*** hands.'
Lk 1:74 Might serve Him ***w*** fear,
6:49 on the earth ***w*** a foundation,
11:42 ***w*** leaving the others undone.
20:28 and he dies ***w*** children, his
20:29 and died ***w*** children.
22:35 When I sent you ***w*** money bag,
Jn 1: 3 and ***w*** Him nothing was made that
8: 7 He who is ***w*** sin among you, let
15: 5 for ***w*** Me you can do nothing.
15:25 They hated Me ***w*** a cause.'
19:23 Now the tunic was ***w*** seam, woven
Acts 5:26 and brought them ***w*** violence,
9: 9 And he was three days ***w*** sight,
10:29 Therefore I came ***w*** objection as
14: 8 a certain man ***w*** strength
14:17 not leave Himself ***w*** witness,
17:23 whom you worship ***w*** knowing,
24:16 have a conscience ***w*** offense
25:17 ***w*** any delay, the next day I sat
27:33 waited and continued ***w*** food,
Rom 1: 9 that ***w*** ceasing I make mention
1:20 so that they are ***w*** excuse,
2:12 For as many as have sinned ***w*** law
2:12 law will also perish ***w*** law,
3: 3 faithfulness of God ***w*** effect?
5: 6 when we were still ***w*** strength,
7: 9 I was alive once ***w*** the law, but
10:14 And how shall they hear ***w*** a
12: 9 Let love be ***w*** hypocrisy.
1 Cor 4: 8 You have reigned as kings ***w*** us—
7:32 But I want you to be ***w*** care.
7:35 serve the Lord ***w*** distraction.
9:18 the gospel of Christ ***w*** charge,
9:21 to those who are ***w*** law,
9:21 as ***w*** law (not being without law
9:21 as without law (not being ***w*** law
9:21 win those who are ***w*** law;
14: 7 Even things ***w*** life, whether
14:10 of them is ***w*** significance.
16:10 he may be with you ***w*** fear;
Eph 1: 4 should be holy and ***w*** blame
2:12 that time you were ***w*** Christ,
2:12 having no hope and ***w*** God in the
5:27 should be holy and ***w*** blemish.
Phil 1:10 may be sincere and ***w*** offense
1:14 to speak the word ***w*** fear.
2:14 Do all things ***w*** complaining and
2:15 children of God ***w*** fault in the
Col 2:11 circumcision made ***w*** hands,
1 Th 1: 3 remembering ***w*** ceasing your work
2:13 we also thank God ***w*** ceasing,
5:17 pray ***w*** ceasing,
1 Tim 2: 8 ***w*** wrath and doubting;
3:16 And ***w*** controversy great is the
5:21 these things ***w*** prejudice,
6:14 keep this commandment ***w*** spot,
2 Tim 1: 3 as ***w*** ceasing I remember you in
3: 3 ***w*** self-control, brutal,
Phm 1:14 But ***w*** your consent I wanted to
Heb 4:15 as we are, yet ***w*** sin.
7: 3 ***w*** father, without mother,
7: 3 ***w*** mother, without genealogy,
7: 3 ***w*** genealogy, having neither
7:20 not made priest ***w*** an oath
7:21 they have become priests ***w*** an
9: 7 not ***w*** blood, which he offered
9:14 Spirit offered Himself ***w*** spot
9:18 covenant was dedicated ***w*** blood.
9:22 and ***w*** shedding of blood there
10:23 of our hope ***w*** wavering,
10:28 Moses' law dies ***w*** mercy
11: 6 But ***w*** faith it is impossible
12: 8 But if you are ***w*** chastening, of
12:14 ***w*** which no one will see the
13: 5 conduct be ***w*** covetousness;
Jas 1: 5 liberally and ***w*** reproach,
2:13 For judgment is ***w*** mercy to the
2:18 Show me your faith ***w*** your
2:20 that faith ***w*** works is dead?
2:26 For as the body ***w*** the spirit is
2:26 so faith ***w*** works is dead also.
3:17 ***w*** partiality and without
3:17 partiality and ***w*** hypocrisy.
1 Pe 1:17 who ***w*** partiality judges
1:19 as of a lamb ***w*** blemish and
1:19 without blemish and ***w*** spot.
3: 1 ***w*** a word, may be won by the
4: 9 to one another ***w*** grumbling.
2 Pe 2:17 These are wells ***w*** water, clouds
3:14 ***w*** spot and blameless;
Jude 12 they feast with you ***w*** fear,
12 They are clouds ***w*** water,
12 late autumn trees ***w*** fruit,
Rev 14: 5 for they are ***w*** fault before the

WITHS (KJV) See BOWSTRINGS

WITHSTAND (13/13) WITHSTOOD

2 Chr 13: 7 inexperienced and could not ***w***
13: 8 And now you think to ***w*** the
20: 6 so that no one is able to ***w***
Esth 9: 2 And no one could ***w*** them,
Eccl 4:12 two can ***w*** him. And a threefold
Jer 49:19 that shepherd Who will ***w*** Me?"
50:44 that shepherd Who will ***w*** Me?"
Lam 1:14 those whom I am not able to ***w***.
Dan 8: 4 so that no animal could ***w*** him;
8: 7 no power in the ram to ***w*** him,
11:15 of the South shall not ***w*** him.
Acts 11:17 who was I that I could ***w*** God?"
Eph 6:13 that you may be able to ***w*** in

WITHSTOOD (4/4) WITHSTAND

2 Chr 26:18 And they ***w*** King Uzziah, and said
Dan 10:13 of the kingdom of Persia ***w*** me

Acts	13: 8	***w*** them, seeking to turn the
Gal	2:11	I ***w*** him to his face, because he

WITNESS (137/119) EYEWITNESSES, WITNESSED, WITNESSES

Gen	21:30	that they may be my ***w*** that I
	31:44	and let it be a ***w*** between you
	31:48	This heap is a ***w*** between you
	31:50	God is ***w*** between you and me!"
	31:52	"This heap is a ***w***,
	31:52	and this pillar is a ***w***,
Ex	20:16	You shall not bear false ***w***
	23: 1	wicked to be an unrighteous ***w***.
Lev	5: 1	of an oath, and is a ***w***,
Num	5:13	and there was no ***w*** against
	17: 7	LORD in the tabernacle of ***w***.
	17: 8	went into the tabernacle of ***w***,
	18: 2	you before the tabernacle of ***w***.
	35:30	but one ***w*** is not sufficient
Deut	4:26	I call heaven and earth to ***w***
	5:20	You shall not bear false ***w***
	17: 6	death on the testimony of one ***w***.
	19:15	One ***w*** shall not rise against a
	19:16	If a false ***w*** rises against any
	19:18	if the ***w*** is a false witness,
	19:18	if the witness is a false ***w***,
	31:19	that this song may be a ***w*** for
	31:21	testify against them as a ***w***;
	31:26	that it may be there as a ***w***
	31:28	and call heaven and earth to ***w***
Josh	22:27	but that it may be a ***w***
	22:28	but it is a ***w*** between you and
	22:34	of Gad called the altar, ***W***,
	22:34	For it is a ***w*** between us that
	24:27	this stone shall be a ***w*** to us,
	24:27	It shall therefore be a ***w*** to
Judg	11:10	The LORD will be a ***w*** between
1 Sam	12: 3	***W*** against me before the LORD
	12: 5	'The LORD is ***w*** against you,
	12: 5	and His anointed is ***w*** this
	12: 5	And they answered, "He is ***w***.
	20:12	LORD God of Israel is ***w***!
1 Ki	21:10	before him to bear ***w*** against
2 Chr	24: 6	Israel, for the tabernacle of ***w***?
Job	16: 8	And it is a ***w*** against me;
	16: 8	up against me And bears ***w*** to
	16:19	Surely even now my ***w*** is in
Ps	89:37	Even like the faithful ***w*** in
Prov	6:19	A false ***w*** who speaks lies,
	12:17	righteousness, But a false ***w***,
	14: 5	A faithful ***w*** does not lie,
	14: 5	But a false ***w*** will utter lies.
	14:25	A true ***w*** delivers souls, But a
	14:25	But a deceitful ***w*** speaks
	19: 5	A false ***w*** will not go
	19: 9	A false ***w*** will not go
	19:28	A disreputable ***w*** scorns
	21:28	A false ***w*** shall perish,
	24:28	Do not be a ***w*** against your
	25:18	A man who bears false ***w***
Isa	19:20	will be for a sign and for a ***w***
	55: 4	I have given him as a ***w*** to
Jer	29:23	Indeed I know, and am a ***w***,
	42: 5	LORD be a true and faithful ***w***
Hos	12:10	given symbols through the ***w*** of
Mic	1: 2	Let the Lord GOD be a ***w*** against
Mal	2:14	Because the LORD has been ***w***
	3: 5	I will be a swift ***w*** Against
Mt	15:19	fornications, thefts, false ***w***,
	19:18	shall not bear false ***w***,
	24:14	in all the world as a ***w*** to all
Mk	10:19	'Do not bear false ***w***,'
	14:56	For many bore false ***w*** against
	14:57	some rose up and bore false ***w***
Lk	4:22	So all bore ***w*** to Him, and
	11:48	you bear ***w*** that you approve the
	18:20	'Do not bear false ***w***,'
Jn	1: 7	This man came for a ***w***,
	1: 7	to bear ***w*** of the Light, that
	1: 8	but was sent to bear ***w*** of
	1:15	John bore ***w*** of Him and cried
	1:32	And John bore ***w***,
	3:11	and you do not receive Our ***w***.
	3:28	"You yourselves bear me ***w***,
	5:31	If I bear ***w*** of Myself,
	5:31	My ***w*** is not true.
	5:32	There is another who bears ***w*** of
	5:32	and I know that the ***w*** which He
	5:33	and he has borne ***w*** to the
	5:36	But I have a greater ***w*** than
	5:36	bear ***w*** of Me, that the Father
	8:13	'You bear ***w*** of Yourself;
	8:13	Your ***w*** is not true."
	8:14	'Even if I bear ***w*** of Myself,
	8:14	My ***w*** is true, for I know where
	8:18	I am One who bears ***w*** of Myself,
	8:18	the Father who sent Me bears ***w***
	10:25	they bear ***w*** of Me.
	12:17	him from the dead, bore ***w***.
	15:27	"And you also will bear ***w***,
	18:23	bear ***w*** of the evil; but if
	18:37	that I should bear ***w*** to the
Acts	1:22	one of these must become a ***w***
	4:33	power the apostles gave ***w*** to
	7:44	had the tabernacle of ***w*** in the
	10:43	To Him all the prophets ***w*** that,
	14: 3	who was bearing ***w*** to the word
	14:17	did not leave Himself without ***w***,
	22: 5	also the high priest bears me ***w***,
	22:15	For you will be His ***w*** to all men
	23:11	so you must also bear ***w*** at
	26:16	to make you a minister and a ***w***
Rom	1: 9	For God is my ***w***, whom I serve
	2:15	their conscience also bearing ***w***,
	8:16	The Spirit Himself bears ***w*** with
	9: 1	my conscience also bearing me ***w***
	10: 2	For I bear them ***w*** that they have
	13: 9	shall not bear false ***w***,
2 Cor	1:23	Moreover I call God as ***w*** against
	8: 3	For I bear ***w*** that according to
Gal	4:15	For I bear you ***w*** that, if
Phil	1: 8	For God is my ***w***, how greatly I
Col	4:13	For I bear him ***w*** that he has a
1 Th	2: 5	for covetousness—God is ***w***.
Heb	2: 4	God also bearing ***w*** both with
	11: 4	through which he obtained ***w***
Jas	5: 3	and their corrosion will be a ***w***
1 Pe	5: 1	I who am a fellow elder and a ***w***
1 Jn	1: 2	and we have seen, and bear ***w***,
	5: 6	it is the Spirit who bears ***w***,
	5: 7	there are three that bear ***w*** in
	5: 8	there are three that bear ***w*** on
	5: 9	If we receive the ***w*** of men,
	5: 9	the ***w*** of God is greater;
	5: 9	for this is the ***w*** of God which
	5:10	in the Son of God has the ***w*** in
3 Jn	6	who have borne ***w*** of your love
	12	And we also bear ***w***,
Rev	1: 2	who bore ***w*** to the word of God,
	1: 5	Jesus Christ, the faithful ***w***,
	3:14	Amen, the Faithful and True ***W***,
	20: 4	had been beheaded for their ***w***

WITNESSED (5/5) WITNESS

Ex	20:18	Now all the people ***w*** the
1 Ki	21:13	and the scoundrels ***w*** against
Rom	3:21	being ***w*** by the Law and the
1 Tim	6:13	and before Christ Jesus who ***w***
Heb	7: 8	of whom it is ***w*** that he lives.

WITNESSES (51/49) WITNESS

Num	35:30	to death on the testimony of ***w***;
Deut	17: 6	the testimony of two or three ***w***;
	17: 7	The hands of the ***w*** shall be the
	19:15	by the mouth of two or three ***w***
	30:19	I call heaven and earth as ***w***
Josh	24:22	You are ***w*** against yourselves
	24:22	And they said, "We are ***w***!"
Ruth	4: 9	You are ***w*** this day that I have
	4:10	You are ***w*** this day."
	4:11	the elders, said, "We are ***w***.
Job	10:17	You renew Your ***w*** against me,
Ps	27:12	For false ***w*** have risen against
	35:11	Fierce ***w*** rise up; They ask me
Isa	3: 9	look on their countenance ***w***
	8: 2	take for Myself faithful ***w*** to
	43: 9	Let them bring out their ***w***,
	43:10	'You are My ***w***,' says the
	43:12	Therefore you are My ***w***,"
	44: 8	declared it? You are My ***w***.
	44: 9	They are their own ***w***;
Jer	32:10	the deed and sealed it, took ***w***,
	32:12	and in the presence of the ***w***
	32:25	for money, and take ***w***"!—yet
	32:44	and seal them, and take ***w***,
Mt	18:16	mouth of two or three ***w***
	23:31	Therefore you are ***w*** against
	26:60	Even though many false ***w*** came
	26:60	But at last two false ***w*** came
	26:65	further need do we have of ***w***?
Mk	14:63	further need do we have of ***w***?
Lk	24:48	And you are ***w*** of these things.
Jn	5:32	that the witness which He ***w*** of
Acts	1: 8	and you shall be ***w*** to Me in
	2:32	of which we are all ***w***.
	3:15	the dead, of which we are ***w***.
	5:32	And we are His ***w*** to these
	6:13	They also set up false ***w*** who
	7:58	And the ***w*** laid down their
	10:39	And we are ***w*** of all things which
	10:41	but to ***w*** chosen before by God,
	13:31	who are His ***w*** to the people.
1 Cor	15:15	and we are found false ***w*** of
2 Cor	13: 1	mouth of two or three ***w***
1 Th	2:10	You are ***w***, and God also,
1 Tim	5:19	except from two or three ***w***.
	6:12	in the presence of many ***w***.
2 Tim	2: 2	have heard from me among many ***w***,
Heb	10:15	But the Holy Spirit also ***w*** to
	10:28	the testimony of two or three ***w***.
	12: 1	by so great a cloud of ***w***,
Rev	11: 3	I will give power to my two ***w***,

WITNESSING (1/1)

Acts	26:22	***w*** both to small and great,

WITS' (1/1)

Ps	107:27	And are at their ***w*** end.

WITTY (KJV) See DISCRETION

WIVES (134/123) WIFE, WIVES'

Gen	4:19	Lamech took for himself two ***w***:
	4:23	Then Lamech said to his ***w***:
	4:23	***W*** of Lamech, listen to my
	6: 2	and they took ***w*** for themselves
	6:18	and your sons' ***w*** with you.
	7: 7	sons, his wife, and his sons' ***w***,
	7:13	Noah's wife and the three ***w*** of
	8:16	and your sons and your sons' ***w***
	8:18	and his wife and his sons' ***w***
	11:29	Then Abram and Nahor took ***w***:
	26:34	he took as ***w*** Judith the
	28: 9	his wife in addition to the ***w***
	30:26	Give me my ***w*** and my children
	31:17	and set his sons and his ***w*** on
	31:50	or if you take other ***w*** besides
	32:22	that night and took his two ***w***,
	34:21	take their daughters to us as ***w***,
	34:29	their little ones and their ***w***
	36: 2	Esau took his ***w*** from the
	36: 6	Then Esau took his ***w***,
	37: 2	sons of Zilpah, his father's ***w***;
	45:19	for your little ones and your ***w***;
	46: 5	their little ones, and their ***w***,
	46:26	body, besides Jacob's sons' ***w***,
Ex	19:15	do not come near your ***w***."
	22:24	your ***w*** shall be widows,
	32: 2	are in the ears of your ***w***,
Num	14: 3	that our ***w*** and children should
	16:27	of their tents, with their ***w***,
	32:26	"Our little ones, our ***w***,
Deut	3:19	'But your ***w***, your little ones,
	17:17	Neither shall he multiply ***w*** for
	21:15	"If a man has two ***w***,
	29:11	"your little ones and your ***w***—
Josh	1:14	'Your ***w***, your little ones,
Judg	3: 6	their daughters to be their ***w***,
	8:30	offspring, for he had many ***w***.
	21: 7	What shall we do for ***w*** for those
	21: 7	give them our daughters as ***w***?
	21:16	What shall we do for ***w*** for those
	21:18	we cannot give them ***w*** from our
	21:23	they took enough ***w*** for their
Ruth	1: 4	Now they took ***w*** of the women of
1 Sam	1: 2	And he had two ***w***:
	25:43	and so both of them were his ***w***.
	27: 3	and David with his two ***w***,
	30: 3	burned with fire; and their ***w***,
	30: 5	And David's two ***w***,
	30:18	and David rescued his two ***w***.
2 Sam	2: 2	and his two ***w*** also, Ahinoam the
	5:13	took more concubines and ***w***
	12: 8	house and your master's ***w*** into
	12:11	and I will take your ***w*** before
	12:11	and he shall lie with your ***w*** in
	19: 5	the lives of your ***w*** and the
1 Ki	11: 3	And he had seven hundred ***w***,
	11: 3	and his ***w*** turned away his
	11: 4	that his ***w*** turned his heart
	11: 8	likewise for all his foreign ***w***,
	20: 3	your loveliest ***w*** and children
	20: 5	your ***w*** and your children";
	20: 7	for he sent to me for my ***w***,
2 Ki	4: 1	A certain woman of the ***w*** of the
	24:15	The king's mother, the king's ***w***,
1 Chr	4: 5	the father of Tekoa had two ***w***,
	7: 4	for they had many ***w*** and sons.
	8: 8	away Hushim and Baara his ***w***.
	14: 3	Then David took more ***w*** in
	23:22	sons of Kish, took them as ***w***.
2 Chr	11:21	of Absalom more than all his ***w***
	11:21	for he took eighteen ***w*** and
	11:23	He also sought many ***w*** for
	13:21	grew mighty, married fourteen ***w***,
	20:13	with their little ones, their ***w***,
	21:14	children, your ***w***, and all your
	21:17	and also his sons and his ***w***,
	24: 3	And Jehoiada took two ***w*** for him,
	29: 9	and our ***w*** are in captivity.
	31:18	little ones and their ***w***,
Ezra	9: 2	some of their daughters as ***w***
	9:12	do not give your daughters as ***w***
	10: 2	and have taken pagan ***w*** from the
	10: 3	our God to put away all these ***w***
	10:10	and have taken pagan ***w***,
	10:11	the land, and from the pagan ***w***.
	10:14	cities who have taken pagan ***w***
	10:17	the men who had taken pagan ***w***.
	10:18	priests who had taken pagan ***w***
	10:19	they would put away their ***w***;
	10:44	All these had taken pagan ***w***,
	10:44	and some of them had ***w*** by
Neh	4:14	sons, your daughters, your ***w***,
	5: 1	of the people and their ***w***
	10:28	to the Law of God, their ***w***,
	10:30	not give our daughters as ***w*** to
	13:25	not give your daughters as ***w***
Esth	1:20	all ***w*** will honor their
Isa	13:16	will be plundered And their ***w***
Jer	6:12	Fields and ***w*** together; For I
	8:10	Therefore I will give their ***w***
	14:16	to bury them—them nor their ***w***,
	18:21	Let their ***w*** become widows
	29: 6	Take ***w*** and beget sons and
	29: 6	and take ***w*** for your sons and
	29:23	with their neighbors' ***w***,
	35: 8	no wine all our days, we, our ***w***,
	38:23	shall surrender all your ***w*** and
	44: 9	the wickedness of their ***w***,
	44: 9	and the wickedness of your ***w***,
	44:15	the men who knew that their ***w***
	44:25	You and your ***w*** have spoken with
Ezek	33:26	and you defile one another's ***w***.
Dan	5: 2	the king and his lords, his ***w***,
	5: 3	the king and his lords, his ***w***,
	5:23	your ***w*** and your concubines,
	6:24	their children, and their ***w***;
Zech	12:12	and their ***w*** by themselves;
	12:12	and their ***w*** by themselves;

12:13 and their **w** by themselves;
12:13 and their **w** by themselves;
12:14 and their **w** by themselves.
Mt 19: 8 permitted you to divorce your **w**,
Lk 17:27 ate, they drank, they married **w**,
Acts 21: 5 with **w** and children, till we
1 Cor 7:29 now on even those who have **w**
Eph 5:22 **W**, submit to your own
5:24 so let the **w** be to their own
5:25 Husbands, love your **w**,
5:28 ought to love their own **w** as
Col 3:18 **W**, submit to your own
3:19 love your **w** and do not be
1 Tim 3:11 Likewise their **w** must be
1 Pe 3: 1 **W**, likewise, be submissive
3: 1 won by the conduct of their **w**,

WIVES' (1/1) WIVES

1 Tim 4: 7 profane and old **w** fables,

WIZARD (KJV) See MEDIUM

WIZARDS (1/1)

Isa 8:19 those who are mediums and **w**,

WOE (111/102)

Num 21:29 **W** to you, Moab! You have
1 Sam 4: 7 **W** to us! For such a thing has
4: 8 **W** to us! Who will deliver us
Job 10:15 **w** to me; Even if I am
Ps 120: 5 **W** is me, that I dwell in
Prov 23:29 Who has **w**? Who has sorrow?
Eccl 4:10 But **w** to him who is alone
10:16 **W** to you, O land, when your
Isa 3: 9 **W** to their soul! For they
3:11 **W** to the wicked! It shall be
5: 8 **W** to those who join house to
5:11 **W** to those who rise early in
5:18 **W** to those who draw iniquity
5:20 **W** to those who call evil good,
5:21 **W** to those who are wise in
5:22 **W** to men mighty at drinking
5:22 **W** to men valiant for mixing
6: 5 **W** is me, for I am undone!
10: 1 **W** to those who decree
10: 5 **W** to Assyria, the rod of My
17:12 **W** to the multitude of many
18: 1 **W** to the land shadowed with
24:16 **W** to me! The treacherous
28: 1 **W** to the crown of pride, to the
29: 1 **W** to Ariel, to Ariel, the city
29:15 **W** to those who seek deep to
30: 1 **W** to the rebellious children,"
31: 1 **W** to those who go down to Egypt
33: 1 **W** to you who plunder, though
45: 9 **W** to him who strives with his
45:10 **W** to him who says to his
Jer 4:13 **W** to us, for we are
4:31 **W** is me now, for my soul is
6: 4 **W** to us, for the day goes
10:19 **W** is me for my hurt!
13:27 **W** to you, O Jerusalem!
15:10 **W** is me, my mother, That you
22:13 **W** to him who builds his house
23: 1 **W** to the shepherds who destroy
45: 3 **W** is me now! For the LORD has
48: 1 **W** to Nebo! For it is plundered,
48:46 **W** to you, O Moab! The people
50:27 **W** to them! For their day has
Lam 3: 5 me with bitterness and **w**.
3:38 That **w** and well-being proceed?
5:16 **W** to us, for we have sinned!
Ezek 2:10 lamentations and mourning and **w**.
13: 3 **W** to the foolish prophets, who
13:18 **W** to the women who sew magic
16:23 '**W**, woe to you!' says the
16:23 **w** to you!' says the Lord GOD—
24: 6 **W** to the bloody city, To the
24: 9 **W** to the bloody city! I too
30: 2 'Wail, '**W** to the day!'
34: 2 **W** to the shepherds of Israel who
Hos 7:13 **W** to them, for they have fled
9:12 **w** to them when I depart from
Am 5:18 **W** to you who desire the day of
6: 1 **W** to you who are at ease in
6: 3 **W** to you who put far off the
Mic 2: 1 **W** to those who devise iniquity,
7: 1 **W** is me! For I am like those
Nah 3: 1 **W** to the bloody city!
Hab 2: 6 **W** to him who increases What is
2: 9 **W** to him who covets evil gain
2:12 **W** to him who builds a town with
2:15 **W** to him who gives drink to his
2:19 **W** to him who says to wood,
Zeph 2: 5 **W** to the inhabitants of the
3: 1 **W** to her who is rebellious and
Zech 11:17 **W** to the worthless shepherd,
Mt 11:21 **W** to you, Chorazin! Woe to you,
11:21 Chorazin! **W** to you, Bethsaida!
18: 7 **W** to the world because of
18: 7 but **w** to that man by whom the
23:13 But **w** to you, scribes and
23:14 **W** to you, scribes and Pharisees,
23:15 **W** to you, scribes and Pharisees,
23:16 **W** to you, blind guides, who say,
23:23 **W** to you, scribes and Pharisees,
23:25 **W** to you, scribes and Pharisees,
23:27 **W** to you, scribes and Pharisees,
23:29 **W** to you, scribes and Pharisees,
24:19 But **w** to those who are pregnant
26:24 but **w** to that man by whom the
Mk 13:17 But **w** to those who are pregnant
14:21 but **w** to that man by whom the
Lk 6:24 But **w** to you who are rich,
6:25 **W** to you who are full, For you
6:25 **W** to you who laugh now,
6:26 **W** to you when all men speak
10:13 **W** to you, Chorazin! Woe to you,
10:13 Chorazin! **W** to you, Bethsaida!
11:42 'But **w** to you Pharisees!
11:43 **W** to you Pharisees! For you love
11:44 **W** to you, scribes and Pharisees,
11:46 '**W** to you also, lawyers!
11:47 **W** to you! For you build the
11:52 **W** to you lawyers! For you have
17: 1 but **w** to him through whom
21:23 But **w** to those who are pregnant
22:22 but **w** to that man by whom He is
1 Cor 9:16 **w** is me if I do not preach the
Jude 11 **W** to them! For they have gone in
Rev 8:13 loud voice, "**W**, woe, woe to
8:13 loud voice, "Woe, **w**, woe to
8:13 **w** to the inhabitants of the
9:12 One **w** is past. Behold, still two
11:14 The second **w** is past.
11:14 the third **w** is coming quickly.
12:12 **W** to the inhabitants of the

WOEFUL (1/1)

Jer 17:16 Nor have I desired the **w** day;

WOES (1/1)

Rev 9:12 still two more **w** are coming

WOLF (6/5) WOLVES

Gen 49:27 "Benjamin is a ravenous **w**;
Isa 11: 6 The **w** also shall dwell with the
65:25 The **w** and the lamb shall feed
Jer 5: 6 A **w** of the deserts shall
Jn 10:12 sees the **w** coming and leaves
10:12 and the **w** catches the sheep and

WOLVES (7/7) WOLF

Ezek 22:27 in her midst are like **w**
Hab 1: 8 And more fierce than evening **w**.
Zeph 3: 3 Her judges are evening **w**
Mt 7:15 inwardly they are ravenous **w**.
10:16 out as sheep in the midst of **w**.
Lk 10: 3 I send you out as lambs among **w**.
Acts 20:29 after my departure savage **w**

WOMAN (395/367) WOMEN

Gen 2:22 taken from man He made into a **w**,
2:23 She shall be called **W**,
3: 1 had made. And he said to the **w**,
3: 2 And the **w** said to the serpent,
3: 4 Then the serpent said to the **w**,
3: 6 So when the **w** saw that the tree
3:12 The **w** whom You gave to be with
3:13 And the LORD God said to the **w**,
3:13 The **w** said, "The serpent
3:15 enmity Between you and the **w**,
3:16 To the **w** He said: "I will
12:11 I know that you are a **w** of
12:14 that the Egyptians saw the **w**,
12:15 And the **w** was taken to
20: 3 a dead man because of the **w**
24: 5 Perhaps the **w** will not be
24: 8 And if the **w** is not willing to
24:14 let it be that the young **w**
24:16 Now the young **w** was very
24:28 So the young **w** ran and told her
24:39 Perhaps the **w** will not follow
24:44 let her be the **w** whom the
24:55 Let the young **w** stay with us a
24:57 We will call the young **w** and ask
34: 3 and he loved the young **w** and
34: 3 and spoke kindly to the young **w**.
34: 4 Get me this young **w** as a wife."
34:12 but give me the young **w** as a
46:10 Shaul, the son of a Canaanite **w**.
Ex 2: 2 So the **w** conceived and bore a
2: 9 So the **w** took the child and
3:22 But every **w** shall ask of her
6:15 Shaul the son of a Canaanite **w**.
11: 2 from his neighbor and every **w**
21:22 and hurt a **w** with child, so
21:28 If an ox gores a man or a **w** to
21:29 that it has killed a man or a **w**,
36: 6 Let neither man nor **w** do any
Lev 12: 2 If a **w** has conceived, and borne
13:29 If a man or **w** has a sore on the
13:38 If a man or a **w** has bright
15:18 when a **w** lies with a man, and
15:19 If a **w** has a discharge, and
15:25 If a **w** has a discharge of blood
15:33 a discharge, either man or **w**,
18:17 uncover the nakedness of a **w**
18:18 Nor shall you take a **w** as a
18:19 you shall not approach a **w** to
18:22 not lie with a male as with a **w**.
18:23 Nor shall any **w** stand before an
19:20 'Whoever lies carnally with a **w**
20:13 with a male as he lies with a **w**,
20:14 If a man marries a **w** and her
20:16 If a **w** approaches any animal and
20:16 you shall kill the **w** and the
20:18 If a man lies with a **w** during
20:27 A man or a **w** who is a medium,
21: 7 is a harlot or a defiled **w**,
21: 7 nor shall they take a **w**
21:14 A widow or a divorced **w** or a
21:14 a divorced woman or a defiled **w**
24:10 Now the son of an Israelite **w**,
Num 5: 6 When a man or **w** commits any sin
5:18 the priest shall stand the **w**
5:19 under oath, and say to the **w**,
5:21 the priest shall put the **w**
5:21 and he shall say to the **w**—
5:22 Then the **w** shall say, "Amen,
5:24 And he shall make the **w** drink
5:26 and afterward make the **w** drink
5:27 and the **w** will become a curse
5:28 But if the **w** has not defiled
5:30 then he shall stand the **w**
5:31 but that **w** shall bear her
6: 2 When either a man or **w**
12: 1 because of the Ethiopian **w**
12: 1 he had married an Ethiopian **w**.
25: 6 to his brethren a Midianite **w**
25: 8 and the **w** through her body.
25:14 was killed with the Midianite **w**,
25:15 And the name of the Midianite **w**
30: 3 Or if a **w** makes a vow to the
30: 9 vow of a widow or a divorced **w**,
31:17 and kill every **w** who has known
Deut 15:12 a Hebrew man, or a Hebrew **w**,
17: 2 a man or a **w** who has been
17: 5 out to your gates that man or **w**
17: 5 stone to death that man or **w**
20: 7 there who is betrothed to a **w**
21:11 the captives a beautiful **w**,
22: 5 A **w** shall not wear anything
22:14 her, and says, 'I took this **w**,
22:15 and mother of the young **w**
22:19 to the father of the young **w**,
22:20 are not found for the young **w**,
22:21 shall bring out the young **w** to
22:22 a man is found lying with a **w**
22:22 die—the man that lay with the **w**,
22:22 lay with the woman, and the **w**;
22:23 If a young **w** who is a virgin
22:24 the young **w** because she did not
22:25 a man finds a betrothed young **w**
22:26 shall do nothing to the young **w**;
22:26 there is in the young **w** no
22:27 and the betrothed young **w**
22:28 If a man finds a young **w** who
28:56 The tender and delicate **w** among
29:18 may not be among you man or **w**
Josh 2: 4 Then the **w** took the two men and
6:21 in the city, both man and **w**,
6:22 and from there bring out the **w**
Judg 4: 9 Sisera into the hand of a **w**.
9:53 But a certain **w** dropped an upper
9:54 A **w** killed him.'" So his young
11: 2 you are the son of another **w**.
13: 3 of the LORD appeared to the **w**
13: 6 So the **w** came and told her
13: 9 the Angel of God came to the **w**
13:10 Then the **w** ran in haste and told
13:11 You the Man who spoke to this **w**?
13:13 Of all that I said to the **w** let
13:24 So the **w** bore a son and called
14: 1 and saw a **w** in Timnah of the
14: 2 I have seen a **w** in Timnah of the
14: 3 Is there no **w** among the
14: 7 went down and talked with the **w**;
14:10 his father went down to the **w**.
16: 4 it happened that he loved a **w**
19: 3 when the father of the young **w**
19:26 Then the **w** came as the day was
20: 4 the husband of the **w** who was
21:11 and every **w** who has known a man
Ruth 1: 5 so the **w** survived her two sons
2: 5 Whose young **w** is this?"
2: 6 It is the young Moabite **w** who
3: 8 a **w** was lying at his feet.
3:11 know that you are a virtuous **w**.
3:14 not let it be known that the **w**
4:11 The LORD make the **w** who is
4:12 will give you from this young **w**.
1 Sam 1:15 I am a **w** of sorrowful spirit.
1:16 your maidservant a wicked **w**,
1:18 So the **w** went her way and
1:23 So the **w** stayed and nursed
1:26 I am the **w** who stood by you
2:20 you descendants from this **w**
15: 3 But kill both man and **w**,
20:30 a perverse, rebellious **w**!
25: 3 And she was a **w** of good
27: 9 he left neither man nor **w**
27:11 would save neither man nor **w**
28: 7 Find me a **w** who is a medium,
28: 7 there is a **w** who is a medium
28: 8 and they came to the **w** by
28: 9 Then the **w** said to him, "Look,
28:11 Then the **w** said, "Whom shall I
28:12 When the **w** saw Samuel, she cried
28:12 And the **w** spoke to Saul,
28:13 And the **w** said to Saul, "I
28:21 And the **w** came to Saul and saw
28:23 servants, together with the **w**,
28:24 Now the **w** had a fatted calf in
2 Sam 3: 8 with a fault concerning this **w**?
11: 2 And from the roof he saw a **w**
11: 2 and the **w** was very beautiful
11: 3 sent and inquired about the **w**.
11: 5 And the **w** conceived; so she sent

11:21 Was it not a **w** who cast a piece
13:17 Put this **w** out, away from
14: 2 and brought from there a wise **w**,
14: 2 but act like a **w** who has been
14: 4 And when the **w** of Tekoa spoke
14: 8 Then the king said to the **w**,
14: 9 And the **w** of Tekoa said to the
14:12 Therefore the **w** said, "Please,
14:13 So the **w** said: "Why then have
14:18 king answered and said to the **w**,
14:18 And the **w** said, "Please, let
14:19 And the **w** answered and said,
14:27 She was a **w** of beautiful
17:19 Then the **w** took and spread a
17:20 servants came to the **w** at the
17:20 So the **w** said to them, "They
20:16 Then a wise **w** cried out from
20:17 the **w** said, "Are you Joab?"
20:21 So the **w** said to Joab,
20:22 Then the **w** in her wisdom went to
1 Ki 1: 2 said to him, "Let a young **w**,
1: 3 sought for a lovely young **w**
1: 4 The young **w** was very lovely;
3:17 And one **w** said, "O my lord,
3:17 this **w** and I dwell in the same
3:18 that this **w** also gave birth.
3:22 Then the other **w** said, "No!
3:22 And the first **w** said, "No!
3:26 Then the **w** whose son was living
3:27 Give the first **w** the living
14: 5 will pretend to be another **w**.
17:17 things that the son of the **w**
17:24 Then the **w** said to Elijah, "Now
2 Ki 4: 1 A certain **w** of the wives of the
4: 8 where there was a notable **w**,
4:12 "Call this Shunammite **w**.
4:17 But the **w** conceived, and bore a
4:25 "Look, the Shunammite **w**!.
4:36 said, "Call this Shunammite **w**.
6:26 a **w** cried out to him, saying,
6:28 This **w** said to me, 'Give your
6:30 king heard the words of the **w**,
8: 1 Then Elisha spoke to the **w** whose
8: 2 So the **w** arose and did according
8: 3 that the **w** returned from the
8: 5 that there was the **w** whose son
8: 5 lord, O king, this is the **w**,
8: 6 And when the king asked the **w**,
9:34 now, see to this accursed **w**,
1 Chr 16: 3 of Israel, both man and **w**,
2 Chr 2:14 (the son of a **w** of the daughters
15:13 or great, whether man or **w**.
24: 7 sons of Athaliah, that wicked **w**,
Esth 2: 4 Then let the young **w** who pleases
2: 7 The young **w** was lovely and
2: 9 Now the young **w** pleased him, and
2:13 each young **w** went to the king,
4:11 know that any man or **w** who
Job 14: 1 Man who is born of **w** Is of
15:14 And he who is born of a **w**,
25: 4 he be pure who is born of a **w**?
31: 1 should I look upon a young **w**?
31: 9 heart has been enticed by a **w**,
Ps 48: 6 as of a **w** in birth pangs,
58: 8 Like a stillborn child of a **w**,
113: 9 He grants the barren **w** a home,
Prov 2:16 deliver you from the immoral **w**,
5: 3 For the lips of an immoral **w**
5:20 be enraptured by an immoral **w**,
6:24 To keep you from the evil **w**,
6:32 commits adultery with a **w**
7: 5 may keep you from the immoral **w**,
7:10 And there a **w** met him,
9:13 A foolish **w** is clamorous;
11:16 A gracious **w** retains honor,
11:22 So is a lovely **w** who lacks
14: 1 The wise **w** builds her house,
21: 9 shared with a contentious **w**.
21:19 with a contentious and angry **w**.
22:14 The mouth of an immoral **w** is a
25:24 shared with a contentious **w**.
27:15 rainy day And a contentious **w**
30:20 is the way of an adulterous **w**:
30:23 A hateful **w** when she is
31:30 But a **w** who fears the LORD,
Eccl 7:26 more bitter than death The **w**
7:28 But a **w** among all these I have
Isa 13: 8 They will be in pain as a **w** in
21: 3 like the pangs of a **w** in labor.
26:17 As a **w** with child Is in pain
42:14 Now I will cry like a **w** in
45:10 you begetting?' Or to the **w**,
49:15 Can a **w** forget her nursing
54: 1 the children of the married **w**,
54: 6 LORD has called you Like a **w**
Jer 4:31 I have heard a voice as of a **w**
6: 2 To a lovely and delicate **w**.
6:24 Pain as of a **w** in labor.
13:21 Like a **w** in labor?
22:23 Like the pain of a **w** in
30: 6 hands on his loins Like a **w**
31: 8 The **w** with child And the one
31:22 A **w** shall encompass a man."
34: 9 female slave—a Hebrew man or **w**—
44: 7 to cut off from you man and **w**,
48:41 Like the heart of a **w** in
49:22 Like the heart of a **w** in
49:24 have taken her like a **w** in
50:43 Pangs as of a **w** in childbirth.
51:22 will break in pieces man and **w**;
Ezek 18: 6 Nor approached a **w** during her
23:44 as men go in to a **w** who plays
36:17 like the uncleanness of a **w** in
44:22 as wife a widow or a divorced **w**,
Hos 3: 1 love a **w** who is loved by a
13:13 The sorrows of a **w** in
Mic 4: 9 pangs have seized you like a **w**
4:10 Like a **w** in birth pangs.
Zech 5: 7 and this is a **w** sitting inside
Mt 5:28 you that whoever looks at a **w**
5:32 and whoever marries a **w** who is
9:20 a **w** who had a flow of blood for
9:22 And the **w** was made well from
13:33 which a **w** took and hid in three
15:22 a **w** of Canaan came from that
15:28 'O **w**, great is your faith!
22:27 Last of all the **w** died also.
26: 7 a **w** came to Him having an
26:10 "Why do you trouble the **w**?
26:13 what this **w** has done will also
Mk 5:25 Now a certain **w** had a flow of
5:33 But the **w**, fearing and
7:25 For a **w** whose young daughter had
7:26 The **w** was a Greek,
10:12 And if a **w** divorces her husband
12:22 Last of all the **w** died also.
14: 3 a **w** came having an alabaster
14: 9 what this **w** has done will also
Lk 2:37 and this **w** was a widow of about
4:26 to a **w** who was a widow.
7:37 a **w** in the city who was a
7:39 know who and what manner of **w**
7:44 Then He turned to the **w** and said
7:44 to Simon, "Do you see this **w**?
7:45 but this **w** has not ceased to
7:46 but this **w** has anointed My feet
7:50 Then He said to the **w**,
8:43 Now a **w**, having a flow of
8:47 Now when the **w** saw that she was
10:38 and a certain **w** named Martha
11:27 that a certain **w** from the crowd
13:11 there was a **w** who had a spirit
13:12 to Him and said to her, "**W**,
13:16 "So ought not this **w**,
13:21 which a **w** took and hid in three
15: 8 Or what **w**, having ten silver
20:32 Last of all the **w** died also.
22:57 But he denied Him, saying, "**W**,
Jn 2: 4 Jesus said to her, "**W**,
4: 7 A **w** of Samaria came to draw
4: 9 Then the **w** of Samaria said to
4: 9 a drink from me, a Samaritan **w**?
4:11 The **w** said to Him, "Sir, You
4:15 The **w** said to Him, "Sir, give
4:17 The **w** answered and said, "I
4:19 The **w** said to Him, "Sir, I
4:21 Jesus said to her, "**W**,
4:25 The **w** said to Him, "I know that
4:27 that He talked with a **w**;
4:28 The **w** then left her waterpot,
4:39 because of the word of the **w**
4:42 Then they said to the **w**,
8: 3 Pharisees brought to Him a **w**
8: 4 this **w** was caught in adultery,
8: 9 and the **w** standing in the
8:10 up and saw no one but the **w**,
8:10 the woman, He said to her, "**W**,
16:21 'A **w**, when she is in labor,
19:26 by, He said to His mother, "**W**,
20:13 Then they said to her, "**W**,
20:15 Jesus said to her, "**W**,
Acts 9:36 This **w** was full of good works
16: 1 the son of a certain Jewish **w**
16:14 Now a certain **w** named Lydia
17:34 a **w** named Damaris, and others
Rom 1:27 the natural use of the **w**,
7: 2 For the **w** who has a husband is
1 Cor 7: 1 good for a man not to touch a **w**.
7: 2 and let each **w** have her own
7:13 And a **w** who has a husband who
7:34 The unmarried **w** cares about the
11: 3 the head of **w** is man, and the
11: 5 But every **w** who prays or
11: 6 For if a **w** is not covered, let
11: 6 But if it is shameful for a **w**
11: 7 but **w** is the glory of man.
11: 8 For man is not from **w**,
11: 8 from woman, but **w** from man.
11: 9 Nor was man created for the **w**,
11: 9 the woman, but **w** for the man.
11:10 For this reason the **w** ought to
11:11 is man independent of **w**,
11:11 nor **w** independent of man, in
11:12 For as **w** came from man, even so
11:12 so man also comes through **w**;
11:13 Is it proper for a **w** to pray to
11:15 But if a **w** has long hair, it is
Gal 4: 4 sent forth His Son, born of a **w**,
1 Th 5: 3 labor pains upon a pregnant **w**.
1 Tim 2:11 Let a **w** learn in silence with
2:12 And I do not permit a **w** to teach
2:14 but the **w** being deceived, fell
5:16 If any believing man or **w** has
Rev 2:20 because you allow that **w**
12: 1 a **w** clothed with the sun,
12: 4 the dragon stood before the **w**
12: 6 Then the **w** fled into the
12:13 he persecuted the **w** who gave
12:14 But the **w** was given two wings of
12:15 mouth like a flood after the **w**,
12:16 But the earth helped the **w**,
12:17 dragon was enraged with the **w**,
17: 3 And I saw a **w** sitting on a
17: 4 The **w** was arrayed in purple and
17: 6 I saw the **w**, drunk with the
17: 7 tell you the mystery of the **w**
17: 9 mountains on which the **w** sits.
17:18 And the **w** whom you saw is that

WOMAN'S (17/17)

Gen 38:20 his pledge from the **w** hand,
Ex 21:22 accordingly as the **w** husband
Lev 24:10 and this Israelite **w** son and a
24:11 And the Israelite **w** son
Num 5:18 uncover the **w** head, and put the
5:25 of jealousy from the **w** hand,
Deut 22: 5 a man put on a **w** garment,
22:15 of the young **w** virginity
22:16 And the young **w** father shall say
22:29 give to the young **w** father
Judg 19: 4 the young **w** father, detained
19: 5 but the young **w** father said to
19: 6 Then the young **w** father said to
19: 8 but the young **w** father said,
19: 9 the young **w** father, said to
1 Ki 3:19 And this **w** son died in the
Esth 2:12 Each young **w** turn came to go in

WOMB (75/73)

Gen 25:23 "Two nations are in your **w**,
25:24 there were twins in her **w**.
29:31 was unloved, He opened her **w**;
30: 2 from you the fruit of the **w**?
30:22 to her and opened her **w**.
38:27 behold, twins were in her **w**.
49:25 of the breasts and of the **w**.
Ex 13: 2 whatever opens the **w** among the
13:12 the LORD all that open the **w**,
13:15 LORD all males that open the **w**,
34:19 All that open the **w** are Mine,
Num 3:12 every firstborn who opens the **w**
8:16 instead of all who open the **w**,
12:12 he comes out of his mother's **w**!
18:15 that first opens the **w** of all
Deut 7:13 also bless the fruit of your **w**
Judg 13: 5 be a Nazirite to God from the **w**;
13: 7 be a Nazirite to God from the **w**
16:17 to God from my mother's **w**.
Ruth 1:11 Are there still sons in my **w**,
1 Sam 1: 5 the LORD had closed her **w**.
1: 6 the LORD had closed her **w**.
Job 1:21 I came from my mother's **w**,
3:10 up the doors of my mother's **w**,
3:11 perish when I came from the **w**?
10:18 You brought me out of the **w**?
10:19 have been carried from the **w**
15:35 Their **w** prepares deceit."
24:20 The **w** should forget him,
31:15 not He who made me in the **w**
31:15 same One fashion us in the **w**?
31:18 And from my mother's **w** I
38: 8 forth and issued from the **w**;
38:29 From whose **w** comes the ice?
Ps 22: 9 He who took Me out of the **w**;
22:10 From My mother's **w** You have
58: 3 wicked are estranged from the **w**;
71: 6 took me out of my mother's **w**.
110: 3 from the **w** of the morning,
127: 3 The fruit of the **w** is a
139:13 covered me in my mother's **w**.
Prov 30:16 The grave, The barren **w**,
31: 2 And what, son of my **w**?
Eccl 5:15 As he came from his mother's **w**,
11: 5 how the bones grow in the **w**
Isa 13:18 no pity on the fruit of the **w**;
44: 2 And formed you from the **w**,
44:24 He who formed you from the **w**:
46: 3 have been carried from the **w**:
48: 8 a transgressor from the **w**.
49: 1 LORD has called Me from the **w**;
49: 5 Who formed Me from the **w** to
49:15 compassion on the son of her **w**?
66: 9 cause delivery shut up the **w**?
Jer 1: 5 Before I formed you in the **w** I
20:17 he did not kill me from the **w**,
20:17 And her **w** always enlarged
20:18 did I come forth from the **w** to
Hos 9:14 Give them a miscarrying **w** And
9:16 kill the darlings of their **w**.
12: 3 brother by the heel in the **w**,
Mt 19:12 thus from their mother's **w**,
Lk 1:15 even from his mother's **w**.
1:31 you will conceive in your **w** and
1:41 that the babe leaped in her **w**;
1:42 is the fruit of your **w**!
1:44 the babe leaped in my **w** for
2:21 He was conceived in the **w**.
2:23 male who opens the **w**
11:27 Blessed is the **w** that bore You,
Jn 3: 4 time into his mother's **w** and
Acts 3: 2 man lame from his mother's **w**
14: 8 a cripple from his mother's **w**,
Rom 4:19 and the deadness of Sarah's **w**.
Gal 1:15 me from my mother's **w** and

WOMBS (2/2)

Gen 20:18 LORD had closed up all the **w**
Lk 23:29 **w** that never bore, and breasts

WOMEN (190/180) WOMAN

Gen 14:16 as well as the **w** and the
24:11 the time when **w** go out to draw

31:35 for the manner of w is with
33: 5 lifted his eyes and saw the w
Ex 1:16 of a midwife for the Hebrew w,
1:19 Because the Hebrew w are not
1:19 are not like the Egyptian w;
2: 7 nurse for you from the Hebrew w,
15:20 and all the w went out after
35:22 They came, both men and w,
35:25 All the w who were gifted
35:26 And all the w whose heart
35:29 all the men and w whose hearts
38: 8 mirrors of the serving w who
Lev 26:26 ten w shall bake your bread in
Num 25: 1 to commit harlotry with the w
31: 9 children of Israel took the w
31:15 Have you kept all the w alive?
31:16 these w caused the children of
31:35 of w who had not known a man
Deut 2:34 we utterly destroyed the men, w,
3: 6 utterly destroying the men, w,
20:14 'But the w, the little ones,
31:12 men and w and little ones, and
Josh 8:25 fell that day, both men and w,
8:35 assembly of Israel, with the w,
Judg 5:24 Most blessed among w is Jael,
5:24 Blessed is she among w in
9:49 about a thousand men and w.
9:51 the city, and all the men and w—
16:27 temple was full of men and w.
16:27 three thousand men and w
21:10 including the w and children.
21:14 and they gave them the w whom
21:14 they had saved alive of the w
21:16 since the w of Benjamin have
21:22 though you have given the w
Ruth 1: 4 Now they took wives of the w of
1:19 and the w said, "Is this
2: 8 but stay close by my young w.
2:22 you go out with his young w,
2:23 stayed close by the young w of
3: 2 whose young w you were with,
4:14 Then the w said to Naomi,
4:17 Also the neighbor w gave him a
1 Sam 2:22 and how they lay with the w who
4:20 the time of her death the w
9:11 they met some young w going out
15:33 As your sword has made w
15:33 mother be childless among w.
18: 6 that the w had come out of all
18: 7 So the w sang as they danced,
21: 4 at least kept themselves from w.
21: 5 w have been kept from us
22:19 of the sword, both men and w,
30: 2 and had taken captive the w and
2 Sam 1:26 Surpassing the love of w.
6:19 both the w and the men, to
15:16 But the king left ten w,
19:35 of singing men and singing w?
20: 3 And the king took the ten w,
1 Ki 3:16 Now two w who were harlots
11: 1 Solomon loved many foreign w,
11: 1 w of the Moabites, Ammonites,
2 Ki 8:12 and rip open their w with
15:16 All the w there who were with
23: 7 where the w wove hangings for
2 Chr 28: 8 brethren two hundred thousand w,
35:25 singing men and the singing w
Ezra 2:65 they had two hundred men and w
10: 1 a very large assembly of men, w,
Neh 7:67 and forty-five men and w
8: 2 the assembly of men and w and
8: 3 before the men and w and those
12:43 the w and the children also
13:23 saw Jews who had married w of
13:26 Nevertheless pagan w caused
13:27 our God by marrying pagan w?
Esth 1: 9 also made a feast for the w
1:17 will become known to all w,
2: 3 eunuch, custodian of the w.
2: 8 and when many young w were
2: 8 of Hegai the custodian of the w.
2: 9 place in the house of the w.
2:12 to the regulations for the w,
2:12 preparations for beautifying w.
2:14 to the second house of the w,
2:15 eunuch, the custodian of the w,
2:17 more than all the other w,
3:13 and old, little children and w,
8:11 both little children and w,
Job 2:10 speak as one of the foolish w
42:15 In all the land were found no w
Ps 45: 9 are among Your honorable w;
Prov 31: 3 Do not give your strength to w,
Song 1: 8 do not know, O fairest among w,
5: 9 beloved, O fairest among w?
6: 1 gone, O fairest among w?
Isa 3:12 And w rule over them. O My
4: 1 And in that day seven w shall
19:16 that day Egypt will be like w,
27:11 The w come and set them on
32: 9 you w who are at ease, Hear my
32:10 be troubled, you complacent w;
32:11 you w who are at ease;
Jer 2:33 have also taught The wicked w
7:18 and the w knead dough, to make
9:17 and call for the mourning w,
9:17 send for skillful wailing w,
9:20 hear the word of the LORD, O w,
38:22 all the w who are left in the
38:22 and those w shall say:
40: 7 and had committed to him men, w,
41:16 mighty men of war and the w
43: 6 men, w, children, the king's
44:15 with all the w who stood by,
44:19 The w also said, "And when
44:20 all the people—the men, the w,
44:24 all the people and to all the w,
50:37 And they will become like w.
51:30 They became like w;
Lam 2:20 Should the w eat their
4:10 hands of the compassionate w
5:11 They ravished the w in Zion,
Ezek 8:14 w were sitting there weeping
9: 6 and little children and w;
13:18 Woe to the w who sew magic
16:34 are the opposite of other w
16:38 And I will judge you as w who
16:41 on you in the sight of many w;
22:10 in you they violate w who are
23: 2 of man, there were two w,
23:10 She became a byword among w,
23:44 Oholah and Oholibah, the lewd w.
23:45 and after the manner of w who
23:48 that all w may be taught not to
Dan 11:17 give him the daughter of w to
11:37 his fathers nor the desire of w,
Hos 13:16 And their w with child ripped
Am 1:13 they ripped open the w with
Mic 2: 9 The w of My people you cast out
Nah 3:13 people in your midst are w!
Zech 5: 9 looked, and there were two w,
8: 4 Old men and old w shall again
9:17 And new wine the young w.
14: 2 rifled, And the w ravished.
Mt 11:11 among those born of w there has
14:21 besides w and children.
15:38 besides w and children.
24:41 Two w will be grinding at the
27:55 And many w who followed Jesus
28: 5 answered and said to the w,
Mk 15:40 There were also w looking on
15:41 and many other w who came up
Lk 1:28 blessed are you among w!"
1:42 "Blessed are you among w,
7:28 among those born of w there is
8: 2 and certain w who had been
17:35 Two w will be grinding
23:27 and w who also mourned and
23:49 and the w who followed Him from
23:55 And the w who had come with Him
24: 1 and certain other w with
24:10 and the other w with them, who
24:22 and certain w of our company,
24:24 and found it just as the w
Jn 11:19 of the Jews had joined the w
Acts 1:14 with the w and Mary the mother
5:14 multitudes of both men and w,
8: 3 and dragging off men and w,
8:12 both men and w were baptized.
9: 2 of the Way, whether men or w,
13:50 up the devout and prominent w
16:13 we sat down and spoke to the w
17: 4 and not a few of the leading w,
17:12 prominent w as well as men.
22: 4 into prisons both men and w,
Rom 1:26 For even their w exchanged the
1 Cor 14:34 Let your w keep silent in the
14:35 for it is shameful for w to
Phil 4: 3 help these w who labored with
1 Tim 2: 9 that the w adorn themselves in
2:10 which is proper for w
5: 2 older w as mothers, younger as
2 Tim 3: 6 and make captives of gullible w
Titus 2: 3 the older w likewise, that they
2: 4 that they admonish the young w
Heb 11:35 W received their dead raised to
1 Pe 3: 5 the holy w who trusted in God
Rev 14: 4 who were not defiled with w,

WOMEN'S (4/4)

Esth 2: 3 into the w quarters, under the
2:11 the court of the w quarters,
2:13 with her from the w quarters
Rev 9: 8 They had hair like w hair, and

WOMENSERVANTS (KJV) See (FEMALE) SERVANTS

WON (7/7)

2 Sam 23:18 and w a name among these
23:22 and w a name among three mighty
1 Chr 11:20 and w a name among these
11:24 and w a name among three mighty
26:27 Some of the spoils w in battles
Mt 23:15 one proselyte, and when he is w,
1 Pe 3: 1 may be w by the conduct of

WONDER (11/11) WONDERFUL, WONDERS, WONDROUS

Deut 13: 1 and he gives you a sign or a w,
13: 2 and the sign or the w comes to
28:46 be upon you for a sign and a w,
2 Chr 32:31 to him to inquire about the w
Ps 71: 7 I have become as a w to many,
Isa 20: 3 three years for a sign and a w
29: 9 Pause and w! Blind yourselves
29:14 A marvelous work and a w;
Jer 4: 9 And the prophets shall w.
Acts 3:10 and they were filled with w and
2 Cor 11:14 And no w! For Satan himself

WONDERED (4/4)

Isa 59:16 And w that there was no
63: 5 And I w That there was no
Acts 5:24 they w what the outcome would
10:17 Now while Peter w within

WONDERFUL (20/20) WONDER, WONDERFULLY

Judg 13:18 ask My name, seeing it is w?
2 Sam 1:26 to me; Your love to me was w,
2 Chr 2: 9 to build shall be great and w.
Job 42: 3 Things too w for me, which I
Ps 40: 5 are Your w works Which You
78: 4 His strength and His w works
107: 8 And for His w works to the
107:15 And for His w works to the
107:21 And for His w works to the
107:31 And for His w works to the
111: 4 He has made His w works to be
119:129 Your testimonies are w;
139: 6 Such knowledge is too w for
Prov 30:18 three things which are too w
Isa 9: 6 And His name will be called W,
25: 1 For You have done w things;
28:29 Who is w in counsel and
Jer 21: 2 according to all His w works,
Mt 21:15 and scribes saw the w things
Acts 2:11 in our own tongues the w works

WONDERFULLY (1/1) WONDERFUL

Ps 139:14 for I am fearfully and w made;

WONDERING (1/1)

Gen 24:21 w at her, remained silent so as

WONDERS (58/58) WONDER

Ex 3:20 and strike Egypt with all My w
4:21 see that you do all those w
7: 3 and multiply My signs and My w
11: 9 so that My w may be multiplied
11:10 Moses and Aaron did all these w
15:11 Fearful in praises, doing w?
Deut 4:34 by trials, by signs, by w,
6:22 the LORD showed signs and w
7:19 eyes saw, the signs and the w,
26: 8 terror and with signs and w.
29: 3 the signs, and those great w.
34:11 in all the signs and w which the
Josh 3: 5 tomorrow the LORD will do w
1 Chr 16:12 works which He has done, His w,
16:24 His w among all peoples.
Neh 9:10 You showed signs and w against
9:17 they were not mindful of Your w
Job 9:10 w without number.
Ps 77:11 Surely I will remember Your w
77:14 You are the God who does w;
78:11 forgot His works And His w
78:43 And His w in the field of
88:10 Will You work w for the dead?
88:12 Shall Your w be known in the
89: 5 the heavens will praise Your w,
96: 3 His w among all peoples.
105: 5 works which He has done, His w,
105:27 And w in the land of Ham.
106: 7 Egypt did not understand Your w;
107:24 And His w in the deep.
135: 9 He sent signs and w into the
136: 4 To Him who alone does great w,
Isa 8:18 We are for signs and w in
Jer 32:20 You have set signs and w in the
32:21 land of Egypt with signs and w,
Dan 4: 2 good to declare the signs and w
4: 3 And how mighty His w!
6:27 And He works signs and w In
12: 6 the fulfillment of these w be?
Joel 2:30 And I will show w in the heavens
Mic 7:15 of Egypt, I will show them w.
Mt 7:22 and done many w in Your name?'
24:24 and show great signs and w to
Mk 13:22 will rise and show signs and w
Jn 4:48 you people see signs and w,
Acts 2:19 I will show w in heaven
2:22 by God to you by miracles, w,
2:43 and many w and signs were done
4:30 and that signs and w may be
5:12 the apostles many signs and w
6: 8 did great w and signs among the
7:36 after he had shown w and signs
14: 3 granting signs and w to be done
15:12 how many miracles and w God
Rom 15:19 in mighty signs and w,
2 Cor 12:12 in signs and w and mighty
2 Th 2: 9 all power, signs, and lying w,
Heb 2: 4 witness both with signs and w,

WONDROUS (16/16) WONDER

Judg 13:19 And He did a w thing while
1 Chr 16: 9 Talk of all His w works!
Job 37:14 still and consider the w works
37:16 Those w works of Him who is
Ps 26: 7 And tell of all Your w works.
71:17 day I declare Your w works.
72:18 Who only does w things!
75: 1 For Your w works declare
78:32 not believe in His w works.
86:10 and do w things; You alone

105: 2 Talk of all His *w* works!
106:22 *W* works in the land of Ham,
119:18 that I may see *W* things from
119:27 I meditate on Your *w* works.
145: 5 And on Your *w* works.
Zech 3: 8 For they are a *w* sign;

WONDROUSLY (1/1)

Joel 2:26 Who has dealt *w* with you;

WONT (KJV) See ACCUSTOMED, CUSTOMARILY, DISPOSED, TENDED, USUALLY

WOOD (128/119) WOODCUTTERS, WOODEN, WOODS

Gen 22: 3 and he split the *w* for the
22: 6 So Abraham took the *w* of the
22: 7 "Look, the fire and the *w*,
22: 9 an altar there and placed the *w*
22: 9 him on the altar, upon the *w*.
Ex 7:19 both in buckets of *w* and
25: 5 red, badger skins, and acacia *w*;
25:10 shall make an ark of acacia *w*;
25:13 shall make poles of acacia *w*,
25:23 also make a table of acacia *w*;
25:28 make the poles of acacia *w*,
26:15 make the boards of acacia *w*,
26:26 you shall make bars of acacia *w*:
26:32 the four pillars of acacia *w*
26:37 five pillars of acacia *w*,
27: 1 shall make an altar of acacia *w*,
27: 6 the altar, poles of acacia *w*,
30: 1 you shall make it of acacia *w*.
30: 5 make the poles of acacia *w*,
31: 5 for setting, in carving *w*,
35: 7 red, badger skins, and acacia *w*;
35:24 with whom was found acacia *w*
35:33 for setting, in carving *w*,
36:20 he made boards of acacia *w*,
36:31 And he made bars of acacia *w*:
36:36 it four pillars of acacia *w*,
37: 1 made the ark of acacia *w*;
37: 4 He made poles of acacia *w*,
37:10 He made the table of acacia *w*;
37:15 he made the poles of acacia *w*
37:25 the incense altar of acacia *w*.
37:28 he made the poles of acacia *w*,
38: 1 of burnt offering of acacia *w*;
38: 6 he made the poles of acacia *w*,
Lev 1: 7 and lay the *w* in order on the
1: 8 and the fat in order on the *w*
1:12 lay them in order on the *w*
1:17 on the *w* that is on the fire.
3: 5 which is on the *w* that is on
4:12 and burn it on *w* with fire;
6:12 And the priest shall burn *w* on
11:32 whether it is any item of *w*
14: 4 and clean birds, cedar *w*,
14: 6 the cedar *w* and the scarlet and
14:49 the house, two birds, cedar *w*,
14:51 "and he shall take the cedar *w*,
14:52 living bird, with the cedar *w*,
15:12 and every vessel of *w* shall be
Num 19: 6 the priest shall take cedar *w*
31:20 hair, and everything made of *w*.
Deut 4:28 *w* and stone, which neither see
10: 1 and make yourself an ark of *w*.
10: 3 "So I made an ark of acacia *w*,
28:36 other gods—*w* and stone.
28:64 have known—*w* and stone.
29:11 from the one who cuts your *w* to
29:17 *w* and stone and silver and
Judg 6:26 a burnt sacrifice with the *w*
1 Sam 6:14 So they split the *w* of the cart
2 Sam 6: 5 kinds of instruments of fir *w*,
24:22 and the yokes of the oxen for *w*.
1 Ki 6:15 he paneled the inside with *w*;
6:23 made two cherubim of olive *w*,
6:31 he made doors of olive *w*;
6:32 The two doors were of olive *w*;
6:33 also made doorposts of olive *w*,
6:34 two doors were of cypress *w*;
7:11 hewn to size, and cedar *w*.
10:11 great quantities of almug *w*
10:12 king made steps of the almug *w*
10:12 never again came such almug *w*,
18:23 in pieces, and lay it on the *w*,
18:23 bull, and lay it on the *w*,
18:33 And he put the *w* in order, cut
18:33 pieces, and laid it on the *w*,
18:33 burnt sacrifice and on the *w*.
18:38 and the *w* and the stones and
2 Ki 19:18 of men's hands—*w* and stone.
1 Chr 21:23 the threshing implements for *w*,
22: 4 from Tyre brought much cedar *w*
29: 2 *w* for things of wood, onyx
29: 2 iron, wood for things of *w*,
2 Chr 2:14 bronze and iron, stone and *w*,
2:16 And we will cut *w* from Lebanon,
9:10 brought algum *w* and precious
9:11 made walkways of the algum *w*
Neh 8: 4 stood on a platform of *w* which
10:34 for bringing the *w* offering
13:31 and to bringing the *w* offering
Job 41:27 And bronze as rotten *w*.
Prov 26:20 Where there is no *w*,
26:21 and *w* to fire, So is a
Eccl 10: 9 And he who splits *w* may be
Song 3: 9 Of the *w* of Lebanon Solomon
Isa 10:15 as if it were not *w*!
30:33 Its pyre is fire with much *w*;
37:19 of men's hands—*w* and stone.
44:19 I fall down before a block of *w*?
45:20 Who carry the *w* of their
60:17 bring silver, Instead of *w*,
Jer 5:14 mouth fire, And this people *w*,
7:18 "The children gather *w*,
28:13 have broken the yokes of *w*,
46:22 axes, Like those who chop *w*.
Lam 4: 8 It has become as dry as *w*.
5: 4 And our *w* comes at a price.
5:13 staggered under loads of *w*.
Ezek 15: 2 how is the *w* of the vine
15: 2 vine better than any other *w*,
15: 3 Is *w* taken from it to make any
15: 6 Like the *w* of the vine among the
20:32 serving *w* and stone.'
21:10 of My Son, As it does all *w*.
24:10 Heap on the *w*, Kindle the
39:10 They will not take *w* from the
41:16 threshold were paneled with *w*
41:22 The altar was of *w*,
41:22 and its sides were of *w*;
Dan 5: 4 bronze and iron, *w* and stone.
5:23 *w* and stone, which do not see
Hab 2:19 Woe to him who says to *w*,
Hag 1: 8 up to the mountains and bring *w*
Lk 23:31 do these things in the green *w*,
1 Cor 3:12 silver, precious stones, *w*,
2 Tim 2:20 but also of *w* and clay,
Rev 9:20 silver, brass, stone, and *w*,
18:12 scarlet, every kind of citron *w*,
18:12 of object of most precious *w*,

WOODCUTTERS (3/3) CUT, WOOD

Josh 9:21 but let them be *w* and water
9:23 *w* and water carriers for the
9:27 And that day Joshua made them *w*

WOODED (1/1)

Josh 17:18 Although it is *w*, you shall

WOODEN (37/37) WOOD

Ex 34:13 and cut down their *w* images
Num 35:18 him with a *w* hand weapon,
Deut 7: 5 and cut down their *w* images,
12: 3 and burn their *w* images with
16:21 as a *w* image, near the altar
Judg 6:25 and cut down the *w* image that
6:28 and the *w* image that was
6:30 he has cut down the *w* image
1 Ki 14:15 they have made their *w* images,
14:23 and *w* images on every high hill
16:33 And Ahab made a *w* image.
2 Ki 13: 6 and the *w* image also remained
17:10 sacred pillars and *w* images
17:16 made a *w* image and worshiped
18: 4 cut down the *w* image and broke
21: 3 and made a *w* image, as Ahab
23: 6 And he brought out the *w* image
23: 7 wove hangings for the *w* image.
23:14 and cut down the *w* images,
23:15 and burned the *w* image.
2 Chr 14: 3 and cut down the *w* images.
17: 6 the high places and *w* images
19: 3 you have removed the *w* images
24:18 and served *w* images and idols;
31: 1 cut down the *w* images,
33: 3 and made *w* images; and he
33:19 places and set up *w* images
34: 3 the *w* images, the carved
34: 4 and the *w* images, the carved
34: 7 altars and the *w* images,
Isa 17: 8 Nor the *w* images nor the
27: 9 *W* images and incense altars
Jer 10: 8 A *w* idol is a worthless
17: 2 altars and their *w* images
Ezek 41:25 A *w* canopy was on the front of
Hos 4:12 counsel from their *w* idols,
Mic 5:14 I will pluck your *w* images from

WOODLAND (1/1)

Mic 7:14 Who dwell solitarily in a *w*,

WOODPILE (1/1)

Zech 12: 6 Judah like a firepan in the *w*,

WOODS (17/17) WOOD

Deut 19: 5 as when a man goes to the *w*
1 Sam 14:26 the people had come into the *w*,
23:16 and went to David in the *w* and
23:18 And David stayed in the *w*,
23:19 with us in strongholds in the *w*,
2 Sam 18: 6 And the battle was in the *w* of
18: 8 and the *w* devoured more people
18:17 him into a large pit in the *w*,
2 Ki 2:24 female bears came out of the *w*
1 Chr 16:33 Then the trees of the *w* shall
Ps 80:13 The boar out of the *w* uproots
83:14 As the fire burns the *w*,
96:12 Then all the trees of the *w*
132: 6 found it in the fields of the *w*.
Song 2: 3 tree among the trees of the *w*,
Isa 7: 2 moved as the trees of the *w*
Ezek 34:25 wilderness and sleep in the *w*.

WOODSMAN (1/1)

Isa 14: 8 No *w* has come up against us.'

WOODSMEN (2/2)

1 Chr 22:15 *w* and stonecutters, and all
2 Chr 2:10 the *w* who cut timber, twenty

WOOF (9/9)

Lev 13:48 it is in the warp or *w* of
13:49 whether in the warp or in the *w*,
13:51 either in the warp or in the *w*,
13:52 the plague, whether warp or *w*,
13:53 either in the warp or in the *w*,
13:56 out of the warp or out of the *w*,
13:57 either in the warp or in the *w*,
13:58 the garment, either warp or *w*,
13:59 linen, either in the warp or *w*,

WOOL (19/19)

Lev 13:48 the warp or woof of linen or *w*,
13:52 in *w* or in linen, or anything
13:59 plague in a garment of *w* or
19:19 a garment of mixed linen and *w*
Deut 22:11 such as *w* and linen mixed
Judg 6:37 I shall put a fleece of *w* on
2 Ki 3: 4 thousand lambs and the *w* of
Ps 147:16 He gives snow like *w*;
Prov 31:13 She seeks *w* and flax,
Isa 1:18 crimson, They shall be as *w*.
51: 8 the worm will eat them like *w*;
Ezek 27:18 wine of Helbon and with white *w*.
34: 3 clothe yourselves with the *w*;
44:17 no *w* shall come upon them while
Dan 7: 9 of His head was like pure *w*.
Hos 2: 5 My *w* and my linen, My oil and
2: 9 And will take back My *w* and My
Heb 9:19 goats, with water, scarlet *w*,
Rev 1:14 and hair were white like *w*,

WOOLEN (1/1)

Lev 13:47 whether it is a *w* garment or

WORD (733/707) WORDS

Gen 15: 1 After these things the *w* of the
15: 4 the *w* of the LORD came to
30:34 it were according to your *w*!"
37:14 and bring back *w* to me."
41:40 be ruled according to your *w*;
44: 2 So he did according to the *w*
44:18 let your servant speak a *w* in
Ex 8:10 it be according to your *w*,
8:13 LORD did according to the *w*
8:31 LORD did according to the *w*
9:20 He who feared the *w* of the LORD
9:21 he who did not regard the *w* of
12:35 had done according to the *w* of
14:12 Is this not the *w* that we told
32:28 of Levi did according to the *w*
Lev 10: 7 they did according to the *w* of
Num 3:16 them according to the *w* of the
3:51 according to the *w* of the
4:45 numbered according to the *w* of
13:26 they brought back *w* to them and
14:20 pardoned, according to your *w*;
15:31 Because he has despised the *w* of
20:24 you rebelled against My *w* at
22: 8 and I will bring back *w* to you,
22:18 I could not go beyond the *w* of
22:20 but only the *w* which I speak to
22:35 but only the *w* that I speak to
22:38 The *w* that God puts in my
23: 5 Then the LORD put a *w* in
23:16 and put a *w* in his mouth,
24:13 I could not go beyond the *w* of
27:21 At his *w* they shall go out,
27:21 and at his *w* they shall come
30: 2 he shall not break his *w*;
36: 5 of Israel according to the *w*
Deut 1:22 and bring back *w* to us of the
1:25 and they brought back *w* to us,
4: 2 You shall not add to the *w* which
5: 5 to declare to you the *w* of the
8: 3 but man lives by every *w* that
9: 5 and that He may fulfill the *w*
18:20 who presumes to speak a *w* in
18:21 How shall we know the *w* which
21: 5 by their *w* every controversy
30:14 But the *w* is very near you, in
32:47 and by this *w* you shall prolong
33: 9 For they have observed Your *w*
34: 5 according to the *w* of the
Josh 1:13 Remember the *w* which Moses the
6:10 nor shall a *w* proceed out of
8:27 according to the *w* of the LORD
8:35 There was not a *w* of all that
14: 6 You know the *w* which the LORD
14: 7 and I brought back *w* to him as
14:10 since the LORD spoke this *w*
19:50 According to the *w* of the LORD
21:45 Not a *w* failed of any good thing
22: 9 obtained according to the *w* of
22:32 and brought back *w* to them.
23:14 not one *w* of them has failed.
Judg 11:35 For I have given my *w* to
11:36 if you have given your *w* to
21:13 the whole congregation sent *w*
1 Sam 1:23 let the LORD establish His *w*.

3: 1 And the **w** of the LORD was rare
3: 7 nor was the **w** of the LORD yet
3:17 What is the **w** that the LORD
3:21 to Samuel in Shiloh by the **w**
4: 1 And the **w** of Samuel came to all
9:27 I may announce to you the **w** of
15:10 Now the **w** of the LORD came to
15:23 you have rejected the **w** of the
15:26 for you have rejected the **w** of
31: 9 and sent **w** throughout the land
2 Sam 3:11 not answer Abner another **w**,
7: 4 night that the **w** of the LORD
7: 7 have I ever spoken a **w** to
7:25 the **w** which You have spoken
12:25 and He sent **w** by the hand of
14:12 maidservant speak another **w**
14:17 The **w** of my lord the king will
15:28 the wilderness until **w** comes
19:14 so that they sent this **w** to
22:31 The **w** of the LORD is proven;
23: 2 And His **w** was on my tongue.
24: 4 Nevertheless the king's **w**
24:11 the **w** of the LORD came to the
24:19 according to the **w** of Gad, went
1 Ki 2: 4 the LORD may fulfill His **w**
2:23 Adonijah has not spoken this **w**
2:27 that he might fulfill the **w** of
2:30 And Benaiah brought back **w** to
2:42 The **w** I have heard is good.'
6:11 Then the **w** of the LORD came to
6:12 then I will perform My **w** with
8:20 the LORD has fulfilled His **w**
8:26 let Your **w** come true, which You
8:56 There has not failed one **w** of
12:15 that He might fulfill His **w**,
12:22 But the **w** of God came to
12:24 Therefore they obeyed the **w** of
12:24 according to the **w** of the
13: 1 from Judah to Bethel by the **w**
13: 2 out against the altar by the **w**
13: 5 man of God had given by the **w**
13: 9 so it was commanded me by the **w**
13:17 For I have been told by the **w** of
13:18 an angel spoke to me by the **w**
13:20 that the **w** of the LORD came to
13:21 you have disobeyed the **w** of
13:26 who was disobedient to the **w**
13:26 according to the **w** of the LORD
13:32 which he cried out by the **w** of
14:18 according to the **w** of the LORD
15:29 according to the **w** of the LORD
16: 1 Then the **w** of the LORD came to
16: 7 And also the **w** of the LORD came
16:12 according to the **w** of the
16:34 according to the **w** of the
17: 1 these years, except at my **w**.
17: 2 Then the **w** of the LORD came to
17: 5 and did according to the **w** of
17: 8 Then the **w** of the LORD came to
17:15 and did according to the **w** of
17:16 according to the **w** of the LORD
17:24 and that the **w** of the LORD in
18: 1 after many days that the **w** of
18:21 the people answered him not a **w**.
18:31 to whom the **w** of the LORD had
18:36 done all these things at Your **w**.
19: 9 the **w** of the LORD came to
20: 9 departed and brought back **w** to
20:33 quickly grasped at this **w**
20:35 said to his neighbor by the **w**
21: 4 and displeased because of the **w**
21:17 Then the **w** of the LORD came to
21:28 And the **w** of the LORD came to
22: 5 Please inquire for the **w** of the
22:13 let your **w** be like the word of
22:13 let your word be like the **w** of
22:19 Therefore hear the **w** of the
22:38 according to the **w** of the LORD
2 Ki 1:16 in Israel to inquire of His **w**?
1:17 died according to the **w** of the
2:22 according to the **w** of Elisha
3:12 The **w** of the LORD is with
4:44 according to the **w** of the
6:18 blindness according to the **w**
7: 1 'Hear the **w** of the LORD.
7:16 according to the **w** of the
9:26 according to the **w** of the
9:36 This is the **w** of the LORD,
10:10 fall to the earth of the **w** of
10:17 according to the **w** of the LORD
14:25 according to the **w** of the LORD
15:12 This was the **w** of the LORD
18:28 Hear the **w** of the great king,
18:36 peace and answered him not a **w**;
19:21 This is the **w** which the LORD
20: 4 that the **w** of the LORD came to
20:16 Hear the **w** of the LORD:
20:19 The **w** of the LORD which you
22: 9 the king, bringing the king **w**,
22:20 So they brought back **w** to
23:16 defiled it according to the **w**
24: 2 according to the **w** of the LORD
1 Chr 10: 9 and sent **w** throughout the land
10:13 because he did not keep the **w**
11: 3 according to the **w** of the LORD
11:10 according to the **w** of the LORD
12:23 according to the **w** of the
15:15 commanded according to the **w**
16:15 The **w** which He commanded,
17: 3 the **w** of God came to Nathan,
17: 6 have I ever spoken a **w** to any
17:23 the **w** which You have spoken

21: 4 Nevertheless the king's **w**
21: 6 for the king's **w** was abominable
21:19 So David went up at the **w** of
22: 8 but the **w** of the LORD came to
2 Chr 6:10 the LORD has fulfilled His **w**
6:17 let Your **w** come true, which You
10:15 the LORD might fulfill His **w**,
11: 2 But the **w** of the LORD came to
12: 7 the **w** of the LORD came to
18: 4 Please inquire for the **w** of the
18:12 Therefore please let your **w** be
18:12 let your word be like the **w**
18:18 Therefore hear the **w** of the
30:12 at the **w** of the LORD.
34:16 the king, bringing the king **w**,
34:21 fathers have not kept the **w** of
34:28 So they brought back **w** to
35: 6 may do according to the **w** of
36:21 to fulfill the **w** of the LORD by
36:22 that the **w** of the LORD by the
Ezra 1: 1 that the **w** of the LORD by the
10: 5 would do according to this **w**.
Neh 1: 8 the **w** that You commanded Your
Esth 1:21 king did according to the **w** of
7: 8 As the **w** left the king's
Job 2:13 and no one spoke a **w** to him,
4: 2 If one attempts a **w** with you,
4:12 Now a **w** was secretly brought to
15:11 And the **w** spoken gently with
Ps 17: 4 By the **w** of Your lips, I have
18:30 The **w** of the LORD is proven;
33: 4 For the **w** of the LORD is
33: 6 By the **w** of the LORD the
56: 4 In God (I will praise His **w**),
56:10 In God (I will praise His **w**),
56:10 LORD (I will praise His **w**),
68:11 The Lord gave the **w**;
89:34 Nor alter the **w** that has gone
103:20 excel in strength, who do His **w**,
103:20 Heeding the voice of His **w**.
105: 8 The **w** which He commanded,
105:19 Until the time that his **w** came
105:19 The **w** of the LORD tested him.
105:28 did not rebel against His **w**.
106:24 They did not believe His **w**,
107:20 He sent His **w** and healed them,
119: 9 taking heed according to Your **w**.
119:11 Your **w** I have hidden in my
119:16 I will not forget Your **w**.
119:17 I may live and keep Your **w**.
119:25 Revive me according to Your **w**.
119:28 me according to Your **w**.
119:38 Establish Your **w** to Your
119:41 salvation according to Your **w**.
119:42 For I trust in Your **w**.
119:43 And take not the **w** of truth
119:49 Remember the **w** to Your
119:50 For Your **w** has given me life.
119:58 to me according to Your **w**.
119:65 O LORD, according to Your **w**.
119:67 astray, But now I keep Your **w**.
119:74 Because I have hoped in Your **w**.
119:76 According to Your **w** to Your
119:81 But I hope in Your **w**.
119:82 fail from searching Your **w**,
119:89 Your **w** is settled in heaven.
119:101 That I may keep Your **w**.
119:105 Your **w** is a lamp to my feet
119:107 O LORD, according to Your **w**.
119:114 my shield; I hope in Your **w**.
119:116 Uphold me according to Your **w**,
119:123 salvation And Your righteous **w**.
119:133 Direct my steps by Your **w**,
119:140 Your **w** is very pure;
119:147 cry for help; I hope in Your **w**.
119:148 That I may meditate on Your **w**.
119:154 Revive me according to Your **w**.
119:158 they do not keep Your **w**.
119:160 The entirety of Your **w** is
119:161 heart stands in awe of Your **w**.
119:162 I rejoice at Your **w** As one who
119:169 according to Your **w**.
119:170 Deliver me according to Your **w**.
119:172 tongue shall speak of Your **w**,
130: 5 And in His **w** I do hope.
138: 2 For You have magnified Your **w**
139: 4 For there is not a **w** on my
147:15 His **w** runs very swiftly.
147:18 He sends out His **w** and melts
147:19 He declares His **w** to Jacob,
148: 8 Stormy wind, fulfilling His **w**;
Prov 12:25 But a good **w** makes it glad.
13:13 He who despises the **w** will be
14:15 The simple believes every **w**,
15: 1 But a harsh **w** stirs up anger.
15:23 And a **w** spoken in due season,
16:20 He who heeds the **w** wisely will
25:11 A **w** fitly spoken is like
30: 5 Every **w** of God is pure;
Eccl 8: 4 Where the **w** of a king is,
Isa 1:10 Hear the **w** of the LORD,
2: 1 The **w** that Isaiah the son of
2: 3 And the **w** of the LORD from
5:24 And despised the **w** of the Holy
8:10 come to nothing; Speak the **w**,
8:20 not speak according to this **w**,
9: 8 The LORD sent a **w** against
16:13 This is the **w** which the LORD
24: 3 the LORD has spoken this **w**.
28:13 But the **w** of the LORD was to
28:14 Therefore hear the **w** of the
29:21 make a man an offender by a **w**,

30:12 "Because you despise this **w**,
30:21 Your ears shall hear a **w** behind
36:21 peace and answered him not a **w**;
37:22 this is the **w** which the LORD
38: 4 And the **w** of the LORD came to
39: 5 Hear the **w** of the LORD of
39: 8 The **w** of the LORD which you
40: 8 But the **w** of our God stands
41:28 asked of them, could answer a **w**.
44:26 Who confirms the **w** of His
45:23 The **w** has gone out of My mouth
50: 4 I should know how to speak A **w**
55:11 So shall My **w** be that goes
66: 2 And who trembles at My **w**.
66: 5 Hear the **w** of the LORD,
66: 5 You who tremble at His **w**:
Jer 1: 2 to whom the **w** of the LORD came
1: 4 Then the **w** of the LORD came to
1:11 Moreover the **w** of the LORD
1:12 for I am ready to perform My **w**.
1:13 And the **w** of the LORD came to
2: 1 Moreover the **w** of the LORD came
2: 4 Hear the **w** of the LORD,
2:31 see the **w** of the LORD!
5:13 For the **w** is not in them.
5:14 "Because you speak this **w**,
6:10 the **w** of the LORD is a
7: 1 The **w** that came to Jeremiah from
7: 2 and proclaim there this **w**,
7: 2 Hear the **w** of the LORD, all
8: 9 they have rejected the **w** of the
9:20 Yet hear the **w** of the LORD,
9:20 let your ear receive the **w** of
10: 1 Hear the **w** which the LORD
11: 1 The **w** that came to Jeremiah from
13: 2 I got a sash according to the **w**
13: 3 And the **w** of the LORD came to
13: 8 Then the **w** of the LORD came to
13:12 you shall speak to them this **w**:
14: 1 The **w** of the LORD that came to
14:17 you shall say this **w** to them:
15:16 And Your **w** was to me the joy
16: 1 The **w** of the LORD also came to
17:15 Where is the **w** of the LORD?
17:20 Hear the **w** of the LORD, you
18: 1 The **w** which came to Jeremiah
18: 5 Then the **w** of the LORD came to
18:18 nor the **w** from the prophet.
19: 3 Hear the **w** of the LORD, O kings
20: 8 Because the **w** of the LORD
20: 9 But His **w** was in my heart
21: 1 The **w** which came to Jeremiah
21:11 Hear the **w** of the LORD,
22: 1 Judah, and there speak this **w**,
22: 2 Hear the **w** of the LORD, O king
22:29 Hear the **w** of the LORD!
23:18 has perceived and heard His **w**?
23:18 Who has marked His **w** and heard
23:28 a dream; And he who has My **w**,
23:28 let him speak My **w** faithfully.
23:29 Is not My **w** like a fire?" says
23:36 For every man's **w** will be his
23:38 LORD: 'Because you say this **w**,
24: 4 Again the **w** of the LORD came
25: 1 The **w** that came to Jeremiah
25: 3 year in which the **w** of the
26: 1 this **w** came from the LORD,
26: 2 to them. Do not diminish a **w**.
27: 1 this **w** came to Jeremiah from
27:18 and if the **w** of the LORD is
28: 7 Nevertheless hear now this **w**
28: 9 when the **w** of the prophet comes
28:12 Now the **w** of the LORD came to
29:10 visit you and perform My good **w**
29:20 Therefore hear the **w** of the
29:30 Then the **w** of the LORD came to
30: 1 The **w** that came to Jeremiah from
31:10 Hear the **w** of the LORD,
32: 1 The **w** that came to Jeremiah from
32: 6 The **w** of the LORD came to me,
32: 8 the prison according to the **w**
32: 8 I knew that this was the **w** of
32:26 Then the **w** of the LORD came to
33: 1 Moreover the **w** of the LORD came
33:19 And the **w** of the LORD came to
33:23 Moreover the **w** of the LORD
34: 1 The **w** which came to Jeremiah
34: 4 'Yet hear the **w** of the LORD,
34: 5 For I have pronounced the **w**,
34: 8 This is the **w** that came to
34:12 Therefore the **w** of the LORD
35: 1 The **w** which came to Jeremiah
35:12 Then came the **w** of the LORD to
36: 1 that this **w** came to Jeremiah
36:27 the **w** of the LORD came to
37: 6 Then the **w** of the LORD came to
37:17 Is there any **w** from the
38:21 this is the **w** that the LORD
39:15 Meanwhile the **w** of the LORD
40: 1 The **w** that came to Jeremiah from
42: 7 after ten days that the **w** of
42:15 Then hear now the **w** of the
43: 8 Then the **w** of the LORD came to
44: 1 The **w** that came to Jeremiah
44:16 As for the **w** that you have
44:24 Hear the **w** of the LORD, all
44:26 Therefore hear the **w** of the
45: 1 The **w** that Jeremiah the prophet
46: 1 The **w** of the LORD which came to
46:13 The **w** that the LORD spoke to
47: 1 The **w** of the LORD that came to
49:34 The **w** of the LORD that came to

50: 1 The **w** that the LORD spoke
51:59 The **w** which Jeremiah the
Lam 2:17 He has fulfilled His **w** Which
Ezek 1: 3 the **w** of the LORD came
3:16 end of seven days that the **w**
3:17 therefore hear a **w** from My
6: 1 Now the **w** of the LORD came to
6: 3 hear the **w** of the Lord GOD!'
7: 1 Moreover the **w** of the LORD came
11:14 Again the **w** of the LORD came
12: 1 Now the **w** of the LORD came to
12: 8 And in the morning the **w** of the
12:17 Moreover the **w** of the LORD
12:21 And the **w** of the LORD came to
12:25 and the **w** which I speak will
12:25 I will say the **w** and perform
12:26 Again the **w** of the LORD came
12:28 but the **w** which I speak will be
13: 1 And the **w** of the LORD came to
13: 2 Hear the **w** of the LORD!'"
13: 6 yet they hope that the **w** may be
14: 2 And the **w** of the LORD came to
14:12 The **w** of the LORD came again
15: 1 Then the **w** of the LORD came to
16: 1 Again the **w** of the LORD came to
16:35 hear the **w** of the LORD!
17: 1 And the **w** of the LORD came to
17:11 Moreover the **w** of the LORD
18: 1 The **w** of the LORD came to me
20: 2 Then the **w** of the LORD came to
20:45 Furthermore the **w** of the LORD
20:47 'Hear the **w** of the LORD!
21: 1 And the **w** of the LORD came to
21: 8 Again the **w** of the LORD came
21:18 The **w** of the LORD came to me
22: 1 Moreover the **w** of the LORD came
22:17 The **w** of the LORD came to me,
22:23 And the **w** of the LORD came to
23: 1 The **w** of the LORD came again to
24: 1 the **w** of the LORD came to me,
24:15 Also the **w** of the LORD came to
24:20 The **w** of the LORD came to me,
25: 1 The **w** of the LORD came to me,
25: 3 Hear the **w** of the Lord GOD!
26: 1 that the **w** of the LORD came
27: 1 The **w** of the LORD came again to
28: 1 The **w** of the LORD came to me
28:11 Moreover the **w** of the LORD
28:20 Then the **w** of the LORD came to
29: 1 the **w** of the LORD came to me,
29:17 that the **w** of the LORD came to
30: 1 The **w** of the LORD came to me
30:20 that the **w** of the LORD came
31: 1 that the **w** of the LORD came
32: 1 that the **w** of the LORD came
32:17 that the **w** of the LORD came to
33: 1 Again the **w** of the LORD came to
33: 7 therefore you shall hear a **w**
33:23 Then the **w** of the LORD came to
33:30 come and hear what the **w** is
34: 1 And the **w** of the LORD came to
34: 7 hear the **w** of the LORD:
34: 9 hear the **w** of the LORD!
35: 1 Moreover the **w** of the LORD came
36: 1 hear the **w** of the LORD!
36: 4 hear the **w** of the Lord GOD!
36:16 Moreover the **w** of the LORD
37: 4 hear the **w** of the LORD!
37:15 Again the **w** of the LORD came
38: 1 Now the **w** of the LORD came to
Dan 3: 2 King Nebuchadnezzar sent **w** to
3:28 have frustrated the king's **w**,
4:17 And the sentence by the **w** of
4:31 While the **w** was still in the
4:33 That very hour the **w** was
5:26 the interpretation of each **w**.
9: 2 the years specified by the **w**
10:11 While he was speaking this **w**
Hos 1: 1 The **w** of the LORD that came to
4: 1 the **w** of the LORD,
Joel 1: 1 The **w** of the LORD that came to
2:11 the One who executes His **w**.
Am 3: 1 Hear this **w** that the LORD has
4: 1 Hear this **w**, you cows of
5: 1 Hear this **w** which I take up
7:16 hear the **w** of the LORD:
8:12 seeking the **w** of the LORD,
Jon 1: 1 Now the **w** of the LORD came to
3: 1 Now the **w** of the LORD came to
3: 3 according to the **w** of the
3: 6 Then **w** came to the king of
Mic 1: 1 The **w** of the LORD that came to
4: 2 And the **w** of the LORD from
Zeph 1: 1 The **w** of the LORD which came
2: 5 The **w** of the LORD is against
Hag 1: 1 the **w** of the LORD came by
1: 3 Then the **w** of the LORD came by
2: 1 the **w** of the LORD came by
2: 5 According to the **w** that I
2:10 the **w** of the LORD came by
2:20 And again the **w** of the LORD
Zech 1: 1 the **w** of the LORD came to
1: 7 the **w** of the LORD came to
4: 6 This is the **w** of the LORD to
4: 8 Moreover the **w** of the LORD
6: 9 Then the **w** of the LORD came to
7: 1 it came to pass that the **w** of
7: 4 Then the **w** of the LORD of
7: 8 Then the **w** of the LORD came to
8: 1 Again the **w** of the LORD of
8:18 Then the **w** of the LORD of
9: 1 The burden of the **w** of the
11:11 knew that it was the **w** of the
12: 1 The burden of the **w** of the LORD
Mal 1: 1 The burden of the **w** of the
Mt 2: 8 bring back **w** to me, that I may
2:13 stay there until I bring you **w**;
4: 4 but by every **w** that
8: 8 my roof. But only speak a **w**,
8:16 cast out the spirits with a **w**,
12:32 Anyone who speaks a **w** against
12:36 to you that for every idle **w**
13:19 When anyone hears the **w** of the
13:20 this is he who hears the **w** and
13:21 arises because of the **w**,
13:22 thorns is he who hears the **w**,
13:22 of riches choke the **w**,
13:23 ground is he who hears the **w**
15:23 But He answered her not a **w**.
18:16 or three witnesses every **w**
22:46 one was able to answer Him a **w**,
26:75 And Peter remembered the **w** of
27:14 But He answered him not one **w**,
28: 8 ran to bring His disciples **w**.
Mk 2: 2 And He preached the **w** to them.
4:14 "The sower sows the **w**.
4:15 by the wayside where the **w** is
4:15 and takes away the **w** that was
4:16 who, when they hear the **w**,
4:18 are the ones who hear the **w**,
4:19 things entering in choke the **w**,
4:20 ground, those who hear the **w**,
4:33 such parables He spoke the **w**
5:36 As soon as Jesus heard the **w**
7:13 making the **w** of God of no effect
8:32 He spoke this **w** openly.
9:10 So they kept this **w** to
10:22 But he was sad at this **w**,
14:72 Then Peter called to mind the **w**
16:20 with them and confirming the **w**
Lk 1: 2 and ministers of the **w**
1:38 it be to me according to your **w**.
2:29 in peace, According to Your **w**;
3: 2 the **w** of God came to John the
4: 4 but by every **w** of God.'
4:32 for His **w** was with authority.
4:36 What a **w** this is! For with
5: 1 about Him to hear the **w** of God,
5: 5 nevertheless at Your **w** I will
7: 7 to come to You. But say the **w**,
8:11 The seed is the **w** of God.
8:12 comes and takes away the **w** out
8:13 receive the **w** with joy;
8:15 having heard the **w** with a noble
8:21 are these who hear the **w** of
10:39 at Jesus' feet and heard His **w**.
11:28 are those who hear the **w** of
12:10 And anyone who speaks a **w**
22:61 And Peter remembered the **w** of
24:19 a Prophet mighty in deed and **w**
Jn 1: 1 In the beginning was the **W**,
1: 1 and the **W** was with God, and the
1: 1 with God, and the **W** was God.
1:14 And the **W** became flesh and
2:22 the Scripture and the **w** which
4:39 in Him because of the **w** of the
4:41 believed because of His own **w**.
4:50 So the man believed the **w**
5:24 he who hears My **w** and believes
5:38 But you do not have His **w**
8:31 Him, "If you abide in My **w**,
8:37 because My **w** has no place in
8:43 are not able to listen to My **w**.
8:51 if anyone keeps My **w** he shall
8:52 If anyone keeps My **w** he shall
8:55 I do know Him and keep His **w**.
10:35 to whom the **w** of God came (and
12:38 that the **w** of Isaiah the prophet
12:48 the **w** that I have spoken will
14:23 loves Me, he will keep My **w**;
14:24 and the **w** which you hear is not
15: 3 already clean because of the **w**
15:20 Remember the **w** that I said to
15:20 If they kept My **w**,
15:25 this happened that the **w**
17: 6 Me, and they have kept Your **w**.
17:14 "I have given them Your **w**;
17:17 Your truth. Your **w** is truth.
17:20 believe in Me through their **w**;
Acts 2:41 who gladly received his **w** were
4: 4 many of those who heard the **w**
4:29 boldness they may speak Your **w**,
4:31 and they spoke the **w** of God
6: 2 that we should leave the **w** of
6: 4 and to the ministry of the **w**.
6: 7 Then the **w** of God spread,
8: 4 went everywhere preaching the **w**.
8:14 Samaria had received the **w** of
8:25 testified and preached the **w**
10:36 The **w** which God sent to the
10:37 that **w** you know, which was
10:44 upon all those who heard the **w**.
11: 1 had also received the **w** of God.
11:16 Then I remembered the **w** of the
11:19 preaching the **w** to no one but
12:24 But the **w** of God grew and
13: 5 they preached the **w** of God in
13: 7 Saul and sought to hear the **w**
13:15 if you have any **w** of
13:26 to you the **w** of this salvation
13:44 came together to hear the **w** of
13:46 It was necessary that the **w** of
13:48 glorified the **w** of the Lord.
13:49 And the **w** of the Lord was being
14: 3 was bearing witness to the **w**
14:25 when they had preached the **w**
15: 7 the Gentiles should hear the **w**
15:27 report the same things by **w** of
15:35 teaching and preaching the **w** of
15:36 where we have preached the **w**
16: 6 Holy Spirit to preach the **w** in
16:32 Then they spoke the **w** of the
17:11 in that they received the **w**
17:13 learned that the **w** of God was
18:11 teaching the **w** of God among
19:10 who dwelt in Asia heard the **w**
19:20 So the **w** of the Lord grew
20:32 you to God and to the **w** of His
22:22 listened to him until this **w**,
28:25 after Paul had said one **w**:
Rom 9: 6 But it is not that the **w** of God
9: 9 For this is the **w** of promise:
10: 8 The **w** is near you, in your
10: 8 the **w** of faith which we
10:17 and hearing by the **w** of God.
15:18 in **w** and deed, to make the
1 Cor 4:19 not the **w** of those who are
4:20 God is not in **w** but in power.
12: 8 for to one is given the **w** of
12: 8 to another the **w** of knowledge
14:36 Or did the **w** of God come
15: 2 if you hold fast that **w** which I
2 Cor 1:18 our **w** to you was not Yes and
2:17 peddling the **w** of God; but as
4: 2 craftiness nor handling the **w**
5:19 and has committed to us the **w**
6: 7 by the **w** of truth, by the power
10:11 that what we are in **w** by
13: 1 or three witnesses every **w**
Gal 5:14 the law is fulfilled in one **w**,
6: 6 him who is taught the **w** share
Eph 1:13 after you heard the **w** of truth,
4:29 Let no corrupt **w** proceed out of
5:26 the washing of water by the **w**,
6:17 which is the **w** of God;
Phil 1:14 much more bold to speak the **w**
2:16 holding fast the **w** of life,
Col 1: 5 you heard before in the **w** of
1:25 to fulfill the **w** of God,
3:16 Let the **w** of Christ dwell in you
3:17 And whatever you do in **w** or
4: 3 open to us a door for the **w**,
1 Th 1: 5 did not come to you in **w** only,
1: 6 having received the **w** in much
1: 8 For from you the **w** of the Lord
2:13 when you received the **w** of God
2:13 you welcomed it not as the **w**
2:13 the **w** of God, which also
4:15 this we say to you by the **w** of
2 Th 2: 2 either by spirit or by **w** or by
2:15 whether by **w** or our epistle.
2:17 establish you in every good **w**
3: 1 that the **w** of the Lord may run
3:14 if anyone does not obey our **w**
1 Tim 4: 5 for it is sanctified by the **w** of
4:12 example to the believers in **w**,
5:17 those who labor in the **w** and
2 Tim 2: 9 but the **w** of God is not
2:15 rightly dividing the **w** of
4: 2 Preach the **w**! Be ready in season
Titus 1: 3 in due time manifested His **w**
1: 9 holding fast the faithful **w** as
2: 5 that the **w** of God may not be
Heb 1: 3 upholding all things by the **w**
2: 2 For if the **w** spoken through
4: 2 but the **w** which they heard did
4:12 For the **w** of God is living and
5:13 of milk is unskilled in the **w**
6: 5 and have tasted the good **w** of
7:28 but the **w** of the oath, which
11: 3 worlds were framed by the **w** of
12:19 who heard it begged that the **w**
13: 7 who have spoken the **w** of God to
13:22 bear with the **w** of exhortation,
Jas 1:18 He brought us forth by the **w**
1:21 with meekness the implanted **w**,
1:22 But be doers of the **w**,
1:23 if anyone is a hearer of the **w**
3: 2 If anyone does not stumble in **w**,
1 Pe 1:23 through the **w** of God which
1:25 But the **w** of the LORD
1:25 Now this is the **w** which by the
2: 2 desire the pure milk of the **w**,
2: 8 being disobedient to the **w**,
3: 1 even if some do not obey the **w**,
3: 1 the word, they, without a **w**,
2 Pe 1:19 And so we have the prophetic **w**
3: 5 that by the **w** of God the
3: 7 are now preserved by the same **w**,
1 Jn 1: 1 concerning the **W** of life—
1:10 and His **w** is not in us.
2: 5 But whoever keeps His **w**,
2: 7 The old commandment is the **w**
2:14 and the **w** of God abides in you,
3:18 let us not love in **w** or in
5: 7 in heaven: the Father, the **W**,
Rev 1: 2 who bore witness to the **w** of
1: 9 is called Patmos for the **w** of
3: 8 little strength, have kept My **w**,
6: 9 who had been slain for the **w**
12:11 blood of the Lamb and by the **w**
19:13 name is called The **W** of God.
20: 4 to Jesus and for the **w** of God,

WORD'S (2/2)

2 Sam 7:21 For Your *w* sake, and according
Mk 4:17 arises for the *w* sake,

WORDS (568/543) WORD

Gen 24:30 and when he heard the *w* of his
24:52 Abraham's servant heard their *w*,
27:34 When Esau heard the *w* of his
27:42 And the *w* of Esau her older son
31: 1 Now Jacob heard the *w* of
34:18 And their *w* pleased Hamor and
37: 8 for his dreams and for his *w*.
39:17 Then she spoke to him with *w*
39:19 when his master heard the *w*
42:16 that your *w* may be tested to
42:20 so your *w* will be verified,
43: 7 told him according to these *w*.
44: 6 he spoke to them these same *w*.
44: 7 "Why does my lord say these *w*?
44:10 let it be according to your *w*;
44:24 that we told him the *w* of my
45:27 when they told him all the *w*
49:21 let loose; He uses beautiful *w*.
Ex 4:15 speak to him and put the *w* in
4:28 So Moses told Aaron all the *w* of
4:30 And Aaron spoke all the *w* which
5: 9 and let them not regard false *w*.
19: 6 These are the *w* which you
19: 7 laid before them all these *w*
19: 8 So Moses brought back the *w*
19: 9 So Moses told the *w* of the
20: 1 And God spoke all these *w*,
23: 8 discerning and perverts the *w*
24: 3 and told the people all the *w*
24: 3 All the *w* which the LORD has
24: 4 And Moses wrote all the *w* of the
24: 8 you according to all these *w*.
34: 1 write on these tablets the *w*
34:27 said to Moses, "Write these *w*,
34:27 to the tenor of these *w* I have
34:28 He wrote on the tablets the *w*
35: 1 These are the *w* which the LORD
Num 11:24 out and told the people the *w*
12: 6 Then He said, "Hear now My *w*:
14:39 Then Moses told these *w* to all
16:31 finished speaking all these *w*,
22: 7 Balaam and spoke to him the *w*
24: 4 of him who hears the *w* of God,
24:16 of him who hears the *w* of God,
Deut 1: 1 These are the *w* which Moses
1:34 LORD heard the sound of your *w*,
2:26 with *w* of peace, saying,
4:10 and I will let them hear My *w*,
4:12 You heard the sound of the *w*,
4:36 and you heard His *w* out of the
5:22 These *w* the LORD spoke to all
5:28 heard the voice of your *w* when
5:28 have heard the voice of the *w*
6: 6 And these *w* which I command you
9:10 and on them were all the *w*
10: 2 will write on the tablets the *w*
11:18 you shall lay up these *w* of
12:28 Observe and obey all these *w*
13: 3 you shall not listen to the *w* of
16:19 of the wise and twists the *w*
17:19 be careful to observe all the *w*
18:18 and will put My *w* in His mouth,
18:19 whoever will not hear My *w*,
27: 3 shall write on them all the *w*
27: 8 on the stones all the *w* of
27:26 does not confirm all the *w* of
28:14 turn aside from any of the *w*
28:58 carefully observe all the *w* of
29: 1 These are the *w* of the covenant
29: 9 Therefore keep the *w* of this
29:19 when he hears the *w* of this
29:29 that we may do all the *w* of
31: 1 Moses went and spoke these *w*
31:12 carefully observe all the *w* of
31:24 had completed writing the *w* of
31:28 that I may speak these *w* in
31:30 the assembly of Israel the *w*
32: 1 O earth, the *w* of my mouth.
32:44 son of Nun and spoke all the *w*
32:45 finished speaking all these *w*
32:46 Set your hearts on all the *w*
32:46 all the *w* of this law.
33: 3 Everyone receives Your *w*.
Josh 1:18 and does not heed your *w*,
2:21 she said, "According to your *w*,
3: 9 and hear the *w* of the LORD
8:34 afterward he read all the *w* of
22:30 heard the *w* that the children
24:26 Then Joshua wrote these *w* in
24:27 for it has heard all the *w* of
Judg 2: 4 of the LORD spoke these *w* to
9: 3 brothers spoke all these *w*
9:30 heard the *w* of Gaal the son of
11:10 do not do according to your *w*.
11:11 and Jephthah spoke all his *w*
11:28 of Ammon did not heed the *w*
13:12 Now let Your *w* come to pass!
13:17 that when Your *w* come to pass
16:16 pestered him daily with her *w*
1 Sam 3:19 him and let none of his *w* fall
8:10 So Samuel told all the *w* of the
8:21 And Samuel heard all the *w* of
11: 5 And they told him the *w* of
15: 1 heed the voice of the *w* of the
15:24 of the LORD and your *w*,
17:11 and all Israel heard these *w*
17:23 spoke according to the same *w*.
17:31 Now when the *w* which David
18:23 Saul's servants spoke those *w*
18:26 his servants told David these *w*
21:12 Now David took these *w* to heart,
24: 7 his servants with these *w*,
24: 9 Why do you listen to the *w* of
24:16 had finished speaking these *w*
25: 9 Nabal according to all these *w*
25:12 came and told him all these *w*.
25:24 and hear the *w* of your
26:19 my lord the king hear the *w* of
28:20 afraid because of the *w* of
28:21 in my hands and heeded the *w*
2 Sam 3: 8 became very angry at the *w* of
7:17 According to all these *w* and
7:28 and Your *w* are true, and You
14: 3 So Joab put the *w* in her
14:19 and he put all these *w* in the
19:11 since the *w* of all Israel have
19:43 Yet the *w* of the men of Judah
19:43 Judah were fiercer than the *w*
20:17 the *w* of your maidservant."
22: 1 David spoke to the LORD the *w*
23: 1 Now these are the last *w* of
1 Ki 1:14 in after you and confirm your *w*.
3:12 I have done according to your *w*;
5: 7 when Hiram heard the *w* of
8:59 And may these *w* of mine, with
10: 6 in my own land about your *w*
10: 7 I did not believe the *w* until
12: 7 and speak good *w* to them, then
13:11 also told their father the *w*
21:27 it was, when Ahab heard those *w*,
22:13 the *w* of the prophets with one
2 Ki 1: 7 meet you and told you these *w*?
6:12 tells the king of Israel the *w*
6:30 when the king heard the *w* of
18:20 for war; but they are mere *w*.
18:27 and to you to speak these *w*,
18:37 and told him the *w* of the
19: 4 your God will hear all the *w*
19: 4 and will rebuke the *w* which the
19: 6 Do not be afraid of the *w* which
19:16 and hear the *w* of Sennacherib,
22:11 when the king heard the *w* of
22:13 concerning the *w* of this book
22:13 fathers have not obeyed the *w*
22:16 all the *w* of the book which the
22:18 Concerning the *w* which you have
23: 2 in their hearing all the *w* of
23: 3 to perform the *w* of this
23:16 who proclaimed these *w*.
23:24 that he might perform the *w* of
1 Chr 17:15 According to all these *w* and
23:27 For by the last *w* of David the
25: 5 Heman the king's seer in the *w*
2 Chr 9: 5 in my own land about your *w*
9: 6 I did not believe their *w*
10: 7 and speak good *w* to them,
11: 4 Therefore they obeyed the *w* of
15: 8 And when Asa heard these *w* and
18:12 the *w* of the prophets with one
29:15 at the *w* of the LORD, to
29:30 praise to the LORD with the *w*
32: 8 were strengthened by the *w* of
33:18 and the *w* of the seers who
34:19 when the king heard the *w* of
34:21 concerning the *w* of the book
34:26 Concerning the *w* which you have
34:27 before God when you heard His *w*
34:30 in their hearing all the *w* of
34:31 to perform the *w* of the
35:22 and did not heed the *w* of Necho
36:16 of God, despised His *w*,
Ezra 7:11 expert in the *w* of the
9: 4 everyone who trembled at the *w*
Neh 1: 1 The *w* of Nehemiah the son of
1: 4 it was, when I heard these *w*,
2:18 and also of the king's *w* that
5: 6 heard their outcry and these *w*.
6:19 and reported my *w* to him.
8: 9 when they heard the *w* of the
8:12 because they understood the *w*
8:13 in order to understand the *w* of
9: 8 You have performed Your *w*,
Esth 3: 4 to see whether Mordecai's *w*
4: 9 returned and told Esther the *w*
4:12 they told Mordecai Esther's *w*.
9:26 because of all the *w* of this
9:30 with *w* of peace and truth,
Job 4: 4 Your *w* have upheld him who was
6: 3 Therefore my *w* have been rash.
6:10 I have not concealed the *w* of
6:25 How forceful are right *w*!
6:26 Do you intend to rebuke my *w*,
8: 2 And the *w* of your mouth be
8:10 And utter *w* from their heart?
9:14 And choose my *w* to reason
11: 2 Should not the multitude of *w* be
12:11 Does not the ear test *w* And
15:13 And let such *w* go out of your
16: 3 Shall *w* of wind have an end?
16: 4 I could heap up *w* against you,
18: 2 long till you put an end to *w*?
19: 2 And break me in pieces with *w*?
19:23 that my *w* were written!
21:34 can you comfort me with empty *w*,
22:22 And lay up His *w* in your
23: 5 I would know the *w* which He
23:12 I have treasured the *w* of His
26: 4 To whom have you uttered *w*?
29:22 After my *w* they did not speak
31:40 The *w* of Job are ended.
32:11 Indeed I waited for your *w*,
32:12 Job, Or answered his *w*—
32:14 not directed his *w* against me;
32:14 will not answer him with your *w*.
32:15 answer no more; *W* escape them.
32:18 For I am full of *w*;
33: 1 And listen to all my *w*.
33: 3 My *w* come from my upright
33: 5 Set your *w* in order before
33: 8 have heard the sound of your *w*,
33:13 an accounting of any of His *w*.
34: 2 'Hear my *w*, you wise men;
34: 3 For the ear tests *w* As the
34:16 listen to the sound of my *w*:
34:35 His *w* are without wisdom.'
34:37 And multiplies his *w* against
35:16 He multiplies *w* without
36: 2 That there are yet *w* to
36: 4 For truly my *w* are not false;
38: 2 By *w* without knowledge?
42: 7 the LORD had spoken these *w*
Ps 5: 1 Give ear to my *w*,
7: LORD concerning the *w* of Cush,
12: 6 The *w* of the LORD are pure
12: 6 words of the LORD are pure *w*,
18: who spoke to the LORD the *w* of
19: 4 And their *w* to the end of the
19:14 Let the *w* of my mouth and the
22: 1 And from the *w* of My
36: 3 The *w* of his mouth are
50:17 And cast My *w* behind you?
52: 4 You love all devouring *w*,
54: 2 Give ear to the *w* of my mouth.
55:21 The *w* of his mouth were
55:21 His *w* were softer than oil,
56: 5 All day they twist my *w*;
59:12 sin of their mouth and the *w*
64: 3 shoot their arrows—bitter *w*,
78: 1 Incline your ears to the *w* of
106:12 Then they believed His *w*;
107:11 they rebelled against the *w* of
109: 3 have also surrounded me with *w*
119:57 said that I would keep Your *w*.
119:103 How sweet are Your *w* to my
119:130 The entrance of Your *w* gives
119:139 enemies have forgotten Your *w*.
138: 4 When they hear the *w* of Your
141: 6 the cliff, And they hear my *w*,
144: 8 Whose mouth speaks vain *w*,
144:11 Whose mouth speaks lying *w*,
Prov 1: 2 To perceive the *w* of
1: 6 The *w* of the wise and their
1:21 in the city She speaks her *w*:
1:23 I will make my *w* known to you.
2: 1 My son, if you receive my *w*,
2:16 who flatters with her *w*,
4: 4 "Let your heart retain my *w*;
4: 5 nor turn away from the *w* of my
4:20 son, give attention to my *w*;
5: 7 And do not depart from the *w*
6: 2 You are snared by the *w* of your
6: 2 You are taken by the *w* of your
7: 1 My son, keep my *w*,
7: 5 who flatters with her *w*.
7:24 Pay attention to the *w* of my
8: 8 All the *w* of my mouth are with
10:19 In the multitude of *w* sin is
12: 6 The *w* of the wicked are, "Lie
15:26 But the *w* of the pure are
16:24 Pleasant *w* are like a
17:27 who has knowledge spares his *w*,
18: 4 The *w* of a man's mouth are
18: 8 The *w* of a talebearer are like
19: 7 He may pursue them with *w*,
19:27 And you will stray from the *w*
22:12 But He overthrows the *w* of the
22:17 your ear and hear the *w* of the
22:21 know the certainty of the *w* of
22:21 That you may answer *w* of truth
23: 8 And waste your pleasant *w*.
23: 9 despise the wisdom of your *w*.
23:12 And your ears to *w* of
26:22 The *w* of a talebearer are like
29:19 will not be corrected by mere *w*;
29:20 you see a man hasty in his *w*?
30: 1 The *w* of Agur the son of Jakeh,
30: 6 Do not add to His *w*,
31: 1 The *w* of King Lemuel, the
Eccl 1: 1 The *w* of the Preacher, the son
5: 2 Therefore let your *w* be few.
5: 3 voice is known by his many *w*.
5: 7 multitude of dreams and many *w*
9:16 And his *w* are not heard.
9:17 *W* of the wise, spoken quietly,
10:12 The *w* of a wise man's mouth
10:13 The *w* of his mouth begin with
10:14 A fool also multiplies *w*.
12:10 sought to find acceptable *w*;
12:10 was upright—*w* of truth.
12:11 The *w* of the wise are like
12:11 and the *w* of scholars are like
Isa 29:11 to you like the *w* of a book
29:18 day the deaf shall hear the *w*
29:21 turn aside the just by empty *w*.
31: 2 And will not call back His *w*,
32: 7 destroy the poor with lying *w*,
36: 5 for war; but they are mere *w*.
36:12 and to you to speak these *w*,
36:13 Hear the *w* of the great king,

36:22 and told him the **w** of the
37: 4 LORD your God will hear the **w**
37: 4 and will rebuke the **w** which the
37: 6 Do not be afraid of the **w** which
37:17 and hear all the **w** of
41:26 is no one who hears your **w**.
51:16 And I have put My **w** in your
58:13 Nor speaking your own **w**,
59: 4 They trust in empty **w** and
59:13 and uttering from the heart **w**
59:21 and My **w** which I have put in
Jer 1: 1 The **w** of Jeremiah the son of
1: 9 I have put My **w** in your mouth.
3:12 Go and proclaim these **w** toward
5:14 I will make My **w** in your mouth
6:19 they have not heeded My **w**,
7: 4 "Do not trust in these lying **w**,
7: 8 you trust in lying **w** that
7:27 you shall speak all these **w** to
11: 2 'Hear the **w** of this covenant,
11: 3 man who does not obey the **w** of
11: 6 Proclaim all these **w** in the
11: 6 Hear the **w** of this covenant and
11: 8 all the **w** of this covenant,
11:10 who refused to hear My **w**,
12: 6 though they speak smooth **w** to
13:10 people, who refuse to hear My **w**,
15:16 Your **w** were found, and I ate
16:10 show this people all these **w**,
18: 2 I will cause you to hear My **w**.
18:18 not give heed to any of his **w**.
19: 2 and proclaim there the **w** that I
19:15 that they might not hear My **w**.
22: 5 if you will not hear these **w**,
23: 9 And because of His holy **w**.
23:16 Do not listen to the **w** of the
23:22 caused My people to hear My **w**,
23:30 who steal My **w** every one from
23:36 for you have perverted the **w** of
25: 8 you have not heard My **w**,
25:13 bring on that land all My **w**
25:30 against them all these **w**,
26: 2 all the **w** that I command you to
26: 5 to heed the **w** of My servants the
26: 7 Jeremiah speaking these **w** in
26:12 this city with all the **w** that
26:15 me to you to speak all these **w**
26:20 land according to all the **w** of
26:21 all the princes, heard his **w**,
27:12 Judah according to all these **w**,
27:14 do not listen to the **w** of the
27:16 Do not listen to the **w** of your
28: 6 the LORD perform your **w** which
29: 1 Now these are the **w** of the
29:19 they have not heeded My **w**,
29:23 and have spoken lying **w** in My
30: 2 a book for yourself all the **w**
30: 4 Now these are the **w** that the
34: 6 the prophet spoke all these **w**
34:18 who have not performed the **w** of
35:13 instruction to obey My **w**?
35:14 The **w** of Jonadab the son of
36: 2 book and write on it all the **w**
36: 4 all the **w** of the LORD which He
36: 6 the **w** of the LORD, in the
36: 8 reading from the book the **w** of
36:10 read from the book the **w** of
36:11 heard all the **w** of the LORD
36:13 declared to them all the **w**
36:16 when they had heard all the **w**,
36:16 tell the king of all these **w**.
36:17 how did you write all these **w**—
36:18 with his mouth all these **w** to
36:20 and told all the **w** in the
36:24 servants who heard all these **w**.
36:27 burned the scroll with the **w**
36:28 write on it all the former **w**
36:32 of Jeremiah all the **w** of the
36:32 added to them many similar **w**.
37: 2 of the land gave heed to the **w**
38: 1 the son of Malchiah heard the **w**
38: 4 by speaking such **w** to them.
38:24 "Let no one know of these **w**,
38:27 them according to all these **w**
39:16 I will bring My **w** upon this
42: 4 your God according to your **w**,
43: 1 to all the people all the **w** of
43: 1 sent him to them, all these **w**,
44:28 shall know whose **w** will stand,
44:29 that My **w** will surely stand
45: 1 when he had written these **w** in
51:60 all these **w** that are written
51:61 see it, and read all these **w**,
51:64 Thus far are the **w** of
Ezek 2: 6 them nor be afraid of their **w**,
2: 6 do not be afraid of their **w** or
2: 7 You shall speak My **w** to them,
3: 4 of Israel and speak with My **w**
3: 6 whose **w** you cannot understand.
3:10 into your heart all My **w** that
12:28 None of My **w** will be postponed
33:31 My people, and they hear your **w**,
33:32 for they hear your **w**,
35:13 Me and multiplied your **w**
Dan 2: 9 to speak lying and corrupt **w**
5:10 because of the **w** of the king
6:14 king, when he heard these **w**,
7: 8 and a mouth speaking pompous **w**.
7:11 of the sound of the pompous **w**
7:20 a mouth which spoke pompous **w**,
7:25 He shall speak pompous **w**
9:12 "And He has confirmed His **w**,
10: 6 and the sound of his **w** like the
10: 9 Yet I heard the sound of his **w**;
10: 9 I heard the sound of his **w** I
10:11 understand the **w** that I speak
10:12 your **w** were heard; and I have
10:12 I have come because of your **w**.
10:15 When he had spoken such **w** to
12: 4 you, Daniel, shut up the **w**,
12: 9 for the **w** are closed up and
Hos 6: 5 I have slain them by the **w** of
10: 4 They have spoken **w**,
14: 2 Take **w** with you, And return to
Am 1: 1 The **w** of Amos, who was among
7:10 is not able to bear all his **w**.
8:11 But of hearing the **w** of the
Mic 2: 7 Do not My **w** do good To him
Hag 1:12 and the **w** of Haggai the
Zech 1: 6 Yet surely My **w** and My
1:13 with good and comforting **w**.
7: 7 you not have obeyed the **w**
7:12 to hear the law and the **w**
8: 9 hearing in these days These **w**
Mal 2:17 wearied the LORD with your **w**;
3:13 Your **w** have been harsh against
Mt 6: 7 will be heard for their many **w**.
10:14 not receive you nor hear your **w**,
12:37 For by your **w** you will be
12:37 and by your **w** you will be
22:22 When they had heard these **w**,
24:35 but My **w** will by no means pass
26:44 third time, saying the same **w**.
Mk 8:38 is ashamed of Me and My **w** in
10:24 were astonished at His **w**.
12:13 to catch Him in His **w**.
13:31 but My **w** will by no means pass
14:39 prayed, and spoke the same **w**.
Lk 1:20 you did not believe my **w** which
3: 4 is written in the book of the **w**
4:22 and marveled at the gracious **w**
9:26 is ashamed of Me and My **w**,
9:44 Let these **w** sink down into your
20:20 that they might seize on His **w**,
20:26 could not catch Him in His **w**
21:33 but My **w** will by no means pass
23: 9 he questioned Him with many **w**,
24: 8 And they remembered His **w**.
24:11 And their **w** seemed to them like
24:44 These are the **w** which I spoke
Jn 3:34 has sent speaks the **w** of God,
5:47 how will you believe My **w**?
6:63 The **w** that I speak to you are
6:68 You have the **w** of eternal life.
8:20 These **w** Jesus spoke in the
8:30 As He spoke these **w**,
8:47 who is of God hears God's **w**;
9:40 who were with Him heard these **w**,
10:21 These are not the **w** of one who
12:47 And if anyone hears My **w** and
12:48 Me, and does not receive My **w**,
14:10 The **w** that I speak to you I do
14:24 not love Me does not keep My **w**;
15: 7 and My **w** abide in you, you will
17: 1 Jesus spoke these **w**,
17: 8 I have given to them the **w**
18: 1 When Jesus had spoken these **w**,
Acts 2:14 be known to you, and heed my **w**.
2:22 "Men of Israel, hear these **w**:
2:40 And with many other **w** he
5: 5 Then Ananias, hearing these **w**,
5:20 speak to the people all the **w**
6:11 heard him speak blasphemous **w**
6:13 cease to speak blasphemous **w**
7:22 and was mighty in **w** and deeds.
10:22 and to hear **w** from you."
10:44 was still speaking these **w**,
11:14 who will tell you **w** by which you
13:42 that these **w** might be preached
15:15 And with this the **w** of the
15:24 us have troubled you with **w**,
15:32 the brethren with many **w**.
16:36 of the prison reported these **w**
16:38 And the officers told these **w** to
18:15 But if it is a question of **w** and
20: 2 and encouraged them with many **w**,
20:35 And remember the **w** of the Lord
20:38 most of all for the **w** which he
24: 4 your courtesy, a few **w** from us.
26:25 but speak the **w** of truth and
28:29 And when he had said these **w**,
Rom 3: 4 be justified in Your **w**,
10:18 And their **w** to the ends
16:18 and by smooth **w** and flattering
1 Cor 1:17 gospel, not with wisdom of **w**,
2: 4 were not with persuasive **w** of
2:13 not in **w** which man's wisdom
14: 9 you utter by the tongue **w** easy
14:19 I would rather speak five **w**
14:19 than ten thousand **w** in a
2 Cor 12: 4 and heard inexpressible **w**,
Eph 5: 6 no one deceive you with empty **w**,
Col 2: 4 deceive you with persuasive **w**.
1 Th 2: 5 time did we use flattering **w**,
4:18 one another with these **w**.
1 Tim 4: 6 nourished in the **w** of faith and
6: 3 does not consent to wholesome **w**,
6: 3 even the **w** of our Lord Jesus
6: 4 disputes and arguments over **w**,
2 Tim 1:13 fast the pattern of sound **w**
2:14 the Lord not to strive about **w**
4:15 he has greatly resisted our **w**.
Heb 12:19 of a trumpet and the voice of **w**,
13:22 I have written to you in few **w**.
2 Pe 2: 3 exploit you with deceptive **w**;
2:18 they speak great swelling **w**
3: 2 you may be mindful of the **w**
3 Jn 10 against us with malicious **w**.
Jude 16 they mouth great swelling **w**,
17 remember the **w** which were
Rev 1: 3 reads and those who hear the **w**
17:17 until the **w** of God are
21: 5 for these **w** are true and
22: 6 These **w** are faithful and
22: 7 who keeps the **w** of the prophecy
22: 9 and of those who keep the **w** of
22:10 Do not seal the **w** of the
22:18 to everyone who hears the **w** of
22:19 if anyone takes away from the **w**

WORE (6/6) WEAR, WEARING

1 Sam 22:18 men who **w** a linen ephod.
2 Sam 13:18 daughters **w** such apparel.
1 Ki 20:32 So they **w** sackcloth around their
1 Chr 15:27 David also **w** a linen ephod.
Neh 4:16 and **w** armor; and the leaders
Lk 8:27 And he **w** no clothes, nor did he

WORK (402/374) WORKED, WORKER, WORKING, WORKMAN, WORKS

Gen 2: 2 the seventh day God ended His **w**
2: 2 the seventh day from all His **w**
2: 3 in it He rested from all His **w**
5:29 comfort us concerning our **w**
39:11 went into the house to do his **w**,
Ex 5: 4 take the people from their **w**?
5: 9 Let more **w** be laid on the men,
5:11 yet none of your **w** will be
5:13 hurry, saying, "Fulfill your **w**,
5:18 "Therefore go now and **w**;
12:16 No manner of **w** shall be done on
14:31 Thus Israel saw the great **w**
18:20 which they must walk and the **w**
20: 9 shall labor and do all your **w**,
20:10 In it you shall do no **w**:
23:12 "Six days you shall do your **w**,
24:10 His feet as it were a paved **w**
25:18 of hammered **w** you shall make
25:31 shall be of hammered **w**.
28:11 With the **w** of an engraver in
28:39 shall make the sash of woven **w**.
31: 4 to **w** in gold, in silver, in
31: 5 and to **w** in all manner of
31:14 for whoever does any **w** on it,
31:15 ***W*** shall be done for six days,
31:15 Whoever does any **w** on the
32:16 Now the tablets were the **w** of
34:10 whom you are shall see the **w**
34:21 "Six days you shall **w**,
35: 2 ***W*** shall be done for six days,
35: 2 Whoever does any **w** on it shall
35:21 the LORD's offering for the **w**
35:24 found acacia wood for any **w** of
35:29 material for all kinds of **w**
35:32 to **w** in gold and silver and
35:33 and to **w** in all manner of
35:35 skill to do all manner of **w** of
35:35 those who do every **w** and those
36: 1 know how to do all manner of **w**
36: 2 stirred, to come and do the **w**.
36: 3 of Israel had brought for the **w**
36: 4 who were doing all the **w** of
36: 4 each from the **w** he was doing,
36: 5 for the service of the **w** which
36: 6 man nor woman do any more **w**
36: 7 was sufficient for all the **w**
37:17 of hammered **w** he made the
37:29 according to the **w** of the
38:24 that was used in all the **w** of
39: 3 to **w** it in with the blue,
39:22 robe of the ephod of woven **w**,
39:32 Thus all the **w** of the
39:42 of Israel did all the **w**.
39:43 Moses looked over all the **w**,
40:33 So Moses finished the **w**.
Lev 11:32 in which any **w** is done, it
16:29 and do no **w** at all, whether a
23: 3 Six days shall **w** be done,
23: 3 You shall do no **w** on it;
23: 7 you shall do no customary **w** on
23: 8 you shall do no customary **w** on
23:21 You shall do no customary **w** on
23:25 You shall do no customary **w** on
23:28 And you shall do no **w** on that
23:30 And any person who does any **w** on
23:31 "You shall do no manner of **w**;
23:35 You shall do no customary **w** on
23:36 you shall do no customary **w**
Num 3: 7 to do the **w** of the tabernacle.
3: 8 to do the **w** of the tabernacle.
3:26 according to all the **w** relating
3:31 and all the **w** relating to them.
3:36 all the **w** relating to them,
4: 3 enter the service to do the **w**
4:23 to do the **w** in the tabernacle
4:30 enters the service to do the **w**
4:35 who entered the service for **w**
4:39 who entered the service for **w**
4:43 who entered the service for **w**
4:47 everyone who came to do the **w**
4:47 the work of service and the **w**
7: 5 may be used in doing the **w** of
8: 4 its flowers it was hammered **w**.

W

8:11 that they may perform the **w** of
8:19 to do the **w** for the children of
8:22 Levites went in to do their **w**
8:24 to perform service in the **w** of
8:25 must cease performing this **w**,
8:25 and shall **w** no more.
8:26 they themselves shall do no **w**.
10: 2 shall make them of hammered **w**;
16: 9 to do the **w** of the tabernacle
18: 4 for all the **w** of the
18: 6 to do the **w** of the tabernacle
18:21 in return for the **w** which they
18:21 the **w** of the tabernacle of
18:23 Levites shall perform the **w** of
18:31 it is your reward for your **w**
28:18 You shall do no customary **w**.
28:25 You shall do no customary **w**.
28:26 You shall do no customary **w**.
29: 1 You shall do no customary **w**.
29: 7 souls; you shall not do any **w**.
29:12 You shall do no customary **w**,
29:35 You shall do no customary **w**.
Deut 2: 7 has blessed you in all the **w**
4:28 the **w** of men's hands, wood and
5:13 shall labor and do all your **w**,
5:14 In it you shall do no **w**:
14:29 God may bless you in all the **w**
15:19 you shall do no **w** with the
16: 8 You shall do no **w** on it.
16:15 your produce and in all the **w**
24:19 God may bless you in all the **w**
27:15 the **w** of the hands of the
28:12 and to bless all the **w** of your
30: 9 make you abound in all the **w**
31:29 Him to anger through the **w** of
32: 4 His **w** is perfect; For all His
33:11 And accept the **w** of his hands;
Judg 2:10 not know the LORD nor the **w**
13:12 boy's rule of life, and his **w**?
19:16 an old man came in from his **w**
Ruth 2:12 "The LORD repay your **w**,
2:19 And where did you **w**?
1 Sam 8:16 donkeys, and put them to his **w**.
14: 6 it may be that the LORD will **w**
2 Sam 9:10 shall **w** the land for him,
12:31 and put them to **w** with saws
1 Ki 5:16 the people who labored in the **w**.
6:35 applied evenly on the carved **w**.
7:14 with all kinds of bronze **w**.
7:14 King Solomon and did all his **w**.
7:22 So the **w** of the pillars was
7:29 oxen were wreaths of plaited **w**.
7:40 Huram finished doing all the **w**
7:51 So all the **w** that King Solomon
9:23 who were over Solomon's **w**:
9:23 over the people who did the **w**.
9:27 to **w** with the servants of
16: 7 Him to anger with the **w** of his
2 Ki 12:11 hands of those who did the **w**,
19:18 but the **w** of men's hands—wood
22: 5 the hand of those doing the **w**,
22: 5 house of the LORD doing the **w**,
22: 9 the hand of those who do the **w**,
1 Chr 4:23 dwelt with the king for his **w**.
6:49 for all the **w** of the Most Holy
9:13 were very able men for the **w**
9:19 were in charge of the **w** of the
9:33 they were employed in that **w**
16:37 as every day's **w** required;
20: 3 and put them to **w** with saws,
22:15 men for every kind of **w**.
23: 4 were to look after the **w** of
23:24 who did the **w** for the service
23:28 of all holy things and the **w**
23:32 Aaron their brethren in the **w**
26: 8 men with strength for the **w**:
27:26 was over those who did the **w**
28:13 for all the **w** of the service of
28:20 you have finished all the **w**
29: 1 and the **w** is great, because
29: 5 and for all kinds of **w** to be
29: 6 the officers over the king's **w**,
29: 7 They gave for the **w** of the house
2 Chr 2: 7 me at once a man skillful to **w**
2:14 skilled to **w** in gold and
2:18 overseers to make the people **w**.
4:11 So Huram finished doing the **w**
5: 1 So all the **w** that Solomon had
8: 9 of Israel servants for his **w**.
8:16 Now all the **w** of Solomon was
15: 7 for your **w** shall be rewarded!"
16: 5 building Ramah and ceased his **w**.
24:12 gave it to those who did the **w**
24:13 and the **w** was completed by
29:34 helped them until the **w** was
31:16 his daily portion for the **w** of
31:17 old and up according to their **w**,
31:21 And in every **w** that he began in
32:19 the **w** of men's hands.
34:12 And the men did the **w**
34:13 overseers of all who did **w** in
Ezra 2:69 gave to the treasury for the **w**
3: 8 began **w** and appointed the
3: 8 old and above to oversee the **w**
4:24 Thus the **w** of the house of God
5: 8 and this **w** goes on diligently
6: 7 Let the **w** of this house of God
6:22 their hands in the **w** of the
10:13 Nor is this the **w** of one or
Neh 2:16 or the others who did the **w**.
2:18 their hands to this good **w**.
3: 5 put their shoulders to the **w**
4: 6 for the people had a mind to **w**.
4:11 and kill them and cause the **w**
4:15 to the wall, everyone to his **w**.
4:19 The **w** is great and extensive,
4:21 So we labored in the **w**,
5:16 I also continued the **w** on this
5:16 were gathered there for the **w**.
6: 3 saying, "I am doing a great **w**,
6: 3 Why should the **w** cease while I
6: 9 hands will be weakened in the **w**,
6:16 for they perceived that this **w**
7:70 fathers' houses gave to the **w**.
7:71 gave to the treasury of the **w**
10:33 and all the **w** of the house of
11:12 Their brethren who did the **w** of
13:10 and the singers who did the **w**
Esth 3: 9 the hands of those who do the **w**,
9: 3 all those doing the king's **w**,
Job 1:10 You have blessed the **w** of his
10: 3 That You should despise the **w**
14:15 You shall desire the **w** of Your
24: 5 They go out to their **w**,
34:11 repays man according to his **w**,
34:19 For they are all the **w** of His
36: 9 Then He tells them their **w** and
36:24 "Remember to magnify His **w**,
37: 7 That all men may know His **w**.
Ps 8: 3 the **w** of Your fingers,
9:16 The wicked is snared in the **w**
28: 4 Give them according to the **w**
33: 4 And all His **w** is done in
58: 2 in heart you **w** wickedness;
62:12 to each one according to his **w**.
64: 9 And shall declare the **w** of
74: 6 they break down its carved **w**,
77:12 also meditate on all Your **w**,
88:10 Will You **w** wonders for the
90:16 Let Your **w** appear to Your
90:17 And establish the **w** of our
90:17 establish the **w** of our hands.
92: 4 made me glad through Your **w**;
95: 9 tried Me, though they saw My **w**.
101: 3 I hate the **w** of those who fall
102:25 And the heavens are the **w** of
104:23 Man goes out to his **w** And to
111: 3 His **w** is honorable and
115: 4 The **w** of men's hands.
135:15 The **w** of men's hands.
141: 4 wicked works With men who **w**
143: 5 I muse on the **w** of Your hands.
Prov 11:18 wicked man does deceptive **w**,
16:11 weights in the bag are His **w**.
18: 9 He who is slothful in his **w** Is
21: 8 for the pure, his **w** is right.
22:29 see a man who excels in his **w**?
24:27 Prepare your outside **w**,
24:29 to the man according to his **w**.
Eccl 2:17 I hated life because the **w**
2:23 and his **w** burdensome; even in
2:26 to the sinner He gives the **w**
3:11 that no one can find out the **w**
3:17 every purpose and for every **w**.
4: 3 Who has not seen the evil **w**
4: 4 all toil and every skillful **w**
5: 6 your excuse and destroy the **w**
7:13 Consider the **w** of God;
8: 9 and applied my heart to every **w**
8:11 the sentence against an evil **w**
8:14 it happens according to the **w**
8:14 it happens according to the **w**
8:17 then I saw all the **w** of God,
8:17 a man cannot find out the **w**
9:10 for there is no **w** or device
12:14 For God will bring every **w** into
Song 7: 1 The **w** of the hands of a
Isa 1:31 And the **w** of it as a spark;
2: 8 They worship the **w** of their
5:12 But they do not regard the **w**
5:19 make speed and hasten His **w**,
10:12 LORD has performed all His **w**
17: 8 The **w** of his hands; He will
19: 9 Moreover those who **w** in fine
19:14 Egypt to err in all her **w**,
19:15 Neither will there be any **w**
19:25 and Assyria the **w** of My hands,
28:21 of Gibeon—That He may do His **w**,
28:21 may do His work, His awesome **w**,
29:14 I will again do a marvelous **w**
29:14 A marvelous **w** and a wonder;
29:23 The **w** of My hands, in his
30:24 and the young donkeys that **w**
31: 2 against the help of those who **w**
32: 6 And his heart will **w** iniquity:
32:17 The **w** of righteousness will be
37:19 but the **w** of men's hands—wood
40:10 And His **w** before Him.
41:24 And your **w** is nothing;
43:13 I **w**, and who will reverse
45:11 And concerning the **w** of My
49: 4 And my **w** with my God.'"
54:16 forth an instrument for his **w**;
60:21 The **w** of My hands, That I may
61: 8 I will direct their **w** in
62:11 And His **w** before Him.'"
64: 8 And all we are the **w** of Your
65: 7 I will measure their former **w**
65:22 My elect shall long enjoy the **w**
Jer 10: 3 The **w** of the hands of the
10: 9 The **w** of the craftsman And of
10: 9 They are all the **w** of
10:15 a **w** of errors; In the time of
17:22 the Sabbath day, nor do any **w**,
17:24 to do no **w** in it,
22:13 gives him nothing for his **w**,
31:16 For your **w** shall be rewarded,
32:19 in counsel and mighty in **w**,
32:30 Me only to anger with the **w** of
48:10 Cursed is he who does the **w** of
50:25 For this is the **w** of the Lord
50:29 Repay her according to her **w**;
51:10 let us declare in Zion the **w**
51:18 a **w** of errors; In the time of
Lam 3:64 According to the **w** of their
4: 2 The **w** of the hands of the
Ezek 15: 4 Is it useful for any **w**?
15: 5 will it be useful for any **w**
44:14 of the temple, for all its **w**,
Hos 13: 2 All of it is the **w** of
14: 3 will we say anymore to the **w**
Mic 2: 1 And **w** out evil on their beds!
5:13 shall no more worship the **w** of
Hab 1: 5 For I will **w** a work in
1: 5 For I will work a **w** in your
3: 2 revive Your **w** in the midst of
Zeph 2:14 He will lay bare the cedar **w**.
Hag 2: 4 says the LORD, 'and **w**;
2:14 and so is every **w** of their
Mt 14: 2 these powers are at **w** in him.
21:28 **w** today in my vineyard.'
26:10 For she has done a good **w** for
Mk 6: 5 Now He could do no mighty **w**
6:14 these powers are at **w** in him.
13:34 his servants, and to each his **w**,
14: 6 She has done a good **w** for Me.
Lk 13:14 days on which men ought to **w**;
Jn 4:34 sent Me, and to finish His **w**.
6:28 that we may **w** the works of
6:29 This is the **w** of God, that you
6:30 What **w** will You do?
7:21 and said to them, "I did one **w**,
9: 4 I must **w** the works of Him who
9: 4 is coming when no one can **w**.
10:33 For a good **w** we do not stone
17: 4 I have finished the **w** which You
Acts 5:38 for if this plan or this **w** is
13: 2 Me Barnabas and Saul for the **w**
13:41 and perish! For I **w** a
13:41 For I work a **w** in
13:41 A **w** which you will by
14:26 to the grace of God for the **w**
15:38 had not gone with them to the **w**.
Rom 2:15 who show the **w** of the law
4: 5 But to him who does not **w** but
7: 5 aroused by the law were at **w**
8:28 And we know that all things **w**
9:28 He will finish the **w** and
9:28 will make a short **w** upon
11: 6 otherwise **w** is no longer work.
11: 6 otherwise work is no longer **w**.
14:20 Do not destroy the **w** of God for
1 Cor 3:13 each one's **w** will become clear;
3:13 the fire will test each one's **w**,
3:14 If anyone's **w** which he has built
3:15 If anyone's **w** is burned, he will
9: 1 Are you not my **w** in the Lord?
15:58 always abounding in the **w** of
16:10 for he does the **w** of the Lord,
2 Cor 9: 8 an abundance for every good **w**.
Gal 6: 4 let each one examine his own **w**,
Eph 4:12 of the saints for the **w** of
4:19 to **w** all uncleanness with
Phil 1: 6 that He who has begun a good **w**
2:12 **w** out your own salvation with
2:30 because for the **w** of Christ he
Col 1:10 being fruitful in every good **w**
1 Th 1: 3 without ceasing your **w** of
4:11 and to **w** with your own hands,
2 Th 1:11 of His goodness and the **w** of
2: 7 of lawlessness is already at **w**;
2:17 you in every good word and **w**.
3:10 you this: If anyone will not **w**,
3:12 Lord Jesus Christ that they **w**
1 Tim 3: 1 a bishop, he desires a good **w**.
5:10 followed every good **w**.
2 Tim 2:21 prepared for every good **w**.
3:17 equipped for every good **w**.
4: 5 do the **w** of an evangelist,
4:18 deliver me from every evil **w**
Titus 1:16 disqualified for every good **w**.
3: 1 to be ready for every good **w**,
Heb 1:10 the heavens are the **w** of
6:10 is not unjust to forget your **w**
13:21 you complete in every good **w**
Jas 1: 4 patience have its perfect **w**,
1:25 hearer but a doer of the **w**,
1 Pe 1:17 according to each one's **w**,
Rev 22:12 to every one according to his **w**.

WORK'S (1/1)

1 Th 5:13 in love for their **w** sake.

WORKED (32/30) WORK

Ex 8:18 Now the magicians so **w** with
28: 6 woven linen, artistically **w**.
36: 8 artisans among them who **w** on
36:35 it was **w** with an artistic
Deut 21: 3 a heifer which has not been **w**
Josh 9: 4 they **w** craftily, and went and
Ruth 2:19 with whom she had **w**,
2:19 The man's name with whom I **w**
1 Sam 14:45 for he has **w** with God this
2 Ki 12:11 carpenters and builders who **w**

2 Chr 24:12 and also those who **w** in iron
34:10 gave it to the workmen who **w**
Neh 4:16 that half of my servants **w** at
4:17 so that with one hand they **w**
9:18 And **w** great provocations,
9:26 And they **w** great provocations.
Ps 78:43 When He **w** His signs in Egypt,
Ezek 23:29 take away all you have **w** for,
29:20 because they **w** for Me,' says
Dan 4: 2 that the Most High God has **w**
Hag 1:14 and they came and **w** on the
Mt 20:12 These last men have **w** only one
Acts 15:12 miracles and wonders God had **w**
18: 3 he stayed with them and **w**;
19:11 Now God **w** unusual miracles by
Gal 2: 8 (for He who **w** effectively in
2: 8 to the circumcised also **w**
Eph 1:20 which He **w** in Christ when He
2 Th 3: 8 but **w** with labor and toil night
Heb 11:33 **w** righteousness, obtained
2 Jn 8 do not lose those things we **w**
Rev 19:20 him the false prophet who **w**

WORKER (8/8) WORK, WORKERS

1 Ki 7:14 was a man of Tyre, a bronze **w**;
Eccl 3: 9 What profit has the **w** from that
Mt 10:10 for a **w** is worthy of his food.
Rom 16: 9 our fellow **w** in Christ,
16:21 Timothy, my fellow **w**,
2 Cor 8:23 he is my partner and fellow **w**
Phil 2:25 my brother, fellow **w**,
2 Tim 2:15 a **w** who does not need to be

WORKERS (35/35) WORKER

1 Chr 4:21 of the house of the linen **w** of
Job 31: 3 And disaster for the **w** of
34: 8 goes in company with the **w** of
34:22 shadow of death Where the **w**
Ps 5: 5 You hate all **w** of iniquity.
6: 8 all you **w** of iniquity; For the
14: 4 Have all the **w** of iniquity no
28: 3 the wicked And with the **w** of
36:12 There the **w** of iniquity have
37: 1 Nor be envious of the **w** of
53: 4 Have the **w** of iniquity no
59: 2 Deliver me from the **w** of
64: 2 From the rebellion of the **w** of
92: 7 And when all the **w** of iniquity
92: 9 All the **w** of iniquity shall be
94: 4 All the **w** of iniquity boast in
94:16 stand up for me against the **w**
125: 5 lead them away With the **w** of
141: 9 And from the traps of the **w** of
Prov 10:29 will come to the **w** of
21:15 will come to the **w** of
Ezek 48:18 shall be food for the **w** of the
48:19 The **w** of the city, from all the
Lk 13:27 all you **w** of iniquity.'
Acts 19:25 them together with the **w** of
Rom 16: 3 my fellow **w** in Christ Jesus,
1 Cor 3: 9 For we are God's fellow **w**;
12:29 Are all **w** of miracles?
2 Cor 1:24 but are fellow **w** for your joy;
6: 1 as **w** together with Him also
11:13 false apostles, deceitful **w**,
Phil 3: 2 of dogs, beware of evil **w**,
4: 3 and the rest of my fellow **w**,
Col 4:11 These are my only fellow **w**
3 Jn 8 that we may become fellow **w** for

WORKING (27/26) WORK

1 Ki 7:14 understanding and skill in **w**
1 Chr 22:16 is no limit. Arise and begin **w**,
Ezra 3: 9 as one to oversee those **w** on
Neh 4:22 guard by night and a **w** party
Ps 52: 2 a sharp razor, **w** deceitfully.
74:12 **W** salvation in the midst of
Ezek 46: 1 shall be shut the six **w** days;
Mk 16:20 the Lord **w** with them and
Jn 5:17 My Father has been **w** until now,
5:17 until now, and I have been **w**.
1 Cor 4:12 **w** with our own hands.
9: 6 have no right to refrain from **w**?
12:10 to another the **w** of miracles, to
2 Cor 4:12 So then death is **w** in us, but
4:17 is **w** for us a far more
Gal 5: 6 but faith **w** through love.
Eph 1:19 according to the **w** of His
3: 7 given to me by the effective **w**
4:16 according to the effective **w** by
4:28 **w** with his hands what is good,
Phil 3:21 according to the **w** by which He
Col 1:29 striving according to His **w**
2:12 Him through faith in the **w** of
2 Th 2: 9 one is according to the **w** of
3:11 not **w** at all, but are
Heb 13:21 **w** in you what is well pleasing
Jas 2:22 Do you see that faith was **w**

WORKINGS (2/1)

Ezek 1:16 of the wheels and their **w** was
1:16 The appearance of their **w** was,

WORKMAN (5/5) WORK, WORKMANSHIP, WORKMEN

Song 7: 1 of the hands of a skillful **w**.
Isa 40:19 The **w** molds an image,
40:20 seeks for himself a skillful **w**
Jer 10: 3 The work of the hands of the **w**,
Hos 8: 6 A **w** made it, and it is not

WORKMANSHIP (16/15) WORKMAN

Ex 28: 8 on it, shall be of the same **w**,
28:15 woven according to the **w** of
31: 3 and in all manner of **w**,
31: 5 to work in all manner of **w**.
35:31 knowledge and all manner of **w**,
35:33 in all manner of artistic **w**.
39: 5 was on it was of the same **w**,
39: 8 artistically woven like the **w**
Num 8: 4 Now this **w** of the lampstand was
1 Ki 7: 8 inside the hall, of like **w**.
7:33 The **w** of the wheels was like
7:33 of the wheels was like the **w**
2 Ki 16:10 pattern, according to all its **w**.
1 Chr 28:21 with you for all manner of **w**,
Ezek 28:13 The **w** of your timbrels and
Eph 2:10 For we are His **w**, created in

WORKMEN (7/7) WORKMAN

2 Ki 12:14 But they gave that to the **w**,
12:15 the money to be paid to **w**,
1 Chr 22:15 Moreover there are **w** with you
2 Chr 24:13 So the **w** labored, and the work
34:10 and they gave it to the **w** who
34:17 hand of the overseers and the **w**.
Isa 44:11 would be ashamed; And the **w**,

WORKMEN'S (1/1)

Judg 5:26 hand to the **w** hammer;

WORKS (250/235) WORK

Ex 23:24 nor do according to their **w**;
31: 4 "to design artistic **w**,
35:32 "to design artistic **w**,
35:35 and those who design artistic **w**.
Num 16:28 has sent me to do all these **w**,
Deut 3:24 can do anything like Your **w**
15:10 will bless you in all your **w**
Josh 24:31 who had known all the **w** of the
Judg 2: 7 who had seen all the great **w** of
1 Sam 8: 8 According to all the **w** which
19: 4 and because his **w** have been
2 Sam 12:31 them cross over to the brick **w**.
1 Ki 13:11 came and told him all the **w**
2 Ki 22:17 Me to anger with all the **w** of
1 Chr 16: 9 Talk of all His wondrous **w**!
16:12 Remember His marvelous **w** which
28:19 all the **w** of these plans."
2 Chr 20:37 the LORD has destroyed your **w**.
32:30 Hezekiah prospered in all his **w**.
34:25 Me to anger with all the **w** of
Neh 6:14 according to these their **w**,
9:35 they turn from their wicked **w**.
Job 23: 9 When He **w** on the left hand, I
33:29 God **w** all these things,
34:25 Therefore he knows their **w**;
37:14 and consider the wondrous **w** of
37:16 Those wondrous **w** of Him who is
Ps 8: 6 to have dominion over the **w** of
9: 1 tell of all Your marvelous **w**.
14: 1 They have done abominable **w**,
15: 2 And **w** righteousness,
17: 4 Concerning the **w** of men,
26: 7 tell of all Your wondrous **w**.
28: 5 they do not regard the **w** of
33:15 He considers all their **w**.
40: 5 are Your wonderful **w** Which
46: 8 behold the **w** of the LORD,
66: 3 'How awesome are Your **w**!
66: 5 Come and see the **w** of God;
71:17 day I declare Your wondrous **w**.
73:28 That I may declare all Your **w**.
75: 1 For Your wondrous **w** declare
77:11 I will remember the **w** of the
78: 4 strength and His wonderful **w**
78: 7 And not forget the **w** of God,
78:11 And forgot His **w** And His
78:32 not believe in His wondrous **w**.
86: 8 Nor are there any **w** like
86: 8 there any works like Your **w**.
92: 4 I will triumph in the **w** of
92: 5 how great are Your **w**!
101: 7 He who **w** deceit shall not dwell
103:22 Bless the LORD, all His **w**,
104:13 with the fruit of Your **w**.
104:24 how manifold are Your **w**!
104:31 May the LORD rejoice in His **w**.
105: 2 Talk of all His wondrous **w**!
105: 5 Remember His marvelous **w** which
106:13 They soon forgot His **w**;
106:22 Wondrous **w** in the land of Ham,
106:35 Gentiles And learned their **w**;
106:39 were defiled by their own **w**,
107: 8 And for His wonderful **w** to
107:15 And for His wonderful **w** to
107:21 And for His wonderful **w** to
107:22 And declare His **w** with
107:24 They see the **w** of the LORD,
107:31 And for His wonderful **w** to
111: 2 The **w** of the LORD are great,
111: 4 He has made His wonderful **w** to
111: 6 His people the power of His **w**,
111: 7 The **w** of His hands are verity
118:17 And declare the **w** of the
119:27 I meditate on Your wondrous **w**.
138: 8 Do not forsake the **w** of Your
139:14 Marvelous are Your **w**,
141: 4 To practice wicked **w** With men
143: 5 I meditate on all Your **w**;
145: 4 generation shall praise Your **w**
145: 5 And on Your wondrous **w**.
145: 9 mercies are over all His **w**.
145:10 All Your **w** shall praise You,
145:17 Gracious in all His **w**.
Prov 8:22 Before His **w** of old.
16: 3 Commit your **w** to the LORD,
26:28 And a flattering mouth **w** ruin.
31:13 And willingly **w** with her
31:31 And let her own **w** praise her
Eccl 1:14 I have seen all the **w** that are
2: 4 I made my **w** great, I built
2:11 Then I looked on all the **w** that
3:22 man should rejoice in his own **w**,
9: 1 and the wise and their **w** are
9: 7 God has already accepted your **w**.
11: 5 So you do not know the **w** of
Isa 26:12 You have also done all our **w**
29:15 And their **w** are in the dark;
41:29 Their **w** are nothing;
44:12 blacksmith with the tongs **w**
44:12 And **w** it with the strength of
57:12 your righteousness And your **w**,
59: 6 cover themselves with their **w**;
59: 6 Their **w** are works of
59: 6 Their works are **w** of
66:18 For I know their **w** and their
Jer 1:16 And worshiped the **w** of their
7:13 you have done all these **w**,
8: 8 pen of the scribe certainly **w**
21: 2 to all His wonderful **w**,
25: 6 anger with the **w** of your hands;
25: 7 anger with the **w** of your hands
25:14 deeds and according to the **w**
44: 8 wrath with the **w** of your hands,
48: 7 you have trusted in your **w** and
Ezek 6: 6 and your **w** may be abolished.
33:13 none of his righteous **w** shall
Dan 4:37 all of whose **w** are truth, and
6:27 And He **w** signs and wonders In
9:14 God is righteous in all the **w**
Am 8: 7 never forget any of their **w**.
Jon 3:10 Then God saw their **w**,
Mic 6:16 All the **w** of Ahab's house are
Mt 5:16 that they may see your good **w**
11: 2 heard in prison about the **w** of
11:20 in which most of His mighty **w**
11:21 if the mighty **w** which were done
11:23 for if the mighty **w** which were
13:54 this wisdom and these mighty **w**?
13:58 Now He did not do many mighty **w**
16:27 reward each according to his **w**.
23: 3 do not do according to their **w**;
23: 5 But all their **w** they do to be
Mk 6: 2 that such mighty **w** are
9:39 for no one who **w** a miracle in
Lk 10:13 if the mighty **w** which were done
19:37 loud voice for all the mighty **w**
Jn 5:20 and He will show Him greater **w**
5:36 for the **w** which the Father has
5:36 the very **w** that I do—bear
6:28 that we may work the **w** of
7: 3 disciples also may see the **w**
7: 7 I testify of it that its **w** are
8:39 you would do the **w** of Abraham.
9: 3 but that the **w** of God should be
9: 4 I must work the **w** of Him who
10:25 The **w** that I do in My Father's
10:32 Many good **w** I have shown you
10:32 For which of those **w** do you
10:37 If I do not do the **w** of My
10:38 not believe Me, believe the **w**,
11:47 For this Man **w** many signs.
14:10 who dwells in Me does the **w**.
14:11 the sake of the **w** themselves.
14:12 the **w** that I do he will do
14:12 and greater **w** than these he
15:24 I had not done among them the **w**
Acts 2:11 own tongues the wonderful **w** of
7:41 and rejoiced in the **w** of their
9:36 This woman was full of good **w**
10:35 nation whoever fears Him and **w**
15:18 God from eternity are all His **w**.
26:20 and do **w** befitting repentance.

Rom 2:10 and peace to everyone who **w**
3:27 Of **w**? No, but by the law of
4: 2 if Abraham was justified by **w**,
4: 4 Now to him who **w**,
4: 6 righteousness apart from **w**:
9:11 not of **w** but of Him who calls),
9:32 by the **w** of the law. For they
11: 6 then it is no longer of **w**;
11: 6 But if it is of **w**,
13: 3 are not a terror to good **w**,
13:12 let us cast off the **w** of
1 Cor 12: 6 the same God who **w** all
12:11 But one and the same Spirit **w**
16:16 and to everyone who **w** and
2 Cor 11:15 will be according to their **w**.
Gal 2:16 justified by the **w** of the law
2:16 in Christ and not by the **w** of
2:16 for by the **w** of the law no
3: 2 receive the Spirit by the **w** of
3: 5 the Spirit to you and **w**
3: 5 does He do it by the **w** of
3:10 For as many as are of the **w** of
5:19 Now the **w** of the flesh are

Eph 1:11 to the purpose of Him who **w**
2: 2 the spirit who now **w** in the
2: 9 not of **w**, lest anyone should
2:10 in Christ Jesus for good **w**,
3:20 to the power that **w** in us,
5:11 with the unfruitful **w** of
Phil 2:13 for it is God who **w** in you both
Col 1:21 in your mind by wicked **w**,
1:29 to His working which **w** in me
1 Th 2:13 which also effectively **w** in you
1 Tim 2:10 godliness, with good **w**.
5:10 well reported for good **w**:
5:25 the good **w** of some are
6:18 that they be rich in good **w**,
2 Tim 1: 9 calling, not according to our **w**,
4:14 repay him according to his **w**.
Titus 1:16 but in **w** they deny Him, being
2: 7 to be a pattern of good **w**;
2:14 people, zealous for good **w**.
3: 5 not by **w** of righteousness which
3: 8 be careful to maintain good **w**.
3:14 also learn to maintain good **w**,
Heb 2: 7 And set him over the **w**
3: 9 And saw My **w** forty
4: 3 although the **w** were finished
4: 4 day from all His **w**";
4:10 himself also ceased from his **w**
6: 1 of repentance from dead **w** and
9:14 your conscience from dead **w** to
10:24 to stir up love and good **w**,
Jas 2:14 has faith but does not have **w**?
2:17 itself, if it does not have **w**,
2:18 "You have faith, and I have **w**.
2:18 me your faith without your **w**,
2:18 will show you my faith by my **w**.
2:20 that faith without **w** is dead?
2:21 our father justified by **w** when
2:22 was working together with his **w**,
2:22 and by **w** faith was made
2:24 that a man is justified by **w**,
2:25 the harlot also justified by **w**
2:26 so faith without **w** is dead
3:13 conduct that his **w** are done
1 Pe 2:12 by your good **w** which they
2 Pe 3:10 both the earth and the **w** that
1 Jn 3: 8 that He might destroy the **w** of
3:12 Because his **w** were evil and his
Rev 2: 2 'I know your **w**, your labor,
2: 5 repent and do the first **w**,
2: 9 'I know your **w**, tribulation,
2:13 'I know your **w**, and where you
2:19 'I know your **w**, love, service,
2:19 patience; and as for your **w**,
2:23 one of you according to your **w**.
2:26 and keeps My **w** until the end,
3: 1 seven stars: "I know your **w**,
3: 2 for I have not found your **w**
3: 8 'I know your **w**. See, I have
3:15 'I know your **w**, that you are
9:20 did not repent of the **w** of
14:13 and their **w** follow them."
15: 3 and marvelous are Your **w**,
18: 6 her double according to her **w**;
20:12 judged according to their **w**,
20:13 each one according to his **w**.

WORLD (252/217) FOREVER, WORLDLY, WORLD'S, WORLDS

1 Sam 2: 8 And He has set the **w** upon
2 Sam 22:16 The foundations of the **w** were
1 Chr 16:30 The **w** also is firmly
Job 18:18 And chased out of the **w**.
34:13 Him over the whole **w**?
Ps 9: 8 He shall judge the **w** in
17:14 From men of the **w** who have
18:15 The foundations of the **w** were
19: 4 their words to the end of the **w**.
22:27 All the ends of the **w** Shall
24: 1 The **w** and those who dwell
33: 8 all the inhabitants of the **w**
49: 1 ear, all inhabitants of the **w**,
50:12 For the **w** is Mine, and all
77:18 The lightnings lit up the **w**;
89:11 The **w** and all its fullness,
90: 2 had formed the earth and the **w**,
93: 1 Surely the **w** is established,
96:10 The **w** also is firmly
96:13 He shall judge the **w** with
97: 4 His lightnings light the **w**;
98: 7 The **w** and those who dwell in
98: 9 He shall judge the **w**,
Prov 8:26 Or the primeval dust of the **w**.
8:31 Rejoicing in His inhabited **w**,
Isa 13:11 I will punish the **w** for its
14:17 Who made the **w** as a wilderness
14:21 And fill the face of the **w**
18: 3 All inhabitants of the **w** and
23:17 with all the kingdoms of the **w**
24: 4 The **w** languishes and fades
26: 9 The inhabitants of the **w** will
26:18 have the inhabitants of the **w**
27: 6 And fill the face of the **w**
34: 1 The **w** and all things that come
38:11 among the inhabitants of the **w**.
62:11 proclaimed To the end of the **w**:
64: 4 since the beginning of the **w**
Jer 10:12 He has established the **w** by
25:26 and all the kingdoms of the **w**
51:15 He has established the **w** by
Lam 4:12 And all inhabitants of the **w**,
Nah 1: 5 the **w** and all who dwell in it.
Mt 4: 8 Him all the kingdoms of the **w**
5:14 "You are the light of the **w**.
13:22 and the cares of this **w** and the
13:35 the foundation of the **w**.
13:38 "The field is the **w**.
16:26 a man if he gains the whole **w**,
18: 7 Woe to the **w** because of
24:14 will be preached in all the **w**
24:21 since the beginning of the **w**
25:34 from the foundation of the **w**:
26:13 is preached in the whole **w**,
Mk 4:19 "and the cares of this **w**,
8:36 a man if he gains the whole **w**,
14: 9 is preached in the whole **w**,
16:15 Go into all the **w** and preach the
Lk 1:70 Who have been since the **w**
2: 1 Caesar Augustus that all the **w**
4: 5 Him all the kingdoms of the **w**
9:25 a man if he gains the whole **w**,
11:50 from the foundation of the **w**
12:30 things the nations of the **w**
16: 8 For the sons of this **w** are more
Jn 1: 9 to every man coming into the **w**.
1:10 He was in the **w**,
1:10 and the **w** was made through Him,
1:10 and the **w** did not know Him.
1:29 takes away the sin of the **w**!
3:16 For God so loved the **w** that He
3:17 not send His Son into the **w** to
3:17 into the world to condemn the **w**,
3:17 but that the **w** through Him
3:19 the light has come into the **w**,
4:42 the Christ, the Savior of the **w**.
6:14 who is to come into the **w**.
6:33 heaven and gives life to the **w**.
6:51 give for the life of the **w**.
7: 4 things, show Yourself to the **w**.
7: 7 The **w** cannot hate you, but it
8:12 "I am the light of the **w**.
8:23 from above. You are of this **w**;
8:23 this world; I am not of this **w**.
8:26 and I speak to the **w** those
9: 5 "As long as I am in the **w**,
9: 5 world, I am the light of the **w**.
9:32 Since the **w** began it has been
9:39 I have come into this **w**,
10:36 sanctified and sent into the **w**,
11: 9 he sees the light of this **w**.
11:27 God, who is to come into the **w**.
12:19 the **w** has gone after Him!"
12:25 he who hates his life in this **w**
12:31 "Now is the judgment of this **w**;
12:31 now the ruler of this **w** will be
12:46 come as a light into the **w**,
12:47 I did not come to judge the **w**
12:47 the world but to save the **w**.
13: 1 He should depart from this **w**
13: 1 loved His own who were in the **w**,
14:17 whom the **w** cannot receive,
14:19 little while longer and the **w**
14:22 to us, and not to the **w**?
14:27 not as the **w** gives do I give to
14:30 for the ruler of this **w** is
14:31 But that the **w** may know that I
15:18 If the **w** hates you, you know
15:19 "If you were of the **w**,
15:19 the **w** would love its own.
15:19 because you are not of the **w**,
15:19 but I chose you out of the **w**,
15:19 therefore the **w** hates you.
16: 8 He will convict the **w** of sin,
16:11 because the ruler of this **w** is
16:20 but the **w** will rejoice; and you
16:21 being has been born into the **w**.
16:28 Father and have come into the **w**.
16:28 I leave the **w** and go to the
16:33 In the **w** you will have
16:33 cheer, I have overcome the **w**.
17: 5 I had with You before the **w**
17: 6 You have given Me out of the **w**.
17: 9 I do not pray for the **w** but for
17:11 "Now I am no longer in the **w**,
17:11 world, but these are in the **w**,
17:12 I was with them in the **w**,
17:13 these things I speak in the **w**,
17:14 and the **w** has hated them
17:14 because they are not of the **w**,
17:14 just as I am not of the **w**.
17:15 should take them out of the **w**,
17:16 "They are not of the **w**,
17:16 just as I am not of the **w**.
17:18 "As You sent Me into the **w**,
17:18 also have sent them into the **w**.
17:21 that the **w** may believe that You
17:23 and that the **w** may know that
17:24 before the foundation of the **w**.
17:25 The **w** has not known You,
18:20 him, "I spoke openly to the **w**.
18:36 "My kingdom is not of this **w**.
18:36 If My kingdom were of this **w**,
18:37 cause I have come into the **w**,
21:25 I suppose that even the **w**
Acts 3:21 His holy prophets since the **w**
11:28 famine throughout all the **w**,
17: 6 These who have turned the **w**
17:24 who made the **w** and everything
17:31 on which He will judge the **w**
19:27 whom all Asia and the **w**
24: 5 all the Jews throughout the **w**,
Rom 1: 8 of throughout the whole **w**.
1:20 For since the creation of the **w**
3: 6 then how will God judge the **w**?
3:19 and all the **w** may become guilty
4:13 he would be the heir of the **w**
5:12 one man sin entered the **w**,
5:13 until the law sin was in the **w**,
10:18 to the ends of the **w**.
11:12 their fall is riches for the **w**,
11:15 is the reconciling of the **w**,
12: 2 do not be conformed to this **w**,
16:25 kept secret since the **w** began
1 Cor 1:20 foolish the wisdom of this **w**?
1:21 the **w** through wisdom did not
1:27 the foolish things of the **w** to
1:27 the weak things of the **w** to
1:28 and the base things of the **w** and
2:12 not the spirit of the **w**,
3:19 For the wisdom of this **w** is
3:22 or the **w** or life or death, or
4: 9 been made a spectacle to the **w**,
4:13 been made as the filth of the **w**,
5:10 immoral people of this **w**,
5:10 would need to go out of the **w**.
6: 2 the saints will judge the **w**?
6: 2 And if the **w** will be judged by
7:31 and those who use this **w** as not
7:31 For the form of this **w** is
7:33 cares about the things of the **w**—
7:34 cares about the things of the **w**—
8: 4 an idol is nothing in the **w**,
11:32 may not be condemned with the **w**.
14:10 kinds of languages in the **w**,
2 Cor 1:12 we conducted ourselves in the **w**
5:19 in Christ reconciling the **w** to
7:10 but the sorrow of the **w**
Gal 4: 3 under the elements of the **w**.
6:14 by whom the **w** has been
6:14 crucified to me, and I to the **w**.
Eph 1: 4 before the foundation of the **w**,
2: 2 to the course of this **w**,
2:12 hope and without God in the **w**.
Phil 2:15 you shine as lights in the **w**,
Col 1: 6 as it has also in all the **w**,
2: 8 the basic principles of the **w**,
2:20 the basic principles of the **w**,
2:20 why, as though living in the **w**,
1 Tim 1:15 Christ Jesus came into the **w**
3:16 Gentiles, Believed on in the **w**,
6: 7 we brought nothing into this **w**,
2 Tim 4:10 me, having loved this present **w**,
Heb 1: 6 brings the firstborn into the **w**,
2: 5 For He has not put the **w** to
4: 3 from the foundation of the **w**.
9:26 since the foundation of the **w**;
10: 5 when He came into the **w**,
11: 7 by which he condemned the **w** and
11:38 of whom the **w** was not worthy.
Jas 1:27 oneself unspotted from the **w**.
2: 5 not chosen the poor of this **w**
3: 6 a **w** of iniquity. The tongue is
4: 4 that friendship with the **w** is
4: 4 wants to be a friend of the **w**
1 Pe 1:20 before the foundation of the **w**,
5: 9 by your brotherhood in the **w**.
2 Pe 1: 4 corruption that is in the **w**
2: 5 and did not spare the ancient **w**,
2: 5 bringing in the flood on the **w**
2:20 escaped the pollutions of the **w**
3: 6 by which the **w** that then
1 Jn 2: 2 only but also for the whole **w**.
2:15 Do not love the **w** or the things
2:15 world or the things in the **w**.
2:15 If anyone loves the **w**,
2:16 For all that is in the **w**—
2:16 of the Father but is of the **w**.
2:17 And the **w** is passing away,
3: 1 Therefore the **w** does not
3:13 if the **w** hates you.
4: 1 have gone out into the **w**.
4: 3 and is now already in the **w**.
4: 4 greater than he who is in the **w**.
4: 5 They are of the **w**.
4: 5 they speak as of the **w**,
4: 5 and the **w** hears them.
4: 9 only begotten Son into the **w**,
4:14 the Son as Savior of the **w**.
4:17 as He is, so are we in this **w**.
5: 4 is born of God overcomes the **w**.
5: 4 victory that has overcome the **w**—
5: 5 Who is he who overcomes the **w**,
5:19 and the whole **w** lies under
2 Jn 7 have gone out into the **w** who
Rev 3:10 shall come upon the whole **w**,
11:15 The kingdoms of this **w** have
12: 9 Satan, who deceives the whole **w**;
13: 3 And all the **w** marveled and
13: 8 from the foundation of the **w**.
16:14 of the earth and of the whole **w**,
17: 8 from the foundation of the **w**,

WORLD'S (1/1) WORLD

1 Jn 3:17 But whoever has this **w** goods,

WORLDLY (1/1) WORLD

Titus 2:12 ungodliness and **w** lusts,

WORLDS (2/2) WORLD

Heb 1: 2 through whom also He made the **w**;
11: 3 faith we understand that the **w**

WORM (11/11) WORMS

Job 17:14 are my father,' And to the **w**,
24:20 The **w** should feed sweetly on
25: 6 And a son of man, who is a **w**?
Ps 22: 6 But I am a **w**, and no man;
Isa 41:14 you **w** Jacob, You men of
51: 8 And the **w** will eat them like
66:24 For their **w** does not die,
Jon 4: 7 the next day God prepared a **w**,
Mk 9:44 'Their **w** does not die,
9:46 'Their **w** does not die,
9:48 'Their **w** does not die,

WORMS (7/7) WORM

Ex 16:20 and it bred **w** and stank.
16:24 nor were there any **w** in it.
Deut 28:39 for the **w** shall eat them.
Job 7: 5 My flesh is caked with **w** and
21:26 the dust, And **w** cover them.
Isa 14:11 under you, And **w** cover you.'
Acts 12:23 And he was eaten by **w** and died.

WORMWOOD (10/9)

Deut 29:18 a root bearing bitterness or **w**;
Prov 5: 4 in the end she is bitter as **w**,
Jer 9:15 feed them, this people, with **w**,
23:15 I will feed them with **w**,
Lam 3:15 He has made me drink **w**.
3:19 The **w** and the gall.
Am 5: 7 You who turn justice to **w**,
6:12 fruit of righteousness into **w**,
Rev 8:11 The name of the star is **W**.
8:11 A third of the waters became **w**,

WORN (4/3) WEAR

Deut 29: 5 Your clothes have not **w** out on
29: 5 and your sandals have not **w** out
Esth 6: 8 be brought which the king has **w**,
Job 16: 7 But now He has **w** me out;

WORRIED (2/2) WORRY

1 Sam 9: 5 about the donkeys and become **w**
Lk 10:41 you are **w** and troubled about

WORRY (9/8) WORRIED, WORRYING

Mt 6:25 do not **w** about your life,
6:28 So why do you **w** about clothing?
6:31 "Therefore do not **w**,
6:34 Therefore do not **w** about
6:34 for tomorrow will **w** about its
10:19 do not **w** about how or what you
Mk 13:11 do not **w** beforehand,
Lk 12:11 do not **w** about how or what you
12:22 do not **w** about your life,

WORRYING (3/3) WORRY

1 Sam 10: 2 the donkeys and is **w** about you,
Mt 6:27 Which of you by **w** can add one
Lk 12:25 And which of you by **w** can add

WORSE (23/22)

Gen 19: 9 now we will deal **w** with you
2 Sam 13:16 evil of sending me away is **w**
19: 7 And that will be **w** for you than
1 Ki 16:25 and did **w** than all who were
Jer 7:26 They did **w** than their fathers.
16:12 And you have done **w** than your
Dan 1:10 he see your faces looking **w**
Mt 9:16 garment, and the tear is made **w**.
12:45 last state of that man is **w**
27:64 So the last deception will be **w**
Mk 2:21 the old, and the tear is made **w**.
5:26 no better, but rather grew **w**.
Lk 11:26 last state of that man is **w**
13: 2 that these Galileans were **w**
13: 4 do you think that they were **w**
Jn 5:14 lest a **w** thing come upon you."
1 Cor 8: 8 if we do not eat are we the **w**.
11:17 for the better but for the **w**.
1 Tim 5: 8 has denied the faith and is **w**
2 Tim 3:13 men and impostors will grow **w**
3:13 impostors will grow worse and **w**,
Heb 10:29 Of how much **w** punishment, do you
2 Pe 2:20 the latter end is **w** for them

WORSHIP (112/105) WORSHIPED, WORSHIPERS, WORSHIPS

Gen 22: 5 lad and I will go yonder and **w**,
Ex 24: 1 of Israel, and **w** from afar.
34:14 (for you shall **w** no other god,
Deut 4:19 you feel driven to **w** them and
8:19 and serve them and **w** them, I
11:16 and serve other gods and **w**
12: 4 You shall not **w** the LORD your
12:31 You shall not **w** the LORD your
26:10 and **w** before the LORD your
30:17 and **w** other gods and serve
1 Sam 1: 3 up from his city yearly to **w**
15:25 that I may **w** the LORD."
15:30 that I may **w** the LORD your
1 Ki 9: 6 go and serve other gods and **w**
12:30 for the people went to **w**
2 Ki 5:18 into the temple of Rimmon to **w**
17:36 you shall fear, Him you shall **w**,
18:22 You shall **w** before this altar in
1 Chr 16:29 **w** the LORD in the beauty of
2 Chr 7:19 serve other gods, and **w** them,
32:12 You shall **w** before one altar and
Ps 5: 7 In fear of You I will **w** toward
22:27 of the nations Shall **w** before
22:29 of the earth Shall eat and **w**;
29: 2 **W** the LORD in the beauty of
45:11 He is your Lord, **w** Him.
66: 4 All the earth shall **w** You
81: 9 Nor shall you **w** any foreign
86: 9 You have made Shall come and **w**
95: 6 let us **w** and bow down; Let us
96: 9 **w** the LORD in the beauty of
97: 7 **W** Him, all you gods.
99: 5 And **w** at His footstool— He
99: 9 And **w** at His holy hill;
132: 7 Let us **w** at His footstool.
138: 2 I will **w** toward Your holy
Isa 2: 8 They **w** the work of their own
2:20 made, each for himself to **w**,
27:13 And shall **w** the LORD in the
36: 7 You shall **w** before this
46: 6 themselves, yes, they **w**.
49: 7 arise, Princes also shall **w**,
66:23 All flesh shall come to **w**
Jer 7: 2 enter in at these gates to **w**
13:10 other gods to serve them and **w**
25: 6 other gods to serve them and **w**
26: 2 which come to **w** in the LORD's
44:19 to **w** her, and pour out drink
Ezek 46: 2 He shall **w** at the threshold of
46: 3 the people of the land shall **w**
46: 9 by way of the north gate to **w**
Dan 3: 5 you shall fall down and **w** the
3: 6 does not fall down and **w** shall
3:10 shall fall down and **w** the gold
3:11 does not fall down and **w** shall
3:12 do not serve your gods or **w**
3:14 you do not serve my gods or **w**
3:15 and you fall down and **w** the
3:15 But if you do not **w**,
3:18 nor will we **w** the gold image
3:28 they should not serve nor **w**
Hos 13: 1 he offended through Baal **w**,
Mic 5:13 You shall no more **w** the work
Zeph 1: 5 Those who **w** the host of heaven
1: 5 Those who **w** and swear oaths
2:11 People shall **w** Him, Each one
Zech 14:16 go up from year to year to **w**
14:17 not come up to Jerusalem to **w**
Mt 2: 2 in the East and have come to **w**
2: 8 that I may come and **w** Him
4: 9 if You will fall down and **w** me.
4:10 You shall **w** the LORD your
15: 9 And in vain they **w** Me,
Mk 7: 7 And in vain they **w** Me,
Lk 4: 7 if You will **w** before me, all
4: 8 You shall **w** the LORD your
Jn 4:20 the place where one ought to **w**.
4:21 in Jerusalem, **w** the Father.
4:22 'You **w** what you do not know;
4:22 do not know; we know what we **w**,
4:23 the true worshipers will **w** the
4:23 the Father is seeking such to **w**
4:24 and those who **w** Him must
4:24 those who worship Him must **w**
12:20 among those who came up to **w**
Acts 7:42 turned and gave them up to **w**
7:43 which you made to **w**;
8:27 and had come to Jerusalem to **w**,
17:23 the objects of your **w**,
17:23 the One whom you **w** without
18:13 fellow persuades men to **w** God
19:27 whom all Asia and the world **w**.
24:11 I went up to Jerusalem to **w**.
24:14 so I **w** the God of my fathers,
1 Cor 14:25 he will **w** God and report that
Phil 3: 3 who **w** God in the Spirit,
Col 2:18 in false humility and **w** of
Heb 1: 6 all the angels of God **w**
Rev 3: 9 I will make them come and **w**
4:10 who sits on the throne and **w**
9:20 that they should not **w** demons,
11: 1 and those who **w** there.
13: 8 who dwell on the earth will **w**
13:12 and those who dwell in it to **w**
13:15 cause as many as would not **w**
14: 7 and **w** Him who made heaven and
14:11 who **w** the beast and his image,
15: 4 all nations shall come and **w**
19:10 And I fell at his feet to **w** him.
19:10 **W** God! For the testimony of
22: 8 I fell down to **w** before the
22: 9 words of this book. **W** God."

WORSHIPED (67/66) WORSHIP

Gen 24:26 man bowed down his head and **w**
24:48 And I bowed my head and **w** the
24:52 that he **w** the LORD, bowing
Ex 4:31 they bowed their heads and **w**.
12:27 people bowed their heads and **w**.
32: 8 and **w** it and sacrificed to it,
33:10 and all the people rose and **w**,
34: 8 head toward the earth, and **w**.
Deut 17: 3 and served other gods and **w**
29:26 and served other gods and **w**
Josh 5:14 on his face to the earth and **w**,
Judg 7:15 its interpretation, that he **w**.
1 Sam 1:19 rose early in the morning and **w**
1:28 So they **w** the LORD there.
15:31 and Saul **w** the LORD.
2 Sam 12:20 the house of the LORD and **w**.
15:32 where he **w** God—there was Hushai
1 Ki 9: 9 and **w** them and served them;
11:33 and **w** Ashtoreth the goddess of
16:31 he went and served Baal and **w**
22:53 for he served Baal and **w** him,
2 Ki 17:16 made a wooden image and **w** all
21: 3 and he **w** all the host of heaven
21:21 father had served, and **w** them.
2 Chr 7: 3 and **w** and praised the LORD,
7:22 and **w** them and served them;
29:28 So all the assembly **w**,
29:29 present with him bowed and **w**.
29:30 they bowed their heads and **w**.
33: 3 and he **w** all the host of heaven
Neh 8: 6 they bowed their heads and **w**
9: 3 fourth they confessed and **w**
Job 1:20 and he fell to the ground and **w**.
Ps 106:19 And **w** the molded image.
Jer 1:16 And **w** the works of their own
8: 2 sought and which they have **w**.
16:11 gods and have served them and **w**
22: 9 and **w** other gods and served
Dan 3: 7 and languages fell down and **w**
Mt 2:11 and fell down and **w** Him.
8: 2 a leper came and **w** Him, saying,
9:18 a ruler came and **w** Him, saying,
14:33 who were in the boat came and **w**
15:25 Then she came and **w** Him, saying,
28: 9 and held Him by the feet and **w**
28:17 they **w** Him; but some doubted.
Mk 5: 6 from afar, he ran and **w** Him.
15:19 bowing the knee, they **w** Him.
Lk 24:52 And they **w** Him, and returned to
Jn 4:20 Our fathers **w** on this mountain,
9:38 I believe!" And he **w** Him.
Acts 10:25 and fell down at his feet and **w**
16:14 city of Thyatira, who **w** God.
17:25 Nor is He **w** with men's hands, as
18: 7 one who **w** God, whose house was
Rom 1:25 and **w** and served the creature
2 Th 2: 4 that is called God or that is **w**,
Heb 11:21 of the sons of Joseph, and **w**,
Rev 5:14 elders fell down and **w** Him who
7:11 faces before the throne and **w**
11:16 fell on their faces and **w** God,
13: 4 So they **w** the dragon who gave
13: 4 and they **w** the beast, saying,
16: 2 of the beast and those who **w**
19: 4 creatures fell down and **w** God
19:20 of the beast and those who **w**
20: 4 who had not **w** the beast or his

WORSHIPER (1/1)

Jn 9:31 but if anyone is a **w** of God and

WORSHIPERS (9/8) WORSHIP

2 Ki 10:19 the intent of destroying the **w**
10:21 and all the **w** of Baal came, so
10:22 out vestments for all the **w** of
10:23 and said to the **w** of Baal,
10:23 but only the **w** of Baal."
Zeph 3:10 the rivers of Ethiopia My **w**,
Jn 4:23 when the true **w** will worship
Acts 17:17 Jews and with the Gentile **w**,
Heb 10: 2 For the **w**, once purified, would

WORSHIPING (4/4)

2 Ki 19:37 as he was **w** in the temple of
2 Chr 20:18 before the LORD, **w** the LORD.
Isa 37:38 as he was **w** in the house of
Ezek 8:16 and they were **w** the sun toward

WORSHIPS (4/4) WORSHIP

Neh 9: 6 The host of heaven **w** You.
Isa 44:15 Indeed he makes a god and **w**
44:17 He falls down before it and **w**
Rev 14: 9 If anyone **w** the beast and his

WORST (1/1)

Ezek 7:24 Therefore I will bring the **w** of

WORTH (12/12) WORTHLESS

Gen 23:15 the land is **w** four hundred
Lev 27:23 shall reckon to him the **w** of
Deut 15:18 for he has been **w** a double
2 Sam 18: 3 But you are **w** ten thousand of
1 Ki 21: 2 I will give you its **w** in
Ezra 8:27 twenty gold basins **w** a thousand
Job 24:25 make my speech **w** nothing?"
Prov 10:20 of the wicked is **w** little.
31:10 For her **w** is far above
Isa 7:23 thousand vines **W** a thousand
Mk 6:37 buy two hundred denarii **w** of
Jn 6: 7 Two hundred denarii **w** of bread

WORTHIES (KJV) See NOBLES

WORTHILY (KJV) See PROSPER

WORTHLESS (18/18) WORTH

Num 21: 5 soul loathes this **w** bread."
Judg 9: 4 hired **w** and reckless men;
11: 3 and **w** men banded together with

1 Sam 15: 9 But everything despised and *w*,
30:22 Then all the wicked and *w* men of
2 Chr 13: 7 Then *w* rogues gathered to him,
Job 13: 4 You are all *w* physicians.
34:18 to say to a king, 'You are *w*,
Ps 119:37 eyes from looking at *w* things,
Prov 6:12 A *w* person, a wicked man,
Isa 40:17 by Him less than nothing and *w*.
41:29 Indeed they are all *w*;
Jer 10: 8 wooden idol is a *w* doctrine.
14:14 a *w* thing, and the deceit of
18:15 have burned incense to *w* idols.
23:16 to you. They make you *w*;
Jon 2: 8 Those who regard *w* idols
Zech 11:17 'Woe to the *w* shepherd,

WORTHLESSNESS (2/2)

Ps 4: 2 How long will you love *w*
Jer 16:19 *W* and unprofitable things."

WORTHY (52/50) UNWORTHY

Gen 32:10 I am not *w* of the least of all
2 Sam 22: 4 who is *w* to be praised;
1 Ki 1:52 If he proves himself a *w* man,
Ps 18: 3 who is *w* to be praised;
Mt 3: 8 Therefore bear fruits *w* of
3:11 whose sandals I am not *w* to
8: 8 I am not *w* that You should come
10:10 for a worker is *w* of his food.
10:11 enter, inquire who in it is *w*,
10:13 "If the household is *w*,
10:13 upon it. But if it is not *w*,
10:37 or mother more than Me is not *w*
10:37 daughter more than Me is not *w*
10:38 and follow after Me is not *w*
22: 8 who were invited were not *w*.
Mk 1: 7 whose sandal strap I am not *w*
Lk 3: 8 Therefore bear fruits *w* of
3:16 whose sandal strap I am not *w*
7: 6 for I am not *w* that You should
7: 7 I did not even think myself *w*
10: 7 for the laborer is *w* of his
15:19 and I am no longer *w* to be
15:21 and am no longer *w* to be called
20:35 But those who are counted *w* to
21:36 that you may be counted *w* to
Jn 1:27 whose sandal strap I am not *w*
Acts 5:41 that they were counted *w* to
13:25 of whose feet I am not *w* to
Rom 8:18 of this present time are not *w*
16: 2 her in the Lord in a manner *w*
1 Cor 15: 9 who am not *w* to be called an
Eph 4: 1 beseech you to walk *w* of the
Phil 1:27 Only let your conduct be *w* of
Col 1:10 that you may walk *w* of the Lord,
1 Th 2:12 that you would walk *w* of God who
2 Th 1: 5 that you may be counted *w* of
1:11 that our God would count you *w*
1 Tim 1:15 is a faithful saying and *w* of
4: 9 is a faithful saying and *w* of
5:17 who rule well be counted *w* of
5:18 The laborer is *w* of his
6: 1 yoke count their own masters *w*
Heb 3: 3 this One has been counted *w* of
10:29 will he be thought *w* who has
11:38 of whom the world was not *w*.
3 Jn 6 on their journey in a manner *w*
Rev 3: 4 Me in white, for they are *w*.
4:11 "You are *w*,
5: 2 Who is *w* to open the scroll and
5: 4 because no one was found *w* to
5: 9 You are *w* to take the scroll,
5:12 '*W* is the Lamb who was slain

WOT, WOTTETH (KJV) See KNOW

WOULD (678/564)

Gen 2:19 to see what he *w* call them.
18:23 *W* You also destroy the righteous
18:24 *w* You also destroy the place
18:28 *w* You destroy all of the city
21: 7 Who *w* have said to Abraham that
21: 7 that Sarah *w* nurse children?
26:10 and you *w* have brought guilt on
29: 3 Now all the flocks *w* be gathered
29: 3 and they *w* roll the stone from
30:15 *W* you take away my son's
31:31 Perhaps you *w* take your
31:42 surely now you *w* have sent me
34:14 for that *w* be a reproach to
38: 9 that the heir *w* not be his;
41:21 no one *w* have known that they
42:21 and we *w* not hear; therefore
42:22 and you *w* not listen?
42:38 then you *w* bring down my gray
43: 7 have known that he *w* say,
43:10 surely by now we *w* have
43:25 for they heard that they *w* eat
44:22 his father *w* die.'
44:34 I see the evil that *w* come
Ex 2: 4 to know what *w* be done to him.
7:16 until now you *w* not hear!
8:26 for we *w* be sacrificing the
8:32 neither *w* he let the people go.
9:15 then you *w* have been cut off
9:35 neither *w* he let the children
10:27 and he *w* not let them go.
14:12 For it *w* have been better
23: 5 and you *w* refrain from helping
32:14 the harm which He said He *w* do
33:11 And he *w* return to the camp,
34:34 he *w* take the veil off until he
34:34 and he *w* come out and speak to
34:35 then Moses *w* put the veil on
39:21 so that it *w* be above the
39:21 and that the breastplate *w* not
39:23 so that it *w* not tear.
40:31 and his sons *w* wash their hands
40:36 the children of Israel *w* go
Lev 10:19 *w* it have been accepted in the
20:19 for that *w* uncover his near of
22: 5 thing by which he *w* be made
22: 5 person by whom he *w* become
Num 9:14 and *w* keep the LORD's
9:17 children of Israel *w* journey;
9:17 the children of Israel *w* pitch
9:18 children of Israel *w* journey,
9:18 of the LORD they *w* camp;
9:20 of the LORD they *w* remain
9:20 of the LORD they *w* journey.
9:21 morning, then they *w* journey;
9:21 they *w* journey.
9:22 the children of Israel *w* remain
9:22 was taken up, they *w* journey.
10:21 (The tabernacle *w* be prepared
11:29 the LORD *w* put His Spirit
12:14 *w* she not be shamed seven days?
14: 3 *W* it not be better for us to
14:30 swore I *w* make you dwell in.
14:31 whom you said *w* be victims, I
15:14 and *w* present an offering made
21:23 But Sihon *w* not allow Israel to
22:29 for now I *w* kill you!"
22:33 surely I *w* also have killed you
24:11 I said I *w* greatly honor you,
Deut 1:26 Nevertheless you *w* not go up,
1:43 yet you *w* not listen, but
1:45 but the LORD *w* not listen to
2:30 But Sihon king of Heshbon *w* not
3:26 and *w* not listen to me.
4:21 and swore that I *w* not cross
4:21 and that I *w* not enter the good
5:29 in them that they *w* fear Me
7: 8 and because He *w* keep the oath
8: 2 whether you *w* keep His
8:20 because you *w* not be obedient
9:20 and *w* have destroyed him;
9:25 had said He *w* destroy you.
21:11 and desire her and *w* take her
23: 5 the LORD your God *w* not
23:21 and it *w* be sin to you.
28:56 who *w* not venture to set the
28:62 because you *w* not obey the
29:20 'The LORD *w* not spare him;
29:20 LORD and His jealousy *w* burn
29:20 written in this book *w* settle
29:20 and the LORD *w* blot out his
29:21 And the LORD *w* separate him
29:22 *w* say, when they see the
29:24 All nations *w* say, 'Why has the
29:25 Then people *w* say: 'Because
32:26 I *w* have said, "I will dash
32:29 That they *w* consider their
Josh 5: 6 swore that He *w* not show them
5: 6 fathers that He *w* give us,
9:27 in the place which He *w* choose,
22:25 So your descendants *w* make
24:10 But I *w* not listen to Balaam;
Judg 1:34 for they *w* not allow them to
2:17 Yet they *w* not listen to their
3: 4 to know whether they *w* obey the
4: 5 And she *w* sit under the palm
6: 3 Midianites *w* come up;
6: 3 people of the East *w* come up
6: 4 Then they *w* encamp against them
6: 5 For they *w* come up with their
6: 5 and they *w* enter the land to
6:31 *W* you plead for Baal? Would you
6:31 *W* you save him? Let the one who
6:31 Let the one who *w* plead for him
8:19 I *w* not kill you."
8:20 But the youth *w* not draw
8:24 I *w* like to make a request of
8:24 that each of you *w* give me the
9:29 Then I *w* remove Abimelech."
9:41 so that they *w* not dwell in
11:17 But the king of Edom *w* not
11:17 but he *w* not consent.
12: 3 So when I saw that you *w* not
12: 5 the men of Gilead *w* say to
12: 6 then they *w* say to him, "Then
12: 6 Shibboleth'!" And he *w* say,
12: 6 Then they *w* take him and kill
13:23 He *w* not have accepted a burnt
13:23 nor *w* He have shown us all
13:23 nor *w* He have told us such
14: 6 lion apart as one *w* have torn
14:18 You *w* not have solved my
15: 1 But her father *w* not permit
15: 7 Since you *w* do a thing like
18: 9 *W* you do nothing? Do not
19:15 for no one *w* take them into
19:25 But the men *w* not heed him.
20:13 of Benjamin *w* not listen
20:38 ambush was that they *w* make
20:39 men of Israel *w* turn in
Ruth 1:13 *w* you wait for them till they
1:13 *W* you restrain yourselves from
1 Sam 1: 4 he *w* give portions to Peninnah
1: 5 But to Hannah he *w* give a double
2:13 the priest's servant *w* come
2:14 Then he *w* thrust it into the
2:14 and the priest *w* take for
2:15 the priest's servant *w* come and
2:16 he *w* then answer him, "No,
2:20 And Eli *w* bless Elkanah and his
2:20 Then they *w* go to their own
2:30 house of your father *w* walk
12:21 for then you *w* go after
13:13 For now the LORD *w* have
13:20 But all the Israelites *w* go down
14:30 which they found! For now *w*
16:23 that David *w* take a harp and
16:23 Then Saul *w* become refreshed
16:23 distressing spirit *w* depart
18: 2 and *w* not let him go home to
20: 9 then *w* I not tell you?"
22:17 servants of the king *w* not lift
22:22 that he *w* surely tell Saul.
25:34 no males *w* have been left
26:23 but I *w* not stretch out my hand
27:10 Then Achish *w* say, "Where have
27:10 And David *w* say, "Against
27:11 David *w* save neither man nor
31: 4 But his armorbearer *w* not,
2 Sam 2:21 But Asahel *w* not turn aside
2:27 the people *w* have given up
4:10 the one who thought I *w* give
6:10 So David *w* not move the ark of
7: 5 *W* you build a house for Me to
11:20 not know that they *w* shoot
12: 8 I also *w* have given you much
12:17 But he *w* not, nor did he eat
12:18 and he *w* not heed our voice.
13:13 you *w* be like one of the fools
13:14 he *w* not heed her voice;
13:16 But he *w* not listen to her.
13:25 but he *w* not go; and he blessed
14: 7 So they *w* extinguish my ember
14:16 of the man who *w* destroy
14:29 but he *w* not come to him.
14:29 second time, he *w* not come.
14:32 It *w* be better for me to
15: 2 Now Absalom *w* rise early and
15: 2 that Absalom *w* call to him and
15: 2 And he *w* say, "Your servant
15: 3 Then Absalom *w* say to him,
15: 4 Moreover Absalom *w* say, "Oh,
15: 4 has any suit or cause *w* come
15: 4 then I *w* give him justice."
15: 5 that he *w* put out his hand and
17:17 so a female servant *w* come and
17:17 and they *w* go and tell King
18:11 I *w* have given you ten shekels
18:12 I *w* not raise my hand against
18:13 Otherwise I *w* have dealt falsely
18:13 and you yourself *w* have set
19: 6 then it *w* have pleased you
20:18 and so they *w* end disputes.
20:19 Why *w* you swallow up the
23:15 that someone *w* give me a drink
23:16 Nevertheless he *w* not drink it,
23:17 Therefore he *w* not drink it.
1 Ki 6: 6 beams *w* not be fastened
8:12 The LORD said He *w* dwell in the
13: 8 I *w* not go in with you; nor
13: 8 nor *w* I eat bread nor drink
14: 2 who told me that I *w* be king
20:33 any sign of mercy *w* c
21: 4 and *w* eat no food.
22:18 Did I not tell you he *w* not
22:49 But Jehoshaphat *w* not.
2 Ki 3:14 I *w* not look at you, nor see
3:27 eldest son who *w* have reigned
4: 8 he *w* turn in there to eat some
5: 3 he *w* heal him of his leprosy."
5:13 *w* you not have done it?
6:22 *W* you kill those whom you have
7: 2 if the LORD *w* make windows in
7:19 if the LORD *w* make windows in
8:14 He told me you *w* surely
8:19 Yet the LORD *w* not destroy
12: 8 that they *w* neither receive
13:14 the illness of which he *w* die.
13:19 then you *w* have struck Syria
13:23 and *w* not yet destroy them or
14:11 But Amaziah *w* not heed.
14:27 did not say that He *w* blot out
17:14 Nevertheless they *w* not hear,
18:12 and they *w* neither hear nor do
22:19 that they *w* become a desolation
24: 4 which the LORD *w* not pardon.
1 Chr 4:10 that You *w* bless me indeed, and
4:10 that Your hand *w* be with me,
4:10 and that You *w* keep me from
10: 4 But his armorbearer *w* not,
11:17 that someone *w* give me a drink
11:18 Nevertheless David *w* not drink
11:19 Therefore he *w* not drink it.
13: 4 said that they *w* do so,
13:13 So David *w* not move the ark
27:23 LORD had said He *w* multiply
2 Chr 4: 6 burnt offering they *w* wash
6: 1 The LORD said He *w* dwell in the
6:20 where You said You *w* put
12:11 the guard *w* go and bring them
12:11 then they *w* take them back into
15:13 and whoever *w* not seek the LORD
18:17 Did I not tell you he *w* not
20:10 whom You *w* not let Israel invade
21: 7 Yet the LORD *w* not destroy the
24:19 but they *w* not listen.
25:13 so that they *w* not go with him

25:20 But Amaziah *w* not heed, for it
33:10 but they *w* not listen.
35:22 Nevertheless Josiah *w* not turn
Ezra 9:14 *W* You not be angry with us
9:14 so that there *w* be no
10: 5 swear an oath that they *w* do
10: 8 and that whoever *w* not come
10: 8 all his property *w* be
10: 8 and he himself *w* be separated
10:19 their promise that they *w* put
Neh 5:12 oath from them that they *w* do
6:11 is there such as I who *w* go
6:14 the prophets who *w* have made
9:29 their necks, And *w* not hear.
9:30 Yet they *w* not listen;
10:30 We *w* not give our daughters as
10:31 we *w* not buy it from them on
10:31 and we *w* forego the seventh
13:19 so that no burdens *w* be
Esth 2:14 She *w* not go in to the king
3: 2 But Mordecai *w* not bow or pay
3: 4 daily and he *w* not listen
3: 4 Mordecai's words *w* stand;
4: 4 but he *w* not accept them.
6: 6 Whom *w* the king delight to honor
7: 4 I *w* have held my tongue,
7: 5 who *w* dare presume in his heart
8:11 province that *w* assault them,
8:13 so that the Jews *w* be ready on
9:27 descendants and all who *w* join
Job 1: 4 And his sons *w* go and feast in
1: 4 and *w* send and invite their
1: 5 that Job *w* send and sanctify
1: 5 and he *w* rise early in the
3:13 For now I *w* have lain still and
3:13 I *w* have been asleep; Then I
3:13 Then I *w* have been at rest
5: 8 I *w* seek God, And to God I
5: 8 And to God I *w* commit my
6: 3 For then it *w* be heavier than
6: 8 That God *w* grant me the thing
6: 9 That it *w* please God to crush
6: 9 That He *w* loose His hand and
6:10 Then I *w* still have comfort;
6:10 I *w* exult, He will not spare;
6:28 For I *w* never lie to your
7:16 I *w* not live forever. Let me
8: 5 If you *w* earnestly seek God
8: 6 Surely now He *w* awake for you,
8: 7 Yet your latter end *w* increase
9:15 I *w* beg mercy of my Judge.
9:16 I *w* not believe that He was
9:20 my own mouth *w* condemn me;
9:20 it *w* prove me perverse.
9:35 Then I *w* speak and not fear
10: 8 Yet You *w* destroy me.
10:19 I *w* have been as though I had
10:19 I *w* have been carried from the
11: 5 that God *w* speak, And open His
11: 6 That He *w* show you the secrets
11: 6 For they *w* double your
11:13 If you *w* prepare your heart,
11:14 And *w* not let wickedness dwell
11:16 Because you *w* forget your
11:17 And your life *w* be brighter
11:17 you *w* be like the morning.
11:18 And you *w* be secure, because
11:18 you *w* dig around you, and
11:19 You *w* also lie down, and no one
11:19 and no one *w* make you afraid;
11:19 many *w* court your favor.
13: 3 But I *w* speak to the Almighty,
13: 5 that you *w* be silent, And it
13: 5 And it *w* be your wisdom!
14:13 that You *w* hide me in the
14:13 That You *w* conceal me until
14:13 That You *w* appoint me a set
16: 5 But I *w* strengthen you with my
16: 5 comfort of my lips *w* relieve
21:27 with which you *w* wrong me.
23: 4 I *w* present my case before
23: 5 I *w* know the words which He
23: 5 words which He *w* answer
23: 5 And understand what He *w* say
23: 6 *W* He contend with me in His
23: 6 No! But He *w* take note of me.
23: 7 And I *w* be delivered forever
24:18 So that no one *w* turn into
30:24 Surely He *w* not stretch out
31:11 For that *w* be wickedness;
31:11 it *w* be iniquity deserving
31:12 For that *w* be a fire that
31:12 And *w* root out all my
31:28 This also *w* be an iniquity
31:28 For I *w* have denied God who
31:35 that the Almighty *w* answer me,
31:36 Surely I *w* carry it on my
31:37 I *w* declare to Him the number
31:37 Like a prince I *w* approach
32:22 Else my Maker *w* soon take me
34:15 All flesh *w* perish together,
34:15 And man *w* return to dust.
34:27 And *w* not consider any of His
36:16 Indeed He *w* have brought you out
36:16 set on your table *w* be full
36:18 For a large ransom *w* not help
37:20 surely he *w* be swallowed up.
40: 8 *W* you indeed annul My judgment?
40: 8 *W* you condemn Me that you may
41:10 so fierce that he *w* dare
41:32 One *w* think the deep had
Ps 14: 7 salvation of Israel *w* come

27:13 I *w* have lost heart,
27:13 I had believed That I *w* see
35:13 And my prayer *w* return to my
35:25 so we *w* have it!" Let them
40: 5 If I *w* declare and speak of
44:21 *W* not God search this out
50:12 I *w* not tell you; For the
51:16 or else I *w* give it; You do
53: 6 the salvation of Israel *w* come
55: 6 I *w* fly away and be at rest.
55: 7 I *w* wander far off, And
55: 8 I *w* hasten my escape From the
56: 1 for man *w* swallow me up;
56: 2 My enemies *w* hound me all day,
57: 3 He reproaches the one who *w*
69: 4 They are mighty who *w* destroy
73:15 I *w* have been untrue to the
78: 6 The children who *w* be born,
81:11 But My people *w* not heed My
81:11 And Israel *w* have none of Me.
81:13 that My people *w* listen to Me,
81:13 That Israel *w* walk in My ways!
81:14 I *w* soon subdue their enemies,
81:15 haters of the LORD *w* pretend
81:15 But their fate *w* endure
81:16 He *w* have fed them also with
81:16 rock I *w* have satisfied you."
84:10 I *w* rather be a doorkeeper in
94:17 My soul *w* soon have settled in
106:23 He said that He *w* destroy
107: 8 that men *w* give thanks to the
107:15 that men *w* give thanks to the
107:21 that men *w* give thanks to the
107:31 that men *w* give thanks to the
119: 6 Then I *w* not be ashamed,
119:57 I have said that I *w* keep Your
119:92 I *w* then have perished in my
124: 3 Then they *w* have swallowed us
124: 4 Then the waters *w* have
124: 4 The stream *w* have gone over
124: 5 Then the swollen waters *W* have
139:18 they *w* be more in number than
139:19 that You *w* slay the wicked, O
Prov 1:25 And *w* have none of my rebuke,
1:30 They *w* have none of my counsel
7:11 Her feet *w* not stay at home.
7:23 He did not know it *w* cost
8:29 So that the waters *w* not
24:28 For *w* you deceive with your
Song 3: 4 I held him and *w* not let him
6:13 What *w* you see in the
8: 1 I *w* kiss you; I would not be
8: 1 I *w* not be despised.
8: 2 I *w* lead you and bring you
8: 2 I *w* cause you to drink of
8: 7 If a man *w* give for love
8: 7 It *w* be utterly despised.
Isa 1: 9 We *w* have become like Sodom,
1: 9 We *w* have been made like
27: 4 Who *w* set briers and thorns
27: 4 I *w* go through them, I would
27: 4 I *w* burn them together.
28:12 Yet they *w* not hear.
30:15 strength." But you *w* not,
42:24 For they *w* not walk in His
44:10 Who *w* form a god or mold an
44:11 Surely all his companions *w* be
48: 8 For I knew that you *w* deal
48:18 Then your peace *w* have been
48:19 Your descendants also *w* have
48:19 His name *w* not have been cut
54: 9 That the waters of Noah *w* no
54: 9 So have I sworn That I *w* not
57:16 For the spirit *w* fail before
58: 5 *W* you call this a fast,
64: 1 that You *w* rend the heavens!
64: 1 That You *w* come down!
Jer 3: 1 *W* not that land be greatly
8:18 I *w* comfort myself in sorrow;
10: 7 Who *w* not fear You, O King of
13:11 but they *w* not hear.'
15: 1 My mind *w* not be favorable
18:10 which I said I *w* benefit it.
22:24 yet I *w* pluck you off;
23:22 Then they *w* have turned them
29:19 neither *w* you heed, says the
36:25 but he *w* not listen to them.
37:10 they *w* rise up, every man in
38:26 that he *w* not make me return to
40:15 to you *w* be scattered, and
43: 4 and all the people *w* not obey
46:13 king of Babylon *w* come and
49: 9 *W* they not leave some
49: 9 *W* they not destroy until they
51: 9 We *w* have healed Babylon,
51:53 Yet from Me plunderers *w* come
51:60 book all the evil that *w* come
Lam 4:12 *W* not have believed That the
4:14 So that no one *w* touch their
Ezek 3: 6 they *w* have listened to you.
6:10 said in vain that I *w* bring
14:14 they *w* deliver only themselves
14:16 they *w* deliver neither sons nor
14:16 only they *w* be delivered, and
14:16 and the land *w* be desolate.
14:18 they *w* deliver neither sons nor
14:18 but only they themselves *w* be
14:20 they *w* deliver neither son nor
14:20 they *w* deliver only themselves
16:15 passing by who *w* have it.
20: 8 against Me and *w* not obey Me.
20:13 Then I said I *w* pour out My

20:15 that I *w* not bring them into
20:21 Then I said I *w* pour out My
20:23 that I *w* scatter them among the
22:30 man among them who *w* make
38:17 in those days that I *w* bring
Dan 1: 8 in his heart that he *w* not
1:10 Then you *w* endanger my head
2: 8 certain that you *w* gain time,
2:29 about what *w* come to pass
6: 2 so that the king *w* suffer no
9: 2 that He *w* accomplish seventy
Hos 7: 1 When I *w* have healed Israel,
8: 7 Aliens *w* swallow it up.
9:16 I *w* kill the darlings of their
10: 3 what *w* he do for us?"
Ob 5 *W* they not have stolen till
5 *W* they not have left some
Jon 3:10 that He had said He *w* bring
4: 5 till he might see what *w* become
Mic 2:11 Even he *w* be the prattler of
Hab 1: 5 in your days Which you *w* not
Zeph 3: 7 So that her dwelling *w* not be
Zech 7:13 proclaimed and they *w* not hear,
7:13 so they called out and I *w* not
8:14 And I *w* not relent,
12: 3 all who *w* heave it away will
Mal 1: 8 *W* he be pleased with you?
1: 8 *W* he accept you favorably?"
1:10 you who *w* shut the doors,
1:10 So that you *w* not kindle fire
Mt 11:21 they *w* have repented long ago
11:23 it *w* have remained until this
12: 7 you *w* not have condemned the
16: 1 Him asked that He *w* show
18: 6 it *w* be better for him if a
18:30 And he *w* not, but went and threw
20:10 supposed that they *w* receive
23:30 we *w* not have been partakers
24:22 no flesh *w* be saved; but for
24:43 what hour the thief *w* come,
24:43 he *w* have watched and not
25:27 and at my coming I *w* have
26:24 It *w* have been good for that
27:34 tasted it, He *w* not drink.
Mk 3: 2 whether He *w* heal him on the
5:10 that He *w* not send them out
6:48 and *w* have passed them by.
9:34 among themselves who *w* be
9:42 it *w* be better for him if a
10:32 them the things that *w* happen
11:13 to see if perhaps He *w* find
11:16 And He *w* not allow anyone to
13:20 no flesh *w* be saved; but for
14:21 It *w* have been good for that
Lk 1:59 and they *w* have called him by
1:62 what he *w* have him called.
2:26 that he *w* not see death before
6: 7 whether He *w* heal on the
7:39 *w* know who and what manner of
8:31 that He *w* not command them
8:32 begged Him that He *w* permit
9:46 them as to which of them *w* be
10:13 they *w* have repented long ago,
12:39 what hour the thief *w* come,
12:39 he *w* have watched and not
15:16 And he *w* gladly have filled his
15:28 But he was angry and *w* not go
16:27 that you *w* send him to my
17: 2 It *w* be better for him if a
17: 6 and it *w* obey you.
17:20 when the kingdom of God *w* come,
18: 4 'And he *w* not for a while;
18:13 *w* not so much as raise his
19:11 the kingdom of God *w* appear
19:40 the stones *w* immediately cry
22:23 which of them it was who *w* do
24:28 and He indicated that He *w* have
Jn 4:10 you *w* have asked Him, and He
4:10 and He *w* have given you living
5:46 you *w* believe Me; for he wrote
6: 6 He Himself knew what He *w* do.
6:64 and who *w* betray Him.
6:71 for it was he who *w* betray Him,
7:39 believing in Him *w* receive;
8:19 you *w* have known My Father
8:39 you *w* do the works of Abraham.
8:42 you *w* love Me, for I proceeded
9:22 he *w* be put out of the
9:41 you *w* have no sin; but now you
11:21 my brother *w* not have died.
11:32 my brother *w* not have died."
11:40 to you that if you *w* believe
11:40 if you would believe you *w* see
11:51 he prophesied that Jesus *w* die
11:52 but also that He *w* gather
12: 4 who *w* betray Him, said,
12:33 by what death He *w* die.
13:11 For He knew who *w* betray Him;
14: 2 I *w* have told you. I go to
14: 7 you *w* have known My Father
14:28 you *w* rejoice because I said,
15:19 the world *w* love its own.
15:22 they *w* have no sin, but now
15:24 they *w* have no sin; but now
18: 4 knowing all things that *w* come
18:30 we *w* not have delivered Him up
18:32 by what death He *w* die.
18:36 My servants *w* fight, so that I
21:19 by what death he *w* glorify
21:23 that this disciple *w* not die.
21:23 to him that he *w* not die,
21:25 the books that *w* be written.

Acts 2:30 He **w** raise up the Christ to sit
3:18 that the Christ **w** suffer, He
5:24 wondered what the outcome **w** be.
7: 6 that his descendants **w** dwell in
7: 6 and that they **w** bring them into
7:25 brethren **w** have understood
7:25 understood that God **w** deliver
7:39 whom our fathers **w** not obey, but
18:14 there **w** be reason why I should
19: 4 believe on Him who **w** come
19:30 the disciples **w** not allow him.
19:31 pleading that he **w** not venture
20:16 so that he **w** not have to spend
20:38 that they **w** see his face no
21:14 So when he **w** not be persuaded,
23:12 saying that they **w** neither eat
24:26 he also hoped that money **w** be
25: 3 that he **w** summon him to
25:22 I also **w** like to hear the man
26:22 and Moses said **w** come—
26:23 that the Christ **w** suffer, that
26:23 that He **w** be the first to rise
26:23 and **w** proclaim light to the
26:29 I **w** to God that not only you,
27:20 all hope that we **w** be saved was
28: 6 expecting that he **w** swell up
Rom 4:13 For the promise that he **w** be
5: 7 for a good man someone **w** even
7: 7 I **w** not have known sin except
7: 7 For I **w** not have known
9:29 We **w** have become like
9:29 And we **w** have been made
1 Cor 2: 8 they **w** not have crucified the
5:10 since then you **w** need to go out
7:14 otherwise your children **w** be
7:28 the flesh, but I **w** spare you.
9:15 for it **w** be better for me to
11:31 For if we **w** judge ourselves, we
11:31 we **w** not be judged.
12:17 where **w** be the hearing?
12:17 where **w** be the smelling?
12:19 where **w** the body be?
14:19 yet in the church I **w** rather
2 Cor 2: 1 that I **w** not come again to you
8: 4 much urgency that we **w** receive
8: 6 so he **w** also complete this
11: 1 that you **w** bear with me in a
Gal 1:10 I **w** not be a bondservant of
2:12 he **w** eat with the Gentiles; but
3: 8 foreseeing that God **w** justify
3:21 truly righteousness **w** have been
3:23 which **w** afterward be revealed.
4:15 you **w** have plucked out your own
4:20 I **w** like to be present with you
5:12 who trouble you **w** even cut
6:12 these **w** compel you to be
Eph 3:16 that He **w** grant you, according
Col 4: 3 that God **w** open to us a door
1 Th 2:12 that you **w** walk worthy of God
3: 4 were with you that we **w** suffer
2 Th 1:11 that our God **w** count you worthy
Phm 1:17 receive him as you **w** me.
Heb 3: 5 of those things which **w** be
3:18 that they **w** not enter
4: 8 then He **w** not afterward have
8: 4 He **w** not be a priest, since
8: 7 then no place **w** have been
9:26 He then **w** have had to suffer
10: 2 For then **w** they not have ceased
10: 2 purified, **w** have had no more
11: 8 the place which he **w** receive
11:15 they **w** have had opportunity to
11:32 For the time **w** fail me to tell
13:17 for that **w** be unprofitable for
Jas 5:17 earnestly that it **w** not rain;
1 Pe 1:10 of the grace that **w** come to
1:11 and the glories that **w** follow.
3:10 'He who **w** love life
2 Pe 2: 6 to those who afterward **w** live
2:21 For it **w** have been better for
1 Jn 2:19 they **w** have continued with us;
Jude 18 that there **w** be mockers
18 in the last time who **w** walk
Rev 6:11 who **w** be killed as they were,
10: 7 the mystery of God **w** be
13:15 as many as **w** not worship

WOUND (20/17) WOUNDED, WOUNDING, WOUNDS

Ex 21:25 **w** for wound, stripe for stripe.
21:25 "burn for burn, wound for **w**,
Deut 32:39 I **w** and I heal; Nor is
1 Ki 20:37 man struck him, inflicting a **w**.
22:35 The blood ran out from the **w**
Job 16:14 He breaks me with **w** upon wound;
16:14 He breaks me with wound upon **w**;
34: 6 My **w** is incurable, though I
Ps 68:21 But God will **w** the head of His
Isa 30:26 heals the stroke of their **w**.
Jer 10:19 My **w** is severe. But I say,
15:18 And my **w** incurable, Which
30:12 Your **w** is severe.
30:14 I have wounded you with the **w**
Hos 5:13 sickness, And Judah saw his **w**,
5:13 Nor heal you of your **w**.
Nah 3:19 Your **w** is severe. All who
1 Cor 8:12 and **w** their weak conscience,
Rev 13: 3 and his deadly **w** was healed.
13:12 whose deadly **w** was healed.

WOUNDED (34/34) WOUND

Judg 9:40 fled from him; and many fell **w**,
1 Sam 17:52 And the **w** of the Philistines
31: 3 and he was severely **w** by the
2 Sam 22:39 destroyed them and **w** them,
1 Ki 22:34 out of the battle, for I am **w**.
2 Ki 8:28 and the Syrians **w** Joram.
1 Chr 10: 3 and he was **w** by the archers.
2 Chr 18:33 out of the battle, for I am **w**.
22: 5 and the Syrians **w** Joram.
24:25 (for they left him severely **w**),
35:23 me away, for I am severely **w**.
Job 24:12 And the souls of the **w** cry
Ps 18:38 I have **w** them, So that they
64: 7 Suddenly they shall be **w**.
69:26 the grief of those You have **w**.
109:22 And my heart is **w** within me.
Prov 7:26 For she has cast down many **w**,
Song 5: 7 they **w** me; The keepers of the
Isa 51: 9 And **w** the serpent?
53: 5 But He was **w** for our
Jer 30:14 For I have **w** you with the
37:10 and there remained only **w** men
51:52 her land the **w** shall groan.
Lam 2:12 As they swoon like the **w** In
Ezek 26:15 when the **w** cry, when slaughter
28:23 The **w** shall be judged in her
30:24 the groanings of a mortally **w**
Zech 13: 6 Those with which I was **w** in the
Mk 12: 4 **w** him in the head, and sent
Lk 10:30 **w** him, and departed, leaving
20:12 and they **w** him also and cast
Acts 19:16 out of that house naked and **w**.
Rev 13: 3 as if it had been mortally **w**,
13:14 an image to the beast who was **w**

WOUNDING (1/1) WOUND

Gen 4:23 For I have killed a man for **w**

WOUNDS (16/16) WOUND

2 Ki 8:29 Jezreel to recover from the **w**
9:15 Jezreel to recover from the **w**
2 Chr 22: 6 Jezreel to recover from the **w**
Job 5:18 bruises, but He binds up; He **w**,
9:17 And multiplies my **w** without
Ps 38: 5 My **w** are foul and festering
147: 3 And binds up their **w**.
Prov 6:33 **W** and dishonor he will get,
23:29 Who has **w** without cause?
27: 6 Faithful are the **w** of a
Isa 1: 6 But **w** and bruises and
Jer 6: 7 Me continually are grief and **w**.
30:17 to you And heal you of your **w**,
Mic 1: 9 For her **w** are incurable.
Zech 13: 6 What are these **w** between your
Lk 10:34 went to him and bandaged his **w**,

WOVE (3/3) WEAVE

Judg 16:14 So she **w** it tightly with the
2 Ki 23: 7 where the women **w** hangings for
2 Chr 3:14 and **w** cherubim into it.

WOVEN (48/38) WEAVE

Ex 26: 1 curtains of fine **w** linen
26:31 You shall make a veil **w** of
26:31 and fine **w** linen. It shall be
26:31 It shall be **w** with an artistic
26:36 **w** of blue, purple, and
26:36 and fine **w** linen, made by a
27: 9 court made of fine **w** linen,
27:16 **w** of blue, purple, and
27:16 and fine **w** linen, made by a
27:18 made of fine **w** linen, and its
28: 4 a skillfully **w** tunic, a turban,
28: 6 and fine **w** linen, artistically
28: 8 And the intricately **w** band of
28: 8 thread, and fine **w** linen.
28:15 Artistically **w** according to the
28:15 and fine **w** linen, you shall
28:27 above the intricately **w** band
28:28 above the intricately **w** band
28:32 it shall have a **w** binding all
28:39 make the sash of **w** work.
29: 5 gird him with the intricately **w**
36: 8 tabernacle made ten curtains **w**
36:35 and fine **w** linen; it was worked
36:37 and fine **w** linen, made by a
38: 9 court were of fine **w** linen,
38:16 around were of fine **w** linen.
38:18 the gate of the court was **w**
38:18 thread, and of fine **w** linen.
39: 2 thread, and of fine **w** linen.
39: 5 And the intricately **w** band of
39: 5 **w** of gold, blue, purple, and
39: 5 and of fine **w** linen, as the
39: 8 artistically **w** like the
39: 8 and of fine **w** linen.
39:20 above the intricately **w** band
39:21 above the intricately **w** band
39:22 robe of the ephod of **w** work,
39:23 with a **w** binding all around
39:24 and of fine **w** linen.
39:27 artistically **w** of fine linen,
39:28 short trousers of fine **w** linen,
39:29 and a sash of fine **w** linen with
Lev 8: 7 with the intricately **w** band
Num 31:20 everything **w** of goats' hair,
Ps 45:13 Her clothing is **w** with gold.
Lam 1:14 They were **w** together by His
Ezek 27:24 in sturdy **w** cords, which were
Jn 19:23 **w** from the top in one piece.

WRANGLINGS (1/1)

1 Tim 6: 5 useless **w** of men of corrupt

WRAP (2/2)

Job 8:17 His roots **w** around the rock
Isa 28:20 so narrow that one cannot **w**

WRAPPED (13/13)

Gen 38:14 with a veil and **w** herself,
1 Sam 21: 9 **w** in a cloth behind the ephod.
1 Ki 19:13 that he **w** his face in his
Ezek 16: 4 not rubbed with salt nor **w** in
Hos 4:19 The wind has **w** her up in its
Jon 2: 5 Weeds were **w** around my head.
Mt 27:59 he **w** it in a clean linen cloth,
Mk 15:46 and **w** Him in the linen.
Lk 2: 7 and **w** Him in swaddling cloths,
2:12 You will find a Babe **w** in
23:53 **w** it in linen, and laid it in a
Jn 11:44 and his face was **w** with a
Acts 5: 6 young men arose and **w** him up,

WRATH (198/194) WRATHFUL

Gen 49: 7 it is fierce; And their **w**,
Ex 15: 7 You sent forth Your **w**;
22:24 and My **w** will become hot, and I
32:10 that My **w** may burn hot against
32:11 why does Your **w** burn hot
32:12 Turn from Your fierce **w**,
Lev 10: 6 and **w** come upon all the people.
Num 1:53 that there may be no **w** on the
11:33 the **w** of the LORD was aroused
16:46 for **w** has gone out from the
18: 5 that there may be no more **w** on
25:11 has turned back My **w** from the
Deut 9: 7 the LORD your God to **w** in the
9: 8 you provoked the LORD to **w**,
9:22 you provoked the LORD to **w**.
29:23 in His anger and His **w**.
29:28 from their land in anger, in **w**,
32:27 Had I not feared the **w** of the
Josh 9:20 lest **w** be upon us because of
22:20 and **w** fell on all the
1 Sam 28:18 LORD nor execute His fierce **w**
2 Sam 11:20 if it happens that the king's **w**
2 Ki 22:13 for great is the **w** of the
22:17 Therefore My **w** shall be aroused
23:26 the fierceness of His great **w**,
1 Chr 27:24 for **w** came upon Israel because
2 Chr 12: 7 My **w** shall not be poured out on
12:12 the **w** of the LORD turned from
19: 2 Therefore the **w** of the LORD
19:10 against the LORD and **w** come
24:18 and **w** came upon Judah and
28:11 for the fierce **w** of the LORD
28:13 and there is fierce **w** against
29: 8 Therefore the **w** of the LORD
29:10 that His fierce **w** may turn away
30: 8 that the fierceness of His **w**
32:25 therefore **w** was looming over
32:26 so that the **w** of the LORD did
34:21 for great is the **w** of the
34:25 Therefore My **w** will be poured
36:16 until the **w** of the LORD arose
Ezra 5:12 provoked the God of heaven to **w**,
7:23 For why should there be **w**
8:22 but His power and His **w** are
10:14 until the fierce **w** of our God
Neh 13:18 Yet you bring added **w** on Israel
Esth 1:18 be excessive contempt and **w**.
2: 1 when the **w** of King Ahasuerus
3: 5 homage, Haman was filled with **w**.
7: 7 Then the king arose in his **w**
7:10 Then the king's **w** subsided.
Job 5: 2 For **w** kills a foolish man,
14:13 me until Your **w** is past,
16: 9 He tears me in His **w**,
19:11 He has also kindled His **w**
19:29 For **w** brings the punishment
20:23 cast on him the fury of His **w**,
20:28 flow away in the day of His **w**.
21:20 And let him drink of the **w** of
21:30 be brought out on the day of **w**.
32: 2 Then the **w** of Elihu, the son of
32: 2 his **w** was aroused because he
32: 3 his three friends his **w** was
32: 5 three men, his **w** was aroused.
36:13 hypocrites in heart store up **w**;
36:18 Because there is **w**,
40:11 Disperse the rage of your **w**;
42: 7 My **w** is aroused against you and
Ps 2: 5 He shall speak to them in His **w**,
2:12 When His **w** is kindled but a
21: 9 shall swallow them up in His **w**,
37: 8 from anger, and forsake **w**;
38: 1 do not rebuke me in Your **w**,
55: 3 And in **w** they hate me.
58: 9 As in His living and burning **w**.
59:13 Consume them in **w**,
76:10 Surely the **w** of man shall
76:10 With the remainder of **w** You
78:31 The **w** of God came against them,
78:38 And did not stir up all His **w**;

78:49 of His anger, *W*, indignation,
79: 6 Pour out Your *w* on the nations
85: 3 You have taken away all Your *w*;
88: 7 Your *w* lies heavy upon me,
88:16 Your fierce *w* has gone over me;
89:46 Will Your *w* burn like fire?
90: 7 And by Your *w* we are
90: 9 days have passed away in Your *w*;
90:11 the fear of You, so is Your *w*.
95:11 So I swore in My *w*,
102:10 of Your indignation and Your *w*;
106:23 the breach, To turn away His *w*,
106:40 Therefore the *w* of the LORD
110: 5 kings in the day of His *w*.
124: 3 When their *w* was kindled
138: 7 out Your hand Against the *w*
Prov 11: 4 do not profit in the day of *w*,
11:23 expectation of the wicked is *w*.
12:16 A fool's *w* is known at once,
14:29 He who is slow to *w* has
14:35 But his *w* is against him who
15: 1 A soft answer turns away *w*,
16:14 of death is the king's *w*,
19:12 The king's *w* is like the
19:19 A man of great *w* will suffer
20: 2 The *w* of a king is like the
21:14 bribe behind the back, strong *w*.
24:18 And He turn away His *w* from
27: 3 But a fool's *w* is heavier
27: 4 *W* is cruel and anger a
29: 8 But wise men turn away *w*.
30:33 So the forcing of *w* produces
Isa 9:19 Through the *w* of the LORD of
10: 6 against the people of My *w* I
13: 9 with both *w* and fierce anger,
13:13 In the *w* of the LORD of hosts
14: 6 He who struck the people in *w*
16: 6 and his pride and his *w*;
54: 8 With a little *w* I hid My face
60:10 For in My *w* I struck you,
Jer 7:29 the generation of His *w*.
10:10 At His *w* the earth will
18:20 To turn away Your *w* from them.
21: 5 in anger and fury and great *w*.
32:37 in My fury, and in great *w*;
44: 8 in that you provoke Me to *w* with
48:30 'I know his *w*," says the
50:13 Because of the *w* of the LORD
Lam 2: 2 He has thrown down in His *w*
3: 1 affliction by the rod of His *w*.
Ezek 7:12 For *w* is on their whole
7:14 For My *w* is on all their
7:19 In the day of the *w* of
13:15 Thus will I accomplish My *w* on
21:31 you with the fire of My *w*,
22:21 on you with the fire of My *w*,
22:31 them with the fire of My *w*;
38:19 and in the fire of My *w* I
Dan 11:36 prosper till the *w* has been
Hos 5:10 I will pour out my *w* on them
13:11 And took him away in My *w*.
Am 1:11 And he kept his *w* forever.
Nah 1: 2 And He reserves *w* for His
Hab 3: 2 In *w* remember mercy.
3: 8 Was Your *w* against the sea,
Zeph 1:15 That day is a day of *w*,
1:18 In the day of the LORD's *w*;
Zech 7:12 Thus great *w* came from the
8:14 your fathers provoked Me to *w*,
Mt 3: 7 warned you to flee from the *w*
Lk 3: 7 warned you to flee from the *w*
4:28 things, were filled with *w*,
21:23 distress in the land and *w*
Jn 3:36 but the *w* of God abides on
Acts 19:28 they were full of *w* and cried
Rom 1:18 For the *w* of God is revealed
2: 5 treasuring up for yourself *w*
2: 5 yourself wrath in the day of *w*
2: 8 —indignation and *w*,
3: 5 Is God unjust who inflicts *w*?
4:15 because the law brings about *w*;
5: 9 we shall be saved from *w*
9:22 wanting to show His *w* and to
9:22 longsuffering the vessels of *w*
12:19 but rather give place to *w*;
13: 4 an avenger to execute *w* on him
13: 5 not only because of *w* but also
2 Cor 12:20 jealousies, outbursts of *w*,
Gal 5:20 jealousies, outbursts of *w*,
Eph 2: 3 were by nature children of *w*,
4:26 let the sun go down on your *w*,
4:31 Let all bitterness, *w*,
5: 6 because of these things the *w*
6: 4 not provoke your children to *w*,
Col 3: 6 Because of these things the *w* of
3: 8 to put off all these: anger, *w*,
1 Th 1:10 who delivers us from the *w* to
2:16 but *w* has come upon them to the
5: 9 For God did not appoint us to *w*,
1 Tim 2: 8 without *w* and doubting;
Heb 3:11 So I swore in My *w*,
4: 3 "So I swore in My *w*,
11:27 not fearing the *w* of the king;
Jas 1:19 hear, slow to speak, slow to *w*;
1:20 for the *w* of man does not
Rev 6:16 on the throne and from the *w*
6:17 For the great day of His *w* has
11:18 and Your *w* has come, And the
12:12 down to you, having great *w*,
14: 8 drink of the wine of the *w* of
14:10 drink of the wine of the *w* of
14:19 the great winepress of the *w*
15: 1 for in them the *w* of God is
15: 7 golden bowls full of the *w* of
16: 1 pour out the bowls of the *w* of
16:19 wine of the fierceness of His *w*.
18: 3 drunk of the wine of the *w* of
19:15 of the fierceness and *w* of

WRATHFUL (2/2) WRATH

Ps 69:24 And let Your *w* anger take hold
Prov 15:18 A *w* man stirs up strife,

WREATH (1/1)

1 Ki 7:30 of cast bronze beside each *w*.

WREATHS (5/4)

1 Ki 7:17 with *w* of chainwork, for the
7:29 the lions and oxen were *w* of
7:36 on each, with *w* all around.
2 Chr 3:16 He made *w* of chainwork, as in
3:16 and put them on the *w* of

WRECKED (2/2)

1 Ki 22:48 for the ships were *w* at Ezion
2 Chr 20:37 Then the ships were *w*,

WREST (KJV) See PERVERT, TWIST

WRESTED (2/2)

2 Sam 23:21 *w* the spear out of the
1 Chr 11:23 *w* the spear out of the

WRESTLE (1/1) WRESTLED

Eph 6:12 For we do not *w* against flesh

WRESTLED (3/3) WRESTLE

Gen 30: 8 great wrestlings I have *w*
32:24 and a Man *w* with him until the
32:25 hip was out of joint as He *w*

WRESTLINGS (1/1)

Gen 30: 8 With great *w* I have wrestled

WRETCHED (2/2)

Rom 7:24 O *w* man that I am! Who will
Rev 3:17 do not know that you are *w*,

WRETCHEDNESS (1/1)

Num 11:15 and do not let me see my *w*!"

WRING (2/2)

Lev 1:15 *w* off its head, and burn it on
5: 8 and *w* off its head from its

WRINGING (1/1)

Prov 30:33 And *w* the nose produces blood,

WRINKLE (1/1)

Eph 5:27 not having spot or *w* or any

WRISTS (5/5)

Gen 24:22 and two bracelets for her *w*
24:30 the bracelets on his sister's *w*,
24:47 nose and the bracelets on her *w*.
Ezek 16:11 put bracelets on your *w*,
23:42 who put bracelets on their *w*

WRITE (89/81) WRITER, WRITES, WRITING, WRITTEN, WROTE

Ex 17:14 *W* this for a memorial in the
34: 1 and I will *w* on these tablets
34:27 *W* these words, for according to
Num 5:23 Then the priest shall *w* these
17: 2 *W* each man's name on his rod.
17: 3 And you shall *w* Aaron's name on
Deut 6: 9 You shall *w* them on the
10: 2 And I will *w* on the tablets the
11:20 And you shall *w* them on the
17:18 that he shall *w* for himself a
27: 3 You shall *w* on them all the
27: 8 And you shall *w* very plainly on
31:19 *w* down this song for
Ezra 5:10 that we might *w* the names of
Neh 9:38 and *w* it; our leaders, our
Esth 8: 8 You yourselves *w* a decree
Job 13:26 For You *w* bitter things against
Prov 3: 3 *W* them on the tablet of your
7: 3 *W* them on the tablet of your
Isa 8: 1 and *w* on it with a man's pen
10: 1 Who *w* misfortune, Which they
10:19 in number That a child may *w*
30: 8 *w* it before them on a tablet,
44: 5 Another will *w* with his hand,
Jer 22:30 '*W* this man down as childless,
30: 2 *W* in a book for yourself all the
31:33 and *w* it on their hearts; and I
36: 2 Take a scroll of a book and *w* on
36:17 how did you *w* all these
36:28 and *w* on it all the former
Ezek 24: 2 *w* down the name of the day,
37:16 a stick for yourself and *w* on
37:16 Then take another stick and *w*
37:20 And the sticks on which you *w*
43:11 *W* it down in their sight, so
Hab 2: 2 *W* the vision And make it plain
Mk 10: 4 Moses permitted a man to *w* a
Lk 1: 3 to *w* to you an orderly account,
16: 6 and sit down quickly and *w*
16: 7 'Take your bill, and *w* eighty.'
Jn 19:21 Jews said to Pilate, "Do not *w*,
Acts 15:20 but that we *w* to them to abstain
25:26 I have nothing certain to *w* to
25:26 place I may have something to *w*.
1 Cor 4:14 I do not *w* these things to
14:37 that the things which I *w* to
2 Cor 9: 1 it is superfluous for me to *w*
13: 2 and now being absent I *w* to
13:10 Therefore I *w* these things being
Gal 1:20 the things which I *w* to you,
Phil 3: 1 For me to *w* the same things to
1 Th 4: 9 have no need that I should *w*
5: 1 have no need that I should *w*
2 Th 3:17 a sign in every epistle; so I *w*.
1 Tim 3:14 These things I *w* to you, though
3:15 I *w* so that you may know how
Phm 1:21 I *w* to you, knowing that you
Heb 8:10 laws in their mind and *w*
10:16 in their minds I will *w*
2 Pe 3: 1 I now *w* to you this second
1 Jn 1: 4 And these things we *w* to you
2: 1 these things I *w* to you, so
2: 7 I *w* no new commandment to you,
2: 8 a new commandment I *w* to you,
2:12 I *w* to you, little children,
2:13 I *w* to you, fathers, Because
2:13 I *w* to you, young men,
2:13 I *w* to you, little children,
2 Jn 12 Having many things to *w* to you,
3 Jn 13 I had many things to *w*,
13 but I do not wish to *w* to you
Jude 3 while I was very diligent to *w*
3 I found it necessary to *w* to
Rev 1:11 *w* in a book and send it to the
1:19 *W* the things which you have
2: 1 of the church of Ephesus *w*,
2: 8 angel of the church in Smyrna *w*,
2:12 of the church in Pergamos *w*,
2:18 of the church in Thyatira *w*,
3: 1 angel of the church in Sardis *w*,
3: 7 of the church in Philadelphia *w*,
3:12 And I will *w* on him the name of
3:12 And I will *w* on him My new
3:14 the church of the Laodiceans *w*,
10: 4 their voices, I was about to *w*;
10: 4 and do not *w* them."
14:13 '*W*: 'Blessed are the dead who
19: 9 '*W*: 'Blessed are those who are
21: 5 '*W*, for these words are true

WRITER (1/1) WRITE

Ps 45: 1 tongue is the pen of a ready *w*.

WRITER'S (2/2)

Ezek 9: 2 with linen and had a *w* inkhorn
9: 3 who had the *w* inkhorn at his

WRITES (3/3) WRITE

Deut 24: 1 and he *w* her a certificate of
24: 3 husband detests her and *w* her
Rom 10: 5 For Moses *w* about the

WRITHE (1/1)

Joel 2: 6 Before them the people *w* in

WRITHES (1/1)

Job 15:20 The wicked man *w* with pain all

WRITING (22/21) WRITE, WRITINGS

Ex 32:16 and the *w* was the writing of
32:16 and the writing was the *w* of
Deut 10: 4 according to the first *w*,
31:24 when Moses had completed *w* the
1 Chr 28:19 LORD made me understand in *w*,
2 Chr 2:11 king of Tyre answered in *w*,
36:22 kingdom, and also put it in *w*,
Ezra 1: 1 kingdom, and also put it in *w*,
Isa 38: 9 This is the *w* of Hezekiah king
Ezek 2:10 and there was *w* on the inside
Dan 5: 7 Babylon, "Whoever reads this *w*,
5: 8 but they could not read the *w*,
5:15 that they should read this *w*
5:16 Now if you can read the *w* and
5:17 yet I will read the *w* to the
5:24 and this *w* was written.
6: 8 the decree and sign the *w*,
6:10 when Daniel knew that the *w*
Lk 1:63 And he asked for a *w* tablet,
Jn 19:19 And the *w* was: JESUS OF
2 Cor 1:13 For we are not *w* any other
Phm 1:19 am *w* with my own hand.

WRITINGS (1/1) WRITING

Jn 5:47 if you do not believe his *w*,

WRITTEN (280/272) WRITE

Ex 24:12 and commandments which I have *w*,
31:18 *w* with the finger of God.
32:15 The tablets were *w* on both
32:15 and on the other they were *w*.
32:32 of Your book which You have *w*.
Deut 9:10 two tablets of stone *w* with
28:58 of this law that are *w* in
28:61 which is not *w* in this Book of
29:20 and every curse that is *w* in
29:21 of the covenant that are *w* in
29:27 on it every curse that is *w* in
30:10 His statutes which are *w* in
Josh 1: 8 do according to all that is *w*
8:31 as it is *w* in the Book of the
8:32 law of Moses, which he had *w*.
8:34 according to all that is *w* in
10:13 Is this not *w* in the Book of
23: 6 to keep and to do all that is *w*
2 Sam 1:18 indeed it is *w* in the Book of
1 Ki 2: 3 as it is *w* in the Law of Moses,
11:41 are they not *w* in the book of
14:19 indeed they are *w* in the book
14:29 are they not *w* in the book of
15: 7 are they not *w* in the book of
15:23 are they not *w* in the book of
15:31 are they not *w* in the book of
16: 5 are they not *w* in the book of
16:14 are they not *w* in the book of
16:20 are they not *w* in the book of
16:27 are they not *w* in the book of
21:11 as it was *w* in the letters
22:39 are they not *w* in the book of
22:45 are they not *w* in the book of
2 Ki 1:18 are they not *w* in the book of
8:23 are they not *w* in the book of
10:34 are they not *w* in the book of
12:19 are they not *w* in the book of
13: 8 are they not *w* in the book of
13:12 are they not *w* in the book of
14: 6 according to what is *w* in the
14:15 are they not *w* in the book of
14:18 are they not *w* in the book of
14:28 are they not *w* in the book of
15: 6 are they not *w* in the book of
15:11 indeed they are *w* in the book
15:15 indeed they are *w* in the book
15:21 are they not *w* in the book of
15:26 indeed they are *w* in the book
15:31 indeed they are *w* in the book
15:36 are they not *w* in the book of
16:19 are they not *w* in the book of
20:20 are they not *w* in the book of
21:17 are they not *w* in the book of
21:25 are they not *w* in the book of
22:13 do according to all that is *w*
23: 3 of this covenant that were *w*
23:21 as it is *w* in this Book of
23:24 words of the law which were *w*
23:28 are they not *w* in the book of
24: 5 are they not *w* in the book of
1 Chr 16:40 do according to all that is *w*
29:29 indeed they are *w* in the book
2 Chr 9:29 are they not *w* in the book of
12:15 are they not *w* in the book of
13:22 and his sayings are *w* in the
16:11 are indeed *w* in the book of the
20:34 indeed they are *w* in the book
23:18 as it is *w* in the Law of
24:27 indeed they are *w* in the
25: 4 but did as it is *w* in the
25:26 indeed are they not *w* in the
27: 7 indeed they are *w* in the book
28:26 indeed they are *w* in the book
30:18 Passover contrary to what was *w*.
31: 3 as it is *w* in the Law of the
31:16 years old and up who were *w* in
31:17 and to the priests who were *w* in
31:18 and to all who were *w* in the
32:32 indeed they are *w* in the
33:18 indeed they are *w* in the book
33:19 indeed they are *w* among the
34:21 do according to all that is *w*
34:24 all the curses that are *w* in
34:31 of the covenant that were *w* in
35: 4 following the *w* instruction of
35: 4 Israel and the *w* instruction
35:12 as it is *w* in the Book of
35:25 and indeed they are *w* in the
35:26 according to what was *w* in
35:27 indeed they are *w* in the book
36: 8 indeed they are *w* in the book
Ezra 3: 2 as it is *w* in the Law of
3: 4 of Tabernacles, as it is *w*,
4: 7 and the letter was *w* in
5: 5 Then a *w* answer was returned
5: 7 in which was *w* thus—To Darius
6: 2 and in it a record was *w* thus:
6:18 as it is *w* in the Book of
8:34 All the weight was *w* down at
Neh 6: 6 In it was *w*: It is reported
7: 5 and found *w* in it:
8:14 And they found *w* in the Law,
8:15 to make booths, as it is *w*.
10:34 the LORD our God as it is *w*
10:36 as it is *w* in the Law, and
12:23 were *w* in the book of the
13: 1 and in it was found *w* that no
Esth 2:23 and it was *w* in the book of the
3: 9 let a decree be *w* that they
3:12 and a decree was *w* according
3:12 name of King Ahasuerus it was *w*,
4: 8 gave him a copy of the *w* decree
6: 2 And it was found *w* that Mordecai
8: 5 let it be *w* to revoke the
8: 8 for whatever is *w* in the king's
8: 9 twenty-third day; and it was *w*,
9:23 as Mordecai had *w* to them,
9:27 to the *w* instructions
9:32 and it was *w* in the book.
10: 2 are they not *w* in the book of
Job 19:23 that my words were *w*! Oh, that
31:35 That my Prosecutor had *w* a
Ps 40: 7 scroll of the book it is *w*
69:28 And not be *w* with the
102:18 This will be *w* for the
139:16 in Your book they all were *w*,
149: 9 on them the *w* judgment—This
Prov 22:20 Have I not *w* to you excellent
Eccl 12:10 and what was *w* was
Isa 65: 6 it is *w* before Me: I will
Jer 17: 1 The sin of Judah is *w* with a
17:13 Shall be *w* in the earth,
25:13 all that is *w* in this book,
36: 6 the scroll which you have *w* at
36:27 the words which Baruch had *w*
36:29 Why have you *w* in it that the
45: 1 when he had *w* these words in a
51:60 all these words that are *w*
Ezek 2:10 and *w* on it were lamentations
13: 9 nor be *w* in the record of the
Dan 5:24 Him, and this writing was *w*.
5:25 is the inscription that was *w*:
6: 9 Darius signed the *w* decree.
9:11 the curse and the oath *w* in
9:13 As it is *w* in the Law of
12: 1 Every one who is found *w* in
Hos 8:12 I have *w* for him the great
Mal 3:16 So a book of remembrance was *w*
Mt 2: 5 for thus it is *w* by the
4: 4 He answered and said, "It is *w*,
4: 6 Yourself down. For it is *w*:
4: 7 It is *w* again, 'You shall not
4:10 with you, Satan! For it is *w*,
11:10 this is he of whom it is *w*:
21:13 And He said to them, "It is *w*,
26:24 indeed goes just as it is *w* of
26:31 of Me this night, for it is *w*:
27:37 over His head the accusation *w*
Mk 1: 2 As it is *w* in the Prophets:
7: 6 of you hypocrites, as it is *w*:
9:12 And how is it *w* concerning the
9:13 as it is *w* of him."
11:17 saying to them, "Is it not *w*,
14:21 indeed goes just as it is *w* of
14:27 of Me this night, for it is *w*:
15:26 of His accusation was *w* above:
Lk 2:23 (as it is *w* in the law of the
3: 4 as it is *w* in the book of the
4: 4 answered him, saying, "It is *w*,
4: 8 behind Me, Satan! For it is *w*,
4:10 it is *w*: 'He shall give
4:17 found the place where it was *w*:
7:27 "This is he of whom it is *w*:
10:20 because your names are *w* in
10:26 'What is *w* in the law?
18:31 and all things that are *w* by
19:46 saying to them, "It is *w*,
20:17 "What then is this that is *w*:
21:22 that all things which are *w* may
22:37 you that this which is *w* must
23:38 And an inscription also was *w*
24:44 must be fulfilled which were *w*
24:46 He said to them, "Thus it is *w*,
Jn 2:17 remembered that it was *w*,
6:31 manna in the desert; as it is *w*,
6:45 It is *w* in the prophets, 'And
8:17 It is also *w* in your law that
10:34 Is it not *w* in your law, 'I
12:14 donkey, sat on it; as it is *w*:
12:16 that these things were *w* about
15:25 might be fulfilled which is *w*
19:20 and it was *w* in Hebrew, Greek,
19:22 answered, "What I have *w*,
19:22 "What I have written, I have *w*.
20:30 which are not *w* in this book;
20:31 but these are *w* that you may
21:25 which if they were *w* one by
21:25 the books that would be *w*.
Acts 1:20 For it is *w* in the book of
7:42 as it is *w* in the book of the
13:29 had fulfilled all that was *w*
13:33 As it is also *w* in the second
15:15 prophets agree, just as it is *w*:
21:25 we have *w* and decided that
23: 5 the high priest; for it is *w*,
24:14 all things which are *w* in the
Rom 1:17 from faith to faith; as it is *w*,
2:15 show the work of the law *w* in
2:24 because of you," as it is *w*.
2:27 even with your *w* code and
3: 4 every man a liar. As it is *w*:
3:10 As it is *w*: "There is none
4:17 it is *w*, "I have made you
4:23 Now it was not *w* for his sake
8:36 As it is *w*: "For Your sake
9:13 As it is *w*, "Jacob I have
9:33 it is *w*: "Behold, I lay
10:15 they are sent? As it is *w*:
11: 8 Just as it is *w*: "God has
11:26 will be saved, as it is *w*:
12:19 place to wrath; for it is *w*,
14:11 For it is *w*: As I live,
15: 3 please Himself; but as it is *w*,
15: 4 For whatever things were *w*
15: 4 were written before were *w* for
15: 9 God for His mercy, as it is *w*:
15:15 I have *w* more boldly to you on
15:21 it is *w*: "To whom He
1 Cor 1:19 is *w*: "I will destroy
1:31 that, as it is *w*, "He who
2: 9 it is *w*: "Eye has not
3:19 it is *w*, "He catches
4: 6 not to think beyond what is *w*,
5:11 But now I have *w* to you not to
9: 9 For it is *w* in the law of Moses,
9:10 our sakes, no doubt, this is *w*,
9:15 nor have I *w* these things that
10: 7 were some of them. As it is *w*,
10:11 and they were *w* for our
14:21 In the law it is *w*:
15:45 it is *w*, "The first man
15:54 to pass the saying that is *w*:
2 Cor 3: 2 You are our epistle *w* in our
3: 3 *w* not with ink but by the
3: 7 *w* and engraved on stones, was
4:13 faith, according to what is *w*,
8:15 As it is *w*, "He who gathered
9: 9 is *w*: "He has dispersed
Gal 3:10 under the curse; for it is *w*,
3:10 in all things which are *w*
3:13 a curse for us (for it is *w*,
4:22 For it is *w* that Abraham had two
4:27 it is *w*: "Rejoice, O
6:11 what large letters I have *w* to
Eph 3: 3 mystery (as I have briefly *w*
Heb 10: 7 of the book it is *w* of
13:22 for I have *w* to you in few
1 Pe 1:16 because it is *w*, "Be holy,
5:12 I have *w* to you briefly,
2 Pe 3:15 given to him, has *w* to you,
1 Jn 2:14 I have *w* to you, fathers,
2:14 I have *w* to you, young men,
2:21 I have not *w* to you because you
2:26 These things I have *w* to you
5:13 These things I have *w* to you who
Rev 1: 3 keep those things which are *w*
2:17 and on the stone a new name *w*
5: 1 sat on the throne a scroll *w*
13: 8 whose names have not been *w* in
14: 1 having His Father's name *w* on
17: 5 on her forehead a name was *w*:
17: 8 whose names are not *w* in the
19:12 He had a name *w* that no one
19:16 robe and on His thigh a name *w*:
20:12 by the things which were *w* in
20:15 And anyone not found *w* in the
21:12 and names *w* on them, which are
21:27 but only those who are *w* in the
22:18 to him the plagues that are *w*
22:19 from the things which are *w*

WRONG (31/29) WRONGED, WRONGFULLY

Gen 16: 5 My *w* be upon you! I gave my
Ex 2:13 said to the one who did the *w*,
Num 5: 8 may be made for the *w*,
5: 8 the restitution for the *w* must
2 Sam 19:19 or remember what *w* your servant
1 Ki 8:47 'We have sinned and done *w*,
2 Ki 18:14 saying, "I have done *w*;
1 Chr 12:17 since there is no *w* in my
16:21 permitted no man to do them *w*;
2 Chr 6:37 'We have sinned, we have done *w*,
Job 1:22 not sin nor charge God with *w*.
19: 7 "If I cry out concerning *w*,
21:27 with which you would *w* me.
24:12 does not charge them with *w*.
36:23 who has said, 'You have done *w*'?
Ps 105:14 permitted no one to do them *w*;
Jer 22: 3 Do no *w* and do no violence to
40: 4 But if it seems *w* for you to
Dan 6:22 I have done no *w* before you."
Mt 20:13 'Friend, I am doing you no *w*.
Lk 23:41 but this Man has done nothing *w*.
Acts 7:24 seeing one of them suffer *w*,
7:26 why do you *w* one another?'
7:27 But he who did his neighbor *w*
25:10 To the Jews I have done no *w*,
1 Cor 6: 7 Why do you not rather accept *w*?
6: 8 you yourselves do *w* and cheat,
2 Cor 7:12 sake of him who had done the *w*,
7:12 the sake of him who suffered *w*,
12:13 Forgive me this *w*!
Col 3:25 But he who does *w* will be repaid

WRONGDOING (3/3)

Deut 19:16 man to testify against him of *w*,
Acts 18:14 If it were a matter of *w* or
24:20 say if they found any *w* in me

WRONGED (8/8) WRONG

Num 5: 7 give it to the one he has *w*.
Judg 11:27 but you *w* me by fighting
Esth 1:16 Queen Vashti has not only *w* the
Job 19: 3 not ashamed that you have *w*
19: 6 Know then that God has *w* me,
Lam 3:59 You have seen how I am *w*;
2 Cor 7: 2 We have *w* no one, we have
Phm 1:18 But if he has *w* you or owes

WRONGFULLY (8/8) WRONG

Gen 43: 6 Why did you deal so *w* with me
Ps 35:19 over me who are *w* my enemies;
38:19 And those who hate me *w* have
69: 4 Being my enemies *w*;
119:78 For they treated me *w* with
119:86 faithful; They persecute me *w*;
Ezek 22:29 and they *w* oppress the
1 Pe 2:19 one endures grief, suffering *w*.

WRONGS (1/1)

Prov 8:36 But he who sins against me *w*

WROTE (62/61) WRITE

Ex 24: 4 And Moses *w* all the words of the
34:28 And He *w* on the tablets the
39:30 and *w* on it an inscription
Num 33: 2 Now Moses *w* down the starting
Deut 4:13 and He *w* them on two tablets of
5:22 And He *w* them on two tablets of
10: 4 And He *w* on the tablets
31: 9 So Moses *w* this law and
31:22 Therefore Moses *w* this song the
Josh 8:32 he *w* on the stones a copy of
18: 9 and *w* the survey in a book in
24:26 Then Joshua *w* these words in
Judg 8:14 and he *w* down for him the
1 Sam 10:25 and *w* it in a book and laid
2 Sam 11:14 it happened that David *w* a
11:15 And he *w* in the letter, saying,
1 Ki 21: 8 And she *w* letters in Ahab's
21: 9 She *w* in the letters, saying,
2 Ki 10: 1 And Jehu *w* and sent letters to
10: 6 Then he *w* a second letter to
17:37 and the commandment which He *w*
1 Chr 24: 6 *w* them down before the king,
2 Chr 26:22 Isaiah the son of Amoz *w*.
30: 1 and also *w* letters to Ephraim
32:17 He also *w* letters to revile the
Ezra 4: 6 they *w* an accusation against
4: 7 the rest of their companions *w*
4: 8 and Shimshai the scribe *w* a
Esth 8: 5 which he *w* to annihilate the
8:10 And he *w* in the name of King
9:20 And Mordecai *w* these things and
9:29 *w* with full authority to
Jer 36: 4 and Baruch *w* on a scroll of a
36:18 and I *w* them with ink in the
36:32 who *w* on it at the instruction
51:60 So Jeremiah *w* in a book all the
Dan 5: 5 of a man's hand appeared and *w*
5: 5 saw the part of the hand that *w*.
6:25 Then King Darius *w*:
7: 1 Then he *w* down the dream,
Mk 10: 5 the hardness of your heart he *w*
12:19 Moses *w* to us that if a man's
Lk 1:63 for a writing tablet, and *w*,
20:28 Moses *w* to us that if a man's
Jn 1:45 law, and also the prophets, *w*—
5:46 for he *w* about Me.
8: 6 But Jesus stooped down and *w* on
8: 8 again He stooped down and *w* on
19:19 Now Pilate *w* a title and put it
21:24 and *w* these things; and we know
Acts 15:23 They *w* this letter by them:
18:27 cross to Achaia, the brethren *w*,
23:25 He *w* a letter in the following
Rom 16:22 who *w* this epistle, greet you
1 Cor 5: 9 I *w* to you in my epistle not to
7: 1 the things of which you *w* to
2 Cor 2: 3 And I *w* this very thing to you,
2: 4 and anguish of heart I *w* to
2: 9 For to this end I also *w*,
7:12 although I *w* to you, I did
2 Jn 5 not as though I *w* a new
3 Jn 9 I *w* to the church, but

WROUGHT (2/2)

Ps 139:15 And skillfully *w* in the
Ezek 27:19 *W* iron, cassia, and cane were

WRUNG (1/1)

Judg 6:38 he *w* the dew out of the fleece,

Y

YAH (4/4) GOD

Ps 68: 4 on the clouds, By His name *Y*,
Isa 12: 2 and not be afraid; 'For *Y*,
26: 4 the LORD forever, For in *Y*,
38:11 I said, "I shall not see *Y*,

YARN (5/5) THREAD

Ex 26: 4 shall make loops of blue *y* on
35:25 were gifted artisans spun *y*
35:26 stirred with wisdom spun *y* of
36:11 He made loops of blue *y* on the
Judg 16: 9 the bowstrings as a strand of *y*

YEA (3/3)

Ps 19:10 are they than gold, *Y*,
23: 4 *Y*, though I walk through
137: 1 Babylon, There we sat down, *y*,

YEAR (366/320) YEARLY, YEARS

Gen 7:11 In the six hundredth *y* of Noah's
8:13 in the six hundred and first *y*,
14: 4 and in the thirteenth *y* they
14: 5 In the fourteenth *y*
17:21 to you at this set time next *y*.
26:12 and reaped in the same *y* a
47:17 for all their livestock that *y*.
47:18 When that *y* had ended, they came
47:18 they came to him the next *y* and
Ex 12: 2 be the first month of the *y*
12: 5 blemish, a male of the first *y*.
13:10 ordinance in its season from *y*
13:10 in its season from year to *y*.
23:11 but the seventh *y* you shall let
23:14 keep a feast to Me in the *y*:
23:16 Ingathering at the end of the *y*,
23:17 Three times in the *y* all your
23:29 out from before you in one *y*,
29:38 altar: two lambs of the first *y*,
30:10 upon its horns once a *y* with
30:10 once a *y* he shall make
34:23 Three times in the *y* all your
34:24 your God three times in the *y*.
40:17 the first month of the second *y*,
Lev 9: 3 a lamb, both of the first *y*,
12: 6 priest a lamb of the first *y*
14:10 one ewe lamb of the first *y*
16:34 for all their sins, once a *y*.
19:24 But in the fourth *y* all its
19:25 And in the fifth *y* you may eat
23:12 a male lamb of the first *y*,
23:18 seven lambs of the first *y*,
23:19 two male lambs of the first *y*
23:41 LORD for seven days in the *y*.
25: 4 but in the seventh *y* there shall
25: 5 for it is a *y* of rest for the
25:10 shall consecrate the fiftieth *y*,
25:11 That fiftieth *y* shall be a
25:13 In this *Y* of Jubilee, each of
25:20 shall we eat in the seventh *y*,
25:21 blessing on you in the sixth *y*,
25:22 you shall sow in the eighth *y*,
25:22 old produce until the ninth *y*;
25:28 him who bought it until the *Y*
25:29 may redeem it within a whole *y*
25:29 within a full *y* he may redeem
25:30 within the space of a full *y*,
25:40 shall serve you until the *Y* of
25:50 from the *y* that he was sold to
25:50 he was sold to him until the *Y*
25:52 but a few years until the *Y* of
25:54 he shall be released in the *Y*
27:17 dedicates his field from the *Y*
27:18 years that remain till the *Y*
27:23 up to the *Y* of Jubilee, and he
27:24 In the *Y* of Jubilee the field
Num 1: 1 in the second *y* after they had
6:12 a male lamb in its first *y* as
6:14 one male lamb in its first *y*
6:14 one ewe lamb in its first *y*
7:15 one male lamb in its first *y*,
7:17 male lambs in their first *y*.
7:21 one male lamb in its first *y*,
7:23 male lambs in their first *y*.
7:27 one male lamb in its first *y*,
7:29 male lambs in their first *y*.
7:33 one male lamb in its first *y*,
7:35 male lambs in their first *y*.
7:39 one male lamb in its first *y*,
7:41 male lambs in their first *y*.
7:45 one male lamb in its first *y*,
7:47 male lambs in their first *y*.
7:51 one male lamb in its first *y*,
7:53 male lambs in their first *y*.
7:57 one male lamb in its first *y*,
7:59 male lambs in their first *y*.
7:63 one male lamb in its first *y*,
7:65 male lambs in their first *y*.
7:69 one male lamb in its first *y*,
7:71 male lambs in their first *y*.
7:75 one male lamb in its first *y*,
7:77 male lambs in their first *y*.
7:81 one male lamb in its first *y*,
7:83 male lambs in their first *y*.
7:87 the male lambs in their first *y*
7:88 and the lambs in their first *y*
9: 1 the first month of the second *y*
9:22 or a *y* that the cloud remained
10:11 second month, in the second *y*,
14:34 you shall bear your guilt one *y*,
15:27 a female goat in its first *y*
28: 3 two male lambs in their first *y*
28: 9 day two lambs in their first *y*,
28:11 seven lambs in their first *y*,
28:14 throughout the months of the *y*.
28:19 seven lambs in their first *y*.
28:27 seven lambs in their first *y*,
29: 2 seven lambs in their first *y*,
29: 8 seven lambs in their first *y*.
29:13 fourteen lambs in their first *y*.
29:17 lambs in their first *y* without
29:20 lambs in their first *y* without
29:23 fourteen lambs in their first *y*,
29:26 lambs in their first *y* without
29:29 lambs in their first *y* without
29:32 lambs in their first *y* without
29:36 seven lambs in their first *y*
33:38 died there in the fortieth *y*
Deut 1: 3 came to pass in the fortieth *y*,
11:12 from the beginning of the *y* to
11:12 year to the very end of the *y*.
14:22 that the field produces *y* by
14:22 the field produces year by *y*.
14:28 At the end of every third *y*
14:28 of your produce of that *y* and
15: 9 heart, saying, 'The seventh *y*,
15: 9 the *y* of release, is at hand,'
15:12 then in the seventh *y* you shall
15:20 before the LORD your God *y* by
15:20 the LORD your God year by *y*
16:16 Three times a *y* all your males
24: 5 he shall be free at home one *y*,
26:12 of your increase in the third *y*—
26:12 the *y* of tithing—and have given
31:10 at the appointed time in the *y*
Josh 5:12 of the land of Canaan that *y*.
Judg 10: 8 From that *y* they harassed and
11:40 of Israel went four days each *y*
17:10 ten shekels of silver per *y*,
1 Sam 1: 7 *y* by year, when she went up to
1: 7 So it was, year by *y*,
2:19 and bring it to him *y* by year
2:19 and bring it to him year by *y*
7:16 He went from *y* to year on a
7:16 He went from year to *y* on a
13: 1 Saul reigned one *y*;
27: 7 the Philistines was one full *y*
2 Sam 11: 1 happened in the spring of the *y*,
14:26 at the end of every *y* he cut it
21: 1 *y* after year; and David
21: 1 for three years, year after *y*;
1 Ki 4: 7 for one month of the *y*.
5:11 Thus Solomon gave to Hiram *y* by
5:11 Solomon gave to Hiram year by *y*.
6: 1 four hundred and eightieth *y*
6: 1 in the fourth *y* of Solomon's
6:37 In the fourth *y* the foundation
6:38 And in the eleventh *y*,
9:25 Now three times a *y* Solomon
10:25 at a set rate *y* by year.
10:25 mules, at a set rate year by *y*.
14:25 It happened in the fifth *y* of
15: 1 In the eighteenth *y* of King
15: 9 In the twentieth *y* of Jeroboam
15:25 over Israel in the second *y* of
15:28 killed him in the third *y* of
15:33 In the third *y* of Asa king of
16: 8 In the twenty-sixth *y* of Asa
16:10 him in the twenty-seventh *y* of
16:15 In the twenty-seventh *y* of Asa
16:23 In the thirty-first *y* of Asa
16:29 In the thirty-eighth *y* of Asa
18: 1 came to Elijah, in the third *y*,
20:22 for in the spring of the *y* the
20:26 it was, in the spring of the *y*,
22: 2 it came to pass, in the third *y*,
22:41 over Judah in the fourth *y* of
22:51 in Samaria in the seventeenth *y*
2 Ki 1:17 in the second *y* of Jehoram the
3: 1 at Samaria in the eighteenth *y*
4:16 About this time next *y* you shall
8:16 Now in the fifth *y* of Joram the
8:25 In the twelfth *y* of Joram the
8:26 and he reigned one *y* in
9:29 In the eleventh *y* of Joram the
11: 4 In the seventh *y* Jehoiada sent
12: 1 In the seventh *y* of Jehu,
12: 6 by the twenty-third *y* of King
13: 1 In the twenty-third *y* of Joash
13:10 In the thirty-seventh *y* of
13:20 the land in the spring of the *y*.
14: 1 In the second *y* of Joash the son
14:23 In the fifteenth *y* of Amaziah
15: 1 In the twenty-seventh *y* of
15: 8 In the thirty-eighth *y* of
15:13 king in the thirty-ninth *y* of
15:17 In the thirty-ninth *y* of
15:23 In the fiftieth *y* of Azariah
15:27 In the fifty-second *y* of
15:30 in his place in the twentieth *y*
15:32 In the second *y* of Pekah the
16: 1 In the seventeenth *y* of Pekah
17: 1 In the twelfth *y* of Ahaz king of
17: 4 as he had done *y* by year.
17: 4 as he had done year by *y*.
17: 6 In the ninth *y* of Hoshea, the
18: 1 it came to pass in the third *y*
18: 9 it came to pass in the fourth *y*
18: 9 which was the seventh *y* of
18:10 In the sixth *y* of Hezekiah,
18:10 the ninth *y* of Hoshea king of
18:13 And in the fourteenth *y* of King
19:29 You shall eat this *y* such as
19:29 And in the second *y* what
19:29 Also in the third *y* sow and
22: 3 in the eighteenth *y* of King
23:23 But in the eighteenth *y* of King
24:12 in the eighth *y* of his reign,
25: 1 it came to pass in the ninth *y*
25: 2 besieged until the eleventh *y*
25: 8 (which was the nineteenth *y*
25:27 to pass in the thirty-seventh *y*
25:27 in the *y* that he began to
1 Chr 20: 1 happened in the spring of the *y*,
26:31 In the fortieth *y* of the reign
27: 1 all the months of the *y*,
2 Chr 3: 2 second month in the fourth *y*
9:24 at a set rate *y* by year.
9:24 mules, at a set rate year by *y*.
12: 2 it happened in the fifth *y* of

13: 1 In the eighteenth *y* of King
15:10 in the fifteenth *y* of the reign
15:19 no war until the thirty-fifth *y*
16: 1 In the thirty-sixth *y* of the
16:12 And in the thirty-ninth *y* of his
16:13 he died in the forty-first *y* of
17: 7 Also in the third *y* of his
22: 2 and he reigned one *y* in
23: 1 In the seventh *y* Jehoiada
24: 5 the house of your God from *y*
24: 5 of your God from year to *y*,
24:23 in the spring of the *y* that
27: 5 of Ammon gave him in that *y*
29: 3 In the first *y* of his reign, in
34: 3 For in the eighth *y* of his
34: 3 and in the twelfth *y* he began
34: 8 In the eighteenth *y* of his
35:19 In the eighteenth *y* of the reign
36:10 At the turn of the *y* King
36:22 Now in the first *y* of Cyrus
Ezra 1: 1 Now in the first *y* of Cyrus
3: 8 second month of the second *y*
4:24 until the second *y* of the
5:13 in the first *y* of Cyrus king of
6: 3 In the first *y* of King Cyrus,
6:15 which was in the sixth *y* of the
7: 7 to Jerusalem in the seventh *y*
7: 8 which was in the seventh *y* of
Neh 1: 1 of Chislev, in the twentieth *y*,
2: 1 in the twentieth *y* of King
5:14 from the twentieth *y* until the
5:14 year until the thirty-second *y*
10:34 at the appointed times *y* by
10:34 the appointed times year by *y*,
10:35 *y* by year, to the house of the
10:35 fruit of all trees, year by *y*,
13: 6 for in the thirty-second *y* of
Esth 1: 3 that in the third *y* of his
2:16 in the seventh *y* of his reign.
3: 7 in the twelfth *y* of King
9:27 these two days every *y*,
Job 3: 6 rejoice among the days of the *y*,
Ps 65:11 You crown the *y* with Your
Isa 6: 1 In the *y* that King Uzziah died,
14:28 the burden which came in the *y*
20: 1 In the *y* that Tartan came to
21:16 has said to me: "Within a *y*,
21:16 according to the *y* of a hired
29: 1 David dwelt! Add *y* to year;
29: 1 David dwelt! Add year to *y*;
32:10 In a *y* and some days You will
34: 8 The *y* of recompense for the
36: 1 to pass in the fourteenth *y* of
37:30 You shall eat this *y* such as
37:30 And the second *y* what springs
37:30 Also in the third *y* sow and
61: 2 To proclaim the acceptable *y* of
63: 4 And the *y* of My redeemed has
Jer 1: 2 in the thirteenth *y* of his
1: 3 the end of the eleventh *y* of
11:23 even the *y* of their
17: 8 will not be anxious in the *y*
23:12 The *y* of their punishment,"
25: 1 in the fourth *y* of Jehoiakim
25: 1 Judah (which was the first *y*
25: 3 From the thirteenth *y* of Josiah
25: 3 this is the twenty-third *y* in
28: 1 And it happened in the same *y*,
28: 1 in the fourth *y* and in the
28:16 This *y* you shall die, because
28:17 the prophet died the same *y* in
32: 1 from the LORD in the tenth *y*
32: 1 which was the eighteenth *y* of
36: 1 it came to pass in the fourth *y*
36: 9 it came to pass in the fifth *y*
39: 1 In the ninth *y* of Zedekiah king
39: 2 In the eleventh *y* of Zedekiah,
45: 1 in the fourth *y* of Jehoiakim
46: 2 defeated in the fourth *y* of
48:44 upon it I will bring The *y* of
51:46 (A rumor will come one *y*,
51:46 in another *y* A rumor will
51:59 to Babylon in the fourth *y* of
52: 4 it came to pass in the ninth *y*
52: 5 besieged until the eleventh *y*
52:12 (which was the nineteenth *y*
52:28 away captive: in the seventh *y*,
52:29 in the eighteenth *y* of
52:30 in the twenty-third *y* of
52:31 to pass in the thirty-seventh *y*
52:31 in the first *y* of his reign,
Ezek 1: 1 came to pass in the thirtieth *y*,
1: 2 which was the fifth *y* of
4: 6 laid on you a day for each *y*.
8: 1 it came to pass in the sixth *y*,
20: 1 came to pass in the seventh *y*,
24: 1 Again, in the ninth *y*,
26: 1 came to pass in the eleventh *y*,
29: 1 In the tenth *y*, in the tenth
29:17 to pass in the twenty-seventh *y*,
30:20 came to pass in the eleventh *y*,
31: 1 came to pass in the eleventh *y*,
32: 1 came to pass in the twelfth *y*,
32:17 to pass also in the twelfth *y*,
33:21 came to pass in the twelfth *y*
40: 1 In the twenty-fifth *y* of our
40: 1 at the beginning of the *y*,
40: 1 in the fourteenth *y* after the
46:13 LORD of a lamb of the first *y*
46:17 it shall be his until the *y* of
Dan 1: 1 In the third *y* of the reign of
1:21 continued until the first *y* of
2: 1 Now in the second *y* of
7: 1 In the first *y* of Belshazzar
8: 1 In the third *y* of the reign of
9: 1 In the first *y* of Darius the son
9: 2 in the first *y* of his reign I,
10: 1 In the third *y* of Cyrus king of
11: 1 Also in the first *y* of Darius
Mic 6: 6 With calves a *y* old?
Hag 1: 1 In the second *y* of King Darius,
1:15 in the second *y* of King Darius.
2:10 in the second *y* of Darius, the
Zech 1: 1 eighth month of the second *y*
1: 7 in the second *y* of Darius, the
7: 1 Now in the fourth *y* of King
14:16 Jerusalem shall go up from *y*
14:16 shall go up from year to *y* to
Lk 2:41 went to Jerusalem every *y* at
3: 1 Now in the fifteenth *y* of the
4:19 proclaim the acceptable *y*
13: 8 let it alone this *y* also, until
Jn 11:49 being high priest that *y*,
11:51 but being high priest that *y* he
18:13 who was high priest that *y*.
Acts 11:26 So it was that for a whole *y*
18:11 And he continued there a *y* and
2 Cor 8:10 and were desiring to do a *y*
9: 2 that Achaia was ready a *y* ago;
Heb 9: 7 priest went alone once a *y*,
9:25 the Most Holy Place every *y*
10: 1 which they offer continually *y*
10: 1 offer continually year by *y*,
10: 3 is a reminder of sins every *y*.
Jas 4:13 spend a *y* there, buy and sell,
Rev 9:15 hour and day and month and *y*,

YEAR'S (2/2)

Ex 34:22 of Ingathering at the *y* end.
Neh 10:31 forego the seventh *y* produce

YEARLY (11/11) YEAR

Lev 25:53 him as a *y* hired servant,
Judg 21:19 there is a *y* feast of the
1 Sam 1: 3 man went up from his city *y* to
1:21 to the LORD the *y* sacrifice
2:19 to offer the *y* sacrifice.
20: 6 for there is a *y* sacrifice
1 Ki 10:14 of gold that came to Solomon *y*
2 Chr 8:13 and the three appointed *y*
9:13 of gold that came to Solomon *y*
Neh 10:32 to exact from ourselves *y*
Esth 9:21 that they should celebrate *y*

YEARNED (3/3) YEARNS

Gen 43:30 Now his heart *y* for his brother;
1 Ki 3:26 for she *y* with compassion for
Song 5: 4 And my heart *y* for him.

YEARNING (1/1)

Isa 63:15 The *y* of Your heart and Your

YEARNS (4/4) YEARNED

Job 19:27 How my heart *y* within me!
Ps 12: 5 in the safety for which he *y*.
Jer 31:20 Therefore My heart *y* for him;
Jas 4: 5 The Spirit who dwells in us *y*

YEARS (528/445) YEAR

Gen 1:14 and seasons, and for days and *y*;
5: 3 lived one hundred and thirty *y*,
5: 4 of Adam were eight hundred *y*;
5: 5 were nine hundred and thirty *y*;
5: 6 lived one hundred and five *y*,
5: 7 lived eight hundred and seven *y*,
5: 8 were nine hundred and twelve *y*;
5: 9 Enosh lived ninety *y*,
5:10 eight hundred and fifteen *y*,
5:11 were nine hundred and five *y*;
5:12 Cainan lived seventy *y*,
5:13 lived eight hundred and forty *y*,
5:14 were nine hundred and ten *y*;
5:15 Mahalalel lived sixty-five *y*,
5:16 eight hundred and thirty *y*,
5:17 eight hundred and ninety-five *y*;
5:18 one hundred and sixty-two *y*,
5:19 Jared lived eight hundred *y*,
5:20 nine hundred and sixty-two *y*;
5:21 Enoch lived sixty-five *y*,
5:22 walked with God three hundred *y*,
5:23 three hundred and sixty-five *y*.
5:25 one hundred and eighty-seven *y*,
5:26 seven hundred and eighty-two *y*,
5:27 nine hundred and sixty-nine *y*;
5:28 one hundred and eighty-two *y*,
5:30 five hundred and ninety-five *y*,
5:31 hundred and seventy-seven *y*;
5:32 And Noah was five hundred *y*
6: 3 be one hundred and twenty *y*.
7: 6 Noah was six hundred *y* old when
9:28 flood three hundred and fifty *y*.
9:29 were nine hundred and fifty *y*;
11:10 Shem was one hundred *y* old,
11:10 and begot Arphaxad two *y* after
11:11 Shem lived five hundred *y*,
11:12 Arphaxad lived thirty-five *y*,
11:13 lived four hundred and three *y*,
11:14 Salah lived thirty *y*,
11:15 lived four hundred and three *y*,
11:16 Eber lived thirty-four *y*,
11:17 lived four hundred and thirty *y*,
11:18 Peleg lived thirty *y*,
11:19 lived two hundred and nine *y*,
11:20 Reu lived thirty-two *y*,
11:21 lived two hundred and seven *y*,
11:22 Serug lived thirty *y*,
11:23 Serug lived two hundred *y*,
11:24 Nahor lived twenty-nine *y*,
11:25 one hundred and nineteen *y*,
11:26 Now Terah lived seventy *y*,
11:32 were two hundred and five *y*,
12: 4 And Abram was seventy-five *y*
14: 4 Twelve *y* they served
15:13 afflict them four hundred *y*.
16: 3 after Abram had dwelt ten *y* in
16:16 Abram was eighty-six *y* old when
17: 1 When Abram was ninety-nine *y*
17:17 to a man who is one hundred *y*
17:17 who is ninety *y* old, bear a
17:24 Abraham was ninety-nine *y* old
17:25 his son was thirteen *y* old
21: 5 Now Abraham was one hundred *y*
23: 1 one hundred and twenty-seven *y*;
23: 1 these were the *y* of the life
25: 7 This is the sum of the *y* of
25: 7 one hundred and seventy-five *y*.
25: 8 age, an old man and full of *y*,
25:17 These were the *y* of the life of
25:17 one hundred and thirty-seven *y*;
25:20 Isaac was forty *y* old when he
25:26 Isaac was sixty *y* old when she
26:34 When Esau was forty *y* old, he
29:18 I will serve you seven *y* for
29:20 So Jacob served seven *y* for
29:27 with me still another seven *y*.
29:30 Laban still another seven *y*.
31:38 These twenty *y* I have been
31:41 been in your house twenty *y*;
31:41 I served you fourteen *y* for
31:41 and six *y* for your flock, and
35:28 were one hundred and eighty *y*.
37: 2 being seventeen *y* old, was
41: 1 pass, at the end of two full *y*,
41:26 seven good cows are seven *y*,
41:26 seven good heads are seven *y*;
41:27 came up after them are seven *y*,
41:27 by the east wind are seven *y*
41:29 Indeed seven *y* of great plenty
41:30 but after them seven *y* of famine
41:34 Egypt in the seven plentiful *y*.
41:35 all the food of those good *y*
41:36 for the land for the seven *y*
41:46 Joseph was thirty *y* old when he
41:47 Now in the seven plentiful *y* the
41:48 up all the food of the seven *y*
41:50 born two sons before the *y* of
41:53 Then the seven *y* of plenty
41:54 and the seven *y* of famine began
45: 6 For these two *y* the famine has
45: 6 and there are still five *y* in
45:11 for there are still five *y* of
47: 9 The days of the *y* of my
47: 9 are one hundred and thirty *y*;
47: 9 have been the days of the *y* of
47: 9 attained to the days of the *y*
47:28 the land of Egypt seventeen *y*.
47:28 one hundred and forty-seven *y*.
50:22 lived one hundred and ten *y*.
50:26 being one hundred and ten *y*
Ex 6:16 And the *y* of the life of Levi
6:18 And the *y* of the life of Kohath
6:20 And the *y* of the life of Amram
7: 7 And Moses was eighty *y* old and
7: 7 old and Aaron eighty-three *y*
12:40 was four hundred and thirty *y*.
12:41 the four hundred and thirty *y*—
16:35 of Israel ate manna forty *y*,
21: 2 servant, he shall serve six *y*;
23:10 Six *y* you shall sow your land
30:14 from twenty *y* old and above,
38:26 in the numbering from twenty *y*
Lev 19:23 Three *y* it shall be as
25: 3 Six *y* you shall sow your field,
25: 3 and six *y* you shall prune your
25: 8 count seven sabbaths of *y* for
25: 8 yourself, seven times seven *y*;
25: 8 time of the seven sabbaths of *y*
25: 8 shall be to you forty-nine *y*.
25:15 According to the number of *y*
25:15 according to the number of *y*
25:16 to the multitude of *y* you
25:16 to the fewer number of *y* you
25:16 to the number of the *y* of
25:21 produce enough for three *y*.
25:27 then let him count the *y* since
25:50 be according to the number of *y*,
25:51 If there are still many *y*
25:52 if there remain but a few *y*
25:52 and according to his *y* he
25:54 he is not redeemed in these *y*,
27: 3 is of a male from twenty *y* old
27: 3 twenty years old up to sixty *y*
27: 5 and if from five *y* old up to
27: 5 five years old up to twenty *y*
27: 6 from a month old up to five *y*
27: 7 and if from sixty *y* old and
27:18 money due according to the *y*
Num 1: 3 from twenty *y* old and above—all
1:18 from twenty *y* old and above,
1:20 from twenty *y* old and above,
1:22 from twenty *y* old and above,

1:24 from twenty y old and above,
1:26 from twenty y old and above,
1:28 from twenty y old and above,
1:30 from twenty y old and above,
1:32 from twenty y old and above,
1:34 from twenty y old and above,
1:36 from twenty y old and above,
1:38 from twenty y old and above,
1:40 from twenty y old and above,
1:42 from twenty y old and above,
1:45 from twenty y old and above,
4: 3 from thirty y old and above,
4: 3 even to fifty y old, all who
4:23 From thirty y old and above,
4:23 even to fifty y old, you shall
4:30 From thirty y old and above,
4:30 even to fifty y old, you shall
4:35 from thirty y old and above,
4:35 even to fifty y old, everyone
4:39 from thirty y old and above,
4:39 even to fifty y old, everyone
4:43 from thirty y old and above,
4:43 even to fifty y old, everyone
4:47 from thirty y old and above,
4:47 even to fifty y old, everyone
8:24 From twenty-five y old and
8:25 and at the age of fifty y they
13:22 (Now Hebron was built seven y
14:29 from twenty y old and above.
14:33 in the wilderness forty y,
14:34 guilt one year, namely forty y,
26: 2 of Israel from twenty y old
26: 4 of the people from twenty y
32:11 from twenty y old and above,
32:13 in the wilderness forty y,
33:39 one hundred and twenty-three y
Deut 2: 7 These forty y the LORD your
2:14 the Zered was thirty-eight y,
8: 2 you all the way these forty y
8: 4 your foot swell these forty y.
15: 1 At the end of every seven y you
15:12 to you and serves you six y,
15:18 servant in serving you six y.
29: 5 And I have led you forty y in
31: 2 am one hundred and twenty y
31:10 "At the end of every seven y,
32: 7 Consider the y of many
34: 7 was one hundred and twenty y
Josh 5: 6 of Israel walked forty y in
13: 1 Joshua was old, advanced in y.
13: 1 "You are old, advanced in y,
14: 7 I was forty y old when Moses
14:10 as He said, these forty-five y,
14:10 eighty-five y old.
24:29 being one hundred and ten y
Judg 2: 8 he was one hundred and ten y
3: 8 Cushan-Rishathaim eight y.
3:11 the land had rest for forty y.
3:14 Eglon king of Moab eighteen y.
3:30 the land had rest for eighty y.
4: 3 and for twenty y he harshly
5:31 the land had rest for forty y.
6: 1 the hand of Midian for seven y,
6:25 the second bull of seven y old,
8:28 country was quiet for forty y
9:22 had reigned over Israel three y,
10: 2 He judged Israel twenty-three y;
10: 3 he judged Israel twenty-two y.
10: 8 of Israel for eighteen y—
11:26 the Arnon, for three hundred y,
12: 7 Jephthah judged Israel six y.
12: 9 He judged Israel seven y.
12:11 He judged Israel ten y.
12:14 He judged Israel eight y.
13: 1 of the Philistines for forty y.
15:20 And he judged Israel twenty y in
16:31 He had judged Israel twenty y.
Ruth 1: 4 they dwelt there about ten y.
1 Sam 4:15 Eli was ninety-eight y old, and
4:18 he had judged Israel forty y.
7: 2 time; it was there twenty y.
13: 1 and when he had reigned two y
17:12 man was old, advanced in y,
29: 3 with me these days, or these y?
2 Sam 2:10 was forty y old when he began
2:10 Israel, and he reigned two y.
2:11 the house of Judah was seven y
4: 4 He was five y old when the news
5: 4 David was thirty y old when he
5: 4 reign, and he reigned forty y.
5: 5 he reigned over Judah seven y
5: 5 he reigned thirty-three y over
13:23 came to pass, after two full y,
13:38 Geshur, and was there three y.
14:28 And Absalom dwelt two full y in
15: 7 it came to pass after forty y
19:32 very aged man, eighty y old.
19:35 'I am today eighty y old.
21: 1 the days of David for three y,
24:13 Shall seven y of famine come to
1 Ki 1: 1 David was old, advanced in y;
2:11 over Israel was forty y;
2:11 seven y he reigned in Hebron,
2:11 he reigned thirty-three y.
2:39 happened at the end of three y,
6:38 So he was seven y in building
7: 1 But Solomon took thirteen y to
9:10 happened at the end of twenty y,
10:22 Once every three y the merchant
11:42 over all Israel was forty y.
14:20 reigned was twenty-two y.
14:21 Rehoboam was forty-one y old
14:21 He reigned seventeen y in
15: 2 He reigned three y in Jerusalem.
15:10 And he reigned forty-one y in
15:25 he reigned over Israel two y.
15:33 and reigned twenty-four y.
16: 8 and reigned two y in Tirzah.
16:23 Israel, and reigned twelve y.
16:23 Six y he reigned in Tirzah.
16:29 Israel in Samaria twenty-two y.
17: 1 not be dew nor rain these y,
22: 1 Now three y passed without war
22:42 Jehoshaphat was thirty-five y
22:42 and he reigned twenty-five y in
22:51 and reigned two y over Israel.
2 Ki 3: 1 of Judah, and reigned twelve y.
8: 1 come upon the land for seven y.
8: 2 land of the Philistines seven y.
8: 3 to pass, at the end of seven y,
8:17 He was thirty-two y old when he
8:17 and he reigned eight y in
8:26 Ahaziah was twenty-two y old
10:36 in Samaria was twenty-eight y.
11: 3 house of the LORD for six y,
11:21 Jehoash was seven y old when he
12: 1 and he reigned forty y in
13: 1 and reigned seventeen y.
13:10 and reigned sixteen y.
14: 2 He was twenty-five y old when he
14: 2 and he reigned twenty-nine y in
14:17 lived fifteen y after the death
14:21 who was sixteen y old, and
14:23 and reigned forty-one y.
15: 2 He was sixteen y old when he
15: 2 and he reigned fifty-two y in
15:17 and reigned ten y in Samaria.
15:23 in Samaria, and reigned two y.
15:27 Samaria, and reigned twenty y.
15:33 He was twenty-five y old when he
15:33 and he reigned sixteen y in
16: 2 Ahaz was twenty y old when he
16: 2 and he reigned sixteen y in
17: 1 and he reigned nine y.
17: 5 and besieged it for three y.
18: 2 He was twenty-five y old when he
18: 2 and he reigned twenty-nine y in
18:10 And at the end of three y they
20: 6 will add to your days fifteen y.
21: 1 Manasseh was twelve y old when
21: 1 and he reigned fifty-five y in
21:19 Amon was twenty-two y old when
21:19 and he reigned two y in
22: 1 Josiah was eight y old when he
22: 1 and he reigned thirty-one y in
23:31 Jehoahaz was twenty-three y
23:36 Jehoiakim was twenty-five y old
23:36 and he reigned eleven y in
24: 1 became his vassal for three y.
24: 8 Jehoiachin was eighteen y old
24:18 Zedekiah was twenty-one y old
24:18 and he reigned eleven y in
1 Chr 2:21 he married when he was sixty y
3: 4 There he reigned seven y and
3: 4 he reigned thirty-three y.
21:12 either three y of famine, or
23: 3 from the age of thirty y and
23:24 from the age of twenty y and
23:27 were numbered from twenty y
27:23 the number of those twenty y
29:27 over Israel was forty y;
29:27 seven y he reigned in Hebron,
29:27 and thirty-three y he reigned
2 Chr 8: 1 to pass at the end of twenty y,
9:21 Once every three y the merchant
9:30 over all Israel forty y.
11:17 of Solomon strong for three y,
11:17 David and Solomon for three y.
12:13 Now Rehoboam was forty-one y
12:13 and he reigned seventeen y in
13: 2 He reigned three y in Jerusalem.
14: 1 the land was quiet for ten y.
14: 6 rest; he had no war in those y,
18: 2 After some y he went down to
20:31 He was thirty-five y old when
20:31 and he reigned twenty-five y in
21: 5 Jehoram was thirty-two y old
21: 5 and he reigned eight y in
21:19 of time, after the end of two y,
21:20 He was thirty-two y old when he
21:20 He reigned in Jerusalem eight y
22: 2 Ahaziah was forty-two y old
22:12 in the house of God for six y,
24: 1 Joash was seven y old when he
24: 1 and he reigned forty y in
24:15 was one hundred and thirty y
25: 1 Amaziah was twenty-five y old
25: 1 and he reigned twenty-nine y in
25: 5 he numbered them from twenty y
25:25 lived fifteen y after the death
26: 1 who was sixteen y old, and
26: 3 Uzziah was sixteen y old when
26: 3 and he reigned fifty-two y in
27: 1 Jotham was twenty-five y old
27: 1 and he reigned sixteen y in
27: 5 him in the second and third y
27: 8 He was twenty-five y old when he
27: 8 and he reigned sixteen y in
28: 1 Ahaz was twenty y old when he
28: 1 and he reigned sixteen y in
29: 1 when he was twenty-five y
29: 1 and he reigned twenty-nine y in
31:16 those males from three y old
31:17 to the Levites from twenty y
33: 1 Manasseh was twelve y old when
33: 1 and he reigned fifty-five y in
33:21 Amon was twenty-two y old when
33:21 and he reigned two y in
34: 1 Josiah was eight y old when he
34: 1 and he reigned thirty-one y in
36: 2 Jehoahaz was twenty-three y old
36: 5 Jehoiakim was twenty-five y
36: 5 and he reigned eleven y in
36: 9 Jehoiachin was eight y old
36:11 Zedekiah was twenty-one y old
36:11 and he reigned eleven y in
36:21 Sabbath, to fulfill seventy y.
Ezra 3: 8 the Levites from twenty y old
5:11 temple that was built many y
Neh 5:14 of King Artaxerxes, twelve y,
9:21 Forty y You sustained them in
9:30 Yet for many y You had patience
Job 10: 5 Are Your y like the days of a
15:20 And the number of y is hidden
16:22 For when a few y are finished,
32: 4 Now because they were y older
32: 6 and said: "I am young in y,
32: 7 And multitude of y should
36:11 And their y in pleasures.
36:26 Nor can the number of His y
42:16 lived one hundred and forty y,
Ps 31:10 And my y with sighing;
61: 6 His y as many generations.
77: 5 The y of ancient times.
77:10 But I will remember the y
78:33 And their y in fear.
90: 4 For a thousand y in Your sight
90: 9 We finish our y like a sigh.
90:10 of our lives are seventy y;
90:10 of strength they are eighty y,
90:15 The y in which we have seen
95:10 For forty y I was grieved with
102:24 Your y are throughout all
102:27 And Your y will have no end.
Prov 4:10 And the y of your life will be
5: 9 And your y to the cruel one;
9:11 And y of life will be added to
10:27 But the y of the wicked will
Eccl 6: 3 children and lives many y,
6: 3 so that the days of his y are
6: 6 even if he lives a thousand y
11: 8 But if a man lives many y And
12: 1 And the y draw near when you
Isa 7: 8 Within sixty-five y Ephraim
16:14 saying, "Within three y,
16:14 as the y of a hired man, the
20: 3 naked and barefoot three y
23:15 will be forgotten seventy y,
23:15 At the end of seventy y it will
23:17 be, at the end of seventy y,
38: 5 will add to your days fifteen y.
38:10 of the remainder of my y.
38:15 shall walk carefully all my y
65:20 child shall die one hundred y
65:20 the sinner being one hundred y
Jer 25:11 the king of Babylon seventy y.
25:12 when seventy y are completed,
28: 3 Within two full y I will bring
28:11 within the space of two full y.
29:10 After seventy y are completed
34:14 At the end of seven y let every
34:14 when he has served you six y,
52: 1 Zedekiah was twenty-one y old
52: 1 and he reigned eleven y in
Ezek 4: 5 For I have laid on you the y of
22: 4 come to the end of your y;
29:11 it shall be uninhabited forty y.
29:12 shall be desolate forty y;
29:13 At the end of forty y I will
38: 8 In the latter y you will come
38:17 who prophesied for y in those
39: 9 fires with them for seven y.
Dan 1: 5 and three y of training for
5:31 being about sixty-two y old.
9: 2 the books the number of the y
9: 2 He would accomplish seventy y
11: 6 And at the end of some y they
11: 8 and he shall continue more y
11:13 come at the end of some y with
Joel 2:25 I will restore to you the y
Am 1: 1 two y before the earthquake.
2:10 And led you forty y through
5:25 In the wilderness forty y,
Hab 3: 2 work in the midst of the y!
3: 2 In the midst of the y make
Zech 1:12 You were angry these seventy y?
7: 3 as I have done for so many y?
7: 5 months during those seventy y,
Mal 3: 4 days of old, As in former y.
Mt 2:16 from two y old and under,
9:20 a flow of blood for twelve y
Mk 5:25 a flow of blood for twelve y,
5:42 for she was twelve y of age.
Lk 1: 7 were both well advanced in y.
1:18 my wife is well advanced in y.
2:36 lived with a husband seven y
2:37 a widow of about eighty-four y,
2:42 And when He was twelve y old,
3:23 ministry at about thirty y
4:25 the heaven was shut up three y
8:42 an only daughter about twelve y
8:43 a flow of blood for twelve y,
12:19 many goods laid up for many y;
13: 7 for three y I have come seeking
13:11 spirit of infirmity eighteen y,
13:16 of it—for eighteen y,

15:29 these many y I have been
Jn 2:20 It has taken forty-six y to
5: 5 had an infirmity thirty-eight y.
8:57 You are not yet fifty y old, and
Acts 4:22 For the man was over forty y old
7: 6 oppress them four hundred y.
7:23 Now when he was forty y old, it
7:30 And when forty y had passed, an
7:36 and in the wilderness forty y.
7:42 sacrifices during forty y
9:33 who had been bedridden eight y
13:18 for a time of about forty y He
13:20 about four hundred and fifty y,
13:21 tribe of Benjamin, for forty y.
19:10 And this continued for two y,
20:31 and remember that for three y
24:10 that you have been for many y
24:17 Now after many y I came to bring
24:27 But after two y Porcius Festus
28:30 Then Paul dwelt two whole y in
Rom 4:19 he was about a hundred y old),
15:23 a great desire these many y to
2 Cor 12: 2 a man in Christ who fourteen y
Gal 1:18 Then after three y I went up to
2: 1 Then after fourteen y I went up
3:17 was four hundred and thirty y
4:10 and months and seasons and y.
1 Tim 5: 9 not let a widow under sixty y
Heb 1:12 And Your y will not
3: 9 And saw My works forty y.
3:17 with whom was He angry forty y?
Jas 5:17 rain on the land for three y
2 Pe 3: 8 one day is as a thousand y,
3: 8 and a thousand y as one day.
Rev 20: 2 and bound him for a thousand y;
20: 3 no more till the thousand y
20: 4 with Christ for a thousand y.
20: 5 live again until the thousand y
20: 6 reign with Him a thousand y.
20: 7 Now when the thousand y have

YELLOW (5/5)

Lev 13:30 there is in it thin y hair,
13:32 and there is no y hair in it,
13:36 need not seek for y hair.
Ps 68:13 her feathers with y gold."
Rev 9:17 hyacinth blue, and sulfur y;

YES (209/204)

Gen 20: 6 God said to him in a dream, "Y,
Deut 33: 3 Y, He loves the people;
Josh 2: 4 and hid them. So she said, "Y,
Judg 5:29 wisest ladies answered her, Y,
1 Sam 9:12 answered them and said, "Y,
24:11 Y, see the corner of your robe
2 Ki 2: 3 you today?" And he said, "Y,
2: 5 So he answered, "Y,
1 Chr 16:21 Y, He rebuked kings for their
Ezra 10:12 Y! As you have said, so we must
Neh 5:15 Y, even their servants bore
Job 1:17 camels and took them away, y,
2: 4 Y, all that a man has he will
5:19 deliver you in six troubles, Y,
6:27 Y, you overwhelm the
6:29 Y, concede, my righteousness
9:10 things past finding out, Y,
11:15 Y, you could be steadfast,
11:18 Y, you would dig around you,
11:19 Y, many would court your
15: 4 Y, you cast off fear,
15: 6 Y, your own lips testify
20: 8 Y, he will be chased away
20:25 Y, the glittering point comes
21: 7 wicked live and become old, Y,
22:25 Y, the Almighty will be your
22:30 Y, he will be delivered by the
30: 8 They were sons of fools, Y,
30: 9 Y, I am their byword.
31: 8 Y, let my harvest be rooted
31:11 Y, it would be iniquity
33:22 Y, his soul draws near the
40: 5 Y, twice, but I will proceed
Ps 7: 5 Y, let him trample my life
7:14 Y, he conceives trouble and
16: 6 Y, I have a good inheritance.
27: 6 His tabernacle; I will sing, y,
29: 5 the LORD breaks the cedars, Y,
31: 9 eye wastes away with grief, Y,
35:10 who is too strong for him, Y,
59:16 Y, I will sing aloud of Your
68: 3 Y, let them rejoice
68:16 Y, the LORD will dwell in it
72:11 Y, all kings shall fall down
78:19 Y, they spoke against God:
78:38 Y, many a time He turned
78:41 Y, again and again they
83:11 like Oreb and like Zeeb, Y,
83:17 Y, let them be put to shame
84: 2 My soul longs, y, even faints
85:12 Y, the LORD will give what
90:17 Y, establish the work of our
102:13 For the time to favor her, Y,
102:26 Y, they will all grow old like
105:14 Y, He rebuked kings for their
109:30 Y, I will praise Him among
116: 5 Y, our God is merciful.
118:11 They surrounded me, Y,
119:127 commandments More than gold, y,
128: 6 Y, may you see your children's
130: 6 Y, more than those who watch
138: 5 Y, they shall sing of the ways
Prov 2: 3 Y, if you cry out for
3:24 Y, you will lie down and your
6:16 six things the LORD hates, Y,
8:19 fruit is better than gold, y,
16: 4 has made all for Himself, Y,
22:10 Y, strife and reproach will
23:16 Y, my inmost being will
23:34 Y, you will be like one
24: 5 A wise man is strong, Y,
29:17 Y, he will give delight to
30:18 are too wonderful for me, Y,
30:21 the earth is perturbed, Y,
30:29 which are majestic in pace, Y,
31:20 her hand to the poor, Y,
Eccl 2: 7 Y, I had greater possessions
12: 9 y, he pondered and sought out
Song 1:16 my beloved! Y, pleasant!
5: 1 Eat, O friends! Drink, y,
5:16 His mouth is most sweet, Y,
Isa 5:29 Y, they will roar And lay
19:21 y, they will make a vow
26: 8 Y, in the way of Your
26: 9 desired You in the night, Y,
26:11 Y, the fire of Your enemies
29: 5 Y, it shall be in an instant,
30:33 was established of old, Y,
32:13 come up thorns and briers, Y,
40: 1 'Comfort, y, comfort My
41:10 I will strengthen you, Y,
41:23 Y, do good or do evil,
42:13 He shall cry out, y,
43: 7 My glory; I have formed him, y,
44:15 Y, he kindles it and bakes
44:19 half of it in the fire, Y,
45:21 Y, let them take counsel
46: 6 They prostrate themselves, y,
47: 3 shall be uncovered, Y,
48:15 Y, I have called him,
55: 1 Y, come, buy wine and milk
56:11 Y, they are greedy dogs
Jer 4:16 mention to the nations, Y,
5:28 Y, they surpass the deeds of
12: 2 You have planted them, y,
12: 2 have taken root; They grow, y,
12: 6 Y, they have called a multitude
14: 5 Y, the deer also gave birth
14:18 Y, both prophet and priest go
23:11 Y, in My house I have found
27:21 'y, thus says the LORD of
31: 3 'Y, I have loved you with an
31:19 on the thigh; I was ashamed, y,
32:41 'Y, I will rejoice over them
46:16 Y, one fell upon another.
51:44 Y, the wall of Babylon shall
Lam 1: 8 Y, she sighs and turns away.
Ezek 6:14 and make the land desolate, y,
16: 6 'Live!' Y, I said to you in
16: 8 Y, I swore an oath to you
16: 9 "Then I washed you in water; y,
16:52 Y, be disgraced also, and bear
22: 2 Y, show her all her
22:21 'Y, I will gather you and
26:18 Y, the coastlands by the sea
28:26 y, they will dwell securely,
32:10 'Y, I will make many peoples
32:28 Y, you shall be broken in
34: 6 y, My flock was scattered
36:12 'Y, I will cause men to walk
Dan 9:11 'Y, all Israel has transgressed
9:21 y, while I was speaking in
10:19 Peace be to you; be strong, y,
11:26 'Y, those who eat of the
Hos 2: 7 Y, she will seek them,
2:19 Y, I will betroth you to Me
7: 9 Y, gray hairs are here and
8:10 Y, though they have hired
9:12 Y, woe to them when I
9:16 Y, were they to bear
12: 4 Y, he struggled with the
Ob 16 Y, they shall drink, and
Jon 3: 8 y, let every one turn from
Mic 2:10 defiled, it shall destroy, Y,
Nah 1: 5 heaves at His presence, Y,
Zeph 2: 1 Gather yourselves together, y,
Zech 6:13 Y, He shall build the temple
7:12 'Y, they made their hearts like
8:22 Y, many peoples and strong
10: 7 Y, their children shall see it
12:10 Y, they will mourn for Him
14: 5 Y, you shall flee As you
14:21 Y, every pot in Jerusalem
Mal 2: 2 Y, I have cursed them
4: 1 an oven, And all the proud, y,
Mt 5:37 Y' be 'Yes,' and your 'No,'
5:37 "But let your 'Yes' be 'Y,'
9:28 this?" They said to Him, "Y,
11: 9 Y, I say to you, and more
13:51 things?" They said to Him, "Y,
15:27 And she said, "Y, Lord, yet
17:25 He said, "Y." And when he
21:16 And Jesus said to them, "Y.
Mk 7:28 answered and said to Him, "Y,
Lk 2:35 (y, a sword will pierce
7:26 Y, I say to you, and more
11:51 Y, I say to you, it shall
12: 5 y, I say to you, fear Him!
12:57 Y, and why, even of
14:26 brothers and sisters, y,
24:22 'Y, and certain women of our
Jn 11:27 She said to Him, "Y,
16: 2 y, the time is coming that
16:32 "Indeed the hour is coming, y,
21:15 to Him, "Y, Lord; You know
21:16 love Me?" He said to Him, "Y,
Acts 3:16 Y, the faith which comes
3:24 'Y, and all the prophets,
5: 8 for so much?" She said, "Y,
10:21 from Cornelius, and said, "Y,
20:34 'Y, you yourselves know that
22:27 are you a Roman?" He said, "Y.
Rom 3:29 Y, of the Gentiles also,
10:18 Y indeed: "Their sound
1 Cor 1:16 Y, I also baptized the
2:10 Spirit searches all things, y,
9:16 y, woe is me if I do not
15:15 Y, and we are found false
2 Cor 1: 9 Y, we had the sentence of
1:17 that with me there should be Y,
1:17 with me there should be Yes, Y,
1:18 our word to you was not Y and
1:19 was not Y and No, but in Him was
1:19 Yes and No, but in Him was Y.
1:20 promises of God in Him are Y,
5: 8 We are confident, y,
8: 3 according to their ability, y,
Gal 4:17 y, they want to exclude you,
Phil 1:18 and in this I rejoice, y,
2:17 Y, and if I am being poured
2 Tim 3:12 Y, and all who desire to live
Phm 1:20 Y, brother, let me have joy
Heb 6: 9 better things concerning you, y,
11:36 of mockings and scourgings, y,
Jas 5:12 other oath. But let your "Y,"
5:12 But let your "Yes," be "Y,
1 Pe 5: 5 Y, all of you be submissive
2 Pe 1:13 Y, I think it is right,
Rev 14:13 'Y," says the Spirit, "that

YESTERDAY (9/9)

Ex 5:14 task in making brick both y
1 Sam 20:27 either y or today?"
2 Sam 15:20 "In fact, you came only y.
2 Ki 9:26 Surely I saw y the blood of
Job 8: 9 For we were born y,
Ps 90: 4 in Your sight Are like y
Jn 4:52 Y at the seventh hour the fever
Acts 7:28 as you did the Egyptian y?
Heb 13: 8 Jesus Christ is the same y,

YESTERNIGHT (KJV) See (LAST) NIGHT

YET (464/449) See APPENDIX

YIELD (28/24) YIELDED, YIELDING, YIELDS

Gen 4:12 it shall no longer y its
49:20 And he shall y royal dainties.
Lev 19:25 that it may y to you its
25:19 Then the land will y its fruit,
26: 4 the land shall y its produce,
26: 4 the trees of the field shall y
26:20 for your land shall not y its
26:20 shall the trees of the land y
Num 20: 8 and it will y its water; thus
Deut 11:17 and the land y no produce, and
22: 9 lest the y of the seed which
2 Chr 30: 8 but y yourselves to the LORD;
Job 6:29 Y now, let there be no
40:20 Surely the mountains y food for
Ps 67: 6 Then the earth shall y her
85:12 And our land will y its
107:37 That they may y a fruitful
Prov 7:21 speech she caused him to y,
Isa 5:10 ten acres of vineyard shall y
5:10 And a homer of seed shall y
Ezek 34:27 the trees of the field shall y
34:27 and the earth shall y her
36: 8 forth your branches and y your
Joel 2:22 The fig tree and the vine y
Hab 3:17 And the fields y no food;
Acts 23:21 But do not y to them, for more
Gal 2: 5 to whom we did not y submission
Jas 3:17 peaceable, gentle, willing to y,

YIELDED (11/11) YIELD

Num 11: 4 who were among them y to
11:34 buried the people who had y to
17: 8 had produced blossoms and y
Dan 3:28 and y their bodies, that they
Hag 2:19 and the olive tree have not y
Mt 13: 8 fell on good ground and y a
27:50 and y up His spirit.
Mk 4: 7 and it y no crop.
4: 8 fell on good ground and y a
Lk 8: 8 and y a crop a hundredfold."
12:16 ground of a certain rich man y

YIELDING (2/2) YIELD

Jer 17: 8 Nor will cease from y fruit.
Rev 22: 2 each tree y its fruit every

YIELDS (12/9) YIELD

Gen 1:11 the herb that y seed, and the
1:11 and the fruit tree that y
1:12 the herb that y seed according
1:12 and the tree that y fruit,
1:29 given you every herb that y

1:29 and every tree whose fruit y
Neh 9:37 And it y much increase to the
Job 24: 5 The wilderness y food for
Prov 12:12 the root of the righteous y
Mk 4:28 For the earth y crops by itself:
Heb 12:11 afterward it y the peaceable
Jas 3:12 Thus no spring y both salt

YOKE (56/50) YOKED

Gen 27:40 That you shall break his y
Lev 26:13 broken the bands of your y and
Num 19: 2 is no defect and on which a y
Deut 21: 3 which has not pulled with a y.
28:48 and He will put a y of iron on
1 Sam 11: 7 So he took a y of oxen and cut
1 Ki 12: 4 Your father made our y heavy;
12: 4 and his heavy y which he put on
12: 9 Lighten the y which your father
12:10 Your father made our y heavy,
12:11 my father put a heavy y on you,
12:11 on you, I will add to your y;
12:14 My father made your y heavy, but
12:14 heavy, but I will add to your y;
19:19 who was plowing with twelve y
19:21 and took a y of oxen and
2 Chr 10: 4 Your father made our y heavy;
10: 4 of your father and his heavy y
10: 9 Lighten the y which your father
10:10 Your father made our y heavy,
10:11 my father put a heavy y on you,
10:11 on you, I will add to your y;
10:14 My father made your y heavy, but
Job 1: 3 five hundred y of oxen, five
42:12 one thousand y of oxen, and one
Isa 9: 4 For You have broken the y of
10:27 And his y from your neck,
10:27 And the y will be destroyed
14:25 Then his y shall be removed
47: 6 On the elderly you laid your y
58: 6 And that you break every y?
58: 9 If you take away the y from your
Jer 2:20 of old I have broken your y
5: 5 have altogether broken the y
27: 8 not put its neck under the y
27:11 bring their necks under the y
27:12 Bring your necks under the y of
28: 2 I have broken the y of the king
28: 4 for I will break the y of the
28:10 the prophet took the y off the
28:11 Even so I will break the y of
28:12 the prophet had broken the y
28:14 I have put a y of iron on the
30: 8 That I will break his y from
51:23 in pieces the farmer and his y
Lam 1:14 The y of my transgressions was
3:27 good for a man to bear The y
Ezek 34:27 broken the bands of their y
Hos 11: 4 to them as those who take the y
Nah 1:13 For now I will break off his y
Mt 11:29 Take My y upon you and learn
11:30 For My y is easy and My burden
Lk 14:19 I have bought five y of oxen,
Acts 15:10 do you test God by putting a y
Gal 5: 1 be entangled again with a y of
1 Tim 6: 1 as are under the y count their

YOKED (2/2) YOKE

1 Sam 6: 7 cows which have never been y,
2 Cor 6:14 Do not be unequally y together

YOKES (5/4)

2 Sam 24:22 threshing implements and the y
Jer 27: 2 for yourselves bonds and y,
28:13 You have broken the y of wood,
28:13 you have made in their place y
Ezek 30:18 When I break the y of Egypt

YONDER (1/1)

Gen 22: 5 the lad and I will go y and

YOU (14479/8372) See APPENDIX

YOU-ARE-THE-GOD-WHO-SEES (1/1) GOD

Gen 16:13 the LORD who spoke to her, Y;

YOUNG (370/350) YOUNGER, YOUNGEST, YOUTH

Gen 4:23 Even a y man for hurting me.
14:24 except only what the y men have
15: 9 turtledove, and a y pigeon."
18: 7 gave it to a y man, and he
19: 4 men of Sodom, both old and y,
22: 3 and took two of his y men with
22: 5 And Abraham said to his y men,
22:19 returned to his y men,
24:14 Now let it be that the y woman
24:16 Now the y woman was very
24:28 So the y woman ran and told her
24:55 Let the y woman stay with us a
24:57 We will call the y woman and ask
31:38 have not miscarried their y,
34: 3 and he loved the y woman
34: 3 woman and spoke kindly to the y
34: 4 Get me this y woman as a wife."
34:12 but give me the y woman as a
34:19 So the y man did not delay to do
38:17 I will send a y goat from the
38:20 And Judah sent the y goat by the
38:23 for I sent this y goat and you
41:12 Now there was a y Hebrew man
44:20 of his old age, who is y;
Ex 10: 9 We will go with our y and our
23:19 You shall not boil a y goat in
24: 5 Then he sent y men of the
29: 1 Take one y bull and two rams
33:11 a y man, did not depart from
34:26 You shall not boil a y goat in
Lev 1:14 of turtledoves or y pigeons.
4: 3 which he has sinned a y bull
4:14 assembly shall offer a y bull
5: 7 turtledoves or two y pigeons:
5:11 turtledoves or two y pigeons,
9: 2 Take for yourself a y bull as a
12: 6 and a y pigeon or a turtledove
12: 8 or two y pigeons—one
14:22 turtledoves or two y pigeons,
14:30 turtledoves or y pigeons,
15:14 turtledoves or two y pigeons,
15:29 turtledoves or two y pigeons,
16: 3 with the blood of a y bull
22:28 do not kill both her and her y
23:18 one y bull, and two rams.
Num 6:10 turtledoves or two y pigeons
7:15 one y bull, one ram, and one
7:21 one y bull, one ram, and one
7:27 one y bull, one ram, and one
7:33 one y bull, one ram, and one
7:39 one y bull, one ram, and one
7:45 one y bull, one ram, and one
7:51 one y bull, one ram, and one
7:57 one y bull, one ram, and one
7:63 one y bull, one ram, and one
7:69 one y bull, one ram, and one
7:75 one y bull, one ram, and one
7:81 one y bull, one ram, and one
7:87 offering were twelve y bulls,
8: 8 Then let them take a y bull with
8: 8 you shall take another y bull
8:12 on the heads of the y bulls,
11:27 And a y man ran and told Moses,
15: 8 And when you prepare a y bull as
15: 9 be offered with the y bull
15:11 be done for each y bull,
15:11 or for each lamb or y goat.
15:24 shall offer one y bull as a
28:11 two y bulls, one ram, and seven
28:19 two y bulls, one ram, and seven
28:27 two y bulls, one ram, and seven
29: 2 one y bull, one ram, and seven
29: 8 one y bull, one ram, and seven
29:13 thirteen y bulls, two rams,
29:17 day present twelve y bulls,
31:18 for yourselves all the y girls
Deut 14:21 You shall not boil a y goat in
22: 6 with y ones or eggs, with the
22: 6 the mother sitting on the y or
22: 6 not take the mother with the y;
22: 7 and take the y for yourself,
22:15 and mother of the y woman
22:15 of the y woman's virginity
22:16 And the y woman's father shall
22:19 the father of the y woman,
22:20 are not found for the y woman,
22:21 shall bring out the y woman
22:23 If a y woman who is a virgin
22:24 the y woman because she did not
22:25 finds a betrothed y woman
22:26 do nothing to the y woman;
22:26 there is in the y woman no
22:27 and the betrothed y woman
22:28 If a man finds a y woman who
22:29 give to the y woman's father
28:50 elderly nor show favor to the y.
32:11 up its nest, Hovers over its y,
32:25 within For the y man
Josh 6:21 y and old, ox and sheep and
6:23 And the y men who had been spies
Judg 6:19 went in and prepared a y goat,
6:25 Take your father's y bull, the
8:14 And he caught a y man of the men
9:54 he called quickly to the y man,
9:54 " So his y man thrust him
12:14 who rode on seventy y donkeys.
13:15 and we will prepare a y goat
13:19 So Manoah took the y goat with
14: 5 a y lion came roaring against
14: 6 have torn apart a y goat,
14:10 for y men used to do so.
15: 1 visited his wife with a y goat.
17: 7 Now there was a y man from
17:11 and the y man became like one
17:12 and the y man became his
18: 3 the voice of the y Levite.
18:15 house of the y Levite man—to
19: 3 the father of the y woman
19: 4 the y woman's father, detained
19: 5 but the y woman's father said
19: 6 Then the y woman's father said
19: 8 but the y woman's father said,
19: 9 the y woman's father, said to
19:19 and for the y man who is with
21:12 four hundred y virgins who
Ruth 2: 5 Whose y woman is this?"
2: 6 It is the y Moabite woman who
2: 8 but stay close by my y women.
2: 9 Have I not commanded the y men
2: 9 and drink from what the y men
2:15 Boaz commanded his y men,
2:21 You shall stay close by my y men
2:22 go out with his y women,
2:23 stayed close by the y women
3: 2 whose y women you were with,
3:10 you did not go after y men,
4:12 give you from this y woman."
1 Sam 1:24 in Shiloh. And the child was y.
2:17 Therefore the sin of the y men
8:16 your finest y men, and your
9:11 they met some y women going out
10: 3 one carrying three y goats,
14: 1 son of Saul said to the y man
14: 6 Then Jonathan said to the y man
16:11 'Are all the y men here?"
16:20 and a y goat, and sent them by
17:56 Inquire whose son this y man
17:58 'Whose son are you, y man?"
20:22 But if I say thus to the y man,
21: 2 And I have directed my y men
21: 4 if the y men have at least kept
21: 5 And the vessels of the y men
25: 5 David sent ten y men; and David
25: 5 and David said to the y men,
25: 8 Ask your y men, and they will
25: 8 Therefore let my y men find
25: 9 So when David's y men came, they
25:12 So David's y men turned on their
25:14 Now one of the y men told
25:25 did not see the y men of my
25:27 let it be given to the y men
26:22 Let one of the y men come over
30:13 I am a y man from Egypt,
30:17 except four hundred y men who
2 Sam 1: 5 So David said to the y man who
1: 6 Then the y man who told him
1:13 Then David said to the y man who
1:15 David called one of the y men
2:14 Let the y men now arise and
2:21 lay hold on one of the y men
4:12 So David commanded his y men,
9:12 Mephibosheth had a y son whose
13:32 they have killed all the y men,
13:34 And the y man who was keeping
14:21 bring back the y man Absalom."
16: 2 and summer fruit for the y men
18: 5 for my sake with the y man
18:12 lest anyone touch the y man
18:15 And ten y men who bore Joab's
18:29 Is the y man Absalom safe?"
18:32 'Is the y man Absalom safe?"
18:32 be like that y man!"
1 Ki 1: 2 Let a y woman, a virgin, be
1: 3 sought for a lovely y woman
1: 4 The y woman was very lovely;
11:28 seeing that the y man was
12: 8 and consulted the y men who had
12:10 Then the y men who had grown up
12:14 to the advice of the y men,
20:14 By the y leaders of the
20:15 Then he mustered the y leaders
20:17 The y leaders of the provinces
20:19 Then these y leaders of the
2 Ki 4:22 Please send me one of the y men
5: 2 back captive a y girl from
5:22 just now two y men of the sons
6:17 opened the eyes of the y man,
8:12 and their y men you will kill
9: 4 So the y man, the servant of
1 Chr 12:28 a y man, a valiant warrior, and
22: 5 Solomon my son is y and
29: 1 is y and inexperienced;
2 Chr 10: 8 and consulted the y men who had
10:10 Then the y men who had grown up
10:14 to the advice of the y men,
13: 7 when Rehoboam was y and
13: 9 himself with a y bull
34: 3 his reign, while he was still y,
35: 7 lay people lambs and y goats
36:17 who killed their y men with the
36:17 and had no compassion on y man
Ezra 6: 9 y bulls, rams, and lambs for the
Esth 2: 2 Let beautiful y virgins be
2: 3 all the beautiful y virgins
2: 4 Then let the y woman who pleases
2: 7 The y woman was lovely and
2: 8 and when many y women were
2: 9 Now the y woman pleased him, and
2:12 Each y woman's turn came to go
2:13 each y woman went to the king,
3:13 both y and old, little children
Job 1:19 and it fell on the y people,
4:10 And the teeth of the y lions
19:18 Even y children despise me;
29: 8 The y men saw me and hid,
31: 1 I look upon a y woman?
32: 6 I am y in years, and you are
33:25 His flesh shall be y like a
38:39 satisfy the appetite of the y
38:41 When its y ones cry to God,
39: 1 the wild mountain goats bear y?
39: 2 know the time when they bear y?
39: 3 They bring forth their y,
39: 4 Their y ones are healthy,
39:16 She treats her y harshly, as
39:30 Its y ones suck up blood;
Ps 17:12 And like a y lion lurking in
29: 6 and Sirion like a y wild ox.
34:10 The y lions lack and suffer
37:25 I have been y, and now am
58: 6 out the fangs of the y lions,

Y

78:63 The fire consumed their **y** men,
78:71 following the ewes that had **y**
84: 3 Where she may lay her **y**—
91:13 The **y** lion and the serpent you
104:21 The **y** lions roar after their
105:34 **Y** locusts without number,
119: 9 How can a **y** man cleanse his
147: 9 And to the **y** ravens that cry.
148:12 Both **y** men and maidens;
Prov 1: 4 To the **y** man knowledge and
7: 7 **y** man devoid of understanding,
20:29 The glory of **y** men is their
30:17 And the **y** eagles will eat it.
Eccl 11: 9 O **y** man, in your youth,
Song 2: 9 is like a gazelle or a **y** stag.
2:17 like a gazelle Or a **y** stag
8:14 like a gazelle Or a **y** stag
Isa 5:29 They will roar like **y** lions;
7:21 a man will keep alive a **y** cow
9:17 will have no joy in their **y**
11: 6 shall lie down with the **y** goat,
11: 6 The calf and the **y** lion and
11: 7 Their **y** ones shall lie down
13:18 bows will dash the **y** men
20: 4 **y** and old, naked and barefoot,
23: 4 Neither do I rear **y** men,
30: 6 on the backs of **y** donkeys,
30:24 the oxen and the **y** donkeys
31: 4 And a **y** lion over his prey
31: 8 And his **y** men shall become
34: 7 And the **y** bulls with the
40:11 lead those who are with **y**.
40:30 And the **y** men shall utterly
62: 5 For as a **y** man marries a
Jer 2:15 The **y** lions roared at him, and
6:11 And on the assembly of **y** men
9:21 And the **y** men—no longer
11:22 The **y** men shall die by the
15: 8 the mother of the **y** men,
18:21 Their **y** men be slain By the
31:12 For the **y** of the flock and the
31:13 And the **y** men and the old,
48:15 Her chosen **y** men have gone
49:26 Therefore her **y** men shall fall
50:30 Therefore her **y** men shall fall
51: 3 Do not spare her **y** men;
51:22 will break in pieces old and **y**;
51:22 break in pieces the **y** man
Lam 1:15 against me To crush my **y** men;
1:18 My virgins and my **y** men Have
2:19 life of your **y** children,
2:21 **Y** and old lie On the ground in
2:21 My virgins and my **y** men Have
4: 3 their breasts To nurse their **y**;
4: 4 The **y** children ask for bread,
5:13 **Y** men ground at the millstones
5:14 And the **y** men from their
Ezek 9: 6 Utterly slay old and **y** men,
17: 4 cropped off its topmost **y** twig
17:22 the topmost of its **y** twigs
19: 2 Among the **y** lions she
19: 3 And he became a **y** lion;
19: 5 cubs and made him a **y** lion.
19: 6 And became a **y** lion;
23: 6 All of them desirable **y** men,
23:12 All of them desirable **y** men.
23:23 All of them desirable **y** men,
30:17 The **y** men of Aven and Pi Beseth
31: 6 the field brought forth their **y**;
32: 2 You are like a **y** lion among the
36:11 they shall increase and bear **y**;
38:13 and all their **y** lions will say
41:19 and the face of a **y** lion toward
43:19 You shall give a **y** bull for a
43:23 shall offer a **y** bull
43:25 they shall also prepare a **y**
45:18 you shall take a **y** bull without
46: 6 it shall be a **y** bull
Dan 1: 4 **y** men in whom there was no
1:10 looking worse than the **y** men
1:13 and the appearance of the **y** men
1:15 in flesh than all the **y** men
1:17 As for these four **y** men, God
Hos 5:14 And like a **y** lion to the house
Joel 2:28 Your **y** men shall see visions.
Am 2:11 And some of your **y** men as
3: 4 Will a **y** lion cry out of his
4:10 Your **y** men I killed with a
8:13 fair virgins And strong **y** men
Mic 5: 8 Like a **y** lion among flocks of
Nah 2:11 feeding place of the **y** lions,
2:13 shall devour your **y** lions;
3:10 Her **y** children also were
Zech 2: 4 speak to this **y** man, saying:
9:17 Grain shall make the **y** men
9:17 And new wine the **y** women.
11:16 who are cut off, nor seek the **y**,
Mt 2: 8 carefully for the **y** Child,
2: 9 stood over where the **y** Child
2:11 they saw the **y** Child with Mary
2:13 take the **y** Child and His
2:13 for Herod will seek the **y** Child
2:14 he took the **y** Child and His
2:20 take the **y** Child and His
2:20 sought the **y** Child's life
2:21 took the **y** Child and His
19:20 The **y** man said to Him, "All
19:22 But when the **y** man heard that
Mk 7:25 For a woman whose **y** daughter had
14:51 Now a certain **y** man followed
14:51 And the **y** men laid hold of him,
16: 5 they saw a **y** man clothed in a
Lk 2:24 or two **y** pigeons."
7:14 **Y** man, I say to you, arise."
15:29 you never gave me a **y** goat,
Jn 12:14 when He had found a **y** donkey,
Acts 2:17 Your **y** men shall see
5: 6 And the **y** men arose and wrapped
5:10 And the **y** men came in and found
7:58 clothes at the feet of a **y** man
20: 9 in a window sat a certain **y** man
20:12 And they brought the **y** man in
23:17 Take this **y** man to the
23:18 asked me to bring this **y** man
23:22 So the commander let the **y** man
Titus 2: 4 that they admonish the **y** women
2: 6 Likewise exhort the **y** men to be
1 Jn 2:13 **y** men, Because you have
2:14 **y** men, Because you are strong,

YOUNGER (32/32) YOUNG

Gen 9:24 and knew what his **y** son had
19:31 Now the firstborn said to the **y**,
19:34 the firstborn said to the **y**,
19:35 And the **y** arose and lay with
19:38 And the **y**, she also bore a
25:23 the older shall serve the **y**.
27:15 them on Jacob her **y** son.
27:42 and called Jacob her **y** son,
29:16 and the name of the **y** was
29:18 for Rachel your **y** daughter."
29:26 to give the **y** before the
43:29 Is this your **y** brother of whom
48:14 Ephraim's head, who was the **y**,
48:19 but truly his **y** brother shall
Judg 1:13 Caleb's **y** brother, took it;
3: 9 Kenaz, Caleb's **y** brother.
15: 2 Is not her **y** sister better
1 Sam 14:49 and the name of the **y** Michal.
1 Chr 24:31 just as their **y** brethren.
Job 30: 1 men **y** than I, Whose fathers I
Ezek 16:46 and your **y** sister, who dwells
16:61 your older and your **y** sisters;
Lk 15:12 And the **y** of them said to his
15:13 the **y** son gathered all
22:26 among you, let him be as the **y**,
Jn 21:18 I say to you, when you were **y**,
Rom 9:12 older shall serve the **y**.
1 Tim 5: 1 **y** men as brothers,
5: 2 **y** as sisters, with all purity.
5:11 But refuse the **y** widows;
5:14 I desire that the **y** widows
1 Pe 5: 5 Likewise you **y** people, submit

YOUNGEST (18/17) YOUNG

Gen 42:13 the **y** is with our father
42:15 place unless your **y** brother
42:20 And bring your **y** brother to me;
42:32 and the **y** is with our father
42:34 And bring your **y** brother to me;
43:33 to his birthright and the **y**
44: 2 the mouth of the sack of the **y**,
44:12 oldest and left off with the **y**;
44:23 Unless your **y** brother comes down
44:26 if our **y** brother is with us,
44:26 man's face unless our **y** brother
Josh 6:26 and with his **y** he shall set up
Judg 9: 5 But Jotham the **y** son of
1 Sam 16:11 said, "There remains yet the **y**,
17:14 David was the **y**. And the three
1 Ki 16:34 and with his **y** son Segub he
2 Chr 21:17 Jehoahaz, the **y** of his sons.
22: 1 made Ahaziah his **y** son king

YOUR (7195/4668) See APPENDIX

YOURS (73/65) See APPENDIX

YOURSELF (257/233) See APPENDIX

YOURSELVES (235/221) See APPENDIX

YOUTH (70/67) YOUNG, YOUTHFUL, YOUTHS

Gen 8:21 man's heart is evil from his **y**;
43:33 the youngest according to his **y**;
46:34 been with livestock from our **y**
Lev 22:13 her father's house as in her **y**,
Num 30: 3 in her father's house in her **y**,
30:16 and his daughter in her **y** in
Judg 8:20 kill them!" But the **y** would
8:20 because he was still a **y**.
1 Sam 17:33 with him; for you are a **y**,
17:33 and he a man of war from his **y**.
17:42 him; for he was only a **y**,
17:55 "Abner, whose son is this **y**?
2 Sam 19: 7 has befallen you from your **y**
1 Ki 18:12 have feared the LORD from my **y**.
Job 13:26 inherit the iniquities of my **y**.
31:18 (But from my **y** I reared him as
33:25 return to the days of his **y**.
36:14 They die in **y**,
Ps 25: 7 not remember the sins of my **y**,
71: 5 You are my trust from my **y**.
71:17 You have taught me from my **y**;
88:15 and ready to die from my **y**;
89:45 The days of his **y** You have
103: 5 So that your **y** is renewed
110: 3 You have the dew of Your **y**.
127: 4 are the children of one's **y**.
129: 1 have afflicted me from my **y**,
129: 2 have afflicted me from my **y**;
144:12 as plants grown up in their **y**;
Prov 2:17 forsakes the companion of her **y**,
5:18 rejoice with the wife of your **y**.
Eccl 4:13 Better a poor and wise **y** Than
4:15 They were with the second **y**
11: 9 O young man, in your **y**,
11: 9 cheer you in the days of your **y**;
11:10 For childhood and **y** are
12: 1 Creator in the days of your **y**,
Isa 47:12 you have labored from your **y**—
47:15 Your merchants from your **y**;
54: 4 will forget the shame of your **y**,
Jer 1: 6 I cannot speak, for I am a **y**.
1: 7 me: "Do not say, 'I am a **y**,
2: 2 The kindness of your **y**,
3: 4 You are the guide of my **y**?
3:24 labor of our fathers from our **y**—
3:25 From our **y** even to this day,
22:21 been your manner from your **y**,
31:19 I bore the reproach of my **y**.
32:30 evil before Me from their **y**.
48:11 has been at ease from his **y**;
Lam 3:27 man to bear The yoke in his **y**.
Ezek 4:14 never defiled myself from my **y**
16:22 not remember the days of your **y**,
16:43 not remember the days of your **y**,
16:60 with you in the days of your **y**,
23: 3 committed harlotry in their **y**;
23: 8 For in her **y** they had lain
23:19 remembrance the days of her **y**,
23:21 the lewdness of your **y**,
Hos 2:15 As in the days of her **y**,
Joel 1: 8 For the husband of her **y**.
Zech 13: 5 me to keep cattle from my **y**.
Mal 2:14 you and the wife of your **y**,
2:15 with the wife of his **y**.
Mt 19:20 things I have kept from my **y**.
Mk 10:20 things I have kept from my **y**.
Lk 18:21 things I have kept from my **y**.
Acts 26: 4 "My manner of life from my **y**,
1 Cor 7:36 if she is past the flower of **y**,
1 Tim 4:12 Let no one despise your **y**,

YOUTHFUL (4/4) YOUTH

Job 20:11 are full of his **y** vigor,
Isa 54: 6 Like a **y** wife when you were
Ezek 23:21 Because of your **y** breasts.
2 Tim 2:22 Flee also **y** lusts; but pursue

YOUTHS (4/4) YOUTH

2 Ki 2:23 some **y** came from the city and
2:24 and mauled forty-two of the **y**.
Prov 7: 7 I perceived among the **y**,
Isa 40:30 Even the **y** shall faint and be

Z

ZAANAIM (1/1)

Judg 4:11 near the terebinth tree at **Z**,

ZAANAN (1/1)

Mic 1:11 The inhabitant of **Z** does not

ZAANANNIM (1/1)

Josh 19:33 from the terebinth tree in **Z**,

ZAAVAN (2/2)

Gen 36:27 the sons of Ezer: Bilhan, **Z**,
1 Chr 1:42 sons of Ezer were Bilhan, **Z**,

ZABAD (8/8)

1 Chr 2:36 Nathan, and Nathan begot **Z**;
2:37 **Z** begot Ephlal, and Ephlal begot
7:21 **Z** his son, Shuthelah his son,
11:41 **Z** the son of Ahlai,
2 Chr 24:26 **Z** the son of Shimeath the
Ezra 10:27 Mattaniah, Jeremoth, **Z**,
10:33 Hashum: Mattenai, Mattattah, **Z**,
10:43 of Nebo: Jeiel, Mattithiah, **Z**,

ZABBAI (2/2)

Ezra 10:28 Bebai: Jehohanan, Hananiah, **Z**,
Neh 3:20 After him Baruch the son of **Z**

ZABBUD (1/1)

Ezra 8:14 the sons of Bigvai, Uthai and **Z**,

ZABDI (6/6)

Josh 7: 1 the son of Carmi, the son of **Z**,
7:17 man by man, and **Z** was taken.
7:18 the son of Carmi, the son of **Z**,
1 Chr 8:19 Jakim, Zichri, **Z**,
27:27 and **Z** the Shiphmite was over
Neh 11:17 the son of Micha, the son of **Z**,

ZABDIEL (2/2)
1 Chr 27: 2 was Jashobeam the son of Z,
Neh 11:14 Their overseer was Z the son

ZABUD (1/1)
1 Ki 4: 5 Z the son of Nathan, a priest

ZABULON (KJV) See ZEBULUN

ZACCAI (2/2)
Ezra 2: 9 the people of Z, seven hundred
Neh 7:14 the sons of Z, seven hundred

ZACCHAEUS (3/3)
Lk 19: 2 there was a man named Z who
19: 5 'Z, make haste and come down,
19: 8 Then Z stood and said to the

ZACCHUR (1/1)
1 Chr 4:26 Z his son, and Shimei his son.

ZACCUR (8/8)
Num 13: 4 of Reuben, Shammua the son of Z;
1 Chr 24:27 Jaaziah were Beno, Shoham, Z,
25: 2 Of the sons of Asaph: Z,
25:10 the third for Z, his sons and
Neh 3: 2 And next to them Z the son of
10:12 Z, Sherebiah, Shebaniah,
12:35 son of Michaiah, the son of Z,
13:13 to them was Hanan the son of Z,

ZACHARIAH (KJV) See ZECHARIAH

ZACHARIAS (9/9) ZECHARIAH
Lk 1: 5 Judea, a certain priest named Z,
1:12 And when Z saw him, he was
1:13 to him, "Do not be afraid, Z,
1:18 And Z said to the angel, "How
1:21 And the people waited for Z,
1:40 and entered the house of Z and
1:59 by the name of his father, Z.
1:67 Now his father Z was filled
3: 2 God came to John the son of Z

ZACHER (KJV) See ZECHER

ZADOK (54/50)
2 Sam 8:17 Z the son of Ahitub and
15:24 There was Z also, and all the
15:25 Then the king said to Z,
15:27 The king also said to Z the
15:29 Therefore Z and Abiathar carried
15:35 And do you not have Z and
15:35 you shall tell to Z and
17:15 Then Hushai said to Z and
18:19 Then Ahimaaz the son of Z said,
18:22 And Ahimaaz the son of Z said
18:27 running of Ahimaaz the son of Z.
19:11 So King David sent to Z and
20:25 Z and Abiathar were the
1 Ki 1: 8 But Z the priest, Benaiah the
1:26 nor Z the priest, nor Benaiah
1:32 Call to me Z the priest, Nathan
1:34 There let Z the priest and
1:38 So Z the priest, Nathan the
1:39 Then Z the priest took a horn of
1:44 The king has sent with him Z the
1:45 So Z the priest and Nathan the
2:35 and the king put Z the priest
4: 2 officials: Azariah the son of Z,
4: 4 Z and Abiathar, the priests;
2 Ki 15:33 was Jerusha the daughter of Z.
1 Chr 6: 8 Ahitub begot Z, and Zadok
6: 8 Zadok, and Z begot Ahimaaz;
6:12 Ahitub begot Z, and Zadok
6:12 Zadok, and Z begot Shallum;
6:53 Z his son, and Ahimaaz his son.
9:11 son of Meshullam, the son of Z,
12:28 Z, a young man, a valiant
15:11 And David called for Z and
16:39 and Z the priest and his
18:16 Z the son of Ahitub and
24: 3 Then David with Z of the sons of
24: 6 Z the priest, Ahimelech the son
24:31 the presence of King David, Z,
27:17 Kemuel; over the Aaronites, Z;
29:22 and Z to be priest.
2 Chr 27: 1 was Jerushah the daughter of Z.
31:10 priest, from the house of Z,
Ezra 7: 2 son of Shallum, the son of Z,
Neh 3: 4 Next to them Z the son of Baana
3:29 After them Z the son of Immer
10:21 Meshezabel, Z, Jaddua,
11:11 son of Meshullam, the son of Z,
13:13 Shelemiah the priest and Z the
Ezek 40:46 altar; these are the sons of Z,
43:19 who are of the seed of Z,
44:15 the Levites, the sons of Z,
48:11 the priests of the sons of Z,
Mt 1:14 Azor begot Z, Zadok begot
1:14 Z begot Achim, and Achim begot

ZADOK'S (1/1)
2 Sam 15:36 Z son, and Jonathan,

ZAHAM (1/1)
2 Chr 11:19 Jeush, Shamariah, and Z.

ZAIR (1/1)
2 Ki 8:21 So Joram went to Z, and all

ZALAPH (1/1)
Neh 3:30 and Hanun, the sixth son of Z,

ZALMON (3/3)
Judg 9:48 Abimelech went up to Mount Z,
2 Sam 23:28 Z the Ahohite, Maharai the
Ps 68:14 It was white as snow in Z.

ZALMONAH (2/2)
Num 33:41 from Mount Hor and camped at Z.
33:42 They departed from Z and camped

ZALMUNNA (12/9)
Judg 8: 5 and I am pursuing Zebah and Z,
8: 6 Are the hands of Zebah and Z
8: 7 has delivered Zebah and Z into
8:10 Now Zebah and Z were at
8:12 When Zebah and Z fled, he
8:12 kings of Midian, Zebah and Z,
8:15 said, "Here are Zebah and Z,
8:15 Are the hands of Zebah and Z
8:18 And he said to Zebah and Z,
8:21 So Zebah and Z said, "Rise
8:21 arose and killed Zebah and Z,
Ps 83:11 their princes like Zebah and Z,

ZAMZUMMIM (1/1)
Deut 2:20 But the Ammonites call them Z,

ZANOAH (5/5)
Josh 15:34 Z, En Gannim, Tappuah,
15:56 Jezreel, Jokdeam, Z,
1 Chr 4:18 and Jekuthiel the father of Z.
Neh 3:13 Hanun and the inhabitants of Z
11:30 Z, Adullam, and their villages;

ZAPHNATH-PAANEAH (1/1)
Gen 41:45 Pharaoh called Joseph's name Z.

ZAPHON (2/2)
Josh 13:27 Beth Nimrah, Succoth, and Z,
Judg 12: 1 together, crossed over toward Z,

ZARA, ZARAH (KJV) See ZERAH

ZAREAH (KJV) See ZORAH

ZAREATHITES (KJV) See ZORATHITES

ZARED (KJV) See ZERED

ZAREPHATH (4/4)
1 Ki 17: 9 'Arise, go to Z, which belongs
17:10 So he arose and went to Z.
Ob 20 of the Canaanites As far as Z.
Lk 4:26 was Elijah sent except to Z,

ZARETAN (3/3)
Josh 3:16 the city that is beside Z.
1 Ki 4:12 which is beside Z below
7:46 molds, between Succoth and Z.

ZARETH-SHAHAR (KJV) See ZERETH (SHAHAR)

ZARHITES (6/5)
Num 26:13 of Zerah, the family of the Z;
26:20 of Zerah, the family of the Z.
Josh 7:17 and he took the family of the Z;
7:17 he brought the family of the Z
1 Chr 27:11 the Hushathite, of the Z;
27:13 the Netophathite, of the Z;

ZARTANAH, ZARTHAN (KJV) See ZARETAN

ZATTU (4/4)
Ezra 2: 8 the people of Z, nine hundred
10:27 of the sons of Z: Elioenai,
Neh 7:13 the sons of Z, eight hundred and
10:14 Parosh, Pahath-Moab, Elam, Z,

ZAVAN (KJV) See ZAAVAN

ZAZA (1/1)
1 Chr 2:33 of Jonathan were Peleth and Z.

ZEAL (22/21) ZEALOT, ZEALOUS
Num 25:11 he was zealous with My **z** among
25:11 the children of Israel in My **z**.
2 Sam 21: 2 sought to kill them in his **z**
2 Ki 10:16 and see my **z** for the LORD."
19:31 The **z** of the LORD of hosts
Ps 69: 9 Because **z** for Your house has
119:139 My **z** has consumed me, Because
Isa 9: 7 The **z** of the LORD of hosts
37:32 The **z** of the LORD of hosts
42:13 He shall stir up His **z** like a
59:17 And was clad with **z** as a
63:15 Where are Your **z** and Your
Ezek 5:13 LORD, have spoken it in My **z**,
Zech 1:14 And for Zion with great **z**.
8: 2 zealous for Zion with great **z**;
Jn 2:17 Z for Your house has eaten
Rom 10: 2 witness that they have a **z** for
2 Cor 7: 7 your **z** for me, so that I
7:11 what vehement desire, what **z**,
9: 2 and your **z** has stirred up the
Phil 3: 6 concerning **z**, persecuting the
Col 4:13 witness that he has a great **z**

ZEALOT (2/2) ZEAL
Lk 6:15 and Simon called the Z;
Acts 1:13 of Alphaeus and Simon the Z;

ZEALOUS (18/17) ZEAL
Num 11:29 'Are you **z** for my sake?
25:11 because he was **z** with My zeal
25:13 because he was **z** for his God,
1 Ki 19:10 I have been very **z** for the LORD
19:14 I have been very **z** for the LORD
Prov 23:17 But be **z** for the fear of the
Joel 2:18 Then the LORD will be **z** for
Zech 1:14 I am **z** for Jerusalem And for
8: 2 I am **z** for Zion with great zeal;
8: 2 With great fervor I am **z** for
Acts 21:20 and they are all **z** for the law;
22: 3 and was **z** toward God as you all
1 Cor 14:12 since you are **z** for spiritual
Gal 1:14 being more exceedingly **z** for
4:17 that you may be **z** for them.
4:18 But it is good to be **z** in a good
Titus 2:14 people, **z** for good works.
Rev 3:19 Therefore be **z** and repent.

ZEALOUSLY (2/2)
Gal 4:17 They **z** court you, but for no
2 Tim 1:17 he sought me out very **z** and

ZEBADIAH (9/9)
1 Chr 8:15 Z, Arad, Eder,
8:17 Z, Meshullam, Hizki, Heber,
12: 7 and Joelah and Z the sons of
26: 2 Z the third, Jathniel the
27: 7 and Z his son after him; in his
2 Chr 17: 8 Levites: Shemaiah, Nethaniah, Z,
19:11 and Z the son of Ishmael, the
Ezra 8: 8 Z the son of Michael, and with
10:20 the sons of Immer: Hanani and Z;

ZEBAH (12/9)
Judg 8: 5 and I am pursuing Z and
8: 6 Are the hands of Z and Zalmunna
8: 7 when the LORD has delivered Z
8:10 Now Z and Zalmunna were at
8:12 When Z and Zalmunna fled, he
8:12 Z and Zalmunna, and routed the
8:15 Here are Z and Zalmunna, about
8:15 Are the hands of Z and Zalmunna
8:18 And he said to Z and Zalmunna,
8:21 So Z and Zalmunna said, "Rise
8:21 So Gideon arose and killed Z
Ps 83:11 all their princes like Z and

ZEBAIM (2/2)
Ezra 2:57 the sons of Pochereth of Z,
Neh 7:59 the sons of Pochereth of Z,

ZEBEDEE (10/9)
Mt 4:21 brothers, James the son of Z,
4:21 in the boat with Z their
10: 2 brother; James the son of Z,
26:37 Him Peter and the two sons of Z,
Mk 1:19 He saw James the son of Z,
1:20 and they left their father Z in
3:17 James the son of Z and John the
10:35 James and John, the sons of Z,
Lk 5:10 James and John, the sons of Z,
Jn 21: 2 Cana in Galilee, the sons of Z,

ZEBEDEE'S (2/2)
Mt 20:20 Then the mother of Z sons came
27:56 and the mother of Z sons.

ZEBINA (1/1)
Ezra 10:43 Jeiel, Mattithiah, Zabad, Z,

ZEBOIIM (4/4)
Gen 10:19 Sodom, Gomorrah, Admah, and Z,
14: 2 of Admah, Shemeber king of Z,

	14: 8	king of Admah, the king of Z,
Hos	11: 8	How can I set you like Z?

ZEBOIM (3/3)

Deut	29:23	and Gomorrah, Admah, and Z,
1 Sam	13:18	that overlooks the Valley of Z
Neh	11:34	in Hadid, Z, Neballat;

ZEBUDAH (1/1)

2 Ki	23:36	His mother's name was Z the

ZEBUL (6/5)

Judg	9:28	and is not Z his officer?
	9:30	When Z, the ruler of the city,
	9:36	saw the people, he said to Z,
	9:36	But Z said to him, "You see
	9:38	Then Z said to him, "Where
	9:41	and Z drove out Gaal and his

ZEBULUN (48/46)

Gen	30:20	So she called his name Z.
	35:23	Levi, Judah, Issachar, and Z;
	46:14	The sons of Z were Sered, Elon,
	49:13	Z shall dwell by the haven of
Ex	1: 3	Issachar, Z, and Benjamin;
Num	1: 9	'from Z, Eliab the son of
	1:30	From the children of Z,
	1:31	were numbered of the tribe of Z
	2: 7	"Then comes the tribe of Z,
	2: 7	the leader of the children of Z.
	7:24	leader of the children of Z,
	10:16	the tribe of the children of Z
	13:10	from the tribe of Z,
	26:26	The sons of Z according to
	34:25	the tribe of the children of Z,
Deut	27:13	to curse: Reuben, Gad, Asher, Z,
	33:18	And of Z he said: "Rejoice,
	33:18	Zebulun he said: "Rejoice, Z,
Josh	19:10	came out for the children of Z
	19:16	of the children of Z according
	19:27	and it reached to Z and to the
	19:34	it adjoined Z on the south side
	21: 7	of Gad, and from the tribe of Z.
	21:34	Levites, from the tribe of Z,
Judg	1:30	Nor did Z drive out the
	4: 6	Naphtali and of the sons of Z;
	4:10	And Barak called Z and Naphtali
	5:14	And from Z those who bear the
	5:18	Z is a people who jeopardized
	6:35	sent messengers to Asher, Z,
	12:12	at Aijalon in the country of Z.
1 Chr	2: 1	Levi, Judah, Issachar, Z,
	6:63	of Gad, and from the tribe of Z.
	6:77	From the tribe of Z the rest of
	12:33	of Z there were fifty thousand
	12:40	as far away as Issachar and Z
	27:19	over Z, Ishmaiah the son of
2 Chr	30:10	and Manasseh, as far as Z;
	30:11	and Z humbled themselves and
	30:18	Manasseh, Issachar, and Z,
Ps	68:27	The princes of Z and the
Isa	9: 1	esteemed The land of Z and
Ezek	48:26	Z shall have one section;
	48:27	"by the border of Z,
	48:33	Issachar, and one gate for Z;
Mt	4:13	in the regions of Z and
	4:15	The land of Z and the land
Rev	7: 8	of the tribe of Z twelve

ZEBULUNITE (2/2)

Judg	12:11	Elon the Z judged Israel.
	12:12	And Elon the Z died and was

ZEBULUNITES (1/1)

Num	26:27	are the families of the Z

ZECHARIAH (45/45) ZACHARIAS

2 Ki	14:29	Then Z his son reigned in his
	15: 8	Z the son of Jeroboam reigned
	15:11	Now the rest of the acts of Z,
	18: 2	name was Abi the daughter of Z.
1 Chr	5: 7	the chief, Jeiel, and Z,
	9:21	Z the son of Meshelemiah was
	9:37	Gedor, Ahio, Z, and Mikloth.
	15:18	brethren of the second rank: Z,
	15:20	Z, Aziel, Shemiramoth, Jehiel,
	15:24	Joshaphat, Nethanel, Amasai, Z,
	16: 5	the chief, and next to him Z,
	24:25	of the sons of Isshiah, Z.
	26: 2	the sons of Meshelemiah were Z
	26:11	Z the fourth; all the sons and
	26:14	they cast lots for his son Z,
	27:21	in Gilead, Iddo the son of Z;
2 Chr	17: 7	leaders, Ben-Hail, Obadiah, Z,
	20:14	came upon Jahaziel the son of Z,
	21: 2	Jehoshaphat: Azariah, Jehiel, Z,
	24:20	the Spirit of God came upon Z
	26: 5	He sought God in the days of Z,
	29: 1	was Abijah the daughter of Z.
	29:13	of Asaph, Z and Mattaniah;
	34:12	and Z and Meshullam, of the
	35: 8	Hilkiah, Z, and Jehiel, rulers
Ezra	5: 1	Then the prophet Haggai and Z
	6:14	of Haggai the prophet and Z
	8: 3	of the sons of Parosh, Z;
	8:11	Z the son of Bebai, and with
	8:16	Jarib, Elnathan, Nathan, Z,
	10:26	the sons of Elam: Mattaniah, Z,
Neh	8: 4	Hashum, Hashbadana, Z,
	11: 4	the son of Uzziah, the son of Z,
	11: 5	son of Joiarib, the son of Z,
	11:12	the son of Amzi, the son of Z,
	12:16	of Iddo, Z; of Ginnethon,
	12:35	Z the son of Jonathan, the son
	12:41	Minjamin, Michaiah, Elioenai, Z,
Isa	8: 2	Uriah the priest and Z the son
Zech	1: 1	the word of the LORD came to Z
	1: 7	the word of the LORD came to Z
	7: 1	the word of the LORD came to Z,
	7: 8	the word of the LORD came to Z,
Mt	23:35	Abel to the blood of Z,
Lk	11:51	of Abel to the blood of Z who

ZECHER (1/1)

1 Chr	8:31	Gedor, Ahio, Z,

ZEDAD (2/2)

Num	34: 8	of the border shall be toward Z;
Ezek	47:15	to Hethlon, as one goes to Z,

ZEDEKIAH (62/61) MATTANIAH

1 Ki	22:11	Now Z the son of Chenaanah had
	22:24	Now Z the son of Chenaanah went
2 Ki	24:17	and changed his name to Z.
	24:18	Z was twenty-one years old
	24:20	Then Z rebelled against the
	25: 2	the eleventh year of King Z.
	25: 7	Then they killed the sons of Z
	25: 7	his eyes, put out the eyes of Z,
1 Chr	3:15	second Jehoiakim, the third Z,
	3:16	were Jeconiah his son and Z
2 Chr	18:10	Now Z the son of Chenaanah had
	18:23	Then Z the son of Chenaanah
	36:10	house of the LORD, and made Z,
	36:11	Z was twenty-one years old
Neh	10: 1	the son of Hacaliah, and Z,
Jer	1: 3	end of the eleventh year of Z
	21: 1	from the LORD when King Z
	21: 3	them, "Thus you shall say to Z,
	21: 7	I will deliver Z king of Judah,
	24: 8	so will I give up Z the king of
	27: 3	who come to Jerusalem to Z
	27:12	I also spoke to Z king of Judah
	28: 1	the beginning of the reign of Z
	29: 3	whom Z king of Judah sent to
	29:21	and Z the son of Maaseiah, who
	29:22	The LORD make you like Z and
	32: 1	LORD in the tenth year of Z
	32: 3	For Z king of Judah had shut him
	32: 4	and Z king of Judah shall not
	32: 5	then he shall lead Z to Babylon,
	34: 2	Go and speak to Z king of Judah
	34: 4	O Z king of Judah! Thus says
	34: 6	spoke all these words to Z
	34: 8	after King Z had made a
	34:21	And I will give Z king of Judah
	36:12	Z the son of Hananiah, and all
	37: 1	Now King Z the son of Josiah
	37: 3	And Z the king sent Jehucal the
	37:17	then Z the king sent and took
	37:18	Jeremiah said to King Z,
	37:21	Then Z the king commanded that
	38: 5	Then Z the king said, "Look, he
	38:14	Then Z the king sent and had
	38:15	Jeremiah said to Z, "If I
	38:16	So Z the king swore secretly to
	38:17	Then Jeremiah said to Z,
	38:19	And Z the king said to Jeremiah,
	38:24	Then Z said to Jeremiah, "Let
	39: 1	In the ninth year of Z king of
	39: 2	In the eleventh year of Z,
	39: 4	when Z the king of Judah and
	39: 5	pursued them and overtook Z in
	39: 6	of Babylon killed the sons of Z
	44:30	as I gave Z king of Judah into
	49:34	the beginning of the reign of Z
	51:59	when he went with Z the king of
	52: 1	Z was twenty-one years old when
	52: 3	Then Z rebelled against the
	52: 5	the eleventh year of King Z.
	52: 8	and they overtook Z in the
	52:10	of Babylon killed the sons of Z
	52:11	He also put out the eyes of Z;

ZEDEKIAH'S (1/1)

Jer	39: 7	Moreover he put out Z eyes, and

ZEEB (6/3)

Judg	7:25	of the Midianites, Oreb and Z.
	7:25	and Z they killed at the
	7:25	killed at the winepress of Z.
	7:25	the heads of Oreb and Z to
	8: 3	princes of Midian, Oreb and Z.
Ps	83:11	nobles like Oreb and like Z,

ZELAH (2/2)

Josh	18:28	Z, Eleph, Jebus (which is
2 Sam	21:14	in the country of Benjamin in Z,

ZELEK (2/2)

2 Sam	23:37	Z the Ammonite, Naharai the
1 Chr	11:39	Z the Ammonite, Naharai the

ZELOPHEHAD (11/9)

Num	26:33	Now Z the son of Hepher had no
	26:33	the names of the daughters of Z
	27: 1	Then came the daughters of Z the
	27: 7	The daughters of Z speak what
	36: 2	inheritance of our brother Z
	36: 6	concerning the daughters of Z,
	36:10	so did the daughters of Z;
	36:11	and Noah, the daughters of Z,
Josh	17: 3	But Z the son of Hepher, the
1 Chr	7:15	of Gilead's grandson was Z,
	7:15	but Z begot only daughters.

ZELOTES (KJV) See ZEALOT

ZELZAH (1/1)

1 Sam	10: 2	the territory of Benjamin at Z;

ZEMARAIM (2/2)

Josh	18:22	Beth Arabah, Z, Bethel,
2 Chr	13: 4	Then Abijah stood on Mount Z,

ZEMARITE (2/2)

Gen	10:18	the Arvadite, the Z, and the
1 Chr	1:16	the Arvadite, the Z, and the

ZEMIRAH (1/1)

1 Chr	7: 8	The sons of Becher were Z,

ZENAN (1/1)

Josh	15:37	Z, Hadashah, Migdal Gad,

ZENAS (1/1)

Titus	3:13	Send Z the lawyer and Apollos on

ZEPHANIAH (10/10)

2 Ki	25:18	Z the second priest, and the
1 Chr	6:36	son of Azariah, the son of Z,
Jer	21: 1	and Z the son of Maaseiah, the
	29:25	to Z the son of Maaseiah the
	29:29	Now Z the priest read this
	37: 3	and Z the son of Maaseiah, the
	52:24	Z the second priest, and the
Zeph	1: 1	of the LORD which came to Z
Zech	6:10	house of Josiah the son of Z.
	6:14	Jedaiah, and Hen the son of Z.

ZEPHATH (1/1)

Judg	1:17	the Canaanites who inhabited Z,

ZEPHATHAH (1/1)

2 Chr	14:10	array in the Valley of Z at

ZEPHI (1/1)

1 Chr	1:36	of Eliphaz were Teman, Omar, Z,

ZEPHO (2/2)

Gen	36:11	of Eliphaz were Teman, Omar, Z,
	36:15	Teman, Chief Omar, Chief Z,

ZEPHON (4/4)

Num	26:15	of Z, the family of the

ZEPHONITES (1/1)

Num	26:15	of Zephon, the family of the Z;

ZER (1/1)

Josh	19:35	fortified cities are Ziddim, Z,

ZERAH (22/22)

Gen	36:13	the sons of Reuel: Nahath, Z,
	36:17	son: Chief Nahath, Chief Z,
	36:33	Jobab the son of Z of Bozrah
	38:30	And his name was called Z.
	46:12	Onan, Shelah, Perez, and Z (but
Num	26:13	of Z, the family of the
	26:20	family of the Parzites; of Z,
Josh	7: 1	the son of Zabdi, the son of Z,
	7:18	the son of Zabdi, the son of Z,
	7:24	him, took Achan the son of Z,
	22:20	Did not Achan the son of Z
1 Chr	1:37	sons of Reuel were Nahath, Z,
	1:44	Jobab the son of Z of Bozrah
	2: 4	bore him Perez and Z.
	2: 6	The sons of Z were Zimri,
	4:24	were Nemuel, Jamin, Jarib, Z,
	6:21	Z his son, and Jeatherai his
	6:41	the son of Ethni, the son of Z,
	9: 6	Of the sons of Z: Jeuel, and
2 Chr	14: 9	Then Z the Ethiopian came out
Neh	11:24	of the children of Z the son of
Mt	1: 3	Judah begot Perez and Z by

ZERAHIAH (5/4)

1 Chr	6: 6	Uzzi begot Z, and Zerahiah
	6: 6	and Z begot Meraioth;
	6:51	Uzzi his son, Z his son,

Ezra 7: 4 the son of Z, the son of Uzzi,
8: 4 Eliehoenai the son of Z,

ZERED (4/3)

Num 21:12 and camped in the Valley of Z.
Deut 2:13 cross over the Valley of the Z.
2:13 over the Valley of the Z.
2:14 over the Valley of the Z was

ZEREDA (1/1)

1 Ki 11:26 of Nebat, an Ephraimite from Z,

ZEREDAH (1/1)

2 Chr 4:17 molds, between Succoth and Z.

ZEREDATHAH (KJV) See ZEREDAH

ZERERAH (1/1)

Judg 7:22 fled to Beth Acacia, toward Z,

ZERESH (4/3)

Esth 5:10 for his friends and his wife Z.
5:14 Then his wife Z and all his
6:13 When Haman told his wife Z and
6:13 his wise men and his wife Z

ZERETH (2/2)

1 Chr 4: 7 The sons of Helah were Z,

ZERETH SHAHAR (1/1)

Josh 13:19 Z on the mountain of the

ZERI (1/1)

1 Chr 25: 3 sons of Jeduthun: Gedaliah, Z,

ZEROR (1/1)

1 Sam 9: 1 the son of Abiel, the son of Z,

ZERUAH (1/1)

1 Ki 11:26 whose mother's name was Z,

ZERUBBABEL (25/24) SHESHBAZZAR

1 Chr 3:19 The sons of Pedaiah were Z and
3:19 The sons of Z were Meshullam,
Ezra 2: 2 Those who came with Z were
3: 2 and Z the son of Shealtiel and
3: 8 Z the son of Shealtiel, Jeshua
4: 2 they came to Z and the heads of
4: 3 But Z and Jeshua and the rest of
5: 2 So Z the son of Shealtiel and
Neh 7: 7 Those who came with Z were
12: 1 the Levites who came up with Z
12:47 In the days of Z and in the days
Hag 1: 1 by Haggai the prophet to Z the
1:12 Then Z the son of Shealtiel,
1:14 stirred up the spirit of Z the
2: 2 Speak now to Z the son of
2: 4 'Yet now be strong, Z,
2:21 'Speak to Z, governor of
2:23 Z My servant, the son of
Zech 4: 6 is the word of the LORD to Z:
4: 7 Before Z you shall become a
4: 9 The hands of Z Have laid the
4:10 plumb line in the hand of Z.
Mt 1:12 and Shealtiel begot Z.
1:13 Z begot Abiud, Abiud begot
Lk 3:27 son of Rhesa, the son of Z,

ZERUIAH (26/25)

1 Sam 26: 6 and to Abishai the son of Z,
2 Sam 2:13 And Joab the son of Z,
2:18 Now the three sons of Z were
3:39 and these men, the sons of Z,
8:16 Joab the son of Z was over the
14: 1 So Joab the son of Z perceived
16: 9 Then Abishai the son of Z said
16:10 I to do with you, you sons of Z?
17:25 daughter of Nahash, sister of Z,
18: 2 hand of Abishai the son of Z,
19:21 But Abishai the son of Z
19:22 I to do with you, you sons of Z,
21:17 But Abishai the son of Z came to
23:18 brother of Joab, the son of Z,
23:37 of Joab the son of Z),
1 Ki 1: 7 with Joab the son of Z and
2: 5 also what Joab the son of Z
2:22 and for Joab the son of Z.
1 Chr 2:16 Now their sisters were Z and
2:16 And the sons of Z were
11: 6 And Joab the son of Z went up
11:39 of Joab the son of Z),
18:12 Moreover Abishai the son of Z
18:15 Joab the son of Z was over the
26:28 and Joab the son of Z had
27:24 Joab the son of Z began a

ZETHAM (2/2)

1 Chr 23: 8 then Z and Joel—three in all.
26:22 Z and Joel his brother, were

ZETHAN (1/1)

1 Chr 7:10 Benjamin, Ehud, Chenaanah, Z,

ZETHAR (1/1)

Esth 1:10 Harbona, Bigtha, Abagtha, Z,

ZEUS (3/3)

Acts 14:12 And Barnabas they called Z,
14:13 Then the priest of Z,
19:35 image which fell down from Z?

ZIA (1/1)

1 Chr 5:13 Sheba, Jorai, Jachan, Z,

ZIBA (16/13)

2 Sam 9: 2 house of Saul whose name was Z.
9: 2 king said to him, "Are you Z?
9: 3 And Z said to the king,
9: 4 And Z said to the king,
9: 9 And the king called to Z,
9:10 Now Z had fifteen sons and
9:11 Then Z said to the king,
9:12 all who dwelt in the house of Z
16: 1 there was Z the servant of
16: 2 And the king said to Z,
16: 2 So Z said, "The donkeys are
16: 3 And Z said to the king,
16: 4 So the king said to Z,
16: 4 And Z said, "I humbly bow
19:17 and Z the servant of the house
19:29 You and Z divide the land.'"

ZIBEON (8/7)

Gen 36: 2 the daughter of Z the Hivite;
36:14 of Anah, the daughter of Z,
36:20 the land: Lotan, Shobal, Z,
36:24 These were the sons of Z:
36:24 the donkeys of his father Z.
36:29 Lotan, Chief Shobal, Chief Z,
1 Chr 1:38 of Seir were Lotan, Shobal, Z,
1:40 The sons of Z were Ajah and

ZIBIA (1/1)

1 Chr 8: 9 his wife he begot Jobab, Z,

ZIBIAH (2/2)

2 Ki 12: 1 His mother's name was Z of
2 Chr 24: 1 His mother's name was Z of

ZICHRI (12/12)

Ex 6:21 were Korah, Nepheg, and Z.
1 Chr 8:19 Jakim, Z, Zabdi,
8:23 Abdon, Z, Hanan,
8:27 and Z were the sons of
9:15 the son of Micah, the son of Z,
26:25 Z his son, and Shelomith his
27:16 was Eliezer the son of Z;
2 Chr 17:16 him was Amasiah the son of Z,
23: 1 and Elishaphat the son of Z.
28: 7 Z, a mighty man of Ephraim,
Neh 11: 9 Joel the son of Z was their
12:17 of Abijah, Z; the son of

ZIDDIM (1/1)

Josh 19:35 And the fortified cities are Z,

ZIDKIJAH (KJV) See ZEDEKIAH

ZIDON, ZIDONIANS (KJV) See SIDON, SIDONIANS

ZIF (KJV) See ZIV

ZIHA (3/3)

Ezra 2:43 The Nethinim: the sons of Z,
Neh 7:46 The Nethinim: the sons of Z,
11:21 And Z and Gishpa were over the

ZIKLAG (15/12)

Josh 15:31 Z, Madmannah, Sansannah,
19: 5 Z, Beth Marcaboth, Hazar Susah,
1 Sam 27: 6 So Achish gave him Z that day.
27: 6 Therefore Z has belonged to the
30: 1 David and his men came to Z,
30: 1 had invaded the South and Z,
30: 1 attacked Z and burned it with
30:14 and we burned Z with fire."
30:26 Now when David came to Z,
2 Sam 1: 1 David had stayed two days in Z,
4:10 him and had him executed in Z—
1 Chr 4:30 Bethuel, Hormah, Z,
12: 1 the men who came to David at Z
12:20 When he went to Z, those of
Neh 11:28 in Z and Meconah and its

ZILLAH (3/3)

Gen 4:19 the name of the second was Z.
4:22 And as for Z, she also bore
4:23 to his wives: "Adah and Z,

ZILLETHAI (2/2)

1 Chr 8:20 Elienai, Z, Eliel,
12:20 Michael, Jozabad, Elihu, and Z,

ZILPAH (7/7)

Gen 29:24 And Laban gave his maid Z to his
30: 9 she took Z her maid and gave
30:10 And Leah's maid Z bore Jacob a
30:12 And Leah's maid Z bore Jacob a
35:26 and the sons of Z,
37: 2 of Bilhah and the sons of Z,
46:18 These were the sons of Z,

ZILTHAI (KJV) See ZILLETHAI

ZIMMAH (3/3)

1 Chr 6:20 Jahath his son, Z his son,
6:42 the son of Ethan, the son of Z,
2 Chr 29:12 Joah the son of Z and Eden the

ZIMRAN (2/2)

Gen 25: 2 And she bore him Z,
1 Chr 1:32 Abraham's concubine, were Z,

ZIMRI (15/13)

Num 25:14 was Z the son of Salu, a
1 Ki 16: 9 Now his servant Z, commander of
16:10 And Z went in and struck him and
16:12 Thus Z destroyed all the
16:15 Z had reigned in Tirzah seven
16:16 Z has conspired and also has
16:18 when Z saw that the city was
16:20 Now the rest of the acts of Z,
2 Ki 9:31 she said, "Is it peace, Z,
1 Chr 2: 6 The sons of Zerah were Z,
8:36 begot Alemeth, Azmaveth, and Z;
8:36 and Zimri; and Z begot Moza.
9:42 begot Alemeth, Azmaveth, and Z;
9:42 and Zimri; and Z begot Moza;
Jer 25:25 all the kings of Z, all the

ZIN (10/9)

Num 13:21 land from the Wilderness of Z
20: 1 came into the Wilderness of Z
27:14 "For in the Wilderness of Z,
27:14 Kadesh in the Wilderness of Z.
33:36 camped in the Wilderness of Z,
34: 3 be from the Wilderness of Z
34: 4 of Akrabbim, continue to Z,
Deut 32:51 Kadesh, in the Wilderness of Z,
Josh 15: 1 of Edom at the Wilderness of Z
15: 3 of Akrabbim, passed along to Z,

ZINA (1/1)

1 Chr 23:10 the sons of Shimei: Jahath, Z,

ZION (160/160)

2 Sam 5: 7 David took the stronghold of Z
1 Ki 8: 1 the City of David, which is Z.
2 Ki 19:21 virgin, the daughter of Z,
19:31 those who escape from Mount Z.
1 Chr 11: 5 David took the stronghold of Z
2 Chr 5: 2 the City of David, which is Z.
Ps 2: 6 My King On My holy hill of Z.
9:11 who dwells in Z! Declare His
9:14 the gates of the daughter of Z.
14: 7 Israel would come out of Z!
20: 2 And strengthen you out of Z;
48: 2 Is Mount Z on the sides of
48:11 Let Mount Z rejoice, Let the
48:12 Walk about Z, And go all
50: 2 Out of Z, the perfection of
51:18 good in Your good pleasure to Z;
53: 6 of Israel would come out of Z!
65: 1 is awaiting You, O God, in Z;
69:35 For God will save Z And build
74: 2 This Mount Z where You have
76: 2 And His dwelling place in Z.
78:68 Mount Z which He loved.
84: 7 one appears before God in Z.
87: 2 The LORD loves the gates of Z
87: 5 And of Z it will be said,
97: 8 Z hears and is glad, And the
99: 2 The LORD is great in Z,
102:13 will arise and have mercy on Z;
102:16 For the LORD shall build up Z;
102:21 the name of the LORD in Z,
110: 2 rod of Your strength out of Z.
125: 1 in the LORD Are like Mount Z,
126: 1 brought back the captivity of Z,
128: 5 The LORD bless you out of Z,
129: 5 Let all those who hate Z Be
132:13 For the LORD has chosen Z;
133: 3 upon the mountains of Z;
134: 3 and earth Bless you from Z!
135:21 Blessed be the LORD out of Z,
137: 1 we wept When we remembered Z.
137: 3 us one of the songs of Z!
146:10 reign forever—Your God, O Z,
147:12 Praise your God, O Z!
149: 2 Let the children of Z be
Song 3:11 Go forth, O daughters of Z,
Isa 1: 8 So the daughter of Z is left as
1:27 Z shall be redeemed with
2: 3 For out of Z shall go forth

3:16 Because the daughters of Z are
3:17 the head of the daughters of Z,
4: 3 that he who is left in Z
4: 4 the filth of the daughters of Z,
4: 5 every dwelling place of Mount Z,
8:18 hosts, Who dwells in Mount Z.
10:12 all His work on Mount Z and on
10:24 "O My people, who dwell in Z,
10:32 the mount of the daughter of Z,
12: 6 and shout, O inhabitant of Z,
14:32 That the LORD has founded Z,
16: 1 the mount of the daughter of Z.
18: 7 the LORD of hosts, To Mount Z.
24:23 of hosts will reign On Mount Z
28:16 I lay in Z a stone for a
29: 8 Who fight against Mount Z."
30:19 the people shall dwell in Z at
31: 4 down To fight for Mount Z and
31: 9 Whose fire is in Z And whose
33: 5 He has filled Z with justice
33:14 The sinners in Z are afraid;
33:20 Look upon Z, the city of our
34: 8 recompense for the cause of Z.
35:10 And come to Z with singing,
37:22 virgin, the daughter of Z,
37:32 those who escape from Mount Z.
40: 9 O Z, You who bring good
41:27 The first time I said to Z,
46:13 I will place salvation in Z,
49:14 But Z said, "The LORD has
51: 3 For the LORD will comfort Z,
51:11 And come to Z with singing,
51:16 of the earth, And say to Z,
52: 1 Put on your strength, O Z;
52: 2 O captive daughter of Z!
52: 7 salvation, Who says to Z,
52: 8 When the LORD brings back Z.
59:20 "The Redeemer will come to Z,
60:14 Z of the Holy One of Israel.
61: 3 console those who mourn in Z,
62:11 "Say to the daughter of Z,
64:10 Z is a wilderness, Jerusalem
66: 8 For as soon as Z was in labor,
Jer 3:14 and I will bring you to Z.
4: 6 Set up the standard toward Z.
4:31 The voice of the daughter of Z
6: 2 have likened the daughter of Z
6:23 against you, O daughter of Z.
8:19 "Is not the LORD in Z?
9:19 of wailing is heard from Z:
14:19 Judah? Has Your soul loathed Z?
26:18 Z shall be plowed like a field,
30:17 outcast saying: "This is Z;
31: 6 'Arise, and let us go up to Z,
31:12 and sing in the height of Z,
50: 5 They shall ask the way to Z,
50:28 land of Babylon Declares in Z
51:10 Come and let us declare in Z
51:24 the evil they have done In Z
51:35 The inhabitant of Z will
Lam 1: 4 The roads to Z mourn Because
1: 6 And from the daughter of Z
1:17 Z spreads out her hands,
2: 1 has covered the daughter of Z
2: 4 the tent of the daughter of Z,
2: 6 Sabbaths to be forgotten in Z.
2: 8 The wall of the daughter of Z.
2:10 elders of the daughter of Z
2:13 you, O virgin daughter of Z?
2:18 "O wall of the daughter of Z,
4: 2 The precious sons of Z,
4:11 He kindled a fire in Z,
4:22 accomplished, O daughter of Z;
5:11 They ravished the women in Z,
5:18 Because of Mount Z which is
Joel 2: 1 Blow the trumpet in Z,
2:15 Blow the trumpet in Z,
2:23 glad then, you children of Z,
2:32 For in Mount Z and in
3:16 LORD also will roar from Z,
3:17 Dwelling in Z My holy
3:21 For the LORD dwells in Z.
Am 1: 2 "The LORD roars from Z,
6: 1 to you who are at ease in Z,
Ob 17 But on Mount Z there shall be
21 saviors shall come to Mount Z
Mic 1:13 of sin to the daughter of Z),
3:10 Who build up Z with bloodshed
3:12 Therefore because of you Z
4: 2 For out of Z the law shall
4: 7 will reign over them in Mount Z
4: 8 stronghold of the daughter of Z,
4:10 bring forth, O daughter of Z,
4:11 And let our eye look upon Z.
4:13 and thresh, O daughter of Z;
Zeph 3:14 O daughter of Z! Shout, O
3:16 Z, let not your hands be
Zech 1:14 for Jerusalem And for Z with
1:17 The LORD will again comfort Z,
2: 7 'Up, Z! Escape, you who dwell
2:10 O daughter of Z! For behold, I
8: 2 I am zealous for Z with great
8: 3 LORD: 'I will return to Z,
9: 9 O daughter of Z! Shout, O
9:13 And raised up your sons, O Z,
Mt 21: 5 "Tell the daughter of Z,
Jn 12:15 not, daughter of Z;
Rom 9:33 I lay in Z a stumbling
11:26 will come out of Z,
Heb 12:22 But you have come to Mount Z and
1 Pe 2: 6 I lay in Z A chief
Rev 14: 1 a Lamb standing on Mount Z,

ZION'S (1/1)
Isa 62: 1 For Z sake I will not hold My

ZIOR (1/1)
Josh 15:54 Arba (which is Hebron), and Z:

ZIPH (10/9)
Josh 15:24 Z, Telem, Bealoth,
15:55 Maon, Carmel, Z, Juttah,
1 Sam 23:14 in the Wilderness of Z.
23:15 was in the Wilderness of Z in
23:24 So they arose and went to Z
26: 2 down to the Wilderness of Z,
26: 2 David in the Wilderness of Z.
1 Chr 2:42 who was the father of Z,
4:16 The sons of Jehallelel were Z,
2 Chr 11: 8 Gath, Mareshah, Z,

ZIPHAH (1/1)
1 Chr 4:16 of Jehallelel were Ziph, Z,

ZIPHION (1/1)
Gen 46:16 The sons of Gad were Z,

ZIPHITES (3/3)
1 Sam 23:19 Then the Z came up to Saul at
26: 1 Now the Z came to Saul at
Ps 54: of David when the Z went and

ZIPHRON (1/1)
Num 34: 9 'the border shall proceed to Z,

ZIPPOR (7/7)
Num 22: 2 Now Balak the son of Z saw all
22: 4 And Balak the son of Z was
22:10 to God, "Balak the son of Z,
22:16 "Thus says Balak the son of Z:
23:18 Listen to me, son of Z!
Josh 24: 9 'Then Balak the son of Z,
Judg 11:25 better than Balak the son of Z,

ZIPPORAH (3/3)
Ex 2:21 and he gave Z his daughter to
4:25 Then Z took a sharp stone and
18: 2 Moses' father-in-law, took Z,

ZITHRI (1/1)
Ex 6:22 were Mishael, Elzaphan, and Z.

ZIV (2/2)
1 Ki 6: 1 over Israel, in the month of Z,
6:37 was laid, in the month of Z.

ZIZ (1/1)
2 Chr 20:16 come up by the Ascent of Z,

ZIZA (2/2)
1 Chr 4:37 Z the son of Shiphi, the son of
2 Chr 11:20 she bore him Abijah, Attai, Z,

ZIZAH (1/1)
1 Chr 23:11 Jahath was the first and Z the

ZOAN (7/7)
Num 13:22 was built seven years before Z
Ps 78:12 of Egypt, in the field of Z.
78:43 His wonders in the field of Z;
Isa 19:11 Surely the princes of Z are
19:13 The princes of Z have become
30: 4 For his princes were at Z,
Ezek 30:14 desolate, Set fire to Z,

ZOAR (10/9)
Gen 13:10 of Egypt as you go toward Z.
14: 2 the king of Bela (that is, Z).
14: 8 king of Bela (that is, Z)
19:22 name of the city was called Z.
19:23 the earth when Lot entered Z.
19:30 Then Lot went up out of Z and
19:30 for he was afraid to dwell in Z.
Deut 34: 3 city of palm trees, as far as Z.
Isa 15: 5 fugitives shall flee to Z,
Jer 48:34 From Z to Horonaim, Like a

ZOBA (2/2)
2 Sam 10: 6 Beth Rehob and the Syrians of Z,
10: 8 the gate. And the Syrians of Z,

ZOBAH (13/13)
1 Sam 14:47 Edom, against the kings of Z,
2 Sam 8: 3 the son of Rehob, king of Z,
8: 5 to help Hadadezer king of Z,
8:12 the son of Rehob, king of Z.
23:36 Igal the son of Nathan of Z,
1 Ki 11:23 his lord, Hadadezer king of Z.
11:24 when David killed those of Z.
1 Chr 18: 3 defeated Hadadezer king of Z
18: 5 to help Hadadezer king of Z,
18: 9 the army of Hadadezer king of Z,
19: 6 from Syrian Maachah, and from Z.
Ps 60: Mesopotamia and Syria of Z,

ZOBEBAH (1/1)
1 Chr 4: 8 and Koz begot Anub, Z,

ZOHAR (5/5)
Gen 23: 8 meet with Ephron the son of Z
25: 9 field of Ephron the son of Z
46:10 Jemuel, Jamin, Ohad, Jachin, Z,
Ex 6:15 Jemuel, Jamin, Ohad, Jachin, Z,
1 Chr 4: 7 sons of Helah were Zereth, Z,

ZOHELETH (1/1)
1 Ki 1: 9 cattle by the stone of Z,

ZOHETH (1/1)
1 Chr 4:20 And the sons of Ishi were Z

ZOPHAH (2/2)
1 Chr 7:35 of his brother Helem were Z,
7:36 The sons of Z were Suah,

ZOPHAI (1/1)
1 Chr 6:26 the sons of Elkanah were Z his

ZOPHAR (4/4)
Job 2:11 and Z the Naamathite. For they
11: 1 Then Z the Naamathite answered
20: 1 Then Z the Naamathite answered
42: 9 and Bildad the Shuhite and Z

ZOPHIM (2/2)
Num 23:14 brought him to the field of Z,

ZORAH (10/10) ZORATHITES, ZORITES
Josh 15:33 In the lowland: Eshtaol, Z,
19:41 of their inheritance was Z,
Judg 13: 2 there was a certain man from Z,
13:25 him at Mahaneh Dan between Z
16:31 up and buried him between Z
18: 2 men of valor from Z and
18: 8 back to their brethren at Z
18:11 from Z and Eshtaol, armed with
2 Chr 11:10 Z, Aijalon, and Hebron, which
Neh 11:29 in En Rimmon, Z, Jarmuth,

ZORATHITES (2/2)
1 Chr 2:53 From these came the Z and the
4: 2 were the families of the Z.

ZOREAH (KJV) See ZORAH

ZORITES (1/1)
1 Chr 2:54 of the Manahethites, and the Z.

ZOROBABEL (KJV) See ZERUBBABEL

ZUAR (5/5)
Num 1: 8 Issachar, Nethanel the son of Z;
2: 5 and Nethanel the son of Z
7:18 day Nethanel the son of Z,
7:23 of Nethanel the son of Z.
10:15 was Nethanel the son of Z.

ZUPH (3/3)
1 Sam 1: 1 the son of Tohu, the son of Z,
9: 5 they had come to the land of Z,
1 Chr 6:35 the son of Z, the son of

ZUR (9/9)
Num 25:15 was Cozbi the daughter of Z;
31: 8 who were killed—Evi, Rekem, Z,
Josh 13:21 of Midian: Evi, Rekem, Z,
15:58 Halhul, Beth Z, Gedor,
1 Chr 2:45 Maon was the father of Beth Z.
8:30 son was Abdon, then Z,
9:36 son was Abdon, then Z,
2 Chr 11: 7 Beth Z, Sochoh, Adullam,
Neh 3:16 of half the district of Beth Z,

ZURIEL (1/1)
Num 3:35 the families of Merari was Z

ZURISHADDAI (5/5)
Num 1: 6 Simeon, Shelumiel the son of Z;
2:12 be Shelumiel the son of Z.
7:36 day Shelumiel the son of Z,
7:41 of Shelumiel the son of Z.
10:19 was Shelumiel the son of Z.

ZUZIM (1/1)
Gen 14: 5 the Z in Ham, the Emim in

ZUZIMS (KJV) See ZUZIM

APPENDIX

APPENDIX

INDEX OF ARTICLES, CONJUNCTIONS, PREPOSITIONS, ETC.

Book, chapter, and verse references in which these frequently appearing words occur are given here in biblical order, but without context lines.

A (8721/6520)

Gen 1:6; 2:6; 7; 8; 10; 18; 20; 21; 22; 24; 3:6; 24; 4:1; 2(2); 12(2); 14(2); 15; 17; 23(2); 25; 26; 5:3; 28; 6:9; 16(2); 7:2(2); 8:1; 7; 8; 11; 21; 9:5; 11; 14; 15; 20(2); 23; 25; 10:8; 9; 11:2; 4(3); 12:1; 2(2); 10; 11; 13:16; 14:20; 23(2); 15:1; 9(5); 12; 13; 15; 17(2); 18; 16:7; 11; 12; 15; 17:4; 5; 8; 11; 16(2); 17(3); 19; 20; 27; 18:4; 5; 7(2); 10; 13; 14; 18; 25; 19:3; 8; 9; 20(2); 26; 28; 30; 37; 38; 20:3(3); 4; 6; 7; 9; 16; 21:2; 7; 8; 13; 14; 16(2); 18; 19(2); 21; 25; 27; 32; 33; 22:2; 6; 7; 8; 13(3); 15; 23:4(3); 6; 9; 18; 20; 24:3; 4; 7; 11; 14; 16; 17; 18; 19; 22(2); 29; 31; 36; 37; 38; 40; 43; 46(2); 55; 65; 25:1; 8; 25; 27(3); 29; 26:1; 8(2); 12; 14; 19; 25; 28; 30; 35; 27:11(2); 12(3); 27; 36; 44; 46; 28:1; 2; 4; 6(3); 11; 12; 18; 20; 22(2); 29:2(2); 9; 14; 20; 22; 24; 29; 32; 33; 34; 35; 30:3; 5; 6; 7; 10; 11; 12; 15; 17; 19; 20; 21; 23; 30; 31:10; 11; 13; 24; 44(2); 45(2); 46; 48; 52(2); 54; 32:13; 18; 24; 33:14; 17; 34:4; 7(2); 8; 12; 14; 31; 35:11(2); 14(3); 16; 20; 36:6; 37:1; 2; 3; 5; 15; 22; 24; 25(2); 31; 33; 38:1; 2(2); 3; 4; 5; 6; 11; 14(2); 15; 17(2); 28; 39:2; 14(2); 20; 40:4; 5; 8; 9; 19; 20; 41:1; 5; 7; 11; 12(2); 15(2); 33; 36; 38(2); 42; 45; 42:7; 25; 43:2; 11(3); 18; 32; 44:7; 15; 18; 19(2); 20(2); 25; 33; 45:7(2); 8(2); 46:3; 10; 29; 47:11; 26; 48:4; 7; 16; 19(2); 49:6; 9(3); 10; 13; 14; 15(2); 17(2); 19; 21; 22(3); 27; 30(2); 50:9; 10; 11; 13; 26; **Ex** 1:8; 16(3); 2:1(2); 2(2); 7; 11; 14(2); 15; 22(3); 3:2(2); 8(2); 12; 17; 19; 4:2; 3; 4; 16; 20; 25(2); 26; 5:1; 21; 6:1(2); 8; 13; 15; 7:9(2); 10; 15; 8:23; 9:3; 4; 5; 8; 24; 10:7; 9; 19; 26; 11:6; 7(2); 12:3(3); 5; 11; 13; 14(3); 16(2); 19(2); 22; 30(2); 38(2); 42(2); 45(2); 48(2); 13:5; 6; 9(3); 13(2); 16; 21(2); 14:20; 21; 22; 29; 15:3; 5; 8; 16; 25(2); 16:4; 14; 23(2); 25; 33; 17:12; 14; 18:3(2); 12; 16; 19:5; 6(2); 13; 16; 18; 20:4; 5; 21:2; 4; 7(2); 8; 12; 13; 14; 16; 18; 20(2); 21; 22; 26; 28(2); 29(2); 30; 31(2); 32; 33(5); 22:1(3); 5(2); 7; 9(2); 10(3); 13; 14; 16(2); 18; 21; 25; 26; 28; 23:1; 2(2); 3; 7; 8; 9(2); 14; 19; 33; 24:10; 14; 15; 17; 25:8; 10(5); 11; 17(4); 23(4); 24; 25(3); 31; 33(2); 35(3); 39; 26:7; 13(2); 14(2); 16(3); 31; 33; 36(2); 27:4(2); 16(2); 21; 28:4(5); 11; 12; 16(3); 17(2); 18(3); 19; 20(2); 21; 28; 29; 32(2); 34(4); 36(2); 37; 43; 29:9; 14; 18(2); 22; 24; 25(2); 26; 28(3); 36(2); 40(3); 41; 42; 30:2(2); 3; 8; 9(3); 10(2); 12; 13(2); 15; 16; 18; 21; 24; 25(2); 31; 35; 31:13; 16; 17; 32:4; 5(2); 8; 9; 10; 11; 17; 21; 29; 30; 31(2); 33:3(2); 5; 11(2); 21; 34:9; 10; 12(2); 14; 15; 20(2); 26; 27; 33; 35:2(2); 5; 22; 29; 36:6; 19(2); 21(2); 35; 37(2); 37:1(5); 2; 6(3); 10(3); 11; 12(3); 19(2); 21(3); 24; 25(2); 26; 38:4; 23; 26(2); 39:9(2); 10(3); 11(3); 12; 13(2); 14; 21; 23(2); 26(4); 28; 29(2); 30; 31; **Lev** 1:3(2); 9(2); 10(2); 13(2); 17(2); 2:1; 2(2); 4; 5(2); 6; 7(2); 9(2); 12; 14; 15; 3:1(2); 5; 6(2); 7; 12; 16; 17; 4:2; 3(2); 12; 14; 20; 21; 22; 23(2); 24; 28(2); 31; 32(2); 33; 5:1(2); 2; 3; 4(2); 6(4); 7(3); 9; 10; 11(2); 12(2); 13; 15(4); 17; 18(2); 19; 6:2(4); 3; 6(2); 11; 13; 15(2); 16; 18; 20; 21(2); 22; 26; 27; 28; 7:5; 6; 9; 12; 14; 16(2); 30; 32; 34; 36; 8:2(2); 21(2); 26; 27; 28; 29; 9:2(4); 3(5); 4(3); 17; 21; 10:9; 13; 14; 15(2); 17; 18; 11:34; 35; 36(2); 37; 38; 12:2(2); 5; 6(7); 7(2); 8(3); 13:2(5); 3; 6; 9; 10; 18; 19(2); 20; 22; 24(2); 25; 27; 28; 29(2); 30; 37; 38(2); 39; 42; 44; 47(4); 49; 57; 58; 59; 14:10; 12(2); 13; 21(3); 22(2); 24; 31(2); 32; 34(2); 55(2); 56(3); 15:2; 13; 15(2); 18(2); 19(2); 25(2); 30(2); 32; 33; 16:3(4); 4; 5(2); 6; 9; 12; 21; 24; 29(3); 31(2); 34; 17:6; 7; 8; 15(2); 18:5; 17; 18(2); 19; 22(2); 19:5(2); 14; 16(2); 19; 20(3); 21(2); 24; 29; 33; 20:12; 13(3); 14(2); 15; 16; 17(2); 18(2); 20; 21; 24; 27(3); 21:4; 7(4); 13; 14(5); 18(3); 19(2); 20(5); 21(2); 23; 22:4(4); 10; 11; 13; 14(2); 18; 19; 20; 21(3); 23(4); 25; 27(3); 28; 29; 23:3(2); 7; 8; 10; 12(2); 13(2); 14; 16; 18(2); 19(3); 20; 21(2); 24(3); 27; 31; 32; 35; 36(2); 37(3); 39(2); 41(2); 24:3; 6; 7; 9(2); 10; 19; 20; 21; 25:2; 4(2); 5; 10; 11; 29(5); 30; 33(2); 35(2); 37; 39; 40(2); 46; 47(2); 50; 52; 53; 26:1(2); 8(2); 25; 33; 36(2); 37; 27:2(2); 3; 4; 5(2); 6(3); 7(2); 8; 11; 12; 14(2); 16(3); 21; 22(2); 23; 24; 28; 31; **Num** 1:2; 4; 49; 3:15; 22; 28; 34; 39; 40; 43; 4:2; 6(2); 7; 8(2); 9; 10(2); 11(2); 12(3); 13; 14; 22; 5:2(2); 6; 13; 15; 18; 19; 21; 23; 24; 26; 27(2); 29; 30; 6:2(2); 6; 11(2); 12(2); 14(3); 15; 17; 20; 7:3; 13; 15; 16; 19; 21; 22; 25; 27; 28; 31; 33; 34; 37; 39; 40; 43; 45; 46; 49; 51; 52; 55; 57; 58; 61; 63; 64; 67; 69; 70; 73; 75; 76; 79; 81; 82; 87; 8:8(2); 11; 12(2); 13; 15; 19; 21; 9:6; 7; 10(2); 13; 14; 20; 22(2); 10:10; 33(2); 11:12(2); 20; 21; 27; 31(3); 33; 12:6(3); 10; 13:2(2); 23(2); 32(2); 14:4; 8; 12; 14(2); 24; 36; 15:3(5); 4(2); 5(2); 6(3); 7(3); 8(5); 9(2); 10(2); 13; 14(2); 19; 20(3); 21; 24(3); 27(3); 30; 32; 38; 16:9; 13(3); 14; 21; 30; 35; 38(2); 39; 40(2); 45; 46; 17:2; 6; 10; 18:6; 7; 8; 10; 17(4); 19; 23; 24; 26(2); 28; 19:2(2); 9(2); 10; 14(2); 16(4); 17; 18(3); 21; 20:5; 15; 16; 20; 21:2; 8(2); 9(3); 28; 22:5; 11; 24(3); 26; 29; 23:2(2); 3; 4(2); 5; 9; 14(2); 16; 19(2); 20; 21; 22; 24(3); 30(2); 24:8; 9(2); 17(2); 18(2); 25:6; 7; 13; 14(2); 15; 18; 26:2; 4; 10; 54(4); 62; 64; 65; 27:4; 7; 8; 11; 16; 18; 28:2; 3; 5(2); 6(2); 7(2); 8; 9; 11; 12(2); 13(2); 14(6); 15; 18; 19; 20(2); 22; 23; 24; 25; 26(2); 27(2); 29:1(2); 2(2); 5; 6; 7; 8(2); 11; 12(2); 13(2); 16; 19; 22; 25; 28; 31; 34; 35; 36(2); 38; 30:2(2); 3(2); 6(2); 9(2); 16(2); 31:4; 16; 17; 18; 28; 29; 35; 49(2); 54; 32:1(2); 4; 5; 14; 29; 33:54(2); 34:6; 22; 23; 24; 25; 26; 27; 28; 35:4; 6; 15; 16; 17(2); 18(2); 21; 23(2); 29; 30(2); 31; **Deut** 1:11; 16; 25; 31; 33; 2:5; 9(2); 10; 19(2); 20; 21; 3:4; 5; 4:6; 12; 16; 19; 23; 24(2); 25; 31; 34(2); 5:2; 8; 9; 15(2); 22; 29; 6:3; 8; 15; 21; 7:6(3); 8; 9; 14; 16; 8:5; 7(2); 8(2); 9(2); 9:2; 3; 6; 12; 13; 14; 16; 26; 10:7; 17; 11:9; 10; 11; 12; 18; 26(2); 13:1(4); 16; 14:2(3); 21(3); 15:1; 3; 7; 9; 12(2); 15; 18; 21; 22(2); 16:8; 10; 12; 15; 16; 19(2); 21; 22; 17:1; 2(2); 8; 14; 15(2); 18(2); 18:3; 6; 10(2); 11(2); 15; 18; 20; 22; 19:5(2); 15; 16; 18; 20:5; 6; 7; 10; 19(2); 21:3(2); 4; 11; 13; 15; 17; 18(2); 20(2); 22(3); 22:5(4); 6; 8(2); 10; 11; 13; 14(2); 17; 19(2); 21; 22(3); 23(4); 25(2); 26; 28(3); 30; 23:5; 12; 17; 18(2); 20; 21; 25; 24:1(3); 3; 5(2); 7; 14; 16; 17(2); 18; 19; 22; 25:1; 2; 5(2); 7; 13(2); 14(2); 15(2); 26:2; 5(2); 8; 9; 15; 19; 27:3; 14; 15; 25; 28:9; 29; 30(3); 33; 36; 37(2); 46(2); 48; 49(2); 50; 65(2); 29:4; 13; 18; 22; 31:15; 19; 21; 24; 26; 32:4; 5; 10(2); 20; 21(2); 22; 28; 30; 47; 49; 33:2; 4(2); 7; 10; 17; 20; 21; 22; 28; 29; 34:6; 10; **Josh** 2:1; 12; 15; 19; 3:4; 13; 16; 4:5; 6; 7; 5:6; 13; 6:5(2); 10; 18; 20; 7:1; 15; 21(2); 26; 8:11; 17; 28(2); 29(2); 32; 35; 9:6(2); 7; 9; 11; 15; 16; 10:2; 8; 10; 13; 14; 16; 20; 11:18; 19; 12:6; 7; 15:13; 18; 19; 17:1(2); 2; 14; 15(2); 17; 18:9; 14; 20:3; 4; 9; 21:13; 21; 27; 32; 38; 44; 45; 22:7(2); 10; 17; 20; 24; 25; 27; 28; 34; 23:1; 10; 24:7; 13; 19(2); 25(2); 26; 27(2); 33; **Judg** 1:14; 15; 24; 26; 2:3; 3:9; 15(2); 16(2); 17; 19; 20; 29; 4:4; 9; 16; 18; 19(3); 21(2); 5:7; 8; 12; 18; 25; 30; 6:8; 17; 19(3); 26; 31; 37; 38; 7:5; 13(5); 14; 16; 8:14; 18; 20; 21; 24; 25; 27; 31; 32; 9:8; 23; 48; 49; 51; 53; 54; 10:1; 3; 11:1(2); 4; 10; 30; 31; 33; 39; 12:2; 13:2; 3; 5(2); 6; 7(2); 15; 16; 19; 23(2); 24; 14:1; 2(2); 3; 5; 6; 8; 10; 12; 16; 18; 15:1(2); 4; 7; 8; 15(3); 16(3); 16:1; 4; 9; 12; 17; 19; 21; 23; 17:1; 2; 3(2); 4(2); 5; 7(2); 8; 9(2); 10(3); 13; 18:10(3); 14(2); 19(6); 22; 23; 27; 19:1(2); 3; 5; 12; 24; 29; 20:10(2); 16(2); 38; 40; 21:1; 5; 11; 12; 15; 17; 18; 19; 21; 22; **Ruth** 1:1(2); 12(2); 2:1(2); 7; 10; 11; 12; 20; 3:8; 9; 11; 12(2); 13; 4:7; 13; 14; 15(2); 16; 17(2); **1 Sam** 1:1; 5; 11(2); 15; 16; 20; 24; 25; 2:13(2); 18(2); 19; 24; 25; 27; 34; 35(2); 36(3); 3:20; 4:7; 10; 12; 13; 17; 20; 5:9; 11; 6:3; 7; 8(2); 14(2); 17; 19; 7:2; 9(2); 10; 12; 16; 8:5; 6; 10; 15; 17; 19; 22; 9:1(3); 2(2); 6; 8; 9(3); 12; 16; 21; 10:1; 3; 5(5); 10; 12(2); 19; 25; 11:1; 2; 7; 13; 12:1; 12; 13; 17; 19; 13:2; 4; 9; 12; 14; 21(2); 14:2; 4(2); 10; 15; 25; 27; 29; 30; 33; 36; 39; 41; 43; 15:5; 12; 18; 28; 29; 16:1; 2; 14; 15; 16(2); 17; 18(4); 20(3); 23; 17:3(3); 4(2); 5(2); 6; 7(2); 8(2); 10; 20; 29; 33(2); 34(3); 38(2); 40(2); 42; 43; 45(3); 46; 49; 50(2); 18:3; 10; 13; 17; 19; 21(2); 23(3); 27; 19:2; 5(2); 8; 12; 13; 16; 20:3; 6; 8; 16; 20; 21; 25; 29; 30; 33; 35; 41; 21:2; 7; 8(2); 9; 22:6; 8; 13; 18; 23:5; 7; 15; 18; 27; 24:3; 4; 14(2); 19; 25:2(2); 3; 8; 16; 17; 29(2); 36(2); 37; 41; 42; 26:8; 12; 13(2); 15; 20(2); 27:5; 10; 28:7(4); 8; 9; 12; 13; 14; 22; 24; 29:1; 30:12(2); 13; 17; 25; 26; 31:4; **2 Sam** 1:2; 2:17; 18; 25(2); 28; 3:1; 7; 8(2); 13; 14; 20; 21; 22; 29(3); 33(2); 34; 38(2); 4:4; 10; 11; 5:3; 11; 20; 6:3; 14; 16; 19(3); 7:2; 5; 6(3); 7(2); 9; 10(2); 11; 13; 19(2); 23(2); 27; 8:2; 8; 13; 9:2; 3; 8; 12; 11:2; 8; 10; 14; 16; 21(3); 27; 12:3; 4; 24; 30; 13:1; 2; 3(2); 6; 18; 25; 14:2(4); 5; 13; 14; 27; 15:2(3); 8; 13; 19; 23; 27; 33; 16:1(3); 5; 8; 22; 17:8(2); 9; 10(2); 13; 17; 18(3); 19; 23; 25; 18:7; 9(2); 10(2); 11; 12; 17(2); 18; 24; 27; 29; 19:4; 9; 16; 17; 18; 26; 32(2); 35; 36(2); 42; 20:1(3); 8(2); 12; 15; 16; 19(2); 21; 22; 26; 21:1; 16; 18; 19; 20; 22:11; 20; 26; 30(2); 31; 32; 35; 44; 23:4; 7; 10; 11(2); 12; 15; 18; 20(4); 21(3); 22; 30; 24:3; 15; 24; **1 Ki** 1:2(2); 3; 39; 41; 42; 52; 2:2; 4; 8(2); 9; 19; 24; 36; 3:1; 4; 5; 6; 7; 8; 12; 15(2); 24(2); 4:5; 5:3; 5; 7; 12; 13; 14; 6:36; 7:3; 6(2); 7; 8; 12; 14(3); 15; 17; 23; 24; 26(3); 29; 31(2); 32(2); 33; 35; 36; 38; 8:9; 13; 16; 17; 18; 20; 21; 25; 41(2); 55; 63; 65(2); 9:5; 7(2); 16; 25; 26; 10:2; 6; 18; 25; 29(2); 11:7; 14; 17; 18; 24; 26; 28; 29; 36; 12:7; 11; 30; 32; 33; 13:1; 2; 3; 7; 18; 24; 14:3; 14; 15; 15:4; 19(2); 22; 16:31; 33; 17:7; 9; 10(3); 11; 12(5); 13; 24; 18:2; 4; 12; 13; 21; 22; 27(2); 32; 34(4); 44(2); 45; 19:2; 4(2); 5; 6(2); 9; 11; 12(2); 13; 21; 20:10; 13; 17; 20; 21; 28; 30; 34; 35; 36(2); 37; 38; 39(3); 42; 21:1; 2(2); 9; 12; 22:7; 10; 21; 22; 23; 34(2); 36; 38; 47; **2 Ki** 1:6; 8(2); 9(2); 10; 12; 13; 2:1; 7; 9; 10; 11(2); 20; 24; 3:4; 15; 18; 25; 27; 4:1; 2; 3; 8; 9; 10(5); 16; 17; 19; 24; 28; 38; 39(2); 42; 5:1(3); 2; 5; 7(2); 8; 10; 12; 14; 15; 19; 22; 6:2(2); 5; 6; 8; 14; 23; 25(3); 26; 32(2); 7:1(3); 6; 9; 10; 16(3); 18(3); 19; 8:1; 6; 8; 9; 11; 13; 15; 19; 20; 9:5; 12; 16; 17(3); 19; 30; 34; 10:2; 6; 8; 18; 19; 20; 21; 27; 11:4; 14; 17; 12:4; 9(2); 20; 13:5; 15(2); 21(2); 14:6; 9; 19; 15:5; 13; 19; 30; 16:8; 17; 17:4; 16(2); 21; 35; 18:17; 21; 23; 28; 31; 32(4); 36; 19:3; 7(2); 29; 31; 32; 35; 20:3; 7; 12; 14; 20(2); 21:3; 7; 13; 22:10; 12; 19(2); 23:3(3); 22; 30; 33(2); 25:1; 8; 17; 23; 28; 30(2); **1 Chr** 1:10; 43; 5:2; 7:16; 23; 9:9; 10:4; 13; 11:3; 11; 13; 14; 17; 20; 22(4); 23(4); 24; 42; 12:1; 4; 14(2); 22; 28(2); 38; 13:7; 14:1; 9; 11; 12; 13; 15; 15:1(2); 27(2); 29; 16:3(3); 15; 17; 17:1; 4; 5; 6(2); 8; 9(2); 10; 12; 17(3); 21(2); 25; 18:8; 19:6; 20:2; 5; 6; 21:3(2); 14; 16; 22:6; 7; 8; 9(2); 10; 23:31; 25:3; 26:14; 27:24; 32(3); 28:2; 3(2); 9(2); 10; 29:9; 15; 16; 19; 21(3); 28; **2 Chr** 1:4; 6; 9; 17(2); 2:1(2); 3; 4; 6(2); 7; 12(3); 13; 14(2); 4:1; 2; 3; 5(3); 5:10; 13; 6:2; 5(2); 7; 8; 13; 16; 32(2); 36; 7:5; 8; 9; 12; 18; 20(2); 9:1; 5; 17; 18; 24; 10:11; 13:5; 8; 9(2); 15; 17; 14:9; 15:3(2); 12; 14; 16:3; 8; 14(2); 17:17; 18:6; 9; 20; 21; 22; 33(2); 19:9; 20:2; 3; 8; 14; 24; 21:6; 7; 8; 12; 14; 15; 17; 22:11; 23:1; 3; 16; 24:8; 9; 24(2); 25:2; 4; 7; 15; 18; 27; 26:19; 21(2); 23; 28:5(2); 7; 9(2); 29:10; 21; 24; 31; 32; 30:3; 5(2); 13; 18; 24(3); 31:3; 32:18; 24; 33:7; 14(2); 34:18; 20; 31; 32; 35:1; 3; 18; 25; 36:3(2); 22; 23; **Ezra** 1:1; 2; 10; 2:61; 63; 3:5; 11; 12; 13; 4:3; 8; 11; 15; 19; 5:5(2); 6; 7; 11; 13; 17(2); 6:1(2); 2(2); 3; 8; 11(3); 12; 17; 7:6; 11; 12; 13; 21; 27; 8:17; 18; 21; 27; 28; 35(2); 9:8(4); 9; 15; 10:1; 3; 7; 12; 19; **Neh** 1:9; 2:6; 8; 10; 12; 17; 3:13; 4:2; 3; 4; 6; 9; 17; 22; 5:1; 7; 11; 6:3; 7; 10; 11; 7:2; 5; 63; 65; 8:4; 18; 9:4; 8; 10; 11; 12(2); 17; 18; 25; 29; 38; 10:29; 31; 32; 38; 11:23(2); 12:22; 47; 13:2; 5; 7; 28; **Esth** 1:3; 5; 6; 9; 19; 2:5(2); 18(3); 19; 23; 3:4; 8; 9; 12; 14; 4:1; 5; 8; 10; 14; 5:9; 14; 6:8(3); 7:5; 8:8; 13(2); 15(2); 17(2); 9:10; 15; 16; 17; 18; 19; 22; **Job** 1:1; 3; 6; 8; 10; 12; 13; 14; 19; 2:1; 3; 4; 8; 13; 3:3; 5; 16; 23; 4:2; 12(2); 15; 16(2); 17(2); 19; 5:2(2); 5; 23; 26(2); 6:15; 22; 26; 7:1(2); 2(2); 6; 7; 12(3); 16; 20; 8:2; 9; 11; 14; 17; 9:2; 3; 17; 19; 25; 27; 32; 10:5(2); 16; 20; 22; 11:2; 12(2); 12:5; 14(2); 18; 24; 25; 13:9; 16; 25; 27; 28(2); 14:2(2); 3; 4; 6; 7; 9; 11; 13; 14; 17; 18(2); 15:2; 14; 22; 23; 24; 33; 16:8; 14; 21(2); 22; 17:3; 6; 18:8(2); 9; 10(2); 19:10; 15; 23; 24; 29; 20:5; 8(2); 19; 24; 29; 21:11; 13; 18; 32; 22:2; 16; 28; 24:3; 9; 14; 20; 24; 25; 25:4; 6(3); 26:10; 14; 27:13; 18(3); 20(2); 28:1(2); 4; 22; 25; 26(2); 29:13; 14(2); 16; 25; 30:5; 15; 24; 29(2); 31:1(2); 9; 12; 18; 23; 30; 35; 36; 37; 32:8; 33:15(2); 23(3); 24; 25; 29; 34:9; 11; 18; 20(2); 23; 29(2); 35:8(2); 36:2; 16; 18; 37:4; 18; 20; 38:3; 14(2); 25(2); 26(2); 28; 39:15(2); 20; 24; 40:7; 9; 17; 21; 24; 41:1(2); 2(2); 4(2); 5; 6; 13; 15; 20; 21; 31(2); 32; 42:8; 11(2); **Ps** 1:3; 2:1; 9(2); 12; 3:3; 4:5:4; 12; 6:7(2); 2; 11; 15; 8:5; 9:9(2); 10:9; 11:1; 6; 12:2; 6; 13:14:15:3; 4; 5; 16:6; 17:1; 12(2); 18:10; 19; 25; 29(2); 30; 31; 34; 43; 19:4; 5(2); 20:21:3; 9; 11; 22:6(2); 13; 15; 30; 31; 23:5; 24:4; 25:26:10; 27:5; 11; 28:29:6(2); 30(2); 5(2);

31:2; 8; 11; 12(2); 20; 21; 32(2); 6(2); 33:3(2); 7; 16; 17(2); 34:18(2); 35:7; 19; 36:4; 6; 37:10; 16(2); 23; 35; 38:4; 13(2); 14; 39:1; 6; 11; 12(2); 40:2(2); 3; 41:42:4(2); 8; 10; 44:13(3); 14(2); 20; 45(2); 1(2); 6; 12; 46(2); 1; 4; 47:2; 5(2); 48(2); 6; 49:4; 7; 20; 50:3; 5; 9; 10; 18(2); 51:10(2); 17(3); 52:2; 8; 53:54:55:6; 13; 56:57:4; 6(2); 58:4; 8(3); 9; 11; 59:6; 14; 60:4; 61(2); 3(2); 62:3(3); 8; 9(2); 63:1; 10; 64:3; 6; 65(2); 66(2); 1; 67(2); 68(2); 5(2); 6; 9; 13; 15(2); 33; 69:4; 8; 11; 22(2); 30; 70:71:7; 72:73:6; 10; 19; 20; 22; 74:18; 75(2); 5; 8; 76(2); 6; 77:13; 17; 20; 78:2; 5(2); 8(2); 13; 14; 19; 21; 38; 39; 50; 52; 57; 65; 66; 79:4(2); 80(2); 1; 6; 8; 81:1; 2; 4(2); 5(2); 82:83(2); 2; 4; 5; 12; 84:3(2); 6; 10(3); 11; 85:86:14; 15; 17; 87(2); 88(3); 4; 89:3; 13; 19; 41; 90:4(2); 5(2); 9; 12; 91:7; 12; 92(2); 6(2); 10; 12(2); 95:10; 96:1; 97:3; 98:1; 5; 6; 100:1; 101:2(2); 4; 5(2); 6; 102:3; 6; 7; 11; 18; 26(2); 103:13; 15; 104:2(2); 4; 6; 9; 18; 105:8; 10; 16; 17(2); 39(2); 41; 106:18; 19; 36; 107:4; 7(2); 27; 33; 34; 35; 36(2); 37; 41; 108(2); 109:2; 3; 6; 9; 19; 23(2); 25; 29; 110:4; 111:10; 112:5; 113:9(2); 114:1; 8(2); 118:5; 12; 119:9; 19; 63; 69; 83; 105(2); 110; 111; 161; 164; 176; 120:2; 121:122:3; 123:2; 124:7; 125:126:127:3(2); 4; 128:3; 129:1; 2; 130:131:2(2); 132:5(2); 17; 133:134:135:12(2); 136:12; 21; 22; 137:3; 4; 138:139:4; 140:3; 5(2); 11; 141:3; 5; 142(2); 3; 143:6; 144:4(2); 8; 9(2); 11; 15; 146:3; 147:10; 148:6; 14; 149:1; 6; **Prov** 1:5(2); 6; 9; 27(2); 2:7; 3:12; 18; 30; 4:1; 9; 24; 5:4; 10; 19(2); 20; 6:1; 5(2); 10(3); 11; 12(3); 17(2); 18; 19; 23(2); 24; 26(3); 27; 30; 32; 34; 7:7; 10(3); 19; 20; 22; 23; 8:27; 30; 9:7(2); 8(2); 9(2); 13; 14; 10:1(3); 4; 5(2); 8; 10; 11; 13; 18; 23(2); 11:1; 7; 12; 13(3); 15; 16; 18; 20; 22(3); 30; 12:2(2); 3; 8(2); 9; 10; 14(2); 15; 16(2); 17; 18; 19(2); 23; 25; 13:1(2); 2; 4; 5(2); 8; 12; 14; 16; 17(2); 18; 19; 22; 14:3(2); 5(2); 6; 7; 10; 12(2); 14; 16(2); 17(2); 25(2); 26; 27; 28(3); 30; 32; 34(2); 35; 15:1(2); 4(2); 5; 12; 13(2); 15(2); 16; 17(2); 18; 19(2); 20(3); 21; 23(2); 30; 16:2; 7; 8; 9; 12; 14; 15; 18(2); 19; 22; 24; 25(2); 27; 28(2); 29(2); 31; 32; 17:1(2); 2(2); 4(2); 7(2); 8(2); 9(2); 10(3); 11; 12(3); 14; 16; 17(2); 18(2); 20(2); 21(2); 22(2); 23(2); 24; 25(2); 27(2); 28; 18:1; 2; 4(2); 6; 7; 8; 9(2); 10; 11; 12; 13; 14(2); 16; 19(3); 20; 22(2); 24(3); 19:1; 2; 3; 5; 6; 9; 10(2); 11(2); 12; 13(3); 14; 15; 19; 21; 22(3); 24; 25; 26; 28; 20:1(2); 2(2); 3(2); 5; 6; 8; 11; 15(2); 16(3); 17; 19; 24(2); 25(2); 26; 27; 21:2; 4(2); 6; 8; 9(4); 14(2); 15; 16; 17; 18; 19; 20; 22; 24; 28; 29; 22:1; 3; 6; 9; 13; 14; 15; 18; 24; 25; 26; 29; 23:1; 2(2); 6; 9; 13(2); 14; 18; 21; 24; 27(4); 28; 32(2); 24:3; 5(2); 6; 7; 8; 14; 16; 25; 26; 28; 33(3); 34; 25:2(2); 11; 12; 13; 15(3); 18(4); 19(2); 20(2); 23; 24(4); 25(2); 26(3); 28; 26:1; 2(3); 3(3); 4; 5; 6(2); 7; 8(3); 9(3); 11(2); 12(2); 13(2); 14; 17(2); 18; 21; 22; 23; 27(2); 28(2); 27:1; 2; 3(2); 4; 6; 7(2); 8(2); 9; 10(2); 12; 13(2); 14(2); 15(3); 17; 19; 21; 22(3); 24; 26; 28:1; 2(2); 3(2); 7(2); 15(3); 16(2); 17(2); 20; 21(2); 22; 23; 24; 25; 26; 29:2; 3; 5(2); 8; 9(2); 11(2); 12; 15; 19; 20(2); 21; 22; 23; 24(2); 25; 30:2; 4; 5; 6; 10; 11; 12; 13; 14; 19(5); 22(2); 23(2); 25; 26; 30; 31(3); 31:10; 15; 16(2); 30; **Eccl** 1:3; 2:16; 19; 21(3); 24; 26; 3:1(2); 2(4); 3(4); 4(4); 5(4); 6(4); 7(4); 8(4); 17; 22; 4:4; 6; 8; 9; 12; 13; 5:3(2); 4; 8; 12; 13; 14; 16; 6:2(2); 3(3); 6; 12(2); 7:3; 5; 6; 7(2); 8; 12(2); 15(2); 20; 28(2); 8:1(3); 4; 5; 6; 9; 12(2); 13; 14; 15; 17(3); 9:4(2); 6; 7; 12(2); 14(2); 15; 17; 10:1(2); 2(2); 3(2); 6; 8(3); 11; 12(2); 14; 16; 19; 20(2); 11:2; 3; 8; 12:4; 5; **Song** 1:13; 14; 2:2; 9(2); 13; 17(2); 3:9; 4:1; 2; 3(2); 4; 5; 12(3); 15(2); 5:11; 13; 6:5; 6; 7; 7:1; 2(2); 3; 5; 7; 13; 8:4; 6(3); 7; 8; 9(3); 10; 11(2); 12; 14(2); **Isa** 1:4(2); 8(5); 9; 14; 21; 30(2); 31; 2:20; 22; 3:6; 7; 16; 17; 24(6); 4:5(3); 6(3); 5:1(3); 2(2); 7; 10; 18; 23; 26; 28; 29; 6:1; 5(2); 6; 11; 13(2); 7:6(2); 8; 11; 13; 14(2); 20; 21(2); 23(2); 25(2); 8:1(2); 3; 11; 12(2); 14(5); 19; 9:2(2); 6(2); 8; 17; 10:7; 13; 14(2); 15(2); 16(2); 17(2); 18; 19; 22; 23; 24; 25; 26; 11:1(2); 6; 10(2); 12; 16; 13:2; 4(2); 5; 8; 12(2); 14; 14:6; 17; 19(2); 23; 29(2); 15:5(2); 16:2; 4; 11; 14; 17:1(2); 7; 9; 11; 12(2); 13; 18:2(3); 3(2); 4; 7(4); 19:1; 4(2); 14(2); 17; 19; 20(4); 21; 23; 24; 20:3(2); 21:1; 2; 3; 5; 6; 7(4); 8; 9(2); 16(2); 22:2(2); 5; 11; 16(4); 18(2); 21; 23(3); 23:3; 11; 16; 24:9; 11; 20(2); 25:2(6); 4(5); 5(2); 6(2); 11; 26:1; 16; 17; 20; 27:2; 10; 11; 28:1; 2(4); 4; 5(2); 6; 10(2); 13(2); 15; 16(5); 19; 22; 27(4); 29:3; 4; 7(2); 8(2); 11; 14(3); 17(3); 21(3); 30:5(3); 6(2); 8(2); 9; 13(3); 14; 17(4); 18; 20; 21; 27; 28; 29(3); 30; 33; 31:4(3); 8(2); 32:1; 2(6); 8; 10; 14(2); 15(2); 18; 33:9; 19(3); 20(2); 21; 34:4(2); 6(2); 13(2); 14; 17; 35:6; 7; 8(3); 36:2; 6; 8; 13; 16; 17(3); 21; 37:3; 7(2); 30; 32; 33; 38:3; 12(2); 13; 14(3); 21(2); 39:1; 3; 40:3; 10; 11; 12(3); 15(3); 16; 20(4); 22(2); 41:12; 15; 18; 28; 42:3; 6(2); 10; 13(2); 14(2); 16; 22; 43:16(2); 17; 19(2); 44:8; 10; 13(3); 14; 15(3); 16; 17; 19; 20(2); 22(2); 45:19; 20; 21(2); 46:1; 6(2); 11(2); 47:1; 3; 7; 8; 9; 14(2); 48:8; 18; 20; 49:2(2); 6(2); 8; 11; 15; 18; 20; 21; 50:2; 4; 7; 9; 11; 51:4; 6; 8; 10; 12(2); 20; 53:2(2); 3; 7(2); 12; 54:6(2); 7; 8(2); 55:4(2); 5; 13; 56:3; 5(2); 7; 57:4; 6(2); 7; 8; 13; 15; 58:1; 2; 5(5); 11(2); 13; 59:5; 15; 17(3); 19(2); 60:8; 15; 22(4); 61:10(2); 62:1; 2; 3(2); 5(2); 7; 10; 12; 63:13; 14(2); 18; 64:6; 10(3); 65:1; 2(2); 3; 5; 8; 10(2); 11(2); 15; 17; 18(2); 20; 22; 66:2; 3(5); 6; 7; 8(2); 12(2); 15; 19; 20; **Jer** 1:5; 6; 7; 11; 13; 18; 2:2; 6(3); 7; 10; 11; 14(2); 21(2); 23; 24; 27(2); 30; 31(2); 32(2); 3:1; 3; 8; 14(2); 19(2); 20; 21; 4:11; 12; 13; 15; 16; 17; 19; 20; 26; 27; 29; 31(2); 5:1; 6(3); 9; 10; 15(3); 18; 19; 22; 23; 26; 27; 29; 6:1; 2; 6; 7; 8; 9(2); 10; 20; 22(2); 24; 27; 7:5; 11; 16; 28; 29; 8:5; 15; 19; 9:1; 2; 9; 10(2); 11(2); 12; 16; 18; 19; 20; 10:3; 5; 8(2); 13; 15; 22(2); 11:5; 9; 14; 16; 19; 12:6; 8; 9; 10; 13:1; 2; 4; 11; 21; 14:8(3); 9(2); 14(2); 17(2); 18; 15:7; 8; 10(2); 14(2); 20; 16:2; 13; 20; 17:1(2); 4; 6(2); 8; 11(2); 12; 16; 17; 22; 27(2); 18:7(2); 9(2); 11(2); 13; 14; 15; 16; 20; 22(3); 19:1; 3; 8; 11; 20:4; 8(2); 9; 11; 15; 21:5; 6; 9; 14; 22:5; 6; 14; 19; 23; 28(3); 30; 23:5(2); 9(2); 10; 14; 16; 19(2); 23(2); 28(2); 29(2); 40; 24:7; 9(4); 25:9; 11; 12; 18(3); 29; 30; 31(2); 32; 34; 36(2); 26:2; 6; 18; 20; 27:10; 14; 15; 16; 28:14; 15; 29:11(2); 18(3); 21; 22; 23; 26; 27; 31; 30:2; 5; 6(2); 11(2); 14; 16; 23; 31:6; 8; 9(2); 10; 12; 15; 20; 22(3); 31; 32; 35(2); 36; 32:20; 21; 22; 31; 33:1; 9(2); 12; 15; 17; 18; 21; 24; 34:8; 9(2); 13; 15; 22; 35:4; 7(2); 19; 36:2(2); 4(2); 9; 22; 37:13; 21; 38:2; 39:18; 40:5; 8; 11; 41:7; 42:2; 5; 18(2); 43:12(2); 44:2; 8(2); 12(2); 15; 22(2); 28; 29; 45:1; 5; 46:7; 8; 10(2); 17; 20; 22; 28(2); 47:7; 48:2; 3; 4; 5; 27; 34; 38(2); 39(2); 41; 42; 45(2); 49:2; 13(4); 14; 18; 19(2); 22; 24; 27; 30; 33(2); 50:2; 3; 5; 11; 12(3); 22; 23(2); 32; 35; 36(2); 37(2); 38; 41(2); 42; 43; 44(2); 51:1; 7; 14; 16; 18; 25; 26(4); 27(2); 29; 33(2); 34; 37(3); 39; 43(4); 46(2); 54; 57; 60; 63; 52:4; 21; 22(2); 32; 34(2); **Lam** 1:1(2); 13; 15; 2:1; 3; 6; 7(2); 8; 18; 22; 3:10(2); 12; 27; 35; 36; 39(2); 44; 47; 52; 65; 4:6; 11; 17; 5:4; 20; **Ezek** 1:4(2); 5; 8; 10(2); 14; 15; 16(2); 24; 25; 26(4); 28(4); 2:3; 5(2); 6; 9(3); 3:5; 9; 12; 13; 17(2); 20(2); 26; 27; 4:1(2); 2(2); 3; 6; 10; 11; 5:1(2); 2; 3; 4; 12; 14(2); 15(3); 6:3; 8; 7:5(2); 7; 11; 23; 26(2); 8:2; 3(2); 7; 8; 11(2); 17; 18; 9:1(2); 2; 4; 10:1(2); 8; 9; 10(2); 14(3); 21; 11:8; 13(2); 15; 16; 19(2); 24; 12:2(2); 3; 6; 11; 16; 23; 13:5; 7; 10; 11; 13(2); 14:7; 8(2); 13; 17; 19; 22; 15:3; 16:3; 7; 8; 11; 12(2); 20; 24(2); 30; 31; 34; 45; 56; 17:2(2); 3; 4(2); 5(2); 6(2); 8; 13; 15; 17(2); 22(2); 23; 18:5; 6; 10(3); 14; 16; 21; 24; 26; 27; 31(2); 19:1; 2; 3; 5; 6; 9; 10; 13; 14(4); 20:6; 11; 12; 13; 20; 21; 33; 34; 41; 47; 21:6; 9(2); 10; 13; 19; 20; 22(3); 23; 28(2); 29; 22:4(2); 18; 20; 22; 24; 25; 30(2); 23:10; 24; 30; 40; 41(2); 42; 44; 24:3(2); 7; 8; 24; 27; 25:4; 5(2); 10; 15; 26:4; 5; 8(3); 10; 14(2); 17; 19; 21; 27:2; 5(2); 32; 36; 28:2(4); 6; 9(3); 12; 16; 19; 24(2); 29:6; 8; 14; 30:3; 8; 10; 16; 18; 21(2); 24; 31:3; 9; 32:2(3); 3; 7; 33:2(2); 7(2); 24; 32(2); 33; 34:8; 12(2); 14; 22; 24; 25; 26; 28; 29; 36:5; 17; 26(3); 37; 38; 37:7(2); 16; 26; 38:4; 7; 9(2); 11(2); 12; 15(2); 16; 19; 21; 39:11; 14(2); 15(2); 17; 40:2(2); 3(3); 5(4); 7; 12; 17; 20; 23; 24; 27; 38; 42(2); 43; 41:8; 10; 18; 19(4); 25; 42:4(2); 7; 11; 12; 20; 43:6; 8; 13(2); 17(2); 19(2); 22(2); 23(2); 24; 25(4); 44:22(2); 25; 30; 45:1(2); 2; 4(3); 5; 7; 11(2); 13(2); 14(5); 15; 18; 21; 22(2); 23(3); 24(2); 46:4; 5(2); 6(2); 7(4); 11(3); 12; 13(2); 14(5); 15; 16; 17; 19; 23; 47:5(2); 9; 20; 48:12; **Dan** 1:5; 2:3; 10; 11; 12; 19; 25; 28; 31; 34; 35; 37(2); 39; 44; 47; 3:4; 6; 10; 11; 15; 29; 4:5; 6; 10; 13(2); 15; 16(2); 19; 23(3); 27; 30; 31; 5:1(2); 5; 7; 11; 16; 18; 29(2); 6:7(2); 12; 13; 17; 20; 26; 7:1; 4(3); 5(2); 6(2); 7; 8(3); 9(2); 10(2); 12(2); 14; 20; 22; 23; 25(2); 8:1; 3; 5(2); 9; 13; 15; 16; 18; 23; 9:12; 15(2); 16; 26; 27; 10:1; 5; 6; 7; 9; 10; 18; 11:3; 5; 7; 10; 11; 13(2); 15(2); 18; 20; 21; 22; 23; 24; 25(2); 34; 38(2); 39; 40; 12:1(2); 7(2); **Hos** 1:2; 3; 4; 6; 8; 2:3(2); 12; 15; 18; 3:1(2); 3; 4:1; 14; 16(2); 5:1(2); 7; 10; 12; 14(2); 6:4; 8; 9; 10; 11; 7:1(2); 3; 4; 6; 8; 11; 16; 8:6; 8; 9; 10; 12; 9:7; 8; 11; 13; 14; 10:3; 4; 6; 7; 11(2); 14; 11:1; 10; 11(2); 12:1; 2; 7; 12(2); 13:2(2); 13:3(2); 7(2); 8(2); 10; 11; 13; 14:7; 8; **Joel** 1:6(3); 8; 14(2); 19; 2:2(3); 3(3); 5(3); 9; 14(3); 15(2); 19; 20; 3:3(3); 8; 16; 18; 19(2); **Am** 1:4; 7; 10; 12; 14(2); 2:2; 5; 6; 7; 13; 15; 3:4(2); 5(3); 6(3); 8; 12(5); 4:5; 10(2); 11; 5:1; 3(3); 19(4); 24; 6:10; 11; 14; 7:7(3); 8(2); 14(4); 17(2); 8:1; 2; 6; 10; 11(3); 9:9; **Ob** 1(2); 7; 18(2); **Jon** 1:3; 4(2); 9; 16; 17; 3:3; 5; 4:2; 5; 6; 7; 8; 10(2); **Mic** 1:2; 4; 6(2); 7(3); 8(2); 14; 2:2(2); 4(3); 11(3); 12(2); 3:11; 12; 4:7(2); 9; 10; 5:1; 8(2); 6:2; 6; 16(2); 7:2; 3; 4(2); 5(2); 6; 8; 14; 17; 18; **Nah** 1:7; 9; 11; 14; 2:8; 3:2; 3(2); 6; 15; 17; **Hab** 1:5; 6; 13; 15; 2:5; 6(2); 12(2); 18; 3:1; 14; **Zeph** 1:7; 10(3); 13; 15(5); 16; 2:9; 13; 15(2); 3:3; 9; 12; 13; 18; **Hag** 1:6; 11; 2:6; 13; 16; 23; **Zech** 1:8(2); 15; 16; 2:1(2); 5; 3:2; 5(2); 8; 4:1; 2(2); 7; 5:1; 2; 6; 7(2); 9; 11; 6:13; 14; 7:14; 8:13(2); 17; 23; 9:3; 6; 7(2); 9(3); 13; 16(2); 10:7; 11:15; 16; 17; 12:2; 3; 6(2); 10; 11; 13:1; 4; 5(2); 14:4; 10; 13; 21; **Mal** 1:6(3); 8; 11; 13; 14(3); 2:2; 7; 11; 15; 3:2; 3(2); 5; 8; 9; 12; 16; 17; 4:6; **Mt** 1:19(2); 20; 21; 23; 2:6; 12; 13; 18; 19; 22; 23(2); 3:4; 16; 17; 4:6; 16; 18; 5:1; 14(2); 15(3); 22; 28; 31; 32; 38(2); 6:2(2); 3; 16; 7:4; 9; 10(2); 17; 18(2); 24; 26; 8:2; 4; 5; 8; 9; 14; 16; 18; 19; 23; 24; 26; 30(2); 9:1; 2(2); 9; 12; 16; 18; 20(2); 32; 10:5; 10; 12; 18; 21; 24(2); 25(2); 29; 34; 35(3); 36; 41(6); 42(2); 11:7; 8; 9(2); 18; 19(3); 12:10(2); 11; 12(2); 20; 29; 32; 33; 35; 38; 39; 41; 42; 43; 13:2; 3; 8(2); 21; 23; 24; 26; 31(2); 32; 33; 34; 44(2); 45; 47; 52; 57; 14:5; 8; 11; 13; 14; 15; 26; 15:5; 11(2); 14; 18; 20(2); 22; 23; 33; 34; 16:1; 4(2); 26(2); 17:1; 5(2); 14; 20; 27(2); 18:2; 6; 12(2); 17(2); 23; 28; 19:3; 5; 7; 23; 24(3); 29; 20:1; 2(2); 9; 10; 13; 28; 29; 21:2(2); 5(3); 8; 13(2); 19; 26; 28; 33(6); 43; 46; 22:2(2); 11(2); 12; 19; 24; 35(2); 46; 23:14; 15; 24(2); 37; 24:14; 31(2); 45; 50; 25:6; 14(2); 15; 19; 21; 23; 24; 32; 35; 38; 43; 44; 26:7; 10; 13; 18; 30; 36; 39; 42; 47; 48; 55; 58; 69; 73; 74; 27:16; 19; 24; 28; 29(2); 32; 33(2); 46; 48(2); 50; 57(2); 59; 60; 65; 28:2; 12; **Mk** 1:4; 6; 10; 11; 16; 19; 23; 26; 30; 35(2); 40; 44; 2:3; 17; 21; 3:1(2); 7; 8; 9; 19; 24; 25; 27; 32; 34; 4:1(2); 3; 8(2); 17; 20; 21(4); 26; 31; 34; 37; 38; 39; 5:2; 7; 11; 21; 24; 25(2); 38; 6:4; 5; 6; 8; 10; 11; 20; 21; 25; 28; 29; 31(2); 32; 34(2); 35; 49; 7:3; 11(2); 15(2); 17; 18; 20(2); 23; 24; 25; 26(2); 8:7; 11; 12; 22; 36; 37; 9:2; 7(2); 14; 17; 36; 39; 41; 42; 10:2; 4(2); 7; 12; 15; 25(3); 30; 45; 46; 11:2; 13; 17(2); 32; 12:1(6); 2; 15; 19; 20; 40; 42; 13:9; 12; 34(2); 14:3; 6; 9; 13(2); 15; 26; 32; 35; 43; 44; 48; 51(2); 54; 68; 70(2); 72; 15:1; 17; 19; 21(2); 22; 34; 36(2); 37; 43; 46(2); 16:5(2); **Lk** 1:1; 5; 13; 17; 22; 26; 27(2); 31; 34; 36; 39; 42; 45; 57; 63; 69; 2:1; 7; 11; 12(2); 13; 16; 24(2); 25; 32; 34; 35; 36(3); 37; 44; 3:3; 22(2); 4:5(2); 11; 25; 26(2); 31; 33(3); 36; 38; 42; 5:3; 4; 6; 8; 12(2); 14; 17; 18(2); 27; 29(2); 31; 36(4); 6:6; 16; 17(3); 39; 40; 43(2); 44; 45; 48(2); 49(3); 7:2; 5; 8; 11(2); 12(3); 16; 24; 25; 26(2); 28; 33; 34(3); 37(2); 39(2); 41; 8:4(2); 5; 8(2); 13; 15; 16(4); 22(2); 23; 24; 27(3); 28; 32; 41(2); 43(2); 9:5; 10; 12; 25; 34; 35; 37; 38; 39; 46; 47; 52; 10:6; 25; 30; 31; 32; 33; 38(2); 39; 11:1; 5; 6; 11(5); 12; 14; 16; 17(2); 21; 22; 24; 27; 29; 30; 31; 32; 33(4); 36; 37; 12:10; 14; 16(2); 33; 46; 50; 54(2); 13:6(2); 11(2); 16; 19(3); 21; 33; 34; 14:2; 5(2); 7; 8; 12(2); 13; 16(2); 18; 20; 28; 32(2); 15:4; 8; 11; 13; 14; 15; 20; 22; 29; 16:1(2); 6; 7; 19; 20; 26; 17:2; 4(2); 6; 7; 12; 15; 16; 18:1; 2(2); 3; 4; 10(2); 12; 13; 17; 18; 25(3); 35; 36; 19:2(2); 4; 7(3); 9; 12(3); 14; 17; 20; 30; 37; 46(2); 20:6; 9(4); 10; 12; 24; 27; 28(2); 29; 47; 21:2; 15; 18; 27; 29; 35; 22:10(2); 12; 24; 29; 36(2); 41; 47; 48; 52; 54; 55; 56; 58; 59; 23:2; 6; 8; 11; 19; 26(2); 27; 46; 47; 49; 50(3); 51; 53; 24:13; 19; 23; 37; 39; 42(2); **Jn** 1:6; 7; 30; 32; 42; 2:1; 15; 16; 3:1(2); 2; 4(2); 25; 27; 4:5; 7(2); 9(3); 10; 14; 19; 27; 29; 44; 46; 5:1; 2; 3; 4; 5; 6; 13; 14; 35; 36; 6:2; 4; 5; 7; 9; 18; 60; 70; 7:20; 22; 23(2); 30; 33; 43; 51; 8:3; 7; 34; 35(2); 40; 44(3); 48(2); 49; 52; 55; 9:1; 11; 14; 16(3); 17; 24; 25; 30; 31; 10:1(2); 5; 12; 13; 19; 20; 21(2); 33(2); 11:1; 38(2); 39; 43; 44; 47; 54; 57; 12:2; 3; 6; 9; 12; 14; 15; 24; 28; 35; 46; 49; 13:4; 5; 16; 26; 33; 34; 14:2; 3; 19; 15:6; 15; 20; 25; 16:16(2); 17(2); 18; 19(2); 21(2); 18:1; 3; 10; 18; 26; 27; 35; 37(2); 39; 40; 19:2(2); 7; 12; 13; 17(2); 19; 23; 29(2); 31; 34; 38; 39(2); 41(2); 20:7; 21:9; 16; **Acts** 1:9; 12; 15; 16; 17; 18; 22; 2:2(2); 22; 30; 3:2; 14; 22; 4:9(2); 16; 36; 5:1(2); 2; 16; 30; 34(3); 36; 6:1; 5(2); 7; 7:3; 5; 6; 11; 16; 27(2); 29; 30(2); 35(4); 37; 41; 46; 47; 57; 58; 60; 8:1; 7; 9; 11; 27(2); 32(2); 9:3; 4; 7; 10(2); 12(2); 15; 25; 26; 33; 36; 43; 10:1(2); 2; 3; 4; 6; 7; 10; 11; 13; 15; 22(3); 26; 28; 30; 32; 39; 48; 11:5(3); 7; 21; 24(2); 26(2); 28; 12:7; 9; 13; 21; 22(2); 13:6(3); 11(2); 18; 21(2); 22; 23; 29; 41(2); 47; 14:1; 3; 5; 8(2); 10; 28; 15:7; 10; 14; 33; 16:1(2); 9(2); 11; 12; 14(2); 16(2); 24; 26; 28; 29; 17:1; 4(2); 5; 12; 15; 18; 31; 34; 18:2; 7; 9; 11; 14; 15(2); 18(2); 20; 24; 19:2; 4; 14; 22; 23; 24(2); 34; 38; 20:9(3); 11; 12; 21:1; 2; 10; 16; 23; 38; 39(2); 40; 22:3; 6; 7; 12(3); 17; 22; 25(2); 26; 27; 28(2); 29; 23:5; 6(2); 7; 9(2); 10; 14; 25; 27; 24:1; 4; 5(3); 10; 14; 15; 16; 18; 22; 25; 27; 25:3; 9; 14(2); 15; 19; 27; 26:5; 13; 14; 16(2); 24; 26; 28; 27:1; 2(2); 5; 8; 12; 14; 26; 28; 34; 39(2); 41; 28:2; 3(2); 4; 6(2); 8; 17; 23; 29; **Rom** 1:1; 10; 14; 28; 2:14; 17; 19(2); 20; 21; 25; 27; 28; 29; 3:4; 5; 7; 25; 28; 4:11; 17; 19; 5:7(2); 14; 7:1; 2; 21; 8:33; 9:9; 28; 29; 33; 10:2; 14; 19(2); 21; 11:5; 8; 9(4); 17(2); 24; 12:1; 3; 20; 13:3; 10; 14:13(2); 15:8; 12; 16; 23(2); 24; 26; 16:1; 2(2); 16; 23; **1 Cor** 1:22; 23; 2:7; 11; 3:10; 14; 18; 4:1; 3(2); 9; 21(2); 5:1; 5; 6; 7; 11(4); 6:1; 5; 15; 16; 18; 20; 7:1(2); 5; 6(2); 10; 11; 12; 13(2); 15(2); 21; 22; 23; 26; 27(3); 28; 34(3); 35; 39; 8:7; 9; 9:5; 7(2); 8; 11; 17(2); 19; 20; 24(2); 25; 11:6(2); 7; 10; 13; 14(2); 15(3); 18; 28; 12:15; 31; 13:1; 11(5); 12; 14:2; 4; 7(2); 11(2); 13; 14; 19; 22; 26(4); 27; 37; 15:38; 44(4); 45(2); 51; 52; 16:7; 9; 12; 20; **2 Cor** 1:10; 15; 22; 2:6; 7; 12; 3:13; 15; 18; 4:17(2); 5:1(2); 5; 17; 6:15; 18; 7:8; 9; 11; 8:2; 10; 11(2); 12; 9:2; 5(2); 7; 10:11; 13; 11:1; 2; 4(2); 9; 16(3); 23; 25(2); 32; 33(2); 12:2(2); 3; 4; 5; 6; 7(2); 11; 13:3; 12; **Gal** 1:6; 10; 2:3; 14; 16; 17; 18; 3:13(2); 15; 19; 20; 21; 25; 4:1(2); 4; 7(3); 18; 22(2); 27; 5:1; 3; 9; 6:1(3); 7; 12; 15; **Eph** 2:21; 22; 3:7; 4:13; 5:2(2); 27; 31; 32; 6:8; 21; **Phil** 1:6; 23; 28; 2:7; 8; 15; 17; 22; 3:5(2); 17; 4:18; **Col** 1:7; 23; 25; 2:1; 15; 16(2); 17; 3:13; 4:1; 3; 7; 9; 11; 12; 13; **1 Th** 2:5; 7; 9; 11; 17; 4:11; 16; 5:2; 3; 4; 8; 26; **2 Th** 1:6; 3:8; 11; 15; 17; **1 Tim** 1:2; 5(2); 9; 13(2); 15; 16; 19; 2:2; 6; 7(2); 11; 12(2); 3:1(4); 2; 5; 6; 7; 9; 13; 4:2; 6; 8; 9; 5:1; 5; 9; 23; 6:5; 9; 10; 19; **2 Tim** 1:2; 3; 7(2); 9; 11(2); 2:3; 4; 11; 15; 20; 21; 22; 24; 3:5; 4:6; **Titus** 1:1; 4; 6; 7(2); 8; 12; 2:7; 3:8; 10; 11; **Phm** 1:1; 9(2); 15; 16(3); 17; 22; **Heb** 1:4; 5(2); 7; 8; 11; 12; 2:2; 3; 6; 7; 9; 17; 3:5(2); 6; 4:1; 4; 7(2); 9; 12; 14; 15; 5:6; 8; 13; 6:13; 7:2; 3; 4; 5; 12; 16; 17; 19; 21; 22(2); 26; 8:1; 2; 4; 6(2); 7; 8; 13; 9:2; 7; 13; 16; 17; 28; 10:1; 3; 5; 20; 21; 22; 26; 27; 29; 31; 32; 33; 34; 37; 11:2; 4; 6; 9; 11; 14; 16(3); 19; 23; 35; 39; 12:1; 7; 10; 19; 20; 28; 29; 13:18; **Jas** 1:1; 6; 8; 10; 11; 18; 23(4); 25(2); 2:2(2); 3; 11; 15; 24; 3:1; 2; 4; 5(3); 6(2); 11; 12(2); 4:4; 11(3); 13(3); 14(2); 5:3; 5; 16; 17(2); 20(3); **1 Pe** 1:3; 6; 19; 22; 2:4; 5(2); 6; 8(2); 9(3); 10; 16; 3:1; 4; 9; 15(2); 16; 20; 21; 4:8; 10; 15(3); 16; 19; 5:1(3); 8; 10; 14; **2 Pe** 1:1; 15; 17; 19(2); 2:3; 5; 11; 14; 16(2); 17; 19; 22(2); 3:8(2); 10(2); 13; **1 Jn** 1:10; 2:4; 8; 22; 27; 3:15; 4:20; 5:10; 16; **2 Jn** 5; 7; 8; **3 Jn** 6; 12; **Jude** 1; 7; 9; 22; **Rev** 1:10(2); 11; 13(2); 14; 15; 16; 2:9; 14(2); 17(2); 18; 20(2); 22; 27; 3:1; 3; 4; 8; 12; 4:1(2); 2; 3(3); 6; 7(5); 5:1; 2(2); 6; 8; 9; 12; 6:1; 2(3); 4; 5(2); 6(4); 8(2); 10; 11(2); 12; 13(2); 14; 7:2; 9; 10; 8:3; 7; 8(2); 9(2); 10(3); 11; 12(5); 13; 9:1; 2; 5(2); 13; 15; 18; 10:1(2); 2; 3(2); 4; 11:1(2); 12(2); 13(2); 12:1(3); 3; 4; 5(2); 6; 8; 10; 12; 14(3); 15; 13:1(2); 2(3); 5; 11(2); 16; 18; 14:1; 2; 3; 7; 9(2); 13; 14(3); 15; 17; 18; 15:2; 16:1; 2; 3; 15; 17; 18(2); 21; 17:3(2); 4; 5; 10; 18:2(4); 10; 15; 17; 21(3); 22; 23; 19:1(2); 5; 6; 11; 12(2); 13; 15(2); 16; 17; 20:1; 2; 3(2); 4; 6; 11; 21:1(2); 2; 3; 10; 11(2); 12; 15; 16; 17; 27; 22:1; 15

ABOVE (234/221)

Gen 1:7; 20; 6:16; 7:17; 27:39; 28:13; 48:22; 49:25; **Ex** 18:11; 19:5; 20:4; 25:20; 22; 26:14; 28:27; 28; 30:14; 36:19; 37:9; 38:26; 39:20; 21; 31; 40:35; 36; 38; **Lev** 3:4; 10; 15; 4:9; 7:4; 11:21; 16:2; 27:7; **Num** 1:3; 18; 20; 22; 24; 26; 28; 30; 32; 34; 36; 38; 40; 42; 45; 3:15; 22; 28; 34; 39; 40; 43; 49; 4:3; 23; 30; 35; 39; 43; 47; 7:89; 8:24; 9:15; 17; 18; 19; 20; 22; 10:11; 34; 11:31; 12:10; 14:14; 29; 16:3; 26:2; 4; 62; 32:11; **Deut** 4:39; 5:8; 7:6; 14; 10:15; 11:21; 14:2; 17:20; 25:3; 26:19; 28:1; 13; 43; 31:15; **Josh** 2:11; **Judg** 9:49; **2 Sam** 22:17; 49; **1 Ki** 7:3; 11; 18; 20; 8:23; **1 Chr** 16:25; 23:3; 24; 27; 28:4; 29:3; **2 Chr** 24:20; 25:5; 34:4; **Ezra** 3:8; **Neh** 8:5; 9:5; 12:39(3); **Esth** 3:1; 5:11; **Job** 3:4; 18:16; 22:14; 28:18; 31:2; 28; **Ps** 8:1; 10:5; 18:16; 48; 27:6; 50:4; 57:5(2); 11(2); 78:23; 95:3; 96:4; 97:9(2); 99:2; 103:11; 104:6; 108:4; 5(2); 113:4(2); 135:5; 136:6; 137:6; 138:2; 144:7; 148:4; 13; **Prov** 8:28; 14:14; 31:10; **Isa** 2:2; 4:5(2); 6:2; 7:11; 14:13; 14; 40:22; 45:8; **Jer** 4:28; 17:9; 31:37; 35:4; 43:10; **Lam** 1:13; **Ezek** 1:22; 25; 26(2); 10:1; 19; 11:22; 19:11; 29:15; 31:5; 41:6; 17; 20; **Dan** 6:3; 11:36; 37; 12:6; 7; **Am** 2:9; **Mic** 4:1; **Hag** 1:10; **Mt** 10:24(2); **Mk** 15:26; **Lk** 3:20; 6:40; **Jn** 3:31(3); 8:23; 19:11; **Acts** 2:19; **Rom** 10:6; 14:5; **2 Cor** 1:8; 11:23; 12:6; 7(2); **Gal** 4:26; **Eph** 1:21; 3:20; 4:6; 10; 6:16; **Phil** 2:9; **Col** 1:22; 3:1; 2; 14; **2 Th** 2:4; **Heb** 9:5; **Jas** 1:17; 3:15; 17; 5:12; **1 Pe** 4:8

AGAINST (1615/1341)

Gen 4:8; 13:13; 14:9(2); 15; 16:12(2); 18:20; 21; 19:9; 13; 20:6; 30:2; 32:25; 34:30; 37:18; 39:9; 42:22; 36; 43:18; 44:18; 50:20; **Ex** 1:10; 4:14; 8:12; 9:17; 10:16(2); 11:7(2); 12:12; 14:5; 25; 15:7; 24; 16:2; 7(2); 8(3); 17:3; 19:22; 24; 20:16; 21:14; 23:33; 32:10; 11; 33; **Lev** 4:2; 13; 22; 27; 5:19; 6:2; 17:10; 19:16; 18; 20:3; 5(2); 6; 26:17; 25; **Num** 5:6; 13; 10:9; 11:33; 12:1; 8; 9; 13:31; 14:2; 9; 27(2); 29; 35; 36; 16:3; 11(2); 19; 38; 41; 42; 17:5; 10; 20:2; 18; 20; 24; 21:1; 5(2); 7(2); 23(2); 26; 33; 22:22; 25(2); 32; 34; 23:23(2); 24:10; 25:3; 26:9(2); 27:3; 14; 30:9; 31:3; 7; 16; 32:13; 14; 23; 35:30; **Deut** 1:26; 41; 43; 44; 2:15; 32; 3:1; 4:26; 5:20; 6:15; 22; 7:4; 24; 8:19; 9:7; 16; 23; 24; 11:17; 25; 13:9; 15:9(2); 17:7; 19:11; 15; 16(2); 18; 20:1; 4; 10; 12; 18; 19(2); 20; 21:10; 22:26; 23:4; 9; 24:15; 28:7(2); 25; 48; 49; 29:7; 20; 27; 30:19; 31:17; 19; 21; 26; 27; 28; 32:24; 51; 33:7; 11; **Josh** 1:18; 7:1; 20; 8:3; 4; 5; 14(2); 22; 9:18; 10:5; 6; 18; 21; 25; 27; 29; 31(2); 34(2); 36; 38; 11:5; 7; 20; 19:47; 21:44; 22:12; 16(2); 18; 19(2); 22; 29; 31; 33; 23:9; 16; 24:9; 11; 22; **Judg** 1:1(2); 3; 5; 8; 9; 10; 11; 22; 2:14; 15; 20; 3:8; 12; 4:7; 24; 5:13(2); 20; 23; 6:2; 3; 4; 31; 32; 7:2; 9; 11; 22; 24; 9:18; 25; 31; 33; 34; 43; 45; 49; 50; 52; 10:7; 9(3); 10; 18; 11:4; 5; 6; 8; 9; 12(2); 20; 25(2); 27(2); 32; 12:1; 3(2); 4; 14:4; 5; 15:9; 10; 14; 16:29; 18:9; 19:2; 20:5; 9; 11; 14; 18; 19; 20(2); 23(2); 25; 28; 30(2); 31; 34; 36; 48; **Ruth** 1:13; 21; **1 Sam** 2:10; 25(2); 3:12; 4:1; 2; 5:9; 7:6; 7; 10; 13; 11:1; 12:3; 5; 9; 12; 14; 15(3); 23; 14:20; 33; 34; 47(6); 15:18; 17:2; 9; 21; 28; 33; 35; 55; 18:17(2); 21; 19:4(3); 5; 20:30; 22:8(2); 13(2); 23:1; 3; 9; 28; 24:6; 7; 10; 11; 12; 13; 25:17(2); 26:9; 11; 19; 23; 27:10(3); 28:15; 29:8; 30:23; 31:1; 3; **2 Sam** 1:16; 5:6; 19; 6:7; 8; 8:10; 10:9(2); 10; 13; 17; 11:23; 25; 12:5; 11; 13; 26; 27; 28; 29; 14:7; 13; 17:21; 18:6; 12; 13(2); 28; 31; 32; 20:15; 21(2); 21:5; 15; 22:30; 40; 49; 23:18; 24:1(2); 4(2); 17(2); **1 Ki** 2:23; 5:3; 6:5(2); 10; 8:31; 33; 35; 44; 46; 50(2); 11:14; 23; 26; 27; 12:19; 21; 24; 13:2; 4; 32(2); 14:25; 15:17; 20; 27; 16:1; 7; 9; 12; 15; 20:1; 22; 23; 25; 26; 27; 21:10; 13(2); 22:6; 15; 23; 32; **2 Ki** 1:1; 3:5; 7(2); 21; 27; 6:8; 7:6; 8:20; 22; 28; 29; 9:14(2); 10:9; 12:17; 13:3; 12; 14:19; 15:10; 19; 25; 30; 37; 16:7; 9; 17:3; 7; 9; 13(2); 15; 18:7; 9; 13; 17; 20; 25(2); 19:8; 20; 22(2); 27; 28; 32; 21:23; 24; 22:13; 17; 19(2); 23:17; 26; 29; 24:1; 2(2); 10; 11; 20; 25:1(3); 4; **1 Chr** 5:20; 10:1; 3; 13; 11:11; 20; 12:19; 21; 13:10; 11; 14:8; 10; 15:13; 18:10; 19:10(2); 11; 14; 17(2); 21:1; 4; 17(2); **2 Chr** 6:22; 24; 26; 34; 36; 39; 10:19; 11:1; 4; 12:2(2); 9; 13:3; 6; 7; 12(2); 14:9; 10; 11(2); 16:1; 4; 17:1; 10; 18:3; 5; 14; 22; 19:10(3); 20:1; 2; 12(2); 16; 17; 22(2); 23; 29; 37; 21:8; 10(2); 16; 22:5; 6; 7; 24:19; 21; 23; 24; 25; 26; 25:10; 15; 27; 26:6; 7(3); 13; 16; 28:12; 13; 30:7; 32:1; 2; 9; 16(2); 17; 19(2); 33:24; 25; 34:27(2); 35:20(2); 21(2); 36:6; 8; 13(2); 16; 17; **Ezra** 4:5; 6; 8; 19; 23; 7:23; 8:22(2); 10:2; **Neh** 1:6; 7; 2:19; 4:9; 5:1; 7; 6:12; 9:10(4); 26(2); 29(2); 30; 34; 13:2; 27; **Esth** 2:1; 4:16; 5:9; 6:13; 7:7; 8:3; 9:24; 25; **Job** 2:3; 6:4; 8:4; 9:4; 10:16; 17; 11:5; 13:26; 14:20; 15:6; 13; 25(2); 26; 16:4; 8(2); 10; 17:8; 19:5(2); 11; 12; 18; 19; 20:22; 27; 21:4; 24:13; 27:7; 22; 30:12; 24; 31:13; 21; 38; 32:2; 3; 14; 33:10; 34:29; 37; 35:6; 39:23; 41:10; 42:7; **Ps** 2:2(2); 3:1; 6; 5:10; 13:4; 15:3; 5; 17:7; 18:29; 39; 48; 21:11; 27:2; 3(2); 12; 31:13; 18; 34:16; 35:1(2); 15; 20; 21; 26; 36:11; 37:12; 38:16; 41:4; 7(2); 9; 43:1; 44:5; 50:7; 20; 51:4; 53:5; 54:3; 55:12; 18(2); 20; 56:2; 5; 59:1; 3; 60:65:3; 69:12; 71:10; 73:9; 74:1; 23; 78:17(2); 19; 21(2); 31; 79:8; 80:4; 81:14; 83:3(2); 5; 86:14; 91:12; 92:11; 94:16(2); 21; 102:8; 105:28; 106:26; 33; 40; 107:11; 109:2(2); 3; 20; 119:11; 23; 69; 124:2; 3; 129:2; 137:7; 9; 138:7; 139:20; 21; 141:5; **Prov** 3:29; 8:36; 14:35; 17:11; 18:1; 19:3; 20:2; 21:30; 23:11; 24:15; 28; 25:18; **Eccl** 8:11; 9:14; 10:4; **Isa** 1:2; 25; 2:4; 3:8; 9; 5:25(2); 30; 7:1(2); 5; 6; 9:8; 11; 21; 10:6(2); 15(3); 24; 13:1; 17; 14:4; 8; 22; 26; 15:1; 17:1; 19:1; 2(5); 12; 17; 20:1; 3; 21:1; 11; 13; 22:1; 23:1; 8; 11; 25:4; 27:4; 29:3(3); 7(2); 8; 30:6; 31:2(2); 4; 6; 32:6; 34:2(2); 36:1; 5; 10(2); 37:8; 21; 23(2); 28; 29; 33; 41:11; 12; 25; 42:13; 24; 43:27; 45:24; 48:14; 54:15; 17(2); 57:4; 59:12; 13; 19; 63:10(2); 66:24; **Jer** 1:15(2); 16; 18(5); 19(2); 2:8; 9(2); 29; 35; 3:13; 25; 4:12; 16(2); 17(2); 5:15; 6:3; 4; 6; 12; 23; 8:14; 11:17(2); 19; 12:8; 9; 14; 13:14; 14:7(2); 20; 15:6; 8(2); 20(2); 16:10(2); 18:8; 11; 18; 23; 19:15; 20:10; 21:2; 4; 5; 10; 13(2); 22:7; 23:2; 30; 31; 32; 25:9(3); 13; 30(3); 26:9; 11; 12(2); 13; 19(2); 20(2); 27:13; 28:8; 16; 29:32; 31:20; 32:24; 29; 33:4; 8(2); 34:1; 7(2); 22; 35:17; 36:2(3); 7; 31; 37:8; 10; 18(3); 19(2); 38:5; 22; 39:1; 40:3; 43:3; 44:7; 11; 23; 29; 46:1; 2; 12; 22; 47:1; 7(2); 48:1; 2; 8; 18; 26; 42; 49:1; 4; 7; 14; 19; 20(2); 23; 28(2); 30(2); 34; 36; 50:1(2); 3; 7; 9(2); 14(2); 15; 21(3); 24; 26; 29(4); 31; 35(3); 36(2); 37(4); 38; 42; 44; 45(2); 51:1(2); 2; 3(2); 5; 11; 12; 14; 25(2); 27(3); 28; 29; 46; 56(2); 60; 62; 52:3; 4(3); **Lam** 1:15; 18; 2:3; 16; 3:3; 46; 60; 61; 62; **Ezek** 2:3(2); 3:8(2); 4:2(5); 3(2); 7; 5:6(2); 8; 16; 17(2); 6:2; 3; 14; 7:3; 11:4; 13:2; 8; 9; 17(2); 20; 14:8; 9; 13(2); 15:7(2); 16:27; 37; 40; 44; 17:15; 20; 18:22; 19:8; 20:8(2); 13; 21(2); 38; 46(2); 21:2(2); 3; 4; 12(3); 15; 22; 31; 23:22(2); 24(2); 25; 46; 24:2; 25:2(2); 3(3); 7; 12; 13; 16; 26:2; 3(2); 7; 8(3); 9; 28:7(2); 21; 22; 23; 29:2(3); 3; 10(2); 18; 30:11; 22; 25; 33:16; 34:2; 10; 35:2(2); 3(2); 11; 12; 13(2); 36:5(2); 38:2(2); 3; 11; 12(2); 16(2); 17; 18; 21(2); 39:1(2); 2; 42:3; 44:12; **Dan** 3:29; 5:6; 23; 6:4; 5(2); 7:21(2); 25; 8:7; 25; 9:7; 8; 9; 11; 12(2); 10:21; 11:2; 14; 16(2); 18; 24; 25(2); 28; 30(2); 32; 36; 39; 40; 42; **Hos** 2:2; 4:1; 7; 12; 7:13(2); 14; 15; 8:1(2); 5; 9:1; 10:9; 10; 12:2; 13:16; **Joel** 1:6; 3:4(2); 19; **Am** 1:8; 3:1(2); 13; 5:1; 6:14; 7:9; 10; 16(2); **Ob** 1; 7; 10; **Jon** 1:2; 13; **Mic** 1:2; 2:3; 4; 3:5; 4:3; 11; 5:1; 5; 9; 6:2; 3; 7:6(2); 9; **Nah** 1:1; 9; 11; 2:13; 3:5; **Hab** 2:6(2); 10; 16; 3:8(2); **Zeph** 1:4(2); 16(2); 17; 2:5; 8; 10; 13; 3:11; **Zech** 1:12; 21; 2:9; 7:10; 8:10; 17; 9:1; 2(2); 13; 10:3; 11:17(2); 12:1; 2; 3; 9; 13:7(3); 14:2; 3; 12; 13; 16; **Mal** 1:4; 3:5(5); 13(2); **Mt** 4:6; 5:11; 23; 10:21; 35(3); 12:14; 25(2); 26; 30; 31; 32(2); 16:18; 18:15; 21; 20:11; 23:13; 31; 24:7(2); 26:55; 59; 62; 27:1; 13; 37; 60; **Mk** 3:6; 24; 25; 26; 29; 6:11; 19; 48; 9:40; 10:11; 11:25; 12:12; 13:8(2); 12; 14:48; 55; 56; 57; 60; 15:4; 46; **Lk** 2:34; 4:11; 5:30; 6:7; 48; 49; 9:5; 50; 10:11; 11:17(2); 18; 23; 12:10(2); 52(2); 53(6); 14:31(2); 15:18; 21; 17:3; 4; 20:19; 21:10(2); 22:52; 65; **Jn** 11:38; 13:18; 18:29; 19:11; 12; **Acts** 4:14; 26(2); 27; 5:39; 6:1; 11; 13; 8:1; 9:1; 5; 29; 13:50; 51; 14:2; 16:22; 18:12; 19:16; 38(2); 20:3; 21:28; 22:24; 23:9; 29; 30; 24:1; 19; 25:2; 3; 7; 8(3); 15; 16; 18; 19; 27; 26:10; 11; 14; 28:17; 19; 22; **Rom** 1:18; 26; 2:2; 7:23; 8:7; 31; 33; 9:20; 11:2; 18; **1 Cor** 4:4; 6; 6:1; 6; 7; 18; 8:12(2); 9:17; **2 Cor** 1:23; 10:2; 5; 13:8; **Gal** 3:21; 5:17(2); 23; **Eph** 6:11; 12(5); **Col** 2:14; 23; 3:13; **1 Tim** 5:11; 19; **2 Tim** 4:16; **Heb** 12:3; 4; **Jas** 3:14; 5:3; 9; **1 Pe** 2:11; 12; 3:12; **2 Pe** 2:11; **3 Jn** 10; **Jude** 9; 15; **Rev** 2:4; 14; 16; 20; 11:7; 13:6; 19:19(2)

AGO (18/18)

1 Sam 9:20; 30:13; **2 Ki** 19:25; **Ezra** 5:11; **Isa** 22:11; 37:26; 48:8; **Lam** 3:6; **Mt** 11:21; **Lk** 10:13; **Acts** 5:36; 10:30; 15:7; 21:38; **2 Cor** 8:10; 9:2; 12:2; **Jude** 4

AM (909/835)

Gen 4:9; 6:7; 17; 15:1; 7; 16:8; 17:1; 18:13; 17; 27; 22:1; 7; 11; 23:4; 24:24; 34; 25:22; 30; 32; 26:24(2); 27:1; 2; 11; 18; 19; 24; 32; 46; 28:13; 15; 20; 29:33; 30:2; 13; 31:11; 13; 32:10; 34:30; 35:11; 37:13; 16; 38:25; 41:44; 43:14(2); 45:3; 4; 46:2; 3; 48:21; 49:29; 50:5; 19; 24; **Ex** 3:4; 6; 11; 14(3); 19; 4:10(2); 6:2; 6; 7; 8; 12; 29; 30; 7:5; 17; 8:22; 29; 10:2; 12:12; 14:4; 18; 15:26; 16:12; 18:6; 20:2; 5; 22:27; 29:46(2); 31:13; 34:11; **Lev** 11:44(2); 45(2); 18:2; 3; 4; 5; 6; 21; 24; 30; 19:2; 3; 4; 10; 12; 14; 16; 18; 25; 28; 30; 31; 32; 34; 36; 37; 20:7; 8; 22; 23; 24; 26; 21:8; 12; 22:2; 3; 8; 30; 31; 32; 33; 23:22; 43; 24:22; 25:17; 38; 55; 26:1; 2; 13; 44; 45; **Num** 3:13; 41; 45; 10:10; 11:13; 14; 21; 13:2; 15:2; 41(2); 18:20; 22:30; 37; 24:14; **Deut** 1:9; 36; 42; 5:6; 9; 31; 29:6; 31:2; 27; 32:39; 52; **Josh** 1:2; 14:10; 11; 23:2; 14; **Judg** 4:19; 6:10; 15; 8:5; 9:2; 13:11; 16:17; 17:9(2); 19:18(2); **Ruth** 1:12; 2:10; 13; 3:9; 12; 4:4; **1 Sam** 1:8; 15; 26; 3:4; 5; 6; 8; 16; 4:16; 9:19; 21; 12:2; 3; 14:7; 16:1; 17:8; 43; 58; 18:18; 23; 22:12; 23:22; 25:19; 28:15; 30:13; **2 Sam** 1:7; 8; 13; 26; 2:20; 3:8; 39; 7:18; 11:5; 14:5; 15:26; 19:20; 22; 35; 20:17(2); 19; 24:14; **1 Ki** 3:7; 13:14; 18; 31; 17:12; 18:12; 22; 36; 19:4; 10; 14; 20:13; 28; 22:4; 34; **2 Ki** 1:10; 12; 2:9; 10; 3:7; 5:7; 16:7; 21:12; **1 Chr** 17:16; 21:13; 17; 29:14; **2 Chr** 2:4; 6; 9; 18:3; 33; 35:23; **Ezra** 9:6; **Neh** 5:10; 6:3; **Esth** 5:12; 7:8; 8:5; **Job** 3:26(2); 7:12; 20; 9:21; 28; 29; 32; 10:7; 15(3); 11:4; 12:3; 4; 13:2; 16:6; 19:7; 10; 15; 17; 21:6; 23:15(2); 30:9(2); 29; 32:6; 18; 33:6; 9(2); 34:5; 6; 40:4; **Ps** 6:2; 6; 13:4; 22:2; 6; 14; 25:16; 28:7; 31:9; 11(2); 12(2); 22; 35:3; 37:25; 38:6(2); 8; 13; 14; 17; 39:4; 10; 12; 13; 40:12; 17; 46:10; 50:7; 52:8; 55:2; 56:3; 69:3; 12; 17; 20; 29; 70:5; 71:18; 73:23; 77:4; 81:10; 86:1; 2; 88:4(2); 8; 15; 102:6(2); 7; 109:22; 23(2); 116:10; 16(2); 119:19; 63; 94; 107; 120; 125; 141; 158; 120:7; 139:14; 18; 142:6; 143:12; **Prov** 8:14; 20:9; 30:2; **Song** 1:5; 6; 2:1; 5; 16; 5:8; 6:3; 7:10; 8:10; **Isa** 1:14; 6:5(2); 8; 8:18; 10:13; 19:11; 24:16; 29:12; 33:24; 38:10; 14; 41:4(2); 10(2); 42:8; 43:3; 5; 10; 11; 12; 13; 15; 25; 44:5; 6(2); 16; 24; 45:3; 5; 6; 18; 22; 46:4; 9(2); 47:8; 10; 48:12(3); 17; 49:21; 23; 26; 51:12; 15; 52:6; 56:3; 58:9; 60:16; 65:1(2); 5; **Jer** 1:6; 7; 8; 12; 15; 19; 2:23; 35; 3:12; 14; 4:19; 6:11(2); 8:21(2); 9:24; 15:6; 16; 20; 18:11; 20:7; 21:13; 23:9; 23; 30; 31; 32; 24:7; 26:14; 29:23; 30:11; 31:9; 32:27; 36:5; 37:14; 38:19; 42:11; 46:28; 50:31; 51:25; **Lam** 1:11; 14; 20; 3:1; 54; 59; 63; **Ezek** 2:3; 4; 4:15; 5:8; 6:7; 10; 13; 14; 7:4; 9; 27; 11:10; 12; 12:11; 15; 16; 20; 25; 13:8; 9; 14; 20; 21; 23; 14:8; 15:7; 16:62; 20:5; 7; 12; 19; 20; 26; 38; 42; 44; 21:3; 22:16; 26; 23:49; 24:24; 27; 25:5; 7; 11; 17; 26:3; 6; 27:3; 28:2; 9; 22(3); 23; 24; 25; 26; 29:3; 6; 9; 10; 16; 21; 30:8; 19; 22; 25; 26; 32:15; 33:29; 34:10; 27; 30; 31; 35:3; 4; 9; 12; 15; 36:9; 11; 23(2); 38; 37:6; 13; 38:3; 16; 23; 39:1; 6; 7; 13; 17; 19; 22; 27; 28; 44:28(2); **Dan** 8:19; **Hos** 2:2; 11:9; 12:9; 13:4; 14:8; **Joel** 2:27(2); 3:10; 17; **Am** 2:13; 7:8; **Jon** 1:9; **Mic** 2:3; 3:8; 7:1; **Nah** 2:13; 3:5; **Hab** 1:6; 2:1; **Zeph** 2:15; **Hag** 1:13; 2:4; **Zech** 1:14; 15; 16; 2:10; 3:8; 4:2; 8:2(2); 15; 10:6; 11:5; 13:5(2); **Mal** 1:6(2); 14; 3:6; **Mt** 3:11; 17; 8:3; 8; 9; 9:28; 11:29; 16:13; 15; 17:5; 18:20; 20:13; 15; 22(2); 23; 22:32; 24:5; 26:61; 27:24; 43; 28:20; **Mk** 1:7; 11; 41; 8:27; 29; 10:38; 39; 12:26; 13:6; 14:62; **Lk** 1:18; 19; 3:16; 22; 5:8; 13; 7:6; 8; 9:18; 20; 12:50; 14:19; 15:19; 21; 16:3; 4; 24; 18:11; 21:8; 22:27; 33; 58; 70; **Jn** 1:20; 21; 23; 27; 3:28; 4:26; 5:7; 6:35; 41; 48; 51; 7:8; 28; 29; 34; 36; 8:12; 14(2); 16(2); 18; 21; 23(2); 24; 28; 58; 9:5(2); 9; 10:7; 9; 11; 14(2); 36; 11:15; 25; 12:26; 32; 13:7; 13; 19; 33; 36; 14:3; 6; 10; 11; 20; 28(2); 15:1; 5; 16:32; 17:10; 11; 14; 16; 24; 18:5; 6; 8; 17; 25; 35; 37; 19:4; 21; 20:17; 21:3; **Acts** 7:32; 9:5; 10; 10:21; 26; 13:25(3); 18:6; 10; 20:26; 21:13; 39; 22:3; 8; 23:6(2); 24:21; 25:11; 26:2; 6; 7; 15; 25; 26; 29; 28:20; **Rom** 1:14; 15; 16; 3:7; 7:14; 15; 24; 8:38; 9:1; 11:1; 3; 13; 14:14; 15:14; 25; 16:19; **1 Cor** 1:12(4); 3:4(2); 4:4; 7:8; 9:1(2); 2(2); 19; 10:19; 30; 12:15(2); 16(2); 13:2; 12; 15:9(2); 10(2); 16:5; 11; 17; **2 Cor** 7:4(2); 14; 8:8; 10:1(3); 2; 11:2; 5; 6(2); 21; 22(3); 23; 29; 31; 12:10(2); 11; 14; 15; 13:1; **Gal** 4:11; 18; **Eph** 3:8; 6:20; 21; **Phil** 1:17; 23; 27; 2:17(2); 3:12; 4:11; 18; **Col** 2:5(2); 4:3; 8; **1 Tim** 1:15; 2:7; 3:15; **2 Tim** 1:5; 12(2); 4:6; **Phm** 1:12; 19; **Heb** 2:13; 12:21; **Jas** 1:13; **1 Pe** 1:16; 5:1; **2 Pe** 1:13; 17; **Rev** 1:8; 11; 17; 18(2); 2:23; 3:11; 17; 16:15; 18:7; 19:10; 21:6; 22:7; 9; 12; 13; 16; 20

AMONG (983/902)

Gen 3:8; 17:10; 12; 23; 23:4(2); 6; 9; 10; 24:3; 41; 30:32(2); 33(2); 35; 41; 33:1; 34:22; 30(2); 35:2; 40:20; 42:5; 47:2; 6; **Ex** 2:5; 7:5; 9:20; 10:2; 12:31; 49; 13:2; 7(2); 13; 15:11; 17:7; 22:25; 23:27; 25:8; 28:1; 29:45; 46; 30:12; 13; 14; 31:14; 32:25; 34:9; 10; 19; 35:5; 10; 36:8; **Lev** 6:18; 22; 29; 7:6; 33; 11:2; 3; 4; 13; 27; 29; 31; 42; 15:31; 16:16; 29; 17:4; 8; 9; 10(2); 12(2); 13; 18:26; 29; 19:16; 34(2); 20:14; 21:1; 4; 10; 15; 22:32; 23:30; 24:10; 25:33; 35; 45; 26:11; 12; 22; 25; 33; 38; 27:29; **Num** 1:47; 49; 2:33; 3:9; 12(2); 41(2); 42; 45; 4:2; 18; 5:21; 27; 8:6; 14; 16; 17; 19(2); 9:7; 13; 14; 11:1; 3; 4; 20; 21; 26; 12:6; 13:2; 14:6; 11; 13; 14; 42; 15:14; 26; 29(2); 30; 16:3; 21; 33; 45; 47; 17:6; 18:6; 20(2); 23; 24; 19:10; 20; 20:13; 21:6; 23:9; 21; 24:20; 25:7; 8; 11; 14; 26:62(2); 64; 27:4(2); 7; 31:16; 17; 32:30; 33:4; 54; 34:17; 29; 35:6; 15; 34; **Deut** 1:13; 42; 2:16; 4:3; 27(2); 6:15; 7:14(2); 20; 21; 13:1; 11; 13; 14; 14:6; 15:4; 7; 9; 16:4; 11; 17:2; 7; 15; 18:2; 6; 10; 18; 19:19; 20; 21:9; 11; 21; 22:21; 24; 23:10; 13; 14; 24:7; 26:11; 28:37; 43; 54; 56; 64; 65; 29:17; 18(2); 30:1; 31:16; 17; 32:26; 34; 46; 51; **Josh** 3:5; 10; 4:6; 7:11; 12; 13; 21; 8:9; 33; 35; 9:7; 10:1; 13:13; 22; 14:3; 15; 15:13; 16:9; 10; 17:4(2); 6; 9; 18:2; 4; 7; 19:49; 20:4; 9; 22:7; 14; 19; 31; 23:7(2); 12; 24:5; 17; 23; **Judg** 1:16; 29; 30; 32; 33; 2:12; 3:5; 5:8; 11; 15; 16; 24(2); 6:27; 10:16; 11:35; 12:4(2); 7; 14:3(2); 18:1; 20; 25; 20:12; 16; 21:5; 12; **Ruth** 2:7; 15; 4:10; **1 Sam** 2:8; 4:3; 17; 6:6; 7:3; 9:2; 22; 10:10; 11(2); 12; 22; 23; 24; 14:15; 30; 34; 39; 15:6(2); 33; 16:1; 19:24; 22:14; 31:9; **2 Sam** 6:19(2); 15:31; 17:9; 19:28; 20:19; 22:50; 23:8; 18; 22; **1 Ki** 2:7; 3:13; 5:6; 6:13; 8:53; 9:7; 11:20; 14:7; 21:9; 12; **2 Ki** 4:13; 9:2; 11:2; 17:25; 26; 33; 18:5; 35; 20:13; 15; 23:9; **1 Chr** 6:60; 7:5; 40; 10:9; 11:20; 24; 12:1; 4; 16:8; 24(2); 31; 21:6; 23:6; 24:4(2); 26:12(2); 19(2); 31(2); 27:6; 28:4; **2 Chr** 7:13; 20; 11:22; 19:4; 20:25; 22:11; 24:16; 23; 26:6; 28:15; 31:19(2); 32:14; 33:19; 35:13; 36:23; **Ezra** 1:3; 2:62; 5:10; 8:15; 10:18; **Neh** 1:8; 6:2; 6; 7:3; 64; 9:17; 10:34; 11:17; 13:26; **Esth** 3:8; 4:3; 9:21; 28(2); 10:3; **Job** 1:6; 2:1; 3:6; 12:9; 15:10; 19; 17:10; 18:17; 19; 22:24; 30:5; 7; 33:23; 34:4; 37; 36:14; 41:6; 42:15; **Ps** 9:11; 12:1; 8; 18:49; 21:10; 22:18; 31:11(2); 35:18; 44:11; 14(2); 45:9; 12; 46:10; 55:15; 57:4(2); 9(2); 66:9; 67:2; 68:13; 17; 18; 25; 74:5; 9; 77:14; 78:45; 49; 60; 79:10; 80:6; 81:9; 82:1; 86:8; 88:5; 89:6; 94:8; 96:3(2); 10; 99:6(2); 104:10; 12; 105:1; 27; 37; 106:27; 29; 47; 108:3(2); 109:30; 110:6; 118:7; 120:5; 126:2; 136:11; **Prov** 1:14; 6:19; 7:7(2); 14:9; 15:31; 17:2; 23:28; 30:14; 30; 31:23; **Eccl** 6:1; 7:28(2); **Song** 1:8; 9; 2:2(2); 3(2); 16; 4:2; 5; 5:9; 10; 6:1; 3; 6; **Isa** 4:3; 5:27; 8:15; 16; 10:4(2); 16; 12:4; 24:13; 29:14; 19; 30:14; 33:14(2); 34:17; 36:20; 38:11; 39:2; 4; 41:28; 42:23; 43:9; 12; 44:4; 14; 48:14; 50:10; 51:18(2); 57:6; 58:12; 61:9(2); 65:4; 66:19(3); **Jer** 3:19; 4:3; 5:26; 6:15; 18; 27; 8:12; 17; 9:16; 10:7; 11:9(2); 12:14; 14:22; 18:13; 24:10; 25:16; 27; 29:18(2); 32; 30:21; 31:7; 8; 32:20; 34:17; 37:4; 10; 12; 39:14; 40:1; 5; 6; 11; 41:8(2); 44:8; 46:18; 48:27; 49:15(2); 50:2; 23; 46; 51:27; 41; **Lam** 1:1(2); 2; 3; 17; 2:9; 4:15; 20; **Ezek** 1:1; 13; 2:5; 6; 3:15; 25; 4:13; 5:9; 10; 14; 15; 6:8; 9; 13; 9:2; 10:2(2); 6(2); 7(2); 11:1; 16(2); 12:10; 12; 15; 16; 13:19; 14:9; 15:2; 6; 16:14; 53; 18:18; 19:2(2); 6; 20:9; 23; 38; 22:15; 26; 30; 23:10; 25:4(2); 10; 27:19; 36; 28:19; 24; 25; 29:12(2); 13; 30:23; 26; 31:3; 10; 14(2); 17; 32:2; 9; 21; 33:6; 33; 34:12; 24; 35:11; 36:19; 21; 22; 23; 24; 30; 37:21; 39:21; 28; 44:9; 47:13; 21; 22(4); 48:29; **Dan** 1:6; 19; 4:35; 7:8; 11:4; 24; **Hos** 5:9; 7:7; 8; 8:8; 10; 9:17; 10:14; 13:15; **Joel** 2:17; 19; 25; 32; 3:2; 9; **Am** 1:1; 4:10; 9:9; **Ob** 1; 2; 4; 14(2); **Mic** 3:11; 5:2; 8(3); 7:2; **Hab** 1:5; **Zeph** 3:18; 20; **Hag** 2:3; 5; **Zech** 1:8; 10; 11; 3:7; 7:14; 8:13; 10:9; 12:8; 14:13; **Mal** 1:10; 11(2); 14; **Mt** 2:6; 4:23; 7:9; 9:35; 11:11; 12:11; 13:7; 22; 25; 49; 16:7; 8; 20:26(2); 27; 21:25; 38; 23:11; 26:5; 27:35; 56; 28:15; **Mk** 1:27; 4:7; 18; 5:3; 6:4; 41; 8:16; 9:33; 34; 10:26; 43(2); 11:31; 12:7; 14:4; 15:31; 40; 16:3; **Lk** 1:1; 25; 28; 42; 61; 2:44; 4:36; 7:16; 28; 8:7; 14; 9:46; 48; 10:3; 30; 36; 11:11; 16:15; 20:5; 14; 22:3; 17; 23; 24; 26(2); 27; 55; 24:5; **Jn** 1:14; 26; 6:9; 43; 52; 7:12; 35(2); 43; 8:7; 9:16; 10:19; 11:54; 56; 12:19; 20; 42; 15:24; 16:17; 19; 19:24(2); 21:23; **Acts** 1:21; 2:45; 3:23; 4:12; 15; 17; 34; 5:12; 6:3; 8; 10:7; 22; 12:18; 13:26; 14:14; 15:7; 12; 19; 22; 17:33; 34; 18:11; 20:18; 25; 28; 29; 30; 32; 21:19; 21; 34; 23:10; 24:5; 21; 25:5; 6; 26:4; 18; 31; 27:22; 28:25; 29; **Rom** 1:5; 6; 13(2); 24; 2:24; 8:29; 11:17; 12:3; 15:9; 26; 16:7; **1 Cor** 1:10; 11; 2:2; 6; 3:3; 18; 5:1(2); 2; 6:5; 11:13; 18; 19(2); 30; 14:25; 15:12; **2 Cor** 1:19; 2:15(2); 6:16; 17; 10:1; 12; 11:6; 26; 12:12; 21; **Gal** 1:16; 2:2; 3:1; 5; **Eph** 2:3; 3:8; 5:3; **Phil** 2:15; **Col** 1:6; 27; 4:16; **1 Th** 1:5; 2:7; 10; 5:12; 13; **2 Th** 1:4; 10(2); 2:10; 3:7; 11; **1 Tim** 3:7; 16; **2 Tim** 1:15; 2:2; **Heb** 5:1; 13:4; **Jas** 1:26; 2:4; 3:6; 13; 4:1; 5:13; 14; 19; **1 Pe** 2:12; 5:1; 2; **2 Pe** 2:1(2); 8; **1 Jn** 4:17; **3 Jn** 9; **Jude** 15; **Rev** 2:13; 7:15; 14:4

AN (1123/1054)

Gen 1:20; 4:3; 22; 6:14; 8:20; 12:7; 8; 13:18; 16:1; 17:7; 8; 13; 19; 21:20; 31; 22:9; 25:8; 26:25; 28; 31; 27:34; 28:3; 33:20; 35:1; 3; 7; 37:36; 38:8; 9; 14; 39:1(2); 41:16; 42:23; 43:12; 16; 32; 44:20; 46:34; 48:4; 49:6; 50:25; **Ex** 2:3; 11; 19; 6:6; 10:13; 12:14; 17; 24; 13:12; 15:25; 16:32; 33; 35; 36(2); 17:15; 19:13; 20:24; 25; 21:6; 28; 33; 22:1(2); 4; 9; 10; 11; 19; 23:1; 20; 22(2); 24:4; 25:2; 10; 33(2); 26:31; 27:1; 28:4; 11; 17; 19(2); 20; 32; 29:18; 25; 33; 40; 41; 30:1; 13; 14; 15; 20; 25; 33; 35; 31:18; 32:4; 5; 34:10; 35:5(2); 22; 24; 36:35; 37:19(2); 38:23; 39:10; 12(2); 13; 23; 30; 40:15; **Lev** 1:2; 9; 13; 17; 2:2; 4; 9; 16; 3:3; 5; 9; 11; 14; 16; 5:1; 2; 4; 11; 6:20; 7:5; 18; 21; 24; 25; 8:21; 28; 11:10; 11(2); 12; 13(2); 20; 23; 35; 41; 42; 13:11; 51; 52; 14:5; 10;

21; 40; 41; 44; 45; 50; 15:16; 18; 16:20; 22; 34; 17:3; 4; 18:22; 23; 19:7; 32; 36(2); 20:13; 15; 21; 22:4; 12; 22(2); 27; 23:8; 13(2); 14; 17; 18; 25; 27; 36(2); 37; 24:5; 7; 8; 10(2); 18; 21; 25:46; 26:1; 27:9(2); 11; 26; 27; **Num** 5:15(2); 17; 21; 6:2; 7:2; 3; 18; 24; 30; 36; 42; 48; 54; 60; 66; 72; 78; 10:8; 9; 12:1; 14:7; 15:3; 4; 6; 9; 10; 13; 14; 15; 25; 18:4; 8; 11; 17; 19; 21; 24; 19:17; 22:4; 22; 25:13; 26:53; 28:5; 6; 7; 8; 9; 12(2); 13(2); 19; 20; 21; 28; 29:3; 6; 9; 13; 14; 36; 30:2; 10(2); 31:50; 32:10; 33:54; 34:2; 17; 35:16; 36:2; 8; **Deut** 1:34; 3:11; 4:20; 21; 34; 38; 5:15; 7:25; 26(2); 10:1; 3; 13:14; 15:4; 17; 17:1; 4; 18:12; 19:10; 20:10; 16; 19; 21:23; 22:5; 10; 23:3; 7(3); 13; 18; 24:4(2); 8; 25:4; 16; 19; 26:1; 8; 14; 27:5(3); 15; 25; 28:37; 29:8; 32:11; **Josh** 1:6; 7:13; 8:2; 14(2); 24; 30; 31(2); 10:20; 11:23; 13:6; 7; 15; 24; 29; 32; 14:1; 13; 17:4(2); 6; 19:49(3); 51(2); 22:10; 11; 16; 19; 23(2); 26; 29; 23:4; 24:25; 32; **Judg** 3:31; 6:19; 24; 26; 8:27; 9:48; 53; 12:5; 14:4; 17:5; 18:1; 14; 19:9; 16; 21:1; 4; 17; 18; **Ruth** 2:17; **1 Sam** 1:1; 4; 2:28; 31; 32(2); 7:17; 9:6; 13:4; 14:3; 14; 28; 35; 48; 17:17; 19:13; 20:3; 36; 21:7; 23:6; 25:28; 26:19; 28:14; 29:9; 30:11; 13; 14; 25; **2 Sam** 1:8; 13(2); 3:35; 15:19; 17:25; 23:5; 21; 24:18; 21; 25; **1 Ki** 1:29; 45; 3:9; 8:13; 31(2); 33; 36; 11:14; 25; 26; 38; 13:11; 14; 18; 14:21; 31; 15:13; 16:32; 18:10; 32; 19:5; 11; 20:25; 30; 22:9; 25; **2 Ki** 6:15; 7:2; 8:3; 9:2; 10:25; 11:4; 12:15; 15:5; 25; 16:10; 11; 17:36; 19:32; 20:10; 25:19; 24; **1 Chr** 2:34; 11:23; 16:17; 29; 21:15; 18; 22; 26; 27:4; 28:8; **2 Chr** 2:4; 6:2; 22(2); 24; 27; 12:13; 13:3; 13; 14:8; 9; 15:14; 16; 18:24; 20:23; 25; 21:18; 26:11; 13; 21; 29:24; 32:8; 21; 36:13; **Ezra** 4:6; 17; 5:11; 8:22; 9:11; 12; 10:5(2); **Neh** 5:12; 18; 6:5; 13; 10:29; **Esth** 2:23; **Job** 2:11; 6:6; 9:26; 10:8; 11:12; 14:4; 15:33; 16:3; 18:2; 19:15; 24; 20:26; 22:11; 28:3; 31:28; 33:13; 38:34; 40:9; 15; 42:15; **Ps** 5:9; 6:7:9; 10:13; 12:24:4; 26:12; 27:3; 33:2; 16; 36:1; 41:8; 43:1; 48:7; 55:12; 64:5; 7; 69:8; 31; 72:16; 78:26; 55; 81:84:88:8; 92:3; 96:8; 102:6; 8; 105:10; 106:20; 26; 109:6; 119:42; 87; 142; 136:12; 145:13; **Prov** 1:6; 3:32; 4:9; 5:3; 20; 6:11; 16; 26; 7:13; 22; 23; 8:5; 7; 23; 10:25; 11:1; 20; 12:4; 22; 13:19; 22; 14:4; 15:8; 9; 26; 16:5; 12; 27; 17:2; 4; 11; 15; 19:14; 15; 20:10; 21; 23; 21:27; 22:14; 24; 23:5; 24:9; 34; 25:12(3); 19; 23; 27:6; 28:9; 10; 22; 29:6; 22; 27(3); 30:19; 20; **Eccl** 3:15; 4:13; 5:6; 6:1; 2; 7:11; 8:3; 11; 9:2(2); 3; 12; 10:5(2); **Song** 2:3; 4:4; 13; 6:4; 10; 7:4; **Isa** 1:13; 6:13; 9:12; 17; 10:6; 14:19; 16:4; 17:6; 9; 19:19; 24:13; 28:4; 29:5; 21; 30:13; 22; 28; 33:1; 37:33; 38:12; 13; 40:19; 41:24; 44:9; 10; 19; 45:17; 23; 48:4; 49:8; 18; 22; 51:20; 53:10; 54:16; 55:3; 13; 56:5; 58:5; 60:15; 19; 61:8; 63:10; 12; 64:6; 65:9; 20(2); 66:3; 17; 20(2); 24; **Jer** 1:11; 18; 2:7; 19; 21; 3:2; 18; 5:15; 16; 30; 6:26; 27; 9:2; 8; 11; 10:14; 19; 15:18; 18:17; 19:4; 21:5; 23:40; 25:9; 11; 18; 26:8; 9; 29:18; 30:14; 17; 31:3; 18; 32:14; 21; 40; 33:9; 40:9; 42:18(2); 44:12(2); 22(2); 27; 46:22; 47:2; 48:40; 49:2; 14; 17; 50:9(2); 51:34; 37(2); 52:25; **Lam** 1:15; 17; 2:4(2); 5; 17; 3:45; 5:10; **Ezek** 1:10(2); 22; 24; 4:3(2); 5:15; 7:2; 6; 10:14; 16:3; 8; 32; 40; 45; 60; 63; 20:5(2); 6; 15; 17; 23; 28; 33; 34; 42; 23:46; 26:7; 13; 33:32; 35:5(2); 36:7; 37:10; 26; 38:10; 41:8; 44:12; 45:2; 5; 6; 10(2); 13(2); 46:7(2); 11(2); 14; 18; 47:13; 14; 22(2); 48:13; 29; **Dan** 2:5; 46; 3:1; 29; 4:3; 34; 5:12; 6:3; 7:14; 27; 8:12; 9:24; 27; 11:6; 7; 18; **Hos** 1:4; 4:15; 7:4; 6; 7; 8:1; 9:10; 13:13; 15; 14:6; **Joel** 2:1; **Am** 3:11; 12; 15; 5:13; 8:10; **Jon** 3:3; **Mic** 1:15; 16; 2:3; 8; 6:10; **Nah** 1:8(2); 9; **Hab** 2:3; **Zech** 6:11; 9:8; **Mal** 1:10; 13; 2:11; 12; 3:3; 5; 4:1; **Mt** 1:20; 2:13; 19; 4:8; 5:38(2); 39; 9:16; 12:35; 39; 43; 13:28; 14:7; 16:23; 17:15; 24:44; 50; 26:5; 7; 72; 28:2; **Mk** 1:23; 2:21; 3:26; 30; 5:2; 6:21; 27; 7:22; 25; 32; 14:2; 3; **Lk** 1:3; 11; 18; 2:9; 4:13; 33; 5:14; 36; 6:7; 45; 7:37; 8:42; 10:34; 11:12; 24; 29; 12:1; 14; 29; 40; 46; 14:5; 16:1; 2; 9; 15; 19:21; 22; 43; 21:13; 22:37; 43; 59; 23:38; **Jn** 1:22; 47; 5:4; 5; 12:29; 13:15; 18:30; **Acts** 2:30; 5:19; 6:15; 7:30; 8:26; 9:37; 10:3; 11; 11:5; 13; 12:7; 21; 23; 13:7; 17; 17:5; 23; 18:24; 20:32; 21:16; 26; 31; 23:9; 12; 21; 25:11; 26:18; 27:6; 16; 23; 28:7; 11; **Rom** 1:1; 23; 2:20; 26; 3:13; 7:3; 11:1; 13; 13:4; **1 Cor** 1:1; 5:11(2); 6:7; 8:4; 7; 10; 9:1; 2; 9; 25; 10:19; 11:27; 29; 12:16; 17; 14:8; 24(2); 26; 15:9; 24; 52; **2 Cor** 1:1; 3:3; 5:12; 6:2; 15; 8:14; 9:8; 11:12; 14; 12:12; **Gal** 1:1; 8; 2:5; 4:7; 14; 5:13; **Eph** 1:1; 11; 5:2; 5; 6:20; **Phil** 4:18; **Col** 1:1; 2:23; **1 Th** 4:16; **2 Th** 3:9; 15; **1 Tim** 1:1; 13; 2:7; 4:12; 5:1; 8; 18; 19(2); **2 Tim** 1:1; 11; 2:9; 4:5; **Titus** 1:1; 2:8; **Heb** 3:12; 6:6; 16(2); 17; 19; 7:16; 18; 20; 21(2); 24; 10:18; 22; 34; 11:7; 8; 12:20; 22; 13:10; **Jas** 3:8; 4:4; 5:10; **1 Pe** 1:1; 4; 2:21; 3:21; 4:5; 15; **2 Pe** 1:11; 2:6; **1 Jn** 2:1; 7; 20; 5:20; **2 Jn** 7; **Jude** 7; 15; **Rev** 2:7; 11; 17; 29; 3:6; 8; 13; 22; 4:3; 8:1; 5; 13; 11:19; 13:9; 14; 19:17; 20:1; 21:17; 27

AND (38260/21831)

Gen 1:1; 2(3); 3; 4(2); 5(2); 6; 7(2); 8(2); 9(2); 10(3); 11(2); 12(3); 13; 14(4); 15(2); 16; 18(4); 19; 20; 21(3); 22(4); 23; 24(3); 25(3); 26(2); 27; 28(4); 29(2); 30(2); 31(2); 2:1(2); 2(2); 3(2); 4(2); 5(2); 6; 7(3); 8; 9(4); 10(2); 12(2); 15(2); 16; 17; 18; 19(3); 20; 21(4); 22; 23(2); 24(3); 25(3); 3:1; 2; 5(2); 6(3); 7(3); 8(3); 9; 10(2); 11; 12; 13(2); 14(2); 15(5); 16(2); 17; 18(2); 19; 20; 21(2); 22(5); 24(2); 4:1(3); 3; 4(3); 5(3); 6; 7(2); 8(2); 10; 12; 13; 14(2); 15(2); 16; 17(5); 18(3); 19; 20(2); 21; 22(3); 23; 25(3); 26(2); 5:2(3); 3(4); 4(2); 5(2); 6(2); 7(3); 8(2); 9; 10(3); 11(2); 12; 13(3); 14(2); 15; 16(3); 17(2); 18(2); 19(2); 20(2); 21; 22(2); 23; 24(2); 25(2); 26(3); 27(2); 28(2); 29(2); 30(3); 31(2); 32(3); 6:1; 2; 3(2); 4(2); 5; 6(2); 7(2); 10(2); 11; 12; 13(2); 14(2); 15(2); 16(3); 17; 18(2); 19(2); 20; 21(4); 7:1; 2(2); 3; 4(2); 5; 7; 8; 9; 10; 11; 12(2); 13(4); 14(2); 15; 16(2); 17(2); 18(2); 19(2); 20; 21(5); 23(3); 24(2); 8:1(4); 2(2); 3(2); 5; 7; 9(3); 10(2); 11(2); 12; 13(5); 14; 16(3); 17(4); 18(3); 19; 20(3); 21; 22(5); 9:1(4); 2(3); 5; 7(3); 8; 9(2); 10(2); 12(3); 13(2); 15(3); 16(2); 17(2); 18(2); 19; 20(2); 21(2); 22(2); 23(4); 24; 26(2); 27(2); 28(2); 29(2); 10:1(2); 2; 3; 4; 6; 7(3); 10(2); 11; 12(2); 14(2); 15; 16; 17; 18; 19(2); 20; 21; 22; 23; 24; 25; 29; 30; 32; 11:1; 2(2); 3(2); 4(2); 5; 6(3); 7; 8; 9; 10; 11(2); 12; 13(3); 14; 15(3); 16; 17(3); 18; 19(3); 20; 21(3); 22; 23(2); 24; 25(3); 26(2); 27; 28; 29(3); 31(6); 32(2); 12:1; 2(2); 3(2); 4(2); 5(4); 6; 7(2); 8(4); 10; 11; 12; 13; 15(2); 16(2); 17; 18(2); 19; 20(2); 13:1(3); 2; 3(2); 4; 5(2); 7(3); 8(3); 10(3); 11(2); 12(2); 13; 14(3); 15; 16; 17; 18(3); 14:1(2); 2; 4; 5(2); 6; 7(3); 8(3); 9; 10(3); 11(3); 12(2); 13(3); 14(2); 15(3); 16(3); 17(2); 18; 19(3); 20(2); 21; 22; 23; 24(2); 15:2; 4; 5(3); 6(2); 8; 9; 10(2); 11; 12(2); 13(2); 14; 17(3); 21; 16:1; 2; 3; 4(2); 5(2); 6; 8(2); 9; 11(2); 12(2); 14; 15; 17:1(2); 2(3); 3; 4; 6(2); 7(4); 8(2); 9(2); 10(2); 11(3); 13(2); 14; 16(3); 17(3); 18; 19(2); 20(4); 22; 23(2); 25; 26; 27; 18:2(4); 3; 4(2); 5; 6(2); 7(3); 8(4); 10(2); 11(2); 13; 14; 15; 16(2); 17; 18(2); 19(2); 20(3); 21(2); 22; 23(2); 24; 27(2); 29(2); 30; 31; 32(2); 33; 19:1(2); 2(5); 3(3); 4; 5(2); 7; 8; 9(3); 10(2); 11(2); 12; 13; 14(2); 15; 16(4); 19(2); 20(2); 21; 24(2); 25; 26; 27; 28(4); 29(2); 30(4); 31; 32; 33(3); 34(2); 35(3); 37; 38(2); 20:1(4); 2(2); 3; 4; 5(2); 6; 7(3); 8(2); 9(3); 11(2); 12; 13; 14(4); 15; 16; 17(2); 21:1(2); 2; 3; 6(2); 8(2); 9; 10; 11; 14(6); 15(2); 16(3); 17(2); 18; 19(4); 20(3); 21; 22(2); 23; 24; 26; 27(3); 28; 30; 32; 33; 34; 22:1(2); 2(2); 3(6); 4; 5(4); 6(4); 7(3); 8; 9(4); 10(2); 11; 12; 13(4); 14; 16(2); 17(3); 19(3); 22; 23; 24; 23:1; 2(2); 3; 4; 5; 7; 8(2); 10; 11; 13(2); 14; 15; 16(2); 17(2); 19; 20; 24:1; 3(2); 4(2); 5; 7(4); 8; 9; 10(3); 11; 12; 13; 14(3); 15; 16(2); 17(2); 18; 19; 20; 21; 22; 23; 25(2); 26; 27(2); 28; 29; 30(3); 31(2); 32(5); 33; 35(7); 36(2); 38(2); 39; 40(3); 42(2); 43(2); 44(2); 45(3); 46(5); 47(3); 48(3); 49(2); 50(2); 51(2); 52; 53(3); 54(5); 55; 56; 57; 58(2); 59(3); 60(3); 61(4); 63(4); 64; 65; 66; 67(3); 25:1; 2(2); 3(3); 4(2); 5; 6; 7; 8(3); 9(2); 10; 11(2); 13; 15; 16(2); 17(4); 21(2); 22; 23(2); 25; 26; 27; 28; 29(2); 30; 32; 33; 34(4); 26:1; 2; 3(4); 4(2); 5(2); 7(2); 8(2); 9(2); 10(2); 12(2); 13; 14(2); 15; 16; 17(2); 18; 19; 21; 22(4); 24(3); 25(3); 26; 27(2); 28(2); 29(2); 30(2); 31(3); 32(2); 34; 35(2); 27:1(3); 3(3); 4(2); 5(2); 7(2); 9(2); 10; 11(2); 12(3); 13; 14(4); 15; 16(2); 17; 18(2); 19; 20; 22(2); 23; 25(4); 26; 27(5); 28(2); 29(3); 30; 31(3); 32; 33(4); 34(2); 35; 36(3); 37(3); 38(3); 39(2); 40(2); 41; 42(3); 44; 45(2); 46; 28:1(3); 2; 3(2); 4(2); 5(2); 6(2); 7(3); 9; 10; 11(4); 12(4); 13(4); 14(4); 15(2); 16(2); 17(3); 18(2); 19; 20(3); 22(2); 29:1; 2(3); 3(2); 4(2); 5; 6(2); 7(2); 8; 10(4); 11(2); 12(3); 13(3); 14(3); 16; 17; 19; 20; 22(2); 23(2); 24; 25; 26; 27; 28; 29; 30(2); 32(2); 33(3); 34(2); 35(3); 30:1; 2(2); 3; 4; 5(2); 6(2); 7(2); 8; 9; 10; 12; 14(2); 15; 16(2); 17(3); 19; 20; 21; 22(2); 23(3); 24; 25(2); 26(2); 27; 28; 29; 30(2); 31(2); 32(5); 33(2); 34; 35(4); 36(2); 37(3); 38; 39(2); 40(3); 41; 42; 43(4); 31:1; 2(2); 3(2); 4(2); 5; 6; 7; 8; 9; 10(4); 11; 12(3); 13(2); 14(2); 15; 16; 17(2); 18(2); 19; 20; 21(2); 22; 23(2); 24; 25; 26(2); 27(4); 28(2); 30; 31; 32; 33(3); 34(2); 35(2); 36(3); 37; 38(2); 40(2); 41(2); 42(3); 43(4); 44(3); 45; 46(3); 48(2); 49; 50; 51(2); 52(3); 53(2); 54(3); 55(5); 32:1; 2; 4(2); 5(3); 6(2); 7(5); 8(2); 9(3); 10(2); 11(2); 12; 13; 14(2); 15(2); 16(2); 17(3); 18; 19; 20(2); 22(4); 23; 24; 25; 26; 28(3); 29(2); 30(2); 31; 33:1(4); 2(5); 3; 4(4); 5(4); 6(2); 7(4); 8; 10(2); 11(2); 12; 13(3); 14; 15; 17(2); 18; 19; 20; 34:2(3); 3(2); 5; 7(3); 9(2); 10(3); 11(2); 12(2); 13(2); 14; 16(3); 17(2); 18(2); 20(3); 21(2); 23(2); 24(2); 25(3); 26(4); 27; 28(2); 29(3); 30(5); 35:1(2); 2(3); 3(3); 4(2); 5(3); 6; 7(2); 8; 9; 10; 11(3); 12(2); 14(2); 15; 16(2); 18; 19; 20; 21; 22(3); 23(2); 24; 25; 26(2); 27; 28; 29(5); 36:3; 4; 5(2); 6(4); 7; 9; 10; 11(2); 12; 13; 14(2); 16; 17; 18(2); 19; 21; 22(2); 23; 24; 25; 26; 27; 28; 30; 32; 33; 35(2); 37; 39(2); 40(2); 43; 37:2(3); 4; 5(2); 7(3); 8(2); 9(4); 10(5); 11; 13; 14(4); 15(2); 17(2); 20(2); 21(2); 22(3); 24(2); 25(4); 26; 27(4); 28(3); 29(2); 30(3); 31; 32(2); 33(2); 34; 35(3); 36; 38:1; 2(3); 3(2); 4(2); 5(3); 6; 7; 8(3); 9; 10; 11(2); 12(3); 13; 14(3); 16; 17; 18(4); 19(3); 20; 21; 22; 23; 24(2); 25(3); 26(2); 28(3); 29; 30; 39:1; 2(2); 3(2); 4(2); 5(3); 6(2); 7(2); 8(2); 9; 11; 12(2); 13(2); 14(2); 15(4); 18(2); 20(2); 21(2); 22; 23; 40:1; 2(2); 4(2); 5(2); 6(3); 8(2); 9; 10(2); 11(3); 12; 13(2); 14(2); 15; 16; 17; 18; 19(2); 20(2); 21; 41:1; 2(2); 3(2); 4(3); 5(3); 7(3); 8(4); 10(2); 11; 12(2); 13(2); 14(4); 15(2); 18(2); 19(2); 20(2); 22(2); 23; 24; 26; 27(3); 30(2); 32(2); 33(2); 34; 35(3); 37; 38; 39; 40; 41; 42(3); 43(2); 44; 45(2); 46(2); 48; 50; 51; 52; 54; 56(3); 42:2(3); 5; 6(3); 7(3); 9; 10; 13(3); 16(2); 18; 19; 20(3); 21; 22(2); 24(5); 25; 26; 27; 28(2); 29; 30; 32; 33; 34(2); 35(2); 36(2); 37; 38; 43:2; 4; 6; 7(2); 8(5); 9; 11(5); 12; 13; 14(2); 15(5); 16(2); 17; 18(2); 20; 21; 22; 23; 24(3); 26(2); 27; 28(3); 29(3); 30(3); 31(3); 32(2); 33(3); 34; 44:1(2); 2; 3; 4(2); 5; 6; 7; 9; 10(2); 11; 12(2); 13(2); 14(3); 15; 16; 17; 18(2); 20(4); 22; 25(2); 28(3); 29; 30; 33; 45:1; 2(3); 4; 6; 7(2); 8(3); 9(2); 10(4); 11(2); 12(2); 13(3); 14(2); 15(2); 16; 17(2); 18(3); 19(2); 21(2); 22; 23(3); 24(2); 25; 26(3); 27; 28; 46:1(2); 2(2); 4(2); 5(2); 6(3); 7(3); 8; 9; 10; 11; 12(3); 13; 14; 15; 16; 17(3); 18; 19; 20(2); 21; 24; 25; 27; 28; 29(4); 30; 31(4); 32(3); 33; 34; 47:1(6); 2(2); 3(2); 4; 5; 6(2); 7(2); 9(4); 10; 11(3); 12; 13; 14(3); 15(2); 16; 17(2); 18(2); 19(5); 21; 22; 23(2); 24(3); 25; 26; 27(3); 28(2); 29(3); 30(2); 31; 48:1(2); 2(3); 3; 4(4); 5(3); 7; 8; 9(3); 10(2); 11; 12; 13(3); 14(2); 15(3); 16(3); 18; 19(3); 20(2); 21; 22; 49:1(2); 2(2); 3(2); 5; 6; 7(2); 9; 10; 11(2); 12; 13; 15(2); 20; 23; 24; 25(2); 26; 27; 28(2); 29; 31(3); 32; 33(3); 50:1(2); 2; 3; 4; 5(2); 6(2); 7(2); 8(2); 9(3); 10(2); 11; 13; 14(3); 15; 17(2); 18(2); 21(3); 22(3); 24(3); 25; 26(3); **Ex** 1:1; 2; 3; 4; 6(2); 7(3); 9(2); 10(3); 11(2); 12(2); 14(2); 15; 16(2); 17; 18(2); 19(2); 20(2); 21; 22; 2:1(2); 2(2); 3(2); 4; 5(2); 6(3); 7; 8(2); 9(3); 10(3); 11(2); 12(3); 13(2); 14(2); 15(2); 16(3); 17(3); 19(3); 20; 21; 22(2); 23(2); 24(2); 25(2); 3:1(2); 2(2); 3; 4(2); 6(2); 7(2); 8(8); 9; 10; 11; 12; 13(2); 14(2); 15(2); 16(4); 17(7); 18(4); 20(2); 21(2); 22(3); 4:1; 3(3); 4(4); 5; 6(2); 7(3); 9(3); 10; 12(2); 14(2); 15(4); 16(2); 17; 18(5); 19; 20(4); 21; 24(2); 25(3); 27(3); 28; 29(2); 30; 31(3); 5:1(2); 2; 3; 4; 5(2); 6; 7; 8(2); 9; 10(3); 13; 14(2); 15; 16(2); 17; 18; 19; 20; 21(3); 22; 6:1; 2(2); 3; 5(2); 6(2); 7; 8(3); 9; 10; 12; 13(3); 14; 15(2); 16(3); 17; 18(4); 19; 20(4); 21; 22(2); 23(2); 24(2); 25; 26; 27; 28; 30; 7:1; 2; 3(3); 4(2); 5(2); 6; 7(2); 8; 9(2); 10(5); 11; 12; 13(2); 15(2); 16; 17; 18(2); 19(4); 20(5); 21; 22(2); 23(2); 25; 8:1(2); 3(2); 4(2); 5(2); 6(2); 7(2); 8(4); 9(3); 10; 11(2); 12(2); 13(2); 14; 15; 16; 17(4); 18; 19; 20(2); 21(3); 22; 23; 24(2); 25(2); 26; 27; 28; 29(2); 30; 31(2); 9:1; 2; 3; 4(2); 6; 7(2); 8(2); 9(3); 10(4); 11(2); 12; 13(2); 14(2); 15(2); 16; 19(5); 20; 21; 22; 23(5); 24; 25(4); 27(6); 28(2); 29; 30; 31(2); 32; 33(3); 34(4); 10:1; 2(3); 3(2); 5(3); 6(3); 8(2); 9(4); 10; 11(2); 12; 13(2); 14(2); 15(2); 16(3); 17; 18; 19(2); 20; 22; 24(2); 25; 26; 27; 28; 29; 11:1(2); 2(3); 3(2); 5(2); 7; 8(3); 10(3); 12:1; 4(2); 7(3); 8; 9; 10; 11(2); 12(3); 13(2); 14; 16; 21(3); 22(4); 23(3); 24(2); 26; 27(2); 28(2); 29(2); 30(2); 31(4); 32(3); 33; 35(2); 36; 38(2); 39(2); 40; 41(2); 43(2); 45; 48(5); 49; 50; 51; 13:2; 3; 5(6); 6; 7; 8; 9; 11(3); 13(2); 15(2); 16; 17; 18; 19(2); 20; 21(3); 14:2(2); 4(3); 5(3); 6; 7; 8(3); 9(3); 10(3); 13(2); 14; 15; 16(3); 17(4); 18; 19(4); 20(3); 21(3); 22(2); 23(3); 24(2); 25(2); 26; 27(2); 28(2); 29(2); 30; 31(2); 15:1(3); 2(4); 4; 7; 8; 14; 16; 17; 18; 19(2); 20(2); 21(2); 22(2); 24; 25(3); 26(3); 27; 16:1(3); 2; 3(2); 4(2); 5(2); 6; 7; 8(2); 10; 11; 12(2); 13(2); 14; 15; 17; 18; 19; 20(3); 21; 22(3); 23(2); 24; 28(2); 31(3); 33(3); 35; 17:1; 2(2); 3(5); 5(3); 6(3); 7(2); 8; 9(2); 10(3); 11(2); 12(6); 13; 14; 15(2); 18:1(2); 4(2); 5(2); 6; 7(3); 8(3); 10(3); 12(2); 13(2); 14; 15; 16(4); 18; 19; 20(4); 21(2); 22; 23(2); 24; 25(3); 27; 19:2; 3(3); 4(2); 5; 6(2); 7(2); 8; 9(2); 10(3); 11; 14(2); 15; 16(3); 17(2); 18; 19(4); 20(2); 21(3); 23; 24(3); 25; 20:1; 5; 6; 9; 11(4); 12; 18(3); 19; 20(2); 24(4); 25; 21:2(2); 4(3); 5; 6(2); 7; 9; 10; 11; 15; 16; 17; 18(2); 19(2); 20; 22(2); 26; 27; 28; 29(3); 32; 33(3); 35(2); 36(2); 22:1(2); 2; 5(3); 6; 7; 9; 10; 11(2); 13; 14(2); 16; 23; 24(3); 27; 29; 30; 31; 23:5; 7; 8(2); 10; 11(3); 12(4); 13(2); 16(2); 20; 21; 22(2); 23(7); 24; 25(3); 27; 28(2); 29; 30; 31(3); 24:1(4); 2; 3(4); 4(4); 5; 6(3); 7(3); 8(2); 9(2); 10(3); 11(2); 12(4); 13; 14(2); 15; 16(2); 18(3); 25:3(2); 4(2); 5; 6(2); 7(2); 8; 9; 10(5); 11(3); 12(2); 13(2); 16; 17(3); 18; 19; 20(2); 21; 22(2); 23(2); 24(2); 25; 26(2); 28(2); 29; 30; 31; 32(2); 33(4); 34; 35(2); 36; 37; 38(2); 40; 26:1(2); 2(2); 3; 4(2); 5; 6(2); 8(2); 9(3); 10; 11(2); 13(3); 14; 15; 16(2); 18; 20; 21; 23; 24; 26; 27; 29; 30; 31(2); 33(2); 35(2); 36(2); 37(3); 27:1(2); 2; 3(4); 4; 6(2); 7; 10(3); 11(3); 12(2); 14; 15(2); 16(3); 17; 18(2); 19; 20; 21; 28:1(3); 2(2); 4(3); 5(2); 6(3); 7; 8(3); 9; 10; 12; 14(2); 15(2); 16; 17(2); 18; 19; 20(2); 21; 23(2); 25(2); 26; 27(2); 28; 30(3); 33(3); 34(2); 35(3); 36; 37; 38; 39; 40(3); 41(2); 42; 43(3); 29:1(2); 2(2); 3(2); 4(3); 5(3); 6; 7(2); 8; 9(4); 10(2); 12(2); 13(4); 14; 15(2); 16(3); 17(3); 18; 19(2); 20(5); 21(9); 22; 23; 24(3); 25; 26(2); 27(3); 28; 29(2); 31(2); 32(2); 33; 34; 35; 36(2); 37(2); 39; 40; 41(3); 43(2); 44(2); 45; 46; 30:2(2); 3(3); 4; 5; 6; 8; 10; 14; 15; 16(2); 18(2); 19(2); 21(3); 23(2); 24; 25; 26; 27(3); 28(2); 30(3); 31; 32; 34(4); 35; 36(2); 31:3(2); 5; 6(2); 7(2); 8; 9(2); 10; 11(2); 12; 13; 17(4); 18; 32:1; 2(3); 3; 4(3); 5(2); 6(4); 7; 8(3); 9(2); 10(2); 11(2); 12(3); 13(4); 15(4); 16; 17; 19(3); 20(3); 21; 24(3); 26(2); 27(5); 28; 29; 31(2); 33; 33:1(3); 2(7); 3; 4(2); 5; 7(3); 8(2); 9(3); 10(2); 11; 12; 13(2); 14(2); 16(2); 17; 18; 19(2); 20; 21(2); 22; 23; 34:1(2); 2(2); 3(2); 4(2); 5(2); 6(5); 7(4); 8(2); 9(3); 10(2); 11(5); 13; 15(4); 16(3); 19; 20(2); 21; 22(2); 24; 27; 28(2); 29; 30(2); 31(3); 32; 33; 34(2); 35; 35:1; 4; 5; 6(2); 7; 8(2); 9(2); 10; 11; 12(2); 13(2); 14; 15; 16(2); 17; 18; 19; 20; 21(3); 22(4); 23(4); 24; 25(3); 26; 27(2); 28(3); 29; 30; 31(3); 32(2); 33; 34(2); 35(6); 36:1(4); 2(3); 3; 5; 6(2); 8(2); 9; 10(2); 12; 13(2); 15; 16; 17(2); 19; 21(2); 23; 25; 26; 29(2); 30; 31; 32; 33; 34; 35(3); 36(2); 37(2); 38(3); 37:1(4); 2(2); 3(2); 4; 5; 6(3); 8; 9; 10(2); 11(2); 12; 13(2); 15(2); 16; 17; 18(2); 19(4); 20(2); 21; 22; 23(2); 25(2); 26(2); 28(2); 29; 38:1(2); 2; 3; 4; 6(2); 8; 10; 11(2); 12(3); 14; 15(3); 17(3); 18(3); 19(3); 20; 23(4); 24(2); 25(3); 26(3); 27(2); 28(2); 29; 30(2); 31; 39:1(2); 2(2); 3(4); 5(3); 6; 8(3); 9; 10(2); 11; 12; 13; 15; 16(2); 17; 18; 19(2); 20; 21(2); 23; 24(2); 25(2); 26(2); 27; 29(2); 30; 31; 32; 33(3); 34; 35; 36; 37; 38; 39; 40(2); 41(2); 43(2); 40:3; 4(3); 5; 7(3); 8; 9(6); 10(2); 11(3); 12(2); 13(2); 14(2); 17; 18; 19(2); 20(2); 21(2); 23; 25; 27; 29(3); 30(2); 31(3); 32; 33(3); 34; 35(2); 38; **Lev** 1:1; 2(2); 4; 5(2); 6(2); 7; 8; 9(2); 11; 12(3); 13(2); 14; 15; 16(2); 17; 2:1(2); 2(2); 3; 4; 6; 8; 9; 10(2); 13; 15(2); 16; 3:2(3); 3; 4(2); 5; 8(3); 9(3); 10(2); 11; 12; 13(2); 14; 15(2); 16; 4:2; 4; 5; 6; 7(2); 8; 9(2); 10; 11(3); 12; 13(3); 14; 15; 17; 18(2); 19; 20(2); 21; 22(2); 24(2); 25; 26(2); 27; 29(2); 30; 31(2); 33; 34; 35; 5:1; 2(2); 3; 4; 5; 6; 7; 8(2); 9; 10(2); 12(2); 13; 15; 16(4); 17(2); 18(3); 6:1; 2; 3(2); 4; 5; 6; 7; 9(2); 10(4); 11; 12(4); 15(2); 16(2); 17; 19; 20(2); 24; 25; 27; 28(2); 7:2; 3(2); 4(2); 5; 8; 9; 14; 18(2); 19; 21; 22; 24(2); 31(2); 33; 34(3); 35; 37; 8:1; 2(3); 3; 4; 5; 6(2); 7(4); 8(2); 9; 10(3); 11(3); 12(2); 13(2); 14(2); 15(5); 16(2); 17; 18(2); 19; 20(3); 21(2); 22(2); 23(3); 24(3); 25(3); 26(4); 27(3); 28; 29(2); 30(5); 31(4); 32; 33; 35(2); 36; 9:1(2); 2(3); 3(3); 4(2); 5(2); 6; 7(5); 8; 9(2); 10; 11; 12(2); 13(2); 14(3); 15(3); 16(2); 17; 18(2); 19(4); 20; 21; 22(2); 23(4); 24(4); 10:1(3); 2(2); 3(2); 4(3); 5; 6(4); 7; 10(3); 11; 12(4); 13; 14(3); 15(3); 16(3); 17; 19(3); 11:1; 3; 7; 8; 9; 10; 13; 14; 16; 17; 18; 19; 22; 25; 27; 28; 29; 30; 32; 33; 34; 35(2); 37; 38; 39; 40(2); 41; 44; 46(3); 47(3); 12:2; 3; 5; 6; 7(2); 8(3); 13:1(2); 2; 3(3); 4(2); 5(3); 6(4); 8; 10(4); 11; 12(2); 13; 15(2); 16; 17(2); 18; 19; 20(2); 21(2); 22; 23(2); 24; 25(2); 26(2); 27; 28; 30(2); 31(2); 32(4); 33; 34(3); 36; 37(2); 39; 42; 43; 45(3); 46; 49(2); 50; 51; 53; 54; 55(2); 56; 58(2); 14:3(3); 4(2); 5; 6(4); 7(3); 8(2); 9(4); 10(2); 11; 12(4); 13; 14(2); 15(2); 16; 17(2); 19; 20(3); 21; 22(2); 24(3); 25(3); 26; 28(2); 30; 31; 33(2); 34; 35(2); 36; 37(2); 38; 39(3); 40; 41(2); 42(3); 43(2); 44(2); 45(3); 47(2); 48(2); 49(2); 51(5); 52(4); 53(2); 54; 55; 56(2); 57; 15:1(2); 2; 3; 4; 5(3); 6(2); 7(3); 8(2); 10(2); 11(4); 12; 13(2); 14(2); 15; 16; 17(3); 18(2); 19(2); 21(2); 22(3); 24(2); 26; 27(2); 28; 29(2); 30(2); 32(2); 33(3); 16:1; 2; 3; 4(3); 5(2); 6(2); 7; 8; 9(2); 10; 11(4); 12; 13; 14(2); 15(2); 16(2); 17; 18(5); 19; 20(2); 21(2); 22; 23; 24(5); 26(3); 27(3); 28(2); 29; 31; 32(3); 33(4); 34; 17:1; 2(2); 4(2); 5; 6(2); 9; 10(2); 11; 13(2); 15(3); 18:2; 3; 4; 5; 17; 21; 25; 26(2); 27; 30; 19:1; 2; 3(2); 5; 6(2); 7; 8; 10(2); 12; 17; 19; 20; 21; 22; 23; 25; 29; 30; 31; 32(2); 33; 34; 36; 37(2); 20:3(2); 4(2); 5(3); 6(3); 7; 8(2); 10; 14(2); 15; 16(2); 17(3); 18(2); 22(2); 23(2); 24(2); 25(3); 26(2);

21:1(2); 2; 6(2); 10; 13; 16; 22; 24(3); 22:2(2); 4; 6; 7(2); 9; 11; 13(2); 14(2); 17; 18(3); 21; 25; 26; 27(2); 28; 29; 31; 23:1; 2; 6; 9; 10(2); 12; 13; 15; 18(3); 19; 21; 22; 25; 26; 27; 28; 30; 32; 36(2); 37(2); 38; 39; 40(3); 24:5(2); 7; 9(3); 10(2); 11(3); 13; 14; 16; 21; 22; 23(2); 25:1; 2; 3(2); 6(3); 7; 8(2); 10(4); 14; 15; 16; 18(3); 19(2); 20; 21; 22(2); 23; 24; 25(2); 27; 28(2); 31; 32; 33; 35; 38; 39(2); 40(2); 41(3); 44(3); 45(2); 46; 47(2); 52(2); 53; 54(2); 26:2; 3(2); 4; 5(2); 6(3); 7; 8; 9(2); 10; 11; 12(2); 13; 14; 15; 16(3); 17(2); 18; 19; 20; 21; 22(2); 23; 24; 25(2); 26(3); 27; 28; 29; 30(2); 31(2); 32; 33(2); 34(2); 36(2); 37; 38; 39; 40(2); 41(3); 42(2); 43(2); 44; 46(3); 27:2; 5(2); 6(2); 7(3); 8; 10(2); 12; 14; 15; 18; 19(2); 22; 23; 25; 27(2); 28; 30; 32; 33(2); **Num** 1:3(2); 4; 17; 18(3); 20; 22; 24; 25; 26; 28; 30; 32; 34; 36; 38; 40; 42; 44; 45; 46(2); 50(3); 51(2); 53; 2:1(2); 3; 4; 5; 6; 7; 8; 9; 10; 11; 12; 13; 14; 15(2); 16(2); 17; 18; 19; 20; 21; 22; 23; 24; 25; 26; 27; 28; 29; 30; 31; 32(2); 34; 3:1; 2(3); 4(3); 5; 6; 7(2); 8; 9(2); 10(2); 13; 15; 17; 18(2); 19(2); 20(2); 21; 22; 24; 26(2); 27; 28; 30; 31; 32; 33; 34(2); 36; 37(2); 38; 39(2); 40(2); 41(2); 43(3); 45; 46(2); 48(2); 49; 50; 51(2); 4:1; 3; 5(3); 6(2); 7(3); 8(2); 9(3); 10; 11(2); 12; 13; 14(3); 15(3); 16; 17; 19(4); 23; 24; 25; 26(3); 27(3); 28; 29; 30; 31; 32(4); 34(3); 35; 36(2); 37; 38(2); 39; 40; 41; 43; 45; 46(2); 47(2); 48; 49; 5:1; 2; 3; 4(2); 6; 7; 10; 11; 12(2); 13(4); 14(2); 15; 16(2); 17(2); 18(2); 19(3); 20(2); 21(3); 22(3); 23; 24(2); 25; 26(2); 27(4); 28(2); 29; 30(2); 6:2; 3; 9(2); 11(4); 12; 14; 15; 16(2); 17(2); 18(2); 19(3); 20(2); 21; 22; 23; 24; 25; 26; 27; 7:1(5); 2; 3(4); 5; 6(2); 7; 8(2); 12; 13(2); 15; 17(2); 19(2); 21; 23(2); 25(2); 27; 29(2); 31(2); 33; 35(2); 37(2); 39; 41(2); 43(2); 45; 47(2); 49(2); 51; 53(2); 55(2); 57; 59(2); 61(2); 63; 65(2); 67(2); 69; 71(2); 73(2); 75; 77(2); 79(2); 81; 83(2); 84; 85(2); 86; 87; 88(2); 8:1; 2; 3; 6; 7(3); 8; 9(2); 10; 11; 12(2); 13(3); 14; 15; 17; 19(3); 20(2); 21(3); 22; 24; 25(2); 9:3; 5; 6(2); 7; 8; 11; 13(2); 14(4); 16; 17; 18; 19; 20; 22; 23; 10:1; 2; 7; 8; 9(2); 10(3); 12; 16; 17(2); 18; 20; 22; 24; 27; 29; 30(2); 31; 32; 33; 34; 35; 36; 11:1(2); 2; 4; 5; 7; 8(3); 9; 10; 11; 15(2); 16; 17(3); 18(2); 20(2); 21; 22; 23; 24(3); 25(4); 26(2); 27(4); 28; 29; 30(2); 31(4); 32(4); 33; 35; 12:1; 2; 4; 5(4); 8(2); 9; 10(2); 11; 14; 15; 16(2); 13:1; 16; 17(2); 18; 20(2); 21; 22(3); 23(2); 25; 26(5); 27(3); 28; 29(3); 30(2); 32(2); 33(2); 14:1(2); 2(3); 3; 4; 5; 6; 7; 8(2); 9; 10; 11; 12(3); 13; 14(4); 17; 18(3); 22(4); 24(2); 25(2); 26(2); 29; 30; 31; 33(2); 34; 35; 36; 38; 39; 40(3); 41; 43(2); 45(3); 15:1; 2; 3; 5; 7; 8; 10; 14(2); 15; 16(2); 18; 22; 23; 24(2); 25(2); 26; 27; 28; 29; 30; 31; 33(3); 36(2); 38; 39(5); 40(3); 16:1(2); 2(2); 3(3); 5(4); 6; 7(2); 9; 10(3); 11(2); 12(2); 13; 14(2); 15; 16(3); 17(4); 18(2); 19; 20(2); 22(2); 24; 25(3); 26; 27(5); 28; 30(3); 32(3); 33(2); 35(3); 37; 38; 39; 40; 41; 42(3); 43; 44; 45; 46(3); 47(3); 48(2); 17:1; 2; 3; 5; 6(2); 7; 8(3); 9(2); 10; 18:1(4); 2(2); 3(3); 4; 5(2); 7(3); 8(2); 9(3); 11(2); 12; 15; 16; 17; 18(2); 19(3); 20; 22; 23; 26; 27(2); 28; 30; 31; 32; 19:1; 2; 3; 4(2); 5; 6(4); 7; 8(2); 9(2); 10(3); 12(2); 13; 14; 15; 17(2); 18; 19(4); 20; 21; 22; 20:1(3); 2; 3(2); 4; 5; 6(3); 8(4); 10(3); 11(4); 12; 13; 15(3); 16(2); 19; 20; 22; 23(2); 25(2); 26(3); 27; 28(3); 21:1; 2; 3(4); 4; 5(4); 6(2); 7(2); 8(2); 9(2); 10; 11(2); 12; 13(2); 15(2); 16; 18; 20; 23(3); 24; 25(2); 26; 29; 32(2); 33(3); 34(2); 35(2); 22:1; 3(2); 4; 5; 6(2); 7(3); 8(2); 9; 11(2); 12; 13; 14(3); 15; 16(2); 17; 18(2); 20(3); 21; 22(3); 23(2); 24; 25(2); 26; 27(2); 28; 29; 30; 31(3); 32; 33(2); 34; 38; 39; 40(3); 41; 23:1(2); 2(4); 3(2); 4(4); 5(2); 6(2); 7(3); 8; 9; 10; 11; 12; 13; 14(3); 15; 16(3); 17(3); 18(2); 19(2); 20; 21; 23; 24(2); 26; 29(2); 30(3); 24:2(3); 3; 7(2); 8; 9(2); 10(3); 13; 14; 15(2); 16; 17(2); 18; 19; 20(2); 21(3); 23; 24(3); 25(2); 25:1; 2(2); 3; 4; 6(3); 7; 8(3); 9; 13(3); 15; 17; 18; 26:1(2); 2; 3; 4(2); 7; 8; 9(3); 10(4); 19(3); 20; 21; 28; 29; 33(2); 34; 36; 40(2); 41; 46; 50; 51(2); 54; 56; 57; 58(2); 59(3); 60(2); 61(2); 62; 63; 64; 65; 27:1(2); 2(3); 3; 6; 7; 8(2); 11(3); 12; 13; 17(2); 18(2); 19(2); 20; 21(2); 22(2); 23(2); 28:2; 3; 5; 7; 8; 9(2); 11; 13; 14; 15; 17; 19(2); 20; 24; 25; 27; 29; 29:1; 2; 4; 6; 8; 10; 11; 12; 13; 15; 16; 18(3); 19; 21(3); 22; 23; 24(3); 25; 26; 27(3); 28; 29; 30(3); 31; 32; 33(3); 34; 37(3); 38; 39(3); 30:3; 4(4); 5; 7(3); 8(2); 11(4); 12; 13; 16(3); 31:1; 3; 6; 7(2); 8; 9(3); 10; 11(3); 12(2); 13(2); 14; 15; 16; 17; 19(4); 20; 22; 23(2); 24(3); 26(3); 27(2); 28(2); 29; 30(3); 31; 32; 35; 36(2); 37(2); 42; 43; 46; 47(3); 48; 49(2); 50(4); 51; 52(3); 54(4); 32:1(3); 2(3); 3; 4; 6(2); 9; 10; 11(2); 12; 13; 14; 15; 16(2); 17; 19; 21; 22(4); 23; 24(2); 25(2); 26; 28; 29(3); 31; 33(2); 34(3); 35(3); 36(2); 37(3); 38(3); 39(3); 40; 41(2); 42(3); 33:1; 2; 5; 6; 7(2); 8(2); 9(2); 10; 11; 12; 13; 14; 15; 16; 17; 18; 19; 20; 21; 22; 23; 24; 25; 26; 27; 28; 29; 30; 31; 32; 33; 34; 35; 36; 37; 38; 39; 41; 42; 43; 44; 45; 46; 47; 48; 51; 52; 53; 54(2); 55(2); 34:2; 4(2); 5; 7; 9; 11; 12; 13; 14(2); 15; 16; 17; 18; 24; 28; 35:1; 2; 3(2); 5(2); 6; 8; 10; 13; 14; 15; 17(2); 18; 24; 25(2); 27(2); 29; 32; 33; 36:1(2); 2(2); 3; 4; 8; 11; 12; 13; **Deut** 1:1; 4; 7(5); 8(3); 9; 10; 11; 12(2); 13(2); 14(2); 15(3); 16(2); 17; 18; 19(2); 20; 21; 22(5); 24(4); 25(2); 27(2); 28(2); 31; 33; 34(3); 36(2); 39(3); 40; 41(3); 42; 43; 44(3); 45; 2:1(2); 2; 4(2); 6; 8(3); 10(2); 12(2); 13; 14; 19; 21(4); 22; 23(2); 24(3); 25(3); 26; 27; 28; 29; 30; 31(2); 32; 33(2); 34(2); 36; 3:1(3); 2(3); 3; 4; 5; 6(2); 7; 8; 9; 10(2); 11; 12(4); 13; 14(2); 16(2); 19; 20; 21; 24(2); 25(2); 26; 27(2); 28(3); 4:1(3); 5; 6(3); 8(2); 9(4); 10(2); 11(3); 12; 13; 14(2); 16; 19(4); 20; 21(2); 22; 23; 25(5); 26; 27(2); 28(2); 29(2); 30(2); 32; 33; 34(3); 36; 37(2); 38; 39(2); 40(3); 42; 43; 45; 46; 47(2); 49; 5:1(4); 5(2); 9; 10; 13; 14; 15(3); 16(2); 21; 22(4); 23; 24(3); 26; 27(4); 28; 29(2); 30; 31(2); 33(2); 6:1(2); 2(4); 3(3); 5; 6; 7(2); 8; 9; 10(2); 11(2); 13(2); 15; 17; 18(4); 20; 21; 22(4); 24; 7:1(8); 2(2); 4; 5(3); 8(2); 9(2); 10; 11; 12(3); 13(7); 15(2); 16; 18; 19(2); 21; 22; 23; 24(2); 26; 8:1(3); 2(2); 3; 6; 7(2); 8(4); 9; 10; 11; 12(3); 13(5); 14; 15(3); 16; 17; 18; 19(3); 9:1(3); 2(2); 3(2); 5(2); 9; 10; 11(2); 13; 14(3); 15(3); 16(2); 17(2); 18(2); 19; 20(2); 21(4); 22(2); 23(2); 25; 26(2); 27; 28; 29(2); 10:1(2); 2(2); 3; 4(2); 5(3); 6(2); 7; 8; 10(2); 11; 12(3); 13(2); 14; 15; 16; 17(2); 18(3); 20(2); 21(2); 22; 11:1(2); 2(3); 3(2); 4(2); 6(4); 8(2); 9(3); 10; 11; 13(3); 14(2); 15(2); 16(3); 17(3); 18(3); 19; 20(2); 21; 22; 23(2); 24; 25; 26; 28; 29; 31(3);

32(2); 12:1; 2(2); 3(3); 5; 6(2); 7(3); 9; 10(2); 11; 12(5); 14; 15(3); 18(5); 20; 21(2); 22(2); 25; 26(2); 27(4); 28(3); 29(2); 30; 31; 13:1; 2(2); 3; 4(5); 5; 6; 9; 10; 11(2); 13(2); 14(3); 15; 16(3); 17(2); 14:2; 5; 6(2); 7; 9; 10(2); 13; 15; 18(2); 23(4); 25; 26(3); 28; 29(6); 15:2; 8; 9(4); 10(2); 11; 12; 13; 14; 15; 16(2); 17(2); 19; 20; 22; 16:1; 2; 4; 7(4); 8; 11(5); 12(2); 13; 14(7); 15; 16(2); 18(2); 19; 20; 17:3(2); 4(4); 5; 7; 8; 9(3); 10; 12; 13(3); 14(3); 17; 19(4); 20(2); 18:1; 3(2); 4(3); 5; 6; 12; 14; 17; 18(2); 19; 21; 19:1(3); 3; 4; 5(4); 6(2); 8; 9(3); 10; 11(2); 12(2); 17; 18(2); 20(3); 20:1(3); 2; 3(2); 5(3); 6(3); 7(4); 8(3); 9; 11(3); 13; 14(2); 17(5); 18; 20; 21:1; 2(2); 3(2); 4; 5(2); 6; 7; 8(2); 10(2); 11(3); 12(2); 13(4); 14; 15(4); 18(2); 19(2); 20(3); 21(2); 22(2); 22:1; 2(2); 3(2); 4; 7(2); 9; 10; 11; 13(2); 14(4); 15(2); 16(2); 17(2); 18; 19(3); 20; 21; 22; 23(2); 24(2); 25(2); 26; 27; 28(3); 29; 23:4(2); 11; 13(4); 14(2); 21; 23; 24:1(4); 2(2); 3(2); 4; 5; 7(2); 8; 11; 12; 13(2); 14; 15(3); 18; 19(2); 20; 21; 22; 25:1(3); 2; 3(3); 5(3); 6; 7; 8(2); 9(2); 10; 11(3); 13; 14; 15(2); 18(3); 26:1(3); 2(2); 3(2); 4; 5(6); 6; 7(4); 8(3); 9(2); 10(2); 11(3); 12(3); 13(2); 14; 15(3); 16(2); 17(4); 19(3); 27:2(2); 3; 4; 5; 6; 7(2); 8; 9(2); 10(2); 11; 12; 13(2); 14(2); 15(3); 16; 17; 18; 19(2); 20; 21; 22; 23; 24; 25; 26; 28:2(2); 3; 4(2); 5; 6; 7; 8(2); 9; 10; 11(2); 12; 13(4); 15(2); 16; 17; 18(2); 19; 20(2); 22; 23(2); 24; 25(2); 26(2); 27; 28(2); 29(3); 31(2); 32(4); 33(3); 35(2); 36(3); 37(2); 39; 41; 42; 43(3); 44; 45(3); 46(3); 47; 48(2); 51(2); 52(2); 53(2); 54(2); 55; 56(4); 57(2); 58; 59(4); 60; 61; 63(4); 64(2); 65(2); 66(2); 67(2); 68(3); 29:2(3); 3; 4(2); 5(2); 7(3); 8(2); 9; 10(3); 11; 12; 13(3); 14; 16; 17(5); 18(2); 19; 20(3); 21; 22(2); 23(4); 26(3); 28(3); 29; 30:1(2); 2(4); 3(2); 4; 5(2); 6(3); 7; 8(2); 9; 10(3); 12(2); 13(2); 14; 15(2); 16(4); 17(3); 18; 19(4); 20(4); 31:1; 2(3); 3; 4(3); 6; 7(3); 8; 9(2); 10; 12(5); 13(2); 14(3); 15; 16(5); 17(5); 18; 19; 20(7); 21; 22; 23(3); 26; 27; 28(3); 29(2); 32:1(2); 2; 4(2); 5; 6(2); 7(2); 10; 12; 13; 14(4); 15(2); 18; 19(2); 20; 22(2); 24; 25; 27; 30(2); 32; 33; 35(2); 36(2); 38(3); 39(3); 40; 41(2); 42(2); 43(2); 44; 46; 47; 50(3); 33:2(3); 5; 6; 7(3); 8(3); 9(2); 10(2); 11(2); 12; 13(2); 16(3); 17(2); 18(2); 19; 20(3); 21; 22; 23(3); 24(2); 25; 26; 27(2); 28; 29(2); 34:1; 2(2); 3; 4; 6; 7; 8(2); 9; 11(2); 12(2); **Josh** 1:2; 4(2); 6; 7; 8(2); 9; 11; 12(2); 13; 14(2); 15(2); 16; 18(2); 2:1(2); 2; 4; 5; 6; 7; 9(2); 10(2); 11(2); 12; 13(3); 14(2); 16; 18(2); 19(2); 20; 21(3); 22(2); 23(3); 24; 3:1(4); 3(3); 4; 5; 6(2); 7; 9; 10(8); 13(2); 15(2); 16(3); 17; 4:1; 3(2); 5(2); 7; 8(4); 9; 10(2); 11; 12(2); 14; 18(3); 19; 20; 5:1(2); 2; 3; 4; 6; 10; 11(2); 12; 13(5); 14(3); 15; 6:1; 2(2); 4(2); 5(2); 6(2); 7(3); 8(2); 9; 11; 12(2); 13(2); 14(2); 15; 16; 17(2); 18(3); 19(3); 20(3); 21(5); 22(2); 23(4); 24(4); 25(2); 26(2); 27; 7:2(3); 3(3); 5(3); 6(3); 7(2); 9(3); 11(4); 13; 14(3); 15(2); 16(2); 17(3); 18; 19(2); 20(3); 21(3); 22(2); 23(3); 24(3); 25(2); 8:1(2); 2(4); 3(3); 4; 5(2); 7; 8; 9(3); 10(3); 11(5); 12(2); 13(2); 14(3); 15(3); 16(2); 17; 18; 19(3); 20(3); 21(3); 22(2); 23; 24(3); 25; 27; 28; 29(3); 31(2); 32; 33(3); 34(2); 35; 9:1(4); 2; 3; 4(4); 5(4); 6(3); 8(2); 9; 10(2); 11(3); 12; 13(4); 15(2); 16; 17(2); 18; 21(2); 22; 23(2); 24(3); 25(2); 26; 27(3); 10:1(5); 2(2); 3; 4(2); 5(5); 6(2); 7(2); 8; 10(2); 11(3); 12(2); 13(2); 14; 15; 16; 17; 18; 19(2); 20; 21; 22; 23(3); 24(3); 25; 26(4); 27(2); 28(2); 29(2); 30(3); 31(3); 32(3); 33(2); 34(3); 35; 36(2); 37(4); 38(2); 39(6); 40(4); 41(2); 42; 43; 11:1; 2(2); 3(2); 4(2); 5(2); 6; 7(2); 8(3); 9; 10(2); 11; 12(2); 14(3); 15; 16(2); 17(3); 20; 21(3); 22; 23; 12:1(2); 2; 3(2); 4(2); 5(3); 6(3); 7(3); 8(2); 13:1(2); 2; 3; 4; 5; 6; 7; 8; 9(2); 11(3); 12(2); 13; 15; 16(2); 17; 20; 21(2); 23(2); 25(2); 26(3); 27(2); 28; 30; 31(2); 14:1; 2; 3; 4(3); 5; 6(2); 7; 9; 10(2); 11; 12(3); 13(2); 15; 15:2; 3; 4(2); 5; 6(2); 7(2); 8; 9(2); 10; 11(3); 14; 16(2); 17; 18; 19; 32; 36; 41; 44; 45; 47(3); 48; 51; 54; 57; 59; 60; 62; 16:3(2); 4; 6(2); 7(2); 8; 10(2); 17:1; 2(2); 3(2); 4(2); 5; 6; 7(2); 9(2); 10(2); 11(9); 13; 14; 15(2); 16(3); 17(3); 18(2); 18:1(2); 3; 4(3); 5(2); 6; 7(2); 8(2); 9(2); 10; 11(2); 12(2); 13; 14; 15(2); 16; 17(3); 18; 19; 24; 28; 19:1; 6(2); 7(2); 8; 10; 11(2); 12; 13(2); 14; 15; 18(2); 21; 22(2); 23; 25; 26; 27(3); 28; 29(3); 30; 33(2); 34(3); 35; 38; 39; 41; 46; 47(4); 50(2); 51; 20:3; 4(4); 6(4); 7; 8(2); 9(2); 21:1; 2; 3; 4(2); 5; 6(2); 7; 8; 9; 11; 12; 16; 17; 18; 20; 22; 23; 24; 25(2); 27; 28; 29; 30; 31; 32(2); 34; 35; 36; 37; 38; 39; 43(2); 44; 22:1; 2(2); 4(3); 5(3); 6(2); 7; 8(2); 9(2); 10(2); 11; 12; 13; 14(2); 15(2); 18; 19; 20(2); 21(2); 22; 25(2); 27(3); 28; 29; 30(2); 31; 32(4); 33(2); 34; 23:2(3); 5(2); 6; 7; 9; 12(4); 13(3); 14(2); 16(4); 24:1(3); 2(3); 3(2); 4(2); 5(2); 6(3); 7(4); 8(3); 9(2); 11(3); 13(3); 14(3); 15(2); 16; 17(3); 18; 20(3); 21; 22; 23; 24(2); 25(2); 26(2); 27; 29; 30; 31; 32; 33; **Judg** 1:2; 3(2); 4(3); 5(4); 6(4); 7(3); 8(2); 9(2); 10(2); 12; 13; 14(2); 15(2); 16(2); 17(3); 18; 19; 20; 22(2); 24(2); 25(2); 26(2); 27(5); 28; 30; 33; 34; 35(2); 36; 2:1(3); 2; 3; 4; 5; 6; 7; 8; 9; 11; 12(4); 13(2); 14(2); 15(2); 17; 18(3); 19(3); 20(2); 3:3; 4; 5; 6(3); 7(2); 8(2); 10(3); 12; 13(3); 16(2); 18; 19(2); 20; 21; 22(2); 23(2); 24; 25(3); 26(2); 27(3); 28; 29; 30; 31; 4:3(2); 5(3); 6(4); 7(3); 8; 9; 10(3); 11; 12; 13; 15(5); 16(2); 17; 18(3); 19; 20(4); 21(5); 22(3); 24(2); 5:1; 4; 6; 10; 12; 14; 15; 17(2); 19; 26; 28; 30(2); 6:2(2); 3; 4(2); 5(3); 6; 7; 8; 9(4); 11; 12(2); 13(2); 14(2); 15; 16(2); 18(3); 19(5); 20(4); 21(6); 24; 25(2); 26(3); 27(2); 28(3); 29(2); 30; 33(3); 34; 35(3); 37; 38(2); 40; 7:1(2); 2; 3(4); 4(2); 5; 6; 7; 8(3); 11(2); 12(2); 13(4); 14(2); 15(3); 16(2); 17(3); 18(3); 19(3); 20(4); 21(4); 22; 23(3); 24(4); 25(5); 8:1; 3(2); 4; 5(2); 6(2); 7(2); 8(2); 10(3); 11(2); 12(4); 14(4); 15(3); 16(4); 17; 18(2); 20; 21(5); 22(2); 25(2); 26(2); 27(3); 28; 29; 31; 32; 33; 9:1(2); 2; 3(2); 4(2); 5; 6(3); 7(4); 8; 9(2); 10; 11(2); 12; 13(2); 14; 15(3); 16(4); 17; 18(2); 19(3); 20(5); 21(4); 23(2); 24(2); 25(3); 26(2); 27(7); 28(2); 29; 31(3); 32(2); 33(4); 34(2); 35(2); 36; 37(2); 38; 39; 40(3); 41(2); 42(2); 43(5); 44(4); 45(3); 47; 48(6); 49(3); 50(2); 51(3); 52(2); 53; 54(3); 55; 57(2); 10:1; 2(2); 3; 5(2); 6(5); 7(2); 8; 9; 10(2); 11(3); 12(4); 13; 14; 15; 16(2); 17(3); 18; 11:1; 2(2); 3(3); 5; 6; 7; 8(3); 9; 10; 11(3); 13(2); 15; 16; 17; 18(4); 19; 20; 21(3); 22; 23; 25; 26(3); 27; 29(4); 30(2); 31; 32; 33(2); 34(2); 35(3); 37(3); 38(3); 39(3); 12:1(2); 2(3); 3(2); 4(3); 5; 6(2); 7(2); 9(2); 10; 12(2); 14; 15; 13:1; 2(2); 3(4); 4; 5(3); 6(3); 7(2); 8(2); 9(2); 10(2); 11(2); 12; 15; 16; 18; 19(3); 20; 21; 22; 23; 24(3);

25(2); 14:1; 2(2); 3(3); 4; 5(2); 6(2); 7(2); 8(2); 9(3); 10; 11; 12(2); 13(2); 14; 15; 16(2); 17; 18(2); 19(4); 20; 15:1; 3; 4(3); 5(3); 6(4); 7; 8(2); 9; 10; 11(2); 13(3); 14(2); 15(2); 17(2); 18(3); 19(4); 20; 16:1(2); 2; 3(4); 5(5); 6; 7(2); 8; 9; 10; 11; 12(3); 13(2); 14(3); 15; 16(2); 17(3); 18(2); 19(3); 20(3); 21(3); 23(2); 24; 25(2); 27(2); 29(3); 30(3); 31(6); 17:2(3); 3; 4(4); 5(3); 7; 9(2); 10(4); 11; 12(2); 18:1; 2(3); 3; 4(2); 6; 7(3); 8(2); 9(2); 10; 11(2); 12; 13(2); 14(2); 15(2); 17; 18(2); 19(4); 20(3); 21(3); 22; 23(2); 24(2); 25(2); 26(2); 27(5); 28(2); 29; 30(2); 19:1; 2(2); 3(4); 4(3); 5(2); 6(3); 7; 8; 9(3); 10(2); 11(4); 13; 14(3); 15; 17(3); 19(4); 20; 21(4); 22; 23; 24(2); 25(4); 26; 27(2); 28(4); 29(2); 30(2); 20:1; 2; 4(2); 5(2); 6(2); 7(2); 10; 13; 15; 16; 18; 19; 20(2); 21; 22(2); 23(3); 25(2); 26(5); 28(2); 30(2); 31(4); 32(2); 33; 34(2); 35; 37(2); 38; 39; 40; 41; 42; 43; 44; 45(3); 47(2); 48(3); 21:2(2); 3; 4(3); 6(2); 8(2); 10(3); 11(2); 12; 13; 14(2); 15; 17; 19; 21(3); 23(4); 24; **Ruth** 1:1(3); 2(4); 3(2); 4(2); 5(2); 7(2); 8(2); 9(2); 10; 12; 14(2); 15(2); 16(2); 17(3); 19(2); 21(2); 22; 2:2(2); 3(3); 4(2); 6; 7(3); 9(3); 10; 11(6); 12; 13; 14(6); 15(2); 16; 17(2); 18(3); 19(3); 20(2); 22(2); 23(2); 3:3(3); 4(3); 5; 6; 7(5); 8(2); 9; 11; 13; 14; 15(3); 17; 4:1(3); 2(2); 4(4); 6; 7(3); 9(4); 10; 11(5); 13(3); 14; 15(2); 16(2); 17; 19; 20; 21; 22; **1 Sam** 1:1; 2(2); 3(2); 4(3); 6; 7; 8; 9; 10(3); 11(4); 12; 15(2); 16; 18(3); 19(5); 20(2); 21(2); 22; 23(2); 24(3); 25; 26; 27; 2:1(2); 3; 4; 5(2); 6(2); 7(2); 8(3); 10; 13; 14; 15; 16(2); 19; 20(3); 21(3); 22(2); 26(3); 27; 28(2); 29(2); 30(2); 31; 32(2); 33(2); 34; 35(2); 36(4); 3:1; 2(2); 3(2); 4; 5(4); 6(2); 8(3); 9(2); 10(3); 13; 14; 15(2); 16(2); 17(2); 18(2); 19(2); 20; 4:1(3); 2; 3; 4(2); 5; 7; 9(2); 10(3); 11(2); 12(2); 13(2); 14(2); 15; 16(2); 17(4); 18(4); 19(4); 20; 21(2); 22; 5:1; 2; 3(2); 4(2); 6(3); 7(2); 8(3); 9(3); 10; 11(4); 12(2); 6:2(2); 3; 4(2); 5(3); 6; 7(2); 8(3); 9; 10(2); 11(3); 12(3); 13(3); 14(2); 15(3); 18(2); 19(2); 20(2); 21; 7:1(3); 2; 3(4); 4(2); 5(2); 6(4); 7; 9(3); 10; 11(3); 12(3); 13(2); 14(2); 15; 16(2); 17; 8:2; 3; 4; 5(2); 7; 8; 9; 11(4); 12(4); 13; 14(3); 15(3); 16(3); 17; 18(2); 19; 20(3); 21(2); 22(2); 9:2(2); 3(3); 4(2); 5; 6(2); 7; 8(2); 11; 12(2); 16; 17; 18; 19(4); 20(2); 21(3); 22(3); 23; 24(2); 26(4); 27; 10:1(3); 2(3); 3(2); 4(2); 5(3); 6(2); 7; 8(3); 9; 10; 11; 12; 13; 14; 15; 18(4); 19(3); 20; 21; 22; 23(2); 24(2); 25(3); 26(2); 27; 11:1(3); 2(2); 3; 4(3); 5(2); 6; 7(5); 8; 9(3); 10; 11(3); 14; 15(3); 12:1; 2(4); 3; 4; 5(2); 6(2); 7; 8(3); 9(3); 10(4); 11(4); 12; 13(2); 14(4); 16; 17(3); 18(4); 19; 21; 23; 24; 25; 13:1; 2(2); 3(2); 4(2); 5(4); 6; 7(3); 8; 9(2); 10; 11(4); 12(2); 13; 14; 15(2); 16; 18; 20; 21(3); 22(2); 23; 14:2; 4(3); 5; 8; 9; 10; 11; 12(3); 13(4); 14; 15(4); 16(3); 17(3); 18; 20(4); 21; 23; 24; 25; 26; 27(3); 28; 32(5); 34(6); 36(3); 38(3); 40(3); 41; 42(2); 43(2); 44(2); 45; 46; 47(2); 48(3); 49(3); 50; 51; 52; 15:3(7); 4(2); 5(2); 7; 8; 9(5); 11(3); 12(3); 13; 14; 15(3); 16(2); 17; 18(3); 19; 20(3); 21; 22(2); 23(2); 24(2); 25; 26; 27(2); 28; 29; 30(2); 31; 32; 33; 34; 35(2); 16:1; 2(3); 3; 4(3); 5(4); 6; 8(2); 9; 10; 11(4); 12(3); 13(3); 14; 15; 16(2); 17; 18(3); 19; 20(3); 21(3); 23(4); 17:1(2); 2(4); 3; 4(2); 5(2); 6(2); 7(2); 8(4); 9(3); 10; 11(2); 12(2); 13; 14; 15; 16(3); 17(2); 18(3); 19(2); 20(4); 21; 22(3); 23; 24(2); 25(2); 26; 27; 28(4); 29; 30(2); 31; 32; 33(2); 34(2); 35(5); 36(2); 37(3); 38; 39(2); 40(4); 41(2); 42(3); 43; 44(3); 45; 46(4); 47(2); 48(3); 49(4); 50(3); 51(5); 52(6); 53; 54(2); 55; 57; 58; 18:1; 2; 3; 4(4); 5(4); 6(2); 7(2); 8(3); 10(2); 11; 13(3); 14(2); 16(2); 17; 18; 20(2); 21; 22(3); 23(2); 24; 27(5); 28(2); 29; 30; 19:1; 2(2); 3(3); 4(2); 5(3); 6; 7(2); 8(5); 9; 10(2); 11(2); 12(3); 13(3); 16; 17(2); 18(6); 20(3); 21(3); 22(4); 23(2); 24(4); 20:1(3); 2; 3(4); 5(2); 11(2); 12(3); 13(3); 14; 18; 19(3); 21(3); 23(3); 24; 25(2); 27(2); 29(4); 30(2); 31; 32(2); 34; 35(2); 37; 38(2); 39; 40; 41(3); 42(5); 21:1(3); 2(3); 4(2); 5(3); 7; 8; 9; 10(2); 11(2); 12; 13; 22:1(3); 2(3); 3(2); 4; 5(2); 6(2); 7(3); 8(2); 9; 10(2); 11(2); 12(2); 13(3); 14(3); 16(2); 17(3); 18(4); 19(4); 20; 21; 23:1; 2(4); 4(2); 5(4); 7(2); 8; 11; 12(2); 13(3); 14(2); 15; 16(2); 17(2); 18(2); 20; 21; 22(3); 23(4); 24(2); 25(3); 26(4); 27; 28; 29; 24:2(2); 3(2); 4(2); 6; 7(3); 8(3); 9; 10(2); 11(3); 12(2); 15(5); 16(2); 18; 20(2); 21; 22(2); 25:1(5); 2(3); 3(5); 5(2); 6(2); 7; 8(2); 9; 10(2); 11(3); 12(3); 13(3); 14; 15; 16; 17(2); 18(3); 19; 20(3); 21; 22; 23; 24(3); 25; 26(3); 27; 28; 29(2); 30(2); 33(3); 34; 35(2); 36(2); 37(2); 38; 39(3); 41; 42(3); 43; 26:2; 3(2); 4; 5(3); 6(3); 7(4); 8; 9(2); 10; 11(2); 12(3); 13; 14(3); 15; 16(2); 17(2); 18; 21; 22(3); 23; 24(2); 25(2); 27:1(2); 2; 3(3); 4; 7; 8(4); 9(3); 10; 11; 28:1(2); 2(2); 3(4); 4(3); 5; 6; 7(2); 8(6); 9; 10; 11; 12; 13(2); 14(5); 15(3); 16; 17(2); 19(2); 20(2); 21(5); 22(2); 23(3); 24(4); 25(3); 29:1; 2(3); 3(2); 4; 5; 6(3); 7; 8(2); 9; 10(2); 11(2); 30:1(3); 2(3); 3(4); 4(2); 5(2); 6; 7; 8(2); 9(2); 10; 11(4); 12(3); 13(3); 14(2); 15(2); 16(4); 17; 18; 19; 20(2); 21(2); 22(4); 23; 25; 31(2); 31:1(2); 2(3); 3; 4(4); 5(2); 6; 7(7); 8; 9(4); 10; 12(5); 13(2); **2 Sam** 1:1; 2(2); 3; 4(4); 5; 6(2); 7(2); 8; 9; 10(4); 11(2); 12(5); 13; 15(3); 17; 18; 22; 23(3); 27; 2:1(2); 2(2); 3; 4(2); 5(2); 6(2); 7(2); 8; 9(2); 10; 11(2); 12; 13(4); 14(2); 15(2); 16(2); 17(2); 18(3); 19; 20; 21(3); 23(3); 24(2); 25(2); 26; 27; 28(2); 29(3); 30(2); 31(2); 32(4); 3:1(4); 5; 6; 7; 8(4); 9; 10(2); 11; 12; 13; 15(2); 16; 18; 19(2); 20(3); 21(4); 22(3); 23(3); 24(2); 25(2); 26; 27; 28; 29(2); 30; 31(3); 32(3); 33(2); 35(2); 36; 37; 38; 39(2); 4:1; 2; 3; 4(5); 5(2); 6(3); 7(3); 8(4); 9(2); 10; 11; 12(4); 5:1(2); 2(3); 3(2); 4; 5(3); 6(3); 8(4); 9(3); 10(2); 11(4); 12; 13(3); 16; 17(2); 18; 19; 20(2); 21(3); 22; 23(2); 24; 25(2); 6:2(2); 3(3); 4(2); 5(2); 6(2); 7(2); 8(2); 9; 11(2); 12(2); 13(2); 14; 15(2); 16(3); 17(2); 18(2); 19(2); 20(2); 21; 22(2); 7:1; 5; 6; 9(3); 10(2); 11; 12(2); 13; 14(2); 16(2); 17; 18(3); 19(2); 21; 23(4); 24; 25(2); 26; 28(3); 29; 8:1(2); 2(2); 4; 6(2); 7(2); 8; 10(4); 11; 12; 13; 14(2); 15(2); 17; 18(2); 9:2(2); 3; 4; 5; 6(2); 7(2); 8; 9(3); 10(4); 12; 13; 10:1; 2; 3(2); 4; 5(2); 6(4); 7; 8(3); 9(2); 10; 11; 12(3); 13(2); 14(2); 16(3); 17(3); 18(3); 19(2); 11:1(4); 2(3); 3(2); 4(4); 5(3); 6; 7(2); 8(3); 9; 11(8); 12(2); 13(3); 14; 15(3); 17(3); 18; 19; 20; 22(2); 23(2); 24(2); 25; 27(4); 12:1(3); 2; 3(6); 4(3); 5; 6(2); 7; 8(4); 9; 10; 11(3); 13; 15(2); 16(3); 17; 18(2); 19; 20(6); 21(2); 22(2); 24(3); 25; 26; 27(3); 28(3); 29(2); 30; 31(6); 13:1; 2; 4; 5(5); 6(3); 7(2); 8(3); 9(3); 10(2); 11; 12; 13(2); 14(2); 15; 17(2); 18(2); 19(3); 20; 22; 23; 24(2); 25; 26; 27; 28(2); 29(2); 30(2); 31(3); 32; 34(3); 35; 36(3); 37(2); 38(2); 39; 14:2(4); 3; 4(3); 5; 6(3); 7(4); 8;

9(4); 10; 11(2); 12; 14; 15; 16(2); 17(2); 18(2); 19(3); 21;
22(3); 23(2); 24; 26; 27; 28; 29; 30(3); 31(2); 32; 33(3);
15:1(2); 2(4); 3; 4; 5(3); 7; 9(2); 11(3); 12; 14(3); 15; 17(2);
18(2); 19(2); 20(3); 21(3); 22(3); 23(3); 24(3); 25(2); 27(2);
29(2); 30(5); 31; 32; 34; 35(3); 36(2); 37; 16:1(2); 2(3); 3(2);
4; 6(5); 8; 9; 11(3); 12; 13(4); 14; 15(2); 16; 18(4); 21(2); 22;
23; 17:1(2); 2(4); 4(2); 5; 6; 8(4); 9; 10(2); 11; 12(3); 13; 14;
15(5); 16(2); 17(4); 18(3); 19(3); 20(4); 21(4); 22(2); 23(5);
24(2); 25; 26; 27; 28(5); 29(5); 18:1(3); 2(2); 4(2); 5(2); 6; 7;
8; 9(3); 10(2); 11(2); 12(2); 13; 14(2); 15(3); 16; 17(3); 18(2);
19; 20; 21; 22; 23; 24(3); 25(4); 26(3); 27(2); 28(3); 29;
30(3); 31; 32(2); 33(3); 19:1(2); 3; 4; 5(3); 6(2); 7(2); 8(2); 9;
11; 12; 13(3); 14; 15(2); 16(2); 17(4); 18; 21; 22; 23; 24;
26(2); 27; 29; 31(2); 32; 33(2); 35(2); 36; 37(2); 38(2); 39(3);
40(3); 41(3); 43(2); 20:1(3); 2; 3(3); 4(2); 6(3); 7(2); 8; 9;
10(4); 11(2); 12(2); 14(4); 15(4); 17; 18; 19(2); 20(2); 21;
22(3); 23(2); 25; 26; 21:1(3); 2(2); 3; 4; 5; 6(2); 7; 8(2); 9(3);
10(2); 11; 12(2); 13(2); 14(2); 15(3); 17(2); 20(2); 22(2);
22:1; 2(3); 3(2); 7(2); 8(2); 9; 10; 11(2); 12; 14; 15(2); 22;
23; 24; 27; 32; 33(2); 34; 38; 39(2); 43; 46; 48; 50; 51(2);
23:1; 2; 4; 5(2); 7(2); 9(2); 10(3); 11; 12(2); 13(2); 14; 15;
16(2); 17; 18; 20; 21(2); 22; 23; 39; 24:1(2); 2; 3(2); 4(2);
5(3); 6(2); 7(3); 8; 9(2); 10; 12; 13(3); 14; 16(3); 17(3); 18(2);
20(3); 21; 22(3); 23; 24; 25(4); **1 Ki** 1:1; 2(3); 3(2); 4(2); 5(3);
6; 7(3); 8; 9(4); 11; 12; 13(2); 14; 15; 16(2); 17; 18; 19(4);
20; 21; 22; 23; 24(2); 25(9); 27; 28(2); 29(2); 30; 31(2);
32(2); 33(2); 34(3); 35(4); 36; 37; 38(3); 39(3); 40(3); 41(2);
42(2); 43; 44(2); 45(2); 47(2); 49(2); 50(2); 51; 53(3); 2:1; 2;
3(3); 4; 5(5); 6; 7; 8(2); 9; 10; 11; 12; 13; 14; 15(2); 16; 19(4);
20; 22(4); 23; 24(2); 25(2); 26(2); 28; 29; 30(4); 31(3); 32(3);
33(3); 34(3); 35; 36(4); 37; 38; 39; 40(3); 41(2); 42(5); 43;
45; 46(3); 3:1(3); 3(2); 5; 6(3); 8; 9; 11; 12; 13(2); 14; 15(4);
16; 17(3); 18; 19; 20(3); 21; 22(3); 23(4); 25(3); 26(2); 27(2);
28(2); 4:2; 3; 4; 5; 6; 7(2); 9; 10; 12; 13; 16; 19; 20(3); 21;
23(2); 24; 25(3); 26; 27(2); 28(2); 29(3); 30; 31(3); 32(2); 33;
34; 5:5; 6(2); 7; 8(2); 9(2); 10; 11(2); 12(3); 13; 14(2); 15;
17(2); 18(3); 6:1(2); 2; 3; 4; 5; 6; 7; 8; 9(3); 10; 12; 13(2);
14; 15(2); 17; 18; 19; 20(2); 21; 24; 25(2); 26; 27(3); 29(2);
30(2); 31; 32(5); 34(2); 35(2); 36(2); 38(2); 7:2(2); 3; 4; 5(3);
6(3); 7; 8; 9(2); 10; 11(2); 12(2); 13; 14(4); 15(2); 16; 17;
18(2); 20; 21(3); 23(2); 25(2); 26; 27; 28(2); 29(3); 30(2);
31(3); 32(2); 33; 34; 35(2); 36(2); 37; 38; 39(2); 40(2); 43;
44; 45; 46; 47; 48; 49(3); 50(3); 51(3); 8:1; 3; 4(2); 5(2); 7(2);
8; 10; 13; 14; 15(2); 20(3); 21; 22; 23(2); 24; 26; 27; 28(3);
29; 30(3); 31(3); 32(3); 33(4); 34(2); 35(3); 36(2); 38; 39(3);
42(3); 43(3); 44(2); 45(2); 46(3); 47(3); 48(4); 49(2); 50(3);
51; 52; 54(2); 55; 58(3); 59(3); 61; 62; 63(4); 64(2); 65(2);
66(4); 9:1(3); 3(4); 4(3); 6(4); 7(2); 8(4); 9(3); 10; 11(2); 13;
14; 15(2); 16(3); 17; 18; 19(3); 20; 22(2); 23; 25(2); 28(4);
10:2(2); 4; 5(2); 6; 7(3); 8(2); 9; 10(2); 11; 12(3); 13(2); 14;
15; 16; 18; 19(2); 21; 22; 23; 25(2); 26(4); 27; 28; 29(4);
11:1; 3(3); 4; 5; 6; 7; 8(2); 10; 11(3); 13; 15; 17; 18(4); 19;
20; 21; 23; 24(4); 25(2); 27(2); 28; 29(2); 30; 31(2); 32;
33(5); 34; 35; 36; 37(2); 38(4); 39; 40(2); 41; 42; 43(2); 12:1;
2; 3(3); 4(2); 5; 6; 7(4); 8; 9; 11; 12; 13; 14; 18; 20(2); 21(2);
23(2); 24; 25(2); 26; 27(2); 28; 29(2); 31; 32(2); 33(3);
13:1(2); 2(3); 3(2); 5; 6(4); 7(2); 10; 11(2); 12; 13; 14(3); 15;
16; 18(2); 19(2); 21(2); 22(2); 23; 24(3); 25(4); 26; 27; 28(3);
29(3); 30; 32; 33; 34(2); 14:2(3); 3(2); 4(3); 5; 6; 7; 8(4); 9(3);
10(2); 11(2); 13(2); 15; 16(2); 17(2); 18(2); 19; 21; 22; 23(2);
24; 26(2); 27; 28; 29; 30(2); 31; 15:3; 4; 5; 6(2); 7(3); 8; 10;
12(2); 13(2); 15(3); 16; 17(2); 18(4); 19(4); 20(2); 21; 22(4);
23; 24; 25; 26(3); 27(2); 28; 29; 30; 31; 32(2); 33; 34(2);
16:2(3); 3(2); 4(2); 5; 6; 7(3); 8; 10(4); 13(2); 14; 15; 16;
17(2); 18(3); 19; 20; 21; 22; 23; 24(2); 25; 26; 27; 28; 29;
31(4); 33; 34; 17:1; 3(2); 4(2); 5(2); 6(4); 7; 9; 10(4); 11(2);
12(5); 13(5); 15(4); 17; 18; 19(3); 20; 21(3); 22(2); 23(4); 24;
18:1(2); 2; 3; 4(3); 5(3); 6; 7(3); 8; 10; 11; 12(3); 13(2); 14;
16(2); 18(3); 19(3); 20; 21(2); 22; 23(4); 24(3); 25(2); 26(2);
27(3); 28(2); 29; 30; 31; 32; 33(5); 34(3); 35; 36(5); 37;
38(5); 39; 40(3); 41; 42(3); 43(4); 44; 45(3); 46(2); 19:1; 2;
3(4); 4(4); 5(3); 6(4); 7(4); 8(4); 9(4); 10(2); 11(6); 12(2);
13(3); 14(3); 15; 16; 17; 18; 19(3); 20(6); 21(7); 20:1(4); 2;
3(2); 4(3); 5(3); 6(4); 7(4); 8(2); 9(2); 10(2); 11; 12(3); 13;
14(2); 15(3); 16; 17(2); 18; 20(3); 21(3); 22(3); 24; 25(4); 26;
27(3); 28(3); 29(2); 30(2); 31(2); 32(4); 33(3); 34(2); 35;
36(2); 37(2); 38(2); 39(4); 40; 41(2); 42; 43(2); 21:1; 2; 4(4);
5; 6(2); 7; 8(3); 9; 10(3); 11; 12; 13(5); 14; 15(2); 16; 19(2);
20; 21(2); 22(2); 23; 24(2); 26; 27(4); 28; 22:1; 3; 6; 7; 8; 9;
10(2); 11; 12(2); 13; 14; 15(3); 17; 18; 19(2); 20(2); 21(2);
22(4); 23; 24(2); 25; 26(2); 27(3); 28; 29; 30(3); 32; 33;
34(2); 35(2); 36; 37(2); 38; 39(2); 42; 43(2); 45; 46; 50(2);
51; 52(3); 53(2); **2 Ki** 1:2(2); 3; 5; 6(2); 7; 8; 9(2); 10(6);
11(2); 12(6); 13(6); 14; 15(2); 2:1; 2; 3(2); 4; 5; 6; 7(2); 8(3);
9; 11(3); 12(5); 13(2); 14(5); 15(2); 16(3); 17; 18; 19; 20(2);
21(2); 23(3); 24(4); 25; 3:1; 2(2); 4(2); 6; 7(2); 8; 9(3); 10;
11; 12(3); 13; 14; 16; 17; 18; 19(4); 20; 21(3); 22(2); 23(2);
24(2); 25(5); 26; 27(3); 4:1(2); 2; 4(3); 5(3); 6; 7(5); 8; 9;
10(4); 11(3); 13; 14(2); 16; 17; 18; 19; 20(2); 21(3); 22(3);
23; 24(2); 25(2); 26(2); 27(2); 29(3); 30(3); 31(2); 33; 34(6);
35(5); 36(3); 37(2); 38(4); 39(4); 40(2); 41(3); 42(3); 43;
44(2); 5:1; 2(2); 4(3); 5(3); 7(4); 8; 9(2); 10(4); 11(6); 12(3);
13(4); 14(3); 15(5); 16; 18(2); 20; 21; 22(2); 23(4); 24(2);
25(2); 26(4); 27(2); 6:1; 2(2); 3; 4; 5(2); 6(3); 7; 8(2); 9; 10;
11(2); 12; 13(3); 14(4); 15(4); 17(5); 18(2); 19; 20(3); 22(4);
23(3); 24(3); 25(3); 27; 28(2); 29(2); 30(2); 31; 32(3); 33(2);
7:1; 2(2); 3; 4(3); 5(2); 6(2); 7(4); 8(12); 9(2); 10(5); 11(2);
12(2); 13(3); 14(2); 15(4); 16(2); 17; 18; 19(2); 20(2); 8:1(4);
2(3); 3(2); 5(3); 6(2); 7(2); 8(3); 9(4); 10; 11; 12(4); 13; 14(2);
15(3); 17; 18(2); 19; 20; 21(4); 22; 23; 24; 26; 27(2); 28; 29;
9:1(3); 2(3); 3(4); 5(3); 6(3); 7; 8(2); 9; 10(3); 11(3); 12(2);
13(2); 14; 15(2); 16(2); 17(5); 18(3); 19(3); 20(2); 21(4); 22;
23(2); 24(3); 25(2); 26(3); 27(3); 28(2); 30(3); 32(2); 33(3);
34(3); 35(2); 36(2); 37; 10:1(3); 2(3); 3; 4; 5(3); 6(2); 7(2);
8(2); 9(3); 11(3); 12(3); 13(2); 14(3); 15(4); 16; 17; 18; 19;
20; 21(2); 22; 23(3); 24(2); 25(5); 26(2); 27(2); 29; 30(2); 32;
33(2); 34; 35; 36; 11:1; 2(3); 4(6); 6; 8(2); 9; 10(2); 11; 12(5);
13; 14(4); 15(3); 16(2); 17(3); 18(5); 19(3); 20; 12:1; 3; 4(2);
5; 7(2); 8; 9(2); 10(3); 11(2); 12(5); 14; 16; 17(2); 18(7); 19;
20(3); 21(2); 13:1; 2(2); 3(2); 4; 5; 6; 7(2); 8; 9; 10; 11; 12;
13; 14(3); 15(3); 16; 17(5); 18(2); 19(2); 20(2); 21(4); 22;
23(3); 25(2); 14:2; 3; 4(2); 7(2); 9(3); 10(3); 11; 12(2); 13(2);
14(5); 15; 16; 19(3); 20; 21(2); 22; 23; 24; 26; 27; 28(3);
15:2; 3; 4; 5; 6; 7; 9; 10(3); 12; 13; 14(3); 15; 16; 17; 18;
19; 20(2); 21; 23; 24; 25(4); 26; 27; 28; 29(3); 30(2); 31; 33;
34; 35; 36; 37; 38; 16:2(2); 4(3); 5(2); 6(2); 7(3); 8(4); 9(2);
10(3); 12(3); 13(3); 14(2); 15(5); 17(4); 18; 20; 17:1; 2; 3(2);
4(3); 5(2); 6(4); 7; 8(2); 9; 10(2); 11; 13(4); 15(4); 16(3);
17(4); 18; 20(2); 21(2); 24(4); 25; 26(2); 27(2); 28(2); 29;
31(4); 32; 34; 35; 36(2); 37(2); 38; 39; 41; 18:2; 3; 4(3); 7(2);
8; 9; 10; 11(3); 12(2); 13(2); 14(2); 15; 16(2); 17(4); 18(2);
20(2); 21; 22(3); 23; 24(2); 25; 26(2); 27(3); 28(2); 31(4);
32(5); 34(3); 36; 37(2); 19:1(2); 2; 3(3); 4; 6; 7(3); 8; 9; 11;
12(3); 13(2); 14(4); 15(2); 16(3); 17; 18(2); 22(2); 23(2);
24(2); 26(3); 27(2); 28(3); 29(3); 30(2); 31; 33; 34; 35(4);
36(2); 37(2); 20:1(4); 2; 3(3); 4; 5; 6(4); 7(2); 8(2); 10; 11;
12; 13(5); 14(2); 15; 17; 18(2); 19; 20(3); 21:1; 2; 3(3); 5;
6(2); 7(2); 8(2); 9; 10; 11; 12; 13(3); 14(2); 15; 17; 18; 19;
20; 21(2); 22; 23; 26; 22:1; 2(2); 5; 6(4); 8(2); 9; 10; 12; 13;
14(2); 16; 17(2); 19(5); 20(2); 23:1; 2(5); 3(6); 4(5); 5(3); 6(3);
8(2); 10; 11; 12(3); 13; 14(3); 15(5); 16(4); 17; 18; 19; 20(2);
22; 24(3); 25; 27(3); 28; 29(2); 30(3); 31; 32; 33(2); 34(4);
35(2); 36; 37; 24:1(2); 2(2); 4; 5; 7; 8; 9; 10; 11; 12(2); 13(3);
14(3); 15(2); 16(3); 17; 18; 20; 25:1(3); 4(2); 5; 6(2); 7; 8; 9;
10; 11; 12; 13(3); 14; 15(2); 16; 17(3); 18(2); 19; 20; 21;
23(3); 24(5); 25(2); 26(4); 28; 29; 30; **1 Chr** 1:4; 5; 6; 7; 8;
9(2); 12; 13; 14; 15; 16; 17; 18; 19; 23; 27; 28; 31; 32(2);
33; 34(2); 35; 36(3); 37; 38; 39(2); 40(2); 41; 42(2); 43; 44;
46; 48; 50(2); 51; 54; 2:2; 3; 4(2); 5; 6; 9; 10; 11; 12; 15;
16(3); 17; 18(2); 20(2); 21; 23(2); 25(2); 27; 28(2); 29(3); 30;
31; 32; 33; 34; 35; 36; 37; 38; 39; 40; 41; 42; 43; 44; 45(2);
46(2); 47(2); 48; 49(2); 51; 52(2); 53(2); 54; 55(2); 3:4(2);
5(2); 8; 9; 14; 15; 16; 17; 18(2); 19; 20(2); 21(2); 22; 23; 24;
4:1; 2(3); 3(2); 4(2); 5(2); 6; 7; 8(2); 9; 10(3); 12(2); 13; 14;
15; 16; 17(3); 18(2); 19; 20(4); 21; 22(2); 23(2); 24; 25;
26(2); 27; 31; 32(2); 33(2); 34; 35; 36; 38; 40(3); 41(3); 42;
43; 5:2; 3; 6; 7(2); 8(2); 10; 11; 12; 13(2); 16(3); 17; 18(4);
19; 20(3); 21(2); 22; 24(2); 25(2); 26(2); 6:1; 2; 3(3); 4; 5; 6;
7; 8; 9; 11; 12; 13; 14; 15; 16; 17; 18; 19; 21; 24; 25; 27;
28; 30; 32; 33; 39; 48; 49(3); 53; 56; 57; 59; 60(2); 62(2);
63; 65(2); 67; 69; 70(2); 71; 72; 73; 74; 75; 76(2); 77; 78;
79; 80; 81; 7:1; 2; 3(2); 4(2); 6; 7(3); 8; 9; 10(2); 11; 12(2);
13; 15; 16(3); 18; 19(2); 21(2); 22; 23(3); 24(2); 25(2); 27;
28(6); 29(5); 30; 31; 32(2); 33; 34; 35(2); 37; 38; 39; 40; 8:2;
5; 6; 7(2); 8(2); 10; 11(2); 12(2); 13(2); 16; 18; 21; 25; 27;
30; 32; 33(2); 34; 35; 36(3); 37; 38; 39(2); 40(2); 9:1; 2(2);
3(3); 5; 6(2); 9(2); 10; 13(2); 15; 16; 17(2); 19; 20; 22(2); 23;
24; 25; 26(2); 27(2); 28; 29(6); 30; 32; 33(2); 37; 38; 39(2);
40; 41; 42(3); 43; 44(2); 10:1(2); 2(3); 3; 4(3); 5(2); 6(2); 7(5);
8; 9(5); 10; 11; 12(5); 13; 14; 11:1; 2(3); 3; 4(2); 6(3); 8; 9(2);
11; 13(2); 14; 15; 16; 17; 18(2); 19; 20; 22; 23(3); 24; 25;
42; 44; 45; 46; 47; 12:1; 2(2); 3(2); 4(2); 5; 6; 7(2); 8(2); 13;
14; 15(2); 16; 17(4); 18(3); 19(2); 20; 21(2); 23; 24; 27; 28;
31; 32; 34(2); 37(3); 38; 39(2); 40(9); 13:1(2); 2(5); 3; 6(2);
7(2); 8(2); 9; 10(2); 11; 14(2); 14:1(2); 3(2); 4; 7; 8(2); 9;
10(2); 11; 12(2); 14(2); 15; 16; 17; 15:1(2); 2; 3; 4; 5(2); 6(2);
7(2); 8; 9; 10(2); 11(4); 12; 14; 15; 16; 17(2); 18(2); 19; 20;
21; 23; 24(3); 25; 26(2); 27; 28(3); 29(4); 16:1(2); 2(2); 3(2);
4(2); 5(3); 6; 7; 11; 12; 16; 17; 19; 20; 22; 25; 27(2); 28; 29;
31(2); 32(2); 35(2); 36(2); 37; 38(2); 39(2); 40(2); 41(3);
42(4); 43; 17:4; 5; 8(3); 9(2); 11(2); 12; 13(2); 14(3); 15;
16(3); 17(3); 19; 21(2); 22; 23(3); 24; 26(2); 27; 18:1(2); 2(2);
3; 4(2); 6(2); 7(2); 8(2); 10(4); 11(2); 13(2); 14(2); 16; 17(2);
19:1; 2; 3(3); 4(2); 5(4); 6(3); 7(3); 8; 9(2); 10(2); 11(2); 13(3);
14(2); 15; 16(2); 17(2); 18(3); 19(2); 20:1(5); 2(3); 3(4); 4; 5;
6(3); 8(2); 21:1; 2(2); 3; 4(2); 5(2); 6; 7; 9; 10; 11; 13; 14;
15(4); 16(3); 17(3); 18; 20(2); 21(4); 23(3); 26(5); 27; 29;
22:1; 2; 3(3); 4(2); 5(3); 6; 7; 8; 9(2); 10(3); 11(2); 12(2);
13(2); 14(5); 15(2); 16(5); 18(3); 19(3); 23:1; 2(2); 3(2); 4; 5;
6; 7; 8; 9; 10(2); 11(2); 12; 13(4); 15; 17; 19; 20; 21(2); 22(3);
23; 24; 26; 27; 28(2); 29(4); 30(2); 31(3); 32(2); 24:1; 2(4);
3; 4(2); 5(2); 6(4); 20; 23; 26; 27; 30; 31(2); 25:1(4); 2; 3(2);
4; 5; 6(2); 7; 8; 9; 10; 11; 12; 13; 14; 15; 16; 17; 18; 19; 20;
21; 22; 23; 24; 25; 26; 27; 28; 29; 30; 31; 26:2; 7(2); 8(2);
9(2); 11; 13; 14; 15; 16; 17; 18; 19; 20; 22; 23; 25(2); 26(4);
28(3); 29(2); 30(2); 31; 32(3); 27:1(4); 2; 3; 4; 6; 7; 23; 25(3);
27(2); 28(2); 29(2); 31; 32(2); 33; 34; 28:1(6); 2(4); 3; 4(2);
5; 6(2); 7; 8(2); 9(3); 10; 11; 12(2); 13(2); 15(3); 16(2); 17(2);
18(3); 20(3); 21(3); 29:1(2); 2; 3(2); 4; 5(2); 6; 7(2); 8; 9;
10(2); 11(4); 12(4); 13; 14(2); 15(2); 16; 17(2); 18(2); 19(4);
20(3); 21(3); 22(4); 23(2); 24(2); 25; 27(2); 28(3); 29(2);
30(3); **2 Chr** 1:1(2); 2(3); 3; 5; 6(2); 7; 8(2); 10(2); 11(3);
12(4); 13; 14(4); 15(2); 16(2); 17(4); 2:1; 2; 3; 4(2); 5; 6; 7(5);
8(3); 9; 10(2); 12(3); 13; 14(9); 15; 16(2); 17(2); 18(2); 3:2;
3; 4(3); 5(2); 6(2); 7(3); 8(2); 9; 10; 11; 12; 13; 14(3); 15;
16(3); 17(2); 4:1; 2; 3; 4(2); 5; 6(2); 7(3); 8(3); 9(3); 11(2);
12; 14; 15; 16; 17; 18; 19; 21(2); 22(2); 5:1(4); 2; 4; 5(2);
6(2); 8(2); 9(2); 11; 12(7); 13(6); 6:2; 3; 4; 6; 10(3); 11; 12;
13(4); 14(2); 15; 17; 18; 19(3); 20; 21(3); 22(3); 23(3); 24(4);
25(3); 26(3); 27(2); 29(2); 30(2); 32(3); 33(3); 34(2); 35(2);
36(3); 37(3); 38(4); 39(3); 40; 41(2); 7:1(3); 2; 3(3); 4; 5(3);
6; 7(2); 8; 9(2); 10(2); 11(3); 12(2); 13; 14(5); 15; 16(3);
17(3); 19(5); 20(3); 21(3); 22(3); 8:1; 2; 3(2); 4; 5(2); 6(5); 7;
9; 10(2); 13(2); 14(3); 15; 17; 18(5); 9:1(2); 3; 4(3); 5; 6(2);
7(2); 8; 9(3); 10(2); 11(4); 12(2); 13; 14(4); 15; 17; 18; 20;
21; 22; 23; 24(2); 25(3); 27; 28(2); 29(2); 31(2); 10:1; 3(4);
4(2); 5; 7(3); 8; 9; 11; 12; 14; 18; 11:1(2); 3(2); 4; 5; 6; 10(2);
11(4); 12(3); 13(2); 14(4); 15; 16; 17(2); 18; 19(2); 20(2);
21(4); 22; 23(3); 12:1(2); 2; 3(3); 4(2); 5(3); 6(2); 9(2); 10;
11(2); 12; 13(2); 14; 15(4); 16; 13:2(2); 4(2); 5; 6; 7(3); 8(3);
9(3); 10(3); 11(4); 12; 13; 14(4); 15(3); 16(2); 17; 18; 19(3);
20(2); 21(2); 22; 14:1; 2; 3(3); 4(2); 5(2); 6; 7(5); 8(5); 9(2);
10; 11(3); 12(2); 13(5); 14; 15(3); 15:2(4); 3; 4; 5; 6; 7; 8(6);
9(3); 11(2); 12; 13; 14(2); 15(4); 16(2); 18(3); 19; 16:1; 2(3);
3(3); 4(2); 5; 6(4); 7(3); 8(2); 9; 10(2); 11(2); 12(2); 14(2);
17:1; 2(3); 4(2); 5(3); 6(2); 7; 8(4); 9(2); 10; 11(3); 12(2); 13;
14; 15(3); 16(2); 17(2); 18(3); 18:1(2); 2(4); 3(2); 4; 5(2); 7;
8; 9(3); 10; 11(2); 12; 13; 14(4); 16; 17; 18(2); 19(2); 20(2);
21(4); 22; 23(2); 24; 25(2); 26(3); 27; 28; 29(3); 31(2); 33(2);
34(2); 19:2(3); 3; 4(2); 6; 7; 8(3); 9(2); 10(3); 11(3); 20:1;
2(2); 3(3); 4; 5; 6(4); 7; 8(2); 9(4); 10(3); 13; 15(3); 16; 17(2);
18(3); 19(2); 20(6); 21(3); 22(3); 23(3); 24; 25(3); 26; 27;
28(2); 29; 31; 32(2); 34; 36(2); 21:1(2); 2; 3(2); 4(2); 5; 6(2);
7(2); 8; 9(4); 11(2); 12; 13(3); 14; 15; 16; 17(5); 19; 20; 22:2;
5(2); 6; 8(3); 9(2); 10; 11(3); 12; 23:1(2); 2(4); 3; 4; 5; 6; 7(3);
8(2); 9(3); 10; 11(4); 12; 13(5); 14(3); 15(2); 16; 17(4); 18;
19; 20(4); 21; 24:1; 3(3); 5(4); 6(3); 7; 8; 9(2); 10(2); 11(6);
12(5); 13(2); 14(5); 15(3); 16(2); 17(2); 18(4); 19; 20; 21;
22(2); 23(4); 25(3); 26; 27(2); 25:1; 2; 5(7); 8; 9; 10; 11(2);
12; 13; 14(2); 15; 16(2); 17; 18(3); 19(2); 21(2); 22(2); 23(2);
24(4); 26; 27(2); 28; 26:1; 2; 3; 4; 5; 6(5); 7; 9(2); 10(3); 11;
13(2); 14; 15(4); 17; 18(2); 19(2); 20(3); 23; 27:1; 2; 3; 4(2);
5(4); 7(3); 8; 9; 28:1(2); 2; 3; 4(3); 5(2); 6; 7; 8(4); 9(2); 10(3);
11; 12; 13(3); 14(2); 15(6); 17; 18(4); 19; 20(2); 21(2); 23;
24; 25(2); 26(2); 27; 29:1; 2; 3; 4(2); 5(2); 6(2); 7; 8(3); 9(2);
11(2); 12(3); 13(2); 14(3); 15(2); 16(3); 17(2); 18(2); 19(2);
20; 21(3); 22(4); 23(2); 24(3); 25(3); 26; 27(2); 28; 29(3);
30(4); 31(5); 32(2); 33; 34; 35; 36; 30:1(4); 2(2); 4(2); 6(4);
7(2); 8(2); 9(3); 10(2); 11(2); 12; 14(3); 15(3); 18; 20(2);
21(2); 22(3); 23; 24(4); 25(2); 27(3); 31:1(4); 2(5); 3(3); 4;
5(4); 6(3); 7; 8(4); 9; 10(4); 11; 12(2); 13(3); 14; 15(2); 16;
17(3); 18(3); 19; 20(3); 21(2); 32:1; 2(2); 3(2); 4(2); 5(4); 6;
7; 8(2); 9(2); 11; 12(4); 13; 15; 16; 17; 18; 19; 20(2); 21(2);
22(3); 23(2); 24(4); 25(2); 26; 27(3); 28(3); 29(2); 30; 32(3);
33(3); 33:1; 3(3); 5; 6(3); 7(2); 8(3); 9; 10(2); 11; 12; 13(3);
14(2); 15(4); 16(2); 18; 19(6); 20; 21; 22; 23(2); 24; 34:1;
2(2); 3(3); 4(5); 5(2); 6(3); 7(2); 8(2); 9(3); 10(2); 11(3); 12(4);
13(3); 15(2); 17(3); 18; 20; 21(2); 22(2); 24; 25(2); 27(5);
28(3); 29(2); 30(5); 31(5); 32(2); 33; 35:1; 2(2); 3; 4; 5(2); 6;
7; 8(4); 9(5); 10(2); 11(2); 12; 13(2); 14(3); 15(2); 16; 17(2);
18(4); 20; 22; 23(2); 24(5); 25(3); 26; 27(2); 36:1; 2; 3(2);
4(4); 5(2); 6; 7; 8(2); 9(3); 10(3); 11; 12; 13(2); 14(3); 15(3);
16; 17; 18(4); 19; 20(2); 22; 23(2); **Ezra** 1:1; 2; 3(2); 4(3);
5(4); 6(4); 7; 8(2); 10(2); 11; 2:1(2); 2; 3; 4; 5; 6(2); 7; 8; 9;
10; 11; 12; 13; 14; 15; 17; 18; 19; 21; 23; 25(2); 26(2); 27;
28(2); 30; 31; 32; 33(2); 34; 35; 36; 37; 38; 39; 40; 41; 42(2);
54; 57; 58(2); 59(2); 60(2); 61(3); 63(2); 64; 65(4); 66(2);
67(3); 69; 70(3); 3:1(2); 2(4); 3(2); 4; 5(3); 7(4); 8(5); 9(3);
10; 11(2); 12(2); 13; 4:1; 2(3); 3(2); 5; 6; 7(3); 8; 9(4); 10(5);
11; 12(4); 13(2); 14; 15(4); 16; 17(2); 19(5); 20(2); 23(2); 24;
5:1(2); 2(3); 3(4); 6(2); 8(3); 9(2); 11(4); 12; 14(3); 15(2);
16(2); 17; 6:1; 2(2); 3(2); 4; 5(4); 6(2); 7; 9(3); 10(2); 11(3);
12; 13; 14(6); 16(2); 17(2); 18; 19; 20(3); 22(2); 7:6; 7; 8; 9;
10(3); 11; 12; 13(2); 14(3); 15(3); 16(3); 17(3); 18(3); 20; 21;
22; 23; 25(3); 26; 28(4); 8:1; 3(2); 4; 5; 6; 7; 8; 9(2); 10(2);
11; 12(2); 13(2); 14(2); 15(4); 16(2); 17(3); 18; 19(3); 20(2);
21(2); 22(2); 23(2); 24(2); 25(5); 26; 27; 28(3); 29(3); 30(3);
31(3); 32; 33(4); 34; 35; 36(3); 9:1(3); 2(2); 3(4); 4; 5(3); 6(3);
7(3); 8(3); 9(2); 10; 12(3); 13(3); 14; 10:1(3); 2(3); 3(3); 4;
5(2); 6(3); 7(2); 8(3); 9(3); 10(2); 11(2); 12; 13; 14(2); 15(3);
16(2); 18(3); 19(2); 20; 21; 22; 23; 24(2); 25(2); 26; 27; 28;
29; 30; 32; 33; 42; 43; 44; **Neh** 1:2(2); 3(3); 4(3); 5(4); 6(4);
7; 9(3); 10(2); 11(3); 2:1(2); 3(2); 5(2); 6(2); 8(3); 9(2); 10;
11; 12; 13(4); 14; 15(3); 16; 17(2); 18(3); 19(3); 20(2); 3:1(3);
2; 3(2); 4; 6(3); 7(2); 8; 9; 10; 11; 12(2); 13(3); 14(2); 15(2);
16; 19; 22; 23; 25; 26; 27; 30; 31(2); 32(2); 4:1(2); 2(3); 3;
4; 5; 6; 7(2); 8(3); 9(2); 10; 11(3); 13(2); 14(7); 15(2); 16(2);
17(2); 18; 19(3); 21; 22(2); 5:1(2); 2(2); 3(2); 4; 5(4); 6(2);
7(2); 8(2); 10(2); 11(3); 12(2); 13(5); 15(2); 16; 17(3); 18(2);
6:1(2); 2; 3; 4; 6(2); 7(2); 9; 10(2); 11(2); 12; 13(2); 14(3);
16(2); 17; 18; 19; 7:1(2); 2(2); 3(5); 4(2); 5(3); 6(2); 7; 8; 9;
10; 11(2); 12; 13; 14; 15; 16; 17; 18; 19; 20; 22; 23; 24;
26(2); 27; 29(2); 30(2); 31; 32(2); 34; 35; 36; 37(2); 38; 39;
40; 41; 42; 43; 44; 45; 56; 59; 60(2); 61(2); 62; 63(2); 65(2);
66; 67(5); 68(2); 69(3); 70(3); 71; 72(2); 73; 8:1; 2(2); 3(3);
4(4); 5(2); 6(3); 7(2); 8(2); 9(3); 10; 12(3); 13; 14; 15(5);
16(4); 17(2); 18(2); 9:1; 2(3); 3(4); 4(2); 5(5); 6(3); 7(2); 8(2);
9; 10(2); 11(2); 12; 13(4); 14(2); 15(2); 16(2); 17(4); 18(2);
19; 20(2); 21; 22(3); 23(2); 24(3); 25(7); 26(3); 27(2); 28(2);
29(4); 30; 31; 32(5); 34; 35; 36(2); 37(3); 38(3); 10:1; 8; 9;
13; 27; 28(3); 29(6); 31(2); 33(2); 34; 35(2); 36(3); 37(2);
38(2); 39(5); 11:1; 2; 3; 4; 5; 6; 7; 8(3); 9; 10; 12(2); 13(3);
14(2); 16; 17; 18; 19(2); 20(2); 21(2); 25(4); 27(2); 28(2);
30(3); 31(2); 35; 12:1(2); 7(2); 8(2); 9; 11; 21; 22(2); 24(3);
25; 26(2); 27(3); 28; 29(2); 30(3); 31; 32; 33; 35; 36(2); 38;
39(2); 40; 41(2); 42; 43(2); 44(4); 45(3); 46(3); 47(3); 13:1;
2; 5(5); 7(2); 8; 9(2); 10; 11(3); 12(2); 13(5); 14(2); 15(4);
16(3); 17; 18(2); 19; 20; 21; 22(4); 23; 24(2); 25(3); 26; 28;
29(2); 30; 31(2); **Esth** 1:1; 3(3); 4(2); 5; 6(7); 7; 10; 11; 12;
13; 14(3); 16(3); 18(2); 19(3); 20; 21(3); 22(2); 2:1; 3(2); 4;
7(3); 8(2); 9(3); 11(2); 12(2); 13; 14(2); 15; 17(3); 18(3); 20;
21(2); 22; 23(3); 3:1(2); 2(2); 4; 7; 8(2); 9; 10; 11(2); 12(3);
13(5); 15(2); 4:1(4); 3(5); 4(4); 5(2); 7(2); 8(3); 9; 10; 11; 13;
14(2); 16(4); 17; 5:1; 2(2); 3; 4; 5; 7(2); 8(4); 9(2); 10(4);
11(2); 12; 14(3); 6:1; 2(2); 3; 5; 6; 7; 8; 9(2); 10(2); 11(3);
12; 13(2); 14; 7:1; 2(2); 3(3); 4(3); 5(2); 6(3); 7; 8:1; 2(2);
3(2); 4(2); 5(4); 7(2); 8(2); 9(5); 10(2); 11(4); 13; 14(2); 15(5);
16(2); 17(5); 9:1; 2; 3(2); 4; 5(2); 6(2); 9; 12(3); 13; 14; 15(2);
16(2); 17(3); 18(3); 19(2); 20(3); 21; 22(3); 24(2); 25(2); 26;
27(4); 28(3); 30(3); 31(4); 32; 10:1(2); 2(3); 3(3); **Job** 1:1(4);
2(2); 3; 4(5); 5(4); 6; 7(5); 8(2); 9; 10(2); 11(2); 12; 13(2);
14(3); 15(2); 16(5); 17(4); 18(3); 19(5); 20(3); 21(3); 2:1;
2(5); 3(3); 4; 5(3); 6; 7; 8; 9; 10; 11(3); 12(5); 13(2); 3:1; 2(2);
3; 5; 9; 13; 14; 17; 19(2); 20; 21; 22; 23; 24; 25; 4:1; 3; 4;
5(2); 6; 8; 9; 10; 11; 12; 14; 5:1; 2; 4; 5; 8; 9; 10; 11; 13;
14; 15; 16; 20; 21; 22(2); 23; 24; 25; 27; 6:1; 2; 9; 11; 13;
16; 18; 20; 21; 24; 26; 27; 7:2; 3; 4; 5(2); 6; 9; 14; 15; 18;
19; 21(2); 8:1; 2; 5; 6(2); 8; 9; 10(2); 12; 13; 14; 16; 17; 19;
21; 22; 9:1; 4(2); 5; 6; 7; 8; 9(2); 14; 16; 17; 19; 22; 27; 30;
31; 32; 34; 35; 10:3; 6; 7; 8; 9; 10; 11(3); 12(2); 13; 14; 16;
17(2); 18; 21; 11:1; 2; 3; 4; 5; 9; 10; 13; 14(2); 15; 16; 17;

18(2); 19; 20(2); 12:1; 2; 4(2); 6; 7(3); 8(2); 10; 11; 12; 13(2); 16(2); 17; 18; 19; 20; 21; 22; 23(2); 24; 25; 13:1; 3; 5; 6; 7; 11; 13; 14; 17; 21; 22; 23(2); 24; 25(2); 26; 27; 14:1; 2(2); 3(2); 7; 8; 9; 10(2); 11(2); 12; 13; 15; 17; 18(2); 19; 20(2); 21(2); 22; 15:1; 2; 4; 5; 6; 10; 11; 12; 13; 14; 15; 16; 19; 20; 24; 25; 27; 30; 32; 33; 34; 35; 16:1; 4; 5; 6; 8(2); 9; 11; 12; 13; 15; 16; 17; 18; 19; 17:2; 6; 7; 8; 9(2); 14(2); 18:1; 2; 3; 5; 6; 7; 8; 9; 10; 11; 12; 14; 16; 17; 18; 21; 19:1; 2; 4; 5; 6; 8; 9; 10; 11; 12; 13; 14; 15; 17; 18; 19; 20(2); 22; 24; 25; 26; 27(2); 20:1; 3; 5; 6; 8; 10; 12; 13; 15; 17; 18; 19; 23; 25; 27; 28; 21:1; 2; 3; 4; 5; 6; 7; 8; 11; 12(2); 13; 15; 18; 20; 23; 24; 26; 27; 28; 29; 31; 32; 22:1; 4; 5; 6; 7; 8; 9; 10; 11; 12; 13; 14; 19(2); 20; 21; 22; 24; 25; 26; 27; 28; 29; 23:1; 4; 5; 7; 8; 11; 13(2); 14; 16; 17; 24:2; 5; 6; 7; 8; 9; 10; 11; 12; 14(2); 15; 19; 20; 21; 23; 25; 25:1; 2; 5; 6; 26:1; 3; 4; 5; 6; 9; 10; 11; 12; 14; 27:1; 2; 3; 6; 7; 13; 14; 15; 16; 17; 19; 21; 22; 23; 28:1; 2; 3(2); 4; 6; 10; 12; 14; 20; 21; 22; 23; 24; 25; 26; 27; 28(2); 29:1; 3; 6; 8(3); 9; 10; 11; 12; 13; 14(2); 15; 16; 17; 18; 19; 20; 21(2); 22; 23; 24; 25; 30:3(2); 4; 6; 9; 11; 12; 15; 16; 17; 19(2); 20; 22; 23; 26; 27; 28; 29; 30; 31; 31:2; 3; 4; 8; 10; 12; 18; 20; 23; 25; 27; 34(2); 36; 38; 40; 32:3; 6(3); 7; 8; 12; 15; 16(2); 20; 33:1; 4; 8; 9; 16; 17; 18; 19; 20; 21; 22; 24; 26; 27(3); 28; 31; 33; 34:1; 8; 10; 11; 14; 15; 18; 20; 21; 24; 25; 27; 29; 33; 37; 35:1; 4; 5(2); 8; 11; 14; 15; 36:1; 2; 7; 8; 9; 10; 11(2); 12; 14; 15; 16; 17; 26; 28; 30; 32; 37:1; 2; 4; 6; 8; 9; 10; 12; 14; 15; 21; 23; 38:1; 3; 7; 8; 9; 10(2); 11; 12; 13; 14; 15; 19; 23; 27; 29; 30; 35; 38; 41; 39:4; 6; 8; 12; 13; 14; 17; 18; 21; 22; 23; 24; 25; 26; 27; 28(2); 30; 40:1; 3; 6; 7; 10(3); 11; 12; 16; 20; 21; 41:17; 18; 20; 21; 22; 23; 27; 42:1; 2; 4(2); 6(2); 7(2); 8(3); 9(3); 10; 11(5); 12; 13; 14(2); 15; 16(3); 17; **Ps** 1:2(2); 3; 2:1; 2(2); 3; 5; 8(2); 11; 12; 3:3; 4; 5; 4:1; 2; 4(2); 5; 7; 8; 5:2; 3; 6; 6:10(2); 7:1; 5(2); 8; 9; 11; 12; 14; 15(2); 16; 17; 8:2(2); 3; 4; 5(2); 7; 8; 9:2; 3; 4; 5; 6; 8; 10; 17; 10:3; 7(3); 14; 15; 16; 18; 11:5; 6(2); 12:2; 3; 13:3; 14:4; 7; 15:2(2); 4; 16:5; 9; 17:3; 6; 12; 14(2); 18(2); 2(3); 4; 6(2); 7(2); 8; 9; 10(2); 11; 12; 13(2); 14(2); 21; 22; 23; 26; 31; 32; 33; 37; 45; 47; 49; 50(2); 19:1; 2; 4; 5; 6(2); 9; 10; 11; 13; 14(2); 20:2; 3; 4; 5; 7; 8(2); 21:1; 2; 4(2); 5; 7; 9; 10; 13; 22:1; 2(2); 4; 5(2); 6(2); 13; 14; 15; 16; 17; 18; 21; 23; 26; 27(2); 28; 29; 31; 23:4; 6(2); 24:1(2); 2; 4; 5; 7(2); 8; 9; 25:5; 6; 8; 9; 10(2); 13; 14; 16(2); 18(2); 19; 20; 21; 26:2(2); 3; 5; 7; 8; 10; 11; 27:1; 2(2); 4; 6; 7; 10; 11; 12; 14; 28:3; 4; 5; 7(3); 8; 9(2); 29:1; 6; 9(2); 10; 30:1; 2; 4; 7; 8; 10; 11; 12; 31:3(2); 7; 8; 9; 10(2); 11; 15; 18; 23; 24; 32:2; 4; 5(2); 8; 9; 11(2); 33:4; 5; 6; 9(2); 19; 20; 34:2; 3; 4(2); 5(2); 6(2); 7; 8; 10; 12; 13; 14(2); 15; 17(2); 18; 21; 22; 35:2(2); 3; 4(2); 5; 6(2); 8; 9; 10; 13; 15(3); 21; 23(2); 24; 26(2); 27(2); 28(2); 36:2; 3(2); 6; 8; 10; 11; 12; 37:2; 3(2); 4; 5; 6; 7; 8; 10; 11; 12; 14(2); 15; 18; 19; 20; 21(2); 23; 25; 26(2); 27(2); 28; 29; 30; 32; 34(2); 35; 36; 37; 40(3); 38:2; 5; 7; 8; 9; 11(2); 12; 13; 14; 17; 19(2); 39:2; 4; 5; 6; 7; 12; 13; 40:1(2); 2(2); 3(2); 4; 5(2); 6(2); 8; 10(2); 11; 14(2); 16; 17(2); 41:2(2); 5; 6; 8; 10; 12; 13; 42:2; 3; 4; 5; 6; 7; 8; 11(2); 43:1(2); 3(2); 4; 5(2); 44:2; 3; 7; 8; 9(2); 10; 11; 12; 13; 15; 16(2); 19; 24(2); 26; 45:3; 4(3); 6; 7; 8(2); 10(2); 12; 15; 17; 46:1; 2; 3; 9; 10; 47:3; 48:1; 5; 6; 12; 14; 49:2(2); 3; 6; 8; 9; 10(2); 13; 14; 50:1; 3(2); 4; 7(2); 10; 11; 12; 14; 15; 17; 18; 19; 20; 21(2); 22; 23; 51:2; 3; 4(2); 5; 6; 7(2); 8; 9; 10; 11; 12; 13; 14; 15; 17; 19; 52(2); 5(2); 6(2); 7; 8; 9; 53:1; 4; 6; 54:1; 3; 7; 55:1; 2(2); 3; 4; 5(2); 6; 7; 8; 9(2); 10(2); 11; 13; 14; 15; 16; 17(4); 19; 22; 23; 57:1; 3(2); 4(2); 7; 8; 10; 58:9; 59:2; 4(2); 6; 11; 12(3); 13; 14(2); 15(2); 16; 60(3); 5; 6; 7; 10; 61:7; 62:2; 3; 6; 7(2); 63:1; 2; 5(2); 64:3; 4; 6; 9; 10(2); 65:1; 4; 5; 7; 8; 9; 11; 12; 66:4; 5; 8; 9; 12; 14; 16(2); 17; 67:1(2); 4(2); 7; 68:4; 12; 13; 20; 23; 27(2); 34; 35; 69:5; 8; 9; 10; 12; 14(2); 15; 17; 18; 19; 20(2); 21; 22; 23; 24; 26; 27; 28; 29; 30; 31; 32(2); 33; 34(2); 35(2); 36; 70:2(2); 4(2); 5(2); 71:2(2); 3; 4; 8; 10; 11; 13(2); 14(2); 15; 17; 18; 20(2); 21; 22; 23; 72:1; 2; 3; 4; 5; 7; 8; 9; 10(2); 12; 13(2); 14(2); 15(3); 16; 17; 19(3); 73:8; 9; 10; 11(2); 13; 14; 21; 22; 24; 25; 26(2); 74:6(2); 11; 14; 15; 16; 17; 18; 21; 75:3; 4; 7; 8(3); 76:2; 3; 4; 5; 6; 7; 8; 11; 77:1; 3(2); 6; 7; 10; 12; 15; 18; 19; 20; 78:3(2); 4(2); 5; 6; 7; 8(3); 9; 11(2); 13(2); 14; 15; 16; 18; 20; 21(2); 22; 23; 24; 26; 28; 29; 31(2); 32; 33; 34(2); 35; 36; 38(2); 39; 40; 41(2); 43; 44; 45; 46; 47; 48; 49; 51; 52; 53; 54; 55; 56(2); 57; 58; 59; 61(2); 62; 63; 64; 66; 67; 69; 70; 71; 72; 79:3; 4; 6; 7; 9(2); 12; 13; 80:2(3); 3; 5; 6; 7; 8; 9(2); 10; 11; 13; 14(2); 15(2); 18; 19; 81:2; 7; 8; 10; 11; 14; 16; 82:2; 3(2); 4; 6; 7; 83:1; 2; 3; 4; 6(2); 7; 11(2); 14; 15; 17(2); 84:2; 3(2); 9; 11(2); 85:4; 7; 8; 10(2); 11; 12; 13; 86:1; 5(2); 6; 9(2); 10; 12; 13; 14(2); 15(3); 16(2); 17(2); 87:4(2); 5(3); 7; 88:1; 3; 5; 7; 8; 10; 12; 13; 15; 18(2); 89:4; 5; 7; 11; 12(2); 13; 14(2); 16; 17; 18; 19; 23; 24(2); 25; 26; 28; 29; 30; 31; 32; 36; 38; 43; 44; 48; 52; 90:2; 3; 4; 6(2); 7; 10(3); 13; 14; 16; 17(2); 91:2; 3; 4(2); 7; 8; 13(2); 15(2); 16; 92:1; 2; 3; 7; 14; 15; 94:4; 5; 6(2); 8; 12; 15; 21; 22; 23; 95:3; 5; 6; 7(2); 10(2); 96:4; 6(2); 7; 8; 11(2); 12; 13; 97:2(2); 3; 4; 6; 8(2); 11; 12; 98:1; 3; 4; 5; 6; 7(2); 9; 99:2; 3; 4; 5; 6(3); 7; 9; 100:3(2); 4(2); 5; 101:1; 5; 102:1; 3; 4; 7; 9; 10(2); 11; 12; 13; 14; 15; 17; 21; 22; 25; 26; 27; 28; 103:1; 2; 4; 6; 8(2); 16(2); 17; 18; 19; 104:1; 14; 15(2); 20; 21; 22; 23; 25(2); 29; 30; 32(2); 35; 105:4; 5; 9; 10; 12; 15; 20; 21; 22; 23; 24; 26; 27; 28(2); 29; 31(2); 32; 33(2); 34; 35(2); 37(2); 39; 40(2); 41; 42; 44; 45; 106:3; 9; 10; 14; 15; 16; 17(2); 19; 25; 27; 28; 29; 30(2); 31; 35; 37; 38(3); 39; 41(2); 42; 43; 45(2); 47; 48; 107:3(3); 5; 6; 7; 8; 9; 10(2); 11; 12; 13; 14(2); 15; 16; 17; 18; 19; 20(2); 21; 22; 24; 25; 27(3); 28; 31; 32; 33; 35; 37(2); 38(2); 39(2); 40; 41; 42(2); 43; 108:1; 2; 3; 4; 5; 6; 7; 11; 109:2; 3; 5; 6; 7; 8; 9; 10; 11; 13; 14; 16; 18; 19; 20; 22(2); 24; 29; 110:4; 111:1; 3(2); 4; 7; 8(3); 9; 112:3(2); 4(2); 5; 10(2); 113:2; 6; 7; 114:2; 3; 115:4; 9; 10; 11; 13; 14(2); 15; 18; 116:1; 3(2); 5; 6; 8; 13; 17; 117:2; 118:5; 14(2); 15; 17; 19; 21; 24; 27; 28; 119:15; 17; 22; 23; 24; 26; 29; 33; 34; 36; 37; 43; 44; 45; 46; 47; 48; 52; 55; 59; 60; 63; 66; 68; 72; 73; 75; 90; 105; 106; 108; 114; 116; 117(2); 120; 121; 123; 124; 131; 132; 133; 135; 137; 138; 141; 142; 143; 144; 146; 147; 151; 153; 154; 157; 158; 160; 163; 165; 166; 167; 168; 174; 175(2); 120:1; 2; 121:2; 8(2); 122:8; 124:7; 8; 125:2; 4; 126:2; 3; 128:2; 5; 129:5; 130:5; 7; 8; 131:2; 3; 132:1; 2; 8; 9; 12; 16; 133:1; 134:2; 3; 135:5; 6(2); 8; 9(2); 10; 11; 12; 14; 15; 136:9; 11; 12; 14; 15; 18; 20; 21; 24; 137:3; 9; 138:2(2); 3; 7; 139:1; 2; 3(2); 5(2); 9; 10; 12; 14(2); 15; 16; 21; 23(2); 24(2); 140:5; 12; 141:4; 5; 6; 7; 9; 142:4; 143:1; 12; 144:1; 2(3); 5(2); 6(2); 7; 8; 11(2); 13; 145:1(2); 2(2); 3(2); 4; 5; 6; 7; 8(2); 9; 10; 11; 12; 13; 14; 15; 16; 19; 21(2); 146:6(2); 9; 147:1; 3; 5; 9; 14; 18(2); 19; 20; 148:3; 4; 5; 6; 7; 8(2); 9(2); 10(2); 11(2); 12(2); 13; 14; 149:1; 3; 6; 7; 8; 150:3; 4(2); **Prov** 1:2; 3; 4; 5(2); 6(2); 7; 8; 9; 12; 16; 22; 24(2); 25; 27(2); 29; 30; 31; 32; 33; 2:1; 2; 3; 4; 5; 6; 8; 9(2); 10; 14; 15; 17; 18; 20; 21; 22; 3:2(2); 3; 4(3); 5; 6; 7; 8; 9; 10; 13; 14; 15; 16; 17; 18; 20; 21; 22; 23; 24; 26; 28(2); 31; 4:1; 3; 4(2); 6(2); 7; 8; 10(2); 12; 14; 15; 16; 17; 22; 24; 25; 26; 5:2; 3; 7; 8; 9; 10; 11(2); 12(2); 14; 15; 17; 18; 19(2); 20; 21; 22; 23; 6:3(2); 5; 6; 8; 11; 19; 20; 22; 23; 26; 27; 28; 33(2); 7:1; 2(2); 4; 7; 8; 9; 10(2); 11; 13; 15; 17; 20; 26; 8:1; 4; 5; 6; 9; 10(2); 11; 12(2); 13(3); 14; 15; 16; 17; 18(2); 19; 30; 31; 33(2); 35; 9:5; 6(2); 7; 8; 9(2); 10; 11; 12; 13; 16; 17; 10:18; 22; 24; 26; 11:7; 8; 10; 24; 25; 29; 30; 31; 12:7; 14; 28; 13:4; 5; 7; 18; 23; 14:6; 10; 13; 16(2); 17; 19; 22; 26; 15:3; 10; 11; 23; 30; 33; 16:3; 6(2); 11; 13; 15; 16; 18; 20; 21; 23; 24; 27; 28; 29; 30; 32; 17:2; 3; 6; 15; 17; 18; 19; 20; 21; 25; 27; 18:3; 6; 7; 8; 10; 11; 12; 13; 15; 16; 17; 18; 19; 21(2); 22; 19:1; 2; 3; 5; 6; 9; 11; 13; 14; 15; 17; 18; 20; 22; 23; 24; 25(2); 26(2); 27; 28; 29; 20:1; 4; 10; 11; 12; 13; 15; 16; 22; 23; 25; 26; 28(2); 29; 21:3; 4; 13; 14; 17; 18; 19; 20; 21(2); 22; 23; 24; 26; 22:1; 2; 3(2); 4(3); 5; 6; 7; 8; 10(2); 11; 16; 17(2); 20; 23; 24; 25; 23:2; 7; 8; 12; 14; 18; 19(2); 21(2); 22; 23(3); 24; 25(2); 26; 27; 28; 32; 33; 24:2; 3; 4; 6; 9; 11; 12; 13; 14; 16; 17; 18(2); 21; 22; 25; 27; 30; 31; 32; 34; 25:3; 4; 5; 6; 9; 10; 12; 14; 15; 16; 17; 18; 19; 20; 21; 22; 23; 26; 26:1; 3; 6; 10; 17; 18; 19; 20; 21; 22; 24; 27; 28; 27:2(2); 3; 4; 9(2); 11; 12(2); 13; 15; 16; 20; 21(2); 23; 25(2); 26; 27; 28:2; 8; 13; 15; 22; 24; 29:1(2); 6; 13; 15; 17; 22; 27; 30:1; 2; 4; 6; 8; 9(4); 10; 11; 13; 14(2); 15; 16; 17(2); 19; 20(2); 23; 28; 30; 31; 33; 31:2(2); 5(2); 6; 7(2); 9(2); 12; 13(2); 15(2); 16; 17; 18; 19; 22; 24(2); 25; 26; 27; 28(2); 30; 31; **Eccl** 1:4; 5(2); 6(2); 9; 13(2); 14(2); 15; 16(2); 17(3); 18; 2:2; 3; 4; 5(2); 7(3); 8(5); 9; 10; 11(3); 12(2); 15; 16; 17; 19(2); 20; 21(2); 22; 23; 24(2); 26(4); 3:2(2); 3(2); 4(2); 5(2); 6(2); 7(2); 8(2); 12; 13(3); 14; 15(2); 16; 17(2); 20; 21; 4:1(2); 4(2); 5; 6; 7; 8(2); 12; 13(2); 16; 5:1; 2(2); 3; 5; 6; 7; 8(3); 15; 16(2); 17(3); 18(3); 19(3); 6:1; 2(3); 3; 4(2); 7; 9; 10; 7:1; 2; 7; 11; 15; 18; 20; 24; 25(3); 26(2); 8:1(2); 4; 5(2); 6; 8(2); 9; 10(2); 12; 15; 16; 9:1(2); 2(3); 3; 5; 6; 7; 8; 9; 11(2); 13; 14(2); 15; 16; 10:1(2); 3; 8; 9; 10; 13; 16; 17(2); 18; 19; 20; 11:2; 3; 4; 6; 7; 8; 9(2); 10(2); 12:1; 2(3); 3(2); 4(2); 5(3); 7; 9(3); 10; 11; 12(2); 13; **Song** 1:4; 8; 17; 2:1; 3; 4; 6; 10(2); 11; 12; 13(2); 14; 16; 17(2); 3:2(2); 4(2); 6; 11; 4:2; 3; 6(2); 7; 8; 10; 11(2); 14(3); 15; 16(2); 5:4; 5; 6; 10; 11; 12; 16; 6:2; 3; 6; 8(2); 9(3); 11; 12; 7:5; 6; 7; 9; 10; 12; 13(2); 8:2; 3; 8; 9; 10; 12; 14; **Isa** 1:1(2); 2(3); 3; 5(2); 6(2); 7; 11; 13(2); 14; 18; 19; 20; 23(2); 24; 25(2); 26; 27; 28(2); 29; 30; 31(2); 2:1; 2(2); 3(4); 4(2); 5; 6; 7(3); 9; 10(2); 11; 12(2); 13(2); 14; 15; 16; 17; 19(2); 20(2); 21(2); 3:1(3); 2(4); 3(3); 4; 5(2); 6; 8(2); 9; 12(2); 13; 14; 15; 16(3); 17; 18; 19; 20; 21; 22; 23(2); 24(2); 25; 26(2); 4:1(2); 2(3); 3(2); 4(2); 5(3); 6(3); 5:2(3); 3(3); 5(4); 6; 7; 9; 10; 12(3); 13; 14(4); 15; 16; 17; 18; 19(3); 20(3); 21; 23; 24(3); 25(2); 26; 28(2); 29(2); 30(3); 6:1(2); 2; 3(2); 4(2); 5; 7(3); 8; 9(2); 10(6); 11(2); 12; 13(2); 7:1; 2(2); 3; 4(4); 5; 6(3); 8; 9; 14(2); 15(2); 16; 17(2); 18(2); 19(4); 20(2); 21; 22; 23; 24(2); 25(3); 8:1; 2(2); 3(2); 4(2); 6(2); 7(3); 8(2); 9; 11; 13; 14(2); 15(3); 17(2); 18(2); 19(3); 20; 21(5); 22(3); 9:1(2); 3; 4; 5(2); 6(2); 7(4); 8; 9(2); 11; 12(2); 14(2); 15; 16; 17(3); 18(2); 19; 20(3); 21; 10:2(2); 3(2); 4; 5; 6(2); 7; 10; 11(2); 12(2); 13(2); 14(2); 16; 17(3); 18(4); 20(2); 24; 25; 26; 27(2); 33; 34; 11:1; 2(3); 3; 4(2); 5; 6(3); 7(2); 8; 10(2); 11(4); 12(2); 13(2); 14(2); 15(2); 12:1(2); 2(2); 4; 6; 13:5; 8(2); 9(2); 10(2); 11(2); 13(2); 14(2); 15; 16; 17; 18; 19(2); 21(2); 22(2); 14:1(3); 2(4); 3(2); 4; 6; 7; 8; 10; 11(2); 16; 17; 20; 21(2); 22(4); 23; 24; 25(2); 26; 27(2); 29; 30(2); 31; 32; 15:1(2); 2(3); 3; 4; 7; 8; 9; 16:5(3); 6(2); 8(2); 9(2); 10; 11; 12; 14(2); 17:1; 2; 3; 4; 5; 7; 9(2); 10(2); 11(2); 12; 13(2); 14(2); 18:2(2); 3(2); 4; 5(3); 6(2); 7(3); 19:1(2); 2; 3(3); 4(2); 5(2); 6(2); 7(2); 8; 9; 10; 12; 14; 16(2); 17; 18; 19; 20(5); 21(4); 22(4); 23(3); 24; 25(2); 20:1(2); 2(4); 3(3); 4(3); 5(2); 6(2); 21:2; 5; 7(3); 9(3); 10; 12; 15; 17; 22:5(3); 6(2); 7; 9; 10; 12(3); 13(4); 15; 16; 17; 18(2); 19; 21(2); 22(3); 23; 24; 25(3); 23:3(2); 12; 13; 17(2); 18(2); 24:1(2); 2; 3; 4(2); 6(2); 12; 17(2); 18(3); 20(4); 21; 22; 23(3); 25:1; 6; 7(2); 8; 9(3); 10; 11(2); 12; 26:1; 6; 8; 10; 11; 14(2); 17; 19(2); 20; 21; 27:1(2); 3; 4; 5; 6(2); 9(2); 10(3); 11(2); 12(2); 13(2); 28:2(2); 4; 5; 6; 7(2); 8; 9; 11; 12; 13(4); 15(2); 17(2); 18; 19(2); 20; 21; 23(2); 24; 25(2); 27; 29; 29:2(2); 3; 4; 5; 6(4); 7(2); 8(5); 9(2); 10(2); 11; 12; 13(2); 14(2); 15(2); 17; 18(2); 19; 20; 21(2); 23(2); 24; 30:1; 2(2); 3; 4; 5; 6(4); 7; 8(2); 10; 12(3); 14; 15(2); 16(2); 17; 18; 20(2); 22; 23(2); 24(2); 25(2); 26(2); 27(2); 28; 29; 30(3); 32(3); 33; 31:1(2); 2(3); 3(4); 4(2); 7; 8(2); 9(2); 32:1; 2; 3; 4; 6(2); 8; 10; 11; 13; 14; 15(2); 16; 17(2); 18; 19; 20; 33:1; 4(2); 5; 6(2); 9(4); 12; 13; 15(2); 21; 24; 34:1(3); 2; 3; 4(2); 5; 6(2); 7(2); 9; 10; 11(4); 12; 13(2); 14(2); 15(3); 16(2); 17; 35:1(3); 2(3); 3; 4; 5; 6(2); 7(2); 8(2); 10(5); 36:1; 2; 3(2); 5; 6; 7(3); 8; 9(2); 10; 11(2); 12(3); 13(2); 16(4); 17(3); 19; 21; 22(2); 37:1(2); 2; 3(3); 4; 6; 7(3); 8; 9; 11; 12(3); 13(2); 14(4); 16; 17(3); 18; 19(2); 23(2); 24(2); 25(2); 27(3); 28(2); 29(3); 30(3); 31(2); 32; 34; 35; 36(3); 37(2); 38(2); 38:1(4); 2; 3(4); 4; 5; 6(2); 7; 9; 15; 16(2); 21(2); 22; 39:1(2); 2(5); 3(2); 4; 6; 7(2); 8; 40:2; 4(3); 5; 6(2); 10(2); 11(2); 12(2); 14(3); 15; 16; 17(2); 19; 22(2); 24(2); 26(2); 27(2); 29; 30(2); 31(2); 41:1; 2; 3; 4(2); 5(2); 6; 9(3); 11(2); 12; 14; 15(2); 16(2); 17; 18(2); 19(4); 20(4); 22(2); 23; 24; 25(2); 26; 27; 28; 29; 42:3; 4; 5(3); 6(2); 8; 9; 10(3); 11; 12; 14(2); 15(3); 16(2); 18; 19; 21; 22(4); 23; 24; 25(2); 43:1; 2; 3; 4(2); 5; 6(2); 8; 9(3); 10(3); 11; 12(2); 13(2); 14; 16; 17(2); 19; 20(2); 22; 25; 27; 28; 44:1; 2(2); 3(2); 5; 6(2); 7(4); 8; 9; 11; 12(3); 13; 14(3); 15(4); 16(2); 17(3); 18; 19(3); 20; 21; 22; 23(2); 24; 25(2); 26(2); 27; 28(2); 45:1; 2(2); 3; 4; 5; 6; 7(2); 8(2); 11(2); 12(2); 13(2); 14(5); 16; 17; 18(2); 20(2); 21(3); 22(2); 23; 24(2); 25; 46:1; 3; 4(3); 5(2); 6(2); 7(2); 8; 9(2); 10(2); 13; 47:1(2); 2; 3; 5; 6; 7; 8; 9; 10(3); 11(2); 12; 13(2); 48:1(2); 2; 3(2); 4(2); 5(2); 6(2); 7(2); 8; 9; 11; 12; 13; 14(2); 15; 16(2); 18; 19; 21(2); 49:1; 2(2); 3; 4(2); 5(2); 6; 7(2); 8(2); 9; 11; 12(2); 13(2); 14; 15; 17; 18(3); 19(3); 21(4); 22(2); 23(2); 25(2); 26(2); 50:1; 2; 3; 5; 6(2); 7; 10(2); 11; 51:1; 2(3); 3(3); 4(2); 5(2); 6(3); 8(2); 9; 11(3); 12; 13(3); 14; 16(2); 17; 19(2); 21; 22; 23(2); 52:1; 3; 5; 10; 12; 13(2); 14; 15; 53:1; 2(2); 3(4); 4(2); 5; 6; 7(2); 8(2); 9; 10; 11; 12(4); 54:1; 2(2); 3(3); 4; 5; 6; 10; 11(2); 12; 13; 14; 16; 17(2); 55:1(4); 2(3); 3(3); 4; 5(2); 7(3); 9; 10(5); 11; 12(3); 13(2); 56:1(2); 2(2); 4(2); 5(3); 6(2); 7(2); 11; 12(2); 57:1; 3; 4; 7; 8(3); 9(2); 11(2); 12; 13; 14; 15(4); 16; 17(3); 18(3); 19(2); 20; 58:1; 2(2); 3(3); 4(2); 5(3); 6; 7(2); 8; 9(3); 10(2); 11(3); 12; 13(2); 14(2); 59:2; 3; 4(2); 5(2); 6; 7(2); 8; 10; 11; 12(2); 13(4); 14(2); 15(2); 16(2); 17(2); 19; 20; 21(2); 60:1; 2(2); 3; 4(2); 5(2); 6(3); 7; 8; 9(3); 10; 11; 12(2); 13(2); 14(2); 15; 16(2); 17(2); 18; 19; 20; 22; 61:1; 2; 4(2); 5(3); 6; 7; 8; 9; 10; 11; 62:1(2); 2; 3; 4(2); 5; 7(2); 8(2); 9; 11; 12(2); 63:2; 3(3); 4; 5(2); 6; 7(2); 9(4); 10(2); 11; 14; 15(4); 16; 17; 64:5(2); 6(2); 7(2); 8(2); 11(2); 12; 65:3; 4(2); 7(2); 8; 9(2); 10; 11; 12(2); 14; 15; 16(2); 17(2); 18(2); 19; 21(2); 22(3); 23; 24; 25(2); 66:1(2); 2(3); 3; 4(2); 9; 10; 11(2); 12(2); 13; 14(2); 15(2); 16(2); 17(3); 18(4); 19(6); 20(3); 21(2); 22(2); 23(2); 24(3); **Jer** 1:7; 9(2); 10(4); 11; 13(3); 15(2); 16; 17(2); 18(3); 2:2; 4; 5; 6(3); 7(2); 8(2); 9; 10(3); 12; 13; 15; 16; 18; 19(4); 20(3); 22; 25(2); 26(4); 27(3); 37; 3:1(2); 2(3); 3; 5; 6(2); 7(2); 8(2); 9(2); 10; 12(2); 13(2); 14(2); 15(2); 16; 17; 18; 19(3); 21; 22; 23; 24(2); 25(3); 4:1; 2(3); 3(2); 4(3); 5(4); 6; 7; 8; 9(3); 10; 11; 13; 15; 16; 18; 20; 21; 22; 23(3); 24(3); 25(2); 26(2); 28(2); 29(3); 30; 5:1(4); 5(2); 7(2); 9; 10; 11; 12; 13; 14(2); 17(5); 19(2); 20; 21(3); 22(2); 23(2); 24; 25; 27; 28; 30; 31(2); 6:1(2); 2; 4; 5(2); 6; 7(2); 10(2); 11; 12(2); 13; 16(3); 18; 20; 21(3); 22; 23(3); 26; 27(2); 28; 7:2(2); 3(2); 5(2); 6(2); 7; 9; 10(3); 12; 13(4); 14(2); 15; 17; 18(2); 20(5); 21; 23(3); 24(3); 25; 28; 29(3); 31(2); 33(2); 34(3); 8:1(4); 2(5); 4(2); 6; 7(2); 8; 9; 10; 13(2); 14(3); 15(2); 16(3); 17; 20; 9:1(2); 2; 3(2); 4(2); 5; 7; 10(3); 12(2); 13(2); 14; 15; 16; 17(2); 18(2); 20(2); 21; 22; 24(2); 26(2); 10:4(2); 5; 6; 7; 8; 9(3); 10(2); 11(2); 12; 13; 14; 16; 18; 19; 20(2); 21(2); 22; 25(3); 11:2(2); 3; 4(2); 5(3); 6(2); 7; 9(2); 10(2); 11; 12(2); 13; 15; 16(2); 17; 18; 19(2); 20; 22; 23; 12:3(2); 4(2); 5(2); 14; 15(3); 16; 17; 13:1(2); 2; 3; 4(2); 5; 6; 7(3); 9; 10(2); 11(2); 12; 13; 14(2); 15; 16(3); 17; 18; 19; 20; 22; 25; 27; 14:2(2); 3(3); 6; 8; 9; 10; 12(3); 14(2); 15(3); 16(2); 17(2); 18(2); 19(2); 20; 15:1(2); 2(4); 3(3); 6; 7; 8; 9(2); 10; 11; 12; 13; 14; 15(2); 16(3); 18; 20(3); 21; 16:3(3); 4(3); 5; 6; 8; 9(3); 10(2); 11(4); 12; 13(2); 15; 16(5); 18(3); 19(3); 21(2); 17:1; 2; 3; 4(2); 5; 6; 7; 8(2); 9; 11; 14(2); 18; 19(3); 20(3); 21; 24; 25(5); 26(6); 27(2); 18:2(2); 3; 4; 7(2); 9(3); 11(4); 12(2); 15(2); 16(2); 17; 18(3); 19; 21(2); 22; 19:1(3); 2(2); 3(2); 4(2); 7(5); 8(2); 9(5); 11(3); 12(2); 13(3); 14(2); 15; 20:2; 3; 4(5); 5(2); 6(5); 7(2); 8(2); 9; 10(2); 11; 12(2); 16(3); 17; 18; 21:1; 4(2); 5(3); 6; 7(7); 8; 9(3); 10(2); 11; 12(2); 13; 14; 22:1; 2(3); 3(3); 4(2); 7; 8(2); 9(2); 12; 13(2); 14(2); 15(3); 16; 17(3); 19; 20(2); 22(2); 25(3); 26(2); 28(2); 30; 23:1; 2; 3(3); 4; 5(3); 6; 8(3); 9(2); 10; 11; 12; 13(2); 14(2); 15; 17; 18(3); 20; 22(2); 23; 24; 28; 29; 31; 32(3); 34(4); 35(2); 36; 37; 38; 39(4); 40(2); 24:1(4); 2; 3(2); 6(4); 7(2); 8(2); 9(2); 10(3); 25:2; 3(2); 4(2); 5(4); 6(3); 9(7); 10(3); 11(3); 12(2); 14(3); 15; 16(3); 17; 18(3); 19; 20; 21; 22; 23; 24; 25; 26(2); 27(2); 28; 29; 30(2); 32; 33; 34(2); 35; 36; 37; 38; 26:2; 3; 4; 5; 6; 7(2); 8(2); 9(2); 10; 11(3); 12(2); 13(2); 14; 15; 16(2); 17; 18(2); 19(3); 20; 21(4); 22; 23(3); 27:2(2); 3(2); 4; 5(3); 6(2); 7(4); 8(4); 10(2); 11(3); 12(3); 13(2); 15(2); 16; 17; 18(2); 19; 20(2); 21(2); 22(2); 28:1(3); 3; 4; 5; 6(2); 7; 8(4); 10; 11(2); 13; 14; 29:1; 2(2); 3; 5(2); 6(6); 7(2); 8; 10(2); 11(2); 12(3); 13(2); 14(3); 16; 17(2); 18(4); 19; 21(2); 22(2); 23(2); 25; 26(2); 28(3); 31(2); 32; 30:3(3); 4; 5; 6(2); 7; 8; 9; 10(3); 11; 16(2); 17; 18(2); 19(3); 20(2); 21(2); 22; 24; 31:1; 4(2); 5; 6; 7(2); 8(3); 9(2); 10(3); 11; 12(5); 13(3); 14; 15; 16(2); 18(2); 19; 23(2); 24(3); 25; 26(2); 27(2); 28(3); 29; 31; 33(3); 34(2); 35(2); 37; 40(3); 32:2; 3(2); 4(3); 5; 6; 8(2); 9; 10(3); 11(2); 12(2); 14(2); 15(2); 17(2); 18; 19(2); 20(4); 21(3); 22; 23(2); 24(3); 25(2); 28; 29(4); 30; 31; 32(2); 33(3); 35(2); 36; 37(2); 38; 39(2); 40; 41(2); 43; 44(3); 33:3(3); 4(2); 5; 6(3); 7(3); 8(2); 9(3); 10(3); 11(3); 12(2); 13; 14; 15(2); 16(2); 18; 19; 20(2); 21; 22; 25(3); 26(3); 34:1(3); 2(3); 3(3); 5; 7(2); 9; 10(3); 11(4); 14; 15(2); 16(5); 17(3); 18(2); 19; 20(2); 21(3); 22(4); 35:2(2); 3(2); 4; 5(2); 10(2); 11; 13(2); 14(2); 15(3); 17(2); 18(3); 36:2(2); 3; 4; 5; 6(2); 7(2); 8; 9; 12(2); 14(2); 15(2); 16; 17; 18; 19(3); 20(2); 21(3); 23(2); 25; 26(3); 28; 29(4); 30(2); 31(3); 32(2); 37:3(2); 4; 5; 8(4); 10(2); 11; 13(2); 14; 15(2); 16(2); 17(3); 20; 21; 38:1; 2(2); 4; 6(3); 8; 9; 10; 11(4); 12(2); 13(2); 14(2); 15; 17(2); 18; 19(2); 20; 22(3); 23(2); 24; 25(4); 27(2); 28; 39:1(2); 3; 4(3); 5(2); 7; 8(3); 9; 10(2); 12(2); 13; 14; 16(3); 17; 18; 40:1; 2(2); 3(2); 4(3); 5(3); 6; 7(4); 8(3); 9(4); 10(4); 11(2); 12(3); 13; 14; 15(3); 41:1(2); 2(3); 3; 4; 5(3); 6; 7(2); 8(2); 10(3); 11; 12(2); 13; 14(2); 15; 16(4); 17(2); 42:1; 2(2); 3; 4; 5; 7; 8; 9; 10(3); 11; 12(2); 14; 15; 16; 17(2); 18(4); 20(2); 21; 22; 43:2; 4; 5; 6(3); 7; 9; 10(4); 11(3); 12(4); 13; 44:1; 2(3); 3; 4; 6(5); 7(2); 8(2); 9(2); 10; 11; 12(7); 13; 14; 15; 17(5); 18(3); 19(3); 20; 21(5); 22(2); 23(2); 24; 25(4); 27(3); 28; 29; 30; 45:3; 4; 5; 46:2; 3(2); 4; 5(2); 6; 8(4); 9(5); 10; 11; 12; 13; 14(3); 16(2); 18; 19; 22; 23; 25(4); 26(2); 27(3); 47:2(4); 4; 6; 7; 48:1(2); 2; 3; 6; 7(3); 8(2); 9; 10; 11(2); 12(2); 14; 15; 16; 17; 18; 19(2); 20; 21(3); 22(2); 23(2); 24; 25; 26; 28(2); 29(3); 31; 32; 33(2); 34; 35; 36; 37(2); 38; 39; 40; 41; 42; 43(2); 44; 45; 46; 49:1; 2; 3(3); 5; 10(3); 11; 12; 13(2); 14(2); 17; 18(2); 19(2); 20; 22(2); 23; 24(2); 26; 27; 28(2); 29(3); 30; 32(2); 36; 37(2); 38(2); 50:1; 2; 3(2); 4(3); 5; 7; 8; 9(2); 10; 11; 12; 13; 16(2); 18; 19(3);

20(2); 21(3); 22; 23; 24(2); 25; 26; 28; 30; 32(3); 34; 35(2); 36(2); 37(3); 38(2); 39; 40(2); 41(2); 42(2); 43; 44(2); 45; 46; 51:2(2); 3; 4; 6; 8; 9(2); 10; 12; 14; 15; 17; 19; 20; 21(2); 22(3); 23(4); 24(2); 25(2); 27; 28; 29(2); 31; 32; 33; 35(2); 36(2); 37; 39(2); 43; 44(2); 45; 46(4); 47; 48(2); 50; 52; 53; 54; 55(2); 56; 57(5); 58(3); 59; 61(3); 63; 64(2); 52:1; 3; 4(3); 7(3); 8; 9(2); 10; 11(2); 13; 14; 15; 16; 17(3); 18; 19(2); 20; 21; 22(2); 24; 25; 26(2); 27; 28; 29; 30; 31; 32(2); 33; 34; **Lam** 1:3; 4; 6; 7(2); 8; 11; 12; 13(3); 14; 18(2); 19; 22(2); 2:1; 2(2); 5(2); 6(2); 8; 9(3); 10(2); 11; 12; 14(2); 15; 16; 17(2); 18; 20(2); 21(3); 22; 3:2(2); 3; 4(2); 5(2); 8; 11; 12; 16; 18(2); 19(2); 20; 26; 28; 30; 37; 38; 40(2); 41; 42; 43(2); 45; 47(2); 49; 50; 53; 57; 62; 63; 66; 4:7; 11; 12(2); 13; 15; 19; 21(3); 5:1; 2; 3; 4; 5; 6; 7; 12; 14; 20; 21; 22; **Ezek** 1:1; 3; 4(3); 5; 6; 7; 8(2); 10; 11; 12(2); 13(2); 14(2); 16(2); 18; 19; 20; 21; 23(2); 24; 26; 27(3); 28; 2:1(2); 2(2); 3(2); 4(2); 6(3); 8; 9; 10(5); 3:1; 2; 3(3); 4; 5; 6; 7; 8; 10; 11(3); 12; 13(2); 14(2); 15(2); 17; 18; 19; 20(3); 21; 22(2); 23(3); 24(3); 25(2); 26; 27(2); 4:1(2); 2(2); 3(4); 4; 5; 6; 7; 8; 9(3); 10; 12(2); 15; 16(3); 17(3); 5:1(4); 2(3); 3; 4(2); 5; 6(2); 8; 9(2); 10(3); 11; 12(4); 13(3); 14; 15(3); 16; 17(4); 6:2; 3(3); 4; 5(2); 6(4); 7; 9; 10; 11(3); 12(2); 13; 14; 7:2; 3(2); 4; 7; 8(2); 9; 13; 14; 15(4); 16; 17; 19(2); 21(2); 22(2); 23; 24(2); 26(2); 27(2); 8:1; 2(4); 3(4); 4; 5; 7; 8; 9(2); 10(3); 11(3); 13(2); 14; 16(4); 17; 18; 9:2(3); 3; 4(3); 5; 6(4); 7(3); 8(3); 9(4); 10; 11; 10:1(2); 2(3); 3; 4(3); 5; 6; 7(4); 9(2); 12(2); 14; 15; 16; 17; 18; 19(4); 20; 21(2); 22(2); 11:1(3); 2(2); 3; 5; 6; 7; 8; 9(3); 12; 13(2); 15; 16; 17; 18(3); 19(3); 20(4); 21; 22; 23(2); 24(2); 12:2; 3; 4; 5; 6; 7(2); 8; 10; 12(2); 13; 14(2); 15; 16; 18(2); 19(3); 20(2); 21; 22; 23(2); 25(2); 27; 13:1; 2; 3; 6; 7; 8; 9; 10(2); 11(2); 13(2); 14(2); 15(2); 16; 18(3); 19(3); 20; 21(2); 22; 23; 14:1; 2; 3; 4(3); 6; 7(2); 8(3); 9(3); 10; 11; 13(2); 14; 15(2); 16; 17(3); 19(3); 20; 21(4); 22(3); 23(3); 15:4; 5; 7; 16:3(3); 6(2); 7(3); 8(4); 9; 10(2); 11; 12(2); 13(5); 15; 16(2); 17(3); 18(3); 19(2); 20(2); 21; 22(3); 24; 25(2); 26; 27; 28; 29; 31; 33; 36(3); 37(2); 38(2); 39(4); 40(2); 41(3); 42(2); 43; 45(4); 46(2); 48; 49(3); 50(2); 51; 52; 53(3); 54; 55(4); 57(2); 58; 60; 61(2); 62; 63(2); 17:1; 2; 3(3); 4; 5(2); 6(3); 7(3); 8; 9(2); 12(3); 13(2); 14; 15(2); 16; 17(2); 18(2); 19; 20(2); 21(2); 22(3); 23(3); 24(4); 18:2; 5(2); 7; 8(2); 9; 11; 12; 14; 16; 17(2); 18; 19(3); 20; 21(2); 23(2); 24(3); 25; 26; 27(2); 28; 29; 30; 31(2); 32; 19:2; 3(2); 4; 5; 6; 7; 8; 9; 10; 11; 12(2); 13(2); 14(2); 20:1; 3; 5(2); 6; 7; 8(2); 10; 11(2); 12; 13; 15; 16; 19; 20(2); 21(2); 22; 23; 24; 25; 26(2); 27; 28(4); 30; 31; 32; 33; 34(2); 35(2); 37; 38; 39(2); 40(2); 41(2); 43(3); 46; 47(4); 21:1; 2; 3(4); 4; 6; 7(3); 9(2); 11(2); 12; 13; 14; 15; 17; 19; 20; 22; 23; 26(2); 27; 28(4); 31; 22:3; 4(3); 5(2); 7(2); 8; 11; 12(2); 13; 14; 15; 18; 20(4); 21(2); 23; 25; 26(4); 27; 28; 29(3); 30; 31; 23:4(4); 5; 6; 7; 8; 10(2); 11; 12; 16; 17(2); 18; 20; 22; 23(2); 24(4); 25(5); 26; 27; 29(3); 32(2); 33(2); 34(2); 35(2); 36; 37(2); 38; 39; 40(3); 41; 42(2); 43; 44; 45(2); 46; 47(3); 49; 24:3(3); 4; 5; 6; 8; 10; 11; 12; 13; 14(2); 17(2); 18(2); 19; 21(2); 22; 23(2); 24; 25(4); 27(2); 25:2; 3(2); 4(3); 5(2); 6; 7(3); 8; 9; 11(2); 12; 13(2); 14(2); 15; 16(2); 17; 26:1; 3; 4(3); 7(2); 8; 9; 10; 11; 12(3); 13; 14; 16(2); 17(3); 19; 20(2); 21; 27:3; 7; 8; 9(2); 10(2); 11; 12; 13(2); 14; 15; 16; 17(2); 18; 19(3); 21(2); 22(2); 23; 25; 27(4); 29; 30; 31(2); 32; 33; 34; 35; 36; 28:2(2); 4(3); 5; 7(2); 8; 9; 12(2); 13(4); 14; 16(2); 18; 19; 21; 22(3); 23; 24; 25; 26(2); 29:2(2); 3; 4(2); 5(2); 7(2); 8(2); 9(3); 10(3); 11; 12(3); 14(2); 17; 18; 19(2); 21; 30:2; 4(3); 5; 6; 7; 8; 9; 11(2); 12(2); 13; 14; 16(2); 17(2); 18(2); 20; 21; 22(3); 23; 24(2); 25; 26; 31:2; 3(2); 4; 5; 6; 7; 8; 10(2); 11; 12(5); 13; 15(2); 16(2); 17; 18(2); 32:1; 2(3); 3; 4(2); 5; 6; 7(2); 8; 10(2); 12; 14; 15; 16; 18(2); 20; 22; 23; 24; 26(2); 28; 29(2); 30(2); 31(2); 32(2); 33:2(3); 3; 4(2); 6(4); 7; 8; 9; 10(2); 11; 13; 14(2); 15; 16; 18; 19(2); 21(2); 22(2); 24; 25; 26; 27(3); 28; 30(3); 31; 32; 33; 34:1; 2; 3; 4; 5; 6(2); 8(2); 10(2); 11; 12(2); 13(4); 14(2); 15; 16(4); 17(3); 18; 19(2); 20; 21(2); 22(3); 23(2); 24(2); 25(3); 26(2); 27(3); 28(2); 29; 30; 31; 35:2; 3(2); 4; 5; 6; 7(2); 8(3); 9; 10(2); 11(2); 13; 36:1(2); 3(4); 4(2); 5(2); 6(3); 8; 9(3); 10(2); 11(4); 12; 13; 17; 18; 19(2); 20; 23(2); 24; 25(2); 26(2); 27(3); 28; 29(2); 30(2); 31(3); 32; 33; 35(3); 36(2); 37:1(3); 2(3); 3; 4; 5; 6(3); 7(3); 8(2); 9(2); 10(3); 11; 12(3); 13; 14(3); 16(4); 17; 18; 19(4); 20; 21(2); 22(2); 23(2); 24(3); 25(3); 26(3); 27; 38:2(2); 3(2); 4(3); 5(2); 6(2); 7(3); 8(2); 9(2); 10; 11; 12(3); 13(3); 14; 15(2); 18; 19; 20(2); 22(4); 23(2); 39:1(3); 2(3); 3; 4(3); 6(2); 7; 8; 9(6); 10(2); 11(2); 13; 14; 15; 17(4); 18(2); 19; 20(2); 21; 23; 24(2); 25(2); 26(2); 27(2); 28; 29; 40:1; 2; 3(3); 4(3); 5(3); 6(3); 7(2); 9; 10(2); 11; 12(2); 14; 16(3); 17(2); 19; 20(2); 21(3); 22(3); 23; 24(3); 25(2); 26(3); 27; 29(3); 30; 31; 32; 33(4); 34(3); 35; 36(2); 37(2); 38; 39(2); 40; 41; 42(4); 43; 44; 47(2); 48(4); 49(3); 41:1(2); 2(4); 3(3); 4(2); 9; 10(2); 11(2); 12; 13(2); 15(2); 16(2); 17(2); 18(3); 19; 20(2); 22(3); 23; 24; 25; 26(3); 42:1(2); 3; 4; 5; 6(2); 7; 10; 11(4); 12; 13(2); 15; 19; 20; 43:2(2); 3; 4; 5(2); 7(2); 8(2); 9(2); 10; 11(7); 13(2); 14; 17(2); 18(2); 20(3); 21; 22; 23; 24; 25; 26(2); 27(3); 44:2(2); 3; 4(2); 5(4); 7(3); 8; 10; 11(3); 12; 13(2); 14; 15(2); 16(2); 17; 18; 19(2); 23(4); 24(3); 27; 29; 30; 45:1; 3; 4; 5; 6; 7(5); 8; 9(3); 10; 11(2); 12; 13; 15(2); 17(3); 18; 19(2); 20; 22(2); 23(2); 24(2); 25; 46:1; 2(2); 3; 4; 5(2); 6; 7; 8; 9; 10; 11(2); 12(3); 14(2); 15; 19; 20(3); 21(2); 22; 23; 24; 47:1; 2(2); 3(2); 4(2); 5; 6; 7; 8; 9(2); 11; 12(3); 14; 16; 17; 18(4); 22(2); 23; 48:8; 9; 10; 12; 13(2); 14; 15(2); 16; 17(5); 18(2); 21(4); 22(2); 29; 31; 32; 33; 34; 35; **Dan** 1:1; 2(2); 3(2); 4(3); 5(3); 6; 7; 9; 10(2); 11; 12(2); 13(2); 14; 15(2); 16(2); 17(4); 19(2); 20(3); 2:1; 2(2); 3(2); 4; 5(3); 6(3); 7(2); 8; 9(2); 10; 11; 12(2); 13(3); 14; 15; 16; 17(2); 18; 20(3); 21(4); 22(2); 23(3); 24(2); 25; 26(2); 27(2); 28(2); 29; 30; 31(2); 32(2); 33; 34(2); 35(4); 37; 38(3); 40(4); 41(2); 42(3); 44(4); 45(3); 46(2); 47(2); 48(3); 49(2); 3:1; 2(2); 3(2); 4; 5(2); 6(2); 7(3); 8; 9; 10(2); 11(2); 12; 13(2); 14; 15(4); 16(2); 17; 19(3); 20(3); 21(2); 22(2); 23(2); 24(3); 25(2); 26(4); 27(4); 28(4); 29(2); 30; 4:1; 2; 3(2); 4; 5(2); 7(2); 8; 9(2); 10(2); 11(2); 12(2); 13; 14(4); 15(3); 16; 17(2); 19(4); 20(2); 21(2); 22(3); 23(6); 24; 25(3); 26(2); 27; 30; 32(4); 33(2); 34(6); 35; 36(4); 37(4); 5:1; 2(3); 3(3); 4(4); 5(2); 6(2); 7(4); 9; 10; 11(5); 12(2); 13; 14(3); 15; 16(5); 17(3); 18(2); 19(4); 20(2); 21(3); 23(10); 24; 25; 26; 27; 28(2); 29(3); 31; 6:1; 2; 3(2); 4; 6(2); 7(3); 8(2); 10(3); 11(2); 12(4); 13; 14(3); 15(2); 16(2); 17(3); 18(2); 19; 20; 22(2); 23(2); 24(6); 25; 26(3); 27(4); 28; 7:1; 2; 3; 4(4); 5(3); 6(2); 7(4); 8(3); 9(2); 10(2); 11(2); 12; 13(2); 14(4); 15; 16(2); 18(2); 19(2); 20(3); 21(2); 22(2); 23(2); 24(2); 25(4); 26(2); 27(4); 28; 8:2(2); 3(4); 4(2); 5(2); 6; 7(4); 8; 9(2); 10(4); 11(2); 12(2); 13(3); 14; 15; 16(2); 17(2); 18; 19; 20; 21; 22; 23; 24(3); 25; 26(2); 27(3); 9:3(2); 4(6); 5(3); 6(2); 7(2); 8; 9; 11(2); 12(2); 13; 14; 15(2); 16(3); 17(2); 18(3); 19(2); 20(3); 23(2); 24(3); 25(4); 26(4); 27(2); 10:1(2); 5(2); 6(2); 7; 8(2); 9; 10; 11(2); 12(2); 13; 15; 16(3); 18; 19(2); 20(2); 11:1; 2(3); 3; 4(2); 5(2); 6(4); 7(2); 8(4); 10(5); 11(3); 12; 13(3); 15(3); 16; 17(2); 18(2); 19(2); 21(2); 22(2); 23(2); 24(3); 25(3); 26; 27; 28; 29; 30(3); 31(3); 32; 33(3); 35(2); 36(2); 38(3); 39(3); 40(4); 41(2); 42; 43(3); 44(2); 45(3); 12:1(2); 2(2); 3(2); 4(3); 5(2); 6; 7(4); 9(2); 10(2); 11(3); 12(2); 13; **Hos** 1:1(2); 2; 3(3); 4; 6(2); 7; 8; 9; 10; 11(3); 2:1; 2; 3(4); 5(3); 6; 7; 8(3); 9(4); 10; 12(3); 13(2); 14; 15; 16(2); 17; 18(2); 19(2); 20; 21; 22; 23(2); 3:1(2); 2(2); 3; 5(3); 4:2(3); 3(2); 5; 9(2); 11; 12(2); 13(3); 14; 19; 5:1; 3; 4; 5; 6; 7; 11; 12; 13(2); 14(3); 6:1; 3; 4; 5; 6(2); 8; 7:1; 3; 7; 9; 10; 14; 15; 8:1; 4; 6; 7; 10; 13(2); 14(2); 9:2(2); 3; 5; 7; 10; 11; 14; 17; 10:3; 5; 6; 8(2); 12; 14; 11:1; 2; 4(2); 6(2); 9(2); 11; 12; 12:1(3); 2; 3; 4(3); 6(2); 8; 10; 12; 13; 14; 13:2(2); 3(2); 4; 6; 8; 10(2); 11; 15; 16; 14:2; 5; 6; 7; 8; **Joel** 1:2; 3; 4; 5(2); 6(2); 7(2); 9; 11; 12(2); 13(2); 14(2); 16; 19; 20; 2:1; 2(3); 3(2); 4; 7; 9; 10(2); 11; 12; 13(4); 14(3); 16(2); 17(2); 18; 19(4); 20(4); 21; 22(2); 23(3); 24(2); 25; 26(3); 27; 28(2); 29(2); 30(4); 31(2); 32(2); 3:1(2); 2(2); 3; 4(3); 5(2); 6; 7; 8(2); 10; 11(2); 12; 15(2); 16(3); 17; 18(3); 19; 20; **Am** 1:1; 2(3); 3; 5(2); 6; 8(2); 9(2); 11(3); 13; 14(2); 15; 2:1; 2(2); 3(2); 4(2); 5; 6(2); 7(2); 8; 9(2); 10; 11; 12; 3:9(3); 10; 11; 12; 13; 14(2); 15; 4:2; 3; 4; 5; 6; 7; 9(2); 11(2); 13(2); 5:3; 4; 5; 6(2); 7; 8(3); 10; 11; 12(2); 14; 16(2); 18; 19(2); 20; 21; 22; 24; 25; 26; 6:1; 2(2); 4; 5; 6; 7; 8(2); 10(2); 11; 12; 14; 7:2; 4(2); 8(2); 9; 11; 12; 13; 14(2); 15; 16; 17(2); 8:2; 3; 4; 5(2); 6; 8(2); 9(2); 10(3); 12(2); 13; 14(2); 9:1(3); 3(3); 4(2); 5(3); 6(2); 7; 8; 9; 11(2); 12; 13(2); 14(3); 15; **Ob** 1(2); 4; 7; 8; 10; 11; 16(2); 17; 18(3); 19(2); 20; 21; **Jon** 1:2; 3(2); 4; 5(3); 6; 7(2); 8(2); 9(2); 10; 12(2); 14(2); 15(2); 16(2); 17(2); 2:2(3); 3(2); 7; 10; 3:2; 3; 4(3); 5; 6(3); 7(3); 8(3); 9(2); 10(2); 4:1; 2(3); 5(2); 6(2); 7; 8(3); 9; 10; 11(4); **Mic** 1:1(2); 2; 3; 4; 5(2); 6; 7(2); 8(3); 16; 2:1; 2(4); 4; 10; 11(2); 13; 3:1(2); 2(2); 3; 6(2); 7; 8(3); 9(2); 10; 11(2); 12; 4:1(2); 2(4); 3(2); 4(2); 5; 6; 7; 8; 10(2); 11; 13(3); 5:4(3); 5(3); 6(2); 8(3); 9; 10(2); 11; 12; 13; 15(2); 6:1; 2(2); 3; 4(2); 5; 6; 8(2); 10; 11; 12; 14; 15; 16(2); 7:2; 3; 4; 9; 10; 11; 12(2); 13; 14; 16; 17; 18; 19; 20; **Nah** 1:2(3); 3(4); 4(4); 5(2); 6(2); 7; 8; 10; 12; 13; 14; 2:2; 3; 5; 6; 7; 10(3); 11(3); 12; 13(2); 3:1; 2; 3; 4; 5; 6; 7; 9(3); 10; 14; 16; 17(2); 18; **Hab** 1:2(2); 3(3); 4; 5; 6; 7(2); 8; 10(2); 11; 13(2); 15(2); 16(2); 17; 2:1(3); 2(2); 3; 5(4); 6(3); 7; 8(3); 10; 11; 13; 16(2); 17(4); 19; 3:2; 3; 4; 5; 6(3); 10(2); 11; 16; 17(2); 19; **Zeph** 1:3(2); 4; 5; 6; 8(3); 9; 10(2); 12(2); 13; 14; 15(4); 16(2); 17(2); 2:4(2); 6; 7; 8(2); 9(4); 10; 13(2); 14; 15(2); 3:1; 7; 11; 12(2); 13(3); 14; 19(2); 20; **Hag** 1:1; 4; 6(2); 8(3); 9; 10; 11(5); 12(3); 14(4); 2:2(2); 3; 4(3); 6(2); 7(3); 8; 9; 12(2); 13(2); 14(4); 15; 17(2); 19; 20; 21; 22(2); 23; **Zech** 1:3; 4; 5; 6(3); 8(4); 10(3); 11(3); 12(2); 13(2); 14; 15; 16; 17; 18(2); 19(2); 21; 2:1(2); 2(2); 3(2); 4; 5; 9; 10(2); 11(2); 12(2); 3:1; 2; 3; 4(3); 5(3); 7(2); 8; 9; 10; 4:1; 2(3); 3; 4; 5(2); 6; 7; 10; 11(2); 12(2); 13(2); 5:1(2); 2(2); 3; 4(3); 5(2); 6; 7; 8(2); 9(4); 11; 6:1(4); 3; 4; 5(2); 6; 7(4); 8(2); 10(3); 11(2); 12; 13(3); 14; 15(2); 7:2; 3(3); 5(3); 6(2); 7(4); 9; 11; 12; 13(2); 8:3; 4; 5; 7; 8(3); 12; 13(3); 14; 15; 16; 17; 19(4); 21(2); 22(2); 9:1(2); 2(2); 3; 4; 5(3); 6; 7(3); 8; 9(2); 10(2); 13(2); 14(2); 15(2); 17(2); 10:2; 3(2); 5; 6(2); 7(2); 8(2); 9(2); 10(2); 11(2); 12(2); 11:5(2); 6(2); 7(2); 8; 9; 10(2); 12; 13(2); 14; 15; 16; 17(2); 12:1; 2; 3; 4(2); 5; 6(2); 7; 8; 10(4); 12(3); 13(2); 14; 13:1(2); 2(2); 3(3); 4; 6; 7; 8(2); 9(3); 14:1; 2; 3; 4(3); 5; 8(3); 9(2); 10(3); 11; 12(2); 13; 14(2); 15(3); 16(2); 17; 18; 19; 21(3); **Mal** 1:3(2); 4(2); 5; 6(2); 8(3); 11; 12; 13(3); 14(2); 2:1; 2(2); 3(2); 5(3); 6(3); 7; 9; 11(2); 12; 13(2); 14(2); 15(2); 17; 3:1(2); 2(2); 3(3); 4; 5(4); 7(2); 8; 10(2); 11; 12; 14; 15; 16(3); 17; 18(2); 4:1(2); 2(2); 4; 5; 6(3); **Mt** 1:2(2); 3(2); 4; 6; 7; 8; 9; 10; 11; 12(2); 13; 14; 15; 16; 17; 19; 21(2); 23(2); 24; 25(2); 2:2; 3; 4(2); 8(5); 9(2); 11(5); 13(2); 14(2); 15; 16(4); 18; 20(2); 21(2); 22; 23(2); 3:2; 4(3); 5; 6; 7; 9; 10(2); 11; 12(2); 14(2); 15; 16(3); 17; 4:2(2); 4; 6(2); 8(2); 9(2); 10; 11(2); 13(3); 15; 16(2); 17; 18(2); 19; 20; 21; 22(3); 23(3); 24(5); 25(2); 5:1(2); 2; 6; 11(2); 12; 13; 15(2); 16; 18; 19(2); 20; 21; 22; 23; 24(3); 25; 29; 30(2); 32; 37; 38; 40; 41; 42; 43; 44(2); 45(3); 47; 6:2; 4; 5(2); 6(2); 7; 12; 13(3); 17; 18; 19(3); 20(2); 24(3); 25; 29; 30; 33(2); 7:2; 3; 4; 5; 6(2); 7(3); 8(2); 12; 13(2); 14(2); 19; 22; 23; 24; 25(4); 26; 27(5); 28; 29; 8:2(2); 3; 4(2); 7(2); 8(2); 9(6); 10; 11(4); 12; 13(2); 15(3); 16(2); 17; 18; 19; 20(2); 21; 22; 24; 25; 26(3); 27; 29; 32(3); 33(2); 34(2); 9:1; 3; 5; 6; 7(2); 8; 9(2); 10(3); 11(2); 13(2); 14; 15(2); 16; 17(2); 18(3); 19(2); 20(2); 22(2); 23(2); 24; 25(2); 26; 27; 28(2); 30(2); 32; 33(2); 35(3); 36; 10:1(3); 2(2); 3(2); 4; 5(2); 7; 11; 12; 14; 15; 16; 17; 18(2); 21(3); 22; 25; 26; 27; 28(2); 29; 35; 36; 37; 38(2); 39; 40; 41; 42; 11:1; 2; 3; 4(3); 5(3); 6; 9; 12(2); 13; 14; 16; 17(3); 18; 19(4); 21(2); 22; 23; 25(4); 27(2); 28(2); 29(3); 30; 12:1(3); 2; 3; 4; 5; 7; 10(2); 11(2); 13(2); 14; 15(2); 18; 20; 21; 22(4); 23(2); 25(2); 27; 29(2); 30; 31; 33(2); 35; 37; 38; 39(3); 40(2); 41(2); 42(2); 43; 44(2); 45(4); 46; 47; 48(2); 49(3); 50(2); 13:1; 2(3); 4(3); 5; 6; 7(3); 8; 10(2); 11; 12; 13; 14(4); 15(3); 16; 17(4); 19(2); 20; 22(3); 23(2); 25(2); 26; 27; 28; 30(2); 31; 32(2); 33; 34; 36(2); 37; 39; 40; 41(2); 42(2); 44(2); 46(2); 47; 48(2); 50(2); 52; 54(3); 55(2); 56; 57; 14:2(2); 3(2); 5; 6; 9(2); 10; 11(3); 12(4); 14(3); 15(2); 17(2); 19(6); 20(2); 21; 22; 23; 26(2); 28(2); 29; 30; 31(3); 32; 33; 35; 36(2); 15:1; 3; 4(2); 8; 9; 10; 12; 13; 14; 15; 17; 18; 21(2); 22(2); 23(2); 24; 25; 26(2); 27; 28(2); 29(2); 30(3); 31(2); 32(3); 34(2); 36(5); 37(2); 38; 39(2); 16:1(2); 2; 3(2); 4(4); 6(2); 7; 9; 10; 11; 12; 14; 16; 17(2); 18(3); 19(3); 21(5); 22; 23; 24(2); 26; 27; 17:1; 2(2); 3(2); 4(2); 5; 6(2); 7(3); 10; 11(2); 12; 14(2); 15(2); 17(2); 18(3); 19; 20(2); 21; 23(3); 24; 25; 27(4); 18:3(2); 6; 8; 9(2); 12(2); 13; 15(2); 17(2); 18; 21(2); 24; 25(3); 26; 27; 28(3); 29(2); 30(2); 31(2); 34(2); 19:1; 2(2); 3; 4(3); 5(4); 7; 9(3); 12(2); 13; 14; 15(2); 16; 19(2); 21(3); 24; 26; 27(2); 29(2); 30; 20:3(2); 4(2); 5(2); 6(3); 7; 8; 9; 10; 11; 12(2); 13; 14; 16; 17; 18(3); 19(4); 20; 21(2); 22(2); 23(2); 24; 25(2); 27; 28; 30; 32(2); 34(3); 21:1; 2(3); 3(2); 5; 6; 7(2); 8(2); 9; 10; 12(4); 13; 14(2); 15(3); 16(3); 17(2); 19(3); 20; 21(3); 22; 23(3); 24; 25; 27(2); 28(2); 29(2); 30(3); 31; 32(4); 33(4); 35(2); 36; 38; 39(2); 41; 42; 43; 44; 45; 22:1(3); 3(2); 4(2); 5; 6(2); 7(2); 9; 10(3); 12; 13(3); 15; 16(2); 18; 20(2); 21(2); 22(2); 23; 24; 25; 26; 29; 32; 33; 35; 37; 38; 39; 40; 46; 23:1; 2; 3(2); 4; 5; 7; 8; 10; 12(2); 13; 14(2); 15(3); 17; 18; 19; 20; 21; 22(2); 23(6); 24; 25(3); 26; 27(2); 28; 29(2); 30; 34(4); 35; 37; 24:1(2); 2; 3(2); 4(2); 5; 6(2); 7(3); 9(2); 10(2); 11; 12; 14(2); 18; 19; 20; 22; 24(3); 27; 29(2); 30(3); 31(2); 32; 35; 36; 38(2); 39(2); 40; 41; 43; 45; 49(3); 50; 51(3); 25:1; 2; 3; 5; 6; 7; 8; 9(2); 10(3); 12; 14; 15(3); 16(2); 17; 18(2); 19; 20; 21; 22; 23; 24(2); 25(3); 26(3); 27; 28; 29; 30(2); 31; 32; 33; 35(3); 36(3); 37(2); 38(2); 39; 40(2); 41; 42(2); 43(4); 44; 46; 26:2; 3; 4(2); 6; 7; 9; 15(2); 18(2); 19; 22(2); 23; 25; 26(4); 27(2); 30; 31; 33; 35; 36(2); 37(4); 38; 39(2); 40(2); 41; 42; 43(2); 44; 45(3); 47(3); 49(2); 50(2); 51(3); 53; 55(2); 56; 57(2); 58(2); 59; 61(2); 62(2); 63(2); 64; 66; 67(2); 69; 71(2); 73(2); 74; 75(2); 27:1; 2(2); 3(2); 4; 5(3); 6; 7(2); 9; 10; 11; 12(2); 16; 20(2); 21; 24; 25(3); 26; 27; 28(2); 29(3); 30(2); 31(2); 33; 35(2); 37; 38; 39; 40(2); 41; 42; 46; 48(3); 50(2); 51(2); 52(2); 53(2); 54(2); 55; 56(2); 58; 60(3); 61(2); 62; 64(2); 66(2); 28:1; 2(4); 3; 4(2); 5; 7(3); 8(2); 9(3); 10(2); 11; 12; 13; 14(2); 15(2); 18(3); 19(3); 20; **Mk** 1:4; 5(2); 6(3); 7(2); 9; 10(2); 13(3); 15(3); 16(2); 17; 18; 19; 20(3); 21(2); 22(2); 23; 25; 26(2); 27; 28; 29(2); 30; 31(4); 32; 33; 34(2); 35(2); 36(2); 39(2); 40; 41(2); 42; 43(2); 44(2); 45(3); 2:1(2); 2; 4; 6(2); 9; 11; 12(2); 13(2); 14(2); 15(3); 16(5); 18(3); 19; 20; 21; 22(2); 23; 24; 25(2); 26(2); 27(2); 3:1(2); 3; 5(3); 6; 7(2); 8(5); 11(2); 13(3); 14; 15(2); 17; 19(2); 22(2); 23; 25; 26(2); 27(2); 28; 31(2); 32(3); 34(3); 35(2); 4:1(4); 2; 4(3); 5; 6; 7(4); 8(3); 9; 11; 12(4); 13; 15(2); 17(2); 19(3); 20(2); 24; 26; 27(4); 32(2); 33; 34; 36; 37(2); 38(2); 39(4); 41(3); 5:2; 3; 4(3); 5(4); 6; 7(2); 9; 13(4); 14(3); 15(5); 16(2); 18; 19(2); 20(3); 21; 22(2); 23(3); 24(2); 26(2); 27; 29; 30(2); 31; 32; 33(3); 34(2); 37(2); 38(3); 39; 40(4); 41; 42(2); 43; 6:1(2); 2(3); 3(4); 4; 5; 6; 7(3); 9; 11(2); 12; 13(3); 14(2); 15; 17(2); 19; 20(4); 21; 22(5); 24(2); 25; 26(2); 27(3); 28(2); 29(2); 30(2); 31(4); 33(3); 34(2); 35(2); 36(2); 37(4); 38(3); 40; 41(5); 42; 43(2); 45; 46; 47; 48; 49(2); 50(2); 51(3); 53; 54; 55; 56(2); 7:1; 3; 4(3); 5; 6; 7; 8(2); 10(2); 13; 14; 19; 20; 23; 24(4); 25(2); 26; 27; 28(2); 30(2); 31; 32(2); 33(4); 34; 35(2); 37(2); 8:1(2); 2; 3; 5; 6(4); 7; 8(2); 9; 10; 11; 12; 13(2); 14; 15; 16; 18(2); 20; 22(2); 23(3); 24(2); 25(3); 27(2); 28; 29; 31(6); 32(2); 33; 34(2); 35; 36; 38(2); 9:1; 2(3); 4(2); 5(3); 7(3); 11; 12(4); 13; 14(2); 15; 16; 17; 18(2); 19; 20(3); 21; 22(3); 24; 25(2); 26(2); 27(2); 28; 29; 30(2); 31(3); 32; 33; 35(3); 36(2); 37; 38; 42; 44; 45; 46; 47; 48; 49; 50; 10:1(3); 2; 3(2); 4; 5(2); 6; 7(2); 8; 11; 12(2); 14(2); 16(2); 17; 19; 20(2); 21(5); 22; 23; 24(2); 26; 27; 28; 29(2); 30(6); 31; 32(4); 33(4); 34(5); 35; 36; 37; 38; 39; 40; 41(2); 42(2); 44; 45; 46; 47(2); 49; 50(2); 51; 52(2); 11:1; 2(3); 3(2); 4(2); 6; 7(2); 8(3); 9; 11(2); 13; 14; 15(4); 16; 18(3); 21; 22; 23(2); 24; 25; 27(2); 28(2); 29(2); 31; 33(3); 12:1(4); 3(3); 4(2); 5(4); 7; 8(2); 9(2); 11; 12(2); 13; 14; 16(2); 17(4); 18; 19(3); 20; 21(3); 22; 24; 26; 28; 30(2); 31; 32; 33(4); 35; 37; 39; 40; 41(2); 42; 43; 13:1; 2(3); 3; 4; 5; 6; 7; 8(4); 9(2); 10; 11; 12(3); 13; 16; 17; 18; 20; 22(3); 24; 25; 26; 27(2); 28; 31; 32; 33; 34(3); 37; 14:1(4); 3(2); 4; 5(2); 7; 11(2); 12; 13(3); 15; 16(3); 18; 19(3); 20; 22(4); 23(2); 24; 26; 27; 31; 32; 33(4); 34; 35(2); 36; 37(2); 38; 39(2); 40(2); 41(2); 43(4); 44; 45(2); 46; 47(3); 48(2); 49; 50; 51; 52(2); 53(3); 54(2); 55; 57; 58; 60(2); 61; 62(2); 63; 64; 65(4); 67(2); 68(2); 69(2); 70(2); 71; 72; 15:1(4); 2; 3; 7; 12; 15; 16; 17(2); 18; 19(2); 20(2); 21(2); 22; 24; 25; 26; 27; 28; 29(3); 30; 32; 34; 36(2); 37(2); 39; 40(2); 41(2); 43(2); 44; 46(3); 47(2); 16:1(2); 3; 5(2); 7; 8(3); 10(2); 11(2); 12; 13(2); 14(2); 15(2); 16; 17; 18(2); 19; 20(3); **Lk** 1:2; 5; 6(2); 7; 10; 12(2); 13(2); 14(3); 15; 16; 17(2); 18(2); 19(4); 20; 21(2); 22(2); 23; 24; 28; 29; 31(3); 32(2); 33(2); 35(3); 36; 38; 39; 40(2); 41(2); 42(2); 46; 47; 49; 50; 52; 53; 55; 56(2); 57; 58; 59; 60; 63(2); 64(2); 65; 66(2); 67; 68; 69; 71; 72; 75; 76; 79; 80(2); 2:1; 4; 7(3); 9(3); 12; 13(2); 14; 15; 16(4); 18; 19; 20(2); 21; 24; 25(4); 26; 27; 28(2); 32; 33(2); 34(3); 36; 37(3); 38(2); 40(3); 42; 43(2); 44(2); 46; 47(2); 48(2); 49; 51(2); 52(4); 3:1(2); 2; 3; 5(3); 6; 8; 9(2); 11(2); 12; 13; 14(2); 15; 16; 17(2); 18; 19; 21; 22(2); 4:1; 2(2); 3; 6(3); 8(3); 9; 11; 12(2); 14; 15; 16(2); 17(2); 18; 20(3); 21; 22(2); 25(2); 27(2); 29(3); 31; 32; 33; 35(3); 36(3); 37; 38(2); 39(4); 40(2); 41(3); 42(4); 44; 5:2(2); 3(3); 4; 5(2); 6(2); 7(3); 9; 10(3); 11; 12(3); 13; 14(3); 15(2); 16; 17(3); 18; 19(2); 21(2); 22; 23; 24; 25; 26(3); 27(2); 28; 29(2); 30(4); 31; 33(3); 34; 36; 37(3); 38; 39; 6:1(2); 2; 3; 4(2); 5; 6(2); 7; 8(4); 10(3); 11; 12; 13(2); 14(3); 15(2); 16; 17(7); 18; 19(2); 20; 22(3); 23; 25; 28; 29; 30; 31; 33; 34; 35(4); 37(3); 38(2); 39; 41; 42; 45; 46; 47(2); 48(3); 49(3); 7:2(2); 3; 4; 5; 6; 7; 8(6); 9(2); 10; 11(2); 12(3); 13; 14(3); 15(2); 16(2); 17(2); 19; 21(3); 22(3); 23; 25; 26; 29; 30; 31(2); 32(3); 33; 34(4); 36(2); 37; 38(5); 39; 40(2); 41; 42; 43(2); 44(2); 49; 8:1(3); 2(3); 3(3); 4(2); 5(3); 6; 7(3); 8; 10(2); 12(2); 13(2); 14(3); 15(2); 17; 18; 19(2); 20(2); 21(3); 22(2); 23(3); 24(6); 25(4); 27(2); 28; 29(4); 30; 31; 32; 33(3); 34(2); 35(4); 37(2); 39(3); 41(4); 42; 43; 44(2); 45(4); 47(2); 48; 50; 51(3); 52; 53; 54; 55(2); 56; 9:1(3); 2; 3(2); 4; 5; 6(2); 7; 8(2); 10(2); 11(3); 12(4); 13(3); 15(2); 16(4); 17(2); 18(2); 19(2); 20; 21(2); 22(5); 23(2); 25; 26(3); 28(2); 29(2); 30(2); 31; 32(3); 33(2); 34(2); 35; 36; 39(3); 41(3); 42(3); 43; 45(2); 47(2); 48(2); 49(2); 52(2); 54(3); 55(2); 56; 58(2); 59; 60; 61(2); 62; 10:1(2); 4; 6; 7(2); 8; 9(2); 10(2); 13(2); 14; 15; 16; 18; 19(3);

21(4); 22(3); 23; 24(4); 25(2); 27(3); 28(2); 29; 30(3); 31; 32(2); 33; 34(4); 35(2); 37(2); 38; 39(2); 40(2); 41(3); 42; 11:4(2); 5(3); 6; 7(4); 8(2); 9(3); 10(2); 14(3); 17; 19; 22(2); 23; 24; 25(2); 26(4); 27(3); 28; 29(2); 31(2); 32(2); 37(2); 39(2); 42(4); 43; 44(2); 45; 46(2); 47; 48; 49(3); 51; 52; 53(3); 54; 12:3; 4(2); 6; 10; 11(2); 15(2); 17; 18(3); 19(2); 21; 23; 24; 25; 27; 28; 29; 30; 31; 33; 35; 36(2); 37(3); 38(2); 39; 42(2); 45(5); 46(3); 47(2); 48; 49; 50; 52; 53(3); 54; 55(2); 56; 57; 58; 13:2(2); 4; 6(2); 7; 8(2); 9; 11(3); 12; 13(3); 14(3); 15(2); 17(2); 18; 19(4); 20; 21; 22(3); 23; 24; 25(5); 26(2); 28(5); 29(3); 30(2); 31; 32(4); 33; 34; 35; 14:2; 3(2); 4(3); 6; 9(4); 10; 11; 12; 14; 16; 17; 18(2); 19(2); 20; 21(6); 22(2); 23(2); 25(2); 26(5); 27(2); 28; 29; 30; 31; 32; 15:1; 2(3); 4; 5; 6(2); 8; 9(2); 12; 13(2); 14; 15(2); 16(2); 17(2); 18(3); 19; 20(6); 21(3); 22(3); 23(4); 24(3); 25(3); 26; 27(3); 28(2); 29(2); 31(2); 32(4); 16:1; 2; 5; 6(3); 7(3); 9; 10; 12; 13(3); 14; 15; 16(2); 17(2); 18(2); 19(2); 21; 22(2); 23(3); 24(3); 25(2); 26(2); 29; 30; 31; 17:2; 3; 4(2); 5; 6(2); 7(2); 8(5); 11; 13(2); 14; 15(2); 16(2); 17; 19; 20; 22; 23; 25; 26; 27(2); 29(2); 31(2); 33; 34; 35; 36; 37(2); 18:1; 3; 4; 7(2); 9; 10; 11; 13; 14; 16(2); 20; 21; 22(3); 24; 26; 28; 30; 31(2); 32(3); 33(2); 34; 36; 38; 40(2); 43(3); 19:1; 2; 3; 4; 5(4); 6(2); 8(2); 9; 10; 11; 12; 13; 14; 15; 17; 18; 21; 22(2); 24(2); 26; 27; 29(2); 30; 31; 32; 34; 35(2); 36; 37; 38; 39; 40; 41; 43; 44(3); 45(2); 47(2); 48; 20:1(2); 2; 3(2); 5; 8; 9; 10; 11(2); 12(3); 15; 16(3); 17; 19(2); 20(2); 21(2); 23; 24(2); 25(2); 26(2); 27; 28(2); 29(2); 30(2); 31(3); 34(3); 35; 36; 37; 39; 41; 46; 47; 21:1(2); 2; 5; 7; 8(2); 9; 10; 11(5); 12(3); 15; 16(3); 17; 21; 23(2); 24(3); 25(4); 26; 27; 28; 29; 30; 33; 34(2); 36(2); 37(2); 22:2(2); 4(2); 5(2); 6; 8(3); 10; 13(2); 14; 17(3); 19(3); 22; 25(2); 26; 29; 30(2); 31; 32; 33; 35(2); 36(3); 37; 38; 39; 41(3); 44; 45; 46; 47(3); 50(2); 51(3); 52(2); 53; 54; 55; 56(2); 58(2); 61(3); 62; 63; 64(2); 65; 66(2); 68; 71; 23:1; 2(2); 3; 4; 7; 8; 10(3); 11(2); 12; 13; 14; 15; 16; 18(2); 19; 22; 23(2); 25(2); 26; 27(3); 28; 29; 30; 33(3); 34(2); 35; 36; 37; 38(2); 39; 41; 43; 44; 45; 46; 48(2); 49; 50; 51; 52; 53; 54; 55(3); 56(3); 24:1; 3; 4; 5; 7(2); 8; 9(2); 10; 11(2); 12(3); 14; 15(2); 17(2); 18(2); 19(3); 20(3); 22; 24(2); 25; 26; 27(2); 28; 29(2); 30(2); 31(2); 32(2); 33(3); 34; 35(2); 36; 37(2); 38(2); 39(3); 40; 41; 42; 43(2); 44(2); 45; 46(2); 47(2); 48; 50(3); 51; 52(2); 53(2); **Jn** 1:1(2); 3; 4; 5(2); 10(2); 11; 14(4); 15; 16(2); 17; 19; 20; 21(2); 25; 29; 32(2); 33; 34(2); 36; 37; 38; 39(3); 40; 41; 42; 43(2); 44; 45(2); 46(2); 47; 48; 49; 50; 51(3); 2:1; 2; 3; 7; 8(3); 9; 10(2); 11(2); 12(2); 13; 14(4); 15(3); 16; 18; 19(2); 20; 22(2); 25; 3:2; 3; 4; 5; 6; 8(2); 9; 10(2); 11(2); 12; 14; 19(2); 20; 22(3); 23(2); 25; 26(3); 27; 29; 31; 32(3); 35; 36; 4:1; 3; 10(3); 11; 12(2); 13; 16; 17; 18; 20; 23(2); 24(2); 27(2); 28; 30; 34; 35(2); 36(3); 37; 38; 39; 40; 41; 42; 43; 46; 47(2); 48; 50; 51(2); 52; 53(2); 5:1; 4; 6; 8; 9(3); 11; 12; 14; 15; 16; 17; 19; 20(2); 21; 24(2); 25(2); 27; 29(2); 30; 32; 33; 35(2); 37; 39; 43; 44; 6:3(2); 5; 9; 11(4); 13; 15; 17(3); 19(2); 21; 22; 24; 25; 26(2); 29; 30; 33; 35(2); 36; 37; 40(3); 42(2); 43; 44; 45(2); 49; 50; 51; 53; 54(2); 55; 56(2); 57; 58; 63; 64; 65; 66; 69; 70; 7:3; 11; 12; 14; 15; 16; 18; 20; 21(2); 22; 26; 28(2); 29; 31(2); 32(2); 33; 34(2); 35; 36(2); 37(2); 42; 45; 51; 52(2); 53; 8:2(3); 3(2); 6; 7; 8(2); 9(2); 10; 11(2); 14(3); 16; 18; 20; 21(2); 23; 25; 26(2); 28; 29; 32(2); 33; 35; 38; 39; 42; 44(3); 46; 48(2); 49; 50(2); 52(2); 53; 55(2); 56(2); 57; 59(2); 9:2; 6(2); 7(3); 8(2); 11(6); 14; 15(2); 16; 18; 19; 20(2); 24; 25; 27; 28; 30; 31; 34(3); 35; 36; 37(2); 38; 39(2); 40; 10:1; 3(3); 4(2); 8; 9(3); 10(3); 12(4); 13; 14(2); 15; 16(4); 18; 20(2); 22; 23; 24; 25; 27(2); 28(2); 29; 30; 33; 35; 36; 38(2); 40(2); 41; 42; 11:1; 2; 5(2); 8; 11; 15; 19(2); 20; 25; 26(2); 28(3); 29; 31(2); 32; 33(2); 34(2); 37; 38; 41(2); 42; 44(4); 45; 46; 47(2); 48(3); 49; 50; 52; 54; 55(2); 56; 57; 12:2; 3(2); 5; 6(2); 9; 11; 13(2); 16; 17; 21; 22(3); 24; 25; 26; 27; 28; 29; 30; 32; 34; 36(2); 38; 40(2); 41; 44; 45; 47(2); 48; 49; 50; 13:2; 3(2); 4(2); 5(2); 6; 7; 9; 10; 12; 13(2); 14; 20; 21(2); 26; 30; 31; 32; 33; 14:3(3); 4(2); 5; 6; 7(2); 8; 9; 10; 11; 12; 13; 16(2); 17; 19; 20(2); 21(4); 22; 23(4); 24; 26; 28; 29; 30; 31; 15:1; 2; 4; 5; 6(4); 7(2); 10; 11; 16(3); 22; 24(2); 27; 16:3; 4; 5; 8(3); 10; 13; 14; 15; 16(3); 17(4); 19(4); 20(2); 22(2); 23; 24; 26; 27; 28(2); 29; 30; 32(2); 17:1; 3(2); 5; 6; 8(3); 10(3); 11; 12; 13; 14; 19; 21; 22; 23(3); 25; 26(3); 18:1; 2; 3(3); 4; 5; 6; 7; 10(2); 12(3); 13; 15(3); 16(2); 18(4); 19; 20(2); 22; 25(2); 27; 28; 29; 30; 31; 33; 35; 37; 38(2); 19:1; 2(3); 3; 4; 5(2); 6(2); 7; 9(2); 10; 13; 14(2); 16; 17; 18(2); 19(2); 20(2); 23(2); 24; 25(2); 26; 27; 29(2); 30; 31; 32(2); 33; 34(2); 35(3); 37; 38(2); 39(2); 40; 41; 20:1; 2(4); 3(2); 4(2); 5(2); 6(2); 7; 8(2); 11(2); 12(2); 13; 14(2); 15; 16; 17(4); 18(2); 19(2); 20; 22(2); 25(2); 26(4); 27(3); 28(3); 29; 30; 31; 21:1; 2; 3(2); 6(3); 7; 9(2); 11(3); 12; 13(3); 17; 18(3); 19; 20; 24(2); 25; **Acts** 1:1; 3; 4; 7; 8(4); 9; 10; 13(6); 14(3); 15(3); 16; 17; 18(2); 19; 20(2); 21; 23(2); 24(2); 25; 26(3); 2:2(2); 3; 4(2); 5; 6(2); 7; 8; 9(4); 10(3); 11; 12; 14(3); 17(2); 18(3); 19(3); 20(2); 21; 22; 23(2); 26; 29(3); 30; 33(2); 36; 37(3); 38(2); 39(2); 40(2); 41; 42(3); 43(2); 44; 45(3); 46(2); 47(2); 3:1; 2; 3; 4; 6(2); 7(4); 8(3); 9(2); 10(2); 11; 13(2); 14(2); 15; 16(2); 19; 20; 23; 24(2); 25(2); 4:1; 2; 3(2); 4; 5(2); 6(2); 7; 8; 10; 13(4); 14; 16; 18(2); 19(2); 20; 23(3); 24(4); 25; 26(2); 27(2); 28; 29; 30(2); 31(2); 32; 33(2); 34; 35(2); 36; 37(2); 5:2(3); 3; 4; 5; 6(3); 8; 9; 10(4); 11; 12(3); 14(2); 15(2); 16(2); 17(2); 18(2); 19(2); 20; 21(5); 22(2); 23; 24; 25(2); 26; 27(2); 28(2); 29(2); 31(2); 32(2); 33; 34; 35; 36(2); 37(2); 38(2); 40(4); 42(3); 6:2(2); 3; 4; 5(5); 6; 7(2); 8(3); 9(2); 10(2); 11; 12(4); 13; 14; 15; 7:2(2); 3(3); 4(2); 5(2); 6(2); 7(3); 8(4); 9; 10(5); 11(3); 13(2); 14(2); 15(2); 16(2); 17; 19; 20(2); 21; 22(3); 24(3); 26(2); 27; 29; 30; 31; 32(3); 34(2); 35(2); 36(3); 38; 39; 41(2); 42(2); 43(2); 46; 49; 51(2); 52(2); 53; 54; 55(2); 56(2); 57; 58(3); 59(2); 60(2); 8:1(2); 2(2); 3(2); 5; 6(2); 7(2); 8; 9; 11; 12(2); 13(3); 14; 17; 18; 22; 23; 24; 25; 26; 27(3); 28; 29; 30(2); 31(3); 32; 33; 34; 35; 36; 37(2); 38(3); 39; 40; 9:1; 2; 3; 4; 5; 6(3); 7; 8(2); 9(2); 10(2); 11(2); 12(2); 14; 15; 17(4); 18(3); 21(2); 22; 24(2); 25; 26(2); 27(4); 28; 29(2); 30; 31(4); 33; 34(2); 35(2); 36; 37; 38(2); 39(3); 40(5); 41(3); 42(2); 10:2(2); 3; 4(3); 5; 7(2); 9; 10; 11(3); 12; 13(2); 15; 16; 17; 18(2); 20; 21; 22(3); 23(2); 24(3); 25(2); 27(2); 30(2); 31(2); 32; 33; 34; 35; 37; 38(2); 39(2); 40; 41; 42(3); 45; 46; 48; 11:1; 2; 3; 5(2); 6(2); 7(2); 10; 12; 13(2); 14; 15; 18; 19; 20; 21(3); 22; 23(2); 24(2); 26(3); 27; 28; 30(2); 12:3; 4; 6(2); 7(4); 8(4); 9(2); 10(4); 11(3); 13; 14; 16(2); 17(4); 19(4); 20(2); 21; 22(2); 23(2); 24; 25(3); 13:1(2); 2(2); 3(2); 4; 5; 7(2); 10(2); 11(4); 13(2); 14(2); 15(3); 16(2); 17(2); 19; 20; 21; 22(2); 25; 26(2); 27; 28; 29; 32; 34; 36; 39; 41; 43(2); 45(2); 46(3); 48(2); 49; 50(4); 51; 52(2); 14:1(2); 2; 3; 4; 5(3); 6(3); 7; 8; 9; 10(2); 12(2); 13; 14(2); 15(3); 17(2); 18; 19(3); 20(2); 21(3); 22; 23; 24; 27(2); 15:1(2); 2(5); 3(2); 4(4); 5; 6; 7(4); 9(2); 12(3); 13(2); 15; 16(2); 20; 22(3); 23(2); 24; 25; 27; 28; 29; 30; 32(2); 33; 35(2); 36(2); 38; 39(2); 40; 41(2); 16:1(2); 2; 3(2); 4(2); 5; 6; 9(3); 11; 12(2); 13(3); 15(3); 17(2); 18(3); 19(2); 20(2); 21; 22(2); 23; 24; 25(3); 26(2); 27(3); 29(2); 30(2); 31(2); 32; 33(4); 34; 35; 36; 37(3); 38(2); 39(3); 40(3); 17:1; 2; 3(3); 4(4); 5(3); 6; 7; 8(2); 9; 10; 11; 12; 13; 14; 15(2); 17(2); 18(3); 19(2); 21; 22; 23; 24(2); 25; 26(3); 27; 28(2); 29; 32; 34(2); 18:1; 2(2); 3; 4(3); 5(2); 6(2); 7(2); 8(2); 9; 10; 11(2); 12; 14; 15(2); 16; 17; 18(3); 19(3); 21; 22(3); 23(2); 24; 25(2); 26(2); 27(2); 19:1(2); 3; 6(3); 8(3); 9(2); 10(2); 12(2); 15(3); 16(2); 17(3); 18(2); 19(3); 20; 21; 22; 23; 25; 26(2); 27(2); 28; 29(2); 30; 32(2); 33(3); 35(2); 36; 38(2); 41; 20:1; 2; 3(2); 4(6); 6; 7; 9(3); 10; 11(2); 12(2); 13; 14(2); 15(2); 17; 18; 19; 20(2); 21(2); 22; 23; 24; 25; 28; 31(2); 32(2); 34; 35; 36(2); 37(2); 38; 21:1(2); 2(2); 3; 4; 5(5); 6; 7(2); 8(3); 10; 11(3); 12; 13; 15(2); 16; 17; 18; 20(3); 24(4); 25(2); 26; 27; 28(3); 30(4); 32(4); 33(4); 34(2); 38; 39; 40(2); 22:1; 2; 3; 4(2); 5(2); 6; 7(2); 8; 9(2); 10(3); 11; 13(3); 14(2); 15; 16(3); 17; 18(2); 19; 20(2); 22(3); 23(2); 24; 25(2); 26; 27; 28; 29(2); 30(4); 23:1; 2; 3; 4; 6(3); 7(3); 8; 9(2); 10(2); 11; 12(2); 14(2); 16(2); 17; 18(3); 19; 20; 21; 22; 23(2); 24(2); 27; 28; 30(2); 31; 32; 33; 34(2); 35; 24:1; 2(2); 3; 5; 6(2); 7; 9; 12; 14; 15; 16; 17; 22; 23(2); 24(2); 25(2); 26; 27; 25:2(2); 4; 5; 6(2); 7; 9(2); 13(2); 15; 16; 17; 19; 20(2); 23(3); 24(3); 25; 26; 27; 26:1; 3; 6(2); 7; 10(2); 11(3); 12; 13; 14(2); 15; 16(3); 18(2); 20(4); 21; 22(2); 23(2); 25; 29(2); 30(2); 31; 27:1(2); 3(4); 5(2); 6; 7; 9; 10(2); 11; 12(3); 15; 16; 17(2); 18; 20; 21(4); 22; 23; 24; 27; 28(4); 29; 30; 31; 32; 33(3); 35(3); 36; 37(2); 38; 40(4); 41(2); 42(2); 43(2); 44(3); 28:2(3); 3(2); 5; 6(2); 7; 8(5); 9; 10; 12; 13(3); 14(2); 15(3); 17(2); 20; 23(2); 24(2); 26(4); 27(3); 28; 29(2); 30; 31; **Rom** 1:4; 5; 7(2); 12; 14(2); 16; 18; 20; 21; 23(4); 25(2); 27; 28; 2:3(2); 4; 5(2); 7; 8(2); 9(2); 10(2); 12; 15; 17(2); 18(2); 19; 20; 27(2); 29; 3:4; 8(2); 9; 14; 16; 17; 19; 21; 22; 23; 26; 30; 4:3; 7; 11; 12; 14; 17; 19(2); 21; 22; 25; 5:2; 3; 4(2); 11; 12(2); 15; 16; 17; 6:13(2); 18; 19; 22(2); 7:6; 9; 10; 11; 12(3); 23; 8:2; 6; 10; 17(2); 22; 28; 30; 34; 9:2; 4; 5; 9; 10; 15; 17; 18; 21; 22; 23; 25; 26; 28; 29(2); 33(2); 10:1; 3; 8; 9; 10; 12; 14(2); 15; 17; 18; 20; 21; 11:3(3); 6; 7; 8; 9(3); 10; 12; 14; 16; 17(4); 20; 22; 23; 24; 26(2); 29; 33(2); 35; 36(2); 12:2(3); 5; 14; 15; 13:1; 2; 3; 9; 11; 12; 13(3); 14; 14:3; 6(3); 7; 8; 9(3); 11; 14; 17(3); 18; 19; 15:1; 4; 5; 6(2); 9(2); 10; 11; 12(2); 13; 18; 19(2); 20; 21; 23; 24; 26; 27; 28; 30; 31; 32; 16:2(2); 3; 7(2); 9; 12; 13(2); 14; 15(4); 17(2); 18(2); 19; 20; 21(2); 23(2); 25; 26; **1 Cor** 1:1; 2; 3(2); 5; 10(2); 14; 19; 22; 23; 24(2); 25; 27; 28(3); 30(3); 2:1; 2; 3; 4(3); 3:1; 2(2); 3(2); 4; 5; 8(2); 10; 13; 16; 20; 23(2); 4:1; 5; 6; 7; 8; 9; 11(4); 12; 17; 19; 21; 5:1; 2(2); 8(2); 6:1; 2; 6; 8(2); 11(2); 13(3); 14(2); 15; 19; 20; 7:2; 3; 4; 5(2); 7; 8; 11; 12; 13; 14; 17; 19; 28; 31; 34(2); 35(2); 36; 37; 40; 8:2; 4; 5; 6(3); 7; 11; 12; 9:4; 5; 6; 7(2); 10; 13; 20; 25; 27; 10:2; 4(2); 7(3); 8; 9; 10; 11; 17; 20(2); 21(2); 26; 27; 28(2); 11:2; 3; 5; 7; 18; 21(2); 22(2); 24(2); 26; 27; 28(2); 29(2); 30(2); 34; 12:3; 6; 11; 12; 13; 16; 19; 21; 23(2); 26; 27; 28; 31; 13:1; 2(4); 3(2); 4; 9; 13; 14:1; 3(2); 10; 11; 15(2); 21(2); 23(2); 24; 25(3); 27; 28(2); 29; 31; 32; 35; 39; 40; 15:1; 4(2); 5; 10; 11; 14(2); 15; 17; 20; 24(2); 30; 32; 34; 35; 37; 38; 39; 40(2); 41; 44; 45; 46; 48; 49; 50; 52(2); 53; 54; 56; 16:3; 6; 9(2); 15; 16(2); 17; 18; 19; **2 Cor** 1:1; 2(2); 3(2); 6(2); 7; 10; 12(2); 15; 16; 17; 18; 19(2); 20; 21; 22; 2:3; 4; 7; 12; 14; 15; 16(2); 3:2; 4; 7; 17; 4:5; 7; 13(3); 14; 17; 5:8; 11; 12; 15(2); 18; 19; 6:2; 7; 8(3); 9(3); 10; 14; 15; 16(3); 17(2); 18(2); 7:1; 3; 7; 13; 15(2); 8:2; 3; 4; 5(2); 7; 10(2); 12; 13; 15; 18; 19(2); 22; 23; 24(2); 9:2; 4; 5(2); 6; 8; 10(3); 13(2); 14; 10:1; 5; 6; 8; 10(2); 12; 16; 11:1; 9(4); 14; 25; 27(3); 29(2); 31; 33; 12:1; 3; 4; 7; 9; 12(2); 14; 15(2); 18; 20; 21(3); 13:2(3); 9(2); 10; 11(2); 14(2); **Gal** 1:1; 2; 3(2); 4; 5; 7; 13; 14; 15; 16; 17; 18; 21; 22; 24; 2:1; 2(2); 4; 9(4); 12; 13; 14; 15; 16; 20(2); 3:5; 6; 8; 16(3); 17(2); 19; 29(2); 4:2; 6; 7; 9; 10(3); 14; 15; 18; 20; 23; 25(2); 27; 30; 5:1; 3; 11; 15; 16; 17(2); 21; 24(2); 6:2; 4(2); 9; 14; 16(3); **Eph** 1:1; 2(2); 3; 4; 8; 10; 15; 17; 19; 20; 21(4); 22(2); 2:1(2); 3(2); 6(2); 8; 12(2); 14; 16; 17(3); 19(2); 20; 3:5; 6; 9; 10; 12; 15; 17; 18(3); 21; 4:2; 4; 6(3); 8; 11(3); 13; 14(2); 16; 17; 21; 23; 24(2); 26; 30; 31; 32; 5:2(3); 3; 5; 9; 11; 14; 18; 19(3); 23; 25; 26; 27; 29; 30; 31(3); 32; 33; 6:2; 3; 4(2); 5; 7; 9(2); 10; 12; 13; 15; 17(2); 18(2); 19; 21(2); 22; 23(2); **Phil** 1:1(2); 2(2); 7(2); 9(3); 10; 11; 13; 14; 15(2); 18(2); 19; 20; 21; 23; 25(3); 27; 28(2); 30; 2:1; 7; 8(2); 9; 10(2); 11; 12; 13; 14; 15(2); 17(3); 18; 25(2); 26; 27; 28; 29; 3:3; 8; 9; 10(2); 13; 15; 17; 18; 19; 4:1(2); 2; 3(2); 6; 7(2); 8; 9(4); 12(4); 15; 16; 18; 19; 20(2); **Col** 1:1; 2(3); 3; 4; 6(2); 9(2); 10; 11; 13; 16(3); 17(2); 18; 20; 21(2); 22(2); 23(2); 24; 26; 28; 2:1(2); 2(2); 3; 5; 7(2); 8(2); 10(2); 13(2); 14; 15; 18; 19(3); 22; 23; 3:3; 5; 10; 11; 12; 13; 15(2); 16(3); 17; 19; 23(2); 25; 4:1; 7; 8; 9; 11; 12; 13(2); 14; 15(2); 16; 17; **1 Th** 1:1(4); 3(2); 5(2); 6(2); 7; 8; 9(2); 10; 2:2; 9(2); 10(3); 11(2); 12; 15(4); 18; 20; 3:2(4); 4; 5; 6(3); 7; 10(2); 11(2); 12(3); 13; 4:1(3); 4; 6(2); 10(2); 11; 12; 14; 15; 16(2); 17(2); 5:1; 3(2); 5; 6; 7; 8(2); 11; 12(3); 13; 15; 23(2); **2 Th** 1:1(2); 2(2); 3; 4(2); 7; 8; 9; 10; 11(2); 12(2); 2:1; 3; 4; 6; 8(2); 9; 10; 11; 13; 15; 16(4); 17(2); 3:1; 2(2); 3; 4(2); 5; 6; 8(2); 12(2); 14(2); **1 Tim** 1:1; 2(2); 4; 5; 9(4); 10; 12; 13; 14(2); 15; 17(2); 19; 20; 2:1; 2(3); 3; 4; 5(2); 7(3); 8; 9; 12; 14; 15; 3:7; 12; 13; 15; 16; 4:1; 3(2); 4; 5; 6; 7(2); 8; 9; 10; 11; 16(2); 5:4(2); 5(4); 7; 8(2); 9; 13(3); 16; 17; 18; 21(2); 23; 25; 6:1; 2(3); 3(2); 4; 5; 7; 8(2); 9(4); 10; 11; 12; 13; 15(2); 16; 20(2); **2 Tim** 1:2(2); 3; 5(2); 7(2); 9(2); 10(2); 11; 12; 13; 15; 16; 17; 18; 2:2; 5; 7; 16; 17(2); 18; 19; 20(3); 21; 23; 24; 26(2); 3:5; 6; 7; 8; 11; 12; 13(3); 14; 15; 16; 4:1(3); 2(2); 4(2); 6; 8; 10; 11; 12; 13; 17(3); 18(3); 19(2); 21; **Titus** 1:1(2); 4(2); 5; 9; 10; 14; 15(2); 16; 2:12(2); 13(2); 14; 15; 3:1; 3(3); 4; 5; 8(2); 9(2); 10; 11; 13; 14; **Phm** 1:1(2); 2; 3(2); 5(2); 7; 9; 11; 16; **Heb** 1:1; 3(2); 5(2); 7(2); 8; 9; 10(2); 11; 12(2); 2:2(2); 3; 4(2); 7(2); 9; 10; 11; 13(3); 14; 15; 17; 3:1; 5; 6; 9; 10(2); 18; 4:4; 5; 6; 12(7); 13(2); 16; 5:1; 2; 4; 7(3); 9; 11; 12(2); 14; 6:1; 2; 3; 4(2); 5(2); 6; 7; 8(2); 10(2); 11; 12; 14; 15; 16; 19(2); 7:1; 2; 5; 6; 11; 15; 18; 20; 21; 26; 27; 8:2(2); 3; 5; 8; 9; 10(3); 11; 12(2); 13; 9:1; 2; 3; 4(2); 5; 7; 9; 10(2); 11; 12; 13(2); 15; 19(4); 21; 22(2); 27; 10:1; 4; 5; 6; 8(2); 11(2); 16; 17; 20; 21; 22; 24(2); 25; 27; 29; 30; 33(2); 34(2); 37(2); 11:4; 5; 6; 7; 8; 9; 10; 11; 12; 13(2); 15; 17; 20; 21; 22; 23; 28; 32(6); 35; 36(3); 37; 38(2); 39; 12:1(2); 2(2); 3; 5; 6; 8; 9(2); 12; 13; 14; 15; 18(4); 19(2); 20; 21(2); 22; 23; 24; 28; 13:4(2); 8; 9; 16; 17(2); 21; 22; 24; **Jas** 1:1; 4; 5(2); 6; 11; 14; 15; 17(2); 21(2); 22; 23; 24; 25(2); 26; 27(4); 2:2; 3(3); 4; 5; 6; 9; 10; 12; 15; 16(2); 18(2); 19; 22; 23(3); 24; 25; 3:3; 4; 5; 6(3); 7(3); 9(2); 10; 11; 12; 13; 14(2); 16(2); 17(2); 4:1; 2(4); 3; 4; 7; 8(2); 9(3); 10; 11(2); 12; 13(3); 14; 15; 17; 5:1; 2; 3(3); 4; 5; 7; 10; 11(2); 12; 14; 15(3); 16; 17(3); 18(3); 19; 20; **1 Pe** 1:1; 2(3); 3; 4(2); 7; 8; 10; 11; 13; 17; 19; 21(2); 23; 24(2); 2:1; 4; 6; 8(2); 11; 14; 18; 20; 25; 3:4; 6; 7; 10(2); 11(2); 12; 13; 14; 15(2); 19; 22(3); 4:3; 5; 7; 8; 11(2); 14; 17; 18; 5:1(2); 4; 5; 10; 11(2); 12; 13; **2 Pe** 1:1(2); 2(2); 3(2); 4; 7; 8; 9; 10; 11; 12; 16; 17; 18; 19(2); 2:1; 2; 3; 4; 5; 6(2); 7; 8; 9; 10(2); 11; 12(2); 13(2); 14(2); 15; 20(2); 22; 3:2(2); 4; 5(2); 7(2); 8; 10(2); 11; 12(2); 13; 14; 15; 16; 18(3); **1 Jn** 1:1; 2(4); 3(3); 4; 5(2); 6(2); 7; 8; 9(2); 10; 2:1; 2(2); 4(2); 8(2); 9; 10; 11(2); 14(2); 16; 17(2); 18; 20; 21; 22; 24; 25; 27(4); 28(2); 3:2; 3; 4; 5(2); 9; 10; 12(3); 15; 16; 17(2); 18; 19(2); 20; 22(2); 23(2); 24(2); 4:3(3); 4; 5; 6; 7(2); 10; 12; 13; 14(2); 15; 16(4); 20; 21; 5:1; 2; 3; 4; 6(3); 7(2); 8(3); 11(2); 13; 15; 16; 17; 18; 19; 20(4); **2 Jn** 1(2); 2; 3(3); 5; 7; 9(2); 10; 12(2); **3 Jn** 2; 3; 5; 10(2); 12(3); 13; 14; **Jude** 1(2); 2; 4(2); 6; 7(3); 8; 10; 11; 15; 16; 22; 24; 25(3); **Rev** 1:1(2); 2; 3(2); 4(4); 5(3); 6(5); 7(2); 8(4); 9(4); 10; 11(5); 12; 13(2); 14(2); 15; 16; 17(2); 18(4); 19(2); 20(2); 2:2(4); 3(4); 5(2); 8(3); 9(3); 10(2); 12; 13(3); 14; 16; 17(2); 18(2); 19(2); 20(2); 21(2); 22; 23(3); 24; 26(2); 28; 3:1(2); 2; 3(3); 4; 5(2); 7(4); 8(2); 9(3); 12(4); 14(2); 16; 17(3); 18(2); 19(2); 20(4); 21; 4:1(3); 2(3); 3(3); 4(2); 5(2); 6(3); 7; 8(4); 9(3); 10(3); 11(4); 5:1(2); 2; 3; 4; 5; 6(5); 7; 8(2); 9(6); 10(3); 11(4); 12(6); 13(10); 14(3); 6:1(2); 2(5); 3; 4(3); 5(3); 6(4); 7; 8(5); 9; 10(3); 11(2); 12(3); 13; 14(2); 15(3); 16(4); 17; 7:2(2); 4(2); 9(3); 10(2); 11(4); 12(6); 13; 14(3); 15(3); 17(2); 8:2(2); 3; 4; 5(3); 7(5); 8(2); 9(2); 10(3); 11; 12(3); 13(2); 9:1; 2(3); 3; 5; 6(2); 7; 8; 9(2); 10; 11; 13; 15(3); 17(5); 18(2); 19(2); 20(2); 21; 10:1(2); 2(2); 3; 4; 5; 6(6); 8(2); 9(4); 10(2); 11(2); 11:1(3); 2(2); 3(3); 4; 5(3); 6(2); 7; 8(2); 9(2); 10(2); 11(2); 12(3); 13(3); 15(4); 16(2); 17(3); 18(7); 19(3); 12:1; 2; 3(3); 4(2); 5(2); 6; 7(4); 9(2); 10(4); 11(3); 12(2); 14(2); 16(2); 17(3); 13:1(4); 2(3); 3(4); 4; 5(3); 6; 7(3); 10; 11(2); 12(3); 14(2); 15; 16(3); 17; 14:1(3); 2(3); 3(3); 4; 5; 6; 7(4); 8; 9(2); 10(2); 11(5); 12; 13; 14(3); 15(2); 16; 18(3); 19(2); 20(2); 15:1; 2(4); 3(3); 4(2); 5; 6(2); 7; 8(2); 16:1; 2(4); 3(2); 4(2); 5(3); 6(2); 7(2); 8; 9(4); 10(2); 11(2); 12; 13(2); 14; 15(2); 16; 17; 18(5); 19(2); 20; 21; 17:1; 2; 3(2); 4(5); 5(2); 6(2); 7(2); 8(6); 10(2); 11(4); 13(2); 14(4); 15; 16(3); 17; 18; 18:1; 2(4); 3; 4(2); 5; 6; 7(4); 8(3); 9(2); 11(2); 12(5); 13(9); 14(3); 15; 16(5); 17; 18; 19(3); 20(2); 21(2); 22(2); 23(2); 24(3); 19:1(3); 2(2); 3; 4(3); 5(2); 6(2); 7(3); 8(2); 9; 10(2); 11(5); 12; 13; 14(2); 15(2); 16(3); 17(2); 18(4); 19(3); 20(2); 21(2); 20:1; 2(2); 3(3); 4(7); 6(3); 8(2); 9(4); 10(5); 11(3); 12(5); 13(3); 14; 15; 21:1(2); 3(4); 4; 5(2); 6(3); 7(2); 8(2); 9; 10(3); 12(3); 13; 14; 15(2); 16(2); 17; 18; 20; 21; 22; 24(3); 26(2); 22:1(2); 2; 3(3); 4; 5(2); 6(2); 8(3); 9(2); 10; 12(2); 13(3); 14; 15(6); 16(2); 17(4); 19(2)

ANY (493/453)

Gen 2:5(2); 3:1; 17:12; 31:14; 36:31; 42:16; 38; 43:34; 47:6; **Ex** 5:19; 12:46; 16:19; 24; 20:4; 21:23; 22:9(2); 10; 20; 22; 23; 25; 24:14; 29:34; 30:32; 33(2); 37; 38; 31:14; 15; 32:24; 34:10; 24; 35:2; 24; 36:6; **Lev** 1:2; 2:11(2); 4:2(2); 13; 22; 27; 5:2; 4; 5; 13; 17; 6:3; 7; 27; 30; 7:15; 18; 19; 21(2); 23; 24; 26(2); 27; 11:10; 24; 25; 26; 27; 28; 32(3); 33(2); 34(2); 35; 36; 37(2); 38; 39; 43; 44; 12:4; 14:54; 15:2; 9; 10; 16; 17(2); 24; 16:2; 17:10; 12; 13; 14; 18:21; 23(2); 24; 26(3); 29; 30; 19:6; 18; 28(2); 20:2; 4; 16; 25; 21:5(2); 9; 11; 17; 18(2); 22:5(2); 6; 18(2); 23; 24; 25; 23:22; 29; 30(2); 24:17; 25:32; 27:31; **Num** 4:15; 5:6; 10; 12; 6:3; 14:23; 18:20; 31; 20:5; 19; 22:38; 23:23; 29:7; 30:9; 31:19(2); 35:11; 26; 36:3; 8; **Deut** 1:17; 2:5; 9; 19; 4:16; 17(2); 18; 32; 33; 5:8; 14; 7:7; 8:19; 12:17; 14:3; 15:7; 21; 16:4; 5; 21; 17:1; 2; 3; 18:6; 19:3; 15(2); 16; 22:3; 6; 13; 23:10; 18; 24; 24:5; 7; 13; 26:14(3); 27:21; 28:14; 55; 29:23; 30:4; 32:28; 39; **Josh** 2:11; 5:1; 6:10; 10:21; 21:45; **Judg** 2:21; 3:1; 4:20(2); 11:25; 12:5; 16:7; 11; 17; 20:8; 21:22; **Ruth** 2:22; **1 Sam** 2:2; 13; 33; 5:5; 9:2; 10:23; 12:3; 4; 13:22; 14:24; 52(2); 18:25; 22:15; 27:1; 30:22; **2 Sam** 2:1; 7:22; 15:4; 19:22; 35; 42; 21:4; 5; **1 Ki** 1:6; 3:12; 6:7; 8:16; 10:20; 18:5; 20:33; 39; **2 Ki** 6:33; 10:24; 12:5; 13; 18:33; 23:25; **1 Chr** 4:27; 17:6; 20; 23:26; 29:25; **2 Chr** 1:12; 2:14(2); 6:5(2); 8:15; 9:9; 19; 23:19; 25:7; 32:13; 15; 34:13; **Ezra** 1:4; 6:12; 7:24; **Neh** 2:12; 5:16; 10:31; **Esth** 4:11; 13; 8:11; **Job** 6:6; 8:12; 9:33; 10:22; 18:19; 22:3; 25:3; 31:7; 19; 32:21; 33:13; 34:27; 37:24; 41:9; **Ps** 4:6; 14:2; 33:17; 34:10; 38:3; 49:7; 53:2; 59:5; 74:9(2); 81:9; 86:8; 91:10; 109:12; 115:17; 135:17; 139:24; 141:4; 147:20; **Prov** 1:17; 14:34; 20:3; 30:2; 30; **Eccl** 1:11; 2:10; **Isa** 7:25; 19:15; 26:18; 27:3; 33:20; 35:9; 36:18; 51:18; 52:14; 53:9; 56:2; 59:4; 62:4; 64:4; **Jer** 9:4; 10:5; 14:22;

17:22; 18:18; 33:26; 35:7; 36:24; 37:17; 44:26; 48:9; **Lam** 1:12; **Ezek** 1:17; 5:11; 9:5; 10:11; 12:24; 28; 15:2; 3(2); 4; 5; 16:5; 18:8; 10; 13; 23; 33:6; 37:23; 39:10; 28; 44:9; 13; 30(2); 46:16; 18; 48:14; **Dan** 2:10; 3:28; 29; 6:4; 5; 7; 12; 8:4; 10:17; 11:37; **Hos** 13:10; **Joel** 2:2; **Am** 6:10; 8:7; **Mic** 4:3; **Zeph** 3:11; **Hag** 2:12; 13; **Zech** 8:10; **Mt** 5:32; 19:3; **Mk** 5:35; 12:21; **Lk** 4:40; 6:4; 8:43; 9:36; 10:19; 11:11; 15:29; 17:18; 24:41; **Jn** 1:18; 5:37; 7:48; 20:23(2); 21:5; **Acts** 4:12; 32; 9:2; 10:28; 11:8; 13:15; 19:39; 24:4; 20; 23; 25:5; 16; 17; 24; 27:12; 34; 42; 28:21(2); **Rom** 6:2; 8:39; 9:11; 11:14; 13:9; 15:18; **1 Cor** 1:16; 6:1; 12; 7:12; 36; 10:27; **2 Cor** 1:4; 13; 12:17; **Gal** 1:8; 9; 2:2; 6:1; **Eph** 5:5; 27; **Phil** 1:28; 2:1(4); 3:11; 4:8; **1 Th** 2:5; 9; **2 Th** 2:3; 3:8; **1 Tim** 1:10; 5:4; 16; **Heb** 3:12; 13; 4:1; 12; 12:15; 16; **Jas** 1:5; 5:12; **1 Pe** 3:6; **2 Pe** 1:20; 3:9; **1 Jn** 4:12; **Rev** 2:10; 7:1; 16; 9:4(2); 12:8; 18:22

ARE (3507/2977)

Gen 2:12; 3:9; 14; 19; 4:6; 11; 7:1; 2; 8; 9:2; 11:6; 12:11; 13; 13:8; 14; 18; 15:5; 16:8; 11; 17:8; 19:5; 15; 20:3; 7; 16; 23:6; 24:13; 23; 47; 25:23; 26:16; 29; 27:18; 21; 22; 24; 32; 41; 46; 28:4; 29:4(2); 8; 14; 15; 21; 31:12; 15; 16; 43(2); 49; 32:6; 17(2); 18; 33:5; 8; 13(3); 14; 15; 34:15; 21; 22; 35:2; 37:13; 15; 16; 38:25; 39:9; 40:12; 18; 41:25; 26(3); 27(2); 35; 42:9; 11(3); 13; 14; 16; 19; 21; 31(2); 32; 33; 34(2); 36; 43:18; 44:16; 18; 45:6; 11; 19; 46:30; 32; 47:1; 3; 8; 9; 48:5; 8; 9; 49:3; 5(2); 8; 12; 28; 50:3(2); 18; **Ex** 1:1; 9; 19(2); 2:13; 3:7; 4:18(2); 19; 25; 26; 5:5; 8; 15; 16; 17; 6:14(2); 15; 16; 19; 24; 25; 26; 27(2); 7:17; 18; 9:27; 32; 10:8(2); 11; 12:13; 13:4; 14:3; 15:4; 16:7; 8(2); 16; 17:4; 18:14; 18(2); 19:6; 21:1; 22:25; 24:14; 25:22; 26; 28:3; 4; 24; 29:33; 30:13; 14; 31:6; 32:2; 22; 33:3; 5; 16; 34:9; 10; 12; 19; 35:1; 10; 39:6; 40:4; **Lev** 4:12(2); 13; 5:17; 7:19; 8:33; 10:14(2); 11:2(2); 8; 9; 10; 13; 27; 31(2); 32; 35; 42; 12:4; 6; 13:21; 26; 39; 16:4; 18:17; 24; 21:2; 22:22; 25; 23:2; 4; 17; 37; 42; 25:7; 23; 33; 42; 44; 45; 51; 55(2); 26:21; 23; 25; 34; 36; 39(2); 41; 44; 46; 27:34; **Num** 1:3; 5; 44; 2:32; 3:1; 2; 3; 9; 13; 18; 20; 26; 46; 4:15(2); 20; 26; 41; 45; 6:5; 13; 20; 8:16; 17; 9:7; 10:29; 31; 11:21; 27; 29; 13:16; 18; 19; 20; 28(2); 30; 31(2); 32; 14:9; 14(2); 33; 35; 40; 43; 15:2; 13; 15; 39; 16:10; 11; 29; 37; 38; 18:2; 6; 17; 18; 19:14; 20:16; 22:5; 6; 9; 12; 24:3; 5; 15; 26:2; 7; 9; 14; 18; 22; 25; 27; 30; 34; 35; 36; 37(2); 41; 42(2); 47; 50; 51; 57; 58; 63; 27:14; 28:19; 31; 29:8; 30:16; 31:49; 33:1; 2; 34:17; 19; 29; 35:33; 36:3; 13; **Deut** 1:1; 10; 11; 28(2); 2:4; 18; 4:4; 8; 20; 30; 32; 45; 5:3(2); 28; 6:1(2); 11; 14; 25; 7:6; 17; 19; 20(2); 23; 8:9; 10; 12; 13; 9:1; 6; 13; 29; 10:5; 11:12; 30; 12:1; 8; 22; 30(2); 13:7; 14:1; 2(2); 4; 7; 9; 21; 24; 29; 16:11; 14; 17:14; 18:12; 20:2; 3; 11; 15(2); 20; 22:5; 17; 20; 28; 23:18; 20; 25:16; 28:10; 13; 20; 21; 23; 24; 45; 51; 58; 61; 29:1; 21; 29; 30:4; 10; 17; 32:4; 5; 15; 18; 20; 21; 28; 32(2); 37; 33:3; 17(2); 27; 29; **Josh** 2:9; 24; 4:9; 21; 5:13; 6:17(2); 19; 7:3; 21; 8:5; 6; 9:8(2); 11; 13; 22; 23; 25; 12:1; 7; 13:1; 14; 17; 30; 32; 14:1; 15:32; 17:3; 9; 14; 15(2); 16(2); 17; 18; 19:35; 21:9; 22:17; 24:22(2); 23; **Judg** 3:1; 4:9; 5:30; 6:2; 13; 7:2(2); 4; 10; 18; 8:5; 6; 15(2); 18; 9:31; 32; 33; 36; 37; 38; 10:4(2); 11:2; 7; 25; 35; 12:4; 5; 13:3; 11; 16:9; 12; 14; 20; 18:3; 14; 18; 19:12; 17; 18; 20:7; 13; 32; 39; **Ruth** 1:11; 2:9; 3:9(2); 10; 11; 4:9; 10; 11; **1 Sam** 2:3; 4(2); 8; 31; 4:8; 17; 6:8; 17; 8:5; 8; 9:13; 12:2; 21; 14:11; 33; 15:13; 18; 16:11; 16; 17:33(2); 58; 19:3; 22(2); 20:21; 22; 21:1; 5; 23:1(2); 3; 21; 24:17; 25:10; 11; 33; 26:11; 14; 15; 28:12; 29:3; 9; 10; 30:13; **2 Sam** 1:4(2); 5; 8; 13; 2:5; 20; 3:25; 28; 39; 5:1; 8; 14; 7:9; 12; 22; 28(2); 9:2; 10:11(2); 11:11(2); 24; 12:7; 13:4; 33; 35; 14:14; 15:2; 13; 15; 19(2); 27; 16:2(2); 8(2); 21(2); 17:2; 8(2); 9; 10(2); 12; 16; 20; 29; 18:3(2); 19:3; 11; 12(3); 13(2); 33; 42; 20:9; 17; 22:28; 29; 23:1; 8; 24:3; 14; 22; **1 Ki** 1:14; 20; 25; 42; 2:9; 26; 39; 4:8; 6:12; 8:8; 33; 35; 51; 9:13(2); 10:8(2); 27; 11:41; 12:28; 13:14; 18; 32; 14:19; 29; 15:7; 23; 31; 16:5; 14; 20; 27; 17:24; 18:9; 22; 25; 36; 37; 19:9; 13; 20:3(2); 4; 17; 23; 31; 22:4; 11; 39; 45; **2 Ki** 1:3; 6; 18; 2:16; 3:7; 4:23; 5:12; 6:9; 16(3); 7:3; 9; 12; 13(3); 8:23; 9:15; 22; 10:2; 5; 6; 9; 13(2); 23; 34; 11:8; 12:4; 19; 13:8; 12; 14:15; 18; 28; 15:6; 11; 15; 21; 26; 31; 36; 16:19; 17:26; 18:20; 21; 23; 26; 34(2); 19:15; 19; 20:17; 20; 21:8; 17; 25; 22:5(2); 23:28; 24:5; **1 Chr** 1:29; 4:22; 6:17; 19; 31; 33; 50; 54; 65; 7:8; 8:6; 9:33; 11:1; 12:15; 18(2); 13:2(2); 14:4; 15:12; 16:14; 26; 27(2); 17:8; 11; 26; 19:12(2); 21:3(2); 13; 22:15; 24:1; 28:21; 29:10; 11; 14; 15(2); 17; 29; **2 Chr** 1:12; 15; 2:7; 5:9; 6:24; 26; 7:14; 8:11; 9:7(2); 27; 29; 10:7; 11:10; 12:15; 13:8(2); 9; 10; 22; 14:11; 15:2; 16:11; 17:14; 18:3; 10; 19:3; 6; 20:2; 6; 7; 10; 11; 12; 34; 23:6; 7; 24:26; 27; 25:26; 26:18; 27:7; 28:10; 26; 29:9; 19; 32:7; 32; 33:8; 18; 19; 34:16; 21; 24; 35:25; 27; 36:8; **Ezra** 2:1; 4:12(2); 16; 5:11(2); 6:6; 8; 9; 7:14; 15; 16; 19; 21; 25; 8:1; 13; 22; 28(3); 9:11; 15(3); 10:4; 13(3); **Neh** 1:3(3); 8; 10; 2:2; 3; 17(2); 19; 4:2(2); 4; 10; 19; 5:2; 5; 9; 6:6; 8; 10; 7:6; 9:6; 7; 8; 17; 31; 33; 36(2); 37; 10:39(2); 11:3; 7; 12:1; **Esth** 1:16; 3:8; 11; 4:16; 8:5; 9:13; 10:2; **Job** 1:19; 3:8; 17; 19; 22; 4:5(2); 9; 10; 11; 19; 20; 5:4(2); 11(2); 6:4(2); 7; 16; 20(2); 21(2); 25; 26; 7:1; 6(2); 8; 16; 8:9; 13; 9:12; 25; 10:5(2); 17; 20; 11:8; 12:2; 6; 13; 16(2); 13:4; 12(2); 23; 14:5; 12; 21; 15:7; 10; 11; 15; 21; 28; 16:2; 22; 17:1; 2; 7; 8; 11(2); 14(2); 18:3; 7; 15; 16; 20(2); 21; 19:3; 13; 22; 20:11; 21:8; 9; 18; 24; 30; 22:3; 10; 12; 19; 20; 23:14; 24:1; 4; 8; 13; 17; 23; 24(4); 25:5; 26:8; 11; 14; 27:5; 14; 28:6; 30:3; 15; 17; 31:24; 40; 32:6; 9; 15; 33:12; 34:18(2); 19; 20(2); 21; 25; 35; 36; 35:5; 6; 7; 36:2; 4; 7(2); 8; 17; 20; 37:10; 16; 17; 24; 38:35; 39:4; 13; 30; 40:17; 18; 41:15; 17; 18; 23(2); 25(2); 29; 30; **Ps** 1:4(2); 2:7; 12; 3:1; 2; 3; 4:6; 5:4; 6:2; 8:4; 9:6; 10:5(2); 8; 14; 11:3; 12:4; 6; 14:1; 2; 5; 16:2; 3(2); 5; 11; 17:2; 14; 19:8; 9; 10; 21:11; 22:1; 3; 9; 14; 23:4; 25:5; 6; 10; 15; 19; 28:1; 31:3; 4; 14; 15; 32:7; 34:15(2); 19; 35:19; 36:3; 6; 8; 12; 37:14; 23; 26; 28; 34; 38:4; 5; 7; 19(2); 20; 39:1; 40:5(2); 12; 41:11; 42:5(2); 11(2); 43:2; 5(2); 44:4; 12; 22(2); 45:2; 5; 8; 9; 49:13; 14; 50:8; 11; 51:17; 53:1; 2; 5; 55:10; 56:2; 5; 8; 12; 57:4(2); 58:3(2); 4; 59:7; 15; 62:9(4); 63:1; 64:6; 65:5; 8; 13(2); 66:3; 68:6; 17; 35; 69:4(2); 5; 19; 70:5; 71:3; 5(2); 6; 7; 13; 24(2); 72:20; 73:1; 4; 5(2); 10; 12(2); 19(2); 27; 74:20; 75:3; 76:4; 7(2); 11; 77:14; 79:4; 11; 82:5; 6(2); 83:18; 84:4; 86:2; 5; 8; 10(2); 15; 87:3; 7; 88:5; 89:11; 14; 15; 16; 17; 26; 49; 90:2; 4; 5(2); 7; 10(2); 92:5(2); 8; 13; 93:2; 5; 94:11; 95:4(2); 7; 96:5; 6(2); 97:2; 9(2); 100:3; 102:3(2); 11; 22; 24; 25; 27; 103:6; 11; 14; 15; 104:1(2); 16; 18(2); 24; 25; 28; 29; 30; 105:7; 106:3; 107:27; 29; 30(2); 39; 109:4; 24; 110:4; 111:2; 7(2); 8; 113:6; 115:4; 8; 16; 116:11; 118:28(2); 119:1; 2; 12; 24; 39; 57; 68; 75; 84; 86; 91; 98; 99; 103; 111; 114; 129; 137(2); 138; 143; 148; 150; 151(2); 156; 157; 168; 172; 120:7; 122:5; 123:3; 4; 125:1; 4(2); 126:3; 127:3; 4; 135:15; 18; 137:8; 139:3; 8(2); 12; 14; 17; 140:6; 141:6(2); 7; 8; 142:5; 6; 143:10; 144:3; 4; 15(3); 145:9; 14; 146:8; **Prov** 1:19; 2:15(2); 3:14; 17(2); 18; 4:22; 5:6; 11; 21; 6:2(2); 16; 18; 23; 7:4; 8:8; 9; 18; 32; 9:12(2); 18(2); 10:6; 11:1; 20(3); 12:5(2); 6; 7(2); 10; 22(2); 14:4; 18; 15:3; 11; 15; 22; 26(2); 16:2; 11(2); 13; 24; 17:6; 15; 24; 18:4; 7; 8; 10; 19; 21; 19:13; 14; 21; 29; 20:7; 10; 15; 18; 23(2); 24; 21:4; 22:3; 4; 5; 23:2; 3; 24:4; 11; 24; 25:1; 26:22; 23; 25; 28; 27:6(2); 12; 15; 20(2); 24; 25; 28:1; 2; 29:2; 16; 30:13(2); 14(2); 15(2); 18(2); 24(3); 25; 26; 29(3); 31; 31:6; 8; 25; **Eccl** 1:8; 11; 14; 2:14; 23; 3:10; 18; 20; 4:2; 9; 5:8; 6:3; 11; 7:26; 8:4; 8; 12; 13; 14(2); 9:1; 3; 10; 12; 16; 10:12; 17; 11:3; 10; 12:2; 3; 4(2); 5; 11(2); **Song** 1:10; 15(2); 16; 17; 4:1(2); 2; 3(2); 5; 7; 11; 13; 5:11; 12; 13(2); 14; 15; 6:4; 6; 7; 8; 7:1(2); 3; 6; 12(2); 13; 8:6; **Isa** 1:4; 7; 14; 15; 18(2); 19; 23; 2:6(3); 13; 14; 3:8; 12; 16; 5:7; 12; 13; 21; 28; 6:11(2); 12; 7:2(2); 8:18; 19; 21; 9:10; 16(2); 10:8; 14; 11:11; 14:12(2); 19(2); 31; 16:4; 7; 8(2); 17:2; 19:11; 12(2); 13(2); 21:3; 22:2(2); 3(3); 23:8(2); 24:6(3); 17; 18(2); 22; 25:1(2); 26:9; 14(2); 15; 27:9; 11; 13(2); 28:1; 7(3); 8; 14; 15; 29:9; 15; 20; 30:17; 18; 27; 31:1(2); 3(2); 32:7; 9; 11; 20; 33:13(2); 14; 35:4; 36:5; 6; 8; 11; 19(2); 37:16; 20; 39:6; 40:7; 11; 15(2); 17(2); 22; 41:8; 9; 23(2); 24; 27; 29(3); 42:17; 22(3); 43:1; 10; 12; 17(2); 44:7; 8; 9(2); 11; 17; 21(2); 45:9; 10; 15; 16; 19; 24; 46:10; 12; 47:8; 13; 48:1; 7; 49:3; 9; 16; 51:9; 10; 12; 16; 20; 52:5; 7; 53:5; 54:1; 55:8(2); 9(2); 56:8; 10(3); 11(2); 57:1; 4; 6; 10; 20; 58:7; 59:3; 6; 7(2); 10; 12(2); 60:8; 61:1; 9; 11; 63:8; 15(2); 16(2); 64:5; 6(2); 8(3); 9; 10; 11; 65:5; 11; 16(2); 24; **Jer** 2:11; 15; 23; 27; 28(2); 31; 3:4; 16; 22; 4:13(2); 17; 20; 22(3); 30; 5:3; 4(2); 6; 7; 10; 16; 26; 27; 28; 6:4; 7(2); 20; 23; 28(3); 29; 7:4; 10; 32; 8:8; 9(2); 20; 9:2; 3; 10(2); 19(2); 25(2); 26(3); 10:2; 3; 5; 6; 8; 9(2); 15; 20(2); 11:16; 12:1(2); 2; 4; 9; 13:16; 23; 14:7; 9(2); 22(2); 15:2(4); 5; 16:3; 14; 17(2); 20; 17:14; 17; 18:6; 19:6; 20:7; 21:4; 7; 22:6(2); 17; 20; 28; 23:5; 7; 10; 11; 14; 26; 24:2; 3; 5; 8; 10; 25:12; 22; 23; 26; 31; 34; 37; 26:19; 27:5; 18(2); 29:1; 8; 10; 17; 22; 25; 30:3; 4; 31:15; 18; 27; 29; 31; 38; 32:19(2); 35; 33:10; 14; 35:7; 14; 36:19; 37:13; 19; 38:22; 39:17; 40:15; 42:2; 11; 43:13; 44:2; 6; 24; 27; 46:27; 5; 15; 21(2); 23; 47:6; 48:12; 14; 17; 33; 41; 49:2; 5; 10; 12; 23(2); 50:2(2); 15; 37; 38; 42; 51:7; 18; 20; 30; 32(2); 43; 47; 51; 52; 56; 60; 64; 52:28; **Lam** 1:2; 4(2); 16; 21; 22; 2:9; 3:22; 23; 4:1; 2; 5; 9; 5:3; 7; 22; **Ezek** 2:4; 5; 6(2); 7; 3:5; 7; 9; 26; 27; 5:2; 6; 7(2); 14; 15; 6:8; 9; 13; 8:6; 9; 13; 9:4; 11:2; 3; 7; 12; 15; 12:2; 3; 9; 10; 14; 19; 20; 22; 23; 13:4; 14:5; 16:3; 32; 34(2); 38; 45(2); 52; 18:2; 4; 25; 29(2); 20:7; 30; 34; 21:7; 24; 31; 22:9(2); 10; 18; 24; 27; 23:45; 26:6; 18; 19; 21; 27:3; 4; 27; 34; 28:2; 3; 19; 24; 25; 29:12(2); 30:4; 5; 7; 8; 31:2; 32:2(2); 23; 26; 27; 29; 30; 33:6; 24(2); 27(2); 30; 32; 34:30; 31(2); 35:8; 12(2); 36:3; 7; 8; 20; 35; 36; 37:11(3); 38:5; 6; 7; 12; 17; 20; 22; 39:4; 19(2); 40:46; 42:13(2); 14; 43:11; 13; 18; 19; 27; 45:14; 46:24; 47:8; 13; 48:1; 11; 22; 29; 30; **Dan** 1:10; 2:20; 26; 37; 38; 3:12; 15; 25; 4:3; 18(2); 35; 37; 5:13; 14; 7:17(2); 24; 8:20; 9:16; 19; 23; 24; 26; 12:3; 9; **Hos** 1:9; 10(2); 2:4; 12; 23(2); 4:2; 4; 6:5; 10; 6:5; 7:2; 4; 7; 9; 16; 8:8; 9:6; 9; 15; 10:2; 11:7; 12:7; 11; 13:9; 13; 14:3; 9; **Joel** 1:6; 7; 12; 13; 17(2); 18; 20; 2:6; 8; 22; **Am** 3:3; 4:1; 6:1; 2; 6; 10; 8:11; 9:7; 8; 12; 13; **Ob** 20; **Jon** 1:8; 4:2; 11; **Mic** 1:5(2); 9; 2:4; 7(2); 5:2(2); 6:10; 12; 16(2); 7:6; 11; **Nah** 1:3; 6; 12; 14; 2:3(3); 6; 10; 3:8; 12(2); 13(2); 17(2); 18; **Hab** 1:3; 6; 7; 8; 9; 10; 12; 13; 15; 2:16; 3:6; **Zeph** 1:8; 11(2); 12; 3:3(2); 4; 6(2); 18; **Hag** 1:6; **Zech** 1:5; 9(2); 10; 19(2); 21(3); 2:2; 3:8; 9; 4:3; 4; 5; 7; 10; 11; 12; 13; 14; 5:10; 6:4; 5; 6(2); 8:16; 17; 9:1; 2; 10:2; 11:2; 9; 16(2); 12:3; 5; 13:6; **Mal** 3:6; 9; 15; **Mt** 1:17(3); 2:6; 18; 20; 3:14; 4:3; 6; 5:3; 4; 5; 6; 7; 8; 9; 10(2); 11; 13; 14; 15; 25; 6:26; 7:13; 14; 15; 8:2; 25; 26; 9:2; 5; 12(2); 17(2); 37; 10:2; 29; 30; 31; 11:3; 5(2); 8; 14; 23; 28; 12:2; 5; 47; 48; 49; 13:15; 16; 38(2); 39; 40; 56; 14:2; 33; 15:14; 16; 20; 16:16; 17; 18; 23(2); 28; 17:26; 18:3; 20; 19:6; 12(3); 26; 30; 20:16; 18; 22(2); 25; 21:16; 23; 22:4(3); 14(2); 16; 21(2); 29; 30(2); 23:8; 13; 25; 27(2); 28; 31(2); 37; 24:6; 8; 16; 19(2); 25:8; 26:15; 33; 45; 63; 70; 73; 27:6; 11; 40; **Mk** 1:11; 24; 40; 2:5; 9; 17(2); 22; 3:11; 32; 34; 4:11; 15; 16; 18(2); 20; 38; 40; 5:9; 6:2; 3; 14; 7:4; 15; 18; 8:29; 33; 9:1; 16; 23; 10:8; 27; 31; 33; 38; 39; 42; 11:3; 5; 28; 12:14; 17(2); 24; 25(2); 27; 34; 13:1; 8; 14; 17(2); 14:29; 36; 37; 41; 61; 68; 70(2); 15:2; **Lk** 1:28; 42; 2:29; 3:22; 4:3; 9; 18; 34; 41; 5:12; 20; 22; 23; 31(2); 38; 6:2; 20; 21(2); 22; 24; 25; 7:19; 20; 22(2); 25(2); 31; 32; 47(2); 48; 8:12; 13; 14(2); 15; 20; 21; 24; 9:12; 27; 55; 61; 10:2; 8; 15; 17; 20(2); 23; 41; 11:7; 21; 28; 41; 44(3); 12:6; 7(2); 24; 26(2); 37; 38; 13:12; 14; 23(2); 25; 27; 30(2); 34; 14:8; 10; 17; 15:31; 16:8; 15; 25; 17:10(2); 17; 31; 18:27(2); 31(2); 19:21; 31; 33; 42; 20:2; 6; 25(2); 34; 35(2); 36(2); 37; 21:7; 21(3); 22(2); 23(2); 24; 26; 30; 22:25; 28; 38; 48; 58; 60; 67; 70; 23:3; 29(2); 37; 39; 40; 24:17; 18; 38; 44; 48; 49; **Jn** 1:19; 21(2); 22; 25; 38; 42; 49(2); 3:2; 10; 26; 4:12; 19; 27; 35(2); 5:28; 39; 40; 6:9; 49; 58; 63(2); 64; 69; 7:3; 7; 23; 47; 52; 8:10; 23(2); 25; 31; 33; 37; 43; 44; 47; 48; 53(2); 57; 9:28(2); 34; 40; 10:8; 16; 21; 24; 26; 30; 34; 36; 11:8; 9; 27; 42; 12:19; 13:6; 10; 11; 17; 35; 36; 14:2; 5; 15:3; 5; 6; 14; 19; 16:5; 15; 19; 29; 30; 17:7; 9; 10(2); 11(2); 14; 16; 21; 22; 18:4; 7; 17(2); 25(2); 33; 34; 37; 19:9; 10; 12; 20:13; 15(2); 23(2); 29; 30; 31; 21:3; 12; 18; 25; **Acts** 2:7; 13; 15; 32; 39; 3:15; 25; 4:9; 24; 5:9; 25; 32; 7:1; 26; 34; 8:23; 30; 9:4; 5(2); 10:19; 31; 33; 39; 12:15; 13:27; 31; 33; 14:15(3); 15:1; 17; 18; 19; 23; 36; 16:17; 21; 28; 17:7; 20; 22; 28; 29; 19:15; 26(2); 37; 38(2); 40; 20:32; 21:20(2); 21; 24; 38; 22:3; 7; 8(2); 10; 16; 27; 23:15; 21; 24:14; 20; 25:9; 24; 26:1; 3; 14; 15(2); 18; 24; 28:27; **Rom** 1:6; 7; 15; 20(3); 28; 29; 32; 2:1(2); 5; 8; 13; 14; 17; 18; 19(3); 25; 27; 3:4; 8; 9(2); 15; 16; 19; 4:4; 7(3); 11; 12; 14(2); 16(2); 6:14; 15; 16; 21; 8:1; 8; 9; 12; 14(2); 16; 18; 28; 36(2); 37; 9:4; 5; 6(2); 7(2); 8(3); 20; 26; 10:15(2); 19; 11:14; 16; 24; 28(2); 29; 33; 36; 12:5; 13:1; 3; 6; 7; 9; 14:4; 8; 15; 20; 15:1; 14; 26; 27; 16:7; 10; 11(2); 14; 15; 18; **1 Cor** 1:2; 11; 18(2); 24; 26; 27; 28(3); 30; 2:6(2); 14(2); 3:2; 3(3); 4; 8; 9(3); 16; 17; 20; 21; 22; 23; 4:8(2); 10(6); 11; 18; 19; 5:2; 4; 7; 12(2); 13; 6:2; 4; 12(3); 15; 19; 20; 7:14; 27(2); 8:5(2); 6(2); 8(2); 9; 9:1; 2; 12(2); 20(2); 21(2); 10:13; 17; 18; 22; 23(3); 11:12; 18; 19; 30; 32(2); 12:4; 5; 6; 12; 20; 22; 27; 29(4); 13:8(2); 14:10; 12; 22; 23(2); 25; 32; 34(2); 37; 15:2; 15; 17; 19; 23; 27; 28; 29(2); 35; 40; 48(4); 16:9; **2 Cor** 1:1; 4(2); 6(2); 7; 13; 14(2); 20; 24; 2:9; 11; 15(3); 16; 17; 3:2; 3; 5; 18; 4:3; 8(2); 11; 15; 18(6); 5:4; 6(3); 8; 11(2); 13(2); 18; 20; 6:12(2); 16; 7:3; 15; 8:23(2); 9:11; 10:4; 7; 10; 11(3); 12; 14; 11:12; 13; 19; 22(3); 23; 13:4; 5(2); 6; 9(3); **Gal** 1:2; 6; 7; 2:15; 17; 3:3(2); 7(2); 9(2); 10(3); 25; 26; 28; 29(2); 4:6; 7; 8; 9; 24(2); 27; 28; 31; 5:17; 18(2); 19(2); 24; 6:1; 10; 13; **Eph** 1:1; 10(2); 18; 2:10; 11; 19; 22; 4:25; 5:4; 8; 12; 13(2); 16; 30; 6:5; **Phil** 1:1; 7; 10; 11; 13; 14; 2:21; 3:3; 13(2); 15; 18; 4:3; 8(6); 21; 22; **Col** 1:2; 16(2); 23; 27; 2:3; 10; 17; 23; 3:1; 5; 8; 4:5; 9; 11(2); 13; 15; **1 Th** 2:10; 14; 15; 20; 3:3; 4:9; 10; 12; 15(2); 17; 5:4; 5(2); 7; 8; 11; 12; 14; **2 Th** 1:3; 7; 2:13; 3:11(2); 12; **1 Tim** 1:14; 16; 20; 2:2; 3:7; 5:3; 16; 20; 24; 25(2); 6:1; 2(3); 17; **2 Tim** 1:13; 15; 2:13; 17; 19; 20; 25; 3:6; 15; **Titus** 1:5; 10; 12; 15(3); 2:1; 3:8; 9; 15; **Heb** 1:5; 10; 12; 14; 2:6; 10(2); 11(2); 18; 3:6; 4:13; 15; 5:2; 5; 6; 14; 6:9; 7:5; 13; 17; 21; 8:1; 4; 8; 9:9; 15; 17; 22; 24; 10:8; 13; 14; 39; 11:3(2); 12:1; 5; 8(2); 23; 27(2); 28; 13:3(2); 11; 18; **Jas** 1:1; 2:7; 9; 16; 3:4(3); 13; 16; 4:11; 12; 5:1; 2(2); 3; **1 Pe** 1:5; 21; 2:5; 7; 9; 10; 14; 20; 3:6(2); 12(2); 14; 4:6; 14(2); 5:1; 9; 14; **2 Pe** 1:8; 12; 2:10(2); 11; 13; 14; 17; 19; 20; 3:7(2); 10; 16; **1 Jn** 2:5; 12; 14; 3:2; 10; 19; 22; 4:1; 4; 5; 6; 17; 5:3; 7(2); 8; 19; 20; **Jude** 1; 7; 12(2); 15; 16; 19; **Rev** 1:3; 4(2); 11; 19; 20(2); 2:2(3); 9(4); 10; 19; 3:1(2); 2; 4; 9(2); 15; 16; 17; 4:5; 11; 5:6; 8; 9; 13(2); 7:13; 14; 15; 8:13; 9:12; 14; 19; 10:6(3); 11:4; 14:4(3); 5; 12; 13; 18; 15:3(2); 4; 16:5; 7; 14; 17:8; 9; 10; 12; 13; 14(2); 15; 17; 18:14; 19:2; 9(3); 20:8; 10; 21:5; 12; 16; 22; 24; 27; 22:6; 14; 15; 18; 19

AROUND (379/354)

Gen 2:13; 35:5; 37:7; 41:42; **Ex** 7:24; 13:18; 16:13; 19:12; 23; 25:11; 24; 25(2); 27:17; 28:32; 33(2); 34; 29:16; 20; 30:3(2); 37:2; 11; 12(2); 26(2); 38:16; 20; 31(2); 39:23; 25; 26; 40:8; 33; **Lev** 1:5; 11; 3:2; 8; 13; 7:2; 8:15; 19; 24; 9:12; 18; 14:41; 16:18; 19:27; 25:31; 44; **Num** 1:50; 53; 3:26; 37; 4:26; 32; 11:24; 31; 32; 16:27; 34; 21:4; 22:4; 35:2; 4; **Deut** 6:14; 13:7; 17:14; 25:19; **Josh** 6:3(2); 4; 7; 11; 14; 15(2); 15:3; 9(2); 11; 12; 16:6; 18:14; 17; 20; 19:8; 14; 21:44; **Judg** 2:12; 14; 7:21; 8:26; 18:23; 20:29; **1 Sam** 15:12; 27; 26:5; 7; **2 Sam** 5:9; 23; 7:1; 22:12; 24:6; **1 Ki** 2:5; 3:1; 4:24; 6:5(3); 6; 29; 7:18; 20; 24(2); 36; 8:14; 18:32; 35; 20:31(2); 32(2); 22:34; **2 Ki** 1:8; 2:24; 6:17; 9:18; 19; 23; 11:11; 17:15; 23:5; 25:1; 4; 10; 17; **1 Chr** 4:33; 9:27; 11:8; 14:14; 22:9; 28:12; **2 Chr** 4:3(2); 6:3; 13:13; 14; 14:7; 14; 15:15; 17:10; 18:33; 20:30; 23:10; 26:6; 34:6; **Ezra** 1:6; **Neh** 5:17; 6:16; 12:28; 29; 13:21; **Job** 1:10(3); 8:17; 11:18; 19:12; 22:10; 24:8; 29:5; 41:14; **Ps** 3:6; 18:11; 27:6; 34:7; 44:13; 48:12; 50:3; 55:10; 59:6; 14; 76:11; 78:28; 79:3; 4; 88:17; 89:7; 128:3; **Prov** 3:3; 6:21; 23:31; **Eccl** 1:6; 9:14; **Song** 3:7; **Isa** 15:8; 29:1; 3; 16; 42:25; 49:18; 60:4; **Jer** 1:15; 4:17; 6:3; 12:9; 13:1; 2; 4; 17:26; 21:14; 25:9; 31:26; 32:44; 33:13; 34:16; 41:14; 46:5; 14; 48:17; 49:5; 50:14; 15; 29; 32; 51:2; 52:4; 7; 14; 22; 23; **Lam** 1:17; 2:3; **Ezek** 1:4; 18; 27(2); 28; 4:2; 5:2; 5; 6; 7(2); 12; 14; 15; 6:5; 13; 8:10; 10:12; 11:12; 12:14; 16:33; 37; 57; 23:15; 24; 27:11(2); 28:24; 26; 31:4; 32:22; 23; 24; 25; 26; 34:26; 36:4; 7; 36; 37:2; 38:4; 39:2; 40:5; 14; 16(2); 17; 25; 29; 30; 33; 36; 43; 41:5; 6; 7; 8; 10; 11; 12; 16; 17; 19; 42:15; 16; 17; 19; 20; 43:13; 17(2); 20; 45:1; 2; 46:23(3); 47:2; 48:35; **Dan** 5:7; 16; 29; 9:16; **Joel** 3:11; **Am** 3:11; **Jon** 2:5(2); **Nah** 3:8; **Zech** 2:5; 7:7; 9:8; **Mt** 3:4; 5; 9:22; 18:6; 21:33; 27:27; **Mk** 1:6; 28; 3:5; 32; 34; 4:10; 5:30; 32; 8:33; 9:8; 14; 42; 10:23; 11:11; 12:1; 38; 14:51; **Lk** 1:65; 2:9; 3:3; 5:15; 6:10; 7:9; 13:8; 17:2; 19:43; 20:46; 22:49; **Jn** 11:19; 20:7; 14; 21:20; **Acts** 9:3; 13:11; 14:20; 22:6; 26:13; **Jude** 7; **Rev** 4:3; 4; 6; 8; 5:11; 7:11

AS (3767/3029)

Gen 4:22; 26; 7:9; 16; 8:21; 9:3; 7; 9; 10:19(6); 30; 11:2; 12:4; 6(2); 19; 13:3(2); 10; 12(2); 16; 14:6(2); 14(2); 15(2); 16(2); 15:15; 16:6; 17:4; 8; 9; 15; 20; 23; 18:1; 5(2); 8; 25(2); 33(2); 19:8; 9; 31; 21:1(2); 4; 22:2; 14; 17(2); 23:9; 18; 20; 24:21; 27; 51; 25:18(3); 20; 31; 33; 26:4; 34; 27:4; 9; 14; 19; 30(2); 37; 28:6; 14; 18; 22; 29:24; 28; 29; 30:4; 9; 31:2; 5; 45; 32:12; 13; 25; 31; 33:10(2); 34:4; 8; 12; 15; 21; 22; 35:18; 36:24; 38:14; 29; 39:10; 18; 40:10; 22; 41:13; 19; 21(2); 36; 38; 39(3); 45; 49; 54; 42:7; 14; 27; 35; 43:6; 17; 18; 34(2); 44:1(2); 3(2); 15; 17; 33; 47:11; 21; 24(2); 30; 48:4; 5; 7; 20(2); 49:4; 9(2); 16; 30; 50:6; 8(2); 12; 13; 20(2); **Ex** 1:17; 2:1; 14; 4:16(2); 5:7; 13; 14; 20; 6:3;

7; 8; 20; 23; 25; 7:1; 6; 10; 13; 20; 22; 8:15; 19; 20; 27; 9:12; 17; 18; 29(2); 30; 35; 10:14; 11:6; 12:14(2); 17; 24; 25; 28; 31; 32; 48; 50; 13:9(2); 11; 16(2); 21; 14:28; 15:16(2); 16:5(2); 10; 14(2); 22; 24; 34; 17:10; 18:21; 21:7; 22(2); 22:13; 26; 23:2; 15; 24:10; 25:27; 26:29; 27:8; 28:1; 3; 4; 12(2); 29; 41; 29:1; 24; 25(2); 26; 36; 40; 41; 44; 30:23; 30; 37; 31:10; 16; 32:1; 13; 17; 19(2); 23; 33:11; 34:4; 9; 10; 18; 32; 35:5; 19; 22(2); 37:14; 27; 38:5; 39:1; 5; 6; 7(2); 21; 26; 29; 31; 41; 43; 40:13; 15(2); 19; 21; 23; 25; 27; 29; 32; **Lev** 1:9; 10; 2:2; 4; 12; 16; 3:5; 6; 7; 9; 11; 14; 16; 4:3; 8; 10; 20(2); 21; 23; 28; 31; 32; 33; 35; 5:6; 7(2); 10; 11; 12; 13; 15(2); 18; 6:6; 15; 17; 20; 7:5; 10(2); 13; 14; 19; 21; 30; 32; 35; 8:2; 4; 9; 13; 17; 18; 21; 27; 29(2); 31; 34; 9:2(2); 3(2); 4; 7; 10; 18; 21(2); 10:3; 5; 15(2); 18; 11:11; 13; 12:2; 5; 6(2); 8(2); 13:5; 40; 43; 14:6; 10; 12(2); 13; 21(2); 22; 24; 30; 31(3); 34; 15:15(2); 25; 26(2); 30(2); 16:3(2); 5(2); 6; 9; 10; 11; 15; 26; 32; 34; 17:5; 18:18; 19(2); 22; 28; 19:16; 18; 20; 21; 23(2); 34(2); 20:13; 25; 21:14; 22:13; 18; 23; 25; 27; 23:12; 18; 19(2); 20; 41; 24:16(2); 19; 20; 23; 25:31; 39; 40; 42; 44; 46(2); 53; 26:34(2); 35(2); 36(2); 37; 27:9; 11; 12; 14; 21; 23; 24; **Num** 1:19; 2:17; 33; 3:3; 4; 16; 42; 51; 4:27; 29; 31; 33; 49; 5:4; 26; 6:11(2); 12; 14(3); 17; 20; 7:13; 15; 16; 19; 21; 22; 23; 25; 27; 28; 31; 33; 34; 35; 37; 39; 40; 41; 43; 45; 46; 47; 49; 51; 52; 53; 55; 57; 58; 59; 61; 63; 64; 65; 67; 69; 70; 71; 73; 75; 76; 77; 79; 81; 82; 83; 87; 8:3; 8; 12(2); 19; 22; 9:18(2); 10:8; 31; 11:12; 12:10(2); 12; 13:21(2); 32; 14:15; 17; 19; 21; 28(2); 32; 45(2); 15:3; 5; 6; 7(2); 8(3); 10(2); 14; 15; 20(2); 24(3); 27; 36; 16:16(2); 31; 38; 39; 40; 47; 17:10; 11; 18:7; 8(2); 11; 17; 18; 19; 21; 24(2); 26; 27(2); 30(2); 20:9; 27; 21:24(2); 26(2); 29; 30(4); 34; 22:4; 8; 22; 23:2; 30; 24:1; 9(2); 26:4; 53; 27:11; 13; 22; 23; 28:2; 3; 5; 7; 8(2); 9; 12(2); 13(2); 15; 19; 22; 24; 27; 29:2; 5; 6; 8; 11; 13; 16; 19; 22; 25; 28; 31; 34; 36; 38; 39(2); 40; 31:7; 9; 19; 29; 31; 41; 47; 54; 32:5; 25; 27; 29; 31; 33:49(2); 54; 56; 34:2; 6; 17; 35:5; 36:2; 10; **Deut** 1:3; 7(2); 10; 11; 17(2); 19; 21; 31; 40; 41; 44; 2:1; 5(2); 9(2); 10(2); 11; 12; 14; 19(2); 20; 21(2); 22; 23(2); 29; 30; 35; 36(2); 3:2; 6; 7; 10(2); 14(2); 16(5); 17(3); 20; 4:5; 7; 8; 19; 20; 21; 33; 38(2); 49(2); 5:12; 14(2); 16; 26; 31; 32; 6:3; 8(2); 16; 19; 24; 25; 8:5; 18; 20; 9:3(2); 18; 21(2); 10:5; 6; 9; 10; 15; 22; 11:4; 10; 18(2); 25; 12:8; 9; 19(2); 20(3); 21(3); 22; 13:6; 11; 17; 14:7; 15:4; 6; 22; 16:10; 17; 21; 17:15; 18:2; 7; 14; 19:5; 8; 10; 19; 20:16; 17; 21:17; 23; 22:11; 16; 26; 24:3; 4; 8; 17; 25:5; 17; 19; 26:1; 15; 18; 19; 27:3; 28:9(2); 29; 49(2); 62; 63; 68; 29:8; 13(3); 15(2); 19; 28; 30:9; 19; 31:3; 4; 13(2); 21; 26; 32:2(4); 10; 11; 40; 49; 50; 33:20; 25; 34:1(2); 2(2); 3(2); 9; **Josh** 1:3; 4(2); 5; 6; 15; 17(2); 2:5; 7(2); 11(2); 3:7; 13(3); 15; 4:8(2); 12; 14; 18; 23; 5:5; 14; 6:22; 7:5(2); 8:2(2); 5; 6; 15; 19(2); 27; 29(2); 31(2); 33(3); 9:21; 25; 10:1; 10(2); 11(3); 28; 30; 39(2); 40; 41(4); 11:4(2); 9; 12; 13; 14; 15; 17(2); 20; 23; 12:2(2); 3(2); 5(2); 6; 7(3); 13:3(3); 4(2); 5(2); 6(4); 7; 8; 9(2); 10(2); 11(2); 14; 25(2); 27(3); 32; 33; 14:1; 2; 5; 7; 10; 11(4); 12; 13; 15:5(2); 16; 17; 47(2); 63; 16:3(2); 5(2); 17:14; 19:8(2); 10(2); 28(2); 33(2); 49; 51; 20:4; 21:8; 12; 22:4; 23:4(2); 5; 8; 9; 10; 15; 24:15; **Judg** 1:7; 12; 13; 20; 2:15(2); 22; 4:16(2); 22; 5:15; 6:4(2); 5(2); 16; 27; 36; 37; 7:5; 12(3); 17; 19; 22(2); 24(4); 8:8; 18; 19; 21; 33(2); 9:15; 16; 33(3); 36; 48; 52(2); 11:13(2); 16(2); 31; 33(2); 13:9; 20; 23; 14:2; 6; 15:5(2); 10; 11; 16:9; 20; 17:8; 13; 19:22; 24; 26; 20:1(3); 8; 11; 30; 31; 32; 39; 43(2); 21:1; 7; 22; **Ruth** 1:8; 3:13; 4:10; **1 Sam** 1:12; 26; 28(2); 2:16(2); 18; 3:10; 20; 4:9; 5:10; 6:6; 8; 12; 14; 17; 18(2); 7:9; 10; 11(2); 9:11; 13(2); 14; 20; 27; 10:7; 12:15; 23; 13:5; 7; 10(2); 14:13; 39; 45; 15:11; 22(2); 23(2); 27; 33; 16:7; 17:20(2); 23; 30; 52(4); 55; 57; 18:1; 3; 6; 7; 10; 17; 19; 27; 19:6; 7; 9; 20; 20:3(2); 13; 17; 20; 21; 23; 25; 31(2); 36; 41(2); 22:8; 13; 14(2); 23:11; 24:4; 13; 25:15(2); 20; 25; 26(3); 29; 34; 39; 26:10; 16; 20; 24; 27:8(3); 28:10; 17; 29:6; 8(2); 9(2); 10(2); 30:24; **2 Sam** 1:6; 2:18(2); 23(2); 27; 3:9; 33; 34; 4:4; 6; 9; 5:12; 25(3); 6:16; 20; 22; 7:10; 15; 23; 25; 8:3; 9:8; 11; 10:2; 11:11(2); 23(2); 25(2); 12:5; 13:13; 29; 35; 36(2); 14:11; 13; 17; 19; 25(2); 15:10(2); 21(2); 26; 30(2); 34; 16:5; 13(2); 19; 20; 23; 17:6; 12(2); 18:33; 19:3; 14; 30; 20:2(2); 8; 21:5; 22:23; 31; 43(2); 44; 45(2); 23:6; 24:7(2); 19; **1 Ki** 1:20; 21; 29; 30; 37; 41; 2:3; 17; 21; 24(2); 31; 38; 44; 3:6; 14; 4:11; 12(2); 15; 20(2); 21(2); 25(2); 5:5; 11; 12; 6:16(2); 7:8; 8:20; 24; 25; 36; 43; 53; 57; 59; 61; 9:2; 4; 5; 8; 11(2); 13; 16; 21; 10:10; 21; 27(4); 11:1(2); 4; 6; 19; 33; 38(2); 12:12; 30(2); 13:6; 18; 20; 34; 14:2; 6; 8; 10; 15; 15:3; 11; 19; 16:2; 9; 11(2); 31(2); 17:1; 11; 12; 13; 18:7; 10; 12(2); 15; 28; 44(2); 19:2; 5; 8(2); 15; 16(2); 20:4; 12; 34; 36(4); 39; 41; 21:11(2); 22:4(3); 14; 17; 36; **2 Ki** 2:2(2); 4(2); 6(2); 11; 19; 23; 3:7(3); 14; 22(2); 27; 4:8(2); 30(2); 40; 5:16; 20; 27(2); 6:5; 26; 30; 7:17; 18; 8:5; 16; 18; 19; 9:17; 22(2); 31; 37; 10:2(2); 15; 25(2); 11:8(2); 12:9; 13:5; 21; 14:3; 5(2); 9; 15:9; 16:2; 8; 17:2; 4; 23(2); 41; 18:8(2); 19:26(2); 29; 37; 21:3; 13; 20; 22:18; 23:16; 21; 27; 24:11; 13; 25:12; 25(2); 30; **1 Chr** 2:19; 35; 4:27(2); 33(2); 39(2); 41; 42; 5:8(2); 9(2); 11(2); 6:10; 26; 66; 7:15; 25(2); 28(2); 9:22; 12:8(2); 40(2); 13:5(2); 14:2; 16(3); 15:15; 27; 29; 16:18; 37; 17:9; 13; 21; 23; 18:3(3); 21:15; 22:7; 11; 23:11; 22; 24; 24:2; 5; 19; 31(2); 25:8(2); 26:13(2); 18; 29; 28:7; 8; 9; 29:11; 14; 15(2); 17; 23; 25; **2 Chr** 1:12; 15(4); 2:3; 16(2); 3:16; 4:6; 22; 5:13; 6:10; 15; 16; 27; 31(2); 33; 7:12; 17(2); 18(2); 21; 8:8; 14; 9:9; 11; 20; 26(2); 27(4); 10:12; 11:14; 16; 18; 22; 12:12; 13:8; 10; 12; 15; 16:3; 17:11; 18:3(2); 13; 16; 20:20; 21; 33; 21:6(2); 23:3; 18(2); 24:22; 25:3(2); 4; 13; 16; 18; 26:5(2); 8(2); 11; 28:1; 5; 29:8; 24; 31(2); 30:7; 8; 10(2); 31:3; 5(2); 15(2); 32:17; 19; 33:14(2); 22; 23; 34:6(2); 26; 35:7(2); 12; 18; 36:21(2); **Ezra** 2:62; 3:1; 2; 4; 9; 4:2; 3; 6:8; 17; 18; 7:25; 27; 28; 8:27; 35; 9:2; 7; 12(2); 13; 15(2); 10:12; 19; **Neh** 1:1; 9; 3:1(4); 8(2); 11(2); 13(2); 15(2); 16(4); 24(2); 26(2); 27(2); 31(4); 32(2); 4:4; 18; 5:5(2); 12; 6:5; 8; 11(2); 7:64; 8:1; 15; 9:10; 11; 23; 24; 10:30; 34; 36; 11:25; 12:37(2); 38(2); 39(2); 13:13; 19; 25; **Esth** 2:7; 15; 20(2); 3:11; 14; 4:2(2); 14; 5:5; 8; 13; 6:10; 7:4; 8; 8:8; 13; 9:18(2); 19; 22(2); 23; 31(2); **Job** 2:10; 3:6; 4:8; 5:7; 8; 14; 26; 6:7; 26; 7:9; 20; 9:32; 10:4; 19; 22(3); 11:16; 12:3(3); 13:9; 24; 14:11; 18(2); 19(2); 16:4; 21; 17:13; 15; 18:3(2); 20; 19:11; 15; 22; 21:4; 33; 23:10; 24:3; 17; 19; 27:2; 3(2); 6(2); 28:5(2); 29:2(2); 4; 18; 22; 23(2); 25(3); 30:5; 14; 15; 18; 31:18; 33; 33:6; 10; 34:3; 26; 35:8; 36:27; 37:18; 22; 23; 39:16; 41:4; 5; 15; 20; 24(4); 27(2); 29; 42:7; 8; 9; 10(2); 15; **Ps** 5:7; 12; 10:5; 9; 11:1; 14:4; 16:3; 17:8; 12; 15; 18:30; 42(2); 44(2); 21:9; 25:10; 26:11; 27:12; 29:10; 31:14; 33:7; 12; 22; 34:18; 35:13; 14(2); 37:2; 6(2); 38:10; 39:5(2); 12; 40:4; 16; 41:12; 42:1; 10; 44:22; 48:3; 6; 7; 8; 53:4; 55:16; 58:3(2); 7(2); 8; 9(2); 61:6; 63:5; 65:3; 66:10; 68:2(2); 14; 17; 69:13; 71:7; 72:5(2); 17(2); 73:1; 2; 5; 6; 19; 20; 74:14; 77:13; 78:65; 79:2; 81:5; 83:9(3); 10; 14(2); 84:6; 89:10; 29; 36; 90:11; 95:8(2); 103:11; 12(2); 13; 15(2); 18; 104:2; 6; 33(2); 105:10; 11; 17; 106:9; 109:17(2); 18(2); 29; 116:2(2); 119:14(2); 70(2); 111; 126; 132; 162; 122:3; 123:2(2); 124:6; 7; 125:2; 5(2); 126:4; 129:6; 135:12; 136:21; 137:8; 139:12; 16; 140:9; 141:2(2); 5; 7; 144:12(2); 147:20; **Prov** 2:4(2); 3:12; 5:4(2); 19; 7:2; 22(2); 23; 8:26; 30; 9:4; 16; 10:26; 11:19; 22; 16:14; 19:24; 20:16; 19; 25; 30; 21:8; 29; 23:7; 28; 24:29; 25:3; 16(2); 25; 26:1; 11; 14; 21; 27:17; 19; 28:1; 4; 29:21; 30:33; **Eccl** 2:13; 15; 16; 3:19; 5:15(2); 16; 19; 7:12; 14(2); 24; 8:13; 9:2(2); 10:5; 11:5; 12:7; **Song** 1:7; 4:11; 5:11; 15; 6:4(4); 10(4); 12; 13; 8:6(6); 10; **Isa** 1:7; 8(3); 18(3); 26(2); 30(2); 31(2); 3:9; 12; 16; 5:18; 24(2); 25; 6:13(2); 7:2; 8:6; 14(2); 9:1; 3; 4; 18; 19; 10:10; 11; 14; 15(3); 18; 20; 22; 25; 26; 30(2); 32; 11:9; 10; 16; 13:6; 8; 14(2); 17; 19; 14:10(2); 17; 24(2); 15:4(2); 16:2; 14; 17:3; 5(2); 9; 19:14; 20:3; 4(2); 21:1; 22:16; 23; 23:15; 24:2(6); 22; 25:4; 5(2); 10; 11; 26:17; 18; 20; 27:7; 28:19(2); 21(2); 29:2; 7; 8(2); 13; 16; 17; 30:17(2); 22; 26(2); 29(2); 31; 31:4; 32:2(3); 15; 33:4; 11; 34:4(2); 35:1; 37:27(2); 30; 38; 38:19; 21; 40:13; 15(3); 17; 41:2(2); 11; 12(2); 25(2); 42:6(2); 19(3); 43:14; 44:7; 47:4; 8; 14; 48:10; 49:6; 8; 18(3); 26; 50:4; 51:4; 9; 23; 52:14; 53:2(2); 3; 7(2); 54:9; 55:4; 9; 10; 56:12; 58:2; 4; 10; 59:10(3); 12; 17(2); 21; 61:10(2); 11(2); 62:1(2); 5(2); 8; 63:10; 13; 14; 64:2(2); 6; 65:8; 15; 18; 22; 66:3(5); 8(2); 13; 20; 22; **Jer** 2:26; 36; 3:5; 18; 20; 4:31(2); 5:2; 9; 19; 22; 26; 27; 29; 6:7; 9(2); 23; 24; 26; 27; 28; 7:14; 15; 8:6; 9:9; 22; 10:6; 11:5; 12:16(2); 13:5; 11; 15:2(4); 13; 18; 19; 17:3; 11; 16; 22; 27; 18:4; 6(2); 17; 19:7; 11; 20:11; 21:7; 9; 22:24; 30; 23:7; 8; 27; 34; 24:8; 25:18; 30; 26:11; 14(2); 27:13; 28:9(2); 30:20; 31:5; 10; 28; 40(2); 32:20; 42; 33:7; 11; 22; 24; 34:5; 11; 38:2; 16; 39:12; 18; 40:3; 10; 41:4; 6(2); 17; 42:2; 18; 43:7(2); 12; 44:6; 13; 16; 17; 22; 23; 30; 45:5; 46:18(3); 26; 48:2; 8; 13; 42; 49:16(2); 18; 50:15; 18; 26; 40; 43; 51:14; 49; 52:16; 34; **Lam** 1:15; 22; 2:6; 7; 12(2); 13; 22; 3:12; 4:2(2); 8(2); 5:10; 21; **Ezek** 1:1; 10; 13; 15; 16; 18; 27(2); 2:5; 4:3; 12; 5:1; 11; 7:17(2); 20; 21(2); 8:1; 9:10; 11; 10:2; 10(2); 13; 22; 11:15; 21; 12:4; 7(2); 11; 23; 13:21; 14:10; 16; 18; 20; 16:4; 19; 29(2); 38; 47; 48(2); 50; 59; 17:16; 19; 18:3; 4(2); 18; 20:3; 31; 33; 36; 39; 41; 21:7; 10; 22:5; 20; 22; 23:4; 16(2); 18; 30; 44; 24:18; 22; 25:4; 7; 10; 26:3; 10; 27:10; 15; 28:2; 6; 16; 29:5; 10(2); 30:9; 18; 31:5; 33:11; 12; 24; 27; 30; 31(2); 32; 34:8; 12; 17; 19; 35:6; 11; 15(3); 36:5; 11; 38; 37:7(2); 8; 10; 16; 39:17; 40:13; 21; 22; 23; 40; 41:7(2); 15(2); 17(2); 21; 25; 42:9; 11(3); 12; 43:22; 24; 44:3; 11; 13; 22; 24; 45:5; 6; 46:5(4); 7(2); 11(2); 12; 15; 47:10; 13; 14; 15; 17; 22(2); 48:8; 11; 21(4); 23; 29; **Dan** 1:13; 17; 2:29; 30; 40(3); 41; 42; 43(2); 45; 4:23; 26; 35; 5:12; 6:10; 7:9; 12; 28; 8:5; 11(2); 18; 22; 9:7; 11; 12; 13; 15; 10:4; 17; 11:5(2); 12:1; **Hos** 1:10; 2:3; 15(3); 4:15; 6:3; 9; 9:9; 10; 11; 13; 10:3; 6; 7; 14; 11:2; 4; 12:9; **Joel** 1:15; 2:32; 3:3; **Am** 2:9(2); 11(2); 13; 3:12; 4:11; 5:8; 14; 19(2); 6:7; 7:15; 8:14(2); 9:9; 11; **Ob** 4(2); 11; 15; 16(2); 20(2); **Jon** 1:14; 4:7; **Mic** 1:7; 2:8(2); 7:14; 15; **Nah** 2:7; **Hab** 1:8; 2:5; 14; 16; **Zeph** 1:8; 2:9; 13(2); **Hag** 1:12; 2:3; 19; **Zech** 1:6; 2:4; 12; 4:1; 7:3; 13; 8:11; 13; 14; 9:11; 15; 16; 10:3; 6; 7; 8; 12:10(2); 13:9(2); 14:3; 5; **Mal** 1:8; 3:3(2); 4(2); 14; 17; **Mt** 1:18; 24; 3:9; 5:48; 6:2; 7; 10; 12; 7:29(2); 8:4; 13; 9:9; 10; 15(2); 32; 10:7; 16(3); 18; 11:7; 12:13(2); 40; 13:4; 40; 43; 14:5; 36(2); 15:9; 28; 17:2(2); 9; 20; 18:3; 4; 25; 33; 19:19; 20:14; 28; 29; 21:6; 18; 23; 26; 22:9(2); 39; 23:15(2); 37; 24:3; 14; 21; 27; 37; 38; 25:32; 40; 45; 26:7; 13; 19; 21; 24; 26; 39(2); 55; 64; 27:10; 11; 32; 65(2); 28:1; 3(2); 6; 9; 15; **Mk** 1:2; 16; 22(2); 29(2); 42(2); 44; 2:14; 15; 19(2); 23; 3:5(2); 10(2); 20; 4:4; 26; 33; 36; 5:36(2); 6:11; 56(2); 7:6; 7; 9:3; 9; 13; 26; 10:1; 15; 17; 32; 46; 11:2(2); 6; 11; 20; 27; 12:23; 31; 33; 13:1; 3; 19; 14:3; 9; 16; 18; 21; 22; 45(2); 48; 66; 15:2; 8; 21; 16:7; 10; 12; 14; **Lk** 1:1; 2; 8; 23(2); 44(2); 55; 70; 2:20; 23; 43; 3:4; 8; 15; 23; 4:16; 5:1; 14(2); 17; 6:10(2); 18(2); 22; 31; 34; 36; 8:5; 6(2); 23; 42; 9:5; 18; 29; 33; 34; 42; 46; 52; 54; 57; 10:3; 7; 8; 27; 33; 38; 11:1(2); 2; 8(2); 27; 30; 36; 37; 41; 53; 13:34; 14:1; 22; 15:25; 30(2); 17:6; 11; 12; 14; 24; 26; 28; 18:11; 13; 17; 35; 19:11; 30; 32; 33; 36; 37; 41; 20:1; 30; 33; 21:5; 13; 35; 22:13; 22; 24; 26(2); 27; 29; 31; 39; 52; 56; 66(2); 23:3; 7(2); 14; 24; 26; 24:4; 5; 17; 24; 30; 36; 39; 50(2); **Jn** 1:12(2); 14; 23; 36; 3:14; 4:12(2); 51; 5:21; 23; 26; 30; 6:11(2); 31; 57; 58; 59; 7:10; 28; 38; 8:6; 20; 28; 30; 9:1; 5(2); 29; 10:15; 26; 11:20(2); 29(2); 56; 12:14; 46; 50; 13:15; 33; 34; 14:27; 31; 15:4; 6; 9; 10; 12; 16:21(2); 17:2(3); 11; 14; 16; 18; 21; 22; 23; 19:40; 20:9; 11; 21; 21:9(2); **Acts** 1:10; 11; 2:2; 3; 4; 15; 22; 39(2); 45; 3:11; 12; 17; 24(2); 4:1; 6(4); 35; 5:42; 6:15; 7:21; 26; 28; 31; 40; 42; 44; 48; 51; 59; 8:3; 12; 16; 32(2); 36; 9:3; 17; 32; 10:9; 25; 27; 29(2); 45(2); 47; 11:15(2); 17; 19(2); 22(2); 12:13; 18(2); 13:2; 5; 17; 22; 25; 33; 47; 48(2); 14:15; 15:8; 11; 15; 16:4; 16; 17:2; 12(2); 23; 25; 28; 19:2; 20:3; 9; 21:10; 31; 37; 22:3; 5; 6; 23; 25; 23:11; 15; 20; 31; 24:10; 25; 25:10; 18; 26:12; 17(2); 24; 29; 30(2); 27:25; 27; 30; 33; 28:10; 15(2); 17; **Rom** 1:13; 15(2); 17; 21; 28; 2:12(4); 24; 26; 3:4; 5; 7; 8(2); 10; 25; 4:4(2); 6; 17(2); 5:12; 18; 19; 21; 6:3(2); 4; 13(3); 19(3); 7:1(2); 2(2); 8:14(2); 26; 36(2); 9:8; 13; 25; 27; 29; 32; 33; 10:15; 11:8; 13; 26; 30; 12:3; 4; 18(2); 13:9; 13; 14:11; 16; 15:3; 7; 9; 15; 21; **1 Cor** 1:6; 31; 2:9; 3:1(3); 5; 10; 15; 4:1; 7; 8; 9; 13; 14; 17; 18; 5:1; 3(2); 7:6(2); 7; 8; 17(2); 25; 26; 29; 30(3); 31; 39(2); 40; 8:2; 5; 7; 9:5; 8; 20(2); 21; 22; 26; 10:6; 7(2); 8; 9; 10; 11; 13; 15; 33; 11:1; 2; 5; 12; 18; 25(2); 26(2); 12:11; 12; 18; 13:11(3); 12; 14:33; 34; 15:8; 22; 38; 48(2); 49; 16:1; 2; 10; **2 Cor** 1:5; 7; 14(2); 18; 22; 23; 2:17(3); 3:1; 5; 6; 18(2); 4:1; 5:5; 20; 6:1; 4; 8; 9(3); 10(3); 13; 16; 7:14; 15; 8:5; 6(2); 7; 11; 15; 9:3; 5(2); 7; 9; 10:2; 7; 14; 15; 11:2; 3; 10; 12; 16; 17; 23; 12:16; 20(2); 13:2; 5; **Gal** 1:9; 2:7; 14(2); 3:1; 6; 10(2); 16(2); 27(2); 4:1(2); 5; 14(2); 28; 29; 5:13; 14; 21; 6:10; 12(2); 16(2); **Eph** 1:4; 5; 2:3; 15; 3:3; 5; 4:4; 17; 21; 32; 5:1; 2; 3; 8; 15(2); 22; 23; 24; 25; 28; 29; 33; 6:5; 6(2); 7; 20; **Phil** 1:7(2); 20; 2:8; 12(2); 15; 17; 22; 23(2); 3:8; 15(2); 17; **Col** 1:6(2); 7; 2:1(2); 6; 7; 20; 3:12; 13; 18; 22; 23; 4:4; **1 Th** 1:5; 2:2; 4(2); 5; 6; 7; 11(2); 13(2); 14; 16; 3:4; 6; 12; 4:1; 6; 11; 13; 5:2; 3; 4; 6; 8; 11; **2 Th** 1:3; 2:2(2); 4; 3:1; 13; 15(2); **1 Tim** 1:3; 16; 3:6; 10; 13; 5:1(2); 2(2); 6:1(2); **2 Tim** 1:3(2); 2:3; 4; 9; 3:8; 9; 4:6; 21(2); **Titus** 1:5; 7; 9; 2:1; **Phm** 1:9; 14; 16; 17(2); 24; **Heb** 1:4; 2:14; 3:2; 3; 5; 6; 7; 8; 15; 4:2(2); 3; 7; 10; 15; 5:3; 4; 6; 10; 6:19; 7:20; 27; 28; 8:5; 6; 9:11; 25; 27; 10:25(2); 11:8; 9; 12(5); 27; 29; 12:5; 7; 10; 20; 27; 13:3; 5; 17; **Jas** 1:10; 2:8; 9; 12; 26; 5:5; 10; **1 Pe** 1:14(2); 15; 19; 24(2); 2:2; 4; 5; 11; 12; 13; 14; 16(3); 3:6; 7(2); 8; 16; 4:10(2); 11(2); 12; 15(2); 16; 19; 5:2; 3; 12; **2 Pe** 1:3; 13(2); 14; 19; 21; 2:1; 13; 3:4; 8(2); 9; 10; 15; 16(2); **1 Jn** 1:7; 2:6; 18; 27(2); 3:2; 3; 7; 12; 23; 4:5; 14; 17; 5:8; **2 Jn** 4; 5; 6; 7; **3 Jn** 2; 3; **Jude** 7(2); **Rev** 1:10; 14(2); 15(2); 17; 2:19; 24(3); 27; 3:3; 19(2); 21; 5:6; 13; 6:11; 12; 13; 14; 9:3; 11; 10:3; 7; 9(2); 10(2); 11:6(2); 12:4(2); 13:3; 15(2); 14:3; 16:3; 15; 18; 17:12(2); 18:6; 7; 17(2); 19:6(3); 20:8; 21:2; 11; 16(3); 22:1

AT (1815/1673)

Gen 3:24; 4:7; 8:3; 6; 13:3; 4; 14:17; 15:15; 17:21; 18:14; 19:11; 21:2; 16; 22; 32; 22:19; 23:9(2); 10; 18; 24:11; 21; 30; 55; 25:11; 27:41; 28:11; 18; 31:10; 33:14; 34:21; 35:27; 38:1; 5; 12; 27; 40:6; 41:1; 21; 42:1; 27; 43:16; 19; 25; 33; 48:3; 49:19; 23; 27; 50:11; **Ex** 2:5; 11; 4:24; 25; 5:23; 8:32; 9:14; 12:6; 9; 18(2); 29; 41; 13:20; 16:6; 12; 13; 18:5; 22; 26; 19:17; 21; 22:23; 23:15; 16; 24:4; 25:18; 19(3); 26; 26:9; 24(2); 27:4; 28:7; 22; 27; 29:39; 41; 42; 30:8; 32:19; 33:8; 9; 10; 34:22; 35:15; 36:29(2); 37:5; 7; 8(3); 13; 38:8; 39:4; 15; 20; 40:8; 28; **Lev** 1:3; 15; 17; 3:2; 4:7(2); 18(2); 24; 25; 29; 30; 33; 34; 5:9; 6:20; 7:18; 8:3; 4; 15; 31; 35; 9:9; 13:7; 22; 27; 35; 37; 14:11; 46; 15:24; 25; 16:2; 7; 29; 17:5; 6; 18:9; 19:7; 20; 23:4; 5; 32; 25:32; 37; 26:32; 27:10; 13; 16; 31; 33; **Num** 2:4; 6; 8; 11; 13; 15; 19; 21; 23; 26; 28; 30; 3:39; 6:18; 8:25; 9:2; 3(2); 5; 7; 11; 13; 18(2); 23(3); 10:3; 10; 11:6; 10; 35; 13:26; 30; 16:18; 19; 27; 34; 50; 18:7; 19:19; 20:24; 21:8; 9; 11; 30; 33; 34; 22:4; 5; 6; 20; 36(2); 38; 23:25(2); 24:1; 25:6; 27:14(2); 21(2); 28:2; 6; 11; 26; 29:39; 33:2; 5; 6; 8; 9; 12; 13; 14; 16; 17; 18; 19; 20; 21; 22; 23; 24; 25; 26; 27; 28; 29; 30; 31; 32; 33; 34; 35; 37; 38; 41; 42; 43; 44(2); 45; 46; 34:5; 9; 12; 35:20; 22; 23; 26; **Deut** 1:4; 6; 9; 16; 18; 2:18; 32; 34; 3:1; 2; 4; 8; 12; 18; 21; 23; 4:3; 11; 14; 15; 46; 5:5; 7:22; 9:11; 18; 19; 20; 22; 10:1; 8; 10(2); 12:8; 14:28; 15:1; 9; 16:4; 6(4); 11; 16(3); 22:15; 23:19; 24; 24:5; 25:18; 28:29; 52(2); 55; 57; 67; 31:10(3); 15; 32:35; 51; 33:3; 8(2); **Josh** 3:16; 5:2; 3; 10; 6:26; 7:7; 8:5; 6; 14; 29; 9:6; 10; 16; 10:6(2); 10; 15; 16; 17; 21; 27; 42; 43; 11:5; 10; 21; 12:4(2); 15:1; 2; 4; 5(2); 7; 8; 11; 21; 63; 16:2; 3; 7; 8; 17:9; 18:1; 9; 12(2); 14; 15; 19(3); 19:22; 29; 33(2); 34; 51; 20:4; 21:2; 3; 22:9; 12; 24:30; 32; **Judg** 1:4; 2:9; 3:2; 19; 29; 4:4; 6; 7; 11; 20; 5:17; 27(2); 7:3; 17; 19; 25(2); 8:10; 18; 32; 9:5; 6; 41; 44; 11:34; 39; 12:6(2); 10; 12; 13:23; 25; 14:4; 16:2; 3; 20; 30; 18:3; 8; 17; 19:2; 16; 26; 27; 20:1; 5; 15; 16; 20; 22; 30; 31; 32; 33; 47; 21:1; 5; 12; 13; 14; 22; 24; **Ruth** 1:22; 2:14; 3:2; 7; 8(2); 10(2); 14; 4:10; 11; **1 Sam** 1:19; 2:1; 11; 22; 29; 3:2; 10; 11; 6:10; 7:6(2); 7; 8:4; 9:8; 10:2; 3; 17; 13:4; 11; 12; 14:18; 15:34; 16:4; 6; 7(4); 17:1; 15; 17; 18:10; 19; 19:18; 19; 22(2); 20:5; 6; 16; 20; 25; 33; 35; 21:4; 22:14; 23:6; 19; 29; 25:1; 24; 40; 26:1; 8; 27:3; 28:4(2); 7; 29:1; 2; 30:21; 31:13; **2 Sam** 2:32; 3:8; 20; 22; 30; 32; 4:5(2); 8; 11; 5:1; 3(2); 8:3; 10; 9:2; 7; 10; 11; 13; 10:4; 5; 8; 11:1(2); 9; 13; 24; 14:26(2); 15:8; 14; 17; 16:6(2); 13; 23; 17:3; 7; 9; 17; 20; 19:28; 32; 42; 20:3; 8(2); 18; 22; 21:15; 18; 19; 20; 22:16(2); 23:8; 13(2); 24:8; **1 Ki** 1:6; 45; 2:7; 8; 19; 26; 27; 39; 40; 3:2; 3; 5; 5:14; 6:7; 16; 7:31; 34; 35; 8:2; 9; 61; 65; 9:2; 6; 10; 26; 10:19; 22; 25; 28; 11:29; 12:27; 32(2); 33; 13:20; 14:1; 15:27; 17:1; 18:19; 27; 36(2); 20:12; 16(2); 33; 22:4; 10(2); 20; 34; 35; 38; 48; **2 Ki** 2:3; 5; 7; 24; 3:1; 6; 14; 21; 4:25; 27; 37; 5:9; 6:32; 7:1; 3; 5; 7; 8:3; 22; 28; 29; 9:2; 7; 10; 24; 27; 31; 32(2); 36; 37; 10:6; 7; 8; 12; 14; 29; 11:6(2); 13:7; 17; 14:10; 11; 13; 20; 16:6; 10; 17:25; 18:10; 14; 16; 33; 19:36; 20:12; 19; 23:6; 8(2); 11; 15; 29; 33; 24:3; 10; 25:4; 6; 20; 21; 23; 25; **1 Chr** 2:55; 4:23; 28; 31; 6:39; 8:29; 9:18; 34; 35; 10:12; 11:1; 3(2); 11; 13; 19; 12:1; 8; 16; 22; 23; 32; 13:3; 15:3; 16:39(2); 18:10; 17; 19:4; 5; 20:1(2); 4(2); 6; 21:19; 22; 28; 29(2); 23:30; 31; 26:18; 31; 28:1; 21; **2 Chr** 1:3; 4; 6; 13; 16; 2:7; 3:1(2); 5:3; 10; 12; 7:8; 8:1; 14; 9:24; 25; 13:14; 18; 14:10; 15:10; 11; 15; 16:7; 10(2); 18:9(2); 19; 33; 19:4; 20:16; 21:10; 22:5; 6; 23:5(2); 13; 19; 24:8(2); 11; 21; 25:19; 21; 23; 26:9(3); 20; 28:15; 16; 29:15; 30:1; 3(2); 5; 10; 12; 13; 21; 31:13; 32:23; 33; 35:15; 17; 36:3; 7; 10; 16; 23; **Ezra** 1:2; 3:8; 4:12; 24; 5:3; 17; 6:2; 3; 8; 17; 8:17(2); 21; 34; 9:4; 5; 10:3; 7; 9; 14; **Neh** 2:12; 19; 3:19; 31; 32; 4:13; 16; 17; 18; 22(2); 5:17; 6:1; 7; 10; 12; 7:3; 8:4(2); 9:37; 10:34; 11:1; 2; 6; 22; 12:25; 27; 44; 13:19(2); 31; **Esth** 1:12; 2:8; 4:8; 14; 5:6; 13; 7:2; 3(2); 9:8; 9; 9:15; 18; 31; **Job** 3:13; 17; 26; 5:14; 22; 23; 26; 6:28; 9:23; 12:5; 14:9; 15:12; 23; 16:4; 9; 10; 12; 14; 17:8; 18:12; 20; 19:25; 21:5; 23; 22:19; 21; 23:15; 26:10; 11; 27:23; 28:9; 29:24; 30:1; 5(2); 12; 17;

31:9; 29; 33:27; 37:1; 21; 39:22; 25; 27; 40:15; 41:9; 29; **Ps** 7:4; 9:3; 10:5; 11:2; 15:5; 16:8; 11; 18:15(2); 22:13; 17; 29:10; 30:4; 34:1; 35:15; 16(2); 26; 37:12; 13; 39:5; 12; 42:7; 45:9; 46:5; 49:5; 52:6; 55:6; 17; 20; 59:6; 8; 14; 62:8; 64:4(2); 7; 68:2; 8(2); 12; 29; 73:12; 74:6; 76:6; 80:16; 81:3(2); 7; 83:9; 10; 91:6; 7(2); 97:5(2); 12; 99:5; 9; 104:7(2); 105:22; 106:3; 32; 107:27; 109:6; 25; 31; 110:1; 5; 114:7(2); 119:20; 37; 45; 62; 162; 121:5; 123:4; 132:7; 141:7; **Prov** 1:21; 23; 26; 5:11; 19; 7:6; 11; 12(3); 19; 8:3(2); 22; 34(2); 9:14; 12:16; 14:9; 19; 16:7; 17:5; 17; 20:21(2); 22:22; 23:30; 32; 34; **Eccl** 5:6; 8; 10:2(2); 17; 12:4; 6(2); **Song** 1:7; 12; 7:13; 8:1; 11; **Isa** 1:26(2); 5:22; 7:3; 9:1; 10:26; 28; 29; 32(2); 13:6; 8; 14:7; 9; 16; 16:2; 4; 17:6; 14; 19:1; 19; 20:2; 21:8; 22:7; 23:5; 15; 17; 27:13; 28:1; 4; 6; 21; 30:4; 17(2); 19(2); 32:9; 11; 33:3; 36:2; 37:37; 39:1; 8; 42:14; 50:2; 51:17; 20; 52:4; 14; 15; 53:9; 59:10(2); 60:4; 14; 64:1; 2; 3; 66:2; 5; 8; **Jer** 1:15; 2:12; 15; 24; 3:17; 4:11; 26; 5:22; 6:4; 15(2); 7:2; 12; 8:1; 12; 16; 10:2(2); 10; 12; 18; 11:12; 14:6; 15:8; 17:11; 18:3; 20:16; 23:23; 32; 25:33; 27:18; 28:1; 29:10; 25; 31:1; 12; 33:7; 11; 15; 34:8; 14; 16(2); 35:11; 36:4; 6; 10; 17; 27; 32; 38:7; 14; 39:10; 40:8; 10; 12; 13; 41:1; 3; 43:9; 44:1(3); 23; 45:1; 46:27; 47:3(3); 48:11; 16; 49:17; 21(3); 50:13; 14; 16; 17; 46; 51:49; 52:7; 9; 26; 27; **Lam** 1:7; 20; 2:15(2); 19(2); 3:53; 63; 4:1; 5:4; 5; 9; 13; 14; **Ezek** 1:15; 3:9; 15; 16; 18; 20; 8:16; 9:2; 3; 6; 11; 10:19; 11:1; 10; 11; 12:4; 6; 7(2); 12; 23; 14:3; 16:25; 31; 18:23; 21:16; 19; 21(3); 22:13(2); 23:14; 34; 24:18; 26:10; 15; 16; 17; 18; 27:3; 28; 35; 36; 28:17; 19; 29:13; 30:18; 31:16; 32:10; 30; 33:6; 8; 34:10; 35:5; 36:11; 38; 38:18; 20; 39:14; 19; 20; 40:1; 40; 44(2); 41:12; 42:4; 7; 9; 43:16; 45:17(2); 25; 46:2; 3; 11; 19(2); 48:1; **Dan** 1:5; 15; 18; 3:5; 7; 8; 15; 4:4; 8; 29; 34; 36; 8:6; 19; 9:21; 23; 10:3; 11:6; 13; 27(2); 29; 40; 43; 12:1(2); 13; **Hos** 5:8; 10:15; 11:7; **Joel** 1:15; 2:1; 9; 3:1; **Am** 3:5; 9; 4:4; 5:12; 13; 6:1; 7; 7:1; 13; 8:9; 9:3; **Ob** 7; 14; **Mic** 1:10; 2:1; 13; 3:4; 5:6; **Nah** 1:3; 5; 3:10; **Hab** 1:10; 2:3; 5; 19; 3:5; 11(2); 16; **Zeph** 1:7; 12; 2:4; 7; 14; 3:19; 20(2); **Zech** 1:15; 3:1; 4:3(2); 11(2); 12:11; 14:7; 14; **Mal** 1:13; 2:8; **Mt** 3:2; 13; 4:17; 5:28; 34; 6:26; 7:3; 28; 8:6; 9:3; 9; 10; 10:7; 11:25; 12:1; 41; 13:30; 40; 49; 57; 14:1; 2; 15:30; 17:12; 18:1; 29; 19:4; 26; 21:1; 22:33; 44; 23:6; 24:33; 41; 44; 50; 25:6; 27; 26:3; 6; 7; 18(2); 45; 46; 58; 60; 64; 27:15; 16; 24; 28:13; **Mk** 1:15; 22; 30; 32; 33; 43; 2:14; 3:5; 34; 5:13; 22; 23; 6:3; 14; 25; 48; 7:25; 8:33; 9:18; 20; 10:21; 22; 24; 27; 11:1; 11; 18; 12:2; 4; 17; 36; 39; 13:29; 35(2); 14:3(2); 42; 54(2); 62; 67; 15:6; 34; 16:14; 19; **Lk** 1:10; 14; 29; 2:18; 33; 41; 47; 3:23; 4:18; 22; 32; 5:5; 8; 9; 27; 6:10; 41; 7:9; 37; 38; 49; 8:35; 41; 9:31; 39; 43(2); 61; 10:14; 32; 39; 11:5; 32; 12:40; 46; 51; 13:1; 25; 14:10; 14; 15; 17; 15:29; 16:20; 17:7; 16; 19:5; 23; 29; 20:10; 17; 26; 42; 46; 21:29; 37; 22:27(2); 30; 54; 56; 61; 23:7; 12; 17; 18; 49; 24:12; 22; 27; 30; 47; **Jn** 1:18; 36; 42; 2:10; 13; 23; 4:27; 35; 45; 46; 47; 52; 53; 5:4; 28; 37; 6:21; 39; 40; 44; 54; 7:2; 11; 8:7; 59; 10:40; 11:24; 32; 49; 12:2; 16; 20; 13:22; 28; 14:20; 16:4; 18:16; 38; 39; 19:11; 39; 19; 27; 21:1; 20; **Acts** 1:6; 2:25; 34; 3:1; 2; 4; 10(2); 12(2); 4:6; 18; 35; 37; 5:2; 9; 10; 15; 19; 6:15; 7:20; 29; 31; 54; 55; 56; 57; 58; 8:1(2); 14; 35; 40; 9:10; 11; 18; 19; 27; 28; 35; 36; 10:11; 25; 30; 11:8; 11; 15; 12:13; 13:1; 9; 12; 15:14; 16:2; 4; 25; 17:13; 16; 18:18; 22; 24; 19:1; 26; 20:5; 6; 14; 15(2); 16; 21:3; 11; 13; 26; 22:3; 6; 13(2); 23:1; 11; 23; 25:4; 8; 10; 23; 24; 26:4; 13; 27:3; 28:11; 12; 23; **Rom** 1:10; 3:9; 26; 4:20; 7:5; 8:34; 9:9; 32; 11:5; 13:12; **1 Cor** 1:2; 6:20; 7:23; 39; 9:7; 13; 11:34; 14:16; 27; 35; 15:6; 23; 29; 32; 52; 16:12; **2 Cor** 1:1; 3:7; 13; 4:18(2); 5:6; 8:14; 10:7; 11:5; 16; **Gal** 4:1; 12; 13; **Eph** 1:20; 2:12; 3:13; **Phil** 2:10; 23; 4:5; 10; **Col** 3:1; **1 Th** 2:2; 5; 19; 3:13; 5:7(2); 13; 23; **2 Th** 2:7; 3:11; **1 Tim** 5:4; **2 Tim** 1:18; 3:11(3); 4:1; 6; 13; 16; **Titus** 3:12; **Heb** 1:1; 3; 13; 2:3; 7:13; 8:1; 9:17; 26; 10:12; 12:2; **Jas** 2:3; 3:4; 5:8; 9; **1 Pe** 1:7; 13; 3:22; 4:7; 17; **1 Jn** 1:5; 2:28; 4:12; **Rev** 1:17; 3:20; 5:3; 4; 7:1; 8:3; 9:14; 18:10; 14; 15; 17; 19:10; 21:12; 25; 22:10

BE (5747/4673)

Gen 1:3; 6; 9; 14(2); 15; 22; 28; 29; 2:18; 23; 24; 3:5(2); 12; 16; 4:7; 12; 14(2); 15; 24; 6:3; 15; 19; 21; 8:17; 9:1; 2; 3; 6; 7; 11(2); 13; 14(2); 16; 20; 25(2); 26(2); 27; 10:8; 11:4; 6; 12:2; 3; 13; 13:8; 16; 14:19; 20; 15:1; 4(2); 5; 13; 15; 16:3; 5; 10; 12(2); 17:1; 4; 5(2); 7; 8; 10; 11(2); 12; 13(2); 14; 15; 16(2); 17; 18:4; 18; 25(3); 29; 30(2); 31; 32(2); 19:14; 15; 17; 20:9; 21:10; 12(2); 30; 22:14; 18; 24:5; 8; 14(2); 27; 41(2); 44; 51; 25:23(2); 26:3; 4; 11; 22; 28; 27:12; 13; 29(3); 33; 39; 45; 46; 28:3; 9; 14(2); 20; 21; 22; 29:3; 7; 15; 26; 30:32; 33; 31:3; 8(2); 24; 29; 44; 32:12; 28; 34:7; 10; 14; 17(2); 22; 23; 30; 35:10(2); 11; 37:27; 35; 38:9; 23; 24; 29; 39:10; 41:30; 31(2); 36(2); 40(3); 52; 42:15; 16(2); 19; 20; 33; 43:9; 11; 23(2); 29; 44:7; 9; 10(3); 17(2); 45:5; 6; 10; 20; 46:33; 47:19(2); 24; 25; 48:5; 6(2); 16; 19(2); 21; 49:6; 7; 8; 10; 17; 20; 26; 29; 50:19; 21; **Ex** 2:4; 3:12(2); 21; 4:8; 9; 12; 14; 15; 16(3); 5:9; 11; 18; 6:7; 7:1; 17; 19; 8:10; 21; 22; 23; 26; 9:3; 16; 22; 28; 29; 10:5; 7; 10; 14; 21(2); 24; 26; 11:6(2); 9; 12:2(2); 5; 13(2); 14; 15; 16(4); 19(2); 26; 32; 33; 46; 48(2); 49; 13:3; 5; 6; 7(3); 9(2); 11; 12; 14; 16; 14:13; 15:9; 14; 15; 16; 16:5(2); 8; 12; 23; 26; 32; 33; 34; 18:10; 19; 21; 22(2); 23; 19:5; 6; 11; 12; 13; 15; 20:12; 20; 23; 26; 21:4; 7; 8; 12; 15; 16; 17; 19(2); 20; 21; 22; 28(3); 29(2); 31; 32; 34; 36; 22:2; 3(2); 5; 8; 9; 11; 16; 19; 20; 24; 25; 27; 30; 31; 23:1; 12; 13(2); 22; 26; 33; 24:7; 12; 25:7; 10; 12; 14; 15(2); 17; 20; 23; 27; 28; 31(2); 33; 34; 35; 36(2); 38; 39; 26:2; 3(2); 5; 6; 7; 8; 11; 16(2); 17; 20; 24(4); 25; 31; 32; 33; 37; 27:1(2); 2; 5; 7(2); 9; 10(2); 11; 12; 13; 14; 15; 16; 17; 18; 19; 21; 28:7; 8; 16(3); 17(2); 18; 20; 21; 30; 32; 35(2); 37(2); 38(3); 43(2); 29:9; 21; 26; 28(2); 29(3); 34; 37(2); 40; 42; 43; 45; 30:2(4); 4; 12; 13; 16; 21; 25; 29(2); 31; 32(2); 33; 34; 36; 37; 38; 31:14(2); 15(2); 33:16(2); 19(2); 22; 23; 34:2; 3; 12; 25; 35:2(3); 9; 27; 29; 36:6; 7; 13; 18; 34; 37:3; 39:21; 40:4; 9; 10; 15; **Lev** 1:4; 15; 2:1; 3; 4; 5; 7; 10; 11; 12; 13; 3:17; 4:2; 12; 13; 15; 20; 22; 26; 27; 31; 35; 5:2; 3(2); 4; 5; 9; 10; 13(2); 16; 17; 18; 6:4; 7; 9(2); 12(2); 13; 16; 17; 18(2); 21; 22; 23(2); 25; 26; 27; 28(2); 30(2); 7:6; 9; 15; 16(2); 17; 18(3); 19(2); 20; 21; 24; 25; 27; 30; 31; 36; 8:5; 10:3(2); 9; 15; 11:11; 12; 13; 20; 23; 24; 25; 26; 27; 28; 29; 31; 32(4); 33; 34; 35(3); 36; 37; 39; 40(2); 41(2); 43; 44; 45(2); 47(2); 12:2(2); 3; 5; 7; 8; 13:2; 3; 4; 5; 6; 7; 9; 14; 15; 19; 34; 37; 45; 46(3); 49; 52; 58(2); 14:2(2); 4; 5; 7; 8(2); 9; 11; 14; 17; 18; 19; 20; 21; 22; 25; 28; 29; 31; 36; 37; 41; 46; 53; 15:3; 4; 5; 6; 7; 8; 9; 10(2); 11; 12(2); 13; 16; 17(2); 18; 19(2); 20(2); 21; 22; 23; 24(2); 25(2); 26(2); 27(2); 28; 16:4(2); 10(2); 17; 27; 29; 30; 34; 17:4(2); 7; 9; 13; 14; 15(2); 18:29; 19:2; 6(2); 7; 8; 15; 20(2); 22; 23(2); 24; 29; 31; 34; 20:2; 7; 9(2); 10; 11(2); 12(2); 13(2); 14(2); 15; 16; 17; 18; 21; 26(2); 27(2); 21:6(2); 8; 9; 22:3; 5(2); 6; 7; 20; 21(3); 23; 25; 27(2); 30; 32; 33; 23:2; 3; 8; 11; 13(2); 14; 15; 17(2); 18; 20; 21; 27(2); 29; 31; 32; 34; 35; 37; 39; 41; 24:3(2); 4; 5; 7; 9; 12; 16(2); 17; 19; 20; 21; 25:4; 6; 7; 8; 10; 11; 12; 23; 28; 30; 31(3); 33; 34; 38; 40; 42; 46; 48; 50(2); 53; 54; 26:12(2); 13; 17; 20; 22; 25; 26; 32; 33; 43; 45; 27:3; 4; 5; 6(2); 7; 9; 10; 12; 14; 15; 16(2); 18; 20; 21(2); 25; 26; 27; 28; 29(2); 32; 33(2); **Num** 1:4; 51(2); 53; 2:3; 5(2); 7; 10(2); 12(2); 14; 16; 18(2); 20; 22; 24; 25(2); 27(2); 29; 3:10; 12; 13; 32; 38; 45; 4:7; 28; 5:8; 9; 10(2); 19; 22; 27; 28; 31; 6:5; 8; 12; 13; 25; 7:5; 8:14; 19; 9:13; 10:7; 8; 9(2); 10; 21; 31; 32(2); 35; 11:16; 22(2); 12:12; 14(3); 13:20; 14:3; 17; 21; 31; 33; 35; 42; 43; 15:9; 11; 15(2); 16; 19; 24; 25; 26; 28; 30; 31(2); 34; 35; 40; 41; 16:7; 16; 22; 26; 38(2); 40; 17:3; 5; 10; 18:2; 4; 5; 7; 9(2); 10; 13; 14; 15; 18; 23; 27; 30; 19:3; 5(2); 7; 8; 9; 10(2); 11; 12(2); 13(2); 14; 16; 17; 19; 20; 21(2); 22(2); 20:24; 26; 21:8; 27(2); 22:6; 11; 23:10; 23; 24:7(3); 18(2); 20; 22; 25:13; 26:53; 54; 55; 56; 27:4; 11; 13; 17; 20; 28:2; 7; 14; 15; 17; 19; 20; 24; 31; 29:3; 8; 9; 13; 14; 31:2; 23(2); 24; 32:5; 17; 22(2); 23; 26; 33:54; 55(2); 56; 34:3; 4; 6; 7; 8; 9; 12; 35:3; 5; 7; 8; 11; 12; 14; 15; 16; 17; 18; 21; 27; 29; 30; 31; 33; 36:3(3); 4(2); 8; **Deut** 1:17; 21; 29; 39; 42; 2:4; 25; 4:6; 20; 26; 27; 5:1; 16(2); 29; 32; 33; 6:2; 3(2); 6; 8; 10; 15; 18; 25; 7:4; 6; 10; 14(2); 16; 18; 21; 22; 24; 25; 26; 8:1; 19; 20; 10:16; 11:8; 13; 15; 16; 17(2); 18; 21; 24(2); 25; 29; 32; 12:1; 11; 23; 27; 32; 13:5; 9; 16(2); 14:2; 19; 29; 15:4; 9(2); 10; 17; 16:4; 8; 12; 17:6(2); 7; 10; 18; 19(2); 20; 18:3; 10; 13; 19; 22; 19:10(2); 15; 21; 20:1; 2; 3(2); 9; 11(2); 21:3; 5; 8; 13(2); 14; 16; 22:6; 7; 9; 19; 29(2); 23:11; 14; 17; 21; 22; 24:4; 5(2); 8; 13; 15; 16(3); 19; 20; 21; 25:2(3); 3; 5; 6(2); 9; 10; 15; 19; 26:1; 12; 16; 17; 18; 19; 27:2; 4; 28:3(2); 4; 5; 6(2); 7; 10; 13(2); 16(2); 17; 18; 19(2); 23(2); 25; 26; 27; 29; 31(4); 32(2); 33; 34; 35; 41; 44(2); 46; 54; 62; 63(2); 68; 29:13; 18(2); 19; 31:6(2); 7; 8(2); 16; 17(2); 19; 21(2); 23(2); 26; 32:20; 24; 25; 38; 46; 50; 33:6; 7(2); 8; 24; 25(2); **Josh** 1:4; 5(2); 6; 7; 9(3); 17; 18(2); 2:14; 17; 19(4); 20; 21; 3:4; 7; 13; 4:6; 7; 6:17; 26; 7:12; 14(2); 15(2); 8:1(2); 4; 8; 9:4; 20; 21; 23; 10:25(3); 11:6; 13:1; 14:9; 12(3); 15:4; 17:18(2); 20:3; 21:27; 22:18(2); 27; 28; 29; 23:4; 6; 13; 24:16; 27(2); **Judg** 1:1; 2:3(2); 3:2; 6; 4:9; 5:31; 6:16; 23; 31; 39(3); 7:4; 11; 9:24(2); 33; 10:18; 11:6; 8; 9; 10; 31(2); 37; 13:4; 5; 7; 8; 12; 13; 14:11; 15:3; 16:6; 7; 10; 11; 13; 17; 17:2; 10; 13; 18:5; 6; 19(4); 25; 19:6(2); 9; 20(2); 28; 21:3; 5; 17(2); 18; 22(2); **Ruth** 1:11; 16; 17; 2:4; 9; 12; 19; 20; 3:1; 4; 13; 14; 4:10; 11; 12; 14(2); 15; **1 Sam** 1:14; 28; 2:9; 10; 28; 30(2); 31; 32; 34; 3:9; 14; 4:9; 19; 5:8; 6:3(2); 8:11(2); 13; 17; 20; 9:20; 10:5; 6; 7; 14; 21; 11:7; 13; 12:15; 23; 25; 13:14; 19; 14:6; 10; 39; 40(2); 15:16; 33; 16:16(2); 17:9(2); 25; 26; 27; 36; 37; 18:17(3); 18; 21(3); 23; 19:2; 6; 11; 20:3; 7(2); 9; 13; 18(2); 23; 29; 31; 32; 42; 21:3; 22:15; 23; 23:17(2); 20; 23; 24:12; 13; 15; 20(2); 25:6; 24; 26; 27; 29; 31; 39; 26:9; 19; 24; 25; 27:12; 28:13; 19; 30:24; **2 Sam** 1:6; 21; 2:7(2); 26(2); 3:12; 17; 29; 5:2; 8; 24; 6:22(3); 7:8; 11; 14(2); 16(2); 26(2); 29; 8:2(2); 10:12(2); 11:15; 12:9; 10; 22; 28; 13:5; 6; 12; 13; 15; 25; 28(2); 14:2; 9(2); 14; 15; 17(2); 32(2); 15:20; 21(2); 34(2); 35; 16:12; 18; 19; 21; 17:3; 9; 11; 12(2); 16; 17; 18:28; 32; 19:7; 21; 22(2); 35; 20:1; 4; 20(2); 21; 21:5; 6; 22:4(2); 47(2); 23:3; 4; 6(2); 7(2); 17; 24:13; 17; 21; **1 Ki** 1:2(2); 5; 21; 30; 35(2); 37; 48; 2:2; 7; 21; 24; 33; 37(2); 45(2); 3:8; 13; 26; 5:6; 7; 6:6; 18; 8:5; 8(2); 15; 16(2); 29(2); 52; 53; 56; 57; 59; 61; 9:3; 7; 8; 10:9; 11:37; 38(2); 12:7(2); 10; 13:2(2); 3; 6; 14:2; 5(2); 6; 15:19; 17:1; 4; 14; 18:27; 31; 36; 19:17; 20:6; 23; 25; 39; 40; 21:7; 22:13; 22; **2 Ki** 1:13; 14; 15; 2:9; 10(2); 21; 3:17; 4:1; 10; 14; 29; 5:6; 10(2); 12; 13; 17; 6:8; 7:1; 2; 18; 19; 9:10; 37; 10:19; 24; 11:5; 6(2); 8(2); 9; 15; 17; 12:15; 14:6(3); 15:19; 16:15; 17:37; 18:29; 30; 19:4; 6; 10; 11; 25; 29; 20:17(2); 18; 19; 22:7; 17(2); 20; 23:27; 25:24(2); **1 Chr** 1:10; 4:10; 11:2; 6; 19; 12:17; 14:15; 15:16; 16:25(2); 30; 31; 36; 38; 17:7; 10; 11(3); 13(2); 14; 23; 24(3); 27; 19:13(2); 21:3; 12; 17(3); 22; 22:5(2); 9(3); 10(2); 11; 13(2); 16; 19; 28:4(2); 6(2); 8; 9; 10; 20(3); 21(2); 29:2(2); 5; 14; 22(2); **2 Chr** 1:9; 2:5; 8; 9; 12; 14; 17; 5:6; 9(2); 13; 6:4; 5(2); 6(2); 20; 40(2); 41; 7:15; 16(2); 21; 9:8(2); 10:7; 10; 11:22; 12:7; 8; 13:9; 15:2; 7(3); 13; 16:3; 18:3; 12; 14; 21; 19:7; 10; 11(2); 20:15; 17; 20; 23:4; 5(2); 7(2); 8; 16; 25:4(2); 5; 8(2); 14; 16; 26:15; 28:10; 29:11; 24; 30:7; 8; 9; 32:7(2); 14; 33:4; 34:25(2); 28; 35:3; 36:22; 23; **Ezra** 1:1; 3; 4:12; 13(2); 15; 16; 21; 5:8; 15; 17; 6:3(2); 4; 5; 8(2); 9; 11(3); 12; 7:16; 17; 20; 21; 23(2); 24; 26(2); 27; 9:12; 14(2); 10:3; 4; 8(2); **Neh** 1:6; 11; 2:3; 6; 7; 17; 4:5; 7; 12; 14; 22; 5:5; 8; 13; 14; 6:6; 7; 9(2); 13; 7:3; 5; 8:11(2); 9:5; 10:38; 11:23; 13:5; 19(4); **Esth** 1:17; 18; 19(2); 22; 2:2; 3; 4; 3:9(2); 14(2); 5:3; 6(2); 14(2); 6:6; 8; 9(2); 11; 7:2(2); 3; 4(3); 8:5; 13(2); 9:1; 12(2); 13(2); 14; 25; 28(2); **Job** 1:5; 21; 3:4; 7; 9; 4:17(2); 5:21(2); 22; 23; 25; 6:3; 6; 14; 28; 29; 7:4; 8; 21; 8:2; 14; 22; 9:2; 24; 11:2(2); 12; 15; 17(2); 18; 12:14(2); 13:5(2); 9; 16; 18; 14:12; 22; 15:14(2); 29; 31; 32(2); 34; 17:9; 18:4(2); 19:29; 20:8(2); 22; 21:2; 4; 5; 30; 32; 33; 22:2(2); 21; 23; 25; 28; 30; 23:7; 24:18(2); 20(2); 25:4(2); 27:5; 7; 14; 15; 19; 28:12; 15(2); 16; 17; 18; 19; 31:6; 8; 11(2); 12; 22; 28; 33:7; 25; 30; 34:10; 30; 35:3; 36:16; 26; 37:20(2); 38:13; 39:9; 40:8; 41:9; 17; 23; 42:2; **Ps** 1:3; 2:10(2); 12; 3:6; 4:4(2); 5:11; 6:10(2); 9:2; 9; 17; 18; 19; 20; 10:2; 6(2); 11:6; 13:2; 14:7; 15:5; 16:4; 8; 17:15; 18:3(2); 46(2); 19:10; 13(2); 14; 21:7; 13; 22:11; 19; 25; 26; 30; 31; 24:7; 25:2; 3(2); 20; 26:11; 27:1; 3; 6; 14; 28:1; 6; 30:6; 10; 12; 31:1; 2; 7; 17(3); 18; 21; 24; 32:6; 9(2); 10; 11; 33:22; 34:1; 2; 21; 22; 35:4(2); 5; 6; 9; 22; 26(2); 27(2); 36:3; 37:1; 2; 9; 10(2); 15; 17; 18; 19(2); 22; 24; 28; 36; 38(2); 38:18; 21; 39:12; 40:5(2); 13; 14(2); 15; 16(2); 41:2; 4; 10; 13; 42:8; 45:14(2); 15; 16; 17; 46:2(2); 3; 5; 10(3); 48:1; 11; 14; 49:14; 16; 50:3; 22; 51:4; 7(2); 13; 19; 53:6; 55:6; 22; 56:1; 11; 57:1(2); 5(2); 11(2); 58:7; 8; 59:5; 12; 13; 60:4; 5; 62:2; 3; 6; 63:5; 10; 11; 64:7; 10; 65:1; 4; 66:8; 9; 20; 67:1; 2; 4; 68:1; 3; 13; 19; 35; 69:6(2); 14; 23; 25; 28(2); 32; 70:2(2); 3; 4(2); 71:1; 3; 6; 8; 12; 13(2); 72:14; 15(3); 16; 17; 18; 19(2); 75:10; 76:7; 8; 11; 77:2; 7; 9; 78:6; 8; 79:5; 10; 80:3; 4; 7; 17; 19; 81:9; 83:1; 4; 17(2); 84:4; 10; 85:5; 86:3; 17; 87:5; 88:11; 12; 89:2; 6(2); 7(2); 21; 24(2); 37; 52; 90:14; 17; 91:4; 5; 15; 92:7; 9; 14; 93:1; 94:8; 96:4(2); 10; 11; 12; 97:1; 7; 98:8; 99:1; 100:4; 101:6; 102:18(2); 26; 28; 104:5; 34(2); 35(2); 106:46; 48; 108:5; 6; 109:7; 8; 9; 10; 12(2); 13(2); 14(2); 15; 17; 19; 20; 28; 29; 110:3; 111:4; 5; 112:2(2); 3; 6(2); 7; 8; 9; 10; 113:2; 3; 115:15; 118:24; 119:6; 46; 58; 74; 76; 78; 80(2); 116; 117; 122; 128; 132; 120:3(2); 121:3; 122:7; 8; 124:6; 125:1; 5; 127:5; 128:2(2); 3; 4; 6; 129:5; 6; 8; 130:2; 4; 132:9; 135:21; 137:8; 139:11; 18; 140:8; 10; 11; 141:2; 5(2); 143:7; 144:1; 12(2); 13; 14(3); 145:3; 149:2; 5; 6; **Prov** 1:9; 31; 33; 2:22(2); 3:7; 8; 10; 22; 24(2); 25; 26; 35; 4:10; 12; 26; 5:10; 16; 17; 18; 19; 20(2); 6:6; 15; 27; 28; 29; 33; 35; 8:5; 11; 33; 9:9; 11(2); 10:24; 27; 28; 30; 31; 11:6; 9; 21; 25(2); 26; 29; 31; 12:3; 8(2); 11; 14(2); 19; 21; 24; 13:4; 9; 11; 13(2); 18; 20(2); 21; 25; 14:11; 13; 14(2); 16:3; 7; 16; 19; 21; 17:11; 18:20(2); 24; 19:2; 20; 23; 20:13; 17; 20; 21; 21:13; 17(2); 18; 22:1; 5; 9; 11; 13; 18; 19; 26; 23:4; 17; 18; 19; 25; 34; 24:1(2); 8; 14(2); 17; 19; 20(2); 28; 25:5; 7; 10; 16; 26:4; 5; 26; 27:11; 14; 18; 23; 28:2; 6; 18; 20; 25; 26; 29:1; 14; 19; 25; 30:6; 9(2); 10; 31:30; **Eccl** 1:9(2); 10; 11; 13; 15(2); 2:16; 19; 3:2; 10; 14(2); 15; 4:11; 12; 13; 14; 5:2(2); 6; 10; 7:9; 14; 16(2); 17(2); 23; 26; 8:3; 12; 13; 15; 17; 9:8; 17; 10:8; 9(2); 14(2); 11:2; 6; 8; 12:12; **Song** 1:4; 7; 2:17; 7:8; 8:1; 7; 14; **Isa** 1:5; 18(2); 20; 26; 27; 28(2); 29(2); 30; 31; 2:2(2); 11(3); 12; 17(3); 3:4; 5(2); 6(2); 10; 11(2); 24(2); 4:1; 2(2); 3; 5; 6; 5:5(2); 6; 9; 15(3); 16(2); 24; 27(3); 29; 6:10; 13(3); 7:4(2); 8(2); 9; 16; 21; 22; 23(2); 25; 8:4; 9(4); 12(2); 13(2); 14; 15(2); 21; 22; 9:1; 5; 6(2); 7; 19; 20(2); 21; 10:2; 17; 18; 19; 22; 24; 27(2); 30; 33(2); 11:5; 9; 10(2); 13; 16(2); 12:2; 13:7; 8(4); 10; 14; 15; 16(2); 19; 20(2); 21; 22; 14:1; 14; 15; 20(2); 25; 29; 31; 15:2; 4(2); 6; 9; 16:2(2); 4; 5; 6; 10(2); 14(2); 17:1; 2; 3; 5(2); 6; 9(2); 11; 13; 18:6; 7; 19:5; 6; 7(2); 9; 10(2); 15; 16(2); 17(2); 18; 19; 20; 21; 22; 23; 24; 20:5; 6; 21:17; 22:7; 14; 18; 20; 21; 25(3); 23:2; 4; 5; 15; 16; 17; 18(3); 24:2; 3; 13(2); 18(2); 20; 22(3); 23; 25:2(2); 5; 9(2); 10; 26:1; 10; 11; 27:9; 10; 11; 12; 13(2); 28:3; 5; 10; 13; 18(2); 19; 21; 22(2); 28; 29:2(2); 4(3); 5(2); 6; 7; 8(2); 9; 14; 16; 17(2); 22; 30:3(2); 5; 8; 13; 14; 15(2); 16; 18(2); 19; 20; 23; 25; 26(2); 28; 30; 31; 32; 31:4(2); 9; 32:2; 3; 4; 5(2); 10; 11; 14(2); 17; 33:1; 2(2); 3; 4; 6; 10; 12(2); 16(3); 20(3); 21; 24; 34:3(2); 4(2); 5; 7; 9; 10; 12(2); 13; 15; 35:1; 2; 4; 5(2); 7; 8(3); 9(2); 36:14; 15; 37:4; 6; 10; 11; 26; 30; 39:6(2); 7; 8; 40:4(2); 5; 9; 24(2); 25; 30; 31; 41:6; 10; 11(2); 12; 23; 42:2; 4; 17(2); 43:2(2); 9(3); 10; 26; 44:8; 9; 11(3); 15; 21; 26(2); 27; 28(2); 45:1; 14; 16; 17(2); 18; 22; 24; 25; 46:5; 13; 47:1; 3(2); 5; 7; 11; 12; 14(3); 15; 48:11; 14; 49:3; 5(3); 6(2); 9; 11; 13; 19(2); 22; 23(2); 24(2); 25(2); 26; 50:7(2); 51:3; 6(2); 7; 8; 12(2); 14; 19; 52:3; 11; 12; 13(2); 53:11; 54:4(3); 9; 10(2); 13(2); 14(2); 55:6; 11; 12; 13(2); 56:1; 5; 6; 7(2); 12; 57:16; 58:8; 10; 11; 12; 60:2; 4; 5; 7; 11(2); 12; 18; 19(2); 20(2); 21(2); 61:3(2); 5; 6; 7; 9; 10; 62:2; 3; 4(4); 12; 64:5; 9; 65:10; 13(3); 17; 18; 19; 20; 22; 23; 25; 66:5(2); 8(2); 10; 11(2); 12(2); 13; 14; 16; 17; 18; 24; **Jer** 1:8; 17; 2:12(3); 36; 3:1; 3; 16; 17(2); 4:1; 7; 9; 11; 14; 27; 28; 29; 5:6; 13; 19; 6:6; 8; 11; 12; 15; 22; 7:20(2); 23(3); 32; 33; 34; 8:2(2); 3; 12; 13; 14; 17; 9:21; 10:2; 5(2); 10; 21; 11:4(2); 5; 11; 19; 23; 12:13; 15; 16(2); 13:10; 12(2); 15; 19(3); 21(2); 27; 14:8; 9; 15(2); 16; 15:1; 2; 8; 11; 18(2); 19; 16:4(5); 6; 10; 14; 17:6; 8(3); 11; 13(2); 14(2); 17; 18(4); 24; 27; 18:14; 16; 20; 21(2); 22; 23; 19:6; 8; 11; 13; 20:6; 10; 11(2); 14(2); 15; 16; 18; 21:9; 10; 22:19; 22; 23; 23:3; 4(2); 6(2); 12(2); 26; 36; 40; 24:2; 3; 7(2); 8; 9; 25:11; 14; 27; 28; 29(2); 32; 33(2); 36; 26:9(2); 18; 27:8; 16; 17; 22(2); 28:9; 29:4; 6; 7; 8; 14(2); 17; 18; 22; 26; 30:7; 10(2); 13; 16; 18; 19; 20(2); 21; 22(2); 31:1(2); 4(2); 6; 12; 14; 15; 16; 30; 33(2); 37; 38; 40(2); 32:4; 5; 15; 36; 38(2); 43; 33:9; 10; 12; 16(2); 20; 21; 22; 24; 26; 34:3; 16; 20; 36:3; 7; 30; 37:17; 20; 38:2; 3; 4; 17; 18; 20; 22; 23(2); 39:16; 17; 18; 40:9(2); 15; 42:2; 4; 5; 6; 11(2); 14; 16; 17; 18(2); 44:8; 12(3); 26; 27; 29; 46:10; 11; 19; 23; 24(2); 26; 27(2); 47:2; 6; 7; 48:2; 3; 4; 6; 7; 8; 9; 13; 26; 28; 34; 37(2); 39; 41; 42; 43; 44; 49:2(3); 5; 10; 13; 17(2); 22; 23; 26; 32; 33; 36; 37; 50:5; 8; 9(2); 10; 12(3); 13(3); 19; 20(3); 26; 30; 36(2); 37; 38; 39(2); 41; 51:2; 6; 8; 26; 29; 35(2); 46; 47; 58(3); 62; 63; 64; **Lam** 2:6; 20; 3:29; 30; 65; 4:21; 5:6; 21; **Ezek** 2:6(3); 8; 3:9(2); 20; 26(2); 4:3(2); 7; 10; 17; 5:12; 13(2); 15; 16; 6:4(2); 6(6); 7:4; 9; 11; 13; 16; 17(2); 18(2); 19(2); 24; 25; 26; 27; 11:11(2); 16; 20(2); 12:3; 11(2); 13; 19; 20; 24; 25; 28(2); 13:6; 9(3); 11; 12; 13; 14(2); 21; 14:3; 10; 11(3); 16(2); 18; 21; 22(3); 15:5(2); 16:16; 20; 25; 34; 42(2); 52; 54; 61; 63; 17:9; 14; 15; 20; 21; 23; 18:13; 20(2); 22; 24; 30; 19:9; 20:3; 9; 12; 14; 20; 22; 31(2); 32(2); 41; 47(2); 48; 21:7(4); 11(3); 12(2); 13; 23(2); 24(2); 27; 32(3); 22:21; 22; 23:25; 29; 32; 33; 48; 24:8; 10; 11(2); 12; 13; 23; 25; 27(3); 25:10; 26:2; 5; 6; 13; 14(2); 16; 17; 20; 21(2); 27:35(3); 36; 28:3; 9; 19; 22; 23; 24; 29:5; 11; 12; 14; 15; 16; 19; 30:3; 4; 7(2); 11; 13; 16(2); 18; 31:14; 18(2);

32:6; 10; 12; 19; 27; 28; 31; 32; 33:4; 5; 12; 13; 16; 27; 28; 34:10; 14; 22; 23; 24; 26; 27; 28; 29; 35:4; 9; 10; 15; 36:9; 10; 12; 25; 28(2); 32(2); 33; 34; 38; 37:19; 20; 22(3); 23(2); 24; 25; 26; 27(3); 38:7(2); 8; 16; 19; 20; 21; 23; 39:4; 8; 12; 13; 16; 20; 25; 41:6; 43:10; 27; 44:2(3); 7; 11; 14; 17; 28; 29; 30; 45:1(2); 2; 3; 4(2); 7; 8; 11(2); 12(2); 15(2); 17; 21; 46:1(3); 2; 4; 5; 6(2); 10; 11; 12(2); 14; 17; 18; 47:5; 9(3); 10(3); 11(2); 12; 15; 17; 19; 20; 22(2); 23; 48:1; 8; 9; 10; 11; 12; 13; 15(2); 16; 17; 18(3); 20; 21(2); 28; 31; 35(2); **Dan** 1:13; 18; 2:5(2); 20; 28; 29; 40; 41(2); 42; 44(2); 3:6; 11; 15; 18; 28; 29(2); 4:1; 11; 15; 16(2); 20; 23; 25; 26; 27(2); 32; 5:7(2); 12; 16(2); 17; 29; 6:1; 7; 8; 12; 15; 17; 25; 26; 7:14; 23(2); 24; 25; 26; 27; 8:13(2); 14; 19; 24; 25; 9:16; 25(2); 26(2); 27; 10:19(3); 11:2; 4(2); 5; 6; 11(2); 12; 17; 19; 20; 22(2); 25; 26; 27(2); 28; 29; 30; 31; 32; 34; 36; 41; 12:1(2); 6; 7(2); 8; 10; 11; **Hos** 1:9; 10(3); 11(2); 2:16; 17; 3:3; 4:3; 9; 14; 19; 5:9; 12; 14; 7:16; 8:4; 6; 9:4(4); 6; 17; 10:6(2); 8; 10; 14; 15(2); 11:5; 12:11; 13:3; 7; 10; 14(2); 15; 16; 14:5; 6; 7(2); **Joel** 1:11; 2:2; 18; 19; 21; 22; 23; 24; 26(2); 27; 31; 32(2); 3:12; 16; 17; 18; 19; **Am** 3:6; 11(2); 12; 14; 4:3; 5:14; 15(2); 16; 17; 18; 19; 6:7; 7:3; 6; 9(2); 11; 17(3); 8:3(2); 5; 9:1; 15; **Ob** 2; 5; 6(2); 9(2); 10; 15; 16; 17(2); 18(2); 21; **Jon** 1:4; 11; 3:4; 7; 8; 4:4; 6; 9(2); **Mic** 1:2; 7(2); 14; 2:11; 3:6; 7; 12; 4:1(2); 10(2); 11; 5:2; 4; 5; 7; 8; 9(2); 10; 6:7; 14(2); 7:4; 8; 10; 11; 13; 16(2); 17; **Nah** 1:10; 12; 14; 2:7(2); 13; 3:11(2); **Hab** 1:5; 2:5; 9; 14; 16(3); 3:17(3); **Zeph** 1:7; 8; 10; 17; 18(2); 2:3(2); 4(2); 5; 6; 7; 9; 11; 12; 14; 3:7; 8; 11(2); 13; 14; 16(2); **Hag** 1:2; 8; 2:4(3); 9; 13(2); **Zech** 1:4; 16(2); 2:4; 5(2); 11; 13; 5:3(2); 11; 6:13(2); 14; 8:3; 5; 6; 8(2); 9(2); 12; 13(2); 19; 9:4; 5(2); 7(2); 10(2); 14; 15; 16; 10:5(2); 6; 7(2); 11; 11:5; 17(2); 12:3; 6; 8(2); 9; 11; 13:1; 2(2); 4(2); 7; 8(2); 14:1; 2(2); 4; 6; 7(2); 8; 9(2); 10(2); 11(2); 12; 13; 14; 15(3); 17(2); 19; 20(2); 21(2); **Mal** 1:4; 8; 9; 11(3); 14(2); 3:4; 5; 10(2); 12; 17; 4:1; 3; **Mt** 1:20; 22; 23; 2:4; 15; 18; 23(2); 3:13; 14; 15; 4:1; 14; 5:4; 6; 9; 12; 13(2); 14; 19(2); 21; 22(3); 24; 25; 29; 30; 37; 45; 48; 6:1; 4; 5(2); 7; 8; 9; 10; 16(2); 18; 21; 22; 23; 24; 33; 7:1; 2(2); 7(2); 8; 26; 8:3; 8; 12(2); 13; 17; 27; 9:2; 15; 21; 22; 29; 10:15; 16; 18; 19; 21; 22(2); 25; 26(2); 36; 11:22; 23; 24; 12:17; 23; 27; 31(2); 32(2); 37(2); 39; 40; 45; 13:12(2); 35; 40; 42; 49; 50; 14:9; 27(2); 15:4; 13; 28; 16:2; 3; 4; 19(2); 21(2); 22; 17:4; 7; 17; 20; 22; 23; 18:6; 8; 9; 16; 17; 18(2); 19; 25(2); 19:5; 21; 25; 30; 20:16; 18; 22; 23; 26(2); 27(2); 28; 31; 33; 21:4; 13; 21(3); 43; 44; 22:13; 28; 23:5; 7; 8; 10; 11; 12(2); 26; 24:2(2); 3(2); 7; 9; 10; 13; 14; 20; 21(2); 22(2); 27; 28; 29(2); 37; 39; 40(2); 41(2); 43; 44; 51; 25:1; 9; 24; 29(2); 30; 32; 26:2(2); 5; 13; 31(2); 33; 37; 42; 46; 54; 56; 27:22; 23; 25; 26; 31; 35; 58; 64(2); 28:5; 10; **Mk** 1:25; 41; 2:20; 22; 3:9; 14; 28; 4:12; 21(2); 22; 24(2); 25(2); 39; 41; 5:18; 23; 28; 34; 36; 43; 6:11; 27; 50(2); 7:10; 24; 27; 34; 8:12; 31(2); 38; 9:5; 12; 19; 34; 35(2); 42; 43; 45(2); 47; 49(2); 10:7; 26; 31; 33; 38; 39; 41; 43(2); 44(2); 45; 48; 49(2); 11:17; 23(3); 12:7; 23; 13:2(2); 4(3); 7; 8(2); 9(2); 10; 12; 13(2); 18; 19(2); 20; 24; 25; 14:2; 9; 19; 27(2); 29; 33; 42; 49; 64; 15:15; 16:6; 16(2); **Lk** 1:13; 15(2); 20(2); 30; 32(2); 33; 34; 35(2); 37; 38; 45; 57; 60; 66; 71; 76; 2:1; 3; 5; 6; 10(2); 12; 23; 34; 35; 49; 3:5(2); 7; 12; 14; 4:7; 35; 5:10; 13; 15; 35; 37(2); 38; 6:17; 21; 35(2); 36; 37(3); 38(3); 40; 7:7; 8:12; 17(2); 18(2); 25; 38; 43; 48; 50(2); 55; 9:22(3); 26; 33; 41; 44; 46; 48; 51; 10:12; 14; 15; 42; 11:2(2); 9(2); 10; 19; 29; 30; 36; 50; 51; 12:2(2); 3(2); 4; 9; 10(2); 19; 20(2); 31; 34; 35; 36; 39; 40; 45; 47; 48(2); 50; 52; 53; 55; 13:14; 16; 24; 28; 30(2); 32; 33; 14:8; 11(2); 12; 14(2); 23; 26; 27; 33; 34; 15:7; 14; 19; 21; 23; 24; 32; 16:2; 13; 21; 31; 17:2; 6(2); 24; 25; 26; 30; 34(3); 35(2); 36(2); 37; 18:13; 14(2); 26; 31; 32(2); 39; 40; 19:7; 15; 19; 26(2); 20:14; 18; 20; 21:6(2); 7(2); 8; 9; 11(2); 12; 15; 16; 17; 18; 22; 23; 24(2); 25; 26; 34; 36; 22:7; 24; 26; 37; 42; 23:23; 24; 31; 32; 43; 24:7(2); 20; 44; 47; **Jn** 1:31; 42; 3:4(2); 7; 9; 14; 17; 20; 21; 4:29; 5:6; 34; 6:20; 45; 7:4; 23; 33; 8:5; 33; 36; 53; 55; 9:3; 22; 39; 10:9; 16; 35; 11:4; 12:23; 26; 31; 34; 38; 42; 13:18; 33; 14:1; 3; 13; 17; 21; 27(2); 15:7; 8; 11; 25; 16:1; 20(2); 24; 32; 33; 17:11; 12; 19; 21(2); 22; 23; 24; 26; 18:9; 28; 32; 36; 19:16; 24(2); 28; 31(2); 36(2); 20:15; 19; 27; 21:25; **Acts** 1:5; 8; 16; 20; 2:14; 20; 21; 24; 25; 38; 40; 3:14; 19(2); 23(2); 25; 4:4; 10; 12; 28; 30; 5:24; 26; 31; 36; 39; 7:7; 35; 8:20; 22; 9:6; 17; 10:42; 47; 48; 11:14; 16; 28; 12:19; 13:11; 28; 38; 39; 42; 46; 47; 14:3; 9; 19; 15:1; 11; 24; 16:15; 22; 30; 31; 17:17; 18; 18:6; 9; 14; 15; 19:27; 36(2); 39; 20:16; 21:13; 14(2); 24; 26; 33; 34; 35; 37; 22:5; 10; 15; 16; 24(2); 23:3; 10; 11; 15; 27; 35; 24:4; 15; 26; 25:4; 6; 9; 10; 17; 19; 20; 21(2); 26:8; 23; 27:20; 22; 24(2); 25; 28(2); 31; 28:28; **Rom** 1:1; 4; 7; 11; 12; 13; 19; 22; 2:12; 13; 26; 3:4(2); 19; 20; 26; 4:11(2); 13; 16(2); 18; 24; 5:9; 10; 19; 6:5; 6(2); 11; 17; 7:3; 4; 8:4; 6(2); 7; 17; 18(2); 21; 26; 29(2); 31; 39; 9:7; 17; 26; 27(2); 33; 10:1; 9; 11; 13; 11:10; 15; 19; 20; 22; 23; 24; 25(2); 26; 35; 36; 12:2(2); 9; 10; 16(2); 21; 13:1; 3; 4; 5; 14:4; 5; 9; 14; 16; 15:5; 12; 16(2); 24; 31(2); 32; 33; 16:19; 20; 24; 27; **1 Cor** 1:1; 2; 8; 10(2); 17; 2:5; 3:13; 15; 18; 4:2; 3; 6; 5:2; 5; 7; 6:2; 5; 7; 9; 12; 7:11; 14; 18; 21(2); 27; 29; 32; 34; 36; 39; 8:10; 9:10; 15(2); 23; 10:1; 13(2); 33; 11:6(3); 16; 19(2); 27; 31; 32; 12:1; 17(2); 19; 22; 23; 25; 13:3; 10; 14:7; 9(2); 10; 11(2); 12; 20(3); 26; 27; 31; 34; 37; 38; 40; 15:9; 22; 26; 28(2); 33; 37; 51; 52(2); 54; 57; 58; 16:2; 6; 10; 13(2); 14; 22; 23; 24; **2 Cor** 1:3; 4; 8; 11; 16; 17; 2:4; 5; 7; 14; 3:8; 4:7; 10; 11; 5:2; 3; 4(2); 8(2); 9; 20; 21; 6:3; 13; 14; 16(2); 17; 18(2); 7:10; 11; 8:10; 11; 13; 14; 16; 9:3(2); 4; 5; 15; 10:2(2); 8; 11; 15; 11:3; 7; 12; 15; 12:6(2); 7(2); 14; 15; 16; 20(2); 13:1(2); 9; 11(3); 14; **Gal** 1:5; 8; 9; 10; 2:3; 6(2); 9; 11; 16(2); 17; 3:8; 22; 23; 24; 4:9; 17; 18; 20; 21; 30; 5:1; 4; 15; 6:1; 3; 7; 12; 16; 18; **Eph** 1:3; 4; 12; 22; 3:6; 10; 16; 18; 19; 21; 4:11; 14; 23; 26; 31; 32; 5:1; 3; 7; 17; 18(2); 24; 27; 31; 6:3; 5; 10; 11; 13; 16; 19; 24; **Phil** 1:10; 20(2); 23; 26; 27; 2:3; 5; 6; 18; 19; 28; 3:9; 16; 21; 4:2; 5; 6(2); 9; 11; 12(3); 20; 23; **Col** 1:9; 12; 2:2; 3:15; 19; 25; 4:6; 11; 18; **1 Th** 2:4; 9; 16; 3:1; 3; 5; 4:13; 17(2); 5:6; 8; 13; 14; 23; 27; 28; **2 Th** 1:5; 9; 10(2); 12; 2:2; 6; 8; 10; 12; 3:1; 2; 8; 14; 16; 18; **1 Tim** 1:7; 17; 2:1; 4; 6; 12; 15; 3:2; 8; 10; 11; 12; 4:3; 4; 6; 12; 15; 5:7; 9; 13; 16; 17; 25; 6:1; 8; 9; 16; 17; 18; 21; **2 Tim** 1:4; 8; 2:1; 2; 6; 15(2); 21; 24; 3:2; 9; 17; 4:2; 4; 5; 9; 16; 17; 18; 22(2); **Titus** 1:7; 9; 11; 13; 2:2; 3; 5(2); 6; 7; 8(2); 9(2); 3:1(2); 2; 8; 12; 14; 15; **Phm** 1:8; 14; 22; 25; **Heb** 1:5(2); 12; 2:3; 17(2); 3:5; 12; 13; 4:11; 5:12; 6:8; 7:11; 8:4; 10(2); 12; 9:16; 23; 10:2; 29; 11:16; 18; 24; 40; 12:5; 9; 10; 11; 13(2); 16; 18; 19; 20; 27; 28; 13:5(2); 9(2); 17(2); 19; 21; 25; **Jas** 1:4; 5; 13; 16; 18; 19; 22; 25; 2:5; 12; 16; 3:10; 4:4; 9; 5:3; 7; 8; 9; 12; 15; 16; **1 Pe** 1:2; 3; 5; 6; 7; 13(2); 15; 16; 2:6; 18; 3:1(2); 3; 4; 7; 8(3); 14(2); 15; 16; 4:6; 7; 9; 11; 13; 16; 17; 5:1; 5(2); 8(2); 11; **2 Pe** 1:2; 4; 8; 10; 11; 12; 15; 2:1; 2; 4; 12; 3:2; 10; 11(2); 12; 14(2); 18; **1 Jn** 1:4; 2:19; 28; 3:1; 2(2); 4:10; **2 Jn** 2; 3; 12; **3 Jn** 2; **Jude** 2; 18; 25; **Rev** 1:6; 17; 2:10(2); 11; 27; 3:2; 5; 18(3); 19; 5:13; 6:11; 7:12; 10:6; 7; 9; 11:5; 9; 18; 12:15; 13:10; 15; 14:10; 16:5; 12; 17:17; 18:8; 21(2); 22(3); 23; 19:7; 8; 20:3; 6; 7; 10; 21:3(3); 4(2); 7(2); 25(2); 22:3(2); 4; 5; 11(4); 21

BECAUSE (1476/1373)

Gen 2:3; 23; 3:10; 14; 17; 20; 5:29; 7:1; 7; 11:9; 12:13; 17; 16:11; 18:20(2); 19:13; 20:3; 11; 18; 21:11; 12(2); 13; 25; 31; 22:16; 18; 25:21; 28; 26:5; 7(2); 9; 20; 22; 27:20; 23; 41; 46; 28:11; 29:15; 20; 33; 34; 30:18; 20; 31:30; 31; 49; 32:32; 33:11(2); 34:7; 13; 19; 27; 35:7; 36:7; 37:3; 38:15; 26; 39:9; 23; 41:31; 32; 57; 43:18(2); 32; 45:5; 26; 46:30; 47:4; 13; 20; 49:4; **Ex** 1:19; 21; 2:10; 23(2); 3:7; 4:26; 5:21; 6:9; 7:24; 8:24; 9:11; 12:39; 13:8; 14:11; 17:7(2); 16; 18:15; 19:18; 23:9; 29:33; 34; 32:35; 40:35; **Lev** 6:4; 10:13; 11:4; 5; 6; 14:48; 15:15; 33; 16:16(2); 19:8; 17; 20; 20:3; 21:23; 22:7; 25; 26:10; 43(2); **Num** 3:13; 5:15; 6:7; 11; 12; 7:9; 9:10; 13; 11:3; 14; 20; 34; 12:1; 13:24; 14:16; 22; 24; 43; 15:26; 31; 34; 16:38; 18:32; 19:13; 20; 20:12; 13; 24; 22:3(2); 22; 29; 32; 25:11; 13; 18; 26:62; 27:4; 30:5; 14; 32:11; 17; 19; 35:28; **Deut** 1:27; 36; 2:5; 9; 19; 25; 4:37; 5:5; 7:7; 8(2); 12; 8:20; 9:4(2); 5(2); 6; 18; 25; 28(2); 12:20; 13:5; 10; 18; 14:8; 29; 15:2; 10; 16; 16:15; 18:12; 19:6; 20:3; 21:14; 22:19; 21; 24(2); 29; 23:4(2); 5; 7; 24:1; 27:20; 28:2; 20; 34; 45; 47; 55; 56; 62; 67(2); 29:25; 31:17; 18; 29; 32:5; 19; 47; 51(2); 33:21; **Josh** 2:9; 11; 24; 5:1; 6; 7; 6:1; 17; 25; 7:12; 13; 15(2); 9:9; 13; 18; 20; 24(2); 10:2(2); 42; 11:6; 14:9; 14; 17:1; 6; 19:47; 20:5; 22:31; 23:3; **Judg** 1:19; 2:18; 20; 3:12; 5:23; 6:2; 6; 7; 27; 30(2); 31; 32; 8:20; 24; 9:5; 18; 10:10; 11:13; 36; 12:4; 13:22; 14:17; 15:6; 18:28; 20:5; 6; 36; 21:15; 22; **Ruth** 1:19; 4:12; **1 Sam** 1:6; 20; 2:1; 25; 3:13; 4:21(2); 6:19(2); 8:18; 9:12; 13; 16; 10:1; 12:10; 22; 13:14; 14:29; 15:23; 24; 16:7; 17:32; 18:3; 12; 16; 19:4(2); 20:17; 18; 34; 21:8; 22:17(2); 24:5; 25:28; 33; 26:12; 16; 21; 28:18; 20; 30:6; 13; 16; 22; **2 Sam** 1:10; 12; 2:6; 3:11; 30; 4:3; 6:8; 12; 8:10; 10:3; 5; 12:6(2); 10; 14; 25; 13:22; 39; 14:15; 26; 16:8; 10; 18:20; 19:9; 21; 26; 42; 21:1(2); 7; 22:8; 20; 23:6; 8; **1 Ki** 2:26(2); 32; 3:2; 6; 11; 19; 5:1; 3; 7:47; 8:11; 33; 35(2); 64; 9:9; 22; 10:9; 11:9; 11; 16; 33; 34(2); 39; 13:21; 14:7; 13; 15; 16; 15:5; 13; 30(2); 16:7(2); 19; 17:7; 19:7; 14; 20:28; 36; 42; 21:2; 4; 6; 20; 22; 25; 29; 22:8; **2 Ki** 1:3; 6; 16(2); 17; 5:1; 8:12; 29; 10:30; 13:4; 23; 15:16; 17:26; 18:12; 19:20; 28; 21:11; 15; 22:7; 13; 17; 19; 23:26; 24:3; 4; 20; **1 Chr** 4:9; 41; 5:1; 9; 20; 22; 7:21; 23; 9:1; 27; 10:13(2); 13:10; 11; 15:13(2); 22; 16:41; 18:10; 19:2; 3; 5; 21:8; 22:8; 23:28; 26:6; 27:23; 24; 28:3; 29:1; 3; 9; **2 Chr** 1:11; 2:11; 5:14; 6:24; 26(2); 7:2; 7; 22; 8:11; 9:8; 11:17; 12:2; 5; 14; 13:18; 14:6; 7; 15:16; 16:7; 8; 10; 17:3; 18:7; 20:15; 25; 37; 21:3; 7; 10; 12; 19; 22:6; 9; 24:16; 18; 20; 24; 25; 25:16; 20; 26:20; 21; 27:6; 28:6; 9; 19; 23; 29:9; 30:3; 32:20; 34:21; 25; 27; 35:14; 15; 36:15; **Ezra** 3:3; 11; 4:14; 5:12; 6:11; 8:22; 9:4; 15; 10:6; 9(2); **Neh** 4:9; 5:3; 9; 15; 18; 6:12; 18; 8:12; 9:37; 38; 13:2; 29; **Esth** 1:15; 8:7; 17; 9:2; 3; 24; 26; **Job** 3:10; 5:5; 6:16; 20; 8:9; 11:16; 18; 17:7; 20:2; 20; 22:4; 23:2; 17; 29:12; 30:11; 16; 31:23; 25(2); 34; 32:1; 2; 3; 4; 16(2); 34:27; 33; 36; 35:9(2); 12; 15; 36:18; 37:19; 38:21(2); 39:11; 17; 24; 41:25; 42:8; **Ps** 5:8; 11; 6:7(2); 7:6; 8:2; 13:6; 16:8; 18:7; 19; 27:11; 28:5; 6; 31:10; 33:21; 37:1; 7(2); 40; 38:3(2); 5; 8; 20; 39:9; 40:15; 41:11; 42:9; 43:2; 44:3; 16(2); 45:4; 11; 48:11; 52:9; 53:5; 55:3(2); 19; 56:9; 60:4; 8; 63:3; 7; 68:29; 69:6(2); 7; 9; 18; 70:3; 78:22; 65; 86:17; 88:9; 91:9; 14(2); 97:8; 102:5; 10; 106:33; 107:11; 17(2); 26; 30; 109:16; 21; 115:1(2); 116:1; 2; 119:53; 56; 62; 74; 100; 136; 139; 158; 164; 122:9; **Prov** 1:24; 25; 29; 20:4; 21:7; 22:22; 23:4; 24:13; 19; 28:2; 21; **Eccl** 2:17; 18; 4:9; 5:20; 8:6; 11; 13; 15; 10:18; 12:3; 9; **Song** 1:3; 6(2); 3:8; **Isa** 1:29; 2:6; 3:8; 16; 5:13; 24; 6:5; 7:5; 24; 8:20; 10:27; 14:20; 21; 29; 15:1(2); 9; 17:9; 10; 19:16; 17; 20; 22:4; 24:5; 26:3; 28:15; 30:12; 31:1(2); 32:14; 37:21; 29; 40:7; 43:20; 47:9; 48:4; 49:7; 50:2; 51:13; 53:9; 12; 54:15; 55:5; 57:11; 60:5; 9; 61:1; 64:7; 12; 65:12; 16(2); 66:4; **Jer** 1:16; 2:35(2); 4:4; 17; 18(2); 19; 28; 31; 5:6; 14; 6:13; 19; 25; 30; 7:12; 13; 8:10; 14; 9:10; 13; 19(2); 10:5; 11:14; 12:4; 11; 13; 13:17; 25; 14:4; 5; 6; 16; 15:4; 13; 17; 16:11; 18; 17:13; 18:15; 19:4(2); 8; 13; 15; 20:8; 17; 21:12; 22:9; 15; 23:9(3); 10; 38; 25:8; 16; 27; 37; 38(2); 26:3; 28:16; 29:15; 19; 22; 23; 31; 32; 30:14; 15(2); 17; 31:15; 19; 32:24; 30; 32; 35:17; 18; 39:18; 40:3; 41:9; 18(2); 44:3; 22(2); 23(2); 46:15; 23; 47:4; 48:7; 26; 42; 45; 50:7; 11(3); 13; 24; 51:11; 51; 55; 56; 58; 52:3; **Lam** 1:4; 5; 8; 16(2); 2:11(2); 3:22; 28; 51; 4:13; 5:9; 10; 17(2); 18; **Ezek** 1:20; 3:7; 20; 21; 4:17; 5:7; 9; 11; 6:9; 7:19; 12:19; 13:8; 10(2); 22; 14:5; 15; 15:8; 16:14; 15; 28; 31; 34; 36(2); 43; 52(2); 61; 63; 18:18; 19; 22; 24(2); 26; 28; 19:10; 20:16; 24; 26; 43; 21:4; 7; 13; 24(2); 22:19; 23:21; 30(2); 35; 45; 24:13; 25:3; 6; 8; 12; 15(2); 26:2; 10; 27:12; 16; 18(2); 30; 31; 28:2; 5; 6; 17; 29:6; 9; 20; 31:5; 7; 10; 15(2); 32:27; 33:12(2); 13; 18; 19; 29; 34:5; 8(2); 21; 35:5; 10; 15; 36:2; 3; 6; 13; 39:10; 11; 23; 41:7; 42:5; 44:2; 3; 7; 12; 47:9; 12; **Dan** 2:8; 30; 3:22; 29; 4:9; 5:10; 19; 6:3; 4; 22; 23; 7:11; 8:12; 9:7; 8; 11; 16; 18(2); 10:12; 16; 11:35; **Hos** 4:6(2); 10; 13; 19; 5:1; 11; 7:13; 8:1; 10; 11; 9:6; 7; 15; 17; 10:3; 5(2); 13; 15; 11:5; 6; 14:1; **Joel** 1:5; 11; 18; 2:20; 3:5; 19; **Am** 1:3; 6; 9; 11; 13; 2:1; 4; 6; 4:12; 5:11; **Jon** 1:10; 12; 2:2; **Mic** 1:16; 2:1; 10; 12; 3:4; 12; 6:13; 7:9; 13; 17; 18; **Nah** 3:4; **Hab** 1:16; 2:3; 5(2); 8(2); 17; **Zeph** 1:17; 2:10; **Hag** 1:9; 2:13; **Zech** 2:4; 8:4; 9:8(2); 11; 10:2; 5; 6; 11:2; 13:3; **Mal** 2:2; 9; 14; 3:5; **Mt** 2:18; 5:36; 7:14; 9:36; 11:6; 20; 12:41; 13:5; 6; 11; 13; 21; 58; 14:4; 5; 9(2); 15:3; 32; 16:7; 8; 17:20; 18:7; 32; 19:8; 20:7; 15; 21:46; 23:29; 24:12; 26:31; 33; 27:6; 18; 19; **Mk** 1:34; 38; 2:4; 3:9; 30; 4:5; 6; 29; 5:4; 6:6; 26(2); 34; 52; 7:19; 8:2; 16; 17; 9:6; 38; 41; 10:5; 11:18; 12:24; 14:27; 15:10; 42; 16:14; **Lk** 1:7; 20; 2:4; 7; 4:18; 43; 5:19; 7:23; 8:6; 19; 30; 9:7; 49; 53; 10:20; 11:8(2); 18; 13:2; 14; 14:14; 15:27; 16:8; 17:9; 18:5; 19:3; 9; 11(2); 17; 21; 31; 44; 21:28; 23:8; **Jn** 1:50; 2:24; 3:18; 19; 23; 29; 4:39; 41; 42; 5:16; 18; 27; 30; 38; 6:2; 18; 26(2); 27; 41; 57(2); 7:1; 7; 23; 30; 39; 43; 8:22; 37; 43; 44; 45; 47; 9:16; 17; 22; 10:13; 17; 19; 26; 33; 36; 11:9; 10; 42; 12:6; 11; 18; 30; 39; 42; 13:29; 14:12; 17; 19; 28; 15:3; 19; 21; 27; 16:3; 4; 6; 9; 10; 11; 16; 17; 21; 27; 32; 17:14; 19:7; 31; 42; 20:13; 29; 21:6; 17; **Acts** 2:6; 24; 4:21; 6:1; 8:11; 20; 10:45; 12:3; 14; 20; 23; 13:27; 14:12; 16:3; 17:18; 31; 18:2; 3; 21:34; 35; 22:29; 30; 24:11; 25:20; 26:2; 3; 27:4; 9; 12; 18; 28:2(2); 3; 18; 20; **Rom** 1:19; 21; 2:24; 3:2; 25; 4:15; 25(2); 5:5; 12; 6:15; 19; 8:7; 10(2); 20; 21; 27; 9:7; 28; 32; 11:20; 13:5; 6; 14:15; 23; 15:15; **1 Cor** 1:25; 2:14; 3:13; 7:2; 5; 26; 8:11; 11:10; 12:15; 16; 15:9; 15; **2 Cor** 1:7; 2:13; 3:7; 10; 14; 5:4; 14; 7:13; 8:22; 9:14; 11:7; 11; **Gal** 2:4; 11; 3:19; 4:6; 13; 16; **Eph** 2:4; 4:18(2); 5:6; 16; **Phil** 1:7; 2:26; 30; **Col** 1:5; 3:6; **1 Th** 2:8; 13; 4:6; **2 Th** 1:3; 10; 2:10; 13; 3:9; **1 Tim** 1:12; 13; 4:10; 5:12; 6:2(2); **2 Tim** 4:3; **Phm** 1:7; **Heb** 3:19; 4:6; 5:3; 7; 6:13; 7:18; 23; 24; 8:8; 9; 11:5; 11; 23; **Jas** 1:10; 4:2; 3; **1 Pe** 1:16; 24; 2:19; 21; 5:8; **2 Pe** 2:2; 3:12; **1 Jn** 2:8; 11; 12; 13(3); 14(2); 21(2); 3:1; 9; 12; 14; 16; 22; 4:1; 4; 13; 17; 18; 19; 5:6; 10; **2 Jn** 2; **3 Jn** 7; **Rev** 1:7; 2:14; 20; 3:10; 16; 17; 5:4; 8:11; 13; 9:2; 11:10; 17; 12:12; 14:8; 16:5; 10; 11; 21; 19:2

BEEN (583/548)

Gen 13:3; 26:8; 28:19; 30:29; 31:5; 38; 41; 42; 34:27; 35:3; 38:26; 39:1; 42:28; 45:6; 46:32; 34; 47:9; **Ex** 2:22; 9:15; 18; 10:14; 14:12; 18:3; 21:29; 34:10; 34; **Lev** 8:35; 10:13; 19; 13:7; 55; 19:20; **Num** 1:17; 11:23; 15:34; 19:20; **Deut** 2:7; 4:32; 9:7; 24; 15:18; 17:2; 4; 21:3; 24:4; 31:27; **Josh** 5:5(2); 7; 6:23; 7:7; 26; 10:14; 17; 27; 23:9; **Judg** 2:10; 6:28; 31; 14:20; 16:11; 17; 22; 19:30; 21:16; **Ruth** 2:11; 18; **1 Sam** 3:20; 4:9; 17(2); 21; 22; 6:7; 9:20; 24; 10:2; 16; 14:30; 15:21; 18:19; 19:4; 20:13; 21:5; 6; 22:6; 25:34; 29:3; 6; 8; 30:3; 5; 21; **2 Sam** 1:26; 3:37; 4:3; 7:9; 8:10; 10:15; 12:8; 13:20; 32; 39; 14:2; 21:13; **1 Ki** 1:27; 37; 2:15; 3:12; 15; 9:21; 10:12; 20; 12:2; 19; 13:17; 14:6; 8; 16:31; 17:7; 19:10; 14; 21:14; 15; **2 Ki** 4:13; 8:16; 22; 9:14; 12:11; 20:12; 22:4; 13; 23:2; 22; **1 Chr** 9:18; 19; 20; 14:8; 17:8; 27; 18:10; 19:16; 28:3; 29:25; **2 Chr** 6:38; 9:19; 10:19; 15:3; 21:10; 28:19; 30:26; 34:30; 35:18; **Ezra** 2:1; 3:6; 4:18; 19(2); 20; 5:16; 8:35; 9:2; 4; 7(2); 8; 10:3; **Neh** 2:1; 18; 5:5; 7:1; 6; 12:22; 13:10; **Esth** 2:1; 6(2); 4:11(2); 6:3(2); 7:4(2); **Job** 3:13(3); 6:3; 7:3(2); 10:19(3); 31:9; 27; 31; 33:6; 38:17; 42:11; **Ps** 22:10; 27:9; 36:12; 37:25; 42:3; 50:18; 59:16; 60:1; 61:3; 63:7; 71:6; 73:14; 15; 79:8; 10; 85:1; 88:15; 89:38; 90:1; 7; 92:10; 94:17; 22; 115:12; 119:54; 71; 92; 122:2; 124:1; 2; 143:3; **Prov** 8:23; 30:32; **Eccl** 1:9; 10; 3:15(2); 6:10; **Isa** 1:6; 9; 5:4; 17:10; 25:4; 26:17; 18(2); 27:7; 30:24; 33:1; 38:9; 39:1; 40:21; 42:14; 43:4; 22; 46:3(2); 48:18; 19(2); 50:1; 52:15; 53:1; 57:11; 60:15; **Jer** 2:10; 31; 3:3(2); 4:17; 5:30; 7:28; 9:19; 11:9; 13:17; 22; 14:17; 15:9; 20:15; 17; 22:21; 28:8; 32:24; 25; 31; 43; 33:4; 34:14; 38:27; 40:7; 12; 42:18; 43:5; 44:10; 18; 48:11(2); 46; 49:14; 50:6; 23; 24(2); 29; 51:8; **Lam** 1:12; 20; 3:10; 5:2; **Ezek** 2:5; 7:13; 9:3; 11:15; 17; 17:7; 20:41; 22:13; 26:10; 29:6; 30:21; 31:14; 33:21; 22; 24; 33; 36:4; 23; 38:8; **Dan** 2:30; 5:2; 3(2); 15; 27; 28; 6:20; 9:11; 12(2); 10:11; 13; 11:36(2); 12:7; **Hos** 5:1; **Joel** 1:5; 9; 2:2; **Ob** 1; 16; **Jon** 2:4; **Mic** 3:4; **Zech** 1:2; 8:9; **Mal** 1:4; 2:11; 14; 3:13; **Mt** 1:6; 2:2; 3:16; 4:12; 5:31; 11:20; 21; 23; 27; 13:11(2); 14:8; 18:31(2); 19:11; 20:6; 23:30; 24:21; 25:23; 26:9; 24(2); 32; 27:3; 8; 28:18; **Mk** 4:11; 22; 5:4(2); 15; 16; 18; 6:16; 9:21; 11:32; 13:19; 14:5; 21(2); 28; 15:44; 46; 16:4; 10; 11; **Lk** 1:1; 70; 2:26; 44; 4:6; 12; 16; 43; 5:25; 7:10; 29; 30; 8:2; 10; 36; 10:13; 22; 12:48; 15:29; 16:11; 12; 16; 22:22; 23:12; 15; 19; 25; 48; **Jn** 3:21; 24; 27; 28; 5:6; 14; 17(2); 6:65; 8:25; 33; 9:18; 32; 11:17; 21; 32; 39; 12:1; 38; 14:9; 15:27; 16:21; 19:11; 41; 20:1; 7; **Acts** 4:9; 13; 14; 16; 21; 22; 8:16; 9:33; 10:17; 21; 31; 45; 11:11; 12:20; 13:1; 12; 26; 40; 48; 14:26; 15:7; 18:25; 19:21; 21:21; 26; 24:10; 19; 25:14; 26:32; 27:9; 28:28; **Rom** 5:1; 5; 9; 10; 6:5; 7; 9; 18; 22; 7:6; 9:29; 11:31; 15:22; 27; 16:2; 26(2); **1 Cor** 1:11; 2:12; 4:9; 13; 9:17; 12:13; 15:12; **2 Cor** 5:3; 7:13(2); 11:6; 25; 12:11; **Gal** 2:7; 9; 20; 3:21(2); 5:13; 6:14; **Eph** 2:5; 8; 13; 20; 3:5; 9; 4:21; **Phil** 1:29; **Col** 1:26(2); 2:7; **1 Th** 2:4; 17; **1 Tim** 5:9; **2 Tim** 1:10; 2:26; 3:14; **Titus** 1:9; 3:7; **Phm** 1:7; **Heb** 3:3; 4:7; 5:9; 7:28; 8:7(2); 9:6; 10:10; 12:11; 13:9; 23; **Jas** 1:12; 3:7; 9; **1 Pe** 1:6; 12; 23; 3:22; **2 Pe** 1:4; 2:3; 21; **1 Jn** 2:19; 3:2; 9(2); 4:12; 17; 18; 5:18; **Rev** 5:6; 6:9; 9:15; 11:2; 12:10; 13; 13:3; 8; 15:4; 20:4

BUT (4309/4075)

Gen 2:6; 17; 20; 3:3; 4:2; 5; 7; 6:8; 18; 8:9; 9:4; 23; 11:5; 30; 12:12; 17; 13:13; 14:22; 15:2; 4; 10; 16; 17:5; 15; 21;

18:15(2); 22; 27; 32; 19:2; 3; 10; 14; 19; 26; 20:3; 4; 7; 12(2); 21:12; 23; 22:7(2); 11; 24:4; 6; 33; 38; 40; 45; 55; 25:6; 22; 27; 28; 31; 26:20; 28; 29; 27:13; 20; 22; 35; 28:19; 29:8; 17; 31; 30:15; 40; 42; 31:5; 7; 24; 29; 30; 33; 34; 35; 43; 47; 32:21; 26; 28; 33:4; 9; 13; 15; 34:8; 12; 13; 15; 17; 31; 35:10; 16; 18; 37:4; 11; 21; 22; 35; 38:7; 9; 20; 39:8; 9; 11; 12; 21; 40:14; 22; 23; 41:8; 15; 24; 30; 54; 42:4; 7; 8; 10; 12(2); 14; 19; 23; 27; 31; 34; 38; 43:3; 5; 7; 21; 23; 34; 44:17; 23; 26; 29; 45:3; 5; 8; 22; 27; 46:12; 47:18; 30; 48:7(2); 11; 19(2); 21; 49:19; 24; 50:20(2); 24; **Ex** 1:7; 12; 16; 17(2); 2:3; 15; 17; 3:2; 11; 19; 22; 4:1; 10; 13; 21; 23; 5:16; 17; 6:3; 9; 30; 7:4; 11; 12; 16; 8:2; 15; 18; 19; 29; 32; 9:6; 7; 12; 16; 21; 30; 32; 10:20; 23; 25; 27; 11:7; 9; 12:9; 16; 44; 13:13; 15; 14:16; 29; 15:19; 16:7; 8; 20; 26; 27; 17:1; 12; 18:22; 26; 19:13; 23; 24; 20:6; 10; 19; 21; 21:5; 13; 14; 18; 23; 28; 29; 34; 22:12; 23:11; 22; 24; 24:2; 11; 29:14; 33; 30:37; 31:15; 32:18(2); 32; 33:11; 12; 20; 23; 34:13; 20; 21; 34; 35:2; 36:38; 40:37; **Lev** 1:9; 13; 17; 2:5; 12; 4:11; 5:8; 11; 6:28; 30; 7:16(2); 20; 24; 31; 8:17; 9:10; 21; 10:6; 11:4; 5; 6; 10; 11; 23; 26; 36; 38; 12:5; 13:4; 7; 14; 21(2); 23; 26(2); 28(2); 31; 33; 35; 37; 40; 41; 53; 57; 14:9; 21; 48; 15:28; 16:10; 17:16; 19:14; 18; 20; 24; 20:24; 21:14; 22:11; 13(2); 23; 32; 23:3; 8; 24:21; 25:4; 17; 26; 28; 30; 34; 36; 43; 46; 52; 26:14; 15; 23; 27; 40; 45; 27:8; 13; 18; 20; 21; 26; 29; **Num** 1:47; 50; 53; 2:33; 3:10; 38; 4:15; 19; 20; 5:8; 20; 28; 31; 6:12; 7:9; 8:26; 9:13; 22; 10:4; 7; 30; 11:6; 20; 26(2); 33; 12:14; 13:31; 14:6; 18; 21; 24; 31; 32; 38; 44; 15:30; 16:12; 30; 18:3; 4; 7; 17; 23; 32; 19:12; 20; 21:23; 30; 22:20; 35; 24:1; 11; 17(2); 20; 24; 26:33; 55; 64; 27:3(2); 30:5; 8; 12; 15; 31:14; 18; 23; 32:17; 23; 27; 30; 32; 33:55; 35:16; 26; 28; 30; 31; 36:6; 9; **Deut** 1:26; 40; 43; 45; 2:11; 12; 20; 21; 30; 3:7; 19; 26; 28; 4:4; 12; 20; 22(2); 26; 29; 5:3; 10; 14; 31; 7:5; 8; 15; 18; 23; 8:3; 9:4; 5; 19; 10:12; 11:7; 11; 28; 12:5; 10; 14; 18; 13:5; 9; 14:7; 12; 24; 15:3; 6(2); 8; 21; 16:6; 17:16; 18:14; 20; 19:11; 13; 20:12; 14; 16; 17; 21:14; 17; 23; 22:20; 25; 26; 27; 23:5; 11; 20; 22; 24; 25; 24:18; 25:7; 8; 26:6; 28:12; 15; 30(3); 31; 38; 39; 40; 41; 44; 65; 68; 29:15; 29; 30:14; 17; 32:15; 21; 34:4; 6; 10; **Josh** 1:8; 14; 2:4; 6; 22; 5:5; 12; 14; 6:4; 13; 15; 19; 22; 24; 7:1; 3; 4; 12; 8:4; 9; 14; 23; 9:3; 8; 12; 14; 18; 21; 10:16; 19; 30; 37; 40; 11:6; 13; 14; 20; 13:13; 33; 14:3; 8; 15:63; 16:10; 17:3(2); 8; 12; 13; 16; 18; 18:2; 7; 20:5; 21:12; 22:3; 5; 7; 18; 19; 24; 27; 28; 23:8; 9; 13; 24:4; 8; 10; 11; 12; 15; 19; 21; **Judg** 1:19; 21; 25; 28; 33; 2:2; 3; 17; 3:15; 19; 26; 4:8; 16; 5:31; 6:10; 13; 27; 31; 34; 39(2); 40; 7:4; 6; 10; 14; 8:4; 20; 23; 9:5; 9; 11; 13; 15; 18; 20; 28; 36; 51; 53; 11:1; 17(2); 18; 20; 27; 13:3; 6; 9; 16; 23; 14:4; 6; 9; 13; 15; 16; 15:1; 12; 13(2); 16:9; 12; 14; 20; 19:2; 5; 8; 12; 18; 23; 24; 25; 28; 20:5; 9; 13; 32; 34; 40; 42; 47; **Ruth** 1:11; 14; 16; 17; 20; 2:8; 3:3; 13; 4:4(2); **1 Sam** 1:2; 5; 11; 13; 15; 22; 2:9; 11; 15; 16; 18; 25; 30; 33; 4:20; 5:6; 6:3; 9; 7:10; 17; 8:3; 6; 7; 19; 9:4(2); 7; 20; 27; 10:12; 16; 19; 21; 27(2); 11:13; 12:10; 12; 15; 20; 23; 25; 13:8; 14; 16; 20; 22; 14:1; 3; 10; 26; 27; 29; 37; 39; 41; 45; 15:3; 9(2); 14; 20; 21; 26; 33; 16:7(2); 14; 17:9; 15; 34; 45; 50; 54; 18:8; 10; 11; 12; 16; 17; 19; 25(2); 19:1; 10; 20:3(2); 5; 7; 9; 13; 15; 22; 25; 39; 41; 21:4; 6; 22:17; 23; 23:3; 14; 24; 27; 24:10; 12; 13; 22; 25:3; 15; 19; 25; 29; 31; 44; 26:3; 11; 19; 23; 27:9; 28:23; 29:2; 4; 8; 30:2; 6; 10; 23; 24; 31:4; **2 Sam** 1:9; 2:8; 21; 31; 3:1; 13; 22; 26; 4:9; 12; 5:6; 6:10; 22; 7:2; 4; 6; 15; 9:10; 10:11; 11:1; 9; 13; 27; 12:3; 4; 12; 17; 21; 23(2); 13:3; 9; 16; 20; 21; 25(2); 27; 37; 14:2; 6; 14; 20; 24(2); 28; 29; 32; 15:3; 16; 26; 34; 16:10; 18; 17:16; 18; 18:3(2); 12; 20; 22; 23; 29; 19:4; 10; 21; 27; 28; 34; 37; 20:2; 3; 5; 10; 12; 21; 21:2(2); 7; 17; 22:19; 28; 42(2); 23:6; 7; 12; 16; 23; 24:3; 10; 14; 17; 24; **1 Ki** 1:1; 4; 8; 10; 19; 26; 52; 2:7; 8; 9; 26; 30; 33; 45; 3:7; 11; 21; 22(2); 23; 26(2); 5:4; 7:1; 31; 8:8; 16; 18; 19; 27; 41; 9:6(2); 12; 22; 24; 11:1; 10; 22(2); 32; 35; 39; 40; 12:8; 10; 11; 14(2); 17; 18; 20; 22; 13:8; 22; 33; 14:4; 9; 15:14; 23; 16:22; 17:13; 18:12; 18; 21(2); 22; 23(2); 25; 26; 29; 19:4; 11(2); 12; 20:6; 9; 23; 28; 30; 21:3; 5; 15; 25; 22:3; 8(2); 16; 18; 28; 30; 31; 48; 49; **2 Ki** 1:3; 4; 6; 14; 16; 2:2; 4; 6; 10; 17(2); 19; 3:2; 5; 11; 13; 15; 25; 26; 4:2; 17; 27(2); 29; 31; 43; 5:1; 11; 16(2); 17; 20(2); 6:5; 12; 19; 22; 29; 32(2); 7:2; 17; 19; 8:13; 15; 9:15; 18; 27; 35; 10:4; 5; 9; 19; 23; 31; 11:2; 8; 12:3; 7; 14; 13:6; 11; 19; 23; 14:6(2); 11; 19; 27; 16:3; 5; 17:2; 14; 18; 19; 36; 39; 40; 18:6; 12; 20; 22; 27; 32; 36; 19:3; 18; 27; 20:10; 21:9; 24; 22:18; 23:9; 23; 35; 25:5; 12; 25; **1 Chr** 4:27; 5:1; 6:49; 56; 7:15; 9:1; 10:4; 14; 11:14; 18; 25; 12:17; 19; 13:13; 15:2; 16:5; 26; 17:1; 3; 5; 19:12; 20:1; 21:3; 6; 8; 13; 17(2); 20; 24; 30; 22:8; 23:11; 17; 22; 27:23; 24; 28:3; 9; 29:1; 14; **2 Chr** 1:4; 11; 2:6; 4:6; 5:9; 6:8; 9; 18; 32; 7:19; 8:9; 10:8; 10; 11; 14(2); 17; 18; 11:2; 12:7; 13:10; 11; 13; 21; 15:2; 4; 5; 7; 17; 16:12; 17:4; 18:6; 7(2); 15; 17; 29; 30; 31; 19:6; 20:10; 12; 15; 37; 21:3; 13; 20; 22:11; 23:6(2); 24:15; 19; 22; 24; 25; 25:2; 4(2); 7; 8; 9; 13; 20; 27; 26:16; 18; 27:2; 28:9(2); 10; 21; 23; 27; 29:34; 30:8; 10; 18; 32:8; 9; 25; 33:2; 10; 17; 22; 23; 25; 34:26; 35:13; 21(2); 22; 36:13; 16; **Ezra** 2:59; 62; 3:12; 4:3(2); 5:5; 12; 16; 8:22; 9:9; 10:13; **Neh** 1:9; 2:2; 14; 19; 20; 3:5; 4:1; 5:15(2); 6:2; 4; 8; 12; 7:4; 61; 64; 9:16; 17(2); 28; 29; 33; 11:3; 21; 13:2; 6; 24; **Esth** 1:12; 16; 17; 2:15; 3:2; 6; 15; 4:4; 11; 14; 5:9; 12; 6:12; 13; 7:7; 9:10; 15; 16; 18; 25; **Job** 1:11; 2:5; 6; 10; 3:9; 21; 4:2; 5; 16; 5:3; 8; 15; 18(2); 6:25; 7:16; 21; 8:15(2); 9:2; 18; 35; 11:5; 20; 12:3; 7; 13:3; 4; 14:10; 16; 18; 22; 16:5; 7; 12; 17:6; 10; 19:16; 20:5; 11; 13; 22:8; 18; 23:6; 8(2); 10; 13; 24:22(2); 26:1; 14; 27:17; 19; 28:5; 12; 30:1; 20; 21; 26; 28; 31:18; 32; 32:8; 33:1; 34:5; 35:10; 12; 36:5; 6; 7; 12; 13; 17; 38:11; 39:13; 40:5(2); 42:5; **Ps** 1:2; 4; 6; 2:12; 3:3; 4:3; 5:7; 11; 6:3; 7:9; 9:7; 20; 10:14; 11:5; 13:5; 14:6; 15:4; 18:18; 27; 41(2); 20:7; 8; 22:2; 3; 6; 9; 19; 24; 26:11; 28:3; 30:5(2); 31:6; 11; 14; 32:10; 34:10; 19; 35:13; 15; 20; 37:9; 10; 11; 17; 20; 21; 22; 28; 36; 38; 39; 38:13; 19; 39:5; 40:17; 41:10; 44:2; 3; 7; 9; 17; 19; 49:15; 50:16; 21; 52:7; 8; 55:13; 21; 23(2); 59:8; 16; 62:4; 63:9; 11(2); 64:7; 66:12; 19; 68:3; 6; 21; 69:13; 20(2); 29; 70:5; 71:7; 14; 73:2; 4; 25; 26; 28; 75:7; 9; 10; 77:10; 78:7; 17; 30; 38; 39; 50; 52; 53; 57; 68; 81:11; 15; 82:7; 85:8; 86:15; 88:13; 89:24; 38; 91:7; 92:8; 10; 94:15; 22; 96:5; 102:12; 26; 27; 103:17; 106:7; 14; 15; 25; 35; 43; 109:4; 16; 21; 28(2); 115:1; 3; 5(2); 6(2); 7(2); 16; 18; 118:10; 11; 13; 17; 18; 119:23; 61; 67; 69; 70; 78; 81; 87; 95; 96; 113; 161; 163; 120:7; 125:1; 127:5; 130:4; 132:18; 135:16(2); 17; 136:15; 138:6; 139:4; 12; 141:8; 145:20; 146:9; **Prov** 1:7; 18; 28(2); 33; 2:22; 3:1; 32; 33; 34; 35; 4:18; 5:4; 8:36; 9:18; 10:1; 2; 3; 4; 6; 7; 8; 9; 10; 11; 12; 13; 14; 17; 19; 21; 23; 25; 27; 28; 29; 30; 31; 32; 11:1; 2; 3; 4; 5; 6; 9; 11; 12; 13; 14; 15; 16; 17; 18; 20; 21; 23; 24; 26; 27; 28; 12:1; 2; 3; 4; 5; 6; 7; 8; 9(2); 10; 11; 12; 13; 15; 16; 17; 18; 19(2); 20; 21; 22; 23; 24; 25; 27; 13:1; 2; 3; 4; 5; 6; 8; 9; 10(2); 11; 12; 13; 15; 16; 17; 18; 19; 20; 21; 22; 24; 25; 14:1; 2; 3; 4; 5; 6; 8; 9; 11; 12; 14; 15; 16; 18; 20; 21; 22; 23; 24; 25; 28; 29; 30; 31; 32; 33; 34; 35; 15:1; 2; 4; 5; 6; 7; 8; 9; 13; 14; 15; 18; 19; 20; 21; 22; 25; 26; 27; 28; 29; 32; 16:1; 2; 9; 14; 22; 25; 33; 17:3; 9; 22; 24; 18:2; 14; 23; 24; 19:4; 12; 14; 16; 20:5; 6; 14; 15; 17; 21:2; 5; 8; 11; 15; 20; 26; 28; 29; 31; 22:3; 12; 23:7; 17; 35(2); 24:16; 25; 25:2; 27:3; 4; 6; 7; 28:1; 2; 4; 5; 7; 10; 11; 12; 13; 14; 16; 18; 19; 20; 25; 26; 27; 28; 29:2; 3; 4; 6; 7; 8; 10; 11; 15; 16; 18; 23; 24; 25; 26; 30:24; 31:29; 30; **Eccl** 1:4; 2:1; 14; 26; 4:1(2); 8; 10; 11; 5:7; 12; 14; 6:2; 3; 6; 7:4; 12; 14; 23; 26; 28(2); 29; 8:13; 9:4; 5; 11; 18; 10:2; 10; 12; 19; 11:8; 9; **Song** 1:5; 6; 3:1; 2; 5:2; 6(3); **Isa** 1:3; 6; 20; 21; 2:18; 5:2; 6; 7(2); 12; 16; 25; 6:9(2); 13; 7:1; 12; 13; 25; 8:9(2); 10(2); 14; 9:10(2); 12; 17; 21; 10:4; 7; 20; 11:4; 14; 13:21; 14:19; 16:6; 12; 14; 17:11; 13; 22:11; 13; 24:16; 26:11; 13; 28:7; 13; 27; 29:8(2); 9(2); 13; 23; 30:1(2); 5; 15; 20; 31:1; 2; 8; 32:8; 33:21; 34:11; 12; 35:8; 9; 36:5; 7; 12; 21; 37:3; 19; 28; 38:17; 40:8; 31; 41:8; 17; 28; 42:19; 20(2); 22; 43:1; 22; 24; 45:17; 46:2; 47:9; 48:1; 10; 49:14; 21; 25; 51:6; 8; 15; 21; 23; 53:5; 9; 54:7; 8; 10; 15; 55:10; 11; 57:3; 13(2); 20; 59:2; 9(2); 11(2); 60:2; 10; 18; 19; 61:6; 62:4; 9; 63:5; 10; 18; 64:6; 8; 65:6; 11; 12; 13(3); 14; 18; 20(2); 66:2; 4; 5; **Jer** 1:7; 19; 2:7; 11; 25; 27; 28; 34; 3:1; 7; 8; 10; 19; 4:22; 5:3(2); 5; 10; 23; 31; 6:16; 17; 19; 7:12; 13(2); 23; 24; 26; 27(2); 32; 8:6; 7; 15; 9:8; 14; 24; 10:8; 10; 19; 24; 11:8(2); 12; 19; 20; 12:2; 3; 13(3); 17; 13:1; 11; 14; 17; 14:5; 12; 13; 19; 15:19; 20; 16:4; 15; 17:6; 8; 11(2); 18(2); 22; 23(2); 24; 27; 18:23; 19:6; 20:3; 9; 11; 12; 21:9; 14; 22:5; 12; 17; 21; 27; 23:3; 8; 22; 38; 25:3; 4; 26:5; 15; 19; 21; 27:11; 18; 28:13; 15; 30:7; 9; 11; 31:30; 33; 32:4; 23; 34; 40; 33:5; 34:3; 11; 14; 35:6; 7; 10; 11; 14; 15; 16; 17(2); 36:20; 25; 26; 31; 37:2; 14; 38:2; 4; 6; 18; 20; 21; 23; 25; 39:5; 10; 12; 17; 18; 40:4; 10; 14; 16; 41:8; 11; 15; 42:2; 13; 14; 21; 43:3; 5; 44:5; 17; 18; 45:5; 46:17; 20; 27; 28; 48:30; 45; 49:6; 10; 12; 19; 39; 50:13; 19; 20(2); 44; 51:9; 26; 62; 52:8; 16; **Lam** 1:17; 19; 21; 2:14; 4:3; 4; 5:7; **Ezek** 1:9; 2:8; 3:5; 7; 14; 18; 19; 20; 27; 7:4; 14; 20; 25; 26; 9:6; 10; 10:11; 11:7; 12; 21; 12:2(2); 16; 23; 28; 13:6; 7; 14:11; 18; 15:7; 16:5; 7; 15; 33; 34; 43; 47; 51; 61; 17:6; 7; 14; 15; 18:5; 7(2); 8; 11; 14; 16; 17; 21; 24; 19:12; 20:8; 9; 14; 16; 18; 21; 24; 38; 39; 21:23; 22:30; 23:14; 45; 24:23; 27:26; 34; 28:9; 29:4; 16; 30:24; 25; 32:27; 33:5(2); 6(2); 8; 9; 11; 13(2); 17; 19; 24; 31(2); 32; 34:3; 4; 8; 16; 28; 36:8; 21; 22; 37:8; 23; 39:28; 41:6; 42:14; 44:1; 8; 13; 15; 20; 22; 45:8; 46:1; 2; 9(2); 17(2); 47:11; **Dan** 1:4; 8; 2:28; 30(2); 39; 43; 49; 3:15; 18; 4:7; 8; 18; 23; 5:8; 15; 20; 22; 6:4; 13; 16; 7:18; 26; 28; 8:3; 4; 7; 8; 17; 18; 22; 24; 25; 27; 9:7; 18; 26; 27; 10:1; 7; 13; 21; 11:4; 6(2); 7; 9; 11; 12; 14; 16; 17; 18; 19; 20(2); 21; 24; 25; 27; 29; 32; 34; 38; 41; 44; 12:4; 10(2); 13; **Hos** 1:6; 2:7(2); 13; 4:10(2); 5:6; 6:1(2); 7:9; 10; 16; 8:4(2); 6; 12; 13; 14; 9:3; 8; 10; 10:11; 11:3; 5; 12; 12:9; 13:1; 4; 9; 14:9; **Joel** 2:20; 3:4; 16; 20; **Am** 1:4; 7; 10; 12; 14; 2:2; 5; 12; 3:8; 4:8; 5:5; 11; 24; 6:6; 14; 7:13; 14; 8:11; 12; **Ob** 12; 17; 18; **Jon** 1:3; 4; 5; 13; 2:9; 3:8; 4:1; 7; 10; **Mic** 1:12; 3:4; 5; 8; 4:4; 5; 12; 5:2; 6:8; 14(2); 15(3); **Nah** 1:8; 2:8; **Hab** 2:3; 4; 20; **Zeph** 1:5; 13(2); 18; 3:5; 7; **Hag** 1:6(3); 9; 2:16(2); 19; **Zech** 1:4; 15; 21; 4:6; 7:11; 14; 8:11; 9:7; 11:6; 16; 12:6; 13:5; 8; 14:2; 7; 11; **Mal** 1:3; 4(2); 7; 9; 12; 14(2); 2:8; 9; 15; 3:2; 7; 8; 4:2; **Mt** 1:20; 2:6; 19; 22; 3:7; 11; 12; 15; 4:4(2); 5:13(2); 15; 17; 19; 22(2); 28; 32; 33; 34; 37; 39(2); 44; 6:3; 6; 13; 15; 17; 18; 20; 23; 33; 7:3; 15; 17; 21; 26; 8:4; 8; 12; 20; 22; 24; 26; 9:4; 6; 12; 13(2); 14; 15; 17; 18; 22; 24; 25; 31; 34; 36; 37; 10:6; 13; 17; 19; 20; 22; 28(2); 30; 33; 34; 11:8; 9; 11; 16; 19; 22; 24; 12:3; 4; 7; 15; 25; 28; 31; 32; 36; 39; 48; 13:6; 8; 11; 12; 16; 20; 21; 23; 25; 26; 29; 30; 32; 38; 48; 57; 14:6; 13; 16; 24; 27; 30; 15:5; 8; 11; 13; 18; 20; 23; 24; 26; 16:3; 8; 11; 12; 15; 17; 23(2); 25; 17:7; 8; 12(2); 16; 18:6; 7; 16; 17; 22; 25; 28; 30; 19:6; 8; 11(2); 13; 14; 17(2); 22; 26(2); 30; 20:10; 13; 16; 22; 23(2); 25; 26; 28; 31; 21:13; 15; 19; 21; 24; 26; 28; 29; 30; 32; 38; 44; 46; 22:5; 7; 8; 11; 14; 18; 30; 31; 32; 34; 23:3; 4; 5; 8; 11; 13; 16; 18; 25; 27; 28; 37; 24:6; 13; 19; 22; 35; 36(2); 37; 43; 48; 25:4; 5; 9(2); 12; 18; 26; 29; 33; 46; 26:5; 8; 10; 11; 24; 29; 32; 39; 41; 50; 52; 56; 58; 60(2); 63; 70; 72; 27:6; 14; 20; 23; 24; 34; 28:5; 17; **Mk** 1:8; 25; 30; 38; 44; 45; 2:7; 8; 10; 17(2); 18; 20; 22; 25; 3:4; 7; 12; 21; 26; 29(2); 33; 4:6; 8; 10; 11; 20; 22; 25; 29; 32; 34; 38; 40; 5:19; 26; 31; 33; 39; 40; 43; 6:4; 9; 16; 19; 33; 37; 38; 50; 7:5; 6; 11; 15; 19; 24; 27; 36; 8:12; 17; 28; 29; 33(2); 35; 9:8; 13; 18; 22; 27; 29; 32; 34; 37; 39; 42; 50; 10:6; 8; 13; 14; 18; 22; 24; 27(2); 31; 38; 40(2); 42; 43; 45; 48; 11:5; 13; 17; 23; 26; 29; 32; 12:7; 12; 14; 15; 25; 26; 27; 32; 34; 44; 13:7(2); 9; 11(3); 13; 17; 20; 23; 24; 31; 32(2); 14:2; 4; 6; 7; 21; 28; 31; 36; 38; 49; 54; 55; 56; 59; 61; 68; 70; 15:3; 5; 9; 11; 14; 23; 16:4; 6; 7; 13; 16; **Lk** 1:7; 13; 20; 22; 29; 43; 61; 2:19; 37; 44; 50; 51; 3:16; 17; 19; 4:4(2); 25; 26; 35; 38; 43; 5:2; 5; 14; 21; 22; 24; 31; 32; 33; 35; 38; 6:3; 4; 8; 11; 24; 27; 32; 35; 40; 41; 46; 49; 7:7; 25; 26; 28; 30; 35; 44; 45; 46; 47; 8:8; 10; 13; 15; 16; 21; 23; 25; 27; 38; 42; 46; 50; 52(2); 54; 56; 9:9; 11; 13; 19; 20; 24; 27; 32; 36; 40; 43; 45; 50; 53; 55; 56; 58; 59; 60; 61; 62; 10:2; 5; 10; 12; 14; 20; 29; 33; 40; 42; 11:4; 15; 17; 20; 22; 28; 33; 34; 39; 41; 42; 12:5; 7; 9; 10; 14; 20; 31; 39; 45; 48; 50; 51; 56; 13:3; 5; 8; 9; 12; 14; 27; 34; 14:4; 10; 13; 18; 34; 35; 15:14; 17; 20; 22; 28; 30; 16:15; 20; 25(2); 30; 31; 17:1; 8; 17; 25; 29; 18:4; 13; 15; 16; 19; 23; 27; 34; 39; 19:3; 7; 14; 25; 27; 33; 40; 42; 46; 47; 20:3; 6; 10; 14; 18; 19; 21; 23; 26; 35; 37; 38; 40; 21:4; 7; 9(2); 12; 13; 18; 20; 23; 33; 34; 37; 22:21; 22; 26; 28; 32; 33; 36; 42; 48; 51; 53; 54; 57; 58; 60; 67; 23:5; 9; 21; 23; 25; 28(2); 35; 40; 41; 49; 24:2; 6; 12; 16; 21; 24; 29; 37; 41; 49; **Jn** 1:8; 12; 13; 17; 20; 26; 31; 33; 2:9; 21; 24; 3:8; 13; 15; 16; 17; 18; 21; 28; 29; 30; 36; 4:2; 4; 14(2); 23; 32; 5:7; 13; 17; 18; 19; 22; 24; 30; 34; 36; 38; 40; 42; 47; 6:6; 9; 20; 22; 26; 27; 32; 36; 38; 39; 64; 68; 7:6; 7; 10(2); 16; 18; 22; 24; 26; 27; 28; 29; 30; 39; 41; 44; 49; 8:1; 5; 6; 10; 12; 14; 16; 26; 28; 35; 37; 40; 42; 45; 49; 55(2); 59; 9:3; 18; 21; 28; 31; 41; 10:1; 2; 5; 6; 8; 12; 18; 26; 33; 38; 39; 41; 11:4; 10; 11; 13; 20; 22; 30; 42; 46; 51; 52; 54; 12:2; 6; 7; 8; 9; 10; 16; 23; 24; 27; 30; 37; 42; 44; 47; 49; 13:7; 9; 10(2); 18; 28; 36; 14:10; 17; 19; 24; 26; 31; 15:15; 16; 19; 21; 22; 24; 25; 26; 16:4; 5; 6; 7; 12; 13; 20(2); 21; 22; 25(2); 33; 17:9; 11; 13; 15; 20; 25; 18:16; 23; 28(2); 36; 39; 40; 19:9; 12; 13; 15(2); 21; 24; 33; 34; 38; 20:7; 11; 17; 27; 31; 21:4; 8(2); 18; 21; 23; **Acts** 1:4; 5; 8; 2:14; 16; 34; 3:6; 14; 18; 4:15; 17; 19; 20; 32; 5:1; 3; 4; 13; 19; 21; 22; 23; 29; 39; 6:4; 7:5; 6; 9; 12; 17; 21; 25; 27; 39; 47; 55; 8:9; 12; 20; 40; 9:7; 8; 15; 22; 24; 26; 27; 29; 37; 40; 10:10; 14; 26; 28; 35; 41; 11:4; 8; 9; 16; 19; 20; 12:5; 9; 14; 15; 17; 19; 20; 24; 13:8; 14; 25; 30; 37; 45; 46; 50; 51; 14:2; 4; 14; 15:5; 11; 20; 38; 40; 16:1; 7; 18; 19; 25; 28; 37; 17:5; 6; 13; 14; 21; 30; 18:6; 9; 15; 17; 19; 21(2); 19:9(2); 15; 22; 26; 27; 34; 39; 20:6; 10; 20; 24; 21:13; 21; 24; 25; 39; 22:3; 9; 28; 23:6; 8; 9; 11; 15; 21; 29; 24:7; 14; 22; 27; 25:4; 9; 11; 19; 21; 25; 26:16; 20; 25(2); 29; 27:10; 14; 21; 22; 39; 41(2); 43; 28:3; 5; 6; 16; 19; 22; **Rom** 1:13; 21; 32; 2:2; 5; 8(2); 10; 13; 25; 29(2); 3:4; 5; 21; 27; 4:2; 4; 5(2); 10; 12; 13; 16; 20; 24; 5:3; 8; 11; 13; 15; 16; 20; 6:10; 11; 13; 14; 15; 17; 22; 23; 7:2; 3; 6; 8; 9; 13; 14; 15; 17(2); 18; 19; 20; 23; 25; 8:1; 4; 5; 6; 9(2); 10; 11; 13; 15; 20; 23; 24; 25; 26; 32; 9:6; 7; 8; 10; 11; 13; 16; 20; 24; 31; 32; 10:2; 6; 8; 16; 18; 19; 20; 21; 11:4; 6; 7; 11; 15; 18(2); 20; 22; 28; 12:2; 3; 4; 16; 19; 21; 13:3; 4; 5; 14; 14:1; 2; 10; 13; 14; 17; 20; 23; 15:3; 21; 23; 25; 29; 16:4; 18; 19; 26; **1 Cor** 1:10; 17; 18; 23; 24; 27; 30; 2:4; 5; 7; 9; 10; 12; 13; 14; 15; 16; 3:1; 5; 6; 7; 10; 15; 4:3; 4; 10(3); 14; 19(2); 20; 5:3; 8; 11; 13; 6:6; 11(3); 12(2); 13(2); 17; 18; 7:4(2); 6; 7; 8; 9; 10; 11; 12; 14; 15(2); 17; 19; 21; 28(2); 29; 32; 33; 34; 35; 36; 37; 38; 39; 40; 8:1; 3; 4; 8; 9; 12; 9:12; 15; 17; 21; 24; 25; 27; 10:5; 13(2); 23(2); 24; 28; 29; 30; 33; 11:3; 5; 6; 7; 8; 9; 12; 15; 16; 17; 28; 32; 34; 12:4; 5; 6; 7; 11; 12; 14; 18; 20; 24(2); 25; 31; 13:1; 2; 3; 6; 8; 10; 11; 12(2); 13; 14:1; 2; 3; 4; 5; 6; 14; 17; 20; 22(3); 24; 28; 30; 33; 34; 38; 15:6; 10(3); 13; 20; 23; 27; 35; 37; 38; 39; 40; 46; 51; 57; 16:4; 7; 8; 11; 12; **2 Cor** 1:9; 12; 18; 19; 24; 2:1; 2; 4; 5(2); 13; 17(2); 3:3(2); 5; 6(2); 7; 14; 15; 18; 4:2(2); 3; 5; 7; 8; 9(2); 12; 17; 18(2); 5:4; 11; 12; 15; 6:4; 12; 7:5; 7; 9; 10; 12; 14; 8:5; 7; 8; 11; 14; 16; 17; 19; 21; 22; 9:6; 12; 10:1; 2; 4; 10; 12; 13; 15; 17; 18; 11:3; 6; 12; 17; 21; 33; 12:6; 14(2); 16; 19; 13:3; 4; 6; 7; 8; **Gal** 1:1; 7; 8; 11; 12; 15; 17; 19; 23; 2:2; 6; 7; 12; 14; 16; 17; 20; 3:11; 12; 16; 18; 20; 22; 23; 25; 4:2; 4; 7; 8; 9; 14; 17; 18; 23; 26; 29; 31; 5:6; 10; 13; 15; 18; 22; 6:4; 8; 13; 14; 15; **Eph** 1:21; 2:4; 13; 19; 4:7; 9; 15; 20; 28; 29; 5:3; 4; 8; 11; 13; 15; 17; 18; 27; 29; 32; 6:4; 6; 12; 21; **Phil** 1:12; 17; 20; 22; 28; 29; 2:3; 4; 7; 12; 19; 22; 24; 25; 27(2); 3:1; 7; 9; 12; 13; 4:6; 10(2); 15; 17; 22; **Col** 1:26; 2:17; 23; 3:8; 11; 14; 22; 25; **1 Th** 1:5; 8; 2:2; 4(2); 7; 8; 13; 16; 17; 18; 3:6; 4:7; 8; 9; 10; 13; 5:1; 4; 6; 8; 9; 15; **2 Th** 2:12; 13; 3:3; 6; 8; 9; 11; 13; 15; **1 Tim** 1:8; 9; 13; 2:10; 12; 14; 3:3; 10; 15; 4:7; 8; 12; 5:1; 4; 6; 8; 11; 13; 23; 24; 6:2; 4; 9; 11; 17; **2 Tim** 1:7; 8; 9; 10; 17; 2:9; 16; 20(2); 22; 23; 24; 3:1; 5; 9; 10; 13; 14; 4:3; 5; 8; 16; 17; 20; **Titus** 1:3; 8; 15(2); 16; 2:1; 10; 3:4; 5; 9; **Phm** 1:11; 14(2); 16(2); 18; 22; **Heb** 1:6; 8; 11; 12; 13; 2:6; 8; 9; 16; 3:4; 6; 13; 18; 4:2; 13; 15; 5:4; 5; 14; 6:8; 9; 12; 7:3; 6; 8; 16; 21; 24; 28; 8:6; 9:7; 11; 12; 23; 24; 26; 27; 10:3; 5; 12; 15; 25; 27; 32; 38; 39(2); 11:6; 13; 16; 12:8; 10; 11; 13; 22; 26(2); 13:4; 14; 16; 19; **Jas** 1:4; 6; 10; 14; 22; 25(2); 26; 2:6; 9; 11; 14; 16; 18; 20; 3:8; 14; 15; 17; 4:6(2); 11(2); 16; 5:12(2); **1 Pe** 1:12; 15; 19; 20; 23; 25; 2:4; 7; 9; 10(2); 16; 18; 20; 23; 25; 3:9; 12; 14; 15; 18; 21; 4:2; 6; 7; 13; 14; 15; 16; 5:2(2); 3; 5; 10; **2 Pe** 1:5; 16; 21; 2:1; 4; 5; 12; 16; 22; 3:7; 8; 9(2); 10; 18; **1 Jn** 1:7; 2:2; 5; 7; 11; 16; 17; 19(2); 20; 21; 22; 27(2); 3:2; 17; 18; 4:1; 10; 18(2); 5:5; 6; 18; **2 Jn** 1; 5; 8; 12; **3 Jn** 9; 11(2); 13; 14; **Jude** 5; 6; 9; 10; 17; 20; 23; **Rev** 1:17; 2:6; 9(2); 14; 25; 3:1; 5; 9; 5:5; 9:4; 5; 11; 20; 10:4; 7; 9; 10; 11:2; 12:8; 14; 16; 17:7; 12; 19:10; 20:3; 5; 6; 21:8; 22; 27(2); 22:3; 15

BY (2852/2453)

Gen 7:9; 15; 9:6; 11; 13:18; 14:6; 13; 15; 16:2; 7(2); 17:16; 18:1; 2; 3; 5; 8; 19:19; 36; 20:3; 21:23; 28; 29; 22:13; 16; 23:20; 24:3; 11; 13; 14; 29; 30; 43; 25:13; 16; 26:18; 27:40; 42; 29:2; 30:3; 27; 40; 31:15; 24; 31; 39(3); 40; 53; 32:16; 33:8; 34:7; 30; 35:4; 36:40; 37:28; 38:16; 18; 20; 21; 24; 25; 39:10; 12; 41:1; 3; 6; 23; 27; 32; 42:15; 16; 33; 43:10; 32(3); 45:1; 7; 47:22; 48:6; 20; 49:13; 17(2); 22; 24; 25(2); **Ex** 2:3; 15; 3:19; 4:4; 13; 6:3; 7:4; 15; 17; 23; 9:35; 12:14; 16; 26; 31; 13:3; 14; 16; 17; 18; 21(3); 22(2); 14:2; 3; 9; 20; 21; 15:16; 27; 16:3(2); 18; 18:18; 19:19; 20:26; 21:3(2); 4; 14; 22:13; 31; 23:30; 25:14; 26:9(2); 24; 36; 27:16; 28:28; 29:11; 18; 25; 28; 32; 38; 41; 43; 30:20; 31:2; 32:13; 33:6; 12; 17; 21; 22(2); 34:7; 35:29; 30; 36:16(2); 29; 37; 37:27; 38:21; 39:9; 21; 29; 40:38(2); **Lev** 1:5; 9; 13; 17; 2:2; 3; 9; 10; 11; 16; 3:3; 4; 5; 9; 10; 11; 14; 15; 16; 4:9; 27; 35; 5:4; 12; 17; 6:2; 17; 18; 7:4; 5; 24(2); 25; 30; 34; 35; 36(2); 8:21; 28; 36; 10:3; 5; 11; 12; 13; 15(2); 11:24; 43; 13:7(2); 24;

15:3; 16:21; 17:15; 18:5; 11; 24; 30; 19:12; 31; 20:25(3); 21:6; 9; 21; 22:2; 4; 5(2); 8; 22; 27; 23:8; 13; 18; 25; 27; 36(2); 37; 24:7; 8; 9(2); 25:39; 47; 26:7; 8; 17; 23(2); 26; 43; 46; 27:2; **Num** 1:2(2); 3; 17; 18(2); 20(2); 22(2); 24(2); 26(2); 28(2); 30(2); 32(2); 34(2); 36(2); 38(2); 40(2); 42(2); 45; 47; 52(2); 2:2; 17; 32; 34(2); 3:15(2); 17; 18; 19; 20(2); 39; 49; 4:2(2); 22(2); 29(2); 32; 34(2); 36; 37; 38(2); 40(2); 42(2); 44; 45; 46(2); 49(2); 5:2; 6:4; 9:6; 7; 16(2); 21(2); 23; 10:13; 34; 13:29; 14:3; 13; 14(2); 18; 25; 30; 36; 37; 42; 43; 15:3; 10; 13; 14; 23; 25; 16:28; 29; 18:6; 17; 19:16; 20:19; 23; 21:4; 18(2); 22; 33; 22:33; 23:3; 6; 15; 17; 24:6(2); 25:18; 26:2; 3; 28; 55; 63(2); 64; 27:2; 21; 23; 28:2; 3(2); 6; 8; 13; 19; 24; 29:6; 13; 18; 21; 24; 27; 30; 33; 36; 37; 30:2; 3; 4; 5; 6(3); 7; 8; 9; 10; 11; 31:12; 33:1; 10; 48; 49; 50; 54(2); 34:13; 35:1; 17; 18; 23; 33; 36:2(2); 13(2); **Deut** 1:2; 22; 33(2); 40; 2:8; 3:12; 4:34(6); 42; 5:15(2); 31; 6:7; 7:19; 22; 25; 8:3(2); 11; 19; 9:29(2); 11:10; 19; 14:22; 15:3; 20; 16:1; 18:1; 19:15; 20:19; 21:5; 17; 23:1; 10; 25:11; 28:10; 68; 29:16; 32:21(4); 22; 24; 47; 33:12; 24; 29; 34:12; **Josh** 2:7; 12; 15; 3:4(2); 10; 5:1; 13; 6:17; 18; 7:14(2); 16; 17; 18; 8:3; 15; 24; 9:18; 19; 10:18; 11:7; 23; 13:6; 14; 16; 22; 32; 14:2(2); 15:8; 16:1; 6; 18:9; 19:29; 34; 51; 20:8; 9; 21:4; 5; 6; 8(2); 9; 40; 22:9; 10; 19; 23:4; 7; 24:26; **Judg** 2:18; 19; 3:1; 4(2); 15; 4:16; 5:17; 19; 6:27(2); 31; 36; 37; 7:1; 5; 7; 12; 22; 8:1; 11; 9:25; 32; 34; 56; 11:27; 15:18; 16:5; 26; 17:2; 18:16; 19:14; 29; 20:9; 21:7; **Ruth** 1:6; 2:8; 12; 21; 23; 4:1; **1 Sam** 1:7; 9; 26; 2:3; 9; 16; 19; 28; 3:14; 21; 4:2; 13; 18; 20; 5:2; 6:3; 8; 9; 10:2; 19(2); 21; 11:7; 9; 13:8; 14:4; 6(2); 33; 34; 36; 15:12; 16:9; 20; 17:23; 26; 35; 43; 18:25; 20:2; 7; 9; 19; 25(2); 33(2); 23:7; 24:3; 21; 25:16; 22; 34; 42; 26:3; 7(2); 11; 12; 16; 27:1; 28:6(3); 8; 10; 15(3); 17; 29:1; 2(2); 30:15; 24; 31:3; **2 Sam** 1:6; 12; 2:13; 15; 16; 24; 27; 3:2; 3; 5; 18; 29; 4:12; 5:8(2); 6:2; 7; 22; 10:2; 8; 15; 19; 11:14; 22; 12:14; 25; 13:31; 32; 15:30; 36; 16:21; 17:9; 11; 22; 18:4(2); 23; 19:7; 20:9; 15; 21; 21:10(2); 22(2); 22:9; 30(2); 23:2; 4; 15; 16; 17; 24:16; **1 Ki** 1:6; 9(2); 17; 27; 30; 2:8; 23; 25; 29; 42; 3:5; 26; 27; 4:20; 5:9(2); 11; 6:8; 22; 7:20; 21; 8:32; 38(2); 43; 53; 9:8; 10:5; 25; 12:15; 13:1(2); 2(2); 5; 9(2); 10; 17(2); 18; 24(2); 25(2); 28; 32; 14:4; 15:4(2); 13; 26; 29; 30; 34; 16:7; 12; 13(2); 26; 17:3; 5; 16; 20; 24; 18:6(2); 24; 19:2; 6; 11; 19; 20:14(2); 35; 38; 39(2); 21:23; 22:8; 19; 28; **2 Ki** 2:1; 7; 11; 13; 3:8; 11; 20; 4:8; 9; 27; 5:1; 6:11; 14; 26; 30; 8:8; 21; 9:27(2); 36; 10:6; 10; 33; 11:11; 14(2); 16; 19; 12:6; 13:25; 14:7; 9; 12; 27; 16:15; 17:4(2); 6; 13(2); 23; 18:11; 17; 31; 19:7; 11; 23(2); 28; 33(2); 20:11; 21:10; 16; 23:3; 11; 24:2; 25:3; 4(3); 30; **1 Chr** 1:36; 2:3; 18(2); 3:1(2); 3(2); 5; 4:38; 41; 5:7; 10; 17; 6:15; 54; 61; 65(2); 7:4; 5; 7; 9; 29; 40; 8:9; 11; 28; 9:1; 22; 23; 28; 10:3; 11:3; 11; 17; 18; 19; 12:19; 22; 31; 14:11; 15:15; 16(2); 16:41; 17:21(2); 18:3; 19:9; 16; 19; 20:8(2); 21:12; 15; 25; 26; 23:24(2); 27; 31; 24:5; 19; 27; 26:17; 25; 27:1; 28:9; 12; 14(2); 15(2); 16; 17(2); 18; 19; 29:5; **2 Chr** 2:16; 3:3; 10; 6:23(2); 29(2); 33; 7:6; 12; 14; 21; 8:14; 18; 9:4; 24; 10:15; 12:7; 13:5; 15:2; 4; 6(2); 15; 16; 18:1; 7; 27; 19:5; 20:11; 16; 21:9; 15(2); 23:10(2); 13(2); 15; 18; 24:11(2); 13; 25:18; 22; 26:11(2); 15; 16; 28:15; 29:9; 25; 30:9; 21(2); 31:15; 16; 17; 19(2); 32:8; 11(2); 30; 33:8; 34:14; 35:6; 20; 36:13; 15; 21; 22; **Ezra** 1:1; 8; 2:61; 62; 3:4; 4:21; 23; 5:17; 6:9; 7:14; 23; 8:15; 18; 20; 30; 33; 9:11; 10:16(2); 17; 44; **Neh** 1:10(2); 2:13; 15(2); 3:15; 23; 25; 4:22(2); 6:16; 7:5; 63; 64; 8:14; 18; 9:9; 12(2); 14; 19(2); 29; 30; 10:29; 34; 35; 11:23; 12:37; 39; 44; 13:17; 18; 25; 26; 27; **Esth** 1:12; 15; 2:14; 20; 3:13; 15; 5:12; 7:7; 8:5; 10; 11; 14; 9:25; 10:3; **Job** 4:9(2); 6:14; 8:8; 9:11; 26; 11:10; 12:4; 6; 15:3; 30; 16:12; 18:8; 9; 19:20; 20:29; 22:16; 30; 26:12; 13; 28:4; 5; 25; 29:3; 7; 30:4; 18; 31:9; 17; 30; 33; 33:18; 36:12; 22; 31; 37:10; 12; 17; 38:2; 24; 37; 39:9; 26; 40:22; 42:5; **Ps** 1:3; 5:10; 9:16; 10:10; 14; 17:4; 7; 18:8; 29(2); 19:11; 22:6; 30:7; 33:6(2); 16(2); 17; 37:22(2); 23; 39:10; 41:11; 44:3; 12; 45:8; 48:4; 49:7; 50:5; 51:12; 54:1(2); 56:7; 57:1; 59:11; 63:10; 11; 65:5; 6; 66:7; 68:4; 71:6; 72:3; 73:10; 23; 74:13; 77:20; 78:17; 18; 26; 49; 55; 64; 72; 80:12; 89:7; 35; 39; 41; 90:7(2); 10; 91:5(2); 94:20; 104:12; 106:7; 22; 39(2); 46; 107:7; 110:7; 111:2; 115:15; 119:9; 93; 133; 121:6(2); 129:8; 134:1; 136:5; 8; 9; 137:1; 140:5; 141:6; 147:4; **Prov** 3:19(2); 20; 29; 5:20; 6:2(2); 26; 7:26; 8:3; 15; 16; 9:11; 14; 15; 10:25; 11:5; 6; 11(2); 12:3; 13; 14; 13:2; 10; 11(2); 14:4; 20; 15:13; 23; 16:6; 12; 20:1; 11; 17; 18(2); 28; 21:6; 22:4; 14; 24:3; 4; 6; 16; 30(2); 25:15; 26:6; 17(2); 26; 28; 27:9; 21; 28:2; 8; 29:4; 6; 19; 31:18; **Eccl** 1:11; 13(2); 4:4; 12; 5:3; 7:3; 23; 26; 9:1; 15; 10:8; 9(2); 12:11; 12; **Song** 1:7; 2:7(2); 3:1; 4; 5(2); 10; 5:4; 12; 7:4; 5; **Isa** 1:7; 20; 3:5(2); 15; 25; 4:1; 4(2); 5(2); 5:30; 6:4; 7:16; 9:1; 16; 10:13(2); 34; 11:3(2); 8; 13:15; 15:5; 18:2; 19:7(3); 18; 22; 20:2; 22:3; 5; 14; 26:9; 13; 27:7; 8(2); 9; 12; 28:7; 18; 19(3); 29:6; 13; 21(2); 31:4; 8; 32:8; 33:21; 36:2; 16; 37:7; 11; 24(2); 29; 34(2); 38:8; 16; 40:17; 26(3); 27; 41:3; 42:16; 43:1; 7; 44:4; 5(2); 21; 24; 45:3; 4; 17; 23; 46:3; 47:14; 48:1(2); 17; 49:10; 50:4; 51:18; 19; 52:12; 53:3; 4; 5; 11; 54:13; 60:19; 62:2; 8(2); 63:12; 19; 64:4; 65:1(3); 15; 16; 66:16(2); **Jer** 2:8; 34; 37; 3:2; 4:26; 5:7(2); 22; 31; 6:5; 25; 29; 7:10; 11; 14; 30; 8:3; 10:5; 12(2); 14; 11:21; 22(2); 12:16(2); 13:5; 24; 14:9; 12(3); 15; 15:16; 16:4(2); 17:2; 8(2); 11; 19(2); 20; 21; 25; 18:16; 21(2); 19:2; 7(2); 8; 20:2; 4; 21:9(3); 22:4; 5; 8; 13(2); 23:6; 13; 27; 32(2); 25:14; 29; 27:3; 5(2); 8; 13(3); 29:3; 14; 19; 22; 31:9; 32; 35(2); 32:17; 34; 36(3); 33:8(3); 16; 34:4; 15; 35:4; 37:2; 38:2(3); 4; 11; 23; 39:4(4); 18; 41:12; 42:5; 17(3); 21; 22(3); 44:12(4); 13(3); 15; 18(2); 26; 27(2); 46:2; 6; 10; 17; 18; 48:19; 49:3; 9; 13; 17; 50:1; 13; 51:5; 13; 14; 15(3); 17; 52:6; 7(3); 34; **Lam** 1:12; 14; 2:15; 21; 3:1; 4:9; 5:12; **Ezek** 1:1; 3; 2:6; 3:15; 23; 4:10; 11; 14; 16(2); 5:6; 12; 14; 6:9(2); 11(3); 12(3); 7:15; 8:3; 10:9(3); 15; 20; 22; 11:10; 24; 12:3; 4; 7; 13:19; 20; 14:3; 5(2); 7; 13; 14; 20; 16:6; 8; 15; 21; 25; 51; 54; 59; 17:5; 8; 9; 14; 15; 18; 21; 18:7; 12; 16; 18; 19:7; 10; 20:3; 11; 13; 21; 25; 27; 31(2); 47; 22:4; 12; 23:17; 25(2); 30; 24:6; 21; 25:12(2); 13; 14; 26:6; 11; 17; 18; 27:33; 34; 28:5; 10; 16; 18(2); 23; 30:5; 6; 10; 12; 17; 31:12; 14; 17; 18; 32:12; 20; 21; 22; 23; 24; 25; 26; 28; 29; 30(2); 31; 32; 33:27; 35:5; 8; 36:3(2); 17; 34; 37:2; 18; 38:17; 39:11; 15; 23; 40:7; 18; 22; 38; 41; 49(2); 41:7; 9; 17; 42:1; 16; 17; 18; 19; 43:3; 4; 7; 8(3); 44:2(2); 3; 4; 25; 31; 45:1; 2; 7; 46:2(2); 8; 9(5); 16; 18; 21; 47:2; 10; 13; 15; 19; 22; 48:2; 3; 4; 5; 6; 7; 8; 12; 15; 20; 24; 25; 26; 27; 28(2); 29; **Dan** 4:17(2); 20; 27(2); 30; 7:2; 8; 16; 8:2; 11; 24; 27; 9:2(2); 3; 5; 10; 12; 18; 19; 10:4; 11:2; 21; 31; 33(2); 34; 12:7; **Hos** 1:2(2); 7(4); 2:17; 3:1; 4:2; 5:11; 6:5(2); 7:4; 16; 8:4; 9; 11:3; 12:3; 6; 10; 13(2); 13:7; 16; **Joel** 2:19; **Am** 2:8; 13; 4:2; 5:3(2); 6:8; 13; 7:4; 8; 11; 17(2); 8:2; 5; 7; 14; 9:1; 10; 12; **Ob** 5; 9; **Jon** 3:7; **Mic** 1:11; 2:2; 5; 8; 13; 3:8; 6:13(2); **Nah** 1:6; 3:8; **Hab** 1:10; 16; 2:4; 5; 12; 3:10; 13; **Zeph** 1:5(2); 18; 2:12; 15; 3:6; **Hag** 1:1; 3; 2:1; 10; 22; **Zech** 1:8; 3:5; 4:3; 6(3); 5:4; 7:12; 8:9; 9:4; 8; 12:12(5); 13(4); 14(2); **Mal** 1:1; 7; 9; 2:10; 14; **Mt** 1:3; 5(2); 6; 22; 2:5; 14; 15; 16; 17; 22; 23; 3:3; 6; 13; 14; 4:1(2); 4(2); 13; 14; 15; 18; 5:13; 18; 20; 26; 34; 35(2); 36; 6:1; 5; 27; 7:13(2); 16; 20; 8:17; 9:25; 34; 10:22; 42; 11:7; 12; 19; 27; 12:17; 24; 27(2); 28; 33; 37(2); 13:1; 4; 19; 35; 14:8; 13(2); 23; 24; 15:6; 17:1; 21; 18:3; 7; 16; 19; 28; 19:12; 20:23; 30(2); 21:4; 19; 23; 24; 27; 22:1; 31; 23:5; 7; 16(2); 18(2); 20(3); 21(3); 22(3); 24:9; 15; 34; 35; 26:4; 24; 52; 63; 73; 27:4; 9; 12; 32; 35; 39; 64; 28:9; **Mk** 1:5; 9; 13; 16; 31; 2:3; 13; 14; 3:5; 22; 4:1; 2; 4; 15; 27(2); 28; 5:4; 7; 21(2); 22; 41; 6:2; 7; 31; 32; 48; 7:26; 8:23; 31; 9:2; 27; 29; 41; 10:1; 15; 46; 11:4; 20; 28; 29; 33; 12:36; 13:13; 14; 30; 31; 14:1; 19; 21; 47; 69; 70; 15:21; 29; 35; 16:11; 18; **Lk** 1:26; 59; 61; 70; 77; 2:8; 18; 21; 26; 27; 3:7; 19; 4:1; 2; 4(2); 15; 5:1; 2; 15; 17; 6:44; 7:24; 30; 35; 8:4; 5; 12; 20; 29; 36; 43; 54; 9:7(2); 8(2); 17; 22; 47; 10:1; 19; 22; 31(2); 32; 11:3; 15; 18; 19(2); 42; 45; 12:25; 13:17; 14:8(2); 16:9; 22; 17:6; 20; 25; 18:5; 17; 31; 35; 36; 37; 19:8; 15; 24; 20:2; 8; 21:16; 17; 19; 20; 24(2); 32; 33; 22:22; 56; 67; 68; 23:8; 15; 24:4; 12; **Jn** 3:2; 34; 4:6; 48; 5:2; 6:13; 15(2); 37; 45; 65; 7:50; 8:9(2); 59; 9:1; 21; 10:1; 2; 3; 5; 9; 14; 11:39; 42; 12:29; 33; 13:35; 14:21; 15:8; 16:30; 17:17; 19; 18:22; 32; 19:25; 26; 39; 20:7; 11; 21:19; 25; **Acts** 1:3(2); 10; 16; 25; 2:16; 22(2); 23(2); 24; 3:7; 12; 18; 21; 4:7(2); 9; 10(2); 11; 12; 25; 30; 36; 5:10; 15; 16; 30; 34; 6:1; 10; 7:25; 35; 45; 53; 8:6; 23(2); 9:8; 25; 39; 10:6; 22; 32; 33; 35; 38; 39; 41; 42; 11:5; 14; 28; 30; 12:5; 7; 9; 20; 23; 13:4; 11; 19; 31; 36; 39(2); 41; 45; 14:3; 5; 15:3; 4; 7; 8; 9; 10; 17; 20; 23; 27; 40; 16:2; 4; 6; 8; 14; 16; 17:10; 13; 29; 31(2); 18:3; 5; 9; 21; 19:11; 13; 25; 20:9; 19; 35; 21:13; 35; 22:11; 20; 25; 30; 23:2; 4; 10(2); 11; 19; 21; 27(2); 31; 24:2; 4; 7; 8; 21; 26; 25:14; 26:2; 6; 7; 8; 18; 27:11(3); 12; 13; 23; 41; 28:16; 24; **Rom** 1:4; 10; 12; 17; 20; 2:7; 12; 14; 16; 3:20(2); 21; 24; 25; 27(2); 28; 30; 4:2; 5:1; 2; 5; 9; 10; 15(2); 17; 19(2); 6:4; 7:2; 5; 6; 8; 11(2); 8:3; 13; 14; 15; 9:10(2); 32(2); 10:5; 17(2); 19(2); 20; 11:6; 14; 20; 24; 12:1; 2; 21; 13:1; 14:14; 18; 19; 21; 15:13; 15; 16; 19; 24; 28; 32; 16:18; 26; **1 Cor** 1:4; 5; 9; 10; 11; 2:12; 15; 3:13; 4:3(2); 4; 6:2; 4; 11; 14; 7:14(2); 39; 8:3; 9:22; 10:9; 10; 29; 11:32; 12:3(2); 9(2); 13; 14:6(4); 9; 24(2); 30; 31; 15:2; 5(2); 6; 7(2); 8(2); 10; 21(2); 31; 16:3; **2 Cor** 1:1; 4; 11; 12; 16(2); 19(2); 24; 2:2; 6; 12; 3:2; 3(2); 18; 4:2; 16; 5:4; 7(2); 6:6(6); 7(3); 8(2); 12(2); 7:6; 7(2); 13; 8:5; 8(2); 14; 19(2); 20; 9:14; 10:1; 2; 9; 11; 12; 15; 11:3; 12:7; 11; 16; 17; 20; 13:1; 4(2); **Gal** 1:11; 22; 2:2(2); 4; 15; 16(5); 17; 20; 3:2(2); 3; 5(2); 8; 11(2); 12; 17; 18; 19; 21; 22; 23; 24; 4:2; 8; 9; 22(2); 5:1; 4; 5; 15; 18; 6:14; **Eph** 1:1; 5; 6; 2:3; 5; 8; 11(2); 13; 18; 3:3; 4; 5; 7; 10; 21; 4:14; 16(2); 21; 30; 5:12; 13; 26; **Phil** 1:11; 14; 20(2); 26; 28; 2:2; 3:9; 11; 16; 21; 4:6; 19; **Col** 1:16; 20(2); 21; 2:11(2); 18; 19; 4:18; **1 Th** 1:4; 2:4; 3:3; 5; 7; 4:9; 15(2); 5:27; **2 Th** 2:2(3); 3; 13(2); 14; 15; 16; **1 Tim** 1:1; 18; 3:16; 4:3; 5; 14; 6:21; **2 Tim** 1:1; 10; 14; 2:26; 3:6; 16; **Titus** 1:9; 3:5; 7; **Phm** 1:6; 7; 14; **Heb** 1:1; 2; 3(2); 4; 2:3(2); 9; 10; 3:4; 16; 5:4; 8; 10; 12; 14; 6:7; 13(2); 16; 17; 18; 7:7; 21; 22; 23; 8:9; 9:15; 26; 10:1; 10; 14; 19; 20; 29; 33; 38; 11:2; 3(2); 4; 5; 7(2); 8; 9; 11; 12; 17; 20; 21; 22; 23(2); 24; 27; 28; 29(2); 30; 31; 12:1; 5; 11; 15; 28; 13:2; 9; 11; 15; **Jas** 1:6; 13(2); 14; 18; 2:7; 9; 12; 17; 18; 21; 22; 24(2); 25; 3:4(2); 6; 7; 13; 18; 5:4; 11; 12(2); **1 Pe** 1:5; 6; 7; 12; 18; 25; 2:4(2); 6; 12; 14; 15; 24; 3:1; 2; 18; 19; 5:2; 9; 10; 12; **2 Pe** 1:1; 3; 4; 13; 21(2); 2:3; 7; 8; 17; 19(2); 3:1; 2; 5; 6; 7; 14; **1 Jn** 2:3; 5; 18; 3:16; 19; 24(2); 4:2; 6; 13; 5:2; 6(3); **3 Jn** 14; **Jude** 1; 12(2); 17; 23; **Rev** 1:1; 2:11; 4:11; 5:9; 6:8; 13; 9:18(2); 20; 10:6; 12:6; 11(2); 15; 13:14(2); 18:15; 17; 19; 23; 19:2; 20; 20:12; 21:25; 27

DOWN (1142/1058)

Gen 11:5; 7; 12:10; 15:10; 11; 12; 17; 18:21; 19:4; 9; 33; 35; 21:16; 23:12; 24:11; 14; 16; 18; 26; 45; 46; 26:2; 27:29(2); 28:11; 33:6; 7(2); 37:7; 9; 10; 25(2); 35; 39:1(2); 42:2; 3; 6; 38(2); 43:4; 5; 7; 11; 15; 20; 22; 26; 28; 44:11; 21; 23; 26(2); 29; 31; 45:9; 13; 46:3; 4; 48:12; 49:8; 9(2); 14; 50:18; **Ex** 2:5; 15; 3:8; 7:10; 12; 9:18; 19; 11:8(2); 14:24; 17:11; 12; 18:7; 19:11; 14; 20; 21; 24; 25; 20:5; 22:26; 23:24(2); 32:1; 6; 7; 15; 34:13; 29(2); **Lev** 9:22; 11:35; 14:45; 47; 22:7; 26:1; 6; 30; **Num** 1:51; 4:5; 10:12; 17; 11:17; 25; 12:5; 13:23; 24; 14:45; 16:30; 33; 20:15; 28; 21:20; 22:27; 23:24; 24:4; 9(2); 16; 25:2; 33:2; 34:11(2); 12; **Deut** 1:25; 5:9; 6:7; 7:5(2); 9:3; 12; 15; 18; 10:5; 22; 11:19; 12:3; 16:6; 19:5; 20:19; 20; 21:4; 22:4; 23:13; 24:13; 15; 25:2; 26:4; 5; 15; 28:24; 43; 52; 31:19; 33:3; 29; **Josh** 1:4; 2:8; 15; 18; 3:13; 16(2); 4:8; 6:5; 20; 7:5(2); 8:21; 22; 29(2); 10:10; 11; 13; 27(2); 11:17; 15:10; 16:3; 7; 17:18; 18:16; 18; 23:7; 16; 24:4; **Judg** 1:9; 34; 2:2; 12; 17; 19; 3:27; 28; 4:14; 21; 5:11; 13(2); 14; 6:25(2); 26; 28(2); 30(2); 31; 32; 7:4; 5(2); 6; 9; 10(2); 11(2); 24; 8:9; 14; 17; 9:36; 37; 48; 49; 12:1; 14:1; 5; 7; 10; 18; 19; 15:8; 11; 12; 16:21; 31; 19:6; 14; 15; 26; 20:21; 25; 31; 43; 45; 48; **Ruth** 2:10; 3:3; 4(2); 6; 7(2); 13; 4:1(3); 2(2); **1 Sam** 2:6; 36; 3:2; 3; 5(2); 6; 9(2); 15; 6:15; 21; 9:25; 27; 10:5; 8(2); 13:12; 20; 14:36; 37; 15:6; 12; 19; 16:11; 17:8; 28(2); 19:12; 24; 20:19; 24; 41; 21:13; 22:1; 23:4; 6; 8; 11(2); 20(2); 25; 24:8; 25:1; 20(2); 23; 26:2; 6(2); 28:14; 29:4; 30:15(2); 16; 24; **2 Sam** 2:13; 16; 23(2); 24; 31; 3:35; 5:17; 8:2; 11:8; 9; 10(2); 13; 15; 13:5; 6; 8; 15:5; 20; 24; 17:18; 18:28; 19:16; 18; 20; 24; 31; 20:15; 21:12; 15; 22:10; 28; 23:13; 20; 21; **1 Ki** 1:23; 25; 33; 38; 53(2); 2:6; 8; 9; 19(2); 25; 29; 31; 32; 46; 5:6; 9; 11:16; 15:13; 16:18; 17:23; 18:30; 40; 42; 44; 19:4; 6; 10; 14; 21:4; 16; 18(2); 22:2; 36; **2 Ki** 1:4; 6; 9; 10(2); 11; 12(2); 14; 15(2); 16; 2:2; 3:12; 19; 25; 4:11; 5:14; 18(2); 21; 6:4; 5; 9; 18; 33; 7:17; 8:29; 9:7; 16; 24; 33(2); 10:13; 27(2); 11:6; 18; 19; 12:20; 13:14; 21; 14:13; 16:17; 17:35; 18:4; 19:23; 37; 20:10; 11; 21:13; 23:7; 8; 12; 14; 15; 25:10; **1 Chr** 7:21; 11:15; 22; 23; 24:6; **2 Chr** 6:13; 7:1; 3; 14:3(2); 15:16; 18:2; 20:16; 22:6; 23:17; 20; 24:17; 25:12; 14; 23; 26:6; 31:1(2); 32:21(2); 33:3; 34:4(2); 7(2); 36:19; **Ezra** 8:34; 9:3; 10:1; 16; **Neh** 1:3; 4; 2:13; 3:15; 4:3; 6:3(2); 9:13; **Esth** 3:15; 8:3; **Job** 2:13; 7:4; 9; 21; 8:12; 11:19; 12:14; 14:7; 12; 17:3; 16; 18:7; 19:10; 20:11; 15; 18; 21:13; 26; 22:16; 20; 29; 27:19; 29:24; 31:10; 33:24; 28; 36:28; 39:3; 40:12; **Ps** 3:5; 4:8; 7:16; 9:15; 14:2; 17:11; 13; 18:9; 27; 20:8; 22:29; 23:2; 28:1; 30:3; 9; 31:2; 35:14; 36:12; 37:2; 14; 24; 38:2; 6; 41:8; 42:5; 6; 11; 43:5; 44:5; 25; 50:1; 53:2; 55:3; 15; 23; 56:7; 57:6; 59:11; 15; 60:1; 12; 62:4; 68:13; 72:6; 11; 73:18; 74:6; 75:7; 8; 78:16; 24; 31; 80:12; 14; 16; 85:11; 86:1; 88:4; 89:23; 40; 44; 90:6; 95:6; 102:19; 104:8; 19; 22; 107:12(2); 23; 26; 108:13; 113:3; 115:17; 119:136; 133:2(2); 136:17; 137:1; 139:2; 3; 143:7; 144:5(2); 145:14; 146:8; 9; 147:6; **Prov** 1:12; 2:18; 3:20; 24(2); 5:5; 7:26; 14:1; 18:8; 21:22; 23:1; 34; 24:31; 25:28; 26:22; **Eccl** 1:5; 3:3; 21; 4:11; 12:3; **Song** 2:3; 4:1; 6:5; 11; 7:9; **Isa** 2:9; 11; 17; 5:5(2); 15; 6:13; 9:10(2); 10:4; 6; 13; 33; 34; 11:6; 7; 14; 14:8; 11; 12; 15; 19; 30; 16:8; 17:2; 18:2; 5; 7; 22:5(2); 10; 19; 25; 24:10; 25:10(2); 11; 12(2); 26:5(2); 6; 27:10; 28:2; 18; 29:4; 30:2; 31; 31:1; 3; 4; 32:19; 33:20; 34:4; 5; 7; 37:24; 38; 38:8(2); 18; 42:10; 43:14; 17; 44:14; 15; 17; 19; 45:8(2); 14; 46:1; 2; 47:1; 49:23; 50:11; 51:23; 52:2; 4; 55:10; 56:10; 58:5; 60:20; 63:6(2); 14; 15; 18; 64:1; 3; 65:10; 12; **Jer** 1:10(2); 2:20; 3:25; 4:26; 6:6; 15; 8:12; 13:17; 18; 15:9; 18:2; 3; 7; 21:13; 22:1; 7; 30; 24:6; 25:37; 26:10; 31:28(2); 40; 33:4; 12; 36:12; 15; 38:6; 11; 39:8; 41:3; 42:10; 45:4; 46:5; 23; 48:2; 15; 18; 20; 39; 49:16; 50:15; 27; 51:25; 40; 52:14; **Lam** 2:1; 2(2); 17; 18; 3:50; 52; 63; **Ezek** 1:24; 25; 6:4; 6; 13:11; 14(2); 16:39(2); 17:24; 19:2; 12; 24:2; 16; 26:4; 9; 12; 16; 20(2); 27:29; 28:8; 30:4; 6; 25; 31:12; 14; 15; 16; 17; 18; 32:18(2); 19; 21; 24(2); 25; 27; 29; 30(2); 34:14; 15; 18; 26; 37:1; 38:20; 22; 39:10; 43:11; 47:8; **Dan** 3:5; 6; 7; 10; 11; 15; 23; 4:13; 14; 23(2); 37; 5:19; 6:10; 14; 7:1; 8:7; 10; 11; 12; 11:12; 26; **Hos** 2:18; 7:12; 10:2; **Joel** 1:17; 2:8; 23; 3:2; 11; 13; **Am** 2:8; 13(2); 5:11; 24; 6:2; 8:9; 9:2; 11; **Ob** 3; 4; **Jon** 1:3(2); 5(2); 2:6; **Mic** 1:3; 4; 6; 12; 3:6; 5:8; 11; 7:10; **Nah** 1:6; 12; **Zeph** 1:11; 2:7; 14; 15; 3:13; **Hag** 2:22; **Zech** 5:8; 10:5; 11; 12; 11:2; **Mal** 1:4; 11; **Mt** 2:11; 3:10; 4:6; 9; 7:19; 8:1; 11; 32; 9:10; 11:23; 13:48; 14:19; 29; 15:29; 30; 35; 17:9; 14; 18:26; 29; 20:20; 21:8; 24:2; 17; 26:20; 27:5; 36; 40; 42; **Mk** 1:7; 40; 2:4; 3:11; 22; 5:13; 33; 6:39; 40; 7:13; 8:6; 9:9; 18; 35; 11:8; 13:2; 15; 15:30; 36; 46; 16:19; **Lk** 1:52; 2:51; 3:9; 4:9; 20; 29; 31; 5:3; 4; 5; 8; 19; 29; 6:17; 38; 7:36; 8:5; 23; 28; 33; 41; 47; 9:14; 15; 37; 42; 44; 54; 10:15; 30; 31; 11:37; 12:18; 37; 13:7; 9; 29; 14:8; 10; 28; 31; 16:6; 17:7; 16; 31; 18:14; 19:5; 6; 21:6; 34; 22:14; 41; 44; 55; 23:53; 24:12; **Jn** 2:12; 3:13; 4:47; 49; 51; 5:4; 7; 6:10(2); 11; 16; 33; 38; 41; 42; 50; 51; 58; 8:2; 6; 8; 10:15; 17; 18(2); 11:32; 13:12; 37; 38; 15:13; 19:13; 20:5; 11; **Acts** 5:5; 10; 7:15; 24; 34; 58; 60; 8:5; 15; 26; 36; 38; 9:25; 30; 32; 40; 10:11; 20; 21; 25; 11:5; 12:10; 19; 13:4; 14; 29; 14:11; 25; 15:1; 16; 16:8; 13; 29; 17:6; 18:22; 19:35; 20:9; 10; 36; 21:5; 10; 32; 22:30; 23:10; 15; 20; 24:1; 22; 25:6; 7; 27:27; 30; 28:6; **Rom** 10:6; 11:3; 10; **1 Cor** 10:7; 14:25; **2 Cor** 4:9; 10:4; 5; 11:33; **Eph** 2:14; 4:26; **2 Tim** 3:6; **Heb** 1:3; 10:12; 11:30; 12:2; 12; **Jas** 1:17; **2 Pe** 2:4; **1 Jn** 3:16(2); **Rev** 1:13; 3:12; 21; 4:10; 5:8; 14; 10:1; 12:10; 12; 13:13; 18:1; 21; 19:4; 20:1; 9; 21:2; 22:8

FOR (8893/7172)

Gen 1:14(2); 15; 29; 30; 2:5; 9; 17; 20; 3:5; 6; 16; 17; 18; 19(2); 21; 4:7; 19; 22; 23(3); 25(2); 26; 5:24; 6:2; 3; 7; 12; 13; 16; 21(3); 7:4; 8:9(2); 21; 9:3; 5; 6; 7; 9; 12; 13; 10:25; 11:3(2); 4; 12:10; 13; 16; 13:6; 8; 11; 15; 17; 14:13; 21; 15:6; 15; 16; 16:10; 13; 17:4; 5; 7; 9; 13; 15; 19; 20; 18:14; 15; 19; 24; 26; 28; 29; 31; 32; 19:13; 14; 17; 21; 22; 30; 20:3; 6; 7(2); 13; 18; 21:1; 2; 7; 10; 12; 16; 17; 18; 21; 22:3; 7; 8(2); 12; 13; 23:2(2); 4; 8; 9; 13; 16; 20; 24:3; 4; 7; 10; 14; 19; 20; 22; 23; 27; 31(2); 32; 37; 38; 40; 41; 44(2); 48; 62; 65; 25:21; 24; 30; 26:3; 7(2); 14; 16; 18; 22(2); 24(2); 27:3; 7; 9; 13; 36(2); 37; 41; 28:15; 29:2; 7; 9; 14; 15; 18; 20(2); 21; 25; 27; 32; 30:13; 15; 16; 26(3); 27(2); 30(2); 31; 33; 37; 31:12; 14; 15; 16; 23; 27; 30; 31; 32; 35; 41(2); 52; 32:10; 11; 12(2); 13; 20; 26; 28; 30; 33:9; 17; 19; 34:8; 10; 14; 21(2); 35:18; 36:7(2); 37:8(2); 17; 27; 28; 34; 35(2); 38:6; 11; 14; 16; 23(2); 27; 39:5; 6; 40:4; 15; 17; 20; 41:8(2); 12; 13; 21; 31; 36(2); 49; 51; 52; 55; 42:2; 4; 5; 18; 19; 21; 23; 25(2); 30; 33; 38; 43:5; 9; 10; 11; 16; 25(2); 30; 32; 44:4; 17; 18; 22; 26; 32(2); 34; 45:3; 5; 6; 7; 11(2); 19; 20; 21; 23(2); 46:3; 32; 34; 47:4(2); 13; 14; 15(2); 16; 17(3); 19; 20(2); 21; 22; 23(2); 24(4); 26; 48:7; 14; 18; 49:6; 7(2); 13; 18; 30; 50:3(4); 5; 10; 12; 13(2); 15; 17; 19; 20(2); 21; **Ex** 1:5; 11; 16; 18; 19; 21; 2:3; 7(2); 9; 19; 22; 3:5; 6; 7; 4:16; 19; 5:7; 8; 18; 23; 6:1; 12; 13(2); 20; 25; 7:9; 12; 24; 8:8; 9(3); 17; 25; 26; 28; 9:2; 8; 11; 14; 16; 19; 27; 28; 30; 31; 32; 10:1; 5; 9; 10; 11; 12; 15; 16; 23; 26; 28; 12:3(2); 4(2); 12; 13; 15; 16; 17; 19; 21(2); 23; 24; 30; 31; 33; 39(2); 42(2); 44; 48; 49(2); 13:3; 8; 9; 16; 17; 19; 14:3; 12(2); 13(2); 14;

18; 25(2); 15:1; 17; 19; 21; 23; 25; 26; 16:3; 4; 7; 8; 9; 15; 16(2); 22; 23; 25; 29(2); 32; 33; 17:1; 3; 14; 16; 18:1(2); 3; 4; 8; 9(2); 11; 14(2); 18(2); 19; 22(2); 19:2; 5; 7; 11(2); 12; 15; 23; 20:4; 5; 7; 11; 20; 23; 24; 25; 21:11; 13; 19(2); 21; 23; 24(4); 25(3); 26; 27; 36; 22:1(2); 2; 3(2); 9(2); 15; 16; 21; 27(3); 23:7; 8; 9; 15; 21(2); 23; 29; 31; 33; 24:14; 25:6(3); 12; 25(2); 26; 27; 29; 33; 37; 26:14; 15; 17(2); 18(2); 19; 20; 22; 23; 24(2); 26; 27(3); 29; 33; 36; 37(2); 27:4; 6; 9(3); 16; 19; 20; 28:2(3); 4; 12; 22; 23; 32; 40(4); 42; 29:1; 9; 22; 27(2); 28(2); 30; 36(2); 37; 41; 30:3; 4(2); 12(2); 15; 16(3); 18; 19; 23; 37(3); 31:5; 10; 11; 13; 14(2); 15; 17; 32:1(2); 7; 23(2); 25; 29; 30; 31; 34(2); 33:3(2); 5; 16; 17; 20; 34:7; 10; 14(2); 16; 17; 18; 24; 27; 35:2(2); 8(3); 14(2); 15; 17; 19(2); 21(3); 24; 28(3); 29; 33; 36:1; 3; 5; 6; 7(2); 14; 19; 20; 22(2); 23(2); 24; 25; 27; 28; 29; 31; 32(2); 34; 36(2); 37; 37:3; 12; 13; 14; 16; 19; 26; 27(2); 38:3; 4; 5(2); 10; 13; 15; 17; 18; 21; 26(3); 27; 28(2); 30(3); 31(4); 39:1(2); 4; 7; 15; 27; 37; 38; 40(3); 41; 40:5(2); 15; 30; 38; **Lev** 1:4; 16; 2:11; 12(2); 14; 3:16; 4:3; 14; 20; 21; 26; 28; 31(2); 35; 5:6(2); 7; 8; 10; 11(2); 13(2); 16(2); 18; 6:2; 4; 7(2); 15; 21; 23(2); 26; 7:7; 8; 12; 15; 19; 25; 33; 34; 35; 8:14(2); 15; 21; 28; 33(2); 34; 35(2); 9:2; 4; 7(3); 8; 15(2); 18; 10:7; 12; 13; 14; 17; 11:35; 42; 44(2); 45(2); 12:6; 7(2); 8; 13:7; 11; 15; 28; 36; 40; 52; 14:2; 4; 6; 13; 18; 19; 20; 21; 23; 29; 31; 32; 53; 54; 55; 56; 15:13(2); 14; 15; 25; 28; 29; 30(2); 32(2); 33(3); 16:2; 6(3); 8(3); 11(4); 15; 16(3); 17(3); 18; 20; 24(2); 27(2); 29; 30(2); 31; 33(5); 34(3); 17:6; 7; 11(4); 14(2); 18:10; 13; 24; 25; 27; 29; 19:2; 4; 10; 20; 22(2); 23; 28; 34; 20:7; 9; 19; 23; 26; 21:1; 2; 3; 6; 7; 8(2); 11; 12; 15; 18; 23; 22:9; 16; 18(2); 20; 23; 23:8; 13; 15; 18; 20; 22(2); 27; 28(2); 29; 34; 36; 39; 40(2); 41; 42; 24:2; 7; 9(2); 18; 20(3); 22(3); 25:4; 5(2); 6(2); 7(2); 8; 10; 12; 16; 17; 21; 23(2); 33; 34; 37; 42; 44; 46; 50; 55; 26:1(3); 9; 16; 18; 20; 24; 28; 35; 36; 44(2); 45; 27:5(2); 6(2); 7; 8; 10(4); 12; 14; 16; 33; 34; **Num** 1:48; 3:25; 26; 41; 46; 47; 4:7; 16; 25; 26(3); 29; 31; 33; 35; 39; 43; 5:7; 8(4); 15(3); 18; 6:5; 7(2); 11; 20; 21; 7:3(2); 10; 11(2); 17; 19; 29; 84; 87; 88(2); 8:12; 16(2); 17; 19(2); 21; 9:14; 10:2(3); 6; 10; 13; 21; 29(2); 33(2); 11:1; 13; 14; 18(3); 20; 21; 22(4); 29; 32; 12:1; 13:30; 31; 14:3; 9; 13; 30; 32; 34; 40; 41; 42; 43; 15:5; 6; 11(3); 15(2); 16(2); 25(3); 28(2); 29(3); 40; 16:3; 28; 34; 37; 38; 46(2); 47; 50; 17:3(2); 6; 18:4; 7(2); 9; 16; 17; 21; 24; 31(2); 19:9(3); 17(2); 21; 20:2; 8; 10; 19; 24; 26; 29; 21:5; 7(2); 13; 24; 26; 28; 34; 22:6(4); 11; 12; 13; 17(2); 29; 34; 37; 23:1(2); 7; 9; 13; 23; 27; 29(2); 25:13(2); 18; 26:62; 65; 27:14; 21; 28:2; 6; 7; 10; 12(2); 13; 14(4); 17; 20(2); 21; 22; 23; 24; 28(2); 29; 30; 29:1; 3(2); 4; 5; 6; 9(2); 10; 11; 14(2); 15; 18(3); 21(3); 24(3); 27(3); 30(3); 33(3); 37(3); 31:2; 3(2); 5; 18; 19; 28; 36; 50(2); 53; 54; 32:1; 4; 9; 12; 15; 16(2); 19; 20; 24(2); 27; 29; 36; 33:4; 14; 53; 34:6(2); 14; 18; 35:3(3); 5; 11; 12; 15(4); 30; 31; 32; 33(3); 34; 36:7; 11; **Deut** 1:15; 17(2); 22; 30(2); 32; 33; 37; 38; 40; 42; 2:1; 5; 7; 9; 15; 19; 22; 28(2); 29; 30; 35; 36; 3:2; 7; 11; 22(2); 24; 27; 28; 4:3; 6; 7(2); 15; 16; 21; 23; 24; 31; 32; 34(2); 40; 43(3); 5:5; 8; 9; 11; 25; 26; 31; 6:15; 24; 25; 7:3; 4; 6(2); 7; 9; 16; 21; 22; 25(2); 26; 8:7; 10; 15; 18; 9:6; 12; 16; 19; 20; 10:1; 13; 17; 18; 19; 21; 11:5; 10; 12; 14; 15; 22; 31; 12:5; 9; 23; 31(2); 13:3; 16; 14:1; 2(2); 7(2); 8; 10; 19; 21; 24; 25; 26(4); 27; 15:4; 6; 8; 10; 11; 18; 16:1; 3; 4; 9; 19; 21(2); 17:1; 8(2); 16(2); 17(2); 18; 18:5; 12; 14(3); 15; 18; 19:2; 3; 7; 9; 11; 21(5); 20:1; 4(2); 14; 18; 19(2); 20; 21:5; 8(2); 11; 14; 17; 23; 22:5; 7; 8; 20; 26; 27; 23:5; 7; 14; 18(2); 21; 23; 24:4; 6; 15; 16(3); 19; 20; 21; 25:16; 26:14(2); 27:2; 28:26; 32; 38; 39; 40; 41; 46; 47; 57(2); 68; 29:13; 16; 20; 21; 26; 30:9(3); 11(2); 12; 13; 20; 31:6; 7; 19(2); 21(2); 23; 27; 29; 32:3; 4; 9; 20; 22; 25; 28; 31; 32; 35; 36; 40; 43(2); 47(2); 33:2; 4; 7; 9; 19; 21; 34:8(2); 9; **Josh** 1:6; 8; 9; 11(2); 2:3; 5; 10(2); 11; 14; 15; 24; 3:4; 5; 12; 15; 4:2; 3; 7; 13(2); 23; 5:2; 3; 5; 6; 7; 13(2); 15; 6:16; 7:1; 3; 5; 9(2); 11; 13; 8:2(2); 6(2); 7; 18; 26; 27; 9:9; 11; 12; 21; 22; 23; 24; 27(2); 10:4; 6; 8; 13; 14(2); 19; 24; 25; 42; 11:6; 10; 13; 14; 20; 13:12; 29; 31(2); 14:2; 3; 4(2); 11(3); 12; 15:18; 63; 16:9; 17:1(3); 2(2); 15(2); 16; 18; 18:4; 6; 7; 8; 10; 19:1(2); 9(2); 10; 17; 24; 32; 40; 50; 20:2; 6; 9(2); 21:2; 4; 10(2); 13; 21(2); 26; 27; 32; 38; 40; 22:16; 17; 24(2); 25; 26(2); 28(2); 29(3); 34; 23:2(5); 3(2); 4; 9(2); 10(2); 13; 14; 24:1(4); 13; 15(2); 17; 18; 19; 22; 25; 27; 31; 32; **Judg** 1:1; 14; 27; 32; 34; 2:7; 10; 15; 18(2); 3:9; 11; 15; 19; 20; 22; 28; 30; 4:3(2); 5; 6; 9(2); 14; 17; 19; 21; 5:11; 13; 16; 25; 30(2); 31; 6:1; 2; 4; 5; 22; 31(3); 7:2(2); 4; 9; 15; 20; 8:5; 7; 10; 14; 20; 21; 22; 24; 28; 30; 35; 9:2; 3; 17(2); 21; 10:8; 11:2; 16; 18; 26; 35; 37(2); 38; 12:6; 9; 13:1; 5(2); 7; 8; 15; 16; 14:2; 3(2); 4; 10; 14; 16:2; 17; 18(2); 19; 24; 25(4); 28; 17:3; 18:1(2); 4; 7; 9; 10; 19; 26; 30; 31; 19:1; 15; 19(4); 20:10; 23; 28; 39; 41; 47; 21:5; 6; 7(2); 9; 14; 15; 16(2); 17; 18; 21; 22(3); 23; **Ruth** 1:6; 12; 13(3); 16; 20; 2:11; 12; 13; 16; 3:1; 9; 10; 11(2); 13(3); 16; 17; 18; 4:4; 6(3); 8; 15; **1 Sam** 1:4; 5; 16; 20; 22; 27; 2:2; 3; 5; 8; 9; 14; 15(2); 17; 20; 23; 24; 25; 30; 32; 35; 36; 3:5; 6; 8; 9; 10; 13(2); 14; 21; 4:7(2); 13(2); 18; 19; 20; 22; 5:7; 11; 6:2; 4; 12; 17(5); 7:3; 5; 8; 9; 17; 8:7; 10; 11; 12; 18; 9:3; 7; 9; 12; 13(2); 16; 19; 20(2); 24(3); 10:2; 7; 14; 11:3; 13; 12:17; 19(3); 21(2); 22(2); 23(2); 24(2); 13:2; 6; 7; 13; 14; 19; 21(2); 14:6(2); 10; 12; 18; 24; 26; 30; 39; 44; 45; 52; 15:2; 6; 11; 12; 15; 23; 24; 26; 29; 35; 16:1(2); 3; 7(2); 11; 12; 22; 17:8(2); 17; 20; 21; 26(2); 27; 28; 31; 33; 39(2); 40; 42; 47; 18:11; 17(2); 19:5(2); 13; 16; 20:4; 6(2); 8(2); 9; 17; 21; 22; 23; 26; 29; 31(2); 34(2); 21:6; 8; 9; 22:3; 8; 10; 13; 15(2); 23; 23:4; 7; 8; 10; 17; 21; 22(2); 23; 26; 27; 24:10; 11; 17; 18; 19(2); 25:1; 8; 11; 17(2); 21; 25; 26; 28(2); 30; 34; 36; 39; 26:9; 12; 15; 18; 19; 20; 21; 23(2); 27:1; 5; 8; 28:1; 3; 8(2); 9; 10; 11(2); 12; 15; 17(2); 20; 29:4(2); 6; 30:6(2); 8; 10; 12(2); 22; 24; 25; 26; 31:4; **2 Sam** 1:9; 12(4); 16; 21; 26; 2:5; 7; 21; 3:9; 14; 17; 18; 20; 22; 27; 31; 37; 39; 4:2; 7; 10; 5:12; 17; 19; 24; 6:6; 7; 17; 22; 7:3; 5; 6; 10; 13; 19; 20; 21; 22; 23(5); 24; 27; 29; 8:4; 10; 9:1; 7(2); 10; 11; 13; 10:11(2); 12(2); 13; 11:4; 25; 26; 12:4(2); 6; 12; 16; 18; 21; 22; 13:2(2); 6; 7; 12; 13(2); 18; 22; 32(2); 33; 37; 39; 14:2; 7; 13; 14; 16; 17; 19; 25; 29; 32; 33; 15:2; 6; 8; 12(2); 19; 34; 16:2(3); 3; 11; 12; 22; 17:8; 10; 11; 14; 17; 21; 29(2); 18:3(2); 5; 8; 12; 13; 16; 18(2); 20; 31; 19:1; 2(3); 6(2); 7(2); 8; 20; 21; 22; 24; 26(2); 28; 32; 33; 37; 38(2); 20:4; 6; 11; 21:1; 2; 3; 4(2); 5; 8; 10; 14; 22:18(2); 22; 23(2); 29; 30; 31; 32; 40(2); 23:5; 9; 24:10; 12; 14; 22(2); 24(2); 25; **1 Ki** 1:2(2); 3; 4; 5; 20; 25; 35; 42; 51; 2:7; 9; 15; 17; 18; 19(2); 20; 22(6); 24; 26; 28; 36; 37(2); 42(2); 3:2; 4; 6; 9; 11(3); 15; 26(2); 28; 4:7(2); 22; 24; 26; 27(2); 28; 31; 5:1; 3; 5(2); 6(3); 7; 9; 11; 6:2; 4; 6; 8; 31; 33; 7:7; 8; 17(3); 18; 40(2); 42(2); 45(2); 48; 50(2); 51; 8:5; 7; 11; 13; 17; 18; 19; 20; 21; 39; 41; 42; 43; 44; 46; 48; 51; 53; 64; 66(3); 9:7; 8; 15; 19(2); 24; 25; 10:3; 12(3); 20; 21; 22; 11:4; 5; 7(2); 8; 12; 13(2); 15; 16; 18; 31(2); 32(2); 34; 36; 38(2); 12:1; 2; 5; 15; 20; 24; 28; 30; 33; 13:6; 9; 12; 13(2); 17; 23; 27; 32; 33; 14:4; 5(2); 6; 9(2); 11; 13(2); 14; 15; 18; 23(2); 15:4; 22; 16:13; 24; 26; 31; 32; 17:5; 9; 12; 13; 14; 15; 18:4; 10; 20; 23; 25(2); 27; 41; 19:3; 4; 7; 10(2); 14; 20; 20:7(2); 9; 10(2); 18(2); 22; 25(2); 29; 34; 38; 39; 42(2); 21:2(2); 4; 6(2); 15(2); 22:5; 6; 11; 12; 15; 34; 43; 48(2); 53; **2 Ki** 2:2; 4; 6; 9; 10; 16; 17; 18; 3:2; 9(2); 10; 13; 17; 26; 4:2; 10; 13(2); 14; 24; 27; 38; 43; 5:3; 17; 6:1; 5; 7; 9; 11; 16; 23; 25(2); 27; 33; 7:1(2); 6; 7; 16(2); 18(2); 20; 8:1(3); 3(2); 5(2); 6; 18; 19; 27; 9:2; 5(3); 8; 16; 20; 25; 34; 10:3; 6; 10; 16; 19(2); 20; 22(2); 24(2); 31; 11:3; 7; 15; 20; 12:7; 12(2); 13; 15; 21; 13:4; 7(2); 17; 14:6(3); 10; 26(2); 28; 15:14; 16:6; 9; 15; 17:4; 5; 7; 9; 10; 12; 16; 21; 22; 32(2); 37; 18:4; 6; 20; 24; 26; 29; 31; 36; 19:3; 4; 8; 18; 25; 31; 34(3); 20:1; 6(2); 10; 12; 19; 21:3(2); 5; 22:13(4); 18; 23:3; 4(3); 7; 13(3); 24:1; 4; 7; 16; 20; 25:3; 16; 26; 30(2); **1 Chr** 1:19; 4:14; 23; 39; 40; 41; 5:20; 22; 6:26; 49(2); 54; 70; 7:4(2); 11; 40; 9:13; 18; 25; 26; 28; 32; 33; 10:4; 13(2); 11:13; 19; 12:8; 18; 19; 21; 22; 23; 24; 25; 37; 39(2); 40; 13:3; 4; 9; 14:2(2); 8; 10; 15; 15:1(3); 2; 3; 11(3); 12; 13; 23; 24; 16:1; 15; 17(2); 21; 25; 26; 33; 34(2); 17:2; 5; 9; 17; 18(2); 19; 21(2); 22; 25; 27; 18:4; 10; 19:6; 7; 12(2); 13(2); 14; 21:6; 8; 10; 11; 12; 13; 23(3); 24(3); 25; 29; 30; 22:1; 3(2); 4; 5(2); 6(2); 7; 8; 9; 10; 14(2); 15; 18; 19; 23:5; 24; 25; 26; 27; 29; 24:5; 6(2); 19; 25:1; 5; 6(2); 8; 9(3); 10; 11; 12; 13; 14; 15; 16; 17; 18; 19; 20; 21; 22; 23; 24; 25; 26; 27; 28; 29; 30; 31; 26:5; 8; 10; 13; 14(3); 16; 17; 18; 30; 32; 27:2; 3; 5; 7; 8; 9; 10; 11; 12; 13; 14; 15; 24; 26; 27; 28:2(2); 3; 4; 5; 6; 8; 9(2); 10(2); 11; 12(2); 13(3); 14(4); 15(4); 16(3); 17(4); 18(2); 20(2); 21(3); 29:1(2); 2(6); 3; 5(3); 7; 9; 11; 14; 15; 16; 17; 19; 21; **2 Chr** 1:3; 4(3); 9; 10; 11; 17(2); 2:1(2); 4(3); 5; 8; 9(2); 12(3); 3:3; 6; 4:6(2); 9; 11(2); 13(2); 16(2); 19; 22; 5:1; 6; 8; 11; 13(2); 14; 6:2; 7; 8; 9; 10; 13; 30; 32; 33; 34; 36; 38; 7:3(2); 6; 7; 9; 10(4); 12; 16; 17; 20; 21; 8:9; 11(2); 13; 14(3); 9:2; 8; 11(3); 19; 20; 21; 25; 10:1; 3; 15; 11:4; 5; 14(2); 15(3); 17(2); 18; 21; 22; 23; 13:8; 9; 10; 11; 12; 14:1; 3; 6; 11(2); 13; 14(2); 15:3; 6; 7; 9; 15; 16:6; 9; 10; 14(2); 17:18; 18:2; 4; 5; 10; 11; 32; 33; 19:6(3); 7; 8(2); 11; 20:8; 9; 12; 15; 17; 21; 23; 25; 26; 27; 30; 33; 21:6; 19(2); 22:1; 3; 4; 7(2); 9; 11; 12; 23:6; 8; 14; 21; 24:3; 6; 7; 14(2); 24; 25; 25:3; 4(3); 6; 7; 8; 13; 20; 26:8; 10(2); 14(2); 15; 16; 18(3); 21; 23; 28:2(2); 6; 11; 13(2); 17; 19(2); 21; 23; 24; 29:6; 9; 11; 21(4); 23; 24(3); 25; 32; 34; 35; 30:2; 3; 5; 9(2); 17(2); 18(3); 24; 26; 31:2; 3(3); 4; 10; 16; 18; 19; 32:7; 15; 25; 26; 27(6); 28(3); 29(2); 33:3(2); 5; 8; 22; 34:3; 11; 21(3); 26; 35:2; 6; 7(2); 8; 9; 14(4); 15; 17; 21; 23; 24; 25; **Ezra** 1:4; 2:68; 69; 3:4; 5(2); 11(2); 12; 13; 4:2; 3; 14; 15; 6:8(2); 9; 10; 17; 20(4); 22; 7:10; 16; 19; 20(2); 23(2); 8:16(2); 17(2); 20; 21; 22(2); 23; 25; 35; 9:2(2); 6; 7; 8; 9; 10; 12; 13(2); 15; 10:1; 4; 6; 13(2); **Neh** 1:4; 6; 9; 11; 2:7; 8(3); 14; 3:17; 4:4; 5; 6; 14; 20; 23; 5:2; 4; 5; 16; 18; 19(2); 6:9; 10; 13(2); 16; 18; 7:2; 8:4; 5; 9; 10(3); 11; 17; 9:3(2); 8; 10(2); 15(2); 18; 20; 30; 31; 33; 35; 10:30; 32(2); 33(6); 34; 37; 39; 11:23(2); 25; 12:29; 43; 44(3); 46; 47(4); 13:5(2); 6; 7(2); 10(2); 13; 14(2); 25; 31; **Esth** 1:3; 4; 5; 8; 9; 11; 13; 17; 20; 2:2; 7; 9; 10; 12(3); 14; 15; 18; 20; 3:2; 4; 6; 8; 14(2); 4:2; 8(2); 10; 14(3); 16(2); 5:4; 8; 10; 6:3(2); 4; 6; 7; 10; 7:4(2); 7(2); 9; 10; 8:1; 6; 8; 13; 9:1; 4(2); 19; 22; 31(2); 10:3; **Job** 1:5; 9; 2:4(2); 8; 11; 13; 3:6; 9; 13; 14; 21(2); 24; 25; 26; 4:11; 5:2; 6; 8; 18; 23; 27; 6:3; 4; 8; 10; 19; 21; 22; 28; 7:1; 2; 4; 16; 21; 8:4; 6; 8; 9; 17; 9:15; 17; 32; 10:6; 11:4; 6; 11; 12; 12:5; 13:7(2); 8(2); 16; 26; 27; 14:7(2); 16; 15:5; 11; 22(2); 23; 24; 25; 31; 34; 16:12; 21(2); 22; 17:1; 3; 4; 10; 13; 15; 18:4; 8; 10(2); 19:21; 25; 27; 29(2); 20:5; 18; 19; 21; 26; 29; 21:4; 14; 19; 21; 28; 30(2); 31; 22:6(2); 26; 28; 23:14(2); 16; 24:5(3); 8; 15; 16; 17; 21(2); 24; 27:8; 14; 28:1; 3; 5; 15(2); 17; 18; 24; 25; 26(2); 29:6; 13; 21; 23(3); 25; 30:4; 23(2); 25(2); 26(2); 28; 31:2; 3(2); 10; 11; 12; 19; 23; 28; 30; 32; 32:11; 18; 22; 33:12; 13; 14; 23; 26; 32; 34:3; 4; 5; 9; 11; 19; 21; 23; 28; 31; 37; 35:3; 9; 14; 36:4; 7; 13; 18; 21; 27; 31; 37:6; 13(3); 19; 23; 38:7; 10; 23(2); 25(2); 39; 41(2); 39:14; 40:20; 41:5; 42:3; 7; 8(4); 9; 10; 11; 12; 16; **Ps** 1:6; 2:8(2); 3:2; 3; 5; 7; 4:3; 8; 5:2; 4; 7; 9; 10; 11; 12; 6:2(2); 4; 5; 8; 7:6; 7; 9; 13; 8:5; 9:4; 7; 8; 9; 10; 18; 10:3; 5; 14; 11:2; 7; 12:1(2); 5(3); 14:5; 16:1; 3; 10; 17:6; 14; 15; 18:17(2); 21; 22; 27; 28; 29; 30; 31; 39(2); 19:4; 21:3; 6; 7; 11; 22:11(2); 16; 18; 24; 28; 23:3; 4; 24:2; 25:5; 6; 7; 11(2); 15; 16; 19; 20; 21(2); 26:1; 3; 11; 27:5; 12; 30:1; 5(4); 11; 31:3(2); 4(2); 7; 9; 10; 13; 14; 16; 17; 19(2); 21; 22; 23; 32:4; 6; 11; 33:1; 4; 9; 17; 20; 21; 35:2; 7(3); 10; 12; 13; 14; 20; 27; 36:2; 9; 37:2; 7; 9; 10(2); 13; 17; 22; 24; 28; 37; 38:2; 4(2); 7; 10; 12; 15; 16; 17; 18; 20; 39:7; 11; 12; 40:1; 12; 41:4; 12; 42:1(2); 2(2); 4; 5(2); 11; 43:2; 5; 44:3; 4; 6; 10; 11; 12; 21; 22(2); 25; 26(2); 46:47:2; 4; 7; 9; 48:4; 14; 49:7; 8; 10; 15; 17; 18(2); 50:6; 8; 10; 12; 51:3; 16; 52:9; 53:5; 54:3; 5; 6; 7; 55:3; 9; 12; 15; 16; 18; 56:1; 2; 5; 6; 9; 13; 57:1; 2; 6; 10; 58:11; 59:3(4); 7; 9(2); 12(2); 15; 16; 17; 60:2; 7; 11; 12; 61:3(2); 5; 62:1; 5(2); 8; 12; 63:1(2); 2; 10; 64:9; 65:3(2); 9; 13; 66:10; 16; 67:4(2); 68:10; 28; 69:1; 3; 6; 7; 9; 13; 16; 17; 20(2); 21(2); 26; 33; 35; 71:3; 5; 10(2); 11; 15; 24(2); 72:12; 15; 73:2; 3; 4; 14; 16; 27(2); 28; 74:4; 12; 20; 75:1; 6; 8; 78:5; 18; 20; 29; 34; 37; 39; 50; 58; 79:2; 7; 8; 9(3); 80:9; 15; 17; 81:4(2); 82:8; 83:2; 5; 12(2); 84:2(2); 3; 10; 11; 85:8; 86:1; 2; 3; 4; 5; 7; 10; 13; 17; 88:3; 10; 89:2; 6; 17; 18; 28; 47; 90:4; 7; 9; 10; 11; 17; 91:11; 92:4; 9(2); 94:13; 14; 16(2); 95:3; 5; 7; 10; 96:4; 5; 13(2); 97:9; 11(2); 98:1; 9; 99:9; 100:5; 102:3; 9; 10; 13; 14; 16; 18; 19; 103:6; 11; 14; 15; 16; 104:8; 14(2); 18(2); 19; 27; 105:8; 10; 14; 16; 32; 38; 39; 42; 106:1(2); 8; 13; 31; 43; 45; 107:1(2); 7; 8(2); 9; 15(2); 16; 21(2); 25; 31(2); 34; 36; 108:4; 8; 12; 13; 109:2; 4; 5(2); 19; 21; 22; 31; 116:7; 8; 12; 117:2; 118:1(2); 7; 12; 21; 29(2); 119:20; 22; 32; 35; 39; 40; 42(2); 43; 45; 50; 66; 71; 76; 77; 78; 81; 83; 85; 91; 93; 94; 95; 98; 99; 102; 110; 111; 115; 118; 120; 122(2); 126(2); 131(2); 147; 153; 155; 166; 168; 171; 172; 173; 174; 176; 120:7(2); 122:5(2); 6; 8; 123:3; 125:3; 5; 126:2; 3; 6; 127:2(2); 130:5; 6(3); 7; 131:1; 132:5(2); 9; 10; 13(2); 14; 16; 17; 133:1; 3; 135:3(2); 4(3); 5; 7; 14; 136:1(2); 2; 3; 4; 5; 6; 7; 8; 9; 10; 11; 12; 13; 14; 15; 16; 17; 18; 19; 20; 21; 22; 23; 24; 25; 26; 137:3; 138:2(2); 5; 139:4; 6; 13; 14; 16; 20; 140:2; 5(2); 9; 12; 141:5; 6; 9; 142:3; 4(2); 6(2); 7; 143:2; 3; 6; 8(2); 10; 11(2); 12; 144:1(2); 146:5; 7; 147:1(2); 8; 13; 20; 148:5; 13; 149:4; 150:2; **Prov** 1:9; 11; 16; 18(2); 19; 22; 32; 2:3(2); 4(2); 6; 7; 18; 21; 3:2; 12; 14; 26; 29(2); 32; 4:2; 13; 16; 17; 22; 23; 5:3; 17; 20; 21; 23; 6:1(2); 3; 23; 26; 34; 7:6; 19; 26; 8:6; 7; 11; 32; 35; 9:4; 7; 11; 12; 14; 16; 10:13; 21; 29; 11:15; 17; 12:6; 19; 26; 13:22; 23; 15:10; 24; 27; 16:4(2); 6; 12(2); 26(2); 17:3(2); 10; 13; 16; 17; 18; 26; 18:6; 16; 19:2; 10(2); 19; 29(2); 20:3; 14; 16(2); 22; 25; 21:8; 12; 15; 18(2); 25; 29; 31; 22:9; 18; 23; 25; 26; 23:3; 5; 7; 9; 11; 13; 17; 18; 21; 27; 28; 24:2; 6; 7; 16; 20(2); 22; 27; 28; 25:3(2); 4; 7; 8; 13; 22; 26:1; 3(3); 12(2); 25; 27:1; 13(2); 21(2); 24; 27(2); 28:8; 21; 29:5; 19; 20(2); 26; 30:18; 21(2); 22; 33; 31:4(3); 8; 10; 15(2); 21(2); 22; 24; **Eccl** 1:14; 17; 2:3; 8; 10; 11; 12; 16; 17(2); 21(2); 22(3); 23; 24; 25; 26(2); 3:1; 12; 17(3); 19(2); 22(2); 4:4(2); 6; 8; 9; 10(2); 14; 16; 5:1; 2; 3; 4; 7; 8; 9; 13; 16; 18(2); 19; 20; 6:2; 4; 7; 8; 9; 10; 12(2); 7:2; 3; 5; 6; 9; 10; 12; 13; 18; 20; 22; 24; 8:2; 3(2); 6; 7; 15; 17; 9:1; 4(2); 5; 7; 9; 10; 12; 10:1; 4; 15; 17(2); 19; 20; 11:1; 2; 6; 7; 8; 9; 10; 12:5; 13; 14; **Song** 1:2; 7; 2:5; 11; 14; 15; 4:4; 5:2(2); 4; 5; 6; 6:5; 7:9; 13; 8:6; 7; 8(2); 11; 13; **Isa** 1:2; 17; 20; 29; 30; 2:3; 6; 12; 20; 22; 3:1; 7; 8; 9; 10; 11; 12; 14; 4:2; 5; 6(3); 5:7(4); 10; 20(4); 22; 23; 25; 6:5(2); 8; 13; 7:4(2); 6; 8; 11; 13; 16; 18(2); 22; 23; 25(3); 8:2; 4; 10; 11; 18; 9:4; 5(2); 6; 12; 13; 16; 17(2); 18; 19; 21; 10:3; 4; 8; 13(2); 17(2); 22; 23; 25; 26; 11:4; 9; 10; 12; 16(2); 12:2; 5; 6; 13:3; 4; 6; 10; 11(2); 17; 14:1; 2; 9; 13; 21; 22; 23; 27; 29; 31; 15:5(3); 6(2); 8; 9; 16:2; 4; 7(2); 8; 9; 11(2); 17:2; 7; 18:4; 5; 6(2); 19:15; 20(3); 20:3; 6; 21:4(2); 6; 15; 16; 17; 22:5; 11(2); 12(4); 13; 14(2); 16; 25; 23:1; 3; 4; 13; 14; 18(4); 24:3; 11; 14; 18; 23; 25:1; 2; 4(2); 6; 8; 9(2); 10(2); 26:1; 4; 5; 8(3); 9; 11; 12(2); 19; 20; 21(2); 27:11; 28:5; 6(2); 8; 10; 11; 15; 16; 19; 20; 21; 22; 26; 27; 29:10; 11; 14; 16; 20(2); 21; 30:4; 7; 8; 15; 16; 18(2); 19; 23; 31; 33(2); 31:1; 4(3); 7(2); 9; 32:6; 10; 12(2); 33:2; 5; 21; 22; 34:2; 5(2); 6; 8(2); 13; 14; 16; 17; 35:1; 6; 8; 36:5; 9; 11; 14; 16; 21; 37:3; 4; 8; 19; 26; 32; 35(3); 38:1; 14; 17(2); 18(2); 39:1; 8; 40:2(2); 3; 5; 10; 16; 20(2); 41:1; 7; 10(2); 13; 17; 28; 42:3; 4; 16; 21; 22(2); 23; 24(2); 43:1; 3(2); 4(2); 5; 7; 14; 21; 23; 25; 44:3; 7; 14(2); 15(2); 17; 18; 21; 22; 23(2); 45:4; 13; 18; 22; 46:9; 13; 47:1; 4; 5; 9; 10; 48:2; 8; 9(2); 11(3); 21; 22; 49:4; 5; 10; 13; 19(2); 20; 21; 22; 23(2); 25; 50:1(2); 7; 51:2; 3; 4; 6; 8; 10; 19; 23; 52:1; 3(2); 4; 5; 8; 9; 12(2); 15; 53:2; 5(3); 8(2); 10; 11; 12; 54:1; 3; 4(3); 5; 6; 7; 8; 9(2); 10; 14(2); 15; 16; 55:2(2); 4; 5; 7; 8; 9; 10; 11; 12; 13(2); 56:1; 4; 7(2); 11; 57:8; 12; 15; 16(2); 17; 21; 58:4; 5; 59:3; 4(2); 9(2); 10; 11(2); 12(3); 14; 16; 17(2); 21; 60:1; 2; 9; 10; 12; 19; 20; 61:3(3); 8(2); 10; 11; 62:1(2); 4; 5; 8(2); 10(2); 63:3; 4; 5; 8; 12; 17; 64:3; 4(3); 5; 7; 65:1; 5; 8(2); 10(2); 11(2); 12; 14(3); 15; 17; 18; 20; 22; 23(2); 66:2; 5; 8; 10(2); 12; 15; 16; 18; 20; 21; 22; 24; **Jer** 1:6; 7; 8; 12; 15; 18; 19; 2:10; 11; 13; 20; 22; 25; 27; 28(2); 37; 3:2; 8(2); 10; 12; 14; 21; 22; 23; 24; 25; 4:3; 6; 8(2); 12(2); 13; 15; 18; 20; 22; 27; 28; 31(2); 5:4; 5; 7; 9; 10; 11; 13; 24; 26; 29; 6:1; 4(2); 6; 11; 12; 16(2); 20; 26(2); 29; 7:5; 16(3); 18; 22; 29; 30; 32; 33(2); 34; 8:11; 14; 15(2); 16; 17; 21; 22; 9:1; 2(2); 3(3); 4; 7; 9; 10(2); 17(2); 18; 19; 21; 24; 26; 10:2; 3(2); 5; 7(2); 13; 14; 16; 18; 19; 21; 25; 11:7; 13; 14(3); 17(2); 18; 20; 23; 12:3(2); 4; 6; 12; 13:7; 10; 11(4); 15; 16; 17; 18; 21; 22; 14:2; 3; 4; 7(2); 8; 11(2); 16; 17; 19(3); 20; 21; 22; 15:2(4); 4; 5; 10(2); 14; 15(2); 16; 17; 20; 16:3; 4(2); 5(2); 6(2); 7(3); 9; 12; 15; 16(2); 17; 18; 20; 17:4; 6; 8; 14; 16; 18:14; 18; 20(4); 22(2); 23; 19:5; 7(2); 20:4; 8; 10(2); 11; 12; 13; 21:2(2); 10(3); 22:4; 6; 10(3); 11; 13; 14; 17(2); 18(2); 20; 22; 30; 23:2; 10(2); 11; 12; 15; 18; 27; 34; 36(2); 24:5; 6(2); 7; 9; 25:12; 14; 15; 29(3); 31; 34; 36; 38; 26:11; 14; 15(2); 16; 27:2; 10; 14; 15; 16; 19; 28:4; 9; 14; 29:6; 7(2); 8; 9; 10; 11; 13; 15; 28; 32; 30:2; 3; 5; 7; 8; 9; 10; 11; 12; 14(2); 17; 21; 31:6; 7(2); 9; 11; 12(2); 13; 15(2); 16; 18; 20(2); 22; 25; 30; 34(2); 35(2); 37; 38; 32:2; 3; 7; 8(2); 15; 17; 19; 25; 27; 30; 31; 39; 42; 44(2); 33:4; 5; 9(2); 11(3); 17; 26; 34:5(3); 7; 20(2); 35:6; 11(2); 14; 36:7; 31; 37:3; 4; 9; 10; 11; 15; 38:4(2); 5; 9; 27; 39:16(2); 18; 40:4(2); 5; 10; 16; 41:8; 9; 18; 42:2(2); 10; 11; 14; 18; 20(2); 43:1; 7; 11(3); 44:11(2); 13; 14; 16; 17; 19; 27(2); 29; 45:3; 5(2); 46:5; 10(2); 12; 14; 19; 21(2); 22; 27; 28(3); 47:3; 4; 48:1; 5(2); 7; 9; 14; 18; 20; 27(2); 31(3); 32; 34; 36(2); 37; 38; 40; 44; 46; 49:3(2); 8; 12; 13; 15; 19; 23; 29; 30; 32(2); 33; 37; 50:3; 9; 14; 15; 16; 20; 23; 25; 27; 29; 31; 38; 42; 44; 51:2; 5; 6; 8(2); 9; 11(2); 12; 16; 17; 19; 20; 24; 26(2); 29; 33; 36; 37; 46; 48; 51; 56; 52:3; 6; 20; 34(2); **Lam** 1:5; 9; 10; 11(2); 13; 16; 18; 19; 20; 22(2); 2:13; 14(2); 16; 19; 3:12; 25; 26; 27; 31; 33; 39; 48; 56; 58; 4:4(3); 9(2); 10; 17(2); 18; 19; 5:4; 16; 20; **Ezek** 1:10; 13; 18; 20; 21; 2:4; 5(2); 7; 3:5; 7; 17; 26; 27; 4:3; 5; 6; 9(2); 5:6; 16; 6:9; 11(2); 7:3; 6; 8; 11; 12; 13(2); 14; 16; 20; 22; 23; 8:12; 14; 17; 9:9; 10; 10:10; 13; 17; 11:5; 12; 16; 21(2); 12:2; 3; 6; 24; 25(2); 27; 13:5; 16; 18; 19(2); 23; 14:7; 21; 15:4(2); 5; 6; 16:4; 5; 14; 16; 17; 24(2); 33; 56; 58; 59; 61(2); 63; 17:20; 18:17; 18(2); 31; 32; 19:1; 11; 14; 20:6; 9; 14; 16; 22; 31; 39; 40;

42; 44; 21:12; 15; 19(2); 20; 21; 22(2); 28(3); 29; 32(2); 22:28; 30; 23:4; 5; 7; 8; 9; 10; 12; 16; 20(2); 28; 29; 34; 37; 39(2); 40(2); 46; 49(2); 24:7; 17; 25:5(2); 6(2); 26:5(3); 7; 14(2); 17; 19; 21; 27:2; 7; 12; 13; 14; 16; 17; 19; 20; 22; 31; 32(2); 28:4; 10; 12; 13; 17; 23; 24; 29:3; 15; 18; 19; 20(2); 30:3; 9; 18; 21; 31:11; 14(2); 15; 32:2; 10; 11; 16(3); 32; 33:7(2); 11; 12; 28; 30; 31; 32; 34:5; 6; 8(2); 10(2); 11(2); 17; 18; 19; 28; 29; 35:6; 36:8; 9(2); 11; 18(2); 21; 22(2); 24; 29; 31; 32(2); 37; 37:16(6); 17; 38:7; 17; 19; 21; 39:5; 9; 12; 13; 17(2); 19; 23; 25; 29; 40:4; 42; 44; 45; 46; 41:6; 24(2); 42:6; 13; 14(2); 43:18(3); 19; 20; 22; 25(2); 26; 44:3; 8; 11; 14(2); 25(3); 26; 28; 45:1; 2(2); 4(2); 14; 15(2); 16; 17; 20(2); 22(3); 23(2); 24(3); 25; 46:5(2); 7(3); 11(3); 12; 18; 47:1; 5; 9; 10; 12(3); 14; 17; 22(2); 48:1; 2; 3; 4; 5; 6; 7; 9; 11; 14; 15(2); 18; 23; 31(3); 32(3); 33(3); 34(3); **Dan** 1:5(2); 10; 12; 17; 2:8; 9(2); 12; 20; 23; 29; 30(2); 37; 3:3; 4:2; 12; 18; 19; 21; 22; 30(2); 36; 5:1; 17; 6:7; 13(2); 23; 7:12(2); 22; 25; 28; 8:14; 19; 22; 26; 27; 9:12; 14; 16(2); 17; 18; 19(2); 20; 23; 24(3); 26; 27; 10:7; 8; 11; 12; 13; 14; 17(2); 19; 11:4(2); 6; 13; 17; 23; 24; 25; 27; 30(2); 33; 35; 36; 37; 39; 12:7; 9; 13; **Hos** 1:2; 4; 6; 9; 11(2); 2:2; 4; 5(2); 7(2); 8(2); 13; 17; 18; 23; 3:1; 2(2); 4; 4:1; 4; 6(2); 9(2); 10; 12; 14; 16; 5:1; 3; 4; 7; 14; 6:1; 4; 6; 9; 11; 7:1; 10; 13; 14; 16; 8:4; 6; 9; 11(3); 12; 13; 14; 9:1(2); 4(2); 6; 11; 15; 10:1; 3(3); 5(3); 6; 7; 10; 12(2); 11:9; 12:8; 12(2); 13:2; 4; 13; 16; 14:1; 2; 3; 4; 9; **Joel** 1:5; 6; 8; 10; 11; 13; 15(2); 17; 19; 20; 2:1(2); 2; 11(3); 13; 14; 18; 21; 22; 23(2); 32; 3:1; 3(3); 8; 9; 12; 13(3); 14; 16; 19; 21(2); **Am** 1:3(2); 6(2); 9(2); 11(2); 13(2); 2:1(2); 4(2); 6(4); 3:2; 5; 10; 14; 4:5; 13; 5:3; 4; 5; 8; 12; 13; 17; 18; 23; 26; 6:5; 6; 10; 13; 7:2; 4; 5; 11; 13; 8:6(2); 8; 10; 11; 9:4(2); 6; 9; **Ob** 1; 7; 10; 11; 15; 16; 18; **Jon** 1:2; 7; 8; 10; 11(2); 12(2); 13; 14(2); 2:3; 4:2; 3(2); 4; 6(2); 8(2); 9(2); 10; **Mic** 1:3; 5(2); 6; 7; 9(2); 12(2); 13; 16; 2:3; 6; 10; 3:1; 3; 6; 7; 11(3); 4:2; 4; 5; 9; 10; 12; 13; 5:4; 7(2); 6:2; 4; 7(2); 12; 16; 7:1; 2; 3; 6; 7; 9; 13; **Nah** 1:2; 10; 13; 14; 15; 2:2(2); 12(2); 3:7; 10; 13; 14; 19; **Hab** 1:3; 4; 5; 6; 9; 10; 12(2); 2:3(3); 5; 9; 11; 14; 17; 3:13(2); **Zeph** 1:7(2); 11; 18; 2:4; 6(2); 7(3); 10; 11; 14; 15; 3:7; 8(2); 9; 11(2); 13; 19; 20; **Hag** 1:4; 9; 11(2); 2:4; 6; 23; **Zech** 1:14(2); 15; 2:5; 6; 8(2); 9(2); 10; 13; 3:8(2); 9; 4:10(2); 5:9; 11; 6:14(2); 7:3; 5(2); 6; 14; 8:2(2); 9; 10(5); 12; 14; 16; 17; 19; 23; 9:1; 3; 5; 7; 8; 11; 13; 16; 17; 10:1(2); 2; 3; 6; 8(2); 10; 11:2(2); 3(2); 4; 5; 6; 7(2); 12; 13; 15; 16(2); 12:3; 10(4); 13:1(4); 5; 14:2; 5; **Mal** 1:3; 11(2); 14; 2:1; 7(2); 11; 14; 16(2); 3:2; 5; 6; 9; 10(2); 11(2); 12; 15; 16; 4:1; 3; 4; **Mt** 1:20; 21; 2:2; 5; 6; 8; 12; 13; 14; 18; 20; 3:2; 3; 9; 15(2); 4:6; 10; 17; 18; 5:3; 4; 5; 6(2); 7; 8; 9; 10(2); 11; 12(2); 13; 18; 20; 28; 29(3); 30(3); 32; 34; 35(2); 37; 38(2); 44; 45; 46; 6:5; 7(2); 8; 13; 14; 16; 19; 20; 21; 24; 26; 32(2); 34(2); 7:2; 8; 9; 10; 12; 13; 25; 29; 8:9; 13; 9:5; 13; 16; 20; 21; 24; 36; 10:10(2); 15(2); 17; 18; 19; 20; 22; 23; 25; 26; 29; 35; 39; 11:3; 10; 13; 17; 18; 21; 22(2); 23; 24(2); 26; 29(2); 30; 12:4(3); 8; 33; 34; 36; 37; 40; 42; 50; 13:12; 15; 16(2); 17; 21(2); 44; 14:3(2); 4; 14; 24; 26; 15:2; 4; 19; 23; 16:2; 3; 17; 23; 25(2); 26(2); 27; 17:4(4); 15(2); 20(2); 27; 18:6; 7; 8; 9; 10; 11; 19; 20; 19:3(2); 5; 9; 12(2); 14; 22; 23; 24(2); 29; 20:1(2); 2; 13; 15; 16; 23(2); 28; 32; 21:26; 32; 46; 22:2; 14; 16; 24; 28; 30; 23:3; 4; 8; 9; 10; 13(2); 14(2); 15; 17; 19; 23; 25; 27; 39; 24:5; 6; 7; 9; 21; 22; 24; 27; 28; 38; 42; 44; 50; 25:8; 9(2); 13; 14; 29; 34; 35; 41; 42; 26:9(2); 10(2); 11; 12(2); 17; 24; 28(3); 31; 43; 52; 73; 27:10; 18; 19; 20; 35; 43; 47; 58; 28:2; 4; 5; 6; 16; **Mk** 1:4; 16; 22; 27; 36; 37; 38; 44; 2:15; 26; 27(2); 3:9; 10; 21; 35; 4:17(2); 19; 22; 25; 28; 5:8; 9; 19; 20; 25; 28; 42; 6:8; 11(2); 14; 17(3); 18(2); 20; 21; 31; 34; 36; 48; 50; 52; 7:3; 8; 10; 12; 21; 25; 27; 29; 8:3; 19; 20; 33; 35(2); 36; 37; 38; 9:5(4); 6; 31; 34; 39; 40; 41; 42; 43; 45; 47; 49; 10:2; 7; 14; 22; 23; 24; 25(2); 27; 29; 35; 36; 40(2); 45(2); 51; 11:13(2); 17; 18; 23; 32; 12:1; 12; 14; 19; 23; 25; 32; 36; 40; 44; 13:6; 7; 8; 9(4); 11; 13; 19; 20; 22; 33; 35; 14:5(2); 6; 7; 8; 15; 21; 24; 27; 36; 40; 56; 70; 15:8; 10; 24; 35; 43(2); 44; 16:3; 4; 8(2); **Lk** 1:13; 15; 17; 18; 21; 22; 30; 36; 37; 44(2); 45; 48(2); 49(2); 57; 63; 68; 69; 76; 2:6; 7; 10; 11; 20; 21; 25; 27; 30; 34(2); 38; 3:3; 8; 13; 19; 4:2; 6; 8; 10; 32; 36; 41; 43; 5:4; 8; 9; 14; 39; 6:4; 19; 20; 21(2); 22; 23(3); 24; 25(2); 26; 28; 32; 33; 34; 35(2); 38; 43; 44(2); 45; 48; 7:4; 5; 6; 8; 19; 20; 28; 30; 32; 33; 39; 44; 47; 8:3; 13; 17; 18; 25; 27; 29(2); 37; 39(2); 40(2); 42; 43; 46; 52; 9:3; 12; 13; 14; 24(2); 25; 26; 33(4); 38; 44; 48; 50; 51; 52; 53; 56; 62; 10:7; 12(2); 13; 14(2); 21; 24; 11:4; 6; 10; 11(2); 12; 30; 31; 32; 42; 43; 44; 46; 47; 48; 52; 54; 12:2; 6; 12; 15; 19; 21; 24; 26; 30; 32; 34; 36; 40; 46; 48; 52; 13:7; 16; 17; 24; 25; 31; 33; 14:11; 14; 17; 24; 28; 35(2); 15:6; 9; 24; 30; 32; 16:2; 3; 8; 9; 13; 15; 17(2); 24; 28; 17:2; 8; 21; 24; 18:3; 4; 14; 16; 23; 24; 25(3); 29; 32; 41; 19:3; 4; 5; 10; 12; 21; 26; 37; 42; 43; 48; 20:6; 9; 19; 22; 28; 33; 36; 38(2); 47; 21:4(2); 8; 9; 12; 13(2); 15; 17; 22; 23; 26; 30; 35; 22:2; 8; 16; 18; 19; 20; 27; 31; 32; 37(2); 59; 71; 23:8(2); 12; 15; 17(2); 19(2); 22; 25; 28(3); 29; 31; 34; 41; 51; 52; 24:29; 39; 41; 46; **Jn** 1:7; 15; 16; 17; 30; 2:17; 25; 3:2; 16; 17; 20; 24; 34(2); 4:8; 9; 18; 22; 23; 35(2); 36; 37; 38; 42; 44; 45; 47; 5:3; 4; 10; 13; 16; 19; 20; 21; 22; 26; 28; 35; 36; 39; 46(2); 6:6; 7; 27(2); 33; 38; 51; 55; 64; 71; 7:1; 4; 5; 8; 13; 29; 39; 52; 8:14; 16; 20; 24; 29; 42; 44; 9:21; 22; 29; 39; 10:4; 5; 11; 15; 32; 33(2); 11:4; 15; 28; 39; 47; 50(2); 51; 52; 12:5; 6; 7; 8; 9; 18; 25; 27; 30; 43; 47; 49; 13:11; 13; 15; 28; 29(2); 35; 37; 38; 14:2; 3; 8; 11; 17; 28; 30; 15:5; 7; 13; 15(2); 21; 22; 16:7; 13; 14; 21; 26; 27; 17:8; 9(4); 19; 20(2); 24; 18:2; 13; 14; 18; 31; 34; 37(2); 19:6; 20; 24(2); 31; 36; 38; 42; 20:9; 17; 19; 21:7; 8; **Acts** 1:4; 5; 7; 17; 20; 2:15; 25(2); 27; 34; 38; 39; 3:3; 14; 22(2); 4:3; 9; 12; 16; 20; 21; 22; 27; 34; 5:3; 8(2); 26; 34; 36; 38; 40; 41; 6:14; 7:5; 16; 20; 25; 33; 37; 40; 46; 49; 8:3; 7; 11; 15; 16; 21; 23; 24; 33; 9:5; 11(2); 15; 16(2); 21; 10:4; 5; 14; 17; 20; 21; 24; 28; 29(3); 38; 46; 11:8; 13; 24; 25; 26; 12:5; 11; 19; 20; 13:2; 7; 8; 11; 15; 18; 20; 21(2); 22; 23; 27; 28; 31; 33; 36; 41; 47(2); 14:26; 15:14; 21; 26; 28; 33; 16:3; 12; 18; 21; 28; 29; 17:2; 15; 16; 20; 21; 23; 27; 28(2); 18:3; 10(2); 15; 18(2); 28; 19:8; 10; 22; 24; 32; 34; 37; 40(3); 20:5; 10; 13; 16(2); 17; 27; 29; 31; 34(2); 38; 21:3; 13(2); 20; 22; 26; 29; 36; 22:10; 11; 15; 18; 21; 22; 25; 26; 30; 23:3; 5; 8; 11(2); 17; 21(3); 23; 30; 24:5; 10(2); 21; 23; 24; 25(2); 26; 25:8; 11; 15; 16; 21; 27; 26:1(2); 2; 6; 7; 14; 16(2); 21; 26(2); 29; 27:20; 22; 23; 25; 29; 34(2); 40; 28:2; 6; 7; 18; 20(3); 22; 27; **Rom** 1:5(2); 8; 9; 11; 16(5); 17; 18; 19; 20; 25; 26(3); 27; 2:1(2); 5; 7; 11; 12; 13; 14; 24; 25; 28; 3:3; 6; 7; 9; 20; 22; 23; 4:2; 3(2); 5; 9(2); 13; 14; 15; 22; 23; 24; 5:6(2); 7(3); 8; 10; 13; 15; 16; 17; 19; 6:5; 7; 10(2); 14(2); 19(2); 20; 21; 23; 7:1; 2; 5; 7; 8; 11; 14; 15(2); 18(2); 19; 22; 8:2; 3; 5; 6; 7; 13; 14; 15; 18; 19(2); 20; 22; 23; 24(3); 25(2); 26(3); 27; 28; 29; 31; 32; 34; 36(2); 38; 9:3(2); 6; 9; 11; 15; 17(2); 19; 21(2); 22; 23; 28; 32; 10:1; 2(2); 3; 4(2); 5; 10; 11; 12(2); 13; 16; 20; 11:1; 4; 12(2); 13; 15; 16; 21; 23; 24; 25; 27; 28(2); 29; 30; 32; 34; 36; 12:3; 4; 17(2); 19; 20; 13:1; 3; 4(4); 5; 6(2); 8; 9; 11; 14; 14:2; 3; 4; 6; 7; 8; 9; 10(2); 11; 15; 17; 18; 19; 20(2); 23; 15:2; 3; 4(2); 8; 9(2); 18; 22; 24(2); 26(2); 27; 30; 31; 16:2; 4; 6; 18; 19; 26; **1 Cor** 1:4; 7; 11; 13; 17; 18; 19; 21; 22; 26; 30; 2:2; 7; 8; 9; 10; 11; 14; 16; 3:2; 3(2); 4; 9; 11; 13; 17; 19(2); 21; 4:4; 6; 7; 9(2); 10; 15(2); 17; 20; 5:3; 5; 7(2); 12; 6:7; 12(2); 13(5); 16; 20; 7:1; 5; 7; 8; 9; 14; 16; 22; 26; 31; 32; 35(2); 8:5; 6(2); 7; 8; 10; 11; 9:2; 9; 10(2); 11; 15(2); 16(2); 17; 19; 23; 25(2); 10:4; 5; 11; 15; 17(2); 23(2); 25; 26; 27; 28(3); 29; 30; 11:5; 6(2); 7; 8; 9(2); 10; 12; 13; 15(2); 17(2); 18; 19; 21; 23; 24; 26; 29; 30; 31; 33; 34; 12:7; 8; 12; 13; 14; 25; 13:9; 12; 14:2(2); 5; 8(2); 9; 12(2); 14; 17; 21; 22(3); 26; 31; 33; 34; 35(2); 15:3(2); 9; 16; 21; 22; 25; 27; 29(2); 32; 34; 41; 52; 53; 16:1; 5; 7; 9; 10; 11(2); 17; 18; **2 Cor** 1:5; 6(3); 7; 8; 11(2); 12; 13; 19; 20; 24(2); 2:2; 4(2); 6; 9; 10(2); 11; 13; 15; 16; 17; 3:6; 9; 10; 11; 14; 4:5(2); 6; 11(2); 15(2); 17(3); 18; 5:1; 2; 4; 5; 7; 10; 12(2); 13(3); 14(2); 15(4); 20; 21(2); 6:2; 13; 14; 16; 7:3; 5; 7; 8(3); 9; 10; 11; 12(3); 13; 14; 15; 8:3; 7; 9(2); 12; 13; 16; 17; 9:1; 2; 7; 8; 10; 11; 12; 13(2); 14(2); 15; 10:3; 4(2); 8(3); 10; 12; 14(2); 18; 11:2(3); 4; 5; 9; 13; 14; 19; 20; 21; 28; 12:1; 4; 6(2); 9(2); 10(2); 11(2); 13; 14(5); 15; 19; 20; 21; 13:4(2); 8(2); 9; 10(2); **Gal** 1:4; 10(2); 12; 13; 14; 2:5; 6; 7(2); 8(2); 12; 16; 18; 19; 20; 21; 3:6; 10(2); 11; 13(2); 18; 20; 21; 23; 26; 27; 28; 4:11(2); 12; 15; 17(2); 19; 20; 22; 24; 25; 27(2); 30; 5:5(2); 6; 13(2); 14; 17; 6:3; 5; 7; 8; 9; 12; 13; 15; 17; **Eph** 1:15; 16; 2:8; 10(2); 14; 18; 22; 3:1(2); 2; 13; 14; 4:12(3); 16; 25; 29; 30; 5:2(2); 3; 5; 6; 8; 9; 12; 13; 20; 23; 25; 29; 30; 31; 6:1; 12; 18; 19; 20; 22; **Phil** 1:4; 5; 7; 8(2); 12; 17; 19(2); 21; 23; 24; 25; 26; 27; 29(2); 2:4(2); 13(2); 18; 20(2); 21; 26; 27; 30; 3:1(2); 3; 7; 8(2); 12; 14; 17; 18; 20(2); 4:6; 10; 11; 16(2); **Col** 1:3; 4; 5; 9(2); 11; 16(2); 19; 24(2); 25; 2:1(3); 5; 9; 3:3; 20; 24; 25; 4:3(3); 8; 11; 12; 13(2); **1 Th** 1:2; 5(2); 8; 9; 10; 2:1; 3; 5(2); 8; 9(2); 13; 14(2); 17; 19; 20; 3:3; 4; 5; 8; 9(4); 4:2; 3; 7; 9; 14; 15; 16; 5:2; 3; 7; 9; 10; 13; 15(3); 18(2); 25; **2 Th** 1:3; 4; 5; 11; 2:3; 7; 11; 13(2); 14; 3:1; 2; 7(2); 10; 11; 13; **1 Tim** 1:9(7); 10(5); 16(2); 2:1; 2; 3; 5; 6; 7; 10; 13; 3:3; 5; 8; 13(2); 4:4; 5; 8(2); 10; 16; 5:4; 8(2); 10; 11; 15; 18; 23; 6:7; 10(2); 19(2); **2 Tim** 1:7; 8; 12(2); 16; 2:9; 10; 16; 20(2); 21(3); 3:2; 6; 9; 15; 16(4); 17; 4:3(2); 6; 8; 10(4); 11(2); 15; 18; **Titus** 1:5; 7(2); 10; 11; 16; 2:1(2); 11; 13; 14(3); 3:1; 3; 9; 12; **Phm** 1:7; 9; 10; 13; 15(3); 22(2); **Heb** 1:5; 14; 2:2; 5; 8; 9(2); 10(3); 11(2); 16; 17; 18; 3:3; 4; 5; 14; 16; 4:2; 3; 4; 8; 9; 10; 12; 15; 5:1(3); 3(3); 12; 13(2); 6:4(2); 6; 7(2); 10; 13; 16(3); 18(2); 20; 7:1; 10; 11; 12; 13; 14; 17; 18; 19; 21; 25; 26(2); 27(4); 28; 8:3; 4; 5; 7(2); 10; 11; 12; 9:2; 7(2); 9; 12; 13(2); 15(2); 16; 17; 19; 24(2); 27; 28(2); 10:1; 2(2); 4; 5; 6; 8; 10; 12; 14; 15; 18; 20; 23; 26(2); 30; 34(2); 36; 37; 11:1; 2; 5; 6; 7; 10(2); 14; 16(2); 26; 27; 30; 32; 40; 12:2; 3; 6; 7; 10(3); 11; 13; 16; 17(3); 18; 20; 25; 29; 13:2; 5; 9; 11(2); 14; 16; 17(4); 18(2); 22; **Jas** 1:6; 7; 11; 12; 13; 20; 23; 24; 2:2; 10; 11; 13; 16; 23; 26; 3:2; 7; 16; 4:1; 14(2); 5:1; 7(2); 8; 14; 16; 17; **1 Pe** 1:2; 4; 5; 6; 16; 20; 2:13; 14(2); 15; 16; 19; 20(2); 21(2); 24; 25; 3:5; 8; 9(2); 10; 12; 14; 15; 17(3); 18(3); 4:1(2); 2(2); 3; 6; 8(2); 14(2); 17(2); 5:2; 5; 7(2); **2 Pe** 1:5; 8; 9; 10; 11; 12; 16; 17; 21; 2:3; 4(2); 8; 9; 16; 17; 18; 19; 20(2); 21(2); 3:4; 5; 7; 12; 13; **1 Jn** 2:2(3); 10; 12; 16; 19; 3:2; 8(2); 9; 11; 16(2); 20; 4:7; 8; 10; 16; 20; 5:3; 4; 7; 9; 16; **2 Jn** 7; 8; 11; **3 Jn** 3; 5(2); 7; 8; **Jude** 3(2); 4(2); 6; 11(2); 13; 21; **Rev** 1:3; 9(2); 2:3; 19; 3:2; 4; 8; 4:11; 5:9; 6:6(2); 9(2); 17; 7:17; 8:1; 9:5; 7; 15; 19(2); 11:2(2); 12:8; 10; 12; 14; 13:5; 18; 14:4; 5; 7; 15(3); 18; 20; 15:1; 4(3); 16:6(2); 14; 17:12; 14; 17; 18:2(2); 3; 5; 6; 7; 8; 9; 10(2); 11; 14; 15; 17; 19; 20; 23(2); 19:2; 6; 7; 8; 10; 17; 20:2; 3; 4(3); 11; 21:1; 2; 4; 5; 22; 23; 22:2; 5; 9; 10; 18

FROM (5170/4336)

Gen 1:4; 6; 7; 14; 18; 2:2; 3; 6; 10; 22; 3:8; 11; 17; 23; 4:1; 10; 11(2); 14(2); 16; 6:7; 16; 17; 7:4; 23; 8:2; 3; 7; 8(2); 10; 11; 13; 21; 9:5(3); 19; 24; 10:5; 11; 14; 19; 30; 32; 11:2; 6; 8; 9; 31; 12:1(2); 4; 8; 13:1; 3; 9; 11; 14(2); 14:17; 23; 15:4; 18; 16:2; 6; 8(2); 17:6; 12; 14; 16; 22; 27; 18:2; 16; 17; 22; 25(2); 19:4; 24; 20:1; 6; 13; 21:16; 21; 30; 22:11; 12; 23:3; 6; 13; 24:3; 5; 7(3); 8; 17; 37; 40(2); 41(2); 43; 46; 50; 62; 64; 25:6; 10; 18; 23; 29; 26:16; 17; 22; 23; 26; 27; 31; 27:9(2); 30(2); 39; 40; 45(2); 28:1; 2; 6(2); 10; 16; 29:3; 4(2); 8; 10; 30:2; 32; 31:1; 16; 27; 31; 39; 40; 49; 32:11(2); 33:10; 18; 19; 34:7; 26; 35:1; 7; 9; 11(2); 13; 16; 36:2; 6; 18; 37:17; 25; 38:1; 17; 20; 39:1; 5; 9; 40:15; 19(2); 41:46; 42:7(2); 24(2); 26; 43:2; 9; 34; 44:5; 7; 8(2); 17; 28; 29; 45:1; 46:5; 26; 34; 47:1; 2; 10; 18; 21; 48:7; 12; 16; 17; 22; 49:9; 10(2); 20; 24; 26; 32; 50:13; 25(2); **Ex** 2:7; 15; 19; 3:2; 4; 8; 4:3; 9(2); 5:4; 5; 19; 20; 6:6(2); 7; 26; 27; 7:5; 8:8(2); 9; 11(4); 12; 29(4); 30; 31(3); 9:8; 10; 15; 33; 10:5; 6; 11; 17; 18; 23; 28; 11:1; 2(2); 5; 8; 12:5(2); 15(3); 19; 29; 31; 35; 37; 41; 13:8; 10; 12; 19; 20; 22; 14:5; 19; 25; 15:22; 16:1(2); 4; 17:1; 14; 16; 18:4; 10; 13; 14; 21; 19:2; 3; 14; 20:22; 21:14; 35; 22:5; 12; 14; 23:5; 7; 13; 16; 25; 28; 29; 30; 31(2); 24:1; 25:2; 3; 15; 22(2); 35; 26:28; 33; 35; 27:21; 28:1; 28; 42; 29:23; 25; 27; 28(3); 30:14; 19; 25; 33; 38; 31:14; 32:1; 4; 12(3); 14; 15; 27; 33:1; 7; 11; 15; 16; 34:11; 18; 29(2); 35:5; 20; 36:3; 4; 6; 33; 37:21; 38:4; 8; 25; 26; 27(2); 28; 39:21; 40:24; 31; 36; **Lev** 1:1; 2:2; 9; 13; 14; 3:3; 9; 14; 4:8; 10; 13; 19; 31; 35; 5:6; 8; 15; 18; 6:2; 6; 15; 22; 30; 7:3; 14(2); 20; 21; 25; 27; 29; 32; 34(3); 35; 8:26; 28; 9:10; 19; 22; 24; 10:2; 4; 7; 14; 11:34; 12:7; 13:12; 28(2); 40; 41; 58; 14:7; 19; 15:2; 19; 31; 16:5; 12; 19; 30; 17:4; 9; 10; 18:29; 19:8; 20:3; 4; 5; 6; 18; 24; 25; 26; 21:7; 22:2; 3; 19(3); 21; 25; 27; 23:15(2); 17; 22; 29; 30; 32; 24:3; 8; 9; 22; 25:12; 14; 15; 33; 36; 41; 44(2); 50; 51; 26:36; 27:3; 5; 6; 7; 17; 18; 24; **Num** 1:3; 4; 5; 6; 7; 8; 9; 10(3); 11; 12; 13; 14; 15; 16; 18; 20; 22(2); 24(2); 26(2); 28(2); 30(2); 32(2); 34(2); 36(2); 38(2); 40(2); 42(2); 45; 2:2; 3:9; 12; 15; 21; 22; 27; 28; 33; 34; 39; 40; 43; 49; 50; 4:2; 3; 13; 18; 23; 30; 35; 39; 43; 47; 5:13; 19; 25; 31; 6:3(3); 4; 18; 19; 7:5; 12; 84; 89(2); 8:4; 6; 11; 14; 16; 19; 24; 9:7; 13; 15; 17; 21; 10:9; 11; 12; 33; 34; 11:31(2); 35; 12:10; 16; 13:2; 3; 4; 5; 6; 7; 8; 9; 10; 11(2); 12; 13; 14; 15; 21; 25; 33; 14:9; 13; 19; 29; 43; 44; 15:3; 23; 30; 16:9; 15; 21; 24; 26; 27; 33; 35; 45; 46(2); 17:2(2); 9; 10; 18:6; 9; 26(2); 28(3); 29; 19:9; 13; 17; 20; 20:6; 9; 14; 17; 21; 22; 28; 21:4; 7; 11; 12; 13(2); 16; 18; 19(2); 20; 22; 24; 26; 28(2); 22:1; 5; 16; 33(2); 41; 23:7(2); 9(2); 13(2); 27; 24:7; 11; 24; 25:4; 7; 11; 26:2; 3; 4; 62; 63; 27:1; 4; 30:6; 12; 14; 31:4; 5(2); 6; 12; 14; 29; 30(3); 32; 42(2); 47(2); 51; 52; 54; 32:7; 8; 11(2); 15; 21; 33:3; 5; 6; 7; 8; 9; 10; 11; 12; 13; 14; 15; 16; 17; 18; 19; 20; 21; 22; 23; 24; 25; 26; 27; 28; 29; 30; 31; 32; 33; 34; 35; 36; 37; 41; 42; 43; 44; 45; 46; 47; 48(2); 49; 50; 52; 55; 34:3; 4; 5; 7; 8; 10; 11; 15; 19; 20; 21; 22; 23(2); 24; 25; 26; 27; 28; 35:1; 2; 4; 8(3); 12; 25; 36:3(2); 4; 7; 9; 13; **Deut** 1:2; 13; 19; 23; 44; 2:6(2); 8(2); 12; 14(2); 15; 16; 22; 23; 26; 36(2); 3:4; 8(2); 12; 16; 17; 4:2; 3; 9; 26; 29; 32; 34; 38; 48; 5:4; 15; 22; 23; 24; 26; 6:12; 15; 19; 23; 7:4; 8(2); 15; 20; 24; 8:3; 14; 9:4; 5; 7(2); 10; 12(2); 14; 15; 16; 21; 23; 24; 28; 10:4; 5; 6; 7(2); 11:10; 11; 12; 17; 23; 24(2); 28; 12:3; 10; 21(3); 29; 30; 32; 13:5(4); 7(2); 10(2); 13; 17; 14:24; 15:7; 11; 12; 13; 14(4); 16; 18; 19; 16:2; 9; 10; 13(2); 17:7; 11; 12; 15; 18; 20; 18:3(2); 6(2); 8; 12; 15(2); 18; 19:5; 12; 13; 19; 20:1; 15; 21:2; 9; 21; 22:1; 4; 8; 21; 22; 24; 23:4; 9; 14; 15; 22; 23; 24:2; 7; 18; 25:9; 11; 19(2); 26:2; 13; 15(2); 28:14; 21; 24; 27; 31; 35; 49(2); 57; 63; 64; 29:11; 18; 20; 21; 22; 28; 30:3(2); 4(2); 31:3; 17; 29; 32:13(2); 14; 20; 26; 39; 42; 49; 33:2(4); 16; 22; 27; 34:1(2); **Josh** 1:4; 7; 8; 2:1; 2; 4; 13; 20; 23; 3:1; 3; 10; 12(2); 13; 14; 16; 4:2(2); 3(2); 4(2); 8; 16; 17; 18; 19; 5:1; 9; 6:18; 22; 7:2; 4; 5; 9; 12; 13; 19; 23; 26; 8:4; 6; 7; 16; 29; 9:6; 8; 9; 12; 22; 23; 24; 10:7; 9; 11(2); 22; 23; 27; 29; 31; 34; 36; 41; 11:2; 17; 21(6); 23; 12:1; 2(2); 3; 7; 13:3; 4; 5; 6(2); 9; 16; 26(2); 30; 14:7; 15; 15:2; 4; 7; 9; 10; 14; 15; 18; 46; 16:1(2); 2; 7; 8; 17:7; 18:4; 13; 14; 17; 19:12; 13; 33; 34(2); 20:3; 6; 8(3); 21:3; 4(3); 5(3); 6(4); 7(3); 9(2); 16; 17; 20; 23; 25; 27; 28; 30; 32; 34; 36; 38; 22:9; 14; 16; 17; 18; 23; 29(2); 32(2); 23:1; 4; 5; 6; 9; 13(2); 15; 16; 24:3; 8; 12; 16; 17; 18; 32; **Judg** 1:11; 14; 16; 20; 36(2); 2:1(2); 12; 17; 19(2); 3:3; 19(2); 20(2); 21; 27; 4:6; 11; 13; 14; 15; 5:4(2); 11; 14(3); 20(2); 6:8; 11; 13; 14; 18; 19; 27; 7:3; 5; 23; 24; 8:8; 13(2); 22; 24; 25; 34; 9:4; 20(3); 27; 35; 36; 37(2); 40; 48; 10:8; 11(4); 12; 16; 11:3; 5; 7; 13; 16; 22(2); 23; 29; 31; 33; 12:9; 13:2; 5; 6; 7; 14; 20; 23; 14:3; 15:13; 14; 17; 16:14(2); 17; 20(2); 25; 17:1; 2; 3; 7; 8; 9(2); 18:2(2); 7; 11(2); 13; 22; 28; 19:1; 2; 16(2); 17; 18(2); 30(2); 20:1(2); 13; 14; 15; 25; 31; 32; 33(2); 34; 38; 40; 48; 21:6; 8(2); 17; 18; 19; 21(2); 23; 24(2); **Ruth** 1:6; 7; 13; 16; 22; 2:4; 6; 7; 8; 9; 16; 4:3; 5(2); 9; 10(2); 12; **1 Sam** 1:3; 14; 20; 2:3; 8(2); 10; 15; 20; 23; 30; 33; 3:12; 17(2); 18; 20; 4:3(2); 4; 8; 12; 16(2); 21; 22; 5:1; 6:3; 5(3); 7; 20; 7:3(2); 8; 14(3); 16; 9:2; 16(2); 25; 10:2; 3; 4; 5; 9; 12; 18(3); 19; 23(2); 11:5; 12:2; 3; 4; 6; 10; 20; 23; 13:8; 11; 15; 14:6; 17; 21; 31; 46; 48; 15:2; 6(2); 7; 11; 15; 23; 26; 28; 16:1; 13; 14(2); 15; 16; 23(2); 17:4(2); 15; 23; 24; 25; 26; 30; 33; 35; 37(3); 40; 46; 53; 57; 18:6; 9; 10; 12; 13; 19:8; 9; 10; 20:1; 2; 9; 15(2); 34; 41; 21:4; 5; 6; 10; 22:1; 3; 15; 23:13(2); 26; 28; 29; 24:1; 2; 7; 13; 21; 25:7; 10; 11; 14; 23; 26(2); 29; 33(2); 34; 35; 37; 39(2); 44; 26:12; 19; 27:8; 28:9; 15; 16; 23; 24; 30:2; 13(2); 16(2); 17; 19; 25; 26; 31:1; 12; **2 Sam** 1:1; 2; 3(2); 4; 13; 22(2); 2:12; 15(2); 19; 21; 22; 26; 30; 3:10(2); 15(2); 18; 22; 26(2); 4:4; 9; 11; 5:9; 13(2); 25; 6:2(2); 12; 7:1; 6; 7; 8(2); 9; 11; 12; 15(3); 23; 8:1; 4; 8(2); 11; 12(6); 13; 9:5; 10:6(2); 14; 11:2(2); 4; 8(2); 10; 15; 20; 21; 24; 12:3; 4(2); 7; 10; 11; 17; 20; 30; 13:5; 6; 9(2); 10; 13; 17; 32; 34; 14:2; 14; 16(2); 18; 19; 25; 32; 15:2(2); 11; 12(2); 14; 18; 19; 24; 28; 35; 16:5(2); 11; 17:11; 27(3); 18:13; 16; 19:7; 9(3); 16; 24; 31; 20:2; 12; 13; 16; 20; 21(2); 22; 21:4(2); 5; 10(2); 12(2); 13; 22:1(2); 3; 4; 7; 9(2); 13; 14; 17; 18(2); 22; 23; 24; 44; 46; 49(2); 23:11; 15; 16; 17; 20; 29; 30; 24:2; 4; 15(2); 16; 21(2); 24; 25; **1 Ki** 1:29; 39; 45; 53; 2:7; 8; 15; 27; 31(2); 33; 36; 40; 41; 3:20; 4:12; 21; 23; 24; 25; 33; 34; 5:6; 9; 16; 6:3; 8; 15; 16; 24; 7:7; 9; 13; 14; 23; 8:1; 8(2); 16; 19; 35; 41; 53; 54(2); 65; 9:6; 7; 12; 21; 24; 28; 10:11(2); 15(4); 28; 29; 11:2; 9; 11; 18(2); 23; 26; 12:2; 15; 24; 25; 28; 31; 13:1; 4; 5; 12; 14; 21; 26; 33(2); 34; 14:7; 8; 10; 15; 15:5; 12; 13; 19; 16:17; 24; 17:3; 4; 6; 13; 23; 18:10; 12(2); 26; 19:19; 21; 20:24; 33; 34; 36; 41; 21:21; 22:24(2); 33; 35; 43; 46; **2 Ki** 1:2; 4; 6; 10(2); 12(2); 14; 16; 2:1; 3; 5; 9; 10; 13; 14; 15; 21; 23(2); 25(2); 3:3; 27; 4:3(2); 5; 27; 39; 42; 5:2; 4; 15; 19; 20(2); 21; 22; 24; 26; 27; 6:2; 27(2); 33; 7:8(2); 13; 8:3; 6; 8; 9; 14; 29; 9:2; 8; 15(2); 10:15; 21; 28; 29(2); 31; 33(2); 11:2(2); 4; 11; 19; 12:5; 7; 8; 13; 15; 16(2); 18; 13:2; 5; 6; 11; 17; 20; 23; 25; 14:13; 24; 25(2); 27; 28; 15:9; 14; 16; 18; 20(3); 24; 28; 16:3; 6; 7(2); 11(2); 12; 14(2); 17(2); 18; 17:7; 8; 9; 13; 18; 20; 21(2); 22; 23; 24(2); 27; 28; 32; 33; 36; 39; 18:6; 8; 14; 16(2); 17(2); 29; 31(2); 33; 34; 35(2); 19:8; 14; 19; 25; 29; 31; 20:6; 9; 14(3); 18; 21:8; 16; 22:4; 23:6; 8(2); 17; 18; 26; 27; 30; 35(2); 24:3; 7; 13; 15; 20; 25:5; 21; 27; 29; **1 Chr** 1:12; 2:23; 53; 55; 4:10; 5:2; 23; 6:60; 61; 62(4);

63(3); 65(3); 66; 70; 71; 72; 74; 76; 77; 78(2); 80; 9:19; 25; 33; 10:1; 11:8; 13; 17; 18; 19; 22; 12:1; 14; 19; 20; 28; 37; 40; 13:5(2); 6; 7; 14:16; 15:25; 16:20(2); 23; 35; 36; 17:5(2); 7(2); 8; 13(2); 21(2); 18:1; 4; 8(2); 11(6); 19:6(3); 7; 20:2; 21:2; 21; 22; 26; 22:4; 9; 23:3; 24; 27; 24:5(2); 29:12; 14; 16; **2 Chr** 1:4; 13(2); 16; 17; 2:8; 16; 3:6; 4:2; 5:2; 9(2); 6:5; 9; 21; 23; 25; 26; 30; 32; 33; 35; 39; 7:1; 8; 14(2); 20; 8:8; 11; 15; 16; 18; 9:10; 26; 28(2); 10:2(2); 15; 11:1; 4(2); 13; 14; 16; 12:8; 12; 13:19; 14:5; 8(2); 15:8(2); 9(2); 11; 16; 17; 16:2; 3; 7; 9; 17:6; 18:23(2); 31; 32; 19:3; 4; 10; 20:2(2); 4(2); 10; 32; 21:12; 22:6; 11(2); 23:2; 10; 20; 24:5(2); 6(2); 14; 23; 25; 25:5; 6; 10; 12; 13; 14; 15; 20; 23; 26; 27; 26:18; 21; 22; 28:8; 11; 12; 15; 21(3); 26; 29:5; 6; 10; 30:5; 6(2); 8; 9; 10; 11; 16; 18; 25(2); 31:1; 10; 16; 17; 32:3; 11; 14(2); 15(2); 17(2); 22(2); 31; 33:8; 15; 34:9(3); 33(2); 35:7(2); 8; 9; 21; 22(2); 27; 36:7; 10; 12; 18; 20; **Ezra** 1:7; 11; 2:1; 59; 62; 3:6; 7(2); 8; 13; 4:9; 11; 12; 14; 5:14(2); 16; 6:4; 5; 6; 8; 11; 21(2); 7:6; 9; 20; 8:1; 21; 31(3); 35; 9:1; 5; 8; 11; 10:1; 2; 6(2); 8(2); 11(2); 14; **Neh** 1:2; 3; 9; 3:15; 20; 21; 24; 25; 4:2; 5; 12; 16; 19; 21; 5:7; 12(2); 13(2); 14(2); 15; 17; 7:3; 6; 61; 64; 8:3(2); 8; 17; 18(2); 9:2; 3; 13; 15; 19; 20; 27(2); 28; 32; 35; 10:28; 31; 32; 37; 11:30; 31; 12:9; 24; 28(2); 29(2); 44; 13:1; 3; 6; 21; 28; **Esth** 1:1; 5; 7; 19; 2:6; 9; 13; 3:8; 10; 4:4; 14; 5:1; 7:7; 8; 8:2; 9; 10; 15; 9:16; 22(3); **Job** 1:7(3); 12; 16; 19; 21; 2:2(3); 7(2); 10; 11; 12; 3:10; 11; 17; 19; 4:2; 13; 20; 5:4; 5; 6(2); 15(3); 20(2); 21; 6:13; 17; 22; 23(2); 7:19; 8:10; 18; 9:34; 10:7; 19; 21; 11:6; 13:20; 21; 14:6; 11; 12; 18; 15:18; 20; 22; 30; 16:16; 17:4; 18:4; 14; 17; 18; 19:9; 13(2); 20:18; 24; 29; 21:9; 14; 16; 22:6; 7; 17; 18; 22; 23; 23:7; 12; 17(2); 24:1; 9(2); 10; 26:4; 27:5(2); 13; 22; 28:2(2); 4(2); 5; 11; 20; 21(2); 28; 29:9; 17; 30:3; 5; 8; 10; 30; 31:2(2); 7; 16; 18(2); 22(2); 23; 33:3; 17(2); 18(2); 21; 24; 28; 30; 34:10(2); 27; 35:7; 36:3; 7; 10; 19; 25; 27; 29; 37:1; 2; 9(2); 22; 38:8; 15; 29; 39:22; 25; 29(2); 41:20; 42:2; **Ps** 2:3; 3:4; 6:8; 7:1; 9:13(2); 12:1; 7; 13:1; 14:2; 16:2; 17:1; 2; 4; 7; 9(2); 13; 14(2); 18(2); 3; 6; 8(2); 12; 13; 16; 17(2); 21; 22; 23; 43; 45; 48(2); 19:6(2); 12; 13; 20:2; 6; 21:4; 10(2); 22:1(2); 10(2); 11; 19; 20(2); 21(2); 24; 24:5(2); 25:6; 27:9; 30:3; 31:11; 15(2); 20(2); 22; 32:7; 33:1; 13; 14; 19; 34:4; 13(2); 14; 16; 35:10(2); 17(2); 22; 36:8; 37:8; 27; 39; 40; 38:9; 10; 11; 21; 39:2; 8; 10; 13; 40:10; 11; 41:13; 42:6(3); 43:1; 44:7; 10; 18; 45:9; 49:14; 15; 50:1; 4; 9; 51:2(2); 9; 11(2); 14; 52:5; 53:2; 55:1; 8; 11; 12; 18; 19; 56:13(2); 57:3; 58:3; 59:1(2); 2(2); 60:11; 61:2; 3; 62:1; 4; 5; 64:1; 2(2); 66:20; 68:10; 18; 20; 22(2); 23; 26; 69:5; 14; 17; 71:5; 6; 12; 17; 20; 72:8(2); 14; 73:27; 74:12; 75:6(3); 76:8; 78:4; 42; 50; 65; 70; 71; 80:14; 18; 81:6(2); 16; 82:4; 83:4; 84:7; 11; 85:3; 11; 86:13; 88:5; 8; 14; 15; 18; 89:19; 33; 48; 90:2; 91:3(2); 93:2(2); 94:13; 96:2; 101:4; 8; 102:2; 19(2); 103:4; 12(2); 17; 104:13; 14; 21; 35; 105:13(2); 106:10(2); 47; 48; 107:2; 3(4); 20; 41; 108:12; 109:10; 15; 17; 24; 31; 110:3; 113:2; 3; 114:1; 115:18; 116:8(3); 118:26; 119:10; 18; 19; 21; 22; 28; 29; 37; 51; 82; 101; 102; 110; 115; 118; 123; 134; 136; 150; 155; 157; 120:2(2); 121:1; 2; 7; 8; 124:7; 125:2; 127:3; 129:1; 2; 130:8; 131:3; 132:11; 134:3; 135:7; 136:11; 24; 138:6; 139:7(2); 12; 15; 19; 140:1(2); 4(2); 141:9(2); 142:6; 143:7; 9; 144:7(2); 10; 11; 148:1; 7; **Prov** 1:15; 2:6; 12(2); 13; 16(2); 22(2); 3:7; 21; 25; 26; 27; 4:5; 15; 21; 24(2); 27; 5:7; 8; 15(2); 6:5(2); 9; 24(2); 7:5(2); 8:6; 23(2); 35; 9:3; 10:2; 11:4; 8; 12:2; 13:14; 19; 14:7; 14; 16; 27; 15:24; 29; 16:1; 6; 17; 33; 17:13; 18:20(2); 22; 19:4; 7; 14(2); 27; 20:9; 21:16; 23; 22:5; 6; 15; 27; 23:13; 14; 24:18; 25:4; 5; 25; 27:8(2); 22; 28:9; 29:21; 26; 30:8; 12; 14(2); 30; 31:14; 16; **Eccl** 1:3; 7; 2:6; 10(3); 24; 3:5; 9; 11; 14; 20; 5:9; 15(2); 7:18; 23; 26; 8:3; 8; 10; 10:5; 11:10(2); **Song** 4:1; 2; 8(6); 15; 5:7; 6:5(2); 6; 8:5; **Isa** 1:6; 12; 15; 16; 2:3; 10; 19; 21; 22; 3:1(2); 4:4; 6(2); 5:23; 26(2); 6:6; 7:3; 11; 17; 20; 22; 8:9; 17; 18; 9:5; 7; 14; 10:2; 3; 27(2); 11:1; 11(4); 12; 16(2); 12:3; 13:5(2); 6; 9; 20; 14:3(2); 9(2); 12; 22; 25(2); 31; 15:9; 16:1; 4; 10; 17:1; 3(2); 18:2; 4; 7(3); 19:5; 23; 20:2; 6; 21:1(2); 10; 15(4); 22:3; 4; 19; 24; 23:1; 7; 24:14; 16; 18(3); 25:4(2); 8(2); 27:12; 28:9(2); 22; 29; 29:13; 15; 30:6; 11(2); 14(2); 27; 31:8; 32:2(2); 15; 33:15(2); 34:1; 3; 4(2); 10; 16; 17; 36:2(2); 16(2); 18; 19; 20(2); 37:8; 14; 20; 26; 30; 32; 38:6; 7; 9; 12(3); 13; 14; 17; 39:3(3); 7; 40:2; 21(2); 27; 41:2; 4; 9(2); 25(2); 26; 42:5; 7(2); 10; 11; 43:5(2); 6(2); 44:2; 8; 24; 45:6; 8; 20; 21(2); 46:3(2); 7; 10(2); 11(2); 12; 47:11; 12; 13; 14; 15; 48:1; 3(2); 5; 6; 7; 8(2); 9; 16(2); 19; 20(2); 21; 49:1(3); 5; 12(3); 17; 24; 50:6; 11; 51:1(2); 4; 8; 52:2(2); 11(2); 53:3; 8(3); 54:8; 10; 14(2); 17; 55:10; 11; 56:2(2); 3; 6; 11; 57:1; 11; 58:7; 9; 12; 13(2); 59:2(2); 5; 9; 11; 13(2); 15; 19(2); 20; 21(4); 60:4; 6; 9; 63:1(2); 3; 15(2); 16; 17(2); 64:7; 65:9(2); 16; 20; 66:6(2); 23(2); **Jer** 1:13; 2:5; 25(2); 35; 37; 3:1; 4; 14(2); 19; 20; 23(2); 24; 25; 4:6; 7(2); 8; 14; 15(2); 16; 28; 29; 5:6(2); 15; 25; 6:1; 8; 13(2); 20(2); 22(2); 7:1; 28; 34(2); 8:10(2); 13; 16; 19; 9:2; 3; 19; 10:3; 9(2); 11(2); 13; 17; 20; 11:1; 4; 15; 19; 12:2; 12; 14; 13:6; 7; 20; 25; 14:18; 15:7; 19; 21(2); 16:5; 9; 14; 15(2); 16; 17(2); 19; 17:5; 8; 12; 13; 16; 26(6); 18:1; 8; 11; 14; 15; 18(3); 20; 22; 23; 19:14; 20:13; 17; 18; 21:1; 2; 7; 22:11; 20; 21; 23:7; 8(2); 14; 15; 16; 22(2); 30; 24:1; 5; 10; 25:3; 10; 15; 17; 28; 30(2); 32(2); 33; 26:1; 3; 10; 23; 27:1; 10; 16; 20; 28:1; 3; 6; 11; 12; 16; 29:1(2); 2; 4; 14(4); 20; 30:1; 3; 8; 10(2); 21(2); 31:8(2); 11; 16(3); 34; 36(2); 38; 32:1; 4; 9; 30; 31(2); 40(2); 33:5; 8; 34:1; 3; 8; 12; 14; 21; 35:1; 15; 36:1; 2(2); 3; 6(2); 7; 8; 9; 10; 11; 14; 16; 21; 29; 37:5(2); 9; 17; 21; 38:9; 10; 11; 14; 18; 23; 25; 39:14; 40:1(3); 4; 41:5(3); 6; 14; 15; 16(3); 42:1; 4; 8; 11; 17; 43:5; 12; 44:5; 7; 12; 28; 46:16; 20; 27(2); 47:4; 48:3; 10; 11(2); 15; 18; 33(3); 34(2); 44; 45; 49:5; 7; 14; 16; 19(2); 32; 36; 38; 50:6; 8; 9(2); 16; 26; 28; 39; 41(2); 44(2); 51:6; 16; 25; 26; 45; 48; 53; 54(2); 64; 52:3; 8; 27; 29; 33; **Lam** 1:6; 13; 16; 2:1; 3; 8; 9; 19; 3:17; 18; 38; 50; 55; 56(2); 66; 5:8; 14; 16; 19; **Ezek** 1:5; 19; 21; 25; 27(2); 3:12; 17(2); 18; 19(2); 20; 4:8; 10; 11; 14; 5:4; 6:9; 7:20; 22; 26(3); 8:2(2); 6; 9:2; 3; 10:2; 4; 6(2); 7; 16(2); 18; 19; 11:15; 17(2); 18; 23; 24; 12:3; 16(3); 27; 13:20; 22; 14:5; 6(2); 7; 8; 9; 11; 13; 17; 19; 21; 15:3(2); 5; 7; 16:3; 17; 33; 37; 42; 17:3; 7; 22; 18:8; 17; 21; 23; 24; 26; 27; 28; 30; 31; 19:8; 14; 20:17; 34; 38; 41; 47; 21:3; 4(2); 19; 22:5; 12; 15; 18; 26; 23:8; 17; 18(2); 22(2); 27; 28; 40; 42; 48; 24:6; 12; 16; 25; 25:7(2); 13(2); 26:4; 7; 16; 20; 27:5(2); 6(2); 7(2); 10; 14; 28:3; 15; 16; 18; 24; 25; 29:8; 10; 13; 18; 30:6; 9; 13(2); 31:12; 32:13; 33:2; 6; 7; 8; 9(2); 11(2); 12; 14; 18; 19; 21; 30; 34:10; 12; 13(2); 25; 27; 35:7; 36:24; 25(2); 29; 33; 37:9; 12; 13; 21(2); 23; 38:6; 8(2); 12; 15; 39:2; 10(2); 17; 22; 23; 24; 27; 29; 40:13; 15; 19; 23; 27; 46; 41:7(2); 16; 17; 20; 42:5(2); 6; 9; 20; 43:2; 6; 9; 14(2); 15; 23; 25; 44:5; 10(2); 15; 30; 45:7; 13(2); 14; 15(2); 46:2; 18(3); 47:1(2); 10; 12; 15; 17; 18; 19; 20; 48:1(2); 2; 3; 4; 5; 6; 7; 8(2); 19; 22; 23; 24; 25; 26; 27; 28; 35; **Dan** 1:6; 2:6; 15; 18; 35; 3:15; 17(2); 26; 4:3; 12; 13; 14(2); 16; 23; 25; 31(2); 32; 33; 34; 5:2(2); 3(2); 13(2); 20(2); 21; 23; 24; 6:13; 18; 20; 27; 7:3(2); 4; 7; 10; 19; 23; 24(2); 8:4; 5; 7; 9:5; 13; 16; 25; 10:12; 11:7; 22; 30; 41; 44; 12:11; **Hos** 1:2; 2:2(2); 10; 15(2); 17; 18; 4:6; 12; 5:3; 6; 7:13; 8:4; 6; 9:12; 15; 10:5; 9; 11:2; 4; 7; 10; 11(2); 12:4; 13:3(2); 9; 14(3); 15; 14:4; **Joel** 1:5; 9; 12; 13; 15; 16; 2:13; 16(2); 20; 3:6; 16(2); 18; 20; **Am** 1:2(2); 5(2); 8(2); 2:3; 10; 14; 3:1; 5; 11; 12; 4:7(2); 11; 5:11(2); 12; 19; 23; 6:2; 4(2); 6; 14; 7:11; 17; 8:12(2); 13; 9:1(2); 2(2); 3(3); 4; 7(3); 8; 14(2); 15; **Ob** 1; 4; 8(2); 9; **Jon** 1:3(2); 8; 10; 15; 2:1; 6; 3:5; 6; 8(2); 9; 10(2); 4:2; 3; 6; **Mic** 1:2; 7; 11; 12; 16; 2:3; 4; 8(2); 9(2); 3:2(2); 3; 4; 7; 4:2; 7; 10(2); 5:2(2); 6; 7; 10; 12; 13; 14; 6:4(2); 5; 7:2; 5; 12(3); 17; 20; **Nah** 1:11; 13; 2:13; 3:7; 11; **Hab** 1:7; 8; 12; 2:9; 11(2); 3:3(2); 4; 13(2); 17; **Zeph** 1:2; 3; 4; 6; 10(3); 2:11; 3:10; 11; **Hag** 2:15(2); 16; 18(3); 19; **Zech** 1:4; 2:6; 13; 3:2; 4(2); 4:12; 6:1; 5; 10(3); 12; 15; 7:12; 8:7(2); 10; 23; 9:5; 7(2); 10(4); 11; 14; 10:4(4); 10(2); 11:6; 13:2(2); 5; 14:2; 4; 5; 8; 10(3); 13; 16; **Mal** 1:10; 11; 13; 2:6; 7; 8; 12; 13; 3:7(2); **Mt** 1:17(3); 21; 24; 2:1; 7; 16(2); 3:7; 9; 13; 16; 17; 4:4; 17; 21; 25(2); 5:18; 29; 30; 37; 42(2); 6:1; 2; 13; 7:4; 5(2); 16(2); 23; 8:1; 11; 30; 34; 9:9; 15; 16; 20; 22; 27; 10:14(2); 29; 11:1; 12; 25; 29; 12:9; 15; 38; 42; 44; 13:12; 35; 49; 53; 14:2; 13(2); 15:1; 5; 8; 18; 21; 22; 27; 28; 29; 16:1; 21(2); 22; 17:9(2); 18; 20; 25(3); 26; 18:8; 9; 35; 19:1; 8; 12; 15; 20; 20:20; 21:8; 11; 25(4); 26; 43; 22:46; 23:34; 35; 24:1; 27; 29; 31(2); 32; 25:28; 29; 32(2); 34; 41; 26:16; 27; 29; 39; 42; 47; 27:40; 42; 45; 51; 55(2); 57; 64; 28:2(2); 7; 8; **Mk** 1:5; 9; 10; 11; 19; 45; 2:20; 21; 3:7(2); 8; 22; 4:25; 5:6; 17; 26; 35; 6:1; 10; 11; 14; 16; 33; 7:1; 4; 6; 11; 15; 17; 18; 21; 23; 24; 28; 31; 33; 8:3; 11(2); 9:9(2); 10; 21; 30; 10:1; 6; 20; 11:8; 12; 13; 14; 20; 30(2); 31; 32; 12:2; 25; 34; 13:27(2); 28; 14:23; 35; 36; 43; 52; 15:30; 32; 38; 40; 45; 16:3; 8; **Lk** 1:2; 3; 15; 38; 45; 50; 52; 71(2); 74; 78; 2:1; 4; 15; 36; 37; 3:7; 8; 22; 4:1; 9; 13; 38; 42; 5:2; 3(2); 8; 10; 35; 36; 6:13; 17(2); 19; 29; 30; 34; 42; 44(2); 7:6; 12; 8:3; 4; 18; 27; 35; 37; 38; 44; 46; 49; 9:4; 5; 7; 33; 37; 38; 39; 45; 54; 10:7; 18; 21; 30; 42; 11:4; 7; 11; 16(2); 22; 24; 27; 31; 50; 51; 12:13; 36; 48; 52; 59; 13:12; 15; 16; 25; 27(2); 29(2); 31; 16:3; 18; 21; 26(2); 30; 31; 17:7; 29; 18:3; 21; 34; 19:8; 24; 26(2); 39; 42; 20:4(2); 5; 6; 7; 35; 21:11; 26; 22:41; 42; 43; 45(2); 71; 23:5; 26; 49; 51; 55; 24:2; 9; 13; 31; 46; 49; 51; **Jn** 1:6; 19; 24; 32; 44; 2:9; 22; 3:2; 8; 13; 27; 31(2); 4:6; 9; 12; 43; 5:24; 34; 41; 44(2); 6:23; 31; 32(2); 33; 38; 41; 42; 45; 46; 50; 51; 58; 64; 66; 7:3; 17; 18; 22(2); 25; 27(2); 28; 29; 40; 42(2); 52; 8:14(2); 23(2); 25; 26; 40; 42; 44(2); 9:1; 16; 29; 30; 33; 10:5; 18(2); 32; 11:37; 41; 53; 54; 55; 12:1; 9; 17; 21; 27; 28; 32; 34; 36; 13:1; 3; 4; 14:7; 31; 15:15; 26(2); 27; 16:22; 27; 28; 30; 17:7; 8; 15; 18:3; 28; 36; 19:9; 11; 12; 23; 27; 20:1; 9; 21:8; 14; **Acts** 1:4(2); 5; 11; 12; 22(2); 25; 2:2; 5; 10; 33; 40; 46; 3:2(2); 5; 15; 19; 22; 23; 24; 26; 4:2; 10; 17; 5:16; 38; 41; 6:3; 5; 9(2); 7:3; 4; 16; 37; 8:10; 26; 33; 36; 9:2; 3; 8; 13; 14; 18; 10:7; 17; 21; 22; 23; 37; 41; 11:4; 5; 9; 11; 20; 27; 12:1; 10; 11(2); 19; 25; 13:4; 8; 13(2); 14; 23; 29; 30; 31; 34; 39(2); 50; 51; 14:8; 15; 17; 18; 19; 26; 15:1; 18; 19; 20(4); 24; 29(5); 33; 38; 39; 16:11; 12; 14; 27; 39; 17:2; 3; 5; 9; 13; 26; 27; 31; 33; 18:1; 2(2); 5; 6; 7; 16; 21; 28; 19:9; 12; 35; 20:6; 9; 15; 17; 18; 20; 24; 30; 21:1(2); 7; 10; 12; 16; 25(4); 27; 39; 22:5; 6; 21; 22; 29; 30; 23:10; 21; 34(2); 24:4; 18; 25:1; 7; 26:4(2); 5; 10; 12; 13; 17(2); 18(2); 22; 23; 27:4; 12; 21(2); 29; 30(2); 34; 43; 28:4; 13; 15; 17; 21; 22; 23(2); **Rom** 1:4; 7; 17; 18; 2:29(2); 3:21; 28; 4:6; 24; 5:9; 14; 16(2); 6:4; 7; 9; 13; 17; 18; 22; 7:2; 3; 4; 6; 8; 24; 8:2; 11(2); 21; 35; 39; 9:3; 5; 21; 10:6; 7; 9; 11:15; 26; 13:1; 3; 14:23(2); 15:19; 22; 26; 31; **1 Cor** 1:3; 30; 2:12; 4:5; 7; 5:2; 13; 6:19; 7:7; 10; 25; 27; 29; 9:6; 14; 19; 10:14; 11:8(2); 12(2); 23; 14:36; 15:12; 20; 41; 47; **2 Cor** 1:2; 10; 16; 2:3; 17; 3:1; 5(2); 18; 5:1; 2; 6; 8; 16; 6:17; 7:1; 9; 11:3; 8; 9(2); 10; 12; 20; 24; 33; 12:6; 8; **Gal** 1:1(2); 3; 4; 6; 8; 12; 15; 2:6; 12; 3:2; 13; 4:1; 24; 5:4(2); 7; 8; 6:17; **Eph** 1:2; 20; 2:12(2); 15; 3:9; 15; 4:16; 18; 31; 5:14; 6:6; 8; 23; **Phil** 1:2; 5; 15(2); 16; 22; 28; 3:9(2); 11; 20; 4:15; 18(2); **Col** 1:2; 7; 13; 18; 23; 25; 26(2); 2:12; 19(2); 20; 3:24; 4:16; **1 Th** 1:1; 8; 9; 10(3); 2:3; 6(3); 13; 14(2); 17; 3:6; 4:1; 3; 16; 5:22; **2 Th** 1:2; 7; 9(2); 2:2; 13; 3:2; 3; 6(2); **1 Tim** 1:2; 5(3); 6; 4:1; 3; 5:13; 19; 6:4; 5; 10; **2 Tim** 1:2; 13; 15; 18; 2:2; 8; 19; 21; 3:5; 14; 15; 4:4; 18; **Titus** 1:4; 14; 2:14; **Phm** 1:3; 20; **Heb** 3:12; 4:3; 4; 10(2); 13; 5:1; 7; 6:1; 7; 7:1; 5(3); 6(2); 13; 14; 23; 26; 8:11; 9:14; 28; 10:13; 22; 11:12; 15; 19(2); 40; 12:3; 25(2); 13:10; 20; 24; **Jas** 1:7; 17(2); 27; 3:11; 15; 17; 4:1(2); 7; 5:19; 20(2); **1 Pe** 1:3; 12; 18(2); 21; 2:11; 3:10(2); 11; 4:1; **2 Pe** 1:9; 17(2); 18; 2:8; 14; 18; 21; 3:4; 17; **1 Jn** 1:1; 5; 7; 9; 2:7(2); 13; 14; 19; 20; 24(2); 27; 3:8; 11; 14; 17; 22; 4:21; 5:21; **2 Jn** 3(2); 4; 5; 6; **3 Jn** 7; 12(2); **Jude** 14; 24; **Rev** 1:4(2); 5(3); 2:5(2); 7; 27; 3:5; 10; 12; 18; 4:5; 6:4; 16(2); 7:2; 13; 17; 8:4; 5; 10; 11; 9:1; 6; 13; 10:1; 4; 8; 11:5; 9; 11; 12; 12:14; 13:8; 13; 14:2; 3; 4; 13(3); 18; 15:8(2); 16:1; 7; 12; 17; 21; 17:8; 18:1; 4; 14(2); 19:5; 21; 20:1; 7; 9; 11; 21:2; 3; 4; 10; 22:1; 19(4)

HAD (2582/2216)

Gen 1:31; 2:2(2); 3; 5(2); 8; 22; 3:1; 5:4; 7; 10; 13; 16; 19; 22; 26; 28; 30; 6:6; 12; 7:9; 16; 8:6; 7; 8; 11; 9:24; 11:1; 3(2); 5; 30; 12:1; 4; 5(2); 7; 16; 20; 13:1; 3; 4; 5; 14; 14:13; 16:1(2); 3; 4; 5; 17:23; 18:8; 11; 33; 19:14; 17; 23; 27; 29; 20:4; 18; 21:1(2); 2; 4; 9; 25; 26; 22:3; 9; 23:16; 24:1; 2; 15; 16; 19; 21; 22; 29; 45; 48; 65; 66; 25:5; 6; 26:8; 14; 15(3); 18(3); 32; 27:17; 30(2); 31; 28:6; 7(2); 9; 11; 18; 19; 29:16; 20; 30:9; 25; 30; 35; 38; 43; 31:18(2); 19(2); 21; 22; 24; 25; 32; 34; 42; 32:23; 33:10; 19; 34:1; 5; 7; 13; 27; 35:16; 27; 36:6; 37:5; 23; 36; 38:15; 30; 39:1(2); 4; 5(3); 6(2); 13; 40:5; 8; 22; 41:1; 11; 15; 21(2); 43(2); 54; 42:9; 29; 43:2(2); 6; 10; 23; 44:2; 4; 45:27(2); 46:1; 5; 6; 47:11; 18; 22; 27; 48:11; 49:33; 50:12; 14; **Ex** 2:6(2); 16; 4:28(2); 30; 31(2); 5:14; 7:13; 22; 25; 8:12; 15; 19; 9:12; 15; 34; 35; 10:10; 14; 15; 23; 12:28; 35(2); 36; 39(2); 13:17; 19; 14:5; 29; 31; 16:3; 18(3); 18:1(2); 2; 6; 8(3); 9(2); 24; 19:1; 2(2); 31:18; 32:20; 25; 33:5; 8; 34:4; 32; 33; 34; 35:22; 25; 29; 36:2; 3; 7; 22; 38:17; 22; 39:1; 5; 7; 21; 26; 29; 31; 32; 42; 43(3); 40:16; 19; 21; 23; 25; 27; 29; 32; **Lev** 8:9; 13; 17; 21; 29; 36; 9:10; 21; 10:1; 5; 19; 14:32; 21:3; 22:4; 24:23; **Num** 1:1; 17; 48; 3:4(2); 7:1; 8:4; 9:1; 11:3; 26(2); 34; 12:1(2); 14; 13:31; 32; 14:2(2); 6; 15:34; 16:39; 40; 42; 47; 50; 17:8(2); 11; 20:3; 21:9; 26(2); 22:2; 33; 23:2; 30; 26:33; 65; 27:3; 4; 31:14; 21; 32; 35; 36; 53; 32:1; 9; 13; 33:4(2); 38; 35:25; **Deut** 1:3; 4; 19; 41; 2:10; 14; 16; 22; 37; 3:3; 5:29; 9:10; 16(4); 21; 25; 10:4; 5; 19:6; 25:10; 29:26; 31:24; 32:27; 30(2); 34:9(2); **Josh** 2:6(2); 7; 23; 3:17; 4:1; 4; 8; 10(2); 11; 12; 14; 18; 23(2); 5:1(2); 4(2); 5(2); 6; 7; 8; 12(2); 6:8; 10; 11; 22(2); 23(2); 25; 7:7; 24; 25; 8:13; 19; 20(2); 21; 24(2); 26; 27; 31; 32; 33; 35; 9:3; 16; 18; 21; 10:1(5); 13; 16; 20; 27; 28; 30; 32; 35; 37; 39(2); 40; 11:5; 9; 12; 14; 15(2); 20; 23; 12:6(2); 13:8(2); 12; 14; 15; 21; 24; 29; 32; 33(2); 14:2; 3(2); 5; 15; 17:3; 6; 8; 11; 18:2; 19:2; 9; 49; 21:4; 5; 6; 7; 8; 20; 42; 43; 44; 45; 22:7; 9; 23:1; 24:31(2); 32(3); **Judg** 1:19; 20; 2:6; 7(2); 10(2); 12; 15(2); 3:1; 2; 4; 11; 12; 18(2); 24; 25; 26; 30; 4:3; 11; 12; 17; 18; 24; 5:31; 6:3; 27; 28; 29; 7:13(2); 19; 8:8; 10; 19; 24; 30(2); 34; 35; 9:22; 46; 56; 10:4(2); 11:34; 39; 12:9; 14; 13:2; 23; 14:4; 6(2); 9; 17; 18; 19; 20; 15:5; 17; 16:18; 19; 20; 22; 30; 31; 17:3(2); 5; 18:1; 7; 14; 17; 27(2); 28; 20:3; 22; 36(2); 39; 41; 21:1; 5(2); 8; 12; 14(2); 15; **Ruth** 1:6(2); 19; 2:17; 18(3); 19; 3:7; 16; 4:1; **1 Sam** 1:2(3); 5; 6; 9; 23; 24; 3:2; 8; 20; 4:3; 6; 18; 21; 5:9; 6:16; 19(2); 7:7; 14; 9:2; 5; 15; 22; 25; 10:9; 13; 16(2); 20; 21; 26; 12:8; 13:1; 4(2); 10; 14:3; 17; 22; 24; 26; 27; 30; 31; 15:35; 17:5; 6; 12; 13; 20; 21; 39; 40; 18:1; 6(2); 12; 26; 19:16; 18; 20:24; 34; 37(2); 41; 21:6; 22:6; 21; 23:7; 13; 15; 24:1; 5; 16; 25:2; 21; 34; 35; 37(2); 40; 44; 26:4; 5; 12; 27:4; 28:3(3); 20; 24; 30:1; 2; 3; 4; 5; 12(2); 16(2); 18; 19; 20; 21(2); 31:7; 11; **2 Sam** 1:1(2); 10; 12; 2:27; 30; 31; 3:7; 17; 22(2); 23; 26; 27; 30; 37; 4:1; 2; 4; 10; 5:12(2); 13; 17; 6:13; 17; 18; 23; 7:1; 8:7; 9; 10(2); 11(2); 9:2; 6; 10; 12; 10:6; 15; 11:7; 22; 27; 12:2; 3(2); 4(2); 6; 8; 13:1; 3; 10; 11; 15; 18; 22; 23; 28; 29; 36; 39; 14:6; 33; 15:2; 18; 24; 30; 32; 16:23; 17:14; 18; 20; 21; 22; 25; 27; 18:5; 18; 33; 19:6(2); 8; 18; 24; 25; 32; 39; 20:3; 5; 17; 21:2(2); 11; 12(3); 13; 20; 22:1; 23:8(2); 9; 11; 20(3); 21; 24:8; 10; **1 Ki** 1:6(2); 38; 2:15; 19; 28(2); 41(2); 3:1; 10; 15; 18; 21(2); 28; 4:7; 11; 24(2); 26; 34; 5:1(2); 12; 15; 6:1; 22; 7:5; 8(2); 20; 28; 30(2); 46; 48; 51(2); 8:54; 66; 9:1; 2; 10; 11; 12; 16(3); 19; 21; 24; 25; 10:4(2); 13; 19; 20; 22; 24; 26; 28; 11:2; 3; 9(2); 10(2); 15(2); 16; 23; 27; 29; 12:1; 2(2); 8(2); 10; 12; 13; 15; 20; 32(2); 33(2); 13:5; 11(2); 12; 20; 23(3); 26; 28; 31; 14:5; 21; 22; 24; 26; 15:3; 5; 12; 13; 15(2); 22; 26; 29(2); 30(3); 34; 16:13(2); 15; 19(2); 26; 31; 32; 34; 17:7; 18:3; 4(2); 5; 26; 31; 19:1(2); 20:33; 21:1; 4(2); 11(2); 15; 26(2); 22:11; 13; 31; 38; 41; 52; 53; **2 Ki** 1:17(2); 2:9; 13; 14(2); 18; 3:2; 3; 21; 4:12; 15; 17(2); 20; 44; 5:1; 2(2); 8; 13; 6:10; 20; 30; 7:5; 6; 15; 17(2); 18; 19(2); 8:1; 5(2); 18; 21; 29; 9:14; 15(2); 16; 29; 30; 34; 10:1; 16; 17; 24(2); 25; 29; 31; 11:10; 15; 20; 12:6; 11(2); 18; 13:2; 6; 7; 14; 19; 23; 25; 14:3; 5; 24; 25; 28; 15:3; 9(2); 18; 24; 28; 34; 16:2; 3; 11; 18; 17:4(2); 7(3); 8(3); 11; 12; 15(3); 20; 23; 28; 29; 34; 35; 18:3; 4; 6; 12; 16; 17; 18; 19:8; 26; 20:4; 11; 12; 21:2; 3(2); 4; 7(2); 9; 16; 20; 21(2); 24; 23:2; 5; 8; 11; 12(2); 13; 15; 19(2); 22; 26; 32; 37; 24:2; 3; 4(2); 7; 9; 13(2); 19; 25:3; 11; 16; 19; 22; 23; **1 Chr** 2:18; 22; 26; 34(2); 52; 4:5; 27; 43; 5:9; 18; 25; 6:32; 49; 7:4; 23; 8:8(2); 38; 40; 9:18; 19; 20; 22; 25; 26; 27; 31; 44; 10:7; 11; 13; 11:10; 11(2); 20; 22(3); 12:15; 29; 32; 39; 13:14; 14:2; 4; 8; 15:3; 15; 16:1; 2; 18:9; 10(2); 11; 19:6; 9; 16; 17; 21:5(2); 19; 28; 29; 23:17; 22; 24:2; 19; 28; 26:9; 10; 26; 28; 30; 27:23; 28:2(2); 12; 29:8; 9(2); 25; **2 Chr** 1:3; 4(3); 5; 12; 14; 16; 2:17; 3:1(2); 4:17; 18; 19; 5:1(2); 10; 11; 6:13(2); 7:1; 2; 6; 7; 10; 8:1; 2; 6; 11; 12; 14; 9:3(2); 12; 18; 19; 23; 25; 10:1; 2; 8(2); 10; 12; 15; 11:14; 15; 12:1(2); 2; 9; 13; 14:6(3); 8; 15:8; 11; 15; 16; 18(2); 16:6; 14; 17:2; 5; 9; 13; 18:1; 10; 12; 30; 20:21; 22; 23; 24; 27; 29; 33; 21:2; 6(2); 7(2); 9; 10; 22:1; 6; 7; 9(2); 23:8; 9; 14; 18; 21; 24:3; 7(2); 9; 10; 14; 16; 22; 24; 25; 25:3; 10; 13; 26:4; 5; 10(2); 11; 19; 20; 27:2; 28:1; 3; 6; 17; 18(2); 19(2); 23; 29:2; 19; 29; 34; 36; 30:2; 3(2); 5; 17(2); 18; 26; 31:1; 10; 12; 32:2; 21; 27; 29; 33:2; 3; 4; 7(2); 9; 15; 22(2); 23; 25; 34:4; 7(2); 8; 9(2); 10; 11; 22; 30; 35:18(2); 20; 24; 36:13; 14; 15; 17; 21; **Ezra** 1:5; 7; 2:1(2); 65; 3:1; 3; 6; 7; 8; 12; 5:14(2); 6:13; 20; 21(2); 7:6; 10; 8:20; 22; 25; 35(2); 9:4; 14; 10:17; 18; 44(3); **Neh** 1:2(2); 2:1; 9; 10; 12; 16(3); 18(2); 4:6; 15; 18; 6:1(2); 12(2); 18; 7:1(2); 5; 6(2); 67; 8:1; 4; 14; 17(2); 9:15; 23; 28(2); 30; 10:28(2); 11:16; 12:22; 29; 43; 13:2; 3; 5(2); 6; 7; 10(2); 23; **Esth** 1:8; 14; 2:1(2); 6(3); 7(2); 10(2); 12; 15; 20(2); 3:2; 4; 6; 4:1; 5; 7(2); 5:5; 11(2); 14; 6:2(2); 4(2); 13; 14; 7:4; 8; 10; 8:1; 2; 3; 16; 17; 9:1; 16; 22; 23(2); 24(2); 25; 26(2); 31(2); **Job** 1:5; 2:11(2); 3:15; 7:4; 10:18(2); 19; 29:12; 30:6; 31:21; 25; 32; 35(2); 32:3(2); 4; 35:3; 41:32; 42:7; 9; 10; 11(2); 12;

13; **Ps** 27:13; 44:20; 51:55:6; 73:2(2); 15; 78:11; 23; 24; 54; 60; 71; 90:2; 94:17; 105:26; 38; 106:21; 23; 34; 119:92; 124:1; 2; **Prov** 8:26; **Eccl** 2:7(2); 11(2); 18; 20; 8:10(2); **Song** 3:4(2); 5:6; 6:11(2); 12; 8:11; **Isa** 1:9; 11; 6:2; 6; 26:13; 37:8; 27; 38:8; 9(2); 17; 21; 22; 39:1(2); 41:3; 48:18; 52:15(2); 53:9; 59:10; 60:10; **Jer** 2:21; 3:3; 7; 8(2); 4:23; 25; 5:7; 6:15; 8:12; 9:2; 11:19; 13:7; 16:15; 19:14; 23:8; 22(2); 24:1(2); 2(2); 25:17; 26:8(2); 19; 28:12; 29:1; 2; 32:3; 16; 34:8; 10; 11; 16; 36:4; 13; 16; 23; 27(2); 32; 37:4; 10; 15; 16; 38:1; 7; 14; 27(2); 39:5; 10; 15; 40:1(2); 5; 7(3); 11(2); 12; 41:2; 4; 9(3); 10; 11; 14; 16(3); 18(2); 43:1(2); 5(2); 6; 44:15; 17; 20; 45:1; 46:21; 52:2; 6; 15; 20; 25; **Lam** 1:7; 9; 4:18; **Ezek** 1:5; 6(2); 8; 10(4); 16; 23(2); 3:6; 8:11; 9:2; 3(3); 11; 10:12; 14; 21; 22; 11:24; 25; 16:14; 17; 49; 17:7; 19:11; 20:6; 9; 14; 15; 22; 24(2); 28; 22:28; 23:8; 10; 18; 19; 39; 41; 43; 33:21; 22(3); 35:5; 36:18(2); 21(2); 38:8; 40:3; 21; 22; 26; 36; 41:18; 23; 24; 42:15; 20; **Dan** 1:4; 9; 11; 17; 18; 2:1; 3; 14; 24; 3:2; 3(2); 7; 27; 4:21; 33; 5:2(2); 3(2); 6:24; 7:1; 4; 5; 6(2); 7(2); 12; 20; 8:3; 5; 6(2); 15; 9:21; 10:1; 13; 15; **Hos** 1:8; 2:23; 13:6; **Joel** 3:21; **Am** 7:2; **Ob** 5(3); 16; **Jon** 1:5(2); 10; 17; 3:10; 4:10; **Nah** 3:8; **Hab** 3:4; **Hag** 1:12; **Zech** 5:9; 7:12; 14; 10:6; 11:10; **Mt** 1:6; 25; 2:4; 7; 9; 11(2); 13; 16; 3:16; 4:2; 12; 7:28; 8:1; 5; 14; 16; 28; 32; 33; 9:8; 20; 28; 31; 10:1; 11:2; 20; 21; 23; 12:7; 9; 10; 13:5; 6; 26; 46(2); 53; 54; 14:3; 4; 10; 21; 23; 29; 34; 15:10; 16:5(2); 17:8; 14; 24; 25; 18:24; 25; 31(2); 32; 33(2); 19:1; 22; 20:2; 8; 11; 34; 21:10; 28; 22:22; 25; 28; 34; 23:30; 24:43; 25:16; 17; 18; 20; 22; 24; 26:1; 19; 20; 24; 30; 48; 57; 71; 75; 27:2; 3; 16; 17; 18; 26; 29; 31; 33; 34; 52; 54; 57(2); 59; 60; 28:11; 12; 16; **Mk** 1:19; 26; 29; 32; 42; 2:4; 3:1; 3; 5; 10; 4:5; 6; 35; 36; 5:2; 3; 4(2); 14; 15(2); 16; 18; 19; 20; 21; 25; 26(3); 30; 32; 33; 40; 6:2; 14; 17(2); 18; 30(2); 41; 44; 46; 52; 53; 7:14; 17; 25; 30; 32; 8:7; 9; 14; 23; 33; 34; 9:8; 9(2); 28; 34; 36; 10:22; 11:6; 11; 12; 19; 12:12; 14; 22; 23; 28; 44; 13:20; 14:16; 21; 23; 26; 44; 45; 72; 15:7; 8; 10; 15; 20; 33; 42; 44; 46; 16:2; 4; 9; 10; 11; 14(2); 19; **Lk** 1:3; 7; 22; 58; 2:15; 17; 20; 26(2); 36; 39; 43; 3:19; 4:2; 13; 16; 17; 33; 35; 40; 5:2; 4; 6; 9; 11; 17; 25; 6:8; 10; 7:10; 13; 20; 24; 39; 41; 42; 8:2(2); 4(2); 8; 27; 29(2); 30; 34; 35(2); 36(2); 38; 39; 42; 43; 47; 56; 9:7; 8(2); 10(2); 11; 36(2); 37; 51; 10:13; 33; 39; 11:14; 38; 12:1; 39; 13:1; 6; 11; 14; 14:2; 15:11; 14; 20; 16:1; 8; 18:40; 19:15(2); 28; 32; 37; 42; 20:19; 33; 21:4; 22:13; 14; 45; 52; 55; 59; 61; 23:8(2); 12; 13; 19; 25; 33; 46; 47; 48; 51; 53; 55; 24:1; 12; 14; 23; 24; 35; 37; 40; **Jn** 2:9(2); 15; 22(3); 25; 3:24; 4:1; 8; 18; 40; 45; 46; 47; 54; 5:4; 5; 6; 13; 15; 16; 6:11; 13; 14; 17; 19; 22(3); 23; 7:9; 10; 30; 8:3; 10; 19; 20; 9:6; 8; 15; 18(2); 22; 35(2); 11:17; 19; 21; 28; 30; 32; 43; 44; 45(2); 57; 12:1(2); 6; 9; 12; 14; 16; 18; 29; 37; 13:1; 3(2); 12; 21; 29(2); 31; 14:7; 15:22; 24; 17:5; 18:1; 18; 22; 38; 19:11; 23; 30; 41; 20:1; 7; 12; 14; 18(2); 20; 22; 21:4; 7; 9; 15; 19; 20; **Acts** 1:2(2); 6; 9; 13; 16; 2:1; 30; 44; 45; 3:10; 12; 4:7; 13; 14; 15; 21(2); 22; 23; 31; 32; 35; 5:7; 27; 40; 6:6; 7:5; 17; 29; 30; 36; 44(2); 60; 8:11; 14; 15; 16(2); 25; 27(2); 9:19; 26; 27(3); 31; 33; 37; 38; 39(2); 41; 10:7; 8; 17(3); 21; 24; 27; 45; 11:1; 13; 20; 23; 26; 12:4; 11; 12; 17; 18; 19; 20; 25; 13:1; 5; 6; 12; 19; 22; 24; 29; 36; 43; 48; 14:8; 9; 11; 21; 23(2); 24; 25; 26(2); 27(3); 15:2; 4(2); 7; 12; 13; 21; 30; 31; 33; 38(2); 16:6; 7; 10(2); 23; 27; 34; 40; 17:1; 3; 9; 18:2(2); 5; 18(2); 22; 23; 25; 27; 19:6; 13; 18; 19; 21; 32; 35; 41; 20:1; 2; 11(2); 13; 16; 18; 36; 21:1; 3; 5; 6; 7; 9; 11; 17; 19(2); 29(2); 33; 35; 40; 22:29; 23:7; 12; 13; 29; 33; 34; 24:10; 19; 25:1; 6; 7(2); 12; 14; 17; 19(2); 23(2); 25(2); 26:14; 30; 31; 32; 27:4; 5; 7; 9; 13; 17; 27; 28; 30; 35(2); 38; 28:1; 3; 6; 9; 11; 17; 18; 19; 23; 25; 29(2); **Rom** 3:25; 4:11; 12; 21; 5:14; 7:7; 9:10; 23; 29; **1 Cor** 1:15; 2:8; 4:7; 7:29; 11:24; **2 Cor** 1:9; 2:13; 3:9; 10; 7:5; 12; 8:5; 6; 15(2); 9:5; **Gal** 2:2; 7; 9; 11; 3:21; 4:4; 22; **Phil** 2:26; 27; **1 Th** 1:9; 2:2; 8; 3:5; **2 Th** 2:2; 12; **Heb** 1:3; 2:14; 17; 4:8; 5:7; 6:15; 7:6; 8:7; 9:1; 4(2); 6; 19; 26; 10:2; 6; 8; 12; 15; 34; 11:5(2); 11; 15(3); 17; 31; 36; 12:9; **1 Pe** 2:10; **1 Jn** 2:7; 19; **2 Jn** 5; **3 Jn** 13; **Rev** 1:16; 4:4; 7; 5:6; 8; 6:2; 5; 9; 8:6; 9:8; 9; 10; 11; 14; 15; 17; 10:2; 10; 12:13; 16; 13:3; 11; 14:18(2); 16:2; 18; 17:1; 18:19; 19:12; 20:4(3); 21:1; 9; 12; 14; 15; 23

HAS (2618/2164)

Gen 3:1; 3; 22; 4:6; 11; 25; 5:29; 6:13; 14:20; 16:2; 11; 17:14; 18:19; 21; 19:13(2); 19; 21:6; 12; 17; 26; 22:20; 23:9; 24:27; 35(3); 36(2); 44; 51; 56; 26:22; 27:27; 35; 36(2); 29:32; 33(2); 30:2; 6(2); 18; 20; 23; 27; 29; 30(2); 31:1(2); 5; 7; 9; 15; 16(2); 42; 33:5; 11; 35:3; 37:20; 33; 38:24; 26; 39:8(2); 9; 14; 41:25; 28; 39; 51; 52; 42:21; 28(2); 43:23; 44:16; 45:6; 8; 9; 46:32; 34; 47:15; 18; 48:9; 11; 15; 16; **Ex** 3:9; 13; 14; 15; 18; 4:1; 5; 11; 5:3; 23; 7:16; 9:18; 10:12; 13:9; 14:3; 15:1(2); 2; 4; 6(2); 21(2); 16:6; 9; 15; 16; 23; 29; 32; 17:16; 18:10(2); 19:8; 20:20; 21:4(2); 8(2); 9; 29(3); 31; 36; 22:3(2); 8; 11; 24:3; 7; 8; 14; 32:1; 23; 24; 29; 33; 35:1; 10; 30; 31; 34; 35; 36:1(2); **Lev** 4:3; 22; 23; 28(2); 35; 5:1; 5; 6; 7; 10; 13; 16; 19; 6:2; 3; 4(3); 5; 10; 7:8; 8:34(2); 10:6; 11; 15; 17; 11:9; 42; 12:2; 7; 13:2; 3; 4(2); 5; 6(2); 7; 8; 10; 12; 13(3); 17(2); 20(2); 21; 23; 25; 26; 27; 28(2); 29; 31; 32; 33; 34; 36; 37; 38; 40; 41; 46; 47; 50; 51; 53; 55(3); 56; 58; 14:39; 43(2); 44; 48; 15:2; 4; 6; 7; 8; 9; 11(2); 12; 13; 16; 19; 25; 32; 33; 16:20; 17:2; 4; 19:8; 20; 22(2); 20:3; 9; 11; 17; 18(2); 20; 21; 24; 27; 21:3; 17; 18(2); 19; 20; 21(2); 23; 22:3; 4(2); 6; 13(2); 20; 23; 24:14; 19; 20; 25:25; 26; 27:20; 22; 28; **Num** 5:2; 7(2); 8; 13; 14(2); 19; 20; 27(2); 28; 6:19; 10:29; 11:23; 12:2(2); 14:3; 9; 24(2); 40; 15:22; 23; 31(2); 16:9; 10; 28; 29; 46(2); 19:2(2); 13; 15; 16; 20(2); 20:14; 21:29; 30; 22:5; 10; 11; 13; 23:7; 8(2); 12; 17; 19(2); 20; 21(2); 22; 23; 24:8; 11; 16; 25:11; 27:8; 9; 10; 11; 30:1; 4(2); 5; 9; 12; 15; 31:17; 19(2); 32:7; 18; 19; 21; 24; 31; 34:13; 14; 35:32; **Deut** 1:10; 11; 21(2); 27; 2:7(2); 3:18; 20; 21; 4:3; 7; 8; 19; 20; 23; 32(2); 5:16; 24; 26; 32; 33; 6:1; 3; 17; 19; 20; 25; 7:1; 6; 8; 8:10; 9:3; 4(2); 28; 10:9; 21; 22; 11:4; 25; 29; 12:7; 12; 15; 20; 21; 13:5; 14:2; 8; 24; 27; 29; 15:2; 14; 18; 21; 16:17; 17:1; 2; 3; 4; 5; 16; 18:5; 14; 21; 22(2); 19:1; 18; 20:5(2); 6(2); 7; 17; 21:3(2); 5; 15; 17; 18; 22; 22:3; 17; 19; 21; 29; 23:15; 23; 24:1; 2; 4; 5(2); 15; 25:5; 19; 26:9(2); 11; 18; 19(2); 27:20; 28:9; 21; 48; 52; 53; 55; 29:4; 13(2); 22; 24; 30:3; 31:2; 3; 7; 32:6; 27; 34:10; **Josh** 1:15; 2:9(2); 14; 24; 6:16; 22; 7:11; 15(3); 26; 8:31; 10:4; 14; 19; 14:9; 10; 17:14; 18:3; 22:4; 25; 23:3(2); 9(2); 13; 14(2); 15(2); 16; 24:20; 27; **Judg** 1:7; 2:20(2); 3:28; 4:6; 14(2); 6:13(2); 25; 29(2); 30(2); 31; 32; 7:2; 14; 15; 8:3; 7; 11:23; 36(2); 13:10; 15:6(2); 10; 16:2; 17; 18; 23; 24; 18:4; 10; 19:23; 30; 20:12; 21:3; 11; **Ruth** 1:13; 15; 20; 21(3); 2:7; 11; 20; 3:3; 18; 4:3; 14; 15; **1 Sam** 1:27; 2:5(3); 8; 4:3; 7(2); 17(3); 21; 22(2); 6:9; 7:12; 9:16; 24; 10:1; 2; 11; 22; 24; 11:13; 12:13; 22; 24; 13:14(2); 14:10; 12; 17; 29(2); 45(2); 15:11(2); 12; 22; 23; 26; 28(2); 33; 16:8; 9; 10; 22; 17:25(2); 36(2); 18:7; 22; 19:4; 17; 20:3; 13; 15; 22; 26; 27; 29(3); 32; 21:2; 11; 22:8(2); 23:7(3); 10; 11; 22; 24:14; 25:21(2); 26; 27; 29; 30(3); 31(2); 34; 39(3); 26:8; 19; 20; 27:6; 12; 28:9(2); 15; 16(2); 17(2); 18; 21; 29:3; 5; 30:23(2); **2 Sam** 1:9; 16; 2:7; 3:9; 18; 23; 24; 29; 38; 4:8; 9; 5:20; 6:12; 7:27; 9:11; 10:3(2); 12:5; 13; 13:20; 24; 30; 32; 14:2; 7; 19; 20; 22; 30; 15:4; 16:8(2); 10; 11; 21; 17:6; 7; 13; 21; 18:19; 28; 31; 19:7; 9; 10; 27; 30; 42; 20:21; 22:21; 25; 36; 23:5; 24:21; 23; **1 Ki** 1:11; 13; 18; 19(3); 25(3); 26; 27; 29; 37; 43; 44; 48; 51; 2:15(2); 23; 24(2); 29; 31; 38; 3:12; 5:4; 6; 7; 8:15; 20; 41; 56(2); 9:8; 9; 10:9; 12; 12:19; 13:3; 26(2); 14:11; 16:16(2); 18:10; 19:18; 21:13; 14; 18; 29(2); 22:23(2); 28; **2 Ki** 1:9; 11; 14; 2:2; 4; 6; 16; 3:7; 10; 13; 4:2; 14; 27(2); 31; 5:20; 22; 6:29; 32; 7:6; 8:1; 4; 7; 9; 10; 13; 22; 10:10; 14:10; 17:26; 18:22; 27; 33; 19:4(2); 9; 16; 21(3); 20:9; 21:11(3); 22:4; 10; 13; 16; **1 Chr** 14:11; 15; 15:2; 16:12; 17:25; 19:3; 21:17; 22:11; 18(2); 23:25; 28:4; 5(2); 10; 29:1; **2 Chr** 2:7; 11; 12; 15; 6:4; 10; 7:21; 22; 8:11; 9:8; 10:19; 14:7; 15:3; 16:7; 18:22(2); 27; 20:37; 21:10; 23:3; 24:20; 25:8; 16; 28:9; 29:8; 11; 30:8; 31:10; 32:12; 34:18; 36:23(2); **Ezra** 1:2(2); 4:3; 18; 19(2); 5:3; 16; 7:27; 28; 9:2; 6; 8; 13; **Neh** 2:5; 9:32; 33; **Esth** 1:16; 4:11(2); 5:5; 8; 6:3(2); 8(3); **Job** 1:10; 11; 12; 21; 2:4; 3:23; 25(2); 6:5; 8:4; 9:4; 10:12; 12:9; 13; 13:1(2); 15:27; 16:7; 11; 12(3); 17:6; 7; 9; 18:17; 19; 19:6(2); 8(2); 9; 10; 11; 13; 21; 20:19(2); 21:31; 23:10; 11; 26:2; 3; 6; 27:2(2); 28:7; 8; 30:2; 11; 15; 19; 25; 31:5; 7; 9; 20; 27(2); 31; 32:14; 19; 33:4; 34:5(2); 9; 31; 35:15; 36:7; 23(2); 25; 37:21; 38:25; 28(2); 36(2); 39:24; 41:11; 42:7; 8; **Ps** 2:7; 4:3; 6:8; 9; 7:15; 9:6; 7; 10:6; 11(2); 13; 13:6; 14:1; 16:7; 18:20; 24; 35(2); 19:4(2); 22:14; 16; 24(2); 31; 24:2; 4(2); 28:6; 31:21; 33:12; 35:8; 27; 36:3; 37:16; 38:10; 40:3; 41:9; 44:15; 17; 18; 45:2; 7; 46:8; 47:5; 50:1; 52:53:1; 3; 5(2); 54:7(2); 55:5; 12; 18; 20(2); 60:6; 62:11; 66:14; 16; 19(2); 20; 68:28; 69:7; 9; 20; 31; 71:11; 72:12; 74:3; 18(2); 77:8(2); 9(2); 78:4; 69; 79:10; 80:15; 83:8; 84:3; 88:4; 16; 89:34; 91:14(2); 92:11; 93:1; 94:22; 23; 98:1; 2(3); 3; 100:3; 101:5; 102:13; 103:10; 12; 19; 104:17; 105:5; 107:2; 16; 108:7; 109:11; 110:4; 111:4; 5; 6; 9(2); 112:9(2); 115:12; 16; 116:1; 2; 7; 118:14; 18(2); 22; 24; 27; 119:50; 53; 56; 139; 120:6; 123:2; 124:6; 7; 126:2; 3; 127:5; 129:4; 132:11; 13(2); 135:4; 142:4; 143:3(3); 146:5; 147:13(2); 20; 148:14; 150:6; **Prov** 3:30; 7:19; 20; 26; 9:1(2); 2(3); 3; 10:4; 13; 18; 23; 25; 12:9; 13:4; 7(2); 14:20; 21; 29; 31; 32; 33; 15:14; 15; 23; 16:4; 22; 17:16; 20(2); 21; 24; 27; 18:2; 24; 19:17(2); 23; 25; 20:12; 14; 22:9; 11; 23:29(6); 24:29; 25:8; 28; 28:11; 30:4(4); 15; **Eccl** 1:3; 9; 10; 13; 16; 2:12; 21; 22(2); 3:9; 11(2); 15(2); 19; 4:3(2); 8; 10; 5:4; 16(2); 17; 19; 6:2; 3; 5(2); 6; 8; 10; 7:13; 14; 22; 8:8(2); 15; 9:7; 9; **Song** 1:4; 6; 2:12; 3:8; 6:1(2); 2; 7:12; 8:8; **Isa** 1:2; 12; 20; 21; 22; 30; 4:4; 5:1; 14; 25; 6:7; 12; 8:18; 9:2; 8; 10:10; 12; 14; 28(3); 29; 31; 12:2; 5; 14:4; 5; 8; 9; 24; 27; 32; 15:2; 6; 8; 16:13; 14; 19:12; 14; 17; 20:3; 21:6; 9; 16; 17; 22:25; 23:4; 8; 9; 11; 24:3; 6; 25:8; 27:7(2); 28:2; 25; 29:10(3); 11; 16; 30:24; 33; 31:4; 33:5; 8(2); 14; 34:2(2); 6; 16(2); 17(2); 36:7; 12; 18; 37:4(2); 9; 17; 22(3); 38:7; 8; 15(2); 40:2; 5; 12; 13(2); 21; 26; 41:4; 20(2); 26; 42:4; 25(2); 44:18; 20; 23(2); 45:9; 18; 21(2); 23; 48:5; 13(2); 14; 20; 49:1(2); 2(3); 7; 10; 13; 14(2); 21(2); 50:1; 4; 5; 10; 51:5; 13; 18(2); 52:9(2); 10; 53:1(2); 2; 4; 6; 10; 54:6; 10; 55:5; 56:3(2); 57:15; 58:14; 59:3; 60:1; 9; 61:1(2); 9; 10(2); 62:8; 11; 63:4; 7(2); 64:4; 65:20; 66:2; 8(2); **Jer** 2:10; 11; 30; 37; 3:3; 6(2); 10; 11; 24; 4:7(2); 8; 17; 5:23; 30; 6:6; 24; 30; 7:11; 28(2); 29; 8:5; 14; 21; 9:12; 21(2); 10:12(3); 22; 11:9; 15(2); 16; 17; 13:15; 17; 14:2; 17; 19; 15:9(4); 16:10; 18:13(2); 20:3; 13; 15; 22:8; 21; 23:9; 15; 17; 18(3); 19; 20; 28(2); 35(2); 37(2); 25:3; 4; 5; 13; 31; 36; 38; 26:11; 13; 15; 16; 27:13; 28:9; 15; 29:15; 26; 28; 31(2); 32; 30:24(2); 31:3; 11; 22; 32:24(2); 25; 31; 43; 33:24(2); 34:14(2); 21; 35:16; 36:7; 28; 37:7; 38:21; 40:2; 3(3); 5; 14; 42:19; 21; 43:2; 3; 44:17; 23; 45:3; 46:10; 12(2); 17; 47:5; 7(2); 48:8; 11(5); 18(2); 19; 21; 32; 39; 49:1(2); 7(2); 14; 16; 20(2); 24(2); 30(2); 31; 50:14; 15(2); 17; 23(2); 25(2); 27; 29(2); 31; 43(2); 45(2); 51:8; 10; 11; 12; 13; 14; 15(2); 30; 34(6); 41; 42; 44; 49; 51; **Lam** 1:1; 2; 3; 5; 6; 8(2); 10(2); 12(2); 13(3); 15(2); 17(2); 2:1; 2(5); 3(3); 4(3); 5(4); 6(4); 7(3); 8(4); 9; 17(6); 3:1; 2; 3; 4; 5; 6; 7(2); 9(2); 10; 11(2); 12; 13; 15(2); 16; 28; 37; 4:1; 8; 11(3); 5:1; 2; 15(2); 16; **Ezek** 2:3; 5; 3:20; 4:14; 5:6; 6:9; 7:2; 3; 5; 6(4); 7(2); 10(4); 11; 12; 13; 8:12; 9:9; 11:15; 12:2; 9; 13:6; 12; 15:5; 18:6; 7(4); 8(2); 9; 11; 12; 13(2); 14; 15; 16(2); 17(2); 19(2); 21; 22(2); 24(2); 26; 19:14(3); 21:11; 25; 29; 22:6; 13; 18; 23:8; 24:6; 12(2); 24; 27; 25:12; 26:2; 10; 29:3; 30:21; 33:13; 15; 16(2); 21; 24; 32; 33; 36:2; 23; 35; 44:2; 14; 45:20; **Dan** 1:10; 2:9; 10; 27; 28; 29; 30; 37; 38(2); 45; 3:5; 4:2; 22; 24; 31; 5:26; 28; 6:20; 27; 9:11(2); 12(3); 13; 14; 11:4; 12; 36(2); 12:7; **Hos** 1:2; 2:5(2); 12; 4:12; 19; 5:6; 6:1(2); 7:8; 12; 8:3; 7; 9; 11; 14(3); 10:1; 5; 11:12; 12:11; 13:16; 14:4; **Joel** 1:2; 4(3); 5; 6(2); 7(2); 11; 12(3); 17; 19(2); 20; 2:2; 20; 21; 23; 25; 26; 32; 3:8; **Am** 3:1; 4(2); 5; 8(2); 4:2; 5:2; 6:8; 7:10; 11; 8:2; 7; 9:6; 11; **Ob** 1; 3; 18; **Jon** 1:2; 7; **Mic** 1:9(2); 2:4(3); 4:4; 9; 5:1; 3; 6:2; 8; 9; 7:2; **Nah** 1:3; 14; 2:1; 3:19(2); **Zeph** 1:7(2); 2:15; 3:2(4); 15(2); **Hag** 1:2; **Zech** 1:2; 6; 10; 2:9; 11; 3:2; 4:9; 10; 6:15; 11:2(2); **Mal** 1:4; 14; 2:10; 11(4); 14; **Mt** 2:2; 4:16; 5:23; 28; 31; 8:20; 9:6; 18; 22; 11:11; 15; 18; 12:11; 28; 13:9; 11(2); 12(2); 21; 28; 43; 44; 15:13; 16:17; 17:12; 18:11; 12; 19:6; 11; 29; 21:3; 42; 24:21; 32; 25:28; 29(2); 26:10; 13; 65; 27:8; 23; 64; 28:18; **Mk** 2:10; 3:22; 26(2); 29; 30; 4:9; 11; 22; 23; 25(2); 29; 5:19(2); 34; 6:16; 7:16; 29; 37; 9:13; 17; 21; 22; 10:9; 29; 52; 11:2; 3; 21; 12:10; 43; 13:19; 28; 14:6; 8(2); 9; 41; 15:44; **Lk** 1:25; 36; 47; 48; 49; 51(2); 52; 53(2); 54; 68; 69; 78; 2:15(2); 3:11(3); 4:6; 12; 18(2); 5:24; 7:5; 16(2); 20; 33; 34; 44; 45; 46; 50; 8:8; 10; 16; 18; 39; 48; 9:19; 58; 10:9; 11; 40; 42; 11:6; 20; 33; 12:5(2); 44; 48; 13:16; 25; 14:5; 28; 29; 33; 34; 35; 15:5; 9; 27(3); 30; 16:16; 17:7; 19; 18:29; 42; 19:7; 9; 10; 16; 18; 24; 25; 26(2); 30; 31; 34; 20:17; 21:3; 8; 22:22; 31; 36(2); 23:15; 22; 41; 24:34; **Jn** 1:18(2); 2:4; 17; 20; 3:13; 18; 19; 27; 29; 32; 33(2); 34; 35; 36; 4:33; 44; 5:17; 22; 24(2); 26(2); 27; 33; 36(2); 37; 6:9; 27; 39; 45; 46(2); 47; 54; 65; 7:6; 8; 31; 38; 42; 52; 8:10; 29; 37; 40; 9:30; 32; 10:20; 21; 29; 11:28; 39; 12:7; 19; 23; 29; 38(2); 40; 48; 50; 13:18; 14:9(2); 21; 30; 15:13; 16:6; 8; 13; 15; 21(4); 32; 17:1; 14; 25; 18:11; 19:11; 35(2); 20:21; **Acts** 1:7; 8; 2:32; 36; 3:16(2); 18; 21; 4:9; 11; 16; 5:3; 31; 32; 7:40; 50; 9:12; 13; 14; 17; 21; 10:15; 22; 28; 31; 11:8; 9; 18; 12:11(2); 13:26; 33(2); 34; 40; 47; 15:14; 16; 21; 17:7; 26(2); 31(3); 19:26; 20:28; 21:28; 22:14; 23:9; 17; 18; 25:16; 26; 27:24; 28:4; 28; **Rom** 1:19; 2:25; 3:1; 7; 26; 4:1; 2; 5:5; 6:7(2); 9; 7:1; 2; 3; 13; 8:2; 9:6; 18; 19; 31; 10:9; 16; 18; 11:1; 2; 7; 8; 11; 25(2); 32; 34(2); 35; 12:3; 13:8; 14:3; 15:8; 18; 16:2(2); 19; 26(2); **1 Cor** 1:11; 20; 27(2); 28; 2:9(2); 10; 16; 3:14; 4:9; 5:1; 2; 3; 7:7; 12; 13; 15; 17(2); 25; 28; 37(2); 9:14; 10:13; 11:14; 15; 12:12; 18; 28; 13:10; 14:26(5); 15:12; 20; 25; 27; 54(2); 16:9; 12; **2 Cor** 1:21; 22; 2:5(2); 4:4; 6; 5:5(2); 10; 18(2); 19; 6:14(2); 15(2); 16(2); 7:13; 8:12; 9:2; 9(2); 13:10; **Gal** 3:1; 13; 22; 25; 4:6; 27(2); 5:1; 11; 6:14; **Eph** 1:3; 6; 2:14(2); 3:5; 9; 4:28; 5:2; 5; **Phil** 1:6; 13; 29; 2:9; 3:12; 4:10; **Col** 1:6(2); 12; 13; 21; 26(2); 2:13; 14; 18; 3:13; 25; 4:13; **1 Th** 1:8(2); 2:16; 3:6; 4:8; **2 Th** 2:16; **1 Tim** 1:12; 5:4; 8; 9; 10(5); 16; 6:16(2); **2 Tim** 1:7; 9; 10(2); 4:10(2); 15; **Titus** 1:3; 9; 2:11; **Phm** 1:18; **Heb** 1:2(2); 4; 9; 13; 2:5; 13; 18; 3:3(2); 4:3; 4; 7; 10(2); 14; 6:20; 7:13; 16; 21; 22; 24; 26; 28; 8:6; 13; 9:17; 20; 24; 26; 10:14; 28; 29; 35; 38; 11:10; 16; 12:2; 26; 13:5; 23; **Jas** 1:11; 12(2); 15; 2:5; 13; 14; 3:7; 5:15; **1 Pe** 1:3; 2:7; 3:22; 4:1(2); 10; 17; **2 Pe** 1:3; 9; 2:3; 22; 3:15; **1 Jn** 2:11; 23; 25; 27; 3:1; 2; 3; 6; 8; 9(2); 15; 17; 24; 4:2; 3; 9; 12(3); 13; 14; 16; 17; 18; 20(2); 5:4; 9; 10(4); 11; 12(2); 18; 20(2); **2 Jn** 9; **3 Jn** 11; 12; **Jude** 6; **Rev** 1:6; 2:7; 11; 12; 17; 18; 29; 3:1; 6; 7; 13; 22; 5:5; 6:17; 9:11; 11:2; 18; 12:6; 10; 12(2); 13:9; 17; 18; 14:7; 8; 15; 16:9; 17:7; 9; 10; 17; 18:2; 5; 6; 10; 14; 20; 19:2(2); 7(2); 16; 20:6(2)

HAVE (4940/3825)

Gen 1:26; 28; 29; 30; 3:11; 13; 14; 17(2); 4:1; 10; 14; 20; 23; 6:7(2); 7:1; 4; 8:21; 9:3; 17; 11:6; 12:18; 19; 14:22; 23; 24; 15:3; 18; 16:8; 13; 17:5; 20(2); 18:3; 5(2); 10; 12(2); 14; 19; 21; 27; 31; 19:8(3); 12(2); 19(2); 21(2); 20:3; 5; 9(4); 10(2); 16; 21:7(2); 23(2); 29; 30; 22:12; 16(3); 18; 24:14(2); 19; 25; 31; 33; 26:10(3); 27(2); 28; 29(3); 32; 27:19; 20; 33; 36; 37(3); 38; 45; 28:15(2); 22; 29:8; 25(2); 34; 30:3; 8(2); 15; 16; 18; 20; 26(2); 27(2); 29; 31:6; 12; 26(2); 27; 28; 30; 32; 36; 37(2); 38(3); 41(2); 42; 43; 51; 32:4; 5(2); 10(2); 28(2); 30; 33:9(2); 10(2); 11; 34:30; 35:3; 17; 37:6; 8; 9; 10; 17; 32; 38:23; 40:8; 15; 41:15(2); 19; 21; 28; 41; 42:2; 9; 10; 12; 36; 43:7(2); 10; 21; 22; 44:4; 5; 15; 19; 20; 28; 45:10; 11; 13; 16; 46:30; 31; 32(2); 47:1; 4(2); 5; 6; 9(2); 23; 25; 26; 29; 30; 48:22; 49:9; 18; 23; 26; 50:4; **Ex** 1:18; 2:18; 20; 22; 3:7(2); 8; 9; 12(2); 16; 17; 4:10; 11; 21; 5:14; 21; 22(2); 23; 6:4; 5(2); 12; 7:1; 9:15; 16; 19; 27; 29; 10:1; 2(2); 6; 16; 29; 12:17; 31; 32; 44; 13:12; 14:5(2); 11(2); 12; 18; 15:5; 7; 13(3); 16; 17(2); 26; 16:3; 12; 17:3; 16; 18:3; 16; 19:4; 20:3; 22(2); 25; 21:8; 23:13; 16(2); 20; 30; 24:12; 26:2; 8; 27:16; 17; 28:3; 7; 21; 32; 29:10; 35; 31:2; 3; 6(3); 11; 32:7; 8(2); 9; 11; 13; 21; 30; 31(2); 32; 34; 33:1; 12(3); 13; 16; 17(2); 19(2); 34:9; 10; 27; **Lev** 4:13; 14; 6:7; 17; 7:7; 8; 33; 34(2); 8:35; 10:13; 17; 18; 19(3); 11:4(2); 5; 6; 10; 12; 21; 23; 14:34; 17:7; 11; 18:27; 19:23; 36; 20:12; 13; 24; 25; 26; 22:22; 23:7; 14; 24; 36; 39; 24:22; 25:28; 31; 44; 26:13; 26; 37; 40; 41(2); **Num** 3:12; 4:15; 5:18; 19; 20(2); 8:16; 18; 19; 9:14; 11:11(3); 15; 18; 20(2); 21; 12:11(2); 13:32; 14:11; 14; 15; 17; 19; 20; 22(3); 27; 28; 29; 31; 35; 40; 43; 15:2; 29; 39; 16:13; 14; 15(2); 28; 30; 41; 18:6; 8(2); 11; 12; 19; 20(2); 21; 23; 24(3); 26; 30; 32; 20:4; 5; 12; 17; 24; 21:5; 7(2); 22; 29; 30; 34; 22:28(2); 29; 30; 32(2); 33; 34; 38(2); 23:4(2); 11(2); 20; 24:10; 19; 27:12; 13; 17; 28:18; 25; 26; 29:1; 7; 12; 35; 31:15; 18; 49; 50; 32:4; 5; 11; 12; 14; 17; 23; 30; 33:51; 53; 34:6; 14; 15; 35:3; 13; 28; **Deut** 1:6; 8; 14; 20; 28(2); 39; 41; 2:3; 5; 7; 9; 19; 24; 31; 3:2; 19(2); 20; 21; 24; 4:3; 5; 9; 25; 33; 5:7; 24(2); 26; 28(3); 6:11; 7:15; 16; 24; 8:10; 12(2); 13; 17; 9:7; 8; 12(3); 13; 20; 23; 24; 26(2); 10:21; 11:2(2); 7; 10; 28; 12:7; 9; 21; 26; 31; 13:2; 6; 13(2); 17; 18; 14:7(2); 9; 10; 16:13; 17:3; 18:1; 2; 8; 17; 20; 19:14; 19; 20:9; 18; 21:7(2); 8; 14(2); 15; 18; 22:3; 9; 23:12; 13; 23; 25:13; 14; 15; 26:3; 10(2); 12(2); 13(5); 14(5); 15; 17; 27:3; 4; 9; 12; 28:20; 31; 33; 36; 40; 51; 64; 65; 66; 29:2; 3; 5(3); 6(2); 19; 25; 30:1; 3; 15; 19; 31:5; 13; 16; 17; 18(2); 20(2); 21(2); 27; 29; 32:5; 18; 21(2); 26; 36; 33:9(2); 34:4; **Josh** 1:3; 8; 9; 15; 2:2; 3(3); 10; 12; 13; 16; 17; 3:4; 8; 5:9; 14; 6:2; 7:7; 11(4); 12; 19; 20(2); 25; 8:1; 6; 8(2); 9:6; 9(2); 13; 19; 22; 24; 10:6; 8; 17; 13:6; 14:9; 15:19; 16:10; 17:14; 16; 17(2); 18; 18:7(2); 22:2(2); 3(2); 11; 16(2); 23; 24(2); 25; 27; 31(2); 23:3; 4(2); 8; 14; 15; 16(2); 24:13; 22; **Judg** 1:2; 7; 15; 2:2(2); 3:19; 20; 5:16; 6:10; 14; 17; 22; 36; 37; 7:9; 13; 8:1; 2; 22; 9:16(3); 18; 19; 31; 48(2);

10:10(2); 13; 14; 15; 11:2; 7; 8; 12(2); 27; 35(2); 36; 12:3; 13:3; 22; 23(3); 14:2; 6; 15; 16(3); 18; 15:10(2); 11(2); 12; 16; 18; 16:10; 11; 13; 15(2); 17; 17:13; 18:3; 4; 9; 23; 24(3); 19:19; 20:10; 21:7; 16; 18; 22; **Ruth** 1:8; 12(3); 2:9(2); 10; 11(3); 12; 13(2); 19; 21; 3:10; 4:9; 10; **1 Sam** 1:15(2); 16; 17; 20; 23; 28; 2:5(2); 29; 3:12; 13; 14; 4:9; 20; 5:10; 6:7; 21; 7:6; 8:7(2); 8(2); 18; 19; 9:7; 8; 16; 20; 10:2(2); 5; 19(2); 11:9; 12:1(2); 2; 3(5); 4(2); 5; 10(2); 13(2); 17; 19; 20; 13:11; 12; 13(3); 14; 14:11; 24; 30; 33; 43; 15:3; 11; 13; 15(2); 20(2); 21; 23; 24(2); 26; 30; 16:1(2); 2; 5; 7; 18; 17:8; 25; 28(2); 29; 39; 45; 18:8(3); 19; 19:4; 17; 20:1; 3; 8; 12; 19; 23; 29; 30; 42; 21:2(2); 3; 4; 5; 8; 14; 15(2); 22:8; 13(3); 22; 23:21; 27; 24:10; 11; 17(2); 18(2); 19; 25:6; 7(2); 11; 21; 31; 33; 34; 35; 26:8; 15; 16(2); 18; 19; 21(2); 27:5; 10; 28:12; 15(2); 21; 22; 29:3; 4; 6(2); 8(3); 9; 10(2); 30:22; **2 Sam** 1:3(2); 4; 10; 16; 19; 25; 26; 27; 2:5(2); 6; 27; 3:7; 8; 24; 4:3; 10; 11; 6:22; 7:6(2); 7(3); 9(4); 11; 18; 19; 21; 22; 24(2); 25(2); 27; 28; 29; 9:9; 10; 10:5; 11:19; 12:8; 9(4); 10(2); 13; 14; 21; 27(2); 13:9; 28; 32; 14:13; 15(2); 21; 22; 31; 32; 15:26; 35; 36; 16:8; 10(2); 19; 17:15; 20; 18:11; 13(2); 18; 21; 22; 19:5(2); 6(2); 11; 20; 22; 28; 29; 34; 41; 42; 43(2); 20:1(2); 21:4; 22:22(2); 36; 38; 39(2); 40(2); 41; 44(3); 49; 24:10(3); 17(3); **1 Ki** 1:6; 11; 24; 27; 33; 35; 44; 45(3); 47; 2:8; 14; 42; 43; 3:6(3); 7; 8; 11(5); 12(2); 13(2); 5:8; 9; 8:13; 16; 20(2); 21; 24(2); 25(2); 26; 27; 33; 35; 36; 43; 44(2); 47(2); 48(2); 50(3); 59; 9:3(4); 4; 5; 6; 7(2); 9; 13; 11:11(3); 13; 22; 32(2); 33(2); 34; 36(2); 12:9; 10; 16(2); 13:17; 21(2); 14:6; 8; 9(3); 15; 15:19; 16:2(2); 17:4; 9; 12; 13; 18(2); 20; 18:5; 9; 12; 18(4); 36; 37; 19:10(2); 14(2); 18(2); 20; 20:4; 5; 13; 18(2); 25; 28; 31; 36; 40; 42; 21:2; 10; 19; 20(3); 22; 22:17(2); **2 Ki** 1:4; 5; 6; 16(2); 2:10; 21; 3:13; 23(2); 27; 4:2; 4; 13; 43; 5:6; 8; 13; 22; 6:22; 7:12(2); 17; 9:3; 5; 6; 12; 18; 19; 10:2; 8; 13; 19; 24; 30(2); 12:7; 13:17; 19(2); 14:10; 17:26; 38; 41; 18:14; 25; 34; 35; 19:3; 6(2); 11(2); 12(2); 15; 17; 18; 20(2); 22(2); 23(2); 24(2); 25; 28; 30; 20:3(2); 5(2); 15(3); 17; 19; 21:7; 8; 15(2); 22:4; 8; 9(2); 13; 17; 18; 19; 23:17; 27(2); **1 Chr** 4:27; 43; 11:19; 12:17; 13:3; 15:12; 17:5(2); 6(3); 8(4); 16; 17(2); 19; 20; 22(2); 23(2); 25; 26; 27(2); 19:5; 21:8(3); 17; 22:8(3); 14(2); 23:11; 28:3(2); 6; 20; 29:2; 3(3); 14; 16; 17(3); 19; **2 Chr** 1:8(2); 9; 11(4); 12(2); 2:3; 8; 13; 6:2; 5; 6(2); 10(2); 11; 15(2); 16(2); 17; 18; 24; 26; 27; 33; 34(2); 37(3); 38(3); 39; 7:12(2); 16; 17; 18; 19; 20(2); 10:9; 10; 16(2); 12:5(2); 7; 13:9; 10; 11; 14:7(2); 11; 16:3; 7(2); 9(2); 18:16(2); 19:3(2); 20:8; 11; 12; 37; 21:12; 13(3); 24:6; 20; 25:9; 15; 16(3); 19; 26:18(2); 28:9; 11; 13; 29:6(3); 7(2); 9; 18; 19; 31; 30:6; 31:10(2); 32:13; 17; 33:7; 8(2); 34:15; 17(2); 21; 24; 25; 26; 27; 35:15; 21(3); **Ezra** 4:2; 12; 14; 15; 16; 19; 20(2); 7:15; 20; 9:1; 2; 6; 7(2); 10; 11; 13(2); 10:2(2); 3; 10(2); 12; 13; 14; **Neh** 1:6(2); 7(2); 9; 10; 2:20; 4:5; 5:3; 4; 5(2); 8; 11; 19; 6:7; 13; 14; 9:6; 8; 33(2); 34; 35; 37(2); 13:14; 29; **Esth** 1:18; 4:11; 14; 5:4; 8; 6:10(2); 13; 7:3; 4(2); 8:5; 7(2); 9:12(2); **Job** 1:5; 8; 10(3); 15(2); 16; 17; 19; 2:3; 3:9; 13(3); 26; 4:3(2); 4(2); 8; 5:3; 16; 23; 27; 6:3; 8; 10(2); 11; 15; 24; 7:3(2); 4; 20(3); 8:4; 18; 10:4; 8; 9; 12; 13; 18; 19(2); 11:4; 16; 12:3; 13:18; 14:5; 15:8; 17; 18; 16:2; 3; 7; 8; 15; 18; 17:4; 6; 16; 19:3(2); 4; 14(2); 19; 20; 21(2); 20:3; 7; 21:3; 15; 29; 33; 22:6; 7(2); 9; 15; 26; 23:11; 12(2); 24:7; 19; 26:2(2); 3(2); 4; 27:12; 28:8; 22; 30:11; 13; 19; 21; 25; 31:1; 5; 9; 13; 16; 19; 21; 24; 25; 26; 28; 29; 30; 31; 32; 33; 39; 32:13; 16; 33:6; 8(2); 24; 27; 32; 34:2; 16; 31; 32; 35:3; 36:9; 16; 21; 23; 24; 37:18; 38:4; 12; 16(2); 17(2); 18; 22(2); 23; 39:6; 19(2); 40:5; 9; 42:3; 5; 7; 8; **Ps** 2:6; 7; 3:1; 6; 7(2); 4:1(2); 7; 5:10; 6:2; 7:3; 4(2); 6; 8:1; 2; 3; 5(2); 6(3); 9:4; 5(3); 6; 10; 13; 15; 10:2; 14; 16; 17; 12:4; 13:4; 5; 14:1; 3(2); 4; 16:2; 6(2); 8; 17:3(5); 4; 6; 10; 11(2); 14; 18:21(2); 35; 37; 38(2); 39(2); 40; 43(3); 48; 19:13; 20:8(2); 21:1; 2(2); 5; 6(2); 22:1; 10; 12(2); 15; 16; 21; 25:16; 17; 26:1(2); 3; 4; 5; 8; 27:4; 7; 9; 12; 13; 30:1(2); 3; 7; 10; 11(2); 31:4; 5; 6; 7(2); 8(2); 9; 17; 19(2); 32:5; 9; 33:21; 34:18(2); 35:7(2); 21; 22; 25(2); 36:12(2); 37:14(2); 25(2); 35; 38:4; 19; 39:5; 40:5; 6; 9; 10(3); 12(2); 41:4; 42:3; 7; 9; 44:1(2); 7(2); 9; 10; 11(2); 17(2); 18; 19; 45:8; 47:9; 48:8(2); 9; 49:14; 50:5; 16; 18; 21; 51:1; 4; 8; 52:9; 53:1; 3; 4; 5; 54:3(3); 55:4; 5; 9; 56:4; 11; 13(2); 57:1; 6(3); 59:8; 16; 60:1(3); 2(2); 3(2); 4; 61:3; 5(2); 62:11; 63:2; 7; 64:6; 65:9; 66:10(2); 12; 14; 68:18(3); 23; 24; 28; 69:1; 2; 4; 7; 8; 9; 26(2); 71:3; 6; 7; 17; 19; 20; 23; 72:8; 73:7; 13; 14; 15; 25; 27; 28; 74:1; 2(3); 7(2); 8; 16; 17(2); 20; 76:5(2); 77:5; 14; 15; 78:3(2); 79:1(3); 2; 3; 4; 7; 8; 12; 80:5; 6; 8(2); 12; 81:11; 16(2); 83:2; 3; 4; 5; 8; 85:1(2); 2(2); 3(2); 10(2); 86:9; 13; 14(3); 16; 17; 88:1; 6; 7; 8(2); 9(2); 13; 15; 16; 18; 89:2; 3(2); 10(2); 11; 12; 13; 19(2); 20(2); 35; 38(2); 39(2); 40(2); 42(2); 43(2); 44; 45(2); 47; 51(2); 90:1; 7; 8; 9; 13; 15(2); 91:9; 92:4; 10(2); 93:3(2); 94:17; 20; 98:1; 3; 99:4(2); 102:9; 10; 13; 27; 104:9; 12; 24; 26; 33; 106:4; 6(3); 109:2(2); 3; 5; 25; 27; 110:3; 111:2; 10; 115:5(2); 6(2); 7(2); 116:8; 16; 118:21(2); 26; 119:4; 10; 11; 13; 14; 22; 26; 30(2); 42; 43; 49; 51; 52; 54; 57; 61(2); 65; 69; 71; 73; 74; 75; 83; 85; 92; 93; 94; 96; 99; 101; 102(2); 106; 110(2); 111; 112; 121; 126; 133; 138; 139; 143; 152(2); 165; 173; 176; 122:2; 123:3(2); 124:3; 4(2); 5; 7; 129:1; 2(2); 130:1; 131:2; 132:14; 135:14; 16(2); 17; 137:8; 138:2; 139:1; 5; 140:4; 5(3); 7; 141:9; 142:3; 143:3; 146:2; 147:20; 149:9; **Prov** 1:14; 24(2); 25; 30; 3:28; 4:11(2); 16; 5:12; 13; 6:1; 3; 31; 7:14(2); 15; 16; 17; 8:14; 23; 9:5; 11:18; 12:20; 13:3; 14:26; 19:19; 20:4; 9; 22:2; 19; 20; 27; 28; 23:8; 35(2); 24:14; 25; 25:7; 16; 26:27; 27:27; 28:13; 19(2); 27; 29:13; 21; 30:2; 3; 20; 27; 32(2); 31:11; 29; **Eccl** 1:14; 16(2); 2:19; 25; 3:10; 19; 4:1(2); 9; 5:4; 11; 13; 18; 6:1; 8; 7:12; 15; 22; 23; 27; 28(2); 29(2); 8:9; 9:5; 6(2); 13; 10:5; 7; 12:1; **Song** 1:6; 9; 15; 2:15; 3:3; 4:1; 2; 9(2); 5:1(4); 3(2); 6:5; 6; 7:13; 8:8; 12; **Isa** 1:2(2); 4(3); 6; 9(2); 11; 29(2); 2:6; 8; 3:6; 9; 14; 4:2; 5:4(2); 13(2); 24; 6:5; 7:5; 17; 8:4; 9:2; 3; 4; 10; 17(2); 10:1; 11; 13(4); 14; 20; 29(2); 13:3(2); 18; 14:1; 10(2); 13; 20; 24(2); 15:7(2); 16:6; 8(2); 9; 10; 17:7; 8; 10(2); 19:13(2); 14; 21:2; 3; 8; 10(2); 22:1; 3(2); 11; 16(3); 23:2; 12; 24:5; 16(3); 25:1; 2; 4; 9(2); 26:1; 8; 9; 12; 13; 14; 15(3); 16; 17; 18(5); 27:11; 28:7(2); 15(4); 22; 29:13; 16; 30:2; 7; 18; 29; 31:6; 7; 33:1(2); 2; 13; 36:10; 19; 20; 37:3; 6(2); 11(2); 12(2); 16; 18; 19(2); 21; 23(2); 24(2); 25(2); 26; 29; 31; 38:3(2); 5(2); 12; 13; 17(2); 39:4(3); 6; 8; 40:21(3); 28(2); 29; 41:8; 9(3); 25; 42:1; 6; 9; 14(2); 16; 24; 43:1(2); 4(2); 7(3); 8(2); 10; 12(2); 21; 22(2); 23(3); 24(4); 27; 44:1; 2; 8; 16; 19(3); 21; 22(2); 45:1; 4(3); 5; 8; 10; 12(2); 13; 19; 20(2); 21; 23; 24; 46:2; 3(2); 4; 11(2); 47:6; 10(4); 12; 15; 48:1; 3; 5(2); 6(2); 7; 10(2); 15(3); 16(2); 18; 19(2); 49:4(2); 8(2); 13; 15; 16; 20(2); 21; 50:1(3); 2; 7; 11(2); 51:13; 16(2); 17(2); 19; 20; 22; 23(2); 52:3; 5; 53:6(2); 54:1(2); 7; 8; 9(2); 16(2); 55:1; 4; 7; 56:11; 57:6(2); 7; 8(5); 10; 11(3); 16; 18; 58:3(3); 5; 6; 59:2(2); 3; 8(2); 21; 60:10; 15; 61:7; 62:6; 8; 9(2); 63:3(3); 6; 17; 18(2); 19; 64:4; 5; 6; 7(2); 65:2; 7; 10; 66:3; 19; 24; **Jer** 1:9; 10; 12; 16; 18; 2:5(4); 11; 13(2); 16; 17(2); 19; 20; 21; 23(2); 25; 27; 28; 29; 30; 31; 32; 33; 34; 35; 3:1; 2(3); 3(2); 5; 6; 13(3); 18; 20; 21(2); 25(2); 4:10(2); 18; 19; 22(3); 28(2); 31; 5:3(6); 5(2); 6; 7; 11; 12; 19; 21(2); 22; 23; 25(2); 27; 28; 31; 6:2; 10; 14; 19; 23; 24; 27; 7:11; 13; 14; 15; 23; 25; 30(2); 31; 8:2(5); 3; 6; 9(2); 11; 13; 14; 16; 19; 9:3; 5; 10; 13(2); 14; 16(2); 19(2); 10:11; 20; 21(2); 25; 11:5; 8; 10(3); 13; 17; 20; 12:2(2); 3(2); 5(2); 6(2); 7(3); 8; 10(3); 11; 12(2); 13(2); 14; 15(2); 13:11; 14; 21; 22(2); 25; 27; 14:3; 7; 10(2); 13; 14; 16; 19(2); 20; 22; 15:5; 6(2); 10(3); 15; 17; 16:2; 5; 10; 11(4); 12; 18(2); 19; 17:4; 13; 16(2); 18:8; 15(3); 20; 22; 19:4(4); 5; 13; 15(2); 20:6; 7; 12; 17; 21:7; 10; 22:9; 12; 23:2; 3; 11; 13; 14; 17; 21(2); 22; 25(4); 36; 38; 24:5; 25:3(2); 4; 7; 8; 13; 35; 26:4; 5; 9; 11; 12; 27:5(2); 6(2); 8; 15; 28:2; 6; 8; 13(2); 14(2); 16; 29:4; 7(2); 9; 14; 15; 16; 18; 19; 20; 23(4); 25; 27; 31; 32; 30:2; 5; 10; 11; 13; 14(3); 15(2); 18; 31:3(2); 18(2); 20; 25(2); 28; 29; 37; 32:17; 20(2); 21; 22; 23(3); 24(2); 25; 29; 30(2); 32; 33(2); 37; 42(2); 33:4; 5; 8(3); 14; 21; 24(3); 25; 26; 34:5; 17; 18(2); 35:7; 8; 9; 10(2); 14; 15(3); 16; 17(5); 18; 36:2; 6; 14; 29(2); 30; 31; 37:18(2); 38:9(3); 19; 22(3); 25(2); 39:18; 40:3; 10; 41:8; 42:4; 10; 12; 18; 19; 21(2); 43:10; 44:2(2); 3; 4; 8; 9; 10(3); 12; 13; 14; 16; 17; 18(2); 23(3); 25(2); 26; 28; 45:4(2); 46:5(2); 12(2); 21; 27; 28; 48:2; 4; 5; 7; 15; 29; 30; 32; 33; 34; 36(2); 38; 46; 49:9; 10(2); 12; 13; 14; 23; 24; 37; 50:6(5); 7(3); 11; 15; 17; 18; 21; 23; 24(3); 33(2); 51:9; 24; 30(3); 32; 50; 51(2); 62; 63; **Lam** 1:2(2); 5(2); 6; 8; 11; 18; 20; 21(4); 22; 2:7; 9; 14(3); 16(5); 20(2); 21(3); 22(3); 3:14; 17(2); 18; 21; 42(2); 43(2); 44; 45; 46; 47; 56; 58(2); 59; 60; 61; 4:10; 12; 14; 5:3; 5; 6; 14; 16; 22; **Ezek** 2:3; 3:6; 8; 9; 17; 19; 21; 4:5; 6(2); 8; 14(2); 5:5; 6(2); 7(2); 9; 11(2); 13(2); 15; 17; 6:8; 10; 7:4; 9; 14; 20; 8:12; 15; 17(3); 18; 9:1; 5; 10; 11; 10:8; 9; 11:5; 6(2); 7; 8; 12(2); 15; 16(3); 17; 12:6; 11; 22; 13:3; 5; 6; 7(3); 8; 10; 14; 15; 22(3); 14:3; 9; 22(2); 23(2); 15:6; 8; 16:5; 15; 17; 21; 48(2); 51(3); 58; 59; 63; 17:21; 24(3); 18:2; 23; 31; 32; 20:3; 27; 32; 41; 43; 44; 48; 21:5; 15; 17; 23; 24(2); 32; 22:4(7); 7(3); 8; 12(2); 13; 14; 18; 19; 22; 25(3); 26(4); 29; 31(3); 23:9; 22; 29; 30(2); 31; 34; 35; 37(2); 38(2); 39; 24:8; 13(2); 14; 22; 26:5; 14; 17; 27:3; 4; 6; 28:4; 5; 6; 10; 19; 25; 29:3; 5; 6; 9; 20; 30:8; 12; 16; 21; 31:10; 11; 12(3); 14; 32:9; 21; 24; 25; 27(2); 30; 32; 33:7; 9; 11; 29(2); 34:4(3); 18(2); 19(2); 21; 24; 27; 35:5(2); 6; 10; 12(2); 13(2); 36:2; 4; 5; 6(2); 7; 20; 22; 23; 36(2); 37:13; 14; 21; 23; 24; 25; 38:12; 13(2); 17; 19; 39:5; 8; 15; 21(2); 24; 25; 26; 27; 29; 40:45; 46; 42:6; 43:8; 11; 23; 44:6; 8(2); 12; 13; 18; 19; 45:5; 7; 10; 47:6; 13; 22; 48:11; 13; 23; 24; 25; 26; 27; **Dan** 2:3; 9; 21; 23(3); 25; 26; 30; 3:10; 12(3); 14; 15; 16; 18; 28; 4:9; 18; 22; 30; 35; 5:7; 14; 15; 16(2); 22; 23(5); 27; 6:7; 12; 13; 22(2); 8:23; 9:5(2); 6; 7(2); 8; 9; 10; 11(2); 13; 14; 15(2); 22; 23; 10:11; 12; 14; 16(2); 19; 20(2); 11:5; 15; 24; 43; **Hos** 1:6; 7; 2:4; 12; 23; 3:3; 4:6(2); 10(2); 12; 5:1; 7(2); 6:5(2); 10; 7:1(2); 2; 5; 7(2); 9; 13(3); 8:1; 9; 10; 11; 12; 9:1(2); 7(2); 10:1; 3; 4; 9; 13(3); 12:8(2); 10(3); 13:2; 14:1; 8(2); **Joel** 1:9; 18; 3:2(2); 3(2); 4; 5(2); 6; 7; 19; **Am** 1:3; 2:4(2); 3:2; 6; 15; 4:6; 8; 9; 10; 11; 5:3(2); 11(2); 14; 6:12; 13; 9:15; **Ob** 1; 5(2); 12(3); 13(2); 14(2); 15; **Jon** 1:10; 14; 2:4; 6; 9; 4:10(2); **Mic** 2:5; 8; 9; 3:4; 6(2); 4:6; 9; 11; 5:12; 15; 6:3(2); 12; 7:9; 19; 20; **Nah** 1:12; 2:2; 3:16; **Hab** 1:12(2); 14; 2:8; 3:2; **Zeph** 1:6(2); 17; 2:3; 8(2); 10(2); 3:4(2); 6(2); **Hag** 1:6(2); 2:19; 23; **Zech** 1:11; 12; 19; 2:6; 3:4; 7; 9; 4:9; 6:8; 10; 7:3; 7; 8:9; 23; 9:8; 13; 10:6; 13:3; 14:18; **Mal** 1:2(3); 3; 4(2); 6; 7; 10; 2:2; 4; 8(3); 9(3); 10; 14; 17(2); 3:7(2); 8(2); 9; 13(2); 14(3); **Mt** 2:2(2); 8; 3:9; 4:16; 5:21; 26; 27; 33; 38; 40; 43; 46; 6:1; 2(2); 5; 6; 8; 16; 7:22; 8:10; 13; 20(2); 29(2); 9:12; 27; 10:8; 23; 25; 35; 11:5; 21; 23; 25(2); 27; 12:3; 5; 7; 18; 13:5; 12(2); 15(2); 27; 51; 14:4; 17; 15:5; 6; 22; 32(3); 34; 16:7; 8; 17:15; 20; 27; 18:15; 26; 29; 33; 19:4; 12; 16; 20; 21(2); 27(2); 28; 20:6; 12(2); 30; 31; 21:13; 16(2); 21; 42; 22:4; 11; 31; 23:23(2); 30; 24:25; 43; 25:20; 22; 23; 24(2); 25; 26(2); 27(2); 29(2); 26:9; 11(2); 24; 25; 32; 35; 50; 55; 65(2); 27:4; 19(2); 43; 46; 65; 28:7; 20; **Mk** 1:24; 38; 2:17; 19; 25; 3:15; 4:5; 17; 25; 40; 5:7; 6:18; 31; 36; 38; 48; 7:4; 11; 13; 8:2(3); 3; 5; 14; 16; 17; 9:22; 50(2); 10:20; 21(2); 23; 28; 47; 48; 11:2; 17; 22; 23; 24; 25; 32; 12:10; 26; 32; 43; 13:23; 14:5; 7(2); 21; 28; 31; 48; 63; 64; 15:34; **Lk** 1:1(2); 14; 30; 59; 62; 70; 2:30; 31; 44; 48(2); 3:8; 4:23; 34; 43; 5:5; 26; 31; 32; 6:3; 24; 7:9; 22(2); 40; 43; 8:13; 14; 18(2); 28; 9:3; 9; 13; 58(2); 10:13; 21; 22; 24(3); 28; 11:5; 6; 41; 42; 52; 12:3(2); 4; 17; 19; 20; 24; 29; 33; 37; 39; 50; 59; 13:7; 14:10; 18(2); 19(2); 20; 15:6; 9; 16; 17; 18; 21; 29; 31; 16:4; 11; 12; 24; 28; 29; 17:6; 8; 10(2); 13; 18:21; 22(2); 24; 28; 38; 39; 19:8; 14; 17; 20; 23; 26; 46; 20:24; 39; 21:4; 22:10; 15; 28; 32(2); 37; 52; 71; 23:14(2); 22; 24:17; 18; 25; 26; 28; 39(2); 41; **Jn** 1:16; 34; 41; 45; 2:3; 4; 10(2); 3:11; 12; 15; 16; 21; 26; 28; 4:9; 10(2); 11; 17(3); 18(2); 32; 38(3); 42; 5:7; 14; 17; 26; 29(2); 30; 36; 37; 38; 39; 40; 42; 43; 6:7; 36; 38; 40; 42; 53; 65; 68; 69; 7:20; 28; 45; 48; 8:6; 12; 19; 25; 26; 33; 38(2); 41; 42; 48; 49; 52; 55; 57; 9:37; 39; 41; 10:10(3); 16; 18(3); 32; 11:21; 32; 34; 37; 41; 12:8(2); 28; 34; 35; 36; 46; 48; 49; 13:8; 12; 14; 15(2); 18; 26; 34; 35; 38; 14:2; 7(2); 9(2); 25; 28; 29; 15:3; 9; 10; 11; 12; 15(2); 22(2); 24(2); 27; 16:1; 3; 4; 6; 12; 22; 24; 25; 27(2); 28; 30; 33(4); 17:2(2); 3; 4(3); 6(3); 7(2); 8(5); 9; 11; 12; 13; 14; 18; 22; 23(3); 24; 25(2); 26; 18:8; 9; 20; 21; 23; 30; 35(2); 37; 39; 19:7; 10; 11; 15; 22(2); 20:2(2); 13(2); 15(2); 17; 25; 29(4); 31; 21:5; 10; **Acts** 1:4; 21; 24; 2:23(2); 28; 3:6(2); 24(2); 4:7; 20; 25; 5:4(2); 9(2); 21; 28; 6:11; 14; 7:25; 34(3); 52; 53(2); 8:21; 24; 9:13; 10:4; 14; 20; 21; 29; 33; 47(2); 13:2; 15; 22; 27; 33; 47; 14:11; 15:24(2); 26; 27; 36; 16:3; 15; 36; 37(2); 17:6(2); 28(2); 18:10; 19:2; 21; 25; 37; 38; 39; 20:16; 25; 27; 33; 34; 35; 21:20; 21; 22; 23(2); 25; 22:15; 23:1; 11; 14(2); 19; 20; 21(2); 22; 35; 24:5; 10; 15; 16; 19; 23; 25; 25:5; 8; 10; 11; 12; 26(3); 26:3; 16(2); 32; 27:21(2); 33; 28:17; 20; 21; 27(2); **Rom** 1:5; 13; 2:12(2); 14; 3:9; 12(2); 13; 17; 23; 4:17; 5:1; 2; 11; 6:5; 14; 21; 22; 7:4; 6; 7(2); 8:9; 23; 9:2; 9; 13(2); 15(4); 17; 20; 21; 29(2); 30; 10:2; 3; 14(2); 16; 18; 21; 11:3; 4(2); 7; 11; 30; 31; 32; 12:4(2); 17; 13:3; 14:22(2); 15:4; 15; 17; 19; 20; 21; 22; 27; 28(2); 16:12; **1 Cor** 2:8; 9; 12(2); 16; 3:10; 4:6; 7; 8; 9; 13; 15(3); 17; 5:2; 3; 11; 12; 6:4; 19; 7:2(2); 4(2); 25; 28(2); 29; 40; 8:1; 10; 9:1; 4; 5; 6; 11; 12; 15(2); 16; 17(2); 19; 22; 27; 10:11; 20; 11:10; 16; 22(2); 12:13; 21(2); 23; 24; 25; 30; 13:1(2); 2(3); 3; 15:6; 15; 18(2); 19; 20; 31; 32; 34; 49; 16:1; 15; **2 Cor** 1:14; 15; 24; 2:3(2); 4; 10(2); 3:4; 12; 4:1(2); 2; 7; 13; 5:1; 12; 16; 17(2); 6:2(2); 11; 7:2(3); 3; 13; 14; 16; 8:11; 12; 18; 22(3); 9:3; 8; 10; 11:2; 4(3); 6; 25; 12:11(3); 21(3); 13:2(2); **Gal** 1:8; 9(2); 13; 2:4; 16; 20; 3:4; 21(2); 27; 4:9; 11; 12; 15; 16; 20; 5:4(2); 10(2); 13; 24; 6:4; 10; 11; 13; **Eph** 1:7; 11; 2:5; 8; 13; 18; 3:2; 3; 12; 4:19; 20; 21(2); 28; 5:11; 6:22; **Phil** 1:7; 12; 2:12; 16; 20; 27; 3:3; 4(2); 7; 8; 12; 13; 15; 16; 17; 18; 4:11; 12; 14; 18; **Col** 1:14; 18; 2:1(2); 6; 7; 23; 3:9; 10; 4:1; 11; 17; **1 Th** 2:4; 6; 15; 3:6; 4:9; 13(2); 5:1; **2 Th** 3:2; 4; 9; **1 Tim** 1:6; 19; 2:12; 3:7; 13; 4:6; 5:11; 12; 15; 6:2; 10; 12; 21; **2 Tim** 1:12(2); 13; 15; 2:2; 18; 3:10; 14(2); 15; 4:3; 7(3); 8; 12; 20; **Titus** 3:5; 8; 12; **Phm** 1:5; 7(2); 10; 20; **Heb** 1:5; 9; 2:1; 7(2); 8; 14; 3:10; 14; 4:1; 3; 8; 14; 15; 5:2; 5; 11(2); 12; 14; 6:4(2); 5; 10(2); 18(2); 19; 7:5(2); 21; 28; 8:1; 3; 7; 9:26; 10:2(2); 5; 7; 9; 10; 26; 34; 36(2); 11:15; 12:4; 5; 8; 9; 11; 18; 22; 28; 13:2; 5; 7; 9(2); 10(2); 14; 18; 22; **Jas** 1:4; 2:4; 6; 11; 14; 17; 18(2); 3:9; 14; 4:2(2); 5:3; 4; 5(2); 6(2); 11; **1 Pe** 1:6; 10; 12(2); 22; 2:3; 10; 25; 4:3; 8; 5:10; 12; **2 Pe** 1:1; 4; 15; 19; 2:14; 15; 18; 20; 21(2); **1 Jn** 1:1(4); 2; 3(2); 5; 6; 7; 8; 10; 2:1; 7; 13(3); 14(4); 18(2); 19; 20; 21; 23; 26; 27; 28; 3:14; 21; 4:1; 3; 4; 14; 16; 17; 21; 5:12(2); 13(2); 14; 15(2); **2 Jn** 1; 4; 5; 6; 7; 9; **3 Jn** 4; 6; 9; **Jude** 4; 11(2); 15(2); 22; **Rev** 1:18; 19; 2:2(2); 3(4); 4(2); 5; 6; 10; 14(2); 15; 20; 24(2); 25; 27; 3:1; 2; 3; 4(2); 8(4); 9; 10; 11; 17(2); 5:9; 10; 7:3; 9:3; 4; 11:6(2); 15; 17; 12:10; 17; 13:8; 14:11; 15:2; 4; 16:5; 6(2); 17:10; 12; 18:3(3); 5; 14; 19:10; 20:7; 21:4; 8; 22:14; 16

HE (10435/7554)

Gen 1:5; 10; 16; 27(2); 31; 2:2(3); 3; 8(2); 19; 21(2); 22(2); 3:1; 6; 10; 11; 15; 16(2); 17; 22; 23; 24(2); 4:5; 9; 10; 17; 20; 21; 26; 5:1; 2; 4(2); 5; 7; 8; 10; 11; 13; 14; 16; 17; 19; 20; 22; 24; 26; 27; 29; 30; 31; 6:3; 6(2); 22; 7:23; 8:6; 7; 8; 9; 10(2); 12; 9:6; 20; 21; 25(2); 26; 27; 29; 10:8; 9; 11; 11:11; 13; 15; 17; 19; 21; 23; 25; 12:4; 7; 8(3); 11(2); 16(2); 20; 13:1(2); 3; 4; 14:13; 14; 15(2); 16; 18; 19; 20; 15:5(2); 6(2); 7; 8; 9; 10(2); 13; 16:4; 8; 12(2); 17:12(2); 13(2); 14; 20; 22; 24; 25; 18:1; 2(3); 7; 8(3); 9; 10; 15; 19(2); 28; 29(2); 30(2); 31(2); 32(2); 33; 19:1(2); 2; 3(2); 9; 14; 16; 17; 21; 25; 27; 28(2); 29; 30(2); 33; 35; 37; 38; 20:4; 5(2); 7(2); 13; 14; 16; 21:1(2); 4; 13; 14; 17; 20; 21; 30; 31; 22:1; 2; 3; 6; 7(2); 9; 11; 12; 23:8; 9(2); 13; 16; 24:2; 7; 10; 11; 12; 15; 27; 30(4); 31; 32; 33(2); 34; 35(2); 36(2); 40; 52; 53; 54(2); 56; 62; 63; 66; 67(2); 25:5; 6(2); 7; 17; 18; 20; 25; 28; 29; 33; 34; 26:7(3); 8; 11; 13; 14; 18; 20; 21; 22(3); 23; 25(2); 30; 33; 34; 27:1(3); 2; 9; 10(2); 14; 18(2); 20; 22; 23(2); 24(2); 25(5); 27(2); 31; 32; 33; 34; 35; 36(5); 45; 28:5; 6(2); 9; 11(3); 12; 17; 18; 19; 29:2; 5; 6(3); 7; 9; 12(2); 13(2); 14; 18; 20; 23(2); 25; 28; 30(2); 31; 33; 30:2; 6; 15; 16; 28; 31; 35; 36; 38(2); 40; 42; 31:1; 8(2); 12; 15; 18(3); 20(2); 21(3); 23(2); 33(2); 35; 49; 32:2(2); 4; 6; 7; 8; 11; 13; 16; 17; 18; 19; 20(2); 21; 22; 23(2); 25(4); 26(2); 27(2); 28; 29(2); 31(2); 32; 33:1; 2; 3(2); 5(2); 8; 11(2); 15; 18(2); 19(2); 20; 34:2; 3; 5; 7; 13; 19(2); 31; 35:6; 7(2); 9; 10; 13; 14(3); 36:6; 24; 37:3(2); 5; 6; 9; 10; 13; 14(3); 15; 16; 18; 21; 22; 27; 29; 30; 33; 35(2); 38:2; 3; 5; 9(3); 10(2); 11(2); 12; 15; 16(2); 17; 18(2); 20; 21; 22; 26; 29; 39:2(2); 3; 4(3); 5(3); 6(5); 8(3); 9; 10; 12; 13; 14(2); 15(2); 18; 20; 21; 23; 40:3; 4; 7; 16; 20(2); 21(2); 22; 41:1; 5; 8; 11; 12(2); 13(3); 14; 25; 28; 42; 43(3); 45; 46; 48(2); 49; 52; 55; 42:2; 4; 6; 7(2); 9; 12; 17; 21; 23; 24(3); 25; 27; 28; 38(2); 43:7; 14; 16; 18; 23(2); 24; 27(2); 28; 29(2); 30; 31(2); 34; 44:1; 2; 5; 6(2); 10(2); 12(2); 14; 16; 17(2); 20; 22; 28; 31(2); 45:1; 2; 4; 8; 14; 15; 21; 22(2); 23; 24(2); 26(2); 27; 46:1; 2; 3; 7; 28; 29; 47:2; 17; 21; 22; 29; 30; 31(2); 48:1; 9; 10(2); 12; 15; 17; 19(3); 20(2); 49:4; 8; 9(2); 11; 13; 15(2); 19; 20; 21; 27(2); 28(2); 29; 33; 50:6; 10; 12; 14(2); 16; 21; 22; 24; 26; **Ex** 1:9; 16; 21; 2:2; 10; 11(2); 12(3); 13(2); 14; 15(2); 18; 19; 20(3); 21; 22(2); 3:1; 2; 4(2); 5; 6(2); 12; 14; 20; 4:2; 3(2); 4; 6(2); 7(2); 13; 14(5); 16(2); 20; 21; 23; 26; 27; 28; 30; 31; 5:3; 17; 23; 6:1(2); 7:13; 14; 15; 20; 22; 8:8; 10(2); 12; 15; 19; 20; 27; 31; 32; 9:7; 12; 20; 21; 34(3); 35; 10:6; 8; 10; 17; 18; 20; 27; 11:1(3); 8; 10; 12:19; 23; 25; 27; 30; 31; 44; 48; 13:5; 11; 19; 22; 14:4; 6; 7; 8; 13; 24; 25; 15:1(2); 2(2); 4; 21(2); 25(4); 16:7; 9; 18(2); 23; 29; 17:7; 11; 12; 16; 18:2; 3; 4; 5; 6; 9; 11; 14(2); 24; 27; 19:13(2); 15; 24; 21:2(2); 3(3); 4; 6(2); 8(3); 9(2); 10(2); 11; 12(2); 13(2); 14; 15; 16(2); 17; 18; 19(3); 20(2); 21(3); 22(2); 26; 27(2); 29; 30; 32; 34; 36; 22:1; 2; 3(3); 4; 5; 6; 7; 8; 11(2); 12; 13(2); 14; 15; 16; 17; 20(2); 27(2); 23:21; 25; 24:1; 4; 5; 6; 7; 11; 14; 16; 28:1; 3; 4; 29; 30; 35(4); 29:21; 30; 30:7(2); 8; 10; 38; 31:15; 17; 18(2); 32:4(2); 5; 12; 14(2); 17; 18; 19(3); 20(2); 27; 29; 33:8; 11; 14; 15; 18; 19; 20; 34:4(2); 9; 10; 28(3); 29(2); 32; 33; 34(4);

35; 35:31; 34; 35; 36:4; 10(2); 11(2); 12(2); 13; 14(2); 16; 17(2); 18; 19; 20; 22; 23; 24; 25; 27; 28; 29; 31; 33; 34; 35; 36(2); 37; 38; 37:2; 3; 4; 5; 6; 7(2); 8; 10; 11; 12; 13; 15; 16; 17(2); 23; 24; 25; 26(2); 27; 28; 29; 38:1; 2(2); 3(2); 4; 5; 6; 7(2); 8; 9; 28; 30; 39:2; 7; 8; 22; 40:13; 16; 19; 20; 21; 22; 23; 24; 25; 26; 27; 28; 29; 30; 33; **Lev** 1:3; 4; 5; 6; 9; 10; 11; 12; 13; 14; 16; 17; 2:1; 2; 8; 3:1(2); 2; 3; 4; 6; 7(2); 8; 9(2); 10; 12; 13; 14; 15; 4:3; 4; 7; 8; 9; 12; 18(2); 19; 20(3); 21(2); 23(2); 24; 26; 28(3); 29; 31; 32(2); 33; 35(2); 5:1(3); 2(2); 3(4); 4(3); 5(3); 6(2); 7(3); 8; 9; 10(2); 11(4); 12; 13; 15; 16(2); 17(2); 18(2); 19; 6:2; 3(2); 4(5); 5(2); 6; 7(3); 10(2); 11; 12; 15; 20; 7:2; 3; 4; 8; 11; 12(2); 13; 14; 15; 16; 20; 29; 30; 33; 36; 38; 8:7(2); 8(2); 9(2); 11; 12; 14; 15(2); 16; 17; 18; 19; 20; 21; 22; 23; 24; 25; 26; 27; 30; 33; 34; 9:2; 9; 10; 11; 12(2); 13; 14; 15; 16; 17; 18(2); 20; 10:1; 16; 20; 11:39; 40(2); 12:7; 13:2; 6; 7(2); 9; 11; 13(2); 14; 16; 17; 33(2); 34; 36; 37; 39; 40(2); 41(3); 44(2); 45; 46(5); 51; 52; 54; 56; 14:2; 6; 7; 8(3); 9(4); 10; 13(2); 18; 19; 20; 21(2); 22; 23; 25; 29; 30(2); 31; 35; 37; 41; 42; 43(2); 45(2); 46; 47(2); 49; 50; 51; 52; 53; 15:4(2); 6(2); 7; 8(2); 9; 10; 11; 12; 13(3); 14; 16; 23(2); 24(2); 27; 16:2; 4(4); 5; 7; 12; 13(2); 14(2); 15(2); 16(2); 17(3); 18; 19; 20(2); 22; 23(2); 24; 25; 26(2); 28(2); 33(3); 34; 17:4; 13; 15(3); 16(2); 18:5; 19:8; 21; 22(2); 20:2; 3; 4; 9; 10; 13; 14; 15; 17(2); 18; 20; 21; 21:3; 4; 8(2); 10; 11; 12; 13; 14(2); 15; 21(2); 22; 23(3); 22:3; 4; 5(2); 6; 7(2); 8; 11; 14; 23:11; 24:4; 8; 16(2); 19; 20; 25:15; 16; 25; 26; 27(2); 28(2); 29(2); 35; 40; 41(3); 48(2); 49(2); 50(2); 51(2); 52(2); 53(2); 54(3); 27:8(2); 10(2); 11; 13(2); 15(2); 17; 18; 19(2); 20(2); 22; 23; 27; 28; 31; 33(3); **Num** 1:19; 3:3; 16; 50; 4:32; 5:7(4); 14(2); 15(2); 21; 23; 24; 27; 30(2); 6:3(3); 4; 5(3); 6(2); 7; 8; 9(3); 10; 11(2); 12; 13; 14; 17; 19; 21(2); 7:1(2); 7; 8; 9; 19; 89(2); 8:3; 4; 9:10; 13; 14; 10:30; 36; 11:3; 24; 30; 32; 34; 12:1(2); 2; 6; 7; 8; 9; 12; 14:8; 16(2); 18; 24(2); 15:4; 14; 27; 28; 30(2); 31; 36; 16:4; 5(3); 10; 26; 31; 40; 47; 48; 17:11; 19:3; 7(2); 11; 12(4); 13; 19(2); 20(2); 21(2); 20:9; 10; 13; 16; 20; 24; 21:1; 7; 8; 9(2); 23; 29; 33; 22:5; 6(2); 8; 22(2); 25; 27; 30; 31(2); 36; 40; 41; 23:3(2); 4; 6(3); 7; 12; 14; 15; 17(2); 18; 19(6); 20; 21(2); 22; 24:1(2); 3; 7; 8(3); 9(4); 10; 15; 20(3); 21(2); 23; 24; 25:7; 8; 11; 13; 15; 27:3(3); 4; 9; 10; 11; 21(2); 22; 23; 30:2(2); 5; 7; 8(2); 12; 14(4); 15(3); 31:6; 32:10; 13; 15; 21; 40; 42; 33:39; 35:12; 16(3); 17(3); 18(3); 19(2); 20(2); 21(4); 22; 23(2); 25(2); 26; 27; 28; 31; 32; **Deut** 1:4; 11; 27; 30(2); 36(3); 38(2); 2:7; 22(2); 30; 3:1; 3; 28(2); 4:13(3); 23; 31(2); 36(3); 37(3); 42; 5:5; 22(2); 24; 6:10; 17; 23(3); 24; 25; 7:8(2); 9; 10(3); 12; 13(3); 24; 8:3(2); 10; 16(2); 18(3); 9:3(2); 5; 25; 28(3); 10:4; 6; 15; 18; 21(2); 11:3; 4(2); 5; 6; 7; 17; 25; 12:10; 12; 15; 20; 31; 13:1; 2; 5; 10(2); 17; 14:21; 23; 27; 29; 15:2; 6; 8; 9; 16(3); 17; 18; 16:16; 17(2); 17:6; 16; 17(2); 18(2); 19(2); 20(3); 18:2; 6; 7; 18; 19; 19:4; 5(2); 6(2); 8(2); 11(2); 12; 15; 19; 20:3; 4; 5; 6; 7; 21:16(2); 17(3); 20(2); 22; 23; 22:3; 16; 17; 19(2); 24; 27; 28; 29(2); 23:1; 7; 10(2); 11(2); 14; 16(2); 24:1(2); 5(3); 6; 13; 15(2); 25:3(2); 7; 8; 18(2); 26:5(2); 9; 18; 19(3); 27:20; 28:8; 9; 21; 44(2); 45; 48(2); 54; 55(3); 60; 29:1; 13(4); 19(2); 25(2); 26; 30:4; 5; 9; 20; 31:2; 3; 4(2); 6(2); 8(3); 11; 23; 32:4(2); 6(2); 7; 8(2); 10(4); 13(3); 15; 19; 20; 36; 37; 39; 43(2); 46; 33:2(3); 3; 5; 7; 8; 9; 12(2); 13; 17; 18; 20(3); 21(3); 22(2); 23; 24; 27; 34:6; 7; **Josh** 1:15; 17; 2:11; 3:1; 10; 4:4; 21; 23; 5:6(2); 7; 13; 14; 6:7; 11; 26(2); 7:6; 15(5); 17(3); 18; 24; 8:4; 10; 12; 14(2); 19; 26(2); 27; 29; 32(2); 33; 34; 9:9; 10; 22; 26; 27; 10:1(2); 7; 12; 28(4); 30(3); 32; 33; 35(2); 37(2); 39(5); 40; 11:1; 9; 11; 12; 15; 17; 20(2); 13:14(2); 33; 14:3; 10; 14; 15:13; 15; 16; 17; 19; 17:1(3); 4; 19:50(2); 20:4(2); 5; 6(3); 9; 21:43; 44; 22:4; 7; 18; 22; 23:3; 10(2); 15; 16(2); 24:7; 10; 17; 18; 19(3); 20(2); 23; 26; 27; 31; **Judg** 1:7; 13; 20; 25; 2:7; 8; 10; 14(2); 20; 21; 23; 3:1; 4(2); 8; 10(2); 13; 17; 18(2); 19(2); 20(2); 22; 24(2); 25; 27(3); 28; 31; 4:3; 10; 18; 19; 20; 21(2); 22; 5:25; 27(7); 6:15; 17; 18; 19(3); 20; 22; 27(2); 30(3); 31; 32(2); 34; 35(2); 38(2); 7:5; 8; 11; 13; 15(2); 16(2); 17; 8:2; 3; 4; 5; 8; 9; 11; 12(2); 14(2); 15; 16(2); 17; 18; 19; 20(3); 26; 30; 31; 35; 9:3; 5(2); 7(2); 16; 18; 21; 28; 29; 31; 33; 36; 40; 43(3); 45(2); 48(2); 50; 52; 54(2); 56; 10:1; 2(2); 3; 4; 7; 18; 11:1; 17; 25(2); 29(2); 33; 34; 35(2); 38(2); 39(2); 12:5; 6(2); 9(3); 11; 14(2); 13:5; 6(2); 7; 11(3); 16; 19; 21; 23(3); 14:2; 4; 6(4); 7; 8(2); 9(5); 14; 15; 16; 17; 18; 19(2); 20; 15:1; 4; 5(2); 6; 8(2); 10; 11; 14; 15; 17(2); 18(2); 19(3); 20; 16:3; 4; 9; 11; 12; 13; 14; 17; 18(2); 20(2); 21; 25(2); 29; 30(3); 31; 17:2; 3; 4(2); 5; 7; 8(3); 9; 18:4(2); 20; 24; 26; 31; 19:1; 3; 4; 5; 7; 8; 9; 10; 13; 15(2); 16; 17(2); 18; 21; 28; 29(2); 21:5; **Ruth** 1:1; 2:14; 20; 21; 3:2(2); 3; 4(3); 7; 9; 10; 13(2); 14; 15(2); 17(2); 18; 4:1; 2; 3; 4; 8; 13; 15; 17; **1 Sam** 1:2; 4; 5(2); 22; 28(2); 2:6; 7; 8(2); 9; 10(2); 14; 15; 16; 22; 23; 35; 3:2; 4; 5(3); 6; 8; 9; 13(2); 16; 17(2); 18; 4:13; 14; 15; 16(2); 18(3); 5:6; 9; 6:5; 6; 9; 19(2); 7:3; 8; 16; 17(3); 8:1; 11(2); 12; 13; 14; 15; 16; 17; 21; 9:2(3); 4(2); 6(4); 9(2); 12(2); 13(3); 16; 17; 26; 27; 10:9; 10; 11; 13(2); 14; 16(2); 21(2); 22; 23(2); 27; 11:6; 7; 8; 12; 12:5(2); 7; 9; 17; 24; 13:1; 2; 7; 8; 9; 10(2); 13; 14:1; 13; 27; 33; 35; 37; 39; 40; 45(2); 47(2); 48; 52; 15:2(3); 8; 11(2); 12(2); 16; 23; 29(2); 30; 35; 16:2; 5(2); 6; 8; 9; 11(3); 12(2); 16; 21(2); 22; 17:5(2); 6; 8; 9; 20; 23(2); 25; 26; 28(2); 30; 31; 33; 36; 37; 38(2); 39; 40(4); 42(2); 47; 49(2); 54; 55; 18:1; 3; 5; 8(2); 10; 11; 13; 15(2); 16; 27(2); 19:4; 5; 6; 7; 9; 10(2); 12; 14; 17(2); 18; 21; 22(2); 23(3); 24; 20:1; 3(2); 6; 7(2); 13; 17(3); 26(3); 29(2); 30; 31; 32(2); 34; 36(2); 42; 21:1; 13; 22:2; 3; 4; 10; 12; 13; 17; 19; 22; 23; 23:6; 7; 9; 11; 13; 17; 22; 23(2); 25(2); 24:3; 5; 6(2); 10; 17; 19; 25:2(2); 3; 14; 17; 21; 25; 29; 30; 36(2); 37; 38; 39; 26:3; 10; 18; 27:3; 4; 9; 11; 12(2); 28:5; 8(2); 9; 11; 14(3); 17; 20; 21; 23(3); 29:3; 4(3); 9; 30:8; 9; 10; 11; 12(2); 13; 15; 16; 21; 25; 26; 31:3; 4; 5; **2 Sam** 1:2(2); 3; 4; 7(2); 8; 9; 10(2); 13; 15(2); 18; 2:1; 9; 10(2); 19; 20; 23(2); 30; 3:11(2); 16; 21; 22(2); 23(2); 24; 26; 27; 28; 30; 4:1; 4(2); 7; 5:4(2); 5(2); 8; 12; 13; 20(2); 23; 25; 6:7; 8; 9; 13; 18; 19; 7:11; 13; 14(2); 18; 8:2(3); 3; 4; 6; 10; 11(2); 13; 14(3); 9:2; 4(2); 6(2); 8; 11; 13(2); 10:3; 5; 7; 9; 10(2); 11; 17; 11:2; 4; 13(4); 15(2); 16(2); 20; 21; 12:1; 3; 4; 5; 6(3); 11; 17(2); 18(2); 19; 20(4); 21; 22; 23(2); 24; 25(2); 30(2); 31(2); 13:2; 4; 8; 9; 11; 13; 14(2); 15(2); 16; 17; 20; 21; 22; 25(3); 26; 27; 32; 36; 39(2); 14:7; 10; 11; 12; 14; 19; 26(4); 29(3); 30(2); 33(2); 15:2; 5; 9; 12; 14; 25; 26; 30(2); 32; 16:3(2); 5(2); 6; 7; 13; 21; 23; 17:2; 5; 6; 9; 10; 12; 13; 23(3); 24; 18:9; 14(2); 18(2); 23(2); 25(2); 26; 27; 28; 30; 33(2); 19:9(2); 14; 18(2); 19; 21; 24(2); 25; 26; 27; 32(3); 39; 42; 20:1; 3; 5; 6; 8; 10(3); 12(2); 13; 14; 17(3); 22; 21:1; 4; 9; 13; 16; 20; 21; 22:2; 7; 8; 10; 11(2); 12; 15(2); 17(3); 18; 20(3); 21; 31; 33; 34; 35; 42; 49; 51; 23:3; 4; 5(2); 8(2); 10; 12; 16; 17(2); 18; 19(3); 20(2); 21(2); 23(2); 24:1; 10; 13; 17; **1 Ki** 1:1; 5; 6; 7; 9; 10; 13; 17; 19(2); 23(2); 24; 25; 26; 30; 35(2); 37; 41; 42; 47; 50; 51(2); 52(2); 53; 2:1(2); 4(2); 5(3); 8; 11(2); 13; 14; 15; 17(3); 22; 24; 25(2); 27(2); 28; 29; 30(2); 31; 32(2); 34; 46(2); 3:1(2); 3; 6; 15; 21(2); 4:11; 15; 19; 24(2); 31; 32; 33(2); 5:1; 5; 7(2); 12; 14; 6:1; 4; 5(2); 6; 9(2); 10; 15(3); 16(2); 19; 20; 21; 22(3); 23; 27; 28; 29; 30; 31; 32(2); 33; 35; 36; 38; 7:1; 2; 6; 7(2); 8(2); 14(3); 15; 16; 17; 18(2); 21(3); 23; 27; 36; 37; 38; 39(2); 40; 51; 8:12; 15; 19; 20; 21(2); 23; 42; 54; 55; 56(2); 57(2); 58(2); 59; 63; 64; 66; 9:1; 2; 11; 13(2); 24; 25(3); 10:3; 4; 5; 9; 17; 26(2); 27; 11:3; 8; 10(2); 14; 15; 16; 17; 19; 22; 24; 25(2); 29; 31; 32; 34; 41; 12:2(2); 4; 5; 6(2); 8; 9; 14; 15; 18; 21(2); 25; 29(2); 31; 32(4); 33(4); 13:2(2); 3; 4(3); 10(2); 11; 12; 13(2); 14(2); 15; 16; 18(3); 19; 21; 23(4); 24; 26(2); 27; 28; 30; 31(2); 32; 33(3); 14:3; 5; 6; 13; 15(2); 16; 18; 19(2); 20; 21(2); 26(3); 29; 15:2; 3(2); 5; 7; 10; 12; 13; 15(2); 17; 19; 20; 21; 23(3); 25; 26(2); 29(5); 30(3); 31; 34(2); 16:5; 7(2); 9; 11(4); 12; 14; 18; 19(2); 20; 23; 24(3); 26(2); 27(2); 31(2); 32(2); 34(3); 17:5(2); 6; 10(3); 11; 15; 16; 19(3); 20; 21; 22; 18:7; 8; 9; 10(2); 12(2); 14; 18; 24; 27(5); 30; 32(2); 33; 34(2); 35; 39(2); 42; 43(2); 44(2); 46; 19:1; 3(2); 4(3); 5; 6(2); 8(2); 9(2); 10; 11; 13; 14; 19(2); 20(2); 21; 20:1; 2; 7; 9; 12(2); 14(3); 15(2); 18; 25; 28; 31; 32(3); 33(2); 34; 36(2); 37; 39(2); 40; 41; 42; 21:4(2); 6(2); 10; 13; 15; 18(2); 20; 26; 27; 29; 22:4; 8; 11; 15(2); 17; 18; 20; 22; 28; 34; 38; 39(3); 42(2); 43(2); 45(2); 46; 52; 53; **2 Ki** 1:2; 5; 7; 8; 9(3); 11(2); 13; 15; 16; 17; 18; 2:3; 4; 5; 6; 10; 12(3); 13; 14(2); 16; 17(2); 18(2); 20; 21; 22; 23(2); 24; 25(2); 3:2(2); 3(2); 4; 7(2); 8(2); 16; 18; 26; 27; 4:3; 6; 7; 8(2); 10(2); 11(2); 12(2); 13; 14; 15(2); 16; 18; 19(2); 20(2); 23; 25; 29; 30; 31; 33; 34(2); 35; 36(3); 38; 41(2); 42; 43; 44; 5:1; 3; 5; 6; 7(2); 8(2); 9; 11; 12; 13; 14(2); 15(3); 16(3); 18; 19(2); 20; 21; 22; 23; 24(3); 25(2); 26; 27; 6:2; 3; 4; 5; 6(3); 7(2); 8; 10(2); 11; 13(3); 14; 16; 17(2); 18; 19; 21; 22; 23(2); 27; 30(3); 31; 32; 33; 7:2; 17(2); 19; 20; 8:1; 5(3); 9; 10; 11(2); 12; 13; 14(3); 15(2); 17(3); 18(2); 19; 21; 23; 26(2); 27(2); 28; 29(2); 9:5(3); 6(2); 10; 11; 12(2); 14; 15; 17(2); 19; 20(2); 22(2); 24; 27(2); 32; 33(2); 34(3); 36(2); 10:5(2); 6; 8; 9; 10; 11; 12; 14(2); 15(5); 16; 17(4); 22(2); 25; 31; 34; 11:2; 3; 4; 5; 8(2); 12; 19(2); 21; 12:1; 18; 19; 21; 13:2(2); 3; 4; 7; 8; 11(2); 12(2); 14; 15; 16(2); 17(4); 18(4); 21; 25; 14:2(3); 3(2); 5; 6; 7; 11; 13; 14; 15(2); 19; 20; 22; 24(2); 25(2); 27(2); 28(3); 15:2(3); 3; 5(2); 6; 9(2); 10; 12; 13; 14; 15; 16(2); 18(2); 21; 24(2); 25; 26; 28(2); 29; 30; 31; 33(3); 34(2); 35; 36; 16:2(3); 3(2); 4; 13(2); 14; 17; 18(2); 19; 17:1; 2; 4(2); 15(2); 20; 21; 22; 23; 26; 34; 37; 39; 18:2(3); 3; 4; 5; 6(2); 7(3); 8; 22; 29; 32; 19:1; 2; 7; 8(2); 9(2); 16; 32; 33(3); 37; 20:2; 7; 9; 11; 12; 15; 19; 20; 21:1(2); 2; 3(3); 4; 5; 6(2); 7(2); 11; 16(2); 17(2); 19(2); 20; 21(2); 22; 25; 26; 22:1(2); 2(2); 4; 8; 11; 23:2; 4; 5; 6; 7; 8(2); 10; 11(2); 14; 15(2); 16(2); 17; 18; 19(2); 20(2); 24; 28; 29; 31(2); 32; 33(2); 34; 35(2); 36(2); 37; 24:1; 2(2); 3; 4(2); 5; 8(2); 9; 13(2); 14; 15(2); 18(2); 19; 20; 25:9(2); 19; 22; 27; 28; 29; **1 Chr** 1:10; 2:3; 21(2); 3:4(2); 4:10; 5:1(2); 6; 20; 26(2); 6:10; 7:23(2); 8:7; 8; 9; 11; 10:3; 4; 5; 13(3); 14(2); 11:8; 11; 13; 19(2); 20; 21(3); 22(2); 23(2); 25(2); 12:1; 18; 19(2); 20; 13:10(3); 14; 14:4; 15:1; 3; 12; 22; 16:2; 3; 4; 12; 14; 15; 16; 21(2); 25; 33; 34; 37; 40; 17:12; 13; 16; 18:2; 3; 4; 6; 10(2); 11; 13(2); 19:3; 5; 8; 10; 11; 12; 17; 20:2; 3; 6; 7; 21:3; 6; 7; 15; 19; 21; 26; 27; 28; 30; 22:2; 6; 10(2); 11; 18(2); 23:1; 2; 13(2); 26:10; 27:3; 23; 24; 28:4(2); 5; 6; 7; 9(2); 12; 14; 16; 17; 20; 29:27(3); 28; **2 Chr** 1:4; 5; 14(2); 15; 2:11(2); 12; 18; 3:2; 4; 5(3); 6; 7(2); 8(2); 9; 10; 14; 15; 16(2); 17(2); 4:1; 2; 6; 7; 8(2); 9(2); 10; 11; 14; 5:1; 13; 6:1; 4(2); 9; 10; 11; 13; 14; 7:3; 7; 10; 22; 8:2; 4(2); 5; 11(2); 12; 14; 9:2; 3; 4; 8; 16; 25; 26; 27; 10:2(2); 4; 5; 6; 8; 9; 14; 15; 18; 11:11(2); 6; 11; 12; 15(2); 20; 21; 22; 23(3); 12:1; 4; 9(2); 12; 13(2); 14(2); 13:2; 20; 14:3; 4; 5; 6(2); 7(2); 9; 15:2(3); 4; 8(3); 9; 15; 16; 18(2); 16:1; 3; 5; 6; 8; 10; 12; 13; 14; 17:2; 3(2); 5; 6; 7; 8; 12; 13; 18:1; 2; 3; 7(2); 10; 14(2); 16; 17; 19; 21; 27; 33; 34; 19:4; 5; 9; 20:15; 21(2); 31(3); 32; 36; 21:2; 3(2); 4; 5(2); 6(3); 7(2); 9; 10; 11; 19; 20(3); 22:2(2); 3; 4; 5; 6(4); 7(2); 8; 9(3); 12; 23:3; 7(2); 10; 19; 20; 24:1(2); 3; 5; 15(3); 16; 19; 20; 22(2); 25; 25:1(2); 2; 3; 4; 5; 6; 11; 14; 15; 16; 20; 21; 23; 24; 27; 26:2; 3(2); 4; 5(2); 6(2); 8; 9; 10(5); 15(3); 16(2); 19(2); 20(2); 21(3); 23; 27:1(2); 2(2); 3(2); 4(2); 5; 6; 8(3); 28:1(3); 2; 3; 4; 5; 9(2); 19; 21(2); 23; 25; 29:1(2); 2; 3; 4; 8; 21; 25; 30:6; 7; 8; 19; 31:4; 20; 21(3); 32:1; 3; 5(2); 6; 9; 17; 21(2); 23; 24(2); 26; 27; 29; 31; 33:1(2); 2; 3(3); 4; 5; 6(3); 7(2); 12(2); 13; 14(3); 15(3); 16; 19(2); 21(2); 22; 23; 34:1(2); 2(2); 3(3); 4(2); 5; 6; 7(2); 8(2); 19; 30; 32; 35:2; 3; 21(2); 22(2); 24(2); 36:2(2); 3; 5(3); 8; 9(3); 11(2); 12; 13(2); 14; 15; 17(2); 18; 20; 22; 23; **Ezra** 1:1; 2; 3; 4; 3:11; 5:12; 14; 15; 7:6; 9(2); 8:23; 31; 9:9; 10:1; 6(3); 8; **Neh** 2:8; 18; 3:12; 14; 15; 4:1; 2; 3(2); 8; 5:13; 6:10; 12; 13; 18; 7:2; 8:3; 5(2); 10; 18; 9:29; 12:8; 13:5; **Esth** 1:3; 4; 10; 20; 22; 2:1; 4; 9(2); 17; 18; 3:4(2); 6; 4:1(2); 2; 4; 5; 8(3); 11(2); 5:5; 9(2); 10; 11; 14; 6:4; 9; 7:5(2); 7; 8; 10; 8:1; 2; 3; 5; 7; 10; 9:25(2); **Job** 1:5; 10; 11(2); 12; 16; 17; 18; 20; 21; 2:3; 4; 5; 6; 8(2); 10; 4:18(2); 5:10; 11; 12; 13; 15; 18(3); 19; 20; 6:9; 10; 14; 7:9; 10; 8:4; 6; 15(2); 16; 18; 20; 21; 9:3; 5(2); 6; 7(2); 8; 9; 10; 11(2); 12; 16(2); 17; 18; 19; 22; 23; 24(2); 32; 11:6; 10; 11(3); 12:4; 13; 14(2); 15(2); 17; 18; 19; 20; 21; 22; 23(2); 24; 25; 13:9; 10; 15; 16; 19; 14:2(2); 5; 6(2); 10(2); 14; 20; 21(2); 15:3(2); 14(3); 22(2); 23(2); 25; 27; 28; 29; 30(2); 33; 16:7; 9(2); 12(3); 13(2); 14(2); 17:3; 5; 6; 9; 18:8(2); 14; 17; 18; 19; 19:8(2); 9; 10(2); 11(2); 13; 16; 25; 20:7(2); 8(2); 12; 13; 15; 16; 17; 18(3); 19(3); 20(3); 22; 23(2); 24; 21:19; 21; 22; 31; 32; 22:2; 4; 13; 14(2); 18; 27; 29; 30(2); 23:5(2); 6(2); 8; 9(2); 10(2); 13(2); 14; 17; 24:14(2); 15; 20; 21; 22; 23; 25:2; 4; 26:7(2); 8; 9; 10; 12(2); 13; 27:7; 8; 10(2); 16; 17; 18; 19(2); 21; 22; 28:4; 9(2); 10; 11(2); 23; 24; 26; 27(3); 28; 30:11; 19; 24(2); 31:4; 14; 15; 20; 32:1; 2; 4; 14; 33:10(2); 11(2); 13; 16; 18; 24; 25; 26(4); 27; 28; 30; 34:9(2); 11; 14(2); 19(2); 21; 23(2); 24; 25(2); 26; 28; 29(2); 33; 37(2); 35:7; 12; 15; 16; 36:5; 6; 7(2); 9; 10; 13; 15; 16; 18; 27; 30; 31(2); 32; 37:3; 4(2); 5; 6; 7; 11(2); 12; 13; 17; 20(2); 22; 23(2); 24; 39:7(2); 8; 9; 10; 21(2); 22(2); 24(2); 25(2); 40:2; 15; 17; 19(2); 21; 23(2); 24; 41:3(2); 4; 10; 25; 27; 29; 30; 31(2); 32; 34(2); 42:10(2); 12; 13; 14; **Ps** 1:2; 3(2); 2:4; 5; 12; 3:4; 7:12(3); 13(2); 14; 15(2); 9:7; 8(2); 12(3); 16; 10:3; 5; 6; 8(2); 9(4); 10(2); 11(3); 13; 11:6; 7; 12:5; 13:6; 15:2; 3(2); 4(2); 5(3); 16:8; 18:6; 7; 9; 10(2); 11; 14(2); 16(3); 17; 19(3); 20; 30; 33; 34; 41; 48; 50; 19:4; 20:2; 3; 4; 6; 21:1; 4; 7; 22:8(2); 9; 24(4); 28; 29; 31; 23:2(2); 3(2); 24:2; 4; 5; 10; 25:8; 9(2); 12(2); 13; 14; 15; 27:5(3); 14; 28:5; 6; 8; 29:6; 31:21; 24; 32:1; 10; 33:5; 7(2); 9(2); 10; 12; 13; 14; 15(2); 20; 34(2); 4; 12; 20; 35:8; 14; 36:2(3); 3; 4(3); 37:4; 5; 6; 13; 23; 24(2); 26; 33; 34; 36(3); 39; 40; 39:6; 40:1; 2; 3; 41:1; 2; 5; 6(4); 8(2); 44:21; 45:11; 46:6; 9(3); 47:2; 3; 4(2); 9; 48:3; 14; 49:9; 10; 12; 15; 17(2); 18(2); 19; 50:4(2); 51:52:5; 54:5; 7; 55:17; 18; 19; 20(2); 22(2); 56:1; 57:3(2); 58:7; 9; 10(2); 11; 60:12; 61:7; 62:2(2); 6(2); 63:64:8; 65:4; 66:5; 6; 7; 16; 17; 19; 68:6; 33; 35; 71:6; 72:2; 4(2); 6; 8; 12(2); 13; 14; 15(2); 75:7; 8; 76:3; 12(2); 77:1; 7; 9; 78:4; 5(2); 11; 12; 13(2); 14; 15; 16; 20(3); 23; 25; 26(2); 27; 28; 29; 33; 34; 38(2); 39; 42; 43; 45; 46; 47; 48; 49; 50(2); 52; 53; 54; 55; 59; 60(2); 62; 66(2); 67; 68; 69(2); 70; 71; 72; 81:5(2); 16; 82:1; 84:11; 85:8; 87:6; 89:26; 41; 48; 91:1; 2; 3; 4; 11; 14(2); 15; 92:12; 15; 93:1(2); 94:9(4); 10(3); 14; 23; 95:5; 7; 96:4; 10; 13(3); 97:10(2); 98:1; 2; 3; 9(2); 99:1; 2; 3; 5; 6; 7(2); 100:3(2); 101:6(2); 7(2); 102:16; 17; 19; 23(2); 103:7; 9(2); 10; 12; 14(2); 15; 104:3; 10; 13; 14(2); 16; 19; 32(2); 105:5; 7; 8(2); 9; 14(2); 16(2); 17; 18; 21; 24; 25; 26(2); 28; 29; 31; 32; 33; 34; 36; 37; 39; 40; 41; 42; 43; 44; 106:1; 3; 8(2); 9(2); 10; 15; 23(3); 26; 33; 40; 41; 43; 44(2); 45; 46; 107:1; 2; 6; 7; 9; 12; 13; 14; 16; 19; 20; 25; 28; 29; 30; 33; 35; 36; 38(2); 40; 41; 108:13; 109:7; 11; 15; 16(2); 17(2); 18; 19; 31; 110:5; 6(3); 7(2); 111:4; 5(2); 6; 9(2); 112:4; 5; 6; 7; 8(2); 9(2); 10; 113:7; 8; 9; 115:3(2); 9; 10; 11; 12(3); 13; 16; 116:1; 2; 6; 118:1; 14; 18; 26; 27; 29; 120:1; 121:3(2); 4; 7; 123:2; 126:6; 127:2; 129:4; 7; 130:8; 132:2; 11; 13; 135:6; 7(3); 8; 9; 10; 14; 136:1; 138:6(2); 142:143:3(2); 145:19(2); 20; 146:4; 5; 9(2); 147:2; 3; 4(2); 6; 9; 10(2); 13(2); 14; 15; 16(2); 17; 18(2); 19; 20; 148:5; 6(2); 14; 149:4; **Prov** 2:7(2); 8; 3:6; 12(2); 19; 29; 30; 33; 34; 4:4; 5:21; 22; 23(2); 6:13(3); 14(2); 15; 29; 30(2); 31(3); 32; 33; 34; 35(2); 7:8; 19; 20; 22; 23; 8:26; 27(2); 28(2); 29(2); 36; 9:7(2); 8(2); 9(2); 18; 10:3; 4; 5(2); 9(2); 10; 17(2); 19; 22; 11:12; 13; 15; 17; 18; 19; 25; 27; 28; 29; 30; 12:1; 2; 8; 9; 11(2); 15; 17; 27; 13:3(2); 11; 13(2); 18; 20; 24(2); 14:2(2); 21(3); 29(2); 31(2); 15:5; 9; 10; 12; 15; 18; 24; 25; 27(2); 29; 32(2); 16:7; 17; 20(2); 30(2); 32(3); 17:5(2); 8(2); 9(2); 15(2); 16; 19(2); 20(2); 21; 27; 28(3); 18:1; 9; 13(2); 20; 22; 19:2; 5; 7; 8(2); 9; 16(2); 17(3); 23(2); 25; 26; 20:4; 11; 14(2); 19; 22; 28; 21:1(2); 11; 17(2); 21; 24; 26; 27; 29; 22:5; 6(3); 8; 9(2); 11; 12; 14; 16(2); 22; 27; 29(2); 23:7(3); 9; 11; 13; 24; 24:7; 8; 12(4); 17; 18; 24; 26; 29; 25:7; 10; 13; 17; 21; 26:5; 6; 8; 17; 24; 25; 27; 27:13; 14; 18; 28:6; 10; 13; 14; 16; 18; 19(2); 20; 23(2); 25(2); 26; 27(2); 29:1; 4; 17(2); 18; 19(2); 21; 24; 27; 30:5; 6; 10; 22(2); 31:11; 23; 28; **Eccl** 1:3; 18; 2:12; 19(2); 21; 22; 24; 26(2); 3:9; 11(2); 4:3; 5; 8(2); 10(2); 14(2); 16; 5:4; 10(2); 12; 14; 15(5); 16(3); 17(2); 18; 20; 6:2(2); 3(2); 6; 10(4); 12; 7:13; 18; 26; 8:3; 5; 7; 13(2); 17(2); 9:2(2); 9; 11; 15; 10:3(3); 8; 9(2); 10; 11:4(2); 12:9(2); **Song** 2:4; 8; 9(2); 16; 3:10; 5:2; 6(2); 16; 6:3; 8:11; **Isa** 1:1; 2:3; 4; 18; 19; 21; 22; 3:7; 4:3; 5:2(3); 7; 14; 25; 26; 6:2(3); 6; 7; 9; 11; 7:13; 15(2); 22; 8:7; 8(3); 14; 9:1; 15(2); 20(2); 10:7; 8; 12; 13; 16; 24; 26; 28(3); 32(2); 34; 11:3; 4(3); 12; 15; 16; 12:2; 5; 13:9; 14:6(2); 15:2; 16:6; 12(2); 17:5; 8(2); 14; 18:3(2); 5; 19:16; 17; 20(2); 22(2); 20:1; 2; 21:4; 6; 7(2); 8; 9(2); 11; 22:8; 16; 18; 19; 21; 22(2); 23; 23:11(2); 12; 24:18(2); 25:7; 8(2); 9; 11(2); 12; 26:3; 5(4); 10(2); 27:1; 5(2); 6; 7(3); 8; 9; 11(2); 28:4; 9(2); 11; 12; 21(2); 24; 25(2); 26; 28; 29:8(5); 10; 11; 12; 16(2); 23; 30:14(2); 18(3); 19(3); 23; 31; 32; 33; 31:2; 3(2); 4; 5(2); 8; 9; 32:6; 7; 8; 33:4; 5(2); 8(3); 15(2); 16; 18(2); 22; 34:2(2); 11; 17; 35:4; 36:2; 7; 14; 37:1; 2; 7; 8(2); 9(3); 17; 33; 34(3); 38; 38:7; 9; 12; 13; 15(2); 19; 21; 39:1(2); 4; 8; 40:6; 11(2); 14; 15; 20; 22; 23(2); 24; 26; 29(2); 41:3; 4; 7(2); 24; 25(3); 26; 42:1; 2; 3(3); 4(2); 13(3); 19; 20; 21; 24; 25(3); 43:1; 10; 13; 25; 44:12(2); 13(3); 14(3); 15(4); 16(4); 17(2); 18; 20(2); 24(2); 28(2); 45:9; 13; 24; 46:4; 6; 48:12; 14; 21(3); 49:1; 2(3); 3; 6; 7; 10(2); 50:4(2); 8; 9; 51:3(2); 12; 13; 14(2); 52:6; 9; 13; 15; 53:2(2); 3(2); 4; 5(2); 7(5); 8(3); 9; 10(3); 11(2); 12(4); 54:5; 55:5; 6(2); 7(2); 57:2; 13; 17; 58:9; 59:2; 5; 15; 16; 17(2); 18(2); 60:9; 61:1; 3; 10(2); 62:7(2); 63:7; 8(2); 9(3); 10(2); 11(3); 65:16(2); 66:3(8); **Jer** 2:14(2); 17; 26; 3:1; 5(2); 4:7; 13; 5:12; 24; 9:8; 12(2); 24; 10:10; 12(2); 13(4); 16; 11:16; 12:4; 13:16(2); 21; 14:10; 22; 15:4; 16:15; 17:6; 8; 11(2); 18:3; 4(2); 19:14; 20:4; 10; 13; 17; 21:7(2); 9(3); 10; 22:10; 11; 12; 16; 19; 28; 23:6; 20; 28; 31; 25:30(2); 31(2); 38; 26:11; 13; 16; 19(2); 21; 27:20; 29:21; 28; 31; 32(3); 30:7; 21; 24(2); 31:10; 11; 20; 32:3; 5(2); 28; 33:1; 15; 21; 24; 34:2; 3; 14; 16; 35:8; 14; 16; 18; 36:4; 12; 13; 18; 21; 25; 30; 37:2(2); 13(2); 14; 17; 38:2(3); 4; 5; 9(2); 10; 26; 27; 28; 39:4; 5; 7; 12; 14(2); 15; 40:1; 3; 11; 15; 41:4; 6(3); 7; 8; 9; 16(3); 42:8; 12; 21; 43:10; 11(2); 12(3); 13(2); 45:1; 46:8; 10; 16; 17; 18; 47:7; 48:10(2); 11(2); 18; 20; 26(2); 27; 29; 42; 44(2); 49:1; 10(2); 19; 20(3); 22; 50:19; 34(2); 44; 45(3); 51:6; 12; 15(2); 16(4); 19; 34(5); 44; 56; 59; 52:1(2); 2; 3; 9; 10; 11; 13(2); 25; 29; 32; 33; **Lam** 1:13(3);

14; 15; 2:1; 2(3); 3(3); 4(3); 5(3); 6(3); 7(2); 8(3); 9; 17(6); 3:2; 3; 4; 5; 6; 7(2); 8; 9(2); 10; 11(2); 12; 13; 15(2); 16; 32(2); 33; 37; 4:11(2); 16; 22(3); **Ezek** 2:1; 2; 3; 10; 3:1; 2; 3; 4; 10; 19(2); 20(3); 21(3); 22; 27(2); 4:15; 16; 6:12(3); 7:13; 20; 8:3; 5; 6; 7; 8; 9; 12; 13; 14; 15; 16; 17; 9:1; 3; 5; 7; 9; 10:2(2); 5; 6(2); 11:2; 12:12(2); 13(3); 27(2); 13:22; 17:4(2); 5(2); 7; 9; 13(2); 15(4); 16(3); 18(2); 19(2); 20(2); 18:6; 7; 8; 9(3); 10; 12; 13(5); 14; 17(2); 18(2); 19; 21(3); 22(3); 23; 24(5); 26(2); 27(2); 28(4); 19:3(3); 4; 6(3); 7; 8; 20:11; 13; 21; 49; 21:11; 21(3); 23; 27; 24:24; 26:8(2); 9(2); 10; 11(2); 29:9; 18; 19; 30:11; 24; 25; 31:11; 32:32; 33:3(2); 5(2); 6; 9(2); 12(3); 13(4); 14; 15(3); 16(3); 18; 19; 22(2); 24; 34:12; 23(2); 37:2; 3; 4; 9; 10; 11; 38:17; 39:15; 40:1; 2; 3(3); 5; 6(2); 8; 9; 11; 13; 14; 17; 19; 20; 23; 24(2); 27; 28(2); 32(2); 35; 45; 47; 48; 41:1; 2; 3; 4(2); 5; 13; 15; 22; 42:1(2); 13; 15(2); 16; 17; 18; 19; 20; 43:1; 7; 18; 44:1; 3(3); 4; 21; 26; 27(2); 45:17; 23; 24; 25; 46:2(2); 5; 7(2); 8; 9(2); 10(2); 11; 12(4); 17; 18; 19; 20; 21; 24; 47:1; 2; 3(2); 4(2); 5; 6(2); 8; **Dan** 1:2(2); 5; 7; 8(4); 10; 14; 20; 2:15; 16; 21(3); 22(2); 24; 28; 29; 38; 48; 49; 3:1; 17; 19; 20; 24; 25; 4:14; 17; 25; 29; 32; 33; 35; 37; 5:2; 7; 12; 19(9); 20; 21(3); 29; 6:4; 10(2); 14(2); 16; 20(2); 23; 26; 27(2); 7:1; 13; 16; 23; 24; 25; 8:4; 6; 7(2); 8; 11; 12(2); 14; 17(3); 18(2); 19; 24(2); 25(5); 9:2; 10; 12(2); 14; 22; 27(2); 10:1; 11(2); 12; 15; 19(2); 20; 11:2; 4(2); 5; 6; 8(2); 10; 12(3); 16(2); 17(3); 18(2); 19(2); 20; 21; 23(2); 24(4); 25(2); 28; 29; 30(2); 32; 36; 37(2); 38(2); 39(3); 40; 41; 42; 43; 44; 45(2); 12:7; 9; 12; **Hos** 1:3; 5:6; 11; 13; 6:1(4); 2(2); 3; 7:4; 5; 9(2); 8:1; 13; 9:9(2); 10:1(2); 2(2); 3; 12; 11:5; 10(2); 12:1; 2; 3(2); 4(4); 7; 12; 13; 13:1(3); 10; 13(2); 15(2); 14:5; **Joel** 1:6; 7(2); 2:13(2); 14; 20; 23(2); **Am** 1:1; 2; 11(2); 15; 2:1; 9; 15(2); 3:4(2); 7; 11; 4:2; 13; 5:2; 6; 8(3); 9; 19; 6:10(2); 11; 7:1; 2; 5; 7; 8:2; 9:1(3); 5; 6; **Jon** 1:3(2); 9; 10(2); 12; 2:2(2); 3:4; 6; 7; 10(3); 4:1; 2; 5(2); 8(2); 9; **Mic** 1:1; 3; 2:4(3); 11; 3:4(2); 4:2; 3; 12; 5:1; 3; 4(2); 5; 6(3); 8; 6:2; 8; 7:9(2); 18(2); 19; **Nah** 1:2; 4; 7; 8; 9; 12; 15; 2:1; 5; **Hab** 1:11(2); 13; 2:1; 2; 5(6); 9(2); 3:4; 6(2); 16(2); 19(2); **Zeph** 1:7; 12; 18; 2:11; 13; 14; 3:5(3); 15; 17(3); **Hag** 1:6; 2:12; **Zech** 1:6; 19; 21; 2:2; 8(2); 13; 3:1; 4(2); 4:2; 6; 7; 13; 14; 5:2; 3; 6(2); 8(2); 11; 6:7; 8; 12(2); 13(3); 7:13; 9:1; 4; 5; 7(2); 9; 10; 10:1; 11; 11:16; 13:3; 4; 5; 6; 14:3; **Mal** 1:8(2); 9(2); 2:5(2); 6; 7; 11(2); 13; 15(2); 16; 17; 3:1(2); 2(2); 3(2); 11; 4:6; **Mt** 1:20; 21; 25; 2:2; 3; 4(2); 7; 8; 14(2); 16(4); 21; 22(3); 23(2); 3:3; 7(2); 11(2); 12(2); 15; 16(2); 4:2(2); 3; 4; 6; 9; 12; 13; 19; 21(2); 24; 5:1(2); 2; 19; 45; 6:24(2); 30; 7:8; 10(2); 21; 29; 8:1; 9(3); 10; 14; 15; 16; 17; 18; 23; 24; 26(2); 28; 32; 9:1; 2; 6; 7; 9(3); 12; 18; 22(2); 24; 25; 28; 29; 34; 36(2); 37; 10:1(2); 22; 25; 37(2); 38; 39(2); 40(2); 41(2); 42; 11:1; 2; 6; 10; 11(2); 14; 15; 18; 20; 12:3(3); 4; 9(2); 11; 13(2); 15(2); 16; 18; 19; 20(3); 22; 26; 29(2); 30(2); 39; 43; 44(3); 45; 46; 48; 49; 13:2; 3; 4; 9; 11; 12(2); 19; 20(2); 21(2); 22(3); 23(2); 24; 28; 29; 31; 33; 34; 37(2); 43; 44(2); 46(2); 52; 53; 54(2); 58; 14:2; 5(2); 7; 9; 10; 13; 14(2); 18; 19(3); 22; 23(3); 29(2); 30(3); 15:3; 4; 6; 10(2); 13; 23; 24; 26; 30; 35; 36; 39; 16:1; 2; 4; 12; 13; 15; 20(2); 21; 23; 26; 27; 17:2; 5; 13; 15(2); 23; 25(2); 18:6; 12; 13(2); 15; 16; 17(2); 24; 25(3); 28; 30(2); 32; 34; 19:1; 2; 4(2); 8; 11; 12; 13; 15; 17; 18; 22(2); 20:2(2); 3; 5; 6; 7; 13; 19; 21; 23; 21:3; 9; 10; 13; 14; 15; 17(2); 18(2); 19; 23(2); 25; 27; 28; 29(2); 30(3); 33; 34; 36; 37; 40; 41; 45; 22:4; 7(2); 8; 11; 12(2); 20; 21; 25; 34; 42; 43; 45; 23:9; 11; 12; 15; 16; 18; 20; 21; 22; 39; 24:3; 13; 26(2); 31; 43; 46; 47; 50(2); 25:12; 15(2); 16; 17; 18; 20; 22; 24; 29(2); 31; 32; 33; 41; 45; 26:1; 7; 10; 16; 18; 20; 21; 23(2); 24; 25; 27; 37(2); 38; 39; 40; 42; 43; 44; 45; 47; 48; 49; 53; 58; 65; 66; 70; 71; 72; 74; 75; 27:3; 5; 12(2); 14; 18; 19; 23; 24(2); 26(3); 34(2); 42(3); 43(3); 59; 60(2); 63; 64; 28:6(3); 7(2); **Mk** 1:6; 7; 8; 10; 13; 16(2); 19(2); 20; 21; 22; 23; 26; 27; 31; 34(2); 35(2); 38; 39; 42(2); 43; 45; 2:1(2); 2; 4; 5; 8; 10; 12; 13(2); 14(4); 15; 16; 17; 23; 25(3); 26; 27; 3:1; 2; 3; 4; 5(3); 8; 9; 10; 12; 13(2); 14(2); 16; 17; 21; 22(2); 23; 26; 27(2); 29; 30; 33; 34; 4:1(2); 2; 4; 9(2); 10; 11; 13; 21; 24; 25; 26; 27; 29; 30; 33; 34(2); 35; 36; 38; 39; 40; 5:2; 4; 5; 6(2); 7; 8; 9(2); 10(2); 18(3); 19; 20; 21; 22(2); 32; 34; 35; 36; 37; 38; 39(2); 40(2); 41; 43; 6:1; 2; 5(2); 6(2); 7; 8; 10; 14; 16(2); 17; 20(4); 23; 26; 27; 31; 34(2); 37; 38; 39; 41(3); 45(2); 46(2); 47; 48(2); 50; 51; 55; 56; 7:6; 9; 10; 14(2); 17; 18; 20; 24(3); 29; 31; 33(2); 34; 35; 36(2); 37(2); 8:5; 6(2); 7; 9; 12; 13; 15; 21; 22; 23(4); 24; 25(2); 26; 27; 29; 30; 31; 32; 33(2); 34(2); 36; 38; 9:1; 2; 6; 9; 12(2); 14(2); 16; 18; 19; 20(2); 21(2); 22; 25; 26(2); 27; 28; 29; 30; 31(3); 33(3); 35(2); 36(3); 38; 40; 41; 42; 10:1(3); 3; 5; 11; 13; 14; 16; 17; 20; 22(2); 32; 34; 36; 46; 47(2); 48; 49; 50; 52; 11:1; 2; 3; 7; 9; 11(2); 12; 13(4); 16; 17; 19; 23(3); 27; 31; 12:1(2); 2(2); 4; 5; 6; 9; 12; 15; 16; 20; 21(2); 27; 28; 32; 34(2); 35; 37; 38; 43; 13:1; 3; 6; 13; 20(2); 21; 27; 36; 14:3; 11(2); 13; 14; 15; 16; 17; 20; 21; 23(3); 24; 31; 32; 33(2); 34; 35; 36; 37; 39; 40(2); 41; 43; 44; 45(2); 52; 54; 61; 68(2); 70; 71; 72(2); 15:2; 3; 6; 8; 10; 11; 14; 15(2); 21; 23; 28; 31(2); 35; 39(2); 41; 44(3); 45(2); 46(2); 47; 16:6(3); 7(2); 9(3); 11; 12; 14(3); 15; 16(2); 19; **Lk** 1:8; 9; 12; 15(2); 16; 17; 21; 22(4); 23; 25; 32; 33; 48; 49; 51(2); 52; 53(2); 54; 55; 60; 62; 63; 64; 68; 70; 73; 2:4; 21; 26(2); 27; 28; 42; 49; 50; 51; 3:3; 7; 11(3); 13; 14; 15; 16; 17(2); 18; 20; 21; 4:2(2); 9; 10; 13; 15; 16(3); 17(3); 18(2); 20; 21; 23; 24; 30; 31; 33; 36; 38; 39; 40; 41(2); 42; 43; 44; 5:1; 3(2); 4(2); 8; 9; 12(2); 13; 14; 16; 17; 20(2); 22; 24; 25(2); 27(2); 28; 34; 36; 39; 6:1; 3(2); 4; 5; 6; 7; 8(2); 10(3); 12; 13(3); 14; 17; 20; 35; 39; 47; 48; 49; 7:1(2); 3(2); 4; 5; 6; 8(3); 9; 11; 12; 13; 14(2); 15(2); 21(2); 23; 24; 27; 28(2); 33; 36; 39(2); 40; 42; 43(2); 44; 48; 50; 8:1; 4; 5; 8(3); 10; 16; 18; 21; 22(2); 23; 24; 25(2); 27(3); 28(2); 29(3); 30; 31; 32(2); 36; 37; 38; 39; 41(2); 42(2); 48; 49; 50; 51(2); 52; 54; 55; 56; 9:1; 2; 3; 7; 9; 10; 11; 13; 14; 16(2); 18(2); 20; 21; 23; 25; 26; 28; 29; 31; 33; 34; 38; 39(2); 42; 43; 48; 49; 50; 51; 55; 59(2); 10:1; 2; 16(3); 18; 23; 26; 27; 28; 29; 31(2); 32; 33(4); 34(2); 35(2); 37(2); 38; 11:1(2); 2; 5; 7; 8(4); 10; 11(3); 12(2); 14; 15; 17; 22(3); 23(2); 24(2); 25(2); 26; 27; 28; 29; 33; 37(2); 38(2); 40; 46; 53; 54; 12:1; 5; 9; 14; 15(2); 16; 17; 18; 21; 22; 28; 36(2); 37(2); 38; 39; 43; 44(2); 46(2); 48; 54; 58; 13:6(2); 7; 8; 10; 12; 13; 14; 17; 18; 20; 22; 23; 25; 27; 32; 35; 14:1; 4; 5; 7(2); 9; 10(2); 11; 12; 15(2); 16; 25; 26; 28; 29; 31; 32; 33; 35; 15:3; 4(2); 5(2); 6(2); 11; 12; 14(2); 15(2); 16; 17(2); 20(2); 24; 25(2); 26; 27(2); 28; 29; 31; 16:1; 2; 5; 6(2); 7(3); 8; 10(2); 13(2); 15; 23; 24(2); 25; 27; 28; 30; 31; 17:1; 2(2); 3; 4; 7; 8; 9(2); 11(2); 12; 14(2); 15(2); 16; 19; 20(2); 22; 25; 31; 37; 18:1; 4(2); 7; 8(2); 9; 14; 15; 21; 22; 23(3); 24(2); 27; 29; 31; 32; 33; 35; 36; 38; 39(2); 40(2); 41; 43; 19:2; 3(2); 4(2); 5; 6; 7; 9; 11(2); 12; 13; 15(4); 17; 19; 22; 24; 25; 26; 28(2); 29(2); 32; 36; 37; 40; 41(2); 45; 47; 20:1; 2; 3; 5; 9; 10; 11; 12; 16; 17; 19; 23; 25; 28; 30; 37; 38; 41; 44; 45; 21:1; 2; 3; 5; 8(2); 10; 29; 37(2); 22:4(2); 6; 8; 10(2); 12; 13; 14; 15; 17; 19; 20; 22; 25; 26(3); 27(3); 31; 33; 34; 35; 36(3); 37; 38; 39(2); 40(2); 41(2); 44; 45(2); 46; 47(2); 51; 56; 57; 59; 60; 61; 67; 70; 23:2; 3; 5; 6; 7(3); 8(4); 9(2); 13; 22(2); 23; 25(2); 26; 35(2); 42; 46(2); 47; 51(2); 53; 24:6(3); 12(2); 17; 19; 21; 23; 25; 27; 28(2); 29; 30(2); 31; 32(2); 35; 38; 40(2); 41; 43; 44; 45; 46; 50(2); 51(2); **Jn** 1:2; 8; 10; 11; 12; 15(3); 18; 20; 21(2); 23; 27; 30(2); 31; 32; 33(2); 36(2); 39(2); 41; 42(2); 43; 51; 2:5; 8; 10; 12(2); 14; 15(2); 16; 21; 22(2); 23(2); 24; 25; 3:3; 4(2); 5; 13; 16; 18(3); 21; 22; 26(2); 29; 30; 31(3); 32(2); 33; 34; 36(2); 4:3; 4; 5; 10; 25(2); 26; 27; 32; 36(3); 39; 40; 43; 45(2); 46; 47(3); 50; 51; 52(2); 53; 54; 5:4; 6(2); 11(2); 16; 18; 19(2); 20(2); 21; 23; 24; 26; 27; 32; 33; 35; 38; 46; 6:2; 3; 5; 6(3); 11(2); 12; 15; 20; 29; 31; 33; 35(2); 39; 41; 42; 46(2); 47; 51; 56; 57; 58; 59(2); 61; 62; 65; 71(2); 7:1; 4; 9(2); 10; 11; 12(2); 17; 18(2); 25; 26; 27; 28(2); 29; 31; 35(2); 36; 38; 39; 50; 51; 8:2(2); 6; 7(2); 8; 10; 12; 20; 22(2); 23; 24; 26; 27; 28; 29; 30; 42; 44(4); 47; 51; 52; 54; 56; 9:1; 2; 6(3); 7(2); 8(2); 9(4); 11; 12(2); 15(3); 16; 17(3); 18; 19; 20; 21(3); 22(2); 23; 25(2); 26(2); 27; 29; 30(2); 31; 33; 35(2); 36(2); 37; 38(2); 10:1; 2; 3; 4(2); 6; 9; 12; 13; 20; 35; 39; 40(2); 11:3; 4; 6(4); 7; 9(2); 10; 11(2); 12(2); 13; 17(2); 24; 25(3); 33; 34; 36; 39; 43(2); 44; 51(2); 52; 56; 57(2); 12:1; 6(4); 9(2); 13; 14; 17; 18; 25(2); 33(2); 35(2); 37; 38; 40; 41; 44; 45; 48; 13:1(2); 3; 5(2); 6; 10; 11(2); 12(2); 16(2); 18; 19; 20(2); 21; 22; 24; 25; 26(2); 28; 29; 30; 31; 14:9; 12(3); 16(2); 17; 21(3); 23; 24; 26; 30; 15:2(2); 5; 6; 16; 23; 26; 16:2; 8(2); 13(6); 14(2); 15; 17; 18(2); 19; 23; 17:2; 18:1(2); 5; 6(2); 7; 8; 9; 13; 17; 22; 25; 30; 32(2); 38(2); 19:7(2); 8; 13; 14; 16; 17; 21; 26(2); 27; 30(2); 33; 35(3); 38(2); 41; 20:5(2); 6; 8; 9; 18; 20(2); 22(2); 25; 27; 21:1; 6; 7(2); 14; 15(2); 16(3); 17(3); 19(4); 22; 23(2); **Acts** 1:2(3); 3; 4(2); 7; 9(2); 10; 17; 18; 22; 25; 26; 2:24; 25; 29; 30; 31; 33; 34; 40; 3:5; 7; 8; 10; 12; 13; 18; 20; 22; 4:9; 32; 5:2; 35; 36; 37; 6:10; 7:2(3); 4(2); 5; 8; 10; 12; 15(2); 20; 21; 23; 24; 25; 26; 27; 29; 31(2); 36(2); 38; 44(2); 55; 59; 60(3); 8:3; 6; 9; 11; 12; 13(2); 16; 18; 27; 28; 31(2); 32(3); 37; 38(2); 39; 40(2); 9:2(2); 3(2); 4; 5; 6; 8; 9; 10; 11; 12(2); 13; 14; 15; 16; 17; 18(2); 19(2); 20(2); 21(2); 26(2); 27(4); 28; 29; 32; 33; 34; 39; 40; 41(3); 43; 10:3; 4(3); 6(2); 8(2); 10(2); 17; 21; 23; 27(2); 28; 32(3); 36; 39; 41; 42(2); 48; 11:13(2); 16; 17; 23(2); 24; 26(2); 12:2; 3(2); 4(2); 7; 8(2); 9(2); 11; 12(2); 17(3); 19(2); 23(2); 13:11; 12; 17; 18; 19(2); 20; 22(3); 25(2); 28; 31; 33; 34(2); 35; 36; 37; 14:9; 10; 12; 17(2); 20(2); 27; 15:8; 41; 16:1; 2; 3; 10; 18; 24; 29; 30; 33(2); 34(3); 17:16; 17; 18(2); 24; 25(3); 26; 27; 31(4); 18:2(2); 3(2); 4; 6; 7; 11; 16; 18(3); 19(2); 20; 21; 22(2); 23(2); 25(2); 26; 27(3); 28; 19:2; 3; 8; 9; 21; 22(2); 25; 31; 34; 35; 41(2); 20:2(2); 3(2); 9(2); 11(2); 13; 14; 16(2); 17; 18; 28; 35; 36(2); 38; 21:11(2); 14; 19(2); 28; 32; 33(3); 34(2); 35(2); 37(2); 40(2); 22:2(2); 8; 13; 14; 21; 22; 24(2); 26; 27; 29(3); 30(3); 23:5; 6; 7; 15(2); 16; 17; 18(2); 20; 23; 25; 27; 29; 34(4); 35(2); 24:2; 6; 22; 23; 24; 25; 26(3); 25:1; 3; 4; 5; 6(3); 7; 8; 12; 20; 22; 24; 25(2); 26:15; 23; 24; 25; 30; 32; 27:6; 35(4); 28:4; 5; 6(2); 8; 15; 17; 23; 29; **Rom** 1:2; 2:27; 28; 29; 3:26; 29(2); 4:2; 10; 11(3); 13; 17; 18; 19(2); 20; 21(2); 6:7; 10(4); 7:1; 2; 8:3; 9; 11; 24; 27(2); 29(3); 30(6); 32(2); 34; 9:15; 18(4); 19; 23(2); 24; 25; 28; 10:21; 11:2(2); 21; 26; 32; 12:3; 7; 8(4); 20; 13:4(3); 8; 14:2(2); 4(2); 6(7); 9; 18; 22(2); 23(3); 15:10; 12; 21; **1 Cor** 1:31; 2:14; 15(2); 16; 3:7(2); 8(2); 10; 14(2); 15(2); 18; 19; 4:4; 5:2; 6:16(2); 17; 18; 7:13; 20; 22(2); 24; 26; 32(2); 33(2); 36(3); 37(2); 38(2); 8:2(3); 9:10(3); 10:12(2); 22; 11:7; 23; 24(2); 25; 26; 29; 12:11; 18; 14:2(2); 3; 4(2); 5(3); 11; 13; 16(2); 24(2); 25; 15:4(2); 5; 6; 7; 8; 12; 15(2); 24(2); 25(2); 27(3); 38; 16:2; 10(2); 11; 12(3); **2 Cor** 1:10; 21; 2:2; 5; 4:14; 5:5; 10; 15; 17; 21; 6:2; 7:7(2); 15; 8:6(2); 9(2); 12; 15(2); 17(2); 23; 9:6(2); 7; 9(2); 10; 10:7(2); 17; 18; 11:4; 12:4; 6; 9; 13:4(2); **Gal** 1:4; 23(2); 2:8; 11; 12(2); 3:5(2); 16; 4:1(2); 23(2); 29; 5:3; 10(2); 6:3(2); 4; 7; 8(2); **Eph** 1:4; 6; 8; 9; 10; 20(2); 22; 2:1; 4; 7; 14; 16; 17; 3:3; 11; 16; 4:8(3); 9(2); 10(2); 11; 28; 5:14; 23; 26; 27; 28; 6:8(2); 22; **Phil** 1:6; 2:8; 22; 26(2); 27; 30; 3:4; 21; **Col** 1:13; 15; 17; 18(2); 21; 2:13; 14; 15; 18; 3:25(2); 4:8; 10; 13; **1 Th** 1:10; 3:13; 4:8; 5:24; **2 Th** 1:10; 2:4(2); 6; 7(2); 14; 3:6; 10; 14; **1 Tim** 1:12; 3:1; 5; 6; 7(2); 5:8; 6:4; 15(2); **2 Tim** 1:12; 16; 17(2); 18(2); 2:4; 5(2); 12; 13(2); 21; 4:11; 15; **Titus** 1:9(2); 2:14; 3:5; 6; **Phm** 1:13; 15; 18; **Heb** 1:2(2); 3; 4; 5(2); 6(2); 7; 8; 13; 2:5; 8(2); 9; 11(2); 14(2); 16(2); 17(2); 18(2); 3:3; 4; 17; 18; 4:3; 4; 7; 8; 10; 5:1; 2(2); 3; 4; 5; 6; 7; 8(3); 9; 13; 6:13(2); 15(2); 7:6; 8(2); 10; 13; 17; 20; 21; 24(2); 25(2); 27(2); 8:4(2); 5(2); 6(2); 8; 13(2); 9:7; 12; 15; 19; 21; 25; 26(2); 28; 10:5(2); 9(3); 12; 14; 15; 17; 20; 23; 29(2); 37; 11:4(3); 5(4); 6(3); 7; 8(4); 9; 10; 16; 17(2); 19; 21; 22; 23(2); 24; 26; 27(2); 28(2); 12:6(2); 10; 17(4); 26; 13:5; 12; 23; **Jas** 1:6; 7; 8; 10; 12(2); 13(2); 14; 18; 23; 24(2); 25(2); 26; 2:5; 10; 11; 14; 21; 23; 3:2; 4:6(2); 7; 8; 10; 11; 5:6; 15(2); 17; 18; 20; **1 Pe** 1:11; 15; 20; 2:6; 7; 23(3); 3:10; 13; 18; 19; 4:1; 2; 14(2); 5:6; 7; 8; **2 Pe** 1:9(2); 17; 2:16; 19; **1 Jn** 1:7; 9; 2:2; 4; 6(3); 9(2); 10; 11(2); 17; 22(2); 23; 25; 28; 29; 3:2(2); 3; 5; 7(2); 8(2); 9(2); 10; 12; 14; 16; 23; 24(4); 4:4(2); 6(2); 8; 10; 13(2); 15; 16; 17; 18; 19; 20(5); 21; 5:5(2); 6; 9; 10(3); 12(2); 14; 15; 16(3); 18; **2 Jn** 9; 11; **3 Jn** 10(2); 11(2); **Jude** 6; 9; **Rev** 1:1; 2; 3; 7; 16; 17; 18; 2:1; 7; 11(2); 12; 17; 23; 26; 27; 29; 3:1; 5; 6; 7(4); 12(2); 13; 20; 22; 4:3; 5:7; 8; 6:2(2); 3; 5(2); 7; 9; 12; 7:2; 14; 15; 8:1; 3(2); 9:2; 11; 10:2(2); 3; 7(2); 9; 11; 11:5; 15; 12:9; 12(2); 13(2); 15; 17; 13:5(2); 6; 10(2); 11; 12; 13(2); 14(2); 15; 16; 14:4; 10(2); 16; 17; 18; 16:15(2); 17:3; 10(2); 14; 15; 18:2; 19:2(2); 9(2); 10; 11(2); 12; 13; 15(3); 16; 17; 20; 20:2; 3(3); 6; 21:3; 5(2); 6; 7(2); 10; 15; 16; 17; 22:1; 6; 7; 9; 10; 11(4); 20

HER (1791/1088)

Gen 2:22; 3:6(2); 15; 8:9(3); 11; 12:15(2); 16; 19(2); 16:2; 3(3); 4(2); 5; 6(3); 7; 9(2); 10; 11; 13; 17:15(2); 16(4); 19:33; 20:4; 6; 7; 13; 21:10; 12; 14(2); 16; 17; 19; 23:2; 24:14; 15(2); 16(2); 17; 18(2); 20; 21; 22; 28; 41; 43; 44; 45(3); 46(2); 47(3); 51(2); 53(2); 55(2); 57; 58; 59; 60; 61; 64(2); 67(2); 25:1; 22; 23; 24(3); 26:9; 27:6; 15(3); 17; 42(2); 29:9; 12(2); 19(2); 20; 21; 23(2); 27; 28; 31; 30:1; 3(2); 4(2); 9(2); 15; 16; 21; 22(2); 31:19; 35; 33:2; 7; 34:2(4); 8; 11(2); 35:17; 18; 20; 38:2(2); 6; 8; 11; 14; 15(2); 16; 18(2); 19(2); 20; 22; 23(2); 24(2); 25; 26(2); 27; 39:10(3); 12; 13; 14; 16; 48:7; **Ex** 2:5(2); 8; 9; 10; 3:22(3); 4:25; 11:2; 15:20(2); 18:2; 3; 6(2); 21:4(2); 8(5); 9(2); 10(3); 11; 22:16(2); 17(2); **Lev** 12:2; 4(2); 5(2); 6; 7(3); 8; 15:19(2); 20; 21; 23; 24(2); 25(4); 26(4); 28; 30(2); 33(3); 18:7; 11; 15; 17(5); 18(2); 19(2); 20; 19:20; 29; 20:14; 17; 18(4); 21:3; 7; 9; 13; 22:13(3); 28(2); **Num** 5:13(3); 15; 16(2); 18; 19; 24; 27(6); 29; 30; 31; 12:12; 13; 14(3); 22:23; 25; 33; 25:8; 30:3(2); 4(4); 5(7); 6(2); 7(4); 8(5); 9; 10; 11(4); 12(6); 13(3); 14(5); 15; 16(2); 36:8; **Deut** 20:7(2); 21:11(2); 12(3); 13(5); 14(5); 15; 22:13(2); 14(3); 16; 17; 19; 21(4); 23(2); 25(3); 27(2); 28(2); 29(3); 24:1(5); 3(5); 4(3); 25:5(4); 8; 11(2); 12(2); 28:30; 56(5); 57(3); 32:22; **Josh** 2:14; 15; 17; 6:17; 22; 23(4); 25; 15:18(3); 19; **Judg** 1:14(3); 15; 4:5; 8; 18; 19; 20; 21; 22; 5:26(2); 27(2); 29(2); 11:34; 35; 37; 38(3); 39(2); 13:3; 6; 9(2); 10; 13; 14(2); 14:2; 3; 8; 16; 17(2); 15:1(2); 2(5); 6(3); 16:1; 5(2); 7; 8; 9; 11; 13; 16; 17(2); 18(2); 19; 19:2; 3(5); 25(4); 26; 27(2); 28(2); 29(2); 20:6(2); **Ruth** 1:3; 5(2); 6; 7(2); 8(2); 9; 10; 14(2); 15(2); 18(2); 22(2); 2:2; 10; 11; 14(2); 15(2); 16(2); 18(2); 19(3); 20(2); 22; 23; 3:1(2); 5; 6(2); 15; 16(3); 4:13(2); 16; **1 Sam** 1:4; 5; 6(4); 7; 8(2); 12; 13(3); 14; 18(2); 19; 22; 23(3); 24; 2:19; 4:19(4); 20(3); 21(2); 18:17; 21; 25:19(2); 20; 23; 35(2); 39; 40; 41; 42; 28:7(2); 10; 13; 14; **2 Sam** 3:15(2); 16(3); 6:16; 23; 11:4(4); 26(2); 27(2); 12:24(2); 13:1; 2; 5; 6; 8; 10; 11(2); 14(3); 15(4); 16; 17; 18(2); 19(5); 20(3); 14:2; 3; 4; 5; 17:8; 20:17; 22; **1 Ki** 1:2(3); 3; 4; 31; 2:19(2); 20; 3:1; 20(2); 26(2); 9:24(2); 10:2; 3(2); 5; 13(3); 14:5(2); 6; 15:13; 17:10; 11; 13; 15; 19(2); 20; 21:6; **2 Ki** 4:2; 5(3); 6(2); 9; 12; 13; 14(2); 15(2); 17; 20; 22; 24; 25; 26(2); 27(3); 30; 36; 37; 5:3; 6:28; 29(2); 8:2; 3(2); 5(3); 6; 9:10; 22; 30(2); 33(4); 34; 35(3); 11:1; 3; 14; 15(3); 16; 19:21; 22:14; **1 Chr** 2:18; 15:29; **2 Chr** 8:11; 9:1; 2(2); 4; 12(2); 11:20; 15:16; 22:10; 23:13; 14(3); 15(2); 34:22; 36:21; **Esth** 1:11(2); 15; 19; 2:1; 7(2); 9(5); 10(2); 11; 13; 14(2); 15(2); 17(2); 20(3); 4:4; 5; 8(3); 5:1; 3; 12; 8:1; **Job** 2:10; 5:16; 31:10; 39:13; 14; 16(2); 17(2); **Ps** 45:13; 14(2); 46:5(2); 48:3(2); 12(2); 13(2); 67:6; 68:13; 31; 80:11(2); 12(2); 84:3; 87:5(2); 102:13; 14(2); 104:17; 123:2; 132:15(2); 16(2); **Prov** 1:20; 21; 2:4(2); 16; 17(2); 18(2); 19; 3:14(2); 15; 16(2); 17(2); 18(2); 4:6(2); 8(2); 13; 5:3; 5(2); 6(2); 8(2); 19(2); 6:6; 8(2); 25(3); 29; 7:5; 8(2); 11; 21(2); 22; 25(2); 26; 27; 8:1; 2; 11; 9:1(2); 2(3); 3; 14; 18; 12:4; 14:1(2); 17:12; 25; 23:25; 27:16; 30:20; 23; 31:10; 11(2); 12; 13; 14; 15(2); 16; 17; 18(2); 19(2); 20(2); 21(2); 22; 23; 25; 26(2); 27; 28(4); 31(4); **Eccl** 7:26(2); 11:5; **Song** 1:6; 2:13; 14; 16; 3:4; 6:9(5); 8:5(2); 9(2); **Isa** 1:27; 3:26; 4:4; 5; 7:16; 9:1(2); 10:11(2); 13:13; 22(2); 16:8; 19:14(2); 21:9; 23:3; 7; 17; 18(3); 24:2; 26:17(2); 21(2); 27:2; 29:7(3); 30:7; 34:15(3); 16; 37:22; 40:2(4); 44:26; 49:15(2); 51:3(3); 18(2); 52:11; 61:10; 62:1(2); 65:18; 19; 66:7; 8; 10(4); 11(2); 12(3); **Jer** 2:23; 24(6); 32(2); 3:1; 7; 8(3); 9; 10(2); 20; 4:17; 31(3); 5:1(2); 10(2); 6:3(2); 4; 5; 6; 7(2); 8:7; 19(2); 9:20; 12:7; 9; 14:2; 15:9(2); 19:15; 20:17; 23:14; 30:17; 31:15(2); 44:17; 18; 19(4); 25; 46:21(2); 22(2); 23; 48:2(2); 4; 9; 15(2); 19; 28; 39(2); 49:2; 4; 14; 19(2); 24(2); 26(2); 50:2(2); 3(2); 9; 10; 13; 14; 15(6); 26(5); 27; 29(3); 30(2); 35(2); 36; 37(2); 38; 44(2); 51:2(3); 3(4); 4; 6(2); 7; 8(2); 9(2); 27(3); 28; 30(2); 33(2); 36(2); 43; 45; 47(3); 48; 52(2); 53(2); 55(2); 56(2); 57(4); 58; 64; **Lam** 1:2(7); 3(2); 4(3); 5(5); 6(2); 7(6); 8(3); 9(4); 10(2); 11; 17(2); 2:5(2); 7; 9(5); 16; 4:6; 7; 13(3); **Ezek** 5:5(2); 6; 12:19; 13:16; 16:2; 32; 46(2); 48; 49; 53(2); 55(2); 57; 18:6; 19:2; 3; 5(2); 11; 12(2); 14(2); 22:2(2); 3(2); 24; 25(3); 26; 27(2); 28; 23:4; 5; 7; 8(5); 9(2); 10(4); 11(4); 14; 16; 17(2); 18(4); 19(2); 20; 31; 42; 43(2); 44; 24:7(2); 8; 12(3); 26:4(4); 6; 17(2); 28:21; 22(2); 23(4); 29:12; 19(3); 30:4(2); 6(2); 7; 8; 18(5); 32:7; 16(4); 18; 20(2); 22(2); 23(3); 24(2); 25(3); 29(2); 33:28; 34:27; 36:17; **Dan** 11:6(4); 7; **Hos** 1:6; 2:2(6); 3(5); 4; 6(2); 7; 8(2); 9; 10(3); 11(5); 12(2); 13(3); 14(3); 15(3); 17; 23(2); 3:2; 3; 4:18; 19; 9:2; 10:7; 11; 14; 13:8; 16; **Joel** 1:8; 2:16; 3:17; **Am** 3:9(2); 4:3; 5:2(2); **Ob** 1; **Mic** 1:6(2); 7(3); 9; 3:11(3); 4:11; 6:12(2); 7:5; 6(2); 10(2); **Nah** 2:5; 7(2); 3:4(2); 7; 8; 9; 10(3); **Zeph** 2:14(2); 15(2); 3:1; 2; 3(3); 4(2); 5; 7(2); **Zech** 2:5(2); 5:8; 8:2; 12; 9:4(2); 5; 12:6; 14:10; **Mt** 1:6; 19(3); 20; 25(2); 2:18; 5:28(2); 31; 32; 8:15(2); 9:18; 22; 25; 10:35(2); 11:19; 14:4; 7; 8; 9; 11; 15:23(2); 28(2); 19:7; 9; 20:20; 21; 21:2; 22:28; 23:37(3); 26:13; **Mk** 1:30; 31(3); 5:23; 29(2); 32; 33; 34; 41; 43; 6:17; 23; 24; 26; 28; 7:26; 27; 29; 30(2); 10:4; 11; 12; 12:21; 22; 23; 44(2); 14:5; 6(2); 9; 16:11; **Lk** 1:5; 28; 30; 35; 36(2); 38; 41; 45; 56(2); 57; 58(3); 61; 2:6; 7; 19; 22; 36; 51; 4:38; 39(2); 7:12; 13(3); 35; 38(2); 44(2); 47; 48; 8:43; 44; 48; 52; 54; 55; 56; 10:38; 40; 41; 42; 11:27; 12:53(2); 13:12(3); 13; 34(3); 15:9; 16:18(2); 18:5(2); 20:30; 31; 33; 21:4; 21(2); **Jn** 2:4; 4:7; 10; 13; 16; 17; 21; 26; 27; 28(2); 8:3; 7; 10; 11; 11:1; 2; 5; 23; 25; 28(2); 31(3); 33(2); 40; 12:3; 7; 16:21; 18:16; 19:27; 20:13; 15; 16; 17; 18; **Acts** 5:8; 9; 10(5); 7:21; 8:27; 9:37(2); 40; 41(3); 12:14; 15;

16:14; 15; 16; 18; 19; 19:27; 21:3; 27:15; **Rom** 7:2(2); 3(2); 9:12; 25; 16:2(2); **1 Cor** 6:16; 7:2; 3(2); 4; 10; 11(2); 12; 13(2); 34; 38(2); 39(2); 11:5(3); 6(2); 10; 13; 15(3); **Gal** 4:25; 30; **Eph** 5:25; 26; 27; 33; **1 Th** 2:7; **2 Pe** 2:22; **2 Jn** 1; **Rev** 2:21(2); 22(2); 23; 12:1(2); 4; 5; 6; 14; 15; 17; 14:8; 18; 16:19; 17:2; 4(2); 5; 6; 7; 16(3); 18:3(3); 4(3); 5(2); 6(4); 7(2); 8(2); 9(3); 10; 11; 15(2); 18; 19; 20(2); 24; 19:2(3); 3; 8; 21:2; 11

HERS (2/2)

2 Ki 8:6; **Job** 39:16

HERSELF (54/50)

Gen 18:12; 20:5; 21:16; 24:65; 38:14(2); 23; **Lev** 15:28; 29; 21:9; **Num** 5:13; 14(2); 27; 28; 29; 22:25; 30:3; 4(2); 5; 6; 7; 8; 9; 10; 11; **Judg** 5:29; **1 Sam** 4:19; **2 Sam** 14:4; 21:10; **Job** 39:18; **Ps** 84:3; **Prov** 31:17; 22; **Song** 1:7; **Isa** 34:14; 61:10; **Jer** 3:11; 4:31; **Ezek** 22:3(2); 23:7; 17; **Hos** 2:13; **Zech** 9:3; **Mt** 9:21; **Mk** 6:22; **Lk** 1:24; 13:11; **Heb** 11:11; **Rev** 2:20; 18:7; 19:7

HIM (6281/4723)

Gen 1:27; 2:15; 18(2); 20; 3:9; 23; 4:8; 15(4); 25; 26(2); 5:1; 3; 24; 6:22; 7:5; 16(2); 23; 8:1; 9; 11; 12; 18; 9:8; 24; 12:3; 4(2); 7; 20(2); 13:1; 14; 14:5; 17(2); 19; 20; 15:4; 5(2); 6; 7; 9; 10; 12; 16:1; 12; 13; 17:1; 3; 19(2); 20(4); 22; 23; 27; 18:1; 2; 9; 10; 18; 19(3); 29; 19:3; 5; 6; 16(3); 21; 26; 30; 32; 34(2); 35; 20:3; 6; 9; 14; 21:2; 3(2); 4; 5; 7; 16(2); 18(2); 21; 22:1; 2; 3(2); 9(2); 11; 12; 13; 23:5; 9; 14; 24:5; 6; 9; 18; 19; 24; 25; 32; 33; 35; 36; 47; 54; 25:2; 9; 33; 26:2; 9; 12; 14; 20; 24; 26; 31; 32(2); 27:1(2); 12; 13; 22; 23(2); 25(2); 26; 27(2); 32; 33; 37(3); 39; 41; 42; 44; 45; 28:1(3); 6(3); 29:5; 13(4); 14(2); 20; 28; 34; 30:4; 16; 20; 27; 29; 31:2; 7; 14; 15; 20; 23(3); 24; 32; 32:1; 3; 6; 7; 11; 19; 20; 21; 24; 25(2); 27; 29; 31; 33:1; 4(3); 11; 13; 34:6; 8; 35:2; 6; 7; 9; 10; 11; 13(2); 14; 15; 18; 26; 29; 36:5; 37:3; 4(3); 5; 8(2); 10(2); 11; 13; 14(2); 15(2); 18(3); 20(3); 21(2); 22(4); 23; 24(2); 27(2); 28(2); 33; 35(2); 36; 38:5; 7; 10; 14; 18; 39:1(2); 3; 4(2); 5; 12; 17; 19; 20(2); 21(2); 23; 40:7; 8; 9; 12; 23; 41:12; 13; 14; 33; 34; 42; 43(3); 45; 50; 42:4; 6; 8; 10; 16; 24; 29; 31; 37(3); 38; 43:3; 5; 7; 9(4); 19; 26(2); 32(2); 33; 34(2); 44:7; 9; 14; 18; 20; 21(2); 24; 28; 29; 32; 45:1(2); 3; 9; 15; 26; 27(2); 28; 46:5; 6; 7; 20; 27; 28(2); 29; 31; 47:7; 18(2); 29; 31; 48:1; 10; 13; 17; 49:9; 10; 19; 23(3); 26; 50:1(2); 3(2); 7; 9; 12; 13(2); 14; 15; 17; 26; **Ex** 1:16; 2:2; 3(2); 4; 6; 9(2); 10(2); 12; 20; 22; 3:2; 4; 18; 4:2; 6; 11; 15; 16; 18; 23; 24(2); 26; 27(2); 28(2); 6:2; 20; 23; 25; 7:15; 16; 8:1; 20; 9:1; 13; 29; 10:1; 3; 7; 28; 12:4; 44; 48; 13:14; 19; 14:6; 15:2(2); 25; 16:8; 17:10; 12; 18:7; 17; 19:3; 7; 13; 19; 24; 20:7; 21:3; 4(2); 6(3); 13; 14(2); 16; 19(2); 22; 26; 27; 30(2); 31; 22:3; 12; 17; 21; 25(2); 26; 23:4; 5; 21(3); 24:2; 14; 28:1; 3; 41; 43(2); 29:5; 7; 21(2); 29; 30:21; 31:3; 6; 18; 32:1(2); 23; 26; 33; 33:15; 34:4; 5; 6; 20; 29; 30; 31; 32; 34; 35; 35:5; 31; 34; 36:3; 38:23; 40:13(2); 16; **Lev** 1:1; 3; 4; 4:3; 26(2); 31(2); 35; 5:6; 10; 13(2); 16(2); 18(2); 6:2; 4; 7; 7:18(2); 8:2; 4; 7(6); 8; 12(2); 30(2); 9:9; 12; 13; 18; 13:3(2); 5(2); 6(2); 8; 10; 11(2); 13; 14; 15; 17(2); 20; 21; 22; 23; 25; 26; 27(2); 28; 30; 34; 36; 37; 44; 14:3; 4; 7(2); 11; 14; 17; 18(2); 19; 20; 21; 25; 28; 29(2); 31; 15:7; 8; 10; 15; 24; 32; 33; 17:10; 18:6; 19:13(2); 17; 22(2); 33; 34; 20:2; 3; 4; 5(2); 6; 9; 21:2; 3; 8; 12; 15; 22:3; 24:9; 11; 12; 14(3); 16(2); 19; 20; 23(2); 25:27; 28; 30; 35; 36; 37(2); 39; 41; 43; 47; 48; 49(3); 50(4); 52(2); 53(2); 54; 27:8(3); 18; 19; 23; 24; **Num** 2:5; 12; 20; 27; 3:6; 9; 42; 4:49; 5:8; 12; 14(2); 6:9; 11; 7:89(3); 8:2; 9:7; 10:30; 11:20; 25(2); 29; 12:6(2); 8; 13:27; 31; 14:24; 36; 15:28(2); 29(2); 31; 33(2); 34(2); 35; 36(2); 16:5(3); 11; 25; 40; 17:6; 11; 19:3; 13(2); 20; 20:9; 18; 19; 21; 21:24; 34(3); 35(2); 22:5; 7; 16; 20; 22(2); 32; 36; 40; 41; 23:4; 6; 9(2); 13; 14; 17(3); 21; 24:2; 4; 8; 9; 16; 17(2); 25:12; 13(2); 27:11; 18; 19(2); 20; 21(2); 22(2); 23(2); 32:15; 16; 21; 33:54; 35:16; 17; 18; 19(2); 20(2); 21(3); 22(2); 23(2); 25; 27; 32; 33; **Deut** 1:3; 16; 36; 38; 2:24; 30; 33(2); 3:2(3); 3; 28(2); 4:7; 25; 29(2); 35; 42; 5:11; 6:13; 16; 7:9; 10(4); 8:6; 9:18; 20; 23; 10:8; 9; 12; 18; 20(2); 11:13; 22; 13:4(3); 8(5); 9(3); 10; 15:8(2); 9; 10(2); 12; 13(2); 14(2); 18; 17:7(2); 19; 18:4; 5(2); 15; 18; 19; 20; 22; 19:4; 6(2); 11(3); 12(2); 13; 16; 19; 20:5; 6; 7; 8; 21:1; 5; 15; 17; 18; 19(2); 21; 22; 23; 22:2(2); 4; 18; 19; 26; 23:16(2); 24:7(2); 13; 15; 25:2; 3(2); 8(2); 9; 10; 11(2); 26:3; 28:44; 29:15(2); 20(2); 21; 30:20; 31:7; 14; 29; 32:10(4); 12(2); 13(2); 15; 16(2); 33:7(2); 11(2); 12(2); 16(2); 24(2); 34:1; 4; 6; 9(2); 11; **Josh** 1:18; 2:19; 23; 4:14; 5:13(3); 14; 6:5; 7; 20; 7:3; 19; 24; 25; 26; 8:11; 14; 23; 9:6; 9; 10:7; 15; 23; 24; 29; 31; 33(2); 34; 36; 38; 43; 11:7; 9; 13:1; 14:6; 7; 13; 15:16; 17; 18(2); 19:50; 20:4(2); 5(2); 22:5(2); 14; 27; 30; 24:3(2); 14; 22; 30; 33(2); **Judg** 1:3; 5; 6(2); 7; 12; 13; 14(2); 15; 24; 2:9; 3:10; 15; 19(2); 20; 23; 27; 28; 31; 4:6; 7; 10; 13; 14; 18(2); 19(2); 21; 22(2); 5:31; 6:12(2); 13; 14; 15; 16; 17; 19; 20; 23; 25; 27; 31(4); 32(2); 34; 35; 7:1; 3; 8; 9; 19; 8:1(2); 3; 4; 8; 14(2); 31; 9:3; 4(2); 16; 19; 24; 25; 26; 28(2); 33; 34; 35; 36; 38(2); 40(2); 44; 48(2); 54(3); 10:3; 6; 11:2; 3; 11; 15; 19; 28; 34; 36; 12:5; 6(3); 8; 11; 13; 13:6; 10; 11; 18; 23; 24; 25; 14:3; 5; 6; 11(2); 13; 16; 17(2); 18; 19; 15:1; 10; 12; 13(3); 14(2); 16:2(2); 5(4); 8; 9; 12(2); 14; 15; 16(2); 19(4); 20; 21(3); 24; 25; 26; 31(3); 17:9(2); 10; 11; 18:3; 5; 15; 19; 25; 26; 27; 19:2(2); 3(4); 4(2); 7; 9; 10(2); 12; 18; 21; 22; 25; 20:23; **Ruth** 2:2; 4; 10; 3:13; 4:15; 16(2); 17; **1 Sam** 1:11; 17; 20; 22; 23(2); 24(3); 27; 28; 2:3; 16(2); 19(2); 25(2); 27; 28; 35; 36; 3:7; 13; 18(4); 19; 6:3; 4; 8; 7:3; 9; 8:5; 10; 9:5; 6; 13(2); 16; 17; 10:1; 9; 10(2); 11; 14; 16; 19; 21; 23; 24(2); 26; 27(2); 11:3; 5; 12:14; 24; 13:7; 8; 10(2); 14; 15; 14:2; 7; 13(2); 17; 20; 34; 37; 39; 43; 52; 15:2; 13; 16; 28; 32; 16:1; 6; 7; 8; 11; 12(2); 13; 14; 15; 17; 18; 21(2); 23; 17:7; 8; 9(2); 13; 20; 24; 25(2); 26; 27(2); 30(2); 31; 32; 33; 38; 41; 42; 50; 51; 57(2); 58; 18:1; 2(2); 3; 4; 5(2); 8; 12; 13(2); 14; 15; 17(2); 20; 21(3); 24; 27; 28; 19:4; 7; 8; 11(3); 15(2); 18(2); 23; 20:2; 7; 17(2); 21; 26; 30; 31; 32; 33(2); 34; 35; 36; 40; 21:1; 5; 6; 11(2); 14; 22:1; 2(2); 4; 6(2); 7; 10(3); 13(3); 15; 17; 23:3; 4; 7; 9; 14(2); 17; 20; 22; 23; 25; 24:1; 4(2); 5; 6; 8; 19; 25:1(2); 5; 6; 12; 17; 21; 22; 25; 35; 36(2); 37(2); 26:2; 3; 5; 7; 8(2); 9; 10; 19; 24; 27:2; 4; 6; 12; 28:3(2); 6; 7; 8; 9; 20; 21; 23; 29:3; 4(4); 6; 30:4; 6; 8; 9; 11(3); 12(2); 13; 15; 16; 21; 31:3; 5; **2 Sam** 1:3(2); 4; 5; 6(2); 7; 8; 10(2); 11; 13; 14; 15(2); 16; 2:1; 3; 5; 8; 9; 20; 21(2); 23; 32; 3:9; 11; 16; 20(2); 22; 23(2); 24; 26; 27(3); 31; 34; 4:4; 6; 7(3); 10(3); 5:10; 12; 14; 25; 6:2; 7; 10; 12; 16; 7:1; 14; 15; 8:4; 10(4); 9:1; 2(2); 4; 5; 7; 9; 10; 10:2; 9; 13(2); 17; 11:1; 4; 7; 8; 13(3); 15; 21; 22; 25; 27; 12:1(2); 3(2); 4(2); 9; 17(2); 18(3); 20; 21; 23(2); 24; 13:4(2); 5(2); 6; 7; 9(2); 11; 12; 16; 17; 25(2); 26; 27(2); 28; 34; 14:3; 6; 7(2); 10; 14; 24(2); 25; 26; 29(2); 31; 32; 33; 15:1; 2; 3; 4; 5(3); 9; 14; 16; 17; 18(2); 22; 24; 26(2); 30; 32; 33; 16:1; 10(2); 11(3); 13(2); 14; 15; 18; 17:2(3); 6; 10; 12(4); 16; 22; 24; 29; 18:1; 9; 11(3); 15; 17(2); 19; 20; 23; 19:17(2); 23; 25; 29; 30; 31; 37(2); 38; 39; 40; 41; 20:5; 6; 7; 9; 10(2); 12(2); 15; 17; 21; 21:4; 15; 17(2); 21; 22:1; 12; 13; 24; 31; 23:9; 10; 11; 21(2); 23; 24:2; 10; 13(3); 18; 20; 22; **1 Ki** 1:1; 2(2); 4; 5; 6(2); 13; 17; 20; 25; 27; 33; 34; 35(2); 38; 40; 41; 42; 44(2); 45; 52(2); 53(2); 2:8; 9(2); 16; 19; 22(2); 25; 29; 30; 31(3); 34; 36; 42; 46; 3:6(2); 11; 16; 19; 20; 21; 26(3); 27; 28; 4:10; 13(2); 24; 5:1; 3; 12; 8:5(2); 32; 62; 65; 9:2; 3; 12(2); 10:1; 2; 11:9; 10; 17; 18(3); 19; 20; 22; 23; 24; 27; 28; 29; 30; 34; 12:1; 3; 7; 8(3); 10(2); 13; 18; 20(3); 13:4(2); 6; 11; 13; 14(2); 15; 18(3); 19; 20; 23; 24(2); 26(5); 29; 30; 31; 33; 14:3; 13(3); 18(2); 22; 15:3; 4(2); 5; 8; 27(2); 28; 29; 16:7; 9; 10(2); 11; 17; 21; 25; 30; 31(2); 33; 17:2; 6; 8; 17; 19(3); 21; 22; 23(2); 18:7(2); 8; 15; 16; 17; 21(3); 30; 19:5(2); 7; 9(2); 13; 15; 18; 19(3); 20; 21; 20:1; 2; 7; 8; 9; 10; 11; 16; 17; 22; 23; 31; 33(4); 34(3); 35; 36(4); 37; 40; 41; 42; 21:4; 5(2); 6; 7; 10(4); 13(4); 19(2); 25; 22:7; 8; 13; 15(2); 16; 21; 22(2); 26; 27; 32; 33; 53; **2 Ki** 1:5; 6(2); 8; 9(3); 10; 11(2); 12; 13(2); 15(3); 16; 2:3; 4; 5; 6; 12; 13; 14; 15(3); 16(3); 17(2); 18; 20; 23(2); 3:11; 12(2); 13; 15; 26(2); 27(2); 4:5; 8; 10; 12; 13; 19; 20(2); 21(2); 23; 27; 29(2); 31(2); 35; 36; 38; 5:1; 3; 5; 6; 7; 8; 10; 13; 15; 16; 19(2); 20(2); 21(3); 23(2); 25; 26; 6:6; 10(2); 13(2); 15; 18; 26; 28; 29(2); 31; 32(5); 33; 7:17(2); 20(2); 8:6; 7; 8; 9(3); 10(2); 14; 19(2); 21(2); 29; 9:1; 2(2); 6; 11; 13; 15; 17(2); 18; 21; 25(3); 26; 27(3); 28(2); 32; 36; 10:3; 4; 7; 8; 9; 11; 15(6); 16; 18; 24; 35; 11:2(2); 4; 8; 12(4); 12:2; 21(2); 13:4; 9; 14; 15; 19; 20; 25; 14:19(3); 20; 21; 15:7; 10(2); 14; 19; 25(4); 30; 16:5; 9; 17:2; 3(2); 4(2); 17; 27(2); 36(3); 18:5(3); 6; 7(2); 15; 21; 36(2); 37; 19:3; 7(2); 21; 37; 20:1(2); 4; 14; 21:6; 11; 23; 22:18; 23:1; 2; 17; 18; 25(4); 26; 29(3); 30(4); 33; 24:1; 2; 12; 25:5(2); 6(2); 7(2); 25; 28(3); 30; **1 Chr** 2:3(2); 4; 9; 19; 21; 24; 29; 35; 3:1; 4; 5; 4:6; 9; 10; 5:2; 20; 7:14; 22; 9:20; 10:3; 9; 14; 11:9; 10(2); 11; 12; 23(2); 25; 42; 12:19; 20; 22; 23; 27; 13:10; 13; 14:1; 2; 10; 14; 16; 17; 15:2; 13; 29; 16:5; 9(2); 27; 29; 30; 17:13(2); 14; 25; 18:4; 10(4); 19:2(2); 10; 14(2); 17; 20:7; 21:11; 12; 20; 26; 28; 22:6; 9; 23:13; 24:19; 25:9; 26:5; 10; 27:7; 28:6; 9(3); 29:22; 23; 25(2); 30; **2 Chr** 1:1(2); 3; 5; 7; 2:3; 4(2); 6(4); 14; 15; 5:6; 6:23; 7:8; 12; 8:18; 9:1; 10:1; 3(2); 7; 8(3); 10(2); 18; 11:13; 19; 20; 22; 12:1; 3; 12(2); 13:3; 5; 7; 10; 11; 19; 20; 14:1; 5; 6; 7; 10; 13; 15:2(4); 4; 9(2); 15; 16:7; 9; 10(2); 14(3); 17:11; 14; 15(2); 16(2); 17; 18(2); 18:2(4); 3; 6; 7; 12; 14; 15; 20(2); 21; 25; 26; 30; 31(3); 32; 19:2; 20:30; 36; 21:7; 9(2); 12; 17; 18; 19; 20; 22:3; 9(4); 11(4); 23:7; 11(4); 24:3; 6; 16; 21(2); 22; 23; 25(6); 26; 27; 25:3; 7; 10; 13; 15(2); 16(2); 23; 27(3); 28(2); 26:1; 5; 7; 17(2); 18; 20(3); 23; 27:5(2); 9; 28:5(3); 16; 20(3); 21; 23(2); 27(2); 29:6(2); 11(3); 29; 30:9; 31:10; 15; 32:3; 6; 7(2); 8; 9; 15; 17; 21; 24(2); 25(2); 29; 31(3); 33(2); 33:6; 11(2); 13(2); 18; 20; 24(2); 34:26; 35:20; 21; 22(2); 24(3); 36:1; 3; 4; 6(3); 8; 10(2); 13; 20; 23(3); **Ezra** 1:2; 3(2); 4; 4:2; 11; 5:7; 15; 6:11; 7:6(2); 9; 26; 8:3; 4; 5; 6; 7; 8; 9; 10; 11; 12; 19; 21; 22(2); 33; 10:1; **Neh** 1:11; 2:1; 6(2); 3:8(2); 10; 12; 16; 17(2); 18; 19; 20; 21; 22; 23; 24; 25; 29; 30(2); 31; 4:3; 6:8; 12(2); 18; 19; 8:4; 9:7(2); 8; 11:8; 13:5; 7; 26(3); 28; **Esth** 1:3; 12; 14; 17; 19; 2:2; 9; 20; 3:1(2); 2; 4; 5; 6; 4:4; 5; 7(2); 8(3); 10; 17; 5:4; 9; 11(2); 14; 6:3(2); 4; 5(2); 6; 9(2); 11(2); 13(4); 14; 7:7; 9; 8:3; 7; 10:2; **Job** 1:2; 8; 10; 2:3(3); 9; 11(3); 12; 13(2); 3:20; 4:4; 6:14; 7:8; 10; 17(2); 18(2); 8:4; 18; 9:3(2); 4; 11(2); 12(2); 13; 14(2); 15; 32; 34(2); 35; 11:10; 13; 12:4; 13; 16; 13:7; 8; 9; 11; 15(2); 16; 14:6; 20(2); 15:21; 22; 24(2); 26; 31; 18:6; 7; 9(2); 10(2); 11(2); 14; 17; 21; 19:16; 28; 20:7; 9(3); 11; 14; 16; 21; 22; 23(2); 24; 25; 26(2); 27; 29; 21:15(2); 19(2); 20; 21; 31; 33(3); 22:3; 4; 14; 21; 27; 23:3; 4; 7; 8; 9(2); 13; 14; 15; 24:1; 20(2); 25:2; 26:2; 6; 14; 27:9; 15; 20(2); 21(2); 22; 23(2); 30:25; 31:14; 18; 29(2); 37(2); 32:8; 13; 14; 33:13; 23; 24(2); 26; 34:13(2); 17; 27; 28; 29; 35:6(2); 7; 14(3); 36:11; 22; 23; 26; 37:16; 18; 19; 23; 24; 39:11(2); 12; 20; 23; 40:2(2); 11; 12; 19; 20; 22(2); 41:4; 5(2); 6(2); 8; 9(2); 10; 11; 13; 22; 23; 26; 28(2); 32; 33; 42:8; 11(6); **Ps** 2:12; 3:2; 4:3(2); 5:12; 7:4; 5; 8:4(2); 5(2); 6; 10:9; 12:5; 13:4; 17:13(2); 18:6; 11; 12; 23; 30; 20:6; 21:2; 3; 4; 5; 6(2); 22:8(5); 23(3); 24(2); 25; 26; 29; 30; 24:6; 25:12; 14; 28:7(2); 32:6; 10; 33:2; 3; 8; 18; 21; 34:5; 6(2); 7; 8; 9; 19; 22; 35:8(2); 10(4); 25; 37:5; 7(2); 12; 13; 22(2); 24; 32; 33(2); 36; 40; 41:1; 2(3); 3(2); 8; 42:5; 11; 43:5; 44:16; 45:11; 49:7; 17; 50:3(2); 18; 23; 51:52:6; 53:5; 55:12; 20; 56:59:61:7; 62:1; 4; 5; 8(2); 63:11; 64:4; 10; 66:6; 17; 67:7; 68:1(2); 4(2); 33; 69:30; 34; 71:11(3); 72:9; 11(2); 12; 15(2); 17(2); 74:14; 76:11(2); 78:17; 34; 36(2); 37; 40(2); 58(2); 70; 71; 81:15; 85:9; 13; 89:7; 20; 21; 22(2); 23; 24; 27; 28(2); 33; 41; 43; 45; 91:2; 14(2); 15(4); 16(2); 92:15; 94:13; 95:2; 96:6; 9; 97:2; 3; 7; 98:1; 100:4; 101:5(2); 103:11; 13; 17; 104:34; 105:2(2); 19; 20(2); 21; 106:10; 23; 29; 31; 32; 107:32(2); 109:6; 7; 12; 17(2); 19(2); 30; 31(2); 111:5; 113:8; 116:2; 117:1; 119:2; 42; 126:6; 130:7; 135:1; 136:4; 5; 6; 7; 10; 13; 16; 17; 140:11; 141:5; 142:2(2); 144:3(2); 145:18(2); 19; 20; 147:11; 148:1; 2(2); 3(2); 4; 14; 149:3; 150:1; 2(2); 3(2); 4(2); 5(2); **Prov** 3:6; 6:16; 7:10; 13(3); 20; 21(2); 8:9; 30(2); 9:4(3); 16(3); 10:13(2); 24; 26; 11:26(2); 27; 12:14; 13:6; 18; 24(2); 14:2; 6; 7; 31; 33; 35; 15:9; 10; 12; 14; 21; 16:7; 13; 22; 26; 29; 17:11; 24; 25; 18:9; 13; 14; 16(2); 17; 19:7(3); 11; 19; 20:2; 7; 21:25; 28; 22:15; 23:13; 14; 24; 24:18(2); 24(2); 29; 25:13; 21(2); 26:4; 12; 15; 25; 27; 27:11; 13; 14; 21; 22; 28:8; 11; 17; 22; 29:20; 21; 23; 30:5; 31; 31:1; 6; 7; 12; **Eccl** 2:26; 3:14; 22(2); 4:10(2); 12; 16; 5:12; 18; 19; 20; 6:2; 10; 12; 7:14; 8:3; 4; 7; 12; 15(2); 9:2(2); 4; 10:12; 14(2); 11:8; **Song** 1:2; 3:1(2); 2(2); 4(3); 11; 5:4; 6(3); 8; 6:1; **Isa** 3:11(2); 5:19; 6:4; 7:4; 8:13(3); 17; 9:11; 13; 10:6(2); 15(2); 20; 26; 11:2; 10; 14:25; 15:4; 9; 16:3; 20:1; 21:6; 14(2); 22:11; 21(2); 23; 24; 25:9(2); 10; 26:3; 27:5; 7(2); 28:6; 26(2); 29:16(2); 21; 30:18; 32; 31:4; 6; 8; 33:16; 36:3; 6; 21(2); 22; 37:3; 7(2); 22; 38; 38:1(2); 39:3; 40:10(3); 13; 14(4); 17(2); 18; 41:2(3); 7; 42:1; 25(3); 43:7(2); 44:3; 7; 10; 20; 45:1(2); 9(2); 10; 13; 24(2); 46:7; 48:14; 15(2); 49:5(2); 7(2); 25; 50:4; 8; 10; 51:2(3); 52:7; 15; 53:2(3); 3(2); 4; 5; 6; 10(2); 12; 55:4; 6; 7(2); 56:6; 8(2); 57:15; 17; 18(3); 19(3); 58:7; 13; 59:15; 16(2); 19; 62:7; 11(2); 63:14; 64:4; 5; 66:2; **Jer** 2:3; 15; 37; 3:1; 4:2(2); 6:11; 9:24; 10:25(2); 11:19; 17:11; 18:18; 19:14; 20:2; 3; 9; 10(2); 15; 16; 21:1; 9; 12; 22:10(2); 12; 13(2); 15; 18(2); 23:24; 28(2); 26:8(2); 19; 21; 22; 23(2); 24(2); 27:6(2); 7(2); 11; 12; 28:14(2); 29:26; 31; 30:10; 21; 31:2; 10(2); 11; 20(4); 32:3; 4(2); 5; 9; 33:13; 34:2; 14(2); 36:4; 8; 15; 22; 31; 37:4; 14(2); 15(2); 17(2); 21; 38:2; 6; 11; 13; 14; 27(2); 39:5(3); 7(2); 9; 12(4); 14(2); 40:1(2); 2; 5(3); 6; 7; 14; 41:2(2); 3; 7; 11; 12; 13; 16; 42:8; 9; 11; 43:1; 44:20; 45:4; 46:25; 27; 48:11; 12(2); 17(2); 19; 26; 27; 49:8(2); 19; 50:16; 17(2); 32(2); 43; 51:44; 52:8; 9(2); 11(3); 31; 32(3); 34; **Lam** 1:17; 2:19; 3:24; 25(2); 28(2); 29; 30(2); **Ezek** 1:3; 2:2; 3:18; 20(2); 27(2); 7:15; 9:4; 5; 12:13(2); 14(2); 14:4(3); 7(4); 8(2); 9(2); 17:6; 7(2); 12; 13(2); 15(2); 16(2); 20(3); 18:13; 22; 19:4(2); 5; 8(2); 9(3); 21:27; 24:27; 28:9(2); 12; 29:2; 20; 30:11; 24; 32:2; 21(2); 33:2; 4; 12; 16; 38:2; 22(3); 40:46; 43:6; 44:26; 46:12; 47:23; **Dan** 2:1; 16; 22; 24; 25; 46; 48(2); 3:28; 4:8(2); 15; 16(2); 19; 23(2); 34; 35; 5:6; 11(2); 17; 19(2); 20; 21; 24; 29; 6:3(2); 4; 5; 6; 14(2); 16; 18(2); 22; 23(2); 7:10(3); 13(2); 14(2); 16; 27; 8:4; 6; 7(5); 11; 9:4; 9; 11; 10:16; 11:1; 5; 6(2); 11; 15; 16(2); 17(4); 18; 22; 23; 25; 26; 30; 31; 40(2); 44; 45; 12:7; **Hos** 1:3; 4; 6; 4:17; 5:6; 7:5; 9; 10; 8:3; 11; 12; 9:4; 17; 11:1; 7; 12:2; 4(2); 14(3); 13:11; 13; 14:2; 4; 8; 9(2); **Joel** 2:14; 20; **Am** 2:3; 5:11; 19(2); 9:13; **Jon** 1:6(2); 8; 10; 11; 15; 4:6; **Mic** 1:4; 2:7; 3:5; 5:5; 6:5; 6; 7:9; **Nah** 1:5; 6; 7; 15; **Hab** 2:4; 6(4); 9; 12; 15(3); 19; 20; 3:5; **Zeph** 1:6; 2:11; 3:9; **Hag** 1:12; **Zech** 1:8; 2:3; 4; 3:1; 4(3); 5; 4:11; 12; 6:12; 9:8(2); 10:4(4); 12:1; 10(2); 13:3(4); 6; **Mal** 2:5(2); 17; 3:16; 17; 18; 4:4; **Mt** 1:20; 24(2); 2:2; 3; 5; 8(2); 11(2); 13; 3:5; 6; 13; 14; 15(2); 16(2); 4:3; 5(2); 6; 7; 8(2); 9; 10(2); 11(2); 20; 22; 24; 25; 5:1; 25; 31; 39; 40; 41; 42(2); 6:8; 7:8; 9; 10; 11; 24; 8:1; 2; 3; 4; 5(2); 7(2); 16; 18; 19; 20; 21; 22; 23; 25(2); 27; 28; 31; 34(2); 9:2; 9(2); 10; 14; 18; 19; 24; 27; 28(2); 31; 32; 10:1; 4; 28; 32; 33; 40; 11:3; 15; 27; 12:2; 3; 4(2); 10(2); 14(2); 15; 16; 18; 22(2); 32(2); 45; 46; 47; 48; 13:2; 9; 10; 12(2); 27; 28; 36; 43; 51; 57; 14:2; 3(2); 4; 5(2); 9; 13; 15; 17; 22; 26; 28; 31(2); 33; 35(2); 36; 15:4; 12; 15; 22; 23; 25; 30; 33; 16:1; 17; 22(2); 24; 17:3; 5; 10; 12(2); 14(2); 16(2); 17; 18; 23; 25; 26(2); 18:2(2); 6; 15(2); 17; 21(2); 22; 24(2); 26; 27(2); 28(3); 29; 30; 32(2); 34(2); 19:2; 3(3); 7; 10; 12; 13; 16; 17; 18; 20; 21; 27; 20:7; 18; 19; 20(2); 21; 22; 26; 27; 29; 33; 34; 21:7; 14; 16; 23; 25; 31; 32(3); 38; 39(3); 41(2); 44; 46(2); 22:12; 13(3); 15; 16; 19; 21; 22; 23(2); 35(2); 37; 42; 43; 45; 46(2); 23:15; 21; 22; 24:1; 3; 15; 17; 18; 47; 50; 51(2); 25:6; 10; 21; 23; 26; 28(2); 29; 31; 32; 37; 44; 26:4; 7; 15(2); 16; 17; 18; 22; 24; 25(2); 33; 34; 35; 37; 48; 49; 50(2); 52; 56; 57; 58; 59; 62; 63; 64; 67(2); 69; 71; 75; 27:1; 2(3); 9; 11(2); 13; 14; 18; 19(2); 22(2); 23; 26; 27; 28(2); 29(2); 30(2); 31(4); 32; 34; 35; 36; 37; 38; 39; 42(2); 43(3); 44(2); 48; 49(2); 54; 55; 58; 64; 28:4; 7; 9(2); 13; 14; 17(2); **Mk** 1:5(2); 10; 12; 13; 18; 20; 25(2); 26(2); 27; 30; 32; 34; 36(2); 37(2); 40(4); 41(2); 42; 43(2); 44; 45; 2:3; 4; 13; 14(2); 15; 16; 18; 24; 25; 26; 3:2(3); 6(2); 7; 8; 9(2); 10(2); 11(2); 12; 13(2); 14; 19; 21; 31(2); 32(2); 34; 4:1; 9; 10(2); 23; 25(2); 36(2); 38(2); 41; 5:2; 3; 4(2); 6; 8; 9; 10; 12; 16; 17; 18(2); 19(2); 20; 21; 22; 23; 24(3); 27; 30; 31; 33(2); 37; 40(2); 6:1; 2(2); 3; 14(2); 17; 19(2); 20(3); 22; 26; 27; 30; 33(2); 35; 37; 45; 49; 50; 54; 56(2); 7:1; 5; 10; 12; 15(2); 16; 17; 18; 25; 26; 28; 32(3); 33; 34; 8:1; 4; 11(3); 19; 22(3); 23(3); 25; 26; 29; 30; 32(2); 34; 38; 9:7; 11; 13(2); 15(3); 18(2); 19(2); 20(4); 21; 22(2); 23(2); 25(2); 26(2); 27(2); 28; 31; 32; 36(2); 37; 38(2); 39; 42; 10:1; 2(2); 10; 13; 17(2); 18; 20; 21(3); 28; 32; 33(2); 34(4); 35; 37; 39; 48; 49(2); 51(2); 52; 11:18(2); 21; 25; 27; 28; 31; 12:3(3); 4(3); 5; 6; 7; 8(3); 12(2); 13(2); 14; 16; 17; 18(2); 26; 28; 29; 32; 33; 34(2); 37(2); 13:1; 2; 3; 15; 16; 14:1(2); 10; 11(2); 12; 13; 19; 21; 29; 30; 33; 35; 40; 44(2); 45(3); 46(2); 50; 51(2); 53; 54; 55; 56; 57; 58; 61(2); 64; 65(5); 67; 69; 72; 15:1(2); 2(2); 3; 4; 8; 10; 12; 13; 14; 15; 16; 17; 18; 19(3); 20(5); 22; 23; 24; 25; 27; 29; 32(2); 36(3); 39; 41(3); 44; 46(3); 16:1; 6; 7; 10; 14; **Lk** 1:11; 12(2); 13; 17; 19; 29; 32; 50; 59; 62; 66; 74; 75; 2:7(2); 17; 22(2); 25; 26; 27; 28; 33; 38; 40; 44(2); 45(2); 46; 47; 48(2); 3:7; 10; 11(3); 12; 14; 19; 22; 4:3; 4; 5(2); 6; 8(2); 9(3); 12; 13; 14; 20; 22; 29(3); 35(5); 37; 38; 40; 42(3); 5:1; 3; 5; 9; 11; 12; 13(2); 14; 15(2); 18; 19(2); 20; 27; 28; 29; 33; 6:3; 4; 7(2); 17; 19(2); 29(2); 30; 7:2; 3(2); 4; 6(2); 9(2); 11; 14; 15; 17; 18; 19; 20; 29; 30; 36(2); 38; 39(2); 40; 42; 43; 49; 8:1; 3; 4; 8; 9; 18(2); 19(2); 20; 24(2); 25; 27; 28; 29; 30(2); 31; 32; 37; 38(3); 39; 40(2); 41; 42; 45; 47(3); 49; 50; 53;

9:7; 9; 10; 11; 12; 18; 23; 26; 30; 32(2); 33; 35; 37; 39(4); 42(3); 45; 47(2); 48; 49; 50(2); 51; 52; 53; 57; 58; 60; 62; 10:16; 22; 25; 26; 28; 30(3); 31; 33; 34(4); 35(2); 36; 37(2); 38; 40; 11:1; 5(2); 6; 8(2); 10; 11(2); 12; 13; 16(2); 22(3); 26; 27; 37(2); 39; 45; 53(2); 54(3); 12:5(2); 8; 10(2); 13; 14; 20; 36; 41; 44; 46(3); 48(2); 58; 13:1; 8; 12; 15; 17; 23; 31; 14:1; 2; 4(3); 5; 6; 8; 9; 12(2); 15(2); 16; 18; 25; 29; 31(2); 35; 15:1(2); 15; 16; 18; 20(2); 21; 22; 27(2); 28; 30; 31; 16:1; 2(2); 5; 6; 7; 14; 27; 29; 31; 17:1; 2; 3(2); 4; 7; 8; 9; 12; 16; 19; 31(2); 37; 18:3; 7; 15; 16; 18; 19; 22; 33(2); 37; 39; 40(3); 42; 43; 19:4; 5(2); 6; 9; 14(2); 15; 17; 19; 22; 24(2); 25; 26(2); 31; 34; 35(2); 39; 47; 48; 20:1; 2; 5; 10(3); 11(3); 12(2); 13(2); 14(2); 15(2); 18; 19; 20(2); 21; 26; 27(2); 38; 40; 44; 21:7; 38(2); 22:2; 4; 5; 6; 9; 10; 14; 26; 33; 36(2); 39; 43(2); 47; 48; 49(2); 51; 52; 54(3); 56(3); 57(2); 58; 59; 61; 63(2); 64(3); 65; 66; 23:1; 2; 3(2); 7; 8(3); 9(2); 10; 11(4); 14(2); 15(2); 16(2); 17; 21(2); 22(3); 26(2); 27(2); 32; 33; 35; 36(2); 38; 39; 40; 43; 49; 55; 24:16; 18; 19; 20(2); 24; 29; 31; 42; 52; **Jn** 1:3(2); 4; 7; 10(2); 11; 12; 15; 18; 19; 21; 22; 25; 29; 31; 32; 33(2); 37; 38; 39; 40; 41; 42(2); 43; 45(2); 46(2); 47(2); 48(2); 49; 50; 51; 2:3; 10; 11; 18; 3:2(2); 3; 4; 9; 10; 15; 16; 17; 18; 26(2); 27; 28; 29; 36; 4:9; 10; 11; 14(3); 15; 19; 23; 24; 25; 30; 31; 33; 34; 39; 40(2); 42; 45; 47(2); 48; 49; 50(2); 51(2); 52(2); 53; 5:6(2); 7; 8; 10; 12; 14(2); 15; 16; 18; 20(2); 23; 24; 27; 38; 43; 6:2; 5; 6; 7; 8; 15(2); 21; 25(2); 27; 28; 29; 30; 34; 38; 40(3); 41; 44(2); 54; 56; 64; 65; 66; 68; 71; 7:1; 3; 5; 11; 12; 13; 18(2); 26; 29(2); 30(2); 31; 32(2); 33; 35; 37; 39; 43; 44(2); 45; 48; 51; 52; 8:2; 3; 4; 6(2); 7(2); 13; 19; 20; 25; 26; 29; 30; 31; 33; 39; 41; 44; 48; 52; 55(4); 57; 59; 9:2; 3; 4; 7; 9; 10; 12; 13; 15; 17; 18(2); 21; 23; 24; 26; 28; 31; 34(2); 35(3); 36; 37(2); 38; 40(2); 10:3; 4; 5; 20; 24(2); 31; 33; 36; 38; 39; 41; 42; 11:3; 8; 10; 11; 15; 16; 20; 24; 27; 29; 30; 32(2); 34(2); 36; 39(2); 44(2); 45; 48(2); 53; 57; 12:2(2); 4; 11; 13; 16(2); 17(2); 18; 19; 21; 26(2); 29; 34; 37; 41; 42(2); 44; 45; 47; 48(2); 13:2; 6; 7; 8(2); 9; 10; 11; 16; 20; 24; 25; 27(2); 28; 29; 31; 32(3); 36(2); 37; 38; 14:5; 6; 7(2); 8; 9; 17(3); 21(2); 22; 23(4); 15:5; 21; 16:5; 7; 19; 29; 17:2(2); 18:2; 4; 5(2); 12; 13; 20; 23; 24; 25; 26(2); 30(2); 31(3); 33; 34; 37; 38(2); 19:1; 2; 3; 4(2); 6(6); 7; 9; 10; 12; 15(3); 16(2); 18(2); 32; 37; 38; 20:2; 6; 13; 15(5); 16; 25; 28; 29; 21:3; 5; 12; 15(2); 16(3); 17(4); 19; 21; 22; 23; **Acts** 1:6; 9; 11; 2:22; 23; 25; 30; 3:4; 7(2); 9; 10; 13; 16(2); 22; 26; 4:10; 5:6(3); 17; 21; 31; 32; 36(2); 37(2); 40; 6:11; 12(3); 14; 15; 7:3; 4; 5(3); 8(2); 9; 10(3); 14; 21(2); 24; 27; 30; 31; 33; 35; 37; 38; 40; 47; 54; 57; 58(2); 8:2; 11; 20; 30(2); 31; 35; 38; 39; 9:2; 3; 4; 6; 7; 8(2); 10; 11; 12; 15; 16; 17; 23; 24; 25(2); 26; 27(3); 29; 30(2); 34; 35; 38(2); 39(2); 10:3; 4(2); 7(2); 11; 13; 15; 19; 21; 23; 25(2); 26; 27; 35(2); 38; 40(2); 41; 43(2); 48; 11:2; 13; 26(2); 12:4(5); 5; 6; 7(2); 8(2); 9; 10; 16; 17; 19(2); 20; 23; 13:9; 11(2); 22; 27(2); 28; 29(3); 30; 31; 34; 39; 14:9; 19(2); 20; 15:21; 16:3(4); 9; 32; 17:15(2); 16; 18; 19(2); 23; 27(2); 28; 31; 34; 18:6; 12; 17; 18; 20; 26(3); 27; 19:2; 4(2); 22; 30; 31; 33; 20:3; 4; 10(3); 14; 18; 37; 38; 21:8; 11; 12; 20; 27(2); 29; 30; 31; 33(2); 34; 36; 40; 22:9; 13; 18; 20; 22; 24(2); 25; 27; 29(3); 30(2); 23:2(2); 3; 9; 10(2); 11; 15(2); 17(2); 18(3); 19; 20; 21(2); 22; 24; 27; 28(2); 29; 30(2); 31; 32; 33; 35; 24:6(2); 7; 8(2); 10; 23(3); 24; 26(4); 25:2(2); 3(3); 5; 15; 16; 18; 19; 21(2); 22; 25; 26(2); 27; 27:3; 28:6; 8(3); 16; 21; 23(2); 30; 31; **Rom** 1:5; 21; 4:3; 4; 5(2); 17; 22; 23; 24; 5:9; 14; 6:4; 6; 8; 9; 7:4; 8:11; 17; 20; 32(2); 37; 9:11; 16(2); 20; 33; 10:9; 11; 12; 14(2); 11:4; 35(2); 36(3); 12:20(2); 13:4; 14:3(5); 4; 14(2); 15:11; 12; 16:25; **1 Cor** 1:5; 30; 31; 2:2; 9; 11; 14; 16; 3:17; 18; 5:3; 6:17; 7:12(2); 13; 15; 17; 18(2); 36; 8:3; 6; 10; 10:12; 11:14; 28; 34; 14:2; 11; 13; 28(2); 37; 38; 15:27(2); 28(3); 16:11(3); 12; 22; **2 Cor** 1:19; 20(2); 2:7; 8; 5:9; 15; 16; 21(2); 6:1; 7:12(2); 14; 15; 8:18; 10:7; 17; 12:18; 13:4(2); **Gal** 1:1; 6; 8; 9; 16; 18; 2:11; 13; 3:6; 4:29; 5:8; 6:6(2); **Eph** 1:4(2); 7; 10; 11(2); 13; 17; 20(2); 22; 23; 2:18; 3:12; 20; 21; 4:15; 21(2); 28(3); 6:9; **Phil** 1:29; 2:9(2); 23; 27(2); 28(2); 29; 3:9; 10; **Col** 1:10; 16(3); 17; 19; 20(2); 28; 2:6; 7; 9; 10; 11; 12(3); 13; 3:4; 10(2); 17; 4:8; 10; 13; **1 Th** 4:14; 5:10; **2 Th** 1:12; 2:1; 3:14; 15(2); **1 Tim** 1:16; 5:1; **2 Tim** 1:12; 18; 2:4(2); 11(2); 12(2); 26; 4:11; 14; 15; 18; **Titus** 1:16; **Phm** 1:12(2); 15; 17; **Heb** 1:5; 6; 2:3; 6(2); 7(3); 8(3); 10; 13; 14; 3:2(2); 4:13; 5:5; 7(2); 9; 6:6; 7:1; 6; 10; 21(2); 25; 9:9; 28; 10:30; 38; 11:5; 6(2); 9; 11; 12; 19(2); 27; 12:2; 3; 5; 25(3); 13:13; 15; **Jas** 1:5(2); 6; 12; 2:3; 5; 14; 23; 3:13; 4:17(2); 5:13(2); 14(3); 15; 19; 20; **1 Pe** 1:8; 21(3); 2:4; 6; 9; 14; 23; 3:6; 10; 11(2); 22; 4:5; 11(2); 16(2); 19; 5:7; 9; 11; 12; **2 Pe** 1:3; 17; 18; 2:19; 3:14; 15; 18; **1 Jn** 1:5(2); 6; 10; 2:3; 4(2); 5(2); 6; 8; 10; 13; 14; 15; 27(2); 28(2); 29; 3:1; 2(2); 3; 5; 6(3); 9; 12; 15; 17(2); 19; 22; 24(2); 4:9; 13; 15; 16; 19; 21; 5:1(3); 10; 14; 15; 16; 18; 20(2); **2 Jn** 10(2); 11; **Jude** 9; 15; 24; **Rev** 1:1; 4; 5; 6; 7(3); 17; 2:7(2); 11; 17(4); 26; 28; 29; 3:6; 12(3); 13; 20(2); 21; 22; 4:9; 10(2); 5:1; 7; 13; 14; 6:2; 4; 8(2); 16; 7:14; 15; 9:1; 10:6; 9; 12:9; 11; 13:2; 4; 7(2); 8; 9; 18; 14:1; 7(2); 15; 18; 16:8; 9; 17:14; 19:5; 7; 10; 11; 14; 19; 20; 21; 20:2; 3(3); 6; 11; 21:6; 22:3; 11(4); 17(3); 18

HIMSELF (545/507)

Gen 4:19; 8:8; 9; 13:11; 18:2; 19:1; 22:8; 23:7; 12; 24:52; 27:42; 28:6; 30:36; 37; 32:21; 33:3; 17; 42:24; 43:31; 32; 45:1(2); 46:29; 47:31; 48:2; **Ex** 4:16; 6:20; 23; 25; 12:3; 21:3(2); 4; 8; 30:12; **Lev** 7:8; 9:8; 13:33; 14:8; 15:13; 14; 16:6(2); 11(3); 17; 24; 20:6; 21:1; 3; 4(2); 11; 22:8; 25:26; 28; 39; 47; 49; 26:46; 27:8; **Num** 6:2; 3; 5; 6; 7; 16:9; 10; 19:12(2); 13; 19; 20; 30:2; 31:53; 35:19; **Deut** 3:22; 4:34; 35; 39; 7:6; 14:2; 17:16; 17(2); 18; 28:9; 29:13; 19; 31:3(2); 33:21; **Josh** 5:3; 22:23; **Judg** 3:13; 16; 19; 4:11; 6:31; 7:5; 9:5; 16:29; 19:1; 21:21; **Ruth** 3:8; **1 Sam** 2:14; 3:21; 10:19; 13:2; 14; 14:52; 15:12; 17:16; 40; 23:7; 25:31; 28:8; 17; 29:4; 30:6; 31; **2 Sam** 1:2; 6:20(2); 7:23(2); 8:13; 9:6; 8; 12:20; 14:22; 33; 15:1; 23; 17:23; 18:18; 21; 20:6; 23:12; **1 Ki** 1:5(2); 47; 52; 8:58; 11:29; 13:4; 14:14; 15:15; 16:9; 18; 17:21; 18:2; 6(2); 19:4; 20:38; 21:25; 29(2); 22:11; 30; **2 Ki** 4:34; 35; 10:24; 13:15; 19:1; **1 Chr** 15:1; 17:21; 29:5; **2 Chr** 2:1; 3; 12; 11:15; 18; 12:1; 12; 13; 13:9; 12; 15:18; 16:9; 14; 17:1; 16; 18:1; 10; 29; 34; 20:3; 35; 36; 21:4; 23:1; 16; 25:11; 28:24; 32:1; 5; 26; 27; 29; 33:12; 23(2); 35:22; 36:12; **Ezra** 10:8; **Neh** 2:20; **Esth** 5:10; **Job** 2:1; 8(2); 4:2; 9:4; 15:2; 31; 17:8; 22:2; 27:10; 32:2; 34:14; 41:25; **Ps** 4:3; 7:13; 10:14; 22:29; 25:13; 35:8; 36:2; 4; 37:35; 49:18; 50:6; 52:7; 55:12; 68:30; 87:5; 93:1; 109:18; 19; 113:6; 132:18; 135:4; **Prov** 6:30; 9:7(2); 11:25; 12:9; 13:7(2); 16:4; 26; 18:1; 24; 21:13; 22:3; 26:24; 27:12; 28:10; 29:15; **Eccl** 6:2; **Song** 3:9; **Isa** 2:9; 20; 7:14; 19:17; 22:16(2); 28:20; 37:1; 38:15; 40:20; 44:5(2); 14(2); 15; 16; 23; 56:3; 59:15; 61:10; 63:10; 12; 64:7; 65:16(2); **Jer** 10:23; 16:20; 23:24; 29:26; 27; 31:18; 43:12; 46:10; 48:26; 42; 49:10; 51:3; 14; 45; **Ezek** 7:13; 14:7; 18:20(2); 27; 33:5; 45:22; **Dan** 1:8(2); 6:3; 14; 8:11; 25; 9:26; 11:36; 37; **Hos** 5:6; 7:8; 10:1; 13:1; **Am** 2:14; 15; 6:8; **Jon** 3:6; 4:5; 8; **Hab** 2:5(2); 6; **Mt** 3:4; 6:4; 8:17; 12:26; 45; 13:21; 14:13; 23; 15:10; 32; 16:24; 18:4; 20:25; 23:12(2); 27:5; 42; 57; **Mk** 3:13; 23; 26; 4:27; 5:5; 30; 6:7; 17; 7:14; 8:34(2); 10:42; 12:36; 37; 43; 14:54; 67; 15:31; 43; **Lk** 3:23; 5:16; 6:13; 7:39; 9:23; 25; 10:1; 29; 11:18; 26; 12:17; 21; 37; 47; 14:11(2); 15:15; 17; 16:3; 18:4; 11; 14(2); 19:12; 20:42; 23:2; 35; 51; 24:12; 15; 27; 36; **Jn** 2:24; 4:2; 12; 44; 53; 5:18; 19; 20; 26(2); 37; 6:6; 15; 61; 7:4; 18; 8:7; 10; 22; 59; 9:21; 11:38; 13:4; 32; 16:27; 18:18; 25; 19:7; 12; 21:1(2); 14; **Acts** 1:3; 2:34; 8:13; 34; 10:17; 12:11; 14:17; 16:27; 18:19; 19:22; 20:1; 13; 25:4; 8; 16; 25; 26:1; 28:16; **Rom** 8:16; 26; 12:3; 14:7(2); 12; 22; 15:3; **1 Cor** 2:15; 3:15; 18; 11:28; 29; 14:4; 8; 28; 37; 15:28; **2 Cor** 5:18; 19; 8:19; 10:7(2); 18; 11:14(2); 20; **Gal** 1:4; 2:12; 20; 6:3(2); 4; **Eph** 1:5; 9; 2:14; 15; 20; 4:11; 5:2; 25; 27; 28; 33; **Phil** 2:3; 7; 8; 3:21; **Col** 1:20; **1 Th** 3:11; 4:16; 5:23; **2 Th** 2:4(2); 16; 3:16; **1 Tim** 2:6; **2 Tim** 2:4; 13; 21; **Titus** 2:14(2); **Heb** 1:3; 2:14; 18; 4:10; 5:2; 3; 4; 5; 6:13; 7:27; 9:7; 14; 25; 26; 12:3; 13:5; **Jas** 1:13; 24; 4:4; **1 Pe** 2:23; 24; **1 Jn** 2:2; 6; 3:3; 5:10; 18; **3 Jn** 10; **Rev** 14:10; 17:11; 19:12; 15(2); 21:3

HIS (7947/5676)

Gen 1:27; 2:2(2); 3; 7; 21; 24(2); 25; 3:8; 15; 20; 21; 22; 4:1; 2; 4(2); 5(2); 8(2); 17(2); 21; 23; 25; 5:3(2); 29; 6:3; 5; 6; 9; 7:2(2); 7(3); 13; 8:9; 18(3); 21(2); 9:1; 6; 8; 21; 22(2); 24(2); 25; 26; 27; 10:5; 10; 15; 25(2); 11:28(2); 31(4); 12:5(2); 8; 11; 12; 17; 20(2); 13:1; 3(2); 10; 12; 18; 14:12; 14(3); 15(2); 16(2); 17; 16:3; 11; 12(2); 15; 17:3; 14(2); 17(2); 19(2); 23(3); 24; 25(2); 26; 27; 18:2; 19(2); 33(2); 19:1; 3; 14(3); 16(3); 26; 30(2); 37; 38; 20:2; 8; 14; 17(2); 21:2; 3; 4; 5; 7; 11; 21; 22; 32; 22:3(3); 4; 5; 6(2); 7; 9; 10(2); 13(2); 19; 21(2); 24; 23:3; 6; 9; 10; 18; 19; 24:2; 7; 9(2); 10(3); 11; 20; 21; 26; 27(2); 30(2); 32; 40; 48; 59; 63; 67(3); 25:6; 8(2); 9; 10; 11; 17(2); 18; 21(3); 25; 26(3); 28; 30; 33; 34(2); 26:7; 8; 11(2); 15(2); 17; 18(2); 25; 26(2); 27:1(2); 5; 10; 11; 13; 14(3); 16(2); 18; 19; 20; 22; 23(2); 26; 27; 30(3); 31(3); 32; 34(2); 37; 38(2); 39; 40; 41(2); 28:7(2); 8; 9; 11; 16; 18; 29:1; 6; 10(3); 11; 13(2); 23; 24(2); 28; 29(2); 32; 33; 34; 35; 30:6; 8; 11; 13; 14; 18; 20; 24; 35; 40; 31:4; 17(2); 18(4); 19; 23; 25(2); 46; 53; 54; 55(2); 32:1; 3; 13(2); 16(2); 20; 22(3); 25; 31; 33:1; 3; 4; 5; 14; 16; 17; 18; 19; 34:3; 4; 5(4); 13; 19; 20; 24(3); 25; 26; 35:2; 7; 10; 18(2); 21; 22; 27; 29(3); 36:2; 6(8); 24; 32; 33; 34; 35(2); 36; 37; 38; 39(3); 37:1; 2(3); 3(2); 4(2); 5; 8(3); 9; 10(3); 11(2); 12; 17; 20; 22; 23(2); 26(2); 27; 29; 30; 34(3); 35(3); 38:1; 3; 4; 5; 6; 9(3); 11(2); 12(2); 13; 16; 20(2); 28(2); 29(3); 30(3); 39:2; 3(2); 4(3); 5; 7; 8; 9; 11; 12(2); 13; 15; 16(2); 18; 19(3); 22; 40:2; 7; 9; 13(2); 20(2); 21; 41:8(2); 10; 11; 12; 14; 37; 38; 42(3); 44; 42:1; 4; 7; 8; 21; 22; 25; 27(4); 28; 35; 37; 38; 43:8; 16; 21; 29(3); 30(3); 31; 33(2); 44:1(2); 2; 4; 11(2); 13; 14; 19; 20(4); 22(3); 30; 33; 45:1; 3(3); 4; 8; 14(2); 15(2); 16; 23(2); 24; 46:1(2); 4; 6; 7(5); 8; 15(3); 18; 25; 26; 29(4); 31(2); 47:2; 3; 7; 11(2); 12(3); 20; 29; 48:1; 9; 12(2); 13(2); 14(3); 17(3); 18(2); 19(3); 49:1; 10; 11(4); 12(2); 13; 15; 16; 22; 24(2); 26; 28; 31(2); 33(4); 50:1; 2(2); 4; 7(2); 8(2); 10; 12; 13; 14(3); 18(2); 22; 24; **Ex** 1:1; 6; 9; 22; 2:4; 7; 10; 11(2); 20; 21; 22; 24; 3:1; 6; 13; 4:4(2); 6(3); 7(4); 14; 15(2); 18; 20(3); 21; 5:2; 21; 6:1; 11; 20; 7:2; 10(2); 12; 20; 23(2); 8:6; 15; 17(2); 24; 29(2); 31(2); 32; 9:20(2); 21(2); 23; 33; 34(2); 10:1(2); 13; 22; 23; 11:2; 5; 10; 12:3; 4(2); 22; 29; 30; 48; 14:4; 5; 6(2); 9(2); 17(3); 18(2); 21; 23(2); 27; 31; 15:3; 4(2); 19(2); 26(3); 16:16; 21; 29(2); 17:11(2); 12(2); 13; 18:1; 5(2); 7; 8; 15; 16; 24; 27(3); 20:7; 17(4); 20; 21:3; 4; 6(3); 7; 9; 13; 14; 15(2); 16; 17(2); 18(2); 19(2); 20(2); 21; 26(2); 27(2); 29; 30; 34; 36; 22:2; 3(2); 4; 5(3); 7; 8(2); 9(2); 10; 11(2); 14; 16; 27(3); 23:3; 4; 6; 21; 22; 24:10; 11; 13; 25:2; 27:21; 28:1; 4; 12; 29; 30; 32; 38; 41; 43(2); 29:4; 6; 7; 8; 9(2); 10; 15; 19; 20; 21(6); 24; 27; 28; 29; 30; 32; 35; 44; 30:19; 21; 30; 33; 38; 31:10; 14; 32:11; 14; 15; 19; 27(5); 29(2); 33:4; 7; 8; 10; 11(2); 34:4; 8; 15; 16(2); 20; 29; 30; 33; 35; 35:19; 34; 39:5; 27; 41; 40:12; 14; 31; **Lev** 1:3(2); 4(2); 10; 14(2); 2:1; 2; 3; 10; 3:1; 2(2); 6; 7; 8(2); 12; 13; 14; 4:3; 4; 6; 17; 22; 23(3); 24; 25; 26; 28(4); 29; 30; 32; 33; 34; 35; 5:4; 6(3); 7; 10(2); 11; 12; 13; 15; 17; 18; 6:2(2); 5; 6; 9; 10(3); 11; 15; 16; 20; 22(2); 25; 7:13(2); 15; 16(2); 18; 20; 21; 25; 27; 29(3); 30; 31; 33; 34; 35; 8:2; 6; 9; 14; 15; 18; 22; 23(2); 27; 30(6); 31(2); 36; 9:1; 9; 22; 10:1; 3; 6; 12; 11:25; 28; 40(2); 12:3; 13:2(3); 3; 4; 6; 7; 11; 12(2); 13; 34; 35; 40; 41; 42(2); 43(2); 44(2); 45(3); 46; 14:2; 8(3); 9(6); 14(2); 15; 16(3); 17(3); 19; 23; 25(2); 26; 27(2); 28(2); 47(2); 15:2(2); 3(7); 5(2); 6; 7; 8; 10; 11(2); 13(4); 15; 16; 21; 22; 27; 16:4(2); 6; 11; 12; 14(2); 17; 19; 21; 24(3); 26(2); 28(2); 32; 17:2; 4; 9; 10; 15; 16(2); 18:6; 14; 19:3(2); 8(2); 21; 22; 20:2; 3(2); 4; 5(2); 6; 9(5); 10; 11(2); 12; 17(6); 19; 20(2); 21(2); 21:1; 2(6); 3; 4; 7; 10(3); 11(2); 12(2); 14; 15(2); 17; 20; 21; 22; 24; 22:2; 5; 6; 7; 11(3); 18(4); 21; 23:29; 30; 24:9; 11; 14; 15(2); 19; 25:10(2); 13; 25(3); 27; 28; 30; 33; 41(3); 48; 49(3); 50; 51; 52(2); 54; 27:14; 15(2); 16; 17; 18; 22; 28; 31; **Num** 1:4; 44; 52(2); 2:2(2); 4; 6; 8; 11; 13; 15; 17; 19; 21; 23; 26; 28; 30; 34; 3:7; 9; 10; 38; 48; 51; 4:5; 15; 19(3); 27; 49(2); 5:7; 9; 10(2); 14(2); 15; 18; 30; 6:4; 5(3); 7(6); 8; 9(3); 11; 12(2); 13; 14; 16(2); 18(2); 19; 21(3); 23; 25; 26; 7:5; 12; 13; 19; 25; 31; 37; 43; 49; 55; 61; 67; 73; 79; 8:13; 19; 22; 9:13(2); 11:1; 10; 28; 29; 12:12; 14:24; 15:4; 30; 31(2); 16:4; 5(2); 17(3); 18; 40; 17:2; 9; 19:4; 5; 7; 8; 10; 13; 19; 21; 20:11(2); 21; 24; 25; 26(3); 28(2); 21:23(2); 24; 26(2); 29(2); 33; 34(2); 35(3); 22:5; 18; 21; 22(3); 23(2); 27; 31(4); 23:6; 7; 10; 16; 17; 18; 21; 24:1; 2; 3; 7(4); 8(2); 10; 13; 15; 18; 20; 21; 23; 25(2); 25:5; 6; 7; 13(2); 27:1; 3; 4; 8(2); 9(2); 10(2); 11(3); 21(2); 23; 30:2(2); 4; 16(2); 31:6; 32:18; 21; 42; 35:21; 23(2); 27; 28(2); 32; 36:2; 7; 8; **Deut** 1:16; 31; 36; 41; 2:24; 30(2); 31(2); 32; 33(2); 34; 3:1; 2(2); 3; 4; 11; 14; 20; 4:13; 20; 30; 36(3); 37(2); 40(2); 42; 47; 5:11; 21(5); 24(3); 6:2(2); 13; 17(2); 22; 7:7; 9; 10; 8:2; 5; 6; 11(3); 18; 9:23; 10:6(2); 8; 9(2); 12; 13; 20; 11:1(4); 2(3); 3(3); 22; 12:5(2); 8; 11; 21; 13:4(2); 17; 18; 14:23; 24; 15:2(3); 8; 17; 16:2; 6; 11; 17:2; 17; 18; 19(2); 20(5); 18:1; 5; 6; 7(2); 8; 10(2); 18; 19:4; 5(3); 6; 9; 11; 12; 18; 19; 20:5; 6; 7; 8(3); 21:16(2); 17(2); 18(2); 19(4); 20; 21; 23; 22:1; 3(2); 4; 19(2); 24; 26; 29(2); 30(2); 23:2; 3; 7; 15(2); 24:1(2); 2; 3(2); 4; 5; 7; 10(2); 12; 13; 15(2); 16; 25:2(2); 5; 6(2); 7(3); 8; 9(5); 10(2); 26:2; 17(5); 18(2); 27:10(2); 16(2); 17; 20(2); 22(3); 23; 24; 28:1; 9; 12; 15(2); 45(2); 54(3); 55; 29:2(2); 12; 19; 20(2); 23(2); 30:2; 8; 10(2); 16(4); 20; 32:4(2); 5; 9(2); 10; 15; 19(2); 36(2); 43(5); 50; 33:1; 2; 3; 6; 7(3); 9(3); 11(2); 12; 13; 16; 17(2); 20; 21; 24(2); 26; 28; 34:6; 7(2); 9; 11(2); **Josh** 2:19(3); 4:5; 14; 5:13(3); 14(2); 6:26(2); 27; 7:6(2); 18; 22; 24(6); 26; 8:1(3); 14; 18; 19; 26; 29; 9:9; 24; 10:21; 33; 11:15; 12:4; 15:17; 17:3; 6; 20:4; 5(2); 6(2); 21:12; 22:5(2); 14; 20; 29; 24:3; 4; 10; 24; 28; 30; 33; **Judg** 1:2; 3; 6; 13; 17; 25; 2:6; 9; 3:10(2); 16(2); 20(2); 21(3); 22(2); 24; 4:2; 7(2); 10; 11; 13; 15(3); 21; 22; 5:11; 15; 17; 22; 26(2); 28(2); 6:11; 13; 21(2); 27(2); 31; 32; 7:5(2); 7; 8; 11; 13; 14(2); 21; 22; 8:20(2); 21; 24; 25; 27(2); 29; 30; 31; 32; 9:1(2); 3; 5(2); 7; 16; 17; 18(2); 19; 21; 24; 26; 28; 30; 31; 41; 43; 48(2); 49; 53; 54(2); 55; 56(2); 10:16; 11:2; 3; 11; 20(2); 21; 23; 32; 34(3); 35; 39; 12:9; 13:2; 5; 6(2); 7; 11; 12; 19; 20; 21; 22; 23; 24; 14:2; 3(2); 4; 5(2); 6(3); 9(2); 10; 19(2); 20(2); 15:1; 6(2); 14(3); 15; 17; 19; 16:3; 5; 9; 12; 14; 16; 17; 18(2); 19(2); 20; 21; 22; 29(2); 30(3); 31(3); 17:2(2); 3(2); 4(2); 5(2); 6; 11; 12; 18:4; 20; 26; 30; 19:2; 3; 4; 5; 7; 9(3); 10; 11; 12; 13; 15; 16; 17; 18; 21; 25; 27(2); 28; 29(2); 20:8(2); 21:1; 24(2); 25; **Ruth** 1:1(2); 2(2); 6; 2:1; 5; 15; 20; 22; 3:4; 7(2); 8; 14; 4:5; 7; 8; 10(3); 13; 14; 17; **1 Sam** 1:1; 3; 4; 11(2); 19; 20; 21(2); 23; 2:9; 10(2); 11; 13; 19; 20; 22; 3:2(2); 9; 12; 13(2); 19; 4:10; 12(2); 13; 15; 18; 19; 5:7; 6:3; 5; 9; 7:1; 15; 17; 8:1; 2(2); 3(2); 11(3); 12(6); 14; 15; 16; 17; 22; 9:2; 3; 5; 7; 10; 14; 15; 22; 10:1(2); 9; 14; 16; 23; 25; 27; 11:6; 7; 12:3; 5; 14; 22(3); 13:2; 14(2); 16; 20(3); 22; 14:1(2); 6; 7; 12(2); 13(3); 14; 17; 20; 26(2); 27(5); 34; 45; 47(2); 49; 50; 15:1; 27; 34; 35; 16:1; 4; 5; 7(2); 10; 13; 16; 17; 20; 21; 23; 17:5; 6(2); 7(2); 13; 15; 17; 22(2); 25(2); 28; 33; 34; 38(2); 39(2); 40(4); 43; 49(5); 51(2); 54(2); 57; 18:1; 2; 3; 4(4); 7(2); 10; 11; 13(2); 14; 22(2); 26; 27(2); 30; 19:1(2); 4(3); 5(2); 7; 9(4); 13; 16; 24; 20:6; 17; 25; 27; 32; 33; 34; 36; 38; 40(2); 41; 21:7; 11(2); 13(3); 14; 22:1(2); 6(3); 7; 11; 15; 23:5; 6; 8; 11; 13; 14; 15; 16; 18; 22; 24; 25; 26(3); 24:2; 3(2); 6; 7(2); 8; 16; 19; 22; 25:1; 2; 3(2); 4; 10; 13(4); 17; 20; 24; 25(2); 36; 37(2); 39(3); 40; 42; 43; 44; 26:5; 7(2); 9; 10; 11; 16; 18; 19; 23(2); 25(2); 27:1(2); 3(3); 8; 11; 12; 28:3; 5; 7(2); 14(2); 18; 23; 25; 29:2; 4; 5(2); 11; 30:1; 3; 6(3); 12; 18; 24(2); 26; 31; 31:2; 4(2); 5(2); 6(3); 7; 8; 9(2); 10(2); 12; **2 Sam** 1:2(2); 4; 5; 6; 10(2); 11; 12; 17; 2:2; 3; 16(3); 21; 23; 29; 32(2); 3:2; 3; 6; 8(2); 12; 27; 29; 30; 32; 38; 39; 4:4(3); 5; 6; 7(3); 8; 9; 10; 11(3); 12; 5:6; 12(2); 21; 6:6; 7; 11; 14; 19; 20(2); 21; 7:1(2); 12; 13; 14; 25; 27; 8:3; 10; 15; 9:3; 6; 9; 11; 13; 10:1(2); 2(3); 3; 10; 12; 11:1; 2; 9(2); 10; 13(3); 27(2); 12:3(4); 4(2); 9(2); 15; 17; 19(2); 20(2); 21; 24(2); 25; 30; 13:2; 8; 17; 18; 22(2); 24; 28; 29; 31(2); 32; 33; 34; 36; 37; 14:7(2); 9; 13; 14; 15; 16; 22(2); 24(2); 25(3); 26(2); 30; 33; 15:5; 12; 14; 16; 18; 22; 25; 30; 32(2); 16:6(2); 9; 11; 12; 13; 18; 19; 22; 17:8; 18; 23(5); 18:9; 14; 17; 18(2); 19; 24; 25; 28; 19:2; 4; 8; 11(2); 17(2); 24(3); 30; 39; 41; 20:1; 3(2); 8; 9; 10(2); 12; 21(2); 22; 21:1; 2; 4; 6; 12; 13; 14(2); 15; 17; 22; 22:1; 7(2); 9(2); 10; 14; 16; 23(2); 25; 31; 51(3); 23:2; 10(2); 18; 21(2); 23; 24:14; 16; 20(2); 21; **1 Ki** 1:2; 6(2); 9; 10; 21; 23; 37; 47; 49; 51; 2:1; 3(5); 4; 5(4); 6; 9; 10; 12(2); 15; 19(2); 22; 23; 32(2); 33(4); 34; 35; 40(3); 3:1; 3; 6; 15; 27; 4:2; 7; 21; 25(2); 26; 27; 28; 31; 32; 34; 5:1(2); 3(3); 10; 11; 7:1(2); 14(2); 51; 8:15(2); 20; 22; 28; 31; 32(3); 38(2); 39; 54(2); 56(3); 58(4); 59(2); 61(2); 66(2); 9:15; 16; 19(3); 22(5); 27; 10:5(5); 24(2); 25; 11:3(2); 4(5); 6; 8; 9; 17; 19; 20; 21; 23; 27; 33; 34(2); 35; 36; 41; 43(4); 12:4; 6; 15; 18; 24; 26; 33; 13:4(2); 11; 12; 13; 19; 24; 27; 28; 30; 31(2); 33; 14:2; 4(2); 8; 18; 20(3); 21(2); 31(5); 15:2; 3(4); 4(2); 5; 6; 8(3); 10; 11; 12; 13; 14; 15; 18; 20; 23(3); 24(5); 26(2); 28; 29; 30; 34; 16:3; 5; 6(3); 7(2); 9(3); 10; 11(3); 13; 19; 26; 28(3); 34(3); 17:17; 19; 23; 18:3; 7(2); 42(2); 43; 46; 19:3(2); 6; 13(2); 19; 21; 20:1; 11; 12; 20; 24; 31; 35; 38; 39; 41; 42(2); 43; 21:4(3); 5; 7; 8; 11(2); 25; 27(2); 29(3); 22:3; 10; 17; 19(3); 22; 31; 34(2); 35; 36(2); 38; 40(3); 42; 43; 46; 50(5); 52(2); 53; **2 Ki** 1:2; 8; 9; 10; 11; 12; 13(2); 16; 17; 2:8; 12; 3:2(2); 27(2); 4:1; 12; 18; 19(2); 20; 25; 32; 34(6); 35; 37; 38; 42; 43; 5:1; 3; 4; 6; 7(2); 8; 9; 11(2); 13; 14; 15; 20; 23; 25; 26; 27; 6:7; 8; 11; 12; 15; 17; 24; 30(2); 32(2); 7:12; 13; 8:11; 14; 15(2); 18; 19(2); 20; 21; 24(4); 26; 9:2; 3; 6; 11(2); 13; 21(2); 24(4); 25(2); 26; 28(3); 36; 10:3; 10; 11(3); 15; 16; 19(2); 24; 31; 34; 35(3); 11:2; 8(2); 9; 11(2); 12:1; 4; 5; 17; 18(2); 20; 21(4); 13:8; 9(3); 12; 13(2); 14; 16(2); 21; 23(2); 24(2); 25; 14:2; 3(2); 5(3); 6; 12; 15; 16(3); 20; 21; 22; 25; 28; 29(3); 15:2; 3; 5; 7(4); 9; 10; 14; 18; 19(2); 22(3); 25(2); 30; 33; 34; 38(5); 16:2(2); 3; 13(4);

15; 20(4); 17:3; 13; 15(3); 18; 20; 23(2); 18:2; 3; 6; 12; 21; 29; 31(3); 19:1; 4; 7(2); 19; 37(4); 20:2; 13(5); 20; 21(3); 21:1; 3; 6; 7; 10; 11; 12; 16; 18(4); 19; 20; 21(2); 22; 23; 24(2); 26(3); 22:1; 2; 11; 23:3(5); 10(2); 18(2); 25(3); 26(2); 29; 30(4); 31; 32; 34(2); 35; 36; 37; 24:1(2); 2; 3; 6(3); 7; 8; 9; 11; 12(5); 15; 17(2); 18; 20; 25:1(2); 5; 7; 29(2); 30(2); **1 Chr** 1:13; 19(2); 43; 44; 45; 46(2); 47; 48; 49; 50(3); 2:4; 13; 18; 19; 35(2); 42; 3:3; 10(3); 11(3); 12(3); 13(3); 14(2); 16(2); 17; 4:9(3); 18; 23; 25(3); 26(3); 27; 5:1(2); 2; 4(3); 5(3); 6; 7; 6:20(3); 21(4); 22(3); 23(3); 24(4); 26(2); 27(3); 29(3); 30(3); 39(2); 49; 50(3); 51(3); 52(3); 53(2); 7:14; 15; 16(3); 18; 20(4); 21(2); 22; 23(3); 24; 25(3); 26(3); 27(2); 35; 8:1; 8; 9; 10; 30; 37(3); 39(2); 9:5; 19(2); 36; 43(3); 10:2; 4(2); 5(2); 6(2); 7; 8; 9(2); 10(2); 12; 13; 11:10; 11; 20; 23; 25; 45; 12:19; 28; 13:6; 9; 10; 14; 14:2(2); 4; 15:5; 6; 7; 8; 9; 10; 17; 16:7; 8(2); 9; 10; 11(2); 12(3); 13(2); 14; 15; 16; 23; 24(2); 27; 29; 34; 37; 38; 39; 41; 43(2); 17:1; 11; 12; 13; 14; 23; 25; 18:3; 10; 14; 19:1(2); 2(2); 3; 7; 11; 13; 15; 19; 20:2; 8; 21:3; 13; 16(2); 20; 21; 23; 27; 22:5; 6; 9(3); 10(2); 17; 18; 23:1; 13(2); 25; 25:5; 9; 10(2); 11(2); 12(2); 13(2); 14(2); 15(2); 16(2); 17(2); 18(2); 19(2); 20(2); 21(2); 22(2); 23(2); 24(2); 25(2); 26(2); 27(2); 28(2); 29(2); 30(2); 31(2); 26:6; 10; 14(2); 15; 22; 25(6); 26; 28; 29; 30; 31; 32; 27:2; 4(2); 5; 6(2); 7(2); 8; 9; 10; 11; 12; 13; 14; 15; 28:1; 2; 6; 7; 11; 19; 20; 29:23; 28(2); 30(2); **2 Chr** 1:1(2); 8; 2:11; 14; 15; 17; 3:1; 2; 4:16; 5:1; 13; 6:4(2); 10; 12; 13(2); 19; 22; 23(3); 29(3); 30; 7:3; 6; 10; 11(2); 8:1; 6; 9(4); 14; 18; 9:4(5); 8; 23(2); 24; 31(4); 10:4; 6; 15; 18; 11:4; 12; 14; 21(2); 22; 23; 12:8; 13(2); 14; 16(3); 13:2; 5; 6; 12; 17; 22(2); 14:1(4); 2; 11; 13; 15:9; 17; 18; 16:4; 5; 12(4); 13(2); 14; 17:1(2); 2; 3; 4(2); 5; 6; 7(2); 18:8; 9; 16; 18(3); 21; 33(2); 34; 19:1; 20:18(2); 20; 21; 25; 30; 31; 32; 21:1(4); 4(2); 7; 8; 9(2); 10(2); 17(3); 18; 19(4); 22:1(2); 2; 3; 4(3); 7; 9; 11; 23:7(2); 8; 10(2); 11; 13; 24:1; 4; 16; 22(2); 25(2); 27(3); 25:1; 3(2); 4; 11; 14; 22; 28; 26:1; 2; 3; 4; 8; 15; 16(3); 19(2); 20; 21(2); 23(4); 27:1; 2; 6(2); 7(2); 9(3); 28:1; 3; 5; 22; 25; 26(2); 27(3); 29:1; 2; 3; 10; 19(2); 25; 30:2; 6; 8(2); 9; 19(2); 27; 31:1; 2; 3; 8; 10; 12; 13; 15; 16(3); 20; 21(2); 32:2; 3; 9; 12(2); 14; 15; 16(2); 17; 21(3); 25; 26; 30; 31; 32; 33(4); 33:3; 6; 7; 10; 12(2); 13(3); 18(2); 19(3); 20(4); 22(2); 23; 24(2); 25(2); 34:2; 3(2); 4; 8(2); 19; 27; 31(6); 33; 35:3; 4; 8; 9; 22; 23; 24(2); 26; 27; 36:1; 4(2); 5; 7; 8(2); 12; 13(2); 15(3); 16(3); 17; 18; 20; 22; 23(2); **Ezra** 1:1; 3(2); 4; 7; 2:1; 3:2(2); 9(2); 11; 4:6; 5:6; 17; 6:10; 11(2); 12; 7:6(2); 9(2); 10; 11; 14; 15; 23; 28; 8:17; 18; 19; 22(2); 25(2); 9:8; 10:8; 11; 18; **Neh** 2:1; 20; 3:1; 10; 12; 17; 23; 28; 29; 30; 4:2; 15; 18(2); 22; 5:7; 13(2); 6:5(2); 11; 18; 19; 7:3(2); 6; 8:4(2); 16; 9:8(2); 10(2); 10:29(2); 11:3; 13; 17; 20; 12:8; 36; 45; 13:10; 26; 30; **Esth** 1:2; 3(2); 4(2); 8; 12(2); 20; 22(2); 2:3; 7(2); 9; 15; 16(2); 17; 18; 3:[illegible](2); 4:1; 4; 17; 5:1; 2(2); 10(2); 11(2); 14(2); 6:6; 12(2); 13(4); 7:5; 7(2); 8:2; 3; 5(2); 7; 9:1; 4; 25(2); 10:2(2); 3(3); **Job** 1:3; 4(2); 10(3); 12; 13; 20(2); 2:3; 4; 5(2); 6; 7(2); 9; 10; 11; 12(2); 13; 3:1(2); 19; 4:9; 17; 18(2); 5:3; 4; 5; 18; 6:9; 14; 7:1; 2; 10(2); 8:15; 16(2); 17; 18; 19; 9:5; 13; 33; 34; 11:5; 12:4; 6; 16; 13:11; 14:5(3); 6; 10; 20; 21; 22(2); 15:15(2); 20; 21; 23; 25; 26; 27(3); 29(2); 30(2); 31; 32(2); 33(2); 16:9(3); 12; 13; 21; 17:5(2); 9; 18:5; 6(2); 7(2); 8; 11; 12(2); 13(2); 14; 15(3); 16(2); 19(2); 20; 19:6; 11(2); 12; 20:6(2); 7; 9; 10(3); 11(2); 12(2); 13; 14(2); 15; 20; 21; 22; 23(2); 25; 26(2); 27; 28(3); 21:17; 19; 20(2); 21(2); 23; 24(2); 25; 31(2); 22:22(2); 23:3; 6; 11(2); 12(2); 13; 15; 24:1; 15; 22; 23; 25:2; 3(2); 5; 26:8; 9(2); 11; 12(2); 13(2); 14(2); 27:1; 8; 9; 14(2); 18; 19; 21; 23; 28:9; 10; 29:1; 3(2); 17; 30:24; 31:20; 23; 30; 31; 32:1; 2; 3(2); 5; 12; 14; 33:10; 13; 17; 18(2); 19(2); 20(2); 21(2); 22(2); 23; 25(2); 26(2); 28(2); 30; 34:11(2); 14(3); 19; 21(2); 27; 29; 35; 36; 37(3); 35:15; 16; 36:7; 22; 23; 24; 26; 29; 30; 32; 33; 37:2(2); 3; 4(2); 5; 6; 7; 11; 12; 13; 15; 39:6; 8; 11; 19; 20; 21; 40:9; 16(4); 17(2); 18(2); 19; 23; 24(2); 41:1; 2(2); 7(2); 12(3); 13; 14(2); 15(2); 18(2); 19; 20; 21(2); 22; 23; 24; 25; 30; 42:10; 11(4); 12; 16; **Ps** 1:2(2); 2:2; 5(2); 12; 3:4; 7:12(2); 13; 16(4); 17; 8:6; 9:7; 11; 16; 10:2; 3; 4(2); 5(3); 6; 7(2); 8; 9(2); 10; 11(2); 13; 15; 16; 11:4(3); 5; 7; 12:2; 14:1; 6; 7; 15:2; 3(3); 4; 5; 17:12; 18:6(2); 8(2); 9; 11(2); 12; 13; 14; 22(2); 24; 30; 50(3); 19:1; 5; 12; 20:6(3); 21:2(2); 3; 5; 9; 22:24; 31; 23:3; 24:3; 4; 5; 25:9; 10(2); 13; 14; 27:4; 5(2); 6; 28:5; 8; 29:2; 9; 11(2); 30:4(2); 5(2); 31:21; 23; 33:4; 6; 11; 12; 14; 18; 21; 34:1; 3; 6; 9; 15; 20; 22; 35:8; 9; 14; 27; 36:1; 2(2); 3; 4; 37:3; 7; 10; 12; 13; 23; 24; 25; 26; 28; 30; 31(3); 33; 34; 38:13; 39:5; 11; 40:4; 41:2; 3(2); 5; 6; 9; 42:5; 8(2); 46:6; 47:8; 48:1; 49:7; 16; 17; 19; 50:4; 6; 23; 52:7(3); 53:1; 6; 55:20(2); 21(3); 56:4; 10(2); 57:3(2); 58:7(2); 9; 10; 59:9; 60:6; 61:6; 62:4; 12; 64:9; 65:6; 66:2(2); 5; 7(2); 8; 20; 67:1; 68:1; 4(2); 5; 21(2); 33; 34(2); 35; 69:33; 36(2); 72:7; 9; 14; 17(2); 19(2); 73:10; 76:1; 2(2); 77:8(2); 9; 78:4(2); 7; 10; 11(2); 20; 22; 26; 32; 37; 38(2); 42; 43(2); 49; 50; 52; 54(2); 56; 61(2); 62(2); 66; 69; 70; 71(2); 72(2); 79:7; 81:6(2); 85:8(2); 9; 13; 87:1; 89:23(2); 24; 25(2); 29(2); 30; 36(2); 39; 40(2); 41; 42(2); 43; 44(2); 45; 48; 91:4(3); 11; 14; 94:14(2); 95:2; 4(2); 5(2); 7(3); 96:2(2); 3(2); 6; 8(2); 13; 97:2; 3; 4; 6(2); 10; 12; 98:1(2); 2(2); 3(2); 99:5; 6(2); 7; 9; 100:2; 3(2); 4(3); 5(2); 101:5; 102:16; 19; 21; 103:1; 2; 7(2); 9; 11; 13; 15; 17; 18(2); 19(2); 20(3); 21(3); 22(2); 104:3(2); 4(2); 13; 15; 23(2); 31; 105:1(2); 2; 3; 4(2); 5(3); 6(2); 7; 8; 9; 18; 19; 21(2); 22(3); 24; 25(2); 26; 27; 28; 37; 42(2); 43(2); 45(2); 106:1; 2; 8(2); 12(2); 13(2); 23(2); 24; 26; 33(2); 40(2); 45(2); 107:1; 8(2); 15(2); 20; 21(2); 22; 24; 31(2); 108:7; 109:6; 7; 8(2); 9(2); 10; 11; 12; 13; 14(2); 18(3); 110:5; 111:3(2); 4; 5; 6(2); 7(2); 9(3); 10(2); 112:1; 2; 3(2); 5; 7; 8(3); 9(2); 10; 113:4; 8; 114:2(2); 116:2; 12; 14; 15; 18; 117:2; 118:1; 2; 3; 4; 29; 119:2; 3; 9; 125:2; 126:6; 127:2; 5; 128:1; 129:7(2); 130:5; 8; 131:2; 132:1; 7(2); 13; 18(2); 133:2; 135:3; 4; 7; 9; 12; 14(2); 136:1; 2; 3; 4; 5; 6; 7; 8; 9; 10; 11; 12; 13; 14; 15(2); 16(2); 17; 18; 19; 20; 21; 22(2); 23; 24; 25; 26; 140:8; 144:4; 10; 145:3; 9(2); 12(2); 17(2); 21; 146:4(3); 5(2); 147:5; 11; 15(2); 17(2); 18(2); 19(3); 20; 148:2(2); 8; 13(2); 14(2); 149:1; 3; 4; 9; 150:1(2); 2(2); **Prov** 2:6; 8; 3:11; 20; 31; 32; 5:21; 22(2); 23; 6:13(3); 14; 15; 26; 27(2); 28; 29; 31; 32; 33; 7:23(2); 8:22(2); 29; 30; 31; 36; 10:1; 9; 15; 19; 11:1; 5(2); 7; 9(2); 12(2); 17(2); 19; 20; 28; 29; 12:4; 8; 10; 11; 13; 14; 15; 22; 26; 13:1; 2; 3(3); 8; 16; 22; 24(2); 25; 14:2(2); 8; 14; 15; 20; 21; 26; 31; 32(2); 35; 15:5; 8; 20; 23; 27; 32; 16:2; 7; 9(2); 10; 11; 15; 17(2); 23(2); 26; 27; 29; 30(2); 32; 17:5; 12; 13; 18; 19; 21; 25; 27; 28(2); 18:1; 2; 6; 7(3); 9; 11(2); 17(2); 20(2); 19:1(2); 2; 3(2); 4; 7; 8; 11; 12; 13; 16(2); 18; 24(2); 26(2); 20:2; 6; 7(2); 8; 11; 14; 17; 19; 20(3); 24; 25; 27; 28; 21:2; 8; 10(2); 13; 23(2); 24; 25; 29(2); 22:5; 8; 9; 11(2); 16; 25; 29; 23:3; 6; 7(2); 14; 24:7; 12; 15; 18; 29; 25:5; 13; 18; 22; 28; 26:4; 5(2); 6; 10(2); 11(2); 12; 14; 15(2); 16; 17; 19; 24; 25; 26(2); 27:8; 14; 16; 17; 18; 22; 28:6(2); 7; 8; 9(2); 10; 11; 13; 14; 16; 18; 19; 24(2); 26; 27; 29:1; 3(2); 5(2); 10; 11; 12; 14; 15; 20; 21; 24; 30:1; 4(3); 6; 10; 17(2); 31:1; 7(2); **Eccl** 1:3; 2:14; 21; 22(2); 23(3); 24(2); 26; 3:13; 22(2); 4:4; 5(2); 8(2); 10; 14; 15; 5:3; 13; 14; 15(3); 17; 18(3); 19(2); 20(2); 6:3(2); 7; 12; 7:15(2); 8:1(2); 3; 5; 9; 12; 13; 15(2); 9:12; 15; 16; 10:2(2); 13(2); 12:5; 13; **Song** 1:2; 4; 12; 2:3(2); 4; 6(2); 16(2); 3:8(2); 11(3); 4:16; 5:1; 4; 11(2); 12; 13(2); 14(2); 15(2); 16; 6:2(2); 3; 12; 7:10; 8:3(2); 7; 10; **Isa** 2:3(2); 10; 19; 20(2); 21; 22; 3:5; 6(2); 8; 11; 14(2); 5:1; 7; 12; 19; 25(4); 6:1; 2(2); 3; 6; 7:2(2); 14; 8:3; 7(3); 8; 17; 9:4(3); 6(2); 7(2); 11; 12(2); 17(2); 19; 20; 21(2); 10:4(2); 7(2); 12(2); 14(2); 16(2); 17(3); 18(2); 19; 24; 26; 27(2); 28; 32; 11:1; 3(3); 4(2); 5(2); 8; 10; 11(2); 15(2); 16; 12:4(3); 13:5; 13; 14(2); 14:17; 18; 21; 25(2); 27; 31; 32; 15:4; 5; 16:6(4); 12; 17:4; 5; 7(2); 8(2); 9; 19:1; 2(2); 14; 22:21; 22; 23; 24; 23:11; 24:2; 23; 25:4; 8; 9; 11; 26:21; 27:1; 8; 9; 28:2; 4; 5; 21(4); 24; 26; 28(2); 29:8(2); 22; 23(2); 30:4(2); 26; 27(4); 28; 30(3); 31:2; 3; 4; 7(2); 8; 9(2); 32:6; 33:6; 15(3); 16(2); 17; 34:2; 16; 17; 36:6; 16(3); 37:1; 4; 7(2); 20; 38(4); 38:2; 9; 39:2(5); 40:10(3); 11(3); 12; 13; 26(2); 28; 41:2(3); 3; 6(2); 42:2(2); 4; 10; 12; 13(2); 21; 24(2); 25; 44:5; 6; 11; 12(2); 13; 17; 19; 20; 26(2); 45:1; 9; 10; 11; 13; 46:7; 47:4; 15; 48:2; 14(2); 15; 16; 19; 20; 49:2(2); 5; 13(2); 50:10(2); 51:14; 15; 17; 22; 52:9; 10; 14(2); 53:5; 6; 7(2); 8; 9(3); 10(4); 11(2); 12; 54:5; 16; 55:7(2); 56:2; 3; 6; 10; 11(2); 57:2; 13; 17(2); 18(2); 58:5(2); 59:1; 2; 16(2); 17; 18(2); 19; 60:2; 62:8(2); 11(2); 63:1(2); 7(2); 9(3); 10; 11(3); 12; 65:15; 20; 66:5; 6; 13; 14(3); 15(3); 16; **Jer** 1:2; 9; 15; 2:3; 15(2); 35; 3:1; 4:7(3); 13(2); 26; 5:8; 6:3; 21; 7:5; 29; 8:6(2); 16(2); 9:4; 5; 8(3); 20; 23(3); 10:10(2); 12(3); 13(2); 14; 16(2); 23; 25; 11:8; 19; 12:15(2); 13:23; 14:8; 16:12; 17:5; 10(2); 11(2); 18:11; 12; 16; 18; 19:3; 9; 20:9(2); 21:2; 7; 9; 22:7; 8; 10; 11; 13(4); 18; 28; 30(2); 23:6(2); 9; 14; 17; 18(2); 20; 27; 30; 34; 35(2); 36; 24:8; 25:4; 5(2); 19(3); 30(3); 31; 38(2); 26:3; 21(2); 23; 27:7(3); 8; 12; 28:11; 29:32; 30:6(2); 8; 18; 21; 24; 31:10; 30(2); 34(2); 35; 32:19(2); 33:2; 11; 21; 26; 34:1(2); 3(2); 9; 10; 14; 15; 16; 17(2); 21; 35:3(2); 14; 15; 18; 36:3; 7; 14; 17; 18; 24; 30; 31(2); 37:2; 10; 12; 17; 38:2; 39:1; 6; 40:3; 42:11; 43:10(2); 12; 44:21; 23(3); 30(4); 46:10; 26; 47:3(3); 48:7(2); 10; 11(4); 12; 16; 17; 25; 26; 29(2); 30(2); 35; 40; 49:1; 2; 3(2); 10(4); 20; 22; 50:16(2); 17; 18; 19(2); 25(2); 28; 32; 34; 43; 45; 51:3(2); 5; 6; 9; 11(2); 15(3); 16(2); 17; 19(2); 23(2); 28; 31; 34; 44; 59; 52:1; 3; 4(2); 8; 10; 11; 31; 33(2); 34(3); **Lam** 1:10; 12; 14; 17; 18; 2:1(3); 2; 3; 4(4); 6(3); 7(2); 8; 17; 3:1; 3; 12; 13; 22; 27; 29; 30; 32; 36; 39; 4:11(2); 20; **Ezek** 1:27(2); 3:12; 18(4); 19(3); 20(4); 7:16; 20; 8:2(2); 11; 12; 9:1; 2(3); 3; 11; 10:7; 12:12(4); 14; 13:22(2); 14:4(3); 7(2); 17:14; 15; 17; 18; 19; 21(2); 18:6(2); 7(2); 8; 11; 12; 13; 14; 15(2); 16; 17(2); 18(4); 21; 23; 24; 26; 30; 19:7; 9; 20:7; 39; 21:22; 22:6; 11(4); 24:2; 26:9(2); 10; 11; 29:3; 18(2); 19; 20; 30:11; 22(2); 24; 31:2; 18; 32:10; 31(2); 32; 33:4(2); 5(2); 6(2); 8(3); 9(3); 11; 12(3); 13(2); 14; 16; 18; 19; 20; 30; 34:12(2); 36:20; 37:16(2); 19; 38:21; 22; 39:11; 40:3; 43:2(2); 44:27; 45:8; 46:2(2); 12(2); 16(3); 17(5); 18(3); 47:3; 23; **Dan** 1:2(3); 3; 8; 20; 2:1(2); 2; 7; 13; 17(2); 18; 20; 46; 3:19; 20; 24; 28(2); 4:3(4); 8; 16; 19; 33(3); 34(2); 35(2); 37; 5:1; 2(4); 3(3); 6(3); 7; 9(2); 10; 20(4); 21(3); 22; 23(2); 29; 6:5; 10(5); 11; 13; 14; 17(2); 18(2); 22; 23; 26(2); 7:1(2); 9(3); 14(2); 20; 25; 26; 27; 8:3(2); 5; 7(2); 11; 24(2); 25(3); 9:2; 4(2); 10(2); 12; 14; 17; 10:6(5); 9(2); 11:2(2); 3; 4(4); 5(2); 6; 7; 9; 10(2); 11; 12; 15; 16(2); 17(2); 18; 19(2); 20; 21; 24(3); 25(2); 26(2); 28(3); 36; 37; 38; 41; 42; 43; 45(2); 12:7(2); **Hos** 1:4; 9; 3:5; 5:5; 13(2); 6:2; 3; 7:5; 9; 10; 8:14(3); 9:8(2); 13; 10:1(4); 6; 11; 11:5; 6(2); 10; 12:2(2); 3(2); 5; 7; 14(3); 13:12; 15(3); 14:5; 6(3); 7; **Joel** 1:6; 2:8; 11(3); 16; 18(2); 19; 20(4); 3:16(2); **Am** 1:2; 11(3); 15; 2:4; 7; 9(2); 14; 3:4; 7(2); 4:2; 13(2); 5:8; 19; 6:8; 7:7; 10; 17; 9:6(3); **Ob** 6; 11(2); 12; **Jon** 1:5; 2:1; 3:6(2); 7; 8(2); 9; 4:6(2); **Mic** 1:2; 3; 2:2(2); 7; 3:4; 8(2); 4:2(2); 4(2); 5; 12; 5:3; 4(2); 6:2; 7:2; 3; 6; 9; 18(2); **Nah** 1:2(2); 3(2); 5; 6(3); 8; 13; 2:3(2); 5; 12(4); **Hab** 1:11(2); 2:4(2); 5; 6; 9(2); 15(2); 20; 3:3(2); 4(3); 5; 6; 14(2); 16; **Zeph** 1:7; 18; 2:3; 11; 13; 15; 3:2; 5; 17; **Hag** 1:9; 2:12; 22; **Zech** 1:21; 2:1; 8; 12; 13; 3:1; 5(2); 10(3); 4:1; 9; 5:4; 6:12; 13(2); 7:2; 9; 10(2); 12; 8:4(2); 10; 16; 9:7(2); 10; 14; 16(2); 10:3(2); 12; 11:6(2); 17(4); 12:10; 13:3(2); 4; 14:4; 9; 13(3); **Mal** 1:3(2); 6(2); 14; 2:6(2); 7; 15; 3:1; 2; 14; 16; 17; 4:2; **Mt** 1:2; 11; 18; 21(2); 23; 24; 25; 2:2; 11; 13; 14; 20; 21; 22; 3:3; 4(2); 7; 12(4); 4:6; 18; 21; 24; 5:1; 2; 22(2); 28; 31; 32; 35; 45; 6:27; 29; 33; 7:9; 24; 26; 28; 8:3(2); 13; 14; 20; 21; 23; 25; 9:1; 7; 10; 11; 19; 20; 21; 37; 38; 10:1; 2(2); 10; 21; 24(2); 25(3); 35; 36; 38; 39(2); 42; 11:1; 2; 20; 12:1; 19; 21; 26; 29(2); 35; 46; 49(2); 13:19; 24; 25(2); 31; 36; 41(2); 52; 54; 55(2); 56; 57(2); 14:2; 3; 11; 12; 15; 22; 31; 36; 15:5; 6; 12; 23; 32; 33; 36; 16:5; 13; 20; 21; 24(2); 25(2); 26(2); 27(3); 28; 17:1; 2(2); 10; 18:6; 15; 23; 25(2); 28; 29(2); 31; 32; 34; 35(3); 19:3; 5(2); 9; 10(2); 13; 15; 23; 25; 28; 20:1; 2; 8; 28; 21:31; 34; 35; 37; 38; 41; 45; 22:2; 3; 5(2); 6; 7; 8; 15; 24(3); 25(2); 33; 45; 23:1; 24:1; 17; 18; 31(2); 43; 45(2); 46; 47; 48(2); 49; 51; 25:14(2); 15; 18; 21; 23; 26; 31(2); 32; 33; 34; 41; 26:1; 7; 8; 23; 39; 45; 48; 51(3); 65(2); 67; 27:3; 19; 24; 25; 29(2); 31; 32; 35; 37; 50; 53; 60; 64; 28:3(2); 7; 8; 9; 13; **Mk** 1:3; 6; 16; 19; 22; 28; 41; 2:8; 15; 16; 23; 3:5; 7; 9; 21(2); 27(2); 31(2); 4:2; 34; 5:3; 15; 22; 27; 28; 31; 6:1(2); 2; 3; 4(3); 5; 14; 17; 21(2); 27; 28; 29(2); 35; 41; 45; 56; 7:2; 11; 12(2); 17; 19(2); 25; 32(2); 33(3); 35(2); 8:1; 4; 6; 10; 12; 23(2); 25(2); 26; 27(2); 33; 34(2); 35(2); 36; 37; 38; 9:3; 18; 21; 28; 31; 36; 41; 42; 10:2; 7(2); 10; 11; 16(2); 23; 24; 45; 46; 50; 52; 11:1; 14; 18; 23; 12:6; 13; 19(4); 37; 38; 43; 13:1; 12; 15; 16; 27(2); 34(3); 14:3; 12; 13; 16; 32; 44; 47(2); 51; 63; 15:7; 17; 20; 21; 24; 26; 27(2); 37; 39; 16:7; **Lk** 1:5; 8; 9; 13; 14; 15; 23(2); 24; 29; 31; 32; 33; 48; 49; 50; 51; 54(2); 55; 59; 60; 62; 63; 64(2); 67; 68; 69; 70; 72; 76; 77; 80; 2:3; 5; 21; 28; 33; 34; 41; 43; 47; 48; 51; 3:1; 4; 17(4); 19; 23; 4:10; 16; 22; 24; 30; 32(2); 40; 5:12; 13; 19; 25; 29; 30; 6:1; 10; 13; 14; 17; 20(2); 40(2); 45(3); 7:1; 3; 11; 12; 15; 16; 19; 38(3); 8:5; 9; 19; 22; 35; 39; 41; 44; 9:1; 14; 18; 23; 24(2); 26(2); 29(2); 31; 32; 42; 43; 51; 52; 53; 54; 58; 62; 10:1; 2; 7; 23; 30; 34(2); 39; 11:1(2); 6; 8(2); 18; 21(2); 22(2); 12:1; 22; 25; 27; 39; 42(2); 43; 45(2); 46; 47(2); 13:6; 7; 13; 15; 17; 19; 14:17; 21(2); 26(2); 27; 15:5; 6; 12(2); 13; 15; 16; 20(3); 22(3); 25; 28; 29; 16:1(2); 5; 18; 20; 21; 23(2); 24; 17:2; 16(2); 24; 31; 33(2); 18:7; 13(2); 14; 43; 19:13; 14; 29; 20:20; 26(2); 28(3); 44; 45; 22:4; 36; 39; 44; 45; 50; 51; 71; 23:11; 34; 46; 49; 55; 24:8; 23; 26; 40(2); 47; 50; **Jn** 1:11(2); 12; 14; 16; 35; 41; 2:2; 5; 11(2); 12(3); 17; 21; 22; 23; 3:4; 16; 17; 20; 21; 22; 32; 33; 35; 4:2; 5; 6; 8; 12(2); 27; 31; 34; 41; 44; 47; 50; 51; 53; 5:9; 18; 28; 35; 37(2); 38; 43; 47; 6:2; 3; 5; 8; 12; 16; 22(3); 24; 27; 52; 53; 60; 61; 66; 7:3; 5; 10; 16; 17; 18; 30; 38; 53; 8:6; 20; 44; 55; 9:2(2); 3; 14; 15; 18(2); 20; 21; 22; 23; 27; 28; 31; 10:3(2); 4(2); 11; 11:2; 12; 13; 16; 32; 41; 44; 51; 54; 12:3; 4; 16; 17; 25(2); 41; 50; 13:1(2); 3; 4; 10; 12; 16; 18; 23; 15:10; 13; 15; 20; 16:13; 17; 29; 32; 17:1; 18:1(2); 2; 10; 19(2); 22; 25; 19:2; 17; 23; 25(2); 26(2); 27; 29; 30(2); 33; 34; 35; 36; 20:7; 20(2); 25(2); 26; 30; 31; 21:2; 7; 14; 20; 24; **Acts** 1:3; 7; 14; 18; 20(2); 22; 25; 2:6; 14; 29; 30(2); 31(2); 41; 3:2; 4; 5; 7; 13; 16(2); 18; 21; 26; 4:26; 32; 5:1; 2; 5; 7; 10; 31; 32; 41; 6:15; 7:4; 5(2); 6; 10(2); 13; 14(2); 20; 23(2); 25(2); 27; 8:1; 2; 11; 28; 32; 33(4); 35; 39; 9:8; 12(2); 17(2); 18(2); 41; 10:2; 7; 22; 24; 25; 34; 43; 11:13; 29; 12:1; 7(2); 11; 15; 17; 21; 13:8; 13; 16; 24; 25; 31; 36(2); 14:3; 8(2); 15:14; 18; 16:1; 3; 27; 32; 33; 34(2); 17:2; 16; 28; 18:2; 6; 8; 14; 18; 19:12; 31; 33(2); 38; 20:7; 10; 28; 32; 38; 21:11; 19; 40; 22:14(2); 15; 20; 30; 23:30; 24:2; 8; 23; 24; 26:1; 24; 26; 27:3; 28:3; 4; 8; 23; 30; **Rom** 1:2; 3; 5; 9; 20(2); 2:4; 6; 18; 26; 3:7; 20; 24; 25(3); 26; 4:5; 13; 19; 23; 5:8; 9; 10(2); 6:3; 5(2); 8:3; 9; 11; 28; 29; 32; 9:19; 22(2); 23; 11:1; 2; 22; 33(2); 34; 12:20; 14:4; 5; 15:2(2); 9; 10; 16:13; 15; **1 Cor** 1:9; 29; 2:10; 3:8(2); 5:1; 5; 6:5; 14; 18; 7:2; 3; 4; 7; 11; 25; 33; 36; 37(4); 9:7; 10; 10:24; 11:4(2); 7; 21; 14:25(2); 15:10; 23(2); 25; 27; 16:11; **2 Cor** 2:11; 14; 3:7; 13; 7:7; 13; 15; 8:9; 17; 9:7; 9; 15; 10:10(3); 11:3; 15; 33; **Gal** 1:15; 16; 2:11; 3:16; 4:4; 6; 5:10; 6:4; 5; 8; **Eph** 1:5; 6; 7(2); 9(2); 11; 12; 14; 18(2); 19(2); 20; 22; 23; 2:4; 7(2); 10; 15; 3:5; 6; 7; 16(2); 4:25; 28; 5:28; 29; 30(3); 31(2); 33; 6:10; **Phil** 1:29; 2:4; 13; 22(2); 30; 3:10(3); 21; 4:19; **Col** 1:9; 11; 13; 14; 20; 22(2); 24; 26; 29; 2:18; 3:9; 4:15; **1 Th** 1:10; 2:11; 12; 19; 3:13; 4:4; 6; 8; **2 Th** 1:7; 9; 10; 11; 2:6; 8(2); **1 Tim** 3:4(2); 5; 5:8(2); 18; 6:1; 15; **2 Tim** 1:8; 9; 2:19; 26; 4:1(2); 8; 14; 18; **Titus** 1:3; 2:14; 3:5; 7; **Heb** 1:2; 3(3); 7(2); 2:4; 8; 17; 3:2; 5; 6; 7; 15; 18; 4:1; 4; 7; 10(3); 13; 5:7(2); 6:10; 17; 7:10; 27; 8:11(2); 9:12; 10:13(2); 20; 30; 11:4; 7; 17; 21; 22; 23; 12:10; 16; 13:12; 13; 15; 21(2); **Jas** 1:8; 9; 10; 11; 14; 18(2); 23; 26(2); 2:21; 22; 3:13; 4:11; 5:20; **1 Pe** 1:3; 2:9(2); 21; 22; 24; 3:10(2); 12; 4:2; 13; 5:10; **2 Pe** 1:3; 9; 16; 2:8; 16; 22; 3:4; 9; 13; 16; **1 Jn** 1:3; 7; 10; 2:3; 4; 5; 9; 10; 11(2); 12; 28; 3:9; 10; 12(3); 14; 15; 16; 17(2); 22(2); 23(2); 24; 4:9; 10; 12; 13; 20(2); 21; 5:2; 3(2); 9; 10; 11; 14; 16; 20; **2 Jn** 6; 11; **3 Jn** 7; 10; **Jude** 14; 24; **Rev** 1:1(3); 4; 5; 6; 14(2); 15(2); 16(3); 17(2); 2:1; 18; 3:5(3); 21; 6:5; 17; 7:15; 10:1(3); 2(3); 5; 7; 11:15; 19(2); 12:3; 4; 5; 7(2); 9; 10; 15; 16; 13:1(2); 2(4); 3(2); 6(3); 12; 17; 18; 14:1; 7; 9(4); 10; 11(2); 14(2); 16; 19; 15:2(3); 8; 16:2(2); 3; 4; 8; 10(2); 12; 15(2); 17; 19; 17:17; 18:1; 19:2(2); 5; 7; 10; 12(2); 13; 15; 16(2); 19; 20(2); 20:1; 4(2); 7; 13; 21:3; 7; 22:3; 4(2); 6(2); 12; 14; 19

HOWEVER (71/71)

Ex 21:13; **Lev** 25:31; **Num** 35:22; **Deut** 12:15; **Judg** 1:27; 4:17; 11:28; 16:22; 18:29; 19:10; 20; 21:18; **Ruth** 3:12; **1 Sam** 8:9; 12:15; **2 Sam** 2:23; 12:14; 13:14; 23:19; **1 Ki** 2:15; 10:7; 11:13; 34; **2 Ki** 3:25; 8:10; 10:29; 12:13; 14:4; 15:35; 17:29; 40; 22:7; **1 Chr** 11:21; 28:4; **2 Chr** 9:6; 21:20; 24:5; 25:4; 32:31; **Ezra** 5:13; **Neh** 9:33; 13:2; **Jer** 44:4; **Ezek** 18:14; **Dan** 2:6; 11:10; **Mt** 17:21; **Mk** 1:45; 5:19; **Lk** 5:15; **Jn** 6:23; 7:13; 27; 11:13; 16:13; **Acts** 4:4; 7:48; 14:20; 15:34; 17:34; 27:26; 28:6; **1 Cor** 2:6; 8:7; 12:2; 14:2; 20; 15:46; 16:12; **2 Cor** 10:13; **1 Tim** 1:16

I (8690/5913)

Gen 1:29; 30; 2:18; 3:10(4); 11; 12; 13; 15; 16; 17; 4:1; 9(2); 13; 14(2); 23; 6:7(4); 13; 17; 18; 7:1; 4(3); 8:21(3); 9:3; 5(3); 9; 11; 12; 13; 14; 15; 16; 17; 12:1; 2(2); 3(2); 7; 11; 13; 19; 13:9(2); 15; 16; 17; 14:22; 23(3); 15:1; 2; 7; 8(2); 14; 18; 16:2; 5(2); 8; 10; 13; 17:1; 2; 5; 6(2); 7; 8(2); 16(2); 19; 20(3); 21; 18:3; 5; 10; 12(2); 13(2); 14; 15; 17(2); 19; 21(2); 26(2); 27; 28(2); 29; 30(3); 31(2); 32(2); 19:8; 19(2); 21(2); 22; 34; 20:5; 6(3); 9; 11; 13; 16; 21:7; 13; 18; 23; 24; 26(2); 30; 22:1; 2; 5; 7; 11; 12; 16; 17(2); 23:4(2); 8; 11(3); 13(2); 24:3(2); 5; 7; 13; 14(4); 19; 24; 31; 33(2); 34; 37; 39; 40; 42(2); 43(2); 44; 45(2); 46(2); 47(2); 48; 49; 56; 58; 25:22; 30; 32; 26:2; 3(4); 4(2); 9(2); 24(3); 27:1; 2(2); 4(3);

6; 7; 8; 9; 11; 12(2); 18; 19(2); 21; 24; 25; 32; 33(2); 37(4); 41; 45(2); 46; 28:13(2); 15(4); 16; 20; 21; 22(2); 29:18; 19(2); 21; 25; 33; 34; 35; 30:1; 2; 3; 8(2); 13; 16; 18; 20; 25; 26(2); 27(2); 28; 29; 30(2); 31(2); 31:3; 5; 6; 10; 11(2); 12; 13; 27; 31(2); 32; 35; 38(2); 39(2); 40; 41(2); 43; 44; 51; 52; 32:4; 5(3); 9; 10(3); 11(2); 12; 20(2); 26; 29; 30; 33:8; 9; 10(3); 11; 12; 14(2); 34:11; 12; 30(3); 35:3(2); 11; 12(3); 37:6; 9; 10; 13(2); 16; 17; 30(2); 35; 38:17; 18; 22; 23; 25; 26(2); 39:9(2); 14; 15; 18; 40:11; 15(2); 16; 41:9; 11; 15(2); 17; 19; 21; 22; 24; 28; 40; 41; 44; 42:2; 14; 18; 22; 33; 34(2); 37(2); 43:9(2); 14(2); 23; 44:15; 17; 21; 28(2); 30; 32(2); 34(2); 45:3; 4; 11; 18; 28(2); 46:2; 3(2); 4(2); 30; 31; 47:16; 23; 29; 30; 48:4(2); 5; 7(2); 9; 11; 19(2); 21; 22(2); 49:1; 7; 18; 29; 31; 50:4; 5(3); 17; 19; 21; 24; **Ex** 2:7; 9; 10; 22; 3:3; 4; 6; 7(2); 8; 9; 10; 11(3); 12(2); 13(2); 14(3); 16; 17(2); 19; 20(2); 21; 4:10(2); 11; 12; 14; 15(2); 21(2); 23(2); 5:2(3); 10; 23; 6:1; 2; 3(2); 4; 5(2); 6(4); 7(3); 8(4); 12; 29(2); 30; 7:1; 2; 3; 4; 5(2); 17(2); 8:2; 8; 9; 21; 22(2); 23; 28; 29(2); 9:14; 15; 16(2); 18; 27(2); 28; 29(2); 30; 10:1(2); 2(3); 4; 10; 16; 29; 11:1; 4; 8; 12:12(3); 13(3); 17; 13:8; 15(2); 14:4(3); 17(2); 18(2); 15:1; 2(2); 9(4); 26(3); 16:4(2); 12(2); 32(2); 17:4; 6; 9; 14; 18:3; 6; 11; 16(2); 19; 19:4(2); 9(2); 20:2; 5; 22; 24(3); 21:5(2); 13; 22:23; 24; 27(2); 23:7; 13; 15; 20(2); 22(2); 23; 25; 26; 27(2); 28; 29; 30; 31(2); 24:12(2); 25:8; 9; 16; 21; 22(3); 28:3; 29:35; 42; 43; 44(2); 45; 46(3); 30:6; 36; 31:2; 3; 6(4); 11; 13; 32:8; 9; 10(2); 13(3); 18; 24(2); 30(2); 32; 33; 34(3); 33:1(2); 2(2); 3(2); 5(2); 12; 13(4); 14; 16(2); 17(2); 19(6); 22(2); 23; 34:1; 9(2); 10(3); 11(2); 18; 24; 27; **Lev** 6:17; 7:34(2); 8:31; 35; 10:3(2); 13; 18; 19; 11:44(2); 45(2); 14:34(2); 16:2; 17:10; 11; 12; 14; 18:2; 3; 4; 5; 6; 21; 24; 25; 30; 19:2; 3; 4; 10; 12; 14; 16; 18; 25; 28; 30; 31; 32; 34; 36; 37; 20:3; 5(2); 6; 7; 8; 22; 23(2); 24(3); 25; 26; 21:8; 12; 15; 23; 22:2; 3; 8; 9; 16; 30; 31; 32(2); 33; 23:10; 22; 30; 43(3); 24:22; 25:2; 17; 21; 38; 42; 55(2); 26:1; 2; 4; 6(2); 9; 11; 12; 13(2); 16(2); 17; 18; 19(2); 21; 22; 24(2); 25(2); 26; 28(3); 30; 31(2); 32; 33; 36; 41; 42(3); 44(3); 45(4); **Num** 3:12; 13(3); 41; 45; 5:3; 6:27; 8:16; 17(2); 18; 19; 9:8; 10:10; 29; 30(2); 11:11; 12(2); 13; 14; 15; 17(2); 21(2); 23; 12:6(2); 8; 13; 13:2; 14:11; 12(2); 17; 19; 20; 21; 22; 23; 24; 27(2); 28(2); 30(2); 31; 35(2); 15:2; 18; 41(2); 16:15(2); 21; 28; 45; 17:4; 5(2); 18:6; 7; 8(2); 11; 12; 19; 20; 21; 24(2); 26; 20:12; 18; 19(2); 24; 21:2; 16; 34; 22:6(2); 8; 11; 17(2); 18; 19; 20; 28; 29(2); 30(3); 32; 33; 34(3); 35; 37(2); 38(3); 23:3(2); 4(2); 8(2); 9(2); 11; 12; 15; 20(2); 26(2); 27; 24:10; 11(2); 12; 13(2); 14(2); 17(2); 25:11; 12; 27:12; 32:8; 11; 33:53; 56(2); 35:34(2); **Deut** 1:8; 9(2); 12; 13; 15; 16; 17; 18; 20; 23; 29; 35; 36; 39; 42; 43; 2:5(2); 9(2); 19(2); 24; 25; 26; 27(2); 28(2); 29; 31; 3:2; 12; 13; 15; 16; 18; 19(2); 20; 21; 23; 25; 4:1; 2(2); 5; 8; 10; 21(2); 22(2); 26; 40; 5:1; 5; 6; 9; 28; 31(2); 6:2; 6; 7:11; 17(2); 8:1; 11; 19; 9:9(3); 12; 13; 14(2); 15; 16; 17; 18(2); 19; 20; 21(2); 23; 24; 25(2); 26; 10:2; 3; 5(2); 10; 11; 13; 11:2; 8; 13; 14; 15; 22; 26; 27; 28; 32; 12:11; 14; 21; 28; 30; 32; 13:18; 15:5; 11; 15; 16; 17:3; 14; 18:16; 18(2); 19; 20; 19:7; 9; 22:14(3); 16; 17; 24:8; 18; 22; 25:8; 26:3(2); 10; 13(3); 14(3); 27:1; 4; 10; 28:1; 13; 14; 15; 68; 29:5; 6; 14; 19(2); 30:1; 2; 8; 11; 15; 16; 18; 19(2); 31:2(2); 5; 14; 16; 17(2); 18; 20(2); 21(3); 23(2); 27(2); 28; 29(2); 32:1; 3; 20(2); 21(2); 23(2); 24; 26(3); 27; 39(6); 40(2); 41(2); 42; 46; 49; 52; 33:9; 34:4(3); **Josh** 1:2; 3(2); 5(3); 6; 9; 2:4; 5; 9; 12(2); 3:7(3); 5:9; 14; 6:2; 10; 7:8; 11; 12; 19; 20(2); 21(2); 8:1; 5; 8; 18; 10:8; 11:6; 13:6(2); 14:7(2); 8; 10; 11; 12; 15:16; 18:4; 6; 8; 20:2; 22:2; 23:2; 4(2); 14; 24:3; 4(2); 5(4); 6; 7; 8(3); 10(2); 11; 12; 13; **Judg** 1:2; 3; 7; 12; 2:1(4); 3(2); 20; 21; 22; 3:19; 20; 4:7(2); 8(2); 9; 19; 22; 5:3(3); 7; 6:8; 9; 10(2); 14; 15(2); 16; 17; 18(3); 22; 37(2); 39; 7:4(3); 7; 9; 13; 17(2); 18(2); 8:2; 3; 5; 7; 9(2); 19; 23; 24; 9:2; 9; 11; 13; 29; 48; 10:11; 12; 13; 11:9; 27; 31(2); 35(2); 37(2); 12:2(2); 3(2); 13:6; 11; 13; 14; 16; 14:2; 12; 16(2); 15:2(2); 3(2); 7(2); 11; 16; 18; 16:7; 11; 15; 17(3); 20; 26; 28(3); 17:2; 3(2); 9(2); 10; 13(2); 18:4; 24(2); 19:18(3); 23; 20:4; 6; 23; 28(3); **Ruth** 1:12(4); 16(2); 17(2); 21; 2:2; 9; 10(2); 13; 19; 3:1; 5; 9; 11; 12(2); 13; 4:4(4); 6(3); 9; 10; **1 Sam** 1:8; 11; 15(2); 16; 20; 22; 26; 27(2); 28; 2:1(2); 16; 23; 24; 27; 28(2); 29; 30(2); 31; 33; 35(2); 36; 3:4; 5(2); 6(2); 8; 11; 12(2); 13(2); 14; 16; 4:16(2); 7:5; 8:7; 8; 9:8(2); 16(2); 17; 19(2); 21; 23(2); 24(2); 26; 27; 10:2; 8(2); 18; 11:2(2); 12:1; 2(2); 3(7); 7; 17; 23(2); 13:11; 12(3); 14:7; 24; 29; 37; 40; 43(2); 15:2; 6; 11(2); 13; 14; 16; 20(2); 24(3); 25; 26; 30(2); 16:1(3); 2(2); 3(2); 5; 7; 18; 17:8; 9; 10; 28; 29; 35(2); 39(2); 43; 44; 45; 46(2); 55; 58; 18:11; 17; 18(2); 21; 23; 19:3(4); 15; 17; 20:1; 3; 4; 5(2); 9(2); 12(2); 13; 14(2); 20(2); 21(2); 22; 23; 29; 30; 36; 21:2(3); 5; 8; 15; 22:3; 9; 12; 15; 22(2); 23:2; 4; 11; 17; 22; 23(2); 24:4; 6; 10(2); 11(2); 17(2); 20; 25:7; 11(3); 19; 21; 22; 25; 35; 26:6; 8; 11; 18; 21(3); 23; 27:1(3); 5(2); 28:2; 7; 8; 11; 13; 15(3); 21; 23; 29:3; 6; 8(3); 9; 30:8(2); 13(2); 15; **2 Sam** 1:3; 6; 7(2); 8(2); 10(3); 13; 16; 26; 2:1(2); 6; 20; 22(2); 3:8(2); 9; 13(2); 14; 18; 21; 28; 35; 39; 4:10(2); 11; 5:19(2); 6:21; 22(2); 7:2; 6(2); 7(3); 8; 9; 10; 11; 12(2); 13; 14(2); 15(2); 18; 27; 9:1; 3; 7; 8; 9; 10:2; 11; 11:5; 11(2); 12; 12:7(2); 8(2); 11(2); 12; 13; 22(2); 23(3); 27(2); 28; 13:4; 5; 6; 10; 13(2); 28(2); 14:5; 8; 15(2); 18; 21; 22; 32(3); 15:4(2); 7; 8(2); 20(3); 25; 26(2); 28; 31; 34(3); 16:4(2); 10; 18(2); 19(4); 17:1; 2(2); 3; 11; 15; 18:2; 4; 10; 11; 12(2); 13; 14; 18; 27; 29(2); 33; 19:6; 7; 20(3); 22(3); 26(2); 28; 29; 33; 34(2); 35(5); 37; 38(2); 20:16; 17(2); 19; 20; 21; 21:3(2); 4; 6; 22:3; 4(2); 7; 22; 23; 24(2); 30(2); 38(2); 39; 41; 43(3); 44; 50; 23:17; 24:2; 10(4); 12(2); 13; 14; 17(3); 24(2); **1 Ki** 1:5; 14; 21; 30(2); 35; 2:2; 7; 8(3); 14; 15; 16; 18; 20(2); 26; 30; 42(2); 43; 3:5; 7(2); 9; 12(2); 13; 14; 17(2); 18; 21(3); 5:5(2); 6; 8(2); 9; 6:12(2); 13; 8:13; 16(3); 20(2); 21; 26; 27; 43; 44; 48; 59; 9:3(2); 4; 5(2); 6; 7(4); 10:6; 7(3); 11:11(2); 12(2); 13(3); 21; 31; 32; 34(3); 35; 36(2); 37; 38(3); 39; 12:11(2); 14(2); 13:7; 8(2); 14; 16(2); 17; 18; 31; 14:2; 6; 7; 10(2); 15:19; 16:2; 3(2); 17:1; 4; 9; 10; 12(3); 18; 20; 21; 24; 18:1; 8; 9; 12(4); 13(2); 15(2); 18; 22; 23; 24; 36(2); 19:2; 4; 10(2); 14(2); 18; 20(2); 20:4(2); 5; 6; 7; 9(2); 13(2); 28(2);

34(2); 42; 21:2(3); 3; 4; 6(3); 7; 20; 21(2); 22; 29(2); 22:4; 6(2); 8; 14; 16; 17; 18; 19; 21; 22; 27; 30; 34; **2 Ki** 1:2; 10; 12; 2:2; 3; 4; 5; 6; 9(2); 10; 18; 21; 3:7(2); 13; 14(3); 4:2; 9; 13(2); 22; 24; 28(2); 30; 43; 5:5; 6; 7; 11; 12; 15; 16(2); 18(2); 20; 6:3; 13; 17; 18; 19; 21(2); 27; 29; 33; 7:13; 8:8; 9; 12; 9:3; 5; 6; 7; 8; 9; 12; 17; 25; 26(2); 10:9; 19; 24; 16:7; 17:13(2); 38; 18:14(2); 23(2); 25; 32; 19:7(2); 19; 20; 23(3); 24(2); 25(3); 27; 28(2); 34; 20:3(2); 5(3); 6(3); 8; 15; 21:4; 7(2); 8(3); 12; 13(2); 14; 22:8; 16; 19(2); 20(2); 23:17; 27(4); **1 Chr** 4:9; 10; 11:19(2); 13:12; 14:10(2); 15:12; 16:18; 17:1; 5(2); 6(3); 7; 8; 9; 10(3); 11(2); 12; 13(3); 14; 16; 19:2; 12; 21:2; 8(4); 10(2); 12; 13; 17(3); 22; 23(2); 24(2); 22:5; 9(2); 10(2); 14(2); 23:5; 28:2; 6(2); 7; 29:2; 3(3); 14; 17(3); 19; **2 Chr** 1:7; 10; 11; 12; 2:4; 5; 6(2); 8; 9; 10; 13; 6:2; 5(3); 6(2); 10(2); 11; 18; 33; 34; 38; 40; 7:12; 13; 14; 16; 17; 18(2); 19; 20(4); 9:5; 6(3); 10:11(2); 14(2); 12:5; 7(2); 16:3; 18:3; 5; 7; 13; 14; 15; 16; 17; 18; 20; 21; 26; 29; 33; 25:9; 16; 28:23; 32:13; 33:7(2); 8(3); 34:15; 24; 27; 28(2); 35:21(3); 23; **Ezra** 4:19; 6:8; 11; 12; 7:13; 21(2); 28(2); 8:15(2); 16; 17(2); 21; 22; 24; 26; 28; 9:3(2); 4; 5(2); 6(2); **Neh** 1:1; 2; 4(3); 5(2); 6(2); 8(2); 9(2); 11(3); 2:1(2); 2; 4; 5(3); 6; 7(2); 8; 9; 11; 12(4); 13; 14; 15(2); 16(3); 17; 18; 20; 4:13(2); 14; 19; 22; 23; 5:6(2); 7(2); 8; 9; 10; 12; 13; 14(2); 15; 16; 18; 19; 6:1(2); 3(4); 4; 8; 10; 11(4); 12; 13; 7:1; 2; 3; 5; 12:31; 38; 40; 13:6(3); 7; 8; 9(2); 10; 11(2); 13; 14; 15(2); 17; 19(2); 21(2); 22; 23; 25; 28; 30(2); **Esth** 3:9; 4:11; 16(4); 5:4; 8(3); 12; 13; 7:3; 4(2); 8; 8:5(2); 6(2); 7; **Job** 1:15; 16; 17; 19; 21(2); 3:3; 11(3); 12; 13(3); 16; 24; 25(2); 26(3); 4:8; 16(2); 5:3(2); 8(2); 6:8(2); 10(3); 11(3); 22; 24(2); 28; 7:3; 4(4); 8; 11(3); 12; 13; 16(2); 19; 20(3); 21(2); 8:18; 9:2; 11(2); 14; 15(3); 16(2); 20(2); 21(3); 22; 27(3); 28(2); 29(2); 30; 32(2); 35; 10:1(2); 2; 7; 9; 13; 14; 15(4); 18; 19(3); 20; 21(2); 11:4; 12:3(2); 4; 13:2(2); 3(2); 14; 15(2); 18(3); 19(2); 20; 22; 14:14; 15; 15:6; 17(3); 16:2; 4(2); 5; 6(3); 12; 15; 22; 17:6; 10; 13(2); 14; 19:4; 7(3); 8; 10; 15; 16(2); 17; 18; 19; 20; 25; 26(2); 27; 20:3; 21:3(2); 4; 6(2); 27; 23:3(3); 4; 5; 7; 8(2); 9(2); 10(2); 11; 12(2); 15(3); 17; 27:5(3); 6(2); 11(2); 29:2; 3; 4; 7(2); 12; 13; 14; 15(2); 16(3); 17; 18(2); 24; 25(2); 30:1(2); 9(2); 19; 20(2); 23; 25; 26(2); 28(2); 29; 31:1(2); 5; 9; 13; 14(2); 16; 18(2); 19; 21(3); 23; 24; 25; 26; 28; 29; 30; 32; 33; 34(2); 35; 36; 37(2); 39; 32:6(2); 7; 10(2); 11(2); 12; 14; 16; 17(2); 18; 20(3); 21; 22; 33:2; 6(2); 8; 9(2); 12; 24; 27; 31; 32; 33; 34:5; 6(2); 31(2); 32(3); 33; 35:3(2); 4; 36:2; 3(2); 37:20; 38:3; 4; 9; 10; 11; 23; 39:6; 40:4(3); 5(3); 7; 14; 15; 41:11; 12; 42:2; 3(3); 4; 5; 6; 8(2); **Ps** 2:6; 7(2); 8; 3:4; 5(2); 6; 4:1; 3; 8; 5:2; 3(2); 7(2); 6:2; 6(3); 7:1; 3; 4; 17; 8:3; 9:1(2); 2(2); 14(2); 10:6(2); 11:1; 12:5(2); 13:2; 3; 4(2); 5; 6; 16:1; 4; 6; 7; 8(2); 17:3; 4; 6; 15(3); 18:1; 2; 3(2); 6; 21; 22; 23(2); 29(2); 37(2); 38; 40; 42(2); 43; 49; 19:13(2); 20:6; 22:2; 6; 10; 14; 17; 22(2); 25; 23:1; 4(2); 6; 25:1; 2; 5; 16; 20; 21; 26:1(3); 3; 4(2); 5; 6(2); 7; 8; 11; 12; 27:1(2); 3; 4(3); 6(3); 7; 8; 13(3); 14; 28:1(2); 2(2); 7(2); 30:1; 2; 3; 6(2); 7; 8(2); 9; 12; 31:1; 5; 6(2); 7; 9; 11; 12(2); 13; 14(2); 17; 22(3); 32:3; 5(4); 8(2); 34:1; 4; 11; 35:3; 11; 13; 14(2); 15; 18(2); 37:25(2); 35; 36; 38:6(3); 8(2); 13(2); 14; 15; 16; 17; 18(2); 20; 39:1(4); 2(2); 3(2); 4(2); 7; 9(2); 10; 12; 13(2); 40:1; 5; 7(2); 8; 9(2); 10(3); 12; 17; 41:4(2); 9; 10; 11; 42:2; 4(4); 5; 6; 9(2); 11; 43:2; 4(2); 5; 44:6; 45:1; 17; 46:10(3); 49:4(2); 5; 50:7(3); 8; 9; 11; 12(2); 13; 15; 21(3); 22; 23; 51:3; 4; 5; 7(2); 13; 16; 52:8(2); 9(2); 54:6(2); 55:2; 6(3); 7; 8; 9; 12(2); 16; 17; 23; 56:3(2); 4(3); 9(2); 10(2); 11(2); 12; 13; 57:1; 2; 4; 7; 8; 9(2); 59:9; 16(2); 17; 60:6(2); 8; 61:2(2); 4(2); 8(2); 62:2; 6; 11; 63:1; 2; 4(3); 6(2); 7; 66:13(2); 14; 15(2); 16; 17; 18; 68:22(2); 69:2(2); 3(2); 4(2); 7; 8; 10; 11(2); 12; 17; 20(3); 29; 30; 70:5; 71:1; 3; 6; 7; 14; 15; 16(2); 17; 18(2); 22(2); 23; 73:3(2); 13; 14; 15(3); 16; 17(2); 21; 22(2); 23; 25(2); 28(2); 75:2(2); 3; 4; 9(2); 10; 77:1; 2; 3(2); 4(2); 5; 6(2); 10(2); 11(2); 12; 78:2(2); 81:5(2); 6; 7(3); 8; 10(2); 12; 14; 16; 82:6; 84:10; 85:8; 86:1; 2; 3; 4; 7; 11; 12(2); 87:4; 88:1; 4(2); 8(2); 9(2); 13; 15(3); 89:1(2); 2; 3(2); 4; 19(2); 20(2); 23; 25; 27; 28; 29; 32; 33; 34; 35(2); 50; 91:2(2); 14(2); 15(3); 16; 92:4; 10; 94:18; 95:10; 11; 101:1(2); 2(2); 3(2); 4; 5(2); 8(2); 102:2; 4; 6(2); 7; 9; 11; 24; 104:33(4); 34; 105:11; 106:5(3); 108:1; 2; 3(2); 7(2); 9(2); 109:4; 22; 23(2); 25; 30(2); 110:1; 111:1; 116:1; 2(2); 3; 4(2); 6; 9; 10(3); 11; 12; 13; 14; 16(2); 17; 18; 118:5; 6; 7; 10; 11; 12; 13; 17; 19(2); 21; 25(2); 28(2); 119:6(2); 7(2); 8; 10; 11(2); 13; 14; 15; 16(2); 17; 18; 19; 22; 26; 27; 30(2); 31; 32; 33; 34(2); 35; 39; 40; 42(2); 43; 44; 45(2); 46; 47(2); 48(3); 51; 52; 55(2); 56; 57(2); 58; 59; 60; 61; 62; 63; 66; 67(3); 69; 70; 71(2); 73; 74; 75; 76; 77; 78; 80; 81; 83(2); 87; 88; 92; 93; 94(2); 95; 96; 97; 99; 100(2); 101(2); 102; 104(2); 106(2); 107; 108; 109; 110; 111; 112; 113(2); 114; 115; 116; 117(2); 119; 120; 121; 125(2); 127; 128(2); 131(2); 134; 141(2); 144; 145(2); 146(2); 147(2); 148; 152; 153; 157; 158; 159; 162; 163(2); 164; 166(2); 167; 168; 173; 174; 176(2); 120:1; 5(2); 7(2); 121:1; 122:1; 8; 9; 123:1; 130:1; 5(2); 131:1; 2; 132:3; 4; 5; 11; 12; 14(2); 15(2); 16; 17(2); 18; 135:5; 137:5; 6(2); 138:1(2); 2; 3; 7; 139:6; 7(2); 8(2); 9; 11; 14(2); 15; 18(3); 21(2); 22(2); 140:6; 12; 141:1(2); 8; 10; 142:1(2); 2(2); 3; 5(2); 6(2); 7; 143:5(3); 6; 7; 8(3); 9; 12; 144:2; 9(2); 145:1(2); 2(2); 5; 6; 146:2(4); **Prov** 1:23(2); 24(2); 26(2); 28; 3:28; 4:2; 3; 11(2); 5:12; 13; 14; 7:6; 7; 14(2); 15(2); 16; 17; 8:4; 6; 12; 13; 14(2); 17; 20; 21(2); 23; 24; 25; 27; 30(2); 9:5; 20:9(2); 22; 22:13; 19; 20; 21; 23:15; 35(4); 24:29(2); 30; 32(3); 26:19; 27:11; 30:2; 3; 7(2); 9(2); 18; 20; **Eccl** 1:12; 13; 14; 16(2); 17(2); 2:1(2); 2; 3(2); 4(2); 5(2); 6; 7(2); 8(2); 9; 10(2); 11(2); 12; 13; 14; 15(3); 17; 18(3); 19(2); 20(2); 24; 25; 3:10; 12; 16; 17; 18; 22; 4:1; 2; 4; 7(2); 8; 15; 5:13; 18; 6:1; 3; 7:15; 23(3); 25; 26; 27; 28(3); 29; 8:2; 9; 10; 12; 14; 15; 16; 17; 9:1(2); 11; 13; 16; 10:5; 7; 12:1; **Song** 1:5; 6(2); 7(2); 9; 2:1; 3; 5; 7; 16; 3:1(4); 2(6); 3(2); 4(5); 5; 4:6; 5:1(4); 2; 3(4); 5; 6(4); 8(2); 6:3; 11; 12; 7:8(3); 10; 12; 13; 8:1(3); 2(2); 4; 5; 10(2); **Isa** 1:2; 11(2); 13; 14; 15(2); 24; 25; 26; 3:4; 7; 5:4(2); 5(2); 6(2); 6:1; 5(4); 8(4); 11; 7:12(2); 8:2; 3; 11; 17(2); 18; 10:6(2); 11(2); 12; 13(4); 14; 12:1; 2; 13:3(2); 11(2); 12; 13; 17;

14:13(3); 14(2); 22; 23(2); 24(2); 25; 30; 15:9; 16:9(2); 10; 18:4(2); 19:2; 3; 4; 11; 21:2; 3(4); 4; 8(2); 10(2); 22:4(2); 19; 20; 21(2); 22; 23; 23:4(2); 24:16(2); 25:1(2); 26:9(2); 27:3(3); 4(2); 28:16; 17; 22; 29:2; 3(3); 11; 12; 14; 30:7; 33:10(3); 13; 24; 36:5; 8(2); 10; 17; 37:7(2); 24(3); 25(2); 26(3); 28; 29(2); 35; 38:3(2); 5(3); 6(2); 8; 10(2); 11(3); 12; 13; 14(3); 15(2); 17; 19; 22; 39:4; 40:6; 25; 41:4(2); 8; 9(2); 10(5); 13(2); 14; 15; 17(2); 18(2); 19(2); 25; 27(2); 28(3); 42:1(2); 6(2); 8(2); 9(2); 14(4); 15(3); 16(4); 19; 43:1(2); 2; 3(2); 4(2); 5(2); 6; 7(3); 10(2); 11(2); 12(3); 13(2); 14; 15; 19(2); 20; 21; 23; 25(3); 28(2); 44:1; 2; 3(2); 5; 6(2); 7(2); 8(2); 16(2); 19(5); 21; 22(2); 24; 26; 27; 45:1; 2(2); 3(2); 4(2); 5(2); 6; 7(3); 8; 12(3); 13(2); 18; 19(4); 21; 22; 23; 24; 46:4(5); 9(2); 10; 11(4); 13(2); 47:3(2); 6(2); 7; 8(3); 10; 48:3(3); 4; 5(2); 6; 7; 8; 9(3); 10(2); 11(2); 12(3); 13; 15(4); 16(2); 17; 49:3; 4(3); 5; 6; 8(3); 11; 15; 16; 18; 20; 21(2); 22; 23; 25(2); 26(2); 50:1(2); 2(5); 3(2); 4; 5(2); 6(2); 7(4); 51:2; 4; 12(2); 15; 16(3); 19; 22; 23; 52:5; 6(2); 53:12; 54:7(2); 8(2); 9(3); 11; 12; 16(2); 55:3; 4; 11(2); 56:3; 5(2); 7; 8; 12; 57:6; 11; 12; 15; 16(3); 17(2); 18(2); 19(2); 58:5; 6; 9; 14; 59:21; 60:7; 10(2); 13; 15; 16; 17(3); 21; 22; 61:8(3); 10; 62:1(2); 6; 8; 63:1; 3(3); 5(2); 6; 7; 65:1(5); 2; 5; 6; 7; 8(2); 9; 12(4); 17; 18(2); 19; 24(2); 66:2; 4(4); 9(2); 12; 13; 18(2); 19(2); 21; 22; **Jer** 1:5(4); 6(3); 7(3); 8; 9; 10; 11(2); 12; 13(2); 15; 16; 17(2); 18; 19; 2:2; 7; 9(2); 20(2); 21; 23(2); 25(2); 30; 31; 34; 35(3); 3:7; 8(2); 12(3); 14(3); 15; 18; 19(3); 22; 4:6; 10; 12; 19(2); 21; 23; 24; 25; 26; 27; 28(3); 31; 5:1; 4; 5; 7(2); 9(2); 14; 15; 18; 29(2); 6:2; 8; 10; 11(3); 12; 15; 17; 19; 21; 27; 7:3; 7(2); 11(2); 12(2); 13(2); 14(3); 15(2); 16; 22(2); 23(3); 25; 31; 34; 8:3; 6(2); 10; 13(2); 17; 18; 21(2); 9:1; 2(2); 7(2); 9(2); 10; 11(2); 13; 15; 16(3); 24(2); 25; 10:18; 19(2); 23; 11:4(4); 5(3); 7(2); 8(2); 10; 11(2); 14; 18; 19(2); 20; 22; 23; 12:1; 7(3); 8; 14(2); 15(2); 17; 13:2; 5; 6; 7(3); 9; 11; 13; 14(2); 24; 26; 27; 14:12(3); 13(2); 14; 15; 16; 18(2); 15:3; 4; 6(2); 7(3); 8(2); 9; 10; 11; 13; 14; 15; 16(2); 17(3); 19; 20(2); 21(2); 16:5; 9; 13(2); 15(2); 16(2); 18; 21(2); 17:3; 4(2); 10(2); 14(2); 16(2); 22; 27; 18:2; 3; 6; 7; 8(3); 9; 10(3); 11; 17(2); 20; 19:2; 3; 5; 7(3); 8; 9; 11; 12; 15(2); 20:4(2); 5(2); 7(3); 8(3); 9(4); 10; 12; 14; 18; 21:4(2); 5; 6; 7; 8; 10; 13; 14(2); 22:5; 6; 7; 14; 21(2); 24(2); 25; 26; 23:2; 3(2); 4; 5; 8; 9; 11; 12; 13; 14; 15; 21(2); 23; 24(2); 25(3); 30; 31; 32(3); 33; 34; 38; 39(3); 40; 24:3; 5(2); 6(4); 7(3); 8; 9(2); 10(2); 25:3; 6; 9; 10; 12(2); 13(2); 14; 15; 16; 17; 27; 29(2); 26:2; 3(2); 4; 5; 6; 14; 27:5; 6(2); 8(2); 10; 11; 12; 15(2); 16; 22(2); 28:2; 3; 4(2); 7; 11; 14(2); 16; 29:4; 7; 9; 10; 11(2); 12; 14(6); 17; 18(3); 19; 20; 21; 23(2); 31; 32(2); 30:2; 3(3); 6; 8; 9; 10; 11(5); 14; 15; 16; 17; 18; 19(2); 20; 21; 22; 31:1; 2; 3(2); 4; 8; 9(3); 13; 14; 18(3); 19(5); 20(3); 23; 25(2); 26; 27; 28(2); 31; 32(3); 33(3); 34(2); 37; 32:3; 5; 8; 9; 10; 11; 12; 13; 16(2); 27; 28; 31; 33; 35; 37(4); 38; 39; 40(3); 41(2); 42(3); 44; 33:3; 5(2); 6(2); 7; 8(2); 9(2); 11; 14(2); 15; 22; 25; 26(3); 34:2; 5; 13(2); 17(2); 18; 20; 21; 22(2); 35:3; 4; 5(2); 14; 15(2); 17(4); 36:2(2); 3(2); 5(2); 18; 31(3); 37:14; 18; 20; 38:14; 15(2); 16(2); 19; 20; 25; 26; 39:16; 17; 18; 40:4(2); 10; 15; 42:4(4); 10(4); 11; 12; 17; 19; 21; 43:10(2); 12; 44:2; 4(2); 10; 11; 12; 13(2); 26; 27; 29; 30(2); 45:3(2); 4(4); 5(2); 46:5; 8(2); 18; 25; 26; 27; 28(6); 48:12; 30; 31(3); 32; 33; 35; 38; 44; 47; 49:2; 5; 6; 8(2); 10(2); 11; 13; 14; 15; 16; 19(2); 27; 32(2); 35; 36; 37(4); 38; 39; 50:9; 18(2); 19; 20(2); 21; 23; 31(2); 32; 44(2); 51:1; 2; 14; 20(2); 21(2); 22(3); 23(3); 24; 25(2); 36(2); 39(2); 40; 44(2); 47; 52; 57; 64; **Lam** 1:11; 14; 16; 18; 19; 20(2); 21; 2:13(4); 22; 3:1; 7; 8; 14; 17; 18; 21(2); 24; 54(2); 55; 57; 59; 63; **Ezek** 1:1(2); 4; 15; 24; 27(2); 28(3); 2:1; 2; 3; 4; 8(2); 9; 3:2; 3(2); 6; 8; 9; 10; 12; 13; 14; 15(2); 17; 18(2); 20(2); 22; 23(3); 26; 27(2); 4:5; 6; 8; 13; 14(3); 15; 16; 5:2; 5; 8(2); 9(3); 10(2); 11(3); 12(2); 13(4); 14; 15(2); 16(3); 17(3); 6:3(3); 4; 5(2); 7; 8; 9; 10(3); 12; 13; 14(2); 7:3(3); 4(3); 8(3); 9(3); 20; 21; 22; 24(2); 27(3); 8:1; 2; 4; 5; 7; 8; 10; 18(3); 9:8(2); 10(2); 11; 10:1; 2; 9; 15; 20(2); 22; 11:1; 5; 7; 8; 9; 10(2); 11; 12; 13(2); 16(3); 17(2); 19(2); 20; 21; 24; 25; 12:6; 7(6); 11(2); 13(2); 14(2); 15(2); 16(2); 20; 23; 25(4); 28; 13:7; 8; 9; 13; 14(2); 15(2); 20(2); 21(2); 22; 23(2); 14:3; 4; 5; 7; 8(3); 9(2); 11; 13(2); 15; 16; 17(2); 18; 19; 20; 21; 22(2); 23(2); 15:6(2); 7(3); 8; 16:6(3); 7; 8(3); 9(3); 10(2); 11; 12; 14; 17; 19(2); 27; 37(2); 38(2); 39; 41; 42(2); 43; 48; 50(2); 53(2); 59; 60(2); 61; 62(2); 63; 17:16; 19(2); 20(2); 21; 22(2); 23; 24(2); 18:3; 23; 30; 32; 20:3(2); 5(3); 6(2); 7(2); 8(2); 9(2); 10; 11; 12(2); 13(2); 14(2); 15(3); 17; 18; 19; 20; 21(2); 22(2); 23(2); 25; 26(3); 28(2); 29; 31(3); 33(2); 34; 35(2); 36(2); 37(2); 38(3); 40(2); 41(3); 42(3); 44(2); 47; 48; 49; 21:3(2); 4; 5; 15; 17(3); 27(2); 30; 31(2); 32; 22:4; 13; 14(2); 15; 16; 19; 20(2); 21; 22; 26; 30(3); 31(3); 23:9; 13; 18(2); 22(2); 24; 25; 27; 28; 30; 31; 34; 43; 48; 49; 24:8; 9; 13(2); 14(5); 16; 18(3); 20; 21; 22; 24; 25; 27; 25:4; 5(2); 7(5); 9; 10; 11(2); 13; 14; 16(2); 17(3); 26:2; 3; 4; 5; 6; 7; 13; 14(2); 19(2); 20(3); 21; 27:3; 28:2(2); 7; 9; 10; 14; 16(2); 17(2); 18(2); 22(4); 23(2); 24; 25(2); 26(2); 29:3(2); 4(2); 5(2); 6; 8; 9(2); 10(2); 12(2); 13; 14; 15; 16; 19; 20; 21(3); 30:8(2); 10; 12(3); 13(2); 14; 15(2); 18; 19(2); 21; 22(2); 23; 24(2); 25(3); 26(2); 31:9; 11(2); 15(4); 16(2); 32:3; 4(3); 5; 6; 7(3); 8; 9(2); 10(2); 12; 13; 14; 15(3); 32; 33:2; 6; 7; 8(2); 11(2); 13; 14; 20; 22; 27(2); 28; 29(2); 34:8; 10(4); 11; 12; 13(2); 14; 15(2); 16(2); 17; 20; 22(2); 23; 24(2); 25; 26(2); 27(2); 29; 30; 31; 35:3(2); 4(2); 6(2); 7; 8; 9(2); 11(4); 12(2); 13; 14; 15(2); 36:5; 6; 7; 9(2); 10; 11(3); 12; 15; 18; 19(2); 21; 22; 23(3); 24; 25(2); 26(2); 27; 28(2); 29(2); 30; 32; 33(2); 36(3); 37(2); 38; 37:3; 5; 6(2); 7(3); 8; 10; 12; 13(2); 14(3); 19(2); 21; 22; 23(2); 25; 26(3); 27; 28; 38:3; 4; 11(2); 16(2); 17(2); 19; 21; 22(2); 23(3); 39:1; 2; 3; 4; 5; 6(2); 7(3); 8; 11; 13; 17; 19; 21(3); 22; 23(2); 24; 25(2); 27(2); 28; 29(2); 40:4(2); 41:8; 43:6(5); 6; 7; 8; 9; 27; 44:4(2); 5; 12; 14; 28(2); 47:5; 7; 14; **Dan** 1:10; 2:3; 8; 9; 23; 24; 25; 26; 30; 3:14; 15; 25; 29; 4:2; 4; 5; 6; 7; 8; 9(2); 10; 13; 18; 30; 34(2); 36; 37; 5:14; 16; 17; 6:22(2); 26; 7:2; 4; 6; 7; 8; 9; 11(2); 13; 15; 16; 19; 21; 28; 8:2(5); 3; 4; 5; 6; 7; 13; 15; 16; 17(2); 18; 19; 27(3); 9:2; 3; 4; 16; 20; 21(2);

22; 23; 10:2; 3(2); 4; 5; 7; 8(3); 9(3); 11(3); 12; 13; 14; 15; 16(2); 19; 20(3); 21; 11:1(2); 2; 12:5; 7; 8(3); **Hos** 1:4; 5; 6(2); 7; 9; 2:2; 3; 4; 5; 6; 7; 8; 9; 10; 11; 12(2); 13; 14; 15; 17; 18(2); 19(2); 20; 21(2); 23(3); 3:2; 3(2); 4:5; 6(2); 7; 9; 14; 5:2; 3; 9; 10; 12; 14(4); 15; 6:4(2); 5(2); 6; 10; 11; 7:1; 2; 12(3); 13; 15; 8:4; 10; 12; 14; 9:10(2); 12(2); 13; 15(3); 16; 10:10(2); 11(2); 11:1(2); 3(2); 4(3); 8(4); 9(4); 11; 12:8(2); 9(2); 10(2); 13:4; 5; 7(2); 8(3); 10; 11; 14(4); 14:4(2); 5; 8(3); **Joel** 1:19; 2:19(2); 20; 25(2); 27(2); 28; 29; 30; 3:1; 2(2); 4; 7; 8; 10; 12; 17; 21(2); **Am** 1:3; 4; 5; 6; 7; 8(2); 9; 10; 11; 12; 13; 14; 2:1; 2; 3; 4; 5; 6; 9(2); 10; 11; 13; 3:1; 2(2); 14(2); 15; 4:6; 7(3); 9; 10(3); 11; 12(2); 5:1; 12; 17; 21(3); 22(2); 23; 27; 6:8(2); 14; 7:2(2); 5(2); 8(3); 9; 14(3); 15; 8:2(2); 7; 9(2); 10(3); 11; 9:1(2); 2; 3(2); 4(2); 7; 8(2); 9; 11(2); 14; 15(2); **Ob** 2; 4; 8; **Jon** 1:9(2); 12; 2:2(2); 4(3); 6; 7; 9(3); 3:2; 4:2(4); 11; **Mic** 1:6(3); 7; 8(3); 15; 2:3; 11; 12(3); 3:1; 8; 4:6(3); 7; 13(3); 5:10; 11; 12; 13; 14(2); 15; 6:3(2); 4(3); 6(2); 7; 11; 13; 14; 16; 7:1; 7(2); 8(3); 9(3); 15; **Nah** 1:12(2); 13; 14(2); 2:13(3); 3:5(3); 6; 7; **Hab** 1:2; 5; 6; 2:1(3); 3:2; 7; 16(3); 18(2); **Zeph** 1:2; 3(3); 4(2); 8; 9; 12; 17; 2:5; 8; 9; 15; 3:6(2); 7(2); 8; 9; 11; 12; 18; 19(3); 20(4); **Hag** 1:8; 9; 11; 13; 2:4; 5; 6; 7(2); 9; 17; 19; 21; 22(3); 23(2); **Zech** 1:3; 6; 8; 9(2); 14; 15(2); 16; 18; 19; 21; 2:1; 2; 5(2); 6; 9; 10(2); 11; 3:4(2); 5; 7; 8; 9(3); 4:2(2); 4; 5; 11; 12; 13; 5:1; 2(2); 4; 6; 9; 10; 6:1; 4; 7:3(2); 13; 14; 8:2(2); 3; 7; 8(2); 10; 11; 12; 13; 14(2); 15; 17; 21; 9:6; 7; 8(2); 10; 11; 12(2); 13; 10:3; 6(7); 8(2); 9; 10(2); 12; 11:5; 6(3); 7(5); 8; 9(2); 10(3); 12; 13; 14(2); 16; 12:2; 3; 4(2); 6; 9; 10; 13:2(2); 5(2); 6; 7; 9(3); 14:2; **Mal** 1:2(2); 3; 4; 6(2); 10(2); 13; 14; 2:2(3); 3; 4; 5; 9; 3:1; 5(2); 6(2); 7; 10; 11; 17(2); 4:3; 4; 5; 6; **Mt** 2:8; 13; 15; 3:9; 11(3); 14; 17; 4:9; 19; 5:17(2); 18; 20; 22; 26; 28; 32; 34; 39; 44; 6:2; 5; 16; 25; 29; 7:23(2); 24; 8:3; 7; 8; 9(2); 10(2); 11; 19; 9:13(2); 21(2); 28; 10:15; 16; 23; 27; 32; 33; 34(2); 35; 42; 11:9; 10; 11; 16; 22; 24; 25; 28; 29; 12:6; 7; 18(2); 27; 28; 31; 36; 44(2); 13:13; 15; 17; 30; 35(2); 14:27; 15:24; 32(2); 16:11; 13; 15; 18(2); 19; 28; 17:5; 12; 16; 17(2); 20; 18:3; 10; 13; 18; 19; 20; 21; 22; 26; 29; 32; 33; 19:9; 16(2); 20(2); 23; 24; 28; 20:4; 13; 14; 15(2); 22(2); 23; 21:21; 24(3); 27(2); 29; 30; 31; 43; 22:4; 32; 44; 23:34; 36; 37; 39; 24:2; 5; 25; 34; 47; 25:12(2); 20; 21; 22; 23; 24; 25; 26(3); 27; 35(3); 36(3); 40; 42(2); 43; 45; 26:13; 15; 18; 21; 22; 25; 29(3); 31; 32(2); 33; 34; 35(2); 36; 39; 42; 48; 53; 55; 61; 63; 64; 70; 72; 74; 27:4; 19; 22; 24; 43; 63; 28:5; 7; 20(2); **Mk** 1:2; 7(2); 8; 11; 17; 24; 38(2); 41; 2:11; 17; 3:28; 5:7(2); 28(2); 41; 6:11; 16; 22; 23; 24; 25; 50; 8:2; 3; 12; 19; 20; 24; 27; 29; 9:1; 13; 17; 18; 19(2); 24; 25; 41; 10:15; 17(2); 20; 29; 38(2); 39(2); 51; 11:23; 24; 29(3); 33(2); 12:15; 26; 36; 43; 13:6; 23; 30; 37(2); 14:9; 14; 18; 19(2); 25(3); 27; 28(2); 29; 30; 31(2); 32; 36; 44; 49; 58(2); 62; 68; 71; **Lk** 1:18(2); 19; 34; 2:10; 48; 49; 3:8; 16(3); 22; 4:6(3); 24; 25; 34; 43(2); 5:5; 8; 13; 24; 32; 6:9; 27; 46; 47; 7:6; 7; 8(2); 9(2); 14; 26; 27; 28; 31; 40; 43; 44; 45; 47; 8:28(2); 46; 9:9(2); 18; 20; 27; 38; 40; 41; 57; 61; 10:3; 12; 18; 19; 21; 24; 25; 35(2); 11:6; 7; 8; 9; 18; 19; 20; 24(2); 49; 51; 12:4; 5(2); 8; 17(2); 18(3); 19; 22; 27; 37; 44; 49(2); 50(2); 51(2); 59; 13:3; 5; 7; 8; 18; 20; 24; 25; 27(2); 32(2); 33; 34; 35; 14:18(3); 19(3); 20(2); 24; 15:6; 7; 9(2); 10; 17; 18(2); 19; 21; 29(3); 31; 16:2; 3(3); 4(2); 9; 24; 27; 28; 17:4; 8; 9; 34; 18:4; 5; 8; 11(2); 12(3); 14; 17; 18; 21; 29; 41; 19:5; 8(3); 13; 20; 21; 22(4); 23; 26; 40; 20:3; 8(2); 13(2); 43; 21:3; 8; 15; 32; 22:11; 15(2); 16(2); 18(2); 27; 29; 32; 33; 34; 35; 37; 53; 57; 58; 60; 67; 68; 70; 23:4; 14; 15; 16; 22(2); 43; 46; 24:39(2); 44(2); 49; **Jn** 1:15; 20; 21; 23; 26; 27; 30; 31(2); 32; 33; 34; 48; 50(2); 51; 2:19; 3:3; 5; 7; 11; 12(2); 28(3); 30; 4:14(2); 15; 17(2); 19; 25; 26; 29; 32; 35; 38; 39; 5:7(2); 17; 19; 24; 25; 30(4); 31; 32; 34(2); 36(2); 41; 42; 43; 45; 6:20; 26; 32; 35; 36; 37; 38; 39; 40; 41; 42; 44; 47; 48; 51(3); 53; 54; 56; 57; 63; 65; 70; 7:7; 8; 17; 21; 23; 28(2); 29(2); 33(2); 34; 36; 8:11; 12; 14(6); 15; 16(3); 18; 21(2); 22; 23(2); 24(2); 25; 26(3); 28(3); 29; 34; 37; 38(2); 40; 42(2); 45; 46; 49(2); 50; 51; 54; 55(5); 58(2); 9:4; 5(2); 9; 11(2); 12; 15(2); 25(4); 27; 36; 38; 39; 10:1; 7(2); 9; 10; 11; 14(2); 15(2); 16(2); 17(2); 18(4); 25(2); 26; 27; 28; 30; 32; 34; 36(2); 37; 38(2); 11:11(2); 15(2); 22; 24; 25; 27; 40; 41; 42(2); 12:24; 26; 27(2); 28; 32(2); 40; 46; 47(2); 48; 49(3); 50(3); 13:7; 8; 12; 13; 14; 15(2); 16; 18(3); 19(2); 20(2); 21; 26(2); 33(4); 34(2); 36; 37(2); 38; 14:2(2); 3(3); 4; 6; 9; 10(3); 11; 12(3); 13; 14; 16; 18(2); 19; 20(2); 21; 25; 26; 27(3); 28(4); 29; 30; 31(2); 15:1; 3; 4; 5(2); 9; 10; 11; 12; 14; 15(4); 16; 17; 19; 20; 22; 24; 26; 16:1; 4(4); 5; 6; 7(5); 10; 12; 15; 16; 17; 19; 20; 22; 23; 25(3); 26(2); 27; 28(2); 32; 33(2); 17:4(2); 5; 6; 8(2); 9(2); 10; 11(2); 12(3); 13(2); 14(2); 15; 16; 18; 19; 20; 21; 22; 23; 24(2); 25; 26(2); 18:5; 6; 8(2); 9; 11; 17; 20(3); 21(2); 23; 25; 26; 35; 36; 37(4); 38; 39; 19:4(2); 6; 10; 15; 21; 22(2); 28; 20:13; 15; 17(2); 21; 25(2); 21:3; 15; 16; 17; 18; 22(2); 23(2); 25; **Acts** 1:1; 2:17; 18; 19; 25(2); 35; 3:6(3); 17; 5:38; 7:3; 7; 32; 34(3); 43; 56; 8:19; 23; 31; 34; 37; 9:5; 10; 13; 16; 10:14; 20; 21; 26; 28; 29(3); 30(2); 33; 34; 11:5(2); 6(2); 7; 8; 11; 15; 16; 17(2); 12:11; 13:2; 22; 25(3); 33; 34; 41; 47; 15:16(3); 19; 16:18; 30; 17:3; 22; 23(3); 18:6(2); 10(2); 14; 15; 21(2); 19:15(2); 21(2); 20:18(2); 20; 22; 24(3); 25(2); 26(2); 27; 29; 31; 32; 33; 35; 21:13; 37; 39(2); 22:3; 4; 5; 6; 7; 8(2); 10(2); 11(2); 13; 17(2); 19(2); 20; 21; 28(2); 23:1; 5; 6(2); 27; 28(2); 29; 30; 35; 24:4; 10(2); 11; 14(2); 15; 16; 17; 20; 21(2); 22; 25(2); 25:8; 10(3); 11(3); 15; 16; 17; 18; 20(2); 21(2); 22; 25(2); 26(3); 26:2(3); 3; 5; 6; 7; 9(2); 10(3); 11(2); 12; 13; 14; 15(2); 16(2); 17(2); 19; 22; 25; 26(2); 27; 29(2); 27:10; 22; 23(2); 25; 34; 28:17(2); 19(2); 20(2); 27; **Rom** 1:8; 9(2); 10; 11(2); 12; 13(3); 14; 15; 16; 3:5; 7; 4:17; 6:19; 7:1; 7(2); 9(2); 10; 14; 15(6); 16(3); 17; 18(2); 19(4); 20(3); 21; 22; 23; 24; 25(2); 8:18; 38; 9:1(2); 2; 3(2); 9; 13(2); 15(4); 17(2); 25; 33; 10:2; 18; 19(3); 20(2); 21; 11:1(2); 3; 4; 11; 13(3); 14; 19; 25; 27; 12:1; 3; 19; 14:11; 14; 15:8; 9; 14; 15; 16; 17; 18; 19; 20(2); 22; 24(4); 25; 28(2); 29(3); 30; 31; 32; 16:1; 4; 17; 19(2); 22; **1 Cor** 1:4; 10; 12(5); 14(2); 15; 16(3); 19; 2:1(2); 2; 3; 3:1; 2; 4(2); 6; 10; 4:3(2); 4(2); 6; 8; 9; 14(2); 15; 16; 17(2); 18; 19(2); 21; 5:3(2); 9; 10; 11; 12; 6:5; 12; 15; 7:6; 7(2); 8(2); 10(2); 12; 17; 25(2); 26; 28; 29; 32; 35(2); 40(2); 8:13(2); 9:1(3); 2(2); 6; 8; 15(2); 16(3); 17(3); 18(3); 19(3); 20(3); 21; 22(4); 23(2); 26(2); 27(3); 10:1; 15(2); 19; 20; 29; 30(3); 33; 11:1; 2(2); 3; 17; 18(2); 22(3); 23(2); 34(2); 12:1; 3; 15(2); 16(2); 21(2); 31; 13:1(2); 2(4); 3(2); 11(6); 12(3); 14:5; 6(3); 11(2); 14; 15(4); 18(2); 19(2); 21; 37; 15:1(2); 2; 3(2); 9(2); 10(4); 11; 31(3); 32; 34; 50; 51; 16:1; 2; 3(2); 4; 5(3); 6(2); 7(2); 8; 10; 11; 12; 15; 17; **2 Cor** 1:13; 15; 17(4); 23(2); 2:1(2); 2; 3(4); 4(2); 8; 9(2); 10(3); 12; 13(3); 4:13(2); 5:11; 6:2(2); 13; 16(2); 17; 18; 7:3(2); 4(2); 7; 8(4); 9; 12(2); 14(2); 16(2); 8:3; 8(2); 10; 13; 9:2(2); 3(2); 5; 6; 10:1; 2(4); 8(2); 9; 11:2(3); 3; 5(2); 6(2); 7(2); 8; 9(5); 11; 12(3); 16(2); 17(2); 18; 21(3); 22(3); 23(2); 24; 25(4); 29(2); 30(2); 31; 33; 12:1; 2(3); 3(2); 5(2); 6(4); 7(2); 8; 9; 10(3); 11(4); 13; 14(3); 15(3); 16(2); 17(2); 18; 20(5); 21(2); 13:1; 2(5); 6; 7; 10(2); **Gal** 1:6; 9; 10(4); 11; 12(2); 13; 14; 16(2); 17(2); 18; 19; 20(2); 21; 22; 2:1; 2(3); 10; 11; 14(2); 18(3); 19(2); 20(4); 21; 3:2; 15; 17; 4:1; 11(2); 12(2); 13; 15; 16(2); 18; 19; 20(2); 5:2; 3; 10; 11(3); 12; 16; 21(2); 6:11; 14(2); 17; **Eph** 1:15(2); 3:1; 3; 7; 8; 13; 14; 4:1; 17; 5:32; 6:19; 20(3); 21; 22; **Phil** 1:3; 7; 8; 9; 12; 17; 18; 19; 20; 22(3); 23; 25(2); 27(2); 2:16(2); 17(2); 19(3); 20; 23(2); 24(2); 25; 27; 28(2); 3:4(2); 7; 8(3); 10; 11; 12(3); 13(2); 14; 18; 4:2(2); 3; 4; 10; 11(3); 12(3); 13; 15; 17(2); 18(2); **Col** 1:23; 24; 25; 29; 2:1(2); 4; 5(2); 4:3; 4(2); 8; 13; **1 Th** 2:18; 3:5(2); 4:9; 13; 5:1; 27; **2 Th** 2:5(2); 3:17; **1 Tim** 1:3(2); 12; 13(3); 15; 16; 18; 20; 2:1; 7(2); 8; 12; 3:14(2); 15(2); 4:13; 5:14; 21; 6:13; **2 Tim** 1:3(3); 4; 5(2); 6; 11; 12(5); 2:7; 9; 10; 3:11; 4:1; 6; 7(3); 12; 13; 17; 20; **Titus** 1:5(2); 3:8; 12(2); **Phm** 1:4; 8; 9; 10(2); 12; 13; 14; 19(2); 21(2); 22(2); **Heb** 1:5(2); 13; 2:12(2); 13(2); 3:10; 11; 4:3; 5:5; 6:14(2); 8:8; 9(3); 10(3); 12(2); 10:7(2); 9; 16(3); 17; 30; 11:32; 12:21; 26; 13:5; 6; 19(2); 22(2); 23; **Jas** 1:13; 2:18(2); **1 Pe** 1:16; 2:6; 11; 5:1(2); 12(2); **2 Pe** 1:12; 13(2); 14; 15; 17; 3:1(2); **1 Jn** 2:1; 4; 7; 8; 13(3); 14(2); 21; 26; 4:20; 5:13; 16; **2 Jn** 1(2); 4(2); 5(2); 12(2); **3 Jn** 1; 2; 3; 4; 9; 10(2); 13(2); 14; **Jude** 3(2); 5; **Rev** 1:8; 9; 10(2); 11; 12(2); 17(3); 18(3); 2:2; 4; 5; 6; 7; 9(2); 10; 13; 14; 15; 16; 17(2); 19; 20; 21; 22; 23(3); 24(2); 25; 26; 27; 28; 3:1; 2; 3(2); 5(2); 8(2); 9(3); 10; 11; 12(3); 15(2); 16; 17; 18; 19(2); 20(2); 21(2); 4:1(3); 2; 4; 5:1; 2; 4; 6; 11(2); 13; 6:1(2); 2; 3; 5(2); 6; 7; 8; 9; 12; 7:1; 2; 4; 9; 14; 8:2; 13(2); 9:1; 13; 16; 17; 10:1; 4(2); 5; 8; 9; 10(2); 11:1; 3; 12:10; 13:1(2); 2; 3; 11; 14:1; 2(2); 6; 13; 14; 15:1; 2; 5; 16:1; 5; 7; 13; 15; 17:1; 3; 6(3); 7; 18:1; 4; 7; 19:1; 6; 10(2); 11; 17; 19; 20:1; 4(2); 11; 12; 21:1; 2; 3; 5; 6(2); 7; 9; 22; 22:7; 8(3); 9; 12; 13; 16(2); 18; 20

IF (1637/1455)

Gen 4:7(2); 24; 8:8; 13:9(2); 16; 15:5; 18:3; 21; 26; 28; 30; 20:7; 23:8; 13; 24:8; 41; 42; 49(2); 25:22; 27:46; 28:20; 30:27; 31; 33; 31:8(2); 50(2); 32:8; 33:10; 13; 34:15(2); 17; 22; 37:14; 26; 42:19; 37; 38; 43:4; 5; 9; 10; 11; 14; 44:22; 26; 29; 32; 34; 47:6; 16; 29; 50:4; **Ex** 1:16(2); 4:8; 9; 23; 8:2; 21; 26; 9:2; 15; 10:4; 12:4; 13:13; 15:26; 18:23; 19:5; 20:25(2); 21:2; 3(2); 4; 5; 7; 8; 9; 10; 11; 13; 14; 16; 18; 19; 20; 21; 22; 23; 26; 27; 28; 29; 30; 32; 33(2); 35; 36; 22:1; 2; 3(2); 4; 5; 6; 7(2); 8; 10; 12; 13; 14; 15(2); 16; 17; 23; 25; 26; 23:4; 5; 22; 33; 24:14; 29:34; 32:32(2); 33:13; 15; 34:9; 20; 40:37; **Lev** 1:3; 10; 14; 2:4; 5; 7; 14; 3:1; 6; 7; 12; 4:2; 3; 13; 23; 27; 28; 32; 5:1(2); 2; 3; 4; 7; 11; 15; 17; 6:2(2); 3; 28; 7:12; 16; 18; 10:19; 11:37; 38(2); 39; 12:2; 5; 8; 13:3; 4; 5; 6; 7; 8; 10; 12; 13; 16; 17; 18; 20; 21; 22; 23; 24; 25; 26; 27; 28; 29; 30; 31; 32; 34; 35; 36; 37; 38; 39; 42; 43; 47; 49; 51; 53; 55; 56; 57; 58(2); 14:3; 21; 37; 39; 43; 44; 48; 15:8; 16; 19; 23; 24; 25(2); 28; 17:16; 18:5; 19:5; 6; 7; 33; 20:4; 12; 13; 14; 15; 16; 17; 18; 20; 21; 21:9; 22:9; 11; 12; 13; 14; 24:19; 25:14; 20; 25(2); 26; 28; 29; 30; 33; 35; 39; 47; 49; 51; 52; 54; 26:3; 14; 15(2); 18; 21; 23; 27; 40; 41; 27:3; 4; 5; 6; 7(2); 8; 9; 10; 11; 13; 15; 16; 17; 18; 19; 20(2); 22; 27(2); 31; 33; **Num** 5:8; 12; 14(2); 19(2); 20(2); 27; 28; 6:9; 9:10; 14; 10:4; 32; 11:15(2); 12:6; 14; 14:2(2); 8; 15; 15:14; 22; 24; 27; 16:29(2); 30; 19:12; 20:3; 19; 21:2; 9; 22:20; 33; 34; 24:13; 27:8; 9; 10; 11; 30:2; 3; 5; 6; 8; 10; 12; 14; 15; 32:5; 15; 20(2); 23; 29; 30; 33:55; 35:16; 17; 18; 20; 22; 26; 36:3; **Deut** 4:29; 5:25; 6:25; 7:17; 8:19; 11:13; 22; 27; 28; 12:21; 13:1; 6; 12; 14; 14:24(2); 15:5; 7; 12; 16; 21(2); 22; 17:2; 4; 8; 18:6; 21; 22; 19:8; 9; 11; 16; 18; 20:11; 12; 19; 21:1; 14; 15(2); 18; 22; 22:2(2); 6; 8; 13; 20; 22; 23; 25; 28; 23:10; 22; 24:3(2); 7; 12; 25:1; 2; 5; 7; 8; 11; 28:1; 9; 13; 15; 58; 30:4; 10(2); 17; 31:27; 32:41; **Josh** 2:14; 19; 20; 8:15; 17:15; 20:5; 22:18; 19; 22(2); 23(3); 23:12; 24:15; 20; **Judg** 4:8(2); 20; 6:13; 17; 31; 36; 37; 7:10; 8:19; 9:15(2); 16(2); 19; 20; 29; 36; 38; 11:9; 10; 30; 36; 12:5; 13:16; 23; 14:12; 13; 18; 15:3; 16:7; 11; 13; 17; **Ruth** 1:12(2); 17; 3:13(2); 4:4(2); **1 Sam** 1:11; 2:16(2); 25(2); 3:9; 17; 6:3; 9(2); 7:3; 9:7; 11:3; 12:14; 15; 25; 14:9; 10; 30; 16:2; 17:9(2); 19:11; 20:6; 7(2); 8; 9; 10; 13; 21; 22; 29; 21:4; 9; 23:3; 23; 24:19; 25:22; 26:19(2); 27:5; 29:4; **2 Sam** 3:9; 35; 7:14; 10:11(2); 11:20; 12:8; 13:26; 14:32; 15:8; 25; 26; 33; 34; 16:23; 17:6; 13; 18:3(2); 25; 33; 19:6; 7; 13; **1 Ki** 1:52(2); 2:4; 23; 3:14; 6:12; 8:25; 9:4(2); 6; 11:38; 12:7; 27; 13:8; 18:21(2); 19:2; 20:10; 18(2); 23; 39; 21:2; 6; 22:28; **2 Ki** 1:10; 12; 2:10(2); 4:29(2); 5:3; 13; 17; 6:27; 31; 7:2; 4(4); 9; 19; 9:15; 10:6; 15; 24; 18:21; 22; 23; 21:8; **1 Chr** 12:17(2); 13:2(2); 19:12(2); 22:13; 28:7; 9(2); **2 Chr** 6:16; 22; 24; 7:14; 17(2); 19; 10:7; 15:2(2); 18:27; 20:9; 25:8; 30:9(2); 33:8; **Ezra** 4:13; 16; 5:17; **Neh** 1:8; 9; 2:5(2); 7; 4:3; 9:29; 10:31; 13:21; **Esth** 1:19; 3:9; 4:14; 16; 5:4; 8(2); 6:13; 7:3(2); 8:5(2); 9:13; **Job** 4:2; 18(2); 8:4; 5; 6; 18; 9:3; 11(2); 12; 16; 19(2); 23; 24; 27; 29; 30; 10:14; 15(2); 16; 11:10; 13; 14; 12:14(2); 15(2); 13:10; 19; 14:7; 14; 15:15; 16:4; 6; 17:13(2); 14; 19:4; 5; 7(2); 28; 21:4; 15; 22:23; 24:17; 25; 25:5; 27:8; 14; 29:24; 30:24; 31:5(2); 7(2); 9(2); 13; 16; 19; 20(2); 21; 24; 25; 26; 29; 31; 33; 38; 39; 33:5; 23; 32; 33; 34:14(2); 16; 32; 35:3; 6(2); 7; 36:8; 11; 12; 37:20; 38:4; 18; **Ps** 7:3(2); 4; 12; 11:3; 14:2; 28:1; 40:5; 41:6; 44:20; 50:12; 53:2; 58:7; 59:15; 62:9; 10; 66:18; 73:15; 81:8; 89:30; 31; 90:10; 94:18; 95:7; 124:1; 2; 130:3; 132:12; 137:5; 6(2); 139:8(2); 9; 11; 18; 24; **Prov** 1:10; 11; 2:1; 3; 4; 3:30; 6:1(2); 30; 9:12(2); 11:31; 16:31; 19:19; 22:18; 27; 23:2; 13; 15; 24:10; 12; 14; 25:21(2); 29:9; 12; 30:4; 32(2); **Eccl** 4:10; 11; 5:8; 6:3; 6; 10:4; 10; 11:3(2); 8; **Song** 1:8; 5:8; 7:12; 8:1; 7; 9(2); **Isa** 1:19; 20; 5:18; 30; 7:9; 8:20; 10:15(3); 21:12; 36:6; 7; 8; 58:9; 10; 13; 59:10; 66:3(4); **Jer** 2:10; 28; 3:1; 4:1(2); 5:1(2); 7:5(2); 6; 12:5(2); 16; 17; 13:17; 22; 14:18(2); 15:1; 2; 19(2); 17:24; 27; 18:8; 10; 22:4; 5; 23:22; 25:28; 26:4; 15; 27:18(2); 31:36; 37; 33:20; 24; 25(2); 38:15(2); 17; 18; 21; 25; 40:4(2); 42:5; 10; 13; 15; 49:9(2); **Lam** 1:12; 2:6; **Ezek** 3:19; 21; 14:9; 14; 15; 17; 19; 16:47; 18:5; 6; 7; 8; 9; 10; 12; 13(2); 14; 21; 20:11; 13; 21; 39; 21:13; 33:3; 4; 6; 9; 10; 14; 15; 43:11; 46:16; 17; **Dan** 2:5; 6; 9; 3:15(2); 17; 18; 5:16; **Hos** 8:7; **Joel** 2:14; 3:4; **Am** 3:4; 5; 6(2); 6:9; **Ob** 5(3); **Jon** 3:9; **Mic** 2:11; 5:8; **Nah** 3:12; **Hag** 2:12; 13; **Zech** 3:7(2); 6:15; 8:6; 9:15; 10:7; 11:12(2); 13:3; 14:18; **Mal** 1:6(2); 2:2(2); 3:10; **Mt** 4:3; 6; 9; 5:13; 23; 29; 30; 40; 46; 47; 6:14; 15; 22; 23(2); 30; 7:9; 10; 11; 8:2; 31; 9:21; 10:13(2); 25; 11:14; 21; 23; 12:7; 11; 26; 27; 28; 14:28; 15:14; 16:24; 26; 17:4; 20; 18:6; 8; 9; 12; 13; 15(2); 16; 17(2); 19; 35; 19:10; 17; 21; 21:3; 21(2); 24; 25; 26; 22:24; 45; 23:30; 24:23; 24; 26; 43; 48; 26:15; 24; 33; 35; 39; 42; 63; 27:40; 42; 43; 49; 28:14; **Mk** 1:40; 3:24; 25; 26; 4:23; 26; 5:28; 7:11; 16; 8:3; 23; 36; 9:22; 23; 35; 42; 43; 45; 47; 50; 10:12; 11:3; 13; 25; 26; 31; 32; 12:19; 13:21; 22; 14:21; 29; 31; 35; 15:36; 44; 16:18; **Lk** 4:3; 7; 9; 5:12; 6:32; 33; 34; 7:39; 9:23; 25; 10:6(2); 13; 11:11(2); 12; 13; 18; 19; 20; 36; 12:26; 28; 38; 39; 45; 13:9(2); 14:26; 34; 15:4; 8; 16:11; 12; 30; 31; 17:2; 3(2); 4; 6; 19:8; 31; 40; 42; 20:5; 6; 28; 22:42; 67(2); 68; 23:6; 31; 35; 37; 39; **Jn** 1:25; 3:12(2); 4:10; 5:31; 43; 46; 47; 6:51; 62; 7:4; 17; 23; 37; 8:14; 16; 19; 24; 31; 36; 39; 42; 46; 51; 52; 54; 55; 9:22; 31; 33; 41; 10:9; 24; 35; 37; 38; 11:9; 10; 12; 21; 32; 40; 48; 57; 12:24; 26(2); 32; 47; 13:8; 14; 17(2); 32; 35; 14:2; 3; 7; 14; 15; 23; 28; 15:6; 7; 10; 14; 18; 19; 20(2); 22; 24; 16:7(2); 18:8; 23(2); 30; 36; 19:12; 20:15; 23(2); 21:22; 23; 25; **Acts** 4:9; 5:38; 39; 8:22; 37; 9:2; 11:17; 13:15; 15:29; 16:15; 18:14; 15; 19:38; 39; 20:16; 23:9; 24:19; 20; 25:5; 11(2); 26:5; 32; 27:12; 39; **Rom** 1:10; 2:25(2); 26; 27; 3:3; 5; 7; 4:2; 14; 5:10; 15; 17; 6:5; 8; 7:2; 3(2); 16; 20; 8:9(2); 10; 11; 13(2); 17(2); 25; 31; 9:22; 10:9; 11:6(2); 12; 14; 15; 16(2); 17; 18; 21; 22; 23; 24; 12:6; 18; 20(2); 13:4; 9; 14:8(2); 15; 23; 15:24; 27; **1 Cor** 3:12; 14; 15; 17; 18; 4:7(2); 19; 6:2; 4; 7:8; 9; 11; 12; 13; 15; 21; 28(2); 36(2); 39; 40; 8:2; 3; 5; 8(2); 10; 13; 9:2; 11(2); 12; 16(2); 17(2); 10:27; 28; 30; 11:5; 6(2); 14; 15; 16; 31; 34; 12:15; 16; 17(2); 19; 26(2); 14:6; 8; 11; 14; 16; 23; 24; 27; 28; 30; 35; 37; 38; 15:2; 12; 13; 14; 15; 16; 17; 19; 29; 32(2); 16:4; 7; 10; 22; **2 Cor** 1:6(2); 2:2; 5; 10; 3:7; 9; 11; 4:3; 5:1; 3; 13(2); 14; 17; 7:8; 14; 8:12; 23(2); 9:4; 10:2; 7; 8; 11:4(2); 15; 16; 20(5); 30; 13:2(2); **Gal** 1:8; 9; 10; 2:14; 17; 18; 21; 3:4; 15; 18; 21; 29; 4:7; 15; 5:2; 11; 15; 18; 25; 6:1; 3; 9; **Eph** 3:2; 4:21; **Phil** 1:22; 2:1(4); 17; 3:4; 11; 15; 4:8(2); **Col** 1:23; 2:20; 3:1; 13; 4:10; **1 Th** 3:8; 4:14; **2 Th** 2:2; 3:10; 14; **1 Tim** 1:8; 10; 2:15; 3:1; 5; 15; 4:4; 6; 5:4; 8; 10(5); 16; 6:3; **2 Tim** 2:5; 11; 12(2); 13; 21; 25; **Titus** 1:6; **Phm** 1:17; 18; **Heb** 2:2; 3; 3:6; 7; 14; 15; 4:7; 8; 6:3; 6; 8; 7:11; 15; 8:4; 7; 9:13; 10:26; 38; 11:15; 12:7; 8; 20; 25(2); 13:3; 23; **Jas** 1:5; 23; 26; 2:2; 8; 9; 11; 14; 15; 17; 3:2; 14; 4:11; 15; 5:15; 19; **1 Pe** 1:6; 17; 2:3; 19; 20(2); 3:1; 6; 13; 14; 17; 4:11(2); 14; 16; 17; 18; **2 Pe** 1:8; 10; 2:4; 20; **1 Jn** 1:6; 7; 8; 9; 10; 2:1; 3; 15; 19; 24; 29; 3:13; 20; 21; 4:11; 12; 20; 5:9; 14; 15; 16; **2 Jn** 10; **3 Jn** 6; 10; **Rev** 1:15; 3:3; 20; 11:5(2); 13:3; 9; 14:9; 22:18; 19

IN (12234/9398)

Gen 1:1; 6; 11; 12; 14; 15; 17; 22; 26; 27(2); 30; 2:3; 4; 5; 8; 9; 15; 17; 21; 3:3; 5; 8(2); 10; 16; 17; 19; 4:3; 8; 16; 20; 22; 5:1(2); 2; 3; 6:4(2); 5; 6; 8; 9; 14; 16; 17; 7:1; 11(2); 15; 16(2); 22; 23; 8:1; 4; 5; 11(2); 13(2); 14; 21; 9:6; 7(2); 13; 14; 16; 21; 27; 10:10; 20(2); 25; 31; 32; 11:2; 4; 28(2); 32; 12:3; 5; 6; 10(2); 13:2(3); 7; 12(2); 17; 18; 14:1; 3; 4; 5(4); 6; 7; 8(2); 12; 14(2); 15:1; 3; 6; 10(2); 13; 15; 16; 16:2; 3; 4(2); 5; 6; 7; 12; 17:7; 8; 11; 12(2); 13(2); 14; 17; 23; 24; 25; 27; 18:1(2); 3; 9; 10; 11; 18; 19; 24; 26; 19:1(2); 2(2); 3; 9; 12; 15; 17; 19; 21; 27; 29; 30(3); 31; 33; 34; 20:1; 3; 5; 6(2); 8(2); 10; 11; 13; 21:2; 7; 11; 12(2); 14(2); 15; 20; 21; 22; 23; 33; 34; 22:3; 6; 9; 13; 14; 18; 23:2(2); 6; 10; 11(2); 13; 16; 17(3); 18(2); 19(2); 20; 24:1(2); 10; 23; 31; 37; 42; 45; 48; 54; 62; 63(2); 65; 25:8; 9(2); 18; 23; 24; 27; 29; 26:1(3); 2; 3; 4; 6; 12(2); 15; 17; 18; 19; 22; 29; 31(2); 27:7; 15; 30; 41; 43; 45; 28:4; 9; 11; 14(2); 16; 18; 20; 21; 29:2; 3; 21; 23(2); 25; 26; 30; 30:2; 3; 4; 14(2); 16(2); 27; 33; 35; 37(2); 38(2); 40; 41; 42; 31:10; 11; 14; 18(2); 20; 23; 24; 25(2); 28; 29; 32; 34; 40; 41; 55; 32:3; 5; 17; 19; 21; 32; 33:2; 8; 10; 14; 15; 18; 34:5; 7(2); 10(2); 11; 19; 21(2); 25; 28(2); 29; 30; 35:3(2); 4(2); 6; 13; 14; 16; 17; 22; 26; 36:5; 6; 8; 9; 16; 17; 21; 24; 30; 31; 32; 33; 34; 35(2); 36; 37; 38; 39; 43; 37:1(2); 7; 11; 12; 13; 15; 17; 22; 24; 29; 31; 35; 36; 38:2; 7; 8; 9; 11(2); 12; 14; 16(2); 18(2); 21; 22; 27; 39:2; 3; 4; 5(2); 6(2); 8; 9; 12; 13; 14(2); 17; 20; 21; 22; 40:3(3); 4; 5(2); 6(2); 7; 9; 10; 11(2); 13; 16; 17; 21; 41:2; 8; 10(2); 11; 16; 17; 18; 19; 22; 30; 31; 34; 35; 36; 37(2); 38; 40; 42; 43; 44; 47; 48(3); 52; 53; 54(2); 56; 57(2); 42:1; 2; 3; 5; 13(2); 15; 16(2); 17; 27; 28; 29; 32; 34; 35; 37; 38; 43:1; 11; 12(3); 15; 18(2); 21(3); 22(2); 23; 26; 28; 33; 44:1; 2; 5; 8; 12; 17(2); 18; 30; 45:3; 6(2); 7; 10; 13; 16; 46:2; 5; 6; 12; 15; 20; 22; 25; 26; 27; 31; 34; 47:1; 4(3); 6(2); 7; 9; 11(3); 12; 13; 14(2); 15(3); 17(2); 18; 24; 25; 27(2); 28; 29(2); 30; 48:3; 5(2); 6; 7; 9; 11; 16; 49:1; 5; 6(2); 7(2); 11(2);

24; 27; 29(2); 30(3); 50:4(2); 5(2); 8; 13; 19; 20; 22; 26(2); **Ex** 1:5; 10; 12; 14(5); 2:3(2); 11; 12; 15; 22; 23; 3:2; 7; 16; 20; 21; 4:2; 4; 6(2); 7(2); 14; 15; 17; 18(2); 19; 20; 21; 30; 5:1(2); 9; 14; 16; 19; 21(3); 23; 6:4; 5; 11; 28; 7:3; 10; 11; 15(2); 16; 17(2); 18; 19; 20(4); 21; 8:9; 11; 14; 20; 22(4); 25; 28; 29; 9:1; 3; 5; 8; 9(2); 10; 13; 14; 16(2); 17; 18; 19(2); 21; 22; 24; 25; 26; 31(2); 10:1; 2(2); 3; 16; 19; 22; 23; 28; 11:2; 3(4); 5; 8; 9; 12:1; 8; 9; 11(2); 12; 18; 19; 20; 22(3); 27; 29(2); 30(2); 33; 34; 36; 40; 46; 13:3; 4; 5; 7; 8; 9; 10; 14; 15; 18; 20; 21(2); 14:3; 11(2); 12(2); 24; 27; 29; 31; 15:4; 6(2); 7; 8; 10; 11(2); 13(2); 17(3); 19; 20; 22; 26; 16:2; 3; 4; 5; 7; 8(2); 10; 12; 13; 16; 24; 25; 29; 32; 33; 17:1; 5; 6(2); 8; 9; 14(2); 18:3; 5; 11(2); 20; 23; 19:1; 2; 9; 11; 16(2); 18(2); 20:4(3); 7(2); 10; 11(2); 24; 21:2; 3(2); 13; 16; 29; 33; 36; 22:2; 4; 5; 6; 12; 21; 23; 27; 31; 23:2; 3; 6; 9; 10; 11; 13; 14; 15(2); 16(2); 17; 19; 20; 21; 23; 26; 29; 33; 24:4; 6; 7; 10; 17; 25:7(2); 12; 15; 21; 22; 37; 26:5; 10; 17; 33; 34; 27:7; 21; 28:10; 11(2); 17; 20; 24; 25; 30(2); 32(2); 38; 43; 29:3(2); 17; 24(2); 29(2); 30(2); 31; 32; 39; 41; 30:18; 19; 36; 31:3(4); 4(3); 5(3); 6; 17; 32:2; 3; 12; 15; 17; 20; 26; 27; 34; 33:3; 5; 10; 12; 13(2); 16; 17; 22; 34:2(2); 4(2); 5; 6; 9; 10(2); 12; 18(2); 21(2); 23; 24; 26; 29; 34; 35; 35:9(2); 19; 27(2); 31(2); 32; 33(3); 34(2); 35; 36:1; 2; 17; 37:3; 38:24; 26; 39:1; 3; 6; 10; 13(2); 17; 18(2); 23(2); 26; 37; 41; 40:3; 4(3); 7; 9; 17; 18; 22; 23; 24; 26(2); 36; 38; **Lev** 1:7; 8; 12; 2:4; 5; 6; 7; 11; 3:17; 4:2; 6(2); 7; 13; 17(2); 18; 22; 27; 5:1; 4; 5(2); 13; 15(2); 16; 18; 6:3(2); 7; 12; 16(2); 18; 20; 21(2); 22; 25; 26(2); 27; 28(3); 30(2); 7:2; 6; 9(3); 24; 26; 38; 8:8; 10; 21; 27(2); 31; 9:9; 10:1; 13; 14; 17; 18; 19; 11:9(4); 10(4); 12; 32(2); 33; 34; 36; 46; 12:4; 4; 5(2); 13:10; 18; 19; 21; 23; 25; 26; 28; 30; 31; 32; 37; 47; 48(3); 49(5); 51(5); 52(4); 53(4); 54; 55; 57(5); 59(3); 14:3; 5; 6; 7; 8; 9; 13(2); 16(2); 17; 18; 27; 28; 29; 34(2); 35; 36(2); 37; 40; 41; 42; 43; 44(2); 47(2); 48(2); 50; 51(2); 53; 15:3; 5; 6; 7; 8; 10; 11(2); 12; 13; 16; 18; 21; 22; 27; 31; 16:2; 4; 16; 17(3); 22; 24; 26; 27(3); 28; 29; 32; 17:3; 5; 11; 15; 18:3; 4; 19; 19:6; 15(2); 17; 24; 25; 28; 33; 34; 35(2); 20:2; 4; 17; 23; 21:5; 13; 17; 20; 22:11; 13; 18; 21; 24; 25(2); 23:3; 14; 21; 24; 29; 31; 39; 41(3); 42(2); 43; 24:3(3); 4; 5; 6(2); 8; 9; 10; 12; 16; 25:4; 7; 11; 13; 18(2); 19; 20(2); 21; 22(2); 24; 28(2); 29; 30(2); 31; 32; 33(3); 45; 49; 53; 54(2); 26:1; 3; 4; 5; 6; 16; 20; 22; 26; 28; 32; 34; 35; 36; 39(3); 40; 44; 45; 27:21; 24; **Num** 1:1(3); 3; 16; 19; 45; 2:17(2); 3:4(2); 13(2); 14; 25; 47; 4:3; 4; 10; 12(2); 15; 16; 19(2); 20; 23; 24; 28; 35; 37; 39; 41; 43; 47; 5:3; 6; 7; 8; 17; 18(2); 23; 6:11; 12; 14(2); 7:5; 15; 17; 21; 23; 27; 29; 33; 35; 39; 41; 45; 47; 51; 53; 57; 59; 63; 65; 69; 71; 75; 77; 81; 83; 87; 88; 8:2; 15; 17; 19; 22(2); 24; 26; 9:1(2); 5; 17; 21; 10:9; 10(2); 11; 12; 31; 11:1; 5; 8(2); 9; 11; 12; 15; 18(2); 25; 26(2); 27; 12:5(2); 6(2); 7; 8; 11(2); 14; 15; 16; 13:18; 19; 22; 26; 28; 29(2); 32; 33(2); 14:2(2); 8; 10; 14(2); 16; 18; 22(2); 24; 25; 28; 29; 30; 31; 32; 33(2); 34; 35; 40; 45; 15:3; 13(2); 27; 32; 38; 16:7(2); 13; 17; 18; 21; 26; 45; 46; 47; 49(2); 17:4; 7; 18:10; 11; 13(2); 14; 20; 21(2); 31(2); 19:2; 4; 5; 7; 8(2); 9; 14(2); 16; 17; 18; 19; 20:1(2); 12; 15; 16; 23; 27; 21:1; 5; 10; 11; 12; 13; 14(2); 20(2); 23; 25(3); 27; 31; 22:1; 5; 7; 13; 21; 22; 23(2); 24; 26; 29; 31(2); 34; 38; 23:5; 12; 16; 21(2); 24:7; 11; 14; 21; 25:1; 4; 6(2); 7; 9; 11; 15; 18(3); 26:2; 3; 9; 19; 59; 63; 64; 65; 27:3(4); 11; 14(2); 17(2); 18; 19; 21; 28:3; 4(2); 7; 8; 9; 11; 19; 24; 27; 29:1; 2; 8; 13; 17; 20; 23; 26; 29; 32; 36; 30:3(2); 10; 16(2); 31:6; 12; 16; 27; 35; 36; 32:5; 13(2); 14; 15; 17; 26; 30; 39; 40; 33:3(2); 8; 11; 15; 36; 38; 40(2); 47; 48; 49; 50; 53; 55(3); 34:29; 35:1; 2; 3; 5; 8; 12; 14; 17; 20; 21; 22; 28; 29; 32; 34; 36:8; 12; 13; **Deut** 1:1(2); 3(2); 4(2); 5; 6; 7(4); 8; 10; 17(2); 25; 27; 30; 31(2); 33(3); 37; 38; 39; 44; 46; 2:4; 7; 8; 9; 10; 12(2); 21; 22(2); 23(2); 24; 25; 29(2); 36; 3:4; 10; 11; 19; 24; 29; 4:1; 5; 6; 8; 10; 14; 16; 17; 18; 22; 23; 25(3); 26; 27; 30(2); 34; 38; 39(2); 40; 42; 43(3); 46(2); 5:1; 2; 8(3); 11(2); 14; 15; 16; 22; 28; 29; 31; 33(2); 6:1; 6; 7; 13; 16; 18(2); 20; 21; 23; 7:7; 13; 17; 8:1; 2(2); 5; 6; 9(2); 12; 15; 16(2); 17; 9:1; 4(2); 5; 7; 8; 10; 15; 18(2); 28; 10:2; 3; 4(2); 5; 6; 8; 10; 11; 12; 14; 15; 19; 20; 22; 11:3; 5; 6(2); 8; 9; 14(2); 15; 18(2); 19; 21; 22; 30(2); 31(2); 12:1; 7(2); 8; 10(2); 13; 14(2); 18(2); 19; 25; 28; 29; 31(2); 13:5(2); 12(2); 15; 17; 18; 14:9; 21; 23; 25; 29; 15:4; 7; 9; 10(2); 11; 12; 15; 18(2); 20; 21; 16:1; 2; 3(2); 4; 7(2); 12; 14; 15(3); 16; 18; 17:2(2); 4; 9; 10; 11; 14; 18; 20(2); 18:5; 7; 16(2); 18; 19; 20(2); 21; 22; 19:1(2); 2; 4; 6; 9; 10; 11; 14(2); 17(2); 20:5; 6; 7; 11; 13; 14; 19; 21:1(2); 4; 5; 6; 9; 13(2); 14; 16; 22:6; 13; 21(2); 23; 24; 25; 26; 27; 23:7; 10; 14; 16(2); 20(2); 24; 24:1(3); 3; 6(2); 8; 13(2); 14; 18; 19(3); 22; 25:2; 3; 5; 7; 9(2); 10; 13; 14; 15; 19; 26:1; 2; 3; 5; 11; 12; 14; 17; 19(3); 27:15; 28:3(2); 6; 8(3); 9; 11(4); 12; 16(2); 19; 20(2); 29(2); 30; 32; 35; 38; 48(4); 52; 53(2); 55(2); 57(2); 58; 61; 62(2); 66; 67; 68; 29:1(2); 2; 5; 9; 11; 16; 19; 20; 21; 23; 27; 28(3); 30:9(4); 10; 12; 14(2); 16(3); 18(2); 20; 31:2; 7; 10; 11(2); 13; 14(2); 15; 17(2); 18(2); 19; 21; 24; 28; 29(2); 30; 32:10(2); 13; 20; 26; 28; 34; 35; 37; 44; 47; 49; 51(2); 33:3; 5; 12; 16; 18(2); 19; 24; 26; 28(2); 34:5; 6(2); 8; 10; 11(3); 12; **Josh** 1:8(2); 11; 14; 17; 18; 2:6; 11(2); 18; 19; 21; 3:1; 7; 8; 13; 15; 16; 17; 4:3; 6; 9(2); 10; 11; 14; 19; 20; 21; 5:1; 4; 5; 6; 7; 8(2); 10; 13; 6:1; 11; 12; 15; 17(2); 21; 23; 24; 25; 7:13; 14; 15; 16; 21(2); 22; 8:4; 9; 10; 12; 16; 17; 18(2); 19; 22; 24(2); 30; 31; 32; 33(2); 34; 9:1(3); 9; 25; 27; 10:6; 12(3); 13(2); 16; 17; 21; 28; 30(2); 32; 35; 37(2); 39; 11:2(4); 3(4); 4; 11; 17; 19; 20; 22(4); 12:2; 7; 8(6); 22; 23; 13:1(2); 9; 10; 12(2); 16; 17; 21(2); 27; 30; 31; 32; 14:1; 4(2); 6(2); 7; 10; 11; 12(2); 15:19; 21; 33; 48; 61; 16:10; 17:11(2); 12; 15; 16; 18:5(2); 6; 8; 9(3); 10; 16; 19:2; 9; 14; 33; 47; 50(2); 51; 20:4; 6(2); 7(4); 8(3); 21:2(2); 6; 11; 21; 27; 32; 38; 39; 43; 22:2; 5; 7; 9; 10; 11; 16; 17; 20(2); 22(2); 24(2); 25; 27(2); 28; 33; 23:1; 2; 6; 12; 13; 14(2); 24:2; 7(2); 13; 14(3); 15; 17(2); 18; 25; 26; 30; 32; 33(2); **Judg** 1:5; 9(3); 10; 15; 16; 21; 27; 29(2); 35(3); 2:3; 9; 11; 17(2); 22; 3:1; 3; 7; 12(2); 16; 20; 22; 24; 27; 4:1; 2(2); 5; 6; 9; 14; 21; 22; 23; 5:2; 6(2); 7(2); 8(2); 10; 11; 14; 19; 21; 24; 25; 28; 31; 6:1; 2; 5;

10; 11(3); 14; 15(2); 17; 19(3); 21; 24; 26; 28; 33; 7:1; 3; 8(2); 11; 12(2); 19; 20(2); 21; 8:2; 3; 4; 6; 8; 9; 11; 15; 27; 28; 29; 31; 32(2); 35; 9:2; 3; 6; 15(2); 16(2); 19(3); 24; 25; 26; 32(2); 33; 34(2); 35(2); 41; 43(2); 44; 45; 48; 51(2); 10:1(2); 2; 4; 5; 6; 8(2); 14; 17(2); 11:2; 3; 7; 11; 12; 17(2); 20; 26(3); 31; 39; 12:2; 3; 7; 9(2); 12; 15(3); 13:1; 9; 10; 20; 14:1; 2; 6; 8; 9; 15; 15:1(3); 8; 9; 19(2); 20; 16:1; 2(2); 4; 9(2); 12(2); 18; 21; 30(2); 31; 17:2; 4; 6(3); 7; 8; 9; 10; 12; 18:1(4); 3; 6; 7(2); 12(2); 14; 19; 21; 22; 28; 31; 19:1(4); 2; 5; 8; 11; 13(2); 15(4); 16(3); 17; 18(2); 20; 27; 20:2; 6(2); 10(2); 13; 19; 20; 22; 27; 28; 29; 30; 31(2); 33(3); 36; 37(2); 38; 39(2); 40(2); 42(2); 21:3(2); 8; 12; 15; 19(2); 20(2); 22; 23; 25(3); **Ruth** 1:1(3); 6; 9; 11; 2:2; 3; 5; 6; 7; 8; 10; 13; 14; 17; 22; 3:2; 4; 10; 13; 4:4; 7(3); 11(2); 13; 14; **1 Sam** 1:3; 9; 10(2); 13; 17; 18; 19; 20; 24; 2:1(3); 9; 10; 13; 14; 26(2); 27(2); 29; 31; 32(2); 33; 34; 35(2); 36(2); 3:1; 2; 3; 9; 11; 12; 21(2); 4:1; 2(2); 6; 8; 5:3(2); 5; 6:1; 8; 13; 15; 18; 7:2; 16; 8:2; 3; 5; 7; 18(2); 21; 9:6; 7; 9; 15; 18; 19; 22; 10:2; 25; 11:4; 7; 8; 11(2); 13; 15; 12:1; 5; 8; 11; 17(2); 23; 24; 13:2(3); 3; 5(2); 6(6); 7; 16(2); 17; 22; 14:2(2); 3; 7; 9; 15(2); 16; 19; 22(2); 27(2); 39; 43; 45; 15:4; 5(2); 12; 14; 17; 19; 21; 22(2); 33(2); 16:12; 13; 18(2); 22; 17:1; 2(2); 12(2); 19; 20; 21; 22; 25; 27; 28; 40(4); 45; 46; 49(2); 50; 54; 57; 18:5(2); 10; 13; 14; 16; 18; 22; 23; 24; 27; 19:1; 2; 3; 5; 7(2); 9(2); 11; 13; 15; 16(2); 18; 19; 22; 23(2); 24; 20:1; 3; 5; 8; 13; 24; 29(2); 34; 35; 42(2); 21:3; 5(2); 6(2); 9(2); 11; 13; 15; 22:2(2); 4; 5; 6(3); 8; 11; 13(2); 14; 15; 23:3; 6; 7; 14(4); 15(2); 16(2); 18; 19(3); 23; 24(2); 25(2); 29; 24:1; 3(2); 10; 11(3); 20; 25:1; 2(3); 3; 4; 5; 6; 7; 8; 9; 15; 21(2); 24; 28; 29; 35; 36; 37; 42; 26:1; 2; 3(2); 6; 7; 15(2); 18; 19; 20; 21; 24(2); 27:1(2); 5(4); 7; 11; 28:1; 3(2); 7; 20; 21; 24; 29:1; 2(2); 3; 4; 5; 6(4); 7; 8; 9; 10(2); 11; 30:6; 11; 14; 24; 27(3); 28(3); 29(3); 30(3); 31; 31:7; 9; 10; **2 Sam** 1:1; 9; 18; 20(2); 23(2); 24; 25(2); 2:3; 11; 16(2); 19; 23; 26; 32(2); 3:2; 5; 7; 17; 19(3); 21; 22(2); 23; 25; 27(2); 29; 30; 32; 38; 4:1; 4; 6; 7; 10; 11; 12(3); 5:2(2); 5(2); 6(2); 9; 14; 18; 22; 23; 24; 6:11; 16; 17(2); 18; 20; 22(2); 7:1; 2; 3; 5; 6(3); 10; 18; 19; 27; 8:6; 13; 14; 9:3; 4(2); 10; 12; 13(2); 10:1; 4; 8(2); 9; 10; 12; 17; 11:1; 11(2); 12; 14; 15(2); 21; 23; 12:1; 3; 9; 11; 16; 24; 30; 31; 13:5; 6; 8; 10; 12; 13; 20; 23; 14:3(2); 6; 13; 17; 19(2); 20; 22(2); 25(2); 28; 32; 15:4; 6; 8; 9; 10; 12; 20; 21(2); 25; 26; 27; 28; 16:2; 3; 4; 8(2); 19(3); 21; 22(2); 23; 17:6; 8(2); 9(2); 11; 12; 16; 18(2); 23(2); 25; 26; 29; 18:3; 6; 9; 10; 12(2); 14(2); 17; 18(3); 25; 33; 19:3; 6; 8(2); 9; 10; 13; 22; 24; 27; 30; 33; 37; 43; 20:1(2); 3(3); 8(3); 9; 10(2); 12(2); 15; 18; 19(2); 22; 24; 21:1; 2; 4; 5; 6; 9(3); 12; 14(3); 20; 22; 22:3; 7; 19; 20; 25; 31; 43; 23:3; 5; 7; 12; 13; 14(2); 17; 20; 21; 39; 24:5(2); 9; 10; 11; 13(2); 14; **1 Ki** 1:1; 2; 14; 19; 22; 23; 25; 30; 35; 41; 42; 45; 52; 2:3(3); 4; 5; 6; 8; 10; 11(2); 34(2); 35(2); 36; 38; 39; 46; 3:3; 5; 6(3); 7; 8; 14; 17(2); 18(2); 19; 20(3); 21(2); 25; 28; 4:8; 9; 10; 11; 12; 13(3); 14; 15; 16; 17; 18; 19(3); 20; 27(2); 31; 5:1; 5; 9; 14(3); 15; 16; 6:1(3); 3; 7; 12(2); 17; 27; 37(2); 38(4); 7:4(2); 5; 6(2); 14; 19(2); 20; 22; 24; 31(2); 46(2); 49; 51(2); 8:1; 2; 4; 6; 8; 9; 12; 13; 16; 17; 18(2); 21; 22; 23; 30; 31; 32; 33; 34; 36(2); 37(2); 39; 40; 43; 45; 47(2); 48; 49; 58; 61; 64; 9:4(2); 11; 16; 18(2); 19(3); 21; 26; 10:2; 5; 6; 9; 10; 17; 21; 23; 24; 26(2); 27(2); 28; 11:2; 6; 12; 14; 15(2); 16; 19; 20(2); 21; 24; 29; 33(2); 36; 38(2); 40; 41; 42; 43(2); 12:2(2); 16(2); 17; 18(2); 19; 25; 26; 27; 29(2); 32; 33(2); 13:4; 8(2); 11(2); 16(2); 19; 22; 25; 30; 31; 32(2); 14:5; 6; 8; 10; 11(2); 13(2); 15; 19; 20; 21(2); 22; 24; 25; 27; 29; 31(2); 15:1; 2; 3; 4; 5(2); 7; 8(2); 9; 10; 11; 17; 18(2); 21; 23(3); 24(2); 25; 26(3); 28(2); 31; 33(2); 34(3); 16:2; 4(2); 5; 6(2); 7(3); 8(2); 9(3); 10(3); 13; 14; 15(2); 16; 19(5); 20; 23(2); 25; 26(2); 27; 28(2); 29(2); 30; 31; 32(2); 34; 17:6(2); 7; 10; 11; 12(3); 17; 24; 18:1; 2; 3; 18; 23; 32; 33(2); 36; 38; 45; 19:8; 9; 11(3); 12; 13(2); 16; 18; 20:6(2); 14; 22; 23; 24; 25; 26; 29; 34(2); 21:1; 2; 8(2); 9; 11; 13(2); 18(2); 19; 20; 21; 24(2); 25; 26; 27; 29(2); 22:2; 3; 16; 17; 20(2); 22(2); 23; 27(2); 28; 35; 37; 38; 39; 40; 41; 42; 43(2); 45; 46; 47; 49; 50(2); 51(2); 52(4); **2 Ki** 1:2; 3; 6; 13; 14; 16; 17(2); 18; 2:18; 20; 21; 24; 3:1; 2; 3; 18; 20; 22; 27; 4:2(2); 4; 8; 10; 11; 15; 27; 29; 33; 35; 36; 37; 38; 40; 41; 42; 5:1; 3; 4; 8; 10; 12(2); 14; 15(2); 18(4); 19; 23; 24; 25; 6:6; 8; 12(2); 13; 25; 32; 7:2(2); 4; 12(2); 13(2); 14; 15; 17; 18; 19(2); 20; 8:2; 8; 11; 15(2); 16; 17; 18(2); 20; 22; 23; 24(2); 25; 26; 27(2); 29; 9:1; 2; 8; 15; 16; 17; 21; 24; 26; 27; 28(3); 29; 34; 37; 10:1; 5(3); 7; 8; 9; 11; 16; 17; 22; 24; 25; 30(3); 31; 32(2); 34; 35(2); 36; 11:2; 3; 4(2); 8(2); 10; 11; 13; 15; 18; 20; 12:1(2); 2(2); 4; 9; 10(3); 18(2); 19; 20; 21(2); 13:1(2); 2; 5; 6(2); 8; 9(2); 10(2); 11(2); 12; 13; 20; 21; 24; 14:1; 2; 3; 5; 6(2); 7; 8; 9(3); 10; 14(2); 15; 16(2); 18; 19; 20; 23(2); 24; 28; 29; 15:1; 2; 3; 5; 6; 7(2); 8(2); 9; 10(2); 11; 13(2); 14(2); 15; 17(2); 18; 20; 21; 22; 23(2); 24; 25(3); 26; 27(2); 28; 29; 30(2); 31; 32; 33; 34; 36; 37; 38(2); 16:1; 2(2); 3; 8(2); 18; 19; 20(2); 17:1(2); 2; 4; 6(3); 8; 9; 14; 17; 19; 22; 24(2); 26; 28; 29(2); 31; 32; 18:1; 2; 3; 4; 5; 9; 10; 11(2); 13; 15(2); 19; 20; 21(2); 22(2); 24; 26(3); 28; 30; 19:7; 10; 12; 27; 28(2); 29(2); 35(2); 37(2); 20:1(2); 3(2); 13(2); 15(2); 17; 18; 19; 20; 21; 21:1; 2; 4(2); 5; 6; 7(3); 15; 16(2); 17; 18(3); 19; 20; 21; 22; 23; 24; 25; 26(3); 22:1; 2(2); 3; 5(2); 8; 9; 14(2); 18; 20; 23:2(2); 3; 4; 5(2); 7; 9; 10; 11; 12; 14; 19(2); 21; 22; 23(2); 24(4); 28; 29; 30(3); 31; 32; 33(3); 34; 36; 37; 24:1; 5; 6; 8; 9; 12; 13(2); 17; 18; 19; 20; 25:1(2); 3; 5; 8; 11; 13(3); 19(2); 21; 22; 24; 25; 27(3); 28; **1 Chr** 1:19; 43; 44; 45; 46(2); 47; 48; 49; 50; 2:3; 6; 7; 21; 22; 24; 3:1; 4(2); 5; 8; 20; 22; 23; 24; 4:9; 22; 38; 41(2); 5:8; 9; 10(2); 11; 12; 13; 16(4); 17(2); 18; 20(2); 22; 23; 6:10(2); 31; 32(2); 54; 55; 62; 67; 71; 76; 78; 80; 7:1; 2(2); 5; 6; 7; 21; 23; 29; 8:8; 28; 32; 40; 9:1; 2(2); 3; 9; 16; 19; 20; 22; 23; 25; 26; 27; 28(2); 31; 32; 33(2); 38; 10:7(2); 9; 10(2); 11:2(2); 5; 7; 10; 14; 15; 16(2); 19; 22; 23; 12:1; 2; 8; 15(2); 17; 21; 33; 40; 13:2(2); 4; 5; 14; 14:3; 4; 14; 15; 15:1; 22; 29; 16:1; 2; 10; 14; 19(2); 27; 29; 32; 35; 40; 17:1(2); 2; 4; 5; 9; 14(2); 16; 17; 19; 25; 18:6; 12; 13; 19:1; 2; 4; 9(2); 10; 11; 13; 17(2); 20:1; 2(2); 3; 8; 21:3; 12; 13; 16(2); 19; 23; 29(2); 22:2; 3(2); 4; 7; 8; 9; 15; 23:8; 9;

12; 13; 23; 25; 28(4); 29; 32; 24:31; 25:5; 6; 7; 26:12; 27; 30; 31; 27:1(2); 2; 4; 5; 6; 7; 8; 9; 10; 11; 12; 13; 14; 15; 21; 24; 25(4); 28; 29(2); 28:2; 8(2); 13; 14(2); 19; 29:2; 11(2); 12(2); 17(2); 18; 21; 25(2); 27(2); 28(2); 29(3); **2 Chr** 1:1; 2; 3; 8; 9; 10; 11; 14(2); 15(2); 16; 2:2; 3; 7(4); 8; 9; 11; 14; 16; 17(2); 18; 3:2; 4; 10; 11; 15; 16; 4:3; 6(3); 7; 8; 17(2); 18; 20(2); 5:1(2); 2; 3; 5; 7; 9; 10; 12; 13; 6:1; 2; 5; 7; 8(3); 11; 12; 13; 14; 16; 22; 24; 27(2); 28(2); 31(2); 32; 37(2); 38; 40; 41; 7:7; 11(2); 15; 18; 8:1; 4(2); 6(3); 8; 11; 17; 9:1(2); 4; 5; 8; 9; 11; 16; 20; 22; 23; 25; 27(2); 29(3); 30; 31(2); 10:2; 16(2); 17; 18(2); 19; 11:3; 5(2); 10; 11; 12; 13; 17; 23; 12:2; 5(2); 10; 12; 13(2); 15; 16(2); 13:1; 2; 3(2); 4; 8; 11; 13; 20; 22; 14:1(3); 2; 6(2); 10(2); 11; 14; 15; 15:4; 5(2); 8; 9; 10(2); 16:1(2); 2; 9; 10; 11; 12(3); 13; 14(4); 17:1; 2(3); 3; 4; 5(2); 6; 7(2); 9; 12; 13(2); 19; 18:1; 2(2); 3; 9; 15; 16; 19(2); 20; 21; 22; 26(2); 27; 34; 19:1; 3(2); 5; 6; 8; 9; 10; 11; 20:2; 5(2); 6(2); 8(2); 9(3); 14; 17; 20(2); 26; 27; 31; 32(2); 34(2); 36; 21:1(2); 3; 5; 6(2); 8; 10; 11; 12(2); 13; 17; 18; 19(2); 20(3); 22:1; 2; 3; 4; 6; 9; 11; 12; 23:1; 3; 5; 6; 7(2); 9; 10; 12; 13; 14; 17; 18(2); 19; 24:1; 2; 6; 9; 11; 12; 14; 16(2); 21; 23; 25(2); 27(2); 25:1; 2; 4(2); 8; 10; 12; 13; 17; 18(3); 24; 26; 27; 28; 26:3; 4; 5(2); 7; 9; 10(5); 15; 17; 19(2); 21; 23(2); 27:1; 2; 4(2); 5(2); 7; 8; 9(2); 28:1(2); 2; 3(2); 6(2); 9; 19; 22; 24(2); 25; 26; 27(3); 29:1; 2; 3(2); 4(2); 6; 7; 9; 10; 16; 17; 18; 19(2); 25; 31; 34; 35(2); 30:2(2); 5; 13; 14; 16; 17; 25; 26(2); 31:1; 2; 3; 4; 5(2); 6(2); 7(3); 11; 12; 15; 16; 17; 18(3); 19(2); 21(4); 32:5(2); 6; 9; 10(2); 13; 18; 21; 23; 24; 26; 29; 30; 31(3); 32(2); 33(2); 33:1; 2; 4(2); 5; 6(2); 7(3); 12; 14(2); 15(2); 18(2); 20(2); 21; 22; 24; 25; 34:1; 2(2); 3(2); 4(2); 6; 8; 10(2); 13; 15; 17; 21(2); 22(2); 24; 26; 28; 30(2); 31(2); 32; 33; 35:1; 2; 3; 5; 10(2); 12; 13(3); 14; 15; 18; 19; 22; 24(2); 25(3); 26; 27; 36:1(2); 2; 5(2); 6; 7; 8(2); 9(2); 11; 12; 14; 17; 22(2); 23; **Ezra** 1:1(2); 2; 3(2); 4(2); 5; 7; 2:42; 68(2); 70(2); 3:1; 2; 4; 8; 10; 4:4; 6(2); 7(2); 8; 10; 15(3); 17; 19(2); 23; 5:1(2); 2; 6; 7; 8(2); 13; 14; 15; 16; 17(2); 6:1(2); 2(3); 3; 5(3); 9; 12; 15; 18(2); 21; 22; 7:1; 6; 7; 8(2); 10; 11; 13; 14; 15; 16(2); 17; 19; 21; 25; 27(2); 8:1; 29(2); 33; 36; 9:2; 8(2); 9(3); 14; 15; 10:2(2); 9; 13; 14(2); **Neh** 1:1(3); 3(2); 11; 2:1(3); 5; 9; 12(2); 15; 17; 20; 3:10; 16; 19; 26(2); 28; 29; 30; 31; 4:2; 21; 22; 5:5; 9; 14; 18; 6:1(2); 2; 4; 5; 6; 7; 8; 9; 10; 11; 15; 16; 17; 18; 7:3; 4; 5(2); 73(2); 8:1(2); 3(2); 5; 7; 8; 13; 14(2); 15(2); 16(3); 9:1; 3; 6; 9; 15; 17(2); 19(2); 21; 23; 24; 25(2); 27; 28; 30; 31; 33; 35(3); 36; 37; 10:29; 34; 36(2); 37; 11:1(2); 3(4); 4; 18; 20(2); 21; 22; 24; 25; 26; 28; 29; 30(2); 31; 32; 33; 34; 35; 36; 12:7; 9; 12; 22; 23; 26(2); 27; 37; 40; 46; 47(2); 13:1(2); 6(2); 7(2); 11; 15(3); 16(2); 19; 23; **Esth** 1:1; 2(2); 3; 4; 5(2); 7(2); 8; 9; 10; 11; 14; 16; 17(2); 19; 22(4); 2:3; 5; 9; 11; 12; 14(4); 15(2); 16(2); 17; 18; 21; 22; 23(2); 3:7(2); 8; 12(2); 13; 14; 15; 4:3(2); 6(2); 8; 11; 13(2); 16; 5:1(2); 2(3); 8; 9; 11; 12; 14; 6:4; 5(2); 6(2); 7:3; 5; 7; 8; 8:5(3); 8(2); 9(5); 10; 11; 12; 13; 14; 15; 17; 9:1(2); 2; 4; 6; 11; 12(2); 13; 14; 15; 16; 19; 20; 32; 10:2; **Job** 1:1; 4; 5(2); 10; 12; 13; 18; 22; 2:6; 8; 10; 3:3; 20; 23; 4:13; 18; 19(2); 20; 5:4; 13; 14(2); 19(2); 20(2); 24; 26; 6:4; 6; 10; 7:11(2); 21; 8:16(2); 17; 9:4(2); 5; 19; 29; 10:1; 13; 11:4; 14(2); 18; 12:5; 6; 10; 24; 25; 13:14(2); 27; 14:8(2); 13; 17; 22; 15:9; 15(2); 21(2); 28(2); 31; 16:4; 9; 15; 17; 19; 17:6; 12; 13; 16; 18:3; 4; 6; 10; 15; 19; 20(2); 19:2; 8; 15(2); 23; 26; 28; 20:11; 12; 13; 14; 20; 22(2); 26; 28; 21:7; 8; 13(2); 16; 17; 21; 23; 25; 26; 34; 22:8; 12; 22; 24; 26; 23:6; 24:5; 6(2); 7; 12; 13; 14; 16(2); 17; 18; 25:2; 5; 26:8; 27:3(2); 10; 15; 20; 28:3; 4; 10; 13; 14; 16(2); 19; 29:2(2); 4; 7; 18; 20; 25; 30:6(2); 10; 17; 25; 27; 28(2); 31:15(2); 21; 26; 32; 33; 32:1; 5; 6; 8; 33:2; 5; 8; 9; 11; 12; 14(2); 15(2); 17; 19; 26; 29; 34:8; 9; 20(2); 23; 24(2); 25; 26; 35:10; 15; 16; 36:4; 5; 8(2); 11(2); 13; 14; 15(2); 20; 31; 37:8; 16; 21; 23(2); 38:8; 16; 26; 32; 36; 38; 40(3); 39:10; 14; 16; 21(2); 40:12; 13(2); 16(2); 21; 24; 41:22; 30; 42:6; 11; 15; **Ps** 1:1(3); 2(2); 3; 5(2); 2:3; 4(2); 5(2); 12(2); 3:2; 4:1; 5; 7(2); 8(2); 5:3(2); 4; 5; 7(2); 8; 9; 10; 11(2); 6:1(2); 5(2); 7:1; 2; 3; 5; 6; 10; 8:1; 9; 9:2; 4; 8(2); 9; 10; 11; 14(2); 15(2); 16; 19; 20; 10:1; 2(2); 4(2); 6(2); 8(2); 9(3); 11; 13; 11:1; 2; 4(2); 12:5; 6; 13:2(2); 5(2); 14:1; 5; 15:1(2); 2; 4; 16:1; 3; 6; 7; 9; 10; 11; 17:3; 5; 7; 11; 12; 14; 15(2); 18:2; 6; 14; 18; 19; 24; 30; 42; 19:4; 11; 14; 20:1; 5(2); 7(2); 21:1(2); 5; 7; 9(2); 13; 22:2(2); 3; 4; 5; 8(2); 22; 25; 23:2; 3; 5; 6; 24:3; 7; 8; 9; 25:2; 5; 8; 9; 12; 13; 20; 26:1(2); 3; 4; 6; 10; 11; 12(2); 27:3; 4(2); 5(3); 6; 9; 11; 13; 28:3; 7; 29:2; 9; 30:5; 6; 9; 31:1(2); 6; 7(2); 8; 9; 14; 15; 17; 19(2); 20(2); 21; 22; 24; 32:2; 6(2); 8; 10; 11(2); 33:1; 4; 7; 8; 18; 19; 21(2); 22; 34:1; 2; 8; 22; 35:7; 9(2); 15; 18; 20; 25; 27; 36:2; 4; 5; 9; 10; 37:3(2); 4; 5; 7(2); 11; 19(2); 23; 29; 31; 33; 35; 39; 40; 38:1(2); 3(2); 7; 14; 15; 18; 39:6; 7; 40:3(2); 5; 7; 9; 16; 41:1; 9; 12; 42:5; 8(2); 11; 43:5; 44:1(2); 6; 8; 19; 45:4; 5; 9; 14; 16; 17; 46:1; 5; 8; 9(2); 10; 48:1(2); 2; 3; 6; 8(2); 9; 49:5; 6(2); 12; 14(3); 20; 50:15; 16; 21; 22; 51:4; 5(2); 6(2); 10; 16; 18; 52:1; 7(2); 8(2); 9; 53:1; 5; 54:5; 55:2; 3; 7; 9; 10; 11; 14; 15; 18; 21; 23; 56(2); 3; 4(2); 6; 7; 8; 10(2); 11; 13; 57:1(2); 58:2(2); 6; 7; 9; 10; 11; 59:3; 7; 8; 12; 13(2); 16(2); 60:6; 8; 61:4(2); 62:4; 7(2); 8; 10(2); 63:1; 2; 4; 6; 7; 11; 64:1; 4; 5; 10(3); 65:1; 4; 5; 8; 66:5; 6; 14; 18; 68:5; 6(2); 10; 14(2); 16(2); 17(2); 21; 23; 26; 30; 34; 69:2; 12; 13(3); 17; 25; 34; 36; 70:4; 71:1; 2; 9; 10; 16; 72:4; 7; 9; 14; 16; 17; 73:1; 4; 5; 11; 12; 13(2); 18; 19; 21; 25; 28; 74:3; 4; 8(2); 12; 13; 14; 75:8; 76:1(2); 2(2); 7; 77:2(2); 6; 9; 13; 18; 19(2); 78:2; 5(2); 7; 9; 10; 12(3); 14; 15(2); 17; 18; 19; 22(2); 26(2); 28; 30; 32(2); 33(2); 37; 40(2); 43(2); 51(2); 52; 55; 63; 79:1; 10; 80:5; 81:5; 7(2); 12; 13; 82:1; 5; 84:4; 5; 7; 10(3); 12; 85:6; 9; 86:2; 5; 7; 11; 15; 87:1; 5; 7; 88:5; 6(3); 11(2); 12(2); 13; 89:2; 5; 6; 7(2); 10; 12; 15; 16(2); 17; 19; 24; 30; 37; 43; 49; 50; 90:1; 4(2); 5; 6(2); 8; 9; 15(2); 91:1; 2; 6; 11; 12; 15; 92:2; 4; 12; 13(2); 14; 15; 94:4; 5; 15; 17; 19; 23; 95:4; 8(3); 10; 11; 96:6; 9; 12; 97:11; 12; 98:2; 4; 7; 99:2; 4; 7; 101:2; 6; 7; 102:2(2); 14; 16; 21(2); 23; 24; 103:8; 19; 20; 22; 104:3; 17; 20; 22; 24; 25; 27; 28; 31; 34; 105:3; 7; 12(2); 16; 18; 23; 27; 30; 31; 32; 35; 36; 39; 41; 106:5; 7; 14(2); 16; 18; 19; 21; 22; 23; 25; 26(2);

27; 43; 47; 107:4(3); 5; 6; 10(3); 13; 14; 16; 19; 23; 24; 28; 32(2); 34; 40; 108:7; 109:4; 13; 16; 17; 110:2; 3(2); 5; 111:1(2); 2; 6; 8; 112:1; 3; 4; 6; 7; 113:6(2); 115:3; 8; 9; 10; 11; 116:9; 11; 14; 15; 18; 19(2); 118:5(2); 8(2); 9(2); 10; 11; 12; 15; 23; 24; 26; 119:1(2); 3; 11; 14(2); 16; 19; 35(2); 37; 40; 42; 43; 47; 50; 51; 54; 55; 70; 74; 75; 81; 83; 89; 92; 109; 114; 147; 161; 120:1; 5; 121:8; 123:1; 124:8; 125:1; 4; 126:4; 5(2); 127:1(2); 4; 5; 128:1; 3; 129:4; 8; 130:5; 7; 131:3; 132:6(2); 11; 133:1; 134:1; 2; 135:2(2); 6(4); 17; 18; 21; 136:10; 13; 15; 23; 137:2; 4; 138:3(2); 7; 139:8; 9; 13; 15(2); 16; 18; 20; 24(2); 140:2; 7; 11; 13; 141:8; 142:3(2); 5; 143:1(2); 2; 3; 8(3); 9; 10; 12; 144:2; 12(2); 13; 14(2); 15; 145:8; 15; 17(2); 18; 146:3(3); 4; 5; 6; 147:5; 10(2); 11(3); 14; 148:1; 149:1; 2(2); 4; 5; 6(2); 150:1(2); **Prov** 1:11; 14; 15; 17(2); 18; 20; 21(2); 22; 2:13; 14(2); 15; 20; 21(2); 3:4; 5; 6; 7; 12; 16(2); 23; 27; 4:3; 7; 11(2); 14; 21; 5:4; 14; 16; 20; 22; 23; 6:1; 8(2); 14; 18; 25; 29; 34; 7:9(3); 12; 8:8; 20; 31; 9:4; 6; 9; 16; 17; 18; 10:5(2); 8; 17; 19; 11:4; 14; 20; 22; 28; 12:4; 6; 15; 20; 25; 27; 28(2); 13:23; 25; 14:2(2); 3; 7; 13; 14; 23; 26; 28(2); 32(2); 33(2); 15:3; 4; 6(2); 22; 23; 16:2; 5; 6; 10; 11; 15; 20; 21; 29; 31; 17:8; 12; 16; 18; 24; 18:2(2); 5; 9; 11; 14; 21; 19:1(2); 20; 21; 22; 23; 24; 20:5; 7; 20; 21:1; 2; 9(2); 10; 14; 16; 19; 20; 22:2; 5; 6; 13; 15; 19; 26; 29; 23:7; 9; 19; 24; 28; 30; 31; 34; 24:6; 7; 10; 15; 23; 27; 25:5; 6(2); 7; 8; 11; 13; 17; 19(2); 20; 24(2); 26:1(2); 5; 7; 8; 9; 12; 13(2); 15; 16; 17; 25; 27:10; 13; 14; 19; 22; 25; 28:6(2); 10; 11; 18; 25; 26; 29:2; 13; 20; 21; 22; 23; 25; 27; 30:4(2); 5; 12; 19(2); 25; 26; 27; 28; 29(2); 32; 31:8; 23; 25; 31; **Eccl** 1:1; 3; 10; 12; 16; 18; 2:1; 3; 5; 7(2); 9; 10; 11; 14(2); 15(2); 16; 18; 19(2); 20; 23; 24; 26; 3:9; 11(2); 12; 16(2); 17; 18; 22; 4:14; 15; 16; 5:2; 4; 7; 8; 14; 15; 17; 18; 19; 6:4(2); 12; 7:4(2); 8(2); 9(2); 14(2); 15(3); 8:8; 9; 10; 11; 15; 9:1(2); 3(2); 6; 9(2); 10; 12(3); 14; 15; 10:6(2); 16; 20(3); 11:3; 5; 6(2); 8; 9(4); 12:1(2); 3; 4; 5; 9; **Song** 1:4; 8; 14; 2:3; 12; 14(2); 3:2(2); 8(2); 4:7; 6:2; 13; 7:1; 4; 11; 12; 8:8; 10; 13; **Isa** 1:1; 6; 7; 8(2); 11; 21; 2:2; 3; 5; 10; 11; 17; 20; 22; 3:6; 7(2); 14; 18; 25; 4:1; 2; 3(3); 6; 5:2(2); 4; 8; 9; 11; 12; 16(2); 17(2); 21(2); 25; 30; 6:1; 5; 6; 12; 13; 7:1; 2; 6; 11(2); 18(3); 19(3); 20; 21; 22; 23; 8:6(2); 9(3); 11; 17; 18(2); 20; 9:1; 2(2); 4; 5; 9; 14; 17; 18; 10:3(2); 5; 7; 17; 19; 20(2); 23; 24(2); 25; 26; 27; 11:3; 8; 9; 10; 11; 15; 16; 12:1; 4; 5; 6; 13:3; 4; 8(2); 10; 13(2); 17; 22(2); 14:1; 2; 3(2); 6(2); 13; 18(2); 20; 25; 28; 30; 31; 32; 15:1(2); 3(2); 5; 16:3; 5(3); 10(2); 17:4; 5; 6(2); 7; 9; 11(3); 18:2; 4(2); 5; 7; 19:1; 3; 9; 14(3); 16; 17; 18(2); 19(2); 20; 21; 23; 24(2); 20:1; 6; 21:1; 3; 5; 8; 13(2); 22:2; 3; 5; 7; 8; 12; 14; 16; 20; 23; 25(2); 23:5; 15(2); 24:6; 10; 11; 12; 13; 15(2); 18; 21; 22(2); 23; 25:4; 5(2); 6; 9(2); 11; 26:1(2); 2; 3(2); 4(2); 8; 9(2); 10; 12; 16; 17(3); 18(2); 19; 27:1(2); 2; 4(2); 6; 8(2); 12; 13(4); 28:4; 5; 6; 7(2); 14; 15; 16; 20; 21; 25(3); 26; 29(2); 29:5; 15; 18; 19(2); 21; 23; 24; 30:2(2); 3; 7; 12; 13(2); 14; 15(2); 19; 21; 23(2); 25; 26; 28; 29; 32(2); 31:1(2); 7; 9(2); 32:1; 2(2); 10; 13; 16(2); 18(3); 19; 33:2; 12; 14; 17; 21; 24; 34:1; 5; 6(2); 11; 13(2); 17; 35:6(2); 7; 36:1; 4; 5; 6(2); 7; 9; 11(3); 13; 15; 37:7; 10; 12; 28; 29(2); 30; 36(2); 38(2); 38:1(2); 3(2); 10; 11; 15; 16; 20; 39:2(2); 4(2); 6; 7; 8; 40:3(2); 11; 12(4); 14; 15; 22; 24; 41:2; 16(2); 18(2); 19(2); 42:1; 2; 4; 6; 7; 10; 12; 14; 16; 17; 22(2); 24; 43:3; 4; 14; 16; 19(2); 20(2); 26; 44:7; 12; 13; 16; 19(2); 20; 23(2); 45:2; 13; 14(2); 16; 18; 19(3); 23; 24; 25; 46:7; 13; 47:1; 5; 8; 9(3); 10(2); 12; 13; 48:1(2); 10; 16; 49:2(2); 3; 4(2); 5; 8(2); 9; 13; 20; 21; 22(2); 50:4; 10(2); 11(3); 51:3; 6(2); 7; 9(2); 14; 16; 20; 52:6; 10; 53:9; 10; 54:6; 14; 16; 17; 55:2; 11; 56:5; 7; 9; 57:2(2); 5; 6; 10; 13; 15; 17; 58:2; 3(2); 10; 11; 12; 14; 59:4; 6; 7; 8; 9; 10; 13; 14; 19; 20; 21; 60:10(2); 11; 18; 22; 61:3; 6; 7(2); 8; 10(2); 11; 62:3(2); 4; 7; 9; 63:1(3); 2; 3(2); 4; 6(2); 9(3); 13; 64:5(2); 65:2; 3; 4(2); 5; 8(2); 12; 16(3); 18; 19(3); 23; 25; 66:3; 4; 7; 8(2); 13; 17; 20(3); **Jer** 1:1(2); 2(2); 3(2); 5; 9; 2:2(3); 5; 17(2); 19; 23(2); 24(3); 27; 28; 30; 3:2; 6; 10; 16(2); 18; 23(2); 25; 4:2(5); 5(3); 9; 11; 19(2); 20; 29; 30; 31; 5:1; 6; 7; 13; 14; 17; 18; 19(2); 20(2); 24(2); 26; 30; 31; 6:1(2); 3; 6; 7; 10; 11; 16(3); 23; 24; 26(2); 29; 7:2(2); 3; 4; 6; 7(2); 8; 10; 11; 12; 14; 17(2); 22; 23; 30(2); 31(2); 32; 8:3; 5; 7; 12; 16(2); 18(2); 19(2); 22; 9:2; 6; 8(2); 23(3); 24(3); 26(3); 10:6; 7; 13; 14; 15; 23(2); 24; 11:4; 6(2); 7; 12; 14; 15; 17; 21; 12:2; 5(3); 8; 12; 16; 13:1; 4(2); 9; 17; 21; 22; 25; 27; 14:4; 5; 6; 8(2); 9; 13; 14; 15(2); 16; 18; 15:4; 7; 11(2); 14; 15; 17; 16:2; 3(2); 6; 7; 9; 19; 17:3; 4(2); 5; 6(3); 7; 8; 11; 13; 17; 19(3); 21; 24; 25; 27; 18:4; 6(2); 10; 15(2); 17; 21; 23; 19:4; 7; 9(2); 10; 11; 14; 20:1; 2(2); 6; 7; 9(3); 14(2); 16; 21:4(2); 5; 7; 9; 12; 14; 22:3; 4; 12; 15; 20; 21; 23(2); 28; 30(2); 23:5; 6; 8; 11; 12(2); 13; 14(2); 18; 19; 20; 22; 24; 25; 26; 29; 24:8(2); 9; 25:1; 3; 5; 13; 23; 24; 34; 26:1; 2(2); 4; 7; 9(2); 10; 14; 15; 16; 18; 20; 27:1; 11(2); 15; 18(2); 19; 21(2); 28:1(5); 5(3); 7(2); 11; 13; 15; 17; 29:5; 7; 8; 9; 15; 16; 21; 22(2); 23(2); 25; 26(3); 28(2); 29; 31(2); 30:2; 6(2); 8; 11; 24; 31:2; 4; 9(2); 10; 12; 13; 15; 17; 21; 22; 23(2); 24(2); 29; 32; 33; 32:1; 2(2); 7; 8(3); 9; 12(3); 14; 15; 19(2); 20(2); 23(2); 34; 35; 37(3); 40; 41; 43; 44(6); 33:1; 5; 10(3); 12(2); 13(6); 15(2); 16; 20; 34:5(2); 6; 9; 10; 13; 15(2); 17; 18; 35:1; 7(2); 8; 9; 10; 15; 36:1; 6(3); 8; 9(3); 10(4); 13; 14(3); 15(2); 16; 18; 20(2); 21(2); 22(2); 23; 28; 29; 32; 37:1; 4; 10; 13; 15(2); 17; 18; 21(2); 38:2; 4; 5; 6(3); 7(2); 9(3); 13; 22(2); 28; 39:1(2); 2(2); 3(2); 5(2); 6; 9; 10; 15; 16; 17; 18; 40:1; 6; 7(2); 9; 10(2); 11(3); 12; 13; 15(2); 41:1(2); 5; 8; 10(2); 12; 17; 18; 42:3; 10; 13; 16(2); 20; 22; 43:4; 5; 8; 9(5); 12(2); 13; 44:1(2); 2; 3; 6(2); 8(2); 9(2); 10(2); 12; 13; 15(2); 16; 17(2); 21(2); 23(3); 24; 26(3); 27; 29; 45:1(2); 3; 5; 46:2(2); 10; 11; 14(4); 19; 21; 25; 26; 47:2; 48:2; 5(2); 6; 7; 9; 11; 18; 20; 26(2); 27; 28(3); 35(2); 38(2); 41(2); 44; 47; 49:1; 2; 4(2); 7; 8; 11; 16; 18(2); 22(2); 24; 26(2); 27; 30; 32; 33; 34; 38; 39; 50:2(2); 4(2); 5; 9; 14; 20(2); 22; 25; 28; 30(2); 32; 37; 39(2); 40; 42; 43; 51:1; 2; 3; 4(2); 6; 7; 10; 13; 16; 17; 18; 20; 21(2); 22(3); 23(3); 24(2); 27; 30; 39; 44; 46(3); 47; 48; 58; 59; 60; 61; 62; 52:1; 2; 3; 4(2); 6; 8; 9; 10; 11(2); 12; 15; 17(3); 25(2); 27; 28; 29; 30; 31(3); 32; **Lam** 1:2; 3; 4; 7(2); 9; 12; 15(2); 19; 20; 2:1(2); 2; 3; 5; 6(2); 7; 11; 12(2); 17; 19; 20; 21(2); 22; 3:2(2); 6; 7; 10(2); 11; 24; 27; 29; 36; 41; 45; 53; 66; 4:3; 5(2); 6; 7(2); 8; 10; 11; 13; 14; 17; 18; 19(2); 20; 21; 5:9; 11(2); **Ezek** 1:1(2); 2; 3; 14; 16; 20; 21; 26; 28; 2:9; 3:3(2); 14(2); 18; 19; 20; 4:12; 16; 5:2(2); 3; 4; 5; 6; 7; 8(2); 10; 12; 13; 14; 15(3); 6:6; 7; 9; 10; 14; 7:4; 7(2); 9; 13; 15(2); 19; 20; 8:1(3); 3; 4; 5; 7; 9; 10; 11(2); 12(2); 18(2); 9:1(2); 2(2); 5; 7; 8; 10:1; 2(2); 3; 5; 6(2); 10; 11; 13; 17; 19; 11:2; 6; 7; 11; 12; 15; 16; 20; 24(2); 25; 12:2; 3(2); 4(2); 5; 6; 7; 8; 10; 13; 19(2); 23; 25; 13:4; 5; 9(2); 13(3); 14; 21; 14:3; 4; 7(2); 14; 16; 18; 19; 20; 22; 23; 15:8; 16:4(2); 6(3); 7; 9; 10; 12(2); 15; 22(2); 24; 31; 34(2); 36; 38; 41; 43; 47(2); 56(2); 60; 17:4; 5; 8; 10; 16(2); 17; 18; 20; 23; 18:3; 9; 17; 26; 32; 19:4; 8; 9(2); 10; 11(2); 12; 13(2); 20:1(2); 5(3); 6; 8; 9; 13(3); 14; 15(2); 16; 17; 18(2); 19; 21(2); 22(2); 23(2); 26; 27; 28; 30; 32(2); 36; 40; 41; 42; 43; 47(2); 21:22; 23; 24(3); 30(2); 32; 22:3; 6; 7(3); 9(3); 10(2); 11; 12; 13; 14; 16; 18; 20(2); 21; 22(2); 24; 25(2); 27; 30; 23:3(2); 6; 8; 11(2); 14; 15; 16; 19(2); 31(2); 32; 39; 43; 44(3); 24:1(2); 4; 5; 6; 7; 10; 11; 12; 13; 17; 18; 23; 25; 25:6; 14; 26:1; 5; 6; 8; 12; 15; 20(3); 27:3; 4; 8; 9(2); 10(2); 11; 20; 21; 24(6); 25; 26; 27(2); 30; 32(2); 34(2); 28:2(2); 5; 8; 9; 12; 13; 14; 15(2); 18; 22(3); 23(2); 25(3); 29:1(2); 3; 4(2); 5; 12; 17(2); 21(2); 30:4(2); 7(2); 8; 9; 12; 13; 14; 16(2); 18; 20(2); 24; 31:1(2); 2; 3; 6(2); 7(2); 8(3); 9; 10(2); 12; 15; 16; 17; 18(3); 32:1(2); 2(2); 3; 10; 15; 17; 19; 20; 23(2); 24; 25(3); 26; 27; 28; 30; 32(2); 33:6; 8; 9; 10; 11; 12(3); 13; 15; 21(2); 22; 24; 27(3); 30; 34:13(2); 14(3); 16; 25(2); 26; 27; 29; 35:8(2); 11; 36:5(2); 6; 7; 11; 17(2); 23(2); 27; 28; 31; 33; 34; 37:1(2); 2; 6; 8; 14(2); 17; 19(2); 20; 22; 23; 24; 25; 26; 28; 38:8; 10; 12; 16(2); 17(2); 18; 19(4); 23; 39:6(2); 7(2); 9; 11(2); 12; 14; 15; 26(2); 27(2); 40:1(2); 2; 3(2); 5; 10; 12; 16(3); 22; 25(2); 26; 29(2); 33(2); 39; 44; 47; 41:6(2); 7; 42:3; 4; 6; 10; 11; 12(2); 14; 43:7; 8; 9; 11; 13; 21; 44:3; 7(4); 9(2); 11; 12; 14; 19(3); 24(2); 27(2); 28(2); 29; 45:3; 8; 16; 18; 20; 21; 25; 46:8; 10(3); 21(2); 22; 23; 47:3; 5; 14; 23; 48:1; 8(3); 9(2); 10(5); 13(2); 15(2); 21; 22; **Dan** 1:1; 4(3); 8; 14; 15; 17(2); 18(2); 20(2); 2:1; 4; 5; 16; 19; 22; 27; 28(2); 34; 40(2); 41; 44(2); 45; 49; 3:1(2); 5; 7; 10; 13; 15; 16; 20; 21; 24; 25; 28; 29; 30; 4:1; 4(2); 6; 7; 8; 9; 10; 12(2); 13; 15(2); 17(2); 18; 21(2); 23(2); 25; 31; 32; 35; 37; 5:1; 2; 3; 5; 7(2); 11(4); 12; 13; 14(2); 15; 16; 20; 21; 23; 27; 29; 6:3; 4; 10; 19(2); 23; 24; 25; 26; 27; 28(2); 7:1; 2; 5; 7(2); 8; 9; 13; 15; 19; 22; 23; 28; 8:1; 2(4); 7; 8; 18; 19; 22; 23; 25(2); 26; 9:1; 2(2); 6; 7; 10; 11; 13; 14(2); 21(2); 24; 25; 27; 10:1; 2; 5; 6; 8(2); 9; 14; 17(2); 21; 11:1; 2; 6; 7; 14(2); 16(2); 20(3); 21(2); 30; 38; 12:1; 2; 6; 7; **Hos** 1:1(2); 4; 5(2); 10; 2:3; 6; 9(2); 10; 15(2); 16; 18; 19(2); 20; 21; 23; 3:5; 4:1; 5(2); 16; 19; 5:2; 4; 5; 8(2); 9; 11; 15; 6:2; 9; 10; 7:1; 2; 5; 6(2); 16; 8:8; 9:2; 3(2); 5(2); 6; 8(2); 9; 10(2); 13; 15; 10:4(2); 9; 12; 13(2); 14(2); 11:6; 9; 11; 12:3(2); 4; 7; 8(2); 9(2); 11(2); 13:1; 5(2); 10; 11(2); 13; 16; 14:3; 8; 9(2); **Joel** 1:2(2); 13; 17; 2:1(2); 5; 6; 7; 8; 9; 15; 23(2); 26; 27; 29; 30(2); 32(2); 3:1; 13; 14(2); 17; 18; 19; 21; **Am** 1:1(2); 13; 14(3); 2:7; 8(2); 16; 3:4; 6(2); 9(4); 10; 12(2); 14; 4:6(2); 5:6(2); 7; 10; 11; 15; 16(2); 17; 20; 25; 6:1(3); 8; 9; 7:7; 8; 10; 17(2); 8:3(2); 8; 9(2); 13; 9:6(2); 9; 11; 15; **Ob** 3(2); 7; 8; 11(2); 12(3); 13(3); 14; 20; **Jon** 1:5; 17; 3:3; 6; 8; 4:2(2); 5; 10(2); 11; **Mic** 1:1; 2; 6; 10(3); 11; 13; 2:1; 4; 5; 11; 12; 3:3(2); 4; 4:1; 2; 5(2); 6; 7; 9(2); 10(3); 13; 5:1; 2; 3; 4(2); 5; 7; 8(2); 10; 15; 6:10; 12; 14; 16; 7:2; 5(3); 8; 10; 11(2); 12; 13; 14(4); 15; 18; **Nah** 1:3(3); 5; 7(2); 12; 2:3(2); 4(2); 5; 10; 12; 13; 3:10; 13; 17; 18; **Hab** 1:5; 15(2); 2:4; 8; 13; 17; 18; 19; 20; 3:2(3); 7; 11; 12(2); 14; 16(2); 17; 18(2); **Zeph** 1:1; 7; 8; 9; 12(2); 18(2); 2:3; 7; 14(2); 15; 3:2; 3; 5; 11(4); 12(2); 13; 15; 16; 17; 19; **Hag** 1:1(2); 4(2); 6; 8; 9; 15; 2:1; 3(3); 9; 10; 12; 15; 17; 19; 22; 23; **Zech** 1:1; 7; 8; 16; 2:1; 4; 5; 10; 11(2); 12; 3:7; 9; 10; 4:10; 5:4; 9; 11; 6:8; 14; 7:1; 3(2); 5; 10; 8:3; 4(2); 5; 6(3); 8(2); 9(2); 10; 11; 15; 16; 17; 22; 23; 9:4; 6; 7; 16; 10:1(2); 2(2); 3; 5(2); 7; 9; 12(2); 11:3(2); 7; 8; 10; 14; 16(2); 12:3(2); 4; 5(2); 6(4); 8(2); 9; 11(3); 13:1; 2; 3; 4; 6; 8(3); 14:1; 3; 4(2); 5; 6; 8(2); 9; 10; 11; 12(2); 13; 14; 15; 18; 20(2); 21(4); **Mal** 1:2; 6; 7; 10(2); 11; 12; 14; 2:6(2); 9; 11(2); 17(4); 3:1; 3; 4(2); 7; 8(2); 10(2); 11; 4:2; 4; **Mt** 1:17(2); 20(2); 2:1(2); 2; 5; 6; 9; 12; 13; 16(2); 18; 19(2); 22; 23; 3:1(2); 3; 4; 6; 12; 17; 4:6; 12; 13(2); 16(2); 21; 23; 5:3; 8; 12; 15; 16; 19(2); 21; 22(3); 28; 45; 48; 6:1; 2(2); 4(2); 5; 6(2); 9(2); 10; 18(2); 19; 20(2); 23; 29; 7:3(2); 4; 6; 11; 13; 15; 21; 22(4); 8:10; 11; 32; 9:4; 10; 25; 31; 33; 35; 10:9; 11; 15; 16; 17; 19; 20; 23; 27(3); 28; 32; 33; 41(2); 42; 11:1; 2; 8(2); 11; 16; 20; 21(3); 22; 23(2); 24; 26; 29; 12:5(2); 6; 18; 19; 21; 32(2); 36; 40(2); 41; 42; 44; 50; 13:3; 10; 13; 14; 19; 21; 24; 27; 30; 31; 32; 33; 34; 35; 40; 43; 44; 54; 57(2); 14:2; 3; 10; 24; 25; 33; 15:9; 33; 16:3; 17; 19(2); 26; 27; 28; 17:5; 22; 27; 18:1; 2; 4; 5; 6(2); 10(2); 14; 18(2); 19; 20(2); 19:21; 28; 20:1; 3; 21; 21:9(2); 12; 14; 15; 18; 22; 28; 32; 33; 41; 42(2); 22:11; 12; 15; 16; 28; 30(3); 36; 43; 23:2; 6; 7; 9; 13(2); 21; 30(2); 34; 39; 24:5; 7; 14; 15; 16; 18; 19; 20; 26(2); 30; 38(2); 40; 45; 48; 51; 25:4; 10; 13; 18; 25; 31; 35; 36; 38; 39; 43(2); 44; 26:6; 12; 13; 23; 29; 52; 55(2); 58; 61; 67; 69; 27:5; 7; 19; 29; 40; 43; 51; 59; 60; 28:18; 19; **Mk** 1:2; 3; 4; 5; 9(2); 11; 13; 14; 15; 19; 20; 23; 35; 39; 45; 2:1; 6; 8(2); 12; 15; 20; 25; 26; 3:23; 34; 4:1; 2; 11; 15; 17; 19; 28; 29; 36; 38; 5:4; 5(2); 13; 14(2); 15; 20; 27; 29; 30(2); 34; 39; 6:2; 4(2); 6; 8; 10; 11; 14; 17; 22; 25; 27; 29; 32; 39; 40(3); 47; 51; 56(2); 7:3; 7; 32; 33; 8:1; 4; 12; 14; 26; 37; 38(2); 9:33; 36(2); 37; 38; 39; 41; 42; 50; 10:10; 16; 21; 24; 30(2); 37; 11:9; 10(2); 14; 15; 20; 22; 23; 25; 26; 27; 12:1; 4; 11; 13; 14; 23; 25(2); 26(2); 35; 38(3); 39; 41; 42; 43; 44(2); 13:6; 8; 9; 11; 14; 16; 17; 18; 19; 24; 25; 26; 32; 35(2); 14:3; 9; 14(2); 17; 20; 25; 49; 60; 66; 15:1; 7; 29; 38; 41; 43; 46(2); 16:2; 5; 12; 17; **Lk** 1:1(2); 4; 5; 6; 7; 8; 15; 17; 18; 19; 20; 21; 22; 25; 26; 28; 31; 36; 39; 41; 44(2); 47; 51; 54; 66; 69; 75; 79; 80(2); 2:1; 7(3); 8(2); 11; 12(2); 14; 16; 19; 21; 23; 24; 25; 27; 28; 29; 34; 38(2); 40; 43; 44; 46(2); 51; 52(2); 3:1; 2; 4(2); 15(2); 17; 20; 22(2); 4:2; 5; 11; 14; 15; 20; 21; 23(2); 24; 25(2); 26; 27(2); 28; 33; 35; 37; 44; 5:7; 12; 18; 19; 22; 29; 35; 6:1; 12(2); 23(3); 35; 41(2); 42(3); 7:1; 9; 25(3); 28; 32; 37(2); 45; 50; 8:10; 13; 23; 27(2); 34(2); 35; 47; 48; 51; 9:12; 14; 26(2); 31; 36; 48; 49; 10:7; 12; 13(3); 17; 20(2); 21(3); 26; 11:1; 2(2); 7; 21; 22; 25; 31; 32; 33(2); 35; 37; 43(2); 48; 52(2); 54(2); 12:1; 3(4); 12; 15; 27; 28; 33; 38(2); 42; 45; 46; 52; 13:4(2); 6; 10; 11; 19(2); 21; 26(2); 28; 29; 35; 14:8; 10(2); 15; 21; 23; 15:4; 7; 10; 14(2); 21; 25; 28; 16:8; 10(4); 11; 12; 15; 19; 23(3); 24(2); 25; 17:4(2); 6; 7; 24; 26(2); 27; 28; 30; 31(3); 34(2); 36; 18:2; 3; 9; 22; 30(2); 19:17; 20; 23; 38(3); 42; 43; 44; 45; 47; 20:1; 20; 21; 26(2); 31; 33; 34; 35; 37; 42; 45; 46(3); 21:2; 3; 4(2); 6; 8; 11; 14; 21(3); 23(2); 25(3); 27; 37(2); 38(2); 22:6; 16; 19; 20; 28; 30; 37; 44; 53; 55; 23:4; 7; 11; 14(2); 19; 22; 29; 31(2); 38; 43; 45; 53(2); 24:1; 3; 4; 6; 18(2); 19; 25; 27; 29; 35; 36; 38; 43; 44; 47; 49; 53; **Jn** 1:1; 2; 4; 5; 10; 12; 18; 23; 28; 45; 47; 2:1; 11(2); 14; 19; 20; 23(2); 25; 3:13; 14; 15; 16; 18(2); 21; 23; 36; 4:14; 18; 20; 21; 23; 24; 31; 37; 39; 44; 45; 53; 5:2(2); 3; 4; 6; 13; 14; 19; 24; 26(2); 28(2); 35; 38; 39; 42; 43(2); 45; 6:10(2); 29; 31; 35; 40; 45; 47; 49; 53; 56(2); 59(2); 61; 7:1(2); 4; 5; 9; 10; 18; 28; 31; 38; 39; 48; 8:2; 3(2); 4(2); 5; 9; 12; 17; 20(2); 21; 24(2); 30; 31; 33; 35; 37; 44(2); 9:3; 5; 7; 34; 35; 36; 10:9; 22; 23(2); 24; 25; 34; 38(2); 42; 11:6; 9(2); 10(2); 13; 17; 20; 24; 25; 26; 30; 31; 33; 38; 45; 48; 52; 56; 12:6; 11; 13; 22; 25; 35; 36; 37; 42; 44(3); 46(2); 48; 13:1; 21; 31; 32(2); 14:1(2); 2; 10(3); 11(2); 12; 13(2); 14; 17; 20(3); 26; 30; 15:2; 4(4); 5(2); 6; 7(2); 9; 10(2); 11; 16; 25; 16:9; 21; 23(2); 24; 25(2); 26(2); 33(2); 17:10; 11(2); 12(2); 13(2); 20; 21(3); 23(3); 26(2); 18:16; 20(3); 26; 38; 19:4; 6; 13(3); 17; 18; 20; 23; 40; 41(3); 20:5(2); 7; 8; 12; 19; 25; 26; 30(2); 31; 21:1; 2; 6; 8; **Acts** 1:2; 7; 8(2); 10; 11; 14; 15(2); 17; 18; 19(2); 20(2); 21; 25; 2:1; 5; 6; 8(2); 9; 11; 14; 17; 18; 19(2); 22; 26; 27; 28; 31; 38; 42(3); 44; 46; 3:6; 11; 13; 16(2); 17; 22; 25; 26; 4:2; 3; 7; 12; 16; 17; 18; 19; 24; 32; 5:4(2); 7; 10; 12; 18; 20; 21; 22; 25(2); 28; 34(2); 37; 40; 42(2); 6:1(2); 7; 15; 7:2(2); 4(2); 5; 6(2); 7(2); 10; 12; 16; 17; 20; 22(2); 29; 30(3); 34; 35; 36(3); 38(2); 39; 41(2); 42(2); 44; 45; 48; 51; 8:8; 9; 16; 21(2); 25; 28; 32; 33; 40; 9:10; 12(2); 13; 20; 21; 22(2); 25; 27; 28; 29; 31(2); 32; 37(2); 38; 43; 10:1; 3(2); 12; 23; 25; 27; 30(2); 31; 32; 34; 35; 39(2); 43; 48; 11:1; 3; 4; 5(2); 13; 22; 26; 27; 28; 29; 12:4; 5; 7; 14; 21; 13:1; 5(2); 13; 14; 17; 18; 19; 27(2); 28; 29; 33(2); 35; 40; 41; 43; 14:1; 3; 8(2); 11(2); 13; 14; 15; 16(2); 17; 22; 23(2); 25; 15:11; 21(2); 23; 35; 36; 38; 16:3; 5(2); 6; 9; 12; 18; 24; 29; 32; 34; 36; 17:2; 5; 11(2); 17(2); 21; 22(2); 24(2); 27; 28; 31; 18:2; 4; 9; 10; 21; 23; 24; 25(2); 26; 19:5; 7; 9; 10; 16; 17; 19; 21; 22; 27; 30; 39; 40(2); 20:6; 8; 9; 10; 12; 16; 18; 22; 23; 29; 35; 21:18; 19; 27; 29; 31; 39; 40; 22:2; 3(2); 5; 17(2); 19; 23:1; 6; 9; 11; 21; 25; 30; 35; 24:3; 12(3); 14(2); 15; 18(2); 20; 24; 25:3; 5; 8; 11; 15; 17; 23; 26:3; 10(2); 11; 14; 18(2); 20(2); 21; 26; 27:12; 21; 27; 31; 35; 37; 40; 28:7; 8; 10; 11; 30; **Rom** 1:2; 7; 9(2); 10; 15(2); 17; 18; 19; 21; 24; 27(2); 28; 2:1; 5(2); 7; 12; 13; 14; 15; 16; 17; 19; 20; 23; 28; 29(2); 3:2; 4; 16; 20; 22; 24; 25; 26; 4:12; 17; 18; 19; 20; 24; 5:2(2); 3; 5; 6; 8; 11; 13; 16(2); 17; 18(2); 21; 6:1; 2; 4; 5(2); 11; 12(2); 19; 20; 21; 23; 7:5(2); 6(2); 8; 13; 17; 18(2); 20; 22; 23(2); 8:1; 2; 3(3); 4; 8; 9(3); 10; 11(2); 18; 20; 24; 26; 37; 39; 9:1(2); 2; 7; 17(2); 25; 26; 28; 33; 10:6(2); 8(2); 9; 14(2); 11:17; 19; 22; 23(3); 25(3); 12:4; 5; 6; 7(2); 8; 10; 11(2); 12(3); 16; 17; 20; 13:4; 9; 13(4); 14:1; 5; 13; 15; 17; 18; 22; 15:12; 13(2); 17(2); 18; 19; 23; 26; 27; 29; 30; 31; 16:1; 2(3); 3; 5; 7; 8; 9; 10; 11; 12(2); 13; 19; 22; **1 Cor** 1:2(2); 5(2); 6; 7; 8; 10(2); 13; 15; 21; 29; 30; 31; 2:3(3); 4; 5(2); 7; 11; 13; 3:1; 16; 18; 19; 21; 4:2; 3; 6; 10; 15(2); 17(3); 20(2); 21; 5:3(2); 4; 5; 9; 6:11; 19; 20(2); 7:7(2); 15; 17; 20(2); 22; 24(2); 25; 28; 34(2); 37(2); 38(2); 39; 8:4; 5; 7; 10; 9:1; 2; 9; 10(2); 18; 24(2); 25; 10:2(2); 5; 8; 25; 33; 11:2; 11; 17; 18; 20; 21; 22(2); 23; 24; 25(3); 27; 29; 34; 12:6; 14; 18; 25; 28; 13:6(2); 9(2); 10; 12(2); 14:2(2); 4; 7; 10; 13; 14; 19(2); 20(3); 21; 23(2); 24; 27(2); 28; 33; 34; 35; 40; 15:1; 2; 10; 15; 17; 18; 19(2); 22(2); 23; 28; 30; 31(2); 32; 41; 42(2); 43(4); 52(2); 54; 58(3); 16:8; 11; 13; 19(2); 24; **2 Cor** 1:1; 4(2); 5; 8; 9(3); 10; 11; 12(2); 14(2); 15; 19; 20(2); 21; 22; 2:1; 3; 9; 10; 13; 14(3); 17(2); 3:2; 9; 10; 14(2); 18; 4:2(2); 6(2); 7; 8; 10(2); 11; 12(2); 5:1; 2; 4; 6; 10; 11; 12(2); 17; 19; 21; 6:1; 2(2); 3; 4(5); 5(6); 13; 16; 7:1; 3; 4; 7; 9(2); 11(4); 12; 13; 14(2); 16(2); 8:2(2); 6; 7(7); 10; 18; 20; 21(2); 22(2); 9:3(2); 7; 8; 11; 14; 10:1; 3; 4; 7(2); 11(2); 15(2); 16(2); 17; 11:1; 3; 6(3); 7; 9(2); 10(2); 12; 17; 21; 23(4); 25; 26(12); 27(5); 30; 32; 33(2); 12:2(2); 3; 5; 7; 9(2); 10(5); 11(2); 12; 13; 18(2); 19; 13:3(2); 4(2); 5(2); 11; **Gal** 1:6; 13; 14(2); 16; 22; 24; 2:2; 4(3); 8(2); 14; 16(3); 20(3); 21; 3:3; 4(2); 8; 10(2); 11; 14; 15; 17; 22; 26; 28; 4:3; 9; 11; 14; 18; 19(2); 25(2); 27; 5:1; 6; 10(2); 14(2); 16; 21; 25(2); 6:1(2); 4(2); 6; 9; 12; 13; 14; 15; 17; **Eph** 1:1(2); 3(2); 4(2); 6; 7; 8; 9; 10(5); 11; 12; 13(2); 15; 16; 17; 18; 20(2); 21(2); 23; 2:1; 2(2); 3; 4; 5; 6(2); 7(3); 10(2); 11(2); 12; 13; 15(3); 16; 21(2); 22(2); 3:4; 5; 6; 9; 10; 11; 12(2); 15; 16; 17(2); 20; 21; 4:2; 3; 4; 6; 14; 15(2); 16; 17(2); 18; 21; 23; 24; 32; 5:2; 5; 8; 9; 12; 18; 19(2); 20; 21; 24; 33; 6:1; 4; 5; 9; 10(2); 12; 13; 18; 20(2); 21; 24; **Phil** 1:1(2); 4; 5; 6; 7(3); 9; 13; 14; 18(4); 20(2); 22; 24; 26; 27; 28; 29; 30(2); 2:1; 3; 5(2); 6; 7; 8; 10; 12(2); 13; 15(2); 16(3); 19; 22; 24; 29(2); 30; 3:1; 3(3); 4(2); 6; 9(2); 14; 15; 17; 19; 20; 4:1; 2; 3(2); 4; 6; 9; 10; 11(2); 12; 14; 15; 16; 19; 21; **Col** 1:2(2); 4; 5(2); 6(2); 8; 9; 10(2); 12; 14; 16; 17; 18; 19; 20; 21; 22(2); 23; 24(3); 27; 28(2); 29; 2:1(2); 2; 3; 5(3); 6; 7(3); 9; 10; 11; 12(3); 13; 15; 16(2); 18; 20; 23; 3:3; 4; 7(2); 10; 11; 15(2); 16(4); 17(2); 18; 20; 22(2); 4:1; 2(2); 3; 5; 7; 12(2); 13(2); 15(2); 16; 17; **1 Th** 1:1; 2; 3(2); 5(4); 6; 7; 8(2); 2:1; 2(2); 3; 13(2); 14(2); 17(2); 19; 3:1; 2; 4; 5; 7; 8; 10; 12; 13; 4:1; 4; 5; 6; 7; 10; 14; 16; 17(2); 5:2; 4; 12; 13; 18(2); **2 Th** 1:1; 4; 8; 10(2); 12(2); 2:2; 4; 6; 12; 13; 17; 3:4; 6; 11; 12; 13; 14; 16; 17; **1 Tim** 1:2; 3; 4; 13; 14; 16; 2:2(2); 3; 6; 7(2); 9(2); 11; 12; 15(2); 3:4; 11; 13(2); 15; 16(4); 4:1; 2; 6(2); 10; 12(6); 14; 16(2); 5:5(2); 6; 17; 20; 22; 6:9; 10; 12; 13; 15; 16; 17(3); 18; **2 Tim** 1:1; 3; 5(3); 6; 8; 9; 13(2); 14; 15; 17; 18; 2:1(2); 4; 5; 7; 10; 20; 25(2); 3:1; 12; 14; 15; 16;

4:2; 5; 20(2); **Titus** 1:2; 3; 4; 5(3); 13; 16; 2:2(3); 3; 7(2); 9; 10; 12; 3:3; 8; 15; **Phm** 1:2; 4; 6(2); 7; 8; 10; 13; 16(2); 20(2); 21; 23; **Heb** 1:1(2); 2; 10; 2:5; 6; 8(3); 10; 12; 13; 14; 17(2); 18; 3:2; 5; 8(3); 10; 11; 12(2); 15; 17; 19; 4:2; 3; 4(2); 5; 7; 15; 16; 5:1; 6; 7; 13; 6:7; 9; 10; 18; 7:10; 15; 19; 8:1; 9(2); 10; 13; 9:2; 4; 5; 7; 9(2); 17; 23; 24; 10:3; 6; 7; 8; 16; 22; 24; 32; 34(2); 38; 11:9(3); 12; 13; 18; 19; 26; 34; 37(2); 38(2); 12:3; 9; 23; 13:3; 18; 21(3); 22; **Jas** 1:6; 8; 9; 10; 11; 23; 25(2); 27; 2:2(3); 3; 5; 10; 16; 3:2(2); 3; 9; 13; 14; 18; 4:1; 5(2); 10; 16; 5:3; 5(2); 10; 14; **1 Pe** 1:1; 2; 4; 5; 6; 11; 14; 15; 17; 20; 21(2); 22(2); 2:6(2); 12; 22; 23; 24; 3:4; 5(3); 15(2); 16; 18; 19; 20(2); 4:1(2); 2; 3(2); 4(2); 6(2); 7; 11; 15; 16; 19; 5:6; 9(2); 12; 13; 14; **2 Pe** 1:2; 4; 8; 12; 13; 17; 19(2); 2:1; 5; 10; 11; 12; 13(2); 14; 18; 20; 22; 3:1; 3; 5; 10(3); 11; 13; 14; 16(3); 18; **1 Jn** 1:5; 6; 7(2); 8; 10; 2:4; 5(2); 6; 8(2); 9(2); 10(2); 11(2); 14; 15(2); 16; 24(4); 27(2); 28; 3:3; 5; 6; 9; 10; 14; 15; 17(2); 18(4); 22; 24(3); 4:2; 3(2); 4(2); 9; 10; 12(2); 13(2); 15(2); 16(3); 17(3); 18(2); 5:7; 10(2); 11; 13(2); 14; 20(2); **2 Jn** 1; 2; 3; 4; 6; 7; 9(2); 11; **3 Jn** 1; 2(2); 3(2); 4; 6; **Jude** 1; 4; 6; 7; 9; 10; 11(3); 12; 15; 18; 20; 21; **Rev** 1:3; 4; 5; 9; 10; 11(2); 13; 15; 16(2); 20; 2:1(2); 7; 8; 12; 13(2); 18; 24; 3:1; 4(2); 5; 7; 12; 18; 20; 4:1; 2(2); 3(2); 4; 6(3); 5:1; 3; 6(2); 13(3); 6:5; 6; 15(2); 7:9; 13; 14; 15; 17; 8:1; 9; 9:6; 10; 11(2); 17; 19(2); 10:2; 6(3); 7; 8; 9; 10; 11:3; 5; 6; 8; 12; 13(2); 15; 19(2); 12:1; 2(2); 3; 7; 8; 10; 12; 13:6(2); 8; 12(2); 13; 14; 14:5; 6; 10(2); 13; 14; 15; 16; 17; 18; 15:1(2); 5; 6; 16:3; 16; 17:3; 4(2); 8; 18:4; 6; 7(3); 8; 10; 16; 17; 19(2); 22(3); 23(2); 24; 19:1; 8; 11; 13; 14(2); 17(2); 20; 20:1; 6; 8; 12; 13(2); 15; 21:8; 10; 22; 23; 24; 27; 22:2; 3; 16; 18; 19

INTO (1457/1339)

Gen 1:9; 2:7; 22; 6:18; 19; 7:1; 7; 9; 15; 8:9(2); 9:2; 10:5(2); 12:14; 14:20; 16:5; 18:6; 19:10; 24:20; 67; 27:17; 30:35; 31:33(3); 32:7; 37:20; 22; 24; 35; 39:11; 20; 23; 40:11; 15; 43:17; 18; 24; 26; 30; 45:4; 47:14; 21; 48:16; 49:33; **Ex** 1:22; 3:18; 4:27; 5:3; 6:8; 7:23; 8:3(5); 21; 24(3); 27; 10:4; 19; 11:4; 12:23; 13:5; 11; 14:21; 22; 23; 27; 28; 15:1; 4; 19; 21; 22; 25; 16:3; 18:7; 21:13; 22:8; 11; 23:19; 20; 31; 24:15; 18(2); 25:14; 16; 26:11; 28:16; 29; 35; 43; 30:20; 32:24; 33:5; 8; 37:5; 38:7; 39:3(3); 40:20; 21; 32; **Lev** 1:6; 12; 16; 6:30; 8:20; 9:23; 10:9; 11:33; 12:4; 14:8; 15; 26; 34; 36; 40; 46; 16:2; 3; 10; 21; 22(2); 26; 28; 19:23; 29; 23:10; 25:2; 35; 26:25; 36; 41; **Num** 5:17; 22; 23; 7:89; 13:17; 14:8; 24; 25; 15:2; 18; 16:14; 30; 33; 38; 47; 17:8; 19:6; 7; 14; 20:1; 4; 12; 21:2; 22; 29; 34; 22:23; 25:8; 27:12; 31:24; 27; 54; 32:7; 9; 32; 33:8; 51; 34:2; 35:10; 36:3; 4; 12; **Deut** 1:22; 24; 27; 40; 41; 43; 2:1; 24; 30; 3:2; 3; 6:10; 7:1; 24; 26; 8:7; 9:9; 21; 11:29; 13:16; 14:6; 18:9; 19:3; 20:13; 21:10; 23:5; 11; 24; 25; 24:10; 26:1; 28:41; 29:12(2); 28; 30:12; 31:23; 32:52; **Josh** 2:18; 19; 24; 3:11; 16; 4:5; 6:2; 11; 19; 20; 22; 24; 7:7; 8:1; 7; 13; 18; 10:8; 19; 27; 30; 32; 11:8; 18:5; 20:4; 5; 21:44; 22:13; 24:8(2); 11; **Judg** 1:2; 4; 16; 34; 2:14(2); 23; 3:8; 10; 21; 28; 4:2; 7; 9; 14; 18; 21(2); 22; 5:15; 6:1; 13; 7:2; 7; 9; 13; 14; 15; 16(2); 8:3; 7; 25; 27; 9:27(2); 42; 43; 10:7(2); 11:19; 21; 30; 32; 12:3; 13:1; 15:1; 5; 12; 13; 18; 16:13; 23; 24; 17:4; 18:10; 18; 19:3; 11; 12; 15; 18; 21; 23; 29; 20:4; 28; **Ruth** 2:18; 3:15; **1 Sam** 2:14; 4:3; 5; 6; 7; 13; 5:2; 5; 6:14; 19; 7:1; 13; 9:13; 14; 22; 25; 10:6; 11:11; 12:8; 9(3); 14:10; 12; 21; 26; 37; 17:46; 47; 49; 19:10; 20:8; 11(2); 35; 42; 21:15; 22:5; 23:4; 7; 11; 12; 14; 20; 24:4; 10; 18; 26:3; 8; 23; 28:19(2); 30:15; 23; **2 Sam** 3:8; 34; 4:6; 7; 5:8; 19(2); 6:10(2); 16; 10:2; 12:8; 20; 13:10; 15:25; 31; 37(2); 16:8; 17:13(2); 17; 18; 18:6; 17; 19:2; 3; 5; 21:9; 22:20; 23:11; 24:14(2); **1 Ki** 1:15; 28; 6:6; 8:6; 10:16; 17; 11:30; 14:28; 15:15; 18; 16:18; 21; 17:3; 5; 23; 18:5; 9; 19:4; 9; 11; 20:2; 13; 28; 30(3); 33; 39; 21:4; 22:6; 12; 15; 25; 30(2); **2 Ki** 2:1; 11; 12; 16; 3:10; 13; 18; 4:4; 32; 39(2); 41; 5:18; 6:5; 23; 7:8; 12; 9:6; 25; 10:15; 21; 23; 24; 25; 11:4; 16; 12:4(2); 9(2); 11; 13; 15; 16; 13:3(2); 17:20; 18:21; 30; 19:1; 10; 18; 25; 32; 33; 37; 20:4; 20; 21:14; 22:4; 5; 7; 9; 23:12; 24:14; 15; **1 Chr** 5:6; 20; 26; 6:15(2); 11:15; 13:13(2); 14:10(2); 17; 16:7; 21:13(2); 22:18; 19; 23:6; 24:19; 29:8; **2 Chr** 3:14; 5:7; 7:11; 9:15; 16; 12:11; 13:16; 15:12; 18; 16:8; 18:5; 11; 14; 24; 29(2); 20:20; 21:17; 22:1; 23:6; 7; 15; 24:7; 10; 24; 25:20; 28:5(2); 9; 27; 29:16; 31; 30:14; 31:10; 32:21; 33:13; 34:7; 9; 14; 17; 36:17; **Ezra** 4:7; 5:8; 12; 14; 8:26; 9:7; 10:6; **Neh** 4:11; 5:5; 6:11; 7:5; 9:11(2); 22; 23; 24; 27; 30; 10:29; 34; 12:44; 13:1; 2; 9; 15; **Esth** 2:3; 8; 16; 23; 3:9(2); 13; 4:1; 7; 11; 7:7; **Job** 3:6; 7; 6:16; 9:24; 31; 10:9; 17:12; 18:8(2); 18; 22:4; 24:16; 18; 30:19; 36:16; 37:8; 39:21; 40:23; **Ps** 5:7; 7:13; 15; 9:17; 10:9; 18:19; 24:3; 30:11; 31:5; 8; 32:4; 35:8; 37:20; 46:2; 55:15; 56:8; 57:6; 63:9; 66:6; 11; 13; 68:6; 24; 69:2; 27; 73:17; 76:5; 6; 78:44; 61(2); 79:1; 12; 88:18; 96:8; 100:4(2); 104:8; 10; 105:23; 29; 106:15; 20; 41; 42; 107:33(2); 34; 35(2); 108:10; 109:18; 114:8(2); 115:17; 119:6; 122:1; 132:3; 7; 135:9; 139:8; 140:10(2); 141:10; 143:2; 7; **Prov** 6:3; 7:25; 13:17; 16:33; 17:20; 18:6; 8; 19:15; 26:9; 22; 27; 28:10; 14; 17; 30:4; **Eccl** 1:7; 10:8; 11:9; 12:14; **Song** 1:4; 3:4; 8:2; **Isa** 2:4(2); 10; 19(2); 21(2); 3:14; 5:13; 14; 8:22; 14:7; 13; 19:1; 4; 8; 23(2); 21:4; 22:18; 21; 23:9; 24:18; 29:17; 30:20; 29; 34:9(2); 36:6; 15; 37:1; 10; 19; 26; 33; 34; 38; 40:9; 41:15; 44:17; 23; 46:2; 47:5; 6; 51:23; 52:4; 9; 54:1; 55:12; 57:2; 63:14; 65:6; 7; 66:20; **Jer** 2:7; 21; 4:5; 29; 6:9; 25; 7:31; 8:6; 10:9; 12:7; 13:16; 15:14; 16:8; 13; 15; 18:4; 19:5; 20:4; 5; 6; 21:7(3); 10; 22:7; 22; 25(2); 26; 28; 23:15; 24:5; 9; 26:23; 24; 27:6; 29:16; 21; 30:16; 32:3; 4; 18; 24; 25; 28(2); 35; 36; 43; 33:11; 34:2; 3; 10; 11; 16; 20(2); 21(3); 35:2(2); 4(2); 11; 36:5; 12; 20; 23; 37:12; 17; 38:3; 6; 9; 11(2); 16; 18; 19; 39:17; 41:7(2); 9; 43:3; 44:12; 14; 21; 30(3); 46:19; 24; 26(2); 47:6; 48:7; 11; 44; 49:3; 51:51; 63; **Lam** 1:3; 5; 7; 13; 14; 18; 2:7; 9; 4:22; 5:15; **Ezek** 3:10; 22; 23; 4:9; 14; 5:4(2); 7:11; 19; 21; 8:8(2); 16; 10:7; 11:5; 9; 24; 12:3(2); 4(2); 7; 11; 13:5; 9; 14:3; 4; 7; 19; 15:4; 16:5; 8; 39; 20:6; 10; 15; 28; 35; 37; 42(2); 21:11; 20; 31; 22:19; 20; 23:9(2); 17; 28(2); 39; 24:3; 25:3; 26:20; 27:26; 27; 28:4; 8; 30:12; 17; 18; 25; 31:11; 16; 32:9; 36:24; 37:5; 10; 12; 17; 21; 22; 38:4; 8; 39:23(2); 28; 40:2; 17; 32; 41:1; 42:1(2); 9; 14; 43:4; 5; 44:12; 13; 45:1; 46:19; 20; 21; 47:8; **Dan** 1:2(3); 9; 2:38; 3:6; 11; 15; 20; 21; 23; 24; 6:7; 12; 16; 24; 7:25; 10:3; 11:11; 24; **Hos** 2:14; 4:7; 9:4; **Joel** 1:14; 2:9; 20; 31(2); 3:2; 5; 8; 10(2); **Am** 1:4; 15; 3:5; 4:3; 10; 5:5; 8; 19; 27; 6:11(2); 12(2); 8:10(2); 9:2; 4; **Jon** 1:3; 5(2); 12; 15; 2:3(2); 7; **Mic** 1:6; 16; 3:5; 4:3(2); 5:5; 6; 7:19; **Nah** 3:10; 12; 14; **Hag** 1:6; **Zech** 4:12; 5:8; 10:10; 11:6(2); 13; 14:2; 10; **Mal** 3:10; **Mt** 2:11; 21; 22; 3:10; 12; 4:1; 5; 18; 5:25; 29; 30; 6:6; 13; 26; 30; 7:19; 8:12; 14; 23; 31; 32(2); 33; 9:1; 17(2); 23; 26; 28; 38; 10:5; 12; 11:7; 12:9; 11; 13:2; 30; 36; 42; 47; 48; 50; 14:15; 22; 32; 35; 15:11; 14; 17; 39; 16:13; 17:15(2); 22; 25; 18:8(2); 9(2); 30; 19:17; 20:2; 4; 7; 21:2; 10; 12; 21; 23; 33; 22:9; 10; 13; 24:43; 25:21; 23; 30; 41; 46(2); 26:18; 41; 45; 27:6; 27; 53; 28:7; 11; 16; **Mk** 1:12; 16; 21; 38; 2:22(2); 26; 3:19; 4:1; 37; 5:13; 18; 6:36; 45; 51; 56; 8:10; 13; 26; 9:22(2); 28; 31; 42; 43(2); 45(2); 47; 11:2; 11(2); 15; 23; 12:1; 41; 13:15; 14:13; 16; 38; 41; 54; 15:16; 16:7; 12; 15; 19; **Lk** 1:9; 39; 79; 2:4; 15; 27; 3:3; 9; 17; 4:1; 16; 37; 42; 5:3; 4; 16; 19; 37; 38; 6:4; 38; 39; 7:11; 24; 8:22; 29; 31; 33; 37; 51; 9:10; 12; 44(2); 10:1; 2; 10; 38; 11:4; 12:5; 28; 39; 58; 14:1; 5; 21; 23; 15:15; 16:4; 9; 16; 17:2; 19:4; 12; 30; 45; 20:9; 21:1; 24; 22:10; 40; 46; 54; 66; 23:19; 25; 42; 46; 24:7; 26; 51; **Jn** 1:9; 3:4; 17; 19; 22; 24; 35; 4:8; 14; 28; 38; 47; 54; 5:4; 7; 24(2); 6:14; 17; 21; 24; 7:3; 14; 8:2; 9:39; 10:36; 11:27; 30; 54; 12:24; 46; 13:2; 3; 5; 15:6; 16:13; 20; 21; 28; 17:18(2); 18:11; 15; 28; 37; 19:9; 20:6; 11; 25(2); 27; 21:3; 7; **Acts** 1:11(3); 13; 2:20(2); 34; 3:3; 5:15; 7:6; 9; 23; 45; 55; 8:38; 9:6; 8; 10:10; 16; 11:10; 13:14; 14:20; 16:7; 19; 23; 24; 34; 37; 17:10; 19:3(2); 8; 22; 27; 29; 31; 20:9; 21:11; 28; 29; 34; 37; 38; 22:4; 10; 11; 23; 24; 23:10; 27:15; 30; 38; 28:5; 17; **Rom** 1:23; 5:2; 6:3(2); 4; 7:23; 8:21; 10:6; 7; 11:24(2); **1 Cor** 1:9; 2:9; 9:27; 10:2; 12:13(2); 14:9; **2 Cor** 3:18; 8:16; 10:5; 11:13; 14; 15; 20; 12:4; **Gal** 1:21; 2:4; 3:27; 4:6; **Eph** 2:21; 4:9; 15; **Col** 1:13; 2:18; **1 Th** 2:12; **2 Th** 3:5(2); **1 Tim** 1:3; 12; 15; 2:14; 3:6; 7; 5:9; 6:7; 9(2); **2 Tim** 3:6; **Heb** 1:6; 9:6; 7; 8; 24; 10:5; 16; 31; 13:11; **Jas** 1:2; 25; 2:2; 6; 5:12; **1 Pe** 1:12; 2:9; 3:22; **2 Pe** 1:11; 2:4; 6; 19; **1 Jn** 4:1; 9; **2 Jn** 7; 10; **Jude** 4; **Rev** 2:10; 22(2); 5:6; 8:8; 9:9; 11:9; 12:6; 14; 13:10(2); 14:10; 19(2); 16:17; 19; 17:3; 17; 18:21; 19:20; 20:3; 10; 14; 15; 21:24; 26; 22:14

IS (6944/5487)

Gen 1:11; 12; 29; 30; 2:4; 9; 11(3); 12; 13(2); 14(3); 18; 23; 3:3; 13; 17; 4:7; 9; 13; 5:1; 6:3; 9; 13; 15; 17(2); 21; 7:15; 8:17; 21; 9:4; 10; 12(2); 15; 16; 17(2); 10:1; 9; 12; 11:4; 6; 9; 10; 27; 12:12; 18; 19(2); 13:9; 14:2; 3; 6; 7; 8; 15; 17; 23; 15:2; 3; 13; 16; 16:6; 14; 17:4; 10; 12(3); 13(2); 14; 17(2); 18:9; 14; 20(2); 19:8; 20(3); 31(3); 37; 38; 20:2; 3; 5(2); 7; 11; 12(2); 13(2); 15; 21:13; 17; 22; 29; 22:7; 14; 17; 23:2; 8; 9; 11; 15(2); 19; 20; 24:8; 23; 51; 65(2); 25:7; 9; 12; 18; 19; 22; 32; 26:7(3); 9(2); 10; 20; 28; 33; 27:11; 20; 22; 27; 33; 36; 28:16; 17(3); 29:6(3); 7(2); 19; 25; 30:3; 15; 33(2); 31:5; 12; 14; 29; 35; 36(2); 43(2); 48; 50(2); 51(2); 52(2); 32:2; 6; 8; 18(2); 20; 27; 29; 30; 32; 33:11; 15; 17; 18; 34:14; 15; 21; 22; 35:6(2); 10; 19; 20; 27; 36:1(2); 8; 9; 19; 37:2; 10; 14; 19; 22; 26; 27; 30; 32; 33(2); 38:11; 13; 18; 21; 24; 39:8; 9; 40:8; 12; 14; 18; 41:15; 16; 25; 28(2); 32; 38; 39; 42:2; 13(2); 14; 16; 22; 28(2); 30; 32(2); 36(2); 38(2); 43:3; 5; 7; 18; 27(2); 28(2); 29; 32; 44:5; 9; 10; 15; 20(3); 26(2); 28; 30(2); 31; 34; 45:12; 20; 26(2); 28(2); 46:33; 34; 47:3; 4; 6; 16; 18(2); 23; 48:1; 2; 7; 18; 49:7(2); 9; 14; 21; 22; 24; 27; 28; 29; 30(2); 32; 50:10; 11(2); 20; **Ex** 1:16(2); 22; 2:6; 14; 18; 20(2); 3:5; 13; 15(2); 16; 4:2; 14(2); 22; 5:2; 16(2); 22; 7:14; 17; 8:10; 19; 26; 9:14; 19(2); 27; 28; 29; 10:5; 7; 10; 11; 11:5; 12:4; 11; 19(2); 22(2); 27; 42(2); 43; 44; 13:2; 8; 12; 14; 14:12; 15:2(2); 3(2); 11(2); 26; 16:1; 15(2); 16; 23(2); 25; 26; 32; 36; 17:3; 7; 18:11; 14; 17; 18; 19:5; 20:4(3); 10(2); 11; 12; 17; 21:16; 18; 21; 30(2); 22:2(2); 4(2); 6; 7(2); 8; 10; 12; 13; 16; 27(2); 23:21; 24:8; 25:3; 9; 26:5; 10; 27:21; 28:8; 26; 28; 29:1; 13; 14; 18(2); 21; 22; 23; 25; 27(4); 28(2); 32; 34; 38; 30:6(2); 10; 13(2); 32; 31:7; 13; 14; 15; 17; 32:4; 5; 8; 9; 17; 18; 26; 33:13; 21; 34:10; 14(2); 35:4; 5; 22; 36:17; 38:21; 24; 26; 40:9; **Lev** 1:3; 5; 8; 10; 12; 13; 14; 17(2); 2:3; 5; 6; 7; 8(2); 9; 10(2); 15; 3:1; 3; 4; 5(2); 6; 9; 10; 12; 14; 15; 16; 4:7(2); 8; 9; 13; 18(3); 21; 22; 24; 27; 31; 35; 5:1; 2(2); 3; 4(2); 5; 7; 8; 9; 11(2); 12; 17; 19; 6:4; 9; 14; 15; 17; 20(2); 21; 22(2); 25(3); 27; 28(2); 29; 30; 7:1(2); 4; 5; 6; 7(2); 9(2); 11; 15; 16; 18; 20; 24; 35; 37; 8:5; 31; 9:6; 10:3; 7; 12; 13; 17; 11:4; 5; 6; 7; 10; 26(2); 28; 32(3); 33; 35; 36; 37; 38; 46; 12:7; 8; 13:3; 4; 6; 8; 9; 10(2); 11(2); 13; 15(2); 17; 18; 20; 21; 22; 23; 25(2); 26; 27; 28(2); 30(2); 31; 32; 36; 37(2); 39(2); 40(2); 41(2); 42(2); 43; 44(3); 45; 46; 47; 48; 49(2); 51(2); 52(2); 54; 55(2); 57(2); 58; 59; 14:3; 4; 7; 8; 11; 13(3); 14; 16; 17; 18(2); 19; 21; 22; 25; 27; 28(2); 29(2); 31(2); 32; 35; 36; 37; 40; 43; 44(2); 46; 48; 54; 57(3); 15:2; 3(2); 4; 8; 13; 17; 18; 19; 23; 24; 28; 31; 32(2); 33(2); 16:2; 6; 11(2); 13; 15; 18; 31(2); 32; 17:2; 11(2); 14(2); 15; 18:6; 7; 8; 10; 11; 12; 13; 14; 15; 16; 17; 18; 19; 22; 23; 25; 27; 19:7(2); 13; 20; 20:14; 16; 17; 21; 27; 21:3; 7(2); 10(2); 12; 20(2); 22:4(2); 7; 8; 11; 12; 13; 24; 25; 27; 28; 23:3(2); 5; 6; 21; 28; 29; 36; 24:9; 16; 25:5; 12; 23; 28; 29; 30; 34; 48; 49(2); 54; 27:3; 4; 7; 8; 9; 11; 12; 14; 21; 22; 26(2); 27(2); 28; 30(2); 33; **Num** 1:51(2); 3:48; 4:4; 15; 16(2); 24; 25; 26; 28; 31; 33; 5:6; 8; 13(2); 15; 17; 18; 28; 29; 6:4; 7; 13; 18; 21(2); 23; 8:24; 9:10(2); 13(2); 10:7; 11:6(2); 14; 17; 20; 12:6; 7; 12; 13:11; 18; 19; 20; 27; 32; 14:7; 9; 18; 42; 15:14; 24; 29; 30; 16:3(2); 5(2); 7; 9; 11; 13; 40; 18:11(2); 13(2); 16; 19; 31; 19:2(2); 9(2); 13; 14; 15; 16; 20(2); 20:5(2); 21:5; 8; 11; 13(2); 14; 16; 20; 22:5; 6(2); 32; 36; 23:19; 21(2); 23; 24:9(2); 21(2); 27:7; 18; 28:3; 6; 10; 14; 16; 17; 23; 29:1; 30:1; 31:21; 49; 32:4; 22; 29; 33:6; 7; 36; 34:2; 13; 35:16; 17; 18; 21; 30; 31; 33; 36:5; 6; **Deut** 1:2; 14; 16; 17(2); 20; 25(2); 2:29; 30; 36(2); 3:11(2); 12; 20; 24; 4:1; 6(2); 7(2); 8; 17; 18; 21; 24; 31; 35(2); 38; 39(2); 40; 44; 48(2); 5:8(3); 14(2); 16; 21; 26; 6:1; 4; 15; 18; 20; 24; 7:9; 21; 25(2); 26; 8:7; 13; 14; 18(2); 9:3; 4(2); 5; 6; 10:9; 14; 15; 17; 21(2); 11:10; 11; 17; 31; 12:1; 8; 9; 10; 12; 18; 21; 23; 25; 28; 13:3; 6; 14; 15; 18; 14:8; 10; 19; 21; 24(2); 27; 15:2(2); 3; 4; 7(2); 9; 12; 21(2); 16:3; 11; 17; 20(2); 17:1; 2; 4(2); 6; 8; 14; 15; 18:2; 3; 9; 17; 22; 19:1; 2; 3; 4; 6(2); 10; 14; 18; 20:1; 4; 5; 6; 7(2); 8(2); 14; 19; 20; 21:1(3); 4; 9; 15(2); 17(2); 20(2); 22; 23(3); 22:2; 20; 22; 23(2); 26(2); 28(2); 23:1; 7; 10; 19; 24:4(2); 7; 12; 14(2); 15; 25:1; 15; 19; 26:1; 2; 3; 11; 27:2; 3; 15; 16; 17; 18; 19; 20; 21; 22; 23; 24; 25; 26; 28:8; 23; 43; 61; 29:11; 15; 20; 23(2); 27; 28; 30:11(2); 12; 13; 14; 20; 31:6; 8; 12; 17; 32:4(3); 6; 9(2); 20; 21; 22; 27(2); 28; 31; 32; 33; 34; 35(2); 36(2); 39(2); 47(2); 49; 33:1; 13; 17; 20; 22; 24; 26; 27; 29; 34:1; 4; **Josh** 1:2; 8; 9; 11; 13(2); 15; 2:11; 19(2); 3:10; 11; 16; 4:24; 5:4; 9; 15; 6:7; 7:2; 13; 15; 20; 8:18; 31; 34; 9:12; 10:13; 11:4; 12:2(2); 9; 13:2; 3(2); 9(2); 16(2); 25; 28; 14:11; 15:7(2); 8(2); 9; 10; 12; 13; 25; 49; 54; 60; 17:16; 18; 18:7; 13; 14; 16; 17; 28; 19:11; 48; 20:6; 7; 21:11; 22:9; 10; 16; 17; 19; 22; 28(2); 29; 31; 34(2); 23:3; 6; 10; 24:17; 18; 19(2); 30; **Judg** 1:26; 3:1; 24; 4:11; 14; 20; 5:9; 18; 24(2); 28; 6:12; 13; 15; 17; 24; 25; 31; 37(2); 7:1; 3; 14; 8:2; 21(2); 9:2; 3; 18; 28(4); 33; 37; 38(2); 10:18; 11:8; 13:17; 18; 14:3; 15(2); 18(2); 15:2; 11; 14; 19(2); 16:2; 15; 17:2; 18:8; 9; 10(2); 12; 19; 19:9(2); 10; 18; 19(2); 24; 20:9; 12; 22; 26; 21:5; 6; 8; 11; 12; 19(2); 22; **Ruth** 1:19; 2:5; 6; 19; 20; 22; 3:2(2); 12(2); 15; 16; 4:4; 11; 15; 17(2); 18; **1 Sam** 1:8; 22; 2:1; 2(3); 3; 24; 35; 36; 3:17; 18; 5:7; 6:3; 4; 9; 20; 9:6(2); 7(2); 9; 11; 12(2); 17; 18; 19; 20(2); 24; 10:1; 2; 5; 7; 11(2); 12(2); 22; 24; 11:3; 9; 12; 12:2; 5(3); 6; 13; 17(2); 13:5; 14:1; 2; 7; 24; 28; 15:7; 14; 22; 23(2); 28; 29; 32; 16:6; 11; 12; 15; 16(2); 18(2); 19; 17:9; 26; 29; 46; 47; 55; 56; 18:17; 18; 19:14; 19; 22; 24; 20:1(2); 2; 3; 5; 6; 7(3); 8; 12(2); 18; 21; 26(2); 37; 21:1; 4(2); 5; 8; 9(3); 11; 14; 22:8(4); 13; 14(3); 17; 23:19(2); 22(2); 23; 24:1; 4; 6; 10; 11; 16; 25:10(2); 17(2); 25(4); 28; 32; 33; 41; 26:1; 3; 15; 16(2); 17(2); 18; 19; 22; 27:1; 28:7(3); 14(3); 29:1; 3; 5; 6; 30:20; 24; 26; **2 Sam** 1:16; 18; 19; 21; 2:7; 16; 24; 3:12; 24; 29; 4:8; 10; 5:7; 6:2; 7:3(2); 18; 19; 22(2); 23; 26; 9:1(2); 3(3); 4(2); 6; 8; 10:12; 11:3; 21; 24; 12:14; 18; 19(2); 21; 23; 13:16; 20; 23; 28; 30; 32; 33; 35; 14:5; 7; 13; 17; 19; 20(2); 30; 32; 15:2; 3(2); 31; 16:3(2); 4; 17; 17:2; 7; 8; 9(2); 10(3); 11; 13; 14; 18:13; 18(2); 20; 25(2); 26; 27(2); 28; 29; 31; 32; 19:1; 2; 8; 26; 27(2); 37; 42; 20:8; 11; 21; 21:1; 22:2; 4; 31(3); 32(2); 33; 48; 51; 23:5(2); 15; 17; 24:5; 16; **1 Ki** 1:9; 16; 23; 41; 45(2); 51; 52; 2:3; 22; 29; 38; 42; 3:6; 8; 9; 22(4); 23(4); 27; 4:12; 5:4; 6; 6:1; 38; 8:1; 2; 21; 23; 24; 28; 31; 35; 37(2); 38; 41; 43; 46; 60(2); 9:8; 15; 21(2); 26; 11:7; 19; 27; 33; 38; 12:24; 28; 13:3; 26; 31; 14:2; 5(2); 10; 13(2); 14; 15; 17:24; 18:7; 8(2); 10(2); 11; 14; 17; 21; 24(2); 27(5); 39(2); 41; 43; 44; 19:4; 7; 20:6; 10; 28(2); 32(2); 39; 21:2; 5; 14; 15; 18; 22:3; 7; 8; 32; **2 Ki** 1:3(2); 6(2); 8; 16(2); 2:14; 19(2); 3:11(2); 12; 18; 23; 4:1(2); 6; 9; 14(2); 23(2); 26(4); 27; 40; 5:3; 4; 8; 15; 21; 22; 26; 6:1; 11; 12; 13(2); 19(2); 28; 32; 33; 7:4; 9; 8:5(2); 12; 13; 9:11; 13; 17; 18(2); 19; 20(2); 22; 27; 31; 32; 36; 10:5; 15:4; 19; 29; 30; 33; 11:5; 12:5; 14:6; 17:23; 18:10; 19; 21; 22; 19:3(2); 4; 13; 21; 26; 20:8; 9; 10; 15(2); 17; 19; 22:13(3); 23:10; 17(2); 21; 25:9; **1 Chr** 1:27; 4:41; 5:1; 23; 26; 11:4; 5; 11; 17; 12:17; 13:2; 6; 11; 16:14; 25(2); 30; 32; 33; 34; 40; 17:1; 2(2); 16; 20(2); 21; 24; 19:13; 21:15; 23; 24; 22:1(2); 5; 14; 16; 18(2); 19; 23:29(2); 28:6; 7(2); 18; 29:1(3); 5; 11(4); 12(2); 16(2); **2 Chr** 2:4; 5; 6; 3:3; 5:2; 13; 6:11; 14; 15; 19; 22; 26; 28(2); 29; 32; 33; 36; 7:3; 13; 21; 8:8(2); 11:4; 12:6; 13:4; 8; 10; 12; 14:7; 11; 15:2; 16:9; 18:6; 7(2); 31; 19:2; 6; 7; 11; 20:2(2); 6(2); 9; 12; 15; 17(2); 34; 22:9; 23:4; 18; 25:4; 7; 9; 19; 26:18; 23; 28:11; 13(2); 22; 29:10; 30:9; 19; 31:3; 10(2); 32:7; 8(2); 34:21(4); 35:12; 21; 36:23(2); **Ezra** 1:2; 3(4); 4(2); 5; 9; 2:68; 3:2; 4; 11; 4:11; 13; 15; 16; 21; 24; 5:2; 6; 8(2); 15; 16(2); 17(2); 6:2; 5(2); 8; 12; 18; 7:11; 14; 15; 23; 27; 8:1; 22; 9:2; 7; 11; 15; 10:2; 4; 13(2); 14; 23; **Neh** 1:3; 2:2(2); 19; 4:10(2); 19; 5:5(2); 7; 9; 6:6; 7; 11; 7:3; 8:9; 10(3); 11; 15; 9:5; 6; 10; 18; 10:34; 36; 13:11; 17; **Esth** 1:19; 20(2); 2:7; 16; 3:7(3); 8(2); 13; 4:16; 5:3; 6(2); 7; 6:4; 5; 13; 7:2(2); 5(2); 6; 9; 8:8; 9; 12; 9:1; 12(2); 24; **Job** 1:8; 12; 2:3; 6; 3:3; 19; 20(2); 23(2); 4:6; 19; 5:1; 4; 7; 17; 24; 27; 6:6; 11; 12(2); 13(2); 14; 17(2); 30; 7:1; 5(2); 7; 17; 8:12; 14; 18; 19; 9:2; 4; 19(2); 22; 24(2); 32; 33; 35; 10:7; 16; 22; 11:4; 9; 12; 18; 12:4; 5(3); 10; 12; 13:19; 28; 14:1(2); 5; 7(2); 10(2); 13; 17; 18; 15:9; 14(2); 16; 20; 22; 23(2); 16:6; 8; 16(2); 17(2); 19(2); 17:1(2); 3; 15; 18:6(2); 8; 10; 12(2); 14; 15; 18; 21; 19:7; 17; 26; 28; 29; 20:5(2); 7; 12; 21; 23(2); 25; 26(2); 29; 21:4; 9; 15; 16(2); 17; 21; 24; 28(2); 22:2; 3(2); 4; 5; 12; 18; 30; 23:2(2); 8; 13; 14; 24:14; 17; 22; 25; 25:3; 4; 6(2); 26:2; 6; 27:3; 8; 11; 13; 14; 19; 21; 28:1(2); 2(2); 5; 11; 12; 13; 14(2); 18; 20; 21; 28(2); 29:19; 20(2); 30:2; 16; 18; 27; 31; 31:2; 3; 23; 28; 31; 35; 32:8; 19(2); 33:9; 12; 19; 23; 24; 34:4; 6; 7; 17; 18; 19; 22; 29; 35:2(2); 10; 14; 36:4(2); 5(2); 16(2); 18; 22; 26; 37:4; 10; 16; 21; 22; 23; 38:2; 15(2); 19(2); 21; 24; 26(2); 30; 39:8; 11; 16; 22; 30; 40:11; 12; 16(2); 19; 23(2); 41:9; 10(2); 11; 16; 24; 33(2); 34; 42:3; 7(2); 8; **Ps** 1:1; 2; 2:12; 3:2; 8; 4:3; 5:9(3); 6:3; 5; 7:2; 3; 10; 11(2); 8:1; 4; 9; 9:15; 16(2); 10:4; 7(2); 16; 11:4(2); 7; 12:4; 8; 14:1(2); 3; 5; 6; 15:4; 16:2; 3; 8; 9; 11; 17:1; 12; 18:2; 3; 30(3); 31(2); 32; 47; 19:3(2); 5; 6(2); 7(2); 8; 9; 11(2); 21:5; 22:11(2); 14; 15; 28; 23:1; 24:1; 6; 8; 10(2); 25:8; 11; 12; 14; 26:3; 10(2); 27:1(2); 28:3; 7; 8(2); 29:3(2); 4(2); 30:5(2); 9; 31:10; 13; 19; 32:1(3); 2(2); 6; 33:1; 4(2); 5; 12(2); 16(2); 17; 18; 20; 34:8(2); 9; 12; 16; 18; 20; 35:10(2); 36:1; 4; 5; 6; 7; 9; 37:13; 16; 26; 31; 33; 37; 39(2); 38:3; 7; 9(2); 14; 17; 20; 39:4; 5(2); 7; 11; 40:4; 7; 8; 41:1; 42:3; 6; 10; 44:15; 25; 45:1(2); 2; 6(2); 11; 13(2);

46:1; 4; 5; 7(2); 11(2); 47:2(2); 7; 9; 48:1; 2; 3(2); 10(2); 14; 49:8; 11; 12; 13; 16; 20(2); 50:6; 10; 12; 51:3; 52:7; 9; 53:1(2); 3; 54:4(2); 6; 55:4; 11; 12(2); 15; 56:9; 57:4; 6; 7(2); 58:4; 11(2); 59:9; 17; 60:2; 7(4); 8; 10; 11; 12; 61:2(2); 62:2(2); 5; 6(2); 7(2); 8; 63:1; 3; 65:1; 4; 9; 66:5; 10; 68:2; 5; 15(2); 16; 17; 20; 27; 34(2); 35; 69:2; 3; 13; 16; 71:11; 18; 19(2); 72:7; 73:1; 4; 11; 25; 26; 28; 74:9(2); 12; 16(2); 75:1; 7; 8(3); 76:1(2); 2; 12; 77:10; 13(2); 79:10; 80:16(2); 81:4; 83:18; 84:1; 5(3); 10; 11; 12; 85:9; 12; 86:8; 13; 87:1; 88:3; 89:7; 8; 10; 11; 13(2); 17; 19; 41; 47; 90:4; 6; 10(2); 11; 91:2; 9; 92:1; 7; 15(3); 93:1(3); 2; 4; 94:12; 13; 95:3; 5; 7; 10; 96:4(2); 10; 12; 13(2); 97:8; 11; 98:9; 99:2(2); 3; 5; 9; 100:3(2); 5(2); 102:4; 103:1; 5; 8; 11; 12; 16; 17; 104:13; 20; 24; 26; 105:7; 106:1; 107:1; 40; 43; 108:1; 4; 8(4); 9; 11; 12; 13; 109:7; 21; 22; 24; 27; 110:5; 111:3; 4; 9; 10; 112:1; 4; 7; 8; 113:3; 4; 5; 115:2; 3; 8; 9; 10; 11; 116:5(2); 15; 117:2; 118:1; 6; 7; 8; 9; 14; 15; 16; 20; 23; 24; 26; 27; 29; 119:38; 50; 64; 70; 71; 72; 77; 85; 89; 96; 97; 105; 109; 118; 126; 132; 140; 142(2); 144; 155; 160; 174; 120:5; 121:5(2); 122:3(2); 123:4; 124:7; 8; 127:2; 3; 5; 128:1; 129:4; 130:4; 7(2); 131:1; 2; 132:14; 133:1; 2; 3; 135:3(2); 5(2); 17; 18; 136:1; 138:5; 6; 139:4; 6(2); 17; 24; 140:3; 141:5; 142:4; 143:2; 4(2); 10; 144:3; 4; 8; 11; 15; 145:3(2); 8; 9; 13; 17; 18; 146:3; 5(2); 6; 147:1(3); 5(2); 148:13(2); **Prov** 1:7; 17; 19; 2:7; 10; 3:13; 15; 16; 18; 27(2); 32(2); 33; 4:7; 13; 16; 18; 19; 5:3; 4; 22; 6:14; 23; 26; 29; 30; 31; 34; 7:19; 27; 8:4; 7; 8; 11; 13; 14; 19; 34; 9:4; 10(2); 13(2); 16; 17(2); 10:1; 5(2); 7; 11; 13(3); 14; 15(2); 17; 18; 19(2); 20(2); 23; 25; 26; 29; 32(2); 11:1; 2; 8; 10; 11(2); 12; 13; 14(2); 15(2); 17; 22; 23(2); 24(3); 30(2); 12:1; 3; 4(2); 8; 9(2); 11; 13; 15(2); 16; 18; 19; 20; 27; 28(2); 13:5; 6; 7; 8; 10; 12; 14; 15; 19(2); 22; 23(2); 14:2; 3; 4; 6; 8(2); 9; 12(2); 16; 17; 20; 21; 23; 24(2); 26; 27; 28(2); 29(2); 30(2); 32; 33(2); 34; 35(2); 15:4; 5; 6(2); 8(2); 9; 10; 13; 15; 16; 17(2); 18; 19(2); 21(2); 23; 27; 29; 33(2); 16:1; 5; 6; 8; 10; 12(2); 13; 14; 15(2); 16; 17; 20; 22(2); 25(2); 27; 29; 31(2); 32(2); 33(2); 17:1; 3; 5; 6; 7; 8; 10; 14; 16; 17; 24; 25; 26; 27; 28(2); 18:4; 5; 7; 9(3); 10; 11; 12(2); 13; 19; 24; 19:1(3); 2; 4; 6; 10; 11; 12(2); 13; 14; 16; 18; 22(3); 26; 20:1(4); 2; 3; 5; 11(2); 14; 15; 16(2); 17; 25; 27; 29(2); 21:1; 2; 3; 5; 6; 8(2); 11(3); 15; 20; 24; 27; 30; 31(2); 22:1; 2; 6; 7; 13; 14(2); 15; 18; 22; 26; 23:1; 5; 7(2); 11; 15; 18; 22; 27(2); 31; 24:3(2); 5; 6; 7; 9(2); 10; 13(2); 14; 23; 25:2(2); 3; 7; 11; 12; 13; 14; 15; 18; 19; 20; 21(2); 24; 25; 26; 27(2); 28; 26:1; 7; 8; 9; 12; 13(2); 16; 17; 19; 20(2); 21(2); 26; 27:3(3); 4(2); 5; 7; 8; 10; 13(2); 21(2); 25; 28:3; 6; 7; 9; 11; 12; 14(2); 15; 16; 18; 21; 24(2); 25; 26; 29:1; 6; 9; 18(2); 20; 24; 27(3); 30:4(2); 5(2); 9; 11; 12(3); 13; 14; 16; 20; 21; 22; 23; 28; 30; 31:4(2); 6; 10; 14; 15; 18; 21(2); 22; 23; 26; 30(2); **Eccl** 1:2; 7; 8; 9(4); 10(2); 11; 13; 14; 15(2); 17; 18; 2:15; 16(2); 17; 19; 21(3); 23; 24; 26(3); 3:1; 2; 12; 13; 15(3); 17; 19; 22(2); 4:1(2); 3(2); 4(2); 8(4); 10; 12; 16; 5:2; 3; 7; 9(2); 10; 12; 13; 14; 16; 18(3); 19; 6:1(2); 2(2); 3(2); 4; 7(2); 9(2); 10(4); 11; 12; 7:1; 2; 3(2); 4(2); 5; 6(2); 8(2); 11; 12(3); 15(2); 18; 20; 24; 26; 27; 8:1(2); 4(2); 6; 8; 9(2); 10; 11(2); 14(2); 16; 17; 9:2(2); 3(3); 4(3); 5; 9; 10; 11; 16(2); 18; 10:2; 3; 5; 6; 10; 11(2); 13; 14; 16; 17; 19; 11:5(2); 7(2); 8(2); 12:4; 5; 6(2); 8; 12(2); 13; **Song** 1:1; 2; 3; 12; 13; 14; 16; 2:2; 3; 6; 9(2); 11(2); 12; 14(2); 16; 3:6; 7; 4:1; 2; 3; 4; 7; 10(2); 11; 12; 5:2(3); 9(2); 10; 11; 14; 15; 16(4); 6:3; 5; 6; 9; 10; 7:2(2); 4(2); 5(2); 7; 10; 8:3; 5; 6; 8; 9(2); 12; **Isa** 1:5; 6; 7(2); 8; 11; 13; 2:7(4); 8; 22(2); 3:7; 8; 14; 4:3(2); 5:7; 8; 14; 16; 25(3); 30; 6:3(2); 5; 7; 11; 13; 7:8(2); 9(2); 13; 18(2); 22; 8:10; 20(2); 9:1; 6(2); 12(2); 15(2); 17(3); 19; 21(2); 10:2; 4(2); 5; 7; 9(3); 29; 11:3; 12:1; 2(2); 4; 5; 6; 13:6; 15(2); 22; 14:6; 7; 9; 11(2); 16; 26(4); 27; 28; 29; 15:1(2); 6; 16:4; 6; 10; 12(2); 13; 17:14(2); 18:1; 5(2); 19:25; 20:6; 21:2; 9(2); 14; 22:5; 15; 25; 23:1(3); 3(2); 7(2); 10; 14; 24:5; 9; 10(2); 11(3); 12(2); 13; 19(3); 25:4; 7; 9(2); 10; 26:3; 4; 7; 8; 11; 17; 19; 20; 27:1; 4; 9; 11; 28:1(2); 4(3); 8; 12(2); 20; 27(3); 29; 29:8(2); 11(3); 12(2); 13; 17; 20(2); 30:9; 14; 18; 21; 27; 28; 29; 33(2); 31:2; 3; 4; 9(2); 32:15(2); 19; 33:5; 6; 9(2); 17; 18(3); 22(3); 23(2); 34:1; 2; 6(2); 8; 36:4; 6; 7; 37:3(2); 4; 13; 22; 27; 38:3; 7; 9; 12; 16; 22; 39:4(2); 6; 8; 40:2(2); 6(2); 10; 16; 20; 22; 26; 27(2); 28(2); 41:7; 17; 24(2); 26(4); 42:8; 10; 19(3); 21; 22; 43:7; 9; 11; 13; 44:3; 6; 8(2); 12(2); 16; 19; 20; 28; 45:5(2); 6(2); 14(3); 18(2); 21(2); 22; 46:9(2); 47:4; 8; 10; 48:2; 22; 49:4; 5; 6; 7; 20; 50:1(2); 2(2); 4; 8(2); 9; 51:5; 7; 13; 15; 18(2); 52:5; 6; 53:2; 3; 7; 54:5(4); 9; 17(2); 55:2(2); 6; 56:1; 2; 57:1; 6; 10; 11; 15; 19(2); 21; 58:5(2); 6; 7; 59:1; 5; 6; 8; 9(2); 11(2); 14(2); 21(2); 60:1; 61:1; 62:11(2); 63:1(2); 2; 3; 4; 5(2); 16; 64:7; 10; 11; 65:2; 4; 6; 8(2); 66:1(4); 2; 3; 24; **Jer** 1:13; 2:6; 8; 14(3); 19(2); 22; 25; 26(3); 34; 3:23(2); 4:7; 18(2); 20(2); 31(2); 5:1; 12; 13; 15(2); 16; 19; 27; 6:6(2); 10(2); 11; 13; 14; 16; 18; 25; 29; 7:10; 11; 14; 23; 28; 30; 31; 32; 8:8; 10; 11; 16; 18; 19(2); 20(2); 22(3); 9:6; 8; 12(2); 19; 10:6(2); 7(2); 8; 9(2); 10(2); 13; 14(4); 16(4); 19(3); 20(2); 23(2); 11:3; 5; 12:8; 9; 11; 13:4; 10; 20; 25; 14:4; 19; 15:10; 14; 18; 16:10(2); 17; 21; 17:1(2); 5; 6; 7(2); 9; 11; 12; 15; 18:6; 12; 23; 19:2; 11; 20:11; 21:12; 22:28(2); 23:6; 9; 10(3); 28; 29; 33; 25:3; 13; 18; 29; 38; 27:18; 29:26; 28; 30:6; 7(3); 12(2); 13; 15; 17; 21; 31:9; 17; 20(2); 33; 35; 32:7(2); 8(3); 14(2); 17; 18; 20; 27; 34; 43; 33:2; 10; 11; 12; 16; 25; 34:8; 15; 36:7; 37:17(2); 38:5; 9(3); 21; 40:4; 41:3; 12; 17; 42:6; 43:9; 44:6; 22(2); 27; 45:3; 4; 46:7; 10; 17; 18(2); 20; 47:2; 5; 48:1(3); 4; 10(2); 15(2); 16; 17; 20(3); 25(2); 29; 30; 38; 39; 41; 47; 49:3; 7; 10; 19(3); 21; 23; 25; 29; 50:2(3); 15; 17; 22; 25; 34(2); 35; 36(2); 37(2); 38(2); 44(3); 46; 51:5; 6; 9(2); 11(2); 16; 17(4); 19(4); 31; 33(2); 41(2); 42; 48; 55(2); 56(2); 57; 52:13; **Lam** 1:1; 4; 9(2); 12(2); 16; 18; 20(3); 22; 2:9; 11(2); 12(2); 13; 15(2); 16; 3:23; 24; 25; 26; 27; 37; 38; 4:3; 6; 8; 22; 5:8; 10; 17; 18; **Ezek** 3:12; 5:5; 6:12(3); 7:7; 12; 14; 15(3); 23(2); 8:17; 9:6; 9(2); 10:20; 11:3(2); 7; 23; 12:12; 22; 27(2); 13:10; 12; 15; 16(2); 14:9; 15:2(2); 3; 4(3); 5; 16:30; 46(2); 17:10; 18:4; 5(2); 9; 10; 18; 19; 21; 24; 25(3); 26; 27; 29(2); 19:2; 13; 14; 20:29(2); 21:7; 9; 11(2); 13; 14; 15(2); 16; 22; 27; 28; 22:22; 24; 25; 23:4(2); 20(2); 37; 45; 24:6(2); 7; 13; 24; 25:8; 26:2(3); 15; 27:27; 32; 28:2; 3; 5; 29:3; 9; 30:3(2); 9; 12; 31:18; 32:15; 16; 20; 22; 23; 24; 29; 33:6; 14; 16; 17(3); 19; 20; 27; 30; 34:12; 18; 37:11; 19; 28; 39:8(2); 40:45; 46; 41:4; 8; 22(2); 42:13; 14; 43:7; 12(3); 13(2); 15; 16; 18; 44:3; 9; 26; 45:3; 13; 14(2); 46:14; 16; 20; 47:16(2); 17(2); 18; 19; 20; 48:12; 14; 29; 35; **Dan** 2:3; 5; 8; 9; 10; 11(3); 15; 22; 28; 36; 45(2); 47; 3:4; 14; 15; 17(2); 25; 29; 4:3(2); 8(2); 9; 17; 18; 22; 24(2); 30; 31; 34(2); 37; 5:11(2); 13; 14; 25; 26; 6:12; 13; 15; 26(2); 7:14; 27; 28; 8:2; 21(3); 26; 9:7; 13; 14; 15; 17; 18; 26; 27(2); 10:4; 17; 21; 11:23; 35; 12:1; 11(2); 12; **Hos** 2:1; 2; 3:1(2); 4:1; 13; 16; 17; 18; 5:1; 3(2); 4; 9; 11; 6:3; 4; 8; 10(2); 11; 7:4; 8; 11; 8:5(2); 6(2); 8(2); 9:7(2); 8(2); 15; 16(2); 10:2; 7; 10; 11; 12; 11:8; 12; 12:1; 5(2); 8; 13:2; 4; 9; 10; 12(2); 13; 14; 15; 16; 14:8; 9(2); **Joel** 1:10(3); 15; 16; 2:1(2); 3; 4; 11(3); 13; 17; 27; 3:13(3); 14; **Am** 2:7; 11; 13; 3:5; 6(2); 4:13(2); 5:2; 8; 13; 18; 20(2); 27; 6:2; 8; 7:2; 5; 10; 13(2); 9:6; 9; **Ob** 3; 7; 15; **Jon** 1:8(3); 12; 2:9; 3:8; 4:3; 4; 8; 9(2); **Mic** 1:2; 3; 5(3); 11; 2:1; 3; 7; 10(2); 3:1; 7; 11; 4:9; 5:3; 6:8; 10; 12; 7:1(2); 2; 4(2); 10(2); 18; **Nah** 1:2(2); 3; 6; 7; 15; 2:5; 6; 7; 9; 10(2); 11; 3:1; 3; 7; 17; 19; **Hab** 1:3; 4; 16; 2:3; 4; 5(2); 6; 13; 18; 19(2); 20; 3:19; **Zeph** 1:7; 14(3); 15; 2:2; 5; 15(2); 3:1; 5; 6; 8; 15; 18; **Hag** 1:4; 6; 9; 2:3(2); 6; 8(2); 13; 14(4); 19; **Zech** 1:7; 11; 2:2(2); 13; 3:2; 4:1; 2; 6; 5:2; 3; 5; 6(4); 7(2); 8; 11; 6:6; 12; 8:6; 23; 9:9(2); 17; 10:2; 3; 5; 10; 11:3(4); 9(2); 12; 12:8; 13:7; 9(4); 14:1; 7; 9; 16; **Mal** 1:5; 6(2); 7; 8(2); 9; 10; 12(2); 14(2); 2:1; 7; 13; 14; 17(2); 3:1; 2; 14(2); 4:1(2); **Mt** 1:16; 20(2); 23; 2:2; 5; 3:2; 3; 9; 10(2); 11(2); 12; 15; 17; 4:4; 6; 7; 10; 13; 17; 5:3; 10; 12; 13; 14; 18; 22; 29; 30; 32; 34; 35(2); 37(2); 48; 6:3; 6; 10; 13; 18; 21; 22(2); 23(4); 25; 30(2); 34; 7:4; 6; 9; 11; 12; 13(2); 14(2); 19; 8:6; 9:5; 15; 16; 17; 24; 37; 10:2; 7; 10; 11; 13(2); 20; 24; 25; 26; 28; 32; 33; 37(2); 38; 11:6(2); 10(2); 11(2); 14(2); 16; 19; 30(2); 12:2; 6; 8; 10; 11; 12(2); 18; 25; 26; 30(2); 33; 41; 42; 45; 48; 50; 13:14; 19; 20; 22; 23; 24; 31; 32(3); 33; 37; 38; 39(2); 44; 45; 47; 52; 55(2); 57; 14:2(2); 4; 15(2); 26; 27; 28; 15:5; 8; 17; 22; 26; 28; 16:2(2); 3; 7; 11; 17; 26; 17:4; 5; 9; 11; 12; 15; 22; 18:1; 4; 8; 9; 10; 12; 14(2); 23; 19:3; 9; 10(2); 12; 14; 17(2); 23; 24; 26; 20:1; 4; 7; 14; 15(2); 23(3); 21:5; 9; 10; 11; 13; 38; 42; 22:2; 8; 17; 20; 23; 32; 36; 38; 39; 42; 45; 23:8; 9(2); 10; 11; 15; 16(2); 17; 18(3); 19; 38; 39; 24:6; 17; 18; 23; 26(2); 28; 32; 33; 42; 44; 45; 46; 48; 50(2); 25:6; 13; 14; 25; 26:2; 13; 18; 22; 24(2); 25; 26; 28(2); 31; 38; 39; 41(2); 45(2); 46; 48; 62; 64; 66; 68; 27:4; 6; 11; 17; 22; 33; 37; 42; 46; 47; 28:6(2); 7(2); 15; **Mk** 1:2; 7; 15(2); 27(2); 37; 2:9; 16; 19; 21; 22; 24; 26; 28; 3:4; 17; 21; 24; 25; 26; 29; 33; 35; 4:15; 21(2); 22; 26; 31(3); 32; 40; 5:9(2); 35; 39; 41; 6:2(2); 3; 4; 14; 15(2); 16; 18; 35(2); 50; 7:2; 6(2); 11(2); 15; 19; 27; 34; 8:16; 17; 21; 38; 9:5; 7; 12(2); 13; 26; 31(2); 40(2); 43; 44; 45; 46; 47; 48; 50; 10:2; 14; 18(2); 23; 24; 25; 27; 29; 40(3); 49; 11:9; 10; 17; 12:7; 11; 14; 16; 18; 27; 28; 29(2); 30; 31(2); 32(2); 33; 35(2); 37; 13:7; 11(2); 15; 16; 21(2); 28; 29; 33; 34; 35; 14:9; 14; 19(2); 20; 21(2); 22; 24(2); 27; 34; 38(2); 41(2); 42; 44; 60; 69; 15:2; 22; 34; 35; 42; 16:6(2); 7; 16; **Lk** 1:13; 18; 28; 35; 36; 42; 43; 45; 49(2); 50; 61(2); 63; 68; 2:4; 11(2); 23; 24; 34; 3:4; 8; 9(2); 13; 16; 17; 4:4; 8; 10; 18; 21; 22; 24; 36; 5:21; 23; 34; 39; 6:2; 4; 5; 9; 20; 23; 32; 33; 34; 35; 36; 40(2); 42(3); 44; 47; 48; 49; 7:23(2); 27(2); 28(3); 35; 39(3); 47; 49; 8:10; 11(2); 17; 25; 26; 30; 49; 52; 9:9; 25(2); 26; 33; 35; 38; 44; 48; 50(2); 62; 10:2; 6; 7; 22(2); 26(2); 29; 42; 11:2; 4; 7; 8; 17; 18; 23(2); 26; 27; 29; 31; 32; 34(5); 35(2); 36; 39; 12:1; 2; 6; 21(2); 23(2); 28(2); 32; 34; 40; 42; 43; 45; 46(2); 48; 50; 54(2); 55; 56; 57; 13:18; 19; 21; 35(2); 14:3; 15; 22(2); 29; 31; 32; 34; 35; 15:4; 10; 24(2); 31; 32(2); 16:2; 3; 10(6); 12(2); 15(2); 16; 17; 18; 25; 26; 17:1; 21; 30; 31(2); 37; 18:16; 19(2); 24; 25; 29; 19:7; 9; 20; 38; 46(2); 20:2; 14; 17(2); 22; 27; 38; 41; 44; 21:20; 30; 31; 22:1; 11; 16; 19(2); 20(2); 21; 22; 26; 27(2); 37; 38; 42; 53; 59; 64; 23:2; 3; 35; 38; 24:6(2); 17; 21; 29(2); 34; 39; 46; **Jn** 1:15; 18; 19; 27(2); 30(2); 33; 34; 38; 41; 42; 47; 3:2; 3; 4; 5; 6(4); 8(2); 13(2); 18(2); 19; 26; 29(2); 31(4); 33; 4:5; 9; 10; 11; 18; 20; 21; 22; 23(3); 24; 25(2); 34; 37; 42; 54; 5:2(2); 7; 10(2); 12; 25(2); 27; 28; 30; 31; 32(2); 45; 6:1; 7; 9; 12; 14(2); 20; 29; 31; 33; 39; 40; 42(2); 45; 46; 50; 51; 55(2); 58; 60; 63; 70; 7:6; 11; 12; 16; 17; 18(2); 20; 22; 25; 26; 27(2); 28; 36; 40; 41; 49; 51; 8:7; 13; 14; 16; 17(2); 19; 26; 29; 34; 39; 44(2); 47; 50; 52; 53; 54(3); 9:4(2); 7; 8; 9(2); 12; 16(2); 17; 19; 20; 21; 23; 24; 25; 29; 30(2); 31; 36; 37(2); 10:1; 2; 12; 13; 20; 29(2); 34; 38; 11:3; 4; 10; 14; 16; 27; 28; 31; 39; 50; 12:13; 14; 15; 27; 31; 34; 35(2); 50; 13:10(2); 16(3); 25; 26; 31(2); 32; 14:8; 21; 22; 24; 28; 30; 15:1; 6(2); 8; 12; 15; 20; 25; 16:2; 7; 11; 14; 17; 18(2); 21; 25; 32(2); 17:3; 12; 17; 18:31; 36(2); 37; 38; 19:13; 17; 30; 35(2); 40; 20:16; 31; 21:7; 14; 20; 22; 23; 24(2); **Acts** 1:7; 12; 19(2); 20; 2:8; 15; 16; 25; 29(2); 39; 3:2; 11; 4:11; 12(2); 16; 19; 24; 36; 5:9; 17; 32; 38; 39; 6:2; 9; 7:33; 35; 37; 38; 42; 49(3); 8:10; 21; 26; 32; 33; 36; 37; 9:5; 11; 15; 20; 21; 22; 36; 10:4; 5; 6(2); 28; 32(2); 35; 36; 42; 11:13; 12:15; 13:8; 9; 11; 33; 38; 39; 15:5; 15; 16:12; 17:3; 7; 19; 24; 25; 27; 29; 18:5; 15; 28; 19:2; 4; 27; 28; 34; 35(2); 20:10; 32; 35; 21:28; 22:22; 25(2); 26; 23:5; 8; 19; 24:2; 11; 21; 25:5; 11; 14; 16; 26:14; 24; 31; 27:5; 33; 34; 28:4; 22; **Rom** 1:8; 9; 12; 15; 16; 17(2); 18; 19; 25; 26; 27; 2:2; 10; 11; 24(2); 25; 28(4); 29(4); 3:1; 4; 5; 8; 10(2); 11(2); 12; 13(2); 14; 18; 20; 21; 22; 24; 27(2); 28; 29(2); 30; 4:5; 8; 14; 15(2); 16(2); 17; 5:13(2); 14; 15; 16; 6:21; 23(2); 7:2(2); 3(2); 7; 12; 13(2); 14; 16; 17; 18(3); 20; 21; 23; 8:1; 6(2); 7(2); 9; 10(3); 24(2); 27; 31; 33; 34(4); 36; 39; 9:5; 6; 8; 9; 13; 14; 16; 33; 10:1; 4; 5; 6; 7; 8(2); 10; 12(2); 15; 20; 11:5; 6(5); 8; 12; 15; 16(3); 23; 24; 26; 27; 12:1; 2; 3; 6; 9(2); 18; 19(2); 20(2); 13:1; 3; 4(2); 9; 10; 11(2); 12(2); 14:1; 2; 4; 11; 14(2); 15; 17; 18; 20; 21(3); 22; 23(3); 15:3; 9; 21; 27; 16:1; 5(2); 19; 25; **1 Cor** 1:2; 9; 13; 18(2); 19; 20(3); 25(2); 31; 2:9; 11; 12; 15(2); 3:5(2); 7; 11(2); 13; 15; 17; 19(2); 23; 4:2; 3; 4; 6; 17; 20; 5:1(3); 6; 11; 6:5(2); 7; 13; 16(2); 17(2); 18; 19(2); 7:1; 8; 9; 10; 11; 12; 13; 14(2); 15; 19(3); 22(4); 26(3); 29; 31; 32; 33; 34(2); 35; 36(2); 39(2); 40(2); 8:3; 4(2); 6; 7(2); 10; 9:3; 6; 9(3); 10; 11; 16(2); 18; 25; 10:7; 13(2); 16(2); 19(3); 25; 26; 27; 28; 29; 11:3(3); 5; 6(2); 7(2); 8; 11; 13; 14; 15(2); 20; 21(2); 24(2); 25; 34; 12:3; 6; 7; 8; 12(2); 14; 15; 16; 26; 13:4(2); 5; 8; 10(2); 13; 14:5; 7; 9; 10; 14; 15; 17; 21; 22; 24(2); 25; 26; 28; 30; 33; 35; 38; 15:12(2); 13(2); 14(3); 16; 17(2); 20; 26; 27(2); 32; 36; 39(2); 40(2); 41; 42(3); 43(4); 44(4); 45; 46; 47; 48; 54(2); 55(2); 56(2); 58; 16:4; 15; 19; **2 Cor** 1:1; 6(3); 7; 12; 18; 21; 2:2(2); 3; 6; 16; 3:3; 5; 11(2); 14; 15; 16; 17(3); 4:3(2); 4; 6; 12; 13; 16(2); 17(2); 5:1; 2; 5; 13(2); 17(2); 19; 6:2(2); 11; 17; 7:4(2); 8:10; 12(2); 15; 18; 19; 20; 23; 9:1; 8; 9; 12; 10:6; 7(3); 10; 15(2); 18; 11:3; 10; 15; 21; 29(2); 31; 12:1; 4; 9(2); 13; 13:3; 5; 7; **Gal** 1:7; 11; 2:16; 17; 20; 3:10(2); 11(2); 12; 13(2); 15(2); 16; 18(2); 20; 21; 28(3); 4:1(2); 2; 9; 18; 19; 22; 24; 25(3); 26(2); 27; 29; 5:3; 10; 14; 22; 23; 6:1; 3; 6; 7; **Eph** 1:14; 18; 19; 21(2); 23; 2:4; 8; 11; 14; 15; 3:9; 13; 15; 18; 20; 4:4; 6; 10; 15; 18; 21; 28; 29; 5:3; 5; 9; 10; 12; 13; 17; 18; 23(3); 24; 32; 6:1; 2; 8; 9(2); 17; **Phil** 1:7; 8; 18; 21(2); 23; 24; 28; 30; 2:1; 9; 11; 13; 3:1(2); 6; 9(3); 19(3); 20; 21; 4:5; 8(2); **Col** 1:5; 6(2); 7; 15; 17; 18(2); 24(2); 27; 2:10; 17; 19; 3:1; 3; 4; 5; 6; 10; 11(2); 14; 18; 20; 25; 4:1; 9; 11; 12; 15; 16(2); **1 Th** 2:5; 13; 19(2); 3:10; 4:3; 6; 5:15; 18; 21; 24; **2 Th** 1:3; 5; 6; 7; 2:3; 4(3); 6; 7(2); 9; 3:1; 3; 17; **1 Tim** 1:4; 5; 8; 9; 10(2); 15; 17; 2:3; 5; 10; 3:1; 13; 15; 16; 4:4(3); 5; 8(3); 9; 10; 14; 5:4; 5; 6; 8; 18; 6:4(2); 5; 6; 7; 10; 15; 20; **2 Tim** 1:1; 5(2); 6; 12; 2:1; 5; 9; 10; 11; 18; 3:15; 16(2); 4:6; 8; 11(2); **Titus** 1:6; 8; 13; 15; 2:8; 3:8; 11; **Phm** 1:6; 8; 11; 12; **Heb** 1:8(2); 2:6; 8; 11; 14; 18; 3:4(2); 13; 15; 4:12(2); 13; 5:1; 2; 3; 4; 13(2); 14; 6:4; 7; 8(2); 10; 16; 18; 7:5; 6; 7; 8; 12; 14; 15; 18; 19; 25; 26; 8:1(2); 3(2); 6; 10; 13(2); 9:2; 3; 11; 15; 16; 17; 20; 22; 27; 10:3; 4; 7; 16; 18(2); 20; 23; 25; 30; 31; 37; 11:1; 6(3); 7; 10; 12; 16(2); 27; 12:1; 7; 13; 29; 13:4; 6; 8; 9; 11; 15; 16; 21; **Jas** 1:6; 8; 12; 13; 14(2); 15; 17(2); 21; 23(2); 25; 26(2); 27; 2:10; 13; 15; 17; 19; 20; 24; 26(2); 3:2; 5; 6(3); 7; 8; 13; 15; 17(2); 18; 4:4; 12(2); 14(2); 16; 17; 5:8; 9; 11; 13(2); 14; **1 Pe** 1:7; 13; 15; 16; 24; 25; 2:3; 6; 7; 15; 19; 20(2); 3:4; 12; 13(2); 15; 17(2); 20; 21; 22; 4:5; 7; 12; 13; 14(2); 18; 5:2; 12; 13; **2 Pe** 1:4; 9; 13; 17; 20; 2:17; 19(2); 20; 3:4; 8; 9(2); 15; **1 Jn** 1:3; 5(3); 7; 8; 9; 10; 2:2; 4(2); 5; 7; 8(3); 9(2); 10; 11(2); 13; 14; 15; 16(3); 17; 18(3); 21; 22(3); 25; 27(2); 29(2); 3:2(2); 3; 4; 5; 7(2); 8; 10(2); 11; 15; 20; 23; 4:2; 3(3); 4(3); 6; 7(2); 8; 10; 15; 16; 17; 18; 20; 5:1(3); 3; 4(2); 5(2); 6(3); 9(2); 11(2); 14; 16; 17(2); 18; 20(3); **2 Jn** 6(2); 7; **3 Jn** 3; 11(3); 12; **Jude** 13; 24; 25; **Rev** 1:3(2); 4(2); 7; 8(2); 9; 2:7; 10; 13; 3:7(2); 4:8(2); 5:2; 12; 13; 6:13; 14; 17; 7:17; 8:11; 9:11; 12; 13; 19; 10:7; 8; 11:2; 8; 14(2); 17(2); 12:14; 13:4(2); 10; 18(3); 14:8(2); 10; 12; 15; 17; 15:1; 16:5(2); 6; 15; 17; 17:8(3); 9; 10; 11(4); 14; 18; 18:2(2); 8; 18; 19; 19:8; 10; 13; 20:2; 5; 6; 8; 12; 14; 21:3; 6; 8; 16(2); 17; 23; 22:7; 10; 11(4); 12

IT (6202/4735)

Gen 1:4; 6; 7; 9; 10; 11; 12; 15; 18; 21; 24; 25; 28; 29; 30; 31; 2:3(2); 5; 10; 11; 13; 14; 15; 17; 18; 3:3(2); 5; 6; 17(2); 18; 19; 4:3; 7; 8; 12; 14; 6:1; 12; 14; 15; 16(2); 21(2); 7:4; 10; 17; 8:6; 13; 9:5; 7; 13; 14; 16; 23; 10:9; 11:2; 12:11; 12; 13; 14; 13:10; 17; 14:1; 15:6; 7; 8; 17(2); 16:14; 17:11; 18:6; 7(2); 8; 15; 21; 24(2); 25(2); 27; 28; 29; 30; 31(2); 32; 19:13; 17; 20(2); 29; 34; 20:13; 15; 21:12; 14(2); 22; 26; 22:1; 6; 13; 14(2); 20(2); 23:8; 9; 11(3); 13(2); 17; 20; 24:14; 15; 22; 30; 43; 52; 65; 25:11; 26:8; 22; 32; 33; 27:1; 4; 5; 7; 10(2); 20(3); 25(2); 30; 31; 33(2); 40; 28:11; 12; 13; 16; 18(2); 29:2; 7(2); 10; 13; 19; 23; 25(3); 26; 30:15; 25; 28; 30; 33; 34; 35; 41; 31:2; 5; 10; 16; 29; 32; 35; 37; 39(2); 44; 45; 47(2); 32:8; 18; 29; 33:11; 20; 34:7; 10(2); 21; 25; 35:8; 14(2); 17; 18; 22(2); 37:5; 9; 10; 14; 21; 23; 24; 32(2); 33(2); 38:1; 9; 13; 17; 24; 27; 28(2); 29; 39:5; 7; 10; 11; 13; 15; 18; 19; 22; 23; 40:1; 8; 10(2); 12; 14; 18; 20; 41:1; 7; 8; 13(2); 15(3); 16; 24; 31; 32; 42; 49; 42:6; 14; 27; 28; 35; 43:2; 11; 12; 18; 21(2); 44:7; 9; 10(2); 17; 24; 31; 45:2; 8; 12; 16(2); 28; 46:33; 47:24; 26; 48:1; 14; 17(2); 49:4; 7(2); 50:9; 20(3); **Ex** 1:10; 16(2); 21; 2:3(3); 5; 6; 11; 18; 20; 23; 3:21; 4:3(4); 4(3); 6; 7(2); 8; 9(2); 24; 25; 5:8; 9; 11; 19; 22; 6:8; 28; 7:9(2); 10; 8:10; 16; 17; 26; 9:8; 9(2); 24(2); 28; 10:13; 11:6(2); 12:2; 4; 5; 6(2); 7(2); 8; 9; 10(2); 11(3); 14(2); 22; 25; 26; 27; 29; 34; 39; 41(2); 42; 43; 44; 45; 46; 47; 48(2); 51; 13:2; 5; 9; 11(2); 13; 14; 15; 16; 17; 14:2; 5; 12; 16; 20(3); 24; 27; 15:7; 23; 25; 16:5(2); 10; 13; 15(3); 16; 18; 19; 20(2); 21(2); 22; 24(3); 25; 26; 27; 31(2); 32; 33(2); 34; 17:3; 6; 11; 12(2); 14; 18:13; 18; 22(2); 19:16; 18; 23; 20:8; 10; 11; 18; 24; 25(3); 26; 21:26; 29(3); 31(2); 33(2); 34; 35(2); 36(2); 22:1(2); 4; 5; 7; 9; 10(2); 11(2); 12(2); 13(2); 14(4); 15(4); 26; 27(2); 30(2); 31; 23:4; 5(2); 11; 13; 15; 33; 24:6; 8; 10(2); 16; 25:2; 9; 11(3); 12; 15; 19; 24; 25; 26; 36; 37(2); 39; 40; 26:6; 11; 13; 24; 31; 32; 27:2(2); 4; 5; 7; 8(3); 16; 21(2); 28:7(2); 8; 15(2); 16; 17; 26; 28; 32(3); 35; 36; 37(3); 38(2); 43; 29:7; 12; 14; 16; 18(2); 20; 21; 22; 25; 26(2); 28(3); 34(2); 36(3); 37; 41; 30:1; 2(2); 3; 4(2); 6; 7(2); 8; 9(2); 10(2); 16(2); 18(2); 19; 21; 25; 26; 32(4); 33(2); 36(3); 37; 38(2); 31:7; 13; 14(3); 17; 32:4; 5(2); 8(2); 9; 13; 18; 19; 20(4); 24(3); 30; 33:1; 7(3); 8; 9; 16; 22; 34:10; 12; 29; 35:2; 5; 24; 36:6; 13; 18; 35; 36; 37:2(2); 3(2); 11(2); 12(2); 13; 21; 22; 24; 25(2); 26(3); 27(2); 38:1; 2(2); 7; 30(2); 39:3(2); 4(3); 5; 9; 10; 19; 21; 23; 30; 31(2); 43(2); 40:3; 4; 7; 9(3); 11; 17; 19; 20; 23; 27; 29; 31; 35; 37; 38; **Lev** 1:3; 4; 6; 11; 12; 13(3); 15(2); 16; 17(4); 2:1(2); 2(3); 3; 4; 5; 6(3); 7; 8(2); 9(2); 10; 15(3); 3:1(2); 2; 5; 6; 7; 8; 12; 13; 14; 4:5; 8; 10; 12(2); 14; 17; 19(2); 20(2); 21(2); 24(2); 25; 26; 30; 31(2); 33; 34; 35(2); 5:1; 2(2); 3(2); 4(2); 5; 8; 9; 10; 11(3); 12(4); 13; 16(3); 17; 18(2); 19; 6:3; 4; 5(3); 9; 12(5); 13; 14; 15(2); 16(3); 17(3); 18(2); 20(2); 21(3); 22(3); 23; 25; 26(3); 27; 28(3); 29(2); 30; 7:1; 3; 5; 6(3); 7(2); 9; 12; 14(2); 15(2); 16(2); 18(5); 19(2); 24; 25; 8:7; 10; 11; 15(3); 19; 21; 23(2); 29(2); 30; 31(2); 9:1; 9; 15(2); 16; 17(2); 24; 10:1(2); 9;

12(2); 13(2); 15; 16; 17(2); 18; 19; 11:4; 5; 6; 7; 26; 28; 32(5); 33; 34; 35(2); 37; 38(2); 41; 12:7; 13:2; 3; 5; 6; 8; 10; 11; 13; 15; 18; 19; 20(3); 21(3); 22(2); 23; 25(4); 26(2); 27(2); 28(2); 30(3); 31(2); 32; 37; 39; 42; 43; 47(2); 48; 49; 51; 52; 53; 54; 55(4); 56(3); 57(2); 58(2); 59(2); 14:6; 7; 12; 13; 14; 15; 21; 25; 35; 36; 43; 44(2); 46; 48; 53; 57(2); 15:3; 17; 23; 25; 16:9; 10(2); 12; 14; 15; 18(2); 19(3); 21(2); 31(2); 17:3; 4; 9(2); 11(2); 13; 14(2); 18:8; 16; 17; 22; 23(3); 25; 28(2); 19:5; 6(3); 7(3); 8; 23(2); 25; 20:14; 16; 17; 21; 24; 21:24; 22:7; 8; 9(2); 11; 13; 14; 20; 21(2); 23; 27(2); 28; 29; 30(2); 23:3(2); 7; 8; 11; 14; 21(3); 25; 27; 28; 31; 32; 35; 36(2); 41(3); 24:3(2); 5; 7; 8; 9(3); 18; 19; 20; 21; 25:5; 10; 11; 12(2); 21; 25; 26(2); 27; 28(3); 29(3); 30(3); 34; 50; 26:1; 16; 32(2); 34; 35(4); 37; 43; 27:4; 7; 9; 10(4); 11; 12(4); 13; 14(4); 15(3); 16; 17; 18; 19(3); 20; 21(2); 24; 26(2); 27(5); 30; 31; 33(6); **Num** 1:50(2); 51(2); 4:5; 6; 7(2); 9; 10(2); 11; 13; 14(2); 16; 25; 5:7(2); 13(2); 15(3); 17; 22; 25; 26; 27; 6:9; 18; 7:1(3); 10; 84; 88; 8:4; 9:3(2); 11(2); 12(2); 15; 16(2); 20; 21; 22(2); 10:11; 29; 32(2); 35; 36; 11:1(2); 8(5); 9; 17; 18; 20; 25; 31; 33; 12:2; 13:18; 23; 27; 30; 32; 14:3; 8; 13; 14; 23; 24; 15:11; 19; 20; 24(2); 25(2); 26(2); 28; 34; 39; 16:4; 7; 9; 13; 17; 18(2); 31; 42(2); 46(3); 47; 17:5; 8; 18:10(3); 11; 13; 19; 23; 26; 27; 28; 30; 31(2); 32(2); 19:3(3); 8; 9; 10; 15; 18(2); 21; 22; 20:5; 8; 19; 21:8(3); 9(2); 14; 17; 27; 28; 22:34; 41; 23:19; 20; 23; 24(2); 27; 24:1; 25:7; 13; 26:1; 27:11(2); 13; 28:6; 8; 24; 29:1; 30:7; 8; 11; 12; 13(2); 31:23(2); 29(2); 54; 32:39(2); 40; 42; 33:53; 55; 56; 34:4; 5; 9; 12; 35:23; 33(2); 36:3(2); **Deut** 1:2; 3; 17; 21; 24; 25(2); 36; 38; 39(2); 2:16; 19; 24; 30; 31; 3:9; 11; 27; 4:2; 7; 26; 32; 35; 38; 39; 40; 5:12; 14; 16; 23; 27; 29; 33; 6:3(2); 10; 18; 24; 25; 7:12; 25(3); 26(4); 8:18(2); 19; 9:2; 4; 5; 11; 21(4); 10:14; 15; 11:10; 12; 13; 29; 31(2); 12:15; 16; 24(2); 25(2); 28; 32(3); 13:14; 15(2); 16(2); 14:8; 10; 21(3); 25; 28; 15:2(3); 3; 9; 16; 17; 18; 20; 21(3); 22(3); 23; 16:3(2); 7; 8; 17:4(3); 14(2); 18; 19(2); 18:3; 19(2); 22; 19:13; 20:2; 5(2); 6(2); 9; 10(2); 11(2); 12; 13(2); 19(2); 20; 21:1; 3; 7; 14; 16; 22:4(4); 7; 8; 23:11; 13; 16; 21(3); 22; 24:1(2); 3; 13; 15(3); 19(2); 20; 21(2); 25:2; 4; 6; 9; 19; 26:1(3); 2; 4; 10; 12; 14(3); 27:2; 4; 6; 15; 28:1; 15; 24; 30; 31; 38; 63; 67(2); 68; 29:8; 19; 22; 23(2); 27; 28; 30:1; 5; 11; 12(4); 13(4); 14; 31:7; 9; 13; 19(2); 21(2); 22; 24; 26(2); 32:19; 22; 27; 47(2); 34:4(2); **Josh** 1:1; 7; 8(2); 15; 2:2; 5(2); 14; 19; 21; 3:2; 3(2); 4(2); 13; 14; 4:1; 7; 11; 18; 24; 5:1; 8; 13; 6:5; 8; 11; 15; 16; 17(2); 18; 20; 24; 7:9; 11; 14; 15; 19; 21; 22(2); 8:2; 5; 7; 8; 14(2); 18; 19; 24(2); 25; 28; 29(2); 31(2); 9:1(2); 12; 16; 25; 10:1(2); 2; 4; 5; 11; 14(2); 17; 18; 20; 24; 27; 28(2); 30(4); 31(2); 32(3); 34(2); 35(3); 36; 37(5); 38; 39(2); 11:1; 11; 20; 23; 12:6; 13:6; 29; 14:7; 12; 15:3; 4; 7; 16; 17; 18; 16:3; 6; 7; 8; 17:9; 10(2); 13; 18(2); 18:4; 5; 8; 12; 14; 17; 18; 19:12; 13; 14(2); 26; 27(2); 33; 34; 47(4); 50; 21:11; 42; 43(2); 22:7; 12; 18; 22; 23(2); 24; 27; 28(2); 29; 30; 34; 23:1; 6; 15; 24:15; 16; 26; 27(2); 29; **Judg** 1:1; 8(2); 12; 13; 14; 17; 28; 2:4; 19; 3:2; 16(2); 21; 27; 4:21; 5:7; 31; 6:3; 5; 7; 11; 17; 18; 24(2); 25(2); 27(2); 28; 30; 37; 38; 39; 40; 7:4; 9(2); 13(3); 15; 8:25; 27(4); 33; 9:25; 33; 42; 45(2); 47; 48(2); 50; 52(2); 11:4; 5; 23; 31(2); 35(2); 39(2); 12:6; 13:16; 18; 19; 20; 14:4; 9; 11; 12; 13(2); 15; 16(3); 17; 15:1; 15(2); 17; 16:2; 4; 9; 14; 16; 22; 25; 30; 17:2(2); 3; 4; 18:2; 9; 10; 12; 19; 28(2); 19:1; 5; 11; 26; 30(3); 20:9; 28; 21:4; 22(2); **Ruth** 1:1; 13; 19; 2:6; 11; 16; 17; 18; 22; 3:1; 4; 8; 12; 13(2); 14; 15(3); 4:4(6); 5; 6(2); 7; 8; **1 Sam** 1:7; 12; 20; 2:14; 16(2); 19; 24; 30; 36; 3:2; 9; 11; 17; 18; 4:3(2); 13; 18; 20; 5:1; 2(2); 3; 4; 7; 9(2); 10; 11(2); 6:2; 3(3); 8(3); 9(3); 13; 15; 16; 20; 21; 7:1; 2(2); 6; 7; 9; 12; 8:1; 15; 9:20; 23; 24(4); 26; 10:1(2); 5; 7; 9; 11; 12; 25(2); 11:7; 9; 11(2); 12:3; 6; 15; 22; 23; 13:3; 4; 10; 22; 14:1; 6; 15; 19; 27; 34; 39; 15:11; 12; 27; 28; 16:2; 6; 16(2); 23(2); 17:25; 27; 35(5); 48; 49; 51(2); 54; 18:4; 6; 10; 19; 23; 26; 30; 19:5; 13(2); 19; 20:2; 4; 7; 9; 13(2); 16; 27; 33; 35; 21:5; 6; 9(4); 22:1; 8; 13; 15; 17; 23:6; 13; 23; 24:1(2); 4; 5; 11; 16; 25:11; 20; 27; 30; 37; 38; 26:12(2); 17; 19; 22; 27:4; 28:1; 14; 17; 24(3); 25; 30:1(2); 3; 25(2); 31:4(2); 8; 9; **2 Sam** 1:1; 2(2); 14; 18; 20(2); 2:1; 23; 26(2); 3:6; 18; 24; 26; 28; 29; 35; 36(2); 37; 4:4; 12; 5:9; 17; 24; 6:3; 4; 6; 10; 12; 13; 17(2); 21; 7:1; 4; 15; 25; 27; 29(3); 8:1; 10:1; 3(2); 7; 17; 11:1; 2; 14(2); 16; 20; 21; 25; 12:3(3); 4; 12; 15; 18; 28(2); 29(2); 30; 31; 13:2; 5(2); 8; 23; 30; 35; 36; 14:15; 26(3); 30; 32; 15:1; 2; 5; 7; 25; 32; 35; 16:12; 16; 17:9(2); 13; 18; 19; 21; 27; 18:10; 18; 29; 19:2; 6; 19; 25; 26; 30; 20:8(2); 10; 15(2); 20(2); 22; 21:1; 10; 18; 22:9; 48; 23:5; 12; 16(4); 17(2); 24:3; 12; 16(2); 24; **1 Ki** 1:11; 18; 21; 41; 48; 51; 2:3; 14; 15; 16; 20; 32; 37; 39; 3:6; 15; 18; 5:7; 6:1; 5; 7(2); 9; 14; 16; 17; 20; 21; 38; 7:3; 7; 23; 24(2); 25; 26(2); 35; 8:10; 15; 17; 18(2); 24(2); 54; 9:1; 8; 10; 16(2); 21; 28; 10:3; 6; 18; 11:4; 11; 12(2); 15; 29; 30; 35; 38; 12:2(2); 10; 20; 28; 13:3; 4(2); 9; 13; 20; 23; 24; 25; 26(2); 27; 29(2); 31; 34; 14:5; 6; 8; 10; 25; 15:13; 21(2); 29; 16:11; 16; 18; 31(2); 17:4; 7; 11; 12(2); 13(2); 17; 18:1; 4; 6; 8; 12; 13; 17; 23(5); 24; 25(2); 26; 27; 33(2); 34(4); 36(2); 38; 39; 44; 45; 19:4; 13(2); 17; 21; 20:1; 6(3); 11; 12; 13; 26; 29; 40; 21:1; 2(5); 6(2); 11; 15; 16; 18; 27; 22:2; 3; 6; 12; 15; 32(2); 33(2); **2 Ki** 1:3; 6; 7; 8; 16; 2:1; 8(2); 9; 10(2); 11; 12; 14; 20(2); 21; 3:5; 14; 15; 20; 25(2); 4:4; 5; 6; 8(2); 10; 11; 18; 23(2); 25; 26(4); 27; 39; 40(3); 41(2); 42; 43; 44; 5:7; 8; 13; 16; 26; 6:5; 6(2); 7(2); 13; 20; 24; 25; 30; 7:2(2); 8(2); 11; 13; 18; 19(2); 20; 8:1; 3; 5; 7; 15(3); 9:3; 13; 15; 17; 18; 19; 22(2); 30; 31; 10:7; 9; 15(2); 20; 24; 25; 27; 11:6; 18; 12:5; 6; 7; 9; 10(2); 11; 14; 16; 17; 13:16; 17; 19; 21; 14:5; 22; 15:12; 16; 16:8; 9; 11; 12; 14; 15; 17(2); 17:5; 7; 23; 25; 18:1; 4(2); 9(2); 10; 16; 21(2); 22; 25(2); 26; 19:1(2); 4; 14(2); 25(3); 26; 32(2); 34; 35; 37; 20:4; 7; 10; 11; 21:12; 13(2); 22:3; 5(2); 8; 9; 10; 11; 23:6(2); 15; 16; 17; 21; 35; 24:2; 11; 25:1(3); 17; 24; 25; 27; **1 Chr** 4:41; 6:10; 9:27; 10:4(2); 8; 11:7; 8; 14; 18(4); 19(3); 12:15; 22; 13:2(2); 3; 13; 14:8; 15; 15:1; 3; 12; 13; 26; 29; 16:1(2); 17; 19; 30; 32; 17:1; 3; 11; 13; 23; 24; 25; 27(3); 18:1; 19:1; 8; 17; 20:1(2); 2(3); 3; 4; 21:2; 10; 15(2); 17; 22(2); 23(2); 24; 30; 22:5; 7; 14; 28:2(2); 6; 7; 8; 10; 20; 29:12; **2 Chr** 1:4(2); 6; 2:4; 16(2); 3:5; 8; 14; 4:2; 3(3); 4; 5(2); 15; 5:11; 13; 6:7; 8(2); 13(2); 15(2); 7:20; 21; 8:1; 3; 8; 16; 18; 9:2; 5; 17; 10:2(2); 10; 14; 12:1; 2; 13:15; 14:11; 15:16; 16:5(2); 18:5; 11; 31(2); 32(2); 19:7; 20:1; 7; 8(2); 32; 21:17; 19; 22:8; 23:17; 18(2); 24:4; 5(2); 8; 11(3); 12; 13; 14; 22; 23; 25:3; 4; 14; 16; 20; 26:2; 18; 28:21; 29:10; 16(3); 22; 30:3; 5; 23; 31:3; 21; 32:5; 12; 33:14(2); 16; 34:4; 10(2); 11; 17; 18; 19; 35:3; 12; 25; 36:22; **Ezra** 1:1; 2:68; 3:2(2); 3; 4; 4:12; 13; 14; 19(2); 24; 5:8; 16(2); 17(2); 6:2; 3; 9; 11; 12(2); 14; 18; 7:10; 18; 20; 21; 23; 24; 26; 9:7; 11; 12; 15; 10:3; 4; 9; 13; **Neh** 1:1; 4; 2:1(2); 5(2); 6; 7; 10; 19; 3:1(2); 13; 14; 15(2); 4:1; 2; 3; 7; 12; 15(2); 16; 5:5; 12; 6:1(2); 3; 6(2); 9; 16(2); 7:1; 4; 5(2); 64; 8:3; 5; 15; 9:6; 8; 10; 36; 37; 38(2); 10:31; 34; 36; 11:23; 13:1; 3; 8; 19(2); **Esth** 1:1; 19(3); 20; 2:8; 10; 23(2); 3:4(2); 7; 8; 9(2); 10; 12; 4:8(2); 5:1; 2; 3; 4; 6(2); 8; 14; 6:2; 9; 11; 7:2(2); 3; 9; 8:2; 5(2); 8; 9; 10; 9:12(2); 13(2); 17; 18; 27; 32; **Job** 1:5(2); 7; 19; 2:2; 3:3; 4(2); 5(3); 6(3); 7; 8; 9; 10; 21(2); 4:5(2); 12; 16; 5:5; 21; 27(2); 6:2; 3; 5; 9; 17(2); 8:12(2); 15(3); 18; 9:2; 7; 19; 20; 22; 24(2); 35; 10:3; 11:11; 14; 16; 12:5; 8; 14; 13:1; 5; 9; 14:7(2); 9; 21(2); 22(2); 15:23; 32; 16:8; 17:15; 18:13; 20:11; 12; 13(3); 14; 18; 23; 25; 26; 21:4; 19; 22:3(2); 4; 8; 19; 28; 24:23; 25; 26:8; 9; 27:5; 6; 12; 14; 17(2); 21; 22; 28:5(2); 6; 7; 8(2); 13; 14(2); 15; 16; 17(2); 19(2); 21; 22; 27(3); 29:11(2); 14; 24; 30:18; 22; 24; 31:3; 11; 17; 26; 36(2); 32:19; 33:14; 27; 34:9; 10; 14; 18; 29; 33(2); 35:3; 13; 36:18; 25(2); 30; 32; 33; 37:3; 4; 13; 21; 38:5; 8; 10; 13(2); 14; 20; 21; 26; 29; 39:12; 28; 29; 30; 40:2; 24; 41:8; 26; 42:7; **Ps** 5:3; 6:7; 7:12; 15; 10:14; 18:8; 32; 47; 21:4; 22:14; 30; 24:2(2); 25:11; 30:9; 33:9(2); 17; 34:2; 14; 35:9; 15; 21; 25; 37:5; 8; 10; 29; 34; 38:10; 39:9(2); 40:3; 7; 41:6; 44:3; 48:5; 8; 13; 49:8; 50:3; 51:16; 52:9(2); 54:6; 55:10(2); 12(3); 13; 57:6; 58:8; 60:2(2); 4; 10; 12; 63:9; 65:9(3); 10; 68:9; 10; 11; 14(2); 16; 69:4; 18; 35; 36(2); 73:16; 28; 74:11; 75:8(2); 80:8; 9(3); 13(2); 16(2); 81:10; 84:6(2); 86:17; 87:5; 89:37; 39; 90:4; 6(2); 10; 91:7; 92:1; 7; 93:1; 94:15; 95:5; 10; 96:10; 12; 98:7; 100:3; 101:3; 103:16(3); 104:5; 6; 20; 32; 105:10; 12; 28; 41; 106:9; 32; 107:34; 42; 108:11; 13; 109:17(2); 18; 19; 23; 27; 112:10; 114:3; 118:8; 9; 23; 24; 119:33; 34; 35; 71; 90; 97; 126; 130; 140; 175; 124:1; 2; 127:1; 2; 128:2; 129:6; 132:6(2); 11; 13; 14; 133:1; 2; 3; 135:3; 136:14; 137:2; 7(2); 139:4; 6(2); 141:5(3); 147:1(2); **Prov** 1:19; 2:21; 22; 3:8; 25; 27(2); 28(2); 4:15(3); 23; 7:23; 8:33; 9:12; 10:22; 11:8; 10; 11; 19; 24; 26; 12:25; 13:12; 19; 14:1; 6; 15:4; 23; 16:12; 14; 22; 27; 31; 17:16; 18:5; 10; 13(2); 21; 19:2; 19; 23; 24; 20:1; 3; 5; 14; 16(2); 25; 21:1; 15; 20; 27; 22:6; 15; 18; 23:23; 31(3); 32; 35; 24:3; 12(2); 13; 14; 18(2); 23; 27; 31; 32(3); 25:2; 4; 7; 10; 16; 24; 27; 26:15(2); 24; 27(2); 28; 27:13; 14; 28:8; 24; 29:4; 30:17(2); 21; 28; 31:4(2); 15; 16; **Eccl** 1:5; 8; 10(2); 2:2; 15(2); 18; 21; 3:13; 14(4); 5:4; 6; 18(2); 19; 6:1; 2(3); 4; 5; 10; 7:2; 5; 12; 18; 23; 24; 8:7; 8; 12; 13; 14(2); 17(4); 9:1; 10; 12; 13; 14(4); 15; 10:1; 8; 9; 11; 11:1; 3; 7; 12:7(2); **Song** 1:7; 2:7; 3:5; 7(2); 5:2; 3; 6:13; 7:2; 8:4; 7(2); 13; **Isa** 1:6; 7; 21(2); 31; 2:2(2); 12; 3:9; 10; 11; 24; 4:3; 5:2(5); 4(3); 5(2); 6(3); 14; 19(2); 29; 6:2; 7; 13(2); 7:1(3); 2; 6; 7(2); 8; 11; 13; 18; 21; 22; 23(2); 25; 8:1; 10(2); 20; 21(2); 9:7(2); 8; 18; 10:7; 12; 13; 15(4); 17; 18; 20; 26; 27; 30; 11:11; 15; 16; 13:6; 9; 14; 17; 20(2); 14:3; 9(2); 23(2); 24(2); 27(2); 30; 32; 16:2; 5; 12(2); 17:1; 4; 5(2); 6; 18:3(2); 19:16; 17(2); 20; 21; 22; 20:1; 21:1; 3(2); 17; 22:5; 7; 9; 11; 14; 20; 25; 23:1(2); 9; 13(2); 15(2); 17; 18; 24:1; 2; 6; 9; 13(2); 18; 20(2); 21; 25:2; 9; 26:5(3); 6; 18; 20; 27:3(4); 8(3); 10; 11; 12; 13; 28:4(2); 15; 18; 19(4); 20; 28(3); 29:2; 5; 8; 11; 16(2); 17; 30:8(3); 14; 19; 21; 23; 32(2); 33(3); 31:5(2); 33:24; 34:1(2); 5; 6; 8; 10(3); 11(3); 13; 16; 17(3); 35:2(2); 8(3); 9(2); 36:1; 6(2); 7; 10(2); 11; 37:1(2); 4; 9; 14(2); 26(3); 27; 33(2); 35; 38; 38:8; 15; 17; 21; 40:5; 7; 9; 19; 21; 22; 41:4; 5; 7(3); 20; 23; 42:5(3); 10; 21; 24; 25(3); 43:9; 13; 19(2); 44:7(2); 8; 12(2); 13(4); 14(2); 15(6); 16; 17(4); 19(3); 23(2); 45:8; 9; 12; 18(4); 21; 46:6; 7(7); 11(4); 13; 47:11(2); 14; 48:3; 5(3); 6; 9; 11; 16; 20; 49:6; 50:1; 2; 51:2; 3; 6; 17; 22; 23; 52:6; 53:3; 10; 54:14; 55:10(2); 11(4); 13; 56:2; 57:1; 11(2); 14(2); 20; 58:5(2); 7; 59:1(2); 11; 15(2); 16; 60:22; 61:11; 62:9(4); 63:5; 18; 65:6; 8(2); 9; 24; 66:18; 23; **Jer** 1:3; 13; 2:19; 34; 3:5; 7; 9; 16(5); 17; 4:4; 9; 11; 18(2); 23; 28; 29; 5:12; 13; 14; 15(2); 19; 20; 22(3); 31; 6:10; 11(2); 16(2); 19; 24; 7:11; 12; 20; 23; 29; 30; 31; 32; 8:16(2); 9:8; 12; 13; 10:4(3); 9; 18; 19; 23; 11:5(2); 16; 18(2); 12:8(2); 11(3); 15; 16; 13:1(2); 2; 4; 5; 6; 7(2); 16(2); 17; 19(2); 14:7; 15:2; 9; 11; 16:10; 14; 17:1; 9; 11; 15; 16; 21; 24(2); 27(2); 18:4(2); 7; 8; 9; 10(3); 16; 19:3; 4; 5; 8; 15; 20:3; 4; 9; 10; 21:10(2); 12; 14(2); 22:14(3); 15; 16; 23:18; 19; 20; 25:12(2); 13; 15; 18; 28; 26:8; 21; 27:5(2); 8; 11(2); 28:1; 10; 29:7; 30:3; 7(3); 8; 23; 24(2); 31:10; 28; 33; 39; 40; 32:3; 7; 8; 10; 20; 23; 24(3); 28; 29; 31(2); 34; 35; 36; 43(2); 33:2(3); 6; 9(2); 10; 34:2; 18; 22(3); 35:11; 36:1; 2; 3; 7; 9; 15(2); 16; 21(2); 23(3); 28; 29; 32(2); 37:8(2); 11; 38:3; 15; 18; 20; 25; 39:1; 4; 40:3; 4(3); 5; 9; 15; 41:1; 4(2); 6; 7; 9; 13; 42:4(2); 6(2); 7; 16; 17; 20; 21; 43:1; 44:6; 21; 22(2); 46:10; 20; 23; 26; 47:2; 7(3); 48:1; 20; 30; 44; 49:2; 12; 17; 18; 23; 27; 33; 39; 50:2; 5; 15; 21; 29; 32; 38; 39(3); 40; 51:11(2); 33; 61; 62(3); 63(3); 52:4(3); 20; 21; 22; 31; **Lam** 1:12; 13; 20; 21; 2:6; 16(2); 3:26; 27; 28; 37(2); 38; 4:4; 8; 11; 5:18; **Ezek** 1:1; 4; 5; 16; 26; 27(3); 28(2); 2:9; 10(2); 3:3; 16; 4:1(2); 2(5); 3(4); 4(2); 7; 9; 10; 12(2); 15; 5:1(2); 2; 13; 15; 7:5; 6(2); 10; 13; 19; 20(3); 21(2); 22(2); 8:1; 17; 9:3; 4; 8; 10:6; 7(3); 10; 11:7; 13; 12:3; 5; 11; 12; 13; 19(2); 23; 25(2); 13:10; 11(3); 12(2); 13; 14(3); 15(2); 14:13(3); 14; 15(2); 16; 17; 18; 19(2); 20; 21(2); 22(2); 23; 15:3(2); 4(3); 5(5); 16:14; 15; 19(2); 23; 57; 17:4(2); 5(3); 6(3); 7(2); 8; 9(3); 10(6); 11; 14; 22(2); 23(3); 24; 18:25; 26(2); 29; 20:1; 9; 14; 22; 47(2); 48(2); 21:5; 7(3); 10(2); 11(3); 12; 13; 14; 15(2); 19; 23; 27(4); 30; 22:14; 20(2); 30; 23:32; 34; 39; 41; 24:3(2); 4(2); 5(3); 6(3); 7(3); 8(2); 11(2); 14(3); 25; 26; 25:3(2); 10; 13(2); 26:1; 5(2); 28:18; 29:3; 9; 11(3); 15(2); 16; 17; 18; 30:3; 9; 12; 20; 21(3); 25; 31:1; 4(3); 5; 7; 8(2); 9(2); 10; 11(3); 12(3); 15(4); 16; 17; 32:1; 15(2); 17; 25(2); 26; 33:12; 17; 18; 19; 21; 33; 34:18; 35:2; 3; 7; 15; 36:10; 17; 18; 29; 32; 36(2); 37:1; 14(2); 16(2); 19; 26; 38:10; 14; 16; 18; 39:8(2); 11(3); 13; 14; 15(2); 40:2; 22(2); 25; 26(2); 29(2); 31; 33(2); 34; 35; 36; 37; 49; 41:8; 10; 15; 18; 19; 42:15; 20(2); 43:3; 11; 17; 18(3); 20(4); 21; 22; 23; 26(2); 27; 44:1; 2(4); 3; 7; 14; 17; 24; 28; 45:1; 2; 3; 4(2); 6; 17; 19; 46:1(2); 6; 13; 14; 16(2); 17(3); 47:5; 8; 9; 10(2); 14(2); 17; 22(2); 23; 48:11; 14(2); 18; 19; 21(2); **Dan** 1:1; 2:11(2); 36; 41; 44(2); 45; 3:1; 4; 14; 18; 19; 4:2; 11; 12(3); 14; 15; 17(2); 22; 23(2); 25; 31; 32; 5:21; 26; 6:1; 5; 8; 15; 17; 7:4(2); 5(2); 6; 7(5); 23(2); 26; 8:2; 8; 10(2); 15; 26; 27; 9:7; 13; 14; 15; 26; 11:17; 27; 29; 35; 12:7; **Hos** 1:5; 10(3); 2:7; 16; 21; 4:9; 6:4; 7:4; 6; 9(2); 8:6(2); 7(3); 13; 14; 9:4(3); 10:5(3); 10; 12; 15; 13:2; **Joel** 1:3; 5; 7(2); 15; 2:1; 11; 28; 32; 3:18; **Am** 1:14; 2:2; 5; 9; 10; 11; 3:5(2); 6; 4:7(2); 5:6(2); 13; 15; 18; 19; 20(2); 6:8; 9; 7:1; 2; 3; 4; 13(2); 8:8(2); 9; 10; 12; 9:3; 4; 5(2); 8; 11; 13; **Ob** 7; 15; **Jon** 1:2; 3; 14; 2:10; 3:2; 7; 10; 4:1; 3; 4; 5; 6(2); 7(2); 8(2); 9(2); 10; **Mic** 1:2; 5; 7; 9(2); 10; 2:1(2); 4; 10(2); 13; 3:1; 4:1(2); 8; 5:10; 6:9; 7:13; **Nah** 1:4; 5; 9; 2:7; 3:1; 7; 9; 15; **Hab** 1:5; 10; 2:2(2); 3(6); 8; 11; 13; 17; 18(2); 19(3); 3:2; **Zeph** 1:8; 12; 14; 2:3; 15; 3:16; **Hag** 1:4; 8; 9(3); 2:3(2); 6; 12; 13(2); 18; **Zech** 1:8; 16; 21; 2:4; 4:2; 3; 7; 9; 5:3; 4(3); 6(2); 11(2); 6:11; 7:1; 7; 13; 8:6(2); 13; 9:2; 5; 10:7; 11:10; 11(2); 12; 13; 12:3(3); 9; 13:2; 3; 4; 8(3); 14:4; 6; 7(3); 8(2); 9; 11; 13; 16; 17; **Mal** 1:8(3); 12; 13; 2:2(2); 3; 13; 16; 3:10; 14(2); **Mt** 1:22; 2:5; 9; 15; 23; 3:15(2); 4:4; 6; 7; 10; 14; 5:13(2); 15(2); 21; 27; 29(3); 30(3); 31; 33; 34; 35(2); 38; 43; 6:10; 7:2; 7(2); 8; 13; 14; 25(2); 27; 28; 8:9; 10; 13; 17; 9:8; 10; 11; 29; 30; 33; 10:11; 12; 13(2); 15; 19; 20; 25; 39(2); 11:1; 10; 12; 14; 16; 22; 23; 24; 26; 12:2; 10; 11(3); 12; 13(2); 15; 17; 24; 32(2); 36; 39; 41; 42; 44; 45; 13:11(2); 17(2); 19; 20; 23; 27; 32(2); 33; 35; 40; 44; 46; 48; 49; 53; 14:4; 9; 11; 12; 13(2); 15; 26; 27; 28; 36; 15:26(2); 28; 16:2(2); 3; 4; 7; 8; 11; 18; 22; 25(2); 26; 17:4; 6; 18; 19; 20; 27; 18:6; 8(3); 9(3); 13; 14; 17; 19; 19:1; 3; 8; 10; 11; 12(2); 23; 24; 25; 20:11; 15; 23(2); 24; 25; 26; 21:4; 13(2); 19(3); 20; 21; 25; 29; 32; 33(3); 42; 43; 44(2); 22:5; 7; 17; 39; 23:16(2); 18(3); 20(2); 21(2); 22; 24:23; 26; 33; 25:28; 40(2); 45(2); 26:1; 7; 8; 10; 12; 22; 24(2); 25(2); 26(2); 27(2); 29; 31; 39; 42; 54; 61; 62; 64; 70; 27:4; 6; 11; 24; 29; 34; 35; 40; 48(3); 59; 60; 65; 28:2; **Mk** 1:2; 9; 45; 2:1; 15; 16; 17; 23; 3:4; 5; 4:1; 4(2); 5(3); 6(3); 7(2); 11; 16; 19; 20; 21; 22; 24; 30; 31(2); 32(2); 33; 37; 40; 5:14(2); 16(2); 43; 6:11; 15(2); 18; 19; 22; 28(2); 29(2); 49; 50; 7:6; 19; 24; 27(2); 36; 8:16; 17; 21; 35(2); 36; 9:5; 12; 13; 18(3); 25; 28; 30; 33; 42; 43(2); 45(2); 47(2); 50; 10:2; 14; 15; 23; 24; 25; 27; 40(2); 41; 42; 43; 47; 11:2(3); 3(2); 4; 7(2); 13(3); 14(2); 17(2); 18; 30; 12:1(2); 11; 14; 15; 16; 31; 35; 13:11; 14; 21; 29; 34; 14:1; 3; 5; 11; 16; 19(2); 20; 21(2); 22(2); 23(2); 25; 27; 35; 41; 60; 68; 70(2); 72; 15:2; 17; 23; 25; 29; 36(2); 42; 16:4; 13; 18; **Lk** 1:3; 8; 23; 38; 41; 59; 2:1; 6; 15; 18; 20; 23; 26; 43; 46; 3:4; 21; 4:4; 6; 8; 10; 12; 17; 20; 35; 39; 42; 5:1; 8; 12; 17; 6:1; 6; 9; 12; 13; 38(2); 48(2); 49; 7:8; 11; 27; 40; 8:1; 5(2); 6(3); 7(2); 10(2); 15; 16(3); 20; 21; 22; 29; 34; 36; 40; 45; 50; 9:7; 11; 18; 24(2); 25; 28; 33(2); 37; 39(2); 40; 45(2); 51; 57; 10:6(2); 12; 14; 21; 24(2); 26; 38; 11:1; 2; 9(2); 10; 14(2); 25; 27; 28; 29(2); 32; 33; 38; 51; 12:10(2); 32; 49; 50; 54; 56; 13:6; 7(2); 8(3); 9(2); 15(2); 16; 18; 19(2); 21(2); 33; 14:1; 3; 18; 22; 28; 29; 34; 35(2); 15:4; 5(2); 8; 9; 22; 23; 32; 16:16; 17; 22; 17:1; 2; 6; 11; 14; 22; 26(2); 28; 29; 30; 33(2); 18:15; 17; 24; 25; 26; 35; 36; 43; 19:7; 15; 23; 24; 29; 30(2); 31(2); 32; 33; 41; 45; 46(2); 20:1; 4; 7; 9; 16; 18(2); 22; 24; 21:5; 13; 14; 35; 22:13; 16(2); 17; 19(2); 22; 23; 27; 36; 38; 42; 66; 71; 23:3; 17; 24; 26; 44; 53(3); 24:4; 10; 15; 21; 24; 29; 30(3); 39; 43; 46(2); 51; **Jn** 1:5; 27; 39; 2:5; 8(2); 9; 17; 19; 20(2); 3:8(4); 27; 4:6; 9; 10; 12; 53; 5:10(2); 13; 15; 6:17; 20; 30; 31; 39; 42; 45; 50; 60; 63; 65; 71; 7:7(2); 10; 17; 22; 51; 8:9; 17; 44; 54; 56; 9:4; 14; 27; 32; 37; 10:10; 17; 18(4); 22(2); 34; 11:2; 4; 38(2); 50; 57; 12:6; 14(2); 24(3); 25(2); 28(2); 29(2); 13:2; 19(2); 24; 25; 26(3); 30; 14:2; 8; 14; 17; 21; 22; 27; 29(2); 15:2; 4; 7; 18(2); 16:7; 14; 15; 17:26; 18:10; 14(2); 18; 25; 28; 31; 19:4(2); 11; 14; 19; 20; 24(3); 29(2); 30; 31; 40; 20:1; 14; 27; 21:4; 6; 7(3); 9; 12; 13; **Acts** 1:7; 19; 20(2); 2:2; 8; 15; 17; 21; 24(2); 3:10; 12; 17; 23; 4:3; 5; 10; 14; 16; 17; 19; 37(2); 5:2(2); 4(4); 7; 9; 38; 39(2); 6:2; 7:5(2); 23; 31; 42; 44; 45; 53; 9:5; 32; 37; 42; 43; 10:4; 12; 28; 42; 11:4; 5; 6; 26; 30; 12:3(2); 15(2); 18; 13:17; 33; 38; 41; 46(2); 14:1; 6; 15:5; 15; 16; 22; 25; 28; 31; 34; 16:16; 35; 17:24; 18:14; 15(2); 19:1; 13; 19; 39; 20:20; 35; 21:1; 3; 20; 22:6; 17; 25; 23:5; 12; 19; 30; 34; 24:3; 11; 21; 25:16; 27; 26:8; 14; 27:1; 8; 17; 25(2); 28(2); 32; 35; 39; 44; 28:8; 17; 19; 22; 28(2); **Rom** 1:16; 17(2); 19; 2:24; 3:4; 10; 19; 27; 4:3; 10; 16(2); 17; 22; 23(2); 24; 6:2; 12; 7:11; 13; 16; 17(2); 20(2); 8:3; 7; 20; 25; 33; 34; 36; 9:6; 12; 13; 16; 20; 26(2); 28; 32(2); 33; 10:8; 15; 11:6(3); 7(2); 8; 26; 35; 12:7; 18; 19; 13:11; 14:6(2); 11; 14; 20; 21; 22; 15:3; 9; 20; 21; 26; 27; **1 Cor** 1:11; 18; 19; 21; 31; 2:9; 3:2; 10(2); 13(3); 14; 19; 4:2; 3; 7(2); 5:1; 6:5; 7; 13; 7:1; 8; 9; 21(2); 26; 31; 36; 8:7; 9:6; 9(3); 10; 11; 15(2); 23; 24; 25; 27; 10:7; 13; 16(2); 28; 11:6; 13; 14; 15; 18; 20; 24; 25; 12:6; 15; 16; 24; 26(2); 13:3; 8; 14:7; 9; 10; 12; 21; 26; 35; 36(2); 15:11; 27; 32; 36; 38; 42; 43(4); 44(2); 45; 16:4; 6; 15; **2 Cor** 1:6(2); 17; 4:3; 6; 5:9; 13(2); 7:8(2); 11; 12; 8:10; 11(2); 12; 9:1; 5(2); 9; 10:14; 11:4; 15; 17; 20; 12:1; 4; 8; 13; 16; **Gal** 1:12(3); 13; 15; 2:6; 20; 3:4; 5; 6; 10; 13; 15(3); 17; 18(2); 19(2); 4:9; 18; 22; 27; 29; **Eph** 2:8; 3:5; 4:9; 29; 5:3; 12; 29; 6:3; 20; **Phil** 1:6; 7; 13; 29; 2:6; 13; 23; 25; 3:1; 21; **Col** 1:6(2); 9; 19; 2:7; 14(2); 15; 3:23; 4:2; 4; 16; 17; **1 Th** 2:3; 13(2); 19; 3:1(2); 4; 5; 5:24; **2 Th** 1:3; 6; 3:1; **1 Tim** 1:8; 13; 4:4; 5; 5:16; 18; 6:7; 21; **2 Tim** 4:16; **Phm** 1:14; **Heb** 2:10; 3:13; 15; 16; 17; 4:1; 2; 6(3); 7; 5:5; 6:4; 7(2); 8(2); 17; 18; 7:8; 11; 14; 15; 8:3; 9:5; 9; 17; 23; 27; 10:4; 7; 31; 11:2; 4; 6; 18; 12:11(2); 17; 19; 20; 13:9; **Jas** 1:2; 5; 11; 15(2); 25; 2:14; 16; 17; 23; 3:6(2); 8;

9(2); 4:3; 14; 17(2); 5:7(2); 17(2); **1 Pe** 1:7; 12; 16; 2:6; 20(3); 3:4; 11; 17(2); 4:4; 10; 11; 12; 17; **2 Pe** 1:13; 2:13; 21(2); 22; 3:10; **1 Jn** 2:17; 18(2); 21; 27; 3:1; 2; 5:6; **2 Jn** 6; **Jude** 3; **Rev** 1:1; 3; 11; 2:17; 3:8; 5:3; 4; 6; 6:2; 4(2); 5; 8; 11; 13; 14; 7:2; 8:3; 5(2); 10; 11; 9:5; 6; 10:6(3); 9(3); 10(3); 11:2(2); 12:4; 13:3; 7; 12; 18; 14:3; 19; 16:3; 6; 17; 17:17; 18:21; 19:6; 8; 15; 20:11; 13; 21:6; 22; 23(2); 24; 26; 27; 22:3

ITS (1350/917)

Gen 1:11; 12(2); 21; 24(2); 25(3); 2:19; 21; 3:6; 4:7; 11; 12; 6:15(2); 16; 20; 7:14(3); 9:4(2); 11:9; 13:17(2); 22:13; 26:21; 22; 28:12; 29:3; 31:48; 40:5; 10(2); 41:8; 49:17; 50:11; **Ex** 3:20; 9:18; 11:7; 12:9(3); 46; 13:10; 13; 14:27; 15:1; 21; 16:31; 17:15; 19:12; 18; 21:28; 29(2); 36; 22:15(2); 30; 23:5; 10; 19; 24:10; 25:9; 10(3); 12; 17(2); 23(3); 26; 29(4); 31(4); 32; 34; 37; 38; 26:19; 30; 27:1; 2(3); 3(7); 4; 10; 11; 18; 19(2); 28:7; 16(2); 21; 27; 28; 32; 33(2); 35; 29:14(2); 16; 17(4); 20; 31; 30:2(4); 3(3); 4(2); 10; 18; 27(2); 28(2); 32; 37; 31:8(2); 9(2); 34:26; 35:11(7); 12; 13(2); 14(2); 15; 16(4); 17; 21; 36:24; 38; 37:1(3); 3; 6(2); 10(3); 13; 16(4); 17(5); 18; 20; 23(3); 24; 25(4); 26(3); 27(2); 38:1(3); 2(2); 3; 4; 8; 18; 39:4; 9(2); 14; 20; 21; 33(6); 35; 36; 37(2); 39(4); 40(4); 40:4; 9; 10; 11; 18(4); **Lev** 1:6; 9(2); 11; 12(3); 15(2); 16(2); 17; 2:16(2); 3:8; 9; 13(2); 4:11(3); 25; 26; 30; 31; 35; 5:8(2); 6:5; 15; 27(2); 7:2; 3; 8:9; 11(2); 17(3); 23; 9:13; 10:18; 11:14; 15; 16; 19; 22(4); 27; 29; 39; 40(2); 42; 13:4; 20; 24; 55; 14:45(2); 16:15; 17:13; 14(3); 18:25(2); 19:24; 25(2); 22:27; 23:10; 13(2); 37; 25:3; 5; 7; 10; 11; 12; 16(2); 19; 22; 27; 26:4(2); 20; 34(2); 43; **Num** 1:50(2); 3:25; 36(4); 4:6; 8; 9(4); 10; 11; 14(2); 16; 25; 31(3); 5:26; 6:12; 14(2); 17(2); 7:1(2); 15; 21; 27; 33; 39; 45; 51; 57; 63; 69; 75; 81; 8:4(2); 8; 9:2; 3(2); 7; 12; 13; 14; 11:7; 8; 13:27; 32; 15:24(2); 27; 16:30; 32; 19:4(2); 5(4); 20:8; 21:25; 32; 26:10; 54; 28:7; 8; 9; 10; 15; 24; 31; 29:6(2); 11; 16(2); 19; 22(2); 25(2); 28(2); 31(2); 34(2); 38(2); 32:33; 41; 42; 34:2; 12; 14; 35:8; 36:9; **Deut** 3:11(2); 12; 9:21; 11:6; 14; 13:15; 16(2); 14:14; 18; 21; 15:23; 20:14; 19; 28:12; 30; 32:11(4); 33:16; **Josh** 3:15; 4:18; 6:2; 26(2); 7:8(2); 8:2(4); 13; 10:1(2); 2; 28; 30(2); 37(2); 39(4); 11:10; 16; 13:17; 27; 15:45; 47(3); 17:10; 11(6); 16; 18; 18:20(2); 21:12; 13(2); 14(2); 15(2); 16(3); 17(2); 18(2); 21(2); 22(2); 23(2); 24(2); 25(2); 27(2); 28(2); 29(2); 30(2); 31(2); 32(3); 34(2); 35(2); 36(2); 37(2); 38(2); 39(2); 42; **Judg** 1:18(3); 26(2); 27(5); 5:23; 7:15; 8:14; 11:26(2); 15:19; **1 Sam** 5:3(2); 4(2); 6; 11; 6:2; 8; 9; 7:12; 14; 9:24; 17:35(2); 51; 21:6; **2 Sam** 6:17; 12:30; 20:8; **1 Ki** 6:2(3); 38(2); 7:2(3); 6(2); 21(2); 23(2); 24; 26; 27(2); 30; 31; 34; 35(2); 36(2); 8:6; 7; 16:34(2); 21:2; **2 Ki** 2:12; 11:18; 12:9; 14:7; 15:16; 16:9; 10(2); 17:24; 29; 18:8; 33; 19:23(4); 22:16; 19; 23:6; 25:21; **1 Chr** 2:23; 5:16; 6:55; 56; 57(2); 58(2); 59(2); 60(3); 67(2); 68(2); 69(2); 70(2); 71(2); 72(2); 73(2); 74(2); 75(2); 76(3); 77(2); 78(2); 79(2); 80(2); 81(2); 7:28(4); 29(4); 8:12; 12:15; 15:3; 15; 16:32; 18:1; 21:27; 23:26; 28:11(4); 15(2); **2 Chr** 3:7; 8(2); 4:1(3); 2(2); 5; 22; 5:7; 8; 13:11; 19(3); 23:17; 24:11; 13; 28:18(3); 29:18(2); 34:24; 27; 28; 36:19(2); **Ezra** 2:68; 3:3; 4:12; 16; 5:15; 6:3(2); 5; 7; 9:9; **Neh** 1:3; 2:3; 13; 17; 3:1; 3(3); 6(3); 13(2); 14(2); 15(2); 4:6; 9:36(2); 11:25(3); 27; 28; 30(2); 13:14; **Esth** 1:22; 3:12; 6:8; 8:9; **Job** 3:9; 4:16; 5:26; 6:5; 9:6(2); 24; 26; 12:11; 14:7; 8(2); 18; 18:4; 24:13(2); 27:22; 28:6; 13; 15; 23(2); 31:38; 39(2); 37:1; 38:5; 6(2); 9(2); 12; 19; 20(2); 32(2); 41; 39:18; 26; 27; 29; 30; **Ps** 1:3(2); 19:5; 6(3); 24:1; 33:17; 34:2; 46:3(2); 50:1; 12; 54:7; 55:10; 11(2); 58:4; 60:2; 65:10(3); 69:15; 72:16; 74:6; 75:3(2); 8; 78:8; 80:10(2); 85:12; 89:9; 11; 96:11; 98:7; 103:16; 104:19; 107:29; 42; 113:3; 137:5; 7; 147:9; **Prov** 1:19; 8:29; 12:28; 14:10(2); 12; 16:25; 33; 17:8; 18:21; 24:31(2); 26:14; 27:8; 18; 28:2; 30:11(2); 12(2); 28; **Eccl** 1:6; 3:11; 6:4; 7:8; **Song** 1:12; 3:10(4); 4:16(2); 7:7; 8; 8:6; 11; 12; **Isa** 1:3(2); 5:2(2); 5(2); 14; 6:13; 7:6; 9:3; 13:9; 10(2); 11; 14:17; 29; 15:8(2); 16:8; 17:6; 19:1; 3; 10; 13; 19; 21:2; 22:11; 23:11; 13(2); 24:1(2); 5; 20; 27:10; 11; 28:25(2); 30:14; 33; 31:4; 33:20(2); 34:9(3); 10; 12(2); 13(2); 14; 36:18; 37:24(4); 40:6; 16; 22; 41:9; 42:11; 44:19; 45:6; 46:7(2); 53:7; 60:22; 61:11; **Jer** 1:15; 18(2); 2:7(2); 11; 4:26; 5:22; 24; 8:1; 11:16; 19; 13:23; 17:8(2); 27; 18:8; 19:8; 12; 20:5(2); 21:14; 25:9; 18(2); 26:15; 27:8; 29:7; 30:18(2); 31:23; 24; 35; 33:12; 34:1; 46:8(2); 48:38; 49:1; 13; 17; 21; 32; 51:21(2); 28(2); 42; 52:21(2); 27; **Lam** 2:2; 4:4; 11; **Ezek** 1:4; 15; 11:6; 7; 9; 11; 15; 18(2); 13:14; 14:13; 15:4; 17:4; 6(2); 7(2); 9(4); 12; 22; 23; 19:7; 20:29; 21:3; 4; 5; 30; 22:21; 22; 23:34; 24:11(3); 25:9; 26:3; 27:9; 31:3; 5(3); 6(3); 7(2); 8(2); 10(3); 11; 12(3); 13(2); 15; 16; 17(2); 32:7; 12; 13(2); 35:8; 36:5; 38; 38:6(2); 40:6; 20(2); 21(5); 22(4); 24; 25(3); 26(2); 29(4); 31(2); 33(4); 34(2); 36(5); 37(2); 38; 41:2(2); 12(2); 13; 15; 22(4); 42:7; 43:11(9); 13; 16; 17(3); 20; 44:5; 14; 45:1(2); 47:8; 11; 48:1(2); 13(2); 16; 18; **Dan** 2:5; 6(2); 7; 9; 26; 31; 32(2); 33(2); 34; 45; 3:1; 4:7; 9; 10; 11; 12(3); 14(4); 18; 19(2); 21; 23; 5:7; 8; 15; 16; 7:4; 5(2); 6; 7; 9; 11; 19(3); 20; 8:21; 22(2); 11:39; **Hos** 2:9(2); 4:19; 9:10; 10:5(3); **Joel** 1:7; 2:22; **Am** 1:3; 6; 7; 9; 10; 11; 13; 14; 2:1; 3(2); 4; 6; 8:10; 9:11(2); **Jon** 1:15; 2:6; **Mic** 1:11; 5:6; **Nah** 1:8; 3:1; **Hab** 2:18(2); 3:10(2); **Zeph** 3:18; **Hag** 1:10; 2:3; **Zech** 2:2(2); 3:9; 4:3; 11; 5:2(2); 4; 8; 11; 8:5; 12; 9:1; 17(2); 12:4; **Mal** 1:11; 12(2); **Mt** 2:16; 5:13; 6:34(2); 7:27; 12:33(3); 13:32; 17:27; 21:34; 24:29; 32; 26:52; **Mk** 4:32; 9:50; 13:24; 28; **Lk** 6:44; 10:10; 13:19; 14:34; 21:20; **Jn** 7:7; 15:19; **Acts** 8:32; 12:10; 15:16; 31; **Rom** 6:12; 13:14; **1 Cor** 9:7; 10:26; 28; 13:5; 15:38; **Gal** 5:24; **Eph** 4:16; **2 Tim** 3:5; **Heb** 7:18; **Jas** 1:4; 11(2); 5:18; **1 Pe** 1:24; **Rev** 1:16; 2:5; 5:2; 5; 9; 6:13; 14; 12:16; 16:12; 21:15(2); 16(3); 17; 18; 22; 23; 24; 25; 22:2(2)

ITSELF (58/52)

Gen 1:11; 12; 32:16; **Ex** 25:34; 37:20; **Lev** 16:22; **Num** 23:9; 24; **Deut** 14:21; **Josh** 22:22; **Judg** 7:2; 18:1; **1 Ki** 7:34; **2 Ki** 19:29; **Job** 10:22; **Ps** 41:6; 68:8; **Prov** 27:25; **Isa** 5:14; 10:15(3); 37:30; 55:2; 60:20; **Jer** 31:24; **Ezek** 1:4; 4:14; 10:17; 17:14; 25:12; 29:15; **Hos** 8:9; **Zech** 12:12(3); 13(2); 14; **Mt** 12:25(2); **Mk** 3:24; 25; 4:28; **Lk** 11:17; **Jn** 15:4; 20:7; 21:25; **Rom** 8:21; 14:14; **1 Cor** 11:14; 13:4; **2 Cor** 10:5; **Eph** 4:16; **Heb** 9:19; 24; **Jas** 2:17; **3 Jn** 12

LIKE (1278/1013)

Gen 3:5; 22; 10:9; 13:10(2); 19:28; 25:22; 25; 27:23; 27; 46; 31:26; 34:31; 38:11; 39:17; 44:18; **Ex** 1:19; 4:6; 7; 7:11; 8:10; 9:14; 24; 11:6(2); 15:5; 7; 8; 10; 11(2); 16:31(2); 19:18; 22:25; 23:11; 24:10; 17; 25:33(2); 34; 28:11; 14; 21; 22; 32; 36; 30:32; 33; 38; 34:1; 4; 37:19(2); 20; 39:8; 14; 15; 23; 30; **Lev** 4:26; 6:17; 7:7; 9:15; 13:2; 25:35; 26:19(2); **Num** 8:11; 13; 15; 21; 9:15; 11:7(2); 8; 15; 13:18; 19; 33; 16:13; 29; 40; 23:10; 22; 24(2); 24:6(4); 8; 27:17; **Deut** 2:11; 3:24; 4:32(2); 7:26; 10:1; 3; 11:10; 21; 12:16; 24; 15:23; 17:14; 18:15; 18; 20:8; 29:23; 32:31; 33:17(2); 26; 29; 34:10; **Josh** 7:5; 10:2; 14; **Judg** 5:31; 8:24; 11:17; 13:6; 15:7; 14; 16:7; 11; 12; 17; 17:11; **Ruth** 2:13; 4:11; 12; **1 Sam** 2:2(2); 4:9(2); 8:5; 20; 9:21; 10:24; 17:7; 36; 19:17; 24; 21:9; 25:36; 37; 26:15; **2 Sam** 5:20; 7:9; 22; 23(2); 9:11; 12:3; 13:13; 14:2; 14; 17:8; 10; 11; 18:27; 32; 19:27; 21:19; 22:34; 43; 23:4(2); **1 Ki** 3:12(2); 13; 4:29; 5:6; 7:8(2); 26(2); 31; 33; 8:23; 10:12; 20; 12:32; 16:3; 7; 20:11; 25; 27; 21:22(2); 25; 22:13; **2 Ki** 3:2; 5:14; 7:13(2); 8:27; 9:9(2); 20; 13:7; 14:3; 17:11; 14; 15; 18:5; 32; 23:25(2); **1 Chr** 11:23; 12:8; 22; 14:11; 17:8; 20; 21; 20:5; 26:12; 27:23; **2 Chr** 1:9; 12; 4:5(2); 6:14; 9:19; 13:9; 18:12; 21:13; 19; 22:4; 30:7; 26; 32:15; 35:18; **Neh** 13:26; **Job** 1:8; 2:3; 3:16(2); 24; 5:25; 6:15(2); 7:1; 2(2); 8:2; 9:26(2); 10:5(2); 9; 10(2); 16; 22; 11:17; 12:25; 13:28(2); 14:2(2); 6; 9; 15:16; 24; 33(2); 16:14; 17:7; 19:10; 20:7; 8(2); 21:11; 18(2); 24:5; 14; 20; 24(2); 27:7(2); 16(2); 18(2); 20; 29:14; 30:15; 19; 31:36; 37; 32:19(2); 33:25; 34:7(2); 36; 36:22; 38:3; 14(2); 30; 39:13; 20; 40:7; 9(2); 15; 17; 18(2); 41:18; 28; 30; 31(2); 33; **Ps** 1:3; 4; 2:9; 7:2; 12:6; 17:12; 18:33; 42; 19:5(2); 22:13; 14(2); 15; 28:1; 29:6(2); 31:12(2); 32:9(2); 35:5; 10; 36:6; 37:2; 20; 35; 38:4; 13(2); 14; 39:6; 11; 44:11; 49:12; 14; 20; 50:21; 52:2; 8; 55:6; 58:4(2); 8(2); 59:6; 14; 62:3; 64:3; 68:13; 71:19; 72:6(2); 16(2); 73:5; 6; 22; 74:5; 77:20; 78:8; 13; 15; 16; 27(2); 52(2); 57(2); 65; 69(2); 79:3; 5; 80:1; 82:7(2); 83:11(3); 13(2); 86:8(2); 88:4; 5; 17; 89:8; 37(2); 46; 90:4(2); 5(3); 9; 92:7; 10; 12(2); 97:5; 102:3(2); 4; 6(2); 7; 9; 11(2); 26(2); 103:5; 15; 104:2; 105:41; 107:27; 41; 109:18(2); 19; 23(2); 113:5; 9; 114:4(2); 6(2); 115:8; 118:12(2); 119:83; 119; 176; 125:1; 126:1; 127:4; 128:3(2); 131:2(2); 133:2; 3; 135:18; 140:3; 143:3; 6; 7; 144:4(2); 147:16(2); 17; **Prov** 1:12(2); 27(2); 4:18; 19; 6:5(2); 11(2); 10:23; 11:28; 12:4; 18; 15:19; 16:15; 24; 27; 17:14; 22; 18:8; 11; 19; 19:12(2); 20:2; 5; 21:1; 23:5; 32(2); 34(2); 24:34(2); 25:11; 12; 13; 14; 18; 19; 20(2); 26; 28; 26:2(2); 4; 7; 8; 9; 17; 18; 22; 23; 27:8; 28:3; 15; 30:14(2); 31:14; **Eccl** 3:18; 6:12; 7:6; 8:1; 9:12(2); 10:7; 12:11(2); **Song** 1:5(2); 2:2; 3; 9; 17; 3:6; 4:1; 2; 3(2); 4; 5; 11; 5:11; 12; 13; 15; 6:5; 6; 7; 7:1; 3; 4(3); 5(2); 7(2); 8(2); 9; 8:1; 10; 14; **Isa** 1:9(2); 18(2); 2:6; 5:24; 28(2); 29(2); 30; 9:18; 10:6; 9(3); 13; 14; 16; 26; 11:7; 13:4; 8; 14:10; 14; 19(3); 15:5; 16:3; 11; 17:6; 12(2); 13(3); 18:4(2); 19:16; 21:3; 22:18; 23:10; 24:13(2); 20(2); 26:19; 27:9; 10; 28:2(2); 4; 29:4; 5(2); 11; 30:13; 14; 27; 28; 33; 31:5; 33:4; 9; 12(2); 34:4; 35:6; 36:17; 38:12(2); 13; 14(2); 40:6; 11; 22(3); 24; 31; 41:15; 42:13(2); 14; 43:17; 44:4; 13; 22(2); 46:9; 48:18(2); 19(2); 49:2; 50:7; 9; 51:3(2); 6(3); 8(2); 12; 20; 23; 53:6; 54:6(2); 9; 57:20; 58:1; 5; 8; 11(2); 59:10; 11(2); 19; 60:8(2); 63:2; 19; 64:6(3); 65:25; 66:12(2); 14; 15; **Jer** 2:30; 3:2; 4:4; 13(2); 17; 5:8; 16; 6:23; 8:2; 9:3; 12; 22; 10:5; 6; 7; 16; 11:19; 12:3; 8; 9; 13:10; 21; 24; 14:6; 8(2); 9(2); 15:18; 16:4; 17:6; 8; 19:12; 13; 20:9; 16; 21:12; 22:23; 23:9(2); 12; 14(2); 29(2); 24:2; 5; 25:34; 38; 26:6; 9; 18(2); 29:17; 22; 30:6; 7; 31:12; 18; 46:7(2); 8(2); 21; 22(2); 48:6; 28; 34; 36(2); 38; 40; 41; 49:19(2); 22(2); 24; 50:8; 9; 11(2); 17; 37; 42(2); 44(2); 51:19; 27; 30; 33; 34; 38(2); 40(2); 55; **Lam** 1:1; 6; 12; 20; 21; 2:3; 4(3); 5; 12; 18; 19; 3:6; 10; 52; 4:3; 7; 5:3; **Ezek** 1:4; 7(2); 13(2); 14; 16; 22; 24(3); 26; 28; 2:8; 3:3; 9; 23; 5:9; 7:16; 19; 20; 8:2(3); 4; 10:1; 5; 12:4; 13:4; 20(2); 15:6; 16:7; 31; 44(2); 57; 17:5; 19:10; 20:32(2); 21:10; 23; 22:25; 27; 23:15; 20(2); 25:8; 26:4; 14; 19; 27:32; 31:2; 8(3); 32:2(2); 14; 36:17; 35; 37; 38(2); 38:9(2); 16; 40:2; 3; 25; 41:7; 42:6; 11; 43:2; 3(3); **Dan** 1:19; 2:35; 40; 3:25; 29; 4:25; 32; 33(3); 5:11; 21(2); 7:4(2); 5; 6; 8; 9; 13; 10:6(5); 11:29; 40; 12:3(2); **Hos** 2:3(2); 3:1; 4:4; 9(2); 16(2); 5:10(2); 12(2); 14(2); 6:3(2); 4(2); 5; 7; 7:4; 6(2); 7; 11; 12; 16; 8:1; 8; 9; 9:1; 4; 10(2); 11; 13; 10:4; 7; 11:8(2); 10; 11(2); 13:3(4); 7(2); 8(2); 14:5(3); 6(2); 7(3); 8; **Joel** 1:2; 8; 2:2(2); 3; 4(2); 5(3); 7(2); 9; **Am** 2:9; 4:11; 5:6; 24(2); 6:5; 8:8(2); 10(2); 9:5(2); 7; **Mic** 1:4(2); 8(2); 16; 2:8; 12(2); 3:3(2); 12(2); 4:9; 10; 12; 5:7(2); 8(2); 7:1(2); 4; 10; 17(2); 18; **Nah** 1:6; 10(3); 2:2; 4(2); 8; 3:15(3); 17(2); **Hab** 1:9(2); 14(2); 2:5; 3:4; 14(2); 19; **Zeph** 1:17(3); 2:2; 9(2); **Hag** 2:23; **Zech** 1:4; 2:6; 5:9; 7:12; 9:3(2); 7(2); 13; 14; 15(2); 16(2); 10:2; 5; 7; 12:6(2); 8(3); 11; 14:20; **Mal** 3:2(2); 4:1; 2; **Mt** 3:16; 6:5; 8; 16; 29; 7:26; 9:33; 36; 10:25(2); 11:16; 13:24; 31; 33; 44; 45; 47; 52; 17:2; 18:5; 17; 23; 20:1; 22:2; 30; 39; 23:27; 25:14; 28:3; 4; **Mk** 1:10; 2:7; 12; 4:31; 6:15; 34; 7:4; 8:24; 9:3; 12:25; 31; 13:34; 15:39; **Lk** 3:22; 6:23; 40; 47; 48; 49; 7:31; 32; 10:18; 11:44; 12:27; 36; 13:18; 19; 21; 15:19; 18:11; 20:31; 22:44; 24:11; **Jn** 1:32; 5:19; 7:46; 8:55; 9:9; 11:48; 18:22; **Acts** 1:11; 3:22; 7:37; 9:18; 10:11; 11:5; 17:29; 20:35; 25:22; **Rom** 1:23; 28; 5:15; 16; 9:20; 29(2); **1 Cor** 3:3; **Gal** 4:12(2); 20; 5:21; **1 Th** 4:5; **1 Tim** 2:9; **2 Tim** 2:17; **Heb** 1:11; 12; 2:17; 7:3; 12:16; **Jas** 1:6; 23; 5:3; 17; **1 Pe** 1:18; 2:25; 5:8; **2 Pe** 1:1; 2:12; **1 Jn** 3:2; **Jude** 10; **Rev** 1:13; 14(2); 15; 16; 2:18(2); 27; 4:1; 3(2); 6; 7(4); 6:1; 12; 8:8; 10; 9:2; 5; 7(3); 8(2); 9(2); 10; 17; 19; 10:1(2); 11:1; 12:15; 13:2(3); 4; 11(2); 14:2(2); 14; 15:2; 16:13; 18:18; 21; 19:12; 21:11(2); 18; 21

MAY (1491/1306)

Gen 2:16; 3:2; 8:17; 9:26; 27(3); 11:7; 12:13(2); 18:5(2); 19(2); 19:2; 5; 8; 32; 34; 21:30; 23:4; 6; 9; 24:14; 49; 55; 56; 60(2); 27:4(2); 7; 10(2); 19; 21; 25; 28; 31; 28:3(2); 4; 29:21; 30:3; 25; 31:37; 49; 32:5; 38:16; 41:36; 44; 42:2; 16; 34; 43:8; 14(2); 18; 44:21; 26; 46:34; 47:19(2); 48:20; 49:1; 50:15; **Ex** 2:7; 20; 3:10; 18; 4:5; 8; 13; 23; 5:1; 9; 7:4; 16; 19; 8:1; 8(2); 9; 10; 16; 20; 22; 28; 29; 9:1; 13; 14; 16(2); 22; 28; 29; 10:1; 2(2); 3; 7; 12; 17; 21(2); 25; 11:7; 9; 12:5; 16; 44; 13:9; 14:4; 12; 26; 16:4; 32; 17:2; 6; 18:19; 19:9; 20:12; 20(2); 26; 21:13; 14; 23:11(2); 12(2); 24:12; 25:8; 14; 28; 26:5; 6; 11; 27:5; 28:1; 3(2); 4; 35; 37; 38(2); 41; 29:46; 30:12; 16; 29; 30; 31:6; 13; 32:10(2); 29; 33:5; 13(2); 40:13; 15; **Lev** 5:3; 4; 6:3; 7; 18; 29; 7:6; 16; 19; 24; 30; 8:35; 10:10; 11; 11:2; 3; 9(2); 21; 22; 34; 39; 47(2); 12:8; 14:8; 36; 16:13; 17; 26; 28; 30; 17:5(2); 13; 19:25(2); 20:14; 22; 21:3; 17; 22; 22:5; 7; 11(2); 12; 13; 23; 23:43; 24:7; 25:25; 27; 29(2); 31; 32; 34; 35; 36; 44(2); 45; 46; 48(2); 49(3); 27:9; 28; 29; **Num** 1:53; 3:6; 4:19; 5:3; 8; 22; 28; 6:20; 7:5; 8:11; 24; 26; 9:8; 10; 11; 11:13; 16; 17; 21; 12:14; 15:39(2); 40; 16:21; 45; 17:10; 18:2; 5; 11; 13; 31; 19:3; 22:19; 23:13; 27; 25:4; 27:17(3); 20; 30:13(2); 31:24; 32:22; 35:6; 11; 12; 15; 28; 32; 36:6; 8; **Deut** 1:11; 2:6(2); 28(2); 31; 3:20; 4:1; 2; 7; 10(2); 40(2); 5:1; 14; 16(2); 27; 31; 33(3); 6:1; 2(2); 3(2); 18(2); 8:1; 18; 9:5; 14; 10:11; 11:8; 9; 14; 15; 21; 12:15(2); 17; 20; 21(2); 22(2); 23; 25; 28; 13:17; 14:4; 6; 9(2); 11; 20; 21(3); 23; 29(2); 15:3; 4; 22(2); 16:3; 5; 20; 17:15; 19; 20(3); 18:7; 19:3; 4; 12; 13; 20:20; 21:13; 22:7(2); 8; 23:8; 11; 12; 14; 16; 20(2); 24; 25; 24:13; 19; 25:1; 3; 6; 15; 26:12; 19; 27:3; 28:58; 29:6; 9; 12; 13(2); 18(2); 19; 29; 30:6; 12; 13; 14; 16; 19; 20(4); 31:5; 12(2); 13; 14; 19; 26; 28; 33:7; **Josh** 1:7(2); 8; 2:5; 16; 3:4; 7; 4:6; 24(2); 9:19; 10:4; 14:12; 18:6; 8; 20:3; 4; 6; 22:24; 27(3); 28; **Judg** 1:3; 2:22; 6:30; 9:7; 33; 11:6; 8; 27; 37; 13:14(2); 17; 14:13; 15; 15:12; 16:5(2); 6; 10; 13; 25; 28; 17:2; 18:5; 19:9(2); 22; 20:10; 13; 21:17; **Ruth** 1:9; 11; 2:2; 16; 3:1; 4:4; 10; 11; 12; 14; 15; **1 Sam** 1:22; 2:16; 36; 4:3; 7:8; 8:20(2); 9:16; 26; 27; 11:2; 3; 10; 12; 12:7; 17; 19; 14:6; 15:25; 30; 17:10; 46; 18:21(2); 19:15; 20:5; 13(2); 14; 42; 24:4; 19; 25:22; 26:19; 23; 25; 27:5; 28:7; 15; 22; 29:4; 7; 8; 30:22; **2 Sam** 2:6; 3:9; 21(2); 7:10; 29; 9:1; 3; 10; 10:12; 11:15; 12:18; 22; 13:5; 6; 10; 14:7; 15; 17; 32; 15:34; 16:4; 11; 12; 17:12; 18:32; 19:26; 37; 20:16; 21:3; 22:28; 24:2; 3(2); 12; 21; 23; **1 Ki** 1:2; 12; 36; 37; 47(2); 2:3; 4; 17; 23; 31; 3:9; 8:29(2); 30; 36; 40; 43(2); 50; 52; 57(2); 58; 59(3); 60; 11:21; 36; 12:26; 13:6; 18; 14:2; 17:10; 12(2); 18:5; 37; 20:34; 21:2; 10; 22:7; 8; 20; **2 Ki** 2:9; 3:11; 17; 4:22; 41; 42; 43; 5:6; 18(2); 6:2; 13; 17; 20; 22; 28; 29; 7:13(2); 9:7; 18:32; 19:4; 19; 22:4; **1 Chr** 4:10; 12:17; 19; 13:2; 15:2; 12; 17:9; 24; 27; 19:13; 21:2; 3; 10; 22(2); 22:11(2); 12(2); 14; 23:25; 28:8; **2 Chr** 1:10; 11; 2:14; 6:6; 20(2); 21; 27; 31; 33(2); 7:16; 12:8; 13:9; 18:6; 7; 19; 23:6; 28:23; 29:10; 30:8; 9; 18; 35:6; 36:23; **Ezra** 1:3; 4:3; 15; 21; 6:10; 12; 7:13; 16; 20(2); 21; 25; 9:8; 12; **Neh** 1:6; 2:3; 5; 17; 4:22; 5:2; 13(2); 6:6; **Esth** 2:3; 4:11; 5:5; 6:9; **Job** 1:5; 3:3; 4(2); 5(3); 6(3); 7(2); 8; 9(2); 9:32; 33; 10:20; 13:13; 14:6; 8(2); 19:29; 21:3; 19; 22:2; 27:7; 8; 17; 31:6; 32:20; 33:14; 30; 34:22; 37:7; 12; 38:11; 20(2); 34; 35; 39:15(2); 40:8; 23; **Ps** 8:2; 9:14; 20; 10:10; 18; 11:2; 12:3; 15:1(2); 17:5; 20:1(2); 2; 3; 4; 5; 9; 24:3(2); 26:7; 27:3; 4; 30:5; 12; 32:6; 34:12; 39:4; 13; 41:10; 48:13; 50:4; 51:4; 8; 56:13; 58:8; 59:13; 60:4; 5; 61:7; 8; 64:4; 65:4; 67:2; 68:23(2); 69:35; 71:3; 73:28; 76:7; 78:6; 7; 8; 83:4; 16; 18; 84:3; 85:6; 9; 86:17; 90:12; 14; 91:7; 92:7; 94:13; 101:6; 8; 102:18; 104:9(2); 14; 27; 31(2); 34; 35; 106:5(3); 107:36; 37; 108:6; 109:15; 27; 113:8; 115:14; 15; 119:17; 18; 71; 73; 77; 80; 88; 101; 116; 125; 134; 148; 122:6; 128:5; 6; 130:4; 142:7; 144:12(2); 13(2); 14; **Prov** 2:20; 3:15; 5:2(2); 6:31; 7:5; 8:11; 21(2); 14:13(2); 15:24; 19:7; 20; 22:19; 21(2); 23:35; 24:16; 27:1; 11; **Eccl** 1:10; 13; 2:26; 3:18; 4:12; 5:15; 8:4; 10:9(2); 11; 20(2); **Song** 4:16; 6:1; 13; 8:12; **Isa** 5:8; 11; 19(2); 7:15; 10:2(2); 19; 13:2; 19:15; 23:16; 24:10; 26:2; 27:5; 28:12; 21; 30:1; 8; 18(2); 37:4; 20; 41:20; 22; 23(2); 26(2); 42:18; 43:9; 10; 26; 44:9; 13; 45:3; 6; 49:9; 15; 20; 51:14; 16; 23; 55:6; 10; 60:11; 21; 61:3(2); 64:2; 65:8; 66:5; 11(2); **Jer** 3:1; 4:14; 6:10; 27; 7:18; 23; 9:12(2); 17(2); 18; 10:18; 11:5; 19; 13:11; 23; 26; 21:2; 26:3; 27:15(2); 28:14; 29:6(2); 30:13; 32:14; 39; 33:21; 35:7; 36:3(3); 7; 42:3; 6; 12; 43:3; 44:8; 29; 46:10; 48:9; 49:19; 50:34; 44; 51:8; 39; **Lam** 1:21; 2:13; 3:29; **Ezek** 4:17; 6:6(4); 8; 7:13; 11:20; 12:3; 16; 19; 13:6; 14:5; 11(3); 15; 16:37; 54; 63; 20:20; 21:5; 11; 15(2); 23; 22:3; 23:48; 24:8(2); 11(4); 25:10; 14; 26:20; 31:14(2); 34:10; 37:9; 38:16; 39:17; 42:14; 43:10; 11; 44:3; 5; 25; 46:18; 48:14; **Dan** 2:30; 4:17; 19; 27; 6:15; **Hos** 6:2; 13:10; **Joel** 3:3; 6; **Am** 5:14; 15; 7:2; 5; 8:5(2); 6; 9:1; 12; **Ob** 9; **Jon** 1:6; 7; 11; 3:9; **Mic** 6:5; 14; 16; 7:3; **Hab** 2:2; 9(2); 15; 3:17(3); **Zeph** 2:3; 3:9; **Hag** 1:8; **Zech** 11:1; **Mal** 1:4; 9; 2:4; 12; 3:3; 10; **Mt** 2:8; 5:16; 45; 6:2; 4; 5; 16; 9:6; 21; 12:36; 14:15; 18:16; 19:16; 20:21; 33; 23:26; 35; 24:20; **Mk** 1:38; 2:10; 3:28; 4:12(2); 32; 5:12; 23; 28; 6:36; 7:9; 10:17; 37; 51; 11:25; 12:15; 13:18; 14:7; 12; 14; 15:32; **Lk** 1:4; 2:35; 5:24; 8:10(2); 16; 9:12; 11:33; 50; 12:36; 14:10; 23; 16:4; 9; 24; 28; 18:41; 20:14; 21:22; 36; 22:8; 11; 30; 31; 40; **Jn** 1:22; 3:21; 4:15; 36; 5:20; 34; 40; 6:5; 7; 28; 30; 40; 50; 7:3; 9:36; 39(2); 10:10(2); 17; 38; 11:4; 11; 15; 16;

25; 42; 12:36; 13:18; 19; 14:3; 13; 16; 29; 31; 15:2; 11(2); 16; 16:4; 24; 33; 17:1; 3; 11; 13; 19; 21(3); 22; 23(2); 24(2); 26; 19:4; 35; 20:31(2); **Acts** 2:25; 3:19(2); 20; 4:29; 30; 6:3; 8:19; 22; 24; 37; 9:17; 15:17; 17:19; 19:27; 40; 20:24; 21:24(2); 37; 24:8; 11; 25:26; 26:18; **Rom** 1:10; 11(2); 12; 19; 3:4(2); 8; 19(2); 6:1; 7:4; 8:17; 9:17(2); 10:1; 11:14; 21; 31; 12:2; 14:2; 19; 15:5; 6; 13(2); 24; 31(2); 32(2); 16:2; **1 Cor** 1:8; 2:16; 3:18; 4:6(2); 5:5; 7; 7:5; 32; 33; 34(2); 35(2); 9:18(2); 23; 24; 10:13; 33; 11:19; 32; 14:1; 5; 10; 13; 19; 31(2); 15:28; 16:2; 6(2); 10; 11; **2 Cor** 1:4; 11; 4:7; 10; 11; 15; 5:4; 10; 12; 6:3; 8:11; 14(3); 9:3; 5; 8; 10; 10:2; 11:2; 3; 4; 12; 16; 12:9; 16; 13:7; 9; **Gal** 4:17; 6:12; 13; **Eph** 1:17; 18; 3:4; 17; 18; 19; 4:15; 28; 29; 6:3(2); 11; 13; 19(2); 20; 21; 22(2); **Phil** 1:9; 10(2); 26; 27; 2:15; 16; 19; 28(2); 3:4; 8; 10; 11; 12; 21; **Col** 1:9; 10; 18; 28; 2:2; 4:4; 6; 8; 12; 17; **1 Th** 2:16; 3:10; 11; 12; 13; 4:12(2); 5:23(2); **2 Th** 1:5; 12; 2:6; 12; 16; 3:1; 2; 5; 14; 16; **1 Tim** 1:3; 18; 20; 2:2; 3:15; 4:15; 5:7; 16; 20; 6:1; 19; **2 Tim** 1:4; 18; 2:4; 7; 10; 25; 26; 3:17; 4:14; 16; **Titus** 1:9; 13; 2:5; 8; 10; 3:13; 14; **Phm** 1:6; **Heb** 4:16; 5:1; 9:15; 10:9; 36; 12:10; 13; 18; 27; 28; 13:6; 19; 20; **Jas** 1:4; 3:3; 4:3; 5:16; **1 Pe** 1:7; 2:2; 9; 12; 15; 3:1; 7; 9; 16; 4:11; 13; 5:6; 8; 10; **2 Pe** 1:4; 3:2; **1 Jn** 1:3; 4; 2:1; 28; 4:17; 5:13(2); 20; **2 Jn** 8; 12; **3 Jn** 2; 8; **Rev** 2:10; 3:11; 18(4); 13:17; 14:13; 19:18; 22:14(2)

ME (4065/3061)

Gen 3:12(2); 13; 4:10; 14(3); 23(2); 25; 6:13; 7:1; 9:9; 12; 13; 15; 17; 12:12; 13; 18(2); 13:8; 9; 14:21; 24; 15:2; 3; 9; 16:2; 5; 13; 17:1; 2; 4; 7; 10; 11; 18:21; 19:8; 19(2); 20; 20:5; 6; 9(2); 11; 13(3); 21:6(2); 16; 23(3); 26; 22:12; 23:4; 8(2); 9(2); 11; 13(2); 15(2); 24:5; 7(3); 12; 17; 23; 27(2); 30; 37; 39; 40; 43; 44; 45; 48; 49(2); 54; 56(2); 25:30; 31; 32; 33; 26:7; 27(3); 27:3; 4(2); 7(2); 9; 12; 13(2); 19(2); 20; 25; 26; 31; 33; 34(2); 36(2); 38(2); 46; 28:20(3); 22; 29:15(2); 19; 21; 25(2); 27; 32; 33; 34; 30:1; 6; 13; 14; 16; 18; 20(2); 24; 25; 26(2); 27; 28; 29; 31(2); 32; 33(2); 31:5(2); 7(2); 9; 11; 13; 26; 27(2); 28; 29; 31; 35; 36; 40; 42(2); 44; 48; 49; 50; 51; 52; 32:9; 11(2); 16; 20(2); 26(2); 29; 33:10; 11; 13; 14; 15(3); 34:4; 11(2); 12(3); 30(4); 35:3(2); 37:9; 14; 16; 38:16(3); 17; 39:7; 8; 9; 12; 14(2); 15; 17(2); 18; 19; 40:8; 9; 14(4); 15; 41:10(2); 13; 16; 24; 51; 52; 42:20; 33; 34; 36(2); 43:6; 8; 9; 16; 29; 44:17; 21; 27; 28; 29; 34; 45:1; 4; 5(2); 7; 8(2); 9(2); 10; 18; 46:30; 31; 47:29(2); 30(3); 31; 48:3(2); 4; 7(2); 9(2); 11; 15; 16; 49:29; 50:5(3); 20; **Ex** 2:9; 14; 3:9; 13(2); 14; 15; 16; 4:1; 18; 23; 25; 5:1; 22; 6:12(2); 30; 7:16(2); 8:1; 8; 20; 28; 9:1; 13; 14; 10:3(2); 17; 28; 11:8(2); 12:32; 13:2; 8; 14:15; 17:2; 4; 18:4; 15; 16; 19:5; 6; 20:3; 5; 6; 23; 24; 25; 22:23; 27; 29; 30; 31; 23:14; 15; 33; 24:12; 25:2; 8; 30; 28:1; 3; 4; 41; 29:1; 44; 30:30; 31; 31:13; 17; 32:2; 10; 23; 24; 26; 32; 33; 33:12(3); 13; 18; 20; 21; 34:2; 20; 40:13; 15; **Lev** 10:3; 19; 14:35; 20:26; 22:2; 25:23; 55; 26:14; 18; 21(2); 23(2); 27(2); 40(2); **Num** 3:41; 8:16; 11:11; 12; 13; 14; 15(3); 16; 14:11(2); 22; 23; 24; 27(2); 29; 35; 16:28; 29; 17:10; 18:9; 20:12(2); 19; 21:22; 22:5; 6(2); 8; 10; 11; 13; 16; 17(2); 18; 19; 28; 29; 32; 33(3); 34; 37; 23:1(2); 3(2); 7(2); 10; 11; 13(2); 18; 27; 29(2); 24:12; 13; 27:14; 28:2(2); 32:11; **Deut** 1:14; 17; 22; 23; 37; 41; 42; 2:1; 2; 9; 17; 27; 28(3); 29; 31; 3:2; 25; 26(4); 4:5; 10(3); 14; 21; 5:7; 9; 10; 22; 23; 28(2); 29; 31; 7:4; 8:17; 9:4; 10; 11; 12; 13; 14; 19; 10:1(2); 4; 5; 10; 11; 12:20; 17:14(2); 18:15; 16(2); 17; 26:10; 13; 14; 28:20; 31:2; 16; 19; 20; 28; 32:21(2); 34; 39; 41; 51(2); **Josh** 2:4; 12(2); 7:19(2); 8:5; 10:4(2); 22; 14:6; 7; 8; 10; 11; 12(2); 15:19(3); 18:4; 6; 8; 19:46; 24:15; **Judg** 1:3; 7; 15(3); 3:28; 4:8(2); 18; 19; 5:13; 6:17(2); 39(3); 7:2(3); 17; 18; 8:5; 15; 24; 9:7; 15; 48; 54(2); 10:12; 13; 11:7(3); 9(2); 12(2); 17; 27(2); 31; 35(2); 36; 37(2); 12:2; 3(3); 5; 13:6(2); 7; 10(2); 16; 14:2; 3(2); 12(2); 13(2); 16(3); 15:1; 11; 12(2); 16:6; 7; 10(3); 11; 13(3); 15(3); 17; 18; 26; 28(2); 30; 17:2; 10(2); 13; 18:4(2); 24; 19:18; 24; 20:5(3); **Ruth** 1:8; 11; 13(2); 16; 17(2); 20(3); 21(4); 2:2; 7; 10; 11; 13(2); 21; 3:5; 17(2); 4:4; **1 Sam** 1:11; 27; 2:28; 29; 30(4); 36; 3:5; 6; 8; 17(2); 8:7; 8; 9:16; 18; 19(2); 21; 10:2; 8; 15; 12:1; 3; 12; 23(2); 13:9; 11; 12; 14:12; 33; 34; 42; 43; 15:1; 11; 16; 20; 25; 30(2); 32; 16:2; 3; 5; 17(2); 19; 22; 17:8; 9(2); 10; 35; 37(2); 43; 44; 45; 18:8; 17; 19:15; 17(3); 20:2(2); 3; 5; 6(2); 8(3); 10; 14; 23; 28; 29(3); 31; 42; 21:2(2); 3; 8; 9; 14; 22:3; 8(5); 13(2); 15; 17; 23(2); 23:11; 12; 21; 23; 24:10; 12(2); 15(2); 17; 18(3); 19; 21(2); 25:19; 21; 24(2); 32; 33; 34(2); 26:6; 8; 19(2); 24; 27:1(3); 5; 28:1; 7; 8(2); 9; 11; 12; 15(6); 16; 17; 19; 21; 22; 29:3(2); 6(2); 30:7; 13; 15(4); 31:4(3); **2 Sam** 1:4; 7(2); 8; 9(5); 26(2); 2:7; 22; 3:8; 12; 14; 35; 39; 4:10; 5:20; 6:9; 21(2); 7:5; 7; 18; 10:2; 11(2); 11:6; 12:10; 22; 23; 13:4; 5; 6; 9; 11; 12; 13; 16(2); 17; 14:9; 10; 15; 16; 18; 19; 32(4); 15:4; 7; 8; 25(2); 26; 28; 33(2); 34; 36; 16:3; 9; 12; 17:1; 18:13; 19; 22; 23; 29; 19:13(2); 19; 22; 25; 26; 33(2); 36; 38(2); 20:4; 20; 22:3; 5(2); 6(2); 17(2); 18(3); 19; 20(3); 21(2); 23; 25; 34; 36(2); 37; 40(3); 41(2); 44(3); 45(2); 48(2); 49(4); 23:2; 3; 5; 15; 17; 24:13; 14; 17; 24; **1 Ki** 1:12; 13; 17; 24; 26(2); 28; 30; 32; 51; 2:4(2); 5; 7; 8(2); 15; 16; 17; 20; 23; 24(3); 30; 31; 42; 3:24; 5:4; 6; 8; 9; 8:25(3); 9:3; 4; 6; 13; 10:7; 11:21; 22(2); 33; 36; 12:5; 6; 9; 12; 24; 27; 13:6(2); 7; 8; 9; 13; 15; 18; 27; 31; 14:2; 8; 9(2); 15:19(2); 16:2; 17:10; 11; 13(2); 18; 19; 18:9; 12; 14; 19; 30; 37(2); 19:2; 20; 20:5; 7; 10(2); 32; 35; 36; 37; 39; 21:2; 6; 20; 22; 29(2); 22:4; 8; 14; 16; 18; 24; 28; 34; **2 Ki** 2:2; 4; 6; 9; 10; 20; 3:7(2); 15; 4:2; 6; 13; 22; 24; 27(2); 28; 5:7(2); 8; 11; 22(2); 6:11; 19; 28; 31; 7:12; 8:4; 9; 10; 13; 14; 9:12; 18; 19; 10:6(2); 15; 16; 19; 16:7(2); 15; 18:14(2); 20; 22; 25; 27; 31(2); 19:6; 20; 27; 28; 20:8; 21:15; 22:10; 13; 15; 17(2); 19; **1 Chr** 4:10(3); 10:4(2); 11:17; 19; 12:17(3); 13:12; 17:4; 6; 12; 16; 17; 19:2; 12(2); 21:2; 12; 13(2); 17; 22(2); 24; 22:7; 8; 28:2; 3; 4(3); 5; 6; 19(2); 29:17; **2 Chr** 1:8; 9; 10; 2:3; 7(2); 8; 9; 6:16(2); 7:17; 9:6; 10:5; 6; 9; 12; 11:4; 12:5; 13:4; 15:2; 16:3(2); 18:3; 7; 15; 17; 23; 27; 33; 20:20; 28:11; 23; 29:5; 34:18; 21; 23; 25(2); 27(2); 35:21(2); 23; 36:23(2); **Ezra** 1:2(2); 4:18; 21; 7:28(3); 8:1; 9:1; 4; **Neh** 1:3; 9; 2:2; 4; 5; 6(2); 7(2); 8(3); 9; 12(2); 14; 18(2); 4:18; 23; 5:15; 18; 19; 6:2(2); 4; 5; 12; 13; 14; 19(2); 12:40; 13:8; 14; 22(2); 28; 31; **Esth** 4:16; 5:12; 13; 6:6; 7:3; **Job** 2:3; 3:12; 25(2); 4:12; 14; 5:8; 6:4(2); 7; 8; 9(2); 13(2); 22(2); 23(2); 24(2); 28; 7:3; 8(3); 12; 13; 14(2); 16; 19(2); 20; 21; 9:11; 16; 17; 18(2); 20(2); 28; 31(2); 34(2); 35; 10:2(3); 8(3); 9(2); 10(2); 11(2); 12; 14(2); 15; 16(2); 17(3); 18(2); 20; 13:13(3); 15; 19; 20; 21(2); 22(2); 23; 24; 26(2); 14:3; 13(4); 15:17; 16:7; 8(3); 9(4); 10(3); 11(2); 12(4); 13; 14(2); 20; 17:1; 2; 3(2); 6; 19:2; 3(2); 4; 5(2); 6(2); 9; 10; 11(2); 12; 13(2); 14; 15; 18(2); 19(2); 21(3); 22; 27; 28; 20:2(2); 3(2); 21:3; 4; 5; 16; 27; 34; 22:18; 23:5(2); 6(2); 10; 14; 16; 24:15; 25; 27:3; 5(2); 6; 7; 28:14(2); 29:2; 5(2); 6; 8; 11(2); 13; 14; 20; 21; 23; 30:1; 2; 10(2); 11(2); 12; 15; 16; 17; 18; 19; 20(2); 21(2); 22(2); 23; 26; 27; 30; 31:6; 8; 13; 15; 20; 23; 29; 35(2); 36; 38; 32:10; 14; 18(2); 21(2); 22; 33:4(2); 5(2); 7; 9; 10(2); 27; 31; 32; 33; 34:2; 10; 32; 34(2); 36:2; 38:3; 4; 18; 40:7; 8; 41:10; 11; 42:3; 4(2); 7; 8; **Ps** 2:7; 8; 3:1(2); 2; 3; 4; 5; 6; 7; 4:1(3); 8; 5:7; 8; 6:1(2); 2(2); 4(2); 8; 7:1(3); 2(2); 4; 5(2); 6; 8(2); 9:13(3); 13:1(2); 2; 3; 4; 6; 16:1; 6; 7(2); 8; 11; 17:3(2); 6(2); 8(2); 9(2); 15; 18:4(2); 5(2); 16(2); 17(3); 18; 19(3); 20(2); 22(2); 24; 32; 33; 35(3); 36; 39(3); 40(2); 43(3); 44(3); 47(2); 48(4); 19:12; 13; 22:1(2); 7(2); 9(2); 11; 12(2); 13; 14; 15; 16(2); 17; 19(2); 20; 21(2); 23:2(2); 3; 4(2); 5; 6; 25:2(2); 4(2); 5(2); 7; 16(2); 17; 19; 20(2); 21; 26:1; 2(2); 11(3); 27:2; 3(2); 5(3); 6; 7(2); 9(3); 10(2); 11(2); 12(2); 28:1(2); 3; 30:1(2); 2; 3; 10; 11(2); 31:1(2); 2(3); 3(2); 4(2); 5; 8; 9; 11(2); 13; 14; 15(2); 16; 17; 21; 32:4; 7(2); 34:3; 4(2); 11; 35:1(2); 3; 7; 11; 12; 13; 15(2); 16; 17; 19(2); 21; 22; 24(2); 26; 36:11(2); 38:1(2); 2(2); 4; 10(2); 12; 16(3); 17; 19; 21(2); 22; 39:1; 3; 4; 8(2); 10; 13; 40:1; 2; 7; 11(2); 12(3); 13(2); 14; 15; 17; 41:4; 5; 6; 7(3); 9; 10(2); 11(2); 12(3); 42:3; 4; 5; 6; 7; 8; 9; 10(2); 11; 43:1(2); 2; 3(2); 5; 44:6; 15(2); 49:5; 15; 50:5(2); 8; 15(2); 23; 51:1; 2(2); 3; 5; 6; 7(2); 8; 10(2); 11(2); 12(2); 14; 54:1(2); 3; 7; 55:2(2); 3(2); 4(2); 5(2); 12(3); 16(2); 18(2); 56:1(3); 2(2); 4; 5; 9; 11; 12; 57:1(2); 2; 3(2); 6; 59:1(3); 2(2); 3; 4; 10(2); 60:5; 8; 9(2); 61:2; 3; 5; 63:8; 64:2; 65:3; 66:19; 20; 69:1; 2; 4(2); 6(2); 9(2); 12; 13(2); 14(4); 15(3); 16(2); 17; 18; 21(2); 29; 70:1(2); 5; 71:1; 2(4); 3; 4; 6; 9(2); 10; 12(2); 17; 18; 20(3); 21; 73:2; 16; 23; 24(2); 28; 77:1; 81:8; 11; 13; 86:1; 3; 7; 11; 13; 14; 16(2); 17(4); 87:4; 88:6; 7(2); 8(2); 14; 16(2); 17(2); 18; 89:26; 36; 91:14; 15; 92:4; 11; 94:16(2); 18; 19; 95:9(2); 101:2; 3; 4; 6(2); 102:2(3); 8(3); 10(2); 24; 103:1; 106:4(2); 108:6; 10(2); 109:2(2); 3(2); 5; 21(2); 22; 25; 26(2); 116:2; 3(2); 6; 12; 118:5(2); 6; 7(3); 10; 11(2); 12; 13(2); 18(2); 19; 21; 119:8; 10; 12; 19; 22; 23; 25; 26(2); 27; 28; 29(2); 30; 31; 33; 34; 35; 37; 40; 41; 42; 49; 50; 51; 53; 58; 61; 64; 66; 68; 69; 71; 72; 73(3); 74; 75; 77; 78; 79; 82; 84; 85; 86(2); 87; 88; 93; 94; 95(2); 98(2); 102; 107; 108; 110; 115; 116(2); 117; 121; 122; 124; 125; 132(2); 133; 134; 135; 139; 143; 144; 145; 146; 149; 153; 154(2); 156; 159; 161; 169; 170; 171; 175; 120:1; 5; 122:1; 129:1; 2(2); 131:1; 2; 138:3(2); 7(2); 8; 139:1(2); 5(2); 6; 10(2); 11(2); 13; 16; 17; 19; 23(2); 24(2); 140:1(2); 4(2); 5(2); 9; 141:1; 4; 5(2); 9(2); 142:3(2); 4(2); 6; 7(2); 143:1; 3; 4(2); 7(2); 8(2); 9; 10(2); 11; 144:2; 7(2); 11(2); **Prov** 1:28(3); 33; 4:4(2); 5:7; 13; 7:14; 24; 8:15; 16; 17(3); 18; 21; 22; 32; 34; 35; 36(2); 9:11; 23:26; 35(2); 24:29; 27:11; 30:7; 8(4); 18; **Eccl** 1:16; 2:7; 9(2); 15; 17; 18; 7:23; 9:13; **Song** 1:2; 4(2); 6(4); 7; 13; 14; 2:4(2); 5(2); 6; 10; 14(2); 3:3; 4; 4:8(2); 5:2; 6; 7(4); 6:5(2); 12; 7:10; 8:2; 3; 6; 12; 13; **Isa** 1:2; 11; 12; 13; 14; 3:7; 5:1; 3; 5; 6:5; 6; 8; 8:1; 3; 5; 11(2); 18; 10:4; 12:1(2); 18:4; 21:3; 4(2); 6; 11; 16; 22:4(2); 24:16; 26:9; 27:4(2); 5(2); 29:2; 13(3); 16; 30:1; 31:4; 36:5; 7; 10; 12; 16(2); 37:6; 21; 28; 29; 38:12(3); 13; 14; 15; 16(2); 20; 39:3; 40:25; 41:1; 43:10(3); 11; 20; 22(2); 23(2); 24(4); 26; 27; 44:6; 7; 8; 17; 21; 22; 45:4; 5(2); 6; 11(2); 19; 21(2); 22; 23; 46:5(2); 8; 9(2); 12; 47:8; 10(2); 48:12; 16(2); 19; 49:1(2); 2(3); 3; 5; 14(2); 16; 20(2); 21; 23; 50:4(2); 6; 7; 8(3); 9(2); 51:1; 4(3); 5; 7; 54:9; 15; 17; 55:2; 3; 11; 56:3; 4; 57:8; 11(2); 13; 16; 58:2(2); 59:21; 60:9; 61:1(3); 10(2); 63:3; 5(2); 15; 65:1(2); 3; 5; 6; 7; 10; 66:1; 22; 23; 24; **Jer** 1:4; 7; 9; 11; 12; 13; 14; 16; 2:1; 2; 5(2); 8(2); 13; 19; 21; 22; 27(2); 29(2); 32; 35; 3:1; 4; 6; 7; 10; 11; 19(2); 20; 4:1; 12; 17; 19; 22; 31; 5:7; 11; 19; 22; 6:7; 20(2); 7:10; 16; 18; 19; 26; 8:18; 19; 21; 9:3; 6; 24; 10:19; 20; 24(2); 11:6; 9; 11; 14; 17; 18(2); 19; 20; 12:1; 3(2); 8(2); 9; 11; 13:1; 3; 5; 6; 8; 11; 22; 25(2); 14:11; 14; 15:1(2); 6; 8; 10(4); 15(4); 16; 17; 18; 19; 16:1; 11(2); 12; 17:13; 14(2); 15; 16; 17; 18(3); 19; 24; 27; 18:5; 15; 19(2); 22; 23(2); 19:4; 20:7(2); 8; 11; 12; 14; 17(2); 22:6; 16; 23:9; 14; 17; 24:1; 3; 4; 7(2); 25:3; 6; 7(2); 15; 17; 26:4; 12; 14(2); 15(2); 27:2; 5; 28:1; 8; 29:12(2); 13(3); 30:20; 21(2); 31:3; 18(2); 26; 34; 36(2); 32:6; 8(2); 25; 27; 29; 30(2); 31; 32; 33; 39; 40; 33:3; 8(2); 9; 18; 22; 34:14; 15; 17; 18; 35:14; 15; 16; 19; 36:18; 37:7(2); 18; 20; 38:14; 15(2); 19(2); 21; 26; 39:18; 40:4(2); 10; 15; 42:9; 20; 21; 44:3; 8; 45:3; 49:4; 11; 19(3); 50:44(3); 51:34(5); 35; 53; **Lam** 1:12; 13(2); 14; 15; 16; 19; 20; 21(2); 22; 2:22; 3:2(2); 3; 5(2); 6; 7; 10; 11(2); 12; 15(2); 16; 20; 52; 53; 60; 61; 62; **Ezek** 2:1; 2(4); 3(3); 9; 10; 3:1; 2; 3; 4; 7; 10; 12(2); 14(3); 16; 17; 22(2); 24(4); 4:15; 16; 6:1; 9(2); 7:1; 8:1(2); 3(3); 5; 6(2); 7; 8; 9; 12; 13; 14; 15; 16; 17(2); 9:9; 10; 11; 11:1(2); 2; 5(2); 14; 24(3); 25; 12:1; 8; 17; 21; 26; 13:1; 19; 14:1(2); 2; 5; 7(2); 11; 12; 13; 15:1; 16:1; 20; 26; 43; 50; 17:1; 11; 20; 18:1; 20:1; 2; 3; 8(2); 12; 13; 20; 21; 27(2); 28; 38; 39; 40; 45; 49; 21:1; 8; 18; 22:1; 12; 17; 18; 23; 30; 23:1; 35(2); 36; 37; 38; 24:1; 15; 19; 20; 25:1; 26:1; 2; 27:1; 28:1; 11; 20; 29:1; 17; 20; 30:1; 9; 20; 31:1; 32:1; 17; 33:1; 7; 21; 22(2); 23; 34:1; 35:1; 13(2); 36:16; 17; 37; 37:1(3); 2; 3; 4; 9; 10; 11; 15; 38:1; 16; 39:23; 26; 40:1(2); 2(2); 3; 4; 17; 24; 28; 32; 35; 45; 48; 41:1; 4; 22; 42:1(2); 13; 15; 43:1; 5(2); 6(2); 7; 8; 9; 18; 19(2); 44:1; 2; 4; 5; 10(2); 13(2); 15(5); 16; 46:19; 20; 21(2); 24; 47:1; 2(2); 3; 4(2); 6(3); 8; **Dan** 2:5; 6(2); 9(4); 23(2); 24; 26; 30(2); 4:2; 5(2); 6(2); 7; 8; 9; 18; 34; 36(4); 5:7; 15(2); 16; 6:22; 7:15; 16(2); 28(2); 8:1(3); 14; 15; 17; 18(3); 9:21; 22(2); 10:7; 8(2); 10(2); 11(2); 12; 13(2); 15; 16(2); 17(3); 18(2); 19(2); 21; **Hos** 2:5; 7; 12; 13; 16(2); 19(2); 20; 3:1; 3; 4:6; 7; 5:3; 15; 6:7; 7:7; 13(3); 14(2); 15; 8:2; 4; 11:7; 8; 12; 12:8; 13:4(2); 6; 9; 10; 14:8; **Joel** 2:12; 3:4(3); **Am** 4:6; 8; 9; 10; 11; 5:4; 22; 23; 25; 7:1; 4; 7; 8; 15(2); 8:1; 2; 9:7; **Ob** 3; **Jon** 1:2; 12(3); 2:2; 3(3); 5(2); 6; 7; 4:3(2); 8; 9; **Mic** 2:4; 5:2; 6:3; 7:1; 7; 8(2); 9(2); 10; **Hab** 1:3(3); 2:1; 2; 3:14; 19; **Zeph** 2:15; 3:7; 8; 11; **Hag** 2:14; 17; **Zech** 1:3; 4; 9(2); 13; 14(2); 19(2); 20; 2:2; 3; 8; 9; 11; 3:1; 4:1(2); 2; 4; 5(2); 6; 8; 9; 13; 5:2; 3; 5(2); 10; 11; 6:4; 5; 8(2); 9; 15; 7:4; 5(2); 8:14; 18; 10:9; 11:8; 11; 12; 13(2); 15; 12:10; 13:5; **Mal** 2:5(2); 6; 3:1; 5; 7; 8; 9; 10; 13; **Mt** 2:8; 3:11; 14; 4:9; 19; 7:4; 21; 22; 23; 8:2; 9; 21; 22; 9:9; 10:32; 33; 37(4); 38(2); 40(3); 11:6; 27; 28; 29; 12:30(3); 14:8; 18; 28; 30; 15:5; 8(3); 9; 22; 25; 32; 16:23(2); 24(2); 17:17; 27; 18:5; 6; 21; 26; 28; 29; 32; 19:14; 17; 21; 28; 20:13; 15; 32; 21:2; 24; 22:18; 19; 23:39; 25:20; 22; 35(3); 36(3); 40; 41; 42(2); 43(3); 45; 26:10; 11; 15; 21; 23(2); 31; 34; 38; 39; 40; 42; 53; 55(2); 75; 27:10; 17; 21; 46; 28:10; 18; **Mk** 1:7; 17; 40; 2:14; 5:7; 31; 6:22; 23; 25; 7:6(2); 7; 11; 14; 8:2; 33; 34(2); 38; 9:19; 37(4); 39; 42; 10:14; 18; 21; 36; 47; 48; 51; 11:29; 30; 12:15(2); 14:6; 7; 18(2); 20; 27; 30; 36; 48; 49; 72; 15:9; 12; 34; **Lk** 1:3; 25(2); 38; 43(2); 48; 49; 2:49; 4:6; 7; 8; 18(3); 23; 5:8; 12; 27; 6:42; 46; 47; 7:8; 23; 42; 44; 45; 8:28; 45(2); 46(2); 9:23(2); 26; 48(3); 59(2); 61; 10:16(4); 22; 40(2); 11:5; 6; 7(2); 23(3); 12:8; 9; 13; 14; 13:27; 35; 14:18; 19; 26; 27; 15:6; 9; 12(2); 19; 29; 31; 16:3; 4; 24; 17:8; 18:3; 5(2); 13; 16; 19; 22; 38; 39; 41; 19:27(2); 20:3; 23; 24; 22:19; 21; 28; 29; 32; 34; 37(2); 42; 53; 61; 68(2); 23:14; 28; 42; 43; 24:39; 44; **Jn** 1:15(3); 27(2); 30(3); 33(2); 43; 48; 2:4; 17; 3:28; 4:7; 9; 10; 15; 21; 29; 34; 39; 5:7(2); 11(2); 24; 30; 32(2); 36(3); 37(2); 39; 40; 43; 46(2); 6:26; 35(2); 36; 37(3); 38; 39(2); 40; 44(2); 45; 47; 56; 57(3); 65; 7:7; 16; 19; 23; 28(2); 29; 33; 34(2); 36(2); 37; 38; 8:12; 16; 18(2); 19(2); 21; 26; 28; 29(3); 37; 40; 42(2); 45; 46(2); 49; 54; 9:4; 11; 10:8; 9; 15; 17; 18; 25; 27; 29; 32; 37; 38(2); 11:25; 26; 41; 42(2); 12:8; 26(3); 27; 30; 44(3); 45(2); 46; 48; 49(2); 50; 13:8; 13; 18(2); 20(3); 21; 33; 36(2); 38; 14:1; 6; 7; 9(2); 10(2); 11(3); 12; 15; 19(2); 20; 21(2); 23; 24(2); 28(2); 30; 31; 15:2; 4(2); 5(2); 6; 7; 9; 16; 18; 20; 21; 23; 24; 25; 26; 27; 16:3; 5(2); 9; 10; 14; 16(2); 17(2); 19(2); 23; 27; 32(2); 33; 17:4; 5; 6(2); 7; 8(2); 9; 11; 12; 18; 20; 21(2); 22; 23(3); 24(4); 25; 26; 18:8; 9; 11; 21(2); 23; 34; 35; 39; 19:10; 11(2); 20:15; 17; 21; 29; 21:15; 16; 17(2); 19; 22; **Acts** 1:4; 8; 2:28(2); 29; 3:22; 5:8; 7:7; 28; 37; 42; 49; 8:19; 24(2); 31; 36; 9:4; 6; 17; 10:28; 29; 30; 11:5; 7; 9; 11; 12(2); 12:8; 11; 13:2; 25; 15:13; 16:15; 20:19; 22; 23; 24; 34; 21:39; 22:5; 6; 7(2); 8; 9(2); 10; 11; 13(2); 18(2); 21; 27; 23:3(2); 11; 18(2); 19; 22; 30; 24:12; 13; 18; 19; 20; 25:5; 9; 11(2); 15; 24; 27; 26:3; 5; 13(2); 14(2); 18; 21(2); 28; 29; 27:21; 23; 25; 28:18(3); **Rom** 1:12; 15; 7:8; 11(2); 13(2); 17; 18(2); 20; 21; 23; 24; 8:2; 9:1; 19; 20; 10:20(2); 12:3; 14:11; 15:3; 15; 18; 30(2); 16:7; **1 Cor** 1:11; 17; 3:10; 4:3; 4; 16; 6:12(2); 7:1; 9:3; 15(2); 16(2); 10:23(2); 11:1; 2; 24; 25; 13:3; 14:11; 21; 15:8; 10(2); 32; 16:4; 6; 9; 11; **2 Cor** 1:17; 19; 2:2(2); 5; 12; 7:7; 9:1; 4; 11:1(2); 10(2); 16(2); 28; 32; 12:1; 6(3); 7(2); 8; 9(2); 11; 13; 21; 13:3; 10; **Gal** 1:2; 11; 15(2); 16; 17; 24; 2:1; 3; 6(2); 7; 8; 9(2); 20(3); 4:12(2); 14; 15; 21; 6:14; 17; **Eph** 3:2; 3; 7; 8; 6:19(2); **Phil** 1:7(2); 12; 21; 26; 30(2); 2:18; 22; 23; 27; 30; 3:1; 7; 12; 4:3; 9; 10; 13; 15; 21; **Col** 1:25; 29; 4:7; 11; **1 Tim** 1:12(3); 16; **2 Tim** 1:8(2); 13; 15; 16; 17(2); 18; 2:2; 3:11(2); 4:8(3); 9; 10; 11(2); 14; 16(2); 17(3); 18(2); **Titus** 1:3; 3:12; 15; **Phm** 1:11; 13(2); 16; 17(2); 19; 20; 22; **Heb** 1:5; 2:13; 3:9(2); 8:11; 10:5; 7; 34; 11:32; 13:6; **Jas** 2:18; **2 Pe** 1:14; **Rev** 1:10; 12; 17(2); 3:4; 18; 20; 21; 4:1; 5:5; 7:13; 14; 10:4; 8; 9(2); 11; 14:13; 17:1(2); 3; 7; 15; 19:9(2); 10; 21:5; 6; 9(2); 10(2); 15; 22:1; 6; 8; 9; 10; 12

MY (4909/3361)

Gen 2:23(2); 4:9; 13; 23(2); 6:3; 18; 9:9; 11; 13; 15; 12:13; 19(2); 13:8; 14:22; 15:2; 3(2); 16:2; 5(2); 8; 17:2; 4; 7; 9; 10; 13; 14; 19; 21; 18:3; 12; 19:2; 7; 8; 18; 19; 20; 34; 20:2; 5(4); 9; 11; 12(4); 13(2); 15; 21:10; 23(2); 30(2); 22:7(2); 8; 18; 23:4(2); 6; 8(2); 11(2); 13; 15; 24:2; 3; 4(3); 6; 7(3); 8; 12(2); 14; 18; 27(3); 33; 35; 36(2); 37(2); 38(3); 39; 40(3); 41(2); 42; 44; 45; 48(3); 49; 54; 56(2); 65; 26:5(5); 7(2); 9; 24; 27:1; 2; 4; 7; 8(2); 11; 12; 13(2); 18(2); 19; 20; 21(2); 24; 25(2); 26; 27; 31; 34; 36(2); 37; 38(2); 41(2); 43(3); 46(2); 28:21(2); 29:4; 14(2); 15; 21(2); 32(2); 34; 30:3(2); 6(2); 8; 15(2); 16; 18(3); 20; 23; 25(2); 26(3); 30(2); 32; 33(2); 31:5; 6; 7; 10; 26; 28(2); 29; 30; 35; 36(2); 37(2); 39; 40(2); 41; 42(3); 43(4); 50(2); 32:4; 5; 9(2); 10; 11; 17; 18; 29; 30; 33:8; 9; 10(2); 11; 13; 14(2); 15; 34:8; 30; 35:3; 37:7(2); 16; 33; 35; 38:11; 26; 39:8(2); 15; 18; 40:9; 11; 16(2); 17; 41:9; 13; 17; 22; 40(2); 51(2); 52; 42:10; 28(2); 37(2); 38(2); 43:3; 5; 9; 16; 29; 44:2; 5; 7; 9; 10; 16(2); 17; 18(2); 19; 20; 21; 22; 23; 24(2); 27(2); 29; 30; 32(2); 33; 34(2); 45:3; 9; 12(2); 13(3); 28; 46:31(2); 47:1(2); 6; 9(3); 18(3); 25; 29; 30; 48:9; 15(2); 16(2); 18; 19; 22(2); 49:3(2); 4; 6(2); 9; 26; 29(2); 50:5(3); 25; **Ex** 3:7; 10; 15(2); 20(2); 4:1; 10; 13; 18; 22(2); 23; 5:1; 6:3; 4; 5; 7; 7:3(2); 4(3); 5; 16; 17; 8:1; 8; 20; 21; 22; 23; 9:1; 13; 14; 15; 16(2); 17; 27; 29; 10:2; 3; 4; 17; 28(2); 11:9; 12:31; 13:15; 19; 15:2(4); 9(3); 16:4; 28(2); 17:9; 18:4(2); 19; 19:5(2); 20:6; 24; 26; 21:5(3); 14; 22:24; 25; 23:18(2); 21; 23; 27; 25:2; 29:43; 31:13; 32:10; 22; 33; 34; 33:2; 12; 14; 17; 19; 20; 22(2); 23(3); 34:9; 25; **Lev** 6:17; 15:31; 17:10; 18:4(2); 5(2); 26(2); 30; 19:3; 12; 19; 30(2); 37(2); 20:3(3); 5; 6; 8; 22(2); 21:23; 22:2; 3; 9; 31; 32; 23:2; 25:18(2); 21; 42; 55; 26:2(2); 3(2); 9; 11(2); 12; 15(4); 17; 30; 42(3); 43(2); 44; **Num** 6:27; 10:30(2); 11:15; 28; 29; 12:6; 7(2); 8; 11; 14:17; 22(2); 24; 28; 34; 15:40; 16:28; 18:8; 20:18; 19; 24; 21:2; 22:18; 29; 38; 23:10; 11; 12; 24:10; 13; 14; 25:11(3); 12; 27:14; 28:2(3); 32:25; 27;

36:2(2); **Deut** 4:5; 10; 5:10; 29; 8:17(2); 9:4; 15; 17; 10:3; 11:13; 18:16; 18; 19(2); 20; 22:16; 17; 25:7(2); 26:5; 13; 14; 29:19; 31:16; 17(2); 18; 20; 27; 29; 32:1; 2(2); 20; 22; 23; 34; 39; 40; 41(3); 42(2); **Josh** 1:2; 7; 2:12; 13(4); 5:14; 7:11; 19; 21; 9:23; 14:7; 8(2); 9; 11(2); 15:16; 22:2; 24:15; **Judg** 1:3; 7; 12; 2:1; 2; 20(2); 4:18; 5:9; 21; 6:10; 13; 15(3); 18; 36; 37; 7:2; 13; 8:7; 19(2); 23; 9:9; 11(2); 13; 15; 17; 18; 29; 11:7; 12; 13; 30; 31; 35(2); 36; 37(2); 12:2; 3(3); 13:8; 18; 14:3; 16(3); 18(2); 15:1; 16:13; 17(3); 28; 17:2(2); 3(2); 9; 18:24; 19:20; 23(2); 24; 20:4; 5; 6; 23; 28; **Ruth** 1:11(2); 12; 13; 16(2); 2:2; 8(2); 13; 21(2); 22; 3:1; 10; 11(2); 16; 18; 4:4; 6(2); 10; **1 Sam** 1:15(2); 16; 26(2); 27; 2:1(3); 24; 28(2); 29(4); 32; 33; 35(3); 3:6; 16; 4:16; 9:5; 16(3); 17; 21; 10:2; 12:2(2); 3; 5; 14:24; 29(2); 39; 40; 42; 43; 15:11; 14; 25; 30; 16:22; 17:46; 18:17(2); 18(2); 21; 19:2; 3(2); 17; 20:1(3); 2(2); 9; 12; 13(2); 15; 29(2); 42; 21:2; 3; 8(2); 15(2); 22:3; 8(3); 12; 15; 23; 23:7; 10; 12; 17(2); 24:6(2); 8; 10(4); 11(4); 12; 13; 15; 16; 21(3); 25:5; 8; 11(4); 24; 25(2); 26(2); 27(2); 28(2); 29; 30; 31(3); 33; 39; 41; 26:11; 17(3); 18(2); 19; 20; 21(2); 23(2); 24(2); 25; 27:12; 28:2; 9; 21(2); 29:6; 8; 9; 30:13; 15; 23; **2 Sam** 1:9; 10; 26; 3:7; 12; 13(2); 14; 18(2); 21; 28; 4:8; 9; 5:2; 19; 20; 6:22; 7:5; 7; 8(2); 10; 11; 13; 14; 15; 18; 9:7; 10; 11(2); 11:11(4); 12:28; 13:4; 5(2); 6(2); 11; 12; 13; 20; 25; 26; 32; 33; 14:5; 7(2); 9(2); 11; 12; 15; 16; 17(2); 18; 19(2); 20; 22; 24; 31; 15:15; 21(2); 16:3; 4; 9; 11(3); 12; 18:5; 12(2); 13; 18; 22; 28; 31; 32; 33(5); 19:4(3); 12(3); 13(2); 19(2); 20; 26(2); 27(2); 28(2); 30; 35; 37(3); 20:9; 22:2(3); 3(6); 4; 7(4); 18; 19(2); 21(2); 22; 24; 25(2); 29(2); 30; 33(2); 34(2); 35(2); 37(2); 38; 39; 41; 44; 47(2); 49; 23:2; 5(3); 24:3(2); 17; 21; 22; 24; **1 Ki** 1:13(2); 17(2); 18; 20(2); 21(2); 24(2); 27(2); 29; 30(2); 31; 33(2); 35(2); 36; 37(2); 48(2); 2:15; 20; 22; 24; 26(2); 31; 32; 38; 44; 3:6; 7(2); 14(3); 17; 20(3); 21(2); 22(2); 23(2); 26; 5:3; 4; 5(3); 6; 9(3); 6:12(4); 13; 8:15; 16(3); 17; 18(2); 19; 20; 24; 25; 26; 28; 29; 9:3(3); 4(2); 6(2); 7(2); 13; 10:6; 7; 11:11(2); 13; 21; 32; 33(4); 34(3); 36(2); 38(5); 12:10(2); 11(2); 14(2); 13:6; 30; 31; 14:7; 8(3); 15:19; 16:2(2); 17:1; 12; 18(2); 20; 21; 18:7; 10; 12; 13; 19:4(2); 10; 14; 20(2); 20:4; 6; 7(4); 9; 32; 34(2); 21:2; 3; 4; 6; 20; 22:4(2); 49; **2 Ki** 1:13; 14; 2:12(2); 19; 3:7(2); 4:1(2); 13; 16; 19(2); 28; 29(2); 5:3; 6; 13; 18(2); 20; 22; 26; 6:8; 12; 15; 21; 26; 28; 29; 32; 8:5; 12; 9:7; 32; 10:6; 9; 15; 16; 30(2); 13:14(2); 14:9; 17:13(3); 18:23; 24; 27; 34; 35(2); 19:12; 23; 24; 28(3); 34(2); 20:5; 6(2); 15(2); 19; 21:4; 7; 8; 14; 15; 22:17; 23:27(2); **1 Chr** 4:10; 11:2(2); 19; 12:17(3); 14:10; 11(2); 16:22(2); 17:4; 6; 7(2); 9; 10; 13(2); 14(2); 16; 25; 21:3(3); 17(2); 23; 22:5; 7(3); 8(2); 10(2); 11; 18; 28:2(3); 3; 4(3); 5(2); 6(3); 7(2); 9; 20; 29:1; 2(2); 3(4); 14; 17(2); 19; **2 Chr** 1:8; 9; 11; 2:3; 4; 7; 8; 13; 14; 15; 6:4; 5(3); 6(2); 7; 8(2); 9; 10; 15; 16(2); 19; 40; 7:13; 14(3); 15(2); 16(3); 17(2); 19(2); 20(3); 8:11; 9:5; 6; 10:10(2); 11(2); 14(2); 12:7; 8; 16:3; 18:3; 13; 25:16; 18; 29:10; 11; 32:13(2); 14(3); 15(3); 17(2); 33:4; 7; 34:25; **Ezra** 7:13; 28; 9:3(3); 5(6); 6(3); 10:3; **Neh** 1:2; 6; 9(2); 2:3(2); 5; 8; 12(2); 18; 4:16; 23(2); 5:10(2); 13; 14; 16; 17; 19; 6:9; 14; 19; 7:2; 5(2); 13:14(3); 19; 22; 29; 31; **Esth** 4:16; 5:7; 8(2); 7:3(4); 4(2); 8:6(2); **Job** 1:5; 8; 21; 2:3; 3:10(2); 24(2); 4:12; 14; 15(2); 16; 5:8; 6:2(2); 3; 4; 7; 8; 11(2); 12(2); 13; 15; 24; 26; 29; 30(2); 7:4; 5(2); 6; 7(2); 11(3); 13(3); 15(2); 16(2); 19; 21(2); 9:14; 15; 16; 17; 18; 19; 20; 21; 25; 27(2); 28; 30; 31; 10:1(4); 6(2); 12; 14; 15(2); 16; 20; 11:4; 13:1(2); 6(2); 14(4); 15; 16; 17(2); 18; 19; 23(3); 26; 27(3); 14:14(2); 16(2); 17(2); 16:4(2); 5(2); 6; 7; 8(2); 9; 12; 13(2); 15(2); 16(2); 17(2); 18(2); 19(2); 20(2); 17:1(2); 2; 7(2); 11(3); 13(2); 14(3); 15(2); 19:2; 4; 5; 8(2); 9(2); 10; 12; 13(2); 14(2); 15(2); 16(2); 17(3); 19; 20(4); 21; 22; 23; 25; 26(2); 27(2); 20:2; 3; 21:2; 4; 6; 23:2(3); 4(2); 7; 11; 12; 16; 17; 24:25; 27:2(2); 3(2); 4(2); 5; 6(2); 7; 29:3; 4(2); 5; 6; 7; 14; 18(2); 19(2); 20(3); 21; 22(2); 24; 30:1; 10; 11; 12(2); 13(2); 15(2); 16(2); 17(2); 18(2); 22; 25; 27; 30(2); 31(2); 31:1; 4(2); 5; 6; 7(4); 8; 9(2); 10; 12; 13; 17; 18(2); 20; 21; 22(3); 24(2); 25(2); 27(3); 30; 31; 32; 33(3); 35(2); 36; 37; 38; 32:6; 10; 17(2); 19; 20; 22; 33:1(2); 2(3); 3(3); 7; 8; 11(2); 34:2; 5; 6(2); 16; 35:2; 10; 36:3(2); 4; 37:1; 38:10; 40:4(2); 8; 42:5; 7(2); 8(3); **Ps** 2:6(2); 7; 3:3(2); 4; 7(2); 4:1(3); 2; 7; 5:1(2); 2(3); 3; 8(2); 6:2; 3; 6(4); 7(2); 8; 9(2); 10; 7:1(2); 3(2); 4; 5(2); 6; 8(2); 10; 9:1; 3; 4(2); 13; 11:1(2); 13:2(3); 3(2); 4; 5; 14:4; 16:1; 2(3); 3; 4; 5(3); 7; 8; 9(3); 10; 17:1(2); 2; 3(2); 5(2); 6; 9; 13; 18:1; 2(8); 3; 6(4); 17; 18(2); 20(2); 21; 23; 24(2); 28(3); 29; 32; 33(2); 34(2); 36(2); 37; 38; 40; 46(2); 48; 19:14(4); 22:1(3); 2; 9; 10(2); 14(2); 15(3); 16(2); 17; 18(2); 19; 20; 22; 25(2); 23:1; 3; 5(3); 6; 25:1; 2(2); 5; 7(2); 11; 15(2); 17(2); 18(3); 19; 20(2); 26:1; 2(2); 3; 6; 9(2); 11; 12; 27:1(3); 2(2); 3; 4; 6(2); 7; 8(2); 9(2); 10(2); 11; 12; 28:1; 2(2); 6; 7(5); 30:1; 2; 3; 6; 7; 9; 10; 11(2); 12(2); 31:1; 2; 3(2); 4; 5; 7(2); 8; 9(3); 10(5); 11(3); 13; 14; 15(2); 22(2); 32:3(2); 4; 5(4); 7; 8; 34:1; 2; 4; 35:1; 2; 3; 4(2); 7; 9; 10; 12; 13(3); 14; 15; 17; 19; 23(4); 24; 26; 27; 28; 36:1; 38:3(3); 4(2); 5(2); 7(2); 8; 9(2); 10(3); 11(4); 12(2); 15; 16; 17; 18(2); 19; 20; 21; 22; 39:1(3); 2(2); 3(2); 4(2); 5(2); 7; 8; 9; 12(4); 40:1; 2(2); 3; 5; 6; 8(2); 9; 10; 12(3); 14; 17(3); 41:4; 5; 7; 9(2); 11; 12; 42:1; 2; 3(2); 4; 5; 6(2); 8; 9; 10(2); 11(3); 43:1; 2; 4(2); 5(3); 44:4; 6(2); 15(2); 45:1(3); 49:3(2); 4(2); 5; 15; 50:5; 7; 16(2); 17; 51:1; 2(2); 3(2); 5; 9(2); 14(2); 15(2); 53:4; 54:2(2); 3; 4(2); 5; 7(2); 55:1(2); 2; 4; 8; 13(3); 17; 18; 56:2; 4; 5; 6(2); 8(2); 9; 11; 13(2); 57:1(2); 4; 6(2); 7(2); 8; 59:1(2); 3(3); 9; 10(3); 11; 16(2); 17(3); 60:7(2); 8(2); 61:1(2); 2; 5; 8; 62:1(2); 2(3); 5(2); 6(3); 7(4); 63:1(3); 3; 4; 5(2); 6; 7; 8; 9; 64:1(3); 66:13; 14(2); 16; 17(2); 18; 19; 20; 68:24(2); 69:1; 3(4); 4(2); 5(2); 7; 8(2); 10(2); 11; 13; 18(2); 19(4); 20; 21(2); 70:2(2); 5(2); 71:1; 3(3); 4; 5(3); 6(2); 7; 8; 9; 10(2); 12; 13(2); 15; 17; 21; 22; 23(2); 24(2); 73:2(2); 13(2); 21(2); 23; 26(4); 28; 74:12; 77:1(2); 2(3); 3; 4; 6(3); 10; 78:1(3); 2; 81:8; 11(2); 13(2); 14; 83:13; 84:2(3); 3(2); 8; 10; 86:2(2); 4; 6(2); 7; 11; 12(2); 13; 14; 87:7; 88:1; 2(2); 3(2); 8; 9(2); 13; 14; 15; 18; 89:1; 3(2); 20(2); 21(2); 24(3); 26(3); 27; 28(2); 30(2); 31(2); 33(2); 34(2); 35; 47; 50; 91:2(3); 9; 14; 16; 92:10; 11(5); 15; 94:17(2); 18; 19(2); 22(3); 95:9; 10; 11(2); 101:2; 3; 6; 7(2); 102:1(2); 2; 3(2); 4(2); 5(3); 8; 9; 11; 23(2); 24(2); 103:1; 2; 22; 104:1(2); 33(2); 34; 35; 105:15(2); 108:1(2); 8(2); 9(2); 109:1; 4(2); 5; 20(2); 22; 24(2); 26; 29; 30; 110:1(2); 111:1; 116:1(2); 4; 7; 8(3); 11; 14; 16; 18; 118:6; 7; 14(2); 21; 28(2); 119:5; 10; 11; 13; 18; 20; 24(2); 25; 26; 28; 32; 34; 36; 37; 39; 43; 48; 50(2); 54(2); 57; 58; 59(2); 69; 76; 77; 80; 81; 82; 92(2); 97; 98; 99(2); 101; 103(2); 105(2); 108; 109(2); 111; 112; 114(2); 115; 116; 120; 121; 123; 129; 131; 133; 136; 139(2); 143; 145; 148; 149; 153; 154; 157(2); 161; 167; 168; 169; 170; 171; 172; 173; 174; 175; 120:1; 2; 6; 121:1(2); 2; 122:8; 123:1; 129:1; 2; 3; 130:2(2); 5; 6; 131:1(2); 2(2); 132:3(2); 4(2); 12(2); 14; 17; 137:5; 6(3); 138:1; 3; 7; 139:2(3); 3(3); 4; 8; 13(2); 14; 15; 16; 22; 23(2); 140:4; 6(2); 7(2); 141:1; 2(2); 3(2); 4; 5(2); 6; 8(2); 142:1(3); 2(2); 3(2); 4(2); 5(2); 6(2); 7; 143:1(2); 3(2); 4(2); 6(2); 7; 8; 9; 10; 11; 12(2); 144:1(3); 2(6); 145:1; 21; 146:1; 2(2); **Prov** 1:8; 10; 15; 23(3); 24; 25(2); 30(2); 2:1(3); 3:1(3); 11; 21; 4:1; 2; 3(2); 4(2); 5; 10(2); 20(3); 5:1(3); 7(2); 12; 13(2); 20; 6:1; 3; 20; 7:1(3); 2(2); 4; 6(2); 14; 16; 17; 19; 24(2); 8:4; 6; 7(2); 8; 10; 19(2); 31; 32(2); 34(2); 9:5; 19:27; 20:9(2); 22:17; 23:15(2); 16; 19; 26(2); 24:13; 21; 27:11(2); 30:9; 31:2(3); **Eccl** 1:13; 16(2); 17; 2:1; 3(3); 4; 7; 9; 10(6); 11; 15(2); 18; 19; 20; 3:17; 18; 7:15; 25; 28; 8:9; 16; 9:1; 12:12; **Song** 1:6(2); 9(2); 12; 13(2); 14; 15; 16; 2:2; 3(2); 6; 8; 9; 10(3); 13(2); 14; 16; 17; 3:1; 4; 4:1; 6; 7; 8; 9(4); 10(2); 11; 12(2); 16(2); 5:1(9); 2(8); 3(2); 4(2); 5(3); 6(3); 7; 8; 10; 16(2); 6:2; 3(2); 4; 9(2); 12(2); 7:9; 10; 11; 12; 13; 8:1(2); 2(2); 3; 10; 12; 14; **Isa** 1:3; 12; 14; 15; 16; 24(2); 25; 3:7; 12(2); 15; 5:1(3); 3; 4; 5; 9; 13; 6:5; 7; 7:13; 8:4(2); 16; 10:2; 5(2); 6; 8; 10; 13(2); 14; 24; 25; 11:9; 12:2(3); 13:3(4); 14:13; 25(2); 15:5; 16:4; 9; 11(2); 18:4(2); 19:25(3); 20:3; 21:3; 4; 8(2); 10(2); 22:4; 14; 20; 25:1; 26:9(2); 19; 20; 27:5; 28:23(2); 29:23(2); 30:1; 2; 32:9(2); 13; 18; 33:13; 34:5(2); 16; 36:8; 9; 12; 19; 20(2); 37:12; 24; 25; 29(3); 35(2); 38:10(2); 12(2); 13; 14; 15(2); 16; 17(3); 20; 39:4(2); 8; 40:1; 27(3); 41:8(2); 9; 10; 25; 42:1(4); 8(3); 14; 19(2); 43:4; 6(2); 7(2); 10(2); 12; 13; 20(2); 21; 25; 44:1; 2; 3(2); 8; 17; 20; 21(2); 28(2); 45:4(2); 11(2); 12; 13(2); 23; 46:10(2); 11; 13(3); 47:6(2); 48:3; 5(3); 9(3); 11(4); 12; 13(2); 18; 49:1(2); 2; 3; 4(4); 5(2); 6(2); 11(2); 14; 16; 21; 22(2); 50:1; 2(2); 4; 5; 6(3); 7; 8; 11; 51:4(3); 5(4); 6(2); 7; 8(2); 16(3); 22; 52:4; 5(2); 6(2); 13; 53:8; 11; 54:8; 10(2); 55:8(2); 9(2); 11(2); 56:1(2); 4(2); 5(2); 6; 7(4); 57:11; 13; 14; 21; 58:1; 2; 13; 59:21(3); 60:7(2); 10(2); 13(2); 21(2); 61:10(2); 62:1; 9; 63:3(4); 4(2); 5(2); 6(2); 8; 65:1; 2; 3; 5; 8; 9(3); 10; 11; 12; 13(3); 14; 15; 16; 19; 22(2); 25; 66:1(3); 2(2); 4; 5; 18; 19(3); 20; **Jer** 1:9(2); 12; 16; 2:7(2); 11; 13; 27; 31; 32; 35; 3:4(2); 12; 13; 15; 19; 4:1; 4; 11; 19(6); 20(2); 22; 31; 5:14; 22; 26; 31; 6:8; 12; 14; 19(2); 26; 27; 7:10; 11; 12(3); 14; 15; 20(2); 23(2); 25; 30(2); 31; 8:7; 11; 18; 19; 21; 22; 9:1(3); 2; 7; 13(2); 10:19(2); 20(5); 11:4(2); 7; 10(2); 15(2); 20; 12:3; 7(3); 8; 9; 10(3); 14(2); 16(4); 13:2; 10; 11; 17(2); 14:14; 15; 17(2); 15:1(2); 6; 7; 10; 14; 15; 16; 18(2); 19; 16:5; 11; 17(3); 18(2); 19(3); 21(3); 17:3; 4; 14; 16; 17; 18:2; 6; 10(2); 15; 20; 22; 19:5; 15; 20:9(2); 10(2); 11; 12; 14; 15; 17(2); 18; 21:10; 12; 22:18(2); 21; 24; 23:1; 2(2); 3; 9(2); 11; 13; 22(3); 25; 27(3); 28(2); 29; 30; 32; 39; 24:6; 7; 25:8; 9; 13; 15; 29; 26:4; 5; 27:5(2); 6; 15; 29:9; 10; 19(2); 21; 23; 32; 30:3; 10; 22; 31:1; 9; 14(2); 18; 19(2); 20(2); 26; 32; 33(2); 32:7; 8(2); 9; 12; 31(3); 34; 35; 37(2); 38; 40; 41(2); 33:5(3); 20(2); 21(3); 22; 24; 25; 26; 34:15(2); 16; 18; 35:13; 15; 36:6; 37:20(2); 38:9; 26; 39:16; 42:18(3); 43:10; 44:4; 6(2); 10(2); 11; 26(2); 29; 45:3(2); 46:27; 28; 48:36(2); 49:25; 37; 38; 50:6; 11; 51:20; 25; 34; 35(2); 45; **Lam** 1:9; 12; 13(2); 14(3); 15(3); 16(4); 18(3); 19(3); 20(2); 21(2); 22(3); 2:11(4); 21(2); 22; 3:4(3); 7; 8; 9(2); 11; 13; 14; 16; 17; 18(2); 19; 20; 21; 24(2); 48(2); 49; 51(3); 52; 53; 54; 56(3); 58(2); 59; 62; 4:3; 6; 10; **Ezek** 1:28; 2:2; 7; 3:2; 3; 4; 10; 14; 17; 23; 24; 4:14(2); 5:6(4); 7(2); 11(2); 13(4); 6:12; 14; 7:3; 4; 8(2); 9; 14; 22(2); 8:1; 3; 5; 6; 14; 18(2); 9:1; 5; 6; 8; 10; 10:13; 19; 11:12(2); 13; 20(3); 12:7(3); 13(2); 28; 13:9(2); 10; 13(2); 15; 18; 19(2); 21; 23; 14:8(2); 9(2); 11; 13; 19; 21; 15:7(2); 16:8; 14; 17(2); 18(2); 19; 21; 27; 42(2); 60; 61; 62; 17:19(2); 20(2); 18:9(2); 17(2); 19; 21; 25; 29; 20:5(2); 6; 8(2); 9; 11(2); 12; 13(4); 14; 15; 16(3); 17; 19(2); 20; 21(5); 22(2); 23; 24(3); 28; 35; 36(2); 39; 40; 42; 44; 21:3; 4; 5; 10; 12(2); 17(2); 31(2); 22:8(2); 13; 20(2); 21; 22; 26(3); 31(2); 23:25; 38(2); 39(2); 41(2); 24:13; 18; 21; 25:3; 7; 13; 14(5); 16; 17; 28:25; 29:3(2); 30:15; 24; 25; 32:3(2); 10; 32; 33:7; 22(2); 31; 34:6(2); 8(5); 10(2); 11; 12; 15; 17; 19; 22; 23; 24; 26; 30; 31(2); 35:3; 36:5(2); 6(2); 7; 8; 12; 18; 20; 21; 22; 23; 27(3); 28; 37:12; 13; 14; 19; 23; 24(3); 25(2); 26; 27(2); 28; 38:14; 16(2); 17; 18(2); 19(2); 20; 21; 39:7(3); 17; 19; 20; 21(3); 23; 24; 25; 29(2); 43:3; 7(3); 8(4); 44:4; 7(4); 8(2); 9; 11; 12; 13; 15; 16(3); 23; 24(5); 45:8(2); 9; 46:18; 47:3; 4(2); 14; 48:11; **Dan** 1:10(2); 2:3; 5; 8; 23; 3:14; 15; 4:4(2); 5(2); 8; 9; 10(2); 13(2); 18; 19; 24; 27; 30(2); 34(2); 36(5); 5:13; 6:22; 26; 7:2; 15(3); 28(3); 8:3; 17; 18; 9:3; 4; 18; 19; 20(5); 10:3; 5; 8; 9(2); 10(2); 15; 16(4); 17(2); 19; 12:8; **Hos** 1:9; 10; 2:1; 2; 5(7); 7; 9(4); 10; 12(2); 16(2); 23(3); 4:6; 8; 12; 5:10; 15(2); 6:5; 11; 7:2; 12; 8:1(2); 2; 5; 12; 13; 9:8; 15; 17; 10:10; 11:1; 7; 8(2); 9; 12:8; 13:11(2); 14; 14:4; **Joel** 1:6; 7(2); 13; 2:1; 25; 26; 27; 28; 29(3); 3:2(3); 3; 5(3); 17; **Am** 1:8; 2:7; 7:8; 15; 8:2; 9:2; 3; 4; 10; 12; 14; **Ob** 13; 16; **Jon** 2:2(2); 5(2); 6(2); 7(2); 4:2; 3; **Mic** 1:9; 2:4; 7; 8; 9(2); 3:2; 3; 5; 6:3; 5; 7(4); 16; 7:1; 7(2); 8; 9; 10(2); **Hab** 1:12(2); 2:1; 3:16(3); 18; 19(4); **Zeph** 1:4; 2:8; 9(2); 12; 3:8(5); 10(3); 11; **Hag** 1:9; 2:5; 23; **Zech** 1:6(3); 9; 16; 17; 18; 2:1; 9; 11; 3:7(4); 8; 4:4; 5; 6; 13; 5:1; 4; 9; 6:1; 4; 8; 8:6; 7; 8; 9:8(2); 13; 10:3; 11:4; 8; 10; 12(2); 14; 12:4; 5; 13:5; 6; 7(3); 9(3); 14:5(2); **Mal** 1:6(3); 7; 10; 11(3); 14; 2:2; 4; 5(2); 9; 3:1; 7; 10; 17; 4:2; 4; **Mt** 2:6; 15; 3:17; 5:11; 7:21; 8:6; 8(2); 9; 21; 9:18; 10:18; 22; 32; 33; 39; 11:10; 27; 29; 30(2); 12:18(4); 44; 48(2); 49(2); 50(2); 13:30; 35; 15:13; 22; 16:17; 18; 25; 17:5; 15; 18:5; 10; 19; 20; 21; 35; 19:20; 29; 20:15; 23(4); 21:13; 28; 37; 22:4(2); 44(2); 24:5; 9; 35; 36; 48; 25:27(3); 34; 40; 26:12(2); 18(2); 26; 28; 29; 38; 39; 42; 46; 53; 27:35(2); 46(2); 28:10; **Mk** 1:2; 11; 3:33(2); 34(2); 35(2); 5:9; 23; 30; 6:23; 8:35; 38; 9:7; 17; 24; 37; 39; 41; 10:20; 29; 40(2); 51; 11:17; 12:6; 36(2); 13:6; 9; 13; 31; 14:8; 14; 22; 24; 34; 42; 15:34(2); 16:17; **Lk** 1:18; 20; 25; 43; 44(2); 46; 47(2); 2:30; 49; 3:22; 6:47; 7:6; 7; 8; 27; 44(2); 45; 46(2); 8:21(2); 9:24; 26; 35; 38(2); 48; 59; 61; 10:22; 29; 40; 11:7; 24; 12:4; 13; 17; 18(3); 19; 45; 14:23; 24; 26; 27; 33; 15:6; 17; 18; 24; 29; 16:3; 5; 24; 27; 17:8; 18:3; 21; 41; 19:8; 23(2); 46; 20:13; 42(2); 21:8; 12; 17; 33; 22:11; 19; 20; 21; 28; 29; 30(2); 42; 23:46; 24:39(2); 49; **Jn** 2:4; 16; 4:34; 49; 5:17; 24; 30(2); 31; 43; 47; 6:32; 38; 51; 54(2); 55(2); 56(2); 65; 7:6; 8; 16; 17; 8:14; 16; 19(2); 28; 31(2); 37; 38; 43(2); 49; 50; 51; 52; 54(2); 56; 9:11; 15; 30; 10:14(2); 15; 16; 17(2); 18; 25; 26; 27(2); 28; 29(2); 30; 32; 37; 11:21; 32; 12:7; 26(2); 27; 47; 48; 49; 13:6; 8; 9(3); 35; 37; 38; 14:2; 7; 10; 12; 13; 14; 15; 20; 21(2); 23(2); 24; 26; 27; 28; 15:1; 7; 8(2); 9; 10(3); 11; 12; 14; 15; 16; 20; 21; 23; 24; 16:10; 23; 24; 26; 17:13; 24; 18:11; 36(4); 37; 19:24(2); 20:13; 17(4); 25(2); 27(2); 28(2); 21:15; 16; 17; **Acts** 2:14; 17; 18(3); 25(2); 26(3); 27; 34(2); 7:34; 49(3); 50; 59; 9:15; 16; 10:30; 11:8; 13:22(2); 33; 15:7; 17; 16:15; 20:24(2); 25; 29; 34; 21:13; 22:1; 24:14; 17; 25:26; 26:4(3); 10; 28:19; **Rom** 1:8; 9(3); 2:16; 3:7; 7:4; 18; 23(3); 9:1; 2; 3(2); 17(2); 25(2); 26; 10:1; 21; 11:3; 13; 14; 27; 15:14; 20; 24(2); 31; 16:3; 4; 5; 7(2); 8; 9; 11; 21(2); 23; 25; **1 Cor** 1:4; 11; 15; 2:4(2); 4:14; 17(2); 5:4; 9; 7:40; 8:13(2); 9:1; 2; 3; 15; 17; 18(2); 27; 10:14; 29; 33; 11:24; 25; 33; 13:3(2); 14:14(2); 18; 19; 15:58; 16:6; 18; 21; 24; **2 Cor** 1:16; 23; 2:3; 13(3); 6:16; 18; 7:4(2); 8; 8:23; 11:26; 28; 30; 12:5; 9(3); 21; **Gal** 1:13; 14(3); 15; 4:14(2); 19; 20; 6:11; 17; **Eph** 1:16; 3:4; 13; 14; 6:10; 19; 21; **Phil** 1:3; 7(2); 8; 13; 14; 16; 19; 20(2); 22; 26; 2:2; 12(3); 25(2); 3:1; 8; 9; 17; 4:1(2); 3; 14; 16; 19; **Col** 1:24(2); 2:1; 4:10; 11; 18(2); **2 Th** 3:17; **1 Tim** 1:11; **2 Tim** 1:3(2); 6; 16; 2:1; 8; 3:10; 4:6; 16; **Phm** 1:4(2); 10(2); 12; 13; 18; 19; 20; 23; 24; **Heb** 1:5; 13; 2:12; 13; 3:9; 10; 11(2); 4:3(2); 5; 5:5; 8:9; 10(2); 10:16; 34; 38; 12:5; 13:6; **Jas** 1:2; 16; 19; 2:1; 3; 5; 14; 18(2); 3:1; 10; 12; 5:10; 12; **1 Pe** 5:13; **2 Pe** 1:14; 15; 17; **1 Jn** 2:1; 3:13; 18; **3 Jn** 4; **Rev** 1:20; 2:3; 13(3); 16; 20; 26; 27; 3:5; 8(2); 10; 12(5); 16; 20; 21(2); 10:10(2); 11:3; 18:4; 21:7; 22:12; 16

MYSELF (146/140)

Gen 3:10; 6:17; 18:27; 31; 22:16; 27:12; 43:9; 50:5; **Ex** 14:18; 19:4; **Num** 3:12; 13; 8:16; 17; 12:6; 17:5; 18:6; 8; **Deut** 9:25(2); **Judg** 16:20; 19:19; **Ruth** 4:6; **1 Sam** 2:27; 35; 16:1; 25:33; **2 Sam** 3:14; 18:2; 19:26; 22:24; **1 Ki** 11:36; 17:12; 18:15; 22:30; **2 Ki** 5:11; **2 Chr** 7:12; 18:29; **Esth** 4:11; **Job** 7:20; 9:21; 30; 13:20; 19:27; 31:17; 29; 42:6; **Ps** 18:23; 35:13; 109:4; 119:16; 47; 52; 131:1; **Prov** 23:15; **Eccl** 2:4(2); 5; 6; 8; 12; 14; 19; 4:8; **Isa** 1:24; 8:2; 33:10; 42:14; 43:21; 44:24; 45:23; **Jer** 5:9; 29; 8:18; 9:9; 21:5; 22:5; 14; 31:19; 49:13; **Ezek** 4:14; 14:3; 7; 20:5; 9; 23:18(2); 29:3; 34:11; 20; 35:11; 38:23(2); **Dan** 10:3; **Hos** 2:23; 3:2; 12:8; **Mic** 6:6; **Hab** 2:1; 3:16; **Zech** 8:21; 11:7; **Lk** 7:7; 24:39; **Jn** 5:30; 31; 7:28; 8:14; 18; 28; 42; 54; 10:18; 12:32; 14:3; 21; 17:19; **Acts** 10:26; 20:24; 24:10; 16; 25:22; 26:2(2); 9; **Rom** 7:25; 9:3; 11:4; 15:14; 16:2; **1 Cor** 4:3; 4; 6; 7:7; 9:19; 27; **2 Cor** 2:1; 10:1; 11:7; 9(2); 12:5; 13; **Gal** 2:18; **Phil** 2:24; 3:13

NO (1676/1556)

Gen 2:5; 4:12; 8:9; 11:30; 13:8; 15:3; 16:1; 17:5; 19; 18:15; 19:2; 18; 31; 23:11; 24:16; 26:29; 30:1; 31:50; 32:28; 33:10; 37:22; 24; 30; 38:21; 22; 39:9; 40:8; 41:8; 15; 21; 24; 39; 44; 42:10; 12; 13; 32; 36(2); 44:23; 45:1; 47:4; 13; **Ex** 2:3; 12; 3:19; 5:7; 16; 18; 8:10; 22; 9:26; 28(2); 29; 10:5; 14; 28; 12:16; 19; 43; 48; 13:3; 7; 14:11; 13; 15:22; 16:18; 19; 29; 17:1; 20:3; 10; 21:8; 22; 22:2; 10; 23:8; 13; 26; 32; 30:12; 33:4; 20; 34:3(2); 7; 14; 17; 35:3; **Lev** 2:11(2); 5:11; 6:30; 7:24; 13:21; 26; 31; 32; 16:17; 29; 17:7; 12; 19:15; 31; 35; 20:14; 21:3; 17; 21; 22:10; 13(2); 21; 23:3; 7; 8; 21; 25; 28; 31; 35; 36; 25:26; 31; 36; 26:17; 36; 37(2); 27:26; 28; 29; **Num** 1:53; 3:4; 5:8; 13; 15(2); 19; 6:5; 8:19; 25; 26; 14:18; 30; 16:40; 18:5; 20; 23; 24; 32; 19:2; 15; 20:2; 21:5(2); 35; 22:26; 30; 23:23; 26:33; 62; 27:3; 4; 8; 9; 10; 11; 17; 28:18; 25; 26; 29:1; 12; 35; 30:7; 11; 14(2); 33:14; 35:31; 32; 33; 36:9; **Deut** 1:39; 2:5; 3:3; 26; 4:12; 15; 39; 5:7; 14; 22; 7:2; 16; 24; 8:15; 10:9; 16; 17; 11:17(2); 25; 12:12; 14:27; 29; 15:4; 19; 16:3; 4; 8; 17:13; 18:1; 2; 21:14; 22:26; 27; 23:14; 17; 24:1; 6; 25:3; 5; 28:26; 29; 31; 32; 65; 66; 68; 31:2; 32:12; 20; 36; 39; 33:26; 34:6; **Josh** 1:5; 5:1; 12; 14; 8:20; 31; 10:14; 21; 11:20; 13:14; 33; 14:3; 4; 17:3; 18:7; 22:25; 27; 33; 23:9; 13; 24:21; **Judg** 2:2; 14; 21; 4:9; 20; 5:19; 6:4; 8:28; 10:13; 16; 11:2; 39; 12:5; 13:2; 3; 5; 7; 21; 14:3; 15:13; 16:17; 17:6; 18:1; 7(2); 10; 28(2); 19:1; 15; 18; 19; 23; 28; 30; 21:8; 25; **Ruth** 1:13; 4:4; **1 Sam** 1:2; 11; 15; 18; 2:2; 3(2); 9; 16; 24; 3:1; 8:19; 9:7; 10:19; 24; 27; 11:3; 11; 12:12; 13:19; 14:26; 15:35; 17:32; 50; 20:2; 15; 21; 34; 21:1; 4; 6; 9; 22:8; 25:31; 34; 26:12; 21; 27:4; 28:10; 20(2); 29:3; 30:4; 12; **2 Sam** 1:21; 6:23; 7:10; 12:6; 13:12(2); 16; 25; 14:6; 19; 25(2); 15:3; 26; 16:18; 18:18; 20; 22; 20:1; 21:4; 17; 24:24; **1 Ki** 1:43; 2:30; 3:2; 18; 22(2); 23; 26; 27; 4:27; 6:7; 18; 8:16; 23; 35; 46; 60; 9:22; 10:5; 12:16; 13:22(2); 17:7; 17; 18:10; 23(2); 25; 26(2); 29(3); 19:4; 21:4; 5; 25; 22:17(2); 31; 47; **2 Ki** 1:3; 6; 16; 17; 2:12; 21; 3:9; 11; 13; 4:14; 16; 5:15; 17; 6:23; 7:5; 10; 9:15; 35; 10:19; 23; 25; 31; 14:26; 17:4; 19:3; 20:10; 21:9; 22:7; 23:10; 18; 25; 25:3; **1 Chr** 2:34; 12:17; 15:2; 16:21; 22; 17:9; 21:24; 22:16; 23:17; 22; 26; 24:2; 28; **2 Chr** 6:5; 14; 26; 36; 7:13; 9:4; 10:16; 14:6; 11; 15:5; 19;

18:16(2); 30; 19:7(2); 20:6; 12; 24; 21:19; 20; 22:9; 23:6; 19; 26:18; 32:15; 35:3; 18; 36:16; 17; **Ezra** 4:16; 9:14; 15; 10:6(2); **Neh** 2:12; 14; 17; 20; 6:1; 8; 13:1; 19; 21; 26; **Esth** 1:19; 4:2; 5:12; 8:8; 9:2; **Job** 2:13; 3:7; 26; 4:18; 20; 5:4; 19; 6:29; 7:8(2); 21; 9:25; 10:7; 18; 11:3; 19; 12:2; 14; 14:4; 12; 15:3; 15; 19; 28; 16:17; 18; 22; 18:17; 19:7; 16; 20:9; 18; 20; 22:6; 23:6; 24:7; 15; 18; 20; 21; 22; 26:2; 3; 6; 27:19; 28:7; 18; 29:12; 30:13; 17; 31:32; 32:3; 5; 15; 16; 19; 33:7; 9; 34:22; 31; 32; 35:10; 36:5; 16; 37:24; 38:11; 26(2); 40:5; 41:10; 16; 42:2; 15; **Ps** 3:2; 5:9; 6:5; 10:18; 14:1; 3; 4; 19:3; 22:6; 23:4; 25:3; 32:2; 9; 33:10; 16; 34:9; 36:1; 37:10(2); 36; 38:3; 7; 14; 39:13; 41:8; 53:1; 3; 4; 5; 58:2; 59:4; 63:1; 69:2; 25; 72:7; 12; 73:4; 74:9; 77:7; 78:64; 79:3; 81:9; 83:4; 84:11; 88:4; 5; 91:10; 92:15; 102:27; 103:16; 104:35; 105:14; 15; 107:4; 40; 119:3; 133; 142:4(2); 143:2; 144:14(2); 146:3; 147:10; **Prov** 1:24; 3:30; 6:4; 7; 35; 8:24(2); 10:22; 25; 11:14; 12:7; 21; 28; 14:4; 17:16; 20; 21; 18:2; 21:10; 30; 22:24; 24:20; 25:28; 26:20(2); 28:1; 3; 17; 24; 29:9; 18; 30:20; 27; 31:7; 11; **Eccl** 1:11; 2:11; 16; 23; 3:11; 19; 4:1(2); 8; 10; 13; 16; 5:4; 6:3; 8:8(3); 16; 9:5; 8; 10; 15; 10:11; 14; 12:1; 12; **Song** 4:7; 5:6; 7:2; 8:8; **Isa** 1:6; 13; 30; 31; 2:7(2); 5:6; 8; 13; 27(2); 29; 8:20; 9:7; 17; 19; 10:14; 13:14; 18; 14:6; 8; 31; 16:10(2); 17:2; 14; 19:7; 22:14; 22(2); 23:1(2); 10; 12(2); 25:2; 26:21; 27:11(2); 28:8; 29:16; 30:7; 16; 19; 32:5; 33:8; 21; 34:10; 35:9; 37:3; 38:11; 40:29; 41:26(3); 28(2); 42:22(2); 43:10; 11; 12; 13; 24; 44:6; 8; 12; 19; 45:5(2); 6; 9; 14(2); 18; 20; 21; 22; 46:9; 47:1; 5; 6; 8; 10(2); 15; 48:22; 50:2(3); 10; 51:18; 22; 52:1; 11; 53:2(2); 9; 54:9; 17; 55:1; 57:1(2); 10; 21; 58:3; 59:4; 8; 10; 15; 16(2); 60:15; 18; 19; 20; 62:4; 7; 8; 63:3; 5(2); 64:7; 65:19; 20; 66:4; **Jer** 2:6(2); 13; 25(2); 30; 31; 3:3; 16; 17; 4:4; 22(2); 23; 25; 6:10; 14; 15; 23; 7:32(2); 33; 8:6; 11; 12; 13; 15; 22(3); 9:10; 12; 21(2); 22; 10:14; 20(2); 11:19; 23; 12:11; 12; 13:19; 14:3; 4; 5; 6; 16; 19(2); 16:12; 14; 17:21; 24(2); 18:23; 19:6; 11; 21:12; 22:3(2); 10; 12; 28; 23:4; 7; 14; 17; 36; 25:27; 35; 30:8; 10; 13(2); 17; 31:12; 15; 29; 34(2); 33:24; 34:9; 10; 35:6(2); 8; 36:19; 30; 38:6; 9; 24; 39:12; 40:15; 41:4; 42:14(2); 18; 44:2; 5; 17; 22; 26; 45:3; 46:25; 27; 48:2; 8; 33; 38; 49:1(2); 5; 7; 10; 18; 33; 36; 50:3; 14; 32; 39; 40; 51:17; 43(2); 52:6; **Lam** 1:3; 4; 6; 7; 9; 17; 21; 2:9(2); 18(2); 22; 4:4; 6; 14; 15; 16; 22; 5:5; 7; **Ezek** 3:18; 7:13; 14; 12:23; 24; 25; 13:10; 15; 16; 21; 23; 14:11; 15; 15:5; 16:5; 34(2); 41; 42; 17:9; 18:3; 7; 32; 19:9; 14; 20:39; 21:13; 27; 22:30; 24:6; 17; 27; 26:13; 21; 27:36; 28:3; 19; 24; 29:16; 30:13; 14; 15; 16; 31:8; 14(2); 32:13; 33:11; 22; 28; 34:5; 6; 8; 10(2); 22; 28(2); 29; 36:12; 14; 29; 37:8; 22; 39:26; 43:7; 44:2; 6; 9; 17; 21; 28; 45:8; **Dan** 1:4; 2:10; 11; 35; 3:16; 27; 29; 4:9; 35; 6:2; 4; 15; 18; 22; 23; 8:4; 7(2); 27; 10:3(2); 8(2); 16; 17; 21; 11:15; 16; 45; **Hos** 1:6; 2:10; 16; 17; 4:1; 4; 5:14; 8:7; 8; 9:11(3); 15; 16; 10:3; 12:8; 13:4(2); **Joel** 1:18; 2:19; 27; 3:17; **Am** 3:4; 5; 5:2(2); 6; 20; 7:14; 9:15; **Ob** 7; 18; **Mic** 2:5; 3:7; 11; 4:4; 9; 5:7; 12; 13; 7:1; 2; **Nah** 1:12; 14; 15; 2:8; 9; 11; 13; 3:8; 18; 19; **Hab** 1:14; 2:19; 3:17(2); **Zeph** 2:5; 3:5(2); 6(2); 11; 13(3); 15; **Hag** 1:6; 2:12; **Zech** 1:21; 4:5; 13; 7:14; 8:10(2); 9:8; 10:2; 10; 11:5; 6; 13:2; 5; 14:6; 11; 17; 18; 21; **Mal** 1:10; **Mt** 2:18; 5:18; 20; 26; 37(2); 6:1; 24; 8:4; 28; 9:12; 16; 30; 36; 10:42; 11:27; 12:39; 13:5; 6; 21; 29; 15:6; 16:4; 7; 8; 20; 17:8; 9; 18:3; 19:6; 17; 20:7; 13; 21:19; 22:23; 24; 25; 46; 23:39; 24:4; 21; 22; 34; 35; 36; 25:3; 9; 42(2); **Mk** 1:45; 2:2; 17; 21; 22; 3:27; 4:5; 6; 7; 17; 40; 5:3; 26; 37; 43; 6:5; 8(3); 7:12; 13; 24; 36; 8:12; 16; 17; 30; 9:3; 8; 9; 25; 39; 41; 10:8; 15; 18; 29; 11:2; 14; 12:14; 18; 19; 20; 22; 31; 32; 34; 13:5; 20; 30; 31; 32; 14:25; 16:18; **Lk** 1:7; 33; 60; 61; 2:7; 3:13; 4:24; 5:14; 31; 36; 37; 39; 7:44; 45; 8:13; 14; 16; 27; 51; 56; 9:13; 21; 36; 62; 10:4; 22; 11:29; 33; 36; 12:4; 17; 33; 13:3; 5; 11; 15:7; 16; 19; 21; 16:2; 13; 30; 17:1; 18:17; 19; 29; 19:30; 20:31; 21:32; 33; 22:16; 36; 67; 68; 23:4; 14; 15; 22; 53; **Jn** 1:18; 21; 47; 2:3; 25; 3:2; 13; 32; 4:9; 17(2); 27; 44; 48; 5:7; 14; 22; 6:22; 37; 44; 53; 65; 66; 7:4; 12; 13; 18; 27; 30; 44; 46; 52; 8:10(2); 11(2); 15; 20; 37; 44; 9:4; 41; 10:5; 18; 29; 41; 11:54; 13:8; 28; 14:6; 19; 30; 15:13; 15; 22(2); 24(2); 16:10; 21; 22; 25; 29; 30; 17:11; 18:38; 19:4; 6; 9; 11; 15; 41; 21:5; **Acts** 1:20; 4:12; 17(2); 21; 5:23; 7:5(2); 11; 8:39; 9:7; 8; 10:34; 11:19; 12:18; 13:28; 34; 37; 41; 15:2; 9; 24; 28; 16:28; 37; 18:10; 17; 19:24; 40; 20:25; 33; 38; 21:25; 39; 23:8(2); 9; 22; 24:11; 25:10; 11; 18; 26:22; 27:20; 22; 28:4; 5; 6; 18; 31; **Rom** 2:11; 3:10; 12; 18; 20; 22; 27; 4:14; 15(2); 5:13; 6:6; 9(2); 7:3; 17; 20; 8:1; 9:6; 10:12; 11:6(4); 12:17; 13:1; 8; 10; 14; 14:7; 15; 15:23; **1 Cor** 1:7; 10; 17; 29; 2:11; 15; 3:11; 18; 21; 6:8; 7:25; 37; 8:4; 9:4; 5; 6; 10; 10:13; 24; 25; 27; 32; 11:16; 12:3(2); 21(2); 22; 24; 25; 13:5; 14:2; 28; 15:12; 13; 16:2; 11; **2 Cor** 1:17(2); 18; 19; 23; 2:13; 3:10; 5:15; 16(2); 21; 6:3; 7:2(3); 5; 8:15; 11:9; 10; 14; 15; 16; 13:7; **Gal** 2:6(2); 16; 20; 3:11; 15; 17; 18; 25; 4:7; 17; 5:10; 23; 6:17; **Eph** 2:12; 19; 4:14; 17; 28; 29; 5:5; 6; 11; 29; 6:9; **Phil** 2:7; 20; 3:3; 4:15; **Col** 2:16; 18; 23; 3:25; **1 Th** 3:1; 3; 5; 4:6; 9; 13; 15; 5:1; 15; **2 Th** 2:3; **1 Tim** 1:3; 4:12; 5:14; 23; 6:16; **2 Tim** 2:4; 14; 3:9; 4:16; **Titus** 2:15; 3:2; **Phm** 1:16; **Heb** 4:13; 5:4; 6:13; 7:13; 8:7; 12; 9:17; 22; 10:2; 6; 17; 18; 26; 38; 12:11; 14; 17; 13:10; 14; **Jas** 1:6; 11; 13; 17; 2:13; 3:8; 12; 5:12(2); **1 Pe** 2:6; 22; 4:2; **2 Pe** 1:20; **1 Jn** 1:5; 8; 2:7; 10; 21; 3:5; 7; 15; 4:12; 18; **3 Jn** 4; **Rev** 2:17; 24; 3:7(2); 8; 11; 12; 5:3; 4; 7:9; 10:6; 11:6; 13:17; 14:3; 5; 11; 15:8; 17:12; 18:7; 11; 14; 22; 19:12; 20:3; 6; 11; 21:1; 4(2); 22; 23; 25; 27; 22:3; 5(2)

NOT (6474/5488)

Gen 2:5; 17; 18; 20; 25; 3:1; 3; 4; 11; 17; 4:5; 7(2); 9; 5:24; 6:3; 8:12; 22; 9:4; 23; 11:7; 12:18; 13:6(2); 9; 14:23; 15:1; 4; 10; 13; 16; 16:10; 17:12; 14; 15; 18:3; 15; 21; 24; 25; 28; 29; 30(2); 31; 32(2); 19:7; 8; 17; 20; 21; 33; 35; 20:4; 5; 6; 7; 9; 11; 12; 21:10; 12; 16; 17; 23; 26(2); 22:12(2); 16; 24:3; 5; 6; 8(2); 21; 27; 33; 37; 39; 41; 49; 56; 26:2; 22; 24; 29; 27:1; 2; 12; 21; 23; 36(2); 28:1; 6; 8; 15; 16; 29:7; 25; 26; 30:31; 33; 40; 42; 31:2; 5; 7; 15; 20; 27; 28; 32(2); 33; 34; 35(2); 38(2); 39; 52(2); 32:10; 25; 26; 32; 34:7; 17; 19; 23; 35:5; 10; 17; 36:7; 37:4; 13; 21; 22; 27; 29; 32; 38:9; 14; 16; 20; 23; 26; 39:6; 8; 10; 23; 40:8; 23; 41:16; 31; 36; 42:2; 4; 8; 11; 15; 20; 21; 22(3); 23; 31; 34; 37; 38; 43:3; 5(3); 8; 9; 10; 22; 23; 32; 44:4; 5; 15; 18; 26; 28; 30; 31; 32; 34; 45:1; 3; 5; 8; 9; 20; 24; 26; 46:3; 47:9; 18; 19(2); 22(2); 26; 29; 48:10; 11; 18; 49:4; 6(2); 10; 50:19; 21; **Ex** 1:8; 17; 19; 3:2; 3; 5; 19(2); 21; 4:1(2); 8; 9; 10; 11; 14; 21; 5:2; 8; 9; 10; 14; 19; 6:3; 9; 12; 7:4; 13; 16; 21; 22; 24; 8:15; 18; 19; 21; 26(2); 28; 29(2); 31; 9:6; 7(2); 11; 12; 17; 18; 19; 21; 30; 32; 33; 10:7; 11; 19; 20; 23; 26(2); 27; 11:6; 9; 10; 12:9; 13; 23; 30(2); 39(2); 45; 46; 13:13; 17; 22; 14:12; 13; 20; 28; 15:23; 16:4; 8; 15; 20; 24; 25; 17:7; 18:17; 18; 19:12; 13(2); 15; 24; 20:4; 5; 7(2); 13; 14; 15; 16; 17(2); 19; 20(2); 23(2); 25; 26; 21:5; 7; 8; 10; 11; 13; 18; 21; 28; 29; 33; 36; 22:8; 11(2); 13; 14; 15; 16; 18; 22; 25(2); 28; 29; 31; 23:1(2); 2; 3; 6; 7(2); 9; 18; 19; 21(2); 24; 29; 33; 24:2; 11; 25:15; 28:28; 32; 35; 43; 29:33; 34; 30:9; 15(2); 32; 37; 32:1; 18; 22; 23; 25; 32; 33:3; 11; 12; 15(2); 23; 34:10; 20; 25; 26; 29; 39:21; 23; 40:35; 37(2); **Lev** 1:17; 2:12; 13; 4:2; 13; 22; 27; 5:1; 7; 8; 11; 17; 18; 6:12; 17; 23; 7:15; 18; 19; 23; 26; 8:33; 35; 10:1; 6; 7; 9; 17; 18; 11:4(2); 5; 6; 7; 8(2); 10; 11; 12; 13; 26(2); 41; 42; 43; 47; 12:4; 8; 13:4(2); 5; 6; 11; 21; 23; 26; 28; 31; 32(2); 33; 34(2); 36; 53; 55(2); 14:36; 48; 15:11; 16:2; 17:4; 9; 14; 16; 18:3(2); 7(2); 8; 9; 10; 11; 12; 13; 14(2); 15(2); 16; 17; 19; 20; 21; 22; 24; 26; 30(2); 19:4; 7; 9; 10; 11; 12; 13(2); 14; 15; 16; 17(2); 18; 19(2); 20(3); 23; 26; 27; 28; 29; 31; 33; 20:4; 19; 22; 23; 25; 21:4; 5; 6; 7; 10; 14; 18; 21; 23; 22:2; 4; 6; 8; 10; 12; 15; 20(2); 22; 23; 24; 25; 28; 32; 23:22; 29; 25:5; 14; 17; 20; 23; 28; 30(2); 34; 37; 39; 42; 43; 46; 53; 54; 26:1; 6; 11; 13; 14(2); 15; 18; 20; 21; 23; 26; 27; 31; 35; 44; 27:10; 11; 20(2); 22; 27; 33(2); **Num** 1:47; 49; 2:33; 4:15; 18; 19; 20; 5:3; 14; 19; 28; 6:6; 7; 9:6; 13(2); 19; 22; 10:7; 30; 31; 11:11; 14; 15; 17; 19; 23; 26; 12:2; 7; 8(2); 11; 12; 14; 15; 13:20; 31; 14:3; 9(2); 11; 16; 22; 23; 41; 42(2); 43; 15:22; 34; 39; 16:12; 14(2); 15(2); 28; 29; 40(2); 18:3; 4; 17; 22; 32; 19:12(2); 13(2); 20(2); 20:5; 12(2); 17(2); 18; 20; 24; 21:22(2); 23; 34; 22:12(2); 18; 30; 33; 34; 37(3); 23:8(2); 9; 12; 13; 19(3); 21; 24; 26; 24:1; 12; 13; 17(2); 25:11; 26:11; 62; 64; 65; 27:3; 17; 29:7; 30:2; 11; 12; 31:18; 35; 49; 32:5; 9; 11; 18; 19; 23; 30; 33:55; 35:12; 23; 27; 30; 33; 34; 36:7; **Deut** 1:9; 17(2); 21; 26; 29; 32; 35; 37; 42(2); 43; 45; 2:5(3); 9(2); 19(2); 30; 36; 37; 3:2; 4(2); 11; 22; 26; 27; 4:2; 21(2); 22; 26; 31; 5:3; 5; 8; 9; 11(2); 17; 18; 19; 20; 21(2); 32; 6:10; 11(3); 14; 16; 7:3; 7; 10; 14; 18; 21; 25; 8:2; 3(2); 4; 11(2); 16; 20; 9:4; 5; 6; 7; 23; 26; 27; 28; 10:10; 11:2(3); 10; 28(2); 30; 12:4; 8; 9; 13; 16; 17; 19; 23(2); 24; 25; 30(2); 31; 32; 13:2; 3; 6; 8; 11; 13; 16; 14:1; 3; 7(2); 8(2); 10(2); 12; 19; 21(2); 24; 27; 15:2; 6(2); 7; 10; 13; 16; 18; 21; 23; 16:5; 16; 19(2); 21; 22; 17:1; 3; 6; 11; 12; 15(2); 16(2); 20(2); 18:9; 10; 14; 16; 19; 20; 21; 22(3); 19:4; 6(2); 13; 14; 15; 20; 21; 20:1; 3(3); 5; 6; 7; 12; 15; 19(2); 20; 21:1; 3(2); 7; 8; 14(2); 16; 18(2); 20; 23(2); 22:1; 2(2); 3; 4; 5; 6; 8; 9; 10; 11; 14; 17; 20; 24; 28; 29; 30; 23:1; 2; 3; 4; 5; 6; 7(2); 10; 15; 16; 18; 19; 20; 21; 22; 24; 25; 24:4(2); 5; 10; 12; 14; 15; 16; 17; 19; 20; 21; 25:4; 5; 6; 7(2); 8; 9; 12; 13; 14; 18; 19; 26:13; 14; 27:5; 26; 28:12; 13(2); 14; 15; 29; 30(2); 31(2); 33; 40; 41; 44; 45; 47; 49; 50; 51; 55; 56; 58; 61; 62; 29:4; 5(2); 6; 14; 15; 18(2); 19; 20; 23; 26(2); 30:11; 12; 17; 18; 31:2; 6(2); 8(2); 13; 17(2); 21; 32:5RE 21; 32:5; 6(2); 17(3); 21(2); 27(2); 31; 34; 47; 51; 52; 33:6; 9; 11; 34:4; 7; 10; **Josh** 1:5; 7; 8; 9(2); 18; 2:4; 5; 22; 3:4(2); 5:5; 6(2); 7; 6:10; 7:3(2); 12; 19; 8:1; 4; 14; 17(2); 26; 35(2); 9:14; 18; 19; 26; 10:6; 8(2); 13(2); 19(2); 25; 11:6; 19; 13:13; 15:63; 16:10; 17:12; 13; 16; 17; 18:2; 20:5(2); 9; 21:44; 45; 22:3; 17(2); 19; 20(2); 22; 26; 27; 28; 31; 23:7(2); 14(2); 24:10; 12; 13(3); 19; **Judg** 1:19; 21; 27; 28; 32; 34; 2:2; 3; 10; 17(2); 19; 20; 22; 3:1; 2; 22; 25; 28; 29; 4:6; 8(2); 14; 16; 18; 5:8; 23; 30; 6:10(2); 13; 14; 18; 23(2); 39; 7:4(2); 8:1; 2; 19; 20; 23; 34; 9:15; 20; 28(2); 38; 41; 10:6; 11; 11:7; 10; 15; 17(2); 18; 20; 24; 26; 27; 28; 12:1; 2; 3; 6; 13:4(2); 6(2); 9; 14; 16(2); 23; 14:4; 6; 9; 14; 15; 16(3); 18(2); 15:1; 2; 11; 12; 13; 16:7; 8; 9; 15(2); 20; 18:1; 9; 25; 19:10; 12(2); 20; 23(2); 24; 25; 20:13; 16; 34; 21:5(2); 7; 8; 9; 12; 14; 17; 22(2); **Ruth** 1:16; 20; 2:8(2); 9(2); 11; 13; 15; 16; 20; 22; 3:1; 2; 3; 10; 11; 13; 14; 17; 18; 4:4; 10; 14; **1 Sam** 1:7; 8(2); 11; 13; 16; 22(2); 2:12; 15; 16; 24; 25; 27; 28(2); 31; 32; 33; 3:2; 5; 6; 7; 13; 14; 17; 4:9; 15; 20(2); 5:7; 11; 12; 6:3(2); 6; 9(2); 12; 7:8; 13; 8:3; 5; 7(2); 18; 9:2; 4(3); 13; 20(2); 21; 10:1; 16; 21; 11:7; 13; 12:4; 5; 14; 15; 17; 19; 20(2); 21; 22; 13:8; 11; 12; 13; 14(2); 14:1; 3; 9; 17; 27; 30; 34; 36; 37; 39; 45(3); 15:3; 11; 17(2); 19; 26; 29(2); 16:7(2); 10; 11; 17:8; 29; 33; 39(2); 47; 55; 18:2; 17; 25; 26; 19:4(2); 6; 11; 20:2(2); 3; 5; 9; 12; 14(2); 15(2); 26; 27; 29; 30; 31; 37; 38; 39; 21:2; 8; 11(2); 22:5; 8; 15; 17(2); 23; 23:14; 17(2); 19; 24:7; 10; 11(2); 12; 13; 18; 21(2); 25:7; 11; 15; 19; 25(2); 28; 26:1; 8; 9; 14; 15(2); 16(2); 20; 23; 28:6; 13; 15; 18; 23; 29:3; 4(2); 5; 6(2); 7; 8; 9; 30:2; 10; 17; 21; 22(2); 23; 31:4; **2 Sam** 1:10; 14; 20(2); 21; 22(2); 23; 2:19; 21; 26; 28; 3:8; 9; 11; 13; 22; 26; 34; 37; 38; 4:11; 5:6; 8; 23; 6:10; 7:6; 7; 15; 9:3; 7; 10:3; 11:3; 9; 10(3); 11; 13; 20; 21; 25; 12:13; 17; 18; 23; 13:4; 12(2); 13; 14; 16; 20; 25(2); 26; 28(2); 30; 32; 33; 14:2; 10; 11(2); 13; 14(2); 18; 24(2); 28; 29(2); 15:11; 14; 20; 27; 35; 16:17; 19; 17:6; 7; 8; 12; 13; 16; 17; 19; 20; 22(2); 23; 18:3(2); 11; 12; 20; 29; 19:7(2); 13(2); 19; 21; 22; 23; 24; 25; 43; 20:3; 10(2); 21; 21:2; 10; 22:22; 23; 37; 39; 42; 44; 23:5(2); 16; 17(2); 19(2); 23; 24:14; **1 Ki** 1:1; 4; 6; 8; 10; 11(2); 13; 18; 19; 26; 27; 51; 52; 2:4; 6; 8; 9; 16; 17; 20(2); 23; 26; 28; 32; 36; 42; 43; 3:7; 11; 12; 13(2); 21; 5:3; 6:6; 13; 7:31; 47(2); 8:5; 8; 11; 19; 25; 41; 46; 56; 57; 9:5; 6; 12; 20; 21; 10:3; 7(2); 21; 11:2; 4; 6; 10(2); 11; 12; 13; 33; 34; 39; 41; 12:15; 16; 24; 31; 13:4; 8; 9; 10; 17; 21; 22; 28; 33; 14:2; 4; 8; 29; 15:3; 5; 7; 14; 23; 29; 31; 16:5; 11; 14; 20; 27; 17:1; 12; 13; 14; 16; 18:5; 10(3); 12; 13; 18; 21; 40; 19:2; 11(2); 12; 18(2); 20:7; 8; 11; 28; 36; 21:4; 6; 15; 29; 22:7; 8(2); 18(2); 28; 33; 39; 43(2); 45; 49; **2 Ki** 1:4; 6; 15; 16; 18; 2:2; 4; 6; 10(2); 16; 17; 18(2); 3:2; 3; 14(2); 17; 26; 4:3; 6; 16; 24; 27; 28(2); 29(2); 30; 31; 39; 40; 5:12(2); 13; 17; 20; 25; 26; 6:9; 10; 11; 16; 19; 22; 27; 32; 7:2; 9; 10; 19; 8:19; 23; 9:3; 18; 20; 37; 10:4; 5; 19; 21(2); 29; 31; 34; 11:2; 15; 12:3; 6; 7(2); 13; 15; 16; 19; 13:2; 6; 8; 11; 12; 23; 14:3; 4; 6(2); 11; 15; 18; 24; 27; 28; 15:4; 6; 9; 16; 18; 20; 21; 24; 28; 35; 36; 16:2; 5; 19; 17:2; 9; 12; 14(2); 15; 19; 22; 25; 26(2); 34; 35; 37; 38; 40; 18:6; 7; 12; 22; 26; 27; 29(2); 30; 31; 32(2); 36(2); 19:6; 10(2); 18; 25; 32; 33; 20:1; 13; 15; 19; 20; 21:8; 17; 22; 25; 22:2; 13; 17; 20; 23:9; 26; 28; 33; 24:4; 5; 7; 25:24; **1 Chr** 4:10; 27; 5:1; 10:4; 13; 14; 11:5; 18; 19; 21; 25; 12:19; 13:3; 13; 14:14; 15:13(2); 16:22; 30; 17:4; 5; 6; 13; 19:3; 19; 21:3; 6; 13; 17(2); 24; 30; 22:8; 13; 18(2); 23:11; 26:10; 27:23; 24; 28:3; 20(2); 29:1; 25; **2 Chr** 1:11; 4:18; 5:6; 9; 14; 6:9; 16; 32; 36; 42; 7:2; 7; 18; 8:7; 8; 9; 11; 15; 9:2; 6(2); 20; 29; 10:15; 16; 11:4; 12:7(2); 12; 14; 15; 13:5; 7; 9(2); 10; 12(2); 20; 14:11; 13; 15:7; 13; 17; 16:7; 8; 12; 17:3; 4; 10; 18:6; 7; 17(2); 27; 32; 19:6; 10; 20:6(3); 7; 10(2); 12; 15(2); 17(2); 32; 33(2); 37; 21:7; 12; 17; 20; 22:11; 23:8; 14; 24:5; 6; 19; 22; 25; 25:2; 4(2); 7(3); 13; 15; 16; 20; 26; 26:18; 27:2; 28:1; 10; 13; 20; 21; 27; 29:7; 11; 34; 30:3(2); 5; 7; 8; 9; 17(2); 18; 19; 32:7; 11; 12; 13; 15(2); 17(2); 25; 26; 33:8; 10; 23; 34:2; 21; 25; 28; 33; 35:15; 21; 22(2); 36:12; **Ezra** 2:59; 62; 63; 3:6; 13; 4:13; 14; 21; 22; 5:5; 16; 6:8; 7:24; 25; 26; 9:1; 9; 12; 14; 10:8; 13; **Neh** 1:7; 2:2; 3; 16(2); 3:5; 4:5(2); 10; 14; 5:5; 9(2); 13; 15; 16; 18; 6:1; 9; 11; 12; 7:3; 4; 61; 64; 65; 8:9; 10; 11; 17; 9:16; 17(2); 19(2); 20; 21(2); 29(2); 30; 31; 32; 35; 10:30; 31; 39; 13:2; 6; 10; 14; 18(2); 19; 24; 25; 26; **Esth** 1:8; 15; 16; 17; 19; 2:10(2); 14; 20; 3:2; 4; 5; 8(2); 4:4; 11(2); 13; 5:9; 6:1; 13; 9:10; 15; 16; 28(2); 10:2; **Job** 1:10; 12; 22; 2:10(2); 12; 3:4; 6(2); 9; 10; 11(2); 16; 18; 21; 26; 4:6; 16; 21; 5:6; 17; 21; 22; 6:10(2); 13; 7:1(2); 9; 11; 16; 19; 21; 8:10; 12; 15(2); 18; 20; 9:3; 5; 7; 11(2); 13; 15; 16; 18; 21; 24; 28; 32; 34; 35(2); 10:2; 7; 10; 14; 19; 20; 21; 11:2; 11; 14; 15; 20; 12:3(2); 9; 11; 13:2; 11; 16; 20(2); 21; 14:2; 7; 12(2); 16; 21(2); 15:6; 9(2); 15; 18; 22; 29; 30; 31; 32; 16:6; 13; 18; 17:2(2); 4; 10; 18:5; 21; 19:3; 7; 22; 27; 20:4; 8; 13; 17; 18; 19; 20; 21; 21:4; 14; 16; 29(2); 22:5; 7; 12; 30; 23:8; 11; 12; 17(2); 24:1(2); 12; 13; 16; 21; 25; 25:3; 5(2); 26:8; 27:4; 5; 6(2); 11; 14; 15; 19; 22; 28:8; 13; 14(2); 29:16; 22; 24(2); 30:10; 20; 24; 25(2); 28; 31:3; 4; 15(2); 17; 20(2); 30; 31(2); 34; 32:6; 9; 12; 13; 14(2); 16; 21; 22; 33:12; 13; 14; 21; 27; 33; 34:19; 23; 27; 30; 32; 33; 35:12; 13; 14; 15; 36:4; 6; 7; 12; 13; 18; 20; 21; 26; 37:4; 23; 39:4; 7; 16; 17; 22; 40:5; 23; 41:9; 12; 42:3(2); 7; 8; **Ps** 1:1; 3; 4; 5; 3:6; 4:4; 5:4; 5; 6:1; 7:12; 9:10; 12; 18(2); 19; 10:4; 6; 12; 13; 14:3; 4; 15:3; 4; 5; 16:4; 8; 10; 17:1; 3; 5; 18:21; 22; 36; 38; 41; 43; 19:3; 13; 21:2; 7; 11; 22:2(2); 5; 11; 19; 24; 23:1; 24:4; 25:2(2); 7; 20; 26:1; 4; 5; 9; 27:3; 9(3); 12; 28:1; 3; 5(2); 30:1; 3; 12; 31:8; 17; 32:2; 5; 6; 9(2); 33:16; 34:5; 10; 20; 35:11; 15(2); 19; 20; 22(2); 24; 25(2); 36:4(2); 11(2); 12; 37:1; 7; 8; 19; 21; 24; 25; 28; 33; 36; 38:1; 9; 13(2); 14; 21(2); 39:6; 8; 9; 12; 40:4; 6(2); 9; 10(2); 11; 12; 17; 41:2; 11; 44:3; 6; 9; 12; 17; 18; 21; 23; 46:2; 5; 49:9; 12; 16; 17; 20; 50:3; 8; 9; 12; 51:11(2); 16(2); 17; 52:7; 53:3; 4; 54:3; 55:1; 11; 12; 19(2); 23; 56:4; 8; 11; 13; 57:58:5; 8; 59:3; 5; 11; 13; 15; 60:10(2); 62:2; 6; 10(2); 64:4; 66:7; 9; 18; 20; 69:5; 6(2); 14; 15(2); 17; 23; 27; 28; 33; 70:5; 71:9(2); 12; 15; 18; 73:5; 74:9; 19(2); 21; 23; 75:4(2); 5(2); 77:19; 78:4; 7; 8(3); 10; 22(2); 30; 32; 37; 38(2); 39; 42; 44; 50; 53; 56; 63; 67; 79:6(2); 8; 80:18; 81:5; 11; 82:5; 83:1(3); 85:6; 8; 86:14; 89:22; 30; 31; 33; 34; 35; 43; 48; 91:5; 7; 92:6; 94:7; 9(2); 10; 14; 95:8; 10; 11; 96:10; 100:3; 101:3; 4; 5; 7(2); 102:2; 17; 24; 103:2; 9; 10; 104:5; 9(2); 105:15; 28; 106:7(2); 11; 13; 23; 24; 25; 34; 107:38; 108:11(2); 109:1; 14; 16; 17; 110:4; 112:7; 8; 115:1(2); 5(2); 6(2); 7(2); 17; 118:6; 17; 18; 119:6; 8; 10; 11; 16; 19; 31; 36; 43; 46; 51; 60; 61; 80; 83; 85; 87; 102; 109; 110; 116; 121; 122; 136; 141; 153; 155; 157; 158; 176; 121:3(2); 6; 124:1; 2; 6; 125:3; 127:5; 129:2; 7; 131:1; 132:3; 4; 10; 11; 135:16(2); 17; 137:6(2); 138:8; 139:4; 12; 15; 21(2); 140:8(2); 10; 11; 141:4(2); 5; 8; 143:2; 7; 146:3; 147:10; 20(2); 148:6; **Prov** 1:8; 10; 15; 28(2); 29; 3:1; 3; 5; 7; 11; 21; 23; 24; 25; 27; 28; 29; 30; 31; 4:2; 5; 6; 12(2); 13; 14(2); 15; 16; 19; 21; 27; 5:6; 7; 8; 13; 17; 6:20; 25; 27; 28; 29; 30; 33; 34; 7:11; 19; 23; 25(2); 8:1; 10; 26; 29; 33; 9:8; 18; 10:3; 19; 30; 11:4; 21; 12:3; 27; 13:1; 8; 14:5; 6; 7; 10; 22; 15:7; 12; 16:10; 29; 17:5; 7; 13; 26; 18:5; 19:2; 5(2); 9; 10; 18; 23; 24; 20:1; 4; 13; 19; 21; 22; 23; 21:13; 17; 26; 22:6; 20; 22; 24; 26; 28; 29; 23:3; 4; 5; 6; 7; 9; 10; 13(2); 17; 18; 20; 22; 23; 31; 35(2); 24:1; 7; 12(4); 14; 15(2); 17(2); 19; 21; 23; 28; 29; 25:6(2); 8; 9; 27(2); 26:1; 2; 4; 17; 25; 27:1(2); 2(2); 10; 22; 24; 28:5; 13; 20; 21; 22; 27; 29:7; 19(2); 30:2; 6; 7; 10; 11; 12; 16; 18; 25; 30; 31:3; 4(2); 12; 18; 21; 27; **Eccl** 1:7; 8; 2:10(2); 21; 4:3; 12; 16; 5:1; 2(2); 4; 5(2); 6; 8; 10; 12; 20; 6:2; 3; 5; 6(2); 7; 7:9; 10(2); 16; 17; 18; 20(2); 21; 28; 8:3(2); 7; 8; 11; 13(2); 17(2); 9:2; 11; 12; 16; 10:4; 10; 11; 15; 17; 20(2); 11:2; 4(2); 5(2); 6(2); 12:2(2); **Song** 1:6(2); 8; 2:7; 3:1; 2; 4; 5; 5:6; 8:1; 4; **Isa** 1:3(2); 6; 11; 15; 23; 2:4; 9; 3:7; 9; 5:4; 6; 12; 25; 6:9(2); 7:1; 4; 7; 8; 9(2); 12; 17; 25; 8:10; 11; 12; 19; 20; 9:1; 12; 13; 17; 20; 21; 10:4; 7(2); 8; 9(3); 11; 15; 24; 11:3; 9; 13(2); 12:2; 13:10(2); 17(2); 18; 22; 14:17; 20; 29; 16:3; 6; 12; 17:8(2); 10; 22:2; 4; 11; 23:4; 13; 18; 24:9; 20; 26:10(2); 11; 14(2); 18; 27:4; 9; 11; 28:12; 15; 16; 18; 22; 25; 27; 28; 29:9(2); 12; 16; 17; 22; 30:1(2); 2; 5; 6; 9; 10(2); 14(2); 15; 20; 31:1; 2; 3(2); 4; 8(2); 32:3; 10; 33:1(2); 19; 20(2); 23(2); 24; 34:10; 16(2); 35:4; 8(2); 9; 36:7; 11; 12; 14(2); 15; 16; 21(2); 37:6; 10(2); 19; 26; 33; 34; 38:1; 11; 39:2; 4; 40:9; 16; 20(2); 21(4); 26; 28(2); 31(2); 41:3; 7; 9; 10(2); 12; 13; 14; 17; 42:2; 3(2); 4; 8; 16(3); 20(2); 24(2); 25(2); 43:1; 2(2); 5; 6; 17; 18; 19; 22; 23(2); 25; 44:2; 8(3); 9; 18; 20; 21; 45:1; 4; 5; 13; 17; 18; 19(2); 21; 23; 46:2; 7; 10; 13(2); 47:3; 7; 8;

11(3); 14(2); 48:1; 6(2); 7(2); 8(3); 9; 10; 11; 16; 19; 21; 49:15(2); 23; 50:5; 6; 7(2); 51:6; 7; 9; 10; 14(2); 21; 52:12; 15(2); 53:3; 7(2); 54:1(2); 2; 4(4); 9; 10; 11; 14(2); 15; 55:2(2); 5(2); 8; 10; 11; 13; 56:3; 5; 57:4; 10(2); 11(3); 12; 16; 58:1; 2; 3; 4; 6; 7(2); 11; 13; 59:1; 2; 6; 8(2); 21; 60:11; 12; 62:1(2); 6; 8; 12; 63:8; 13; 16; 64:3; 4; 9; 65:1(3); 2; 5; 6; 8(2); 12(3); 17; 20; 22(2); 23; 25; 66:4(2); 9; 19; 24(2); **Jer** 1:7; 8; 17; 19; 2:2; 8(3); 11(2); 17; 19; 20; 23(2); 24; 27; 34; 35; 37; 3:1; 2; 4; 7; 8; 10; 12(2); 13; 16; 19; 25; 4:1; 3; 6; 8; 11; 22; 27; 28; 29; 5:3(2); 4; 7; 9(2); 10(2); 12; 13; 15; 18; 19; 21(2); 22(2); 24; 28(2); 29(2); 6:8; 15; 16; 17; 19; 20; 25; 29; 7:4; 6(2); 9; 13(2); 16(2); 17; 19; 20; 22; 24(2); 26; 27(2); 28; 31; 8:2; 4(2); 6; 7; 12; 19(2); 20; 9:3(2); 4; 5; 9(2); 13; 23(2); 10:2(2); 4; 5; 7; 10; 11; 16; 21(2); 23(2); 24; 25(2); 11:3; 8(2); 11(2); 12; 14(2); 19; 21; 12:4; 6; 13; 17; 13:1; 11; 12; 14; 15; 17; 21; 27; 14:9; 10(2); 11; 12(2); 13; 14; 15(2); 17; 18; 21(3); 22; 15:1; 7; 14; 15; 17; 19; 20; 16:2; 4; 5; 6; 8; 11; 13(2); 17; 20; 17:4; 6(2); 8(2); 11(2); 16; 17; 18(2); 23(2); 27(3); 18:6; 10; 15; 17; 18(2); 19:5; 15; 20:3; 9(2); 11(2); 14; 16; 17; 21:7; 10; 22:5; 6; 10; 11; 15; 16; 18(2); 21(2); 26; 27; 28; 30; 23:2; 10; 16(2); 20; 21(2); 23; 24(2); 29; 32(2); 38; 40; 24:2; 6(2); 25:3; 4; 6(3); 7; 8; 29; 33; 26:2; 4; 5; 16; 19; 24; 27:8(2); 9(2); 13; 14(2); 15; 16; 17; 18; 20; 28:15; 29:6; 8; 9; 11; 16; 19; 23; 27; 31; 32; 30:5; 10; 11(2); 14; 19(2); 24; 31:9; 32; 40; 32:4; 5; 23; 33(2); 35; 40(2); 33:3; 20; 21; 24; 25(2); 26; 34:3; 4; 14; 17; 18; 35:7; 13; 14(2); 15(2); 16; 17(2); 19; 36:24; 25(2); 31; 37:4; 9(2); 14(2); 19; 20; 38:4; 15(2); 16; 17; 18(2); 20; 23; 24; 25(2); 26; 27; 39:16; 17; 18; 40:3; 5; 7; 9; 14; 16; 41:8(2); 42:5; 10(2); 11(2); 13; 19; 21; 43:2(2); 4; 7; 44:3; 4; 5; 10(2); 16; 21(2); 23; 27; 45:5; 46:5; 6; 11; 15; 21; 27(2); 28(3); 47:3; 48:11(2); 27; 30; 33; 49:9(2); 10; 12(2); 25; 36; 50:2; 5; 7; 13; 20; 24; 42; 51:3; 5; 6; 9; 19; 26; 39; 44; 50; 57; 64; **Lam** 1:9; 10; 14; 2:1; 2; 8; 14; 17; 21; 3:2; 22(2); 31; 33; 36; 37; 38; 42; 43; 44; 49; 56; 57; 4:12; 15; 16; 17; 18; 5:12; **Ezek** 1:9; 12; 17; 2:6(2); 8; 3:5; 6; 7(2); 9; 19; 20(2); 21(2); 26; 5:6; 7; 11; 6:10; 7:4; 7; 9; 12; 13(2); 19(2); 8:12; 18(2); 9:5; 6; 9; 10:11(2); 16; 11:3; 11; 12; 12:2(2); 9; 13; 13:5; 6; 7(3); 9; 12; 19(2); 22(2); 16:4(2); 16; 22; 28; 29; 31; 43(2); 47; 51; 56; 61; 17:9; 10; 12; 14; 18; 18:6; 7; 8; 12; 13; 14; 15; 16; 17(2); 18; 19; 20; 21; 23; 24; 25(3); 28; 29(3); 30; 20:3; 7; 8(2); 9; 13; 14; 15; 16; 17; 18; 21(2); 22; 24; 25(2); 31; 38; 39; 44; 47; 48; 49; 21:5; 32; 22:24; 26; 28; 30; 23:27; 48; 24:6; 7; 8; 12; 13(2); 14; 17(2); 19; 22; 25; 25:10; 26:15; 19; 28:2; 9; 29:5; 15; 30:21; 31:8(3); 32:7; 9; 27; 33:4; 5; 6(2); 8; 9; 12(2); 15; 17(2); 20; 31; 32; 34:2; 3; 4; 8; 35:6; 36:22; 31; 32; 37:18; 23; 38:14; 39:7; 10; 29; 41:6; 42:6; 14; 44:2; 8; 13; 18; 19; 22; 25; 31; 46:2; 9; 18; 20; 47:5(2); 11; 12(2); 48:11; 14(2); **Dan** 1:8(2); 2:5; 9; 10; 11; 18; 24; 30; 43(2); 44; 3:6; 11; 12(2); 14; 15; 18(2); 24; 25; 27(2); 28; 4:7; 18; 19; 30; 5:8; 10; 15; 22; 23(2); 6:5; 8; 12(2); 13; 17; 22; 26; 7:14(2); 8:22; 24; 9:10; 11; 13; 14; 18; 19; 26; 10:7; 12; 19; 11:4; 6; 12; 15; 17; 19; 20; 21; 24; 25; 27; 29; 38; 42; 12:8; **Hos** 1:7; 9(2); 10; 2:2; 4; 7(2); 8; 23(2); 3:3; 4:10(2); 14(2); 15(2); 5:3; 4(2); 6; 6:6; 7:2; 9(2); 10; 14; 16; 8:4(2); 6; 13; 9:1; 2; 3; 4(2); 17; 10:3; 9; 11:3; 5; 9(4); 13:13; 14:3(2); **Joel** 1:16; 2:7; 8(2); 13; 17; 21; 22; 3:21; **Am** 1:3; 6; 9(2); 11; 13; 2:1; 4(2); 6; 11; 12; 14; 15(2); 3:6(2); 8; 10; 4:6; 7; 8(2); 9; 10; 11; 5:5; 11(2); 14; 18; 20(3); 21; 22; 23; 6:6; 10; 13; 7:3; 6; 8; 10; 16(2); 8:2; 8; 11; 12; 9:1(2); 4; 7(2); 8; 9; 10; **Ob** 5(2); 8; 12; 13(2); 14; **Jon** 1:6; 13; 14(2); 3:7; 9; 10; 4:2; 10; 11; **Mic** 1:5(2); 10(2); 11; 2:6(3); 7; 10; 3:1; 4; 11; 4:3; 12; 5:15; 6:14(2); 15(3); 7:5(2); 8; 18; **Nah** 1:3; 9; 3:17; 19; **Hab** 1:2(2); 5; 6; 12(2); 2:3(2); 4; 5; 6(2); 7(2); 13; 3:17; **Zeph** 1:6; 12; 13(2); 3:2(4); 3; 7; 11; 16(2); **Hag** 1:2; 6(2); 2:3; 5; 17; 19; **Zech** 1:4(2); 6; 12; 3:2; 4:5; 6; 13; 7:6; 7; 10; 11; 13(2); 14; 8:11; 13; 14; 15; 17; 9:5; 10:6; 11:5; 6; 9; 12; 16; 12:7; 13:3; 4; 14:2; 17; 18(2); 19; **Mal** 1:2; 8(2); 10; 2:2(3); 6; 9; 10(2); 13; 15; 16; 3:5; 6(2); 7; 10(2); 11; 18; **Mt** 1:19; 20; 25; 2:6; 12; 3:9; 10; 11; 4:4; 7; 5:17(2); 21; 27; 33; 34; 39; 42; 46; 47; 6:1; 2; 3; 5; 7; 8; 13; 15; 16; 18; 19; 20; 25(2); 26; 29; 30; 31; 34; 7:1(2); 3; 6; 19; 21; 22; 25; 26; 29; 8:8; 10(2); 9:13(2); 14; 24; 10:5(2); 13; 14; 19; 20; 23; 24; 26(3); 28; 29(2); 31; 34(2); 37(2); 38(2); 11:6; 11; 17(2); 20; 12:2; 3; 4; 5; 7(2); 11; 16; 19; 20(2); 24; 25; 30(2); 31; 32; 13:5; 11; 12; 13(2); 14(2); 17(2); 19; 27; 34; 55(2); 56; 57; 58; 14:4; 16; 27; 15:2; 6; 11; 13; 17; 20; 23; 24; 26; 32; 16:9; 11(2); 12; 17; 18; 22; 23; 28; 17:7; 12; 16; 19; 21; 24; 18:10; 12; 13; 14; 16; 22; 25; 30; 33; 35; 19:4; 6; 8; 10; 14; 18(4); 20:13; 15; 22; 23; 26; 28; 21:21(2); 25; 27; 29; 30; 32(2); 22:3; 8; 11; 16; 17; 29; 31; 32; 23:3(2); 4; 8; 9; 10; 30; 37; 24:2(3); 6(2); 17; 18; 20; 21; 23; 26(2); 29; 36; 39; 42; 43; 44; 50(2); 25:9; 12; 24(2); 26(2); 29; 43(3); 44; 45(2); 26:5; 11; 24; 29; 35; 39; 40; 55; 70; 72; 74; 27:6; 13; 14; 24; 34; 28:5; 6; 10; **Mk** 1:7; 22; 34; 2:2; 4; 17; 18; 24; 26; 27; 3:12; 20; 4:5; 12(2); 13; 21; 22; 25; 27; 34; 38; 5:3; 7; 10; 19; 36; 39; 6:3(2); 4; 9; 11; 18; 19; 26; 31; 34; 50; 52; 7:3; 4; 5; 18; 19; 24; 27; 8:14; 17; 18(3); 21; 33; 9:1; 6; 18; 28; 30; 32; 37; 38(2); 39; 40; 44(2); 46(2); 48(2); 10:9; 14; 15; 19(5); 27; 30; 38; 40; 43; 45; 11:13; 16; 17; 23; 26; 31; 33; 12:10; 14(2); 15; 24(2); 26; 27; 34; 13:2(2); 7(2); 11(2); 14; 15; 16; 18; 19; 21; 24; 32; 33; 35; 14:2; 7; 29; 31; 36; 37; 40; 49; 56; 59; 71; 15:23; 16:6(2); 11; 13; 14; 16; **Lk** 1:13; 20(2); 22; 30; 34; 2:10; 26; 37; 43; 45; 49; 50; 3:8; 9; 14; 15; 16; 4:4; 12; 22; 35; 41; 5:10; 19; 32; 36; 6:2; 3; 4; 29; 30; 37(4); 39; 40; 41; 42; 43; 44; 46; 48; 7:6(3); 7; 9(2); 13; 23; 28; 30; 32(2); 45; 46; 8:10(2); 17(2); 18; 19; 28; 31; 43; 47; 49; 50; 52(2); 9:3; 5; 27; 33; 40; 45(2); 49; 50(2); 53; 55; 56; 10:6; 7; 10; 20; 24(2); 40; 42; 11:4; 7; 8; 23(2); 35; 38; 40; 44(2); 46; 52; 12:2(2); 4; 6(2); 7; 10; 11; 15; 21; 22; 26; 27; 29; 32; 33(2); 39; 40; 46(2); 47; 48; 51; 56; 57; 59; 13:9; 14; 15; 16; 24; 25; 27; 34; 35; 14:5; 6; 8; 12; 26; 27; 28; 29; 30; 31; 33; 15:4; 8; 13; 28; 16:11; 12; 31; 17:8; 9; 17; 18; 20; 22; 23; 31(2); 18:1; 2; 4(2); 7; 11; 13; 16; 17; 20(4); 30; 34; 19:3; 14; 21(2); 22(2); 23; 26; 27; 44(2); 20:5; 7; 16; 21; 22; 26; 38; 40; 21:6(2); 8(2); 9(2); 14; 15; 18; 21; 22:18; 26; 27; 32; 34; 40; 42; 53; 57; 58; 60; 23:28; 34; 40; 51; 24:3; 6; 11; 16; 18; 23; 24; 26; 32; 39; 41; **Jn** 1:5; 8; 10; 11; 13; 20(2); 21; 25; 26; 27; 31; 33; 2:4; 9; 12; 16; 24; 3:7; 10; 11; 12; 15; 16; 17; 18(3); 20; 24; 28; 34; 36(2); 4:2; 15; 18; 22; 32; 35; 38; 42; 5:10; 13; 18; 23(2); 24; 28; 30; 31; 34; 38(2); 40; 41; 42; 43; 44; 45; 47; 6:7; 17; 20; 22; 24; 26; 27; 32; 36; 38; 42; 43; 46; 50; 58; 64(2); 70; 7:1; 5; 6; 8(2); 10; 16; 19; 22; 23; 24; 25; 28(2); 30; 34; 35; 36; 39(2); 42; 45; 49; 8:6; 12; 13; 14; 16; 20; 23; 24; 27; 29; 35; 40; 41; 43(2); 44; 45; 46; 47(2); 48; 49; 50; 55(2); 57; 9:8; 12; 16(2); 18; 21(2); 25(2); 27; 29; 30; 31; 33; 39; 10:1; 5; 6; 8; 10; 12(2); 13; 16; 21; 25; 26(2); 33; 34; 37(2); 38; 11:4; 9(2); 10; 15; 21; 30; 32; 37; 40; 50; 51; 52; 56; 12:5; 6; 8; 9; 15; 16; 30; 35; 37; 39; 42; 44; 46; 47(3); 48; 49; 13:7; 8; 9; 10; 11; 16; 18; 37; 38; 14:1; 2; 5; 9; 10(2); 18; 22(2); 24(3); 27(2); 15:2; 6; 15; 16; 19; 20; 21; 22; 24; 16:1; 3; 4; 7(2); 9; 13; 16; 17; 18; 19; 26; 32; 17:9; 14(2); 15; 16(2); 20; 25; 18:11; 17(2); 25(2); 26; 28; 30(2); 31; 36(3); 40; 19:10(2); 12; 21; 24; 31; 33; 36; 20:2; 5; 7; 9; 13; 14; 17(2); 24; 25; 27; 29; 30; 21:4; 6; 8; 11; 18; 23(3); 25; **Acts** 1:4; 5; 7; 2:7; 15; 24; 25; 27; 31; 34; 3:6; 23; 4:18; 5:4(3); 7; 22; 28(2); 40; 42; 6:2; 10; 13; 7:5; 18; 19; 25; 32; 39; 40; 48; 50; 52; 53; 60; 8:21; 32; 9:21; 26; 38; 10:14; 15; 28; 41; 47; 11:8; 9; 12:9; 14; 19; 22; 23; 13:10; 11; 25(2); 27; 35; 39; 14:17; 15:19; 38(2); 16:7; 21; 17:4; 5; 6; 12; 24; 27; 29; 18:9(2); 15; 20; 19:2; 9; 26(2); 27; 30; 31; 32; 35; 20:10; 12; 16; 22; 27; 29; 31; 21:4; 12; 13; 14; 21; 34; 38; 22:9; 11; 18; 22; 23:5(2); 9; 21; 24:4; 23; 25:7; 11; 16; 24; 27; 26:19; 25; 26; 29; 32; 27:7; 10; 12; 14; 15; 21; 24; 34; 39; 28:4; 19; 25; 26(2); **Rom** 1:13; 16; 21; 28(2); 32; 2:4; 8; 13; 14(2); 21(2); 22; 26; 27; 28; 29(2); 3:3; 4; 6; 8; 9; 10; 12; 17; 29; 31; 4:2; 4; 5; 8; 10; 12; 13; 16; 17; 19(2); 20; 23; 5:3; 5; 11; 13; 14; 15; 16; 6:2; 3; 12; 13; 14(2); 15(2); 16; 7:1; 6; 7(4); 13; 15(2); 16; 18; 19(2); 20; 8:1; 3; 4; 7; 9(3); 12; 15; 18; 20; 23; 24; 25; 26; 32(2); 9:1; 6(2); 8; 10; 11(2); 14; 16; 21; 24; 25(2); 26; 30; 31; 32; 33; 10:2; 3; 6; 11; 14(2); 16; 18; 19(2); 20(2); 11:1; 2(2); 4; 7; 8(2); 10; 11; 18(2); 20; 21(2); 23; 25; 12:2; 3; 4; 11; 14; 16(2); 19; 21; 13:3; 4; 5; 9(5); 13(3); 14:1; 3(4); 6(4); 13(2); 15; 16; 17; 20; 22; 23(2); 15:1; 3; 18(2); 20; 21(2); 31; 16:4; 18; **1 Cor** 1:16; 17(2); 20; 21; 26(3); 28; 2:1; 2; 4; 5; 6; 8; 9; 12; 13; 14; 3:1; 2(3); 3; 4; 16; 4:3; 4; 6; 7(2); 14; 15; 18; 19; 20; 5:1; 2; 6(2); 8; 9; 10; 11(2); 12; 6:1; 2; 3; 5(2); 7(2); 9(3); 12(2); 13; 15(2); 16; 19(2); 7:1; 4(2); 5(2); 6; 10(2); 11; 12(3); 13(2); 15; 18(2); 21; 23; 27(2); 28(2); 30(3); 31; 35; 36; 38; 8:7; 8(2); 10; 9:1(4); 2; 7(2); 8; 9; 12(3); 13; 16; 18; 21; 24; 26(2); 10:1; 5; 6; 7; 13; 16(2); 18; 20(2); 23(2); 27; 28; 29; 33; 11:6; 7; 8; 14; 17(2); 20; 22(2); 29; 31; 32; 12:1; 14; 15(3); 16(3); 13:1; 2; 3; 4(3); 5(3); 6; 14:2; 11; 16; 17; 20; 21; 22(2); 23; 33; 34; 39; 15:9; 10(2); 13; 14; 15(2); 16(2); 17; 29; 32; 33; 34(2); 36; 37; 39; 46; 51; 58; 16:7; 22; **2 Cor** 1:8; 9; 12; 13; 18; 19; 24; 2:1; 4; 5(2); 11; 13; 17; 3:3(2); 5; 6; 7; 8; 13; 4:1; 2; 4; 5; 7; 8(2); 9(2); 16; 18(3); 5:1; 3; 4; 7; 12(2); 19; 6:1; 3; 9; 12; 14; 17; 7:3; 7; 8; 9; 10; 12; 14; 8:5; 8; 10; 12(2); 13; 17; 19; 21; 9:4; 5; 7; 12; 10:2; 3; 4; 8(2); 12(2); 13; 14(2); 15; 16; 18; 11:4(3); 5; 6; 11; 17; 29(2); 31; 12:1; 2(2); 3; 4; 5; 6; 13; 14(3); 16; 18(2); 20(2); 21; 13:2; 3; 5; 6; 7; 10; **Gal** 1:1; 7; 10; 11; 16; 20; 2:3; 5; 14(2); 15; 16(2); 17; 21; 3:1; 10; 12; 16; 20; 21; 4:1; 8(2); 12; 14; 18; 21; 27(2); 30; 31; 5:1; 8; 13; 16; 17; 18; 21; 26; 6:4; 7(2); 9(2); 12; 13; **Eph** 1:16; 21; 2:8; 9; 3:5; 13; 4:20; 26(2); 30; 5:3; 4; 7; 15; 17; 18; 27; 6:4; 6; 7; 12; **Phil** 1:16; 28; 29; 2:4; 6; 12; 16; 21; 27; 30; 3:1; 9; 12; 13; 4:11; 17; **Col** 1:9; 23; 2:1; 8; 18; 19; 21(3); 3:2; 9; 19; 21; 22; 23; **1 Th** 1:5; 8(2); 2:1; 3; 4; 8; 9; 13; 15; 17; 19; 4:5(2); 7; 8; 13; 5:3; 4; 5; 6; 9; 19; 20; **2 Th** 1:8(2); 2:2; 3; 5; 10; 12; 3:2; 6; 7; 8; 9(2); 10; 11; 13; 14(2); 15; **1 Tim** 1:9; 20; 2:7; 9; 12; 14; 3:3(5); 5; 6; 8(3); 11; 4:14; 5:1; 8; 9(2); 13(2); 16; 18; 19; 22; 6:1; 2; 3; 17; **2 Tim** 1:7; 8; 9; 12; 16; 2:5; 9; 14; 15; 20; 24; 4:3; 8; 16; **Titus** 1:6; 7(5); 11; 14; 2:3(2); 5; 9; 10; 3:5; 14; **Phm** 1:14; 19; **Heb** 1:12; 14; 2:5; 8(2); 11; 16; 3:8; 10; 11; 15; 16; 17; 18(2); 19; 4:2(2); 3; 5; 6; 7; 8; 15; 5:5; 12; 6:1; 10; 12; 7:6; 11; 16; 20; 21; 27; 8:2; 4; 9(2); 9:7; 8; 11(2); 12; 18; 24; 25; 10:1; 2; 4; 5; 8; 25; 35; 37; 39; 11:1; 3; 5(2); 7; 8; 13; 16; 23; 27; 31(2); 35; 38; 39; 40; 12:4; 5; 7; 8; 9; 13; 18; 19; 20; 25(3); 26; 13:2; 6; 9(3); 16; 17; **Jas** 1:7; 16; 20; 22; 23; 25; 26; 2:1; 4; 5; 6; 7; 11(3); 14; 16; 17; 21; 24; 25; 3:1; 2; 10; 14; 15; 4:1; 2(3); 3; 4; 11(2); 14; 17; 5:6; 9; 12; 17(2); **1 Pe** 1:4; 8(2); 12; 14; 18; 23; 2:10(2); 16; 18; 23(2); 3:1; 3; 6; 7; 9; 14; 21; 4:4; 12; 16; 17; 5:2(2); 4; **2 Pe** 1:12; 16; 2:3(2); 4; 5; 10; 11; 12; 21; 3:8; 9(2); **1 Jn** 1:6; 8; 10(2); 2:1; 2; 4(2); 11; 15(2); 16; 19; 21(2); 23; 27(2); 28; 3:1(2); 2; 6; 9; 10(3); 12; 13; 14; 18; 21; 4:1; 3(2); 6(2); 8(2); 10; 18; 20(2); 5:3; 6; 10(2); 12(2); 16(3); 17; 18(2); **2 Jn** 1; 5; 7; 8; 9(2); 10(2); 12; **3 Jn** 9; 10(2); 11(2); 13; **Jude** 5; 6; 9; 10; 19; **Rev** 1:17; 2:2; 3; 9; 10; 11; 13; 21; 24(2); 3:2; 3(2); 4; 5; 8; 9; 17; 18; 4:8; 5:5; 6:6; 7:1; 3; 16; 8:12; 9:4(2); 5; 6; 20(3); 21; 10:4; 11:2; 9; 12:8; 11; 13:8; 15; 14:4; 15:4; 16:9; 11; 18; 20; 17:8(3); 10; 11; 18:7; 21; 22(2); 23(2); 19:10; 20:4(2); 5; 15; 21:25; 22:9; 10

NOW (2142/2106)

Gen 2:10; 23; 3:1; 22; 4:1; 2; 8; 11; 6:1; 7:17; 9:18; 10:1; 11:1; 6; 26; 12:1; 10; 19; 13:6; 14; 14:10; 14; 21; 15:5; 12; 15; 16:1; 2; 7; 18:3; 11; 21; 27; 31; 19:1; 2; 4; 8; 9; 19; 20; 31; 20:2; 7; 21:5; 23; 22:1; 2; 12; 20; 23:10; 24:1; 14; 16; 29; 37; 42; 49; 62; 25:12; 21; 29; 26:8; 15; 22; 28; 29; 27:1; 2; 3; 5; 8; 9; 26; 30; 36; 37; 43; 28:10; 29:3; 9; 16; 18; 23; 32; 34; 35; 30:1; 14; 20; 30; 37; 31:1; 12; 13; 16; 19; 25; 28; 30; 34; 42; 44; 32:4; 10; 25; 33:1; 10; 15; 34:1; 5; 25; 35:8; 17; 22; 28; 36:1; 4; 12; 31; 37:1; 3; 5; 15; 18; 20; 36; 38:12; 27; 39:1; 6; 40:13; 20; 41:8; 12; 33; 47; 42:6; 22; 43:1; 10; 18; 30; 44:10; 30; 33; 45:5; 8; 16; 19; 46:8; 30; 34; 47:4; 13; 29; 48:1; 5; 10; 17; 50:4; 5; 17; 21; **Ex** 1:1; 8; 2:11; 16; 23; 3:1; 3; 9; 10; 18; 4:6; 12; 15; 5:5; 18; 6:1; 20; 7:16; 8:18; 9:15; 18; 19; 31; 10:1; 11; 17; 11:2; 12:1; 6; 13; 35; 40; 14:1; 5; 24; 15:23; 16:10; 27; 36; 17:8; 18:6; 11; 19; 19:5; 18; 20:18; 21:1; 24:1; 16; 28:1; 29:38; 32:1; 10; 16; 25; 30(2); 32; 34; 33:5; 13(2); 34:5; 9; 29; **Lev** 1:1; 4:1; 13; 11:1; 13:45; 14:43; 16:1; 24:10; 25:47; 27:1; **Num** 1:1; 20; 3:1; 12; 6:13; 7:1; 10; 89; 8:4; 9:1; 6; 15; 10:11; 29; 11:1; 4; 6; 7; 15; 23; 26; 31; 12:3; 6; 13:4; 20; 22; 26; 14:10; 15; 17; 19; 22; 25; 36; 41; 15:32; 16:1; 8; 26; 31; 42; 49; 17:8; 19:1; 20:2; 10; 14; 16; 29; 21:10; 22:2; 4; 11; 19; 23; 29; 33; 34; 36; 38; 23:23; 24:1; 11; 14; 17; 25:1; 7; 14; 26:33; 62; 27:12; 28:1; 30:14; 31:17; 25; 43; 32:1; 7; 33:2; 40; 50; 35:6; 36:1; 3; **Deut** 1:3; 2:13; 4:1; 32; 44; 5:25; 6:1; 10:6; 12; 22; 11:29; 17:12; 19:8; 20:12; 22:17; 26:10; 27:1; 28:1; 29:2; 30:1; 31:15; 19; 32:39; 33:1; 34:9; **Josh** 1:2; 2:1; 8; 12; 3:12; 4:19; 5:10; 14; 6:1; 10; 17; 7:2; 19(2); 8:1; 11; 14; 21; 30; 9:6; 11; 12; 17; 19; 23; 25; 10:1; 13:1; 7; 14:10(2); 11; 12; 15:13; 18; 17:14; 18:1; 11; 21; 21:4; 22:4(2); 7; 11; 26; 30; 31; 23:1; 24:14; 23; 29; **Judg** 1:1; 8; 10; 14; 16; 36; 2:8; 3:1; 16; 17; 20; 4:4; 11; 6:11; 13; 17; 22; 25; 39; 7:3; 8; 12; 8:1; 2; 6; 10; 15; 26; 32; 9:7; 16; 26; 32; 38(2); 46; 10:4; 11:1; 7; 8; 12; 13; 23; 25; 12:4; 13:2; 3; 4; 7; 10; 12; 14:1; 2; 5; 14; 17; 15:9; 18; 16:1; 9; 10; 13; 23; 27; 17:1; 3; 7; 13; 18:14; 24; 19:4; 9; 18; 24; 20:3; 7; 9; 13; 17; 38; 39; 21:1; **Ruth** 1:1; 4; 19; 22; 2:4; 7; 14; 3:2; 8; 11; 12; 4:1; 7; 18; **1 Sam** 1:1; 9; 13; 16; 21; 24; 2:12; 16; 22; 30; 34; 3:7; 10; 4:1; 6; 13; 19; 6:1; 7; 13; 7:7; 10; 8:1; 5; 9; 9:3; 6; 9; 12; 13; 15; 22; 10:2; 19; 11:5; 12:1; 2; 7; 10; 13; 16; 13:4; 10; 12; 13; 14; 19; 14:1; 16; 17; 19; 25; 29; 30; 31; 36; 43; 52; 15:1; 3; 10; 18; 25; 30; 16:1; 12; 16; 17; 17:1; 7; 12; 17; 19; 28; 29; 31; 52; 18:1; 6; 8; 12; 20; 22; 26; 19:1; 9; 19; 20:17; 25; 29; 31; 36; 21:1; 3; 7; 12; 22:5; 6; 7; 12; 20; 23:6; 20; 24:1; 5; 20; 21; 25:2; 7; 14; 17; 21; 23; 26(2); 27; 36; 26:1; 5; 8; 11; 13; 16; 19; 20; 27:1; 5; 7; 28:1; 3; 15; 22; 24; 29:7; 10; 30:1; 6; 21; 26; 31:1; 11; **2 Sam** 1:1; 7; 2:6; 7; 12; 14; 18; 25; 3:1; 6; 17; 18; 27; 36; 4:2; 11; 5:8; 14; 17; 6:12; 16; 7:1; 2; 8; 20; 25; 28; 29; 9:1; 6; 10; 10:7; 11:13; 12:10; 23; 24; 26; 28; 13:3; 7; 11; 13; 18; 20; 25; 28(2); 33; 14:6; 7; 15(2); 17; 25; 32; 15:2; 7; 13; 32; 34; 16:5; 8; 11; 14; 23; 17:1; 5; 9; 16; 17; 21; 23; 27; 18:3(2); 5; 10; 18; 19; 24; 19:7(2); 9(2); 10; 18; 24; 32; 38; 40; 20:3; 6; 8; 21:1; 2; 10; 18; 23:1; 18; 24:2; 3; 10; 11; 13; 16; 20; 22; **1 Ki** 1:1; 12; 15; 18(2); 41; 50; 2:1; 9; 13; 16; 22; 24; 39; 3:1; 4; 7; 16; 4:22; 5:1; 4; 6; 6:2; 7:13; 8:1; 17; 25; 26; 9:4; 10; 25; 10:1; 13; 24; 29; 11:14; 29; 41; 12:4; 11; 16(2); 20; 26; 30; 13:11; 20; 26; 14:5; 14; 19; 22; 29; 15:7; 16; 21; 25; 31; 16:5; 9; 14; 16; 20; 27; 30; 17:17; 24; 18:3; 7; 11; 14; 19; 25; 39; 43; 45; 19:4; 20:1; 27; 31; 33; 35; 39; 21:7; 22:1; 11; 13; 24; 31; 34; 39; 45; **2 Ki** 1:2; 4; 14; 18; 2:3; 5; 8; 15; 16; 3:1; 4; 15; 20; 23; 4:6; 8; 9; 13; 18; 26; 27; 31; 38; 40; 5:1; 5; 6; 15(2); 22; 25; 6:1; 8; 19; 21; 30; 7:3; 4; 9; 12; 17; 19; 8:5; 6; 16; 23; 28; 9:2; 12; 14; 17; 22; 24; 26; 30; 34; 10:1; 2; 6; 10; 15; 19; 24; 25; 34; 11:13; 12:6; 7; 19; 13:8; 12; 19; 24; 14:5; 15; 18; 28; 15:6; 11; 15; 21; 26; 31; 36; 16:10; 19; 17:5; 18:1; 9; 19; 21; 23; 25; 19:19; 25; 37; 20:3; 20; 21:17; 25; 22:3; 11; 23:1; 19; 25; 28; 33; 24:5; 25:1; 23; 27; **1 Chr** 1:32; 43; 2:16; 18; 21; 34; 3:1; 4:9; 22; 42; 5:1; 10; 6:19; 31; 50; 54; 66; 7:5; 24; 28; 8:1; 29; 9:3; 28; 10:1; 11:6; 10; 13; 15; 12:1; 23; 14:1; 8; 16:42; 17:1(2); 7; 23; 26; 27; 18:9; 19:8; 16; 20:4; 21:1; 8; 12; 15; 20; 22:5(2); 11; 19; 23:3; 14; 24:1; 7; 25:9; 28:1; 6; 8; 10; 29:2; 13; 17; 20; 29; **2 Chr** 1:1; 5; 9; 10; 2:13; 15; 3:1; 5:2; 6:7; 16; 17; 40; 41; 7:15; 16; 8:11; 16; 9:1; 12; 29; 10:4; 11; 16(2); 11:1; 21; 12:1; 7; 13; 13:8; 12; 22; 15:1; 16:5; 9; 17:3; 18:10; 12; 30; 33; 19:7; 20:10; 13; 22; 34; 21:4; 22:10; 23:12; 24:4; 17; 27; 25:3; 14; 17; 19; 26; 26:1; 6; 22; 27:7; 28:10; 11; 22; 26; 29:5; 10; 11; 17; 31; 30:8; 13; 31:1; 11; 32:15; 20; 32; 33:12; 18; 34:14; 35:1; 3; 26; 36:3; 8; 22; **Ezra** 1:1; 2:1; 3:8; 4:1; 13; 14; 21; 22; 23; 5:16; 17; 6:6; 15; 7:1; 17; 8:15; 33; 9:8; 10; 12; 10:1; 2; 3; 11; **Neh** 1:6; 10; 2:1; 9; 4:3; 7; 5:5; 8; 11; 18; 6:1; 7; 9; 7:4; 8:1; 13; 9:1; 32; 10:1; 28; 11:1; 12:1; 12; 27; 13:4; 20; **Esth** 1:1; 2:9; 15; 20; 3:4; 5:1; 6:4; 6; 7:9; 8:3; 9:1; 12; 10:2; **Job** 1:6; 11; 13; 2:5; 11; 3:13; 4:5; 7; 12; 5:1; 6:21; 28; 29; 7:21; 8:6; 9:25; 12:7; 13:6; 18; 19; 14:16; 16:7; 19; 17:3; 22:21; 24:25; 30:1; 9; 16; 32:4; 14; 33:2; 35:15; 37:21; 38:3; 40:7; 15; 16; 42:5; 8; 12; **Ps** 2:10; 12:5; 17:11; 20:6; 27:6; 30:6; 37:25; 39:7; 41:8; 50:22; 71:18; 74:6; 116:14; 18; 118:2; 3; 4; 25(2); 119:67; 122:8; 124:1; 129:1; **Prov** 5:7; 7:24; 8:32; **Eccl** 2:1; 16; 9:6; 15; 12:1; **Song** 3:2; 7:8; **Isa** 1:18; 21; 2:2; 5:1; 3; 5; 7:1; 3; 13; 8:7; 16:14; 19:12; 22:1; 23:15; 28:22; 29:22(2); 30:8; 31:3; 33:10(3); 36:1; 4; 5; 8; 10; 37:20; 26; 38; 38:3; 21; 42:14; 43:1; 19; 44:1; 47:8; 12; 13; 48:7; 16; 49:5; 19; 52:5; 64:8; **Jer** 2:18; 4:12; 31; 5:1; 21; 24; 7:12; 13; 11:18; 13:6; 14:10; 17:15; 18:11(2); 13; 20:1; 21:8; 23:6; 25:5; 26:8; 13; 20; 27:6; 16; 18; 28:7; 12; 15; 29:1; 27; 29; 30:4; 6; 32:16; 36; 34:10; 35:15; 36:1; 9; 15; 16; 17; 22; 27; 37:1; 3; 4; 19; 20; 38:1; 7; 22; 25; 28; 39:11; 40:3; 4; 5; 41:1; 6; 9; 42:1; 15; 22; 43:1; 44:7; 45:3; 50:17; 51:63; 52:4; 12; 21; 31; **Lam** 1:18; 4:8; **Ezek** 1:1; 5:5; 2:9; 3:16; 4:14; 6:1; 7:3; 8; 8:5; 6; 9:3; 10:3; 11:13; 12:1; 27; 14:1; 16:35; 17:12; 18:25; 19:13; 21:25; 22:2; 23:11; 43; 26:2; 18; 27:2; 31:1; 32:24; 33:22; 36:35; 38:1; 8; 39:25; 40:5; 42:5; 15; 43:9; 44:6; 46:12; 19; 48:1; **Dan** 1:6; 9; 18; 2:1; 23; 36; 3:15; 4:18; 37; 5:8; 12; 15; 16; 6:8; 10; 18; 8:18; 9:15; 17; 20; 22; 10:4; 11; 14; 17; 20; 11:2; 14; 34; **Hos** 1:8; 2:7; 10; 4:4; 16; 5:3; 7; 7:2; 8:8; 10; 13; 10:2; 3; 13:2; **Joel** 2:12; **Am** 6:7; 7:16; **Jon** 1:1; 17; 3:1; 3; 4:3; **Mic** 3:1; 9; 4:1; 7; 9; 10; 11; 5:1; 4; 6:1; 5; 7:4; 10; **Nah** 1:13; 2:8; **Hag** 1:5; 2:2; 3; 4; 11; 15; 18; **Zech** 1:4; 3:3; 4:1; 5:5; 6:14; 7:1; 8:11; 9:8; **Mal** 1:9; 2:1; 3:10; 15; **Mt** 1:18; 2:1; 13; 3:10; 15; 4:3; 12; 6:30; 8:5; 14; 23; 30; 9:8; 10; 10:2; 11:2; 21; 11:1; 12; 12:9; 24; 13:22; 53; 58; 14:21; 23; 24; 25; 15:32(2); 38; 16:5; 17:1; 9; 22; 19:1; 16; 20:2; 17; 29; 21:1; 18; 23; 34; 45; 22:25; 24:3; 32; 25:2; 26:1; 17; 21; 29; 48; 53; 59; 65; 69; 27:11; 15; 32; 42; 43; 45; 57; 28:1; 11; **Mk** 1:6; 14; 23; 29; 35; 40; 2:15; 23; 4:18; 36; 5:11; 21; 25; 6:5; 14; 35; 44; 47; 48; 7:2; 8:2; 9; 14; 27;

9:2; 9; 38; 10:17; 30; 32; 46; 11:1; 12; 20; 12:2; 20; 34; 41; 13:3; 12; 28; 14:12; 18; 44; 51; 55; 66; 15:6; 25; 32; 33; 42; 16:1; 9; **Lk** 1:24; 26; 36(2); 39; 57; 67; 2:8; 15; 17; 22; 29; 36; 46; 3:1; 9; 15; 23; 4:13; 33; 38; 42; 5:10; 17; 6:1; 6; 12; 21(2); 25; 7:1; 11; 39; 8:1; 11; 14; 22; 32; 38; 43; 47; 52; 9:7; 28; 37; 49; 51; 57; 10:31; 38; 11:1; 7; 39; 12:11; 52; 13:10; 14:1; 15; 17; 25; 15:25; 16:14; 25; 17:11; 20; 18:3; 18; 19:2; 11; 37; 41; 42; 20:1; 10; 29; 42; 21:28; 30; 22:1; 24; 36; 55; 63; 23:8; 26; 44; 50; 24:1; 13; 30; 36; 51; **Jn** 1:19; 24; 39; 42; 44; 2:2; 6; 8; 10; 13; 23; 3:23; 4:6; 18; 23; 42; 43; 51; 5:2; 5; 17; 25; 6:4; 10; 16; 7:2; 14; 25; 44; 8:2; 5; 40; 52; 9:1; 14; 19; 21; 25; 31; 41; 10:22; 11:1; 5; 18; 22; 30; 43; 51; 57; 12:9; 20; 27; 31(2); 13:1; 7; 19; 23; 27; 31; 33; 36; 37; 14:7; 29; 15:22; 24; 16:5; 12; 19; 22; 24; 29; 30; 31; 32; 17:5; 7; 11; 13; 18:6; 14; 15; 18; 25; 36; 40; 19:14; 19; 23; 25; 28; 29; 41; 20:1; 14; 24; 21:4; 6; 7; 14; **Acts** 1:5; 9; 18; 2:33; 37; 44; 3:1; 11; 17; 4:1; 13; 17; 29; 32; 5:7; 24; 38; 6:1; 7:4; 11; 23; 34; 52; 8:1; 14; 26; 36; 39; 9:10; 23; 32; 10:5; 17; 24; 33; 11:1; 10; 19; 12:1; 3; 7; 11; 16; 20; 13:1; 2; 6; 11; 13; 18; 29; 43; 48; 14:1; 11; 25; 27; 15:6; 10; 32; 36; 37; 16:6; 10; 14; 16; 34; 36; 37; 17:1; 16; 30; 18:6; 9; 24; 19:7; 11; 28; 20:2; 7; 11; 22; 25; 32; 21:1; 9; 12; 27; 31; 22:1; 6; 16; 17; 23:10; 13; 15; 21; 24:1; 13; 17; 25(2); 25:1; 26:6; 17; 24; 27:9(2); 20; 22; 27; 28:1; 16; **Rom** 1:10; 13(2); 3:19; 21; 4:4; 23; 5:5; 9; 11; 6:8; 19; 21; 22; 7:6; 17; 20; 8:1; 9; 22; 27; 11:12; 30; 31; 13:11(2); 15:5; 8; 13; 14; 23; 25; 30; 33; 16:17; 25; 26; **1 Cor** 1:10; 12; 2:12; 3:2(2); 8; 12; 4:6; 7; 13; 18; 5:11; 6:7; 13; 7:1; 10; 14; 25; 29; 8:1; 7; 9:23; 25; 10:6; 11; 11:2; 17; 12:1; 18; 20; 27; 13:12(2); 13; 14:6; 15:12; 20; 28; 50; 16:1; 5; 7; 10; 12; **2 Cor** 1:6; 13; 21; 2:10; 14; 3:17; 5:5; 16(2); 18; 20; 6:2(2); 13; 7:9; 8:11; 14; 22; 9:1; 10; 10:1; 12:14; 13:2; 7; **Gal** 1:9; 10; 20; 23; 2:11; 20; 3:3; 16; 20; 4:1; 9; 20; 25; 28; 29; 5:19; 6:17; **Eph** 2:2; 13; 19; 3:5; 10; 20; 4:9; 5:8; **Phil** 1:5; 20; 30; 2:12; 3:18; 4:10; 15; 20; **Col** 1:21; 24; 26; 2:4; 3:8; 4:16; **1 Th** 3:6; 8; 11; 5:14; 23; **2 Th** 2:1; 6; 7; 16; 3:5; 12; 16; **1 Tim** 1:5; 17; 4:1; 8; 5:5; 6:6; **2 Tim** 1:10; 3:8; **Phm** 1:9; 11; **Heb** 2:8; 3:17; 7:4; 7; 8:1; 6; 13; 9:5; 6; 24; 26; 10:18; 38; 11:1; 16; 12:11; 26; 27; 13:20; **Jas** 2:11; 3:18; 4:13; 16; 5:1; **1 Pe** 1:6; 8; 12; 25; 2:10(2); 25; 3:21; 4:18; **2 Pe** 3:1; 7; 18; **1 Jn** 2:3; 9; 18; 28; 3:2; 24; 4:3; 5:14; **2 Jn** 5; **Jude** 14; 24; 25; **Rev** 2:24; 5:8; 6:1; 9:16; 10:4; 11:11; 12:1; 10; 13; 13:2; 14:13; 16:19; 19:11; 15; 20:7; 21:1; 14; 22:8

O (996/903)

Gen 24:12; 31; 42; 27:34; 38; 32:9; 43:20; 44:18; 49:18; **Ex** 4:10; 13; 15:6(2); 11; 16; 17(2); 32:4; 8; 34:9; **Num** 10:35; 36; 12:13; 16:22; 21:17; 29; 24:5(2); **Deut** 3:24; 4:1; 5:1; 6:3; 4; 9:1; 26; 20:3; 21:8; 26:10; 27:9; 32:1(2); 6; 43; 33:23; 29; **Josh** 7:8; 13; **Judg** 3:19; 5:3(2); 12; 21; 31; 6:13; 15; 22; 13:8; 16:28(2); 21:3; **1 Sam** 1:11; 26; 17:55; 23:10; 11; 20; 26:17; **2 Sam** 1:21; 24; 7:18; 19(2); 22; 25; 27; 28; 29; 14:4; 9; 22; 15:31; 34; 16:4; 18:33(2); 19:4(2); 26; 20:1; 22:29; 50; 23:17; 24:10; 23; **1 Ki** 1:13; 20; 24; 3:7; 17; 26; 8:26; 28; 53; 12:16(2); 28; 13:2; 17:18; 20; 21; 18:17; 26; 37; 20:4; 21:20; **2 Ki** 6:12; 26; 8:5; 13:14; 19:15; 16(2); 19; 20:3; **1 Chr** 11:19; 12:18(2); 16:13; 28; 35; 17:16; 17(2); 19; 20; 23; 25; 27; 21:17; 29:11(2); 16; 18; **2 Chr** 1:9; 6:17; 19; 41(2); 42; 10:16(2); 13:12; 14:11(2); 20:6; 12; 17; 20; 25:7; **Ezra** 9:6; 10; 15; **Neh** 1:5; 11; 4:4; 6:9; 13:14; 22; 29; 31; **Esth** 7:3; **Job** 7:20; 16:18; 19:21; 37:14; **Ps** 2:10; 3:3; 7(2); 4:1; 2; 8; 5:1; 3; 8; 10; 12; 6:1; 2(2); 3; 4; 7:1; 3; 6; 8; 8:1; 9; 9:1; 2; 6; 13; 19; 20; 10:1; 12(2); 12:7; 13:1; 3; 16:1; 2; 5; 17:1; 6; 7; 13; 14; 18:1; 15; 49; 19:14; 21:1; 13; 22:2; 19(2); 24:7; 9; 25:1; 2; 4; 6; 7; 11; 22; 26:1; 2; 6; 27:7; 9; 11; 28:1; 29:1; 30:1; 2; 3; 8; 10; 12; 31:1; 5; 9; 14; 17; 33:1; 22; 35:1; 22(2); 24; 36:5; 6; 7; 38:1; 15(2); 21(2); 22; 39:12; 40:5; 8; 9; 11; 13(2); 17; 41:10; 42:1; 5; 6; 11; 43:1; 4; 5; 44:1; 4; 23; 45:3; 6; 10; 48:9; 10; 50:7(2); 51:1; 10; 14; 15; 17; 52:1; 54:1; 2; 6; 55:1; 9; 23; 56:1; 2; 7; 12; 57:1; 5; 7; 9; 11; 58:6(2); 59:1; 3; 5; 8; 9; 11; 17; 60:1; 10(2); 61:1; 5; 62:12; 63:1; 64:1; 65:1; 2; 5; 66:10; 67:3; 5; 68:7; 9; 10; 24; 28; 35; 69:1; 5; 6(2); 13(2); 16; 29; 70:1(2); 5(2); 71:1; 4; 5; 12(2); 17; 18; 19(2); 22(2); 72:1; 74:1; 10; 18; 22; 75:1; 76:6; 77:13; 16; 78:1; 79:1; 9; 12; 80:1; 3; 4; 7; 14; 19; 81:8(2); 82:8; 83:1(2); 13; 16; 84:1; 3; 8(2); 9; 12; 85:4; 86:1; 3; 4; 6; 8; 9; 11; 12; 14; 15; 87:3; 4; 88:1; 13; 89:5; 8(2); 15; 51; 90:3; 13; 92:1; 5; 9; 93:3; 5; 94:1(2); 2; 5; 12; 18; 96:7; 97:8; 99:8; 101:1; 102:1; 12; 24; 103:1; 2; 22; 104:1(2); 24; 35; 105:6; 106:4; 47; 108:1; 3; 5; 11(2); 109:1; 21; 26; 113:1; 114:5(2); 6(2); 7; 115:1; 9; 10; 116:4; 7; 16; 19; 118:25(2); 119:12; 31; 33; 41; 52; 55; 57; 64; 65; 75; 89; 107; 108; 126; 137; 145; 149; 151; 156; 159; 169; 174; 120:2; 122:2; 123:1; 3; 125:4; 126:4; 130:1; 3; 7; 131:3; 132:8; 135:1; 9; 13(2); 19(2); 20; 137:5; 7; 8; 138:4; 8; 139:1; 4; 17; 19; 21; 23; 140:1; 4; 6; 7; 8; 141:3; 8; 142:5; 143:1; 7; 9; 11; 144:5; 9; 145:1; 10; 146:1; 10; 147:12(2); **Prov** 1:2; 6:9; 8:4; 5; 24:15; 31:4; **Eccl** 3:1; 5:2; 10:16; 17; 11:9; **Song** 1:5; 7; 8; 2:7; 14; 3:5; 11; 4:11; 16(2); 5:1(2); 8; 9; 16; 6:1; 4; 13; 7:1; 6; 8:4; 12; **Isa** 1:2(2); 2:5; 3:12; 5:3; 7:13; 8:8; 9; 10:22; 24; 30(2); 12:1; 6; 14:12; 31(2); 16:4; 9; 21:2(2); 13; 14; 22:17; 23:4; 10; 12; 24:17; 25:1; 26:7; 8; 13; 15; 17; 27:12; 33:2; 37:16; 17(2); 20; 38:3; 14; 16; 40:9(2); 27(2); 41:1; 43:1(2); 22(2); 44:1; 2; 21(2); 23(2); 45:15; 46:3; 8; 47:1(2); 5; 48:1; 12; 49:1; 3; 13(3); 51:4; 9; 17; 52:1(2); 2(2); 54:1; 11; 62:6; 63:16; 17; 64:8; 9; 12; **Jer** 2:4; 12; 28; 31; 3:14; 20; 4:1; 14; 19(2); 5:3; 15; 21; 6:1; 8; 18; 19; 23; 26; 9:20; 10:1; 6; 7; 17; 23; 24; 11:13; 20; 12:1; 3; 13:27; 14:7; 8; 9; 20; 22; 15:5; 15; 16; 16:19; 17:3; 13; 14; 18:6(2); 19; 19:3; 20:7; 12; 21:12; 13; 22:2; 23; 29; 30:10(2); 31:4; 7; 10; 21; 22; 23; 32:25; 34:4; 37:20; 42:15; 19; 45:2; 46:9(2); 11; 19; 27(2); 28; 47:6; 48:2; 18; 19; 32; 43; 46; 49:3; 4; 8; 16; 30; 50:24; 31; 42; 51:13; 25; 62; **Lam** 1:9; 11; 20; 2:13(2); 18; 20; 3:55; 58; 59; 61; 64; 4:21; 22(2); 5:1; 19; 21; **Ezek** 3:25; 6:3; 8:15; 17; 11:4; 5; 12:25; 13:4; 11; 16:35; 18:25; 29; 30; 31; 20:31; 39; 44; 21:25; 26:3; 17(2); 27:3; 8; 28:16; 22; 29:3(2); 33:8; 10; 11; 12; 20; 34:9; 17; 35:3; 15; 36:1; 4; 8; 22; 32; 37:3; 4; 9; 12; 13; 38:3; 16; 39:1; 44:6; 45:9; **Dan** 2:4; 23; 29; 31; 37; 3:4; 9; 10; 12; 16; 17; 18; 24; 4:22; 24; 27; 5:10; 18; 6:7; 8; 12; 13; 15; 21; 22; 9:4; 7; 8; 15; 16; 18; 19(3); 22; 10:11; 19; **Hos** 5:1(3); 3; 8; 6:4(2); 11; 8:5; 9:1; 14; 10:9; 15; 13:9; 14(2); 14:1; **Joel** 1:19; 2:17; 21; 3:4; 11; **Am** 2:11; 3:1; 4:12(2); 5:1; 25; 6:14; 7:2; 5; 8:14; 9:7; **Ob** 9; **Jon** 1:14(2); 2:6; 4:3; **Mic** 1:2; 13; 15; 2:12; 3:1; 4:8; 10; 13; 5:1; 6:2; 3; 5; 8; **Nah** 1:15; 3:18; **Hab** 1:12(3); 3:2(2); 8; **Zeph** 2:1; 5; 3:14(3); **Zech** 1:12; 2:10; 3:8; 4:7; 8:13; 9:9(2); 13(2); 11:1; 2(2); 13:7; **Mal** 2:1; 3:6; **Mt** 6:30; 8:26; 14:31; 15:22; 28; 16:8; 17:17; 20:30; 31; 23:37; 26:39; 42; **Mk** 9:19; 12:29; **Lk** 5:8; 9:41; 12:28; 13:34; 24:25; **Jn** 17:5; 25; **Acts** 1:1; 24; 7:42; 13:10; 18:14; 26:13; **Rom** 2:1; 3; 7:24; 9:20; 15:10; **1 Cor** 7:16(2); 15:55(2); 16:22; **2 Cor** 6:11; **Gal** 3:1; 4:27; **1 Tim** 6:11; 20; **Heb** 1:8; 10:7; 9; **Jas** 2:20; **Rev** 4:11; 6:10; 11:17; 12:12; 15:3; 4; 16:5; 18:20

OF (31661/17357)

Gen 1:2(3); 6; 10; 14; 15; 17; 20(3); 24; 25; 26(2); 27; 28(2); 29; 30(2); 2:1; 4; 5(2); 6; 7(3); 9(5); 10; 11(2); 12; 13(2); 14(2); 15; 16(2); 17(4); 19(3); 20(2); 21; 23(3); 3:1(3); 2(2); 3(3); 5; 6; 7(2); 8(4); 11; 12; 14(2); 17(5); 18; 19(2); 20; 21; 22(3); 23(2); 24(3); 4:2(2); 3(3); 4(3); 10; 14; 16(3); 17(2); 19(2); 20; 21; 22(2); 23; 25; 26; 5:1(3); 4; 8; 11; 14; 17; 20; 23; 27; 29(2); 31; 6:1; 2(3); 4(4); 5(3); 7(2); 8; 9; 13; 14; 15; 16; 17; 19(3); 20(5); 21; 7:2(2); 3(3); 4; 7(2); 8(4); 10; 11(4); 13; 14; 15(2); 16; 18; 22(2); 23(2); 8:2(2); 3; 4(2); 5(2); 6(2); 8; 9(2); 13(3); 14; 16; 17; 19; 20(2); 21; 9:2(5); 5(4); 6; 10(4); 11; 12; 13; 15; 16; 17; 18(3); 19; 21; 22(2); 23; 25; 26; 27; 29; 10:1(2); 2; 3; 4; 5; 6; 7(2); 10(2); 18; 19; 20; 21(3); 22; 23; 25; 29; 30; 31; 32(2); 11:2; 4; 5; 8; 9(2); 10; 27; 28; 29(5); 31(3); 32; 12:1; 3; 5(2); 6(2); 8(2); 11; 13; 15; 17; 13:4(2); 7(2); 10(3); 11; 12(2); 13; 16(2); 18; 14:1(5); 2(5); 3; 6; 7; 8(6); 9(4); 10(3); 11; 13(3); 15; 17(3); 18(2); 19(2); 20; 21; 22(2); 24; 15:1; 2(2); 4; 7(2); 16; 18; 16:2; 3; 7(2); 8; 9; 10; 11; 12; 13; 17:4; 5; 6; 8; 11(2); 14; 16(2); 23(2); 24; 25; 27; 18:1(2); 5; 6; 10; 11; 14; 18; 19; 25; 28(2); 29; 31; 32; 19:1; 4(2); 8; 11; 12; 13; 14; 15; 16(2); 22; 24; 25; 26; 28(3); 29(3); 30; 31; 32; 34; 36; 37; 38(3); 20:2(2); 3; 5(2); 6; 11(2); 12(2); 13; 16; 18(3); 21:2; 3; 9; 10; 11; 12(2); 13(2); 14(2); 15; 16(2); 17(4); 19; 21(2); 22; 25(2); 26; 27; 28; 29; 31; 32(2); 33; 34; 22:2(3); 3(2); 6(2); 8; 9; 11; 13; 14(2); 15(2); 17(2); 18; 21; 23:1(2); 2; 3; 4; 5; 6(2); 7(2); 8(2); 9(2); 10(4); 11(2); 12; 13(2); 15; 16(4); 17; 18(3); 19(3); 20; 24:2; 3(3); 7(2); 9; 10(2); 11; 12; 13(3); 15(2); 22; 24; 27(2); 30; 31; 32; 37; 42; 43; 47; 48(3); 53(2); 60(3); 62; 25:3; 4(2); 6(2); 7(2); 8; 9(3); 10; 11; 12; 13(3); 16; 17(2); 18(2); 19; 20(3); 22; 26; 27; 28; 31; 33; 34; 26:1(2); 2; 4(2); 7(2); 8; 9; 10; 14(3); 15; 17; 18(3); 19; 20(2); 24; 25; 26(2); 29; 33; 34(2); 35; 27:2; 7; 9; 15; 16(3); 17; 19; 22; 25; 27(3); 28(5); 30; 31; 33; 34; 39(4); 41(2); 42; 45; 46(6); 28:1; 2(3); 3; 4; 5(3); 6; 8; 9(2); 11(2); 12; 13(2); 14(2); 17(2); 18; 19(2); 22; 29:1(2); 2(2); 5; 10(3); 16(2); 17; 20; 22; 30:2(2); 14(2); 16; 33; 35; 36; 37(2); 40; 41; 31:1; 2; 3; 5; 9; 11; 13(3); 18; 21; 23; 25; 29; 32(2); 33; 35; 37; 38; 39; 42(4); 53(4); 32:1; 2; 3(2); 9(2); 10(3); 11(2); 12; 16; 17; 22; 24; 25(3); 30; 32(2); 33:8; 10; 15(2); 17; 18(2); 19(3); 34:1(2); 2(2); 3; 6; 7; 8; 13; 15; 19; 20(2); 23; 24(4); 25(2); 26; 27; 30; 35:1; 3; 5(2); 6; 7; 8; 11; 14; 15; 20; 21; 22; 23; 24; 25; 26(2); 28; 29; 36:1; 2(4); 3; 5(2); 6(3); 7; 9(2); 10(5); 11; 12(2); 13(2); 14(3); 15(4); 16(3); 17(4); 18(2); 19; 20; 21(3); 22; 23; 24(2); 25(2); 26; 27; 28; 29; 30(2); 31(2); 32(2); 33(2); 34(2); 35(3); 36; 37; 38; 39(4); 40(2); 43(3); 37:1; 2(4); 3(2); 14(2); 20; 21; 22; 23(2); 25; 28(2); 31; 32; 36(2); 38:2; 7; 12(2); 19; 20; 21; 22; 39:1(2); 2; 4; 5(2); 11(2); 14; 21(2); 22; 23; 40:1(3); 3(2); 4; 5(3); 7; 8; 12; 14(2); 15; 17(2); 18; 20(2); 41:1; 2; 3(2); 5; 8; 10(2); 11(2); 12(2); 14; 15; 16; 17; 18; 19; 25; 27; 29(2); 30(2); 31; 33; 34(3); 35(2); 36(2); 37(2); 38; 41; 42; 43; 44; 45(3); 46(3); 48(3); 49; 50(3); 51; 52(2); 53(2); 54(2); 55; 56(2); 42:5(2); 6; 7; 9; 12; 13(2); 15; 16(2); 19(2); 21; 22; 27(2); 29; 30(2); 32(2); 33(3); 35(2); 43:11(2); 12; 16; 18; 19(2); 21; 23; 27; 29; 34; 44:1(2); 2(2); 4; 8(2); 9; 16; 20(2); 24; 31; 33; 45:2; 8(2); 9; 10; 11; 12; 13(2); 16; 17; 18(3); 19(2); 20(2); 21(2); 22(4); 23; 25(2); 26; 27; 46:1; 2; 3(2); 5; 6; 8(2); 9; 10(2); 11; 12(3); 13; 14; 15; 16; 17(2); 18; 19; 20(3); 21; 22; 23; 24; 25; 27(3); 28; 31(2); 34; 47:1(2); 4(2); 6(3); 9(8); 11(3); 13(3); 14(2); 15(2); 17; 18(2); 19; 20(2); 21(2); 22; 24; 25; 26(2); 27(2); 28(2); 30; 31; 48:3; 4(2); 5; 6; 7; 10; 16(2); 17(2); 19; 21; 22; 49:2; 3(3); 5; 8; 10; 11; 13; 15; 16(2); 24(4); 25(5); 26(6); 28; 29; 30(3); 32; 50:4(3); 5; 7(4); 8(2); 10(2); 11(3); 13(3); 17(4); 19; 23(2); 24(2); 25; **Ex** 1:1(2); 5; 7; 9(2); 10(2); 12(2); 13; 14; 15(4); 16; 17; 18; 2:1(3); 3; 5; 6; 10; 11; 15(3); 16; 19; 23(5); 25; 3:1(4); 2(3); 4; 6(4); 7(2); 8(3); 9(2); 10(2); 11(2); 12; 13(2); 14; 15(5); 16(5); 17(3); 18(3); 19; 21; 22(4); 4:5(4); 7; 8(2); 10(2); 13; 14; 20(2); 25(2); 26(2); 27; 28; 29(2); 30; 31; 5:1; 3; 4; 5; 6; 8; 10; 11; 12(2); 14(2); 15(2); 18; 19(2); 21(2); 6:1; 4(2); 5(2); 6(2); 7; 9(3); 11(3); 12(2); 13(5); 14(4); 15(3); 16(4); 17; 18(3); 19(2); 20(2); 21; 22; 23(2); 24(2); 25(4); 26(2); 27(2); 28; 29; 30; 7:2(2); 3; 4(3); 5; 11; 16; 18; 19(5); 20(2); 21(2); 22; 24; 8:3; 5; 6(2); 7; 9; 13(4); 16(2); 17(3); 19; 21(4); 22(3); 24(5); 26(2); 29; 31(2); 9:1; 3; 4(4); 6(4); 7(3); 8(2); 9(2); 11; 12; 13; 20(2); 21; 22(3); 23; 24; 25(3); 26(2); 29; 33; 35(2); 10:1(2); 2; 3; 5(3); 6(2); 10; 12(3); 13; 14(2); 15(5); 19; 20; 21; 22; 23; 26; 11:1; 2(3); 3(4); 4; 5(4); 6; 7(2); 9; 10(2); 12:1; 2(2); 3(3); 4; 5; 6(3); 7(2); 10(2); 12(3); 13; 16; 17(3); 18(2); 19(2); 21; 22(4); 27(3); 28; 29(4); 31; 33; 35(4); 36; 37; 38; 39(3); 40(2); 41(3); 42(5); 43; 46(2); 47; 48; 50; 51(3); 13:2(2); 3(5); 5; 8; 9; 11; 13(2); 14(4); 15(4); 16(2); 17(2); 18(5); 19(2); 20; 21(2); 22(2); 14:2; 3(2); 5(2); 7(2); 8(4); 9; 10(2); 11; 13; 15; 16(2); 17; 19(3); 20(2); 22(2); 23; 24(3); 25; 27; 28(2); 29(2); 30(2); 15:1; 3; 7; 8(2); 14(2); 15(4); 16; 17; 19(4); 20; 22; 23(2); 26(2); 27; 16:1(5); 2(2); 3(4); 6(3); 7; 9(2); 10(3); 12(2); 14(2); 15; 16; 17; 19; 20(2); 22; 27; 29; 31(2); 32(2); 33; 35(3); 36; 17:1(4); 3; 5(2); 6(3); 7(4); 9(2); 10; 12; 13; 14(2); 18:1(3); 3(2); 4(3); 5; 9(2); 10(5); 12; 15; 16; 21(5); 24; 25(5); 19:1(4); 2; 3(2); 6(2); 7; 8; 9; 11; 16; 17(2); 18; 19; 20(2); 21; 20:2(4); 4; 5(2); 7; 10; 18; 22; 23(2); 24; 25(2); 21:9; 19; 26(2); 27(2); 28; 30; 32; 34; 22:5(2); 7; 8; 9(3); 11(2); 12; 14; 17; 21; 25; 28; 29(2); 23:5; 6; 8; 9(2); 11(2); 12; 13(2); 15(3); 16(5); 18(2); 19(3); 21; 25; 26; 29; 31; 24:1(2); 3; 4(3); 5(3); 7(2); 8; 9(2); 10(2); 11(2); 12; 13; 16(3); 17(5); 18; 25:2; 9(2); 10; 11; 12; 13; 14; 15; 17; 18(3); 19(2); 20; 21; 22(2); 23; 24; 25; 26; 28; 29; 31(3); 32(5); 33; 35(3); 36(3); 37; 38; 39(2); 26:1(2); 2(3); 4(5); 5(2); 6; 7; 8(2); 9; 10(3); 12(3); 13(5); 14(2); 15; 16(2); 17; 19(2); 20; 21(2); 22; 23; 24; 25; 26(2); 27(3); 28; 29; 31(2); 32(2); 33; 34; 35; 36(2); 37(3); 27:1; 2; 3; 4; 5; 6; 7; 9(2); 10; 11(4); 12(2); 13; 14; 15; 16(2); 17(3); 18(3); 19(3); 20(2); 21(3); 28:1; 3; 6; 8(3); 9(2); 10(2); 11(5); 12(2); 13; 14; 15(3); 17(2); 21(3); 22; 23(2); 24(2); 25(2); 26(4); 27(2); 28(3); 29(3); 30(3); 31(2); 32(2); 33(2); 34; 36(2); 37; 38(2); 39(3); 43; 29:2; 4(2); 5(2); 10(2); 11(2); 12(4); 14; 15; 19; 20(7); 21(3); 22(2); 23(2); 24(2); 26(2); 27(5); 28(3); 29; 30; 31; 32(3); 34(3); 38; 40(6); 42(2); 43; 44; 45; 46(2); 30:1; 2; 3; 5; 6; 10(2); 12(2); 13; 16(5); 18(3); 20; 23(2); 24(3); 25; 26(2); 27; 28; 31; 33; 34; 35(2); 36(3); 31:2(4); 3(2); 5; 6(4); 7(3); 8; 9; 10(2); 13; 15; 16; 17; 18(4); 32:1(3); 2; 4(2); 7(2); 8(3); 10; 11(2); 12; 13(2); 15; 16(2); 17(2); 18(5); 19(2); 20; 22; 23(3); 26(2); 27; 28(3); 31; 32; 33; 34; 35; 33:1(3); 5; 6(2); 7(2); 9(2); 10; 11; 16; 19; 22; 34:1; 2; 4(2); 5; 7; 10; 12; 15(3); 16; 18(4); 20(2); 22(4); 23; 25(3); 26(3); 27; 28; 29(2); 30(2); 31; 32; 34; 35(3); 35:1(2); 2; 4(2); 5; 12; 15; 16; 17(2); 18(2); 19(2); 20(3); 21(2); 22(2); 23; 24(2); 25; 26; 29(3); 30(5); 31(2); 33; 34(3); 35(3); 36:1(2); 3(3); 4; 5; 6; 8(3); 9(2); 11(5); 12(3); 13; 14; 15(2); 17(3); 19(2); 20; 21(2); 22; 24(2); 25; 26(2); 27; 28; 29; 30(2); 31(2); 32(2); 34; 35(2); 36(3); 37; 37:1; 2; 3(2); 4; 5; 6; 7(3); 8; 9; 10; 11; 12(2); 13; 15; 16; 17(3); 18(5); 19; 21(3); 22(3); 23; 24(2); 25(2); 26; 27; 28; 29(2); 38:1(2); 2; 3; 4; 5; 6; 7; 8(5); 9(2); 10; 11; 12(2); 14(2); 15(2); 16(2); 17(4); 18(4); 19(2); 20(2); 21(6); 22(4); 23(5); 24(3); 25(2); 26; 27(3); 29; 30(2); 39:1(2); 2(2); 5(4); 6(3); 7(2); 8(3); 10; 13; 14(2); 15; 16(2); 17(2); 18(2); 19(4); 20; 21(3); 22(3); 23(2); 24(3); 25(2); 26; 27; 28(3); 29; 30(3); 32(4); 34(3); 35; 39; 40(3); 41; 42; 40:2(3); 3; 5(3); 6(4); 7; 10; 12(2); 17(2); 19(2); 20(2); 21(2); 22(2); 24(2); 26(2); 28; 29(4); 30; 32; 33; 34(2); 35(2); 36; 38(3); **Lev** 1:1; 2(5); 3(4); 4; 5(2); 7; 10(3); 11; 14(3); 15; 2:1; 2(2); 3(2); 4; 5; 7; 8; 10(2); 12; 13(3); 14(3); 16(2); 3:1(2); 2(3); 3; 6(2); 8(2); 9; 13(2); 4:2(4); 4(2); 5(2); 6(3); 7(9); 8; 10(3); 13(4); 14; 15(2); 16(2); 17; 18(7); 22(2); 23; 24; 25(6); 26(2); 27(3); 28; 29(2); 30(4); 31; 33; 34(5); 35(2); 5:1(2); 2(4); 3; 4(2); 5; 6; 9(5); 11(2); 12; 13; 15(3); 16; 17(2); 6:3; 5; 7; 9(2); 10; 12; 14(2); 15(2); 16(3); 17; 18; 20(5); 21; 25; 26(2); 30(2); 7:1; 8; 10; 11(2); 12(2); 13(2); 14; 15(3); 16(2); 17(2); 18(4); 19; 20(2); 21(2); 23(2); 24(2); 25(2); 26(2); 29(3); 32; 33(2); 34(5); 36; 37(2); 38(2); 8:2; 3(2); 4(2); 7; 11; 12; 14; 15(2); 18; 22(2); 23(4); 24(4); 26(2); 29(2); 30(4); 31(3); 32(2); 33(3); 35(3); 36; 9:1; 3(3); 5; 6; 7; 8; 9(3); 10; 17(2); 18; 23(2); 10:1; 4(3); 5; 6; 7(4); 9; 11(2); 12; 13; 14(5); 15(3); 16(2); 17; 19; 11:2; 9; 21; 24(2); 25(3); 26; 27; 32(2); 33; 35; 36; 37; 38; 40; 45(2); 46(2); 12:2(2); 3; 4(2); 5; 6(4); 7; 13:2(3); 3(2); 4; 10; 11; 12; 19; 20; 23; 24; 25; 30; 38; 39; 43(3); 48(2); 49; 51; 52; 53; 56(4); 57; 58; 59(3); 14:2(2); 3; 5; 6; 10(4); 11(2); 12; 14(6); 15(3); 16; 17(7); 18(2); 21(3); 23(2); 24(2); 25(7); 26(2); 27; 28(7); 29(2); 30; 34(2); 37; 38(2); 39; 42; 45; 50; 51; 52; 55(2); 57; 15:2; 7; 10; 12(2); 13; 14(2); 15; 16; 18; 25(5); 26(3); 28; 29(2); 30; 31; 33; 16:1(2); 3(2); 5(3); 7(2); 11; 12(3); 13; 14(3); 15(2); 16(6); 17(2); 18(5); 19(3); 20(2); 21(5); 23; 24; 25; 29(2); 31; 33(2); 34; 17:2; 3(2); 4(4); 5(3); 6(3); 8(3); 9(2); 10(3); 11; 12; 13(3); 14(4); 15; 18:2; 3(4); 6(2); 7(2); 8; 9(3); 10; 11; 12(2); 13(2); 14; 15; 16; 17(2); 21(2); 24; 25; 26(2); 27; 29; 30; 19:2(2); 3; 5(2); 8; 9(3); 10; 12; 13; 15; 16; 17; 18; 19; 21(2); 22; 23; 27(2); 29; 32; 34; 35; 36(2); 20:2(6); 3; 4(2); 11; 12; 13; 17; 18(2); 19(3); 23; 25; 21:1; 5; 6(3); 8; 9; 12(4); 14; 17(2); 21(3); 22; 24; 22:2(2); 3(2); 4(3); 12; 15(2); 16; 18(6); 19; 21; 22; 24; 25(2); 29(2); 30; 32; 33(2); 23:2(2); 3(2); 4; 5; 6(2); 10(3); 12; 13(4); 15; 17(3); 18; 19(3); 20; 22(2); 24(4); 27(2); 28; 31; 32(2); 34(3); 37; 38; 39(3); 40(4); 43(3); 44(2); 24:2(2); 3(3); 4; 5; 8; 9; 10(3); 11(4); 12; 15; 16(2); 19; 20; 23(2); 25:2; 4; 5(4); 6; 8(3); 9(3); 10(2); 11(2); 13(2); 15(3); 16(4); 22; 24(2); 25(2); 28(2); 30; 31(2); 32(2); 33(3); 34(2); 35; 38(3); 39; 40; 41; 42(2); 45; 46; 47(2); 48; 49; 50(4); 51; 52(2); 54; 55(3); 26:4; 5(2); 6; 8(2); 10; 13(3); 16; 19; 20; 22; 25(2); 26; 29(2); 30; 31; 36(3); 38; 39; 40; 41; 44; 45(4); 46(2); 27:2; 3(3); 6(2); 8; 15(2); 16(4); 17; 18; 19(2); 21; 22; 23(2); 24; 25; 26; 28(2); 30(5); 31; 32(2); 34; **Num** 1:1(5); 2(4); 4; 5(2); 6; 7; 8; 9; 10(3); 11; 12; 13; 14; 15; 16(2); 18(2); 19; 20(2); 21(2); 22(3); 23(2); 24(2); 25(2); 26(2); 27(2); 28(2); 29(2); 30(2); 31(2); 32(3); 33(2); 34(2); 35(2); 36(2); 37(2); 38(2); 39(2); 40(2); 41(2); 42(2); 43(2); 44; 45(2); 49(3); 50; 52; 53(5); 54; 2:2(4); 3(6); 5(4); 7(4); 9; 10(4); 12(4); 14(4); 16; 17(3); 18(4); 20(4); 22(4); 24; 25(4); 27(4); 29(4); 31; 32(3); 33; 34; 3:1; 2(2); 3(2); 4(2); 6; 7(3); 8(5); 9; 12(3); 13; 14; 15; 16; 17; 18(2); 19; 20(2); 21(3); 22(2); 23; 24(3); 25(5); 26(2); 27(5); 28(2); 29(3); 30(4); 31; 32(4); 33(2); 34; 35(5); 36(3); 37; 38(4); 39(2); 40(3); 41(6); 42; 43(3); 45(4); 46(5); 47(3); 48; 50(3); 51; 4:2(3); 3; 4(3); 5; 6(2); 7; 8; 9; 10; 11; 12(2); 14(2); 15(4); 16(4); 18(2); 19; 22(2); 23; 24(2); 25(5); 26(3); 27(2); 28(6); 29; 30(2); 31(2); 33(6); 34(2); 35; 37(5); 38(2); 39; 41(6); 42(3); 43; 45(5); 46(2); 47(3); 49(2); 5:2(2); 3; 4(2); 6; 7; 8; 9(3); 12; 13; 14(4); 15(3); 17(2); 18; 21; 25; 26; 29; 30(2); 6:2(2); 4; 5(4); 8; 9; 10(2); 12; 13(4); 15(2); 17(2); 18(3); 19(2); 20(2); 21(2); 23; 27; 7:2(3); 3; 5(2); 7; 8(3); 9(2); 11; 12(2); 13(5); 14(2); 16; 17(3); 18(2); 19(5); 20(2); 22; 23(3); 24(3); 25(5); 26(2); 28;

29(3); 30(3); 31(5); 32(2); 34; 35(3); 36(3); 37(5); 38(2); 40; 41(3); 42(3); 43(5); 44(2); 46; 47(3); 48(3); 49(5); 50(2); 52; 53(3); 54(3); 55(5); 56(2); 58; 59(3); 60(3); 61(5); 62(2); 64; 65(3); 66(3); 67(5); 68(2); 70; 71(3); 72(3); 73(5); 74(2); 76; 77(3); 78(3); 79(5); 80(2); 82; 83(3); 84; 85(2); 86(3); 87; 88; 89(3); 8:2; 3; 4; 6; 7; 8; 9(3); 10; 11(2); 12; 14; 15; 16(4); 17(2); 18(3); 19(6); 20(3); 22; 24(2); 25; 26; 9:1(4); 2; 3; 4; 5(3); 7(2); 10(3); 11; 12(3); 13; 14(2); 15(2); 16; 17(2); 18(3); 19(2); 20(2); 22; 23(5); 10:2(2); 3(3); 4(2); 8; 10(3); 11(2); 12(3); 13(2); 14(4); 15(4); 16(4); 17(2); 18(3); 19(4); 20(4); 22(4); 23(4); 24(4); 25(5); 26(4); 27(4); 28(3); 29(2); 33(4); 34; 36; 11:1(2); 3(2); 4; 7; 8(2); 10(2); 11; 16(4); 17(2); 18; 20(2); 22; 24(3); 25; 26(2); 28(2); 30; 31; 33; 34; 12:1; 3; 4; 5(2); 8; 9; 12; 14; 15; 16; 13:2(3); 3(5); 4(2); 5(2); 6(2); 7(2); 8(2); 9(2); 10(2); 11(3); 12(2); 13(2); 14(2); 15(2); 16(2); 17; 20(4); 21(2); 22; 23(4); 24(3); 26(4); 28; 29(2); 32(3); 33; 14:2(2); 5(3); 6(2); 7(2); 9; 10(3); 12; 14(3); 15; 17; 18; 19(2); 21; 23(2); 25; 27; 29(2); 30(2); 33; 34; 36; 38(3); 39; 40; 41; 44(2); 15:2; 4(5); 5(2); 6(4); 7(2); 9(4); 10; 15; 18; 19(2); 20(3); 21(2); 23; 24(2); 25(2); 26(2); 29; 31; 32; 38(3); 39; 41(2); 16:1(6); 2(5); 3(2); 7; 8; 9(4); 10; 12; 13; 14(2); 15; 17; 18(2); 19(3); 22(2); 24; 25; 26(2); 27(2); 28; 29; 37(2); 38(2); 40(2); 41(3); 42(2); 43; 47; 50(2); 17:2; 3(2); 4; 5(4); 6(3); 7; 8(4); 9; 12; 13; 18:2(4); 3(2); 4(3); 5(3); 6(3); 8(3); 9(2); 11(3); 12(2); 15(3); 16(3); 17(3); 19(3); 20; 21(3); 22(2); 23(3); 24(3); 26(3); 27(2); 28; 29(3); 30(3); 31; 32(4); 19:2(2); 4(4); 6; 9(4); 10(2); 11; 13(3); 16; 17(2); 20(2); 21(2); 20:1(2); 4; 5(2); 6(4); 8; 10; 12(2); 13(2); 14; 16(2); 19(2); 22; 23(2); 24(2); 26; 27; 28(2); 29; 21:1(2); 3(2); 4(3); 5; 6(2); 10; 11; 12; 13(3); 14(3); 15(3); 17; 20(2); 21; 24(5); 25; 26(3); 27; 28(4); 29(2); 31; 33; 34; 35; 22:1(3); 2; 3(3); 4(4); 5(4); 6; 7(3); 8; 10(2); 11(2); 13; 14; 16; 18(3); 21; 22; 23(2); 24; 25; 26; 27; 28; 31; 32; 34; 35(2); 36(2); 41(2); 23:6; 7(2); 9; 10(3); 13; 14(2); 17; 18; 19; 21; 22; 23(2); 24; 28; 24:2; 3(3); 4(3); 8; 13(3); 15(3); 16(4); 17(4); 19(2); 24; 25:1; 2; 3(2); 4(2); 5(3); 6(8); 7(2); 8(4); 11(4); 12; 13(2); 14(3); 15(4); 18(6); 26:1; 2(3); 3; 4(4); 5(6); 6(4); 7(2); 8; 9(3); 11; 12(7); 13(4); 14; 15(7); 16(4); 17(4); 18(3); 19(2); 20(7); 21(5); 22(2); 23(5); 24(4); 25(2); 26(7); 27(2); 28; 29(5); 30(5); 31(4); 32(4); 33(3); 34(2); 35(7); 36(3); 37(4); 38(7); 39(4); 40(5); 41(2); 42(4); 43(2); 44(7); 45(6); 46(2); 47(3); 48(5); 49(4); 50(2); 51(2); 53; 54; 55(2); 57(7); 58(6); 59(2); 62(3); 63(2); 64(3); 65(4); 27:1(8); 2(2); 3; 4; 7(3); 8; 11(2); 12; 14(4); 16(2); 17; 18; 20(3); 21(2); 23; 28:2; 5(4); 7; 9(2); 11; 12(4); 13(3); 14(4); 15; 16(2); 17; 20(2); 21(2); 23; 24; 26(2); 28(2); 29; 30; 29:1(2); 3; 4; 5; 7; 9(2); 10; 11; 12; 14(4); 15; 16; 19; 25; 40; 30:1(2); 2; 5; 9; 31:2; 3; 4(2); 5; 6; 8(4); 9(2); 11; 12(3); 13; 14; 16(4); 20(3); 21(2); 23; 26(2); 28(3); 30(4); 32; 35; 37; 38; 39; 40; 42; 47(4); 48(3); 49(3); 50(2); 52(3); 53; 54(4); 32:1(5); 2(3); 4; 6(2); 7(2); 9(3); 11(2); 12(2); 13; 14(2); 17(3); 18(2); 19(2); 24; 25(2); 26; 28(4); 29(3); 30; 31(2); 32(3); 33(9); 34; 37; 39(2); 40; 41; 33:1(5); 2(2); 3(3); 5; 6; 7; 8(2); 9; 11; 12; 15; 16; 36; 37(2); 38(5); 40(5); 44; 47; 48(2); 49; 50; 51(2); 52; 53; 54; 55; 34:2(3); 3(3); 4(3); 5; 8(2); 11(3); 13; 14(7); 15; 17(2); 18; 19(3); 20(3); 21(2); 22(3); 23(4); 24(3); 25(3); 26(3); 27(3); 28(3); 29(2); 35:1; 2(2); 4(2); 6; 8(3); 10(2); 11; 12; 13(2); 14(3); 15; 19; 20; 21; 24; 25(4); 26(2); 27(5); 28(4); 29; 30; 31(2); 32(2); 33; 34(2); 36:1(10); 2(2); 3(7); 4(5); 5(4); 6(2); 7(6); 8(7); 9(2); 10; 11(2); 12(4); 13(3); **Deut** 1:1; 2; 3(2); 4(2); 5(2); 7(2); 10; 11; 15(5); 19; 20; 21; 22(3); 23; 24; 25(2); 26; 27(3); 28; 29; 34; 35(3); 36; 38; 39; 40; 41(2); 43; 2:1(2); 4(3); 5; 7; 8(4); 9(2); 12(2); 13(2); 14(4); 15(2); 16; 18; 19(5); 20; 22; 24; 25(3); 26(3); 29; 30; 34; 35; 36; 37(3); 3:1; 2; 3; 4(2); 6(2); 7; 8(3); 10(3); 11(5); 12; 13(5); 14(3); 16(3); 17(3); 18(2); 20; 26(2); 27; 4:1; 2; 3; 4; 6; 9; 11(2); 12(3); 13; 15(2); 16(2); 17(2); 18(2); 19; 20(2); 23(2); 25(2); 28; 31; 32; 33(3); 34; 36(3); 37; 41(2); 42; 44; 45(2); 46(5); 47(6); 48; 49(3); 5:3; 4; 5(2); 6(4); 8; 9(2); 11; 14(2); 15; 22(2); 23(2); 24; 25; 26(3); 28(3); 6:2; 3; 7; 9; 10; 11; 12(3); 14; 15(2); 17; 18(2); 20; 21(2); 23; 7:4; 6; 7; 8(3); 13(5); 15(2); 18; 19; 21; 22; 25; 8:1; 3; 6; 7(4); 8(3); 9; 14(3); 15; 17; 20; 9:2(3); 4(3); 5(4); 6; 7; 9(2); 10(4); 11(3); 12; 14; 15; 17; 18(2); 19; 23; 26; 27; 10:1(2); 3(2); 4(2); 6(2); 7(2); 8(3); 12; 13; 16; 17(2); 19; 22; 11:2; 3(2); 4(2); 6(3); 7; 10; 11(2); 12(3); 18; 19; 20; 21(3); 24; 25(2); 27; 28; 30(3); 12:1; 3; 5; 6(2); 11; 14; 15(3); 17(8); 25; 27(3); 28; 13:1; 2; 3(2); 5(4); 6(2); 7(4); 9; 10(3); 12; 13; 15(3); 16; 17(2); 18(2); 14:1(2); 2; 7; 9; 21; 22; 23(3); 28(3); 29; 15:1(2); 2(2); 3; 5; 7(2); 9; 15; 19(2); 16:1(3); 3(6); 4; 5; 6(2); 10(2); 13; 15; 16(3); 17; 19(2); 17:2(2); 3(2); 4; 6(3); 7(2); 8(2); 9(2); 11; 18(2); 19(2); 20; 18:1(2); 4(3); 5(2); 6(2); 7; 8; 9; 12; 16(3); 19; 20; 22(2); 19:2; 3; 4; 5; 6(2); 10(2); 11; 12(3); 13; 14; 15; 16; 20:1(2); 2; 3(2); 6(2); 8; 9; 10; 11; 13; 15(2); 16(2); 19(2); 21:3; 4; 5(2); 6; 8; 9(2); 13; 15; 16(2); 17(4); 18(2); 19(3); 20(2); 21; 22; 23; 22:3; 8; 9(3); 11; 12; 15(3); 17(2); 18; 19(3); 20; 21(2); 22; 24; 26; 29; 23:1; 2(4); 3(3); 4(3); 8(2); 14; 16; 17(4); 18(4); 21; 24; 24:1(2); 3(2); 7(3); 8; 9; 14(2); 19; 21; 22; 25:2; 5(3); 6(2); 7; 8; 9; 10; 11(2); 17; 19; 26:2(3); 4(2); 7; 8; 10; 12(2); 14(4); 27:1; 3(2); 5; 6; 8; 9; 10; 14; 15(2); 21; 22(2); 26; 28:1(2); 2; 4(5); 9; 10(3); 11(5); 12; 13; 14; 15; 18(4); 20(2); 24; 25; 26(2); 27; 28; 31; 33(2); 34; 35(2); 39; 42; 45; 47(2); 48(2); 49; 50; 51(4); 53(2); 54(2); 55(2); 56(3); 57; 58; 60(2); 61; 62(2); 64; 65(2); 66; 67(2); 68; 29:1(3); 2; 7(2); 8; 9; 10(2); 16; 18; 19(2); 20; 21(3); 22(2); 23; 24; 25(4); 27; 29; 30:4; 6; 8; 9(4); 10(2); 20; 31:4; 6(2); 7(2); 9(4); 10(3); 12; 14(2); 15(3); 16(2); 18; 19(2); 20; 21(3); 22; 23(4); 24; 25(2); 26(3); 28; 29(2); 30(3); 32:1; 3; 4; 5; 7(2); 8(4); 9; 10; 13(2); 14(5); 15; 18; 19(2); 22; 24(3); 25; 26; 27; 28; 32(5); 33(2); 35; 38(2); 42(3); 43; 44(3); 46; 49(4); 51(5); 52; 33:1(2); 2; 4(2); 5(2); 7(2); 8(2); 9; 11(3); 12(2); 13(3); 14(2); 15(2); 16(5); 17(4); 18; 19(4); 20(2); 21(2); 22; 23(3); 24(2); 26; 28(2); 29(2); 34:1(3); 2(3); 3(3); 4; 5(3); 6; 8(3); 9(4); 11; 12; **Josh** 1:1(3); 2; 3; 4(2); 5; 6; 8; 9; 10; 12; 13; 14(2); 15(3); 18; 2:1(2); 2(2); 3; 6; 9(3); 10(4); 11; 14(2); 17(2); 18; 19; 20; 23; 24(2); 3:1; 3(2); 6(2); 7; 8(3); 9(2); 11(3); 12; 13(6); 14; 15(3); 16; 17(3); 4:3(2); 4; 5(6); 7(5); 8(5); 9(3); 10; 11(2); 12(4); 13; 14(2); 16; 18(5); 19(2); 20; 21; 23; 24(2); 5:1(7); 2; 3(2); 4(3); 5; 6(4); 9(2); 10(3); 11(2); 12(4); 14(2); 15; 6:1(2); 2; 3; 4; 5(2); 6(4); 7; 8(3); 10; 11; 12; 13(3); 15; 18(2); 19(2); 20; 21; 23; 24(3); 7:1(9); 2; 3; 4; 5(2); 6(2); 7(2); 9; 11; 12; 13; 15; 16; 17(3); 18(5); 19; 20; 21(3); 23(2); 24(3); 26(4); 8:1(2); 3(2); 4; 8; 9; 10; 11(2); 12; 13(3); 14(2); 15; 19; 20(2); 21(2); 22(3); 23; 24(4); 25; 26; 27(2); 29(4); 30; 31(5); 32(4); 33(9); 34(2); 35(2); 9:1(2); 3; 5; 6; 7; 9(3); 10(3); 11; 12; 13; 14(3); 15; 16; 17; 18(3); 19; 20; 23(2); 24(2); 26(3); 27; 10:1(2); 2; 3(5); 4; 5(6); 6(2); 7(2); 8; 11(2); 12(3); 13(2); 14; 18; 20(2); 21(2); 22; 23(5); 24(4); 25; 27(2); 28(3); 30(3); 32(2); 33; 35; 37; 39; 40; 41; 42; 11:1(4); 2(2); 3; 5; 6(2); 7(2); 8(3); 10; 11; 12(3); 13; 14(3); 15; 16(2); 17; 19(2); 20; 21(2); 22(3); 12:1(4); 2(5); 3(3); 4(3); 5(4); 6(4); 7(5); 9(2); 10(2); 11(2); 12(2); 13(2); 14(2); 15(2); 16(2); 17(2); 18(2); 19(2); 20(2); 21(2); 22(2); 23(4); 24; 13:2(2); 3(3); 4(2); 5; 6(2); 7; 8; 9(3); 10(4); 11; 12(3); 13; 14(3); 15(2); 16(2); 19; 20; 21(5); 22(2); 23(5); 24(2); 25(2); 26; 27(6); 28(2); 29(3); 30(3); 31(7); 32(2); 33(2); 14:1(7); 2; 3(2); 4; 5; 6(3); 7; 8; 12; 13; 14(3); 15; 15:1(5); 2; 3(3); 4; 5(3); 6(3); 7(4); 8(7); 9(4); 10; 11; 12(3); 13(4); 14(2); 15(2); 17(2); 19; 20(3); 21(4); 47; 62; 63(3); 16:1(2); 2; 3(2); 4; 5(3); 6(2); 8(3); 9(3); 17:1(5); 2(10); 3(5); 4(2); 5(2); 6(3); 7(3); 8(3); 9(4); 11(4); 12(2); 13; 14; 15(2); 16(6); 17; 18:1(3); 2; 3(2); 5; 7(3); 10; 11(6); 12(2); 13(2); 14(2); 15(3); 16(6); 17(3); 18; 19(2); 20(2); 21(3); 28(2); 19:1(4); 8(4); 9(8); 10(2); 11; 12; 13; 14(2); 16(2); 17; 23(3); 24(2); 27; 29(2); 31(3); 32(2); 39(3); 40(2); 41; 47(6); 48(3); 49(3); 50(2); 51(8); 20:2(3); 3; 4(6); 5; 6; 7(3); 8(4); 9(3); 21:1(7); 2; 3(2); 4(6); 5(6); 6(6); 7(4); 8(2); 9(4); 10(5); 11(2); 12(2); 13(2); 17; 19(2); 20(6); 21(2); 23; 25; 26(3); 27(5); 28; 30; 32(2); 33; 34(4); 36; 38(2); 40(3); 41(3); 42; 43(2); 44; 45(2); 22:1; 2; 3(2); 4(3); 5; 7(3); 8; 9(9); 10(5); 11(8); 12(4); 13(6); 14(5); 15(4); 16(2); 17(2); 18; 19(4); 20(2); 21(5); 22(2); 24; 25(2); 27; 28(2); 29; 30(6); 31(7); 32(6); 33(4); 34(2); 23:3; 5; 6(2); 7(2); 10; 12; 14(3); 16(2); 24:1(2); 2(4); 3(2); 4; 6; 8(2); 9(3); 10; 11; 12; 13; 14; 15(2); 17(3); 23; 26(3); 27; 29(2); 30(3); 31(3); 32(9); 33(2); **Judg** 1:1(2); 8(2); 9; 10; 11(2); 13; 15; 16(4); 17; 19(2); 20; 21(2); 22; 23(2); 24; 25; 26; 27(4); 30(2); 31(3); 32; 33(4); 34; 35(2); 36(2); 2:1(2); 2; 4(2); 5; 6; 7(3); 8(2); 9(3); 11(2); 12(4); 14(3); 15; 16(2); 17; 18(4); 20; 21; 22; 23; 3:1; 2(2); 3(2); 4(2); 5; 7(2); 8(4); 9(3); 10(2); 11; 12(4); 13(3); 14(2); 15(4); 17; 22; 23; 24; 25; 27(2); 28; 29(2); 30; 31(2); 4:1(2); 2(3); 3(3); 4; 5(3); 6(6); 7; 9; 11(3); 12; 13; 15; 16(2); 17(4); 19; 20(2); 23(3); 24(4); 5:1; 3; 4; 5; 6(3); 9; 11(3); 12; 15(3); 16(2); 18(2); 19(3); 21(2); 22; 23(3); 24; 28(2); 30(4); 6:1(3); 2(3); 3; 4; 6(2); 7(2); 8(4); 9(4); 10; 11; 12(3); 13; 14(2); 19; 20; 21(5); 22(2); 24; 25(2); 26(2); 27; 28(2); 29; 30(2); 33(2); 34; 37; 38(2); 7:1(4); 3(2); 4(2); 6(2); 8(2); 11; 12; 13(2); 14(3); 15(3); 17; 18(3); 19(2); 20(2); 22; 23; 24(2); 25(5); 8:1; 2(3); 3; 5(3); 6(2); 7; 8(2); 9; 10(3); 11(2); 12; 13(2); 14(3); 15(2); 16(3); 17(2); 18(2); 19; 22(2); 24(2); 26(3); 28(2); 29; 32(3); 33; 34(2); 35; 9:1(3); 2(4); 3(2); 4(2); 5(2); 6(2); 7(2); 15(2); 17(2); 18(2); 20(2); 21; 23(3); 24(3); 25(2); 26(2); 27; 28(4); 30(3); 31; 35; 36(2); 37; 39; 40; 43; 44(2); 46(4); 47(2); 49(3); 51(2); 52; 54; 55; 56; 57(4); 10:1(4); 4; 6(8); 7(4); 8(4); 9(2); 10; 11(2); 14; 15; 16; 17(2); 18(3); 11:1(2); 2; 3; 4; 5(3); 6; 7; 8(3); 9(2); 10; 11; 12(2); 13(4); 14(2); 15(3); 17(3); 18(7); 19(2); 21(4); 22(2); 23; 24; 25(2); 26; 27(2); 28(2); 29(4); 30; 31(3); 32; 33(2); 36(3); 39; 40(2); 12:1(2); 2(2); 3; 4(3); 5(2); 6; 7; 8; 12; 13; 15(3); 13:1(3); 2(2); 3; 5(2); 6(3); 7; 8; 9(2); 12; 13(2); 15; 16(2); 17; 18; 20(2); 21(2); 25; 14:1(2); 2(2); 3; 4; 5; 6; 8(3); 9(3); 12(3); 13; 14(2); 16; 17; 18; 19(3); 15:1; 4; 5; 6; 8(2); 10; 11(3); 12; 14; 15; 16(2); 18(3); 20; 16:2; 3(4); 4; 5(3); 8; 9(2); 13(2); 14; 18(2); 19; 22; 23; 24; 27(2); 29; 31; 17:1; 2; 3; 4(2); 5; 7(2); 8(3); 10(2); 11; 12; 18:1(2); 2(5); 3(2); 5; 6; 7; 10; 11(3); 12; 13(2); 14; 15(2); 16(4); 17(2); 19; 21; 22(3); 23; 25(2); 26; 27; 29(3); 30(6); 31; 19:1; 3(2); 5; 6; 8; 11; 12(3); 13; 15; 16(2); 17; 18(2); 19; 22(2); 23; 26; 27(2); 29(2); 30(2); 20:1(2); 2(4); 3(3); 4; 5(2); 6(3); 7(2); 8; 10(4); 11; 12(2); 13(3); 14(2); 15(2); 17(3); 18(5); 19; 20(2); 21(3); 22; 23(3); 24(2); 25(2); 26(2); 27(4); 28(3); 30(2); 31(4); 32(2); 33(2); 35; 36(2); 37; 38(2); 39(3); 40; 41(2); 42(3); 43; 44(2); 45(3); 46(2); 47(2); 48(3); 21:1(2); 3; 5(2); 6; 8; 9(2); 10(3); 12(2); 13(2); 14(2); 15; 16(2); 17; 18; 19(4); 20; 21(3); 22(2); 23; 24; **Ruth** 1:1(2); 2(5); 4(4); 6(2); 7; 9; 13; 19(2); 22(2); 2:1(4); 2; 3(3); 5; 6(2); 10; 11(2); 12; 13; 14(2); 17; 19; 20(3); 23(2); 3:7(2); 10; 11; 13; 15; 17; 4:1; 2(2); 3(2); 4(2); 5(3); 6; 9; 10(3); 11; 12(2); 15(2); 17(2); 18; **1 Sam** 1:1(7); 2(2); 3(3); 7; 9(2); 10; 11(3); 15; 16(2); 17(2); 20; 24(3); 27; 2:3; 4; 8(2); 9; 10(3); 12; 17(2); 22(2); 23; 25; 27(2); 28(5); 29(2); 30(2); 31; 33(3); 34; 36(4); 3:1; 3(3); 7; 11; 14(2); 15(2); 17; 19; 20; 21; 4:1; 2; 3(4); 4(6); 5(2); 6(4); 8; 9; 10; 11(2); 12; 13; 14(2); 17; 18(3); 19; 20; 21(2); 22; 5:1; 2(2); 3(2); 4(4); 5(2); 6(2); 7(3); 8(7); 9(2); 10(4); 11(4); 12; 6:1(2); 2; 3(2); 4(3); 5(3); 8(2); 11(2); 12(2); 13; 14(3); 15(3); 16; 18(6); 19(3); 20; 21(2); 7:1(4); 2; 3(2); 4; 6; 7(5); 8(2); 11(2); 13(3); 14; 15; 8:2(2); 4; 7; 8; 9; 10; 11; 12; 14; 15; 17; 18; 19; 21(2); 22; 9:1(6); 2(2); 3(2); 4(4); 5; 6; 7; 8(3); 9; 10; 12(2); 16(2); 17; 20; 21(6); 22; 23; 25; 26(3); 27(3); 10:1; 2; 3(3); 4; 5(2); 6; 8; 10(2); 11; 16; 18(5); 20(2); 21(3); 22; 23; 25; 11:1; 3(2); 4(2); 5(2); 6; 7(4); 8(2); 9(2); 10; 11(3); 15(2); 12:6; 7; 8; 9(6); 10; 11(2); 12; 14; 15(3); 17; 19; 13:2(4); 3(2); 4; 5; 6; 7(2); 13; 15; 16; 17(3); 18(2); 19; 21; 22(3); 23(2); 14:1; 2; 3(3); 4(2); 5; 6; 11(3); 12(2); 14; 16(2); 18(3); 19; 22(2); 24(2); 25; 27; 28; 29; 30(2); 34; 36; 37(2); 38; 41; 43; 45; 47(2); 48; 49(4); 50(5); 51(3); 52; 15:1(2); 2; 4; 5; 6(2); 7; 8(2); 9; 10; 13(2); 14(2); 15; 17(2); 19(2); 20(2); 21(2); 22(2); 23(2); 24; 26; 27; 28(2); 29; 30; 32(2); 34; 35; 16:4; 7; 10; 13(3); 14; 18(4); 20; 17:2(2); 4; 5(3); 7; 8(2); 10; 11; 12(3); 13(2); 17; 18(2); 19(2); 22; 23(2); 24; 25; 26; 28; 32; 33; 34; 36(2); 37(3); 38; 44(2); 45(4); 46(4); 50; 51; 52(4); 53; 54; 55; 57(2); 58; 18:1(2); 5(3); 6(3); 12; 15; 17; 21; 23; 24; 25(2); 27; 29; 30(2); 19:4; 6; 13; 16; 20(3); 23; 20:6; 8; 11; 12; 14; 15(3); 16(2); 19; 21; 23; 27(2); 28; 30(3); 31; 34; 39; 42; 21:3; 5; 7(3); 9(2); 10; 11(3); 12(2); 13; 15; 22:1; 3(2); 4; 5(2); 7(4); 8(3); 9(3); 10(2); 11; 12; 13(2); 15(3); 17(3); 19(3); 20(3); 22(2); 23:2; 3; 4; 5; 6; 10; 11(2); 12(2); 14; 15; 17; 18; 19(2); 20; 21; 23(2); 24(2); 25(2); 26(2); 28; 24:1; 2; 3; 4(3); 6; 8; 9; 11(2); 13; 14; 15; 20; 25:1; 3(5); 9; 10; 14; 18(5); 20; 21; 22(2); 24; 25; 28(2); 29(4); 31; 32; 34; 36; 39(3); 40; 41(2); 42(2); 43(2); 44; 26:1; 2(3); 3; 5(2); 6(2); 11; 12; 13; 14; 15; 16; 19(3); 20(2); 22; 24(2); 27:1(5); 2(2); 6; 7; 8(3); 10(3); 11; 28:2; 3; 5; 6; 7; 13; 17; 18; 19(3); 20(2); 22(2); 29:2; 3(4); 4(3); 5; 6; 7; 8; 9(2); 11; 30:5; 6(2); 8; 12(3); 13; 14(4); 15; 16(3); 17(2); 19; 22(2); 26(4); 27; 29(2); 31:1; 7(4); 9(2); 10(2); 11; 12(3); **2 Sam** 1:1(2); 3; 4; 11; 12(2); 13; 15; 18(3); 19; 20(3); 21(4); 22(4); 24(2); 25; 26; 27; 2:1(3); 2; 3; 4(3); 5(2); 7; 8(3); 10; 11; 12(3); 13(5); 15(3); 16; 17(2); 18(2); 21; 23(2); 24(2); 25(2); 30; 31(2); 3:1(3); 3(4); 4(2); 6(3); 7; 8(3); 10(2); 13; 14; 15; 17; 18(4); 19(3); 22; 23; 25; 26; 27; 28(3); 29(2); 32; 36; 37; 39; 4:2(7); 5(3); 8(4); 9; 12(2); 5:1; 3; 6; 7(2); 8; 9; 10; 11; 12; 14; 17; 18; 19; 20(2); 22; 23(2); 24(3); 6:1; 2(2); 3(4); 4(3); 5(3); 6(2); 7(2); 8(2); 9(2); 10(3); 11(2); 12(6); 13; 15(3); 16(2); 17(2); 18(2); 19(4); 20(5); 21(2); 22; 23(2); 7:2(2); 4; 6; 7(3); 8; 9; 10(2); 13; 14(3); 19(2); 26(2); 27(2); 29(2); 8:1; 3(2); 4; 5(3); 6; 7(2); 8(2); 9(2); 10(3); 12(4); 13; 16(2); 17(2); 18; 9:1(2); 2(2); 3(4); 4(2); 5(3); 6(2); 7; 11; 12(2); 10:1(2); 2(4); 3(2); 4; 6(5); 7(2); 8(3); 9; 10(3); 11; 12(2); 14(2); 16; 18(2); 19; 11:1(2); 2; 3(2); 8; 9(2); 11; 13; 14; 15; 17(4); 19; 21(2); 23; 24; 26; 12:3; 7(2); 8; 9(3); 10; 11; 14; 17; 18; 20; 25(2); 26(2); 28; 30(2); 31(2); 13:1(2); 3; 6; 11; 13; 16; 18; 19; 21; 29; 30; 32(2); 37(2); 14:1; 4; 7; 9; 11(2); 13; 15(2); 16(2); 17(2); 19(2); 20(3); 22; 25(2); 26(3); 27; 15:2; 3; 6(2); 10(2); 13(2); 14; 23; 24(3); 25(2); 27; 28; 29; 30(2); 31; 32; 34; 16:1(6); 3(2); 5(3); 6; 8(3); 9; 10; 15; 18; 19; 21; 22(2); 23(3); 17:4; 8(2); 9; 10; 12; 14(4); 15; 16; 18; 21; 22; 24; 25(5); 26; 27(4); 29; 18:1(2); 2(5); 3(2); 6(2); 7(3); 8; 9(2); 11; 12; 14; 17; 19(2); 22; 23; 27(3); 31; 32; 19:5(3); 6; 8; 9(4); 11(2); 13(2); 14(3); 16(2); 17(3); 18; 20(2); 21; 22; 24; 27; 29; 35; 37; 38; 40(2); 41(2); 42(3); 43(6); 20:1(2); 2(3); 3; 4; 5; 6; 7(2); 10; 11; 12; 13; 14; 15; 17; 19; 21(2); 22(2); 23(2); 24(2); 21:1(3); 2(6); 3; 5(2); 6(2); 7(4); 8(5); 9(3); 10(4); 11(2); 12(4); 13(3); 14(3); 16(3); 17(3); 18(2); 19(3); 20; 21; 22(2); 22:1(3); 3(2); 5(2); 6(2); 8; 11; 12; 13; 16(5); 17; 19; 21; 22; 31; 34; 35; 36; 41; 43; 44(2); 47; 51; 23:1(5); 2; 3(3); 4(2); 6; 7; 8; 9(3); 11(3); 12; 13(4); 14; 15(2); 16(2); 17(2); 18(3); 19; 20(4); 21; 22; 24(4); 26; 29(4); 30; 32(2); 33; 34(3); 36(2); 37(2); 24:1; 2(3); 3; 4(4); 5(3); 6; 7(2); 8; 9(3); 10; 11; 12; 13; 14(2); 15; 16(2); 18; 19; 22; 24; **1 Ki** 1:3; 5; 7; 8; 9(2); 11(2); 12; 19(2); 20(2); 25; 26; 27; 30; 32; 33; 36(2); 37; 38; 39; 41; 42; 44; 46; 47; 48; 50(3); 51(3); 52; 2:1; 2; 3(2); 4; 5(7); 7; 8; 10; 12; 13(2); 16; 20; 22; 24; 25(2); 26(2); 27(2); 28(3); 29(2); 30; 31; 32(6); 33(2); 34; 35(2); 39(4); 43; 45; 46(2); 3:1(3); 2; 3; 6; 7; 8; 9; 11; 15(2); 18; 20; 28(2); 4:2; 3(2); 4; 5(2); 6; 7; 8; 10; 11(2); 12(2); 13(3); 14; 15; 16; 17; 18; 19(6); 21(3); 22(2); 24(2); 25; 26; 29; 30(3); 31; 33(7); 34(4); 5:1(2); 3(3); 5; 7; 11(2); 12; 13; 14; 16; 17; 6:1(6); 3(5); 5(2); 6(2); 8; 9; 11; 13; 15(4); 16; 17; 18; 19(2); 20; 21(2); 23; 24(4); 25; 26; 27(4); 29(2); 30; 31(3); 32(2); 33(3); 34; 36(2); 37(3); 38; 7:2(3); 6(3); 7; 8; 9; 10; 12(5); 14(4); 15(3); 16(4); 17(2); 18; 19(2); 20; 21; 22(3); 23(2); 26; 27(2); 28; 29; 30(2); 32(2); 33(3); 34(2); 35(4); 36; 37(2); 38(2); 39(3); 40; 41(2); 42(2); 45(2); 46; 47; 48(3); 49(3); 50(5); 51(3); 8:1(7); 2(2); 3; 4(2); 5; 6(4); 7; 8(2); 9(4); 10(2); 11(3); 14(2); 15; 16(2); 17(3); 20(4); 21(3); 22(3); 23; 25(2); 26; 27; 28; 29; 30(2); 34; 36; 37; 38; 39(2); 41; 42; 43; 46; 47; 48; 51(2); 52(2); 53(2); 54; 55; 56; 59(3); 60; 63(3); 64(5); 65(2); 66; 9:1; 4; 5(2); 7; 9(2); 10(2); 11(2); 13(2); 14; 15(2); 16; 18; 19; 20(3); 21; 22(4); 23; 24; 26(3); 27; 28; 10:1(4); 4(2); 5(3); 7; 9; 10(3); 11(2); 12(2); 13; 14(2); 15(3); 16(2); 17(4); 18; 19(3); 20; 21(4); 22; 23; 24; 25; 29(3); 11:1(2); 2(2); 4; 5(2); 6; 7(4); 9; 12(3); 13(2); 14; 15; 17; 18; 19(3); 20(2); 21; 23(2); 24(2); 25(2); 26; 27; 28(3); 29; 30; 31(3); 32(4); 33(4); 34(3); 35; 39(2); 40(2); 41(4); 43; 12:2(2); 3; 4; 14; 15(2); 16; 17(2); 18; 19; 20(2); 21(4); 22(2); 23(4); 24(3); 25; 26; 27(4); 28(2); 31(3); 32(2); 33(2); 13:1(2); 2(3); 4(2); 5(2); 6(3); 7; 8; 9; 11; 12; 14(2); 17; 18; 20; 21(2); 22(2); 26(3); 29(2); 31; 32(2); 33(3); 34(3); 14:1; 2; 3(2); 4(2); 5; 6(2); 7; 8; 10(3); 11; 13(3); 14; 16(2); 17; 18; 19(5); 21(3); 22; 24(2); 25(2); 26(3); 27(3); 28; 29(5); 31; 15:1(2); 2; 3(2); 5(3); 6; 7(5); 8; 9(2); 10; 11; 13; 15; 16; 17(2); 18(7); 19(2); 20(3); 22(2); 23(6); 24; 25(3); 26(2); 27(3); 28(2); 29(2); 30(4); 31(5); 32; 33(3); 34(2); 16:1(2); 2(2); 3(4); 4; 5(5); 7(6); 8(3); 9(3); 10(2); 11(3); 12(2); 13(3); 14(5); 15(2); 16; 18; 19(3); 20(5); 21(3); 22; 23(2); 24(5); 25; 26(3); 27(5); 29(4); 30(2); 31(4); 32; 33(2); 34(3); 17:1(3); 2; 5; 8; 10; 11; 12(2); 14(3); 15; 16(3); 17; 18; 19; 22(2); 24(2); 18:1; 3; 4; 5; 9; 12; 13(2); 15; 17; 18; 19(2); 20; 22; 24(2); 25(2); 26; 29(2); 30; 31(4); 32(2); 36(3); 38; 40(2); 41(2); 42; 44; 46(3); 19:2(2); 6; 7; 8(2); 9; 10(2); 13; 14(2); 15; 16(3); 17(2); 19(2); 21; 20:1; 2; 4; 6; 7(2); 9; 10(2); 11; 13; 14; 15(2); 17(2); 19(2); 20; 21; 22(3); 23(3); 26; 27(3); 28(4); 29(2); 30; 31(3); 32; 33; 35(3); 36; 39(2); 40; 41(2); 42; 43; 21:1(2); 3; 4(2); 7; 11(2); 13; 15(2); 16(2); 17; 18(3); 19; 20; 22(5); 23; 24; 25; 26; 28; 29; 22:2(2); 3(4); 4; 5(2); 6(2); 7(2); 8(3); 9(2); 10(4); 11(2); 13(3); 15; 16; 18; 19(2); 22; 23(2); 24; 26(2); 27(2); 29(2); 30(2); 31(3); 32(2); 33(2); 34(4); 35; 38; 39(5); 41(3); 42; 43(2); 44; 45(5); 46(2); 47; 49; 50; 51(3); 52(5); 53; **2 Ki** 1:1; 2(3); 3(5); 6(2); 7; 9(3); 10(2); 11(2); 12(2); 13(5); 14; 15(2); 16(3); 17(4); 18(5); 2:3; 5; 6; 7(3); 8; 9; 11(3); 12(2); 13(2); 14(2); 15(2); 16; 19(2); 21; 22; 24(3); 3:1(3); 2(2); 3(2); 4(3); 5(2); 6; 7(2); 8(2); 9(3); 10(2); 11(7); 12(3); 13(5); 14(3); 15; 16; 18; 19(2); 20; 24; 25(3); 26(2); 4:1(3); 2; 7; 9; 13; 16; 17; 21(2); 22(3); 25(2); 27(2); 28; 29; 30; 31(2); 33; 34; 38(2); 39(2); 40; 42(3); 44; 5:1(5); 2; 3; 4; 5(5); 6(2); 7(2); 8(2); 9; 11; 12(2); 14(3); 15; 17; 18(3); 20(2); 22(5); 23(4); 27; 6:1; 6; 8; 9(2); 10(3); 11(4); 12(2); 15(2); 17(3); 18; 20; 21; 23(2); 24; 25(4); 26; 30; 31(2); 32(3); 7:1(4); 2(2); 3; 4; 5(2); 6(7); 8; 9; 10; 12(2); 13(4); 14; 15; 16(4); 17(2); 18(4); 19(2); 8:2(3); 3(2); 4(2); 6; 7(2); 8(2); 9(3); 11; 12; 16(6); 18(5); 19; 21; 23(5); 24; 25(5); 26(2); 27(6); 28(2); 29(4); 9:1(3); 2(2); 3; 4; 5(2); 6(2); 7(5); 8; 9(5);

10; 11; 13; 14(3); 15; 16; 17(2); 20(2); 21(3); 22; 25(2);
26(4); 27(2); 28; 29(2); 30; 31; 33; 35(2); 36(3); 37(2); 10:1;
3; 5(2); 6(2); 8(2); 10(3); 11(2); 12; 13(5); 14(2); 15; 17;
19(3); 21(3); 22(2); 23(5); 24(2); 25(4); 26(2); 27(2); 29(2);
30(2); 31(3); 32(2); 33; 34(5); 11:1; 2(3); 3; 4(4); 5; 6(2); 7(3);
9(2); 10(2); 11(2); 13(2); 14; 15(3); 16; 18(4); 19(6); 20;
12:1(2); 2; 4(3); 5; 6(2); 7(2); 8; 9(2); 10; 11(4); 12(2); 13(5);
14; 16; 17; 18(5); 19(5); 20; 21(3); 13:1(4); 2(3); 3(5); 4(2);
5(2); 6(2); 7(3); 8(5); 10(3); 11(3); 12(6); 13; 14(3); 16; 17(2);
18; 19; 20; 21(3); 22(2); 23; 24; 25(6); 14:1(5); 2; 3; 6(3); 7;
8(3); 9(2); 11(2); 13(6); 14(2); 15(6); 16; 17(5); 18(5); 20;
21(2); 23(5); 24(3); 25(6); 26; 27(3); 28(5); 29; 15:1(4); 2; 3;
5(2); 6(5); 7; 8(3); 9(3); 10(2); 11(5); 12(2); 13(3); 14(2);
15(5); 17(3); 18(3); 19(2); 20(3); 21(5); 23(3); 24(3); 25(4);
26(5); 27(3); 28(3); 29(4); 30(4); 31(5); 32(5); 33; 34; 35(2);
36(5); 37(2); 38; 16:1(4); 2; 3(4); 5(3); 6(2); 7(5); 8(3); 9(2);
10(2); 13; 14(3); 15(4); 17(2); 18(3); 19(5); 20; 17:1(4); 2(2);
3; 4(4); 5; 6(4); 7(5); 8(4); 9; 12; 13; 14; 16(2); 17; 18; 19(2);
20(2); 21(2); 22(2); 23; 24(5); 25(2); 26(6); 27(4); 28; 29;
30(3); 31; 32(2); 33; 34; 36; 39; 18:1(5); 2; 3; 4; 5(2); 7; 9(5);
10(4); 11(3); 12(2); 13(3); 14(6); 15(2); 16(4); 17; 18(2); 19;
20; 21(2); 23; 24(2); 26(2); 28(2); 30(2); 31(4); 32(3); 33(4);
34(2); 35; 37(3); 19:1; 2(2); 3; 4(2); 5; 6(3); 8; 9; 10(3); 11;
12(2); 13(4); 14(2); 15(3); 16; 17; 18; 19; 20(3); 21(2); 22;
23(4); 24(2); 25; 26; 29(2); 30(2); 31(3); 32; 35(2); 36; 37(2);
20:1; 4; 5(3); 6(3); 7; 8; 11; 12(2); 13; 16; 18(3); 19; 20(5);
21:2(3); 3(2); 4(2); 5(3); 6; 7(4); 8; 9; 11; 12(2); 13(3); 14(3);
15; 16; 17(5); 18(2); 19(2); 20; 22(2); 23; 24(2); 25(5); 26;
22:1(2); 2(2); 3(4); 4; 5(4); 7; 8(2); 9(2); 11(2); 12(3); 13(4);
14(4); 15; 16(2); 17; 18(3); 23:1; 2(6); 3; 4(5); 5(3); 6(2); 7(2);
8(5); 9(2); 10(2); 11(4); 12(4); 13(8); 14; 15; 16(3); 17(4); 18;
19(3); 20; 21; 22(4); 23; 24(3); 25; 26(2); 27; 28(5); 29(3);
30(2); 31(2); 32; 33(4); 34(2); 35(2); 36(2); 37; 24:1; 2(6);
3(3); 4; 5(5); 7(5); 8(2); 9; 10(2); 11; 12(4); 13(6); 14(2); 15;
16; 17; 18(2); 19; 20(3); 25:1(3); 2; 3(2); 4(3); 5(2); 6; 7(2);
8(6); 9(3); 10(3); 11(4); 12(3); 13(2); 15(2); 16(2); 17(4); 18;
19(8); 20(2); 21(2); 22(4); 23(6); 24(3); 25(3); 26(2); 27(6);
28; 29; 30; **1 Chr** 1:5; 6; 7; 8; 9(2); 17; 19; 23; 28; 29; 31;
32; 33(2); 34; 35; 36; 37; 38; 39; 40(2); 41(2); 42(2); 43(4);
44(2); 45(2); 46(3); 47; 48; 49; 50(3); 51; 54; 2:1; 3(4); 4; 5;
6(2); 7(2); 8; 9; 10(2); 16; 17; 18; 21(2); 22; 23(3); 24; 25(2);
26; 27(2); 28(2); 29(2); 30; 31(2); 32(2); 33(2); 42(5); 43; 44;
45(2); 47; 49(4); 50(4); 51(2); 52(3); 53; 54(2); 55(3); 3:1;
2(4); 5; 9(2); 15; 16; 17; 19(2); 21(5); 22(2); 23; 24; 4:1; 2(2);
3(3); 4(5); 5; 6; 7; 8(2); 10; 11(2); 12(2); 13(2); 14; 15(3); 16;
17(2); 18(5); 19(4); 20(2); 21(8); 22; 24; 26; 27(2); 31; 34;
35(3); 37(5); 39(2); 41(2); 42(4); 43; 5:1(4); 3(2); 4; 6(2); 7;
8(3); 9(3); 10(2); 11(2); 13; 14(8); 15(3); 16; 17(4); 18(2);
21(4); 23(2); 24(3); 25(3); 26(6); 6:1; 2; 3(2); 15; 16; 17(2);
18; 19(2); 20; 22; 25; 26; 28; 29; 31(2); 32(3); 33(4); 34(4);
35(4); 36(4); 37(4); 38(4); 39(2); 40(3); 41(3); 42(3); 43(3);
44(4); 45(3); 46(3); 47(4); 48(4); 49(4); 50; 54(3); 55; 56(2);
57(3); 60; 61(4); 62(5); 63(4); 64; 65(6); 66(4); 67(3); 70(4);
71(3); 72; 74; 76; 77(3); 78(3); 80; 7:1; 2(5); 3(3); 5(2); 6;
7(3); 8(2); 9(2); 10(2); 11(3); 12(2); 13(2); 14(3); 15(2); 16(2);
17(4); 19; 20; 21; 29(4); 30; 31(2); 33(2); 34; 35; 36; 38; 39;
40(3); 8:3; 6(4); 8; 10; 12; 13(4); 16; 18; 21; 25; 27; 28; 29;
34; 35; 38; 39; 40(3); 9:1(3); 3(5); 4(7); 5; 6(2); 7(5); 8(6); 9;
10; 11(6); 12(8); 13(4); 14(6); 15(3); 16(6); 18(2); 19(8); 20;
21(4); 23(4); 26(2); 27(2); 28(2); 29(2); 30(3); 31(2); 32(4);
33(2); 34(2); 35; 40; 41; 44; 10:1; 7; 9(2); 10(2); 12(2); 13;
14(2); 11:3(2); 4; 5(3); 6; 7; 8; 9; 10(2); 11(3); 12(2); 13(2);
14; 15(4); 16; 17(2); 18(2); 19(2); 20(2); 21; 22(4); 23(2); 24;
26(3); 28; 30; 31(4); 32(2); 34(2); 35(2); 37; 38(2); 39(2); 41;
42(2); 43; 44; 45; 46; 12:1; 2; 3(2); 7(2); 8(2); 14(2); 16(2);
17; 18(3); 19; 20(2); 21(2); 22; 23(3); 24(2); 25(3); 26(2); 27;
29(5); 30(3); 31(2); 32(3); 33(2); 34; 35; 36; 37(5); 38(3);
40(3); 13:1; 2(3); 3(2); 4; 5(2); 6; 7(2); 10; 11; 12(2); 13(2);
14(3); 14:1; 2; 4; 8; 9; 10; 11(2); 14(2); 15(3); 16; 17(2);
15:1(2); 2(2); 3; 4; 5(3); 6(3); 7(3); 8(3); 9(3); 10(3); 12(4);
14(2); 15(3); 16(2); 17(6); 18; 19; 22(2); 24; 25(4); 26(2); 27;
28(3); 29(3); 16:1(2); 2; 3(4); 4(3); 6(2); 7; 9; 10; 12; 13(2);
18(2); 23; 26; 28; 29; 33; 35; 36; 37(2); 38; 39; 40(2); 42(2);
17:1(3); 3; 6(3); 7; 8; 9(2); 11; 17(3); 18; 24(3); 27; 18:1; 3;
4; 5(3); 6; 7(2); 8(3); 9(3); 10(2); 11; 12(2); 15(2); 16(2); 17;
19:1(2); 2(3); 3(2); 6(3); 7(2); 8(2); 9(2); 10; 11(3); 12; 13(2);
15; 16; 18(2); 19(2); 20:1(3); 2(2); 3(2); 4(2); 5(3); 6; 7; 8(2);
21:2(2); 3; 5(2); 8; 10; 12(5); 13(2); 14; 15(3); 16; 18(2);
19(2); 22; 25; 26; 28; 29(2); 30(4); 22:1(2); 2(2); 3(2); 6; 7;
8; 9; 10; 11; 12; 13; 14(3); 15(2); 16; 17; 18; 19(5); 23:1; 2;
3(2); 4(3); 6; 7; 8; 9(3); 10(2); 12; 13; 14(3); 15; 16(2); 17(3);
18(2); 19(2); 20(2); 21(2); 22; 23; 24(6); 25; 26; 27; 28(7);
29; 31; 32(7); 24:1(3); 3(5); 4(8); 5(5); 6(5); 19(4); 20(6);
21(2); 22(3); 23(2); 24(4); 25(3); 26(2); 27; 28; 29(2); 30(2);
31(4); 25:1(6); 2(5); 3(3); 4(2); 5(2); 6(5); 7(2); 26:1(5); 2; 4;
6; 7; 8(3); 10(2); 11; 12(2); 19(3); 20(4); 21(5); 22(3); 23;
24(3); 26(3); 27(2); 28(4); 29; 30(5); 31(5); 32(3); 27:1(5); 2;
3(4); 4(2); 5(2); 7; 9; 10(2); 11; 12; 13; 14(2); 15; 16(3); 17;
18(2); 19(2); 20(4); 21(3); 22(3); 23(2); 24(4); 25(2); 26(2);
27(2); 28; 29; 32; 34(2); 28:1(6); 2(4); 3; 4(6); 5(3); 8(4); 9(2);
11; 12(8); 13(6); 14(4); 15(4); 16(2); 17; 18(4); 19; 20(3);
21(5); 29:2(8); 3(3); 4(5); 5(4); 6(5); 7(6); 8(3); 10; 14; 17;
18(4); 20; 22; 23(2); 24; 25; 26; 28; 29(4); 30; **2 Chr** 1:1;
2(3); 3(2); 4; 5(3); 6; 9; 10; 11; 12; 13; 17(3); 2:1; 3; 4(2); 6;
10(4); 11; 12; 14(5); 15; 17; 18(2); 3:1(2); 2(2); 3; 4(2); 8(2);
9(2); 11(4); 12(3); 13; 14; 15(3); 16(3); 17(2); 4:2(2); 3; 5; 7;
8; 9; 11; 12(2); 13; 16(2); 17; 18; 19(2); 20(2); 21(2); 22(4);
5:1(3); 2(7); 3; 4; 5; 6; 7(4); 8; 9(3); 10(2); 11; 12(2); 13(2);
14(3); 6:3(2); 4; 5(3); 7(3); 10(4); 11(2); 12(3); 13(2); 14;
16(2); 17; 18; 19; 21(2); 25; 27; 28; 30(2); 32(2); 33; 37; 38;
41; 42(2); 7:1; 2(2); 3(2); 5(2); 6(2); 7(4); 8(2); 9; 10(2); 11(2);
12; 18; 20; 22(3); 8:1(2); 2; 6(2); 7(2); 8; 9(4); 10(2); 11(5);
12; 13(4); 14(4); 15; 16(5); 17; 18(3); 9:1(3); 3(2); 4(3); 6(3);
9(2); 10(2); 11(3); 12; 13(2); 14(2); 15(2); 16(4); 17; 18(3);
19; 20(4); 21; 22; 23(2); 24; 26(2); 29(6); 31; 10:2(2); 4; 13;
14; 15(3); 16; 17(2); 18(2); 19; 11:1; 2(2); 3(2); 4; 11; 16(3);
17(3); 18(5); 20; 21; 22; 23(2); 12:1; 2(2); 3; 4; 5(3); 6; 7(2);
8(2); 9(4); 10(3); 11; 12; 13(2); 15(3); 16; 13:1; 2(2); 3(2); 4;
5(2); 6(3); 7; 8(3); 9(4); 10; 11(2); 12(2); 13; 15(2); 16; 17;
18(3); 20; 22(3); 14:1; 2; 3; 4; 5; 8(2); 9; 10; 14; 15:1(2); 4;
5; 8(5); 10(2); 12; 13; 16(2); 17; 18; 19(2); 16:1(4); 2(4); 3;
4(3); 6; 7(4); 9(2); 10(2); 11(3); 12; 13; 14(2); 17:2(3); 3; 4(2);
6; 7(2); 9(3); 10(2); 11; 13(3); 14(3); 16(2); 17(2); 18:3(2);
4(2); 5; 6(2); 7(3); 8(3); 9(4); 10(2); 12(3); 15; 17; 18(2); 19;
21; 22(2); 23; 25(2); 26(2); 28(2); 29(2); 30(3); 31(2); 32(2);
33(4); 34(2); 19:1; 2(2); 4(2); 5; 7(2); 8(4); 9; 10; 11(4);
20:1(2); 4; 5(2); 6(2); 7(2); 10(3); 11; 14(8); 15(3); 16(3); 17;
18; 19(5); 20(2); 21; 22; 23(4); 25; 26(3); 27(2); 28; 29(3);
30; 31; 32(2); 33; 34(6); 35(2); 37(2); 21:1; 2(3); 3; 4(3); 6(5);
7(2); 9; 10; 11(2); 12(4); 13(6); 15(2); 16; 17; 19(3); 20(2);
22:1(3); 2; 3(2); 4(3); 5(3); 6(4); 7(2); 8(3); 9(2); 10(3); 11(5);
12; 23:1(6); 2(2); 3(3); 4(2); 5(3); 6(3); 9(2); 10(2); 12(2); 13;
14(2); 15(2); 17(2); 18(6); 19(2); 20(5); 21; 24:1; 2(2); 4; 5(2);
6(5); 7(4); 8(2); 9; 11; 12(5); 13; 14(5); 15; 16; 17(2); 18(3);
20(3); 21(3); 23(4); 24(3); 25(5); 26(2); 27(4); 25:1; 2; 4; 5(2);
6(2); 7(4); 9(3); 11(3); 12(3); 13(2); 14(3); 15(2); 17(4); 18(2);
20(2); 21(2); 23(6); 24(2); 25(5); 26(4); 28; 26:1(2); 3; 4; 5(2);
6(3); 8; 9; 11(3); 12(3); 13; 16(2); 17; 18(2); 19; 20; 21(3);
22(3); 23; 27:1; 2(2); 3(3); 4; 5(6); 7(4); 9; 28:1; 2(2); 3(4);
5(5); 6(2); 7; 8(2); 9(2); 10; 11; 12(7); 15; 16; 18(3); 19(2);
20; 21(4); 22; 23(5); 24(7); 25(2); 26(3); 27(2); 29:1; 2; 3(3);
5(2); 6(2); 7(2); 8; 9; 10; 12(11); 13(4); 14(4); 15(3); 16(5);
17(5); 18(3); 19; 20(2); 21(2); 25(5); 26; 27(3); 30(2); 31(2);
32; 35(3); 30:1(2); 3; 5; 6(6); 7; 8; 10; 12(4); 13; 15(2); 16(3);
17(2); 18; 19(2); 21(2); 22(2); 24(2); 25(2); 26(3); 31:1(2);
2(3); 3(2); 4; 5(5); 6(4); 10(2); 11; 12; 13(4); 14(3); 15; 16(2);
18; 19(3); 21(2); 32:1(2); 4; 5; 6; 7; 8(3); 9(2); 10; 11(2);
13(4); 14; 15(2); 17(4); 18; 19(4); 20(2); 21(5); 22(4); 23(2);
26(4); 27; 28(2); 29; 30(3); 31(2); 32(6); 33(3); 33:2(3); 3;
4(2); 5(3); 6(3); 7(4); 8(2); 9(2); 11(3); 12; 14(4); 15(4); 16(2);
18(7); 19; 22; 25(2); 34:2(2); 3(3); 4(3); 5; 6; 7; 8(5); 9(3);
10(4); 11; 12(7); 13(3); 14(3); 15(2); 17(2); 19; 20(3); 21(4);
22(4); 23; 24; 25; 26(3); 29; 30(6); 31; 32(3); 33(2); 35:1;
2(2); 3(2); 4(3); 5(4); 6(2); 7; 8(2); 9; 12(3); 14(2); 15(2);
16(3); 17(2); 18(4); 19(2); 20; 21; 22(3); 24(3); 25; 26(3);
27(2); 36:1(2); 3(4); 4; 5; 6; 7(2); 8(4); 9; 10(2); 12(2); 13;
14(3); 15; 16(2); 17(2); 18(5); 19(2); 20(2); 21(2); 22(6);
23(4); **Ezra** 1:1(6); 2(3); 3(3); 4(2); 5(3); 6; 7(3); 8(3); 9; 10;
11; 2:1(3); 2(3); 3; 4; 5; 6(3); 7; 8; 9; 10; 11; 12; 13; 14; 15;
16(2); 17; 18; 19; 20; 21; 22; 23; 24; 25; 26; 27; 28; 29; 30;
31; 32; 33; 34; 35; 36(3); 37; 38; 39; 40(3); 41; 42(7); 43(3);
44(3); 45(3); 46(3); 47(3); 48(3); 49(3); 50(3); 51(3); 52(3);
53(3); 54(2); 55(4); 56(3); 57(5); 58; 59; 60(3); 61(7); 63; 65;
68(4); 69; 70; 3:1; 2(6); 3(2); 4; 5(2); 6(3); 7(2); 8(9); 9(3);
10(5); 11(2); 12(3); 13(4); 4:1(4); 2(3); 3(5); 4(2); 5(4); 6(3);
7(3); 9(3); 10(2); 11(2); 15(3); 17; 22; 23(2); 24(5); 5:1(3);
2(4); 3; 4; 5(2); 6(2); 8(2); 10; 11(3); 12(3); 13(3); 14(4); 15;
16(2); 17; 6:2; 3(3); 4(2); 5(3); 6; 7(5); 8(3); 9(3); 10(3); 11;
12; 13; 14(7); 15(4); 16(5); 17(4); 18(2); 19(2); 20(2); 21(4);
22(6); 7:1(5); 2(3); 3(3); 4(3); 5(4); 6(3); 7(3); 8; 9(3); 10;
11(4); 12(4); 13(2); 14; 15; 16(3); 17(2); 18(2); 19(3); 20;
21(4); 22(4); 23(4); 24(3); 25; 26(3); 27(2); 28(2); 8:1(3);
2(6); 3(4); 4(3); 5(2); 6(3); 7(3); 8(3); 9(3); 10(2); 11(3); 12(3);
13(2); 14(2); 15(2); 16; 17; 18(6); 19(2); 20(3); 21; 22(3);
24(3); 25; 26(2); 27; 28; 29(5); 30; 31(4); 33(6); 34; 35(2);
36; 9:1(3); 2(3); 3(2); 4(4); 7(3); 8; 9(3); 11(2); 12; 15(2);
10:1(2); 2(5); 3(3); 4; 5; 6(5); 7; 8(2); 9(6); 10; 11(2); 13(2);
14(3); 15(2); 16(4); 17; 18(4); 19; 20(2); 21(2); 22(2); 23;
24(2); 25(3); 26(2); 27(2); 28(2); 29(2); 30(2); 31(2); 33(2);
34(2); 43(2); 44; **Neh** 1:1(3); 2; 3; 4; 5; 6(4); 9(2); 11(3);
2:1(2); 2; 3; 4; 5; 7; 8(3); 9; 10(3); 13; 17; 18(3); 19; 20;
3:1(2); 2(2); 3; 4(5); 5; 6(2); 7(3); 8(3); 9(3); 10(3); 11(3);
12(3); 13(2); 14(3); 15(6); 16(6); 17(3); 18(4); 19(3); 20(3);
21(6); 22; 23(2); 24(2); 25(3); 26; 27; 28; 29(4); 30(4); 31(4);
4:2(2); 4; 7; 8; 9; 10; 13; 14(2); 15; 16(2); 18; 19; 20; 21;
23; 5:1; 3; 5(2); 7; 9(3); 11; 13; 14(2); 15(3); 18(3); 6:1; 2;
10(5); 14; 15; 16; 17(2); 18(4); 7:2(2); 3(3); 5(2); 6(3); 7(3);
8; 9; 10; 11(3); 12; 13; 14; 15; 16; 17; 18; 19; 20; 21(2); 22;
23; 24; 25; 26; 27; 28; 29; 30; 31; 32; 33; 34; 35; 36; 37;
38; 39(3); 40; 41; 42; 43(4); 44; 45(6); 46(3); 47(3); 48(3);
49(3); 50(3); 51(3); 52(3); 53(3); 54(3); 55(3); 56(2); 57(4);
58(3); 59(5); 60; 61; 62(3); 63(6); 65; 67; 70(2); 71(3); 72;
73(2); 8:1(3); 2(2); 3(3); 4; 5; 8; 9; 10; 13(3); 14(2); 15(2);
16(6); 17(4); 18(2); 9:1(2); 2(2); 3(3); 4; 6(2); 7(2); 8; 9; 10;
11; 12; 14; 15; 17; 18; 19(2); 22(6); 23; 24(2); 25; 27(3); 28;
30(2); 32(2); 37; 38; 10:1; 9(3); 14; 28(3); 29(2); 30; 31(2);
32(3); 33(3); 34(2); 35(4); 36(4); 37(5); 38(4); 39(6); 11:1(3);
3(3); 4(12); 5(7); 6; 7(8); 9(2); 10(2); 11(7); 12(7); 13(5);
14(3); 15(5); 16(5); 17(6); 20(3); 22(10); 24(4); 25(2); 30; 31;
35; 36(2); 12:1; 7(2); 12(4); 13(2); 14(2); 15(2); 16(2); 17(3);
18(2); 19(2); 20(2); 21(2); 22(4); 23(5); 24(4); 25; 26(5);
27(2); 28(2); 29(2); 31; 32(2); 35(7); 36(2); 37(5); 38(2);
39(4); 40(2); 43; 44(2); 45(3); 46(4); 47(3); 13:1(3); 2; 4(2);
5; 6(2); 7(2); 8(2); 9(2); 10; 11; 12; 13(3); 14; 15; 16(3); 17;
19(2); 20(2); 22; 23; 24(4); 25; 26(2); 27; 28(4); 29; 30; **Esth**
1:1; 2; 3(3); 4(2); 5(2); 6(3); 7; 8; 10(2); 14; 15; 16; 18(3);
19; 21; 22; 2:1; 3(3); 4; 5(3); 6(2); 8(3); 9; 11(3); 12(2); 14(2);
15(4); 16(2); 17; 18(2); 20; 21; 23(2); 3:1; 6(4); 7(3); 8; 9(2);
10(2); 12(3); 13(2); 14; 15; 4:1; 2; 5; 6; 7; 8; 9; 11; 5:1(2);
2; 6; 8; 11(3); 6:1(2); 2(2); 4; 9(2); 10; 13; 7:2; 7; 8(2); 9(2);
8:1(2); 2; 3; 5; 6; 7; 9(2); 10; 11; 12(3); 13; 15(5); 17(3);
9:1(2); 2(2); 3(2); 5; 10(3); 11; 12(2); 15(2); 16(2); 17(4);
18(2); 19(3); 20; 21(2); 22(2); 24(2); 26(2); 28(2); 29; 30(3);
31(2); 32(2); 10:1; 2(6); 3(2); **Job** 1:1; 3(3); 5(2); 6; 10; 12;
15; 16; 17; 19; 21; 2:1; 7(3); 8; 10; 11; 3:1; 5(2); 6(2); 9(2);
10; 14; 18; 20; 4:6; 9(2); 10(3); 11(2); 12; 13; 19; 5:1; 12;
13; 15; 17; 20; 21(2); 22(2); 23(2); 25; 26; 6:3; 4(2); 6; 10;
12; 14; 15; 16; 18; 19(2); 23; 26; 7:1(2); 3; 4; 8; 11(2); 20;
8:2; 8; 13(2); 19(2); 22; 9:3; 6; 8; 9; 13; 15; 19(2); 23; 24(2);
28; 34; 10:1; 3(2); 4; 5(2); 14; 15; 18; 21(2); 22; 11:2(2); 6;
7(2); 20(2); 12:5; 6; 7; 8; 9; 10(2); 12; 17; 18; 20(2); 22(2);
24(3); 13:4; 6; 11; 12(2); 21; 26; 27; 14:1(3); 4; 5; 9; 14; 15;
19(2); 15:5; 8; 11; 13; 14; 20; 23; 30; 34(2); 16:3; 5; 11; 16;
22; 17:5; 6; 7; 10; 11; 12; 16; 18:5(2); 7; 9; 13(2); 14(2); 15;
17; 18; 21(2); 19:9; 11; 17; 20; 21; 28; 29(2); 20:2; 3; 4;
5(2); 8; 10; 11; 15; 16; 18; 22; 23; 25(2); 28(2); 21:6; 9; 12;
14; 16; 17; 20(2); 21; 24(2); 25; 28(2); 30(2); 33; 22:4(2); 6;
9; 11; 12; 14; 18; 24(2); 30; 23:2; 6; 12(2); 15; 17; 24:3; 4;
6; 8(2); 12; 15; 17(3); 18(2); 22; 24(2); 25:4; 6; 26:9; 10(2);
11; 14(3); 27:3; 8; 11; 12; 13(2); 21; 23; 28:3; 6; 12; 13; 16;
17; 18(2); 19; 20; 21(2); 24; 28; 29:4(2); 6; 10(2); 13; 17;
24; 30:1; 2; 6(2); 8(2); 12; 16(3); 18; 21; 24; 27; 29(2); 31;
31:2(2); 3; 11; 13; 16; 17; 19; 20; 23; 28; 29; 31; 34(2); 37;
40(3); 32:2(4); 5; 6; 7; 8; 12; 18; 33:4(2); 6; 7; 8; 13(2); 15;
16; 19; 25; 30; 34:8; 10; 16; 19; 20; 21; 22(2); 26; 27; 28(2);
34; 36; 35:8; 9(4); 11(2); 12(2); 15; 36:5; 6; 8; 16(2); 17; 24;
26; 27; 29; 30; 37:2; 3; 6; 7; 9(2); 10; 12; 14; 15; 16; 19;
24; 38:1; 4; 7; 13(3); 16(2); 17(3); 18; 19; 21; 22(2); 23(2);
27; 28; 29; 30; 31(2); 33; 34; 37; 39; 41; 39:5; 7(2); 8; 13;
17; 21; 25(2); 28; 40:6; 11; 17; 18(2); 19(2); 20; 21; 41:6;
9(2); 14; 15; 18; 19(2); 20; 21; 23; 25; 29; 31; 34; 42:2; 5(2);
7; 8; 11(2); 12(2); 14(3); 15; 17; **Ps** 1:1(3); 2; 3; 5; 6(2); 2:2;
6; 8(2); 9; 10; 3:2; 6(2); 7; 4:1; 2; 5; 6; 5:2; 5; 7(2); 8; 10;
6:5; 7(2); 8(2); 7(2); 6(2); 7; 9; 10; 13; 17; 8(2); 2(3); 3; 4(2);
6; 7; 8(3); 9(3); 1; 9; 12; 13; 14(3); 16; 18; 10:1; 3; 4; 5; 7;
8; 14; 15; 16; 17; 18; 11:4; 6; 12:1; 5(2); 6(2); 8; 13:3; 14:2;
4; 5; 6; 7(3); 15:16:4; 5; 11(2); 17:4(3); 8(2); 14(2); 18(5); 2;
4(2); 5(2); 7; 10; 11; 12; 13; 15(4); 16; 18; 20; 21; 24; 30;
33; 34; 35; 40; 43(2); 44; 46; 19:1; 4; 5; 6; 7(2); 8(2); 9(2);
13; 14(2); 20:1(3); 2; 5; 6; 7; 21:2; 3(2); 4; 7; 9; 10; 22(2);
1; 3; 6; 9; 12; 14; 15; 16; 20; 21; 22; 23(2); 24; 25; 27(2);
29; 30; 23:3; 4(2); 5; 6(2); 24:3; 5; 6; 7; 8; 9; 10(3); 25:5; 6;
7; 10; 14; 15; 17(2); 22; 26:5; 7(2); 8; 10; 27:1(2); 4(4); 5(2);
6; 9; 10; 11; 12; 13(2); 14; 28:2; 3; 4(2); 5(2); 6; 8; 29:2;
3(2); 4(3); 5(2); 7(2); 8(2); 9; 30(2); 4(2); 31:2(2); 4; 5; 8; 10;
12; 13; 15; 19(2); 20(3); 22; 24; 32:4; 5; 6; 7; 33:2; 3; 4;
5(2); 6(3); 7; 8(2); 10(3); 11(2); 13; 14(2); 16; 18; 34:2; 6; 7;
11; 15; 16(2); 17; 19(2); 20; 22(2); 35:2; 5; 6; 12; 27; 28(2);
36(2); 1(2); 3; 7(2); 8(2); 9; 11(2); 12; 37:1(3); 4; 7(2); 11;
14; 16; 17; 18; 19; 20(2); 23; 28; 30(2); 31(2); 37; 38; 39(2);
38:3(2); 5; 7; 8(2); 10; 12; 39:4; 8; 10; 40:2(2); 5; 7(2); 9;
12; 15; 41:1; 2; 3; 5; 13; 42(2); 4(2); 5; 6(2); 7; 8; 9(2); 10;
11; 43:2(3); 4; 5; 44(2); 1; 3(2); 14; 15; 16(3); 19(2); 20; 21;
45(3); 1; 2; 4; 5; 6(2); 7; 8; 12; 14; 16; 46(2); 2; 4(3); 5(2);
7(2); 8; 9; 11(2); 47(2); 1; 4; 5; 7; 9(4); 48(2); 1; 2(3); 6(2);
7; 8(3); 9; 10(2); 11(2); 49(2); 1; 3; 5; 6; 7; 8; 13(2); 15; 16;
19; 50:1; 2(2); 9; 10; 11(2); 13(2); 15; 23; 51:1; 12; 14(3);
17; 18; 19; 52(2); 1; 5(2); 7; 8(2); 9; 53:2; 3; 4; 5; 6(3); 54:2;
7; 55:3(4); 4; 10; 14; 19; 21; 23; 56:13; 57:1; 4; 6; 58:1; 2;
4; 5; 6; 8; 10; 59:2; 4; 5(2); 10; 12(2); 13; 16(3); 17; 60(4);
3; 4; 6; 8; 11; 61:2; 4; 5; 62:3; 7; 9(2); 63(2); 7; 9; 11; 64:1;
2(3); 5; 6; 9; 65:4(2); 5(4); 7(3); 8(2); 9(2); 12; 66:2; 3; 5(2);
8; 15(2); 19; 67:7; 68:2; 5(2); 8(3); 11; 12; 13; 15(4); 16;
17(2); 19; 20; 21(2); 22; 23; 24; 26; 27(3); 29; 30(4); 31; 32;
33(2); 35; 69:4; 6(4); 9; 12; 13(2); 14(2); 16; 18; 20; 24;
26(2); 28(2); 30; 35; 36; 70:3; 71:4(4); 6(2); 9; 13; 15; 16(3);
20; 22; 24; 72:4(2); 7; 8; 10(3); 13; 15; 16(4); 18; 20(2);
73:3(2); 10; 15; 17; 26; 74:1; 2(2); 4; 7; 8; 11; 12(2); 13; 14;
17; 19(2); 20(3); 23(2); 75:8(2); 9; 10(2); 76:3(2); 4; 5(2); 6;
9; 10(2); 12(2); 77:2; 5(2); 10(2); 11(2); 12; 15; 18; 20; 78:1;
2; 4; 7; 9(2); 10; 12(3); 14; 16; 18; 23; 24(2); 27; 28; 30;
31(3); 32; 38; 41; 43; 45; 49(2); 51(2); 55; 60; 65; 67(2); 68;
72(2); 79:2(4); 9(2); 10(2); 11(2); 13; 80:1; 4(2); 5; 7; 8;
13(2); 14; 16; 17(2); 19; 81(2); 1; 3; 4(2); 5; 7(2); 10(2); 11;
15; 16; 82:1; 4; 5; 6(2); 7; 83:4; 6; 7; 8; 12; 84(3); 1; 2; 3;
6; 8(2); 9; 10(2); 12; 85(2); 1; 2; 3; 4; 11; 86:4; 6; 7; 13; 14;
15; 16; 87(2); 2(2); 3(2); 4; 5; 88(3); 1; 3; 9; 11; 12; 89:1(2);
5; 6; 7; 8; 9; 14; 15; 17; 18; 22; 26; 27(2); 29; 34; 39; 42;
43; 45; 47; 48; 50(2); 51; 90(2); 3; 8; 10(2); 11(2); 12; 17(3);
91:1(2); 2; 3; 5(2); 6(2); 8; 92:3; 4; 7; 9; 13(2); 93:2; 4(2);
94:2; 4; 7; 11; 12; 13; 16; 19; 20; 21; 22; 95:1; 4(2); 7(2);
8; 96:2; 5; 7; 9; 12; 97:1; 2; 5(3); 7; 8(2); 10(3); 12; 98:2;
3(3); 5; 6; 100:3; 101:1; 3; 6; 8(2); 102:2; 5(2); 6(2); 10; 12;
15(2); 17; 19; 20; 21; 24; 25(3); 28; 103:7; 15; 17; 20; 21;
22; 104:3(2); 4; 5; 7; 11; 12; 13; 14; 15; 16(3); 20; 24; 30;
31; 105:2; 3; 5; 6(2); 11(2); 16; 19; 20; 21(2); 23; 27; 30;
31; 33; 35; 36; 38; 40; 44(2); 106:2; 5(2); 7; 10(2); 11; 16;
17; 20; 22; 25; 28; 32(2); 38(2); 40; 41; 45; 48; 107:2(2); 3;
6; 8; 10; 11(2); 13; 14(2); 15; 16(2); 17(2); 18(2); 19; 21; 22;
24; 25; 26; 28; 31; 32(2); 34; 35; 43; 108:7; 12; 109:1; 2(2);
3; 14(2); 15; 24; 31; 110:2(3); 3(4); 4; 5; 6; 7; 111:1; 2; 4;
5; 6(2); 7; 10(2); 112:2; 4; 7; 10; 113:1(2); 2; 3; 7(2); 8; 9;
114:1(3); 7(3); 8(2); 115:1(2); 4; 10; 12(3); 16; 116:3(3); 4;
9; 13(2); 14; 15(2); 16; 17(2); 18; 19(2); 117:2; 118:3; 10;
11; 12(2); 15(3); 16(2); 17; 19; 20; 26(2); 27; 119:1; 7; 13;
14; 27; 29; 30; 32; 33; 35; 43(2); 46; 52; 53(2); 54; 61; 62;
63(2); 64; 72(3); 84; 87; 88; 96; 108; 111; 115; 116; 119;
120(2); 130; 134; 136; 144; 147; 152; 160(2); 161; 164;
172; 120:4(2); 5; 121:122(2); 1; 4(3); 5(2); 6; 8; 9(2);
123:2(4); 4(2); 124(2); 7; 8; 125:3; 5; 126:1; 127(2); 2; 3;
4(2); 5; 128:2; 3; 5(3); 129:4; 8(2); 130:1; 2; 131(2); 132:2;
3(2); 5; 6(2); 8; 10; 11; 17; 133(2); 2(2); 3(2); 134:1(2);
135:1(2); 2(3); 7(2); 8(2); 9; 11(3); 15(2); 19(2); 20; 21;
136:2; 3; 14; 19; 20; 26; 137:1; 2; 3(3); 6; 7(2); 8; 138:4(2);
5(3); 7(2); 8; 139:9(2); 15; 16; 17; 140:3; 4; 6; 7(2); 8; 9(2);
12; 141:2; 3; 4; 5; 6; 7; 9(2); 142:5; 7; 143:5(2); 10; 11;
144:3(3); 7(2); 8; 9; 11(2); 13; 145:5; 6(2); 7(2); 8; 11(3);
12(2); 15; 16; 19; 21; 146:3; 5; 8; 9; 147:2; 4; 10(2); 13;
148:3; 4; 5; 11(2); 13; 14(4); 149:1; 2; 6; 8; 150:3; **Prov**
1:1(3); 2; 3; 5; 6; 7(2); 8(2); 13; 17; 19(2); 21; 25; 29; 30;
31; 32(2); 33; 2:5(2); 8(2); 12; 13(2); 14; 17(2); 19; 20(2);
3:2; 3; 4; 9; 11; 14; 16; 17; 18(2); 25(2); 27; 31; 33(3); 35;
4:1; 3; 5; 9(2); 10; 11; 13; 14(2); 17(2); 18; 19; 21; 23(2);
26; 5:3; 5; 6; 7; 8; 10; 13; 14(2); 16; 18; 20; 21(2); 22; 23(2);
6:2(2); 3; 5(2); 10; 20; 23(2); 24; 26(2); 31; 34; 7:2; 3; 6; 7;
10; 16; 18; 20; 22; 24; 27; 8:2; 3(2); 4; 5; 6(2); 8; 13; 16;
20(3); 22(2); 26; 27; 28; 29; 31; 34; 9:3; 5(2); 6; 10(3); 11;
14(2); 18; 10:1(2); 2; 3; 4; 6(2); 7(2); 11(3); 13(3); 14; 15;
16(2); 17; 19; 20(2); 21(2); 22; 23; 24(2); 27(2); 28(2); 29(2);
31; 32(2); 11:3(2); 4; 5; 6; 7; 11(2); 12(2); 13; 14; 20; 21;
22; 23(2); 26; 29; 30(2); 12:2; 3; 4; 5(2); 6(2); 7; 8; 10(2);

11; 12(2); 13; 14(2); 15; 18(2); 20(2); 23; 24; 25; 26; 28; 13:2(2); 4(2); 8; 9(2); 12; 14(3); 15; 20; 22; 23(2); 25(2); 14:3(3); 4; 7(2); 8(2); 11(2); 12; 13; 17; 19; 24(2); 26(2); 27(3); 28(3); 33(2); 15:2(2); 3; 4; 6(2); 7(2); 8(2); 9; 11(2); 13; 14(2); 15(2); 16; 17; 19(3); 21(2); 22; 23; 24; 25(2); 26(2); 28(2); 29; 30; 31; 33(2); 16:1(2); 2; 4; 6; 10; 13; 14; 15(2); 17; 19; 21; 22(2); 23; 25; 28; 31(2); 17:1; 6(2); 8; 12; 14; 15; 16(2); 18; 21; 23; 24(3); 27(2); 18:4(2); 7; 8; 10; 12; 14; 15(2); 19; 20(2); 21; 19:3; 6; 7; 11; 12; 13(2); 16; 19; 23; 27; 28; 29; 20:2(2); 4; 5(2); 8; 15(2); 16; 24; 27(3); 29(2); 30; 21:1(2); 2; 4; 5(2); 6; 7; 8; 9; 10; 12; 13; 15; 16(2); 20; 22; 25; 27; 31(2); 22:2; 4; 5; 8; 9; 11; 12(2); 14; 15(2); 17; 20; 21(3); 23; 26(2); 23:4; 6; 9(2); 10; 12; 17; 20; 24; 29; 30; 34(2); 24:1; 2; 5; 6; 9; 10; 14; 15; 19(2); 20; 30(3); 33; 25:1(3); 2(2); 3; 6(2); 7; 11(2); 12(2); 13(3); 14; 17; 19(2); 22; 24; 26:6; 7(2); 9(2); 22; 27:3; 6(2); 9; 10; 13; 17; 20; 21; 23; 25; 26; 27(2); 28:2(3); 7; 19; 21; 25; 29:3; 7; 13; 25; 30:1(2); 2; 3; 4; 5; 7; 9; 17; 19(5); 20; 33(2); 31:1; 2(2); 5; 6; 8; 9; 11(2); 12; 21; 23; 26; 27(2); 31(2); **Eccl** 1:1(2); 2(2); 8; 10; 11(2); 13; 2:2(2); 3(2); 5; 6; 7; 8(5); 16(2); 20; 22; 24; 26; 3:8(2); 10; 13(2); 15; 16(2); 18(2); 19; 21(3); 4:1(2); 8; 14; 16; 5:1(2); 6(2); 7; 8(2); 9; 12(2); 18(2); 19(2); 20(2); 6:2(2); 3; 7; 9(2); 12; 7:1(2); 2(3); 4(4); 5(2); 6(2); 8; 9; 12; 13; 14(2); 15; 19; 25(3); 8:1(2); 2; 4; 6; 8; 10; 11(2); 14(2); 15; 17; 9:1; 3(3); 5; 9(2); 11(2); 12; 17(3); 18; 10:4; 12(2); 13(2); 15; 17; 18(2); 20; 11:3; 5(3); 8; 9(3); 12:1; 3; 4(3); 5(2); 8; 10; 11(2); 12; 13; **Song** 1:1; 2; 3(2); 4(2); 5(3); 6; 7; 8; 10(2); 11(2); 13; 14(2); 17(2); 2:1(2); 3(2); 5; 7(2); 8; 12(2); 14(2); 17; 3:4(2); 5(2); 6(2); 7(2); 8; 9(2); 10(4); 11(4); 4:1; 2(2); 3(2); 4(2); 5; 6(2); 8(3); 9(2); 10; 11(2); 13; 14; 15(2); 5:2(2); 4; 5; 7; 8(2); 12; 13(2); 14; 15(2); 16(2); 6:2; 5; 6; 7; 9(2); 11(2); 12; 13; 7:1(3); 2; 3; 4(2); 5; 7; 8(3); 9(2); 8:2(5); 4; 6; 7; 9(2); 14; **Isa** 1:1(4); 4(2); 6; 8(2); 9; 10(4); 11(6); 13; 14; 15; 16; 19; 20; 21; 23(2); 24(3); 26; 28(2); 29(2); 31; 2:1; 2(2); 3(5); 5(2); 6(2); 7(2); 8(2); 10(2); 11(2); 12(2); 13(2); 16; 17(2); 19(4); 20(2); 21(4); 22; 3:1(3); 2; 3; 6(2); 7; 8; 10; 11; 12; 14(2); 15(2); 16; 17(3); 24(6); 4:1; 2(3); 4(5); 5(2); 6; 5:1; 3(2); 7(4); 8; 9; 10(2); 12(2); 15; 16; 17; 18; 19(2); 24(4); 25(2); 26; 27; 29; 30; 6:1; 3(2); 4(2); 5(4); 6; 8; 10; 12; 7:1(7); 2(3); 3; 4(3); 5; 6; 8(2); 9(2); 13; 17; 18(3); 19(2); 20(2); 22; 23; 25; 8:2; 4(3); 6; 7(2); 8(2); 11; 12; 13; 14(4); 17; 18; 19; 22; 9:1(4); 2(2); 3; 4(4); 5; 6; 7(5); 9(2); 11; 13; 16; 18; 19(2); 20; 10:2(2); 3; 5; 6(2); 10(2); 12(4); 13(2); 14; 16(2); 17; 18(2); 19(2); 20(4); 21; 22(2); 23(2); 24(3); 26(4); 27; 29; 30; 31; 32(3); 33(2); 34; 11:1(2); 2(6); 3(3); 4(3); 5(2); 9(2); 10; 11(2); 12(3); 13(2); 14(3); 15(2); 16(2); 12:3; 6(2); 13:1; 2; 4(5); 5(2); 6; 8; 9; 10; 11(2); 12; 13(4); 18; 19(2); 21(2); 14:1; 2(2); 4; 5(2); 8; 9(2); 11; 12; 13(3); 14; 15; 17; 18(2); 19(3); 20; 21(3); 22; 23(3); 24; 27; 29(2); 30; 31; 32(2); 15:1(2); 3; 4; 5(3); 6; 7; 8; 9(3); 16:1(3); 2(3); 3; 4(2); 5; 6(3); 7; 8(3); 9(2); 14(2); 17:2; 3(4); 4(2); 5(2); 6(3); 7; 8; 9(2); 10(3); 11(2); 12(4); 13(2); 14(2); 18:1; 2(2); 3; 4(2); 6(4); 7(5); 19:1(2); 3; 4(2); 6; 7; 10; 11(3); 12; 13(3); 16(4); 17(5); 18(4); 19(2); 20(3); 24(2); 25(2); 20:1; 2; 4(2); 5; 6(2); 21:1; 3(2); 7(3); 9(3); 10(3); 11(3); 13; 14(2); 15; 16(2); 17(5); 22:1; 2; 4(3); 5(4); 6; 7; 8(3); 9(2); 10; 11; 12; 14(2); 15; 18; 19; 20; 21(2); 22(2); 24(2); 25; 23:1(2); 2(2); 3(2); 4; 5; 6; 8; 9(3); 10; 12; 13(2); 14; 15(3); 17(3); 24:4; 6; 8(3); 10; 11; 13(3); 14; 15(3); 16; 17; 18(3); 21(2); 23; 25:1; 2; 3; 4; 5(3); 6(6); 7; 8; 10; 11; 12(2); 26:1; 6(2); 7(2); 8(3); 9; 10(2); 11(2); 13; 15; 17; 18; 19; 21(2); 27:2; 5; 6; 7; 8; 9(3); 11; 12(3); 13(2); 28:1(3); 2(2); 3(2); 4; 5(4); 6; 7(2); 8; 13; 14; 17; 21; 22; 29; 29:4(4); 5(2); 6(2); 7(2); 8; 10; 11; 13; 14(2); 16(2); 18(4); 19; 22; 23(3); 30:1(2); 2(2); 3(2); 5; 6(4); 9; 11(2); 12; 14; 15; 17(3); 18; 19; 20(2); 22(4); 23(2); 25(2); 26(6); 27(2); 28(2); 29(3); 30(3); 31; 32(2); 33(3); 31:1; 2(2); 4(3); 5; 6; 7(2); 8(2); 9; 32:2(2); 3(2); 4(2); 6; 7; 13; 14(2); 17(2); 20; 33:1; 2; 3; 4(2); 6(3); 7; 12; 15(2); 16(2); 19(2); 20(3); 21; 23; 34:2; 4; 5; 6(5); 8(3); 11(2); 13; 14(2); 16(2); 35:2(4); 4; 5(2); 6; 7(2); 8; 10; 36:1(3); 2; 3(2); 4; 5; 6(2); 8; 9(2); 11; 13(2); 15(2); 16(4); 17(2); 18(4); 19(2); 20; 22(3); 37:1; 2(2); 3; 4(2); 5; 6(3); 8; 9; 10(3); 11; 12(2); 13(4); 14(2); 16(4); 17; 18; 19; 20; 21(3); 22(2); 23; 24(3); 25(2); 26; 27; 30(2); 31(2); 32(3); 33; 36(2); 37; 38(2); 38:1; 4; 5; 6(2); 8; 9(2); 10(4); 11(2); 12; 13; 15; 16; 17; 20(2); 21; 22; 39:1(2); 2; 5(2); 7(3); 8; 40:3(2); 5(2); 6; 7; 8; 9; 12(2); 13; 14(2); 21; 22; 23; 26(2); 28(2); 41:5; 6; 8; 9; 14(2); 16; 17; 18(3); 20(2); 21; 22; 25; 28; 42:9; 10(2); 11(2); 13; 22; 25(2); 43:3; 6; 13; 14; 15; 18; 20; 22; 24; 28; 44:5(2); 6(2); 9; 12; 13(2); 14; 15; 16; 17; 19(3); 23; 25; 26(3); 28; 45:1; 2(2); 3(3); 6; 9; 11(3); 13; 14(4); 15; 16(2); 19(2); 20; 22; 23; 25; 46:3(3); 6; 7; 9; 11; 47:1(2); 4(2); 5(2); 7; 8; 9(4); 12; 13; 14; 48:1(6); 2(2); 7; 10; 13; 14; 17; 18; 19(2); 20(2); 49:1(2); 2; 5; 6(3); 7(4); 8; 10; 11; 12; 15; 16; 19; 23; 24; 25(2); 26; 50:1(2); 2; 4; 10(2); 11; 51:1; 3(2); 4; 7(2); 9(2); 10(2); 11; 12(3); 13(4); 15; 16(2); 17(4); 20(4); 22(5); 23; 52:2(2); 7(2); 9; 10(3); 11(2); 12; 14; 53:1; 2; 3; 6; 8(2); 10; 11; 12; 54:1(2); 2(2); 4(2); 5(3); 9(2); 10; 12(3); 13; 15; 17(2); 55:3; 5(2); 12; 13(2); 56:2; 3; 5; 6(2); 7(2); 8; 9; 57:3(2); 4(2); 5; 6; 10(2); 11(2); 13; 14(2); 15(2); 17(2); 19; 58:1; 2(3); 3; 4; 6; 8; 9; 11; 12(3); 13; 14(3); 59:5; 6(2); 7; 8; 13; 17(2); 19(3); 21(2); 60:1; 3; 5(2); 6(3); 7(3); 9(3); 10; 11; 13(3); 14(5); 15; 16(3); 17(4); 20; 21(2); 61:1(2); 2(3); 3(5); 4; 5; 6(3); 7(2); 10(2); 62:2; 3(3); 6; 8(2); 11(2); 12; 63:1; 4(2); 7(4); 9(2); 11(3); 12; 14; 15; 16; 17; 19; 64:4; 7(2); 8; 12; 65:3; 4; 7; 9; 10(2); 14(3); 16(2); 19(2); 22(3); 23(2); 66:1; 2; 5; 6(2); 9; 11(2); 12; 14; 15; 16; 20(3); 21; 24; **Jer** 1:1(4); 2(5); 3(8); 4; 8; 11(2); 13; 14(2); 15(5); 16; 18(2); 2:1; 2(3); 3; 4(4); 6(5); 10; 13; 16(2); 18(2); 19(2); 20; 21(2); 24; 26; 27; 28(2); 31(2); 34(2); 36(2); 3:4; 6; 8; 16(2); 17(3); 18(4); 19(2); 20; 21(2); 23(2); 24; 25; 4:1; 3; 4(5); 7; 8; 9(2); 11(2); 16; 17; 19(2); 21; 25; 26; 29; 30; 31(5); 5:1; 4(2); 5(2); 6; 11(2); 14; 15; 18; 20; 22; 24; 27(2); 28(3); 6:1(3); 2; 4; 6(2); 9(2); 10; 11(5); 12; 13(2); 14; 17; 19; 22; 23(2); 24(3); 25(2); 26; 7:2(3); 3(2); 4(3); 11; 12(2); 15(2); 17(2); 18; 19; 20(2); 21(2); 22(2); 24; 25(2); 28; 29; 30; 31(3); 32(3); 33(3); 34(6); 8:1(8); 2(2); 3(3); 6; 7(2); 8(2); 9; 11(2); 12; 14; 15; 16(3); 19(2); 21(3); 22(2); 9:1(3); 2; 6; 7(2); 10(3); 11(3); 12; 14; 15(3); 17; 19(2); 20(2); 22; 26(2); 10:1; 2(2); 3(3); 5; 7(2); 9(4); 13(3); 15(2); 16(4); 17; 18; 22(4); 23; 11:2(3); 3(2); 4(2); 6(3); 7(2); 8(2); 9(2); 10(3); 12(3); 13(3); 14; 16(2); 17(5); 18; 19; 20; 21(2); 22; 23(3); 12:1; 3; 4(2); 5(2); 6; 7(2); 9; 12(3); 13(3); 14(2); 16(2); 13:2; 3; 8; 9(2); 10; 11(3); 12; 13(2); 16; 18; 19(2); 22; 24; 25; 27; 14:1; 2; 8(2); 14; 16(2); 17; 19; 20; 21; 22; 15:1; 3(3); 4(4); 6; 7(2); 8(2); 9; 10(3); 11(2); 13; 16(2); 17(2); 21(2); 16:1; 4(3); 5; 7; 8; 9(6); 12; 13; 14(2); 15(2); 16(2); 18; 19(2); 17:1(5); 3; 4; 8; 10; 11; 12; 13(2); 15; 16; 17; 18; 19(4); 20(3); 21; 22; 24; 25(4); 26(4); 27(2); 18:4(2); 5; 6(2); 8; 11(2); 12; 13; 14(2); 17; 18; 19; 21(2); 23; 19:1(4); 2(3); 3(6); 4(2); 5; 6(3); 7(4); 8; 9(3); 10; 11; 13(6); 14; 15(2); 20:1(2); 2(2); 3; 4(3); 5(4); 8; 9(2); 12; 13(2); 21:1(2); 2(2); 4(4); 6(2); 7(6); 8(2); 10(2); 11(3); 12(5); 13(2); 14; 22:1(2); 2(3); 3(2); 4(2); 6(3); 9; 11(3); 16; 18(2); 19(2); 23(2); 24(2); 25(5); 29; 30(2); 23:1; 2(2); 3(2); 5; 7(2); 8(2); 9(3); 10(4); 12; 13; 14(3); 15(3); 16(4); 17; 18; 19(2); 20(2); 22; 26(3); 33; 34; 35; 36(3); 38(3); 39; 24:1(6); 4; 5(3); 8(3); 9; 25:1(6); 2(2); 3(4); 5; 6; 7; 8; 9(2); 10(6); 11; 12(2); 14; 15(2); 16; 18; 19; 20(5); 21; 22(3); 24(2); 25(3); 26(4); 27(3); 28; 29(2); 30; 31; 32(2); 33(3); 34(2); 35; 36(3); 37(2); 38(3); 26:1(4); 2(2); 3(2); 5; 6; 7; 8; 9(2); 10(4); 13; 16; 17(3); 18(8); 19; 20(4); 22; 23; 24(3); 27:1(4); 3(7); 4(2); 6(3); 7; 8(3); 9; 11(2); 12(3); 13; 14(2); 16(2); 17; 18(5); 19(2); 20(4); 21(6); 28:1(7); 2(4); 3(2); 4(5); 5(3); 6; 7; 8(2); 9(2); 11(5); 12(2); 13(2); 14(6); 16; 29:1(2); 2; 3(5); 4(2); 7; 8(2); 11(2); 16; 17; 18; 20(2); 21(6); 22(3); 25(3); 26(2); 27; 29; 30; 30:2; 5(3); 7(2); 8; 10; 11(2); 14(3); 15(2); 16; 17; 18; 19(2); 23(2); 24(2); 31:1(2); 3; 4(2); 5; 7(2); 8; 9; 10; 11; 12(3); 14; 16; 19; 21; 23(5); 27(4); 31(2); 32(2); 33; 34(2); 35(2); 36; 37(2); 38; 40(3); 32:1(3); 2(3); 3(3); 4(4); 6; 7(2); 8(5); 9(2); 12(5); 14(2); 15(2); 16; 18(3); 19(3); 20; 21(2); 22; 23(2); 24(2); 25; 26; 27; 28(3); 30(4); 31; 32(6); 35(3); 36(4); 37; 39; 43(2); 44(5); 33:1(2); 4(4); 5; 6; 7(2); 9(2); 10(3); 11(10); 12(2); 13(6); 14(2); 15; 17(2); 19; 22(3); 23; 25; 26(3); 34:1(2); 2(4); 3(2); 4(2); 5; 6; 7(4); 12; 13(5); 14; 16; 17; 18(2); 19(4); 20(4); 21(5); 22; 35:1(3); 2(3); 3(3); 4(9); 5(3); 6; 7; 8(2); 11(5); 12; 13(4); 14(2); 16(3); 17(3); 18(4); 19(3); 36:1(3); 2(2); 3; 4(4); 5; 6(4); 8(2); 9(4); 10(7); 11(3); 12(4); 13; 14(5); 16; 20(2); 21(2); 24; 26(2); 27(2); 28; 29(2); 30(4); 31(2); 32(4); 37:1(5); 2(2); 3(2); 5; 6; 7(3); 10; 11(3); 12(2); 13(4); 15; 17(2); 19; 20; 21(3); 38:1(4); 3(2); 4(4); 6(2); 7(2); 8; 10; 11; 13(2); 14(2); 16; 17(3); 18(2); 19; 20; 22(2); 23(2); 24; 28; 39:1(3); 2(2); 3(5); 4(5); 5(3); 6(4); 8(2); 9(3); 10(2); 11(2); 13(2); 14(3); 15(2); 16(2); 17(2); 40:1; 2; 5(5); 6; 7(4); 8(5); 9(3); 11(4); 12(2); 13(2); 14(3); 15(2); 16(2); 41:1(6); 2(4); 3; 5; 6(2); 7(3); 8; 9(5); 10(4); 11(4); 12; 13(2); 14; 15; 16(6); 17; 18(5); 42:1(3); 2; 6(2); 7; 8(2); 9; 11(4); 13; 14(2); 15(4); 16(2); 17; 18(3); 19; 21; 43:1; 2(2); 3(2); 4(4); 5(4); 6(4); 7(2); 8; 9(2); 10(3); 11; 12(3); 13(4); 44:1(2); 2(3); 3; 6(2); 7(3); 8(3); 9(7); 11(2); 12(3); 13; 14(4); 15; 16; 17(5); 18; 19; 21(3); 22(3); 23; 24(2); 25(3); 26(5); 27(2); 28(4); 30(6); 45:1(5); 2; 46:1; 2(6); 10(4); 11; 12; 13(2); 16; 17; 18; 21(2); 24(3); 25(3); 26(5); 27; 28(2); 47:1; 2(2); 3(4); 4(3); 5; 6; 48:1(2); 2; 3; 5(3); 10; 13(3); 15; 16; 18; 19; 24(2); 25; 27; 28; 29(4); 31; 32(3); 33; 34(2); 36; 38; 41; 43; 44(2); 45(8); 46; 47(2); 49:2(3); 3; 5; 6(2); 7; 8(2); 12(2); 16(3); 18(2); 19(2); 20(3); 21; 22(3); 25(2); 26(2); 27(2); 28(3); 30(2); 32; 33; 34(4); 35(3); 36(2); 39; 50:1; 3; 4(2); 7(2); 8(3); 9(2); 11; 12; 13(2); 15; 16; 17(2); 18(4); 20(2); 21(2); 22(2); 23; 25(4); 26(2); 27; 28(4); 29(2); 30; 31; 33(3); 34(2); 35; 38; 40; 41; 42; 43(3); 44(2); 45(3); 46(2); 51:2; 4; 5(2); 6(2); 10; 11(3); 12(2); 13; 14; 16(3); 18(2); 19(4); 20; 23; 24; 28(2); 29(2); 30(2); 31; 32; 33(4); 34; 35(2); 41; 42; 43; 44(2); 45(3); 47; 49(2); 51; 53; 54(2); 55; 56(2); 57; 58(3); 59(4); 64; 52:1(2); 2; 3(3); 4(3); 5; 6(2); 7(4); 8(2); 9(2); 10(3); 11(3); 12(5); 13(3); 14(3); 15(5); 16(3); 17(2); 19; 20(2); 21(2); 22(3); 24; 25(9); 26(2); 27(2); 29; 30(3); 31(9); 32; 33; 34(3); **Lam** 1:1; 5(2); 6; 7(3); 12; 14(2); 15; 21; 2:1(3); 2(3); 3; 4(2); 5; 6; 7(4); 8(2); 10(3); 11(4); 12; 13(2); 15(3); 17(2); 18(2); 19(4); 20; 21; 22; 3:1; 6; 13; 14; 26; 30; 32; 33; 34; 35; 38; 39; 45; 48(3); 51(2); 62; 64; 66; 4:1(2); 2(3); 3; 4(2); 6(5); 9(3); 10(3); 12(3); 13(4); 16; 19; 20(3); 21(2); 22(3); 5:9(2); 10(2); 11; 13; 15; 17(2); 18; 21; **Ezek** 1:1(2); 2(2); 3(4); 4(5); 5(2); 7(3); 8(2); 10(8); 11; 13(4); 14; 16(4); 17; 18(2); 20; 21; 22(3); 23; 24(4); 26(3); 27(5); 28(6); 2:1; 3(2); 6(4); 8; 9; 3:1(2); 3; 4(2); 5(3); 6(2); 7(2); 9; 10; 11; 12; 13(3); 14(2); 16(2); 17(2); 22; 23; 25; 26; 4:1; 3; 4(3); 5(4); 6(2); 7; 8; 9(2); 11; 12; 13; 14; 15; 16(2); 17; 5:1; 2(2); 3(2); 4(3); 5; 7; 8; 9(2); 10; 12(2); 14; 16(2); 6:1; 2(2); 3(2); 5(2); 9; 11(2); 7:1; 2(3); 7(2); 11(4); 16(2); 19(3); 20(2); 21(2); 23(2); 24(2); 27; 8:1(3); 2(4); 3(7); 4(2); 5(3); 6(2); 7; 8; 10(3); 11(5); 12(4); 14(2); 15; 16(4); 17(2); 9:2; 3(3); 4(3); 8; 9(4); 10:1(3); 2; 3; 4(4); 5(3); 7(2); 8; 9; 10; 11; 12; 14(4); 17; 18(2); 19(4); 20; 21(2); 22; 11:1(5); 2; 4; 5(2); 7(2); 9(2); 10; 11; 12; 13(3); 14; 15(3); 17; 19(2); 22(2); 23(3); 24; 25; 12:1; 2(2); 3; 6; 8; 9(2); 10; 13; 16; 17; 18; 19(6); 21; 22(2); 23; 24; 26; 27(3); 28; 13:1; 2(4); 5(2); 9(4); 14; 16(2); 17(3); 18(3); 19(2); 21; 22(2); 23; 14:1(2); 2; 3(2); 4(3); 5; 6; 7(4); 8; 10(2); 11; 12; 13(2); 15; 15:1; 2(3); 4; 6(3); 16:1; 2; 3; 5; 8; 10; 13(2); 14; 15; 16; 19; 20; 22(2); 25(2); 26; 27(3); 29(2); 30; 31; 32; 34; 35; 36(2); 39; 41; 43; 45; 46(2); 49(4); 51; 53(3); 56; 57(5); 60; 61; 63; 17:1; 2(2); 3(2); 4(2); 5(2); 6; 9; 11; 12; 13; 16; 22(3); 23(3); 24; 18:1; 2; 4(2); 6(2); 10(2); 11; 13; 15(2); 17; 19; 20(4); 22(2); 24(3); 25(2); 26; 29(3); 30; 31; 32; 19:1; 3; 4(2); 5; 7; 9(2); 10(2); 11; 14; 20:1(4); 2; 3(4); 4(2); 5(3); 6(3); 7(2); 8(3); 9(2); 10(2); 13; 15; 17; 18; 22; 26; 27(2); 30(2); 31(3); 34; 35; 36(2); 37; 38(2); 39(2); 40(4); 41; 42; 43; 44; 45; 46; 47(2); 49; 21:1; 2(2); 3(2); 4; 5; 6; 7; 8; 9; 10; 11; 12(2); 14; 15; 18; 19(5); 20; 21(3); 23; 25; 28; 29; 30; 31(2); 32; 22:1; 2; 4; 5; 6; 7; 16; 17; 18(3); 19; 20; 21; 22; 23; 24(2); 25; 29; 30; 31; 23:1; 2(2); 6; 7(2); 9(2); 12; 14; 15(4); 17; 19(2); 20(2); 21(2); 23(3); 24; 26; 27; 28(2); 29; 31; 32; 33(2); 35; 36; 39; 42(2); 45(2); 24:1(2); 2(3); 4; 5; 7; 8; 13; 15; 16(2); 17; 20; 21(3); 22; 25(2); 25:1; 2; 3(3); 4; 6; 8; 9(4); 10; 12(2); 14; 15; 16; 26:1(2); 2(2); 4(2); 5; 7(2); 10(3); 11; 12; 13(2); 14; 15(2); 16; 18; 20(3); 27:1; 2; 3(2); 4; 5; 6(3); 7; 8; 9(2); 10; 11(2); 12; 13; 14; 15(2); 16(2); 17(2); 18(4); 21; 22(2); 23; 24; 25(3); 26; 27(3); 28(2); 29; 30; 31(2); 32; 33; 34; 35; 28:1; 2(5); 5; 6; 7(2); 8(2); 9; 10(2); 11; 12(4); 13(2); 14(2); 16(4); 17(2); 18(3); 20; 21; 24; 25(2); 29:1(2); 2(2); 3(2); 4(3); 5(3); 6(3); 7; 9; 10(2); 11(2); 12(2); 13; 14(3); 15; 16(3); 17(2); 18(2); 19(2); 20; 21(2); 30:1; 2; 3(3); 5; 6; 7(2); 9; 10(3); 11; 12(2); 13(2); 15(2); 17; 18; 20(2); 21(3); 22(2); 24(3); 25(6); 31:1(2); 2(2); 3; 4; 5(3); 6(2); 7; 8(2); 9(3); 11(2); 12(3); 13(2); 14(2); 15(3); 16(4); 18(4); 32:1(2); 2(2); 3; 4(2); 6(2); 8; 9; 10(2); 11(2); 12(4); 13(2); 15(2); 16; 17(2); 18(4); 20; 21(2); 22; 23(3); 24(3); 25(4); 26(2); 27(5); 28; 30(2); 32(2); 33:1; 2(3); 4; 5; 7(2); 10(2); 11(2); 12(7); 13(2); 15; 16; 17(2); 18; 19; 20(3); 21(2); 22; 23; 24(2); 27; 28; 29; 30(3); 32; 34:1; 2(3); 5; 6; 7; 8; 9; 13(2); 14(2); 18(2); 25; 26; 27(3); 28; 29(2); 30; 31; 35:1; 2; 5(4); 12; 15(4); 36:1(4); 2; 3(3); 4(3); 5; 6(2); 8; 10(2); 12(2); 13; 15(2); 16; 17(3); 20(3); 21; 22(2); 24; 26(3); 30(3); 32; 34(2); 35; 37(2); 38; 37:1(4); 3; 4; 9; 11(2); 12; 15; 16(4); 18; 19(4); 21; 22; 23; 26; 38:1; 2(4); 3; 4; 5; 6; 8(4); 11(2); 12; 13; 14; 15(2); 17(2); 18; 19(2); 20(4); 23; 39:1(2); 2; 3(2); 4(4); 7; 8; 9; 11(3); 12; 13; 14(2); 15; 16; 17(4); 18(7); 20; 22; 23(2); 25(2); 27(2); 28; 29; 40:1(4); 2(3); 3(2); 4(2); 5(2); 6; 7(3); 8; 9(2); 10; 11(2); 12; 13(2); 15(3); 16; 18(2); 19(2); 22(2); 23; 26; 38; 39; 40(4); 41; 42; 43; 44(2); 45; 46(3); 47; 48(3); 49; 41:1; 2(2); 3; 5(2); 6; 7(3); 8; 9(4); 10; 11(2); 12; 14(2); 15(2); 19(2); 20; 21(2); 22(2); 25(2); 26(2); 42:3(2); 4(2); 5; 6; 7; 8; 10(2); 11; 12(3); 14; 43:2(4); 3; 4(2); 5; 7(8); 9; 10(3); 11(2); 12(2); 13(3); 14(2); 17; 18; 19(2); 20(3); 21(2); 22; 44:1; 2; 3(2); 4(4); 5(3); 6(3); 7; 8(2); 9; 11(2); 12; 13; 14; 15(3); 17(2); 22(4); 30(4); 45:1; 2; 4(2); 5; 6(3); 7(2); 8(2); 9; 11(3); 13(4); 14(2); 15(2); 16; 17(3); 18; 19(7); 20; 21(2); 22; 23(2); 24(2); 25; 46:1(2); 2(3); 3; 5; 6; 7(2); 8(2); 9(6); 11; 13(2); 14(3); 16(3); 17(4); 18(2); 19(2); 21(2); 22; 23(3); 24(2); 47:1(5); 2; 6(2); 7; 9; 10(2); 12(2); 13; 15; 16(3); 17(2); 18(2); 19; 21; 22(2); 48:1(4); 2; 3; 4; 5; 6; 7; 8(2); 10; 11(3); 12(2); 13; 14(2); 15; 17; 18(4); 19(2); 20; 21(4); 22(5); 23; 24; 25; 26; 27; 28(2); 29; 30; 31(2); 35; **Dan** 1:1(4); 2(7); 3(5); 4; 5(4); 6(2); 7; 8(3); 9(2); 10; 11; 13(2); 15(2); 16; 18(2); 20; 21; 2:1; 10; 12; 14(2); 18(3); 19; 20; 23(2); 24(2); 25(2); 27; 28; 30; 32(3); 33(3); 34; 35; 36; 37(2); 38(4); 39; 41(3); 42(3); 43; 44(2); 45; 47(3); 48(2); 49(3); 3:1(3); 2(2); 3(2); 5(2); 6; 7(2); 10(2); 11; 12(2); 15(3); 19; 20; 21; 22; 23; 24; 25(3); 26(3); 27(2); 28; 29; 30; 4:5; 6(2); 8(2); 9(3); 10(2); 11; 12(2); 13; 15(4); 16(2); 17(4); 18(2); 21(2); 22; 23(4); 24; 25(3); 26; 27; 29(2); 30; 32(2); 33; 34; 35(3); 36; 37(2); 5:1(2); 3(2); 4; 5(4); 6; 7(2); 10(2); 11(4); 13; 14(2); 15; 16(2); 19; 21(3); 23(3); 24; 26; 29; 30; 6:2; 5; 7(2); 8; 12(2); 13; 14; 15; 16; 17(2); 19; 20; 23(2); 24(2); 26(2); 27; 28(2); 7:1(3); 2; 6; 8(2); 9(2); 11(2); 12; 13(3); 15; 16(3); 17; 18; 19(2); 22(3); 25; 27(2); 28; 8:1(2); 2; 5; 8(2); 9(2); 10(3); 11(2); 12; 13(2); 15; 16; 17(2); 19; 20; 21; 22; 23; 25; 26; 9:1(5); 2(4); 6; 7(4); 8; 10; 11(2); 13; 15(2); 16; 17; 18(2); 20(2); 21; 23; 24; 25; 26(3); 27(2); 10:1(3); 4(2); 5; 6(4); 9(2); 10; 12; 13(4); 16(3); 17; 18; 20(2); 21; 11:1; 2; 4; 5(2); 6(5); 7(3); 8(2); 9(3); 10; 11(3); 12; 13(2); 14(3); 15(2); 17(2); 19; 21; 22(2); 23; 24; 25(2); 26(2); 31; 33; 35(3); 36; 37(2); 38; 40(3); 41; 42; 43(2); 45; 12:1(2); 2(2); 3; 4; 6(2); 7(2); 8; 9; 10; 11; 13; **Hos** 1:1(7); 2(2); 3; 4(4); 5(2); 6; 7; 10(4); 11(4); 2:4; 10; 12(2); 13; 15(4); 17; 18(4); 3:1(3); 2(2); 4; 5; 4:1(4); 3(3); 6(2); 8; 12; 19; 5:1(2); 4; 5; 9(2); 10; 12; 13; 14; 6:3; 5; 6; 8; 9(2); 10(2); 11; 7:1(3); 5; 10; 12; 16(2); 8:1; 6; 10(3); 12; 13; 9:4(2); 5(2); 6(2); 7(4); 8(2); 9; 15(2); 16; 10:1(2); 4; 5(3); 6; 8(2); 9(2); 13(2); 14; 15(2); 11:1; 4; 5; 6; 9; 11; 12; 12:5; 6; 9(2); 10; 11; 12; 13; 14; 13:2(4); 4; 5; 8; 12; 13; 14; 15(2); 14:1; 2; 3; 7; 9; **Joel** 1:1(2); 2(2); 5(2); 6(2); 8; 9; 11; 12(2); 13; 14(2); 15; 16; 18(2); 19; 20; 2:1(2); 2(3); 3; 4; 5; 6; 7; 11; 13; 22; 23; 24; 26; 27; 30; 31(2); 32; 3:1; 2(2); 4; 6(2); 7; 8(2); 9; 12; 14(3); 16(2); 18(3); 19(2); 21(2); **Am** 1:1(7); 2(2); 3(2); 4(2); 5(3); 6; 7; 8; 9(2); 10; 11; 12; 13(2); 14(3); 2:1(3); 2; 4(2); 5; 6(2); 7(3); 8(2); 9; 10(2); 11(3); 13; 15; 16; 3:1(2); 2(2); 4; 9(2); 12(5); 13(2); 14(2); 15; 4:1(2); 3; 5(2); 6(2); 10(2); 11; 13(2); 5:1; 2; 3; 4; 6; 8(3); 11; 14; 15(2); 16; 18(2); 20; 23(2); 25; 26; 27; 6:1; 2; 3(2); 4(2); 5; 6; 7; 8(2); 10(3); 12; 14(4); 7:1; 2; 8; 9(3); 10(4); 12; 14(2); 16(2); 8:1; 2; 3; 4; 6; 7(2); 8(2); 11(3); 12; 14(2); 9:1(2); 3(2); 5(3); 6(2); 7(3); 8(3); 9; 10; 11(2); 12; 13; 14; **Ob** 1; 3(2); 7; 8; 9; 11; 12(5); 13(4); 14; 15; 17; 18(5); 19(3); 20(6); 21; **Jon** 1:1(2); 3(2); 5; 8; 9; 10; 12; 17; 2:2(3); 3; 4; 6; 9(2); 3:1; 3; 5(2); 6; 7; 4:5(3); **Mic** 1:1(4); 3(2); 5(5); 6; 7(2); 9; 11(2); 12(2); 13(4); 14(2); 15(2); 16; 2:1; 4; 5; 7(2); 9; 11(2); 12(5); 3:1(3); 3; 8(3); 9(4); 12(4); 4:1(2); 2(5); 4(2); 5(2); 8(5); 10(2); 12; 13(2); 5:1(2); 2(3); 3(2); 4(4); 6(2); 7(3); 8(4); 11; 13; 6:2; 4(2); 5(3); 7(4); 8; 10(2); 11; 12; 13; 16(3); 7:1; 4(2); 5; 6; 7; 9; 13(2); 14(3); 15(2); 16; 17(3); 18(2); 19; 20; **Nah** 1:1(2); 3; 4; 6; 7; 8; 9; 14(2); 15; 2:2(2); 3(2); 6; 7; 8(2); 9(4); 10; 11(2); 13(2); 3:1; 2(4); 3(2); 4(4); 5; 10; 12; 13(2); 16; 18; 19; **Hab** 1:6; 13; 14; 15; 2:8(4); 9; 13(2); 14(2); 16(2); 17(4); 18(2); 3:1; 2(2); 3; 7(3); 8; 10; 11(2); 13(2); 14; 15; 16; 17; 18; **Zeph** 1:1(8); 2; 3(3); 4(3); 5; 6; 7(2); 8; 10; 11; 14(3); 15(5); 16; 18(3); 2:2; 3(2); 5(4); 7(3); 8(3); 9(5); 10(2); 11(2); 14(2); 3:8(2); 9; 10(2); 11; 12; 13; 14(2); 15; 20; **Hag** 1:1(6); 2; 3; 5; 7; 9(3); 11; 12(6); 14(9); 15(2); 2:1(2); 2(4); 4(3); 5; 6; 7(2); 8; 9(3); 10(3); 11; 12; 13(2); 14; 15; 16; 17; 18(2); 20(2); 21; 22(3); 23(3); **Zech** 1:1(5); 3(3); 4; 6; 7(5); 11; 12(3); 14; 16; 17; 21(2); 2:4(2); 5; 6(2); 7; 8(2); 9; 10; 11; 12; 3:1; 5; 6; 7(2); 9(2); 10; 4:1; 2(2); 3; 6(2); 7; 8; 9(3); 10(3); 11; 12; 14; 5:3(3); 4(4); 9; 11; 6:1; 5(2); 9; 10(2); 11(2); 12(2); 13(2); 14(2); 15(3); 7:1(3); 2; 3(2); 4(2); 5; 8; 9; 10; 12(2); 13; 8:1(2); 2; 3(4); 4(3); 5(2); 6(4); 7(3); 8; 9(4); 11(2); 12; 13(2); 14(2); 15; 17; 18(2); 19(6); 20(2); 21(2); 22; 23(3); 9:1(5); 3; 6; 8(2); 9(3); 10; 11(2); 12; 13; 15(2); 16(2); 10:1(2); 3(2); 5; 6(2); 7; 10(2); 11(4); 11:2; 3(3); 6(2); 7; 11(2); 12; 13(2); 15; 16; 12:1(4); 2; 3; 4(2); 5(3); 6; 7(6); 8(3); 10(3); 11; 12(4); 13(3); 13:1(2); 2(2); 3; 4(2); 6; 7; 14:1; 2(2); 3; 4(4); 5(2); 8(2); 10(3); 13; 14; 16(3); 17(3); 18(2); 19(3); 20; 21(3); **Mal** 1:1(2); 3; 4(2); 5; 6; 7; 8; 9; 10; 11(2); 12; 13; 14; 2:2; 3; 4; 5; 6; 7(3); 8(2);

10; 11; 12(2); 13; 14; 15(2); 16(2); 17(2); 3:1(2); 2; 3(2); 4(2); 5; 6; 7(2); 10(2); 11(2); 12; 14; 16; 17; 4:1; 2; 3(2); 4; 5(2); 6(2); **Mt** 1:1(4); 6; 16(2); 18(2); 20(3); 24; 2:1(2); 2; 4(2); 5; 6(3); 13; 15(2); 19; 20; 21; 22(2); 3:1; 2; 3(3); 7(2); 8; 10; 16; 4:3; 4; 5; 6; 8; 13; 15(4); 16; 17; 18; 19; 21; 23(3); 5:3; 9; 10; 11; 13; 14; 19(4); 20(2); 21(2); 22(3); 26; 27; 29; 30; 31; 33; 35; 45; 6:5; 8; 22(2); 23; 26(2); 27; 28; 29; 30(2); 33; 7:15; 21(2); 24; 26; 8:11; 12(2); 20(2); 21; 26; 28(2); 29; 30; 31; 32(2); 9:2; 3; 6; 12; 14; 15; 16; 20(2); 22; 26; 27; 34; 35; 38; 10:1(2); 2(2); 3; 5(2); 6(2); 7; 10; 15(2); 16; 17; 20; 23(2); 25(2); 29; 30; 31; 36; 37(2); 38; 41(2); 42(3); 11:2(2); 6; 10; 11(2); 12(2); 19(2); 20; 22; 24(2); 25; 12:1; 4; 8(2); 11; 12; 23; 24; 28(2); 32; 34(3); 35(3); 36(2); 38; 39; 40(3); 41(2); 42(3); 43; 45; 50; 13:1; 5; 11(2); 14; 15(2); 18; 19; 21; 22(2); 24; 27; 30; 31; 32(2); 33(2); 35; 36(2); 37; 38(2); 39; 40; 41(2); 42(2); 43; 44; 45; 46; 47(2); 49; 50(2); 52(2); 58; 14:3(2); 6; 9(2); 20; 24; 25; 27; 29; 31; 33; 34; 35; 36; 15:2; 3(2); 6(2); 9; 11; 14; 18; 19; 21; 22(2); 24(2); 29; 31; 37; 39; 16:3(2); 4; 6(2); 8(2); 9; 10; 11(2); 12(4); 13(2); 14; 16; 18; 19(2); 23(3); 27(2); 28; 17:5; 9; 12; 13; 18; 20; 22(2); 25; 27; 18:1; 2; 3; 4; 6(2); 7; 10(2); 11; 12; 14(2); 16; 19; 20; 23; 27; 28; 35; 19:1; 7; 8(2); 10; 12; 14(2); 23; 24(2); 28(3); 20:1; 8; 12; 13; 18; 20; 21; 25; 28; 29; 30; 31; 21:1; 3; 5(2); 9(2); 11; 12(3); 13(2); 15; 16(2); 17; 23; 25; 31(3); 32; 37; 39; 40; 43(2); 45; 22:2; 5; 13; 16(2); 27; 28; 29; 30; 31; 32(5); 35; 42; 23:4; 5; 13; 15; 16; 22; 23(2); 25(2); 26(2); 27; 28; 29(2); 30(2); 31; 32; 33(2); 34(2); 35(3); 39; 24:1; 3(4); 6(2); 8; 12; 14; 15(2); 17; 21; 27(2); 29(2); 30(5); 31(2); 36(2); 37(3); 39(2); 43; 44; 50(2); 51; 25:1; 2; 8; 13; 14; 19; 21; 23; 30; 31(2); 34(2); 40(2); 45(2); 26:2; 3(2); 6; 7; 10; 14; 15; 17(2); 21; 22; 24(3); 27; 28(2); 29(2); 30; 31(3); 33; 37; 45(2); 47(2); 51(2); 53; 56; 57; 61; 63; 64(3); 65; 66; 67; 69; 71; 73; 75; 27:1; 3; 5; 6; 8; 9(4); 11; 18; 19; 21; 24(2); 27; 29(2); 32; 33; 37; 40; 42; 43; 47; 48; 51; 52; 53; 54; 56(2); 57; 58; 60(2); 62; 28:1; 2; 4; 11; 12; 19(4); 20; **Mk** 1:1(3); 3(2); 4(2); 5; 9; 14(2); 15; 16; 17; 19; 24(2); 25; 26; 29(2); 2:4; 6; 10; 12; 14; 17; 18(4); 19; 21; 23; 26(2); 28(2); 3:5; 9; 11; 17(3); 18; 21(2); 22; 28; 35; 4:4; 5; 11(2); 19(2); 26; 30; 32; 5:1(2); 2(2); 7; 8; 10; 11; 22(2); 23; 25; 29(2); 30; 34; 35; 36; 37; 38(2); 40; 42; 6:3(2); 6; 11; 14; 15; 17(2); 21; 23; 24; 25; 26(2); 29; 37; 43(2); 47; 48; 50; 53; 54; 56; 7:1; 2; 3; 4; 5; 6; 7; 8(3); 9; 13(2); 15; 20; 21(2); 24; 26; 29; 31(4); 35; 8:3; 8; 10; 15(3); 17; 19; 20; 23; 27; 28; 31; 33(3); 38(4); 9:1; 7; 9; 12; 13; 17; 24; 25; 26; 31(2); 35(2); 36; 37; 39; 41; 42; 47; 10:1(2); 4; 5(2); 6; 14(2); 15; 23; 24; 25(2); 33; 35; 44(2); 45; 46(2); 47(2); 48; 49; 11:1(2); 3; 5; 9; 10(2); 15(2); 17(2); 19; 30; 12:2(2); 8; 9; 13; 14(2); 22; 24; 26(4); 27(2); 28(2); 29; 34; 35; 38; 44(2); 13:1(3); 3; 7(2); 8; 14(2); 15; 19; 25; 26; 27(2); 32; 35(2); 14:1; 2; 3(3); 10; 12; 13(2); 14; 18; 20; 21(3); 24; 25(3); 26; 27(2); 41(2); 43; 47(2); 51; 54; 61; 62(3); 63; 64; 65; 66(2); 67; 69; 70; 71; 15:2; 3; 9; 10; 12; 17; 18; 21(2); 22; 26(2); 32; 35; 36; 38; 39; 40(2); 43(3); 46(2); 47; 16:1; 2; 3; 6; 9(2); 12; 14; 19; **Lk** 1:1; 2; 3; 4; 5(6); 6; 8; 9(2); 10(2); 11(3); 15; 16(2); 17(3); 19; 23; 26; 27(2); 29; 32(2); 33(2); 35(2); 38; 39; 40; 41; 42; 43; 44; 45; 48; 51; 54; 59; 65; 66(2); 68; 69(2); 70; 71; 74; 75; 76(2); 77(2); 78; 79(2); 80; 2:4(5); 9(2); 10; 11; 13; 21; 22(2); 23; 24(2); 25; 27; 31; 32; 33; 34; 35; 36(4); 37; 38; 39; 40; 41; 42; 46; 3:1(7); 2(2); 3(2); 4(4); 6; 7; 8; 9; 23(3); 24(5); 25(5); 26(5); 27(5); 28(5); 29(5); 30(5); 31(5); 32(5); 33(5); 34(5); 35(5); 36(5); 37(5); 38(4); 4:3; 4; 5(2); 9(2); 14(2); 17; 18(2); 19; 20; 22; 25; 26(2); 27(2); 29(2); 30; 31; 33; 34(2); 35(2); 38; 40; 41(2); 43; 44; 5:1(2); 3; 6; 9; 10; 12; 15; 17(4); 19; 24; 29; 31; 33(2); 34; 36; 6:1; 2; 4; 5(2); 15; 16; 17(4); 20; 22; 26; 30; 35; 45(6); 49; 7:1; 3; 11; 12(2); 18; 19; 21; 23; 24; 27; 28(2); 29; 30; 31; 34(2); 36; 37; 38; 39; 42; 44; 8:1(2); 2(2); 3; 5; 10(2); 11; 12; 13; 14; 19; 21; 22; 24; 26; 28; 29; 32; 33; 35; 37(2); 41; 42; 43; 44(2); 47; 48; 49; 51; 9:2; 5; 7; 8; 9; 11(2); 14; 17; 19; 20; 22; 26(4); 27; 29; 31; 35; 36; 43; 44(2); 46; 47; 52; 55(2); 56; 58(2); 60; 62; 10:2; 6; 7; 9; 11(2); 19; 21; 26; 30; 34; 35; 36; 11:1; 5; 6; 8; 11; 15(2); 20(2); 24; 26; 28; 29; 30; 31(4); 32(2); 34(3); 36(3); 39(2); 41; 42(2); 44; 45; 46; 47; 48; 49(2); 50(3); 51(3); 52; 12:1(4); 4; 6; 7(2); 8(2); 9; 10; 15(2); 16; 20; 24; 25; 27; 28; 30; 31; 39; 40; 42; 46; 48(2); 54; 56(2); 57; 13:7; 10; 11; 14; 15; 16(2); 18; 19; 20; 21; 25; 27; 28(2); 29; 33; 35; 14:1(3); 5; 10; 14; 15(2); 18; 19; 21(2); 24; 28; 32; 33; 15:4(2); 10(2); 12(2); 15; 17; 19; 26; 30; 16:2; 4; 5; 6; 7; 8(2); 14; 15; 16; 17; 20; 24; 28; 17:2; 7; 11; 15; 20(2); 21; 22(3); 24(2); 26(3); 28; 29; 30; 18:8; 12; 16(2); 17; 24; 25(2); 29(2); 31; 34; 37; 38; 39; 19:3(2); 8; 9; 10; 11; 13; 22; 27; 29; 31; 33; 34; 37(3); 38; 39; 44; 46(2); 47; 20:1; 4; 10(2); 13; 15(2); 20; 21; 26; 27; 32; 34; 36(2); 37(3); 38(2); 39; 41; 42; 45; 46; 21:4(2); 5; 9; 16; 18; 21; 22; 24(2); 25; 26(2); 27; 31; 34; 35; 36; 22:1; 6; 7; 10; 11; 16(2); 18(3); 19; 21; 22; 23; 24; 25; 30; 39; 44; 47; 48; 50(2); 52; 53; 55; 58; 61; 66; 69(3); 70; 23:1; 3; 6; 11; 14; 15; 23(2); 26; 27; 28; 35; 37; 38(2); 39; 41; 45; 51(2); 52; 53; 24:1; 3; 7(2); 10; 13; 14; 17; 19; 22; 23; 24; 25; 35; 36; 42; 44; 47; 48; 49(2); **Jn** 1:4; 7; 8; 12; 13(6); 14(3); 15(2); 16; 18; 19; 23(2); 29(2); 30; 34; 35; 36; 40; 42; 44; 45(3); 46; 47; 49(2); 51(2); 2:1(2); 3(2); 6(3); 8; 9(2); 11(2); 13; 15(2); 16; 21(2); 25; 3:1(2); 3; 5(2); 6(2); 8(2); 10; 13; 14; 18(2); 22; 25; 29(3); 31(2); 34; 36; 4:5(2); 7; 9; 10; 13; 14(2); 22; 30; 32; 34; 39(4); 41; 42(2); 46; 47(2); 52; 54; 5:1; 3(2); 4(2); 19; 25(2); 27; 29(2); 30(2); 31; 32(2); 36; 37; 39; 42; 6:1(2); 4; 7(2); 8; 11; 13; 22; 25; 26; 27; 28; 29; 33; 35; 38; 39(2); 40; 42; 48; 50; 51(2); 53(2); 57(2); 60; 62; 64; 66; 68; 69; 70; 71(3); 7:2; 7; 13(2); 14; 18; 19; 23; 25; 28; 31; 37; 38(2); 41; 42(2); 43; 44; 48; 50; 52; 8:1; 6; 10; 12(2); 13; 14; 17; 18(2); 23(2); 27; 28(2); 34; 39; 41(2); 42; 44(3); 46(2); 47(2); 54; 59(2); 9:3; 4; 5; 6; 7; 11; 16; 18; 21; 22; 23; 31; 32(2); 35; 40; 10:2; 5; 7; 16; 18; 19; 20; 21(2); 22; 25; 26; 28; 29; 32; 35; 36(2); 37; 39; 11:1(2); 4(2); 9; 13; 19; 22; 27; 37(2); 39; 40; 42; 45; 46; 49; 52; 55; 12:2; 3(4); 4; 7; 9; 11(2); 13(3); 15; 17; 21; 23; 24; 30; 31(2); 34(2); 36; 38(2); 41; 42(2); 43(2); 13:1; 2; 10; 18; 21; 23; 24; 26(2); 27; 30; 31; 14:11; 17; 30; 15:3; 4; 19(3); 26(2); 16:2; 4; 5; 8(3); 9; 10; 11(2); 13; 14; 15; 17; 29; 33; 17:6; 12(2); 14(2); 15; 16(2); 24; 18:3; 5; 7; 9; 12(2); 13; 15; 17; 18; 22(2); 23; 25; 26(3); 32; 33; 36(2); 37; 39; 19:2; 3; 5; 7; 14; 17; 19(2); 20; 21(3); 25(2); 29; 32(2); 34; 36; 38(5); 39; 40(3); 42; 20:1; 2; 12; 19(2); 23(2); 24; 25(2); 30; 31; 21:1; 2(3); 6(3); 9; 10; 11; 12; 15; 16; 17; 24; **Acts** 1:1; 3(2); 4; 8; 9; 11; 13(2); 14; 15(2); 16; 18; 19; 20; 21; 22(3); 24(2); 2:1; 2; 3(2); 10; 11; 13; 14; 15; 17; 19; 20(2); 21; 22(2); 23; 24; 28(2); 29; 30(2); 31; 32; 33(2); 36; 37; 38(4); 42; 46; 3:1; 2; 6(2); 10; 12; 13(3); 15(2); 16; 18; 19(2); 21(3); 25(3); 26; 4:1; 4(2); 6(2); 8(2); 10(3); 13; 15; 18; 19; 21(2); 22; 25; 26; 27; 30; 31; 32(3); 33; 34(2); 36(3); 5:2(2); 3(2); 9(2); 12; 13; 14; 15(2); 17; 19; 20; 21(2); 24; 30; 31; 34; 35; 36; 37(2); 38; 39; 40; 41; 6:1; 2(2); 3(2); 4; 5; 7(3); 8; 9; 14; 15; 7:2; 3; 4(2); 8; 10(3); 11; 16(3); 17; 22; 23; 24; 26; 29; 30(3); 31; 32(4); 34; 35; 36; 37; 40(3); 41; 42(3); 43(2); 44; 45(2); 46; 49; 52(3); 53; 55(3); 56(2); 58(2); 8:1; 3; 5; 7; 9; 10; 12(2); 14; 16(2); 18; 20; 21; 22(2); 24; 25(2); 26; 27(4); 34(3); 37; 39(2); 9:1; 2(2); 11(2); 15(2); 20; 26; 27; 29; 31(2); 32; 36; 10:1; 3(2); 7; 12(3); 22; 28; 31; 32; 36(2); 38; 39(2); 42; 43; 45(2); 48; 11:1; 2; 5; 6(2); 16; 20; 21; 22(2); 23(2); 24(2); 28(2); 30; 12:2; 3; 4; 7; 10; 11(2); 12(2); 13; 14; 17; 18; 20; 22(2); 23; 24; 13:1; 5(2); 7; 10(4); 11; 12; 15(3); 16; 17(3); 18; 19; 21(3); 22; 24(2); 25; 26(3); 27; 34; 36; 38; 39; 42; 43(2); 44; 46(2); 47; 48; 49; 50; 14:1(3); 3; 4; 6(2); 11; 13(2); 19; 22(2); 26; 27; 15:1; 2; 3; 5(3); 7; 10; 11; 14; 15; 16; 17; 22; 23; 26; 27; 35; 36; 40; 16:1; 2; 3; 6; 9; 12(2); 13; 14(2); 16; 17(2); 18(2); 19; 26; 27; 32; 33; 36; 40(2); 17:1; 4(3); 5(2); 6; 7; 8; 10; 12(2); 13; 18; 19; 22(2); 23; 24; 26(3); 27; 28; 29; 30; 31; 32(2); 18:3; 7; 8(2); 11; 12; 14; 15(2); 17(2); 18; 21; 23; 25(3); 26; 19:4; 5; 8(2); 9(2); 10; 11; 12; 13(2); 14; 16; 17; 19(4); 20; 22; 24; 25; 27(3); 28(2); 31(2); 32; 33; 34; 35(4); 37(2); 40; 20:4(4); 6; 7; 16; 17; 19; 24(3); 25; 26(2); 27; 28; 32; 35; 38; 21:5(2); 6; 8(2); 11; 13; 14; 16(2); 20; 24; 26(3); 28; 30; 31; 34; 35(2); 36; 39; 22:3(3); 5; 8; 9; 11(2); 14(2); 15; 16; 18; 20(2); 23:5(2); 6(2); 9; 11; 12; 16; 17; 21; 23; 29(2); 24:5(3); 7; 8; 10; 13; 14; 15(2); 18; 21; 22; 23; 25:2; 8; 11(2); 15; 16; 18; 20; 21; 23; 24; 25; 26:2; 4; 5; 6; 9(2); 10; 16(2); 18(2); 20; 25; 26; 31; 27:1; 2(3); 4; 5; 7; 8; 10; 11; 12; 16; 21; 22(2); 23; 30; 32; 34(2); 35; 41; 42; 44; 28:2(2); 3(2); 7(2); 8(2); 9; 16; 17(3); 19; 20; 21(2); 23(3); 27(2); 28; 31; **Rom** 1:1(2); 3(2); 4(2); 6; 7; 8; 9(2); 10; 12; 16(3); 17; 18(2); 19; 20; 23; 24; 25; 27(2); 29; 30(2); 32(3); 2:2; 3; 4(2); 5(3); 9(3); 13(3); 15; 16; 18; 20(3); 24(2); 25; 26; 27; 29; 3:1; 2; 3; 5; 7; 13; 14; 17; 18; 20(2); 21; 22; 23(2); 26; 27(2); 28; 29(3); 4:6; 11(4); 12(3); 13(2); 14(2); 16(5); 17(2); 18; 19; 20; 25(2); 5:2(2); 5; 10; 14(3); 15(2); 17(3); 18; 6:3; 4(2); 5(2); 6(2); 13(2); 16(2); 17(2); 18; 19(5); 20; 21(2); 22; 23(2); 7:2; 4; 6(2); 8; 22; 23(2); 24; 25(2); 8:2(3); 3(2); 4; 5(2); 7; 9(2); 10(2); 11; 13; 14(2); 15(2); 16; 17; 18; 19(3); 20; 21(3); 23(2); 27(2); 29; 34; 35; 39; 9:4(2); 5; 6(2); 7; 8(3); 9; 11(3); 16(3); 22; 23(2); 24(2); 26; 27(3); 29; 30; 31(2); 32; 33; 10:3(2); 4; 5; 6; 8; 13; 14; 15(3); 17; 18; 11:1(4); 2; 5; 6(2); 8; 14; 15; 17(3); 20; 22; 24; 25(2); 26; 28; 29; 33(3); 34; 36; 12:1; 2(2); 3(2); 5; 13; 16; 17; 20; 13:2; 3; 5; 6; 10; 11; 12(2); 14:7; 9; 10; 12(2); 14; 15; 16; 17; 20(2); 15:1; 2; 3; 4; 5; 6; 7; 8; 12; 13(2); 14; 15; 16(3); 18(2); 19(3); 27; 28; 29(3); 30; 32; 33; 16:1; 2(4); 4; 5; 7; 10(2); 11(2); 16; 18; 20(2); 23(2); 24; 25(2); 26; **1 Cor** 1:1(2); 2(2); 4; 6; 7; 8; 9; 10; 11; 12(5); 13; 14; 16; 17(3); 18(2); 19(2); 20(2); 21(2); 24(2); 25(2); 27(2); 28; 30; 2:1(3); 4(3); 5(2); 6(3); 7; 8(3); 9; 10; 11(4); 12; 14(2); 16(2); 3:4(2); 10; 13; 16(2); 17(2); 19; 20; 4:1(3); 5(2); 6(2); 13(2); 17; 19; 20; 21; 5:4(2); 5(2); 8(2); 10(2); 6:1; 9; 10; 11(3); 12; 15(3); 19; 7:1; 2; 5(2); 19; 23; 26; 31; 32; 33; 34(2); 36; 40; 8:4; 6; 7; 9; 10; 11; 9:2; 5; 7(3); 9; 10; 12(2); 13(4); 15; 16; 18; 23; 10:4; 5; 7; 8; 9; 10; 11; 13; 16(5); 17; 18(2); 21(5); 27; 28; 29; 30; 31; 32; 33; 11:3(3); 7(2); 10(2); 11(2); 16; 18; 21; 22; 24; 25; 27(3); 28(2); 12:3; 4; 5; 6; 7(2); 8(2); 9; 10(4); 12; 15(2); 16(2); 18; 21(2); 22; 23; 27; 28(2); 29; 30; 13:1(2); 2; 13; 14:10(2); 11; 12; 16(2); 21; 23; 25; 26; 32; 33(3); 36; 37; 15:3; 6; 8(2); 9(2); 10(2); 12; 13; 15(2); 19; 20; 21; 32; 34; 39(5); 40(2); 41(3); 42; 47(2); 48(2); 49(3); 50; 52; 56(2); 58; 16:1; 2(2); 10; 15(3); 17; 19; 23; **2 Cor** 1:1(3); 3(3); 5; 7(2); 8(2); 9; 12(2); 14; 16; 19; 20(2); 2:3; 4(2); 5; 10; 11(2); 13; 14; 15; 16(2); 17(3); 3:1(2); 3(5); 5(2); 6(3); 7(5); 8; 9(2); 10; 12; 13(2); 14; 17; 18(2); 4:2(4); 4(5); 6(5); 7(3); 10(2); 11; 13; 15; 17; 5:10; 11; 13; 14; 18(2); 19; 21; 6:1; 2(2); 4; 7(3); 16(2); 7:1(2); 4; 6; 7; 10; 11; 12(3); 13; 15; 8:1(2); 2(3); 4; 5; 8(2); 9; 11(2); 16; 17; 19; 21(2); 22; 23(2); 24(2); 9:2; 3; 4; 5(2); 7; 10; 12(2); 13(3); 14(2); 10:1; 2; 4; 5(2); 13; 14; 15; 16; 11:7(2); 10(2); 12; 13; 14; 15; 17; 22; 23; 26(4); 31; 32; 12:1; 2; 3; 5(2); 6; 7(2); 9; 12; 17(2); 18; 20; 21; 13:1; 3; 4(2); 11(3); 14(3); **Gal** 1:2; 4; 6; 7; 10; 12; 13(2); 14(2); 19; 21; 22; 2:2; 4; 5; 9; 12; 13; 14(2); 15; 16(3); 17; 20; 21; 3:2(2); 5(2); 7(2); 9; 10(3); 11; 12; 13; 14(2); 15; 16(2); 17; 18(2); 19(2); 21; 26; 27; 4:1; 3; 4(2); 6; 7; 13; 14; 23(2); 26; 28; 30(2); 31(2); 5:1; 5; 11; 16; 19; 20; 21(2); 22; 6:1; 2; 8(2); 10(2); 12; 14; 16; 17; 18; **Eph** 1:1(2); 3; 4; 5; 6(2); 7(2); 9; 10(2); 11(2); 12; 13(3); 14(3); 15; 16; 17(4); 18(4); 19(2); 23; 2:2(4); 3(4); 4; 7; 8(2); 9; 12(2); 13; 14; 15; 19(2); 20; 22; 3:1; 2(3); 4; 5; 6(2); 7(4); 8(2); 9(2); 10; 14; 16; 19(2); 4:1(2); 3(2); 4; 6; 7(2); 9; 12(4); 13(7); 14(3); 16(2); 17(2); 18(4); 23; 25(2); 29; 30(2); 5:1; 4; 5; 6(3); 8; 9; 11; 12; 17; 20; 21; 23(3); 26; 30(3); 33; 6:4; 5; 6(2); 10; 11(2); 12(3); 13; 14; 15(2); 16(2); 17(3); 19; **Phil** 1:1; 3; 4; 6(2); 7(3); 8; 10; 11(2); 12; 14; 17(2); 19(2); 25(2); 27(4); 28(2); 29; 2:1(2); 2(2); 3; 4(2); 6; 7(3); 8(2); 10(4); 11; 15(2); 16(2); 17; 21; 30; 3:2(3); 5(5); 8(3); 10(2); 12(2); 14(2); 16; 18(3); 4:2; 3(2); 7; 8; 9; 15; 22; 23; **Col** 1:1(2); 3; 4(2); 5(4); 6; 7; 9; 10(2); 12(2); 13(3); 14; 15; 18; 20; 22; 23(2); 24(2); 25(2); 27(3); 2:2(6); 3; 5; 8(2); 9; 10; 11(3); 12; 13; 14(2); 15; 17(2); 18(2); 20; 22; 23(4); 3:1; 6(3); 8; 10; 12; 14; 15; 16; 17; 22; 24; 4:3; 9; 10; 11(2); 12(3); 16; **1 Th** 1:1; 2; 3(4); 5; 6(3); 8; 9; 2:2; 6; 8; 9(2); 11; 12; 13(3); 14(2); 16; 19(2); 3:2(2); 6(2); 13; 4:3; 4; 5; 6(2); 15(2); 16(2); 5:2; 5(4); 8(3); 18; 22; 23(2); 28; **2 Th** 1:1; 3(2); 4(2); 5(4); 8; 9(2); 11(3); 12(2); 2:1; 2; 3(2); 4; 7(2); 8(2); 9(2); 10; 14(2); 3:1; 5(2); 6; 8(2); 9; 16; 17; 18; **1 Tim** 1:1(2); 5; 7; 9(2); 11; 14; 15(2); 20; 2:1(2); 3; 4; 7; 3:1; 2(2); 5(2); 7; 9; 12; 15(3); 16; 4:1; 4; 5; 6(3); 8(2); 9; 10(2); 14(2); 5:8; 9; 17; 18; 20; 24; 25; 6:1(2); 3; 5(4); 10(3); 11; 12(2); 13; 15(2); 20; **2 Tim** 1:1(3); 4; 6(2); 7(4); 8(4); 10; 11; 13; 16(2); 2:3; 4; 6; 8(2); 9(2); 10; 14(2); 15; 17; 18; 19(2); 20(2); 22; 24; 26; 3:2(2); 3; 4(2); 5; 6(2); 7; 8; 10; 11; 14; 16; 17; 4:2; 5; 6; 8; 15; 17(2); 19; **Titus** 1:1(4); 2; 3; 6(2); 7; 8; 10; 11; 12(2); 14; 2:3; 5; 7; 8; 10; 11; 13; 3:2; 4; 5(3); 7; **Phm** 1:1; 4; 5; 6(2); 7; 9; 25; **Heb** 1:2; 3(4); 5; 6; 7(2); 8(2); 9; 10(2); 13; 2:4; 5; 6(3); 7; 9(2); 10; 11; 12; 14(2); 15; 16; 17; 3:1(2); 3; 5; 6; 8; 12(2); 13(2); 14(2); 16; 19; 4:1(3); 3; 4; 6; 8; 9; 11; 12(5); 13; 14; 16(2); 5:3; 6; 7(2); 9; 10; 11(2); 12(2); 13(2); 14(2); 6:1(4); 2(7); 4; 5(2); 6; 9; 10; 11(2); 16; 17(2); 18; 19; 20; 7:1(3); 2(4); 3(3); 4; 5(3); 8; 10; 11(2); 12(2); 13; 14; 15; 16(2); 17; 18(2); 19; 21; 22; 28; 8:1(3); 2(2); 5; 6; 8(2); 9(2); 10; 11(3); 9:1; 3(2); 4(2); 5(2); 6; 8; 10; 11(2); 12; 13(3); 14; 15(4); 16(2); 19; 20; 21; 22; 23; 24(2); 25; 26(3); 28; 10:1(2); 2; 3; 4; 7(2); 10(2); 12; 18; 19; 21; 22; 23; 25(2); 26; 27; 28; 29(4); 31; 33; 34; 36(2); 39(3); 11:1(2); 3(2); 4; 6; 7(3); 9(2); 12; 13; 18; 21(3); 22(3); 23; 24(2); 25(2); 26; 27; 28; 30; 32(2); 33; 34(4); 36(2); 38(2); 12:1; 2(3); 5; 8; 9; 10; 11; 15(3); 16; 19(2); 22(2); 23(3); 24(3); 27(2); 13:7(2); 11; 15(2); 20(3); 22; **Jas** 1:1(2); 3; 5(2); 6; 10; 12; 17(2); 18(4); 20(2); 21; 22; 23; 24; 25(2); 2:1(2); 5(2); 10; 11; 12; 15; 16; 23; 3:1; 6(2); 7(3); 8; 9; 10; 13; 17; 18; 4:4(2); 10; 11(4); 5:4(4); 5; 7(2); 8; 10(2); 11(2); 14(2); 15; 16; 20(2); **1 Pe** 1:1(2); 2(4); 3(2); 5; 7(2); 8; 9(2); 10(2); 11(3); 13(2); 17; 19(2); 20; 22; 23(2); 24(2); 25; 2:2; 8(2); 9(2); 10; 12; 13; 14(2); 15(2); 16; 19; 25; 3:1; 4(3); 7(2); 8(2); 12(2); 13; 14; 17; 20; 21(4); 22; 4:2(3); 3(2); 4(2); 7; 8; 10(2); 11; 13; 14(3); 15; 17(3); 19; 5:1(3); 2; 4; 5; 6; 10; 12; 14; **2 Pe** 1:1(2); 2(2); 3; 4; 8; 11; 12; 15; 16(2); 20(2); 21(2); 2:2(2); 4; 5(3); 6; 7; 9(2); 10(2); 12; 13; 14; 15(3); 16; 17; 18(2); 19; 20(2); 21; 3:1(2); 2(4); 4(2); 5(3); 7(2); 10; 11; 12(3); 15; 16(2); 17; 18; **1 Jn** 1:1; 7; 2:5; 14; 15; 16(5); 17(2); 19(4); 21; 29; 3:1(2); 2; 8(3); 9(2); 10(3); 12; 17; 19; 23; 4:1; 2(2); 3(2); 4; 5(2); 6(4); 7(2); 9; 13; 14; 15; 17; 5:1(2); 2; 3; 4; 5; 9(4); 10(2); 12; 13(4); 15; 18(2); 19(2); 20; **2 Jn** 2; 3; 4; 9(2); 13; **3 Jn** 3; 6(2); 10; 11; **Jude** 1(2); 4; 5(2); 6; 7; 8; 9; 10; 11(3); 13(2); 14; 15(2); 17; 21(2); 23; 24; **Rev** 1:1; 2(2); 3; 5; 7(2); 9(3); 10; 13(2); 14; 15; 16; 18(2); 20(2); 2:1(3); 6; 7(3); 8; 9(2); 10(3); 12; 14(2); 15; 16; 17; 18(3); 21; 22; 23; 24; 27; 3:1(2); 5; 7(2); 9(2); 10; 12(5); 14(4); 16; 17; 18; 4:4; 5(2); 6(3); 8; 5:1; 5(4); 6(4); 7(2); 8(2); 9; 11(3); 6:1(2); 5; 6(3); 7; 8(3); 9(2); 11(2); 12; 13; 14; 15(2); 16(2); 17; 7:1(2); 2; 3; 4(4); 5(6); 6(6); 7(6); 8(6); 9; 13; 14(2); 15; 17(2); 8:3; 4(2); 7; 8; 9(2); 10(2); 11(2); 12(5); 13(5); 9:2(4); 3(2); 4(2); 5; 7(3); 9(3); 11; 13; 15; 16(3); 17(4); 18(2); 20(4); 21; 10:1; 7(3); 8; 10; 11:1; 4; 6; 7; 8; 11; 13(2); 15(3); 18; 19(2); 12:1; 4(2); 5; 9; 10(3); 11(2); 12; 14(2); 15; 16; 17(3); 13:1(2); 2(2); 3; 8(3); 10; 11; 12; 13; 14; 15(3); 17(2); 18(2); 14:2(3); 5; 6; 7(2); 8(3); 10(6); 11(2); 12(3); 14; 15(2); 17; 18(2); 19(3); 20; 15:1; 2(4); 3(4); 5(2); 6; 7(3); 8(2); 16:1(2); 2; 3; 4; 5; 6; 9; 10(3); 11(3); 12; 13(6); 14(5); 17(2); 19(4); 21(3); 17:1(2); 2(3); 3(2); 4(2); 5(3); 6(3); 7(2); 8(3); 11; 13; 14(2); 17(2); 18; 18:2; 3(6); 4(2); 9(2); 10; 11; 12(6); 13; 15(2); 18; 22(3); 23(3); 24(2); 19:1; 2; 6(3); 7; 8; 9(2); 10(4); 12; 13; 15(4); 16(2); 17(2); 18(6); 19; 20(2); 21; 20:2(2); 4(2); 5; 6(2); 8(2); 9(3); 10; 12; 14; 15(2); 21:2; 3; 6(3); 9; 10; 11; 12(3); 14(3); 17(2); 18(2); 19(3); 21(2); 23(3); 24(2); 26; 27; 22:1(4); 2(5); 3(2); 5; 6; 7(2); 8; 9(3); 10(2); 14; 16; 17; 18(2); 19(3); 21

OH (104/100)

Gen 17:18; 30:34; **Ex** 16:3; 32:31; **Num** 11:29; 12:11; 23:23; **Deut** 5:29; 28:67(2); 32:29; **Josh** 7:7; **2 Sam** 15:4; 23:15; **1 Chr** 4:10; 11:17; 16:8; 29; 34; **Job** 3:7; 6:2; 8; 7:7; 10:18; 11:5; 13:5; 14:13; 16:21; 19:23(2); 23:3; 29:2; 31:35(2); 34:36; **Ps** 6:4; 7:9; 14:7; 31:19; 23; 34:3; 8; 9; 36:10; 43:1; 3; 47:1; 53:6; 55:6; 60:1; 61:7; 66:8; 67:4; 68:32; 73:19; 74:19; 21; 79:8; 81:13; 86:16; 90:14; 95:1; 6; 96:1; 9; 98:1; 101:2; 105:1; 106:1; 4; 107:1; 8; 15; 21; 31; 109:26; 118:1; 29; 119:5; 8; 10; 97; 136:1; 2; 3; 26; 139:19; **Prov** 30:13; **Song** 8:1; **Isa** 21:10; 48:18; 64:1; **Jer** 9:1; 2; 44:4; 51:41(2); **Am** 7:2; 5; **Ob** 5; 6; **Mal** 1:13; **Rom** 11:33; **2 Cor** 11:1

ON (4232/3472)

Gen 1:2; 11; 15; 17; 22; 25; 26; 28; 29; 30; 2:2(2); 5; 21; 3:14; 4:12; 14; 15(2); 16; 26; 6:1; 4; 6; 12; 17(2); 7:3; 4; 6; 8; 10; 11; 12; 13; 14; 17; 18(2); 19; 21(2); 22; 23; 24; 8:4; 5; 9; 14; 17(3); 19; 20; 9:2(5); 16(2); 17; 23; 10:8; 32; 12:8(3); 9; 13:3; 4; 15:11; 18; 16:7; 17:3; 17; 18:3; 16; 19:2; 24; 25; 31; 34; 20:9(2); 11; 21:8; 14; 33; 22:2; 4; 6; 9; 12; 17; 24:15; 27; 30; 33; 45; 47(2); 61; 26:9; 10; 25; 27:12; 13; 15; 16(2); 28:12(2); 13; 18; 20; 29:1; 2; 3; 32; 30:3; 31:12; 17; 22; 34; 46; 54(2); 32:1; 21; 31(2); 32; 33:4; 14(2); 16; 34:15; 22; 25; 35:14(2); 19; 20; 37:22; 23; 25; 34; 38:9; 14; 19; 28; 30; 39:5; 7; 40:16; 17; 19; 20; 41:3; 5; 17; 22; 42; 45; 50; 44:14; 21; 45:14(2); 46:4; 20; 29(2); 47:31; 48:2; 7(2); 14(2); 17; 18; 49:8; 26(2); 50:1; 23; **Ex** 1:16; 2:6; 3:12; 22(2); 4:3(2); 9(2); 20; 24; 27; 31; 5:8; 9; 21; 22; 6:28; 7:4; 5; 8:3(2); 4(3); 5; 7; 17; 18; 21(3); 9:3(6); 6; 9; 10; 11(2); 14(2); 19; 22(3); 23; 33; 10:6; 13; 14; 15(2); 11:1(2); 5; 12:3; 7(2); 8; 11(2); 12; 13(2); 15; 16(3); 17; 18; 23(2); 29; 34; 37; 41; 51; 13:4; 6; 9; 16; 14:16; 22(3); 26(2); 29(3); 30; 15:9; 16; 19; 26(2); 16:1; 5; 14(2); 22; 26; 27; 29(2); 30; 17:1; 5; 6; 9; 12(3); 18:8; 13; 19:1; 4; 11; 16(2); 20; 20:5; 24; 25; 26; 21:22; 30(2); 22:3; 30; 23:12; 24:6; 8; 11; 12; 16(2); 17; 18; 25:11; 12(2); 14; 21; 22; 26; 30; 33(2); 34; 40; 26:4(3);

5(2); 10(2); 13(4); 26; 27; 30; 35(2); 27:2; 4; 7; 8; 12; 13; 14; 15; 21; 28:8; 9; 10(2); 12(2); 23; 24; 25; 26(3); 27; 29; 36; 37(3); 38(2); 41(2); 43(2); 29:5; 6(2); 7; 8; 9; 10; 12; 13(2); 15; 16; 18; 19; 20(5); 21(5); 22; 25; 30; 38; 30:1; 4(2); 7(2); 8; 9(2); 32; 33; 31:7; 14; 15; 17; 18; 32:6; 15(3); 16; 20; 22; 26; 27; 29; 30; 33:3; 4; 19; 21; 34:1(2); 2; 21; 28; 32; 33; 35; 35:2; 3; 36:8; 11(3); 12(3); 17(2); 31; 32(2); 37:3(2); 8(2); 13; 16; 19(2); 20; 27; 38:2; 7; 9; 11; 12; 15; 39:5; 7; 16; 17; 18; 19(3); 20; 24; 25; 30; 31; 40:2; 4; 13; 17; 19; 20; 22; 24; 27; **Lev** 1:4(2); 5; 7(2); 8(2); 9; 11(2); 12(2); 13; 15; 16; 17(3); 2:1(2); 2; 6; 9; 12; 14; 15(2); 3:2(2); 3; 4; 5(3); 8(2); 9; 10; 11; 13(2); 14; 15; 16; 4:3; 4; 7; 8; 9; 10; 12; 15; 18; 19; 24; 25; 26; 29; 30; 31; 33; 34; 35; 5:9; 10; 11(2); 12; 6:5; 9(2); 10(3); 11; 12(5); 13; 14; 15(2); 20; 27(2); 7:2; 4; 5; 16; 17; 18; 31; 35; 36; 38(2); 8:7(3); 8; 9(3); 11; 12; 13(2); 14; 15; 16(2); 18; 19; 21; 22; 23(3); 24(4); 25; 26(2); 28(2); 30(5); 9:1; 9; 10; 12; 13; 14; 17; 18; 20(2); 24(2); 10:1; 11:2; 20; 21(2); 27(2); 29; 32; 35; 37; 38(2); 41; 42(3); 44; 46; 12:3; 13:2(2); 3(2); 4; 5(2); 6(2); 8; 9; 10; 11; 14; 24; 27; 28; 29; 32; 34; 38; 39(2); 41; 42(2); 43(3); 44; 45; 51; 14:7; 9; 10; 14(3); 17(4); 18; 20; 23; 25(3); 28(4); 29; 37; 39(2); 15:4(2); 6(2); 8; 9; 14; 17; 20(2); 22; 23(3); 24(2); 26(2); 29; 16:2; 4(2); 9; 10; 13(2); 14(2); 15; 18; 19; 21(2); 22; 23; 24; 25; 29; 30; 32; 17:6; 19:6; 7; 28; 20:25; 21:5; 10; 22:20; 22; 25; 28; 30; 23:3; 5; 6; 7(2); 8; 11(2); 12; 21(2); 24; 25; 28; 29; 30; 32; 35(2); 36(2); 37; 39(3); 40; 24:4; 6; 7(2); 14; 25:1; 9(2); 21; 26:9; 21; 30; 35; 46; 27:23; 34; **Num** 1:1; 18; 53; 2:3; 10; 18; 25; 3:1; 13; 29; 35; 38; 4:6; 7(3); 10; 12; 14(2); 25; 5:15(2); 17; 26; 6:7; 9(2); 10; 18; 27; 7:9; 12; 18; 24; 30; 36; 42; 48; 54; 60; 66; 72; 78; 89; 8:7; 10; 12; 17; 9:3; 5; 6; 10; 11; 13; 15; 10:5; 6; 11; 12; 33; 11:8; 9(2); 11; 21; 31(2); 12:3; 11; 13:23; 14:5; 18; 15:30; 32; 38; 16:1; 4; 18; 22; 39; 41; 45; 46; 17:2; 3; 8; 18:5; 17; 19:2; 12(4); 13(2); 15; 17; 18(4); 19(3); 20; 20:6; 16; 19; 26; 28(2); 21:1; 4; 8; 9; 10; 13; 15; 20; 22:1; 22; 24(2); 30; 31; 36; 23:2; 4; 14; 30; 24:20; 21; 27:18; 23; 28:9; 16; 17; 18; 25; 26; 29:1; 7; 12; 17; 20; 23; 26; 29; 32; 35; 30:5; 7; 8; 12; 14; 31:2; 3; 19(2); 24; 28; 32:10; 19(2); 32; 33:3(2); 4; 6; 37; 38; 39; 34:4(2); 11; 15; 35:5(4); 14; 30; 33; **Deut** 1:1; 3; 5; 7; 19; 36; 41; 2:28; 36; 3:8; 24; 26; 4:10; 13; 17; 18; 32; 36; 39; 41; 43; 46; 47; 48; 49; 5:4; 22; 6:8; 9(2); 7:6; 7; 15; 16; 25; 8:4; 9:9; 10(2); 27(2); 10:1; 2(2); 4; 11:12; 18; 20(2); 24; 29(2); 30; 12:1; 2(2); 16; 24; 27(2); 13:17; 14:2; 15:23; 16:8(2); 17:6(2); 18; 20:2; 3; 21:8; 16(2); 22; 23; 22:5; 6(3); 8; 12; 14; 19; 23:4; 19; 25; 24:4; 9; 15(2); 25:17; 18; 26:6; 7; 27:2; 3; 4; 5; 6; 8; 11; 12; 13; 28:8; 20; 24; 35; 46; 48; 56; 60; 29:5(2); 20; 22; 27; 30:3; 7(2); 32:2(2); 11; 22; 23(2); 36; 41; 46; 50(2); 33:2; 10; 16(2); 26; 34:9; **Josh** 1:14; 15; 2:6; 8; 9; 10; 11; 15(2); 19(3); 3:17(2); 4:5; 14; 19(2); 22; 5:1; 4; 5; 7; 10(2); 11(2); 12; 14; 6:13; 15(2); 7:2; 5; 6(2); 7; 10; 8:8; 9; 11; 12; 13(2); 19; 20; 22(2); 29; 31; 32; 33; 9:1; 4; 5(2); 12; 17; 10:11(2); 24(2); 26(2); 28; 32; 35; 11:2; 4; 13; 12:1; 2; 7(2); 13:9; 16; 19; 27; 32; 14:3; 9; 11; 15:3; 5; 7; 10(2); 16:1; 5; 6(2); 17:5; 8; 9; 10(2); 18:5(2); 7; 12(2); 13; 15; 16(2); 20; 19:13(2); 14; 27; 34(2); 20:8(2); 22:4; 7; 11(2); 20; 23(2); 23:13; 24:2; 8; 14; 15; 30; **Judg** 1:8; 2:9; 3:16; 25; 4:15; 17; 23; 5:1; 10; 17; 18; 21; 6:20; 26; 28; 32; 37(3); 39(2); 40(2); 7:1; 5; 6; 9; 18; 25; 8:11; 21; 26; 34; 9:5; 7; 18; 24(2); 25; 42; 48; 49; 53; 57(2); 10:4; 8; 11:18; 35; 37; 38; 12:1; 14; 13:19; 20; 14:15; 16; 17(2); 18; 15:5; 7; 14; 16:3; 19; 26; 27; 28; 29(2); 30; 17:2; 9; 18:5; 6; 10; 19:5; 8; 12; 14; 22; 27; 20:21; 22; 24; 25; 30; 36; 45; 21:4; 19; **Ruth** 1:7; 2:9; 10; 3:3; 15(2); 4:5; 16; **1 Sam** 1:9; 11; 2:34; 4:12; 13; 5:3; 4(2); 5; 6; 9; 6:4(2); 8; 11; 15; 18; 7:1; 16; 9:12; 14; 20(3); 25; 26(2); 27(2); 10:1; 3; 11:2(2); 7; 11; 12:11; 13:5; 12; 22; 14:1; 4(2); 13; 24; 25; 32(2); 40(2); 47; 15:2; 12; 16; 18; 19; 20(2); 16:16; 17:3(4); 5; 6; 38; 49; 18:4; 10; 25; 19:2; 23; 20:19; 21; 25(2); 31; 41; 21:2(2); 3; 4; 6; 8; 13(2); 22:18; 23:19; 21; 24; 26(2); 24:2; 7; 12; 25:8; 12; 13(3); 18; 19; 20; 23; 24(2); 39; 42; 26:12; 13; 25; 27:11; 28:8; 20; 22; 23; 30:1; 17; 31:1; 4; 5; 7(2); 8; **2 Sam** 1:2(2); 6(2); 10(2); 16; 19; 24; 2:13(2); 21; 23; 25; 29; 3:6; 12; 29(3); 4:5; 7; 11; 5:8; 10; 6:3(2); 4; 5(6); 7:9; 23; 9:6; 11:2; 13; 21; 12:16; 18; 30; 13:5; 18; 19(3); 29; 30; 31; 34; 14:2; 4; 7; 9(2); 12; 14; 22; 26; 30(2); 31; 33; 15:32; 33; 16:1; 2; 6(2); 12; 22; 17:12(2); 14; 19; 18:9(2); 19:19; 26; 40(2); 20:8; 10; 13; 21:9; 10(3); 20(2); 22:1; 28; 34; 23:1; 2; 20; 24:5; 18; **1 Ki** 1:1; 13; 17; 20(2); 24; 27; 30; 33; 35; 38; 44; 46; 47; 48; 2:4; 5(3); 12; 15; 19; 24; 32; 37(2); 42; 44; 3:4; 6; 19; 4:24(3); 29; 5:3; 4; 5; 6:8; 32(3); 35(2); 7:2; 3; 9; 16; 17; 18; 19; 20(2); 21(2); 25; 29(3); 31; 35(2); 36(3); 38; 39(3); 41(2); 42; 43; 48; 49(2); 8:20; 23; 25; 27; 32; 36; 50; 54; 64; 66; 9:5; 9; 25(2); 26; 10:5; 9; 19; 20; 11:7; 29; 30; 12:4; 9; 10; 11; 31; 32(2); 33(3); 13:2(3); 3; 13; 24(2); 25; 28; 29; 32; 14:10; 23; 16:11; 24; 17:14; 19; 20; 21; 18:1; 7(2); 19; 20; 23(2); 24(2); 25; 26; 27; 28; 33(3); 39; 42; 19:6; 11; 15; 19; 20:11; 20; 29; 30; 21:4; 21; 27; 29; 22:10(2); 17; 19(3); 24; 25; 30; 43; **2 Ki** 1:9; 13; 2:2; 4; 6(2); 8; 11; 15; 24; 3:9; 11; 22(2); 25; 4:7; 10; 13; 20; 21; 29(2); 31(2); 32; 34(5); 35; 38; 5:2(2); 11; 18; 23; 6:26; 29; 30(2); 31; 7:2; 17; 8:12; 15; 29; 9:3; 6; 10; 13; 15; 17; 21; 26; 30; 32; 33(2); 36; 37; 10:3; 12; 24; 30; 11:5(2); 7; 8; 9(3); 12; 19; 12:3; 9; 11; 13:13; 16(3); 21; 23; 14:4; 20; 15:4; 12; 35; 16:4(2); 12; 13; 14; 15(2); 17; 18; 17:10; 11; 29; 18:14; 17; 21; 23(2); 26; 27; 19:22; 26; 35; 20:5; 7; 11; 22:16(2); 20; 23:5; 6; 12; 13; 16(2); 20(2); 33; 25:1; 6; 8; 17; 27; **1 Chr** 1:10; 4:10; 6:44; 49(2); 78(2); 9:18; 10:1; 4; 5; 8; 11:9; 22; 12:8; 18; 40(2); 13:7; 8(4); 14:9; 13; 15:15; 21; 16:7; 40; 17:8; 21; 18:7; 20:2; 6(2); 21:16; 18; 22; 26(2); 28; 22:8; 18; 23:31(3); 26:16; 17(3); 18(2); 30; 28:5; 29:3; 15; 21; 22; 23; 25(2); **2 Chr** 1:6; 7; 2:4(3); 3:1(2); 2; 5; 7; 13; 15; 16(2); 17(4); 4:4; 6(2); 7(2); 8(2); 10; 12(2); 13; 14; 19; 6:10; 13(2); 14; 16; 18; 23(2); 27; 7:3(2); 9; 10; 22; 8:12; 17; 9:4; 8; 18; 19; 10:4; 9; 10; 11; 12; 11:12; 12:7; 13:4; 11; 18; 14:7; 11; 15:5; 16:7(2); 8; 9(2); 17:10; 18:9; 16; 18(2); 23; 24; 29; 20:24; 25; 26; 29; 22:8; 23:4; 7; 8(3); 11; 20; 24:4; 9; 22; 25; 25:28; 26:11; 15; 16; 19; 20; 27:3; 28:4(2); 15; 29:6; 17(3); 21; 22(3); 23; 24; 27; 30:12; 15; 32:12; 18; 22; 33:14; 16; 17; 34:4; 5; 21; 24(2); 25; 28; 35:1; 3; 16; 36:3; 15(2); 17(2); **Ezra** 3:2; 3(2); 9; 5:8; 15; 6:7; 8; 11; 15; 19; 7:9(2); 17; 24; 26; 8:22; 31; 33; 9:5; 10:9; 16; **Neh** 2:12; 14; 3:25; 26; 4:3; 4; 16; 17; 19; 5:4; 15; 16; 18; 6:15; 8:2; 4; 13; 16; 18; 9:1(2); 4; 6; 11; 12; 13; 19; 32; 10:1; 31(3); 34; 12:31(2); 37; 38; 13:1; 15(3); 16; 18(3); 19; 21(3); **Esth** 1:2; 6(2); 10; 2:21; 23; 3:6; 7; 12; 13; 4:1; 5:1(3); 14; 6:2; 3; 4; 8(2); 9; 11; 7:2; 9(2); 10; 8:1; 7(2); 9; 10(2); 12(2); 13(2); 14(2); 9:1(2); 2; 10; 11; 13; 15(2); 16; 17(2); 18(3); 22; 25(2); 10:1(2); **Job** 1:4; 7(2); 8; 10; 12; 19; 2:2(2); 3; 12; 13; 3:3; 5; 4:13; 15; 5:10(2); 11; 6:2; 30; 7:1; 17; 8:9; 15; 9:8; 26; 33; 10:3; 12:4; 21; 13:13; 14:3; 20; 16:9; 10; 13; 16; 19; 17:2; 18:10; 11; 15; 19:10; 21(2); 24; 25; 20:4; 23(2); 21:22; 30; 22:28; 23:9; 24:2; 18; 20; 21; 23(2); 26:7; 10; 27:10; 28:9; 29:9; 14; 19; 22; 30:22; 31:2; 6; 30; 36(2); 33:7; 15; 19; 34:14; 21; 36:2; 7; 16; 25; 28; 37:6; 12; 38:14; 26; 39:14; 18; 27; 28(2); 40:11; 12; 41:8; 23; 33; **Ps** 2:6; 3:7; 4:1; 4; 6:2; 7:7; 16; 8:9:4; 13; 10:8; 11:2; 12:8; 14:4; 16:3; 4; 17:2; 18:33; 21:12; 22:9; 25:3; 5; 16; 18; 27:14(2); 30:10; 31:9; 13; 33:14; 18(2); 34:15; 35:17; 36:4; 37:3; 9; 34; 41:2; 3(2); 43:4; 47:8; 48:2; 9; 49:4; 14; 50:10; 51:19; 52:9; 55:10; 22; 57:4; 59:10; 61:62:9; 10; 63:6(2); 65:12(2); 66:6; 11; 67:2; 4; 68:4; 18; 21; 25; 33; 69:9; 15; 29; 71:21; 72:16; 75:5; 76:77:12; 78:24; 27; 49; 53; 79:6(3); 81:3; 83:10; 14; 84:5; 86:16; 87:7; 90:13; 91:14; 92:3(3); 8; 11(2); 93:4; 94:23; 99:8; 101:6; 102:7; 13; 103:17; 104:3; 32; 106:32; 107:23; 40; 41; 112:2; 113:5; 118:5; 6; 7; 119:15; 23; 27; 48; 78; 84; 87; 148; 123:2; 3(2); 124:1; 2; 125:3; 129:3; 6; 133:2(2); 135:14; 138:6; 139:4; 11; 142:4; 143:5(2); 144:9; 145:5(2); 147:7; 8; 149:5; 7(2); 9; **Prov** 1:9; 23; 28; 3:3; 5; 33; 4:9; 15(2); 5:14; 6:11; 28; 7:3(2); 19; 20; 8:2; 27; 9:14; 15; 10:6; 13; 11:26; 31; 13:2; 14:21; 31; 15:3; 14; 16:10; 26; 27; 17:10; 24; 19:12; 17; 18; 20:8; 22:3; 11; 23:5; 31; 24:32; 25:20; 22; 26:14(2); 27; 27:12; 15; 18; 30:19; 24; 32; 31:26; **Eccl** 1:6; 2:3; 11(2); 4:1; 5:2; 20; 7:20; 8:14; 16; 10:7(2); 11:2; **Song** 2:12; 3:1; 8; 11; 4:4; 5:3; 5; 15; 8:14; **Isa** 1:24; 2:2; 3:9; 26; 5:1; 6; 27; 6:1; 9(2); 7:3; 19; 8:1; 17; 19; 9:8; 11; 17; 20(2); 10:12(2); 20(2); 26; 11:14; 13:2; 18; 14:1; 13(2); 25; 15:2; 3; 9; 16:5; 12; 18:2; 3(2); 6(2); 19:1; 8; 21:8; 22:16; 22; 24; 25; 23:3; 17; 24:18; 21(2); 23; 25:6(2); 7; 10; 26:3; 5; 27:11(2); 28:20; 29:10; 30:6(2); 8(2); 12; 16(2); 17(2); 18; 25(2); 32; 31:1; 32:11; 13(2); 15; 19; 33:5; 16; 18; 34:5(2); 35:9; 10; 36:2; 6; 8(2); 11; 12; 37:23; 27; 38:8(3); 21; 40:15; 24; 26; 31; 41:25; 42:5(2); 25(2); 44:3(4); 19; 20; 45:12; 46:1(2); 6; 7; 47:1; 6; 48:2; 14; 49:9; 10; 13; 15; 16; 18; 22; 51:5; 6; 9; 11; 52:1(2); 53:6; 54:8; 10; 55:7; 56:2; 7; 57:7; 17; 58:4; 13; 14; 59:17(3); 60:7; 10; 62:6; 63:7(2); 64:7; 65:3; 7(2); 66:2(2); 4; 12(2); 20(3); **Jer** 1:14; 2:17; 20; 34(2); 37; 3:6; 12; 21; 4:7; 29; 5:3; 9; 10; 29; 6:11(2); 19; 21; 23(2); 25; 7:20(5); 29; 8:2; 13(2); 9:3; 9; 21; 22; 10:25(3); 11:11; 16; 20; 23; 12:12; 15; 13:13; 16; 27; 14:16; 15:5; 8; 15; 16:4; 17; 17:1(2); 2; 18; 21; 22; 24; 25(2); 27; 18:15; 19:3; 13; 15(2); 20:3; 10(2); 12; 22:2; 4(2); 24; 30; 23:12(2); 19; 24:6; 25:13; 26; 29(2); 30; 33; 26:3; 15(3); 27:2; 5; 28:14; 29:16; 17; 30:6; 18; 23; 31:5; 6; 19; 20; 29; 30; 33; 32:10; 29; 42(2); 33:17; 21; 26; 35:17(2); 36:2; 4; 6; 22; 23(2); 28; 30; 31(3); 32; 39:2; 5; 40:2; 4; 41:4; 17; 42:12; 18(2); 43:12; 44:2(2); 45:5; 46:4; 10; 25; 48:11; 21(2); 22; 23; 24(2); 32; 37(2); 38; 41; 49:23; 29; 50:6; 15; 19(2); 42; 51:12; 31; 47; 52; 52:4; 6; 9; 12; 22; 23(2); 31; **Lam** 1:2; 12; 21; 2:4; 7; 10(2); 11; 21; 3:28; 55; 57(2); 4:19; 5:18; **Ezek** 1:1; 2; 8; 10(2); 15; 26; 28(2); 2:1; 2; 10(3); 3:23; 24; 25; 4:1; 4(2); 5; 6(2); 9; 6:13(2); 7:12; 14; 16; 18(2); 8:1; 10; 9:4; 6; 8(2); 10; 10:3; 11:9; 13; 21; 23(2); 12:6; 7; 12; 13:5; 15(2); 18; 14:13; 17; 19; 21; 15:3; 16:4; 5(2); 11(2); 12; 14; 15; 16; 41; 43; 17:19; 22; 23; 18:2; 6; 11; 15; 19:8; 9; 20:1; 5; 6; 8; 13; 21; 24; 40(2); 21:29; 31; 22:9; 20; 21; 22; 24; 30; 31(2); 23:6; 10; 12; 14; 15; 23; 37; 38; 39; 41(2); 42(2); 45; 24:1; 3(2); 6; 7(2); 8; 10; 11; 17(2); 23(2); 25; 26; 27; 25:9; 12; 14; 17; 26:1; 16; 17; 18; 27:3; 11(2); 27; 29; 30; 28:13; 14; 23; 26; 29:1; 5; 7; 17; 18; 30:9(2); 15; 19; 20; 21; 31:1; 12; 13; 32:1; 4(3); 5; 17; 27; 33:4; 21; 26; 32; 34:6; 12(2); 13; 14(2); 35:8; 36:3; 12; 18(2); 25; 33; 38; 37:6; 9; 16(2); 20; 22; 38:8; 10; 14; 15; 20(2); 22(3); 39:2; 5; 6(2); 9; 13; 14; 17; 21; 25; 29; 40:1(2); 2(2); 4; 9; 10(3); 12(4); 16(3); 20; 21(2); 26(3); 27; 31; 34(3); 37(3); 39(3); 40; 41(3); 42; 43; 48(4); 49(2); 41:1(2); 2(2); 5; 6; 10; 11; 15(2); 17; 19(2); 20; 25(3); 26(5); 42:9; 14; 20; 43:3; 7; 14; 17; 18(3); 20(3); 22; 24; 27(2); 44:4; 17; 18(2); 19; 27; 30; 45:7(4); 18; 19(3); 20; 21; 22; 23; 25; 46:1(2); 3; 4; 6; 9; 12; 47:2(2); 7; 12; 15; 16; 18; 48:10(4); 21(2); 28; 30; 32; 33; 34; **Dan** 2:10; 29; 34; 46; 3:19; 27(2); 4:5; 10; 13; 15; 5:5; 6:10; 14; 17; 23; 27; 7:1; 4; 5; 6; 20; 23; 8:17; 9:11; 17; 27(2); 10:4; 9; 10(2); 11:18; 20; 27; 12:5(2); **Hos** 1:4; 6; 7; 2:4; 23; 4:8; 13(2); 5:1; 10; 6:2; 9; 7:9; 12; 9:1; 10; 10:7; 8(2); 12; 11:7; 12:1; 6; 14:3; **Joel** 2:9; 28; 29(2); 32; 3:2; **Am** 2:7; 8; 3:5; 9; 12; 14; 4:1; 7; 5:2; 8; 19; 6:4(2); 12; 7:7; 8:10(2); 11; 9:1; 3; 4; 6; 8; 11; **Ob** 11; 12; 13(2); 16; 17; **Jon** 1:4(2); 6; 7; 3:4; 5; 4:5; 8; 10; **Mic** 1:3; 2:1; 3:6; 11; 4:1; 7; 5:1; 7; 15; 7:19; **Nah** 1:2; 15; 3:17; 18; **Hab** 1:13(2); 2:1; 2; 9; 15; 16; 3:1; 8; 10; 14; 17; 19; **Zeph** 1:5; 10; 2:14; 3:8; 9; **Hag** 1:1; 11(5); 14; 15; 2:1; 10; 20; **Zech** 1:7; 8; 12(2); 3:5(3); 4:2(2); 5:11; 6:11; 13(2); 7:1; 9:1; 2; 9; 10:5; 6; 11:11; 13; 12:4; 6(2); 10(3); 13:9; 14:4(2); 12; 15(3); 17; 20; **Mal** 1:7; 10; 2:3; 6; 3:16; 17; 4:3; **Mt** 4:5; 8; 21; 5:1; 14; 15; 25; 39; 45(4); 6:5; 10; 19; 25; 7:24; 25(2); 26; 27; 8:24; 9:2; 6; 9; 16; 18; 27; 10:27; 34; 12:1; 2; 5; 10; 11; 12; 13:1; 2; 5; 8; 20; 23; 14:8; 11; 13; 19; 23; 25; 26; 28; 29; 15:22; 29; 32(2); 35; 16:18; 19(2); 17:1; 6; 15; 18:18(2); 19; 28; 33(2); 19:13; 15; 28(2); 20:17; 21(2); 23(2); 30; 31; 21:5; 7(2); 8(2); 19(2); 44(2); 46; 22:11; 40; 46; 23:4; 9; 18; 20; 22; 35(2); 24:3; 17; 20; 30; 50; 25:15; 31; 33(2); 34; 41; 26:7; 12; 17; 29; 39; 50; 64; 27:19; 25(2); 28; 29; 30(2); 31; 38(2); 48; 55; 62; 28:2; 18; **Mk** 1:21; 2:4; 10; 21; 23; 24; 3:2; 4; 13; 4:1(2); 5; 8; 16; 20; 21; 26; 31(2); 35; 38; 5:19; 23; 6:5; 9; 21; 25; 28; 33; 39; 47; 48; 49; 55; 7:30; 32; 8:2; 3; 6; 23(2); 25; 27; 9:2; 3; 20; 22; 33; 34; 40; 10:16; 17; 32; 34; 37(2); 40(2); 47; 48; 52; 11:2; 4; 7(2); 8(2); 13; 12:12; 13:3; 15; 14:3; 12; 35; 46; 65; 68; 15:17; 19(2); 20; 27(2); 36; 40; 16:2; 5; 9; 18; **Lk** 1:11; 25; 50; 59; 65; 78; 2:14; 4:5; 9; 16; 20; 29; 31; 40; 5:10; 12; 17; 18; 19; 24; 25; 36; 6:1; 2; 6; 7; 9; 17; 29; 48(2); 49; 7:13; 8:6; 8; 13; 15; 16; 22; 23; 27; 32; 43; 9:28; 37; 38; 50; 57; 10:6; 19; 31; 32; 34(2); 35; 37; 11:2; 6; 33; 12:3; 22; 46; 49; 51; 52; 13:4; 6; 7; 10; 13; 14(4); 15; 16; 31; 14:1; 3; 5; 15:5; 20; 22(3); 16:24; 17:13; 16; 29; 31; 18:8; 38; 39; 19:28; 30; 35(2); 36; 43; 20:1; 18(2); 19; 20; 21:12; 14; 25; 26; 34; 35(2); 37; 22:21; 26; 30; 64; 69; 23:26; 30; 33(2); 35; 56; 24:1; 32; 35; 49; **Jn** 1:33; 2:1; 3:36; 4:20; 21; 5:16; 6:2; 3; 19; 22(2); 25; 27; 57; 7:12; 17; 22; 23(2); 30; 37; 44; 8:6; 8; 20; 9:6; 15; 11:51; 53; 12:11; 14; 15; 49; 13:23; 25; 14:7; 10; 16:13; 17:4; 19:2(2); 12; 18; 19; 29; 31(2); 37; 20:1; 22; 21:4; 6; 7; 9; 20; **Acts** 1:26; 2:17; 18(2); 21; 30; 3:4; 11; 4:3; 5; 17; 22; 29; 5:15(2); 18; 28; 30; 6:6; 7:5; 8; 38; 59; 8:17; 18; 19; 39; 9:12; 14; 17(2); 21; 27; 42; 10:7; 9(2); 23; 39; 40; 45; 11:17; 12:7; 8(2); 21(2); 13:3; 11; 14; 15; 44; 14:10; 15:3; 10; 16:3; 13; 23; 31; 17:26; 31; 32; 18:6; 8; 19:4(2); 6; 16; 17; 20:7; 10; 13(2); 14; 16; 37; 21:3; 5(2); 8; 18; 27; 40; 22:16; 19; 23:2; 24; 32; 24:22; 25:6; 17; 26:16; 27:6; 17(2); 19; 20; 26; 29; 37; 44(2); 28:3(2); 8; 9; **Rom** 2:9; 17; 3:22; 31; 4:5; 7:7; 8:3; 5; 9:15(2); 18; 23; 33; 10:11; 13; 14; 11:22; 32; 12:16; 18; 20; 13:2; 4; 12; 14; 15:3; 15; 20; 24(2); 16:19; **1 Cor** 1:2; 3:10(2); 12; 14; 4:6; 7:29; 35; 8:5; 11:10; 23; 12:23; 14:25; 15:53(2); 54(2); 16:2; 6; 7; 11; 17; **2 Cor** 1:11; 16; 2:7; 3:3(2); 7; 15; 4:4; 8; 5:12; 16; 20; 6:7(2); 7:4; 5; 8:1; 24; 11:20; **Gal** 2:7; 3:13; 27; 6:17; **Eph** 1:10; 2:20; 4:8; 24; 26; 6:3; 11; 14; **Phil** 1:22; 29; 2:10; 17; 27(3); 3:12; 19; 4:8; **Col** 1:7; 16; 20; 3:2(3); 5; 10; 12; 14; **1 Th** 5:8; **2 Th** 1:8(2); **1 Tim** 1:16; 3:16; 4:14; 15; 5:22; 6:12; 19; **2 Tim** 1:6; 2:22; 4:8; **Titus** 3:6; 13; **Phm** 1:13; 18; **Heb** 1:3; 4:4; 5:2; 6:1; 2; 7:18; 19; 8:4; 5; 6; 10; 9:4; 10:28; 34; 11:13; 21; 12:25; **Jas** 2:21; 3:6(2); 4:3; 5:5; 17; **1 Pe** 1:17; 2:6; 24; 3:3; 9; 12; 4:14(2); **2 Pe** 1:18; 2:1; 5; 3:12; **1 Jn** 3:1; 23; 5:8; **3 Jn** 6; **Jude** 15; 20; 22; **Rev** 1:9; 10; 17; 2:17; 24; 3:10; 12(2); 21(2); 4:2; 4(2); 9; 10; 5:1(2); 3; 7; 10; 13(2); 6:2; 4; 5; 8; 10(2); 16(2); 7:1(3); 3; 10; 11; 15; 8:10(2); 9:4; 7; 17; 10:1; 2(2); 5(2); 8(2); 11:10(2); 11(2); 16(2); 12:1; 3; 13:1(3); 8; 13; 14(2); 16(2); 14:1(2); 6; 9(2); 13; 14(2); 15; 16(2); 15:2; 16:1; 3; 4; 8; 10; 12; 18; 17:1; 3; 5; 8; 9; 16; 18:17; 19(2); 20; 24; 19:2; 4; 11; 12; 14; 16(2); 18; 19; 21; 20:3; 4(3); 9; 11; 21:5; 12; 13(4); 14; 22:2; 4

OR (1407/1104)

Gen 13:9; 17:12; 27; 19:33; 35; 21:12; 23; 22:12; 24:21; 49; 50; 26:11; 27:21; 30:1; 31:14; 39; 43; 50; 35:27; 37:8; 32; 39:10; 41:44; 42:16; 44:8; 16; 19; 45:5; **Ex** 4:1; 9; 11(2); 5:3; 8:21; 10:4; 15; 11:7; 12:5; 19; 13:22; 16:4; 17:7; 19:12; 13(2); 20:4(3); 23; 21:4; 6; 15; 16; 17; 18; 20; 21; 26; 27; 28; 29; 31; 32; 33(2); 36; 22:1(2); 4(2); 5; 6; 7; 9(2); 10(2); 14; 22; 23:4; 26; 28:43; 29:34; 30:9(2); 20; 33; 34:19; 35:24; **Lev** 1:10; 14; 2:4; 3:1; 6; 4:23; 28; 5:1; 2(3); 3; 4(2); 6; 7; 11; 6:2(3); 3; 4(3); 5; 7:9; 10; 12; 16; 21; 23(2); 26; 10:9; 11:4; 9; 10(2); 12; 26; 32(3); 35; 36; 42; 12:6(2); 7; 8; 13:2(2); 16; 19; 24(2); 29(2); 30; 38; 42(2); 43; 47; 48(3); 49(4); 51(2); 52(3); 53(2); 55; 56(2); 57(2); 58(2); 59(4); 14:22; 30; 37; 15:3; 14; 23; 25; 29; 33; 16:29; 17:3(3); 8(2); 10; 13(2); 15(2); 16; 18:7; 9(2); 10; 17; 26; 19:26; 35; 20:2; 9(2); 17; 25(2); 27(2); 21:7; 11; 14(3); 18(2); 19; 20(6); 23; 22:4(2); 5(2); 8; 10; 13; 16; 18(2); 19; 21(2); 22(5); 23(2); 24(3); 27(2); 28; 25:14; 26; 35; 36; 47(3); 49(4); 26:15; 27:10(2); 12; 14; 20; 26; 27; 28(2); 30; 32; 33; **Num** 5:6; 14; 30; 6:2; 3; 7(2); 10; 9:10(2); 21; 22; 11:8; 22; 23; 13:18(2); 19(2); 20(2); 14:2; 15:3(4); 5; 6; 8(2); 11(2); 14; 30; 16:29; 18:15; 17; 19:16(3); 18(2); 20:5(3); 17(2); 19; 21:22; 22:18; 26; 23:10; 19; 24:13; 30:2; 3; 6; 9; 10; 12; 13; 14; 35:18; 20; 21; 22; 23(2); **Deut** 1:16; 21; 29; 2:19; 37(2); 3:24; 4:16; 17; 18; 32; 34; 5:8(2); 21; 32; 7:14(2); 25; 8:2; 9:5; 27(2); 12:17(4); 13:1(2); 2; 3; 5; 6(2); 7; 8(2); 14:7; 8; 21; 24; 26(2); 15:2; 12; 21(2); 22; 17:1(2); 2; 3(2); 5(2); 6; 8(3); 11; 12; 20; 18:3; 10(5); 11(4); 20; 22; 19:15(2); 20:3; 21:18; 22:1; 2; 4; 6(3); 23:1; 3; 17; 18; 19(2); 24:3; 5; 6; 7; 14; 17; 27:15; 16; 22; 28:14; 51(4); 29:6; 18(4); 32:36; 33:9; **Josh** 1:7; 5:13; 6:10; 7:3; 8:17; 20; 22; 10:14; 13:13; 20:3; 22:22; 23(3); 28; 29; 23:6; 12; 24:12; 15; **Judg** 1:27(4); 30; 31(3); 33; 2:22; 5:8; 30; 9:2; 13:4; 7; 14; 14:3; 6; 15; 16; 18:19; 19:13; 30; 20:28; 21:22; **Ruth** 1:16; 3:10; **1 Sam** 2:14(3); 3:14; 6:12; 12:3(3); 4; 21; 13:19; 14:6; 52; 16:7; 17:34; 18:18; 20:2; 10; 12; 27; 21:2; 3; 8; 22:8; 15(2); 25:31; 36; 26:10(2); 12(2); 18; 27:10(2); 28:6(2); 20; 29:3; 30:19(3); **2 Sam** 2:19; 21; 3:29(3); 35; 14:19; 15:4; 14; 21; 17:9; 19:19; 35; 42; 20:20; 21:4(2); 24:13(2); **1 Ki** 1:10; 3:7; 8; 6:7(2); 8:5; 23; 37(4); 38; 46; 9:6; 15:17; 18:10(2); 27(3); 20:8; 39; 21:2; 6; 22:6; 15; 31; **2 Ki** 2:16; 21; 4:13; 5:17; 6:10; 27; 7:13; 9:15; 32; 12:13; 13:19; 23; 14:26; 17:34(2); 20:9; 13; 22:2; 23:10; **1 Chr** 5:23; 21:12(2); 23:26; **2 Chr** 1:11(3); 5:6; 6:14; 24; 28(4); 29; 36; 7:13(2); 8:15; 11:4; 14:11; 15:13(2); 16:1; 18:5; 14; 30; 19:10(3); 20:9; 17; 21:12; 29:7; 32:15(3); 34:2; 36:17(2); **Ezra** 2:59; 4:13; 6:12(2); 7:24(2); 26(3); 9:12; 14; 10:13; **Neh** 2:16(2); 20(2); 5:8; 8:16(2); 9:35(2); 10:31(2); 13:1; 20; 24; 25; **Esth** 2:10; 3:2; 5; 4:11; 16; 5:9; 6:3; 8:6; 11; 9:12; **Job** 3:12; 15; 16; 4:7; 6:5; 6; 12; 22; 23(2); 7:12; 8:3; 10:4; 12:8; 13:9; 22; 15:3; 7; 16:3; 18:4; 22:3; 11; 25:4; 28:16; 18; 31:5; 7(2); 9; 13; 16; 17; 19; 24; 26; 29; 39; 32:12; 33:14; 34:13; 29; 35:6; 7; 36:19; 23; 37:13(2); 38:5; 6; 8; 16; 17; 21; 22; 24; 25; 28; 31; 32; 36; 37; 39; 40; 39:1; 2; 10; 11; 15; 40:9; 24; 41:1; 2; 5; 7; 12; 26; **Ps** 7:4; 24:3; 32:9; 35:14; 44:20; 50:8; 13; 16; 51:16; 69:31; 88:11; 90:2; 120:3; 132:3; 4; 139:7; 144:3; 14; **Prov** 4:27; 6:7; 7:22; 8:8; 26(2); 18:5; 20:20; 21:30(2); 23:20; 34; 27:10; 28:24; 29:9; 30:4; 9; 32; **Eccl**

1:18; 2:19; 25; 5:12; 6:3; 5; 8:16; 9:5; 10(3); 11:3; 5; 6(2); 12:6(3); 14; **Song** 2:7; 9; 17; 3:5; 8:14; **Isa** 1:6(2); 11(2); 5:6; 27(2); 6:13; 7:4; 11; 10:15(2); 17:6(2); 19:15(2); 27:5; 7; 28:28; 29:8; 16; 30:5(2); 14; 21; 34:10; 38:14; 39:2; 40:13; 18; 25; 41:22; 23; 42:19; 43:9; 44:10; 45:9; 10; 17; 48:1; 49:24; 50:1; 2; 53:2; 57:11; 60:11; 62:6; 65:17; 66:8; **Jer** 2:18; 31; 32; 4:11; 5:12; 7:6; 16; 22(2); 24; 26; 32; 10:20; 11:8; 14(2); 13:23; 14:22; 15:5(2); 16:2; 5; 7; 10(2); 19:5; 6; 21:7(2); 13; 22:3; 18(2); 23:32; 33(2); 25:33(2); 27:9; 31:40; 32:23; 43; 34:9; 35:8; 9; 36:23; 37:18; 19; 40:5; 42:6; 17; 21; 43:3; 44:5; 10; 14; 23(2); 28; 48:24; **Lam** 2:22; 3:36; **Ezek** 2:5; 6; 7; 3:11; 4:14; 12:24; 14:7; 17; 19; 15:3; 16:38; 17:9; 18:10; 11; 12; 13; 17; 22:14; 24; 28:24; 29:5; 34:6; 43:7; 44:9; 17; 22(2); 25(3); 31(2); 45:14; 20; 46:12; 48:14; **Dan** 2:10(2); 38; 3:12; 14; 29; 4:19; 34; 35; 5:8; 23(2); 6:4(2); 7; 12; 13; 15; 26; 10:3; 11:17; 20; 29; **Hos** 1:7(2); 10; 3:4(3); 4:1(2); 4; **Joel** 1:2; **Am** 3:12; 4:8; 5:19; 6:2; 11; **Jon** 3:7; **Nah** 2:9; **Zeph** 2:2; **Hag** 2:12(3); **Zech** 7:10(2); 14; 8:10; **Mal** 2:17; **Mt** 5:17; 18; 36; 6:24; 25; 31(2); 7:4; 9; 10; 16; 9:5; 17; 10:11; 14; 19; 37(2); 11:3; 12:5; 25; 29; 32; 33; 13:21; 15:4; 5; 6; 16:9; 14; 26; 17:25(2); 18:8(3); 16(2); 20; 19:29(7); 20:15; 21:25; 22:17; 23:17; 19; 24:20; 23; 26; 25:37; 38; 39(2); 44(5); 26:53; 27:17; **Mk** 2:9; 21; 22; 3:4(2); 33; 4:17; 21; 30; 6:15; 56; 7:10; 11; 12; 8:37; 10:29(7); 11:30; 12:14; 15; 13:11; 21; 35; **Lk** 2:24; 3:14; 15; 5:23; 37; 6:9(2); 42; 7:19; 20; 8:16; 9:25; 11:11; 12; 33; 12:11(2); 14; 29; 38; 41; 47; 13:4; 15; 14:5; 12; 31; 32; 15:8; 16:13; 17:7; 21; 23(2); 18:11; 29(4); 20:2; 4; 22; 21:15; 22:27; 68; **Jn** 2:6; 4:27; 6:19; 7:17; 48; 9:2; 21; 25; 13:29; 14:11; 18:34; **Acts** 1:7; 3:12(2); 4:7; 34; 5:38; 7:49; 8:34; 9:2; 10:14; 28(2); 11:8; 16:21; 17:21; 29(2); 18:14; 19:12; 20:33(2); 23:8; 9; 29; 24:12; 20; 23; 25:11; 26:31; 28:6; 17; 21; **Rom** 2:4; 15; 3:1; 29; 4:9; 10; 13; 6:3; 16; 7:1; 8:35(6); 9:11; 10:7; 11:2; 34; 35; 12:7; 14:4; 8; 10; 13; 21(2); **1 Cor** 1:12(3); 13; 2:1; 3:22(7); 4:3; 21; 5:10(3); 11(5); 6:16; 19; 7:11; 15; 16; 8:5; 9:6; 7; 8; 10; 10:19; 22; 31(2); 32(2); 11:4; 5; 6; 22; 27; 12:13(2); 26; 13:1; 14:6; 7(2); 23; 24; 27; 29; 36(2); 37; 15:11; 37; 16:6; **2 Cor** 1:6; 13; 17; 3:1(2); 5:9; 10; 13; 6:15; 8:23; 9:7; 10:12; 11:4(2); 12:2; 3; 6; 13:1; **Gal** 1:8; 10(2); 2:2; 3:2; 5; 15; 4:9; 14; **Eph** 3:20; 5:3; 27(2); 6:8; **Phil** 1:18; 20; 27; 2:3; 16; 3:12; **Col** 1:16(3); 20; 2:16(4); 3:17; **1 Th** 2:6; 19(2); 5:10; **2 Th** 2:2(3); 4; 15; **1 Tim** 2:9(3); 12; 5:4; 16; 19; 6:16; **2 Tim** 2:11; **Titus** 1:6; 3:12; **Phm** 1:18; **Heb** 2:6; 10:28; 12:16; 20; **Jas** 1:17; 2:3; 15; 3:12; 4:5; 13; 15; 5:12(2); **1 Pe** 1:11; 18; 2:14; 3:3; 9; 4:15; **1 Jn** 2:15; 3:18; **Rev** 2:5; 16; 3:15; 4:8; 5:3(3); 4; 7:1; 3; 9:4(2); 21(3); 13:16; 17(3); 14:9; 11; 20:4(2); 21:23; 27(2)

OUR (1158/896)

Gen 1:26(2); 5:29(2); 19:31; 32(2); 34; 23:6; 24:60; 29:26; 31:1(2); 14; 15; 16(2); 32; 33:12; 34:9; 14; 16; 17; 21; 31; 37:26; 27(3); 41:12; 42:13; 21; 32(2); 43:4; 7; 8; 18(2); 21(3); 22(3); 28; 44:8; 25; 26(2); 31; 46:34(2); 47:3; 18(4); 19(3); 25; **Ex** 1:10; 3:18; 5:3; 8; 8:10; 26; 27; 10:9(6); 25; 26(2); 12:27; 17:3(2); 34:9(2); **Lev** 25:20; **Num** 10:31; 11:6(2); 13:33; 14:3; 9; 20:3; 4; 15(2); 16; 21:5; 27:3; 4(2); 31:49; 32:16(2); 17; 18; 19; 26(4); 32; 36:2; 3(2); 4; **Deut** 1:6; 19; 20; 25; 28(2); 41; 2:8; 29; 33; 36; 37; 3:3(2); 4:7; 5:2; 3; 24; 25; 27(2); 6:4; 20; 22; 23; 24(2); 25; 21:7(2); 20; 26:3; 7(5); 15; 29:15; 18; 29(2); 31:17; 32:3; 27; 31(2); **Josh** 2:11; 13; 14; 19; 24; 5:13; 7:9; 9:11(2); 12(2); 13(2); 24; 17:4; 18:6; 21:2; 22:19; 24; 25; 27(5); 28(2); 29; 24:17(3); 18; 24; **Judg** 6:13; 9:3; 10:10; 11:2; 6; 8; 19; 24; 13:23; 16:23(3); 24(5); 19:19; 21:7; 18; 22; **Ruth** 2:20; 3:2; 4:3; **1 Sam** 2:2; 4:3; 5:7; 10; 11; 7:8; 8:20(2); 9:7; 8; 12:10; 19; 14:9; 10; 16:16; 17:9; 47; 20:29; 23:20; 25:14; 17; 29:4; 30:23; **2 Sam** 7:22; 10:12(2); 12:18; 18:12; 19:9; 41; 43; 22:32; **1 Ki** 1:2(2); 11; 43; 47; 8:21; 40; 53; 57(2); 58(2); 59; 61; 65; 12:4; 10; 20:31(2); **2 Ki** 18:22; 19:19; 22:13; **1 Chr** 12:17; 19; 13:2(2); 3; 15:13; 16:14; 35; 17:20; 19:13(2); 28:2; 8; 29:10; 13; 15(2); 16; 18; **2 Chr** 2:4; 5; 6:31; 10:4; 10; 13:10; 11; 12; 14:7; 11(2); 19:7; 20:6; 7; 9; 12(2); 28:13(3); 29:6(2); 9(4); 32:8(2); 11; 34:21; **Ezra** 4:3; 5:12; 7:27; 8:17; 18; 21(3); 22; 23(2); 25; 30; 31; 33; 9:6(3); 7(4); 8(4); 9(3); 10; 13(4); 15; 10:2; 3(2); 14(3); **Neh** 4:4; 9(2); 11; 15; 20; 22; 23; 5:2(2); 3; 4; 5(8); 8(2); 9(2); 6:1; 16(2); 8:10; 9:9; 16; 32(6); 34(4); 36; 37(3); 38(3); 10:29; 30(2); 32; 33; 34(3); 35; 36(6); 37(5); 38; 39; 13:2; 4; 18; 27; **Job** 8:9; 22:20; 28:22; **Ps** 8:1; 9; 12:4(3); 17:11; 18:31; 20:5(2); 7; 22:4; 33:20(3); 21; 35:21; 40:3; 44:1(2); 5; 7; 9; 13; 18(2); 20(2); 24(2); 25(2); 26; 46:1; 7; 11; 47:3; 4; 6; 48:1; 8; 14(2); 50:3; 59:11; 60:10; 12; 65:3; 5; 66:8; 9(2); 11; 12; 67:6; 68:19; 20; 74:9; 77:13; 78:3; 5; 79:4; 9(2); 10; 12; 80:6(2); 81:1; 3; 84:9; 85:4; 9; 12; 13; 89:17; 18(2); 90:1; 8(2); 9(2); 10; 12; 14; 17(3); 92:13; 94:23; 95:1; 6; 7; 98:3; 99:5; 8; 9(2); 103:10(2); 12; 14; 105:7; 106:6; 7; 47; 108:11; 13; 113:5; 115:3; 116:5; 118:23; 122:2; 9; 123:2(2); 4; 124:1; 2; 4; 5; 7; 8; 126:2(2); 4; 135:2; 5; 136:23; 24; 137:2; 141:7; 144:12(2); 13(3); 14(2); 147:1; 5; 7; **Prov** 1:13; 7:18; **Song** 1:16; 17(2); 2:9; 12; 15; 7:13; 8:8; **Isa** 1:10; 3:6; 4:1(3); 20:6; 25:9; 26:8; 12; 13; 28:15; 33:2; 20; 22(3); 35:2; 36:7; 37:20; 38:20; 40:3; 8; 42:17; 47:4; 52:10; 53:1; 3; 4(2); 5(3); 55:7; 58:3; 59:12(4); 13; 61:2; 6; 63:16(3); 17; 18; 64:6(2); 7; 8(2); 11(3); **Jer** 3:22; 23; 24(2); 25(6); 5:19; 24; 6:24; 8:14; 9:18(2); 19; 21(2); 11:21; 12:4; 14:7(2); 9; 20(2); 22; 16:10(3); 19; 17:12; 18:12; 20:10; 21:13; 23:6; 36; 26:16; 31:6; 33:16; 35:6; 8(5); 10; 36:15; 37:3; 38:16; 42:2; 6(2); 20; 43:2; 44:17(4); 19; 25; 46:16(2); 50:28; 51:10(2); 51; **Lam** 3:40; 41; 46; 4:17(3); 18(5); 19; 20; 5:1; 2(2); 3; 4; 5; 6; 7; 9(2); 10; 15(2); 16; 17(2); 21; **Ezek** 33:10(2); 21; 36:2; 37:11(2); 40:1; **Dan** 1:13; 2:30; 3:17; 9:6(3); 8(3); 9; 10; 12; 13(3); 14; 15; 16(2); 17; 18(3); **Hos** 7:5; 14:2; 3(2); **Joel** 1:16(2); **Am** 6:13; **Mic** 2:4; 4:5; 11; 5:5(2); 6(2); 7:17; 19(2); 20; **Zech** 1:6(2); 9:7; **Mt** 3:9; 6:11; 12(2); 8:17(2); 20:33; 21:42; 23:30; 25:8; 27:25; **Mk** 9:40; 11:10; 12:11; 29; **Lk** 1:55; 71; 72; 73; 74; 75; 78; 79; 3:8; 7:5; 9:50; 11:3; 4; 13:26; 17:5; 10; 23:41; 24:20; 22; 32; **Jn** 3:11; 4:12; 20; 6:31; 7:51; 8:39; 53; 9:20; 11:11; 48; 12:38; 14:23; 19:7; **Acts** 2:8; 11; 39; 3:12; 13; 25; 5:30; 7:2; 11; 12; 15; 19(2); 38; 39; 44; 45(2); 13:17; 14:17; 15:10; 25; 26; 36; 16:20; 17:20; 28; 19:25; 20:21; 21:5; 6; 7; 22:3; 14; 24:6; 7; 26:5; 6; 7; 27:10; 19; 28:17(2); 25; **Rom** 1:3; 7; 3:5; 4:1; 12; 24; 25(2); 5:1; 5; 11; 21; 6:6; 11; 23; 7:5; 25; 8:16; 23; 26; 39; 9:10; 10:16; 12:6; 7; 13:11; 14:13; 15:4; 6; 16:1; 9; 18; 20; 24; **1 Cor** 1:1; 2; 3; 7; 8; 9; 10; 2:7; 4:12; 5:4(2); 7; 6:11; 9:1; 10(2); 10:1; 6; 11; 12:23; 24; 15:3; 14; 31; 57; 16:12; 23; **2 Cor** 1:1; 2; 3; 4; 5; 7; 8; 11; 12(2); 18; 22; 3:2(2); 5; 4:3; 6; 10; 11; 16; 17; 5:1; 2; 9; 12; 6:3; 11; 7:3; 4; 5; 12; 14; 8:9; 22; 23; 24; 9:3; 10:4; 8; 14; 15; 11:21; 31; 12:18; **Gal** 1:3; 4(2); 2:4; 3:24; 6:14; 18; **Eph** 1:2; 3; 14; 17; 2:3; 14; 3:11; 14; 5:20; 6:22; 24; **Phil** 1:2; 3:20; 21; 4:20; 23; **Col** 1:1; 2; 3; 7; 3:4; **1 Th** 1:1; 2; 3(2); 5; 2:1; 2; 3; 4; 8; 9; 19(2); 20; 3:2(2); 5; 7; 9; 11(3); 13(2); 5:9; 23; 28; **2 Th** 1:1; 2; 8; 10; 11; 12(2); 2:1(2); 14(2); 15; 16(2); 3:6; 12; 14; 18; **1 Tim** 1:1(2); 2(2); 12; 14; 2:3; 6:3; 14; **2 Tim** 1:2; 8; 9; 10; 4:15; **Titus** 1:3; 4(2); 2:10; 13; 3:4; 6; 14; **Phm** 1:1(2); 2; 3; 25; **Heb** 1:3; 3:1; 14; 4:14; 15; 7:14; 10:22(2); 23; 12:2; 10; 29; 13:15; 20; 23; **Jas** 2:1; 21; 3:6; 9; **1 Pe** 1:3; 2:24; 4:3; 5:12; **2 Pe** 1:1; 2; 8; 11; 14; 16; 3:15(2); 18; **1 Jn** 1:1(2); 3; 9(2); 2:2; 3:5; 16; 19; 20(2); 21; 4:10; 5:4; **2 Jn** 12; **3 Jn** 12; 14; **Jude** 3; 4(2); 17; 21; 25; **Rev** 1:5; 5:10; 6:10; 7:3; 10; 12; 11:8; 15; 12:10(3); 19:1; 5; 22:21

OURS (18/18)

Gen 26:20; 31:16; 34:23; **Deut** 21:20; **Josh** 2:14; 20; 9:12; **Judg** 14:15; **Ruth** 2:20; **2 Sam** 19:42; **1 Ki** 22:3; **Mk** 12:7; **Lk** 20:14; **Acts** 19:27; **1 Cor** 1:2; **2 Cor** 1:14; **Jas** 5:17; **1 Jn** 2:2

OURSELVES (62/54)

Gen 11:4(2); 43:7; 44:16; **Num** 31:50; 32:17; **Deut** 2:35; 3:7; **Josh** 22:23; 26; **1 Sam** 12:19; 14:8; **Ezra** 8:21; **Neh** 10:32(2); **Job** 34:4(2); **Ps** 83:12; 100:3; **Prov** 7:18; **Isa** 7:6; 28:15; 56:12; **Jer** 26:19; 35:9; 50:5; **Ezek** 37:11; **Am** 6:13; **Lk** 22:71; **Jn** 4:42; **Acts** 6:4; 23:14; **Rom** 8:23(2); 15:1; **1 Cor** 11:31; **2 Cor** 1:4; 9(2); 12; 3:1; 5(2); 4:2; 5(2); 5:12; 13; 6:4; 7:1; 10:12(2); 14; 12:19; **Gal** 2:17; **Eph** 2:3; **1 Th** 2:10; **2 Th** 1:4; 3:9; **Titus** 3:3; **Heb** 10:25; **1 Jn** 1:8

OUT (2498/2294)

Gen 2:9; 10; 19; 23; 3:19; 22; 23; 24; 4:10; 14; 16; 8:7; 8; 9; 10; 12; 16; 17; 18; 19; 9:10; 18; 11:31; 12:1; 14:8; 17; 18; 15:7; 14; 19:5; 6; 8; 10; 12; 14(2); 16; 24; 29; 30; 21:10; 17; 22:10; 15; 23:4; 8; 16; 24:11; 13; 15; 29; 43; 45; 53; 63; 25:25; 26; 27:3; 30; 28:10; 29:2; 30:16(2); 31:13; 33; 32:25; 34:1; 6; 24(2); 26; 37:14; 21; 22; 28; 38:24; 25; 28(2); 29; 30; 39:14; 15; 18; 40:14; 17; 41:2; 3; 14; 18; 43; 45; 46; 43:23; 31; 44:4; 16; 28; 45:1(2); 19; 25; 46:28; 47:10; 30; 48:14; 50:24; **Ex** 1:10; 2:10; 11; 13; 23; 3:8; 10; 11; 12; 17; 20; 4:4(2); 6; 7; 14; 5:8; 10; 15; 20; 6:1; 6; 7; 11; 13; 26; 27; 7:2; 4; 5(2); 15; 19; 8:5; 6; 12(2); 13(3); 16; 17; 20; 29; 30; 9:9; 10; 15; 22; 23; 29(2); 33(2); 10:5; 6; 11; 12; 13; 18; 21; 22; 11:1; 4; 8(3); 10; 12:17; 21; 22; 31; 33; 39(2); 41; 42; 51; 13:3(3); 4; 9; 14(2); 16; 18; 14:8; 10; 11; 16; 21; 26; 27; 30; 15:12; 20; 22; 25; 16:3; 4; 6; 27; 29; 32; 17:1; 3; 4; 6; 9; 14; 18:1; 7; 9; 10(2); 18; 25; 19:1; 17; 22; 24; 20:2(2); 21:2; 3(2); 4; 5; 7; 11; 27; 22:6; 7; 23:15; 28; 29; 30; 31; 24:16; 25:11; 20; 32(3); 33; 28:35; 29:46; 32:1; 4; 7; 8(2); 11; 12; 19; 23; 24; 27; 32; 33; 33:1; 2; 7; 8; 34:11; 18; 24; 34(2); 37:9; 18(3); 19; 40:19; **Lev** 1:15; 4:12(2); 5:9; 6:12; 13; 9:23; 24; 10:2; 4; 5; 7; 11:45; 13:12; 20; 25; 42; 56(4); 14:3; 38; 41; 43; 16:17; 18; 24; 17:13; 18:24; 25; 28(2); 19:36; 20:22; 23; 21:12; 22:33; 23:43; 24:10; 25:38; 42; 55; 26:10; 13; 33; 45; **Num** 1:1; 2:17(2); 5:2; 3; 9:1; 10:12; 13; 14; 17; 18; 21; 22; 25; 29; 33; 34; 35; 11:2; 20(2); 24; 26; 31; 32; 12:4(2); 12; 13; 14; 15; 13:2; 16; 17; 21; 25; 32; 14:6; 7; 25; 34; 36; 38; 15:41; 16:13; 14; 27; 35; 37; 39; 46; 17:9; 20:5; 8; 10; 11; 16(2); 18; 20; 21:5; 23; 28; 32(2); 33; 22:6; 11(2); 23; 32; 36; 23:22; 24:6; 8; 17(2); 19; 25:4; 26:4; 27:17(2); 21; 28:7; 30:2; 31:27; 28; 36; 32:21; 23; 24; 33:1; 3; 38; 52; 55; 34:7; 8; 10; 35:20; **Deut** 1:22; 24; 27; 33; 44; 2:32; 3:1; 4:12; 15; 20(2); 33; 36(2); 37; 38; 45; 46; 5:6(2); 15; 6:12; 19; 21; 23; 7:1; 8; 19; 22; 8:4; 7; 9; 14; 15; 9:3; 4(2); 5; 12; 14; 17; 26; 28; 29; 11:23; 12:5; 27; 13:5; 10; 13; 14; 14:28; 15:9; 16:1; 3(2); 6; 17:5; 18:5; 12; 20:1; 21:2; 10; 19; 22:15; 21; 24(2); 27; 28; 23:4; 9; 12; 19; 24:1; 3; 5; 9; 11; 15; 25:4; 6; 11; 17; 19; 26:4; 7; 8; 28:6; 7; 19; 25; 38; 57; 29:5(2); 7; 20; 25; 30:4; 31:2; 32:11; 33:18; 27; **Josh** 2:1; 2; 3(2); 5; 7; 10; 3:1; 3; 10; 14; 4:3; 20; 5:4(2); 5(2); 6; 6:1; 10; 22(2); 23(2); 25; 7:2(2); 23; 8:5; 6; 9; 14; 17; 18(2); 19(2); 22; 26; 9:26; 10:22; 23; 24; 11:4; 13:6; 12; 13; 14:7; 11; 12; 15:3; 4; 11; 14; 63; 16:2; 6; 7; 8; 10; 17:12; 13; 18; 18:4; 11; 15; 17; 19:1; 10; 12; 17; 24; 32; 34; 40; 21:4; 22:31; 23:5; 9; 13; 24:5; 6; 7; 10; 12; 17; 18; 32; **Judg** 1:19(2); 21; 23; 24; 27; 28; 29; 30; 31; 32; 33; 2:3; 12; 15; 16; 18; 21; 23; 3:9; 10; 15; 19; 22(2); 23; 24; 4:3; 14; 18; 22; 5:4; 25; 28; 31; 6:6; 7; 8; 9(3); 18; 19; 20; 21(3); 30; 38; 7:21; 8:25; 9:7; 15; 17; 27; 29; 33; 35; 38; 39; 41; 42; 43; 10:10; 12; 14; 11:2; 3; 13; 31; 34; 36; 39; 12:2; 13:5; 14:9; 14(2); 15:15; 18; 19; 16:5; 14; 20; 21; 18:2; 14; 17; 23; 19:22; 23; 24; 25; 27; 20:1; 10(3); 20; 21; 25; 28; 31; 37; 42; 21:10; 21(2); 24; **Ruth** 1:7; 13; 21; 2:17; 18; 22; 3:18; **1 Sam** 1:15; 16; 2:5; 28; 3:3; 4:1; 13; 5:9; 10; 7:6; 8; 9; 11; 8:8; 18; 20; 9:11; 14; 10:18; 11:2; 3; 7(2); 10; 12:8(2); 10; 11; 13:10; 17; 23; 14:11; 27; 15:6; 11; 16:16; 17:4; 8(2); 20; 34; 35; 49; 51; 55; 18:5; 6; 13; 16; 30(2); 19:3; 8; 20:11(2); 12; 35; 37; 38; 21:5; 23:15; 22; 24:6; 8(2); 10; 14; 15; 25:29; 26:4; 9; 10; 11; 14(2); 19; 20; 23; 24; 27:1; 28:1; 3; 12; 13; 17; 29:6; 30:16; 21; **2 Sam** 2:12; 13; 23; 3:25; 4:5; 5:2; 24; 6:3; 4; 6; 20; 9:5; 10:3; 8; 16; 11:1; 13; 17; 23; 12:30; 31; 13:9(3); 17; 18; 15:5; 16; 17; 16:5; 7(2); 17:21; 18:2(2); 3; 4; 6; 25; 28; 19:4; 7(2); 28; 20:7(2); 8; 10; 16; 22; 21:17; 22:7; 15; 17; 20; 43; 23:4; 16; 21; 24:4; 7; 16; 20; **1 Ki** 2:30; 36; 37; 42; 46; 3:7; 4:33; 5:13; 6:1; 27; 7:9; 8:9; 10; 16; 21; 22; 38; 44; 51(2); 53; 9:7; 9; 11:12; 29; 31; 32; 34; 35; 12:25; 13:2; 3; 4(3); 5; 21; 32; 14:21; 24; 15:17; 16:2; 17:19; 20; 21(2); 18:28; 44; 19:11; 13; 20:16; 17(3); 18(2); 19; 21; 31; 33; 39(2); 42; 21:10; 26; 22:3; 22(2); 32; 34; 35; **2 Ki** 2:3; 12; 21; 24; 3:6; 4:1; 5; 18; 21; 34; 35; 37; 39; 40; 5:2; 11; 27; 6:5; 7; 15; 26; 7:11; 12(2); 16; 9:11; 19; 21(2); 24; 32; 10:9; 22(2); 25(2); 26; 11:8; 12; 14; 12:11; 12; 13:25; 14:11; 27; 16:3; 17:7; 8; 23; 18:18; 28; 31; 19:9; 27; 31; 35; 20:4; 11; 21:2; 7; 15; 23:4; 6; 16; 24:7; 12; 13; 20; 25:7; 19; **1 Chr** 5:20; 7:11; 8:13; 9:28; 11:2; 18; 23; 12:17; 33; 36; 13:2; 9; 14:8; 15(2); 17; 15:13; 17:21; 19:3; 9; 20:1(2); 2; 3; 4; 21:16; 21; 25:9; 26:14; 16; 27:1; 28:8; **2 Chr** 1:10; 5:10; 11; 6:5; 12; 13; 29; 34; 7:20; 22; 12:3; 7; 11; 13; 13:9; 14; 14:9; 10; 11; 15:2; 5; 16:1; 18:21(2); 31; 33; 19:2; 4; 20:7; 9; 10; 11; 17; 20(2); 21; 21:9; 15; 19; 22:7; 23:7; 11; 14; 24:5; 25:21; 26:6; 11; 18; 19; 20(2); 28:3; 9; 29:5; 7; 16(2); 23; 31:1; 32:13; 18; 20; 33:2; 7; 15; 34:14; 21; 25; 35:20; 24; **Ezra** 1:7; 8(2); 3:8; 8:25; 9:3; 5; **Neh** 1:9; 2:13; 4:5; 5:13(3); 8:15; 16; 9:4; 7; 15; 18; 21; 28; 11:1; 12:27; 13:8; 14; 25; **Esth** 1:19; 3:15; 4:1(2); 6; 11; 5:2; 9; 8:4; 14; 15; **Job** 1:11; 12; 2:5; 7; 3:24; 5:1; 12; 27; 7:5; 8:16; 19; 9:3; 6; 8; 10; 10:6; 10; 18; 11:7(2); 13; 12:15; 22; 13:9; 14:4; 15:13; 25; 30; 16:7; 13; 20; 18:5; 6; 16; 18; 19:7; 20:15; 25(2); 21:17; 30; 24:5; 11; 12; 24(2); 26:7; 27:21; 23; 28:10; 27; 29:6; 7; 12; 16; 19; 30:5; 16; 20; 24(2); 28; 31:8; 12; 34; 38; 32:11; 33:6; 21; 35:9(2); 12; 36:16; 37:18; 38:1; 13; 14; 32; 35; 37; 39:29; 40:6; 41:1; 19(2); 20; 21; **Ps** 5:10; 7:15; 8:2; 9:5; 10:5; 15; 16; 14:7; 15:5; 18:6; 14; 16; 19; 41; 42; 19:4; 5; 20:2; 22:7; 9; 14(2); 25:15; 17; 22; 27:12; 30:2; 8; 31:4; 12; 22; 34:6(2); 17(2); 19; 35:3; 36:2; 40:2(2); 41:6; 42:4; 43:3; 44:2(2); 9; 20; 21; 45:8; 50:2; 9; 51:1; 9; 52:5; 53:6; 54:7; 55:23; 56:9; 57:2; 58:2; 6; 60:6; 10; 62:8; 66:2; 12; 68:6; 7; 31(2); 33; 69:14(2); 24; 28; 71:4(2); 6; 74:11; 75:8; 77:1; 2; 17(2); 78:16; 20; 55; 79:6; 80:8(2); 11; 13; 81:10; 84:2; 85:11; 88:1; 8; 9; 13; 89:34; 94:12; 97:10; 102:104:2; 23; 105:37; 41; 43; 106:29; 107:3; 6(2); 13(2); 14; 19(2); 28(2); 108:7; 11; 109:13; 14; 110:2; 113:7(2); 114:1; 119:43; 145; 146; 121:8; 125:3; 128:5; 130:1; 135:7; 21; 136:6; 11; 138:3; 7; 141:1(2); 142:1; 2; 5; 7; 143:6; 11; 144:6; 7(2); 14; 147:15; 17; 18; **Prov** 1:21; 23; 24; 2:3; 4:23; 7:15; 8:1; 3; 12; 29; 9:1; 3(2); 10:31; 13:9; 20:5; 20; 26; 22:10; 24:20; 25:2; 19; 26:20; 28:11; 30:17; 31:18; 19; 20; **Eccl** 1:13; 3:11; 4:14; 7:14; 24; 25; 27; 29; 8:17; 12:9; **Song** 3:6; 4:16; **Isa** 1:15; 2:3; 5:2; 25(2); 6:4; 7:3; 8:8; 9:12; 17; 21; 10:4; 11:1; 12:6; 13:13; 14:19; 26; 27; 29; 15:4(2); 5; 16:2; 4; 8; 10; 17:10; 21:11; 22:19; 23:11; 25:11(2); 26:16; 17; 19; 21; 28:7(2); 19; 20; 27; 29:4(4); 10; 18(2); 30:11; 31:3; 32:20; 34:3; 11; 36:3; 13; 16; 37:9; 28; 32; 36; 40:2; 6; 22(2); 26; 42:2; 5; 7; 13; 43:8; 9; 13; 25; 44:13(2); 22; 24; 45:12; 23; 46:6; 7(2); 48:13; 21; 49:13; 50:6; 51:13; 17; 22; 52:11(2); 12; 53:2; 12; 54:2; 55:12(2); 57:4; 13; 14; 58:5; 7; 59:5; 62:10; 12; 63:11; 65:2; 66:5; 20; **Jer** 1:10; 14; 2:6; 26; 3:18; 4:1; 5:6; 6:1; 11; 12; 25; 7:15(2); 18; 20; 22; 25; 8:1(2); 9:8; 19; 10:12; 13; 18; 22; 25; 11:4; 7; 11; 12; 14; 12:3; 8; 14(2); 15; 14:16; 18; 15:1; 6; 19; 16:13; 16; 17:8; 16; 19; 22; 18:21; 23; 19:2; 13; 20:3; 8; 21:9; 12; 22:3; 14; 19; 20; 26; 28; 23:3; 15; 39; 24:5; 27:10; 15; 29:16; 30:7; 19; 31:24; 32; 37; 32:9; 21; 29; 37; 34:13(2); 36:30; 37:12; 17; 38:8; 10; 13; 39:4(2); 7; 40:12; 41:6; 42:18(2); 43:12; 44:6; 7; 17(2); 18; 19(2); 25; 47:2; 48:31; 44; 45; 49:5; 20; 29; 50:3; 8; 25; 45; 51:15; 16; 25; 34; 44; 45; 63; 52:3; 7; 11; 25; 31; **Lam** 1:17; 2:4; 8; 12; 18; 19(2); 3:7; 8; 40; 4:11; 15; **Ezek** 1:4(3); 13; 22; 23; 2:9; 3:22; 23; 25; 5:2; 4; 12; 6:14; 7:8; 10; 8:3; 9:1; 7(2); 8(2); 10:7(2); 19; 11:7; 9; 19; 12:4; 5; 6; 7(2); 12(2); 14; 13:2; 17; 21; 23; 14:9; 13; 19; 22(2); 15:7; 16:5; 14; 15; 27; 36; 17:22; 19:14; 20:6(2); 8; 9; 10; 13; 14; 21; 22; 28; 33; 34(3); 38; 41(2); 21:3; 4; 5; 31; 22:22; 31; 23:8; 24:6; 25:7; 13; 16; 27:33; 28:16; 29:4; 30:22; 25; 31:4; 5; 11; 32:4; 7; 21; 34:11; 12(2); 13; 35:3; 36:18; 20; 24; 26; 37:1; 38:4; 8; 12; 15; 39:3(2); 9; 27; 29; 42:1; 14; 15; 44:3; 5; 19; 46:2; 8; 9(3); 10(2); 12(2); 20; 21; 47:2(2); 3; 18; **Dan** 2:13; 14; 34; 45; 3:26; 4:14; 6:20; 23(2); 7:8; 17; 8:9; 22; 9:11; 15; 23; 27; 11:11; 32; 42; 44; **Hos** 1:11; 5:10; 7:5; 14; 9:13; 11:1; 12:13; **Joel** 1:14; 19; 20; 2:16; 28; 29; 3:7; **Am** 3:4; 12; 4:3; 5:3(2); 6; 8; 6:4; 10; 8:3; 9:6; **Ob** 6; **Jon** 1:2; 4; 5; 14; 2:2(2); 4; 3:4; 4:5; **Mic** 1:3; 11; 2:1; 9; 13(2); 4:2; 5:2; 7:15; **Nah** 1:6; 14; 2:2; **Hab** 1:2; 2:11; 3:14; **Zeph** 1:4; 14; 17; 2:4; 13; 3:15; 19; **Hag** 2:5; 16; **Zech** 1:16; 17; 21; 2:3(2); 4:1; 5:3; 4; 5; 6:5; 7; 12; 7:13; 8:10; 9:4; 11:12; 12:1; **Mal** 3:10; 4:2; **Mt** 2:6; 15; 3:5; 12; 5:13; 26; 29; 7:22; 8:3; 12; 16; 28; 29; 31; 32; 34; 9:26; 27; 32; 33; 34; 38; 10:1; 5; 8; 11; 16; 11:7; 8; 9; 12:11; 13(2); 14; 19; 24; 26; 27(2); 28; 34; 35(2); 43; 49; 13:1; 3; 41(2); 52; 14:14; 26; 29; 30; 31; 35; 15:11; 18; 19; 21; 22; 23; 17:5; 18; 19; 21; 18:9; 28; 20:1; 3; 5; 6; 29; 30; 31; 21:9; 12; 15; 16; 17; 39; 22:3; 4; 7; 10; 23:24; 24:1; 17; 26; 25:1; 6; 8; 26:15; 30; 51; 55; 71; 75; 27:23; 32; 46; 50; 53; 60; 28:8; **Mk** 1:5; 23; 25; 26(2); 29; 34; 35; 39; 41; 45; 2:12; 13; 3:5(2); 6; 11; 14; 15; 21(2); 22; 23; 4:3; 5; 32; 5:2(2); 5; 7; 8; 10; 13; 14; 30; 6:1; 7; 12; 13; 24; 34; 38; 49; 54; 7:15; 20; 21; 26; 29; 30; 8:11; 23; 27; 9:7; 18; 24; 25; 26(2); 28; 29; 38; 47; 10:17; 46; 47; 48; 11:9; 11; 12; 15; 19; 12:8; 44(2); 13:1; 9; 15; 14:13; 16; 26; 48; 68; 15:13; 14; 20; 21; 34; 37; 39; 45; 46; 16:8; 9; 17; 20; **Lk** 1:22; 42; 2:1; 4; 8;

3:7; 17; 4:14; 22; 29; 33; 35(2); 36; 37; 41(2); 5:3; 4; 13; 17; 27; 36; 6:10; 12; 19; 22; 45(3); 7:12; 24; 25; 26; 8:2; 5; 12; 14; 22; 27; 28; 29; 31; 33; 35; 46; 9:5; 35; 38; 39; 40; 49; 10:2; 3; 10; 35; 11:14(2); 15; 18; 19(2); 20; 24; 12:54; 13:28; 31; 32; 14:5; 21; 23; 35; 15:22; 28; 16:4; 17:24; 29; 18:7; 38; 39; 19:22; 40; 45; 20:12; 15; 21:4(2); 13; 37; 22:39; 52; 62; 23:18; 20; 46; 53; 24:50; **Jn** 1:15; 46; 2:3; 8; 10; 15(2); 4:30; 47; 54; 6:37; 7:28; 37; 38; 41; 52; 8:9; 53; 59; 9:22; 34; 35; 10:3; 4; 9; 28; 29; 39; 11:31; 44; 12:13(2); 17; 31; 42; 44; 13:30; 31; 15:6; 19; 16:2; 17:6; 15; 18:1; 16; 29; 38; 19:4(2); 5; 6; 12; 13; 15; 17; 34; 20:2; 3; 21:3; 18; 23; **Acts** 1:9; 18; 21; 2:17; 18; 33; 3:19; 4:15; 30; 5:6; 9; 10; 15; 19; 6:3; 7:3; 4; 7; 10; 12; 21; 36; 40; 45; 57; 58; 60; 8:7; 39; 9:28; 30(2); 40; 10:45; 11:22; 12:1; 6; 9; 10; 17; 13:4; 17; 42; 14:14; 19; 15:14; 24; 16:13; 17; 18(2); 30; 37(2); 39; 40; 17:5; 6; 11; 19:12; 16; 28; 33; 34(2); 21:5; 28; 30; 36; 38; 22:18; 23; 29; 23:6; 29; 24:7; 21; 25:24; 26; 26:1; 27:13; 30; 38; 28:1; 3; **Rom** 2:18; 5:5; 8:15; 9:27; 10:18; 21; 11:24; 26; 33; 13:11; **1 Cor** 5:7; 10; 9:9; 14:23; 15:8; **2 Cor** 2:4; 4:6; 6:17; 8:11; 12:2; 3; **Gal** 2:4; 4:6; 15; 30; **Eph** 4:29; 5:10; **Phil** 1:12; 17; 19; 2:4; 12; 17; **Col** 2:14(2); 3:8; **1 Th** 1:8; **2 Th** 2:7; **1 Tim** 5:18; 6:7; **2 Tim** 1:17; 2:22; 3:11; 4:2; 6; 17; **Titus** 3:6; **Heb** 3:16; 8:9; 11:8(2); 15; 34; 13:17; **Jas** 2:25; 3:10; 5:4; **1 Pe** 2:9; **2 Pe** 2:9; 3:5; **1 Jn** 2:19(2); 4:1; 18; **2 Jn** 7; **3 Jn** 10; **Jude** 4; 5; 23; **Rev** 1:16; 3:5; 12(2); 16; 5:6; 7; 9; 6:2; 4; 14; 7:10; 14; 9:2; 3; 17; 18; 10:3; 10; 11:2; 7; 12:2; 7; 9(2); 15; 16; 13:1; 11; 14:10; 15; 17; 18; 20; 15:6; 16:1; 2; 3; 4; 8; 10; 12; 13(3); 14; 17(2); 17:8; 18:4; 18; 19; 19:15; 20:8; 9; 21:2; 10; 16

OVER (1022/895)

Gen 1:2; 18(2); 26(5); 28(3); 3:16; 4:7; 8:1; 9:14; 11:4; 8; 9; 24:2; 25:25; 26:21; 22; 27:29; 32:10; 16; 21; 22; 23(2); 31; 33:3; 36:31; 37:8(2); 41:33; 34; 40; 41; 43; 45; 56; 42:6; 45:15; 26; 47:6; 26; 49:22; 50:1; **Ex** 1:8; 11; 2:14; 5:14; 7:19(5); 8:5(3); 6; 10:12; 13; 14; 21; 12:13; 23; 27; 14:4(2); 7; 16; 17(2); 18; 21; 26; 27; 15:16(2); 16:18; 18:21; 25; 26:7; 9; 12; 13; 28:29; 30(2); 30:6; 36:14; 39:43; 40:19; 38; **Lev** 13:7; 12; 22; 27; 34; 35; 36; 14:5; 6; 50; 16:21; 25:43; 46; 53; 26:16; 17; 37; **Num** 1:50(3); 3:32; 49; 4:6; 8; 11; 13; 7:2; 10:10(2); 14; 15; 16; 18; 19; 20; 22; 23; 24; 25; 26; 27; 11:13; 16; 16:13; 33; 23:15; 27:16; 31:14(2); 48; 32:5; 7; 21; 27; 29; 30; 32; **Deut** 1:13; 15; 2:13(2); 14; 18; 24; 31; 33; 3:18; 25; 27; 28; 4:14; 21; 22(2); 26; 6:1; 7:2; 16; 23; 9:1; 3; 11:8; 11; 31; 12:10; 15:6(2); 17:14; 15(3); 19:12; 21:6; 23:14; 24:20; 27:2; 3; 4; 12; 28:23; 36; 63(2); 30:9(2); 13; 18; 31:2; 3(2); 5; 32:11; 47; 34:4; **Josh** 1:2; 11; 2:23; 3:1; 6; 11; 14; 16; 17(2); 4:1; 3; 5; 7; 8; 10; 11(2); 12; 13; 22; 23(2); 5:1; 7:7; 26; 8:29; 31; 10:12; 12:5(4); 18:13; 22:19; 24:11; **Judg** 3:10; 22; 28; 6:33; 8:4; 22; 23(3); 9:2(2); 8(2); 9; 10; 11; 12; 13; 14; 15; 18; 22; 26; 10:9; 18; 11:8; 11; 12:1(2); 3; 5; 14:4; 15:11; 18:19; **1 Sam** 8:1; 7; 9; 11; 12(2); 19; 9:16; 17; 10:1; 19; 11:12; 12:1; 12; 13; 14; 13:1; 7; 13; 14; 14:1; 4; 6; 8; 38; 47; 15:1(2); 17; 26; 35; 16:1; 17:50; 51; 18:5; 13; 19:20; 20:6; 22:2; 9; 23:17; 25:30; 26:13; 22; 27:2; 30:16; **2 Sam** 1:9; 10; 17(2); 24; 2:4; 7; 8; 9(6); 10; 11; 15; 29; 3:10(2); 17; 21; 33; 34; 5:2(2); 3; 5(2); 12; 17; 6:21(2); 7:8(2); 11; 26; 8:15; 16; 18; 10:17; 11:27; 12:7; 31; 13:2; 15:22(2); 23(3); 24; 16:9; 17:16; 19; 20; 21; 22(2); 24; 18:1; 8; 17; 24; 33; 19:10; 17; 18; 22; 37; 38; 39(2); 42; 20:12; 21; 23(2); 22:30; 23:3; 23; 24:5; 16; **1 Ki** 1:34; 35; 2:11; 15; 35; 4:1; 4; 5; 6(2); 7; 21; 24(2); 5:7; 6:1; 8:7; 16; 9:5; 23(2); 11:24; 25; 28; 37(2); 42; 12:17; 20; 13:30; 14:2; 7; 14; 15:1; 9; 25(2); 33; 16:2; 8; 16; 22; 23; 29(2); 19:15; 16; 20:38; 39; 21:7; 22:41; 51(2); **2 Ki** 2:3; 5; 8; 9; 14; 3:1; 4:43; 44; 5:11; 8:13; 15; 20; 9:3; 6(2); 12; 29; 10:36; 11:3; 5; 18; 13:1; 10; 14; 15:5; 8; 17; 23; 27; 18:18; 37; 19:2; 21:13; 25:22; **1 Chr** 1:43; 5:2; 6:31; 9:11; 20; 26; 29(3); 31; 10:14; 11:2; 3; 25; 12:4; 14(2); 23; 38; 14:2; 8; 15:25; 17:7; 10; 18:14; 15; 17; 19:17; 21:16; 22:10; 23:1; 26:20(2); 22; 26(2); 29; 32; 27:2; 4; 6; 16(3); 17(2); 18(2); 19(2); 20(2); 21(2); 22; 25(2); 26; 27(2); 28(2); 29(2); 30(2); 31(2); 28:1(3); 4(2); 5; 29:3; 6; 11; 12; 26; 27; **2 Chr** 1:9; 11; 13; 2:11; 5:8; 6:5; 6; 8:10; 9:8; 26; 30; 10:17; 13:1; 5; 15:9; 19:11; 20:6; 27; 31; 21:4; 8; 22:9; 12; 23:4; 14; 25:5; 26:21; 28:7; 31:14; 32:1; 6; 11; 25(2); 34:13; 36:4; 10; **Ezra** 4:20(2); 5:1; 6:18; **Neh** 5:15; 9:28; 37(2); 11:9; 21; 12:44(2); 13:4; 13; 26; **Esth** 1:1; 3:12; 8:2; **Job** 6:5; 7:12; 14:16; 22(2); 16:11; 15; 21:5; 32; 26:7; 9; 28:8; 29:2; 4; 31:10; 34:13(2); 38:24; 33; 40:4; 41:34; **Ps** 8:6; 12:4; 13:2; 18:29; 19:13; 22:28; 23:5; 25:2; 29:3(2); 30:1; 35:19; 24; 38:4; 16; 18; 41:11; 42:7; 47:2; 8; 49:14; 60:8; 64:8; 66:12; 68:34; 78:50; 62; 81:12; 83:18; 88:16; 89:25(2); 91:11; 103:16; 19; 104:8; 9; 106:41; 108:9(2); 109:6; 118:18; 119:133; 124:4; 5; 141:3(2); 145:9; 146:9; **Prov** 17:2; 19:10; 20:26; 22:7; 25:28; 28:15; 31:27; **Eccl** 1:12; 2:19; 3:19; 4:16; 5:8(2); 8:8; 9; **Song** 2:4; 11; **Isa** 3:4; 12; 4:5; 7:6; 8:7(3); 8; 9:7; 11:15(2); 14:2; 8; 26; 15:2(2); 16:8; 9; 19:4; 16; 22:15; 23:6; 11; 12; 25:7(2); 26:13; 28:19; 27; 31:4; 5; 9; 34:2; 11; 35:8; 36:3; 22; 37:2; 40:27; 41:2; 45:14(2); 51:10; 23(2); 52:5; 60:2; 62:5(2); 63:19; **Jer** 1:10(2); 5:6; 22; 6:12; 17; 13:21; 26; 15:3; 4; 14; 23:4; 29:26; 31:28(2); 39; 32:41; 33:26; 38:2; 40:5; 11; 41:2; 10; 43:10; 44:27; 48:12; 32; 40; 49:19; 22; 50:44; 51:42; 48; **Lam** 1:10; 2:17; 3:54; 4:18; 21; 5:2; 8; **Ezek** 1:22; 25; 26; 4:15; 5:1; 9:1; 4; 10:2; 4; 18; 12:13; 16:8; 17:20; 19:8; 20:33; 26:2; 29:15; 32:3; 8; 18; 31; 34:6; 23; 37:8; 22; 24; 43:27; 47:11; **Dan** 1:11; 2:38; 39; 48(2); 49; 3:12; 4:16; 17; 23; 25; 32; 5:21; 6:1(2); 2; 3; 8:12; 9:1; 11:5; 39; 43(2); 12:1; **Hos** 11:8; **Joel** 2:2; 5; 17; **Am** 5:5; 6:2; 13; **Ob** 12; **Jon** 2:3; 4:6; **Mic** 4:7; 6:14; 7:8; 16; 18; **Nah** 3:3; 5; 19; **Hab** 1:14; 3:9; **Zeph** 1:9; 3:17(2); 18; **Zech** 1:16; 5:3; 8; 9:14; 16; 14:9; **Mt** 2:9; 22; 4:6; 5:25; 9:1; 10:1; 13:44; 14:34; 18:13(2); 20:25(2); 24:45; 47; 25:21(2); 23(2); 26:36; 27:18; 36; 37; 45; **Mk** 4:35; 5:21; 6:7; 53; 10:42(3); 15:10; 33; **Lk** 1:33; 2:8; 4:10; 29; 39; 6:38; 8:22; 9:1; 10:19; 11:44; 12:14; 42; 44; 13:11; 15:7(2); 10; 19:14; 17; 19; 27; 41; 22:25(2); 23:38; 44; **Jn** 6:1; 13; 17; 17:2; 18:1; **Acts** 4:22; 6:3; 7:10; 11; 27; 8:2; 11:19; 15:31; 16:9; 17:16; 18:23; 19:13; 20:2; 21:2; 27:5; 9; **Rom** 1:28; 3:25; 5:14; 6:9; 14; 7:1; 9:5; 21; 10:12; 14:1; 15:12; **1 Cor** 7:4(2); 37; 9:12; 10:30; 15:6; **2 Cor** 1:24; 2:3; 3:13; 8:15; **Eph** 1:22; 4:19; **Col** 1:15; 2:15; **1 Th** 5:12; **1 Tim** 2:12; 6:4; **Heb** 2:7; 3:6; 10:21; 13:7; 17; 24; **Jas** 2:13; 5:14; **1 Pe** 5:3; **Jude** 7; **Rev** 1:5; 2:26; 6:8; 9:11; 11:6; 10; 13:7; 14:18; 15:2(4); 16:9; 17:18; 18:11; 20; 20:6

SHALL (7231/4686)

Gen 1:29; 2:17(2); 23; 24(2); 3:1; 3(2); 14(2); 15(2); 16(3); 17(2); 18(2); 19(2); 4:12(2); 14(2); 15; 24; 6:3(2); 15(2); 16(3); 17; 18; 19(2); 21(3); 7:2; 8:22; 9:2; 3; 4; 6; 11(2); 13; 14(2); 15; 16; 25; 12:2; 3; 15:4(2); 5; 8; 14; 15(2); 16; 16:2; 10; 11(2); 12(3); 17:4; 5(2); 6; 9; 10(2); 11(2); 12; 13; 14; 15(2); 16(2); 17(2); 19(2); 20; 21; 18:10; 12; 13; 14; 17; 18(2); 25; 19:20; 20:7(2); 21:10; 12; 22:2; 14; 17; 18; 24:4; 7; 37; 38; 40; 43; 25:23(3); 26:2; 4; 11; 22; 27:10; 12(2); 33; 37; 39; 40(4); 28:1; 6; 14(3); 21; 22; 30:24; 30; 31(2); 32; 31:8(2); 32:18; 19; 28; 34:10(2); 30; 35:10(2); 11(2); 37:8(2); 10; 20(2); 30; 35; 38:18; 41:36(2); 40(2); 42:15(2); 16; 20; 34; 38; 43:3; 5; 9; 44:10(2); 16(3); 17; 23; 29; 32; 34; 45:10(2); 13(2); 46:33; 34; 47:23; 24(3); 30; 48:5; 6; 19(4); 49:1; 4; 8(3); 9; 10(2); 13(3); 16; 17(2); 19(2); 20(2); 26; 27(2); 50:5; 17; 25; **Ex** 1:16(2); 22(2); 2:7; 3:12(2); 13; 14; 15; 18(2); 21(2); 22(3); 4:9(2); 12; 15(2); 16(3); 17(2); 22; 5:7; 8(2); 18(2); 19; 6:1; 7; 12; 30; 7:1; 2(2); 5; 9; 15(2); 16; 17(2); 18(2); 19; 8:3(2); 4; 9; 11(2); 21; 22; 23; 28; 9:4; 19(2); 28; 10:5(3); 6; 7; 14; 26(2); 28; 11:5; 6(2); 7; 8; 12:2(2); 3; 4; 5; 6(2); 7; 8(2); 10(2); 11(2); 13(2); 14(3); 15(3); 16(3); 17(2); 18; 19(2); 20(2); 22(2); 24; 25; 26; 27; 33; 43; 45; 46(3); 47; 48(2); 49; 13:3; 5(2); 6(2); 7(3); 8; 9; 10; 11; 12(2); 13(3); 14(2); 16; 19; 14:2; 13; 14; 16; 17; 18; 15:9(2); 18; 24; 16:4; 5(3); 6; 7; 8; 12(3); 26; 17:4; 6; 18:20; 21; 22(2); 19:3; 5; 6(2); 12(2); 13(4); 20:3; 4; 5; 7; 9; 10; 13; 14; 15; 16; 17(2); 22; 23(2); 24(2); 25; 26; 21:1; 2(2); 3(2); 4(2); 6(4); 7; 8(2); 9; 10; 11; 12; 14; 15; 16; 17; 19(3); 20; 21; 22(2); 23; 26; 27; 28(3); 29(2); 30; 31; 32(2); 34(3); 35(2); 36(2); 22:1; 2; 3(2); 4; 5; 6; 7; 8; 9(2); 11(3); 12; 13(2); 14; 15; 16; 17; 18; 19; 20; 21; 22; 24; 25(2); 26; 28; 29(2); 30(3); 31(3); 23:1; 2(2); 3; 4; 5; 6; 8; 9; 10; 11(2); 12(2); 14; 15(3); 17; 18(2); 19(2); 24(2); 25; 26; 28; 31; 32; 33; 24:2(3); 25:2; 3; 9; 10(2); 11(3); 12(2); 13; 14; 15(2); 16; 17(2); 18(2); 19; 20(3); 21(2); 23(2); 24; 25(2); 26; 27; 28; 29(2); 30; 31(3); 32; 33; 34; 35; 36(2); 37(2); 38; 39; 26:1(2); 2(2); 3(2); 4(2); 5(2); 6; 7(2); 8(2); 9(2); 10; 11; 12; 13; 14; 15; 16(2); 17(2); 18; 19; 20; 22; 23; 24(4); 25; 26; 28; 29; 30; 31(2); 32(2); 33(3); 34; 35(2); 36; 37(3); 27:1(3); 2(3); 3(2); 4(2); 5; 6; 7(2); 8(2); 9(2); 10(2); 11; 12; 13; 14; 15; 16(2); 17(2); 18; 19; 20; 21(2); 28:2; 3; 4(2); 5; 6; 7(2); 8; 9; 11(2); 12(2); 13; 14; 15(3); 16(3); 17(3); 18; 20; 21(2); 22; 23; 24; 25; 26; 27; 28; 29; 30(3); 31; 32(2); 33; 35; 36; 37(2); 38(2); 39(3); 40(3); 41(2); 42(2); 43(2); 29:1; 2; 3; 4(2); 5; 6; 7; 8; 9(3); 10(2); 11; 12; 13; 14; 15(2); 16(2); 17; 18; 19(2); 20; 21(2); 22; 24(2); 25; 26(2); 27; 28(2); 29; 30; 31; 32; 33(2); 34(2); 35(2); 36(3); 37(2); 38; 39(2); 40; 41(2); 42; 43; 46; 30:1(2); 2(4); 3(2); 4(2); 5; 6; 7(2); 8; 9(2); 10(2); 12; 13(2); 14; 15(2); 16(2); 18(3); 19; 20; 21(2); 25(2); 26; 29; 30; 31(2); 32(3); 33; 34; 35; 36(2); 37(3); 38; 31:11; 13; 14(3); 15(2); 16; 32:1; 13; 23; 34; 33:16; 20; 21; 22; 23(2); 34:3; 10; 13; 14; 17; 18(2); 20(4); 21(3); 22; 23; 25(2); 26(2); 35:2(3); 3; 10; 36:1; 40:2; 3; 4(2); 5; 6; 7; 8; 9(3); 10(2); 11; 12; 13; 14; 15(2); **Lev** 1:2; 3; 4; 5(2); 6; 7; 8; 9(2); 10; 11(2); 12(2); 13(2); 14; 15(2); 16; 17(3); 2:1(2); 2(3); 3; 4; 5; 6; 7; 8(2); 9; 10; 11(2); 12(2); 13(3); 14; 15; 16; 3:1; 2(2); 3; 4; 5; 6; 7; 8(2); 9(2); 10; 11; 12; 13(2); 14; 15; 16; 17(2); 4:4; 5; 6; 7(2); 8; 9; 10; 12(2); 14; 15(2); 16; 17; 18(2); 19; 20(4); 21; 23; 24; 25; 26(3); 28; 29; 30; 31(4); 32; 33; 34; 35(4); 5:2; 3; 4; 5(2); 6(2); 7; 8(3); 9(2); 10(3); 11(3); 12(2); 13(3); 15; 16(4); 17; 18(3); 6:4(2); 5; 6; 7(2); 9(2); 10(3); 11; 12(4); 13(2); 14; 15(2); 16(3); 17; 18; 20; 21(3); 22(2); 23(2); 25; 26(2); 27; 28(2); 30(2); 7:2(2); 3; 4; 5; 6; 7; 8; 9; 10; 11; 12; 13; 14(2); 15(2); 16; 18(4); 19(2); 20; 21; 23; 24; 25; 26; 27; 29; 30(2); 31(2); 32; 33; 8:31; 32; 33(2); 35; 9:3; 10:7; 9; 13; 14; 15(2); 11:4; 8(2); 11(3); 12; 13(2); 20; 23; 24(2); 25; 26; 27; 28; 29; 31; 32(3); 33(2); 35(3); 36; 39; 40(2); 41(2); 42; 43(2); 44(3); 45; 12:2(2); 3; 4(2); 5(2); 6; 7(2); 8; 13:2; 3(2); 4; 5(2); 6(3); 7; 8; 9; 10; 11(2); 13(2); 14; 15; 16; 17(2); 19; 20; 21; 22; 23; 25(2); 26; 27(2); 28; 30(2); 31; 32; 33(3); 34(3); 36; 37; 39; 43; 44; 45(2); 46(4); 49; 50; 51; 52(2); 54(2); 55(2); 56; 57; 58(2); 14:2(2); 3(2); 4; 5; 6; 7(3); 8(3); 9(4); 10; 11; 12; 13; 14(2); 15; 16(2); 17; 18(2); 19(2); 20(3); 21; 22; 23; 24(2); 25(2); 26; 27; 28; 29; 30; 31; 36(2); 37; 38; 39; 40(2); 41(2); 42(2); 44; 45(2); 46; 47(2); 48; 49; 50; 51; 52; 53(2); 15:3; 4; 5; 6; 7; 8; 9; 10(2); 11; 12(2); 13(2); 14; 15(2); 16; 17; 18; 19(2); 20(2); 21; 22; 23; 24(2); 25(2); 26(2); 27(2); 28(2); 29; 30(2); 31; 16:3; 4(4); 5; 6; 7; 8; 9; 10; 11(2); 12; 13; 14(2); 15; 16(2); 17; 18(2); 19; 20; 21(2); 22(2); 23(3); 24; 25; 26; 27(2); 28; 29(2); 30; 31; 32; 33(3); 34; 17:4(2); 6; 7(2); 8; 9; 12(2); 13; 14(2); 15(2); 16; 18:3(3); 4; 5(2); 6; 7(2); 8; 9; 10; 11; 12; 13; 14(2); 15(2); 16; 17(2); 18; 19; 20; 21(2); 22; 23(2); 26(2); 29; 30; 19:2; 3; 5; 6(2); 7; 8(2); 9(2); 10(3); 11; 12(2); 13(2); 14(2); 15(3); 16(2); 17(2); 18(2); 19(4); 20(2); 21; 22(2); 23(3); 24; 26(2); 27(2); 28; 30; 32; 33; 34(2); 35; 36; 37; 20:2(3); 8; 9(2); 10; 11(2); 12(2); 13(2); 14; 15(2); 16(2); 17(2); 18; 19(2); 20(2); 21; 22; 23; 24; 25(2); 26; 27(3); 21:1; 4; 5(2); 6(2); 7(2); 8(2); 9; 10; 11; 12; 13; 14(2); 15; 18; 21(2); 23; 22:3; 4; 6(2); 7; 8; 9; 10(2); 13; 14; 15; 19; 20(2); 21; 22; 23; 24(2); 25(2); 27(2); 30(2); 31; 32; 23:2; 3(2); 4; 7(2); 8(3); 10; 11(2); 12; 13(2); 14(2); 15(2); 16; 17(3); 18(2); 19; 20(2); 21(3); 22(3); 24; 25(2); 27(3); 28; 29; 31(2); 32(3); 34; 35(2); 36(4); 37; 39(2); 40(2); 41(3); 42(2); 24:3(2); 4; 5(2); 6; 7; 8; 9(2); 15(2); 16(3); 17; 18; 19; 20; 21(2); 22; 25:2; 3(2); 4(2); 5; 6; 7; 8(2); 9(2); 10(4); 11(2); 12(2); 13; 14; 15(2); 16(2); 17(2); 18; 20(2); 22(2); 23; 24; 28(3); 30(2); 31(2); 33; 35; 37; 39; 40(2); 41(3); 42; 43(2); 45; 46(2); 50(3); 51; 52(2); 53(2); 54; 26:1(3); 2; 4(2); 5(3); 6; 7; 8(3); 10; 11; 12; 16(3); 17(3); 20(3); 22(2); 25; 26(3); 29(2); 30; 32; 33; 34(2); 35; 36(3); 37(2); 38(2); 39(2); 43; 44; 27:3; 4; 5; 6(2); 7; 8(3); 9; 10(2); 11; 12(2); 14(2); 15; 16(2); 17; 18(2); 19; 20; 21(2); 23(2); 24; 25; 26; 27(3); 28; 29(2); 31; 32; 33(4); **Num** 1:3; 4; 5; 49; 50(3); 51(3); 52; 53(2); 2:2(2); 3(2); 5(2); 7; 9; 10(2); 12(2); 14; 16; 17(2); 18(2); 20; 22; 24; 25(2); 27(2); 29; 31; 3:7; 8; 9; 10(3); 12; 13; 15; 41; 45; 47(2); 48; 4:5(2); 6(2); 7(2); 8(2); 9; 10; 11(2); 12; 13; 14(2); 15(2); 19; 20; 23; 25; 26; 27(2); 28; 29; 30; 32; 5:3(2); 7(2); 9; 10(2); 15(3); 16; 17; 18(2); 19; 21(2); 22; 23(2); 24(2); 25(2); 26; 27; 28; 30(2); 31(2); 6:3(3); 4; 5(3); 6; 7; 8; 9(2); 10; 11(2); 12(2); 13; 14; 16; 17(2); 18(2); 19; 20; 23; 27; 7:5; 11; 8:2; 7; 8; 9(2); 10(2); 11; 12(2); 13; 14(2); 15(2); 25; 26(2); 9:3(2); 11; 12(2); 13(2); 14; 10:2(2); 3; 4; 5; 6(2); 7; 8(2); 9; 10(2); 32(2); 11:17; 18(3); 19; 22(2); 23; 13:2; 14:21; 23(2); 24; 27; 29; 30; 31; 32; 33; 34(2); 35(2); 43; 15:4; 5; 6; 7; 9; 10; 11; 12; 13; 14; 15(2); 16; 19; 20(2); 21; 24; 25(3); 26; 27; 28(2); 29; 30; 31(2); 35; 39; 16:7; 22; 28; 38; 17:3(2); 4; 5; 13; 18:1(2); 3(2); 4(2); 5; 7(3); 9(2); 10(3); 13; 14; 15(3); 16; 17(2); 18; 20(2); 22; 23(4); 24; 26; 27; 28(2); 29; 30(2); 32(2); 19:3(2); 4; 5(2); 6; 7(4); 8(2); 9(2); 10(2); 11; 12; 13(2); 14; 16; 17(2); 18; 19(3); 20; 21(3); 22(2); 20:8; 12; 18; 20; 24(2); 26; 21:8(2); 34; 22:6; 11; 12(2); 20; 35; 23:5; 8(2); 13(2); 16; 24; 24:7(4); 8(2); 9; 17(2); 18(2); 19; 20; 22; 23; 24(3); 25:13; 26:53; 54(3); 55(2); 56; 65; 27:7; 8(2); 9; 10; 11(3); 13; 20; 21(4); 28:2; 3(2); 4(2); 7(2); 8(2); 11; 14; 15; 17; 18(2); 19; 20(2); 21; 23; 24(2); 25(2); 26(2); 27; 31; 29:1(2); 2; 3; 7(3); 8; 9; 12(3); 13(2); 14; 35(2); 36; 39; 30:2(2); 4(2); 5; 7(2); 8; 9; 11(2); 12; 15; 31:2; 4; 23(4); 24; 30; 32:6; 11; 22; 29; 30; 32; 33:52; 53; 54(5); 55(3); 56; 34:2; 3(2); 4(2); 5(2); 6(2); 7(2); 8(2); 9(3); 10; 11(2); 12(3); 13; 17; 18; 35:2; 3(2); 4(2); 5(3); 6(2); 7(2); 8(4); 11; 12; 13; 14(2); 15; 16; 17; 18; 19(2); 21(2); 24; 25(3); 27; 29; 30; 31(2); 32; 33; 36:7(2); 8; 9(2); **Deut** 1:17(3); 22; 35; 36; 37; 38(2); 39(2); 2:6(2); 25(2); 28; 3:2; 18; 19; 27; 28(2); 4:2; 22; 40; 5:7; 8; 9; 11; 13; 14; 17; 18; 19; 20; 21(2); 25; 31; 32(2); 33(2); 6:5; 6; 7(2); 8(2); 9; 10; 13(2); 14; 16; 17; 18; 21; 7:2(2); 3(2); 5(2); 11; 12; 14(2); 16(3); 18(2); 19; 21; 24; 25(2); 26(2); 8:2; 3; 6; 10; 18; 19(2); 20; 9:3; 10:2; 20(3); 11:1; 8; 13; 18(2); 19; 20; 24(2); 25; 29(2); 32; 12:1; 2(2); 3(2); 4; 5(2); 6; 7(2); 8; 11; 12; 14(2); 16(2); 18; 24(2); 25; 26; 27(3); 31; 32; 13:3; 4(2); 5(2); 8(3); 9(2); 10; 11; 14; 15; 16(3); 17; 14:1; 3; 7; 8; 10; 12; 19; 21(2); 22; 23; 25; 26(3); 27; 28; 15:1; 2(2); 3; 6(4); 7; 8; 10; 11; 12; 13; 14(2); 15; 17(3); 18; 19(2); 20; 21; 23(2); 16:2; 3(2); 4(2); 6; 7(2); 8(3); 9; 10(2); 11; 12(2); 13; 14; 15; 16(2); 17; 18(2); 19(2); 20; 21; 22; 17:1; 4; 5(2); 6(2); 7(2); 8; 9(2); 10(2); 11(2); 12(2); 13; 15(2); 16(2); 17(2); 18(2); 19(2); 18:1(2); 2; 3(2); 4; 8; 9; 10; 13; 15; 18; 19; 20; 21; 22; 19:2; 3; 5; 7; 9; 12; 13(2); 14; 15(2); 17; 18; 19(2); 20(2); 21(2); 20:2(2); 3; 5; 8; 9(2); 11(2); 12; 13; 14(2); 15; 16; 17; 19; 21:2; 3; 4(2); 5(2); 6; 7; 8; 9; 12(2); 13(2); 14(4); 16; 17; 19; 20; 21(3); 23(2); 22:1(2); 2(3); 3(3); 4(2); 5(2); 6; 7; 8; 9; 10; 11; 12; 15; 16; 17; 18; 19(2); 21(3); 22(2); 24(3); 25; 26; 29(3); 30; 23:1; 2(2); 3(2); 6; 7(2); 10(2); 11(2); 12; 13(2); 14; 15; 16; 17; 18; 19; 20; 21; 22; 23; 24; 25; 24:4; 5(2); 6; 7(2); 8(2); 10; 11(2); 12; 13(2); 14; 15; 16(3); 17; 18; 19(2); 20(2); 21(2); 22; 25:2; 4; 5(2); 6; 8; 9(2); 10; 12(2); 13; 14; 15; 19(2); 26:1; 2(2); 3; 4; 5; 10; 11; 13; 16; 27:2(2); 3; 4(3); 5(2); 6; 7(2); 8; 10; 12; 13; 14; 15; 16; 17; 18; 19; 20; 21; 22; 23; 24; 25; 26; 28:1; 2; 3(2); 4; 5; 6(2); 7; 10(2); 12(2); 13; 14; 15; 16(2); 17; 18; 19(2); 22; 23(2); 24; 25(2); 26(2); 29(4); 30(6); 31(6); 32(3); 33(2); 34; 36; 37; 38(2); 39(3); 40(3); 41(3); 42; 43(2); 44(4); 45; 46; 48; 51(2); 52(2); 53(2); 55; 57; 60; 62; 63(2); 64; 65(2); 66(2); 67(2); 68(2); 29:19; 30:1; 5; 18(2); 31:2; 3; 7; 11; 17(3); 21; 23; 32:22(2); 24; 25(2); 35; 42; 46; 47; 52(2); 33:10(2); 12(2); 17; 19(3); 22; 25(2); 28(2); 29(2); 34:4; **Josh** 1:4; 5; 6; 8(2); 14(2); 15; 18; 2:14; 19(3); 3:3; 4; 8(2); 10; 13(4); 4:3; 7(2); 22; 6:3(3); 4(3); 5(3); 10(3); 17(2); 19; 26(2); 7:8; 14(5); 15(2); 8:2(2); 4; 5; 7; 8(2); 9:23; 10:8; 11:6; 14:9; 12; 15:4; 17:17; 18(4); 18:4; 5(3); 6; 20:3; 4; 5; 6; 22:18; 23:5; 7(2); 8; 10; 13; 15; 16; 24:27(2); **Judg** 1:1; 2; 2:2(2); 3(2); 4:20; 5:11(2); 6:14; 16; 23; 26; 37(2); 7:4(4); 5; 11(2); 17; 8:23(2); 9:33(2); 10:18; 11:2; 9; 31; 13:3; 5(4); 7(2); 8; 22; 14:13; 15:3; 18; 16:7; 11; 17; 20:18; 23; 28(2); 21:1; 5; 7; 11(2); 16; 22; **Ruth** 1:16; 2:21; 3:1; 4(3); 13; **1 Sam** 1:11; 28; 2:9(2); 10; 30; 32; 33(2); 34(2); 35(2); 36; 3:9; 14; 5:8; 6:2; 4; 5(2); 9; 20; 8:9; 9:7; 16; 17; 19; 10:2; 3; 4; 5; 8(2); 11:7; 9(2); 12; 13; 12:12; 25; 13:14; 14:37; 39; 44; 45(2); 15:33; 16:3(2); 16(2); 17:9; 25; 26; 27; 47; 18:21; 25; 19:6; 20:2; 8; 14; 15; 31(2); 21:15; 22:16; 23; 23:2; 17(3); 20; 23; 24:12; 13; 20(2); 25:6; 11; 29(2); 30; 26:10(3); 25; 27:1(2); 28:8; 10; 11; 29:9; 30:8(3); 23; 24(2); **2 Sam** 2:1(2); 26; 3:12; 13; 39; 4:11; 5:2; 6; 8(2); 19; 23; 24(2); 7:8; 10; 13; 14; 15; 16(2); 9:7; 10(3); 11; 10:11; 11:11; 21; 25; 12:5; 6; 10; 11; 13; 14; 23(2); 14:10; 11; 15:10; 14; 21; 35; 36; 16:10; 17:6; 12; 13; 18:3; 20(3); 19:21; 22; 23; 38; 20:18; 21:3(2); 4; 17; 22:4; 29; 44; 23:4; 6; 7; 24:13(3); **1 Ki** 1:13(2); 17(2); 24(2); 30(2); 35(3); 52(2); 2:4; 24; 33(2); 37(3); 42; 45(2); 3:5; 12; 13; 5:5; 9(2); 8:19(2); 25; 29; 9:5; 11:2; 32; 37(2); 38; 12:10(2); 24; 13:2(3); 3(2); 9; 17; 22; 14:5; 11(2); 12; 13(2); 14; 16:4(2); 17:1; 4; 14(2); 18:12; 31; 19:16(2); 17; 20:5; 6(2); 13; 25; 28; 36; 39(2); 40; 42; 21:19(3); 23; 24(2); 22:6(2); 11; 15(2); 16; 22; 25; **2 Ki** 1:2; 4(2); 6(2); 16(2); 2:10(2); 16; 21; 3:8; 17(3); 19(2); 4:2; 4; 16; 43(2); 5:8; 10(2); 27; 6:15; 21(2); 22; 7:1; 2(2); 4(3); 12; 18; 19(2); 8:8; 9; 10; 9:7; 8; 10(2); 36; 37(2); 10:10; 19; 24; 30; 11:5(2); 6(2); 7; 8; 14:6(3);

15:12; 16:15; 17:12; 35; 36(3); 37(2); 38(2); 39; 18:22; 29; 30; 19:6; 7; 10(2); 11; 29(2); 30; 31; 32; 33(2); 20:1; 5; 8; 9; 17(2); 18(2); 21:14; 22:17(2); 18; 20(2); 23:27; 25:24; **1 Chr** 11:2; 5; 6; 19; 14:10; 14; 15(2); 16:30; 33; 17:4; 7; 9; 11; 12; 13; 14; 27; 19:12; 21:22; 22:8; 9(3); 10(2); 23:26; 28:3; 6; **2 Chr** 1:7; 12; 2:9; 6:9(2); 16; 7:18; 8:11; 10:10(2); 11:4; 12:7; 13:12; 15:7; 16:9; 18:5(2); 10; 14(3); 15; 21; 24; 19:9; 10; 20:20(2); 23:3; 4(2); 5(2); 6; 7; 25:4(3); 8; 9; 26:18; 28:13; 32:12; 33:4; 34:26; 28(2); 35:3; **Ezra** 6:8; 7:24; 9:10; **Neh** 9:29; 10:38(2); 39; 13:25; **Esth** 1:15; 19; 5:3; 6(2); 6:6; 9; 11; 7:2(2); 9:12(2); **Job** 1:21; 2:10(2); 5:19(2); 20; 21(2); 22(2); 23(2); 24(2); 25(2); 26; 7:4; 8; 10(2); 8:13; 14; 10:21; 11:20; 13:16; 18; 14:14; 15(2); 16:3; 22; 17:10; 16; 18:4(2); 19:25; 26; 27(2); 28; 20:26; 21:30; 32; 33(2); 23:10; 27:6; 14; 15(2); 23(2); 28:18; 29:18; 31:14(2); 33:25(2); 26(2); 28; 35:3; 36:11; 12(2); 38:3; 40:2; 4; 7; 41:9; 42:4; 8; **Ps** 1:3(3); 5; 6; 2:4(2); 5; 9(2); 5:3; 4; 5; 6; 7:7; 8; 16(2); 9:3; 7; 8(2); 17; 18(2); 10:6(2); 11:6; 12:7(2); 13:2; 5; 15:5; 16:4; 8; 17:3; 15; 18:3; 43; 19:13(2); 21:1(2); 7; 9(3); 10; 22:25; 26; 27(2); 29(2); 30; 23:1; 6; 24:5; 7; 9; 25:12; 13(2); 15; 26:1; 27:1(2); 3; 5(3); 6; 14; 28:5; 30:6; 31:20(2); 24; 32:6(2); 7(2); 10(2); 33:17; 21; 34:1; 2(2); 10; 21(2); 22; 35:9(2); 10; 28; 37:2; 4; 5; 6; 9(2); 10(2); 11(2); 15(2); 17; 18; 19(2); 20(3); 22(2); 24; 28; 29; 31; 34(2); 38(2); 40(2); 42:2; 5; 8; 11; 43:5; 44:6; 45:4; 14(2); 15(2); 16(2); 17; 46:4; 5(2); 49:3(2); 8; 14(3); 15; 17(2); 19(2); 50:3(4); 4; 15; 51:7(2); 13; 14; 15; 19(2); 52:5(2); 6(2); 55:16; 17; 22(2); 23(2); 56:7; 57:3(2); 58:9; 10(2); 59:8(2); 10(2); 60:12; 61:7; 62:2; 3; 6; 63:3; 5(2); 9; 10(2); 11(3); 64:7(2); 8; 9(3); 10(2); 65:1; 4; 66:3; 4(2); 67:4; 6(2); 7(2); 69:31; 32(2); 36(2); 71:6; 15; 20; 21; 23; 24; 72:5; 6; 7; 8; 11(2); 14; 15(2); 16(2); 17(4); 73:20; 27; 75:8; 10; 76:10(2); 12; 80:3; 7; 19; 81:9(2); 82:7; 8; 85:11(2); 13; 86:9(2); 87:5; 88:10; 11; 12; 89:2(2); 21(2); 22; 24(2); 26; 28; 36; 37; 91:1; 3; 4(3); 5; 7; 8; 10(2); 11; 12; 13(2); 15; 92:9(2); 12(2); 13; 14(2); 94:9(2); 10; 20; 23(2); 95:11; 96:10(2); 13; 98:9; 101:3; 4; 6(2); 7(2); 102:12; 15; 16(2); 17(2); 108:13; 109:31; 110:2; 3; 5; 6(3); 7(2); 112:10; 116:12; 118:7; 17; 20; 119:27; 32; 33; 34(2); 42; 44; 117(2); 144; 171; 172; 175; 120:3(2); 121:4; 6; 7(2); 8; 125:3; 5; 126:5; 6; 127:5(2); 128:2(2); 3; 4; 130:8; 132:12(2); 16; 18; 137:4; 138:4; 5; 139:10(2); 11(2); 12; 140:13(2); 141:5(2); 142:7(2); 144:5; 145:4(2); 6; 7(2); 10(2); 11; 21(2); 146:10; 148:6; **Prov** 1:13(2); 31; 3:6; 35(2); 5:23(2); 6:11; 15(2); 29; 12:19; 21; 13:2; 3; 4; 21; 25; 18:20(2); 19:9; 21:18; 28; 22:13; 23:14; 35; 24:14; 16; 34; 26:2; 27:27; 29:25; 31:25; 30; **Eccl** 3:14; 17; 5:15(2); 16; 7:26(2); 10:12; 11:3; **Song** 8:8; **Isa** 1:18(2); 19; 20; 26; 27; 28(2); 29(2); 30; 31(2); 2:2(4); 3(3); 4(4); 11(3); 12(2); 17(2); 18; 19; 3:4; 10(2); 11(2); 24; 25; 26(2); 4:1; 2(2); 3; 5:5(2); 6(2); 9; 10(2); 14; 15(3); 16(2); 17(2); 26; 6:8; 13; 7:7(2); 9; 14(2); 15; 16; 18; 21; 22; 23; 8:4; 13; 15(2); 21; 9:11; 12; 18(2); 19(2); 20(3); 21(2); 10:4(2); 11; 12; 15(2); 20; 22; 24; 27; 11:1(2); 2; 3; 4(3); 5; 6(3); 7(3); 8(2); 9(2); 10(4); 11(2); 13(4); 14(4); 13:14; 14:3; 10; 15; 20; 24(2); 25; 32; 15:4; 5; 16:2(2); 6; 7(3); 11; 12; 17:4; 5(2); 19:25; 20:4; 5; 6; 22:7(3); 18(2); 20; 21; 22(4); 23:15; 17; 24:2; 3; 9; 13(2); 14(3); 18(3); 20(3); 21; 25:10; 26:6; 11; 19(3); 27:5; 6(2); 9; 12; 13(2); 29:2(2); 4(5); 5(2); 7; 8(2); 14(2); 16(3); 17; 18(2); 19(2); 22(2); 30:3(2); 6; 7; 13; 14(3); 15(2); 16(2); 17(2); 19(2); 20; 21; 28; 29; 31:7; 8(4); 9(2); 32:8; 12; 33:3(2); 4(2); 7(2); 11(3); 12(2); 14(2); 34:3(3); 4(3); 5(2); 7(2); 9(2); 10(4); 11(3); 12(3); 13(2); 14(3); 15(2); 16(2); 17(2); 35:1(2); 2(3); 5(2); 6(2); 7(2); 8(5); 9(4); 10(3); 36:7; 37:6; 7; 10(2); 11; 30(2); 31; 32; 33; 34(2); 38:1; 10; 11(2); 15(2); 19(2); 21; 22; 39:6(2); 7(2); 40:4(2); 5(2); 6; 10(2); 24(3); 25; 30(2); 31(4); 41:11(3); 12(2); 15; 16(4); 25(3); 42:4; 13(4); 17(2); 43:2(3); 10; 17(2); 19(2); 21; 44:7; 9; 11(2); 15; 19(2); 26(2); 28(3); 45:9(2); 13; 14(5); 16(2); 17(2); 23(3); 24(3); 25(2); 46:7; 10; 13(2); 47:1; 3; 5; 7; 8(2); 9(2); 11(5); 13; 14(4); 15(3); 48:14(2); 49:5(2); 7(2); 9(2); 10(2); 11; 12; 17(2); 18; 22(2); 23(3); 24; 25; 26(2); 50:11(2); 51:11(3); 22; 52:1; 3; 6(2); 8(3); 10; 12; 13(2); 15(4); 53:2; 10(3); 11(3); 12; 54:3; 10(3); 13(2); 14(4); 15(2); 17(2); 55:3; 5(2); 11(4); 12(3); 13(4); 56:5; 7; 57:2(2); 13(2); 14; 58:8(4); 9(2); 10(2); 11; 12(3); 13; 14; 59:8; 19; 21; 60:2; 3; 4(2); 5(4); 6(4); 7(3); 9; 10(2); 11(2); 12(2); 13; 14(3); 16(2); 18(2); 19(2); 20(3); 21(2); 22; 61:4(3); 5(2); 6(4); 7(4); 9(2); 10; 62:2(2); 3; 4(4); 5(2); 6; 8; 9(2); 12(2); 65:9(2); 10; 12; 13(6); 14(2); 15; 16(2); 17; 19; 20(3); 21(2); 22(4); 23(2); 24; 25(4); 66:5; 8(2); 9(2); 12(2); 13; 14(3); 16; 17; 18(2); 19; 20; 22(2); 23(2); 24(2); **Jer** 1:7(2); 14; 15; 19; 2:35; 36; 3:16(5); 17(3); 18(2); 19; 4:1; 2(3); 9(4); 10; 13; 14; 27; 28; 29(4); 5:6(3); 7; 9(2); 12; 13; 14; 17(4); 19(2); 29(2); 6:3(3); 9; 10; 11; 12; 15(2); 21(2); 7:23; 27(2); 28; 34; 8:1; 2(3); 3; 4; 12(2); 13(3); 17; 9:7; 9(2); 22(2); 10:11(2); 15; 21(2); 11:4; 22(2); 23; 12:12(2); 15; 16(2); 13:10; 12(2); 13; 18; 19(4); 14:13(2); 15(2); 16; 17; 15:2(2); 14; 19(2); 20; 16:2(2); 4(6); 6(3); 7(2); 8; 10; 11; 13; 14; 16(2); 19; 21; 17:4(2); 6(3); 8; 13(2); 14(2); 24; 25(2); 26; 27(2); 18:18; 20; 19:6; 9(2); 10; 11; 13; 20:4(3); 6(3); 21:3; 6; 7(2); 8; 9(3); 10(2); 13(2); 14; 22:4; 5; 7; 10; 11; 12(2); 15; 18(2); 19; 22(2); 26; 27; 30(2); 23:3; 4(2); 5; 7; 8; 12(2); 17(2); 24; 32; 33; 35; 36; 37; 40; 24:7(2); 9; 25:11(2); 14; 26; 27; 28(3); 29; 32(2); 33(3); 34; 26:4; 9(2); 18(2); 27:4; 7(2); 8; 9; 11; 14; 22(2); 28:14; 16; 29:21; 22; 24; 32(2); 30:3; 7; 8(2); 9; 10(2); 16(3); 18(2); 19(3); 20(2); 21(3); 22; 31:1; 4(3); 5(2); 6; 8; 9(2); 12(3); 13; 14; 16(2); 17; 22; 23; 24; 28; 29; 30(2); 33; 34(2); 36; 38; 39(2); 40(2); 32:3; 4(3); 5(3); 15; 28; 29; 36; 38; 33:9(3); 10; 12; 13; 15; 17; 18; 21; 34:2; 3(5); 4; 5(2); 14; 20; 35:6; 7(2); 19; 36:6; 29; 30(2); 37:7; 8; 17; 38:2(4); 3(2); 17(3); 18(3); 20(3); 22(2); 23(4); 24; 26; 39:16; 17; 18(2); 40:9; 16; 42:4; 14; 16(4); 17(3); 18(2); 22; 43:11; 12(3); 13(2); 44:12(4); 14(2); 26; 27; 28(2); 29; 45:4; 46:10(2); 11; 18; 19; 22(2); 23; 24(2); 26; 27(2); 47:2(4); 4; 48:2(2); 3; 7(2); 8(4); 9; 12; 13; 26(2); 34; 36(2); 37(2); 39(2); 40; 41; 42; 43; 44(2); 45(2); 49:2(3); 3; 5; 10; 12(2); 13(2); 17; 18(2); 19; 20(2); 22(2); 26(2); 27; 28; 29(3); 32; 33(2); 36; 39; 50:3(4); 4(2); 5; 9(4); 10(2); 12(3); 13(3); 16(2); 19(2); 20(3); 30(2); 32; 39(4); 40; 41(2); 42(4); 44; 45; 51:2(2); 4; 6; 14; 18; 26(2); 29; 37; 38(2); 44(2); 47(2); 48(2); 49; 52; 57; 58(3); 62(3); 63(2); 64(3); **Lam** 2:13(3); 4:15; 20; 21(2); **Ezek** 2:4; 7; 3:18(2); 19; 20(3); 21; 22; 26; 27; 4:3(2); 4; 5; 6; 7(3); 9; 10(2); 11(2); 12; 13; 15; 16(2); 5:2(3); 3; 10(2); 12(2); 13(2); 15; 16; 17; 6:4(2); 6(2); 7(2); 10; 11; 12(3); 13; 14; 7:4; 9; 11(2); 13(2); 21; 22; 24; 25; 27; 11:7; 10(2); 11(2); 12; 16; 20; 12:3; 4(2); 6(2); 11(2); 12(3); 13(3); 15; 16; 19; 20(3); 23; 24; 13:9(3); 11(2); 13; 14(2); 21(2); 23(2); 14:8; 10(2); 21; 22; 23; 15:7(2); 16:39(2); 40(2); 41(2); 42; 43; 62; 17:16; 18; 20; 21(3); 24; 18:3; 4; 9; 13(4); 17(2); 18; 19; 20(4); 21(2); 22(2); 24(3); 28(2); 20:11; 13; 21; 31; 32; 38; 40; 42; 43(2); 44; 47(3); 48(2); 21:4; 5; 7(3); 13; 19; 24; 25; 26; 27; 29; 32(3); 22:14; 16(2); 21; 22(2); 23:24(3); 25(5); 26; 29; 32(2); 34(2); 35; 47(2); 49(3); 24:14; 16(2); 21; 22(2); 23(3); 24(2); 27(2); 25:4(3); 5; 7; 11; 13; 14; 17; 26:2; 4; 5(2); 6(2); 13; 14(2); 20; 21; 28:7; 8(2); 9; 10; 19; 22; 23(2); 24(2); 26; 29:5(2); 6; 9; 11(2); 12; 14; 15(2); 16(2); 19; 21; 30:4(2); 5; 6(3); 7(2); 9(2); 11(2); 13; 16(3); 17(2); 18(4); 19; 25(2); 26; 31:11; 18(2); 32:7; 10(2); 11; 12(2); 13(2); 15; 16(3); 20; 21; 28; 29; 32; 33:4; 5; 7; 8(2); 9; 12(3); 13(3); 14; 15(2); 16(2); 18; 19; 27(2); 28(2); 29; 34:10; 14(2); 17; 22; 23(2); 26; 27(4); 28(4); 29; 30; 35:4(3); 6(2); 8; 9(2); 10; 12; 15(2); 36:7; 8; 9; 10; 11(2); 12(3); 14; 15; 23; 25; 28(2); 33; 34; 36; 38(2); 37:5; 6(2); 13; 14(2); 22(3); 23(2); 24(3); 25(3); 26; 27(2); 38:10; 19; 20(4); 23; 39:4; 5; 6; 7; 8; 15; 16; 18; 19; 20; 21; 22; 23; 28; 29; 42:13(2); 14(3); 43:7; 19; 20(2); 21; 22(2); 23; 24; 25(2); 26; 27(2); 44:2(4); 3; 9; 10; 11(3); 12; 13(2); 15(2); 16(3); 17(3); 18(2); 19(2); 20(2); 21; 22; 23; 24(3); 25; 26; 28(2); 29(2); 30(2); 31; 45:1(3); 2; 3(2); 4(2); 5(2); 6(2); 7(2); 8(3); 10; 11(2); 12(2); 13(2); 15(2); 16; 17(2); 18; 19; 20(2); 21(2); 22; 23; 24; 25; 46:1(3); 2(5); 3; 4; 5; 6(2); 7; 8; 9(4); 10(3); 11; 12(4); 13(2); 14; 15; 16; 17(4); 18(2); 20(2); 24; 47:9; 10; 13(2); 14(2); 15; 17; 18; 19; 20; 21; 22(3); 23(2); 48:1; 8(2); 9(2); 10(2); 11; 12; 13(2); 14; 15(2); 16; 17; 18(3); 19; 20(2); 21(4); 22; 23; 24; 25; 26; 27; 28; 29; 31; 35(2); **Dan** 2:5(2); 6; 9; 39(2); 40; 41(2); 42; 44(4); 3:5; 6; 10; 11; 15; 29(2); 4:25(5); 26; 32(4); 5:7(2); 16(2); 6:5; 7; 12; 26(2); 7:14(2); 18; 23(3); 24(4); 25(4); 26(2); 27(2); 8:14; 19(2); 22; 23; 24(4); 25(5); 9:25(2); 26(3); 27(3); 11:2(2); 3(2); 4(2); 5(3); 6(5); 7(2); 8(2); 9(2); 10(3); 11(3); 13; 14(3); 15(3); 16(3); 17(4); 18(4); 19(2); 20(2); 21(2); 22; 23(2); 24(4); 25(4); 26(3); 27(3); 28(2); 29(2); 30(3); 31(3); 32(2); 33(2); 34(2); 35; 36(5); 37(2); 38(2); 39(3); 40(3); 41(3); 42(2); 43(2); 44(2); 45(2); 12:1(3); 2; 3; 4(2); 6; 7(2); 8; 10(4); 11; 13; **Hos** 1:5; 10(3); 11(2); 2:10; 12; 15; 16; 17; 20; 21(2); 22(2); 23; 3:3(3); 4; 5(2); 4:5(2); 9; 10(2); 19; 5:6; 7; 9; 14; 6:4(2); 7:16(2); 8:1; 6; 7; 10; 13; 14; 9:2(2); 3(3); 4(6); 6(4); 11; 16; 17; 10:6(3); 8(3); 10; 11(2); 14(2); 15(2); 11:5(2); 6; 10(2); 11; 12:8; 11; 13:3; 4; 8; 13; 15(5); 16(2); 14:3; 5; 6(2); 7(3); 8; **Joel** 1:15; 2:3; 24(2); 26(2); 27(2); 28(4); 31; 32(3); 3:17(3); 18(4); 19; 20; **Am** 1:4; 5; 7; 8; 10; 12; 14; 15; 2:2(2); 5; 14(3); 15(3); 16; 3:11(3); 12; 14; 15(2); 4:2; 5:3(2); 5(2); 11(2); 16(3); 17; 6:7(2); 9(2); 7:3; 6; 9(2); 11(2); 17(5); 8:3(2); 8(2); 9; 12(3); 13; 14; 9:1(2); 2; 3; 4; 5; 9; 10(2); 13(3); 14(3); 15; **Ob** 2; 6(2); 7(3); 9; 10(2); 15(2); 16(3); 17(3); 18(4); 19(4); 20(2); 21(2); **Jon** 1:11; 3:4; **Mic** 1:7(3); 14(2); 15; 16; 2:3; 4; 6(2); 10; 12; 3:6(4); 7(2); 12(2); 4:1(4); 2(3); 3(4); 4(2); 8(2); 10(4); 13; 5:2; 3(2); 4(3); 5; 6(2); 7; 8; 9(2); 10; 12; 13; 6:6(2); 7; 9; 11; 14(3); 15(2); 16; 7:4; 11; 12; 13; 16(3); 17(4); **Nah** 1:10; 14; 15; 2:7(3); 13(2); 3:7(2); 13; **Hab** 1:2; 12; 17; 2:4; 8; 19; **Zeph** 1:8; 10; 12; 13(3); 14; 17(2); 18(2); 2:4(3); 5; 6; 7(3); 9(3); 10; 11; 12; 14(4); 15; 3:8; 10; 11(2); 12; 13(4); 15; 16; **Hag** 2:7; 9; 13; 22; **Zech** 1:16(2); 17; 2:4; 9; 11(2); 3:7; 4:7(2); 9; 5:3(2); 4(2); 6:12(2); 13(5); 14; 15(3); 8:3; 4; 5; 8(2); 12(4); 13(2); 16; 19; 20; 21; 22; 23; 9:5(4); 6; 7(2); 8; 10(3); 15(3); 16; 17; 10:5(3); 6; 7(4); 8; 9(3); 11(4); 12; 11:6; 17(3); 12:3; 5; 6(2); 7; 8(2); 9; 11; 12; 13:1; 2(2); 3(3); 4; 8(3); 14:2(3); 4(2); 5(3); 6; 7(2); 8(3); 9(2); 10(2); 11(3); 12(4); 13; 14; 15(2); 16(2); 17; 18(2); 19; 20(2); 21(3); **Mal** 1:4; 5(2); 11(3); 2:4; 3:7; 11; 17; 18; 4:1; 2(2); 3(2); **Mt** 1:21; 23(2); 2:6; 23; 4:4; 6(2); 7; 10(2); 5:4; 5; 6; 7; 8; 9; 13; 19(2); 21; 22(3); 27; 33(2); 36; 43; 48; 6:5; 31(3); 33; 7:21; 9:21; 10:41(2); 42; 11:16; 24; 12:27; 45; 13:14; 16:4; 18; 22; 28; 17:17(2); 18:21; 19:5(2); 16; 18(4); 19; 27; 29; 20:26; 21:3; 13; 22:24; 37; 39; 23:11; 39; 24:2(2); 13; 21; 51; 25:1; 27:22; **Mk** 4:30(2); 5:28; 6:24; 37; 8:12; 9:19(2); 35; 43; 45; 10:7; 8; 17; 30; 43(2); 44; 11:17; 12:15(2); 30; 31; 13:2(2); 13; 19; **Lk** 1:13; 15; 18; 31; 60; 2:23; 3:5(2); 6; 10; 12; 14; 4:4; 8(2); 10; 11; 12; 6:21(2); 25(2); 37(2); 7:31; 9:27; 41; 10:19; 25; 27; 11:5; 51; 12:17; 31; 47; 48; 59; 13:18; 20; 32; 35; 14:14; 15; 24; 34; 16:3; 17:4; 18:7; 18; 30; 19:31; 20:13; 21:6(2); 18; 22:11; 34; 49; **Jn** 1:42; 51; 3:36; 4:14(2); 5:24; 45; 6:5; 28; 35(2); 45; 51(2); 68; 7:17; 33; 35; 8:12; 32(2); 36; 51; 52; 55; 10:28(2); 11:25; 26; 47; 12:27; 13:8; 26; 33; 36; 38; 15:7; 26; 16:26; 18:11; 19:15; 24; 36; 37; **Acts** 1:5; 8(2); 2:17(4); 18; 20; 21(2); 37; 38; 3:22; 23(2); 25; 4:16; 7:7; 37; 11:16; 13:11; 15:11; 19:39; 21:11; 22:10; 23:5; 25:12; 22; 26:2; 28:26; **Rom** 1:17; 3:5; 4:1; 8; 18; 24; 5:9; 10; 6:1(2); 2; 5; 8; 14; 15; 7:7(2); 8:18; 31; 32; 33; 35(2); 39; 9:7; 9; 12; 14; 26(2); 30; 10:5; 13; 14(3); 15; 11:35; 13:9(6); 14:10; 11(2); 12; 15:12(3); 21(2); 24; 28; 29; **1 Cor** 4:21; 6:3; 15; 16; 8:11; 9:9; 11:22(2); 13:12; 14:6; 11; 15:22; 37; 49; 51(2); 52; 54; **2 Cor** 5:3; 6:16; 18; 10:8; 15; 11:10; 12:20(2); 21; 13:1; 4; **Gal** 2:16; 3:8; 11; 12; 4:30; 5:10; 14; 16; 6:5; 9; **Eph** 5:31(2); **Phil** 1:20; 22; 25; 2:24; 4:19; **1 Th** 4:17(2); 5:3; **2 Th** 1:9; 3:10; **1 Tim** 5:18; 6:8; **2 Tim** 2:11; 12; **Phm** 1:22; **Heb** 1:5; 2:3; 3:11; 4:3; 5; 8:10; 11(2); 9:14; 10:38; 11:18; 32; 12:9; 20; 25; 13:23; **Jas** 2:8; 10; 3:1; 4:15; **1 Jn** 3:2(3); 19; **3 Jn** 14; **Rev** 2:11; 23; 27(2); 3:4; 5; 10; 12; 5:10; 7:16(2); 11:15; 13:10; 14:10(2); 15:4(2); 18:14; 21(2); 22(3); 23(2); 20:6(2); 21:3; 4(2); 7(2); 8; 24; 25(2); 26; 27; 22:3(3); 4(2); 5(2); 19

SHE (973/719)

Gen 2:23(2); 3:6(2); 12; 20; 4:1; 2; 17; 22; 25; 8:9; 11:30; 12:14; 18; 19; 16:1; 4(3); 5(2); 6; 8; 13(2); 17:16; 18:15; 19:26; 33(2); 35(2); 38; 20:2; 3; 5(3); 12(3); 16; 21:7; 9; 10; 14; 15; 16(3); 19(2); 24:14; 16; 18(2); 19(2); 20; 24(2); 25; 36; 44; 45; 46(2); 47; 55; 58; 64(2); 65(2); 67; 25:2; 21; 22(2); 26; 26:7(3); 9(2); 27:16; 17(2); 42; 29:9; 12; 32(2); 33(2); 34; 35(3); 30:1; 3(2); 4; 6; 8; 9(2); 11; 13; 15; 17; 18; 20; 21; 23; 24; 31:35; 34:1; 35:8; 16; 17; 18(2); 36:12; 14; 38:3; 4(2); 5(2); 14(3); 15(2); 16(2); 17; 18(2); 19; 24; 25(3); 26; 28; 29; 39:7; 10; 12; 13; 14; 16; 17; 46:15; 18; 25; **Ex** 1:16; 2:2(2); 3(2); 5(2); 6(3); 7; 10(2); 22; 4:26; 6:20; 23; 25; 21:4; 7; 8; 11; 22; **Lev** 12:2(2); 4(2); 5(3); 6; 7; 8(3); 15:19; 20(2); 22; 23; 25; 26(2); 28(3); 29; 18:7; 11; 12; 13; 14; 15; 19; 19:20; 20:17; 18; 21:9(3); 22:12; 13; **Num** 5:13(2); 14; 27; 28; 12:10; 14(2); 22:25; 27; 28; 33; 26:59; 30:4(2); 5; 6(2); 7; 8(3); 9; 10; 11; **Deut** 21:12; 13(2); 22:14; 19; 21; 24; 29; 24:1; 2; 4; 25:6; 28:57(2); **Josh** 2:4; 6(2); 8; 15(2); 16; 21(3); 6:17(2); 22; 23; 25(3); 15:18(3); 19; **Judg** 1:14(3); 15; 4:5; 6; 9; 18; 19; 5:24; 25(2); 26(4); 29; 11:34; 36; 37; 38; 39(2); 13:9; 14(2); 14:3; 7; 17(3); 15:2; 16:8; 9; 14; 15; 16; 18; 19(2); 20; 19:3; 20:5; **Ruth** 1:3; 6(3); 7(2); 9; 15; 18(3); 20; 2:2; 3(2); 7(3); 10; 13; 14(2); 15; 16; 17(2); 18(5); 19(2); 23(2); 3:5; 6; 7; 9; 14(2); 15(2); 16(3); 17; 18; 4:13(2); **1 Sam** 1:7(3); 10; 11; 12; 13; 18; 22; 23; 24(2); 26; 2:5; 19; 21; 4:19(2); 20(2); 21; 22; 18:19; 21; 19:14; 25:3; 19(2); 20(3); 23; 24; 35; 36; 41; 42; 28:12; 14; 24(2); 25; **2 Sam** 4:4; 6:16; 11:4(3); 5; 26; 27; 12:24; 13:2; 8; 9; 10; 11; 12; 14; 16; 18; 14:4; 5; 11; 27; 20:17; 18; 21:8(2); 10; **1 Ki** 1:4; 17; 22; 28; 2:13; 14; 16; 19; 20; 21; 3:17; 19; 20; 26(2); 27; 10:1; 2(3); 6; 10; 13(4); 14:4; 5(2); 6; 17; 15:13; 17:11; 12; 15(2); 18; 21:8; 9; 11; **2 Ki** 4:2; 5(2); 6; 7; 8; 9; 12; 13; 14; 15; 16; 21; 22; 23; 24; 25; 26; 27(2); 28; 36; 37(2); 5:2; 3; 6:28; 29; 8:2; 3; 6(2); 9:30; 31; 34; 11:1; 13; 14; 16(2); 22:14; 15; **1 Chr** 2:21; 26; 29; 35; 49; 7:16; 23; 15:29; **2 Chr** 9:1(3); 5; 9; 12(5); 11:19; 20; 15:16; 22:10; 11(2); 23:12; 13; 15; 34:22; 23; 36:21(2); **Esth** 1:11; 15; 17; 19; 2:1; 7; 9; 12; 13(2); 14(3); 15; 17; 20; 4:4; 5; 5:2; 12; **Job** 39:14; 15; 16; 18(2); **Ps** 45:14; 46:5; 68:12; 80:11; 84:3; **Prov** 1:20; 21(2); 3:15; 18; 4:6(2); 8(2); 9(2); 13; 5:4; 7:11; 12; 13(2); 21(2); 26; 8:2; 3; 9:1; 2(3); 3(2); 4; 13; 14; 16; 12:4; 23:22; 28; 30:20; 23; 31:12; 13; 14(2); 15; 16(2); 17; 18; 19; 20(2); 21; 22; 24; 25; 26; 27; 30; **Song** 6:10; 8:2; 5; 8(2); 9(2); **Isa** 3:26; 8:3; 23:3; 17; 26:17; 40:2; 51:18(2); 66:7(3); 8; **Jer** 3:1; 6; 7(2); 9; 4:17; 31; 6:6; 7; 15:9(3); 33:16; 46:24; 48:9; 39; 49:24; 50:9; 12; 13(2); 14; 15(2); 29(2); 51:8; 9; 42; 53; **Lam** 1:1; 2(2); 3(2); 4; 7; 8(2); 9(2); 10; **Ezek** 5:6; 16:49(2); 19:2(2); 3; 5(3); 11(2); 12(2); 13; 14; 22:3; 23:5(2); 7(3); 8; 9; 10; 11(2); 12; 13; 14(2); 16; 17; 18; 19(2); 20; 43; 24:7(2); 12; 26:2(3); 17; 32:20; **Dan** 11:6(2); 17; **Hos** 1:3; 6; 8(2); 2:2; 3; 5(2); 6; 7(3); 8; 12; 13(3); 15(2); 13:16; **Am** 5:2(2); **Mic** 1:7; 13; 5:3; 7:10(2); **Nah** 2:7(2); 10; 3:10(2); **Zeph** 2:15; 3:2(4); **Zech** 9:4; **Mal** 2:14; **Mt** 1:18; 21; 25; 8:15; 9:18; 21; 12:42; 14:7; 8; 11; 15:23; 25; 27; 20:21; 22:28; 26:7; 10; 12; **Mk** 1:31; 5:23(2); 26(2); 27(2); 28; 29(2); 42; 6:19; 24(2); 25; 7:25; 26; 28; 30(2); 10:12; 12:23; 44(2); 14:3; 6; 8(3); 67(2); 16:10; **Lk** 1:24; 29(2); 42; 45; 57; 2:7; 36; 38; 4:39; 7:12; 37; 38(2); 39; 44; 47; 8:42; 47(5); 50; 52; 53; 55(2); 10:39; 40; 11:31; 13:13; 15:8(2); 9(2); 18:3; 5; 20:33; 21:4(2); **Jn** 8:11; 11:20; 27; 28(2); 29(2); 31; 32; 12:7; 16:21(3); 20:2; 11(2); 12; 13; 14(2); 15; 16; 18; **Acts** 5:8; 10; 9:36; 37; 39; 40(3); 12:14(2); 15; 16:14; 15(3); 18; **Rom** 7:2; 3(5); 16:2(2); **1 Cor** 7:11; 12; 28; 34(3); 36; 39(2); 40(3); **Gal** 4:27; **Eph** 5:27; 33; **1 Tim** 2:15; 5:5; 6(2); 9; 10(5); **Heb** 11:11(3); 31; **Jas** 2:25; **1 Pe** 5:13; **Rev** 2:21; 12:2; 5; 6; 14(2); 14:8; 18:6(2); 7(2); 8; 19; 21:12

SO (3469/3349)

Gen 1:5; 7; 8; 9; 11; 13; 15; 19; 21; 23; 24; 27; 30; 31; 2:20; 3:6; 10; 14; 24; 4:6; 11; 5:5; 8; 11; 14; 17; 20; 23; 27; 31; 6:7; 12; 22; 7:7; 16; 23; 8:6; 9; 12; 17; 18; 9:1; 24; 29; 11:8; 32; 12:4; 5; 9; 14; 20; 13:6; 8; 16; 14:16; 15:5; 9; 16:2; 4; 6; 10; 15; 17:23; 18:2; 6; 8; 9; 25; 26; 28; 29; 30; 31; 33; 19:3; 6; 7; 9; 11; 14; 17; 25; 33; 20:8; 17; 21:8; 14; 16; 20; 27; 32; 22:3; 6; 8; 11; 13; 19; 23:2; 15; 17; 20; 24:2; 9; 18; 21; 22; 24; 28; 30; 34; 46; 47; 56; 57; 59; 61; 65; 67; 25:22; 24; 25; 26; 27; 32; 33; 26:6; 9; 11; 14; 20; 21; 22; 25; 28; 30; 33; 27:1; 6; 18; 20; 22; 23; 25(2); 32; 41; 42; 28:5; 9; 11; 21; 29:1; 6; 12; 13; 18; 20; 25; 26; 28(2); 32; 30:3; 8; 11; 13; 18; 20; 24; 29; 31; 33; 35; 38; 39; 42; 31:4; 9; 21; 25; 28; 36; 45; 32:1; 7; 13; 19; 21; 27; 33:1; 5; 11; 16; 34:4; 5; 10; 12; 19; 35:4; 6; 8; 10; 14; 18; 19; 29; 36:8; 37:6; 8; 10; 13; 14; 16; 17; 23; 26; 28; 31; 38:3; 14; 16; 17; 18; 19; 22; 24; 26; 28; 39:4; 5; 10; 13; 16; 18; 19; 40:3; 4; 7(2); 8; 18; 41:4; 7; 13; 16; 21; 24; 31; 37; 43; 45; 48; 55; 57; 42:3; 8; 17; 20(2); 26; 28; 34; 43:6; 11; 15; 18; 21; 24; 30; 32; 34; 44:2; 5; 6; 12; 14; 17; 24; 31; 45:1; 4; 8; 13; 16; 21; 24; 46:1; 3; 6; 29; 33; 47:10; 13; 15; 17; 20; 25; 27; 28; 31; 48:10; 12; 17; 18; 20; 49:17; 50:2; 7; 12; 16; 22; 26; **Ex** 1:10; 13; 18; 21; 22; 2:2; 6; 8; 9; 10; 12; 14; 18; 20; 24; 3:2; 4; 8; 12; 20; 22; 4:2; 3; 7; 11; 14; 16; 18; 21; 23; 26; 27; 28; 31; 5:3; 6; 12; 22; 6:9; 7:1; 4; 6(2); 10(2); 11; 14; 20(2); 21; 22; 24; 8:3; 6; 7; 10; 13; 16(2); 17; 18(2); 24; 26; 30; 9:4; 6; 8; 24(2); 29; 33; 35; 10:3; 5; 8; 11; 13; 15(2); 18; 22; 11:9; 10; 12:11; 14; 17; 27; 28(2); 30; 34; 36; 50; 13:14; 18; 20; 21; 14:4(2); 6; 9; 10; 11; 17; 20(2); 22; 25; 27; 28; 30; 31; 15:22; 25; 27; 16:13; 15; 17; 18; 21; 22; 24; 30; 34; 17:4; 6; 7; 10; 11; 12; 13; 18:7; 13; 14; 17; 19; 22; 23; 24; 26; 19:2; 7; 8; 9; 14; 16; 25; 20:20; 21; 21:12; 20; 22; 29; 35; 22:2; 6; 23:2; 25; 24:3; 11; 13; 18; 25:9; 33; 37; 26:6; 25; 27:8; 28:3; 4; 7; 12; 28(2); 29; 30; 32; 38; 41; 29:9; 44;

30:21; 32:3; 5; 14; 19(2); 21; 22; 24; 28; 30; 35; 33:6; 8; 11; 16; 17; 22; 34:2; 4; 8; 28; 29; 30; 36:3; 6; 30; 37:19; 39:21; 23; 32; 42; 43; 40:16; 18; 33; **Lev** 4:20; 26; 31; 35; 5:6; 10; 16; 18; 6:7; 8:4; 34; 35(2); 36; 9:5; 10:2; 3; 5; 13; 20; 12:8; 14:13; 18; 20; 31; 15:15; 24; 16:16(2); 18:30; 23:44; 24:11; 19; 20; 23; 25:18; 26:15; 27:12; 14; **Num** 1:19; 45; 54; 2:17; 34(2); 3:4; 10; 16; 42; 49; 4:26; 5:4(2); 22; 6:21; 27; 7:1; 6; 10; 8:3; 4; 7; 10; 15; 20; 22; 9:4; 5; 6; 14; 16; 20; 21; 10:13; 31; 33; 35; 11:1; 3; 4; 11; 16; 24; 25; 28; 34; 12:2; 4; 7; 9; 11; 13; 15; 13:3; 21; 33; 14:1; 4; 28; 35; 15:12; 14; 15; 20; 25; 28; 36; 16:4; 18; 23; 27; 33; 39; 46; 47; 48; 50; 17:6; 11; 12; 20:2; 6; 9; 19; 20; 21; 27; 21:2; 3; 6; 7; 9(2); 23; 25; 33; 35; 22:4; 7; 8; 10; 13; 21; 23; 25; 27; 30; 35; 39; 41; 23:3; 6; 12; 14; 17; 26; 28; 24:12; 15; 24; 25; 25:3; 5; 8; 11; 26:3; 65; 27:5; 22; 29:40; 31:3; 5; 31; 41; 51; 32:9; 10; 13; 23; 28; 31; 33; 40; 33:9; 41; 35:7; 16; 20; 21; 23; 25; 33; 36:3; 4; 7; 8; 10; **Deut** 1:15; 19; 23; 43; 46; 2:5; 13; 16; 33; 3:3; 21; 26; 29; 4:7; 13; 5:23; 6:10; 7:4; 19; 8:3; 5; 20; 9:3; 8; 15; 20; 10:3; 11:17; 12:10; 22; 13:5; 11; 17; 14:24; 16:15; 17:7; 12; 18:6; 19:5; 11; 19; 20:2; 9; 21:9; 21; 23; 22:3; 5; 21; 22; 24; 26; 24:8; 25:9; 26:8; 11; 12; 28:14; 34; 55; 63; 29:18; 19; 22; 24; 30:17; 31:9; 14; 17; 24; 32:12; 44; 33:25; 34:5; 8; 9; **Josh** 1:5; 16; 17; 2:1; 3; 4; 14; 17; 19; 21; 23; 3:2; 6; 7; 9; 14; 16; 4:8; 10; 5:1; 3; 8; 14; 15; 6:8; 11; 14; 20; 23; 25; 27; 7:1; 2; 4; 10; 16; 22; 25; 26; 8:3; 12; 16; 17; 19; 20; 22(2); 25; 28; 9:7; 9; 15; 24; 26(2); 10:1; 7; 10; 13(2); 18; 23; 24; 27; 36; 39; 40; 11:4; 7; 9; 12; 15(2); 23; 14:5; 9; 11; 15:1; 17; 18(2); 19; 16:4; 17:15; 18:9; 19:51; 20:7; 21:3; 9; 40; 43; 22:6; 9; 25; 33; 23:5; 15; 24:7; 10; 16; 22; 25; 28; **Judg** 1:3; 7; 13; 15; 17; 19; 21; 23; 25; 29; 30; 32; 2:4; 7; 14(2); 17; 22; 3:2; 7; 11; 12; 14; 17; 20; 24; 25; 28; 30; 4:2; 9; 13; 14; 19; 21; 23; 5:15; 28; 31; 6:1; 3; 6; 15; 19; 20; 22; 24; 27; 29; 36; 38; 40; 7:1; 5; 8; 13; 15; 19; 8:2; 7; 9; 18(2); 21(3); 25; 28; 33; 9:4; 27; 29; 34; 37; 39; 41; 43; 45; 49(2); 52; 54; 10:7; 9; 11; 16; 11:5; 7; 9; 14; 17; 20; 24; 32; 36; 38; 39; 12:3; 13:6; 11; 13; 19; 24; 14:2; 5; 10(2); 14; 15; 16; 17; 18; 19; 15:6; 8; 10; 11; 13; 17; 18; 19; 16:6; 8; 9; 11; 14; 16; 18; 20; 25(2); 26; 30; 17:3; 9; 10; 12; 18:2(2); 4; 5; 7; 9; 15; 20; 23; 24; 27; 28; 31; 19:3; 4; 6; 7; 8; 9; 10; 13; 18; 21; 23; 25; 28; 30; 20:1; 4; 5; 6; 8; 11; 19; 24; 27; 31; 33; 36; 46; 21:4; 10; 12; 14; 23; 24; **Ruth** 1:5; 17; 22; 2:2; 6; 7; 10; 14; 17; 18; 19; 23; 3:6; 9; 14; 16; 4:1(2); 2; 8; 13; **1 Sam** 1:7; 9; 14; 18; 20; 23; 28; 2:3; 14; 21; 23; 31; 3:2; 5; 6; 9; 15; 17; 19; 4:4; 5; 7; 10; 15; 17; 5:3; 8; 9; 10; 11(2); 6:3; 10; 14; 16; 21; 7:2; 4; 6; 8; 10; 13; 8:6; 8; 10; 22; 9:4; 6; 10; 14; 24(2); 10:9; 14; 16; 23; 24; 27; 11:4; 7(2); 11(2); 15; 12:18; 13:9; 22; 14:7; 11; 15; 19; 23; 24; 31; 33; 34; 37; 41; 42; 43; 44; 45; 47; 15:4; 6; 12; 17; 28; 31; 32; 33; 16:4; 6; 8; 12; 13; 17; 21; 23; 17:20; 23; 25; 27; 38; 39; 41; 43; 48; 49; 50; 56; 58; 18:5; 7; 9; 10; 18; 21; 23; 26; 29; 30(2); 19:2; 6; 7; 10; 12; 14; 17; 18; 22; 23; 20:2(2); 4; 11; 13; 16; 28; 34; 35; 38; 41; 42; 21:2; 6; 9; 13; 22:2; 4; 5; 11; 14; 18; 22; 23:5; 7; 13(2); 15; 18; 24; 26; 28; 24:3; 7; 16; 22; 25:9; 12; 13; 20; 21; 22; 24; 25; 35; 37; 39; 42; 43; 26:5; 7; 12; 15; 20; 24; 25; 27:1; 3; 4; 6; 12; 28:4; 8; 14; 23; 25; 29:4; 8; 11; 30:3; 8; 9; 10; 12; 15; 18; 21(2); 23; 24; 25; 31:6; 8; **2 Sam** 1:2; 3; 5; 8; 10; 11; 14; 15; 16; 2:2; 3; 5; 13; 15; 16; 17; 19; 22; 23(2); 28; 30; 3:6; 7; 9; 14; 16; 20; 21; 27; 30; 32; 34; 35; 4:12; 5:10; 12; 19; 20; 25; 6:3; 10; 12; 13; 15; 17; 19; 21; 7:17; 26; 8:2; 15; 9:2; 4; 7; 11; 13; 10:2; 13; 14; 19; 11:3; 5; 8; 10; 12; 16; 20; 21; 22; 25; 12:5; 13; 17; 20; 24; 25; 29; 31; 13:2; 5; 8; 15; 16; 20; 23; 27; 29; 31; 35; 36; 38; 14:1; 3; 7; 10; 13; 14; 17; 19; 23; 24; 30; 32; 33; 15:2; 5; 6; 9; 14; 22; 30; 34; 37; 16:2; 4; 8; 10(2); 11; 14; 16; 17; 19; 22; 23; 17:7; 12(2); 14; 15(2); 17; 20; 22; 26; 18:4; 6; 9; 11; 16; 21; 22; 23; 27; 30; 32; 19:2; 8; 11; 13; 14(2); 25; 29; 42; 20:2; 3; 5; 7; 14; 18(2); 21(2); 22; 21:2; 4; 8; 9; 13; 14; 21; 22:4; 35; 37; 39; 41; 23:5; 16; 21; 24:2; 8; 10; 13; 15; 19; 20; 24; 25; **1 Ki** 1:3; 6; 11; 15; 18; 23; 28; 30; 32; 36; 37; 38; 40; 45(2); 49; 50; 53; 2:7; 10; 13; 18; 19; 21; 23; 25; 27; 28; 30; 32; 34; 38(2); 40; 46; 3:12; 13; 14; 20; 24; 27; 4:1; 21; 5:7; 12; 18; 6:6; 7; 9; 14; 21; 26; 27; 33; 38; 7:1; 12; 14; 18; 22; 40; 47; 51; 8:3; 8; 11; 20; 54; 63; 9:13; 25; 10:3(2); 13; 23; 11:4; 9; 19; 21; 22; 24; 37; 12:2; 5; 12; 15; 16; 19; 32; 33; 13:4(2); 6; 9; 10; 13; 19; 23; 27; 29; 31; 34; 14:4; 6; 20; 31; 15:8; 19; 20; 24; 29; 16:6; 16; 22; 28; 17:5; 10; 12; 15; 17; 18; 19; 18:2; 4; 5; 6; 9; 12; 16; 20; 24; 26; 27; 28; 30; 35; 40; 42; 43; 44; 45; 19:2; 6; 8; 10; 13; 19; 21; 20:7; 10; 11; 14; 16; 18; 20; 24; 25; 26; 29; 32; 33; 34(2); 37; 40; 43; 21:2; 4; 5; 11; 13; 16; 20; 27; 22:4; 6; 8; 12; 16; 20; 22(2); 26; 29; 30; 32; 34; 37; 40; **2 Ki** 1:2; 4; 6; 8; 9; 10; 12; 15; 17; 2:2; 4; 5; 6; 8; 9; 10(3); 12; 20; 22; 24; 3:6; 9; 11; 12; 17; 24(2); 27; 4:2; 5; 6; 8; 10; 14; 15; 19; 23; 25(2); 28; 30; 36; 37; 39; 41; 44; 5:5; 8; 12; 14; 17; 19; 21; 23; 6:2; 4; 6(2); 7; 13; 16; 18; 20; 23; 29; 31; 7:2; 6; 10; 12; 13; 15; 16; 18; 20; 8:2; 6; 9; 13; 15; 21; 24; 9:4; 9; 12; 14; 15; 16; 18(2); 20; 22(2); 27; 32; 33; 35; 37; 10:7; 9; 11; 13; 14; 15; 16; 20; 21(2); 22; 24; 35; 11:2; 3; 9; 14; 16; 20; 12:6; 7; 10; 21; 13:4; 5; 9; 13; 15; 16; 18(2); 21; 14:10; 11; 16; 29; 15:5(2); 7; 12; 20; 22; 30; 38; 16:7; 9; 11; 13; 20; 17:4; 7; 16; 23; 25; 26; 32; 41; 18:5; 15; 21; 19:1; 5; 9; 36; 20:7; 11; 14; 15; 19; 21; 21:14; 18; 21; 22:9; 14; 20; 23:17; 18; 35; 24:6; 25:2; 3; 6; 20; 29; **1 Chr** 2:3; 4:10; 39; 41; 5:1; 23; 26; 6:64; 9:1; 23; 10:6; 8; 13; 11:14; 18; 12:18; 13:4; 5; 7; 13; 14:2; 11; 16; 15:14; 17; 25; 26; 16:1; 37; 17:15; 24; 18:6; 14; 19:2; 7; 14; 15; 17; 19; 20:3; 7; 21:2; 8; 11; 14; 16; 19; 25; 27; 22:2; 5; 14; 23:1; 25:7; 29:14; 20; 22; 25; 28; **2 Chr** 1:13; 2:3; 4:11; 5:1; 4; 9; 14; 6:10; 7:5; 8:14; 16; 9:2(2); 12; 22; 26; 10:2; 5; 12; 15; 16; 19; 11:5; 17; 12:6; 9; 12; 16; 13:9; 13; 17; 20; 14:1; 7; 10; 12; 13; 15:6; 10; 16:3; 4; 13; 17:9; 10; 12; 18:3; 7; 11; 15; 19; 21(2); 28; 29; 31; 32; 33; 19:4; 20:4; 6; 20; 24; 25; 28; 31; 37; 21:9; 17; 19; 22:1; 9; 11(2); 23:8; 13; 15; 19; 21; 24:6; 11; 13; 20; 21; 23; 24; 25; 25:8; 10; 12; 13; 14; 16; 21; 26:15; 17; 20; 23; 27:6; 9; 28:14; 15; 24; 27; 29:22; 28; 30; 31; 34; 35; 36; 30:5; 7; 9; 10; 21; 26; 31:21; 32:17; 21; 23; 26; 33; 33:9; 20; 34:6; 16; 22; 28; 32; 35:6; 10; 12; 16; 22(2); 24; 36:22; **Ezra** 1:1; 2:70; 3:13; 4:10; 11; 17; 5:2; 5; 17; 6:8; 14; 7:12; 28; 8:23; 30; 32; 36; 9:2; 3; 14; 10:5; 9; 12; 16; **Neh** 1:4; 2:2; 4; 6; 11; 15(2); 18; 20; 4:1; 6; 10; 12; 16; 17; 21; 23; 5:7; 12; 13; 15; 6:3(2); 7; 13; 15; 7:73; 8:2; 4; 8; 11; 17(2); 9:10; 11; 22; 24; 25; 28; 12:31; 40; 43; 13:3; 11; 19(2); 21; 25; **Esth** 1:8; 17; 19; 2:4; 8; 9; 16; 17; 22; 3:2; 10; 15; 4:4; 6; 9; 12; 16; 17; 5:2; 4; 5; 9; 13; 14; 6:1; 4; 6; 10; 11; 7:1; 5; 6; 10; 8:2; 4; 9; 13; 15; 9:14; 23; 26; 32; **Job** 1:3; 5; 7; 9; 12; 2:2; 4; 7; 13; 5:12; 16; 7:3; 9; 15; 20; 8:13; 9:2; 35; 13:15; 14:5; 12; 19; 19:8; 22:11; 14; 28; 24:18; 19; 25; 29:25; 31:17; 27; 34; 32:1; 6; 14; 33:20; 34:28; 41:10; 16; 42:7; 9; 15; 17; **Ps** 1:4; 7:7; 10:10; 18:3; 34; 36; 38; 40; 22:1; 26:6; 35:25; 40:12; 42:1; 45:11; 48:5; 8; 10; 55:6; 58:5; 11; 61:8; 63:2; 64:8; 65:9; 68:2(2); 69:23; 73:20; 22; 77:4; 13; 78:20; 21; 29; 53; 60; 72; 79:13; 80:12; 81:12; 83:15; 90:11; 12; 93:1; 95:11; 102:4; 15; 103:5; 11; 12; 13; 15; 104:5; 106:9; 32; 33; 40; 107:2; 29; 30; 109:17(2); 18; 115:2; 8; 119:27; 42; 44; 88; 123:2; 125:2; 127:2; 4; 135:18; **Prov** 1:19; 2:2; 20; 3:4; 10; 22; 27; 6:3; 11; 29; 32; 7:13; 15; 8:29; 10:26; 11:19; 22; 15:7; 11; 17:21; 19:24; 22:19; 23:7; 24:14; 34; 25:3; 22; 25; 27; 26:1; 2; 11; 14; 21; 27:17; 18; 19; 20; 30:33; 31:11; **Eccl** 2:9; 15; 3:19; 22; 5:11; 16; 6:2; 3; 7:6; 14; 8:7; 10; 15; 9:1; 2; 12; 10:1; 11:5; **Song** 2:2; 3; 5:9; **Isa** 1:8; 3:24; 5:2; 24; 6:5; 13; 7:2; 8; 22; 10:7(2); 13; 17; 19; 26; 14:24(2); 16:2; 6; 18:4; 20:2; 4; 21:1; 22:19; 22; 23:1; 24:2(6); 10; 26:17; 27:13; 28:20; 29:8; 30:14; 31:4; 5; 36:6; 37:1; 5; 9; 37; 38:8; 13; 14; 16; 39:3; 4; 8; 41:7; 44:12; 18(2); 45:1; 47:7; 48:9; 49:5; 51:11; 52:14; 15; 53:7; 54:9; 55:9; 11; 59:2; 15; 19; 60:15; 61:11; 62:5(2); 63:8; 10; 14; 65:8; 16; 22; 66:4; 13; 22; **Jer** 2:26; 36; 3:9; 20; 4:4; 5:19; 27; 31; 6:7; 7:28; 8:9; 9:10; 12; 10:4; 18; 11:4; 5; 14; 12:1; 13:2; 5; 11; 14:19; 16:12; 17:11; 18:4; 6; 10; 12; 19:11; 21:12; 22:8; 26; 23:14; 24; 33; 24:2; 3; 5; 8(2); 25:13; 26:7; 16; 24; 27:7; 28:6; 11; 17; 29:6; 17; 26; 30:6; 7; 31:28; 32:9; 11; 31; 40; 42; 33:20; 21; 22; 26; 34:5; 35:11; 36:14; 15; 18; 21; 37:14; 38:6(2); 11; 12; 13; 16; 20; 23; 27; 39:4; 13; 14; 40:5; 15; 41:7; 8; 13; 42:5; 17; 18; 20; 43:4; 7; 44:6; 14; 22; 46:18; 48:39; 50:15; 40; 51:49; 60; 62; 52:5; 6; 9; 33; **Lam** 3:7; 4:14; 18; 5:20; **Ezek** 1:18; 28(2); 3:2; 3; 14; 23; 25; 26; 4:5; 8; 9; 13; 14; 5:15; 17; 6:6; 8; 14; 8:5; 7; 10; 14; 16; 9:6; 8; 11:22; 25; 12:6; 7; 11; 12; 19; 13:14(2); 22; 14:15; 15:6; 16:8; 19; 23; 42; 17:6; 18:30; 19:14; 20:15; 29; 31; 36; 21:24; 22:20; 22; 26; 30; 23:17; 27; 24:18; 19; 26:20; 29:15; 31:9; 14; 33:7; 22; 28; 31; 34:5; 12; 35:15; 36:3; 19; 30; 35; 38; 37:3; 7; 10; 38:16; 20; 39:7; 22; 40:4; 41:9; 13; 19; 43:11; 26; 44:4; 45:3; 11; 20; 46:18; 20; **Dan** 1:5; 11; 13; 14; 2:1; 2; 13; 15; 16; 18; 19; 35; 42; 3:3; 7; 13; 4:19; 5:6; 6:2; 4; 6; 8; 13; 16; 22; 23; 28; 7:16; 8:2; 4; 17; 9:11; 10:7; 19; 11:15; 28; 30; **Hos** 1:3; 2:6; 12; 3:2; 3; 4:9; 6:9; 9:13; 11:2; 12:6; 13:7; **Joel** 2:4; 13; 25; 3:17; **Am** 2:11; 3:12; 4:8; 5:9; 14; 7:2; 3; 6; 8:2; **Ob** 16; **Jon** 1:3; 4; 6(2); 7; 9; 15; 2:10; 3:3; 5; 9; 4:2; 5; 6; 7; 8; **Mic** 2:2; 6; 12; 3:7; 4:7; 7:3; **Zeph** 2:5; 3:7; **Hag** 1:14; 2:5; 13; 14(3); **Zech** 1:6(2); 9; 11; 14; 19; 21(2); 2:2; 3:5; 4:2; 4; 6; 14; 5:2; 6; 10; 6:7; 13; 7:3; 11; 13; 14; 8:13; 15; 10:12; 11:7; 11; 12; 13; 12:7; 14:15; **Mal** 1:10; 2:5; 13; 3:11; 15; 16; **Mt** 1:17; 22; 2:5; 3:15; 5:12; 16; 19; 47; 6:18; 28; 30; 7:17; 28; 8:13; 15; 24; 27; 28; 31; 32; 9:1; 9; 19(2); 11:26(2); 12:22; 40; 45; 13:2; 15; 27; 32; 40; 49; 54; 57; 14:8; 10; 20; 29; 15:16; 31; 35; 37; 16:14; 17:16; 20; 18:14; 29; 31; 35; 19:6; 8; 17; 28; 20:4; 8; 16; 23; 26; 32; 34; 21:6; 11; 20; 21; 27; 39; 22:10; 12; 19; 23:28; 24:27; 33; 37; 39; 46; 25:20; 27; 26:16; 19; 35; 44; 75; 27:11; 14; 54; 64; 66; 28:8; 9; 15; **Mk** 1:27; 31; 45; 2:2; 4; 12; 14; 3:2(2); 9; 10; 20(2); 23; 4:1; 12; 17; 32; 37; 40; 5:12; 14; 24; 6:12; 24; 32; 34; 40; 42; 7:18; 8:6; 8; 21; 23; 28; 9:10; 18; 21; 26; 29; 10:8; 11; 18; 29; 39; 43; 49; 51; 11:4; 6; 11; 15; 22; 33; 12:8; 12; 16; 22; 32; 43; 13:14; 29; 14:11; 16; 15:5; 11; 13; 15; 28; 39; 45; 16:8; 19; **Lk** 1:8; 21; 23; 59; 62; 63; 80; 2:3; 6; 15; 27; 39; 45; 46; 48; 3:10; 14; 4:16; 22; 28; 39; 5:1; 7(2); 10; 11; 16; 28; 6:7; 10; 26; 7:3; 15; 40; 8:32; 40; 9:6; 9; 15; 17; 19; 39; 40; 45; 10:21(2); 27; 34; 36; 11:2; 9; 14; 30; 37; 12:1; 18; 21; 28; 38; 43; 54; 13:16; 14:7; 10; 21; 33; 15:3; 12; 26; 29; 16:2; 5; 6; 7; 8; 22; 26; 17:6; 10; 14(2); 17; 24; 26; 30; 37; 18:13; 19; 22; 29; 37; 40; 19:4; 6; 13; 15; 32; 20:7; 15; 20; 21:3; 7; 31; 22:4; 6; 9; 13; 26; 35; 38; 62; 70; 23:4; 24; 47; 24:15; 16; 19; 33; 42; **Jn** 2:18; 3:8; 14; 16; 4:5; 40; 45; 46; 50; 53; 5:21; 26; 6:9; 10; 12(2); 19; 57; 7:23; 43; 8:7; 22; 59; 9:7; 11; 24; 10:15; 11:6; 17; 12:37; 40; 50; 13:12; 13; 31; 33; 14:2; 9(2); 31; 15:8; 18:11; 15; 36; 19:1; 16; 30; 35; 38; 42; 20:4; 21; 25; 21:6; 11; 15; **Acts** 1:11; 19; 2:12; 46; 3:5; 8; 12(2); 19; 4:17; 21; 24; 5:5; 8(2); 11; 15; 25; 32; 41; 7:1; 8; 15; 19; 51; 8:25; 27; 30; 32; 34; 38; 39; 9:2; 6; 11; 12; 19; 21; 28; 35; 43; 10:4; 8; 14; 30; 33; 11:8; 26; 12:4; 8; 9; 12; 15(2); 21; 13:4; 8; 21; 42; 47; 14:1; 23; 28; 15:3; 8; 17; 30; 39(2); 16:5; 8; 15; 26; 31; 36; 40; 17:9; 11; 15; 27; 33; 18:3; 18; 26; 19:2(2); 3; 10; 12; 14; 16; 20; 22; 27; 29; 20:13; 16; 24; 32; 21:11; 14; 24; 34; 40; 22:8; 10; 19; 24(2); 23:11; 16; 18; 22; 24:9; 14; 16; 23; 25:10; 23; 26; 26:1; 15; 27:2; 15; 17; 38; 44; 28:4; 9; 14; 17; 23; 25; 27; **Rom** 1:11; 15; 20; 4:16; 18(2); 5:18; 19; 21(2); 6:4; 19; 7:3(2); 6; 13; 25; 8:8; 9:16; 10:17; 11:5; 10; 16; 26; 31; 12:5; 20; 14:12; 15:19; 20; **1 Cor** 1:7; 2:11; 3:7; 15; 4:1; 5:3; 6:5; 7:5; 17(2); 29; 37; 38; 9:14; 15; 11:12; 28; 12:12; 13:2; 14:9; 10; 12; 25; 15:11(2); 22; 42; 45; 48(2); 54; 16:1; **2 Cor** 1:5; 7; 8; 10; 2:4; 7; 17; 3:7; 13; 4:12; 5:6; 7:7; 14; 8:6(2); 11; 9:7; 10:7; 11:3; 9; 22(3); **Gal** 1:6; 9; 2:13; 3:3; 4; 9; 4:3; 29; 31; 5:17; 6:2; **Eph** 2:15; 4:20; 5:24; 28; 33; **Phil** 1:13; 20; 27; 2:16; 3:4; 17; 4:1; **Col** 2:6; 16; 3:13; **1 Th** 1:7; 8; 2:4; 8; 6; 3:13; 4:10; 14; 5:2; 4; **2 Th** 1:4; 2:4; 7; 3:17; **1 Tim** 3:15; 6:1; **2 Tim** 2:25; 3:8; 4:17; **Heb** 1:4; 2:3; 3:11; 19; 4:3; 5:3; 5; 6:15; 7:9; 22; 9:28; 10:25; 33; 36; 11:3; 5; 29; 12:1(2); 13; 19; 20; 21; 13:2; 6; 17; **Jas** 1:11; 19; 2:12(2); 26; 3:4; 5; 6; 10; **1 Pe** 1:21; 5:13; **2 Pe** 1:11; 19; **1 Jn** 2:1; 4:11; 17; **2 Jn** 12; **Rev** 1:7; 3:16; 5:4; 6:5; 8; 7:14; 8:6; 12; 9:2; 15; 10:9; 11:6; 12:9; 15; 13:4; 13; 14:16; 19; 16:2; 7; 12; 17:3; 20:3; 22:20

THAN (515/458)

Gen 3:1; 14(2); 4:13; 18:28; 19:9; 25:23; 26:16; 28:17; 29:19; 30; 34:19; 37:3; 4; 38:26; 39:9; 41:40; 48:19; 49:12(2); **Ex** 1:9; 14:12; 18:11; 30:15; 36:5; **Lev** 13:3; 4; 20; 21; 25; 26; 30; 31; 32; 34; 15:25; **Num** 3:46; 5:20; 12:3; 13:31; 14:12; 22:15; 24:7; **Deut** 1:11; 28; 4:38; 7:1; 7; 17; 9:1; 14; 11:23; 20:1; 30:5; **Josh** 10:2; 11; **Judg** 2:19; 8:2; 11:25; 14:18(2); 15:2; 16:30; **Ruth** 3:10; 12; 4:15; **1 Sam** 1:8; 2:29; 9:2(2); 10:23; 15:22(2); 28; 18:30; 24:17; 27:1; **2 Sam** 1:23(2); 6:22; 13:14; 15; 16; 17:14; 18:8; 19:7; 43(2); 20:5; 6; 23:23; 24:3; **1 Ki** 1:37; 47(2); 2:32; 4:31(2); 12:10; 14:9; 22; 16:25; 30; 33; 19:4; 20:23(2); 25; 21:2; **2 Ki** 5:12; 6:16; 9:35; 21:9; 11; 25:28; **1 Chr** 4:9; 11:21; 25; 21:3; 24:4; **2 Chr** 2:5; 9:12; 10:10; 11:21; 20:25; 21:13; 25:9; 29:34; 32:7; 33:9; **Ezra** 9:6; 13; **Neh** 7:2; **Esth** 1:19; 2:17(2); 4:13; 6:6; **Job** 3:21; 4:17(2); 6:3; 7:6; 15; 9:25; 11:6; 8(2); 9(2); 17; 15:10; 23:12; 30:1; 32:2; 4; 33:12; 34:19; 35:2; 3; 5; 11(2); 36:21; 42:12; **Ps** 4:7; 8:5; 19:10(3); 37:16; 40:5; 12; 45:2; 7; 51:7; 52:3(2); 55:21(2); 61:2; 62:9; 63:3; 68:35; 69:4; 31; 73:7; 76:4; 84:10(2); 87:2; 93:4(2); 105:24; 118:8; 9; 119:72; 98; 99; 100; 103; 127(2); 130:6(2); 139:18; 142:6; **Prov** 3:14(2); 15; 5:3; 8:10; 11; 19(3); 11:24; 12:9; 15:16; 17; 16:8; 16(2); 19; 32(2); 17:1; 10; 12; 18:19; 24; 19:1; 22; 21:3; 9; 19; 22:1(2); 25:7; 24; 26:12; 16; 27:3; 5; 10; 28:6; 23; 29:20; 30:2; **Eccl** 1:16; 2:7; 9; 16; 24; 25; 3:12; 22; 4:2; 3; 6; 9; 13; 5:1; 5; 6:3; 5; 8; 9; 10; 7:1(2); 2; 3; 5; 8(2); 10; 19; 26; 8:15; 9:4; 16; 17; 18; **Song** 1:2; 4; 4:10(2); 5:9(2); **Isa** 13:12(2); 40:17; 52:14(2); 54:1; 55:9(3); 56:5; 57:8; 65:5; **Jer** 3:11; 4:13; 5:3; 7:26; 8:3; 15:8; 16:12; 20:7; 31:11; 13; 46:23; 52:32; **Lam** 4:6; 7(3); 8; 9; 19; **Ezek** 3:9; 5:6(2); 7; 6:14; 8:15; 15:2; 16:47; 51; 52(2); 23:11(2); 28:3; 36:11; 42:5; 6; **Dan** 1:10; 15; 20; 2:30; 3:19; 7:20; 8:3; 11:2; 8; 13; **Hos** 2:7; 6:6; **Am** 6:2(2); **Jon** 4:3; 8; 11; **Mic** 7:4; **Nah** 3:8; 16; **Hab** 1:8(2); 13(2); **Hag** 2:9; **Zech** 12:7; **Mt** 3:11; 5:29; 30; 37; 47; 6:25(2); 26; 10:15; 31; 37(2); 11:9; 11(2); 22; 24; 12:6; 12; 41; 42; 45(2); 13:32; 18:8; 9; 13; 19:24; 21:36; 26:53; 27:64; **Mk** 1:7; 4:31; 32; 6:11; 8:14; 9:43; 45; 47; 10:25; 12:31; 33; 43; 14:5; **Lk** 3:13; 16; 7:26; 28(2); 9:13; 10:12; 14; 11:22; 26(2); 28; 31; 32; 12:7; 23(2); 24; 13:2; 4; 14:8; 15:7; 16:8; 17; 17:2; 18:14; 25; 21:3; **Jn** 1:50; 3:19; 4:1; 12; 5:20; 36; 7:31; 8:53; 10:29; 12:43; 13:16(2); 14:12; 28; 15:13(2); 20; 21:15; **Acts** 4:19; 5:29; 15:28; 17:11; 20:35; 23:13; 21; 24:11; 25:6; 26:13; 22; 27:11; **Rom** 1:25; 3:9; 8:37; 12:3; 13:11; **1 Cor** 1:25(2); 3:11; 7:9; 9:15; 10:22; 14:5; 18; 19; 15:10; **2 Cor** 1:13; **Gal** 1:8; 9; 4:27; **Eph** 3:8; **Phil** 2:3; **1 Tim** 1:4; 5:8; **2 Tim** 3:4; **Phm** 1:16; 21; **Heb** 1:4(2); 9; 2:7; 9; 3:3(2); 4:12; 7:26; 9:23; 11:4; 25; 26; 12:24; **Jas** 1:11; **1 Pe** 1:7; 3:17; **2 Pe** 2:20; 21; **1 Jn** 3:20; 4:4; **3 Jn** 4; **Rev** 2:19

THAT (7380/6205)

Gen 1:4; 10; 11(2); 12(3); 18; 21(2); 25(2); 26; 28; 29; 30; 31; 2:4; 9; 12; 17; 18; 19; 3:5; 6(2); 7; 11(2); 4:3; 8; 14; 5:1; 5; 6:2(2); 5(2); 6; 7; 17; 21; 22; 7:1; 2; 4; 5; 8(2); 10; 11; 14; 16; 21(2); 22; 8:1; 6; 11; 13; 17(3); 9:2; 3; 4; 10(2); 12; 14; 16; 17; 10:11; 12; 11:2; 6; 7; 12:1; 5; 11(2); 12; 13(2); 14(2); 18; 20; 13:1; 6(2); 10; 16; 14:2(2); 3; 5; 7; 8; 14; 17; 23(3); 15:8; 13(2); 17(2); 16:4; 5; 10; 17:14; 18; 23; 26; 18:5(2); 19(3); 21; 24; 25; 19:5; 11; 17; 21; 29; 32; 33; 34(2); 35; 20:6; 7; 9(2); 10; 13(2); 21:7; 8; 22(3); 23(3); 30(2); 31; 22:1; 12; 20; 23:2; 4; 6; 8; 9; 11; 15; 17; 19; 20; 24:2; 3; 6; 14(3); 15; 22; 30; 36; 43; 49; 52; 55; 56; 66; 25:5; 11; 30; 26:1; 8; 12; 21; 28; 29; 32; 27:1(2); 4(2); 7; 10(2); 19; 20; 21; 25; 30; 31; 40; 28:3; 4; 6(2); 7; 8; 11(2); 18; 19(2); 20; 21; 22; 29:2; 10; 12(2); 13; 19(2); 21; 23; 25(2); 31; 33; 30:1; 3; 9; 15; 16; 25(2); 27; 33; 34; 35(4); 38; 41(2); 31:1; 5; 6; 10; 12; 19; 20(2); 21; 22; 24; 26; 29; 32; 35; 36; 37; 39; 43; 52; 32:2; 5; 7; 13; 20; 21; 22; 25; 29; 32(2); 33:11; 13; 14; 16; 34:5; 14; 25; 29; 35:2; 5; 6; 17; 18; 19; 22(2); 27; 37:4; 10; 22; 23(2); 38:1(2); 9(2); 14; 16(2); 18; 21; 24; 27; 28; 29; 39:3(2); 4; 5(4); 6; 7; 8; 10; 12; 13; 14; 15(2); 18; 19; 23; 40:1; 6; 15; 16; 20; 41:1; 8; 15; 21; 35; 36(2); 42:1; 2(3); 16; 23; 28; 29; 33; 34(2); 35; 43:2; 7; 8; 12; 14; 15; 18(2); 21; 25; 32; 44:2; 7; 15; 17; 21; 24; 27; 31(2); 34; 45:10; 11; 12(2); 13; 15; 24; 46:1; 32; 34(2); 47:1; 13; 14; 17; 18(2); 19(2); 24; 26; 29; 48:1; 7; 10; 17; 20; 49:1; 15(2); 17(2); 25; 29; 30; 32; 50:15; **Ex** 1:6; 10; 21; 2:2; 7; 11; 12; 18; 20(2); 23; 3:4; 8; 10; 11(2); 12; 18; 19; 20; 21; 4:2; 5(2); 8; 9; 14; 21(2); 23; 24; 31(2); 5:1; 2; 9; 19; 6:7; 29(2); 7:2; 4; 5; 16; 17(2); 18; 19; 20(2); 21; 8:1; 8(2); 9; 10(2); 15; 16; 20; 22(4); 28; 29; 9:1; 4; 9; 10; 13; 14(2); 16(2); 17; 19; 22; 24; 25; 28; 29(2); 30; 34; 10:1; 2(3); 3; 5; 6; 7(2); 8; 11; 12(2); 13(2); 15; 17; 21; 25; 11:7(2); 8; 9; 12:8; 12; 15; 16(2); 19; 22(2); 25; 27; 29; 33; 36; 41(2); 42; 51(2); 13:5; 8; 9; 12(4); 14; 15(2); 17(2); 14:2; 4(3); 5(2); 12(3); 18; 20(2); 21; 24; 25; 26; 28; 30; 16:3; 4; 5; 6; 7; 10; 12; 13; 22; 23; 25; 27; 32; 17:2; 6; 11; 14; 18:1(2); 8(2); 11; 13; 14(2); 17; 19; 22; 24; 19:8; 9; 12; 16(2); 20:4(3); 11; 12; 17; 20(2); 22; 26; 21:12; 14; 20; 22; 29; 35; 36; 22:2; 6; 11(2); 27(2); 23:11; 12; 13; 22; 24:7; 12; 25:2; 8; 9(2); 14; 21; 26; 28; 33; 35; 37; 40; 26:5(2); 6; 10; 11; 12(2); 13; 14; 27:5; 20; 28:1; 3(2); 4; 28(2); 32; 35; 37; 38(2); 41; 43; 29:13(2); 21; 22; 23; 27(2); 28; 30; 32; 35; 46(2); 30:6(2); 12; 16; 29; 30; 31:6(2); 7; 11; 13(2); 14; 32:1(2); 4; 8; 10; 13; 19; 21; 22; 23; 25; 28; 29; 30; 33:5; 7; 8; 9; 13(3); 16; 17; 22; 34:1; 3; 10; 19; 29(2); 32; 35; 35:10; 22; 36:1; 13; 17; 18; 19; 37:8; 13; 38:15; 22; 24(2); 26; 39:5; 21(2); 23; 32; 42; 40:4; 9; 13; 15; 16; 17; 37; **Lev** 1:5; 8; 12; 17; 2:8; 3:3(2); 4; 5; 9(2); 10; 14(2); 15;

4:8; 9; 35; 5:4; 5(3); 8; 13; 16; 6:3; 4; 5; 7; 27; 7:3; 4; 8;
9(2); 16; 19; 20(2); 21(2); 24; 27; 30; 36; 8:10; 16; 25; 26;
28; 31; 35; 36; 9:1; 10:10; 11; 12; 20; 11:2; 3; 4(2); 9(2);
10(2); 12; 20; 21; 27; 29; 31; 34; 41; 42; 43; 44; 46(2); 47(2);
13:8; 39; 50; 52; 54; 57; 14:5; 6; 8(2); 16; 18; 27; 28; 29;
35; 36(3); 40; 41; 15:10; 12; 20(2); 22; 24; 28; 31; 16:13(2);
15; 17; 18; 30(2); 17:4(2); 5(2); 9; 10; 11; 13; 18:28; 30(2);
19:8; 25; 20:3; 5; 6; 14; 19; 22; 25; 26; 22:2(2); 3; 22; 23;
23:12; 14; 15; 21; 28; 29; 30(2); 43(2); 24:2; 7; 12; 25:7;
11; 27; 33; 35; 36; 44; 50; 26:13; 15; 25; 40; 41; 44; 45;
27:9(2); 18; 23; 28(2); **Num** 1:50; 53; 54; 2:34; 3:6; 13; 4:6;
16; 19; 25; 26; 5:2; 3; 6(2); 13; 17; 18; 19; 22; 24(2); 27(2);
31; 6:4; 6; 11; 20; 21; 7:1; 5; 89; 8:11; 15; 17; 19; 20; 22;
9:4; 5; 6(3); 8; 13(2); 15; 17; 22; 10:5; 6; 11; 32; 35; 11:11;
12; 13; 16; 17(2); 21; 25(2); 29(2); 32; 34; 13:11; 32; 14:1;
3; 14(2); 45; 15:12; 19; 23; 24; 30; 31; 39(2); 40; 16:5; 7;
9; 10; 11; 13(2); 21; 28; 30(2); 31; 40(2); 42; 45; 17:5; 8;
10; 18:2; 5; 15; 23; 19:2; 3; 13; 20; 20:4; 14; 29; 21:1; 3;
7; 8; 13; 15; 20; 22:2; 4; 6; 19; 20; 24; 28; 35(2); 36; 38(2);
41(2); 23:19(2); 26(2); 27; 28; 24:1; 6; 15; 25:4; 11; 26:1;
10; 27:17; 20; 30:2; 5; 7; 8; 14(2); 31:23(2); 26; 52; 32:1;
9; 10; 13; 33:55; 56; 34:2; 35:2; 8; 11; 12; 15; 16; 20; 21;
23; 32; 33; 36:8; **Deut** 1:3(2); 9; 16; 17; 18; 19; 31; 32; 35;
44; 46; 2:6(2); 17; 20; 28(2); 30; 31; 34; 36; 3:4; 8; 12; 18;
19; 21(2); 23; 26; 4:1; 2; 5; 7; 8; 10(2); 14(2); 17(2); 18(2);
21(2); 22; 26; 32(2); 34; 35(2); 36; 39; 40(2); 42(2); 48; 5:1;
5; 8(3); 14; 15; 16(2); 21; 23; 24; 27(2); 28; 29(3); 31; 33(3);
6:1; 2(2); 3(2); 18(2); 23; 24; 7:9; 12; 16; 25; 8:1; 2; 3(3); 5;
7; 11; 13; 15; 16(2); 18; 19; 9:3; 4; 5(3); 6; 7; 8; 11; 14; 19;
21; 24; 10:1; 2; 8; 10; 11; 14; 11:2; 6; 8; 9; 13; 14; 15; 17;
21; 29; 12:1; 3; 10; 11; 13(2); 14; 19; 23; 25; 28; 30(2); 31;
13:3(2); 5(2); 14; 15(2); 17; 14:6; 7; 9(2); 19; 21(2); 22; 23;
24; 26; 28; 29; 15:15; 16; 18; 19; 16:3(2); 12; 15; 20; 17:1;
4; 5(3); 10(2); 12; 14; 16; 18; 19; 20(3); 18:18; 19; 20; 22;
19:3; 4; 5; 11; 12; 13; 14; 15; 20:2; 9; 11; 14; 16; 20; 21:3;
4; 6; 13; 16; 17; 23(2); 22:5; 7(2); 8; 18(2); 22; 24; 23:11;
14; 19; 20; 23; 24:1; 4; 7; 8(2); 13; 18; 19; 22; 25:1; 2; 6(2);
15; 19; 26:2(2); 3; 12; 14; 17(2); 18; 19(2); 27:2; 3; 4; 28:1;
10; 15; 20; 55; 58(2); 63; 67(2); 29:2; 6(2); 9(2); 12; 13(2);
16(2); 18(2); 19; 20(2); 21; 22(2); 26(2); 27; 29; 30:2; 3; 6;
12(2); 13(2); 14; 16(2); 17; 18; 19(2); 20(4); 31:5; 12(2); 13;
14; 17(3); 18(2); 19; 21; 25; 26; 28; 29; 32:13; 17; 29(3);
36; 39; 48; 33:11; 34:12; **Josh** 1:1; 3; 7(2); 8(2); 16; 18; 2:5;
9(3); 12; 13; 14; 19; 23; 3:2; 4; 7(2); 10(2); 13(2); 16(3); 4:1;
6; 7; 10(2); 11; 14; 18; 24(3); 5:1(2); 2; 6(2); 8; 12; 13; 6:5;
8; 15(2); 16; 17; 20; 21; 22; 23; 24; 25; 26; 7:7; 14; 15(2);
24; 26; 8:5; 8; 9; 13(2); 14(2); 18(2); 20; 21(2); 22(2); 24;
25(2); 27; 29(2); 33; 34; 35; 9:2; 9; 10; 16(2); 24; 26; 27;
10:2; 4; 10; 11; 14(2); 20; 24; 27; 28; 32; 35(3); 37; 40; 11:1;
4; 10; 13; 15; 19; 20(4); 21; 23; 12:2; 13:2(2); 4; 9; 16; 17;
14:9; 11; 12(4); 15:2; 8; 18; 46; 16:1; 17:7; 12; 13; 18:6; 8;
13; 14; 16; 19:8; 9; 11; 20:3; 4(2); 6; 9; 21:44; 22:2(2);
16(3); 18(2); 20; 27(3); 28(2); 29; 30; 31; 34; 23:1; 3; 4(2);
6; 11; 12; 13; 14; 15; 24:8; 15; 16; 17; 22; 25; 26; 29; **Judg**
1:1; 3; 14; 27; 28; 2:4; 5; 10; 14; 19; 22; 3:1(2); 2; 4; 19;
27; 29; 30; 4:4; 12; 23; 5:1; 21; 6:8; 17; 21; 22; 25(3); 28;
30(2); 32; 37; 40; 7:1(2); 4; 9; 13; 15; 19; 8:3; 6; 15; 21; 24;
26(2); 28; 33; 9:2(3); 6; 7; 24; 25; 28; 33; 38; 41; 42; 44;
45; 46; 47; 49; 55; 10:8; 9; 11:4; 5; 6; 8(2); 12; 21; 26; 31;
35; 37; 39; 40; 12:3; 6; 13:13; 14(2); 17; 21; 14:3; 4(3); 9;
11; 13; 15(3); 17; 15:1; 2; 7; 11; 12(2); 14(2); 17(2); 19;
16:3; 4; 5; 11; 16; 17; 18; 20; 25(2); 26; 28; 30; 17:2; 13;
18:1; 5; 10; 12; 14; 19; 23; 26; 28; 31; 19:1; 5; 9(2); 10(2);
22; 30(2); 20:3; 5; 10(2); 12; 13; 15; 21; 22; 26(2); 34; 35;
36; 38; 41; 46; 21:3; 4; 7; 11; 14; 17; 19; 22; 24; **Ruth** 1:1;
6(2); 9; 11; 13; 18; 19; 2:10; 11; 16; 22(2); 3:1; 4; 5; 6; 8;
10; 11(2); 12; 13; 14; 15; 16(2); 4:4; 9(3); 10; **1 Sam** 1:7;
12; 20; 22; 2:13; 14; 20; 21; 24; 30; 31(2); 34; 36(2); 3:2(2);
4; 8; 9; 12(2); 13; 14; 17(2); 20; 4:3; 4; 5; 6; 9; 15; 18; 19(2);
5:9; 10; 11; 6:5; 6; 9(2); 15; 7:2; 6; 7; 8; 10(2); 8:1; 7(2); 8;
18(2); 20(2); 9:6(2); 8; 16; 19; 20; 24; 26(2); 27; 10:5(2); 7;
9(2); 11(3); 14; 16; 24; 11:2; 3; 5; 11(3); 12; 12:1; 5; 7; 12;
17(2); 18; 19; 23; 13:3; 4(2); 6; 10(2); 11(3); 18; 22; 14:1(2);
3; 6; 7; 14; 15; 18; 19; 21; 22; 23; 24; 27; 31; 34; 35; 37;
43; 15:3; 9(2); 11; 25; 29; 30; 35; 16:6; 13; 16; 23; 17:10;
12; 25; 26; 43; 46(2); 47; 48; 49; 51; 18:2; 4; 6; 9; 10; 15;
18; 19; 21(2); 27; 28(2); 30(2); 19:1; 10; 15; 17; 18; 22;
24(2); 20:1; 3; 5; 6; 7; 9; 13; 14; 26; 27; 30; 33; 35; 21:7;
9(2); 10; 15; 22:4; 6; 8(2); 13(2); 18; 21; 22(2); 23:6; 7(2);
9; 10; 13; 15; 17; 23; 25; 28; 24:1; 4; 5; 6; 10; 11(2); 16;
20(2); 21(2); 25:4; 6; 7; 11; 17; 20; 21(3); 30; 31(3); 37; 38;
39; 26:3; 4; 11(2); 16(2); 17; 27:1; 4; 5; 6; 7; 28:1(2); 7; 14;
15; 21; 22; 25; 29:4; 7; 8; 9; 30:1; 10; 15; 18; 21; 22(2); 23;
25; 31:5; 6; 7(2); 8; **2 Sam** 1:2(2); 5; 10(3); 15; 2:1; 11; 16;
17; 23(2); 26; 29; 3:6; 8; 19; 21(3); 22; 23; 24; 25(2); 27;
37(2); 38; 4:1; 4; 5:7; 8; 12(2); 17; 20; 6:9; 12; 13; 17; 7:2;
3; 4(2); 6; 10; 11(2); 18; 22; 29; 8:1; 4; 7; 9; 11; 9:1; 8; 9;
10; 11; 10:1; 3; 6; 9; 10; 14; 15; 19; 11:1; 2; 12; 14; 15; 16;
20(2); 21; 22; 26; 27; 12:8; 15; 18(3); 19(2); 21; 22; 13:2;
5; 6; 10; 15; 16; 19; 23; 30; 32; 33; 36; 14:1; 7(2); 13; 14;
15; 18; 19; 20; 22(2); 32; 15:1; 2; 4; 5; 7; 35; 16:4(2); 12(2);
16; 21; 17:7; 8; 9; 10; 11(3); 13; 14; 21; 23; 27; 18:7; 8; 32;
19:2(2); 3; 6(3); 7(2); 14; 19(2); 20; 22(2); 25; 26; 34; 37;
20:10; 12(2); 16; 20; 21; 21:3; 5; 7; 14(2); 18; 22:28; 35;
39; 41; 23:10; 15; 16; 17; 24:2; 12; 18; 21; 24; **1 Ki** 1:2;
11; 12; 20; 21; 40; 45(2); 51; 2:1; 3(2); 4; 5(2); 11; 15(2);
17; 27; 31; 39; 41; 42; 43; 44; 3:3; 4(2); 9; 10; 12; 13; 18;
28; 4:33; 5:1; 6; 7; 6:1; 6; 7; 22; 27; 7:3; 18; 29; 40; 41; 42;
51; 8:1; 4; 5; 8; 10; 11; 16(2); 18; 25; 29(2); 36; 40(2); 43(3);
50; 52; 54; 56; 58; 59; 60(2); 64(2); 65; 66; 9:2; 3; 4; 11;
19; 21; 25; 10:2(2); 3; 4; 14; 15; 29; 11:4; 7; 10; 17; 19(2);
21(3); 22; 25; 28; 29(2); 30; 36; 38; 41; 42; 12:3; 15; 16;
20; 21; 32(2); 13:4(2); 6; 11(2); 18; 20; 23; 32; 14:1; 2(2);
5; 20; 22; 25; 29; 15:5; 7; 12; 17; 18; 19; 21; 23; 29(2); 31;
16:7; 11; 14; 16; 18(2); 27; 31; 17:4; 7; 10; 12(2); 17(2);
24(2); 18:1; 4; 5; 7; 9; 10; 12; 17(2); 18; 27; 30; 36(3); 37(3);
38; 44; 45; 19:1; 3; 4; 8; 9; 13; 17; 18; 20:4; 6; 9; 12; 13;
25; 26; 28; 29; 31; 21:1; 2; 3; 5; 10; 13; 15(2); 16(2); 26;
27; 22:2; 3; 7; 14; 16; 17; 20(2); 25; 32; 33(2); 35; 39(2);
45; 53; **2 Ki** 1:3; 6; 2:1; 3; 5; 8(2); 9; 11; 13; 14(2); 3:2; 5;
6; 9(2); 11; 14; 15; 17(2); 20; 21; 24; 26; 4:1; 6; 8; 9; 11;
18; 22; 25; 40; 41; 42; 43; 5:6(2); 7(2); 8(3); 15; 6:9; 12; 13;
17; 20(2); 22; 24; 28; 29; 30; 7:12; 13; 19; 8:3; 5; 6(2); 10;
12; 13(2); 15(2); 22; 23; 9:2; 7; 22; 25; 37; 10:7; 9; 10; 21;
23; 25; 29(2); 30; 34; 36; 11:1; 2; 9; 10; 17; 12:4(2); 6; 8;
10(3); 12; 14; 18; 19; 13:5; 8; 12; 21; 14:5; 9(3); 10(2); 14;
26; 27; 28; 15:3; 4; 5; 6; 19; 21; 26; 31; 34; 36; 16:6; 8; 10;
11; 16; 17; 17:7; 9; 15(2); 25; 38; 18:1; 3; 4; 5; 9; 10; 12;
15; 16; 20; 32; 35; 19:1; 4(2); 8; 19(2); 25(2); 33; 35; 37;
20:4; 8(2); 9; 12(2); 13(2); 15(2); 17; 21:7; 8(2); 12; 17(2);
21(2); 22:3; 4; 9; 11; 13(3); 17; 19; 23:3; 4; 7; 10; 11; 12;
13; 15(2); 16; 17; 19; 24(3); 28; 32; 33; 37; 24:3; 4; 5; 7; 9;
10; 19; 20; 25:1; 3; 9; 13(2); 23; 25; 27(2); **1 Chr** 4:10(4);
33; 5:1; 23; 26; 6:10; 49; 7:21; 9:31; 33; 10:5; 7(2); 8; 11;
11:5; 14; 17; 18; 19; 12:22; 23; 13:2; 4; 11; 12; 14; 14:2;
8; 11; 15:12; 26; 29; 16:1; 7; 32; 39; 40; 17:1; 2; 3(2); 5; 9;
10(2); 11; 16; 20; 24; 25; 27; 18:1; 4; 7; 9; 11; 19:1; 3; 6;
10; 15; 16; 19; 20:1; 4; 21:2; 10; 17; 18; 22(2); 24; 28(2);
29; 22:12; 19; 23:13; 25; 32; 26:28; 27:28; 29(2); 28:8; 12;
18(2); 29:3; 11; 14; 16; 17; 22; 27; 30; **2 Chr** 1:3; 5; 7; 10;
11; 13; 2:6; 8; 3:1; 4; 15; 4:11; 12; 13; 18; 5:1; 2; 5; 6; 9;
13; 14; 6:5(2); 6; 8; 16; 20(2); 27; 31; 33(3); 7:7; 8; 10; 11;
16; 17; 8:2; 6(2); 8; 9:1(2); 2; 3; 13; 10:2; 15; 16; 11:1; 12:1;
2; 7; 8; 13:5; 9(2); 15; 18; 15:8; 9; 11; 18(2); 16:1; 3; 5; 7;
10; 11; 17:10(2); 18:6; 13; 15; 16; 19(2); 24; 31; 32(2); 34;
19:3; 20:1; 6; 12; 26; 29; 37; 21:7; 10; 17(2); 19; 22:8; 10;
11; 23:8; 9; 16; 19; 24:4; 5; 7; 9; 11(3); 20; 23; 25:3; 10;
12; 13; 14; 16(2); 18(3); 19(2); 20; 24; 27; 26:4; 13; 20; 27:2;
5; 28:9(2); 22; 23; 29:2; 10; 11; 16; 24; 31; 34; 36; 30:1; 5;
7; 8; 9; 14; 25; 31:4; 21; 32:2(2); 4; 5; 7; 10; 14(3); 18; 23;
26; 31(3); 33:8; 13; 15; 34:9; 14; 16; 17; 19; 21(3); 22; 24;
25; 31; 33; 35:6; 12; 17; 18; 22; 24(2); 36:22(2); **Ezra**
1:1(2); 6; 2:63; 3:5; 13; 4:1; 11; 12; 13; 15(3); 16(2); 19; 21;
22; 5:5; 6; 8; 10; 11; 14; 15; 16; 17; 6:2; 8; 10; 11; 7:11;
13; 16; 19; 21; 24; 8:15; 17; 21; 34; 9:2; 8; 12; 13; 14; 10:5;
7; 8; 9; **Neh** 1:2; 4; 6; 8; 2:1; 5(2); 7; 8(2); 10; 17(2); 18;
19; 3:15; 25; 4:1(2); 2; 7(2); 10; 12; 15(3); 16(2); 17; 22; 23;
5:2; 3; 11; 12; 14; 18; 19; 6:1(3); 2; 3; 6(2); 12(2); 13(4);
16(2); 7:2; 5; 65; 72; 8:1; 3; 12; 14; 15; 17; 9:6; 10; 11; 17;
18; 24; 28; 29; 32; 33; 35; 36; 11:23; 12:43(2); 13:1(2); 3;
7; 10; 14; 17; 19(3); 21; 22(2); **Esth** 1:3; 8; 17; 18; 19(2);
22; 2:3; 7; 8; 3:4(2); 5; 7; 9; 12; 14(2); 4:1; 6; 7(2); 8(2);
11(2); 13; 17; 5:1; 2(2); 4; 5(2); 9(2); 12; 14; 6:1; 2; 4(2); 9;
10; 13; 7:7; 10; 8:1; 6; 9(2); 11; 13(2); 9:1(3); 11; 21; 22;
24; 25(2); 27; 28(3); **Job** 1:1; 3; 5(2); 8; 10; 11; 12; 2:3; 4;
11; 13; 3:4; 6; 7; 12; 5:12; 24; 25; 6:2; 8(3); 9(2); 11(2); 15;
7:7; 12; 15; 17(2); 18; 20; 9:16; 28; 32(2); 10:3(2); 6; 7; 9;
13; 18; 20; 11:5; 6(2); 16; 12:9; 13:5; 18; 28; 14:5; 6; 7(2);
13(3); 15:9(2); 13; 14(2); 22; 23; 16:3; 21; 19:3; 6; 8; 23(2);
24; 25; 26; 29; 20:3; 5; 9; 18; 21:3; 15; 18; 19; 22:3(2); 4;
11; 14; 23:3(2); 10; 13; 24:18; 26:2; 27:5; 28:7; 28; 29:2;
16; 30:23; 31:6; 11; 12(2); 17; 27; 31; 34; 35(3); 32:5; 19;
20; 33:20; 30; 34:9; 23; 28; 30; 36; 36:2; 9; 10; 37:2; 7; 12;
20; 38:13; 20(2); 34; 35; 39:2; 15(2); 40:8; 14; 41:10; 11;
16; 42:2(2); 7; 11; **Ps** 1:3; 4:3; 7; 8:2; 4(2); 8; 9:14; 17; 20;
10:10; 18; 11:2; 12:3; 14:7; 17:2; 3; 5; 18:34; 38; 40; 20:6;
22:31; 25:12; 26:7; 27:4(2); 13; 30:3; 12; 34:8; 12; 35:8(2);
11; 36:4; 37:13; 16; 37; 39:4; 13; 40:4; 12; 41:8; 10; 11;
42:4; 46:10; 48:13; 49:9; 11; 12; 20; 50:4; 21; 51:4; 8; 53:6;
55:6; 18; 56:13; 58:4; 8; 11; 59:13(2); 60:4; 5; 61:2; 8;
62:11; 64:4; 65:4; 67:2; 68:18; 23; 69:10; 23; 34; 35; 72:6;
73:25; 28; 74:18(2); 75:1; 77:4; 78:4; 5; 6(2); 7; 8; 11; 20;
35; 39(2); 44; 53; 60; 71; 79:6(2); 80:12; 15; 81:13(2); 83:4;
16; 18(2); 85:6; 9; 86:17; 87:5; 89:34; 90:12; 14; 91:5; 6(2);
92:7; 15; 93:1; 94:11; 13; 95:10; 96:12; 100:3; 101:6; 8;
102:2; 4; 11; 18; 103:1; 5; 14; 104:5; 9(2); 14; 15; 26; 27;
105:19; 45; 106:5(3); 8; 20; 23; 31; 32; 33; 40; 107:7; 8;
15; 21; 29; 31; 36; 37; 108:6; 109:11; 15; 16; 27(3); 113:6;
8; 114:5(2); 6; 118:13; 119:5; 11; 17; 18; 57; 71(2); 73;
75(2); 77; 80; 88; 101; 106; 116; 125; 134; 148; 152;
120:5(2); 122:3; 130:4; 135:5; 138:8; 139:14; 19; 140:10;
12; 142:7; 144:3(2); 12(2); 13(2); 14(3); 146:4; 6; 147:9;
150:6; **Prov** 2:2; 4:18; 5:2; 6:17; 18(2); 7:5; 8:21(2); 29;
9:18(2); 14:12; 15:24; 31; 16:25; 29; 19:20; 21; 20:30;
22:19; 21(2); 23:5; 35; 25:7(2); 26:7; 9; 27:8; 11; 28:22;
29:1; 30:11; 12; 15; 16; 17; 31:3; 18; **Eccl** 1:9(2); 11; 13;
14; 17; 2:11; 13; 14; 16; 17; 24(2); 26; 3:9; 11(2); 12; 13;
14(2); 15; 18(2); 22(3); 4:1; 3; 4; 5:1; 6; 6:2; 3(2); 5; 10; 11;
7:2; 12; 14(2); 18; 22; 24; 29; 8:8; 9; 12; 14(2); 16; 17(2);
9:1(2); 3(3); 5; 9; 11; 15; 10:3; 11:6; 8; 9; 12:3; **Song** 1:13;
2:15; 4:16; 5:8; 9; 6:1; 13; 8:1; **Isa** 1:30; 2:1; 2; 8; 11; 13;
14; 17; 20; 3:7; 10; 18; 4:1; 2; 3; 5:4; 6; 11; 19(3); 30; 6:1;
7:1; 8; 15; 16; 17(2); 18(4); 21(2); 22; 23(2); 8:6; 11; 12; 21;
9:7; 10:2(2); 12; 14; 19; 20(2); 27(2); 32; 11:10; 11(2); 16;
12:1; 4(2); 13:2; 4; 14; 14:4; 25; 26(2); 28; 29; 32; 16:12(2);
13; 14; 17:4(2); 7; 9; 12; 18:7; 19:16; 18; 19; 21; 23; 24;
20:1; 6; 21:10; 22:1; 7; 8; 9; 12; 16; 20(2); 25(3); 23:1;
15(2); 16; 17; 24:10; 18; 21(2); 25:7; 9; 26:1; 2; 27:1(3); 2;
5; 9; 12(2); 13; 28:5; 13; 20; 21; 29:5; 11; 18; 30:1; 8; 9;
18(2); 23; 24; 26; 31:7; 33:17; 19; 20; 34:1(2); 36:1; 5; 20;
37:1; 4(2); 8; 20(2); 26(2); 34; 38; 38:7; 17; 22; 39:1(2); 2(2);
4(2); 6; 40:2(2); 20(2); 41:3; 7; 20(2); 22; 23(4); 26(2); 42:5;
8; 10; 11; 18; 43:9; 10(2); 12; 26; 44:7; 8; 9; 10; 13; 18(2);
45:1; 3(2); 6(2); 19; 20; 21; 23; 46:5; 10; 47:7; 48:4; 8; 9;
16; 18; 49:5; 6(2); 9; 23; 26; 50:2; 4; 7; 51:9; 10; 12; 14(3);
16; 23; 52:5; 6(2); 53:2; 54:9(2); 55:10; 11; 13; 56:5(2);
57:1; 11(2); 58:2; 5; 6(2); 7(2); 59:1(2); 2; 5; 8; 15; 16(2);
60:11; 15; 16; 21; 61:3(2); 9; 11; 62:1; 63:5; 7; 13; 64:1(3);
2; 65:1; 2; 5; 8; 12; 16; 24; 66:1; 4; 5; 11(2); 18; 23; **Jer**
1:17; 2:3; 5; 6; 8; 13; 17; 19(2); 24; 28; 3:1; 8; 9; 13; 16;
17; 18; 4:4; 9(2); 11; 14; 16; 5:7; 19; 22; 6:10; 27; 7:1; 7;
8; 18; 22; 23(2); 25; 28; 8:1; 16; 9:1(2); 2(2); 10; 12(2);
17(2); 18; 24(2); 25; 10:4; 11; 18; 11:1; 4; 5; 13; 14; 19(2);
12:15; 17; 13:4; 6; 11; 12; 20; 24; 26; 14:1; 19; 22; 15:10;
15; 18; 16:10; 12; 13; 14; 21; 17:11; 23; 18:4; 8(2); 10; 12;
20; 19:2; 3; 6; 15(2); 20:1; 2; 3; 16; 17; 18; 21:2; 4; 12; 22:5;
21; 23:5; 7; 14; 29; 34; 39; 24:2; 7; 10; 25:1; 5; 7; 12(2);
13(2); 16; 33; 26:2; 3; 8(2); 12; 13; 15; 24; 27:5; 8(2); 11;
13; 15(2); 18; 19; 21; 22; 28:1; 3; 7; 14; 29:1; 6(2); 11; 17;
26(2); 32; 30:1; 2; 3(2); 4; 7(2); 8(2); 13; 31:17; 27; 28;
32(2); 33; 37; 38; 32:1; 8(2); 11(2); 14; 23; 31; 35; 39; 40(2);
42; 33:9(2); 10; 14(2); 15; 20; 21; 26; 34:7; 8; 9(2); 10(2);
13; 35:7; 8; 10; 11; 17; 18; 36:1; 2; 3(3); 7(2); 8; 9; 13; 16;
23(3); 28; 29; 31; 37:12; 15; 18; 21(2); 38:1; 7; 9; 21; 25;
26; 27; 28; 39:4; 14; 16; 17; 40:1; 4; 7; 10; 11(2); 13; 14;
15; 41:1; 3; 5; 6; 7; 11(2); 12; 13; 16; 42:3; 4; 6; 7; 10; 12;
16; 17; 19; 20; 22; 43:2; 3; 10; 13; 44:1; 2; 3; 4; 8(2); 10;
14; 15; 16; 20; 21; 25; 26; 29(3); 45:1; 4; 46:10; 13; 47:1;
2; 4; 48:9; 12; 20; 41; 49:2; 8; 13; 19(2); 20(2); 22; 26; 31;
34; 50:1; 4; 5; 20; 21; 30; 31; 34; 44(2); 45(2); 51:7; 31; 39;
46(2); 47; 48; 52; 60(2); 62; 63; 64; 52:2; 4; 6; 13; 17(2);
31; **Lam** 1:1; 6(2); 7; 17; 20; 21(3); 2:13; 15; 22; 3:7; 26;
38; 44; 4:12; 14; 17; 18; **Ezek** 1:1; 25; 2:3; 5; 8; 3:2; 3; 10;
13; 16; 18; 21; 25; 26; 4:4; 8; 9; 17; 5:6; 7(2); 13; 14; 15;
6:6; 7; 8; 10(2); 13; 14; 7:4; 9; 27; 8:1; 4; 6; 13; 9:4; 8; 10:1;
6; 7; 12; 11:5; 10; 12; 13; 20; 24; 12:3; 6; 12; 15; 16(2); 19;
20(2); 22; 27; 13:6; 9; 11; 14(2); 16; 21; 22; 23; 14:3; 5;
8(2); 9; 11(2); 15; 17; 19; 22(2); 23(2); 15:7; 16:21; 24; 34;
37; 47; 54(2); 62; 63; 17:7; 14(2); 15; 21; 24; 18:23(2); 24;
26; 30; 19:5(2); 9; 14; 20:1; 6(2); 9; 12(2); 14; 15; 20(2); 22;
23; 25; 26(4); 38; 42; 43; 44; 48; 21:5(2); 7; 11; 14(3); 15;
23; 24(2); 22:3; 16; 22; 24; 26; 30; 23:13; 27; 48; 49;
24:8(2); 11(3); 19; 24(2); 25; 26; 27(2); 25:5; 7; 10; 11; 14;
17; 26:1; 6; 10; 19; 20; 28:3; 17; 22; 23; 24; 26; 29:6; 9;
12(2); 15; 16; 17; 19; 21(2); 30:7; 8; 9; 12; 19; 20; 22; 25;
26; 31:1; 3; 9(2); 14(2); 16; 32:1; 15(2); 17; 33:8; 11; 12(2);
13(2); 21; 28; 29; 30; 33; 34:10; 18(2); 27; 30; 35:4; 9; 12;
15; 36:3; 4; 7(2); 11; 23; 28; 30; 31; 33; 35; 36; 38; 37:6;
9; 13; 14; 25; 28; 38:7; 10(2); 12; 14; 16(2); 17; 18; 19;
20(2); 23; 39:6; 7; 11(2); 13; 17; 22(2); 23; 28; 40:4; 10;
12(2); 21; 24; 26; 34; 37; 39; 41; 48(2); 49; 41:6; 8; 12; 19;
22; 42:8; 12; 14; 15; 43:1; 10; 11(2); 27; 44:5; 12; 14; 17;
18; 27; 28; 31; 45:11; 22; 46:1; 4; 12; 18; 20; 47:2; 5(2);
9(2); 10; 12; 22; 23; 48:9; 12; 15; 35; **Dan** 1:5(2); 8(2); 16;
18; 2:1; 8(2); 9; 11; 16; 18(2); 30; 35(2); 40(2); 45(2); 46;
3:3(2); 5(2); 7; 8; 10; 14; 17; 18; 19; 28; 29; 4:1; 2; 6; 9(2);
16; 17(2); 20; 25; 26; 30; 32; 33; 5:2; 3; 5; 6; 13; 14(2); 15;
16; 19; 21; 25; 29; 30; 6:2(2); 7; 8; 10(2); 12; 13(2); 15(2);
17; 22; 23; 25; 26; 7:7; 14; 20(2); 8:1; 2(2); 4(2); 6; 7; 13;
15; 17; 21; 22(2); 9:2; 13; 25; 10:4; 7; 11; 12; 12:1(3); 5; 7;
11; **Hos** 1:1; 5(2); 2:6; 8; 12; 16(2); 18; 21(2); 6:2; 5; 7:2;
8:4; 9:10; 10:11; 11:3; 12:5; 8; 13:3; 10; **Joel** 1:1; 2:5; 17;
25; 27; 28; 32; 3:1; 3; 6; 17; 18(2); **Am** 1:13; 2:16; 3:1; 14;
5:3(2); 9; 13; 14; 15; 6:8; 9; 7:2(2); 5; 8:3; 5(2); 6; 9(2); 11;
13; 9:1; 11; 12; **Ob** 8; 9; 11(2); **Jon** 1:2; 4; 5; 6; 7; 10; 11;
12; 3:2(2); 8; 9; 10(2); 4:2; 6; 7; 8(2); 11; **Mic** 1:1; 2; 2:4;
3:4; 4:1; 6; 5:3; 7; 10(2); 15; 6:5; 10; 16; 7:3; 11; 12; **Nah**
3:7; 8(2); **Hab** 1:6; 8; 14; 2:2; 9(2); 13; 15; 18(2); 3:8; 16;
Zeph 1:8; 10; 12(2); 15; 2:3; 15(2); 3:3; 7; 9; 11; 16; 19;
20; **Hag** 1:2; 8; 9; 2:5; 18; 23; **Zech** 1:19; 21(3); 2:9; 11(2);
3:9(2); 10; 4:9; 12; 5:3(2); 5; 6; 6:7; 15; 7:1; 11; 13; 14; 8:9;
13; 17; 23; 9:12; 16; 11:1; 9; 10; 11(2); 13; 14; 16(2);
12:3(2); 4; 6; 7(2); 8(2); 9(3); 11; 14; 13:1; 2(2); 3; 4(2); 8;
14:4; 6(2); 7; 8(2); 9; 13(2); 15; 16; 17; 19; 20; 21; **Mal** 1:9;
10; 12; 2:4(2); 5; 16(2); 17; 3:3; 10(2); 11; 14(2); 17; 4:1; 3;
Mt 1:20; 22; 2:8; 12; 15; 16; 22; 23; 3:9; 4:3; 4; 12; 14; 17;
5:14; 16; 17; 20; 21; 22; 23; 27; 28; 29; 30; 32; 33; 38; 43;
45; 6:1; 2; 4; 5; 7; 16; 18; 23(2); 29; 32; 7:1; 13; 19; 22; 25;
27; 28; 8:4(2); 8; 11; 13; 17; 24; 27; 28(2); 9:6(2); 10; 12;
22; 26; 28; 30; 31; 10:14; 15; 19; 25; 26(2); 34; 11:1; 24;
25(2); 12:1; 5; 6; 10; 17; 22; 36; 45; 13:2; 15; 17; 32; 35;
41; 44(2); 46; 47; 53; 54; 14:1; 20; 30; 35(2); 36; 15:12;
17; 22; 28; 37; 16:1; 11; 12; 13; 15; 18; 20(2); 21(2); 17:10;
12; 13; 18; 27(2); 18:1; 7; 10(2); 11; 12; 13(2); 14; 16; 19(2);
25(3); 27; 28; 31; 32; 34; 19:1; 4; 13; 16; 17; 22; 23; 28;
20:10; 21; 22(2); 23; 25; 30; 31; 33; 21:4; 15; 31; 34; 45;
22:16; 21(2); 24; 34; 46; 23:3; 17; 18; 19; 26; 31; 35; 24:2;
4; 6; 20; 32; 33; 36; 38; 43; 46; 47; 48; 50(2); 25:26; 26:1;
2; 16; 24(2); 29; 34; 53; 54; 55; 56; 27:3; 4; 8; 14; 16; 18;
19; 20; 24(2); 33; 35; 46; 47; 54; 63; 64; 28:5; 7; 11; 20;
Mk 1:9; 27; 38; 44; 45; 2:1; 2; 8; 10(2); 12; 15; 16; 23; 3:2;
9; 10; 12; 14(2); 17; 20; 24; 25; 4:1; 4; 8; 12; 15; 22; 28;
32; 37; 38; 40; 41; 5:7; 10; 12; 14; 18; 20; 23; 26; 29; 30;
36; 43(2); 6:2; 5; 10; 11; 12; 20; 36; 55; 56; 7:2; 9; 11; 15(2);
18; 20; 34; 36; 8:27; 29; 30; 31; 9:1; 9; 11; 12; 13; 18; 25;
26; 43; 45; 10:13; 17; 18; 32; 37; 38(2); 39; 42; 47; 51;
11:10; 23; 24; 25; 12:2; 14; 15; 17(2); 19; 26; 28; 34(2);
35(2); 43; 44; 13:2; 5; 11(2); 18; 24; 28; 29; 32; 14:12; 21(2);
25; 30; 35; 72; 15:5; 10; 11; 32; 35; 39; 42; 44; 16:1; 4; 7;
11; 12; **Lk** 1:4; 8; 21; 22; 23; 35; 41; 43; 59; 71; 74; 2:1(2);
6; 15(2); 20; 26; 35; 38; 46; 49; 3:7; 8; 20; 21; 4:29; 40; 41;
5:1; 7; 12; 17; 24(2); 36; 6:1; 6; 7; 12; 23; 32; 33; 34; 38;
42(3); 48; 49; 7:4; 6; 9; 11; 21; 22; 37; 8:1; 10; 14; 15; 16;
17(2); 22; 31; 32; 38; 40; 47; 53; 55; 9:5; 7(2); 8(2); 10; 12;
18(2); 19; 20; 28; 33; 37; 39; 45; 51; 57; 10:11; 12(3); 20;
21(2); 24; 31; 38; 40; 42; 11:1; 14; 26; 27(2); 28; 33; 35;
38; 48; 50; 54; 12:1; 2(2); 4(2); 12; 30; 33; 36; 37; 39; 42;
43; 44(2); 45; 46; 47; 51; 13:1; 2; 4; 9; 17; 31; 32; 33; 14:1;
5; 10; 21; 23; 24; 33; 15:7; 12; 14; 15; 16; 29; 31; 32; 16:1;
4; 9; 16; 22; 24; 25; 26; 27; 28; 17:1; 2; 9(2); 11; 14; 15;
24; 27; 29; 31; 34; 18:1; 3; 8; 9; 11; 12; 15; 19; 22; 24; 31;
35; 37; 39; 41; 19:4; 10; 15(2); 22; 23; 26; 29; 40; 42; 20:1;
6; 7; 10; 14; 17; 18; 19; 20; 21; 25(2); 27; 28; 35; 37; 40;
41; 21:3; 4; 6; 8; 20; 22; 30; 31; 34; 36(2); 22:8; 22; 30; 31;
32; 34; 37; 40; 70; 23:2; 7(2); 12; 23; 24; 26; 29; 48; 53;
54; 24:4; 13; 15; 16; 17; 21; 23; 25; 28; 30; 33; 35; 39; 44;
45; 47; 51; **Jn** 1:3; 7; 8(2); 9; 22; 31; 34; 39; 2:9; 17; 22;
25; 3:2(2); 6(2); 7; 13; 15; 16(2); 17; 19; 21(2); 28; 32; 33;
4:1(2); 5; 9; 11; 14(2); 15; 18; 19; 20; 25; 27; 29; 36; 38;
39(2); 42; 44; 47; 50; 53; 5:6(2); 9; 13; 15; 18; 20(2); 23;
32; 34; 36(2); 40; 42; 44; 45; 6:5; 7; 12(2); 14; 15; 22(3);

24; 28; 29; 30; 36; 37; 39; 40; 42; 46; 50; 51; 61; 63; 65; 66; 69; 7:3(2); 7; 22; 23; 26; 35; 36; 37; 42; 49; 8:5; 6; 17; 24(2); 27; 28(2); 29; 37; 48; 52; 54; 9:2; 3; 8; 18; 20(2); 22(2); 24; 25; 29; 30; 31; 32; 35; 36; 39(2); 10:10(2); 17; 25; 38(2); 41; 11:2; 4(2); 6; 11(2); 13; 15(2); 16; 17; 20; 22; 24; 27; 29; 31; 40; 41; 42(3); 49; 50(3); 51(2); 52(2); 53; 56; 57(2); 12:6; 9(2); 12(2); 16(2); 18; 19; 23; 29; 34; 36; 38; 40; 46; 48(2); 50; 13:1(2); 3(2); 5; 15; 18; 19(2); 29(2); 34(2); 35; 14:3; 10(2); 11; 12; 13(2); 16; 20(2); 22; 26; 29; 31(2); 15:2(3); 8; 11(2); 12; 15; 16(3); 17; 18; 20; 25; 16:1; 2(2); 4(2); 7; 15(2); 17; 18; 19; 20; 21; 23; 24; 26(2); 27; 30(3); 32; 33; 17:1; 2; 3; 7; 8(2); 11; 12; 13; 15(2); 19; 21(4); 22; 23(3); 24(2); 25; 26; 18:4; 8; 9; 13; 14(2); 15; 22; 28; 32; 36; 37(2); 39; 19:4(2); 8; 10; 13(2); 24; 27(2); 28(2); 31(4); 33; 35(2); 36; 38; 20:1; 7; 9; 14; 18(2); 31(3); 21:3; 4; 7(2); 12; 15; 16; 17; 22(2); 23(4); 24; 25(3); **Acts** 1:1; 19(2); 21; 22; 25; 2:8; 17; 21; 24; 25; 29; 30(2); 31; 36; 41; 3:10; 17; 18; 19(2); 20; 23(2); 4:2; 5; 10; 13(2); 16; 17(2); 23; 24(2); 29; 30; 32; 34; 5:9; 15(2); 21; 40; 41; 6:2; 14; 7:3; 6(2); 7; 12; 16; 19; 25(2); 37; 44; 8:1; 8; 9; 14; 15; 18; 19; 20; 23; 24; 37; 39; 9:2; 12; 17; 20; 21(2); 22; 26; 27; 32; 37; 38; 43; 10:28; 34; 37; 42; 43; 47; 11:1; 11; 17; 19; 23; 26; 28; 12:1; 3; 6; 9; 10; 11; 14; 15; 19; 13:1; 20; 28; 29; 32; 33; 34; 38; 42; 46; 47; 14:1(2); 9; 15(2); 17; 21; 27(2); 15:2; 4; 7(2); 11; 17; 19; 20; 24; 29; 38; 39; 16:3(2); 10; 12(2); 16; 18; 19; 26; 38; 17:3; 11; 13; 16; 22; 27(2); 29; 18:5; 28; 19:1; 4(2); 10; 12; 16(2); 23; 25; 26(2); 31; 34; 35; 20:2; 16; 18; 20; 22; 23(2); 24; 25; 26; 29; 31; 34; 35(2); 38; 21:1; 12; 21(2); 22; 24(4); 25(2); 29; 31; 22:2; 11; 13; 14; 17; 19; 24(2); 26; 29; 23:5; 6; 8; 12; 14; 15; 19; 20; 21; 22; 27; 29; 30; 34; 24:2; 9; 10; 11; 14; 15; 26(2); 25:3; 4(2); 24; 25(2); 26; 26:5; 8; 18; 20; 23(2); 26; 27; 29; 27:1; 10; 13; 20; 25; 27; 43; 44; 28:1; 2; 6(2); 7; 8; 17; 19; 22; 27; 28; **Rom** 1:8; 9; 11(2); 12(2); 13(2); 20(2); 32; 2:2; 3; 4; 18; 19; 21; 28; 29; 3:4; 8(2); 9; 19(2); 24; 25; 26; 28; 4:1; 9; 11(2); 13; 16(2); 18; 21; 23; 5:3(2); 8; 11; 16; 20; 21; 6:1; 3; 4; 6(3); 8; 9; 10(2); 12; 16(2); 17(2); 7:1; 3(2); 4(2); 6; 13(2); 14; 15(2); 16; 17; 18(2); 19(2); 20; 21; 24; 8:3; 4; 16; 17; 18; 22; 23; 24; 28; 29; 38; 9:2; 3; 6; 8; 11; 17(2); 23; 30; 32; 10:1; 2; 6; 7; 8; 9(2); 11:8(2); 10; 11; 18; 19; 25(2); 31; 32; 12:1; 2(2); 6; 13:1; 11; 14:9; 14; 15:4; 6; 8; 9; 13; 14; 16(2); 19; 29; 30; 31(2); 32; 16:2; 5; **1 Cor** 1:5; 7; 8; 10(3); 11; 12; 14; 15; 26; 28; 29; 31; 2:5; 12(2); 16; 3:11; 16(2); 18; 20; 4:2; 3; 6(2); 7; 8; 9; 5:1(2); 2; 5; 6; 7; 6:2; 3(2); 5; 6; 7; 9; 15; 16; 18; 19; 7:5(2); 7(2); 24; 26(2); 29; 34; 35(2); 37; 8:1; 2; 4(2); 7; 9:10; 13; 14; 15(2); 18(2); 19; 20(2); 21; 22(2); 23; 24(2); 10:1; 4(3); 6; 13; 17; 19; 20; 29; 33; 11:2; 3; 5; 14; 18; 19; 23(2); 32; 12:2; 3(2); 12; 24; 25(2); 28; 13:2; 10(2); 14:1; 5(2); 12; 13; 19; 21; 23; 25; 31; 36; 37; 15:2; 3(2); 4(2); 5; 6; 7; 12(2); 15; 26; 27; 28; 37(2); 50; 54; 58; 16:2; 4; 6(2); 10; 11; 14; 15(2); 16; 19; **2 Cor** 1:4; 7; 8(2); 9; 10; 11; 12; 14; 15; 17; 23; 24; 2:1; 3; 4(2); 7; 9; 10; 3:3; 5; 7; 10; 13; 4:7; 10; 11; 14; 15; 5:1; 4; 6; 10; 12; 14; 15; 19(2); 21; 6:3; 7:3; 7; 8; 9(3); 11; 12; 16; 8:2; 3; 4; 6; 7; 9(2); 11; 13; 14(3); 19; 20; 9:2; 3; 5; 8; 10:2(2); 5; 7(2); 11; 14; 15(2); 11:1; 2; 3; 5; 7; 12; 16; 18; 21(2); 31; 12:8; 9; 13; 16; 19; 20; 13:2; 5; 6(2); 7(3); 9; **Gal** 1:4; 6; 11; 16; 2:2; 4; 5; 7; 9(2); 10; 13; 14; 16(2); 19; 3:1; 7; 8; 11; 14(2); 17(3); 22; 24; 4:1; 5; 9; 13; 15; 17; 22; 5:2; 3; 10; 12; 17(2); 21; 6:7; 12; 13; 14; **Eph** 1:4; 10; 12; 17; 18; 21(2); 2:7; 8; 10; 11; 12(2); 15; 16; 3:3; 6; 8; 10; 13; 16; 17(2); 19; 20(2); 4:9; 10; 14; 17; 18; 22; 24; 28; 29; 5:5; 13; 15; 26; 27(2); 33; 6:3; 8; 9; 11; 13; 19(2); 20; 21; 22(2); **Phil** 1:6; 9; 10(3); 12; 13(2); 17; 18; 19; 20; 25; 26; 27(2); 28; 2:10; 11(2); 15; 16(2); 19; 22; 24; 26; 28; 3:8; 9; 10; 12(3); 16; 18; 21; 4:10; 11; 14; 15; 17(2); **Col** 1:9; 10; 16(2); 18; 19; 28; 2:2; 14; 19; 3:24; 4:1; 3; 4; 6; 8; 12; 13; 15; 16(2); 17; **1 Th** 1:7; 8; 2:1; 9; 12; 16; 3:3(2); 4; 6(2); 10; 13; 4:1; 3; 4; 6; 9; 10; 11; 12(2); 14; 15; 5:1; 2; 4; 10; 15; 27; **2 Th** 1:4(2); 5; 10; 11; 12; 2:3; 4(4); 5; 6; 10; 11; 12; 3:1; 2; 4; 6; 8; 11; 12; 14(2); **1 Tim** 1:3(2); 8; 9; 10; 15; 16; 18; 20; 2:1; 2; 8; 9; 3:15; 4:1; 8(2); 14; 15; 5:7; 14; 16; 20; 21; 25; 6:1; 5; 14; 18; 19; **2 Tim** 1:4; 5; 12(2); 14; 15; 18(2); 2:1; 2; 4; 8; 10; 18; 23; 25; 26; 3:1; 15; 17; 4:8; 13; 17(2); **Titus** 1:5(2); 9; 13; 2:2; 3; 4; 5; 8(2); 10; 11; 12; 14; 3:7; 8; 11; 13; 14; **Phm** 1:6; 12; 13; 14; 15; 18; 19; 21; 22; **Heb** 2:6(2); 8(2); 9; 14(2); 17; 18; 3:10; 18; 19; 4:3; 6; 11; 14; 16; 5:1; 14; 6:7; 9; 10; 11; 12; 18; 7:5; 8; 11; 14; 8:3; 5; 7; 9; 10; 13; 9:4(2); 8; 11; 15; 23; 25; 10:4; 9; 10; 13; 16; 20; 34; 36; 11:3(2); 4; 5(2); 6(2); 13; 14; 15; 16; 19; 35; 40; 12:1; 2; 10; 13; 17; 18(2); 19(2); 21; 24(2); 25; 27(3); 13:9; 12; 15; 17; 18; 19; 20; 23; **Jas** 1:3; 4; 7(2); 18; 2:7; 19; 20; 22; 24; 3:1; 3; 6; 13; 17; 4:1; 3; 4; 5; 14; 15; 5:1; 11; 16; 17; 20; **1 Pe** 1:4; 7(2); 10; 11; 12; 13; 18; 21; 2:2; 3; 9; 12; 15; 21; 24; 3:1; 7; 9(2); 15; 16; 18; 20; 4:2; 4; 6; 11; 13(2); 5:1; 4; 6; 9; 12; **2 Pe** 1:3; 4(2); 9; 14; 15; 19; 20; 2:8; 14; 3:2; 3; 5; 6; 8; 9(2); 10; 15; **1 Jn** 1:1; 2; 3(2); 4; 5; 6; 8; 10; 2:1; 3; 5; 16; 18(2); 19(2); 21; 22; 24; 25; 27; 28; 29(2); 3:1; 2; 5; 8; 11(2); 14; 15; 19; 22; 23; 24; 4:2(2); 3(2); 9(2); 10(2); 13; 14; 15; 16; 17; 21; 5:1; 2; 3; 4; 5; 7; 8; 10; 11; 13(3); 14(2); 15(3); 16(2); 18; 19; 20(2); **2 Jn** 4; 5(2); 6(2); 8(2); 12; **3 Jn** 2; 3; 4; 8; 10; 12; **Jude** 5; 18; **Rev** 1:2; 9; 12; 2:2; 4; 6; 10; 20; 23; 3:1(2); 2; 9; 11; 15; 17; 18(4); 5:13; 6:4; 11; 7:1; 8:3; 12; 9:20; 10:6(4); 11:6; 7; 18(2); 12:6; 9; 12; 13; 14; 15; 13:13; 15; 17; 14:3; 8; 13; 16:12; 14; 21; 17:7; 8(2); 11; 18; 18:7; 10(2); 14; 16(2); 19; 19:10(2); 12; 15; 17; 18; 20:2; 3; 21:17; 27; 22:9(2); 14; 18

THE (61782/23845)

Gen 1:1(3); 2(6); 4(3); 5(5); 6(4); 7(5); 8(4); 9(3); 10(3); 11(4); 12(3); 13(3); 14(4); 15(3); 16(5); 17(3); 18(4); 19(3); 20(5); 21; 22(3); 23(3); 24(3); 25(3); 26(7); 27; 28(6); 29(2); 30(3); 31(3); 2:1(3); 2(2); 3; 4(7); 5(6); 6(3); 7(4); 8(2); 9(8); 10; 11(4); 12(2); 13(4); 14(6); 15(3); 16(3); 17(3); 18; 19(4); 20(3); 21(2); 22(3); 25; 3:1(5); 2(5); 3(4); 4(2); 5; 6(3); 7; 8(9); 9; 10; 11; 12(3); 13(4); 14(4); 15; 16; 17(4); 18(2); 19(2); 20; 21; 22(3); 23(3); 24(5); 4:1; 2; 3(4); 4(2); 6; 7; 8; 9; 10(2); 11; 12(2); 13; 14(3); 15(2); 16(4); 17(3); 19(3); 20; 21(2); 22; 26(2); 5:1(4); 2; 4; 5; 8; 11; 14; 17; 20; 23; 27; 29(3); 31; 6:1(2); 2(2); 3; 4(4); 5(4); 6(2); 7(4); 8(2); 9; 11(2); 12(2); 13(3); 14; 15(2); 16(3); 17(3); 18; 19; 20(2); 7:1(2); 3(4); 4(3); 5; 6(2); 7(3); 8; 9; 10(3); 11(7); 12(2); 13(3); 14; 15(2); 16; 17(5); 18(5); 19(4); 20(2); 21(2); 22(3); 23(5); 24(2); 8:1(4); 2(4); 3(5); 4(5); 5(7); 6(3); 7(2); 8(3); 9(7); 10(2); 11(4); 12; 13(10); 14(4); 16; 17(3); 19(2); 20(2); 21(4); 22; 9:1; 2(7); 3; 5(4); 6; 7; 10(5); 11(3); 12(2); 13(4); 14(3); 15; 16(4); 17(3); 18(3); 19(2); 21; 22(2); 23; 26(2); 27; 28; 29; 10:1(3); 2; 3; 4; 5(2); 6; 7(2); 8; 9(3); 10(2); 12; 14; 16(3); 17(3); 18(5); 19(2); 20; 21(4); 22; 23; 25(2); 29; 30(2); 31; 32(5); 11:1; 2(2); 4(3); 5(4); 6(2); 8(4); 9(6); 10(2); 27; 28; 29(5); 31(3); 32; 12:1; 3(2); 4; 5(3); 6(5); 7(2); 8(6); 9; 10(3); 12; 14(2); 15(2); 17; 13:1; 3(3); 4(4); 6; 7(5); 9(5); 10(5); 11; 12(3); 13(2); 14(2); 15; 16(4); 17; 18(2); 14:1; 2; 3(2); 4; 5(5); 6(2); 7(3); 8(6); 10(4); 11; 13(3); 16(3); 17(5); 18; 21(3); 22(3); 24(3); 15:1(2); 2; 4(2); 5; 6; 7(2); 10(3); 11(2); 12; 14; 16(3); 17; 18(5); 19(3); 20(3); 21(4); 16:2(2); 3(2); 5; 7(5); 8; 9(2); 10(2); 11(3); 12; 13(2); 14; 17:1; 8(2); 11(2); 14(2); 23(2); 24; 25; 27(2); 18:1(5); 2(2); 4; 6; 7; 8(2); 9; 10(2); 11; 13; 14(3); 16(2); 17; 18(2); 19(3); 20(2); 21; 22(2); 23(2); 24(3); 25(6); 26(3); 27; 28(2); 29; 30; 31(2); 32(2); 33; 19:1(4); 2(3); 4(5); 5; 6(2); 8(2); 9(2); 10(3); 11(4); 12(2); 13(4); 14; 15(4); 16(4); 17(2); 19; 22(2); 23(2); 24(3); 25(4); 27(3); 28(5); 29(5); 30; 31(5); 32; 33; 34(4); 35; 36; 37(3); 38(3); 20:1; 3; 5; 6; 7; 8(2); 11; 12(2); 18(3); 21:1(2); 2; 3; 8(2); 9(2); 10; 11; 12; 13(2); 14(3); 15(4); 16(2); 17(5); 18; 19(2); 20(2); 21(2); 22; 23(2); 27; 28; 29; 31; 32(3); 33(3); 34(2); 22:2(2); 3(4); 4(2); 5(2); 6(4); 7(3); 8(2); 9(4); 10; 11(2); 12; 13; 14(4); 15(2); 16; 17(5); 18(2); 21; 23:1(2); 2; 3; 5; 6; 7(3); 8; 9(3); 10(5); 11(4); 12(2); 13(4); 15; 16(4); 17(6); 18(3); 19(3); 20(3); 24:1; 2; 3(6); 5(3); 7(2); 8; 9(2); 10(2); 11(2); 13(4); 14(2); 15; 16(2); 17; 20(2); 21(2); 22(2); 24; 26(2); 27(4); 28; 29(2); 30(7); 31(3); 32(6); 35; 37(2); 39; 40; 42(2); 43(2); 44(2); 45; 46; 47(3); 48(4); 49(2); 50(2); 51; 52(2); 53; 54(2); 55; 56; 57; 60(2); 61(3); 62(2); 63(3); 65(3); 66(2); 25:3; 4(2); 6(4); 7(2); 9(4); 10(2); 11; 12(2); 13(3); 16; 17(2); 18; 19; 20(4); 21(2); 22(2); 23(4); 25; 27(2); 29; 26:1(4); 2(2); 3; 4(3); 7(4); 8; 10; 12(2); 13; 14; 15(3); 17; 18(5); 19; 20(4); 22(2); 24(3); 25(2); 26; 28; 29(2); 31; 32(2); 33(2); 34(4); 27:2; 3; 5; 7(2); 9(2); 15(2); 16(4); 17(3); 20; 22(3); 27(4); 28(3); 30; 33; 34; 39(3); 41(2); 42; 46(4); 28:1; 2(2); 4(2); 5(4); 6; 8; 9(3); 11(2); 12(2); 13(4); 14(8); 16; 17(2); 18(2); 19(2); 21; 29:1(3); 2(3); 3(6); 5; 6; 7(2); 8(4); 10(5); 13; 16(4); 20; 22(2); 23; 25; 26(2); 27; 31; 32; 33; 35; 30:2(3); 13; 14(2); 16(2); 24; 27; 30; 32(5); 33(3); 35(5); 36; 37(3); 38(5); 39(3); 40(5); 41(6); 42(3); 43; 31:1; 2; 3(2); 4; 5; 8(4); 9; 10(4); 11; 12(2); 13(3); 18; 19; 20; 21(2); 22; 23; 24; 25(2); 26; 29; 32; 33; 34(3); 35(2); 38; 39; 40(3); 42(4); 46; 49; 53(4); 54(2); 55; 32:1; 2; 3(2); 6; 7(2); 8(2); 9; 10(3); 11(4); 12(2); 16; 17; 19(3); 20; 21(2); 22; 23; 24; 25(2); 26; 30(2); 31; 32(5); 33:1(2); 2; 3; 5(2); 6; 8; 10; 13(4); 14(2); 15(2); 17(2); 18(3); 19(2); 34:1(3); 2(3); 3(3); 5; 6; 7(3); 8; 10; 12; 13; 19(3); 20(2); 21(2); 22; 24(2); 25(4); 26(2); 27(3); 28(2); 29; 30(4); 35:1; 2; 3(2); 4(3); 5(3); 6(2); 7(2); 8(2); 12; 13; 14; 15(2); 17; 19; 20; 21; 22; 23; 24; 25; 26(2); 28; 36:1; 2(6); 5(2); 6(3); 7; 9(3); 10(5); 11; 12(2); 13(2); 14(3); 15(4); 16(3); 17(4); 18(3); 19; 20(3); 21(4); 22; 23; 24(5); 25(2); 26; 27; 28; 29(2); 30(3); 31(3); 32(2); 33; 34(2); 35(3); 38; 39(4); 40(2); 43(4); 37:1(2); 2(5); 3; 7; 9(3); 10; 11; 13; 14(2); 15(2); 17; 22; 23; 24; 27; 28(3); 29(2); 30; 31(3); 32; 35; 36(2); 38:7(3); 9(2); 10(2); 12(3); 14; 16; 17; 19; 20(4); 21(3); 22(2); 24; 25(2); 27; 28(2); 30; 39:1(2); 2(3); 3(2); 5(7); 6; 8; 11(3); 14; 17; 19; 20(3); 21(4); 22(4); 23(4); 40:1(4); 2(2); 3(5); 4(2); 5(4); 6; 7; 9; 10; 11(2); 12(2); 13; 15(3); 16(2); 17(3); 18(2); 19; 20(4); 21(2); 22; 23; 41:1(2); 2(2); 3(4); 4(2); 6; 7(2); 8(2); 9; 10(4); 11; 12(2); 14; 17(2); 18(2); 19; 20(3); 21; 23; 24(3); 25; 26(3); 27(3); 28; 29; 30(4); 31(3); 32(2); 33; 34(4); 35(3); 36(5); 37(3); 38; 40; 41; 43(3); 44; 45(2); 46(2); 47(2); 48(7); 49(2); 50(2); 51(2); 52(3); 53(2); 54(3); 55(3); 56(7); 57; 42:5(3); 6(4); 7; 9(3); 12(2); 13(3); 15; 16; 18; 19; 21; 22; 25; 26; 27(2); 29; 30(3); 32(2); 33(4); 34; 35; 38(2); 43:1(2); 2; 3; 5; 6; 7; 8; 9; 11(3); 12(2); 13; 14; 15; 16; 17(3); 18(3); 19(3); 20; 21(2); 23; 24(2); 25; 26(3); 27; 31; 32(4); 33(3); 44:1(3); 2(5); 3(2); 4(2); 5; 8(3); 11; 12(3); 13; 14; 16(2); 17(2); 22; 24; 26; 28; 29; 30(2); 31(3); 32(2); 33(2); 34(2); 45:2(2); 6(2); 7; 8; 10; 12; 16; 17; 18(4); 19; 20(2); 21(3); 23(2); 24; 25; 26; 27(3); 46:1; 2(2); 3; 5(2); 6; 8(2); 9; 10(2); 11; 12(3); 13; 14; 15(2); 16; 17(2); 18; 19; 20(2); 21; 22; 23; 24; 25; 26; 27(3); 28(2); 31; 32; 34(2); 47:1(2); 4(4); 6(4); 9(8); 11(4); 12; 13(5); 14(5); 15(5); 16; 17(5); 18(2); 19; 20(4); 21(4); 22(3); 23(2); 24(2); 25; 26(3); 27(2); 28(2); 29; 31(2); 48:2; 3; 5; 6; 7(3); 10; 12; 14(2); 15; 16(5); 17; 18; 21; 22(2); 49:1; 3(3); 8; 9; 10(3); 11(3); 13(2); 15; 16; 17(3); 22; 23; 24(5); 25(5); 26(7); 27(3); 28; 29(3); 30(5); 32(3); 33; 50:2(2); 3(2); 4(3); 5; 7(4); 8(2); 10(2); 11(7); 13(5); 15; 17(4); 19; 23(3); 24; 25; **Ex** 1:1(2); 7(2); 9(2); 10(2); 12(3); 13(2); 14; 15(5); 16(3); 17(3); 18(3); 19(4); 20(2); 21; 22; 2:1; 2; 3(3); 5(5); 6(3); 7(2); 8(2); 9(2); 10(2); 12(2); 13(3); 14; 15(2); 16(2); 17; 19(3); 20; 21; 23(5); 25; 3:1(6); 2(5); 3; 4(3); 5; 6(4); 7(2); 8(9); 9(4); 10; 11; 12; 13(2); 14; 15(5); 16(3); 17(8); 18(6); 19; 21(2); 22; 4:1; 2; 3(2); 4(2); 5(4); 6; 8(4); 9(5); 10; 11(6); 13; 14(3); 15; 16; 17; 19(2); 20(2); 21(2); 22; 24(3); 25; 26; 27(3); 28(3); 29(2); 30(5); 31(3); 5:1(2); 2(2); 3(5); 4(2); 5(2); 6(3); 7; 8; 9; 10(3); 12(2); 13; 14(2); 15(2); 16; 17; 18; 19(2); 21(3); 22; 6:1; 2; 4(2); 5(3); 6(4); 7(3); 8(2); 9; 10; 11; 12(2); 13(4); 14(4); 15(3); 16(4); 17; 18(3); 19(2); 20(2); 21; 22; 24(3); 25(4); 26(4); 27(3); 28(3); 29(2); 30; 7:1; 2; 3; 4(2); 5(3); 6; 8; 10; 11(3); 13; 14(2); 15(4); 16(3); 17(5); 18(6); 19(3); 20(8); 21(7); 22(2); 24(4); 25(2); 8:1(2); 3(2); 4; 5(5); 6(3); 7(2); 8(4); 9(3); 10; 11(2); 12(2); 13(6); 14; 15; 16(4); 17(5); 18; 19(3); 20(4); 21(3); 22(4); 24(5); 25; 26(5); 27(2); 28(2); 29(4); 30; 31(3); 32; 9:1(3); 3(8); 4(4); 5(3); 6(5); 7(4); 8(3); 9(2); 10; 11(5); 12(3); 13(4); 14; 15; 16; 19(3); 20(4); 21(3); 22(4); 23(4); 24(2); 25(6); 26(2); 27; 28; 29(5); 30; 31(5); 32(2); 33(6); 34(3); 35(3); 10:1(2); 2(3); 3(2); 5(6); 6(5); 7(2); 8(2); 9; 10; 11; 12(6); 13(5); 14(3); 15(11); 16; 17; 18; 19(4); 20(2); 21(2); 22; 23; 24; 25; 26(2); 27; 28; 11:1; 2(2); 3(9); 4(2); 5(8); 6; 7(3); 8; 9(2); 10(2); 12:1(2); 2(2); 3(3); 4(5); 5(3); 6(4); 7(4); 8; 11; 12(5); 13(5); 14; 15(3); 16(2); 17(2); 18(5); 19(2); 21(2); 22(7); 23(8); 25(2); 27(6); 28(2); 29(8); 30(2); 31(2); 33(3); 34; 35(3); 36(5); 37; 39; 40(2); 41(5); 42(4); 43(3); 46(2); 47; 48(3); 49(2); 50(2); 51(3); 13:1; 2(3); 3(3); 4; 5(7); 6(2); 8; 9(2); 11(3); 12(4); 13; 14(2); 15(8); 16; 17(4); 18(5); 19(2); 20(2); 21(2); 22(3); 14:1; 2(3); 3(3); 4(2); 5(4); 7; 8(4); 9(3); 10(4); 11; 12(4); 13(4); 14; 15(2); 16(4); 17(2); 18(2); 19(3); 20(7); 21(5); 22(5); 23(3); 24(7); 25(4); 26(4); 27(8); 28(5); 29(4); 30(5); 31(5); 15:1(5); 2; 3(2); 4(2); 5(2); 6; 7; 8(6); 9(2); 10(2); 11; 12; 13; 14(2); 15(3); 16(2); 17(3); 18; 19(8); 20(4); 21(3); 22(3); 23(2); 24; 25(4); 26(5); 27; 16:1(6); 2(3); 3(6); 4(2); 5; 6(3); 7(4); 8(6); 9(3); 10(6); 11; 12(4); 13(4); 14(4); 15(3); 16(3); 17; 21; 22(3); 23(2); 25(2); 26(2); 27(2); 28; 29(4); 30(2); 31(2); 32(5); 33; 34(2); 35(3); 17:1(6); 2(2); 3(2); 4; 5(4); 6(5); 7(6); 9(3); 10(2); 12(4); 13(2); 14(4); 16(2); 18:1(2); 3; 4(4); 5(2); 7; 8(5); 9(4); 10(7); 11(3); 12; 13(3); 14(3); 15; 16; 17; 19(2); 20(4); 21; 22(2); 24; 25; 26(2); 19:1(5); 2(3); 3(4); 4; 5; 6(2); 7(3); 8(5); 9(6); 10(2); 11(5); 12(3); 13(2); 14(3); 15(2); 16(7); 17(4); 18(3); 19(2); 20(6); 21(3); 22(3); 23(3); 24(4); 25; 20:2(3); 4(3); 5(5); 7(3); 8; 10(3); 11(7); 12(2); 18(7); 20; 21(2); 22(2); 21:1; 2; 4; 5; 6(3); 7; 9; 18; 19; 22(2); 26(2); 27(2); 28(3); 29(2); 32(2); 34(3); 35(3); 36(2); 22:2; 3; 4; 5(2); 6(2); 7(2); 8(4); 9(3); 11(2); 12; 14; 16; 17; 20; 21; 24; 26; 29(2); 30; 31(2); 23:1; 5; 6; 7(2); 8(3); 9(2); 11(4); 12(3); 13; 14; 15(3); 16(8); 17(2); 18(2); 19(4); 20(2); 23(6); 25(2); 26; 27; 28(3); 29(3); 30; 31(6); 24:1(2); 2(2); 3(7); 4(6); 5(2); 6(3); 7(5); 8(5); 9; 10(2); 11(2); 12(3); 13; 14; 15(2); 16(6); 17(7); 18(4); 25:1; 2; 3; 6(3); 7(2); 9(3); 12; 14(5); 15(3); 16(2); 18(2); 19(5); 20(5); 21(4); 22(5); 25; 26(2); 27(4); 28(2); 30(2); 31; 32(3); 33(3); 34; 35(8); 40(2); 26:1; 2(4); 3; 4(6); 5(6); 6(2); 7; 8(4); 9(3); 10(5); 11(3); 12(6); 13(6); 14; 15(2); 16(2); 17(2); 18(3); 19(2); 20(3); 21; 22(2); 23(2); 24(3); 26(2); 27(7); 28(3); 29(3); 30(2); 32; 33(8); 34(4); 35(9); 36(2); 37; 27:1; 4; 5(4); 6; 7(5); 8; 9(4); 10(2); 11(4); 12(3); 13(3); 14(2); 15; 16(2); 17(2); 18(4); 19(4); 20(3); 21(5); 28:1; 3; 4; 5; 6; 8(3); 9(2); 10; 11(5); 12(5); 14(2); 15(3); 17(2); 18; 19; 20; 21(5); 22(2); 23(4); 24(4); 25(6); 26(5); 27(5); 28(7); 29(5); 30(7); 31(2); 32(2); 34(2); 35(2); 36(2); 37(3); 38(4); 39(3); 42(2); 43(3); 29:3(3); 4(2); 5(8); 6(3); 7; 9(2); 10(4); 11(4); 12(7); 13(7); 14(3); 15(2); 16(2); 17; 18(4); 19(3); 20(9); 21(4); 22(10); 23(3); 24(3); 25(3); 26(3); 27(6); 28(4); 29; 30(2); 31(3); 32(6); 33; 34(5); 36; 37(3); 38(2); 39(2); 40; 41(5); 42(3); 43(2); 44(2); 45; 46(3); 30:4(2); 5; 6(5); 7; 8(2); 10(3); 11; 12(3); 13(4); 14; 15(3); 16(6); 17; 18(2); 20(3); 22; 24(2); 25(2); 26(3); 27(3); 28(2); 31; 34; 35(2); 36(2); 37(2); 31:1; 2(3); 3; 6(3); 7(6); 8(3); 9(2); 10(4); 11(2); 12; 13(2); 14; 15(4); 16(3); 17(5); 18(2); 32:1(5); 2(2); 3(2); 4(2); 5; 6(2); 7(2); 8(2); 9; 11(2); 12(4); 13; 14(2); 15(6); 16(5); 17(3); 18(5); 19(6); 20(4); 22(2); 23(2); 24; 25; 26(4); 27(2); 28(3); 29; 30(3); 31; 33; 34(3); 35(3); 33:1(4); 2(6); 3; 4; 5(2); 6; 7(6); 8(3); 9(5); 10(4); 11(4); 12; 16(3); 17; 19(2); 21(2); 22(2); 34:1(4); 2(4); 3; 4(4); 5(4); 6(3); 7(7); 8; 10(4); 11(6); 12(2); 14; 15(3); 16(2); 18(4); 19; 20(2); 21; 22(4); 23(3); 24(3); 25(4); 26(4); 27(2); 28(5); 29(4); 30(2); 31(2); 32(2); 34(3); 35(4); 35:1(4); 2(2); 3; 4(4); 5(2); 8(3); 9(2); 10; 11; 12(4); 13(2); 14(4); 15(7); 16(2); 17(5); 18(4); 19(5); 20(3); 21(4); 22; 24(2); 25; 26; 27(4); 28(3); 29(5); 30(5); 31; 34(3); 35(4); 36:1(4); 2(2); 3(5); 4(4); 5(4); 6(4); 7(2); 8(2); 9(4); 10; 11(6); 12(5); 13(2); 14(2); 15(4); 17(5); 18; 19; 20; 21(2); 22(2); 23(2); 24(2); 25(3); 26; 27(2); 28(2); 29(3); 30; 31(2); 32(6); 33(3); 34(3); 37; 37:1; 3; 5(5); 6; 7(2); 8(5); 9(5); 10; 12; 13(2); 14(4); 15(2); 16(2); 17(3); 18(3); 19(3); 20; 21(7); 25; 27; 28; 29(4); 38:1; 2; 3(7); 4(2); 5(3); 6; 7(5); 8(5); 9(4); 10(2); 11(4); 12(3); 13(2); 14(2); 15(3); 16(2); 17(7); 18(7); 19; 20(3); 21(9); 22(4); 23(2); 24(7); 25(4); 26(3); 27(6); 28(2); 29; 30(7); 31(8); 39:1(4); 2; 3(3); 5(3); 6(2); 7(4); 8(3); 9; 10; 11; 12; 13; 14(3); 15(2); 16(3); 17(4); 18(6); 19(5); 20(5); 21(8); 22(2); 23(4); 24(2); 25(5); 26(3); 29; 30(4); 31(2); 32(5); 33(2); 34(4); 35(3); 36(2); 37(3); 38(5); 39(2); 40(8); 41(4); 42(3); 43(2); 40:1; 2(4); 3(4); 4(3); 5(7); 6(5); 7(3); 8(3); 9(2); 10(4); 11; 12(2); 13; 16; 17(5); 18; 19(5); 20(7); 21(7); 22(5); 23(3); 24(5); 25(3); 26(3); 27; 28(3); 29(7); 30(3); 32(3); 33(6); 34(5); 35(5); 36(3); 37(2); 38(5); **Lev** 1:1(2); 2(5); 3(4); 4(2); 5(8); 6; 7(5); 8(7); 9(3); 10(3); 11(5); 12(4); 13(5); 14(2); 15(5); 16(3); 17(5); 2:1; 2(5); 3(4); 4; 8(4); 9(4); 10(3); 11(2); 12(4); 13(2); 14(3); 16(4); 3:1(2); 2(6); 3(7); 4(6); 5(5); 6(2); 7; 8(3); 9(9); 10(6); 11(3); 12; 13(3); 14(5); 15(6); 16(4); 4:1; 2(3); 3(3); 4(7); 5(3); 6(6); 7(13); 8(7); 9(6); 10(6); 11; 12(4); 13(6); 14(4); 15(7); 16(3); 17(4); 18(10); 19(2); 20(3); 21(4); 22(2); 23; 24(5); 25(7); 26(5); 27(3); 28; 29(5); 30(6); 31(6); 33(4); 34(8); 35(9); 5:1(2); 2(3); 6(4); 7(2); 8(2); 9(8); 10(3); 12(5); 13(3); 14; 15(6); 16(6); 17(2); 18(3); 19; 6:1; 2; 4(2); 5; 6(3); 7(2); 8; 9(7); 10(6); 11(2); 12(6); 13; 14(5); 15(6); 16(3); 17(2); 18(4); 19; 20(4); 21(3); 22(2); 23; 24; 25(6); 26(3); 28; 29(2); 30(4); 7:1(2); 2(4); 3(3); 4(6); 5(3); 6; 7(3); 8(3); 9(3); 10(2); 11(3); 12; 13(2); 14(4); 15(3); 16(4); 17(4); 18(4); 19(2); 20(5); 21(5); 22; 23; 24(2); 25(4); 28; 29(5); 30(6); 31(4); 32(3); 33(5); 34(8); 35(5); 36(3); 37(8); 38(5); 8:1; 2(3); 3(3); 4(4); 5(2); 7(7); 8(4); 9(5); 10(2); 11(3); 12; 13; 14(5); 15(7); 16(6); 17(3); 18(4); 19(2); 20(4); 21(6); 22(4); 23(3); 24(6); 25(8); 26(4); 27; 28(3); 29(4); 30(5); 31(5); 32(2); 33(3); 34; 35(4); 36(3); 9:1(2); 2; 3(3); 4(2); 5(3); 6(4); 7(5); 8(3); 9(8); 10(7); 11(3); 12(3); 13(2); 14(4); 15(5); 16(2); 17(4); 18(5); 19(8); 20(4); 21(3); 22(3); 23(5); 24(5); 10:1(2); 2(2); 3(2); 4(4); 5; 6(4); 7(5); 8; 9; 11(4); 12(4); 13(2); 14(6); 15(7); 16(3); 17(4); 18; 19(4); 11:1; 2(4); 3(3); 4(3); 5(2); 6(2); 7(3); 9(4); 10(4); 12; 13(4); 14(2); 16(4); 17(3); 18(3); 19(4); 21; 22(4); 24; 25; 26(3); 29(5); 30(5); 38; 41; 42; 44(2); 45(2); 46(5); 47(4); 12:1; 2(2); 3(2); 4(3); 5; 6(5); 7(3); 8(2); 13:1; 2(4); 3(9); 4(6); 5(6); 6(6); 7(4); 8(4); 9(2); 10(5); 11(2); 12(6);

13(3); 15(3); 16(2); 17(4); 18(2); 19(3); 20(4); 21(3); 22(2); 23(4); 24(3); 25(6); 26(4); 27(4); 28(6); 29(2); 30(5); 31(6); 32(6); 33(4); 34(7); 35(2); 36(4); 37(3); 38(2); 39(5); 40; 41; 42; 43(6); 44; 45(2); 46(3); 48; 49(6); 50(3); 51(8); 52(3); 53(5); 54(3); 55(6); 56(6); 57(4); 58(2); 59(3); 14:1; 2(4); 3(5); 4; 5(2); 6(8); 7(3); 8; 9(2); 10(2); 11(5); 12(3); 13(7); 14(8); 15(3); 16(4); 17(9); 18(6); 19(3); 20(5); 22; 23(5); 24(6); 25(9); 26(3); 27(3); 28(10); 29(5); 30; 31(5); 32(2); 33; 34(3); 35(3); 36(7); 37(5); 38(5); 39(5); 40(4); 41(3); 42(2); 43(4); 44(4); 45(4); 46; 47(2); 48(7); 49; 50; 51(8); 52(8); 53(4); 54; 55; 57; 15:1; 2; 4; 6; 7(2); 8; 9; 11(2); 12(2); 14(5); 15(5); 19; 25(3); 26(3); 29(4); 30(6); 31; 32; 16:1(4); 2(7); 3(2); 4(3); 5(3); 6; 7(4); 8(4); 9(2); 10(6); 11(4); 12(3); 13(6); 14(6); 15(8); 16(5); 17(3); 18(8); 19(3); 20(4); 21(8); 22(3); 23(3); 24(3); 25(3); 26(3); 27(7); 28; 29(3); 30(2); 32(3); 33(6); 34(2); 17:1; 2(3); 3(3); 4(6); 5(8); 6(8); 7; 8(2); 9(3); 10(2); 11(6); 12; 13(2); 14(4); 18:1; 2(2); 3(4); 4; 5; 6; 7(2); 8; 9(3); 10; 11; 12; 13; 14; 15; 16; 17; 18; 21(3); 24; 25(3); 27(3); 28(2); 29; 30; 19:1; 2(3); 3; 4; 5; 6(4); 7; 8(2); 9(3); 10(3); 12(2); 13; 14(3); 15(3); 16(2); 18(2); 21(3); 22(5); 23; 24(2); 25(2); 26; 27(2); 28(2); 29(2); 30; 31; 32(3); 34(3); 36(2); 37; 20:1; 2(5); 4(3); 6; 7; 8; 10(3); 11; 15; 16(2); 17; 18; 19; 22; 23(2); 24(2); 25; 26(2); 21:1(4); 5; 6(4); 7; 8(2); 9(2); 10(3); 12(5); 15; 16; 17; 21(5); 22(3); 23(3); 24; 22:1; 2(3); 3(4); 4(2); 6(2); 7(2); 8; 9; 10(3); 11; 12(2); 13; 14(2); 15(3); 16(2); 17; 18(4); 19(3); 21(3); 22(3); 24; 25; 26; 27(2); 28; 29; 30(2); 31; 32(2); 33(2); 23:1; 2(3); 3(3); 4(2); 5(3); 6(4); 7; 8(2); 9; 10(4); 11(5); 12(3); 13; 14; 15(5); 16(3); 17(2); 18(4); 19(2); 20(7); 21; 22(5); 23; 24(4); 25; 26; 27(3); 28(2); 32(2); 33; 34(4); 35; 36(3); 37(3); 38(3); 39(8); 40(5); 41(3); 43(3); 44(3); 24:1; 2(3); 3(4); 4(3); 6(2); 7(2); 8(2); 9(2); 10(3); 11(5); 12(2); 13; 14(2); 15; 16(7); 22(3); 23(4); 25:1; 2(4); 4(3); 5(2); 6(3); 7; 8(2); 9(6); 10(2); 11; 12(2); 15(3); 16(5); 17; 18; 19; 20; 21; 22(3); 23(2); 24(2); 26; 27(3); 28(3); 30(4); 31(4); 32(5); 33(8); 34(2); 38(3); 40; 41; 42; 44; 45(2); 46; 47(2); 50(5); 51(2); 52(2); 54; 55(3); 26:1; 2; 4(3); 5(4); 6(3); 7; 8; 10(3); 13(3); 16; 19; 20(2); 25(4); 29(2); 30; 31; 32; 33; 34(2); 35; 36(2); 38(2); 40; 41; 42; 43; 44(2); 45(5); 46(4); 27:1; 2(2); 3(2); 8(4); 9(2); 10; 11(3); 12(2); 14(3); 15; 16(2); 17; 18(5); 19(2); 20(2); 21(5); 22(2); 23(4); 24(4); 25(3); 26(4); 28(3); 29; 30(8); 32(6); 33; 34(3); **Num** 1:1(7); 2(3); 4; 5(3); 6; 7; 8; 9; 10(3); 11; 12; 13; 14; 15; 16(2); 18(4); 19(2); 20(2); 21; 22(2); 23; 24(2); 25; 26(2); 27; 28(2); 29; 30(2); 31; 32(3); 33; 34(2); 35; 36(2); 37; 38(2); 39; 40(2); 41; 42(2); 43; 44(2); 45; 47; 48; 49(2); 50(5); 51(5); 52; 53(8); 54(2); 2:1; 2(3); 3(8); 5(4); 7(4); 9; 10(6); 12(4); 14(4); 16(2); 17(5); 18(6); 20(4); 22(4); 24(2); 25(6); 27(4); 29(4); 31; 32(3); 33(3); 34(2); 3:1(2); 2(3); 3(3); 4(4); 5; 6(2); 7(5); 8(6); 9(2); 10; 11; 12(5); 13(6); 14(2); 15; 16(2); 17; 18(2); 19; 20(3); 21(6); 22(2); 23(3); 24(4); 25(8); 26(8); 27(10); 28(3); 29(4); 30(5); 31(8); 32(5); 33(5); 34(2); 35(6); 36(5); 37(2); 38(7); 39(4); 40(4); 41(9); 42(3); 43(2); 44; 45(7); 46(6); 47(4); 48(2); 49(2); 50(5); 51(3); 4:1; 2(2); 3(3); 4(4); 5(4); 7(6); 8; 9(2); 11; 12(2); 13(2); 14(6); 15(8); 16(11); 17; 18(4); 19; 20; 21; 22; 23(3); 24(3); 25(7); 26(8); 27(3); 28(7); 29; 30(3); 31(3); 32(3); 33(7); 34(4); 35(2); 37(7); 38; 39(2); 41(6); 42(2); 43(2); 45(6); 46(2); 47(3); 49(4); 5:1; 2(2); 3(2); 4(4); 5; 6(2); 7(2); 8(8); 9(3); 10; 11; 12; 13; 14(2); 15(3); 16(2); 17(5); 18(8); 19(2); 21(7); 22(2); 23(2); 24(4); 25(6); 26(5); 27(3); 28; 29; 30(4); 31; 6:1; 2(3); 4(2); 5(6); 6(2); 8(2); 9(2); 10(4); 11(3); 12(3); 13(5); 14; 16(2); 17(4); 18(7); 19(6); 20(8); 21(6); 22; 23(2); 24; 25; 26; 27; 7:1(2); 2(4); 3(3); 4; 5(3); 6(3); 7; 8(4); 9(3); 10(5); 11(3); 12(4); 13(3); 16; 17(3); 18(2); 19(3); 22; 23(3); 24(3); 25(3); 28; 29(3); 30(3); 31(3); 34; 35(3); 36(3); 37(3); 40; 41(3); 42(3); 43(3); 46; 47(3); 48(3); 49(3); 52; 53(3); 54(3); 55(3); 58; 59(3); 60(3); 61(3); 64; 65(3); 66(3); 67(3); 70; 71(3); 72(3); 73(3); 76; 77(3); 78(3); 79(3); 82; 83(3); 84(3); 85(4); 86(5); 87(6); 88(7); 89(6); 8:1; 2(3); 3(4); 4(4); 5; 6(2); 9(4); 10(4); 11(5); 12(6); 13(2); 14(3); 15(2); 16(4); 17(5); 18(3); 19(9); 20(6); 21(2); 22(4); 23; 24(3); 25; 26(2); 9:1(5); 2(2); 3; 4(2); 5(6); 6; 7(3); 8; 9; 10(2); 11(2); 12(2); 13(4); 14(6); 15(8); 16(2); 17(6); 18(7); 19(5); 20(6); 21(4); 22(3); 23(9); 10:1; 2(3); 3(3); 4(3); 5(3); 6(5); 7(2); 8(3); 9(3); 10(5); 11(6); 12(4); 13(4); 14(4); 15(4); 16(4); 17(4); 18(3); 19(4); 20(4); 21(3); 22(4); 23(4); 24(4); 25(6); 26(4); 27(4); 28(2); 29(5); 31; 32(2); 33(6); 34(3); 35; 36; 11:1(7); 2(3); 3(4); 4(2); 5(6); 7(2); 8(3); 9(4); 10(4); 11(2); 12; 14; 16(5); 17(4); 18(4); 20; 21; 22(2); 23(2); 24(7); 25(6); 26(7); 27; 28; 29(2); 30(2); 31(7); 32(4); 33(6); 34(2); 35; 12:1; 2(2); 3(3); 4(3); 5(4); 6; 8(2); 9(2); 10(2); 13; 14(2); 15(2); 16(2); 13:1; 2(2); 3(4); 4(2); 5(2); 6(2); 7(2); 8(2); 9(2); 10(2); 11(3); 12(2); 13(2); 14(2); 15(2); 16(4); 17(3); 18(2); 19(2); 20(6); 21(3); 22(2); 23(2); 24(4); 25; 26(6); 27; 28(4); 29(11); 30; 31(2); 32(4); 33(3); 14:1(2); 2(3); 3(2); 5(3); 6(3); 7(3); 8; 9(4); 10(5); 11(2); 12; 13(2); 14; 15; 16(3); 17; 18(6); 19(2); 20; 21(3); 22(3); 23; 24; 25(6); 26; 27(2); 28; 29; 30(3); 31; 33(3); 34(3); 35; 36(4); 37(4); 38(4); 39(2); 40(5); 41(2); 42; 43(5); 44(5); 45(2); 15:1; 2(2); 3(4); 4; 5(2); 7; 8; 9; 10(2); 12; 13; 14; 15(4); 16; 17; 18(2); 19(3); 20(2); 21(2); 22; 23(4); 24(6); 25(5); 26(4); 28(3); 29(2); 30(2); 31(2); 32(3); 33; 35(4); 36(3); 37; 38(4); 39(4); 41(3); 16:1(5); 2(3); 3(4); 5; 7(4); 9(6); 10(2); 11; 12; 13; 14; 15; 16; 17; 18(2); 19(6); 20; 22(3); 23; 24(2); 25; 26(2); 27(2); 28; 29(2); 30(4); 31; 32(2); 33(3); 34; 35(2); 36; 37(5); 38(4); 39(3); 40(3); 41(5); 42(5); 43; 44; 46(4); 47(6); 48(3); 49(2); 50(3); 17:1; 2; 3(2); 4(2); 5(4); 6(2); 7(3); 8(4); 9(3); 10(3); 11; 12; 13(2); 18:1(4); 2(3); 3(5); 4(4); 5(5); 6(5); 7(3); 8(3); 9(2); 11(3); 12(6); 13; 15(4); 16(3); 17(5); 18(2); 19(5); 20(2); 21(5); 22(2); 23(4); 24(5); 25; 26(5); 27(4); 28(4); 29(3); 30(7); 31; 32(3); 19:1; 2(4); 3(2); 4(2); 5; 6(4); 7(3); 8; 9(6); 10(5); 11; 12(5); 13(4); 14(3); 16; 17(2); 18(7); 19(5); 20(5); 21(2); 22(2); 20:1(5); 2; 3(2); 4(2); 6(6); 7; 8(5); 9(2); 10(2); 11(2); 12(4); 13(3); 14(2); 15; 16(3); 17(3); 18; 19(2); 22(2); 23(3); 24(3); 27(3); 28(3); 29(2); 21:1(4); 2; 3(4); 4(6); 5(2); 6(4); 7(5); 8; 9; 10; 11(2); 12; 13(8); 14(5); 15(4); 16(3); 18(5); 20(4); 21; 22; 23; 24(7); 25(2); 26(4); 27; 28(4); 29; 31(2); 32; 33; 34(2); 22:1(4); 2(2); 3(2); 4(5); 5(6); 6; 7(4);

8(2); 10; 11(2); 12; 13(3); 14; 16; 18(3); 19; 20(2); 21(2); 22(3); 23(9); 24(3); 25(5); 26(4); 27(4); 28(3); 29; 30; 31(4); 32(2); 33; 34(3); 35(5); 36(5); 38; 40; 41(4); 23:3; 4; 5; 6; 7(3); 8; 9(4); 10(3); 12; 13; 14(2); 15; 16; 17(2); 21(2); 24(3); 26; 28(2); 24:1(2); 2; 3(4); 4(4); 6(3); 8; 11; 13(3); 14; 15(4); 16(6); 17(2); 19(2); 20; 21(2); 24; 25:1(2); 2(3); 3(2); 4(8); 5; 6(7); 7(4); 8(6); 9; 10; 11(5); 13; 14(5); 15(4); 16; 17; 18(5); 26:1(4); 2(2); 3(3); 4(4); 5(6); 6(4); 7(2); 8; 9(5); 10(2); 11; 12(7); 13(4); 14(2); 15(7); 16(4); 17(4); 18(2); 19(2); 20(7); 21(5); 22; 23(5); 24(4); 25; 26(7); 27(2); 28; 29(5); 30(5); 31(4); 32(4); 33(3); 34; 35(7); 36(3); 37(3); 38(7); 39(4); 40(5); 41; 42(4); 43(2); 44(7); 45(5); 46(2); 47(2); 48(5); 49(4); 50; 51; 52; 53(2); 55(3); 56(3); 57(7); 58(12); 59(2); 61; 62(2); 63(4); 64(3); 65(4); 27:1(8); 2(5); 3(3); 4; 5; 6; 7(2); 8; 11(3); 12(3); 14(6); 15; 16(4); 17(2); 18(3); 19(2); 20(2); 21(6); 22(3); 23(2); 28:1; 2; 3(2); 4(4); 6; 7(2); 8(4); 9; 10(2); 11(2); 12; 13; 14(3); 15(3); 16(4); 17(2); 18; 19; 21; 23(2); 24(4); 25; 26(3); 27; 28; 29; 30; 31; 29:1(4); 2; 3(2); 4; 5; 6(4); 7; 8; 9(2); 10; 11(3); 12(3); 13; 14(2); 15; 16(2); 17; 18(4); 19(2); 20; 21(4); 22; 23; 24(4); 25(2); 26; 27(4); 28; 29; 30(4); 31; 32; 33(4); 34; 35; 36; 37(4); 38; 39; 40(2); 30:1(5); 2; 3; 4; 5(2); 7; 8(2); 12(3); 14(2); 16(2); 31:1; 2(2); 3(3); 4(2); 5; 6(6); 7(3); 8(5); 9(2); 10; 11(2); 12(9); 13(4); 14(4); 15; 16(6); 17; 18; 19(3); 21(6); 22(6); 23(2); 24(2); 25; 26(4); 27(3); 28(6); 29(2); 30(9); 31(2); 32(3); 36(2); 37(2); 38(2); 39(2); 40(2); 41(4); 42(2); 43(2); 47(5); 48(3); 49; 50(2); 51(3); 52(4); 53; 54(6); 32:1(5); 2(5); 4(3); 5; 6(2); 7(4); 8; 9(6); 10; 11(2); 12(4); 13(5); 14(2); 15; 17(4); 18; 19(3); 20(2); 21(2); 22(4); 23; 25(2); 26; 27; 28(5); 29(6); 30; 31(3); 32(4); 33(11); 34; 37; 38; 39(3); 40; 41; 33:1(4); 2(3); 3(8); 4(3); 5; 6(2); 8(4); 10; 11(2); 12; 14; 15; 16; 36; 37(2); 38(8); 40(6); 44; 47; 48(3); 49(3); 50(3); 51(3); 52(2); 53(3); 54(4); 55(3); 34:1; 2(4); 3(4); 4(3); 5(3); 6(2); 7; 8(3); 9; 11(5); 12(3); 13(5); 14(7); 15(4); 16; 17(5); 18(2); 19(4); 20(3); 21(2); 22(3); 23(4); 24(3); 25(3); 26(3); 27(3); 28(3); 29(5); 35:1(3); 2(5); 3; 4(5); 5(8); 6(2); 7(2); 8(7); 9; 10(3); 11; 12(3); 13; 14(2); 15(3); 16; 17(2); 18; 19(2); 21(3); 24(3); 25(9); 26(3); 27(4); 28(6); 30(3); 31; 32(3); 33(5); 34(4); 36:1(10); 2(5); 3(7); 4(6); 5(5); 6(3); 7(5); 8(5); 9; 10(2); 11(2); 12(4); 13(7); **Deut** 1:1(4); 3(6); 4; 5(2); 6; 7(12); 8(3); 10(2); 11; 14; 15; 16(2); 17(4); 18; 19(4); 20(3); 21(3); 22(3); 23; 24(2); 25(3); 26(2); 27(4); 28(4); 30; 31(3); 32; 33(4); 34(2); 36(3); 37; 38; 40(3); 41(3); 42; 43(3); 44; 45(2); 46; 2:1(4); 2; 4(3); 7(3); 8(4); 9(2); 10(2); 11(2); 12(4); 13(4); 14(8); 15(4); 16(2); 17; 18; 19(4); 20; 21(2); 22(2); 23(2); 24(2); 25(4); 26; 27(3); 29(5); 30; 31; 33; 34; 35(3); 36(5); 37(6); 3:1; 2(2); 3; 4(2); 6; 7(3); 8(6); 9(2); 10(3); 11(4); 12(4); 13(6); 14(5); 16(9); 17(8); 18(2); 20(4); 21(3); 22; 23; 25(2); 26(2); 27(5); 28; 29; 4:1(4); 2(3); 3(3); 4; 5(2); 6(2); 7; 9(2); 10(6); 11(4); 12(5); 13; 14(2); 15(3); 16(2); 17(4); 18(5); 19(7); 20(2); 21(4); 22; 23(4); 24; 25(4); 26(2); 27(4); 28; 29; 30(2); 31(2); 32(4); 33(3); 34(2); 35; 36(2); 39(2); 40(2); 41(3); 42; 43(5); 44(2); 45(4); 46(5); 47(5); 48(2); 49(6); 5:1; 2; 3; 4(4); 5(5); 6(3); 8(3); 9(5); 11(3); 12(2); 14(3); 15(4); 16(3); 22(6); 23(5); 24(3); 25(2); 26(4); 27(2); 28(5); 31(4); 32(3); 33(3); 6:1(4); 2(2); 3; 4(2); 5; 7; 9; 10(2); 12(3); 13; 14(2); 15(5); 16; 17(2); 18(4); 19; 20(5); 21; 22; 23; 24(2); 25; 7:1(9); 2; 4(2); 6(5); 7(2); 8(5); 9(2); 11(3); 12(3); 13(5); 15(2); 16(2); 18; 19(8); 20(2); 21(2); 22(3); 23; 25(3); 8:1(2); 2(3); 3(2); 5; 6(2); 7; 10(2); 11; 14(3); 15; 16(2); 17; 18; 19; 20(4); 9:1; 2(3); 3(2); 4(4); 5(5); 6; 7(5); 8(2); 9(6); 10(9); 11(5); 12(2); 13; 15(4); 16(3); 17; 18(4); 19(3); 20(2); 21(3); 22; 23(4); 24(2); 25(2); 26; 27; 28(4); 10:1(3); 2(4); 3(3); 4(10); 5(4); 6(2); 8(6); 9(2); 10(4); 11(3); 12(3); 13(2); 14(3); 15; 16; 17(2); 18(3); 19(2); 20; 22(2); 11:1; 2(2); 3; 4(4); 5; 6(5); 7; 8; 9(2); 10(2); 11(2); 12(7); 13; 14(3); 17(5); 19; 20; 21(6); 22; 23; 24(5); 25(4); 27(3); 28(4); 29(4); 30(7); 31(3); 32; 12:1(5); 2(4); 3; 4; 5(2); 6(2); 7(2); 9(3); 10(3); 11(4); 12(2); 14(2); 15(6); 16(2); 17(3); 18(5); 19; 20; 21(3); 22(4); 23(5); 24; 25(2); 26(3); 27(8); 28(2); 29(2); 31(3); 13:2(2); 3(3); 4; 5(6); 6(2); 7(5); 9(2); 10(3); 12; 13; 15(5); 16(4); 17(3); 18(4); 14:1(4); 2(5); 4(4); 5(7); 6(3); 7(5); 8(2); 9; 12(3); 13(3); 15(4); 16(3); 17(3); 18(4); 21(2); 22(2); 23(5); 24(5); 25(3); 26; 27; 28(2); 29(6); 15:1; 2(3); 4(3); 5(2); 6; 7(2); 9(3); 10; 11(2); 12; 14; 15(2); 17; 18; 19(4); 20(3); 21; 22(2); 23; 16:1(5); 2(6); 3(5); 4(2); 5(2); 6(6); 7(3); 8(2); 9(4); 10(4); 11(7); 13; 14(4); 15(5); 16(6); 17(2); 18(2); 19(4); 20(2); 21(2); 22; 17:1(2); 2(3); 3(2); 6(2); 7(6); 8(2); 9(4); 10(2); 11(6); 12(5); 13; 14(3); 15; 16(2); 18(4); 19(3); 20(4); 18:1(5); 2; 3(6); 4(3); 5(3); 6(3); 7(4); 8; 9(3); 10; 11; 12(2); 13; 14; 15; 16(5); 17; 20(2); 21(2); 22(6); 19:1(3); 2(2); 3(2); 4(2); 5(5); 6(4); 8(2); 9; 10(2); 12(3); 13; 14(3); 15(2); 17(4); 18(2); 19; 20:1(2); 2(3); 3; 4; 5(3); 6; 7; 8(3); 9(4); 11; 12; 13(3); 14(6); 15(2); 16(2); 17(7); 18; 19(3); 20(2); 21:1(3); 2(3); 3(3); 4(4); 5(5); 6(4); 8(2); 9(3); 10; 11; 13; 15(4); 16(6); 17(6); 18(2); 19(2); 20; 21(2); 23(3); 22:3; 4; 5; 6(7); 7(2); 9(3); 12(2); 15(7); 16(2); 17(4); 18; 19(2); 20(2); 21(5); 22(4); 23; 24(5); 25(3); 26(2); 27(2); 29(2); 23:1(2); 2(5); 3(5); 4(2); 5(4); 8(4); 9; 10(3); 11(2); 12; 14(2); 15; 16; 17(2); 18(5); 20(2); 21(2); 23; 25; 24:3(2); 4(3); 6(2); 7(2); 8(2); 9(2); 11(2); 12; 13(3); 14; 15(2); 16; 17(2); 18; 19(6); 20(4); 21(4); 22; 25:1(3); 2(2); 4; 5(4); 6(2); 7(4); 8; 9(3); 10; 11(4); 15(2); 16; 17; 18(2); 19(4); 26:1(2); 2(6); 3(4); 4(4); 5; 6; 7(2); 8; 10(4); 11(3); 12(7); 13(6); 14(3); 15; 16; 17; 18; 19; 27:1(3); 2(4); 3(4); 4; 5; 6(3); 7; 8(2); 9(4); 10(2); 11(2); 12(2); 14(2); 15(6); 16(2); 17(2); 18(4); 19(5); 20(2); 21(2); 22(4); 23(2); 24(2); 25(2); 26(3); 28:1(4); 2(2); 3(2); 4(5); 7; 8(4); 9(3); 10(3); 11(6); 12(4); 13(5); 14(3); 15(2); 16(2); 18(4); 20(2); 21(3); 22(2); 23; 24(3); 25(3); 26(4); 27(4); 28; 33(2); 34; 35(5); 36(2); 37; 38(2); 39(3); 40; 42; 43; 44(2); 45(2); 47(2); 48; 49(4); 50(2); 51(4); 52; 53(4); 54(3); 55(2); 56(4); 57; 58(2); 59; 60; 61(2); 62(3); 63(3); 64(3); 65(2); 67(3); 68(2); 29:1(6); 2(2); 3(2); 4; 5; 6; 8(3); 9; 10(2); 11(3); 12(2); 15; 16(2); 18(2); 19(4); 20(4); 21(5); 22(5); 23(3); 24(2); 25(3); 27(2); 28; 29(3); 30:1(4); 2; 3(3); 4(2); 5(2); 6(3); 7; 8(2); 9(6); 10(4); 13(2); 14; 16(3); 18(2); 20(4); 31:2; 3(2); 4(3); 5; 6(2); 7(3); 8(2); 9(6); 10(4); 11(2); 12(4); 13(3); 14(4); 15(5); 16(5); 18; 19(2); 20; 21(3); 22(2); 23(3); 24; 25(4); 26(4); 27; 28;

29(5); 30(3); 32:1; 2(4); 3(2); 4; 6; 7(2); 8(7); 9(2); 10(2); 12; 13(6); 14(6); 15; 18(2); 19(2); 22(4); 24(3); 25(4); 26; 27(3); 30; 32(2); 33(2); 35(2); 36; 37; 38(2); 42(6); 43; 44(4); 46(2); 47(2); 48; 49(4); 50; 51(5); 52(3); 33:1(3); 2; 3; 4; 5(3); 7; 8; 11(2); 12(3); 13(4); 14(4); 15(4); 16(8); 17(7); 19(5); 20(2); 21(5); 23(4); 26(3); 27(3); 28; 29(3); 34:1(4); 2(3); 3(4); 4(2); 5(5); 6; 8(3); 9(4); 10; 11(3); 12(2); **Josh** 1:1(5); 2(2); 3; 4(8); 5; 6; 7(3); 8; 9; 10(2); 11(4); 12(3); 13(4); 14(2); 15(7); 17; 2:1(3); 2(3); 3(3); 4(3); 5(3); 6(3); 7(5); 8; 9(6); 10(7); 11; 12; 14(3); 15(3); 16(3); 17; 18(2); 19(3); 21(2); 22(4); 23(3); 24(4); 3:1(3); 2(2); 3(6); 4; 5(2); 6(7); 7(2); 8(7); 9(3); 10(8); 11(5); 12; 13(12); 14(6); 15(9); 16(7); 17(8); 4:1(3); 2; 3(5); 4(2); 5(7); 7(9); 8(8); 9(7); 10(7); 11(6); 12(4); 13(2); 14(3); 15; 16(4); 17(2); 18(11); 19(5); 20; 21; 23(5); 24(5); 5:1(12); 2(3); 3(3); 4(5); 5(4); 6(8); 7; 8(2); 9(4); 10(5); 11(5); 12(7); 14(3); 15(3); 6:1; 2(2); 3(2); 4(5); 5(7); 6(6); 7(4); 8(8); 9(7); 10(2); 11(5); 12(4); 13(9); 14(3); 15(6); 16(6); 17(5); 18(3); 19(4); 20(11); 21(3); 22(4); 23(2); 24(6); 25(2); 26(2); 27(2); 7:1(10); 2(3); 3(3); 4(2); 5(5); 6(4); 7(5); 9(4); 10; 11; 12(2); 13(3); 14(7); 15(3); 16(2); 17(5); 18(4); 19; 20; 21(4); 22(2); 23(4); 24(5); 25; 26(4); 8:1(3); 2; 3; 4(3); 5(3); 6(2); 7(3); 8(4); 9(2); 10(4); 11(3); 12(2); 13(8); 14(5); 15(2); 16(2); 17; 18(4); 19(2); 20(6); 21(5); 22(3); 23; 24(8); 25; 26(2); 27(4); 29(6); 30; 31(6); 32(4); 33(10); 34(6); 35(4); 9:1(12); 3; 5; 6(2); 7(2); 9(2); 10(3); 11(2); 12; 13; 14(2); 15(2); 16; 17(2); 18(6); 19(3); 20; 21(3); 23; 24(4); 26(2); 27(4); 10:1; 2; 4; 5(7); 6(5); 7(2); 8; 10(2); 11(5); 12(7); 13(6); 14(3); 15; 17(2); 18(2); 19; 20; 21(3); 22(3); 23(6); 24(4); 25; 26; 27(6); 28(5); 30(6); 32(6); 35(3); 37(4); 39(3); 40(6); 41; 42; 43; 11:1(2); 2(7); 3(10); 4(2); 5; 6; 7(2); 8(4); 9; 10(2); 11(3); 12(5); 13; 14(5); 15(2); 16(6); 17(2); 19(4); 20(2); 21(4); 22(3); 23(3); 12:1(9); 2(7); 3(7); 4(3); 5(4); 6(8); 7(8); 8(12); 9(2); 10(2); 11(2); 12(2); 13(2); 14(2); 15(2); 16(2); 17(2); 18(2); 19(2); 20(2); 21(2); 22(2); 23(4); 24(2); 13:1; 2(4); 3(9); 4(6); 5(4); 6(5); 7(2); 8(6); 9(6); 10(4); 11(2); 12(3); 13(6); 14(3); 15(2); 16(6); 17; 19(2); 20; 21(6); 22(4); 23(7); 24(2); 25(3); 26; 27(8); 28(3); 29(3); 30(2); 31(4); 32(4); 33(2); 14:1(9); 2(4); 3(6); 4(3); 5(3); 6(6); 7(3); 8(3); 9(2); 10(3); 11; 12(5); 13; 14(4); 15(4); 15:1(6); 2(3); 3(3); 4(3); 5(10); 6(4); 7(7); 8(11); 9(7); 10(3); 11(5); 12(5); 13(5); 14(2); 15(2); 17(2); 19(3); 20(3); 21(6); 32; 33; 46; 47(2); 48; 61; 62; 63(5); 16:1(7); 2(2); 3(4); 4; 5(4); 6(5); 7; 8(6); 9(5); 10(3); 17:1(4); 2(10); 3(5); 4(6); 5(3); 6(3); 7(3); 8(3); 9(8); 10(3); 11(4); 12(3); 13(2); 14(2); 15(5); 16(6); 17; 18(2); 18:1(4); 2; 3(3); 4; 5(3); 6(3); 7(8); 8(4); 9(4); 10(3); 11(6); 12(7); 13(5); 14(6); 15(6); 16(12); 17(4); 18; 19(8); 20(4); 21(3); 28(2); 19:1(5); 8(5); 9(8); 10(3); 11(2); 12(2); 13; 14(3); 16(2); 17(2); 22(2); 23(4); 24(3); 26; 27(3); 29(5); 31(3); 32(3); 33(3); 34(5); 35; 39(4); 40(3); 41; 46; 47(6); 48(3); 49(3); 50(5); 51(11); 20:1; 2; 3(2); 4(6); 5(2); 6(5); 7(3); 8(7); 9(6); 21:1(9); 2(2); 3(4); 4(9); 5(6); 6(6); 7(4); 8(4); 9(4); 10(5); 11(3); 12(3); 13(3); 17; 19(3); 20(7); 21(2); 23; 25; 26(4); 27(5); 28; 30; 32(2); 33(2); 34(5); 36; 38(2); 40(5); 41(4); 43(2); 44(2); 45(2); 22:1(3); 2(2); 3(3); 4(6); 5(5); 7(3); 8; 9(10); 10(7); 11(9); 12(3); 13(7); 14(4); 15(4); 16(5); 17(3); 18(3); 19(8); 20(3); 21(5); 22(3); 23(2); 24; 25(4); 27(3); 28(3); 29(4); 30(9); 31(10); 32(8); 33(5); 34(4); 23:1; 3(2); 4(3); 5(2); 6(4); 7; 8; 9; 10; 11; 12; 13(2); 14(4); 15(4); 16(5); 24:1(2); 2(6); 3(3); 4; 6(3); 7(4); 8(4); 9(2); 11(9); 12(3); 13; 14(5); 15(7); 16(2); 17(5); 18(5); 19(2); 20; 21(2); 22(2); 23(2); 24(2); 25; 26(5); 27(3); 28; 29(3); 30(3); 31(6); 32(6); 33(2); **Judg** 1:1(4); 2(2); 3; 4(3); 5(2); 8(4); 9(5); 10(2); 11(2); 13; 15(3); 16(7); 17(3); 19(4); 20; 21(4); 22(2); 23(3); 24(4); 25(6); 26(3); 27(5); 28; 29(2); 30(3); 31(2); 32(4); 33(6); 34(4); 35(3); 36(3); 2:1(3); 2; 4(4); 5(2); 6(3); 7(7); 8(3); 9(3); 10(2); 11(4); 12(5); 13(2); 14(4); 15(4); 16(2); 17(4); 18(7); 19; 20(2); 21; 22(2); 23(2); 3:1(3); 2(2); 3(5); 4(3); 5(7); 7(5); 8(4); 9(5); 10(3); 11(2); 12(6); 13(2); 14; 15(6); 17; 18(3); 19; 21; 22(5); 23(3); 24(3); 25(4); 26; 27(4); 28(4); 30(2); 31(2); 4:1(3); 2(3); 3(3); 4; 5(3); 6(4); 7(2); 9(3); 11(5); 12; 13(2); 14(3); 15(3); 16(5); 17(5); 18; 20(2); 21(2); 22(2); 23(2); 24(2); 5:1; 2(2); 3(2); 4(4); 5(3); 6(5); 8; 9(3); 10; 11(9); 13(5); 14; 15(3); 16(4); 17(2); 18(3); 19(3); 20(2); 21(2); 22(2); 23(7); 24(2); 26(2); 28(4); 30(3); 31(2); 6:1(5); 2(7); 3(2); 4(2); 5; 6(3); 7(3); 8(4); 9(3); 10(3); 11(6); 12(3); 13(5); 14(3); 15(2); 16(2); 19(3); 20(4); 21(11); 22(4); 23; 24(2); 25(5); 26(5); 27(3); 28(7); 29; 30(4); 31; 33(4); 34(4); 37(3); 38(4); 39(3); 40(2); 7:1(7); 2(3); 3(3); 4(5); 5(4); 6(3); 7(4); 8(4); 9(3); 10; 11(4); 12(6); 13(2); 14(3); 15(5); 16(2); 17(2); 18(5); 19(8); 20(7); 21(2); 22(6); 23(2); 24(7); 25(6); 8:1(2); 2(3); 3; 4(2); 5(2); 6(2); 7(3); 8(3); 9; 10(4); 11(4); 12(2); 13(2); 14(2); 15(2); 16(4); 17(3); 18; 19(2); 20; 21; 22(2); 23; 24; 25; 26(5); 27; 28(3); 29; 32(3); 33(3); 34(3); 35(2); 9:1(3); 2(3); 3(2); 4; 5(2); 6(3); 8(2); 9; 10(2); 11; 12(2); 13; 14(2); 15(4); 17; 18(2); 20(2); 23(2); 24(4); 25(3); 26(2); 27(2); 28(4); 30(4); 31(2); 32(2); 33(4); 34; 35(4); 36(5); 37(3); 38; 39; 40(2); 42(3); 43(3); 44(6); 45(4); 46(5); 47(2); 48(3); 49(5); 51(6); 52(3); 54; 55; 56; 57(4); 10:1(3); 4; 6(13); 7(6); 8(6); 9(3); 10(3); 11(6); 12; 14; 15(2); 16(3); 17(2); 18(6); 11:1(2); 2; 3; 4; 5(3); 6; 7; 8(3); 9(3); 10(2); 11(3); 12(2); 13(6); 14(2); 15(3); 16(2); 17(3); 18(10); 19; 21(4); 22(6); 23(2); 24; 25; 26(3); 27(4); 28(3); 29(3); 30(2); 31(3); 32(2); 33(2); 35; 36(3); 37; 38; 39; 40(3); 12:1(2); 2; 3(2); 4(4); 5(5); 6(2); 7(2); 11; 12(2); 13(2); 15(5); 13:1(6); 2(2); 3(3); 5(4); 6(3); 7(3); 8(3); 9(4); 10(3); 11(2); 12; 13(3); 14; 15(2); 16(5); 17(2); 18(2); 19(4); 20(7); 21(4); 23; 24(3); 25(2); 14:1(2); 2(2); 3(2); 4(3); 5; 6(3); 7; 8(4); 9(3); 10; 12(2); 14(3); 15(2); 16; 17(4); 18(4); 19(4); 15:1; 3; 4; 5(7); 6(4); 8(2); 9; 10; 11(3); 12(2); 13; 14(4); 16(2); 17; 18(4); 19; 20(2); 16:2(5); 3(6); 4; 5(2); 8(2); 9(4); 12(2); 13(3); 14(6); 18(5); 19; 20(2); 21(2); 22; 23(2); 24(3); 25(2); 26(4); 27(4); 28(2); 29(3); 30(5); 31; 17:1; 2(3); 3(3); 4(3); 5; 7; 8(4); 10; 11(3); 12(3); 13; 18:1(3); 2(5); 3(3); 5; 6(3); 7(6); 8; 9(2); 10; 11(2); 13(2); 14(2); 15(3); 16(4); 17(10); 18(5); 19; 20(5); 21(3); 22(4); 23; 24; 25(2); 26; 27(5); 28(2); 29(5); 30(8); 31(2); 19:1; 2; 3(2); 4; 5(3); 6(3); 7; 8(3); 9(5); 10(2); 11(3); 12; 13; 14; 15(3); 16(4); 17(4); 18(3); 19; 20(3); 21; 22(7); 23(3); 24; 25(3); 26(4); 27(6); 28(3); 29; 30(3); 20:1(4); 2(6);

3(3); 4(4); 5(2); 6(2); 8; 9; 10(3); 11(2); 12(2); 13(6); 14(2); 15(3); 17(2); 18(4); 19(2); 20(2); 21(3); 22(5); 23(5); 24(3); 25(4); 26(5); 27(4); 28(4); 30(4); 31(8); 32(4); 33(2); 34(2); 35(3); 36(4); 37(5); 38(4); 39(3); 40(4); 41(2); 42(5); 43(3); 45(3); 46; 47(3); 48(5); 21:1; 2(2); 4(2); 5(5); 6; 7; 8(4); 9(2); 10(5); 11; 12(3); 13(3); 14(2); 15(3); 16(3); 17; 18(2); 19(3); 20(2); 21(4); 22(2); 23(2); 24; **Ruth** 1:1(4); 2(5); 4(5); 5; 6(3); 7(3); 8(2); 9(2); 13(2); 17; 19(3); 20; 21(3); 22(3); 2:1; 2(2); 3(5); 4(3); 5; 6(4); 7(3); 9(4); 10; 11(2); 12(2); 14(3); 15; 16; 17; 18; 19(2); 20(3); 21; 23(2); 3:2; 3(2); 4; 6; 7(2); 8; 10(3); 11; 13(5); 14(2); 15(2); 16; 18(3); 4:1(2); 2(2); 3(3); 4(3); 5(8); 6; 7(2); 8; 9(3); 10(7); 11(7); 12(3); 13; 14(2); 16; 17(3); 18; **1 Sam** 1:1(5); 2(3); 3(4); 4; 5; 6; 7(2); 9(5); 10; 11(3); 12; 15; 16; 17; 18; 19(3); 20(2); 21(3); 22(2); 23(2); 24(3); 25; 26(2); 27; 28(3); 2:1(2); 2; 3(2); 4(2); 5(2); 6(2); 7; 8(9); 9(2); 10(6); 11(3); 12(2); 13(4); 14(4); 15(4); 16(2); 17(5); 18; 19; 20(3); 21(3); 22(3); 23; 24; 25(3); 26(2); 27(2); 28(4); 29(2); 30(3); 31(2); 32; 33(2); 36; 3:1(4); 3(4); 4; 6; 7(3); 8(4); 10; 11; 13; 14(2); 15(4); 17(3); 18; 19(2); 20; 21(4); 4:1(3); 2(4); 3(9); 4(8); 5(5); 6(9); 7(2); 8(5); 9; 10; 11(2); 12(2); 13(5); 14(4); 16(3); 17(4); 18(5); 19(2); 20(2); 21(3); 22(2); 5:1(2); 2(3); 3(5); 4(7); 5(2); 6(3); 7(3); 8(8); 9(5); 10(5); 11(6); 12(4); 6:1(4); 2(5); 3(2); 4(5); 5(2); 6(2); 7(2); 8(4); 9; 10(2); 11(6); 12(8); 13(3); 14(6); 15(9); 16(3); 17(3); 18(9); 19(7); 20; 21(4); 7:1(7); 2(3); 3(7); 4(4); 5; 6(3); 7(6); 8(4); 9(3); 10(4); 11(2); 12; 13(6); 14(5); 15; 17; 8:2(2); 4; 5; 6(2); 7(3); 8(2); 9(2); 10(3); 11(2); 14; 18; 19(2); 20; 21(4); 22(2); 9:1(4); 2(2); 3(3); 4(5); 5(2); 6; 7(3); 8(2); 9; 10(2); 11(3); 12(2); 13(4); 14(3); 15(2); 16(3); 17(2); 18(2); 19(2); 20; 21(5); 22(2); 23(2); 24(3); 25(4); 26(4); 27(4); 10:1; 2(3); 3; 5(4); 6(2); 7; 10(2); 11(4); 12; 13; 14; 16(3); 17(2); 18(5); 19; 20(2); 21(3); 22(4); 23(2); 24(5); 25(4); 11:1(2); 2; 3(2); 4(5); 5(5); 6; 7(5); 8(2); 9(6); 10; 11(7); 12(2); 13; 14(2); 15(4); 12:2; 3; 5; 6(3); 7(3); 8(2); 9(7); 10(4); 11(2); 12(2); 13(2); 14(5); 15(6); 16; 17(4); 18(4); 19(3); 20(3); 22(2); 23(3); 24; 13:2(3); 3(6); 4(3); 5(4); 6(3); 7(4); 8(2); 9; 10; 11(3); 12(2); 13(3); 14(3); 15; 16(2); 17(4); 18(5); 19(3); 20(2); 21(7); 22(3); 23(3); 14:1(4); 2(2); 3(5); 4(6); 5(2); 6(4); 10; 11(5); 12(4); 15(6); 16(2); 17(3); 18(3); 19(5); 20(2); 21(5); 22(4); 23(2); 24(4); 25(3); 26(5); 27(4); 28(4); 29; 30(3); 31(2); 32(5); 33(3); 34(4); 35(3); 36(3); 37(2); 38; 39(2); 40(2); 41(2); 43(2); 45(4); 46(2); 47(3); 48(2); 49(6); 50(5); 51(3); 52(2); 15:1(4); 2(2); 4; 5; 6(5); 7(2); 8(4); 9(6); 10(2); 11; 12; 13(3); 14(3); 15(7); 16; 17(2); 18(3); 19(5); 20(5); 21(5); 22(4); 23(3); 24(3); 25; 26(3); 27; 28(2); 29; 30(2); 31; 32(2); 33; 35(2); 16:1(2); 2(2); 3(2); 4(3); 5(3); 6; 7(6); 8; 9; 10; 11(3); 12(2); 13(4); 14(3); 16(2); 18(3); 19; 23(2); 17:1; 2(3); 3(2); 4(2); 5(2); 7; 8(2); 10(2); 11; 12(3); 13(6); 14(2); 16; 17; 18; 19(3); 20(7); 21; 22(3); 23(5); 24(2); 25(3); 26(5); 27(2); 28(4); 30(2); 31; 34; 35; 36(2); 37(7); 40(2); 41(3); 42; 43(2); 44(5); 45(5); 46(9); 47(3); 48(3); 49(3); 50(3); 51(2); 52(8); 53(2); 54(2); 55(3); 56; 57(4); 58(2); 18:1(2); 4; 5(4); 6(4); 7; 8(2); 10(3); 11(2); 12; 13; 14; 17(3); 18; 19(2); 20; 21(2); 22(2); 23; 24; 25(5); 26(2); 27(3); 28; 30(3); 19:3; 4; 5(2); 6(2); 8; 9(2); 10(4); 11; 13; 15(2); 16(3); 20(3); 21; 22; 23; 24; 20:3; 5(4); 6; 8; 11(2); 12(2); 13(2); 14(2); 15(4); 16(3); 18; 19(4); 20; 21(3); 22(3); 23(2); 24(4); 25(2); 27(4); 29(2); 30(2); 31(2); 34(3); 35(3); 36(2); 37(5); 38(2); 39(2); 40; 41(3); 42(4); 21:1; 2(3); 4(2); 5(5); 6(4); 7(4); 8; 9(5); 10; 11(3); 12; 13(2); 14; 15; 22:1; 3; 4(3); 5(4); 6; 7; 8; 9(4); 10(3); 11(5); 13; 14(2); 15(2); 16; 17(8); 18(4); 19(6); 20(2); 21; 22(3); 23:1(2); 2(3); 3(2); 4(3); 5(2); 6; 8; 9(2); 10; 11(2); 12(3); 13; 14(3); 15; 16; 17; 18(3); 19(4); 20(2); 21; 22; 23(3); 24(3); 25(3); 26(3); 27(2); 28(2); 24:1(2); 2(2); 3(4); 4(3); 6(4); 7; 8(3); 9; 10(3); 11(2); 12(2); 13(3); 14; 15; 18; 19; 20; 21; 22; 25:1(2); 2; 3(5); 4; 5; 7; 9; 10; 13; 14(2); 15(2); 16(2); 20(2); 21; 22; 23(2); 24; 25; 26(2); 27; 28(4); 29(6); 30(2); 31; 32; 34; 36; 37(2); 38; 39(5); 40; 41(3); 42; 44; 26:1(2); 2(2); 3(4); 5(6); 6(3); 7(4); 8(2); 9; 10(2); 11(4); 12(3); 13(2); 14(3); 15(3); 16(4); 19(7); 20(5); 21; 22(2); 23(3); 24(2); 27:1(3); 2(2); 3(2); 5(2); 6; 7(3); 8(6); 9(6); 10(5); 11(3); 28:1; 3(3); 4; 5(2); 6(3); 8(2); 9(4); 10(2); 11; 12(2); 13(3); 14; 15; 16; 17(3); 18(3); 19(7); 20(2); 21(2); 22; 23(3); 24(2); 29:1(2); 2(3); 3(5); 4(7); 6(4); 7(2); 8(2); 9(3); 10(2); 11(4); 30:1(3); 2; 3; 4; 5(3); 6(4); 7(3); 8; 9(2); 10; 11; 14(4); 15; 16(5); 17(2); 18; 20; 21(4); 22(2); 23(2); 24(2); 26(5); 27; 29(4); 31; 31:1(3); 2(2); 3(3); 7(8); 8(3); 9(4); 10(3); 11(2); 12(4); 13; **2 Sam** 1:1(3); 2(2); 3; 4(4); 5; 6(2); 10(2); 11; 12(4); 13(2); 14; 15; 16; 18(4); 19(2); 20(5); 21(3); 22(6); 25(3); 26; 27(2); 2:1(3); 2(3); 3(2); 4(4); 5(2); 6; 7; 8(2); 9; 10; 11(2); 12(3); 13(7); 14; 15(2); 16(2); 17(2); 18; 19(2); 21; 22; 23(6); 24(4); 25; 26(3); 27; 28; 29(2); 30; 31; 3:1(3); 2; 3(5); 4(4); 5; 6(3); 7; 8(3); 9; 10(3); 12; 14; 15; 17; 18(5); 19(3); 20; 21; 22; 23(3); 24; 25; 26; 27(3); 28(3); 29(3); 30; 31(2); 32(3); 33; 34; 35(2); 36(3); 37(3); 38; 39(3); 4:2(6); 3; 4; 5(5); 6(3); 7(2); 8(6); 9(3); 10; 11; 12(3); 5:1; 2(2); 3(3); 6(6); 7(2); 8(7); 9(3); 10; 12(2); 14; 17(3); 18(2); 19(4); 20(2); 22(2); 23(2); 24(6); 25(2); 6:1; 2(5); 3(5); 4(4); 5(2); 6(2); 7(3); 8(3); 9(3); 10(5); 11(5); 12(6); 13(2); 14; 15(5); 16(4); 17(5); 18(3); 19(5); 20(5); 21(4); 22; 23(2); 7:1(2); 2(3); 3(2); 4(2); 5; 6(2); 7(2); 8(3); 9(3); 10; 11(2); 13; 14(3); 18; 19; 23(3); 25; 26(3); 29(2); 8:1(3); 2(2); 3(2); 4; 5(2); 6(2); 7(2); 9; 11(3); 12(4); 13; 14(2); 16(3); 17(4); 18(3); 9:1; 2(2); 3(4); 4(4); 5(2); 6(2); 7; 9; 10(2); 11(4); 12; 13; 10:1(2); 2(4); 3(3); 4; 5(2); 6(5); 7(2); 8(5); 9(2); 10(4); 11(2); 12(2); 13(3); 14(4); 15; 16(3); 17(2); 18(3); 19(3); 11:1(4); 2(4); 3(4); 5; 6; 7(2); 8(2); 9(3); 11(3); 12; 13; 14(2); 15(3); 16; 17(5); 18(2); 19(4); 20(3); 21(4); 22; 23(5); 24(4); 25(3); 26; 27(2); 12:1(2); 2; 3; 4(4); 5(3); 6; 7(3); 8; 9(6); 10(3); 11(2); 12; 13(2); 14(3); 15(2); 16(2); 17(2); 18(6); 19(2); 20(3); 21(2); 22(3); 24; 25(3); 26(2); 27; 28(4); 29; 30(2); 31(5); 13:1(2); 3; 4; 5; 6(2); 8; 9; 10(4); 13(2); 15(2); 16; 17; 18(2); 23; 24(2); 25; 26; 27; 29(2); 30(2); 31(2); 32(5); 33(3); 34(3); 35(2); 36(2); 37; 14:1(2); 2; 3(2); 4(3); 5; 6(4); 7(4); 8(2); 9(4); 10; 11(5); 12(2); 13(4); 14; 15(5); 16(4); 17(5); 18(4); 19(8); 20(3); 21(2); 22(4); 24(2); 25(2); 26(4); 28; 29(2); 30; 32(2); 33(5); 15:2(3); 3; 4; 6(3); 7(3); 8(2); 9;

10(3); 12(3); 13(2); 14(3); 15(3); 16(3); 17(3); 18(4); 19(3); 21(4); 22(2); 23(7); 24(6); 25(5); 27(4); 28(2); 29; 30(3); 31(2); 32(3); 34(2); 35(3); 37; 16:1(3); 2(7); 3(4); 4; 5(3); 6(3); 8(6); 9(3); 10(2); 11; 12(2); 13(2); 14(2); 15(2); 16(3); 18(2); 19; 21(2); 22(3); 23(3); 17:2(2); 3(3); 4(2); 5; 7; 8(2); 9(2); 10; 11(2); 12(3); 13; 14(8); 15(2); 16(4); 17; 19(3); 20(4); 21(2); 22(3); 24(2); 25(3); 26; 27(4); 29(4); 18:1; 2(8); 3(2); 4(4); 5(5); 6(4); 7(2); 8(5); 9(5); 11(2); 12(4); 13; 14(2); 16(3); 17; 18(2); 19(4); 20(3); 21(3); 22(2); 23(2); 24(5); 25(3); 26(4); 27(6); 28(6); 29(3); 30; 31(4); 32(6); 33(3); 19:1; 2(4); 3(2); 4(2); 5(5); 7(2); 8(7); 9(7); 10; 11(6); 12(2); 13; 14(4); 15(5); 16(2); 17(4); 18(4); 19(4); 20(3); 21(2); 23(2); 24(5); 25(2); 26; 27(3); 28(2); 29(2); 30(2); 31(4); 32; 33; 34(2); 35(3); 36(3); 37(2); 38; 39(4); 40(4); 41(6); 42(4); 43(8); 20:1(2); 2(3); 3(4); 4(2); 5(2); 6; 7(4); 8; 9; 10(4); 12(6); 13(3); 14(2); 15(4); 16; 17(2); 19(3); 21(6); 22(6); 23(4); 24; 25; 26; 21:1(4); 2(8); 3(3); 4; 5(3); 6(3); 7(5); 8(7); 9(7); 10(8); 11(2); 12(6); 13(3); 14(6); 15(2); 16(3); 17(4); 18(4); 19(6); 20; 21; 22(3); 22:1(6); 2; 3(2); 4; 5(2); 6(2); 7; 8(2); 10; 11(2); 12; 13; 14(2); 16(8); 19(2); 21(2); 22(2); 25; 26; 27(2); 28(2); 29; 31(2); 32; 34; 36; 40; 41; 42; 43(3); 44(3); 45; 46; 47(2); 48; 49; 50; 51; 23:1(6); 2(2); 3(3); 4(5); 6; 7(2); 8(5); 9(5); 10(4); 11(5); 12(4); 13(4); 14(3); 15(3); 16(6); 17(3); 18(2); 19(2); 20(3); 21(3); 22; 23(2); 24(3); 25(2); 26(3); 27(2); 28(2); 29(4); 30; 31(2); 32(2); 33(3); 34(5); 35(2); 36(2); 37(3); 38(2); 39; 24:1(2); 2(7); 3(6); 4(8); 5(5); 6; 7(4); 8(2); 9(6); 10(3); 11(4); 12; 14(3); 15(4); 16(9); 17(3); 18(3); 19(2); 20(3); 21(5); 22(3); 23(3); 24(4); 25(5); **1 Ki** 1:2(3); 3(3); 4(3); 5; 7(2); 8(4); 9(4); 10(2); 11(2); 12; 14; 15(5); 16(2); 17; 18; 19(5); 20(3); 21; 22(2); 23(5); 25(4); 26(2); 27(3); 28(2); 29(2); 30; 31(2); 32(4); 33(2); 34(3); 36(4); 37(3); 38(5); 39(4); 40(4); 41(4); 42(2); 44(7); 45(4); 46(2); 47(4); 48(2); 49; 50(2); 51(3); 52; 53; 2:1; 2(2); 3(3); 4(2); 5(7); 6; 7(2); 8(5); 9; 10; 11; 12; 13(2); 15(3); 17; 18; 19(2); 20; 21; 22(4); 23; 24(2); 25(2); 26(4); 27(4); 28(4); 29(4); 30(4); 31(3); 32(8); 33(3); 34(2); 35(6); 36; 37(2); 38(3); 39(2); 42(4); 43(3); 44(3); 45(2); 46(4); 3:1(4); 2(4); 3(3); 4(2); 5; 8; 10(2); 11; 13; 15(3); 16; 17(2); 18(4); 19; 20(2); 21(2); 22(7); 23(6); 24(2); 25(3); 26(4); 27(3); 28(4); 4:2(2); 3(3); 4(3); 5(4); 6(3); 7(2); 8; 10; 11(2); 12(2); 13(3); 14; 15; 16; 17; 18; 19(6); 20(2); 21(5); 23; 24(4); 25; 28(2); 29(2); 30(4); 31(3); 33(3); 34(3); 5:3(5); 4; 5(4); 6; 7(2); 8(2); 9(2); 12(2); 13; 14; 15; 16(3); 17(3); 18(2); 6:1(8); 2(2); 3(9); 4; 5(6); 6(8); 7(3); 8(7); 9(2); 10(2); 11(2); 13; 14; 15(8); 16(5); 17; 18(2); 19(5); 20(2); 21(4); 22(4); 23; 24(6); 25(2); 26(2); 27(11); 28; 29(3); 30(3); 31(4); 32(3); 33(3); 34(2); 35; 36; 37(5); 38(4); 7:2(3); 3; 5; 6; 7(2); 8(2); 9(4); 10; 12(6); 14(2); 15; 16(5); 17(3); 18(4); 19(4); 20(5); 21(7); 22(5); 23(2); 24(3); 25(5); 26; 27; 28(3); 29(4); 30; 31(5); 32(6); 33(3); 34(2); 35(6); 36; 37(2); 38; 39(8); 40(6); 41(6); 42(3); 43(2); 44; 45(5); 46(2); 47(3); 48(6); 49(7); 50(12); 51(10); 8:1(9); 2(4); 3(3); 4(7); 5(2); 6(9); 7(5); 8(5); 9(5); 10(5); 11(6); 12(2); 14(3); 15; 16; 17(3); 18; 19(2); 20(6); 21(4); 22(4); 25; 27(2); 28(3); 29(2); 30; 32(2); 34(2); 35; 36(2); 37(2); 38; 39(2); 40(2); 43(2); 44(3); 46(3); 47(2); 48(3); 51; 52(2); 53(2); 54(3); 55; 56; 57; 59(4); 60(3); 61; 62(2); 63(5); 64(14); 65(3); 66(5); 9:1(3); 2(2); 3; 5(2); 7; 8; 9(3); 10(5); 11(2); 12; 13; 14; 15(6); 16(2); 18(2); 19(2); 20(3); 21(2); 22; 23(3); 24(2); 25(5); 26(3); 27(3); 10:1(4); 3; 4(3); 5(5); 6; 7(3); 9(3); 10(2); 11; 12(6); 13(2); 14; 15(5); 17(3); 18; 19(7); 20; 21(4); 22(3); 23(2); 24(2); 26(2); 27(3); 28(2); 29(3); 11:1(2); 2(3); 4(2); 5(4); 6(3); 7(4); 9(2); 10; 11(2); 12(2); 13(3); 14(3); 15(3); 19(3); 20(2); 21(2); 23; 25(2); 26(2); 27(4); 28(5); 29(5); 30; 31(4); 32(4); 33(6); 34(3); 35; 36; 39; 40; 41(4); 42; 43; 12:2(2); 3; 4; 5; 6; 8(3); 9; 10; 12(4); 13(4); 14(2); 15(7); 16(4); 17(2); 18; 19; 20(3); 21(5); 22(2); 23(4); 24(6); 25; 26(2); 27(3); 28(3); 29; 30(2); 31(2); 32(7); 33(6); 13:1(3); 2(7); 3(5); 4(4); 5(7); 6(7); 7(2); 8(2); 9(3); 10; 11(4); 12; 13(2); 14(2); 17(3); 18(2); 20(4); 21(6); 22(3); 23(2); 24(5); 25(6); 26(9); 27; 28(7); 29(6); 30; 31(2); 32(7); 33(3); 34(4); 14:1; 2(2); 3; 4; 5(2); 6(2); 7(2); 8(2); 10(3); 11(6); 12(2); 13(4); 14(3); 15(4); 16; 17(3); 18(3); 19(5); 20; 21(4); 22(2); 24(5); 25; 26(6); 27(5); 28(5); 29(5); 31; 15:1(2); 2; 3(3); 4; 5(5); 6; 7(5); 8; 9; 10; 11(2); 12(3); 13; 14(2); 15(4); 18(9); 20(3); 22; 23(7); 24; 25(2); 26(3); 27(3); 28; 29(4); 30(2); 31(5); 33(2); 34(3); 16:1(3); 2(2); 3(4); 4(5); 5(5); 7(9); 8(2); 9; 10; 11; 12(4); 13(3); 14(5); 15(3); 16(5); 18(4); 19(4); 20(6); 21(3); 22(3); 23; 24(6); 25(2); 26(3); 27(6); 29(3); 30(3); 31(4); 32; 33(2); 34(3); 17:1(3); 2(2); 3(2); 4(2); 5(4); 6(4); 7(2); 8(2); 10(2); 12; 14(6); 15; 16(4); 17(3); 19; 20(2); 21(2); 22(4); 23(3); 24(4); 18:1(4); 3; 4(2); 5(4); 6; 9; 10(2); 12(3); 13(3); 15; 18(3); 19(2); 20(2); 21(3); 22(2); 23(3); 24(5); 25(2); 26(3); 28; 29(3); 30(4); 31(5); 32(4); 33(5); 35(3); 36(4); 37; 38(8); 39(3); 40(2); 41; 42(2); 43; 44(3); 45(2); 46(3); 19:1(2); 2(2); 4; 7(4); 8(2); 9(3); 10(3); 11(11); 12(4); 13(2); 14(3); 15(2); 16(2); 17(2); 19(2); 20; 21(2); 20:1; 2; 4; 5; 6; 7(3); 8(2); 9(4); 10(2); 11(3); 12(3); 13(2); 14(4); 15(4); 16(2); 17(2); 19(3); 20(3); 21(3); 22(5); 23(4); 24; 25(2); 26(3); 27(4); 28(7); 29(4); 30(4); 31(3); 32; 33(2); 34; 35(5); 36(2); 37; 38(3); 39(4); 40; 41(3); 42; 43; 21:1(2); 3(2); 4(3); 6; 7(2); 8(4); 9(2); 10; 11(3); 12; 13(5); 15(2); 16(2); 17(3); 18; 19(4); 20(2); 22(5); 23(3); 24(5); 25(2); 26(3); 28(3); 29(3); 22:2(3); 3(3); 4; 5(3); 6(5); 7; 8(4); 9(2); 10(5); 11(3); 12(3); 13(5); 14(2); 15(5); 16(4); 17(2); 18; 19(4); 20; 21; 22(3); 23(3); 24(4); 26(4); 27; 28; 29(2); 30(2); 31(3); 32(3); 33(3); 34(4); 35(7); 36(2); 37(2); 38(5); 39(7); 41(2); 42; 43(6); 44; 45(6); 46(4); 47; 48; 49(2); 50; 51(2); 52(6); 53; **2 Ki** 1:1; 2(2); 3(6); 4(2); 5; 6(4); 8; 9(3); 10; 11; 12; 13(2); 14; 15(3); 16(3); 17(4); 18(5); 2:1; 2(2); 3(3); 4(2); 5(3); 6(4); 7(4); 8(2); 11; 12; 13(3); 14(4); 15(4); 16(2); 19(5); 21(4); 22(2); 23(2); 24(4); 3:1(2); 2(3); 3(2); 4(2); 5(2); 7; 8; 9(5); 10(3); 11(6); 12(4); 13(6); 14(2); 15(3); 16; 17; 18(3); 20(3); 21(3); 22(6); 23(2); 24(3); 25(5); 26(3); 27; 4:1(5); 2(2); 4(2); 5(2); 6(2); 7(3); 10; 11; 13(3); 15; 17(2); 18(2); 21(3); 22(3); 23(2); 24; 25(3); 26; 27(5); 29(2); 30(3); 31(4); 32(2); 33(3); 34(4); 35(3); 37; 38(6); 39(2); 40(3); 41(3); 42(3); 43(2); 44(2); 5:1(4); 2(2); 3; 4(2); 5(2); 6(2); 7(2); 8(3); 9; 10; 11(4); 12(4); 13; 14(4);

15(2); 16; 17; 18(5); 20(3); 21; 22(3); 24(3); 26; 27; 6:1(3); 2; 4; 5(2); 6(3); 8; 9(3); 10(3); 11(3); 12(3); 14; 15(3); 17(4); 18(3); 19(3); 20(2); 21; 23(2); 26(2); 27(3); 28; 29; 30(5); 31(2); 32(8); 33(4); 7:1(4); 2(3); 3(2); 4(5); 5(4); 6(11); 7; 8(2); 9; 10(4); 11(2); 12(7); 13(4); 14(3); 15(5); 16(5); 17(7); 18(3); 19(2); 20(2); 8:1(3); 2(5); 3(5); 4(4); 5(5); 6(7); 7; 8(3); 10; 11; 12(3); 13; 15; 16(3); 18(6); 19(2); 21(4); 23(5); 24; 25(3); 26; 27(7); 28(2); 29(4); 9:1(3); 2(2); 3(3); 4(3); 5(2); 6(5); 7(7); 8(2); 9(5); 10(3); 11(2); 12; 13(2); 14(2); 15(3); 17(2); 18(4); 19; 20(4); 21(2); 22; 24; 25(4); 26(7); 27(3); 28(2); 29(2); 31; 32; 33(2); 35(3); 36(5); 37(4); 10:1(2); 3; 5(4); 6(5); 7(2); 8(4); 9(2); 10(6); 11; 12(2); 13(6); 14; 15(2); 16; 17(2); 18; 19(3); 21(4); 22(3); 23(5); 24(4); 25(9); 26(2); 27(2); 29(3); 30(4); 31(3); 32(2); 33(3); 34(5); 36; 11:1(2); 2(4); 3(3); 4(9); 5(2); 6(5); 7(6); 8(2); 9(6); 10(5); 11(8); 12(4); 13(6); 14(6); 15(9); 16(2); 17(6); 18(8); 19(13); 20(5); 12:1; 2(4); 3(3); 4(8); 5(3); 6(4); 7(6); 8(4); 9(10); 10(6); 11(9); 12(4); 13(5); 14(3); 15(2); 16(7); 18(6); 19(5); 20(2); 21(3); 13:1(3); 2(4); 3(5); 4(4); 5(4); 6(3); 7(3); 8(5); 10(2); 11(4); 12(5); 13; 14(3); 16(3); 17(5); 18(3); 19; 20(4); 21(4); 22; 23; 25(6); 14:1(3); 3(2); 4(3); 5(2); 6(5); 7; 8(2); 9(3); 13(5); 14(6); 15(5); 16; 17(3); 18(5); 20; 21; 22; 23(3); 24(4); 25(8); 26(2); 27(4); 28(5); 29; 15:1(2); 3(2); 4(3); 5(7); 6(5); 7; 8(2); 9(4); 10(2); 11(5); 12(4); 13(2); 14(2); 15(6); 16; 17(2); 18(4); 19(2); 20(5); 21(5); 23(2); 24(4); 25(3); 26(5); 27(2); 28(4); 29(2); 30(4); 31(5); 32(3); 33; 34(2); 35(6); 36(5); 37(2); 38; 16:1(3); 2(2); 3(7); 4(2); 5; 6(2); 7(4); 8(6); 9(2); 10(3); 11(2); 12(5); 13(2); 14(9); 15(13); 16; 17(5); 18(6); 19(5); 20; 17:1(2); 2(3); 4(3); 5(2); 6(6); 7(4); 8(5); 9(2); 11(4); 12; 13(3); 14(2); 15(2); 16(3); 17(3); 18(2); 19(3); 20(3); 21(3); 22(2); 23(2); 24(3); 25(3); 26(9); 27(5); 28(2); 29(4); 30(3); 31(3); 32(4); 33(3); 34(5); 35; 36(2); 37(4); 38; 39(2); 41; 18:1(3); 2; 3(2); 4(5); 5(2); 6(2); 7(2); 8; 9(3); 10(3); 11(5); 12(4); 13(2); 14(2); 15(5); 16(6); 17(8); 18(6); 19(3); 21; 22; 23; 24; 25(2); 26(5); 27(3); 28(4); 29; 30(4); 31(2); 32; 33(4); 34(2); 35(3); 36(2); 37(7); 19:1(2); 2(6); 3; 4(8); 5; 6(4); 7; 8(2); 9; 10(2); 11; 12(3); 13(4); 14(6); 15(5); 16(2); 17(2); 18(2); 19(3); 20(2); 21(5); 22; 23(6); 24(2); 26(5); 28; 29(4); 30(2); 31(2); 32(2); 33(3); 35(6); 37(3); 20:1(3); 2(2); 4(3); 5(6); 6(3); 7; 8(5); 9(5); 10(2); 11(4); 12; 13(3); 14; 16(2); 17(2); 18(2); 19(2); 20(6); 21:2(6); 3(2); 4(3); 5(4); 6(3); 7(3); 8(3); 9(3); 10(2); 11; 12; 13(3); 14(2); 15; 16(2); 17(6); 18(2); 19; 20(2); 21(2); 22(3); 23(2); 24(4); 25(5); 26; 22:1; 2(5); 3(7); 4(6); 5(10); 6; 7; 8(7); 9(9); 10(4); 11(4); 12(6); 13(6); 14(7); 15(2); 16(4); 17; 18(4); 19(2); 20(2); 23:1(2); 2(13); 3(6); 4(10); 5(9); 6(7); 7(6); 8(12); 9(4); 10(3); 11(11); 12(10); 13(10); 14(3); 15(6); 16(8); 17(5); 18(2); 19(6); 20(3); 21(5); 22(5); 23(2); 24(9); 25(2); 26(3); 27(2); 28(5); 29(3); 30(3); 31; 32(2); 33(2); 34; 35(6); 36; 37(2); 24:2(5); 3(3); 4(2); 5(5); 7(5); 8; 9(2); 10(2); 11; 12(3); 13(9); 14(5); 15(4); 16(2); 17; 18; 19(2); 20(3); 25:1(4); 2(2); 3(6); 4(8); 5(4); 6(2); 7(2); 8(7); 9(6); 10(5); 11(9); 12(4); 13(8); 14(6); 15(5); 16(5); 17(8); 18(5); 19(11); 20(2); 21(2); 22(4); 23(8); 24(4); 25(6); 26(4); 27(6); 28; 29(2); 30(2); **1 Chr** 1:5; 6; 7; 8; 9(2); 10; 12(2); 14(3); 15(3); 16(3); 17; 19(2); 23; 28; 29; 31; 32(2); 33(2); 34; 35; 36; 37; 38; 39; 40(2); 41(2); 42(2); 43(5); 44; 45(2); 46(3); 49; 50(3); 51; 54; 2:1; 3(6); 4; 5; 6; 7(3); 8; 9; 10; 13(2); 14(2); 15(2); 16; 17(2); 18; 21(2); 22; 23(3); 24; 25(3); 26; 27(2); 28(2); 29(2); 30; 31(2); 32(2); 33(2); 42(5); 43; 44; 45(2); 47; 49(4); 50(4); 51(2); 52(2); 53(7); 54(4); 55(8); 3:1(5); 2(5); 3(2); 5; 9(3); 15(5); 16; 17; 19(2); 21(5); 22(2); 23; 24; 4:1; 2(3); 3(3); 4(5); 5; 6; 7; 8(2); 10; 11(2); 12(2); 13(2); 14; 15(3); 16; 17(2); 18(5); 19(5); 20(2); 21(8); 22(2); 23(2); 24; 26; 27; 31; 33; 34; 35(3); 37(5); 39(3); 40; 41(2); 42(2); 43(2); 5:1(7); 2; 3(2); 4; 6; 7(2); 8(3); 9(4); 10(3); 11(2); 12(2); 14(8); 15(2); 16(2); 17(2); 18(4); 19; 20(2); 22(2); 23(3); 24; 25(5); 26(6); 6:1; 2; 3(2); 10; 15(2); 16; 17(2); 18; 19(3); 22; 25; 26; 28(3); 29; 31(5); 32(4); 33(6); 34(4); 35(4); 36(4); 37(4); 38(4); 39(2); 40(3); 41(3); 42(3); 43(3); 44(5); 45(3); 46(3); 47(4); 48(3); 49(5); 50; 54(3); 55; 56(3); 57(2); 60; 61(5); 62(5); 63(4); 64(2); 65(6); 66(3); 67(2); 70(4); 71(3); 72; 74; 76; 77(3); 78(6); 80; 7:1; 2(3); 3(2); 5; 6; 7; 8(2); 10(2); 12(2); 13(2); 14(3); 15(2); 16(2); 17(4); 19; 20; 21; 28(2); 29(4); 30; 31(2); 33(2); 34; 35; 36; 38; 39; 40(2); 8:1(2); 2(2); 3; 6(4); 8; 12; 13(2); 16; 18; 21; 25; 27; 28; 29; 34; 35; 38; 39(3); 40; 9:1(2); 2(2); 3(3); 4(6); 5(2); 6; 7(4); 8(6); 10; 11(7); 12(8); 13(3); 14(5); 15(3); 16(7); 17(2); 18(4); 19(10); 20(3); 21(3); 22; 23(5); 24(3); 26(2); 27(2); 28; 29(8); 30(4); 31(6); 32(3); 33(4); 34(2); 35; 40; 41; 44; 10:1(3); 2(2); 3(3); 7(3); 8(3); 9(5); 10(2); 11; 12(4); 13(3); 14(3); 11:2(2); 3(5); 4(3); 5(3); 6(2); 7(2); 8(5); 9; 10(4); 11(4); 12(3); 13(3); 14(3); 15(6); 16(3); 17(2); 18(6); 19(3); 20; 21(3); 22(3); 23(3); 24; 25(2); 26(3); 27(2); 28(3); 29(2); 30(3); 31(3); 32(2); 33(2); 34(4); 35(3); 36(2); 37(2); 38(2); 39(4); 40(2); 41(2); 42(3); 43(2); 44(3); 45(2); 46(3); 47; 12:1(4); 2(3); 3(5); 4(4); 5; 6; 7; 8(4); 9(3); 10(2); 11(2); 12(2); 13(2); 14(4); 15(6); 16(2); 17; 18(3); 19(3); 20; 21(2); 22; 23(5); 24; 25; 26; 27(2); 29(3); 30; 31; 32(2); 35; 37(5); 38; 13:1; 2(4); 3(2); 4(4); 5(2); 6(3); 7(3); 9(2); 10(3); 11; 12; 13(4); 14(4); 14:2(2); 4; 8(2); 9(2); 10(2); 11; 13(2); 14; 15(4); 16(2); 17(3); 15:1(2); 2(4); 3(2); 4(2); 5(2); 6(2); 7(2); 8(2); 9(2); 10(2); 11(2); 12(6); 13(3); 14(4); 15(5); 16(4); 17(5); 18(2); 19(2); 21; 22(2); 23; 24(4); 25(6); 26(4); 27(5); 28(5); 29(4); 16:1(3); 2(5); 4(4); 5; 6(4); 7(2); 8(2); 10(2); 11; 12; 14(2); 15; 16; 18(2); 23(3); 24; 25; 26(4); 28(3); 29(4); 30(2); 31(4); 32(2); 33(4); 34; 35; 36(3); 37(4); 38; 39(5); 40(4); 41(2); 42(2); 43; 17:1(4); 3; 4; 5; 6; 7(3); 8(3); 9; 10(2); 16; 17; 18; 21(2); 23; 24(3); 27; 18:1(3); 2; 3; 4; 5(2); 6(2); 7(2); 8(3); 9; 11(4); 12(2); 13(2); 15(3); 16(4); 17(4); 19:1(2); 2(3); 3(3); 4; 5(3); 6(2); 7(2); 8(2); 9(5); 10(2); 11(4); 12(2); 13(2); 14(3); 15(3); 16(4); 17(2); 18(4); 19(3); 20:1(6); 2(2); 3(4); 4(4); 5(5); 6; 7; 8(3); 21:2(3); 3(2); 4; 5(5); 6; 8; 9; 10; 11; 12(8); 13(3); 14; 15(7); 16(3); 17(2); 18(5); 19(3); 20; 21(2); 22(5); 23(5); 24(2); 25; 26(3); 27(2); 28(3); 29(6); 30(3); 22:1(3); 2(3); 3(4); 4; 5(2); 6; 7(2); 8(3); 10; 11(3); 12(3); 13(2); 14(2); 16; 17; 18(5); 19(10); 23:2(3); 3(3); 4(3); 5; 6; 7; 8(2); 9(3); 10(2); 11(2); 12; 13(4); 14(3); 15; 16(2); 17(3); 18(2); 19(5); 20(3); 21(2); 22; 23; 24(9); 25;

26(3); 27(2); 28(10); 29(5); 30; 31(6); 32(9); 24:1(3); 3(3); 4(4); 5(4); 6(10); 7(2); 8(2); 9(2); 10(2); 11(2); 12(2); 13(2); 14(2); 15(2); 16(2); 17(2); 18(2); 19(5); 20(4); 21(2); 22(2); 23(5); 24(2); 25(2); 26(2); 27; 29; 30(3); 31(6); 25:1(6); 2(5); 3(3); 4; 5(3); 6(8); 7(3); 8(4); 9(2); 10; 11; 12; 13; 14; 15; 16; 17; 18; 19; 20; 21; 22; 23; 24; 25; 26; 27; 28; 29; 30; 31; 26:1(5); 2(5); 3(3); 4(6); 5(3); 7; 8(2); 10(4); 11(4); 12(5); 13(2); 14(3); 15(2); 16(4); 17(4); 18(4); 19(4); 20(5); 21(4); 22(4); 23(4); 24(3); 26(6); 27(3); 28(5); 29; 30(8); 31(5); 32(5); 27:1(7); 2(3); 3(5); 4(3); 5(5); 6(3); 7(3); 8(3); 9(4); 10(4); 11(4); 12(4); 13(4); 14(4); 15(3); 16(6); 17(3); 18; 19(2); 20(4); 21(3); 22(3); 23(4); 24(4); 25(8); 26(4); 27(6); 28(5); 29(5); 30(4); 31(3); 32(2); 33(3); 34(3); 28:1(13); 2(4); 4(6); 5(4); 8(6); 9(4); 10(2); 11(4); 12(10); 13(10); 15(5); 16(3); 17(5); 18(7); 19(2); 20(5); 21(7); 29:1(4); 2; 3(3); 4(3); 5(4); 6(6); 7(2); 8(5); 9(2); 10(2); 11(6); 17(2); 18(3); 19; 20(6); 21(3); 22(5); 23(2); 24(3); 25(2); 26; 27; 29(7); 30(3); **2 Chr** 1:1(2); 2(4); 3(6); 4(2); 5(6); 6(3); 9(2); 11; 12(2); 13(2); 14(2); 15(3); 16(2); 17(3); 2:1(2); 2; 4(8); 5; 6; 7; 9; 10; 11; 12(2); 14(3); 15(4); 17(3); 18(2); 3:1(6); 2(3); 3(5); 4(6); 5; 6(2); 7(3); 8(3); 9(3); 10; 11(8); 12(6); 13; 14; 15(3); 16(3); 17(11); 4:2(2); 3(4); 4(5); 5; 6(5); 7(3); 8(3); 9(4); 10(3); 11(5); 12(6); 13(3); 14(2); 16(5); 17(2); 18(2); 19(5); 20(3); 21(3); 22(10); 5:1(9); 2(9); 3(4); 4(3); 5(6); 6(2); 7(9); 8(5); 9(6); 10(4); 11(3); 12(4); 13(7); 14(5); 6:1(2); 3(3); 4; 5(2); 7(3); 8; 9(2); 10(7); 11(4); 12(4); 13(2); 16; 18(2); 19(3); 20(2); 21; 23(2); 25(2); 26; 27(2); 28(2); 30(2); 31; 32; 33(2); 34; 36; 37(2); 38(3); 40; 41; 42(2); 7:1(5); 2(6); 3(8); 4(3); 5(3); 6(6); 7(10); 8(3); 9(4); 10(5); 11(5); 12; 13(2); 18; 21; 22(2); 8:1(3); 2(2); 4(2); 6(5); 7(2); 8(2); 9; 10(2); 11(7); 12(4); 13(8); 14(8); 15(4); 16(7); 17(2); 18(3); 9:1(2); 3(3); 4(5); 5; 6(3); 8(2); 9(2); 10(2); 11(6); 12(2); 13; 14(3); 16(3); 17; 18(5); 19; 20(4); 21(3); 22(2); 23(3); 25(2); 26(5); 27(3); 29(9); 31; 10:2(2); 4; 5; 6; 8(3); 9; 10(2); 12(4); 13(3); 14(2); 15(7); 16(4); 17(2); 18; 19; 11:1(2); 2(3); 3; 4(3); 11; 13(2); 14(2); 15(3); 16(4); 17(3); 18(4); 20; 21; 22; 23; 12:1(3); 2(2); 3(2); 4; 5(4); 6(3); 7(4); 8(3); 9(6); 10(5); 11(5); 12(3); 13(3); 14; 15(4); 16; 13:1; 2; 3; 4; 5(2); 6(3); 7; 8(5); 9(5); 10(5); 11(6); 12(2); 13; 14(4); 15(2); 16; 18(3); 20(2); 22(4); 14:1(2); 2(2); 3(5); 4(3); 5(4); 6(2); 7(2); 9; 10(2); 11; 12(3); 13(3); 14(4); 15; 15:1(2); 2; 3; 4; 5(4); 8(10); 9; 10(3); 11(2); 12; 13; 14; 15(2); 16(3); 17(2); 18(2); 19(2); 16:1(2); 2(4); 4(3); 6; 7(5); 8(3); 9(3); 10(2); 11(3); 12(3); 13; 14(2); 17:2(3); 3(3); 4(2); 5(2); 6(3); 7(2); 8(2); 9(5); 10(4); 11(2); 13(2); 14(2); 15; 16(2); 19(3); 18:2; 3; 4(3); 5(3); 6; 7(4); 8(2); 9(4); 10(3); 11(3); 12(5); 13; 14(2); 15(4); 16(2); 17; 18(4); 19; 20(2); 21(2); 22(3); 23(4); 25(4); 26; 27; 28(2); 29(2); 30(4); 31(4); 32(3); 33(4); 34(4); 19:1; 2(6); 3(2); 4(3); 5(2); 6(3); 7(3); 8(4); 9(2); 10; 11(9); 20:1(3); 2; 3; 4(3); 5(4); 6(2); 7(2); 10(2); 13; 14(9); 15(2); 16(4); 17(3); 18(4); 19(6); 20(3); 21(5); 22(2); 23(3); 24(3); 25(2); 26(5); 27; 28(2); 29(4); 30; 31; 32(3); 33(3); 34(6); 36; 37(3); 21:1; 2(2); 3(2); 4(3); 6(6); 7(3); 8; 9(3); 10; 11(2); 12(4); 13(6); 14; 15; 16(5); 17(3); 18; 19(3); 20(3); 22:1(6); 2; 3(2); 4(4); 5(2); 6(3); 7(3); 8(3); 9(4); 10(3); 11(8); 12(2); 23:1(7); 2(3); 3(6); 4(4); 5(7); 6(7); 7(4); 8(6); 9(5); 10(8); 11(4); 12(6); 13(8); 14(7); 15(3); 16(3); 17(4); 18(11); 19(4); 20(14); 21(4); 24:2(4); 4(2); 5(5); 6(9); 7(6); 8(4); 9(4); 10(3); 11(7); 12(9); 13(3); 14(8); 16(2); 17(4); 18(2); 19; 20(7); 21(5); 22(3); 23(7); 24(4); 25(6); 26(5); 27(6); 25:2(2); 3(2); 4(5); 7(3); 8; 9(5); 10; 11(2); 12(5); 13(3); 14(3); 15(4); 16(3); 17(2); 18(3); 19; 20(2); 23(6); 24(5); 25(3); 26(4); 27(2); 28; 26:1; 2; 4(2); 5(3); 6(5); 7(3); 8(2); 9(4); 10(5); 11(5); 12(2); 13(2); 14; 15(2); 16(4); 17(2); 18(5); 19(5); 20(3); 21(6); 22(4); 23(2); 27:1; 2(5); 3(4); 4(2); 5(5); 6; 7(4); 9; 28:1(2); 2(3); 3(7); 4(2); 5(5); 6(2); 7(4); 8(2); 9(3); 10(2); 11(3); 12(7); 13(2); 14(5); 15(5); 16(2); 17; 18(4); 19(2); 21(7); 22(2); 23(4); 24(7); 25; 26(3); 27(3); 29:1(2); 2(2); 3(5); 4(3); 5(4); 6(4); 7(5); 8(2); 9; 10; 11; 12(10); 13(2); 14(2); 15(6); 16(12); 17(10); 18(5); 19(3); 20(4); 21(6); 22(10); 23(4); 24(5); 25(8); 26(4); 27(7); 28(4); 29; 30(5); 31(4); 32(4); 33; 34(7); 35(7); 36(3); 30:1(4); 2(4); 3(2); 4(3); 5(3); 6(9); 7; 8(3); 9(2); 10(2); 12(6); 13(2); 14(3); 15(8); 16(6); 17(5); 18(3); 19(3); 20(2); 21(6); 22(5); 23(2); 24(3); 25(5); 26(2); 27(3); 31:1(6); 2(7); 3(9); 4(5); 5(6); 6(5); 7(2); 8(3); 9(3); 10(7); 11(2); 12(5); 13(5); 14(8); 15(4); 16(4); 17(3); 18(2); 19(7); 20; 21(4); 32:1(3); 3(3); 4(4); 5(4); 6(3); 7(2); 8(3); 9; 11(3); 12; 13(3); 14; 15; 16; 17(4); 18(3); 19(5); 20(2); 21(5); 22(5); 23(2); 24; 25; 26(5); 28; 30(4); 31(4); 32(7); 33(3); 33:2(6); 3(3); 4(3); 5(4); 6(5); 7(3); 8(6); 9(4); 10; 11(4); 12(2); 13; 14(6); 15(9); 16(3); 17(3); 18(8); 19(2); 22(3); 23; 25(4); 34:2(5); 3(7); 4(7); 5(2); 6; 7(5); 8(10); 9(7); 10(9); 11(3); 12(7); 13(2); 14(7); 15(6); 16(3); 17(6); 18(4); 19(3); 20(5); 21(7); 22(7); 23(2); 24(4); 25; 26(4); 27; 28(2); 29(2); 30(13); 31(5); 32(3); 33(5); 35:1(4); 2(4); 3(6); 4(2); 5(7); 6(4); 7(4); 8(7); 9(3); 10(4); 11(5); 12(7); 13(4); 14(6); 15(6); 16(7); 17(3); 18(6); 19(2); 20(2); 21; 22(3); 23(2); 24(2); 25(3); 26(4); 27(2); 36:1(3); 3(2); 4; 5(2); 7(3); 8(5); 9(2); 10(5); 12(5); 13; 14(7); 15; 16(3); 17(6); 18(7); 19(2); 20(3); 21(4); 22(6); 23(4); **Ezra** 1:1(6); 2(3); 3(2); 4(3); 5(6); 7(4); 8(3); 9; 11(2); 2:1(4); 2(3); 3; 4; 5; 6(2); 7; 8; 9; 10; 11; 12; 13; 14; 15; 16; 17; 18; 19; 20; 21; 22; 23; 24; 25; 26; 27; 28; 29; 30; 31(2); 32; 33; 34; 35; 36(3); 37; 38; 39; 40(3); 41(2); 42(8); 43(4); 44(3); 45(3); 46(3); 47(3); 48(3); 49(3); 50(3); 51(3); 52(3); 53(3); 54(2); 55(4); 56(3); 57(4); 58(2); 59; 60(3); 61(7); 62; 63(3); 64; 68(5); 69(2); 70(6); 3:1(4); 2(7); 3(4); 4(3); 5(4); 6(6); 7(5); 8(13); 9(4); 10(9); 11(6); 12(4); 13(8); 4:1(5); 2(3); 3(5); 4(3); 5(2); 6(3); 7(4); 8(2); 9(9); 10(6); 11(4); 12(4); 13(3); 14(3); 15(5); 16(3); 17(6); 18; 19; 20(2); 21(2); 22(2); 23(3); 24(4); 5:1(5); 2(4); 3(4); 4(2); 5(3); 6(8); 7; 8(5); 10(2); 11(3); 12(4); 13; 14(5); 15(2); 16(3); 17(3); 6:1(2); 2(2); 3(5); 4(2); 5(5); 6(4); 7(5); 8(6); 9(4); 10(3); 12; 13(2); 14(8); 15(5); 16(7); 17(3); 18(4); 19(5); 20(6); 21(6); 22(7); 7:1(4); 2(3); 3(3); 4(3); 5(5); 6(5); 7(7); 8(3); 9(5); 10(2); 11(6); 12(3); 13(2); 14(2); 15(3); 16(6); 17(2); 18(4); 19(4); 20(2); 21(8); 23(5); 24; 25(4); 26(3); 27(4); 28(4); 8:1(3); 2(3); 3(2); 4(2); 5; 6(2); 7(2); 8(2); 9(2); 10; 11(2); 12(2); 13; 14; 15(4); 17(5); 18(4); 19; 20(4); 21(2); 22(5); 24(2); 25(6); 28(5); 29(7); 30(6); 31(7); 33(12); 34(2); 35(4); 36(7); 9:1(15); 2(4); 3; 4(4); 5(2); 6; 7(5); 8; 9(3); 11(5); 12(2); 14; 10:1(2); 2(4); 3(3); 5(3); 6(5); 7(2); 8(4); 9(7); 10(2); 11(4); 12; 13(2); 14(3); 15(3); 16(8); 17(3); 18(5); 19; 20; 21; 22; 23(2); 24(2); 25; 26; 27; 28; 29; 30; 31; 33; 34; 43; **Neh** 1:1(5); 2(3); 3(4); 4; 6(4); 7(3); 8(2); 9(3); 11(4); 2:1(4); 2; 3(4); 4(2); 5(3); 6(3); 7(5); 8(9); 9(6); 10(4); 12(2); 13(4); 14(3); 15(4); 16(7); 17(2); 18(2); 19(4); 20; 3:1(6); 2(2); 3(2); 4(5); 5(2); 6(3); 7(7); 8(4); 9(2); 10(2); 11(4); 12(2); 13(4); 14(3); 15(8); 16(7); 17(3); 18(3); 19(5); 20(6); 21(6); 22(3); 23(2); 24(4); 25(7); 26(5); 27(3); 28(2); 29(4); 30(3); 31(7); 32(5); 4:1(2); 2(3); 3; 5; 6(3); 7(5); 10(3); 11; 12; 13(4); 14(5); 15; 16(6); 17(2); 18(3); 19(6); 20(2); 21(4); 22(2); 23(2); 5:1; 3; 4; 5; 7; 8; 9(3); 11(4); 12; 13(4); 14(5); 15(4); 16(2); 17; 18(2); 6:1(5); 2(2); 3; 4; 5; 6(3); 7; 9; 10(7); 11; 14(3); 15(2); 16; 17(2); 18(4); 7:1(5); 2(3); 3(4); 4(3); 5(5); 6(4); 7(3); 8; 9; 10; 11(2); 12; 13; 14; 15; 16; 17; 18; 19; 20; 21; 22; 23; 24; 25; 26; 27; 28; 29; 30; 31; 32; 33(2); 34(2); 35; 36; 37; 38; 39(3); 40; 41; 42; 43(3); 44(2); 45(7); 46(4); 47(3); 48(3); 49(3); 50(3); 51(3); 52(3); 53(3); 54(3); 55(3); 56(2); 57(4); 58(3); 59(4); 60(2); 61; 62(3); 63(6); 64; 65(3); 66; 70(5); 71(4); 72(2); 73(8); 8:1(7); 2(5); 3(7); 4(2); 5(5); 6(5); 7(4); 8(4); 9(9); 10(4); 11(3); 12(2); 13(8); 14(5); 15; 16(8); 17(6); 18(7); 9:1(2); 2; 3(5); 4(3); 5(2); 6(5); 7(3); 8(7); 9(2); 10; 11(6); 12; 14; 15(2); 19(6); 21; 22(4); 23(2); 24(7); 27(3); 28; 30(3); 32(5); 35(2); 36; 37; 10:1(3); 8; 9(3); 14(2); 28(10); 29(3); 30(2); 31(6); 32(2); 33(10); 34(9); 35(4); 36(6); 37(10); 38(9); 39(13); 11:1(5); 2(2); 3(3); 4(9); 5(7); 6; 7(8); 9(3); 10(2); 11(7); 12(8); 13(5); 14(2); 15(5); 16(5); 17(9); 18(2); 19(2); 20(3); 21(2); 22(10); 23(2); 24(5); 25(2); 30; 31; 35; 36; 12:1(3); 7(3); 8(2); 12(4); 17; 22(4); 23(7); 24(5); 25(3); 26(7); 27(4); 28(5); 29(3); 30(4); 31(5); 32; 35(7); 36(3); 37(7); 38(7); 39(9); 40(4); 41; 42(2); 43(3); 44(12); 45(6); 46(2); 47(8); 13:1(4); 2(2); 3(2); 4(3); 5(8); 6(3); 7(3); 8(2); 9(5); 10(5); 11(2); 12(5); 13(6); 14; 15(3); 16(2); 17(2); 18; 19(6); 20; 21(3); 22(4); 24(4); 28(4); 29(4); 30(2); 31(2); **Esth** 1:1(2); 2(2); 3(5); 4(2); 5(6); 6; 7(3); 8(4); 9(2); 10(4); 11(3); 12(2); 13(4); 14(3); 15(2); 16(6); 17; 18(4); 19(5); 20; 21(5); 22(2); 2:1; 2(2); 3(8); 4(3); 5(4); 6(2); 7; 8(7); 9(5); 11(2); 12(3); 13(3); 14(9); 15(8); 16(3); 17(4); 18(4); 19; 20; 21(2); 22(2); 23(5); 3:1(3); 2(3); 3(3); 6(4); 7(8); 8(4); 9(4); 10(5); 11(3); 12(8); 13(6); 14; 15(6); 4:1(2); 2(3); 3(2); 4; 5; 6(2); 7(3); 8(2); 9; 11(9); 13(2); 14(2); 16(3); 5:1(8); 2(6); 3(2); 4(3); 5(3); 6(3); 8(6); 9; 11(4); 12(3); 13(2); 14(6); 6:1(5); 2(2); 3(2); 4(6); 5(3); 6(4); 7(3); 8(2); 9(7); 10(5); 11(5); 12; 14(2); 7:1; 2(4); 3; 4(2); 6(2); 7(4); 8(10); 9(6); 10(2); 8:1(4); 2(2); 3(5); 4(3); 5(8); 6(2); 7(4); 8(5); 9(10); 10(2); 11(3); 12(4); 13(2); 14(4); 15(3); 16; 17(5); 9:1(10); 2(2); 3(7); 4(2); 5(3); 6(2); 10(5); 11(3); 12(6); 13(3); 14(2); 15(4); 16(4); 17(4); 18(5); 19(5); 20(2); 21(2); 22(4); 23(2); 24(6); 25(3); 26(2); 27(3); 28(2); 29(2); 30(3); 31; 32(2); 10:1(3); 2(7); 3(4); **Job** 1:1; 3(3); 5(3); 6(2); 7(3); 8(2); 9; 10(2); 12(3); 14(2); 15(4); 16(3); 17(5); 19(4); 20; 21(4); 2:1(3); 2(3); 3(2); 4; 6; 7(4); 8(2); 10; 11(3); 13; 3:1; 3(2); 4; 5(3); 6(4); 8; 9(3); 10; 11; 12(2); 14; 17(2); 18(3); 19(2); 20; 22; 25; 4:1; 4; 6; 7; 8; 9(2); 10(6); 11(3); 13(2); 15; 19; 5:1; 3; 4; 5(2); 6(2); 7; 10(2); 12(2); 13(3); 14(2); 15(4); 16; 17(3); 20(2); 21(2); 22(2); 23(4); 25(2); 26; 6:2; 3(2); 4(3); 5(2); 6; 8; 10(2); 12; 14(2); 15(2); 16(2); 18; 19(2); 23(2); 26; 27; 30; 7:1; 2; 4; 8; 9(2); 11(2); 21; 8:1; 2; 3; 5; 8(2); 11(2); 13(3); 16; 17(2); 19(2); 20(2); 22(2); 9:5; 6; 7(2); 8(3); 9(4); 13(2); 22(2); 23(3); 24(4); 31; 10:1; 3(3); 5(2); 18; 19(2); 21(3); 22(2); 11:1; 2; 6; 7(3); 9(2); 17; 20(2); 12:2; 4; 5; 6; 7(3); 8(3); 9(2); 10(2); 11(2); 15(2); 16(2); 17; 18; 19; 20(3); 21; 22; 24(4); 25; 13:3; 6; 11; 21; 26; 27(2); 14:5; 8(2); 9; 11; 12; 13; 14; 15; 19(3); 15:1; 2; 5(2); 7(2); 8; 10(2); 11(2); 15; 19; 20(3); 21; 25; 29; 30(2); 34(2); 16:5; 10; 11(3); 13; 15; 16; 22; 17:1; 5; 6; 8(2); 9; 11; 12(3); 13(2); 14; 16(2); 18:1; 4(2); 5(3); 6; 7; 9(2); 10(2); 13; 14(2); 17(3); 18; 20(2); 21(3); 19:9; 17; 20; 21; 25; 28(2); 29(3); 20:1; 2; 3(2); 5(4); 6(2); 8; 9; 10(2); 11; 16(2); 17(2); 18; 19; 23; 24; 25(2); 27(2); 28(2); 29(2); 21:7; 9; 12(3); 13; 14; 15; 16(2); 17(3); 18; 20(2); 21; 24; 25; 26; 27; 28(5); 29; 30(3); 32(2); 33(2); 22:1; 3; 6; 7(2); 8(3); 9(2); 12(2); 13; 14; 15; 17; 18(2); 19(2); 20; 23; 24(4); 25; 26; 29; 30; 23:5; 7; 9(2); 10; 12(2); 16; 17; 24:1; 3(3); 4(4); 5(2); 6(3); 7(2); 8(3); 9(3); 10(3); 12(4); 13; 14(4); 15(3); 16(3); 17(5); 18(4); 19(2); 20(2); 21(2); 22; 24(2); 25:1; 5(2); 26:2; 5(2); 7(2); 8(2); 9; 10(3); 11; 12(2); 13(2); 14(2); 27:2; 3; 7(2); 8(2); 10; 11(2); 13(3); 14; 17(3); 19; 20; 21; 28:2; 3(2); 5; 6; 7; 8(2); 9(3); 10; 11; 12; 13(2); 14(2); 16; 18; 19; 20; 21(3); 24(3); 25(2); 26(2); 28(2); 29:2; 4(2); 5; 6; 7(3); 8(2); 9; 10(2); 11(2); 12(3); 13(2); 15(2); 16(2); 17(3); 18; 19(2); 23(2); 24; 25(2); 30:1; 2; 3; 4; 6(4); 7(2); 8; 12; 14; 15; 16; 18; 19; 21; 22; 23; 25; 28(2); 31; 31:2(3); 3(2); 7; 13; 15(3); 16(3); 17; 18; 20; 21(2); 22; 26(2); 29; 31; 32(2); 34(3); 35; 37; 40; 32:2(4); 5; 6(2); 8(2); 9; 18; 33:4(3); 8; 11; 15; 16; 18(2); 22(2); 24; 25; 28(2); 30(2); 34:3(2); 8; 10; 12; 13(2); 16; 19(3); 20(4); 21; 22; 25; 26; 28(4); 30(2); 36; 35:5(2); 9(3); 10; 11(3); 12; 13; 36:6(3); 7(2); 8; 12; 13; 14; 15; 17(2); 19; 20; 26; 27; 28; 29(2); 30(2); 31; 33(2); 37:2(2); 3(3); 6(4); 7; 8; 9(5); 10(2); 11; 12(2); 14; 15; 16; 17(2); 18; 19; 21(3); 22; 23; 38:1(2); 4(2); 5; 7(2); 8(2); 9; 12(2); 13(3); 15(2); 16(3); 17(3); 18(2); 19(2); 20; 21; 22(2); 23(2); 24(2); 25(2); 27(2); 28(2); 29(2); 30(3); 31(3); 32; 33(3); 34; 36(2); 37(2); 38(2); 39(4); 41; 39:1(3); 2(2); 5(3); 6(2); 7(4); 8(2); 9; 10(3); 13(3); 14(2); 18; 19; 21(2); 22; 23(2); 24(2); 25(4); 26(2); 27; 28(4); 29; 30; 40:1; 2(2); 3; 6(2); 11; 12; 13; 15; 17; 19(2); 20(3); 21; 22(3); 23(2); 41:6; 8; 9; 14; 18(2); 23; 24; 25; 26; 28; 29; 30; 31(2); 32; 34; 42:1; 5(2); 7(3); 9(5); 10(2); 11(2); 12(2); 14(6); 15(2); **Ps** 1:1(6); 2(2); 3; 4(3); 5(4); 6(5); 2:1(2); 2(4); 4(2); 7(2); 8(3); 10; 11; 12(2); 3:3; 4; 5; 7(3); 8; 4:3(2); 5(2); 6; 7; 5:2; 3(2); 5; 6(2); 7; 10; 12; 6:5; 8(2); 9(2); 7(2); 5(3); 6(2); 7(2); 8(2); 9(5); 10; 11; 14; 15; 17(3); 8(2); 1(2); 2(3); 3(3); 4; 5; 6; 7(2); 8(6); 9; 9(3); 4; 5(2); 7; 8(2); 9(2); 11(2); 12(2); 13; 14(2); 15(3); 16(4); 17(2); 18(3); 19; 20; 10:2(3); 3(3); 4; 8(5); 9(2); 10; 12; 13; 14(3); 15(3); 16(2); 17(2); 18(4); 11:1; 2(3); 3(2); 4(3); 5(4); 6(2); 7(2); 12:1(3); 3(2); 5(6); 6(2); 8(2); 13:3; 6; 14:1; 2(2); 4(2); 5(2); 6(3); 7(3); 15:2; 4; 5; 16:2; 3(3); 5; 6; 7(2); 8; 11; 17:2; 3; 4(4); 8(2); 9; 11; 13; 14(2); 18(9); 2(2); 3; 4(2); 5(2); 6; 7(3); 9; 10(2); 11; 12; 13(2); 14; 15(6); 18(2); 20(2); 21(2); 24(2); 25; 26(2); 27; 28; 30(2); 31; 33; 35; 39; 40; 41; 42(3); 43(4); 44; 45; 46(2); 47; 48; 49; 19:1(3); 4(4); 6; 7(6); 8(6); 9(4); 10; 14(2); 20:1(4); 2; 5(2); 6(2); 7(2); 9; 21:1; 2; 3; 7(4); 9(3); 10(2); 22(3); 1; 2(2); 3; 6; 7(2); 8; 9; 15; 16(2); 20(3); 21(3); 22(2); 23; 24(2); 25; 26(2); 27(5); 28(3); 29(3); 30(2); 23:1; 2; 3; 4(2); 5; 6(3); 24:1(3); 2(2); 3(2); 5(2); 6; 7; 8(2); 9; 10(2); 25:5(2); 7; 8(2); 9(2); 10(2); 12(3); 13; 14(2); 15(2); 17; 26:1; 5(2); 7; 8(2); 12(2); 27:1(3); 2; 4(6); 5(2); 6; 10; 12; 13(4); 14(2); 28:1; 2; 3(2); 4(2); 5(3); 6(2); 7; 8(2); 29:1(2); 2(4); 3(5); 4(4); 5(5); 7(3); 8(5); 9(4); 10(3); 11(2); 30(2); 3(2); 4(2); 5; 8; 9(2); 12; 31:4; 6; 8(2); 13; 15; 17(2); 18(2); 19(2); 20(3); 21; 22; 23(4); 24; 32:2(2); 3; 4; 5(2); 8; 9(2); 10(2); 11; 33:1(2); 2(2); 4(2); 5(3); 6(5); 7(3); 8(4); 10(5); 11(3); 12(3); 13(2); 14(3); 16; 18(2); 20; 34:1; 2(3); 3; 4; 6; 7(2); 8(2); 9; 10(2); 11(2); 12; 15(3); 16(4); 17(2); 18; 19(3); 21(2); 22(2); 35:3; 5(3); 6(2); 9; 10(3); 12; 17; 18; 19; 20(2); 27(2); 28; 36(3); 1(2); 3; 5(2); 6; 7(2); 8(2); 9; 10; 11(3); 12; 37:1; 2(2); 3(2); 4(2); 5; 6(2); 7(2); 9(2); 10; 11(3); 12(2); 13; 14(3); 16; 17(4); 18(3); 19(2); 20(5); 21(2); 22; 23(2); 24; 25; 28(3); 29(2); 30(2); 31; 32(2); 33; 34(3); 35; 37(3); 38(3); 39(4); 40(2); 38:6; 8; 10; 12; 39:1; 3; 4; 8(2); 10; 40:1; 2; 3; 4(2); 7(2); 9(2); 10; 12; 16; 17; 41:1(2); 2(3); 3; 13; 42(2); 1(2); 2; 4(3); 5; 6(4); 7; 8(4); 9(2); 11; 43:1; 2(3); 4(2); 5; 44(2); 1; 2(2); 3(2); 10; 11; 14(3); 15; 16(3); 19(2); 20; 21(2); 22; 25(2); 45(3); 1(2); 2; 5(3); 6; 7; 8; 9; 11; 12(3); 13(2); 14(2); 15; 16; 17; 46(2); 2(4); 3; 4(4); 5(2); 6(3); 7(2); 8(3); 9(6); 10(2); 11(2); 47(2); 1; 2(2); 3(2); 4; 5(2); 7(2); 8; 9(6); 48:1(2); 2(6); 4; 7; 8(3); 9; 10(2); 11; 13; 49(2); 1; 3; 4; 5(2); 6; 8; 9; 10(2); 12; 13; 14(4); 15(2); 16; 19; 20; 50:1(5); 2; 4(2); 6; 10(2); 11(4); 12; 13(2); 14; 15; 16; 23; 51(2); 1; 6(2); 8; 12; 14(2); 17; 18; 19; 52(3); 1; 5(2); 6; 7(2); 8(2); 9; 53:1; 2; 4; 5; 6(2); 54(2); 2; 4; 55:3(4); 4; 7; 8; 9; 10; 14(2); 16; 18; 21; 22(2); 23; 56(3); 7; 10; 13(2); 57(2); 1; 3; 4; 5(2); 6; 8; 9(2); 10(2); 11(2); 58:2(2); 3(2); 4(2); 5; 6(2); 8; 9; 10(4); 11(2); 59(3); 2; 3; 5(2); 6; 8; 12(3); 13(2); 14; 16(2); 60(3); 2; 3; 4; 6; 7; 9; 11; 61:2(3); 3; 4; 5; 6; 62:7; 9; 63:2; 6; 7; 9(2); 10; 11(2); 64:1; 2(4); 4; 6(2); 9; 10(3); 65:1; 4(2); 5(4); 6; 7(5); 8(3); 9(2); 11; 12(3); 13(2); 66:1; 2; 3; 4; 5(2); 6(2); 7(2); 8; 9; 11; 15; 18; 19; 67:3(2); 4(3); 5(2); 6; 7(2); 68:2(3); 3; 4; 5; 6(2); 7; 8(5); 10; 11(3); 12; 13(2); 14; 15(2); 16(2); 17(3); 18(2); 19(2); 20(2); 21(3); 22(3); 23; 24(2); 25(3); 26(3); 27(3); 30(6); 32(2); 33; 34; 35; 69(2); 1; 2; 4; 9; 12(3); 13(3); 14(2); 15(3); 16; 26(2); 28(3); 30; 31; 32; 33(2); 34; 35; 36; 70:71:3; 4(4); 8; 9; 15; 16(2); 20(2); 22(2); 24; 72:1(2); 3(3); 4(5); 5; 6(2); 7(2); 8(3); 9(2); 10(3); 12(2); 13(3); 15; 16(5); 17; 18(2); 19; 20(2); 73:3(3); 9(2); 11; 12; 15; 17; 26; 28; 74:1; 2; 3(3); 4; 5; 7(2); 8(2); 10(2); 12(2); 13(4); 14(3); 15(2); 16(4); 17(2); 18; 19(3); 20(4); 21(2); 22; 23(2); 75:2; 3; 4(3); 6(3); 7; 8(5); 9; 10(4); 76:3(3); 4; 5(3); 6; 8; 9(2); 10(2); 11; 12(3); 77:2(3); 5(2); 6; 7; 10(3); 11(2); 13; 14(2); 15; 16(3); 17(2); 18(5); 19(2); 20; 78:1; 4(3); 6(2); 7; 9(2); 10; 12(3); 13(2); 14(3); 15(3); 16; 17(2); 18; 19; 20(3); 21; 23(2); 24; 25; 26(2); 27(3); 28; 31(3); 35; 40(2); 41; 42(2); 43; 46(2); 48; 49; 50; 51(3); 52; 53; 55(2); 56; 60(2); 61; 62; 63; 64; 65; 67(2); 68; 69(2); 70; 71; 72(2); 79:1; 2(6); 6(2); 9; 10(4); 11(3); 80(2); 1; 4; 5; 8; 9; 10(2); 11(2); 12; 13(4); 15(2); 16; 17(2); 81:1; 2(3); 3(4); 4; 5; 6(2); 7(2); 10(2); 15(2); 16(2); 82:1(3); 2; 3(2); 4(3); 5(2); 6; 7; 8; 83:4; 6(3); 7; 8; 9; 10; 12; 13(3); 14(4); 18(3); 84(2); 2(3); 3(2); 5; 6(2); 9; 10(2); 11(2); 12; 85(2); 1; 2; 3; 8; 11; 12; 86:4; 6; 7; 8; 13; 14; 16; 87:1; 2(3); 5; 6(2); 7(2); 88(3); 3; 4; 5(3); 6(2); 10(2); 11(2); 12(2); 13; 89:1(2); 2; 5(3); 6(5); 7(2); 9(2); 11(3); 12(2); 14; 15(3); 17; 18(2); 19; 22(2); 25(2); 26; 27(3); 29; 32; 34; 36; 37(3); 39(2); 41; 42; 43(2); 44; 45; 47; 48(2); 50(3); 51; 52; 90:2(3); 4; 5; 6(2); 8; 10; 11(2); 15(2); 17(4); 91:1(4); 2; 3(3); 5(2); 6(2); 8(2); 9(2); 13(4); 92:1; 2; 3(2); 4; 7(2); 9; 11; 12; 13(3); 15; 93:1(3); 3(3); 4(4); 94:2(2); 3(2); 4; 6(3); 7(2); 8; 9(2); 10; 11(2); 12; 13(3); 14; 15; 16(2); 17; 19; 20; 21(2); 22(2); 23; 95:1(2); 3(3); 4(4); 5(2); 6; 7(2); 8(3); 96:1(3); 2(2); 3; 4; 5(4); 7(3); 8(2); 9(3); 10(4); 11(3); 12(4); 13(3); 97:1(3); 2; 4(2); 5(6); 6(2); 8; 9; 10(4); 11(2); 12(2); 98:1(2); 2(3); 3(4); 4(2); 5(4); 6(3); 7(2); 8(3); 9(3); 99:1(4); 2(2); 4; 5; 6; 7(2); 9(2); 100:1; 2; 3(2); 5; 101:3; 5; 6(2); 8(5); 102(2); 2(2); 5; 6(2); 7; 12; 13(2); 15(5); 16; 17(2); 18(2); 19(3); 20(2); 21(2); 22(3); 23; 24; 25(4); 27; 28; 103:1; 2; 5; 6; 7; 8; 11(2); 12(2); 13; 15; 16; 17(2); 19; 20(2); 21; 22(2); 104:1; 2; 3(5); 5(2); 6(3); 7; 8(3); 9; 10(3); 11(2); 12(3); 13(3); 14(4); 15; 16(3); 17(3); 18(4); 19(2); 20(2); 21; 22; 23; 24; 26; 30(2); 31(3); 32(2); 33; 34; 35(4); 105:1(2); 3(2); 4; 5; 7(2); 8; 9; 11(2); 16(2); 19(3); 20(3); 23; 27; 30; 33; 35(2); 36(2); 38; 39; 40(2); 41(2); 44(4); 45; 106:1(2); 2(2); 4; 5(2); 7(3); 9(3); 10(3); 11; 14(2); 16(3); 17(2); 18(2); 19; 20; 22(2); 23; 24; 25(2); 26; 27(2); 28; 29; 30; 32; 34(2); 35; 38(3); 39; 40(2); 41(2); 45; 47; 48(3); 107:1; 2(4); 3(5); 4; 6; 7; 8(2); 9(2); 10; 11(3); 13; 14; 15(2); 16(2); 18; 19; 21(2); 22; 23; 24(3); 25(3); 26(2); 28; 29; 31(2); 32(4); 33; 34; 36; 40; 41; 42; 43(2); 108:2; 3(2); 4(2); 5(2); 7; 8; 10; 12; 109:2(4); 11; 13; 14(3); 15(3); 16(2); 19; 20; 21; 30(2); 31(2); 110:1; 2(3); 3(5); 4(2); 5(2); 6(3); 7(3); 111:1(5); 2(2); 4; 6(3); 7; 10(3); 112:1(3); 2(2); 4(2); 6; 7; 9; 10(3); 113:1(4); 2(3); 3(3); 4(2); 5; 6(3); 7(4); 8; 9(2); 114:1; 3; 4(2); 7(4); 8(2); 115:2; 4; 9; 10; 11(2); 12(3); 13; 14; 15; 16(5); 17(2); 18(2); 116:1; 3(2); 4(2); 5; 6(2); 7; 9(3); 12; 13(3); 14(2); 15(3); 16; 17(3); 18(2); 19(4); 117:1; 2(3); 118:1; 3; 4; 5(2); 6; 7; 8; 9; 10(2); 11(2); 12(2); 13; 14; 15(5); 16(4); 17(2); 18; 19(2); 20(3); 22(3); 23; 24(2); 26(4); 27(4); 29; 119:1(4); 2; 13; 14; 19; 21(2); 25; 27; 29; 30; 32; 33(2); 35; 43; 49; 51; 53; 54; 55; 61(2); 64; 69; 72; 78; 84; 85; 88; 90; 95; 96; 97; 100; 108; 110; 111; 112; 113; 115; 119(2); 122; 130(2); 134; 144; 147(2); 148; 155; 158; 160; 120:1; 4(2); 5; 121:1; 2; 5(2); 6(2); 7; 8; 122:1(2); 4(6); 5(2); 6; 8; 9(2); 123:1; 2(5); 4(3); 124:1; 2; 4(2); 5; 6; 7(3); 8(2); 125:1; 2(2); 3(4); 5(2); 126:1(2); 2(2); 3; 4(2); 127:1(5); 2; 3(3); 4(2); 5(2); 128:1; 2; 3; 4(2); 5(3);

129:3; 4(3); 6(2); 7; 8(4); 130:1; 2; 5; 6(3); 7(2); 131:3; 132:2(2); 3(2); 5(2); 6(2); 8; 10; 11(2); 13; 17; 133:2(5); 3(4); 134:1(4); 2(2); 3; 135:1(4); 2(4); 3(2); 4; 5; 6(2); 7(5); 8; 9; 11(2); 14; 15(3); 19(2); 20(3); 21(2); 136:1; 2; 3; 5; 6(2); 8; 9; 13; 14; 15; 16; 19; 26; 137:1; 2(2); 3; 4; 6; 7(2); 8; 9(2); 138:1; 3; 4(3); 5(4); 6(3); 7(2); 8(2); 139:9(4); 11(2); 12(5); 15(2); 16; 17; 18; 19; 24; 140:3; 4(2); 5(2); 6(2); 7(3); 8(2); 9(2); 10; 11(2); 12(4); 13(2); 141:2(2); 3; 5(3); 6(2); 7(3); 8; 9(3); 10; 142:1(2); 3; 5(2); 7; 143:3(2); 5(2); 7; 8(2); 10; 144:1; 2; 3; 5; 7; 10(2); 11; 15(3); 145:3; 5; 6; 7; 8; 9; 11; 12(2); 14; 15; 16; 17; 18; 19; 20(2); 21(2); 146:1(2); 2; 5(2); 6; 7(4); 8(6); 9(5); 10(2); 147:1; 2(2); 3; 4(2); 6(4); 7(2); 8(3); 9(2); 10(3); 11; 12; 13; 14; 15; 16; 18; 20; 148:1(4); 4; 5(2); 7(3); 11(2); 13(3); 14(4); 149:1(3); 2; 3(2); 4(2); 5; 6; 7(2); 9(2); 150:1; 3(3); 4; 6(2); **Prov** 1:1(2); 2; 3; 4(2); 6(2); 7(3); 8(2); 11; 12; 15; 17(2); 19(2); 20; 21(4); 29(2); 31(2); 32(3); 2:5(3); 6; 7; 8(2); 12(2); 13(2); 14(2); 16(2); 17(2); 18; 19; 20(2); 21(3); 22(3); 3:3; 4; 5; 7; 9(2); 11(2); 12(2); 13(2); 14; 15; 19(3); 20(2); 25; 26; 27; 31; 32(3); 33(6); 34(2); 35(2); 4:1; 3(2); 5; 7; 10; 11; 14(3); 17(2); 18(4); 19(2); 21; 23; 26; 27(2); 5:3; 4; 7; 8; 9; 10; 13; 14(3); 16; 18; 20; 21(3); 22(2); 23; 6:2(2); 3; 5(4); 6; 8(2); 10; 16; 20; 23(3); 24(2); 31; 34; 7:2; 3; 5(2); 6; 7(2); 8(2); 9(3); 10; 12; 20; 22(3); 23; 24; 27(2); 8:2(4); 3(5); 4; 6; 8; 11; 13(4); 16(2); 20(3); 22(2); 23; 25(2); 26(4); 27(3); 28(3); 29(4); 31; 34(2); 35; 9:3(2); 5; 6; 10(5); 14(3); 18(2); 10:1(2); 3(4); 4(2); 6(4); 7(4); 8; 10; 11(4); 13(2); 14(2); 15(3); 16(4); 17; 19; 20(4); 21(2); 22(2); 24(4); 25(3); 26(3); 27(4); 28(4); 29(4); 30(3); 31(3); 32(4); 11:1; 2; 3(4); 4; 5(3); 6(3); 7(2); 8(2); 9(2); 10(3); 11(5); 14(2); 17; 18; 20(2); 21(3); 23(4); 25; 26(2); 28; 29(3); 30(2); 31(4); 12:2; 3(2); 4; 5(4); 6(4); 7(3); 9; 10(3); 12(4); 13(3); 14(2); 15; 18(3); 19; 20; 21(2); 22; 23; 24(3); 25; 26(3); 27; 28; 13:2(3); 4(3); 6; 8(2); 9(4); 10; 12(2); 13(2); 14(3); 15(2); 19; 20; 21; 22(3); 23(2); 25(4); 14:1(2); 2; 3(3); 4(2); 7(2); 8(3); 9; 10; 11(4); 12; 13(2); 14; 15(2); 18(2); 19(5); 20(2); 21; 24(3); 26(2); 27(3); 28(2); 30(2); 31(2); 32(2); 33(2); 35; 15:2(3); 3(4); 4; 6(4); 7(4); 8(5); 9(3); 10; 11(3); 12; 13(2); 14(2); 15(2); 16(2); 19(4); 22; 23; 24(2); 25(5); 26(5); 28(4); 29(4); 30(4); 31(3); 33(3); 16:1(5); 2(3); 3; 4(3); 5; 6(2); 7; 9; 10(2); 11(3); 13; 14; 15(3); 17(2); 19(3); 20(2); 21(2); 22; 23(2); 24(2); 25; 26; 28; 31(2); 32; 33(3); 17:2; 3(4); 5; 6(2); 8; 14; 15(3); 16(2); 21; 22; 23(2); 24(4); 26; 18:3; 4(2); 5(2); 7; 8(2); 10(3); 11; 12; 14; 15(4); 17; 18; 19; 20(2); 21(2); 22; 23(2); 19:1; 3(2); 4; 6(2); 7(2); 11; 12(3); 13(2); 14; 16; 17(2); 21; 23(2); 24; 25; 27; 28(2); 29; 20:2(2); 4; 5; 7; 8; 10; 12(3); 14; 15; 16; 21(2); 22; 23; 24; 26(2); 27(4); 28; 29(2); 30(2); 21:1(4); 2(2); 3; 4(2); 5(2); 6; 7(2); 8(2); 10(2); 11(3); 12(4); 13(2); 14; 15(2); 16(3); 18(4); 19; 20(2); 22(3); 25(2); 26; 27(2); 28; 29; 30; 31(3); 22:2(4); 3; 4(2); 5(2); 6; 7(4); 8; 9; 10; 11; 12(4); 13(2); 14(2); 15(2); 16(2); 17(2); 19; 21(2); 22(3); 23(2); 28; 23:6; 8; 9(2); 10(3); 17(3); 19; 21(2); 23; 24(2); 28; 30; 31(2); 32; 34(4); 24:4; 7; 9(2); 10; 11; 12; 13; 14; 15(2); 16; 18; 19; 20(3); 21(2); 22; 23; 24(2); 25; 26; 27; 29; 30(4); 33; 25:1; 2(2); 3(3); 4(2); 5(2); 6(4); 7(2); 8; 9; 13(2); 22; 23; 26; 26:3(3); 6; 7(3); 9(2); 10(3); 13(3); 14; 15(2); 16; 17; 19; 20; 22(2); 26; 27:6(2); 7; 9(2); 10; 12; 13; 14; 16; 17; 18; 19; 20; 21(2); 23; 25(4); 26(3); 27(2); 28:1(2); 2; 3; 4(3); 5; 6; 7; 8; 9; 10(2); 11(2); 12(2); 14; 23; 24; 25; 27; 28(2); 29:2(3); 4(2); 6; 7(4); 9; 10(3); 13(4); 14(2); 15; 16(2); 18(2); 21; 23; 24; 25(2); 26(2); 27(3); 30:1(2); 2; 3; 4(4); 8; 9(2); 14(3); 15; 16(4); 17(4); 19(7); 20; 21; 24; 25(2); 26(2); 27; 28; 33(3); 31:1(2); 5(3); 8(2); 9(2); 11; 12; 14; 19(2); 20(2); 23(3); 24; 26; 27(2); 30; 31(2); **Eccl** 1:1(3); 2; 3; 4; 5(3); 6(4); 7(5); 8(2); 9; 12; 13; 14(3); 17; 2:3(2); 6(2); 8(4); 11(4); 12(2); 14(3); 15; 16(4); 17(3); 18(2); 19; 20(2); 22(2); 23; 24; 26(3); 3:9; 10(2); 11; 13(2); 16(3); 17(2); 18(2); 19(2); 20; 21(5); 4:1(5); 2(2); 3(2); 4; 6; 7; 15(3); 16(2); 5:1(2); 6(2); 7; 8(4); 9(4); 11; 12(3); 13; 16; 18(3); 19; 20(2); 6:1; 3; 5; 7(2); 8(4); 9(4); 11; 12(2); 7:1(2); 2(4); 3; 4(5); 5(3); 6(3); 7; 8(3); 9; 10; 11; 12; 13; 14(4); 18; 19(2); 25(2); 26(2); 27(3); 8:1(2); 2(2); 4; 6; 8(3); 9; 10(3); 11(3); 13; 14(4); 15(3); 16; 17(3); 9:1(3); 2(7); 3(4); 4; 5(3); 6; 9(5); 10; 11(5); 12; 13; 15; 16; 17(2); 10:1; 3; 4(2); 5(2); 6; 7; 10(2); 11; 12(2); 13(2); 15(2); 16; 17(2); 18(2); 20(4); 11:1; 2; 3(6); 4(2); 5(5); 6(2); 7(3); 8; 9(3); 12:1(3); 2(6); 3(6); 4(5); 5(5); 6(6); 7(3); 8; 9(2); 10; 11(3); 12; 13(2); **Song** 1:1(2); 2; 3(2); 4(5); 5(2); 6(3); 7(2); 8(3); 10; 11; 12; 14(2); 15; 17; 2:1(4); 2(2); 3(5); 4; 7(4); 8(3); 9(2); 11(2); 12(5); 13(3); 14(4); 15(4); 16; 17(4); 3:1; 2(4); 3(3); 4(3); 5(4); 6(2); 7; 8; 9(2); 10; 11(5); 4:2; 4; 5; 6(4); 8(5); 10; 11(3); 14; 15; 16; 5:1; 2(3); 4(2); 5(2); 7(4); 8; 9; 11; 12; 15; 16; 6:1; 2(2); 3(2); 6; 9(7); 10(4); 11(5); 12(2); 13(5); 7:1(3); 4(3); 5; 8(3); 9(5); 11(2); 12(4); 13; 8:2(3); 5(3); 6; 7(3); 8; 9; 11; 12; 13(3); 14; **Isa** 1:1(3); 2; 3(2); 4(2); 5(2); 6(3); 8; 9; 10(3); 11(4); 13(4); 16; 17(3); 18; 19(2); 20(3); 21; 23(3); 24(3); 26(4); 28(2); 29(2); 31(2); 2:1(2); 2(6); 3(7); 4; 5(2); 6(3); 8; 10(5); 11(3); 12(2); 13(2); 14(2); 16(2); 17(3); 18; 19(8); 20; 21(8); 3:1(6); 2(6); 3(5); 5(5); 6; 7; 8(2); 9; 10(2); 11(2); 12; 13(2); 14(5); 15(3); 16(2); 17(5); 18(5); 19(3); 20(5); 21(2); 22(4); 23(4); 25(2); 26; 4:2(4); 3; 4(6); 5(3); 6(2); 5:2; 6; 7(4); 8(2); 9; 11; 12(6); 15(2); 16; 17(3); 19(2); 23(2); 24(8); 25(5); 26(3); 27(2); 29; 30(5); 6:1(4); 3(2); 4(4); 5(3); 6(3); 8(2); 10; 11(3); 12(4); 13; 7:1(4); 2(5); 3(6); 4(2); 5; 6; 7; 8(2); 9(2); 10; 11(3); 12; 14(2); 15(2); 16(4); 17(3); 18(6); 19(3); 20(8); 22(2); 24; 25; 8:1; 2(2); 3(2); 4(4); 5; 6; 7(4); 8(3); 10; 11(2); 13; 14(2); 16(2); 17(2); 18(3); 19(2); 20(2); 22; 9:1(7); 2(3); 3(3); 4(4); 5; 6; 7(4); 8; 9(2); 10(2); 11(2); 12(2); 13(2); 14; 15(4); 16; 17; 18(4); 19(5); 20(3); 10:2(3); 3(2); 4(2); 5(2); 6(5); 10(2); 12(5); 13(4); 14(3); 15(2); 16(3); 17; 18; 19(2); 20(4); 21(3); 22(3); 23(3); 24(3); 25; 26(5); 27(2); 29; 31; 32(3); 33(4); 34(3); 11:1; 2(7); 3(4); 4(7); 5(2); 6(7); 7(4); 8(4); 9(5); 10(2); 11(5); 12(5); 13(2); 14(6); 15(5); 16(3); 12:2; 3; 4(2); 5(2); 6; 13:1(2); 2(3); 4(5); 5(3); 6(3); 9(3); 10(3); 11(6); 12; 13(5); 14; 15; 17; 18(3); 19(3); 20(2); 21; 22; 14:1(3); 2(3); 3(3); 4(3); 5(5); 6(2); 7; 8(2); 9(5); 11(2); 12(3); 13(5); 14(3); 15(2); 16(2); 17(2); 18(2); 19(3); 20; 21(4); 22(3); 23(3); 24; 25; 26(4); 27; 28(2); 29(2); 30(3); 31; 32(4); 15:1(3); 2(2); 3; 4; 5(2); 6(3); 7(3); 8(2); 9(3); 16:1(6); 2(4); 3(4); 4(5); 5(2); 6; 7; 8(6); 9(2); 10(3); 12; 13(2); 14(4); 17:1; 2; 3(6); 4(2); 5(4); 6(4); 7; 8(4); 9; 10(2); 11(4); 12(5); 13(6); 14(3); 18:1(2); 2(2); 3(3); 4(2); 5(6); 6(6); 7(5); 19:1(4); 3(5); 4(4); 5(3); 6(3); 7(5); 8(3); 11(4); 12; 13(3); 14; 15; 16(3); 17(3); 18(4); 19(4); 20(4); 21(4); 22(2); 23(4); 24(2); 25(2); 20:1(2); 2(4); 3; 4(4); 6(2); 21:1(5); 2(2); 3; 4; 5(3); 6; 8(2); 9(2); 10(3); 11(3); 12(3); 13(2); 14; 15(4); 16(3); 17(5); 22:1(3); 2; 3; 4(2); 5(4); 6(2); 7(2); 8(4); 9(4); 10(3); 11(3); 12; 14(2); 15(2); 17; 18; 20; 21(2); 22(2); 24(5); 25(5); 23:1(2); 2(2); 3(4); 4(3); 5(2); 6; 8(3); 9(4); 10; 11(3); 13(3); 15(4); 16; 17(6); 18(2); 24:1(2); 2(10); 3(2); 4(4); 5(4); 6(4); 7(3); 8(6); 10; 11(3); 12(2); 13(6); 14(3); 15(6); 16(5); 17(3); 18(9); 19(3); 20; 21(5); 22(2); 23(3); 25:3(3); 4(7); 5(4); 6(3); 7(3); 8(4); 9; 10(3); 11; 12(4); 26:1; 2(3); 4(2); 5(3); 6(5); 7(4); 8(3); 9(4); 10(4); 11; 15(4); 17; 18(3); 19(3); 20; 21(4); 27:1(4); 3; 6(2); 7; 8(2); 9(4); 10(3); 11; 12(4); 13(5); 28:1(4); 2(2); 3(2); 4(5); 5(2); 6(2); 7(4); 9(2); 12(3); 13(2); 14(2); 15; 16; 17(6); 18; 19; 20(2); 21(2); 22(2); 24(2); 25(6); 27(4); 29; 29:1; 4(4); 5(3); 6(2); 7(2); 8(2); 10(4); 11(2); 12; 13(2); 14(2); 15(2); 16(4); 17; 18(5); 19(4); 20(2); 21(2); 22(2); 23(3); 30:1(2); 2(2); 3(2); 6(7); 7; 9(2); 10(2); 11(3); 12; 14(4); 15(2); 17(2); 18(2); 19(2); 20(3); 21(3); 22(2); 23(4); 24(4); 25(3); 26(11); 27(2); 28(5); 29(4); 30(4); 31(3); 32(2); 33(3); 31:1(2); 2(2); 3(2); 4(2); 5; 6; 8; 9(2); 32:2(3); 3(2); 4(4); 5(2); 6(5); 7(4); 10(2); 12(2); 13(3); 14(3); 15(3); 16(2); 17(2); 19(2); 20(3); 33:2; 3(4); 4(3); 5; 6(4); 7; 8(4); 9; 10; 12(3); 14(3); 15; 16; 17(2); 18(2); 20; 21; 22(3); 23(4); 24(2); 34:1(2); 2(3); 3; 4(4); 5; 6(7); 7(3); 8(4); 11(6); 12; 14(5); 15(2); 16(2); 17; 35:1(4); 2(5); 3(2); 4; 5(4); 6(5); 7(3); 8(3); 9; 10(2); 36:1(2); 2(6); 3(5); 4(3); 6; 7; 8; 9; 10(2); 11(5); 12(3); 13(4); 14; 15(4); 16(2); 18(5); 19(2); 20(2); 21; 22(7); 37:1(2); 2(6); 3; 4(8); 5; 6(4); 7; 8(2); 9; 10(2); 11; 12(3); 13(4); 14(6); 15; 16(4); 17(2); 18(2); 19(2); 20(3); 21(2); 22(5); 23; 24(5); 25(2); 27(5); 29; 30(4); 31(2); 32(2); 33(2); 34(3); 36(6); 38(3); 38:1(3); 2(2); 4(2); 5(2); 6(2); 7(3); 8(6); 9; 10(3); 11(5); 12; 15; 16; 17; 18; 19(4); 20(4); 21; 22(3); 39:1; 2(3); 3; 5(2); 6(2); 7(2); 8(2); 40:2; 3(5); 4(2); 5(4); 6(3); 7(5); 8(3); 9(2); 10; 11; 12(6); 13(2); 14(2); 15(4); 19(3); 21(3); 22(3); 23(3); 24(2); 25; 26(2); 27; 28(5); 29; 30(2); 31; 41:1; 2(3); 3; 4(5); 5(3); 7(5); 8; 9(2); 13; 14(2); 15(2); 16(4); 17(3); 18(4); 19(9); 20(3); 21(2); 22(2); 23; 25(4); 26; 27; 42:1; 2; 4(2); 5(4); 6(3); 7(2); 8; 9; 10(4); 11(5); 12(2); 13; 15(3); 16; 17; 19; 20; 21(2); 23; 24(2); 25(2); 43:1; 2(4); 3(2); 5(2); 6(4); 8(2); 9(2); 10; 11; 12; 13; 14(3); 15(2); 16(3); 17(3); 18(2); 19(2); 20(6); 23; 24; 28(3); 44:2(2); 3; 4(2); 5(4); 6(5); 7(2); 11; 12(4); 13(5); 14(5); 16(2); 17; 19(2); 23(3); 24(5); 25(2); 26(3); 27; 28; 45:1(4); 2(3); 3(3); 5; 6(3); 7(2); 8(3); 9(4); 10; 11(3); 12(2); 13; 14(3); 15; 17; 18(4); 19(3); 20(2); 21; 22; 23; 24; 25(2); 46:1(3); 2; 3(3); 6(2); 7; 9; 10(2); 11(2); 47:1(3); 2(4); 4(2); 5(2); 6; 7; 8; 9(3); 12; 13(4); 14(3); 48:1(5); 2(3); 3(2); 5; 7; 8; 10; 12(2); 13(3); 14(2); 16(3); 17(4); 18(2); 19(3); 20(4); 21(5); 22(2); 49:1(3); 2; 4; 5(4); 6(5); 7(6); 8(5); 9(2); 10; 12(3); 13; 14; 15; 16; 18; 19(2); 20(3); 22(3); 23(3); 24(4); 25(5); 26(2); 50:1(2); 2(2); 3; 4(4); 5; 6; 7; 9(2); 10(4); 11(2); 51:1(4); 3(4); 4; 5(2); 6(4); 7; 8(2); 9(5); 10(7); 11(2); 12; 13(8); 14(2); 15(3); 16(4); 17(5); 18(3); 20(5); 22(5); 23(3); 52:1(3); 2(2); 3; 4(2); 5(2); 7(2); 8; 9; 10(6); 11(3); 12(2); 14; 53:1(2); 5; 6(2); 7; 8(3); 9(2); 10(3); 11; 12(6); 54:1(5); 2(2); 3(4); 4(2); 5(4); 6; 8; 9(3); 10(3); 13(2); 16(4); 17(4); 55:1; 3; 4(2); 5(2); 6; 7(3); 8; 9(2); 10(5); 11; 12(4); 13(5); 56:1; 2(3); 3(5); 4(2); 6(6); 8(2); 9(2); 57:1(2); 3(3); 4; 5(4); 6(2); 8; 9; 10(2); 13(2); 14(3); 15(6); 16(2); 17(2); 19(3); 20(2); 21; 58:1; 2(2); 3; 4; 5; 6(4); 7(3); 8(3); 9(4); 10(4); 11; 12(5); 13(4); 14(6); 59:1; 5; 6; 8; 10(2); 13(2); 14; 15; 17; 18; 19(8); 20(2); 21(4); 60:1(2); 2(4); 3(2); 5(4); 6(4); 7(3); 9(5); 10; 11(2); 12; 13(6); 14(5); 16(5); 19(3); 20(2); 21(3); 22; 61:1(8); 2(3); 3(5); 4(4); 5(2); 6(5); 8; 9(4); 10(3); 11(5); 62:2(3); 3(3); 4; 5(2); 6; 7; 8(4); 9; 10(6); 11(4); 12(3); 63:1; 2; 3(2); 4(2); 6(2); 7(8); 9(2); 11(3); 12(2); 13(2); 14(3); 15; 17; 64:1(2); 2; 3; 4(5); 6; 8(2); 65:4(4); 5; 7(4); 8(3); 10; 11; 12(2); 13; 15; 16(5); 17; 19(2); 20(2); 22(3); 23(3); 25(6); 66:1(3); 2; 5(3); 6(5); 8; 9(3); 11(2); 12(3); 14(2); 15; 16(3); 17(5); 19(4); 20(5); 21; 22(3); 23; 24(2); **Jer** 1:1(4); 2(5); 3(7); 4(2); 5(2); 7; 8; 9(2); 10(2); 11(2); 12; 13(4); 14(4); 15(7); 16; 18(4); 19; 2:1(2); 2(5); 3(3); 4(4); 5; 6(4); 8(5); 9; 10; 12; 13; 15; 16(2); 17(2); 18(5); 19(3); 20; 21; 22; 23(2); 24(2); 26(2); 27; 28(2); 29; 31(2); 33; 34(3); 37; 3:1(2); 2(4); 3; 4; 5; 6(4); 8(2); 9; 10; 11; 12(3); 13(2); 14; 16(5); 17(6); 18(5); 19(2); 20; 21(3); 22; 23(4); 24; 25(3); 4:1; 2(2); 3(2); 4(3); 5(3); 6(2); 7(2); 8(2); 9(7); 10(2); 11(3); 16(2); 17; 19(3); 20; 21(3); 23(2); 24(2); 25(2); 26(3); 27(2); 28(2); 29(4); 31(3); 5:1(2); 2; 3; 4(3); 5(6); 6(2); 7(2); 9; 10; 11(3); 12; 13(2); 14; 15; 17; 18; 19; 20; 22(4); 24(5); 28(7); 29; 30; 31(3); 6:1(3); 2; 3; 4(3); 6(2); 9(3); 10(2); 11(7); 12(3); 13(4); 14; 15(2); 16(4); 17(2); 19; 21(4); 22(4); 23; 24; 25(4); 26; 29(5); 30; 7:1(2); 2(5); 3(2); 4(6); 6(3); 7; 11; 12(2); 13; 14; 15; 17(2); 18(5); 19(2); 20(5); 21(2); 22(2); 23; 24(2); 25(3); 28(2); 29(3); 30(3); 31(4); 32(5); 33(5); 34(9); 8:1(10); 2(5); 3(3); 4; 6(2); 7(8); 8(4); 9(3); 10(4); 11(2); 12(2); 13(5); 14(3); 16(6); 17; 19(4); 20(2); 21(2); 22(2); 9:1(2); 2; 3(3); 5; 6(2); 7(2); 9; 10(8); 11; 12(4); 13; 14(2); 15(2); 16; 17(2); 19; 20(3); 21(3); 22(4); 23(4); 24(3); 25(3); 26(5); 10:1(2); 2(5); 3(7); 7(3); 9(5); 10(6); 11(4); 12(3); 13(6); 15; 16(4); 17(2); 18(3); 21(2); 22(4); 23; 25(2); 11:1(2); 2(3); 3(3); 4(3); 5; 6(4); 7(2); 8(2); 9(3); 10(3); 11; 12(4); 13(3); 14; 15; 16(2); 17(4); 18; 19(4); 20(2); 21(4); 22(3); 23(2); 12:1(2); 3(2); 4(4); 5(4); 6; 7(2); 8; 9(3); 11; 12(8); 13(2); 14(3); 16(3); 17; 13:1; 2(2); 3(3); 4(3); 5(2); 6(3); 7(4); 8(2); 9(3); 10; 11(5); 12; 13(6); 14(3); 15; 16(3); 17; 18(3); 19(2); 20(2); 22; 23(2); 24(2); 25(2); 27(3); 14:1(3); 2(2); 3; 4(3); 5(2); 6(3); 8(2); 10(2); 11; 12(3); 13(2); 14(3); 15(2); 16(4); 17; 18(3); 19; 20; 21; 22(3); 15:1; 2(7); 3(7); 4(2); 6; 7(2); 8(4); 9(3); 10; 11(4); 12(2); 16; 17(2); 19(3); 20; 21(4); 16:1(2); 3(2); 4(6); 5(3); 6(2); 7(2); 8; 9(8); 10(2); 11; 12; 14(5); 15(5); 16(3); 18; 19(4); 21; 17:1(4); 2(2); 3; 4; 5(3); 6(3); 7(3); 8(3); 9; 10(4); 11; 12(2); 13(4); 15(2); 16; 17; 18; 19(6); 20(3); 21(3); 22(2); 24(4); 25(4); 26(8); 27(4); 18:1(2); 2; 3(2); 4(4); 5(2); 6(3); 7; 8; 9; 10; 11(3); 12; 13(3); 14(4); 15; 17(4); 18(6); 19; 21(4); 23; 19:1(5); 2(5); 3(4); 4(3); 5; 6(5); 7(7); 9(5); 10(3); 11; 12; 13(6); 14(4); 15(3); 20:1(4); 2(5); 3(3); 4(5); 5(4); 8(2); 11; 12(2); 13(5); 14(2); 15; 16(5); 17; 18; 21:1(5); 2(3); 4(6); 6; 7(10); 8(3); 9(2); 10(3); 11(4); 12(5); 13(3); 14(2); 22:1(3); 2(3); 3(7); 4(2); 5; 6(4); 7; 8; 9(2); 10; 11(2); 12; 16(3); 18(2); 19(2); 22; 23(2); 24(3); 25(5); 27; 29(2); 30(2); 23:1(3); 2(4); 3; 4; 5(3); 6; 7(5); 8(5); 9(2); 10(4); 11; 12(3); 13; 14(2); 15(5); 16(5); 17(2); 18(2); 19(3); 20(4); 22; 23; 24(2); 25; 26(3); 28(4); 29(2); 30(2); 31(2); 32(2); 33(5); 34(5); 35(2); 36(5); 37(3); 38(7); 39; 24:1(6); 2(2); 3(3); 4(2); 5(4); 7; 8(5); 9(2); 10(4); 25:1(5); 2(3); 3(5); 4(2); 5(2); 6; 7(2); 8; 9(4); 10(10); 11; 12(4); 13; 14; 15(2); 16; 17(4); 18; 20(7); 21; 22(5); 23; 24(4); 25(4); 26(7); 27(3); 28(2); 29(4); 30(4); 31(6); 32(3); 33(6); 34(3); 35(3); 36(5); 37(3); 38(3); 26:1(4); 2(6); 3(2); 4; 5(2); 6(2); 7(5); 8(5); 9(5); 10(7); 11(4); 12(4); 13(4); 15; 16(6); 17(4); 18(7); 19(4); 20(4); 21(3); 22(2); 23(4); 24(4); 27:1(4); 2; 3(8); 4(2); 5(4); 6(4); 7; 8(8); 9; 11(4); 12(2); 13(6); 14(3); 15(2); 16(5); 17; 18(8); 19(6); 20(2); 21(7); 22(2); 28:1(12); 2(4); 3(2); 4(5); 5(8); 6(5); 7(2); 8; 9(5); 10(3); 11(7); 12(6); 13(2); 14(5); 15(3); 16(4); 17(3); 29:1(8); 2(6); 3(4); 4(2); 7(3); 8(2); 9; 10; 11(2); 14(5); 15; 16(4); 17(4); 18(4); 19(3); 20(3); 21(5); 22(4); 23; 24; 25(6); 26(5); 29(3); 30(2); 31(2); 32(5); 30:1(2); 2(2); 3(4); 4(2); 5; 7; 8; 9; 10(2); 11; 12; 14(3); 15; 17; 18(4); 19; 21; 23(4); 24(4); 31:1(4); 2(4); 3; 4; 5(2); 6(2); 7(4); 8(7); 9; 10(3); 11(2); 12(6); 13(4); 14(3); 15; 16(4); 17; 18; 19(2); 20; 21(2); 22(2); 23(4); 25; 27(6); 28; 29(2); 30; 31(4); 32(5); 33(3); 34(4); 35(7); 36(2); 37(5); 38(6); 39(2); 40(9); 32:1(4); 2(5); 3(3); 4(4); 5(2); 6(2); 7(2); 8(9); 9(3); 10(3); 11(2); 12(9); 14(2); 15(2); 16(3); 17(2); 18(6); 19(3); 20; 21; 24(6); 25(4); 26(2); 27(2); 28(4); 29(2); 30(5); 31; 32(5); 33(2); 34; 35(4); 36(7); 39; 42(2); 43(2); 44(10); 33:1(4); 2(3); 4(7); 5(2); 6; 7(3); 9(4); 10(3); 11(16); 12; 13(12); 14(4); 15; 16(2); 17(3); 18(2); 19(2); 20(3); 21(2); 22(5); 23(2); 24(2); 25(2); 26(2); 34:1(5); 2(5); 3(2); 4(4); 5(4); 6; 7(3); 8(3); 10(3); 11; 12(3); 13(5); 14; 15; 17(5); 18(5); 19(8); 20(6); 21(4); 22(2); 35:1(4); 2(5); 3(4); 4(11); 5(3); 6; 7; 8(2); 11(5); 12(2); 13(5); 14(2); 15(2); 16(3); 17(4); 18(5); 19(3); 36:1(3); 2(4); 3(2); 4(4); 5(2); 6(8); 7(4); 8(6); 9(7); 10(13); 11(5); 12(9); 13(4); 14(9); 16(2); 18; 19; 20(8); 21(8); 22(4); 23(7); 24; 25(2); 26(7); 27(6); 28(3); 29(2); 30(6); 31(3); 32(6); 37:1(3); 2(5); 3(6); 4; 5; 6(3); 7(3); 8; 9(2); 10(3); 11(3); 12(2); 13(6); 14(2); 15(4); 16(2); 17(5); 19; 20(3); 21(8); 38:1(6); 2(3); 3(3); 4(7); 5(2); 6(6); 7(6); 8(2); 9(5); 10(4); 11(5); 12(2); 13(3); 14(6); 16(3); 17(4); 18(3); 19(3); 20(2); 21(2); 22(4); 23(3); 25(3); 26; 27(3); 28(3); 39:1(2); 2(5); 3(6); 4(7); 5(3); 6(4); 8(5); 9(7); 10(5); 11(2); 13(3); 14(5); 15(4); 16(3); 17(3); 18(2); 40:1(4); 2(3); 3(2); 4(2); 5(7); 6(3); 7(8); 8(6); 9(5); 10; 11(6); 12(2); 13(4); 14(4); 15(4); 16(2); 41:1(7); 2(7); 3(3); 4; 5(2); 6(2); 7(5); 8; 9(7); 10(9); 11(5); 12(3); 13(4); 14(2); 15(2); 16(11); 17; 18(5); 42:1(7); 2(2); 3(3); 4(3); 5(2); 6(4); 7(2); 8(6); 9(2); 10; 11(2); 13(2); 14(3); 15(4); 16(3); 17(3); 18(3); 19; 20(3); 21(2); 22(2); 43:1(4); 2(4); 3(3); 4(7); 5(5); 6(7); 7(3); 8(2); 9(5); 10(3); 11(3); 12(3); 13(5); 44:1(4); 2(4); 4; 6(2); 7(3); 8(4); 9(7); 11(2); 12(7); 13(2); 14(3); 15(4); 16(3); 17(3); 18(2); 19(2); 20(4); 21(6); 22(3); 23(3); 24(5); 25(3); 26(7); 27(3); 28(5); 29; 30(4); 45:1(6); 2(2); 3; 4; 5; 46:1(4); 2(4); 3; 4(3); 5; 6(4); 7; 8(3); 9(6); 10(6); 11; 12(4); 13(4); 14; 15; 16(2); 17; 18(4); 20; 21(2); 23; 24(4); 25(2); 26(5); 27; 28(2); 47:1(4); 2(7); 3(5); 4(6); 5; 6; 7(2); 48:1(3); 2; 5(3); 6(2); 8(4); 10(2); 12(3); 13; 14; 15(3); 16; 17(2); 18; 19; 21; 24(2); 25(2); 26; 28(5); 29(2); 30; 31; 32(4); 33(3); 34(2); 35(3); 36(2); 37(2); 38(2); 40; 41(3); 42; 43(3); 44(6); 45(6); 46; 47(4); 49:1(2); 2(4); 3; 4; 5; 6(3); 7(2); 8(3); 12(3); 13; 14(2); 16(7); 18(2); 19(4); 20(5); 21(4); 22(4); 23; 25(2); 26(2); 27(2); 28(4); 30(2); 31(2); 32(3); 34(5); 35(3); 36(3); 37(2); 38(3); 39(3); 50:1(5); 2; 3; 4(4); 5(2); 6; 7(4); 8(5); 9; 10; 12(2); 13(2); 14(2); 15(2); 16(3); 17(2); 18(4); 20(3); 21(3); 22; 23(3); 24; 25(6); 26; 27(2); 28(5); 29(4); 30(2); 31(2); 32; 33(3); 34(3); 35(3); 36; 37; 38; 39(3); 40; 41(3); 42(4); 43(2); 44(4); 45(6); 46(5); 51:1; 2; 3; 4(3); 5(2); 6(3); 7(4); 9; 10(3); 11(9); 12(7); 13; 14; 15(3); 16(6); 17; 18; 19(4); 20; 21(2); 22(2); 23(2); 24(3); 25(3); 26; 27(7); 28(4); 29(3); 30(2); 31; 32(3); 33(4); 34; 35(3); 36; 39; 40; 41(3); 42(2); 44(2); 45(3); 46(3); 47(2); 48(5); 49(3); 50(2); 51(2); 52(3); 53(2); 54(3); 55(2); 56(3); 57(2); 58(5); 59(7); 60; 63; 64(2); 52:1; 2(2); 3(3); 4(4); 5(2); 6(7); 7(9); 8(4); 9(3); 10(3); 11(3); 12(7); 13(6); 14(5); 15(10); 16(4); 17(8); 18(7); 19(9); 20(6); 21(2); 22(4); 23(3); 24(5); 25(12); 26(3); 27(2); 28(2); 29; 30(5); 31(7); 32; 33(2); 34(3); **Lam** 1:1(4); 2; 3; 4(2); 5(4); 6(2); 7(5); 9; 10(2); 12(2); 13; 14(3); 15(3); 16(2); 17; 18; 19; 20; 21; 2:1(5); 2(6); 3; 4(2); 5(2); 6(4); 7(7); 8(4); 9(4); 10(5); 11(7); 12(3); 13; 15(5); 16; 17(2); 18(2); 19(7); 20(5); 21(4); 22(3); 3:1(2); 3; 6; 12; 13; 14(2); 18; 19(2); 22; 24; 25(2); 26(2); 27; 29; 30; 31; 32; 33; 34(2); 35(3); 36; 37; 38(2); 39; 40; 45(2); 48(2); 50; 51; 53; 54; 55; 57; 58; 62(2); 64; 66(2); 4:1(5); 2(4); 3(3); 4(4); 5; 6(5); 8; 9(3); 10(4); 11; 12(6); 13(4); 14; 15; 16(5); 19(4); 20(4); 21(2); 22; 5:4; 6(2); 9(3); 10; 11(3); 13; 14(3); 15; 16; **Ezek** 1:1(7); 2(3); 3(9); 4(4); 5(2); 7(3); 8(2); 9; 10(10); 12; 13(6); 14; 15(2); 16(6); 18; 19(5); 20(6); 21(5); 22(5); 23(3); 24(5); 25; 26(5); 27(5); 28(7); 2:2; 3; 4; 10(2); 3:1; 4; 5; 7(2); 11(3); 12(3); 13(5); 14(4); 15(2); 16(3); 17; 18(2); 19; 21(2); 22(3); 23(5); 24; 26; 27; 4:3(2); 4(4); 5(5); 6(2); 7; 8; 9; 13(3); 16; 5:1; 2(6); 3; 4(4); 5(4); 6(2); 7(4); 8(3); 9; 10; 11; 12(3); 13; 14(2); 15(2); 16(2); 17(2); 6:1(2); 2; 3(7); 5(2); 6(2); 7(2); 8(3); 9(3); 10; 11(4); 12(3); 13(2); 14(3); 7:1(2); 2(5); 3; 4; 5; 6; 7(3); 9; 10(2); 12(4); 13(3); 14; 15(5); 16(2); 19(4); 20(2); 21(3); 23(2); 24(4); 26(3); 27(5); 8:1(7); 2(4); 3(7); 4(4); 5(4); 6(2); 7(3); 8(2); 9; 10(3); 11(3); 12(7); 14(3); 16(12); 17(4); 9:1; 2(3); 3(7); 4(7); 5(2); 6(3); 7(4); 8; 9(7); 11(2); 10:1(5); 2(5); 3(6); 4(10); 5(5); 6(4); 7(6); 8(2); 9(3); 10; 11(2); 12(2); 13; 14(8); 15(3); 16(5); 17(5); 18(5); 19(8); 20(3); 21(2); 22(4); 11:1(8); 2; 3(3); 5(4); 6; 7(4); 8(2); 9; 10(3); 11(2); 12(3); 13(2); 14(2); 15(3); 16(4); 17(4); 19; 21(2); 22(4); 23(7); 24(3); 25(2); 12:1(2); 2; 5; 6(2); 7; 8(3); 9(2); 10(3); 12(3); 13(2); 14; 15(3); 16(3); 17(2);

19(6); 20(3); 21(2); 22(2); 23(3); 24; 25(4); 26(2); 27(2); 28(3); 13:1(2); 2(3); 3(2); 4; 5(4); 6(3); 7; 8(2); 9(6); 12(2); 13; 14(4); 15(2); 16(2); 17; 18(4); 20(3); 21; 22(4); 23; 14:1; 2(2); 4(5); 5; 6(2); 7(3); 8(2); 9(2); 10(5); 11(2); 12(2); 14; 15(2); 16(2); 17; 18; 20; 21(2); 22; 23; 15:1(2); 2(5); 4(2); 5; 6(7); 7; 8(2); 16:1(2); 3(2); 4; 5(2); 7; 8(2); 14(2); 15; 16; 17; 19(2); 21; 22; 23; 25; 26; 27(3); 28(3); 29(2); 30(2); 31; 34(2); 35(2); 36(2); 41(2); 43(2); 45; 46(2); 48; 49(3); 51; 52; 53(3); 56; 57(5); 58; 59(3); 60; 62; 63; 17:1(2); 2; 3(3); 5(2); 7; 9; 10(2); 11(2); 12(2); 13(3); 14; 16(4); 17; 18(2); 19; 20; 21(2); 22(4); 23(2); 24(8); 18:1(2); 2(3); 3; 4(5); 6(3); 7(3); 9; 11; 12(3); 14; 15(3); 16(2); 17(2); 19(4); 20(11); 22(2); 23(2); 24(5); 25(2); 26; 27; 28; 29(3); 30; 31; 32(2); 19:1; 2(2); 4(2); 6; 7(2); 8(2); 9(2); 10; 11(2); 12(3); 13; 20:1(6); 2(2); 3(3); 4; 5(6); 6(2); 7(3); 8(4); 9(2); 10(2); 12; 13(3); 14; 15(3); 17; 18(2); 19; 20; 21(2); 22(2); 23(3); 26(2); 27(2); 28(3); 30(3); 31(2); 32(2); 33; 34(2); 35(2); 36(3); 37(3); 38(4); 39; 40(5); 41(3); 42(3); 43; 44(2); 45(2); 46(4); 47(8); 48; 21:1(2); 2(2); 3(2); 5; 7(2); 8(2); 9; 10; 11(2); 12(2); 13(4); 14(5); 15(3); 16; 17; 18(2); 19(6); 20(2); 21(8); 22(3); 23; 24; 26(6); 28(2); 29(3); 30(2); 31(2); 32(4); 22:1(2); 2; 3(2); 4(4); 6; 7(3); 9; 12; 13(2); 14(2); 15(2); 16(3); 17(2); 18(2); 19(2); 20; 21; 22(2); 23(2); 24; 25(2); 26(4); 27; 28(2); 29(4); 30(2); 31(2); 23:1(2); 2; 4; 5(2); 9(3); 10; 12; 13; 14; 15(3); 17(2); 19(3); 20(2); 21(2); 22; 23(3); 25; 27; 28(3); 29; 30; 31; 32(2); 33(2); 34; 35(2); 36; 37; 38; 39(2); 42(3); 44(2); 45(2); 46; 47; 48; 49; 24:1(6); 2(3); 3(2); 4(2); 5(3); 6(3); 7; 9(3); 10(5); 11(2); 12; 14(2); 15(2); 16; 17; 18(3); 19; 20(2); 21(5); 24; 25(2); 27; 25:1(2); 2; 3(6); 4(2); 5; 6(2); 7(4); 8(3); 9(4); 10(5); 11; 12(2); 13(2); 14(2); 15(3); 16(5); 17; 26:1(5); 2(2); 3(2); 4(2); 5(4); 6(3); 7(2); 8(2); 10(5); 11(3); 12(2); 13(2); 14(3); 15(5); 16(3); 18(4); 19(2); 20(7); 21; 27:1(2); 3(4); 4(2); 6(2); 7; 9(2); 11; 14; 15(2); 16; 17; 18(2); 21; 22(2); 23; 25(3); 26(3); 27(4); 28(3); 29(5); 32(2); 33(2); 34(4); 35(2); 36(2); 28:1(2); 2(6); 6(2); 7(3); 8(5); 9; 10(4); 11(2); 12(3); 13(4); 14(3); 15; 16(4); 17(2); 18(4); 19; 20(2); 22(2); 23(3); 24(2); 25(5); 26; 29:1(6); 3(2); 4(3); 5(7); 6(3); 7; 8; 9(3); 10(2); 12(7); 13(4); 14(3); 15(3); 16(3); 17(6); 18; 19(3); 20(2); 21(3); 30:1(2); 2(2); 3(5); 4(2); 5(4); 6(4); 7(4); 8; 9(2); 10(2); 11(5); 12(7); 13(5); 15(2); 17(2); 18(2); 19; 20(6); 21; 22(4); 23(3); 24(3); 25(7); 26(4); 31:1(6); 3(2); 4(4); 5(3); 6(4); 7; 8(5); 9(2); 10(2); 11(3); 12(8); 13(4); 14(6); 15(6); 16(7); 17(2); 18(8); 32:1(6); 2(3); 3; 4(6); 5(2); 6(4); 7(3); 8(3); 9(3); 10; 11(3); 12(5); 13(2); 14; 15(3); 16(4); 17(5); 18(6); 19; 20(3); 21(5); 22; 23(5); 24(6); 25(8); 26(3); 27(6); 28(3); 29(3); 30(7); 31(2); 32(6); 33:1(2); 2(4); 3(4); 4(3); 5(2); 6(6); 7; 8(2); 9; 10; 11(4); 12(9); 13(2); 14; 15(3); 17(3); 18; 19; 20(2); 21(5); 22(5); 23(2); 24(3); 25(2); 26; 27(8); 28(2); 29(2); 30(6); 34:1(2); 2(6); 3(4); 4(2); 5(2); 6(3); 7(2); 8(3); 9(2); 10(4); 11; 12(2); 13(6); 14(2); 15; 16(3); 17; 18(4); 20(3); 21; 24(2); 25(3); 26; 27(6); 28(2); 29(3); 30(3); 31(2); 35:1(2); 3; 4; 5(5); 6; 7(2); 8(2); 9; 10; 11(2); 12(2); 14(2); 15(3); 36:1(3); 2(3); 3(6); 4(11); 5(3); 6(8); 7(2); 10(3); 11; 13; 14; 15(5); 16(2); 17(2); 18(2); 19(2); 20(3); 21(2); 22(3); 23(4); 24; 26; 28; 29; 30(4); 32; 33(4); 34(2); 35(2); 36(4); 37(2); 38(3); 37:1(6); 2; 4(2); 5; 6; 7; 8(3); 9(4); 11; 12(2); 13; 14(2); 15(2); 16(3); 18; 19(5); 20; 21(3); 22(2); 25; 28(2); 38:1(2); 2(2); 3(2); 6(2); 8(5); 9; 10; 12(4); 13; 14; 15; 16(3); 17(2); 18(3); 19(2); 20(12); 21; 22; 23(2); 39:1(2); 2(2); 3(2); 4(4); 5(2); 6(2); 7(4); 8(2); 9(5); 10(4); 11(3); 12(2); 13(4); 14(4); 15(4); 16(3); 17(3); 18(5); 20(2); 21(2); 22(2); 23(4); 25(3); 27(2); 28(2); 29(2); 40:1(10); 2(4); 3(2); 4(2); 5(6); 6(4); 7(5); 8(2); 9(6); 10(6); 11(5); 12(2); 13(5); 14(4); 15(5); 16(5); 17(3); 18(6); 19(7); 20; 21(2); 22(2); 23(3); 24; 27(2); 28(3); 31; 32(2); 34; 35; 37; 38(3); 39(5); 40(7); 41(3); 42(4); 43(3); 44(9); 45(2); 46(6); 47(3); 48(6); 49(5); 41:1(5); 2(5); 3(4); 4(4); 5(4); 6(5); 7(8); 8(3); 9(7); 10(2); 11(7); 12(4); 13(3); 14(4); 15(8); 16(6); 17(3); 19(4); 20(5); 21(4); 22(3); 23(2); 24(2); 25(5); 26(6); 42:1(7); 2(3); 3(3); 4(2); 5(4); 6(5); 7(4); 8(4); 9(4); 10(6); 11(3); 12(6); 13(12); 14(4); 15(3); 16(3); 17(2); 18(2); 19(2); 20(3); 43:1(3); 2(6); 3(7); 4(5); 5(5); 6; 7(7); 8; 9; 10(3); 11(2); 12(6); 13(6); 14(9); 15(2); 16; 17(2); 18(4); 19(4); 20(5); 21(5); 22(4); 23; 24(3); 25; 26; 27(4); 44:1(3); 2(2); 3(6); 4(7); 5(6); 6(3); 7(2); 9(2); 10; 11(5); 12(2); 13; 14; 15(7); 17(5); 19(5); 21; 22(2); 23(5); 27(5); 29(3); 30(4); 31; 45:1(4); 2; 3(3); 4(6); 5(3); 6(5); 7(12); 8(4); 9(2); 11(6); 12; 13; 14(2); 15(2); 16(3); 17(11); 18(5); 19(11); 20(3); 21(4); 22(3); 23(4); 25(8); 46:1(8); 2(9); 3(6); 4(4); 5(3); 6(2); 7; 8(4); 9(10); 10; 11(4); 12(6); 13(2); 14(2); 15(3); 16(2); 17(2); 18(2); 19(6); 20(7); 21(4); 22(3); 23(2); 24(5); 47:1(11); 2(4); 3(5); 4(3); 5; 6(2); 7(3); 8(4); 9(2); 10(3); 12(3); 13(4); 15(5); 16(3); 17(6); 18(7); 19(7); 20(4); 21; 22(3); 23(2); 48:1(7); 2(3); 3(3); 4(3); 5(3); 6(3); 7(3); 8(10); 9(2); 10(9); 11(4); 12(2); 13(3); 14(2); 15(6); 16(4); 17(6); 18(10); 19(3); 20(4); 21(16); 22(10); 23(4); 24(3); 25(3); 26(3); 27(3); 28(7); 29(3); 30(3); 31(4); 32; 33; 34; 35(4); **Dan** 1:1(2); 2(7); 3(5); 4(3); 5(5); 6; 7(3); 8(5); 9(3); 10(5); 11(3); 13(4); 15(4); 16(2); 18(5); 19(2); 20(2); 21; 2:1; 2(8); 3(2); 4(4); 5(3); 6(2); 7(2); 8; 9(3); 10(3); 11(3); 12(2); 13(2); 14(3); 15(4); 16(3); 17; 18(3); 19(2); 20; 21(3); 22; 23; 24(6); 25(4); 26(2); 27(9); 28(2); 30(3); 34; 35(10); 36(3); 37; 38(5); 39; 40(2); 41(5); 42(3); 43; 44(3); 45(10); 47(3); 48(3); 49(5); 3:1(3); 2(11); 3(12); 5(4); 6; 7(5); 8; 10(3); 11; 12(3); 13(2); 14; 15(6); 16; 17(2); 18; 19(2); 20; 21(2); 22(4); 23(2); 24(3); 25(5); 26(5); 27(5); 28(2); 29; 30(2); 4:1(2); 2(2); 5(2); 6(3); 7(5); 8(4); 9(4); 10(3); 11(4); 12(4); 13; 14(3); 15(8); 16; 17(9); 18(4); 19(3); 20(3); 21(4); 22(3); 23(8); 24(4); 25(5); 26(3); 27; 29(3); 30(2); 31(3); 32(4); 33(2); 34(3); 35(5); 36(2); 37; 5:1(3); 2(5); 3(4); 4; 5(9); 6(2); 7(8); 8(3); 10(5); 11(7); 12(2); 13(4); 14; 15(4); 16(3); 17(4); 18; 19; 21(6); 23(4); 24(2); 25; 26; 27; 28; 29(3); 30; 31(2); 6:1(2); 2(2); 3(3); 4(2); 5; 6; 7(5); 8(4); 9; 10; 12(7); 13(3); 14(3); 15(5); 16(4); 17(5); 18(2); 19(3); 20(4); 21; 22; 23(3); 24(6); 25; 26(4); 27(2); 28(3); 7:1(3); 2(2); 3(2); 4(2); 6; 7(3); 8(4); 9(2); 10(2); 11(5); 12(2); 13(4); 14; 15; 16(2); 17; 18(4); 19(4); 20(2); 21(2); 22(6); 23(2); 24(2); 25(4); 26; 27(7); 28(3); 8:1(4); 2(5); 3(4); 4; 5(5); 6(2); 7(5); 8(3); 9(3); 10(4); 11(4);

12(3); 13(6); 14; 15(3); 16(3); 17(3); 18; 19(4); 20(3); 21(4); 22(2); 23(2); 24(2); 25; 26(4); 27(2); 9:1(6); 2(8); 3; 4; 6(3); 7(4); 9; 10(3); 11(4); 12; 13(2); 14(4); 15; 16; 17(2); 18; 20(3); 21(5); 23(4); 24(2); 25(5); 26(8); 27(5); 10:1(5); 4(5); 6(3); 7(3); 9(3); 10; 11; 12; 13(4); 14(2); 15; 16(3); 18(2); 20(2); 21; 11:1(2); 2(3); 4; 5(2); 6(7); 7(3); 8(2); 9(5); 11(6); 12; 13(4); 14(3); 15(4); 16; 17(2); 18(3); 19; 20; 21(2); 22(3); 23; 24(4); 25(4); 26; 27(3); 28; 29(4); 30(2); 31(3); 32(2); 33; 35(3); 36(3); 37(2); 39(2); 40(7); 41(2); 42(2); 43(3); 44(2); 45(3); 12:1(3); 2(2); 3(3); 4(4); 5; 6(4); 7(5); 8; 9(3); 10(3); 11(3); 12; 13(3); **Hos** 1:1(6); 2(4); 3; 4(5); 5(2); 6; 7(2); 10(6); 11(4); 2:3; 4; 5; 10; 12(2); 13(3); 14; 15(4); 16; 17(2); 18(7); 20; 21(3); 22; 23; 3:1(6); 3; 4; 5(4); 4:1(6); 3(7); 4; 5(3); 6; 7(2); 8; 10; 11; 12(2); 13(2); 14; 15(2); 16; 19; 5:1(2); 2; 4(2); 5; 6; 7; 8(2); 9(2); 10; 12; 14; 6:1; 2; 3(6); 4; 5(2); 6; 7; 9(2); 10(2); 11; 7:1(2); 4(2); 5; 6; 8; 10(2); 12; 16(4); 8:1(3); 3(2); 6; 7(3); 8; 10(3); 12; 13(2); 9:1; 2(3); 3; 4(3); 5(4); 7(5); 8(3); 9; 10(4); 12; 13; 15; 16; 17; 10:1(3); 3; 4(2); 5(2); 6; 7; 8(5); 9(3); 12; 13(2); 14; 15; 11:2; 4; 5(2); 6; 7; 9(2); 10(2); 11(2); 12(2); 12:1(3); 2; 3(2); 4; 5(2); 6; 9(4); 10(3); 11(2); 12; 13; 14; 13:2(3); 3(2); 4(2); 5(2); 7; 8; 12; 13; 14(2); 15(4); 16; 14:1; 2(2); 3(2); 5(2); 7; 9(3); **Joel** 1:1(3); 2(2); 4(6); 5; 6(2); 8; 9(6); 10(5); 11(4); 12(8); 13(4); 14(6); 15(4); 16(2); 17(3); 18(3); 19(3); 20(4); 2:1(5); 2(3); 3(2); 4; 5(2); 6; 7; 8; 9(4); 10(4); 11(4); 12; 13; 14; 15; 16(6); 17(6); 18; 19(2); 20(3); 21; 22(5); 23(6); 24(2); 25(5); 26(2); 27(2); 30(2); 31(5); 32(5); 3:1; 2(2); 4; 6(3); 7; 8(4); 9(3); 10; 12(3); 13(4); 14(4); 15(2); 16(5); 17; 18(6); 19; 21(2); **Am** 1:1(6); 2(4); 3; 4(2); 5(7); 6(2); 7; 8(6); 9(3); 10; 11(2); 12; 13(3); 14(4); 15; 2:1(3); 2; 3(2); 4(3); 5; 6(3); 7(7); 8(3); 9(4); 10(4); 11; 12(2); 14(3); 15(2); 16(2); 3:1(3); 2(2); 4; 5(2); 6(2); 7(2); 8; 9(5); 10; 11(2); 12(5); 13(3); 14(5); 15(5); 4:1(3); 2(2); 3; 5(2); 6; 7(2); 8; 9(2); 10(3); 11(2); 13(5); 5:3(3); 4(2); 6(2); 7; 8(8); 9(2); 10(3); 11; 12(3); 13; 14; 15(3); 16(4); 17; 18(4); 19(2); 20(2); 23(2); 25; 26; 27(2); 6:1(2); 2(2); 3(2); 4(3); 5; 6(2); 7(2); 8(4); 10(7); 11(3); 12; 14(4); 7:1(5); 2(2); 3(2); 4(4); 6(2); 7; 8(3); 9(4); 10(4); 11; 12; 13(2); 15(3); 16(3); 17(3); 8:1; 2(2); 3(3); 4(3); 5(5); 6(3); 7(2); 8(3); 9(3); 11(5); 12(2); 13; 14(2); 9:1(7); 3(3); 4; 5(4); 6(7); 7(5); 8(7); 9(3); 10(3); 11(2); 12(3); 13(7); 14(2); 15(2); **Ob** 1(4); 2; 3(4); 4(3); 7(3); 8(3); 9(2); 11(3); 12(5); 13(4); 14(2); 15(3); 16; 17; 18(5); 19(5); 20(7); 21(3); **Jon** 1:1(3); 3(5); 4(4); 5(7); 6; 7; 9(4); 10(4); 11(2); 12(2); 13(2); 14; 15(2); 16(3); 17(3); 2:1(2); 2(2); 3(4); 5(2); 6(4); 7; 9(2); 10(2); 3:1(3); 2; 3(2); 4(2); 5(3); 6; 7(2); 8; 10; 4:2; 4; 5(5); 6(2); 7(2); 8(2); 9; 10(2); **Mic** 1:1(3); 2(2); 3(3); 4(3); 5(5); 6(2); 7(3); 8(2); 9; 10; 11; 12(3); 13(5); 14(2); 15; 2:1; 3; 4; 5(2); 7(3); 8(2); 9; 11; 12(3); 13(3); 3:1; 2(2); 3(3); 4; 5(2); 6(3); 7(2); 8(2); 9(2); 11(2); 12(4); 4:1(6); 2(7); 4(2); 5(3); 6(3); 7(3); 8(6); 10(4); 12(3); 13(3); 5:1(2); 2(2); 3(3); 4(7); 5; 6(4); 7(5); 8(5); 10; 11; 13; 15; 6:1(3); 2(3); 4(2); 5(3); 6(2); 7(3); 8; 9(3); 10(4); 11(2); 14; 15; 16(3); 7:1; 2(2); 3(3); 4(3); 5; 6; 7(2); 8; 9(3); 10(2); 11(2); 12(3); 13(2); 14(2); 15(2); 16; 17(3); 18(2); 19(2); **Nah** 1:1(4); 2(3); 3(7); 4(3); 5(4); 6(2); 7(2); 9; 11; 12; 14(4); 15(3); 2:1(2); 2(4); 3(5); 4(3); 5; 6(3); 7; 10(2); 11(6); 12; 13(4); 3:1; 2(2); 3; 4(3); 5(3); 8(4); 10; 11; 12(2); 13(2); 14(4); 15(4); 16(2); 17(3); 18(2); **Hab** 1:1(2); 4(3); 5; 6(3); 8; 9; 13; 14; 2:1; 2(2); 3(2); 4(2); 8(5); 9; 11(4); 13(3); 14(6); 16(2); 17(5); 18(3); 20(2); 3:1; 2(4); 3(3); 4; 6(4); 7(3); 8(3); 9; 10(4); 11(3); 12(2); 13(4); 14(2); 15(2); 16(3); 17(8); 18(2); 19(2); **Zeph** 1:1(8); 2(3); 3(9); 4(4); 5(3); 6(2); 7(5); 8(4); 9(2); 10(5); 11; 12(2); 14(6); 16(2); 17; 18(5); 2:2(5); 3(4); 5(7); 6; 7(5); 8(3); 9(5); 10(2); 11(5); 13(2); 14(8); 15; 3:1; 2; 4(2); 5(2); 8(5); 9(3); 10(2); 12(2); 13; 15(3); 17(2); 18; 19; 20(4); **Hag** 1:1(10); 2(4); 3(3); 5; 7; 8(3); 9; 10(3); 11(7); 12(13); 13(4); 14(11); 15(3); 2:1(6); 2(5); 4(5); 5; 6(2); 7(2); 8(3); 9(4); 10(6); 11(3); 12(3); 13; 14; 15(2); 16(2); 17(2); 18(5); 19(6); 20(4); 22(6); 23(4); **Zech** 1:1(7); 2; 3(3); 4(3); 5; 6(2); 7(9); 8(2); 9; 10(5); 11(5); 12(3); 13(2); 14(2); 15; 16(2); 17(2); 19(2); 20; 21(5); 2:3; 4; 5(2); 6(5); 7; 8(3); 9; 10; 11(2); 12(2); 13; 3:1(3); 2(4); 3; 4; 5(3); 6(2); 7; 8(2); 9(4); 10; 4:1; 2(2); 3(3); 4; 5; 6(3); 7; 8(2); 9(3); 10(6); 11(2); 12(3); 14(3); 5:3(4); 4(7); 5; 6; 7; 8(2); 9(3); 10(2); 11(2); 6:1; 2(2); 3(2); 4; 5(3); 6(6); 7(4); 8(2); 9(2); 10(5); 11(4); 12(5); 13(4); 14(4); 15(5); 7:1(5); 2(3); 3(5); 4(2); 5(4); 7(6); 8(2); 9; 10(4); 12(5); 13; 14(3); 8:1(2); 2; 3(6); 4(2); 5(2); 6(4); 7(5); 8; 9(8); 10; 11(3); 12(5); 13; 14(2); 15; 16(2); 17; 18(2); 19(10); 20; 21(3); 22(2); 23(3); 9:1(6); 3(3); 4(2); 5; 6(2); 7(2); 8; 9; 10(7); 11(2); 12; 13(2); 14(4); 15(3); 16(3); 17(2); 10:1(5); 2(3); 3(5); 4(3); 5(5); 6(3); 7; 9; 10(2); 11(7); 12(2); 11:2(3); 3(4); 4(2); 5; 6(5); 7(6); 8; 10(2); 11(4); 13(6); 14; 15(2); 16(4); 17(2); 12:1(8); 2; 3; 4(3); 5(3); 6(6); 7(6); 8(6); 9; 10(3); 11(2); 12(5); 13(3); 14; 13:1(2); 2(7); 3(2); 6; 7(5); 8(2); 9(3); 14:1(2); 2(8); 3(2); 4(6); 5(5); 6; 7; 8(2); 9(3); 10(6); 11; 12(3); 13(2); 14(2); 15(6); 16(4); 17(4); 18(5); 19(4); 20(7); 21(3); **Mal** 1:1(3); 2(2); 3(2); 4(5); 5(2); 6(2); 7(2); 8(3); 9; 10(2); 11(5); 12(2); 13(5); 14(4); 2:2; 3; 4; 6; 7(4); 8(4); 9(2); 10(2); 11(2); 12(4); 13(4); 14(2); 15(2); 16(2); 17(4); 3:1(5); 2; 3(2); 4(3); 5; 6; 7(2); 10(4); 11(5); 12; 13; 14; 15; 16(3); 17(2); 18(2); 4:1(4); 2; 3(4); 4(2); 5(4); 6(6); **Mt** 1:1(4); 6(3); 11; 16; 17(4); 18(2); 20(2); 22(2); 23; 24(2); 2:1(3); 2(2); 3; 4(3); 5; 6(3); 7(2); 8; 9(4); 10; 11(2); 13(3); 14; 15(3); 16(4); 17; 19; 20(3); 21(2); 22; 23; 3:1(2); 2; 3(5); 5(2); 6; 7(2); 10(4); 11; 12(2); 13; 16(3); 4:1(3); 3(2); 4; 5(4); 6; 7; 8(3); 10; 11; 13(2); 14; 15(6); 16(2); 17; 18(2); 21(2); 22; 23(3); 25; 5:1; 3(2); 5(2); 7; 8; 9; 10; 12; 13(3); 14(2); 15; 17(2); 18; 19(3); 20(3); 21; 22(2); 23; 24; 25(4); 26; 33; 35(3); 37; 39; 45(4); 46(2); 47; 6:2(3); 5(4); 6; 7; 8; 13(4); 16; 18; 22(3); 23; 24(4); 25; 26(2); 28(2); 30(3); 32; 33; 34; 7:2; 3(2); 4; 5(2); 6; 12(2); 13(3); 14(2); 19; 21(2); 24; 25(4); 26; 27(3); 28; 29; 8:1; 4(2); 8; 11; 12(2); 13; 15; 16; 17; 18; 20(2); 22; 24(3); 26(2); 27(3); 28(4); 29; 31(2); 32(5); 33(2); 34; 9:2; 3; 6(2); 8; 9; 10(2); 11; 13; 14(2); 15(5); 16(3); 17(3); 20; 22; 23(3); 24; 25(3); 26; 28(2); 31; 33(3); 34(3); 35(4); 36; 37(2); 38(2); 10:2(3); 3(2); 4; 5(3); 6(2); 7; 8(3); 13; 14; 15(2); 16; 18; 20; 22; 23(2); 25(2); 27(4); 28(2); 29; 30; 41(2); 42; 11:2; 3; 4; 5(7); 7(3); 11(2); 12(4); 13(2); 16; 17; 19; 20; 21; 22; 23; 24(2); 25; 27(6); 12:1(2); 2(2); 4(3); 5(5);

6; 7; 8(2); 10; 11; 12; 13(2); 14; 17; 18; 19; 22; 23(2); 24(3); 28(2); 29; 31(2); 32(3); 33(2); 34(3); 35(2); 36; 38; 39(2); 40(5); 41(3); 42(6); 45(2); 46; 48; 50; 13:1(3); 2(2); 4(2); 6; 7; 10; 11(2); 14; 15; 18(2); 19(4); 20(2); 21; 22(5); 23(2); 24; 25; 26(2); 27(2); 28; 29(2); 30(5); 31; 32(5); 33; 34; 35(3); 36(5); 37(2); 38(8); 39(7); 40(3); 41; 42; 43(3); 44; 45; 47(2); 48(2); 49(5); 50; 52; 55; 14:1(2); 2(2); 3; 5; 6; 8; 9(2); 11; 12; 13(2); 15(3); 19(8); 20; 22(3); 23(2); 24(5); 25(3); 26(2); 28; 29(2); 30; 32(2); 33(2); 34; 35; 36; 15:1; 2(2); 3; 6; 9; 10; 11(2); 12; 14(3); 17(2); 18(2); 19; 20; 21; 24(2); 26(2); 27(2); 29(2); 30; 31(6); 32(2); 33; 35(2); 36(4); 37; 39(3); 16:1; 2; 3(6); 4(2); 5; 6(3); 9(2); 10(2); 11(2); 12(3); 13(2); 14(2); 16(3); 18; 19(2); 20; 21(2); 23(2); 26; 27(2); 28; 17:2(2); 5; 6; 9(4); 10; 12; 13(2); 14; 15(2); 18(2); 19; 22(2); 23; 24(2); 25(3); 26; 27(2); 18:1(2); 2; 3; 4(2); 6(2); 7(2); 8; 10; 11; 12(3); 13; 14; 16; 17(2); 20; 23; 26; 27(2); 28; 30; 34; 19:1(2); 3; 4; 5; 8(2); 10(2); 12; 13; 14(2); 17; 20; 21; 22; 23; 24(2); 28(4); 30; 20:1(2); 2; 3(2); 4; 5(2); 6; 7; 8(5); 9; 10; 11; 12(3); 14; 16(2); 17(2); 18(3); 19(2); 20; 21(2); 22(2); 23; 24(2); 25(2); 28; 30; 31(2); 21:1; 2; 3; 4; 5(2); 6; 7(2); 8(3); 9(5); 10; 11(2); 12(5); 14(3); 15(5); 16; 17; 18(2); 19(2); 20(2); 21(2); 23(4); 25; 26; 28; 30; 31(4); 32; 34; 35; 36; 38(3); 39; 40(2); 41; 42(5); 43(2); 45; 46; 22:2; 3; 4; 6; 7; 8; 9(2); 10(2); 11(2); 13(2); 15; 16(3); 19; 21(2); 23(2); 25; 26(3); 27; 28(2); 29(2); 30; 31(2); 32(6); 33; 34(2); 36(2); 37; 38; 39; 40(2); 41; 42(2); 43; 44; 23:1; 2(2); 5; 6(3); 7; 8; 10; 13; 16(3); 17(3); 18(2); 19(3); 20; 21; 22; 23(3); 25(2); 26(3); 29(4); 30(3); 31; 32; 33; 35(6); 37(2); 39(2); 24:1(3); 3(5); 5; 6; 8; 12; 13; 14(4); 15(3); 16; 17; 18; 20; 21(2); 22; 23; 24; 26(2); 27(5); 28(2); 29(6); 30(6); 31(2); 32; 33; 36; 37(3); 38(4); 39(3); 40(2); 41(2); 43(3); 44; 49; 50; 51; 25:1(2); 4; 5; 6; 8(2); 9; 10(3); 11; 13(3); 14; 16; 18; 19; 21; 23; 24; 25; 27; 28; 30(2); 31(3); 32(2); 33(3); 34(4); 37; 40(2); 41(3); 45; 46; 26:2(2); 3(6); 5(2); 6(2); 7; 9; 10; 11; 13; 14(2); 17(5); 18(3); 19(2); 20; 23; 24(2); 26; 27; 28(2); 29; 30; 31(3); 34; 35; 36; 37; 40; 41(2); 44(2); 45(3); 47(3); 48; 51(2); 52(2); 54; 55(2); 56(3); 57(3); 58(3); 59(3); 61; 62; 63(4); 64(4); 65; 67; 68; 69; 71; 72; 74; 75(2); 27:1(2); 2; 3(2); 5(2); 6(4); 7; 8; 9(4); 10(2); 11(4); 12; 14; 15(3); 19; 20(2); 21(2); 23(2); 24(2); 25; 27(4); 29(2); 30(2); 31; 35; 37(3); 38(2); 40(3); 41(2); 42(2); 43; 44(2); 45(3); 46; 49; 51(4); 52(2); 53(2); 54(4); 56(2); 58(2); 59; 60(3); 61(2); 62(3); 64(6); 66(3); 28:1(5); 2(3); 4; 5(2); 6(2); 7; 8; 9; 11(4); 12(2); 14; 15(2); 16(2); 19(5); 20(2); **Mk** 1:1(3); 2; 3(4); 4(2); 5(2); 8; 9; 10(3); 12(2); 13(3); 14(2); 15(3); 16(2); 19(2); 20(2); 21(2); 22; 24; 26; 27; 28; 29(2); 31(2); 32; 33(2); 34; 35; 38; 42; 44; 45(2); 2:1; 2(2); 4(4); 5; 6; 9; 10(2); 12(2); 13(2); 14(2); 16(2); 17; 18(4); 19(4); 20(2); 21(3); 22(4); 23(3); 24(2); 26(5); 27(2); 28(2); 3:1; 2; 3(2); 4; 5(3); 6(2); 7; 8; 9; 11(2); 13; 16; 17(3); 18(2); 20; 22(3); 27; 28; 29; 35; 4:1(5); 4(3); 6; 7; 10(2); 11(2); 13; 14(2); 15(4); 16(2); 17; 18(3); 19(4); 20(2); 24; 26(2); 27; 28(5); 29(3); 30; 31(2); 32(2); 33; 35(2); 36(2); 37(2); 38; 39(3); 41(2); 5:1(4); 2(2); 3; 4(2); 5(2); 7; 8; 10; 11; 12(2); 13(6); 14(3); 15(2); 16; 18; 19; 21(2); 22(2); 23; 27; 29(2); 30; 31; 33(2); 35(3); 36(3); 37; 38(3); 39; 40(4); 41(2); 42; 6:2(2); 3(2); 6; 7; 8; 11(2); 14(2); 15(2); 16; 17; 21(2); 22(2); 24(2); 25(3); 26(2); 27; 28(2); 30; 32; 33(2); 35(2); 36; 39; 41(4); 43; 44; 45(3); 46; 47(4); 48(4); 49; 51(2); 52; 53; 54(2); 56(4); 7:1(2); 3(4); 4(2); 5(3); 7; 8(3); 9; 13; 14; 15(2); 17(2); 21; 24; 26(2); 27(3); 28(3); 29; 30(2); 31(4); 33; 35; 36(2); 37(2); 8:1; 2; 3; 4; 6(4); 10(2); 11; 13(2); 14(2); 15(3); 19(2); 20(2); 23(3); 26(2); 27(2); 28(2); 29; 31(2); 33(2); 34; 35; 36; 38(3); 9:1; 7; 9(4); 10(2); 11; 12; 14; 15; 16; 17; 18; 20(3); 22(2); 24(2); 25(2); 26; 27; 28; 31(3); 33(2); 34(2); 35; 36; 42; 43; 44; 45; 46; 47; 48; 50; 10:1(3); 2; 5; 6(2); 8; 10(2); 13; 14(2); 15; 17; 19; 21(2); 23; 24(2); 25(2); 29; 30; 31; 32(3); 33(4); 34; 35; 37; 38(2); 39(2); 41; 42; 45; 46(2); 48; 49; 51; 52; 11:1; 2; 3; 4(3); 5; 7; 8(3); 9(2); 10(4); 11(3); 12; 13; 15(5); 16; 18(2); 19; 20(3); 21; 23; 27(4); 30; 32; 12:1; 2(4); 4; 7(2); 8; 9(4); 10(3); 11; 12(2); 13(2); 14(2); 17(2); 20; 21(2); 22(2); 23; 24(2); 25; 26(6); 27(4); 28(2); 29(4); 30(2); 31; 32(2); 33(5); 34; 35(4); 36(2); 37; 38(2); 39(3); 41(3); 43; 13:1; 3(2); 4; 7; 8; 9; 10(2); 11; 13; 14(4); 15(2); 16; 19(2); 20(3); 21; 22; 24(2); 25(3); 26(2); 27(3); 28; 29; 32(3); 33; 34; 35(6); 14:1(4); 2(2); 3(4); 5; 7; 9; 10(2); 12(3); 13; 14(5); 16(2); 17(2); 20(2); 21(2); 23; 24; 25(3); 26; 27(2); 30; 35(2); 38(2); 39; 41(4); 43(4); 44; 47(2); 49(2); 51; 52; 53(4); 54(4); 55(2); 60(2); 61(4); 62(4); 63; 64; 65(2); 66(3); 68; 69; 72(3); 15:1(4); 2(2); 3; 6; 7; 8; 9(2); 10; 11(2); 12(2); 14; 15; 16(3); 18; 19(2); 20; 21(2); 22; 25; 26(3); 27; 28(2); 29; 30; 31(2); 32(3); 33(3); 34; 38(2); 39(2); 40(2); 42(3); 43(2); 44; 45(2); 46(4); 47; 16:1(2); 2(5); 3(3); 4; 5(2); 6; 8; 9(2); 12; 13; 14(2); 15(2); 18; 19(2); 20(3); **Lk** 1:2(2); 3; 4; 5(4); 6(2); 8; 9(4); 10(3); 11(3); 13; 15(3); 16(2); 17(8); 18; 19(2); 20; 21(2); 22; 23; 25(2); 26(2); 27(2); 28(2); 30; 32(4); 33; 34; 35(5); 36; 38(3); 39; 40; 41(3); 42; 43; 44(2); 45; 46; 48; 51(2); 52(2); 53(2); 58; 59(3); 65; 66(2); 67; 68; 69; 70(2); 71; 72; 73; 74; 75; 76(4); 77; 78(2); 79(2); 80(3); 2:1; 4(3); 6; 7; 8(2); 9(3); 10; 11(2); 12; 13(2); 14; 15(3); 16; 17; 18; 20(2); 21(5); 22(3); 23(4); 24(2); 25(2); 26(2); 27(6); 31; 32(2); 34; 35; 36(2); 37; 38; 39(2); 40(2); 41(2); 42(2); 43(2); 44; 46(3); 50; 3:1(3); 2(3); 3(3); 4(7); 5(2); 6; 7(2); 9(4); 10; 14; 15(2); 16; 17(2); 18; 19(2); 21(2); 22; 23(2); 24(5); 25(5); 26(5); 27(5); 28(5); 29(5); 30(5); 31(5); 32(5); 33(5); 34(5); 35(5); 36(5); 37(5); 38(4); 4:1(4); 2; 3(2); 5(3); 6; 8; 9(3); 12; 13; 14(3); 16(2); 17(4); 18(7); 19(2); 20(4); 22; 25(3); 26; 27(3); 28; 29(4); 30; 31; 33; 34; 35; 36; 37(2); 38; 39; 40; 41(3); 42; 43(2); 44; 5:1(3); 2(2); 3(4); 4; 5; 7(2); 9; 10; 13; 14; 15(2); 16; 17(3); 19(4); 21(2); 24(2); 27; 30; 32; 33(2); 34(3); 35(2); 36(4); 37(3); 39; 6:1(4); 2(2); 4(3); 5(2); 6; 7(2); 8(2); 9; 10(2); 12; 15(2); 16; 17; 19; 20; 22; 23; 26; 29(2); 33; 35(2); 38; 39(3); 41(2); 42(4); 45(4); 46; 48(5); 49(3); 7:1(2); 3; 4; 6(2); 7; 9; 10(2); 11; 12(4); 13; 14; 17; 18; 19; 20(3); 22(8); 24(4); 28(2); 29(3); 30(2); 31(2); 32(2); 33; 34; 36(2); 37(3); 38(2); 39; 41; 43; 44(2); 45; 47; 49; 50; 8:1(3); 3; 5(3); 7; 10(3); 11(3); 12(4); 13(3); 14; 15(3); 16; 19; 21; 22(2); 23; 24(3); 25; 26(2); 27(3); 28; 29(5); 31;

32; 33(6); 34(2); 35(3); 37(4); 38(2); 39; 40; 41; 42; 44; 45; 47(4); 49(3); 51(3); 54; 9:2(2); 3; 5; 6(2); 7(2); 8; 10(2); 11(2); 12(4); 16(4); 17; 18; 19(2); 20; 22(3); 25; 26(2); 27; 28; 29; 32; 34; 35; 36(2); 37(2); 38; 39; 42(3); 43(2); 44(2); 47; 51; 52; 53; 56; 57; 58(2); 60(2); 62(2); 10:1; 2(4); 4; 7(2); 9(2); 11(2); 13; 14; 17(2); 19(3); 20; 21(2); 22(6); 23(2); 26; 27; 31; 32(2); 35(2); 36; 11:4; 7; 13; 14(3); 15(2); 20(2); 26(2); 27(3); 28; 29(3); 30(2); 31(7); 32(3); 33; 34(3); 35; 36(2); 38; 39(3); 40(2); 42(2); 43(3); 44; 45; 46; 47(2); 48; 49; 50(4); 51(4); 52; 53(2); 12:1(3); 3(4); 4; 7; 8(2); 9; 10(2); 11; 12; 13(2); 15(2); 16; 22; 23; 24(2); 26(2); 27; 28(3); 30(2); 31; 32; 33; 36; 37; 38(2); 39(3); 40; 42; 45; 46(2); 48; 49; 54(2); 55; 56(3); 58(6); 59; 13:1; 4; 7(2); 10(2); 14(5); 15(3); 16; 17(2); 18; 19(2); 20; 22; 24; 25(4); 28(2); 29(5); 32; 33; 34(2); 35(3); 14:1(4); 3(2); 5; 7; 8; 9; 10(3); 13(4); 14(2); 15(2); 18; 21(8); 22; 23(3); 28; 29; 32; 34; 35(2); 15:1(2); 2; 4(3); 8; 9; 10(2); 12(2); 13; 16(2); 21; 22(2); 23; 25(2); 26; 27; 30; 16:3(2); 4; 5; 8(4); 11(2); 13(4); 14; 15; 16(3); 17; 21(3); 22(3); 24; 29; 30; 31(2); 17:1; 2; 5(2); 6(3); 7; 9; 11; 14; 17; 20(3); 21; 22(4); 24(3); 26(3); 27(3); 28; 29; 30(2); 31(4); 34(2); 35(2); 36(3); 37(2); 18:6(2); 8(2); 10(2); 11; 13; 14; 15; 16(2); 17; 20; 22; 24; 25(2); 27; 29(2); 30; 31(3); 32; 33; 34; 35; 39; 43; 19:3; 5; 8(2); 10; 11; 15(2); 16; 18; 23; 24; 29; 30; 31; 33(3); 34; 35; 36; 37(5); 38(4); 39(2); 40; 41; 42; 44(2); 45; 47(5); 48; 20:1(6); 4; 6; 9; 10(4); 13(2); 14(3); 15(3); 16; 17(3); 19(3); 20(3); 21; 25(2); 26(2); 27; 29; 30; 31(2); 32; 33; 34; 35(2); 36(2); 37(6); 38(3); 39; 41(2); 42(2); 45(2); 46(5); 21:1(2); 4; 5; 6; 8; 9; 12; 21(3); 22; 23; 24(4); 25(6); 26(3); 27; 29(2); 31; 35(2); 36; 37(3); 38(3); 22:1; 2(3); 3; 4; 6(2); 7(2); 8; 10(2); 11(5); 13; 14(2); 16; 17; 18(3); 20(2); 21(2); 22; 24; 25(2); 26(2); 27(3); 30; 31; 34; 37(2); 39; 40; 44; 47; 48; 49; 50(2); 52(3); 53(2); 54; 55(2); 56; 60; 61(4); 63; 64(2); 66(2); 67; 69(3); 70; 23:1; 2; 3(2); 4(2); 5(2); 6; 10; 13(3); 14; 17; 19; 22; 23(2); 25; 26(2); 27; 29(2); 30(2); 31(2); 33(5); 35(4); 36; 37(2); 38(2); 39(2); 40(2); 41; 44(3); 45(3); 47; 48; 49; 51(2); 52; 53; 54(2); 55(2); 56(2); 24:1(5); 2(2); 3(2); 5(3); 7(3); 9(3); 10(3); 12(2); 18(3); 19(2); 20; 21; 22; 24(2); 25; 26; 27(3); 28; 29; 30; 32(2); 33; 34; 35(3); 36; 44(4); 45; 46(3); 49(2); 53; **Jn** 1:1(4); 2; 4(2); 5(3); 7; 9(2); 10(3); 12; 13(3); 14(4); 17; 18(3); 19(2); 20; 21; 23(5); 24; 25(2); 28; 29(4); 32; 33(2); 34; 35; 36; 37; 39; 40; 41(2); 42; 43; 44; 45(3); 48; 49(2); 50; 51(2); 2:1(2); 2; 3; 5; 6(2); 7(2); 8(2); 9(8); 10(5); 13(2); 14(2); 15(5); 18; 20; 21; 22(3); 23(3); 3:1(2); 3; 5(2); 6(2); 8(3); 10; 13; 14(3); 16; 17(3); 18(2); 19(3); 20(2); 21(2); 22; 25; 26; 28; 29(5); 31(2); 34(2); 35(2); 36(3); 4:1(2); 5; 6(2); 8; 9; 10; 11(2); 12; 14(2); 15; 17; 18; 19; 20; 21(2); 22; 23(4); 25; 28(3); 29; 30; 31; 33; 34; 35(2); 37; 39(3); 40; 42(4); 43; 45(4); 46; 47; 49; 50(2); 52(3); 53(2); 54; 5:1; 2; 3(2); 4(4); 7(3); 9(2); 10(2); 12; 13; 14; 15(2); 16(2); 18(3); 19(3); 20(2); 21(3); 22(2); 23(4); 25(4); 26(2); 27; 28(2); 29(2); 30(2); 32; 33; 35; 36(4); 37; 39; 42; 44(2); 45; 6:1(2); 3; 4(2); 10(3); 11(4); 12; 13(2); 14(3); 15; 16; 17(2); 18; 19(2); 21(3); 22(5); 23(2); 24; 25(2); 26(2); 27(4); 28; 29; 31(2); 32(2); 33(2); 35; 37(2); 38; 39(3); 40(3); 41(2); 42; 44(2); 45(2); 46(2); 48; 49(2); 50; 51(4); 52; 53(2); 54; 57(2); 58(2); 59; 62; 63(3); 64; 67; 68; 69(3); 70; 71(2); 7:1; 2; 3; 4; 7; 10; 11(2); 12(3); 13; 14(3); 15; 17; 18(2); 19(2); 20; 22(2); 23(3); 26(2); 27; 28; 31(2); 32(4); 35(4); 37(2); 38; 39(2); 40(2); 41(2); 42(4); 43; 45(2); 46; 47; 48(2); 49; 8:1; 2(3); 3(2); 4; 5; 6; 8; 9(4); 10; 12(3); 13; 15; 16; 17; 18; 20(2); 22; 25; 26; 27; 28; 29; 32(2); 35; 36; 39; 40; 41; 44(5); 45; 46; 48; 52(2); 53; 57; 59(2); 9:3; 4(2); 5(3); 6(5); 7; 8; 11; 13; 14; 15; 16(2); 17; 18(2); 22(3); 24(2); 30; 32(2); 35; 40; 10:1(3); 2(3); 3(2); 4; 5; 6; 7(2); 8; 9; 10; 11(3); 12(6); 13(2); 14; 15(3); 19; 21(3); 22; 23; 24(2); 25; 31; 33; 35(2); 36(3); 37; 38(2); 40(2); 41; 11:1; 2; 3; 4(2); 6; 7; 8(2); 9(3); 10(2); 16; 17; 19(2); 20; 24(2); 25(2); 27(3); 28; 30(2); 31(3); 33(2); 36; 37(2); 38; 39(2); 40; 41(3); 42; 45(2); 46(2); 47(2); 48; 50(2); 51; 52; 54(3); 55(4); 56(2); 57(2); 12:1(2); 2; 3(4); 5; 6(2); 7; 8; 9(2); 10; 11; 12(2); 13(2); 17(2); 18; 19(2); 20; 23(2); 24; 29; 31(2); 32; 34(4); 35(2); 36(2); 38(4); 42(3); 43(2); 46; 47(2); 48(2); 49; 50; 13:1(5); 2(2); 3; 5(2); 18; 22; 26(2); 27; 28; 29(3); 30; 31; 33; 38; 14:4; 5; 6(4); 8; 9(2); 10(5); 11(4); 12; 13(2); 16; 17(2); 19; 22; 24(2); 26(3); 27; 28; 30; 31(3); 15:1(2); 3; 4(2); 5(2); 6; 9; 16; 18; 19(5); 20; 24; 25; 26(4); 27; 16:2(2); 3; 4(2); 7(2); 8; 11; 13; 15; 16; 17; 20; 21(3); 23; 25(2); 26; 27; 28(4); 32(2); 33(2); 17:1; 3; 4(2); 5(2); 6(2); 8; 9; 11(2); 12(3); 13; 14(3); 15(2); 16(2); 18(2); 19; 21; 22; 23; 24(2); 25; 26; 18:1; 2; 3; 6; 9; 10(2); 11(2); 12(4); 13; 14(2); 15(3); 16(4); 17(2); 18; 19; 20(3); 22(3); 23; 24; 26(3); 28(3); 31; 32; 33(3); 35; 36; 37(3); 38; 39(3); 19:2; 3; 5(3); 6; 7(2); 8; 9; 11(2); 12; 13(2); 14(4); 15; 17; 18; 19(4); 20(3); 21(6); 23(4); 24(2); 25(2); 26; 27; 28; 30; 31(5); 32(4); 34; 35; 36; 38(3); 40(4); 41(2); 42(2); 20:1(5); 2(3); 3(2); 4(2); 5; 6(2); 7(2); 8(2); 9(2); 10; 11(2); 12(4); 15; 18(2); 19(7); 20(2); 21; 22; 23(2); 24(2); 25(6); 26(2); 30; 31(2); 21:1(2); 2(2); 3; 4(3); 6(4); 7(3); 8(3); 10; 11(2); 12(2); 13(2); 14(2); 17(2); 20(3); 23; 24; 25(2); **Acts** 1:1; 2(3); 3(2); 4(2); 5; 6; 7; 8(3); 12; 13(4); 14(2); 15(3); 16(2); 18(2); 20; 21(2); 22; 24; 26(2); 2:1; 2; 4(2); 6; 10; 11; 14; 15(2); 16; 17; 19; 20(5); 21(2); 23; 24; 25; 28; 29; 30(3); 31(2); 33(4); 34(2); 36; 37(3); 38(4); 39(2); 42(2); 43; 46; 47(3); 3:1(3); 2(3); 3; 6; 7; 8; 9; 10(2); 11(3); 12; 13(3); 14(2); 15(2); 16(2); 18(2); 19(2); 21(3); 22(2); 23; 24; 25(4); 4:1(5); 2(3); 3; 4(3); 5; 6(3); 7; 8(2); 10(3); 11(2); 13; 14; 15; 17; 18; 19; 20; 21; 22; 23; 24; 25(3); 26(4); 27(2); 30; 31(3); 32(2); 33(3); 34(2); 35; 36(2); 37(2); 5:2(2); 3(3); 6; 8; 9(4); 10; 11; 12(3); 13(2); 14; 15(3); 16; 17(3); 18(2); 19(2); 20(3); 21(7); 22(2); 23(3); 24(5); 25(3); 26(3); 27(2); 29; 30; 32; 34(4); 37(2); 40(2); 41(2); 42(2); 6:1(5); 2(4); 3; 4(2); 5(3); 6; 7(5); 8; 9(2); 10(2); 12(4); 13; 14; 15(2); 7:1; 2; 4(2); 7; 8(3); 9; 10; 11; 13(2); 16(3); 17(3); 22(2); 23; 24; 26; 28; 29; 30(2); 31(3); 32(4); 33(2); 34; 35(4); 36(3); 37(2); 38(5); 40; 41(2); 42(4); 43(2); 44(3); 45(4); 46; 48(2); 49(2); 51; 52(4); 53(2); 54; 55(3); 56(3); 58(3); 8:1(3); 3; 4; 5; 6(3); 9(2); 10(3); 12(3); 13; 14(2); 15; 16(2); 17; 18(3); 19; 20; 21; 22; 24(2); 25(4); 26(3); 27(2); 28; 29; 30; 32(3); 33; 34(2); 36(2); 37; 38(3); 39(4); 40; 9:1(3); 2(2); 4; 5(2); 6(2); 7; 8(2); 10; 11(3); 14; 15(2); 17(4); 19; 20(3); 21; 22(3); 23; 24; 25(2); 26; 27(4); 29(3); 30; 31(5); 32(2); 34; 35; 38; 39(3); 40; 41; 42; 10:1; 2; 3(2); 6; 7; 9(4); 11(2); 12(2); 15; 16; 17(2); 19(2); 21; 22(3); 23; 24; 30; 31; 32(2); 33; 36(2); 37; 38(3); 39(2); 40; 41(2); 42(3); 43; 44(2); 45(4); 47; 48(2); 11:1(3); 2; 4; 5; 6(2); 9; 11; 12(2); 15(2); 16(3); 17(2); 18; 19(3); 20(2); 21(3); 22(2); 23(2); 24(2); 26(2); 28(3); 29(2); 30(2); 12:1(2); 2(2); 3(2); 4; 5; 6(3); 7(3); 8; 9; 10(5); 11(4); 12(2); 13(2); 14(2); 16; 17(3); 18; 19; 20(3); 22(2); 23; 24; 13:1(2); 2(3); 4; 5(3); 6; 7(2); 8(3); 9; 10(3); 11(4); 12(3); 14(2); 15(6); 17(3); 18; 19; 20; 21(2); 22; 23; 24(2); 25; 26(2); 27(2); 29; 30; 31; 32; 33; 34(2); 36; 38; 39; 40; 42(4); 43(3); 44(3); 45(3); 46(2); 47(4); 48(3); 49(3); 50(4); 51; 52(2); 14:1(4); 2(3); 3(2); 4(4); 5; 6; 7; 11(4); 12; 13(3); 14(2); 15(5); 18; 19(2); 20(3); 21; 22(4); 23; 25; 26(2); 27(3); 28; 15:1(2); 2; 3(4); 4(3); 5(3); 6; 7(3); 8(2); 10(2); 11(3); 12(2); 14(2); 15(2); 16; 17(4); 19; 21; 22(3); 23(5); 24; 26; 27; 28; 30(2); 32; 33(2); 35(2); 36(2); 38(2); 39; 40(2); 41; 16:1; 2; 3; 4(3); 5(2); 6(3); 7; 9; 10(3); 11; 12; 13(4); 14(3); 15; 17(3); 18(2); 19(2); 20; 22(2); 23; 24(2); 25; 26(3); 27(4); 31; 32(2); 33(2); 35(2); 36(3); 38(2); 39; 40(3); 17:1; 2; 3(3); 4(2); 5(6); 6(3); 7; 8(3); 9; 10(3); 11(2); 12; 13(3); 14(2); 16; 17(4); 18; 19; 21(2); 22(2); 23(3); 24; 26(3); 27(2); 29(2); 31(3); 32(2); 34; 18:2; 3; 4; 5(3); 6; 7(2); 8(4); 9(2); 11; 12(2); 13; 14; 16; 17(4); 18; 19(2); 22; 23(2); 24; 25(5); 26(2); 27(2); 28(3); 19:1; 2; 4; 5(2); 6; 7; 8(3); 9(4); 10(2); 11; 12(3); 13(4); 15; 16(2); 17(2); 19(2); 20(2); 21; 23; 24; 25; 27(3); 28; 29(2); 30(2); 31(2); 32; 33(3); 34; 35(6); 38; 39; 41; 20:1(2); 3; 4; 6; 7(4); 8; 9; 12; 13; 15(3); 16; 17(2); 18; 19(3); 22(2); 23; 24(4); 25; 26; 27; 28(3); 29; 30; 32; 35(3); 38(2); 21:1; 3(2); 4; 5(3); 6; 7; 8(4); 11(5); 13(2); 14(2); 16; 17; 18(2); 19; 20(2); 21(3); 22; 24; 25; 26(5); 27(4); 28(4); 29(3); 30(4); 31(2); 32(3); 33; 34(4); 35(4); 36(2); 37(2); 38(3); 39; 40(3); 22:2(2); 3(2); 4; 5(4); 7; 9(2); 10; 11(2); 12(2); 14(3); 16(2); 17; 20(2); 21; 22; 23; 24(2); 25; 26(2); 27; 28; 29; 30(3); 23:1; 2(2); 3(2); 5; 6(5); 7(3); 8; 9(2); 10(3); 11(2); 12; 14; 15(2); 16; 17(2); 18(2); 19(2); 20(2); 21; 22(2); 23(2); 24; 25; 26; 27(2); 28; 30(3); 31; 32(3); 33(2); 34; 24:1(3); 5(4); 6; 7; 9; 10(2); 12(4); 13; 14(4); 15(3); 18(2); 20; 21(2); 22(3); 23; 24; 25; 27; 25:1; 2(3); 3; 6(2); 7; 8(3); 9; 10; 12; 14; 15(3); 16(5); 17(3); 18; 21; 22; 23(5); 24(3); 26; 27; 26:2(2); 3; 4(2); 5(2); 6(2); 7; 8; 9; 10(2); 12; 13(2); 14(3); 16(2); 17(2); 18; 19; 20(2); 21(2); 22; 23(5); 25; 26; 27; 30(2); 27:1(2); 2; 3; 4(2); 5; 6; 7(2); 8; 9; 10; 11(5); 12(3); 13; 15(2); 16(2); 17(2); 18(2); 19(2); 21; 22; 23; 27(3); 29(2); 30(5); 31(3); 32(3); 33; 34; 35; 37; 38(3); 39(2); 40(5); 41(5); 42(2); 43; 44(2); 28:1; 2(3); 3(2); 4(3); 5(2); 7(2); 8; 9(2); 11(2); 13(2); 15; 16(5); 17(5); 19; 20; 21; 23(3); 24; 25(2); 27; 28(2); 29; 31(3); **Rom** 1:1; 2; 3(2); 4(4); 5; 6; 7; 8; 9; 10; 12; 13; 15; 16(4); 17(2); 18(2); 20(3); 23(2); 24; 25(4); 26; 27(4); 32(2); 2:1; 2; 3(2); 4(2); 5(2); 8; 9(2); 10(2); 12(2); 13(5); 14(4); 15(2); 16(2); 17; 18(2); 19; 20(3); 23(2); 24(2); 25(2); 26(2); 27(3); 28; 29(3); 3:1(2); 2; 3; 5; 6; 7; 13; 17; 19(3); 20(4); 21(4); 22; 23; 24; 25; 26(3); 27; 28(2); 29(5); 30(2); 31(3); 4:1; 3; 4; 5; 6(2); 8(2); 9(2); 11(4); 12(4); 13(5); 14(2); 15; 16(5); 17(2); 18; 19; 20; 24; 5:2; 5(2); 6; 10; 11; 12; 13(2); 14(2); 15(7); 16(4); 17(4); 18; 20(2); 6:4(3); 5(2); 6; 9; 10(2); 13; 17; 19; 21(2); 22; 23(2); 7:1(2); 2(4); 4(3); 5(3); 6(5); 7(4); 8(2); 9(2); 10; 11; 12(2); 13; 14; 16; 19(2); 21; 22(2); 23(2); 25(4); 8:1(2); 2(3); 3(4); 4(4); 5(6); 7(2); 8; 9(4); 10(2); 11(3); 12(2); 13(4); 14; 15(2); 16; 18(2); 19(4); 20; 21(4); 22; 23(4); 26(2); 27(5); 28; 29(2); 34; 35; 36; 39; 9:1(2); 3; 4(7); 5(3); 6; 7; 8(6); 9; 11(2); 12(2); 17(2); 20; 21(3); 22; 23(2); 24(2); 26(2); 27(5); 28(3); 29; 30; 31(2); 32(2); 10:3; 4(2); 5(3); 6; 7(2); 8(2); 9(2); 10(2); 11; 12; 13(2); 15(2); 16; 17; 18(3); 11:1(2); 2; 4(2); 5; 7(2); 11; 12(2); 13; 15(3); 16(4); 17(3); 18(3); 21; 22; 24; 25(2); 26; 28(4); 29(2); 31; 33(3); 34(2); 12:1; 2; 3; 4(2); 6; 11; 13(2); 16(2); 17; 19; 13:1(2); 2(2); 3(2); 4; 8; 9; 10(2); 11; 12(4); 13; 14(2); 14:1; 6(4); 8(3); 9(2); 10; 11; 14; 15; 17(2); 19(2); 20(3); 15:1(2); 3; 4(2); 5; 6; 7; 8(4); 9(2); 11; 12(2); 13(3); 15; 16(5); 17; 18; 19(3); 20; 25; 26(2); 27; 29(3); 30(3); 31; 32; 33; 16:1; 2(2); 4(2); 5(2); 7; 8; 10; 11(2); 12(3); 13; 14; 15; 16; 17; 18(2); 20(2); 22; 23(4); 24; 25(4); 26(4); **1 Cor** 1:1; 2(2); 3; 4; 6; 7; 8(2); 9; 10(4); 13; 16; 17(2); 18(3); 19(4); 20(4); 21(4); 23(2); 24(2); 25(2); 26; 27(6); 28(5); 31; 2:1; 4; 5(2); 6(2); 7(3); 8(2); 9(2); 10(2); 11(5); 12(4); 13; 14(3); 16(3); 3:5; 6; 7; 10(2); 13(2); 16(2); 17(2); 19(2); 20(3); 22; 4:1; 4; 5(5); 6; 9(2); 11; 13(3); 15; 17; 19(3); 20; 5:1; 4(2); 5(4); 6; 7; 8(3); 10(3); 13; 6:1(2); 2(4); 4; 9(2); 10; 11(3); 12; 13(6); 14; 15; 16; 17; 18; 19(2); 7:1; 3(3); 4(4); 8(2); 10(2); 12(2); 14(4); 15; 17(2); 19; 20; 22(2); 25(2); 26; 28; 29; 31; 32(3); 33(2); 34(5); 35; 36; 39; 40; 8:4(2); 6; 7; 8(2); 10; 11; 12; 9:1; 2(2); 5(3); 7(2); 8(2); 9(2); 12; 13(6); 14(3); 16(2); 18(3); 19; 20(4); 22(2); 23; 24; 25; 26; 10:1(2); 2(2); 3; 4; 5; 6; 7; 10; 11(2); 13(2); 16(6); 18(3); 20(2); 21(5); 22; 24; 25; 26(2); 28(4); 29; 30; 31; 32(3); 33; 11:2; 3(3); 5; 7(2); 9(2); 10(2); 11; 16; 17(2); 20; 22; 23(2); 25(3); 26; 27(3); 28(2); 29; 32(2); 34; 12:3(2); 4; 5; 6; 7(3); 8(4); 9(2); 10(2); 11; 12(2); 14; 15(3); 16(3); 17(4); 18(2); 19; 21(4); 22; 23; 24; 25(3); 26(2); 27; 28; 31; 13:1; 2; 3; 6; 13; 14:2; 4; 5; 7; 8; 9(2); 10; 11(2); 12(2); 15(5); 16(3); 17; 19; 21(2); 23; 25; 27; 29; 30; 32(3); 33(3); 34(2); 36; 37(3); 15:1; 3; 4(2); 5; 6(2); 7; 9(3); 10(2); 12(2); 13; 15; 16; 19; 20(2); 21(2); 23; 24(3); 26; 28; 29(3); 31; 32(2); 34; 35; 39; 40(4); 41(3); 42(3); 45(2); 46(3); 47(4); 48(2); 49(4); 50; 52(4); 54; 56(3); 57; 58(3); 16:1(3); 2(2); 6; 7(2); 10(2); 11; 12; 13; 15(4); 17; 19(3); 20; 21; 22; 23; **2 Cor** 1:1(3); 2; 3(2); 4; 5; 6; 7(2); 9(2); 11; 12(3); 13; 14(2); 17(2); 19; 20(2); 22; 2:2; 3; 4; 6; 7; 9; 10; 12; 14; 15; 16(4); 17(2); 3:3(3); 6(5); 7(4); 8(2); 9(2); 10; 13(2); 14(4); 16(2); 17(4); 18(5); 4:2(4); 4(5); 5; 6(5); 7(2); 10(4); 11; 13; 14; 15(2); 16; 18(4); 5:1; 5; 6(2); 8(2); 10(3); 11(2); 14; 16(2); 18; 19(2); 21; 6:1; 2(3); 6; 7(5); 13; 16(3); 17; 18; 7:1(2); 6(2); 7; 8; 10(2); 12(4); 13; 15; 8:1(2); 2(2); 4(4); 5(2); 8(2); 9; 11; 16(2); 17; 18(3); 19(3); 21(3); 22; 23(2); 24(2); 9:1(2); 2(2); 3; 5; 9; 10(3); 12(3); 13(3); 14; 10:1; 2; 3(2); 4; 5(2); 7; 8; 13(2); 14; 16(2); 17; 18; 11:3(2); 5; 7; 9; 10(2); 12(2); 17; 18; 20; 22; 24; 25; 26(4); 28(2); 30; 31; 32(4); 33; 12:1; 2(3); 3(2); 6; 7(3); 8; 9; 11; 12; 14(5); 15(2); 18(2); 21; 13:1(2); 2(2); 4(2); 5; 8(2); 10(2); 11; 13; 14(5); **Gal** 1:1(2); 2(2); 3; 4; 6; 7; 11; 12; 13; 14; 16; 19(2); 20; 21; 22; 23; 2:2; 5(2); 7(5); 8(3); 9(4); 10(2); 12(2); 13(3); 14(4); 15; 16(6); 19(2); 20(3); 21(2); 3:1; 2(4); 3(2); 5(4); 8(4); 10(5); 11(3); 12(2); 13(2); 14(4); 15; 16; 17(3); 18(2); 19(4); 21(3); 22(2); 23(2); 24; 29; 4:1; 2(2); 3(2); 4(3); 5(2); 6; 9; 13(2); 15; 16; 21(2); 22(2); 23(3); 24(2); 26(2); 27; 29(2); 30(6); 31(2); 5:1; 3; 5(2); 7; 9; 10; 11(2); 13; 14; 16(3); 17(5); 18(2); 19(2); 21(2); 22(2); 24; 25(2); 6:2; 6; 8(3); 10; 12(2); 13; 14(3); 16; 17(2); 18; **Eph** 1:1(2); 2; 3(2); 4(2); 5; 6(3); 7(2); 9; 10(3); 11(2); 12; 13(3); 14(4); 15(2); 17(4); 18(5); 19(2); 20(2); 22; 23; 2:2(6); 3(5); 6; 7(2); 8; 11(3); 12(3); 13; 14; 15(3); 16(2); 18; 19(2); 20(3); 21(2); 22; 3:1; 2(2); 3; 4; 5(2); 6(3); 7(3); 8(4); 9(4); 10(5); 11; 14; 15; 16(2); 18(2); 19(2); 20; 21; 4:1(3); 3(3); 7; 9(2); 10(2); 12(5); 13(7); 14(2); 15(2); 16(4); 17(4); 18(3); 21; 22(2); 23; 24; 26; 27; 29; 30(2); 5:5; 6(2); 8; 9(2); 10; 11; 13; 14; 16(2); 17(2); 18; 19; 20(2); 21; 22; 23(5); 24(2); 25; 26(2); 29(2); 31; 32; 33; 6:1; 2; 3; 4(2); 5; 6(2); 7; 8(2); 9; 10(2); 11(3); 12(3); 13(2); 14; 15(2); 16(3); 17(4); 18(2); 19(2); 21; 23(3); **Phil** 1:1(2); 2; 5(2); 6; 7(2); 8; 10(2); 11(2); 12(3); 13(2); 14(3); 16; 17(3); 19(2); 22; 23; 24; 27(3); 30; 2:1; 2; 4; 6; 7(2); 8(3); 9; 10(2); 11(2); 15(2); 16(2); 17; 18; 19; 21; 22; 24; 25; 28; 29; 30; 3:1(2); 2; 3(3); 4(2); 5(5); 6(3); 8(3); 9(2); 10(2); 11(2); 14(3); 16(3); 18(2); 20(2); 21; 4:1; 2(2); 3(3); 4; 5; 7; 9(2); 10; 15(2); 17(2); 18; 21; 22; 23; **Col** 1:1; 2(2); 3; 4; 5(4); 6(3); 8; 9(2); 10(2); 12(4); 13(3); 14; 15(3); 18(7); 19(2); 20; 22; 23(3); 24(3); 25(2); 26; 27(4); 2:1; 2(4); 3; 5(2); 6; 7; 8(3); 9(2); 10; 11(5); 12(3); 13; 14(3); 17; 19(3); 20(3); 22(2); 23(3); 3:1(2); 2; 5; 6(2); 9; 10(2); 12; 14; 15; 16(2); 17(3); 18; 20; 22; 23; 24(4); 4:3(2); 5; 7(2); 10; 11(2); 12; 14; 15(2); 16(3); 17(2); **1 Th** 1:1(5); 3; 5; 6(3); 8(2); 9; 10(2); 2:2; 4; 8; 9; 13(3); 14(3); 15; 16(3); 19; 3:2; 5; 8; 9; 12; 13; 4:1; 2; 3; 5; 6(2); 10; 15(4); 16(4); 17(4); 5:1(2); 2(3); 5(2); 8(3); 12; 14(2); 18; 19; 23(2); 26; 27(2); 28; **2 Th** 1:1(3); 2; 3; 4; 5(2); 7; 8; 9(3); 11(2); 12(3); 2:1; 2; 3(3); 4; 7(2); 8(4); 9(3); 10(2); 11; 12; 13(4); 14(2); 15; 3:1(2); 3(2); 4(2); 5(3); 6(2); 16(2); 17; 18; **1 Tim** 1:1(2); 2; 5(2); 7(2); 8; 9(4); 11(2); 12; 14; 15; 17; 18(2); 19; 2:3; 4(2); 5; 7(2); 8; 9; 14; 3:1; 2; 5; 6(2); 7(2); 9(2); 12; 13; 15(5); 16(5); 4:1(2); 3; 5; 6(3); 8; 10(2); 12; 14(4); 16; 5:8; 9(2); 10(2); 11; 14(3); 16; 17(2); 18(3); 20(2); 21(2); 25; 6:1(2); 3(2); 5; 10(2); 12(3); 13(2); 15(2); 17; 19; 20; 21; **2 Tim** 1:1(2); 2; 5; 6(2); 8(4); 10(2); 11; 13; 14; 16(2); 18(2); 2:1; 2; 4; 5; 6(2); 7; 8(2); 9(2); 10(3); 14(3); 15; 18(3); 19(3); 21(2); 22; 24; 25; 26(2); 3:1; 7(2); 8(2); 11; 14; 15; 17; 4:1(3); 2; 3; 4; 5; 6; 7(3); 8(3); 13(3); 14(2); 17(5); 18; 19; 21; 22; **Titus** 1:1(3); 3; 4(2); 5; 6; 9; 10; 11; 13; 14; 15; 2:1; 2; 3; 4; 5; 6; 10; 11; 12; 13; 3:4(2); 5(2); 7; 9; 10; 12; 13; 15; **Phm** 1:2(2); 3; 5(2); 6(2); 7(2); 9; 13; 16(2); 20(2); 25; **Heb** 1:1(2); 2; 3(5); 4; 5; 6(3); 7; 8(2); 9; 10(5); 12; 13; 2:1(2); 2; 3(2); 4; 5; 6; 7(2); 9(3); 10; 12(2); 13; 14(4); 16; 17(2); 3:1(2); 3(2); 6(4); 7; 8(3); 12; 13; 14(2); 15; 17; 4:2(2); 3(3); 4(2); 9; 11; 12(4); 13; 14(2); 16; 5:3; 6; 7; 8; 9; 10; 12(2); 13; 6:1(3); 2(2); 4(2); 5(3); 6; 7(2); 10; 11(3); 12; 15; 16; 17(2); 18; 19(3); 20(2); 7:1(3); 3; 4(2); 5(5); 6; 7(2); 10; 11(5); 12(2); 13; 15; 16(2); 17; 18(2); 19(3); 21(2); 25; 26; 27; 28(5); 8:1(6); 2(3); 4(2); 5(5); 8(4); 9(5); 10(3); 11(3); 13; 9:1(2); 2(5); 3(4); 4(7); 5(2); 6(4); 7(3); 8(4); 9(3); 10; 11(2); 12(2); 13(5); 14(3); 15(7); 16(2); 17; 18; 19(5); 20(2); 21(3); 22; 23(4); 24(3); 25(2); 26(5); 27; 28; 10:1(4); 2; 4; 5; 7(2); 8; 9(2); 10(2); 11; 12; 15; 16(2); 19(2); 20; 21; 23; 25(4); 26(2); 27; 28; 29(4); 30(2); 31(2); 32; 34; 36(2); 38; 39(2); 11:1(2); 2; 3(3); 7(3); 8; 9(3); 10; 11; 12(4); 13(2); 17; 19; 21(2); 22(2); 23; 24; 25(2); 26(3); 27(2); 28(3); 29(2); 30; 31(2); 32(2); 33; 34(5); 37; 38(2); 39; 12:1(2); 2(6); 5(3); 6; 9; 11(2); 12(2); 14; 15; 17; 18; 19(3); 20; 21; 22(3); 23(4); 24(3); 26(2); 27(2); 13:3(2); 4; 6; 7(2); 8; 9; 10; 11(4); 12(2); 13; 14; 15(2); 19; 20(5); 22; 24; **Jas** 1:1(2); 3; 6(2); 7; 9; 10(2); 11(3); 12(3); 17; 18; 20(2); 21; 22; 23; 25(2); 27(2); 2:1(2); 3(3); 5(2); 6(3); 8(2); 9; 10; 11; 12; 13; 16(2); 19; 21; 23(2); 25(2); 26(2); 3:2; 4; 5; 6(4); 7; 8; 9; 10; 11; 13; 14; 17; 18; 4:4(2); 5(2); 6(2); 7; 10(2); 11(4); 15; 5:3; 4(6); 5; 6; 7(6); 8(2); 9(2); 10(3); 11(4); 14(4); 15(3); 16; 17; 18(2); 19; 20; **1 Pe** 1:1(2); 2(4); 3(3); 5(2); 7(2); 9(2); 10(2); 11(3); 12(3); 13(3); 14; 17(2); 19; 20(2); 21; 22(3); 23; 24(4); 25(4); 2:2(2); 3; 6; 7(3); 8; 9; 10; 11; 12(2); 13(2); 14(2); 15(2); 17(2); 18(2); 24; 25; 3:1(2); 3; 4(4); 5; 7(3); 9; 12(5); 15(2); 17; 18(4); 19; 20(3); 21(5); 22; 4:1(3); 2(4); 3(2); 4; 5(2); 6(3); 7; 10; 11(4); 12; 13; 14(2); 17(4); 18(3); 19; 5:1(3); 2; 3; 4(2); 5(2); 6; 8; 9(3); 10; 11(2); 12; **2 Pe** 1:1; 2; 3; 4(3); 8; 11; 12; 16; 17(2); 18; 19(3); 21(2); 2:1(2); 2; 4; 5(4); 6; 7(2); 9(4); 10(2); 11; 12; 13(2); 15(4); 16(2); 17; 18(3); 20(6); 21(2); 22(2); 3:2(5); 3; 4(3); 5(4); 6; 7(4); 8; 9; 10(7); 12(4); 15(2); 16(2); 17(2); 18(2); **1 Jn** 1:1(2); 2(2); 3; 5; 6; 7(3); 8; 2:1(2); 2(2); 4; 5; 7(4); 8(2); 9; 10; 11; 13(3); 14(3); 15(6); 16(8); 17(3); 18(3); 20; 21(2); 22(3); 23(4); 24(4); 25; 27(2); 3:1(2); 8(6); 10(3); 11(2); 12; 13; 14; 16; 17; 19; 23; 24; 4:1(2); 2(2); 3(4); 4; 5(3); 6(2); 9(2); 10; 14(3); 15; 16; 17; 5:1; 2; 3; 4(3); 5(2); 6(2); 7(3); 8(3); 9(3); 10(3); 11; 12(2); 13(4); 14; 15; 18; 19(3); 20(2); **2 Jn** 1(3); 2; 3(4); 4; 5; 6(2); 7(2); 9(4); 13; **3 Jn** 1(2); 3(2); 5; 6; 7; 8; 9(2); 10(2); 12; 14; **Jude** 1; 3(2); 4(2); 5(3); 6(3); 7(2); 8; 9(4); 11(3); 12(2); 13(2); 14(2); 15; 17(2); 18; 19; 20; 21(2); 23(3); 24; **Rev** 1:1; 2(2); 3(2); 4(2); 5(6); 7(2); 8(6); 9(4); 10(2); 11(5); 12; 13(5); 15; 16; 17(2); 18; 19(3); 20(8); 2:1(5); 5; 6(2); 7(5); 8(4); 9; 10(2); 11(3); 12(3); 13; 14(2); 15(2); 16; 17(4); 18(3); 19(2); 23(2); 24(2); 26(2); 27; 28; 29(2); 3:1(4); 2; 5; 6(2); 7(3); 9; 10(3); 12(5); 13(2); 14(7); 18(2); 20(2); 22(2); 4:1; 2(2); 3; 4(2); 5(3); 6(4); 7(4); 8; 9(2); 10(3); 5:1(3); 2; 3(3); 4; 5(5); 6(7); 7(3); 8(6); 9; 10; 11(5); 12; 13(5); 14(2); 6:1(3); 3(2); 4(2); 5(2); 6(4); 7(3); 8(4); 9(5); 10; 11; 12(3); 13(2); 14; 15(9); 16(5); 17; 7:1(7); 2(6); 3(4); 4(3); 5(3); 6(3); 7(3); 8(3); 9(2); 10(2); 11(5); 13; 14(4); 15(2); 16; 17(3); 8:1; 2; 3(5); 4(5); 5(4); 6(2); 7(3); 8(3); 9(3); 10(3); 11(4); 12(6); 13(6); 9:1(4); 2(7); 3(4); 4(3); 5; 7(3); 9(2); 11(3); 13(3); 14(4); 15(2); 16(4); 17(5); 18(3); 20(2); 10:1; 2(2); 4(3); 5(3); 6(5); 7(5); 8(6); 9(2); 10(2);

11:1(3); 2(4); 4(4); 6(2); 7(2); 8(2); 9; 10(2); 11(2); 13(5); 14(2); 15(3); 16; 17; 18(6); 19(2); 12:1(2); 4(4); 6(2); 7(2); 9(4); 10(3); 11(4); 12(4); 13(4); 14(4); 15(3); 16(5); 17(5); 13:1(3); 2(4); 3(2); 4(4); 7; 8(5); 10(5); 11; 12(4); 13(2); 14(6); 15(6); 17(4); 18(3); 14:2(3); 3(5); 4(4); 5; 6(3); 7(2); 8(2); 9; 10(7); 11(3); 12(4); 13(3); 14(2); 15(5); 16(3); 17; 18(5); 19(6); 20(4); 15:1(2); 2(4); 3(5); 5(3); 6(3); 7(3); 8(5); 16:1(5); 2(5); 3(3); 4(2); 5(3); 6; 7; 8(2); 9; 10(4); 11; 12(5); 13(6); 14(4); 16; 17(4); 18; 19(6); 20; 21(3); 17:1(4); 2(5); 3(2); 4(2); 5(4); 6(5); 7(6); 8(7); 9(3); 10; 11(3); 12(2); 13; 14(2); 15(2); 16(3); 17(2); 18(3); 18:1; 2; 3(8); 6; 7(2); 8; 9(3); 11(2); 14(2); 15; 17; 18; 19; 21(2); 22(2); 23(5); 24(2); 19:1; 2(3); 4(3); 5; 6(4); 7(2); 8(3); 9(3); 10(3); 13; 14; 15(3); 17(5); 18(5); 19(4); 20(5); 21(5); 20:1(2); 2(2); 3(3); 4(3); 5(4); 6(2); 7; 8(5); 9(5); 10(4); 11(2); 12(5); 13(3); 14(2); 15(2); 21:1(2); 2; 3; 4; 5; 6(6); 8(3); 9(5); 10(3); 11; 12(4); 13(4); 14(5); 15; 16(3); 17; 18(2); 19(7); 20(8); 21(3); 22(2); 23(5); 24(3); 26(3); 27; 22:1(2); 2(7); 3(2); 5(2); 6(3); 7(2); 8(2); 9(2); 10(3); 13(6); 14(4); 16(4); 17(3); 18(3); 19(5); 21

THEIR (3904/2783)

Gen 1:21; 4:4; 6:12; 20(2); 7:14; 8:19; 9:23(4); 10:5(3); 20(4); 30; 31(4); 32(2); 11:7; 12:5; 13:6; 14:6; 11(2); 24; 17:7; 8; 9; 23; 18:20; 26; 19:10; 33; 35; 36; 20:8; 22:17; 24:52; 59; 25:13(2); 16(4); 31:38; 43; 53; 32:15; 33:2; 6; 34:13; 18; 20(2); 21; 23(2); 27; 28(3); 29(3); 35:4(2); 36:7(2); 19; 30; 40(3); 43(2); 37:4; 12; 16; 21; 22; 25(3); 32; 40:1; 42:6; 24; 25; 26; 28; 29; 35(2); 36; 43:2; 11; 15; 24(2); 26; 27; 28; 44:3; 13; 45:25; 27; 46:5(3); 6(2); 17; 32(3); 47:1(2); 4; 9; 12; 17(2); 22(2); 30; 48:6(2); 49:5; 6(4); 7(2); 28; 50:8(3); 15; 17; **Ex** 1:11; 14(2); 2:11; 16; 17; 18; 23; 24; 3:7(3); 4:5; 31(2); 5:4; 5; 6; 10; 21; 6:4; 6; 14; 16; 17; 19; 25; 26; 7:11; 12; 19(4); 22; 8:7; 18; 26; 10:7; 23; 12:27; 34(4); 42; 51; 13:17; 20; 14:10; 22(2); 25; 26(2); 29(2); 17:1; 18:7; 23; 19:10; 14; 21:32; 34; 22:23; 23:24(3); 27; 32; 33; 25:20(2); 36(2); 38; 26:21; 25; 29; 32; 37; 27:10(2); 11(2); 12(2); 14(2); 15(2); 17(2); 21; 28:10(2); 12; 21; 38; 42; 29:10; 15; 19; 20(2); 25; 28(2); 45; 46(2); 30:12; 19(2); 21(3); 31:16; 32:3; 4; 25(2); 32; 34; 33:6; 34:13(3); 15(2); 16(2); 35:17; 18; 25; 36:26; 30; 34; 36; 38(4); 37:9(2); 22(2); 38:10; 11(2); 12(2); 14(2); 15(2); 17(2); 19(4); 28; 39:13; 14; 40:15(3); 31(2); 36; 38; **Lev** 4:15; 6:17; 7:34; 36; 38; 8:14; 16; 18; 22; 24(3); 25; 28; 9:24; 10:5; 19(2); 11:8(2); 11(2); 21; 15:31(2); 16:16(3); 21(2); 22; 27(3); 34; 17:5; 7(2); 18:3; 9; 10; 29; 19:23; 20:4; 11; 12; 13; 16; 17; 18; 19; 20; 24; 27; 21:5(3); 6(3); 22:16; 25; 23:4; 18(2); 24:14; 25:32; 33; 34(2); 45; 26:4; 13; 20; 36(2); 39(2); 40(3); 41(3); 43(2); 44(2); 45(3); **Num** 1:2(2); 3; 16; 18(2); 20(3); 22(3); 24(3); 26(3); 28(3); 30(3); 32(3); 34(3); 36(3); 38(3); 40(3); 42(3); 45; 47; 52(2); 2:3; 9; 10; 16; 17; 18; 24; 25; 31; 32(2); 34(2); 3:4; 10; 15(2); 17; 18; 19; 20(2); 26; 31; 37(3); 39; 40; 45; 51; 4:2(2); 22(2); 26(2); 27(4); 28; 29(2); 31; 32(3); 33; 34(2); 36; 38(2); 40(2); 42(2); 44; 46(2); 5:3; 6:15(2); 7:2; 3; 7; 8; 9; 10; 11; 17; 23; 29; 35; 41; 47; 53; 59; 65; 71; 77; 83; 87(2); 88; 8:7(2); 10; 12; 21; 22; 26(2); 9:17; 10:5; 6(2); 12; 14(2); 18(2); 21; 22(2); 25(2); 28(2); 11:10; 12; 33; 13:2; 4; 33; 14:1; 5; 6; 9; 23; 15:12; 25(3); 38(2); 16:15; 22; 26; 27(4); 32(2); 34; 38; 45; 17:2(2); 6(3); 10; 18:11; 12; 13; 17(2); 18; 20; 23; 20:6; 8(2); 11; 21:2; 3; 18; 22:7; 24:2; 8; 25:2(2); 18(2); 26:2; 12; 15; 20; 23; 26; 28; 35; 37; 38; 41; 42(2); 44; 48; 50; 55; 56; 57; 59; 27:5; 7(2); 14; 19; 28:2; 3; 9; 11; 14; 19; 20; 27; 28; 31; 29:2; 3; 6(2); 8; 9; 11; 13; 14; 17; 18(3); 19; 20; 21(3); 23; 24(3); 26; 27(3); 29; 30(3); 32; 33(3); 36; 37(3); 31:9(4); 10; 29; 32:17; 38; 33:1; 2(3); 4(2); 52(3); 34:14(3); 15; 35:2; 3(4); 7; 36:3; 4(2); 6; 11; 12(2); **Deut** 1:8; 25; 2:5; 9; 12(2); 21; 22; 23; 4:10; 37; 38; 5:29; 7:3(2); 5(4); 10; 16; 24(2); 25; 9:5; 14; 27(2); 10:11; 15; 11:4(2); 6(3); 9; 12:2; 3(5); 29; 30(2); 31(3); 13:13; 14:8(2); 13; 15; 18:2(2); 18; 19:1(2); 20:18(2); 21:5; 6; 8; 23:6(2); 24:16(2); 29:8; 17(2); 25; 28; 31:4; 7; 11; 13; 19; 20; 21(2); 28; 32:5; 8; 20; 21; 27; 29; 30; 31; 32(3); 33; 35(2); 36; 37; 38(2); 33:29; **Josh** 1:6; 3:14; 4:18; 21; 5:1; 6; 7(2); 8; 7:6; 11; 12(3); 16; 8:19; 33; 9:4; 5(2); 14; 16; 17(2); 10:5; 13; 19(2); 24(2); 40; 42; 11:4; 6(2); 9(2); 12; 13; 17; 20; 21; 23(2); 12:7; 13:8; 14; 15; 16; 23(2); 24; 25; 28(2); 29; 30; 31; 33; 14:2; 4(3); 15:1; 2; 12; 20; 32; 36; 41; 44; 46; 51; 54; 57; 59; 60; 62; 16:4; 5(2); 8; 9; 17:2(2); 4; 18:2; 4; 5(2); 7(2); 10; 11(2); 12; 20; 21; 24; 28(2); 19:1(2); 2; 6; 7; 8; 9; 10(2); 11; 15; 16(2); 17; 18; 22(2); 23(2); 24; 25; 30; 31(2); 32; 33; 38; 39(2); 40; 41; 47; 48; 49; 21:2; 3(2); 7; 8; 19; 20; 26; 33(2); 40(2); 41; 43; 44(4); 22:6; 7(2); 9; 23:1; 2(4); 5; 7; 24:1(3); 8; **Judg** 1:4; 7; 2:2; 3; 4; 10; 12; 14(2); 17(2); 18(2); 19(3); 20; 22; 3:4; 6(5); 7; 24; 25; 5:18; 20; 6:5(3); 9; 7:2; 6(3); 8(2); 12; 19; 20(2); 8:3; 10; 21; 26; 28; 33; 34(2); 9:3; 24(2); 26; 27(2); 57; 10:12; 12:2; 13:20; 14:17; 19(2); 15:13; 16:18; 23; 24; 25; 18:1; 2(2); 8(2); 14; 16; 26; 29; 19:14; 21; 20:13; 14; 15; 33(2); 42(2); 21:2; 6; 10; 21; 22(2); 23(2); **Ruth** 1:9; 14; **1 Sam** 1:19; 2:20; 25; 33; 6:6; 7; 10; 11; 13(2); 8:9; 22; 9:16; 10:4; 12; 21; 11:4; 12:9; 14:30; 46; 15:24; 17:1; 18; 51; 53; 18:27; 21:13; 22:17(2); 23:5; 25:12; 28:1; 23; 29:1; 30:2; 3(3); 4; 31:9; 13; **2 Sam** 1:23(2); 2:25; 26; 27; 3:18; 30; 4:12; 5:21; 7:10; 23; 24; 10:3; 4(3); 18; 12:30; 13:31; 36; 15:30; 36; 17:8; 18:28; 20:2; 3; 22:46; 23:7; 17; 19; **1 Ki** 1:40; 2:4(3); 15; 33; 4:8; 27; 6:27; 7:25; 33(4); 8:7; 23; 25; 34; 35; 37(2); 44; 45(3); 48(5); 49(3); 50; 66; 9:9(2); 21; 10:5; 29; 11:2; 8; 12:16; 27; 13:11; 12; 14:15(2); 22(2); 27; 30; 15:16; 32; 16:2; 13; 26; 18:28; 37; 39; 19:21; 20:6; 23; 24; 25; 32(2); 22:10; **2 Ki** 1:14; 3:24; 27; 5:24; 6:20; 22; 23; 7:5; 7(4); 15; 8:12(4); 21; 10:7; 11:12; 13:3; 5; 14; 14:6(2); 16:15(2); 17:7; 9(2); 14(3); 15; 16; 17; 19; 23; 25; 31; 33; 34(2); 40; 41(4); 18:12; 27; 35; 36; 37; 19:17; 18; 26; 21:8; 14(2); 15; 22:7; 17; 23:2; 4; 9; 12; 14; 25:13; 23(2); 24; **1 Chr** 1:29; 2:16; 3:9; 19; 4:3; 27; 31; 32; 33(2); 38(2); 39; 41(3); 42; 5:7(2); 9; 10(2); 13(2); 15; 16; 20(3); 21(5); 22; 23; 24(2); 25; 6:19; 32(2); 33; 44; 48; 54(3); 60(2); 62; 63; 64; 65; 66; 7:2(3); 4(2); 5(2); 7(2); 9(2); 11; 21; 22; 28; 30; 32; 40(2); 8:10; 13; 28; 32(2); 9:1; 2(2); 6; 9(3); 13(2); 17; 19; 22(3); 23; 25(2); 32; 34; 38(2); 10:7; 9; 10; 12; 11:19(2); 21; 12:30; 32(3); 39; 13:2(2); 8; 14:12; 15:15; 16; 17; 18; 16:21; 17:9; 22; 19:4(2); 7; 20:2; 21:16; 23:22; 24(2); 28; 32; 24:2; 3; 4(2); 19(3); 30; 31(2); 25:1; 3; 6; 7; 8; 26:6; 8(2); 12; 13; 21; 27:1(2); 28:15; 18; 29:18; 20(2); 21; **2 Chr** 1:17; 3:13; 4:4; 7; 16; 20; 5:8; 11; 12(2); 13; 6:14; 16; 25; 26; 28(2); 34; 35(3); 37; 38(5); 39(3); 7:3; 6(2); 10; 14(3); 22; 8:8; 14(3); 9:4(2); 6; 10:16; 11:13(2); 14(2); 16(2); 12:10; 15; 13:10; 14; 16; 18; 14:4; 15:4; 12(3); 15(2); 17:14(2); 18:9; 19:4; 10; 20:13(3); 24; 25; 27; 33(2); 21:3; 22:5; 24:10; 18(2); 23; 24(2); 25:4(3); 5; 10; 15; 20; 26:11; 13; 28:6; 8; 15; 29:6(2); 15; 23; 24; 30; 34; 30:7; 16(2); 22; 27(2); 31:1; 2; 6; 15; 17(3); 18(4); 19; 32:13; 17; 33:17; 34:5; 12; 25; 30; 32; 33(2); 35:2; 10(2); 11; 15(3); 25; 36:15; 17(2); **Ezra** 2:59(2); 61; 62; 65; 66(2); 67(2); 69; 70(2); 3:8(2); 9(2); 10; 12; 4:5; 7; 9; 17; 23; 5:3; 5; 8; 10; 6:12; 13; 18(2); 20; 22; 7:16; 17(2); 8:1; 19; 24; 26; 9:2(2); 11(2); 12(3); 10:14; 19(3); **Neh** 2:18; 3:5(3); 18; 23; 4:3; 4(2); 5(2); 11; 13(4); 15; 5:1(2); 5; 6; 11(4); 14; 6:6; 9; 14; 16; 7:61(2); 63; 64; 67; 68(2); 69; 73(2); 8:6(3); 7; 12; 15; 16; 9:1; 2(3); 3(3); 4; 6; 9; 11; 15(2); 16; 17(3); 20(2); 21(2); 23(2); 24(2); 26; 27(3); 28; 29(2); 35(2); 37; 10:1; 10; 28(3); 29(2); 30; 11:3; 9; 12; 14(2); 19; 25; 30; 31; 12:7; 9(2); 22; 24; 27; 45; 13:11; 13(2); 24; 25(3); **Esth** 1:17(2); 20; 22; 2:12; 3:8; 12; 13; 4:8; 8:9(2); 11(2); 13; 9:2(2); 5; 16(3); 22; 27; 28; 31(3); **Job** 1:4(2); 5(2); 13; 18; 2:12(2); 3:15; 4:21; 5:5; 12(2); 13; 15; 6:4; 17; 18; 8:4; 8; 10; 11:3; 9; 20; 12:18; 14:12; 15:18; 35; 16:10; 17:2; 4; 19:12; 15; 21:8(4); 9; 10(2); 11(2); 13; 16(2); 17; 29; 22:6; 16; 18; 20; 24:5(2); 6; 11; 18(2); 23; 27:15; 23; 29:9(2); 10(2); 23; 30:2(2); 4; 9(2); 12; 31:16; 39; 33:15; 16; 34:24; 25; 36:9(2); 10; 11(2); 14; 15(2); 20; 37:8; 38:15; 33; 40(2); 39:3(2); 4; 40:12; 13; 22; 42:15(2); **Ps** 2:3(2); 12; 4:7; 5:9(4); 10(2); 11; 7:7; 9:5; 6; 10; 15; 10:17; 11:2(2); 6; 16:4(3); 17:10(2); 11; 14(3); 18:45; 19:3; 4(2); 21:10(2); 12(2); 22:13; 25:22; 28:3(2); 4(3); 8; 33:15(2); 19; 34:5; 15; 17; 35:6; 7; 16; 17; 21; 25; 36:7; 37:14; 15(3); 18; 39; 40:15; 44:1; 3(2); 49:6(2); 8; 10; 11(5); 13(2); 14(2); 54:5; 55:9; 15; 23; 56:5; 57:4; 58:4; 6(2); 59:7(2); 12(3); 62:4; 64:3(3); 8; 65:7; 9; 68:23; 27(2); 69:22(2); 23(2); 25(2); 27; 70:3; 71:15; 72:14(2); 73:4(2); 6; 7; 9(2); 17; 20; 74:4; 8; 76:5(2); 78:4; 5; 6; 7; 8; 12; 18(2); 28(2); 29; 30(3); 33(2); 35(2); 36(2); 37; 38; 44(2); 46(2); 47(2); 48(2); 50(2); 51; 53; 55; 57; 58(2); 63(2); 64(2); 79:3; 10; 12(2); 81:12(2); 14(2); 15; 83:2; 11(2); 16; 85:2; 89:17; 32(2); 90:10; 16; 91:12; 93:3(2); 94:23(2); 95:10; 98:8; 99:8; 102:17; 28; 104:11; 12; 17; 21(2); 22; 27; 29(2); 105:14; 24; 25; 29(2); 30(2); 31; 32; 33(3); 35(2); 36(2); 106:11; 15(2); 18; 20; 21; 25; 27; 29; 35; 36; 37(2); 38; 39(2); 42(2); 43(2); 44(2); 45; 107:5; 6(2); 12; 13(2); 14; 17(2); 18; 19(2); 20; 26; 27; 28(2); 30; 38; 41; 109:10(2); 13; 25; 29; 115:2; 4; 7; 9(2); 10(2); 11(2); 119:70; 118; 123:2; 124:3; 6; 125:3; 4; 5; 127:5; 129:3; 132:12; 135:12; 17; 136:10; 21; 140:2; 3(2); 9; 141:4; 6; 10; 144:12; 145:15; 19; 147:3; 149:2(2); 5; 6(2); 8(2); **Prov** 1:6; 15; 16; 18(2); 22; 31(2); 2:15; 4:16; 22; 8:21; 9:15; 10:15; 11:6; 20; 14:24; 17:6; 26; 20:29(2); 21:12; 22:23; 23:11(2); 24:2(2); 22; 29:16; 30:5; 13(2); 25; 26; **Eccl** 2:3; 3:11; 12; 4:1; 9; 5:11; 13; 9:1; 3; 6(3); **Isa** 2:4(2); 7(4); 8(3); 3:4; 8(2); 9(3); 10; 12; 16; 17; 5:12; 13(2); 14(3); 17; 21(2); 24(2); 25; 27(2); 28(3); 29; 6:10(5); 8:12; 19; 21(2); 9:17(2); 10:2; 13; 25; 11:7; 14; 13:8; 10(2); 11; 16(4); 18(2); 20; 21; 22(2); 14:1; 2(2); 9; 21; 25; 15:2; 3(3); 4; 16:10; 18:2; 7; 19:3; 20:4; 5(2); 21:14; 24:14; 25:11(3); 26:11; 14; 21; 29:13(4); 14(2); 15(2); 19; 30:6(2); 26; 31:3; 4(2); 32:12; 33:2; 7; 9; 23; 24; 34:2; 3(4); 4; 7(2); 35:10; 36:12; 20; 21; 22; 37:18; 19; 27; 40:24; 26; 31; 41:1; 17; 29(2); 42:11; 15; 43:9; 14; 44:9(2); 18(2); 25; 45:12; 20; 46:1; 47:9; 49:7; 9; 22(2); 23(2); 26(2); 50:2; 3; 51:7; 11; 52:8(2); 15; 53:11; 54:17; 55:12; 56:7(2); 11; 57:2; 8(3); 58:1(2); 2; 59:5; 6(4); 7(3); 8; 18; 60:8; 9(2); 10; 11; 61:6; 7(2); 8; 9(2); 62:6; 63:3; 6; 8; 9; 65:2; 4; 6; 7(2); 21; 22; 23; 66:3(3); 4(2); 18(2); 24(2); **Jer** 1:8; 16(2); 17; 2:11; 26(4); 27(3); 3:17; 21(2); 24(4); 4:16; 5:3; 4; 5; 6(3); 16; 24; 27; 31; 6:3(2); 10; 12; 19; 23; 27; 7:19; 24(2); 26(3); 28(2); 30; 31(2); 8:1; 7; 10(2); 12; 19; 9:3(2); 5; 8; 14(2); 16; 10:7; 9; 15; 21; 11:8; 10(2); 12; 14; 18; 22(2); 23; 12:2(2); 14; 13:10; 14:3(4); 4; 6; 10(3); 11; 12; 14; 16(4); 15:7; 8; 9; 16:3(2); 4; 7(2); 15(2); 17(2); 18(3); 17:1; 2(3); 23(2); 25; 18:15; 16; 17; 21(6); 22; 23(3); 19:4; 5; 7(3); 9(4); 15; 20:4; 5; 11; 21:7(2); 22:9; 23:3; 8; 10(2); 11; 12(2); 16; 22(2); 26; 27(2); 31; 32(2); 24:5; 7(2); 9; 10; 25:12; 14(2); 36; 38; 26:3; 27:4; 11(2); 28:13; 29:5; 23; 28; 30:3; 9(2); 10; 20(2); 21(3); 31:12; 13; 17; 23; 32; 33(3); 34(2); 32:18; 22; 30(2); 32(4); 34; 35(2); 38; 39; 40; 44; 33:5; 8(2); 12; 20; 26; 34:11; 14; 16; 20(3); 21(2); 35:14; 16; 36:3(2); 6; 7; 15; 24; 31; 37:7; 38:4; 18; 19; 23; 40:7; 8; 9; 41:5(3); 8; 17; 42:17; 43:1(2); 44:3; 5(2); 9; 12; 15; 46:5; 10; 21(2); 25(2); 26; 27; 47:3; 5; 48:13; 34; 44; 49:7; 18; 20; 21; 29(5); 32(3); 35; 37(2); 50:4; 5; 6(2); 7(2); 9; 27(2); 34(2); 37(2); 38; 40; 42; 45; 51:5; 18; 30(2); 39(2); 55; 56; 52:17; **Lam** 1:11; 19(2); 22; 2:10(2); 12(3); 15(2); 16(2); 18; 20; 3:14; 46; 60(2); 61(2); 62; 63(3); 64; 4:3(2); 7; 8(3); 10; 14; 20; 5:7; 8; 12; 14; **Ezek** 1:5; 7(2); 8(2); 9; 10; 11(3); 13; 16(2); 18(2); 22; 23; 24(2); 25(2); 26; 2:3; 6(3); 3:8(2); 9; 4:4; 5; 12; 13; 17; 5:10(2); 6:5; 9(4); 13(4); 14; 7:11; 12; 14; 18; 19(7); 20(2); 24(2); 27; 8:11; 16(2); 17; 9:10(2); 10:8; 10; 11; 12(4); 16; 19; 21; 22(3); 11:19; 20; 21(4); 22; 12:3(2); 4(2); 5; 6; 7; 16(2); 19(2); 13:2; 3; 17; 18; 14:3(2); 5(2); 10; 11(2); 14; 20; 22(2); 23(2); 16:39; 40; 45; 47(2); 53; 55(2); 19:4; 7(2); 8(2); 20:4; 8; 16(2); 18(3); 24(2); 26(2); 28(4); 30; 21:6; 14; 15; 23; 28; 22:10(2); 26; 31(2); 23:3(3); 4(2); 7; 8; 15(3); 17; 24; 30; 36; 37(3); 39(2); 42(2); 45; 47(4); 24:25(7); 25:4(2); 26:10; 16(3); 17; 27:9; 11; 29; 30(2); 32; 35(2); 28:7; 25; 26; 29:7(2); 14; 16; 21; 30:11; 31:4; 6(3); 14(2); 32:2; 10; 14(2); 22; 24(2); 25(2); 26(3); 27(5); 29; 30(2); 33:2(2); 17; 29; 31(3); 34:10(2); 13; 14; 23; 24; 26; 27(3); 30; 35:5(2); 36:7; 12; 17(3); 18; 19(2); 23(2); 37; 37:10; 20; 21; 23(5); 25(3); 26; 27; 28; 38:13; 16; 39:22; 23(2); 24(2); 26(3); 27; 28(2); 40:16; 41:7; 16(2); 21; 42:4; 11(2); 14; 43:7(4); 8(2); 9(3); 10; 11; 44:10(2); 12(2); 13(2); 18(2); 19(2); 20(3); 28(3); 45:4; 8; 11; 46:10; 16; 18; 19; 47:10(2); 12(5); 48:29; 34; **Dan** 1:15; 16; 3:21(4); 27(2); 28(2); 29; 4:21; 6:24(3); 7:12(2); 8:23(2); 25; 11:8(3); 32; 38; **Hos** 1:7; 2:5; 17; 3:5(2); 4:7; 8(2); 9(2); 12(3); 13; 18; 19; 5:4(3); 5; 6; 7; 15(2); 7:2(3); 3(2); 6(2); 7(2); 10; 12; 14(2); 15; 16(3); 8:4; 13(2); 9:4(3); 6(2); 9(2); 11; 12; 15(3); 16(2); 10:2(3); 8; 10; 11:3; 4; 6; 11; 12:11; 13:2(2); 6; 8; 16(2); 14:4; 7; **Joel** 1:3(2); 2:4; 10; 17; 22; 3:6; 13; 15; 19; **Am** 1:13; 15; 2:4(2); 8; 3:10; 14; 6:2; 7:11; 8:7; 9:4; 15; **Ob** 12; 13(5); 17; **Jon** 1:2; 2:8; 3:10(2); 4:11(2); **Mic** 2:1(2); 9(2); 12; 13(2); 3:2; 3(2); 4; 5(2); 7; 4:3(2); 13(2); 6:12(2); 16; 7:4; 13; 16(4); 17; **Nah** 2:2; 5; 7; 10; 3:19; **Hab** 1:7(2); 8(3); 9; 15(2); 16(4); 17; 2:7; 3:11; 14; **Zeph** 1:9; 12; 13(3); 17(2); 18(2); 2:7(3); 8; 10; 14; 3:6(3); 7; 13(2); **Hag** 1:12(2); 14; 2:14; 22; **Zech** 1:21; 2:9; 5:6; 9; 6:5; 7:11(2); 12; 8:8; 12; 9:16; 10:2; 5; 6; 7(3); 9; 11:3; 5; 6; 8; 16; 12:5(2); 12(2); 13(2); 14; 14:12(6); **Mal** 4:6; **Mt** 1:21; 2:11; 12; 3:6; 4:6; 8; 20; 21(2); 22; 23; 6:2; 5; 7; 14; 15; 16(2); 7:6; 16; 20; 8:22; 34; 9:2; 4; 29; 30; 35; 10:17; 11:1; 16; 12:9; 25; 13:15(5); 43; 54; 58; 14:14; 15:2; 8(3); 27; 17:6; 8; 12; 25; 18:10; 31; 19:12; 20:8; 34(2); 21:7; 8; 41; 22:5; 7; 16; 18; 22; 23:3; 4; 5(3); 25:1; 3; 4(2); 7; 26:43; 67; 27:39; **Mk** 1:5; 18; 19; 20; 23; 39; 2:5; 6; 3:5; 4:12; 15; 5:17; 6:6; 8; 52; 7:3; 6(2); 8:3; 9:44; 46; 48; 10:42; 11:4; 7; 8; 12:15; 44; 14:40; 46; 56; 59; 65; 15:29; 16:14; **Lk** 1:16; 20; 51; 52; 66; 77; 2:8; 39; 44; 3:15; 4:6; 11; 15; 29; 35; 5:2; 6; 7; 11; 15; 20; 22; 30; 6:1; 8; 17; 23; 26; 8:3; 12; 9:47; 60; 11:17; 48; 12:36; 42; 13:1; 16:4; 8; 17:13; 19:32; 35; 36; 20:23; 21:1; 4; 12; 22:66; 23:25; 48; 51; 24:5; 11; 16; 31(2); 43; 45; **Jn** 3:19; 4:38; 8:9; 10:39; 11:19; 12:40(4); 13:12; 15:22; 25; 17:19; 20; 18:8; 19:3; 31; 20:10; **Acts** 1:9; 19; 26; 2:45; 46; 4:5; 23; 24; 26; 29; 5:18; 6:1; 7:19; 34; 39; 41; 54; 57; 58; 9:24; 10:9; 12:20(2); 25; 13:5; 18; 19; 27; 33; 50; 51; 14:2; 3; 5; 11; 13; 14; 16; 15:3; 9; 22; 26; 16:19; 22; 24; 33; 17:21; 26(2); 19:18; 19; 21:21; 24(2); 22:22; 23; 30; 23:16; 28; 29; 25:19; 26:18; 27:13; 43; 28:6; 27(5); **Rom** 1:21(2); 24(2); 26; 27(2); 28; 2:15(3); 3:3; 8; 13(3); 15; 16; 18; 8:5; 10:3; 18(2); 11:9; 10(2); 11; 12(3); 15(2); 24; 27; 30; 13:7; 15:27(3); 16:4; 5; 18; **1 Cor** 3:19; 8:7; 12; 10:5; 14:35; 16:19; **2 Cor** 3:14; 15; 5:19; 6:16; 8:2(3); 3(2); 14(2); 9:14; 11:15; **Gal** 2:13; **Eph** 4:17; 18(2); 5:24; 28(2); **Phil** 2:21; 3:19(3); **Col** 2:2; **1 Th** 2:15; 16; 5:13; **2 Th** 3:12; **1 Tim** 3:11; 12(2); 4:2; 5:4; 12; 6:1; 10; **2 Tim** 2:17; 26; 3:9; 4:3; 4; **Titus** 1:12; 15; 2:4(2); 5; 9; 3:13; **Heb** 2:10; 15; 3:10; 5:14; 7:5; 8:9; 10(3); 12(3); 10:16(2); 17(2); 11:16; 35; 13:7; **Jas** 1:27; 3:3; 5:3; **1 Pe** 3:1; 5; 12; 14; 4:14; 19; **2 Pe** 2:2; 3(2); 8; 12; 13; 3:3; 16; **3 Jn** 6; **Jude** 6(2); 13; 15; 16; 18; **Rev** 2:22; 3:4; 4:4; 10; 6:11(2); 7:3; 9; 11; 14; 17; 9:4; 5; 7(2); 8; 9; 10(2); 17; 18; 19(4); 20; 21(4); 10:3; 4; 11:5(2); 6; 7; 8; 9(2); 11; 12; 16(2); 12:11(2); 13:16(2); 14:1; 2; 5; 11; 13(2); 15:6; 16:6; 10; 11(3); 17:13; 17(2); 18:11; 19; 19:19; 21; 20:4(3); 12; 21:3; 4; 8; 24; 22:4

THEIRS (20/20)

Gen 15:13; 34:23; 43:34; **Ex** 29:9; **Lev** 18:10; **Num** 7:9; 16:26; 18:9; **Josh** 21:10; **1 Sam** 30:19; **Isa** 61:7; **Jer** 44:28; **Ezek** 16:52; 44:29; 46:17; **Hab** 1:6; **Mt** 5:3; 10; **1 Cor** 1:2; **2 Tim** 3:9

THEMSELVES (316/295)

Gen 3:7; 8; 6:2; 21:28; 29; 30:40; 34:30; 43:28; 32(2); **Ex** 5:7; 12:39; 18:22; 26; 19:22; 26:9(2); 32:7; 8; 26; 31; 33:6; 36:16(2); **Lev** 20:5; 22:2; **Num** 8:7; 21; 26; 11:32; **Deut** 7:20; 9:12; 31:14; 20; 32:5; 31; **Josh** 8:27; 9:5; 10:16; 11:14; 24:1; **Judg** 5:2; 9; 6:2; 9:51; 15:9; 18:30; 31; 19:22; 20:2; 20; 22(2); 30; 33; **1 Sam** 2:5; 3:13; 4:2; 5:8; 14:11; 21:4; **2 Sam** 5:18; 22; 10:6; 8(2); 17; 16:14; **1 Ki** 8:47; 14:23; 18:23; 28; **2 Ki** 7:12; 8:20; 12:5; 17:9; 10; 16; 17; 32; **1 Chr** 11:10; 14; 15:14; 19:6(2); 7; 9(2); 11; 21:20; 29:20; 24; **2 Chr** 5:11; 6:37; 7:14; 12:6; 7(2); 13:7; 20:25; 21:8; 29:15; 34(2); 30:3; 11; 15; 17; 18; 24; 31:4; 18; 35:14(2); **Ezra** 6:20(2); 21; 9:1; 2; **Neh** 4:2; 17; 8:16; 9:2; 18; 25; 10:28; 11:2; 12:29; 30; 13:22; **Esth** 8:13; 9:1; 27; 31; **Job** 1:6; 2:1; 3:14; 24:16; 34:22; 41:25; **Ps** 2:2; 3:6; 9:20; 35:26; 37:11; 38:16; 39:6; 44:10; 57:6; 59:4; 64:5; 66:3; 7; 80:6; 94:4; 106:28; 109:29; **Prov** 23:5; 28:12; 28; **Eccl** 3:18; 11:3; **Isa** 3:9; 15:3; 22:7; 30:2; 46:2; 6; 47:14; 48:2; 56:6; 59:6; 8; 66:17(2); **Jer** 2:13; 24; 4:2; 5:7; 7:19; 9:5; 10:5; 11:17; 12:13; 16:6(2); 18:15; 41:5; 49:29; 50:9; **Lam** 2:10; 4:14; **Ezek** 6:9; 14:14; 18; 20; 26:16; 27:31(2); 31:14; 34:2; 8; 10; 36:5; 37:23; 44:18; 25(2); **Dan** 10:7; 11:14; **Hos** 1:11; 4:14; 8:4; 9:10; 13:2; **Am** 9:3; **Hab** 1:7; 2:13; **Zech** 12:12(2); 13(2); 14; **Mt** 9:3; 14:15; 16:7; 17:1; 19:12; 21:25; 38; 23:4; **Mk** 1:27; 2:8; 4:17; 6:32; 36; 51; 8:16; 9:2; 8; 10; 34; 10:26; 11:31; 12:7; 14:4; 15:31; 16:3; **Lk** 4:36; 7:30; 49; 18:9; 20:5; 14; 22:23; 24:12; **Jn** 6:52; 7:35; 11:55; 56; 12:19; 14:11; 16:17; 17:13; 18:18; 28; 19:24; **Acts** 4:15; 15:32; 16:37; 19:13; 20:30; 21:25; 23:12; 21; 24:15; 20; 26:31; 27:36; 28:25; 29; **Rom** 1:24; 27; 2:14; 15; 13:2; **1 Cor** 16:15; **2 Cor** 5:15; 8:5; 10:12(5); 11:13; 15; **Gal** 5:12; **Eph** 4:19; **1 Th** 1:9; **1 Tim** 2:9; 3:13; 6:10; 19; **2 Tim** 3:2; 4:3; **Heb** 6:6; 9:23; **1 Pe** 1:12; 3:5; **2 Pe** 2:1; 19; **Jude** 7; 10; 12; **Rev** 6:15; 8:6

THEN (3990/3913)

Gen 1:3; 6; 9; 11; 14; 16; 20; 24; 26; 28; 31; 2:3; 15; 22; 3:4; 7; 9; 12; 17; 22; 4:2; 9; 16; 19; 23; 24; 26; 6:5; 7:1; 8:1; 4; 7; 11; 15; 20; 21; 9:8; 21; 25; 10:19; 11:3; 29; 12:5; 6; 7; 13:1; 7; 9(2); 11; 16; 18; 14:7; 11; 13; 18; 15:3; 5; 7; 10; 13; 16:3; 5; 10; 13; 17:3; 15; 16; 17; 19; 22; 18:1; 9; 16; 22; 26; 27; 30; 32; 19:2; 3; 9; 12; 18; 24; 28; 30; 35; 20:10; 14; 16; 17; 21:4; 14; 16; 17; 19; 25; 29; 33; 22:2; 4; 7; 9; 13; 15; 23:3; 7; 12; 24:8; 10; 12; 18; 20; 26; 32; 41; 47; 50; 53; 54; 58; 61; 64; 67; 25:8; 13; 33; 34; 26:2; 9; 12; 17; 21; 23; 26; 31; 27:2; 10; 15; 17; 21; 24; 26; 33; 37; 39; 41; 45; 28:1; 12; 16; 18; 20; 21; 29:5; 7; 8; 11; 13; 15; 21; 25; 28; 30; 33; 35; 30:4; 6; 8; 11; 13; 14; 19; 22; 28; 36; 40; 31:3; 8(2); 11; 14; 16; 17; 23; 31; 33; 36; 46; 51; 54; 55; 32:3; 6; 8; 9; 16; 18; 24; 29; 33:3; 6; 8; 10; 12; 18; 20; 34:6; 11; 16; 17; 30; 35:1; 3; 9; 13; 16; 21; 27; 36:6; 37:7; 9; 12; 14; 19; 24; 25; 28; 29; 32; 34; 38:6; 11; 16; 18(2); 21; 23; 29; 39:4; 9; 17; 20; 40:5; 9; 11; 21; 41:1; 3; 6; 9; 14; 17; 19; 23; 25; 36; 39; 42; 53; 55; 42:7; 9; 18; 21; 24; 25; 28; 29; 33; 35; 37; 38; 43:8; 9; 11; 17; 23; 25; 27; 29; 31; 34; 44:8; 11; 13; 16; 18; 21; 26; 27; 32; 45:1; 3; 4; 14; 21; 25; 28; 46:2; 5; 28; 31; 47:1; 3; 5; 6; 7; 12; 16; 20; 23; 31; 48:3; 8; 10; 14; 21; 49:4; 29; 50:1; 10; 18; 25; **Ex** 1:15; 16(2); 2:5; 7; 9; 14; 17; 21; 23; 3:3; 5; 13; 18; 4:1; 4; 8; 10; 20; 22; 25; 26; 29; 30; 31; 5:4; 15; 20; 6:1; 7; 12; 13; 7:6; 8; 9; 19; 22; 8:5; 8; 12; 19; 20; 25; 26; 29; 9:1; 5; 7; 10; 13; 15; 22; 33; 10:7; 10; 12; 16; 21; 24; 28; 11:4; 6; 8; 12:6; 8; 21; 28; 31; 37; 44; 48; 13:1; 13; 17; 14:4; 11; 18; 21; 26; 28; 15:1; 15; 20; 22; 27; 16:2; 4; 6; 9; 17; 23; 25; 32; 17:1; 14; 18:2; 9; 12; 22; 23; 27; 19:5; 8; 10; 16; 20; 24(2); 20:19; 22; 21:3; 6; 8; 11; 13; 19; 23; 28; 30; 35; 22:3; 8; 11; 13; 23:22; 24:5; 7; 9; 12; 15; 25:1; 26:33; 28:9; 24; 29:5; 8; 11; 17; 20; 26; 32; 34; 30:11; 12; 17; 31:1; 32:4; 6; 11; 20; 26; 29; 31; 33:1; 12; 15; 16; 19; 23; 34:4; 9; 20; 27; 31; 35; 35:1; 21; 36:2; 4; 8; 19; 37:1; 38:7; 9; 28; 39:30; 43; 40:1; 6; 12; 34; 37; **Lev** 1:4; 8; 13; 14; 17; 2:9; 16; 3:3; 7; 9; 12; 14; 4:3; 5; 14; 15; 17; 21; 28; 30; 33; 35; 5:3; 4; 7; 9; 11; 12; 14; 15; 6:4; 8; 11; 7:12; 28; 8:6; 8; 13; 14; 15; 16; 18; 19; 21; 22; 24; 25; 28; 30; 9:6; 9; 13; 15; 17; 20; 22; 23; 10:1; 8; 16; 11:32; 12:1; 2; 4; 5; 7; 8; 13:2; 3; 4; 5; 6(2); 8; 9; 13; 17; 19; 21; 22; 25; 26; 27; 30(2); 31; 34; 36; 39; 43; 54; 55; 56; 58; 14:1; 4; 11; 13; 16; 19; 21; 25; 27; 36; 38; 40; 42; 44; 48; 50; 53; 15:8; 13(2); 15; 16; 28; 30; 16:8; 12; 15; 19; 23; 28; 33; 17:15; 16; 18:1; 19:23; 20:1; 5; 22:1; 14; 23:10; 16; 19; 23; 33; 24:1; 12; 14; 15; 23; 25:2; 9; 19; 21; 25; 27; 28; 29; 30; 33; 35; 41; 52; 54; 26:4; 18; 21; 24; 28; 34(2); 42; 27:3; 4; 5; 6; 7; 8; 10; 11; 13; 14; 15; 16; 18; 19; 23; 27(2); 33; **Num** 1:17; 2:7; 14; 22; 29; 3:11; 14; 40; 44; 4:1; 6; 10; 12; 15; 17; 21; 5:5; 7; 15; 18; 21; 22; 23; 25; 27; 28; 30; 31; 6:1; 5; 9; 10; 16; 18; 7:2; 4; 8:5; 8; 12; 13; 21; 23; 9:9; 21; 10:4; 5; 6; 9; 12; 17; 21; 25; 11:2; 10; 17; 18; 25; 29; 12:1; 5; 6; 8; 10; 14; 13:17; 23; 27; 30; 14:5; 8; 11; 13; 15; 20; 39; 45; 15:4; 9; 19; 24; 27; 35; 16:3; 8; 15; 19; 22; 25; 29; 30; 34; 36; 43; 47; 17:4; 9; 18:1; 20; 25; 26; 30; 19:5; 7; 9; 12; 20:1; 7; 11; 12; 18; 19; 20; 22; 28; 21:1; 2; 4; 8; 17; 21; 24; 30; 32; 34; 22:1; 5; 9; 15; 18; 22; 24; 26; 28; 31; 35; 37; 40; 23:1; 3; 5; 11; 13; 16; 18; 25; 27; 29; 24:3; 10; 20; 21; 23; 25:4; 10; 16; 26:52; 27:1; 8; 9; 10; 11; 15; 30:1; 4; 5; 7; 11; 12; 14; 15; 31:6; 12; 21; 48; 32:16; 20; 22; 23; 29; 31; 42; 33:5; 38; 52; 55; 34:1; 3; 4; 8; 13; 35:9; 11; 24; 36:3; 4; 5; **Deut** 1:16; 19; 29; 41; 45; 2:1; 9; 32; 3:1; 18; 20; 23; 4:11; 41; 5:25; 28; 6:12; 21; 23; 25; 7:12; 8:10; 17; 19; 9:9; 10; 12; 17; 21; 23; 10:5; 11; 11:14; 23; 12:11; 21; 13:14; 14:25; 15:12; 17; 18; 16:10; 17:4; 5; 8; 18:7; 19:9; 12; 17; 19; 20:5; 10; 11; 12; 21:2; 5; 7; 12; 14; 16; 19; 21; 22:2(2); 8; 15; 18; 21; 22; 24; 25; 29; 23:9; 10; 24:4; 7; 25:2; 7; 8; 9; 12; 26:4; 7; 10; 13; 27:9; 28:10; 59; 64; 29:20; 25; 27; 30:5; 31:1; 7; 14; 17; 20; 21; 23; 27; 30; 32:15; 48; 33:28; 34:1; 4; 10; **Josh** 1:8(2); 10; 15; 2:4; 7; 15; 20; 21; 3:1; 3; 6; 17; 4:4; 7; 9; 11; 15; 21; 22; 5:7; 9; 12; 15; 6:5; 6; 10; 11; 13; 20; 26; 7:6; 9; 15; 18; 24; 26; 8:5; 7; 10; 18; 22; 33; 9:7; 14; 17; 19; 22; 10:12; 15; 20; 22; 25; 29; 31; 33; 38; 43; 11:11; 23; 14:6; 11; 15; 15:3; 7; 9; 10; 11; 15; 16:2; 6; 7; 17:14; 15; 18:3; 8; 10; 14; 16; 18; 19; 19:12; 14; 27; 29; 20:5; 6; 21:1; 22:1; 13; 15; 19; 21; 31; 23:16; 24:1; 3; 6; 7; 9; 11; 20; 26; **Judg** 1:4; 6; 7; 10; 12; 20; 2:1; 5; 11; 20; 3:11; 13; 20; 21; 23; 28; 4:6; 8; 9; 14; 19; 21; 22; 5:1; 8; 11; 13; 19; 22; 6:1; 4; 13; 14; 17(2); 21; 23; 30; 33; 34; 37; 39; 7:1; 4; 7; 11; 14; 16; 18; 20; 24(2); 8:3; 5; 7; 8; 11; 13; 15; 17; 19; 22; 24; 27; 29; 9:1; 5; 10; 12; 14; 15; 19(2); 28; 29; 33; 38; 41; 44; 48(2); 50; 51; 54; 10:6; 17; 11:3; 6; 11; 17; 19; 23; 29; 31; 37; 12:1; 3; 6(3); 7; 10; 15; 13:8; 10; 15; 17; 21; 14:3; 7; 12(2); 13; 16; 17; 19; 15:4; 6; 8; 11; 12; 14; 16; 18; 16:3; 7; 10; 11; 15; 17; 19(2); 21; 26; 28; 30; 17:4; 8; 11; 13; 18:8; 12; 14; 17; 21; 26; 30; 19:3; 5; 6; 8; 16; 26; 20:3; 12; 18; 21; 23; 26; 29; 33; 45(2); 21:2; 13; 16; 19; 21(2); 22; 23; **Ruth** 1:3; 5; 6; 9; 14; 2:3; 5; 8; 13; 18; 20; 3:1; 4; 10; 13; 14; 15; 16; 18; 4:3; 4; 5; 14; 16; **1 Sam** 1:8; 11(2); 17; 19; 22; 25; 2:11; 14; 16(2); 20; 27; 35; 3:1; 6; 8(2); 11; 16; 18; 21; 4:2; 6; 12; 16; 18; 21; 5:1; 6:3; 4; 6; 8(2); 9(2); 10; 12; 14; 15; 19; 7:1; 3(2); 9; 12; 14; 8:4; 9:4(2); 7; 10; 18; 21; 10:1; 3; 6; 10; 12; 14; 17; 25; 11:1; 3(2); 6; 9; 12; 14; 12:5; 6; 8; 10; 14; 15; 20; 21; 13:3; 5; 6; 8; 12; 15; 17; 14:6; 7; 8; 9; 10; 12; 17; 20; 28; 33; 35; 36; 40; 43; 46; 15:6; 13; 14; 16; 19; 22; 24; 30; 32; 34; 16:3; 5; 9; 11; 13; 18; 22; 23; 17:8; 9(2); 17; 23; 26; 30; 32; 40; 45; 47; 49; 53; 57; 18:3; 8; 17; 25; 27; 30; 19:3; 5; 7; 10; 15; 17; 20; 21; 22; 23; 20:1; 3; 6; 7; 9; 10; 12; 13; 18; 20; 21; 24; 30; 33; 36; 40; 42; 21:5; 10; 14; 22:3; 7; 9; 13; 15; 17; 23:1; 3; 4; 8; 10; 12; 13; 16; 19; 26; 29; 24:2; 4; 17; 25:1; 10; 11; 13; 18; 26; 31; 32; 38; 41; 26:2; 6; 8; 14; 15; 17; 21; 25; 27:2; 5; 10; 28:4; 7; 9(2); 11; 16(2); 20; 23; 25; 29:1; 3; 6; 9; 30:4; 7; 11; 13; 17; 20; 22; 31:2; 4; 10; 13; **2 Sam** 1:4; 6; 13; 15; 17; 2:4; 14; 20; 22; 26(2); 27; 29; 32; 3:8; 12; 16; 18; 19; 21; 24; 31; 34; 38; 4:5; 6; 7; 5:1; 9; 11; 22; 24(2); 6:5; 7; 14; 17; 19; 20; 7:3; 18; 8:2; 6; 10; 9:3; 5; 6; 8; 11; 10:2; 5; 8; 11(3); 16; 18; 11:2; 4; 6; 11; 12; 17; 18; 21; 23; 25; 12:1; 7; 15; 18; 20; 21; 24; 30; 31; 13:6; 8; 9; 10; 15; 17; 19; 24; 25; 26; 28; 29; 32; 34; 14:5; 8; 11; 13; 18; 22; 31; 33; 15:3; 4; 8; 10(2); 12; 16; 18; 19; 22; 25; 31; 33; 34; 16:3; 9; 10; 20; 21; 17:3; 5; 13; 15; 19; 23; 24; 18:2; 4; 9; 14; 17; 19; 21; 23; 25; 26; 28; 31; 33; 19:5; 6; 8; 12; 15; 18; 19; 30; 35; 39; 41; 42; 43; 20:9; 10; 15; 16; 17; 22(2); 21:5; 12; 16; 17; 18; 22:1; 8; 16; 43; 23:11; 13; 14(2); 24:6; 7; 9; 17; 21; 24; **1 Ki** 1:5; 7; 13; 14; 16; 17; 22; 28; 31; 35; 39; 43; 47; 52; 2:12; 15; 17; 20; 23; 28; 29; 31; 36; 42; 43; 3:1; 11; 14; 15; 18; 22; 24; 26; 5:2; 8; 9; 10; 13; 6:11; 12; 16; 27; 29; 35; 7:7; 16; 21; 38; 8:4; 6; 12; 14; 22; 32; 34; 36; 39; 45; 49; 55; 62; 9:5; 7; 9; 11; 12; 14; 24; 27; 10:6; 10; 11:7; 18; 20; 22; 26; 30; 38(2); 43; 12:3; 5; 6; 7; 10; 13; 18; 25; 27; 13:2; 4; 6; 7; 13; 14; 15; 25; 28; 30; 31; 14:17; 20; 27; 28; 31; 15:8; 18; 22; 24; 27; 16:1; 6; 11; 17; 21; 24; 28; 32; 17:2; 8; 20; 22; 24; 18:15; 17; 22; 24; 26; 30; 32; 34; 38; 41; 42; 44; 46; 19:2; 5; 6; 11; 15; 19; 20; 21; 20:2; 5; 10; 14; 15; 19; 21; 23; 25; 28; 30; 31; 33; 34; 36; 38; 40; 42; 21:7; 10; 13; 14; 17; 22:2; 6; 9; 13; 15; 17; 19; 21; 36; 38; 40; 47; 49; 50; **2 Ki** 1:7; 9; 10; 11; 16; 2:2; 4; 6; 11; 14; 16; 19; 21; 23; 25; 3:7; 8; 13; 15; 22; 25; 27; 4:3; 4; 7; 12; 14; 16; 20; 22; 24; 29; 35; 37; 40; 41; 42; 5:3; 5; 6; 9; 13; 17; 19; 24; 26; 6:3; 10; 17; 23; 26; 28; 31; 33; 7:1; 8; 9; 16; 19; 8:1; 4; 7; 11; 14; 21; 24; 29; 9:3(2); 6; 11; 13; 19; 21(2); 23; 25; 27; 31; 33; 34; 10:4; 6; 8; 16; 18; 21; 23; 25; 27; 35; 11:5; 11; 17; 19(2); 12:9; 11; 17; 18; 21; 13:3; 5; 9; 13; 14; 16; 17; 18; 19; 20; 24; 14:8; 13; 16; 20; 29; 15:5; 7; 10; 16; 22; 25; 30; 38; 16:5; 6; 11; 15; 20; 17:21; 24; 27; 28; 18:11; 14; 17; 19; 24; 26; 28; 37; 19:2; 8; 15; 20; 37; 20:2; 7; 9; 14; 16; 21; 21:18; 23; 24; 26; 22:8; 10; 12; 15; 23:3; 5; 7; 11; 13; 17; 21; 30; 34; 24:1; 6; 12; 17; 20; 25:4; 7; 11; 21; 22; **1 Chr** 1:29; 5:12; 21; 7:22; 8:30; 9:18; 36; 10:2; 4; 7; 10; 11:1; 3; 5; 7; 9; 16(2); 12:3; 16; 18; 29; 13:1; 4; 8; 10; 14:3; 9; 11; 13; 15; 17; 15:2; 4; 16; 16:1; 3; 5; 33; 43; 17:2; 16; 18:2; 6; 19:2; 5(2); 9; 12(3); 18; 20:2; 3; 21:3; 5; 16; 21; 22; 24; 22:1; 6; 13; 23:8; 24:3; 26:14; 27:34; 28:2; 11; 29:5; 6; 9; 20; 23; **2 Chr** 1:3; 2:1; 3; 6; 11; 17; 3:17; 4:2; 11; 5:5; 7; 6:1; 3; 12; 23; 25; 27; 30; 33; 35; 39; 7:4; 12; 14; 18; 20; 22; 8:12; 17; 9:5; 31; 10:3; 6; 10; 13; 18; 11:15; 18; 12:5; 10; 11; 16; 13:4; 7; 15; 17; 14:1; 9; 14; 15:9; 12; 14; 16; 16:2; 6; 10; 17:1; 18:5; 8; 12; 14; 16; 18; 20; 23; 25; 27; 19:1; 5; 20:2; 5; 14; 19; 27; 30; 37; 21:1; 19; 22:1; 6; 9; 23:3; 10; 11; 16; 20; 24:5; 8; 10; 20; 27; 25:9; 11; 16; 23; 28; 26:9; 14; 19; 21; 23; 27:9; 28:5; 12; 15(2); 27; 29:4; 12; 16; 17; 18; 20; 21; 23; 27; 31; 36; 30:6(2); 15; 23; 27; 31:1; 9; 12; 32:6; 18; 21; 26; 33; 33:13; 14; 20; 24; 25; 34:10; 15; 18; 20; 23; 29; 31; 35:3; 7; 12; 14; 36:1; 4; 8; 19; **Ezra** 1:5; 3:2; 9; 11; 4:4; 5:1; 4; 5; 9; 16; 6:1; 13; 16; 21; 8:16; 18; 21; 31; 9:4; 10:5; 6; 10; 12; 16; **Neh** 2:4; 6; 9; 12; 14; 15; 17; 18; 3:1(2); 4:10; 19; 5:8; 9; 12; 13(2); 6:5; 8; 12; 7:1; 5; 8:3; 6; 10; 16; 9:2; 4; 12:30; 13:6; 9; 12; 17; 19; 21; 27; **Esth** 1:13; 22; 2:2; 4; 9; 18; 3:3; 8; 12; 4:4; 5; 10; 15; 5:2; 5; 7; 8; 11; 14(2); 6:3; 9(2); 10; 7:3; 7; 8; 9; 10; 8:7; 17; 9:13; 29; **Job** 1:8; 20; 2:3; 9; 3:13; 4:1; 15; 16; 6:1; 3; 10; 7:14; 21; 8:1; 18; 9:1; 14; 29; 35; 10:14; 18; 11:1; 10; 11; 15; 12:1; 13:13; 20; 22(2); 15:1; 16:1; 17:15; 18:1; 19:1; 6; 20:1; 21:1; 34; 22:1; 24; 26; 29; 23:1; 24:24; 25:1; 4; 27:12; 28:20; 27; 29:11(2); 18; 30:26; 31:1; 8; 10; 14; 22; 40; 32:2; 33:16; 24; 27; 34:29(2); 36:9; 38:1; 21; 40:3; 6; 10; 14; 41:10; 42:1; 11; **Ps** 2:5; 18:7; 15; 42; 19:13; 27:10; 39:3; 40:7; 43:4; 51:13; 19(2); 55:12(2); 56:9; 67:6; 73:17; 78:34; 35; 65; 80:18; 89:19; 32; 96:12; 106:12; 24; 30; 107:6; 13; 19; 28; 30; 116:4; 119:6; 92; 124:3; 4; 5; 126:2(2); 142:3; **Prov** 1:28; 2:5; 9; 3:23; 8:30; 11:2; 20:14; 24; **Eccl** 2:11; 12; 13; 15(2); 18; 4:1; 7; 8:10; 17; 9:16; 10:10; 12:7; **Song** 8:10; **Isa** 4:5; 5:4; 17; 6:6; 8; 11; 7:3; 13; 8:3(2); 22; 10:19; 14:2; 25; 17:14; 19:21; 20:3; 5; 21:8; 9; 22:14; 20; 24:23; 28:18; 29:12; 30:23; 31:8; 32:16; 33:23; 35:5; 6; 36:2; 4; 9; 11; 13; 22; 37:2; 8; 15; 21; 36; 38; 38:2; 39:3; 5; 40:18; 25; 41:1; 7; 44:7; 15; 48:18; 49:4; 21; 23; 52:4; 58:8; 9; 10; 14; 59:15; 60:5; 63:11; 66:12; 20; **Jer** 1:4; 6; 9; 12; 14; 2:21; 3:8; 11; 16; 4:1; 10; 5:7; 19; 6:16; 7:7; 10; 34; 8:3; 22; 11:6; 12; 15; 12:5(2); 15; 16; 13:7; 8; 13; 23; 14:11; 13; 18(2); 15:1; 2; 19; 16:11; 17:25; 27; 18:3; 5; 10; 18; 19:10; 14; 20:2; 3; 9; 10; 21:3; 22:4; 9; 15; 16; 22; 23:22; 33; 24:3; 7; 25:12; 17; 28; 26:6; 12; 13; 17; 22; 27:7; 22; 28:5; 10; 15; 29:12; 30; 30:19; 21; 31:13; 36; 39; 32:2; 5; 8(2); 13; 26; 39; 33:9; 21; 26; 34:6; 15; 16; 35:3; 5; 12; 15; 36:4; 10; 12; 13; 19; 32; 37:5; 6; 14; 17(2); 21; 38:5; 10; 12; 14; 17(2); 18; 24; 26; 27; 39:3; 6; 9; 14; 40:6; 8; 12; 15; 41:2; 10; 14; 16; 42:4; 8; 10; 15; 16; 43:8; 44:15; 17; 20; 47:2; 49:1; 2; 51:48; 62; 64; 52:3; 7; 10; 15; 27; **Ezek** 1:4; 2:2; 10; 3:4; 12; 15; 22; 24; 4:6; 13; 15; 5:1; 2; 4; 6:4; 9; 13; 14; 7:4; 9; 26; 27; 8:2; 5; 8; 12; 15; 17; 9:1; 7; 9; 11; 10:2; 4; 6; 18; 11:1; 5; 10; 13; 19; 24; 12:15; 16; 20; 13:9; 14; 21; 14:4; 7; 8; 22; 15:1; 7; 16:9; 23; 29; 35; 53; 55; 61; 62; 17:5; 18:13; 19:8; 20:2; 4; 7; 8; 13; 21; 29; 38; 42; 44; 49; 21:10; 22:3; 16; 22; 23:13; 17; 18; 36; 43; 49; 24:11; 20; 25:5; 26:6; 16; 20; 28:20; 23; 24; 25; 26; 29:6; 9; 16; 21; 30:8; 19; 26; 31:18; 32:4; 14; 15; 33:4; 10; 23; 25; 26; 29; 33; 34:27; 35:4; 9; 12; 15; 36:11; 25; 28; 31; 36; 38; 37:2; 6; 11; 13; 14; 16; 17; 21; 23; 25; 38:15; 23; 39:3; 6; 7; 9; 28; 40:6; 9; 13; 17; 19; 28; 35; 45; 48; 41:1; 42:1; 13; 14; 43:6; 21; 44:1; 7; 45:17; 46:2; 10; 12(2); 21; 47:1; 6; 8; **Dan** 1:3; 10; 13; 19; 2:2; 4; 14; 15; 17; 19; 25; 35; 39; 46; 48; 3:4; 13; 19; 21; 24; 26(2); 30; 4:7; 19; 5:3; 6; 9; 13; 17; 21; 24; 29; 6:3; 5; 11; 15; 17; 19; 21; 23; 25; 7:1; 11; 14; 19; 25; 27; 8:3; 6; 13; 14; 15; 9:3; 27; 10:12; 16; 18; 20; 11:3; 10; 19; 31; 36; 12:5; 7; 8; **Hos** 1:4; 6; 9; 11; 2:7(2); 23(2); 3:1; 5:13; 15; 7:1; 11:10; 13:15; **Joel** 2:18; 23; 27; 3:17; **Am** 6:2; 9; 10; 7:5; 8; 10; 12; 14; 15; 8:2; **Ob** 9; 21; **Jon** 1:5; 8; 10; 11; 12; 16; 2:1; 4; 3:4; 6; 10; 4:4; 8; 9; **Mic** 3:4; 5:3; 5; 7; 7:10; **Hab** 1:11; 2:2; **Zeph** 3:9; 11; **Hag** 1:3; 12; 13; 2:12; 14; **Zech** 1:9; 12; 18; 20; 2:1; 9; 11; 3:1; 4; 6; 7; 4:5; 9; 11; 13; 5:1; 3; 5; 8; 9; 6:1; 4; 7; 9; 12; 15; 7:4; 8; 8:18; 9:14; 10:11; 11:9; 12; 14; 12:10; 13:3; 6; 7; 14:3; 5; **Mal** 1:6; 8; 2:4; 3:4; 16; 18; **Mt** 1:19; 24; 2:7; 12; 16; 17; 21; 3:5; 13; 15; 4:1; 5; 10; 11; 19; 24; 5:2; 13; 24; 7:5; 11; 23; 8:3; 13; 19; 21; 25; 26; 33; 9:2; 6; 14; 15; 29; 35; 37; 11:20; 12:11; 12; 13; 14; 22; 26; 29; 38; 44; 45; 47; 13:3; 19; 26; 27; 28; 36; 43; 52; 56; 14:12; 19; 33; 15:1; 6; 12; 15; 21; 25; 28; 30; 33; 16:1; 6; 12; 20; 22; 24; 27; 17:4; 10; 13; 17; 19; 26; 18:1; 2; 21; 27; 32; 19:6; 7; 13; 23; 25; 27; 20:20; 31; 21:1; 9; 12; 14; 17; 25; 30; 37; 22:8; 13; 15; 35; 43; 45; 23:1; 32; 24:1; 9; 10; 11; 14; 16; 21; 23; 30(2); 40; 45; 25:1; 7; 16; 24; 31; 34; 37; 41; 44; 45; 26:3; 14; 25; 27; 31; 36; 38; 40; 45; 50; 54; 56; 65; 67; 74; 27:3; 5; 9; 13; 22; 23; 26; 27; 30; 35; 38; 51; 58; 28:10; 16; **Mk** 1:5; 11; 17; 21; 27; 34; 41; 2:3; 13; 18; 20; 3:4; 6; 14; 20; 27; 31; 4:2; 13; 24; 28; 30; 39; 5:1; 9; 13; 15; 17; 38; 41; 6:1; 6; 21; 30; 39; 48; 51; 7:1; 5; 12; 29; 32; 34; 36; 8:4; 11; 15; 22; 25; 26; 30; 9:5; 12; 17; 20; 26; 30; 33; 36; 10:1; 8; 13; 21; 23; 26; 28; 32; 35; 48; 49; 52; 11:7; 9; 15; 17; 27; 29; 31; 12:1; 13; 18; 28; 35; 37; 38; 42; 13:1; 14; 21; 26; 27; 14:3; 10; 15; 23; 27; 32; 34; 37; 41; 46; 48; 50; 57; 59; 63; 65; 71; 72; 15:2; 4; 8; 12; 14; 16; 19; 21; 23; 36; 38; 46; 16:19; **Lk** 1:11; 30; 34; 38; 42; 65; 2:10; 20; 34; 51; 3:7; 10; 12; 4:1; 5; 9; 14; 20; 24; 30; 31; 36; 5:3; 13; 18; 29; 33; 35; 36; 6:9; 20; 42; 7:6; 14; 16; 18; 31; 36; 44; 48; 50; 8:9; 12; 19; 24; 26; 33; 35; 37; 55; 9:1; 10; 14; 16; 23; 33; 41; 42; 46; 59; 10:2; 17; 23; 30; 37; 11:13; 26; 36; 39; 41; 45; 12:13; 16; 20; 22; 26; 28; 41; 42; 54; 13:7; 15; 18; 23; 26; 14:5; 9; 10; 12; 16; 21; 23; 15:1; 11; 15; 16:3; 7; 24; 27; 17:1; 12; 22; 18:1; 6; 15; 26; 28; 31; 35; 39; 42; 19:1; 8; 15; 16; 20; 23; 35; 37; 45; 20:5; 9; 13; 17(2); 21; 27; 31; 39; 44; 45; 21:5; 10; 20; 21; 27; 29; 38; 22:3; 7; 11; 12; 15; 17; 23; 34; 36; 43; 44; 46; 52; 59; 70(2); 23:1; 3; 9; 11; 13; 22; 30; 34; 39; 42; 45; 53; 56; 24:3; 5; 9; 18; 25; 28; 31; 44; 46; **Jn** 1:21; 22; 25; 38; 2:10; 17; 20; 3:25; 4:9; 11; 28; 30; 35; 42; 48; 52; 5:4; 12; 19; 6:2; 5; 10; 14; 18; 21; 28; 30; 32; 34; 41; 42; 53; 62; 67; 7:6; 10; 11; 28; 33(2); 35; 45; 47; 8:3; 9; 12; 19; 21; 25; 28(2); 31; 41; 48; 52; 57; 59; 9:12; 15; 19; 26; 28; 38; 40; 10:7; 24; 31; 41; 11:7; 12; 14; 16; 20; 21; 31; 32; 36; 38; 41; 45; 47; 53; 56; 12:1; 3; 4; 14; 16; 21; 28; 35; 44; 13:6; 14; 22; 25; 27; 30; 16:17; 18:3; 7; 10; 12; 16; 17; 19; 24; 27; 28; 29; 31; 33; 37; 40; 19:1; 3; 4; 5; 10; 12; 16; 20; 23; 27; 32; 40; 20:2; 6; 8; 10; 13; 19; 20; 27; 21:5; 9; 13; 20; 23; **Acts** 1:12; 2:3; 7; 38; 41; 43; 3:6; 10; 4:8; 5:5; 9; 10; 17; 26; 34; 6:2; 7; 9; 11; 7:1; 4; 8; 14; 29; 33; 42; 57; 60; 8:5; 13; 17; 24; 29; 35; 37; 9:1; 4; 5; 6; 8; 13; 19; 21; 25; 31; 34; 39; 41; 10:10; 21; 23; 28; 29; 34; 46; 48; 11:12; 16; 18; 22; 25; 28; 29; 12:2; 8; 18; 23; 13:3; 9; 12; 16; 46; 14:13; 19; 15:12; 22; 36; 39; 16:1; 22; 29; 32; 39; 17:2; 10; 14; 18; 22; 18:8; 17; 18; 19:3; 4; 13; 16; 31; 20:13; 37; 21:13; 22; 26; 33; 37; 22:2; 12; 14; 21; 22; 23; 27; 29; 23:1; 3; 5; 9; 17; 19; 31; 24:10; 25:2; 12; 22; 26:1; 20; 28; 32; 27:21; 29; 32; 36; 28:1; 21; 30; **Rom** 3:1; 6; 9; 27; 31; 4:1; 9; 10; 5:9; 6:1; 15; 21; 7:3; 7; 13; 16; 21; 25; 8:8; 17; 31; 9:14; 16; 19; 30; 10:14; 17; 11:1; 5; 6; 7; 11; 19; 12:6; 14:12; 15:1; **1 Cor** 3:5; 7; 4:5; 5:10; 6:4; 15; 7:38; 9:18; 10:19; 12:28; 13:10; 12(2); 14:15; 26; 15:5; 7; 8; 13; 14; 16; 18; 24; 28; 29; 54; **2 Cor** 2:2; 4:12; 5:14; 20; 6:1; 8:5; 12:10; **Gal** 1:18; 2:1; 21; 3:9; 19; 21; 29; 4:7; 8; 15; 29; 31; 5:11; 16; 6:4; **Eph** 5:15; **Phil** 1:18; **Col** 3:1; 4; **1 Th** 4:1; 17; 5:3; **2 Th** 2:8; **1 Tim** 2:13; 3:2; 10; **Phm** 1:17; **Heb** 2:14; 4:8; 14; 7:2; 27; 8:7; 9:1; 21; 26; 10:2; 7; 9; 17; 12:8; 26; **Jas** 1:15; 19; 2:24; 3:17; 4:14; **2 Pe** 2:9; 3:6; **Rev** 1:12; 3:16; 5:2; 7; 11; 14; 6:11; 14; 7:2; 13; 8:3; 5; 8; 10; 12; 9:1; 3; 13; 10:8; 10; 11:1; 9; 15; 19; 12:2; 6; 10; 13:1; 6; 11; 14:1; 6; 9; 13; 14; 17; 15:1; 7; 16:1; 3; 4; 8; 10; 12; 17; 20; 17:1; 15; 18:21; 19:5; 9; 17; 20; 20:1; 4; 11; 14; 21:2; 5; 9; 17; 22:6; 9

THERE (2223/2002)

Gen 1:3(2); 6; 14; 30; 2:5; 8; 10; 11; 12; 20; 6:4; 9:11; 11:2; 7; 8; 9(2); 31; 12:7; 8(2); 10(2); 13:4(2); 7; 8; 18; 14:10; 15:17; 18:16; 22; 24; 28(2); 29(2); 30(2); 31; 32; 19:20; 22(2); 31; 20:1; 21:31; 33; 22:2; 9; 13; 23:13; 24:6; 7; 8; 23; 30; 45; 63; 25:10; 24; 26:1; 8(2); 17(2); 19; 22; 23; 25(3); 28; 27:9; 45; 28:2; 6; 11; 12; 29:2; 3; 30:32; 31:14; 40; 46; 32:4; 13; 29; 33:1; 15; 20; 35:1(2); 3; 7(2); 16; 37:7; 15; 24; 25; 26; 38:2; 21; 22; 39:1; 9; 20; 22; 40:8; 16; 41:2; 8; 12(2); 15; 24; 39; 54; 42:1; 2(2); 16; 26; 27; 28; 43:21; 25; 30; 44:14; 45:6(2); 11(2); 46:3; 47:13; 18; 27; 48:7(2); 49:24; 31(3); 32; 50:5; 9; 10; **Ex** 1:8; 5:13; 16; 20; 7:19; 21; 8:10; 15; 18; 22; 9:14; 22; 24(2); 26; 28; 29; 10:14(2); 15; 19; 21; 22; 26; 11:6; 12:16(2); 30(3); 13:6; 14:11; 15:25(2); 27(2); 16:14; 24; 26; 17:1; 3; 6; 19:2; 16; 21:30; 22:2; 3; 24:10; 12; 25:22; 35; 26:20; 25; 33; 27:9; 11; 16; 28:32; 29:43; 30:12; 34; 32:17; 34:2; 5; 28; 36:30; 37:19; 21; 38:10; 12; 19; 39:14; 23; 40:30; **Lev** 7:7; 8:31; 10:16; 11:36; 13:10; 19; 21; 26; 30; 31; 32; 37; 42; 14:35; 15:17; 18; 16:17; 23; 19:20; 20:14; 22:21; 23:35; 39; 25:4; 19; 51; 52; **Num** 1:4; 53; 3:22; 28; 4:14; 5:13; 8:19; 9:6; 17; 11:6; 16; 17; 34; 12:6; 10; 13:20(2); 22; 23; 24; 28; 33; 14:35; 43; 17:3; 18:5; 19:2; 18; 20:1(2); 2; 5; 26; 28; 21:5; 12; 13; 16; 32; 35; 22:26; 29; 41; 23:6; 9; 13; 15; 17; 23; 27; 26:62; 64; 65; 31:5; 16; 32:26; 33:9; 14; 38; 54; 35:11; 15; 25; **Deut** 1:28; 37; 38; 39; 46; 2:10; 20; 36; 3:4; 24; 4:7; 8; 28; 29; 35; 39; 42; 5:15; 26; 6:23; 7:14; 8:15; 10:5; 7; 11:17; 12:5; 6; 7; 11(2); 14(2); 13:1; 14:26; 15:4; 7; 9; 21; 16:6; 8; 17:2; 9; 12; 18:7; 10; 19:3; 4; 12; 20:5; 6; 7; 8; 21:4; 22:26; 27; 23:10; 17; 24:18; 25:1; 26:5(2); 27:5; 7; 28:32; 36; 64; 65; 68; 29:18(2); 23; 30:4(2); 31:26; 32:12; 25; 28; 36; 39(2); 52; 33:19; 21; 26; 34:4; 5; 10; **Josh** 2:1; 11; 16; 22; 3:1; 4; 4:8; 9; 5:1; 6:22; 7:3; 4; 13; 21; 22; 26; 8:14; 17; 32; 35; 10:11; 14; 19; 11:11; 19; 13:1; 14:12; 15:4; 14; 15; 17:1; 2; 15; 18:1; 2; 10; 13; 19:13; 34; 20:3; 9; 22:10; 17; 24:26; **Judg** 1:7; 11; 20; 2:5; 3:25; 4:9; 17; 20; 22; 5:8; 11; 15;

27; 6:24; 28; 37; 39; 40; 7:4; 13; 8:8; 27; 9:21; 43; 51(2); 10:1; 11:34; 12:6; 13:2; 14:3; 10; 16:1; 27; 17:1; 6; 7(2); 18:1; 2; 7(2); 10; 11; 12; 13; 14; 15; 17; 28(2); 19:1(2); 2; 4; 7; 15; 18(2); 19; 27; 28; 20:26; 27; 40; 21:2; 3; 4; 5; 8; 9; 10; 17; 19; 24(2); 25; **Ruth** 1:1; 2; 4; 11; 17; 2:1; 3:8; 12; 4:1; 4; 17; **1 Sam** 1:1; 3; 22; 28; 2:2(2); 14; 31; 32; 3:1; 4:4(2); 10(2); 13; 17; 5:3; 4; 11(2); 6:14(2); 7:2; 6; 14; 17(3); 9:1; 2; 4; 6(2); 7; 12(2); 14; 17; 22; 10:3(2); 5; 10(2); 12; 22; 23; 24; 11:3; 5; 14; 15(3); 13:19; 22; 14:4; 15; 16(2); 17; 20; 25; 26; 30; 34; 52; 16:11(2); 17:23; 29; 46; 50; 18:10; 19:8; 16; 23; 20:3; 6(2); 8; 12; 21(2); 29; 21:4(2); 6(2); 7; 8; 9(3); 22:1(2); 2; 3; 8(2); 22; 23:22; 29; 24:3; 11; 25:2; 7; 10; 20; 36; 26:7; 27:1; 5; 28:7; 20; 30:2; 3; 16; 31:12; **2 Sam** 1:6; 21(2); 2:2; 4; 17; 18; 23; 30; 3:1; 6; 27; 29; 4:3; 6; 5:20; 21; 6:2; 7(2); 7:22(2); 9:1; 2; 3(2); 10:18; 11:16; 12:1; 13:34; 38; 14:2; 6; 25(2); 30; 32(2); 15:3; 21; 24; 29; 32; 35; 36; 16:1; 5(2); 14; 17:9; 12; 13(2); 18:7(2); 8; 11; 13; 24; 25; 26; 31; 19:8; 17; 20:1(2); 21:1; 13; 18; 19; 20(2); 22:42; 23:9; 11; 24:3; 9; 13; 25; **1 Ki** 1:14; 34; 42; 45; 2:29; 33; 36(2); 3:2; 4; 12; 13; 21; 4:27; 5:4; 6; 9; 12; 6:18; 19; 7:4; 20; 34; 36; 47; 8:8; 9; 16; 21; 23; 29; 35; 37(2); 46; 56; 60; 64; 9:3(2); 28; 10:3; 5; 10; 12; 19; 20; 11:16; 24; 36; 12:20; 25(2); 13:17; 25; 14:2; 13; 21; 24; 30; 15:6; 7; 16; 19(2); 32; 17:1; 4; 7; 9(2); 10; 17; 18:2; 10; 26; 29; 40; 41; 43; 44; 45; 19:3; 6; 9; 19; 20:15; 39; 40; 21:18; 25; 22:7; 8; 47; **2 Ki** 1:3; 6; 9; 16; 2:16; 21(2); 23; 25(2); 3:9; 11; 27; 4:6; 8(2); 10(2); 11(2); 31; 32; 38; 40; 41; 5:8; 15; 18; 6:2(2); 6; 9; 10; 14; 15; 20; 25; 30; 33; 7:3; 4; 5; 8; 10; 8:5; 9:2; 5; 10; 16; 27; 10:15; 21; 11:14; 16; 12:9; 10; 13; 14:19; 26; 15:16(2); 20; 16:6; 17:11; 18; 25; 27(3); 19:3; 32; 35; 20:13; 15; 19; 22:7; 23:12; 16; 20; 25; 27; 34; 24:13; 25:3; 30; **1 Chr** 3:4; 6; 4:23; 40; 41(3); 43; 7:11; 11:13(2); 23; 12:17; 33; 39; 40; 13:6; 10; 14:11; 12; 16:37; 17:20(2); 20:2; 5; 6(2); 21:26; 28; 22:15; 16; 24:4; 5; 26:18; 31; **2 Chr** 1:3; 5; 6; 2:17; 5:9; 10; 6:5; 6; 11; 14; 26; 28(2); 36; 7:7; 13; 16(2); 8:2; 18; 9:2; 4; 9; 11; 18; 19; 12:13; 15; 13:2; 14:14; 15:5; 19; 16:3(2); 18:6; 7; 19:7; 20:6; 24; 25; 26; 21:17; 23:13; 15; 24:11; 25:27; 26:20; 28:9; 13; 18; 29:19; 30:17; 26(2); 31:19; 32:7; 14; 21; 35:18; 36:16; **Ezra** 2:65; 4:20; 5:17; 6:6; 12; 7:23; 8:15(2); 21; 32; 9:14; 10:2; 6; 13(2); **Neh** 1:3; 9; 2:11; 12; 14; 4:10; 20; 5:1; 2; 3; 4; 16; 6:1; 7; 11; 7:67; 8:17; 18; 12:46; 13:16; 26; **Esth** 1:6; 18; 2:5; 3:8; 4:3; 6:5; **Job** 1:1; 6; 8; 13; 21; 2:1; 3; 3:17(2); 18; 19; 4:16; 5:1; 4; 6:6; 20; 29; 30; 7:1; 9:33; 10:7; 11:18; 12:14; 14:7; 19:7; 29; 23:7; 8; 24:13; 25:3; 28:1; 31:31; 32:5; 8; 33:9; 23; 34:22; 35:12; 36:2; 16; 18; 38:26(2); 39:29; 30; 40:20; 41:33; **Ps** 3:2; 4:6; 5:9; 6:5; 7:2; 3; 14:1(2); 2; 3; 5; 18:41; 19:3; 6; 11; 22:11; 30:9; 32:2; 34:9; 36:1; 12; 38:3; 7; 46:4; 48:6; 50:22; 53:1(2); 2; 3; 5; 55:18; 56:2; 58:11; 63:1; 66:6; 68:18; 27; 69:2; 20; 35; 71:11; 72:16; 73:4; 11; 25; 74:9(2); 75:8; 76:3; 79:3; 10; 81:9; 86:8(2); 87:4; 6; 92:15; 104:26(3); 105:31; 37; 106:11; 107:12; 36; 40; 109:12(2); 112:4; 122:5; 130:4; 7; 132:17; 133:3; 135:17; 137:1; 3; 139:4; 8(2); 10; 16; 24; 142:4; 144:14(2); 146:3; **Prov** 7:10; 8:23; 24(2); 27; 9:18; 11:10; 14(2); 24(2); 12:18; 28; 13:7; 23; 14:9; 12; 23; 26; 15:6; 16:25; 17:16; 18:24; 19:18; 21; 20:15; 21:20; 30; 22:13; 14; 23:18; 24:6; 14; 20; 31; 26:12; 13; 20(2); 25; 28:12; 29:9; 18; 20; 30:11; 12; 13; 14; 15; 18; 24; 29; **Eccl** 1:7; 9; 10; 11(2); 2:11; 16; 21; 3:1; 16(2); 17(2); 4:1; 8(2); 16; 5:7; 13; 14; 6:1; 11; 7:15(2); 20; 8:4; 6; 8; 9; 14(3); 9:4; 10; 14; 15; 10:5; 11:3; 12:12; **Song** 4:7; 6:8; 7:12; 8:5(2); **Isa** 1:6; 2:7(2); 3:24; 4:5; 6; 5:6; 8; 7:23; 24; 25; 8:20; 9:7; 10:14; 11:1; 10; 16; 13:20(2); 21(3); 15:6; 16:10(2); 17:9; 19:15; 19; 23; 22:14; 18(2); 23:1; 10; 12; 24:11; 27:10(2); 28:10; 13; 29:2; 30:14; 25; 28; 33:21; 34:12; 14; 15(2); 35:7; 8; 9(3); 37:3; 33; 36; 39:2; 4; 8; 41:17; 26(3); 27; 28(2); 43:10(2); 11; 12; 13; 44:6; 8(2); 19; 20; 45:5(2); 6(2); 14(2); 18; 21(2); 22; 46:9(2); 47:8; 10; 48:16; 22; 49:21; 50:2(3); 51:18(2); 52:4; 11; 53:2; 55:10; 57:7; 10; 21; 59:8; 9; 11; 15; 16(2); 63:5(2); 64:7; 65:9; 20; **Jer** 2:10; 25; 3:3; 6; 4:25; 5:1; 6; 6:14; 7:2; 32; 8:11; 14; 15; 22(4); 10:6; 7; 13; 14; 20; 11:23; 12:4; 13:4; 6(2); 7; 14:4; 5; 6; 19(3); 22; 16:13; 17:16; 18:2; 3; 19:2; 11; 20:6(2); 22:1; 26; 27; 24:1; 26:20; 27:22; 29:6; 26; 30:13; 31:6; 8; 17; 24; 32:5; 17; 24; 27; 33:10; 12; 20; 36:12; 32; 37:10; 12; 13; 16; 17(2); 20; 38:6; 9; 11; 26; 28; 40:4; 41:1; 3; 42:14; 15; 16(3); 17; 43:2; 12; 44:12; 14; 27; 28; 46:17; 47:7; 49:16; 18; 23; 33; 36; 38; 50:9; 20; 39; 40; 51:16; 17; 52:6; 23; 34; **Lam** 1:12; 2:22; 3:29; 5:8; **Ezek** 1:3; 20; 2:9; 10; 3:15; 22(2); 23; 5:4; 7:11; 25; 8:1; 2; 4; 5; 7; 8; 9; 10; 11; 14; 16; 10:1(2); 9; 11:1; 18(2); 12:13; 24; 13:10; 11; 13; 16; 20; 14:22; 17:7; 20; 20:28(2); 35; 40(3); 43; 22:20; 23:2; 3(2); 40; 28:3; 24; 26; 29:14; 30:13; 18; 32:22; 24; 26; 29; 30; 34:5; 8; 14; 26; 35:10; 37:2; 7; 8; 25; 38:19; 39:11(2); 40:1; 3(2); 5; 12; 16(2); 17; 24; 25; 27; 29; 30; 33; 38; 42; 49; 41:26; 42:10; 11; 12; 13; 14; 45:2; 46:19; 21; 23; 47:1; 2; 7; 9(2); 23; 48:1; 35; **Dan** 1:4; 2:9; 10; 11; 28; 3:12; 29; 4:13; 27; 5:11; 6:4; 7:6; 8(2); 8:3; 4; 7(2); 15; 9:25; 10:13; 11:20; 31; 12:1(2); 5; 11; **Hos** 1:10; 2:15(2); 4:1; 3; 6:7; 10; 7:9; 9:15; 10:9; 12:4; 13:4; 8; **Joel** 2:2; 27; 32; 3:2; 11; 12; **Am** 3:5; 6; 4:7; 5:2; 16; 17; 6:2; 10; 7:12(2); 9:2(2); 3(2); 4; 5; **Ob** 4; 17(2); **Jon** 1:4; 4:5; **Mic** 3:7; 4:9; 10(2); 6:10; 7:1; 2; **Nah** 2:9; 3:3; 15; **Hab** 1:3; 2:19; 3:4; 17; **Zeph** 1:10; 14; 2:5; 7; 15; 3:6; **Hag** 2:14; 16(2); **Zech** 1:18; 2:3; 4:2; 5:1; 9; 11; 8:10(2); 10:2; 11:3(2); 12:11; 14:6; 11; 17; 21; **Mal** 1:10; 3:10(2); **Mt** 2:13; 15; 22; 4:21; 5:23; 24; 26; 6:21; 7:9; 13; 14; 8:12; 26; 28; 30; 9:9; 27; 10:11; 26; 11:1; 11; 12:6; 9; 10; 11; 15; 45; 13:42; 50; 53; 58; 14:13; 23; 15:21; 29(2); 16:28; 17:20; 18:20; 19:2; 12(3); 15; 21:17; 33; 22:11; 13; 23; 25; 24:7; 21; 23; 28; 51; 25:9; 25; 30; 26:5; 36; 71; 27:36; 45; 47; 55; 57; 61; 28:2; 7; 10; **Mk** 1:7; 13; 19; 23; 35; 38; 2:2; 6; 15; 3:1; 4:22; 39; 5:2; 11; 13; 6:1; 5; 10; 11; 31; 33; 53; 7:4; 15; 24; 9:1; 30; 10:1; 29; 11:5; 12:18; 20; 31; 32(2); 13:8(2); 19; 21; 14:2; 4; 15; 15:7; 33; 40; 16:7; **Lk** 1:5; 33; 45; 61; 2:6; 7; 8; 11; 13; 25; 36; 4:25; 33; 5:17; 29; 6:6; 7:28; 41; 8:24; 27; 32; 41; 9:4(2); 14; 27; 10:6; 9; 11:26; 12:2; 18; 34; 55(2); 59; 13:1; 11; 14; 23; 28; 30(2); 14:2; 22; 15:7; 10; 13; 14; 16:1; 19; 20; 26(2); 17:12; 17; 18; 21; 23; 34; 37; 18:2; 3; 29; 19:2; 20:27; 29; 21:7; 11(2); 23; 25; 22:12; 24; 23:32; 33; 44; 50; 24:18; **Jn** 1:6; 26; 2:1(2); 6(2); 12; 3:1; 22; 23(2); 25; 4:6; 35; 40; 43; 46; 5:1; 2; 5; 6; 32; 45; 6:3; 9; 10; 22(2); 24; 64; 7:12; 43; 8:44; 50; 9:16; 10:16; 19; 40; 42; 11:8; 9; 15; 31; 39; 54(2); 12:2; 9; 20; 26; 13:23; 14:3; 18:1; 2; 3; 18; 19:25; 29; 41; 42; 20:5; 6; 14; 21:9; 11; 25; **Acts** 2:2; 3; 5; 4:12(2); 34; 6:1; 9; 7:4; 12; 8:8; 9; 9:10; 18; 33; 36; 38; 10:1; 18; 11:28; 12:18; 19; 13:1; 4; 25; 14:3; 7; 19; 26; 28; 15:7; 33; 34; 16:1; 12; 13; 26; 17:1; 7; 13; 14; 17; 21; 18:7; 11; 14; 19; 23; 19:2; 14; 21; 23; 35; 38; 40; 20:8; 13; 15; 22; 21:1; 3; 4; 20; 40; 22:5; 10; 12; 23:8; 9; 10; 13; 24:15; 25:4; 5; 9; 11; 14(2); 20; 27:4; 6; 12(2); 22; 23; 28:7; 13; 15; 18; **Rom** 2:11; 3:10; 11(2); 12; 18; 22; 30; 4:15(2); 5:13; 8:1; 9:14; 26; 10:12; 11:5; 13:1; 9; 14:14; 15:12; 24; **1 Cor** 1:10; 11; 3:3; 5:1; 6:5; 7:34; 8:4; 5(2); 6; 7; 11:18; 19; 12:4; 5; 6; 20; 25; 13:8(3); 14:10; 23; 27; 28; 15:12; 13; 39; 40; 41; 44(2); 16:2; 9; **2 Cor** 1:17; 3:17; 8:11(2); 12; 14; 12:20; **Gal** 1:7; 3:21; 28(3); 5:23; **Eph** 4:4; 6:9; **Phil** 2:1; 4:8(2); **Col** 3:11; 25; **2 Th** 3:11; **1 Tim** 1:10; 2:5; **2 Tim** 2:20; 4:8; **Titus** 1:10; 3:12; **Heb** 3:12; 4:9; 13; 7:8; 11; 12; 15; 18; 19; 23; 8:4; 9:16(2); 22; 10:3; 18(2); 26; 12:7; 16; **Jas** 1:17; 2:2(2); 3; 19; 3:16; 4:12; 13; **1 Pe** 3:21; **2 Pe** 2:1(2); **1 Jn** 2:10; 3:5; 4:18; 5:7; 8; 16; 17; **Jude** 18; **Rev** 2:14; 4:3(2); 6; 6:4; 12; 8:1; 5; 9:10; 10:6; 11:1; 13; 15; 19; 12:6; 16:18(2); 17:10; 20:11; 21:1; 4(2); 25(2); 27; 22:3; 5(2)

THEREFORE (1356/1340)

Gen 2:24; 3:23; 4:15; 10:9; 11:9; 12:12; 19; 16:14; 18:12; 19:22; 20:6; 7; 21:10; 23; 31; 25:30; 26:33; 27:3; 8; 28; 43; 29:15; 32; 33; 34; 35; 30:6; 15; 31:44; 48; 32:32; 33:17; 34:21; 37:20; 38:10; 29; 41:33; 42:21; 22; 44:30; 33; 45:5; 47:4; 22; 50:5; 11; 21; **Ex** 1:11; 20; 3:9; 10; 4:12; 5:8; 17; 18; 6:6; 9:19; 10:17; 12:17; 13:10; 15; 15:23; 16:29; 17:2; 19:5; 20:11; 31:14; 16; 32:10; 34; 33:5; 13; **Lev** 8:35; 9:8; 11:44; 45; 13:25; 52; 16:4; 17:12; 14; 18:5; 25; 26; 30; 19:8; 37; 20:7; 22; 23; 25; 21:6; 8; 22:9; 31; 25:17; **Num** 3:12; 11:18; 14:16; 16:11; 38; 18:7; 24; 30; 20:12; 21:7; 14; 27; 22:6; 17; 19; 34; 24:11; 25:12; 31:17; 50; 32:5; 35:34; **Deut** 2:4; 4:6; 37; 39; 40; 5:15; 25; 32; 6:3; 7:9; 11; 8:6; 9:3; 6; 26; 10:9; 16; 19; 11:1; 8; 18; 15:11; 15; 16:2; 18:2; 19:7; 23:14; 24:18; 22; 25:19; 26:16; 27:4; 10; 28:48; 29:9; 30:19; 31:19; 22; **Josh** 1:2; 2:12; 3:12; 4:17; 5:9; 7:5; 12; 14; 26; 8:6; 9; 9:6; 11(2); 19; 23; 24; 10:3; 5; 9; 13:7; 14:12; 14; 17:1; 4; 18:6; 19:9; 22:4; 26; 28; 23:6; 11; 15; 24:10; 14; 23; 27; **Judg** 2:3; 23; 3:8; 25; 6:32; 7:3; 9:16; 32; 10:13; 11:13; 27; 13:4; 14:2; 15:2; 19; 16:12; 17:3; 18:12; 14; 20:13; 42; 21:20; **Ruth** 1:7; 3:3; 4:8; **1 Sam** 1:7; 13; 28; 2:17; 30; 3:9; 14; 5:5; 8; 10; 6:5; 7; 8:9; 9:13; 10:12; 19; 22; 11:10; 12:7; 13; 16; 13:12; 14:27; 41; 15:1; 25; 16:19; 17:51; 18:13; 15; 21; 22; 27; 19:2; 24; 20:8; 29; 31; 21:3; 22:1; 23:2; 20; 23; 25; 28; 24:15; 19; 21; 25:8; 17; 26; 36; 26:4; 8; 19; 27:6; 12; 28:2; 15; 18; 22; 29:7; 10; 31:4; **2 Sam** 1:11; 2:7; 16; 23; 4:11; 5:3; 8; 20; 23; 6:21; 23; 7:8; 22; 27; 29; 9:10; 10:4; 12:10; 16; 19; 28; 13:13; 33; 14:12; 15; 21; 29; 32; 15:29; 35; 17:11; 16; 19:7; 10; 20; 23; 27; 28; 43; 21:3; 22:25; 50; 23:17; 19; 24:4; **1 Ki** 1:2; 2:2; 6; 9; 19; 24; 33; 44; 3:9; 5:6; 8:2; 25; 61; 9:9; 10:9; 11:11; 40; 12:4; 18; 24; 28; 13:26; 14:10; 12; 18:19; 23; 20:9; 23; 28; 42; 22:19; 23; 32; **2 Ki** 1:4; 6; 16; 2:17; 3:23; 4:31; 33; 5:7; 15; 27; 6:7; 11; 14; 7:4; 7; 9; 12; 14; 9:26; 36; 10:19; 12:7; 14:11; 15:16; 17:4; 18; 25; 26; 18:23; 19:4; 18; 19; 26; 28; 32; 21:12; 22:17; 20; **1 Chr** 10:4; 14; 11:3; 7; 19; 21; 13:11; 14:11; 14; 17:7; 25; 19:4; 21:4; 7; 18; 22:19; 23:11; 24:2; 28:8; 29:10; 13; **2 Chr** 2:7; 15; 5:3; 6:16; 41; 7:22; 9:8; 10:4; 18; 11:4; 12:5; 7; 14:7; 16:7; 9; 17:5; 18:12; 18; 22; 31; 19:2; 7; 20:26; 22:4; 24:18; 25:10; 15; 28:5; 11; 29:8; 34; 30:17; 32:15; 25; 33:11; 34:25; 35:14; 24; 36:17; **Ezra** 2:62; 4:14; 5:17; 6:6; 7:17; 9:12; 10:3; 11; **Neh** 2:2; 20; 4:13; 5:2; 6:6; 7; 9; 7:64; 9:27; 28; 30; 32; 13:8; 28; **Esth** 1:12; 3:8; 9:19; 26; **Job** 5:17; 6:3; 28; 7:11; 9:22; 11:6; 17:4; 20:2; 21; 22:10; 23:15; 32:6; 10; 34:10; 25; 33; 35:16; 37:24; 42:3; 6; 8; **Ps** 1:5; 2:10; 7:7; 16:9; 18:24; 49; 21:12; 25:8; 27:6; 28:7; 31:3; 36:7; 40:12; 42:6; 45:2; 7; 17; 46:2; 55:19; 59:5; 63:7; 73:6; 10; 78:21; 33; 91:14; 106:23; 26; 40; 107:12; 110:7; 116:2; 10; 118:7; 119:104; 119; 127; 128; 129; 140; 139:19; 143:4; **Prov** 1:31; 4:7; 5:7; 6:15; 34; 7:24; 8:32; 17:11; 14; 20:19; **Eccl** 2:1; 17; 20; 4:2; 5:2; 8:11; 11:10; **Song** 1:3; **Isa** 1:24; 2:9; 3:17; 5:13; 14; 24; 25; 7:14; 8:7; 9:11; 14; 17; 10:12; 16; 24; 12:3; 13:7; 13; 15:4; 7; 16:7; 9; 11; 17:10; 21:3; 22:4; 24:6(2); 15; 25:3; 26:14; 27:9; 11; 28:14; 16; 22; 28; 29:13; 14; 22; 30:3; 7; 12; 13; 16(2); 18(2); 36:8; 37:4; 19; 20; 27; 29; 33; 38:20; 42:25; 43:4; 12; 28; 47:8; 11; 50:7(2); 51:21; 52:5; 6(2); 53:12; 57:10; 59:9; 16; 60:11; 61:7; 63:5; 65:7; 12; 13; **Jer** 1:17; 2:9; 19; 33; 3:3; 5:4; 6; 14; 27; 6:11; 15; 18; 21; 7:14; 16; 20; 27; 32; 8:10; 12; 9:7; 15; 10:21; 11:8; 11; 21; 22; 12:8; 13:12; 24; 26; 14:10; 15; 17; 22; 15:6; 19; 16:13; 14; 21; 18:11; 13; 21; 19:6; 20:11; 22:18; 23:2; 7; 12; 15; 30; 32; 38; 39; 25:8; 27; 30; 26:13; 27:9; 14; 28:16; 29:16; 20; 27; 32; 30:10; 16; 31:3; 12; 20; 32:23; 28; 36; 34:12; 17; 35:17; 19; 36:6; 14; 30; 37:15; 20; 38:4; 40:3; 42:22; 44:7; 11; 22; 23; 26; 48:11; 12; 31; 36(2); 49:2; 20; 26; 50:18; 30; 39; 45; 51:7; 36; 47; 52; **Lam** 1:8; 9; 2:8; 3:21; 24; **Ezek** 3:17; 4:7; 5:7; 8; 10; 11(2); 7:20; 24; 8:18; 11:4; 7; 16; 17; 12:3; 23; 28; 13:8(2); 13; 20; 23; 14:4; 6; 15:6; 16:27; 34; 37; 50; 17:19; 18:30; 32; 20:10; 25; 27; 30; 21:4; 6; 12; 14; 24; 22:4; 13; 19(2); 31; 23:9; 22; 31; 35(2); 24:6; 9; 25:4; 7; 9; 13; 16; 26:3; 28:6; 7; 16; 29:8; 10; 19; 30:22; 31:5; 10; 11; 32:3; 33:7; 10; 12; 25; 34:7; 9; 20; 22; 35:6(2); 11; 36:3; 4; 5; 6; 7; 14; 18; 22; 37:12; 38:14; 39:11; 23; 25; 41:7; 42:6; 43:8; 44:2; 12; **Dan** 1:8; 19; 2:6; 9; 10; 24; 3:8; 22; 29; 4:6; 27; 6:9; 8:8; 26; 9:11; 14; 17; 23; 25; 10:8; 11:30; 44; **Hos** 2:6; 9; 14; 4:3; 5; 13; 14; 5:5; 12; 6:5; 10:14; 12:14; 13:3; 6; **Joel** 2:12; **Am** 2:14; 3:2; 11; 4:12; 5:11; 13; 16; 27; 6:7; 8; 7:16; 17; **Jon** 1:14; 4:2; 3; **Mic** 1:6; 8; 14; 2:3; 5; 3:6; 12; 5:3; 6:13; 16; 7:7; **Hab** 1:4(2); 15; 16; 17; **Zeph** 1:13; 2:9; 3:8; **Hag** 1:5; 10; **Zech** 1:3; 16; 7:13; 8:19; 10:2; **Mal** 2:9; 15; 16; 3:6; **Mt** 3:8; 10; 5:19; 23; 48; 6:2; 8; 9; 22; 23; 25; 31; 34; 7:12; 20; 24; 9:38; 10:16; 26; 31; 32; 12:12; 27; 31; 13:13; 18; 40; 52; 14:2; 7; 18:4; 23; 26; 19:6; 27; 21:40; 43; 22:9; 17; 21; 28; 23:3; 14; 20; 31; 34; 24:15; 26; 42; 44; 25:13; 28; 27:8; 17; 64; 28:19; **Mk** 2:28; 6:14; 19; 10:9; 11:24; 12:6; 9; 23; 24; 27; 37; 13:35; **Lk** 1:35; 3:8; 9; 4:7; 6:36; 7:7; 42; 47; 8:18; 10:2; 40; 11:19; 34; 35; 49; 12:3; 7; 22; 40; 13:14; 14:20; 15:28; 16:11; 27; 19:12; 20:15; 25; 33; 44; 21:8; 14; 36; 23:16; 20; 22; **Jn** 1:31; 2:22; 3:29; 4:1; 6; 33; 5:10; 18; 6:13; 15; 24; 30; 43; 45; 52; 60; 65; 7:3; 22; 30; 40; 8:13; 24; 36; 47; 9:8; 10; 16; 23; 41; 10:17; 19; 39; 11:3; 33; 54; 12:17; 19; 29; 39; 50; 13:11; 24; 15:19; 16:15; 18; 22; 18:4; 8; 25; 31; 37; 39; 19:6; 8; 11; 13; 21; 24(2); 26; 31; 20:3; 25; 21:7; **Acts** 1:6; 21; 2:26; 30; 33; 36; 3:19; 6:3; 8:4; 22; 10:20; 29; 32; 33; 11:17; 12:5; 13:35; 38; 40; 14:3; 15:2; 10; 19; 27; 16:11; 36; 17:12; 17; 20; 23; 29; 19:32; 36; 38; 20:26; 28; 31; 21:23; 23:15; 24:26; 25:5; 17; 26; 26:3; 19; 22; 27:25; 34; 28:20; 28; **Rom** 1:24; 2:1; 21; 26; 3:20; 28; 4:16; 22; 5:1; 12; 18; 6:4; 12; 7:4; 12; 8:1; 12; 9:18; 11:22; 12:1; 20; 13:2; 5; 7; 10; 12; 14:8; 13; 16; 19; 15:7; 17; 28; 16:19; **1 Cor** 3:21; 4:5; 16; 5:7; 8; 13; 6:7; 20; 7:26; 8:4; 13; 9:26; 10:12; 14; 31; 11:20; 27; 33; 12:3; 15; 16; 14:11; 13; 22; 23; 39; 15:11; 58; 16:11; 18; **2 Cor** 1:17; 2:8; 3:12; 4:1; 13(2); 16; 5:9; 11; 16; 17; 6:17; 7:1; 12; 13; 16; 8:24; 9:5; 11:15; 12:9; 10; 13:10; **Gal** 2:17; 3:5; 7; 24; 4:7; 16; 5:1; 6:10; **Eph** 1:15; 2:11; 19; 3:13; 4:1; 8; 17; 25; 5:1; 7; 14; 17; 24; 6:13; 14; **Phil** 2:1; 9; 12; 23; 28; 29; 3:15; 4:1; **Col** 2:6; 20; 3:5; 12; **1 Th** 2:18; 3:1; 7; 4:8; 18; 5:6; 11; **2 Th** 1:11; 2:15; **1 Tim** 2:1; 8; 5:14; **2 Tim** 1:6; 8; 2:1; 3; 10; 21; 4:1; **Titus** 1:13; **Phm** 1:8; 12; **Heb** 1:9; 2:1; 17; 3:1; 7; 10; 4:1; 6; 9; 11; 16; 6:1; 7:11; 25; 8:3; 9:18; 23; 10:5; 19; 35; 11:12; 16; 12:1; 12; 28; 13:12; 13; 15; **Jas** 1:21; 4:4; 6; 7; 17; 5:7; **1 Pe** 1:13; 2:1; 6; 7; 13; 4:1; 7; 19; 5:6; **2 Pe** 1:10; 3:11; 14; 17; **1 Jn** 2:24; 3:1; 4:5; **3 Jn** 8; 10; **Rev** 2:5; 3:3(2); 19; 7:15; 12:12; 18:8

THESE (1285/1210)

Gen 9:19(2); 10:5; 20; 29; 31; 32(2); 14:3; 15:1; 10; 19:8; 20:8; 21:29; 30; 22:1; 20; 23; 23:1; 24:28; 25:4; 13; 16(2); 17; 26:3; 4; 27:36; 46; 29:13; 30:32; 31:16; 38; 43(3); 32:17; 33:5; 8; 34:21; 35:26; 36:5; 10; 12; 13(2); 14; 15; 16; 17(3); 18(3); 19(2); 20; 21; 23; 24; 25; 26; 27; 28; 29; 30; 31; 40; 43; 38:25(2); 39:7; 17; 40:1; 42:36; 43:7; 16(2); 44:6; 7; 45:6; 23; 46:8; 15; 18(2); 22; 25(2); 48:1; 8; 49:28; **Ex** 1:1; 4:9; 6:14(2); 15; 16; 19; 24; 25; 26; 27(2); 10:1; 11:8; 10; 18:18; 19:6; 7; 20:1; 21:1; 11; 24:8; 25:39; 28:4; 29:24; 30:25; 34; 35; 32:31; 34:1; 27(2); 35:1; **Lev** 2:8; 5:4; 5; 13; 17; 6:3; 7; 8:27; 11:2; 4; 9; 13; 21; 22; 24; 29; 31; 42; 16:4; 18:24(2); 26; 27; 29; 30; 20:23; 21:14; 22:25; 23:2; 4; 37; 25:54; 26:14; 23; 46; 27:34; **Num** 1:5; 16; 17; 44; 2:9; 32; 3:1; 2; 3; 17; 18; 20; 21; 27; 33; 35; 4:15; 26; 37; 41; 45; 5:23; 7:5; 10:8; 11:11; 12; 13; 14; 13:4; 16; 14:11; 13; 14; 15; 22(2); 39; 15:13; 22; 16:14; 26; 28; 29; 30; 31; 38; 21:25; 22:9; 28; 32; 33; 24:10; 26:7; 9; 14; 18; 22; 25; 27; 30; 34; 35; 36; 37(2); 41; 42(2); 47; 50; 51; 53; 57; 58; 63; 64; 27:1; 14; 28:23; 29:39; 30:16; 31:16; 32:15; 33:1; 2; 34:17; 19; 29; 35:6; 7; 15; 24; 29; 36:13; **Deut** 1:1; 35; 2:7; 3:5; 21; 4:6; 30; 42; 45; 5:22; 6:1; 6; 24; 25; 7:12; 17; 8:2; 4; 9:4; 5; 10:21; 11:18; 22; 23; 12:1; 28; 30; 14:4; 7; 9; 12; 15:5; 16:12; 17:19; 18:12(2); 14; 19:5; 9(2); 11; 20:15; 16; 22:17; 23:18; 25:3; 26:16; 27:4; 12; 13; 28:2; 15; 45; 29:1; 18; 30:1; 7; 31:1; 3; 17; 28; 32:45; **Josh** 2:11; 4:6; 7; 21; 9:13(2); 10:16; 24; 42; 11:1; 5; 14; 12:1; 6; 7; 13:12; 32; 14:1; 10; 17:2; 3; 9; 19:8; 16; 31; 47; 48; 51; 20:9; 21:3; 8; 9; 42(2); 22:3; 23:3; 4; 7(2); 12(2); 13; 24:26; 29; **Judg** 2:4; 3:1; 9:3; 38; 13:23(2); 16:15; 18:14; 18; 19:13; 20:17; 25; 35; 44; 46; **Ruth** 3:17; **1 Sam** 4:8(2); 6:17; 10:7; 14:6; 8; 49; 16:10; 17:11; 17; 18; 30; 39; 18:26; 19:7; 21:12; 23:2; 24:7; 16; 25:9; 12; 37; 29:3(3); 4; 31:4; **2 Sam** 3:5; 39; 5:14; 7:17; 21; 8:11; 13:21; 14:19; 16:2; 21:22; 23:1; 8; 17; 18; 22; 24:17; 23; **1 Ki** 4:2; 8; 27; 7:9; 45; 8:59; 9:13; 21; 10:8; 11:2; 12:6; 7; 27; 17:1; 17; 18:36; 20:19; 21:1; 22:11; 17; 23; **2 Ki** 1:7; 13; 3:10; 13; 6:20; 7:8; 10:9; 17:41; 18:27; 20:14; 21:11; 23:16; 17; 24:16; 25:16; 20; **1 Chr** 1:23; 29; 31; 33; 43; 54; 2:1; 3; 18; 23; 33; 50; 53; 55; 3:1; 4; 5; 9; 4:2; 3; 4; 6; 12; 18; 23; 31; 33(2); 38; 41; 5:14; 17; 24; 6:17; 19; 31; 33; 50; 54; 64; 65; 7:8; 11; 17; 29; 33; 40; 8:6; 10; 28(2); 38(2); 40; 9:9; 33; 34; 44(2); 10:4; 11:10; 19(2); 20; 24; 12:1; 14; 15; 23; 38; 14:4; 17:15; 19; 18:11(2); 20:8; 21:17; 23:4; 9; 10; 24; 24:1; 30; 31; 25:5; 6; 26:8; 12; 19; 27:1; 22; 31; 28:19; 29:17; 19; **2 Chr** 3:13; 4:9; 18; 8:8; 9:7; 11; 10:6; 7; 14:7; 8; 15:8; 17:14; 19; 18:10; 16; 22; 21:2; 24:26; 29:12; 32; 32:1; 35:7; 36:18; **Ezra** 1:11; 2:1; 59; 62; 4:21; 5:9; 15; 6:8(2); 7:1; 8:1; 13; 9:1; 14; 10:3; 44; **Neh** 1:4; 10; 4:2; 5:6; 6:6; 7; 14; 16; 7:6; 61; 64; 10:8; 29; 11:3; 7; 12:1; 7; 26; 13:26; **Esth** 1:5; 2:1; 3:1; 4:11; 8:11; 9:20; 26; 27; 28(2); 31; 32; **Job** 8:2; 10:13; 12:3; 9; 19:3; 26:14; 32:1; 5; 33:29; 36:31; 42:7; **Ps** 15:5; 42:4; 50:21; 51:17; 57:1; 73:12; 104:27; 107:43; **Prov** 6:16; 24:23; 25:1; **Eccl** 7:10; 28; 11:9; 12:12; **Isa** 3:6; 7:4; 8:6; 29:13; 24; 34:16; 36:12; 20; 38:16(2); 39:3; 40:26; 42:16; 44:7; 21; 45:7; 47:7; 9; 48:14; 49:12(2); 18; 21(3); 51:19; 57:6; 60:8; 64:5; 12; 65:5; **Jer** 2:34; 3:7; 12; 4:12; 18; 5:4; 5; 9; 19; 25; 29; 7:2; 4(2); 10; 13; 27; 9:9; 24; 26; 10:11; 11:6; 13:22; 14:22; 16:10; 17:20; 20:1; 22:2; 5; 23:21; 33; 24:5; 25:9; 11; 30; 26:7; 10; 15; 27:6; 12; 28:14; 29:1; 30:4; 15; 31:21; 32:14; 33:24; 34:6; 7; 35:7; 36:16; 17; 18; 24; 38:9; 12; 16; 24; 27; 43:1; 10; 45:1; 51:60; 61; 52:20; 26; 28; **Lam** 1:16; 4:9; 5:17; **Ezek** 1:21(2); 8:15; 11:2; 14:3; 14; 16; 18; 16:5; 20; 30; 43; 17:12; 18; 18:10; 13; 23:30; 24:19; 27:24;

30:17; 35:10(2); 36:20; 37:3; 4; 5; 9; 11; 18; 40:24; 28; 29; 32; 33; 35; 42; 46; 43:13; 18; 27; 45:15; 46:24; 47:9; 13; 48:1; 10; 16; 29; 30; **Dan** 1:17; 2:28; 44(2); 3:12; 13; 21; 23; 27; 4:10; 6:2; 5; 6; 11; 14; 15; 7:16; 10:21; 11:4; 27; 41; 12:6; 7; 8; **Hos** 2:12; 14:9; **Am** 6:2; **Mic** 2:7; **Hab** 2:6; **Hag** 2:13; **Zech** 1:9; 10; 12; 19(2); 21(2); 3:7; 4:4; 5; 10; 11; 12; 13; 14; 6:4; 5; 8:6; 9(2); 10; 12; 15; 16; 17; 13:6; **Mt** 1:20; 3:9; 4:3; 9; 5:19; 37; 6:29; 32(2); 33; 7:24; 26; 28; 9:18; 10:2; 5; 42; 11:25; 13:34; 51; 53; 54; 56; 14:2; 15:8; 20; 18:6; 10; 14; 19:1; 20; 20:12; 21; 21:16; 23; 24; 27; 22:22; 40; 23:23; 36; 24:2; 3; 6; 8; 33; 34; 25:40; 45; 46; 26:1; 62; **Mk** 2:8; 4:15; 16; 18; 20; 6:2; 14; 7:23; 8:4; 9:37; 42; 10:20; 11:28(2); 29; 33; 12:31; 40; 13:2; 4(2); 8; 29; 30; 14:60; 16:17; **Lk** 1:19; 20; 65; 2:19; 51; 3:8; 4:28; 5:27; 7:9; 18; 8:8; 13; 21; 9:13; 28; 44; 10:1; 21; 36; 11:27; 42; 45; 53; 12:27; 30(2); 31; 13:2; 17; 14:6; 15; 21; 15:26; 29; 16:14; 17:2; 18:21; 22; 34; 19:11; 15; 40; 20:2; 8; 47; 21:4; 6; 7(2); 9; 12; 22; 28; 31; 36; 23:23; 31; 49; 24:9; 10; 14; 18; 21; 26; 36; 44; 48; **Jn** 1:28; 50; 2:16; 18; 3:2; 9; 10; 22; 5:3; 16; 20; 34; 39; 6:1; 5; 59; 7:1; 4; 9; 31; 32; 8:20; 28; 30; 9:6; 22; 40; 10:19; 21; 11:11; 28; 43; 12:16(3); 36; 41; 13:17; 21; 14:12; 25; 15:11; 17; 21; 16:1; 3; 4(2); 6; 25; 33; 17:1; 11; 13; 20; 25; 18:1; 8; 22; 19:24; 36; 20:18; 31; 21:1; 15; 24(2); **Acts** 1:9; 14; 21; 22; 24; 2:7; 15; 22; 3:24; 4:16; 5:5(2); 11; 24; 32; 35; 38; 7:1; 50; 54; 10:8; 44; 47; 11:12; 18; 22; 27; 12:17; 13:42; 14:15(2); 18; 15:17; 28; 29; 16:17; 20; 36; 38; 17:6; 7; 8; 11(2); 20; 30; 18:1; 17; 19:21; 36; 37; 41; 20:5; 24; 34; 36; 21:12; 23:22; 24:1; 8; 9; 22; 25:9; 11(2); 20; 26:21; 26(2); 29; 30; 27:31; 35; 28:29; **Rom** 2:14; 8:14; 30(3); 31; 37; 9:8; 11:24; 31; 14:18; 15:23(2); **1 Cor** 2:13; 4:6; 14; 6:8; 9:8; 15(2); 10:6; 11; 11:17; 12:2; 11; 23; 28; 13:13(2); **2 Cor** 2:16; 7:1; 13:10; **Gal** 4:24; 5:17; 6:12; **Eph** 5:6; **Phil** 3:7; 4:3; 8; 9; **Col** 2:23; 3:6; 8; 14; 4:11; **1 Th** 3:3; 4:18; **2 Th** 1:9; 2:5; **1 Tim** 3:10; 14; 4:6; 11; 15; 5:7; 21; 6:2; 8; 11; **2 Tim** 1:12; 2:2; 14; 3:8; **Titus** 2:15; 3:8(2); **Heb** 1:2; 7:13; 9:5; 6; 23(2); 10:1; 18; 11:13; 39; **Jas** 3:10; **1 Pe** 1:20; 4:4; **2 Pe** 1:4; 8; 9; 10; 12; 15; 2:12; 17; 3:11; 14; 16; **1 Jn** 1:4; 2:1; 26; 5:7; 8; 13; **Jude** 7; 8; 10(2); 12; 14; 16; 19; **Rev** 2:1; 8; 12; 18; 3:1; 7; 14; 4:1; 7:1; 9; 13; 14; 9:12; 18; 20; 11:4; 6; 10; 14:4(3); 15:5; 16:5; 9; 17:13; 14; 16; 18:1; 15; 19:1; 9; 20; 20:3; 21:5; 22:6; 8(2); 16; 18; 20

THEY (6961/5169)

Gen 2:4; 24; 25; 3:7(3); 8; 4:8; 5:2; 6:2(3); 4; 19; 7:9; 14; 15; 23; 8:17; 9:2; 23; 11:2(3); 3(3); 4; 6(3); 7; 8; 31(2); 12:5(4); 12(3); 20; 13:6(2); 11; 14:2; 4(2); 7; 11; 12; 13; 15:13; 14(2); 16; 16:10; 18:5; 8; 9; 19; 21; 19:2; 3(2); 4; 5; 8; 9(3); 11(2); 16; 17; 33; 35; 20:11; 17; 21:30; 32(2); 22:9; 19; 24:19; 41; 54; 57; 58; 59; 60; 61; 25:18; 25; 26:15; 18; 20; 21(2); 22; 28; 30; 31(2); 32; 35; 29:2; 3; 4; 5; 6; 8(2); 20; 30:38(2); 41; 31:37; 43; 46(2); 54; 32:18; 33:4; 6; 7(2); 34:5; 7; 14; 22; 23; 25; 26; 28; 29(2); 30; 31; 35:4; 5(2); 16; 36:7; 16; 37:4; 5; 8; 16; 17; 18(2); 19; 23; 24; 25(2); 28; 31; 32(2); 38:21; 39:22; 40:4; 6; 8; 15; 41:2; 14; 18; 21(3); 43; 42:7; 8; 10; 13; 20; 21; 23; 26; 28; 29; 35(3); 43:2(2); 7; 15(2); 18(2); 19(2); 24; 25(3); 26; 28(2); 32; 33; 34; 44:1; 3; 4; 7; 13; 14; 45:3; 4; 24; 25; 26; 27; 46:6(2); 28; 32(2); 47:1(2); 3; 4; 9; 14; 17; 18; 22(2); 25; 27; 48:5; 6; 9; 49:6(2); 26; 31(2); 50:8; 10(2); 11; 15; 16; 17(2); 18; 26; **Ex** 1:10(2); 11(2); 12(3); 14(2); 19; 2:16(2); 18; 19; 23; 3:13; 18; 4:1(2); 5; 8(2); 9; 18; 31(2); 5:1; 3; 8(3); 9; 16; 19; 20(2); 21; 6:4; 9; 7:6; 7; 10; 11; 12; 16; 17; 19; 24; 8:1; 8; 9; 11; 14; 17; 18; 20; 21; 26; 9:1; 10(2); 13; 19; 32; 10:3; 5(3); 6(2); 7; 11; 12; 14(2); 15(2); 23; 12:7(2); 8(2); 28; 33(2); 35; 36(3); 39(4); 50; 13:17; 20; 14:2; 3; 4; 5; 10; 11; 17; 25; 15:5; 10; 16; 22(2); 23(3); 27(2); 16:1(2); 4; 5(3); 10; 15(2); 18; 20; 21; 22; 24; 27; 32; 35(3); 17:4; 7; 12; 18:7(2); 11; 16(2); 20(2); 22(3); 26(3); 19:1; 2; 13; 14; 17; 21; 20:18; 19; 21:35(2); 22:23; 23:11; 33(2); 24:2; 7; 10; 11(2); 25:2; 10; 15; 20; 37(2); 26:24(3); 27:8; 20; 28:3; 4(2); 5; 6; 20; 21; 28; 30; 38; 41; 42; 43(4); 29:33(2); 46; 30:4; 20(4); 21(2); 29; 30; 31:6; 11; 32:4; 6; 8(2); 13; 15; 17; 20; 22; 23; 24; 35; 33:4; 34:15; 30; 35:21; 22; 25; 36:3(2); 5; 6; 7; 8; 29; 37:9; 39:1; 3; 4; 6(2); 9; 10; 13; 15; 16; 17; 18; 19; 20; 21; 24; 25; 27; 30; 31; 32; 33; 43(2); 40:15; 32(3); 37; **Lev** 2:12; 4:13; 14; 24; 33; 6:16; 20; 7:2(2); 8:28; 9:5; 13; 20; 24; 10:2; 5; 7; 14; 15; 19; 11:8; 10; 11; 13(2); 31; 32; 35; 42; 13:54; 14:36; 40(2); 41(2); 42; 15:18; 31(2); 16:1; 27; 17:5(2); 7(2); 18:17; 19:20; 20:4; 12; 13; 14(2); 16; 17; 19; 20(2); 21; 23; 27; 21:5(2); 6(3); 7(2); 22:2(3); 9(3); 15(2); 16; 18; 25; 23:17(3); 18; 20; 24:2; 9; 11; 12; 23; 25:31(2); 42(2); 45(2); 46; 55; 26:7; 26; 36(2); 37; 39; 40(3); 41; 43(2); 44; 27:11; **Num** 1:1; 18(2); 50(2); 54; 2:2; 16; 17(2); 24; 31; 34(2); 3:4(2); 6; 7; 8; 9; 10; 13; 31; 4:5; 6(2); 7; 8(2); 9(2); 10; 11(2); 12(2); 13; 14(3); 15(2); 19(2); 20(2); 25; 26; 31; 49(2); 5:2; 3; 9; 6:7; 20; 27; 7:3(2); 5; 9; 11; 8:11; 16; 22; 25; 26(2); 9:1; 4; 5; 6(2); 11(2); 12(2); 18(2); 20(2); 21(2); 22; 23(3); 10:3; 4; 6; 10; 13; 28; 33; 34; 11:13; 16; 17; 21; 25(2); 26(2); 32; 34; 12:2; 5; 13:19(2); 21; 22; 23(3); 25; 26(2); 27; 31; 32(2); 14:4; 7; 9; 11; 12; 14(2); 23; 31; 35(2); 40; 44; 15:25; 32; 34; 16:2; 3; 12; 16; 22; 27; 29; 30; 33(2); 34; 37; 38(3); 39; 42; 45; 17:5; 9; 10; 18:2; 3(4); 4; 6; 9; 12; 13; 15; 17; 21; 22; 23(2); 24(2); 19:2; 9; 17; 20:2; 6; 27; 21:3; 4; 6; 11; 12; 13; 16; 18; 32; 33; 35(2); 22:3; 5; 6; 7; 11; 12; 15; 16; 39; 24:24; 25:2; 18(2); 26:9; 10; 55; 61; 62; 64; 65; 27:2; 21(2); 28:19; 31; 29:8; 13; 31:7(2); 8(2); 10(2); 11; 12; 49; 52; 32:1; 5; 9(3); 11; 12; 16; 30(2); 38(2); 33:3; 6; 7(2); 8; 9(2); 10; 11; 12; 13; 14; 15; 16; 17; 18; 19; 20; 21; 22; 23; 24; 25; 26; 27; 28; 29; 30; 31; 32; 33; 34; 35; 36; 37; 41; 42; 43; 44; 45; 46; 47; 48; 49; 55; 35:2; 3; 12; 36:2; 3(2); 4; 6(2); 12; **Deut** 1:24; 25(2); 39(2); 2:4; 11; 15; 21; 22; 3:20; 4:9; 10(3); 45; 46; 47; 5:28(3); 29(2); 31; 6:8; 7:4; 23; 9:12(2); 13; 14; 29; 10:5; 7; 11; 11:4; 18; 30; 12:30; 31(2); 14:7(2); 19; 15:6; 16:16; 18; 17:9; 10(2); 11(3); 18:1; 2; 3; 8; 17; 19:20; 20:9; 11; 18(2); 21:4; 7; 15; 18; 20; 22:17; 19; 21; 28; 23:4(2); 25:1(2); 26:12; 28:7; 10; 22; 41(2); 46; 51(3); 52(2); 60; 29:22; 25; 26(2); 31:12(2); 16(2); 17(2); 18(2); 20(3); 24; 30; 32:5(2); 7; 16(2); 17(2); 20; 21(2); 24; 27; 28; 29(3); 37; 33:3; 9; 10(2); 11; 17(2); 19(3); **Josh** 1:15; 16; 2:1; 3; 4; 7; 8; 13; 21; 22; 23; 24; 3:1(2); 3; 6; 7; 13; 4:8; 9; 14(2); 19; 20; 5:4; 5; 6; 7(2); 8(3); 11; 12(2); 6:5; 11; 14(2); 15(2); 19; 20; 21; 23; 24(2); 7:3; 4; 5; 6; 11(3); 12; 21; 22; 23; 24; 25(2); 26; 8:5; 6(3); 9; 11; 13; 15; 16; 17; 19(2); 20(2); 21; 22(3); 23; 24(3); 29; 31; 33; 9:2; 4(2); 6; 8; 9; 13; 14; 16(3); 24; 26; 10:2; 5; 11(2); 20; 23; 24(2); 26; 27(2); 29; 31; 34; 35; 36; 37; 38; 39; 11:4(2); 5; 7; 8(2); 11; 14(3); 19; 20(2); 22; 12:1; 14:4; 5; 16:10; 17:4; 13; 18; 18:4; 5; 9; 19:2; 47(2); 49; 50; 51; 20:3; 4; 5; 7; 8; 21:2; 9; 11; 12; 13; 20; 21; 27; 43; 22:6; 9; 10; 15(2); 28; 33; 23:12; 13; 24:1; 2; 7; 8; 22; 30; 32; 33; **Judg** 1:4; 5(2); 6; 7; 8; 10; 11; 16; 17; 19(3); 20; 24; 25(2); 28; 32; 33; 34; 35; 2:3; 5(2); 9; 12(4); 13; 14; 15(2); 17(4); 19(2); 22; 3:4(2); 6(2); 7; 12; 24; 25(3); 26; 28; 29; 4:12; 24; 5:8; 11; 19; 20; 23; 30; 6:4; 5(3); 29(3); 33; 35; 7:11; 19(2); 20(2); 25(4); 8:1; 5; 18(3); 19; 24(2); 25(2); 28; 35; 9:3; 4(2); 6; 7; 8; 9; 25; 27(2); 31; 36; 41; 42; 46; 51; 55; 10:4; 6; 8; 16; 11:2; 6; 13; 16; 17; 18(2); 21; 22; 12:4; 6(2); 13:20; 14:9; 11(2); 13; 14; 15; 15:6; 10; 11; 12; 13(2); 16:2(2); 7; 11; 21; 23; 24(2); 25(3); 17:4; 18:2(2); 3(3); 5; 7(4); 9; 12(2); 13; 15; 17; 19; 21; 22; 23(2); 26; 27(2); 28(2); 29; 31; 19:4; 5; 6; 8; 11; 14; 15; 21; 22(2); 25(2); 20:5(2); 6; 10(3); 18; 22; 26(2); 31; 32; 36(3); 38; 39(2); 41; 42(2); 43; 45(3); 47; 48(2); 21:2; 5; 8; 12(2); 14(3); 17; 19; 20; 23(4); 24; **Ruth** 1:2; 4(2); 7; 9; 10; 11; 13; 14; 19(2); 22; 2:4; 9; 21; 4:2; 17; **1 Sam** 1:9; 19; 25; 28; 2:12; 14; 15; 16; 20; 22; 25; 27; 34; 4:2; 4; 6(2); 7(2); 9; 5:2; 3; 4; 7; 8(3); 9; 10(2); 11; 6:3; 4(2); 6(2); 10; 11; 12; 13; 14; 16; 18; 19; 21; 7:6(2); 7; 10; 13; 8:2; 3; 6; 7(3); 8(3); 19; 9:4(4); 5; 10; 11(2); 12; 14(2); 20; 25; 26; 27; 10:2; 4; 5; 10; 14; 21; 22; 23; 27; 11:5(2); 7; 9(2); 11; 15(2); 12:4; 5; 9(2); 10; 21; 13:5; 6; 22; 14:9; 10; 11; 13; 16; 17; 20; 21; 22(2); 30; 31; 33; 36; 15:3; 6; 9; 15; 18; 16:6; 17:1; 2; 11; 19; 24; 31; 51; 53; 18:6; 7; 8(2); 20; 27; 30; 19:1; 8; 20(2); 21(2); 22; 24; 20:41(2); 21:11; 22:1; 4; 11; 17; 23:1(2); 12; 13; 24; 25; 28; 25:7; 8; 9; 11; 12; 16; 40; 26:12(2); 19(2); 27:11; 28:4; 8; 25(2); 29:5; 30:2; 4; 10; 11(3); 12; 16(2); 19; 20; 21(3); 22(2); 24; 31:7; 8; 9; 10(2); 12; 13; **2 Sam** 1:12(2); 23(3); 2:3; 4(2); 13; 15; 16; 24; 28; 29; 32(2); 3:21; 23; 32; 4:6(2); 7(2); 8; 12(2); 5:3; 8; 11; 17; 21; 6:3; 4; 6; 17; 7:10; 9:2; 10:5; 6; 13; 14; 15(2); 16; 19(2); 11:1; 10; 20; 12:18; 19; 20; 13:9; 30; 32; 36; 14:7(2); 11; 15:11; 24; 29; 30; 36; 16:14; 22; 17:8(2); 17(2); 18; 20(4); 21(2); 29; 18:3(2); 17; 19:3; 8; 14; 17; 20:3; 7; 8; 14; 15(2); 18(3); 22(2); 21:5; 9(2); 13; 14(2); 22:18; 19; 38; 39(2); 42; 45(2); 23:6; 7; 9; 24:5; 6(2); 7(2); 8(2); 13; 17; **1 Ki** 1:1; 3; 7; 23; 25(2); 32; 39; 41; 44; 45; 2:7; 39; 3:22; 24; 28(2); 4:21; 28; 5:1; 6; 14; 18; 6:8; 10; 27; 7:28; 8:1; 4; 8(2); 9; 25; 30; 33(2); 35(2); 36; 40(2); 42; 43; 44; 46(2); 47(2); 48; 50(2); 51; 52; 66; 9:9(2); 12; 13; 22; 28; 10:29; 11:2(2); 18(2); 24; 33; 41; 12:3; 7(2); 20; 24; 27; 13:11; 13; 20; 25; 27; 30; 14:2; 15; 18; 19; 22(2); 23; 24; 29; 15:7; 8; 22; 23; 31; 16:5; 13(2); 14; 17; 20; 27; 18:6; 10(2); 26(4); 28; 29; 34(2); 39(2); 40; 19:10; 14; 21; 20:6(2); 12; 16; 17; 18(2); 23(2); 25; 27; 29; 32; 33; 21:12; 13; 14; 22:6; 11; 32(2); 33; 37; 39; 45; 48; **2 Ki** 1:6; 8; 18; 2:2; 4; 9; 11; 15(2); 16; 17(3); 18; 20; 3:9; 21; 22; 23; 24(3); 25(3); 26; 27; 4:39(2); 40(4); 41; 42; 43(2); 44; 5:23; 24; 6:4(2); 14; 20(4); 22; 23(2); 25; 7:3; 4(2); 5(2); 6; 7(2); 8(2); 9; 10; 11; 12(3); 13(2); 14; 15; 8:23; 9:12; 13; 21; 27; 33; 35(2); 36; 37; 10:4; 7; 8; 13; 14; 16; 20; 21; 24; 25; 26; 27; 34; 35; 11:2; 12(2); 16; 17; 18; 19; 20; 12:8; 10; 11(2); 14(2); 15(3); 19; 21; 13:5; 6; 8; 9; 12; 20; 21(3); 14:15; 18; 19(2); 20; 28; 15:6; 7; 11; 15; 16; 21; 26; 31; 36; 16:5; 18; 19; 17:7; 8; 9; 10; 11(2); 12; 14; 15(3); 16; 17; 19; 21; 22; 24; 25; 26(3); 28(2); 29; 32(2); 33(2); 34(3); 40(2); 18:10; 12(2); 17(3); 18; 20; 34; 19:3; 18(2); 26(2); 37; 20:7; 14(2); 15(2); 18(2); 20; 21:8; 9; 14; 15; 17; 25; 22:7; 14; 17(2); 19; 20; 23:9; 18; 28; 24:5; 25:1; 5; 6(2); 7; 14; 23(3); 26; **1 Chr** 4:14; 23; 28; 33; 39; 40; 41(2); 43(2); 5:9; 10(2); 19; 20(3); 21; 22; 24; 25; 6:32(2); 54; 55; 56; 57; 61; 62; 63; 65; 67; 78; 7:4; 7(2); 9; 21; 40; 8:32; 40; 9:1; 13; 18; 22; 23; 26(2); 27(3); 28; 33; 34; 38; 10:7(2); 8; 9; 10; 12; 11:3; 7; 14; 19; 12:1; 2; 15; 19; 21(3); 22; 39; 13:2; 4; 7; 9; 14:11(2); 12(2); 16; 15:26; 16:1(2); 20; 17:9; 19:6; 7; 11; 14; 15; 16(2); 17; 19(2); 20:4; 8; 21:3(2); 17(2); 23:11; 24; 25; 26; 32; 24:4; 5; 25:8; 26:6; 8; 13; 14; 27; 31; 29:7; 9(2); 21; 22(2); 29; **2 Chr** 1:17(2); 3:13(2); 4:6(2); 5:2; 5; 9(2); 10; 13; 6:16; 21; 24; 26(2); 27; 31(2); 32; 33; 34; 36(2); 37(2); 38(2); 7:3; 9(2); 22(2); 8:15; 18; 9:28; 29; 10:3; 7(2); 11:4; 17(2); 12:2; 6; 7(2); 8(2); 11; 15; 13:11(2); 13; 14; 18; 14:1; 7; 10; 13(3); 14(2); 15; 15:4; 9(2); 10; 11(2); 12; 14; 15; 16:4; 6; 14(3); 17:9(2); 10; 18:5; 9; 10; 14; 29; 31(2); 32; 19:8; 10; 20:2; 4; 8; 10(2); 11; 16; 20(2); 21; 22(2); 23(2); 24; 25(4); 26(2); 27; 28; 29; 34; 36; 37; 21:17; 20; 22:4; 9(4); 23:2(2); 6(2); 11; 15(2); 16; 17; 20; 21; 24:8; 9; 11(2); 12; 13; 14(4); 16; 18; 19(2); 21(2); 23; 24(2); 25(4); 27; 25:10; 12; 13(2); 20; 26; 27(2); 28; 26:18; 20; 23(2); 27:7; 9; 28:5; 6; 8; 15(4); 18; 23(2); 26; 27(2); 29:6; 7; 15; 16; 17(4); 18; 19; 21; 22(3); 23(2); 24; 29; 30(2); 34; 30:1; 3; 5(3); 9; 10; 14(2); 15; 16; 18; 22; 23; 31:1; 4; 5; 6; 7(2); 8; 11; 12; 16; 18; 32:3; 18(2); 19; 31; 32; 33; 33:8; 10; 18; 19; 20; 34:4; 9(3); 10(2); 11; 14; 16; 17; 22; 24; 25(2); 28; 33; 35:1; 6; 11; 12(3); 13(2); 14; 15; 24; 25(2); 27; 36:8; 16; 19; 20; **Ezra** 2:59(2); 62(2); 63; 65; 68; 69; 3:3(2); 4; 5; 6; 7(2); 11(2); 4:2; 4; 6; 11; 13; 15; 23; 5:5; 7; 11; 14; 6:3; 8; 9; 10; 14(2); 17; 18; 20; 22; 8:17(2); 18; 36(2); 9:2; 10:5(2); 7(2); 16; 17; 19(3); 44; **Neh** 1:3; 2:7; 10; 18(2); 19; 3:1(2); 3; 6; 8; 13; 4:2(4); 3; 5; 7; 11; 12(2); 17; 22; 5:8(2); 12(2); 6:2; 4; 9; 10(2); 13(2); 16(2); 19; 7:3; 5; 61(2); 64; 65; 67; 8:1; 4; 6; 8(2); 9; 12; 14; 15; 18; 9:2; 3(2); 10; 11; 12; 16; 17(4); 18; 19; 21; 22; 24(2); 25(2); 26(2); 27; 28(4); 29(2); 30; 35(2); 37; 11:30; 12:27; 37; 39; 43; 47; 13:1; 2; 3(2); 5; 13; 15(2); 19; 21; 22(2); 29; **Esth** 1:7; 8; 17(2); 18; 2:3; 3:4(2); 6; 7; 8; 9; 14; 4:12; 6:1; 14; 7:8; 10; 8:7; 9:5; 10(2); 12; 14; 15; 16; 17; 18; 21; 22; 23; 26(2); 27; 31; 10:2; **Job** 1:15; 19; 2:11; 12(2); 13(2); 3:18; 22; 4:9(2); 20(2); 21; 5:4; 14; 6:7; 17(2); 18; 20(3); 8:10; 9:5; 25(2); 26; 11:6; 8; 20; 12:7(2); 15(2); 25; 14:12; 21; 15:24; 35; 16:10(3); 17:12(2); 16; 18:14; 15; 19:12; 18; 23; 24; 21:11; 12; 13; 14; 18; 19; 26; 30; 22:12; 17; 29; 24:2; 3(2); 4; 5; 6; 7; 8; 10(2); 11; 13; 16(3); 17; 18; 23; 24(5); 28:4(2); 29:22; 23(2); 24(2); 30:1; 3; 5(2); 6; 7(2); 8(2); 10(3); 11; 12(2); 13(3); 14(2); 15; 24; 31:13; 32:3; 4; 15; 16(2); 34:19; 20; 25; 27; 28; 35:5; 9(2); 12; 36:7(2); 8; 9; 10; 11(2); 12(3); 13; 14; 37:12(2); 38:35; 40; 39:2(2); 3(3); 4(2); 16; 41:6; 17(2); 23; 25; 42:11; **Ps** 3:1(2); 2; 5:9; 10; 7:2; 9:3; 15(2); 10:2; 11:2(2); 12:2(2); 14:1(2); 3(2); 4; 5; 16:3; 17:10(2); 11(2); 14; 18:17; 18; 37; 38(2); 41; 44(2); 19:10; 20:8; 21:11(3); 22:4; 5(2); 7(2); 13; 16; 17; 18(2); 31; 23:4; 25:6; 19(2); 27:2; 28:4; 5; 31:4; 13(2); 32:6; 9; 34:5; 35:7(2); 11; 12; 13; 15(2); 16; 20(2); 21; 36:8; 12; 37:2; 9; 19(2); 20; 28; 40; 38:4; 16(2); 19; 20; 39:6; 40:5; 12; 41:7; 8; 42:3; 10; 44:3; 45:8; 15(2); 48:4; 5(4); 49:11; 14; 19; 51:19; 53:1; 3; 4; 5; 54:3; 55:3(2); 10; 19(2); 21; 56:5; 6(4); 7; 8; 57:6(3); 58:3(2); 4; 8; 59:3; 4; 6(2); 7(2); 12; 13; 14(2); 15(2); 62:4(4); 9(2); 63:10(2); 64:4(2); 5(3); 6; 7; 9; 65:8; 12; 13(2); 66:4; 6; 68:12; 24; 69:4; 21(2); 23; 26; 35; 71:24(2); 72:5; 73:5(2); 7; 8(2); 9; 11; 12; 19(2); 74:4; 5; 6; 7(2); 8(2); 76:5; 77:16; 78:5; 6; 7; 10(2); 17; 18; 19(2); 22; 29; 30; 32; 34(2); 35; 36(2); 37; 39; 40; 41; 42; 44; 53; 56; 57; 58; 79:1(2); 2; 3; 7; 12; 80:16; 82:5(3); 83:3; 4; 5(2); 8; 16; 18; 84:4; 6(2); 7; 88:17(2); 89:15; 16(2); 31; 51; 90:5(2); 10; 91:12; 92:7; 14(2); 94:4; 5; 6; 7; 11; 21; 95:9(2); 10; 11; 99:6; 7; 101:6; 102:26(3); 104:7(2); 8(2); 9(2); 10; 11; 12; 22; 28(2); 29(2); 30; 32; 105:12; 13; 18; 27; 28; 38; 44; 45; 106:7; 12(2); 13(2); 16; 19; 20; 21; 24(2); 28; 29; 32; 33; 34; 35; 36; 37; 38; 39; 42; 43; 107:4(2); 6; 7; 11; 12; 13; 18; 19; 24; 26(2); 27; 28; 30(2); 36; 37; 38; 39; 43; 109:2; 3; 4; 5; 25(2); 27; 28; 111:8; 115:5(4); 6(4); 7(5); 118:11(2); 12(2); 119:3(2); 74; 78; 86; 87; 91; 98; 111; 126; 150(2); 155; 158; 120:7; 122:1; 6; 124:3; 126:2; 127:1; 5; 129:1; 2(2); 3; 135:16(4); 17(2); 138:4; 5; 139:16; 18; 20; 140:2; 3; 5(2); 8; 10; 141:6(2); 9; 142:3; 6; 144:5; 145:7; 11; 147:20; 148:5; **Prov** 1:9; 11; 16; 18(2); 28(3); 29; 30; 31; 2:19; 3:2; 22; 4:16(3); 17; 19; 22; 6:22(3); 7:5; 8:9; 11:21; 14:22; 15:22; 16:5; 13; 18:8; 19:7; 20:10; 21:7; 23:3; 5; 35(2); 26:22; 28:28; 30:24; 25; 26; 27; 31:5; **Eccl** 1:7; 13; 3:18(2); 19; 4:1(2); 9; 10; 11; 15; 5:1(2); 11; 7:29; 8:10(2); 9:1; 3(2); 5(2); 6; 10:15; 11:3; 8; 12:3; 5; **Song** 1:4; 6; 3:8; 5:7(2); 6:5; 9; **Isa** 1:2; 4(3); 6; 14; 18(3); 23; 29; 2:4(2); 6(3); 8; 19; 20; 3:9(3); 10; 16; 5:6; 8(2); 11; 12; 13; 24; 26; 29(3); 30; 6:10; 7:19; 22; 8:15; 19(2); 20; 21(3); 22(2); 9:3(2); 12; 13; 18; 21; 10:1; 2; 4(2); 18; 29(2); 11:9; 14(3); 13:2; 5; 8(3); 17; 18; 14:1; 2(2); 7; 10; 21; 32; 15:3; 5(2); 7(3); 16:7; 8; 17:2; 3; 9; 13; 18:6; 19:3; 8; 12; 13; 14; 20; 21; 22; 20:5; 21:14; 15; 22:3(2); 24; 23:5; 13(2); 24:5; 9; 14(3); 22(2); 26:11(2); 14(4); 16(2); 19; 27:11; 13(2); 28:7(5); 12; 13; 29:9(2); 15; 23; 30:1; 5; 6; 31:1(2); 3; 33:1(2); 12; 17; 23(2); 34:12; 17(2); 35:2; 10; 36:5; 19; 21; 37:3; 19(2); 27(2); 38; 39:3(2); 4(2); 7(2); 40:17; 24(3); 31(3); 41:5; 11; 20; 22; 27; 29; 42:9; 16(2); 17(2); 22(2); 24(2); 43:2; 9; 17(4); 21; 44:4; 9(3); 11(3); 18(3); 45:6; 14(5); 16(2); 20; 46:2(3); 6(4); 7(2); 47:9; 14(2); 15(2); 48:2; 3(2); 7; 13; 21; 49:9; 10; 15; 21; 22; 23(2); 26; 50:9; 51:5; 11; 20(2); 52:6; 8(2); 15(3); 53:9; 54:15; 56:10(3); 11(3); 57:2; 6(2); 12; 58:2(3); 3; 59:4(2); 5; 6; 7; 8(2); 19; 60:4(2); 6(2); 7; 11; 14; 21; 61:3; 4(3); 6; 7(2); 9; 62:6; 12; 63:8; 10; 13; 15; 65:16; 21(2); 22(2); 23(2); 24(2); 25; 66:3; 4(2); 5; 18; 19; 20; 24(2); **Jer** 1:15; 16; 19(2); 2:5; 6; 13; 15; 24; 26; 27(2); 28; 30; 3:1; 16(3); 17; 18; 21(2); 4:2; 17; 22(5); 23; 24; 29; 30; 5:2(2); 3(4); 4(2); 5; 7; 8; 10; 12; 15; 16; 17(4); 22(3); 23; 24; 26(3); 27; 28(6); 6:3; 9; 10(3); 14; 15(6); 16; 17; 19; 23(3); 28(3); 7:17; 18(2); 19(2); 24; 26(2); 27(2); 30; 31; 32; 8:1; 2(8); 4; 5(2); 6; 9(3); 11; 12(6); 16; 17; 19; 9:2; 3(4); 5(2); 6; 10(2); 13; 14; 16; 17(2); 10:4(2); 5(6); 8; 9; 15(2); 18; 20; 21; 25; 11:8(2); 10(2); 11(2); 12(2); 14; 17; 19; 12:2(3); 4; 5(2); 6(3); 10(2); 11; 13(2); 16(3); 17; 13:11(2); 12; 14:2; 3(3); 4; 6; 10(2); 12(2); 14; 16(2); 18; 15:2; 7; 20(2); 16:4(5); 6; 10; 11; 16(2); 17; 18(2); 21; 17:13; 15; 19; 23(2); 25; 26; 18:12; 15(2); 18; 20; 22; 19:4(3); 5; 11; 13; 15(2); 20:4; 10; 11(2); 21:6; 22:7; 9(2); 12; 18(2); 27(2); 28(2); 23:3; 4(2); 7; 8; 12; 13; 14(2); 16(2); 17(2); 21(2); 22(2); 26; 32; 24:2; 3; 7(2); 8; 10; 25:5; 16; 28; 33(2); 26:10; 23; 24; 27:10; 11; 14; 15; 16; 18; 22(2); 28:14(2); 29:6; 9; 17; 19; 23; 30:3; 9; 14; 17; 19(2); 31:1; 9(2); 12(2); 15; 16; 23; 29; 32; 33; 34; 37; 32:14; 23(3); 24; 29; 31; 32(2); 33(2); 34; 35(2); 38; 39; 40; 33:5; 8(3); 9; 24(2); 34:5; 10; 11(2); 18(2); 22; 35:6; 14; 17(2); 36:7; 9; 15; 16(2); 17; 20(2); 24(2); 31; 37:4; 5; 9; 10; 15(2); 21(2); 38:6(2); 7; 9(2); 13; 18; 19(2); 20; 22; 23; 25; 27; 39:4; 5(2); 14; 16; 40:7; 8(2); 12; 41:1; 7; 12(2); 13; 17(2); 18; 42:5; 17; 43:3; 5; 7(3); 44:2; 3(4); 5; 6; 9; 10(3); 12(4); 14(2); 46:5; 6; 12; 15; 16; 17; 21(3); 22; 23(2); 47:2; 48:2; 5; 32; 34; 36; 39; 49:9(3); 23(2); 29(3); 50:3(2); 4(2); 5; 6(3); 7; 9; 20; 33; 36(2); 37(2); 38(2); 42(3); 51:2; 14; 18(2); 24; 26; 30(3); 32; 38(2); 39; 57; 58; 64; 52:4; 7; 8; 9; 18; **Lam** 1:2; 8; 11(2); 14; 19(2); 21(3); 2:7; 8; 10; 12(2); 14; 15; 16(2); 20; 3:23; 53; 4:2; 7; 8; 10; 14(2); 15(3); 18; 19; 5:5; 11; **Ezek** 1:5; 7; 9; 12(3); 17(4); 18(2); 20; 24(3); 25(2); 2:3; 4; 5(4); 6; 7(3); 3:6; 7; 9; 11(2); 15; 25; 26; 27; 4:16; 17; 5:6(2); 13; 17; 6:9(3); 10; 11; 13; 14; 7:14; 18; 19(2); 20; 21; 22; 24; 25; 26; 27(2); 8:6; 9; 12; 13; 16; 17(4); 18; 9:2; 6; 7; 8; 9; 10:11(6); 13; 19(2); 20; 22; 11:7; 16; 18(2); 20(2); 12:2; 3(2); 11; 12; 15; 16(3); 19; 23; 13:6(2); 9(2); 10(2); 21; 14:5; 10; 11; 14; 15; 16(2); 18(2); 20(2); 22; 23; 15:7; 8; 16:37; 39(2); 40(2); 41; 47; 50; 51; 52; 17:15; 17; 23; 19:4; 9(2); 20:8(3); 9; 12; 13(3); 16; 20; 21(2); 24; 25; 26(2); 28(3); 38(2); 49; 21:7; 23; 29(2); 22:7(3); 9; 10; 12; 18(2); 25(3); 26(3); 29; 23:3(2); 4(2); 8; 10(2); 17; 24(3); 25(3); 26; 29; 37(3); 38(2); 39(3); 40; 43; 44(2); 45; 47; 49; 24:14; 25; 27; 25:3; 4(3); 11; 14(2); 17; 26:4; 6; 12(3); 16(2); 17; 27:5(2); 6; 8; 10(2); 11(2); 12; 13; 15; 16; 17; 21; 22; 30(3); 31; 32; 28:7; 8; 17;

22; 23; 24; 25(2); 26(3); 29:6; 7(2); 9; 13; 14; 15; 16(2); 18; 20; 21; 30:4; 7; 8; 11; 19; 25; 26; 31:14; 17; 32:3; 10; 12; 15; 16(2); 20; 21(2); 24; 25(2); 26; 27(2); 29; 30(2); 33:24; 29(2); 30; 31(5); 32(2); 33; 34:5(3); 10; 12; 14; 19(2); 22; 25; 27(2); 28(2); 29; 30(2); 35:12(2); 15; 36:3; 8; 11; 12; 13; 17; 18(2); 19; 20(5); 21; 35; 38; 37:2; 9; 10; 11; 17; 19; 21; 22(2); 23(3); 24(2); 25(3); 27; 38:8; 23; 39:6; 9; 10(3); 11(2); 13; 14(2); 16; 23(2); 26(3); 28; 40:38; 41; 42(2); 41:6(2); 25; 42:6; 11; 13; 14(6); 43:7; 8(3); 10; 11(3); 22(2); 24; 25; 26; 44:7; 10; 11(3); 12(2); 13(3); 15(2); 16(3); 17(3); 18(2); 19(4); 20(2); 22; 23; 24(3); 25(2); 26; 29; 45:5; 8; 46:6; 10(2); 15; 20(2); 47:9; 10; 11; 12; 22(2); 48:14(2); **Dan** 1:4; 5; 16; 18; 19; 2:2; 7; 13(2); 18; 43(2); 46; 3:3; 9; 12; 13; 19; 24; 25; 27; 28(2); 4:6; 7; 25(3); 26; 32(2); 5:3; 4; 8; 15(2); 20; 21; 23; 29; 6:4; 12; 13; 16; 22; 23; 24(3); 7:5; 12; 13; 26; 8:20; 9:7; 10:7; 11:6; 14; 21; 22; 25; 27; 31(2); 33; 34(2); **Hos** 1:11; 2:4; 8; 17; 21; 22; 23; 3:5; 4:2; 7(2); 8(2); 10(3); 12; 13; 14(2); 18; 19; 5:4(2); 6(2); 7(2); 15(3); 6:7(2); 9; 7:1; 2(2); 3; 4; 6(2); 7; 10; 11(2); 12; 13(3); 14(4); 15; 16(2); 8:1; 4(4); 5; 7; 8; 9; 10(2); 11; 12; 13(2); 9:3; 4; 6; 9; 10(3); 12; 16(2); 17(2); 10:1; 2; 3; 4; 8; 9; 11:2(3); 3; 5; 7; 10; 11; 12:1; 8; 11(2); 13:2(2); 3; 6(4); 16; 14:7; **Joel** 1:18; 2:4; 5; 7(3); 8(3); 9(4); 17; 3:2(2); 3(2); 8; 19; **Am** 1:3; 6; 9; 13(2); 2:4; 6; 7; 8; 3:3; 10; 4:8; 5:10(2); 16(2); 6:7; 9; 14; 7:2; 8:3; 12(2); 14; 9:2(2); 3(2); 4; 12; 14(3); 15; **Ob** 5(3); 16(3); 18; 19; **Jon** 1:7(2); 8; 11; 13; 14; 15; 3:10; **Mic** 1:5; 7; 16; 2:1; 2(2); 6(2); 8; 12; 13; 3:4(2); 5; 7; 11; 4:3(2); 12(2); 5:1; 4; 6; 7:2; 3(2); 12; 16; 17(3); **Nah** 1:10; 12(2); 2:4(3); 5(2); 8(2); 3:3; 10; 12(2); 17(2); **Hab** 1:7; 8; 9(2); 10(3); 15(3); 16; 17; 2:7; 3:11; 14; **Zeph** 1:13(2); 17(2); 2:4; 7(2); 8; 10(2); 3:4; 7; 9; 12; 13; 19; **Hag** 1:14; 2:7; 14; **Zech** 1:4; 5(2); 6(2); 9; 11; 15; 2:9; 11; 3:5(2); 8; 4:10; 5:9(2); 10; 6:7(2); 7:11(2); 12; 13(2); 14(2); 8:8(2); 9:2; 15(3); 16; 10:2(2); 5(2); 6; 8(2); 9(3); 12; 11:6; 12; 13; 12:2; 6; 10(3); 13:2; 4; 9; 14:12; 18(2); **Mal** 1:4(2); 3:3; 5; 15; 17; 4:3; **Mt** 1:11; 12; 18; 23; 2:5; 9(3); 10(2); 11(4); 12(2); 13; 18; 4:6; 18; 20; 22; 24; 5:4; 5; 6; 7; 8; 9; 11; 12; 15; 16; 6:2(2); 5(3); 7(2); 16(3); 26(2); 28(2); 7:6; 15; 8:16; 29; 32(2); 33; 34(2); 9:2; 8; 11; 15; 17(2); 24; 28; 31(2); 32(2); 36; 10:17; 19; 23; 25(2); 11:7; 18; 19; 20; 21; 12:2; 10(2); 14; 24; 27; 36; 41; 45; 13:5(3); 6(3); 13(3); 15(3); 16(2); 41; 48(2); 51; 54; 56; 57; 14:5; 13; 15; 16; 17; 20(2); 26(2); 32; 34(2); 35; 36; 15:2(2); 9; 12; 14; 18; 30; 31(2); 32(2); 34; 37(2); 16:5; 7; 12; 14; 20; 28; 17:6; 8(2); 9; 12(2); 14; 16; 22; 23(2); 24; 18:19; 31; 19:6; 7; 25; 20:4; 7; 9; 10(3); 11(2); 18; 22; 24; 29; 30; 31(2); 33; 34; 21:1; 7; 15; 20; 25; 27; 31; 34; 36; 37; 38; 39; 41; 45; 46(3); 22:3; 5; 10; 15; 16; 19; 21; 22(2); 28; 30; 33; 34; 42; 23:3(2); 4(2); 5(2); 6; 25; 24:9; 26; 30; 31; 38; 25:5; 10; 44; 26:5; 8; 15; 19; 21; 22; 26; 30(2); 50; 60; 66; 67; 27:2(2); 4; 6; 7; 9(2); 13; 15; 16; 17; 18; 20; 21; 22; 23; 28; 29(3); 30; 31(2); 32(3); 33; 34; 35(3); 36; 37; 47; 53; 54; 66; 28:8; 9(2); 10; 11; 12(2); 15(2); 17(2); **Mk** 1:16; 18; 20; 21; 22; 27(3); 29(2); 30; 32; 34; 37(2); 45; 2:3; 4(4); 8; 15; 16; 18; 19(2); 20; 23; 24; 3:2(2); 4; 6; 8; 9; 11; 12; 13; 14; 19; 20; 21(2); 28; 30; 31; 32; 4:12(3); 15; 16; 17(2); 18; 33; 34; 36(2); 38; 41; 5:1; 14(2); 15(2); 17; 40; 42; 6:3; 12; 13; 29; 30(2); 31; 32; 33; 34; 36(2); 37; 38(2); 40; 42; 43; 49(2); 50; 51; 52; 53(2); 54; 55; 56(2); 7:2(2); 3; 4(4); 7; 32(2); 36(2); 37; 8:2; 3; 5; 6; 7; 8(2); 14; 16; 19; 20; 22; 28; 30; 9:1; 4; 6; 8(2); 9(3); 10; 11; 13(2); 15; 18(2); 20; 30; 31; 32; 34(2); 10:4; 8; 13; 26; 32(4); 33; 34; 37; 39; 41; 46; 49; 11:1; 4(2); 6(2); 7; 12; 15; 18(2); 20(2); 27; 28; 31; 32; 33; 12:3; 4; 5; 6; 8; 12(3); 13; 14(2); 16(2); 17; 18; 23; 25(2); 26; 44; 13:9; 11; 26; 14:1; 2; 5; 11(2); 12; 16; 18; 19; 22; 23; 26(2); 31; 32; 40; 46; 50; 53; 64; 15:1; 4; 6; 7; 13; 14; 16; 17(2); 19(2); 20(2); 21; 22; 23; 24(2); 25; 27; 35; 16:1; 2; 3; 4(2); 5(2); 6; 8(4); 10; 11(2); 12; 13(2); 14(2); 17(2); 18(4); 20; **Lk** 1:6; 7(2); 22; 58; 59(2); 61; 62; 63; 2:6; 9; 16; 17(2); 20; 22; 39(2); 42; 43(2); 44; 45(2); 46; 48(2); 50; 4:2; 11; 22; 28; 29(2); 32; 36(2); 38; 41; 5:6(2); 7(3); 9; 11(2); 18; 19(3); 26(2); 33; 35; 6:7; 11(2); 18; 22; 39; 44; 7:4(2); 16; 20; 31; 32; 42; 8:4; 10(2); 12; 13; 14; 22; 23(2); 24(2); 25(2); 26; 31; 32; 34; 35(2); 36; 37; 40; 53; 9:6; 10(2); 11; 12; 13; 15; 17; 19; 27; 32(2); 33; 34(2); 36(2); 37; 40; 43; 45(3); 52(2); 53; 54; 56; 57; 10:7; 8; 10; 13; 38; 11:19; 26; 32; 48; 49; 54; 12:1; 4; 11; 24; 27(2); 36; 48; 13:2; 4; 29; 14:1; 4; 6; 7; 12; 14; 18; 15:24; 16:4; 9; 14; 28; 29; 30; 31(2); 17:1; 13; 14(2); 21; 23; 27(4); 28(6); 37; 18:9; 15(2); 33; 34(2); 37; 43; 19:7(2); 11(2); 25; 33; 34; 35(3); 37; 42; 44; 20:5; 6; 7(2); 10; 11; 12; 13(2); 14; 15; 16(2); 19(2); 20(2); 21; 24; 26(2); 31; 36(2); 40; 41; 21:7; 12; 16; 24; 27; 30; 22:2(2); 5; 9; 13(2); 23; 35; 38; 49; 54; 55; 64; 65; 70; 71; 23:2; 5; 12; 18; 21; 23; 24; 25; 26(3); 29; 30; 31; 33(2); 34(3); 55; 56(2); 24:1(2); 2; 3; 4; 5(2); 8; 9; 11; 14; 15; 16; 19; 23(3); 24; 28(2); 29; 31; 32; 33; 35; 36; 37(2); 41; 42; 45; 52; **Jn** 1:21; 22; 25; 37; 38; 39; 2:3(2); 7; 8; 12; 22; 23; 3:21; 23; 26; 4:27; 30; 35; 40; 42; 45; 52; 5:12; 23; 39; 6:2; 9; 11; 12; 13; 14; 15; 19(3); 21(2); 23; 24; 25(2); 28; 30; 34; 42; 45; 60; 63; 64; 7:25; 26; 30; 40; 52; 8:3; 4; 6(2); 7; 19; 25; 27; 33; 39; 41; 59; 9:10; 12; 13; 17; 18; 19; 22; 24; 26; 28; 34(2); 35; 10:4; 5(2); 6; 10(2); 16; 25; 27; 28; 39; 11:13; 31; 34; 41; 42; 53; 56(2); 57; 12:2; 9(2); 12; 16(2); 18; 21; 37; 39; 40(2); 42(2); 43; 15:6(2); 20(4); 21(2); 22(2); 24(2); 25; 16:2; 3(2); 9; 18; 19; 17:3; 6(2); 7; 8(2); 9; 11; 13; 14; 16; 19; 21(2); 22; 23; 24(2); 18:5; 6; 7; 13; 18; 21; 25; 28(4); 30; 40; 19:2; 3(2); 6; 15; 16; 18; 23; 24(3); 29; 31; 33(2); 37(2); 40; 42; 20:2(2); 4; 9; 13(3); 20; 23(2); 21:3(3); 5; 6(2); 8; 9(2); 15; 25; **Acts** 1:6(2); 9; 10; 12; 13(3); 23; 24; 26; 2:1; 2; 4; 7; 12; 13; 18; 37(2); 42; 46; 3:2; 10(2); 4:1; 2; 3; 7(2); 13(5); 14; 15(2); 17; 18; 21(3); 23; 24(2); 29; 31(4); 32; 35; 5:9; 12; 15; 16; 17; 21(2); 22; 24; 26(2); 27(2); 33(2); 40(4); 41(2); 42; 6:5; 6(3); 10; 11; 12(2); 13; 7:6; 7(2); 16; 19; 25; 26; 35; 39; 41; 52; 54(3); 57; 58; 59; 8:1; 10; 11; 12; 14; 15(2); 16; 17(2); 25(2); 36(2); 39; 9:8; 24; 26; 29; 30; 31; 37(2); 38; 39; 10:9; 10; 18; 22; 24; 39; 46; 48; 11:18(3); 20; 22; 23; 26; 30; 12:10(3); 15(2); 16(2); 19; 20(2); 25(2); 13:2; 3; 4(2); 5(3); 6(2); 13; 14(2); 17; 21; 27; 28(2); 29(2); 45(2); 48; 51; 14:1; 3; 6; 7; 11; 12; 14; 18; 19; 21(2); 23(3); 24(2); 25(2); 26(3); 27(2); 28; 15:2; 3(2); 4(3); 11; 13; 23; 30(4); 31(2); 33(2); 36; 38; 39; 16:3; 4(2); 6(2); 7(2); 8; 19; 20; 21; 23(2); 31; 32; 37(2); 38(3); 39; 40(3); 17:1(2); 6(2); 8(2); 9(2); 10(2); 11; 13; 15; 19; 27(2); 32; 18:3; 6; 20; 26; 19:2; 3; 4; 5(2); 6; 16; 19; 26; 28(2); 32; 33; 34; 20:8; 12(2); 18; 37; 38(2); 21:4; 5; 6; 20(4); 21(2); 22; 24(2); 25(2); 29(2); 31; 32(2); 22:2(2); 9; 18; 19; 22(2); 23; 24; 25; 23:12(2); 14; 20; 21(3); 28; 31; 32; 33(2); 24:12; 13(2); 14; 15; 19(2); 20; 25:2; 3; 7; 14; 17; 18; 26:5(2); 10; 18; 20; 31(2); 27:1; 12; 13(2); 17(4); 18; 27; 28(3); 29; 30; 36; 38(2); 39(3); 40(2); 41; 44; 28:1(2); 2; 4; 6(3); 10(2); 15; 17; 18; 21; 23; 25(2); 27(3); 28; **Rom** 1:20; 21(2); 22; 28; 29; 3:9(2); 12(2); 13; 17; 4:11; 17; 9:6; 7(2); 26; 32(2); 10:1; 2; 3; 14(5); 15(2); 16; 18; 11:3(2); 8(2); 10; 11(2); 20; 23(2); 28(2); 31; 13:6; 15:21; 27; **1 Cor** 2:8(2); 14(2); 3:20; 7:8; 9; 14; 29; 30(3); 9:25; 10:4; 6; 11; 20; 33; 12:19; 13:8(2); 14:7(2); 21; 23; 34(2); 35; 15:10; 11; 29(2); 35; 16:4; 15; 17; 18; **2 Cor** 6:16; 8:3; 5; 23; 9:13; 10:10; 12; 11:12; 22(3); 23; 12:21; **Gal** 1:23; 24; 2:4; 6; 7; 9(2); 10; 12; 14; 4:17(2); 6:12; 13(2); **Phil** 3:18; **Col** 3:21; 4:9; 11; **1 Th** 1:9; 2:14; 15; 16; 5:3(2); **2 Th** 2:10(2); 11; 12; 3:12; **1 Tim** 1:3; 7(2); 20; 2:15; 5:7; 11(2); 12; 13(2); 6:2; 18; 19; **2 Tim** 2:10; 16; 18; 23; 25; 26; 3:9; 4:3(3); 4; **Titus** 1:11; 13; 16(2); 2:3; 4; 10; 3:9; 13; 14; **Heb** 1:4; 11(2); 12; 14; 3:10(2); 11; 18; 19; 4:2; 3; 5; 6:6(2); 7:5; 21; 23; 8:9; 10; 10:1; 2; 11:13; 14; 15(3); 16; 23(2); 29; 30; 35; 37(3); 38; 40; 12:10; 20; 25; 13:17; **Jas** 2:7; 3:3; 4(2); 4:1; **1 Pe** 1:12; 2:8(2); 12(3); 3:1; 2; 16; 4:4; 5; 6; **2 Pe** 1:21; 2:3; 10(2); 12; 13(2); 14; 15; 18(2); 19(2); 20(2); 3:4; 5; 16; **1 Jn** 2:19(6); 4:1; 5(2); **3 Jn** 7; **Jude** 10(3); 11; 12(2); 15; 16; 18; **Rev** 1:7; 2:2; 9; 22; 24; 27; 3:4(2); 9; 4:4; 8; 11; 5:9; 6:9; 10; 11(2); 7:13; 15; 16; 8:7; 9:4; 5; 6; 8; 9; 10; 11; 19; 20; 21; 11:2; 3; 6(2); 7; 11; 12(2); 18; 12:6; 8; 11(2); 13:4(2); 14:3; 4; 5; 11; 13; 15:3; 16:4; 6; 9(2); 10; 11; 14; 15; 16; 17:8; 12; 13; 18:9; 18; 19; 19:3; 20:4(2); 6; 9; 10; 13; 21:3; 26; 22:4; 5(2); 14

THIS (2814/2598)

Gen 2:4; 23; 3:13; 14; 4:2; 14; 5:1; 29; 6:9; 15; 7:1; 9:12; 17; 10:1; 11:6; 10; 27; 12:7; 12; 18; 15:4; 7; 18; 17:10; 21; 18:25; 19:8; 9; 12; 13; 14(2); 20; 21(2); 37; 38; 20:5; 6; 10; 11; 13; 16; 21:10(2); 26; 30; 22:14; 16; 23:19; 24:5; 7; 8; 9; 12; 14; 41; 42; 58; 65; 25:7; 12; 19; 22; 31; 32; 33; 26:3; 10; 11; 33; 28:15; 16; 17(3); 20; 22; 29:25; 27; 33; 34; 30:31; 31:1; 13; 43(2); 48(2); 51(2); 52(5); 32:2; 10; 19; 32; 33:8; 34:4; 14; 15; 22; 35:12; 17; 20; 36:1; 9; 24; 37:2; 6; 9; 10; 19; 22; 32; 38:21; 22; 23; 28; 29; 39:9(2); 11; 19; 40:12; 14; 18; 41:9; 24; 28; 34; 38; 39; 42:15(2); 18; 21; 28; 32; 33; 43:10; 11; 29; 44:5; 15; 29; 45:17; 19; 47:23; 26; 48:4; 9; 15; 18; 49:28; 50:11; 20; 24; **Ex** 1:18; 2:6; 9; 12; 14; 15; 3:3; 5; 12(2); 15(2); 21; 4:17; 5:22; 23; 7:17; 23; 8:19; 23; 32; 9:5; 6; 14; 16; 18; 27; 10:6; 7; 17(2); 12:2; 3; 14; 17(2); 24; 25; 26; 42; 43; 13:3(2); 4; 5(2); 8; 10; 14; 14:5; 12; 15:1; 16:3(2); 8; 15; 16; 23; 32; 17:4; 14; 18:14; 18; 23(2); 21:31; 24:8; 25:3; 26:13; 28:17; 29:1; 38; 42; 30:13; 31; 32:1; 4; 8; 9; 12; 13; 21; 23; 24; 29; 33:4; 12; 13; 17; 34:11; 35:4; 37:8; 38:15; 21; **Lev** 3:17; 6:9; 14; 20; 25; 7:1; 11; 35; 36; 37; 8:5; 34; 9:6; 10:3; 19; 11:46; 12:7; 13:59; 14:2; 32; 54; 57; 15:3; 32; 16:29; 34; 17:2; 7; 19:20; 23:27; 34; 24:10; 25:13; 26:16; 18; 27; **Num** 4:4; 19; 24; 28; 31; 33; 5:19; 22; 29; 30; 6:13; 21; 23; 7:17; 23; 29; 35; 41; 47; 53; 59; 65; 71; 77; 83; 84; 88; 8:4; 24; 25; 9:3; 11:6; 15; 31; 12:11; 13:17; 27; 14:2; 3; 8; 14; 16; 19(2); 27; 29; 32; 35(3); 41; 15:13; 16:6; 21; 28; 45; 18:9; 11; 19:2; 14; 20:4; 5; 10; 12; 13; 21:2; 5; 17; 22:4; 6; 17; 24; 30(2); 24:14; 23; 27:12; 28:3; 10; 14; 17; 24; 29:7; 30:1; 31:21; 32:5; 19; 20; 22; 32; 34:2; 6; 7; 9; 12; 13; 15; 35:5; 14; 36:6; **Deut** 1:1; 5(2); 6; 31; 35; 2:3; 7; 18; 22; 25; 30; 3:8; 12; 14; 18; 26; 27; 28; 4:6(2); 8(2); 20; 22; 26; 32; 38; 39; 41; 44; 46; 47; 5:3; 24; 25; 28; 6:1; 24; 8:17; 18; 19; 9:4; 6; 7; 13; 27; 10:8; 15; 11:4; 5; 13:11; 15:2; 10; 15; 17:18; 19; 18:3; 16; 19:4; 21:7; 20; 22:14; 16; 26; 24:18; 22; 25:3; 26:9(2); 16; 27:3; 8; 9; 26; 28:14; 58(3); 61; 29:4; 7; 9; 14(2); 19; 20; 21; 24(2); 27(2); 28; 29; 30:10; 11; 31:2; 7; 9; 11; 12; 16; 19(2); 21; 22; 24; 26; 30; 32:27; 29; 34; 44; 46; 47; 49; 33:1; 7; 34:4; 6; **Josh** 1:2(2); 4; 6; 8; 11; 13; 14; 15; 2:14; 17; 18; 20; 3:4; 7; 10; 4:6; 9; 22; 5:4; 9(2); 6:3; 25; 26; 7:7; 20; 25; 26(2); 8:20; 22; 28; 29; 9:1; 12; 20; 24; 27; 10:13; 27; 11:6; 16; 12:7; 13:2; 7; 13; 23; 28; 14:10(2); 11; 12; 14; 15:1; 4; 12; 20; 63; 16:8; 10; 18:14; 19; 20; 28; 19:8; 16; 23; 31; 39; 48; 22:3; 7; 16(3); 17; 18; 22; 28; 29; 31(2); 23:8; 9; 13; 14; 15; 24:15; 27; **Judg** 1:21; 26; 2:2(2); 20; 3:2; 4:14; 5:5; 6:13; 14; 20; 24; 26; 29(2); 7:4(2); 14; 8:1; 7; 9; 9:18; 19; 29; 10:4; 15; 11:27; 37; 12:3; 13:11; 20; 23; 15:3; 6; 7; 11; 18; 19; 16:28; 18:3; 12; 19:11; 23(2); 24; 30; 20:3; 9; 12; 16; 21:3; 11; 22; **Ruth** 1:19; 2:5; 20; 3:13; 18; 4:7(2); 9; 10; 12; 14; 18; **1 Sam** 1:3; 27; 2:20; 34; 4:6; 14; 5:5; 6:9; 18; 20; 8:8; 11; 9:6; 12; 13; 16; 17; 21; 24; 10:11; 27; 11:2; 6; 13; 12:2; 5; 8; 16; 20; 14:10; 28; 29; 33; 35; 38; 45(2); 15:14; 16:8; 9; 12; 17:10; 17; 25; 26(2); 27; 32; 33; 36; 37; 46(2); 47; 55; 56; 18:24; 19:17; 20:2; 3; 21; 21:5; 11; 15(2); 22:8; 13; 15; 24:4; 6; 10; 16; 18; 19; 25:21; 24; 25; 27; 31; 32; 33; 26:8; 16; 19; 21; 24; 27:6; 28:10; 18(2); 29:3(2); 4; 5; 6; 8; 30:8; 15(2); 20; 24; 25; **2 Sam** 1:17; 2:1; 5; 6(2); 3:8; 38; 4:3; 8; 6:8; 22; 7:6; 17; 18; 19(2); 27(2); 28; 8:1; 10:1; 11:3; 11; 25; 12:5; 6; 11; 12; 14; 21; 13:1; 12; 16; 17; 20; 32; 14:3; 13; 15; 19; 20(2); 21; 15:1; 6; 16:9; 11; 12; 17; 18; 17:6; 7; 16; 25; 18:18; 20; 31; 19:7; 14; 21; 42; 22:1; 23:5; 17(2); 24:3; **1 Ki** 1:27; 30; 45; 48; 2:23; 26; 3:6(2); 9; 10; 11; 17; 18; 19; 23; 4:24(2); 5:7(2); 6:12; 7:8; 28; 8:8; 24; 27; 29(2); 30; 31; 33; 35; 38; 42; 43; 54; 61; 9:3; 7; 8(3); 9; 13; 15; 21; 10:12; 20; 21; 11:10; 11; 27; 39; 12:9; 10; 19; 24; 27; 30; 13:3; 8; 16; 33; 34; 14:2; 14; 15; 17:21; 24; 18:36; 37; 19:2; 20:6; 7; 9; 12; 13; 24; 28; 33; 34; 39; 22:20; 27; **2 Ki** 1:2; 2:8; 14; 19; 21; 22; 3:16; 18; 23; 4:9; 12; 13; 16; 36; 43; 5:6; 7; 18(2); 20; 6:9; 11; 18; 19(2); 24; 28; 32; 33; 7:1; 2; 9; 18; 8:5(2); 8; 9; 13; 22; 9:1; 11; 25; 26; 27; 34; 36; 10:2; 6; 27; 11:5; 14:7; 15:12; 16:6; 17:12; 23; 34; 41; 18:19; 21; 22; 25(2); 30; 19:3; 21; 29(2); 31; 32; 33; 34; 20:6(2); 9; 17; 21:7; 15; 22:13(2); 16; 17; 18; 19; 20; 23:3(2); 17; 21; 23; 27; 24:3; 20; **1 Chr** 4:41; 43; 5:9; 26; 9:26; 11:11; 19; 13:11; 16:7; 17:5; 15; 16; 17; 19; 26; 18:1; 19:1; 21:3; 7; 8; 22; 22:1(2); 24:19; 26:26; 27:6; 24; 28:7; 8; 19; 29:5; 14; 16; 18; **2 Chr** 1:10(2); 11; 2:4; 3:3; 5:9; 6:15; 18; 20(2); 21; 22; 24; 26; 29; 32; 33; 34; 40; 7:12; 15; 16; 20; 21(3); 22; 8:8; 9:19; 20; 10:9; 19; 11:4; 14:11; 16:9; 10; 18:19; 26; 19:10; 20:1; 7; 9(2); 12; 15; 17; 26; 35; 21:10; 18; 23:4; 24:4; 25:9; 16; 27:5; 28:22; 29:9; 28; 30:9; 26; 31:1; 10; 32:9; 15; 20; 30; 33:7; 14; 34:21; 24; 25; 26; 27; 28; 31; 35:19; 20; 21; 25; **Ezra** 1:9; 3:12; 4:8; 11; 13; 15(2); 16; 19; 21; 22; 5:3(2); 4; 5; 6; 8; 9; 12; 13; 17(2); 6:7(2); 8(2); 11(2); 12; 16; 17; 7:6; 11; 17; 24; 27; 8:1; 23; 35; 9:2; 3; 7(2); 10; 13; 15(2); 10:2; 4; 5; 9; 13(2); 14; 15; **Neh** 1:11(2); 2:2; 18; 19; 5:10; 11; 12; 13(2); 16; 18(2); 19; 6:4; 12; 13; 16; 8:9; 10; 9:1; 10; 18; 32; 38; 13:4; 6; 14; 17; 18(2); 22; 27; **Esth** 1:1; 13; 18; 2:4; 4:5; 14(2); 5:7; 13; 6:3; 9; 7:6; 9:4; 14; 17; 25; 26(2); 29; **Job** 1:3; 22; 2:10; 11; 3:1; 5:27; 8:19; 10:13; 12:9; 13:1; 17:8; 18:21; 19:26; 20:4; 29; 21:2; 23:15; 27:13; 31:28; 33:12; 34:16; 35:2; 36:21; 37:1; 14; 38:2; 11; 18; 42:3; 16; **Ps** 7:3; 12:7; 17:14; 18:22:31; 24:6; 8; 10; 27:3; 32:6; 34:6; 35:22; 41:11; 44:17; 21; 48:14; 49:1; 13; 50:22; 51:4; 56:9; 62:11; 68:16; 69:31; 32; 71:17; 18; 73:16; 74:2; 18; 77:10; 78:21; 32; 54; 59; 80:14; 81:4; 5; 87:4; 5; 6; 92:6; 102:18; 104:25; 109:20; 27; 113:2; 115:18; 118:20; 23; 24; 119:50; 56; 91; 121:8; 125:2; 131:3; 132:14; 149:9; **Prov** 6:3; 22:2; 24:12; 29:13; 30:1; 20; **Eccl** 1:10; 13; 17; 2:1; 10; 15; 19; 21; 23; 24; 26; 4:4; 8; 16; 5:10; 16; 19; 6:2; 5; 9; 7:6; 10; 18; 23; 29; 8:9; 10; 14; 15; 9:1; 3; 13; 11:6; 12:13; **Song** 3:6; 5:16(2); 7:7; 8:5; **Isa** 1:12; 5:25; 6:7; 9; 10; 8:11; 12; 20; 9:7; 12; 16; 17; 21; 10:4; 12:5; 14:4; 16; 26(2); 28; 16:13; 17:14; 20:6; 22:14; 15; 23:7; 8; 13; 24:3; 25:6; 7; 9(2); 10; 26:1; 27:9(2); 28:11; 12(2); 14; 29; 29:11; 12; 14; 30:9; 12; 13; 21; 36:4; 6; 7; 10(2); 15; 37:3; 22; 30(2); 32; 33; 34; 35; 38:6(2); 7(2); 9; 19; 39:6; 41:20; 42:22; 23; 43:9; 21; 44:16; 45:21; 46:8; 47:8; 48:1; 6(2); 7; 16; 20; 50:11; 51:21; 54:9; 17; 56:2; 58:4; 5; 6; 59:21(2); 63:1(2); 66:2; 14; **Jer** 1:10; 18; 2:12; 17; 3:4; 10; 25; 4:8; 10; 11; 18; 28; 5:7; 9; 14(2); 20; 21; 23; 29; 6:6; 19; 21; 7:2; 3; 6; 7; 10; 11; 14; 16; 20; 23; 25; 28; 33; 8:3; 5; 9:9; 12; 15; 24; 10:7; 18; 19; 11:2; 3; 5; 6; 7; 8; 14; 13:9; 10(2); 12; 13; 25; 14:10; 11; 13; 15; 17; 15:1; 20; 16:2; 3(2); 5; 6; 9; 10(2); 13; 21; 17:24; 25(2); 18:6; 19:3; 4(2); 6; 7; 8; 11(2); 12(2); 15; 20:5; 21:4; 6; 7; 8; 9; 10; 22:1; 3; 4(2); 5; 8(2); 11; 12; 16; 21; 28; 30; 23:6; 26; 32; 38; 24:5; 6; 8; 25:3(2); 9; 11; 13; 15; 18; 26:1; 6(2); 9(2); 11(2); 12(2); 15; 16; 20(2); 27:1; 16; 17; 19; 22; 28:3(2); 4; 6; 7; 15; 16; 29:2; 10; 16; 28; 29; 32; 30:17; 21; 31:23; 26; 33; 32:3; 8; 14(2); 15; 20(2); 22; 23; 28; 29(2); 31(2); 35; 36; 37; 41; 42(2); 43; 33:4; 5; 10; 12; 16; 34:2; 8; 22; 35:14; 16; 36:1; 2; 7; 29(2); 37:8; 18; 19; 38:2; 3; 4(4); 17; 18; 21; 23; 39:16; 40:2(2); 3; 4; 16; 42:2; 10; 13; 18; 19; 21; 44:2; 4; 6; 7; 10; 22; 23(2); 29(2); 45:4; 46:7; 10; 50:17; 25; 51:6; 62; 63; 52:3; **Lam** 2:15; 16; 20; 3:21; 5:17; **Ezek** 1:5; 28; 2:3; 3:1; 3; 4:3; 5:5; 6:10; 8:5; 15; 17; 10:15; 20; 11:2; 3; 6; 7; 11; 15; 12:10; 22; 23; 16:44; 49; 17:7; 18:2; 3; 19:14; 20:27; 29(2); 31; 21:11; 23:11; 38; 24:2(2); 24; 31:18; 32:16; 33:33; 36:22; 32; 35; 37; 39:8; 40:10; 12(2); 18; 21; 26; 34; 37; 39; 41; 45; 48(2); 49; 41:2; 4; 22; 43:7; 12(2); 13; 44:2; 45:2; 3; 13; 16; 46:3; 14; 20; 47:6; 8; 12; 14; 15; 17; 18; 19; 20; 21; 48:12; 14; 29; **Dan** 1:14; 2:12; 18; 29; 30; 31; 32; 36; 38; 45; 47; 3:16; 29; 4:17; 18; 24(2); 28; 30; 5:7; 12; 15; 22; 24; 25; 26; 6:3; 5; 28; 7:6; 7; 8; 16; 24; 28; 8:12; 16; 9:7; 13; 15; 10:8; 11; 17; 11:18; 12:5; **Hos** 5:1; 7:10; 16; 8:6; **Joel** 1:2(2); 3:9; **Am** 3:1; 4:1; 5; 12; 5:1; 16; 7:3; 6(2); 8:4; 8; 9:12; **Ob** 20; **Jon** 1:7; 8; 10; 12; 14; 4:2; **Mic** 1:5; 2:3(2); 10; 11; 3:9; 5:5; **Nah** 1:12; **Hab** 1:11; **Zeph** 1:4; 2:10; 15; **Hag** 1:2; 4; 2:3(2); 7; 9(2); 14(2); 15; 18; 19; **Zech** 2:4; 3:2; 4:6; 9; 5:3(2); 5; 6; 7; 8; 6:15; 8:6; 11; 12; 13:9; 14:12; 15; 19; **Mal** 1:9; 13; 2:1; 4; 12; 13; 3:9; 10; 4:3; **Mt** 1:22; 2:3; 3:3; 17; 6:9; 11; 7:12; 8:9(2); 27; 9:3; 13; 26; 28; 33; 10:23; 11:10; 16; 23; 12:6; 7; 23; 24; 32; 41; 42; 45; 13:15; 19; 20; 22; 28; 40; 54(2); 55; 56; 14:2; 15; 15:11; 12; 15; 16:17; 18; 22; 17:5; 20; 21; 18:4; 5; 19:5; 11; 26; 20:14; 21:4; 10; 11; 21; 23; 38; 42; 44; 22:20; 33; 38; 23:36; 24:14; 21; 32; 34; 43; 26:8; 9; 12; 13(2); 26; 28; 29; 31; 34; 39; 42; 56; 61; 71; 27:8; 24; 37; 47; 54; 58; 28:14; 15(2); **Mk** 1:27(2); 38; 2:7(2); 12; 3:21; 4:13; 19; 41; 5:32; 39; 6:2(2); 3; 16; 35; 7:6; 29; 8:12(2); 32; 38; 9:7; 10; 21; 29; 32; 10:5; 7; 22; 30; 11:3; 23; 28; 12:7; 10; 11; 16; 30; 31; 43; 13:19; 28; 30; 14:4; 9(2); 22; 24; 27; 30; 36; 58; 69; 71; 15:39(2); **Lk** 1:18; 29; 34; 36; 43; 61; 66; 2:2; 11; 12; 15; 17; 25; 34; 37; 48; 3:20; 4:3; 6(2); 21; 22; 23; 36; 43; 5:6; 21; 6:3; 7:4; 8; 17; 27; 31; 39(3); 44; 45; 46; 49; 8:9; 11; 25; 9:9; 21; 34; 35; 45(2); 48; 54; 10:5; 11; 20; 28; 11:29; 30; 31; 32; 50; 51; 12:18; 20; 39; 41; 56; 13:6; 7; 8; 16(2); 14:9; 30; 15:2; 3; 24; 30; 16:1; 2; 8; 24; 26; 28; 17:6; 18; 25; 18:5; 9; 11; 14; 23; 30; 34; 19:9; 14; 28; 42; 20:2; 9; 14; 17; 19; 34; 21:3; 23; 32; 34; 22:15; 17; 19(2); 20; 23; 34; 37; 42; 51; 53; 56; 59; 23:2; 4; 5; 14(2); 18; 38; 41; 46; 47; 52; 24:4; 17; 21; 40; **Jn** 1:7; 15; 19; 30; 33; 34; 2:11; 12; 19; 20; 22; 3:2; 19; 29; 4:13; 15; 20; 21; 27; 29; 37; 42; 54; 5:1; 16; 28; 6:6; 14; 29; 34; 39; 40; 42; 50; 51; 52; 58(2); 60(2); 61(2); 7:8(2); 15; 25; 26; 27; 31; 36; 39; 40(2); 41; 46; 49; 8:4; 6; 23(2); 40; 9:2; 3; 8; 9; 16; 19; 20; 24; 29; 30; 33; 39; 10:6; 16; 18; 41; 11:4; 7; 9; 26; 37(2); 39; 42; 47; 48; 51; 12:5; 6; 7; 18(2); 25; 27(3); 30; 31(2); 33; 34; 13:1; 7; 28; 35; 14:30; 15:8; 12; 13; 25; 16:11; 17; 18; 30; 17:3; 18:17; 29; 34(2); 36(2); 37(2); 38; 40; 19:12; 20; 28; 38; 20:14; 20; 22; 30; 21:1; 14; 19(2); 21; 23(2); 24; **Acts** 1:6; 11; 16; 17; 18; 25; 2:6; 12; 14; 16; 29; 31; 32; 33; 36; 37; 40; 3:12(2); 16(2); 4:7; 9; 10; 11; 17; 22; 5:4; 20; 28(2); 33; 37; 38(2); 6:3; 13(2); 14(2); 7:4; 6; 7; 19; 20; 29; 35; 37; 38;

40; 60(2); 8:10; 19; 21; 22; 26; 29; 32; 34; 35; 9:13; 21(2); 22; 36; 10:16; 17; 30; 11:10; 30; 12:12; 13:7; 17; 23; 26; 33; 38; 48; 14:9; 14; 15:2; 6; 15; 16; 23; 16:17; 18; 17:3; 18; 19; 23; 31; 32; 18:10; 13; 21; 25; 19:5; 10; 17; 25; 26; 27; 28; 40; 20:26; 29; 35; 21:9; 11; 28(3); 22:3; 4; 22; 26; 28; 23:1; 7; 9; 13; 17; 18; 27; 24:2; 5; 10; 14; 16; 21(2); 25:5; 24; 26:7(2); 10; 16; 22; 26; 31; 32; 27:10; 21; 23; 34; 28:4; 9; 20(2); 22; 26; 27; **Rom** 1:26; 2:3; 4:9; 5:2; 6:6; 7:24; 8:18; 24; 9:9(2); 10; 17; 20; 10:6; 11:5; 8; 25; 27; 12:2; 13:6(2); 9; 11; 14:9; 13; 15:9; 22; 28(2); 16:22; **1 Cor** 1:12; 20(2); 2:6(2); 8; 3:12; 18; 19; 4:4; 17; 5:2; 3; 10; 6:3; 4; 5; 7:6; 7; 26; 29; 31(2); 35; 8:3; 9; 9:3; 10; 12(2); 17; 23; 10:28; 11:10; 22; 24(2); 25(2); 26(2); 27(2); 30; 14:21; 15:19; 34; 50; 53(2); 54(2); 16:12; **2 Cor** 1:12; 15; 17; 2:1; 3; 6; 9; 3:10; 14; 15; 4:1; 4; 7; 5:1; 2; 4; 5; 7:3; 11(2); 8:6; 7; 10; 14; 19; 20(2); 9:3; 4; 6; 12; 13; 10:7; 11; 11:10; 17; 12:8; 13; 13:1; 9; **Gal** 1:4; 2:4; 3:2; 17; 4:25; 5:8; 14; 6:16; **Eph** 1:21; 2:2; 3:1; 8; 14; 4:9; 17; 5:5; 31; 32; 6:1; 12; 18; 22; **Phil** 1:6; 7; 9; 18; 19; 22; 25; 2:5; 3:15(2); **Col** 1:9; 27; 29; 2:4; 3:20; 4:8; 16; 18; **1 Th** 2:13; 3:3; 5; 4:3; 6; 8; 15; 5:4; 18; 27; **2 Th** 1:11; 2:11; 3:10; 14; **1 Tim** 1:9; 15; 16; 18; 2:3; 3:1; 4:9; 10; 16; 5:4; 6:7; 14; 17; **2 Tim** 1:12; 15; 2:4; 11; 17; 19; 3:1; 6; 4:10; **Titus** 1:5; 13; 3:8; **Phm** 1:15; **Heb** 3:3; 4:4; 5; 5:3; 4; 12; 6:3; 9; 19; 7:1; 4; 27; 8:1; 3; 10; 9:8; 11; 15; 20; 27; 10:12; 16; 11:5; 12:15; 27; 13:19; **Jas** 1:25; 26; 27; 2:5; 3:15; 4:15; **1 Pe** 1:6; 10; 25; 2:15; 19; 20; 21; 3:5; 9; 4:6; 16; 5:12; **2 Pe** 1:5; 12; 13; 17; 18; 20; 3:1; 3; 5; 8; 17; **1 Jn** 1:5; 2:3; 5; 25; 3:3; 8; 10; 11; 16; 17; 19; 23; 24; 4:2; 3; 6; 9; 10; 13; 17(2); 21; 5:2; 3; 4; 6; 9; 11(2); 14; 20; **2 Jn** 6(2); 7; 10; **Jude** 4; 5; **Rev** 1:3; 19; 2:4; 6; 24; 4:1; 11:5; 15; 18:18; 20:5; 14; 22:7; 9; 10; 18(2); 19(2)

THOSE (1508/1349)

Gen 4:20; 21; 6:4(2); 7:16; 23; 12:3; 15:17; 19:25; 24:60; 27:29; 41:35; 42:5; 45:1; 46:31; 47:24; 50:3; **Ex** 1:5; 2:11; 4:21; 15:7; 16:16; 20:5; 6; 29:33; 30:13; 14; 35:35(2); 38:25; **Lev** 10:3; 11:4(2); 21; 27; 14:11; 42; 15:10; 27; 22:22; 26:17; 36; 39; **Num** 1:21; 22; 23; 25; 27; 29; 31; 33; 35; 37; 39; 41; 43; 2:3; 5; 12; 27; 3:22(2); 32; 34; 38; 43; 49(2); 4:36; 38; 40; 42; 44; 48; 7:2; 9:7; 10:35; 11:26; 14:6; 23; 37; 15:33; 16:33; 39; 49(2); 18:16; 21:27; 25:9; 26:7; 18; 22; 25; 27; 34; 37; 41; 43; 47; 50; 51; 54; 57; 62; 63; 64; 27:3; 31:8; 27; 36; 33:55; **Deut** 3:25; 5:3; 9; 10; 7:9; 10; 15; 20; 22; 14:7; 17:9; 18:3; 9; 19:17; 20; 26:3; 28:65; 29:3; 29; 30:7; 32:21; 41; 33:11(2); **Josh** 2:7; 3:15; 4:20; 8:19; 10:20; 22; 23; 24; 11:10; 12; 18; 13:22; 17:12; 16(2); 18:8; 20:4; 6; 21:16; 24:17; **Judg** 2:16; 18; 23; 3:2; 5:14(2); 31; 7:6; 8; 8:11; 11:13; 35; 14:19; 17:6; 18:1(2); 19:1; 20:27; 28; 21:7; 16; 23; 25; **1 Sam** 2:4; 5; 30(2); 3:1; 7:16; 9:13; 22; 10:9; 18; 11:11; 14:48; 17:28; 18:23; 25:26; 27:8; 28:1; 30:2; 9; 20; 22; 27(3); 28(3); 29(3); 30(3); 31; 31:7; **2 Sam** 5:14; 6:13; 8:2(2); 16:2; 23; 17:10; 18:31; 19:28; 21:13; 22:18; 40; 41; 49; **1 Ki** 2:7; 3:2; 8:47; 50; 11:24; 21:27; **2 Ki** 4:4; 6:16(2); 22; 7:13; 10:1; 5; 32; 11:9; 12:11; 15:37; 18:4; 19:12; 31; 20:1; 21:24; 22:5(2); 9; 23:5; 24; 25:28; **1 Chr** 4:23; 9:22; 12:15; 20; 36; 40; 16:10; 22:4; 27:23; 26; **2 Chr** 5:12; 9:9; 11:16; 14:6; 11; 15:5; 9; 16:9; 17:19; 19:2; 20:21; 29; 21:13; 23:6; 8; 13; 24:12(2); 28:12; 30:9; 25; 31:16; 32:13; 14; 24; 33:25; 34:4; 21; 22; 36:20; **Ezra** 1:6; 2:1; 2; 62; 3:3; 5(2); 8; 9; 5:9; 14; 7:13; 25; 8:1; 22(2); 35; 9:2; 4; 10:3(2); 6; 8; 14; **Neh** 1:5; 4:17(2); 5:2; 4; 17; 6:17; 7:5; 6; 7; 64; 8:3; 10; 17; 9:2; 10:1; 28; 13:15; 23; **Esth** 1:2; 14; 2:21; 3:9; 9:1; 2; 3; 5; 11; **Job** 3:8(2); 4:8; 19; 5:11(2); 8:22; 12:5; 6; 18:20(2); 19:15; 19; 20:7; 21:22; 29; 24:1; 13; 19; 26:5(2); 27:15; 30:31; 34:36; 37:16; 42:11; **Ps** 2:12; 5:6; 11(2); 7:1; 9:10(2); 13; 13:4; 15:4; 17:7(2); 18:17; 39; 40; 48; 21:8; 22:7; 25; 26; 29; 24:1; 6; 25:3; 14; 28:1; 31:6; 11; 15; 19(2); 33:18(2); 34:7; 9; 10; 16; 18; 21; 22; 35:1(2); 3; 4(2); 36:10; 37:9; 14; 22(2); 38:12(2); 19; 20; 40:16; 44:5; 7; 10; 13; 49:6; 13; 50:5; 54:4; 55:20; 59:1; 60:4; 61:5; 63:9; 11; 68:1; 6; 11; 69:4; 6(2); 9; 12; 14; 26; 36; 70:4(2); 71:10; 72:9; 16; 73:27(2); 74:23; 79:4; 11; 83:2; 84:4; 11; 85:9; 86:5; 17; 87:4; 88:4; 89:7; 23; 92:13; 98:7; 99:6; 101:3; 102:8; 20; 103:11; 13; 17; 18; 105:3; 106:3; 41; 46; 107:10; 23; 34; 109:20; 31; 111:5; 10; 115:8; 13; 118:4; 7(2); 119:2; 63; 74; 79(2); 84; 118; 132; 165; 123:4; 125:1; 4(2); 126:1; 5; 129:5; 8; 130:6(2); 135:18; 137:3(2); 139:21; 140:9; 143:3; 7; 12; 145:19; 146:8; 147:11(2); **Prov** 1:12; 2:7; 13; 3:18; 27; 4:22; 5:13; 8:9; 17(2); 21; 32; 36; 9:15; 10:26; 11:20; 12:20; 22; 14:22; 18:21; 21:5; 6; 22:21; 23; 26(2); 23:30(2); 24:11(2); 21; 22; 25; 25:13; 26:28; 28:4; 5; 30:5; 31:6; **Eccl** 1:11; 4:16; 5:14; 7:11; 12; 8:8; 12; 12:3; **Song** 8:12; **Isa** 1:28; 3:12; 4:2; 5:8; 11; 18; 20; 21; 7:20; 8:19; 9:2; 16; 10:1; 10; 15; 33; 13:3; 14:16; 19; 17:14(2); 19:8; 9(2); 13; 23:2; 18; 24:6; 9; 26:5; 27:6; 7(2); 28:1; 6; 9(2); 29:15; 24; 30:16; 18; 31:1; 2; 32:3(2); 35:4; 37:12; 32; 38:1; 18; 40:11; 29; 31; 41:11(2); 12(2); 42:5; 7; 44:9; 49:9; 12; 17; 19; 26; 50:6(2); 51:6; 23(2); 52:5; 56:8; 57:8; 58:12; 59:20; 60:6; 12; 14(2); 61:1; 3; 62:9(2); 63:19(2); 65:1(2); 11; 66:2(2); 17; 19; **Jer** 2:8; 24; 3:16; 18; 5:7; 18; 6:15; 8:3; 10; 12; 16; 12:1; 4; 13:20; 14:15; 18(2); 17:13; 18:19; 19:7; 9; 21:7; 22:25(2); 23:17; 32; 24:5; 8; 25:30; 31; 29:31; 30:16(2); 19; 31:4; 24; 29; 33; 36; 33:7; 11(2); 15; 16; 34:20; 21; 38:22; 39:9; 43:11(3); 44:13; 14; 30; 46:22; 25; 26; 47:2; 48:39; 45; 49:5(2); 12; 32; 36; 37; 50:4; 9; 20(2); 28; 51:1; 4; 52:32; **Lam** 1:10; 14; 17; 2:22; 3:25; 4:5(2); 9(2); 15; **Ezek** 1:21(3); 6:9; 7:16; 9:1; 11:15; 21; 24; 25; 12:4; 19; 13:2; 11; 15(2); 16:27; 37(2); 57; 17:21; 18:11; 20:23; 38; 21:23; 22:5(2); 9; 23:28(2); 26:20(2); 27:10; 14; 28:26; 30:6(2); 31:16; 17(2); 18; 32:18; 20; 21; 24; 25; 28; 29(2); 30(2); 32; 33:24; 27(2); 34:4; 27; 35:8; 38:8; 17; 39:6; 9; 10(2); 11; 14; 40:22; 25; **Dan** 1:6; 2:21; 3:22; 4:19; 37; 6:24; 7:16; 17; 9:4(2); 7(2); 16; 10:2; 11:6(2); 14; 26; 30; 32; 33; 35; 12:2; 3(2); **Hos** 2:23; 4:4; 5:10; 11:4; 14:7; **Joel** 2:29; 3:1; **Am** 6:7; 8:14; **Ob** 7; 14(2); **Jon** 2:8; **Mic** 2:1; 6; 8; 4:6; 6:11; 7:1(2); 13; **Nah** 1:7; **Hab** 1:13; **Zeph** 1:5(2); 6; 9; 11; 18; 3:11; 18; 19; **Hag** 2:16; 22; **Zech** 3:4; 6:8; 15; 7:5; 8:23; 10:7; 11:5; 9; 16(3); 13:6; 14:3; 15; **Mal** 3:5(2); 15; 16(2); **Mt** 2:20; 3:1; 4:16; 24; 5:4; 6; 10; 21; 27; 33; 44(3); 46; 7:11; 8:10; 33; 9:12(2); 10:25; 28; 36; 11:8; 11; 12:3; 4; 13:41; 14:9; 21; 33; 15:18; 38; 17:24; 19:11; 20:9; 23; 25; 21:9; 12(2); 40; 41; 22:3; 4; 7; 8; 10; 23:13; 31; 37; 24:16; 19(3); 22(2); 29; 25:3; 7; 9; 10; 19; 34; 41; 26:51; 57; 71; 73; 27:39; 47; 54; **Mk** 1:5; 9; 32; 36; 44; 2:17(2); 20; 25; 26; 3:8; 13; 34; 4:10; 11; 20; 5:14; 16; 38; 40; 6:22; 26; 44; 55; 7:15; 8:1; 9; 10:13; 23; 24; 40; 42; 11:5; 9(2); 15(2); 23; 12:7; 43; 13:14; 17(3); 19; 20; 24; 14:47; 69; 70; 15:29; 32; 35; 16:10; 14; 17; **Lk** 1:1; 2; 4; 24; 39; 45; 50; 66; 79; 2:1; 18(2); 33; 38; 4:2; 18; 28; 40; 5:31(2); 33; 35; 6:3; 4; 12; 18; 27; 28(2); 32(2); 33; 34; 7:10; 14; 25; 28; 49; 8:12; 13; 14; 15; 16; 34; 45; 9:11; 32; 36; 11:13; 28; 33; 52; 12:4; 20; 37; 38; 13:4; 34; 14:7; 10; 15; 17; 24; 16:15; 26(2); 17:10; 18:24; 26; 39; 19:24; 27; 32; 45; 20:1; 16; 35; 21:21(3); 23(3); 26; 35; 22:25; 28; 49; 23:14; 24:24; 33; **Jn** 1:12; 22; 24; 2:14; 16; 4:24; 5:25; 29(2); 6:2; 11; 13; 14; 7:39; 8:9; 10; 26; 29; 31; 9:8; 39(2); 10:32; 12:2; 20; 13:29; 17:9; 11; 12; 20; 18:9; 21; 20:29; **Acts** 1:15; 16; 19; 2:9; 18; 41; 47; 3:2; 18; 24; 4:4; 32; 5:5; 9; 16; 17; 21; 32; 6:1; 9; 7:41; 52; 8:4; 9:21; 37; 10:7; 44; 45; 11:2; 19; 13:26; 27; 31; 15:19; 21; 16:35; 17:11; 15; 17; 18:27; 19:13; 19; 22; 20:32; 34; 21:5; 12; 15; 19; 24; 22:5; 9; 11; 19; 20; 29; 23:2; 4; 24:20; 25:5; 26:13; 18; 20; 22; 30; 27:24; 43; 28:9; **Rom** 1:28; 32(2); 2:2; 3; 7; 8; 19; 3:19; 4:7; 11; 12; 14; 16(2); 17; 5:14; 17; 6:21; 7:1; 8:1; 5(2); 8; 28(2); 9:8; 10:5; 15; 19; 20(2); 11:14; 22; 12:14; 15(2); 13:2; 15:3; 18; 21; 26; 31; 16:10; 11; 17; 18; **1 Cor** 1:2; 11; 18; 21; 24; 2:6; 9; 4:19; 5:12(2); 13; 6:4; 7:29; 30(3); 31; 8:9; 10; 9:3; 13(2); 14; 20(2); 21(2); 24; 10:18; 27; 11:19; 22; 12:22; 23; 14:22(2); 23; 15:18; 20; 23; 48(2); **2 Cor** 1:4; 2:3; 15(2); 4:3; 5:12; 15; 10:12; 11:12; 12:17; 13:2; **Gal** 1:17; 2:2; 6(2); 12; 18; 3:7; 9; 22; 4:5; 8; 5:12; 21; 24; 6:10; 13; **Eph** 2:17; 5:12; 6:5; 24; **Phil** 2:10(3); 3:13(2); 17; 4:22; **Col** 2:1; 18; 3:1; 4:5; 13(2); **1 Th** 4:12; 13; 14; 15; 5:7(2); 12; 14; **2 Th** 1:6; 8(2); 10; 2:10; 3:12; **1 Tim** 1:16; 3:7; 13; 4:3; 10; 16; 5:8; 16; 17; 20; 24; 25; 6:2(2); 9; 17; **2 Tim** 1:15; 2:19; 22; 25; 3:6; **Titus** 1:9; 10; 15; 3:8; 15; **Heb** 1:14; 2:3; 11; 15; 18; 3:5; 17; 18; 4:2; 6; 5:2; 14(2); 6:4; 7; 12; 7:5; 25; 27; 8:10; 9:15; 28; 10:1; 3; 14; 16; 33; 39(2); 11:6; 14; 31; 12:11; 19; 27; 13:3; 7; 9; 10; 11; 17(2); 24(2); **Jas** 1:12; 2:5; 12; 3:18; **1 Pe** 1:12; 2:7; 14(2); 3:12; 16; 4:6; 17; 19; 5:3; **2 Pe** 1:1; 2:6; 10; 13; 18; **1 Jn** 2:26; 3:22; 5:16; **2 Jn** 1; 8; **3 Jn** 10; **Jude** 1; 5; **Rev** 1:3(2); 2:2(2); 9; 10; 14; 15; 22; 3:9; 10; 6:9; 10; 7:4; 9:4; 6; 17; 11:1; 9; 10(2); 11; 18(2); 13:6; 12; 14(3); 14:6; 12; 15:2; 16:2; 17:8; 14; 19:5; 9; 18; 20(2); 20:4; 21:24; 27; 22:9; 14

THROUGH (525/472)

Gen 6:13; 12:6; 13:17; 19:6; 26:8; 30:32; 38:29; 42:23; **Ex** 12:12; 23; 14:16; 24; 19:21; 24; 26:28; 36:33; 40:20; **Lev** 18:21; 26:6; **Num** 12:2(2); 13:22; 32; 14:7; 16:40; 20:17(3); 18; 19; 20; 21; 21:22(2); 23; 25:8(2); 31:16; 23(2); 33:8; **Deut** 1:19; 2:4; 7; 27; 28; 30; 3:21; 8:15; 9:26; 15:17; 18:10; 29:16; 31:29; **Josh** 1:11; 2:15; 18; 3:2; 16:1; 18:4; 8; 9; 12; 20:2; 21:2; 24:17; **Judg** 2:22; 3:23; 5:26; 28(2); 9:54; 11:16; 17; 18; 19; 20; 29(2); 20:12; **Ruth** 4:5; 10; **1 Sam** 9:4(4); 19:12; 31:4(2); **2 Sam** 2:29(2); 4:7; 5:20; 6:16; 18:14; 20:14; 23:16; 24:8; **1 Ki** 8:56; 10:29; 14:6; 18; 16:34; **2 Ki** 1:2; 3:26; 9:30; 14:25; 16:3; 17:17; 21:6; 23:10; 25:4; **1 Chr** 10:4; 11:18; 14:11; 15:29; **2 Chr** 1:17; 23:20; 30:10; 32:4; 33:6; **Ezra** 6:14; **Neh** 2:7; 13; 9:11; **Esth** 6:9; 11; **Job** 20:24; 22:13; 29:3; 41:2; **Ps** 8:8; 19:4; 21:7; 23:4; 32:3; 44:5(2); 59:4; 60:12; 66:3; 6; 12(2); 68:7; 73:9; 78:13; 84:6; 92:4; 106:9(2); 107:39; 108:13; 109:24; 115:7; 118:19; 20; 119:98; 104; 148; 136:14; 16; **Prov** 7:6; 11:9; 12:13; 24:3; **Eccl** 5:3; 14; 10:8; 18; 12:3; **Song** 2:9(2); **Isa** 8:8; 21; 9:19; 13:15; 14:19; 16:8; 21:1; 23:10; 27:4; 28:7(4); 15; 18; 30:6; 31; 34:10; 43:2(3); 16; 47:2; 48:21; 60:15; 62:10(2); 63:13; **Jer** 2:6(4); 3:9; 5:1; 9:6; 10; 12; 21; 17:24; 32:35; 51:4; 43; 52:7; **Lam** 3:22; 44; **Ezek** 5:17; 6:8; 9:4(2); 5; 12:5(2); 7; 12(2); 14:15(2); 17; 16:14; 21; 40; 20:26; 31; 23:37; 29:11(2); 33:28; 34:6; 39:14; 15; 40:28; 42:15; 46:9(2); 19; 47:3; 4(2); **Dan** 8:25; 9:2; 11:2; 10; 40; **Hos** 12:10; 13:1; **Joel** 3:17; **Am** 2:10; 4:3; 5:17; **Mic** 2:13; 5:8; **Nah** 1:12; 15; 3:4(2); **Hab** 1:6; 3:12; 14; 15(2); **Zech** 1:17; 7:7; 12; 14; 9:8; 10:11; 13:3; 9; 14:5; **Mt** 1:22; 2:15; 10:23; 12:1; 43; 19:24; **Mk** 2:4; 23; 6:55; 7:13; 31; 9:30; 10:25; 11:16; 16:20; **Lk** 1:78; 2:35; 4:14; 30; 5:19; 6:1; 8:1; 9:6; 11:24; 13:22; 24; 17:1; 11; 18:25; 19:1; **Jn** 1:3; 7; 10; 17(2); 3:17; 4:4; 8:59; 11:4; 14:6; 17:11; 20; **Acts** 1:2; 2:22; 43; 3:16(2); 4:16; 30; 5:12; 8:18; 40; 9:25; 32; 10:36; 43; 13:6; 38; 14:22; 24; 15:3; 11; 12; 41; 16:4; 6; 17:1; 23; 18:27; 19:1; 21; 20:3; 21:4; 19; 24:2; 28:25; **Rom** 1:2; 5; 8; 2:23; 3:7; 22; 24; 25; 30; 31; 4:13(2); 20; 5:1; 2; 9; 10; 11(2); 12(2); 16; 17(2); 18(2); 21(2); 6:4; 7:4; 7; 13(2); 25; 8:3; 11; 37; 11:11; 30; 31; 36; 12:3; 15:4; 18; 30(2); 16:27; **1 Cor** 1:1; 21(2); 2:10; 3:5; 15; 4:15; 8:6(2); 10:1; 11:12; 12:8(2); 15:57; 16:5(2); **2 Cor** 1:5; 11; 20; 2:14; 3:4; 4:15; 5:18; 20; 8:9; 9:11; 12; 13; 11:33; **Gal** 1:1(2); 12; 15; 2:19; 21; 3:14; 19; 26; 4:7; 23; 5:5; 6; 13; **Eph** 1:7; 2:8; 16; 18; 3:6; 9; 12; 16; 17; 4:6; **Phil** 1:19; 2:3; 3:9; 4:7; 13; **Col** 1:14; 16; 20; 22; 2:8; 12; 3:17; **1 Th** 4:2; 5:9; **2 Th** 2:13; 3:12; **1 Tim** 6:10; **2 Tim** 1:6; 10; 3:15; 4:17; **Titus** 1:3; 3:5; 6; **Phm** 1:22; **Heb** 1:2; 2:2; 10; 14; 15; 3:13; 4:14; 6:12; 7:9; 11; 19; 25; 9:14; 10:10; 20; 11:4(2); 29; 33; 39; 13:20; 21; **1 Pe** 1:3; 5; 12; 21; 22; 23; 2:5; 3:20; 21; 4:11; **2 Pe** 1:3; 4(2); 2:18(2); 20; **1 Jn** 4:9; **Rev** 8:13; 18:3; 22:14

THUS (766/738)

Gen 1:7; 2:1; 6:22; 9:11; 19:36; 20:16; 21:32; 24:30; 25:34; 30:43; 31:8(2); 41; 32:4(2); 37:35; 39:6; 42:25; 45:9; 47:17; 48:20; 50:17; **Ex** 3:14; 15; 4:22; 5:1; 10; 15; 6:9; 7:17; 8:1; 20; 9:1; 13; 10:3; 11:4; 12:11; 36; 50; 14:20; 31; 19:3; 20:22; 26:17; 24; 29:35; 32:27; 36:22; 29; 39:32; 40:16; **Lev** 4:20; 15:31; 16:3; 18:27; 25:50; **Num** 1:54; 2:34; 4:49; 7:89; 8:7; 14; 20; 26; 10:28; 15:11; 17:5; 11; 18:26; 28; 20:8; 14; 21; 21:31; 22:16; 23:5; 16; 32:8; 36:9; **Deut** 7:5; 9:25; 19:10; 20:15; 32:6; **Josh** 7:10; 13; 10:25; 11:16; 16:5; 21:13; 42; 22:16; 24:2; **Judg** 3:5; 5:31; 6:8; 8:28; 34; 9:56; 11:15; 21; 33; 17:4; 18:4; **1 Sam** 2:27; 7:12; 9:9; 10:18; 11:9; 14:9; 10; 15:2; 16:10; 18:25; 28; 19:4; 20:7; 22; 25:6; 26:18; 27:11(2); **2 Sam** 7:5; 8(2); 11:25; 12:7; 11; 15:26; 16:7; 17:15(2); 21; 18:33; 20:10; 23:1(2); 24:12; **1 Ki** 1:48; 2:30(3); 46; 3:22; 4:30; 5:11; 6:5; 7:18; 37; 48; 9:8; 10:29; 11:31; 12:10(2); 24; 13:2; 21; 14:5(2); 7; 16:12; 17:14; 20:2; 5; 13; 14; 28; 42; 21:19(2); 22:11; 27; **2 Ki** 1:4; 6; 11; 16; 2:21; 3:16; 17; 4:43; 5:4(2); 6:10; 7:1; 8:22; 9:3; 6; 12(3); 18; 19; 10:28; 16:16; 18:19; 29; 31; 19:3; 6(2); 10; 20; 32; 20:1; 5; 21:12; 22:15; 16; 18; 25:21; **1 Chr** 15:28; 17:4; 7(2); 21:10; 11; 24:4; 5; 29:26; **2 Chr** 1:17; 4:19; 7:11; 21; 10:10(2); 11:4; 12:5; 13; 13:18; 18:10; 26; 19:9; 20:15; 21:10; 12; 24:11; 20; 22; 29:25; 31:20; 32:4; 10; 22; 34:19; 23; 24; 26; 33; 36:23; **Ezra** 1:2; 4:24; 5:3; 7; 9; 11; 6:2; **Neh** 5:13; 13:18; 30; **Esth** 1:18; 2:12; 13; 6:9; 11; 9:5; **Job** 1:5; **Ps** 38:14; 63:4; 73:15; 21; 106:20; 29; 39; 109:5; 128:4; 147:20; **Isa** 7:7; 8:11; 10:24; 21:6; 16; 22:15; 24:13; 28:16; 29:22; 30:12; 15; 31:4; 36:4; 14; 16; 37:3; 6(2); 10; 21; 33; 38:1; 5; 42:5; 43:1; 14; 16; 44:2; 6; 24; 45:1; 11; 14; 18; 47:15; 48:17; 49:7; 8; 22; 25; 50:1; 51:22; 52:3; 4; 56:1; 4; 57:15; 65:8; 13; 66:1; 12; **Jer** 2:2; 5; 4:3; 27; 5:13; 14; 6:6; 9; 16; 21; 22; 7:3; 20; 21; 8:4; 9:7; 15; 17; 22; 23; 10:2; 11; 18; 11:3; 11; 21; 22; 12:14; 13:1; 9; 12; 13; 14:10(2); 15; 15:2; 19; 16:3; 5; 9; 17:5; 19; 21; 18:11; 13; 23; 19:1; 3; 11; 12; 15; 20:4; 21:3; 4; 8; 12; 22:1; 3; 6; 11; 18; 30; 23:2; 15; 16; 35; 37; 38; 24:5; 8; 25:8; 15; 27; 28; 32; 26:2; 4; 18; 27:2; 4(2); 16; 19; 21; 28:2; 11; 13; 14; 16; 29:4; 8; 10; 16; 17; 21; 25; 31; 32; 30:2; 5; 12; 18; 31:2; 7; 15; 16; 23; 35; 37; 32:3; 14; 15; 28; 36; 42; 33:2; 4; 10; 12; 17; 20; 24; 25; 34:2(2); 4; 13; 17; 35:8; 13; 17; 18; 19; 36:29; 30; 37:7(2); 9; 21; 38:2; 3; 4; 17; 39:16; 42:9; 15; 18; 43:10; 44:2; 7; 11; 25; 30; 45:2; 4(2); 47:2; 48:1; 40; 47; 49:1; 7; 12; 28; 35; 50:18; 33; 51:1; 4; 33; 36; 58; 64(2); 52:27; **Ezek** 1:11; 2:4; 3:11; 27; 5:5; 7; 8; 13; 6:3; 11; 12; 7:2; 5; 11:5(2); 7; 16; 17; 12:10; 19; 23; 28; 13:3; 6; 8; 13; 15; 18; 20; 14:4; 6; 21; 15:6; 8; 16:3; 13; 36; 59; 17:3; 9; 19; 22; 20:3; 5; 27; 30; 39; 47; 21:3; 9; 24; 26; 28; 22:3; 19; 28; 23:7; 21; 22; 27; 28; 32; 35; 39; 44; 46; 48; 24:3; 6; 9; 21; 24; 27; 25:3; 6; 8; 12; 13; 15; 16; 26:3; 7; 15; 19; 27:3; 28:2; 6; 12; 22; 25; 29:3; 8; 13; 19; 30:2; 6; 10; 13; 19; 22; 25; 31:7; 10; 15; 32:3; 11; 33:10; 25; 27(2); 34:2; 10; 11; 17; 20; 30; 35:3; 7; 13; 14; 36:2; 3; 4; 5; 6; 7; 13; 22; 33; 37; 37:5; 9; 12; 19; 21; 38:3; 10; 14; 17; 23; 39:1; 16; 17; 25; 41:19; 43:18; 20; 44:6; 9; 45:9; 18; 20; 46:1; 15; 16; 47:13; 17; 21; **Dan** 1:16; 21; 2:24; 25; 4:14; 6:6; 7:5; 23; 11:17; 39; **Hos** 10:4; 15; **Am** 1:3; 6; 9; 11; 13; 2:1; 4; 6; 3:11; 12; 4:12; 5:3; 4; 7:1; 4; 7; 11; 17; 8:1; **Ob** 1; **Mic** 2:3; 3:5; 5:6; 14; **Nah** 1:12; **Hag** 1:2; 5; 7; 2:6; 11; **Zech** 1:3; 4; 14; 16; 17; 2:8; 3:7; 6:12; 7:9; 12; 14; 8:2; 3; 4; 6; 7; 9; 14; 19; 20; 23; 11:4; 11; 12:1; 14:5; **Mal** 1:4; 13; **Mt** 2:5; 3:15; 15:6; 19:12; 26:54; **Mk** 2:8; 7:18; 19; **Lk** 1:25; 18:11; 19:31; 24:46(2); **Jn** 4:6; **Acts** 3:18; 13:34; 21:11; 26:12; 24; **Rom** 5:12; **1 Cor** 7:36; 8:12; 9:26(2); 14:25; **2 Cor** 5:14; 16; **Eph** 2:15; **1 Th** 4:17; **Heb** 6:17; 9:6; **Jas** 2:17; 3:12; **Rev** 2:15; 9:17; 18:21

TO (20825/13908)

Gen 1:11; 12(2); 14; 15; 16(2); 17; 18(2); 21(2); 24(2); 25(3); 26; 28; 29; 30(3); 2:5(2); 9; 10; 15; 18; 19(2); 20(4); 21; 22; 24; 3:1; 2; 4; 6(3); 9(2); 12; 13; 14; 16; 17; 19(2); 22; 23; 24(2); 4:3(2); 6; 8; 9; 10; 11; 12; 13; 15; 18; 23(2); 26(2); 6:1(3); 4(2); 13; 16; 17; 19; 20(2); 21; 22; 7:1; 3; 4; 5; 9; 10; 15; 8:1; 6; 7; 8; 9(2); 11; 12; 13; 15; 19; 20; 9:1; 8(2); 11; 15; 16; 17; 20; 24; 25; 10:1; 5(2); 8; 11; 20(2); 21; 25; 31(3); 32; 11:2; 3; 5; 6(2); 31(3); 12:1(2); 4; 5(3); 6; 7(4); 8(2); 10(2); 11(3); 15(2); 18; 13:1; 3; 4; 6; 8; 9(3); 14; 15; 17; 18; 14:1; 7; 10; 17; 21; 22(2); 23; 15:1; 4; 5(2); 6; 7(3); 9; 10; 13; 15; 17; 18(2); 16:2(2); 3(2); 4; 5; 6(2); 7; 9(2); 10; 11; 13; 16; 17:1(2); 7(2); 8; 9; 15; 17; 18; 21; 23; 18:1; 2(2); 5; 6; 7(3); 9; 10(2); 13; 14(2); 16; 19(3); 21(2); 25(2); 27(2); 29; 31(2); 33; 19:1(2); 2; 3; 5(4); 6; 8(3); 9(2); 11; 12; 13; 14(3); 15; 16; 17(2); 18; 19; 20(2); 21; 27; 29; 30; 31(3); 34; 37; 38; 20:1; 3(2); 5; 6; 9(4); 10; 13(3); 14(2); 16; 17; 21:2; 3(2); 5; 7; 9; 10; 12(3); 14; 16; 17(2); 22(2); 23(5); 27; 32; 22:1(2); 2; 3; 5(2); 7; 9; 10; 11; 12; 14; 15; 19(2); 20(2); 23; 23:2(2); 3; 5; 7; 9; 11(2); 13; 14; 15; 16; 18; 20; 24:2; 4(2); 5(4); 6; 7(3); 8; 9; 10(2); 11; 12; 13; 14(2); 15; 16(2); 17; 18; 20(2); 21; 23; 24(2); 25(2); 27; 29; 30(3); 32(2); 33; 36(2); 38(2); 39; 40; 41; 42; 43(4); 44; 45(2); 47; 48; 49(2); 50; 52(2); 53(3); 54; 56(2); 58; 60; 63; 65(2); 25:5; 6(2); 8; 11; 12; 13; 16; 17; 22; 23; 24; 30; 32(2); 33(3); 26:1; 2(2); 3(2); 4; 7(2); 8(2); 9; 10; 11; 13; 16; 23; 24; 26; 27(2); 29; 32(2); 33; 35; 27:1(2); 3; 4; 5(4); 6(2); 8; 9; 10; 11; 12(2); 13; 14; 18; 19; 20(2); 21; 22; 25(2); 26; 29(2); 31(2); 32; 33; 34; 37(2); 38; 39; 40; 42(3); 43; 45; 46(2); 28:1; 2(2); 4(2); 5(2); 6(2); 7; 9(3); 11(2); 12; 13; 14(2); 15(2); 20(2); 21; 22; 29:1; 4; 5; 6; 7; 10; 13(3); 14; 15; 19(2); 20; 21(2); 23(3); 24; 25(3); 26; 29; 30; 34; 30:1; 3; 4; 9; 14; 15; 16(2); 17; 18; 22; 24; 25(4); 27; 29; 30; 33; 34; 38(2); 41; 31:3(3); 4(2); 5; 7; 9; 11; 12; 13(2); 14; 16; 18(2); 19; 20(2); 24(3); 26(2); 28; 29(3); 31; 35; 36; 39; 43(3); 46; 51; 52(2); 54; 55; 32:3; 4;

5; 6(3); 8; 9(3); 13; 16(2); 17; 18; 19; 27; 30; 32; 33:3(2); 4; 8; 11; 13; 14(2); 16; 17; 18; 34:1(2); 3(2); 4; 6(2); 7; 8; 9(2); 11(2); 12(2); 14(4); 15; 16(2); 19; 20; 21; 22(2); 23; 25; 30; 35:1(4); 2(2); 3(2); 6; 7; 9; 10; 11; 12(2); 16(2); 17(2); 19; 20; 26; 27; 29; 36:4; 5; 6; 7; 12; 14; 30; 40; 43; 37:2; 4; 5; 6; 7; 8; 9(2); 10(4); 12; 13(3); 14(3); 17; 18; 19; 22(2); 23(2); 25(3); 26; 27; 28(2); 29; 30; 32; 33; 35(3); 36; 38:1; 2; 8(3); 9(3); 11; 12; 13(2); 14(2); 16(3); 18(2); 20; 22; 24; 25(2); 26; 27; 39:1; 3; 7; 8(2); 10(3); 11; 14(6); 17(4); 19(2); 22; 40:1; 6; 8(4); 9(2); 12; 13(2); 14(2); 16; 20; 21; 22; 41:1; 8; 9; 11; 12(2); 13(2); 14; 15(2); 17; 24(2); 25(2); 28(2); 32(2); 34; 38; 39; 40(2); 41; 44; 50(2); 52; 54; 55(4); 56; 57(2); 42:1; 2; 3; 5; 6(2); 7(4); 9(2); 10(2); 12(2); 14(2); 16; 18; 19; 20; 21; 22; 23; 24; 25(4); 27; 28(3); 29(2); 30; 31; 33; 34(2); 36(2); 37(3); 38; 43:2(2); 3; 5; 6; 7; 8; 9; 11; 13; 15; 16(2); 18; 19; 20; 21; 22; 23; 26; 29(2); 30; 32; 33(2); 34; 44:2; 4(2); 6; 7; 8; 10; 11; 13; 14; 15; 16; 17; 18; 20; 21(2); 22; 23; 24; 27; 28; 29; 30; 31; 32(2); 33; 34; 45:1; 3; 4(2); 5; 7(2); 8; 9(3); 10; 11; 12; 17(3); 18; 21; 22(3); 23; 24; 25(2); 27(2); 46:1(2); 2; 3(2); 4; 5; 6; 7; 8; 15; 18(2); 20(2); 22; 25(2); 26; 27(2); 28(4); 29(3); 30; 31(4); 32; 34; 47:2; 3(2); 4(2); 5(2); 8; 9(2); 12; 15; 17; 18(2); 21; 22; 23; 24(2); 26; 29; 31(2); 48:1; 2; 3(2); 4(2); 5(2); 7(3); 9(2); 11(2); 12; 15; 17(2); 18; 21(2); 22; 49:2; 4(2); 6; 10; 11(2); 15; 26; 28(2); 29(3); 33; 50:2; 4; 7; 10; 13; 14(2); 15; 16; 17(3); 19; 20(2); 21; 23; 24(5); **Ex** 1:1; 9; 11; 15; 18; 19(2); 2:4(2); 5(2); 7; 8; 9; 10; 11(2); 13; 14; 15; 16; 18; 20; 21(2); 23; 3:1(2); 2; 4(2); 6; 8(5); 9; 10; 11(2); 12; 13(6); 14(3); 15(4); 16(3); 17(2); 18(3); 4:1(2); 2; 4; 5; 6; 9; 10(2); 11; 14; 15; 16(2); 18(4); 19(2); 20; 21(2); 22; 23(2); 24(2); 25; 27(2); 30; 5:1; 2; 3; 4(2); 7; 8; 10; 12; 13; 15; 16(2); 17; 20; 21(3); 22; 23(3); 6:1(2); 2(2); 3(4); 4; 6; 8(3); 9; 10; 11; 13(2); 16; 17; 19; 23; 25; 26(2); 27(2); 28(2); 29(3); 7:1(2); 2(2); 7; 8; 9(2); 10; 14(2); 15(4); 16(2); 17; 18; 19(2); 20; 24; 8:1(3); 2; 5(3); 8; 9(2); 10; 12; 13; 16(2); 18; 19; 20(3); 25; 26(2); 27; 28; 29(2); 31; 9:1(2); 2; 4; 8; 12; 13(2); 14; 18; 20; 22; 23; 27; 29(2); 33; 10:1(2); 3(3); 4; 5(2); 6; 7(2); 8(2); 9; 10; 12; 21; 24; 25; 26; 28(2); 11:1; 5; 8(2); 9; 12:1; 2; 3(2); 4(3); 13; 14(2); 21(2); 23(3); 25(2); 26; 29(2); 35; 37; 41(2); 42; 43; 48(2); 51(2); 13:1; 2; 3; 5(2); 6; 9; 10; 11(2); 12; 14(2); 15(2); 17(2); 21(3); 14:1; 2; 10; 11(3); 12; 13; 15(3); 20(2); 21; 22; 24; 26; 27; 29; 15:1(2); 5; 13; 21; 23; 25; 26; 27; 16:1; 3(3); 4; 6; 8(2); 9(2); 10(2); 11; 12; 15(3); 16(2); 18; 21; 23(3); 25; 27; 28(2); 32; 33(2); 34; 35(2); 17:1(2); 2; 3; 4(2); 5; 9; 10(2); 14; 16; 18:5; 6(2); 7; 8(2); 12(3); 13; 15(3); 16; 17; 18; 19(2); 21; 22; 23(2); 26; 27; 19:1; 2; 3(3); 4(2); 5; 6(2); 8; 9(3); 10(2); 12(3); 14; 15; 16; 17; 20; 21(2); 23(2); 24(3); 25(2); 20:5(2); 6(2); 8; 19; 20(2); 22(2); 23; 24; 26; 21:6(3); 7; 8(3); 9(2); 12; 14; 15; 16; 17; 18; 19; 28; 29(3); 30; 31(2); 32; 34; 36; 22:5; 7(2); 8(2); 9(2); 10(2); 12; 13; 16; 17(3); 18; 19; 20(2); 23; 25(2); 26; 27; 29(2); 30; 31(2); 23:1; 2(3); 3; 4; 13; 14; 20(2); 22(2); 23; 24(2); 27(2); 31(2); 33; 24:1(2); 4; 5; 8; 12(2); 13; 14(3); 16; 25:1; 2; 7; 9; 22; 27(2); 35; 40(2); 26:3(2); 5; 7; 13; 17; 28; 30; 27:3; 7; 20(2); 21; 28:1; 3(3); 4; 14; 15; 21(2); 25; 28; 36; 41; 42(2); 43(2); 29:1(3); 4; 13; 18(2); 22; 25; 28; 29(2); 30; 33(2); 35(2); 36; 41; 42; 44(2); 30:1; 4; 10; 11; 12; 13(2); 14; 15(2); 16; 17; 20(3); 21(2); 22; 24; 25; 30; 31(2); 32(2); 34; 35; 36; 37(2); 38; 31:1; 4(2); 5; 10; 11; 12; 13; 14(2); 15(2); 16; 32:1(2); 2(2); 3; 5; 6(2); 7; 8; 9; 12(4); 13(3); 14; 17; 20; 21(2); 23; 24(2); 25; 26(2); 27(2); 28; 29; 30(3); 31; 33; 34(2); 33:1(4); 3; 5(4); 7(2); 8; 9; 11(4); 12(2); 15; 17; 19; 34:1; 2(2); 7; 12; 15; 24; 26; 27(2); 30; 31(2); 34(2); 35; 35:1(2); 2(2); 4; 5(2); 9; 19; 22; 27; 29(3); 30; 32(2); 33; 34; 35; 36:1(3); 2; 3; 5(2); 6; 7; 10(2); 12; 13; 18; 22; 24; 33(2); 34; 37:3; 5; 14(2); 15; 21; 27; 29; 38:7; 18; 21; 24; 25; 26; 39:3; 4; 14(3); 21; 26; 30; 31(2); 32; 33; 41(2); 42; 40:1; 4; 12; 13; 15; 16; 17; 35; **Lev** 1:1(2); 2(3); 4; 9; 13; 14; 15; 17; 2:1; 2(2); 3; 8(3); 9; 10; 11(2); 12; 13; 14; 16; 3:3; 4; 5; 6; 9(2); 10; 11; 14; 15; 4:1; 2(2); 3; 4; 5; 9; 12; 16; 23; 27; 28; 31; 35(2); 5:4(2); 6; 7(2); 8; 10; 11; 12(3); 14; 15(3); 16(3); 17; 18; 6:1; 2(2); 4; 5(2); 6(2); 8; 11; 15; 18; 19; 20; 21; 22; 24; 25(2); 30; 7:4; 5; 10(2); 11; 14(2); 18(2); 20; 21; 22; 23; 25; 28; 29(3); 30; 32; 34(2); 35(3); 36(2); 38(2); 8:1; 5(2); 11; 12; 15; 16; 21; 25; 28; 31; 34(2); 9:1; 2; 3; 4(2); 6(2); 7(2); 8; 9; 12; 13; 16; 18; 19; 23; 10:3; 4; 6(2); 7; 8; 11; 12(3); 13; 15; 17(3); 19; 11:1(2); 2; 4; 5; 6; 7; 8; 10; 11; 12; 20; 21; 23; 26; 27; 28; 29; 31; 35; 37; 38; 45; 47; 12:1; 2; 6(2); 8; 13:1; 2(2); 3; 4; 5; 9; 12; 15; 16; 19; 37; 49; 59(2); 14:1; 2; 4(2); 7; 8; 11; 14; 17; 18; 19; 21(2); 22; 23(2); 25; 28; 29(2); 31(2); 33; 35; 36(2); 37; 38; 41; 45; 49; 57; 15:1; 2(2); 3; 14(2); 26; 29(2); 16:1; 2(2); 10(3); 17; 18; 22; 27; 30; 32; 34; 17:1; 2(4); 4(4); 5(4); 6; 7; 8; 9(3); 11(2); 12; 14; 18:1; 2(2); 3(2); 4; 6(2); 12; 13; 17(2); 18(2); 19; 20; 21; 23(2); 19:1; 2(2); 4; 5; 11; 15; 20(2); 21(2); 23; 24; 25; 29(2); 31(2); 34; 20:1; 2(3); 3(2); 4; 5; 6(2); 9; 10; 11; 12; 13; 15; 16; 22; 24(3); 26; 27; 21:1(3); 2; 3; 4; 6; 7; 8; 10; 16; 17(2); 21(3); 24(2); 22:1; 2(2); 3(2); 8; 12; 13; 14(2); 15; 16; 17; 18(4); 21(3); 22(2); 24; 26; 27; 29; 33; 23:1; 2(3); 6; 8; 9; 10(4); 11; 12; 13; 14; 16(2); 17; 18(2); 20; 21; 23; 24; 25; 26; 27; 28; 32(2); 33; 34(2); 36(2); 37(3); 38; 41; 44; 24:1; 2(2); 7; 9; 11; 12; 13; 15; 16(2); 17; 19; 20; 21; 23; 25:1; 2(3); 4; 8; 9(2); 10(3); 11; 12; 13; 14; 15(3); 16(4); 25; 26(2); 27(3); 28(3); 30; 38(2); 39(2); 41(2); 46; 47(4); 49; 50(3); 51; 52; 55; 26:1(2); 5; 8; 16; 21(3); 23; 24; 27; 28; 31; 32; 36; 37; 40(2); 41; 44; 27:1; 2(4); 3(2); 5; 6; 8(2); 9(2); 11; 13(2); 14(2); 15(2); 16(2); 17; 18(2); 19(3); 20(2); 21; 22; 23(3); 24(2); 25(2); 27(3); 28(2); 29(2); 30; 31(2); 32; **Num** 1:1; 2; 3(2); 18; 20(3); 22(3); 24(3); 26(3); 28(3); 30(3); 32(3); 34(3); 36(3); 38(3); 40(3); 42(3); 45(2); 48; 50(2); 51(3); 52; 54; 2:1; 3; 5; 9; 10; 12; 16(2); 18; 20; 24(2); 25; 27; 32; 34(2); 3:3; 5; 7(2); 8(3); 9(2); 10(2); 11; 13; 14; 16; 22; 23; 26(2); 28; 29; 31; 32; 34; 35; 36; 38(4); 40; 43; 44; 48; 50; 51(2); 4:1; 3(2); 4; 5; 15(3); 17; 19(2); 20; 21; 23(3); 27; 30(2); 32; 35; 37; 39; 41; 43; 45; 47(2); 49(3); 5:1; 4; 5; 6; 7; 8(3); 9; 11; 12(2); 15(2); 19(2); 21; 24; 25; 6:1; 2(5); 4; 5; 6; 7; 8; 10(2); 11; 12; 13; 14; 17; 21(4); 22; 23(2); 25; 7:1; 4; 5(3); 6; 7(2); 8(2); 9; 11; 13; 19; 25;

31; 37; 43; 49; 55; 61; 67; 73; 79; 85; 86; 89(3); 8:1; 2(2); 3; 4(2); 5; 7(2); 12(2); 13; 15; 16; 17; 19(3); 20(3); 21; 22(2); 23; 24(2); 26(3); 9:1; 3; 5; 7; 8; 9; 10; 12; 13; 14(2); 20(2); 10:1; 4; 6; 7; 8; 9; 11; 13; 14; 18; 22; 25; 28; 29(3); 30(3); 31; 32(2); 33; 36; 11:2(2); 4(2); 11; 12(3); 13(3); 14; 16(4); 18(2); 20; 22(2); 23(2); 25; 26; 29; 30; 34; 35; 12:4(2); 6(2); 8(2); 11; 13; 14; 13:1; 2(2); 3; 16; 17(3); 22; 23; 26(3); 27; 30; 31; 14:2; 3(4); 4(2); 7(2); 8; 10; 11; 13; 14(2); 16(3); 18; 19; 20; 22; 23; 26; 28(2); 29; 34; 35; 36; 38; 39; 40(2); 44(2); 15:1; 2(4); 3(4); 4; 7; 8(2); 10; 12(2); 13; 14; 17; 18(3); 19; 21; 22; 24(2); 25; 28; 33(2); 34; 35(2); 37; 38(3); 39; 41; 16:3; 5(5); 8; 9(6); 10; 12; 13; 15; 16; 19; 20; 23; 24; 25; 26; 28; 30; 31; 36; 37; 38; 40(4); 44; 46(2); 50; 17:1; 2(2); 6(2); 8; 9; 10(2); 12; 18:1(2); 3; 4; 5; 6(2); 7(3); 8(2); 9; 10; 11; 12(2); 13; 15; 16(2); 17; 19(2); 20; 24(3); 25; 26(3); 27; 28(2); 29; 30(2); 19:1; 2; 3; 10(2); 20:5(3); 6(2); 7; 8(2); 10; 12(2); 14; 15; 16; 17(2); 18; 19; 21; 22; 23; 24(2); 25; 26; 27; 21:1; 2; 3; 4; 5; 7(2); 8; 15; 16(2); 17; 18; 19(2); 20; 21; 23(2); 24; 27; 29(2); 30; 32; 33(2); 34(3); 22:2; 4; 5(3); 6; 7(2); 8(3); 9; 10(2); 11; 12; 13(4); 14(2); 16(3); 17; 18(3); 19; 20(4); 23; 26(3); 28(2); 29; 30(4); 32(2); 34; 35(2); 36; 37(4); 38(3); 39; 40(2); 41; 23:1; 3(3); 4; 5; 6; 11(3); 12; 13(2); 14(2); 15; 16; 17(2); 18; 20; 25; 26; 27(2); 28; 29; 24:1(3); 2; 10(2); 11; 12(3); 13(2); 14(2); 25; 25:1; 2(2); 3; 4; 5(2); 6; 10; 12; 13; 16; 26:1(2); 2(2); 12; 15; 18; 20; 22; 23; 25; 26; 27; 28; 35; 37(2); 38; 41; 42(2); 43; 44; 47; 48; 50; 52; 53(2); 54(3); 55; 56; 57; 59(2); 60; 62; 27:6; 7(2); 8(3); 9; 10; 11(2); 12(2); 13; 14; 15; 18; 20; 28:1; 2(4); 3(2); 6; 7; 8; 11; 13; 15; 19; 22; 24; 26; 27; 30; 29:2; 5; 6(2); 8; 12; 13; 18; 21; 24; 27; 30; 33; 36; 37; 39; 30:1; 2(3); 3; 7; 11; 13; 14(3); 31:1; 2; 3(2); 4; 6(2); 12(4); 13; 15; 16; 21(2); 25; 27; 28; 29(2); 30; 36; 41; 43; 47; 48; 49; 50; 52; 32:2(3); 5; 6(3); 8; 9; 11; 14; 16; 17(2); 18; 19; 20; 25; 27; 28(3); 29; 31; 33(3); 38; 39; 40; 33:2; 7; 9; 14; 38; 50; 51(2); 53; 54(4); 56(3); 34:1; 2(3); 3; 4(3); 5; 7; 8; 9; 10; 11(3); 13(3); 14(2); 16; 18; 29; 35:1; 2; 3; 5; 6(3); 7; 8(2); 9; 10(2); 11; 16; 17; 18; 19(2); 21(2); 24; 25; 28; 29; 30; 31; 32(2); 36:2(4); 3(2); 4; 5; 7; 9; 11; **Deut** 1:1; 2; 3(4); 5; 6; 7(4); 8(4); 9(2); 14; 17; 19(2); 20(2); 21; 22(2); 24; 25(2); 27(2); 28; 29; 30; 31; 33(3); 35(2); 36; 38; 39; 41(2); 42; 43; 44; 45(2); 46; 2:1; 2; 4; 5; 9(2); 12; 14(2); 15; 17; 18; 19; 22; 24; 25; 26; 27(3); 29; 31(4); 32; 33; 36; 37; 3:1(2); 2(3); 6; 8; 11; 12; 13; 14; 15; 16; 18; 20(3); 21(2); 24; 26(3); 27; 28; 4:1(2); 2; 4; 5(2); 6; 7(2); 9(2); 10(3); 11; 12; 13(2); 14(2); 15(2); 19(3); 20; 23; 25(2); 26(2); 30; 31; 32; 34(2); 35; 38(2); 42; 45; 48; 5:1(2); 4; 5(2); 9(2); 10(2); 12; 15; 22(2); 23; 27; 28(3); 30(2); 31(2); 32(3); 6:1(2); 2; 3; 7; 10(3); 18; 19; 20; 21; 23(2); 24(2); 25; 7:1; 2(2); 3; 4; 6(2); 8; 10(3); 11; 12(3); 13(2); 16(2); 18(2); 19; 22; 23; 24; 25; 26; 8:1(2); 2(2); 3; 6(2); 16; 18(2); 20; 9:1(3); 3; 4; 5(3); 6; 7(2); 8(2); 9; 10(2); 11; 12; 13; 18(2); 19(2); 22; 26; 28(3); 10:1(2); 4(3); 6; 7(2); 8(6); 10; 11(3); 12(4); 13; 14; 15; 20; 22; 11:3(2); 4(3); 5; 6; 8; 9(2); 10; 11; 12; 13; 16; 19; 21(2); 22(5); 24; 25(2); 28; 29; 31; 32; 12:1(2); 5; 7; 9; 10; 11(2); 13; 15; 18; 19; 20; 21; 26; 29; 30(2); 31(3); 32(2); 13:2(2); 3(2); 4; 5(4); 7(2); 8(2); 9(2); 10; 12; 17; 18(3); 14:2(2); 21(3); 23(2); 24(2); 25; 15:2; 3; 4; 5; 6; 8; 9; 10(3); 11(2); 12; 14; 16; 17(2); 18; 19; 21; 16:1; 2(2); 6; 7; 8; 9(3); 10; 11; 12; 15; 17; 18; 21; 17:1(2); 5(2); 6(2); 7(2); 8(2); 9(2); 10(3); 11(4); 12; 14; 16(4); 19(2); 20(2); 18:2; 3; 5(2); 6; 8; 9; 12; 14; 16; 17; 18; 20(2); 22; 19:2; 3; 5(4); 8(3); 9(2); 11; 12; 14; 16; 19(3); 20:1; 2; 3; 4(2); 5(2); 6; 7(2); 8(2); 9(2); 10(2); 11(2); 15; 18(2); 19(2); 20; 21:1; 2; 3; 4; 5(3); 6; 8; 10; 12; 13; 16(2); 19(2); 20; 21; 22; 22:1; 2(2); 5(2); 6; 13; 14; 15; 16(2); 19; 21(3); 22; 23; 24(2); 26; 27; 29(2); 23:2; 3; 4; 5; 8; 14(2); 15(2); 16; 18(2); 19; 20(4); 21(3); 22; 23; 24:4; 5(2); 8(2); 9; 10; 11(2); 13(2); 15(2); 16(3); 18; 19; 22; 25:1; 2(3); 5(3); 6; 7(5); 8(2); 9(2); 11; 16; 17; 19; 26:2(2); 3(6); 5(2); 7; 9; 11; 12; 13(2); 14; 15; 16(2); 17; 18; 19; 27:2; 5; 6; 9; 12; 13; 14; 15; 18; 25; 28:1(2); 7; 8; 9(2); 11(2); 12(5); 13; 14(3); 15(2); 20; 21(2); 24; 25(2); 31(3); 32; 35; 36; 38; 44(2); 45; 50; 56(3); 60; 63(4); 64; 68(3); 29:1; 2(4); 4(4); 7(2); 8(3); 11; 13(4); 18; 21; 24; 26; 27; 29(3); 30:1(2); 2(2); 4; 5; 6; 10(2); 12; 13; 16(4); 18(2); 20(4); 31:1; 2(2); 4(2); 5(3); 7(5); 9(2); 11; 12; 13(2); 14; 16(2); 18; 19; 20(3); 21(2); 22; 23; 28(2); 29(2); 32:3; 8(2); 16(2); 17(4); 21(4); 22; 26; 30; 35; 40; 41; 43; 45; 46(3); 47; 48; 49; 50; 52; 33:7; 17; 19; 26; 29; 34:1(2); 4(4); 5; 6; 10; 11; **Josh** 1:1(2); 2(2); 3; 4; 5; 6(3); 7(4); 8(2); 11(3); 12; 15; 18; 2:1(2); 2; 3(3); 4; 6; 7(2); 8; 9; 10; 12(2); 16(2); 17; 18; 21; 22; 23; 24; 3:1; 5; 6; 7(2); 8; 9; 13; 14; 15; 4:1(2); 5(2); 6(2); 7; 8(3); 9; 10(3); 11; 12; 13; 15; 16; 18(2); 21(2); 23; 5:2; 6(2); 9(2); 13(3); 14(3); 15; 6:2; 5; 6; 7; 8; 10; 14; 15; 16; 17; 19; 22(2); 25(2); 7:2(2); 3(2); 6; 7(2); 10; 12; 14(2); 19(3); 22; 23(2); 24; 26(2); 8:1(2); 2(2); 3; 8; 9; 10; 14; 16; 18; 19; 20(3); 23; 24(2); 27; 28; 29; 30; 31; 34; 9:1; 2; 3; 4; 6(4); 7; 8(2); 9; 10(2); 11(3); 12(2); 15(2); 17; 18; 19(2); 20(2); 21; 22; 24(2); 25(2); 26; 27; 10:1(3); 3; 4; 6(2); 8; 10; 12; 13; 15; 18; 19; 21(2); 22; 23; 24(2); 25(2); 28(2); 29; 30(2); 31; 32(2); 33; 34; 35(2); 36; 37(2); 38; 39(3); 43; 11:1(4); 2; 3; 5; 6; 8(3); 9; 17; 20; 23(4); 12:1; 3; 5; 6; 7(3); 13:1(2); 4(2); 5; 6; 7; 14(2); 15(2); 23; 24(3); 26(2); 28; 29(2); 31; 33(2); 14:1; 3; 4(2); 6(3); 7(2); 10; 12; 13; 14; 15:1; 3(5); 4; 6(2); 8(2); 9(3); 10(4); 11(4); 12; 13(3); 15; 16; 18(3); 20; 46; 63; 16:1(4); 2(2); 3(2); 5; 6; 7(2); 8(2); 10; 17:2(2); 4(2); 5; 7(2); 8; 9(2); 12; 13; 14(2); 15; 17(2); 18:3(2); 4(2); 6; 8(3); 9; 10(2); 11; 12; 13(2); 14; 15; 16(4); 17(2); 18; 19; 20(2); 21; 28; 19:1; 8; 10; 11(2); 13; 16; 17(2); 18; 22; 23; 24; 26; 27(3); 29(3); 31; 32(2); 34; 39; 40; 47; 48; 49(2); 50; 20:1; 2(2); 4; 6(2); 21:1(3); 2(3); 3; 7; 8; 12; 13; 27; 33; 34; 40; 43(3); 44(2); 45(2); 22:2; 3; 4(3); 5(7); 6; 7(3); 8(2); 9(4); 10; 12(2); 13(3); 15(4); 16; 19; 21; 23(3); 24(3); 26; 27(2); 28(3); 29; 31; 32(3); 33; 23:1(2); 2; 3; 4(2); 6(4); 7(2); 8(2); 9(2); 11; 12(3); 13; 14; 15; 16; 24:1; 2; 4(4); 5; 6(2); 7; 9(2); 10(2); 11; 15(2); 16; 19; 21; 22(2); 23; 24; 27(4); 28; 29; 33(2); **Judg** 1:1(3); 3(3); 7(2); 9; 12; 14(3); 15; 20; 21; 23; 24(2); 25; 26(2); 27; 28; 33; 34(2); 35; 2:1(3); 3; 4; 5; 6(2); 10; 12(2); 15; 17(2); 18; 19(3); 22; 3:2; 3; 4; 6(2); 9; 10; 13;

15(2); 17; 20; 24(3); 26; 28(3); 4:3; 5; 6; 8; 9; 10; 12(2); 13; 14; 17; 18(3); 19(2); 20; 21; 22(2); 5:3(2); 11; 16; 18; 23(2); 26(2); 30; 6:5; 6; 7(2); 8(2); 10; 11(2); 12(2); 13(2); 14; 15; 16; 17; 18; 19; 20; 22; 23; 24(2); 25(2); 26; 27(2); 29; 30; 31(2); 35(2); 36; 39; 7:2(2); 4(4); 5(3); 6(2); 7(2); 8; 9; 10(2); 11(2); 13(3); 15; 17(2); 19; 22; 25; 8:1(3); 2; 3; 4; 5(2); 6; 8(2); 9; 15(2); 18; 20; 22; 23; 24(2); 27(2); 35; 9:1(2); 3; 5; 7(3); 8(2); 9(2); 10; 11(2); 12; 13(2); 14; 15; 16; 21; 24; 26; 29; 31(2); 33; 35; 36(2); 38; 40; 48(2); 50; 51; 52; 54(2); 55; 56; 10:1; 4; 9; 10; 11; 12; 14; 15(3); 18; 11:2; 4; 5; 6; 7(2); 8(2); 9(3); 10(2); 12(2); 13; 14; 15; 16; 17(2); 18; 19(2); 20; 22(2); 24; 30; 31; 32; 33; 34(2); 35(2); 36(4); 37; 39; 40; 12:1(3); 2; 3(2); 5; 6; 13:3(2); 4(2); 5(2); 6; 7(3); 8(2); 9(2); 10(3); 11(3); 12; 13(2); 15; 16(2); 17(2); 18; 19; 20; 21; 22; 23(2); 25; 14:1; 3(2); 4; 5(3); 8(2); 9(2); 10(2); 11; 12(3); 13(2); 14(2); 15(4); 16(5); 17; 18(2); 19(3); 20; 15:1(2); 2; 3; 4; 6; 7; 10(4); 11(6); 12(4); 13; 14; 18; 19; 16:1(2); 3; 5(3); 6(2); 7; 8; 9; 10; 11; 12; 13(2); 14; 15; 16(2); 17(2); 18; 19(2); 21; 22; 23(3); 26; 28; 17:2; 3(4); 4(2); 8(3); 9(4); 10(2); 11(2); 13; 18:1(2); 2(4); 3; 4; 5; 6; 7(2); 8(2); 9(2); 10; 12; 13(2); 14(2); 15(2); 17; 18; 19(5); 23(2); 24; 25; 26; 27(3); 28; 29; 30; 19:1; 2; 3(3); 5(3); 6(2); 7; 8; 9(3); 10(2); 11; 12(2); 13(2); 14; 15(3); 18(3); 21; 22(2); 23(2); 24; 25(2); 27; 28(2); 20:1; 3; 4(2); 5; 8(2); 9; 10(2); 13(2); 14(3); 18(3); 20(2); 21; 25; 26; 28; 31(3); 32; 36; 39; 40(2); 45(2); 47; 48(2); 21:1; 2; 3; 5(3); 8(4); 12; 13(2); 18; 19; 21(2); 22(5); 23; 24(2); **Ruth** 1:1(2); 2; 7(2); 8(2); 10(2); 12; 14; 15(2); 16(2); 17; 18(2); 19(2); 20; 22; 2:2(3); 3(3); 4; 5; 8(2); 9(2); 10(2); 11(3); 13; 14(2); 15; 18; 19; 20(3); 21; 22; 23; 3:1; 3(2); 5(2); 6(2); 7; 13; 14; 16; 17(2); 4:1; 3(2); 4(2); 5; 7(2); 8; 9; 10; 11; 12; 13; 14; 15(2); 16; 17; **1 Sam** 1:3(2); 4(3); 5; 6; 7; 8(2); 10; 11; 14; 19; 20; 21(2); 22; 23(2); 24; 25; 26; 28(2); 2:5; 6; 8; 10; 11(2); 14; 15(2); 16; 19(3); 20(2); 22; 23; 25; 27(3); 28(5); 29; 34; 35; 36(2); 3:1; 2(2); 5; 6; 7; 8; 9; 11; 12; 14; 15; 17(3); 18; 19; 20; 21; 4:1(2); 3; 4; 7; 8; 9; 10; 12; 16; 19; 20; 5:1; 3; 4; 5; 8(2); 10(4); 11; 12; 6:2; 3(2); 4(2); 5; 7; 8; 9(3); 10; 12(3); 13; 14; 15; 16; 17; 18(3); 20(2); 21; 7:1; 3(2); 5(2); 8(3); 9(2); 10; 14(2); 16(2); 17(2); 8:1; 4; 5(2); 6(2); 7(2); 8(3); 10; 11; 12(2); 13; 14; 15; 16; 19; 22(3); 9:3; 5(2); 6(2); 7(3); 8(2); 9(2); 10(2); 11(3); 12; 13(2); 14(2); 16; 17(2); 18; 19; 21; 23(2); 26; 27(4); 10:2(2); 3(2); 5(2); 7; 8(4); 9(2); 10(2); 11; 13; 14(4); 15; 16; 17; 18; 19; 20; 21; 24; 25(2); 26; 11:1; 3(4); 4; 7(2); 9(3); 10(2); 12(2); 13; 14(2); 15; 12:1(2); 2; 3(2); 5; 6; 7; 8; 10; 12; 17; 18; 19(3); 20; 22; 23; 13:2; 4(2); 5(2); 7; 8(2); 9; 10; 12; 13; 14; 15; 17(3); 18(3); 19; 20(2); 21; 23; 14:1(2); 4(2); 6(2); 7(2); 8(2); 9(3); 10(2); 11; 12(3); 17; 18; 19(3); 20; 23; 25; 26; 27; 31; 33; 34; 35(2); 36(2); 40(3); 41; 43; 45(2); 46; 15:1(2); 2; 5; 6(2); 7; 9; 10; 11; 12(3); 13(2); 15(2); 16(3); 20; 21(2); 22(2); 24; 26; 27; 28(2); 32(2); 34(2); 35; 16:1(2); 2(2); 3(2); 4; 5(4); 7; 10; 11(2); 13; 15; 16; 17(2); 19; 20; 21; 22; 17:1(2); 8(4); 9; 13(4); 15; 17(2); 18; 20(2); 22; 23; 25; 26; 28(2); 31; 32; 33(3); 34(2); 37; 39(3); 40; 41; 43(2); 44(3); 45(3); 46; 48(2); 49; 52(2); 54; 55; 58; 18:1(2); 2; 4(2); 6; 8(2); 11; 17(2); 18(2); 19(2); 21(3); 23(2); 25(3); 26; 27; 30; 19:1(2); 2; 4(2); 5; 7; 10(2); 11(3); 14; 15(2); 17(2); 18(2); 20; 22(2); 23(2); 20:1; 2; 4; 5(3); 6; 8; 9; 10; 11; 12(2); 13(3); 17; 18; 19; 20; 21; 22; 24; 26; 27(2); 28(2); 29(2); 30(3); 31; 32; 33(2); 36; 37; 38; 40(3); 41; 42; 21:1(3); 2(3); 5; 6; 7; 8; 9; 10; 11(2); 12; 14(2); 15; 22:1(2); 2; 3(2); 5(2); 7; 8(3); 9(2); 11(2); 13(2); 15(3); 17(3); 18; 22; 23:2; 3(2); 4; 5; 6; 7; 8(3); 9; 10(3); 15; 16; 17(2); 18; 19; 20(3); 23; 24; 25(2); 26(2); 27; 24:2; 3(3); 4(4); 6(3); 7; 8(2); 9(2); 10; 11; 16; 17; 19; 21; 22(2); 25:1; 5(3); 6(4); 8(3); 9(2); 11; 13; 14; 15; 16; 17; 19; 21; 22(2); 23(2); 26; 27(2); 29; 30(2); 31(2); 32(2); 33; 34(2); 35(2); 36; 39(2); 40(5); 41(2); 44; 26:1; 2(2); 5; 6(3); 7; 8(3); 9; 10(2); 13; 14(3); 15(2); 16; 20(2); 25(2); 27:1(2); 2; 4; 5; 6(2); 8; 9; 11(2); 28:1(3); 2(2); 7(3); 8(2); 9(3); 10; 12; 13(2); 14(2); 15(2); 17; 18; 21(3); 24; 29:3(3); 4(4); 5; 6(3); 8(2); 9(2); 11(4); 30:1; 2; 3; 4; 7(3); 9; 11; 12; 13(2); 14; 15(4); 21(4); 24; 25; 26(3); 27; 31(2); 31:4; 8; 9; 10; 11; 12; **2 Sam** 1:1; 2(2); 3(2); 4; 5; 6; 7; 8; 9; 10; 13; 14(3); 16; 18; 26(2); 2:1(3); 5(4); 6; 8; 10; 12; 14; 19(2); 21(3); 22(2); 23(2); 24(2); 26(2); 29; 32; 3:2; 5; 7(2); 8(4); 9(2); 10(2); 12(3); 13; 14(2); 16(2); 17; 19(2); 20; 21(2); 23; 24(2); 25(3); 27(2); 29; 31(2); 35(3); 37; 38; 39; 4:3; 4; 5; 6; 8(2); 9; 10; 5:1; 2; 3; 4; 6(2); 11; 13; 14; 17(2); 19; 20; 24; 6:2; 6; 8; 9; 12(2); 19(2); 20(2); 21(2); 23; 7:1; 2; 3; 4; 5; 6; 7(2); 8(2); 11(2); 17(3); 19; 20; 21(2); 22; 23(3); 27(3); 28; 29; 8:1; 2(4); 3; 5; 7(2); 10(2); 11; 15; 9:2(2); 3(2); 4(2); 6; 7(2); 9(5); 10; 11(2); 10:2(3); 3(6); 5; 6; 14; 16; 17; 19(2); 11:1; 2; 4(2); 6(2); 7; 8(2); 9; 10(3); 11(4); 12; 13(2); 14; 16; 19; 20(2); 23(2); 25(2); 27; 12:1(3); 3; 4(5); 5; 7; 9(2); 10; 11; 13(2); 14(3); 15(2); 17(2); 18(3); 19; 20; 21; 22; 23(2); 24; 27; 29; 31(4); 13:2(2); 4(2); 5(4); 6(3); 7(2); 8; 9; 10(2); 11(3); 13; 15; 16(3); 20(2); 22; 23; 24; 25(2); 26; 28; 29; 30(2); 33(2); 35; 37; 38; 39(2); 14:2(3); 3(2); 4(2); 5; 6; 7; 8(2); 9; 10(2); 11(2); 12; 15(3); 18; 19(2); 20(3); 21; 22; 23(2); 24(2); 25; 26; 27; 29(3); 30; 31(2); 32(4); 33(3); 15:1; 2(3); 3(2); 4; 5(2); 6; 7(4); 8; 9(2); 13; 14(2); 15(2); 16; 19; 22; 25; 26(2); 27(2); 28; 29; 32(2); 33(2); 34(2); 35; 16:2(5); 3(2); 4(2); 5; 9; 10(2); 11; 15; 16(2); 17(2); 18; 20(2); 21(3); 22; 17:1; 3; 6(2); 7; 11(3); 13; 14(2); 15; 18; 20(3); 21(2); 23(2); 24; 25; 27; 29; 18:2; 3; 4(2); 11(2); 12(2); 17; 18(2); 19; 20; 21(2); 22; 23; 24(2); 26; 28(2); 32(2); 33; 19:5; 7; 8; 11(6); 12; 13(2); 14; 15(5); 16; 18(2); 19(3); 20(3); 21; 22(3); 23(2); 24; 25(3); 26; 27; 28(2); 29; 30(2); 31; 33; 34(3); 35; 37; 38; 39; 40; 41(2); 43(2); 20:1(2); 2; 3(4); 4; 5; 6; 7; 9(2); 12; 13; 14; 15; 16; 17(2); 18; 19; 21(2); 22(4); 21:2(3); 3; 4; 6; 8; 9; 10; 17(3); 20; 22; 22:1; 4; 7; 21(2); 25(2); 31; 35; 42(2); 45; 50(2); 51(3); 23:3; 10(2); 13; 16(2); 19; 21; 23; 24:1; 2(2); 3(2); 4; 6(4); 7(3); 8; 9; 10; 11; 12; 13(4); 14; 15; 16(2); 17; 18(3); 19; 20; 21(4); 22(2); 23(2); 24(2); 25; **1 Ki** 1:2; 3; 5; 8; 11; 13(3); 15; 16; 17(2); 23; 28; 30; 31(2); 32; 33(2); 35; 38; 40; 42; 43; 47; 48; 51(2); 52; 53(3); 2:3(2); 4(2); 5(3); 6(2); 7(2); 8(4); 9(3); 13; 14(2); 16; 17; 18; 19(5); 20; 21; 22; 23; 24; 26(4); 27; 28(4); 29; 30(3); 31; 36; 38; 39; 40(2); 41; 42(2); 44(2); 3:1;

4(2); 5; 6(2); 7; 8; 9(3); 11(2); 12; 14; 15; 16; 21; 25(2); 26; 28; 4:10; 12; 13(2); 21; 24; 27; 28(2); 33; 34; 5:1; 2; 5(2); 6(2); 8; 9(3); 10; 11; 14; 17(2); 18; 6:1(2); 8(2); 10; 11; 12; 15; 16; 18; 19; 24; 38; 7:1; 3; 7; 9(3); 11; 14; 16; 18; 20; 23; 24; 32; 40; 42; 8:1; 6(2); 8; 10; 13; 15; 16(2); 17; 18(2); 25(2); 26; 28; 31; 32; 33(2); 34(2); 36; 39(2); 40; 43(2); 44(2); 46(2); 47(2); 48(3); 52(4); 53; 54(2); 56(2); 58(3); 61(2); 63; 64; 65; 66; 9:1(2); 2(2); 3(2); 4(2); 5; 8(2); 12; 13; 15; 16; 19; 21(2); 24; 27; 28(2); 10:1; 2(2); 3; 5; 6; 9; 10; 12; 13(2); 14; 24; 29; 11:2(2); 4; 8; 9; 11(2); 13; 15; 17(2); 18(3); 21(2); 22(3); 24(2); 27(2); 31(2); 33; 35; 36(2); 38(2); 40(3); 12:1(3); 3; 5(2); 6; 7(3); 9(2); 10(4); 11; 12(2); 14(3); 15(2); 16(4); 18(2); 19; 20(2); 21(3); 22; 23(3); 24(2); 26; 27(3); 28(3); 30; 32; 13:1(2); 2; 4(2); 5; 6(3); 7; 8(2); 10; 11; 12; 13; 14; 15; 18(4); 20; 21; 22(2); 26(4); 27; 29(3); 31; 32; 34; 14:2(2); 3; 4(2); 5(4); 6(2); 8(2); 9(2); 11; 12; 13; 15(2); 17(2); 18; 21; 22; 24; 27; 15:3; 14; 17; 18; 27(2); 29(2); 30; 16:1; 2(2); 4; 7; 11(2); 12; 13; 15; 19; 21; 26; 31(2); 33(2); 34; 17:1; 2; 4; 5; 8; 9(3); 10(3); 11(2); 13(2); 15; 16; 18(6); 19(2); 20; 21(2); 22; 23; 24; 18:1(3); 2(2); 4; 5(5); 6; 9; 10; 12(2); 13(2); 15; 16(2); 17; 19; 21; 22; 25; 30(3); 31(2); 32; 36; 37; 40(2); 41; 42(2); 43; 44(2); 45; 46; 19:2(2); 3(2); 5; 9(2); 10; 13; 14; 15(2); 18; 20(2); 21; 20:2(2); 5(2); 6; 7; 8; 9(3); 10(2); 12(2); 22(2); 23; 25; 26(2); 28; 30; 31(2); 32; 33(2); 34; 35(2); 36; 39(2); 40; 41; 42(2); 43(2); 21:1(2); 2(3); 3(2); 4; 5(2); 6(3); 7; 8; 10; 11(2); 14; 15(3); 16; 17; 18(2); 19(2); 20(2); 22; 24; 25; 26; 28; 22:2(2); 3(2); 4(3); 5; 6(2); 8; 12; 13(2); 14; 15(3); 16; 17; 18; 20; 22; 24(2); 25; 26(2); 29; 30; 32; 34; 36(2); 37; 38; 48(2); 49; 53(2); **2 Ki** 1:2; 3(4); 4; 5(2); 6(7); 7(2); 9(3); 10; 11(2); 12; 13; 15(2); 16(4); 17; 2:1(2); 2(3); 3(2); 4(3); 5(2); 6(2); 9; 15(2); 16; 18(3); 19; 20; 21; 22(2); 23(2); 25(2); 3:7(2); 10; 12; 13(5); 21(2); 23; 24; 26(2); 27; 4:1(3); 2; 5; 6(3); 8(3); 9; 10; 11; 12; 13(5); 14; 16; 18(2); 19(3); 20; 22(2); 23; 24; 25(2); 26(2); 27(2); 29; 31; 33; 36; 37; 38(2); 39; 40(2); 41; 42; 43; 44; 5:1; 3; 5; 6(3); 7(3); 8(2); 10(2); 11(2); 13(3); 14; 15; 16; 17(2); 18; 19; 21; 22; 23; 24; 25; 26(4); 27; 6:1; 2; 3; 4; 9; 10; 11; 15; 18(3); 19(3); 20; 21; 22; 23; 26; 28(2); 29; 31; 32(3); 33; 7:3; 4; 5(4); 6(3); 8; 9; 10(2); 11; 12(3); 15; 16; 17(2); 18; 20; 8:1(2); 2; 3(3); 5(4); 7; 8(2); 9(2); 10(2); 12; 14(3); 16; 19(2); 21(2); 22; 25; 28; 29(3); 9:1(2); 2; 4; 6; 10; 11(4); 12; 13; 15(3); 16(2); 17; 18(3); 19(2); 20; 21; 23; 25; 26; 27(2); 28; 30; 34; 35; 10:1(4); 2; 4; 5; 6(2); 7(2); 9; 10; 12; 13; 15(3); 17(4); 18; 19; 21; 22; 23; 24; 25(2); 27; 30(3); 31; 32; 11:4; 8(2); 9(3); 10; 11; 13; 14; 15; 18; 19; 12:4(2); 7; 11; 12(3); 14; 15(2); 16; 17(2); 18; 20; 13:4; 14; 15; 16; 18; 23; 14:6(4); 7; 8; 9(3); 11; 12; 13(2); 14; 19(2); 22; 25(2); 28; 15:3; 12(2); 14; 19; 20(2); 29; 32; 34; 37; 16:1; 3; 5(2); 6(2); 7; 8; 9; 10(4); 11; 15; 16; 17:4(2); 5; 6; 9; 11(2); 12; 13(2); 17(4); 23(2); 26; 29; 31; 33; 34; 35(2); 36; 37; 41; 18:1(2); 3; 4; 6; 8; 9; 11; 14; 16; 17(3); 18(2); 19(2); 21; 22(2); 23(2); 25(2); 26(3); 27(5); 29; 31(2); 32(2); 37; 19:2; 3(3); 4; 5; 6(2); 7(2); 9(2); 10; 11; 14; 16; 20(2); 21; 23(3); 25; 28; 29; 34; 35; 37; 20:1(2); 2; 4; 5; 6; 8(2); 9; 10; 11; 12; 13; 14(3); 16; 17; 19; 21:2; 6(2); 7(2); 8(3); 9; 14; 15(2); 16; 22:2(2); 3(2); 4; 5(2); 6(3); 8(2); 9; 13(2); 14; 15(2); 17(2); 18(2); 20(3); 23:1(2); 2; 3(3); 4(2); 5(6); 6(2); 8(2); 9; 10; 11(2); 15; 16; 19(4); 20; 21; 25(2); 29(2); 30; 32; 34(2); 35(6); 37; 24:2(2); 3(2); 7(2); 9; 12; 15(2); 16; 17; 19; 25:1; 6; 7; 8; 11; 13; 20; 21; 23; 24; 26; 27(2); 28; **1 Chr** 1:10; 19; 32; 2:3; 9; 21; 23; 35; 3:1; 4; 5; 4:39(2); 41; 42; 43; 5:1(2); 11; 18(3); 20; 23(2); 25; 26(2); 6:19; 31; 32; 48; 49(2); 54; 56; 57; 61; 62; 63; 64; 7:4; 9; 11; 21; 22; 23; 28(2); 8:6(2); 7; 9:1; 9; 19; 22; 24; 25(2); 10:4; 8; 9; 11; 12; 14; 11:1; 2; 3(2); 4; 5; 8; 10(2); 15(2); 18(2); 21; 23; 25; 12:1; 15(3); 16; 17(6); 18(2); 19(3); 20(2); 22(2); 23(4); 29; 31; 32(2); 33; 36(2); 38(3); 40; 13:2(5); 3; 5(2); 6(4); 9(2); 10; 11; 12; 14:1(2); 8; 10; 11; 14; 15(2); 15:2(2); 3(2); 12(2); 14; 15; 16(3); 19; 20; 21; 24; 25; 29; 16:3(2); 4(4); 5; 7; 8; 9(2); 16; 17(2); 18; 20(2); 21; 23(2); 25(2); 28(2); 29; 33; 34; 35(3); 36; 37; 38; 40(4); 41(2); 42; 43(2); 17:1(2); 2; 3; 4; 5(3); 6(2); 7(2); 10; 11; 15(3); 17(2); 18; 19; 20; 21(2); 25(2); 26; 27; 18:1; 3; 5; 7; 10(2); 11; 14; 19:2(5); 3(6); 5; 6(2); 7; 15; 19; 20:1; 2; 3(3); 6; 8; 21:1; 2(4); 4; 5; 6; 8; 9; 10; 11(2); 12(2); 13; 15(3); 17(2); 18(3); 21(2); 22(3); 23(2); 24; 26; 27; 30; 22:2(3); 4; 5; 6; 7(3); 8; 9(2); 11; 13; 14(2); 17; 19(3); 23:4; 13(4); 14; 25; 26; 28; 30(2); 31(2); 32; 24:3; 7(2); 8(2); 9(2); 10(2); 11(2); 12(2); 13(2); 14(2); 15(2); 16(2); 17(2); 18(2); 19; 30; 25:2; 3(2); 5; 26:6; 12; 13; 14; 15(2); 16; 27; 31; 32; 27:1; 28:2(3); 3; 4(3); 5; 6(2); 7; 8; 10; 15; 20; 29:1; 2(2); 3; 4; 5(3); 8; 9; 12(3); 14; 16; 17(2); 19(3); 20; 21(2); 22(2); 24; 30(3); **2 Chr** 1:2(4); 3; 4; 6; 7(2); 8(2); 9; 11; 12; 13; 17; 2:1; 2(3); 3(3); 4(4); 6(2); 7(2); 8; 9(2); 10; 11; 14(4); 15; 16(3); 17; 18; 3:1(2); 2; 3; 8; 4:2; 3; 6(2); 7; 11; 13; 20; 22; 5:7(2); 9; 11(2); 13(3); 6:2; 4; 5(2); 6; 7; 8(2); 16(2); 17; 19; 22; 23; 25(2); 27; 29; 30(2); 31(2); 33(2); 34(2); 36(2); 37(2); 38(2); 40; 41; 7:3; 6(2); 7; 8; 10; 11; 12(2); 13; 15; 17; 18; 21; 8:1; 2; 3; 6; 8; 11(2); 12; 13(2); 14(2); 15; 17; 18(2); 9:1(3); 2; 4; 5; 8(3); 9; 12(3); 13; 14; 18; 21; 23; 26; 28; 10:1(3); 3; 5(2); 6; 7(3); 9(2); 10(4); 11; 12(2); 14(3); 15(2); 16(4); 18(2); 19; 11:1(3); 2; 3(2); 4; 14(2); 16(4); 22(2); 23; 12:1; 4; 5(2); 7; 10; 12; 13; 14; 13:5(2); 7; 8; 9; 10(2); 11(2); 12; 13; 14(2); 14:4(2); 7; 9; 11(2); 13; 15; 15:2(2); 4; 5(2); 9; 11; 12; 13(2); 16:1; 2; 7(2); 9(3); 17:4; 5; 7; 14; 15; 16(2); 18; 18:2(3); 3; 4; 5(2); 7; 11; 12(2); 14(3); 15; 16; 17; 19; 20; 23(2); 24; 25(2); 28; 29; 31; 33; 19:1; 2(2); 3; 4(2); 6(2); 8; 10; 20:1; 3; 4(2); 6; 7; 9; 11(2); 12; 15; 17; 18; 19; 21; 22(2); 23(2); 24; 25; 27(2); 28(2); 33; 36(3); 37(2); 21:3; 7(3); 10; 11; 12; 13; 17; 20; 22:3; 4; 5; 6(3); 7(2); 9(2); 23:2; 3; 7(2); 8(2); 9(2); 10; 12; 14; 17; 18(2); 20; 24:5(4); 6(3); 7; 9(2); 11(2); 12(3); 13; 17(2); 19(3); 20; 22; 23(2); 25:4(2); 5(4); 7; 8(2); 9(3); 10(2); 11; 12; 13(2); 14(2); 15; 16(2); 17; 18(3); 19; 21; 22; 23(2); 24; 26; 27(2); 26:2; 4; 8; 11(2); 13; 14; 15(2); 16(2); 18(4); 19; 20; 22; 23; 27:2; 5; 28:3; 5; 7; 8; 9(3); 10(2); 13(4); 15(2); 16(2); 19; 20; 21; 22; 23(2); 25(3); 26; 29:2; 5; 7; 8(3); 10; 11(3); 15(2); 16(3); 17(2); 18; 20; 21; 24; 25; 27; 30(2); 31; 32; 30:1(5); 2; 5(4); 6(3); 7; 8; 9(3); 10; 11; 12(2); 13; 15;

16(2); 17(2); 18; 19(2); 20; 21; 22(2); 23; 24(2); 27(2); 31:1(3); 2(5); 4(2); 6; 10(2); 11; 14(2); 15(3); 16; 17(4); 18; 19(3); 21; 32:1(2); 2; 3; 5; 6; 8(2); 9(3); 11(2); 13(2); 14; 15; 17(2); 18(2); 20; 21; 23(2); 24(2); 25; 30; 31(3); 33:2; 6(3); 7(2); 8(2); 9; 10; 11; 13(2); 14; 16; 17; 18(2); 22; 34:2(2); 3(2); 4; 7; 8; 9(2); 10(2); 11(3); 12; 15(2); 16(2); 21(2); 22(3); 23; 25(2); 26(2); 28(3); 30; 31(3); 32; 33; 35:1; 3(2); 4(2); 5(2); 6; 7; 8(4); 9; 10; 12(3); 13; 15(2); 16(3); 20; 21(3); 22; 23; 24; 25; 26; 27; 36:4(2); 6(2); 7; 10; 13; 14; 15; 18; 20(2); 21(2); 23; **Ezra** 1:2; 3; 5; 8; 11; 2:1(3); 63; 68(2); 69(2); 3:1; 2; 3; 5; 6(2); 7(6); 8(3); 9; 10(2); 11; 4:2(3); 3(3); 4; 5; 7; 8; 11; 12(2); 13; 14; 15; 17(4); 18; 20; 21; 22(2); 23; 5:1; 2; 3(3); 5; 6; 7(2); 8(2); 9(3); 10; 12(2); 13; 14; 15(2); 17(2); 6:5(3); 8(3); 9; 10; 12(3); 13; 14(2); 17; 18(2); 21; 22; 7:6; 7; 8; 9(2); 10(3); 11; 12; 13(2); 14(2); 15(2); 16; 17; 18(3); 19; 20; 21; 22; 24; 25; 27; 28(2); 8:15; 17; 21; 22(3); 25; 28(3); 30(3); 31(2); 32; 35(2); 36(2); 9:1(2); 4; 5; 6(3); 7(5); 8(3); 9(5); 11(2); 12(2); 10:1; 2; 3(4); 5; 7; 8; 10(2); 11; 13; 16; **Neh** 1:1; 3; 9(3); 11(3); 2:1(2); 2; 3; 4(2); 5(3); 6(2); 7(4); 8(5); 9; 10; 11; 12; 13; 14(3); 17; 18(2); 20; 3:2(2); 4(3); 5(2); 7; 8(2); 9; 10(2); 12; 16; 17; 19(2); 20; 21; 24; 27; 4:4; 5; 6(2); 7; 8; 9; 10; 11; 13; 14(3); 15(4); 19; 20; 22; 5:5(2); 7; 8(5); 11; 12; 13; 14; 17; 19; 6:2(2); 3(2); 5; 6(2); 7(2); 8; 9; 10(3); 11; 14; 17(2); 18; 19(2); 7:2; 3; 5; 6(2); 65; 70(2); 71; 8:1; 3; 6; 7; 8; 9(2); 10(3); 12(3); 13(2); 15(2); 18; 9:4; 8(3); 12; 14; 15(3); 17(5); 19(2); 20; 23; 26(2); 27(2); 28(2); 29; 36(2); 37; 10:28; 29(2); 30; 31; 32; 33; 34(2); 35(2); 36(3); 37(5); 38(2); 39; 11:1(3); 2; 30; 12:24(2); 27(3); 31; 44; 45; 46; 13:2; 5(2); 6; 7; 9; 10; 12; 13(3); 16; 17; 19(2); 21; 22(2); 24; 25; 26; 30(2); 31; **Esth** 1:1(2); 5; 7; 8; 9; 11(4); 12; 13; 14(2); 15(3); 17(2); 18; 19; 21; 22(3); 2:3; 8; 9(2); 10; 11(2); 12(3); 13(3); 14(3); 15(2); 16; 18; 21; 22; 3:2; 3; 4(4); 6(2); 7; 8(2); 9; 10; 11(4); 12(7); 13(4); 14; 15; 4:4; 5(2); 6; 7(3); 8(6); 10; 11(5); 13; 14; 15(2); 16; 17; 5:2; 3(3); 4; 5; 6(2); 8(2); 12(2); 14(3); 6:1; 2; 4; 5; 6(2); 7; 9(4); 10; 11(2); 12(2); 13(3); 14(2); 7:1; 2(2); 4(3); 5(2); 8; 9; 8:1; 2; 3(2); 5(3); 6(3); 7(2); 9(6); 11(3); 13(2); 9:1(2); 2; 11; 12(2); 13(3); 14; 19; 20; 21; 22(4); 23; 24(2); 26; 27(2); 28; 29; 30(2); 31; 10:2; 3(2); **Job** 1:2; 4; 5; 6; 7(2); 8; 11; 12; 14; 15; 16; 17; 19; 20; 2:1(2); 2(2); 3(3); 5; 6; 7; 8; 9(2); 10; 11(2); 13; 3:8; 20(2); 23; 25; 4:12; 5:1; 7; 8; 11; 26; 6:7(2); 9; 14; 17; 22; 24; 26; 28(2); 7:3; 9; 10; 20(2); 8:5; 22; 9:3; 12; 14; 16; 18; 32; 10:1; 2; 3; 15; 19; 21(2); 11:10; 12:3; 8(2); 22; 13:2; 3(2); 17(2); 20; 22; 25; 14:3; 21; 15:8; 19; 28; 16:8; 11(2); 12; 20; 17:5; 9; 14(2); 16; 18:2; 11; 19:17(2); 20(2); 20:3; 6(2); 21; 23; 29; 21:2; 12(2); 13; 14; 15; 31; 32; 33; 22:2(2); 3(2); 7; 15; 17(2); 21; 23; 26; 27; 23:3; 5; 9; 11; 24:4; 5; 10; 17; 25:2; 3; 26:3; 4; 28:3; 4; 11; 24; 25; 28(2); 29:7; 10; 13; 15(2); 16; 19; 21; 30:1; 2; 3; 6; 10; 20; 21; 22(2); 23(2); 26; 31(2); 31:5; 7; 12; 16; 23; 24; 30; 32(2); 35; 37; 39; 32:4(2); 6; 10; 11(2); 12; 19; 21; 22; 33:1; 17; 22; 23; 24(2); 25; 26(2); 28; 30; 31; 32(2); 33; 34:2; 10(3); 11(3); 14; 15; 16; 18(3); 19; 28(2); 31; 33; 34(2); 36; 37; 35:3; 5; 6; 13; 36:2; 3; 6; 10; 21; 24; 32; 37:3; 6(2); 13; 14; 15; 19; 20(2); 24; 38:6; 12; 17; 19; 20(2); 26(2); 27(2); 34; 35; 36; 40; 41; 39:4; 9; 11; 12(2); 24; 40:14; 41:3(2); 10; 17; 28; 42:7(2); 8(2); 11; **Ps** 2:5; 7; 9; 3:4; 8; 4:2; 3; 5:1; 2(2); 3; 6:7:2; 4; 5; 6; 8(2); 9; 17(2); 8:6; 9(2); 2; 11; 20; 10:9; 14(2); 17; 18(2); 11:1(2); 12:13:6; 14:2; 15:3; 4; 16:2; 6; 10; 17:1(2); 6; 11; 12; 18(2); 3; 6(2); 20(2); 24(2); 30; 34; 41(2); 44; 49(2); 50(3); 19:4; 5; 6; 10; 20:4; 21:4; 11; 22(2); 5; 11; 15(2); 19; 22; 24; 27; 29; 30; 31; 23:2; 24:4; 25:1; 7; 10; 16; 26:11; 27:2; 4(2); 6; 8; 12; 28:1(4); 2; 3; 4(4); 29:2; 11; 30:2; 3; 4; 8(2); 9; 12(3); 31:2(2); 13; 18; 22; 32:2; 5(2); 6; 10; 33:2; 3; 10; 11; 19(2); 34:5; 9; 11; 15; 16; 18; 35:3; 4(3); 12; 13; 23(2); 24; 26; 36:3(2); 5; 10(2); 12; 37:5(2); 7; 14(2); 32; 34; 38(2); 17; 22; 39(2); 4; 12; 40:1; 3; 4; 5; 8; 12; 13(2); 14(3); 15; 41:2; 4; 6(2); 8; 10; 13; 42:3; 4(2); 8; 9; 10; 43:3(2); 4(2); 44:7; 9; 12; 13(2); 20; 25(2); 45(2); 14(2); 17; 46:9; 47:1; 6(2); 9; 48:1; 10(2); 13; 14; 49:4; 7; 9; 10; 11; 19; 50:1; 4(2); 5; 14(2); 16(2); 19; 22; 23; 51(3); 1(2); 6; 12; 13; 18; 52(3); 53(2); 2; 5; 54(3); 2; 6; 55:1; 2; 14; 22; 23; 56(2); 1; 4; 9; 11; 12(2); 57(2); 1(2); 2(2); 9; 58(2); 59(3); 4; 5(2); 10; 13; 17; 60(2); 4; 9(2); 61:1; 2(2); 8; 62(2); 4; 11; 12(3); 63:2; 9; 64:3; 65:1; 2; 4; 66:1; 3(2); 4(2); 8; 9; 12(2); 17; 19; 67:1(2); 68:4(2); 16; 20; 29; 31; 32(2); 33; 34; 35; 69(2); 1; 8(2); 11; 13; 16(2); 18; 20; 21; 27; 70(3); 1(2); 5; 71:1; 2(2); 3(2); 7; 11; 12; 17; 18(3); 22; 23; 24; 72:1; 3; 4; 8(2); 15; 73:1(2); 15; 16; 18; 19; 24; 28(2); 74:3; 7(2); 14; 19; 20; 75(2); 1; 4(2); 9; 76:7; 8; 9(2); 11(3); 12; 77(2); 1(3); 2; 6; 9; 78:1(2); 4(2); 5; 6(2); 8; 10; 13; 16; 24; 25; 26; 36; 46(2); 48(2); 50; 54; 58(2); 62; 66; 71; 72; 79:2; 3; 4(2); 8; 11(2); 12; 13; 80(2); 3; 5; 6; 7; 9; 11(2); 19; 81:1(2); 8; 12(2); 13; 15; 82:2; 3; 83:17; 84:7; 85:1; 4; 5; 8(3); 9; 86:3(2); 4; 5(2); 6(2); 11; 16(2); 87:4; 88(2); 2; 3; 4; 8; 9; 13; 15; 89:1; 3; 4; 6(2); 7(2); 18(2); 19(2); 26; 29; 33; 35; 39; 40; 41; 44; 49; 90:2; 3; 12; 15; 16(2); 91:11; 92:1(4); 2; 15; 94:1(2); 2; 15; 95:1(2); 2; 96:1(2); 2(2); 4(2); 7(2); 8; 13; 97:7; 98:1; 3; 4; 5; 9; 99:7; 8; 100:1; 4; 5; 101:1; 2; 3; 102:1; 2; 4; 5; 12; 13; 14; 18(2); 20(3); 21; 22; 103:7(2); 8; 10(2); 17(2); 18(3); 104:8; 9; 11; 14; 15; 23(2); 26; 29; 33(2); 34; 105:1; 2(2); 9; 10(2); 11; 13(2); 14; 19; 22; 25(2); 39; 106:1; 23; 26; 27(2); 28(2); 29; 31(2); 36; 37; 38; 45; 46; 47(3); 48; 107:1; 4; 6; 7; 8(2); 12; 13; 15(2); 18; 19; 21(2); 23; 26(2); 27; 28; 30; 31(2); 40; 108:3; 4; 10; 109:4; 12(3); 16; 17; 19; 20(2); 25; 26; 31; 110:1; 4; 111:4; 5; 6; 9; 112:9; 113:3(2); 6; 115:1; 16; 116:2; 7; 12; 14; 17; 18; 118:1; 6; 8(2); 9(2); 18; 19; 27; 29; 119:4; 5; 9; 25(2); 28; 31(2); 33; 36(2); 38(2); 41(2); 48; 49(2); 58(2); 59; 60; 62(2); 65; 72; 76(2); 77; 79; 85; 88; 90; 91; 95; 103(2); 105(2); 107; 112(2); 116; 121; 124; 126; 128; 130; 132; 146; 149(2); 154; 156; 159; 165; 169; 170; 120:1; 3(2); 121:1; 3; 122:1; 4(3); 123:2(3); 124:6; 125:3(2); 4(2); 5; 127:2(3); 129:5; 130:1; 2; 132:2(2); 3; 4(2); 8; 11; 133:1; 135:3; 7; 12; 136:1; 2; 3; 4; 5; 6; 7; 8; 9; 10; 13; 16; 17; 22; 25; 26; 137:6; 7; 8; 138:1; 139:12; 17; 140:4; 6; 11; 13; 141:1(4); 4(2); 142:1(2); 5; 6; 143:1; 3; 6; 8(3); 10; 144:9(2); 10; 145:3; 4; 8; 9; 12(2); 15; 18(2); 146:2; 4; 7(2);

10; 147:1(2); 6; 7(2); 8; 9(2); 15; 18; 19(2); 148:14; 149:1; 3; 7; 8; 9; 150:2; **Prov** 1:2; 3; 4(3); 6; 11; 12; 16(2); 23; 31; 33; 2:2(2); 7; 10; 12; 13; 16; 18(2); 19; 20; 3:2; 8(2); 18; 22(2); 27(2); 28; 32; 34; 4:1; 4; 9; 20(2); 22(2); 27; 5:1(2); 5; 9(2); 10; 13; 6:4(2); 6; 10; 16; 18; 24; 26; 27; 29; 30; 31; 7:4; 8; 13; 15(2); 21; 22(2); 23; 24(2); 25; 27(2); 8:4(2); 7; 9(2); 13; 21; 29; 32; 34; 9:4; 9; 11; 15(2); 16; 10:3; 16(2); 23(2); 26(3); 29; 11:1; 8; 19(2); 20; 24; 27; 29; 12:8; 14; 22; 24; 13:1; 5; 14; 18; 19(3); 21; 22; 25; 14:6; 8; 12; 22; 23; 27; 29; 30(2); 34; 15:8; 9; 12; 18; 21; 26; 28; 16:1; 3; 5; 7; 12; 16(3); 17; 19(2); 22; 23; 24(2); 25; 30; 32; 17:4(2); 7(2); 15; 21; 23; 25(2); 26(2); 18:5(3); 9; 10; 13; 17; 18; 19; 19:2; 6; 10; 11(2); 17; 19; 20; 23; 24; 27; 20:2; 3; 10; 13; 17; 23; 25(2); 21:3(2); 5(2); 7; 9; 13; 15(2); 19; 25; 22:1; 7; 9; 16(3); 17; 20; 21(2); 27; 23:1; 2(2); 4; 7; 12(2); 21; 22; 24:1; 8; 9; 11; 12(2); 13; 14; 21; 23(2); 24; 29(4); 33; 25:2(2); 4; 7; 8(2); 9; 12; 13; 20; 21(2); 24; 25; 27(2); 26:4; 5; 8; 11; 15(2); 21(3); 27:4; 7; 10; 14; 23(2); 24; 28:10; 20; 21; 24; 27; 29:12; 13; 15(2); 17; 24; 27(2); 30:1(2); 5; 6; 8; 10; 14; 17; 31:3(2); 4; 6(2); 8; 19; 20(2); 25; **Eccl** 1:5; 6; 7; 11; 13(2); 17(2); 2:3(3); 6; 12; 14; 15(2); 16; 17; 18; 21; 26(3); 3:2(4); 3(4); 4(4); 5(4); 6(4); 7(4); 8(2); 10; 11; 12(2); 14; 15; 19(2); 20(2); 21; 22; 4:8; 10(2); 14; 5:1(3); 4(2); 5(2); 6; 11; 12; 13; 15; 18(2); 19(3); 6:2(2); 6; 8; 7:2(5); 5(2); 9; 11; 12; 21; 25(3); 27(2); 8:2; 3; 4; 8(2); 9(2); 11; 14(4); 15; 16(2); 17(3); 9:2(4); 3(2); 4; 10; 11(6); 13; 10:1(2); 14; 15(2); 16; 11:2(2); 3; 7; 12:5; 7(2); 10; 12; **Song** 1:6; 9; 13; 14; 2:3(2); 4; 10; 16; 3:4; 4:6(2); 16; 5:1(2); 5; 6:2(4); 11(3); 7:8; 11; 12; 8:2(3); 5; 11(3); **Isa** 1:4; 6; 9; 10; 11(2); 12(2); 13; 14; 16; 17; 2:2(2); 3(2); 7(2); 19; 20(2); 21(2); 3:4; 8; 9; 10; 11; 12; 13(2); 4:1; 3; 5:1; 2; 4(2); 5; 8(3); 11; 18; 20; 21; 22(2); 26(2); 30; 6:3; 6; 7:1(3); 2; 3(3); 4; 7; 10; 13; 15; 16; 18; 25(2); 8:1; 2; 3(2); 4; 5; 8; 10; 11; 14(2); 19; 20(3); 22; 9:3; 7; 13; 16; 10:1; 2(2); 3; 5; 6(3); 7; 11(2); 12; 20; 21; 27; 28(2); 30; 11:10; 11(2); 12:5; 13:2; 5; 9; 10; 14(2); 16; 18; 20; 22; 14:1; 2; 3(2); 9; 10; 11; 12; 15(2); 19; 24; 15:2(3); 4; 5; 7; 8(2); 16:1(3); 4; 8; 12(3); 17:4; 7; 8; 11(2); 12(2); 18:1; 2(2); 4; 7(3); 19:11; 14; 17; 19(2); 20(2); 21(2); 22; 23; 20:1; 4; 6; 21:2(2); 6; 9; 10; 11; 14; 16(2); 22:1; 4; 5; 7; 8; 9; 10; 11; 14; 15(2); 21(2); 23; 24; 23:1; 6; 7; 9(3); 11; 12; 13; 15(3); 17; 18; 24:9; 16(2); 20; 21; 25:2; 4(2); 11; 12(2); 26:5(2); 10; 14; 21; 27:2; 6; 7; 9; 12(2); 13; 28:1(3); 2; 5; 6(2); 9; 11; 12(2); 13; 15; 19; 20; 21; 24; 29:1(3); 2; 11(2); 12; 15(2); 20; 24; 30:1(2); 2(4); 4; 6; 7; 8; 10(4); 11; 13(2); 14(2); 18; 19; 21(2); 22; 28(3); 29(2); 30; 31:1(3); 4(2); 6; 9; 32:4; 5; 6(4); 7; 9; 33:1; 2; 4; 34:1; 2; 10; 12; 14; 17; 35:2; 4; 10; 36:1; 2(2); 3; 4(2); 6; 7(2); 8(2); 10(2); 11(3); 12(4); 14; 16(2); 17; 22; 37:2; 3(3); 4; 5; 6(2); 7(2); 9(2); 10; 11; 14; 15; 17; 21(2); 22; 24(3); 26; 29; 30; 35; 38; 38:1(2); 2; 4; 5; 7; 10; 15; 18; 19; 20; 22; 39:1; 3(4); 5; 6; 8; 40:2(2); 9; 16; 18(2); 20; 22; 23; 25(2); 29(2); 41:2(3); 6; 9; 13; 22(2); 23; 27(2); 42:1; 2; 5(2); 6(2); 7(2); 8(2); 9; 10(2); 12; 17; 23(2); 24(2); 25; 43:6(2); 14; 20(2); 23; 28(2); 44:7; 13; 15(2); 17; 19; 22; 26(2); 27; 28(2); 45:1(4); 6; 9(2); 10(3); 11; 14(3); 18; 19; 20; 22; 23; 24; 46:1; 3; 4(2); 5; 7; 8; 11; 12; 47:7; 8; 9; 11; 12; 14(2); 15(2); 48:3(2); 5(3); 11; 12; 13; 16; 17; 20; 21; 49:1; 3; 5(4); 6(4); 7(3); 8(4); 9(2); 18; 21; 22; 23(2); 50:1; 2(2); 4(3); 6(2); 51:1(3); 2(2); 4(2); 6; 7; 8; 10; 11; 13; 16; 18; 19; 23; 52:1; 4; 7; 8; 53:1; 6; 7; 10(2); 54:3(2); 4; 9; 16; 55:1; 2; 3; 4; 5; 7(2); 10(2); 11; 13; 56:1(2); 3; 4; 5; 6(4); 7; 8(2); 9; 10; 11; 57:1; 6; 7; 8(2); 9(2); 11; 15(2); 18(2); 19(2); 58:2; 4(2); 5(4); 6(3); 7(2); 10; 12; 14; 59:7(2); 18(3); 20(2); 60:3(2); 4; 5(2); 7(2); 8; 9(3); 10; 11; 13(2); 14; 19(2); 61:1(6); 2(2); 3(2); 11(2); 62:11(2); 63:1; 5(2); 6; 7(3); 12; 14(2); 64:2(3); 5; 7; 65:1; 2(2); 3(2); 5; 10; 12; 15; 17; 24; 66:8(2); 9; 12; 14(2); 15; 17(2); 19(3); 20(2); 23(4); 24; **Jer** 1:2; 4; 5; 7(3); 8; 9; 10(6); 11; 12(2); 13; 14; 16; 17; 19; 2:1; 3; 7; 10; 18(4); 24; 27(4); 28; 31(2); 33; 36; 3:1(2); 2; 3; 4; 5; 6; 7; 9; 10; 11; 12; 13; 14(2); 15; 16(2); 17(3); 18(2); 22; 25; 4:1; 3; 4; 7; 9; 10; 11(4); 13; 16; 18; 22(2); 5:1; 3(2); 5(2); 7; 13; 19; 22; 31; 6:1; 2; 3; 4; 6; 10(2); 12; 13(3); 15; 17; 20(2); 7:1; 2; 3; 6; 7(2); 9; 10; 12(2); 13; 14(4); 16; 18(3); 19(2); 21; 22; 25; 27(2); 28; 30; 31; 34; 8:4; 5(2); 6; 10(5); 12; 14(2); 19; 9:3; 4; 5(2); 6; 8; 12; 13; 14; 15; 21(2); 10:1; 10; 11; 13; 14; 20; 22; 23; 24; 11:1; 2(2); 3; 4; 5(2); 6; 8; 9; 10(3); 11(3); 12(2); 13(5); 14; 15; 17(3); 19; 20; 12:6; 8; 9(2); 11(2); 12; 13; 14; 15(2); 16(2); 13:1; 2; 3; 4; 6(4); 7; 8; 10(2); 11(3); 12(2); 13; 16; 18(2); 20; 21(2); 23; 27; 14:1; 3; 8; 10(2); 11; 13; 14(3); 16(2); 17; 18; 15:1; 2(5); 3(3); 4(2); 5; 8(2); 9; 10; 11; 16; 18(2); 19(2); 20(2); 16:1; 5; 7(2); 8(2); 9; 10; 11; 12; 15; 19; 21(2); 17:4; 10(3); 15; 17; 18; 19; 20; 21; 24(2); 26; 27; 18:1; 2(2); 3; 4(2); 5; 7(3); 8; 9(2); 11(2); 12; 15(3); 16; 18; 19(2); 20(2); 21(2); 22; 23; 19:2; 4; 5(2); 7; 9(2); 11(2); 12(2); 13(2); 14(2); 20:3; 4(3); 5; 6(2); 8; 13; 15(2); 18; 21:1(2); 2; 3(2); 8; 9(2); 14; 22:1; 3; 6(2); 8(2); 13; 20; 21; 27(3); 23:1; 2(2); 3; 5; 12; 13; 14; 16(2); 17(3); 21; 22; 27; 28; 32; 33; 35(2); 37; 38; 24:1; 3; 4; 6; 7(2); 9(2); 10; 25:1; 2(2); 3(3); 4(2); 5; 6(2); 7(3); 12; 14(2); 15(3); 17; 18; 27; 28(3); 29; 30; 31(2); 32; 33; 35(2); 36; 26:2(4); 3; 4(3); 5(2); 6; 8(2); 10; 11(2); 12(2); 14; 15(3); 16(3); 17; 18; 19; 20; 21(3); 22(2); 23; 24(2); 27:1; 2; 3(3); 4(3); 5(2); 6; 9(2); 10(2); 12(2); 14(3); 15; 16(5); 17; 18(2); 20; 22(2); 28:1; 3(2); 4(2); 5; 6(2); 9; 12; 15; 29:1(3); 3(2); 4(3); 6; 7(2); 8(2); 9; 10(2); 11; 12(2); 14(2); 18(2); 19; 20; 21; 24; 25(3); 27; 28; 30; 31(3); 32; 30:1; 2; 3(3); 8; 11; 13; 15; 17; 18; 21(2); 31:2; 3; 6(2); 9(2); 12; 13; 15; 17; 21; 26; 28(8); 32(3); 34; 38; 40(2); 32:1; 4(2); 5; 6; 7(2); 8(3); 9; 11; 12; 16(2); 18; 19(4); 20; 22(2); 23(2); 24(2); 25; 26; 29(5); 30; 31(2); 32(2); 33(2); 34; 35(5); 37(2); 41; 44; 33:1; 2; 3; 4; 5(2); 6; 7; 9(2); 11; 12; 14(2); 15(2); 17; 18(3); 19; 21; 22; 23; 26(2); 34:1; 2; 3(2); 6; 8(3); 12; 14; 15; 16; 17(7); 22(2); 35:1; 2(3); 5; 8; 9(2); 10; 11(2); 12; 13; 14(3); 15(2); 17(2); 18(2); 19; 36:1(2); 2(3); 3; 4; 8; 9(4); 12; 13; 14(2); 15; 16(2); 18; 19; 20; 21; 25(2); 26; 27; 29(2); 30(2); 32(2); 37:2; 3(2); 6; 7(6); 12(2); 13; 14(3); 18; 19; 20; 21; 38:1; 2(2); 4(3); 8; 9(2); 11; 12; 14(2); 15(4); 16(2); 17(2); 18; 19(2); 20; 21; 22; 23(2); 24; 25(6); 26(3); 27(2); 39:5(2); 7(2); 9(2); 11; 12(2); 14(2); 15;

16; 18; 40:1(2); 2; 4(6); 5(2); 6(2); 7(2); 8; 9; 10; 12(2); 13; 14(2); 15(2); 16; 41:1(2); 5(2); 6(3); 8; 10(3); 12; 14; 15; 17; 42:1; 2(3); 4(4); 5(2); 6; 7; 8; 9(3); 11; 12(2); 14; 15(2); 17(3); 19; 20(4); 21; 22(2); 43:1(2); 2(4); 3(3); 4; 5; 7; 8; 9; 10; 11(3); 44:1; 3(4); 4; 5(3); 7(2); 8(3); 10; 12(3); 14(4); 15; 16(2); 17(3); 18(2); 19(4); 20; 23; 24(2); 25(3); 27; 28(3); 29; 45:1; 2; 3; 4; 5; 46:1; 3; 11; 13; 16(2); 19; 28; 47:1; 4(2); 48:1; 4; 9(2); 11; 15; 27; 32; 33; 34(3); 35(2); 39; 46; 49:2; 3; 9; 10; 12; 14(2); 24; 28; 29; 31; 32; 34; 37; 39; 50:5(2); 6; 9; 15; 16(2); 19; 21; 27(2); 29(3); 33; 34; 39; 51:2; 9(3); 11; 16; 17; 27; 29; 31(3); 33; 35; 40; 44; 48; 49; 50; 53(4); 59; 61; 62; 63; 52:2; 4; 9; 11; 12; 15; 17; 26; 27; 31; 32; **Lam** 1:2; 4(2); 7; 10; 11; 12; 14; 15; 19; 22(2); 2:1; 2; 4; 6(2); 8(2); 10; 12; 13; 14; 17; 18; 20; 22; 3:10; 13; 21; 25(2); 27; 30; 32; 34; 35; 37; 40; 41; 51; 64; 4:3; 4; 6; 8; 15; 16; 21; 5:2(2); 6(2); 8; 16; 19; 21; **Ezek** 1:1; 3; 12; 20; 2:1(2); 2(2); 3(4); 4(2); 7; 8; 9; 3:1(2); 2; 3; 4(3); 5(2); 6(3); 7(2); 10(2); 11(3); 15; 16(2); 18(3); 22; 24; 26(2); 27; 4:3; 4; 5; 8; 10; 11; 15; 16; 5:1; 7; 10; 12; 13; 15; 16; 6:1; 3(4); 6; 13; 7:1; 2; 3; 7; 8; 9; 13; 14; 19; 20; 21; 24; 27(3); 8:1; 3(3); 5; 6(2); 7; 8; 9; 12; 13; 14(2); 15; 17(6); 9:3(2); 4; 5; 7; 9; 10:2; 7; 8; 9; 16; 11:1; 2; 3; 5; 12; 14; 15; 24; 25; 12:1; 2(2); 3; 6; 8; 9; 10; 11(2); 12; 13(2); 14(2); 17; 19(3); 21; 23(2); 25; 26; 28; 13:1; 2; 3; 5(2); 11; 12; 13(2); 14; 15; 18(2); 19(2); 22; 14:1; 2; 3; 4(5); 6; 7(3); 9; 12; 15; 21; 22; 15:1; 3(2); 6; 16:1; 2; 3; 4; 5(2); 6(2); 8; 13; 20(3); 21(2); 23; 25(2); 26(2); 27; 33(4); 34; 36; 37; 42; 43; 46(2); 47; 55(3); 61; 17:1; 2; 3; 4; 8; 9(2); 11; 12(3); 15; 17; 20; 21; 18:1; 6; 7(2); 12; 15; 16; 24; 30; 19:3; 4; 6; 9; 12; 20:1(2); 2; 3(3); 4; 5(4); 6(2); 7; 9(2); 12; 13; 15; 18; 21; 23; 25; 26; 27(3); 28; 29(3); 30(2); 31; 35; 42(2); 44(2); 45; 47(2); 21:1; 3; 4; 7(2); 8; 10(2); 11(2); 17; 18; 19(2); 20(3); 21; 22(6); 23(2); 24(2); 25; 27; 29(2); 30; 31; 22:1; 3; 4(4); 6; 9; 12; 17; 18; 20(2); 23; 24; 27(3); 23:1; 16; 17; 19; 21; 24(2); 27; 30; 32; 36(2); 37(2); 38; 39; 40(2); 44(3); 46; 48(2); 24:1; 3(2); 6(2); 7; 9; 13; 14(3); 15; 18; 19(2); 20; 21; 24(2); 26(2); 27(2); 25:1; 3; 4; 7(2); 10; 14(2); 15; 26:1(2); 2; 3(2); 11; 13; 15; 17(2); 20(2); 27:1; 3; 5; 9(2); 10; 28:1; 2; 11; 12; 17; 18; 20; 25; 29:1; 4(3); 5(2); 6; 10; 14(3); 16; 17(2); 18; 19; 21(2); 30:1; 2; 6; 9; 10; 11; 13; 14; 20(2); 21(3); 31:1(2); 2(2); 4; 7; 13; 14(5); 15(2); 16; 17; 18(2); 32:1(2); 2; 4; 6; 12; 17(2); 18(2); 20; 21; 24(2); 25; 27; 29; 30; 33:1; 2(2); 8(2); 9; 10; 11; 12(2); 13; 14; 20; 21(2); 22; 23; 24; 25; 27(3); 30(2); 31; 32; 33; 34:1; 2(3); 10; 13; 18(2); 20; 25; 26; 35:1; 3; 5; 11(2); 12(2); 15; 36:1; 4(2); 5(2); 6; 8(2); 9; 12; 13; 15; 16; 17; 19; 20; 22; 27; 28; 32; 33; 37; 37:2; 3; 4(3); 5(2); 7; 9(3); 11; 12(2); 15; 17; 18; 19; 21; 25; 38:1; 10; 11; 12(3); 13(6); 14; 16; 18; 20; 22; 39:3; 4(3); 11; 12; 14(2); 17(3); 23; 24(2); 26; 28; 40:4(3); 6; 11; 13; 14; 15; 18; 19; 23; 24; 26; 27; 28(2); 29; 31; 32; 33; 34; 35(2); 37; 39; 40; 45; 46(2); 48; 49; 41:4; 6; 7(2); 16; 17; 20; 22; 42:7; 11; 12; 13; 19; 20; 43:1; 3; 6; 7; 10; 11; 14(2); 18; 19(3); 24; 44:1; 2; 3; 4; 5(2); 6(2); 7(2); 8; 11(2); 12(2); 13(2); 14; 15(4); 16(2); 19(3); 23; 24; 27(2); 28; 30(3); 45:4(3); 5; 6(2); 7; 8(2); 11; 15; 17(2); 23; 25; 46:3; 4; 5; 7; 9; 11; 12; 13; 14(3); 16(2); 17(3); 20(2); 21; 24; 47:1; 2; 3(2); 4(2); 6(2); 8; 10; 11; 14(3); 15(2); 16; 17; 19(2); 20; 21; 22; 48:1(3); 2; 3; 4; 5; 6; 7; 8(2); 10(2); 12; 14; 17(4); 18(3); 21(5); 22(2); 23; 24; 25; 26; 27; 28(2); **Dan** 1:1; 2; 3; 4(2); 7(4); 10; 11; 12(2); 16; 2:2(2); 3(2); 4; 5(2); 9(2); 11; 12; 13; 14; 15(2); 16; 17(2); 19; 21(2); 23(2); 24(3); 25(2); 26(3); 27; 28; 29(3); 30(2); 39; 43; 44; 45(2); 46; 3:2(3); 4; 9; 12; 13; 14; 16(2); 17; 18; 20; 24(2); 4:1(2); 2; 3; 6(2); 7; 8; 9; 11(2); 17; 18(2); 20; 22(2); 25; 26(3); 27(2); 31; 32; 34(3); 35(2); 36(5); 37; 5:2; 7(2); 8; 10; 13; 15; 16; 17(3); 28; 6:1(2); 2; 3; 4; 6; 7(2); 8; 12; 14(2); 15; 16; 18; 19; 20(4); 21; 24; 25(2); 26; 7:4(2); 5; 6; 10; 11; 13; 14; 16(2); 19; 22; 25; 26; 27; 8:1(3); 4; 6; 7(2); 10(2); 12(3); 13(2); 14; 17(2); 18; 19; 25; 26; 9:3; 4; 6(2); 7(5); 8(2); 9; 10; 11; 12; 16(2); 17; 21; 22(2); 23; 24(6); 25; 26; 27; 10:1; 7; 8; 9; 11(4); 12(3); 13; 14(4); 15; 16; 19(2); 20(2); 11:1; 3; 4; 6(2); 8; 9(2); 10; 15; 16; 17(2); 18(2); 21; 25; 28(2); 35; 36; 39; 44; 45; 12:1; 2(2); 3; 4; 6; 7; 12; 13; **Hos** 1:1; 2(2); 4(2); 5; 6; 10(3); 2:1(2); 7; 9; 11; 13; 14; 18; 19(2); 20; 21; 23; 3:1(2); 3; 4:12; 15(2); 17; 5:1; 4; 5; 6; 12(2); 13(2); 14(2); 15; 6:1; 3(2); 4(2); 9; 7:10(2); 11(2); 12; 13(2); 14; 16; 8:1; 2; 5; 6; 9; 13; 9:3; 4(3); 10(2); 12(2); 13; 16; 10:1(2); 6; 8(2); 11; 12; 15; 11:2(2); 3; 4; 5(2); 7; 12:1; 2(2); 4; 7; 12; 14; 13:2; 7; 10; 14:1; 2(2); 3; 5; 8; **Joel** 1:1; 9; 13; 14; 19; 20; 2:9; 12; 13(2); 17(2); 19; 23; 25; 26; 27; 28; 32; 3:2; 4; 6; 7; 8(2); 11; 12(2); 18; 20; **Am** 1:5; 6(2); 9; 2:1; 7(2); 10; 12; 3:7; 10; 14; 4:1; 4; 6; 7; 8(3); 9; 10; 11; 12(3); 13; 5:2; 3; 4; 5(2); 6; 7(2); 15; 16(2); 18(2); 6:1(2); 2(3); 3(2); 5; 9; 10(2); 14; 7:8; 10(2); 12(2); 14; 15(2); 8:2; 9; 12(3); 9:2; 7; 9; **Ob** 3; 5(2); 7; 9; 14; 15; 21(2); **Jon** 1:1; 2; 3(6); 4; 5(2); 6(2); 7; 8; 9; 10; 11(2); 12; 13(3); 14; 16; 17; 2:1; 2; 5; 6; 7; 9; 10; 3:1; 2(2); 3(2); 4; 5; 6; 7; 8; 4:2(3); 3(2); 4; 6; 8(2); 9(4); **Mic** 1:1; 7(2); 9(3); 11; 12; 13(2); 14(2); 15(2); 2:1; 4; 5; 6(2); 7; 11; 3:1; 4; 8(3); 4:1(2); 2(2); 8; 10(2); 12; 13(2); 5:2(2); 3; 4; 6:3; 5; 8(3); 9; 14; 7:1; 7; 8; 9; 10; 11; 12(4); 20(3); **Nah** 1:3; 2:5; 3:1; 7; 10; **Hab** 1:2; 3; 6; 8; 11; 13; 16(2); 17; 2:1(2); 5; 6(2); 9; 10; 12; 13; 15(4); 17; 18; 19(3); 3:13; 14; 16; 19; **Zeph** 1:1; 12; 18; 2:5; 11(2); 15; 3:1(2); 2; 4; 5; 8(3); 9(2); 16; 18; 19; **Hag** 1:1(2); 4(2); 6; 8; 9(2); 13; 2:2(3); 5; 7; 16(3); 17; 20; 21; **Zech** 1:1; 3(3); 4; 6(4); 7; 9; 10(2); 11; 13; 14; 16; 19; 21(4); 2:2(3); 3; 4(2); 8; 11(2); 3:1; 2; 4(2); 7; 4:2(2); 4; 5; 6(2); 7; 8; 9; 10(2); 11; 12; 5:2; 3(3); 5; 10; 11(2); 6:4; 5; 6; 7(4); 8(3); 9; 12; 15(2); 7:1(2); 2(2); 3; 4; 5(2); 8; 9; 11; 12; 8:3; 12; 13; 14(2); 15(3); 16; 18; 21(2); 22(2); 9:9; 10(3); 12(2); 10:5; 11:12(2); 13(2); 15; 17; 12:2; 9; 13:2; 3(2); 4; 5; 6; 8; 14:2; 4; 5; 6; 7; 10(3); 13; 16(4); 17(2); 18; 19; 20; 21; **Mal** 1:1; 6; 8; 9; 11(2); 14(2); 2:2(4); 4; 5; 8; 12; 15; 16; 3:1; 3; 4; 7(2); 10; 11; 14; 16; 4:2; 6(2); **Mt** 1:11; 12; 17; 18; 19(2); 20(3); 24; 2:1; 2; 4; 5; 8(2); 11; 12; 13(3); 16(2); 18; 19; 20; 22; 3:5; 7(4); 9(5); 10; 11; 13(2); 14(3); 15(3); 16; 4:1; 3; 6; 7; 9; 10; 11; 12; 17(2); 19; 24; 5:1; 13; 15; 17(3); 18; 20; 21; 22(2); 23; 24; 25(2); 26; 27; 28(2); 29(2); 30(2); 32(2); 33(2); 34; 39(2); 40; 41; 42(2); 44(2); 6:1; 2; 5(2); 6; 16(3); 18(3); 24; 25; 27; 29; 33; 7:2; 4; 5; 6; 7(2); 8; 11(3); 12(3); 13; 14; 15; 21; 22; 23; 24; 8:4(3); 5; 7; 9(3); 10(2); 11; 13; 16; 18(2); 19; 20(2); 21; 22; 25; 26; 28(2); 29(2); 31; 32; 33; 34(2); 9:1; 2(2); 5(2); 6(3); 7; 8; 9; 11; 12; 13(2); 14; 15; 18; 21; 24; 28(4); 29(2); 32; 37; 38; 10:1(3); 6; 13; 15; 17; 18(2); 19; 21(3); 22; 23(2); 28; 29; 34(2); 35; 42; 11:1(3); 3; 4; 5; 7(3); 8; 9(2); 11; 14(2); 15; 16(2); 17; 20; 21(2); 22; 23(2); 24; 25; 27(3); 28; 12:1(2); 2(2); 3; 4; 6; 10; 11; 12; 13; 16; 18; 20; 22; 25(2); 31; 32; 36; 38; 39(2); 42; 44; 46(2); 47(2); 48; 13:2; 3(2); 9; 10(2); 11(4); 12; 13; 17(3); 24; 27; 28(3); 30(2); 31; 33; 34(2); 36(2); 37; 43; 48; 51(2); 52; 53; 54; 57; 14:2; 4(2); 5(2); 7; 9(2); 11(2); 13; 15; 16(3); 17; 18; 19(4); 22; 23; 25; 27; 28(2); 29(2); 30; 31; 34; 35; 15:1; 3; 4; 5(2); 8; 10(2); 12; 15(2); 20; 21; 22; 24; 26(2); 28(2); 30; 32(3); 33(2); 34; 35; 36(2); 39; 16:2; 3; 4; 5(2); 6; 8; 11(2); 12; 15; 17(2); 18; 21(3); 22(2); 23(2); 24(2); 25; 26; 27; 28; 17:3; 4(2); 9; 11; 12(3); 13; 14(3); 16; 17; 19; 20(4); 22(2); 24(2); 26(2); 27(2); 18:1; 2; 3; 6; 7(2); 8(3); 9(3); 10; 11; 12(2); 13; 17(4); 18; 19; 21(2); 22(4); 23; 24(2); 25; 32; 34(2); 35; 19:1(2); 3(3); 4; 5; 7(3); 8(2); 9; 10(2); 11(2); 12; 13; 14; 16; 17(2); 18; 20; 21(3); 23(3); 24(3); 26; 27; 28(2); 20:1; 4; 6; 7(2); 8(2); 12; 14(3); 15; 17(2); 18(4); 19(4); 20; 21(2); 22(3); 23(3); 25; 26; 27; 28(3); 32; 33; 21:1; 2(2); 3; 5; 9; 13; 14; 15; 16(2); 17; 18; 19(2); 21(4); 24; 25; 27; 28; 30; 31(3); 32; 33; 34; 36; 37; 40; 41(3); 42; 43(2); 44; 46; 22:1; 3(3); 4; 5(2); 8; 9; 11; 12; 13; 16; 17(2); 20; 21(4); 23; 25; 26; 29; 31; 37; 42; 43; 44; 46; 23:1(2); 3(2); 4; 5; 7; 13(2); 14; 15(2); 16(2); 18; 23(2); 25; 27; 28; 29; 34; 35; 36; 37(2); 38; 39; 24:1; 2(2); 3; 4; 6; 9; 13; 14; 16; 17; 18; 19(2); 23; 24; 26; 27; 31; 34; 43; 45; 47; 49(2); 25:1(2); 6; 8; 9; 10(2); 11; 12; 14(2); 15(5); 20; 21; 22; 23; 24; 26; 27; 28; 29; 34; 36; 39; 40(4); 41; 44; 45(3); 26:1(2); 2; 4; 7; 9; 10; 13(2); 14; 15(3); 16; 17(4); 18(2); 21; 22(2); 24; 25; 26; 27; 29; 30; 31(2); 32; 33(3); 34(2); 35(2); 36(2); 37; 38(2); 40(2); 45(2); 49; 50; 52; 53; 55(2); 57; 58(2); 59(2); 61(2); 62; 63; 64(2); 68; 69; 71(2); 73; 74; 75; 27:1(2); 2; 3; 4(2); 6; 7; 8; 11; 13; 15(2); 17(3); 19(2); 21(3); 22(2); 24; 26(2); 31; 32; 33(2); 34; 48(2); 49; 51; 53; 55; 58(3); 62; 64; 65; 28:1(2); 5; 8; 9; 10(3); 11; 12; 14; 16; 18(2); 20(2); **Mk** 1:5; 7; 9; 13; 14; 17; 24(2); 32; 34; 35; 37; 38; 40(3); 41; 44(4); 45(3); 2:2(2); 3; 5; 8; 9(3); 10(2); 11(2); 13; 14; 16; 17(3); 18; 19; 23; 24; 25; 26(2); 27; 3:3; 4(5); 5; 7; 8; 10; 13(2); 14; 15(3); 16; 17; 21; 23(2); 28; 29; 31; 32; 4:1(2); 2; 3; 9(2); 11(4); 13; 21(3); 22; 23; 24(3); 25; 30; 33(2); 34(2); 35(2); 38; 39; 40; 41; 5:1(2); 7; 8; 12; 14; 15; 16; 17(2); 19(2); 20; 21(2); 31; 32; 33; 34; 36; 37; 38; 39; 41(2); 43; 6:1; 2(2); 4; 7(2); 8; 9(2); 10; 11; 18(2); 19; 22(2); 23(2); 24; 25(2); 26; 27; 28(2); 30; 31(3); 32; 33; 34; 35; 36; 37(4); 38; 39; 41(3); 45(2); 46(2); 48; 50; 51; 53; 55(2); 7:1; 5; 6; 9; 10; 11(2); 14(2); 16; 18; 24(2); 26; 27(3); 28; 29; 30; 31; 32(2); 34(2); 37(2); 8:1(3); 2; 3; 6(3); 7; 10; 11; 12(3); 13; 14; 17; 19; 21; 22(3); 26; 27(2); 29(2); 31; 32; 34(3); 35; 9:1(2); 4; 5(2); 6; 10; 13(2); 14; 15; 18; 19; 20; 21; 22; 23(2); 25; 29; 30; 31; 32; 33; 35(2); 36; 41(3); 42; 43(4); 45(3); 47(3); 10:1(2); 2; 3; 4(2); 5; 7; 11; 13; 14(2); 15; 18; 20; 21(2); 23(2); 24(2); 25(2); 28(2); 29; 30; 32(3); 33(5); 35(2); 36(2); 37; 38(2); 39(2); 40(2); 41; 42(2); 43; 44; 45(3); 46; 47; 48; 49(2); 50; 51(3); 52; 11:1; 2; 3; 5; 6; 7; 11; 13(2); 14; 15(2); 16; 17; 21; 22; 23(2); 24; 27(2); 28(2); 29; 32; 33(2); 12:1(3); 2; 6; 9; 12; 13(2); 14(3); 15; 16(2); 17(3); 18; 19; 24; 26; 32; 33(2); 34; 36; 38(2); 43(4); 13:1; 2; 5; 9(2); 10; 12(3); 13; 14; 15; 16; 17(2); 21; 22; 27; 30; 34(4); 37(2); 14:1; 5; 8; 9(2); 10(3); 11; 12(2); 13; 14; 16; 18; 19(3); 20; 21; 22; 23; 24; 25; 26; 27(2); 28; 29(2); 30(2); 31; 32(2); 33; 34(2); 37; 40; 41; 45(2); 48(2); 53; 55(2); 61; 64; 65(5); 69(2); 70; 71; 72(2); 15:1; 2; 6(2); 8(2); 9(2); 11; 12(2); 14; 15(3); 18; 20; 21; 22; 23; 24; 36(3); 38; 41(2); 43; 45; 16:2; 6; 7; 8; 9; 12; 13; 14; 15(2); 19; **Lk** 1:1; 2; 3(3); 9(2); 11; 13; 16; 17(4); 18; 19(3); 20; 22(2); 23; 25; 26; 27(2); 28; 30; 34; 35(2); 38(2); 39; 43(2); 50; 55(3); 56; 57; 58; 59; 61; 62; 72(3); 73; 74; 76; 77(2); 79(3); 80; 2:1; 3(2); 4; 5; 6; 10(2); 11; 12; 14; 15(4); 22(4); 23; 24(2); 26; 27(2); 29; 32(2); 34; 38(2); 39(3); 41; 42(2); 44; 45; 46; 48(2); 49; 50; 51(2); 3:2; 7(4); 8(5); 9; 11(2); 12(2); 13; 14; 16(2); 18; 21; 4:3(2); 6(3); 8; 9(2); 10; 12; 14; 16(2); 18(7); 19; 20; 21(2); 22; 23(2); 24; 26(3); 29; 31; 34(2); 40; 41; 42(2); 43(2); 5:1; 3; 4; 5; 7(3); 10; 11; 14(3); 15(2); 17; 18; 20; 21; 22; 23(2); 24(4); 25; 27; 31; 32(2); 33; 34; 36; 6:2(2); 4(2); 5; 8; 9(5); 10; 11; 12(4); 13; 17; 19; 23; 24; 25(2); 26(2); 27(2); 29; 30; 31(3); 32; 33(3); 34(5); 35; 38(2); 39; 42(2); 47; 7:2(2); 3(2); 4; 6(2); 7(2); 8(3); 9(2); 10; 13; 14; 15(2); 18; 19(2); 20(2); 21; 22(2); 24(3); 25; 26(2); 28; 31; 32(2); 36(3); 38; 39; 40(3); 42; 43; 44(2); 45; 47(2); 48; 49(2); 50; 8:1; 4; 5; 8; 10(3); 14; 17; 18(2); 19; 20; 21; 22(2); 24; 25(2); 26; 28; 29; 31; 32; 35(2); 37; 39; 41(2); 47; 48; 49; 51; 55; 56; 9:1; 2(2); 3; 9; 10; 11; 12(2); 13(2); 14; 16(3); 20; 21(2); 23(2); 24; 25; 28(2); 31; 33(2); 40; 42; 43; 44; 45; 46; 48; 50; 51(4); 52; 53; 54(2); 56(3); 57; 58(2); 59; 60; 62(2); 10:1; 2(2); 5; 6; 7; 9(2); 11; 12; 13(2); 15(2); 17; 18; 19; 20; 21; 22(3); 23; 24(2); 25; 26; 28; 29(2); 30; 34(2); 35(2); 36; 37; 40(2); 41; 11:1(3); 2; 4; 5(3); 6(2); 7; 8(2); 9(3); 10; 13(3); 17(2); 24; 27; 29(2); 30(2); 31; 37(2); 39; 41; 42(2); 43; 44; 45; 46(2); 47; 51(2); 52; 53(3); 54; 12:1(2); 4; 5(2); 8; 10; 11; 12; 13(2); 14; 15; 16; 17; 19; 20; 22(2); 25; 26; 27; 31; 32; 36; 37(2); 39; 41(3); 42; 44; 45(2); 47; 48(2); 49; 50; 51; 54; 58(4); 13:2; 7; 8; 12(2); 14(2); 15; 17; 18; 20; 23(2); 24(3); 25(2); 26; 31(2); 32; 34(2); 35(2); 14:1; 3(2); 7(2); 8; 9(3); 10; 12; 15; 16; 17(2); 18(3); 19(2); 21(2); 23(2); 24; 25; 26; 28(2); 29(2); 30(2); 31(2); 35; 15:1(2); 3; 6; 7; 10; 12(3); 13; 14; 15(2); 17(2); 18(2); 19; 20; 21(2); 22; 24; 25; 27; 29; 31; 16:1(2); 2; 3; 4; 5(2); 6; 7(2); 9; 11; 13; 15; 17(2); 21; 22; 26(3); 27; 28(2); 29; 30; 31; 17:1(2); 3; 4; 5; 6; 7(2); 8; 10; 11; 14(2); 18(2); 19; 22(2); 23; 24; 31; 33; 37(2); 18:1(2); 3; 7; 9; 10(2); 13(2); 14; 15; 16(2); 17; 18; 19; 22(2); 24; 25(2); 29(2); 30; 31(2); 32; 40(2); 41; 42; 43; 19:3; 4(2); 5(2); 7; 8(2); 9(2); 10(2); 12(2); 13(2); 14; 15(3); 17; 19; 22; 24(2); 25; 26(2); 27; 28; 29(2); 31; 32; 33; 35; 37; 39; 40; 44; 45; 46; 47; 48(2); 20:2; 3; 8; 9(2); 10; 15; 16; 18; 19; 20(3); 22(2); 23; 25(3); 27; 28; 34; 35; 36; 38; 41; 42; 45; 46; 21:3; 7; 9; 10; 12; 14; 15; 16; 21; 23(2); 28; 29; 32; 34; 36(3); 38(2); 22:4; 5; 6(2); 9(2); 10; 11(2); 13; 15(2); 16; 18; 19; 22; 23; 24; 25; 32; 33(4); 35; 36; 37; 38; 39; 40(2); 43; 44; 45; 46; 47(2); 48; 49(2); 52(2); 53; 61; 67; 70; 23:1; 2(3); 4; 5; 7(2); 8(2); 11; 14(2); 15; 17(2); 18; 20(2); 22; 25(2); 28; 30(3); 32(2); 33; 42; 43(2); 48; 51; 52; 56; 24:1; 5(2); 6; 9(2); 10; 11; 12(2); 13; 17; 18; 19(2); 20(2); 21; 24; 25(2); 26(2); 27; 28; 29; 30(2); 32(2); 33; 34; 35; 36(2); 38; 41; 44(2); 46(3); 47; 51; 52; **Jn** 1:7; 8; 9; 11; 12(3); 19; 22(2); 27; 31; 33(2); 38(3); 39; 41; 42; 43(3); 45; 46(2); 48(2); 49; 50(2); 51(2); 2:2; 3; 4(2); 5(2); 6; 7(2); 8(2); 10; 12; 13; 16; 18(2); 19; 20; 22; 24; 3:2(2); 3(2); 4; 5; 7; 9; 10; 11; 13; 17; 20; 21; 26(4); 27; 4:3; 4; 5(2); 7(2); 8; 9; 10(2); 11(2); 13; 15(2); 16; 17; 19; 20; 21; 23; 25; 26(2); 28; 30; 32(2); 33(2); 34(3); 35; 38; 40(2); 42; 43; 45(2); 46; 47(2); 48; 49; 50(2); 52; 53; 5:1; 6(2); 7; 8; 10(2); 11; 12; 14; 16; 18; 19(2); 21(2); 22; 24; 25; 26; 27; 29(2); 33(2); 35; 36; 40(2); 45; 6:5; 6; 8; 11(2); 12; 14; 15(3); 16; 17; 20; 24; 25; 26; 27; 28; 29; 30; 31; 32(2); 33; 34; 35(2); 36; 37(2); 38; 43; 44; 45; 47; 52; 53(2); 61; 63; 65(3); 67(2); 68; 69; 7:1(2); 3; 4(2); 6; 8(2); 9; 10; 17; 19; 20; 21; 24; 25; 26; 30; 32; 33(2); 35(3); 37; 44; 45(2); 50(2); 52; 53; 8:1; 2; 3; 4; 6; 7; 9; 10; 11; 12; 13; 14; 15; 19; 21; 23; 24; 25(3); 26(3); 27; 28; 31; 33; 34; 37; 39(2); 40; 41; 42; 43(2); 44; 48; 51; 52; 53; 56; 57; 58(2); 59; 9:7; 10; 11(2); 12; 13; 15; 17; 24; 26(2); 27(2); 29; 30; 34; 35; 37; 40; 41; 10:1; 3; 6; 7(2); 10(3); 18(2); 20; 24; 26; 29(2); 31; 35; 39; 40; 41; 11:3; 7(2); 8(2); 11; 14; 15; 16; 19; 21; 23; 24; 25; 27(2); 29; 31(2); 32; 34; 38; 39; 40(2); 44; 45; 46; 49; 53(2); 54; 55(2); 56; 12:1; 5; 6; 10(2); 12(2); 13; 16; 20; 21(2); 24; 27; 29; 32; 35; 38; 47(2); 13:1(2); 2; 3; 5(2); 6(2); 7; 8; 9; 10(2); 12(2); 14; 15; 16; 19; 20; 21; 24(2); 25; 26(2); 27; 28; 29(2); 33(2); 34; 36; 37; 38; 14:2; 3; 5; 6(2); 8; 9; 10; 12(2); 18; 21; 22(3); 23(2); 25; 26(2); 27(2); 28(3); 29; 15:3; 11; 13; 15; 20; 21; 22; 26; 16:1(2); 3; 4; 5; 6; 7(3); 10; 12(2); 13; 14; 15; 16; 17(2); 19(2); 20; 21; 23; 25(2); 26; 28; 29; 32; 33; 17:1; 2; 4; 6(2); 8; 11; 13; 26; 18:4; 5; 6(2); 11; 13; 15; 16(2); 17; 20; 21; 24; 25; 28; 29; 30(2); 31(5); 33; 35; 36; 37(2); 38(3); 39(3); 19:4(2); 5; 6; 7(2); 9; 10(4); 11; 12; 14; 15; 16(2); 17; 21; 23; 26; 27(2); 29; 33; 39; 40; 20:1; 2(3); 3; 4; 8; 10; 13(2); 15(3); 16(3); 17(7); 18; 19; 21(2); 22; 25(2); 26; 27; 28; 29; 21:1; 3(2); 5; 6(2); 7; 9; 10; 11; 12; 13; 14; 15(3); 16(3); 17(4); 18; 19; 21; 22(2); 23(2); **Acts** 1:1; 2; 3(2); 4(2); 6; 7(2); 8(2); 12; 16(2); 19; 22; 25(2); 2:3; 4; 7; 12; 14(2); 17; 21; 22; 23; 27; 28; 29(2); 30(3); 33; 34; 37(2); 38; 39(3); 41; 46; 47; 3:1; 2; 3; 5; 10; 11(2); 12; 13; 14(2); 20; 22(2); 25; 26(2); 4:1; 4; 5; 8; 9; 10(2); 15; 16(2); 17; 18; 19(4); 23(2); 24; 28(2); 29; 30; 33; 35; 5:3(2); 4(2); 9(2); 14; 16; 20; 21(2); 28(2); 29; 31(4); 32(2); 33; 34; 35(3); 36(2); 38(2); 39; 41; 6:4(2); 7; 10; 11; 12; 13; 14; 7:2; 3(2); 4; 5(4); 7; 13(2); 14; 15; 16; 17; 20; 23; 26(2); 28; 30; 31(2); 33; 34(2); 35(2); 37; 38(3); 39; 40(2); 41; 42; 43; 44(2); 46; 54; 8:1; 2; 3; 5(2); 10(2); 14; 20; 24; 25; 26(2); 27(2); 29; 30; 31; 32; 35; 36; 38; 40; 9:1; 2(2); 4(2); 5; 6(2); 10; 11(2); 13; 14; 15(2); 17; 21; 23; 24(2); 26(2); 27(3); 29; 30(2); 32(2); 34; 35; 38(3); 39; 40; 10:2(2); 3; 4; 5; 7; 8(2); 9; 10; 11(2); 13; 15; 19; 21(2); 22(3); 28(3); 32(2); 33(3); 36; 41(3); 42(4); 43; 48(2); 11:2; 3; 4; 5; 7; 11; 12; 13(2); 15; 18(2); 19; 20(2); 21; 22(2); 24; 25; 26; 27; 28; 29(3); 30; 12:1; 3; 4(3); 5; 6; 8(2); 10(3); 11; 12; 13; 15; 17(6); 19(2); 20; 21; 23; 13:2(3); 4(2); 6; 7; 8; 11; 13(2); 14; 15; 19; 22; 23; 24; 25; 26; 28; 31(2); 32(2); 34(2); 35; 38(2); 41(2); 42; 43(2); 44; 46(2); 47(2); 48; 51; 14:1; 3(2); 5; 6(2); 9; 11; 13(2); 15(2); 16; 18; 19; 20; 21(2); 22; 23; 24; 25; 26(2); 27; 15:1; 2(2); 3; 4; 5(3); 6; 7; 8; 10; 12; 13; 14; 18; 19; 20(2); 22(2); 23; 24; 25(3); 28(3); 29; 30; 33; 34(2); 36; 37; 38; 39; 40; 16:1; 3; 4(2); 6; 7(2); 8; 9(2); 10(4); 11(2); 12; 13(2); 14; 15(3); 16; 17; 18(2); 19; 20; 21; 22; 23; 25(2); 27; 30; 32(2); 36(2); 37; 38; 39; 17:1; 2; 3(2); 5(2); 6; 7; 10; 11; 14(2); 15(3); 16; 17; 18(3); 19; 20(2); 21(2); 23(2); 25; 26; 29; 30; 31; 18:1; 2(2); 5; 6(2); 7; 9; 10; 12; 13(2); 14(2); 15(2); 19; 20; 21; 22; 24; 26(2); 27(3); 19:1; 2(2); 3; 4; 12; 13; 17; 21(2); 22; 24; 30(2); 31; 33(2); 36; 39; 40; 20:1(3); 2; 3(3); 4; 7(3); 13(4); 14; 15; 16(3); 17; 18(3); 19; 20(2); 21(2); 22(2); 24(3); 26; 27(2); 28(3); 30; 31; 32(3); 35(2); 38; 21:1(4); 2; 3(2); 4(2); 5; 7; 8; 11; 12(2); 13(2); 15; 16; 17; 18; 20; 21(4); 25; 26; 31(2); 32; 33; 34; 35; 37(3); 39(2); 40(2); 22:2; 3; 4; 5(5); 7(2); 8; 9; 10(2); 12; 13(2); 15; 17; 18; 20; 21(2); 22(2); 24; 25(2); 27; 29; 30(2); 23:2; 3(5); 9; 10(2); 14; 15(4); 17(3); 18(6); 19; 20(3); 21; 22; 23(2); 24(2); 26; 27; 28; 30(2); 31; 32(2); 33(3); 35; 24:1; 2; 4(3); 6(3); 8(2); 10(2); 11(2); 14(2); 16; 17(2); 19(2); 23(4); 25; 27; 25:1(2); 3(2); 5; 6(2); 9(3); 10(2); 11(3); 12(2); 13(2); 16(5); 17; 19; 20(2); 21(3); 22(2); 24; 25(2); 26(3); 27(3); 26:1(2); 3(2); 5(2); 6; 7(2); 9; 10; 11(2); 12; 14(3); 16(3); 17; 18(4); 19; 20(3); 21; 22(2); 23(3); 28(2); 29; 32(2); 27:1(2); 2(2); 3(2); 4; 5; 6; 7; 8; 12(2); 13; 17; 21; 22; 23; 28(2); 29; 30; 31; 33(2); 34; 35(2); 39; 40; 42; 43(2); 44; 28:4(2); 6; 8; 13; 14; 15; 16(3); 17(2); 18(2); 19(3); 20; 21; 22; 23(2); 25; 26; 28(2); 30; **Rom** 1:1(2); 3; 4(2); 5; 7(3); 10(2); 11(2); 13(3); 14(4); 15(2); 16; 17; 19; 22; 24(2); 26; 28(3); 30; 2:2; 4; 6(2); 7; 8; 10(3); 14; 16; 19(2); 3:2; 7; 15; 19; 22; 25; 26; 4:1; 2; 3; 4; 5; 6; 8; 9; 11; 12; 13(2); 16(4); 17; 18(2); 20; 21; 22; 23; 24; 5:5; 7; 10; 12; 14(3); 15; 18(2); 21; 6:2; 10(2); 11(3); 13(3); 16(4); 17; 19; 20; 22; 7:1; 2; 4(4); 5(2); 6; 10(2); 13; 15; 16; 18(2); 19(2); 20; 21; 22; 23; 8:1(3); 4(2); 5(2); 6(2); 7; 11; 12(3); 13(2); 15; 18; 20; 27; 28(3); 29(2); 31; 38; 39; 9:3; 4; 5; 11; 12; 15; 17; 19; 20(2); 21; 22(2); 26(2); 30; 31; 33; 10:1; 2; 3(2); 4; 6; 7; 11; 12; 18(2); 19(2); 20; 21(2); 11:4(2); 5; 8; 9; 11(3); 13(2); 14; 23; 24; 25; 30; 32; 35(2); 36(2); 12:1; 2; 3(6); 6(3); 9; 10(2); 13(2); 19; 13:1; 3(3); 4(2); 6; 7(5); 8; 10; 11; 14; 14:1; 4(4); 6(4); 7(2); 8(2); 9; 11(2); 12; 13(2); 14(3); 18; 21; 22; 15:1(2); 2; 5(2); 7; 8(3); 9(2);

12; 14; 15(2); 16; 17(2); 18(2); 19; 20; 21; 22; 23(2); 24(4); 25(3); 26; 27(2); 28(2); 29; 30; 31; 32; 16:1; 4; 5; 17; 19(2); 25(4); 26(3); 27; **1 Cor** 1:1; 2(3); 3; 4; 8; 11; 17(2); 18(2); 19; 21; 23(2); 24; 26; 27(4); 28(2); 2:1(2); 2; 6; 10; 12; 14; 3:1(4); 2; 5; 8; 10(2); 18; 22; 4:5; 6(2); 9(4); 11; 14; 17; 18; 19; 21; 5:5; 9(2); 10; 11(3); 12; 6:1; 2; 3; 4(2); 5(2); 6; 7; 8; 16; 17; 7:1(2); 3(2); 5; 8(2); 9(2); 10(2); 11(2); 12(2); 13; 15; 17; 26; 27(2); 32; 39(2); 40; 8:1; 2; 4; 7; 8; 9; 10(2); 9:2(2); 3; 4; 5; 6; 7; 15(2); 16; 19; 20(2); 21; 22(2); 25; 27; 10:1; 6; 7(2); 11; 13(3); 15; 19; 20(3); 22; 27(2); 28(2); 31; 32(3); 11:2; 3; 6; 7; 10; 13(2); 14; 15(2); 16; 20; 22(2); 23; 29; 33; 12:1; 2; 3; 7; 8(2); 9(2); 10(5); 11; 13; 21(2); 22; 23; 24; 13:3(2); 12; 14:2(2); 3; 6(2); 9; 11(2); 12; 21; 22(2); 28(2); 30; 32; 34(2); 35(2); 37(2); 39(2); 15:1(2); 2; 3(2); 4; 6; 9; 24(2); 28(2); 32; 34(2); 38; 54; 57; 16:1; 3(2); 5; 7(2); 9; 11; 12(3); 15; 16(2); **2 Cor** 1:1; 2; 4; 8(2); 11; 13(2); 15(2); 16(5); 17; 18; 20; 23(2); 2:1; 3(2); 4; 5(2); 7; 8(2); 9(2); 12(3); 14; 15; 16(4); 3:1(2); 5; 15; 16; 18; 4:2; 3; 6(2); 11; 13; 15(2); 5:2; 4; 8(2); 9(2); 10; 11; 12(2); 16(2); 18; 19(3); 20; 21; 6:1; 11; 13; 18; 7:2; 3(3); 5; 9; 10(2); 11; 12(2); 14(3); 8:1; 3; 4; 5(2); 10(3); 11; 12(2); 16; 17; 19(3); 24; 9:1(3); 2; 4; 5(3); 8; 9; 10; 11; 12; 13; 15; 10:2(2); 3; 5; 6; 7; 9; 14(2); 16(2); 11:2(2); 5; 7; 8(2); 9(2); 12(2); 15; 17; 18; 21; 29; 32; 12:1(2); 2; 4; 6(2); 7(2); 9; 11; 13(2); 14(4); 17; 19; 13:1; 2(2); 5; 7; 10; **Gal** 1:2; 3; 4; 5; 6; 7; 8(2); 9; 10; 11(2); 13; 16; 17(4); 18(2); 20; 22; 23; 2:1; 2(2); 3; 4; 5; 6(5); 7(2); 8; 9(4); 10; 11(3); 14(2); 17; 19(2); 3:2; 5; 6; 8; 10; 15; 16(3); 18; 19; 22; 24(2); 29; 4:5; 9(3); 12; 13; 15; 17; 18; 20(2); 21; 23; 24; 25; 29(2); 5:2; 3(2); 4; 13; 17; 6:3; 8(2); 10(2); 11; 12(2); 13; 14(2); 16; **Eph** 1:1; 2; 5(3); 6; 7; 8; 9(2); 11(2); 12; 14; 16; 17; 19; 21; 22(2); 2:2(2); 7; 15; 16(2); 17(2); 18; 3:2; 3; 5(2); 7(2); 8; 9; 10(2); 11; 14; 16(2); 18; 19; 20(3); 21(2); 4:1; 3; 7(2); 8; 11; 13(3); 14; 16; 19(2); 22; 24; 27; 28; 29; 32; 5:2; 10; 12; 19(2); 20; 21; 22(2); 24(2); 27; 28; 31; 6:4; 5(3); 7(2); 9; 11; 13(2); 16; 18; 19(2); 20; 21; 22; 23; **Phil** 1:1; 2; 7; 11; 12(2); 13(2); 14; 16(2); 20; 21(3); 23; 24; 26; 28(2); 29(3); 2:6; 8; 11; 13(2); 19(2); 23; 25(3); 30(2); 3:1(2); 7; 10; 11; 13(2); 15; 16; 21(4); 4:2; 5; 6; 11(2); 12(6); 17; 18; 19; 20; **Col** 1:2(2); 3; 6; 8; 9(2); 11; 12(2); 20(2); 22; 23; 25(3); 26; 27(2); 29(2); 2:1; 2(2); 5; 8(3); 14(2); 17; 19; 20; 22; 3:5; 8; 9; 10; 15; 16; 17; 18; 20; 22; 23(2); 4:3(2); 4; 6; 8; 9; 10; 11(2); 17(2); **1 Th** 1:1(2); 2; 5; 7; 8; 9(3); 10(2); 2:1; 2(2); 4; 8(3); 9(2); 15; 16(4); 17; 18(2); 3:1; 2; 3; 5; 6(3); 9; 11; 12(3); 4:1(2); 4; 7; 9(2); 11(3); 13; 15; 17; 5:1; 9(2); 12; 13; 15; 27; **2 Th** 1:1; 2; 3; 6; 7; 10(2); 12; 2:1; 2; 9; 13(2); 14; 3:6; 7; 8; 9; **1 Tim** 1:2; 4; 6; 7; 10; 11(2); 15; 16(2); 17(2); 18(2); 20(2); 2:4(3); 6; 12(3); 3:2; 3; 5; 8; 14(3); 15; 4:1; 3(3); 4; 8; 10; 12; 13(3); 14; 15(2); 16(2); 5:4(2); 11(2); 13(2); 14(2); 24; 6:3(2); 9; 12; 13; 16; 17(3); 18(2); 19; 20; **2 Tim** 1:1; 2; 4; 5; 6; 8; 9(3); 10; 11; 12(2); 14; 16; 18(2); 2:2(2); 5; 6; 8; 9; 14(3); 15(3); 16; 24(2); 26(2); 3:2; 7(2); 9; 11; 12; 15; 4:3; 4; 8(3); 9(2); 11; 12; 14; 18; 21; **Titus** 1:1; 3(2); 4; 7; 9; 14; 15(2); 16; 2:3; 4(2); 5(2); 6; 7; 8; 9(3); 11; 3:1(4); 2(3); 5; 7; 8(3); 12(4); 14(2); **Phm** 1:1; 2(2); 3; 8; 9; 10; 11(3); 13(2); 14; 16(2); 19(2); 21; 22; **Heb** 1:1; 2; 5(3); 8; 13; 14; 2:1; 3(2); 4; 5(2); 10(2); 11; 12(2); 15; 16(2); 17(3); 18; 3:2; 6; 14; 18(2); 4:1; 2(2); 6; 11(2); 12; 13(2); 16(2); 5:1; 2; 3; 4; 5(2); 6; 7(2); 9; 10; 11(2); 12(3); 14(2); 6:1; 5; 6(3); 8(2); 10(2); 11; 13; 17(2); 18(2); 20; 7:2; 4; 5(2); 9; 11(2); 13; 16(2); 17; 19; 21(2); 25(4); 27; 8:3(2); 4; 5(2); 9(2); 11; 12; 13; 9:9; 11; 14(2); 19(2); 22; 24; 26(2); 27; 28(2); 10:1; 2; 7; 8; 9; 15; 19; 24; 31; 39(2); 11:4; 6(2); 7; 8(2); 11; 15(2); 16; 19; 20; 24; 25(2); 26; 29; 32; 34; 35; 12:4; 5(2); 9; 10; 11(2); 17; 18(2); 19; 22(3); 23(3); 24(2); 13:2; 6; 7; 10; 13; 14; 15(2); 16(2); 18; 19(2); 21(2); 22(2); **Jas** 1:1; 5(2); 12; 15; 19(3); 21; 27(2); 2:3(3); 5(2); 8; 13; 16; 20; 23; 3:2; 10; 17; 4:4; 6; 7; 8(2); 9(2); 12(3); 13; 15; 17(3); 5:16; **1 Pe** 1:1; 2(2); 3(2); 4; 5; 7; 10; 12(6); 13(2); 14; 17; 25; 2:4(2); 5(2); 6; 7(2); 8(2); 13(2); 14(2); 15; 18(3); 21; 23; 24; 25; 3:1; 5; 7(2); 9; 12; 15(2); 17; 18(2); 19; 22; 4:4; 5(2); 6(3); 9; 10; 11; 12(2); 13; 17; 19(3); 5:3(2); 5(3); 10; 11; 12; 14; **2 Pe** 1:1; 2; 3(2); 4; 5(2); 6(3); 7(2); 9; 10; 11; 12; 13; 15; 16; 17; 19; 2:4(2); 6(2); 8; 9(2); 10(2); 12; 13; 21(3); 22(4); 3:1; 3; 9; 11; 13; 14(2); 15(3); 16(2); 18; **1 Jn** 1:2(2); 3; 4; 5; 9(2); 2:1; 6; 7; 8; 12; 13(3); 14(2); 21; 26(2); 3:5; 14; 16; 4:10; 11; 5:13(2); 14; 16(3); 17; **2 Jn** 1; 5; 6; 8; 10; 12(6); **3 Jn** 1; 4; 8; 9(2); 10(2); 13(3); 14(3); **Jude** 1; 2; 3(6); 5; 7(2); 11; 15(2); 16(2); 18; 24(3); 25; **Rev** 1:1(2); 2(3); 4(3); 5; 6(2); 8; 11(8); 12; 13; 17; 2:1; 5; 7(3); 8(2); 10(2); 11; 12; 13; 14(4); 16; 17(3); 18; 20(3); 21; 23(2); 24(2); 26; 27; 29; 3:1; 2; 6; 7; 9; 10(2); 13; 14; 18; 20; 21(2); 22; 4:8; 9; 11; 5:2(2); 3(2); 4(2); 5(3); 9(3); 10; 12; 13(2); 6:2(2); 4(3); 8(2); 11(2); 13; 16; 17; 7:2(3); 10(2); 12; 13; 14(2); 17; 8:2; 5; 6; 7; 13(2); 9:1(3); 3; 4; 5(2); 6; 10; 14; 15; 10:4(2); 5; 7(2); 8; 9(3); 11; 11:2; 3; 5(2); 6(4); 9; 10; 12(2); 13; 17; 12:2; 4(3); 5(2); 9; 11; 12(2); 13(2); 14; 15; 17; 13:4(2); 5; 6; 7(3); 12; 14(3); 15(3); 16; 14:4(2); 6(3); 7; 13; 15(2); 18; 20; 15:7; 8; 16:1; 5; 6; 8(2); 14(3); 16; 19; 17:1; 7; 8; 11; 13; 15; 17(4); 18:5; 6(3); 17; 19:1; 8(2); 9(3); 10(2); 17; 19; 20:1; 4(2); 8(3); 12; 13; 21:5; 6(2); 9; 10; 15; 17; 23; 22:6(2); 8; 9; 10; 12(3); 14; 16(2); 18(3); 20

TOO (78/74)

Gen 18:14; 36:7; **Ex** 12:4; 18:18; 23:29; 36:7; **Lev** 21:18; 22:23(2); 27:8; **Num** 11:14; 16:3; 7; 22:6; **Deut** 1:17; 2:36; 7:22; 12:21; 14:24(2); 17:8; 30:11; **Josh** 17:15; 19:9; **Judg** 6:27; 7:2; 4; 18:26; **Ruth** 1:12; **2 Sam** 3:39; 10:11(2); 12:8; 17:5; 22:18; **1 Ki** 1:36; 3:8; 8:64; 12:28; 13:18; 19:7; **2 Ki** 3:26; 6:1; **1 Chr** 19:12(2); **2 Chr** 29:34; **Ezra** 9:6; **Job** 15:11; 32:17; 42:3; **Ps** 18:17; 35:10; 38:4; 73:16; 120:6; 131:1; 139:6; **Prov** 24:7; 30:18; **Isa** 28:20; 40:20; 49:6; 19; 20; **Jer** 4:12; 32:17; 27; **Ezek** 16:47; 20:27; 24:9; 34:18; 47:5; **Hos** 3:3; **Mk** 7:9; **Acts** 17:6; **2 Cor** 2:5; 7; 11:21

UNTO (23/17)

Ps 19:2(2); 29:1(2); 2; 42:7; 57:10(2); 112:4; 115:1(2); 123:1; **Prov** 4:18; **Isa** 9:6(2); 53:12; **Mt** 3:11; **Jn** 11:4; **Rom** 10:10(2); **Phil** 2:27; **Heb** 12:2; **Jude** 21

UP (1937/1783)

Gen 2:6; 21; 4:8; 7:11; 17; 8:7; 13; 13:1; 17:22; 19:14; 28; 30; 20:18; 21:15; 18; 22:13; 23:3; 7; 24:16; 26:15; 18; 23; 27:38; 28:12; 18; 29:11; 31:45; 35:1; 3; 13; 14; 37:28; 38:8; 12; 13; 40:13; 20; 41:2; 3; 4; 5; 6; 18; 19; 20; 21; 22; 23; 27; 35; 48(3); 43:2; 44:4; 17; 24; 30; 33; 34; 45:9; 25; 46:4; 29; 31; 47:14; 48:2; 49:4(2); 9; 26; 33; 50:5; 6; 7(2); 9; 14; 23; 25; **Ex** 1:10; 2:17; 23; 3:8; 17; 7:12; 20; 8:3; 4; 5; 6; 7; 9:16; 10:5; 14; 12:34; 38; 13:8; 18; 19; 14:11; 16; 16:13; 23; 24; 33; 34; 17:3; 10; 11; 19:3; 12; 20; 23; 24(2); 20:26; 24:1; 2; 9; 12; 13; 15; 18; 26:30; 27:5; 29:46; 32:1; 6; 30; 33:1; 3(2); 5; 12; 15; 34:2; 3; 4; 24; 40:2; 5; 8(2); 17; 18(3); 21; 28; 33(2); 36; 37(2); **Lev** 6:10; 10:16; 11:45; 13:37; 14:38; 46; 15:3; 26:1(2); 38; 27:3; 5; 6; 23; **Num** 1:51(2); 6:26; 7:1; 9:15; 17; 21(2); 22; 10:11; 35; 11:6; 20; 32; 13:17(2); 21; 22; 30; 31(2); 14:1; 13; 40(2); 42; 44; 15:19; 20(2); 16:2; 12; 13; 14; 30; 32; 34; 37; 39; 18:24; 26; 29; 30; 32; 19:9; 20:4; 5; 16; 25; 27; 21:3; 5; 17; 33; 22:4(2); 41; 23:7; 18(2); 24; 24:3; 15; 20; 21; 23; 26:10; 27:12; 31:26; 32:9; 11; 33:38; **Deut** 1:21; 22; 24; 26; 28(2); 41(2); 42; 43; 3:1; 27; 5:5; 6:7; 8:14; 9:1; 9; 23; 10:1; 3; 11:6; 17; 18; 19; 14:28; 15:3; 16:22; 17:8; 18:11; 15; 18; 20:1; 22:4; 25:7(2); 9; 27:2; 4; 15; 29:22; 32:11(2); 34(2); 49; 34:1; **Josh** 2:6; 8; 10; 3:6(2); 4:5; 8; 9; 16; 17; 19; 20; 23(2); 5:1; 7; 6:1; 5; 6; 12; 20; 26(2); 7:2(2); 3(2); 4; 10; 13; 8:1; 3; 10(2); 11; 10:4; 5; 6; 12; 33; 36; 14:8; 15:3; 6(2); 7; 8(2); 15; 16:1; 17:15; 18:1; 11; 12(2); 19:47; 22:3; 24:17; 26; 32; **Judg** 1:1; 2; 3; 4; 16; 22; 2:1(2); 4; 16; 18; 3:9; 15; 4:5; 10(2); 12; 14; 6:3(2); 5; 8; 13; 35; 8:8; 11; 27; 9:18; 32; 33; 48; 51; 11:2; 13; 16; 31; 12:3; 13:20; 14:2; 19; 15:5; 6; 9; 10(2); 13; 16:3; 5; 8; 18(2); 31; 18:9; 12; 17; 30; 31; 19:28(2); 30(2); 20:3; 9; 13; 18(2); 23(2); 26; 28; 30; 31; 38; 40; 45; 21:2; 5(2); 8; 19; **Ruth** 1:9; 14; 2:15; 18; 4:1; **1 Sam** 1:3; 7; 21; 22; 24; 2:6; 7; 14; 19; 35; 5:12; 6:9; 10; 20; 21; 7:7; 10; 12; 8:8; 9:11; 13(2); 14(2); 19; 24; 26; 10:3; 18; 25; 11:1; 4; 12:6(2); 13:5; 15; 14:9; 10(2); 12(2); 13; 21; 15:2; 6; 11; 12; 34; 17:2; 8; 21; 23; 25(2); 19:15; 20:38; 22:8; 23:19; 29; 24:7; 16; 22; 25:5; 35; 26:19; 27:8; 28:8; 11(2); 14; 15; 29:9; 10; 11; 30:4; **2 Sam** 2:1(3); 2; 3; 27; 32; 3:10; 32; 4:4; 5:8; 17; 19(2); 22; 23; 6:2; 12; 15; 7:6; 12; 12:3; 11; 17; 13:36; 14:7; 14; 15:20; 24; 30(4); 16:13; 17:6; 16; 21; 18:18; 24; 28; 33; 19:34; 20:3; 15; 19; 20; 21:8; 12; 13; 22:9; 49; 23:1; 24:18; 19; 22; **1 Ki** 1:35; 40; 45; 2:19; 34; 3:15; 5:13; 6:8; 7:21(3); 8:1; 3; 4(2); 35; 54; 9:16; 24; 10:5; 11:14; 15; 23; 12:8; 10; 24; 27; 28(2); 29; 13:29; 14:14; 16; 25; 15:4; 17; 16:17; 32; 34; 17:7; 14; 16; 18:38; 41; 42(2); 43(2); 44; 46; 20:1; 22; 26; 33; 34; 21:16; 25; 22:6; 12; 20; 29; 35; 38; **2 Ki** 1:3; 4; 6(2); 7; 9; 13; 14; 16; 2:1; 8; 11; 13; 16; 23(4); 3:7; 8; 19; 21; 22; 24; 25; 4:21; 34; 35; 36; 37; 6:7; 24; 9:2; 16; 20; 25; 32; 10:4; 15; 12:10; 17(2); 14:10; 15:14; 16:5; 7(2); 9; 17:3; 4; 5; 7; 10; 36; 18:9; 13; 17(2); 25(2); 19:4; 14; 22; 23; 24; 28; 20:5; 8; 21:3; 22:4; 23:2; 9; 24:1; 10; 25:6; **1 Chr** 5:26; 11:6; 11; 20; 13:6(2); 14:8; 10(2); 11; 14; 15:3; 12; 14; 25; 28; 17:5; 11; 19:17(2); 21:1; 19; **2 Chr** 1:4; 6; 2:16; 3:17; 5:2; 4; 5(2); 13; 6:26; 7:13; 8:11; 9:4; 10:8; 10; 11:4; 12:2; 9; 13:3; 6; 16:1; 18:2; 5; 11; 19; 28; 34; 20:16; 19; 23; 21:16; 17; 24:23; 25:14; 19; 26:16; 28:9; 12; 15; 24; 29:7; 8; 20; 30:7; 27; 31:16; 17; 32:5(2); 25; 33:3; 19; 34:30; 35:20; 36:6; 15; 22; 23; **Ezra** 1:1; 3; 5; 2:59; 4:12; 23; 5:2; 7:6; 7; 13; 22; 28; 8:1; 9:6(2); 10:2; 6; 10; **Neh** 2:15; 18; 3:1; 4:3; 6; 7:5; 61; 8:5; 6; 9:3; 5; 18; 10:38; 12:1; 31; 37; **Esth** 2:7; 20; 5:3; 6; 7:2; **Job** 1:16; 3:10; 4:15; 5:5; 18; 7:9; 8:11; 10:15; 11:15; 12:15; 14:11; 17; 16:4; 8(2); 12; 17:8; 19:8; 12; 20:6; 15; 27; 21:19; 22:22; 23; 26; 24:22; 26:8; 12(2); 27:7; 16(2); 17; 19; 28:5; 11; 30:13; 20; 22; 28; 31:14; 29; 36:13; 27; 37:20; 38:34; 39:27; 30; 41:10; 15; 25; 42:8; **Ps** 3:1; 3; 4:6; 5:3; 7:6(2); 9:13; 10:12; 14:4; 15:3; 16:4; 17:7; 10; 18:8; 35; 39; 48; 20:5; 21:9; 22:15; 24:4; 7(2); 9(2); 25:1; 27:2; 6; 28:2; 5; 9; 30:1; 3; 31:8; 19; 33:7; 35:2; 11; 23; 25; 39:2; 6; 40:2; 12; 41:8; 9; 10; 44:5; 11; 47:5; 53:4; 54:3; 56:1; 57:3; 59:1; 15; 63:4; 69:1; 9; 15; 29; 71:20; 74:3; 4; 5; 8; 15; 23; 75:3; 4; 5; 77:9; 18; 78:13; 21; 38; 48; 80:2; 83:2; 86:4; 88:8; 89:2; 4; 90:5; 6; 91:12; 92:7; 11; 93:3(3); 94:2; 16(2); 18; 97:3; 102:10; 16; 104:8; 105:35; 106:9; 17; 18; 26; 30; 107:25; 26; 110:7; 116:13; 119:48; 117; 121:1; 122:4; 123:1; 124:2; 127:2(2); 129:6; 132:3; 134:2; 139:2; 21; 140:10; 141:2; 7; 143:8; 144:12; 145:14; 147:2; 3; 6; **Prov** 2:3; 7; 3:20; 6:31; 8:1; 10:12; 14; 13:22; 15:1; 18; 16:27; 22:6; 15; 23:8; 25:7; 26:24; 28:25; 29:22; 30:13; 21; 31:28; **Eccl** 3:3; 4:10(2); 10:12; 12:4; **Song** 2:7; 10; 13; 3:5; 4:2; 12; 5:6; 6:6; 7:8; 12; 13; 8:4; 5; **Isa** 1:2; 6; 2:3; 4; 12; 13; 14; 3:13; 14; 5:2; 6; 13; 26; 6:1; 7:1; 6; 8:7(2); 8; 16; 9:11; 18; 19; 10:15(2); 24; 26(2); 29; 30; 11:12; 16; 13:2; 14; 17; 14:4; 8; 9(2); 21; 22; 15:2; 5(2); 7; 18:3; 19:5; 6; 21:2; 22:1; 23:4; 13(2); 18; 24:10; 14; 18; 22; 25:8; 26:11; 28:4; 7; 21; 30:26; 28; 32:9; 13; 33:3; 10; 12; 34:4; 13; 35:9; 36:1; 10(2); 37:4; 14; 23; 24; 25; 29; 38:22; 40:9(3); 15; 26; 31; 41:2; 25; 42:11; 13; 15(2); 43:6; 44:4; 11; 26; 27; 45:8; 13; 47:13; 48:13; 49:6; 18; 19; 21; 22; 23; 50:2; 9; 51:6; 8; 10; 17; 18; 52:8; 53:2; 55:13(2); 57:7; 8(2); 14(2); 20; 58:1; 12; 59:19; 60:4; 10; 61:4; 62:10(3); 63:11; 64:7; 11; 66:9; **Jer** 2:6; 3:2; 6; 4:3; 6; 7; 13; 29; 5:10; 17(3); 6:1; 4; 7(2); 7:13; 16; 25; 29; 9:10(2); 12; 18; 10:17; 20; 25; 11:7; 13; 14; 12:17; 13:19; 20; 14:2; 16:14; 15; 18:7; 21; 20:9; 22:20(2); 22; 23:4; 7; 8; 10; 24:6; 8; 25:32; 26:5; 10; 17; 27:22; 29:15; 19; 22; 30:9; 13; 31:6; 21; 28; 40; 32:2; 3; 33; 33:1; 15; 35:11; 15; 37:5; 7; 10; 38:13; 39:5; 15; 42:10; 45:4; 46:4; 7; 8(2); 9; 11; 47:6; 48:15; 49:14; 19; 22; 28; 31; 50:2; 3; 9; 21; 26; 32; 38; 41; 44; 51:1; 3; 9; 11; 12(2); 14; 27(2); 34; 36; 42; 53; 52:9; 31; **Lam** 2:2; 5(2); 7; 16; 22; 3:12; 63; 4:5; 5:12; **Ezek** 1:19(2); 21(2); 3:12; 14; 4:2; 7:11; 8:3; 11; 9:3; 10:4; 15; 16; 17(2); 19; 11:1; 22; 23; 24(2); 13:5; 14:3; 4; 7; 15:6; 16:21; 27; 40; 17:9(2); 14; 17; 24; 18:6; 19:1; 3; 12; 20:25; 28; 21:22(2); 23:8; 22; 46(2); 24:8; 10; 26:3(2); 8; 17; 27:2; 32; 28:2; 5; 12; 17; 29:4; 5; 31:10; 14; 32:2; 3; 33:25; 34:4; 16; 18; 29; 36:3(2); 37:12; 13; 38:11; 16; 39:2; 15; 40:6; 26; 31; 34; 37; 40; 49; 41:7(2); 42:6; 43:5; 24; 47:3; 4(2); **Dan** 2:21; 44; 3:1; 2; 3(2); 5; 7; 12; 14; 18; 22; 5:19; 20; 23; 6:23(2); 7:2; 3; 4; 5; 8; 20; 8:3; 8; 10; 22; 26; 9:24; 11:1; 2; 4; 6; 10(2); 12; 14; 23; 25(2); 12:1; 4; 7; 9; 11; **Hos** 1:11; 2:6; 15; 4:8; 15(2); 19; 6:1; 2; 8:4; 7; 8; 9; 9:6; 12; 16; 10:4; 12; 11:8; 13:12(2); 15(2); **Joel** 1:6; 10; 12; 20; 2:20; 22; 3:2; 9(2); 12; **Am** 1:6; 9; 2:10; 11; 3:1; 5; 10; 4:10; 5:1; 2; 6:8; 10; 14; 8:4; 9:2; 7; 11(2); 15; **Ob** 1; 14; **Jon** 1:2; 4; 12; 15; 2:6; 7; 4:6; 10; **Mic** 2:4; 8; 13; 3:10; 4:2; 3; 5:3; 6:4; **Nah** 1:4; 9; 2:1; 7; 3:15; **Hab** 1:6; 10; 15; 2:5; 6; 7; 3:16; **Zeph** 3:8; **Hag** 1:8; 14; **Zech** 1:21(2); 2:6(2); 7; 5:7; 9; 9:3; 5; 13; 10:11; 12; 11:16; 14:10; 16; 17; 18(2); 19; **Mal** 3:15; 4:1; **Mt** 3:9; 12; 16; 4:1; 5; 6; 8; 5:1; 6:19; 20; 9:6; 10:17; 19; 21(2); 11:5; 12:41; 42; 13:5; 6; 7; 28; 29; 14:19; 20; 23; 15:29; 37; 16:9; 10; 24; 17:1; 8; 23; 27; 18:21; 22(2); 20:17; 18; 22:7; 24; 23:13; 32; 24:1; 9; 11; 26:2; 49; 73; 27:37; 50; **Mk** 1:10; 31; 2:9; 11; 12; 3:13; 26; 4:5; 6; 7; 8; 32; 5:29; 6:23; 41; 43; 51; 7:34; 8:8; 19; 20; 24; 25; 34; 9:2; 27; 10:16; 21; 32; 33; 11:20; 12:19; 13:9; 11; 12; 14:45; 57; 60; 15:11; 41; 16:4; 18; 19; **Lk** 1:69; 2:4; 28; 42; 3:8; 20; 4:5; 11; 16(2); 25; 29; 5:19; 23; 24; 25(2); 28; 6:20; 7:15; 16; 8:6; 7; 8; 9:16; 17; 23; 28; 51; 10:25; 11:31; 32; 12:19; 21; 13:7; 11; 25; 14:10; 16:23; 17:6; 13; 18:10; 31; 19:4; 5; 28; 20:28; 21:1; 12; 28(2); 22:45; 23:5; 24:33; 50; 51; **Jn** 2:7; 13; 17; 19; 20; 3:14(2); 4:14; 35; 5:1; 4; 7; 8; 9; 11; 12; 6:3; 5; 12; 13; 39; 40; 44; 54; 7:8(2); 10(2); 14; 8:7; 10; 28; 59; 10:1; 31; 11:11; 31; 41; 55; 12:20; 32; 34; 13:18; 17:1; 18:30; 19:30; 21:11; **Acts** 1:2; 9; 10; 11(2); 13; 15; 22; 2:14; 24; 30; 32; 3:1; 6; 7; 8; 13; 22; 26; 5:6; 17; 30; 34; 36; 37; 6:12; 13; 7:20; 21; 37; 42; 43; 8:31; 39; 9:40; 41; 10:4; 9; 16; 26(2); 40; 11:2; 10; 28; 12:7; 13:1; 16; 18; 22; 23; 31; 33; 37; 43; 50(2); 14:2; 10; 20; 15:2; 5; 7; 16; 16:22; 17:13; 18:12; 22; 19:19; 20:9; 11; 30; 32; 21:4; 12; 15; 27; 38; 22:3; 13; 24:11; 25:1; 9; 18; 26:10; 30; 27:20; 27; 41; 28:6; **Rom** 1:24; 26; 2:5; 4:24; 25; 8:32; 9:17; 10:7; 13:9; **1 Cor** 4:6; 18; 19; 5:2; 6:14(2); 8:1; 10:7; 13:4; 15:15(2); 35; 54; 16:2; **2 Cor** 2:7; 4:14(2); 5:4; 9:2; 11:4; 19; 20; 12:2; 4; 14; **Gal** 1:17; 18; 2:1; 2; **Eph** 2:6; 4:15; 6:4; 9; 13; **Col** 1:5; 24; 2:7; 18; **1 Th** 2:16; 4:17; **1 Tim** 2:8; 3:6; 16; 5:10; 6:19; **2 Tim** 1:6; 4:3; 8; **Heb** 1:12; 5:7; 7:27(2); 10:24; 11:17(2); 19; 12:15; 13:20; **Jas** 4:10; 5:3; 15; **1 Pe** 1:13; 2:5(2); **2 Pe** 1:13; 3:1; 10; **1 Jn** 3:17; **Jude** 12; 13; 20; **Rev** 4:1; 6:14; 8:7(2); 10:4; 5; 11:12; 12:5; 16; 13:1; 11; 14:20; 16:12; 18:21; 19:3; 20:3; 9; 13(2)

UPON (627/574)

Gen 6:12; 15:12(2); 16:5; 18:27; 31; 19:23; 22:9; 31:10; 34:25; 27; 35:5; 37:27; 38:29; 42:21; 43:18; 44:34; 47:20; 48:16; 49:19; **Ex** 2:25; 3:6; 5:3; 10:12; 14:24; 26; 15:19; 18:8; 19:11; 18; 20; 20:12; 26:32(2); 34; 28:33; 34; 35; 30:10(2); 32:21; 34; 33:16; 34:7; 40:23; 29; **Lev** 1:8; 12; 3:5; 6:9; 10:6; 7; 11:34; 16:10; 17:11; 18:25; 19:19; 20:9; 11; 12; 13; 16; 27; 21:12; 22:3; **Num** 5:14(2); 30(2); 6:5; 19; 25; 26; 11:17(2); 25(3); 26; 29; 15:31; 39; 16:3; 7; 24:2; **Deut** 2:25; 4:7; 30; 5:9; 7:23; 11:25; 17:9; 10; 11; 19:10; 28:2; 15; 45; 46; 59; 61; 30:1; 31:17; 21; 32:35; **Josh** 1:3; 9:20; 10:9; 13; 23:15(2); 24:7; **Judg** 3:10; 6:34; 9:33; 44; 11:29; 13:5; 19; 25; 14:6; 19; 15:14; 16:9; 12; 14; 17; 20; 18:25; 20:34; 37; 41; **1 Sam** 1:11; 2:8; 28; 34; 4:19; 7:10; 9:16; 10:6; 10; 11; 11:6; 16:13; 16; 23; 18:10; 19:9; 20; 23; 20:9; 28:10; 18; **2 Sam** 1:9; 21; 5:23; 9:8; 15:14; 16:8; 17:2; 12; 20:12; 22:4; 7; 11(2); 24:15; **1 Ki** 2:33(4); 7:25; 16:18; 18:46; **2 Ki** 2:9; 16; 3:15; 27; 4:21; 7:9; 8:1; 9:25; 19:7; 21:12; 24:3; **1 Chr** 7:23; 12:18; 14:14; 17; 16:8; 19:17; 21:14; 27:24; 28:19; **2 Chr** 4:4; 14:14; 15:1; 19:2; 7; 10; 20:9; 12; 14; 24:18; 20; 28:11; 29:8; 32:26; 33:11; **Ezra** 3:3; 5:5; 7:6; 9; 28; 8:18; 22; 31; 9:13; **Neh** 2:8; 18; 4:12; 9:32; **Esth** 2:17; 8:17; 9:2; 3; 27; **Job** 2:11; 3:4; 25; 4:5; 14; 5:13; 7:8; 13:11; 15:21; 16:14; 20:25; 21:9; 17; 25:3; 27:9; 29:3; 13; 30:15; 31:1; 33:15; 36:30; 38:5; 42:11; **Ps** 3:8; 4:6; 7:16; 11:6; 14:2; 17:6; 18:3; 6; 10(2); 21:3; 5; 22:10; 24:2(2); 27:5; 7; 31:16; 17; 32:4; 33:22; 35:8; 40:2; 17; 44:17; 45:2; 3; 50:15; 51:1; 53:2; 4; 54:7; 55:3; 4; 5; 16; 56:12; 67:1; 69:24; 72:6; 73:25; 80:17(2); 18; 84:9; 86:5; 7; 88:7; 9; 90:17; 91:13; 14; 15; 99:6(2); 105:1; 38; 112:8; 116:2; 4; 13; 17; 119:49; 132; 135; 125:5; 128:6; 129:8; 132:11; 12; 18; 133:2; 3; 135:9; 137:2; 139:5; 140:10; 141:8; 145:18(2); **Prov** 1:27; 6:21; 26; 10:24; 22:18; 24:25; 28:22; **Eccl** 9:12; 11:1; 3; **Song** 1:6; 2:8(2); 17; 4:16; 6:13; 8:5; 6(2); 9; **Isa** 2:12(2); 13(2); 14(2); 15(2); 16(2); 3:9; 7:17; 9:1; 2; 6; 7; 11:2; 14; 12:4; 15:9(2); 24:17; 20; 26:16; 28:10(4); 13(4); 22; 32:12; 15; 33:4; 20; 37:7; 40:7; 42:1; 43:22; 47:9; 11(3); 13; 50:10; 51:5; 52:7; 53:5; 55:6; 59:21; 60:1; 2; 61:1; 63:3; 66:24; **Jer** 2:3; 4:20; 5:12; 6:26; 11:8; 13:22; 15:14; 18:8; 22; 22:23; 23:17; 40; 29:12; 30:16; 18; 32:23; 36:3; 38:22; 39:16; 40:3; 42:10; 17; 46:16; 21; 47:5; 48:43; 44(2); 49:5; 8; 37; 51:35(2); 60; 64; **Lam** 1:14; 3:47; 65; 5:1; **Ezek** 1:3; 3:14; 22; 4:4; 5:13(2); 16; 6:10; 12; 7:2; 3; 8(2); 26(2); 8:1; 11:5; 8; 14:22(2); 16:8; 38; 18:13; 20(2); 23:8; 24:13; 25:11; 17; 26:19; 28:18; 23; 29:8; 30:4; 9; 32:8; 11; 33:2; 3; 5; 10; 22; 36:10; 11; 29; 37:1; 6; 8; 10; 39:4; 40:1; 44:17; **Dan** 2:28; 4:24; 28; 9:12; 13; 14; 10:7; **Hos** 4:2; 7:7; 14; 8:14; 10:14; 12:14(2); 13:13; **Joel** 3:4; 7; **Am** 1:7; 10; 12; 2:2; 5; 4:2; 7; 5:9(2); 8:2; **Ob** 15(2); **Jon** 1:7; 8; 3:10; **Mic** 3:11; 4:11; **Nah** 3:6; 7; 19; **Zeph** 1:17;

2:2(2); **Hag** 2:15; **Zech** 3:9; **Mal** 2:2; **Mt** 3:16; 4:16; 10:13; 11:29; 12:18; 28; 23:36; 24:2; **Mk** 1:10; 13:2; **Lk** 1:12; 35; 2:25; 40; 3:22; 4:18; 7:16; 11:20; 22; 18:32; 19:43; 44; 21:6; 23; 22:29(2); 24:49; **Jn** 1:32; 33; 51; 5:14; 18:4; **Acts** 1:8; 2:3; 43; 4:1; 33; 5:5; 11(2); 6:12; 8:16; 24; 10:44; 11:15(2); 13:11; 40; 15:28; 18:6; 19:6; 13; 24:2; **Rom** 4:9(2); 9:28; 10:12; **1 Cor** 9:16; 10:11; **2 Cor** 11:28; 12:9; **Gal** 3:14; 6:16(2); **Eph** 5:6; **Phil** 1:3; 2:27; **Col** 3:6; **1 Th** 2:16; 5:3(2); **Heb** 6:7; **Jas** 5:1; **1 Pe** 1:13; 4:14; 5:7; **1 Jn** 1:1; **Rev** 3:3(2); 10; 8:3; 9:3; 16:2(2); 21

US (1447/1095)

Gen 1:26; 3:22; 5:29; 11:3; 4(2); 7; 19:5; 13; 31; 32; 34; 20:9; 23:6(3); 24:23; 55; 65; 26:10(2); 16; 22; 28(3); 29; 31:14; 15; 37; 44; 50; 53; 32:18; 20; 33:12(2); 34:9(2); 10; 14; 16; 17; 21(4); 22(2); 23(2); 35:3; 37:8(2); 17; 20; 21; 27; 39:14(2); 17; 41:11; 12(2); 13; 42:2; 21(2); 22; 28; 30(2); 33; 43:2; 3; 4; 5; 7; 18(3); 44:7; 25; 26(2); 27; 30; 31; 47:15; 19(2); 25; 50:15(2); **Ex** 1:10(2); 2:14; 19(2); 3:18(2); 5:3(3); 8; 16; 17; 21(2); 8:26; 27; 10:7; 25; 26; 13:14; 15; 16; 14:5; 11(3); 12(2); 25; 16:3; 7; 8; 17:2; 3(2); 7; 9; 19:23; 20:19(2); 24:14; 32:1(3); 23(3); 33:15(2); 16; 34:9(2); 36:5; **Num** 10:29; 32(2); 11:4; 13; 18(2); 12:2; 11; 13:27; 30; 14:3(2); 4; 8(3); 9; 16:13(3); 14(2); 34; 20:5(2); 14; 15; 16; 17; 21:5; 7; 22:4; 14; 27:4; 31:49; 32:5; 19; 32; **Deut** 1:6; 14; 19; 20; 22(4); 25(3); 27(4); 41; 2:29; 30; 32; 33; 36(2); 37; 3:1; 4:7; 5:2; 3(2); 24; 25; 27; 6:21; 23(3); 24(2); 25(2); 9:28; 13:2(2); 6; 13; 26:3; 6(3); 8; 9(2); 15; 29:7; 15(2); 29; 30:12(2); 13(2); 31:17(2); 33:4; **Josh** 1:16(2); 2:9; 14; 17; 18; 20; 24; 4:23; 5:6; 13; 7:7(2); 9; 25; 8:5; 6(2); 9:6; 7; 11(2); 20; 22(2); 25(2); 10:6(4); 17:4; 14(2); 16; 21:2; 22:17; 19(2); 22; 25; 26; 27(2); 28(2); 29; 31; 34; 24:16; 17(2); 18; 27(2); **Judg** 1:1; 24; 6:13(6); 8:1(2); 21; 22(2); 9:8; 10; 12; 14; 10:15(2); 11:8; 10; 19; 24; 12:1; 13:8(2); 15; 23(3); 14:15(2); 15:10(2); 11(2); 16:5; 25; 18:9; 19(2); 25; 19:11; 13; 28; 20:3; 8; 18; 32(2); 39; 21:1; 22; **1 Sam** 4:3(5); 7; 8(2); 5:7(2); 10(2); 11; 6:2; 9(3); 20; 7:8(2); 12; 8:5(2); 6(2); 19; 20(2); 9:5(2); 6(2); 8; 9; 10; 27; 10:16; 19; 27; 11:1; 3; 10; 12; 14; 12:4(2); 10; 12; 14:1; 6(2); 8; 9; 10(2); 12; 17; 36(3); 17:9; 20:11; 21:5; 23:19; 25:7; 15; 16; 40; 26:11; 27:11; 29:4; 9; 30:22; 23(3); **2 Sam** 2:14; 5:2; 10:12; 11:23(2); 13:25; 26; 15:14(3); 19; 20; 17:5; 18:3(5); 19:6; 9(2); 10; 42; 43; 20:6(2); 21:4; 5(2); 6; 17; 24:14; **1 Ki** 3:18(2); 5:6; 8:57(3); 12:4; 9; 10; 18:23; 26; 20:31; **2 Ki** 1:6(2); 4:9; 10(3); 13; 6:1; 2(2); 11; 16; 7:4(3); 6(2); 9(2); 12; 13; 9:5; 12; 10:5; 14:8; 18:26; 30; 32; 19:19; 22:13(2); **1 Chr** 13:2(2); 3(2); 15:13; 16:35(3); 19:13; **2 Chr** 10:4; 9; 10; 13:10; 12; 14:7(3); 11; 20:9; 11(3); 12; 25:17; 29:10; 32:7; 8(2); 11; 34:21; **Ezra** 4:2(2); 3(2); 12; 14; 18; 5:11; 17; 8:17; 18(2); 21; 22; 31(2); 9:8(3); 9(4); 13(3); 14(2); 10:3; 13; 14; **Neh** 2:17; 18; 19(2); 20; 4:12(2); 15(2); 20(2); 5:2; 8; 10; 17(2); 6:2; 7; 9; 10(2); 16; 9:32; 33; 37; 13:18; **Job** 9:33(2); 15:9; 10; 21:14; 22:17; 31:15; 34:4(2); 37; 35:11(2); 37:19; **Ps** 2:3(2); 4:6(2); 12:4; 17:11; 20:9; 33:22; 34:3; 40:5; 44:1; 5; 7(2); 9(2); 10(2); 11(2); 13(2); 14; 17; 19(2); 23; 26; 46:7; 11; 47:3; 4; 54:60:1(3); 3; 10; 11; 62:8; 65:5; 66:10(2); 11; 12; 67:1(3); 6; 7; 68:19; 28; 74:1; 8; 9; 78:3; 79:4; 8(2); 9(2); 80:2; 3; 6; 7; 18; 19; 83:4; 12; 85:4(2); 5; 6; 7(2); 90:12; 14; 15(2); 17(2); 95:1(2); 2(2); 6(2); 100:3; 103:9; 10(2); 12; 106:47(2); 108:11; 12; 115:1(2); 12(2); 117:2; 118:27; 119:4; 122:1; 123:2; 3(2); 124:2; 3(2); 4; 6; 126:3; 132:7(2); 136:23; 24; 137:3(4); 8; **Prov** 1:11(3); 12; 14(2); 7:18(2); **Eccl** 1:10; 12:13; **Song** 2:15; 5:9; 7:11(2); 12(2); **Isa** 1:9; 18; 2:3(2); 5; 4:1; 6:8; 7:6(2); 8:10; 9:6(2); 14:8; 10; 17:14(2); 22:13; 25:9; 26:12(2); 13; 28:15; 29:15(2); 30:10(2); 11; 32:15; 33:2; 14(2); 21; 22; 36:11; 15; 18; 37:20; 41:1; 22(2); 43:9; 26; 50:8; 53:6; 59:9(2); 11; 12(2); 63:7; 16(2); 17; 64:6; 7(2); 12; **Jer** 2:6(2); 27; 3:25; 4:5; 8; 13; 5:12; 19; 24(2); 6:4(2); 5(2); 24; 26; 8:8; 14(4); 9:18; 11:19(2); 14:7; 9; 19(2); 21(2); 16:10; 18:18(3); 21:2(4); 13; 26:16; 29:15; 28; 31:6; 35:6; 8; 10; 11; 36:17; 37:3; 9; 38:25(2); 40:10; 41:8; 42:2; 3; 5(2); 6; 20(2); 43:3(4); 44:16; 46:16; 48:2; 50:5; 51:9; 10; **Lam** 3:40; 41; 43; 45; 46; 47; 4:15; 17(2); 19(2); 5:1; 8(2); 16; 20(2); 21; 22(2); **Ezek** 8:12; 11:15; 24:19(2); 33:10; 24; 35:12; 37:18; 44:6; **Dan** 1:12; 2:23; 3:17(2); 9:7; 8; 10; 11; 12(3); 13; 14; 16; **Hos** 6:1(3); 2(2); 3(3); 10:3; 8(2); 12:4; 14:2; 3; **Am** 4:1; 9:10; **Ob** 1; **Jon** 1:6; 7(2); 8(2); 11; 14(2); **Mic** 3:11(2); 4:2(2); 5:1; 6; 7:19; **Zech** 1:6(2); 8:21; 23; **Mal** 1:2; 9; 2:10; **Mt** 1:23; 3:15; 6:11; 12; 13(2); 8:25; 29; 31(2); 9:27; 13:28; 36; 56; 15:15; 23; 17:4(2); 20:7; 12; 30; 31; 21:25; 38; 22:17; 25; 24:3; 25:8; 9; 11; 26:17; 46; 63; 68; 27:4; 25; 49; **Mk** 1:24(2); 38; 4:35; 5:12; 6:3; 9:5(2); 22(2); 38(2); 40; 10:35; 37; 12:7; 19; 13:4; 14:12; 15; 42; 15:36; 16:3; **Lk** 1:1; 2; 69; 71; 74; 78; 2:15(2); 48; 4:34(2); 7:5; 16; 20; 8:22; 9:33(2); 49; 50; 54; 10:11; 17; 11:1; 3; 4(4); 45; 12:41; 13:25; 15:23; 16:26(2); 17:13; 19:14; 20:2; 6; 14; 22; 28; 22:8; 9; 67; 23:18; 30(2); 39; 24:22; 24; 29; 32(3); **Jn** 1:14; 22; 2:18; 4:12; 25; 6:34; 52; 8:5; 9:34; 10:24(2); 11:7; 15; 16; 50; 14:8(2); 9; 22; 31; 16:17; 17:21; 18:31; 19:24; **Acts** 1:17; 21(2); 22(2); 2:29; 3:4; 12; 4:17; 5:28; 6:14; 7:27; 38; 40(3); 10:41; 42; 11:13; 15; 17; 13:33; 47; 14:11; 17; 15:7; 8; 9; 24; 25; 28; 36; 16:9; 10; 14; 15(2); 16; 17(2); 21; 37(4); 17:27; 20:5; 14; 21:5; 11; 16; 17; 18; 23:9; 24:4; 25:24; 27:2; 6; 7; 20; 28:2(2); 7(2); 10; 15(2); **Rom** 3:8; 4:16; 24(2); 5:5; 8(2); 6:3; 8:4; 18; 26; 31(2); 32(2); 34; 35; 37; 39; 9:24; 29; 12:6(3); 7; 13:12(2); 13; 14:7; 12; 13; 19; 15:2; 7; 16:6; **1 Cor** 1:18; 30; 2:10; 12; 4:1; 6; 8; 9; 5:7; 8; 6:14; 7:15; 8:6; 8; 10:8; 9; 15:32; 57; 16:16; **2 Cor** 1:4; 5; 8; 10(3); 11(2); 14; 19; 20; 21(2); 22(2); 2:11; 14(2); 3:3; 6; 4:7; 12; 14(2); 17; 5:5(2); 14; 18(2); 19; 20; 21; 6:12; 7:1; 2; 6; 7; 9; 8:4; 5; 7; 19(2); 20(2); 9:11; 10:2; 8; 13; **Gal** 1:4; 23; 2:4; 3:13(2); 24; 4:26; 5:1; 25; 26; 6:9; 10; **Eph** 1:3; 4; 5; 6; 8; 9; 19; 2:4; 5; 6(2); 7; 3:20; 4:7; 5:2(2); **Phil** 3:15; 16(2); 17; **Col** 1:8; 12; 13(2); 2:14(2); 4:3(2); **1 Th** 1:6; 9; 10; 2:8; 13; 15; 16; 18; 3:6(4); 4:1; 7; 8; 5:6(2); 8; 9; 10; 25; **2 Th** 1:7; 2:2; 16(2); 3:1; 6; 7; 9; **1 Tim** 6:17; **2 Tim** 1:7; 9(3); 14; 2:12; **Titus** 2:12; 14(2); 3:5; 6; 15; **Heb** 1:2; 2:3; 4:1; 2; 11; 14; 16; 6:1; 18; 20; 7:26; 9:24; 10:15; 20; 22; 23; 24; 11:40(2); 12:1(4); 9; 10; 28; 13:13; 15; 18; **Jas** 1:18; 3:3; 4:5; **1 Pe** 1:3; 12; 2:21(2); 3:18; 21; 4:1; 17; 5:10; **2 Pe** 1:1; 3(2); 4; 3:2; 9; **1 Jn** 1:2; 3; 7; 8; 9(2); 10; 2:19(5); 25; 3:1(2); 16; 18; 20; 21; 23; 24(2); 4:6(2); 7; 9; 10; 11; 12(2); 13(2); 16; 17; 19; 5:11; 14; 15; 20; **2 Jn** 2(2); **3 Jn** 9; 10; **Rev** 1:5(2); 6; 5:9; 10; 6:16(2); 19:7

VERY (290/280)

Gen 1:31; 4:5; 7:13; 12:14; 13:2; 17:23; 26; 18:20; 20:8; 21:11; 24:16; 26:13; 34:7; 41:19; 31; 49; 47:13; 50:9; 10; **Ex** 1:20; 8:28; 9:3; 14; 18; 24; 10:14; 19; 11:3; 12:41; 51; 14:10; 18:11; 19:16; 24:10; 30:36; **Num** 6:9; 11:33; 12:3; 13:28; 14:37; 16:15; 21:4; 32:1; **Deut** 9:20; 21; 11:12; 20:15; 27:8; 28:54; 29:4; 30:14; 32:48; **Josh** 1:7; 3:16; 5:11; 8:4; 9:9; 13; 22; 24; 10:20; 27; 11:4; 13:1; 22:8(2); 23:6; **Judg** 3:17; 9:40; 11:33; 35; 13:6; 15:18; 18:9; **Ruth** 1:13; 20; **1 Sam** 2:3; 17; 22; 4:10; 5:9; 11; 14:8; 15; 20; 31; 18:8; 15; 19:4; 20:7; 21:12; 23:22; 25:2; 15; 36; **2 Sam** 1:26; 2:17; 3:8; 7:24; 11:2; 13:3; 21; 36; 18:17; 19:11; 32(2); 24:10; **1 Ki** 1:4; 6; 15; 2:18; 10:2(2); 19:10; 14; 21:26; **2 Ki** 14:26; 15:20; 17:18; 21:16; **1 Chr** 9:13; 16:19; 17:22; 21:8; 13; 23:17; **2 Chr** 7:8; 9:1; 11:12; 14:13; 16:8; 14; 20:35; 21:15; 24:24; 30:13; 32:27; 29; 33:14; **Ezra** 9:7; 10:1(2); **Neh** 1:7; 4:1; 7; 5:6; 6:16; 8:17; **Esth** 1:18; **Job** 1:3; 2:13; 32:6; **Ps** 35:8; 46:1; 50:3; 71:19; 79:8; 89:2; 92:5; 93:5; 104:1; 105:12; 119:107; 112; 138; 140; 128:3; 137:7; 139:14; 142:6; 146:4; 147:15; **Prov** 27:15; **Isa** 1:9; 5:1; 10:25; 16:6; 14; 24:16; 29:17; 30:19; 31:1; 33:17; 40:15; 47:6; 48:8; 52:13; 64:12; **Jer** 2:12; 4:19; 5:11; 14:17; 18:13; 20:15; 24:2(2); 3(2); 38:16; 46:20; **Lam** 1:20; 5:22; **Ezek** 2:3; 16:7; 26; 24:2(2); 27:25; 33:32; 37:2(2); 40:1; 2; 47:7; 9; **Dan** 2:12; 4:33; 5:30; 6:19; 8:8; 11:25; **Joel** 2:11(2); **Am** 5:20; **Jon** 4:6; **Zech** 1:2; 9:2; 5; 12:3; 14:4; **Mt** 10:30; 15:28; 17:18; 18:31; 21:8; 26:7; **Mk** 8:1; 14:3; 16:2; 4; **Lk** 1:3; 7:21; 9:5; 10:11; 12:7; 12; 59; 13:31; 18:23(2); 24; 19:17; 48; 20:19; 23:12; 24:1; 33; **Jn** 5:36; 8:4; 12:3; **Acts** 10:10; 11:11; 12:20; 16:18; 17:22; 25:10; **Rom** 9:17; 10:20; 11:8; 13:6; **1 Cor** 4:3; **2 Cor** 2:3; 5:5; 7:11; 12:15; **Gal** 2:10; **Eph** 6:22; **Phil** 1:6; **Col** 4:8; **1 Th** 5:13; **2 Tim** 1:17; 18; **Phm** 1:8; **Heb** 10:1; **Jas** 3:4; 5:11; **1 Pe** 3:4; **2 Pe** 1:5; **Jude** 3

WAS (4346/3555)

Gen 1:2(3); 3; 4; 7; 9; 10; 11; 12; 15; 18; 21; 24; 25; 30; 31; 2:5(2); 9; 19; 20; 23; 3:1; 6(2); 10(2); 20; 23; 4:2(2); 5; 18; 19(2); 20; 21(2); 22; 26; 5:24; 32; 6:5(2); 6(2); 9; 11(2); 12; 7:6; 12; 17; 22(2); 8:2; 11; 13; 14; 9:18; 19; 21; 10:9; 10; 19; 25(3); 30; 11:10; 29; 30; 12:4; 10(2); 11; 14(2); 15; 18; 13:2; 6; 7; 10; 14:10; 14; 18; 15:12; 17; 16:1; 14; 16; 17:1; 24(2); 25(2); 26; 18:1; 10(2); 15; 19:1; 22; 30; 20:16; 21:3; 4; 5(2); 8(2); 11; 15; 20; 22:13; 20; 24; 23:17(3); 24:1; 15; 16; 22; 29; 33; 36; 45; 67; 25:1; 6; 8; 10; 17; 20; 21; 25; 26(2); 27(2); 29; 30; 26:1(2); 7; 8; 34; 27:1; 5; 28:12; 17; 29:2; 9(2); 12(2); 16(2); 17; 25(2); 31(2); 34; 30:2; 30; 37; 31:1(2); 2; 22; 31; 36; 39; 40; 48; 32:7; 24; 25; 33:1; 34:3; 19; 24; 28(2); 29; 35:4; 5; 8(2); 16; 17; 18(2); 19; 29; 36:12; 22; 24; 32; 35; 39(2); 43; 37:1; 2(2); 3; 15; 23; 24(2); 25; 29; 38:1; 2; 5; 6; 7; 12; 13; 14(3); 15; 16; 21(2); 22; 24; 25; 28(2); 29; 30; 39:2(3); 3; 5(2); 6; 10; 11; 13; 19(2); 20; 21; 22; 23(2); 40:2; 3; 9; 10; 11; 15; 16(2); 20; 41:7; 8(2); 10; 12; 24; 32; 37; 46; 49; 54(2); 55; 56; 57; 42:1; 5; 6(2); 27; 35; 43:1; 12(2); 18; 21; 26; 34; 44:12; 14; 16; 17; 24; 45:8; 16; 46:8; 23; 47:13(2); 14; 20; 28; 48:1; 2; 7; 14(2); 49:15(2); 26; 33; 50:9; 11; 15; 26; **Ex** 1:5; 7; 14; 15; 21; 2:2; 11; 21; 3:1; 2(2); 6; 4:6; 7; 14; 5:13; 19; 6:3; 7:7; 15; 21; 23; 8:15; 24; 9:7; 24(2); 25; 26; 31(2); 33; 35; 10:13; 15; 22; 11:3; 6; 12:29; 30(3); 34; 39; 40; 13:15; 17; 14:5(2); 20; 15:23; 16:13; 14; 15; 20; 22; 31(2); 17:1; 11; 18:3; 4(2); 5; 11; 13; 19:16; 18; 20:21; 21:36; 22:13; 15(2); 24:10(2); 17; 18; 25:40; 27:8; 29:33; 31:17; 32:16; 19; 33:7; 8; 34:28; 29; 35:21(2); 23; 24; 36:2; 4; 7; 9; 15; 21; 35; 37:1; 6; 10; 21; 22; 25(3); 38:1(3); 17; 18(3); 19; 21; 23; 24(2); 25; 29; 39:4; 5(2); 9; 10; 19; 23; 32; 40:17; 35; 36; 37(2); 38(2); **Lev** 4:10; 6:2; 3; 4; 27; 8:4; 10; 16; 21; 25; 26; 28; 29; 30; 9:8; 15; 10:16(2); 18; 20; 13:5; 14:6; 48; 15:10; 16:27; 17:15; 19:20; 21:10; 24:10; 11; 25:28; 33; 50; 51; 27:24; **Num** 2:4; 6; 8; 11; 13; 15; 19; 21; 23; 26; 28; 30; 3:16; 24; 30; 32; 35; 38; 5:13(2); 6:12; 7:9; 10; 12; 13(2); 17; 19; 23; 25(2); 29; 31(2); 35; 37(2); 41; 43(2); 47; 49(2); 53; 55(2); 59; 61(2); 65; 67(2); 71; 73(2); 77; 79(2); 83; 84(2); 88(2); 89; 8:4(2); 9:15(2); 16; 17; 20(2); 21(3); 22(2); 10:11; 14; 15; 16; 17; 18; 19; 20; 22; 23; 24; 25; 26; 27; 28; 34; 35; 11:1; 2; 7; 8; 10(2); 18; 25; 26; 33(3); 12:3; 9; 10; 15(2); 13:20; 22; 24; 14:16; 15:25; 16:15; 48; 17:6; 19:13; 20:1; 2; 13(2); 29; 21:1; 3; 9; 24; 26; 35; 22:3(2); 4; 22(2); 26; 27; 30; 36; 41; 23:6; 17; 24:10; 20; 25:3(2); 8; 11; 13; 14(3); 15(3); 18; 26:5; 8; 46; 59(2); 62; 64; 65; 27:3; 13; 28:6; 31:14; 16; 26; 32; 36; 37; 38; 39; 40; 41; 43; 52; 32:1; 10; 13(2); 33:14; 39; 35:23; 25; 36:2; **Deut** 1:34; 37; 2:14(2); 15; 16; 20; 36; 3:4; 11; 13; 26; 4:21; 35; 5:23(2); 8:2; 15; 9:8; 19(2); 20; 21; 28; 10:6; 11:6; 13:14; 19:6; 21:6; 22:14; 17; 27; 26:5; 29:27; 31:24; 32:12; 50; 33:5; 16; 21; 34:7; 9; **Josh** 1:5; 17; 2:2; 5(2); 15; 3:2; 7; 14; 4:10; 5:1(2); 8; 13; 6:1; 8; 21; 24; 27; 7:16; 17; 18; 22; 8:13; 14; 17; 18; 25; 29; 33; 35; 9:5; 10; 10:2(2); 17; 24; 27; 11:10; 11; 19; 20; 12:2; 4(2); 13:1; 16; 23(2); 25; 29; 30; 33; 14:2; 7(2); 11; 15(2); 15:1(2); 5; 12; 13; 15; 18; 20; 16:5(2); 8; 17:1(4); 2; 7; 9; 10(4); 18:1; 14; 19; 20(2); 28; 19:1; 8; 9(2); 10; 16; 23; 27; 31; 39; 41; 21:10; 11; 22:14; 17; 23:1; 24:26; 33; **Judg** 1:10; 11; 17; 19; 22; 23; 28; 36; 2:4; 8; 14; 15; 18(2); 19; 20; 3:2; 8; 16; 17; 20; 25; 30; 31; 4:1; 2; 4; 16; 17; 21; 5:8(2); 15; 6:3; 6; 11; 21; 22; 28(4); 30; 38; 40(2); 7:1; 6; 8; 13; 15; 8:3; 20(2); 26; 28(2); 31; 32; 33(2); 9:3; 5; 6; 25; 30; 44; 47; 51; 55; 10:2; 5; 7; 9; 11:1(2); 5; 18; 34(2); 39; 12:7; 10; 12; 15; 13:2(3); 6(2); 9(2); 16; 21; 14:4(2); 19; 20; 15:17; 16:4; 9; 16; 27; 17:1(2); 6(2); 7(3); 11; 18:1(2); 20; 28(3); 29(2); 31; 19:1(2); 2; 3; 10(2); 11; 16(2); 26(3); 27; 28; 30; 20:4; 27; 34(2); 38; 40; 21:4; 9; 25(2); **Ruth** 1:1; 2(2); 3; 4; 7; 18; 19; 2:1(2); 3; 5; 6; 14; 17; 3:7; 8(2); 4:7(2); 9(2); **1 Sam** 1:1(2); 2; 7; 9; 10; 13(2); 18; 24; 2:13(2); 17; 20; 22; 3:1(2); 2; 3(2); 7; 15; 19; 4:2; 10(2); 11; 13; 15; 18(2); 19(2); 5:3; 4(2); 6; 7; 9(2); 10; 11(2); 6:1; 4; 14; 15; 7:2(2); 10; 13; 14; 17; 8:1; 2; 9:1(2); 2(3); 5; 9; 10; 14; 24(2); 26; 10:9; 10; 20; 21(2); 23; 11:5; 6; 11; 12:12; 15; 13:3; 7; 19; 21; 22; 14:2; 3; 4(2); 14; 15(2); 16; 18; 19; 20(2); 25; 26; 27; 35; 38; 42; 43; 50(2); 51(2); 52; 15:9; 12; 16:6; 12; 23(2); 17:4; 5(2); 7; 12(3); 14; 20; 23; 28; 40; 42; 48; 50; 51; 18:1; 4; 5; 6; 8; 10; 12(2); 14; 15; 19; 28; 29; 30; 19:7; 8; 9; 16; 19; 21; 23; 20:9; 25; 27; 30; 33; 34; 35(2); 37; 21:1; 5; 6(2); 7(2); 12; 22:2(3); 4; 6; 9; 22; 23:7; 13; 15; 24:1; 3; 16; 25:2(4); 3(4); 4; 7; 20; 21; 36(3); 37; 39; 44; 26:16; 21; 24; 27:4; 7; 11; 28:5; 14; 20(2); 21; 30:3; 6(2); 19; 25; 31:3; 4; 5; **2 Sam** 1:2; 6; 10(3); 14; 25; 26; 2:10; 11(2); 16; 17; 18; 23; 24; 32; 3:1; 2; 6(3); 7; 22; 35; 4:1; 2(2); 4(3); 5; 7; 5:2; 4; 10; 6:3; 4; 7; 9; 12; 13; 14; 20; 21; 7:1; 19; 8:16(2); 17; 18; 9:2(2); 12; 13; 10:9; 17; 11:2; 4; 7; 16; 21; 26; 27; 12:3; 5; 18(2); 19; 21; 22; 30(2); 13:1; 2(3); 3(2); 8; 15; 19; 21; 34; 36; 38; 39; 14:1; 6; 25(3); 26; 27(2); 15:2; 5; 24; 32; 34; 16:1(2); 5(2); 15; 16; 23(2); 17:19; 22; 23(2); 25(2); 18:6; 8; 9(2); 14; 24(2); 29; 33; 19:1; 2; 16; 25; 32(2); 20:1; 8(3); 10; 13; 23(2); 24(2); 25; 26; 21:1; 7; 11; 16(3); 18(2); 19(2); 20(3); 22:8; 11; 19; 24; 42; 23:2; 8; 9; 10; 11(2); 14(2); 16; 18; 19; 20; 23; 24; 24:1; 2; 16(2); 17; 25; **1 Ki** 1:1; 4; 6; 15(2); 22; 42; 50; 51; 2:5; 10; 11; 12; 15(2); 26; 29; 34; 41; 46; 3:2; 4; 17; 18; 21(2); 26; 28; 4:1; 19(2); 22; 27; 31(2); 5:7; 12; 13; 14; 6:2; 3; 6(3); 7(4); 8; 17; 18(3); 20; 22; 24; 25; 26(2); 37; 38(2); 7:2; 3; 4; 5; 6(3); 7; 10; 12; 14(3); 16(2); 20; 22; 23(2); 24; 25; 26(2); 27; 28; 29; 31(2); 32; 33; 35; 36; 38(2); 40; 47; 48; 51; 8:9; 14; 17; 18(2); 54; 57; 64(3); 9:25; 10:2; 3; 5; 6; 7; 14; 19; 21(2); 29; 11:4(4); 14; 15; 17; 20; 21; 25; 26; 28(2); 30; 40; 42; 43; 12:2; 15; 18; 20; 32; 13:5; 6; 9; 18; 23; 24(2); 26; 31; 34; 14:6; 8; 20; 21(2); 30; 31(2); 15:2; 3(2); 5; 6; 7; 10; 11; 14; 16; 18; 19; 22; 23; 24; 29; 32; 16:6; 9; 11; 18; 28; 17:10; 11; 16; 17(2); 19; 18:2; 3; 4; 7; 13; 26(2); 27; 28; 29(2); 30; 38; 45; 19:6; 11(2); 12; 13; 19(2); 20:26; 29(2); 40(2); 21:1; 11; 15; 16(2); 25; 27; 22:32; 33; 35; 36; 37; 42(2); 43; 47; 50; **2 Ki** 1:2; 7; 9; 2:1; 8; 9; 14; 17; 23; 3:4; 9; 20(2); 22; 26; 27; 4:8(2); 25; 31; 32; 38; 41; 5:1(2); 8; 14(2); 6:5(2); 8; 10; 11; 13; 15; 17; 20; 25(2); 26; 32; 33(2); 7:5; 10; 15; 16; 8:5(2); 6; 7(2); 11; 17; 18; 24; 26(2); 27; 29; 9:16; 21; 34; 10:5(2); 7; 9; 21(2); 30; 36; 11:1; 2; 3; 14; 16; 20; 21; 12:1; 2; 6; 10(3); 12; 16; 13:3; 13; 19; 21(2); 23; 14:2(2); 3; 5; 9(3); 12; 16; 20; 21; 25; 26(2); 15:2(2); 3; 5(2); 12(2); 33(2); 34; 38; 16:2(2); 8; 10; 14; 20; 17:7; 18(2); 23; 25; 18:2(2); 3; 5; 7; 9; 10; 15; 17; 18; 36; 37; 19:1; 2; 37; 20:1; 3; 13(3); 21:1(2); 18; 19(2); 26; 22:1(2); 2; 9; 19; 23:11; 15; 23; 25; 26; 31(2); 36(2); 24:8(2); 10; 18(2); 25:2; 3; 4(2); 5; 8; 16; 17(4); 21; 30; **1 Chr** 1:19(3); 29; 39; 41; 43; 46; 50(2); 2:3; 7; 8; 17; 21; 26(2); 29; 31(3); 34; 42; 45(2); 49; 3:1; 10(2); 22; 4:3; 4(2); 9; 11; 15; 40; 41; 5:1(2); 2; 6; 7; 12; 15; 22; 6:10; 39; 7:2; 3; 10; 12; 15(2); 16; 17; 24; 25; 31; 40; 8:29; 30; 34; 9:1(2); 17; 20; 21; 35; 36; 40; 10:3; 4; 5; 11:2; 9; 12(2); 13(2); 16(2); 18; 20; 21; 22; 23; 25; 12:1; 3; 14(2); 19; 22; 40; 13:4; 10; 12; 14:2; 15:22(2); 26; 27; 16:39; 17:1; 13; 17; 18:15(2); 16; 17; 19:10; 17; 20:2; 4; 5(2); 6(3); 21:6; 7; 15(2); 17; 30; 22:7; 23:1; 3; 11; 13; 16; 17; 18; 19; 20; 28; 24:19; 21; 23; 25:1; 7; 26:10; 20; 24; 28; 31; 27:2; 3; 4(2); 5(2); 6(4); 7; 8; 9; 10; 11; 12; 13; 14; 15; 16; 24; 25(2); 26; 27(2); 28(2); 29(2); 30(2); 31; 32(2); 33(2); 34(2); 28:4; 29:27; **2 Chr** 1:1(2); 3(2); 6; 11; 13; 2:14; 3:3; 4(3); 6; 8; 9; 11(2); 12(2); 15(2); 4:1; 2(2); 3(2); 4; 5(2); 6; 11; 18; 19; 5:1; 3; 10; 13; 6:3; 7; 8(2); 7:7(2); 8:16(3); 9:1; 2; 4; 5; 6; 13; 20(2); 31; 10:2; 15; 18; 12:13(2); 16; 13:2(2); 7; 13; 14; 14:1; 2; 5; 14; 15:4; 5(2); 6; 8; 9; 13; 15; 17; 19; 16:3; 10(2); 12; 14; 17:3; 15; 16; 18; 18:31; 32(2); 20:25; 26; 29; 30; 31(3); 32; 21:1; 3; 4; 5; 17; 20; 22:2(2); 6; 7; 8; 9; 10; 11; 12; 23:13; 18; 19; 21; 24:1(2); 2; 11(3); 13; 15(2); 25:1(2); 2; 3; 10; 14; 15; 16; 18(3); 22; 26:1; 3(2); 4; 12; 13; 15; 16(2); 19; 20; 21(4); 27:1(2); 2; 8; 28:1(2); 5; 7; 9(3); 29:1(2); 2; 25; 28; 32; 34; 35; 30:12; 17; 18; 26; 27; 31:1; 5; 12; 14; 20; 32:2; 5; 14; 15; 23; 24; 25(2); 31(2); 33:1; 12; 13; 19; 21; 34:1; 2; 3; 9; 14; 16; 17; 27; 35:10; 16; 19; 24; 26; 36:2; 5; 8; 9; 11; 16; **Ezra** 1:6; 2:61; 64; 3:11; 12; 13; 4:7; 14; 15; 19; 23; 24; 5:1; 5(2); 7; 11; 14; 17; 6:1; 2(2); 15(2); 7:6; 8; 28(2); 8:22; 31; 33; 34; 35; 10:1(2); 9; **Neh** 1:1; 4(2); 11; 2:1; 11; 12; 14; 3:12; 25; 4:1; 3; 6; 12; 15; 16; 18; 5:1; 14; 18(3); 6:6; 10; 13; 15; 16; 18; 7:1(2); 2; 4; 63; 64; 66; 72; 8:1; 3; 5; 9; 17; 18; 10:29; 11:9(2); 11; 14; 22; 23; 24; 12:22; 38; 43; 13:1; 3; 4; 6; 13(2); 19; 26(2); 28; **Esth** 1:1; 2; 8; 10; 11; 12; 13; 2:5(2); 7; 8(2); 11; 13; 16; 20; 23(3); 3:4; 5; 12(2); 14; 15(2); 4:3; 4; 5; 6; 8; 5:2(2); 9; 6:1; 2; 7:6; 7; 8; 8:1; 9; 13; 14; 15; 9:4; 11; 14; 17; 22; 32; 10:3(2); **Job** 1:1(3); 3; 5; 6; 13; 16; 17; 18; 2:1; 13; 3:3(2); 16; 4:4; 12; 16(2); 8:7; 9:16; 10:13; 15:7; 19; 16:12; 20:4; 22:9; 23:17; 29:4(2); 5; 10; 14; 15(2); 16; 30:25; 31:20; 25; 32:1; 2(2); 3; 5(2); 6; 33:27; 42:7; **Ps** 7:4; 18:7; 11; 18; 23; 41; 22:10; 30:7; 32:4(2); 33:9; 35:13; 37:36; 39:2(2); 3(2); 9(2); 44:3; 50:21; 51:5; 53:5; 55:13; 18; 21; 63:66:14; 17; 68:8; 9; 11; 14; 69:20; 73:3; 16; 21(2); 22(2); 76:8; 77:2; 3(2); 18; 19; 78:8; 21(2); 30; 35; 37; 59; 62; 79:3; 87:4; 6; 95:10; 99:6; 105:17; 18; 37; 38; 106:11; 18; 30; 31; 38; 40; 107:12; 116:6; 118:23; 119:67; 122:1; 124:1; 2; 3; 126:2; 139:15(2); 142:3; **Prov** 4:3; 5:14; 7:11; 12; 8:23; 24; 25; 27; 30(2); 31; 23:35; 24:31(3); 26:19; **Eccl** 1:12; 2:1; 3; 10; 11(2); 15;

17(2); 24; 3:16(2); 4:14; 16(2); 5:6; 7:23; 9:14; 15; 12:7; 9; 10(2); **Song** 2:3; 4; 5:6; 6:12; 8:11; **Isa** 1:21; 6:4; 7:2; 10:14; 26; 11:16; 21:3(2); 22:9; 14; 25; 23:13; 26:16; 28:13; 30:33; 36:3; 21; 22; 37:1; 2; 38; 38:1; 17; 20; 39:2(3); 41:28(2); 42:24; 43:10; 12; 13; 47:6; 48:4; 8; 16(2); 49:21; 50:2(2); 5; 52:14; 53:3; 5(3); 7(3); 8(3); 9; 12; 57:17(2); 59:15; 16(2); 17; 63:3; 5(2); 9; 16; 65:1(3); 66:7; 8; **Jer** 2:3; 3:21; 4:23; 25; 26; 7:12; 8:15; 16; 11:19; 13:7(2); 20; 14:4; 5; 6; 19(2); 15:9; 16; 17:16; 18:3; 4; 20:1; 2; 7; 8; 9(2); 14; 22:15; 16(2); 25:1; 26:20; 21; 24; 28:1; 29:3; 31:15; 18; 19(2); 26; 32; 32:1; 2(2); 8; 9; 11(2); 33:1; 34:15; 35:4; 36:22; 23(3); 37:4; 13(3); 21; 38:6(2); 7(2); 28(3); 39:2; 4; 15; 41:7; 9; 13; 46:2; 5; 48:13; 27(2); 49:12; 51:5; 7; 59; 52:1(2); 5; 6; 7(2); 8; 12; 19(2); 20; 21(3); 22(3); 27; 34; **Lam** 1:1(2); 9; 14; 2:5; 22; 4:6; 18; 20; **Ezek** 1:1; 2; 3; 4(2); 5; 13(2); 15; 16(2); 20; 21; 22; 25; 26(2); 28(2); 2:9(2); 10; 3:3; 14; 22; 4:14; 6:9; 8:2; 3; 4; 5; 7; 8; 9:2; 8(2); 10:1; 4(2); 5; 7; 11; 14; 15; 17(2); 19; 21; 22; 11:13; 22; 12:7; 15:5; 16:3; 4; 8; 13; 14; 19; 23; 34; 36; 45; 49; 56; 57(2); 17:7; 8; 19:4; 5; 7; 8; 10; 11; 12(2); 23:3; 5; 13; 17; 40; 42; 24:18; 25:3(2); 26:2; 17; 27:7(2); 12; 16; 18; 20; 28:13(2); 15; 17; 29:18; 30:22; 31:3(2); 4; 5; 7; 8; 10; 32:25(2); 33:22(2); 24; 34:4(2); 5; 6(2); 8; 16(3); 35:10; 15; 36:17; 35; 36; 37:1; 7(2); 8; 40:1(2); 2; 3(2); 5(2); 6(2); 7(3); 9; 12; 13; 15; 18(2); 20; 21; 22(2); 23; 24; 25; 26; 27; 29; 33; 36; 38; 43; 47; 48; 49; 41:2; 5; 8; 9; 10; 11; 12(2); 13; 14; 18; 19(2); 21(2); 22; 25; 42:1(2); 2(3); 3; 4; 6; 7(2); 8(2); 9; 11(2); 12; 43:2; 3; 44:1; 31; 46:19(2); 21; 23; 47:1(2); 2; 5(2); **Dan** 1:4; 19; 2:1; 12; 19; 26; 31(2); 32; 34; 35; 45; 3:1; 19(2); 22; 24; 27(2); 4:4; 10(2); 12(2); 13; 19(2); 21; 29; 31; 33(3); 36(2); 5:9(2); 13; 20(3); 21(4); 24; 25; 30; 6:2; 3; 4(2); 10(2); 14; 17; 22; 23(3); 7:4(3); 5; 6(2); 7(2); 8(2); 9(4); 10; 11(2); 13; 14; 15; 19; 20; 21(2); 22; 8:2(3); 3(2); 4; 5; 7(3); 8; 11; 12; 13; 15; 17; 18(2); 26; 27(2); 9:1; 20; 21; 10:1(4); 2; 4; 5; 6; 8(2); 9; 11; 19; 12:1(2); 6; 7; **Hos** 1:10; 2:3; 7; 7:1; 11:1; 4; 12:13; 13:6; **Am** 1:1; 2:9(3); 10; 4:7; 7:1; 2; 14(3); **Jon** 1:4(2); 5(2); 11; 17; 3:3; 4:2(2); 6; **Mic** 1:13; **Nah** 2:8; 3:8(3); 9; 10; **Hab** 3:2; 3; 4(2); 8(2); 9; 14; **Hag** 2:15; 18; **Zech** 1:15; 2:3(2); 3:3(2); 8:9; 10; 11:11(2); 13:6; **Mal** 1:2; 2:5(2); 6(2); 3:16; **Mt** 1:16; 18(3); 19; 22(2); 2:1; 3; 4; 9; 15(2); 16(2); 17(2); 18; 19; 22(2); 23; 3:3; 4(2); 4:1; 2; 14; 5:1; 21; 27; 33; 38; 43; 6:29; 7:25; 27; 28; 8:3; 13; 17; 24(2); 26; 30; 9:22; 25; 33(2); 36; 10:3; 12:3; 4; 10; 13; 17; 22(2); 40; 46; 13:6; 19; 33; 35; 47; 48; 14:6; 9; 11; 14; 15; 23; 24(2); 30(2); 15:24; 28; 16:20; 17:2; 5; 18; 18:11; 24; 25; 27; 34(2); 19:8; 20:30; 21:4(2); 10; 18; 21; 23; 25; 33; 42; 45; 22:7; 10; 12; 31; 46; 25:5; 6; 10; 25; 35(3); 36(3); 42(2); 43; 26:3; 6; 10; 25; 47; 56; 71; 27:3; 9(3); 12; 15; 19; 24; 35; 45; 51; 54; 61; 63; 28:2; 3; 5; **Mk** 1:6; 9; 13(2); 14; 23; 33; 39; 42; 45; 2:1(2); 2; 3; 4(2); 15; 25; 27; 3:1; 5; 8; 32; 4:1(2); 6(2); 10; 15; 36; 37; 38; 39; 5:5; 11; 14; 21; 26; 29(2); 35; 36; 40; 42; 6:20; 26; 34; 35; 47(2); 48; 49; 52; 55; 7:26; 32; 35; 8:25; 9:2; 33(2); 10:1; 14; 17; 22; 32; 47; 11:11; 12; 13; 27; 30; 12:11; 14:1; 4; 32; 43; 49; 66; 15:6; 7(2); 21; 25; 26; 28(2); 33; 38; 39; 41; 42; 43; 44; 47; 16:1; 4; 6; 11; 19; **Lk** 1:5(3); 7; 8(2); 10; 12; 19; 23; 26; 27(2); 29(2); 36; 41; 59; 64; 66; 67; 80; 2:2; 4; 5; 6; 7; 13; 15; 17; 20; 21(2); 25(4); 36(2); 37; 40; 42; 46; 51; 3:15; 21(2); 23; 4:1; 2; 16; 17(2); 25(2); 26(2); 27; 29; 31; 32; 33; 38; 40; 41; 42; 44; 5:1; 3; 6; 12(2); 17(2); 18; 24; 36; 6:3; 6(2); 10; 13; 48; 49; 7:2(2); 4; 6; 12(3); 15; 37; 41; 8:5; 20; 24; 29(2); 32; 36; 40; 41; 42; 47(2); 49; 53; 9:7(3); 18; 29; 31; 34; 36; 42; 45; 53; 10:1; 33; 36; 40; 11:1; 14(3); 50; 12:27; 13:10; 11(2); 13; 21; 14:2; 30; 15:6; 20; 24(2); 25; 28; 32(3); 16:1(3); 19(2); 20(2); 22(3); 17:10; 14; 15; 16; 20; 26; 28; 18:2; 3; 23; 34; 35; 37; 19:2(3); 3(2); 4; 10; 11; 15; 22; 37; 47; 20:4; 6; 7; 21:5; 37; 22:3; 23; 24; 37; 39; 41; 47(2); 49; 53; 56; 59; 60; 66; 23:7; 8; 17; 26; 38; 44(2); 45(2); 47; 50; 51(2); 53; 54; 55; 24:6; 10; 13; 15; 18; 19; 21(2); 23; 35; 44; 46; 51; **Jn** 1:1(3); 2; 3(2); 4(2); 6(2); 8(2); 9; 10(2); 15(2); 17; 28; 30; 39(2); 40; 44; 2:1(2); 9; 13; 17; 21; 23; 25; 3:1; 23(2); 26; 4:6(2); 46(2); 47; 51; 53; 5:1; 4; 5; 9(2); 10; 13(2); 15; 18; 35; 6:4; 10; 17; 18; 21; 22; 24; 62; 71; 7:2; 12; 39(2); 42; 43; 8:4; 9; 44; 56; 58; 9:1; 2; 8; 13; 14; 16; 19; 20; 22; 24; 25; 32; 10:19; 22(2); 40; 11:1; 2(2); 6(2); 13; 15; 18; 20(2); 30; 32; 33; 38; 39; 41; 44; 55; 57; 12:1; 2; 3; 5; 6(2); 9; 12; 16; 21; 36; 13:3; 5; 21; 23; 24; 30; 16:4; 17:5; 12; 18:1; 10; 13(2); 14(2); 15; 16; 18; 28; 37; 40; 19:8; 14; 19; 20(3); 23; 29; 31(2); 32; 33; 41(2); 42; 20:1; 14; 24; 21:4; 7; 11; 12; 14; 17; **Acts** 1:2; 9; 11; 15; 17; 22; 23; 26; 2:16; 24; 26; 31; 3:2; 10; 11; 13; 20; 4:3; 11; 22; 31; 32; 33; 34; 36; 5:4(3); 7; 36; 6:1; 7:2; 4; 9; 12; 13; 20(3); 21; 22(2); 23; 24; 38; 59; 8:1(2); 8; 9(2); 13(2); 18; 28(2); 32(2); 33; 40; 9:9; 10; 18; 19; 26; 28; 33; 36(2); 38(2); 39; 43; 10:1(2); 4; 16(2); 18(2); 22; 24; 25; 29; 30; 37; 38; 42; 44; 11:5; 10; 11; 17; 21; 23; 24; 26; 28; 12:3; 5(2); 6(2); 9(3); 12; 15; 18(2); 20; 23; 25; 13:1(2); 6; 7; 25; 29; 31; 32; 36; 46; 49; 14:3; 4; 5; 8; 12; 13; 15:22; 37; 16:1(2); 2; 3; 13; 14; 19; 26; 27; 35; 17:1; 2; 13; 16(2); 23; 18:3; 5; 7; 12; 14; 19:1; 16; 17; 29; 32; 34; 20:3; 9(3); 16; 20; 21:3; 8; 30; 31; 33; 37; 40; 22:3; 17(2); 20(2); 28; 29(2); 30; 23:5; 7; 12; 27(3); 29; 30; 34(2); 24:2; 24; 25; 25:4; 15; 20(2); 23; 24; 26:4; 19; 26; 27:1; 2; 9(2); 11; 12; 15; 20; 25; 33; 39; 41; 42; 44; 28:1; 2; 6; 7(2); 9; 11; 16; 17; 18; 19; **Rom** 1:3; 13; 27; 4:2; 3; 9; 10(2); 13; 18; 19; 20; 21; 22; 23(2); 25(2); 5:5; 13; 14; 6:4; 6; 7:4; 8; 9; 10; 13; 8:3; 20; 9:12; 25; 26; 10:20(2); 15:20; 21; **1 Cor** 1:4; 6; 13; 2:3; 3:10; 5:7; 7:18(2); 20; 24; 10:4; 5; 28; 11:9; 23; 13:11; 14:36; 15:4; 5; 6; 7; 8; 10(2); 11; 47; 48; 16:12; 17; **2 Cor** 1:17; 18; 19(3); 2:6; 12; 3:7(2); 10; 11; 13; 5:19; 7:7; 14; 8:9; 11; 19; 9:2; 10:14; 11:9(2); 25(3); 32; 33; 12:2; 4; 7; 11; 13; 13:4; **Gal** 1:11; 12; 22; 2:3(2); 7; 10; 11; 13; 3:1; 4; 6; 17(2); 19(3); 24; 4:14; 15; 23(2); 28; 29(2); **Eph** 3:2; 5; 8; 4:7; 24; **Phil** 2:5; 26(3); 27; 30; **Col** 1:23; 25; 2:14(2); **1 Th** 2:1; 3; **2 Th** 1:10; 2:5; **1 Tim** 1:11; 13; 14; 2:7; 13; 14; 3:16; 4:14; 6:20; **2 Tim** 1:9; 11; 14; 16; 2:8; 3:9; 4:17; **Titus** 1:3; **Phm** 1:11; **Heb** 2:3; 9; 10; 3:2(2); 5; 10; 16; 17(2); 4:2; 6; 15; 5:4; 5; 7(2); 8; 7:4; 10; 11; 20; 26; 8:5(2); 6; 9:2(2); 8(2); 9; 18; 23; 28; 10:29; 11:4; 5(3); 8(2); 11; 17; 18; 19; 21; 22; 23(3); 38; 12:2; 17; 20; 21; **Jas** 1:24; 2:21; 22(2); 23(3); 25; 5:17; **1 Pe** 1:11(2); 12; 20(2); 25; 2:22; 23; 3:20; 4:6; **2 Pe** 1:9; 2:7; 16; **1 Jn** 1:1; 2(3); 3:5; 8; 12; 4:3; 9; **Jude** 3(2); **Rev** 1:4; 8; 9; 10; 16; 18; 2:8; 13(2); 4:1; 2; 3(2); 6; 7(2); 8; 5:3; 4; 11; 12; 6:2; 4(2); 8(2); 11(3); 12; 14; 7:2; 8:1; 3(2); 7; 8; 11; 12; 9:1; 3; 5; 7; 9; 10; 16; 18; 10:1(2); 4; 10; 11:1; 8; 13; 17; 19(2); 12:4(2); 5(2); 8; 9(2); 14; 17; 13:2; 3; 5(2); 7(2); 12; 14(2); 15; 14:5; 16; 20; 15:5; 8(2); 16:5; 8; 12; 18; 19(2); 21; 17:3; 4; 5; 8(2); 11; 18:1; 16; 24; 19:8; 11; 13; 20; 20:4; 10; 11; 12; 15; 21:1; 11; 18(2); 19; 21(2); 22:2

WE (1826/1311)

Gen 3:2; 11:4; 13:8; 19:2; 5; 9; 13; 32(2); 34; 20:13; 22:5; 24:25; 50; 57; 26:16; 22; 28(2); 29(2); 32; 29:4; 5; 8(2); 27; 31:15; 49; 32:6; 34:14; 15(2); 16(4); 17; 37:7; 20(2); 26; 32; 38:23; 40:8; 41:11; 12; 38; 42:2; 11(2); 21(3); 31(3); 32; 43:4; 5; 7(2); 8(3); 10(2); 18; 20; 21(3); 22(2); 44:8(3); 9; 16(5); 20(2); 22; 24(2); 26(4); 46:34; 47:3; 4; 15; 18; 19(4); 25; 50:15; 18; **Ex** 1:9; 3:18; 8:26(2); 27; 10:9(3); 25; 26(4); 12:33; 14:5(2); 12(3); 15:24; 16:3(3); 7; 8; 17:2; 19:8; 20:19(2); 24:3; 7; 14; 32:1; 23; 33:16; 34:9; **Lev** 25:20(2); **Num** 9:7(2); 10:29(2); 31; 32; 11:5(2); 13; 20; 12:11(2); 13:27; 28; 30; 31(2); 32(2); 33(3); 14:2(2); 7; 40(3); 16:12; 14; 17:12(3); 13; 20:3; 4; 10; 15; 16(2); 17(5); 19; 21:7(2); 22(4); 30(2); 31:50; 32:5; 16; 17(2); 18; 19; 31; 32; **Deut** 1:19(2); 22(2); 28(3); 41(2); 2:1(2); 8(2); 13; 14(2); 33; 34(3); 35(2); 3:1; 3; 4(2); 6(2); 7; 8; 12; 29; 4:7; 5:24(2); 25(3); 26; 27; 6:21; 25; 12:8; 18:21; 26:7; 29:7; 8; 16(2); 29; 30:12; 13; **Josh** 1:16(2); 17(2); 2:10; 11; 14; 17; 18; 19; 20; 4:23; 5:1; 6:17; 7:7; 8:5; 6(2); 9:6; 7; 8; 9; 11; 12(2); 13; 19(2); 20(3); 22; 24; 25; 10:4; 17:14; 22:17; 23; 24; 26; 27; 28(2); 29; 31; 24:15; 16; 17(2); 18; 21; 22; 24(2); **Judg** 1:3; 24; 8:6; 15; 25; 9:28(2); 38; 10:10(2); 15(2); 11:6; 8; 10; 24; 12:1; 13:8; 15; 17; 22(2); 14:13; 15; 15:10; 12(2); 13(2); 16:2; 5(2); 18:5(2); 9; 19:12(2); 18; 19; 22; 20:9(2); 10; 13; 21:7(3); 16; 18; 22(2); **Ruth** 1:10; 4:11; **1 Sam** 5:8; 6:2(2); 4; 9; 7:6; 8:19; 20; 9:6; 7(3); 10:14(2); 11:1; 3(2); 10; 12; 12:10(3); 19(2); 14:8; 9(2); 10; 12; 15:15; 16:11; 17:9; 10; 20:42; 23:3(2); 25:7; 8; 15(4); 16; 30:14(2); 22(2); **2 Sam** 5:1; 7:22; 11:23; 12:18(2); 13:25; 14:7(2); 14; 15:14; 15; 16:20; 17:6; 12(2); 13; 18:3; 19:10; 42; 43(3); 20:1(2); 21:4; 5; 6; **1 Ki** 3:18; 8:47(2); 12:4; 9; 16(2); 17:12; 18:5(2); 20:23(3); 25(2); 31; 22:3; 7; 8; 15(2); **2 Ki** 3:8; 11; 6:1; 2; 15; 28(2); 29(2); 7:3(2); 4(7); 9(3); 10; 12(2); 10:4; 5(3); 13(2); 18:22; 26; **1 Chr** 11:1; 12:18(2); 13:3; 15:13; 17:20; 29:13; 14(2); 15; 16; **2 Chr** 2:16(2); 6:37(2); 10:4; 9; 16(2); 13:10; 11; 14:7(2); 11(2); 18:3; 5; 6; 7; 14; 20:9; 12(2); 25:9; 16; 28:13; 29:18; 19; 31:10; **Ezra** 4:2(2); 3; 14(2); 16; 5:4; 8; 9; 10(2); 11(2); 7:24; 8:15; 21; 22; 23; 31; 32; 9:7(2); 9; 10(2); 14; 15(2); 10:2; 4; 12; 13; **Neh** 1:6; 7; 2:17(2); 20; 4:1; 4; 6; 9(2); 10; 11; 19; 21; 5:2(2); 3(2); 4; 5; 8; 12(2); 16; 9:33; 36(2); 37; 38; 10:30; 31(2); 32; 34; 35; 39; 13:27; **Esth** 1:15; 7:4(2); **Job** 2:10(2); 5:27; 8:9; 9:32; 15:9; 17:16; 18:2; 3; 19:28; 21:14; 15(3); 26:14; 28:22; 32:13; 36:26; 37:5; 19(2); 23; 38:35; **Ps** 12:4; 20:5(2); 7; 8; 9; 21:13; 33:21; 22; 35:25(2); 36:9; 44:1; 5(2); 8; 17(2); 20; 22(2); 46:2; 48:8(2); 9; 55:14; 60:12; 64:6; 65:4; 66:6; 12; 74:9; 75:1(2); 78:3; 4; 79:4; 8; 13(2); 80:3; 7; 14; 18(2); 19; 90:7(2); 9; 10; 12; 14; 15; 95:7; 100:3(2); 103:14; 106:6(3); 108:13; 115:18; 118:24; 26; 123:3; 124:7; 126:1; 3; 129:8; 132:6(2); 137:1(3); 2; 4; **Prov** 1:13(2); 24:12; **Song** 1:4(3); 11; 6:1; 13; 8:8(2); 9(2); **Isa** 1:9(2); 2:3; 4:1; 5:19(2); 8:18; 9:10(2); 14:10; 16:6; 20:6(2); 22:13; 24:16; 25:9(3); 26:1; 8; 13; 17; 18(4); 28:15(4); 30:16(2); 33:2; 36:7; 11; 38:20; 41:22; 23(2); 26(2); 42:24; 46:5; 51:23; 53:2(2); 3(2); 4; 5; 6(2); 56:12; 58:3(2); 59:9(2); 10(5); 11(2); 12; 63:19; 64:3; 5(3); 6(2); 8(2); 9; 66:5; **Jer** 2:31(2); 3:22; 25(3); 4:13; 5:12; 6:16; 17; 24; 7:10; 8:8; 14(2); 15; 20; 9:19(4); 13:12; 14:7; 9; 19; 20(2); 22; 15:2; 16:10; 18:12(2); 20:10(3); 26:19; 30:5; 35:6; 8(2); 9; 10; 11(2); 36:16; 38:25; 41:8; 42:2; 3(2); 5; 6(3); 13; 14(3); 20; 44:16; 17(4); 18(2); 19(2); 25(2); 48:14; 29; 50:7; 51:9; 51(2); **Lam** 2:16(4); 3:22; 42; 4:17; 18; 20(2); 5:3; 4(2); 5; 6; 7; 9; 16; 21; **Ezek** 11:3; 20:32; 21:10; 33:10(2); 24; 35:10; 37:11; **Dan** 2:4; 7; 23; 36; 3:16; 17; 18(2); 24; 6:5(2); 9:5(2); 6; 8; 9; 10; 11; 13(2); 14; 15(2); 18; **Hos** 6:2; 8:2; 10:3(2); 14:2; 3(2); **Am** 6:10; 13; 8:5(2); 6; **Ob** 1; **Jon** 1:6; 7; 11; 14; 3:9; **Mic** 2:4; 4:2; 5; 5:5; **Hab** 1:12; **Zech** 1:11; 8:23; **Mal** 1:4(2); 6; 7; 2:10(2); 17; 3:7; 8; 13; 14(2); 15; **Mt** 2:2; 3:9; 6:12; 31(3); 7:22; 8:25; 29; 9:14; 11:3; 17(2); 12:38; 14:17; 15:33; 16:7; 17:19; 27; 19:27(2); 20:18; 22; 21:25; 26(2); 27; 22:16; 23:30(2); 25:37; 38; 39; 44; 26:65; 27:42; 63; 28:13; 14; **Mk** 1:24; 2:12; 4:30(2); 38; 5:9; 12; 6:37; 8:16; 9:28; 38(2); 10:28; 33; 35(2); 37; 39; 11:31; 32; 33; 12:14; 15(2); 14:58; 63; 15:32; **Lk** 1:71; 74; 3:8; 10; 12; 14; 4:23; 34; 5:5; 26; 7:19; 20; 32(2); 8:24; 9:12; 13(2); 49(2); 10:11; 11:4; 13:26; 15:32; 17:10(2); 18:28; 31; 19:14; 20:5; 6; 21; 22:8; 49; 71(2); 23:2; 41(2); 24:21; **Jn** 1:14; 16; 22; 41; 45; 3:2; 11(3); 4:22(2); 42(3); 6:5; 28(2); 30; 42; 68; 69; 7:27; 35; 8:33; 41(2); 48; 52; 9:20; 21(2); 24; 28; 29(2); 31; 40; 41; 10:33; 11:16; 47; 48; 12:21; 34; 13:29; 14:5(2); 23; 16:18; 30(2); 17:11; 22; 18:30; 19:7; 15; 20:2; 25; 21:3; 24; **Acts** 2:8(2); 11; 32; 37; 3:12; 15; 4:9; 12; 16(2); 20(2); 5:23(3); 28; 29; 32; 6:2; 3; 4; 11; 14; 7:40; 10:33; 39; 47; 11:12; 17; 13:32; 46; 14:15; 22; 15:10; 11(2); 19; 20; 24(2); 27; 36; 16:10; 11; 12; 13(2); 16; 28; 17:19; 20; 28(2); 29(2); 32; 19:2; 13; 25; 40(2); 20:6(2); 13; 14; 15(3); 21:1(2); 2; 3(2); 4; 5(4); 6(2); 7(2); 8; 10; 12(2); 14; 15; 16; 17; 23(2); 25; 23:9; 14(3); 15; 24:2; 3; 5; 6; 8; 26:14; 27:1; 2; 3; 4(2); 5(2); 7(2); 8; 15; 16; 18; 19; 20; 26; 27; 29; 37; 28:10; 11; 12; 13(2); 14(2); 16; 21; 22(2); **Rom** 1:5; 2:2; 3:5; 8(2); 9(2); 19; 28; 31(2); 4:1; 9; 5:1; 2(2); 3; 6; 8; 9; 10(3); 11(2); 6:1(2); 2; 4(2); 5(2); 6; 8(3); 15(2); 7:4; 5; 6(3); 7; 14; 8:12; 15; 16; 17(2); 22; 23(2); 24; 25(3); 26(3); 28; 31; 36(2); 37; 9:14; 29(2); 30; 10:8; 12:4; 5; 13:11; 14:8(6); 10; 15:1; 4; **1 Cor** 1:23; 2:6; 7; 12(2); 13; 16; 3:9; 4:8; 9; 10(3); 11(2); 12(3); 13(2); 6:3; 8:1(2); 4; 6(2); 8(4); 9:4; 5; 11(2); 12(3); 25; 10:6; 16(2); 17(2); 22(2); 11:16; 31(2); 32(3); 12:13; 23(2); 13:9(2); 12; 15:11; 15(2); 19(2); 30; 32; 49(2); 51(2); 52; **2 Cor** 1:4(2); 6(3); 7; 8(3); 9(2); 10; 12; 13; 14; 24; 2:11; 15; 16; 17(2); 3:1(2); 4; 5; 12(2); 18; 4:1(3); 2; 5; 7; 8(2); 11; 13(2); 16; 18; 5:1(2); 2; 3; 4(2); 6(3); 7; 8; 9; 10; 11(2); 12; 13(2); 14; 16(3); 20(2); 21; 6:1; 3; 4; 9; 11; 7:2(3); 5(2); 13(2); 14; 8:1; 4; 5; 6; 18; 22(3); 9:4; 10:2; 3(2); 7; 11(4); 12; 13; 14(2); 15; 11:4; 6; 12; 21; 12:18(2); 19(3); 13:4(2); 6; 7(2); 8; 9(3); **Gal** 1:8(2); 9; 2:4; 5; 9; 10; 15; 16(2); 17(2); 3:14; 23; 24; 25; 4:3(2); 5; 28; 31; 5:5; 25; 6:9(2); 10; **Eph** 1:4; 7; 11; 12; 2:3; 5; 10(2); 18; 3:12; 20; 4:13; 14; 25; 5:30; 6:12; **Phil** 3:3; 16; 20; **Col** 1:3; 4; 9(2); 14; 28(2); **1 Th** 1:2; 5; 8; 9; 2:2(2); 4(2); 5; 6(2); 7; 8; 9(2); 10; 11; 13; 17; 18; 3:1(2); 3; 4(3); 6; 7; 8; 9(2); 10; 12; 4:1; 2; 6; 10; 11; 14; 15(2); 17(2); 5:5; 10(2); 12; 14; **2 Th** 1:3; 4; 11; 2:1; 13; 3:2; 4(2); 6; 7; 8(2); 9; 10(2); 11; 12; **1 Tim** 1:8; 2:2; 4:10(2); 6:7(2); 8; **2 Tim** 2:11(2); 12(3); 13; **Titus** 2:12; 3:3; 5; 7; **Phm** 1:7; **Heb** 2:1(3); 3(2); 5; 8; 9; 3:6(2); 14(2); 19; 4:3; 13; 14; 15(2); 16; 5:11; 6:3; 9(2); 11; 18; 19; 7:19; 8:1(2); 9:5; 10:10; 26(2); 30; 39; 11:3; 12:1(2); 9(3); 10; 25(2); 28(2); 13:6; 10; 14(2); 18(2); **Jas** 1:18; 3:1; 2; 3(2); 9(2); 4:13; 15; 5:11; **1 Pe** 2:24; 4:3(2); **2 Pe** 1:16(2); 18(2); 19; 3:13; **1 Jn** 1:1(3); 2; 3(2); 4; 5; 6(3); 7(2); 8(3); 9; 10(3); 2:1; 3(3); 5(2); 18; 28; 3:1; 2(5); 11; 14(3); 16(2); 19(2); 21; 22(3); 23; 24; 4:6(2); 9; 10; 11; 12; 13(2); 14; 16; 17(2); 19; 21; 5:2(3); 3; 9; 14(2); 15(5); 18; 19(2); 20(3); **2 Jn** 4; 5(2); 6; 8(3); **3 Jn** 8(2); 12; 14; **Rev** 5:10; 7:3; 11:17

WERE (2813/2362)

Gen 1:5; 7(2); 8; 13; 19; 23; 31; 2:1; 4; 25(2); 3:7(2); 11; 19; 4:8; 5:2; 4; 5; 8; 11; 14; 17; 20; 23; 27; 31; 6:1; 2; 4(3); 7:6; 10; 11(2); 19; 20; 23(3); 8:1; 2; 5; 9; 13; 9:18; 19; 23; 29; 10:1; 2; 3; 4; 5; 6; 7(2); 18; 20; 21; 22; 23; 25; 29; 31; 32(2); 11:32; 12:6; 13:6; 13; 14:5; 13; 14; 17; 17:23(2); 27; 18:2; 11; 24(2); 28; 19:11; 30; 36; 20:8; 23:1; 17(3); 20; 24:10; 32; 54; 63; 25:3; 4(2); 13; 16(2); 17; 24(2); 26:35; 27:1; 15; 23; 42; 28:12; 29:2; 17; 30:34; 35(2); 42(2); 31:10; 19; 32:7; 33:1; 10; 34:5; 7; 25; 35:2; 4(2); 5; 6; 22; 23; 24; 25; 26(3); 28; 36:5(2); 7(2); 10; 11; 12; 13(2); 14; 15(2); 16(2); 17(3); 18(2); 19(2); 20; 21; 22; 23; 24; 25; 26; 27; 28; 29; 30; 31; 40; 43; 37:7; 38:27; 39:20; 22; 40:4; 5; 6; 7; 10; 13; 16; 17; 41:21; 48; 50; 53; 42:28; 35; 43:18(2); 34; 44:3; 4; 45:3; 46:8; 9; 10; 11; 12(2); 13; 14; 15(2); 16; 17(2); 18; 19; 20; 21; 22(2); 24; 25; 26; 27(3); 31; 48:5; 10; 49:24; 32; 50:3; 4; 23; **Ex** 1:5(2); 7; 12; 2:13; 5:12; 14(2); 19; 6:4; 14; 15; 16; 17; 18(2); 19; 20; 21; 22; 24; 7:20(3); 21; 8:18; 9:11; 26; 31; 32; 10:6; 8; 11; 14; 12:39; 14:10; 11; 21; 22; 27; 29; 15:8; 23; 25; 27; 16:24; 17:12; 19:16(2); 22:21; 23:9; 24:10; 26:30; 32:3; 15(3); 16; 25; 34:1; 29; 30; 35:25; 29; 36:4; 6; 9; 15; 29; 30; 38; 37:9; 13; 14; 16; 17; 19; 20; 22; 25; 38:2; 9; 10(2); 11(2); 12(2); 13; 14; 15; 16; 17(2); 19(2); 20; 25; 27; 39:6; 13; 14; **Lev** 8:28; 9:18; 10:12; 16; 18:27; 28; 30; 19:34; 26:37; 40; **Num** 1:16; 20; 21(2); 22(2); 23(2); 24; 25(2); 26; 27(2); 28; 29(2); 30; 31(2); 32; 33(2); 34; 35(2); 36; 37(2); 38; 39(2); 40; 41(2); 42; 43(2); 44; 45(2); 46(2); 47; 2:9; 16; 24; 31; 32(3); 33; 3:17; 21; 22(3); 23; 27; 28; 29; 33; 34(2); 35; 38(2); 39(2); 43(2); 49(2); 4:36(2); 37(2); 38; 40(2); 41; 42; 44(2); 45; 46; 48(2); 49(2); 7:2(2); 87; 88; 9:6(2); 11:4; 26; 29; 12:3; 8; 13:3; 4; 22; 33(2); 14:6; 29; 15:32; 16:34; 35; 39(2); 49; 18:27; 19:18; 21:32; 22:3; 18; 22; 29; 40; 23:17; 24:13; 25:5; 6; 9; 26:5; 7(2); 9; 12; 15; 18; 19; 20; 21; 22; 23; 25; 26; 27; 28; 33; 34(2); 37; 38; 40; 41(2); 43(2); 44; 47; 48; 50(2); 51; 54; 57; 60; 62(3); 63; 64; 27:1; 31:5; 8; 38; 39; 40; 48; 32:39; 33:4; 9; 36:11; 12; **Deut** 1:41; 2:11; 15; 3:5; 8; 4:32; 47; 5:5; 15; 6:21; 7:7(2); 8:15; 9:10; 15; 10:2; 19; 15:15; 22; 16:12; 23:7; 24:18; 22; 25:17; 18; 28:60; 62; 67(2); 29:17; 31:24; 30; 32:29; 33:5; 34:7; **Josh** 2:4; 10; 3:16; 4:7(2); 5:1(2); 4; 6(2); 7; 8; 8:11; 15; 16(3); 22; 24; 25; 33; 35; 9:1; 10; 13; 16; 17; 24(2); 10:1; 2; 11(2); 26; 28; 30; 32; 35; 37(2); 39; 11:2; 11; 22; 13:21; 22; 31; 14:4; 12(2); 15:21; 16:9; 17:2; 5; 12; 18:21; 19:8; 15; 30; 51; 20:9; 21:4; 10(2); 19; 26; 33; 40; 41; 42; 22:30; 24:15; **Judg** 1:27; 30; 33; 35(2); 2:12; 15; 3:4; 19; 24; 25; 4:13; 5:6; 14(2); 15(2); 6:5; 7:1; 11; 12(2); 19(2); 8:4; 10(2); 18(2); 19; 21; 24; 26(2); 30; 9:29; 34; 35; 36; 43; 44; 45; 47; 48(2); 10:8; 11:33; 12:2; 14:8; 15:14; 16:2(2); 9; 12; 25; 27; 30(2); 17:2; 4; 18:3; 7(3); 16; 17; 22(2); 26; 30; 19:10; 11; 16; 22; 20:11; 16(2); 17; 31; 36; 44; 46(2); 48; 21:9; 13; **Ruth** 1:2; 13; 3:2; 4:11; **1 Sam** 1:3; 2:5; 12; 27; 4:4; 7; 15; 19; 5:4; 12; 6:13; 15; 7:7; 10; 13; 14; 8:2; 9:3; 4; 14; 20; 22(2); 27; 10:14; 11:8; 9; 11(2); 13:2(2); 4; 6(2); 8; 11; 22(2); 14:2(2); 17(2); 20; 21(2); 24; 28; 31; 41; 49(2); 15:9; 17(2); 17:1; 2; 11; 13; 19; 24; 31; 18:6; 22:2; 6; 11; 23:24; 26; 24:3; 25:7(2); 15(3); 16(2); 20; 43; 26:12; 27:2; 8; 29:4; 30:2; 4; 9(2); 10; 16; 21; 27(3); 28(3); 29(3); 30(3); 31(2); 31:7(3); **2 Sam** 1:11; 14; 23(4); 2:3; 4; 17; 18; 30; 3:2; 5; 17; 20; 23; 31; 34; 4:2; 7; 5:2; 13; 14; 6:2; 8:17; 18; 9:12; 10:5; 8; 13; 14; 16; 19(3); 11:7; 16; 12:1; 18; 19; 31; 13:30; 34; 14:27; 15:4; 14; 22; 30; 16:6; 14; 17:22; 29; 18:1; 7; 12; 19:9; 17; 28; 43(2); 20:3; 8; 14; 15; 25; 21:2; 9; 15; 22; 22:8; 9; 13; 16(2); 18; 23; 38; 23:9; 17; 24:9(2); **1 Ki** 1:8; 41; 49(2); 2:5; 26; 3:16; 18; 4:2; 20; 32; 5:3; 14; 6:10; 25; 31; 32; 34; 7:3; 4; 9; 11; 12; 17; 18; 19(2); 20; 22; 24(2); 28; 29(3); 30; 31(2); 32(2); 33; 34(2); 35; 37; 41(2); 42; 45; 47; 8:4; 5(2); 47; 9:20(2); 21; 22; 23(2); 10:19; 21(2); 11:29; 12:21; 31; 13:8; 14:4; 9; 24; 15:14; 16:15; 16; 21; 25; 30; 33; 20:1; 12; 15; 16; 23; 27; 30; 33; 21:8; 11; 22:43; 48; **2 Ki** 2:3; 5; 15; 3:14; 21(2); 4:6; 38; 39; 40; 5:3; 6:20; 32; 7:3; 9:5; 25; 10:4; 6(2); 29; 11:2; 9(2); 10; 14(2); 12:3; 13; 13:21; 14:4; 14; 15:4; 16(2); 25; 35; 16:17; 17:2; 9; 15; 33; 18:5; 19:12; 18; 26(2); 35; 21:11; 23:3; 4; 7; 8(2); 12; 13(2);

16; 19; 20; 24(2); 24:11; 16; 25:4; 10; 13(2); 17; 19(2); 25; 26; 28; **1 Chr** 1:5; 6; 7; 8; 9(2); 17; 19; 23; 28; 31; 32(2); 33(2); 34; 35; 36; 37; 38; 39; 40(2); 41; 42(2); 43; 51; 54; 2:1; 3(2); 4; 5; 6; 9(2); 16(2); 18; 25; 27; 28(2); 30; 32; 33(2); 42; 43; 47; 50(2); 53; 54; 55(2); 3:1(2); 4; 5; 6; 9; 15; 16; 17; 19(2); 21; 22; 23; 24; 4:1; 2; 3; 4; 6; 7; 12; 13(2); 14; 15; 16; 17; 18; 19; 20(2); 21; 23; 24; 26; 31; 32; 33(2); 38; 41; 5:3; 4; 14; 17; 20(3); 24(2); 25; 6:1; 2; 3(2); 16; 18; 19; 20; 22; 25; 26; 28; 29; 32; 33; 44; 48; 54; 60; 66; 71; 77; 78; 7:1; 2(2); 3(2); 4; 5; 6; 7(3); 8; 9; 10; 11(2); 12; 13; 16; 17; 19; 20; 21; 28; 29; 30; 31; 33(2); 34; 35; 36; 38; 39; 40(2); 8:3; 6; 10; 12; 13; 16; 18; 21; 25; 27; 28; 35; 38(2); 39; 40(2); 9:1; 2; 9; 13; 17; 19; 22(2); 23; 24; 26(2); 27; 28; 29; 31; 32; 33(2); 34; 41; 44(2); 10:7(2); 11:2; 4; 10; 13; 19; 26; 12:1(2); 2; 8(2); 14; 20(2); 21(2); 23(2); 31; 32(2); 33; 38; 39; 40(2); 14:12; 15:19; 23; 24; 27; 16:19; 41(2); 42; 18:7; 16; 17; 19:5; 9; 14; 15; 16; 19(2); 20:2; 3; 4; 8; 21:20; 29; 22:2; 23:3; 4(2); 5; 9; 10; 11; 14; 15; 17; 21(2); 23; 24(2); 27; 24:1; 4(3); 5(2); 26; 27; 30(2); 25:2; 5; 6(2); 7(2); 26:2; 4; 6(2); 7(2); 8; 11; 12; 17; 18; 19; 22; 25; 26; 31(2); 32; 27:2; 4; 5; 7; 8; 9; 10; 11; 12; 13; 14; 15; 22; 28; 29; 31; 29:15; **2 Chr** 1:12; 2:17(2); 3:11; 4:3; 12(2); 13; 22; 5:5; 6(2); 11; 12; 13; 6:37; 8:7(2); 8; 9; 10; 9:9; 11; 18(2); 20(2); 11:1; 13; 12:5; 15; 13:13; 18; 14:8; 13(3); 15:17; 16:8; 17:10; 13; 18:2; 30; 20:21; 22; 24; 25; 33; 37(2); 21:2; 13; 16; 17; 22:4; 11; 23:8(2); 9; 13(2); 14; 25:12; 24; 26:17; 28:15(2); 23; 29:29; 31; 32; 33; 34(2); 35; 30:8; 14; 15; 17; 21; 31:1; 6; 13; 15; 16; 17; 18; 19(4); 32:3; 8; 9; 13; 18; 34:4; 12(2); 13(3); 31; 32; 33; 35:3; 7(2); 14; 15(2); 17; 18; **Ezra** 1:6; 11(2); 2:2; 58; 59(2); 62(3); 65; 66; 3:1; 5; 4:1; 20; 5:1; 2; 4; 6; 10; 14; 6:1; 20; 8:3; 20; 25; 33(2); 9:1; 9; 10:16; 18; **Neh** 1:9; 2:10; 13(2); 4:1; 7(2); 16; 5:2; 3; 4; 8(2); 15; 16; 17; 18; 6:1; 9; 16; 18; 7:4(2); 7; 60; 61(2); 64(2); 67; 68; 73; 8:3; 12; 13; 9:1; 17; 25; 26; 10:1; 8; 11:1; 6; 12; 13; 14; 18; 19; 20; 21; 36; 12:7; 8; 12; 23; 24; 25; 44; 46; 13:5; 13; 15; **Esth** 1:5(2); 6(2); 2:8(2); 9; 12; 19; 23; 3:1; 2; 3; 6; 12(2); 13; 6:1; 14; 8:9; 11; 9:11; 15; 18; 20; **Job** 1:2; 3; 13; 14; 18; 4:7; 6:2; 20; 8:6; 9; 9:15; 20(2); 11:14; 17; 15:7; 16:4; 19:23(2); 24; 21:4; 22:16(2); 29:2; 5; 6; 30:5; 8(2); 32:4; 33:21; 34:36; 37:20; 38:4; 6; 21; 39:16; 42:15; **Ps** 18:7; 8; 15(2); 17; 22; 37; 22:5(2); 33:6; 34:5(2); 35:13; 14; 39:12; 46:6; 48:5; 50:12; 55:18; 20; 21(3); 68:25; 33; 76:5; 6; 77:16; 19; 78:29; 30; 37; 39; 57; 63; 80:10; 81:6; 87:5; 90:2; 99:6; 8; 105:12; 106:39; 42; 43; 107:17; 118:12; 119:5; 126:1; 139:16(2); 148:5; **Prov** 3:20; 7:26(2); 8:24(2); 25; **Eccl** 1:16; 2:7; 9; 4:2; 15; 7:10; 8:10; **Song** 1:6; 6:13; 8:1; **Isa** 5:25; 6:4; 7:2; 10:15; 12:1; 14:2; 3; 8; 26:18; 20; 27:7; 30:4; 5; 37:12; 19; 27(2); 36; 41:5; 11; 22; 42:24; 43:4; 46:1(2); 48:4; 8; 49:21; 51:1(2); 52:14; 53:3; 54:6; 57:10; 63:19; **Jer** 1:1; 5; 2:36; 3:5; 4:26; 5:8; 6:15(2); 8:12(2); 9:1; 11:13; 14:3; 4; 15:16; 20:2; 22:24; 26; 24:1; 2; 26:9; 28:6; 29:1; 4; 34:5; 7; 8; 36:12; 24; 28; 32; 37:5; 15; 40:1(2); 4; 6; 7; 11(2); 13; 41:2; 3(2); 7; 8; 10; 11; 13(3); 16; 18; 42:8; 16; 20; 44:6; 17; 50:11; 24; 33; 51:53(2); 52:7; 14; 17(2); 20; 23(2); 25(2); 30; 32; **Lam** 1:14; 2:4; 6; 4:5; 7(2); 18; 19; 5:12(2); **Ezek** 1:1; 7(2); 8; 11; 16; 18(3); 19(2); 20; 21(2); 27(2); 2:10; 8:14; 16(2); 9:6; 8; 10:3; 9; 10; 12; 13; 15; 19; 20; 11:1; 14:14; 16; 18; 20; 16:4(3); 5(3); 7(2); 13(2); 20; 22; 27; 28(2); 29; 31; 47; 50; 52; 17:6; 19:12; 20:8; 9; 21; 24; 25; 43; 21:30; 23:2; 3; 4; 6; 42; 24:13; 27:8(2); 9(2); 10; 11(2); 13; 15(2); 17; 19; 21; 22; 23; 24(2); 25(2); 28:12; 13(2); 14(2); 15(2); 29:13; 31:5; 8(2); 9; 15; 16; 17; 34:4; 5(2); 12; 36:19; 31; 37:2(2); 38:8; 39:23; 26; 40:4; 10(3); 12; 16(3); 17; 25; 29(2); 30; 31(2); 33(2); 34(2); 37(2); 39; 40(2); 41; 42; 43; 44; 49; 41:2; 6(2); 16(2); 20; 21; 22; 25(2); 26; 42:5; 6; 10; 11(3); 12; 43:3; 46:22(2); 23; 47:7; **Dan** 1:6; 16; 20; 2:28; 31; 35; 42; 3:20; 21(2); 27; 4:10; 12; 21; 5:6; 9; 11; 12; 24; 6:18; 7:2; 4; 7; 8(2); 9; 10; 12; 20; 8:3; 11; 10:3; 7; 12; **Hos** 2:23; 8:12; 9:16; 13:6(2); **Am** 4:7; 8; 11; **Ob** 11; **Jon** 1:5; 10; 2:5; **Mic** 1:13; **Nah** 3:9(2); 10(2); **Hab** 1:5; 3:6; 8; 9; **Zeph** 3:19(2); **Hag** 2:16(2); **Zech** 1:8; 12; 18; 5:9; 6:1(2); 2; 7:3; 7(2); 8:10; 13; 11:11; **Mt** 1:11; 12; 2:16; 3:6; 16; 4:18; 24(2); 5:12; 7:28; 8:16(2); 9:30; 36; 11:21; 23; 12:1; 3; 4; 23; 13:2; 6; 54; 57; 14:20; 21; 26; 33; 35; 36; 15:1; 12; 37(2); 38; 17:6; 22; 23; 18:6(2); 31; 19:12(2); 13; 25; 20:9; 24; 21:15; 22:3(2); 8(2); 25; 33; 41; 23:37; 24:22; 37; 38; 25:2(2); 3; 10; 21; 26:8; 21; 22; 26; 43; 51; 57; 69; 71; 27:38; 44; 51; 52(2); 54; 55; 56; 28:11; 15; **Mk** 1:5; 16; 19; 22; 27; 32(2); 34; 36; 2:6; 12; 15; 18; 26; 4:33; 34; 36; 5:13; 15; 40; 42; 6:2; 3; 13; 31; 34; 42; 44; 50; 51; 55; 56; 7:35; 37; 8:8; 9; 9:4; 6; 15; 32; 42(2); 10:24; 26; 32(3); 11:18; 12:20; 41; 14:4(2); 11; 22; 35; 40; 53; 67; 15:32; 40(2); 16:5; 8(2); **Lk** 1:2; 4; 6; 7; 23; 45; 65; 2:6(2); 8; 9; 18; 21; 22; 33; 47; 48; 3:2; 15; 21; 4:20(2); 25; 27; 28; 32; 36; 40; 5:2; 9(2); 10(2); 17; 26(2); 29; 6:3; 11; 18(2); 7:10; 39; 8:1; 23(2); 25; 35; 37; 40; 56; 9:14; 17(2); 30; 32(2); 33; 34; 43; 45; 10:13; 11:29; 52; 12:49; 13:1; 2; 4; 17(2); 34; 14:7; 17; 24; 16:14; 16; 17:2(2); 9; 12; 14; 17; 18; 27; 18:9; 34; 19:17; 32; 33; 48(2); 20:29; 22:5; 23:5; 6; 23; 32; 39; 24:4; 5; 13; 16; 21; 24; 28; 31; 33; 37; 44; 53; **Jn** 1:3; 13; 24(2); 28; 48; 2:2; 6; 3:19; 23; 5:35; 6:2; 12; 13; 15; 19; 21; 22; 26; 64; 7:10; 8:39; 41; 42; 9:10; 33; 34; 40; 41; 10:41; 11:31; 52; 12:16; 17; 20; 13:1; 14:2; 15:19; 17:6; 18:30; 36; 19:28; 36; 20:3; 19(2); 20; 26; 21:2; 6; 8; 11; 18; 25; **Acts** 1:13; 2:1; 2; 4; 5; 6; 7; 8; 12; 37; 41(2); 43; 44; 47; 3:10; 4:6(2); 13; 26; 27; 31(2); 32; 34(2); 5:12(2); 14; 16(2); 17(2); 33; 36; 37; 41; 6:1; 7; 10; 7:16; 26; 54; 8:1; 4; 7(3); 12; 13; 14; 9:2; 8; 21; 23; 26; 31(2); 10:12; 38; 45; 11:1; 10; 19; 20; 24; 26; 12:6; 10; 12; 16; 13:1; 41; 45; 48; 52; 14:7; 15:4; 10; 30; 33; 16:2; 3; 4; 5; 6; 12; 15; 25(2); 26(3); 32; 33; 38(2); 17:4; 5; 11(2); 21; 18:3; 8; 14; 18; 19:3; 5; 7; 9; 12; 14; 21; 28; 31; 20:8(2); 12; 34; 21:5; 8; 16; 18; 24; 27; 30; 31; 22:5; 9(2); 11; 20; 29; 23:6; 13; 15; 20; 31; 24:9; 26:5; 10; 27:4; 17; 18; 27(2); 30; 36; 37; 28:6; 9; 10; 14; 24(2); **Rom** 1:21(2); 3:2; 25; 5:6; 8; 10(2); 19; 6:3(2); 4; 17(2); 20(2); 7:5(3); 6; 8:24; 9:3; 25; 32; 11:7; 17(2); 19; 20; 24(2); 30; 15:4(2); 16:7; **1 Cor** 1:5; 9; 13; 2:4; 3:2; 4:18; 5:3; 6:11(4); 20; 7:7; 21; 23; 10:1; 2; 5; 7; 9; 10; 11; 11:5; 12:2(2); 13; 17(2); 19; **2 Cor** 1:8; 3:14; 5:20; 7:5(3); 9(2); 8:3; 10; 11:17; 21; 12:12; 13; 13:2; **Gal** 1:17; 22; 23; 2:2; 6; 12; 14; 3:16; 23; 27; 4:3(2); 5; **Eph** 1:13; 2:1; 3; 5; 12; 13; 17(2); 4:1; 4; 30; 5:8; **Phil** 3:7; **Col** 1:16(2); 21; 2:11; 12; 3:1; 15; **1 Th** 1:5; 2:2(2); 7; 8; 3:4; 7; **2 Th** 2:15; 3:7; 10; **1 Tim** 6:12; **Titus** 3:3; **Phm** 1:14; **Heb** 2:15; 4:3; 6:4; 7:11; 23(2); 8:4; 9:4; 5; 10:32; 33(2); 11:3(2); 12; 13(2); 23; 29; 30; 34; 35; 37(4); **1 Pe** 1:12; 18; 2:8; 10; 21; 24; 25; 3:9; 20(2); **2 Pe** 1:16; 18; 21; 2:1; 3:2; 4; 5; **1 Jn** 2:19(2); 3:12; **Jude** 4; 17; **Rev** 1:14; 15; 3:15; 4:4; 5; 6; 8; 11; 5:9; 6:11; 7:4(2); 5(3); 6(3); 7(3); 8(3); 8:2; 5; 7(2); 9; 12; 9:2; 4; 5; 7(2); 8; 10; 15; 17; 20; 11:13(2); 15; 18; 19; 12:9; 13:2; 14:3(2); 4(2); 15:8; 16:9; 18(2); 20; 17:2; 18:23(2); 24; 19:6; 12(2); 20; 21(2); 20:3; 5; 12(3); 13(3); 14; 21:14; 19; 21; 22:2

WHEN (2863/2675)

Gen 2:4; 3:6; 4:8; 12; 6:1; 4; 7:6; 9:14; 12:4; 11; 12; 14; 14:14; 15:11; 12; 17; 16:4; 5; 6; 16; 17:1; 24; 25; 18:2; 19:1; 15; 17; 23; 29(2); 33(2); 35(2); 20:13; 21:4; 5; 24:11; 19; 22; 30(2); 36; 41; 43; 52; 64; 25:20; 24; 26; 26:8; 34; 27:1; 5; 34; 40; 29:10; 13; 31; 30:1; 9; 16; 25; 30; 33; 38; 42; 31:10; 49; 32:2; 17; 19; 25; 33:18; 34:2; 7; 25; 35:1; 7; 9; 16; 17; 22; 36:33; 34; 35; 36; 37; 38; 39; 37:4; 18; 23; 38:5; 9; 15; 25; 28; 39:11; 13; 15; 19; 40:13; 14; 16; 41:10; 21; 46; 55; 42:1; 21; 35; 43:2; 16; 19; 21; 26; 44:4(2); 24; 30; 31; 45:27(2); 46:33; 47:15; 18; 29; 48:7(2); 17; 49:33; 50:4; 11; 15; 17; **Ex** 1:16; 2:2; 3; 5; 6; 11; 12; 13; 15; 18; 3:4; 12; 13; 21; 4:6; 14; 21; 31; 5:13; 7:5; 7; 9; 15; 8:9; 15; 9:34; 10:10; 13; 11:1; 12:13(2); 23; 25; 26; 27; 44; 48; 13:5; 8; 11; 14; 15; 17(2); 14:10; 18; 27; 15:23; 25; 16:3(2); 8; 14; 15; 18; 21; 32; 17:11(2); 18:14; 16; 19:9; 13; 19; 20:18; 22:27; 23:16; 28:29; 30; 35(3); 43(2); 29:30; 36; 30:7; 8; 12(3); 15; 20(2); 31:18; 32:1; 5; 17; 25; 34; 33:4; 9; 34:24; 29(2); 30; 33; 39:9; 40:32; **Lev** 1:2; 2:1; 8; 3:1; 4:14; 22; 5:3; 4; 5; 6:20; 21; 27; 7:35; 38; 9:24; 10:9; 20; 11:31; 32; 12:6; 13:2; 9; 14; 20; 14:34; 57(2); 15:2; 13; 18; 23; 31; 16:1; 17; 20; 23; 18:28; 19:9; 23; 20:4; 22:7; 16; 27; 29; 23:10; 12; 22(2); 39; 43; 24:16; 25:2; 26:17; 25; 26; 35; 36; 37; 44; 27:2; 14; 21; **Num** 1:51(2); 3:1; 4; 4:5; 15(2); 19; 5:6; 21; 27; 29; 30; 6:2; 7; 13; 7:1; 10; 84; 89; 8:2; 19; 9:19; 20; 21(2); 22; 10:3; 5; 6; 7; 9; 28; 34; 36; 11:1; 2; 9; 25; 12:10; 12; 15:2; 8; 18; 19; 28; 16:4; 42; 18:16; 26; 30; 32; 19:14; 20:3; 16; 29; 21:8; 9; 22:25; 27; 36; 24:1; 23; 25:7; 26:9; 10(2); 61; 64; 27:13; 28:26; 32:1; 8; 9; 33:39; 51; 34:2; 35:10; 19; 21; 36:4; **Deut** 1:41; 2:8; 16; 19; 22; 4:10; 15; 19; 25; 30(2); 5:23; 28; 6:7(4); 10; 11; 20; 7:1; 2; 8:10; 12; 13; 14; 9:9; 23; 11:19(4); 29; 12:10; 20; 25; 28; 29; 14:24; 15:4; 10; 13; 18; 16:13; 17:14; 18; 18:9; 22; 19:1; 5; 20:1; 2; 9; 10; 13; 19; 21:9; 10; 18; 22:8; 14; 26; 23:4; 9; 11(2); 13; 21; 24; 25; 24:1; 2; 5; 9; 10; 13; 19; 20; 21; 25:18; 19; 26:1; 12; 14; 27:2; 3; 4; 12; 28:6(2); 19(2); 29:7; 19; 22; 25; 30:1; 31:4; 11; 14; 20; 21; 24(2); 32:8(2); 19; 36; 33:5; 34:7; **Josh** 2:5; 10; 14; 18; 3:3; 8; 14; 4:1; 6; 7; 11; 18; 21; 5:1; 8; 13; 6:5(2); 8; 16; 18; 20(2); 7:8; 21; 8:5; 8; 13; 14; 20; 21; 24(2); 9:1; 3; 22; 10:1; 12; 24; 11:1; 5; 14:7; 15:18; 17:13; 19:49; 20:4; 22:7; 10; 12; 28; 30; 23:16; **Judg** 1:14; 24; 28; 35; 2:4; 6; 8; 10; 18; 19; 21; 3:9; 15; 18; 24; 27; 4:1; 18; 22; 5:2(2); 4(2); 31; 6:7; 28; 29; 38; 7:13; 15; 17; 18; 22; 8:1; 3; 4; 7; 9; 12; 9:7; 30; 33; 35; 36; 46; 55; 11:2; 5; 7; 13; 16; 31; 34; 35; 12:2; 3; 5; 13:11; 17; 20; 21; 14:8; 9; 11; 15:5; 14; 17; 16:2(2); 9; 15; 16; 18; 24; 25; 17:3; 18:10; 18; 22; 26; 19:1; 3; 7; 9; 15; 17; 25; 27; 29; 20:10; 40; 41; 21:9; 21; 22; **Ruth** 1:1; 18; 19; 2:9; 15; 3:4; 15; 16; 4:13; **1 Sam** 1:7; 24; 2:13; 19; 27; 3:2; 4:2; 3(2); 5; 6; 13(2); 14; 18; 19; 5:2; 3; 4; 7; 6:6; 16; 7:7(2); 8:1; 6; 9:5; 9; 17; 25; 10:2; 5; 7; 9; 10; 11; 13; 14; 20; 21(2); 23; 11:6; 8; 12:8; 9; 12(2); 13:1; 6; 11; 14:17; 22; 26; 52; 15:2; 6; 12; 17; 16:6; 16; 17:11; 24; 28; 31; 34; 35; 42; 48; 51; 55; 18:1; 6; 15; 19; 26; 19:14; 16; 20; 21; 20:12; 15; 19; 24; 37; 21:1; 6; 22:1; 6; 17; 22; 23:6; 9; 25(2); 24:1; 8; 16; 18; 25:4; 9; 11; 15; 23; 30; 31; 37; 39; 40; 26:20; 28:5; 6; 12; 22; 30:1; 12; 16; 21; 26; 31:5; 7; 8; 11; **2 Sam** 1:1; 2; 7; 2:10; 24; 30; 3:13; 23; 26; 27; 28; 35; 4:1; 4; 7; 10; 11; 5:2; 4; 17; 24; 6:6; 13; 18; 7:1; 12; 8:5; 9; 13; 9:2; 6; 10:5; 6; 7; 9; 14; 15; 17; 19; 11:1; 7; 10; 13; 19; 20; 26; 27; 12:19; 20; 21; 13:5; 6; 11; 21; 28(2); 14:4; 26(2); 29; 33; 15:32; 16:1; 5; 7; 16; 17:3; 6; 9; 20(2); 23; 27; 18:5; 29; 19:3; 18; 25; 39; 20:8; 12(2); 13; 17; 21:15; 21; 22:1; 5; 23:4; 9; 24:8; 11; 16; 17; **1 Ki** 1:21; 23; 41; 2:7; 8; 3:21(2); 5:7; 6:7; 7:24; 8:9(2); 10; 21; 30(2); 31; 33(2); 35(2); 37(2); 38; 42; 44(2); 46; 47; 48; 53; 54; 9:1; 10; 10:1; 2; 4; 11:4; 15; 21; 24; 29; 12:2; 16; 20; 21; 13:4; 24; 26; 31; 14:5; 6; 12; 17; 21; 15:21; 29; 16:11; 18; 17:10; 18:10; 12; 13; 17; 29; 39; 19:3; 13; 15; 20:12; 21:15; 16; 27; 22:25; 32; 33; 42; **2 Ki** 1:5; 2:1; 9; 10; 14; 15; 17; 18; 3:5; 15; 20; 21; 24; 26; 4:4; 6; 12; 15; 17; 20; 25; 27; 32; 36; 5:6; 7; 8; 13; 18(2); 21; 24; 26; 6:4; 15; 18; 20; 21; 30; 32; 7:5; 8; 12; 17; 8:6; 17; 26; 29; 9:2; 5; 15; 22; 25; 27; 30; 34; 10:7; 15; 17; 11:1; 13; 14; 21; 13:21; 14:2; 15:2; 33; 16:2; 12; 18:2; 17; 18; 19:1; 35; 20:17; 21:1; 19; 22:1; 11; 19; 23:29; 31; 36; 24:8; 18; 25:23; **1 Chr** 1:44; 45; 46; 47; 48; 49; 50; 2:19; 21; 5:7; 6:15; 7:23; 10:5; 7; 8; 11; 11:2; 12:15; 19; 20; 13:9; 14:8; 12; 15; 15:26; 16:2; 19; 20; 17:1; 11(2); 18:5; 9; 19:6; 8; 10; 15; 16; 17(2); 19; 20:7; 21:28; 23:1; **2 Chr** 4:3; 5:10(2); 11; 13(2); 6:21(2); 26(2); 28(2); 29; 32; 34(2); 36; 37; 38; 7:1; 3; 13; 9:1(2); 3; 10:2; 16; 11:1; 12:1; 7; 12; 13; 13:7; 14; 15:4; 8; 9; 16:5; 18:24; 31; 32; 19:8; 20:10; 21; 22; 23; 24; 25; 29; 31; 21:4; 5; 20; 22:2; 6; 7; 8; 9; 10; 23:7(2); 12; 13; 24:1; 11(2); 14; 15; 25; 25:1; 26:3; 16; 27:1; 8; 28:1; 29:1; 27; 29; 31:1; 8; 32:2; 21; 33:1; 12; 21; 34:1; 7; 8; 9; 14; 19; 27; 35:20; 36:2; 5; 9; 11; **Ezra** 2:68; 3:1; 10; 11; 12; 4:1; 23; 9:1; 3; 10:6; **Neh** 1:4; 2:1; 3; 6; 10; 19; 4:1; 7; 12; 15; 5:6; 6:1; 16; 7:1(2); 73; 8:5; 9; 9:18; 27; 28; 10:38; 13:3; **Esth** 1:2; 4; 5; 10; 17; 20; 2:1; 7; 8(2); 15; 19; 20; 23; 3:4; 5; 4:1; 5:2; 9; 6:13; 7:8; 9:25; **Job** 1:5; 6; 13; 15; 2:1; 11; 12; 3:11; 22; 4:13; 5:21; 6:5; 17(2); 7:4(2); 13; 9:5; 11:3; 12; 13:9; 16:22; 20:23; 21:6; 21; 22:29; 23:9(2); 10; 15; 27:9; 28:26; 29:2; 3(2); 4; 5(2); 6; 7(2); 11(2); 30:24; 26(2); 31:13; 14(2); 21; 26; 29; 32:5; 33:15; 34:29(2); 36:13; 20; 37:4; 15; 17; 21(2); 38:4; 7; 8; 9; 10; 11; 38; 40; 41; 39:1(2); 2; 18; 41:25; 42:10; **Ps** 2:12; 3:4:1; 3; 8:3; 9:3; 12; 10:9; 12:8; 13:4; 14:7; 17:15; 20:9; 22:24; 27:2; 7; 8; 10; 28:2(2); 30:9; 31:22; 32:3; 6; 34:35:13; 36:2(2); 37:33; 34; 38:16; 39:11; 41:5; 6; 42:2; 4; 48:7; 49:5; 16(2); 17; 18; 50:18; 51:4(2); 52:53:6; 54:56:6; 9; 57:58:7; 10; 59:60:61:2; 63:6; 66:14; 68:7(2); 9; 14; 69:10; 71:9; 18; 23; 72:12; 73:3; 16; 20(2); 75:2; 76:7; 9; 78:34; 42; 43; 59; 81:5; 87:6; 89:9; 90:4; 92:7(2); 94:8; 95:9; 101:2; 102:22; 104:22; 105:12; 13; 38; 106:16; 44; 107:39; 109:7; 23; 25; 28; 114:1; 119:6; 7; 74; 82; 84; 120:7; 122:1; 124:2; 3; 126:1; 128:2; 137:1; 138:3; 4; 139:15; 16; 18; 141:1; 7; 142:3; **Prov** 1:26; 27(2); 2:10; 3:24; 25; 27; 28; 4:3; 8; 12(2); 5:11; 6:9; 22(3); 30; 31; 8:24(2); 27(2); 28(2); 29(2); 10:25; 11:2; 7; 10(2); 13:12; 14:7; 16:7; 17:28(2); 18:3; 20:14; 16; 21:11(2); 27; 22:6; 23:1; 16; 22; 31(3); 35; 24:17(2); 32; 25:8; 26:25; 27:13; 25; 28:1; 12(2); 28(2); 29:2(2); 16; 30:22(2); 23; 31:23; **Eccl** 4:10; 5:1; 4; 11; 14; 8:7; 16; 9:12; 10:3; 11; 16; 17; 12:1; 3(2); 4(2); 5; **Song** 3:4; 5:6; 8:8; **Isa** 1:12; 15; 2:19; 21; 3:6; 4:4; 5:4; 6:13; 8:19; 21; 9:1; 3; 10:12; 18; 13:19; 16:12; 17:5; 18:3(2); 5; 20:1; 21:3(2); 23:5; 24:13(2); 26:9; 11; 16; 17; 27:9; 11; 28:15; 18; 25; 29:8(2); 23; 30:19; 25; 29(2); 31:3; 4; 32:7; 33:1(2); 3; 37:1; 9; 36; 38:9; 39:6; 40:24; 41:28; 43:2(2); 48:13; 21; 50:2(2); 51:13; 52:8; 53:2; 10; 54:6; 57:13; 20; 58:7; 59:19; 64:3; 65:12(2); 66:4(2); 14; **Jer** 2:2; 7; 17; 20; 26; 3:16; 4:30; 5:7; 19; 6:14; 15; 7:32; 8:11; 12; 10:13; 11:15; 12:1; 13:21; 14:12(2); 16:10; 17:6; 8; 27; 18:22; 20:8; 21:1; 22:23; 23:33; 25:12; 26:8; 10; 21(2); 27:20; 28:9; 29:13; 31:2; 6; 23; 31; 32:16; 34:1; 7; 10; 14; 18; 35:11; 36:11; 13; 16; 23; 37:5; 11; 13; 16; 38:7; 28; 39:4; 5; 40:1; 7; 11; 41:4; 7; 11; 13; 42:6; 18; 20; 43:1; 11; 44:19; 45:1; 51:16; 33; 59; 61; 63; 52:1; **Lam** 1:7; 3:8; 37; 4:15; **Ezek** 1:9; 12; 17(2); 19(2); 21(3); 24(2); 28; 2:2; 9; 3:18; 20; 27; 4:6; 5:2; 13; 15; 16; 6:8; 13; 8:7; 8; 10:3; 5; 6; 9; 11(3); 16(2); 17(2); 19; 12:15; 13:10; 12; 16; 14:13; 21; 23; 15:5(2); 7; 16:5; 6; 8; 22; 53; 54; 55; 61; 63; 17:10; 17; 18:2; 24; 26; 27; 19:5; 20:5; 28; 31; 32; 41; 42; 44; 21:7(2); 22:14; 28; 23:19; 21; 24:24; 25; 25:3(3); 17; 26:10; 15(2); 19(2); 27:33; 28:22; 25; 26; 29:7(2); 16; 30:4; 8; 18; 25; 31:15; 16; 32:7; 9; 10; 15(2); 33:2; 3; 8; 13; 14; 18; 19; 22; 29; 33; 34:5; 27; 35:5; 11; 14; 36:17; 20(2); 23; 37:13; 18; 28; 38:14; 16; 18; 39:15; 26; 27; 42:14; 15; 43:3; 8; 18; 23; 24; 27; 44:7(2); 10; 15; 19; 21; 45:1; 46:8; 9; 10(2); 12; 47:3; 7; 8; 48:11; **Dan** 1:18; 3:7; 5:20; 6:10; 14; 20; 8:8; 15; 17; 23; 10:8; 15; 19; 20; 11:4; 12; 34; 12:7(2); **Hos** 1:2; 8; 2:15; 4:14(2); 5:13; 6:11; 7:1; 14; 9:12; 10:10(2); 11:1; 10; 13:1(2); 6; **Joel** 3:1; **Am** 3:4; 4:2; 7; 9; 6:10; 7:2; 8:5; 9:13; **Ob** 11; **Jon** 2:7; 4:2; 8; **Mic** 5:5(2); 6(2); 7:8(2); 11; 15; **Nah** 1:12; 3:17; **Hab** 1:13; 2:1; 3:16(2); **Zeph** 3:20; **Hag** 1:9; 2:5; 16(2); **Zech** 5:11; 7:2; 5; 6(2); 7; 8:14; 12:2; 13:3; 4; **Mal** 1:8(2); 3:2; **Mt** 2:3; 4; 7; 8; 9; 10; 11(2); 13; 14; 16; 19; 22; 3:7; 16; 4:2; 3; 12; 5:1; 11; 6:2; 3; 5; 6(2); 7; 16; 17; 7:28; 8:1; 5; 10; 14; 16; 18; 23; 28; 32; 34; 9:2; 8; 11; 12; 15; 22; 23; 25; 27; 28; 31; 33; 36; 10:1; 12; 14; 19; 23; 11:1; 2; 12:2; 3; 9; 15; 24; 43; 44; 13:6; 19; 21; 26; 32; 46; 48; 53; 54; 14:6; 13(2); 14; 15; 23(2); 26; 29; 30; 32; 34; 35; 15:2; 10; 12; 31; 16:2; 5; 13; 17:6; 8; 14; 24; 25; 27; 18:24; 31; 19:1; 22; 25; 28; 20:2; 8; 9; 10; 11; 24; 30; 21:1; 10; 15; 20; 23; 32; 34; 38; 40; 45; 46; 22:7; 11; 22; 33; 34; 23:15; 24:3; 15; 32; 33; 46; 50; 25:31; 37; 38; 39; 44; 26:1; 6; 8; 10; 20; 29; 30; 71; 27:1; 2; 17; 24; 26; 29; 31; 33; 34; 47; 54; 57; 59; 28:12; 17; **Mk** 1:19; 26; 32; 37; 2:4(2); 5; 8; 16; 17; 20; 25; 3:5; 8; 21; 4:6; 10; 15; 16; 17; 29; 31; 32; 34; 35; 36; 5:2; 6; 18; 21; 22; 27; 39; 40; 6:2; 11; 16; 20; 21; 22; 29; 34; 35; 38; 41; 46; 47; 49; 53; 54; 7:2; 4; 14; 17; 30; 8:19; 20; 23; 33; 34; 38; 9:8; 14; 15; 20; 25; 28; 33; 36; 10:14; 41; 47; 11:1; 11; 12; 13; 19; 24; 12:14; 23; 25; 34; 13:4(2); 7; 11; 14; 28; 29; 33; 35; 14:11; 12; 23; 25; 26; 40; 67; 72; 15:20; 24; 33; 35; 39; 41; 42; 45; 16:1; 2; 4; 9; 11; **Lk** 1:9; 12; 22; 25; 29; 41; 58; 2:15; 17; 21; 22; 27; 39; 42; 43; 45; 48; 3:21; 4:2; 13; 17; 25; 28; 35; 40; 42; 5:4; 6; 8; 11; 12; 19; 20; 22; 35; 6:3; 10; 13; 22(2); 26; 42; 48; 7:1; 3; 4; 6; 9; 12; 13; 20; 24; 29; 37; 39; 42; 8:4; 8; 13; 14; 16; 27; 28; 34; 40; 45; 47; 50; 51; 9:5; 10; 11; 12; 26; 32; 36; 37; 51; 54; 10:31; 32; 33; 35(2); 11:1; 2; 14; 21; 22; 24; 25; 33; 34(2); 36; 38; 12:1; 11; 36(2); 37; 43; 46(2); 55; 58; 13:12; 17; 25; 28; 35; 14:7; 8; 10(2); 12; 13; 15; 15:5; 6; 9; 14; 17; 20; 16:4; 9; 17:7; 10; 14; 15; 20(2); 22; 30; 18:8; 15; 22; 23; 24; 40; 43; 19:5; 7; 15; 28; 29; 43; 20:13; 14; 16; 37; 21:7(2); 9; 20; 28; 30; 31; 22:7; 10; 14; 32; 35; 40; 45; 49; 53; 55; 23:6; 8; 13; 33; 42; 46; 47; 24:6; 23; 40; **Jn** 1:19; 38; 42; 48; 2:3; 9; 10; 15; 22; 23(2); 3:4; 4:1; 21; 23; 25; 40; 45; 47; 52; 54; 5:6; 7; 25; 6:11; 12; 14; 15; 16; 19; 22; 24; 25(2); 60; 61; 7:9; 10; 27; 31; 40; 8:3; 7; 10; 28; 44; 9:4; 6; 14; 35; 10:4; 11:4; 6; 17; 28; 31; 32; 33; 43; 12:12; 14; 16; 17; 41; 13:1; 12; 19; 21; 26; 31; 14:29; 15:26; 16:4; 8; 13; 21; 25; 18:1; 6; 22; 38; 19:6; 8; 13; 23; 26; 30; 33; 20:14; 19; 20(2); 22; 24; 21:4; 7; 15; 18(2); 19; **Acts** 1:6; 8; 9; 13; 22; 2:1; 6; 37; 3:12; 13; 4:7; 13; 15; 21; 24; 31; 5:7; 21; 22; 23; 24; 27; 33; 40; 6:1; 6; 7:2; 4; 5; 12; 17; 21; 23; 30; 31; 54; 60; 8:12; 13; 14; 15; 18; 25; 39; 9:8; 19; 26; 30; 37; 39; 40; 41; 10:4; 7; 8; 32; 11:2; 6; 17; 18; 20; 23; 26; 12:4; 6; 10; 11; 12; 14; 16; 19; 25; 13:5; 6; 12; 13; 14; 17; 19; 22; 29; 42; 43; 45; 48; 14:5; 11; 14; 20; 21; 23; 25; 27; 15:2; 4; 7; 30(2); 31; 16:6; 15; 19; 23; 34; 35; 38; 40; 17:1; 6; 8; 9; 10; 13; 16; 32; 18:5; 6; 12; 14; 20; 22; 26; 27(2); 19:2; 5; 6; 9; 21(2); 28; 30; 34; 35; 41; 20:2; 3; 7; 11; 14; 18; 36; 21:1; 3; 5; 6; 7; 11; 12; 14; 17; 19; 20; 27; 32; 34; 35; 40(2); 22:2; 17; 20; 26; 23:6; 7; 10; 12; 16; 28; 30; 33; 34(2); 35; 24:2; 22(2); 24; 25; 25:1; 6; 7; 12; 14; 15; 17; 18; 21; 23; 25; 26:10; 14; 30; 31; 27:1;

4; 5; 7; 9; 13; 15; 17; 20; 27; 28; 30; 35(2); 38; 39; 28:1; 3; 4; 9; 10; 15(2); 16; 17; 18; 19; 23; 25; 29; **Rom** 2:14; 16; 3:4; 5:6; 10; 13; 6:20; 7:5; 9; 9:10; 11:27; 13:11; 15:28; 29; **1 Cor** 2:1; 3:4; 5:4; 8:12; 9:18; 27; 11:18; 20; 24; 32; 33; 34; 13:10; 11(2); 14:7; 15:24(2); 27; 28; 54; 16:2; 3; 5; 12; **2 Cor** 1:17; 2:3; 12; 3:15; 16; 7:5; 7; 10:2; 6; 11(2); 11:9; 12:10; 20; 21; 13:9; **Gal** 1:15; 2:7; 9; 11; 12; 14; 4:3; 4; 8; 18; 6:3; **Eph** 1:20; 2:5; 3:4; 4:8; **Phil** 2:19; 28; 4:15; **Col** 3:4; 7; 4:16; **1 Th** 2:6; 13; 3:1; 4; 5; 5:3; **2 Th** 1:7; 10; 2:5; 3:10; **1 Tim** 1:3; 5:11; **2 Tim** 1:5; 17; 4:3; 13; **Titus** 3:4; 12; **Heb** 1:3; 6; 5:7; 6:13; 7:10; 27; 8:5; 8; 9; 9:6; 19; 10:5; 11:8; 11; 17; 21; 22; 23; 24; 31; 12:5; 17; **Jas** 1:2; 12; 13; 14; 15(2); 2:21; 25; **1 Pe** 1:11; 2:12; 20(2); 23(2); 3:2; 16; 20; 4:3; 13; 5:4; **2 Pe** 1:16; 17; 18; 2:18; **1 Jn** 2:28; 3:2; 5:2; **3 Jn** 3; **Jude** 9; **Rev** 1:17; 5:8; 6:1; 3; 5; 7; 9; 12; 13; 14; 8:1; 9:5; 10:3(2); 4; 7; 10; 11:7; 12:13; 17:6; 8; 10; 18:9; 18; 20:7; 22:8

WHICH (2908/2594)

Gen 1:7(2); 21; 29; 30; 2:2(2); 3; 11; 13; 14; 22; 3:1; 3; 11; 17; 23; 24; 4:11; 5:29; 6:17; 7:15; 23; 8:6; 7; 12; 9:12; 15; 17; 11:5; 13:4; 15; 18; 14:6; 15; 17:8; 10; 18:8; 10; 19:19; 21; 28; 29; 21:2; 23; 25; 29; 22:2; 3; 9; 17; 23:9(2); 16; 17(4); 24:5; 42; 25:6; 7; 9; 10; 18; 26:2; 3; 15; 18(2); 32; 27:15; 17; 27; 41; 28:4(2); 13; 22; 29:27; 30:26; 37; 38; 31:10; 12; 16; 18(2); 39; 51; 32:8; 10; 12; 32; 33:8; 13; 14; 18; 34:7; 35:3; 4(3); 6; 12; 20; 36:6; 37:6; 22; 38:10; 14; 39:6; 19; 40:20; 41:27; 28; 36; 43; 48(2); 53; 42:9; 38; 43:2; 18; 26; 44:5(2); 8; 45:6; 27(2); 46:5; 6; 47:14; 22; 26; 48:22; 49:30(2); 50:5; 10; 11; 13; 15; 24; **Ex** 1:14; 3:9; 20; 4:9; 17; 21; 28; 30; 5:8; 6:4; 8; 7:15; 17; 8:3; 12; 21; 22; 9:19; 10:2; 5(2); 6; 15; 19; 21; 12:16; 25; 39; 13:3; 5; 12; 14:13; 31; 15:17(2); 26; 16:1; 8; 15; 16; 26; 32(2); 17:5; 18:9; 11; 20; 19:6; 7; 20:12; 21:1; 22:9; 23:16; 20; 28; 24:3; 8; 12; 25:3; 16; 22(2); 40; 26:30; 27:21; 28:4; 8; 24; 26; 38; 29:27(4); 33; 30:4; 37; 32:2; 3; 8; 14; 20; 32; 34; 35; 33:1; 7; 34:1; 35:1; 4; 29; 36:3; 5; 37:16; 27; 38:7; 21; 39:19; **Lev** 2:11; 3:5; 9; 4:2; 3; 7(2); 8; 13; 14; 18(3); 22; 23; 27; 28(2); 5:3; 6; 7; 8; 10; 17; 18; 6:3; 4(2); 5; 7; 10; 15; 20; 27; 28; 30; 7:8; 11; 25; 38; 8:30; 9:6; 8; 12; 15; 18(2); 10:1; 6; 11; 14; 11:2; 10; 21(2); 23; 26; 32(2); 33; 34; 35; 36; 37; 39; 13:20; 50; 52; 54; 57; 14:34; 37; 40; 15:4(2); 6; 9; 17; 23; 24; 26; 16:2; 6; 9; 10; 11(2); 15; 16; 23; 17:2; 5; 18:5; 24; 30; 19:22(2); 20:23; 25; 22:3; 5; 15; 18; 23:2; 4; 10; 37; 38; 25:2; 31; 45; 51; 26:16; 22; 39; 40; 46; 27:11; 22(2); 26; 34; **Num** 3:26; 31; 48; 4:9; 12; 14; 15; 26; 5:3; 7; 8; 9; 18; 6:5; 18; 21; 7:9; 13; 19; 25; 31; 37; 43; 49; 55; 61; 67; 73; 79; 8:4; 10:29; 11:5; 12; 12:11(2); 13:2; 24; 32(2); 14:8; 11; 15; 16; 22; 23; 27; 30; 31; 34; 40; 15:2; 18; 22; 39; 16:39; 17:5; 18:9; 12; 13; 15; 16; 19; 21; 24; 26; 28; 19:2(3); 15; 20:12; 24; 21:11; 13; 16; 20; 30; 22:5; 20; 30; 36; 23:13; 25:18; 27:12; 17; 28:3; 6; 23; 30:1; 4(2); 5; 6; 7; 8(2); 9; 11; 16; 31:21; 32; 38; 39; 40; 41; 42; 32:4; 7; 9; 11; 38; 33:6; 7; 36; 34:13(2); 35:4; 6(2); 8; 13; 14; 17; 18; 23; 34(2); 36:3; 4; 13; **Deut** 1:1; 8; 14; 18; 19; 20; 22(2); 25; 35; 36; 2:12; 29; 35; 36; 3:4; 12(2); 19; 20(2); 21; 28; 4:1(2); 2(2); 5; 8; 13; 14; 19; 21; 23(2); 26; 28; 31; 32; 40(2); 44; 45; 48; 5:1; 16; 28; 31(2); 33(2); 6:1(2); 2; 6; 10(2); 11(3); 17; 18; 20; 23; 7:1; 8; 11; 12; 13; 15; 19(2); 8:1(2); 3; 9(2); 10; 11; 15; 16; 18; 20; 9:5; 9; 10; 12; 16; 18; 19; 21; 23; 28(2); 10:2; 4; 5; 11; 13; 21; 11:3; 7; 8(2); 9; 10(2); 11(2); 12; 13; 17; 21; 22; 24; 27; 28(2); 29; 31; 32; 12:1(2); 2; 7(2); 9; 10; 11; 14; 15; 17; 18(2); 21; 26(2); 28; 29; 31; 13:2(2); 5; 6; 7; 12; 13; 18; 14:4; 25; 29; 15:4; 5; 7; 10; 20; 16:3; 4; 5; 7; 10; 15; 16; 17; 18; 20; 21; 22; 17:1; 2; 3; 8(2); 10(2); 11(3); 14; 18:6; 9; 14; 19; 20; 21; 22; 19:2; 3; 8; 9; 10; 14(2); 20:14; 15(2); 16; 18; 20; 21:1; 3(2); 4; 23; 22:3; 9; 12; 23:16; 20(2); 23; 24:4; 25:6; 15; 19; 26:1; 2; 3; 10; 11; 13; 15; 19; 27:1; 2; 3; 4; 10; 28:1; 8(2); 11; 13; 14; 15; 20; 21; 23(2); 27; 34; 35; 36; 45; 50; 52(2); 53; 55; 57(2); 60; 61; 63; 64; 67(2); 68; 29:1(2); 3; 12; 16; 17; 22; 23; 25; 29; 30:1; 5; 8; 10; 11; 16; 18; 20; 31:5; 7; 11; 13; 16; 18; 20; 21; 23; 29; 32:37; 46(2); 47; 49(2); 50; 52; 33:1; 34:1; 4; 11; 12; **Josh** 1:2; 6; 7; 11; 13; 14; 15(2); 2:6; 17; 18; 20; 3:4; 16; 4:20; 23; 5:6; 7:2; 11; 14(3); 8:26; 27; 31; 32; 35; 9:13; 20; 27; 10:27; 11:13; 12:2(2); 7(2); 9; 13:3(2); 8; 9; 16; 25; 30; 32; 14:1(2); 6; 12; 15:7(2); 8(2); 9; 10; 13; 25; 49; 54; 60; 17:5; 18:2; 3; 7; 13; 14; 16; 17; 28; 19:13; 27; 50; 51; 20:2; 6; 7; 21:9; 10; 11; 43; 45; 22:4; 5; 9(2); 10; 17; 28; 29; 23:13; 14; 15(2); 16(2); 24:12; 13(3); 14; 15; 23; 27; 30; 31; 32(3); 33; **Judg** 1:16; 26; 2:1; 7; 10; 17; 20; 21; 3:1; 4; 4:11; 14; 6:2; 11(2); 13; 26; 28; 8:26; 9:2; 4; 9; 13; 38; 56; 10:4(2); 14; 11:28; 39; 15:19; 16:26; 29; 17:2; 18:5; 24; 31; 19:14; 20:4; 9; 18; 31; 21:12; 19; **Ruth** 2:9; 4:3; 12; **1 Sam** 1:17; 27; 2:29; 32; 3:11; 13; 6:4; 7; 8; 15; 17; 18(2); 7:14; 8:8(2); 9:23(2); 10:2; 4; 12:3; 7; 16; 17; 21; 13:5; 13; 14:2; 4; 14; 19; 30; 15:7; 14; 20; 21; 17:1; 31; 40; 20:23; 33; 36; 37; 21:2; 6; 23:19; 24:4; 25:27; 26:3; 28:21; 29:1; 4; 30:14; 16; 19; **2 Sam** 2:16; 24; 32; 6:3; 4; 7:25; 8:11; 12:3; 13:10; 15(2); 23; 14:14; 15:7; 16:23; 18:9; 18; 20:5; 8; 23:15; 24:5; 24; **1 Ki** 1:9; 2:4; 27; 31; 3:28; 4:12; 5:3; 8; 6:1; 2; 12(2); 38; 7:17; 19; 20; 41; 45; 48; 51; 8:1; 2; 9; 16; 20; 21(2); 26; 27; 28; 29(2); 34; 36(2); 40; 43(2); 44(2); 48(3); 50; 56; 58; 59; 63; 9:1; 3; 6; 7(2); 8; 12; 13; 15; 24; 25; 26; 10:5; 6; 7; 11; 24; 27; 11:11; 13; 32; 36; 12:4; 8; 9; 13; 15; 28; 32; 33(2); 13:3; 4; 5; 11; 12(2); 21; 22; 26(2); 32(2); 14:15; 18; 21; 22; 24; 26; 15:3; 15(2); 22; 23; 26; 27; 29; 30(3); 34; 16:12; 13(2); 15; 19(2); 24; 26; 27; 32; 34; 17:3; 5; 9; 16; 18:26(2); 19:3; 20:19; 34; 21:1; 4; 11; 15; 22; 22:24; 38; 39; **2 Ki** 1:4; 6; 16; 17; 18; 2:22; 3:8; 4:17; 5:6; 6:10; 11; 7:13; 15; 8:29; 9:5; 15; 27; 36; 10:10; 17; 33; 11:10; 12:2; 11; 20; 13:12; 14; 25; 14:6; 11; 15; 25; 15:12; 15; 16:14; 18; 19; 17:8; 12; 13(2); 15; 19; 22; 25; 29; 34; 37; 18:6; 9; 16; 17; 19; 21; 19:4; 6(2); 16; 21; 28; 20:9; 11; 19; 21:3; 4; 7(2); 8; 16; 25; 22:4(2); 16; 18; 20; 23:2; 8(2); 10; 12(2); 13(2); 15; 16; 17; 19; 24; 26(2); 27(2); 24:2; 4; 13; 25:4; 8; 14; 16; **1 Chr** 6:65; 10:13; 11:4; 17; 13:6; 15:3; 16:12; 15; 16; 40; 17:23; 18:8; 20:4; 21:19; 24; 29; 22:13; 23:5; 26:26; 29:19; **2 Chr** 1:3; 6; 15; 2:5; 9; 11; 14; 15; 17; 3:3; 5; 4:12; 19; 5:1; 2; 3; 10; 6:5; 10; 11(2); 17; 18; 19; 20; 25; 27(2); 31; 33(2); 34(2); 38(3); 7:6; 7; 19; 20(2); 21; 8:1; 2; 4; 11; 12; 9:4; 5; 6; 18; 23; 27; 10:4; 8; 9; 15; 11:10; 15; 12:9; 13; 13:4; 8(2); 15:8; 16:6; 14(2); 17:2; 18:23; 20:2; 11; 25; 34; 22:6; 23:9; 24:22; 25:9; 13; 15; 21; 26:23; 28:23; 29:19; 32; 30:8; 31:6; 32:3; 33:3; 4; 7(3); 8; 22; 34:4; 9(2); 11; 24; 26; 28; 30; 35:3; 21; 36:8; 14; 23; **Ezra** 1:2; 3(2); 4; 5; 7; 2:68; 3:7; 4:15; 18; 24; 5:2; 7; 8; 11; 14; 16; 17; 6:5(3); 12; 15; 7:6; 8; 14; 15; 20; 27; 8:25; 9:11(3); **Neh** 1:6(2); 7; 9; 2:8; 12; 13(2); 18; 3:25; 5:18; 7:72; 8:1; 4; 14; 9:5; 12; 15; 23; 29; 34; 35; 10:29; 13:5; 15(2); 17; **Esth** 1:2; 9; 20; 2:16; 3:7(2); 13; 4:8; 16; 5:8; 11; 6:8(3); 14; 7:9; 8:2; 3; 5; 9; 12; 9:22(2); 23; 25; 10:2; **Job** 2:8; 3:3(2); 4:14; 5:1; 6:16(2); 26; 10:21; 15:3; 28(2); 20:18; 19; 21:27; 22:15; 23:5; 24:16; 27:18; 33:21; 36:24; 27; 28; 37:5; 38:23; 26; 40:15; 41:1; 33; 42:3; **Ps** 1:4; 7:15; 8:3; 9:15(2); 10:2; 12:5; 17:1; 19:5; 21:11; 31:4; 18; 19(2); 32:9(2); 35:7; 40:5; 45:8; 50:8; 58:5; 7; 8; 59:12; 61:7; 66:14; 68:16; 33; 69:31; 71:3; 23; 74:2(2); 78:3; 5; 45(2); 54; 68; 69; 79:10; 12; 80:15; 89:49; 51(2); 90:5; 15(2); 94:20; 104:8; 15; 16; 20; 25; 26; 105:5; 8; 9; 106:36; 107:25; 109:19(2); 118:20; 22; 119:39; 47; 48; 49; 85; 138; 125:1; 129:6; 7; 132:12; 138:8; 142:3; 143:8; 148:6; **Prov** 6:7; 22:27; 28; 23:5; 24:13; 25:1; 28:3; 30:18(2); 24; 29(2); 30; 31:1; 3; **Eccl** 1:3; 7; 9(2); 10; 13; 2:6; 11; 18; 19(2); 20; 22; 3:9; 10; 15; 21(2); 5:13; 15; 18(2); 6:1; 12; 7:24; 28; 8:9; 13; 14; 15; 9:9(2); 11:6; **Song** 1:1; 3:11; 4:2(2); 4; 5; 6:6; 7:4; 13; **Isa** 1:1; 29(2); 2:8; 20; 6:6; 7:25; 10:1; 3; 13:1; 14:3; 28; 16:8; 13; 17:2; 9; 18:1; 2; 19:15; 16; 17; 21:4; 10; 23:13; 26:2; 28:1; 4(2); 12; 29:11; 30:6; 14; 23; 24; 28; 32; 31:7; 33:21; 36:4; 6; 37:4; 6(2); 17; 22; 29; 38:7; 8(2); 39:8; 42:5; 47:11; 12; 50:1; 51:1(2); 54:17; 55:11; 56:11; 57:16; 59:5; 21; 60:12; 62:2; 8; 63:7; 64:3; 65:12; 66:4; 22; **Jer** 2:11; 3:8; 5:17(2); 7:10; 11; 12; 14(3); 30; 31(2); 8:2(5); 17; 9:13; 14; 10:1; 11:4; 5; 8(2); 10; 11; 17; 12:5; 14; 13:4; 6; 10; 15:14(2); 18; 16:15; 20; 17:4(3); 6; 8; 19(2); 18:1; 10; 14; 23; 19:2; 5; 9; 11; 20:2; 14(2); 16; 21:1; 4; 22:6; 27; 28(2); 23:6; 27; 40; 24:2; 3; 8; 25:1; 2; 3; 13(2); 22; 26; 27; 29; 26:2; 3; 4; 19; 27:8(2); 18; 20; 28:6; 29:8; 14; 19; 23; 31:9; 21; 32; 32:1; 2; 7; 8; 11(2); 14(2); 22; 32; 34; 35(2); 36; 43; 33:3; 4; 8(3); 10; 12; 14; 16; 24; 34:1; 15; 18; 21; 35:1; 4; 14; 15; 16; 36:3; 4; 6; 14; 27; 28; 32; 37:2; 7; 38:3; 6; 20; 41:9; 17; 42:3; 5; 8; 16(2); 21; 43:1; 9; 44:3; 9; 14; 22; 46:1; 2(2); 28; 48:28; 38; 49:28; 31; 50:3; 51:43; 59; 52:7; 12; 18; 20(2); **Lam** 1:12(2); 2:17; 4:6; 5:18; **Ezek** 1:2; 23(2); 3:20; 23; 4:10; 5:9; 16(2); 6:9(3); 8:3; 9; 17; 9:2; 10:22; 11:1; 12; 23; 12:2; 22; 25; 28; 13:12; 20; 14:3; 15:2; 6; 16:14; 17; 19(2); 36; 51; 52; 17:19(2); 20; 18:14; 21; 22(2); 24(3); 25(2); 26; 27; 28; 29(2); 31; 20:7; 8; 11; 13; 15; 21; 25; 28; 29; 42; 43; 22:4(2); 13(2); 23:41; 24:6; 25; 26:6; 27:24; 27; 28:25; 29:18; 31:14; 18; 32:9; 16; 30; 33:16; 17; 29; 35:11; 12; 36:4; 18; 21; 22; 23(2); 36; 37:19; 20; 23; 38:8; 39:8; 17; 19; 21(2); 26; 40:6(2); 39; 41; 42; 45; 46; 49; 41:6; 42:1(2); 7; 11; 13; 14(2); 43:3(3); 4; 8; 44:1; 13; 19; 45:13; 46:9; 17; 19(2); 47:5; 13; 16(2); 48:8; 22; 29; **Dan** 1:2; 5; 8; 20; 2:26; 27; 34; 39; 44; 3:2; 7; 12; 14; 15; 18; 29; 4:5; 20(2); 21(2); 24; 5:2(2); 3; 23; 6:8; 12; 15; 26; 7:6; 11; 14(2); 17(2); 19(2); 20(4); 23; 8:2; 3; 6; 9; 20; 26; 9:7(2); 10; 12; 14; 17; 18; 27; 10:10; 11:4; 38; 39; **Hos** 1:10; 2:8; 12; 13; 8:8; **Joel** 2:25; 3:7; **Am** 1:1; 4; 7; 10; 12; 2:4; 7; 3:1; 5:1; 3; 26; 9:11; **Jon** 4:10(2); 11; **Mic** 1:1; 2:3; 7:1; 20; **Nah** 3:17; **Hab** 1:1; 5; 6; 2:17; **Zeph** 1:1; 2:8; 3:7; 11; **Zech** 1:6; 7; 12; 2:8; 4:10; 12; 7:12; 12; 14; 9:2; 11:10; 13:6; 14:4; 7; 12; 16; 18; **Mal** 2:11; 4:1; 4; **Mt** 1:20; 22; 23; 2:9; 15; 16; 23; 3:10; 4:13; 14; 6:27; 30; 7:14; 8:17; 9:5; 11:4; 20; 21; 23; 12:4; 17; 44; 13:14; 31; 32; 33; 35; 44; 48; 15:13; 18; 20; 27; 18:11; 19:18; 21:4; 24; 31; 42; 22:36; 23:17; 19; 27; 25:13; 26:28; 27:21; 35; 60; 62; 28:16; **Mk** 1:44; 2:4; 9; 26; 4:22; 31; 5:41; 6:2; 7:4; 13; 15(2); 11:2; 21; 12:10; 28; 42; 13:19; 14:14; 24; 32; 15:22; 28; 34; 46; **Lk** 1:1; 4; 20; 45; 73; 78; 2:4; 10; 15; 17; 18; 31; 33; 34; 50; 3:9; 19; 22; 4:22; 29; 5:3; 9; 23; 6:4; 46; 49; 7:42(2); 47; 8:26; 9:31; 43; 46; 10:11; 13; 23; 36; 42; 11:5; 22; 24; 27; 35; 44; 50; 12:1; 20; 24; 25; 28; 33; 13:14; 19; 21; 14:5; 28; 15:4; 6; 9; 16:21; 17:7; 10; 18:27; 34; 19:10; 20; 30; 20:17; 21:6(2); 15; 22; 26; 22:1; 10; 19; 20; 23; 24; 37; 23:14; 29(2); 24:1; 13; 14; 18; 44(2); **Jn** 1:9; 38; 41; 42; 2:22; 23; 3:6(2); 4:5; 32; 38; 53; 5:2; 28; 32; 36; 39; 6:1; 2; 13; 22; 27(3); 41; 50; 51(2); 58; 7:31; 8:6; 26; 40; 46; 9:7; 10:6; 16; 32; 12:38; 48; 13:5; 14:24; 15:3; 24; 25; 17:4; 5; 7; 8; 22; 24; 26; 18:1; 9; 11; 32; 19:17; 24; 41; 20:16; 30; 21:10; 25; **Acts** 1:2; 4; 7; 12; 16; 24; 25; 2:8; 22; 32; 33; 3:2; 11; 15; 16; 18; 21; 25; 4:11(2); 12; 20; 36; 5:17; 6:10; 14; 7:4; 17; 43; 45; 52; 8:1; 6; 13; 24; 26; 32; 9:36(2); 39; 10:17; 36; 37(2); 39; 11:14; 28; 12:10; 13:2; 27; 32; 39; 41; 14:26; 15:10; 16; 16:4; 12; 21; 17:19; 31; 19:26; 35; 40; 20:19; 24; 28(2); 32; 38; 21:19; 24; 26; 22:10; 24:8; 13; 14(2); 15; 18; 21; 25:7; 11; 26:2; 3; 4; 16(2); 22; 27:5; 39; 28:11; 19; 24; 31; **Rom** 1:2; 27; 28; 2:28; 4:11; 12; 17; 5:2; 16(3); 6:17; 21; 7:5; 10; 23; 8:18; 26; 39; 9:23; 10:5; 8; 11:24; 12:1; 14:19(2); 21; 15:17; 18; 16:17; **1 Cor** 1:2; 4; 27; 28(2); 2:7; 8; 9; 11; 13(2); 3:10; 11(2); 14; 17; 6:20; 7:1; 20; 24; 10:16(2); 20; 30; 11:23(2); 24; 12:22; 23; 24; 13:10(2); 14:37; 15:1(3); 2(2); 3; 10; 31; **2 Cor** 1:1; 4; 6(2); 8; 2:4; 6; 3:7; 4:17; 18(4); 5:2; 7:7; 8:19; 20; 22; 9:2; 5; 11; 10:2; 8; 13(2); 11:4(2); 12; 30; 12:4; 13; 21; 13:10; **Gal** 1:7; 11; 20; 22; 23; 2:2; 4; 10; 18; 20; 3:10; 17; 21; 23; 4:8; 9; 14; 24(3); 25; 26; 5:1; 19; 21; **Eph** 1:6; 8; 9; 10(2); 20; 21; 23; 2:2; 4; 10; 3:2; 4; 5; 7; 9; 11; 13; 19; 4:1; 16; 22; 24; 5:4; 12; 18; 6:2; 16; 17; 20; **Phil** 1:11; 12; 23; 28; 30; 2:5; 9; 21; 3:6; 9(3); 12; 13(2); 20; 21; 4:7; 9; **Col** 1:5(2); 6; 23(3); 24; 25(2); 26; 27; 29; 2:12; 14; 17; 18; 22(2); 3:1; 5(2); 7; 14; 15; 4:3; 9; 17; **1 Th** 2:13(2); 14; 3:9; **2 Th** 1:5(2); 2:14; 15; 3:6; 17; **1 Tim** 1:4(2); 6; 7; 11; 14; 19; 2:7; 10; 3:13; 15; 4:3; 6; 8; 14; 5:13; 6:3; 4; 9; 10; 12; 15; **2 Tim** 1:1; 5; 6; 9; 11; 13(2); 14; 2:9; 10; 3:11; 14; 15(2); 4:8; **Titus** 1:1; 2; 3; 11; 2:1; 3:5; **Phm** 1:5; 6; **Heb** 1:5; 13; 2:3; 5; 11; 3:5; 4:2; 5:8; 6:7; 10; 18; 19; 7:13; 14; 19; 28; 8:2; 6; 9:2(2); 3; 4(2); 7; 9(2); 20; 24; 10:1; 8; 11; 20; 27; 29; 32; 35; 11:3(2); 4; 7(2); 8; 10; 12; 15; 19; 12:1; 5; 8; 12; 14; 27; 28(2); 13:9; 10; **Jas** 1:1; 12; 21; 2:5; 7; 16; 23; 5:4; **1 Pe** 1:12(2); 23; 25; 2:7; 8; 11; 12; 3:4; 20; 21; 4:11; 12; 5:2; 12; **2 Pe** 1:4; 18; 19; 3:1; 2; 6; 7; 10; 12; 13; 16(2); **1 Jn** 1:1(4); 2; 3; 5; 2:7(2); 8; 18; 24; 27; 4:3; 5:9; 16; **2 Jn** 2; 5; **3 Jn** 10; **Jude** 3; 15(2); 17; **Rev** 1:1(2); 3; 4; 11; 19(3); 20(2); 2:6; 7; 10; 13; 15; 17; 3:2; 10; 12; 4:1(2); 5; 5:6; 8; 13; 6:9; 7:9; 8:3; 9:13; 18; 20; 10:4; 8(2); 11:2; 8; 12:16; 13:2; 14; 14:10; 17; 16:14; 17:3; 7; 9(2); 12; 15; 16; 18; 18:6; 14; 19; 19:20; 21; 20:8; 12(2); 21:8(2); 12; 22:2; 6; 19

WHO (6045/4885)

Gen 3:11; 4:14; 20; 21; 6:4; 7:23; 9:18; 12:3(2); 7; 13:5; 14:7; 12; 13; 14; 17; 20; 24; 15:4; 7; 16:13(2); 17:12(3); 13(2); 14; 17(2); 23(2); 18:27; 19:5; 8; 11; 14; 15; 20:7; 16; 21:3; 6; 7; 26; 23:10; 18; 24:2; 7(2); 15; 27; 32; 48; 54; 60; 65; 26:11; 27:18; 29(2); 32; 33(2); 46; 30:2; 32:9; 19; 33:5; 15; 34:14; 24(2); 35:1; 2; 3; 6; 26; 36:1; 5; 18; 19; 20; 24; 31; 35; 38:21; 30; 39:1; 22; 40:5; 7; 41:8; 15; 24; 42:5; 6; 30; 43:22; 32; 44:20; 45:1; 8; 46:8; 22; 26(2); 27(2); 31; 48:5; 8; 14; 15; 16; 49:9; 25(2); 26; 50:3; 14; **Ex** 1:1; 5; 8; 22; 2:13; 14; 3:7; 11; 14; 22; 4:11(2); 18; 19; 28; 5:2; 20; 6:7; 27; 9:20; 21; 10:8; 11; 11:5(2); 8; 12:27; 29(2); 40; 44; 49; 14:19; 15:7; 11(2); 26; 16:16; 18(2); 18:10(2); 18; 19:16; 22; 20:2; 5; 6; 7; 10; 21:8; 12; 15; 16; 17; 19; 22:6; 16; 20; 25; 23:5; 24:5; 25:2; 28:3; 29:30; 46; 30:13; 14; 31:6; 13; 14; 32:1; 23; 33:7; 16; 35:10; 22; 24; 25; 35(2); 36:4; 8; 38:8; 25; **Lev** 5:8; 11; 6:18; 22; 26; 27; 7:7; 8; 9; 14; 18(2); 19; 20; 21(2); 25; 29; 33; 10:3; 12; 16; 11:26; 39; 40(2); 45; 12:7; 13:4; 12; 13; 17; 31; 33; 14:4; 7; 8; 11(2); 14; 17; 18; 19; 25; 28; 29; 31; 32(2); 35; 46; 47(2); 15:4; 6(2); 7(2); 8(2); 9; 10; 11; 12; 13; 32(2); 33(4); 16:26; 28; 29; 32; 17:3(2); 8(2); 10(3); 12; 13(2); 15; 18:6; 26; 27; 29; 19:8; 13; 20(2); 34; 36; 20:2(2); 5; 6; 8; 9; 10(2); 11; 24; 27(2); 21:2; 3(2); 7; 8; 10(2); 17; 18(2); 19; 20; 21; 22:3; 4(2); 6; 10; 11; 18; 32; 33; 23:29; 30; 42; 24:14(2); 16; 23; 25:6; 28; 30; 38; 39; 45(2); 47; 49; 50; 26:13; 17; 32; 36; 39; 27:8; 15; 19; 24; 29; **Num** 1:3; 5; 17; 20; 21; 22(2); 23; 24; 25; 26; 27; 28; 29; 30; 31; 32; 33; 34; 35; 36; 37; 38; 39; 40; 41; 42; 43; 44; 45(2); 46; 51; 2:5; 9; 12; 16; 24; 27; 31; 32(2); 3:10; 12; 22(2); 32; 34; 38(2); 39; 43; 46; 49(2); 4:3; 23; 30; 35; 36; 37(2); 38; 39; 40; 41(2); 42; 43; 44; 45; 46; 47; 48; 5:2; 14; 6:21; 7:2(2); 12; 8:16; 9:6; 13; 10:9; 35; 11:4(2); 18; 20; 26; 32; 34; 12:3; 13:3; 18; 28; 31; 14:6(2); 22; 23; 27; 29(2); 35; 36; 37; 38; 45; 15:4; 13; 15; 16; 26; 28; 29(3); 30; 33; 41; 16:5(2); 34; 35; 38; 39; 40; 49(2); 18:7; 11; 13; 19:8; 9; 10(2); 11; 13; 14(2); 16(2); 18(2); 20; 21(2); 22; 21:1; 8; 26; 27; 32; 34; 22:9; 40; 23:10; 24:4(3); 9(3); 16(3); 23; 25:5; 6; 9; 14(2); 15; 18; 26:2; 4; 7; 9; 18; 22; 25; 27; 34; 37; 41; 43; 47; 50; 51; 54; 57; 59; 62; 63(2); 64; 27:3; 17(2); 21; 31:8; 14; 17; 18; 21; 27(2); 28; 30; 35; 36; 42; 47; 48; 49; 32:11; 39; 33:1; 40; 34:17; 35:11; 15; 21; 25; 31; 32; 33; 36:8; **Deut** 1:4(2); 16; 30; 33; 38; 39(2); 44; 2:4; 8; 22; 23(2); 25; 29(2); 3:2; 8; 24; 4:3; 4; 6; 42; 46; 47; 5:3(2); 6; 9; 10; 11; 14; 26(2); 6:12; 14; 7:9(2); 10(2); 15; 20(2); 8:14; 15(2); 16; 18; 9:2; 3; 10:17; 21; 11:2(2); 30; 12:12; 18; 13:5; 6; 10; 14:2; 21; 27; 29; 15:2; 16:11(2); 14; 17:2; 3; 5; 12(2); 15; 18:3; 7; 10(3); 11(2); 12; 20(2); 19:4; 17; 18; 20; 20:1; 4; 5; 6; 7; 8; 11; 21:1; 15; 18(2); 23; 22:5; 23; 25; 28(2); 29; 23:1; 10; 15; 24:3; 4; 14(2); 25:9; 10; 16(2); 26:3; 11; 27:15; 16; 17; 18; 19; 20; 21; 22; 23; 24; 25; 26; 28:7; 43; 56; 29:11(3); 15(2); 22(2); 30:7(2); 12; 13; 31:6; 8; 9; 12; 13; 25; 32:6; 15; 18(2); 21; 27; 38; 39; 41; 33:9; 11(2); 12; 16(2); 20; 26; 29; **Josh** 2:3(2); 7; 10; 3:8; 13; 15(2); 17; 4:9; 10; 16; 18; 5:1(2); 4(2); 5; 6(2); 6:7; 9; 17(2); 22; 23; 26; 7:15; 8:5; 11; 16; 17; 20; 25; 33(2); 35; 9:1; 8; 10(2); 16; 10:6; 11; 20; 24; 28; 30; 32(2); 35; 37(2); 39; 11:2; 8; 11; 12:2; 4(2); 13:10; 12(2); 21(2); 22; 14:8; 15:16; 16:10; 17:16(3); 18:8; 20:3; 6; 9; 21:4; 10; 22:30; 23:3; 7; 10; 24:8; 17(2); 18; 31(2); **Judg** 1:1; 9; 10; 17; 21; 29; 2:7(2); 10; 12(2); 14; 16(2); 18; 3:1; 2; 3; 9; 18; 19; 31; 4:2(2); 13; 5:9; 10(3); 14; 18; 31; 6:8; 9; 17; 29; 31(2); 35; 7:1; 2; 5(2); 6; 7; 11; 18; 19; 8:4; 5; 10; 11; 30; 31; 34; 9:24(2); 25; 28(2); 32; 33; 34; 35; 38; 44; 45; 48(2); 10:4; 8; 18(2); 11:21; 35; 12:5; 14; 13:8; 10; 11; 14:19; 20; 15:6; 16:24; 26; 30; 17:5; 18:3; 7(2); 14; 16; 17(2); 22; 27; 29; 19:12; 16; 18; 19; 22; 30; 20:2; 4; 13; 15(2); 16; 17; 46(2); 48; 21:5(3); 7; 8; 11; 12; 13; 16; 18; 23; **Ruth** 1:22; 2:3; 5; 6(2); 19; 20; 3:9; 4:3; 11(3); 14; 15(2); **1 Sam** 1:26; 2:4; 5(2); 14; 15; 22; 25; 30(2); 35; 36; 3:11; 4:2; 4; 8(2); 16; 20; 5:5; 12; 6:20; 8:9; 10; 11; 9:5; 9; 13; 22; 10:11; 12; 18; 19; 11:9; 11; 12(2); 12:6(2); 8; 14; 13:22; 14:1; 2; 6; 17(2); 20; 21(3); 22; 24; 28; 39; 45; 48; 15:28; 16:16(2); 17; 18; 19; 17:12; 13; 25(2); 26(3); 27; 37; 41; 18:18; 20:10; 21:7; 22:2(3); 6; 7; 8(2); 9; 11; 14(3); 17; 18; 23; 23:22; 24:9; 25:6; 10(3); 22; 26; 27; 32; 34; 39; 44; 26:6; 9; 14; 15; 27:2; 28:7(2); 29:3; 10; 30:2; 4; 9(2); 10; 17; 21(2); 22; 23; 24(3); 27(3); 28(3); 29(3); 30(3); 31; 31:7(2); **2 Sam** 1:5; 6; 8; 11; 13; 24(2); 2:3; 4; 31; 3:20; 26; 29(3); 31; 4:2; 4; 5; 8; 9; 10; 5:2; 6; 8; 14; 6:2(2); 21; 7:9; 12; 18; 23; 9:1; 3; 12; 10:13; 16; 18; 19; 11:21(2); 12:4(3); 5; 14; 22; 31; 13:17; 34; 14:2; 7; 13; 16; 25; 15:2; 4; 6; 14; 18; 22; 30; 16:1; 2; 10; 11; 14; 21; 17:2; 9; 10(2); 12; 16; 18; 22(2); 25; 29; 18:1; 11; 15; 28(2); 31; 32; 19:3; 5; 16; 28; 20:12; 15; 21:5; 12; 13; 16(2); 18; 20; 22:4; 18; 31; 32(2); 40; 41; 48; 49; 23:3; 7; 9; 17; 20; 24:2; 9; 13; 16; 17; **1 Ki** 1:8; 20; 27; 29; 41; 48; 49; 2:7; 8; 24(2); 3:9; 16; 23; 4:7; 19; 27; 34; 5:6; 15(2); 16(2); 8:5; 15; 19; 23(2); 41; 46; 47; 48; 50(2); 56; 9:8; 9; 16; 20(2); 21; 23(3); 27; 10:8; 9; 11:8; 9; 18; 23; 12:6; 8(2); 9; 10(2); 17; 18; 20; 21; 31; 13:2; 4; 12; 14; 20; 21; 26(2); 14:2; 8(2); 9; 13; 14;

16(2); 27; 15:18; 16:16; 22(2); 25; 30; 33; 17:17; 18:3; 19; 24; 19:19; 20:10; 11(2); 14; 30; 21:8; 11; 18; 25; 22:13; 20; 46; 52; **2 Ki** 1:6; 7; 2:3; 5; 15; 3:3; 11; 21; 26; 27; 4:5; 9; 5:3; 4; 6:12; 16(2); 7:13; 17; 8:14; 21; 9:19; 32(2); 10:1; 5(3); 6; 9; 11; 13; 17; 21; 29; 31; 11:2; 5; 7; 9(2); 12:9; 11(3); 13:2; 6; 11; 14:5; 21; 24; 25; 15:9; 16(2); 18; 24; 28; 16:7; 17:2; 7; 14; 15; 32; 36; 18:5; 18; 21; 26; 27(2); 35; 37; 19:2; 12; 15; 30; 31; 20:18; 21:11; 24; 22:5(2); 9(2); 15; 18; 23:5; 11; 15; 16; 17; 18; 20; 22; 24; 25; 24:16; 25:10; 11(2); 19(4); 22; 25; 28; **1 Chr** 1:27; 43; 46; 2:7; 9; 19; 22; 42; 55(2); 3:1; 4:11; 14; 22; 23; 41; 43; 5:8; 10; 18; 20; 6:10; 33; 39; 7:21; 24; 31; 8:6(2); 7; 12; 13(2); 32; 9:2; 16; 33; 10:7; 11:2; 10; 12; 19; 22; 12:1; 8; 15; 20(2); 31; 32; 33(2); 35; 36; 38; 40; 13:2(2); 6; 15:26; 27; 16:10; 41(2); 17:8; 11; 13; 16; 21; 19:7; 9; 14; 16; 20:3; 4; 21:5(2); 12; 15; 17(2); 20; 22:2; 9; 23:24; 24:28; 25:1; 2; 3; 7(2); 26:6; 27:5; 6; 26; 28:1; 6; 29:5; 14(2); 17; **2 Chr** 1:10; 12; 2:6(2); 7(2); 10; 12(2); 17; 5:6; 11; 12; 6:4; 9; 14(2); 32(2); 36; 39; 7:14; 21; 22; 8:7(2); 8; 10; 18; 9:7; 8; 10; 10:6; 8(2); 9; 10(2); 17; 18; 11:1; 13; 12:3; 5; 10; 13:10; 14:8(2); 11; 13; 15:5(2); 9; 16:2; 17:16; 18:2; 12; 19; 30; 19:2; 6; 10; 20:7; 17; 21(2); 22; 35; 21:9; 13; 16; 22:1; 8; 9; 11; 23:6; 8(2); 13; 14; 19; 24:12(2); 20; 26; 25:3; 5; 15; 26:1; 5; 7; 11; 18; 28:5; 7; 12; 15(2); 29:29; 30:6; 7; 9; 17(2); 19; 21; 22; 25(2); 31:1; 4; 6; 16(2); 17; 18; 19(3); 32:4; 9; 14; 18; 21; 33:11; 18; 25; 34:4; 9; 10(2); 13; 21; 23; 26; 32; 33; 35:3(2); 7; 17; 18; 21; 36:12; 13; 17; 20; 23; **Ezra** 1:3; 6; 11; 2:1(3); 2; 59; 61; 62; 3:5; 8; 12; 4:2; 12; 17; 20; 5:1(2); 3; 4; 6; 9; 10; 12; 6:6; 9; 12(2); 21(2); 7:13; 21; 25(3); 27; 8:1; 22(2); 25; 35(2); 9:4(2); 10:3(2); 13; 14; 17; 18; **Neh** 1:2(2); 3; 5(2); 11; 2:16; 3:26; 4:12; 17(2); 18; 23; 5:2; 3; 4; 8; 13; 15; 17; 6:10; 11(2); 14; 7:5; 6(3); 7; 61; 63; 64; 8:2; 3; 9(2); 17; 9:7; 26; 27(2); 32; 10:1; 28(2); 36; 39; 11:2; 3; 6; 12; 17; 19; 12:1; 8; 22; 44; 13:10; 16; 23; 26; **Esth** 1:1; 5; 10; 13(2); 14(2); 16; 19; 2:2; 4; 6; 14; 15(2); 22; 3:1; 2; 3; 6; 9; 12; 4:11(2); 14; 16; 6:2; 3; 4; 10; 7:5(2); 9; 8:5; 11; 14; 9:1; 2; 5; 11; 13; 15; 18; 19; 20; 27; **Job** 1:1; 8; 2:3; 3:8(2); 14; 15(2); 16; 20; 21; 22; 4:2; 4; 7; 8; 19(2); 5:1; 9; 11(2); 6:14; 7:2(2); 8; 9; 8:13; 22; 9:4; 12(2); 19; 24; 33; 10:7; 11:10; 12:3; 4(2); 5; 6; 9; 13:19(2); 14:1; 4; 15:7; 14; 16(2); 17:3(2); 5; 9; 15; 18:4; 15; 21; 19:15; 20:7; 26; 21:15; 29; 31(2); 22:2; 16; 30; 23:13; 24:1; 13; 19; 21; 25; 25:4; 6(2); 26:2; 3; 14; 27:2(2); 7; 15; 29:12(2); 25; 30:4; 25; 31; 31:15; 28; 29; 31; 34:2; 7; 8; 13(2); 17(2); 29(2); 34; 35:10; 11; 36:4; 22; 23(2); 37:16; 24; 38:2(2); 5(2); 6; 8; 25; 28; 29; 36(2); 37(2); 41; 39:5(2); 40:2(2); 11; 12; 19; 41:10; 11; 13(2); 14; 42:3(2); 11; **Ps** 1:1; 2:4; 12; 3:1(2); 2; 3; 6; 4:3; 6(2); 5:4; 6; 11(2); 6:5; 7:1; 4; 10; 8:1; 9:10(2); 11; 13(2); 11:5; 12:4(2); 13:4; 14:1; 2(2); 3; 4; 15:1(2); 2; 3; 4(2); 5(2); 16:3; 4; 7; 17:7(3); 9(2); 14; 18:3; 17; 30; 31(2); 32; 39; 40; 47; 48; 19:12; 21:8; 22:7; 9; 23; 25; 26; 29(2); 31; 24:1; 3(2); 4(2); 6(2); 8; 10; 25:3(2); 12; 14; 28:1; 3; 31:6; 11; 15; 19(2); 24; 32:6; 10; 33:18(2); 34:7; 8; 9; 10; 12(2); 16; 18; 21; 22; 35:1(2); 3; 4(2); 10(3); 14; 19(2); 26(2); 27(2); 36:10; 37:7(2); 9; 14; 38:12(2); 13; 14; 19; 20; 39:6; 9; 40:4; 14(2); 15; 16; 41:1; 7; 9; 44:5; 7; 10; 16; 45:14; 46:8; 49:6; 13(2); 20; 50:5; 22; 23; 52:7; 53:1; 2(2); 3; 4; 5; 54:4; 55:12(3); 19; 20; 56:2; 57:2; 3; 4; 58:11; 59:1; 7; 60:4; 9(2); 10(2); 12; 61:5; 63:9; 11(2); 64:3; 5; 8; 65:2; 5; 6; 7; 8; 66:9; 16; 20; 68:1; 4; 6; 11; 12; 19; 21; 30; 33; 35; 69:4(2); 6(2); 9; 12; 14; 32; 36; 70:2(2); 3; 4(2); 71:6; 10; 13(2); 18; 19(2); 20; 24; 72:9; 12; 18; 73:12; 27(2); 74:5; 9; 23; 76:7; 11(2); 77:13; 14; 78:6; 65; 79:4; 11; 80:1(2); 12; 81:10; 83:2; 10(2); 12; 84:4; 11; 12; 85:9; 86:2; 5; 17; 87:4; 88:4(2); 5(2); 89:6(2); 8; 10; 15; 19; 23; 41; 90:11; 91:1; 9; 92:11; 13; 94:9(2); 10(2); 16(2); 95:10; 97:7(2); 10; 98:7; 99:6; 100:3; 101:3; 5; 6; 7(2); 102:8; 103:3(2); 4(2); 5; 6; 11; 13; 17; 18; 20(2); 21; 104:2(2); 3(2); 4; 5; 105:3; 17; 106:2(2); 3(2); 10; 21; 41; 46; 107:10; 23(2); 34; 108:10(2); 11(2); 13; 109:20; 31; 111:2; 5; 10; 112:1(2); 113:5(2); 6; 114:8; 115:8(2); 11; 13; 15; 17; 118:4; 7(2); 26; 119:1; 2(2); 21; 38; 42; 53; 63(2); 74; 79(2); 84; 118; 132; 150; 162; 165; 120:6; 121:2; 3; 4; 122:6; 123:1; 4; 124:1; 2; 6; 8; 125:1; 4(2); 126:1; 5; 6; 127:1; 5; 128:1(2); 4; 129:5; 7; 8; 130:3; 6(2); 134:1; 3; 135:2; 18(2); 20; 21; 136:4; 5; 6; 7; 10; 13; 16; 17; 23; 25; 137:3(2); 7; 8(2); 9; 139:21(2); 140:2; 4; 9; 141:4; 142:4; 143:3; 7; 12; 144:1; 2; 10(2); 15; 145:14(2); 18(2); 19; 20; 146:5; 6(2); 7(2); 8; 147:8(3); 11(2); 17; **Prov** 1:12; 19; 2:7; 12; 13; 14; 15; 16; 17; 19; 3:13(2); 18(2); 4:22; 5:13; 6:19(2); 29; 32; 7:5; 26; 8:9(2); 17(2); 21; 32; 34; 36(2); 9:4; 7(2); 15(2); 16; 10:4; 5(3); 9(2); 10; 13(2); 17(2); 19; 26; 11:12; 13; 15(2); 17; 18; 19; 20; 22; 24(2); 25; 26(2); 27(2); 28; 29; 30; 12:1; 4; 8; 9(2); 11(2); 15; 17; 18; 20; 22; 13:3(2); 7(2); 11; 13(2); 18(2); 20; 24(2); 14:2(2); 6; 21(2); 22(2); 29(2); 31(2); 33; 35; 15:5; 9; 10(2); 12; 14; 15; 18; 21; 27(2); 32(2); 16:13; 17; 20; 22; 26; 32(3); 17:2; 5(2); 9(2); 15(2); 19(2); 20(2); 21; 24; 25; 27; 18:1; 9(2); 13; 14; 21; 22; 24(2); 19:1(2); 2; 5; 6; 8(2); 9; 16(2); 17; 23; 25; 26(2); 20:6; 8; 9; 16; 19(2); 21:5; 6; 16; 17(2); 21; 28; 22:5; 8; 9; 11; 14; 16(2); 21; 23; 26(2); 29; 23:22; 24; 25; 29(6); 30(2); 34(2); 24:8; 11; 12(2); 22; 24; 25; 26; 25:10; 13; 18; 20(2); 26; 26:6; 8(2); 10; 16; 17(2); 18; 19; 24; 27; 28; 27:4; 8; 11; 13; 14; 18; 28:3; 4; 5; 6; 8(2); 9; 11; 13; 14(2); 16(2); 18; 19(2); 20; 23(2); 25(2); 26; 27(2); 29:1; 4; 5; 14; 18; 21; 27; 30:4(4); 5; 9; 23; 31:6(2); 8; 10; 30; **Eccl** 1:11; 16; 18; 2:7; 9; 12; 18; 19; 21; 25(2); 26(2); 3:21; 22; 4:2(2); 3(2); 10; 13; 15(2); 16; 5:10(2); 11; 16; 6:8; 10; 12(2); 7:11; 12; 13; 15(2); 18; 20; 24; 26; 8:1(2); 4; 5; 7; 8; 10; 12(2); 9:2(4); 4; 10:8; 9(2); 14; 11:4(2); 5(2); 12:7; **Song** 1:7; 3:3; 4; 6; 5:7; 6:9; 10(2); 8:1; 2; 5(2); 10; 12; 13; **Isa** 1:4; 12; 28; 3:12; 4:2; 3(2); 5:8; 11(2); 14; 16; 18; 20(3); 21; 23; 6:4; 8; 7:22; 8:17; 18; 19(2); 9:1; 2(2); 9; 13; 15; 16; 10:1(2); 14; 15(3); 20; 24; 11:10; 11; 16; 13:3; 15(2); 17; 14:6(2); 12; 16(3); 17(2); 19(2); 27(2); 15:9; 16:3; 17:5; 12; 14(2); 19:8(2); 9(2); 10; 13; 17; 21:14(2); 22:2; 3; 11; 15; 16(2); 23:2; 8; 18; 24:6; 9; 18(2); 26:5; 19; 27:4; 6; 7(2); 11(2); 13(2); 28:1; 2; 6(2); 14(2); 29; 29:7(2); 8; 11; 12; 15(3); 16(2); 20; 21(2); 22; 24(2); 30:1(2); 2; 5; 6; 9; 10; 16; 18; 31:1(3); 2; 3(2); 32:3(2); 9; 11; 20(2); 33:1(2); 13(2); 14(2); 15(4); 18(2); 24; 35:4; 36:3; 6; 11; 12(2); 20; 22; 37:2; 12; 16; 31; 32; 38:18; 39:7; 40:9(2); 11; 12; 13; 14(2); 22(2); 26(2); 29; 31; 41:2(4); 3; 4; 7(2); 11(2); 12(2); 24; 26(4); 27; 28; 42:5(4); 7; 10; 17(2); 19(3); 23(2); 24; 43:1(2); 7; 8(2); 9; 13(2); 14; 16; 17; 25; 44:2(2); 3; 7; 9; 10; 24(4); 25(2); 26(2); 27; 28; 45:3; 9(2); 10; 15; 16; 18(6); 20(2); 21(2); 24; 46:3(2); 11; 12; 47:8(3); 48:1(2); 14; 17(2); 49:5; 7; 9; 10; 17; 19; 21(2); 23; 25; 26; 50:4; 6(2); 8(3); 9(2); 10(3); 11(2); 51:1(2); 2; 6; 7; 10; 12(4); 13; 15; 17; 18; 19; 22; 23(3); 52:5; 6; 7(5); 11; 53:1; 8; 54:1(2); 10; 16(2); 55:1(2); 5; 56:2(3); 3; 4; 6(2); 8(2); 11; 57:13; 15(2); 19(2); 58:7; 59:5; 15; 20; 21; 60:8(2); 14(2); 61:1; 2; 3; 9; 62:6; 9(2); 63:1(4); 2; 8; 11(2); 12; 13; 19; 64:4(2); 5(2); 7(2); 65:1(2); 2; 3(2); 4(2); 5; 7; 10; 11(4); 16(2); 20; 66:2(2); 3(4); 5(3); 6; 8(2); 9; 10(2); 17; 19(3); 24; **Jer** 1:1; 2:6(2); 8; 24(2); 3:15; 4:31; 5:1(2); 6; 21(2); 22; 24; 26; 6:11; 15; 7:2; 8:3(2); 10; 12; 16; 9:12(3); 24; 25; 26(2); 10:7; 23; 25(2); 11:3; 10; 17; 20; 21; 12:1; 4; 14; 13:10(2); 13; 20; 23; 14:8; 9; 15(2); 15:5(3); 9; 16:3(3); 14; 15; 17:5; 7; 9; 11; 13(2); 16; 18; 20; 18:13; 16; 19; 19:7; 8; 9; 10; 20:1; 5; 6; 12; 15; 21:4; 7; 9(3); 12; 13(3); 22:2(2); 4; 10; 11(2); 13(2); 14; 25; 26; 30; 23:1; 2; 4; 7; 8; 16; 17(2); 18(2); 25; 26; 27; 28(2); 30; 31; 32; 34; 24:5; 8(2); 25:23; 24; 30; 31; 26:20(2); 22; 23; 27:3; 9; 14; 15; 16; 28:1; 4; 5; 6; 8; 9; 29:1; 4; 8; 16(3); 21; 22; 25; 26; 27; 30:16(3); 19; 20; 21(2); 31:2; 4; 8; 10; 30; 35(2); 32:9; 12(2); 24; 29; 33:2(2); 9; 11(2); 13; 22; 34:5; 8; 10; 14; 18(2); 19; 20; 21; 36:6; 9; 21; 24; 32; 37:5; 7; 10; 19; 38:2(2); 4; 7; 16(2); 19; 22; 39:9(3); 10; 40:1(2); 6; 7(2); 10; 11(2); 15; 41:2; 3(2); 7; 8; 10(2); 13(2); 42:17; 43:5; 44:1(2); 12; 13; 14(2); 15(3); 20; 24; 26; 27; 28(2); 30(2); 46:7; 9(2); 22; 25; 26; 47:2; 4; 48:10(2); 12; 17(2); 19(2); 28; 35; 44(2); 45; 49:4(2); 5(2); 12; 16(2); 17; 19(5); 37; 50:7; 10; 12; 13; 14; 16; 28; 29; 33; 37; 44(5); 51:1; 2; 13; 25; 50; 52:12; 14; 15(2); 25(4); 32; **Lam** 1:1; 8; 12; 16; 2:4; 13; 15; 19; 3:1; 25(2); 30; 37(2); 4:5(2); 9; 13; 21; **Ezek** 2:2; 3:15; 27(2); 5:10; 14; 6:8; 9; 12(3); 7:7; 9; 13; 16; 9:1; 3; 4; 6; 11; 10:7; 11:2; 3; 12:4; 10; 12; 14; 19(2); 13:2(2); 3; 9(2); 11; 15(2); 16(2); 17; 18; 19(3); 14:4(2); 7(2); 10; 22; 16:15; 25; 27(2); 32; 38; 44; 45; 46(2); 52; 57; 59; 17:15; 16; 21; 18:4; 10(2); 14; 15; 17; 20; 32; 20:12; 38; 21:23; 31; 22:9(2); 10; 30; 23:6; 42; 43; 44; 45; 24:26; 27; 26:2; 17(2); 20(2); 27:3; 27; 29; 28:9(2); 14; 18; 19; 24(2); 26; 29:3(2); 30:5; 6; 31:14; 16; 17; 32:15; 18; 21; 23; 24(3); 25; 27(2); 29(2); 30(2); 33:5; 21; 22; 24; 27(3); 32; 34:2; 4; 27; 35:7(2); 8; 36:5; 34; 38:11; 12(2); 17; 20; 22; 39:4; 6; 9; 10(2); 11; 28; 40:45; 46(2); 42:13; 43:19(2); 44:5(2); 9; 10(2); 15; 45:4; 20; 47:22(2); 48:11(3); **Dan** 1:4; 10(2); 13; 15; 20; 2:10; 11; 14; 21; 25; 28; 29; 30; 3:10; 15(2); 20; 22; 28(2); 29; 4:19; 22; 34; 37; 5:13; 23; 6:12; 13; 24; 27; 7:16; 24; 8:13; 16; 23; 9:1; 4(3); 6; 12; 15; 26; 27; 10:7; 16; 11:3; 6(3); 7; 11; 16; 20; 26; 30; 32(2); 33; 12:1(2); 2; 3(2); 6; 7(2); 12; **Hos** 2:5(2); 23(2); 3:1(2); 4:3; 4; 14; 5:10; 9:4; 11:4; 12; 13:2; 14:7; 9(2); **Joel** 1:9; 13(2); 2:11(2); 14; 17; 26; **Am** 1:1; 5; 8; 2:9; 10; 15(2); 3:8(2); 10; 12; 4:1(4); 13(3); 5:7; 10(2); 18; 6:1; 3(2); 4; 5; 6; 7; 10; 13(2); 8:4; 8; 14(2); 9:1(2); 5(2); 6(2); 10; 12(2); 13; **Ob** 3(3); 7; 14(2); 20; **Jon** 1:9; 2:8; 3:9; 4:2; 11; **Mic** 2:1; 6; 7(2); 8; 13; 3:2(2); 3; 5(4); 9; 10; 4:11; 5:3; 8; 6:9; 7:1(2); 5; 10(2); 13; 14; 18; **Nah** 1:5; 6(2); 7; 11; 15(2); 2:1; 3:4; 7(2); 19; **Hab** 1:13; 2:2; 6(2); 7; 8; 9; 12(2); 15; 17; 19; **Zeph** 1:5(3); 6; 9(2); 11; 12(2); 18; 2:3; 15; 3:1; 11; 18(2); 19(2); **Hag** 1:6; 2:3(2); 13; 22; **Zech** 1:9; 10; 11; 13; 14; 19; 2:3; 4; 7; 8; 3:2; 4; 7; 8; 4:1(2); 4; 5; 7; 10; 14; 5:4; 5; 10; 6:4; 5; 8; 10; 7:3; 8:9(2); 9:7; 8(2); 10:5; 11:5; 11; 16(2); 17; 12:1; 3; 8; 13:3(2); 7; 14:12; 16; 18; 21; **Mal** 1:6; 10(2); 14; 2:12(2); 17; 3:2(2); 5(2); 15; 16(3); 17; 18(2); 4:1; 2; **Mt** 1:6; 16; 2:2; 6; 16; 20; 3:3; 7; 11; 4:16(2); 24(2); 5:4; 6; 10; 12; 15; 32; 42(2); 44(3); 46; 6:4; 6(2); 18(2); 7:8(3); 9; 11(2); 13; 14; 15; 21(2); 23; 24; 26(2); 8:10; 16(2); 27; 33; 9:8; 12(2); 20; 10:2; 4; 11; 20(2); 22; 28(2); 32; 33; 37(2); 38; 39(2); 40(3); 41(2); 11:6; 8; 10; 11; 14; 15; 23; 28; 12:3; 4; 10; 11; 22; 30(2); 32; 48(3); 13:9; 19; 20(2); 22(2); 23(3); 24; 37; 39; 41; 43; 46; 52; 14:9; 21; 33; 35; 15:1; 4; 38; 16:13; 15; 17; 28; 17:24; 18:1; 6; 10; 14; 23; 24; 28; 19:4; 9; 12(4); 25; 28; 29; 30; 20:1; 9; 12; 25; 21:9(3); 10; 12(2); 23; 33; 41; 22:2; 3; 4; 8; 11; 23; 23:9; 11; 12; 13; 16; 20; 21(2); 22(2); 24; 31; 37(2); 39; 24:13; 16; 17; 18; 19(2); 45; 25:1; 3; 9; 10; 14; 16; 17; 18; 20; 22; 24; 28; 29(2); 26:3; 23; 25; 51; 52; 57; 68(2); 71; 73; 75; 27:9; 17; 22; 39; 40; 44; 47; 52; 54; 55; 57; 28:5; **Mk** 1:2; 7; 19; 24; 32(2); 34; 36; 2:3; 7; 17(2); 26; 3:1; 3; 19; 22; 29; 33; 34; 4:9; 11; 16; 18; 20; 24; 41; 5:3; 14; 15; 16(2); 18; 30; 31; 32; 35; 38; 40; 6:13; 22; 26; 44; 55; 7:10; 32; 8:9; 27; 29; 9:1; 17; 23; 34; 37; 38; 39; 40; 42; 10:13; 23; 24; 26; 29; 30; 31; 42; 11:5; 9(3); 15(2); 28; 12:18; 38; 40; 41; 43; 13:11; 13; 14; 15; 16; 17(2); 34; 14:4; 18; 20; 47; 69; 70; 15:7; 29(2); 32; 35; 39; 41(2); 43; 16:3; 6; 10; 14; 16(2); 17; **Lk** 1:2; 19; 35; 36; 45; 49; 50; 61; 65; 66; 70; 71; 79; 2:5; 11; 18; 23; 37; 38; 47; 3:7; 11(3); 4:18; 20; 26; 33; 34; 40; 5:9; 10; 12; 17; 18; 21(3); 24; 29; 31(2); 6:3; 8; 16; 17; 18; 21(2); 24; 25(2); 27(2); 28(2); 29(2); 30(2); 32(2); 33; 40; 48; 49(2); 7:2; 10(2); 14; 15; 23; 25; 27; 28; 37; 39(3); 41; 49(3); 8:2; 3; 8; 12; 13(2); 14; 15; 16; 20; 21; 25; 27; 34; 36(2); 43; 45(2); 9:9; 11; 18; 20; 27; 30; 31; 32; 48(2); 50; 61; 10:15; 16(4); 22(2); 29; 30; 36; 37; 39; 11:4; 10(3); 13; 23(2); 28; 33; 40; 44; 51; 52; 12:4; 5; 9; 10(2); 14; 21; 36; 42; 47; 48; 13:1; 4; 11; 23; 30(2); 34(2); 35; 14:2; 7; 9; 10(2); 11; 12; 15(2); 17; 24; 29; 31; 35; 15:7(2); 10; 30; 16:1; 10(2); 11; 12; 14; 15; 18; 19; 20; 26; 17:12(2); 18; 31(2); 18:2; 7; 9; 14(2); 24; 26(2); 29; 30; 39; 19:2; 3; 7; 24(2); 26(2); 27; 32; 38; 45; 20:2(2); 20; 27; 35; 46; 47; 21:21(3); 23(2); 35; 22:3; 23; 25; 26(3); 27(5); 28; 36(2); 47; 52; 63; 64(2); 23:7; 14; 19; 25; 26; 27; 39; 48; 49; 51; 55; 24:10; 19; 21; 22; 23; 24; 33; **Jn** 1:12; 13; 15; 18; 19; 22(2); 24; 27; 29; 30; 33(2); 40; 2:9; 14; 16; 3:8; 13(2); 18(2); 21; 26; 29(2); 31(3); 33; 36(2); 4:10(2); 12; 24; 25; 26; 29; 34; 36(3); 39; 5:5; 10; 11; 12(2); 13(2); 15; 23(2); 24(2); 25; 28; 29(2); 30; 32; 37; 44; 45; 6:2; 9; 13; 14; 22; 33; 35(2); 37; 38; 39; 40(2); 44; 45; 46; 47; 56; 57; 58; 60; 63; 64(4); 71; 7:16; 18(3); 20; 28; 33; 38; 45; 50; 8:7; 9; 12; 16; 18(2); 25; 26; 29; 31; 40; 47; 50; 53; 54; 9:1; 2; 4; 8(2); 13; 16; 18; 19; 21; 24; 32; 36; 37; 39(2); 40; 10:1; 2; 8; 12(2); 21; 29; 11:2; 16; 25; 27; 31; 33; 37; 39; 42; 44; 45; 52; 12:1; 2; 4; 13; 17; 20; 21; 25(2); 29; 34; 35; 38; 44(2); 45(2); 48; 49; 13:1; 10; 11; 16(2); 18; 20(3); 24; 25; 14:9; 10; 12; 21(3); 24(2); 15:5; 21; 23; 26; 16:5; 17:20; 18:2; 5; 13; 14; 16(2); 17; 18; 21; 22; 37; 19:11; 32; 35; 39; 20:8; 29; 21:12; 20(3); 24; **Acts** 1:11(2); 16(2); 21; 23; 24; 2:7; 14; 39; 41; 44; 47; 3:2; 3; 10; 11; 20; 23; 24; 4:4; 14; 16; 24; 25; 32; 34(2); 36; 5:5; 9; 11; 16; 17; 32; 36; 37; 6:13; 15; 7:18; 24; 27(2); 34; 35(2); 37; 38(3); 40; 46; 52; 53; 8:4; 7(2); 9; 14; 15; 27; 33; 9:2; 5; 7; 14; 17; 21(3); 22; 32; 33; 35; 10:2(2); 7(2); 17; 21; 22; 27; 38(2); 41; 42; 44; 45; 47; 11:1; 13; 14; 17; 19; 20; 13:1(2); 7; 9; 16; 22; 25; 26; 27; 31(2); 39; 43; 14:3; 8; 15; 16; 15:5; 8; 17(2); 19; 21; 22; 23; 24; 26; 27; 38; 16:1; 2; 3; 13; 14; 16; 17; 32; 17:5; 6; 15; 17; 21; 24; 18:2; 7; 27; 19:4; 10; 13; 14; 15; 18; 19; 22; 24; 31; 35; 37; 20:9; 32; 34; 21:8(2); 9; 11; 20; 21; 23; 25; 28; 33; 38; 22:5; 8; 9(2); 11; 12; 19; 20; 25(2); 29; 23:2; 4; 13; 21; 24:20; 24; 25:5; 7; 19; 24; 26:13; 15; 18; 29; 30; 27:24; 43; 28:7; 9; 16; 18; 21; 30; **Rom** 1:3; 7; 15; 16; 18; 25(2); 32(3); 2:1(2); 2; 3; 6; 7; 8; 9; 10; 14; 15; 19; 21(2); 22(2); 23; 27; 28; 29; 3:5; 11(2); 12; 19; 22; 26; 30; 4:4; 5(2); 11; 12(2); 14; 16(3); 17; 18; 24(2); 25; 5:5; 14(3); 16; 17; 6:2; 7; 7:1; 2; 4; 17; 20; 21; 24; 8:1(2); 4; 5(2); 8; 11(3); 20; 23; 27; 28(2); 31; 32; 33(2); 34(5); 35; 37; 9:4; 5; 6; 8; 11; 16(3); 19; 20(2); 25(2); 30; 10:4; 5; 6; 7; 12; 15(2); 16; 19; 20(2); 11:4; 14; 22; 24; 34(2); 35; 12:3; 7; 8(4); 14; 15(2); 13:2; 4; 8; 14:1; 2; 3(4); 4; 6(4); 14; 18; 20; 22; 23; 15:1; 3; 12; 21; 26; 31; 16:1; 4; 5; 6; 7(2); 10; 11(2); 12(2); 14; 15; 17; 18; 22; 25; **1 Cor** 1:2(2); 8; 18(2); 21; 24; 30; 31; 2:6(2); 9; 12; 15; 16; 3:5(2); 7(3); 8(2); 4:4; 5; 7; 17(2); 19; 5:2; 3; 11; 12(2); 13; 6:4; 5; 16; 17; 18; 19; 7:12; 13(2); 22(2); 29; 30(3); 31; 32; 33; 34; 37; 38(2); 8:9; 10(2); 9:3; 6; 7(3); 10(2); 13(2); 14; 20(2); 21(2); 24; 25; 26; 10:12; 13; 18; 27; 28; 11:5; 19; 22; 29; 12:6; 14:2; 3; 4(2); 5(2); 8; 11(2); 13; 16; 22(2); 23; 30; 15:9; 18; 20; 23; 27; 28; 29; 48(2); 57; 16:16; **2 Cor** 1:1; 4(2); 9; 10; 19; 21; 22; 2:2(3); 14; 15(2); 16; 3:6; 13; 4:3; 4(2); 6(2); 11; 14; 5:4; 5(2); 12; 15(2); 18; 21; 7:6; 12(2); 8:15(2); 16; 19; 9:6(2); 10; 14; 10:1; 2; 12; 17; 18; 11:4; 9; 12; 29(2); 31; 12:2; 21; 13:2; 3; **Gal** 1:1; 2; 4; 6; 7; 15; 17; 23; 2:2; 3; 4; 6(2); 8; 9; 12; 15; 20(2); 3:1; 5; 7; 9; 10; 12; 13; 16; 22; 4:5; 21; 23; 27(3); 29(2); 5:3; 4; 7; 8; 10; 12; 21; 24; 6:1; 6(2); 8(2); 10; 13; **Eph** 1:1; 3; 11; 12; 14; 19; 23; 2:1; 2; 4; 11; 13; 14; 17(2); 3:8; 9; 20; 4:6; 10(2); 15; 19; 28(2); 5:5; 14; 28; 6:5; 24; **Phil** 1:1; 6; 2:6; 13; 20; 25; 3:3; 17; 19; 21; 4:3; 13; 21; 22; **Col** 1:2; 7; 8; 12; 18; 21; 2:10; 12; 3:4; 10(2); 25; 4:5; 9; 11(2); 12; 13; 15; **1 Th** 1:7; 10; 2:4; 10; 12; 13; 15; 4:5; 8(2); 10; 12; 13(2); 14; 15(2); 17; 5:7(2); 8; 10; 12; 14; 24(2); **2 Th** 1:6; 7; 8(2); 10; 2:4; 7; 10; 12; 16; 3:3; 6; 11; 12; **1 Tim** 1:12; 16; 17; 2:2; 4; 6; 3:4; 7; 13; 4:3; 10(2); 16; 5:3; 5; 6; 16; 17(2); 20; 6:2(2); 5; 9; 13(2); 15; 16; 17(2); **2 Tim** 1:9; 10; 14; 2:2; 4; 15; 18; 19(2); 22; 25; 3:6; 12; 4:1; 8; **Titus** 1:2; 9; 11; 14; 15; 2:8; 14; 3:8; 15(2); **Phm** 1:11; **Heb** 1:1; 3; 7; 14; 2:3; 9; 11(2); 14; 15; 18; 3:2(2); 3; 4; 16(2); 17; 18; 4:2; 3; 10; 14; 15; 5:2; 4; 5; 7(2); 9; 13; 14(2); 6:4; 12; 18; 7:1; 5(2); 6; 9; 16; 21; 25; 26; 27; 28(2); 8:1; 4; 5; 9:9; 14; 15; 28; 10:1; 14; 23; 28; 29; 30; 33; 37; 39(2); 11:6(2); 11; 14; 17; 27; 28; 31; 33; 12:2; 3; 9; 11; 16; 19; 23; 25(4); 13:3; 7(2); 9; 10; 17(2); 20; 24; **Jas** 1:5; 6; 12(2); 25; 2:5; 11; 12; 13; 3:9; 13; 18; 4:5; 11; 12(2); 13; 17; 5:4; 10; 11; 20; **1 Pe** 1:3; 5; 10; 11; 12; 15; 17; 21(2); 2:6; 7(2); 9; 10(2); 14(2); 22; 23(2); 24; 3:5; 10; 12; 13(2); 15; 16; 20; 22; 4:1; 5; 6; 17; 19; 5:1(2); 10; 13; 14; **2 Pe** 1:1; 3; 9; 2:1(2); 4; 6; 7; 10; 11; 13; 15; 18(2); **1 Jn** 2:4; 6; 9; 10; 11; 13; 14; 17; 22(3); 23; 26; 29; 3:3; 7; 8; 10; 12; 14; 24; 4:4(2); 6(2); 7; 8; 16; 18; 20; 21; 5:1(3); 5(3); 6(2); 10(2); 12(2); 13; 16; 18; 20(2); **2 Jn** 1; 7; 9; 11; **3 Jn** 6; 9; 10; 11(2); **Jude** 1; 4(2); 5; 6; 15; 18; 19; 24; 25; **Rev** 1:2; 3(2); 4(4); 5; 7; 8(3); 18; 2:1(2); 2(2); 7(2); 8; 9; 11(2); 12; 13; 14(2); 15; 17(3); 18; 20; 22; 23; 24; 26; 29; 3:1; 4; 5; 6; 7(4); 9; 10; 12; 13; 21; 22; 4:3; 8; 9(2); 10(2); 5:1; 2; 7; 12; 13; 14; 6:2; 4; 5; 8; 9; 10; 11; 16; 17; 7:4; 10; 13; 14; 15; 17; 8:2; 6; 13; 9:4; 14(2); 15; 17; 20; 10:6(2); 8; 11:1; 10(2); 11; 16; 17(3); 18(2); 12:4; 5; 9; 10; 12; 13; 17; 13:4(3); 6; 8; 10(2); 12; 14(3); 17; 18; 14:3; 4(2); 6; 7; 11; 12; 13; 15; 16; 18(2); 15:2; 4; 7; 16:2(2); 5(3); 9; 15; 17:1(2); 8; 12; 14; 18:8; 9; 15; 17; 19; 24; 19:2; 4; 5; 9; 10; 11; 18; 19; 20(3); 21; 20:2; 4(2); 6; 10; 11; 13(2); 21:5; 6; 7; 9; 15; 24; 27; 22:7; 8; 9; 11(4); 14; 17(2); 18; 20

WHOM (761/710)

Gen 2:8; 3:12; 4:25; 6:2; 7; 10:14; 12:5; 15:14; 16:15; 17:21; 20:3; 21:3; 9; 22:2; 24:3; 14; 24; 40; 44; 47; 25:12; 30:26; 31:43; 32:17; 33:5; 34:1; 38:25; 39:17; 41:38; 50; 43:27; 29; 44:10; 16; 45:4; 46:15; 18; 20; 25; 48:6; 9; 15; 49:8; **Ex** 1:15; 5:14; 6:5; 26; 14:13; 15:13; 16; 18:3; 9; 23:27; 28:3; 32:7; 11; 13; 33:1; 12; 19(2); 34:10; 35:23; 24; 36:1; **Lev** 2:2; 13:45; 17:7; 22:5; 25:27; 42; 44; 55; 26:45; 27:24; **Num** 1:44; 3:3; 39; 4:37; 41; 45; 46; 5:8; 11:16; 21; 12:1; 13:16; 32; 14:31; 36; 16:5; 7; 17:5; 22:6(2); 23:8(2); 24:12; 27:18; 33:4; 55; 36:6; **Deut** 4:46; 7:16; 19; 9:2(2); 12; 26(2); 29; 17:15; 21:8; 24:5; 11; 28:33; 36; 48; 53; 54; 55; 57; 32:20; 33:8(2); 34:10; **Josh** 2:10; 4:4; 5:6; 7; 6:25; 10:25; 12:1; 13:21; 24:15; 17; **Judg** 4:22; 7:4; 8:15; 18; 9:38; 13:8; 20:36; 21:14; 23; **Ruth** 2:11; 19(2); 4:1; 12; **1 Sam** 2:33; 6:20; 8:18; 9:17; 20; 10:24; 12:3(2); 13(2); 17:28; 45; 21:9; 24:14(2); 25:25; 28:11; 29:5; 30:13; 21; **2 Sam** 3:14; 6:22; 7:7; 15; 23(2); 9:3; 14:7; 16:18; 19; 21; 17:3; 19:10; 20:3; 21:6; 8(2); 22:3; 23:8; **1 Ki** 2:5; 3:8; 21; 5:5; 7:8; 8:51; 9:21; 10:26; 11:2; 20; 34; 13:23; 17:1; 20; 18:15; 31; 20:14; 42; 21:26; 22:8; **2 Ki** 3:14; 5:16; 6:19; 22; 8:5; 10:24; 16:3; 17:8; 11; 15; 26; 27; 28; 33; 34; 35;

18:20; 19:4; 10; 12; 22(2); 20:18; 21:2; 9; 23:5; 25:22; **1 Chr** 1:12; 2:21; 4:18; 5:6; 25; 6:31; 11:10; 11; 14:4; 17:6; 21(2); 26:32; 29:1; **2 Chr** 1:11; 14; 2:7; 8:8; 9:25; 18:7; 20:10; 22:7; 23:18; 28:3; 11; 32:31; 33:2; 9; 34:12; **Ezra** 2:1; 65; 4:10; 5:14; 8:20; 10:44; **Neh** 1:10; 7:6; 67; 8:10; **Esth** 2:6; 4:5; 11; 6:6(2); 7; 9(2); 11; 13; **Job** 3:23; 5:17; 15:19; 19:19; 27; 25:3; 26:4; **Ps** 16:3; 18:2; 27:1(2); 32:2; 41:9; 45:16; 47:4; 73:25; 80:17; 86:9; 88:5; 89:21; 94:1(2); 12; 105:26; 106:34; 38; 107:2; 144:2; 146:3; **Prov** 3:12(2); 27; 25:7; **Eccl** 4:8; 16; 5:19; 6:2; 8:14(2); 9:9; **Song** 1:7; **Isa** 6:8; 8:18; 10:3; 19:25; 22:16; 23:2; 28:9(2); 12; 31:6; 36:5; 37:4; 10; 12; 23(2); 39:7; 40:14; 18; 25(2); 41:8; 9; 42:1(2); 19; 24; 43:7; 10; 44:1; 2; 46:5; 47:15; 49:3; 7(2); 50:1(2); 51:19; 53:1; 57:4(2); 11; 61:9; 63:19; 66:13; **Jer** 1:2; 7; 6:10; 7:9; 9:12; 16; 11:12; 14:15; 16; 18:8; 19:4; 20:6; 23:9; 24:5; 25:15; 17; 26:5; 27:5; 28:9; 29:1; 3; 4; 20; 22; 30:9; 33:5; 34:11; 16; 37:1; 38:9; 39:17; 40:5; 41:2; 9; 10; 14; 16(2); 18; 42:6; 9; 11; 43:6; 44:3; 50:20; 52:28; **Lam** 1:10; 14; 2:20; 22; 4:20; **Ezek** 9:6; 11:1; 7; 15; 13:22; 16:20; 37; 20:9; 23:7; 9; 22; 28; 37; 40; 24:21; 28:25; 29:13; 31:2; 32:19; 38:17; **Dan** 1:4(2); 11; 2:24; 3:12; 17; 5:11; 12; 13; 6:2; 16; 20; 7:8; 9:21; 11:21; **Hos** 13:10; **Joel** 2:2; 32; 3:2; 21; **Am** 6:1; **Mic** 4:6; **Nah** 3:19; **Zeph** 3:18; **Zech** 1:4; 10; 12:10; **Mal** 1:4; 2:14; 3:1(2); **Mt** 1:16; 3:17; 11:10; 27; 12:18(2); 27; 17:5; 25; 18:7; 19:11; 20:23; 22:10; 23:35; 24:45; 46; 26:24; 27:9; 15; 17; 56; **Mk** 1:11; 3:16; 17; 6:16; 10:40; 13:20; 14:21; 71; 15:12; 40; 16:9; **Lk** 5:18; 6:13; 14; 34; 47; 7:4; 27; 43; 47; 8:2; 35; 38; 9:9; 10:22; 11:19; 12:5; 37; 42; 43; 48(2); 13:4; 16; 17:1; 19:15; 22:22; **Jn** 1:15; 26; 30; 33; 45; 47; 3:26; 34; 4:18; 5:21; 38; 45; 6:29; 68; 7:25; 28; 39; 8:53; 54; 10:35; 36; 11:3; 12:1; 9; 38; 13:18; 22; 23; 24; 26; 14:17; 26; 15:26; 17:3; 6; 9; 11; 12; 24; 18:4; 7; 9; 19:26; 37; 20:2; 15; 21:7; 20; **Acts** 1:2; 3; 2:24; 36; 3:2; 13; 15; 16; 21; 4:10(2); 22; 27; 5:25; 30; 32; 6:3; 6; 7:7; 35; 39; 45; 52; 8:10; 19; 34; 9:5; 10:21; 39; 13:22; 37; 14:23; 15:24; 17:3; 23; 31; 19:13; 16; 27; 20:25; 21:16; 29; 22:5; 8; 25:15; 19; 24; 26:15; 17; 26; 27:23(2); 28:4; 23; **Rom** 1:6; 9; 3:25; 4:6; 8; 17; 5:2; 11; 6:16(2); 8:15; 29; 30(3); 9:4; 5(2); 18(2); 24; 10:14(2); 11:2; 36; 13:7(4); 14:15; 15:21; 16:4; **1 Cor** 1:9; 3:5; 6:19; 7:25; 39; 8:6(3); 11; 10:11; 15:6; 15; **2 Cor** 1:10; 2:3; 10; 8:22; 10:18; 11:4; 12:17; **Gal** 1:5; 2:5; 3:19; 4:19; 6:14; **Eph** 1:13; 2:3; 21; 22; 3:12; 15; 4:16; 30; 6:22; **Phil** 2:15; 3:8; 18; **Col** 1:14; 2:3; 19; 4:10; **1 Th** 1:10; **2 Th** 2:8; **1 Tim** 1:15; 20(2); 6:16(2); **2 Tim** 1:3; 12; 15; 3:14; **Titus** 3:6; **Phm** 1:10; 13; **Heb** 1:2(2); 2:10(2); 13; 3:17; 18; 4:6; 13; 5:11; 6:7; 7:2; 4; 8; 13; 11:18; 38; 12:6(2); 7; 13:21; 23; **Jas** 1:17; **1 Pe** 1:8; 3:19; 4:11; 5:8; **2 Pe** 1:17; 2:2; 17; 19; **1 Jn** 3:24; 4:20(2); **2 Jn** 1; **3 Jn** 1; **Jude** 13; **Rev** 7:2; 10:5; 17:2; 18

WHOSE (295/267)

Gen 1:11; 12; 29; 7:22; 11:4; 16:1; 22:24; 24:23; 29; 37; 47; 32:17; 38:1; 2; 25; 44:17; **Ex** 34:14; 35:21(2); 26; 29; 36:2(2); **Lev** 13:40; 41; 16:27; 21:10; 24:10; **Num** 12:12; 24:3; 15; **Deut** 8:9(2); 19:1; 21:6; 28:49; 29:18; **Josh** 12:1; 24:15; **Judg** 5:14; 6:10; 8:31; 13:2; 16:4; 17:1; **Ruth** 2:2; 5; 12; 3:2; **1 Sam** 9:1; 2; 10:26; 12:3(3); 17:4; 12; 55; 56; 58; 25:2; **2 Sam** 3:7; 12; 6:2; 9:2; 12; 13:1; 3; 14:27; 16:5; 8; 17:10; 25; 20:1; 21:16; 19; **1 Ki** 3:26; 8:39; 11:26; 19:18; **2 Ki** 7:2; 17; 8:1; 5; 12:15; 18:22(2); **1 Chr** 2:26; 34; 7:15; 8:29; 38; 9:35; 44; 12:8; 20:5; 26:7; **2 Chr** 6:30; 16:9; 28:9; **Ezra** 1:5; 7:15; 8:13; **Esth** 2:5; **Job** 1:1; 3:23; 4:19; 8:14(2); 12:5; 10; 17:6; 22:16; 26:4; 30:1; 38:29; 39:6; **Ps** 1:3; 15:4; 17:14; 26:10(2); 32:1(2); 2; 33:12; 38:14; 46:4; 57:4; 78:8; 83:18; 84:5(2); 144:8(2); 11(2); 15; 146:5; **Prov** 2:15; 13:6; 30:14(2); 31; **Eccl** 2:21; 7:26(2); **Isa** 1:30; 2:22; 5:28; 6:13; 10:5; 10; 14:2; 18:2; 7; 23:7(2); 8(2); 26:3; 28:1; 30:13; 31:9(2); 36:7(2); 45:1; 51:7; 15; 57:15; 20; 58:11; **Jer** 5:15; 17:5; 7; 19:13; 22:25; 32:18; 29; 33:5; 37:13; 44:28; 46:7; 18; 48:15; 49:12; 51:57; **Ezek** 3:6; 11:21; 17:16(2); 20:9; 14; 22; 21:25(2); 27; 29(2); 23:20(2); 24:6(2); 40:3; **Dan** 2:11; 26; 31; 3:1; 27; 4:19; 20; 21(2); 37; 7:20; 10:1; 5; **Am** 2:9; 5:27; **Ob** 3; **Jon** 1:7; 8; **Mic** 5:2; **Nah** 3:8(2); **Zech** 6:12; 11:5; **Mt** 3:11; 10:3; 22:20; 28; 42; **Mk** 1:7; 7:25; 12:16; 23; **Lk** 1:27; 2:25; 3:16; 6:6; 12:20; 13:1; 20:24; 33; 24:18; **Jn** 1:6; 27; 4:46; 6:42; 11:2; 18:26; 19:24; **Acts** 10:5; 6; 18; 32; 11:13; 12:12; 25; 13:6; 25; 14:13; 18:7; 28:7; 11; **Rom** 2:29; 3:14; 4:7(2); **2 Cor** 4:4; 8:18; 11:15; **Gal** 3:1; **Phil** 3:19(3); 4:3; **Titus** 1:11; **Heb** 3:6; 17; 6:8; 7:6; 11:10; 12:26; 13:7; 11; **1 Pe** 2:24; 3:6; **Rev** 9:11; 13:8; 12; 17:8; 20:8; 11

WILL (6401/4478)

Gen 2:18; 3:4; 5(2); 15; 16; 4:7; 14(2); 5:29; 6:7; 13; 18; 20; 7:4(2); 8:21(2); 9:5(3); 15; 16; 11:6; 12:1; 2(2); 3(2); 7; 12(4); 13:9(2); 16; 14:23(2); 15:2; 4; 8; 13(3); 14; 16:10; 17:2(2); 6(2); 7; 8; 16(2); 19; 20(3); 21; 18:5; 10; 14; 21(2); 26; 28; 29; 30(2); 31; 32(2); 19:2; 9; 13; 14; 21; 32; 20:4; 7; 11; 21:6; 13; 18; 23(2); 24; 30; 22:5(2); 8; 17(2); 23:6; 13(3); 24:3(2); 5; 7; 8; 14(2); 19; 33; 39; 40; 41(3); 42; 44; 46; 49; 57; 58(2); 26:3(2); 4(2); 24; 29; 27:9; 12; 25; 41; 45; 46; 28:13; 15(3); 20; 22; 29:18; 27(2); 32; 34; 35; 30:3; 13; 15; 20; 28; 31(2); 33(2); 31:3; 52(2); 32:8; 9; 12; 20(3); 26; 33:12; 13; 14; 34:11; 12; 15(2); 16(4); 17(2); 22; 23(2); 30; 35:3; 17; 37:13; 20; 38:16; 17(2); 40:13(2); 19(2); 41:16; 29; 30(3); 31(2); 32; 40; 42:20; 33; 34; 37; 43:4; 5(2); 8; 9; 16; 44:9; 26; 31(3); 45:6; 11; 18(2); 28; 46:3; 4(3); 31; 47:16; 18; 19; 25; 30; 48:4(2); 6; 9; 20; 21; 49:7; 25(2); 50:5; 15; 21; 24; 25; **Ex** 2:9; 3:3; 10; 12; 17; 18; 19; 20(3); 21; 4:1; 8; 9; 12; 14; 15(2); 21(2); 23; 5:2; 10; 11; 6:1(3); 6(3); 7(2); 8(2); 7:3; 4; 17; 18; 8:2; 8; 21(2); 22; 23; 26; 27(2); 28; 29; 9:3; 4; 5; 9(2); 14; 17; 18; 28; 29(3); 30; 10:3; 4; 5; 9(2); 29; 11:1(3); 4; 8; 9; 12:12(3); 13; 17; 23(2); 25(2); 13:13; 19; 14:3; 4(3); 13; 14; 17(2); 15:1; 2(2); 9(4); 14(2); 15(3); 16(2); 17; 26; 16:4(2); 23(2); 25; 26; 17:6(2); 9; 14; 16; 18:18; 19(2); 22(3); 23(2); 19:5; 8; 11; 20:7; 19; 24(2); 21:5; 13; 22:23; 24(2); 27(3); 23:7; 21; 22; 23(2); 25(2); 26; 27(3); 28; 29; 30; 31(2); 33; 24:3; 7; 12; 25:16; 21; 22(3); 28:35; 29:42; 43; 44(2); 45(2); 30:4; 6; 36; 32:10; 13; 30; 32; 33; 34; 33:1; 2(2); 3; 12; 14(2); 16; 17; 19(6); 22(2); 23; 34:1; 10(2); 20; 24(2); **Lev** 1:3; 4; 9:4; 6; 12:8; 16:2; 17:10(2); 19:5; 20:3(2); 5(2); 6; 24; 22:19; 29; 32; 23:30; 25:18; 19(2); 21(2); 26:4; 6(4); 7; 9; 11; 12; 16(2); 17; 18; 19(2); 21; 22; 24(2); 25(3); 28(2); 30; 31(2); 32; 33; 36; 42(3); 43(2); 44; 45; **Num** 5:27(4); 6:27; 9:8; 10:9(2); 29(2); 30(2); 32(2); 11:4; 17(3); 18(2); 21; 23; 14:8; 11(2); 12(2); 13; 14; 15; 24; 28; 31; 35; 40; 41; 43; 15:19; 24; 16:5(3); 12; 14(2); 28; 30; 17:5(2); 19:12(2); 20:8; 17(4); 19(2); 21:2(2); 16; 22(3); 22:4; 8; 17(2); 19; 34; 23:3(3); 19(2); 27(2); 24:13; 14(2); 30:5; 8; 12; 32:7; 15(2); 16; 17(2); 18; 19; 23; 25; 26; 27; 31; 32; 33:56; 35:6; 7; 8; 14; 36:3(3); 4(2); **Deut** 1:13; 17; 30; 39(2); 41; 2:4; 5; 9; 19; 25; 27(2); 3:21; 28; 4:6; 10; 26(3); 27(3); 28; 29(2); 31; 5:11; 25; 27; 31; 6:25; 7:4(2); 10(2); 12; 13(2); 15(3); 16; 20; 22(2); 23(2); 24(2); 8:9(2); 9:3; 14; 10:2; 11:14; 15; 23(2); 25; 31(2); 12:11; 30; 15:4; 6; 10; 11; 16; 18; 16:15; 17:12; 14; 18:14; 15; 18(2); 19(2); 19:14; 20:12; 21:3; 18(2); 20; 23:21; 25:2; 6; 7; 9; 19; 26:17(2); 19; 28:1; 7; 8(2); 9; 11; 12; 13; 15; 20; 21; 22; 24; 25; 27; 28; 35; 36; 37; 48(2); 49(2); 54; 55(2); 56; 57; 59; 60; 61; 63; 64; 65; 68(2); 30:3; 4(2); 5(2); 6; 7; 8; 9(2); 12; 13; 16; 31:3; 4; 5; 6; 8(2); 16(3); 17(3); 18; 20(2); 21(2); 23; 29(3); 32:1; 7(2); 20(3); 21(2); 23(2); 24; 26(2); 36; 37; 41; 42; 43(2); 33:27(2); 34:4; **Josh** 1:3; 5(2); 8(2); 11; 16(2); 17; 2:12; 14; 17; 19; 20; 3:5; 7(2); 10; 6:5; 7:9(2); 12; 25; 8:5(2); 6(3); 7; 8; 18; 9:20(2); 10:25; 11:6; 13:6; 14:12; 15:16; 18:3; 4; 22:18; 28; 23:5; 13; 15; 16; 24:15(2); 18; 19; 20; 21; 24(2); **Judg** 1:3; 12; 24; 2:1; 3; 21; 22; 4:7(2); 8(4); 9(3); 22; 5:3(2); 6:16; 18; 36; 37; 7:4(2); 7; 8:7; 9; 23; 25; 9:23; 38; 10:13; 18; 11:10; 24(2); 30; 31(2); 12:1; 13:8; 12; 15; 16; 14:12; 15; 15:7(2); 12; 13(2); 16:2; 5; 17; 20; 17:3; 10; 13; 18:5; 10; 19:12(2); 18; 20:8(2); 9(2); 10; 28; 21:7; 22; **Ruth** 1:10; 11; 16(2); 17(2); 2:8(2); 3:4; 5; 11; 13(2); 18(2); 4:4(3); 12; **1 Sam** 1:11(3); 14; 22; 2:9; 10(3); 15; 16; 25(2); 30; 31(2); 32; 34; 35(2); 36; 3:11(2); 12; 13; 4:8; 6:3(2); 5; 7:3; 5; 8:9; 11(4); 12(2); 13; 14; 15; 16; 17(2); 18(2); 19; 9:8; 13(4); 16; 19(2); 10:2(2); 3; 4; 5(3); 6(2); 8; 11:1; 2; 3; 10; 12:3; 10; 14; 15; 16; 17(2); 22; 23; 13:12; 14:6; 8; 9; 10(2); 12; 37; 40; 15:2; 16; 26; 29; 16:1; 2; 3; 11; 16; 17:9; 25(2); 32; 36; 37; 44; 46(3); 47; 18:11; 17; 21; 19:3(3); 5; 11; 20:2; 4; 7; 10; 13; 18(2); 20; 21; 21:9; 22:3; 7; 23:4; 11(3); 12(2); 23(2); 24:4; 10; 19; 21(2); 25:8; 17; 28; 31; 26:6(2); 8; 21; 27:1; 12; 28:1; 2; 19(3); 23; 30:15(2); 22; 24; **2 Sam** 2:6; 26(2); 3:13; 18; 21; 5:6; 19(2); 24; 6:21; 22(3); 7:10(2); 11; 12(3); 13; 14(2); 27; 9:7(2); 11; 10:2; 11; 11:11; 12; 12:11(2); 12; 22; 13:4; 13; 14:7; 8; 14; 15(2); 16; 17; 15:8; 21; 25; 28; 33; 34(2); 35; 16:3; 12(2); 18(2); 19; 21(2); 17:1; 2(3); 3(2); 8; 9(2); 10; 12(2); 13; 18:2; 3(2); 4; 22; 19:7(2); 26; 33; 36; 38(2); 20:6; 21(2); 21:4(2); 6(2); 22:3; 4; 26(2); 27(2); 28; 50; 23:5; 24:24(2); **1 Ki** 1:5; 14; 20; 21(2); 30; 51; 2:8; 17; 18; 20; 26; 30; 32; 38; 44; 3:14; 5:5; 6(2); 8; 9(2); 6:12; 13(2); 8:19; 27; 42; 9:3; 5; 7(3); 8(2); 9; 11:2; 11; 12(2); 13(2); 31(2); 34; 35; 36; 37; 38(2); 39; 12:4; 7(2); 11(2); 14(2); 27(2); 13:7; 32; 14:3(2); 5(2); 10(3); 14; 15(3); 16; 15:19; 16:3(2); 17:4; 18:1; 5; 12(2); 14; 15; 21; 23; 24; 19:17(2); 20; 20:6(2); 9; 13; 14; 22; 23; 25(2); 28; 31; 34(2); 21:2(2); 4; 6(2); 7; 21(3); 22; 29(2); 22:4; 6; 12; 14; 15; 20; 21; 22; 30; **2 Ki** 2:2; 3; 4; 5; 6; 3:7(2); 18; 4:10; 30; 5:5; 11; 16; 17; 20; 6:3; 8; 11; 19; 28; 7:4; 9; 8:1; 10; 12(4); 13; 9:8; 9; 26; 10:5(2); 6; 18; 13:19; 17:39; 18:14; 21; 23; 24; 27; 30; 32; 19:4(2); 7(2); 23(2); 28(2); 31; 34; 20:5; 6(3); 8; 9; 18(2); 19; 21:4; 7; 8; 12; 13(2); 14; 22:16; 20(2); 23:27(2); **1 Chr** 12:17; 14:10(2); 16:18; 17:9(2); 10(2); 11(3); 12; 13(2); 14; 25; 19:2; 12; 21:24(2); 22:5; 9(2); 10(2); 13; 28:6; 7; 9(2); 20(2); 21(2); **2 Chr** 1:12; 2:5; 8; 10; 12; 16(3); 6:9; 18; 7:14(3); 15; 16; 18; 20(3); 21; 22; 10:4; 7; 11(2); 14(2); 12:7(2); 8; 15:2(2); 16:3; 18:3(2); 5; 11; 13; 19; 20; 21; 29; 19:10; 11(2); 20:9(2); 12; 16(2); 17; 21:14; 15; 28:23; 30:6; 9(2); 32:11; 15; 17; 33:7; 8; 34:24; 25; 28(2); **Ezra** 4:3; 13(2); 15; 16(2); 7:18; 26; 10:11; **Neh** 1:8; 9; 2:6(2); 8; 19; 20(2); 4:2(4); 3; 11; 12; 20; 5:8; 12(3); 6:7; 9(2); 10; 11; 10:39; 13:21; **Esth** 1:17(2); 18(2); 19; 20(2); 3:9; 4:13; 14(2); 16(2); 5:8(2); 6:13(2); 7:8; 8:6; **Job** 1:11; 2:4; 5; 4:2; 5:1(2); 6:10; 24; 7:7; 8; 11(3); 13(2); 19; 21(3); 8:2; 10; 18; 19; 20(2); 21; 22(2); 9:13; 18; 19; 27(2); 28; 31(2); 10:1(2); 2; 9; 14; 11:11; 12; 20; 12:2; 7(2); 8(2); 13:7; 8(2); 9; 10; 11; 15(2); 19; 20; 22; 25(2); 14:7(2); 9; 12; 14; 15; 22(2); 15:17(2); 22; 29(3); 30(3); 31; 32(2); 33; 34(2); 17:3; 4; 5; 9(2); 16; 18:2; 19:2; 20:7(2); 8(2); 9(2); 10(2); 11; 16(2); 17; 18(3); 20; 21; 22(2); 23(2); 24(2); 26; 27(2); 28(2); 22:15; 21; 23(2); 24; 25; 26; 27(3); 28(3); 29(2); 30(2); 24:15; 25; 27:4; 5; 6; 9; 10(2); 11(2); 17(2); 19; 30:23; 32:10; 13; 14; 17(2); 20; 33:7(2); 12; 26; 28; 31; 33; 34:12(2); 17; 31; 32; 35:3; 4; 13(2); 36:2; 3(2); 19; 38:3; 39:9(2); 10; 11(2); 12; 40:5(2); 7; 14; 41:3(2); 4(2); 5(2); 6(2); 12; 42:4; 8; **Ps** 2:7; 8; 3:6; 4:2(2); 3; 6; 8; 5:2; 3(2); 7(2); 12(2); 6:5; 9; 7:12; 17(2); 9:1(2); 2(2); 9; 10; 14; 10:11; 13; 17(2); 11:6; 12:4; 5(2); 13:1(2); 2; 6; 16:4; 7; 9; 10(2); 11; 17:6; 15; 18:1; 2; 3; 25(2); 26(2); 27(2); 28(2); 49; 20:5(2); 6; 7; 21:8(2); 12(2); 13; 22:22(2); 25; 26; 30; 31(2); 23:4; 6; 25:14; 26:4; 5; 6(2); 11; 12; 27:3; 4; 6(3); 8; 10; 12; 28:1; 7; 29:11(2); 30:1; 9(2); 12; 31:7; 32:5; 8(2); 9; 34:1; 11; 35:17; 18(2); 37:10; 33; 38:15; 18(2); 39:1(2); 6; 40:3(2); 8; 41:1; 2(4); 3(2); 5; 8; 42:6; 8; 9; 43:4(2); 44:5(2); 6; 45:11; 12(2); 17; 46:2; 10(2); 47:3; 4; 48:8; 14; 49:4(2); 11; 15; 18; 50:2; 7(2); 8; 9; 13; 15; 21; 23; 51:6; 13; 17; 52:9(2); 54:5; 6(2); 55:16; 17; 19; 23; 56:3; 4(2); 9; 10(2); 11; 12; 57:1; 2; 7; 8; 9(2); 58:5; 11; 59:9; 16(2); 17; 60:6(2); 8; 9(2); 12; 61:2; 4(2); 6; 8; 62:3; 63:1; 4(2); 7; 64:5; 8; 65:2; 3; 5; 66:6; 13(2); 15(2); 16; 18; 68:13; 16; 21; 22(2); 29; 31(2); 69:30(2); 35; 71:14(2); 16(2); 22(2); 72:2; 3; 4(3); 9(2); 10(2); 12; 13(2); 14; 15(2); 16; 73:15; 24; 74:10(2); 75:2; 9(2); 10; 77:7(2); 10; 11(2); 12; 78:2(2); 4; 79:5(2); 13(2); 80:4; 18(2); 81:8(2); 10; 82:2; 84:4; 11(2); 85:5(2); 6; 8(3); 12(2); 13; 86:7(2); 11; 12(2); 87:4; 5; 6; 88:10; 89:1(2); 4; 5; 23; 25; 27; 28; 29; 32; 33; 34; 35; 46(2); 91:2(2); 14(2); 15(3); 16; 92:4; 94:3(2); 8; 14(2); 15(2); 16(2); 18; 95:7; 96:12; 101:1(2); 2(3); 3; 4; 5(2); 8; 102:13; 18; 26(5); 27; 28(2); 103:9(2); 104:33(2); 34; 105:11; 107:43(2); 108:1; 2; 3(2); 7(2); 9(2); 10(2); 13; 109:30(2); 110:4; 111:1; 5; 112:2(2); 3; 5; 6(2); 7; 8; 9; 10(2); 115:12(3); 13; 18; 116:2; 9; 13; 14; 17(2); 18; 118:6; 10; 11; 12; 19(2); 21; 24; 28(2); 119:7; 8; 15; 16(2); 32; 45; 46(2); 47; 48(2); 62; 69; 74; 78; 82; 84; 93; 95; 106; 115; 145; 146; 121:1; 3(2); 122:8; 9; 132:3; 4; 11(2); 12; 14; 15(2); 16; 17(2); 18; 135:14(2); 138:1(2); 2; 7(3); 8; 139:14; 140:12; 143:10; 144:9(2); 145:1(2); 2(2); 5; 6; 19(2); 20; 146:2(2); 149:4; **Prov** 1:5(2); 9; 22; 23(2); 26(2); 28(4); 32(2); 33(2); 2:5; 9; 11(2); 21(2); 22(2); 3:2; 8; 10(2); 22; 23(2); 24(3); 26(2); 28; 4:6(2); 8(2); 9(2); 10; 12(2); 6:9(2); 22(3); 26; 33(2); 34; 35(2); 7:20; 8:6(2); 7; 17; 9:8; 9(2); 11(2); 12; 10:3; 7; 8(2); 9; 10; 24(2); 27; 28(2); 29; 30(2); 31; 11:3(2); 5(2); 6(2); 7; 9; 15; 18; 21(2); 25(2); 26(2); 27; 28(2); 29(2); 31; 12:2; 6; 7; 8(2); 11; 13; 14(2); 21; 24(2); 13:9; 11(2); 13(2); 18(2); 20(2); 14:3; 5; 11(2); 14(2); 19; 26; 15:10; 12; 25(2); 27; 31; 16:3; 5; 14; 20; 21; 17:2(2); 5; 11; 13; 18:14; 21; 19:5(2); 8; 9; 15; 16; 17; 19(2); 21; 23(2); 24; 25(2); 27; 20:4(2); 5; 6; 13; 17; 20; 21; 22(2); 21:7; 13; 15; 16; 17(2); 28; 22:5; 6; 8(2); 9; 10(2); 11; 14; 15; 16; 23; 29(2); 23:5; 8; 9; 11; 13; 15; 16; 18; 21(2); 24(2); 33(2); 34; 24:6; 8; 12; 14; 20(2); 22; 24(2); 25(2); 29(2); 25:4; 5; 8; 22(2); 26:26; 27(2); 27:14; 18(2); 22; 26; 28:2; 8; 10(2); 13(2); 14; 16; 17; 18(2); 19(2); 20(2); 21; 22; 23; 25; 26; 27(2); 29:1; 14; 16; 17(2); 19(2); 21; 23(2); 30:17(2); 31:11; **Eccl** 1:9(2); 11(2); 2:1; 16; 18; 19(2); 3:22; 4:10; 11; 13; 16; 5:10; 12; 20; 6:12; 7:2; 14; 18; 23; 8:5; 7(2); 8; 12; 13(2); 15; 17(2); 9:5; 6; 10:8(2); 14; 11:1; 2; 4(2); 6(2); 8; 9; 12:7(2); 14; **Song** 1:4(3); 11; 3:2(2); 4:6; 7:8(2); 12; 8:9(2); **Isa** 1:5; 15(2); 24; 25; 26; 31; 2:3; 17; 20; 3:4; 5(2); 7; 14; 17(2); 18; 24; 4:1; 3; 5(2); 6; 5:5(2); 6(2); 24(2); 26(2); 27(3); 28; 29(5); 30; 6:8; 13(2); 7:8(2); 9; 12(2); 13; 14; 16; 17; 18; 19(2); 20(2); 21; 22(2); 23; 24(2); 25(2); 8:2; 4; 7; 8(4); 10(2); 14; 17(2); 21(2); 22(2); 9:1; 5; 6(2); 7(2); 9; 10(2); 14; 17; 10:3(4); 6(2); 12(2); 16(2); 17(2); 18(2); 19; 20(2); 21; 22; 23; 25(2); 26(2); 27(2); 32(2); 33(3); 34(2); 11:12(2); 15(2); 16(2); 12:1(2); 2; 3; 4; 13:6; 7(2); 8(5); 9; 10(3); 11(3); 12; 13(2); 14(2); 15(2); 16(2); 17(3); 18(3); 19; 20(4); 21(4); 22(2); 14:1(4); 2(3); 4; 13(3); 14(2); 16; 20; 22; 23(2); 25; 27(2); 29(2); 30(4); 31(2); 32; 15:2(2); 3(2); 4(3); 5(3); 6; 7; 9(2); 16:5(2); 9(2); 10(3); 12(2); 14(2); 17:1(2); 2(2); 3(2); 4; 6; 7(2); 8(2); 9(2); 10; 11(3); 13(3); 18:4(2); 5; 6(3); 7; 19:1(3); 2(2); 3(3); 4(2); 5(2); 6(3); 7; 8(3); 9; 10(2); 15; 16(2); 17(2); 18(2); 19; 20(4); 21(4); 22(4); 23(3); 24; 20:6; 21:12; 13; 16; 17; 22:4; 14; 17(2); 18; 19(2); 20; 21(2); 22; 23(2); 24; 25(2); 23:5; 12(2); 15(2); 17(2); 18(3); 24:20; 21; 22(3); 23(2); 25:1(2); 2; 3(2); 5(2); 6; 7; 8(3); 9(3); 10; 11(2); 12; 26:1(2); 3; 9(2); 10(3); 11(2); 12; 14(2); 21(2); 27:1(2); 9; 10(3); 11(3); 12(2); 13(2); 28:2; 3; 5; 9(2); 11; 15; 16; 17(3); 18(3); 19(3); 21(2); 29:2; 3(3); 6; 14; 23; 24(2); 30:6; 9; 16(2); 18(2); 19(2); 20; 22(3); 23(3); 24; 25; 26(2); 30; 31; 32(2); 31:2(3); 3(3); 4(2); 5(3); 32:1(2); 2; 3(2); 4(2); 5; 6(3); 10(3); 13; 14(3); 16; 17; 18; 33:1(2); 6; 10(3); 16(4); 17(2); 18; 19; 20(4); 21(2); 22; 24(2); 35:4(2); 36:6; 8; 9; 12; 14; 15(2); 18; 37:4(2); 7(2); 24(2); 29(2); 32; 35; 38:5; 6(2); 7; 8; 16; 20; 39:7(2); 8; 40:11(2); 18(2); 20(2); 24(3); 25; 41:10(3); 13(2); 14; 15; 17(2); 18(2); 19(2); 22; 27; 42:1; 2; 3(3); 4; 6(2); 8; 14(2); 15(3); 16(4); 21; 23(2); 43:2; 4; 5; 6; 13; 14; 19(2); 20; 25; 28(2); 44:2; 3(2); 4; 5(3); 15; 21; 26; 27; 45:1; 2(2); 3; 5; 13; 14; 46:4(4); 5; 10; 11(2); 13; 47:3(3); 11; 12(2); 48:6; 9(2); 11(2); 15; 49:3; 6; 8; 10(2); 11; 13; 15; 19(2); 20(2); 21; 22; 23; 25(2); 26; 50:7(3); 8; 9(4); 51:3(4); 4(2); 5(3); 6(5); 8(3); 12(2); 19(2); 23; 52:12(2); 53:8; 12; 54:3; 4(4); 7; 8; 11; 12; 55:3; 7(2); 56:5(2); 7(2); 8; 12(3); 57:12(2); 13(2); 16(2); 18(2); 19; 58:4; 9(2); 11; 14; 59:2; 6(2); 18(2); 19; 20; 60:2(2); 7; 9; 12; 13; 15; 17(3); 19; 20; 22; 61:8(2); 10; 11; 62:1(2); 2; 8; 63:7; 8; 64:12(2); 65:6(2); 7; 8; 9; 12; 15; 19; 24(2); 66:1; 2; 4; 12; 13; 15; 16; 18; 19(2); 21; 22; **Jer** 1:16; 19; 2:3(2); 9(2); 19(2); 20; 24(2); 25; 27; 29; 31; 35; 37(2); 3:4; 5(2); 12(2); 14(2); 15(2); 16; 22; 4:1(2); 6; 7; 11; 12(2); 21; 27; 28(2); 30(4); 5:1; 5; 6; 12; 14; 15; 18; 19; 22; 31; 6:11; 12; 16(2); 17; 19; 21; 22; 23; 26; 30; 7:3; 7; 9; 14; 15; 16; 20(2); 23; 27(2); 32(2); 33(2); 34; 8:4(2); 10(2); 13; 17; 9:4(2); 5(2); 7; 10; 11(2); 15; 16(2); 25; 10:4; 10(2); 18(2); 11:4; 8; 11(3); 12(2); 14; 22; 23; 12:4(2); 5; 14; 15; 16; 17; 13:9; 12(2); 13; 14(3); 17(3); 21(2); 24; 26; 27; 14:10; 12(3); 13; 16(2); 22; 15:3; 4; 5(3); 6; 7(3); 8(3); 9; 11(2); 13; 14; 18; 19; 20(2); 21(2); 16:9; 13(2); 15; 16(2); 18; 20; 21(2); 17:3; 4; 8(4); 11(2); 27(2); 18:2; 8; 10; 12(2); 14(2); 16; 17(2); 19:2; 3(2); 7(3); 8(2); 9; 11; 12; 15; 20:4(2); 5(3); 9; 10(3); 11(5); 21:2; 4(2); 5; 6; 7; 14(2); 22:5; 6; 7; 8(2); 9; 14; 21; 22; 23; 25; 26; 23:2; 3; 4(2); 5; 6(3); 12; 15; 19; 20(2); 26; 33; 34; 36; 39(2); 40; 24:5; 6(4); 7(2); 8; 9; 10; 25:6; 9(3); 10; 12(3); 13; 14; 16(2); 27; 29; 30(3); 31(3); 35; 36; 26:3; 4; 6(2); 8; 13; 15; 27:8(3); 10(2); 11; 13(2); 16; 22; 28:3; 4(2); 9; 11; 16; 29:7; 10; 12(2); 13; 14(4); 17(2); 18(2); 21; 32(2); 30:3(2); 8(2); 9; 10; 11(3); 16; 17; 18; 19(2); 20; 21; 22; 23; 24(2); 31:1; 4; 6; 8; 9(2); 10; 13(2); 14; 18; 20; 22; 27; 28; 31; 33(3); 34(2); 37; 32:3; 7; 28; 31; 37(3); 38; 39; 40(4); 41(2); 42; 43; 44(2); 33:3; 5; 6(2); 7(2); 8(2); 11(3); 14; 15; 16(3); 20; 22; 26(4); 34:2; 17; 18; 20; 21; 22(3); 35:6; 13; 15; 17; 36:3; 7(2); 16; 29; 31(2); 37:7; 9(2); 19; 38:14; 15(2); 16(2); 25; 39:16; 17; 18; 40:4; 10; 15(2); 42:4(3); 6; 10(3); 12; 13; 14(2); 17; 18; 20; 43:10(3); 12; 44:11; 12; 13; 16; 17; 25(2); 27; 28; 29(2); 30; 45:4(2); 5(2); 46:6; 8(2); 11; 25; 26; 27; 28(4); 47:3; 5; 48:12; 31(3); 32; 33; 35; 44; 47; 49:2; 4; 5(2); 6; 8(2); 11; 12; 15; 16; 17(2); 19(3); 27; 32(2); 35; 36(2); 37(3); 38(2); 39; 50:5; 9; 18; 19; 20; 31; 32(3); 34; 36(2); 37(2); 38; 44(3);

45; 51:1; 2; 14; 20(2); 21(2); 22(3); 23(3); 24; 25; 29; 31; 33; 35(2); 36(2); 39(2); 40; 44(2); 46(3); 47; 52; 56; 57; 58; 64; **Lam** 3:31; 32; 4:22(3); 5:21; **Ezek** 2:1; 5; 3:7(2); 18; 20; 21; 25; 26; 27; 4:3; 8; 13; 16; 5:2; 4; 8; 9(2); 10(2); 11(3); 12(2); 13(2); 14; 16(2); 17(3); 6:3(2); 4; 5(2); 8; 9(2); 12; 14; 7:3(3); 4(4); 8(3); 9(4); 13; 15(2); 16; 17(2); 18(3); 19(4); 21; 22(2); 24(3); 25; 26(4); 27(5); 8:6; 13; 15; 18(4); 9:8; 10(3); 11:8; 9; 10; 11; 13; 17(2); 18(2); 19(2); 20; 21; 12:3; 13(2); 14(2); 16; 23; 25(3); 28(2); 13:9; 11(2); 12; 13; 14(3); 15(2); 18; 19; 20; 21; 23; 14:4; 7; 8(2); 9; 13(2); 22(4); 23; 15:5; 6; 7(2); 8; 16:27; 37(3); 38(2); 39; 41; 42(2); 43; 44; 53; 55; 59; 60(2); 61(2); 62; 17:9(4); 10(3); 15(2); 17; 19; 20(2); 22(3); 23(4); 18:30(2); 20:3; 4(2); 8; 20; 31; 32; 33; 34; 35(2); 36; 37(2); 38(3); 39; 40(2); 41(2); 47; 21:3; 4; 7(4); 12(2); 17(2); 23(2); 27(2); 30; 31(2); 22:2(2); 5; 14; 15; 19; 20(2); 21; 23:22(2); 24; 25; 27(2); 28; 29; 30; 31; 33; 36; 43; 45; 48; 24:9; 13; 14(5); 19; 21; 25; 26; 27(2); 25:4; 5; 7(4); 9; 10; 11; 13; 14; 16(2); 17; 26:3; 4; 7; 8(2); 9(2); 10(2); 11(3); 12(3); 13; 14; 15; 16(3); 17; 20(2); 21(2); 27:27; 28; 29; 30(3); 31; 32; 34; 35(3); 36(2); 28:7; 9; 22; 23; 25; 26(2); 29:4(3); 5; 8; 9; 10; 12(2); 13; 14; 15(2); 16; 19(2); 21(2); 30:3; 8; 10; 12(2); 13(2); 14; 15(2); 19; 22(2); 23; 24(3); 25; 26; 31:11; 13(2); 18; 32:3(2); 4(3); 5; 6(2); 7(2); 8; 9; 10; 12; 13; 14; 27; 31; 33:5; 6; 8; 20; 27; 28(2); 33(2); 34:10(3); 11; 12; 13(3); 14; 15(2); 16(2); 20; 22(2); 23; 24; 25(2); 26(2); 29; 35:3; 6; 7; 8; 9; 10; 11(2); 14; 15; 36:9; 10; 11(2); 12; 15; 23; 24; 25(2); 26(2); 27(2); 28; 29(2); 30; 31(2); 33; 35; 36; 37(2); 37:5; 6; 12; 14(2); 17; 18; 19(3); 20; 21(2); 22; 23(3); 26(3); 27; 28; 38:4; 8(2); 9; 10(2); 11(3); 13; 14; 15; 16(3); 18(2); 21(2); 22(2); 23(2); 39:2; 3; 4; 6; 7(2); 9(2); 10(3); 11(5); 12; 13(2); 14(2); 15; 16; 21; 25(2); 29; 43:7; 9; 24; 27; 44:14; 47:9(4); 10(3); 11(2); 12(5); 22; **Dan** 2:4; 7; 24; 25; 28; 29; 36; 40; 43(2); 44; 45; 3:15; 17; 18; 4:17; 35; 5:12; 17; 6:16; 8:4; 13; 10:14; 20; 21; 11:2(2); 3; 12(3); 13; 16; 21; 27; 36; 45; 12:13; **Hos** 1:4; 5; 6(2); 7(3); 9; 11; 2:4; 5; 6; 7(4); 9(2); 10; 11; 12(2); 13; 14(2); 15; 16; 17; 18(2); 19(2); 20; 21(2); 23(3); 3:3; 4:3(3); 5; 6(2); 7; 9; 14(2); 16; 5:6; 10; 12; 14(3); 15(3); 6:1(2); 2(2); 3; 7:12(3); 8:2; 3; 10; 13; 14; 9:5; 9(2); 12; 13; 14; 15(2); 17; 10:2(2); 10; 11; 11:9(3); 10; 11; 12:2(2); 9; 14; 13:7(2); 8(3); 10; 14(4); 14:2; 3(2); 4(2); 5; **Joel** 2:2; 14; 18; 19(4); 20(4); 23; 25; 28; 29; 30; 3:2(2); 4(2); 7(2); 8(2); 12; 15(2); 16(3); 18; 21; **Am** 1:3; 4; 5; 6; 7; 8(2); 9; 10; 11; 12; 13; 14; 2:1; 2; 3; 4; 5; 6; 3:2; 4(2); 5(2); 6(2); 8; 14; 15; 4:2; 3(2); 12(2); 5:2; 14; 15; 17; 18; 19; 22(2); 23; 27; 6:8; 10(4); 11; 14(2); 7:8; 9; 8:2; 5; 7; 9(2); 10(3); 11; 9:1; 2; 3(2); 4(2); 8(2); 9(2); 11(2); 14; 15; **Ob** 2; 3; 4; 5; 8; **Jon** 1:6; 12; 2:4; 9(2); 3:9; **Mic** 1:3; 4(2); 6(3); 7; 8(3); 15; 2:5; 11; 12(3); 13(3); 3:4(3); 4:2; 5; 6(2); 7(2); 10; 12; 13(3); 5:1; 5; 10; 11; 12; 13; 14(2); 15; 6:2; 7; 13; 14; 7:7(3); 8(2); 9(3); 10(4); 15; 19(3); 20; **Nah** 1:2; 3; 8(2); 9(2); 12(2); 13; 14(2); 2:2; 13(2); 3:5(2); 6; 7(2); 11(3); 15(3); 19; **Hab** 1:2(2); 5; 2:1(3); 3(4); 6; 7(3); 11(2); 14; 16(2); 17; 3:16; 18(2); 19(2); **Zeph** 1:2; 3(3); 4(2); 8; 9; 12(3); 17; 18; 2:3; 5; 7; 11(2); 13; 14; 3:5; 7(2); 9; 11; 12; 17(4); 18; 19(3); 20(2); **Hag** 2:6; 7(2); 9; 12; 13; 19; 21; 22(3); 23(2); **Zech** 1:3; 9; 12; 17(2); 2:5(2); 9(2); 10; 11(2); 12(2); 3:4; 7(3); 9(2); 10; 4:9; 5:4; 11; 8:3; 6; 7; 8(2); 11; 12; 13; 21; 9:4(3); 6; 7; 8; 10; 11; 12; 14(3); 15; 16; 10:1(2); 3(3); 6(4); 8(2); 9; 10(2); 12; 11:6(3); 9; 16(3); 12:2; 3(2); 4(3); 6; 7; 8; 9; 10(3); 13:2(2); 3; 4(2); 5; 6(2); 7(2); 9(6); 14:1; 2; 3; 4; 5; 6(2); 7; 12; 13(2); 14; 15; 17; 18; **Mal** 1:4(3); 9; 10; 2:2(4); 3(2); 3:1(2); 3(2); 4; 5(2); 7; 8; 10(2); 11(2); 12(2); 17; 4:1(2); 5; 6; **Mt** 1:21(2); 2:6; 13; 3:11; 12(2); 4:9(2); 19; 5:18; 20; 21; 26; 6:4; 6; 7; 10; 14; 15; 18; 21; 22; 23; 24(2); 25(3); 30; 34; 7:2(2); 5; 7(3); 8; 9; 10; 11; 16; 20; 21; 22; 23; 24; 26; 8:7; 8; 11; 12(2); 19; 9:15(3); 18; 10:14; 15; 17; 18; 19; 21(2); 22(2); 23; 25; 26(2); 29; 32; 33; 36; 39(2); 11:10; 22; 23; 28; 29; 12:11; 18(2); 19(2); 20(2); 21; 25; 26; 29; 31(2); 32(2); 36; 37(2); 39; 40; 41; 42; 44; 50; 13:12(3); 14(2); 30; 35(2); 40; 41(2); 42(2); 43(2); 49(2); 50; 15:13; 14; 16:2; 3; 18; 19(3); 25(2); 26; 27(2); 17:11; 20(3); 23(2); 27; 18:3; 14; 16; 18(2); 19; 26; 29; 35; 19:21; 28; 30; 20:4; 7; 16; 18(2); 19; 23; 21:2; 3; 21(2); 22; 24(2); 25; 27; 29; 31; 37; 40; 41(2); 43; 44(2); 22:13; 28; 23:4; 12(2); 14; 34(2); 36; 24:3(2); 5(2); 6; 7(2); 9(2); 10(3); 11; 12(2); 14(2); 21; 22; 24; 27; 28; 29(4); 30(3); 31(2); 34; 35(2); 37; 39; 40(2); 41(2); 46; 47; 50; 51; 25:21; 23; 29(3); 30; 31; 32(2); 33; 34; 37; 40; 41; 44; 45; 46; 26:2; 13; 18; 21; 23; 29; 31(3); 32; 33; 34; 35; 39(2); 42; 52; 53; 64; 75; 27:42; 43; 49; 63; 64; 28:7; 10; 14; **Mk** 1:2; 8; 17; 2:20(3); 3:27; 28; 35; 4:13; 22; 24(2); 25(2); 5:23; 6:11(2); 22; 23; 8:3; 35(2); 36; 37; 38; 9:1; 31(2); 41; 49(2); 50; 10:15; 21; 31; 33(2); 34(2); 39(2); 11:2; 3; 23(2); 24; 26; 29(2); 31; 33; 12:6; 7; 9(2); 23; 40; 13:4(3); 6(2); 8(3); 9(3); 11; 12(2); 13; 19; 22; 24(2); 25(2); 26; 27; 30; 31(2); 14:9; 13; 15; 18; 25; 27(3); 28; 29; 30; 31; 36(2); 58(2); 62; 72; 15:36; 16:3; 7; 16(2); 17(3); 18(4); **Lk** 1:13; 14(2); 15(2); 16; 17; 20(2); 31; 32(3); 33(2); 35(3); 37; 45; 48; 66; 76(2); 2:10; 12(2); 34; 35; 3:16; 17(2); 4:6; 7(2); 23; 5:5; 10; 35(3); 37(2); 6:9; 35(2); 37; 38(3); 39; 40; 42; 47; 7:7; 27; 30; 42; 8:17(2); 18(2); 50; 9:5; 24(2); 26; 48; 57; 61; 10:6(2); 12; 14; 15; 28; 35; 42; 11:2; 7; 8(2); 9(3); 10; 11(2); 12; 13; 18; 19; 24; 29; 30; 31; 32; 36; 49(2); 12:2(2); 3(2); 5; 8; 9; 10(2); 12; 18(3); 19; 20(2); 22(2); 28; 34; 36; 37(3); 42; 43; 44; 46(2); 47(2); 48(2); 52; 53; 55; 13:3; 5; 24(2); 25; 26; 27; 28; 29; 30(2); 14:5; 10; 11(2); 14; 15:7; 18(2); 16:11; 12; 13(2); 30; 31; 17:7; 8(2); 21; 22(3); 23; 24; 26; 30; 33(2); 34(3); 35(2); 36(2); 37; 18:5; 8(2); 14(2); 17; 22; 31; 32(2); 33(2); 19:14; 22; 26(2); 30; 43(2); 44; 20:3; 5; 6; 8; 13(2); 15; 16; 18(2); 47; 21:6; 7(2); 8; 9; 10; 11(2); 12(2); 13; 14; 15(2); 16(2); 17; 21; 23; 24(2); 25; 26; 27; 32; 33(2); 35; 36; 22:10; 12; 16; 18; 34; 42(2); 61; 67; 68; 69; 23:16; 22; 25; 29; 30; 31; 43; **Jn** 1:13(2); 50; 2:19; 20; 3:12; 4:13; 14(2); 21; 23; 25; 34; 48; 5:20; 21; 25(2); 28; 30(2); 43; 47; 6:27; 30(2); 37(2); 38(2); 39; 40(2); 44; 51; 54; 57; 58; 7:17; 31; 34; 36; 38; 41; 8:21(2); 22; 24(2); 28; 33; 9:21; 31; 10:5(2); 9(2); 16(2); 11:12; 22; 23; 24; 48(2); 56; 12:25(2); 26(2); 28; 31; 32; 48; 13:7; 21; 32; 33; 35; 37; 38; 14:3; 12(2); 13; 14; 16(2); 17; 18(2); 19(3); 20; 21(2); 22; 23(3); 26(2); 30; 15:7; 8; 10; 20(2); 21; 26; 27; 16:2(2); 3; 7(2); 8; 13(4); 14(2); 15; 16(2); 17(2); 19(2); 20(4); 22(3); 23(2); 24; 25(2); 26; 32(2); 33; 17:20; 26; 20:15; 25; 21:6; 18(2); 22; 23; **Acts** 1:6; 11; 2:17; 18; 19; 26; 27(2); 28; 39; 3:22; 23; 5:9; 38; 6:4; 14; 7:3; 7(2); 34; 37; 43; 49; 8:33; 9:6; 16; 10:6; 32; 43; 11:14(2); 13:10; 22(2); 34; 35; 36; 41; 15:16(4); 27; 29; 16:31; 17:31; 32; 18:6; 10; 21; 20:22; 25; 29; 30; 21:14; 22; 22:10; 14; 15; 18; 21; 23:3; 14; 21; 35; 24:15; 22; 25; 26:16; 17; 27:10; 22; 25; 34; 28:26(2); 28; **Rom** 1:10; 2:3; 6; 12(2); 13; 16; 18; 26; 27; 3:3; 6; 20; 30; 5:7; 17; 19; 7:3; 15; 16; 18; 19(2); 20; 24; 8:11; 13(2); 21; 27; 9:9; 15(4); 19(2); 20; 25; 27; 28(2); 33; 10:6; 7; 9; 11; 19(2); 11:15; 19; 22; 23; 24; 26(3); 12:2; 19; 20; 13:2; 3; 14:4; 15:9; 18; 32; 16:20; **1 Cor** 1:1; 8; 19; 3:8; 13(4); 14; 15(2); 17; 4:5(2); 17; 19(2); 6:2(2); 5; 9; 10; 12; 13; 14; 7:16(2); 28; 37(2); 8:10; 13; 9:17; 10:13(2); 11:27; 34; 13:8(3); 10; 14:7; 8; 9(2); 11; 15(4); 16; 21(2); 23; 25; 15:26; 28; 29; 35; 52(2); 16:3; 4; 5; 6; 8; 12; **2 Cor** 1:1; 7; 10; 13; 3:8; 4:14(2); 6:16(2); 17; 18; 8:5; 9:6(2); 10:11; 13; 11:9; 12; 15; 18; 30; 12:1; 5(2); 6(2); 9; 14; 15; 21; 13:1; 2; 6; 11; **Gal** 1:4; 5:2; 10; 21; 6:4; 7; 8(2); **Eph** 1:1; 5; 9; 11; 5:14; 17; 6:6; 8; 16; 21; **Phil** 1:6; 15; 18; 19; 20; 22; 2:13; 20; 3:15; 21; 4:4; 7; 9; **Col** 1:1; 9; 3:4; 24; 25; 4:7; 9; 12; **1 Th** 4:3; 14; 15; 16(2); 5:18; 24; **2 Th** 2:3; 7; 8(2); 11; 3:3; 4; 10; **1 Tim** 2:15; 3:5; 4:1; 6; 16; 6:15; **2 Tim** 1:1; 2:2; 12; 16; 17; 21; 25; 26; 3:1; 2; 9(2); 12; 13; 4:1; 3(3); 4; 8; 18; **Phm** 1:19; 21; **Heb** 1:5; 11(2); 12(3); 14; 2:4; 12(2); 13; 3:7; 15; 4:7; 6:3; 14(2); 7:21; 8:8; 10(3); 12(2); 9:28; 10:7; 9; 10; 16(3); 17; 27; 29; 30(2); 36; 37(2); 12:14; 13:4; 5; 6; 21; **Jas** 1:5; 7; 10; 11; 12; 18; 25; 2:12; 18(2); 4:7; 8; 10; 13; 14; 5:3(2); 15(3); 20; **1 Pe** 2:6; 15; 3:13; 17; 4:2; 3; 5; 8; 17; 18; 19; 5:1; 4; **2 Pe** 1:8; 10; 11; 12; 15; 21; 2:1(2); 2(2); 3; 12; 13; 3:3; 10(4); 11; 12(2); **1 Jn** 2:17; 24; 27; 5:14; 16(2); **2 Jn** 2; 3; **3 Jn** 6; 10; **Rev** 1:7(2); 19; 2:5; 7; 10(2); 16(2); 17(2); 22; 23(2); 24; 26; 28; 3:3(4); 5(2); 9(2); 10; 12(3); 16; 20; 21; 4:1; 11; 7:15; 17(2); 9:6(4); 10:9(2); 11:2; 3(2); 7; 8; 9; 10; 13:8; 17:1; 7; 8(2); 13; 14(2); 16; 18:7; 8(2); 9; 11; 15; 19:15; 20:7; 8; 10; 21:3(2); 4; 6; 7; 9; 22:18

WITH (6200/5081)

Gen 1:20; 21; 3:6; 12; 4:8; 5:22; 24; 6:3; 9; 11; 13(2); 14; 16; 18(2); 19; 7:2; 7; 13; 23; 8:1; 16; 17(2); 18; 9:4; 8; 9(2); 10(3); 11; 12; 11:31; 12:4; 8; 13; 17; 20; 13:1; 5; 14:2; 5; 13; 17; 24; 15:14; 18; 16:6; 11; 17:3; 4; 12; 13; 19(2); 21; 22; 23; 27(2); 18:16; 23; 25; 33; 19:1; 9(2); 10; 11; 30; 32; 33; 34(2); 35; 36; 20:16; 21:6; 10(2); 18; 19; 20; 22; 23(3); 32; 22:3; 5; 23:8(2); 24:15; 32; 40; 45; 49; 54; 55; 58; 25:21; 30; 26:3; 10; 15; 20(2); 24; 26; 28(2); 31; 27:15; 34; 35; 37; 41; 44; 28:4; 15; 20; 29:6; 9(2); 14; 19; 27; 30; 30:8(2); 15; 16(2); 20(2); 29; 33; 40; 31:3; 5; 6; 21; 23; 25; 26; 27(2); 32(2); 35; 38; 42; 50; 32:4; 6; 7; 9; 10; 11; 15; 20; 24; 25; 28(2); 33:1; 5; 7; 10; 11; 13; 15(2); 34:2; 5; 6; 7; 8; 9; 10; 16; 20; 21; 22; 23; 26; 35:2; 3; 6; 13; 14; 15; 22; 37:2(2); 14(2); 25; 38:14; 24; 25; 39:2; 3; 7; 8; 10(2); 12; 14(2); 15; 16; 17; 18; 21; 23; 40:2; 4; 5; 7; 14; 41:10; 12; 42:4; 6; 13; 21; 24; 25; 26; 32; 33; 38(2); 43:3; 4; 5; 6; 8; 16(2); 18; 19; 23; 32(2); 34; 44:1; 5; 9; 10; 12(2); 16; 23; 26(2); 29; 30; 31(2); 33; 34; 45:1; 5; 15; 23(2); 46:1; 4; 6; 7; 15; 26; 34; 47:12; 17; 29; 30; 48:1; 10; 12; 13(2); 21; 22; 49:25; 29; 30; 50:7; 9; 10; 13; 14; **Ex** 1:1; 7; 10; 11; 13; 14(2); 20; 2:3; 21; 24(3); 3:2; 8; 9; 12; 17; 18; 20; 4:12; 15(2); 17; 5:3(3); 15; 6:1(2); 4; 6(2); 7:11; 17; 22; 8:2; 5; 7; 17; 18; 9:15; 24; 10:9(3); 10; 24; 26(2); 12:8(2); 9(2); 10; 11; 22; 38; 48; 13:5; 9; 13; 19(2); 14:6; 7; 8; 11; 25; 15:8; 10; 19; 20(2); 16:3; 12; 20; 31; 32(2); 17:2(2); 3; 4; 5(2); 8; 9(2); 10; 13; 16; 18:3; 5; 6(2); 12(2); 18; 19; 22; 19:9; 13; 17; 24; 20:19(2); 22; 23; 21:3; 6; 8; 9; 14; 18(3); 19; 20; 22; 29; 22:14; 15; 16; 19; 24; 30(2); 23:1; 5; 11; 18; 32(2); 24:2; 3; 8; 13; 14; 25:2; 11; 13; 19; 20; 22(2); 24; 28(2); 33(2); 34; 39; 26:1(2); 6; 25; 29(2); 31; 32; 37; 27:2(2); 6; 8; 11; 12; 14; 15; 28:1; 3; 11(2); 21; 41; 29:2(2); 3; 4; 5; 9; 12; 14(2); 17(2); 21(2); 23; 33; 34; 40(2); 41; 42; 43; 30:2; 3; 4; 5; 6; 10; 18; 20; 26; 28; 34; 36; 31:3; 6; 8; 9; 18(2); 32:4; 11(3); 35; 33:3; 9; 12; 14; 15; 16; 22; 34:3; 5; 10; 12; 15(2); 16(2); 20; 25; 27(2); 28; 29; 31; 32; 33; 34; 35; 35:12; 16; 23; 24; 25; 26; 31; 35; 36:8; 13; 34(2); 35; 36(2); 38(2); 37:2; 4; 8; 9; 11; 15; 19(2); 20; 24; 25; 26; 27; 28; 38:2(2); 6; 7(2); 10; 11; 12; 14; 15; 19; 23; 30; 39:3; 6; 10; 14; 21; 23; 29; 35; 37; 39; 40:3; 12; 14; 31; **Lev** 1:9; 12; 13; 16; 2:2; 4(2); 5; 7; 11; 13(2); 16; 4:11; 12; 20(3); 25; 30; 34; 5:3; 4; 15; 16; 18; 6:6; 15; 16; 17; 21; 7:7; 10; 12(4); 13; 17; 19; 30; 8:2; 6; 7(4); 13; 15; 16; 17; 26; 30(2); 31; 32; 9:4; 11; 13; 14; 10:9; 14; 15(2); 16; 11:21; 43(2); 44; 13:57; 14:10; 16; 21; 27; 31; 37; 52(2); 15:3; 17; 18; 24; 33; 16:3; 4(2); 12; 14(2); 15(2); 19; 24; 17:13; 18:20(2); 22(2); 23(3); 24; 19:13; 19(2); 20; 22; 26; 33; 20:2; 5(2); 6; 10(2); 11; 12; 13(2); 14; 15; 16; 18; 20; 24; 27; 21:9; 22:6; 8; 10; 11; 27; 23:13; 17; 18(2); 20(2); 24:5; 23; 25:6; 23; 35; 36; 40; 41; 43; 45; 46; 50; 51; 52; 53(2); 54; 26:9; 39; 40; 42(3); 44; **Num** 1:4; 5; 44; 2:3; 9; 10; 16; 17; 18; 24; 25; 31(2); 3:1; 25; 31; 32; 37; 48; 4:5; 8; 9(2); 10; 11; 12(2); 14; 16; 25; 32(2); 5:8; 13; 19; 20; 6:15(3); 17; 20; 7:13; 19; 25; 31; 37; 43; 49; 55; 61; 67; 73; 79; 87; 89; 8:8(2); 26; 9:11; 10:9; 29; 32; 11:8; 16; 17(2); 18; 33; 12:7; 8; 13:23; 27; 31; 14:8; 9; 10; 11; 12; 21; 27; 43; 15:4; 5; 6; 9(2); 12; 14; 15; 16; 24; 35; 36; 16:1; 2; 10; 13; 14; 17; 18; 22; 27; 30; 32(3); 33; 17:4; 18:1(3); 2(3); 4; 7; 11(2); 19(3); 19:4; 12; 20:3; 11; 13; 18; 20(2); 21:18; 24; 34; 22:3; 7; 8; 9; 12; 13; 14; 20; 21; 22; 23; 24; 27; 31; 35(2); 39; 40; 23:13; 17; 21; 24:4; 8; 16; 25:1; 11; 14; 18; 26:3; 10; 27:3; 18; 21; 28:5; 9(2); 10; 12(2); 13; 20; 28(2); 31(2); 29:3; 6(2); 9; 11; 14; 19; 30:4; 8; 10; 31:6(2); 8(2); 9; 10; 14(2); 23; 32:19; 29; 30; 32; 33; 33:3; 34:12; 35:7; 16; 17; 18; 21; 25; **Deut** 1:16; 37; 2:5; 6(2); 7; 9; 19; 26; 35; 3:3; 5; 13; 17; 23; 26; 27; 4:11(2); 21; 23; 29(2); 37(2); 40(2); 5:2; 3(2); 4; 16; 22; 23; 24; 29(2); 33; 6:3(2); 5(3); 18; 21; 7:2; 3; 5(2); 8; 9; 10; 12; 15; 25; 8:3; 16; 9:8; 9; 10; 15; 19(2); 20; 21; 26; 10:9; 12(2); 14; 22; 11:2; 9; 13(2); 12:3; 4; 12; 23; 25; 28; 13:3(2); 10; 15(2); 16; 14:6; 27; 29; 15:5; 14; 16; 19; 16:3(2); 10; 18; 17:5; 19; 18:1; 6; 19:5(2); 13; 20:1; 3; 4; 12; 13; 20; 21:3; 4; 21; 22:2; 3(3); 6(3); 7; 9; 10; 12; 14; 17; 21; 22(2); 23; 24; 25(2); 28; 29; 23:4; 11; 13; 16; 23; 25; 24:5; 25:2; 3; 26:8(4); 9; 15; 16(2); 27:1; 2; 3; 4; 6; 14; 16; 20; 21; 22; 23; 28:22(7); 27(4); 28; 30; 32; 35; 40; 47; 29:1(2); 12(2); 14; 15(4); 19; 25; 30:2(2); 6(2); 10(2); 31:6; 7; 8; 16(3); 20; 23; 27; 32:6; 12; 14(2); 16(2); 22; 24(2); 25; 34; 42(2); 43; 44; 33:1; 2; 8(2); 13(2); 14(2); 15(2); 16; 17; 21(2); 23; 34:4; **Josh** 1:5(2); 9; 17(2); 2:6; 14; 19; 3:7(2); 14; 4:3; 8; 5:6; 13; 6:5(2); 10; 13; 17; 20; 21; 24; 26(2); 27; 7:12; 15(2); 21; 22; 24; 25(3); 8:1; 5; 11; 24; 26; 33; 35; 9:2(2); 6; 7; 11(2); 15(2); 16; 25; 10:1; 4(2); 7; 10; 11; 15; 20; 24; 28; 29; 30; 31; 32; 34; 35; 36; 37; 38; 39; 43; 11:4(2); 6; 7; 9; 10; 11(2); 12; 14; 18; 19; 21; 13:8; 21; 22; 27; 14:4; 8; 12; 15:32; 36; 41; 44; 45; 46; 47(3); 51; 54; 57; 59; 60; 62; 63; 16:9; 18:24; 28; 19:15; 16; 22; 30; 31; 38; 46; 47; 48; 21:2; 8; 11; 13(2); 14(2); 15(2); 16(3); 17(2); 18(2); 19; 21(2); 22(2); 23(2); 24(2); 25(2); 26; 27(2); 28(2); 29(2); 30(2); 31(2); 32(3); 33; 34(2); 35(2); 36(2); 37(2); 38(2); 39(2); 41; 22:5(2); 8(8); 14; 15; 18; 24; 27(3); 30; 23:4; 12; 24:6; 8; 12(2); 25; **Judg** 1:3(3); 7; 8; 16; 17; 18(3); 19; 21; 22; 25; 2:1; 2; 17; 18; 3:21; 27; 31; 4:6; 7; 8(2); 9(2); 10(2); 13; 14; 15; 18(2); 22; 5:9(2); 14; 15; 6:5; 12; 13; 16; 17; 23; 26; 39(2); 7:1; 2; 4(3); 5; 10; 11; 16; 18; 19; 8:1; 2; 3; 4; 7(2); 10; 16; 27; 33; 35; 9:1(2); 4; 9; 16; 19(2); 23; 26; 32; 33; 34; 35; 38(2); 39; 44; 45; 48(2); 52; 11:3(2); 8; 11; 33; 34; 38; 39; 12:1(2); 2; 13:9; 19; 14:5; 7; 11; 15; 18; 15:1; 6; 8; 13; 14; 15; 16(2); 16:6; 7; 8; 9; 10; 11; 12; 13; 14; 15; 16; 21; 28; 30(2); 17:2; 10; 11; 18:6; 7; 11; 16; 17(2); 19; 25; 27(2); 28; 19:3; 4; 5; 10(2); 19; 20; 24; 27; 20:37; 48; 21:5; 10; **Ruth** 1:6; 7; 8(3); 10; 11; 18; 20; 22; 2:4; 6; 19(2); 22; 23; 3:1; 2; **1 Sam** 1:24(2); 2:4; 13(2); 19; 22; 26; 29; 3:19; 4:4; 8; 12; 19; 5:6; 7; 8; 9; 12; 6:2; 3; 11; 15; 19; 21; 7:3; 10; 8:8; 9:3; 5; 19; 24(2); 25; 10:5; 6; 7; 26; 11:1; 2; 7(2); 10; 12:2; 3; 7; 20; 24; 13:2(2); 5; 15; 16; 22(2); 14:2; 7; 13; 17; 18; 20; 21(3); 27; 28; 32; 33; 34(2); 43; 45; 52; 15:6; 8; 25; 26; 30; 16:1; 2; 5; 12; 16; 18; 19; 20; 23; 17:3; 5; 9; 19; 20; 23; 25; 28; 32; 33; 37; 38(2); 39; 43; 45(3); 47; 50; 51; 57; 18:4; 6(3); 10; 12; 14; 22; 28; 19:3; 8(2); 9(2); 10; 13; 16; 20:5; 8(2); 13(2); 16; 35(2); 21:1; 8; 22:2; 3; 4; 6(2); 8; 17; 19(2); 23(2); 23:5(2); 6; 19; 23(2); 24:7; 8; 17(2); 18; 19; 25:7; 13(2); 16; 25; 26; 29; 31; 33; 26:2; 5; 6(2); 7; 8; 27:2(2); 3(3); 5; 28:1(2); 8; 12; 14(2); 19(2); 23; 29:2; 3; 4(4); 6; 8; 9; 10(2); 30:1; 3; 4; 9; 14; 21; 22(2); 23; 31:4; 5; **2 Sam** 1:2; 11; 17; 21; 24; 2:3(2); 23; 3:8; 12(2); 13; 16; 17; 20(2); 21; 22(2); 23; 27; 31(2); 5:3; 10; 6:2(2); 10; 12; 14; 15(2); 7:3; 7; 9; 12; 14(2); 22; 29; 8:2(3); 10(2); 11; 10:13; 17; 19; 11:1; 4; 5; 9; 11; 13; 17; 12:3(2); 9(2); 11; 16; 17; 24; 30; 31; 13:11; 14; 15(2); 20; 24; 26(2); 27; 28; 31; 14:2; 6; 17; 19; 15:1; 11; 12; 13; 14(2); 16; 17; 19(2); 20(2); 22; 23; 24; 27; 30; 31; 32; 33; 35; 36; 16:1; 2; 10; 12; 14; 15; 17; 18; 21; 23(2); 17:2; 8; 10; 12; 16; 22; 24; 29; 18:1; 2; 5; 14; 27; 28; 19:4; 7; 16; 17(2); 22; 25; 31; 32; 33(2); 34; 36(2); 37; 38; 40; 41; 20:7; 8; 9; 10; 15; 16; 21:3; 15(2); 17; 18; 19; 22:10; 26(2); 27(2); 40; 23:5(2); 6; 7(2); 9; 15; 21(2); 24:2; 20; 24; **1 Ki** 1:7(2); 8; 14; 21; 22; 23; 31; 33; 37(2); 40(2); 41; 44; 49; 51; 2:4(2); 8(3); 9; 10; 32; 3:1; 6; 18; 26; 4:13; 5:6; 6:4; 7; 9; 10; 12; 15(3); 16; 18; 20; 21(2); 22(2); 28; 29; 30; 32; 35; 36; 7:2; 3; 4; 6; 7; 9; 12; 14(2); 17; 36; 49; 8:2; 5(2); 9; 15(2); 21; 23(2); 24(2); 46; 48(2); 54; 55; 57(2); 59; 62; 65; 9:11; 16; 25; 27(2); 10:1; 2(3); 7; 18; 22; 26; 11:2(2); 9; 16; 17; 18; 21; 22; 29; 38; 43; 12:8; 10; 11(2); 14(2); 18; 21; 13:7; 8; 15; 16(3); 18; 19; 14:3; 6; 8; 20; 22; 31(2); 15:8; 19; 20; 22; 24(2); 30; 16:2; 6; 7; 13; 17; 18; 26; 28; 34(2); 17:18; 20; 18:4; 13; 28; 32; 33; 35; 45; 19:1; 10; 14; 19(2); 20:1(2); 19; 20; 21; 34(2); 38; 21:8(2); 9; 12; 13; 22; 22:4; 11; 13; 27; 31(2); 40; 44; 49; 50(2); **2 Ki** 1:9; 11; 13(2); 14; 15(2); 2:1; 11; 16; 3:7; 9; 12; 13; 17; 19; 20; 26; 4:13; 26(3); 5:3; 5; 7; 9; 23; 26; 6:1; 3; 4; 8; 15; 16(2); 18(2); 22; 32; 33; 7:2; 14; 19; 8:2; 4; 9; 12(2); 21; 24(2); 28; 9:15; 18; 19; 24; 28; 10:2; 6; 13; 16; 19; 23; 25; 31; 35; 11:3; 4; 8(2); 9; 11; 15; 20; 12:14; 21; 13:4; 9; 12; 13(2); 14; 19; 23; 14:10(2); 15; 16(2); 20; 22; 29; 15:7(2); 16; 19; 22; 25(2); 38(2); 16:15; 20(2); 17:15; 18; 35; 36; 38; 18:7; 17; 27; 28; 31; 37; 19:1; 2; 6; 9; 24; 32; 37; 20:3; 21; 21:11; 18; 22:7; 14; 17; 23:2(2); 3; 11; 14; 18; 25(3); 26(2); 24:4; 6; 25:7; 9; 10; 11; 14; 17; 24; 25(2); 28; **1 Chr** 2:23; 4:10; 23; 5:10; 18; 19; 20; 6:32; 33; 55; 57(2); 58(2); 59(2); 60(3); 64; 67(2); 68(2); 69(2); 70(2); 71(2); 72(2); 73(2); 74(2); 75(2); 76(3); 77(2); 78(2); 79(2); 80(2); 81(2); 7:4; 8:12; 32; 9:20; 25; 38; 10:4; 11:3; 9; 10(2); 13; 17; 23(2); 42; 12:2(2); 17; 19; 27; 33; 34(2); 37; 38; 39; 13:1(2); 2; 8(3); 13; 14; 14:1; 12; 15:16; 18; 20; 21; 25; 27(2); 28(5); 16:5(2); 16; 38; 41; 42(2); 17:2; 6; 8; 11; 20; 18:8; 10(2); 11; 19:7; 14; 17; 19; 20:3(3); 4; 5; 6; 21:7; 12(2); 20; 21; 24; 22:11; 13; 15; 16; 18; 23:2; 5; 29(4); 24:3; 25:1; 3; 6; 7; 8; 9; 26:8; 16; 27:32; 28:1; 4; 9(2); 20; 21; 29:2; 6; 9; 17; 21; 22; 30; **2 Chr** 1:1; 3(2); 14; 2:3(2); 7(2); 8; 12; 13; 14(2); 3:4; 5(2); 6; 7; 8; 9; 10; 4:9; 20; 21; 5:3; 6; 10; 12(3); 13(2); 6:4(2); 11; 14(2); 15(2); 18; 36; 38(2); 41; 7:6; 8; 18; 8:5; 18; 9:1(2); 6; 17; 18; 21; 25; 31; 10:8; 10; 11(2); 14(2); 18; 11:13; 12:1; 3(2); 16; 13:3(2); 8; 9; 11; 12(2); 17; 19(3); 14:1; 9; 11(2); 13; 15:2(2); 6; 9(2); 12(2); 14(2); 15(2); 16:3; 6; 8; 10; 13; 14; 17:3; 8(2); 9; 14; 15; 16; 17(2); 18; 18:1; 2(2); 3(2); 10; 12; 26; 30(3); 19:6; 7; 9; 11; 20:1(2); 13; 17(2); 18; 19; 21; 27(2); 28; 35; 36; 37; 21:1(2); 3; 4; 7; 9(2); 14; 15; 18; 22:1; 5; 7; 9; 12; 23:1; 3; 7(2); 8; 10; 13; 14; 18(2); 21; 24:21; 24; 25:2; 7(3); 13; 16; 19(2); 24; 28; 26:2; 13; 17; 19; 23(2); 27:5; 9; 28:5; 9; 18(3); 27; 29:8; 10; 18(2); 25(3); 26(2); 27(2); 29; 30(2); 35(2); 30:6; 9; 21; 23; 31:21; 32:3; 7(3); 8(2); 9; 18; 21; 33; 33:11(2); 20; 34:6; 12; 25; 30; 31; 35:11; 12; 13; 18; 21(4); 22; 36:10; 17; 19; 23; **Ezra** 1:3; 4(2); 5; 6(3); 11; 2:2; 63; 3:9(3); 10(2);

11; 12; 13; 4:2; 3; 5:2; 8; 6:4; 16; 21; 22; 7:13; 14; 16; 17(2); 18; 28; 8:1; 3; 4; 5; 6; 7; 8; 9; 10; 11; 12; 13; 14; 18; 19; 24; 33(2); 34; 9:1; 2; 11(3); 14(2); 10:3; 4; 12; 14; 16; **Neh** 1:2; 3; 5; 2:3; 9; 12(2); 13; 17; 3:1; 3; 6; 13; 14; 15; 4:13; 17(2); 5:10; 6:5; 7:7; 65; 8:2; 6; 13; 9:1(2); 4; 6; 8; 12(2); 13; 24(2); 30; 34; 10:29; 38; 11:17; 25; 12:1; 24(2); 27(3); 35; 36; 38; 40; 41; 42; 43; 13:2; 4; 9; 11; 15; 17; 25; **Esth** 1:6; 7; 8; 10; 2:6(2); 12(2); 13; 3:1; 5; 11; 12; 4:1; 2; 3; 5:9(2); 12(2); 14; 6:12; 14; 7:1; 8:3; 8(2); 10; 15; 9:5(3); 19; 29(2); 30; **Job** 1:4; 15; 17; 22; 2:7; 8; 10; 11; 13; 3:14; 15(2); 4:2; 18; 20; 5:14; 23(2); 6:2; 7:5; 14(2); 8:21(2); 22; 9:3; 14; 17; 18; 30(2); 35; 10:2; 11(2); 13; 17; 12:2; 12(2); 13; 16; 18; 13:3; 13; 17; 19; 14:3; 5; 15:2(2); 3(2); 11; 20; 26; 27(2); 16:5; 9; 10; 14; 21; 17:2; 3(2); 19:2; 4; 6; 16; 22; 24; 20:11; 17; 26; 21:3; 8; 25; 27; 34; 22:4; 18; 21; 23:4; 6; 7; 14; 24:8; 12; 14; 22; 26:12; 27:11; 12; 13; 14; 28:14; 22; 29:5; 6; 30:1; 21; 30; 31:1; 5; 20; 31; 32:14; 33:13; 19(2); 26; 29; 30; 34:8(2); 35:4; 36:2; 4; 7; 17; 18; 32; 37:4; 5; 11; 18; 22; 38:8; 32; 39:4; 10; 17; 19; 24; 40:2; 9; 10(2); 15; 22; 24; 41:1(2); 2; 4; 5(2); 7(2); 13; 14; 15; 42:8; 11; **Ps** 2:9; 11(2); 3:4; 4:5:4; 9; 12(2); 6:6(2); 7:4; 11; 8:5; 9:1; 12:2(2); 4; 13:6; 14:5; 15:3; 17:10; 13; 14(3); 18:9; 12; 25(2); 26(2); 32; 39; 20:6; 21:3; 6; 22:13; 23:4; 5; 25:14; 19; 26:4(2); 5; 7; 9(2); 27:7; 28:3(2); 7; 29:11; 30:11; 31:9; 10(2); 32:7; 8; 9; 33:2(2); 3; 34:3; 35:1(2); 13; 16(2); 19; 26; 36:8; 9; 37:12; 24; 39:1(2); 2; 3; 11; 12; 41:11; 42:4(4); 8; 10; 44:1; 2; 9; 17; 19; 45:1; 3; 7; 8; 12; 13; 15; 46:3; 7; 11; 47:1; 5(2); 7; 48:7; 50:5; 18(2); 51:7; 19(2); 54(2); 4; 55:20; 58:9; 59:7; 60:5; 10; 62:4; 63:5(2); 64:7; 65:4; 6; 10; 11(2); 13(2); 66:13; 15(2); 17(2); 68:13(2); 16; 19; 30(2); 69:3; 10; 28; 30(2); 71:8(2); 13; 22(2); 72:2(2); 19; 73:7; 19; 23; 24; 74:6; 75:5; 76:10; 77:1(2); 15; 78:14(2); 36(2); 37; 47(2); 58(2); 62; 79:12; 80:5; 10(2); 16; 81:2; 16(2); 83:5; 7; 8; 9(4); 15(2); 16; 84:6; 85:5; 86:12; 87:4; 88:4; 7; 89:1; 3; 10; 20; 21; 24; 28; 32(2); 38; 45; 51(2); 90:14; 91:4; 8; 15; 16; 92:3; 10; 93:1(2); 94:20; 95:2(2); 10; 96:13(2); 98:5(2); 6; 9(2); 100:2(2); 4(2); 101:2; 6; 102:9; 103:4; 5; 9; 10; 104:1; 2(2); 6(2); 13; 28; 105:9; 18; 25; 30; 37; 40; 43(2); 106:4(2); 5; 6; 29; 32; 33; 35; 38; 107:9; 12; 22; 108:1; 6; 11; 109:2; 3; 18(2); 19; 21; 29(3); 30; 110:6; 111:1; 112:5; 9; 113:8(2); 116:7; 118:27; 119:2; 7; 10; 13; 17; 20; 34; 58; 65; 69; 78; 98; 124; 145; 120:4; 6; 123:3; 4(2); 125:5; 126:2(2); 6(2); 127:5; 128:2; 129:7; 130:4; 7(2); 131:1(2); 2; 132:9; 15; 16; 18; 136:12(2); 138:1; 3; 139:3; 18; 22; 141:4; 142:1(2); 7; 143:2; 147:7; 8; 14; 20; 149:3(2); 4; 8(2); 150:3(2); 4(2); 5(2); **Prov** 1:11; 13; 15; 31; 2:16; 3:5; 9(2); 10(2); 15; 28; 30; 32; 4:23; 5:10; 17; 18; 19; 6:3; 12; 13(2); 22; 25; 32; 7:5; 10; 13; 14; 16; 17; 18; 20; 21(2); 8:8; 11; 12; 18; 24; 31; 10:9; 10; 22; 11:2; 9; 10; 12:11; 14; 21; 13:10; 16; 20; 14:1; 14; 18; 15:16(2); 17; 16:7; 8; 19(2); 17:1(2); 18:3; 19:2; 7; 23; 20:8; 13; 17; 19(2); 21:9; 19; 24; 27; 22:24(2); 27; 23:1; 7; 13; 14; 20(2); 21; 24:1; 4; 21; 28; 31(2); 25:9; 16; 24; 26:23(2); 24; 27:14; 16; 22(2); 28:4; 17; 20; 22; 23; 29:9; 14; 24; 30:8; 16; 19; 22; 28; 31; 31:13; 17; 21; 26; **Eccl** 1:8(2); 16; 2:1; 3(2); 9; 21; 22; 3:10; 4:6(2); 8; 15; 5:2; 10(2); 11; 20; 6:3; 4; 10; 7:11; 8:12; 13; 15; 9:7(2); 9; 10; 14; 10:13; 11:5; **Song** 1:2; 6; 10(2); 11; 2:3; 5(2); 13; 3:6(2); 7; 10; 11(2); 4:8(2); 9(2); 13(2); 14(2); 5:1(3); 2(2); 5(2); 12; 14(2); 6:1; 4; 10; 7:2; 6; 8:9; **Isa** 1:4; 6; 7; 22; 27(2); 2:6(2); 3:10; 11; 14; 16(2); 17; 5:2; 13; 18(2); 26; 6:2(3); 4; 6; 7; 10(3); 7:2; 20(3); 24; 25; 8:1; 10; 11; 9:7; 10(2); 12; 10:14; 15(2); 22; 24; 33; 34; 11:4(4); 6(2); 15; 12:1; 3; 13:9; 14:1; 6; 19; 20; 21; 23; 30; 15:3; 5; 16:4; 9(2); 14; 17:5; 18:1; 5; 19:23; 24; 20:4; 21:3; 7(2); 9; 14; 22:2; 6; 12; 21(2); 23:17; 24:2(12); 9; 12; 25:11; 26:9; 17; 18; 19; 27:1; 5(2); 6; 8; 28:1; 2; 11; 12; 15(2); 18(2); 27(3); 28(2); 29:3; 6(2); 9(2); 13(2); 30:23; 24; 27; 28; 29; 30(2); 31; 32(2); 33; 32:1; 7; 33:1(2); 5; 14(2); 15; 21; 34:3; 6(4); 7(4); 14; 15; 17; 35:2; 4(2); 7; 10(2); 36:2; 12; 13; 16; 22; 37:1; 2; 6; 9; 25; 33; 38; 38:3; 8; 20; 39:2; 40:9; 10(2); 11(2); 12; 14; 19; 31; 41:3; 4; 7(2); 10(2); 11; 12; 15; 43:2; 5; 23(3); 24(4); 44:5; 12(3); 13(3); 16; 45:9(2); 17; 47:3; 6; 12; 15; 48:20; 49:4(2); 18; 23; 25(2); 26(3); 50:2; 3; 8; 11; 51:11(2); 16; 21; 52:8; 12; 53:3; 9(2); 12(3); 54:1; 7; 8(2); 9; 11(3); 55:3; 12(2); 56:12; 57:5; 8; 9; 15; 58:4; 7; 14; 59:3(2); 6; 12; 17; 21; 60:5; 7; 9; 61:8; 10(4); 62:11; 63:1; 3; 11; 12; 64:11; 65:23; 66:10(3); 11(2); 15(4); **Jer** 1:8; 19; 2:22; 29; 37; 3:1; 2(2); 9; 10; 15; 18; 20; 4:8; 30(3); 5:11; 17; 6:3; 7(2); 11(2); 7:23; 8:8; 19(2); 9:4; 7; 8; 15; 18(2); 25; 10:3; 4(2); 24; 11:5; 10; 15; 16; 19; 12:1(2); 5(2); 6; 13:12(2); 13; 17; 14:3; 17(3); 18; 21; 15:7; 11(2); 14; 17; 20; 16:8; 18; 17:1(2); 18; 18:6; 10; 17; 18; 19; 23; 19:4; 5; 9; 10; 20:4; 11; 17; 18; 21:2; 4; 5(2); 7; 10; 22:7; 14(3); 15; 19; 23:15; 24:1; 7; 25:6; 7; 26; 31(2); 26:11; 12; 14; 21; 22; 23; 24; 27:8; 18; 28:4; 29:13; 16; 18(3); 23; 30:6(2); 11; 14(2); 23; 31:3(2); 4; 7; 8(2); 9(2); 14(2); 24; 27; 31(2); 32; 33; 32:4; 5; 21(3); 22; 29; 30; 40; 41(2); 33:5(2); 20(2); 21(2); 25; 34:2; 3; 8; 13; 22; 36:18(2); 22; 23; 27; 37:8; 10; 15; 38:6; 10; 11; 13; 17; 18; 20; 23; 25; 27; 39:3; 7; 8; 9; 40:4(2); 5; 6; 9; 41:1; 2(2); 3(2); 5(2); 7; 9; 11; 12; 13(2); 15; 16; 42:6; 8; 11; 17; 43:6; 12; 13; 44:8; 15; 25(2); 46:4; 10; 22(2); 25; 28; 47:5; 48:5; 32; 33; 39; 49:2; 3(2); 20; 50:4; 5; 33; 38; 39; 45; 51:5; 14(2); 20(2); 21(2); 22(3); 23(3); 28; 32; 34; 40; 42; 58; 59; 52:13; 14; 18; 22(2); 32; **Lam** 1:2; 7; 16; 2:1; 4; 10; 11; 13; 3:5; 9; 15; 16(2); 43; 44; 48; 4:6; 14; 5:6; 18; 22; **Ezek** 1:4; 15; 20; 21; 26; 27(2); 2:6; 3:3; 4; 10; 22; 24; 25; 27; 4:16(2); 17; 5:2(2); 11(2); 12; 7:18; 23; 27; 8:1; 16; 17; 18; 9:1(2); 2(2); 3; 6; 7; 11; 10:2(2); 4; 7; 12; 11:6; 13; 22; 12:7; 12; 18(2); 19(2); 13:10; 11; 12; 14; 15; 22; 14:11; 16:4; 8; 9; 10(2); 11; 13; 17; 26; 28(2); 36(2); 37; 40(2); 41; 43; 46; 59; 60(2); 61; 62; 17:3; 7; 12; 13; 16; 17; 21; 18:7; 16; 19:4; 7; 9; 20:6; 7; 15; 18; 28; 31; 33(3); 34(3); 35; 36(2); 39; 40; 43; 44; 21:6(2); 22; 23; 31; 22:4; 11; 14; 21; 28; 31; 23:7(3); 8; 10; 15; 17; 23; 24(2); 25; 29; 33; 37; 40; 41; 42(2); 43(2); 47(3); 24:4; 7; 12; 16; 23; 26; 25:6; 10; 15; 17; 26:7(4); 8; 9; 11; 16; 20(2); 27:6; 11; 14; 18(2); 21; 31(2); 33; 28:4; 13; 16; 29:7; 30:5; 11(2); 24; 31:3; 4; 9; 11; 16; 17(2); 18(2); 32:2; 3; 4; 5; 6; 7; 16; 18; 19; 21(2); 22; 24; 25(3); 26; 27(2); 28; 29(2); 30(3); 32; 33:25; 31; 34:3; 4; 18(2); 19(2); 21(2); 25; 29; 30; 35:8; 13; 36:5; 18; 38; 37:6; 19(2); 23(3); 26(2); 27; 38:4(2); 5(2); 6; 9; 15; 22(2); 39:4; 9; 10; 14; 20(3); 24; 40:4(2); 42; 41:13; 15; 16; 18; 42:16; 43:2; 7; 8; 13; 15; 17; 22; 44:5(2); 18; 45:2; 7; 24; 46:5; 7; 11; 14; 47:3; 14; 22; 48:8; 20; 34; **Dan** 1:2; 8(2); 13; 14; 2:11; 14; 18; 22; 41; 43(3); 3:5; 7; 10; 15; 4:15(3); 23(3); 25(2); 32; 33; 5:7; 16; 21(3); 29; 6:10; 14; 17(2); 20; 7:7; 13; 19(2); 8:6; 7; 18(2); 22; 9:3; 4(2); 15; 22; 26; 27; 10:5; 7; 9; 13; 17; 20; 11:3; 4; 6(3); 7(2); 8; 11(3); 13; 16; 17(3); 18; 22; 23(2); 25(2); 28; 32; 34(2); 38(2); 39; 40(2); 44; **Hos** 2:3; 6; 13; 18(3); 22(3); 3:3; 4:2; 3; 4; 5; 14(2); 5:5; 6; 7; 6:7; 8; 7:3(2); 5(2); 14; 9:1; 8; 11:4(2); 9; 12(4); 12:1; 3; 4; 13:16; 14:2; 8; **Joel** 1:8; 2:5; 12(4); 20; 24; 26; 3:2; 4; 18(3); **Am** 1:3; 11; 13; 2:2(2); 3; 3:15; 4:2(2); 5; 9; 10(2); 5:6; 14; 20; 6:6; 10(2); 12; 7:7(2); 9; 9:1; 13(2); **Ob** 7; **Jon** 1:3; 14; 2:6; 9; 3:6; 8; **Mic** 1:7; 2:4; 8; 10; 13; 3:5; 10(2); 5:1; 6; 6:2; 6(3); 7; 8; 11(2); 15; 7:2; 3; 14; **Nah** 1:8; 2:3; 7; 12(2); 3:3; 12; **Hab** 1:15; 2:6; 12; 14; 16; 19; 3:8; 9; 13; 14; 15; 16; 19; **Zeph** 1:3; 4; 8; 9; 12; 2:6; 8; 9; 3:6; 8; 9; 14; 17(3); 19; **Hag** 1:6(2); 12; 13; 2:3; 4; 5; 7; 12; 17; **Zech** 1:2; 6; 9; 13; 14(2); 15(2); 16; 19; 2:1; 3; 7; 3:3; 4; 4:1; 2(2); 4; 5; 7; 5:4; 5; 9; 10; 6:2(2); 3(2); 4; 6; 7:2; 14; 8:2(2); 4; 23(2); 9:8; 13; 14; 15(3); 10:5; 7; 9; 11; 11:10; 12:4(3); 13:6; 14:5; 12; 18; **Mal** 1:8; 2:3; 4; 5; 6; 10; 13(3); 14; 15; 16; 17; 3:9; 4:2; 4; 6; **Mt** 1:18; 23(2); 2:3; 10; 11; 3:4; 11(2); 12; 4:10; 21; 24; 5:22; 25(2); 28; 41; 6:16; 7:2(2); 8:5; 11; 14; 16; 24; 29; 9:10; 11; 15; 36; 12:3; 4; 30(2); 41; 42; 45(2); 46; 47; 13:15(3); 20; 29; 56; 14:7; 9; 14; 15:8(2); 20; 30; 32; 16:27; 17:3; 17(2); 18:9; 16; 23; 25; 26; 27; 29; 19:10; 26(2); 20:2; 8; 13; 15; 20; 22(2); 23(2); 24; 21:2; 22:10; 16; 25; 37(3); 23:4; 30; 24:30; 31; 49; 51; 25:3; 4; 10; 16; 19; 27(2); 31; 26:11; 18; 20; 23; 29; 35; 36; 37; 38; 40; 47(2); 51; 53; 55(2); 58; 67; 69; 71; 72; 27:7; 19; 22; 34; 38; 41; 44(2); 46; 48; 50; 54; 28:8; 12; 20; **Mk** 1:6(2); 8(2); 13; 20; 23; 24; 26; 27; 29; 30; 34; 36; 41; 2:15; 16(2); 19(2); 25; 26; 3:5; 6; 7; 14; 4:10; 16; 24; 30; 33; 36; 5:2; 3; 4; 5; 7(2); 17; 18; 24; 40; 42; 6:3; 13; 22; 25; 26; 34; 50; 7:2(2); 5; 6; 8:2; 4; 10; 11; 14; 34; 38; 9:1; 4(2); 8; 12; 14; 16; 19(2); 24; 47; 49(2); 50; 10:27(3); 30; 38(2); 39(2); 41; 46; 11:11; 12:30(4); 33(4); 13:26; 14:7; 14; 17; 18; 20; 31; 33; 43(2); 48; 49; 53; 54; 58; 62; 65; 67; 15:1; 7; 12; 17; 19; 23; 27; 28; 31; 32; 34; 37; 41; 16:10; 17; 20; **Lk** 1:15; 25; 28; 30; 37; 39; 41; 42; 51; 53; 56; 58; 66; 67; 78; 2:5(2); 13; 16; 36; 37; 40; 51; 52; 3:14; 16(2); 17; 18; 4:1; 28; 32; 33; 34; 36; 38; 40; 5:9; 10; 19; 26; 29; 30; 34; 6:3; 4; 11(2); 17(2); 18; 38; 7:3; 6; 11; 12; 29; 36; 38(3); 42; 44(2); 46(2); 49; 8:1; 7; 13; 14; 15(2); 16; 22; 23; 28(2); 29; 37; 38; 45; 9:30; 32(3); 39; 41(2); 49; 10:17; 27(4); 40; 11:7; 20; 23(2); 26; 31; 32; 37; 46(2); 12:13; 46; 47; 48; 50; 58(2); 13:1; 14; 14:9; 10; 15; 18; 25; 31(2); 15:2; 6; 9; 13; 16; 17; 28; 29; 30; 31; 16:21; 17:15; 20; 18:7; 11; 27(2); 19:7; 23; 37; 20:1; 21:5; 25; 27; 34; 22:4; 11; 14; 15(2); 21; 28; 33; 37; 48; 49; 52; 53; 56; 59; 23:9; 11(2); 12(2); 18; 23; 32; 35; 43; 46; 55; 24:1; 10; 15; 17; 24; 29(2); 30; 32; 33; 44; 49; 52; **Jn** 1:1; 2; 26; 31; 33(2); 35; 39; 2:4; 7; 15; 3:2; 22; 26; 4:9; 11; 27(2); 40; 5:18; 6:3; 13; 22; 66; 7:23; 24; 33; 8:6; 9; 16; 29; 38(2); 9:6(2); 37; 40; 11:2(2); 16; 31; 33; 43; 44(2); 54; 12:2; 3(2); 8; 17; 35; 40(2); 13:5(2); 8; 18; 33; 14:9; 16; 17; 23; 25; 27; 30; 15:27; 16:4; 32; 17:5(3); 12; 24; 26; 18:1; 2; 3; 5; 15; 18; 22; 26; 19:3; 15(2); 18; 29; 32; 34; 40; 20:7; 19; 24; 26; 21:3; 8; **Acts** 1:4; 5(2); 14(3); 17; 18; 22; 26; 2:1; 4(2); 14; 29; 30; 40; 46(2); 47; 3:4; 8; 10; 25; 4:8; 13; 14; 24; 27; 29; 31(2); 33; 5:1; 12; 17(2); 21(2); 26; 28; 40; 6:9; 7:9; 19; 38(2); 45; 48; 54; 57(2); 60(2); 8:6; 7; 11; 13; 20(2); 31; 37; 9:7; 17; 19; 28; 39(2); 43; 10:2; 6; 20; 23; 27; 28; 38(3); 41; 45; 46; 11:2; 3; 12; 16(2); 21; 23(2); 26; 12:2; 6; 17; 20(3); 25; 13:1; 7; 9; 16; 17; 18; 31; 36; 45; 52(2); 14:4(2); 5; 10; 13; 15; 17; 18; 20; 23; 27; 28; 15:2; 4; 15; 22(2); 24; 25(2); 32; 33; 35; 37; 38(2); 16:3; 9; 16; 22; 28; 34; 39; 17:2; 11; 15; 17(3); 23; 24; 25; 34; 18:2; 3; 8; 10; 12; 14; 18; 19; 20; 19:4; 6; 25; 26; 29(2); 33; 34; 20:2; 19(2); 24; 28; 31; 34; 36; 21:5; 7; 8; 12; 16(3); 18; 24; 26; 29; 33; 36; 40; 22:9; 11; 12; 22; 25; 28; 23:15; 27; 32; 24:1; 3; 7; 12; 18(2); 24; 26; 25:5; 12; 23(2); 24; 26:3; 12; 13; 24; 30; 27:2; 7; 8; 10; 16; 19; 24; 39; 28:14; 16; 20(2); 27(3); 31; **Rom** 1:4; 9; 12; 27; 29; 2:5; 11; 27; 3:13; 5:1; 6:4; 6(2); 8(2); 7:16; 18; 21; 25(2); 8:16; 17(2); 18; 22; 25; 26; 32; 9:14; 22; 10:9; 10(2); 11:2; 17; 27; 12:8(3); 10; 15(2); 16; 18; 21; 14:15; 20; 15:1; 6; 10; 13; 14; 30; 32(2); 33; 16:14; 15; 16; 20; 24; **1 Cor** 1:2; 10; 17; 2:1; 3; 4; 13; 3:2(2); 12; 19; 4:3; 8; 12; 21; 5:4(2); 8(3); 9; 10(2); 11(2); 12; 6:16; 17; 7:5; 9; 12; 13; 24; 8:7; 9:17; 23; 26; 10:5; 13; 20; 30; 11:5; 13; 32; 12:26(2); 30; 13:1; 14:5(2); 6; 15(4); 16; 18; 19; 21; 23; 39; 15:10; 32; 35; 16:4; 6; 7; 10; 11; 12; 14; 16; 19; 20; 21; 23; 24; **2 Cor** 1:1; 4(2); 12; 17; 21; 2:4; 7; 3:3; 18; 4:14(2); 5:1; 2; 8; 6:1(2); 14(3); 15(2); 16; 7:4; 7; 8; 15; 8:4; 18; 19(2); 22; 9:4; 13; 10:1; 2; 12; 14; 11:1(2); 2; 4; 9; 19; 20; 25; 29; 32; 12:8; 12; 18; 13:4; 11; 12; 14; **Gal** 1:2; 16; 18; 2:1(2); 3; 5; 12; 13(2); 20; 3:9; 4:18; 20; 25; 30; 5:1; 24; 6:6; 11(2); 18; **Eph** 1:3; 13; 2:4; 5; 19; 3:12; 16; 18; 19; 4:1; 2(3); 14; 19; 25; 28; 31; 5:6; 7; 11; 18(2); 26; 6:2; 3; 5; 6; 7; 9; 14; 15; 16; 18(2); 23; 24; **Phil** 1:1; 4; 7; 8; 11; 20; 23; 25; 27; 2:6; 12; 17; 18; 22(2); 23; 29; 4:3(2); 6; 9; 15; 21; 23; **Col** 1:9; 11(2); 2:4; 5; 7; 11; 12(2); 13; 19; 20; 22; 3:1; 3; 4; 9; 13; 16; 22; 4:2; 6(2); 9; 10; 18; **1 Th** 1:6; 2:4; 17; 3:4; 9; 13; 4:11; 14; 16(3); 17(2); 18; 5:10; 14; 26; 28; **2 Th** 1:6(2); 7(2); 9; 11; 2:5; 8(2); 9; 10; 3:1; 8; 10; 14; 16; 17; 18; **1 Tim** 1:14; 2:9(2); 10; 11; 15; 3:4; 6; 9; 4:2; 3; 4; 14; 5:2; 21; 6:3; 4; 6; 8; 10; 21; **2 Tim** 1:3; 4; 8; 9; 2:4; 10; 11(2); 12; 22; 3:6; 4:2; 11(2); 13; 16; 17; 22(2); **Titus** 1:1; 2:15; 3:13; 15(2); **Phm** 1:13; 19; 25; **Heb** 1:9; 2:4(2); 7; 9; 3:10; 17(2); 4:2; 15; 5:7; 7:21; 8:8(3); 9; 10; 9:4; 10; 11(2); 12(2); 19; 21; 22; 23(2); 24; 25; 10:1; 16; 22(2); 32; 11:7; 9(2); 25; 31(2); 37; 12:1; 7(2); 14; 17; 18; 20; 28; 13:3; 5; 9(3); 12; 16; 17(2); 22; 23; 25; **Jas** 1:6; 11; 17; 21; 2:1; 2; 4; 22; 3:9(2); 4:4(2); 5:12; 14; 17; **1 Pe** 1:8; 18; 19; 22; 2:18; 3:4; 6; 7(2); 15; 4:1; 4; 11; 13; 17; 5:5; 13; 14; **2 Pe** 1:1; 18; 2:3; 13; 16; 3:6; 8; 10(2); 12; 17; **1 Jn** 1:1; 2; 3(3); 6; 7; 2:1; 19; **2 Jn** 2; 3; 5; 12; **3 Jn** 10(2); 13; **Jude** 9; 12; 14; 23; 24; **Rev** 1:7; 12; 13(2); 2:16; 22; 23; 27; 3:4; 18; 20(2); 21(2); 4:1; 5:1; 2; 12; 6:1; 8(4); 10; 7:2; 9(2); 10; 8:3; 4; 5; 7; 8; 13; 9:9; 19; 10:1; 3; 11:6; 12:1(2); 2; 5; 7; 9; 17(2); 13:4; 7; 10(2); 14:1; 4; 7; 9; 10; 15; 18; 15:2; 6; 8; 16:8; 9; 17:1; 2(2); 4; 6(3); 12; 14(2); 16; 18:1; 2; 3; 8; 9; 16; 21; 19:2; 13; 15(2); 17; 20(2); 21(2); 20:4; 6; 21:3(3); 8; 9(2); 12; 15; 16; 19; 22:12; 21

YET (464/449)

Gen 6:3; 8:10; 12; 15:16; 18:29; 21:13; 31:7; 38:5; 40:23; 44:4; **Ex** 5:11; 18; 9:17; 30; 34; 10:7; 11:1; 21:22; 32:32; 33:12; **Lev** 5:17; 11:7; 21; 26:24; 44; **Num** 11:21; 26; **Deut** 1:32; 43; 5:24; 9:29; 12:9; 14:8; 22:17; 29:4; 31:27; 32:52; **Josh** 3:4; 13:1; 2; 14:11; 17:12; 18:2; **Judg** 1:35; 2:17; 10:13; 16:7; 8; 20:28; 21:14; **1 Sam** 3:6; 7(2); 10:22; 12:20; 15:30; 16:11; 24:11; 25:29; **2 Sam** 7:19; 14:14; 19:28; 43; 21:20; 23:5; **1 Ki** 8:28; 47; 14:8; 19:18; **2 Ki** 3:17; 5:18; 8:19; 13:23; 14:3; 17:13; 33; 41; **1 Chr** 5:2; 17:17; 20:6; **2 Chr** 6:6; 19; 37; 13:6; 14:7; 16:8; 12; 20:33; 21:7; 24:19; 30:18; **Ezra** 3:12; 9:9; 10:2; **Neh** 1:9; 2:16; 5:5; 18; 9:19; 28; 29; 30(2); 13:18; 26; **Esth** 4:11; 14; 5:13; **Job** 5:7; 8:7; 12; 21; 9:21; 31; 10:8; 13:15; 14:9; 17:9; 20:7; 14; 21:14; 32; 22:18; 24:11; 12; 23; 26:8; 29:5; 32:3; 33:10; 14; 34:19; 35:14; 36:2; 40:23; **Ps** 2:6; 37:10; 25; 36; 40:17; 42:5; 11; 43:5; 44:22; 49:20; 55:21; 71:14; 78:23; 56; 90:10; 94:7; 102:18; 107:41; 119:51; 83; 109; 110; 141; 143; 157; 129:2; 138:6; 139:16(2); **Prov** 6:31; 8:26; 11:24; 13:7(2); 19:7; 27:22; 30:12; 25; 26; 27; 31:15; **Eccl** 1:7; 2:14; 19; 21; 4:3; 8; 16; 6:2; 7; 8:12; 17; 9:15; 11:8; **Isa** 6:13; 10:7; 25; 32; 14:15; 17:6; 26:10; 27:10; 28:12; 29:2; 17; 30:20; 31:2; 42:25(2); 44:1; 11; 46:7; 10; 49:4; 15; 53:4; 7; 10; 56:8; 57:10; 58:2; **Jer** 2:9; 21; 22; 32; 35; 3:1; 8; 10; 4:27; 5:22(2); 28; 7:24; 26; 9:20; 11:8; 12:1; 14:9; 15:9; 18:23; 22:6; 17; 24; 23:21(2); 32; 25:7; 27:15; 30:11; 31:5; 32:25; 33; 34:4; 36:24; 28; 37:4; 40:5; 41:4; 44:28; 48:47; 51:33; 53; **Lam** 3:29; 32; **Ezek** 2:5; 3:19; 6:8; 11:16; 12:13; 13:6; 14:22; 16:31; 18:19; 25; 29; 20:13; 23:19; 44; 24:16; 28:2; 29:13; 18; 31:18; 32:25; 33:17; 20; 36:20; 44:11; **Dan** 2:41; 5:17; 7:12; 9:13; 10:9; 14; 11:33; 45; **Hos** 1:7; 10; 5:13; 7:9; 13; 15; 9:12; 13:4; **Am** 2:9(2); 4:6; 8; 9; 10; 11; 5:11; 6:12; 9:8; 9; **Jon** 2:4; 6; 3:4; **Mic** 1:15; 3:11; 5:2; 6:10; 7:13; **Nah** 1:12; 3:10; **Hab** 2:3; 19; 3:18; **Hag** 2:4; 17; 19; **Zech** 1:6; 8:20; **Mal** 1:2(2); 6; 2:12; 14(2); 17; 3:7; 8; 13; **Mt** 6:26; 29; 12:6; 16; 13:21; 15:17; 27; 16:9; 20:26; 24:6; **Mk** 6:26; 7:28; 8:17; 10:43; 13:7; 14:29; **Lk** 11:8; 12:27; 48; 15:29; 18:5; 22:27; **Jn** 2:4; 3:24; 4:27; 5:34; 6:36; 7:6; 8(2); 19; 30; 39(2); 8:16; 20; 55; 57; 9:30; 10:5; 11:30; 14:9; 15:19; 16:32; 19:41; 20:5; 9; 17; 29; 21:4; 12; 23; **Acts** 3:17; 5:13; 8:16; 12:15; 26:16; 28:4; 17; **Rom** 5:7; 6:17; 8:37; 9:11; 11:30; 14:15; **1 Cor** 2:6; 15; 3:15; 4:4; 15; 5:10; 7:10; 25; 8:2; 6; 9:2; 12:20; 31; 14:19; 21; 15:10; **2 Cor** 4:8; 16; 5:16; 6:8; 9(2); 10(3); 8:9; 9:3; 11:6; 12:5; 13:4; **Gal** 2:3; 3:12; 15; **Phil** 1:22; 2:25; 3:8; **Col** 1:21; 2:5; **2 Th** 3:15; **Phm** 1:9; **Heb** 2:8; 4:15; 5:8; 7:15; 9:8; 10:37; 11:7; 12:4; 26; 27; **Jas** 2:10; 4:2; **1 Pe** 1:8; 2:16; 4:16; **1 Jn** 3:2; **Jude** 9; **Rev** 17:8; 10; 12

YOU (14479/8372)

Gen 1:29(2); 2:16; 17(3); 3:1; 3(3); 4; 5(2); 9; 11(5); 12; 13; 14(4); 15(2); 16(2); 17(4); 18(2); 19(5); 4:6; 7(5); 10; 11; 12(3); 14; 6:15; 16(3); 18(4); 19(2); 20; 21(3); 7:1(2); 2(2); 8:16(2); 17(2); 9:2(2); 3(2); 4; 7; 9(2); 10(2); 11; 12(2); 15; 10:19(2); 30; 12:1; 2(3); 3(3); 11; 12(2); 13(2); 18(2); 19; 13:8; 9(3); 10; 14; 15(2); 17; 14:23; 15:2; 3; 5; 7(2); 15(3); 16:5(2); 6; 8(2); 11(3); 17:2(2); 4(2); 5; 6(3); 7(4); 8(3); 9(4); 10(4); 11(2); 12; 15; 16; 18; 19(2); 20; 21; 18:5(4); 10; 14; 15; 23; 24; 25(2); 28; 19:2; 5; 8(3); 9; 12(2); 15; 17(2); 19(2); 21(2); 22; 34; 20:3(2); 4; 6(3); 7(5); 9(4); 10(2); 13; 15(2); 16(2); 21:12; 17; 22(2); 23(4); 26; 29; 30; 22:2(2); 5; 12(2); 16; 17; 18; 23:4(2); 6(3); 9; 11(3); 13(2); 15; 24:3(2); 4; 5; 6; 7(2); 8(2); 14(2); 23; 31; 37; 38; 40(2); 41(4); 42; 47; 49; 50; 51; 58; 60; 25:18; 26:2; 3(3); 9; 10(2); 16; 24(2); 27(3); 28(3); 29(5); 27:4; 7; 8; 10(2); 18; 19; 20; 21(2); 24; 25; 28; 29(5); 32; 33; 36; 37; 38; 40(4); 42(2); 45(4); 28:1; 3(4); 4(5); 6; 13(2); 14(2); 15(6); 22(2); 29:4; 5; 14; 15(2); 18; 19; 25(3); 27(2); 30:2; 15(3); 16(2); 26(3); 29(2); 30(2); 31(3); 33; 31:3; 6; 12; 13(2); 16; 24; 26(2); 27(2); 28(2); 29(2); 30(3); 31; 32(2); 35; 36; 37(2); 38; 39(2); 41(2); 42(2); 43; 44(2); 48; 49; 50(3); 51; 52(2); 32:6; 9; 10; 12(2); 17(5); 18; 19(2); 26(2); 28; 29; 33:5; 8; 9; 10; 11; 12; 15; 34:10(2); 11; 12; 15(3); 16(2); 17; 30; 35:1(2); 2; 11; 12(2); 17; 37:8(2); 10(2); 13; 15; 32; 38:16(3); 17(2); 18; 23; 29(2); 39:9(2); 17; 40:7; 13(3); 14; 19(3); 41:15(2); 39(2); 40(2); 41; 55; 42:1; 7; 9(2); 12; 14(2); 15(2); 16(4); 19(2); 20; 22(2); 33; 34(4); 36(2); 37(2); 38(3); 43:3(2); 4(2); 5(3); 6(2); 7; 8; 9(3); 14; 23(2); 27; 29(2); 44:4(2); 5; 8; 10; 15(2); 17; 18; 19; 21; 23(3); 27; 29(2); 32; 45:4; 5(2); 7(2); 8; 10(4); 11(3); 12; 13(3); 18(2); 19; 24; 46:3; 4(2); 30; 33; 34(2); 47:5; 6(2); 8; 16; 23(3); 24; 25; 30(2); 48:2; 4(4); 5(2); 6; 20(2); 21(2); 22; 49:1(2); 2; 3; 4(3); 8(2); 9; 25(2); 50:5; 6; 17(3); 20(2); 21; 24(2); 25(2); **Ex** 1:16(2); 18; 22(2); 2:7(2); 9; 13; 14(3); 18; 20; 3:5; 10(2); 12(5); 13; 14(2); 15(2); 16(2); 17; 18(3); 19; 20; 21(2); 22(2); 4:1; 5; 8; 9(2); 10; 12(2); 13; 14(2); 15(3); 16(2); 17(2); 21(2); 22; 23(2); 25; 26; 5:4; 5; 7; 8(2); 10; 11; 14; 15; 17(2); 18(2); 19; 21(2); 22(2); 23; 6:1; 6(3); 7(3); 8(2); 29; 7:1; 2(2); 4; 9(2); 15(2); 16(3); 17; 8:2; 4; 9(2); 10; 11; 21(2); 22; 28(3); 29; 9:2; 14; 15(2); 16(2); 17(2); 19; 28(2); 29; 30(2); 10:2(2); 3; 4; 5(2); 7; 10(3); 11(2); 16; 24; 25; 28(2); 29; 11:1(3); 7; 8; 9; 12:2; 4; 5; 6; 10(2); 11(2); 13(5); 14(3); 15(2); 16(2);

17(2); 18; 20(2); 22(2); 23; 24(2); 25(3); 26(2); 27; 31(2); 32; 44; 46(2); 48; 49; 13:3(2); 4; 5(3); 6; 7(2); 8; 9(2); 10; 11(3); 12(2); 13(4); 14(2); 19(3); 14:2; 11(2); 12; 13(3); 14(2); 15; 15:7(3); 10; 11(2); 12; 13(3); 16; 17(2); 26(3); 16:3; 4; 6(2); 7(2); 8(2); 12(3); 15; 23(2); 25; 26; 28; 29(2); 32(2); 17:2(2); 3; 5(2); 6(2); 18:6; 10; 14(3); 17; 18(4); 19(3); 20; 21; 22(3); 23(3); 19:3; 4(3); 5(2); 6(2); 9(3); 12(2); 23; 24(2); 20:2; 3; 4; 5; 7; 9; 10(2); 12; 13; 14; 15; 16; 17(2); 19; 20(3); 22(3); 23(2); 24(4); 25(4); 26; 21:1; 2; 13; 14; 23; 22:18; 21(2); 22; 23; 24; 25(4); 26(2); 28; 29(2); 30(2); 31(3); 23:1; 2(2); 3; 4(2); 5(4); 6; 8; 9(3); 10; 11(2); 12(2); 13; 14; 15(4); 16(2); 18; 19(2); 20(3); 22; 23(2); 24(2); 25(2); 27(3); 28(2); 29(2); 30(3); 31(2); 32; 33(3); 24:1; 8; 12(2); 14(2); 25:2; 3; 9(2); 11(2); 12; 13; 14; 16(2); 17; 18(2); 19; 21(3); 22(3); 23; 24; 25(2); 26; 28; 29(2); 30; 31; 37; 40(2); 26:1(2); 4(2); 5(2); 6; 7(2); 9(2); 10; 11; 14; 15; 17; 18; 19; 22; 23; 26; 29; 30(2); 31; 32; 33(3); 34; 35(2); 36; 37(2); 27:1; 2(2); 3(2); 4(2); 5; 6; 8(2); 9; 20(2); 28:2; 3; 9; 11(2); 12; 13; 14; 15(3); 17; 22; 23; 24; 25; 26; 27; 30; 31; 33; 36; 37; 39(3); 40(3); 41(2); 42; 29:1; 2; 3; 4(2); 5; 6; 7; 8; 9(2); 10; 11; 12; 13; 14; 15; 16(2); 17; 18; 19; 20; 21; 22; 24(2); 25; 26; 27; 31; 34; 35(3); 36(4); 37; 38; 39(2); 41(2); 42(2); 30:1(2); 3(2); 4(2); 5; 6(2); 9(2); 12(3); 15; 16; 18(3); 25; 26; 29; 30; 31; 32(2); 35; 36(3); 37(3); 31:6; 11; 13(4); 14(2); 32:4; 7; 8; 10; 11; 13; 21(2); 22; 29; 30; 32(2); 34(2); 33:1(2); 2; 3(2); 5(3); 12(6); 13; 14(2); 16; 17(3); 19(2); 20; 21; 22(2); 23; 34:1; 3; 10(2); 11(2); 12(2); 13; 14; 15(3); 16; 17; 18(4); 20(4); 21(3); 22; 24(2); 25; 26(2); 27; 35:1; 2; 3; 5; 10; 40:2; 3; 4(2); 5; 6; 7; 8; 9(2); 10; 11; 12; 13; 14; 15(2); **Lev** 1:2(2); 2:4; 6; 8; 11(2); 12; 13(3); 14(2); 15; 3:17; 6:21(2); 27; 7:23; 24; 26; 32; 8:32; 33(2); 34; 35(2); 9:3; 4; 6(2); 10:6; 7(3); 9(4); 10; 11; 13; 14(3); 15; 17(2); 18; 11:2; 3; 4(2); 5; 6; 7; 8(3); 9(2); 10; 11(3); 12; 13; 20; 21; 22; 23; 24; 26; 27; 28; 29; 31; 33; 35; 38; 39; 42; 43(3); 44(3); 45(2); 13:55; 57; 58; 14:34(2); 15:31; 16:29(3); 30(3); 31(2); 34; 17:8(2); 10; 11; 12(2); 13; 14; 18:3(5); 4; 5; 6; 7(2); 8; 9; 10; 11; 12; 13; 14(2); 15(2); 16; 17(2); 18; 19; 20; 21(2); 22; 23; 24; 26(2); 27; 28(3); 30(4); 19:2; 3; 5(2); 6; 9(3); 10(3); 11; 12(2); 13(2); 14; 15(3); 16(2); 17(2); 18(2); 19(4); 23(3); 25(2); 26(2); 27(2); 28(2); 30; 32; 33(2); 34(5); 35; 36(2); 37; 20:2; 8(2); 14; 15; 16; 19; 22(3); 23(2); 24(4); 25(3); 26(3); 21:8(3); 22:19; 20; 22; 23; 24(2); 25; 29; 30; 31; 32(2); 33; 23:2; 3; 4; 6; 7(2); 8(2); 10(3); 12(2); 14(2); 15(2); 16; 17; 18; 19; 21(3); 22(5); 24; 25(2); 27(2); 28(2); 31; 32(3); 35; 36(4); 37; 38; 39(2); 40(2); 41(2); 42; 24:2; 5; 6; 7; 15; 22; 25:2(2); 3(2); 4; 5; 6(3); 8(2); 9(2); 10(4); 11(2); 12(2); 13; 14(2); 15(2); 16(3); 17(2); 18(2); 19; 20; 21; 22(2); 23; 24; 35(3); 36; 37; 38(2); 39(3); 40(2); 41; 43(2); 44(3); 45(3); 46(3); 47(2); 26:1(3); 2; 3; 4; 5; 6(2); 7(2); 8(3); 9(4); 10; 11(2); 12(2); 13(3); 14; 15(2); 16(3); 17(6); 18(2); 21(2); 22(3); 23; 24(2); 25(4); 26; 27; 28(2); 29(2); 30; 33(2); 34; 35; 36; 37; 38(2); 39; 27:12; **Num** 1:3; 4; 5; 49; 50; 3:9; 10; 15; 41; 47(2); 48; 4:23; 27; 29; 30; 32; 5:3(2); 19(2); 20(3); 21; 6:23; 24(2); 25(2); 26(2); 7:5; 8:2; 7; 8; 9(2); 10; 12; 13; 14; 15; 26; 9:3(2); 8; 10; 14(2); 10:2(2); 3; 4; 5; 6; 7; 8; 9(5); 10(2); 29(2); 31(2); 32(2); 35(2); 11:11(2); 12(2); 15; 16(2); 17(4); 18(5); 19; 20(3); 21; 23(2); 29; 12:4; 6; 8; 13:2; 27; 14:12; 13; 14(3); 15; 17; 19; 28(2); 29(2); 30(2); 31(2); 32; 34(3); 41; 42(2); 43(4); 15:2(3); 3; 5; 6; 7; 8; 10; 12(2); 14(3); 15(3); 16(2); 18(2); 19(2); 20(2); 21; 22; 23; 29; 39(3); 40; 41; 16:3(2); 7(2); 8; 9(3); 10(4); 11(2); 13(2); 14(2); 16(2); 17(2); 22; 26; 28; 30; 41; 17:3; 4(2); 5; 10; 18:1(4); 2(5); 3; 4(2); 5; 6; 7(4); 8(2); 9; 10(2); 11(2); 12; 15(2); 16; 17(2); 19(4); 20(2); 26(3); 27; 28(3); 29; 30(2); 31(2); 32(4); 19:2; 3; 20:4; 5; 8(2); 10(2); 12(2); 14; 18(2); 20; 24; 21:2; 5; 7; 17; 29(2); 34(2); 22:6(2); 8; 9; 12(2); 13; 16; 17(2); 19; 20(3); 28(2); 29(2); 30(2); 32(2); 33; 34(2); 35(2); 37(4); 38; 23:3; 5; 11(3); 13(2); 16; 26; 27(2); 24:9(2); 10(2); 11(2); 12; 14; 22; 25:5; 18(2); 26:54(2); 27:7; 8(2); 9; 10; 11; 13(2); 14; 18; 20; 28:2; 3(2); 4(2); 7; 8(2); 11; 18(2); 19; 20; 21; 22; 23; 24; 25(2); 26(3); 27; 30; 31; 29:1(3); 2; 5; 7(3); 8; 12(3); 13; 35(2); 36; 39; 31:2; 4; 15; 19; 23(2); 24(2); 26; 30; 32:6; 7; 14; 15(2); 20(2); 22; 23(3); 29(3); 30(2); 33:51; 52(2); 53(2); 54(4); 55(5); 56; 34:2(2); 6; 7; 8; 10; 13; 17; 18; 35:2; 4; 5; 6(3); 7(2); 8(3); 10; 11(2); 12; 13(2); 14(2); 29; 31; 32; 33(2); 34; **Deut** 1:6; 8; 9(2); 10(2); 11(4); 13; 14(2); 15; 17(4); 18(2); 19; 20(2); 21(2); 22; 26; 27; 29; 30(3); 31(4); 32; 33(4); 37; 38; 39; 40; 41(3); 42(2); 43(2); 44(3); 45(2); 46(2); 2:3; 4(2); 5; 6(4); 7(3); 9; 18; 19(2); 25(3); 28; 31(2); 37; 3:2(2); 18(3); 19(2); 20(3); 21; 22(2); 24; 27; 28; 4:1(3); 2(4); 3; 4(2); 5(3); 8; 9; 10; 11; 12(3); 13(2); 14(3); 15(2); 16; 19(3); 20(3); 21; 22; 23(3); 25; 26(4); 27(3); 28; 29(3); 30(3); 31(2); 32; 33; 34; 35(2); 36(4); 37; 38(4); 40(6); 5:1; 4; 5(4); 6; 7; 8; 9; 11; 12; 13; 14(3); 15(3); 16(3); 17; 18; 19; 20; 21(2); 23(2); 24; 27(2); 28(2); 31(3); 32(3); 33(6); 6:1(3); 2(3); 3(3); 5; 6; 7(5); 8; 9; 10(3); 11(4); 12(2); 13; 14(2); 15(3); 16(2); 17(2); 18(3); 19; 20(2); 21; 7:1(4); 2(3); 3(2); 4(2); 5(2); 6(2); 7(4); 8(3); 11(2); 12(2); 13(4); 14(2); 15(4); 16(4); 17; 18(2); 19(2); 20; 21(2); 22(3); 23; 24(3); 25(3); 26(3); 8:1(3); 2(5); 3(5); 4; 5(2); 6; 7; 9(3); 10(3); 11(2); 12; 13; 14(2); 15(2); 16(4); 17; 18(2); 19(3); 20(3); 9:1; 2(2); 3(4); 4(2); 5(2); 6(2); 7(4); 8(3); 9; 10; 12; 14; 16(3); 18; 19(2); 21; 22; 23(4); 24(2); 25; 26(2); 28; 29; 10:2(2); 4; 10; 12; 13; 15; 19; 20(3); 21; 22; 11:1; 4; 5(2); 8(4); 9; 10(3); 11; 13(2); 14(2); 15; 16; 17(3); 18; 19(5); 20; 22(2); 23(2); 25(5); 26; 27(2); 28(3); 29(3); 31(3); 32(2); 12:1(3); 2(2); 3(2); 4; 5(2); 6; 7(5); 8; 9(2); 10(4); 11(3); 12(3); 13(2); 14(3); 15(2); 16(2); 17(2); 18(4); 19(2); 20(4); 21(5); 22; 23(2); 24(2); 25(4); 26(2); 27(2); 28(4); 29(3); 30(3); 31; 32(2); 13:1(2); 2(2); 3(3); 4(2); 5(6); 6(3); 7(3); 8(2); 9; 10(3); 11; 12(2); 13(2); 14(2); 15; 16; 17(3); 18(2); 14:1(2); 2(2); 3; 4; 6; 7(2); 8(2); 9(2); 10(2); 11; 12; 19; 20; 21(5); 22; 23(2); 24(4); 25; 26(4); 27(2); 28; 29(3); 15:1; 3(2); 4(3); 5(2); 6(6); 7(3); 8; 9(3); 10(4); 11(2); 12(4); 13(3); 14(3); 15(4); 16(4); 17(2); 18(6); 19(2); 20; 21; 22; 23(2); 16:1; 2; 3(5); 4(2); 5(2); 6(2); 7(2); 8(2); 9(2); 10(3); 11(3); 12(3); 13(2); 14(2); 15(3); 17; 18(2); 19(2); 20(3); 21(2); 22; 17:1; 2(2); 4(3); 5; 7(2); 8(2); 9(2); 10(4); 11(5); 12; 14(2); 15(6); 16(2); 18:4; 9(3); 10; 12; 13; 14(3); 15(2); 16; 18; 21; 22; 19:1(2); 2(2); 3(2); 7(2); 8; 9(3); 10(2); 13(2); 14(3); 19(3); 20; 20:1(4); 2; 3; 4(3); 10; 11(3); 12(3); 13; 14(3); 15(2); 16(2); 17(2); 18(2); 19(3); 20(3); 21:1; 8; 9(3); 10(2); 11; 12; 13; 14(5); 21(2); 22; 23(3); 22:1(2); 2(5); 3(5); 4(2); 6(2); 7(3); 8(3); 9(2); 10; 11; 12(2); 21(2); 22; 24(4); 26; 23:4(4); 5(2); 6; 7(3); 10; 12(2); 13(3); 14(4); 15(2); 16(2); 18; 19; 20(5); 21(4); 22(2); 23(3); 24(3); 25(3); 24:4(2); 7(2); 8(3); 9; 10(2); 11(3); 12; 13(3); 14; 15(3); 17; 18(4); 19(3); 20(2); 21(2); 22(3); 25:4; 12; 13; 14; 15(2); 17(2); 18(2); 19(4); 26:1(3); 2(3); 3; 5; 10(2); 11(4); 12; 13(2); 14; 15(2); 16(2); 17(3); 18(3); 19(2); 27:1; 2(3); 3(5); 4(4); 5(2); 6; 7; 8; 9; 10(2); 12; 28:1(3); 2(3); 3(2); 6(4); 7(3); 8(4); 9(3); 10(2); 11(2); 12(3); 13(4); 14(2); 15(4); 16(2); 19(4); 20(5); 21(3); 22(3); 23; 24(2); 25(3); 27(2); 28; 29(4); 30(4); 31(4); 33(2); 34; 35; 36(5); 37(2); 38; 39(2); 40(2); 41; 43(3); 44(3); 45(5); 46; 47; 48(3); 49(2); 51(3); 52(4); 53(3); 54; 55; 56; 57; 58(2); 59; 60(3); 61(2); 62(3); 63(8); 64(3); 65(2); 66(2); 67(2); 68(5); 29:2; 4; 5(2); 6(3); 7; 9(2); 10; 12(2); 13(3); 14; 16(2); 17; 18(2); 22; 30:1(4); 2(3); 3(4); 4(3); 5(4); 6; 7(2); 8(2); 9(2); 10(2); 11(2); 12; 13; 14(2); 15; 16(4); 17; 18(4); 19(3); 20(4); 31:2; 3(4); 5(3); 6(3); 7(2); 8(4); 11; 13(2); 14; 16; 23(2); 26; 27(2); 29(4); 32:6(4); 7(2); 14; 15(3); 18(3); 38; 46(2); 47(3); 50; 51(2); 52(3); 33:7; 8(2); 10; 26; 27; 29(4); 34:4(2); **Josh** 1:2; 3; 5(4); 6; 7(4); 8(4); 9(3); 11(2); 13(3); 14(2); 15(3); 16(2); 17(2); 18; 2:3; 5; 9(3); 10(4); 11; 12(3); 14(2); 16(2); 17; 18(3); 19; 20(2); 3:3(2); 4(4); 5; 7(2); 8(3); 10(3); 11; 4:3(3); 5; 6(2); 7; 22; 23(2); 24; 5:9; 13; 15; 6:3(4); 4; 5; 10(3); 16; 18(3); 22; 7:7; 9; 10; 12(3); 13(3); 14; 19(2); 25(2); 8:1; 2(3); 4(2); 7; 8(4); 9:7(2); 8(2); 11; 12; 22(3); 23(2); 24(3); 10:8; 25; 11:6; 13:1; 6; 14:6(2); 9; 12; 15:18; 19; 17:14; 15(2); 17(2); 18(2); 18:3(2); 4; 6(2); 7; 8; 20:2; 22:2(3); 3; 4; 5; 16(3); 18(2); 24; 25(3); 27(2); 28; 31(2); 23:3(3); 4; 5(3); 6; 7(4); 8(2); 9(3); 10(3); 11; 12(3); 13(4); 14(3); 15(5); 16(5); 24:5; 6; 7(2); 8(4); 9; 10(2); 11(2); 12(2); 13(6); 15(3); 19; 20(4); 22(2); 23; 27(2); **Judg** 1:3; 14; 15; 24; 2:1(3); 2(4); 3(2); 3:19; 20; 4:6; 7; 8(2); 9(3); 14; 20(2); 22(2); 5:4(2); 10; 14; 16; 6:8(2); 9(4); 10(3); 12(2); 14(2); 16(2); 17; 18(3); 23(2); 26; 31(2); 36(2); 37(2); 7:2; 4(6); 5; 7; 10; 11; 17; 18; 8:1(2); 2; 3; 15; 18(2); 19(2); 22(2); 23(3); 24(2); 9:2(3); 7(2); 10; 12; 14; 15(2); 16(2); 17(2); 18; 19(2); 31; 32(2); 33(4); 36; 38(3); 48; 10:10; 11; 12(3); 13(2); 14(2); 15; 11:2(2); 7(3); 8(2); 9; 12(2); 23; 24(2); 25; 26; 27(2); 30; 35(2); 36(2); 12:1(3); 2(2); 3(2); 4; 5; 13:3(2); 5; 7; 8; 11; 15(2); 16(3); 17; 18; 14:3; 12(3); 13(2); 15(2); 16(5); 18(2); 15:2; 7(2); 10; 11(2); 12(3); 13(3); 18; 16:5; 6(2); 9; 10(2); 12; 13(3); 14; 15(3); 20; 17:2(3); 3; 9; 10; 18:3(3); 6; 9; 10(2); 14(2); 18; 19(2); 23(2); 24(4); 25(2); 19:9; 17(2); 20; 23; 24; 20:7; 12; 21:11(2); 22; **Ruth** 1:8(2); 9; 10; 11; 13(2); 16(4); 17(2); 21; 2:4(2); 8(2); 9(2); 10; 11(3); 12(2); 13; 19(3); 21; 22(2); 3:1(2); 2; 4(4); 5; 9(2); 10(3); 11(3); 13(3); 15; 16; 18; 4:4(5); 5(2); 6; 9; 10; 11; 12; 14; 15(3); **1 Sam** 1:8(3); 11; 14(2); 17; 23(2); 26; 2:2; 15; 16(2); 20; 23; 24; 29; 32; 34; 3:5; 6; 8; 9(2); 17(4); 4:9(3); 20; 6:3(4); 4; 5(3); 6; 8; 21; 7:3(3); 5; 8:5; 7(2); 8; 9; 11; 17; 18(3); 9:3; 12; 13(3); 16(2); 17; 19(3); 20; 21; 23(2); 24(2); 26; 27(2); 10:1; 2(5); 3(2); 4(3); 5(3); 6(2); 7(3); 8(6); 14; 15; 18(2); 19(3); 24; 11:1; 2; 3; 9(2); 10(3); 12:1(2); 2(3); 3; 4(2); 5(2); 7(2); 10; 11(2); 12(3); 13(3); 14(3); 15(2); 17(2); 20; 21; 22; 23(2); 24; 25(3); 13:11(2); 13(3); 14(2); 14:7; 9; 12; 33; 36; 37; 38; 40(2); 43; 44; 15:1; 6(2); 13; 16; 17(3); 18; 19(2); 23(2); 26(3); 28(2); 16:1(2); 2; 3(4); 4; 15; 16(3); 17:8(2); 9; 25; 28(3); 33(2); 37; 43; 45(3); 46(3); 47; 58; 18:17; 21; 22(2); 23; 25; 19:2; 3(3); 4(2); 5(2); 11(2); 17(2); 20:2; 4(2); 8(4); 9(3); 10; 12(2); 13(5); 14; 15; 18; 19(2); 21(2); 22(2); 23(2); 30(2); 31; 37; 42; 21:1(2); 2(2); 3; 9(2); 14(2); 15; 22:3; 7(3); 8(2); 13(3); 16(2); 18; 23; 23:12; 17(3); 21(2); 23; 24:4(3); 9; 10(3); 11(3); 12(3); 13; 14; 15; 17(3); 18(3); 19(2); 20; 21(2); 25:6(3); 7; 8; 17; 19; 25; 26; 28; 29; 30(2); 31(2); 32; 33(2); 34(2); 40(2); 26:6; 14(2); 15(3); 16(3); 19; 21; 23; 25(2); 27:5; 8; 10; 28:1(3); 2(2); 8; 9(2); 10; 11; 12(2); 13; 15(3); 16(2); 18(2); 19(2); 21; 22(3); 29:4; 6(3); 7; 8(2); 9; 10(2); 30:8; 13(2); 15(3); 23; 24; 26; **2 Sam** 1:3; 5; 8; 13; 14; 16; 21; 24; 26(2); 2:5(2); 6(3); 20; 22; 26(2); 27; 3:7; 8(2); 12(2); 13(5); 17(2); 21(2); 24(3); 25(3); 34; 38; 4:11; 5:2(3); 6(2); 19; 23; 24(3); 6:22; 7:3; 5; 7; 8(2); 9(4); 11(3); 12(2); 15; 16; 18; 19; 20(2); 21; 22(3); 23; 24(2); 25(2); 26; 27(3); 28(2); 29(3); 9:2; 7(3); 8; 10(2); 10:3(3); 11(3); 11:10(2); 11; 12; 19; 20(4); 21(2); 25(2); 12:7(3); 8(3); 9(3); 10; 11; 12; 13; 14(2); 21(3); 13:4(2); 5; 13(3); 16; 20; 25; 26; 28(2); 14:5; 8; 10(2); 13; 17; 18; 19(2); 32(2); 15:2; 3; 10(2); 19(2); 20(3); 26; 27(2); 28; 33(2); 34(2); 35(4); 36(2); 16:2; 4; 7(2); 8(4); 10(3); 17; 21(2); 17:3(2); 8; 11(2); 21; 18:2; 3(3); 4; 11(3); 12; 13; 14; 20(3); 21; 22(2); 31(2); 32; 19:5; 6(4); 7(4); 10; 11; 12(3); 13(2); 14; 22(3); 23; 25; 28; 29(2); 33(2); 37; 38(3); 41; 42; 43(2); 20:9; 16; 17; 19(2); 21; 21:3(2); 4(3); 17(2); 22:3; 26(2); 27(2); 28(2); 29; 30; 36; 37; 40(2); 41; 44(2); 49(2); 50; 24:12(2); 13(3); 21; 23; 24; **1 Ki** 1:6; 11; 12(2); 13; 14(2); 17; 18; 20(3); 24; 27; 30; 33; 35; 42; 45; 2:3(3); 4; 5; 8(3); 9(2); 13; 14; 15; 16; 17; 18; 20(2); 22; 26(4); 31; 37(2); 42(5); 43(2); 44(2); 3:5; 6(5); 7; 8; 11; 12(5); 13(3); 14; 5:3; 6(3); 8(2); 9(3); 6:12(3); 8:13(2); 18; 19; 23(2); 24(3); 25(3); 26; 27; 28; 29(2); 30(2); 33(3); 34; 35(2); 36(2); 39(2); 40(2); 43(2); 44(2); 46(2); 47; 48(4); 50(2); 51; 52; 53(3); 9:3(2); 4(3); 5; 6(2); 13; 10:8; 9(3); 11:2(2); 11(3); 22(2); 31; 35; 37(3); 38(5); 12:4; 6; 7; 9; 10(4); 11(3); 14(2); 24; 28(2); 13:2(3); 7; 8(2); 9(2); 14; 16(3); 17(2); 18(2); 21(2); 22(2); 14:2; 3(2); 5(2); 6(2); 7(2); 8(2); 9(3); 15:19(2); 16:2(3); 17:4(2); 9; 13; 18(2); 20; 24; 18:7; 9; 10(2); 11; 12(3); 14; 17; 18(2); 21; 24; 25; 36; 37(3); 44; 19:7; 9; 13; 15; 16(2); 20(2); 20:4; 5(2); 6; 9; 13(2); 14; 22(2); 25(2); 28; 34(2); 36(3); 39; 40; 42; 21:2(3); 3; 4; 5; 6(3); 7(2); 10; 15; 19(3); 20(3); 21; 22; 22:3; 4(2); 11; 16(2); 18; 22; 23; 24; 25(2); 28(2); 30; **2 Ki** 1:3; 4(3); 5; 6(5); 7(2); 10; 12; 16(4); 2:2; 3(2); 4; 5(2); 6; 9(2); 10(4); 16; 18; 23(2); 3:7(2); 13; 14(2); 17(3); 19; 4:1; 2(2); 4(3); 7; 13(3); 16; 23; 24; 26; 29(2); 30; 5:6(3); 8; 10(2); 13(3); 25; 26(2); 27; 6:1; 9; 11; 12; 19(2); 22(3); 27(2); 28; 32; 7:2(2); 12; 19(2); 8:1(2); 9; 10; 12(4); 13; 14(2); 9:2; 3; 5(2); 6; 7; 11(2); 12; 15; 18; 19; 25; 26; 10:2(3); 5; 6; 9; 13; 23; 30; 11:5(2); 6; 7; 8(2); 12:7; 13:17(2); 19(4); 14:10(6); 17:12; 13; 26; 27; 35; 36(4); 37(3); 38(3); 39(2); 18:14; 19; 20(3); 21; 22(2); 23(3); 24; 27(2); 29(2); 30; 31(2); 32(3); 19:6(2); 9; 10(3); 11(2); 15(3); 19(2); 20; 21(2); 22(2); 23; 25(2); 28(2); 29(2); 20:1; 3; 5(2); 6; 9; 14; 18(2); 19; 22:15; 18(3); 19(4); 20(2); 23:17; 25:24; **1 Chr** 4:10(2); 11:2(3); 5; 12:17(2); 18(2); 13:2; 14:10; 14; 15(3); 15:12(3); 13; 16:13; 18; 19; 17:2; 4; 6; 7(2); 8(4); 10(2); 11(2); 13; 16; 17; 18(2); 19; 20(2); 21; 22(2); 23(2); 24; 25(3); 26; 27(3); 19:3(3); 12(3); 21:10(2); 12; 22; 23; 22:8(3); 9; 11(3); 12(3); 13(2); 14; 15; 16; 18(2); 28:3(2); 8(2); 9(5); 10; 20(4); 21; 29:10; 11; 12(2); 13; 14(2); 15; 16; 17(2); 18; **2 Chr** 1:7; 8; 9; 11(4); 12(4); 2:3; 11; 16(3); 6:2(2); 8; 9; 14(2); 15(3); 16(3); 17; 18; 19; 20(3); 21(2); 24(2); 25; 26(2); 27(2); 30(2); 31(2); 33(2); 34(3); 36(2); 37; 38(3); 39; 41; 7:17(4); 18; 19(2); 9:6; 7; 8(3); 10:4; 6; 7; 9; 10(4); 11(3); 14(2); 11:4; 12:5(2); 13:5; 8(4); 9; 11; 12(2); 14:11(4); 15:2(6); 7; 16:3(2); 7; 8; 9(2); 18:3(3); 10; 15(2); 17; 21; 22; 23; 24(2); 27(2); 29; 19:2(2); 3(2); 6(3); 7; 9; 10(4); 11(2); 20:2; 6(3); 7; 8; 9(2); 10; 11; 12(2); 15(4); 16; 17(3); 20(3); 37; 21:12; 15; 23:4(2); 7; 24:5; 6; 20(4); 25:7; 8(2); 9; 15; 16(4); 19(6); 26:18(3); 28:9; 10(2); 11(2); 13(2); 29:8; 11(2); 31; 30:6; 7; 8; 9(3); 32:10(2); 11; 12; 13; 14; 15(3); 34:23; 26(3); 27(5); 28(2); 35:21(3); 36:23; **Ezra** 1:3; 4:2(2); 3; 12; 15; 16; 18; 22; 5:3; 9; 10; 6:8; 7:13; 14; 15; 16; 18; 19; 20; 21; 24; 25; 8:28; 29; 9:6; 11(2); 12; 13; 14(2); 15(3); 10:4; 10; 12; **Neh** 1:5(2); 6(3); 7(2); 8(3); 9(2); 10; 2:2; 4; 5; 6; 17; 19(2); 20; 4:5(2); 12; 20; 5:7; 8; 9(2); 11; 12; 6:3; 6(3); 7(2); 8(2); 10(2); 9:6(4); 7; 8(4); 9; 10(3); 11(2); 12; 13; 14; 15(2); 17(2); 18; 19; 20; 21; 22; 23(2); 24; 26; 27(4); 28(5); 29; 30(2); 31(2); 32; 33(2); 34; 35(3); 36; 37; 13:17(2); 18; 21(3); 25; **Esth** 3:3; 11(2); 4:13; 14(3); 5:3(2); 6; 6:10(2); 13(2); 7:2; 8:8(2); 9:12; **Job** 1:7; 8; 10(2); 11; 15; 16; 17; 19; 2:2; 3(2); 5; 9; 10; 4:2(2); 3(2); 4; 5(4); 5:1(2); 19(2); 20; 21(2); 22(2); 23(2); 24(2); 25; 26; 6:21(2); 26; 27(2); 7:12; 14; 17(2); 18; 19; 20(2); 21(2); 8:2; 5; 6(2); 10(2); 18; 22; 9:12; 28; 31; 10:2; 3(3); 4(2); 6; 7; 8; 9(2); 10; 12; 13(2); 14; 16(2); 17; 18; 11:3(2); 4; 5; 6(2); 7(2); 8(2); 13; 14; 15(2); 16; 17(2); 18(3); 19(2); 12:2(2); 3(2); 7(2); 8(2); 13:2(2); 4(2); 5; 7; 8(2); 9(2); 10(2); 11(2); 20; 21; 22; 24; 25(2); 26; 27(2); 14:3; 5(2); 13(3); 15(3); 16; 17; 19; 20(2); 15:4; 5; 6(2); 7(2); 8(2); 9(2); 11(2); 12; 13; 17; 16:2; 3(2); 4(3); 5; 7; 8; 17:4(2); 10(2); 14(2); 18:2; 4(2); 19:2; 3(3); 5; 21; 22; 28; 29; 20:4; 21:27; 28; 29(2); 34; 22:3(2); 4(2); 6; 7(2); 9; 10(2); 11(2); 13; 15; 21; 23(3); 24; 26; 27(3); 28(2); 29(2); 26:2(2); 3(2); 4(2); 27:5; 11; 12(2); 30:20(3); 21(2); 22(2); 23; 31:24; 32:6(2); 11; 12(2); 13; 33:5; 7(2); 8; 12(2); 13; 32(2); 33; 34:2(2); 10; 16; 17; 18(2); 33(3); 35:2(2); 3(2); 4(2); 5; 6(3); 7(2); 8; 14(3); 36:2; 4; 16; 17(2); 18(2); 19; 21; 23; 37:15; 16; 18; 38:3(2); 4(2); 5; 11; 12; 16(2); 17(2); 18(2); 20(2); 21(2); 22(2); 31; 32(2); 33(2); 34(2); 35(2); 39; 39:1(2); 2(2); 9; 10(2); 11(2); 12; 19(2); 20; 40:4; 7(2); 8(3); 9(2); 14(2); 15; 41:1(2); 2; 3(2); 4(2); 5(2); 7; 42:2(2); 3; 4(3); 5(2); 7(2); 8(3); **Ps** 2:7(2); 8; 9(2); 10; 12; 3:3; 7(2); 4:1; 2(3); 7; 8; 5:2; 3(2); 4(2); 5; 6; 7; 10; 11(3); 12(2); 6:3; 5(2); 8; 7:1; 6; 7; 8:2(2); 3; 4(2); 5(2); 6(2); 9:1; 2; 4(2); 5(3); 6; 10(3); 13; 10:1(2); 13; 14(4); 15; 17(3); 11:1; 12:7(2); 13:1(2); 14:6; 16:1; 2(3); 5(2); 10(2); 11; 17:3(3); 6(2); 7(2); 14; 18:1; 25(2); 26(2); 27; 28; 29; 35; 36; 39(2); 40; 43(2); 48(2); 49; 20:1(2); 2(2); 4; 21:2; 3(2); 4(2); 5; 6(2); 8; 9; 10; 11; 12(2); 22:1(2); 2; 3; 4(2); 5(2); 9(2); 10(2); 15; 19; 21; 22; 23(3); 25; 27; 23:4; 5(2); 24:7(2); 9(2); 25:1; 2; 3; 5(2); 20; 21; 27:8(2); 9; 28:1(2); 2; 29:1; 30:1(2); 2(2); 3(2); 4; 7(2); 8; 9; 11(2); 12(2); 31:1; 3; 4; 5; 7(2); 8; 14(2); 17; 19(4); 20(2); 22(2); 23; 24; 32:5(2); 6(2); 7(3); 8(4); 9; 11(2); 33:1; 22; 34:9; 11(2); 35:10; 17; 18(2); 22; 36:6; 8; 9; 10; 37:4; 10; 34(2); 38:9(2); 15(2); 39:5(2); 7; 9; 11(2); 12; 40:5(2); 6(3); 9; 16(2); 17; 41:2; 3; 4; 10; 11; 12; 42:1; 5(2); 6; 9; 11(2); 43:2(2); 4; 5(2); 44:1; 2(3); 3; 4; 5; 7; 9(2); 10; 11; 12; 13; 14; 17; 19; 23; 24; 45:2(2); 4; 5; 7(2); 8; 14; 16; 17; 47:1; 48:7; 13; 49:18(2); 50:7; 8; 12; 15(2); 16; 17(2); 18(2); 19; 20(2); 21(4); 22(2); 51:4(5); 6(2); 8; 13; 16(2); 17; 19; 52:1; 3; 4(2); 5(4); 9(2); 53:5(2); 54:6; 55:13; 22; 23(2); 56:3; 8; 9; 12(2); 13(2); 57:1; 9(2); 58:1(4); 2(2); 59:5; 8(2); 9(2); 16; 17; 60:1(3); 2(2); 3(2); 4(2); 10(2); 61:2; 3; 5(2); 6; 62:3(3); 8; 12(2); 63:1(4); 2; 3; 4; 5; 6(2); 7; 8; 65:1(2); 2(2); 3; 4(2); 5(2); 7; 8; 9(4); 10(4); 11; 66:3; 4(2); 8; 10(2); 11(2); 12(2); 13; 15; 16; 67:3(2); 4; 5(2); 68:7(2); 9(2); 10; 13(2); 16(2); 18(3); 28; 29; 32; 35; 69:5(2); 6(2); 9; 13; 19(2); 26(2); 32; 70:4(2); 5; 71:1; 3(2); 5(2); 6(3); 7; 14; 17; 19(2); 20; 21; 22(2); 23(2); 72:5; 73:18(2); 20(2); 22; 23(2); 24; 25(2); 27(3); 74:1; 2(3); 11; 13(2); 14; 15(2); 16; 17(2); 22; 23; 75:1; 76:4; 7(2); 8; 10(2); 77:4; 14(2); 15; 16(2); 20; 79:5; 6; 11; 12; 13; 80:1(2); 4; 5; 6; 8(2); 9; 12; 14; 15; 17; 18; 81:7(4); 8(2); 9(2); 10; 16; 82:2; 6(2); 7; 8; 83:2; 5; 18; 84:4; 5; 12; 85:1(2); 2(2); 3(2); 5(2); 6(2); 86:2(2); 3; 4; 5(2); 7(2); 8; 9(2); 10(2); 12; 13; 14; 15; 17; 87:3; 7; 88:1; 2; 5; 6; 7; 8(2); 9(2); 10(2); 13(2); 14(2); 18; 89:2; 8(2); 9(2); 10(2); 11; 12; 13; 17; 19; 26; 38(2); 39(2); 40(2); 42(2); 43; 44; 45(2); 46; 47; 49; 90:1; 2(2); 3; 5; 8(2); 11; 15; 91:3; 4(2); 5; 7; 8; 9; 10; 11(2); 12(2); 13(2); 92:4; 8; 10; 93:2; 94:8(3); 12; 13; 20; 95:7; 97:7; 9(2); 10; 12; 99:4(2); 8(3); 100:1; 101:1; 2; 102:1; 10; 12; 13; 25; 26(2); 27; 28; 103:4; 20; 21(2); 104:1(2); 5; 6; 8; 9; 20; 24; 26; 27(2); 28(2); 29(2); 30(2); 105:6; 11; 106:4; 108:3(2); 11(2); 109:21; 27; 28; 110:3; 4; 114:5(3); 6; 115:11; 14(2); 15; 116:4; 7; 8; 16; 17; 19; 117:1(2); 118:13; 21(2); 26; 28(4); 119:4; 7; 10; 11; 12; 21; 26; 32; 38; 49; 57; 62; 63; 65; 68; 74; 75; 79; 82; 84; 90; 93; 98; 102; 114; 115; 118; 119; 120; 126; 137; 138; 146; 151; 152; 164; 168; 169; 170; 171; 175; 120:3(3); 121:3; 6; 7; 122:6; 8; 123:1(2); 127:2; 128:2(3); 5(2); 6; 129:8(2); 130:1; 3; 4(2); 132:8; 134:1; 3; 135:1; 2; 9; 20; 137:5; 6; 8(2); 138:1(2); 2; 3; 4; 7(2); 139:1; 2(2); 3; 4; 5; 8(2); 12(2); 13(2); 14; 15; 18; 19(2); 20; 21(2); 140:6; 7; 141:1(2); 2; 8(2); 142:3; 5(2); 7; 143:6(2); 8(2); 9; 10; 144:3(2); 9(2); 145:1; 2; 10(2); 15(2); 16; 147:13; 14; 148:3; 4(2); 7; **Prov**

1:10; 22(2); 23(2); 24; 25; 27; 2:1(2); 2; 3; 4; 5; 9; 11(2); 12; 16; 20; 3:2; 3; 15; 23; 24(3); 28(2); 29; 30; 4:2; 6(2); 8(3); 9; 11(2); 12(3); 24(2); 25; 5:2; 6(2); 9; 11; 17; 19; 20; 6:1(2); 2(2); 3; 6; 9(2); 11; 22(6); 24; 25; 35; 7:1; 4; 5; 15(2); 8:4; 5(2); 9:8(2); 11; 12(4); 14:7; 19:19(2); 20; 27; 20:13(2); 22; 22:18(2); 19(2); 20; 21(3); 25; 27(2); 29; 23:1(2); 2; 5; 7(2); 8(2); 11; 13; 14; 22; 25; 34; 24:6; 10; 12; 14; 24; 28; 25:7(2); 8(2); 16(3); 17(2); 22(2); 26:4; 12; 27:1; 2; 22; 27; 29:17; 20; 30:4; 6(2); 7; 9; 10(2); 32(2); 31:29; **Eccl** 2:1; 5:1; 2; 4(2); 8; 7:10; 16; 17; 18; 21(2); 22; 8:4; 9:9(3); 10; 10:4; 16; 17; 11:1; 2; 5(2); 6; 9(2); 12:1; **Song** 1:3; 4(3); 7(3); 8; 9; 11; 15(3); 16; 2:7; 3:3; 5; 4:1(3); 7(2); 9(2); 5:8(3); 9; 6:1; 4; 13(2); 7:5; 6; 12; 13; 8:1(3); 2(3); 4; 5(4); 12; 13; **Isa** 1:5(2); 10(2); 12; 15(3); 19(2); 20(2); 25; 26; 29(3); 30; 2:6; 3:6(2); 12(2); 14; 15; 5:5; 7:3; 5; 9(2); 13(2); 14; 16; 17; 25; 8:9(2); 13; 19; 9:3(2); 4; 10:3(3); 24(2); 12:1(4); 3; 4; 14:3(2); 4; 8(2); 9(3); 10(3); 11(2); 12(3); 13; 15; 16(3); 19; 20(2); 29(2); 31; 16:4; 7; 9; 17:10(2); 11(2); 18:3(2); 19:11; 12; 21:5; 10; 12; 13(2); 22:1(2); 2; 3; 8; 9(2); 10(2); 11(3); 14; 16(3); 17(2); 18(2); 19(2); 23:1; 2(2); 6; 12(3); 14; 16(2); 24:17; 25:1(3); 2; 3(2); 4; 5; 26:3(3); 7; 8(2); 9(2); 12(2); 13(2); 14; 15(4); 16; 19; 20; 27:8; 12(2); 28:12; 14; 15; 18; 19; 29:3(3); 4(2); 6; 10; 11; 16; 30:12; 13; 15(2); 16(3); 17(2); 18(2); 19(3); 20; 21(3); 22(3); 23; 29; 32:9(2); 10(2); 11(2); 20; 33:1(8); 2; 3; 11(3); 13(2); 19(2); 34:1(2); 35:4; 36:4; 5(3); 6; 7(2); 8(3); 9; 12(2); 14(2); 15; 16(2); 17; 18; 37:6(2); 9; 10(3); 11(2); 16(3); 20(2); 21; 22(2); 23(2); 24; 26(2); 29(2); 30(2); 38:1; 3; 6; 7; 12; 13; 16; 17(2); 18(2); 19; 39:3; 7(2); 8; 40:9(2); 18(2); 21(4); 25; 27; 28(2); 41:8; 9(5); 10(4); 11(2); 12(3); 13(2); 14(3); 15(2); 16(2); 23; 24(2); 42:6(3); 9; 10(3); 17; 18(3); 20; 23; 43:1(5); 2(6); 4(4); 5(2); 10(2); 12(2); 19; 22(2); 23(4); 24(4); 26; 44:2(4); 8(2); 17; 21(4); 22; 23(2); 24; 26(2); 28; 45:2; 3(3); 4(3); 5(2); 8; 9; 10(2); 11; 14(5); 15; 17; 20; 22; 46:4(2); 5; 8; 12; 47:1; 5; 6(2); 7(2); 8; 9(2); 10(4); 11(6); 12(3); 13(3); 15(3); 48:4; 5(3); 6(4); 7(2); 8(3); 9(2); 10(2); 14; 17(3); 18; 49:1; 3; 6(3); 7; 8(4); 9; 15; 16; 17(2); 18(3); 19; 20(2); 21; 23(2); 25; 26; 50:1(2); 10; 11(4); 51:1(4); 2; 7(2); 9; 10; 12(3); 13(2); 16(2); 17(2); 19(3); 21; 22; 23(4); 52:1; 3(2); 9; 11; 12(2); 14; 53:10; 54:1(2); 3; 4(3); 6(2); 7(2); 8(2); 9(2); 10(2); 11; 14(4); 15; 17(3); 55:1; 2; 3; 5(5); 12(2); 56:9(2); 57:3(2); 4(3); 6(2); 7(2); 8(5); 9(2); 10(4); 11(3); 12; 13(2); 58:3(3); 4(3); 5; 6; 7(3); 8; 9(3); 10; 11(2); 12(3); 13; 14(3); 59:2(2); 12; 21; 60:1; 2(2); 4; 5(3); 7(2); 9; 10(3); 11; 12; 13; 14(4); 15(3); 16(2); 18; 19(2); 61:6(4); 7; 62:2; 3; 4(3); 5(2); 6; 8; 12; 63:14; 16(2); 17; 19; 64:1(2); 3(2); 4; 5(3); 7(2); 8(2); 11; 12(2); 65:5; 11; 12(4); 13(3); 14; 15(2); 66:1; 5(3); 10(2); 11(2); 12(2); 13(2); 14; **Jer** 1:5(5); 7(4); 8(2); 10; 11; 12; 13; 17(2); 18; 19(4); 2:2(2); 7(3); 9; 17(3); 19(4); 20(2); 21(2); 22; 23(3); 25; 27(2); 28(2); 29(2); 31; 33(2); 35(3); 36(3); 37(2); 3:1; 2(3); 3(2); 4(2); 5(2); 6; 12; 13(2); 14(3); 15(2); 16; 19(3); 20; 22(3); 4:1(3); 2; 4; 10(2); 14(2); 18; 19; 30(7); 5:1; 3(2); 7; 14; 15(3); 17; 18; 19(4); 22(2); 25; 31; 6:1; 8(2); 16; 17; 18; 23; 27(2); 7:2; 3; 5(2); 6; 7; 8; 9(2); 13(5); 14(2); 15; 16; 17; 23(3); 25; 27(4); 28; 8:4; 8; 17(2); 10:1; 6(2); 7(2); 11; 24; 25; 11:4(2); 13; 15(3); 17(2); 18; 20(2); 21; 12:1(3); 2(2); 3(4); 5(6); 6(3); 13:4; 6; 12(2); 13; 16; 17; 20; 21(5); 22; 23; 25; 27(2); 14:7; 8; 9(2); 13(3); 14; 17; 19(2); 20; 22(3); 15:2(2); 5(3); 6(4); 10; 11; 14(3); 15; 17; 18; 19(7); 20(6); 21(2); 16:2(2); 8; 10(2); 11; 12; 13(5); 19; 17:4(5); 13; 14; 16(3); 17; 20; 24; 27; 18:2; 6(2); 11; 20; 22; 23(2); 19:2; 10(2); 20:4; 6(5); 7(2); 12(2); 15; 21:3; 4(2); 5; 8(2); 9; 13; 14; 22:2(2); 4; 5; 6(2); 7; 15(2); 21(3); 22; 23(2); 24; 25(2); 26(4); 23:2(2); 16(2); 17(2); 20; 33(3); 35; 36(2); 37(2); 38(3); 39(4); 40; 24:3; 25:3(2); 4(2); 5; 6; 7(2); 8; 15; 27(2); 28(2); 29(2); 34(2); 26:2; 4(3); 5(2); 8; 9; 11; 12; 13; 14; 15(3); 27:4; 9(2); 10(4); 13(2); 14(3); 15(4); 16(2); 28:6; 8; 13(2); 15(2); 16(3); 29:6; 7(2); 8(2); 9; 10(3); 11(2); 12(2); 13(2); 14(6); 15; 16; 19; 20; 21; 22; 24; 25; 26(2); 27(2); 31(2); 30:2; 10; 11(6); 13(2); 14(3); 15(2); 16(3); 17(3); 22; 24; 31:3(2); 4(3); 5; 18(2); 21; 22(2); 23; 32:3; 5(2); 7; 17(2); 18; 19; 20(2); 21; 22(2); 23(2); 24(2); 25; 36; 43; 33:3(3); 10; 20; 24; 34:3(3); 4(2); 5(4); 14(3); 15(2); 16(2); 17(3); 21; 35:6(2); 7(4); 13; 14(2); 15(4); 18(2); 36:2(2); 6(3); 14; 17; 19(2); 29(3); 37:7(3); 10(2); 13; 17; 18(2); 19(2); 20; 38:5; 10; 14; 15(4); 16(2); 17(2); 18(2); 20(3); 21; 22(2); 23(2); 24; 25(6); 26; 39:12; 16; 17(3); 18(4); 40:3(2); 4(6); 5; 9; 10(2); 14(2); 15(2); 16(2); 42:2(2); 4(3); 5; 6; 9; 10(6); 11(4); 12(3); 13; 15; 16(5); 18(4); 19(2); 20(2); 21(3); 22(2); 43:2(2); 3; 44:2; 3; 4; 7(2); 8(3); 9; 10; 11; 16(2); 21(2); 22; 23(3); 25(2); 29(4); 45:2; 3; 4; 5(3); 46:4; 11(2); 14; 19; 27; 28(5); 47:5; 6(2); 48:2(2); 7(2); 14; 17(2); 18; 27(3); 28; 32; 43; 46; 49:3; 4; 5(3); 9; 12(3); 15; 16(4); 30(2); 50:11(5); 12; 14; 21; 23; 24(4); 29; 31(2); 42; 51:13; 14(2); 20(3); 21(2); 22(3); 23(3); 25(4); 26(2); 36; 46; 50; 61; 62(2); 63(2); 64; **Lam** 1:10; 12(2); 21(2); 22(2); 2:13(5); 14(2); 15; 16; 17; 20; 21(2); 22; 3:17; 42; 43(2); 44; 45; 56; 57(2); 58(2); 59; 60; 61; 4:21(3); 22; 5:19; 20; 21; 22; **Ezek** 2:1; 3; 4(2); 6(3); 7; 8(3); 3:1; 3; 5; 6(3); 7; 10; 17; 18(2); 19(2); 20; 21(2); 22; 25(4); 26; 27(2); 4:1(2); 3(2); 4(2); 5(2); 6(3); 7(2); 8(3); 9(2); 10(2); 11(2); 12; 15(2); 5:1; 2(3); 3; 7(3); 8; 9; 10(2); 11(2); 12(2); 14(2); 15(2); 16(2); 17(4); 6:3; 7; 8(2); 9; 13; 7:2; 3(4); 4(2); 6; 7(2); 8(4); 9(2); 8:6(2); 12; 13; 15(2); 17; 9:8; 11; 11:5; 6(2); 7(2); 8(2); 9(3); 10(3); 11(2); 12(3); 13; 17(4); 12:2; 3; 4(2); 6(4); 9(2); 11; 20; 22; 13:5; 7(3); 8(2); 9; 11; 12(2); 14(3); 15; 18; 19; 20(2); 21; 22(2); 23(2); 14:8; 22(3); 23(3); 15:7; 16:4(4); 5(6); 6(4); 7(3); 8(6); 9(2); 10(4); 11; 13(3); 14; 15; 16; 17(2); 18(2); 19(3); 20(3); 21; 22(2); 23; 24; 25(2); 26; 27(3); 28(3); 29(2); 30; 31(3); 32; 33(2); 34(5); 36; 37(4); 38(2); 39(3); 40(3); 41(3); 42(2); 43(2); 44; 45(2); 46(2); 47(2); 48; 51(2); 52(4); 54(3); 55; 57; 58; 59(2); 60(2); 61(4); 62(2); 63(3); 17:12; 21; 18:2(2); 3; 19; 25; 30; 31(3); 20:3(2); 4(2); 7; 20(2); 29; 30; 31(4); 32(2); 33; 34(3); 35(2); 36; 37(2); 38(2); 39(3); 41(5); 42(2); 43(4); 44(2); 47(2); 21:3(2); 4; 7(3); 14; 24(3); 25; 28; 29(3); 30(2); 31(3); 32(2); 22:2(2); 4(5); 5(2); 6; 7(2); 8; 9(2); 10(2); 11; 12(3); 13; 14; 15(3); 16(2); 19(2); 20(3); 21(3); 22(3); 24; 23:21; 22(3); 24(3); 25(2); 26; 27(2); 28(3); 29(3); 30(3); 31; 32(2); 33; 34(2); 35(2); 36; 40(2); 41(2); 49(3); 24:13(4); 14; 16(2); 19(2); 21; 22(2); 23(2); 24(3); 25; 26(2); 27(2); 25:3; 4(3); 5; 6; 7(6); 26:3(2); 8(3); 10; 14(3); 15; 16; 17(3); 19(3); 20(3); 21(4); 27:3(2); 5; 7(2); 8; 9(2); 10(2); 12; 15; 16(2); 18; 21; 25; 26(2); 27; 30; 31(2); 32(2); 33(2); 34; 35; 36(2); 28:2(3); 3(2); 4; 5; 6; 7; 8(2); 9(4); 10; 12; 13(3); 14(4); 15(3); 16(4); 17(4); 18(4); 19(3); 22; 29:3; 4; 5(5); 7(4); 8(2); 10; 31:2; 10; 18(3); 32:2(2); 3(2); 4(4); 6; 8; 9; 10(2); 11; 19; 28; 33:7(3); 8(2); 9(2); 10(2); 11; 12; 14; 20(2); 25(3); 26(4); 30(2); 31(2); 32; 34:3(3); 4(3); 7; 17; 18(3); 19(2); 21; 31(2); 35:3(3); 4(2); 5; 6(4); 9(2); 10; 11(2); 12(2); 13; 14; 15(3); 36:1; 2; 3(4); 6; 7; 8(2); 9(3); 10; 11(4); 12(4); 13(2); 14; 15(2); 22(2); 23(2); 24(3); 25(3); 26(3); 27(3); 28(2); 29(2); 30; 31(2); 32; 33(2); 36; 37:3; 5(2); 6(6); 12(2); 13(2); 14(4); 16; 18(3); 20; 38:3; 4(2); 6; 7(2); 8(2); 9(3); 10; 11; 13(3); 14; 15(3); 16(3); 17(2); 39:1(2); 2(4); 4(4); 5; 17(3); 18; 19(4); 20; 40:4(4); 43:19; 20(2); 21; 22; 23(2); 24; 25; 27; 44:5; 7(2); 8(3); 28; 30; 45:1(2); 3; 6; 10; 13(2); 18; 20(2); 21; 46:13(2); 14; 47:6; 13; 14(2); 18; 21; 22(5); 23; 48:8; 9; 20; 29; **Dan** 1:10; 13(2); 2:5(2); 6(2); 8(2); 9(4); 23(5); 26; 29(2); 30; 31(2); 34; 37(2); 38(2); 39; 41(2); 43; 45; 47; 3:4; 5(2); 10; 12(3); 14; 15(6); 16; 18(2); 4:1; 9(2); 18(3); 19(2); 20; 22; 25(5); 26(2); 27; 31(2); 32(4); 35; 5:10; 13; 14(3); 16(4); 22(2); 23(5); 27; 6:7; 12(2); 13(2); 16(2); 20(2); 22; 25; 8:19; 20; 9:7(3); 8; 18; 22; 23(2); 10:11(2); 12; 14; 17; 19(2); 20(2); 21; 11:2; 12:4; 13(2); **Hos** 1:9; 10(2); 2:16; 19(2); 20(2); 23(2); 3:3(4); 4:1; 5(2); 6(3); 15; 5:1; 3; 8; 13(2); 6:4(2); 11; 8:2; 9:1(2); 5; 14; 10:9; 12; 13(4); 15; 11:8(4); 12:6; 9; 13:4; 5; 9; 10(2); 11; 14:1; 2; 3(2); **Joel** 1:2(2); 5(2); 11(2); 13(3); 19; 20; 2:19(3); 20; 22; 23(3); 25(2); 26(2); 27; 3:4(3); 5; 6(2); 7; 11; 17; **Am** 2:10(2); 11; 12; 13; 3:1; 2(2); 11; 4:1; 2(2); 3(2); 5(2); 6(2); 7; 8; 9(2); 10(2); 11(3); 12(2); 5:1; 7; 11(5); 14(3); 17; 18(2); 22; 25; 26(2); 27; 6:1; 2; 3; 10; 12; 13; 14(2); 7:8; 10; 12; 16; 17; 8:2; 4; 9:7; **Ob** 2(2); 3(3); 4(3); 5(3); 7(5); 10(2); 11(2); 12(3); 13(2); 14(2); 15(2); 16; **Jon** 1:6; 8(2); 10; 11; 12; 14(2); 2:2; 3; 6; 7; 9; 3:2; 4:2; 4; 9; 10(2); **Mic** 1:2(2); 11(2); 13; 14; 15; 16; 2:3(2); 4; 5; 6(2); 7; 8(2); 9(2); 11; 12; 3:1(2); 2; 6(2); 9; 12; 4:8(2); 9(2); 10(5); 11; 13; 5:2(3); 12; 13; 6:2(2); 3(2); 4(3); 5; 8(2); 13(3); 14(3); 15(2); 16(3); 7:12; 15; 17; 18; 19; 20(2); **Nah** 1:9; 11; 12(2); 13; 14(2); 15; 2:13; 3:5; 6(3); 7(3); 8; 11(3); 15(3); 16; 19(2); **Hab** 1:2(3); 3; 5(2); 12(3); 13(2); 14; 2:7(2); 8(2); 10; 15; 16(3); 17; 3:8(2); 9; 10; 12(2); 13(2); 14; 15; **Zeph** 1:11; 2:2(2); 3(2); 5(2); 12(2); 3:7(2); 11(3); 15; 17(3); 18; 19; 20(3); **Hag** 1:4; 6(5); 9(3); 10; 13; 2:3(2); 4(2); 5(3); 17(2); 19; 23(3); **Zech** 1:3; 9; 12(2); 2:2; 6; 7; 8(2); 9; 11(2); 3:2(2); 4(2); 7(4); 8(2); 4:2; 5; 7(2); 9(2); 13; 5:2; 6:15(3); 7:5(2); 6(3); 7; 10; 8:9; 13(3); 14; 16; 17; 23(2); 9:9; 11; 12(2); 13; 11:9; 12; 13:3(2); 14:5(4); **Mal** 1:2(3); 5; 6(2); 7(2); 8(4); 9; 10(3); 12(2); 13(4); 2:1; 2(4); 3; 4(2); 8(3); 9(2); 13(2); 14(3); 16; 17(3); 3:1(2); 5; 6; 7(3); 8(3); 9(2); 10(2); 11; 12(2); 13(2); 14; 18; 4:2(2); 3; 5; **Mt** 1:20; 21; 2:6(2); 8; 13; 3:7; 9; 11(2); 14(2); 4:3; 6(4); 7; 9(2); 10(3); 19; 5:11(3); 12; 13; 14; 18; 20(2); 21(2); 22(2); 23(2); 25(4); 26(3); 27(2); 28; 29(3); 30(3); 32; 33(2); 34; 36(2); 38; 39(2); 40; 41; 42(2); 43(2); 44(5); 45; 46(3); 47(2); 48; 6:1(2); 2(3); 3; 4; 5(3); 6(4); 7; 8(2); 14(2); 15; 16(2); 17(2); 18(2); 23; 24; 25(4); 26; 27; 28; 29; 30(2); 32; 33; 7:1; 2(4); 3; 4; 5; 6; 7(3); 9; 11; 12(2); 15; 16; 20; 23(2); 8:2(2); 4; 8; 10; 11; 13(2); 19(2); 26(2); 29(3); 31; 9:2; 4; 5; 6; 22; 28; 29; 10:7; 8; 11(2); 12; 13; 14(2); 15; 16; 17(2); 18; 19(4); 20(2); 22; 23(3); 27(2); 31; 40; 42; 11:3; 4; 7; 8; 9(2); 10; 11; 14; 17(4); 21(3); 22(2); 23(2); 24(2); 25(2); 28(2); 29(2); 12:3; 5; 6; 7(2); 11; 28; 31; 34; 36; 37(2); 38; 47; 13:10; 11; 14(2); 17(3); 27; 28; 29(2); 51; 14:4; 16; 28(2); 31(2); 33; 15:3; 5(2); 6; 7; 12; 16; 17; 28(2); 34; 16:2; 3(2); 8(3); 9(2); 10; 11(2); 15; 16; 17(2); 18(2); 19(3); 22(2); 23(2); 28; 17:4(2); 12; 17(2); 20(4); 25; 27(3); 18:3(3); 8(3); 9(3); 10(2); 12; 13; 15(4); 16; 17; 18(3); 19(2); 22; 26; 28; 29; 32(3); 33(2); 35(2); 19:4; 8; 9; 17(2); 18(4); 19; 21(3); 23; 24; 27; 28(2); 20:4(2); 6; 7(2); 12; 13(2); 14; 21; 22(3); 23; 25; 26(2); 27; 32(2); 21:2(2); 3(2); 5; 13; 16(3); 19; 21(4); 22(2); 23(2); 24(3); 25; 27; 28; 31(2); 32(4); 42; 43(2); 22:9; 12; 16(3); 17; 18(2); 29; 31(2); 37; 39; 42; 23:3; 8(2); 11; 13(4); 14(3); 15(3); 16; 23(3); 25(2); 27(2); 28(2); 29(2); 31(2); 33; 34(3); 35(2); 36; 37; 38; 39(3); 24:2(2); 4; 6(2); 9(3); 15; 23; 25; 26; 32; 33(2); 34; 42; 44(2); 47; 25:9; 12(2); 13; 20; 21(2); 22; 23(2); 24(3); 25; 26(2); 27; 34(2); 35(3); 36(3); 37(3); 38(3); 39(2); 40(3); 41; 42(2); 43(3); 44(2); 45(3); 26:2; 10; 11(3); 13; 15(2); 17(2); 21(2); 25; 27; 29(2); 31; 32; 33; 34(2); 35(2); 39; 40; 41; 45; 50; 53; 55(3); 62(2); 63(2); 64(3); 65; 66; 68; 69; 70; 73(2); 75; 27:4; 11(2); 13(2); 17(2); 21(2); 24; 40(2); 46; 65(2); 28:5; 7(3); 14; 20(2); **Mk** 1:2; 8(2); 11; 17; 24(3); 37; 40(2); 44; 2:5; 8; 9; 10; 11; 25; 3:11; 28; 32; 4:11; 13(2); 24(4); 38; 40(2); 5:7(3); 19(2); 31(3); 34; 41; 6:10(2); 11(4); 18; 22(2); 23(2); 25; 37; 38; 7:6; 8(2); 9(2); 11(2); 12; 13(2); 18(2); 8:5; 12; 17(3); 18(3); 19; 20; 21; 29(2); 33; 9:1; 5; 13; 16; 17; 19(2); 22; 23; 25; 33; 41(3); 43(2); 45(2); 47(2); 50; 10:3; 5; 15; 18; 19; 21(3); 28; 29; 35; 36(2); 38(3); 39(2); 42; 43(2); 44; 49; 51(2); 52; 11:2(3); 3(2); 5; 14; 17; 21; 23; 24(5); 25(3); 26; 28(2); 29(2); 31; 33; 12:10; 14(2); 15; 24(2); 26; 27; 30; 31; 32; 34; 43; 13:2; 5; 7; 9(3); 11(5); 13; 14; 21; 23; 28; 29(2); 30; 33; 35; 36; 37; 14:6; 7(5); 9; 12(2); 13; 15; 18(2); 25; 27; 28; 30(2); 31(2); 36(2); 37(2); 38; 41; 48; 49(2); 60(2); 61; 62; 64(2); 67; 68; 70(2); 71; 72; 15:2(2); 4(2); 9(2); 12(2); 29; 34; 16:6; 7(3); **Lk** 1:3; 4(2); 13(2); 14; 19(2); 20(2); 28(2); 30; 31; 35(2); 42; 76(2); 2:10; 11; 12(2); 29; 31; 48(2); 49(2); 3:7; 8; 13; 16(2); 22(2); 4:3; 6; 7; 8(2); 9; 10(2); 11(2); 12; 23; 24; 25; 34(3); 41; 5:10; 12(2); 20; 22; 23; 24(2); 30; 34; 6:2; 3; 9; 20; 21(4); 22(4); 24(2); 25(4); 26(2); 27(2); 28(2); 29; 30; 31(3); 32(3); 33(3); 34(3); 35; 37(3); 38(3); 41; 42(3); 46; 47; 7:6; 7; 9; 14; 19; 20(2); 22; 24; 25; 26(2); 27; 28; 32(4); 33; 34; 40; 43; 44(2); 45; 46; 47; 50; 8:10; 18; 20; 28(2); 39; 45(2); 48; 9:4; 5(2); 13; 20; 27; 33; 38; 41(2); 48; 54; 55(2); 57(2); 60; 61; 10:3; 5; 6; 8(3); 9; 10(2); 11(2); 12; 13(3); 14; 15; 16(2); 19(2); 20; 21(2); 23; 24(3); 27; 28(2); 35(2); 36; 40; 41; 11:2; 5; 7; 8; 9(4); 11; 13; 18; 20; 27(2); 35; 36; 39; 41(2); 42(3); 43(2); 44(2); 45; 46(3); 47(2); 48(3); 51; 52(4); 12:3(2); 4; 5(3); 7; 8; 11(3); 12(2); 14; 19; 20(2); 22(3); 24; 25; 26(2); 27; 28(2); 29(2); 30; 31; 32; 33; 36; 37; 40(2); 41; 44; 51(2); 54(2); 55(2); 56(2); 57; 58(4); 59(3); 13:2; 3(3); 4; 5(3); 9; 12; 15; 24; 25(4); 26(2); 27(4); 28; 31; 34; 35(4); 14:5; 8(2); 9(3); 10(5); 12(3); 13; 14(3); 18; 19; 22; 24; 28; 33; 15:4; 7; 10; 18; 29(2); 30; 31; 16:2(2); 5; 7; 9(3); 11; 12(2); 13; 15; 25(2); 26(2); 27(2); 17:3; 4(3); 6(3); 7; 8; 10(3); 19; 21; 22(2); 23; 34; 18:8; 11; 14; 17; 19; 20; 22(3); 28; 29; 41(2); 42; 19:17; 19; 21(5); 22(3); 23; 26; 30(3); 31(3); 33; 40; 42(2); 43(4); 44(4); 46; 20:2(2); 3; 5; 8; 21(2); 23; 39; 21:3; 6; 8; 9; 12(4); 13; 14; 15; 16(2); 17; 20; 30; 31(2); 32; 34; 36; 22:9; 10(2); 11(2); 12; 15; 16; 18; 19; 20; 26(2); 27; 28; 29; 30; 31(2); 32(2); 33; 34(3); 35(2); 37; 40; 46(2); 48; 52; 53(2); 58; 60; 61; 64; 67(3); 68(2); 70(2); 23:3(2); 14(2); 15; 37; 39; 40(2); 42; 43(2); 24:5; 6; 17(2); 18(2); 36; 38; 39; 41; 44(2); 48; 49(2); **Jn** 1:19; 21(2); 22(2); 25(2); 26(2); 33; 38(2); 42(2); 48(4); 49(2); 50(4); 51(2); 2:5; 10; 18(2); 20; 3:2(2); 3; 5; 7(2); 8; 10; 11(2); 12(4); 26(2); 28; 4:9; 10(4); 11(2); 12; 17; 18(3); 19; 20; 21; 22(2); 26; 27(2); 32; 35(2); 38(3); 42; 48(2); 5:6; 10; 12; 14(2); 19; 20; 24; 25; 33; 34; 35; 37; 38(3); 39(3); 40(2); 42(3); 43(2); 44; 45(3); 46(2); 47(2); 6:25; 26(4); 27; 29; 30(3); 32(3); 36(2); 47; 53(4); 61; 62; 63; 64; 65; 67; 68; 69; 70(2); 7:3; 4; 7; 8; 19(3); 20(2); 21; 22(2); 23; 28(3); 33; 34(2); 36(2); 45; 47; 52; 8:5; 7; 10; 11; 13; 14; 15; 19(3); 21(2); 22; 23(2); 24(4); 25(2); 26; 28(2); 31(2); 32(2); 33(2); 34; 36(2); 37(3); 38(2); 39(2); 40(2); 41; 42; 43(2); 44(2); 45; 46(2); 47(2); 48; 49; 51; 52(2); 53(2); 54; 55(2); 57(2); 58; 9:17; 19; 26; 27(4); 28; 30; 34(2); 35; 37(2); 41(3); 10:1; 7; 20; 24(2); 25(2); 26(3); 32(2); 33(2); 34; 36(2); 38(2); 11:3; 8(2); 15; 21; 22(2); 26; 27; 28; 32; 34; 40(3); 41(2); 42(2); 49; 50; 56; 12:8(3); 19(2); 24; 34; 35(3); 36(2); 13:6; 7(2); 8(3); 10(2); 11; 12(2); 13(2); 14; 15(3); 16; 17(3); 18; 19(2); 20; 21(2); 27; 33(4); 34(4); 35(2); 36(3); 37; 38(3); 14:1; 2(2); 3(3); 4(2); 5; 7(3); 9(3); 10(2); 12; 13; 14; 15; 16(2); 17(3); 18(2); 19(2); 20(3); 22; 24; 25(2); 26(2); 27(3); 28(5); 29(2); 30; 15:3(2); 4(3); 5(2); 7(5); 8(2); 9; 10(2); 11(2); 12(2); 14(3); 15(3); 16(6); 17(2); 18(3); 19(4); 20(2); 21; 26; 27(2); 16:1(2); 2(2); 3; 4(5); 5(2); 6; 7(3); 10; 12(2); 13(2); 14; 15; 16(2); 17(2); 19(3); 20(3); 22(3); 23(4); 24(2); 25(3); 26(3); 27(2); 29; 30(3); 31; 32; 33(3); 17:1; 2(2); 3(2); 4(2); 5; 6(2); 7(2); 8(3); 9; 11(2); 12; 13; 15(2); 18; 21(3); 22; 23(3); 24(3); 25(3); 26; 18:4; 7; 8(2); 9; 17(2); 21; 22; 23; 25(2); 26; 29; 30; 31; 33; 34(2); 35(2); 37(2); 39(4); 19:4(2); 6; 9; 10(4); 11(3); 12(2); 35; 20:13; 15(4); 19; 21(2); 23(2); 26; 29(2); 31(2); 21:3; 5; 6; 10; 12; 15(3); 16(3); 17(5); 18(9); 20; 22(2); 23; **Acts** 1:4; 5; 6; 7; 8(3); 11(3); 24(2); 2:14; 15; 22(2); 23; 27(2); 28(2); 29; 33; 36; 38(2); 39; 3:6; 12; 13; 14(2); 16(2); 17; 20; 22(3); 25; 26(3); 4:7; 10(3); 11; 19(2); 24; 27; 5:4(2); 8; 9(2); 25; 28(2); 30; 35; 38; 39(2); 6:3; 7:3; 4; 26(2); 27; 28(2); 33; 34; 35; 37(2); 42; 43(3); 49; 51(3); 52; 8:20(2); 21; 22; 23; 24; 30(2); 34; 37(2); 9:4; 5(3); 6(3); 17(3); 34; 10:6(2); 15; 19; 21(2); 22(2); 28; 29; 32; 33(3); 37; 11:3; 9; 14(2); 16; 12:15; 13:10(3); 11(2); 15; 16; 25; 26(2); 32; 33(2); 34; 35; 38(2); 39; 40; 41(3); 46(2); 47(2); 14:15(4); 15:1(2); 7; 10; 24(2); 25; 28; 29(3); 16:15; 18; 31(2); 36; 17:3; 19; 20; 22; 23(2); 32; 18:10(3); 14; 21; 19:2(2); 3; 13; 15; 25; 26; 36; 37; 39; 20:18(2); 20(2); 25; 26; 27; 28; 29; 32(3); 34; 35(2); 21:13; 20; 21(2); 22; 23; 24(2); 37(2); 38; 39; 22:1; 3; 7; 8(2); 10(2); 14(2); 15(2); 16; 19; 21; 25; 26; 27; 23:3(4); 4; 5; 11(2); 15(3); 18(2); 19; 20; 21; 22; 30(2); 35; 24:2; 4(2); 8(2); 10; 11; 14; 19; 21; 25; 25:5; 9; 10; 12(2); 22; 24; 26(2); 26:1; 2; 3(2); 8; 14(2); 15(2); 16(4); 17(2); 24(2); 27(2); 28; 29; 27:21; 22(2); 24(3); 31; 33; 34(2); 28:20(3); 21(2); 22(2); 26(2); 28; **Rom** 1:6; 7; 8; 9; 10; 11(3); 12(2); 13(3); 15; 2:1(5); 3(3); 4(2); 5; 17; 19; 21(4); 22(4); 23(2); 24; 25(2); 27; 3:4(2); 4:17; 6:3; 11; 12; 14(2); 16(4); 17(3); 18; 19; 20(2); 21(2); 22; 7:1; 4(2); 7; 8:9(2); 10; 11(2); 13(4); 15(2); 9:17(2); 19; 20(2); 26; 10:8; 9(2); 19(2); 11:2; 13; 17; 18(3); 19; 20; 21; 22(3); 24; 25(2); 30; 31; 12:1(2); 2; 3; 14; 18; 20; 13:3(2); 4(2); 5; 6; 9(6); 14:4; 10(2); 15; 22; 15:3; 5; 6; 9; 11(2); 13(2); 14(2); 15(2); 22; 23; 24(3); 28; 29; 30(2); 32(2); 33; 16:1; 2(2); 16; 17(2); 19; 20; 21; 22; 23(2); 24; 25; **1 Cor** 1:3; 4(2); 5; 6; 7; 8(2); 9; 10(4); 11(2); 12; 13(2); 14; 26; 30; 2:1(2); 2; 3; 3:1; 2(3); 3(3); 4; 5; 9(2); 16(3); 17; 18; 23; 4:3; 6(2); 7(6); 8(5); 10(3); 14(2); 15(3); 16; 17(2); 18; 19; 21(2); 5:1; 2(2); 4; 6; 7(2); 9; 10; 11; 12; 6:1; 2(3); 3; 4(2); 5; 7(4); 8(2); 9; 11(4); 15; 16; 19(4); 20; 7:1; 5(2); 16(4); 21(2); 23; 27(2); 28(3); 32; 35(2); 8:10; 12(2); 9:1; 2(2); 9; 11; 12; 13; 23; 24(2); 10:1; 13(4); 20; 21(2); 27(3); 28(2); 31(2); 11:2(3); 3; 14; 17(2); 18(2); 19(2); 20; 22(5); 23; 24; 25; 26(2); 30; 33; 34; 12:1; 2(3); 3; 21(2); 27; 31; 14:1; 5(2); 6(3); 9(3); 12(3); 16(2); 17; 18; 23; 25; 26(2); 31; 36(2); 37; 15:1(4); 2(4); 3; 11; 12; 17; 31; 36; 37(2); 51; 16:1; 2; 3; 5; 6(2); 7(2); 10; 12; 14; 15(2); 16; 19(2); 20; 23; 24; **2 Cor** 1:2; 7(3); 8; 11; 12; 13(3); 14(2); 15(2); 16(3); 18; 19; 21; 23; 24; 2:1; 2; 3(3); 4(4); 5; 7; 8; 9(2); 10; 3:1(2); 2; 3; 4:12; 14; 5:12(3); 13; 20; 6:1; 2(2); 11; 12(2); 13; 16; 17; 18(2); 7:3; 4; 7; 8(2); 9(3); 11(3); 12(3); 13; 14(2); 15(3); 16; 8:1; 6; 7(2); 9(2); 10; 11(2); 13; 16; 17; 22; 23; 9:1; 2; 3(2); 4(2); 5(2); 8(2); 10; 11; 14(3); 10:1(3); 2; 7; 9; 13; 14(2); 15; 16; 11:1(2); 2(3); 4(4); 6; 7(2); 8; 9(2); 11; 19(2); 20(5); 12:9; 11(2); 12; 13(2); 14(3); 15; 16(2); 17(2); 18; 19(2); 20(3); 21; 13:1; 2; 3(3); 4; 5(4); 6; 7(2); 9(2); 11; 13; 14; **Gal** 1:3; 6(2); 7; 8(2); 9(2); 11; 13; 20; 2:5; 14(2); 3:1(3); 2(2); 3(2); 4; 5(2); 8; 26; 27; 28; 29(2); 4:6; 7; 8(2); 9(3); 10; 11(2); 12(3); 13(2); 14(2); 15(3); 16; 17(3); 18; 19; 20(2); 21(2); 27(2); 5:2(3); 4(3); 7(2); 8; 10(3); 12; 13; 14; 15(2); 16; 17(2); 18(2); 21(2); 6:1(2); 11; 12; 13; **Eph** 1:2; 13(3); 16(2); 17; 18; 2:1; 2; 5; 8; 11; 12; 13; 17; 19; 22; 3:1; 2(2); 4(2); 13(2); 16; 17; 19; 4:1(2); 4; 6; 17; 20; 21; 22; 24; 25; 30; 31; 32; 5:3; 5; 6; 8(2); 14(2); 15; 33; 6:3(2); 4; 9; 11; 13; 16; 21(2); 22(2); **Phil** 1:2; 3; 4; 6; 7(3); 8; 10(2); 12; 24; 25; 26; 27(2); 28; 29; 30; 2:4; 5; 12; 13; 15(2); 17; 18; 19; 22; 25; 26(2); 28(2); 3:1(2); 15(2); 17; 18(2); 4:3; 9(2); 10(2); 14(2); 15(2); 16; 18; 21; 22; 23; **Col** 1:2; 3; 5(2); 6(3); 7; 9(2); 10; 21; 22; 23(2); 24; 25; 27; 2:1(2);

4; 5; 6; 7; 8; 10; 11; 12; 13(2); 16; 18; 20(2); 3:1; 3; 4; 7(2); 8; 9; 13(2); 15; 16; 17; 23; 24(2); 4:1; 6(2); 7; 8; 9(2); 10(3); 12(4); 13; 14; 16(2); 17(2); 18; **1 Th** 1:1; 2(2); 5(3); 6; 7; 8; 9(2); 2:1(2); 2(2); 5; 6; 7; 8(3); 9(3); 10(2); 11(2); 12(2); 13(4); 14(2); 17; 18; 19; 20; 3:2(2); 3; 4(3); 5; 6(3); 7; 8; 9; 11; 12(2); 4:1(3); 2(2); 3; 4; 6; 9(3); 10(3); 11(2); 12(2); 13(2); 15; 5:1(2); 2; 4(2); 5; 11; 12(4); 14; 18; 23; 24; 27; 28; **2 Th** 1:2; 3(2); 4(2); 5(2); 6; 7; 10; 11(2); 12(2); 2:1; 3; 5(3); 6; 13(2); 14; 15; 17; 3:1; 3(2); 4(3); 6(2); 7(3); 8; 9; 10(2); 11; 13; 16(2); 18; **1 Tim** 1:3(2); 18(3); 3:14(2); 15(2); 4:6(3); 14(2); 16(2); 5:18; 21(2); 6:11; 12; 13; 14; 21; **2 Tim** 1:3; 4; 5(2); 6(2); 13; 14; 15; 18; 2:1; 2; 3; 7; 3:10; 14(3); 15(2); 4:1; 5; 11; 13; 15; 21; 22; **Titus** 1:5(3); 2:1; 8; 15; 3:8; 12; 15(2); **Phm** 1:3; 4; 5; 6; 7; 8; 9; 10; 11(2); 12; 15; 16; 17(2); 18; 19(2); 20; 21(2); 22; 23; **Heb** 1:5(2); 9(2); 10; 11; 12(2); 2:6(2); 7(2); 8; 12; 3:7; 12; 13; 15; 4:1; 7; 5:5(2); 6; 11; 12(4); 6:9; 10(2); 11; 12; 14(2); 7:17; 21; 8:5(2); 9:20; 10:5(2); 6; 8; 25; 29; 32(2); 33(2); 34(2); 36(3); 12:3; 4; 5(3); 7(2); 8(2); 17; 18; 22; 25; 13:3; 5(3); 7(2); 17(2); 19(2); 21(2); 22(2); 23; 24(2); 25; **Jas** 1:2; 4; 5; 26; 2:3(3); 4; 6(3); 7; 8(3); 9(2); 11(3); 16(2); 18(2); 19(2); 20; 22; 24; 3:1; 13; 14; 4:1; 2(5); 3(3); 4; 5; 7; 8(3); 10; 11(2); 12; 13; 14; 15; 16; 5:1(2); 3(2); 4; 5(2); 6(3); 8; 9; 11; 12; 13; 14; 16; 19; **1 Pe** 1:2; 4; 6(2); 8(3); 10; 12(2); 13; 15(2); 17; 18; 20; 22; 25; 2:2; 3; 5; 7; 9(3); 11; 12; 15; 20(4); 21(2); 24; 25; 3:6(2); 8; 9(2); 13(2); 14(2); 15(2); 16; 4:4(2); 12(2); 13(2); 14(3); 15; 5:1; 2; 3; 4; 5(2); 6; 7; 10(2); 12(2); 13(2); 14; **2 Pe** 1:2; 4; 8; 10(2); 11; 12(2); 13(2); 15; 16; 19; 2:1; 3; 13; 3:1; 2; 11; 15; 17(3); **1 Jn** 1:2; 3(2); 4; 5; 2:1(2); 7(3); 8(2); 12(2); 13(6); 14(6); 18; 20(2); 21(3); 24(5); 26(2); 27(7); 29(2); 3:5; 7; 11; 13; 15; 4:2; 3; 4(2); 5:13(4); **2 Jn** 3; 5(2); 6(2); 10; 12(2); 13; **3 Jn** 2; 3(2); 5(2); 6(2); 12; 13; 14(3); **Jude** 2; 3(3); 5(2); 9; 12; 17; 18; 20; 24(2); **Rev** 1:4; 11; 19; 20(2); 2:2(2); 3; 4(2); 5(3); 6(2); 9; 10(5); 13(3); 14(2); 15; 16; 20(2); 23; 24(2); 25; 3:1(3); 3(5); 4; 8(2); 9; 10(2); 11; 15(2); 16(2); 17(2); 18(4); 4:1; 11(2); 5:9(2); 6:10; 7:14; 10:11; 11:17(2); 18; 12:12(2); 14:15; 15:4(3); 16:5(2); 6; 17:1; 7(2); 8; 12; 15; 16; 18; 18:4(2); 6; 14(3); 20(2); 22(3); 23(2); 19:5; 10; 18; 21:9; 22:9; 16; 21

YOUR (7195/4668)

Gen 3:5; 10; 14(2); 15(2); 16(4); 17(3); 19; 4:6; 9; 10; 11(2); 14; 6:18(3); 7:1; 8:16(3); 9:2; 5; 9; 12:1(3); 2; 7; 13; 18; 19(2); 13:8; 14; 15; 16(2); 14:20(2); 15:1(2); 4(3); 5; 13; 15; 18; 16:5; 6(2); 9; 10; 11; 17:5(2); 7(2); 8; 9; 10; 11; 12(3); 13(3); 15; 19; 18:3(2); 4; 5(2); 9; 10; 19:2(3); 12(2); 15(2); 17; 19(3); 20:6; 13; 16; 21:12(3); 13; 18; 22:2(2); 12(3); 16(2); 17(2); 18; 20; 23:6(2); 8; 11; 15; 24:2; 5; 7; 14(3); 17; 19; 23; 40; 43; 44; 46; 51; 60; 25:23(2); 31; 26:3(2); 4(3); 9; 10; 24(2); 27:3(3); 6(2); 9; 10; 13; 19(2); 20; 29(2); 31; 32(2); 35(2); 37; 39; 40(3); 42; 44; 45; 28:2(2); 4; 13(2); 14(2); 29:15; 18; 30:14; 15; 27(2); 28; 29; 31; 32; 34; 31:3(2); 5; 6; 7; 8(2); 9; 12; 13; 29; 30; 31; 32; 37(2); 38(3); 41(3); 32:4; 5; 6; 9(2); 10; 12; 18; 20; 27; 28; 29; 33:5; 10(2); 34:8; 9; 11; 16; 35:1; 2; 10(3); 11; 12; 37:7; 10(2); 13; 14; 32; 38:8(2); 11; 13; 18(3); 24; 39:19; 40:13(2); 19(2); 41:40; 44; 42:10; 11; 13; 15; 16(2); 19(3); 20(2); 33(2); 34(2); 43:3; 5; 7(2); 11; 12(3); 13; 14; 23(4); 27; 28; 29; 44:7; 8; 9; 10; 16; 17; 18(3); 21; 23(2); 24; 27; 30; 31(2); 32; 33; 45:4; 7; 9; 10(4); 11; 12; 17(2); 18(2); 19(3); 20; 46:3; 4; 30; 33; 34; 47:3(2); 4(2); 5(2); 6; 15; 16(2); 19; 23; 24(4); 29(2); 48:1; 2; 4; 5; 6; 11(2); 18; 21; 22; 49:2; 4; 8(4); 18; 25; 26; 50:4; 6; 16; 17(2); 18; 21; **Ex** 2:9; 13; 3:5(2); 6; 13; 15; 16; 18; 22(2); 4:2; 4; 6(2); 7(2); 9; 10; 12; 14; 15; 16; 17; 19; 21; 23(2); 5:4; 11; 13(2); 14; 15; 16(3); 19; 23(2); 6:7(2); 7:1(2); 2; 9; 15; 19(2); 8:2; 3(7); 4(2); 5(2); 9(3); 10; 11(3); 16; 21(3); 23; 25; 28; 9:3; 14(3); 15; 19; 22; 30; 10:2(2); 4; 6(4); 8; 10; 12; 16; 17; 21; 24(3); 29; 11:8; 12:2; 4; 5; 11(5); 14; 15; 17(2); 19; 20; 21; 23; 24; 26; 32(2); 13:5; 7; 8; 9(3); 11; 13; 14; 16(2); 14:14; 16(2); 26; 15:6(2); 7(2); 8; 10; 12; 13(3); 16(2); 17(3); 26; 16:7; 8(2); 9; 12; 32; 33; 17:5(2); 18:6(2); 19:15; 20:2; 5; 7; 9; 10(8); 12(4); 16; 17(3); 24(4); 25; 26; 22:24(2); 26; 28; 29(3); 30(2); 23:1; 4; 6; 10; 11(3); 12(4); 13; 16(2); 17; 19(2); 21; 22(2); 25(3); 26(2); 27; 31(2); 33; 28:1; 2; 4; 41; 29:12; 26; 42; 30:8; 10; 31; 31:13; 32:2(3); 4; 7; 8; 11(2); 12(2); 13(4); 30; 32; 33:1; 3; 5(2); 13(4); 15; 16(3); 18; 34:9(2); 10; 12; 16(2); 19; 20; 23; 24(3); 26(2); 35:3; **Lev** 1:2; 2:5; 7; 13(4); 14(2); 3:17(2); 5:15; 18; 6:6; 18; 7:26; 32; 8:33; 9:7(2); 10:4; 6(3); 9(2); 13(2); 14(4); 15; 11:44; 45; 14:34; 16:2; 29(2); 30; 31; 17:11; 15; 18:2; 4; 7(3); 8(2); 9(3); 10(3); 11(3); 12(2); 13(2); 14(2); 15(2); 16(2); 20; 21(2); 26; 30; 19:2; 3; 4; 5; 9(3); 10(3); 12; 13; 14; 15; 16(2); 17(3); 18(2); 19(2); 25; 27(2); 28; 29; 31; 32; 33; 34; 36; 20:7; 19(2); 24; 21:8; 17; 22:3(2); 19; 20; 24; 25(2); 29; 33; 23:3; 10; 11; 14(3); 17; 21(2); 22(4); 27; 28; 31(2); 32(2); 38(3); 40; 41; 43(2); 24:3; 22(2); 25:3(2); 4(2); 5(2); 6(2); 7(2); 9; 11; 14(2); 15; 17(2); 19; 24; 25; 35; 36(2); 37(2); 38(2); 39; 43; 44; 45(2); 46(3); 47; 53; 55; 26:1(2); 5(3); 6; 7; 8; 12; 13(2); 15; 16(2); 17; 18; 19(3); 20(2); 21; 22(3); 24; 25; 26(3); 28; 29(2); 30(4); 31(3); 32; 33(2); 34; 35; 37; 38; 39; 27:2; 3(2); 4; 5; 6(2); 7; 8; 13; 15; 16; 17; 18; 19; 23(2); 25; 27(2); **Num** 5:19; 20(2); 21(3); 22(3); 9:10; 10:8; 9(3); 10(7); 35; 11:11(2); 12; 15; 20; 14:13; 14; 15; 19; 20; 29; 31; 32; 33(3); 34; 42; 15:3; 14; 15; 20; 21(2); 23; 39(2); 40; 41(3); 16:6; 10; 11; 16; 18:1(4); 2(3); 3; 6; 7(3); 8; 9; 11(2); 13; 16; 19(2); 20(2); 23; 26; 27; 28; 29; 31(3); 20:8; 14; 16; 17(2); 19; 21:22(2); 34; 22:13; 30; 32(2); 23:3; 15; 24:5(2); 11; 12; 14; 21(2); 27:13(2); 18; 20; 28:11; 26; 29:7; 39(7); 31:2; 19; 24; 49; 32:4; 5(2); 6; 8; 14; 21; 22; 23; 24(3); 25; 27; 31; 33:54(2); 55(2); 34:3(2); 4; 6; 7(2); 8; 9; 10; 12; 35:29(2); **Deut** 1:7; 8; 10; 11; 12(3); 13; 15(2); 16(2); 21(2); 23; 26; 27; 30(2); 31; 32; 33; 34; 35; 37; 39(2); 40; 42; 45; 2:4; 7(4); 24(2); 27; 30(2); 3:2; 18(2); 19(4); 20(2); 21(2); 22; 24(5); 26; 27(2); 4:1; 2; 3(2); 4; 6(2); 9(5); 10; 19(2); 21(2); 23(2); 24; 25; 26; 29(3); 30; 31(2); 34(2); 37; 39; 40(3); 5:1; 6; 9; 11; 12; 13; 14(12); 15(2); 16(5); 20; 21(3); 22; 23(2); 28; 30; 32; 33(2); 6:1; 2(5); 3; 5(4); 6; 7(2); 8(2); 9(2); 10(2); 13; 15(2); 16; 17; 18; 19; 20; 21; 7:1; 2; 3(2); 4; 6(2); 8; 9; 12(2); 13(8); 14; 16(2); 17; 18; 19(3); 20; 21; 22; 23; 24; 25; 26; 8:1; 2(2); 3; 4(2); 5(2); 6; 7; 10; 11; 13(4); 14(2); 16; 17; 18(2); 19; 20; 9:3; 4(2); 5(4); 6(2); 7; 12; 16; 17; 18; 21; 23; 26(3); 27; 29(4); 10:9; 11; 12(5); 13; 14; 15; 16; 17; 20; 21(3); 22(2); 11:1; 2(2); 7; 9(2); 10; 12(2); 13(3); 14(4); 15(2); 16; 18(4); 19(2); 20(2); 21(3); 22; 24(2); 25; 27; 28; 29; 31; 12:1; 4; 5(2); 6(7); 7(4); 9; 10(2); 11(6); 12(5); 13; 14(2); 15(3); 17(9); 18(9); 19; 20(3); 21(5); 25; 26; 27(4); 28(2); 29; 31; 13:3(4); 4; 5(3); 6(8); 8; 9; 10; 12(2); 16; 17(2); 18(2); 14:1(2); 2; 21(2); 22; 23(7); 24(2); 25(2); 26(4); 27; 28(2); 29(3); 15:3(2); 4; 5; 6; 7(6); 8; 9(3); 10(4); 11(5); 12; 14(3); 15; 16; 17(2); 18; 19(5); 20(2); 21; 22; 16:1(2); 2; 3; 4; 5(2); 6; 7(2); 8; 10(3); 11(7); 13(2); 14(6); 15(4); 16(2); 17; 18(3); 20; 21; 22; 17:1(2); 2(3); 5; 8(2); 12; 14; 15(3); 18:4(4); 5(2); 6; 9; 12; 13; 14; 15(3); 16; 21; 19:1(2); 2(2); 3(2); 8(4); 9; 10(2); 13; 14(3); 21; 20:1(2); 3(2); 4(2); 11; 13(2); 14; 16; 17; 18; 21:1; 2(2); 5; 8(2); 10(3); 11; 12; 13(2); 23; 22:1(2); 2(3); 3; 4; 5; 7; 8(2); 9(2); 17; 23:5(3); 6; 7; 9; 13(2); 14(4); 16(2); 18(2); 19; 20(3); 21(2); 23(3); 24(4); 25(3); 24:4; 9; 10; 13; 14(3); 18; 19(4); 20; 21; 25:3(2); 12; 13; 14; 15(2); 16; 18(2); 19(3); 26:1; 2(3); 3; 4(2); 5; 10(2); 11(2); 12(2); 13(3); 15(2); 16(3); 17; 19; 27:2; 3(2); 5; 6(2); 7; 9; 10; 28:1(2); 2; 4(5); 5(2); 7(2); 8(3); 9; 11(4); 12(2); 13; 15; 17(2); 18(4); 20(2); 23(2); 24; 25; 26; 29; 31(5); 32(4); 33(2); 34; 35(2); 36; 40(2); 42(2); 45; 46; 47; 48(2); 51(4); 52(6); 53(5); 55(2); 57(2); 58; 59; 62; 64; 65; 66; 67(2); 68; 29:2; 3; 5(3); 6; 10(5); 11(5); 12(2); 13; 22; 30:1; 2(4); 3(2); 4; 5(3); 6(6); 7(2); 9(6); 10(4); 14(2); 16(2); 17; 18; 19; 20(4); 31:3; 6; 11; 12(2); 13; 16; 26; 27(2); 28(2); 29; 32:6; 7(2); 17; 38; 46(2); 47(2); 50(2); 33:3(3); 8(3); 9(2); 10(3); 18(2); 25(3); 27; 29(3); 34:4(2); **Josh** 1:3; 4; 5; 8(2); 9; 11; 13; 14(5); 15(3); 17; 18(2); 2:3; 11; 16; 18(5); 19; 20; 21; 3:3(2); 9; 4:5; 6; 21; 22; 23(2); 24; 5:15(2); 6:2; 10(2); 7:9; 10; 13(2); 14; 8:1; 7(2); 18(2); 9:8; 9(2); 11; 24(2); 25; 10:6; 8; 19(3); 24; 25; 14:9(3); 15:4; 18:3; 20:3; 22:3(2); 4(4); 5(3); 8(3); 19; 24; 25; 27; 23:3(2); 4; 5(3); 8; 10; 11; 13(4); 14(3); 15(2); 16; 24:2; 3; 6(2); 7; 8; 11; 12(2); 14; 15; 19(2); 23; 27; **Judg** 1:3; 2:1; 3; 3:28(2); 4:7; 14; 5:12; 14; 31; 6:10; 17; 25(2); 26; 30; 7:7; 9; 10; 11; 15; 8:3; 6(2); 7; 15(2); 22(2); 9:2; 18; 29; 38; 54; 10:14; 11:9; 10; 17; 19; 24; 36(3); 12:1; 13:12; 16; 17(2); 14:3; 13; 15(2); 15:2; 18; 16:6; 15(2); 17:10; 18:6; 8; 10; 19(2); 25(3); 19:5(2); 6; 8; 9(2); 19(2); 20; 22; 20:7; 28; 21:22; **Ruth** 1:10; 11; 13; 15(2); 16(2); 2:9; 10; 11(5); 12; 13(3); 14; 3:3; 9(3); 17; 4:11; 12; 15(2); **1 Sam** 1:8; 11(3); 14; 16; 17; 18(2); 26; 2:1; 3; 16; 23; 27; 28; 29; 30(2); 31(3); 32; 33(4); 34; 36; 3:9; 10; 4:17; 6:4; 5(4); 6; 7:3(2); 8:5(2); 11; 13; 14(3); 15(2); 16(4); 17; 18; 9:19; 20(2); 26; 10:2; 19(5); 11:2; 12:1; 6; 7; 8(2); 11; 12(2); 14; 15; 16; 17; 19(2); 20; 24; 25; 13:13(2); 14; 14:7(2); 19; 28; 15:15; 17; 21; 24; 30; 33(2); 16:1; 16; 19; 17:9; 17(2); 18; 28(2); 32; 34; 36; 44; 46; 55; 58; 19:2; 11; 20:1; 3(3); 6; 7; 8(3); 10; 15; 18; 22; 29; 30(2); 31; 42; 22:14(3); 15; 16; 22; 23; 23:4; 10; 11(2); 20; 24:4(2); 9; 10; 11(2); 15; 16; 18; 20; 25:6; 7; 8(5); 24(3); 25; 26(3); 27; 28(2); 29(3); 31; 33; 35(3); 41; 26:8(2); 15(2); 16; 17; 21; 24; 27:5(2); 28:1; 2; 16; 17(2); 19; 21(2); 22(2); 29:6(3); 8; 10; 31:4; **2 Sam** 1:14; 16(3); 19; 24; 25; 26; 2:5; 7(2); 21(2); 22; 3:8; 12; 21; 25(2); 31; 34(2); 4:8(2); 11; 5:1(2); 19; 6:21; 7:3; 9; 11; 12(4); 16(3); 19(2); 20; 21(3); 23(3); 24(2); 25; 26(2); 27(2); 28(2); 29(3); 9:2; 6; 7(2); 8; 9; 10(4); 11; 10:3; 5; 11:8(2); 10; 11; 21; 24(2); 25; 12:8(3); 9; 10(2); 11(5); 13; 13:5(2); 7; 10; 20(3); 24(2); 35; 14:6; 7; 8; 11(2); 12; 15; 17(2); 19(2); 20; 22(2); 31; 15:2; 3; 8; 15; 19; 20; 21; 27(2); 34(3); 16:3; 4; 8(2); 17(3); 19(2); 21(2); 17:8(2); 10; 18:28; 29; 33; 19:5(5); 6(2); 7(2); 14; 19; 20; 26(2); 27(2); 28(2); 29; 35(2); 36; 37(2); 20:6; 17; 22:28; 36(2); 50; 24:3; 10; 13(3); 16; 17; 23; **1 Ki** 1:2; 12(2); 13(2); 14; 16; 17(3); 19; 26(2); 27; 30; 33; 47(2); 53; 2:3; 4; 6; 7(2); 21; 26; 37(2); 38; 39; 44(3); 3:6; 7; 8(2); 9(2); 11; 12; 13; 14(2); 20; 22(2); 23(2); 5:5(3); 6(2); 6:12; 8:18(2); 19(2); 23(2); 24(3); 25(2); 26(2); 28(2); 29(2); 30(3); 31; 32; 33(2); 34; 35; 36(4); 38; 39; 41(2); 42(3); 43(4); 44(2); 48; 49; 50; 51(2); 52(3); 53(2); 61; 9:3(2); 4; 5(2); 6; 10:6(2); 7; 8(3); 9; 11:2; 11; 12(3); 13; 22; 37; 12:4(2); 7; 9; 10; 11; 14(2); 16(2); 24; 28; 13:6; 8; 18; 21; 22(2); 14:9; 12(2); 15:19(2); 16:3; 17:11; 12; 13; 19; 23; 24; 18:8; 9; 10; 11; 12; 14; 18; 24; 25; 31; 36(2); 44; 19:2; 10(3); 14(3); 15; 16; 20:3(3); 5(4); 6(3); 9; 13; 28; 31; 32; 33; 34; 39(2); 40(2); 42(3); 21:2; 5; 6; 7; 19; 21; 22; 22:4(2); 13; 30; 49; **2 Ki** 1:10; 12; 13; 14; 2:2; 3; 4; 5; 6; 9; 16(2); 3:7(2); 13(2); 17(2); 18; 4:1(2); 2; 3; 4; 7(2); 13; 16; 26; 29(2); 30; 36; 5:8; 10; 15; 17(2); 18(2); 25; 27; 6:3; 12; 22(2); 28; 29; 7:2; 19; 8:1; 8; 9; 13; 9:1; 7; 22; 31; 10:2; 3(2); 5(2); 6; 15(3); 24; 30; 12:7; 13:16; 14:9; 10; 15:12; 16:7(2); 17:13(2); 39(2); 18:23; 24; 26; 27; 32; 19:4(3); 6; 10; 16(2); 21; 22(2); 23; 27(4); 28(4); 20:1; 3; 5(3); 6; 15; 17(2); 18; 22:9; 19(2); 20(3); 23:21; **1 Chr** 4:10; 10:4; 11:1(2); 2; 12:18(3); 14:10; 15:12; 16:18; 35(2); 17:2; 8; 10; 11(4); 17(2); 18(2); 19(2); 21(2); 22(2); 23; 24(2); 25(2); 26; 27; 19:3; 5; 21:8; 12(2); 15; 17(2); 22:11; 12; 18; 19(3); 28:6; 8(2); 9; 21; 29:12(2); 13; 14; 16(3); 17; 18; 19(3); 20; **2 Chr** 1:9; 11(2); 2:8(2); 10; 14(2); 6:8(2); 9(2); 14(2); 15(3); 16(2); 17(2); 19(2); 20(3); 21(3); 22; 23; 24(2); 25; 26; 27(4); 29; 30; 31; 32(4); 33(4); 34(2); 38; 39(2); 40(2); 41(4); 42(2); 7:12; 17; 18(2); 9:5(2); 6; 7(3); 8(3); 10:4(2); 7; 9; 10; 11; 14; 16(2); 11:4; 13:12; 14:11; 15:7(2); 16:3(2); 7(2); 8; 18:3; 12; 14; 29; 19:3; 10(2); 20:6; 7(2); 8; 9(2); 11; 20; 37; 21:12(2); 13(2); 14(4); 15(2); 24:5; 25:15; 18; 19; 28:9(2); 10(2); 11; 29:5; 8; 30:7(2); 8(2); 9(3); 32:14; 15; 33:8; 34:16; 27(2); 28(3); 35:3(2); 4(2); 5; 6; **Ezra** 4:2; 11; 15; 6:6; 7:14(2); 17; 18(2); 19; 20; 25(2); 26; 8:28; 9:10; 11; 12(3); 14; 10:4; 11; **Neh** 1:5(2); 6(4); 7; 8; 10(4); 11(5); 2:2; 5(2); 6; 4:14(5); 5:8; 6:8; 8:9; 10(2); 9:5(2); 8; 14(2); 16; 17; 18; 19; 20(2); 25; 26(2); 27; 28; 29(3); 30(2); 31; 32; 34(3); 13:18; 22; 25(2); 27; **Esth** 3:8; 4:13; 14; 5:3; 6(2); 7:2(2); 3; 9:12(2); **Job** 1:11(2); 12; 18; 2:5(2); 6; 9; 4:4; 6(4); 5:24(2); 25(2); 6:22; 25; 27; 28; 7:8; 17; 20; 8:2; 4; 5; 6; 7(2); 21(2); 10:3; 5(2); 7; 8; 12; 13; 17(2); 11:3; 4; 6(2); 13(2); 14(2); 15; 16; 17; 18; 19; 13:5; 12(2); 13; 17; 21; 24(2); 14:3; 13; 15; 15:5(2); 6(2); 10; 12(2); 13(2); 16:4; 5; 18:3; 21:2; 5(2); 14; 27; 34; 22:3; 4; 5(2); 6; 22; 23; 24; 25(2); 26(2); 27(2); 28; 30; 30:21; 32:11(2); 14; 33:5(2); 6; 8; 31; 33; 34:33; 35:4; 6; 7; 8(2); 36:16; 19; 37:17; 38:11; 12; 21; 34; 39:9; 11; 12(2); 26; 27; 40:11; 14; 41:5; 6; 8; 42:7; 8; **Ps** 2:8(2); 3:8(2); 4:4(2); 5; 6; 5:5; 7(3); 8(2); 11; 6:1(2); 4; 7:6; 8:1(2); 2; 3(2); 6; 9; 9:1; 2; 3; 10; 14(2); 19; 10:5; 12; 14; 17; 11:1; 13:1; 5(2); 15:1(2); 16:10; 11(2); 17:2(2); 4; 5; 6; 7(2); 8(2); 13; 14(2); 15(2); 18:15(2); 35(3); 49; 19:11; 13; 14; 20:3(2); 4(2); 5(2); 21:1(2); 5; 6; 8(3); 9; 12(2); 13(2); 22:22; 26; 23:4(2); 24:6; 7; 9; 25:4(2); 5; 6(2); 7(2); 11; 26:3(2); 6; 7; 8(2); 27:8; 9(2); 11; 14; 28:2; 9(2); 30:7(2); 9; 31:1; 2; 3; 5; 7; 15; 16(3); 19; 20; 22; 24; 32:4; 33:22; 34:13(2); 35:3; 24; 28(2); 36:5(2); 6(2); 7(2); 8(2); 9; 10(2); 37:4; 5; 6(2); 38:1(2); 2(2); 3; 39:10(2); 13; 40:5(2); 8(2); 10(5); 11(3); 16; 41:12; 42:3; 7(2); 10; 43:3(4); 44:2; 3(3); 5; 8; 12; 17; 18; 22; 24; 26; 45:2; 3(4); 4(2); 5; 6(2); 7(2); 8; 9(2); 10(3); 11(2); 12; 16(2); 17; 47:1; 48:9(2); 10(3); 11; 50:7; 8(2); 9(2); 14; 16; 19(2); 20(2); 21; 51:1(2); 4; 9; 11(2); 12(2); 13; 14; 15; 18; 19; 52:2; 5; 9(2); 54:1(2); 5; 6; 55:22; 56:8(2); 57:1; 5; 10(2); 11; 58:2; 9; 59:11; 16(2); 60:3; 5(2); 61:4(2); 5; 8; 62:8; 10; 63:2(2); 3; 4; 7; 8; 65:4(3); 8; 11(2); 66:3(3); 4; 13; 67:2(2); 68:7; 9; 10(2); 23(3); 24; 28(2); 29; 35; 69:7; 9; 13(2); 16(2); 17(2); 24(2); 27; 29; 32; 70:4; 71:2(2); 8(2); 15(2); 16; 17; 18(2); 19; 22; 24; 72:1(2); 2(2); 73:15; 24; 28; 74:1(2); 2(2); 3; 4(2); 7(2); 10; 11(3); 13; 18; 19(2); 21; 22; 23; 75:1(2); 5; 76:6; 7; 11; 77:11; 12(2); 13; 14; 15(2); 17; 18; 19(3); 20; 78:1; 79:1(2); 2(2); 5; 6(2); 8; 9(2); 10; 11; 13(3); 80:2; 3; 4; 7; 15; 16; 17(2); 18; 19; 81:10(2); 83:1; 2; 3(2); 15(2); 16; 84:1; 3; 4; 9; 10; 85:1; 2; 3(2); 4; 5; 6; 7(2); 86:1; 2; 4; 8; 9; 11(3); 12; 13; 16(3); 88:2; 5; 7(2); 11(2); 12(2); 14; 15; 16(2); 89:1; 2; 4(2); 5(2); 8; 10(2); 12; 13(2); 14(2); 15; 16(2); 17; 19; 38; 39; 46; 49(2); 50; 51(2); 90:4; 7(2); 8; 9; 11(2); 13; 14; 16(3); 91:4; 7(2); 8; 9; 10; 11; 12; 92:1; 2(2); 4(2); 5(2); 9(2); 93:2; 5(2); 94:5(2); 12; 18; 19; 95:8; 9; 97:8; 99:3; 102:2(2); 10(2); 12; 14; 15; 24; 25; 27; 28; 103:3(2); 4; 5(2); 104:7(2); 13; 24(2); 28; 29; 30; 105:11; 106:4(2); 5(3); 7(2); 47(2); 108:4(2); 5; 6(2); 109:21(2); 26; 27; 28; 110:1(2); 2(2); 3(3); 5; 115:1(3); 14; 116:7; 16(3); 119:4; 5; 6; 7; 8; 9; 10; 11; 12; 13; 14; 15(2); 16(2); 17(2); 18; 19; 20; 21; 22; 23(2); 24; 25; 26; 27(2); 28; 29; 30; 31; 32; 33; 34; 35; 36; 37; 38(2); 39; 40(2); 41(3); 42; 43; 44; 45; 46; 47; 48(2); 49; 50; 51; 52; 53; 54; 55(2); 56; 57; 58(2); 59; 60; 61; 62; 63; 64(2); 65(2); 66; 67; 68; 69; 70; 71; 72; 73(2); 74; 75; 76(3); 77(2); 78; 79; 80; 81(2); 82; 83; 84; 85; 86; 87; 88(2); 89; 90; 91(2); 92; 93; 94; 95; 96; 97; 98; 99; 100; 101; 102; 103; 104; 105; 106; 107; 108; 109; 110; 111; 112; 113; 114; 116; 117; 118; 119; 120; 122; 123(2); 124(3); 125(2); 126; 127; 128; 129; 130; 131; 132(2); 133; 134; 135(3); 136; 137; 138; 139; 140(2); 141; 142(2); 143; 144; 145; 146; 147; 148; 149(2); 150; 151; 152; 153; 154; 155; 156(2); 157; 158; 159(2); 160(2); 161; 162; 163; 164; 165; 166(2); 167; 168(2); 169; 170; 171; 172(2); 173(2); 174(2); 175; 176(2); 121:3; 5(3); 7; 8(2); 122:2; 7(2); 9; 128:2; 3(4); 5; 6; 130:2; 132:8(2); 9(2); 10(2); 11(2); 12(2); 134:2; 135:13(2); 137:9; 138:2(6); 4; 7(2); 8(2); 139:5; 7(2); 10(2); 14; 16(2); 17; 20(2); 140:13(2); 142:7; 143:1(2); 2(2); 5(2); 7; 8; 10(2); 11(2); 12(2); 144:5; 6; 7; 145:1; 2; 4(2); 5(2); 6(2); 7(2); 10(2); 11(2); 13(2); 16; 146:3; 10; 147:12; 13(2); 14; **Prov** 1:8(2); 9(2); 14; 15; 26(2); 27(2); 2:2(2); 3; 10(2); 3:1; 3(2); 5(2); 6(2); 7; 8(2); 9(2); 10(2); 21; 22(2); 23(2); 24; 26(2); 27; 28; 29; 4:4; 7; 9; 10; 12; 13; 20; 21(2); 23; 25(2); 26(2); 27; 5:1; 2; 8; 9(2); 10(2); 11(2); 15(2); 16; 17; 18(2); 6:1; 2(2); 3(2); 4(2); 9; 11(2); 20(2); 21(2); 25; 7:2; 3(2); 4; 15; 25; 9:11; 16:3(2); 19:18(2); 20; 20:13; 22:17(2); 18; 19; 25; 27; 28; 23:2; 4; 5; 8; 9; 12(2); 15; 16; 17; 18; 19; 22(2); 25(2); 26(2); 33(2); 24:6; 10; 12; 13; 14(2); 17(2); 27(2); 28(2); 34(2); 25:7; 8; 9(2); 10(2); 17; 21; 27:2(2); 10(4); 23(2); 26; 27(3); 29:17(2); 30:32(2); 31:3(2); 8; 9; **Eccl** 5:2(3); 6(4); 7:9; 17; 18; 21; 22; 8:2; 3; 9:7(3); 8(2); 9(3); 10(2); 10:4; 16(2); 17(2); 20(3); 11:1; 6(2); 9(5); 10(2); 12:1(2); 6; **Song** 1:2; 3(2); 4; 7(2); 8; 10(2); 2:14(4); 4:1(2); 2; 3(4); 4; 5; 9(2); 10(3); 11(3); 13; 5:9(2); 6:1(2); 5(2); 6; 7(2); 7:1(2); 2(2); 3; 4(3); 5(3); 6; 7; 8(2); 9; 8:5; 6(2); 13; **Isa** 1:7(4); 11; 12; 14(2); 15(2); 16; 18; 22(2); 23; 25(2); 26(2); 2:6; 3:6; 7; 12; 14; 25(2); 4:1; 6:7(3); 7:3; 11; 17(2); 8:8; 13(2); 10:3; 22; 27(2); 30; 12:1; 6; 13:2(2); 14:3(2); 9; 11(2); 13; 19; 20(2); 30(2); 16:3; 9(2); 17:10(2); 11(2); 19:12; 20:2(3); 22:2; 3; 7; 14; 18(2); 19(2); 21(3); 23:7; 10; 14; 25:1(2); 12; 26:8(2); 9; 11(2); 13; 16; 17; 19(2); 20(2); 28:18(2); 22; 29:4(3); 5; 10(2); 30:3(2); 15; 19; 20(3); 21; 22(2); 23(2); 31:7; 32:11; 33:4; 6; 11; 17; 18; 20; 23; 35:4; 36:8; 9; 11; 12; 17; 37:4(3); 6; 10; 17(2); 22; 23(2); 24; 28(4); 29(4); 38:1; 3; 5(4); 17; 18; 19; 39:4; 6(2); 7; 40:1; 9(2); 26; 41:10; 13(2); 14; 21(2); 24; 26; 42:6; 43:1; 3(4); 4; 5; 14(2); 15(2); 23(2); 24(3); 25(2); 26; 27(2); 44:3(2); 22(2); 24; 27; 28; 45:3; 4; 9; 21; 46:1; 4; 47:2; 3(2); 6(2); 8; 9(2); 10(4); 12(3); 13; 15(2); 48:4(2); 8; 17(2); 18(2); 19(2); 49:16; 17(2); 18; 19(2); 20; 21; 22(2); 23(3); 25; 26(2); 50:1(4); 11; 51:2; 6; 13; 15; 16; 20(2); 22(3); 23; 52:1(2); 2; 7; 8; 12; 54:2(4); 3; 4(2); 5(3); 6; 8; 11(2); 12(3); 13(2); 15; 55:2(2); 3(2); 5; 8(2); 9(2); 57:6(2); 7; 8(2); 9(2); 10(2); 11; 12(2); 13; 58:1; 3(2); 4; 7(3); 8(4); 9; 10(3); 11(2); 13(5); 14; 59:2(3); 3(4); 21(4); 60:1; 3(2); 4(4); 5; 6; 9(2); 10; 11; 14; 16(2); 17(2); 18(4); 19(3); 20(4); 21; 61:5(3); 7; 62:2(2); 3; 4(3); 5(2); 6; 8(3); 11; 63:2(2); 14; 15(5); 16; 17(4); 18(2); 19; 64:1; 2(3); 3; 5; 7(2); 8; 9; 10; 12; 65:7(2); 15; 66:5(2); 9; 14(2); 20; 22(2); **Jer** 1:9; 2:2(2); 5; 9; 16; 17; 19(3); 20(2); 22; 23; 25(2); 28(4); 30(3); 33(2); 34; 36; 37(3); 3:2(3); 13(3); 18; 22; 4:1; 3; 4(2); 7(2); 14(2); 18(4); 30(3); 5:3; 7; 14; 17(8); 19; 25(2); 6:9; 16; 20(2); 7:3(2); 5(2); 6; 7; 11; 14; 15; 21(2); 22; 23; 25; 29; 9:6; 20(2); 10:6; 7; 17; 24; 25(2); 11:4(2); 5; 7; 13(2); 16; 20; 21; 12:1; 6(2); 13; 13:1; 4; 16(2); 17; 18(2); 20(2); 22(4); 25(2); 26(3); 27(4); 14:7; 9; 19; 21(3);

15:11; 13(4); 14; 15(2); 16(3); 17; 16:9(2); 11; 12; 13; 17:1; 3(4); 4(2); 22(2); 18:11(2); 20; 23(2); 20:3; 4(2); 6(2); 12; 21:4; 12; 14; 22:2(2); 7; 15; 17(3); 20(2); 21(3); 22(3); 23; 25; 26; 23:2; 39; 25:4; 5; 6; 7(2); 28; 34(2); 26:11; 13(3); 14; 15; 27:2; 4; 9(5); 10; 12; 13; 16; 28:6; 7; 29:6(2); 8(4); 13; 14; 16; 21; 25; 30:8(2); 10; 12(2); 13; 14(3); 15(4); 16; 17; 22; 31:4; 7; 16(3); 17(2); 21(2); 32:7; 17; 19; 21; 23(2); 34:3; 5; 13; 14; 16; 35:6; 7; 15(3); 18; 36:14; 37:18; 19; 38:5; 12; 16; 17(2); 20; 22(2); 23; 39:18(2); 40:2; 4; 10(2); 42:2; 3; 4(2); 5; 9; 12; 13; 15; 20(3); 21; 43:9; 44:3; 8; 9(3); 10; 21(3); 22(2); 25(5); 45:5; 46:4; 12(2); 15; 27; 47:6; 48:6; 7(2); 18(2); 27; 32(3); 46(2); 49:4; 11(2); 16(3); 50:12; 31; 51:13(2); 24; 36; 46; 50; **Lam** 1:10; 2:13; 14(3); 16; 17; 18; 19(3); 21; 3:23; 55; 56; 65; 66; 4:22(3); 5:19; **Ezek** 2:1; 8; 3:3(2); 8(2); 9; 10(2); 11; 18; 19; 20; 21; 24; 26(2); 27; 4:3; 4; 6; 7(2); 8; 9; 10; 15; 5:1(2); 3; 8; 9; 10; 11(2); 12; 16; 6:2; 3; 4(4); 5(2); 6(5); 7; 11(2); 7:3(2); 4(3); 8(2); 9(3); 8:5; 9:5; 8; 10:2; 11:5; 6; 7; 11; 15(3); 12:3(2); 4; 5; 6(2); 18(2); 25; 13:4; 17(2); 19; 20(2); 21(3); 23; 14:6(3); 16:3(4); 4(2); 6(3); 7(2); 8(2); 9; 11(2); 12(3); 13; 14(2); 15(3); 16; 17; 18; 20(3); 22(3); 23; 25(3); 26(2); 27(2); 29; 30; 31(2); 33(3); 34; 36(6); 37(3); 39(4); 41; 43(4); 45(4); 46(2); 47; 48(2); 49; 51(3); 52(4); 53; 54; 55(3); 56(3); 57; 58(2); 60; 61(3); 63(2); 18:25; 29; 30(2); 19:2; 10(2); 20:5; 7; 18; 19; 20; 27; 30; 31(3); 32; 36; 39(2); 40(3); 42; 43(3); 44(2); 46; 21:2; 12; 14; 16(2); 24(4); 30; 32; 22:4(2); 7; 9; 12; 13; 14(2); 15; 23:21(3); 22; 25(6); 26(2); 27(3); 29(3); 31(2); 32; 33; 34; 35(3); 40; 48; 49(2); 24:13(2); 14(2); 16(2); 17(5); 21(4); 22; 23(5); 26; 27; 25:2; 4(2); 6(3); 26:8; 9(2); 10(2); 11(3); 12(7); 13(2); 15; 18(2); 27:4(3); 5; 6(2); 7; 8(3); 9(2); 10; 11(5); 12(3); 13(2); 14; 15(2); 16(2); 17(2); 18(2); 19(2); 20; 21; 22(2); 23; 24(2); 25; 26; 27(6); 28; 33(3); 34(2); 28:2(2); 4(3); 5(4); 6; 7(2); 13(2); 15; 16; 17(4); 18(4); 21; 22; 29:2; 4(6); 5; 10; 21; 31:2; 32:2(2); 5(2); 6; 7; 8; 9; 10; 12; 33:2; 8; 9; 11; 12; 17; 25(2); 26; 30; 31; 32; 34:18(3); 19(2); 21; 31; 35:2; 4; 8(3); 9; 11(2); 12; 13(2); 36:8(2); 11; 13; 14; 15; 22; 24; 25(2); 26; 28(2); 29; 30(2); 31(5); 32(2); 33; 37:12(2); 13(2); 14; 17; 18; 20; 25; 38:2; 4(2); 7; 9; 10; 12; 13; 15; 39:3(2); 4; 40:4(3); 43:27(2); 44:5(2); 6; 7; 30(3); 45:12; 47:14(2); **Dan** 1:10(3); 12; 13; 2:4; 5; 28(3); 29(2); 30; 38; 47; 3:12; 17; 18; 4:19; 22(2); 25; 26; 27(3); 32; 5:10(2); 11(4); 16; 17(2); 18; 22; 23(5); 26; 28; 6:16; 20; 9:5(2); 6(2); 11(2); 13; 15; 16(6); 17(3); 18(4); 19(4); 23; 24(2); 10:12(4); 14; 21; 11:14; 12:1(2); 9; 13(2); **Hos** 1:9; 2:1(2); 2; 6; 4:4; 5; 6(2); 13(2); 14(2); 5:13; 6:4; 5; 8:1; 5; 9:1; 7; 10; 10:12; 13(2); 14(2); 15; 11:9; 12:6(2); 9; 13:4; 9; 10(3); 14(2); 14:1(2); 8; **Joel** 1:2(2); 3(2); 5; 13; 14; 2:12; 13(3); 14; 17(2); 23; 26; 27; 28(4); 3:4(2); 5; 7(2); 8(2); 10(2); 11; 17; **Am** 2:11(2); 3:2; 11(2); 4:1; 2; 4(2); 6(2); 9(4); 10(4); 12; 5:12(2); 21(2); 22(2); 23(2); 26(3); 6:2; 4; 10; 7:17(3); 8:10(2); 14; 9:15; **Ob** 3(2); 4; 7(2); 9; 10; 12; 15(2); **Jon** 1:6(2); 8(2); 2:3(2); 4(2); 7; **Mic** 1:16(3); 2:3; 10; 4:9(2); 10; 13(2); 5:9(3); 10(3); 11(2); 12; 13(4); 14(3); 6:1(2); 8; 9; 13; 14; 16; 7:4(2); 5(3); 10; 11; 14(3); **Nah** 1:13; 14(3); 15(2); 2:1(3); 13(4); 3:5(4); 9; 12; 13(5); 14(2); 16; 17(2); 18(3); 19(3); **Hab** 1:5; 13; 2:7; 10(2); 15; 16; 3:2(2); 8(4); 9(2); 11(2); 13(2); 15; **Zeph** 3:11(3); 12; 14; 15(3); 16; 17(2); 20(2); **Hag** 1:4; 5; 7; 11; 2:3; 17; **Zech** 1:2; 4(3); 5; 6; 2:10; 11; 3:4; 8; 5:5; 6:15; 8:9; 13; 14; 16; 17(2); 9:9; 11(2); 13(2); 11:1(2); 13:6; 14:1(2); **Mal** 1:5; 6; 8; 9; 10; 13; 2:2; 3(3); 13; 14(3); 15; 16; 17; 3:7; 11(2); 13; 4:3; **Mt** 1:20; 4:6; 7; 10; 5:12; 16(3); 20; 23(2); 24(4); 25(2); 29(3); 30(3); 33; 36; 37(2); 39; 40(2); 43(2); 44; 45; 47; 48; 6:1(2); 3(2); 4(2); 6(4); 8; 9; 10(2); 14; 15(2); 17(2); 18(2); 21(2); 22(2); 23(2); 25(2); 26; 32; 7:3(2); 4(3); 5(2); 6; 11(2); 22(3); 8:4; 13; 9:2; 4; 5; 6(2); 11; 14; 18; 22; 29; 10:9; 10; 13(2); 14(2); 20; 29; 30; 11:10(2); 26; 29; 12:2; 13; 27(2); 37(2); 47(2); 13:16(2); 27; 15:2; 3; 4(2); 6; 28; 17:16; 20; 24; 18:8; 9; 14; 15(2); 33; 19:8(2); 19(3); 20:14; 15; 21(2); 26; 27; 21:5; 22:37(4); 39; 44(2); 23:8; 9(2); 10; 11; 32; 34; 37; 38; 24:3; 20; 42; 25:8; 21; 23; 25; 26:18; 42; 52; 73; 27:65; **Mk** 1:2(2); 44(2); 2:5; 8; 9(2); 11(2); 18; 3:5; 32(2); 5:9; 19; 23; 34(2); 35; 6:11; 18; 7:5; 9; 10(2); 13; 29(2); 8:17; 9:18; 38; 43; 45; 47; 10:5; 19(2); 21; 37(3); 43; 52(2); 11:25(2); 26(2); 12:30(5); 31; 36(2); 13:18; 14:70; **Lk** 1:13(2); 31; 36; 38; 42; 44; 61; 2:29(2); 30; 32; 35; 48; 3:14; 4:8; 11; 12; 21; 23; 5:4; 5; 14; 20; 22; 23; 24(2); 6:10; 22; 23; 24; 27; 29(2); 30; 35(2); 36; 38; 41(2); 42(5); 7:27(2); 44; 48; 50; 8:20(2); 25; 30; 39; 48; 49; 9:5; 40; 41; 44; 49; 10:3; 6; 11; 17; 20; 21; 26; 27(6); 11:2(3); 13(2); 19(2); 34(4); 36; 39; 46; 47; 48; 12:7; 19; 20; 22; 30; 32; 34(2); 35(2); 58; 13:12; 26; 34; 35; 14:12(3); 15:19(2); 21(2); 27(2); 29; 30; 32; 16:2; 6; 7; 11; 12; 15; 25(2); 17:3; 19(2); 18:20(2); 42(2); 19:5; 16; 18; 20; 22; 39; 42(3); 43; 44(2); 20:43(2); 21:14; 15; 18; 19(2); 28(2); 34; 22:32(2); 42; 53; 23:14; 28; 42; 46; 24:38; **Jn** 2:4; 17; 4:16; 18; 35; 50(2); 51; 53; 5:8; 10; 11; 12; 6:49; 58; 7:3; 6; 8:13; 17; 19; 21; 24(2); 38; 41; 42; 44(2); 54; 56; 9:10; 17; 19; 26; 41; 10:34; 11:15; 23; 12:15; 28; 30; 13:14(2); 37; 38; 14:1; 26; 27; 15:11; 16; 16:6; 7; 20; 22(2); 24; 17:1(2); 6(2); 11; 12; 14; 17(2); 26; 18:11; 31; 35; 19:14; 15; 26; 27; 20:17(2); 27(2); 21:18; **Acts** 2:17(4); 22; 27; 28; 35(2); 39; 3:17; 19; 22(2); 25; 26; 4:25; 27; 28(2); 29(2); 30(2); 5:3; 4(3); 9; 28; 7:3(2); 32; 33(2); 37(2); 43; 51; 52; 8:20; 21; 22(2); 37; 9:13; 14; 17; 34; 10:4(2); 31(2); 11:14; 12:8(2); 13:35; 41; 14:10; 15:24; 16:31; 17:23; 28; 18:6(2); 15; 19:37; 22:13; 16; 18; 20; 23:5; 35; 24:2; 4; 22; 26:16; 27:34; **Rom** 1:8; 2:5(2); 17; 23; 25; 27; 3:4; 4:18; 6:12; 13(2); 19(3); 22; 8:11; 36; 9:7; 10:6; 8(2); 9(2); 11:3(2); 25; 28; 12:1(2); 2; 16(2); 20; 13:9; 14:10(2); 15(3); 16; 21; 15:9; 24; 16:19(2); 20; **1 Cor** 1:26; 2:5; 4:6; 5:6; 6:5; 8; 15; 19(2); 20(2); 7:5; 14; 16(2); 35; 8:11; 9:11; 10:29; 14:16; 23; 34; 15:14; 17(2); 34; 55(2); 58; 16:3(2); 17; **2 Cor** 1:6(2); 14; 24(2); 2:8; 10; 4:5; 15; 5:11; 6:12; 7:2; 4; 7(3); 9; 13; 8:7; 8; 9; 10; 14(2); 19; 24(2); 9:2(2); 5; 10; 13(2); 10:6; 8; 15; 11:3; 12:15; 19; **Gal** 3:16; 4:6; 15; 16; 5:14; 6:13; 18; **Eph** 1:13; 15(2); 18; 3:13; 17; 4:4; 22; 23; 26; 29; 5:19; 22; 25; 6:1; 2; 4; 5; 9; 14; 15; 22; **Phil** 1:5; 9; 19; 25; 26; 27(2); 28; 2:12; 17; 19; 20; 25; 30; 4:5; 6; 7; 10; 17; 19; **Col** 1:4(2); 7; 8; 21; 2:5(2); 13(2); 18; 3:2; 3; 5; 8; 15; 16; 18; 19; 20; 21; 22; 4:1; 6; 8(2); **1 Th** 1:3; 4; 5; 8; 2:14; 17; 3:2; 5; 6; 7; 9; 10(2); 13; 4:3; 11(2); 5:23; **2 Th** 1:3; 4(2); 2:17; 3:5; **1 Tim** 4:12; 15; 5:23(2); 6:20; **2 Tim** 1:4; 5(2); 4:5; 21; 22; **Phm** 1:2; 5; 6; 7; 13; 14(2); 19; 21; 22; 25; **Heb** 1:8(2); 9(2); 10; 12; 13(2); 2:7; 12; 3:8; 9; 15; 4:7; 6:10; 9:14; 10:7; 9; 34; 35; 11:18; 12:3; 13; 13:5; 17; **Jas** 1:3; 21; 2:2; 8; 18(2); 3:14; 4:1(2); 3; 8(2); 9(2); 14; 16; 5:1; 2(2); 3(2); 4; 5; 8; 12(2); 16; **1 Pe** 1:7; 9(2); 13(2); 14; 15; 17; 18(2); 21; 22; 2:12(2); 18; 20; 25; 3:1; 2; 3; 7; 15; 16; 4:7; 14; 5:5; 7; 8; 9; **2 Pe** 1:5; 10; 19; 3:1; 17; **1 Jn** 1:4; 2:12; **2 Jn** 4; 10; 13; **3 Jn** 2; 6; **Jude** 12; 20; **Rev** 1:9; 2:2(3); 4; 5; 9; 13; 19(3); 23; 3:1; 2; 8; 9; 11; 15; 18(2); 4:11; 5:9; 10:9(2); 11:17; 18(3); 14:15; 18; 15:3(2); 4(2); 16:7; 18:10; 14; 23(2); 19:10(2); 22:9(2)

YOURS (73/65)

Gen 14:23; 20:7; 31:32; 45:20; 48:6; **Lev** 10:15; **Num** 18:9; 11; 13; 14; 15; 18(2); 22:30; **Deut** 11:24; 28:41; **Josh** 2:14; 17; 17:18(2); **Judg** 6:14; **1 Sam** 15:28; **2 Sam** 16:4; **1 Ki** 3:9; 26; 20:4; 21:19; 22:23; **2 Ki** 1:13; **1 Chr** 12:18; 21:24; 29:11(3); **2 Chr** 1:10; 18:22; 20:15; **Job** 42:2; **Ps** 71:16; 74:16(2); 89:11(2); 119:94; **Song** 7:7; **Isa** 45:14; **Jer** 5:19; 32:7; 8(2); **Dan** 2:39; **Hos** 5:1; **Mt** 6:13; 20:14; 25:25; **Lk** 4:7; 5:33; 6:20; 15:30; 31; 22:42; **Jn** 8:10; 15:20; 17:6; 9; 10(2); **1 Cor** 3:21; 22; 8:9; 16:18; **2 Cor** 12:14; **2 Pe** 1:8

YOURSELF (257/233)

Gen 6:14; 21(2); 14:21; 16:9; 28:2; 33:9; **Ex** 9:17; 10:3; 28; 18:18; 20:4; 23:7; 30:23; 34:2; 12; **Lev** 9:2; 7; 18:20; 23; 19:18; 34; 25:8; **Num** 5:20; 10:2; 11:17; **Deut** 4:9(2); 5:8; 9:1; 10:1(2); 12:13; 19; 30; 16:9; 21(2); 19:2; 3; 7; 9; 20:14; 22:1; 3; 4; 7; 12; 23:9; 28:40; **Josh** 5:2; 17:15; **Judg** 8:21; **Ruth** 3:3(3); 4:6; 8; **1 Sam** 20:4; 8; 25:26; **2 Sam** 2:21; 7:23; 14:2; 18:13(2); 20:4; 22:26(2); 27(2); 24:12; **1 Ki** 2:2; 36; 3:11(3); 11:31; 13:7; 14:2; 9; 17:13; 18:1; 20:22; 34; 40; 21:20; **2 Ki** 4:29; 6:7; 9:1; 22:19; **1 Chr** 17:21; 21:10; 11; 23; **2 Chr** 1:11; 20:37; 21:13; 34:27(2); **Neh** 9:10; 26; **Job** 5:27; 10:16; 14:3; 15:8; 17:3; 18:4; 22:21; 38:3; 40:7; 10(2); **Ps** 7:6; 18:25(2); 26(2); 25:16; 35:23; 37:4; 40:9; 49:18; 55:1; 76:7; 10; 80:15; 17; 89:46; 104:2; 119:102; **Prov** 6:3(2); 5; 9:12; 24:27; 25:6; 30:32; **Eccl** 7:16; **Isa** 7:11; 26:20; 33:3; 45:15; 52:2(2); 57:8; 58:7; 14; 63:14; 64:12; 65:5; **Jer** 1:17; 2:17; 22; 4:8; 30(3); 13:1; 17:4; 20:4; 22:15; 30:2; 32:8; 20; 45:5; 46:19; 47:5; 6; **Lam** 2:18; 3:43; 44; 4:21; **Ezek** 3:24; 4:3; 9(2); 16:5; 16; 17; 24(2); 25; 21:19; 22:4; 16; 23:22; 28; 40(2); 28:4; 37:16; 17; 38:7; **Dan** 5:17; 23; 9:15; 10:12; **Hos** 1:2; **Mic** 1:10; 16; 5:1; **Nah** 3:15(2); **Zech** 11:15; **Mt** 4:6; 8:4; 19:19; 22:39; 27:40; **Mk** 1:44; 12:31; 15:30; **Lk** 4:9; 23; 5:14; 6:42; 7:6; 10:27; 17:8; 23:37; 39; **Jn** 1:22; 7:4; 8:13; 53; 10:33; 14:22; 17:5; 18:34; 21:18; **Acts** 5:3; 12:8; 15; 16:28; 21:24; 24:8; 26:1; 24; **Rom** 2:1; 5; 19; 21; 13:9; 14:22; **Gal** 5:14; 6:1; **1 Tim** 3:15; 4:7; 15; 16(2); 5:22; 6:5; **2 Tim** 2:15; **Titus** 2:7; **Jas** 2:8

YOURSELVES (235/221)

Gen 18:4; 34:9; 10; 35:2; 45:5; **Ex** 5:11; 7:9; 9:8; 12:21; 16:23; 18:18; 19:12; 20:23; 30:15; 16; 37; 32:29; 34:17; **Lev** 11:43(2); 44(2); 18:24; 30; 19:4; 20:7; 25; 23:15; 40; 26:1(2); **Num** 11:18; 16:3(2); 7; 21; 31:3; 18; 19; 32:20; **Deut** 2:4; 4:15; 16; 23(2); 7:25; 9:16; 11:16; 23; 14:1; 27:2; 31:14; 19; **Josh** 1:11; 3:5; 12; 4:2; 3; 7:13; 8:2; 10:19; 20:2; 22:16; 19; 23:11; 24:15; 22(2); **Judg** 15:12; 21:22; **Ruth** 1:13; **1 Sam** 2:29; 4:9(2); 8:18; 10:19; 12:17; 14:34; 16:5; 17:8; **2 Sam** 3:31; **1 Ki** 18:25; **1 Chr** 15:12; **2 Chr** 13:9; 20:17; 29:5; 31; 30:8; 32:11; 35:4; 6; **Ezra** 6:6; 10:11; **Neh** 13:25; **Esth** 8:8; **Job** 19:5; 29; 42:8(2); **Isa** 1:16(2); 2:22; 8:9(2); 29:9; 31:7; 32:11(2); 45:20; 46:8; 48:14; 49:9; 18; 50:1; 11; 52:3; 57:5; **Jer** 2:28; 4:4; 5; 6:1; 8:14; 13:18; 17:21; 26:15; 27:2; 37:9; 44:7; 8; 46:14; 49:3; 50:14; **Ezek** 13:18; 18:31; 20:7; 18; 30; 31; 43; 34:3; 36:31; 39:17; 47:21; 22; **Hos** 10:12; **Joel** 1:13; **Am** 5:26; 6:5; 6; **Mic** 6:15; **Zeph** 2:1; **Hag** 1:4; 6; **Zech** 7:6; **Mt** 3:9; 6:19; 20; 16:8; 23:13; 15; 31; 25:9; **Mk** 6:31; 9:33; 50; 13:9; **Lk** 3:8; 11:46; 52; 12:33; 36; 57; 13:28; 16:9; 15; 17:3; 14; 21:30; 34; 22:17; 23:28; **Jn** 3:28; 6:43; 16:19; **Acts** 2:22; 5:35; 13:46; 15:29; 18:15; 20:10; 28; 30; 34; **Rom** 6:11; 13; 16; 12:19; **1 Cor** 5:13; 6:7; 8; 7:5; 10:15; 11:13; **2 Cor** 7:11(2); 11:19; 13:5(3); **Eph** 2:8; **Col** 2:20; 3:7; 8; **1 Th** 2:1; ; **1 Th** 2:1; 3:3; 4:9; 5:2; 13; 15; **2 Th** 3:7; **Heb** 10:34; 13:3; **Jas** 1:22; 2:4; 4:10; **1 Pe** 1:14; 17; 2:13; 4:1; 5:5; 6; **1 Jn** 5:21; **2 Jn** 8; **Jude** 20; 21